Symbols and Language Abbreviations used in the Etymologies

* hypothetical
‡ foreign word or phrase
< derived from
? perhaps; possibly; uncertain
\+ plus
& and

Abyss., Abyssinian
Afr., African
Alb., Albanian
Am., American
Am. Fr., American French
Am. Ind., American Indian
Am. Sp., American Spanish
Anglo-Fr., Anglo-French
Anglo-Ind., Anglo-Indian
Anglo-Ir., Anglo-Irish
Anglo-L., Anglo-Latin
Anglo-N., Anglo-Norse
Anglo-Norm., Anglo-Norman
Ar., Arabic
Aram., Aramaic
Arm., Armaric
AS., Anglo-Saxon
Assyr., Assyrian

Bab., Babylonian
Beng., Bengali
Bohem., Bohemian
Braz., Brazilian
Bret., Breton
Brit., British
Bulg., Bulgarian

Canad., Canadian
Canad. Fr., Canadian French
Catal., Catalonian
Celt., Celtic
Ch., Chaldean; Chaldee
Chin., Chinese
Corn., Cornish
Cym., Cymric

D., Dutch
Dan., Danish; Daniel

Early Mod. D., Early Modern Dutch
Early Mod. Eng., Early Modern English
E.Fris., East Frisian
Egypt., Egyptian
E.Ind., East Indian
Eng., English
Esk., Eskimo
Eth., Ethiopic

Finn., Finnish
Fl., Flemish
Fr., French
Frank., Frankish; Franconian
Fris., Frisian

G., German
Gael., Gaelic
Gaul., Gaulish
Gmc., Germanic
Goth., Gothic
Gr., Greek

Haw., Hawaiian
Heb., Hebrew
Hind., Hindi; Hindu; Hindustani
Hung., Hungarian

Ice., Icelandic
Idg., Indo-Germanic
IE., Indo-European
Ind., Indian
Ir., Irish
Iran., Iranian
It., Italian

Japan., Japanese
Jav., Javanese

Kor., Korean

L., Latin
Late Anglo-Fr., Late Anglo-French
Late Gr., Late Greek
Late ME., Late Middle English
LG., Low German
LGr., Late Greek
Lith., Lithuanian
LL., Late Latin; Low Latin
LWS., Late West Saxon

MD., Middle Dutch
ME., Middle English
Med., Medieval
Mex., Mexican
MFl., Middle Flemish
MFr., Middle French
MGr., Medieval Greek; Middle Greek
MHG., Middle High German
MIr., Middle Irish
MIt., Middle Italian
ML., Medieval Latin
MLG., Middle Low German
MnE., Modern English
Mod. Gr., Modern Greek
Mod. L., Modern Latin
Mod. Pr., Modern Provencal
Mongol., Mongolian
MScand., Middle Scandinavian
MScot., Middle Scottish

N., Norse
Norm., Norman
Norw., Norwegian

O, Old
OAr., Old Arabic
OCelt., Old Celtic
OCym., Old Cymric
OD., Old Dutch
ODan., Old Danish
OFr., Old French
OFris., Old Frisian
OHG., Old High German
OIr., Old Irish
OIt., Old Italian
OLG., Old Low German
ON., Old Norse
ONorm.Fr., Old Norman French
OPer., Old Persian
OS., Old Saxon
OSlav., Old Slavic
OSerb., Old Serbian
OSp., Old Spanish
OW., Old Welsh

Per., Persian
Peruv., Peruvian
Phoen., Phoenician
Pid.Eng., Pidgin English
Pol., Polish
Port., Portuguese
Pr., Provençal
Pre-AS., Pre-Anglo-Saxon
Prov. Eng., Provincial English
Prov. Scot., Provincial Scottish

Russ., Russian

S.Afr.D., South African Dutch
Sans., Sanskrit
Scand., Scandinavian
Scot., Scottish
Sem., Semitic
Serb., Serbian
Singh., Singhalese
Slav., Slavic; Slavonic
Sp., Spanish
Sw., **Swed.**, Swedish
Syr., Syrian; Syriac

Tag., Tagalog
Tart., Tartar
Tibet., Tibetan
Turk., Turkish

W., Welsh
W.Afr., West African
W.Fl., West Flemish
W.Gmc., West Germanic
W.Ind., West Indian
W.S., West Saxon

Yid., Yiddish

COLLEGE EDITION

WEBSTER'S NEW WORLD DICTIONARY

OF THE AMERICAN LANGUAGE

COLLEGE EDITION

WEBSTER'S NEW WORLD DICTIONARY

OF THE AMERICAN LANGUAGE

THE WORLD PUBLISHING COMPANY

Cleveland and New York

Webster's New World Dictionary, College Edition
is based upon and includes material from
Webster's New World Dictionary, Encyclopedic Edition

57R11WP1065

Library of Congress Catalog Card Number: 64-12965

PRINTED IN THE UNITED STATES OF AMERICA

CONTENTS

EDITORIAL STAFF

General Editors

DAVID B. GURALNIK JOSEPH H. FRIEND

Supervising Associate Editor

Samuel Solomon

Associate Editors

Frederic E. Reeve Jean L. McKechnie

Etymological Editors

Harold E. Whitehall William E. Umbach

Special Consulting Editor

Mitford M. Mathews

Assistant Editors

Fannie Biebel, Robert Campbell, Bryant M. French, Thomas H. Layman, Clark C. Livensparger, Donald Lloyd, Mary S. Shulman, Andrew N. Sparks, Bruce Thomas, Laura Robinson Whitehall

Special and Contributing Editors

Herman Briscoe, Orah C. Briscoe, Dorothy Charpie, John Cowley, Raymond Early, Isidore Edelman, Herman Epstein, Gerald Graham, Josephine McCarter Gunther, James Holly Hanford, Muriel Hughes, Robert A. Hume, Juda A. Joffe, Austin Johnson, Allen Kellogg, Charlton Laird, Lucy Preston, Goldie Rimson, Oscar Rimson, Martha Rosen, Myrtle Sokolsky, Edward N. Teall, Edith Weisskopf, Alice Whitehall

Contributors and Consultants

Katherine Austin, Blair Banister, Richard L. Barrett, Orfea Barricelli, Andrew Bugosh, Miriam A. Cramer, Julian DeVries, Ruth Elliott, Helen M. Focke, Ann Frankenberry, Dorothe French, Robert Gault, Leopold H. Gergely, Robert Gorrell, Hugo Gunther, Ursula Hanford, Gertrude K. Heberlein, Horace Hilb, Jane G. Hilb, Jobe Jenkins, Helen Jung Kittsley, Helene Laird, Richard Looser, David Marrin, Alice Monroe, Helga Preisman, Doris Shankroff, Douglas Slocum, George F. Sowers, Lloyd Swift, Janet Thomas, Elizabeth Weed, Kenneth Whelan, Irving Wolfson, Arthur Yaspan

Research and Office Assistants

Nora Carlson, Bernice Eaton, Margaret T. Ellis, Jack E. Goodman, Helen Hutchins, Elizabeth Jones, F. John Julyan, Irene Kauffman, Rita L. Mayo, Frances B. Mehlek, Esther Meltzer, Maxine Ogle, Dorothy Ormiston, Dorothy Pacholik, Eleanor Rickey, Evelyn Robison, Ruth Roser, Margaret Soltis, Eleanor Stamm, Jerome Stone, Eulalia Sturtevant, Sol Witkewitz, Lenora C. Zearfoss

Illustrator

Joseph M. Guerry

Design and Production

Abe Lerner and Joseph Trautwein

FOREWORD

As this edition of *Webster's New World Dictionary* is being prepared to go to press, the editors are systematically including in the plate proofs the death dates of recently deceased notables, new terms and senses resulting from the latest technological advancements, and such other changes and additions as last-minute developments make necessary.

This final gesture in the interest of up-to-dateness is a rather symbolic one, a logical extension of the lexicographic principles that have guided the editors in the preparation of this work. For just as historical events and scientific concepts refuse to remain fixed, unyielding entities, so too a living language will not permit itself to be immutably pinned down. The excellent dictionaries of Dr. Johnson and Nathaniel Bailey, remarkable though they were in their days, have little more pertinence for the present-day reader of the *New York Times* than the alchemical writings of Roger Bacon have for a nuclear physicist.

Not only could the earlier dictionaries have no knowledge of *dilantin, snorkel, betatron, cortisone, ACTH, cybernetics,* and *vibraphone,* but they would be of no help in uncovering the meanings of *extrapolate, parking meter, iron curtain, cold war, simulcast,* and *hot-foot.* Moreover, even those senses of words that have had continued currency from the time of Dr. Johnson to the present are in the earlier dictionaries defined in a language that falls strangely on 20th-century American ears.

The 100 scholars, specialists, and editorial workers who compiled this dictionary set out to create a new work that would be built in the light of contemporary linguistics, psychology, and the allied sciences. Recognizing that modern lexicography is a disciplined science, they were, nevertheless, determined to avoid the dogmatism that led Ambrose Bierce to define a *dictionary* as "a malevolent literary device for cramping the growth of a language and making it hard and inelastic." This dictionary was not to create the impression that it was authoritarian, laying down the law about usage; it was to play, rather, the role of a friendly guide, pointing out the safe, well-travelled roads.

Webster's New World Dictionary derives from the best traditions in British and American lexicography and is based especially on the broad foundations laid down for American dictionaries by Noah Webster. It is neither an abridgment nor a revision of some earlier work. It is a new dictionary in which every definition has been written afresh in the simplest language consistent with accuracy and fullness. The editors have tried to avoid wherever possible the "essence" type of definition, which merely states the class of things to which the thing being defined belongs and the differences that distinguish it from other members of this class. Instead, the reader is given the necessary additional connotative information, even if it means devoting a good deal of space to doing so (see, for example, the definitions of *Aryan, blood,* and *epic*).

In choosing the words to be entered and defined, the editors used as their criterion the frequency of occurrence in contemporary American usage and in readings generally required of college and university students, insofar as it could be determined. As a result, this dictionary contains over 142,000 vocabulary entries, more than any other comparable American desk dictionary. All entries are arranged in a single alphabetical list, so that there is no need to leaf through numerous supplements and prefatory lists, as well as the dictionary proper, to find entries such as *Isaiah, Charlemagne, Atlantic, John Bull, viz., F.O.B., OHG., a priori,* and *coup de grâce.*

In addition to the customary literary, scientific, and technical wordstock, the *New World* contains with a fullness unknown in previous general desk dictionaries colloquialisms and slang, the informal and vulgate words that are so rich and characteristic a feature of American English. Thus, along with the well-established entries, such as *dead beat, double cross, flophouse, sob sister,* and *jerk,* there are included a large number of widely used terms that have been overlooked by other dictionaries, such as *fungo, cover girl, double take, big time, comic book, hot rod, sixty-four dollar question,* and *whoops.* Particular care has been devoted to the phrasal units and compounds whose meaning cannot be inferred from the definitions of the individual components (for example, *act of God, black market, drive-in, hard up*) and to the important idiomatic phrases that are such a vital part of English (see, for example, the lists after *do, make,* and *run*). Many abbreviations have been entered as well as words and phrases in other languages that one is likely to encounter in an English context. While retaining all such obsolete, archaic, and Scottish and British dialectal terms and senses as appeared justified, the editors have placed special emphasis on providing full treatment of the hundreds of important new terms and new senses of older terms that have come into both scientific and general use in recent years. Trade-marks which have become generic terms or have passed into wide general usage have also been entered, invariably with a careful indication of their proprietary nature.

This dictionary contains no run-on forms, that is, words entered after the definition of a related term, often syllabified and pronounced, but having no other useful purpose, except, perhaps, to increase the vocabulary count. Too often, the meaning of such a word is not self-evident. Full acquaintance with the word *career* does not in itself make possible an understanding of the very particular meaning of the derived *careerist.* Other conventional space-saving short-cuts have been sacrificed to increase usefulness to the reader. Alternative pronunciations, plurals whose spelling may present some difficulty, irregular comparatives, superlatives, principal parts of verbs, and so forth, have been entered in their full forms.

Following many of the key entries in the dictionary will be found a paragraph in smaller type in which words that are related to, or apparently synonymous with, the entry are carefully discriminated from one another as to precise meaning. Illustrative examples are supplied wherever these are helpful in showing the distinctions (see the synonymies following ***happy*** and ***trite***).

The pronunciations here recorded are those of General American, the speech of the great majority of the inhabitants of the United States. As many variant pronunciations as space would permit have been included, but artificial, "platform" speech has been ignored. (For a more detailed discussion of pronunciation, see pp. x-xii.)

Dr. Whitehall and Dr. Umbach, who were in charge of the etymological research for this dictionary, have related the etymologies to the definitions in such a way that the "semantic flow" of the word—its evolution from earlier forms and its sense development—as well as its kinship to other words in English and related languages, is immediately made clear. The history of each word, except for certain names, obvious derivatives, and the like, has been traced back as far as present linguistic knowledge allows. For native English words Dr. Whitehall has regularly followed the thread of development back to the hypothetical base in Indo-European, the reconstructed language from which most of the languages of the Western world are believed to have descended. It is the editors' conviction that the detailed care accorded to the etymologies will have been justified if they succeed in helping students to achieve a deeper understanding of their language.

Data such as population and area figures are conservative and have been carefully checked with authoritative sources. Unofficial estimates of population figures have been avoided; only the latest official counts or estimates available were considered reliable. For values of foreign monetary units, the latest exchange figures are given, except where current fluctuation is such that these would be meaningless.

The illustrations, which were specially prepared for this dictionary by Joseph M. Guerry, were selected and designed for maximum usefulness to the reader. Tools and instruments are depicted in use, so that their function and relative size are made clear. Actual sizes of animals and plants have been given in preference to reduction ratios. Small outline maps appear throughout as an aid in locating many places of historical, literary, or current political importance. Modern typography and format have been selected to combine ease of reading with attractive appearance. For example, several different type faces have been used and the part-of-speech designations have been printed in slightly bolder type to make it easy for the reader to find what he is looking for. The design and production of this dictionary were the responsibility of Mr. Abe Lerner and Mr. Joseph Trautwein. For valuable cooperation in solving many problems of typography, thanks are due to Mr. Joseph Schwartz, of Westcott and Thomson, Inc.

One could not expect maximum efficiency from a new technological apparatus if he did not first read the operating instructions. Each user of this dictionary is, therefore, urged to read the *Guide to the Use of the Dictionary* on the following pages.

The Editors

GUIDE TO THE USE OF THE DICTIONARY

I. *The entry words*

A. *Arrangement of entries*

All entries, including proper nouns, abbreviations, combining forms, and compounds of two or more words, have been entered in strict alphabetical order. All the elements in bold-face type are to be regarded as of equal value, with the following exceptions: in biographical entries, only the last, or family, name (that part preceding the comma) has been considered in alphabetization, but where there are two or more persons with the same family name, the first, or given, names have determined the order of entries.

John of Gaunt (gônt), Duke of Lancaster, 1340–1399; son of Edward III.

John·son, Andrew (jon′s'n), 1808–1875; seventeenth president of the United States (1865–1869).

Johnson, James Wel·don (wel′d'n), 1871–1938; American writer and diplomat.

Johnson, Samuel, 1709–1784; English writer, critic, and lexicographer; known as *Dr. Johnson.*

Johnson City, a city in northeastern Tennessee: pop., 25,000.

If two or more variant spellings of a single word exist, each is entered in its proper place and the definition and variant spellings are given with the form most frequently used, the others being cross-referred to this.

cas·si·mere (kas′ə-mêr′), ***n.*** [< *Kashmir;* cf. CASHMERE (wool)], a thin, twilled woolen cloth, used for men's suits: also spelled **casimere, casimire.**

In some few cases, where usage is about evenly divided, full definitions are given with each form. Where the variant spellings are so nearly alike that they would normally appear in consecutive or nearly consecutive order, and where they are pronounced alike, the less frequent form or forms are entered directly after the main entry word, preceding the pronunciation.

en·am·el·er, en·am·el·ler (i-nam′'l-ẽr), ***n.*** a person or thing that enamels.

Idiomatic phrases listed after a main entry have also been entered alphabetically within each group, all elements in bold-face type, again, being given equal weight. Such phrases have been entered wherever possible under the key word.

few (fū), ***adj.*** [ME. *fewe, few;* AS. *feawe, feawa, pl.;* akin to OFris. *fē,* Goth. *fawai, pl.;* IE. base **pōu-,* etc., small, little, as also in L. *paucus,* little (cf. PAUCITY)], not many; of small number. ***pron. & n.*** not many; a small number.

quite a few, [Colloq.], a rather large number; a good many.

the few, the minority: contrasted with *the many.*

Biographical entries have been given with the most familiar form of the person's name, fuller forms, pseudonyms, maiden names, etc. being identified in parentheses following the pronunciation.

Henry, O., (pseudonym of *William Sydney Porter*), 1862–1910; American short-story writer.

Dick·ens, Charles (dik′'nz, dik′inz), (pseudonym *Boz*), 1812–1870; English novelist.

Prefixes and initial combining forms are indicated by a hyphen following the entry form.

in·tra- (in′trə), [L. < *intra,* within, inside < **intera;* akin to *interior, inter*], a combining form meaning *within, inside of,* as in *intramural, intravenous.*

Suffixes and terminal combining forms are indicated by a hyphen preceding the entry form.

-ice (is), [ME. *-ice, -ise, -is;* OFr. *-ice;* L. *-itius,* masc., *-itia,* fem., *-itium,* neut.], a suffix meaning *the condition, state,* or *quality of,* as in *justice, malice.*

Such affixes and combining forms have been pronounced only where it is feasible to pronounce the element in isolation.

B. *Syllabification*

The syllabifications used in this dictionary, indicated by centered dots in the entry words, are those adopted by printers in the 18th century and in general use since then to indicate the points at which words may conveniently be divided at the end of a written or printed line.

ox·i·diz·a·ble (ok′sə-dīz′ə-b'l), ***adj.*** that can be oxidized.

In adopting this traditional syllabification, the editors are fully aware of its inconsistencies, of its total failure to conform to any scientific principles. They are also aware that to upset the system by adopting one based on the etymological or descriptive, formative elements in words would be to instigate a major revolution in printing practice. (See p. xx, par. 2.4.)

C. *Derived forms*

Every word entered in this dictionary has been fully defined. Nothing has been left to supposition or guesswork. Wherever a common derived form, such as an adverb from an adjective or a noun from a verb, shows the slightest deviation in spelling or pronunciation or offers the slightest doubt as to meaning, such a form generally has been entered, pronounced, and defined.

It is possible in English to form an almost infinite number of derived forms simply by adding certain prefixes or suffixes to the base word. In very many such cases it is possible to understand immediately the meanings of such derived words, if the meanings of the base word and of the affixes (the most common of which have been entered in this dictionary) are understood. For example, if the suffix *-able* is clearly understood to mean "that can be ——ed" or "capable of being ——ed," the meanings of such derived forms as *contradictable, recallable,* and *moldable* are immediately apparent. An analogous situation exists for words compounded with *-er, -less, -like, -ly, -ness,* etc. Space for less easily understood forms is therefore conserved by omitting many such words.

For some of the more common prefixes, such as *re-* and *non-,* sample lists of words compounded with such forms have been entered under the proper prefix or suffix merely to indicate the frequency with which such words occur in usage.

For adjectives ending in *-ic* having alternative forms in *-ical,* the derived adverbs (ending in *-ically*) have generally not been entered where such forms mean only "in (the specified) manner." Where the alternative form in *-ical* does not exist, the derived adverb has been entered.

The names of many sciences or studies ending in *-logy* (as, *psychology, histology*) form nouns of agent by replacing the *-y* with *-ist* (as, *psychologist, histologist*). In such cases, the derived form is not always entered but can easily be inferred.

D. *Foreign terms*

Words and phrases borrowed from other languages and not regarded as completely naturalized English terms are indicated by a double dagger (‡) preceding the entry word. The language from which such a word is borrowed is indicated in its etymology and the foreign pronunciation is given first.

‡moi·ré (mwȧ′rā′; Eng. mwä-rā′, mō′rā′), ***adj.*** [Fr., pp. of *moirer,* to water < *moire;* see MOIRE], having

II. *Pronunciation*

A. *General introduction and key*

With pronunciation, as with all other aspects of lexicography, it cannot be repeated too often that dictionaries are not the lawmakers—they are merely the law-recorders. A pronunciation is not "correct," or standard, because it is given in a dictionary; rather, it should be found in a dictionary because good usage has already made it standard. There is no single hypothetically "correct" standard for all speakers of American English (in the sense that Received Standard is the guide for British English), since the usage of the cultivated speakers in any region or locality constitutes a standard for that area. Hence, since the scope of a desk dictionary prohibits the inclusion of every possible acceptable variant, the editors of such a dictionary are justified in recording those pronunciations used by the greatest numbers of cultivated speakers. Thus, the pronunciations given in this dictionary are those observed among literate speakers of the Central variety of General American English (see p. xvii, par. 1.15). These are symbolized, however, in as broad a manner as is consistent with accuracy, so that speakers of other varieties of American English can readily read their own pronunciations into the symbols used here. In addition, the principal differentiating features of the language as spoken in the East and South are given in variant pronunciations, where these also occur as occasional forms in General American. Thus (häf) as well as (haf), (glō′ri) as well as (glôr′i), and (tūn) as well as (to͞on) are entered. As a result, the reader can be assured that although no single standard exists for the whole nation, the kind of pronunciation here indicated is acceptable anywhere in the United States.

One of the prime frustrations besetting the editors of a dictionary is the necessity for recording in isolation pronunciations that almost invariably occur in context. Thus, the word *and*, regarded as a unique phenomenon existing independently of the phrases and clauses of which it is always an element, could simply be recorded as (and). In actual practice such a pronunciation occurs only when the particle is deliberately emphasized in speaking (as, "The boys *and* the girls are invited."). In all other instances, the loss of stress results in a neutralization of the vowel to (ə) or even in a total loss of vowel to the following consonant, which becomes syllabic (see Key to Pronunciation, p. xi), and in extreme cases to an additional loss of the final *d*. Hence *ham and eggs* becomes (ham′ ənd egz′), or (ham′ ′nd egz′) or even (ham′ ′n egz′). In addition to causing phonemic change, loss, and gain, the context in which a word is used often serves to alter its stress pattern. In this way *semifinal* (sem′i-fī′n′l) often becomes (sem′i-fī′n′l round′). Wherever practicable, such contextual variants have been indicated in one way or another. The general principle of the editors has been to record the speech of the unstudied, informal conversation of cultivated speakers. Such words as hardly ever occur in normal conversation necessarily have no colloquial pronunciation except where analogy would inevitably lead to one.

Key to Pronunciation

An abbreviated form of this key appears at the bottom of every alternate page of the vocabulary.

Symbol	Key Words	IPA
a	fat, lap	[æ]
ā	ape, date	[e]
â	bare, care	[e → ɛ → æ]
ä	car, father	[ɑ → a]
e	ten, let	[ɛ]
ē	even, meet	[i]
ê	here, dear	[ɪ → i]
ẽr	over, under	[ər *or* ɚ]
i	is, hit	[ɪ]
ī	bite, mile	[ɑɪ]
o	lot, top	[ɑ]
ō	go, tone	[o]
ô	horn, fork	[ɔ → ɒ]
o͞o	tool, troop	[u]
oo	book, moor	[ʊ]
oi	oil, boy	[ɔɪ]
ou	out, doubt	[aʊ]
u	up, cut	[ʌ]
ū	use, cute	[ju → ɪu]
ũr	fur, turn	[ər *or* ɜ]
ə	a *in* ago e *in* agent i *in* sanity o *in* comply u *in* focus	[ə]
b	bed, dub	[b]
d	did, had	[d]
f	fall, off	[f]
g	get, dog	[g]
h	he, ahead	[h]
j	joy, jump	[dʒ]
k	kill, bake	[k]
l	let, ball	[l]
m	met, trim	[m]
n	not, ton	[n]
p	put, tap	[p]
r	red, dear	[r]
s	sell, pass	[s]
t	top, hat	[t]
v	vat, have	[v]
w	will, always	[w]
y	yet, yard	[j]
z	zebra, haze	[z]
ch	chin, arch	[tʃ]
ŋ	ring, drink	[ŋ]
sh	she, dash	[ʃ]
th	thin, truth	[θ]
th	then, father	[ð]
zh	azure, leisure	[ʒ]
′	**[see explanatory note on p. xi]**	

Foreign Sounds **(see explanatory notes on p. xi)**

Symbol	Key Words	IPA
à	Fr. *bal*	[a]
ë	Fr. *coeur*	[œ]
ö	Fr. *feu*	[ø]
ô	Fr. *coq*	[o → ɑ → ɔ]
ü	Fr. *duc*	[y]
n	**[see explanatory note on p. xi]**	
H	G. *ich*	[ç]
kh	G. *doch*	[x]

This simplified Key to Pronunciation was evolved on the assumption that the reader is already familiar with the qualities of almost all the symbols as they occur in the key words. A few explanatory notes on the more complex of these symbols follow to give the fullest understanding of the pronunciations recorded. It should be recognized that certain concessions have of necessity been made to practicality and convenience; notably, a few symbols are deliberately intended to cover a relatively narrow range of vowel sounds to allow for regional and individual differences, and several symbols duplicate in essence others to allow a minimum distortion of the orthography in respelling.

ä This symbol represents essentially the low back vowel of *far* (IPA [ɑ]) but may also represent the low central vowel occasionally heard in New England for *bath* (IPA [a]).

â This symbol is used, always followed, and hence colored, by *r*, to represent the range of sounds (ā, e, a) heard variously in such words as *care* and *prayer*.

ê Like (â), this symbol followed, and hence colored, by *r*, represents a range of sounds (i through ē) heard variously in such words as *here* and *dear*.

i This symbol, representing essentially the vowel in *hit*, has also been used to indicate the neutralization of vowel in the unstressed syllables of such words as *garbage* (gär′bij), *goodness* (good′nis), and *preface* (pref′is). In some persons' pronunciation of such words, total neutralization is heard; hence, (gär′bəj) (good′nəs), and (pref′əs) can be assumed as possible variants.

o This symbol represents sounds that are essentially identical with those of (ä), but has been used where the original spelling has an *o* to avoid, as was mentioned above, too great distortion of the orthography.

ô This symbol, representing essentially the vowel in *fork* (IPA [ɔ]), has also been used to represent the sound midway between (ä) and (ô) heard in an Eastern variant of *fob* (IPA [ɒ]).

This symbol, called the schwa, is borrowed from the International Phonetic Alphabet, and has been used to represent the reduced, weakened, and dulled vowel of neutral coloration heard in the unstressed syllables of *ago*, *agent*, *sanity*, *comply*, and *focus*. Although it must be recognized that the degree and quality of the dulling of such vowels will vary from word to word and from speaker to speaker, it must also be remembered that in modern conversational English, *all* totally unstressed vowels are neutralized either to (ə) or to (i).

ũr and ẽr These two symbols represent respectively the stressed and unstressed r-colored vowels heard successively in the two syllables of *murder* (mũr′dẽr) and indicated by IPA [ər or ɜ] and [ər or ɚ]. Where these symbols are given, Southern and Eastern speakers will, as a matter of course, pronounce them without the r-coloration, that is, by "dropping their *r*'s," as represented by IPA [ɜ] and the schwa [ə].

ŋ This symbol, also borrowed from the International Phonetic Alphabet, represents the back-tongue nasal sound indicated in spelling by the *-ng* of *sing* and occurring also for *n* before the back consonants *k* and *g*, as in *drink* (driŋk) and *finger* (fiŋ′gẽr).

' The apostrophe occurring before an *l*, *m*, or *n* indicates that this consonant has become a sonant, or syllabic consonant; that is, it has formed a syllable with no appreciable vowel sound, as in *apple* (ap′'l) or *season* (sē′z'n). In some persons' speech such syllabic consonants are often replaced with syllables containing neutralized vowels, as (sē′zən); such variants, though not entered here, can, of course, be inferred.

The apostrophe has also been used after final *l* and *r*, in certain French words, to indicate that they are voiceless after an unvoiced consonant, as in *par exemple* (pȧr′ eg′zän′pl'), *lettre* (let′r'). In such cases the final *l* and *r* often tend to be lost entirely in French speech.

In some Russian words where certain consonants are followed by the "soft sign" in the Cyrillic spelling, this has been indicated by (y'). The sound can be approximated by pronouncing an unvoiced (y) directly after the consonant involved.

B. *Foreign sounds*

Although virtually no two sounds of different languages can be scientifically regarded as precisely identical, sufficient similarity exists, for all practical purposes, to permit the use of most of the preceding symbols in the recording of foreign pronunciation. The eight additional symbols that follow fill adequately the gaps in the main phonetic key. Several of these symbols are, again, intended to convey varying sounds in differing languages, where the similarities are sufficient to permit the use of a single symbol.

ȧ This symbol, representing the *a* in French *bal* (bȧl), can perhaps best be described as intermediate between (a) and (ä), corresponding closely to IPA [a].

ë This symbol represents the sound of *eu* in French *leur* (lër) and can be approximated by rounding the lips for (ô) and trying to pronounce (e).

ö This symbol represents the sound of *eu* in French *feu* (fö) or *ö* (*oe*) in German *Göthe* (*Goethe*) (gö′tə) and can be approximated by rounding the lips for (ō) and trying to pronounce (ā).

ô This symbol represents a range of sounds varying from (ō) to (ô) and heard with such varying quality in French *coq* (kôk), German *doch* (dôkh), Russian *gospodin* (gôs′pô-dēn′), Italian *poco* (pô′kô), etc.

ü This symbol represents the sound of *ü* in French *duc* (dük) and German *grün* (grün) and can be approximated by rounding the lips for (o͞o) and trying to pronounce (ē).

kh This symbol represents the unvoiced velar or uvular fricative, as in German *doch* (dôkh) or Scottish *loch* (lokh) and can be approximated by arranging the speech organs as for (k) but allowing the breath to escape in a continuous stream, as in pronouncing (h).

H This symbol represents a sound similar to the preceding but formed forward in the mouth, as in German *ich* (iH), and frequently misheard by English speakers as (sh).

n This symbol indicates that the vowel sound immediately preceding it is nasalized; that is, the nasal passage is left open so that the breath passes through both the mouth and the nose in voicing the vowel [examples: Fr. *mon* (mō*n*), *en passant* (ä*n*′ pȧ′sä*n*′)].

C. *Stress*

A primary, or strong, stress is indicated by a heavy stroke (′) immediately following the syllable so stressed. A secondary, or weak, stress is indicated by a lighter stroke (′) following the syllable so stressed.

qual·i·ta·tive (kwäl′ə-tā′tiv), ***adj.*** [LL. *qualitativus*], having to do with quality or qualities: distinguished from *quantitative*.

In addition to such accents, some syllables in English receive what may be termed reduced secondary stresses. Such stresses are not indicated but may be inferred where an apparently unstressed syllable retains an unneutralized vowel.

Words of one syllable are regarded, in isolation, as receiving a primary stress, although this is not indicated. In contextual usage such words often receive a secondary stress or no stress at all.

Words of two or more syllables may be characterized by rising stress (i.e., by secondary stress on an early syllable and primary stress on a later one), by falling stress (i.e., by the reverse of this situation), or by level stress (i.e., by primary stress on two syllables). Where such words are characterized by all three of these patterns, space has often been conserved by indicating only the level stress.

D. *Variants*

Where two or more pronunciations for a single word are given, the order in which they are entered does not necessarily mean that one is preferred to, or "better" than, the others. In most cases the order indicates that, in the opinion of the editors, the form given first is the most frequent in general use. Where usage is about evenly divided, since one form must be given first, the editors' preference generally prevails. Unless a variant is qualified, however, as by "now rarely" or "less commonly," it is understood that all pronunciations here entered represent standard uses.

In order to save space, where variants exist for two or more syllables of a word, a telescoped system has been used whereby two or more forms indicate four or more variants. Thus, for example, where *nucleolate* has (no͞o-klē′ə-lit, nū-klē′ə-lāt′), by substituting the variant syllables the following pronunciations may also be inferred: (. . . no͞o-klē′ə-lāt′, nū-klē′ə-lit).

Where specific parts of speech have variant pronunciations, these are indicated by italicized notes in the pronunciation proper.

re·tic·u·late (ri-tik′yoo-lit; *also, and for v. always,* ri-tik′yoo-lāt′), ***adj.*** [L. *reticulatus* < *reticulum;* see RETICULE], like a net or network; netlike; specifically, in *botany*, having the veins arranged like the threads of a net: said of leaves. ***v.t.*** [RETICULATED (-id), RETICU-

In some few instances, where the entry was relatively short and it was felt that the pronunciation would not be overlooked, it was entered directly with the part of speech to which it had reference.

Every word used in this dictionary is pronounced in its main entry. Where it occurs in a phrase, the pronunciation is not repeated, unless it was felt that its contextual use created sufficient differences to warrant recording. Where the same family name exists for two or more biographical entries, the pronunciation and syllabification are given only with the first entry.

Math·er, Cot·ton (kot′'n math′ẽr), 1663–1728; American clergyman and writer.

Mather, In·crease (in′krēs), 1639–1723; father of *Cotton;* American clergyman and writer.

Complete pronunciations are given throughout for every main entry. Where truncated forms are given with irregular inflections, it is understood that the part of the form not pronounced is identical in quality and stress with the similar part of the main entry.

fish·y (fish′i), ***adj.*** [FISHIER (-i-ẽr), FISHIEST (-i-ist)], 1. of or full of fish. 2. like a fish in odor, taste, etc.

Words borrowed from foreign languages but completely naturalized in English use are given Anglicized pronunciation. Where the foreign pronunciation is also still heard, it has been given in second place, properly labeled.

hors d'oeu·vre (ôr′dũrv′, ôr′duv′; Fr. ôr′dö′vr'), [*pl.* HORS D'OEUVRES (-dũrvz′, -duvz′; Fr. -dö′vr')], [Fr.,

The designation *sp. pronun.* (*spelling pronunciation*) indicates that the variant so labeled has resulted from an attempt to conform with the spelling, which may not be properly phonetic, and in this way deviates from the historical or established pronunciation (cf. **hist**).

For words beginning with the combination *wh-*, where the pronunciation (hw) has been given, as in *why* (hwī), *while* (hwīl), and *white* (hwīt), alternative, unaspirated pronunciations are heard today with increasing frequency, as (wī), (wīl), and (wīt). Such variants have not been given with each word, but on those pages of the vocabulary containing words beginning with *wh-*, a note has been added to the bottom of the page indicating their occurrence. Compounds derived from such words and found elsewhere in the vocabulary should also be understood to have such variants.

III. *Inflected forms*

Inflected forms regarded as irregular or offering difficulty in spelling or pronunciation are entered in brackets immediately following the part-of-speech labels.

en·ti·ty (en′tə-ti), ***n.*** [*pl.* ENTITIES (-tiz)], [Fr. *entité;* ML. *entitas* < L. *ens, entis,* ppr. of *esse,* to be], 1. being; ex-

Where variant inflected forms exist, all such forms are entered. If the inflected form is so altered in spelling (as by internal inflection) that it would appear at some distance from the main form in the alphabetized list, it is entered additionally in its proper place in the vocabulary.

rode (rōd), past tense and archaic past participle of **ride.**

Forms regarded as regular inflections, and hence not normally entered, include:

a) Plurals formed by adding *-s* to the singular (or *-es* after *s, x, z, ch,* and *sh*), as *ships, brushes.*

b) Present tenses formed by adding *-s* to the verb (or *-es* after *s, x, z, ch,* and *sh*), as *sorts, marches.*

c) Past tenses and participles formed by simply adding *-ed* to the verb with no other change in the verb form, as *sorted, marched.*

d) Present participles formed by simply adding *-ing* to the verb with no other change in the verb form, as *sorting, marching.*

e) Comparatives and superlatives formed by simply adding *-er* and *-est* to the adjective or adverb with no other change in the positive form, as *taller, tallest.*

Where two inflected forms are given for a verb, the first is the form for the past tense and the past participle, and the second is the form for the present participle.

make (māk), ***v.t.*** [MADE (mād), MAKING], [ME. *maken;* AS. *macian;* akin to G. *machen;* IE. base **maĝ-*, to

Where three forms are given, separated from one another by commas, the first represents the past tense, the second the past participle, and the third the present participle.

blow (blō), ***v.i.*** [BLEW (blōō), BLOWN (blōn), BLOWING], [ME. *blowen;* AS. *blawan;* akin to G. *blähen;* IE. base

Where there are alternative, obsolete, or archaic forms, these are given and properly indicated.

ride (rīd), ***v.i.*** [RODE (rōd), or *archaic* RID (rid), RIDDEN (rid′′n) or *archaic* RID OR RODE, RIDING], [ME. *riden;* AS. *ridan;* akin to G. *reiten;* IE. base **reidh-*, to go,

In the interest of conserving space, where an irregularly inflected verb is simply compounded from another verb with the addition of a prefix, the inflected forms are not always repeated with the derived word, particularly if the base verb is used in the definition.

IV. *Etymology*

Etymology has deliberately been made one of the strong features of this dictionary. During the years of preparation, the etymologies of all the entries were restudied in light of recent publication, early dated quotations, and the chief new etymological dictionaries. The results of this survey, often original in character, are here presented with a fullness altogether unparalleled in any previous American dictionary. A striking innovation is the exhaustive treatment accorded to words of native origin, hitherto comparatively neglected in most English dictionaries. While it is undoubtedly easier to etymologize words borrowed into English from the Classical languages, the native word-stock deserves the attention accorded it here on the grounds that it comprises much of the everyday vocabulary of the English language. On semantic grounds alone, it is probably more important that the reader should understand the ultimate origins of such words as *arm* (of the body), *left* (hand, etc.), and *hen* than that he should recognize the constituents which make up such borrowed words as *attention* and *adventure.* The careful attention given the native vocabulary is paralleled in the painstaking care given to borrowings from Norse and Low German sources.

Wherever the semantic history of the entries can be illuminated by the procedure, etymologies are carried back to the Indo-European base and correlated through this with other words, both native and of Classical or Romance origin, which are also ultimately derived from it. A typical example of this treatment is that of *light:*

light (līt), ***n.*** [ME. *liht;* AS. *leoht;* akin to G. *licht;* IE. base **leuq-*, to shine, bright, seen also in L. *lucere,* to shine, *lux, lumen,* light (cf. LUCID, LUMINOUS), *luna,* moon (cf. LUNAR), etc.], 1. *a*) that which makes it

The first section of this etymology provides typical Middle English and Anglo-Saxon forms representing the history of the word *within* English itself. Next comes a cognate form from another Germanic language (in this case, German) introduced by the words *akin to.* The final section of the etymology gives the reconstructed Indo-European base (its hypothetical character is indicated by *), its generalized meaning or meanings, a selected group of Latin words also derived from this base, and cross references to borrowings or derivatives of these found in English. The intention behind this elaborate apparatus is not to present a mere list of historically related forms; it is to elucidate the semantic background of the entry, link it with other words of similar descent and meaning, and prepare the way for the more recent semantic history of the entry represented in the definitions. In short, the editors have thought of the etymologies as a vital part of definition and as a guide to the correct focusing of the definitions proper. Particularly in the longer and more complex words, they have aimed at an organization which flows smoothly from the etymology to the last sense recorded.

Because of the ample space devoted to etymology, the reader will not need to master a long list of abbreviations. He need merely understand the abbreviations for the various languages (see the list of abbreviations, p. xxxv) and remember that the symbol < means "(derived) from," that * indicates a hypothetical, reconstructed base, that "*prob.*" indicates strong scholarly opinion or editorial conviction in favor of what follows, and that "?" indicates uncertainty or unverifiable hypothesis. Where two hypotheses regarding the origins of a word are in conflict, both are usually briefly mentioned. Where the ultimate etymology is uncertain, the most promising direction of approach is given.

For words compounded in Modern English from a base word and an affix or affixes, the etymology contains only these elements. Detailed etymologies can be found with the main entries for such bases and affixes.

fix·a·tive (fik′sə-tiv), ***adj.*** [*fix* + *-ative*], that can or tends to make permanent, prevent fading, etc. ***n.*** a sub-

Where the definition makes the compounding elements of such a word perfectly obvious, no etymology is required.

V. *The definitions*

A. *Arrangement and styling of senses*

Semantic order from the etymology through the most recent sense of a word has been the guiding principle determining the order of senses within any given entry (cf. **common**). In this way, it has been possible to give a logical, progressive flow that permits the reader to see quickly and clearly the development of a word and the relationship of its senses to one another. In longer entries, where the treatment would not seriously disturb the semantic flow, technical senses have been entered, with suitable field labels properly alphabetized, at the end of the entry, to facilitate their being found quickly. For the same reason, archaic, obsolete, colloquial, slang, and dialectal senses are entered just before the technical senses, unless they are firmly anchored on one of the general meanings.

foul (foul), ***adj.*** [ME.; AS. *ful;* akin to G. *faul,* rotten, putrid, lazy; IE. base **pū-*, **pu-*, etc., to stink (? < exclamation of disgust), seen also in *pus, putrid*], 1. so offensive to the senses as to cause disgust; stinking; loathsome: as, a *foul* odor. 2. extremely dirty; dis-

. . . . .

treacherous; dishonest. 11. [Archaic], ugly. 12. [Colloq.], unpleasant, disagreeable, etc. 13. in *baseball,* relating to or having to do with foul balls or foul lines. 14. in *printing,* full of errors or changes: as, *foul* copy. ***n.*** anything foul; specifically, *a*) a collision

Obsolete senses that bridge the gap between the etymology and the definitions proper often occur first. Such senses are generally preceded by "originally" or "formerly" rather than by a formal usage label.

Where a primary sense of a word can easily be subdivided into several closely related meanings, this has been done; such meanings are indicated by italicized letters after the pertinent numbered sense.

ell (el), ***n.*** 1. the letter L. 2. something shaped like an L; specifically, *a)* an extension or wing at right angles to the main structure. *b)* an L-shaped joint of piping or tubing.

Where a basic word has very many senses that can conveniently be arranged under a few major headings, such a division has been made (cf. **hand, go**). The sections, indicated by Roman numerals, are then further subdivided into numbered (and, where necessary, lettered) senses (cf. **go**).

Synonyms, in addition to being entered separately in discriminative synonymies (see p. xiv), are also incorporated in the definition treatment at those points where their relevance is most easily apparent. Antonyms are frequently indicated following definitions by ***opposed to. . .*** or ***distinguished from. . .***

grand opera, opera, generally on a serious theme, in which the whole text is set to music: distinguished from *operetta, comic opera.*

If a word is capitalized in all its meanings, the entry word itself is printed with a capital letter.

Eur·a·sian (yoo-rā′zhən, yoo-rā′shən), ***adj.*** 1. of Eurasia. 2. of mixed European and Asiatic descent. ***n.*** 1. a person of mixed European and Asiatic descent. 2. a member of a people of both Europe and Asia.

If it is capitalized in most of its meanings, a lower-case letter in brackets occurs immediately after the numeral or part of speech of any sense not capitalized.

Her·cu·les (hũr′kyoo-lēz′), ***n.*** [L.; Gr. *Hēraklees* < *Hēra*, Hera + *kleos*, glory], 1. in *Greek & Roman mythology*, the son of Zeus and Alcmene, renowned for feats of strength, particularly the twelve labors imposed on him by Hera. 2. [h-], any very large, strong man. 3. a northern constellation: see **constellation**, chart.

Where it is capitalized in only one or two of the senses, the word is entered with a lower-case letter, and a capital letter in brackets occurs after the numeral or part of speech of each pertinent sense. In some instances these designations are qualified by the self-explanatory "often," "sometimes," or "usually."

or·i·en·tal (ôr′i-en′t′l, ō′ri-en′t′l), ***adj.*** [ME. *orientale*], 1. eastern. 2. [O-], of the Orient, its people, or their culture; Eastern. ***n.*** [usually O-], a native of the Orient or a member of a people native to that region. Opposed to *occidental, Occidental*. Abbreviated **Or.**

The designation *pl.* (or ***often pl., usually pl.***, etc.) before a definition means that the definition applies to the plural form of the entry word.

gill (gil), ***n.*** [ME. *gile, gille;* prob. < Anglo-N.; cf. ON. *gjǫlnar*, jaws, gills, older Dan. (*fiske*) *gæln*, Sw. *gäl;* IE. base **ghelunā-*, jaw, seen also in Gr. *chelynē*, lip, jaw], 1. the organ for breathing of most animals that live in water, as fish, lobsters, etc. 2. *often pl. a)* a red flap of flesh hanging below the beak of a fowl; wattle. *b)* the flesh under and about the chin and lower jaw of a person. 3. *pl.* the thin, leaflike, radiating plates on the undersurface of a mushroom.

The designation ***used in pl.*** (or ***often in pl., usually in pl.***, etc.) means that although the definition applies to the given singular form of the entry word, the word is used (or often used, usually used, etc.) in the plural.

hand·cuff (hand′kuf′), ***n.*** *usually in pl.* either of a pair of connected rings that can be locked about the wrists of a prisoner to keep him from using his hands, or to fasten him to a policeman.

The designations *sing.*, ***in sing.***, etc. are similarly used.

A colon after a definition generally means that the material that follows is not part of the definition proper but is additional information enlarging upon the factual content, examining the connotations, or indicating the usage of the term in the preceding sense.

fig·ur·a·tive (fig′yoor-ə-tiv), ***adj.*** [LL. *figurativus* < L.

. . . . .

another that may be thought of as analogous with it; metaphorical: to call a fierce fighting man a tiger is a figurative use of *tiger:* abbreviated **fig.** 4. containing or using figures of speech.

If instead of a colon there is a period followed by a capitalized word, the additional information applies to all the preceding senses (in that part of speech).

hy·dro- (hī′drō, hī′drə), [< Gr. *hydōr*, water], a combining form meaning: 1. water, as in *hydrostatic, hydrometer.* 2. in *chemistry, the presence of hydrogen,* as in *hydrocyanic*. Also, before a vowel, **hydr-.**

Examples of the use of a term or sense have been liberally supplied, also set off from the definition proper by a colon and preceded, generally, by the word *as.*

gar·nish (gär′nish), ***v.t.*** [ME. *garnischen* < base of OFr. *garnir, guarnir, warnir*, to protect; prob. < MHG. *warnen*, to equip oneself, prepare, protect], 1. to decorate; adorn; embellish; trim. 2. to decorate (food) with something that adds color or flavor: as, a steak is often *garnished* with parsley. 3. in *law*, to bring

The part-of-speech labels are entered in bold-face italics after the pronunciation, if any. All the senses following such a label (until the next part of speech or the end of the entry) are for that part of speech. In some instances where it was feasible to combine several parts of speech (e.g., ***n. & adj.*** or ***v.t. & v.i.***), this was done, so that the senses that follow apply to each part of speech.

Erse (ũrs), ***adj. & n.*** [Scot. var. of *Irish*], 1. formerly, Scottish Gaelic. 2. in *linguistics*, Irish Gaelic.

In definitions of transitive verbs the specific or generalized objects of the verb, where given, are enclosed in parentheses since such objects are not strictly part of the definition.

ex·hale (eks-hāl′, ig-zāl′), ***v.i.*** [EXHALED (-hāld′, -zāld′), EXHALING], [Fr. *exhaler;* L. *exhalare; ex-*, out + *halare*, to breathe], 1. to breathe forth air; expire. 2. to be given off or rise into the air as vapor; evaporate. ***v.t.*** 1. to breathe forth (air or smoke). 2. to give off (vapor, fumes, etc.).

Where certain verbs are, in usage, invariably or usually followed by a specific preposition or prepositions, this has been indicated in either of the following two ways: the preposition has been worked into the definition, italicized and enclosed in parentheses, or a note has been added after the definition indicating that the preposition is so used.

earth (ũrth), ***n.*** [ME. *erthe;* AS. *eorthe;* akin to G. *erde;* IE. base **er-t*, as also in MIr. *ert*, ground], 1. the

. . . . .

etc. ***v.t.*** 1. to embed in or cover (*up*) with soil for protection, as seeds, plants, or roots. 2. to chase (an

gloat (glōt), ***v.i.*** [prob. via dial. < AS. **glotian* or cognate ON. *glotta*, to grin scornfully; akin to G. *glotzen*, Eng. dial. *glout*, to stare; IE. base **ghlud-* < **ĝhel-*, etc., to shine, as in *glass, glow*], to gaze or meditate with malicious pleasure, exultation, or avarice (often with *over*).

In general the aim of the editors has been, wherever possible, to define in such terms that the definition could conceivably replace in context the word being defined.

It is theoretically possible to use almost any word as whatever part of speech is required, although most such uses would be only for the nonce. Thus any transitive verb can be used absolutely as an intransitive verb, with the object understood (e.g., he *defined* the word; you must *define* carefully). Such absolute uses are entered only when they are relatively common. In the same way nouns used as adjectives (e.g., a *cloth* cover; a *family* affair) are indicated only for the most frequent uses.

B. *Usage labels*

There is no universally accepted system of labeling the various levels of usage in English. It is generally understood that usage varies according to locality, degree of urbanization, level of education, occupation, etc., but any attempt to assign a specific label to every sense of every term entered would be highly complicated by the overlapping of categories and by the fact that most of the basic vocabulary of the language (as *run, house, man, pretty*) occurs at all levels of usage.

The best current practice recognizes that usage labels must be descriptive rather than authoritarian or condemnatory. In this light, the following labels could adequately describe the three basic levels: *formal* (for technical, scientific, and academic writing and for certain restricted types of platform address), *informal* (for the usual writing and speaking of most educated people, as most novels and plays, newspaper and magazine articles, and ordinary conversation), and *vulgate* (for slang and certain restricted shoptalk). It cannot be repeated too often, however, that such classification has no direct connection with *good* (or *standard*) *usage* and *bad* (or *substandard*) *usage.* What is good usage in a literary essay may not be the best usage in ordering groceries; what is good usage in a letter to a friend may not be the best usage in a scientific dissertation. Some slang often falls properly into *informal usage,* and some magazine articles often lean heavily upon *formal usage.*

After much deliberation, the editors of this dictionary decided that the familiarity of the more conventional usage designations makes their use advisable *if the meaning of these labels is clearly understood in advance.* The labels, and what they are intended to indicate, are given below. If the label, which is placed in brackets (and often abbreviated), occurs directly after a part-of-speech label, it applies to all the senses of that part of speech; if it occurs after a numeral, it applies only to the sense so numbered.

Colloquial: The term or sense is generally characteristic of conversation and informal writing. It is not to be regarded as substandard or illiterate.

Slang: The term or sense is not generally regarded as standard usage but is used, even by the best speakers, in occasional, highly informal contexts. Slang terms are generally short-lived but may survive and become part of the colloquial or informal vocabulary.

Obsolete: The term or sense is no longer used but occurs in earlier writings.

Archaic: The term or sense is rarely used today except in certain restricted contexts, as in church ritual, but occurs in earlier writings.

Poetic: The term or sense is used only in poetry or, occasionally, in prose where a poetic quality is desired.

Dialect: The term or sense is used regularly only in certain geographical areas.

British: The term or sense is characteristic of British, rather than American, English. When preceded by *especially*, it indicates an additional, though less frequent, American usage. Since this dictionary was prepared from the American point of view, terms and senses originating in or restricted to the United States are not so indicated. *British dialect* indicates that the term or sense is used regularly only in certain geographical areas of Great Britain, usually in northern England.

In addition to the above usage labels, supplementary information is often given after the definition, indicating whether the term or sense is generally regarded as obscene, vulgar, profane, or derogatory, used with ironic, familiar, or hyperbolic connotations, etc.

VI. *The Synonymies*

Synonyms are words that have nearly identical or closely related meanings in one or more of their senses. They are sometimes, but by no means always, interchangeable with one another in these senses. More often, the subtle differences that distinguish them are of greater importance to precision in language than their apparent equivalence. In this dictionary, such synonyms, or related words, are discriminated in a short paragraph entered after that word which may generally be considered the basic or most comprehensive one of the group. Distinctions in the meanings of the words are briefly stated and typical examples of usage given wherever these will be helpful.

SYN.—**happy** generally suggests a feeling of great pleasure, contentment, etc. (a *happy* marriage); **glad** implies more strongly an exultant feeling of joy (your letter made her so *glad*), but both **glad** and **happy** are commonly used in merely polite formulas expressing gratification (I'm *glad*, or *happy*, that you could come); **cheerful** implies a steady display of bright spirits, optimism, etc. (he's always *cheerful* in the morning); **joyful** and **joyous** both imply great elation and rejoicing, the former generally because of a particular event, and the latter as a matter of usual temperament (the *joyful* throngs, a *joyous* family). See also **lucky.**—***ANT.*** sad.

Each of the words discriminated in the example above is cross-referred to the entry for **happy,** where this synonymy appears. Thus, following the entry for **glad,** there is a note "***SYN.*** see **happy.**"

Whenever the basic word of a list is treated in another of its senses elsewhere, a cross reference is given to indicate this. Thus, "See also **lucky**" in the paragraph above means that the word **happy,** in its sense of "lucky" or "fortunate" is treated in the synonymy for **lucky.**

In many cases antonyms are given at the end of the synonymy and these, in turn, may receive discriminative treatment themselves. Thus, the antonym **sad** heads a synonymy that includes **melancholy, dejected, depressed,** and **doleful,** all antonymous to **happy.**

THE ENGLISH LANGUAGE

by Harold Whitehall

I. MODERN AMERICAN ENGLISH

A. Pronunciation

1.1 To most of us, the smallest practical unit of language is the *word*. All who can read, however, assume that words are built up from a limited number of distinctive "sounds" roughly corresponding to the letters of our alphabet. We are aware that they do not correspond exactly. When pressed for a description of these "sounds," we have to amplify such vague alphabetical indications as "the long *ī* of *bite*" or "the short *a* of *bat*" with further details intended to convey impressions to the ear: "the soft *g* of *gin*," "the hard *s* of *sits*," etc. Because modern spelling reflects the pronunciation of the 15th rather than that of the 20th century, such descriptions are of limited usefulness. A more scientific procedure is to separate our "sounds" from their surroundings and to study the details of their formation as we prolong or slow down their articulation.

1.2 The mechanism by which speech sounds are produced is best thought of as an extremely flexible wind instrument comparable in some respects to the bassoon, in others to the bagpipe. It comprises a bellows (the LUNGS), an inner resonator (the PHARYNX, or UPPER THROAT) with a double reed (the VOCAL BANDS) at its base, and two outer resonators, one fixed (the NASAL CAVITY) and one modifiable (the ORAL CAVITY, or MOUTH). Speech sounds result when an outflowing stream of air is pumped through this instrument by the bellows action of the lungs and is impeded or modified in various ways as it passes through the resonators toward the outer air. It should be noted that the primary purpose of this apparatus is not the production of sounds at all; its parts possess functions more closely connected with breathing and eating than with speaking. There are no vocal organs as such.

FIG. I

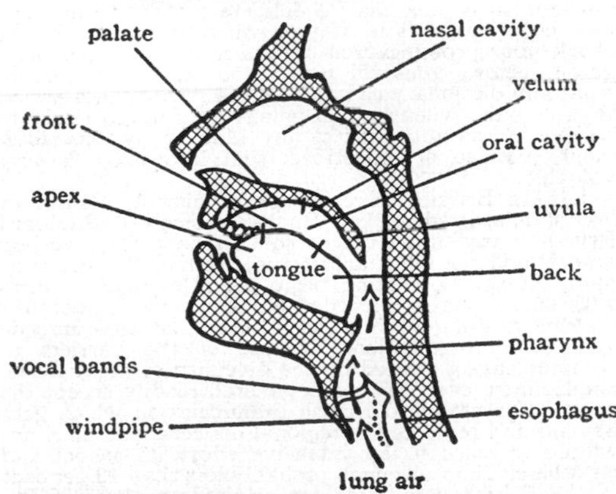

1.3 The double reed of the speech mechanism consists of two bands of membrane set in the top of the windpipe behind the thyroid cartilage (the Adam's apple of the male) and known as the VOCAL CORDS, or better, VOCAL BANDS. The modifiable outer resonator, the ORAL CAVITY, can be altered in shape, partially blocked, or completely blocked by action of the lips and tongue. Either of the two outer resonators can be shut off from the other by raising or lowering the VELUM, or SOFT PALATE, the soft, fleshy part at the rear of the roof of the mouth.

1.4 As outflowing breath streams upward from the lungs through the windpipe, it can first encounter the double-reed apparatus of our mechanism—the vocal bands. In ordinary breathing, these are drawn back transversely toward the left- and right-hand sides of the top of the windpipe; the GLOTTIS, or space between them, is widely opened; and the breath can pass by them without being checked or impeded. Sounds formed with the glottis thus opened are known as VOICELESS SOUNDS. If, however, the vocal bands are pulled close together and the glottis reduced to a mere slit, pressure of the upward-moving breath stream will induce a sinuous vibration of such sort that slight openings and closings of the edges of the vocal bands follow each other in rapid succession. This vibration is communicated to the moving breath stream itself and thence, in increasingly amplified form, to the moving column of air in the resonating chambers of the upper throat, mouth, and/or nasal cavity. The amplified vibration is heard as VOICE, a musical hum characteristic of VOICED SOUNDS. All English vowels and many English consonants are voiced; other consonants are voiceless: cf. voiced (z) in *zee* with voiceless (s) in *see*, voiced (v) in *vast* with voiceless (f) in *fast*, voiced (b) in *bit* with voiceless (p) in *pit*, etc. The distinction between voiced and voiceless, of primary importance in classifying sounds, reflects the first basic possibility of our vocal instrument. Another possibility is to narrow the glottis gradually toward the position for voice just before articulating certain other voiced sounds. This gradual narrowing is basic in producing the sound which we associate with the English letter *h*.

1.5 After the outflowing breath stream leaves the region of the glottis, it can next be diverted by the soft, fleshy part at the rear of the roof of the mouth—the VELUM, or SOFT PALATE. If the velum is so raised as to shut off the breath stream from the nasal cavity, the breath will escape through the mouth; if the velum is lowered and the breath stream blocked in the mouth by action of the lips or tongue, it will escape through the nasal cavity and the nostrils. The raising or lowering of the velum, therefore, gives us another phonetic possibility: when the breath escapes through and is further worked on in the mouth, we get ORAL SOUNDS; when the breath is blocked in the mouth and escapes through the nose, we get NASAL SOUNDS (cf. oral *b* in *bat* with nasal *m* in *mat*, oral *d* in *dash* with nasal *n* in *gnash*, etc.).

1.6 From the foregoing, it is clear that the vocal bands, velum, and nasal cavity, whatever their importance in the over-all activity of speaking, do not account solely for most individual speech sounds. The one exception in English is the unusually simple sound *h*, produced, as described above, by a progressive narrowing of the glottis. Most of our sounds are not so much articulated as co-articulated—produced by several simultaneous muscular movements working in concert. In sound production, the opening or closing of the glottis and the raising or lowering of the velum are of primary importance, but most of the audible distinctions between English sounds result from further modification of the outflowing breath stream caused by further muscular adjustments in the mouth. These movements, designed to produce various kinds of CAVITY FRICTION (i.e., the passage of the breath stream over the entire surface of cavities or chambers), LOCAL FRICTION, or MIXED FRICTION (cavity plus local friction) depend upon the action of the tongue and lips.

1.7 Within the mouth, the outflowing breath stream may be further modified in five principal ways. (1) It may be allowed to produce cavity friction in the resonance chambers molded by the positions of tongue, lips, and jaw. The resulting sounds, which add various mixtures of overtones to the basic voice hum according to the varying shapes assumed by the chambers, are commonly known as VOWELS. (2) The breath may be stopped completely along the center line of the tongue but allowed to escape along both sides: sounds thus formed, known as LATERALS, are exemplified by English (l), as in *let*. When the back of the tongue is also somewhat elevated as in the Middle Western (l) of *feel*, such sounds combine local friction with cavity friction. (3) The outflowing breath may be forced, with characteristic local frictional noises, through a narrow slit or groove formed between the teeth and lower lip or between the upper parts of the mouth and various parts of the tongue. Such sounds, which include English (f), (v), (s), (z), (th), (*th*), (sh), (zh), are known as FRICATIVES (SPIRANTS). (4) The breath may be stopped for a moment by movements of the lower lip or some part of the tongue and then released with some degree of local friction. Such sounds, as English (p), (b), (t), (d), (k), (g), are known as STOPS. (5) The breath may be lightly, rapidly, and intermittently stopped in such a manner that the tongue (or uvula), protruding elastically, executes either a single swift flip or a succession of flips under pressure of the breath stream. Sounds of this type, known as TRILLS and FLIPS, are known in American English only by the variety of (t) in Middle Western *water, butter*, etc. (6) Finally, the breath stream may be stopped in the mouth, so that pressure is built up behind the point of stoppage, and the main current of the outflowing air is allowed to escape, with cavity friction, through the nasal cavity. The sounds produced in this way (strictly, nasalized voiced stops) are known as NASALS: cf. (b) and (m), (d) and (n), (g) and (ŋ).

1.8 The capacities of the breath-stream mechanism so briefly described above are almost endless. We have seen how it resembles, in some points, the bassoon and bagpipe. We might add that few musical instruments of any kind can produce so many varied noises (SOUNDS) as this physiological instrument of ours. But after all, the primary purpose of speaking is communication, or, as Leonard Bloomfield phrases it, "to connect the speaker's stimulus with the hearer's response": if we used too many of these noises in speech the purpose of speaking would be defeated. In practice, every language has evolved its own particular system of sound-signals based not on all but on very few of the breath-stream mechanism's phonetic possibilities. Although the total number of these signals seldom exceeds forty in any language, it should be remembered that any particular signal may actually comprise several sounds closely related in articulation, and that one or more of these closely related sounds may serve as distinctive signals in other languages—that is, may be used to differentiate words and forms. Thus, the English sound signal (l) includes the purely consonantal (l) of *lit* and the vowellike, mixed-friction (l) of *feel;* in Polish, these two variants of our English signal (l) occur as two distinct sound signals used to differentiate words from each other. Similarly, the Spanish sound signal (ô) comprises two variants which resemble the distinctive English signals (ō) and (ô) heard in *boat* and *bought.* We may readily realize that a distinctive signal of one language may not occur in another (cf. the vowel (ü) of French *lune,* the consonant (kh) of German *Nacht*), that distinctive signals in one language or dialect may be merely variant forms of a single signal in another, and that the whole system of signals in one language or dialect may differ basically from the system of another. In examining any language or dialect, therefore, the first constructive step is to discover its distinctive sound signals—its PHONEMES, as we shall henceforth call them—and the system which they compose (PHONEMIC SYSTEM).

1.9 On pages xviii and xix is given one possible chart of the phonemes of North Central American English, both in symbols used by this dictionary and in those of the International Phonetic Association (IPA). Each phoneme is embodied within a short illustrative word. Whenever dialects, languages, or historical states of languages are to be contrasted or compared, the IPA symbols, which apply to the bundles of articulation features forming a speech sound irrespective of the spelling, are much to be preferred. In the chart, a new *sound* is conceived to have been made every time an articulator is moved either to constrict or to release the breath stream; but the phonemes (ch), (j), as the IPA symbols [tʃ], [dʒ] clearly show, actually involve two articulation movements. Similarly, the complex vowel phonemes known as DIPHTHONGS (not shown in the chart) involve a vowel articulation followed immediately by a glide of the articulator to an ending position which is that of another vowel: thus English (ī) can be thought of as (ä + i), IPA [aɪ]; English (ou) as (ä + oo), IPA [aʊ]; English (oi) as (ô or ō + i), IPA [ɔɪ] or [oɪ].

1.10 The chart is actually a graph of physiological sound-production, to be read horizontally from right to left for the action of articulating organs from glottis to lips and vertically, bottom to top, for the types of articulation from least to greatest total constriction (STRICTURE) of the breath stream. To describe the chief characteristics (PHONETIC FEATURES) of any phoneme, one needs only to read from right to left along the appropriate line and reproduce the column and line labels. Following this procedure, we find that the phoneme (s) is a voiceless, oral, tongue apex (apical) groove fricative; that (m) is a voiced, nasal, lip phoneme; and that (o͞o) is a voiced, oral, tongue-back, rounded, high-vowel phoneme. Similar descriptions for all the other phonemes can easily be made.

1.11 Implicit in the discussion of phonemes (see **1.9** above) is the notion that each one tends to appear in variant forms (ALLOPHONES) according to the environment in which it occurs. Phonemes are, after all, seldom encountered as individual utterances; they are realized as segments of a larger continuum of sound in words and word groups. It is natural enough, therefore, that they should be influenced by whatever is in close contact with them, whether it be other phonemes, pauses in the speech flow, or conditions of stress and the like. Whatever it be, all phonemes show some degree of positional variation caused by the environments in which they occur, just as signals formed by a semaphorist show slight variations of form according to the context of signals in which they occur. It is true that most of the variations are almost imperceptible except to a trained phonetician. The differences, for instance, between the (t) of *top*, which is aspirated (i.e., followed by a puff of breath) and the (t) of *stop*, which is not, become noticeable only when we listen with the utmost care. Yet these slight differences are important because they sometimes indicate boundaries between words and because what we call SOUND-CHANGE, whereby one phoneme may eventually become merged with, or change to, another, often starts from the weakest (i.e., least characteristic) positional variant of a phoneme. It is no accident that the distinction between *that's tough* and *that stuff* depends chiefly upon the aspirated initial (t) in the former, or that the weakly articulated flip (t) of *letter, water, patter, batter*, etc. has now become, in some parts of the Middle West, an allophone of the phoneme (d). If we wish to possess more than a cursory knowledge of our own speech, we need to know something about the allophones of our phonemes as well as about the phonemes themselves.

1.12 Every American belongs to one speech minority or another. The fact that we do not possess any single, accepted American standard pronunciation means, among other things, that different speakers use different allophones and even different phonemes in pronouncing the same words. Not that these differences seriously impede communication between us. The United States is actually one of the few large countries in the world where one may travel from border to border without changing language or running the risk of being seriously misunderstood. A *calf* is still a *calf* whether pronounced (kaf), IPA [kæf] or (käf), IPA [kaf or kɑf]. Even so, it is well to recognize that every reader of this dictionary has, in one sense or other, his own dialect, and that the pronunciation symbols of the dictionary, deliberately conceived with the widest possible applications, will mean different things to different readers. Even speakers from the central area of the country, who might be expected to feel particularly at home with the pronunciations entered here, will find divergencies of detail between what they actually say and what we indicate they might say. Such matters are not adequate grounds for social shame, linguistic fear, or self-condemnation. The dictionary is not intended as an instrument of torture or an arbiter of "correctness" but as a *generalized record of observed fact.* The truth is that nobody knows how he pronounces his own language until he has made a deliberate effort to find out how he pronounces it. If you will take the trouble to check your pronunciation system with the details suggested below, you will foster your understanding of what any dictionary can and cannot record. In a period such as ours, when human beings are far too ready to believe in the authority of any kind of written statement, justified or unjustified, that knowledge is very valuable.

1.13 In Britain, there is such a thing as a more or less standardized spoken English (Received Standard British) based upon the speech of the great boarding schools and the older universities. But in Britain, very many of the population begin their linguistic careers with one of the regional dialects as their sole speech—dialects so different from each other that they impede general communication. Because of the barriers to communication created by the diversity of the dialects, Englishmen, even Britons in general, readily accept the notion of a standard British pronunciation which goes beyond and replaces the regional dialects; and they are willing to learn it, by intensive effort, in school and elsewhere. Thus, although probably less than 10 per cent of the British population are original speakers of Received Standard British, it is universally accepted as desirable by educational authorities, by radio performers, and by the mass of the population. A dictionary of British English, therefore, can automatically adopt Received Standard British for its pronunciations.

1.14 In this country, the situation is otherwise. As previously mentioned, ours is probably the only nation on earth in which one can travel three thousand miles without encountering serious difficulties of oral communication. Regional differences in speech undoubtedly exist here: the speech of Maine is not like that of Georgia, nor is the speech of Texas like that of Minnesota. Yet, unless we deliberately exaggerate them for social or other reasons, our regional speech differences offer no great barrier to the free exchange of opinions and ideas. They consist more of flavor than of substance. Precisely for that reason, all the pressures ever exerted for the official adoption of a Received Standard American English comparable in scope with Received Standard British have proved unavailing. The practical necessity simply does not exist. In the affairs of American life, one may speak a Southern, Middle Atlantic, Chicago-Great Lakes, or Eastern New England English without any real disadvantage. The important thing is that we should speak, in a forceful, clear, and literate fashion, the variety of English of our upbringing.

1.15 The pronunciation recorded in this dictionary is largely that of General American, especially as used by literate speakers in the central part of the country. It represents a type of American English used, with relatively minor variations, in the whole of the Central, the Middle Western, the Northwestern Middle Western, the Western New England, and the Middle Atlantic States. It is the native speech of most of the editors of the dictionary. Since, however, many users of this book will speak other regional varieties of American English than the one we employ, and will undoubtedly read their own pronunciation patterns into the highly generalized symbols used by this dictionary, we shall give here a brief sketch of the principal types of American English as spoken on a literate level.

a) *Eastern New England* (*Coastal Northeastern*). In its most characteristic form, this type is confined to speakers native to the New England States east of the Connecticut River. In origins, it seems to be an American development of the middle-class speech of East Anglia, London, and the Home Counties in the 17th and 18th centuries. Since Received Standard British has much the same origin, it shares many features with the speech of Eastern New England. Especially notable are the following characteristics:

(1) Loss of final (r) and of (r) before consonants ("*r*-coloring") in such words as *far, farm, heard, sir, firm, force, course, beard, chair,* etc.

(2) Use of (r) as a link between contiguous vowels and between vowels and consonants in loose contact: *cloth* (klôrth), *law-and-order* (lôr ənd ôdə), etc.

(3) Use of either a low central vowel or a low back unrounded vowel (ä), IPA [ɑ or a], before the voiceless fricatives (f, s, th) and before (n) followed by a voiceless fricative or stop: *after* (äftə), *glass* (gläs), *path* (päth), *dance* (däns), *plant* (plänt), etc. This same sound is usually heard also in such words as *half* and *calf*.

(4) Use of a low back rounded vowel, IPA [ɒ], in *hot, rock, college, cot, rod,* etc., as well as in such words as *caught, salt, saw*.

(5) Use of (ä), or (o), as the first vowel of *horror, sorry, orange,* etc.

b) *Coastal and General Southern*. This type of American speech, often called, in its eastern Virginia and South Carolina forms, *Plantation Southern*, seems to be based on the upper-class London and Home Counties speech of the late 17th and early 18th centuries. Its chief characteristics are the following:

(1) Loss of final (r) and of (r) before consonants in such words as *far, farm, sir, heard, form, force, course, beard, chair,* etc. In *sir, heard,* etc., the vowel is usually a tense mid-central phoneme, IPA [ɜ], often made into the diphthong [ɜɪ] before a consonant. In *far, farm,* the vowel is usually a lengthened, low back rounded phoneme, IPA [ɒ].

(2) Loss or distinct weakening of the final vowel in the diphthongs of *dine, white, oil, toil*.

(3) Use of the general Southern diphthong (aoo), IPA [æʊ], in such words as *out, cow, house*. In Eastern Virginia, a circumflex diphthong (əo͞o), IPA [əu], occurs before voiceless consonants, while a falling diphthong (aoo), IPA [æʊ], normally appears before voiced consonants.

(4) Centralization or fronting of (o͞o), (oo) in such words as *moon, spoon,* and *book, good,* (IPA [mün], [spün], [bük], [güd]).

(5) Consistent occurrence of the semivowel (y) before (o͞o)—rendered (ū) in this dictionary—in such words as *due* (dū), *tune* (tūn), *news* (nūz).

(6) The breaking of the vowels (i, e, a, o, oo) into diphthongs, especially at points of pitch change: thus, *bid, bed, bad, rod* are normally (biəd, beəd, baəd, roəd).

c) *Southern Mountain* (*Highland Southern, South Midland*). This speech type appears to be a Southern Appalachian blend of General Southern with Pennsylvania speech. Today, however, it is heard over the central lower Mississippi valley (sometimes in local competition with General Southern), and in East Texas, Arkansas and parts of Oklahoma, Eastern Kansas, Missouri, Southern Illinois, Southern and Central Indiana, Southern Ohio, and Southern Pennsylvania. Its range is furthest north in Central Indiana. Southern Mountain speech shares characteristics 2, 3, 4, 5, 6 in *b* above with General Southern, but retains *r* (more accurately, an "*r*-coloring" of the vowel) in such words as *far, farm, heard, sir, form, force, chair,* etc. Other features, some shared with other dialects, but specially significant for the contrast with the speech of the Central Middle Western States, are as follows:

(1) Raising and diphthongization of (e) before *g*, as in *egg* (āig), *leg* (lāig), *keg* (kāig). This usually accompanies a related lengthening of (i), and a distinct diphthongization of (a), before *g*.

(2) The front vowel (e) often appears as (i) before nasals, especially in such words as *ten, tennis, penny, pen,* etc. Among cultivated speakers in the northern part of the Southern Mountain area, this is now regarded as substandard.

(3) The front vowel (i) is usually lowered and diphthongized to (āi) or (ei) before (ŋ), as in *thing, think, ink,* etc.

(4) The *s* of *greasy, absorb,* is usually (z).

(5) The vowel of *dish, fish,* and the final vowel of *city, charity,* etc. occurs as (ē) in many parts of the area.

(6) The word *wash* is often pronounced (wôrsh) or (wärsh).

(7) The vowel (ō) often appears as a diphthong with a fronted first element parallel with the fronting in *spoon, good,* etc. Example: *boat* (bəōt). Because of the migration of workers from the South in World War II, Southern Mountain speech is now heard sporadically in such Northern industrial cities as Chicago, Detroit, and Cleveland.

d) *General American* (*North Midland, North Central, Western*). Since this is the type of pronunciation recorded in this dictionary, it deserves fairly detailed attention here. Its general phonemic system, or rather, one of its systems, has been illustrated in section 1.9 above. The following details are significant:

(1) Final (r) and (r) before consonants ("*r*-coloring") are everywhere retained in such words as *far, farm, heard, sir, firm, force, course, beard,* and *chair*.

(2) The vowel (o), IPA [ɑ] or [a], in *hot, rock, college, cot, rod,* etc., contrasts with the vowel (ô), IPA [ɔ] of such words as *caught, salt, all, law*. (But cf. *Western Pennsylvania* below.)

(3) The vowel in such words as *horror, sorry, orange* is usually (ô), IPA [ɔ], in contrast to the (o), IPA [ɑ], of the Coastal East and General Southern. (But cf. *Middle Atlantic* below.)

(4) The diphthongs (ou), (ī), (oi) occur as [ɑʊ] or [aʊ], [ɑɪ] or [aɪ], and [ɔɪ] or [oɪ].

(5) After the apical consonants (t), (d), (n) the vowel (o͞o) is not normally preceded by the semivowel (y) as in the Southern dialects.

(6) The vowels (i, e, a, o, oo) completely lack the diphthongization heard in the Southern dialects.

(7) The phonemes (ā) and (ō) are less obviously diphthongized than in other regional varieties of American speech.

(8) The vowels in the classes of words represented by *Mary, marry, merry* have generally coalesced under the same sound, usually (e), IPA [ɛ].

(9) The back vowels (o͞o), (oo), and (ō) are not centralized or fronted. (But cf. *Middle Atlantic* below.)

(10) The vowel in *after, pass, path, dance,* etc. is (a), IPA [æ], not (ä), IPA [a, ɑ], as in Eastern New England speech.

(11) The vowel (e) is not raised and diphthongized before *g* as it is in Southern Mountain speech.

(12) The *s* in *greasy, absorb* is usually (s), rather than (z) as in the South and in Eastern New England.

In its widest geographical sense, General American includes several subtypes. As research progresses, we are likely to discover more of them and to discard the use of the term General American itself. (1) The *Middle Atlantic* type is chiefly characterized by the fronting of (o͞o) and (ō) and by its low back unrounded vowel (o), IPA [ɑ], in *horror, sorry, orange*. (2) The *Western Pennsylvania* type often possesses the low back unrounded vowel, IPA [ɑ], both in *hot, rock, college, rod,* etc. and in *caught, salt, law,* etc. This is obviously a mixed dialect, reproduced further west in some of the Ohio River towns and in the Southwest. (3) The *West Central* type, spoken in Chicago and on the southern shores of the Western Great Lakes area, has (ä), both in *hot, rock, college, rod,* etc. and in *father, balm, alms*.

1.16 This brief survey of the four principal varieties of American speech does some injustice to the varied and subtle regional modifications of the American language. Several of the large cities, notably New York City, have developed or are in the process of developing their own characteristic speech patterns, while the Southern Piedmont possesses a variety of speech quite distinct from either General Southern or Southern Mountain, although it incorporates features found in both. Our present knowledge of the allophonic, and sometimes of the phonemic, variations present in American speech is the measure of our comparative ignorance rather than of our knowledge of the subject.

Syllables

2.1 Thus far, we have been chiefly concerned with phonemes as isolated sound-signal units. It is time to put them into the contexts of actual speech and to study them in combination with the various contextual factors (PROSODIC FEATURES) which influence them.

2.2 When we study a succession of phonemes in an utterance, the first thing that strikes us is a marked variation of prominence (SONORITY) between them. For instance, in the word *limitation* (limətāshən),

FIG. II

THE DISTINCTIVE SOUND-SIGNAL UNITS (PRIMARY PHONEMES) OF NORTH CENTRAL AMERICAN ENGLISH

A. In the pronunciation symbols of this dictionary

← RELATIVE INCREASE OF OVER-ALL STRICTURE — RELATIVE INCREASE IN SONORITY →

TYPE OF ARTICULATION		ARTICULATOR: LIP	TONGUE APEX	TONGUE FRONT	TONGUE CENTER	TONGUE BACK	CO-ARTICULATION: VELUM—In position for:	GLOTTIS—In position for:
STOP	Local Friction	(**p**)in (**b**)in	(**t**)in (**d**)in			(**k**)in (**g**)ive	oral oral	voiceless voiced
FRICATIVE Breath release through: 1. Slit 2. Groove	Local Friction	(**f**)in (**v**)im	(**th**)in (***th***)en (**s**)in (**z**)inc	(**sh**)in a(z)ure (**zh**)			oral oral oral oral	(**h**)im—voiceless voiced voiceless voiced
AFFRICATE (= stop & neighboring fricative)	Local Friction		(**ch**)est [= **t** + **sh**] (**j**)est [= **d** + **zh**]				oral oral	voiceless voiced
LATERAL	Mixed Friction		(**l**)imb				oral	voiced
NASAL	Mixed Friction	(**m**)an	(**n**)an			sa(ng) (**ŋ**)	nasal	voiced
SEMIVOWEL (= vowellike sound used as consonant)	Mixed Friction			(**y**)ield	(**r**)eeled	(**w**)ield	oral	voiced
VOWEL Relative tongue position:	Cavity Friction	co-articulation					oral (all vowels)	voiced! (all vowels)
1. High	Cavity Friction	(o͞o) rounded (oo) rounded		b(ee)t (**ē**) b(i)t (**i**)		b(oo)t (**o͞o**) b(oo)k **oo**		
2. Mid	Cavity Friction	(ō) rounded (ô) rounded		b(ai)t (**ā**) b(e)t (**e**)	{b(u)tt (**u**) sof(a) (**ə**)}	b(oa)t (**ō**) b(ou)ght (**ô**)		
3. Low	Cavity Friction			b(a)t (**a**)	f(a)ther (**ä**)	b(o)x (**o**)		

FIG. II

THE DISTINCTIVE SOUND-SIGNAL UNITS (PRIMARY PHONEMES) OF NORTH CENTRAL AMERICAN ENGLISH

B. In the symbols of the International Phonetic Alphabet (IPA)

← RELATIVE INCREASE OF OVER-ALL STRICTURE —— RELATIVE INCREASE IN SONORITY →

TYPE OF ARTICULATION		ARTICULATOR: LIP	ARTICULATOR: TONGUE APEX	ARTICULATOR: TONGUE FRONT	ARTICULATOR: TONGUE CENTER	ARTICULATOR: TONGUE BACK	CO-ARTICULATION: VELUM—In position for:	CO-ARTICULATION: GLOTTIS—In position for:
STOP	Local Friction	pɪn bɪn	tɪn dɪn			kɪn gɪv	oral oral	voiceless voiced
FRICATIVE Breath release through: 1. Slit 2. Groove	Local Friction	fɪn vɪm	θɪn ðɛn sɪn zɪŋk	šɪn [ʃ] æžər [ʒ]			oral oral oral oral	(h)ɪm—voiceless voiced voiceless voiced
AFFRICATE (= stop & neighboring fricative)	Local Friction		čɛst [tʃ] ǰɛst [dʒ]				oral oral	voiceless voiced
LATERAL	Mixed Friction		lɪm				oral	voiced
NASAL	Mixed Friction	mæn	næn			sæŋ	nasal	voiced
SEMIVOWEL (= vowellike sound used as consonant)	Mixed Friction			jild	rild	wild	oral	voiced
VOWEL Relative tongue position:	Cavity Friction	co-articulation					oral (all vowels)	voiced (all vowels)
1. High	Cavity Friction	(u) rounded (ʊ) rounded		bit bɪt		but bʊk		
2. Mid	Cavity Friction	(o) rounded (ɔ) rounded		bet bɛt	{bʌt {sofə	bot bɔt		
3. Low	Cavity Friction			bæt	faðər	bɑks		

[lɪmətešən], phonemes 2, 4, 6, 8, are obviously more prominent in their relative sonority than the others; in *oscillator* (osəlātĕr), [ɑsəletər], this same prominence occurs in phonemes 1, 3, 5, 7. On further analysis, we find that all of these prominent phonemes, (i), (ə), (ā), (o), etc. are cavity friction sounds (i.e., vowels) bordered either by less prominent phonemes possessing mixed or local friction, or by silence. In essence, then, any speech flow consists of a series of peaks and troughs of prominence with sonorous cavity-friction phonemes at the peaks and less sonorous phonemes or silence (pause) at the troughs. A glance at Fig. II makes it clear that this variation in the sonority of phonemes depends upon the relative degree of stricture. In the chart, sonority decreases from the bottom of the diagram, where the breath stream is represented as least constricted, to the top, where it is most constricted. If we use the symbol 1 to characterize the most sonorous (cavity-friction) sounds, 2 to indicate the less sonorous (mixed-friction) sounds, and 3 to symbolize the least sonorous (local-friction) sounds, then the peaks and troughs of sonority in our examples may be easily diagrammed:

21 2131 312 13121312
(limə tā shən), (osə lāt ĕ r).

Now reference to the syllabification in this dictionary will immediately show that the words *limitation, oscillator,* i.e., *lim/i/ta/tion, os/cil/la/tor,* possess just as many 1's as they possess syllables. In other terms, the most obvious thing about syllables is that they are *peaks of prominence bordered by troughs of less prominence.* The phonemes at the peaks are called SONANTS; those at the troughs are called CONSONANTS.

2.3 This explanation, however, does not completely account for syllables. As can be easily seen if we prolong (ä), [ɑ], and at the same time hit the chest repeatedly with a fist, the pumping action of the lungs (CHEST PULSE) is a vital factor in syllable formation. Further, since the less sonorous phonemes constrict the breath stream, hence slow down expiration, and thus retard lung action, that action is relatively slow at the troughs, and relatively fast at the peaks, of sonority. Like everything else in speech, the syllable is relatively complex in its mechanical formation.

2.4 No one is likely to have much trouble in counting the number of syllables in a word. To decide where one syllable ends and another begins, however, is a matter of such difficulty that linguistic science is still unable to provide a simple formula for syllable division in English. Neither the system of division used in this dictionary nor any other yet devised really squares with the observable facts of the English language. *The separation of syllables in this and similar books is merely a graphic convenience,* intended to help printers to be consistent. Its virtues are esthetic, not linguistic. Perhaps the only scientific method of practical syllabification would depend upon the etymological and formative elements present in words. Meanwhile, we continue to use, and, unfortunately, to have represented to us as factual, a system which is neither logical in itself nor based in any degree on the ascertained characteristics of our language.

2.5 In our consideration of syllables, it is well to remember that the details of their formation may vary considerably in different languages. In English, the phonemes at the peaks of sonority are all, according to one conventional interpretation, cavity friction sounds (VOWELS). Phonetically, however, the pronunciation of such words as *battle, bottle, border,* and *batten* as

313 2 313 2 312 3 2 313 2
(bat′l, bot′l, bôr′dĕr, bat′n)

shows the possibility of employing such mixed-friction phonemes as (l), (r), (n) as sonants. We find them thus employed in several languages. Similarly, the vowel in *bird, sir, stir, curd,* etc., symbolized in this dictionary by (ŭr), IPA [ər] or [ɜ˞] may be regarded with equal justification as an "*r*-vowel" to be symbolized as in Czech by simple *r*:

323 32 332 323
(brd), (sr), (str), (krd).

The unusual English exclamation *pst!* acquaints us with the possibility, actually used in some languages, of employing the more sonorous fricatives as peaks of sonority in syllables.

2.6 Similar differences between various languages are also apparent at the troughs of sonority. Among languages other than English, some begin syllables only with sonants, some end them only with sonants, some begin or end them only with single consonants, and some permit only a single consonant between syllables. English syllables can commence and end with sonants, with single consonants, and with clusters of as many as three consonants (we shall disregard inflectional endings) before and after the peak of the syllable: cf. *strict, quartz.* Any possible combination of these may occur between syllables.

2.7 The exceptionally flexible structure of the English syllable is not difficult to understand once we realize that the essential nucleus, the sonant, stands at a peak of sonority, which may be attained or departed from either swiftly or gradually. The presence of consonant clusters implies gradual ascent or descent in relative sonority, i.e., it has somewhat the same effect as that of initial (h) on the voicing of a following vowel.

2.8 It must not be thought that any consonant may adjoin any other consonant in the above scheme. The permissible clusters of consonants are in part conditioned by historical but chiefly by physiological factors. These include the following: (1) whether two phonemes which might adjoin in the same cluster have the same articulator; (2) whether they have the same type of articulation; (3) whether they are both voiced or voiceless; (4) whether they have the same or varying conditions of stricture; (5) whether, especially in phonemes of the same articulation type, one is slightly more *prominent* than the other. Thus *r*, an apical consonant, is never preceded by *s*, also apical; stops do not combine initially with stops, etc. In initial clusters, and in some dialects in final clusters, English appears to insist upon a certain degree of differentiation between contiguous consonants.

Stress and Related Phenomena

3.1 Our consideration of the syllable has shown that in any *series of phonemes* within an utterance, certain phonemes are more prominent than others. Those prominent phonemes, we have seen, are the chief determinants of what we call syllables. When we come to consider a *series of syllables* in an utterance, we likewise find that certain syllables are more prominent than others. In *limitation, oscillator,* for instance, the syllables *-tā-* and *os-* obviously carry more relative prominence than any others in these two words, and, if we listen closely to our own pronunciation, we shall find that *lim-* and *-lāt-*, although less prominent than *-tā-* and *os-*, are still more prominent than the other syllables surrounding them. In conventional dictionary terms, we should say that the prominent syllables are *stressed,* i.e., pronounced with more vigor or intensity of articulation, than the remaining *unstressed* syllables. In short, we should regard stress, the relative loudness or intensity of syllables conditioned by the relative energy of articulation, as the factor producing differences of prominence between successive syllables. This dictionary distinguishes between *primary,* or *strong,* stress, here marked by superscript (**′**) *after* the syllable to which it applies, and *secondary,* or *light,* stress, marked by superscript (′) *after* the syllable to which it applies, *reduced secondary* stress, to be inferred when an apparently unstressed syllable has any other vowel than (ə), and *unstress,* or *zero* stress, which is left unmarked. Thus *lim′i-ta′tion* (lim′ə-tā′shən), *os′il-la′tor* (os′ə-lā′-tĕr), etc. The reader should be warned that the individual perception of stress varies greatly. Most users of this dictionary will have little difficulty in distinguishing between the four stress levels mentioned above, but some may find it difficult to discriminate between reduced secondary stress and zero stress, or even between secondary and primary stress. The laboratory phonetician can perceive additional stress levels by means of his instruments.

3.2 In English, the placing of stress is phonemic, i.e., significant for the expression of meaning. All our words except monosyllabic words have a definite stress pattern or, more occasionally, patterns, which play an important role in our recognition of them. Notice that the hearing recognition of *insight* as compared with *incite* depends upon the primary stress of its first syllable (in′sīt′) as compared with the stress on the second syllable of the latter (in-sīt′). Among most speakers, such words as *inlay, impact, address, import, imprint, increase, contrast, contract, insult, insert, contest, protest, convert, converse, convict, protect, conflict, rebel, transfer* are stressed on the first syllable when used as nouns, on the second when used as verbs. This alternation of stress pattern, however, is not uniformly applied in the English-speaking world, and the number of words affected by it varies somewhat from region to region. In New England, for instance, a *selectman* is often called a (sē′lek-man′); in many parts of the country you *po-lice′* the town but call in the *po′lice.* Because stress patterns in English are meaningful, it is often necessary to memorize these patterns for relatively unfamiliar words. Our native words of Anglo-Saxon and Germanic origin present little difficulty since the stress almost invariably falls upon the most important formative element in them (the BASE): *man, man′ly, man′li-ness, un-man′, un-man′ly,* etc. But in the other part of our vocabulary, comprising words chiefly of Latin, French, or Greek origin, many words show a change in stress pattern when formative elements (suffixes) are added to them: *ha′bit, ha-bit′ual, e′qual, e-qual′i-ty,* etc. The realistic method of looking at this phenomenon is to think of such words as existing in two forms: (1) a word-form. (2) a combining form (stem-form). Thus, we might contrast the word-forms *ha′bit, e′qual, pho′to-graph′,* etc. with the combining forms *ha-bit′-, eq-ual′-, pho-tog′raph-,* used in forming derivatives. Since, in many words, the fixed stress patterns of the native English tradition come into conflict with the shifting patterns of the Greco-Latin tradition, different speakers may stress certain words in different ways. Not the least important function of a dictionary is to indicate those variants in stress pattern which are used by well-informed speakers of the language, and, by implication, to suggest those which are not so used.

3.3 We have said that any English word spoken individually possesses a definite stress pattern (RESIDUAL STRESS PATTERN); when words are uttered in contexts, however, this pattern may or may not be preserved or left unmodified. The primary stresses of an utterance tend to occur at somewhat regular time intervals, usually on the key modifiers and nouns in the subject, on the noun complements of the sentence, and on the kernel words of phrases. The more words intervene between these strong stresses, the more their syllables tend to be crushed together and the word stresses to be weakened or suppressed. Thus, the *lexical* stress pattern apparent when a word is pronounced singly or in one of the rhythmically stressed positions of a phrase or sentence often fails to correspond exactly with the stress pattern of the same word as it occurs in the unstressed positions of continuous utterance. A dictionary, naturally enough, indicates the *lexical stress pattern* of the word rather than the modified variants which may occur in actual speaking. You need not be surprised, nor accuse yourself of careless speaking, if you occasionally find that the form used in one of your utterances does not exactly coincide with the form given by this book. English spoken without the natural rhythm of English is scarcely English at all. Moreover, one of the characteristics of our language is an extra-strong stress (EMPHATIC STRESS) which may be applied to any syllable in an utterance for special emphasis of meaning irrespective of the natural stress patterns possessed by the words as individual units. This also tends to modify somewhat the stress patterns of words next to it.

3.4 In addition to STRESS, two other factors affect the relative prominence of certain syllables, particularly in spoken contexts. The more important of these is PITCH, i.e., the relative lowness or highness of the frequency of voice hum in the enunciation of sonants and voiced consonants. The other is LENGTH, i.e., the relative duration of sonants and some consonants. Generally speaking, syllables under stress tend to have higher pitch and longer duration of the sonant than those not stressed. Pitch, however, is chiefly important as indicating the *attitudes* of speakers to what they are saying in continuous utterances and as representing the nonconventional element underlying English punctuation. Length is seldom meaningful in American English, except to speakers who may discriminate *balm* as [baam] from *bomb* as [bam] or those who, through assimilation, pronounce such words as *nests*, *rests* as [nɛss], [rɛss], with a lengthened final consonant. Thus, although this dictionary, following common practice, distinguishes the vowel (o͞o) of *spoon* from the vowel (oo) of *good*, and the vowel (ā) of *cane* from the vowel (a) of *can* by using the (¯) which is the conventional diacritic applied to long vowels, the reader should understand that it refers not to length but to a difference of quality between the sounds thus discriminated. We do not indicate pitch at all, although single words spoken as individual utterances show definite patterns of falling pitch: (1) In monosyllabic words, the pitch normally glides downward during the articulation of the vowel: *bad. good. house. home.* (2) In words of two syllables of which the first is stressed, the down glide of the pitch occurs at the point of syllable juncture: *blackbird. holy.* etc. You can best recognize this falling pitch by contrasting it with the rising pitch heard when the same words are used as questions: *bad? good? blackbird?* Nowadays, linguists are pretty well agreed that English is spoken on four levels of pitch of which two (high and extra high pitch) are above the usual voice level and one (low pitch) below it. Of these, however, the extra high pitch may well be a variant of the high pitch, one used when an utterance is surcharged with emotion, while the normal voice level seems to be nondistinctive in itself. Perhaps the best way to understand the pitch schemes of English is to consider that any *change* from the normal voice level, in combination with a following optional or obligatory pause, signifies something about the sentence in which it occurs: it may mark a center of attention within the sentence, or indicate the end of the sentence, or, according to its direction of change, distinguish the sentence as being a statement, question, or the like. Pitch changes reinforce the stress patterns of the language and help to produce the relatively even-timed rhythm which characterizes continuous utterance in spoken English. The principal domain of pitch, however, is the sentence, while that of stress is the word and the phrase. (For further information on pitch, the reader is referred to Kenneth L. Pike, *The Intonation of American English* [Ann Arbor, Michigan, University of Michigan Press, 1945].)

B. The Chief Grammatical Features

4.1 To a person who speaks English the statement "man dog chase" would seem strange and unsatisfactory. The individual words, it is true, are symbolically related to two objects and to an event, and the two objects in question and the event referred to are commonly encountered in our everyday world. Thus we cannot say that "man dog chase" does not possess "meaning." Yet taken together the three words do not, for us who speak English, make a satisfactory statement. Why not? Because the three words suggest a whole range of practical possibilities, no one of which could be isolated with any confidence from the context. For example, did the dog chase the man? Is the man chasing the dog? Will the man chase the dog? To limit these possibilities, to make the context understandable—in short, to put the sentence into the form of a grammatical statement in English—other linguistic features are required:

A dog chased the man.

4.2 This is a much more satisfactory statement, more satisfactory in that it includes certain relations between our original three words that are necessary for the meaning, yet relations that the three words are incapable of expressing in themselves. As we see when we contrast the two forms of the statement, these relations are expressed through certain specific linguistic devices:

(a) *Man dog chase*

(b) *A dog chased the man.*

(1) The relation between *dog* as the actor, *chase* as the action, and *man* as the goal of the action is indicated by arranging our three original words in a one, two, three order. (2) The time of the event described in relation to the time at which the writer is describing it is indicated by adding *-d* (pronounced t) to *chase.* (3) The relation of the objects *dog* and *man* to the writer's previous experience of them is indicated by placing *a* before *dog* and *the* before *man.* Notice that the final effect of expressing these relations through these specific devices is to select from a bundle of possible suggestions the particular ones relevant to a single actual situation. If we are willing to accept "a dog chased the man" as a grammatical statement of something not grammatically expressed in the series "man dog chase," then the function of the devices of grammar becomes plain. They show themselves to be an apparatus for limiting the suggestions of juxtaposed words. The trouble with "man dog chase," was, as we saw, that it could express *too many* situations. The grammatical devices limit the suggestions of the words to a single situation.

4.3 In a sense, our example illustrates the nature of all linguistic expression, and especially that of English. All utterances and written symbolizations of utterance include elements like *man, dog,* and *chase* which are symbolically correlated with objects, processes, events, and so forth in the world around us. Such elements possess what might be called *practical* meaning. But utterances also include certain features, whether expressed through words or through lesser units, which merely serve to indicate various kinds of relations between the elements of *practical* meaning—features not correlated symbolically with anything in the outside world, and possessing only *grammatical* meaning. Thus, the *-d* added to *chase* indicates "past time"; *the,* as placed before *man,* implies something like "previously noticed, mentioned, identified, or experienced"; *a,* as placed before *dog,* means "not previously noticed, mentioned, identified, or experienced"; the order of the words *dog chase man* shows that *dog* is the actor, *chase,* the action, and *man,* the goal to which the action is directed. Even the apparently insignificant period at the end of the sentence possesses grammatical meaning, since it symbolizes the final pause and the marked fall of pitch by which we mark the end of the spoken declarative sentence. It indicates "end of statement." A complete paraphrase of our simple example in such terms as these would give the following total linguistic meaning: (*a previously, unidentified*) *DOG* (*actor*) *CHASE* (*action*) + (*past time*) (*a previously identified*) *MAN* (*goal of the action*) (*end of statement*). Thus, what seemed to be logically simple turns out to be linguistically complex.

4.4 Such individual paraphrases, however interesting, are not systematically rewarding. No matter how varied may be those elements of language that possess *practical meaning,* the elements used to express relations between them, and the relations so expressed are relatively few. Words for objects, events, and qualities refer to everything we know about the world and ourselves; *practical meaning* encompasses the whole of human knowledge, but the features of *grammatical meaning* can apply only to a mere handful of relations and relational concepts. For instance, the element *-d,* which we added to *chase* to imply "past time," occurs also in *looked, hooked, stepped, shipped, ripped, asked,* and a host of other English verbal forms, always with the same grammatical meaning; and *the* and *a,* in the meanings assigned to them, are commonplaces of English expression. It is convenient, therefore, to work out serviceable descriptions of such features, and to define, as accurately as will serve our purposes, the grammatical relations they express. The result will be a descriptive grammar. From this standpoint, English grammar is merely a survey of devices used to indicate customary grammatical relations, together with a summary of the relations themselves.

4.5 Before proceeding further, we must clearly understand that what we call grammar varies from language to language—that very few grammatical relations are common to all languages, and that the grammatical devices of one language need not necessarily recur in another. There is no such thing as universal grammar. In our example, *A dog chased the man*(.), the order of the words is of primary importance, for *A man chased the dog*(.) would also refer to an entirely real-life situation. Yet Latin allows *pater filio librum dat, librum dat filio pater*, etc. (*the father gives the son a book*), without changing the grammatical relations or altering anything except the relative emphasis on the words of the sentence. At the same time, the Latin sentence is a perfectly satisfactory Latin statement even though it lacks equivalents for English *the* or *a* in association with the nouns *pater, filius*, and *liber*, whereas *father son book gives* would be impossible in English. English grammar, then, involves a certain grammatical device—the use of *the* and *a* employed to express a certain grammatical relationship (definiteness versus indefiniteness)—that Latin, for the most part, can dispense with. Conversely, Latin gets along perfectly well without another grammatical device (fixed word order) that English cannot dispense with.

4.6 This simple instance of the contrast of two grammatical resources in English and Latin could be multiplied. Of the two or three thousand languages that are spoken or have been spoken on earth, relatively few possess or have possessed a primary grammatical device of fixed word order comparable to that in Modern English. Many languages indicate the grammatical relations expressed by our prepositions through changes in the form of words; such *case forms*, as they are called, vary in number from the five or six of the Latin noun to the twenty-three of the noun of Georgian (the South Caucasian language spoken natively by Joseph Stalin) and to the possible forty-eight to fifty-two of a few little-studied languages. English nouns are officially classified as *masculine, feminine*, and *neuter* according to the sexual status of the objects, processes, etc. to which they refer. Yet French knows only the masculine and feminine genders, Latin could use either *flumen* (neuter) or *fluvius* (masculine) for river, and in both German and Anglo-Saxon the word for *woman* (German *Weib*, Anglo-Saxon *wīf*) is of neuter gender. To take more extreme cases, Eskimo has no gender system at all, while Bantu arranges its nouns according to a system of seventeen to twenty-three classes quite dissociated from anything approaching sex. There are languages which have tenseless verbs and languages which have tense verbs; languages with singular, dual, and plural number; languages with a single third-person singular masculine pronoun, and languages with three of them, all serving a definite grammatical purpose. Language is as pigheaded and stubborn about its grammatical relationships and classifications as the human minds that have evolved it—and as illogical. It follows, therefore, that the grammar of any given language must be studied in terms of that language itself. Attempts to make any one language conform to the details of another lead either to total failure or to a "grammar" which, like the Procrustean bed, encourages the lopping off of that which it cannot contain. No language has a strictly logical grammar. No language has a perfectly unambiguous internal structure. Yet of any language we can say what Louis Chevrolet reputedly said when he invented the automobile clutch, "It's brutal! But it works!"

4.7 Amid the welter of varied linguistic features, two important grammatical relations seem to be held in common by all known languages: (1) some kind of actor-action-goal (or, in more conventional terms, subject-predicate-object) relation; (2) some kind of relation between names of objects and modifying qualities. If, in real life, a *big man* and a *white dog* are involved in an act of *following*, the essential minimum of information needed to describe the act would be that telling (a) which did the *following* and which was *followed*, and (b) which was *big* and which was *white*. The manner in which this necessary information is linguistically indicated represents the irreducible minimum grammar of any language. Further information, such as when the act took place (*tense*), how the reporter regards it emotionally (*mood* or *mode*), whether he thinks of it as a finished action or as one proceeding in the past (*aspect*), whether he has previous recognition of the man and/or the dog (*definiteness*), whether the dog is male or female (*gender*), etc., might be helpful, but, for basic comprehension of the reported situation, not indispensable. Hence, the amount of further information given grammatically would tend to vary according to the pattern of the language in which the action happened to be expressed.
In Modern English, both the obligatory subject-predicate-object relation and the obligatory noun-modifier relation are expressed through the device of fixed word-order, our principal and indispensable grammatical device:

A big man followed the white dog.

Here, the subject (*actor*) *man* precedes the predicate verb (*action*) *followed*, and the object (*action-goal*) *dog* follows the action; similarly, the modifiers *big* and *white* immediately precede the words they modify, *man* and *dog*. Modern English, then, is basically a word-order language.

4.8 In many other languages, the irreducible minimum of grammatical relation would be normally expressed by the device of what has been called "like signaling"—that is, by the addition of signal-elements (called *inflections*) to the ends of word-elements. In Latin we might encounter such a sentence as *vir magnus illUM canEM albUM sequebatur*, "A big man followed that white dog," where the elements *-EM. -UM* show that all the words thus signalized are parts of the object of the sentence, and (b) that the modifiers *ill*(*um*) and *alb*(*um*) are associated with *can*(*em*). In Anglo-Saxon, the lineal ancestor of Modern English, our sentence about the man and the dog would owe its structure to the same signaling device:

Se greata mann thone hwitan hund folgode,

or

Folgode thone hund hwitan se greata mann,

or

Thone hwitan hund folgode se greata mann.

In terms of linguistic meanings indicated by signals (*inflections*), the first of these might be paraphrased as: THE (in subject-masculine-definite determiner) GREAT (in subject-masculine-modifier) MAN (in subject) THE (in object-masculine-definite-determiner) WHITE (in object-masculine-modifier) DOG (in object) FOLLOW (past time, hence, verb). Latin and Anglo-Saxon, then, like Greek, Sanskrit, and a great many other languages whose grammar is best known, are basically "like-signaling" or inflectional languages; that is, they express the obligatory grammatical relations not through word order but through inflection.

4.9 Now the grammar of an inflectional language will no more mix with that of a word-order language than oil with water; yet in the past, descriptions of English grammar have been modeled after those of the grammars of Latin and Greek—the two languages whose structure Western civilization first came to know. This fact may account for the difficulty which modern students frequently have with "English grammar," for, although nowadays the normal English speaker has had no Latin at all or has had only a superficial acquaintance with Latin, he has been compelled to look at his own language through the forms of another language of a radically different structure.

4.10 In modeling descriptions of English grammar after those of Latin and Greek, many important features have naturally been neglected. At this we need not be surprised—the surprise is that the transfer of grammatical form and terminology ever worked at all. It did work, and, in the absence of a real descriptive grammar (i.e., a grammar undertaking to describe the structure of English as such), worked beneficially. It was able to do so for three rather accidental reasons.

a) A tremendous number of English words have been borrowed from Greek and Latin, and a study of the principles of word formation in Latin could serve for the English student the practical purpose of elucidating these loan words.

b) Since Latin and English are after all both descended from the same Indo-European parent language, they have in common an unusual number of parts of speech. The study of Latin, therefore, had at least the indirect value of acquainting the student with comparable parts of speech in English.

c) The common descent of Latin and English also accounts for the fact that the two languages have in common a good many nonobligatory grammatical relations. The study of these in Latin allowed the student to become acquainted by analogy with such relations in English.

Since nonobligatory grammatical relations form an important area of English grammar, it will be worth while to examine their general nature.

NUMBER

4.11 In English, *number* is the most important of the nonobligatory grammatical relations. This is true (1) partly because of the peculiar distinctiveness of the noun number forms as compared with those of languages in which the word form expresses both number and gender, and (2) partly because number is expressed to some degree by verbs, pronouns, and adjectives as well as nouns. Certain North American Indian, Dravidian, and Australian languages show, in comparison with English, a sharp restriction in the expression of number. But in English, number patterns are emphasized, often to an illogical extent.

Every one of these agents *was* honest.
Neither of the students *was* excellent.
None was granted the required permission.
Everybody took off *his* hat.

4.12 Ostensibly, English distinguishes only between the *singular* (one, or a group considered as one) and the *plural* (more than one); whereas certain other languages reveal a *singular*, a *dual* (two), and a *plural* (more than two). Thus, Sanskrit sharply differentiates *sá vṛkas*, "that wolf," from *tâu vṛ́kau*, "those two wolves," as well as from *té vṛ́kās*, "those more than two wolves." Similarly, the final vowel of Anglo-Saxon *doru* (English *door*) and *nosu* (English *nose*) indicates that those words once referred to a "pair of doors" and a "pair of nostrils." Anglo-Saxon even had a set of dual personal pronouns, *wit* (*uncer, unc, uncit*) and *git* (*incer, inc, incit*). Actually, the dual number, expressed in a less formal manner, is still relatively prominent in English:

1. With nouns: a *pair* of trousers
a *pair* of shoes
a *pair* of scissors

2. With pronouns: *both* of us
both of you
both of them
we *two*
us *two*
you *two*
they *two*

With adjectives: the so-called comparative degree, as, the *larger* of these
the *smaller* of the two
the *higher* hill

DEFINITENESS

4.13 In common with most Western European languages of the Germanic and Romance groups, English expresses an important grammatical relation called *definiteness*, or *identification*. Consider, for instance, the use of *a* and *the* in the following context:

One day, *a* child met *a* man. *The* child immediately trusted *the* man and went up to him.

In the first sentence, both *child* and *man* are indefinite, that is, they are felt as being previously unidentified or unnoticed. In the second sentence, since previous mention has identified them, we use the determiner *the* instead of *a*, i.e., we use a definite article instead of an indefinite article. *The* and *a* are not the only English words used to express this relation. In addition to *the*, the words *this* (*these*), *that* (*those*), and any possessive form (*Dick's, my*, etc.) can be used to establish the definiteness of nouns following them. In addition to *a* (*an*), the words *any, each, either, neither, every, no, one, somewhat, whatever, which, whichever, many a, such a, what a*, although some of these indicate either distributive or number reference, can be used to establish the indefiniteness of following nouns. A simple rule of thumb for distinguishing between these two classes of words is to note that the former group (*determiners*) can be preceded by *all*:

all *the* men
all *that* cake
all *this* year
all *those* children
all *Dick's* toys
all *my* life

But never:

all *a* man
all *some* food
all *each* night, etc.

In many languages, neither the relation of definiteness nor any means of expressing it is an important part of grammar.

4.14 We often use the relation of *definiteness* as a means of expressing our emotional attitude toward nouns just as we use the so-called *verbal auxiliaries* as a device for expressing our emotions toward action. Furthermore, the written language suggests we have developed an apparatus for expressing *explicit indefiniteness* and *explicit definiteness*, as well as the normal *indefiniteness* and *definiteness* contrast:

One day, *a certain* man met *a certain* child. *The* child immediately trusted *the* man and went up to him.
One Mr. Jones was arraigned in court yesterday.
Have they *a* mother? No, *the* mother died when they were born.

I translated from German.
I translated from *the* German.

Is breakfast ready?
Is *the* breakfast ready?

Recognition of purely emotional connotations in the definiteness relation seems to underlie the following significant quotations:

> The dentist, therefore, with no great difference of meaning, but with great difference of effect, says, "Close *the* mouth," instead of "Shut *your* mouth."
>
> Mildred L. Lambert in *American Speech*, *III*, 180, (1928)

> "You're all very devoted to *that* child," she said. . . "I don't know that Maggie's so desperately keen on *the* infant," he said. "She's not like you about him, that's sure!" Mrs. Hamps admitted. And she went on in a tone that was only superficially casual, "I wonder *the* mother doesn't come down to him." Not "his" mother—"the" mother. Odd, the effect of that trifle! Mrs. Hamps was a great artist in phrasing.
>
> Arnold Bennett, *Clayhanger*, ch. IV.

GENDER

4.15 The word *gender* is so obviously associated with discriminations on the basis of sex that we fail, for the most part, to understand its original function. In the widest sense, it reflects an attempt to classify words descriptive of the phenomena of the universe (*nouns*) according to the terms of classification which any particular culture has ever held regarding them. Some languages, notably Modern English, Modern Armenian, and Modern Persian, have found the formal classifying factor in logical sex distinctions. In these languages, masculine nouns symbolize male creatures, feminine nouns, female creatures, and neuter nouns, objects or things considered sexless. This is called *natural gender*. Actually, of course, trees and plants are not sexless, and a modern zoologist could distinguish sexes among them if there were any point in making gender distinctions in our names for them. But gender, as this example indicates, is invariably a throwback to the prescientific past, even when, as in English, it has all but shaken itself loose from tradition.

4.16 Most languages using sex as an index of classification possess what is called *grammatical gender;* i.e., the correlation of nouns with sex distinctions does not agree with the logical sex differentia of phenomena as we know them, but is predetermined by some particular suffix, or some particular article, or by factors not immediately analyzable. Thus, Latin *fluvius*, "river," is marked as masculine by the suffix *-us*, in much the same fashion that French *sentinelle*, plainly referring to a masculine "sentry," takes the feminine article *la* because of its association with the large group of feminine nouns ending in *-elle*. In both German and Anglo-Saxon, the word for "woman" (German *Weib*, Anglo-Saxon *wīf*, English *wife*) is shown to be of neuter gender by the form of the definite article that accompanies it (German *das Weib*, Anglo-Saxon *thaet wīf*). In Greek and Latin, the word for *sun* is masculine and the word for *moon* feminine, in German, *moon* (*der Mond*) is marked as masculine by *der* and *sun* (*die Sonne*) as feminine by *die*. All these apparent illogicalities go back to a primitive classification of phenomena into animate (active) and inanimate (passive).

4.17 In conventional grammatical terms, English possesses a natural gender scheme of *masculine, feminine*, and *neuter*. On the basis of pronoun reference, however, we are obliged to consider the primary classification as *nonpersonal*, and *personal*, with *masculine* and *feminine* as subdivisions of the latter. Notice that the reference pronouns *who, which* reveal no masculine-feminine distinction, and that the nonpersonal pronoun of the third person, *it*, is often so employed that this distinction is submerged:

I hadn't recognized him as Jones until then. Immediately the name was mentioned, I knew *it* was Jones.
There's a man at the door. I think *it's* a clergyman.

Furthermore, emotional considerations often transform the nonpersonal into the personal. We treat the thing in our warmth of feeling as a person. For example:

Do you know the willow in *his* natural state? He's a really picturesque tree.
The salmon gave me a real struggle before I landed *him*.
The seas jarred the schooner and wrecked *her* steering gear.

Moreover, side by side with the conventional natural gender of English exists a traditional "hidden" system of gender of an entirely different kind. In this, smaller animals, body parts, features of the botanical world, cities and societies and corporations personified, countries and states as localities, and unnamed small watercraft are usually "it," while larger animals, dogs, eagles, and turkeys are frequently "he," and cats, wrens, personified countries and states, nature, automobiles, trains, named boats, sailboats, and powerboats are commonly "she." The process by which this hidden gender system arose must have been remarkably similar to that by which our remote linguistic ancestors evolved the classifications which have become *grammatical gender.*

CASE

4.18 Case is the relationship between a noun and a pronoun and some other noun or pronoun in the same clause or phrase. The word *case* means, etymologically, "a falling," (Latin *casus*) and owes its application to the Latin conception that all other cases fall away from the nominative:

Nominative	homo
Accusative	hominem
Genitive	hominis
Dative	homini
Ablative	homine

Since, in actuality, the Latin nominative is a truncated form of the word-base ***homin-*** to which a nominative marker *-o* has been added, our use of the word *case* has no validity beyond that of custom. The number of case forms as marked by inflection in the Latin manner varies a great deal from language to language, from the twenty-three in Georgian to the two or three in English and the one in French. To attempt to catalogue all possible customary relations between one noun (or pronoun) and another noun (or pronoun) would require at least thirty-six marked case forms. Probably no language in the world actually possesses this number, and all languages with a case system indicated by word inflections show the merging of several relations under a single marked form. The Latin accusative case, for instance, expresses at least two customary relations, and the dative at least four. Case systems such as those of Latin and Greek reflect a confusion rather than an explicit expression of the grammatical relations they are supposed to indicate.

4.19 In English, none of our nouns possess distinctive case endings. We attribute ***nominative*** versus ***objective*** case to them on the analogy of the pronouns which can substitute for them: ***I, he, she, it, we, they*** as compared with ***me, him, her, it, us, them.*** The so-called "possessive case" of English nouns is most conveniently thought of as a method of transforming the noun into a ***determiner*** (cf. 4.13 above), although such constructions as ***this book of hers, this pen of John's*** may reveal a genuine "possessive case" for the pronoun.

4.20 Detailed discussion of the various cases found in Latin and Greek is irrelevant to the structure of English, which, through its tremendous battery of prepositions, explicitly expresses far more than the five named relations of the former and the seven of the latter language. It is important to remember that any conceivable grammatical relationship between substantive expressions can be expressed in English by means of word order, prepositions, or prepositional phrases. Only in our pronoun system do we also indicate the basic relation of the subject to the object by means of actual changes in word forms. What might be called the purely relational cases, expressed somewhat imperfectly in Latin, Greek, Sanskrit, and many other languages through word forms, are expressed in English, perhaps less systematically, but more subtly and often more accurately, by means other than changing the word forms. In a sense, therefore, it is unfair to our language to say that it possesses only two or three cases. Through its prepositions it is capable of expressing very many case notions indeed.

PERSON

4.21 Life situations that involve language establish a linguistic relation between a ***speaker,*** a ***hearer,*** and ***someone or something spoken about.*** This is the grammatical relation of ***person,*** expressed chiefly in the subjects of sentences and reflected elsewhere through verbal forms and pronouns. By conventional terminology, the person of the ***speaker*** is the ***first person,*** that of the ***hearer,*** the ***second person,*** and that of ***what is spoken about,*** the ***third person.*** In most languages, person is closely associated with number, as in the English verbal forms ***call-s, run-s, see-s,*** where the *-s* indicates both ***third person*** and ***singular number.*** In English, the relation of person is transmitted chiefly through the ***personal pronouns,*** a system of person markers involving ***person, number, gender,*** and ***case.***

SINGULAR

1st person	I (me)
2nd person	you (you)
3rd person	he, she, it, (him, her, it)

PLURAL

we	(us)
you	(you)
they	(them)

In many languages, the personal pronouns, especially in the first person dual and plural, possess distinct ***inclusive*** and ***exclusive*** forms. In such languages, ***we*** might be represented both by a form expressing ***I and you*** (inclusive) or by a form expressing ***I and someone not you*** (exclusive). The virtual replacement of the original second person singular ***thou*** by ***you*** in English is paralleled in many languages by the development of a ***formal*** second person pronoun which contrasts in function with the original pronoun (German ***Sie,*** originally third person plural, as contrasted with the original ***du,*** second person singular, and ***Ihr,*** second person plural). Although nouns are normally in agreement with the third person forms of verbs, English personal names and nouns without determiners are occasionally understood as indicating the second person:

John, give me a match!
Hey, sailor, give me a match!

TENSE

4.22 ***Tense*** times a happening with reference to the time at which an utterance about it is made. If the two times coincide—that is, if something is happening at the time of talking about it—the tense is ***present tense.*** If the happening preceded the time of talking about it, the tense is ***past tense.*** If the happening is not yet in process, the tense is ***future*** or ***potential tense.*** In English, these simple tense relations are expressed, with a minimum of disturbance from other factors, in what may be termed the ***simple tense forms: I go*** (present), ***I went*** (past). Some languages do not express such tense relations at all. Among those that do, this scheme of time reference is often complicated by the intrusion of other factors, some of them stylistic, some emotional. Thus Latin used the ***present*** tense forms to give special vividness to ***past*** happenings; and indeed this "historical present" is not unknown in English ("Then I pitch him a close one inside. He takes a half swing and then holds up. The umpire calls it a strike."). In English, the simple present ***I go*** in "Tomorrow I go to Boston" combines with the time-adverb to express a future happening. The English simple present is, in fact, not so much a "present" as a "non-past": it does not indicate present time as such but any time which is thought of as not being dissociated from the present:

Few persons ***remember*** how they learned to walk.
Trees ***grow*** up just as we do.

Similarly, the simple past ***I went*** in "When I was young, I went to school" suggests not only a past happening but also one that was constantly repeated in a segment of past time. The hastiest of examinations of English sentences will reveal that many of our alleged tenses, including all the so-called "progressive forms" (***I am going, I was going,*** etc.), do not acquire their real significance from tense alone but either from two other grammatical relations (***aspect*** and ***mood***) or from the total syntactical construction in which they appear. Moreover, English possesses another kind of tense dimension, best described as indicating an ***immediate*** versus ***proximate*** (i.e., remoter, less immediate) time relation, which is quite distinct from the one mentioned above:

General future: ***I am to go*** (time in the future unspecified)
Immediate future: ***I am about to go*** (time in the immediate future is specified)
Proximate future: ***I am going to go*** (time in a less immediate future is specified).

This same tense relation, working on the plane of immediate versus less immediate probability, possibility, etc., underlies the use of ***I will*** compared with ***I would, I can*** compared with ***I could, I may*** compared with ***I might,*** etc. It is a highly important element in the English tense system.

ASPECT

4.23 Translating the Russian grammatical term ***vid*** as applied to Slavic verbs, the term ***aspect*** refers to the status of a happening as completed or non-completed, occurring once or several times, having a result or no result, and the like. This verbal relation was first pointed out as early as the 1st century B.C. by the Latin grammarian Varro, and is actually referred to in the terms ***perfect, imperfect*** (Varro's ***perfectum, infectum***) as applied to tenses in various Western European languages. The original application to the Latin verb may be thus illustrated: ***perfect aspect*** in ***dīxī,*** "I have said," ***dīxeram,*** "I had said," and ***dīxerō,*** "I am to have said"; ***imperfect aspect*** in ***dīco,*** "I am saying," ***dīcebam,*** "I was saying," and ***dīcam,*** "I am to be saying." The aspect distinction here depends on whether a happening is thought of as ***completed*** (perfect aspect) or ***incomplete*** and ***continuing*** (imperfect aspect) at any one of the three tense levels. Aspects of a somewhat similar character are encountered in the Semitic languages (including Biblical Hebrew), in the Hamitic languages, in various African languages, and in the Slavic group of European languages. They are also found in English.

4.24 The simple tense forms of English (***I say, I said; I go, I went***) are not complicated by aspect; they are, in short, indefinite as to aspect, or, if the total aspect system of our language is considered, they may be considered as belonging to an *indefinite* aspect. *Definite* aspects appear when the verb takes the form of a verbal word group or verbal phrase, as follows: (1) a *perfect* or *completive* aspect is indicated by the use of a past participle in the phrase, as in *I have said, I have gone, I am gone;* (2) an *imperfect* or *durative* aspect is indicated by the use of a present participle (*-ing* form) in the verbal phrase, as in *I am saying, I am going, I have been going,* etc.; (3) an *iterative* or *repetitive* aspect is indicated by the use of *keep* with a present participle, as in *I keep saying, I kept going,* etc.; (4) an *inceptive* or *commencement* aspect is indicated by the use of *get* with a present participle, as in *get going;* (5) an *effective* aspect is indicated by the use of *get* with a past participle, as in *he gets gone, he gets seen.* Traces of other possible aspects are also present in the language. When the whole aspectual system of English is considered, it will be seen that the primary contrast is between the *perfect* or *completive* aspect on the one hand and the *imperfect* or *durative* on the other. The other aspects are particularizations of these, the *iterative* and *inceptive* being variants of the imperfect and the *effective* a variant of the perfect. Notice also that the two chief aspects are marked by the final suffix (*-ing, -ed, -t,* or *-en*) of the verbal phrase, while their particularizations are marked by the verbal auxiliaries *keep* and *get.* These, then, are our *aspect-markers.*

MOOD

4.25 The grammatical relation of *mood* or *mode* establishes the speaker's feeling about the actuality of a happening. The indicative mood, for instance, indicates that the speaker regards what he says as representing a fact or an alleged fact, whereas the so-called subjunctive mood implies that he is doubtful or uncertain about it. In Modern English, the subjunctive mood has tended to disappear, yet the few forms surviving still carry the implication of doubt, uncertainty, or unreality:

If John *finish* the work in time, I shall thank him.
If his health *be* really bad, he ought to quit work.
If he *were* here, I would know what to say to him.

But though the subjunctive is dying out, English is very rich in devices for expressing one's attitude toward his statement. For example, English syntactical constructions can be used to mark a nonactual happening as a probability, a prediction, an obligation, a necessity, a hope, etc. Consider, for example, the following methods of expressing the same basic linguistic situation:

Tomorrow, I go to Indianapolis.
Tomorrow, I will (*or* shall) go to Indianapolis.
Tomorrow, I am going to Indianapolis.
Tomorrow, I am going to go to Indianapolis.
Tomorrow, I am to go to Indianapolis.
Tomorrow, I may go to Indianapolis.
Tomorrow, I must go to Indianapolis.
Tomorrow, I can go to Indianapolis.
Tomorrow, I could go to Indianapolis.
Tomorrow, I've got to go to Indianapolis.
Tomorrow, I should go to Indianapolis.
Tomorrow, I ought to go to Indianapolis.
Tomorrow, I have to go to Indianapolis.

The modal apparatus suggested by this array of grammatical possibilities indicates that in the use of verbs, the speaker's attitudes are of paramount importance. The verb is, as a matter of fact, one of the two principal emotion-carriers in the sentence (the other is the apparatus for conveying *definiteness*).

VOICE

4.26 Abstractly speaking, the relation of *voice* indicates whether the subject acts (*active voice*) or is acted upon (*passive voice*), or performs the action for itself (*dynamic voice*), or turns the action upon itself (*reflexive voice*). In English, all such notions can be expressed, but the normal distinction, that between *active* and *passive,* is best described as a special feature of word-order emphasis designed to accent what would normally be the recipient of an action. The *effective* aspect, as in *he gets seen,* is in some respects closer to the passive voice of other languages. In many languages, particularly in French, the so-called "passive" is actually a derivative of the reflexive: French *il se trouve* (it is found); French *ils se marient* (they get married). In some languages, specifically in Latin, a particular form of the verb expresses the passive relation: *pater amat,* which will translate "father loves," as compared with *pater amatur,* "father is loved."

COMPARISON

4.27 By *comparison* we mean the expression of equality or inequality between objects:

He is *as* good *as* I am.
He is *better* than I am.

This is *as* valuable a jewel *as* I have ever seen.
This is the *more* valuable jewel.
This is the *most* valuable jewel of them all.

He was a famous man.
He was a *less* famous man.

I moved quickly; she moved *more* quickly.
The cat moved *most* quickly of all.

The second degree of comparison (usually called the *comparative degree*) reflects a lingering sense of the dual number. Even among literate speakers, the superlative is sometimes used instead, particularly when the dual notion is expressed by *two*:

The *highest* of the two hills.

4.28 To summarize the bearings of the grammatical relations even as briefly as they are summarized here may seem a putting of the cart before the horse. But it must be remembered that the entire grammatical apparatus of a language, complex and subtle in some points, relatively simple in others, exists only to express these and similar relations. A language does not exist as an abstraction, but as an instrument for the expression of practical, and sometimes of artistic, situations. As long as human beings need to establish relations between the meaningful elements of their discourse, every language will possess a fair number of customary relations and methods of expressing them. In terms of practical necessity, we may deplore the undue complication, the confusions of pattern and form, the conflicting details, which mask rather than reveal the indications of grammatical relations in most vernaculars known to linguistic science. But to deplore them thus is to ignore processes of linguistic growth. Any language is merely the product of the forces of change and of the sociological conditions that shaped it. We cannot expect, from any language thus evolved, the man-made simplicities of Basic English and Esperanto.

4.29 The grammatical relations briefly examined above are expressed in English through three specific grammatical devices illustrated by the sentence, "A big man followed the white dog." (Cf. **4.7**). The first device is that of fixed word order, which establishes, by mere position, the actor (subject), ***man,*** the action (predicate) *followed,* and the action-goal (object) *dog,* as well as the fact that *the white* modifies *dog* and *the big* modifies *man.* This is the obligatory grammatical device of Modern English, used to express the indispensable grammatical relations of the subject-predicate-complement and of noun modification. The second device is that involving the use of relation words, exemplified in our example by *the.* One type of relation words (*prepositions*) expresses the relation known in other languages as *case,* another (*verbal auxiliaries*) expresses the grammatical relations of *mood* and *aspect,* and another (*conjunctions*), the various relationships between phrases, sentences, etc. Word order and the use of relation words are thus the principal grammatical devices of Modern English. A third device, that of changing the word form (e.g., *followed* rather than *follows* in our illustrative example) to express number, gender, tense, or comparison, and, in the use of pronouns, to express the relationships between elements of contiguous sentences or parts of sentences, is of comparatively minor grammatical but of great social importance. Since both the device of word order and the devices of using relation words create grammatical groupings larger than the individual word, it follows that the *essential grammar* of Modern English applies to word groups rather than to the word as such. In normal Modern English, word groups express the substance and words the coloration of expression. That is why our language, whether of British or American extraction, is described as an *analytical,* or better, as a primarily *syntactical,* language.

C. American English and British English

5.1 The American national language, originally a nondistinctive variety of English, has been so molded by the sociological, historical, geographical, and ethnological conditions of its North American environment that it has acquired a distinctiveness of its own. Before we attempt to examine this distinctiveness, it is well to state at once that it is of a kind easy to overestimate and difficult to view dispassionately from either side of the Atlantic. When a native speaker of English, whether American or British, engages a Frenchman or German in conversation, he is usually willing to meet him halfway; he expects, as a matter of course, to be forced to adjust his mental attitude in relation to the alien terms of his companion. But when he converses with another native speaker of English of different nationality from his own, whether it be American or British, he demonstrates no such willingness, no such halfway *rapprochement.* Differences of background, education, manners, and experience go unregarded merely because the basic language is the same; differences in pronunciation, vocabulary, idiom, and syntax become a source of irritation, ridicule, or misunderstanding. Our imagined speaker is in any case as full of linguistic shibboleths as an egg is full of meat. In various devious ways, he has become persuaded that a dropped preconsonantal *r* is "effete," or, alternatively, that it symbolizes social distinction—that a "broad *a*" is esthetic, or, alternatively, an "affectation,"—that the pronunciation (et) for *ate* is "cultured," or, alternatively, "vulgar." To the primary *matter* of language, which is the symbolization of experience, he adds a secondary symbolization, built up during the last two hundred years from confused notions of propriety, esthetics, snobbery, subconscious fear, national pride, and personal egotism, and expressed through the *manner* of language. It is no wonder, therefore, that the distinctive features of American English loom far larger than they actually are. The century-old controversies over "Americanisms" and "Briticisms," the charges of "corruption" or "effeteness" hurled back and forth across the ocean, the barriers of distrust between two friendly nations—these are inevitable consequences of linguistic intolerance.

5.2 At their widest, the real distinctions between literate American English and literate British English are quite insufficient to impede seriously the communication of ideas. When they do impede, the impediment is caused less by difficulties in understanding than by a deliberate desire not to understand. Not language but imagination is at fault. Formal American English and formal British English, although they are separated by 3,000 Atlantic miles and 160 years of national divergencies, actually vary far less than the local dialects of Dewsbury and Howden, two English towns in Yorkshire some forty miles apart. Even if we take the furthest poles of differentiation, and contrast informal conversational American with informal conversational British speech, we are still well within the limits of mutual understanding—far more so, indeed, than if we happened to be inhabitants of Dewsbury buying shoes in Howden.

5.3 The point is, of course, that until recently Dewsbury people seldom bought shoes or anything else in Howden; they bought them in Dewsbury. For a thousand years they had been buying them in Dewsbury. And because there are in the British Isles thousands of towns like Dewsbury, towns whose inhabitants for centuries stayed close to home in their own speech-communities, the Isles form a crisscross pattern of distinctive dialects as quilt-crazy as the little English fields. In the United States, dialect distinctions of the same intensity within such relatively small areas are almost unknown. Three hundred years of settlement is too brief a time; the American people, lured to wandering by the shifting frontiers of the last 150 years, have moved too constantly. And in the whole of American history, there has never been so complete a severance of communication with England as formerly existed between Dewsbury and Howden. Instead, there has been a steady flood of linguistic influence across the Atlantic, first—up to about 1914—from England to this country, and since then from this country to the British Isles. Now that the cultural importer has become, in a far wider sense, a cultural exporter, American and British English are on a much closer conversational footing than they ever were. The Americanization of British English is proceeding at a far brisker pace than the Anglicization of American English ever achieved.

5.4 Behind all this lie the basic facts of linguistic history. Up to about 1830, both American and British English shared an identical development; both owe their present accepted national forms to the effects of authoritarianism working on bourgeois credulity; both succumbed, in the period of the Industrial Revolution, to a process of "refinement" at the hands of grammarian and lexicographer. But there the resemblance begins to break down. The American English which emerged from the crucible, chiefly a literary language smelted down from good New England ore, was immediately forged by John Adams, Noah Webster, and their like into an instrument for national unity and national aspiration. The British English, which was both a literary and a spoken language, was molded to the purposes of a powerful ruling class.

5.5 Theoretically, American English has derived from Noah Webster and the long tradition of popular education, a regimentation much more rigid than that of British English, and it is true that its traditional elevated style sometimes borders on the stilted. Yet except among a few New England speakers, the spoken language has always veered so sharply from the prescribed norm that its development has been comparatively untrammeled. American colloquial speech, constantly vitalized by the swiftly changing patterns of American life, has served the linguistic inventiveness of the American people as an inexhaustible reservoir. In the last fifty years, thanks to a heightened national self-consciousness, this reservoir has been tapped more and more by American literature, and today the floodgates are opening wide.

Spelling

5.6 The first American spelling reformer was Benjamin Franklin; the second, and most influential, Noah Webster. Present differences between American and British spelling are due to a compromise selection of certain forms and principles first sponsored by Webster on the basis of Franklin's theories. In his *Scheme for a New Alphabet and a Reformed Mode of Spelling* (1768), Franklin argued for thoroughgoing phonetic spelling, sketched a plan for the most scientific of early phonetic alphabets, and left us a remarkably accurate transcript of his own late-18th-century pronunciation. Webster was much more restrained in his innovations, and became increasingly restrained in his later works. Even so, his *American Dictionary* (1828) carries the phonetic principle much farther than it is carried in normal American orthography of today. Our present compromise with Webster's suggestions has been strongly influenced by the very conservative *Worcester's Dictionary* of 1846.

5.7 Of accepted peculiarities of American spelling, the following are most notable: (1) *-or* for British *-our* in *honor, favor*, etc.; (2) *-er* for British *-re* in *fiber, theater*, etc.; (3) a single consonant for the British double consonant in *traveler, traveled, wagon, riveted*, etc.; (4) *-s-* for British *-c-* in *offense, defense*, etc.; (5) preferred *-z-* for British *-s-* in *-ize, -ization*, etc. (but cf. *advertise, exercise*, etc.); (6) *e* for *ae* or *æ* in such words as *anesthesia, esthetic, etiology, medieval*, etc., and in such prefixes as *hemo-, hemato-*, etc.; (7) *bark* for British *barque, check* for *cheque, connection* for *connexion, cipher* for *cypher, draft* for *draught, fuse* for *fuze, gray* for *grey, hostler* for *ostler, jail* for *gaol, kilogram* for *kilogramme, curb* for *kerb, lackey* for *lacquey, mold* for *mould, molt* for *moult, pigmy* for *pygmy, plow* for *plough, program* for *programme, quartet* for *quartette, reflection* for *reflexion, story* for *storey, sty* for *stye*, etc. In estimating these features, however, it must be remembered that many British authors use some American spellings, and that certain American authors occasionally prefer British spellings.

Vocabulary

5.8 Americans have always lived on a frontier, physical, spiritual, or political. Just as certainly as there was a physical frontier in the West during the 19th century, its locale in the 18th lay in western Massachusetts, northwestern Maine, Vermont, northwestern Connecticut, New York State, western Pennsylvania, Kentucky, and Tennessee. Before that, the Coastal Colonies had themselves been a frontier, physical, spiritual, and political, for the British Isles. The frontier is the most important factor in the formation of the American vocabulary. If *adobe, alcalde, canyon*, and *mesa* symbolize adjustment to the new environment of the Southwest, *alewife, basswood, clearing*, and *chickadee* symbolize, just as definitely, the first adjustments of the original Colonists to the environment of the Coastal East. Throughout the three hundred years of American history, there have always been new things to name, new concepts to express, new conditions to communicate. It is no wonder, therefore, that American English has developed an inventiveness and verbal virtuosity all its own. The colloquial geniuses who first talked of an *anxious seat, bandwagon, crimp*, and *crowbait* (a worthless horse) were merely exercising linguistic ingenuity under the same pressure of environment as the unknown Colonist who first applied *bell* to "a stretch of country," *gut* to "a narrow water gap," and *land office* to a typically American institution. Sometimes, as in *succotash, bayou, calaboose, boss, prairie*, a word conveniently existent in another language was borrowed; but far more often native English elements, put to service under pressure of necessity, emerged in new combinations, new extensions of meaning, new connotations: *selectman, mass meeting, alarmist, lightning rod, ground hog, windfall, officeholder, clingstone, crosstown, panfish, locate, legislate, store, haul*, and the like. A great number of well-publicized differences between British and American words are of this origin: American *bill* beside British *banknote, coal oil* beside *paraffin (oil), dry-goods store* beside *draper's, shoulder* (of a road) beside *verge, cracker* beside *biscuit, sidewalk* beside *footpath, business suit* beside *lounge suit*.

5.9 Not all the verbal inventions or modifications are as direct or as pithy as these. There is a strong current of formality in American English. To the natural Puritan solemnity and liking for sonorous abstractions, the conditions of early settlement added a legalistic and administrative vocabulary sometimes pretentious, sometimes half playful, and sometimes plainly desperate. Democracy implies active participation in formal processes of taxation, organization, and government; it implies the development of an active vocabulary through which such matters may be discussed in public. In other lands, the terminologies of law and administration belong chiefly to the professional jargons of experts; in this country they have been from the beginning a part of the practical vocabulary of the ordinary citizen. Words such as *admittance, amendable, appreciation, apportionment, advisory, assembly, bureau, endorser, insubordinate, deputize, infraction*, and *prescriptive* are as indigenous to the American soil as *angel-food;* and if today a real-estate dealer becomes a *realtor*, and a cleaner's a *pantorium*—if an automobile is *repossessed* and *reconditioned* and a veteran *rehabilitated*—an old

American verbal tradition merely demonstrates that it is still at work.

II. THE DESCENT, RELATIONSHIPS, AND HISTORY OF THE ENGLISH LANGUAGE

6.1 The ultimate origins of English, as modern scholarship sees them, can best be grasped from some such table as that on the back end paper of this book.

6.2 Whatever the demerits of this diagram, it at least suggests the connection of English with the West Germanic subbranch of the Germanic branch of a parent language (*Indo-European*), established by the methods of comparative and geographical linguistics. It also suggests that English is closely connected with Dutch and Frisian, more remotely with German, more remotely still with Latin, Greek, Welsh, and Russian, and very remotely with Sanskrit and Iranian. Consideration of series of cognate forms like English *brother*, Dutch *broeder*, German *bruder*, Old Saxon *brōthar*, Lithuanian *broter-*, Greek *phrātēr*, Latin *frāter*, Irish *brāthair*, Sanskrit *bhrātar-* underlines these relationships and gives a hint of the comparative method by which their existence was originally established. See further the many Indo-European bases cited in the etymologies of this dictionary.

6.3 The significant history of the English language, however, goes back no further than the 5th century A.D., when tribes from the northwestern Continental fringe, speaking a form of Low German, invaded and conquered Romano-Celtic England. To trace the development of the English language is to trace the process by which the dialects spoken by this handful of invaders became the mighty instrument of communication, emotion, and literature now used by upward of 250 million of the world's inhabitants. And the more we trace this phenomenon, the more we shall realize that the history of our language is merely one aspect of the social and cultural history of the invaders' descendants.

The Principal Periods of English

6.4 The origins of the English language lie in a social dislocation, i.e., the emigration of certain groups from the Continent to England, with the consequent breaking of communication between these groups and their Continental kinsfolk. The next great dislocation occurred during the Norman Conquest (1066–c.1120). Between the two events extends a period which, although marred by internecine wars and the incursions of Scandinavian invaders (850–1042), shows comparative social stability and an apparent if largely fictitious linguistic equilibrium. To the English language of this period, roughly from 450 to about 1150, we may give the name *Anglo-Saxon* (AS.), or *Old English* (OE.).

6.5 Irrespective of their tribal origins, the Germanic invaders of England seem to have called their language *Englisc* (from *Engle*, "the Angles"; cf. *Anglian*). As a spoken language it was not entirely uniform. Dialectal differences already developed on the Continent probably increased rather than decreased on English soil, where the conditions of settlement tended further to split up the original communities. These original differences, seconded by the Scandinavian invasions and the differentiation natural to some fifteen centuries of untrammeled development, have much to do with the complexities of Modern English dialectal speech. Yet Anglo-Saxon writings, our chief source of information about the language, show a quite remarkable uniformity. The eventual national ascendancy of the West-Saxon kingdom, centered around the capital at Winchester, gave the written dialect of Wessex the importance of a written standard language; and the great bulk of literature was either written originally in West-Saxon or was transcribed into it from its original Northumbrian and Mercian sources.

6.6 The next great period of the language, that of *Middle English* (ME.), cannot be fitted as neatly between dates as the preceding period. Time was needed to absorb the great historical shock of the Norman Conquest, and the terminal date for Middle English can be fixed only in the most arbitrary manner. The adoption of the limits 1150–1475 is dependent upon the emerging of a distinctive Post-Conquest literature and upon the social effects of the invention of printing.

6.7 It would be an error to regard the Conquest as producing a clean break in the history of English; it merely released and accelerated tendencies toward differentiation that must already have been in operation. Its most immediate result was to replace English, as an authoritative language, first by Latin and then by the Norman-French of the conquerors for well over two hundred years. In the meantime, the effects upon the English language itself were threefold: (1) the social prestige of Norman-French and the extension in the ecclesiastical, administrative, and scholarly use of Latin brought into English an enormous number of words borrowed from these languages; (2) the loss of the West-Saxon written standard allowed free play to the dialectal peculiarities and disturbed the linguistic equilibrium of English; (3) the influence of French and Latin spelling did much to revise the traditional orthography of English.

6.8 The first part of the Middle English period is something like linguistic chaos. Important literary works were written in half a dozen dialects sufficiently diverse in themselves, and made doubly diverse by the individual spelling expedients of their authors. Early Middle English is not one but a group of dialects, each of which must be mastered separately by the student. The resolution of this confusion, which was the adoption of London English as a basis for a new *written* standard language, came about under the pressure of many disparate factors: (1) the breakdown of direct English authority over Normandy (1204–65); (2) the gradual establishment of nationalism (1272–1400); (3) the rise in importance of the middle and laboring classes (1348–85); (4) the growing centralization of administration at the capital, accompanied by the rise of an administrative English (London Official English) based on the speech of London; (5) the timely appearance of important works by Chaucer, Lydgate, and Occleve, all of whom wrote London or South Eastern English. By 1420, at the latest, a written form of the South East Midland dialect used in and around London was on its way to becoming a written standard for the entire country. Although much fine literature continued to be produced in the rival literary dialects of the Northwest and the North, the predominance of written London English was never afterward seriously challenged. When in the years 1476–90 Caxton chose to use it for his printed books, the ground had already been fully prepared for him.

6.9 The third and last period of English, extending from about 1476 to the present, actually consists of two distinct phases of the language. In the earlier phase, which ends in the full tide of the Industrial Revolution about 1780, the principal pressures exerted on the language result from the invention of printing, the vast extension of literacy, the intellectual ferment of the Renaissance, and, above all, from a continuous social struggle between the rising middle classes and the dominant aristocracy. Theoretically, the wide diffusion of the printed word should have worked toward linguistic stability and uniformity. Actually, the converse is true. Its immediate result was to produce self-conscious awareness—awareness of ideas and ideologies, awareness of the implications of language, awareness of class and society. There were thus rapid accretions of foreign words, particularly of Latinic abstract words, that greatly modified the English vocabulary. And in spite of the normalizing tendencies of the printed language, in spite of the efforts of many self-conscious grammarians and orthoëpists, this phase of English is one of extremely rapid linguistic change. At its beginning, the vowel system of English was Continental, i.e., the vowel symbols had more or less the same phonetic values as in Italian, Spanish, French, or German. At its end, the vowel distribution of English had undergone so thorough a regrouping that the sounds were completely divorced from the Continental values of the symbols and consequently from the system of orthography—still the basis of modern English spelling—fixed by Caxton and his followers.

6.10 Changes as violent as this are likely to have violent social causes. Insofar as any single *social* cause can be considered responsible, it would appear to lie in the dislocation of the community along vertical lines, the clash of phonemic system against phonemic system resulting from the clash of the aristocratic and middle classes. As early as 1400, the powerful bourgeoisie of England's first industrial stronghold, East Anglia, had developed a kind of generalized *lingua franca*, based on the local spoken dialects of that region, through which they were enabled to carry out their business affairs. Wherever industry later extended, this *lingua franca*, no longer purely regional, seems to have followed. In the 17th century, the settlement of the New England Colonies by immigrants drawn principally from South Eastern England brought this type of English to the New World, where it formed the basis for the Northeastern Coastal American speech of today.

6.11 Yet for all its wide distribution, the middle-class *lingua franca* had the phonemic system of the East Anglian dialects; and that system varied greatly from the system used by the London aristocracy. Thus during the entire period (1476–1780)—the so-called period of Early Modern English (EMnE.)—we have the spectacle of two important class dialects existing, often in the same localities, side by side, and influencing the formative years of each successive youngest generation from two directions at once. By the unconscious attempts of each youngest generation to reconcile the conflicting signaling-systems of the two class dialects, to achieve a workable synthesis between them, the Great Vowel Shift of the Early Modern English period may well have been strongly influenced.

6.12 Within the limits of the Early Modern period itself, no such synthesis was achieved. The social struggle went on. Linguistic change lost nothing of its rapidity. The two great class dialects of English not only held their ground, but even gained; for if the middle-class type became standard for the New England Colonies, the aristocratic type became standard in the Southern Colonies, where it formed the original basis of the General Southern American of today. The final phase of the English language, the phase of Late Modern English (LMnE.), was not ushered in until the Industrial Revolution, by securing enormous material gains for the middle classes, had secured their social, political, and economic victory, and an authoritative predominance for their type of English. Upon that type, pruned and "regularized" by grammarians and lexicographers between 1750 and 1850, both the cultivated British and the cultivated American of today are firmly rooted. As spoken English, the older aristocratic type lingers in Tidewater Virginia and a few other Southern localities. From England, it has disappeared almost without a trace. Thus the history of English between 1750 and 1850 is not the history of an evolution but the history of a replacement.

6.13 Within the actual limits of the Late Modern phase of English, from 1780 to the present, something like linguistic equilibrium has been re-established. Apart from certain necessary phonological generalizations, change has been slight and gradual. Individual, regional, and to some extent, class divergencies still exist; but the written word, fostered by democratic social institutions, by popular education, and by the accessibility of grammars and dictionaries, has come to be of paramount importance. Even today, however, the continued diphthongization of (ā) and (ō) and various other developments warn us that the development of the English phonemic system is still under way.

Characteristics of English in the Anglo-Saxon Period (450–1150)

6.14 Anglo-Saxon differs considerably from Modern English in pronunciation, vocabulary, and grammar. Yet many of the characteristics and a good many of the words of MnE. are clearly recognizable in their AS. form, and the difficulties of AS. may easily be overstressed.

(a) *Spelling and Pronunciation*

Although AS. had the so-called "Continental" values for its vowel symbols, and although many of its sounds have since been modified by sound-change, one of its chief difficulties is the actual form of AS. spelling. As a result of palatalizations that occurred after the spelling system was already fixed, a single consonantal symbol may represent several sounds. Moreover, the priests who originally reduced AS. to writing tended to be too careful in expressing the vowels, even to the point of rendering the allophonic variations of the vowel phonemes. The following summary should aid recognition:

(1) c = MnE. *k* in *cynn* "kin," *munuc* "monk," and MnE. *ch* (= AS. *ky-* and *ty-*) in *cild* "child," *ceorl* "churl." (2) g = MnE. *y* in *gēar* "year," *gīet, gēt* "yet," *fæger* "fair," MnE. *g* in *grund* "ground," *gold* "gold," and German fricative *g* (not unlike MnE. *w*) in *boga* "bow," *folgian* "follow." (3) h = MnE. written *-gh* (no longer pronounced) in *niht* "night," and *sōhte* "sought," but had the phonetic values of *ch* in G. *ich* and *Nacht.* (4) cg (= AS. *dy*) = MnE. *-dge* in *brycg* "bridge"; sc = MnE. *sh* (it was phonemically *sy*) in *sciþ* "ship," *Englisc* "English." (5) f = MnE. *f* in *fētor* "fetter," but had the allophonic value of MnE. *v* in *heofon* "heaven," *æfre* "ever." (6) MnE. *th,* as in *with, then* was expressed indifferently by the Runic symbols *þ, ð,* as in *wiþ* "with," *ðū* "thou." (7) *y,* a vowel with the sound of *u* in Fr. *une,* corresponds chiefly to MnE. *i* as in *fyr* "fire," occasionally to MnE. *u* as in *bysig* "busy," *cycgel* "cudgel," and very occasionally to MnE. *e* (from Kentish dialect) as in *cnyll* "knell." (8) æ = MnE. *a* in *bæk* "back," but *ǣ* may correspond to MnE. *ea* as in *dǣlan* "to deal," or to MnE. *ee* as in *dǣd* "deed." (9) Certain diphthongs, like the *ea* of *earm* "arm," and *eall* "all," are no more than ultra-accurate recordings of the simple vowel before the retroflex *r* and the "dark" *l* heard in modern General American; others, like the *ie* of *stiele* "steel," and the *ea* of *ceald* "cold," are found only in West Saxon and have no influence on the later history of our forms for such words, which are derived from Anglian *stēle, cāld,* etc. All diphthongs, irrespective of origin, became mere allophones of long vowels in late AS., were simplified in ME. writing, and are of little importance in the general development of English.

(b) *Vocabulary*

About 85 per cent of the Anglo-Saxon vocabulary has been lost to Modern English chiefly because of later replacements from French and Latin. In estimating this loss, however, we should not forget that the AS. words which managed to survive—the bulk of our prepositions, pronouns, auxiliaries, and conjunctions, as well as our words for fundamental concepts—occur more frequently in spoken and written MnE. than most other elements in our vocabulary. Moreover, much of this lost vocabulary consists of synthetic compounds of which the individual elements still survive. *Dōm-bōc* (law-book), *eorþcræft* (geometry), and *gaderscipe* (marriage) may be gone, yet *doom, book, earth, craft, gather* are still with us and *-ship* is still an active formative suffix. The flexible formation of compounds from words and particles in current use, a feature still operative in German, is rightly considered to be one of the distinguishing marks of AS. vocabulary. Yet formations like *steamboat, motorcar, ice cream, fire insurance* still keep alive the method by which AS. *mōdcearu* (mind care, sorrow) was formed. Although MnE. compounds usually result from the crystallization of phrases, they probably represent as important a segment of the MnE. vocabulary as that of the AS. compounds in AS.

(c) *Grammar and Morphology*

AS. was what is usually termed an "inflected" or "synthetic" language like Modern German; i.e., the functional correlation between meaningful words was largely expressed by suffixes which served to denote such relationships as number, gender, case, tense, and voice. Like most Indo-European languages, AS. possessed "grammatical gender," a device only remotely connected with sex (cf. 4.16 above), which served to classify nouns for inflection. Thus *mægden* (maiden) was neuter, *swāt* (sweat) masculine, and *tīd* (time, tide) feminine. Theoretically, the noun and adjective had inflections for four cases in the singular and the plural, and the latter had, in addition, forms for each of the three genders and variant forms according to whether it was accompanied by the article or not. The pronoun, the keystone to any system based upon inflectional agreement, was even more complex: it possessed not only distinctive forms for all genders, persons, and cases, but also preserved, in addition to the normal singular and plural, a dual number. The practical purpose of this serried array of inflections simply amounted to this: that the relation between meaningful words expressed in MnE. chiefly through word order and the use of words empty of meaning—prepositions like *on, of, to,* or words like *concerning, according* used as prepositions—was expressed in AS. by the addition of suffixes (cf. 4.8 above) to the meaningful word. In AS. I should write *Hē wæs ān þara twelfa;* in MnE., *He was one of the twelve.* I might write *Lēof, þaes mē þyncþ þū eart wītega;* in MnE., to express the same relationship, I should have to write *Dear one,* according to *that* (or from *that*) *it seems to me you are a prophet.* Since inflections are phonemic elements, any phonetic changes which level and confuse them may finally result in a complete breakdown of the entire system and its replacement by the analytical expression of relationship that we find in MnE. That is precisely what happened. From the first written records onward, the inflections of noun and adjective lacked clarity and distinction; when final vowels became weakened, these inflections were rendered practically useless. Those of the pronoun (with the exception of the dual number) and, to some extent, those of the verb, still retained sufficient distinction to continue their usefulness in ME. and MnE.

Characteristics of English in the Middle English Period (1150–1475)

6.15 Consideration of the bewildering diversity of the Middle English dialects lies outside the scope of this discussion. Even the great Northern literary dialect, lineal ancestor of the language of Burns, and that of the Northwest used by the *Gawain* poet must be passed over in silence. For the historian of English, the one important variety of ME. is that of the South Eastern Midland area, particularly as written by Chaucer.

(a) *Spelling and Pronunciation*

If the ME. of Chaucer resembles MnE. more closely than AS., the fact is due partly to a series of orthographic adaptations brought about by the influence of French. The most important of these are: (1) the use of *ch* for *c,* as in *child,* AS. *cild;* (2) the use of *qu* for *cw,* as in *quene, queen,* AS. *cwen;* (3) the partial displacement of *þ, ð* by *th,* as in *with,* AS. *wiþ;* (4) the introduction of *v* for medial voiced *f,* as in *love,* AS. *lufu;* (5) the use of *sh, ssh* for *sc,* as in *shal,* AS. *sceal,* and in *wasshe,* AS. *wascan;* (6) the use of *k* before front vowels for *c,* as in *kepen,* AS. *cēpan* (keep), beside the retained *c* before back vowels, as in *cot;* (7) the eventual introduction of consonantal *y* for *g,* as in *yere,* AS. *gēar* (year), etc.; (8) the use of *ou* for AS. *ū* to discriminate it from Fr. *u* and AS. *ȳ* spelled *u,* as in *mouth,* AS. *mūþ* beside *muchel,* AS. *mycel* (much); the use of *o* for the sake of clarity in the neighborhood of *v, u, m, n, w,* as in *monk,* AS. *munuc,* and *sone,* AS. *sunu* (son); (9) in the latest ME., the use of *ea* and *oa,* imported from the Low Countries, in such words as *deal, boat* to distinguish the vowels from those of *deed, boot,* which had a different pronunciation; (10) the replacement of AS. *æ* by ME. *a,* as in *that,* AS. *þæt* (it is uncertain whether this change is merely orthographic or a symbol of a sound-change); (11) the equally uncertain replacement of AS. *ǣ* in *hǣlan* (to heal) by ME. *e,* as in *helen.*

Actual phonetic changes, as distinct from mere changes of orthography, are also apparent: (1) AS. *ā*, as in *hām* (home), *stān* (stone), etc., shifted to the sound of the vowel (ô) in MnE. *law* and was spelled *o, oo*, as in ME. *home, hoom, stone, stoon;* (2) the AS. diphthongs, where they survived in Late AS. itself, became simple vowels, as in ME. *depe, deep* (AS. *dēop*) and ME. *streem* (AS. *strēam*); (3) AS. *ȳ*, as in *hȳll, fȳr*, became *i* in South East Midland, as in *hill, fire;* (4) AS. fricative *g*, as in *boga*, already closely analogous to *w*, became and was written *w*, as in ME. *bowe;* (5) vowels of unstressed syllables lost their distinct character and became leveled, for the most part, under a sound usually written *e*, pronounced (ə) in the Western and (i) in the Eastern dialects; (6) long vowels were shortened before two or more consonants (whence MnE. *kept* beside *keep, depth* beside *deep*), and when they occurred in the first syllable of trisyllabic words (whence *holiday* and *halidame* beside *holy*); (7) the short vowels *a, e, o* were lengthened in open syllables, as in AS. *năma*, ME. & MnE. *name*, and AS. *mĕte*, ME. *mēte*, MnE. *meat.*

(b) *Vocabulary*

The ME. vocabulary differs from that of AS. by the accretion of a vast number of words borrowed from other languages and by the consequent loss of many AS. words. The process had already commenced during the 10th and 11th centuries, i.e., during the latter part of the AS. period, with borrowings from the Scandinavian settlers resident in Eastern and Northern England who spoke Anglo-Norse (referred to as Anglo-N. in this dictionary). Because of the rigid traditions of the West-Saxon written language, comparatively few such borrowings appear in AS.; we first realize their number and importance only after the Conquest. Permanent additions to the English language from this source include common nouns like *axletree, bull, dirt, law, leg, root, skin, want, window*, adjectives like *ill, rotten, tight, weak*, and verbs like *call, crawl, die, raise, scowl, take.*

Much more impressive, however, are the borrowings of words of Romance origin from the Norman conquerors, more especially during the years after about 1240, when the Norman-French were forced by political circumstances to reconcile themselves to their English neighbors. There are few periods of the language that show the accession of so many alien, and on the whole, useful, words as the period 1250–1450. Among them were the mundane *air, bacon, bucket, fry, gum, pork, push, sound, stew, stubble*, and *trip*, as well as the more abstract *beauty, color, heritage, honor, judgment, noble*, and *tragedy*. Some, like *abbey, cardinal, clerk, image, parson, penance*, and *piety*, are drawn from the special vocabulary of the Church; some, like *assize, attorney, fine, forfeit, pillory, plea, suit*, from that of the law, some from medicine, like *anatomy, balm, ointment, poison, stomach;* some from the army, like *ambush, archer, lance;* some from the table, like *appetite, taste, veal;* some from the home, like *basin, lamp, towel.*

Side by side with these French words, many of which were ultimately of Latin origin, occur direct borrowings from Latin itself. But whereas the French words bear in many cases the stamp of actual usage, actual speech, most of the Latin words were plainly literary and scholarly borrowings: *custody, genius, immune, lucrative, necessary, private, rational, subjugate, temperate*, etc.

(c) *Grammar and Morphology*

The eventual result of the weakening of unstressed final vowels, described above in 6.15 (a) was the disintegration of the complicated AS. inflectional system. In the English of Chaucer, "grammatical" is completely replaced by "natural" gender (cf. 4.15 above); the complex AS. article has become the invariable *þe, the;* the adjective is indeclinable except for a nonnominative *-e;* inflectional expression of noun cases is limited to the genitive singular; a single suffix *-es* has largely superseded the great variety of endings once used to indicate the genitive singular and the plural. To trace these changes in detail would require a volume of paradigms. Here, the practical results can be summarized in a single sentence. AS. was a "synthetic," while Late ME. is an "analytical," language. Of the once highly organized inflectional system of article, noun, and adjective, all that is left in MnE. is a group of fossil forms: *for the nonce, Atterbury, Nash, Noakes*, and *Nelm* (*for þen ones, æt þære byrig, at þen asche, at þen okes, at þen elme*).

The pronoun and verb also underwent considerable phonetic modification during the ME. period, but partly because of adaptation and partly because of their importance in determining the grammatical relationships within the analytical sentence, their main features are remarkably well preserved. In the pronoun, the outstanding developments were: (1) loss of the dual; (2) replacement of the masculine third person accusative *hine* by the dative *him;* (3) appearance of a feminine *she* (from AS. *sēo*, the nominative feminine of the article) due to the reduction of *ēo* to *ē* in Eastern dialects and replacing the original *hēo* except in those of the West; (4) intrusion of the Scandinavian plurals *they, their, them* to replace the English *hi, he, hir, hem*, which had become indistinguishable from the personal singulars. Most of these changes were very gradual; Chaucer, for instance, still retains *hir, hem*, and the latter has still a kind of fictitious survival in MnE. *'em*. The net result of all the changes was to level off distinctions no longer needed and at the same time to reinforce distinctions that phonetic change threatened to obliterate.

Similarly with the verb. AS. had two great classes of verbs, usually distinguished as *weak* and *strong*. In the first class the preterit and past participle were formed by adding to the present stem the dental suffixes *-ede, -ode, -de*, and *-ed, -od, -d;* in the second, tense change was indicated by a modification (ablaut, gradation, or "internal inflection") of the stem vowel itself. Compare MnE. *talk—talked* or *drop—dropped* with *sing—sang—sung*. In the strong verbs, never important in numbers but extremely frequent in occurrence, the phonetic changes of the Early ME. period brought about the loss of distinction between past singular and past plural, and seriously weakened the distinction between past plural and past participle. In the weak verbs, the operation of the sound-change that weakened the vowels of final unstressed syllables obliterated the distinction between the class which added the suffixes *-ede, -ed*, and that which added *-ode, -od* to indicate tense changes. By the end of the ME. period, therefore, the verb was fairly close to its modern development. One other important change concerns the personal ending of the third person singular indicative. The *-eth* that would be the regular development of AS. *-aþ* still lingers on in verse, but during the Late ME. period it had already been replaced in the common usage of the Eastern dialects by the ending *-es, -s*, borrowed from the Northern dialect via the East Anglian towns and London Middle-class dialect.

6.16 *Illustrative Survivals and Modifications of English Inflection*

A. The Personal Pronouns in AS.

	1st person		2nd person		3rd person			Common plural for all genders
	sing.	*plural*	*sing.*	*plural*	*M.*	*F.*	*N.*	
Nom.	ic	wē	þū	gē	hē	hēo	hit	hīe
Acc.	mē	ūs	þē	ēow	hine	hīe	hit	hīe
Gen.	mīn	ūre	þīn	ēower	his	hire	his	hira, heora
Dat.	mē	ūs	þē	ēow	him	hire	him	heom

B. The Personal Pronouns in Late ME.

Nom.	I	we	thou	ye	he	**she**	hit	**they**
Acc.	me	us	thee	you	**him**	hir(e)	hit	hem/**them**
Gen.	my, myn	oure	thy(n)	your	his	hir(e)	his	hir(e)/**their**
*Dat.	me	us	thee	you	him	hir(e)	hit	hem/**them**

C. The Personal Pronouns in MnE.

Nom.	I	we	—	**you**	he	she	it	they
Acc.	me	us	—	you	him	her	it	them
Gen.	my, mine	our, ours	—	your, yours	his	her, hers	**its**	their, theirs
*Dat.	me	us	—	you	him	her	it	them

D. The Interrogative Pronoun Masc. and Fem.

	AS.	*ME.*	*MnE.*
Nom.	hwa	who	who
Acc.	hwone	**whom**	whom
Gen.	hwæs	whos	whose
Dat.	hwæm, hwām	**whom**	whom

Characteristics of English in the Early Modern English and Late Modern English Periods (1476–)

6.17 After the end of the ME. period, the English language does not lend itself to any such schematic treatment as we have attempted for Anglo-Saxon and Middle English. The varied and flexible instrument used by Shakespeare, Milton, and, eventually, by ourselves, is altogether too gigantic to be compressed neatly into mnemonic schedules. Moreover, most of us have read the great authors of the Early Modern English period, and we are at least aware of the external appearance of EMnE. To proceed further, to delve beneath the spelling in order to explore the progress of the Great Vowel Shift during the 16th, 17th, 18th, and 19th centuries, would require the use of some such probe as the alphabet of the International Phonetic Association. And even if we familiarized ourselves with such an alphabet, we might well end by knowing at once too much and too little. While it is easy to visualize the phonetic direction of the changes—to state, in phonetic terms, that long low-tongue and mid-tongue vowels were raised, long high-tongue vowels diphthongized, short vowels lowered or centralized—the complicated correlations of vowel with vowel during the period of the changes would still elude us.

6.18 With the fixation of English spelling, which commenced with Caxton and was achieved about 1650, the English language acquired its modern external form. With the introduction of thousands of new words from various sources during the same period, it completed most of the circle of its vocabulary. Thanks to these facts, the modern reader may approach most English authors from Dryden onward without being conscious of too marked a sense of archaism. This annihilation of time is perhaps the greatest benefit conferred on humanity by standard written language.

(a) *Spelling and Pronunciation*

6.19 If a great written national language is ever to perform its proper functions in the world, its spelling will eventually be stabilized once and for all. When, therefore, the stabilization of English spelling sometime around 1650–1700 is regarded as calamitous—as in some respects it is—we should not be blinded to the advantages that standardization has brought us. Nor should we forget that the spelling reformers, such men as Thomas Smith (1568), Richard Mulcaster (1582), William Bullokar (1580), Charles Butler (1634), Edward Phillips (1658), Owen Price (1668), and the anonymous author of *Right Spelling* (1704), faced a situation of near chaos, calling for immediate remedy. And they faced it without knowledge of the continuous phonetic development of English which was to heighten, from decade to decade, the discrepancy between the spoken language and its written form. A similar discrepancy exists in French and several other languages; it is indeed unavoidable in all cases where the conservative forces of a powerful language are arrayed against natural phonemic change. And the change in the spelling of the spoken language, if it ever comes, is bound to be too late to catch up with the progress of linguistic development. Meanwhile, it is comforting for readers of today to be able to peruse books written in 1650 with no more discomfort than a slight feeling of strangeness caused by occasional final *e*'s, double consonants, contracted past participles, and rare forms like ***musick*** and ***publick***.

6.20 For the historian of English, however, spelling standardization has undoubted disadvantages in that it masks completely the continuous phonetic change of the English vowels precisely at the period when they were undergoing their most remarkable development. As a result, our knowledge of these changes has serious gaps. Lacking evidence hidden under the spellings of cultivated literature in the EMnE. period, we have to rely upon various kinds of indirect evidence: the spelling lapses of less literate authors; the rhymes of the poets; the descriptions of pronunciation found in early writings on English phonetics; the condemnation of certain pronunciations by early writers on English grammar; our knowledge of trends of development in MnE.; our study of the various British dialects and American speech varieties. Taken together, these sources supply a not inconsiderable body of evidence, particularly since we know the starting point (the South Eastern Middle English vowel system) and the ending points of the series of vowel changes. It is one of the ironies of the English language that our quite impractical spelling system, by reflecting, for the most part, the pronunciation of the Late Middle English (South East Midland) vowel system, gives us a firm point of departure.

6.21 If we take a series of key words containing the requisite vowels (excluding diphthongs), the positions that the vowels held phonetically in Late Middle English would be as in Chart A on the facing page.

6.22 In EMnE., as stabilized from about 1600 to about 1700, the situation is roughly as it appears in Chart B on the facing page. (The arrows indicate directions of allophonic changes.)

In brief, the long high-tongue vowels have been converted to rising diphthongs with a center-tongue first element, the other long vowels of ME. have each been raised or (in the case of ā) fronted a single degree, the short vowels have tended to be lowered, and the gap in the low back area of the system has been filled by the simplification of former diphthongs, chiefly those which developed before *-gh* (IPA [X]) and "dark" *l* (IPA [ɫ]), and by the retraction of ME. *a* after *w*. Since all evidences indicate the diphthongization of the ME. vowels (ē) and (o͞o) in *bite* and *bout* as the earliest of these changes, we can assume that the difficulty of maintaining a proper distinction between long and short phonemes in the high vowel position furnishes a mechanical explanation of the start of these vowel changes (but cf. 6.11 above).

6.23 The further changes in the vowel system revealed by a comparison of EMnE. with contemporary English seem to be due partly to the further progression of the tendencies sketched above, and partly to a restricted blending of the two chief class dialects. To the former, we can attribute the development of the modern diphthongs in *bite* and *bout* (ī), (ou), IPA [aɪ], [aʊ], generalized from the EMnE. [əi], [əu] in positions before voiced consonants, and also the eventual unrounding and centralization of the vowel of *butt*. To the latter, we can probably attribute the raising of the vowel of *beat* until it coalesces with that of *beet*, a change that, in turn, encouraged the raising of the vowel of *bate* to approximately its present position. A tendency to diphthongize the reflexes of the original ME. long vowels seen in *beet, beat, bate, boat, boot*, which arose in the late 18th century, has now extended to most varieties of English on both sides of the Atlantic. More recently, both Received Standard British and the Southern and Coastal varieties of American English have revealed a further tendency to centralize the first element of these diphthongs as they appear in *boot* and *boat*. Obviously the degree to which these various changes have operated on the regional varieties of MnE. goes a long way toward accounting for many of the chief differences in contemporary pronunciation.

(b) *Vocabulary*

6.24 If the English of the 16th and 17th centuries seems in every respect to have passed through a stage of flux, the fact is nowhere more apparent than in the state of the vocabulary. During earlier periods, borrowing from French and Scandinavian had been aided by the presence of alien populations living and talking side by side with the English. Even the borrowings from Latin had received impetus from the use of spoken Anglo-Latin as a scholarly and legal tongue. In the EMnE. period, however, the bulk of the early borrowings were bookish, directly attributable to the great rising interest in learning, translation, philosophy, the classics, and contemporary foreign language that grew out of the ferment of the Renaissance. The early borrowings were principally from Latin or from Greek through Latin: ***antipathy, appendix, comprehensible, denunciation, dogma, emanate, emphasis, epitome, implacable, lexicon, monopoly, obstruction, pathetic, pretext, reliance, submerge, tantalize***, etc. Later, as the early voyagings and foreign travel seconded the actual physical extension of the British Empire, words of other origins began to flood into the language: Italian words such as ***cameo, grotto, violin;*** Arabic and American Indian words borrowed via Spanish, such as ***apricot, cocoa, embargo, potato***, and ***tobacco;*** French words, first of the type of ***chocolate, detail, equipment, ticket***, and ***explore***, later supplemented by such words of the polite world as ***coquette, pique, soubrette***, and ***coiffure***. But the rapidly growing position of the British Isles as a center of world commerce is best revealed by the borrowings from more exotic sources: ***calico*** and ***dinghy*** from India; ***mammoth*** and ***sable*** from Russia; ***gingham, bantam***, and ***indigo*** from Siam and the Malay Coasts; ***caravan*** from Persia; ***tea*** from China; ***tulip*** from Turkey; ***alpaca*** from South America; ***boorish*** from the Dutch of South Africa. There are few languages that have not been laid under contribution, and many of the words of most distant origin are among those we now use in our everyday affairs.

(c) *Grammar*

6.25 Compared with parallel changes taking place in pronunciation and vocabulary, EMnE. developments in grammar appear to be of comparatively minor importance. Most of them, indeed, are covered in 6.16 above. If Shakespeare could apparently make English a more malleable and flexible instrument of expression than anything we write today, his advantages lie less in relative grammatical freedom than in the narrower gap between the written and spoken language of his time, and, most of all, in his masterly use of the instrument he found ready to his hand. Written language relies principally upon the sentence as its unit of expression; spoken language relies upon the phrase, and especially upon the spontaneous juxtaposition of phrases.

CHART A

	Tongue Front		Tongue Center		Tongue Back	
	Long	*Short*	*Long*	*Short*	*Long*	*Short*
High	**bite** (ē) IPA [i:]	**bit** (ē) short [i]			**bout** (ōō) IPA [u:]	**butt** (ōō) short [u]
Higher Mid	**beet** (ā) IPA [e:]	**bet** (ā) short [e]			**boot** (ō) IPA [o:]	**bott** (ō) short [o]
Lower Mid	**beat** (e) long IPA [ɛ:]				**boat** (ô) long IPA [ɔ:]	
Low			**bate** (ä) IPA [a:]	**bat** (ä) short [a]		

CHART B

	Tongue Front		Tongue Center		Tongue Back	
	Long	*Short*	*Long*		*Long*	*Short*
High	**beet** (ē) IPA [i:]	**bit** (i) [ɪ]	**bite** (iē) IPA [ɪi]	**bout** (ooōō) [ʊu]	**boot** (ōō) IPA [u:]	**butt** (oo) [ʊ]
Higher Mid	**beat** (ā) IPA [e:]	**bet** (ā) or	or (əē) IPA [ə̯i]	or (əōō) [ə̯u]	**boat** (ō) IPA [o:]	**bott** (ō) or
Lower Mid	**bate** (e) long IPA [ɛ:] or	**bet** (e) [ɛ]			**bought** (ô) long IPA [ɔ:] or	**bott** (ô) [ɔ] or
Low	**bate** (a) long IPA [æ:]	**bat** (a) [æ]			(o) long IPA [ɑ:]	**bott** (o) IPA [ɑ]

The great vitality of some types of Elizabethan written English seems to spring from their proximity to the spoken norm.

The following are the most obvious grammatical developments of the EMnE. period: (1) complete replacement of the singular pronouns *thou, thee, thy* except in poetry, by Quakers, and in religious observances; (2) replacement of the nominative plural personal pronoun *ye* by the *you* of the accusative; (3) gradual intrusion of *who* and *which* as relative pronouns beside *that*, the almost invariable relative of ME.; (4) extension of the use of *more* and *most* to form the comparatives and superlatives of adjectives consisting of two or more syllables; (5) a marked loss of impersonal constructions of the type *it likes me;* (6) a great extension, especially during the 18th and 19th centuries, in the use of such "progressive" verb forms as *I am singing, he was going, he is being killed*, etc. (see 4.23 above); (7) a rapid development in the use of the new neuter genitive *its* in place of the *his* of ME.

For the most part, these developments do not appear to have obliterated any distinctions that the English grammatical system vitally needs. In Southern American English, however, the popularity of the plural *you-all* at least suggests a subconscious need for differentiation between the forms of singular and plural for the pronoun of the second person. Of all the EMnE. grammatical changes, the increasing development of "progressive" verbal forms marking the imperfect aspect may in the long run prove to be of most importance.

III. THE DEVELOPMENT OF THE ENGLISH DICTIONARY

7.1 The evolution of the English dictionary is rooted in the general evolution of the English language. In this development the chief pressures were exerted by the steady increase in the word stock of English from the 50,000–60,000 words of Anglo-Saxon through the 100,000–125,000 words of the Middle-English vocabulary to the huge total of some 650,000 words which could theoretically be recorded in an exhaustive dictionary of contemporary English. Such an overall increase as this made the dictionary *necessary*. The pressure of vocabulary, however, has always been influenced and reinforced by the intellectual climate of each successive period of the language. A dictionary is not exactly a work of art, yet it bears as strongly as an artistic production the impress of the age that bore it. For that reason, the history of the dictionary is a fascinating chapter in the history of ideas.

The beginnings of dictionary history are neither national nor concerned with any of the national languages. They are concerned with the international language of medieval European civilization: Latin. Our first word books are lists of relatively difficult Latin terms, usually those of a Scriptural nature, accompanied by glosses in easier or more familiar Latin. Very early in the Anglo-Saxon period, however, we find glosses containing native English (i.e., Anglo-Saxon) equivalents for the hard Latin terms, and it may be that two of these—the *Leiden* and *Erfurt Glosses*—represent the earliest written English we possess. Such glosses, whether Latin-Latin or Latin-English, continued to be compiled during the entire Anglo-Saxon and most of the Middle-English period.

7.2 The next stage of development, attained in England around 1400, was the collection of the isolated glosses into what is called a *glossarium*, a kind of very early Latin-English dictionary. As it chances, our first example of the glossarium, the so-called *Medulla Grammatica* written in East Anglia around 1400, has never been printed; but two later redactions were among our earliest printed books, and one of these, the *Promptorium Parvulorum sive clericorum*, issued by Wynkyn de Worde in 1499, was the first work of a dictionary nature ever to be printed on English soil. Significantly enough, this version of the *Medulla* places the English term first and its Latin equivalent second.

7.3 The first onset of the Renaissance worked against rather than in favor of the native English dictionary. The breakdown of Latin as an international language and the rapid development of international trade led to an immediate demand for foreign-language dictionaries. The first of such works, Palsgrave's *Lesclaircissement de la Langue Francoyse* (1523), was rapidly followed by Salesbury's Welsh-English dictionary (1547), Percival's English-Spanish dictionary (1591), and finally, by the best known of all such works, Florio's Italian-English dictionary (1599). Meanwhile, the first great classical dictionary, Cooper's *Thesaurus* (1565), had already appeared. The history of dictionaries is larded with strange occurrences: we are not surprised, therefore, that the publication of Cooper's work was delayed five years because his wife, fearing that too much lexicography would kill her husband, burned the first manuscript of his magnum opus. It should be noted, in passing, that none of these various word books of the 16th century actually used the title *dictionary* or *dictionarium*. They were called by various kinds of fanciful or half-fanciful names, of which *hortus* "garden," and *thesaurus* "hoard" were particularly popular.

7.4 During the late 16th century, the full tide of the Renaissance had been sweeping a curious flotsam and jetsam into English literary harbors. Constant reading of Greek and Latin bred a race of Holofernes pedants who preferred the Latin or Greek term to the English term. Their principle in writing was to use Latino-Greek polysyllabics in a Latino-English syntax. Their strange vocabulary—studded with what some critics call "inkhorn" terms—eventually affected English so powerfully that no non-Latinate Englishman could ever hope to read many works in his own language unless he was provided with explanations of elements unfamiliar to him. The "Dictionary of Hard Words," the real predecessor of the modern dictionary, was developed to provide precisely such explanations. It is significant that the first English word book to use the name *dictionary*, Cokeram's *The English Dictionary* (1623), is subtitled "An Interpreter of Hard Words." Among those explained on its first few pages are *Abequitate, Bulbulcitate*, and *Sullevation*. In point of time, the first "dictionary of hard words" was Robert Cawdrey's *Table Alphabeticall of Hard Words* (1604). Of the various works of the same class appearing after this date may be mentioned John Bullokar's *English Expositor* (1616) and Edward Phillip's *New World of Words* (1658), both of which reveal a strong interest in the reform of spelling, Blount's *Glossographia* (1656) containing the first etymologies ever to appear in a printed English dictionary, and Thomas Kersey's *Dictionarium Anglo-Brittanicum* (1708), which also includes legal terms, provincialisms, and archaisms. If the 16th was the century of the foreign-language dictionary, the 17th was the century of the dictionary of hard words.

7.5 Between 1708 and 1721, hard-word dictionaries began to be replaced by word books giving ever-increasing attention to literary usage. The Latino-Greek borrowings of the earlier century had been either absorbed into the language or sloughed away. The French influence, from 1660 onwards, had replaced Renaissance stylistic ideas with notions of a simple elegance in syntax and a quiet effectiveness in vocabulary. These stylistic virtues were actually achieved in the works of Swift, Addison, Steele, and lesser writers. The literary mind of the early 18th century, therefore, was convinced that English had finally attained a standard of purity such as it had never previously known; it was also convinced that the brash outgrowth of mercantile expansionism, later to be reinforced by the infant Industrial Revolution, might very well destroy this hard-won standard of literary refinement. What more natural than that the standard should be enshrined in a dictionary for the admiration and guidance of posterity?

7.6 The first word book to embody the ideals of the age was Nathaniel Bailey's *Universal Etymological Dictionary of the English Language*, originally published in 1721, and then, in a beautiful folio volume with illustrations by Flaxman, in 1731. This, one of the most revolutionary dictionaries ever to appear, was the first to pay proper attention to current usage, the first to feature etymology, the first to give aid in syllabification, the first to give illustrative quotations (chiefly from proverbs), the first to include illustrations, and the first to indicate pronunciation. An interleaved copy of the 1731 folio edition was the basis of Samuel Johnson's *Dictionary* of 1755; through Johnson, it influenced all subsequent lexicographical practice. The position of dictionary pioneer, commonly granted to Johnson or to Noah Webster, belongs in reality to one of the few geniuses lexicography ever produced: Nathaniel Bailey.

7.7 Johnson's *Dictionary* (1755) enormously extends the techniques developed by Bailey. Johnson was able to revise Bailey's crude etymologies on the basis of Francis Junius' *Etymologicon Anglicanum* (first published in 1743), to make a systematic use of illustrative quotations, to fix the spelling of many disputed words, to develop a really discriminating system of definition, and to exhibit the vocabulary of English much more fully than had ever been attempted before. In his two-volume work, the age and following ages found their ideal word book. Indeed, a good deal of the importance of the book lies in its later influence. It dominated English letters for a full century after its appearance and, after various revisions, continued in common use until 1900. As late as the '90's, most Englishmen used the word *dictionary* as a mere synonym for Johnson's *Dictionary;* in 1880 a Bill was actually thrown out of Parliament because a word in it was not in "the Dictionary."

7.8 One of the tasks taken upon himself by Johnson was to remove "improprieties and absurdities" from the language. In short, he became a linguistic legislator attempting to perform for English those offices performed for French by the French Academy. From this facet of his activities we get the notion, still held by many dictionary users, and fostered by many dictionary publishers, that the dictionary is a "supreme authority" by which to arbitrate questions of "correctness" and "incorrectness." The dictionaries of the second half of west of the Appalachians, was issued in Chicago by George W. Ogilvie, a publisher who carried on his own private guerrilla "war of the dictionaries" against the Merriam Company between 1904 and circa 1917. At the moment, the most important advances in lexicography are taking place in the field of the abridged collegiate-type dictionaries.

7.16 Meanwhile, the scholarly dictionary has not been neglected. Once the *New English Dictionary* was published, scholarly opinion realized the need to supplement it in the various periods of English and particularly in American English. The first of the proposed supplements, edited by Sir William Craigie and Professor J. R. Hulbert, is the *Dictionary of American English on Historical Principles*, completed in 1944. This was followed by a *Dictionary of Americanisms*, edited by Mitford M. Mathews and published in 1951. A *Middle English Dictionary*, a *Dictionary of the Older Scottish Tongue*, and a *Dictionary of Later Scottish* are in preparation, and work on the *American Dialect Dictionary* of the American Dialect Society is now finally under way.

the 18th century extended this notion particularly to the field of pronunciation. By 1750, the increasing wealth of the middle classes was making itself felt in the social and political worlds. Those who possessed it, speakers, for the most part, of a middle-class dialect, earnestly desired a key to the pronunciations accepted in polite society. To provide for their needs, various pronunciation experts—usually of Scottish or Irish extraction—edited a series of pronunciation dictionaries. Of these, the most important are James Buchanan's *New English Dictionary* (1769), William Kenrick's *New Dictionary of the English Language* (1773), Thomas Sheridan's *General Dictionary of the English Language* (1780), and, above all, John Walker's *Critical Pronouncing Dictionary and Expositor of the English Language* (1791). In such works, pronunciation was indicated by small superscript numbers referring to the "powers" of the various vowel sounds. Despite the legislative function exercised by the authors of almost all of these works, we must admit that they did indicate contemporary pronunciation with great accuracy, and when Walker's pronunciations were combined with Johnson's definitions the result was a dictionary which dominated the word-book field, both in England and the United States, until well after 1850.

7.9 If the chief contributions of the 18th century to dictionary making were (1) authoritative recording of literary vocabulary and (2) accurate recording of pronunciation, those of the 19th were unmistakably (1) the recording of word history through dated quotations and (2) the development of encyclopedic word books. Already in 1755, Samuel Johnson had hinted in his preface that the sense of a word "may easily be collected entire from the examples." During the first twenty-five years of the century, the researches of R. K. Rask, J. L. C. Grimm, and F. Bopp clearly defined the historical principle in linguistic. It was only a question of time, therefore, before someone combined Johnson's perception with the findings of the new science of historical linguistics. That person was Charles Richardson, who, in this *New Dictionary of the English Language* (1836), produced a dictionary completely lacking definitions but one in which both the senses and the historical evolution of the senses were accurately indicated by dated defining quotations. Richardson's work leads directly to the great *New English Dictionary on Historical Principles*, first organized in 1858, begun under Sir James Murray in 1888, and completed under Sir William Craigie in 1928. With its supplement (1933), the *New English Dictionary* or *Oxford English Dictionary* (N.E.D. or O.E.D.) covers the vocabulary of English with a completeness of historical evidence and a discrimination of senses unparalleled in linguistic history. No other language has ever been recorded on anything approaching this scale, and no dictionary of English since the *New English Dictionary* was completed has failed to reveal a profound debt to this monumental work. As compared with the effort represented by the N.E.D., the attempt to record the technological vocabularies of the language as first seen in John W. Ogilvie's *Universal Dictionary of the English Language* (1850) seems to be of minor importance, although it has had great practical effect on subsequent American dictionaries.

7.10 Since the publication of the O.E.D., the only important British dictionary has been Henry Cecil Wyld's *Universal Dictionary of the English Language* (1932), a work of somewhat restricted vocabulary coverage but one which may well point the way to the dictionary of the future. Wyld has discarded the older logical definitions for definitions of a more functional nature; his examples delve deeply into idiom; his etymologies are of a completeness and modernity unparalleled until this present dictionary in any medium-sized word book. The failure of Wyld's book to achieve much popularity on this side of the Atlantic underlines the fact that the typical American dictionary of the English language is a work *differing in kind* from any of those so far mentioned. It differs because the conditions of American life and culture differ from those of English life and culture.

7.11 The modern American dictionary is typically a single compact volume published at a relatively modest price containing: (1) definitive American spellings, (2) pronunciations indicated by diacritical markings, (3) strictly limited etymologies, (4) numbered senses, (5) some illustrations, (6) selective treatment of synonyms and antonyms, (7) encyclopedic inclusion of scientific, technological, geographical, and biographical items. It owes its development, within the general framework of the evolution sketched above, to the presence of a large immigrant population in this country, to the elaborate American system of popular education, and to the vast commercial opportunities implicit in both of these.

The first American dictionaries were unpretentious little schoolbooks based chiefly on Johnson's *Dictionary* of 1755 by way of various English abridgments of that work. The earliest of these were Samuel Johnson Junior's *School Dictionary* (1798), Johnson and Elliott's *Selected Pronouncing and Accented Dictionary* (1800), and Caleb Alexander's *Columbian Dictionary* (1800). The most famous work of this class, Noah Webster's *Compendious Dictionary of the English Language* (1806) was an enlargement of Entick's *Spelling Dictionary* (London, 1764), distinguished from its predecessors chiefly by a few encyclopedic supplements and emphasis upon its (supposed) Americanism. The book was never popular and contributed little either to Webster's own reputation or to the development of the American dictionary in general.

7.12 The first important date in American lexicography is 1828. The work that makes it important is Noah Webster's *An American Dictionary of the English Language* in two volumes. Webster's book has many deficiencies—etymologies quite untouched by the linguistic science of the time, a rudimentary pronunciation system actually inferior to that used by Walker in 1791, etc.—but in its insistence upon American spellings, in definitions keyed to the American scene, and in its illustrative quotations from the Founding Fathers of the Republic, it provided the country with the first *native* dictionary comparable in scope with that of Dr. Johnson. It was not, as is often claimed, the real parent of the modern American dictionary; it was merely the foster-parent. Because of its two-volume format and its relatively high price it never achieved any great degree of popular acceptance in Webster's own lifetime. Probably its greatest contribution to succeeding American dictionaries was the style of definition writing—writing of a clarity and pithiness never approached before its day.

7.13 The first American lexicographer to hit upon the particular pattern that distinguishes the American dictionary was Webster's lifelong rival, Joseph E. Worcester. His *Comprehensive, Pronouncing, and Explanatory Dictionary of the English Language* (1830), actually a thoroughly revised abridgment of Webster's two-volume work of 1828, was characterized by the addition of new words, a more conservative spelling, brief, well-phrased definitions, full indication of pronunciation by means of diacritics, use of stress marks to divide syllables, and lists of synonyms. Because it was compact and low priced, it immediately became popular—far more popular, in fact, than any of Webster's own dictionaries in his own lifetime. As George P. Krapp, in his *The English Language in America*, says: "If one balances the faults of the Webster of 1828 against the faults of the Worcester of 1830, the totals are greatly in the favor of Worcester." One might feel the same about its merits as compared with those of Webster's own revision of his *American Dictionary* (1841), which featured the inclusion of scientific terms compiled by Professor W. Tully. The first Webster dictionary to embody the typical American dictionary pattern was that of 1847, edited by Noah Webster's son-in-law, Chauncey A. Goodrich, and published by the Merriams.

7.14 Temperamentally the flamboyant Noah Webster and the cautious Joseph Worcester were natural rivals. Their rivalry, however, was as nothing compared with that which developed between the rival publishers of the Webster and Worcester dictionaries. By 1845, the great flood of immigration and the vast extension of the school system had suddenly lifted dictionary making into the realm of big business. In a "war of the dictionaries" that reflects the rudimentary business ethics of the period, the rival publishers used every device of advertisement and every stratagem of high-powered salesmanship to drive each other off the market. Unsavory as this war appears in retrospect, it certainly helped to force rapid improvement of the dictionaries that these publishers controlled. Worcester's initial advantages were surpassed in the Merriam-Webster of 1847; the innovations in Worcester's edition of 1860 were more than paralleled in the Merriam-Webster of 1864, one of the best dictionaries ever to appear, but one from which almost everything really characteristic of Noah Webster himself was deleted. The battle was finally decided in favor of the Webster dictionaries, chiefly because the popularity of Webster's "Little Blue Back Speller" had put their name in every household, partly because of the death of Joseph Worcester, and partly because of the merit of the Merriam product from 1864 onwards.

7.15 Since about 1870, the climate of American dictionary making has been much more peaceful. In the field of unabridged dictionaries, the most important accretion is the *Century Dictionary* (1889), edited by the great American linguist, William Dwight Whitney, and issued in six volumes. Unfortunately, this magnificent work, considered by many authorities to be basically the finest ever issued by a commercial publisher, has lost much of its popularity because of inadequate subsequent revision. The fact that it was not in a one-volume format undoubtedly also worked against its popular success. The only other new unabridged dictionaries that have appeared in the period are Webster's *Imperial Dictionary of the English Language* (1904), and Funk and Wagnalls *New Standard Dictionary* (1893). The first of these, the only unabridged dictionary ever published

ABBREVIATIONS AND SYMBOLS USED IN THIS DICTIONARY

abbrev., abbreviated; abbreviation
abl., ablative
Abyss., Abyssinian
acc., accusative
act., active
A.D., anno Domini
adj., adjective
adv., adverb
Afr., African
Alb., Albanian
Am., American
a.m., A.M., ante meridiem
Am. Fr., American French
Am. Ind., American Indian
Am. Sp., American Spanish
Anglo-Fr., Anglo-French
Anglo-Ind., Anglo-Indian
Anglo-Ir., Anglo-Irish
Anglo-L., Anglo-Latin
Anglo-N., Anglo-Norse
Anglo-Norm., Anglo-Norman
Ar., Arabic
Aram., Aramaic
Arm., Armoric
art., article
AS., Anglo-Saxon
Assyr., Assyrian
at. no., atomic number
at. wt., atomic weight
Bab., Babylonian
B.C., before Christ
Beng., Bengali
Bohem., Bohemian
Braz., Brazilian
Bret., Breton
Brit., British
Bulg., Bulgarian
c., circa (about, approximately); **century**
Canad., Canadian
Canad. Fr., Canadian French
Catal., Catalonian
caus., causative
Celt., Celtic
cf., *confer* (compare)
Ch., Chaldean; Chaldee
Chin., Chinese
Chron., Chronicles
coed., coeducational
Col., Colossians
Colloq., colloq., colloquial
comb., combination
comp., compound
compar., comparative
conj., conjunction.
contr., contracted; contraction
Cor., Corinthians
Corn., Cornish
Cym., Cymric
D., Dutch
Dan., Danish; Daniel
dat., dative
def. art., definite article
deriv., derivative
Deut., Deuteronomy
Dial., dial., dialect; dialectal; dialectic
dim., diminutive
Early Mod. D., Early Modern Dutch
Early Mod. Eng., Early Modern English
Eccles., Ecclesiastes
E.Fris., East Frisian
e.g., *exempli gratia* (for example)
Egypt., Egyptian
E.Ind., East Indian
Eng., English
envir., environment
Eph., Ephesians
equiv., equivalent
Esk., Eskimo
esp., especially
est., estimated
Esth., Esther
etc., et cetera (and others, and so forth)
Eth., Ethiopic
etym., etymology
Ex., Exodus
Ez., Ezra
Ezek., Ezekiel
fem., feminine
ff., following
fig., figurative; **figuratively**
Finn., Finnish
Fl., Flemish
fl., flourished
Fr., French
Frank., Frankish; **Franconian**
freq., frequentative
Fris., Frisian
ft., feet
fut., future
G., German
Gael., Gaelic
Gal., Galatians
Gaul., Gaulish
Gen., Genesis
genit., genitive
Gmc., Germanic
Goth., Gothic
Gr., Greek
grad., graduate
Hab., Habakkuk
Hag., Haggai
Haw., Hawaiian
Heb., Hebrew; **Hebrews**
Hind., Hindi; Hindu; **Hindustani**
Hos., Hosea
Hung., Hungarian
Ice., Icelandic
Idg., Indo-Germanic
IE., Indo-European
i.e., *id est* (that is)
in., inches
Ind., Indian
indef. art., indefinite **article**
indic., indicative
inf., infinitive
intens., intensified; **intensifier; intensive**
interj., interjection
IPA, **International Phonetic Alphabet**
Ir., Irish
Iran., Iranian
irreg., irregular
Isa., Isaiah
It., Italian
Ja., James
Japan., Japanese
Jav., Javanese
Jer., Jeremiah
Josh., Joshua
Judg., Judges
Kor., Korean
L., Latin
Lam., Lamentations
Late Anglo-Fr., Late **Anglo-French**
Late Gr., Late Greek
Late ME., Late Middle English
Lev., Leviticus
LG., Low German
LGr., Late Greek
L.Heb., Late Hebrew
lit., literally
Lith., Lithuanian
LL., Late Latin; **Low Latin**
LWS., Late West Saxon
Mal., Malachi
masc., masculine
Matt., Matthew
MD., Middle Dutch
ME., Middle English
Med., Medieval
Mex., Mexican
MFl., Middle Flemish
MFr., Middle French
MGr., Medieval Greek; **Middle Greek**
MHG., Middle High German
mi., mile; miles
Mic., Micah
MIr., Middle Irish
MIt., Middle Italian
ML., Medieval Latin
MLG., Middle Low German
MnE., Modern English
Mod., mod., modern

Mod. Gr., Modern Greek
Mod. L., Modern Latin
Mod. Pr., Modern Provençal
Mong., **Mongol.**, Mongolian
MScand., Middle Scandinavian
MScot., Middle Scottish
N., Norse
n., noun
Nah., Nahum
naut., nautical
Neh., Nehemiah
neut., neuter
nom., nominative
Norm., Norman
Norw., Norwegian
n.pl., noun plural
Numb., Numbers
O, old
OAr., Old Arabic
Ob., Obadiah
Obs., **obs.**, obsolete
occas., occasionally
OCelt., Old Celtic
OCym., Old Cymric
OD., Old Dutch
ODan., Old Danish
OFr., Old French
OFris., Old Frisian
OHG., Old High German
OIr., Old Irish
OIt., Old Italian
OL., Old Latin
OLG., Old Low German
ON., Old Norse
ONorm.Fr., Old Norman French
OPer., Old Persian
orig., origin; original; originally
OS., Old Saxon
OSlav., Old Slavic
OSerb., Old Serbian
OSp., Old Spanish
OW., Old Welsh
p., page
pass., passive
Per., Persic; Persian
perf., perfect
pers., person; personal
Peruv., Peruvian
Phil., Philippians; Philemon
Phoen., Phoenician
phr., phrase
Pid.Eng., Pidgin English
pl., plural
p.m., **P.M.**, post meridiem
Pol., Polish
pop., population
Port., Portuguese
poss., possessive
pp., pages; past participle
ppr., present participle
Pr., Provençal
Pre-AS., Pre-Anglo-Saxon
prec., preceding
prep., preposition
pres., present
prin. pts., principal parts
prob., probable; probably
prof., professional
pron., pronoun
pronun., pronunciation
Prov., Proverbs
prov., provincial
Prov. Eng., Provincial English
Prov. Scot., Provincial Scottish
Ps., Psalms
p.t., past tense
redupl., reduplication; reduplicative
refl., reflexive
resp., respelling
Rev., Revelation
Rom., Romans
Russ., Russian
S.Afr.D., South African Dutch
Sam., Samaritan; Samuel
Sans., Sanskrit
Scand., Scandinavian
Scot., Scottish
Sem., Semitic
Serb., Serbian
sing., singular
Singh., Singhalese
Slav., Slavic; Slavonic
S. of Sol., Song of Solomon
Sp., Spanish
sp., spelling
sq., square
subj., subjunctive
superl., superlative
Sw., **Swed.**, Swedish
syn., synonymy
Syr., Syrian; Syriac
t., tense
Tag., Tagalog
Tart., Tartar
Thess., Thessalonians
Tibet., Tibetan
Tim., Timothy
Tit., Titus
transl., translation
Turk., Turkish
ult., ultimate; ultimately
unc., uncertain
undergrad., undergraduate
v., verb
var., variant
v.aux., verb auxiliary
v.i., verb intransitive
v.imp., verb impersonal
v.t., verb transitive
W., Welsh
W.Afr., West African
W.Fl., West Flemish
W.Gmc., West Germanic
W.Ind., West Indian
W.S., West Saxon
Yid., Yiddish
Zech., Zechariah
Zeph., Zephaniah

* hypothetical
‡ foreign word or phrase
< derived from
? perhaps; possibly; uncertain
+ plus
& and

A

A, a (ā), ***n.*** [*pl.* A's, a's, As, as (āz)], 1. the first letter of the English alphabet: from the Greek *alpha*, a borrowing from the Phoenician: see **alphabet**, table. 2. a sound of A or a: in English, the low front vowel, IPA [æ], of *hat;* the low central or low back vowel, IPA [a] or [ɑ], of *father, barn;* and the mid front vowel, IPA [e], of *bake.* 3. a type or impression for A or a. 4. *a symbol for* the first in a sequence or group. ***adj.*** 1. of A or a. 2. first in a sequence or group; hence, 3. first-class; A 1: see **A one.**

A (ā), ***n.*** 1. an object shaped like A. 2. in *chemistry, the symbol for* argon. 3. in *education,* a grade first in quality: as, an *A* in history. 4. in *music, a)* the sixth tone or note in the scale of C major, or the first in the scale of A minor. *b)* a key, string, etc. producing this tone. *c)* the scale having A as the keynote. ***adj.*** shaped like A.

a (ə; *stressed,* ā), ***adj., indefinite article*** [form of *an* before consonants; see AN, *adj.*], 1. one; one sort of. 2. each; any one. *A* connotes a thing not previously noted or recognized, in contrast with *the,* which connotes a thing previously noted or recognized. 3. [orig. a prep. < AS. *an, on,* in, on, at], to each; in each; for each; per: as, once *a* day. Before words beginning with a consonant sound or a sounded *h, a* is used (*a* child, *a* home, *a* uniform, *a* eunuch); before words beginning with a vowel sound or a silent *h, an* is used (*an* eye, *an* ultimatum, *an* honor).

a (ə), ***prep.*** [AS. *of,* from, of], of: as, Anthony *a* Wood.

a (ə) ***pron.*** [Dial.], 1. he. 2. she. 3. it. 4. they. 5. I.

a (ə) ***prep.*, a-** (ə), ***prefix*** [weakened form of AS. *an, on,* in, on, at], 1. in, into, on, at, to, as in *aboard, ashore, abed.* 2. in the act or state of, as in *asleep, a-crying, a-wishing.* The prefix, hyphenated or unhyphenated, is now in general use, but the preposition is found only occasionally, as in *a fishing.*

a, a' (ô, ä), ***adj.*** [Scot.], all.

a- (ə), a prefix of various origins and meanings: 1. [AS. *a-, ar-,* out of, up], *up, out,* as in *awake, arise:* now generally used as an intensive. 2. [AS. *of-, af-,* off, of], *off, of,* as in *akin.* 3. (ā, a, ə), [Gr. *a-, an-,* not], *not, without,* as in *amentia, agnostic:* before vowels *an-* is used, as in *anesthetic.* 4. [L.], ab-: used before *m, p, v,* as in *aversion.* 5. [L.], ad-: used before *sc, sp, st,* as in *ascription.*

a, in *algebra,* a symbol representing a known quantity or a constant.

A., 1. Absolute. 2. Academy. 3. acre. 4. America. 5. American. 6. angstrom unit. 7. April. 8. Artillery.

A., angstrom unit.

A., a., [L.], 1. *anno,* in the year. 2. *ante,* before.

a., 1. about. 2. acre; acres. 3. active. 4. adjective. 5. alto. 6. ampere. 7. anonymous. 8. answer. 9. are (in the metric system).

A.A., 1. antiaircraft. 2. antiaircraft artillery.

AAA, Agricultural Adjustment Administration.

A.A.A., 1. Amateur Athletic Association. 2. American Automobile Association. 3. Automobile Association of America.

A.A.A.A., Associated Actors and Artists of America: an A.F. of L. labor union.

A.A.A.L., American Academy of Arts and Letters.

A.A.A.S., 1. American Academy of Arts and Sciences. 2. American Association for the Advancement of Science.

Aa·chen (ä'kən, ä'khən), ***n.*** a city in the Rhine Province, Germany: pop., 163,000: French name, *Aix-la-Chapelle.*

A.A.E., American Association of Engineers.

A.A.E.E., American Association of Electrical Engineers.

A.A.F., Army Air Forces.

A.A.G., Assistant Adjutant General.

Aal·borg (ôl'bôr), ***n.*** a seaport in northern Denmark: pop., 55,000.

Aalst (älst), ***n.*** Alost: the Flemish name.

A.A.P.S.S., American Academy of Political and Social Sciences.

Aar (är), ***n.*** a river in Switzerland, flowing into the Rhine: length, 181 mi.

aard·vark (ärd'värk'), ***n.*** [D., earth pig, earth farrow; see FARROW], a burrowing African mammal that feeds on ants and termites.

aard·wolf (ärd'woolf'), ***n.*** [*pl.* AARDWOLVES (-woolvz')], [D., earth wolf], a South African flesh-eating mammal somewhat like the hyena and the civet.

Aar·hus (ôr'hōōs), ***n.*** a seaport in eastern Jutland, Denmark: pop., 100,000.

Aar·on (âr'ən, ar'ən), [LL.; Gr. *Aarōn;* Heb. *aharōn,* lit., the exalted one], a masculine name. ***n.*** in the *Bible,* the older brother of Moses and first high priest of the Hebrews: Ex. 4.

Aa·ron·ic (âr-on'ik), ***adj.*** 1. of or characteristic of Aaron. 2. Levitical.

Aaron's rod, 1. in the *Bible,* the rod used by Aaron to perform miracles: Numb. 17:8. 2. any of several plants with flowers on a long stem, as the goldenrod and the common mullein: also **Aaron's-rod.** 3. in *architecture,* a long, straight molding with scroll and leaf ornament.

A.A.S., 1. *Academiae Americanae Socius,* [Mod. L.], Fellow of the American Academy. 2. American Academy of Sciences.

A.A.U., Amateur Athletic Union.

A.A.U.P., American Association of University Professors.

A.A.U.W., American Association of University Women.

Ab (äb, ab; Heb. ôv), ***n.*** [Heb.], the eleventh month of the Jewish year: see **Jewish calendar.**

ab- (ab, əb), [L.], a prefix meaning *away, from, from off, down,* as in *abdicate:* shortened to *a-* before *m, p, v;* often *abs-* before *c* or *t,* as in *abstract.*

Ab, in *chemistry,* alabamine.

ab., about.

A.B., *Artium Baccalaureus,* [Mod.L.], Bachelor of Arts.

A.B., a.b., able-bodied (seaman).

a·ba (ä'bə), ***n.*** [Ar.], 1. a woven fabric of camel's or goat's hair. 2. a loose, sleeveless robe worn by Arabs.

a·ba·cá (ä'bə-kä'), ***n.*** [Tag.], 1. a kind of hemp. 2. the Philippine plant that produces it.

a·back (ə-bak'), ***adv. & adj.*** [AS. *on bæc,* at or on the back], 1. [Archaic], backward; back. 2. in *navigation,*

a) backward against the mast, as the sails of a square-rigged vessel in a wind from straight ahead. b) in an unmanageable condition because of a sudden shift of wind striking the sails from the side opposite that to which they are trimmed.

taken aback, surprised; startled and confused.

ab·a·cus (ab'ə-kəs), *n.* [*pl.* ABACUSES (-iz), ABACI (-sī')], [L. < Gr. *abax,* counting board], 1. a frame with beads or balls sliding back and forth on wires or in slots, for doing or teaching arithmetic. 2. in *architecture,* a slab atop the capital of a column.

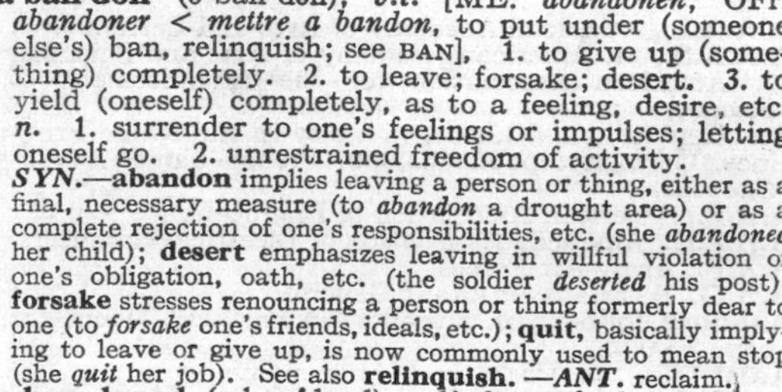

ABACUS

A·bad·don (ə-bad'ən), *n.* [Heb., destruction, abyss], in the *Bible,* 1. the place of lost souls; hell; bottomless pit. 2. the angel of this place, Apollyon: Rev. 9:11.

a·baft (ə-baft'), *adv.* [AS. *on-be-æftan; on,* on + *be,* by + *æftan,* behind], on or toward the stern or rear of a ship; astern; aft. *prep.* in *nautical usage,* behind; back of.

ab·a·lo·ne (ab'ə-lō'ni), *n.* [Sp.], a sea mollusk with an oval, somewhat spiral shell perforated along the rim and lined with mother-of-pearl.

ab·am·pere (ab-am'pêr), *n.* [*ab*solute + *ampere*], a C.G.S. electromagnetic unit, 10 amperes.

a·ban·don (ə-ban'dən), *v.t.* [ME. *abandonen;* OFr. *abandoner* < *mettre a bandon,* to put under (someone else's) ban, relinquish; see BAN], 1. to give up (something) completely. 2. to leave; forsake; desert. 3. to yield (oneself) completely, as to a feeling, desire, etc. *n.* 1. surrender to one's feelings or impulses; letting oneself go. 2. unrestrained freedom of activity.
SYN.—**abandon** implies leaving a person or thing, either as a final, necessary measure (to *abandon* a drought area) or as a complete rejection of one's responsibilities, etc. (she *abandoned* her child); **desert** emphasizes leaving in willful violation of one's obligation, oath, etc. (the soldier *deserted* his post); **forsake** stresses renouncing a person or thing formerly dear to one (to *forsake* one's friends, ideals, etc.); **quit,** basically implying to leave or give up, is now commonly used to mean stop (she *quit* her job). See also **relinquish.** —*ANT.* reclaim.

a·ban·doned (ə-ban'dənd), *adj.* [pp. of *abandon*], 1. given up; forsaken; deserted. 2. given up to wickedness; immoral and shameless. 3. unrestrained.

a·ban·don·ment (ə-ban'dən-mənt), *n.* 1. an abandoning. 2. the fact or condition of being abandoned.

‡à bas (å' bä'), [Fr.], down with: an expression of disapproval: opposed to *vive.*

a·base (ə-bās'), *v.t.* [ABASED (-bāst'), ABASING], [OFr. *abaissier;* LL. *abassare,* to lower, bring down; see A- & BASE (low)], to humble; humiliate: as, he *abased* himself before the king. —*SYN.* see **degrade.**

a·base·ment (ə-bās'mənt), *n.* the fact or state of being abased; humiliation; degradation.

a·bash (ə-bash'), *v.t.* [ME. *abassen;* OFr. *esbahir,* to astonish < L. *ex* + *bah* (interj. of surprise)], to make ashamed and uneasy; make self-conscious and embarrassed; disconcert. —*SYN.* see **embarrass.**

a·bash·ment (ə-bash'mənt), *n.* the fact or state of being abashed; feeling of shame and uneasiness.

a·bat·a·ble (ə-bāt'ə-b'l), *adj.* that can be abated.

a·bate (ə-bāt'), *v.t.* [ABATED (-id), ABATING], [ME. *abaten;* OFr. *abattre,* to beat down; see A- & BATTER (to beat)], 1. to make less in amount, degree, force, etc. 2. to deduct. 3. in *law,* to put a stop to; end; quash. *v.i.* to become less in amount, degree, force, etc.; diminish; subside. —*SYN.* see **wane.**

a·bate·ment (ə-bāt'mənt), *n.* [ME.; OFr.; see ABATE], 1. lessening; reduction. 2. in *law,* the act of putting an end to; quashing. 3. the amount abated.

a·bat·er (ə-bāt'ēr), *n.* a person or thing that abates.

ab·a·tis (ab'ə-tis), *n. sing. & pl.* [Fr. < *abattre,* to beat down; see ABATE], 1. a barricade of felled trees with branches facing the enemy. 2. a barbed-wire entanglement for defense. Also spelled **abattis.**

a·ba·tor (ə-bā'tēr), *n.* in *law,* a person who abates.

A battery, an electric battery of low voltage used to light the filament of certain radio tubes, etc.

ab·at·toir (ab'ə-twär', ab'ə-twär'), *n.* [Fr. < *abattre,* to beat down, fell; see ABATE], a slaughterhouse.

ab·ax·i·al (ab-ak'si-əl), *adj.* [*ab-,* from + *axial*], away from the axis: as, an *abaxial* ray of light.

ab·ba (ab'ə), *n.* [Aram.], 1. father: title of a bishop in the Syriac, Coptic, and Ethiopic Christian churches. 2. [A-], in the *New Testament,* God: Mark 14:36.

ab·ba·cy (ab'ə-si), *n.* [*pl.* ABBACIES (-siz)], [LL. *abbatia* < L. *abbas;* see ABBOT], an abbot's position, jurisdiction, or term of office.

Ab·bas·sid (ə-bas'id, ab'ə-sid), *n. & adj.* Abbasside.

Ab·bas·side (ə-bas'īd, ab'ə-sīd'), *n.* any caliph of the dynasty that ruled at Bagdad (750–1258 A.D.) and claimed descent from Mohammed's uncle, Abbas. *adj.* of this dynasty.

ab·ba·tial (ə-bā'shəl), *adj.* [Fr.; LL. *abbatialis* < *abbatia;* see ABBACY], of an abbot or abbey.

ab·bé (ab'ā; Fr. å'bā'), *n.* [Fr.; L. *abbas;* see ABBOT], in France, a title of respect given to a priest, minister, etc.

ab·bess (ab'is, ab'es), *n.* [ME. & OFr. *abbesse* < LL. *abbatissa,* fem. of *abbas;* see ABBOT], a woman who is the superior, or head, of a nunnery: abbreviated **abb.**

ab·bey (ab'i), *n.* [*pl.* ABBEYS (-iz)], [ME. *abbeie;* OFr. *abaie* < L. *abbatia;* see ABBACY], 1. a monastery headed by an abbot or a nunnery headed by an abbess. 2. the monks or nuns in such a place, collectively. 3. a church or building belonging to an abbey. Abbreviated **abb.** —*SYN.* see **cloister.**

Ab·bey, Edwin Austin (ab'i), 1852–1911; American painter.

ab·bot (ab'ət), *n.* [AS. *abbod;* LL. & Gr. *abbas;* Aram. *abba,* father], a man who is head of a monastery; father superior: abbreviated **abb.**

Ab·bot, Charles Gree·ley (grē'li ab'ət), 1872– ; American astrophysicist.

Ab·bots·ford (ab'əts-fērd), *n.* the estate (1812–1832) of Sir Walter Scott, on the Tweed River in Scotland.

Ab·bott, Jacob (ab'ət), 1803–1879; American clergyman and author.

Abbott, Lyman, 1835–1922; son of *Jacob;* American clergyman, editor, and author.

abbr., abbrev., 1. abbreviated. 2. abbreviation.

ab·bre·vi·ate (ə-brē'vi-āt'), *v.t.* [ABBREVIATED (-id), ABBREVIATING], [< L. *abbreviatus,* pp. of *abbreviare* < *ad-,* to + *breviare* < *brevis,* short], 1. to make shorter. 2. to shorten (a word or phrase) by leaving out or substituting letters. —*SYN.* see **shorten.**

ab·bre·vi·a·tion (ə-brē'vi-ā'shən), *n.* [Fr.; L. *abbreviatio;* see ABBREVIATE], 1. a making shorter. 2. the fact or state of being made shorter. 3. a shortened form of a word or phrase, as *N.Y.* for *New York, Mr.* for *Mister, lb.* for *pound, CIO* for *Congress of Industrial Organizations,* etc. Abbreviated **abbr., abbrev.**

ab·bre·vi·a·tor (ə-brē'vi-ā'tēr), *n.* one who abbreviates.

A B C (ā' bē' sē'), *n.* [*pl.* A B C's (-sēz')], 1. *usually pl.* the alphabet; hence, 2. the basic or simplest elements (of a subject); rudiments.

ABC, American Broadcasting Company.

ab·cou·lomb (ab-kōō-lom'), *n.* [*ab*solute + *coulomb*], a C.G.S. electromagnetic unit, 10 coulombs.

A B C Powers, Argentina, Brazil, and Chile.

Abd-el-Ka·dir (əb-dool-kä'dir), *n.* Algerian leader in wars against the French; lived 1807?–1883.

Abd-el-Krim (əb-dool-krēm'; Eng. ab'del-krim'), *n.* leader of a revolt of the Moors in the Rif region, Morocco (1919–1926); born c. 1880.

Abd-er-Rah·man Khan (äb'dēr-rə-män' khän'), 1830?–1901; amir of Afghanistan (1880–1901).

Ab·di·as (ab-dī'əs), *n.* Obadiah: form used in the Douay Bible.

ab·di·ca·ble (ab'də-kə-b'l), *adj.* that can be abdicated.

ab·di·cant (ab'də-kənt), *adj.* [L. *abdicans,* ppr. of *abdicare;* see ABDICATE], abdicating. *n.* an abdicator.

ab·di·cate (ab'də-kāt'), *v.t. & v.i.* [ABDICATED (-id), ABDICATING], [< L. *abdicatus,* pp. of *abdicare,* to deny, renounce; *ab-,* off + *dicare,* to proclaim], to give up formally (a high office, throne, authority, etc.); surrender (a power or function).
SYN.—**abdicate** most commonly refers to the formal giving up by a sovereign of his throne, but sometimes describes a surrender of any prerogative; **renounce,** often interchangeable with **abdicate,** is the more frequent usage when the voluntary surrender of any right, claim, title, practice, etc. is meant, and often suggests sacrifice (she *renounced* the pleasures of society); **resign** is applied to the deliberate giving up of a position, unexpired term, etc. by formal notice. —*ANT.* assume.

ab·di·ca·tion (ab'də-kā'shən), *n.* [L. *abdicatio;* see ABDICATE], the act of giving up a high office, authority, or function, especially that of a king.

ab·di·ca·tor (ab'də-kā'tēr), *n.* [Mod. L.; see ABDICATE], a person who abdicates.

Ab·di·el (ab'di-əl), *n.* [Heb., lit., servant of God], the angel in Milton's *Paradise Lost* who resists Satan's attempts to incite a revolt against God.

ab·do·men (ab'də-mən, ab-dō'mən), *n.* [L.], 1. in higher vertebrates, the part of the body situated between the diaphragm and the pelvis, and containing the stomach, intestines, etc.; belly. 2. in insects and crustaceans, the posterior or hind part of the body, below the thorax.

ab·dom·i·nal (ab-dom'ə-n'l), *adj.* [Mod. L. *abdominalis* < *abdomen*], of, in, or for the abdomen.

ab·du·cent (ab-dōō'sənt, ab-dū'sənt), *adj.* [L. *abducens,* ppr. of *abducere;* see ABDUCT], in *physiology,* abducting: opposed to *adducent.*

ab·duct (ab-dukt', əb-dukt'), *v.t.* [< L. *abductus,* pp. of *abducere,* to lead away; *ab-,* away + *ducere,* to lead], 1. to take (a person) away unlawfully and by force; kidnap. 2. in *physiology,* to move or pull (a part of the body) away from the median axis or from another part: as, a muscle that *abducts* the thumb.

ab·duc·tion (ab-duk′shən, əb-duk′shən), ***n.*** [L. *abductio;* see ABDUCT], 1. an abducting or being abducted. 2. in *law,* the unlawful carrying off of a person, especially a woman for sexual purposes. 3. in *physiology,* *a)* the moving of a part of the body away from the median axis or from another part. *b)* the changed position resulting from this.

ab·duc·tor (ab-duk′tẽr, əb-duk′tẽr), ***n.*** [Mod. L.; see ABDUCT], 1. a person who abducts; kidnaper. 2. in *physiology,* a muscle or nerve that abducts.

Abd·ul-A·ziz (äb′dül-ä-zēz′), ***n.*** sultan of Turkey (1861–1876); lived 1830–1876; deposed.

Abd·ul-Ha·mid II (äb′dül-hä-mēd′), 1842–1918; sultan of Turkey (1876–1909); deposed.

Abd·ul-Me·jid (äb′dül-me-jēd′), ***n.*** sultan of Turkey (1839–1861); lived 1823–1861.

a·beam (ə-bēm′), ***adv.*** [*a-*, on + *beam*], 1. at right angles to a ship's length or keel. 2. opposite a ship's side (with *of*).

a·be·ce·dar·i·an (ā′bi-si-dâr′i-ən), ***n.*** [ML. *abecedarius* < *A, B, C, D*], 1. a person learning the alphabet; beginner. 2. a person teaching the alphabet or the basic elements of a subject. ***adj.*** 1. of the alphabet; hence, 2. elementary.

a·be·ce·da·ry (ā′bi-sē′də-ri), ***adj. & n.*** [*pl.* ABECEDARIES (-riz)], abecedarian.

a·bed (ə-bed′), ***adv.*** [*a-*, on, in + *bed*], in bed; on a bed.

A·bed·ne·go (ə-bed′ni-gō′), ***n.*** [Heb., prob. < *abed nebo,* servant of Nebo], in the *Bible,* one of the three captives who came out of the blazing furnace miraculously unharmed: Dan. 3.

A·bel (ā′b'l), [L.; Gr. *Abel;* Heb. *hebel,* lit., breath], a masculine name. ***n.*** in the *Bible,* the second son of Adam and Eve: he was killed by Cain: Gen. 4.

Ab·é·lard, Pierre (ab′ə-lärd′; Fr. à′bā′lår′), 1079–1142; French scholastic philosopher, teacher, and theologian: see also **Héloïse.**

a·bele (ə-bēl′, ā′bəl), ***n.*** [D. *abeel;* OFr. *abel, aubel;* LL. *albellus,* dim. of L. *albus,* white], the white poplar.

a·bel·mosk (ā′b'l-mosk′), ***n.*** [Ar. *abu al misk,* lit., father of musk], a plant of the mallow family: its seeds are used to make perfume.

Ab·er·deen (ab′ẽr-dēn′), ***n.*** 1. a city in eastern Scotland, on the North Sea: pop., 186,000. 2. a city in northeastern South Dakota: pop., 23,000. 3. a city in western Washington: pop., 19,000. 4. a town in northeastern Maryland: pop., 10,000: site of Aberdeen Proving Ground of the United States Army.

Ab·er·deen An·gus (ab′ẽr-dēn′ aŋ′gəs), [after *Aberdeen,* Scotland + *Angus,* a proper name], any of a breed of black, hornless cattle, originally from Scotland.

Ab·er·do·ni·an (ab′ẽr-dō′ni-ən), ***adj.*** of Aberdeen. ***n.*** a native or inhabitant of Aberdeen.

ab·er·rance (ab-er′əns), ***n.*** [L. *aberrantia* < *aberrans*], the quality or state of being aberrant; deviation.

ab·er·ran·cy (ab-er′ən-si), ***n.*** [*pl.* ABERRANCIES (-siz)], aberrance.

ab·er·rant (ab-er′ənt), ***adj.*** [L. *aberrans,* ppr. of *aberrare,* to go astray; *ab-*, from + *errare,* to wander], deviating from what is true, correct, normal, or typical.

ab·er·ra·tion (ab′ẽr-ā′shən), ***n.*** [L. *aberratio* < *aberrare;* see ABERRANT], 1. a departure from what is right, true, correct, etc. 2. a deviation from the normal or the typical. 3. mental derangement or lapse. 4. in *astronomy,* *a)* a small apparent change in position of a heavenly body, caused by the motion of the earth and of light. *b)* the amount of such change. 5. in *optics,* *a)* the failure of light rays from one point to converge to a single focus. *b)* an error in a lens or mirror causing such failure: see **chromatic aberration, spherical aberration.**

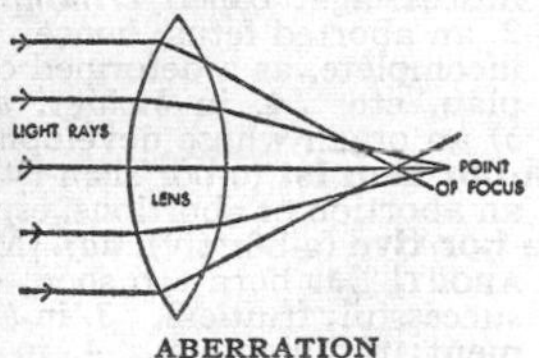

ABERRATION

a·bet (ə-bet′), ***v.t.*** [ABETTED (-id), ABETTING], [ME. *abetten;* OFr. *abeter,* to incite; *a-*, to + *beter,* to bait], to incite, sanction, or help, especially in wrongdoing.

a·bet·ment (ə-bet′mənt), ***n.*** an abetting.

a·bet·tal (ə-bet′'l), ***n.*** abetment.

a·bet·tor (ə-bet′ẽr), ***n.*** [Anglo-Fr. *abettour* < OFr. *abeter*], a person who abets: also spelled **abetter.**

a·bey·ance (ə-bā′əns), ***n.*** [Anglo-Fr. *abeiance;* OFr. *abeance,* expectation < *bayer,* to gape, wait expectantly < LL. *badare,* to gape], 1. temporary suspension, as of an activity or function. 2. in *law,* a state of not having been determined or settled, as of lands awaiting proof of ownership.

ab·far·ad (ab-far′əd, ab-far′ad), ***n.*** [*ab*solute + *farad*], a C.G.S. electromagnetic unit, 10^9 farads.

ab·hen·ry (ab-hen′ri), ***n.*** [*ab*solute + *henry*], a C.G.S. electromagnetic unit, 10^{-9} henry.

ab·hor (əb-hôr′, ab-hôr′), ***v.t.*** [ABHORRED (-hôrd′), ABHORRING], [L. *abhorrere; ab-*, away, from + *horrere,* to shudder], to shrink from in fear, disgust, or hatred. —***SYN.*** see **hate.**

ab·hor·rence (əb-hôr′əns, ab-hor′əns), ***n.*** [< *abhorrent*], 1. an abhorring; loathing; detestation. 2. something abhorred; something repugnant. —***SYN.*** see **aversion.**

ab·hor·rent (əb-hôr′ənt, ab-hor′ənt), ***adj.*** [L. *abhorrens,* ppr. of *abhorrere;* see ABHOR], 1. causing fear, disgust, etc.; detestable. 2. feeling abhorrence. 3. opposed (*to* one's principles, reason, etc.). —***SYN.*** see **hateful.**

A·bib (ā′bib; Heb. ä-vēv′), ***n.*** [Heb.], Nisan: the early Hebrew name: see **Jewish calendar.**

a·bid·ance (ə-bīd′'ns), ***n.*** an abiding.

a·bide (ə-bīd′), ***v.i.*** [ABODE (-bōd′) or ABIDED (-id), ABIDING], [AS. *abidan* < *bidan,* to remain], 1. to stand fast; remain; go on being. 2. [Archaic or Poetic], to stay; reside (with *in* or *at*). ***v.t.*** 1. to await. 2. to submit to; put up with. —***SYN.*** see **continue, stay.**
  abide by, 1. to live up to (a promise, agreement, etc.). 2. to submit to and carry out, as a decision.

a·bid·ing (ə-bīd′iŋ), ***adj.*** [ppr. of *abide*], continuing without change; enduring; lasting.

Ab·i·gail (ab′i-gāl′, ab′i-g'l), [Heb. *abīgayil,* lit., father is rejoicing], a feminine name: diminutives, *Abby, Gail.* ***n.*** 1. in the *Bible,* the wife of Nabal and later of David: I Sam. 25. 2. [a-], [< *Abigail,* name of a maid in *The Scornful Lady* by Beaumont and Fletcher (1616)], a lady's maid.

Ab·i·lene (ab′ə-lēn′), ***n.*** a city in central Texas: pop., 90,000.

a·bil·i·ty (ə-bil′ə-ti), ***n.*** [*pl.* ABILITIES (-tiz)], [ME. *abilite;* OFr. *habilité;* L. *habilitas,* ableness (to hold) < *habere,* to have, hold], 1. a being able; power to do (something physical or mental). 2. talent. 3. *usually in pl.* special skill. 4. seaworthiness.

-a·bil·i·ty (ə-bil′ə-ti), [*pl.* -ABILITIES (-tiz)], [L. *-abilitas*], a suffix used to form nouns from adjectives ending in *-able,* as in *durability.*

‡ab in·i·ti·o (ab in-ish′i-ō), [L.], from the beginning: abbreviated **ab init.**

‡ab in·tra (ab in′trə), [L.], from within.

ab·i·o·gen·e·sis (ab′i-ō-jen′ə-sis), ***n.*** [Gr. *a-*, without; + *biogenesis*], in *biology,* spontaneous generation; production of living organisms from lifeless matter: a former theory, now rejected.

ab·i·o·ge·net·ic (ab′i-ō-jə-net′ik), ***adj.*** of or by abiogenesis.

a·bi·o·ge·net·i·cal·ly (ab′i-ō-jə-net′i-k'l-i), ***adv.*** in an abiogenetic manner; by spontaneous generation.

ab·i·og·e·nist (ab′i-oj′ə-nist), ***n.*** a person who believes in abiogenesis.

ab·ir·ri·tant (ab-ir′ə-tənt), ***adj.*** relieving or lessening irritation; soothing. ***n.*** something, especially a medicine or drug, that relieves or lessens irritation.

ab·ir·ri·tate (ab-ir′ə-tāt′), ***v.t.*** [ABIRRITATED (-id), ABIRRITATING], in *medicine,* to relieve or lessen irritation in.

ab·ject (ab-jekt′, ab′jekt), ***adj.*** [L. *abjectus,* pp. of *abjicere,* to throw away < *ab-*, from + *jacere,* to throw], 1. miserable; wretched: as, *abject* poverty. 2. lacking self-respect; degraded. —***SYN.*** see **base.**

ab·jec·tion (ab-jek′shən), ***n.*** [Fr.; L. *abjectio;* see ABJECT], the state of being abject; degradation.

ab·ju·ra·tion (ab′joo-rā′shən), ***n.*** [L. *abiuratio* < *abjurare;* see ABJURE], an abjuring or being abjured.

ab·jur·a·to·ry (əb-joor′ə-tôr′i, ab-joor′ə-tō′ri), ***adj.*** of, or having the nature of, abjuration; abjuring.

ab·jure (əb-joor′, ab-joor′), ***v.t.*** [ABJURED (-joord′), ABJURING], [L. *abjurare; ab-*, away, from + *jurare,* to swear], 1. to give up (rights, allegiance, etc.) on oath; renounce. 2. to give up (opinions) publicly; recant.

Ab·kha·zi·an Autonomous Soviet Socialist Republic (äb-khä′zi-än), a division of the Georgian S.S.R., on the Black Sea: area, 3,358 sq. mi.; pop., 400,000.

ab·lac·ta·tion (ab′lak-tā′shən), ***n.*** [L. *ablactatio* < *ab-*, from + *lac,* milk], the act or process of weaning.

ab·la·tion (ab-lā′shən), ***n.*** [LL. *ablatio* < L. *ablatus;* see ABLATIVE], 1. removal, especially the surgical removal of a part of the body. 2. in *geology,* a wearing or wasting away, as of a glacier or rock.

ab·la·tive (ab′lə-tiv), ***n.*** [L. *ablativus* < *ablatus* (pp. of *auferre*), carried away], in *linguistics,* 1. the case expressing removal, deprivation, and direction from. 2. a word or phrase in this case. 3. in Latin, the case expressing source, cause, agency, and instrument, as well as deprivation. 4. a Latin word or phrase in this case. ***adj.*** of or in the ablative. Abbreviated **abl.**

ablative absolute, in *Latin grammar,* a grammatically independent phrase in the ablative case, used to express time, cause, or circumstance: sometimes applied to English constructions thought to resemble the Latin.

ab·laut (ab′lout; G. äp′lout), ***n.*** [G.; *ab-*, off, from + *laut,* sound], in *linguistics,* patterned change of the root vowels in verbal forms, expressing changes of tense, aspect, etc., as in *drink, drank, drunk:* also called *gradation.* ***adj.*** of or characterized by ablaut.

a·blaze (ə-blāz′), *adv.* [*a-*, on + *blaze* (a fire)], on fire. *adj.* 1. flaming; gleaming. 2. greatly excited; eager.

a·ble (ā′b'l), *adj.* [ABLER (-blẽr), ABLEST (-blist)], [ME.; OFr. *hable;* L. *habilis,* suitable, handy < *habere,* to have, hold], 1. having enough power, skill, etc. (*to* do something). 2. having much power of mind; skilled; talented. 3. in *law,* legally qualified or authorized to do a specified act. 4. in *nautical usage,* seaworthy.
SYN.—**able** implies power or ability to do something (*able* to make payments) but sometimes suggests superior power or skill (an *able* orator); **capable** usually implies the mere meeting of ordinary requirements (a *capable* machinist); **competent** and **qualified** both imply the possession of the requisite qualifications for the specified work, situation, etc., but **qualified** stresses compliance with specified requirements (a *competent* critic of modern art, a *qualified* voter). —*ANT.* inept.

-a·ble (ə-b'l), [Fr.; L. *-abilis*], a suffix used to form adjectives, and meaning: 1. *able to,* as in *durable.* 2. *capable of being,* as in *drinkable.* 3. *worthy of being,* as in *lovable.* 4. *having qualities of,* as in *comfortable.* 5. *tending or inclined to,* as in *peaceable.* Also **-ible, -ble.**

a·ble-bod·ied (ā′b'l-bod′id), *adj.* healthy and strong.

able-bodied seaman, a trained, skilled sailor: abbreviated **A.B., a.b.**: now often **able seaman.**

ab·le·gate (ab′li-gāt′), *n.* [L. *ablegatus,* pp. of *ablegare,* to send away; *ab-,* away + *legare,* to send, depute], a special envoy sent by the Pope to a foreign land.

a·bloom (ə-bloom′), *adv. & adj.* [*a-,* in + *bloom*], in bloom; in flower.

ab·lu·ent (ab′loo-ənt), *adj.* [L. *abluens* < *abluere,* to wash off], that makes clean. *n.* any substance used for cleaning; detergent.

ab·lu·tion (ab-loo′shən, əb-loo′shən), *n.* [ME. *ablucioun;* L. *ablutio* < *ab-,* off + *luere,* to wash], 1. a washing of the body, especially as a religious ceremony. 2. the liquid used for such washing.

ab·lu·tion·ar·y (ab-loo′shən-er′i, əb-loo′shən-er′i), *adj.* of or for ablution.

a·bly (ā′bli), *adv.* in an able manner; skillfully.

-a·bly (ə-bli), a suffix used to form adverbs corresponding to adjectives ending in *-able.*

ab·ne·gate (ab′ni-gāt′), *v.t.* [ABNEGATED (-id), ABNEGATING], [< L. *abnegatus,* pp. of *abnegare; ab-,* away, from + *negare,* to deny], to deny and refuse; give up (rights, claims, etc.); renounce.

ab·ne·ga·tion (ab′ni-gā′shən), *n.* [L. *abnegatio;* see ABNEGATE], a giving up of rights, etc.; self-denial; renunciation.

ab·ne·ga·tor (ab′ni-gā′tẽr), *n.* one who abnegates.

Ab·ner (ab′nẽr), [L.; Heb. *'abnēr,* lit., the father is a light], a masculine name.

ab·nor·mal (ab-nôr′məl, əb-nôr′məl), *adj.* [earlier *anormal* < Fr. *anormal, anomal* < Gr. *anōmalos* (see ANOMALOUS); influenced by L. *abnormis* < *ab-,* from + *norma,* rule], not normal; not average; not typical; not usual; irregular; unnatural. —*SYN.* see **irregular.**

ab·nor·mal·i·ty (ab′nôr-mal′ə-ti), *n.* 1. the quality or condition of being abnormal. 2. [*pl.* ABNORMALITIES (-tiz)], an abnormal thing; malformation.

ab·nor·mal·ly (ab-nôr′mə-li, əb-nôr′mə-li), *adv.* 1. in an abnormal manner; irregularly. 2. to an abnormal degree, exceptionally: as, he is *abnormally* clever.

abnormal psychology, the study of the behavior of abnormal people, especially that of the neurotic, psychotic, or feeble-minded.

ab·nor·mi·ty (ab-nôr′mə-ti), *n.* [*pl.* ABNORMITIES (-tiz)], [L. *abnormitas* < *abnormis;* see ABNORMAL], 1. abnormality. 2. monstrosity.

Å·bo (ō′boo), *n.* Turku, a city in Finland: Swedish name.

a·board (ə-bôrd′, ə-bōrd′), *adv.* [*a-,* on + *board;* also < Fr. *à bord*], on board; on, in, or into a ship, airplane, etc. *prep.* 1. on board of; on; in. 2. alongside.
all aboard! 1. get on! get in!: a warning to passengers that the train, car, airplane, etc. will start soon. 2. everyone (is) aboard!: a signal to the driver or pilot that he may start.

a·bode (ə-bōd′), *n.* [ME. *abad, abood* < AS. *abidan;* see ABIDE], 1. a staying in a place; sojourn. 2. a place where one lives or stays; home; house; residence.

a·bode (ə-bōd′), alternative past tense and past participle of **abide.**

ab·ohm (ab-ōm′), *n.* [*ab*solute + *ohm*], a C.G.S. electromagnetic unit, 10^{-9} ohm.

a·bol·ish (ə-bol′ish), *v.t.* [Fr. *abolir;* L. *abolere,* to retard, destroy; formed, with *ab-,* from, to contrast with *adolere,* to increase, grow; later associated and contrasted with *adolescere* (see ADOLESCENT), in the sense "to burn," and hence used to mean "to burn away"], to do away with completely; put an end to; make (a law, etc.) null and void.
SYN.—**abolish** denotes a complete doing away with something, as an institution, custom, practice, condition, etc. (to *abolish* slavery, ignorance, etc.); **annul** and **abrogate** stress a cancelling by authority or formal action (the marriage was *annulled,* the law *abrogated* certain privileges); **rescind, revoke,** and **repeal** all agree in describing the setting aside of laws, orders, permits, etc. (to *rescind* an order, *revoke* a charter, *repeal* an Amendment). —*ANT.* establish.

ab·o·li·tion (ab′ə-lish′ən), *n.* [Fr.; L. *abolitio;* see ABOLISH], 1. an abolishing or being abolished; complete destruction; annulment. 2. [sometimes A-], the abolishing of Negro slavery in the United States.

ab·o·li·tion·ar·y (ab′ə-lish′ən-er′i), *adj.* of or for abolition.

ab·o·li·tion·ism (ab′ə-lish′ən-iz'm), *n.* the doctrine of abolitionists.

ab·o·li·tion·ist (ab′ə-lish′ən-ist), *n.* 1. a person in favor of abolishing some law, custom, or institution. 2. [sometimes A-], a person who favored the abolition of Negro slavery in the United States.

ab·o·ma·sum (ab′ə-mā′səm), *n.* [L. *ab-,* from + *omasum,* bullock's tripe], the fourth or digesting chamber of the stomach of a cud-chewing animal, as the cow: see **ruminant,** illus.

ab·o·ma·sus (ab′ə-mā′səs), *n.* an abomasum.

A-bomb (ā′bom′), *n.* an atomic bomb.

a·bom·i·na·ble (ə-bom′ə-nə-b'l), *adj.* [ME.; OFr.; L. *abominabilis* < *abominari;* see ABOMINATE], 1. nasty and disgusting; vile; loathsome. 2. disagreeable; highly unpleasant; very bad: as, he shows *abominable* taste. —*SYN.* see **hateful.**

a·bom·i·na·bly (ə-bom′ə-nə-bli), *adv.* in an abominable manner.

a·bom·i·nate (ə-bom′ə-nāt′), *v.t.* [ABOMINATED (-id), ABOMINATING], [< L. *abominatus,* pp. of *abominari,* to regard as an ill omen; see AB- & OMEN], 1. to have feelings of hatred and disgust for; loathe; abhor. 2. to dislike very much.

a·bom·i·na·tion (ə-bom′ə-nā′shən), *n.* 1. an abominating; hatred and disgust (for a thing or person); loathing. 2. anything hateful and disgusting.

a·bom·i·na·tor (ə-bom′ə-nā′tẽr), *n.* a person who abominates.

‡à bon mar·ché (à′ bōn′ màr′shā′), [Fr.], at a good bargain; cheap.

ab·o·rig·i·nal (ab′ə-rij′ə-n'l), *adj.* [< *aborigines*], 1. existing (in a place) from the beginning or from earliest days; first; indigenous. 2. of or characteristic of aborigines. *n.* an aboriginal animal or plant; aborigine. —*SYN.* see **native.**

‡ab o·ri·gi·ne (ab ō-rij′i-nē′), [L.], from the origin or beginning.

ab·o·rig·i·nes (ab′ə-rij′ə-nēz′), *n.pl.* [*sing.* ABORIGINE (-nē′)], [L., first inhabitants < *ab-,* from + *origine,* the beginning; see ORIGIN], 1. the first or earliest known inhabitants of a region; natives. 2. the native animals or plants of a region.

a·bort (ə-bôrt′), *v.i.* [< L. *abortus,* pp. of *aboriri,* to miscarry; *ab-,* from + *oriri,* to arise], 1. to give birth before the fetus is viable; have a miscarriage; hence, 2. to come to nothing. 3. in *biology,* to fail to develop; stay rudimentary. *v.t.* 1. to cause to have an abortion. 2. to check (a disease) before fully developed.

a·bor·ti·cide (ə-bôr′tə-sīd′), *n.* [< L. *abortus* (see ABORT) + *cidium* < *caedere,* to kill], 1. destruction of the fetus in the womb. 2. an abortifacient.

a·bor·ti·fa·cient (ə-bôr′tə-fā′shənt), *adj.* [< L. *abortio,* miscarriage (see ABORT) + ppr. of *facere,* to make], causing abortion. *n.* something that causes abortion.

a·bor·tion (ə-bôr′shən), *n.* [L. *abortio;* see ABORT], 1. expulsion of a fetus from the womb before it is viable; miscarriage: called *criminal abortion* when unlawful. 2. an aborted fetus; hence, 3. anything immature and incomplete, as a deformed creature, a badly developed plan, etc. 4. in *biology, a*) arrest of development. *b*) an organ whose development has been arrested.

a·bor·tion·ist (ə-bôr′shən-ist), *n.* a person who performs an abortion or abortions, especially a criminal abortion.

a·bor·tive (ə-bôr′tiv), *adj.* [ME. *abortif;* L. *abortivus;* see ABORT], 1. born too soon. 2. coming to nothing; unsuccessful; fruitless. 3. in *biology,* arrested in development; rudimentary. 4. in *medicine, a*) causing abortion. *b*) halting a disease process. —*SYN.* see **futile.**

A·bou·kir (ä′boo-kir′, ə-boo′kẽr), *n.* Abukir.

a·bou·li·a (ə-boo′li-ə), *n.* abulia.

a·bound (ə-bound′), *v.i.* [ME. *abounden;* OFr. *abonder;* L. *abundare,* to overflow; *ab-* + *undare,* to rise in waves < *unda,* a wave], 1. to be plentiful; exist in large numbers or amounts. 2. to have plenty; be wealthy (*in*): as, a land that *abounds* in grain. 3. to be filled; teem (*with*): as, woods that *abound* with game.

a·bout (ə-bout′), *adv.* [ME. *aboute(n)* < AS. *abutan, onbutan,* around < *on,* on + *be,* by + *utan,* outside < *ut,* out: all senses develop from the sense of "around"], 1. on every side; all around: as, look *about.* 2. here and there; in all directions; as, travel *about.* 3. in circumference; around the outside: as, ten miles *about.* 4. near: as, standing somewhere *about.* 5. in the opposite direction; to a reversed position: as, turn it *about.* 6. in succession or rotation: as, play fair—turn and turn *about.* 7. nearly; approximately: as, *about* four years old. 8. [Colloq.], all but; almost: as, just *about* ready. *adj.* (used predicatively) 1. astir; on the move: as, he is up and *about* again. 2. in the vicinity; prevalent: as, typhoid is *about. prep.* 1. around; on all sides of. 2. here and there in; everywhere in. 3. near to. 4. with; on (one's person): as, have your wits *about* you. 5. concerned with; attending to: as, go *about* your business. 6. intending; on the point of (followed by an infinitive or a gerund): as, I am *about* to say something. 7. having to do with; concerning. 8. in connection with. Abbreviated **a., ab., abt.**

a·bout-face (ə-bout′fās′), *n.* 1. a turning or facing in the opposite direction; hence, 2. a reversal of attitude or opinion. *v.i.* (ə-bout′fās′), to turn or face in the opposite direction.

a·bout-ship (ə-bout′ship′), *v.i.* to put a ship on the other tack.

a·bove (ə-buv′), *adv.* [ME. *aboven;* AS. *abufan, onbufan,* overhead, above < *on-,* intens. + *bufan* < *be,* by + *ufan,* over, on high], 1. in or at a higher place; overhead; up. 2. in heaven. 3. before or earlier (in a book or printed passage): often used in combinations like *above-mentioned.* 4. higher in power, status, etc. *prep.* 1. higher than; over; on top of. 2. beyond; past: as, the road *above* the village. 3. superior to; better than: as, *above* the average. 4. in excess of; more than: as, *above* fifty dollars. *adj.* placed, found, mentioned, etc. above or earlier. *n.* something that is above.

above all, most of all; mainly.

a·bove·board (ə-buv′bôrd′, ə-buv′bōrd′), *adv. & adj.* [*above* + *board* (table): orig. a cardplayer's term], in plain view; without dishonesty or concealment: as, be open and *aboveboard* with me.

a·bove·ground (ə-buv′ground′), *adv. & adj.* not buried; not dead.

‡ab o·vo (ab ō′vō), [L., from the egg], from the beginning, or origin.

abp., archbishop.

abr., 1. abridge. 2. abridged. 3. abridgment.

ab·ra·ca·dab·ra (ab′rə-kə-dab′rə), *n.* [L.], 1. a word supposed to have magic powers as a charm against diseases, and hence used in incantations, on amulets, etc. 2. a magic spell or formula. 3. gibberish; jargon.

ab·ra·dant (ə-brā′dənt), *adj.* [OFr. < L. *abradere;* see ABRADE], abrading. *n.* an abrasive.

ab·rade (ə-brād′), *v.t.* [ABRADED (-id), ABRADING], [L. *abradere; ab-,* away + *radere,* to scrape], to scrape or rub off; wear away by scraping or rubbing.

A·bra·ham (ā′brə-ham′), [Heb., lit., father of many: the original form, *Abram,* means "father is exalted"; see Gen. 17:5], a masculine name: diminutive, *Abe. n.* in the *Bible,* the first patriarch and ancestor of the Hebrews: Gen. 12–25.

in Abraham's bosom, 1. at rest with one's dead ancestors; hence, 2. in a state of heavenly bliss, peace, etc.

A·bram (ā′brəm), Abraham.

a·bran·chi·an (ā-braŋ′ki-ən), *adj. & n.* abranchiate.

a·bran·chi·ate (ā-braŋ′ki-it, ā-braŋ′ki-āt′), *adj.* [< Gr. *a-,* not + *branchia,* gills], in *zoology,* without gills. *n.* an animal without gills.

ab·ra·sion (ə-brā′zhən), *n.* [ML. *abrasio* < L. *abradere;* see ABRADE], 1. a scraping or rubbing off, as of skin. 2. a wearing away by rubbing or scraping, as of rock by wind, water, etc. 3. an abraded spot or area.

ab·ra·sive (ə-brā′siv, ə-brā′ziv), *adj.* [L. *abrasus,* pp. of *abradere* (see ABRADE); + *-ive*], causing abrasion. *n.* a substance used for grinding, polishing, etc., as sandpaper or emery.

ab·re·act (ab′ri-akt′), *v.t.* [back-formation < *abreaction*], in *psychoanalysis,* to relieve (a repressed emotion), as by talking about it.

ab·re·ac·tion (ab′ri-ak′shən), *n.* [*ab-* + *reaction,* after G. *abreagierung*], in *psychoanalysis,* the relieving of a repressed emotion, as by talking about it.

a·breast (ə-brest′), *adv. & adj.* [*a-,* on + *breast*], side by side (in going or facing forward).

abreast of (or **with**), in line with; not behind.

a·bridge (ə-brij′), *v.t.* [ABRIDGED (-brijd′), ABRIDGING], [ME. *abreger;* OFr. *abregier;* L. *abbreviare;* < *ad-,* to + *breviare* < *brevis,* short], 1. to reduce in scope, extent, etc.; shorten. 2. to shorten by lessening the number of words but keeping the main contents. 3. to lessen; curtail. 4. to deprive of (rights, privileges, etc.). Abbreviated **abr.** —*SYN.* see **shorten.**

a·bridg·ment, a·bridge·ment (ə-brij′mənt), *n.* [OFr. *abregement* < *abregier;* see ABRIDGE], 1. an abridging or being abridged; reduction. 2. a curtailment, as of rights. 3. an abridged or condensed form of a book, etc. Abbreviated **abr.**

SYN.—**abridgment** describes a work condensed from a larger work by omitting the less important parts, but keeping the main contents more or less unaltered; an **abstract** is a short statement of the essential contents of a book, court record, etc. often used as an index to the original material; **brief** and **summary** both imply a statement of the main points of the matter under consideration (the *brief* of a legal argument), **summary,** especially, connoting a recapitulating statement; a **synopsis** is a condensed, orderly treatment, as of the plot of a novel, that permits a quick general view of the whole; a **digest** is a concise, systematic treatment, generally more comprehensive in scope than a synopsis, and, in the case of technical material, often arranged under titles for quick reference; an **epitome** is a statement of the essence of a subject in the shortest possible form. —*ANT.* expansion.

a·broach (ə-brōch′), *adv. & adj.* [ME. *abroche; a-,* on + OFr. *broche,* a spit], 1. broached; opened so that the liquid contents can come out. 2. astir.

a·broad (ə-brôd′), *adv.* [*a-,* on + *broad*], 1. broadly; far and wide. 2. current; in circulation: as, a report is *abroad* that we have won. 3. outside one's house; outdoors: as, stroll *abroad.* 4. outside one's own country; to or in foreign countries. 5. wide of the mark; in error. *n.* a foreign land or lands (preceded by *from*).

ab·ro·ga·ble (ab′rə-gə-b'l), *adj.* that can be abrogated.

ab·ro·gate (ab′rə-gāt′), *v.t.* [ABROGATED (-id), ABROGATING], [< L. *abrogatus,* pp. of *abrogare,* to repeal; *ab-,* away + *rogare,* to ask, propose], to abolish; repeal; annul; cancel. —*SYN.* see **abolish.**

ab·ro·ga·tion (ab′rə-gā′shən), *n.* [L. *abrogatio*], an abrogating or being abrogated; repeal (of a law, etc.).

ab·ro·ga·tive (ab′rə-gā′tiv), *adj.* abrogating.

ab·ro·ga·tor (ab′rə-gā′tẽr), *n.* a person who abrogates.

a·brupt (ə-brupt′), *adj.* [L. *abruptus,* pp. of *abrumpere,* to break off; *ab-,* off + *rumpere,* to break], 1. sudden; hasty; unexpected. 2. sudden and short in behavior or speech; gruff; brusque. 3. very steep. 4. jumping from topic to topic without proper transitions; jerky and disconnected: as, *abrupt* writing. 5. in *geology,* suddenly cropping out: as, *abrupt* strata. —*SYN.* see **steep, sudden.**

a·brup·tion (ə-brup′shən), *n.* [L. *abruptio;* see ABRUPT], a sudden breaking away (of parts of a mass).

A·bruz·zi, Duke of the (ä-brōōt′tsē), (*Prince Luigi Amedeo*), 1873–1933; Italian naval officer and explorer.

A·bruz·zi e Mo·li·se (ä-brōōt′tsē e mô′lē-ze), a department of central Italy, on the Adriatic.

abs- (abs), ab-: used before *t* or *c,* as in *abstract, abscond.*

abs., 1. absent. 2. absolute. 3. abstract.

Ab·sa·lom (ab′sə-ləm), *n.* [L.; Heb. *'abshālōm,* lit., the father is peace], in the *Bible,* David's favorite son, killed after rebelling against his father: II Sam. 18.

ab·scess (ab′ses), *n.* [L. *abscessus* < *abscidere,* to go from < *ab(s)-,* from + *cedere,* to go: the notion was formerly held that humors *go from* the body into the swelling], a swollen, inflamed area in body tissues, in which pus gathers. *v.i.* to form an abscess.

ab·scessed (ab′sest), *adj.* [pp. of *abscess*], having an abscess or abscesses.

ab·scis·sa (ab-sis′ə), *n.* [*pl.* ABSCISSAS (-əz), ABSCISSAE (-ē)], [L. *abscissa* (*linea*), (a line) cut off; fem. of *abscissus,* pp. of *abscindere,* to cut off; *ab-,* from, off + *scindere,* to cut], in *geometry,* the line or part of a line drawn horizontally on a graph, by which a point is located with reference to a system of co-ordinates: distinguished from *ordinate.*

ABSCISSA
OP′, abscissa of P; OP″, ordinate of P

ab·scis·sion (ab-sizh′ən, ab-sish′ən), *n.* [L. *abscissio;* see ABSCISSA], 1. a cutting off, as by surgery. 2. an abrupt stopping, as in the middle of a sentence, for rhetorical effect.

ab·scond (ab-skond′, əb-skond′), *v.i.* [L. *abscondere; ab(s)-,* from, away + *condere,* to hide; see RECONDITE], to go away hastily and secretly; run away and hide, especially in order to escape the law.

ab·sence (ab′s'ns), *n.* [ME.; OFr.; L. *absentia;* see ABSENT, *adj.*], 1. a being absent; being away. 2. the time of being away. 3. a being without; lack: as, in the *absence* of evidence.

absence of mind, a being absent-minded; preoccupation.

ab·sent (ab′s'nt; *for v.,* ab-sent′), *adj.* [ME.; OFr.; L. *absens,* ppr. of *absum, abesse; ab-,* away + *esse,* to be], 1. not present; away. 2. not existing; lacking. 3. not attentive; absorbed in thought. *v.t.* [Fr. *absenter;* L. *absentare* < *absens*], to take or hold (oneself) away: as, he *absents* himself from classes. Abbreviated **abs.**

ab·sen·tee (ab′s'n-tē′), *n.* a person who is absent, as from home, school, work, etc. *adj.* of the nature of an absentee; by an absentee: as, *absentee* ownership.

ab·sen·tee·ism (ab′s'n-tē′iz'm), *n.* the condition of being absent, as from home, school, work, etc.; especially, such absence when deliberate or habitual.

absentee landlord, a person who owns land, buildings, etc. in some city or region other than that in which he lives: often implying neglect of tenants or workmen.

‡ab·sen·te re·o (ab-sen′ti rē′ō), [L.], in the absence of the defendant: abbreviated **abs. re.**

ab·sent·ly (ab′s'nt-li), *adv.* in an absent or preoccupied manner; inattentively.

ab·sent-mind·ed (ab′s'nt-mīn′did), *adj.* 1. so dreamy or lost in thought as not to pay attention to what one is doing or what is going on around one; hence, 2. habitually forgetful.

SYN.—**absent-minded** suggests an aimless wandering of the mind away from the immediate situation, often implying a habitual tendency of this kind (the *absent-minded* professor);

abstracted suggests a withdrawal of the mind from the immediate present, and a serious concern with some other subject; **preoccupied** implies that the attention cannot be readily turned to something new because of its concern with a present matter; **absorbed** implies a total concentration of one's attention; **distrait** suggests inability to concentrate, often emphasizing such a condition as a mood; **distraught** implies a similar inability to concentrate, specifically because of worry, grief, etc.; **inattentive** implies a failure to pay attention, emphasizing such behavior as a lack of discipline.

absent without leave, in *military usage*, absent from duty without official permission but with no intention of deserting: abbreviated **A.W.O.L., a.w.o.l.**

ab·sinthe, ab·sinth (ab′sinth), *n.* [Fr.; L. *absinthium*, wormwood; Gr. *apsinthion*], 1. wormwood or its essence. 2. a green, bitter alcoholic liquor with the flavor of wormwood and anise.

ab·sinth·ism (ab′sinth-iz'm), *n.* a diseased condition caused by habitually drinking too much absinthe.

‡**ab·sit o·men** (ab′sit ō′men), [L.], may there be no (ill) omen (in it).

ab·so·lute (ab′sə-lōōt′), *adj.* [ME. *absolut;* L. *absolutus*, pp. of *absolvere*, to loosen from; see ABSOLVE], 1. perfect. 2. complete; whole. 3. not mixed; pure. 4. not limited; not conditional; unrestricted: as, an *absolute* ruler. 5. positive; certain; definite. 6. actual; real: as, an *absolute* truth. 7. not dependent on anything else; considered without reference to anything else. 8. in *grammar*, *a)* forming part of a sentence, but not in the usual relations of syntax: in the sentence "The weather being good, they went," *the weather being good* is an *absolute* construction. *b)* used without an explicit object: said of a verb usually transitive, such as *steal* in the sentence "Thieves steal." *c)* with the noun understood: said of a pronoun or an adjective, such as *ours* and *brave* in the sentence "Ours are the brave." 9. in *law*, not encumbered. 10. in *physics*, of the absolute temperature: abbreviated **A.** *n.* something that is absolute. Abbreviated **abs.**

the Absolute, in *philosophy*, that which is thought of as existing in and by itself, without relation to anything else.

absolute alcohol, ethyl alcohol containing not over one per cent by weight of water.

absolute ceiling, the greatest altitude above sea level at which aircraft can keep normal horizontal flight.

absolute monarchy, a kingdom in which the king's powers are unlimited.

absolute music, music that does not try to tell a story, describe a scene, etc.: distinguished from *program music*.

absolute pitch, 1. the pitch of a tone as determined by its rate of vibration. 2. the ability to recognize the pitch of any tone heard, or to reproduce a given tone without having it sounded beforehand.

absolute temperature, temperature measured from absolute zero.

absolute zero, a point of temperature, theoretically equal to − 273.18° C. or − 459.72° F.: the hypothetical point at which a substance would have no molecular motion and no heat.

ab·so·lu·tion (ab′sə-lōō′shən), *n.* [ME. *absoluciun;* OFr. *absolution;* L. *absolutio* < *absolvere*, to loosen from; see ABSOLVE], 1. a formal freeing (*from* guilt or obligation); forgiveness. 2. remission (*of* sin or penalty for it); specifically, in some churches, such remission formally given by a priest after penance by the sinner. 3. the saying or formula of such remission.

ab·so·lut·ism (ab′sə-lōōt′iz'm), *n.* 1. the doctrine or system of government in which the ruler has unlimited powers; despotism. 2. the quality of being absolute, or certain; positivism. 3. in *philosophy*, any doctrine involving the existence of an absolute. 4. in *theology*, predestination.

ab·so·lut·ist (ab′sə-lōōt′ist), *n.* a person who believes in or advocates absolutism. *adj.* of or characterized by absolutism.

ab·sol·u·to·ry (əb-sol′yoo-tôr′i, ab-sol′yoo-tō′ri), *adj.* [L. *absolutorius* < *absolvere;* see ABSOLVE], absolving; that serves to absolve.

ab·solve (ab-solv′, əb-zolv′), *v.t.* [ABSOLVED (-solvd′, -zolvd′), ABSOLVING], [L. *absolvere; ab-*, from + *solvere*, to loose], 1. to pronounce free from guilt or blame; acquit. 2. to give absolution to (in the religious sense). 3. to free (*from* a promise, etc.).

SYN.—**absolve** implies a setting free from responsibilities or obligations (*absolved* from her promise) or from the penalties for their violation; **acquit** means to release from a specific charge by a judicial decision, usually for lack of evidence; to **exonerate** is to relieve of the blame or consequence for a wrongdoing; to **pardon** is to release from punishment for an offense (the prisoner was *pardoned* by the governor); **forgive** implies giving up all claim to punishment as well as any resentment or vengeful feelings; to **vindicate** is to clear (a person or thing under attack) through evidence of the unfairness of the charge, criticism, etc. —*ANT.* blame.

ab·sol·vent (ab-sol′vənt, əb-zol′vənt), *adj.* absolving. *n.* a person who absolves.

ab·sorb (əb-sôrb′, ab-zôrb′), *v.t.* [L. *absorbere; ab-*, from + *sorbere*, to drink in, suck], 1. to suck up; drink in. 2. to engulf wholly. 3. to take up fully the attention, energy, or time of; interest greatly. 4. to take in and incorporate; assimilate. 5. in *physics*, to take in and not reflect; take in and change into heat: as, light rays are *absorbed* by black surfaces.

ab·sorb·a·bil·i·ty (əb-sôrb′ə-bil′ə-ti, ab-zôrb′ə-bil′ə-ti), *n.* the quality or state of being absorbable.

ab·sorb·a·ble (əb-sôrb′ə-b'l, ab-zôrb′ə-b'l), *adj.* that can be absorbed.

ab·sorbed (əb-sôrbd′, ab-zôrbd′), *adj.* [pp. of *absorb*], 1. taken in; sucked up. 2. engulfed. 3. assimilated. 4. greatly interested; wholly occupied: as, *absorbed* in reading. —*SYN.* see **absent-minded.**

ab·sor·be·fa·cient (əb-sôrb′ə-fā′shənt, ab-zôrb′ə-fā′shənt), *adj.* [< L. *absorbere* (see ABSORB) + ppr. of *facere*, to make, cause], in *medicine*, inducing absorption of fluids. *n.* a drug that induces absorption.

ab·sorb·en·cy (əb-sôrb′ən-si, ab-zôrb′ən-si), *n.* the quality of being absorbent.

ab·sorb·ent (əb-sôrb′ənt, ab-zôrb′ənt), *adj.* [L. *absorbens*, ppr. of *absorbere;* see ABSORB], capable of absorbing moisture, light rays, etc. *n.* a thing or substance that absorbs moisture, light rays, etc.

absorbent cotton, raw cotton made absorbent by the removal of its wax: used for surgical dressings, etc.

ab·sorb·ing (əb-sôrb′iŋ, ab-zôrb′iŋ), *adj.* [ppr. of *absorb*], 1. taking in, sucking in, etc. 2. very interesting.

ab·sorp·tion (əb-sôrp′shən, ab-zôrp′shən), *n.* [L. *absorptio* < *absorbere;* see ABSORB], 1. an absorbing or being absorbed. 2. the fact or state of being much interested or engrossed. 3. assimilation. 4. in *biology*, the passing of nutrient material into the blood stream or lymph. 5. in *physics*, *a)* a taking in and not reflecting. *b)* partial loss in power of light or radio waves passing through a medium.

ab·sorp·tive (əb-sôrp′tiv, ab-zôrp′tiv), *adj.* [L. *absorptus*, pp. of *absorbere* (see ABSORB); + *-ive*], 1. able to absorb. 2. relating to absorption.

ab·sorp·tiv·i·ty (ab′sôrp-tiv′ə-ti, ab′zôrp-tiv′ə-ti), *n.* 1. the quality of being absorptive. 2. in *physics*, the fraction of a radiant energy absorbed by the surface that it strikes.

abs. re., *absente reo*, [L.], in the absence of the defendant.

ab·stain (əb-stān′, ab-stān′), *v.i.* [ME. *abstenen;* OFr. *abstenir;* L. *abstinere*, to keep from < *ab(s)-*, from + *tenere*, to hold], to keep oneself back; voluntarily do without; refrain: as, he *abstains* from alcoholic liquor. —*SYN.* see **refrain.**

ab·stain·er (əb-stān′ẽr, ab-stān′ẽr), *n.* a person who abstains, especially from drinking alcoholic liquor.

ab·ste·mi·ous (ab-stē′mi-əs, əb-stē′myəs), *adj.* [L. *abstemius*, abstaining from alcoholic liquor < *ab(s)-*, from + *temetum*, strong drink], moderate in eating and drinking; not self-indulgent; temperate.

ab·sten·tion (ab-sten′shən, əb-sten′shən), *n.* [L. *abstentio* < *abstinere;* see ABSTAIN], an abstaining.

ab·sten·tious (ab-sten′shəs, əb-sten′shəs), *adj.* [< *abstention*], abstaining.

ab·sterge (ab-stũrj′, əb-stũrj′), *v.t.* [ABSTERGED (-stũrjd′), ABSTERGING], [L. *abstergere; ab(s)-*, away + *tergere*, to wipe], 1. to wipe away; clean. 2. to purge.

ab·ster·gent (ab-stũr′jənt, əb-stũr′jənt), *adj.* [L. *abstergens*, ppr. of *abstergere;* see ABSTERGE], cleansing. *n.* a cleansing substance.

ab·ster·sion (ab-stũr′shən), *n.* [< L. *abstersus*, pp. of *abstergere;* see ABSTERGE], 1. a cleansing. 2. a purging.

ab·ster·sive (ab-stũr′siv), *adj.* [< L. *abstersus*, pp. of *abstergere*, to wipe off; see ABSTERGENT], abstergent.

ab·sti·nence (ab′stə-nəns), *n.* [ME.; OFr.; L. *abstinentia* < ppr. of *abstinere;* see ABSTAIN], 1. an abstaining from some or all food, drink, or other pleasures. 2. the act of giving up drinking any alcoholic liquors: also called *total abstinence*.

ab·sti·nent (ab′stə-nənt), *adj.* practicing abstinence.

ab·stract (ab-strakt′, ab′strakt), *adj.* [L. *abstractus*, pp. of *abstrahere*, to draw from, separate; *ab(s)-*, from + *trahere*, to draw], 1. thought of apart from any particular instances or material objects; not concrete. 2. expressing a quality thought of apart from any particular or material object: as, beauty is an *abstract* word. 3. not easy to understand; abstruse; hence, 4. loosely, theoretical; not practical. 5. in *art*, characterized by design or form that is geometric or otherwise not representational. *n.* (ab′strakt), 1. a brief statement of the essential thoughts of a book, article, speech, court record, etc.; summary. 2. that which is abstract: as, the *abstract* fascinates his mind. Abbreviated **abs.** *v.t.* (ab-strakt′), 1. to take away; remove. 2. to think of (a quality) apart from any particular instance or material object that has it; form (a general idea) from particular instances. 3. (ab′-strakt), to summarize; make an abstract of. —*SYN.* see **abridgment.**

in the abstract, in theory as apart from practice.

ab·stract·ed (ab-strak′tid), *adj.* [pp. of *abstract*], 1. removed or separated (*from* something); hence, 2. withdrawn in mind; preoccupied; absent-minded. —*SYN.* see **absent-minded.**

ab·strac·tion (ab-strak′shən), *n.* [L. *abstractio;* see ABSTRACT], 1. an abstracting or being abstracted;

removal. 2. formation of an idea, as of the qualities or properties of a thing, by mental separation from particular instances or material objects. 3. an idea so formed, or a word or term for it: as, "honesty" and "whiteness" are *abstractions*. 4. an unrealistic or impractical notion. 5. mental withdrawal; preoccupation; absent-mindedness. 6. an abstract quality; abstract character. 7. in *art*, a picture, statue, etc. that is wholly or partly abstract, or not representational.

ab·strac·tion·ism (ab-strak'shən-iz'm), *n.* the theory and practice of the abstract, especially in art; cult of abstract pictures, statues, etc.

ab·strac·tion·ist (ab-strak'shən-ist), *n.* 1. a person who deals with abstractions. 2. a person who makes, or is in favor of, abstract paintings, statues, etc.

ab·strac·tive (ab-strak'tiv), *adj.* [ML. *abstractivus;* see ABSTRACT], abstracting. *n.* something that abstracts.

abstract noun, a noun naming an abstract idea.

abstract of title, a brief history of the ownership of a piece of real estate.

ab·stric·tion (ab-strik'shən), *n.* [< L. *ab*, from, off + *strictio*, a binding], in *botany*, the cutting off of spores from a spore-bearing branch by the formation of dividing tissues (septa), as in certain fungi.

ab·struse (ab-strōōs', əb-strōōs'), *adj.* [L. *abstrusus*, pp. of *abstrudere*, to thrust away; *ab(s)-*, away + *trudere*, to thrust], hard to understand; deep; recondite.

ab·surd (əb-sũrd', ab-zũrd'), *adj.* [Fr. *absurde* < L. *absurdus*, not to be heard of; *ab-*, intens. + *surdus*, dull, deaf, insensible], clearly untrue or unreasonable, and therefore laughable, ridiculous, etc.

SYN.—**absurd** means laughably inconsistent with what is judged as true or reasonable (an *absurd* hypothesis); **ludicrous** is applied to what is laughable from incongruity or exaggeration (a *ludicrous* facial expression); **preposterous** is used to describe anything flagrantly absurd or ludicrous; **foolish** describes that which shows lack of good judgment or of common sense (don't take *foolish* chances); **silly** and **ridiculous** apply to whatever excites amusement or contempt by reason of its extreme foolishness, **silly** often indicating an utterly nonsensical quality. —*ANT.* sensible, logical.

ab·surd·i·ty (əb-sũr'də-ti, ab-zũr'də-ti), *n.* [Fr. *absurdité;* L. *absurditas* < *absurdus;* see ABSURD], 1. the quality or state of being absurd; foolishness; nonsense. 2. [*pl.* ABSURDITIES (-tiz)], an absurd idea or thing.

A·bu-Bakr (ə-bōō'bak'ẽr), *n.* first caliph (632–634 A.D.) after Mohammed, in Mecca; lived 573–634 A.D.; father of Aisha.

A·bu-Bekr (ə-bōō'bek'ẽr), *n.* Abu-Bakr.

A·bu·kir (ä'bōō-kêr', ə-bōō'kẽr), *n.* a bay near Alexandria, Egypt, at the mouth of the Nile: site of the victory (1798) of the British under Nelson over the French: also spelled **Aboukir.**

a·bu·li·a (ə-bū'li-ə, ab'yoo-lē'ə), *n.* [Mod. L.; Gr. *aboulia*, indecision < *a-*, without + *boulē*, will, determination], in *psychology*, loss of the ability to exercise will power and come to decisions: also spelled **aboulia.**

a·bun·dance (ə-bun'dəns), *n.* [ME.; OFr.; L. *abundantia* < ppr. of *abundare;* see ABOUND], 1. great plenty; more than sufficient quantity. 2. wealth.

a·bun·dant (ə-bun'dənt), *adj.* [L. *abundans*, ppr. of *abundare;* see ABOUND], 1. very plentiful; more than sufficient; ample. 2. rich (*in* something). —*SYN.* see **plentiful.**

‡ab ur·be con·di·ta (ab ũr'bi kon'di-tə), [L.], from the founding of the city (Rome, founded c. 753 B.C.).

a·buse (ə-būz'; *for n.*, ə-būs'), *v.t.* [ABUSED (-būzd'), ABUSING], [ME. *abusen;* Fr. *abuser* < L. *abusus*, pp. of *abuti*, to misuse; *ab-*, away, from + *uti*, to use], 1. to use wrongly; misuse. 2. to hurt by treating badly; mistreat. 3. to use insulting, coarse, or bad language about or to; scold harshly; revile. 4. [Archaic except in the passive], to deceive. *n.* 1. wrong, bad, or excessive use. 2. mistreatment; injury. 3. a bad, unjust, or corrupt custom or practice. 4. insulting or coarse language. 5. [Archaic], deception. —*SYN.* see **wrong.**

a·bu·sive (ə-bū'siv), *adj.* [Fr. *abusif;* L. *abusivus* < *abusus;* see ABUSE], 1. abusing; mistreating. 2. coarse and insulting in language; scurrilous; harshly scolding.

a·but (ə-but'), *v.i.* [ABUTTED (-id), ABUTTING], [ME. *aboutien;* OFr. *abouter*, to join end to end < *a-*, to + *bout, but*, end], to touch at one end; border; terminate (with *on, upon*, or *against*). *v.t.* to end at; border upon; support or lean on by abutment.

a·bu·ti·lon (ə-bū'ti-lon), *n.* [Mod. L.; Ar. *aubūtīlūn*], any of a number of related plants or shrubs of the mallow family, with showy flowers of white, yellow, or red.

a·but·ment (ə-but'mənt), *n.* 1. an abutting. 2. something that abuts or borders upon something else. 3. the point of contact between a support and the thing supported. 4. *a*) in *architecture*, a part that supports an arch or strut. *b*) the structure supporting the extreme ends of a bridge.

ABUTMENTS

a·but·tal (ə-but''l), *n.* 1. an abutment. 2. *pl.* the parts in which land abuts on other land; boundaries.

a·but·ter (ə-but'ẽr), *n.* the owner of an abutting, or adjacent, piece of land.

a·buzz (ə-buz'), *adj.* [*a-*, in + *buzz*], 1. filled with buzzing; hence, 2. full of activity.

ab·volt (ab-vōlt'), *n.* [*ab*solute + *volt*], a C.G.S. electromagnetic unit, 10^{-8} volt.

ab·watt (ab-wôt', ab-wot'), *n.* [*ab*solute + *watt*], a unit of power, 10^{-7} watt.

a·by, a·bye (ə-bī'), *v.t.* [ABOUGHT (-bôt')], [AS. *abycgan*, to pay for], [Archaic], to pay for; atone for. *v.i.* [Archaic], to last; endure.

A·by·dos (ə-bī'dos, ə-bī'dəs), *n.* 1. an ancient Egyptian city. 2. an ancient city in Asia Minor.

a·bysm (ə-biz''m), *n.* [OFr. *abisme;* ML. *abismus;* L. *abyssus;* see ABYSS], [Poetic], an abyss.

a·bys·mal (ə-biz'm'l), *adj.* of or like an abysm or abyss; bottomless; unfathomable; immeasurable.

a·bys·mal·ly (ə-biz'm'l-i), *adv.* to an abysmal degree.

a·byss (ə-bis'), *n.* [L. *abyssus;* Gr. *abyssos; a-*, without + *byssos*, bottom], 1. the primeval great deep or chaos. 2. a bottomless gulf; deep fissure in the earth; chasm. 3. anything too deep for measurement; profound depth: as, an *abyss* of shame, of time, etc. 4. the ocean depths.

a·byss·al (ə-bis''l), *adj.* [*abyss* + *-al*], 1. too deep to be measured; unfathomable. 2. of the ocean depths.

Ab·ys·sin·i·a (ab'ə-sin'i-ə), *n.* Ethiopia.

Ab·ys·sin·i·an (ab'ə-sin'i-ən), *adj.* of Abyssinia, its people, language, culture, etc.; Ethiopian. *n.* 1. a native of Abyssinia. 2. the language of the Abyssinians. Abbreviated **Abyss.**

ac- (ak, ək), ad-: used before *c* or *q*, as in *accept, acquire.*

-ac (ak, ək), [Fr. *-aque;* L. *-acus;* Gr. *-akos*], an adjective-forming suffix meaning: 1. *characteristic of*, as in *elegiac, demoniac.* 2. *of, relating to*, as in *cardiac, coeliac.* 3. *affected by* or *having*, as in *maniac.* The resulting adjectives are sometimes used as nouns.

Ac, in *chemistry*, actinium.

A.C., 1. Air Corps. 2. *Ante Christum*, [L.], before Christ. 3. Armored Corps. 4. Army Corps.

A/C, a/c, in *bookkeeping*, 1. account. 2. account current.

A.C., a.c., in *electricity*, alternating current.

a·ca·cia (ə-kā'shə), *n.* [L.; Gr. *akakia*, shittah tree, thorny tree; prob. < *ake*, a point], 1. any of several trees or shrubs of the mimosa family, with clusters of yellow or white flowers: some types yield gum arabic or dyes. 2. the flower. 3. gum arabic. 4. the locust tree: also **false acacia.**

acad., 1. academic. 2. academy.

Ac·a·deme (ak'ə-dēm', ak'ə-dēm'), *n.* [< Gr. *akadēmeia*, the grove of *Akadēmos*, figure in ancient Greek legend], 1. the grove near ancient Athens where Plato taught. 2. [a-], [Poetic], a school.

ac·a·dem·ic (ak'ə-dem'ik), *adj.* [L. *academicus* < *academia;* see ACADEMY], 1. of schools or colleges and their learning; scholastic; scholarly. 2. having to do with general or liberal rather than technical or vocational education. 3. of or belonging to a learned society. 4. too far from immediate reality; not practical enough; too speculative. 5. formal; pedantic. Abbreviated **acad.** *n.* 1. a person belonging to a college or university. 2. *pl.* purely theoretical discussions.

ac·a·dem·i·cal (ak'ə-dem'i-k'l), *adj.* academic.

ac·a·dem·i·cal·ly (ak'ə-dem'i-k'l-i), *adv.* 1. in relation to an academy. 2. in an academic manner; pedantically. 3. from an academic point of view.

ac·a·dem·i·cals (ak'ə-dem'i-k'lz), *n.pl.* traditional clothing worn in some colleges; cap and gown.

academic freedom, freedom of a teacher (or student) to express his beliefs (political, economic, etc.) without arbitrary interference.

a·cad·e·mi·cian (ə-kad'ə-mish'ən, ak'ə-də-mish'ən), *n.* [Fr. *académicien*], 1. a member of an academy (sense 5). 2. [A-], a member of the French Academy, the English Royal Academy, or the American Academy of Arts and Letters.

ac·a·dem·i·cism (ak'ə-dem'ə-siz'm), *n.* the quality of being academic; formal or pedantic quality, spirit, etc.

a·cad·e·mism (ə-kad'ə-miz'm), *n.* academicism.

a·cad·e·my (ə-kad'ə-mi), *n.* [*pl.* ACADEMIES (-miz)], [Fr. *académie;* L. *academia;* Gr. *akadēmeia;* see ACADEME], 1. [A-], Academe; hence, Plato's followers or philosophy. 2. a place of higher learning. 3. a private secondary or high school. 4. any school for special instruction or training. 5. an association of scholars, writers, artists, etc., for advancing literature, art, or science. Abbreviated **acad., A.**

A·ca·di·a (ə-kā'di-ə), *n.* 1. [Poetic], a French colony (1604–1713) that included what is now Nova Scotia. 2. a parish of Louisiana settled by Acadian exiles.

A·ca·di·an (ə-kā'di-ən), *adj.* of Acadia or its people; Nova Scotian. *n.* a native or inhabitant of Acadia.

Acadia National Park, a national park of granite

mountains on Mount Desert Island, Maine: area, 38 sq. mi.
ac·a·leph (ak'ə-lef), *n.* [Gr. *akalēphē*, a nettle], a jellyfish, sea nettle, or other related coelenterate.
ac·a·lephe (ak'ə-lēf'), *n.* an acaleph.
ac·an·tha·ceous (ak'ən-thā'shəs), *adj.* [*acanth(o)-* + *-aceous*], in *botany*, 1. spiny; prickly. 2. belonging to a large family of plants having spines or thorns.
a·can·thine (ə-kan'thin, ə-kan'thīn), *adj.* of or resembling an acanthus.
a·can·tho- (ə-kan'thə), [< Gr. *akantha*, thorn < *akis*, spine], a combining form meaning *thorn, like a thorn*, as in *acanthocephalan:* also, before a vowel, **acanth-**.
a·can·tho·ceph·a·lan (ə-kan'thə-sef'ə-lən), *n.* [*acantho-* + Gr. *kephalē*, head], any of a number of related parasitic, threadlike worms having a proboscis covered with thornlike hooks.
a·can·thoid (ə-kan'thoid), *adj.* [*acanth-* + *-oid*], spiny; spine-shaped.
ac·an·thop·ter·yg·i·an (ak'ən-thop'tẽr-ij'i-ən), *adj.* [< *acantho-* + Gr. *pterygion*, a fin], of a group of bony, spiny-finned fishes. *n.* such a fish, as a perch or bass.
a·can·thous (ə-kan'thəs), *adj.* acanthoid.
a·can·thus (ə-kan'thəs), *n.* [*pl.* ACANTHUSES (-iz), ACANTHI (-thī)], [L.; Gr. *akanthos;* see ACANTHO-], 1. a plant with prickles and large leaves, found in the Mediterranean region. 2. in *architecture*, a motif or conventional representation of the leaf of this plant, used especially on the capitals of Corinthian columns.
‡a cap·pel·la (ä' kä-pel'lä; Eng. ä'kə-pel'ə), [It. < L. *ad*, to, according to + *capella*, chapel], in chapel style; without instrumental accompaniment: said of choral singing.
‡a ca·pric·cio (ä' kä-prēt'chô), [It.; *a*, at + *capriccio;* see CAPRICE], in *music*, at pleasure; at whatever tempo and with whatever expression the performer likes.
A·ca·pul·co (ä'kä-pōōl'kô), *n.* a seaport in southwestern Mexico: pop., 6,500.
ac·a·ri·a·sis (ak'ə-rī'ə-sis), *n.* [Mod. L. < Gr.], infestation by acarids.
ac·a·rid (ak'ə-rid), *n.* [Gr. *akari*], a mite, tick, or similar arachnid.
a·car·i·dan (ə-kar'ə-dən), *adj.* of the acarids. *n.* an acarid.
ac·a·roid (ak'ə-roid'), *adj.* like an acarid.
acaroid resin (or **gum**), a resin taken from some kinds of grass tree, used in varnish, etc.
a·car·pel·ous, a·car·pel·lous (ā-kär'p'l-əs), *adj.* [*a-*, without + *carpel* + *-ous*], in *botany*, without carpels.
a·car·pous (ā-kär'pəs), *adj.* [*a-*, not + *-carpous*], in *botany*, bearing no fruit; sterile.
a·cat·a·lec·tic (ā-kat'ə-lek'tik), *adj.* [LL. *acatalecticus;* Gr. *akatalēktos*, incessant < *a-*, without + *katalēgein*, to stop], in *prosody*, having the full number of syllables or metrical feet. *n.* an acatalectic line or verse.
a·cau·dal (ā-kô'd'l), *adj.* [*a-*, not + *caudal*], having no tail.
a·cau·date (ā-kô'dāt), *adj.* acaudal.
ac·au·les·cent (ak'ô-les'ənt), *adj.* [*a-*, not + *caulescent*], in *botany*, 1. having no stem. 2. having only a very short stem.
a·cau·lous (ā-kô'ləs), *adj.* [Mod. L. *acaulis;* L. *a*, without + *caulis*, a stalk, stem], acaulescent.
acc., 1. acceptance. 2. accepted. 3. accompanied. 4. accompaniment. 5. according. 6. account. 7. accountant. 8. accusative.
Ac·cad (ak'ad), *n.* Akkad.
ac·cede (ak-sēd'), *v.i.* [ACCEDED (-id), ACCEDING], [L. *accedere* < *ad-*, to + *cedere*, to yield], 1. to enter upon the duties (of an office); attain (with *to*). 2. to give assent; give in; agree (with *to*). —*SYN.* see **consent**.
ac·ced·ence (ak-sēd'əns), *n.* an acceding.
ac·cel·er·a·ble (ak-sel'ẽr-ə-b'l), *adj.* capable of acceleration.
ac·cel·er·an·do (ak-sel'ẽr-an'dō; It. ät-che'le-rän'dô), *adv. & adj.* [It.], in *music*, with gradually quickening tempo: abbreviated **accel.**
ac·cel·er·ant (ak-sel'ẽr-ənt), *adj.* [L. *accelerans*, ppr. of *accelerare;* see ACCELERATE], accelerating. *n.* 1. something that increases the speed of a process. 2. in *chemistry*, a catalyst.
ac·cel·er·ate (ak-sel'ẽr-āt'), *v.t.* [ACCELERATED (-id), ACCELERATING], [< L. *acceleratus*, pp. of *accelerare* < *ad-*, to + *celerare*, to hasten], 1. to increase the speed of. 2. to hasten the working of. 3. to cause to happen sooner. *v.i.* to increase in speed; go faster.
ac·cel·er·a·tion (ak-sel'ẽr-ā'shən), *n.* [L. *acceleratio*], 1. an accelerating or being accelerated. 2. change in velocity, either increase (*positive acceleration*) or decrease (*negative acceleration*). 3. the rate of such change.
acceleration of gravity, the acceleration of a freely falling object, caused by the force of gravity: it is expressed in terms of the rate of increase of velocity per second (32+ ft. per second per second).
ac·cel·er·a·tive (ak-sel'ẽr-ā'tiv), *adj.* of, causing, or increasing acceleration.
ac·cel·er·a·tor (ak-sel'ẽr-ā'tẽr), *n.* 1. a person or thing that accelerates or increases the speed of something. 2. a device, such as the foot throttle of an automobile, for increasing the speed of a machine. 3. in *anatomy*, a nerve or muscle that speeds up a motion. 4. in *chemistry*, a substance that speeds up a reaction. 5. in *photography*, a chemical that speeds up developing.
ac·cel·er·om·e·ter (ak-sel'ẽr-om'ə-tẽr), *n.* [< *accelerate* + *-meter*], an instrument for measuring and recording the acceleration of an aircraft.
ac·cent (ak'sent, ak's'nt), *n.* [Fr.; L. *accentus* < *ad-*, to + *canere*, to sing; a L. rendering of Gr. *prosōdia* (see PROSODY), orig. referring to the pitch scheme of Gr. verse], 1. the emphasis (by stress, pitch, or both) given to a particular syllable or word in speaking it. 2. a mark used in writing or printing to show the placing and kind of this emphasis, as in the primary (') and secondary (') accenting of English (*ac-cel'er-a'tor, ac'a-dem'i-cal-ly*, etc.). 3. a mark used to distinguish between various sounds of the same letter: as, in French there are acute (´), grave (`), and circumflex (^) *accents*. 4. the pitch contour of a phrase. 5. tone of the voice; hence, 6. a distinguishing regional or national manner of pronouncing: as, Irish *accent*, Southern *accent*. 7. *pl.* speech; words; utterance. 8. a distinguishing style of expression: as, the *accent* of Beethoven. 9. a striking or prominent feature of any artistic composition: as, the classical *accent* of a pillar. 10. a mark used with a number or letter, as in mathematics to indicate a variable (a'), or in measurement of length (10'5'', ten feet five inches) or of time (3' 16'', three minutes sixteen seconds). 11. in *music*, *a)* emphasis or stress on a note or chord. *b)* a mark showing this. 12. in *music & prosody*, rhythmic stress or beat. *v.t.* (ak'sent, ak-sent'), 1. to pronounce (a syllable, word, or phrase) with special stress. 2. to stress or emphasize. 3. in *writing & printing*, to mark with an accent.
ac·cen·tu·al (ak-sen'choo-əl), *adj.* [< L. *accentus* (see ACCENT); + *-al*], 1. of accent. 2. having rhythm based on stress: as, German poetry is basically *accentual*.
ac·cen·tu·ate (ak-sen'choo-āt'), *v.t.* [ACCENTUATED (-id), ACCENTUATING], [< ML. *accentuatus*, pp. of *accentuare* < L. *accentus;* see ACCENT], 1. to pronounce with an accent or stress. 2. to mark (a letter, etc.) with an accent. 3. to emphasize; heighten the effect of.
ac·cen·tu·a·tion (ak-sen'choo-ā'shən), *n.* [ML. *accentuatio;* see ACCENTUATE], an accentuating or accenting.
ac·cept (ək-sept', ak-sept'), *v.t.* [ME. *accepten;* OFr. *accepter;* L. *acceptare* < *accipere* < *ad-*, to + *capere*, to take], 1. to take (what is offered or given); receive (something) willingly. 2. to receive favorably; approve. 3. to agree to; acquiesce in; consent to. 4. to believe in. 5. to respond to in the affirmative: as, he will *accept* an invitation. 6. in *business*, to agree, as by a signed promise, to pay (a bill or draft). 7. in *law*, to receive in person, as service of a writ. 8. in *parliamentary procedure*, to receive (a committee report) as satisfactory. —*SYN.* see **receive**.
ac·cept·a·bil·i·ty (ək-sep'tə-bil'ə-ti, ak-sep'tə-bil'ə-ti), *n.* the quality of being acceptable.
ac·cept·a·ble (ək-sep'tə-b'l, ak-sep'tə-b'l), *adj.* [ME.; OFr.; L. *acceptabilis* < *acceptare;* see ACCEPT], worth accepting; satisfactory; agreeable; pleasing to receive.
ac·cept·a·bly (ək-sep'tə-bli, ak-sep'tə-bli), *adv.* in an acceptable manner.
ac·cept·ance (ək-sep'təns, ak-sep'təns), *n.* [OFr. < *accepter;* see ACCEPT], 1. an accepting or being accepted. 2. approving reception; approval. 3. belief in; assent. 4. in *business*, *a)* a promise to pay. *b)* a signed bill of exchange or draft showing this. Abbreviated **acc.**
ac·cept·an·cy (ək-sep'tən-si, ak-sep'tən-si), *n.* acceptance.
ac·cept·ant (ək-sep'tənt, ak-sep'tənt), *adj.* [Fr. < *accepter;* see ACCEPT], accepting; receiving.
ac·cep·ta·tion (ak'sep-tā'shən), *n.* [ML. *acceptatio;* see ACCEPT], 1. the generally accepted meaning (of a word or expression). 2. [Archaic], acceptance.
ac·cept·ed (ək-sep'tid, ak-sep'tid), *adj.* [pp. of *accept*], generally regarded as true, valid, proper, etc.; conventional; approved: abbreviated **acc.**
ac·cept·er (ək-sep'tẽr, ak-sep'tẽr), *n.* one who accepts.
ac·cep·tor (ək-sep'tẽr, ak-sep'tôr), *n.* [L.; see ACCEPT], 1. a person who accepts, or receives. 2. a person who signs a promise to pay a draft or bill of exchange.
ac·cess (ak'ses), *n.* [ME. & OFr. *acces;* L. *accessus*, pp. of *accedere;* see ACCEDE], 1. a coming toward or near to; approach. 2. a way or means of approach. 3. the right to come into, approach, or use (with *to*); admittance. 4. increase; growth. 5. an outburst; paroxysm: as, an *access* of anger. 6. in *medicine*, the onset of a disease; attack.
ac·ces·sa·ry (ak-ses'ə-ri), *adj. & n.* [*pl.* ACCESSARIES (-riz)], accessory.
ac·ces·si·bil·i·ty (ak-ses'ə-bil'ə-ti), *n.* [Fr.; L. *accessibilitas*], the condition or quality of being accessible.
ac·ces·si·ble (ak-ses'ə-b'l), *adj.* [Fr.; LL. *accessibilis* < L. *accedere;* see ACCEDE], 1. that can be approached or entered. 2. easy to approach or enter. 3. that can be got; obtainable. 4. open to the influence of (with *to*): as, he is not *accessible* to pity.
ac·ces·si·bly (ak-ses'ə-bli), *adv.* so as to be accessible.
ac·ces·sion (ak-sesh'ən), *n.* [Fr.; L. *accessio* < pp. of

accedere; see ACCEDE], 1. a coming to; attaining (the throne, power, etc.): as, the *accession* of a new king. 2. assent. 3. *a*) increase by addition. *b*) an addition. 4. in *law*, *a*) addition to property by improvements or natural growth. *b*) the owner's right to the increase in value due to such additions.

ac·ces·so·ri·al (ak'sə-sôr'i-əl, ak'sə-sō'ri-əl), *adj.* [< L. *accessorius* (see ACCESSORY); + *-al*], of or like an accessory; supplementary.

ac·ces·so·ry (ak-ses'ə-ri), *adj.* [L. *accessorius* < *accessus*, pp. of *accedere;* see ACCEDE], 1. additional; extra; helping in a secondary or subordinate capacity. 2. in *law*, acting as an accessory; helping in an unlawful act. *n.* [*pl.* ACCESSORIES (-riz)], 1. something extra; thing added to help in a secondary way. 2. any article of clothing worn to complete one's outfit, as purse, gloves, stockings, etc. 3. equipment, usually demountable and replaceable, for convenience, comfort, safety, or completeness: as, the *accessories* of an automobile. 4. in *law*, a person who, though absent, helps another to break or escape the law; accomplice.

accessory before (or **after**) **the fact**, a person who, though absent at the commission of a felony, aids or abets the accused before (or after) its commission.

‡**ac·ciac·ca·tu·ra** (ät-chäk'kä-tōō'rä), *n.* [It. < *acciaccare*, to crush], 1. in *music*, a short grace note sounded very quickly just before a principal note: it has a small line through the stem, and is shown as smaller. 2. in *phonetics*, the unemphatic first sound in a rising diphthong.

ac·ci·dence (ak'sə-dəns), *n.* [for *accidents*, inflections; see ACCIDENT; cf. CASE], 1. the part of grammar, or of a grammar book, that deals with the inflection of words: distinguished from *word formation*, *syntax*. 2. the elementary or first parts of a subject; rudiments.

ac·ci·dent (ak'sə-dənt), *n.* [ME.; Fr. < L. *accidens*, falling, ppr. of *accidere*, to happen < *ad-*, to + *cadere*, to fall], 1. a happening that is not expected, foreseen, or intended. 2. an unfortunate occurrence or mishap; sudden fall, collision, etc., usually resulting in physical injury: as, a traffic *accident*. 3. fortune; chance. 4. an attribute or quality that is not essential. 5. in *geography* & *geology*, an irregular formation. 6. in *law*, an unforeseen event that is not anyone's fault.

ac·ci·den·tal (ak'sə-den't'l), *adj.* [ML. *accidentalis;* see ACCIDENT], 1. occurring by chance; fortuitous. 2. belonging but not essential; attributive; incidental. 3. in *music*, of an accidental. *n.* 1. a nonessential quality or attribute. 2. in *music*, a sign used after the key signature to show a change of pitch in the note before which it is placed; a sharp, flat, natural, double sharp, or double flat.

SYN.—**accidental** describes that which occurs by chance (an *accidental* encounter) or outside the normal course of events (an *accidental* attribute); **fortuitous**, which frequently suggests a complete absence of cause, now usually refers to chance events of a fortunate nature; **casual** describes the unpremeditated, random, informal, or irregular quality of something (a *casual* visit, remark, dress, etc.); **incidental** emphasizes the nonessential or secondary nature of something (an *incidental* consideration); **adventitious** refers to that which is added extrinsically and connotes a lack of essential connection.

ac·ci·den·tal·ly (ak'sə-den't'l-i), *adv.* in an accidental manner; by chance.

accident insurance, insurance against injury due to accident.

ac·cip·i·ter (ak-sip'i-tẽr), *n.* [*pl.* ACCIPITRES (-trēz')], [L., a hawk], a hawk, eagle, or related bird of prey.

ac·cip·i·trine (ak-sip'i-trin, ak-sip'i-trīn'), *adj.* of or like an accipiter.

ac·claim (ə-klām'), *v.t.* [L. *acclamare* < *ad-*, to + *clamare*, to cry out], 1. to greet with loud approval; applaud. 2. to announce or acknowledge with applause; hail: as, they *acclaimed* him president. *v.i.* to shout approval. *n.* loud applause, approval, or welcome. —*SYN.* see **praise.**

ac·cla·ma·tion (ak'lə-mā'shən), *n.* [L. *acclamatio*, a shouting; see ACCLAIM], 1. an acclaiming or being acclaimed. 2. loud applause, approval, or welcome. 3. a vote by voice; especially, an enthusiastic approving vote without counting: as, elected by *acclamation*.

ac·clam·a·to·ry (ə-klam'ə-tôr'i, ə-klam'ə-tō'ri), *adj.* of or by acclamation.

ac·cli·mate (ə-klī'mit, ak'li-māt'), *v.t.* & *v.i.* [ACCLIMATED (-id), ACCLIMATING], [Fr. *acclimater;* see AD- & CLIMATE], to accustom or become accustomed to a new climate or different environment.

ac·cli·ma·tion (ak'li-mā'shən), *n.* [< *acclimate* + *-ion*], acclimatization.

ac·cli·ma·ti·za·tion (ə-klī'mə-ti-zā'shən), *n.* an acclimatizing or being acclimatized.

ac·cli·ma·tize (ə-klī'mə-tiz'), *v.t.* & *v.i.* [ACCLIMATIZED (-tīzd'), ACCLIMATIZING], [< *acclimate* + *-ize*], to acclimate.

ac·cliv·i·ty (ə-kliv'ə-ti), *n.* [*pl.* ACCLIVITIES (-tiz)], [L. *acclivitas* < *ad-*, to + *clivus*, hill], an upward slope of ground: opposed to *declivity*.

ac·cli·vous (ə-klī'vəs), *adj.* [L. *acclivus* < *ad-*, to + *clivus*, hill], sloping upward.

ac·co·lade (ak'ə-lād', ak'ə-läd'), *n.* [Fr.; It. *accollata* < *accollare*, to embrace < L. *ad*, to + *collum*, neck], 1. an embrace, formerly used in conferring knighthood. 2. a touch on the shoulder with the flat side of a sword, now used in conferring knighthood; hence, 3. an approving or praising mention; award. 4. in *music*, a vertical line joining two or more staves.

ac·com·mo·date (ə-kom'ə-dāt'), *v.t.* [ACCOMMODATED (-id), ACCOMMODATING], [< L. *accommodatus*, pp. of *accommodare* < *ad-*, to + *commodare*, to fit < *com-*, with + *modus*, a measure], 1. to make fit; adjust; adapt (often used reflexively). 2. to reconcile. 3. to supply or help by supplying (*with* something). 4. to do a service or favor for. 5. to have space for; find room for; lodge. *v.i.* to become adjusted, as the lens of the eye in focusing on objects at various distances. —*SYN.* see **adapt, contain.**

ac·com·mo·dat·ing (ə-kom'ə-dāt'iŋ), *adj.* [ppr. of *accommodate*], having a willing disposition; obliging; complaisant.

ac·com·mo·da·tion (ə-kom'ə-dā'shən), *n.* [Fr.; L. *accommodatio;* see ACCOMMODATE], 1. an accommodating or being accommodated; adaptation (*to* a purpose); adjustment. 2. reconciliation of differences. 3. willingness to do favors or services. 4. a help or convenience. 5. *pl.* lodgings; room and board. 6. *pl.* traveling space, as in a railroad train or airplane; seat, berth, etc. 7. in *business*, *a*) a loan. *b*) an accommodation bill. 8. in *physiology*, the self-adjustment of the lens of the eye for focusing on objects at various distances.

accommodation bill (or **note**), a bill of exchange or a note made or endorsed without consideration by one or more persons to enable the drawer to get credit or raise money on it.

accommodation ladder, a ladder or stairway hung over a ship's side, usually at the gangway.

accommodation train, a railroad train that stops at all or most stations.

ac·com·mo·da·tive (ə-kom'ə-dā'tiv), *adj.* accommodating or disposed to accommodate.

ac·com·pa·ni·ment (ə-kum'pə-ni-mənt, ə-kump'ni-mənt), *n.* [Fr. *accompagnement* < *accompagner;* see ACCOMPANY], 1. anything that accompanies something else; thing added, usually for order or symmetry. 2. in *music*, a part, usually instrumental, played together with the main part for richer effect; obbligato: as, the *accompaniment* to a vocal solo: abbreviated **acc.**

ac·com·pa·nist (ə-kum'pə-nist), *n.* a person who plays or sings an accompaniment.

ac·com·pa·ny (ə-kum'pə-ni), *v.t.* [ACCOMPANIED (-nid), ACCOMPANYING], [Fr. *accompagner* < L. *ad*, to + LL. **companio;* see COMPANION], 1. to send with; add to; supplement: as, *accompany* words with acts. 2. to go with; be together with; attend. 3. in *music*, to play or sing an accompaniment for or to. *v.i.* to perform a musical accompaniment; be an accompanist.

SYN.—**accompany** means to go or be together with as a companion, associate, attribute, etc., and usually connotes equality of relationship (he *accompanied* her to the theater); **attend** implies presence either in a subordinate position or to render services, etc. (Dr. Jones *attended* the patient); **escort** and **convoy** are both applied to the accompanying, as by an armed guard, of persons or things needing protection (**convoy**, especially in the case of sea travel and **escort** in the case of land travel); **escort** also implies an accompanying as a mark of honor or an act of courtesy; **chaperon** implies accompaniment, for reasons of propriety, of young unmarried people by an older or married person.

ac·com·plice (ə-kom'plis), *n.* [< ME. *a complice;* the article *a* is merged, after *accomplish;* OFr. *complice* < LL. & L. *complex*, accomplice; see COMPLEX], a person who helps another in an unlawful act; partner in crime. —*SYN.* see **associate.**

ac·com·plish (ə-kom'plish), *v.t.* [ME. *acomplissen;* OFr. *acomplir;* LL. *accomplere* < L. *ad*, to + *complere*, to complete, fill up], to do; succeed in doing; complete (a task, time, or distance). —*SYN.* see **perform, reach.**

ac·com·plished (ə-kom'plisht), *adj.* [pp. of *accomplish*], 1. done; done successfully; completed. 2. trained; skilled; proficient. 3. trained in social arts and manners; educated and polished.

ac·com·plish·ment (ə-kom'plish-mənt), *n.* [Fr. *accomplissement* < *accomplir;* see ACCOMPLISH], 1. an accomplishing or being accomplished; completion. 2. something accomplished or done successfully; work completed; achievement. 3. social art or skill.

ac·cord (ə-kôrd'), *v.t.* [ME. *acorden;* OFr. *acorder;* LL. *accordare* < L. *ad*, to + *cor, cordis*, heart], 1. to make agree or harmonize; reconcile. 2. to grant; bestow on. *v.i.* to be in agreement or harmony (usually followed by *with*). *n.* 1. mutual agreement; harmony. 2. an informal agreement between countries. 3. harmony of sound, color, etc. —*SYN.* see **agree.**

of one's own accord, voluntarily, without being told or asked by anyone else.

with one accord, all agreeing; with no one dissenting.

ac·cord·ance (ə-kôr′d'ns), *n.* [ME.; OFr. *acordance* < *acordant;* see ACCORDANT], 1. agreement; harmony; conformity: as, he did it in *accordance* with the suggestion. 2. an agreeing. 3. a granting.

ac·cord·ant (ə-kôr′d'nt), *adj.* [ME.; OFr. *acordant,* ppr. of *acorder;* see ACCORD], in agreement or harmony (usually with *to* or *with*).

ac·cord·ing (ə-kôr′diŋ), *adj.* agreeing; in harmony. *adv.* accordingly. Abbreviated **acc.**

according as, 1. to the degree that; in proportion as. 2. depending on whether.

according to, 1. in a way consistent with. 2. in proportion to. 3. on the authority of; as stated by.

ac·cord·ing·ly (ə-kôr′diŋ-li), *adv.* 1. in agreement with what has preceded; correspondingly. 2. therefore.

ac·cor·di·on (ə-kôr′di-ən), *n.* [invented word (1829) < It. *accordare;* + *-ion* as in *clarion,* etc.; see ACCORD], a musical instrument with keys, metal reeds, and a bellows, which is alternately pulled out and pressed together between the player's hands to force air through the reeds and thus produce tones.

ACCORDION

ac·cor·di·on·ist (ə-kôr′di-ən-ist), *n.* a person who plays the accordion.

accordion pleats, narrow pleats like the folds in the bellows of an accordion.

ac·cost (ə-kôst′, ə-kost′), *v.t.* [Fr. *accoster* < L. *accostare,* to bring side by side < *ad-,* to + *costa,* rib, side], 1. to approach and speak to; greet first, before being greeted. 2. to solicit for sexual purposes: said of prostitutes, etc.

ac·couche·ment (ə-ko͞osh′mənt; Fr. ä′ko͞osh′mäṅ′), *n.* [Fr. < *accoucher,* to put to bed, to give birth < *à,* to + *coucher;* see COUCH], childbirth; confinement.

ac·cou·cheur (a′ko͞o-shũr′; Fr. å′ko͞o′shër′), *n.* [Fr.; see ACCOUCHEMENT], a medical man who attends childbirth cases; expert in obstetrics.

ac·cou·cheuse (a′ko͞o-sho͞oz′; Fr. å′ko͞o′shöz′), *n.* [Fr., fem. of *accoucheur*], a midwife.

ac·count (ə-kount′), *v.t.* [ME. *acounten;* OFr. *aconter; a-,* to + *conter,* to tell < *compter* < L. *computare;* see COMPUTE], to consider or judge to be; deem; value. *v.i.* 1. to furnish a reckoning (*to* someone) of money received and paid out. 2. to make satisfactory amends (*for* something): as, he will *account* for his crime. 3. to give satisfactory reasons for; explain (with *for*): as, can he *account* for his actions? 4. to dispose of, as by killing; put out of action (with *for*): as, he *accounted* for five of the enemy. *n.* 1. a counting; calculation. 2. *often pl.* a record of business transactions; statement of money received, paid, or owed. 3. a business relation, especially one in which credit is used; charge account: abbreviated **A/C, a/c, acct., acc.** 4. worth; importance: as, a thing of small *account.* 5. an explanation. 6. a report; description; story.

call to account, 1. to demand an explanation of; hence, 2. to reprimand.

give a good account of oneself, to acquit oneself creditably.

on account, 1. on a charge account; on the installment plan. 2. as partial payment.

on account of, 1. because of. 2. for (someone's) sake.

on (a person's) account, for (a specified person's) sake.

on no account, not under any circumstances.

take account of, 1. to take into consideration; allow for. 2. to take notice; note.

take into account, to take into consideration.

turn to account, to make profitable; get use from.

ac·count·a·bil·i·ty (ə-koun′tə-bil′ə-ti), *n.* the condition of being accountable, liable, or responsible.

ac·count·a·ble (ə-koun′tə-b'l), *adj.* 1. liable to be called to account; responsible. 2. capable of being accounted for; explicable. —*SYN.* see **responsible.**

ac·count·a·bly (ə-koun′tə-bli), *adv.* in a manner that can be accounted for.

ac·count·an·cy (ə-koun′t'n-si), *n.* the keeping or inspecting of commercial accounts; work of an accountant.

ac·count·ant (ə-koun′t'nt), *n.* a trained person whose work is to inspect, keep, or adjust accounts: see **certified public accountant**: abbreviated **acc.**

ac·count·ant·ship (ə-koun′t'nt-ship′), *n.* [see -SHIP], the work or position of an accountant.

account book, a book in which business accounts are set down.

account current, a record of business dealings showing money owed: abbreviated **A/C, a/c** (no period).

ac·count·ing (ə-koun′tiŋ), *n.* [ME. *acounting* < *acounten;* see ACCOUNT], 1. the system, science, or art of keeping, analyzing, and explaining commercial accounts. 2. a statement of debits and credits. 3. a settling or balancing of accounts.

ac·cou·ple·ment (ə-kup′'l-mənt), *n.* [Fr. < *accoupler,* to couple up], 1. [Obs.], a coupling, or joining, of one thing to another. 2. something that couples; specifically, in *carpentry,* a brace or tie.

ac·cou·ter (ə-ko͞o′tẽr), *v.t.* [Fr. *accoutrer,* earlier *accoustrer;* ? < *à* + **coustrer* < L. *consuere,* to sew, knit together; see COUTURE], to outfit; equip, especially for military service: also spelled **accoutre.**

ac·cou·ter·ments (ə-ko͞o′tẽr-mənts), *n.pl.* [*sing.* ACCOUTERMENT], [Fr. *accoutrements;* see ACCOUTER], 1. personal outfit; clothes; dress. 2. a soldier's equipment except clothes and weapons. 3. *sing.* an accoutering or being accoutered. Also spelled **accoutrements.**

ac·cou·tre (ə-ko͞o′tẽr), *v.t.* [ACCOUTRED (-tẽrd), ACCOUTRING], to accouter.

Ac·cra (ak′rə), *n.* the capital of Ghana, on the Gulf of Guinea: pop., 133,000: also spelled **Akkra.**

ac·cred·it (ə-kred′it), *v.t.* [Fr. *accréditer,* to give credit or authority < *à,* to + *crédit;* see CREDIT], 1. to bring into credit or favor. 2. to authorize; give credentials to. 3. to believe in; take as true. 4. to certify as coming up to a set standard. 5. to attribute. 6. to give (someone) credit for or consider (someone) as having (followed by *with*). —*SYN.* see **authorize.**

ac·cred·it·a·tion (ə-kred′i-tā′shən), *n.* an accrediting or being accredited.

ac·crete (ə-krēt′), *v.i.* [ACCRETED (-id), ACCRETING], [< L. *accretus,* pp. of *accrescere;* see ACCRETION], 1. to grow by being added to. 2. to grow together; adhere. *adj.* in *botany,* grown together.

ac·cre·tion (ə-krē′shən), *n.* [L. *accretio* < *accrescere,* to increase < *ad-,* to + *crescere,* to grow], 1. growth in size, especially by addition or accumulation. 2. a growing together of parts normally separate. 3. accumulated matter: as, the *accretion* of earth on the shore. 4. a whole resulting from such growth or accumulation.

ac·cre·tive (ə-krē′tiv), *adj.* of or by accretion.

ac·cru·al (ə-kro͞o′əl), *n.* 1. an accruing. 2. the amount that accrues.

ac·crue (ə-kro͞o′), *v.i.* [ACCRUED (-kro͞od′), ACCRUING], [< Fr. *accrue, n.* < *accrû,* pp. of *accroître,* to increase; L. *accrescere;* see ACCRETION], 1. to come as a natural growth or advantage (with *to*). 2. to be added as a natural increase: said especially of interest on money.

ac·crue·ment (ə-kro͞o′mənt), *n.* accrual.

acct., account.

ac·cul·tu·ra·tion (ə-kul′chẽr-ā′shən), *n.* [< *ac-* + *culture* + *-ation*], in *sociology,* 1. the process of conditioning a child to the cultural patterns. 2. the process of becoming adapted to new cultural patterns.

ac·cum·ben·cy (ə-kum′bən-si), *n.* the state of being accumbent; accumbent position.

ac·cum·bent (ə-kum′bənt), *adj.* [L. *accumbens,* ppr. of *accumbere* < *ad-,* to + *cubare,* to recline], 1. lying down. 2. in *botany,* lying against some other part.

ac·cu·mu·la·ble (ə-kūm′yoo-lə-b'l), *adj.* that can be accumulated.

ac·cu·mu·late (ə-kūm′yoo-lāt′), *v.t. & v.i.* [ACCUMULATED (-id), ACCUMULATING], [< L. *accumulatus,* pp. of *accumulare* < *ad-,* to + *cumulare,* to heap], to pile up; collect; gather.

ac·cu·mu·la·tion (ə-kūm′yoo-lā′shən), *n.* [L. *accumulatio*], 1. an accumulating or being accumulated; collection. 2. accumulated or collected material; heap. 3. the addition to capital of interest or profits.

ac·cu·mu·la·tive (ə-kūm′yoo-lā′tiv), *adj.* 1. resulting from accumulation; cumulative. 2. tending to accumulate. 3. acquisitive.

ac·cu·mu·la·tor (ə-kūm′yoo-lā′tẽr), *n.* [L.; see ACCUMULATE], 1. a person or thing that accumulates. 2. an apparatus that collects and stores energy; specifically, [British], a storage battery.

ac·cu·ra·cy (ak′yoo-rə-si), *n.* 1. the quality or state of being accurate or exact; precision. 2. [*pl.* ACCURACIES (-siz)], an instance of this.

ac·cu·rate (ak′yoo-rit), *adj.* [L. *accuratus,* pp. of *accurare* < *ad-,* to + *curare,* to take care < *cura,* care], 1. careful and exact. 2. free from mistakes or errors; precise. —*SYN.* see **correct.**

ac·curs·ed (ə-kũr′sid, ə-kũrst′), *adj.* [pp. of obs. v. *accurse;* ME. *acursien; a-* + *cursien;* see CURSE], 1. under a curse; ill-fated. 2. damnable; abominable.

ac·curst (ə-kũrst′), *adj.* accursed.

accus., accusative.

ac·cus·al (ə-kūz′'l), *n.* accusation.

ac·cu·sa·tion (ak′yoo-zā′shən), *n.* [ME. *acusacioun;* OFr. *acusation;* L. *accusatio* < pp. of *accusare;* see ACCUSE], 1. an accusing or being accused. 2. what a person is accused of; charge of wrongdoing.

ac·cu·sa·ti·val (ə-kū′zə-tī′v'l), *adj.* of the accusative case.

ac·cu·sa·tive (ə-kū′zə-tiv), *adj.* [L. *accusativus* < *accu-*

sare; see ACCUSE: L. mistranslation of Gr. grammatical term correctly rendered *causitivus*, causitive, by Priscian: the goal or terminating point of an action was orig. considered to be its cause], of or in the accusative or objective case. *n.* 1. the accusative or objective case. 2. a word in this case. Abbreviated **acc., accus.**

accusative case, in *linguistics*, the case expressing the goal of an action or motion, as, in *Latin grammar*, the case occurring in the direct object of a verb and after certain prepositions, or, in *English grammar*, the objective case, a relational case shown in the changed forms of the pronouns *me, us, him, her, them,* and *whom.*

ac·cu·sa·to·ri·al (ə-kū'zə-tôr'i-əl, ə-kū'zə-tō'ri-əl), *adj.* [L. *accusatorius;* see ACCUSE], of an accuser.

ac·cu·sa·to·ry (ə-kū'zə-tôr'i, ə-kū'zə-tō'ri), *adj.* accusing; making or containing an accusation.

ac·cuse (ə-kūz'), *v.t.* [ACCUSED (-kūzd'), ACCUSING], [ME. *acusen;* OFr. *acuser;* L. *accusare*, to call to account < *ad-*, to + *causa*, a cause, case, or lawsuit], 1. to find at fault; blame. 2. to bring charges against (*of* doing wrong, breaking the law, etc.).

SYN.—**accuse** is used with reference to finding fault for offenses of varying gravity (to *accuse* one of murder, to *accuse* one of carelessness); **charge** usually implies an accusation of a legal or formal nature; **indict** describes the action of a grand jury, etc. in finding a case against a person and ordering him brought to trial; **arraign** refers to the actual process of calling the person before the court and informing him of the charges against him; **impeach** is applied to charging a public official with misconduct of office, but in nonlegal usage denotes a challenging of a person's motives, etc.

ac·cused (ə-kūzd'), *n. sing. & pl.* [see ACCUSE], in *law*, the person or persons against whom a charge of crime or misdemeanor is brought (with *the*).

ac·cus·tom (ə-kus'təm), *v.t.* [OFr. *acostumer* < *a-*, to + *costume;* see CUSTOM], to make familiar by custom, habit, or use; habituate (*to* something).

ac·cus·tomed (ə-kus'təmd), *adj.* [pp. of *accustom*], 1. customary; usual; characteristic: as, he spoke with *accustomed* ease. 2. wont or used (*to*): as, he is *accustomed* to obeying orders. —*SYN.* see **usual.**

ace (ās), *n.* [ME. *as, aas* < L. *as*, unit, pound], 1. a unit; "one" in dice, playing cards, or dominoes. 2. a playing card, domino, etc. marked with one spot. 3. a point, as in tennis, won by a single stroke. 4. a single point or particle: as, I was within an *ace* of confessing. 5. an expert in any activity, especially in combat flying: so called from the fact that in many card games the ace is the highest card. *adj.* [Colloq.], first-rate; expert: as, an *ace* salesman. *v.t.* [ACED (āst), ACING], to score a point against by a single stroke, as in tennis.

-a·ce·a (ā'shi-ə, ā'shə), [L., neut. pl. of *-aceus*], a plural suffix used in forming the zoological names of classes or orders; see **-aceous.**

-a·ce·ae (ā'si-ē'), [L., fem. pl. of *-aceus*], a plural suffix used to form botanical names of families; see **-aceous.**

a·ce·di·a (ə-sē'di-ə), *n.* [LL. < Gr. *akēdia* < *a-*, not + *kēdos*, care], spiritual sloth and indifference.

ace in the hole, 1. in *stud poker*, an ace dealt and kept face down until the deal is over; hence, 2. [Slang], any advantage held in reserve until needed.

A·cel·da·ma (ə-sel'də-mə), *n.* [L.; Gr. *Akeldama;* Aram. *ōkēl damō*, field of blood], 1. in the *Bible*, the potter's field near Jerusalem bought with the money given Judas for betraying Jesus: Acts 1:19, Matt. 27:8. Judas committed suicide there. 2. a place of bloodshed.

a·cen·tric (ā-sen'trik, ə-sen'trik), *adj.* [*a-* + *centric*], having no center; off center.

-a·ceous (ā'shəs), [L. *-aceus*], a suffix meaning *of the nature of, like, belonging to, characterized by,* as in *crustaceous:* used to form adjectives corresponding to zoological and botanical nouns ending in *-acea, -aceae.*

a·ceph·a·lous (ā-sef'ə-ləs, ə-sef'ə-ləs), *adj.* [L. *acephalus;* Gr. *akephalos* < *a-*, without + *kephalē*, head], 1. headless. 2. leaderless. 3. in *zoology*, having no part of the body differentiated as the head.

a·ce·quia (ə-sā'kyə; Sp. ä-se'kyä), *n.* [Sp. < Ar.], an irrigation canal.

ac·er·ate (as'ẽr-it, as'ẽr-āt'), *adj.* [L. *aceratus*, needlelike < *acus, aceris*, a pin, needle], in *botany*, needle-shaped.

ac·er·bate (as'ẽr-bāt'), *v.t.* [ACERBATED (-id), ACERBATING], [< L. *acerbatus*, pp. of *acerbare*, to make harsh or bitter], 1. to make sour or bitter. 2. to irritate; vex.

a·cer·bi·ty (ə-sũr'bə-ti), *n.* [*pl.* ACERBITIES (-tiz)], [Fr. *acerbité;* L. *acerbitas* < *acerbus*, sharp], 1. a sour, astringent quality. 2. sharpness, bitterness, or harshness of temper, words, etc.

ac·er·ose (as'ẽr-ōs'), *adj.* [< L. *acus, aceris*, a needle; form influenced by next entry], in *botany*, shaped like a needle; having a sharp, stiff point: see **leaf**, illus.

ac·er·ose (as'ẽr-ōs'), *adj.* [L. *acerosus*, full of chaff < *acus, aceris*, chaff], 1. like chaff. 2. mixed with chaff.

a·cer·vate (ə-sũr'vit, ə-sũr'vāt), *adj.* [L. *acervatus*, pp. of *acervare*, to heap up < *acervus*, heap], in *botany*, heaped up; growing in clusters.

a·ces·cence (ə-ses'əns), *n.* [Fr.; see ACESCENT], the process of becoming sour.

a·ces·cent (ə-ses'ənt), *adj.* [Fr. < L. *acescens*, ppr. of *acescere*, to turn sour], becoming sour; likely to sour.

a·cet- (ə-sēt', ə-set', as'it), aceto-.

ac·e·tab·u·lar (as'ə-tab'yoo-lẽr), *adj.* of or like an acetabulum.

ac·e·tab·u·lum (as'ə-tab'yoo-ləm), *n.* [*pl.* ACETABULA (-lə)], [L., orig., vinegar cup < *acetum*, vinegar], 1. in *anatomy*, the cup-shaped socket of the hip bone, into which the thigh bone fits. 2. in *zoology*, a sucker of a leech, octopus, etc.

ac·e·tal (as'ə-tal'), *n.* [*acet-* + *-al*], a colorless, slightly soluble, volatile liquid, $C_6H_{14}O_2$, formed by the imperfect oxidation of alcohol and used in medicine as a hypnotic.

ac·et·al·de·hyde (as'ə-tal'də-hīd'), *n.* [*acet-* + *aldehyde*], a colorless, soluble, volatile liquid, C_2H_4O, used as a solvent and in making various organic compounds.

ac·et·am·id (as'ə-tam'id, ə-set'ə-mid), *n.* acetamide.

ac·et·am·ide (as'ə-tam'īd, ə-set'ə-mīd', as'ə-tam'id), *n.* [*acet-* + *amide*], a white, crystalline organic substance, CH_3CONH_2, the amide of acetic acid.

ac·et·an·i·lid (as'ə-tan''l-id), *n.* acetanilide.

ac·et·an·i·lide (as'ə-tan''l-īd', as'ə-tan''l-id), *n.* [*acet-* + *aniline* + *-ide*], a white, crystalline organic substance, $CH_3CONHC_6H_5$, produced by the action of acetic acid on aniline: used as a drug to lessen pain and fever.

ac·e·tate (as'ə-tāt'), *n.* [*acet-* + *-ate*], a salt or ester of acetic acid: as, cellulose *acetate.*

ac·e·tat·ed (as'ə-tā'tid), *adj.* treated with acetic acid.

a·ce·tic (ə-sē'tik, ə-set'ik), *adj.* [< L. *acetum*, vinegar], of, like, containing, or producing acetic acid or vinegar.

acetic acid, a sour, colorless, liquid compound, CH_3COOH, having a sharp odor: it is found in vinegar.

acetic anhydride, a colorless liquid, $C_4H_6O_3$, decomposable by water to acetic acid, used as a reagent in organic synthesis.

a·cet·i·fi·ca·tion (ə-set'ə-fi-kā'shən), *n.* an acetifying.

a·cet·i·fy (ə-set'ə-fī'), *v.t. & v.i.* [ACETIFIED (-fīd'), ACETIFYING], to change into vinegar or acetic acid.

ac·e·tim·e·ter (as'ə-tim'ə-tẽr), *n.* an acetometer.

ac·e·to- (ə-sē'tō, as'ə-tō), [< L. *acetum*, vinegar], a combining form meaning *of* (or *from*) *acetic acid* or *acetyl:* also, before a vowel, **acet-.**

ac·e·tom·e·ter (as'ə-tom'ə-tẽr), *n.* [*aceto-* + *-meter*], an instrument used to find the amount of acetic acid in a definite quantity of vinegar or other liquid.

ac·e·tone (as'ə-tōn'), *n.* [*acet-* + *-one*], a colorless, inflammable, volatile liquid, CH_3COCH_3, used as a paint remover and as a solvent for certain oils and other organic compounds: also called *dimethyl ketone.*

acetone body, a ketone body.

ac·e·ton·ic (as'ə-ton'ik), *adj.* derived from acetone.

ac·e·tose (as'ə-tōs'), *adj.* acetous.

ac·e·tous (as'ə-təs, ə-sē'təs), *adj.* [*acet-* + *-ous*], of, producing, or like vinegar; sour.

a·ce·tum (ə-sē'təm), *n.* [L. < *acere*, to be sour], in *pharmacy*, vinegar.

ac·e·tyl (as'ə-til), *n.* [*acet-* + *-yl*], the radical CH_3CO, derived from acetic acid: found only in compounds.

a·cet·y·late (ə-set''l-āt'), *v.t.* [ACETYLATED (-id), ACETYLATING], [*acetyl* + *-ate*], to combine an acetyl radical with (an organic compound).

ac·e·tyl·cho·line (as'ə-til-kō'lēn, as'ə-til-kol'in), *n.* [*acetyl* + *choline*], an alkaloid, $C_7H_{17}O_3N$, extracted from ergot and used in medicine to lower blood pressure and increase peristalsis.

a·cet·y·lene (ə-set''l-ēn'), *n.* [*acetyl* + *-ene*], a colorless, poisonous, highly inflammable gaseous hydrocarbon, C_2H_2, produced by the reaction of water and calcium carbide: it is used as the starting material in the synthesis of many organic compounds, for lighting, and, with oxygen in a blowtorch, for welding, etc.

ac·e·tyl·sal·i·cyl·ic acid (as'ə-til-sal'ə-sil'ik, ə-sē't'l-sal'ə-sil'ik), aspirin.

ace·y-deuc·y (ā'si-dōō'si, ā'si-dū'si), *n.* [< *ace* + *deuce*], a variation of the game of backgammon.

A·chae·a (ə-kē'ə), *n.* Achaia.

A·chae·an (ə-kē'ən), *adj.* of Achaia, its people, or its culture; Greek. *n.* 1. a native or inhabitant of Achaia. 2. a Greek: so used in Homer. The Achaeans are thought to have migrated from the northern Danube region into Greece c. 1300 B.C.

A·cha·ia (ə-kā'ə, ə-kī'ə), *n.* a province of ancient Greece, in the Peloponnesus.

A·cha·ian (ə-kā'ən, ə-kī'ən), *adj. & n.* Achaean.

A·cha·tes (ə-kā'tēz), *n.* [L.], 1. in Virgil's *Aeneid*, a loyal friend and companion of Aeneas; hence, 2. a loyal friend.

ache (āk), *v.i.* [ACHED (ākt), ACHING], [orig. *ake* < ME. *aken;* AS. *acan;* akin to LG. *äken*, to smart, MD. *akel*, sorrow, shame < IE. base **agos-*, fault, guilt, sin; now *ache* through confusion with the *n.*], 1. to have or give dull, steady pain. 2. [Colloq.], to yearn or long (with *for* or an infinitive). *n.* (āk; *before 1700,* āch), [ME.; AS. *æce* < the *v.*], a dull, continuous pain.

a·chene (ā-kēn′), *n.* [Gr. *a-*, not + *chainein,* to gape], any small, dry fruit with one seed, whose thin outer covering (pericarp) does not burst when ripe.

a·che·ni·al (ā-kē′ni-əl), *adj.* of an achene.

Ach·er·on (ak′ēr-on′), *n.* [L.; Gr.], 1. in *Greek & Roman mythology,* the river in Hades across which Charon ferried the dead; hence, 2. Hades; infernal regions.

Ach·e·son, Dean Good·er·ham (dēn good′ēr-ham′ ach′i-s′n), 1893– ; American lawyer and statesman; secretary of state (1949–1953).

A·cheu·le·an, A·cheu·li·an (ə-shōō′li-ən), *adj.* [Fr. *Acheulien* < *St. Acheul,* France, where remains were found], denoting or of a type of paleolithic culture characteristic of the Heidelberg and Piltdown man.

‡**à che·val** (å′ shə-vål′), [Fr.], 1. on horseback; astraddle; hence, 2. straddling (an issue).

a·chiev·a·ble (ə-chēv′ə-b'l), *adj.* that can be achieved.

a·chieve (ə-chēv′), *v.t.* [ACHIEVED (-chēvd′), ACHIEVING], [ME. *acheven;* OFr. *achever,* to finish < *a-*, to + *chief,* end, head < L. *caput,* the head], 1. to do; do successfully; accomplish. 2. to get or reach by exertion; attain; gain. *v.i.* to effect a desired result. —*SYN.* see **perform, reach.**

a·chieve·ment (ə-chēv′mənt), *n.* [Fr. *achèvement;* see ACHIEVE], 1. an achieving. 2. a thing achieved, especially by skill, work, courage, etc.; feat; exploit.

achievement quotient, in *educational psychology,* the ratio of a person's achievement age (as shown by testing what has been learned) to his mental age: also called *accomplishment quotient:* abbreviated **A.Q.**

A·chil·les (ə-kil′ēz), *n.* [L.; Gr. *Achilleus*], in Homer's *Iliad,* the Greek hero of the Trojan War, who killed Hector and was killed by Paris with an arrow that struck his only vulnerable spot, his heel.

Achilles' heel, (one's) vulnerable or susceptible spot.

Achilles' tendon, the tendon connecting the back of the heel to the muscles of the calf of the leg.

A·chit·o·phel (ə-kit′ə-fel′), *n.* Ahithophel.

ach·la·myd·e·ous (ak′lə-mid′i-əs), *adj.* [< *a-*, not + Gr. *chlamys, chlamydos,* a cloak or coat], in *botany,* having neither sepals nor petals; without a perianth.

ach·ro·mat·ic (ak′rə-mat′ik), *adj.* [Gr. *achrōmatos* < *a-*, without + *chrōma,* color], 1. colorless. 2. refracting white light without breaking it up into its component colors. 3. forming visual images whose outline is free from prismatic colors. 4. in *biology, a)* staining poorly with the usual stains. *b)* made of achromatin. 5. in *music,* without accidentals: as, an *achromatic* scale. *n.* an achromatic lens.

FLINT GLASS
CROWN GLASS

ACHROMATIC LENS
(of microscope)

a·chro·ma·tin (ə-krō′mə-tin), *n.* [*a-*, not + *chromatin*], in *biology,* that material of the cell nucleus not easily colored by the usual stains.

a·chro·ma·tism (ə-krō′mə-tiz'm), *n.* the condition or quality of being achromatic; lack of color.

a·chro·ma·tize (ə-krō′mə-tīz′), *v.t.* [ACHROMATIZED (-tīzd′), ACHROMATIZING], to make achromatic; rid of color.

a·chro·ma·tous (ā-krō′mə-təs, ə-krō′mə-təs), *adj.* [Gr. *achrōmatos;* see ACHROMATIC], 1. without color. 2. without enough color: as, *achromatous* blood.

a·chro·mic (ā-krō′mik, ə-krō′mik), *adj.* [< Gr. *achrōmos* (see ACHROMOUS); + *-ic*], without color.

a·chro·mous (ā-krō′məs, ə-krō′məs), *adj.* [Gr. *achrōmos,* colorless; *a-*, not + *chrōma,* color], without color.

a·cic·u·la (ə-sik′yoo-lə), *n.* [*pl.* ACICULAE (-lē′)], [L., dim. of *acus,* a pin, needle], in *biology & geology,* a needlelike spine, prickle, or crystal.

a·cic·u·lar (ə-sik′yoo-lēr), *adj.* of or like an acicula; bristly; spiny; needlelike.

a·cic·u·late (ə-sik′yoo-lit), *adj.* 1. having aciculae. 2. having marks like scratches made by a needle.

a·cic·u·lat·ed (ə-sik′yoo-lā′tid), *adj.* aciculate.

a·cic·u·lum (ə-sik′yoo-ləm), *n.* [*pl.* ACICULUMS (-ləmz), ACICULA (-lə)], [Mod. L. < *acicula*], 1. an acicula. 2. in *zoology,* a bristlelike part; seta.

ac·id (as′id), *adj.* [L. *acidus,* sour < base *ac-*, sharp], 1. sour; sharp and biting to the taste; tart. 2. of or like an acid; having the properties of an acid. *n.* 1. a sour substance. 2. in *chemistry,* any compound that can react with a base to form a salt, the hydrogen of the acid being replaced by a positive ion; according to modern theory, a compound which yields hydrogen ions (protons) to a base in a chemical reaction: in water solution, an acid tastes sour, turns blue litmus red, and, according to the dissociation theory, produces free hydrogen ions. —*SYN.* see **sour.**

ac·id-fast (as′id-fast′), *adj.* not readily decolorized by acids when stained, as the tubercle bacillus.

ac·id-form·ing (as′id-fôrm′iŋ), *adj.* 1. forming an acid in chemical reaction; acidic. 2. yielding a large acid residue in metabolism: said of foods.

a·cid·ic (ə-sid′ik), *adj.* 1. acid-forming. 2. containing an excess of an acid-forming substance: rocks containing much silica (an acidic oxide) are called *acidic* rocks.

a·cid·i·fi·a·ble (ə-sid′ə-fī′ə-b'l), *adj.* that can be acidified.

a·cid·i·fi·ca·tion (ə-sid′ə-fi-kā′shən), *n.* an acidifying or being acidified.

a·cid·i·fi·er (ə-sid′ə-fī′ēr), *n.* anything that acidifies; any substance producing an acid effect.

a·cid·i·fy (ə-sid′ə-fī′), *v.t. & v.i.* [ACIDIFIED (-fīd′), ACIDIFYING], 1. to make or become sour or acid. 2. to change into an acid.

ac·i·dim·e·ter (as′i-dim′ə-tēr), *n.* [< *acid* + *-meter*], an instrument or solution used to find the amount of acid present in a definite weight or volume of a solution or other mixture.

a·cid·i·ty (ə-sid′ə-ti), *n.* [*pl.* ACIDITIES (-tiz)], [Fr. *acidité;* L. *aciditas* < *acidus*], 1. acid quality or condition; sourness. 2. the degree of this. 3. hyperacidity.

ac·id·ly (as′id-li), *adv.* in a sour, biting manner.

ac·i·doph·i·lic (as′i-dof′ə-lik), *adj.* [< *acid* + *-phile* + *-ic*], staining readily with acid dyes, as some bacteria.

ac·i·doph·i·lus milk (as′i-dof′ə-ləs), milk with acidophilic bacteria added: used for medicinal purposes.

ac·i·do·sis (as′i-dō′sis), *n.* in *medicine,* a condition in which the alkali reserve (blood bicarbonates) of the body is below normal: loosely called *autointoxication.*

ac·i·dot·ic (as′i-dot′ik), *adj.* of or having acidosis.

acid test, a crucial, final test of the value or quality of a thing or person: originally, a test of gold by acid.

a·cid·u·late (ə-sij′oo-lāt′), *v.t.* [ACIDULATED (-id), ACIDULATING], [< L. *acidulus,* slightly sour; + *-ate*], to make somewhat acid or sour.

a·cid·u·lous (ə-sij′oo-ləs), *adj.* [L. *acidulus,* dim. of *acidus;* see ACID], somewhat acid or sour. —*SYN.* see **sour.**

ac·i·er·ate (as′i-ēr-āt′), *v.t.* [ACIERATED (-id), ACIERATING], [Fr. *acier,* steel; + *-ate*], to change into steel.

ac·i·form (as′i-fôrm′), *adj.* [< L. *acus,* needle; + *-form*], needle-shaped; sharp.

ac·i·nac·i·form (as′i-nas′i-fôrm′), *adj.* [L. *acinaces,* short sword; Gr. *akinakēs,* of Per. origin; + *-form*], in *botany,* shaped like a scimitar.

a·cin·i·form (ə-sin′i-fôrm′), *adj.* [< L. *acinus,* grape, grapestone; + *-form*], 1. shaped like a cluster of grapes. 2. full of little kernels, like a grape.

ac·i·nose (as′i-nōs′), *adj.* acinous.

ac·i·nous (as′i-nəs), *adj.* [L. *acinosus*], composed of, containing, or resembling an acinus or acini.

ac·i·nus (as′i-nəs), *n.* [*pl.* ACINI (-nī′)], [L., a grape, grapestone], 1. any of the small parts (drupelets) composing such fruits as the raspberry, blackberry, etc. 2. a grape or any berry. 3. a grape seed or berry seed. 4. in *anatomy,* one of the small sacs of a compound or racemose gland.

-a·cious (ā′shəs), [< L. *-ax, -acis;* + *-ous*], an adjective-forming suffix meaning *characterized by, inclined to, full of,* as in *tenacious, fallacious.*

-ac·i·ty (as′ə-ti), [Fr. *-acité* < L. *-acitas*], a suffix used to form nouns corresponding to adjectives in **-acious,** as in *tenacity.*

Ack-Ack, ack-ack (ak′ak′), *n.* [echoic; prob.telephonic expansion of abbrev. *A.A.,* antiaircraft artillery], [Slang], 1. an antiaircraft gun. 2. its fire.

ac·knowl·edge (ək-nol′ij, ak-nol′ij), *v.t.* [ACKNOWLEDGED (-ijd), ACKNOWLEDGING], [earlier *aknowledge* < ME. *knowlechen, cnawlechen* < *knowleche* (see KNOWLEDGE); influenced by ME. *aknowen,* AS. *oncnawan,* to understand, know, and with Latinized prefix], 1. to admit to be true or as stated; confess. 2. to recognize the authority or claims of. 3. to recognize and answer (a greeting or introduction). 4. to express thanks for. 5. to state that one has received (a letter, gift, favor, etc.). 6. in *law,* to recognize as genuine; certify in legal form: as, *acknowledge* a deed.

SYN.—**acknowledge** implies the reluctant disclosure of something one might have kept secret (he *acknowledged* the child as his); **admit** describes assent that has been elicited by persuasion and implies a conceding of a fact, etc. (I'll *admit* you're right); **own** denotes an informal acknowledgment of something in connection with oneself (to *own* to a liking for turnips); **avow** implies an open, emphatic declaration, often as an act of affirmation; **confess** is applied to a formal acknowledgment of a sin, crime, etc., but in a weakened sense is used interchangeably with **admit** in making simple declarations (I'll *confess* I don't like him). —*ANT.* deny.

ac·knowl·edg·ment, ac·knowl·edge·ment (ək-nol′ij-mənt, ak-nol′ij-mənt), *n.* 1. an acknowledging or being acknowledged; admission; avowal. 2. recognition of the authority or claims of. 3. a recognizing and answering, as to a greeting. 4. an expression of thanks or appreciation. 5. something given or done in return, as for a letter, a favor, etc. 6. a legal avowal or certificate.

a·clin·ic (ā-klin′ik, ə-klin′ik), *adj.* [Gr. *aklinēs* < *a-*, not + *klinein;* see INCLINE], not dipping: said of a magnetic needle.

aclinic line, an imaginary line around the earth near

the equator, where the magnetic needle does not dip.

A.C.L.U., American Civil Liberties Union.

ac·me (ak′mi, ak′mē), ***n.*** [Gr. *akmē*, a point, top, age of maturity], the highest point; point of culmination.—***SYN.*** see **summit.**

ac·ne (ak′ni, ak′nē), ***n.*** [Mod. L; ? < Gr. *akmē*; see ACME], a common skin disease characterized by chronic inflammation of the sebaceous glands, usually causing pimples on the face, back, and chest.

ac·node (ak′nōd), ***n.*** [< L. *acus*, a needle, point (cf. ACUTE); + *node*], in *mathematics*, the point of a curve where the curve turns sharply back on itself: it is a double point, at which the curve has two imaginary tangents, and is consecutive to no real point on the curve.

a·cock (ə-kok′), ***adv. & adj.*** [*a-*, on + *cock*], in a cocked or tilted fashion: as, with hat *acock*.

a·cock·bill (ə-kok′bil′), ***adv.*** [*acock* + *bill* (a point)], with the ends cocked or tilted up: said of the flukes of a catted anchor or a ship's yards angled to the deck.

ac·o·lyte (ak′ə-līt′), ***n.*** [ME. *acolit;* ML. *acolytus;* Gr. *akolouthos*, follower], 1. in the *Roman Catholic Church*, a member of the highest of the four minor orders, whose duty is to serve at Mass. 2. in the *Anglican Church*, a layman who has similar duties. 3. an altar boy. 4. an attendant; follower; helper.

A·con·ca·gua (ä′kôn-kä′gwä), ***n.*** a volcanic mountain of the Andes in western Argentina: height, 23,080 ft.: highest peak in South America.

ac·o·nite (ak′ə-nīt′), ***n.*** [L. *aconitum;* Gr. *akoniton*], 1. a poisonous plant of the crowfoot family, with blue, purple, or yellow hoodlike flowers; monkshood; wolfsbane. 2. a drug made from dried roots of monkshood, used as a cardiac and respiratory sedative.

a·co·ni·tum (ak′ə-nī′təm), ***n.*** aconite (in both senses).

a·corn (ā′kôrn, ā′kẽrn), ***n.*** [ME. *akern;* AS. *æcern*, nut, mast of trees; akin to Goth. ***akran,*** ON. ***akarn*** < IE. base *ə*g-*, to grow; form influenced by supposed connection with *corn*], the fruit of the oak tree; oak nut.

acorn squash, a kind of squash shaped like an acorn.

ACORNS AND LEAVES

a·cot·y·le·don (ā′kot-'l-ē′d'n, ə-kot″l-ē′d'n), ***n.*** [*a-*, without + *cotyledon*], any plant without cotyledons, as a moss, lichen, or fern; cryptogam.

a·cot·y·le·don·ous (ā′kot-'l-ē′d'n-əs, ə-kot″l-ē′d'n-əs), ***adj.*** without cotyledons; cryptogamous.

a·cous·tic (ə-kōōs′tik, ə-kous′tik), ***adj.*** [Fr. *acoustique;* Gr. *akoustikos*, of or for hearing < *akouein*, to hear], having to do with hearing, heard sound, or the science of heard sound.

a·cous·ti·cal·ly (ə-kōōs′ti-k'l-i, ə-kous′ti-k'l-i), ***adv.*** with reference to acoustics; from the standpoint of acoustics.

ac·ous·ti·cian (ak′ōōs-tish′ən, ak′ous-tish′ən), ***n.*** 1. an expert in acoustics. 2. a person who fits the hard of hearing with hearing aids.

a·cous·tics (ə-kōōs′tiks, ə-kous′tiks), ***n.pl.*** 1. the qualities of a room, theater, etc. that have to do with how clearly sounds can be heard or transmitted in it. 2. [construed as sing.], the science of heard sound.

‡**à cou·vert** (å′ kōō′vâr′), [Fr.], under cover; secure.

A.C.P., American College of Physicians.

ac·quaint (ə-kwānt′), ***v.t.*** [ME. *acointen;* OFr. *acointier* < ML. *adcognitare* < L. *ad*, to + *cognitus*, pp. of *cognoscere*, to know thoroughly < *con-*, with + *gnoscere*, to know], 1. to familiarize (oneself *with* a thing). 2. to inform (followed by *with* or *that*). —***SYN.*** see **notify.**

ac·quaint·ance (ə-kwān′t'ns), ***n.*** [ME. *aqueintance;* OFr. *acointance* < *acointier;* see ACQUAINT], 1. knowledge (of something) got from personal experience or study of it: as, an intimate *acquaintance* with art. 2. knowledge (of a person) got by casual personal contact: less intimate than *friendship*. 3. a person or persons whom one knows only slightly.

ac·quaint·ance·ship (ə-kwān′t'ns-ship′), ***n.*** [*acquaintance* + *-ship*], 1. personal knowledge. 2. the relation between people who are acquaintances.

ac·quaint·ed (ə-kwān′tid), ***adj.*** [pp. of *acquaint*], having personal knowledge of a thing, or slight personal knowledge of a person; having acquaintanceship.

ac·qui·esce (ak′wi-es′), ***v.i.*** [ACQUIESCED (-est′), ACQUIESCING], [Fr. *acquiescer*, to yield to; L. *acquiescere* < *ad-*, to + *quiescere*, to be at rest], to accept or consent quietly without protesting (with *in*); assent without enthusiasm. —***SYN.*** see **consent.**

ac·qui·es·cence (ak′wi-es′'ns), ***n.*** [Fr.; see ACQUIESCE], an acquiescing; unprotesting assent or consent.

ac·qui·es·cent (ak′wi-es″nt), ***adj.*** [L. *acquiescens*, ppr. of *acquiescere;* see ACQUIESCE], acquiescing; consenting or assenting without protest.

ac·quir·a·ble (ə-kwīr′ə-b'l), ***adj.*** that can be acquired.

ac·quire (ə-kwīr′), ***v.t.*** [ACQUIRED (-kwīrd′), ACQUIRING], [ME. *aqueren;* OFr. *aquerre;* L. *acquirere* < *ad-*, to + *quaerere*, to seek], 1. to get or gain by one's own efforts or actions. 2. to get possession of; get as one's own. —***SYN.*** see **get.**

acquired characteristic, in *biology*, a modification of structure or function caused by environmental factors: now generally regarded as not inheritable: also **acquired character.**

ac·quire·ment (ə-kwīr′mənt), ***n.*** 1. an acquiring or being acquired. 2. something acquired, as a skill, etc.

ac·qui·si·tion (ak′wə-zish′ən), ***n.*** [L. *acquisitio* < pp. of *acquirere;* see ACQUIRE], 1. an acquiring or being acquired. 2. an acquired or added thing or person: often in a favorable sense, as, he is a distinct *acquisition* to the team.

ac·quis·i·tive (ə-kwiz′ə-tiv), ***adj.*** [< L. *acquisitus*, pp. of *acquirere;* see ACQUIRE], eager to acquire; good at getting and holding (money, ideas, etc.); grasping. —***SYN.*** see **greedy.**

ac·quit (ə-kwit′), ***v.t.*** [ACQUITTED (-id), ACQUITTING], [ME. *aquiten;* OFr. *aquiter*, to free < ML. *acquitare*, to settle a claim < L. *ad*, to + *quietare*, to quiet], 1. to pay (a debt or claim). 2. to release from a duty, obligation, etc. 3. to declare (a person) not guilty (*of* something); exonerate. 4. to bear or conduct (oneself); behave. —***SYN.*** see **absolve, behave.**

ac·quit·tal (ə-kwit″l), ***n.*** 1. an acquitting; discharge (of duty, obligation, etc.). 2. in *law*, a setting free or being set free.

ac·quit·tance (ə-kwit″ns), ***n.*** [ME.; OFr. *aquitance* < *aquiter;* see ACQUIT], 1. a settlement of, or release from, debt or liability. 2. a record of this; receipt in full.

ac·quit·ter (ə-kwit′ẽr), ***n.*** a person who acquits.

A·cre (ä′kẽr, ā′kẽr), ***n.*** a seaport in western Israel, prominent during the Crusades: pop., 9,000.

a·cre (ā′kẽr), ***n.*** [AS. *æcer*, field, cultivated land, tract plowable in a day; akin to Goth. *akrs*, OHG, *ackar*, G. *acker;* IE. base **agros*, field, lit., place to which cattle are driven < **agō-* (L. *agere*), to drive, do; cf. Sans. *ájrah*, plain, country, Gr. *agros*, country, L. *ager*, field, etc.; cf. AGRICULTURE], 1. a measure of land, 43,560 sq. ft.: abbreviated **A., a.** 2. a field: now only in the phrase *God's acre*, a graveyard. 3. *pl.* lands; estate.

a·cre·age (ā′kẽr-ij, ā′krij), ***n.*** [*acre* + *-age*], 1. the number of acres in a piece of land; acres collectively. 2. land sold or distributed by the acre.

a·cred (ā′kẽrd), ***adj.*** consisting of or owning many acres: often used in hyphenated compounds, meaning *having* (a specified number or quantity of) *acres*, as, a *many-acred* farmer.

a·cre-foot (ā′kẽr-foot′), ***n.*** the quantity of water (43,560 cu. ft.) that would cover one acre to a depth of one foot.

a·cre-inch (ā′kẽr-inch′), ***n.*** one twelfth of an acre-foot, or 3,630 cubic feet.

ac·rid (ak′rid), ***adj.*** [L. *acer, acris*, sharp; form influenced by *acid*], 1. sharp, bitter, stinging, or irritating to the taste or smell. 2. bitter or caustic in speech, etc.

ac·ri·dine (ak′ri-dēn′, ak′ri-din), ***n.*** [*acrid* + *-ine*], a colorless, crystalline compound, $C_{13}H_9N$, found in coal tar: certain dyes and drugs are made from it.

a·crid·i·ty (a-krid′ə-ti, ə-krid′ə-ti), ***n.*** 1. the quality or state of being acrid. 2. [*pl.* ACRIDITIES (-tiz)], an acrid remark.

Ac·ri·lan (ak′ri-lan′), ***n.*** a synthetic acrylic fiber used in clothing, carpeting, etc.: a trade-mark.

ac·ri·mo·ni·ous (ak′rə-mō′ni-əs), ***adj.*** [LL. *acrimoniosus;* see ACRIMONY], bitter and caustic in temper, manner, or speech.

ac·ri·mo·ny (ak′rə-mō′ni), ***n.*** [*pl.* ACRIMONIES (-niz)], [L. *acrimonia*, sharpness < *acer*, sharp], bitterness or harshness of temper, manner, or speech; asperity.

a·crit·i·cal (ā-krit′i-k'l), ***adj.*** [*a-*, not + *critical*], 1. not critical; having no tendency to criticism or critical judgment. 2. in *medicine*, showing no signs of a crisis.

ac·ro- (ak′rō, ak′rə), [< Gr. *akros*, at the point, end, or top; highest; outermost < base *ak-*, pointed], a combining form meaning: 1. ***pointed,*** as in *acrocephaly*. 2. ***highest, topmost, at the extremities,*** as in *acrospire*.

ac·ro·bat (ak′rə-bat′), ***n.*** [Fr. *acrobate;* Gr. *akrobatos*, walking on tiptoe < *akros* (see ACRO-) + *bainein*, to walk, go], an expert performer of tricks on the trapeze, tightrope, etc.; skilled gymnast or tumbler.

ac·ro·bat·ic (ak′rə-bat′ik), ***adj.*** 1. of an acrobat. 2. like or characteristic of an acrobat or his tricks.

ac·ro·bat·i·cal·ly (ak′rə-bat′i-k'l-i, ak′rə-bat′ik-li), ***adv.*** in an acrobatic manner.

ac·ro·bat·ics (ak′rə-bat′iks), ***n.pl.*** 1. an acrobat's tricks. 2. tricks like these: as, mental *acrobatics*.

ac·ro·car·pous (ak′rə-kär′pəs), ***adj.*** [*acro-* + *-carpous*], bearing fruit at the end of the stalk.

ac·ro·ce·phal·ic (ak'rō-sə-fal'ik), *adj.* of or having acrocephaly. *n.* a person who has acrocephaly.
ac·ro·ceph·a·lous (ak'rō-sef'ə-ləs), *adj.* acrocephalic.
ac·ro·ceph·a·ly (ak'rō-sef'ə-li), *n.* [< *acro-* + Gr. *kephalē*, head], an abnormal condition in which the skull is pointed.
ac·ro·drome (ak'rə-drōm'), *adj.* [*acro-* + *-drome*], in *botany*, having the veins ending at the tip of the leaf.
a·crod·ro·mous (ə-krod'rə-məs), *adj.* acrodrome.
ac·ro·gen (ak'rə-jən), *n.* [*acro-* + *-gen*], a plant, such as a fern or moss, having a perennial stem with the growing point at the tip.
a·crog·e·nous (ə-kroj'ə-nəs), *adj.* in *botany*, 1. growing at the tip. 2. of the acrogens.
a·cro·le·in (ə-krō'li-in), *n.* [*acr*id + L. *ole*re, to smell; + *-in*], a yellowish or colorless, pungent liquid, C_3H_4O, a decomposition product of glycerol and glycerides, used as a tear gas in chemical warfare, etc.
ac·ro·lith (ak'rə-lith'), *n.* [L. *acrolithus;* Gr. *akrolithos* < *akros* (see ACRO-) + *lithos*, stone], a statue with stone head, hands, and feet, and a wooden trunk.
ac·ro·me·gal·ic (ak'rō-mi-gal'ik), *adj.* of or having acromegaly. *n.* a person who has acromegaly.
ac·ro·meg·a·ly (ak'rō-meg'ə-li), *n.* [< *acro-* + Gr. *megas*, *megalē*, large], a disease in which there is permanent enlargement of the bones of the head, hands, and feet, caused by abnormal activity of the pituitary gland.
a·cro·mi·on (ə-krō'mi-ən), *n.* [Mod. L.; Gr. *akrōmion* < *akrōmia*, point of the shoulder < *akros*, at the end, topmost < *akē*, a point + *ōmos*, the shoulder], in *anatomy*, the outer extremity of the shoulder blade.
a·cron·i·cal, a·cron·y·cal (ə-kron'i-k'l), *adj.* [Gr. *akronychos*, at sunset < *akros* (see ACRO-) + *nyx*, night], in *astronomy*, happening at sunset or in the evening: also spelled **acronichal, acronychal.**
ac·ro·nym (ak'rə-nim), *n.* [*acro-* + homo*nym*], a word formed from the first (or first few) letters of several words, as *radar*, from *ra*dio *d*etecting *a*nd *r*anging.
a·crop·e·tal (ə-krop'ə-t'l), *adj.* [*acro-* + *petal*], in *botany*, developing upward from the base toward the apex: said of certain types of inflorescence.
ac·ro·pho·bi·a (ak'rə-fō'bi-ə), *n.* [*acro-* + *phobia*], a fear of high places.
a·crop·o·lis (ə-krop'ə-lis), *n.* [Gr. *akropolis* < *akros* (see ACRO-) + *polis*, city], the fortified upper part of an ancient Greek city; especially, [A-], that of Athens, on which the Parthenon was built.
ac·ro·spire (ak'rə-spīr'), *n.* [< *acro-* + Gr. *speira*, twisted thing], the spiral primary bud of germinating grain.
a·cross (ə-krôs', ə-kros'), *adv.* [*a-*, on, in + *cross;* prob. after Fr. *encroix*], 1. crossed; crosswise. 2. from one side to the other. 3. on or to the other side. *prep.* 1. from one side to the other of. 2. on or to the other side of; over; through. 3. into contact with: as, he came *across* an old friend.
a·cros·tic (ə-krôs'tik, ə-kros'tik), *n.* [L. *acrostichis;* Gr. *akrostichos* < *akros* (see ACRO-) + *stichos*, line of verse], a verse or arrangement of words in which certain letters in each line, such as the first or last, when taken in order spell out a word, motto, etc. *adj.* of or like an acrostic.
a·cros·ti·cal·ly (ə-krôs'ti-k'l-i, ə-kros'tik-li), *adv.* in the manner of an acrostic.
ac·ro·tism (ak'rə-tiz'm), *n.* [< Gr. *a-*, without + *krotos*, a beat; + *-ism*], in *medicine*, absence or imperceptibility of the pulse beat.
a·cryl·ic (ə-kril'ik), *adj.* [*acr*olein + *-yl* + *-ic*], 1. designating or of a colorless, pungent acid, $C_3H_4O_2$, obtained by the oxidation of acrolein. 2. designating or of a series of olefin acids with the general formula $C_nH_{2n-2}O_2$.
acrylic fiber, any of a group of synthetic fibers derived from a compound of hydrogen cyanide and acetylene, and made into fabrics.
acrylic resin, any of a group of transparent thermoplastic resins formed by polymerizing esters of acrylic acid or methacrylic acid.
act (akt), *n.* [Fr. *acte;* L. *actus*, a doing or moving, *actum*, thing done; pp. of *agere*, to do], 1. a thing done; deed. 2. an action; doing. 3. a decision (of a court, legislature, etc.); law; decree. 4. a document formally stating what has been done, made into law, etc. 5. one of the main divisions of a drama or opera. 6. a short performance on a program, as in vaudeville; hence, 7. [Colloq.], a piece of affected or feigned behavior. *v.t.* [< L. *actus;* see the *n.*], 1. to play the part of. 2. to perform in (a play); hence, 3. to behave like; simulate: as, don't *act* the child. *v.i.* 1. to perform on the stage; play a role; be an actor. 2. to be suited to performance: said of a play or a role. 3. to behave; comport oneself. 4. to do a thing; function. 5. to have an effect (often with *on*): as, acids *act* on metal. 6. to appear or pretend to be: as, he *acted* very angry.
  act as, to perform the functions of.
  act for, 1. to do the work of. 2. to act in behalf of.
  act on, 1. to act in accord with; obey. 2. to act in regard to. 3. to have an effect on.
  act up, [Colloq.], 1. to be playful. 2. to misbehave.
act., active.
act·a·bil·i·ty (ak'tə-bil'ə-ti), *n.* the quality of being actable.
act·a·ble (ak'tə-b'l), *adj.* that can be acted: said of a play, a role, etc.
Ac·tae·on (ak-tē'ən), *n.* [L.; Gr. *Aktaion*], in *Greek mythology*, the hunter who made Artemis angry by watching her bathe: she changed him into a stag, and he was torn to pieces by his own dogs.
‡Ac·ta Sanc·to·rum (äk'tä säŋk-tō'rəm, ak'tə saŋk-tôr'əm), [L., Acts of the Saints], in the *Roman Catholic Church*, a collection of lives of the saints and martyrs.
actg., acting.
ACTH, [< *a*drenocorti*c*o*t*ropic *h*ormone], a pituitary hormone used experimentally in the treatment of rheumatoid arthritis and certain other diseases.
ac·tin- (ak'tin), actino-.
ac·ti·nal (ak'ti-n'l, ak-tī'n'l), *adj.* [*actin-* + *-al*], in *zoology*, of the oral region of a radiate animal, the region from which the rays or tentacles grow.
act·ing (ak'tiŋ), *adj.* [ppr. of *act*], 1. performing or adapted for performance: as, an *acting* version of a play. 2. functioning. 3. temporarily taking over the duties or position of someone else: as, the *acting* chairman. Abbreviated **actg.** *n.* 1. the act of performing on the stage; art or occupation of an actor; hence, 2. affected or simulated behavior. —*SYN.* see **temporary.**
ac·tin·i·a (ak-tin'i-ə), *n.* [*pl.* ACTINIAE (-ē'), ACTINIAS (-əz)], [Mod. L. < Gr. *aktis*, *aktinos*, a ray], 1. a sea anemone. 2. any animal related to it.
ac·tin·i·an (ak-tin'i-ən), *adj.* [see ACTINIA], of or like a sea anemone. *n.* any sea anemone.
ac·tin·ic (ak-tin'ik), *adj.* having to do with actinism.
actinic rays, light rays of short wave length, occurring in the violet and ultraviolet parts of the spectrum, that produce chemical changes, as in photography.
ac·ti·nide series (ak'ti-nīd'), [< *actinium*], a group of radioactive chemical elements from element 89 (actinium) through 103 (?): see group III of **periodic table.**
ac·tin·i·form (ak-tin'i-fôrm'), *adj.* [< *actin-* + *-form*], having radial form; rayed.
ac·tin·ism (ak'tin-iz'm), *n.* [*actin-* + *-ism*], in *chemistry*, that property of ultraviolet light, X rays, etc. by which chemical reactions are produced.
ac·tin·i·um (ak-tin'i-əm), *n.* [Mod. L. < Gr. *aktis*, *aktinos*, ray], a radioactive chemical element, found with uranium and radium in pitchblende and other minerals: symbol, Ac; at. wt., 227 (?); at. no., 89.
ac·ti·no- (ak'ti-nō, ak-tin'ə), [< Gr. *aktis*, *aktinos*, ray], a combining form meaning: 1. in *chemistry, of actinism* or *actinic rays*, as in *actinograph*. 2. in *biology, of radiated structure*, as in *actinomycosis*. Also **actin-.**
ac·tin·o·gram (ak-tin'ə-gram'), *n.* an actinograph.
ac·tin·o·graph (ak-tin'ə-graf', ak-tin'ə-gräf'), *n.* [*actino-* + *-graph*], in *photography*, an actinometer.
ac·ti·noid (ak'ti-noid'), *adj.* [*actin-* + *-oid*], having a radial form, as an actinozoan.
ac·tin·o·lite (ak-tin'ə-līt'), *n.* [*actino-* + *-lite*], a greenish type of amphibole: asbestos is the fibrous variety.
ac·ti·nol·o·gy (ak'ti-nol'ə-ji), *n.* [*actino-* + *-logy*], the science of light rays and their chemical effects.
ac·ti·nom·e·ter (ak'ti-nom'ə-tẽr), *n.* [*actino-* + *-meter*], 1. in *physics*, an instrument for measuring the intensity of the sun's rays, or the actinic effect of light rays. 2. in *photography*, an exposure meter.
ac·ti·nom·e·try (ak'ti-nom'ə-tri), *n.* the measurement of the intensity of radiation by using an actinometer.
ac·ti·no·mor·phic (ak'ti-nə-môr'fik), *adj.* [*actino-* + *-morphic*], in *biology*, having radial symmetry, as a flower or a starfish.
ac·ti·no·mor·phous (ak'ti-nə-môr'fəs), *adj.* actinomorphic.
ac·ti·no·my·cete (ak'ti-nō-mī-sēt') *n.* [*actino-* + *-mycete*], any of a large group of moldlike, parasitic microorganisms, important in the development of antibiotics.
ac·ti·no·my·co·sis (ak'ti-nō-mī-kō'sis), *n.* [*actino-* + *mycosis*], a fungus infection of cattle, hogs, and people, that affects the mouth, jaw, skin, bones, and viscera.
ac·ti·no·zo·an (ak'ti-nə-zō'ən), *n.* [< *actino-* + Gr. *zōion*, an animal], an anthozoan.
ac·tion (ak'shən), *n.* [ME. *accion;* OFr. *action;* L. *actio* < pp. of *agere*, to do, drive], 1. the doing of something; being in motion or operation. 2. an act or thing done. 3. *pl.* behavior; habitual conduct. 4. the influence or effect of something (on something else): as, the *action* of a drug. 5. the way of moving, working, etc., as of a machine. 6. the moving parts or mechanism, as of a gun, piano, etc. 7. the sequence of happenings in a story or play. 8. a legal process; lawsuit. 9. a military encounter; combat. 10. the appearance of animation in a painting, sculpture, etc. —*SYN.* see **battle.**
  bring action, to start a lawsuit.
  in action, 1. active; in motion or operation. 2. participating. 3. in combat.
  see action, to participate in military combat.
  take action, 1. to become active. 2. to start a lawsuit.
ac·tion·a·ble (ak'shən-ə-b'l), *adj.* in *law*, that gives cause for an action, or lawsuit.
Ac·ti·um (ak'ti-əm, ak'shi-əm), *n.* a cape on the western coast of ancient Greece: the forces of Mark Antony and

Cleopatra were defeated by those of Octavian under Agrippa in a naval battle near Actium (31 B.C.).
ac·ti·vate (ak′tə-vāt′), *v.t.* [ACTIVATED (-id), ACTIVATING], 1. to make active; cause to engage in activity; hence, 2. to create or organize (a military unit, governmental bureau, etc.). 3. to make radioactive. 4. to make capable of reacting or of accelerating a chemical reaction. 5. to treat (sewage) with air so that aerobes will become active in it, thus purifying it.
ac·ti·va·tion (ak′tə-vā′shən), *n.* an activating or being activated.
ac·ti·va·tor (ak′tə-vā′tẽr), *n.* 1. a thing or person that activates. 2. in *chemistry*, a catalyst.
ac·tive (ak′tiv), *adj.* [ME. & OFr. *actif;* L. *activus* < base *act-* as in *actus*, pp. of *agere;* see ACT], 1. acting; functioning; working; moving. 2. capable of acting, functioning, etc. 3. causing action, motion, or change. 4. characterized by much action or motion; lively; busy; agile; quick: as, an *active* mind. 5. necessitating action or work. 6. in *business*, producing profit or interest: as, *active* funds. 7. in *grammar*, *a)* indicating the voice or form of a verb whose subject is shown as performing the action of the verb: opposed to *passive*. *b)* in or of the active voice. *c)* showing action rather than state of being: said of verbs like *throw* and *walk*. *n.* 1. an active member of an organization. 2. in *grammar*, the active voice. Abbreviated **act., a.**
SYN.—**active** implies a state of motion, operation, etc., ranging from cases of normal functioning to instances of quickened activity (he's still *active* at eighty, an *active* market); **energetic** suggests a concentrated exertion of energy or effort (an *energetic* workout); **vigorous** implies forcefulness, robustness, and strength as an inherent quality (a *vigorous* plant); **strenuous** is applied to things that make trying demands on one's strength, energy, etc. (a *strenuous* trip); **brisk** implies liveliness and vigor of motion (a *brisk* walk). See also **agile.**
active immunity, immunity (to a disease) due to the production of antibodies in the body tissues.
active list, a list of officers serving in or available for service in the armed forces.
active service, service on the active list or in the armed forces in wartime.
ac·tiv·ism (ak′tiv-iz'm), *n.* the doctrine or policy of being active or doing things with energy and decision.
ac·tiv·i·ty (ak-tiv′ə-ti), *n.* [*pl.* ACTIVITIES (-tiz)], 1. the quality or state of being active; action; motion; doing; use of energy. 2. normal power of mind or body; energetic action; liveliness; alertness. 3. an active force. 4. any specific action or pursuit: as, outside *activities*.
ac·tiv·ize (ak′tə-vīz′), *v.t.* [ACTIVIZED (-vīzd′), ACTIVIZING], to make active; activate.
act of God, in *insurance & law*, a happening for which no one is liable, because no one could foresee or prevent it; accident due to natural causes.
act of war, an act of aggression by one nation, group of nations, etc. against another without declaring war.
ac·tor (ak′tẽr), *n.* [L., a doer, advocate < base *act-;* see ACT], 1. a person who does a thing. 2. a person who acts in plays, moving pictures, etc.
bad actor, [Slang], 1. a person who misbehaves. 2. an unscrupulous or dangerous person; criminal.
ac·tor-ac·tion construction (ak′tẽr-ak′shən), a sentence or clause containing both subject (actor) and predicate (action).
ac·tress (ak′tris), *n.* [< *actor* + *-ess*], a woman or girl who acts in plays, moving pictures, etc.
Acts (akts), *n.pl.* [construed as sing.], a book of the New Testament, ascribed to Luke, and describing the beginnings of the Christian church: full title, **Acts of the Apostles.**
ac·tu·al (ak′chōō-əl), *adj.* [ME. *actuel*, active; Fr. *actuel;* LL. *actualis*, active, practical < *actus*, pp. of *agere*, to do], 1. existing in reality or in act; not merely possible, but real. 2. existing at the present moment. —*SYN.* see **true.**
ac·tu·al·i·ty (ak′chōō-al′ə-ti), *n.* 1. the state of being actual; reality. 2. [*pl.* ACTUALITIES (-tiz)], an actual thing or condition; fact.
ac·tu·al·i·za·tion (ak′chōō-əl-i-zā′shən), *n.* an actualizing or being actualized.
ac·tu·al·ize (ak′chōō-əl-īz′), *v.t.* [ACTUALIZED (-īzd′), ACTUALIZING], 1. to make actual or real; realize in action. 2. to make realistic.
ac·tu·al·ly (ak′chōō-əl-i, ak′choo-li), *adv.* [*actual* + *-ly*], really; as a matter of fact.
actual sin, in *theology*, any sin committed by a person of his free will, as distinguished from original sin.
ac·tu·ar·i·al (ak′chōō-âr′i-əl), *adj.* [< *actuary* + *-al*], 1. of actuaries or their work. 2. calculated by actuaries.
ac·tu·ar·y (ak′chōō-er′i), *n.* [*pl.* ACTUARIES (-iz)], [L. *actuarius*, clerk < *actus;* see ACT], a person whose work is to calculate risks, premiums, etc. for insurance.
ac·tu·ate (ak′chōō-āt′), *v.t.* [ACTUATED (-id), ACTUATING], [< ML. *actuatus*, pp. of *actuare* < L. *actus;* see ACT], 1. to put into action or motion. 2. to impel to action: as, what motives *actuated* him?
ac·tu·a·tion (ak′chōō-ā′shən), *n.* an actuating or being actuated; impulse.
ac·tu·a·tor (ak′chōō-ā′tẽr), *n.* a person or thing that actuates.
ac·u·ate (ak′ū-it), *adj.* [< L. *acus*, a needle; + *-ate*], having a point; sharp at the end.
a·cu·i·ty (ə-kū′ə-ti), *n.* [*pl.* ACUITIES (-tiz)], [Fr. *acuité;* ML. *acuitas* < L. *acus*, a needle], acuteness; keenness, as of thought or vision.
a·cu·le·ate (ə-kū′li-it, ə-kū′li-āt′), *adj.* [L. *aculeatus*], in *botany & zoology*, having an aculeus or aculei.
a·cu·le·us (ə-kū′li-əs), *n.* [*pl.* ACULEI (-ī′)], [L., dim. of *acus*, a needle], 1. in *botany*, a prickle. 2. in *zoology*, a sting.
a·cu·men (ə-kū′mən), *n.* [L., a point, sting, mental acuteness < *acuere*, to sharpen], keenness and quickness of mind; sharp insight.
a·cu·mi·nate (ə-kū′mi-nit), *adj.* [L. *acuminatus*, pp. of *acuminare*, to sharpen], pointed; tapering to a point: as, an *acuminate* leaf: see **leaf,** illus. *v.t.* (ə-kū′mi-nāt′), [ACUMINATED (-id), ACUMINATING], to sharpen.
a·cu·mi·na·tion (ə-kū′mi-nā′shən), *n.* 1. an acuminating or acuminate condition. 2. a tapering point.
ac·u·punc·ture (ak′yoo-puŋk′chẽr), *n.* [< L. *acus*, a needle + *punctura*, a pricking], in *medicine*, the insertion of a needle into a part of the body. *v.t.* (ak′yoo-puŋk′chẽr), to perform an acupuncture on.
a·cute (ə-kūt′), *adj.* [L. *acutus*, pp. of *acuere*, to sharpen; cf. ACUITY], 1. sharp-pointed. 2. keen or quick of mind; shrewd. 3. sensitive to impressions. 4. severe and sharp, as pain, jealousy, etc. 5. severe but of short duration; not chronic: said of some diseases. 6. critical; crucial. 7. shrill; high in pitch. 8. under 90 degrees: said of angles.

ACUTE ANGLE

SYN.—**acute** suggests severe intensification of an event, condition, etc. that is sharply approaching a climax (an *acute* shortage); **critical** is applied to a turning point which will decisively determine an outcome (the *critical* battle of a war); **crucial** comes into contrast with **critical** where a trial determining a line of action rather than a decisive turning point is involved (a *crucial* debate on foreign policy). See also **sharp.**
acute accent, a mark (′) used to show: 1. the quality or length of a vowel, as in *idée*. 2. primary stress, as in *týpewriter*. 3. any stress on a spoken sound or syllable, as in scanning poetry. 4. high rising tone or pitch, as in the Chinese language.
A.C.W.A., Amalgamated Clothing Workers of America: a C.I.O. labor union.
-a·cy (ə-si), [variously < Fr. *-atie;* L. *-acia, -atia;* Gr. *-ateia*], a suffix used in forming abstract nouns, meaning *quality, condition, position*, etc., as in *celibacy, curacy*.
a·cy·clic (ā-sī′klik, ā-sik′lik), *adj.* [*a-*, not + *cyclic*], 1. not cyclic; not in cycles. 2. in *chemistry*, having the structure of an open chain rather than a closed ring.
ad (ad), *n.* [Colloq.], an advertisement.
ad (ad), *n.* [short for *advantage*], in *tennis*, advantage: said of the first point scored after deuce.
ad in, server's advantage.
ad out, receiver's advantage.
ad- (ad, əd), [L. *ad-*, to, at, toward; akin to *at*], a prefix meaning, in general, *motion toward, addition to, nearness to*, as in *admit, adjoin, adrenal:* through assimilation in Latin, it is spelled *ac-* before *c* or *q*, as in *accept; af-* before *f*, as in *affect; ag-* before *g*, as in *aggrade; al-* before *l*, as in *allure; an-* before *n*, as in *annihilate; ap-* before *p*, as in *approve; ar-* before *r*, as in *arrive; as-* before *s*, as in *assimilate; at-* before *t*, as in *attempt; a-* before *sc, sp*, and *st*, as in *ascend*. Many apparent English occurrences of this prefix are Latinizations, often erroneous, of French or even of English words: see **advance, admiral, accursed, acknowledge.**
-ad (ad), [Gr. *-as, -ad*], a suffix meaning *of* or *relating to*, used in forming: 1. the names of collective numerals, as in *monad*. 2. the names of some poems, as in *Iliad*. 3. the names of some plants, as in *cycad*.
-ad (-əd), [Fr. *-ade*], -ade: shortened form, as in *ballad*.
ad., 1. adverb. 2. [*pl.* ADS.], advertisement.
A.D., 1. active duty. 2. *Anno Domini*, [L.], in the year of the Lord; of the Christian era: used with dates.
a.d., 1. after date. 2. *ante diem*, [L.], before the day.
A·da (ā′də), [Heb. *'ādāh*, beauty], a feminine name: also spelled **Adah.**
A.D.A., 1. American Dental Association. 2. Americans for Democratic Action: also **ADA** (no period).
a·dac·ty·lous (ā-dak′t'l-əs), *adj.* [*a-* (without) + *dactyl* + *-ous*], congenitally lacking fingers or toes.
ad·age (ad′ij), *n.* [Fr. < L. *adagium, adagio* < *ad-*, to + *aio*, I say], an old saying or proverb; maxim. —*SYN.* see **saying.**
a·da·gio (ə-dä′jō, ə-dä′ji-ō′), *adv.* [It. *ad agio*, lit., at

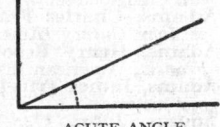

ease], in *music & dancing*, slowly and leisurely. ***adj.*** slow. ***n.*** [*pl.* ADAGIOS (-jōz, -ōz′)], 1. a slow movement or part in music. 2. a slow ballet dance requiring skillful balancing.

Ad·a·line (ad′ə-lin′), a feminine name: see **Adeline.**

Ad·am (ad′əm), [Heb. < *ādām*, a human being], a masculine name. *n.* in the *Bible*, the first man: Gen. 1–5.

not know (a person) from Adam, not know (a person) at all.

the old Adam, the supposed human tendency to sin.

Ad·am (ad′əm), ***adj.*** [after Robert and James *Adam*, 18th-c. British architects, its originators], relating to a style of English furniture and architecture with straight lines and ornamentation of garlands, etc.

Ad·am-and-Eve (ad′əm-ən-ēv′), ***n.*** a kind of orchid bearing clusters of yellowish-brown flowers and one leaf at the base; puttyroot.

ad·a·mant (ad′ə-mant′, ad′ə-mənt), ***n.*** [ME.; OFr.; L. *adamas, adamantis*, the hardest metal < Gr. *adamas, adamantos* < *a-*, not + *daman*, to subdue], 1. a very hard stone or substance. 2. [Poetic], unbreakable hardness. ***adj.*** 1. too hard to be broken. 2. unyielding; firm. —***SYN.*** see **inflexible.**

ad·a·man·tine (ad′ə-man′tin, ad′ə-man′tēn, ad′ə-man′-tin), ***adj.*** [ME.; L. *adamantinus*, hard as steel; Gr. *adamantinos* < *adamas*], 1. made of adamant. 2. like adamant; very hard; unbreakable; unyielding; firm.

A·dam·ic (ə-dam′ik), ***adj.*** of or like Adam.

Ad·am·ic, Louis (ad′ə-mik), 1899–1951; American writer, born in Yugoslavia.

Ad·am·ite (ad′əm-it′), ***n.*** 1. a human being; person thought of as descended from Adam. 2. a person who goes naked in imitation of Adam, as did members of an early religious sect.

Ad·ams, Charles Francis (ad′əmz), 1807–1886; son of *John Quincy;* American diplomat and lawyer.

Adams, Henry Brooks, 1838–1918; son of *Charles Francis;* American historian and writer.

Adams, James Trus·low (trus′lō), 1878–1949; American historian.

Adams, John, 1735–1826; second president of the United States (1797–1801).

Adams, John Quin·cy (kwin′si), 1767–1848; son of *John;* sixth president of the United States (1825–1829).

Adams, Maude, (born *Maude Kiskadden*), 1872–1953; American actress.

Adams, Mount, 1. a mountain of the Cascade range, southern Washington: height, 12,470 ft. 2. a peak of the White Mountains, New Hampshire: height, 5,800 ft.

Adams, Samuel, 1722–1803; American statesman and Revolutionary leader.

Adam's apple, the projection formed in the front of the throat by the thyroid cartilage, seen chiefly in men.

ad·ams·ite (ad′əmz-it′), ***n.*** [< Major Roger *Adams* (1889–), Am. army officer who invented it], a yellow, odorless crystalline compound, $NH\cdot(C_6H_4)_2\cdot AsCl$, used in a vaporous form as a lung-irritant in chemical warfare: symbol, DM (no period).

Ad·am's-nee·dle (ad′əmz-nē′d'l), ***n.*** the yucca plant.

A·da·na (ä′dä-nä), ***n.*** a city in southern Turkey: pop., 100,000 (1945).

a·dapt (ə-dapt′), ***v.t.*** [Fr. *adapter;* L. *adaptare; ad-*, to + *aptare*, to fit; see APT], 1. to make suitable or more suitable, especially by changing. 2. to change (oneself) so that one's behavior, attitudes, etc. will conform to new or changed circumstances.

***SYN.*—adapt** implies a modifying so as to suit new conditions and suggests flexibility (to *adapt* oneself to a new environment); **adjust** describes the bringing of things into proper or harmonious relation through the use of skill or judgment (to *adjust* brakes, to *adjust* differences); **accommodate** implies a subordinating of one thing to the requirements of another and suggests concession or compromise (he *accommodated* his walk to the halting steps of his friend); **conform** means to bring or act in harmony with some standard, pattern, principle, etc. (to *conform* to specifications).

a·dapt·a·bil·i·ty (ə-dap′tə-bil′ə-ti), ***n.*** the quality of being adaptable.

a·dapt·a·ble (ə-dap′tə-b'l), ***adj.*** 1. that can be adapted or made suitable. 2. able to change without difficulty so as to conform to new or changed circumstances.

ad·ap·ta·tion (ad′əp-tā′shən, ad′ap-tā′shən), ***n.*** [Fr.; LL. *adaptatio;* see ADAPT], 1. an adapting or being adapted. 2. a thing resulting from adapting: as, this play is an *adaptation* of a novel. 3. in *biology*, a change in structure, function, or form that produces better adjustment of an animal or plant to its environment. 4. in *physiology*, the power that the eye has of adjusting to variations in light. 5. in *sociology*, a change in behavior to conform to cultural patterns.

a·dapt·er (ə-dap′tẽr), ***n.*** 1. a person or thing that adapts. 2. a contrivance for adapting apparatus to new uses. 3. a connecting device. Also spelled **adaptor.**

a·dap·tion (ə-dap′shən), ***n.*** adaptation.

a·dap·tive (ə-dap′tiv), ***adj.*** 1. showing adaptation. 2. able to adapt.

A·dar (ə-där′, ô′där), ***n.*** [Heb.], the sixth month of the Jewish year: see **Jewish calendar.**

Adar She·ni (shā′ni), [Heb., lit., second Adar], Veadar: see **Jewish calendar.**

‡**ad as·tra per as·pe·ra** (ad as′trə pẽr as′pə-rə), [L.], to the stars through difficulties.

a·day, a-day (ə-dā′), ***adv.*** [*a-*, on + *day*], daily.

A.D.C., Aide-de-camp.

‡**ad cap·tan·dum vul·gus** (ad kap-tan′dəm vul′gəs), [L.], for catching the crowd; to please the people.

add (ad), ***v.t.*** [ME. *adden* < L. *addere*, to add < *ad-*, to + *dare*, to give], 1. to join or unite (*to*) so as to increase the quantity, number, size, etc. 2. to state further. 3. to combine (numbers) into a sum; calculate the total of. ***v.i.*** 1. to cause an increase of (with *to*): as, this *adds* to my pleasure. 2. to find a sum; do addition in arithmetic.

add up to, 1. to reach a total of. 2. to mean; signify.

add·a·ble (ad′ə-b'l), ***adj.*** addible.

Ad·dams, Jane (ad′əmz), 1860–1935; American social worker; founder of Hull House.

ad·dax (ad′aks), ***n.*** [L. < native Afr. word], a large antelope of northern Africa and Arabia, with long, twisted horns.

ADDAX (4 ft. high at shoulder)

added line, in *music*, an extra line above or below the staff, for showing high or low notes that cannot be shown on the staff: also called *ledger line.*

ad·dend (ad′end, ə-dend′), ***n.*** [< *addendum*], in *mathematics*, a number or quantity to be added to another.

ad·den·dum (ə-den′dəm), ***n.*** [*pl.* ADDENDA (-də)], [L., gerundive of *addere*, to add, place], 1. a thing added or to be added. 2. an appendix or supplement to writing. 3. the part of a gear tooth that projects beyond the pitch circle. 4. the addendum circle.

addendum circle, a circle touching the points of the teeth of a gear wheel.

ad·der (ad′ẽr), ***n.*** [ME. *adder, addre* < *nadder*, by faulty separation of *a nadder*, an adder; AS. *nædre* < IE. base **nətr*, **nētr* (cf. L. *natrix*, watersnake)], 1. a small, poisonous snake of Europe; common viper. 2. a large, poisonous snake of Africa; puff adder. 3. any of several harmless snakes of North America, as the milk adder.

ad·der's-mouth (ad′ẽrz-mouth′), ***n.*** any of a number of related orchids with greenish flowers.

ad·der's-tongue (ad′ẽrz-tuŋ′), ***n.*** 1. the dogtooth violet. 2. a fern with a narrow spike somewhat resembling a snake's tongue.

add·i·ble (ad′ə-b'l), ***adj.*** that can be added.

ad·dict (ə-dikt′; *for n.*, ad′ikt), ***v.t.*** [< L. *addictus*, pp. of *addicere*, to give assent; *ad-*, to + *dicere*, to say], to give (oneself) up habitually (with *to*). ***n.*** a person addicted to some habit, as to the use of a drug.

ad·dict·ed (ə-dik′tid), ***adj.*** [pp. of *addict*], devoted or given up (*to* a practice or habit, especially a bad habit).

ad·dic·tion (ə-dik′shən), ***n.*** the condition of being addicted (*to* a habit); habitual inclination.

adding machine, a machine that prints numbers and automatically adds them as the operator presses its keys: some adding machines can also subtract, multiply, and divide.

Ad·dis A·ba·ba (ad′dis ä′bə-bə, ä′dis ä′bə-bə), the capital of Ethiopia (Abyssinia): pop., 200,000 (est. 1948).

Ad·di·son, Joseph (ad′ə-s'n), 1672–1719; English essayist, poet, and statesman.

Ad·di·so·ni·an (ad′ə-sō′ni-ən), ***adj.*** of or like Joseph Addison; specifically, of or like his literary style, characterized by clarity, restraint, urbanity, etc.

Ad·di·son's disease (ad′ə-s'nz), [after Dr. Thomas *Addison* (1793–1860) of England, its discoverer], a disease of the adrenal glands, characterized by anemia, peculiar skin discoloration, etc.

ad·dit·a·ment (ə-dit′ə-mənt), ***n.*** [L. *additamentum*], a thing added; addition.

ad·di·tion (ə-dish′ən), ***n.*** [ME. *addicion;* OFr. *addition;* L. *additio* < *addere;* see ADD], 1. an adding of numbers to get a number called the sum. 2. a joining of a thing to another thing. 3. a thing or part added; increase. 4. in *law*, an identifying title or mark of status after a person's name, as in *John Smith, M.D.*

ad·di·tion·al (ə-dish′ən-'l), ***adj.*** added; more; extra.

ad·di·tion·al·ly (ə-dish′ən-'l-i), ***adv.*** in addition.

ad·di·tive (ad′ə-tiv), ***adj.*** [L. *additivus;* see ADD], 1. showing or relating to addition. 2. to be added.

ad·dle (ad′'l), ***adj.*** [ME. *adel* in *adel-eye*, addle-egg, a transl. of L. *ovum urinae*, egg of urine, confused form of *ovum urinum* (a rendering of Gr. *ourion ōon*, windegg); AS. *adela;* akin to MLG. *adele*, G. *adel*, mire, mud, filth], 1. rotten: said of an egg. 2. muddled; confused; empty: now usually in compounds, as *addlebrained.* ***v.t.*** [ADDLED (-'ld), ADDLING], 1. to make rotten. 2. to muddle; confuse. ***v.i.*** 1. to become rotten. 2. to become muddled or confused.

ad·dle·brained (ad′'l-brānd′), ***adj.*** having an addle brain; muddled; stupid: also **addleheaded, addlepated.**

ad·dress (ə-dres′), ***v.t.*** [ME. *adressen*, to adorn; OFr. *adresser; a-*, to + *dresser* < LL. *directiare*, to direct < *dirigere*, to lay straight], 1. to direct (spoken or written words *to*). 2. to speak to or write to (sometimes used reflexively). 3. to write the destination on (a letter or parcel). 4. to use a proper form in speaking to: as, *address* the judge as *Your Honor.* 5. to apply (oneself); direct (one's energies): with *to.* 6. in *golf,* to take a stance and aim the club at (the ball). 7. in *law,* to remove (a judge) from office by executive action following a formal request by a legislative body. *n.* (ə-dres′ *or, for 2 & 3,* ad′res), 1. a written or spoken speech. 2. the place to which mail, etc. can be sent to one; place where one lives. 3. the writing on an envelope, parcel, etc. showing its destination. 4. skill and tact in handling situations. 5. conversational manner. 6. *pl.* wooing; attentions in courting. —*SYN.* see **speech.**

ad·dress·ee (ad′res-ē′), *n.* the person to whom mail, etc. is addressed.

ad·dress·er (ə-dres′ẽr), *n.* a person who addresses.

addressing machine, a machine for automatically printing addresses on letters, etc.

ad·dress·o·graph (ə-dres′ə-graf′, ə-dres′ə-gräf′), *n.* [< *address* + *-graph*], an addressing machine: a trademark (**Addressograph**).

ad·dres·sor (ə-dres′ẽr), *n.* an addresser.

ad·duce (ə-do͞os′, ə-dūs′), *v.t.* [ADDUCED (-do͞ost′, -dūst′), ADDUCING], [L. *adducere,* to lead or bring to; *ad-,* to + *ducere,* to lead], to give as a reason, proof, or example.

ad·du·cent (ə-do͞o′s'nt, ə-dū′s'nt), *adj.* [L. *adducens,* ppr. of *adducere;* see ADDUCE], in *physiology,* adducting.

ad·duc·i·ble, ad·duce·a·ble (ə-do͞o′sə-b'l, ə-dū′sə-b'l), *adj.* that can be adduced.

ad·duct (ə-dukt′), *v.t.* [< L. *adductus,* pp. of *adducere;* see ADDUCE], in *physiology,* to move or pull (a part of the body) toward the median axis or toward another part: opposed to *abduct.*

ad·duc·tion (ə-duk′shən), *n.* [Fr.; ML. *adductio* < L. *adductus,* pp. of *adducere;* see ADDUCE], 1. an adducing or citing. 2. in *physiology, a)* an adducting. *b)* the position (of a part) resulting from adducting.

ad·duc·tive (ə-duk′tiv), *adj.* 1. adducting. 2. of adduction.

ad·duc·tor (ə-duk′tẽr), *n.* a muscle that adducts.

Ade, George (ād), 1866–1944; American humorist.

-ade (ād; *occasionally,* äd, ad), [Fr. *-ade;* Pr., Port., or Sp. *-ada;* It. *-ata;* L. *-ata,* fem. ending of pp. of verbs of the first conjugation], a suffix meaning: 1. *the act of,* as in *blockade.* 2. *the result* or *product of,* as in *pomade.* 3. *participant in an action,* as in *brigade.* 4. [after *lemonade,* etc.], *drink made from,* as in *limeade.*

Ad·e·la (ad′'l-ə), a feminine name: diminutive, *Della;* variant, *Adelia;* Fr. *Adèle:* see **Adelaide.**

Ad·e·laide (ad′'l-ād′), [Fr. *Adélaïde;* G. *Adelheid;* OHG. *Adalheit,* lit., nobility; *adal,* nobility, noble family + *-heit,* noun suffix akin to Eng. *-hood*], a feminine name: diminutive, *Addie;* variants, *Adeline, Adela. n.* the capital of South Australia: pop., 594,000.

Ad·el·bert (ə-del′bẽrt, ad′'l-bẽrt), a masculine name: see **Albert.**

A·dele (ə-del′), a feminine name: see **Adela.**

A·de·li·a (ə-dē′li-ə, ə-dēl′yə), a feminine name: see **Adela.**

Ad·e·li·na (ad′'l-ī′nə, ad′'l-ē′nə), a feminine name: see **Adeline.**

Ad·e·line (ad′'l-īn′, ad′'l-ēn′), a feminine name: variants, *Adelina, Aline:* also spelled **Adaline:** see **Adelaide.**

a·demp·tion (ə-demp′shən), *n.* [Early Mod. Eng. < L. *ademptionem,* a taking away < *adimere,* to take away, snatch; cf. REDEEM], in *law,* a revoking of some grant or bequest; specifically, the invalidating of a legacy, as by the disposal of the specific bequest before the testator's death.

A·den (ä′d'n, ā′d'n), *n.* 1. a region of southwestern Arabia, under British control: area, 112,000 sq. mi.; pop., c. 1,000,000: see **Saudi Arabia,** map. 2. a British colony in this region: area, 75 sq. mi.; pop., 155,000. 3. the capital of this colony: seaport: pop., 80,000. 4. a gulf of the Arabian Sea, between the southern coast of Arabia and eastern Africa.

A·de·nauer, Kon·rad (kôn′rät ä′də-nour′; Eng. ad′ə-nour′), 1876– ; German statesman; chancellor of the Federal Republic of Germany (1949–1963).

a·den- (ad′'n), adeno-.

ad·e·nec·to·my (ad′n-ek′tə-mi), *n.* [*aden-* + *-ectomy*], the surgical removal of a gland.

ad·e·nine (ad′ə-nēn′, ad′ə-nin, ad′ə-nīn′), *n.* [*aden-* + *-ine*], a white, crystalline purine base, $C_5H_5N_5$, derived from nucleic acid formed in the pancreas, spleen, etc.

ad·e·ni·tis (ad′'n-ī′tis), *n.* [*aden-* + *-itis*], glandular inflammation.

ad·e·no- (ad′'n-ō, ad′'n-ə), [< Gr. *adēn,* gland], a combining form meaning *of a gland* or *glands,* as in *adenology:* also, before a vowel, **aden-.**

ad·e·noid (ad′'n-oid′), *adj.* [*aden-* + *-oid*], 1. glandlike; glandular. 2. of or like lymphoid tissue.

ad·e·noi·dal (ad′'n-oi′d'l), *adj.* 1. adenoid. 2. having adenoids; hence, 3. having the characteristic mouth-breathing, nasal tone, etc. due to adenoids.

ad·e·noids (ad′'n-oidz′), *n.pl.* growths of adenoid tissue in the upper part of the throat, behind the nose: they can swell up and obstruct breathing and speaking.

ADENOIDS

ad·e·nol·o·gy (ad′'n-ol′ə-ji), *n.* [*adeno-* + *-logy*], the study of glands.

ad·e·no·ma (ad′'n-ō′mə), *n.* [*aden-* + *-oma*], a benign tumor of glandular origin, or with a glandlike cell arrangement.

ad·ept (ə-dept′), *adj.* [L. *adeptus,* pp. of *adipisci,* to arrive at < *ad-,* to + *apisci,* to pursue: orig. used of alchemists claiming to have arrived at the philosopher's stone], highly skilled; expert. *n.* (ad′ept, ə-dept′), an expert.

ad·e·qua·cy (ad′ə-kwə-si), *n.* the quality or state of being adequate.

ad·e·quate (ad′ə-kwit), *adj.* [L. *adaequatus,* pp. of *adaequare; ad-,* to + *aequare,* to make equal < *aequus,* level, equal], 1. equal to a requirement or occasion; sufficient; suitable. 2. barely satisfactory; acceptable but not remarkable. —*SYN.* see **sufficient.**

‡**Ad·es·te Fi·de·les** (äd-es′tə fi-dā′lās, ad-es′tə fi-dē′lis), [L.], a Latin hymn (O Come All Ye Faithful).

‡**à deux** (à′ dö′), [Fr.], 1. for two; of two; hence, 2. intimate. 3. intimately.

‡**ad ex·tre·mum** (ad eks-trē′məm), [L., at the extreme], at last; finally.

ad fin., *ad finem,* [L.], to the end; at the end.

ad·here (əd-hêr′, ad-hêr′), *v.i.* [ADHERED (-hêrd′), ADHERING], [L. *adhaerere; ad-,* to + *haerere,* to stick], 1. to stick fast; become attached. 2. to give allegiance or support (with *to*). —*SYN.* see **stick.**

ad·her·ence (əd-hêr′əns, ad-hêr′əns), *n.* [Fr.; L. *adhaerentia* < ppr. of *adhaerere;* see ADHERE], an adhering; attachment (*to* a person, cause, party, idea, etc.); devotion and support.

ad·her·ent (əd-hêr′ənt, ad-hêr′ənt), *adj.* [Fr. < L. *adhaerens,* ppr. of *adhaerere;* see ADHERE], sticking fast; attached. *n.* a supporter or follower (*of* a cause, party, etc.). —*SYN.* see **follower.**

ad·he·sion (əd-hē′zhən, ad-hē′zhən), *n.* [Fr.; L. *adhaesio* < pp. of *adhaerere;* see ADHERE], 1. a sticking (*to* something) or being stuck together. 2. adherence; devoted attachment. 3. a thing that adheres. 4. in *medicine, a)* the growing together of normally separate tissues. *b) pl.* the bands of fibrous tissue by which such tissues are connected. 5. in *physics,* the force that holds together the unlike molecules of substances whose surfaces are in contact: distinguished from *cohesion.*

ad·he·sive (əd-hē′siv, ad-hē′siv), *adj.* [Fr. *adhésif* < L. *adhaesus,* pp. of *adhaerere;* see ADHERE], 1. sticking; clinging. 2. gummed; sticky. *n.* an adhesive substance.

adhesive tape, tape with a sticky substance on one side, variously used, as for holding bandages in place.

ad·hib·it (ad-hib′it), *v.t.* [< L. *adhibitus,* pp. of *adhibere,* to summon < *ad-,* to + *habere,* to have], 1. to let in; admit. 2. to affix. 3. to administer, as a remedy.

‡**ad hoc** (ad′ hok′), [L., to this], for this specific purpose; for this case only.

‡**ad ho·mi·nem** (ad hom′ə-nem′), [L., lit., to the man], 1. appealing to one's prejudices, selfish interests, etc. rather than to reason. 2. attacking one's opponent rather than dealing with the subject under discussion.

ad·i·a·bat·ic (ad′i-ə-bat′ik), *adj.* [Gr. *adiabatikos,* not able to go through < *a-,* not + *dia,* through + *bainein,* to go], of or denoting change in volume or pressure without loss or gain of heat.

ad·i·an·tum (ad′i-an′təm), *n.* [L.; Gr. *adianton,* maidenhair < *a-,* not + *diainein,* to make wet], any of a number of related ferns with dark, wiry branches and wedge-shaped leaflets; maidenhair fern.

ad·i·aph·o·rous (ad′i-af′ə-rəs), *adj.* [Gr. *adiaphoros; a-,* not + *diaphoros,* different < *diapherein,* to differ; *dia-,* through + *pherein,* to bear], 1. morally neutral or indifferent; neither wrong nor right. 2. in *medicine,* neither harmful nor helpful.

ad·i·a·ther·man·cy (ad′i-ə-thũr′mən-si), *n.* [< Gr. *a-,* not + *dia,* through + *thermē,* heat], the quality of being impervious to heat waves.

a·dieu (ə-dū′, ə-do͞o′; Fr. à′dyö′), *interj. & n.* [*pl.* ADIEUS (-dūz′, -do͞oz′); Fr. ADIEUX (-dyö′)], [Fr. < OFr. < L. *ad,* to + *Deum,* accus. of *Deus,* God], good-by; farewell.

A·di·ge (ä′dē-je), *n.* a river in northern Italy, flowing into the Gulf of Venice: length, c. 220 mi.

ad in·fi·ni·tum (ad in′fə-nī′təm), [L., to infinity], endlessly; forever; without limit: abbreviated **ad inf.**

‡**ad i·ni·ti·um** (ad i-nish′i-əm), [L.], at the beginning: abbreviated **ad init.**

ad in·te·rim (ad in′tə-rim), [L.], 1. in the meantime. 2. temporary. Abbreviated **ad int.** —*SYN.* see **temporary.**

‡**a·dios** (ä-dyôs′), *interj.* [Sp. < L. *ad* + *Deum;* see ADIEU], good-by; farewell.

ad·i·po·cere (ad′ə-pə-sêr′), *n.* [Fr. *adipocire* < L. *adeps, adipis,* fat + *cera,* wax], a fatty or waxy substance produced in decomposing dead bodies exposed to moisture.

ad·i·pose (ad′ə-pōs′), *adj.* [LL. *adiposus* < L. *adeps, adipis,* fat], of animal fat; fatty. *n.* fat in the connective tissue throughout an animal's body.

ad·i·pos·i·ty (ad′ə-pos′ə-ti), *n.* 1. an adipose state; fat; obesity. 2. a tendency to become obese.

Ad·i·ron·dacks (ad′ə-ron′daks), *n.pl.* a mountain range of the Appalachians, in northeastern New York: highest peak, Mt. Marcy: also **Adirondack Mountains.**

ad·it (ad′it), *n.* [L. *aditus,* pp. of *adire,* to approach; *ad-,* to + *ire,* to go], 1. an approach. 2. entrance. 3. an almost horizontal passageway into a mine.

Adj., Adjutant.

adj., 1. adjective. 2. adjourned. 3. adjudged.

ad·ja·cence (ə-jā′s'ns), *n.* adjacency.

ad·ja·cen·cy (ə-jā′s'n-si), *n.* [LL. *adjacentia;* see ADJACENT], 1. the quality or state of being adjacent; nearness. 2. [*pl.* ADJACENCIES (-siz)], an adjacent thing.

ad·ja·cent (ə-jā′s'nt), *adj.* [L. *adjacens,* ppr. of *adjacere,* to lie near; *ad-,* to + *jacere,* to lie, lit., cast oneself down], near or close (*to* something); adjoining.

SYN.—**adjacent** things may or may not be in actual contact with each other but they are not separated by things of the same kind (*adjacent* angles, *adjacent* farmhouses); that which is **adjoining** something else touches it at some point or along a line (*adjoining* rooms); things are **contiguous** when they touch along the whole or most of one side (*contiguous* farms); **tangent** implies contact at a single, nonintersecting point with a curved line or surface (a line *tangent* to a circle); **neighboring** things lie near to each other (*neighboring* villages).

adjacent angles, two angles having the same vertex and a line in common.

ad·jec·ti·val (aj′ik-tī′-v'l, aj′ik-ti-v'l), *adj.* 1. of an adjective. 2. having the nature or function of an adjective. 3. added to an adjective base: as, an *adjectival* suffix.

ad·jec·ti·val·ly (aj′ik-tī′v'l-i, aj′ik-ti-v'l-i), *adv.* as an adjective.

A C B D

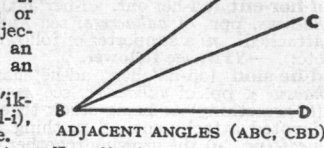

ADJACENT ANGLES (ABC, CBD)

ad·jec·tive (aj′ik-tiv), *n.* [L. *adjectivus,* that is added < *adjectus,* pp. of *adjicere,* to add to < *ad-,* to + *jacere,* to throw], 1. any of a class of words used to limit or qualify a noun or other substantive: as, *good, every,* and *Aegean* are *adjectives.* 2. any phrase or clause similarly used. *adj.* 1. of an adjective. 2. having the nature or function of an adjective. 3. dependent or subordinate. Abbreviated **adj., a.**

ad·join (ə-join′), *v.t.* [ME. *ajoinen;* Fr. *ajoindre;* L. *adjungere; ad-,* to + *jungere,* to join], 1. to be next to; be close to; be contiguous to. 2. to unite or annex (*to* a person or thing). *v.i.* to lie close together; be in contact or proximity.

ad·join·ing (ə-join′iŋ), *adj.* [ppr. of *adjoin*], neighboring; adjacent; contiguous. —*SYN.* see **adjacent.**

ad·journ (ə-jũrn′), *v.t.* [ME. *ajournen;* OFr. *ajurner;* LL. *adjurnare,* to set a day < L. *ad,* to + *diurnus,* of a day < *dies,* day], to put off until a future day; suspend (proceedings) for the day. *v.i.* 1. to suspend business (of a legislature, etc.) for a time. 2. [Colloq.], to go away from a place (*to* another place): as, let's *adjourn* to the veranda.

SYN.—**adjourn** is applied to the action of a deliberative body, etc. in bringing a session to a close, with the intention of resuming at a later date; **prorogue** applies to the formal dismissal of a parliament by the crown, subject to reassembly; to **dissolve** is to end the existence of an assembly as constituted, so that an election must be held to reconstitute it; **postpone** implies the intentional delaying of an action until a later time; **suspend** denotes the breaking off of proceedings, privileges, etc. for a time, sometimes for such an indefinite time as to suggest cancellation (to *suspend* a sentence).

ad·journ·ment (ə-jũrn′mənt), *n.* 1. an adjourning or being adjourned. 2. the time during which a legislature, etc. is adjourned.

Adjt., Adjutant.

ad·judge (ə-juj′), *v.t.* [ADJUDGED (-jujd′), ADJUDGING], [ME. *ajugen;* OFr. *ajugier;* L. *adjudicare; ad-,* to + *judicare,* to judge, decide], 1. to judge or decide by law. 2. to declare or order by law. 3. to condemn; sentence judicially (with *to*): as, the criminal was *adjudged* to jail. 4. to give or award by law, as costs, etc. 5. [Rare], to regard; deem.

ad·ju·di·cate (ə-jōō′di-kāt′), *v.t.* [ADJUDICATED (-id), ADJUDICATING], [< L. *adjudicatus,* pp. of *adjudicare;* see ADJUDGE], in *law,* to hear and decide (a case); adjudge. *v.i.* to act as judge; give judgment (*in* or *on* a matter, dispute, etc.).

ad·ju·di·ca·tion (ə-jōō′di-kā′shən), *n.* [L. *adjudicatio*], 1. an adjudicating. 2. in *law, a*) a judge's decision; court's finding. *b*) a decree in bankruptcy.

ad·ju·di·ca·tive (ə-jōō′di-kā′tiv, ə-jōō′di-kə-tiv), *adj.* adjudicating.

ad·ju·di·ca·tor (ə-jōō′di-kā′tẽr), *n.* [LL.], a person who adjudicates; judge.

ad·junct (aj′uŋkt), *n.* [L. *adjunctus,* pp. of *adjungere;* see ADJOIN], 1. a thing added to something else, but secondary or not essential. 2. a person connected in a relatively subordinate capacity with another person; associate. 3. in *grammar,* a modifying word or phrase. 4. in *logic,* a nonessential attribute.

ad·junc·tive (ə-juŋk′tiv), *adj.* [L. *adjunctivus*], having the character of an adjunct.

ad·ju·ra·tion (aj′oo-rā′shən), *n.* [L. *adjuratio,* a swearing to < pp. of *adjurare;* see ADJURE], 1. a solemn charge or command. 2. an earnest entreaty.

ad·jur·a·to·ry (ə-joor′ə-tôr′i, ə-joor′ə-tō′ri), *adj.* [L. *adjuratorius;* see ADJURE], adjuring.

ad·jure (ə-joor′), *v.t.* [ADJURED (-joord′), ADJURING], [ME. *adjuren;* L. *adjurare; ad-,* to + *jurare,* to swear], 1. to command or charge solemnly on oath or under penalty. 2. to entreat solemnly; appeal to earnestly.

ad·jur·er, ad·ju·ror (ə-joor′ẽr), *n.* a person who adjures.

ad·just (ə-just′), *v.t.* [OFr. *ajouster* < L. *ad,* to + *juxta,* near; influenced by OFr. *juste* < L. *justus,* just], 1. to alter so as to make fit or correspondent. 2. to regulate; make accurate, as a watch. 3. to settle or arrange rightly. 4. to decide how much is to be paid in settling (an insurance claim). 5. in *military usage,* to correct (the gun sight, one's aim, etc.) in firing. *v.i.* to come into conformity; become suited or fit. —*SYN.* see **adapt.**

ad·just·a·ble (ə-jus′tə-b'l), *adj.* that can be adjusted.

ad·just·a·bly (ə-jus′tə-bli), *adv.* so as to be adjustable.

ad·just·er, ad·jus·tor (ə-jus′tẽr), *n.* 1. a person who adjusts something, as insurance claims. 2. a thing or device that adjusts something, as in a machine.

ad·just·ment (ə-just′mənt), *n.* [Fr. *ajustement;* see ADJUST], 1. an adjusting or being adjusted. 2. a means or device by which parts are adjusted to one another: as, the *adjustment* on a micrometer. 3. the settlement of how much is to be paid in cases of loss or claim. 4. a lowering of price, as of damaged or soiled goods.

ad·ju·tan·cy (aj′ə-tən-si), *n.* [*pl.* ADJUTANCIES (-siz)], the rank or office of a military adjutant.

ad·ju·tant (aj′ə-tənt), *n.* [L. *adjutans,* ppr. of *adjutare,* to aid < *adjuvare,* to help, assist], 1. an assistant. 2. an army staff officer who helps the commanding officer by handling correspondence, distributing orders, etc.: abbreviated **adj., adjt.** 3. a large stork of India and Africa: also **adjutant crane, adjutant stork.**

ADJUTANT STORK (60 in. high)

adjutant general, [*pl.* ADJUTANTS GENERAL, ADJUTANT GENERALS], 1. an officer in the army who is the main assistant of the commanding general of a corps or higher echelon. 2. an officer in charge of the militia of a State or Territory of the United States. 3. [A-G-], in the *United States Army,* the general in charge of the department that handles all records, circulars, correspondence, etc.: abbreviated **A.G., Adj. Gen., Adjt. Gen.**

ad·ju·vant (aj′ə-vənt), *adj.* [Fr.; L. *adjuvans,* ppr. of *adjuvare,* to assist], helping; aiding; auxiliary. *n.* 1. a person or thing that helps. 2. a substance added to a drug to aid its action.

‡**ad Ka·len·das Grae·cas** (ad kə-len′dəs grē′kəs), [L.], 1. at the Greek Calends; hence, 2. never: the Greeks did not reckon dates in the Roman way, by calends.

Ad·ler, Alfred (äd′lẽr), 1870–1937; Austrian psychologist and psychiatrist.

Ad·ler, Felix (ad′lẽr), 1851–1933; American educational reformer; founder of the Ethical Culture Society.

ad-lib (ad′lib′), *v.t. & v.i.* [AD-LIBBED (-libd′), AD-LIBBING], [< *ad libitum*], [Colloq.], to improvise (words, gestures, etc. not in the script); extemporize.

ad lib·i·tum (ad lib′i-təm), [L.], 1. at pleasure; as one pleases; as much as one pleases. 2. in *music,* freely: a direction to the performer that he may change tempo, interpretation, etc., or omit passages, to suit himself. Abbreviated **ad lib., ad libit.**

‡**ad lit·ter·am** (ad lit′ẽr-əm), [L., lit., to the letter], literally; exactly.

ad loc., *ad locum,* [L.], at or to the place.

Adm., 1. Admiral. 2. Admiralty.

adm., administrator.

ad·meas·ure (ad-mezh′ẽr), *v.t.* [ADMEASURED (-ẽrd), ADMEASURING], [ME. *amesuren;* OFr. *admesurer;* LL. *admensurare;* see AD- & MEASURE], to apportion.

ad·meas·ure·ment (ad-mezh′ẽr-mənt), *n.* [OFr. *amesurement;* see ADMEASURE], 1. a measuring. 2. size or dimensions. 3. an apportioning.

Ad·me·tus (ad-mē′təs), *n.* [L.; Gr. *Admētos*, lit., wild, unbroken], in *Greek legend*, a king of Thessaly whose wife, Alcestis, sacrificed her life for him but was brought back from Hades by Hercules.

ad·min·i·cle (ad-min′i-k'l), *n.* [L. *adminiculum*, support, orig. a support for the hand; dim. < *ad-*, to + *manus*, hand], 1. a thing that helps. 2. in *law*, corroborative evidence; proof that explains.

ad·mi·nic·u·lar (ad′mi-nik′yoo-lẽr), *adj.* [< L. *adminiculum;* see ADMINICLE], 1. helping. 2. corroborative.

ad·min·is·ter (əd-min′ə-stẽr, ad-min′ə-stẽr), *v.t.* [ME. *aministren;* OFr. *aministrer;* L. *administrare; ad-*, to + *ministrare*, to serve], 1. to manage; conduct; direct. 2. to give out or dispense, as punishment or justice. 3. to give or apply (medicine, etc.). 4. to give or tender (an oath, pledge, etc.). 5. in *law*, to act as executor of (an estate). *v.i.* 1. to act as manager or administrator. 2. to furnish help or be of service (with *to*): as, *administer* to an invalid's needs. —*SYN.* see **govern.**

ad·min·is·tra·ble (əd-min′ə-strə-b'l, ad-min′ə-strə-b'l), *adj.* that can be administered.

ad·min·is·trant (əd-min′ə-strənt, ad-min′ə-strənt), *adj.* [L. *administrans*, ppr. of *administrare;* see ADMINISTER], executive. *n.* a person who administers.

ad·min·is·trate (əd-min′ə-strāt′, ad-min′ə-strāt′), *v.t.* [ADMINISTRATED (-id), ADMINISTRATING], to administer.

ad·min·is·tra·tion (əd-min′ə-strā′shən, ad-min′ə-strā′shən), *n.* [ME. *administracioun;* OFr. *administration;* L. *administratio* < pp. of *administrare;* see ADMINISTER], 1. management. 2. the management of governmental or institutional affairs. 3. [often A-], the executive officials of a government or institution and their policy. 4. their term of office. 5. the administering (*of* punishment, medicine, a sacrament, an oath, etc.). 6. in *law*, the management and settling (*of* an estate).

ad·min·is·tra·tive (əd-min′ə-strā′tiv, ad-min′ə-strā′tiv), *adj.* [L. *administrativus;* see ADMINISTER], of administration; connected with management; executive.

ad·min·is·tra·tor (əd-min′ə-strā′tẽr, ad-min′ə-strā′tẽr), *n.* [L.; see ADMINISTER], 1. a person who administers; person who has executive work or ability. 2. a person appointed by a law court to settle an estate; executor. Abbreviated **adm.**

ad·min·is·tra·tress (ad-min′ə-strā′tris), *n.* a woman administrator.

ad·min·is·tra·trix (ad-min′ə-strā′triks), *n.* [*pl.* ADMINISTRATRIXES (-iz), ADMINISTRATRICES (-strā′tri-sēz′, -strə-tri′sēz)], [ML.], a woman administrator.

ad·mi·ra·ble (ad′mə-rə-b'l), *adj.* [Fr.; L. *admirabilis* < *admirari*], 1. deserving admiration. 2. excellent.

ad·mir·a·bly (ad′mə-rə-bli), *adv.* in an admirable manner.

ad·mi·ral (ad′mə-rəl), *n.* [ME. *admirail, amirail;* OFr. *admiral, amiral* < Ar. *amir al*, ruler of; sp. influenced by *admirable*], 1. the commanding officer of a navy or fleet. 2. a naval officer of the highest rank: abbreviated **Adm.** 3. in the *United States Navy*, a full admiral: see **full admiral, rear admiral, vice-admiral, Admiral of the Fleet.** 4. a vessel carrying the admiral; flagship. 5. [orig. *admirable*], any of various colorful butterflies with very small forelegs.

Admiral of the Fleet, the highest rank in the United States Navy, having the insigne of five stars.

ad·mi·ral·ship (ad′mə-rəl-ship′), *n.* [see -SHIP], the rank or position of an admiral.

ad·mi·ral·ty (ad′mə-rəl-ti), *n.* [*pl.* ADMIRALTIES (-tiz)], [ME.; OFr. *admiralté* < *amiral;* see ADMIRAL], 1. the rank, position, or authority of an admiral. 2. [often A-], the governmental department or officials in charge of naval affairs, as in England. 3. maritime law or court. 4. [A-], the building in London in which British naval affairs are administered. Abbreviated **Adm.**

Admiralty Islands, a group of small islands in the Bismarck Archipelago: pop., 13,700: also **Admiralties.**

Admiralty Range, a mountain range in Antarctica, northwest of the Ross Sea.

ad·mi·ra·tion (ad′mə-rā′shən), *n.* [Fr.; L. *admiratio* < *admirari;* see ADMIRE], 1. an admiring; wonder, delight, and pleased approval at anything fine, skillful, beautiful, etc. 2. high esteem. 3. a thing or person inspiring such feelings. 4. [Archaic], a wondering.

ad·mire (əd-mīr′), *v.t.* [ADMIRED (-mīrd′), ADMIRING], [OFr. *amirer;* L. *admirari; ad-*, at + *mirari*, to wonder], 1. to regard with wonder, delight, and pleased approval. 2. to have high regard for. 3. [Archaic], to marvel at. 4. [Dial. or Colloq.], to like or wish (*to* do something). —*SYN.* see **regard.**

ad·mir·er (əd-mīr′ẽr), *n.* 1. a person who admires. 2. a man who admires, or is in love with, a woman; suitor.

ad·mis·si·bil·i·ty (əd-mis′ə-bil′ə-ti, ad-mis′ə-bil′ə-ti), *n.* the quality or condition of being admissible.

ad·mis·si·ble (əd-mis′ə-b'l, ad-mis′ə-b'l), *adj.* [Fr.; ML. *admissibilis* < L. *admissus*, pp. of *admittere;* see ADMIT], 1. that can be accepted or allowed: as, *admissible* evidence. 2. having the right to be admitted.

ad·mis·si·bly (əd-mis′ə-bli, ad-mis′ə-bli), *adv.* in an admissible manner.

ad·mis·sion (əd-mish′ən, ad-mish′ən), *n.* [L. *admissio* < *admissus*, pp. of *admittere;* see ADMIT], 1. an admitting; allowing to enter. 2. the fact of being allowed to enter. 3. right of entry; access. 4. an entrance fee. 5. a conceding; granting. 6. an acknowledging; confessing. 7. a thing conceded, acknowledged, or confessed.

Admission Day, any of several legal holidays celebrated individually by certain States commemorating their admission into the Union.

ad·mis·sive (əd-mis′iv, ad-mis′iv), *adj.* [L. *admissivus;* see ADMIT], admitting or tending to admit.

ad·mit (əd-mit′, ad-mit′), *v.t.* [ADMITTED (-id), ADMITTING], [ME. *admitten;* L. *admittere; ad-*, to + *mittere*, to send], 1. to permit to enter or use; let in. 2. to entitle to enter: as, the ticket *admits* one. 3. to allow; leave room for. 4. to have room for; hold: as, the hall *admits* 2,500 people. 5. to concede; grant. 6. to acknowledge; confess. 7. to permit to practice certain functions: as, he was *admitted* to the bar. *v.i.* 1. to give entrance (*to* a place). 2. to allow or warrant (with *of*). —*SYN.* see **acknowledge, receive.**

ad·mit·tance (əd-mit′'ns, ad-mit′'ns), *n.* 1. an admitting or being admitted. 2. permission to enter; right of entry. 3. in *electricity*, the current divided by the voltage; reciprocal of impedance.

ad·mit·ted·ly (əd-mit′id-li, ad-mit′id-li), *adv.* by admission or general agreement; confessedly.

ad·mix (ad-miks′, əd-miks′), *v.t. & v.i.* [back-formation, after *mix* < *admixt*, mixed with; L. *admixtus;* see ADMIXTURE], to mix (a thing) in; mix with something.

ad·mix·ture (ad-miks′chẽr, əd-miks′chẽr), *n.* [< L. *admixtus*, pp. of *admiscere; ad-*, to + *miscere*, to mix], 1. a mixture. 2. a thing or ingredient added in mixing.

ad·mon·ish (əd-mon′ish, ad-mon′ish), *v.t.* [ME. *amonesten;* OFr. *amonester* < L. *admonere; ad-*, to + *monere*, to warn], 1. to warn; caution against specific faults. 2. to reprove mildly. 3. to advise; exhort. 4. to inform or remind, by way of a warning. —*SYN.* see **advise.**

ad·mon·ish·ment (əd-mon′ish-mənt, ad-mon′ish-mənt), *n.* an admonishing or being admonished.

ad·mo·ni·tion (ad′mə-nish′ən), *n.* [ME. *amonicioun;* OFr. *amonition, admonition;* L. *admonitio* < *admonere*], 1. an admonishing. 2. a mild rebuke; reprimand.

ad·mon·i·tor (əd-mon′ə-tẽr, ad-mon′ə-tẽr), *n.* [L. < *admonere;* cf. ADMONISH], a person who admonishes.

ad·mon·i·to·ry (əd-mon′ə-tôr′i, ad-mon′ə-tō′ri), *adj.* [LL. *admonitorius*], admonishing; warning; rebuking.

ad·nate (ad′nāt), *adj.* [L. *adnatus*, pp. of *adnasci*, to be born, grow to], in *botany* & *zoology*, congenitally joined together: said of unlike parts.

ad·na·tion (ad-nā′shən), *n.* the condition of being adnate.

‡**ad nau·se·am** (ad nô′shi-am′, ad nô′zi-əm), [L., to nausea], to the point of disgust; to a sickening extreme.

ad·nom·i·nal (ad-nom′ə-n'l), *adj.* [*ad-* + *nominal;* cf. ADNOUN], of, or having the nature of, an adnoun.

ad·noun (ad′noun′), *n.* [*ad-* + *noun*, after *adverb*], in *grammar*, an adjective, especially one used as a noun: as, "the lame, the halt, and the blind" are *adnouns.*

a·do (ə-dōō′), *n.* [ME. *ado* < northern dial. inf. *at do*, to do], fuss; trouble; stir; pother.

a·do·be (ə-dō′bi), *n.* [Sp.], 1. unburnt, sun-dried brick. 2. the clay of which this brick is made. 3. a building made of adobe.

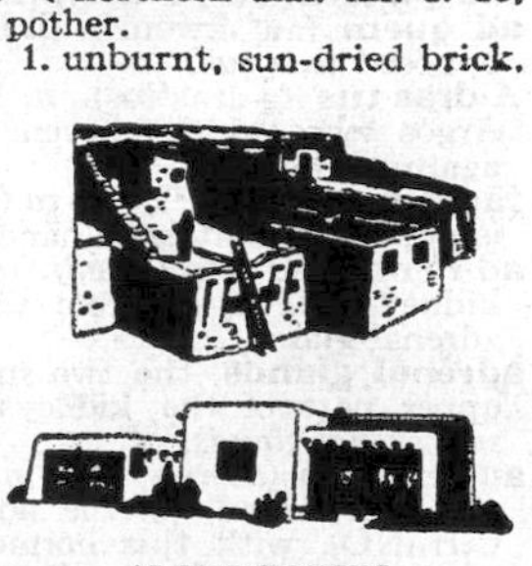

ADOBE HOUSES

ad·o·les·cence (ad′'l-es′'ns), *n.* [Fr.; L. *adolescentia* < *adolescens;* see ADOLESCENT], 1. the quality of being youthful; adolescency. 2. the time of life between puberty and maturity; youth.

ad·o·les·cen·cy (ad′'l-es′'n-si), *n.* [L. *adolescentia;* see ADOLESCENCE], the quality of being adolescent; youthful condition.

ad·o·les·cent (ad′'l-es′'nt), *adj.* [Fr.; L. *adolescens*, ppr. of *adolescere*, to come to maturity, be kindled, burn < **adalescere; ad-*, to + *alescere*, to increase, grow up < *alere*, to feed, sustain; akin to AS. *alan*, to nourish, ON. *ala*, to produce, Goth. *alan*, to grow], 1. growing up; developing from childhood to maturity. 2. of or characteristic of adolescence; youthful. *n.* a boy or a girl from puberty to adulthood; person in his teens. —*SYN.* see **young.**

Ad·olph (ad′olf, ā′dôlf, ə-dolf′), [L. *Adolphus;* OHG. *Adolf, Adulf*, lit., noble wolf < *adal*, nobility + *wolf*, wolf], a masculine name: equivalents, L. *Adolphus*, Fr. *Adolphe*, G. *Adolf.*

Ad·o·na·i (a′də-nā′ī; Heb. ä′dō-noi′), *n.* [Heb., my Lord; ? < Phoen. *adōn*, lord], God; Lord: used in

fat, āpe, bâre, cär; ten, ēven, hêre, ovẽr; is, bīte; lot, gō, hôrn, tōōl, look; oil, out; up, ūse, fũr; get; joy; yet; chin; she; thin, *th*en; zh, leisure; ŋ, ring; ə for *a* in *ago*, *e* in *agent*, *i* in *sanity*, *o* in *comply*, *u* in *focus;* ' as in *able* (ā′b'l), Fr. bål; ë, Fr. coeur; ö, Fr. feu; Fr. mon; ô, Fr. coq; ü, Fr. duc; H, G. ich; kh, G. doch. See pp. x–xii. ‡ foreign; * hypothetical; < derived from.

Hebrew reading as a substitute for the "ineffable name" JHVH (see **Jehovah**).
A·don·ic (ə-don'ik), *adj.* [Fr. *adonique;* ML. *adonicus;* see ADONIS], of, like, or characteristic of Adonis. *n.* a line of verse consisting of a dactyl followed by a spondee or trochee: supposedly first used in laments for Adonis.
A·do·nis (ə-dō'nis, ə-don'is), *n.* [L. < Gr. *Adōn, Adōnis;* prob. < Phoen. *adōn,* lord], 1. in *Greek mythology,* a young man loved by Aphrodite because he was so handsome: he was killed by a wild boar. 2. any very handsome young man.
a·dopt (ə-dopt'), *v.t.* [Fr. *adopter;* L. *adoptare; ad-,* to + *optare,* to choose], 1. to choose and bring into a certain relationship, especially that of a member of one's own family. 2. to take into one's own family by legal process and treat as one's own child. 3. to take and use as one's own: said of an idea, a word, etc. 4. to choose and follow (a course). 5. to vote to accept (a committee report, motion, etc.).
a·dopt·a·ble (ə-dop'tə-b'l), *adj.* that can be adopted; fit for adoption.
a·dop·tion (ə-dop'shən), *n.* [ME. *adopcioun;* L. *adoptio* < *adoptare;* see ADOPT], an adopting or being adopted.
a·dop·tive (ə-dop'tiv), *adj.* [L. *adoptivus* < *adoptare;* see ADOPT], 1. adopted. 2. adopting.
a·dor·a·bil·i·ty (ə-dôr'ə-bil'ə-ti, ə-dōr'ə-bil'ə-ti), *n.* the quality or state of being adorable.
a·dor·a·ble (ə-dôr'ə-b'l, ə-dōr'ə-b'l), *adj.* [Fr.; L. *adorabilis* < *adorare;* see ADORE], 1. worthy of adoration or love. 2. [Colloq.], delightful; charming.
a·dor·a·bly (ə-dôr'ə-bli, ə-dōr'ə-bli), *adv.* in an adorable manner.
ad·o·ra·tion (ad'ə-rā'shən), *n.* [Fr.; L. *adoratio* < pp. of *adorare;* see ADORE], 1. a worshiping or paying homage, as to a divinity. 2. great love, devotion, and respect.
a·dore (ə-dôr', ə-dōr'), *v.t.* [ADORED (-dôrd', -dōrd'), ADORING], [Fr. *adorer;* L. *adorare,* to worship; *ad-,* to + *orare,* to speak < *os, oris,* a mouth], 1. to worship as divine. 2. to love greatly; idolize; honor highly. 3. [Colloq.], to like very much. —*SYN.* see **revere.**
a·dor·er (ə-dôr'ẽr, ə-dōr'ẽr), *n.* 1. a person who adores; worshiper. 2. a devoted lover; warm admirer.
a·dorn (ə-dôrn'), *v.t.* [ME. *adornen;* OFr. *adorner* < L. *adornare; ad-,* to + *ornare,* to deck out], 1. to serve as an ornament to; add beauty, splendor, honor, or distinction to. 2. to put decorations on; ornament.
SYN.—**adorn** is used of that which adds to the beauty of something by gracing it with its own beauty (roses *adorned* her hair); **decorate** implies the addition of something to render attractive what would otherwise be plain or bare (to *decorate* a wall with pictures); **ornament** is used with reference to accessories which enhance the appearance (a crown *ornamented* with jewels); **embellish** suggests the addition of something highly ornamental or ostentatious for effect; to **beautify** is to lend beauty to, or heighten the beauty of; **bedeck** emphasizes the addition of showy things (*bedecked* with jewelry).
a·dorn·ment (ə-dôrn'mənt), *n.* 1. an adorning or being adorned. 2. a decoration or ornament.
A·do·wa (ä'dō-wä'), *n.* Aduwa.
a·down (ə-doun'), *adv. & prep.* [AS. *of dune,* from the hill, downward], [Poetic], down.
‡**ad pa·tres** (ad pā'trēz), [L.], to (one's) fathers; dead.
ad quem (ad' kwem'), [L.], to or at which or whom: opposed to *a quo.*
A·dras·tus (ə-dras'təs), *n.* in *Greek legend,* a king of Argos who led the Seven against Thebes: see **Seven against Thebes.**
‡**ad rem** (ad' rem'), [L., to (the) thing], to the point at issue; to the matter in hand.
ad·re·nal (ad-rē'n'l), *adj.* [*ad-* + *renal*], 1. near the kidney. 2. of or from the adrenal glands. *n.* an adrenal gland.
adrenal glands, the two small ductless glands on the upper part of the kidneys in mammals: also called *suprarenal glands.*
ad·ren·al·in (ad-ren''l-in), *n.* [*adrenal* + *-in*], 1. a hormone produced by the adrenal glands. 2. a drug, $C_9H_{13}NO_3$, with this hormone in it, made from the adrenal glands of animals or synthetically, and used to raise blood pressure, stop bleeding, etc.: a trade-mark (**Adrenalin**). Also called *epinephrine.*
ad·ren·al·ine (ad-ren''l-in, ad-ren''l-ēn'), *n.* adrenalin.
A·dri·an (ā'dri-ən), [L. *Adrianus, Hadrianus* < *Adria, Hadria,* name of two Italian cities], a masculine name. *n.* the Roman emperor Hadrian.
Adrian IV, (*Nicholas Breakspear*), 1100?–1159; Pope (1154–1159): he was the only English Pope.
A·dri·an·o·ple (ā'dri-ən-ō'p'l, ad'ri-ən-ō'p'l), *n.* a city in northwestern Turkey: pop., 45,000: officially called *Edirne:* former name, *Adrianopolis:* site of a battle (378 A.D.) in which the Visigoths defeated the Romans.
A·dri·an·op·o·lis (ā'dri-ən-op'ə-lis), *n.* Adrianople.
A·dri·at·ic (ā'dri-at'ik, ad'ri-at'ik), *n.* a sea between Italy and Yugoslavia: it is an arm of the Mediterranean. *adj.* in or of the Adriatic.
a·drift (ə-drift'), *adv. & adj.* [*a-,* on + *drift*], drifting; floating without mooring or direction; untied: often used figuratively.
a·droit (ə-droit'), *adj.* [Fr., *à,* to + *droit,* right < L. *directus,* pp. of *dirigere;* see DIRECT], skillful and clever. —*SYN.* see **dexterous.**
‡**à droite** (å' drwåt'), [Fr.], to the right; on the right.
ads., advertisements.
ad·sci·ti·tious (ad'si-tish'əs), *adj.* [< L. *adscitus,* pp. of *adsciscere,* to receive with knowledge, approve; *ad-,* to + *sciscere,* to seek to know < *scire,* to know], added; supplemental; adventitious.
ad·script (ad'skript), *adj.* [L. *adscriptus,* pp. of *adscribere; ad-,* to + *scribere,* to write], written after.
ad·scrip·tion (ad-skrip'shən), *n.* an ascription.
ad·sorb (ad-sôrb', ad-zôrb'), *v.t.* [< L. *ad-,* to + *sorbere,* to drink in, suck], to collect (a gas, liquid, or dissolved substance) in condensed form on a surface.
ad·sorb·ent (ad-sôrb''nt, ad-zôrb''nt), *adj.* adsorbing. *n.* a thing or substance that adsorbs.
ad·sorp·tion (ad-sôrp'shən, ad-zôrp'shən), *n.* [< *adsorb,* after *absorption*], an adsorbing or being adsorbed; adhesion of the molecules of a gas, liquid, or dissolved substance to a surface.
ad·sorp·tive (ad-sôrp'tiv, ad-zôrp'tiv), *adj.* 1. able to adsorb. 2. relating to adsorption. *n.* an adsorbent.
ad·su·ki bean (ad-sōō'ki, ad-zōō'ki), adzuki bean.
‡**ad·sum** (ad'sum), [L.], I am present.
ad·u·lar·i·a (aj'ə-lâr'i-ə), *n.* [Mod. L. < *Adula,* a group of mountains in Switzerland], a translucent kind of feldspar; moonstone.
ad·u·late (aj'ə-lāt'), *v.t.* [ADULATED (-id), ADULATING], [< L. *adulatus,* pp. of *adulari,* to fawn upon], to praise too highly or flatter servilely.
ad·u·la·tion (aj'ə-lā'shən), *n.* [L. *adulatio;* see ADULATE], servile flattery or excessive praise.
ad·u·la·tor (aj'ə-lā'tẽr), *n.* [L.], a person who adulates.
ad·u·la·to·ry (aj'ə-lə-tôr'i, aj'ə-lə-tō'ri), *adj.* [L. *adulatorius;* see ADULATE], servilely flattering.
a·dult (ə-dult', ad'ult), *adj.* [L. *adultus,* pp. of *adolescere;* see ADOLESCENT], 1. grown up; mature in age, size, strength, etc. 2. of or for grown men and women. *n.* 1. a mature person; man or woman. 2. an animal or plant that is grown up. 3. in *law,* a person who has come of age. —*SYN.* see **ripe.**
a·dul·ter·ant (ə-dul'tẽr-ənt), *n.* [L. *adulterans,* ppr. of *adulterare,* to falsify], a substance that adulterates. *adj.* adulterating; making inferior or impure.
a·dul·ter·ate (ə-dul'tẽr-āt'), *v.t.* [ADULTERATED (-id), ADULTERATING], [< L. *adulteratus,* pp. of *adulterare,* to falsify < *adulter,* an adulterer < *ad-,* to + *alter,* other, another], to make inferior, impure, not genuine, etc. by adding a poor or improper substance. *adj.* (ə-dul'tẽr-it), 1. guilty of adultery; adulterous. 2. illegitimate through adultery. 3. adulterated; not genuine.
a·dul·ter·a·tion (ə-dul'tẽr-ā'shən), *n.* [L. *adulteratio;* see ADULTERATE], 1. an adulterating or being adulterated. 2. an adulterated substance, commodity, etc.
a·dul·ter·a·tor (ə-dul'tẽr-ā'tẽr), *n.* [L., a counterfeiter; see ADULTERATE], a person who adulterates.
a·dul·ter·er (ə-dul'tẽr-ẽr), *n.* [altered, after L. *adulterare,* from ME. *avowterer, avouter;* OFr. *avoutre* < *avoutrer,* to commit adultery; L. *adulterare;* see ADULTERATE], a person (especially a man) guilty of adultery.
a·dul·ter·ess (ə-dul'tẽr-is, ə-dul'tris), *n.* [ME. *avoutres;* OFr. *avotresse,* fem. of *avoutre;* see ADULTERER], a woman guilty of adultery.
a·dul·ter·ine (ə-dul'tẽr-in, ə-dul'tẽr-īn'), *adj.* [L. *adulterinus* < *adulter;* see ADULTERATE], 1. of adultery. 2. due to adulteration.
a·dul·ter·ous (ə-dul'tẽr-əs), *adj.* 1. relating to adultery. 2. guilty of, or given to, adultery.
a·dul·ter·y (ə-dul'tẽr-i), *n.* [*pl.* ADULTERIES (-iz)], [L. *adulterium* < *adulter;* see ADULTERATE], sexual intercourse between a married man and a woman not his wife, or between a married woman and a man not her husband.
a·dult·hood (ə-dult'hood), *n.* the state of being adult.
ad·um·bral (ad-um'brəl), *adj.* [see ADUMBRATE], in shadow; shady.
ad·um·brate (ad-um'brāt, ad'əm-brāt'), *v.t.* [ADUMBRATED (-id), ADUMBRATING], [< L. *adumbratus,* pp. of *adumbrari,* to shade < *ad-,* to + *umbra,* shade], 1. to outline in a shadowy way; sketch. 2. to foreshadow. 3. to overshadow.
ad·um·bra·tion (ad'əm-brā'shən), *n.* [L. *adumbratio;* see ADUMBRATE], 1. a faint outline or sketch. 2. a foreshadowing; advance sign. 3. an overshadowing.
ad·um·bra·tive (ad-um'brə-tiv), *adj.* adumbrating; faintly indicative.
a·dunc (ə-duŋk'), *adj.* [L. *aduncus; ad-,* to + *uncus,* hooked, a hook], curving inward, as a parrot's beak.
a·dun·cous (ə-duŋ'kəs), *adj.* adunc.
a·dust (ə-dust'), *adj.* [L. *adustus,* pp. of *adurere,* to burn up; *ad-,* to + *urere,* to burn], 1. scorched; burnt. 2. parched. 3. sunburnt. 4. sallow and melancholy.
A·du·wa (ä'doo-wä'), *n.* a town in Ethiopia: pop., 5,000: also spelled **Adowa.**
Adv., 1. Advent. 2. Advocate.
adv., 1. ad valorem. 2. adverb. 3. adverbial. 4. *adversus,* [L.], against. 5. advertisement.
ad va·lo·rem (ad və-lôr'əm, ad və-lō'rəm), [L.], in proportion to the value: a phrase applied to certain duties

levied on imports according to their invoiced value: abbreviated **adv., ad val.**

ad·vance (əd-vans′, ad-väns′), *v.t.* [ADVANCED (-vanst′, -vänst′), ADVANCING], [ME. *avancen;* OFr. *avancer,* to forward < L. **abantiare* < *ab-,* from + *ante,* before: the *a-* was made *ad-* on the supposition that it came from L. *ad-,* to, toward], 1. to bring forward; move forward. 2. to suggest. 3. to further; help; promote. 4. to cause to happen earlier. 5. to raise the rate of. 6. to pay (money) before due. 7. to lend. *v.i.* 1. to go forward; move ahead. 2. to improve; make progress; develop. 3. to rise in rank, quality, importance, etc. *n.* 1. a moving forward. 2. an improvement; progress. 3. a rise in value or cost. 4. *pl.* approaches to get favor, become acquainted, etc.; overtures (*to* someone). 5. a payment made before due, as of wages. 6. a loan. *adj.* 1. in front: as, *advance* guard. 2. beforehand: as, *advance* information.

in advance, 1. in front. 2. before due; ahead of time.

SYN.*—advance** is used to describe assistance in hastening the course of anything or in moving toward an objective; to **promote** is to help in the establishment, development, or success of something (to *promote* good will); **forward** emphasizes the idea of action as an impetus (concessions were made to *forward* the pact); **further** emphasizes assistance in bringing a desired goal closer (to *further* a cause). —ANT.*** retard, check.

ad·vanced (əd-vanst′, ad-vänst′), *adj.* [pp. of *advance*], 1. in advance; moved forward; in front. 2. far on in life; old. 3. ahead of the times; very progressive or unconventional: as, *advanced* ideas. —***SYN.*** see **liberal.**

advanced standing, credits toward a degree allowed to a student by a college for courses taken elsewhere.

advance guard, a detachment of troops sent ahead to reconnoiter and protect the line of march.

ad·vance·ment (əd-vans′mənt, ad-väns′mənt), *n.* 1. an advancing or being advanced. 2. promotion; success. 3. progress; improvement; furtherance.

ad·van·tage (əd-van′tij, ad-vän′tij), *n.* [ME. *avantage, avauntage;* OFr. *avantage* < *avant,* before < L. *ab ante,* from before], 1. a more favorable position; superiority (often with *of* or *over*). 2. a favorable or beneficial circumstance, event, etc. 3. gain or benefit. 4. in *tennis,* the first point scored after deuce: often shortened to *ad* or *vantage. v.t.* [ADVANTAGED (-tijd), ADVANTAGING], to give an advantage to; be a benefit or aid to.

have the advantage of, to have an advantage over.

take advantage of, 1. to make use of for one's own benefit or for a selfish purpose. 2. to impose upon.

to advantage, to good effect.

ad·van·ta·geous (ad′vən-tā′jəs), *adj.* [Fr. *avantageux* < *avantage;* see ADVANTAGE], favorable; useful; profitable.

ad·vec·tion (ad-vek′shən), *n.* [L. *advectio,* a conveying < *advectus,* pp. of *advehere,* to convey; *ad-,* to + *vehere,* to carry], the transference of heat by horizontal currents of air. *adj.* of or due to advection.

Ad·vent (ad′vent), *n.* [< L. *adventus,* pp. of *advenire; ad-,* to + *venire,* to come], 1. the period including the four Sundays just before Christmas: abbreviated **Adv.** 2. Christ's birth. 3. Christ's second coming to earth, on Judgment Day: also called the **Second Advent.** 4. [a-], a coming or arrival.

Ad·vent·ism (ad′ven-tiz'm), *n.* [*Advent* + *-ism*], the belief that Christ's second coming to earth and the Last Judgment will soon occur.

Ad·vent·ist (ad′ven-tist), *n.* a member of a Christian sect based on Adventism. *adj.* of Adventism or Adventists.

ad·ven·ti·tious (ad′ven-tish′əs), *adj.* [L. *adventicius,* coming from abroad; see ADVENT], 1. added from outside; not inherent; accidental. 2. in *botany,* occurring in unusual or abnormal places: as, *adventitious* leaves. —***SYN.*** see **accidental.**

ad·ven·tive (ad-ven′tiv), *adj.* [L. *adventus* (see ADVENT); + *-ive*], in *botany,* not native to the environment. *n.* a plant that is not native to the environment.

Advent Sunday, the first Sunday in Advent.

ad·ven·ture (əd-ven′chẽr), *n.* [ME. *aventure;* OFr. *aventure;* L. *adventura,* lit., a happening < *advenire;* see ADVENT], 1. the encountering of danger. 2. an exciting and dangerous undertaking. 3. an unusual, stirring experience, often of romantic nature. 4. a business venture or speculation. 5. a liking for danger, excitement, etc.: as, he is full of *adventure. v.t.* [ADVENTURED (-chẽrd), ADVENTURING], to risk; venture on. *v.i.* 1. to engage in daring undertakings. 2. to take risks.

ad·ven·tur·er (əd-ven′chẽr-ẽr), *n.* 1. a person who has or likes to have adventures. 2. a soldier willing to fight for the side that pays the most; soldier of fortune. 3. a speculator. 4. a person who tries to become rich, socially accepted, etc. by dubious schemes.

ad·ven·ture·some (əd-ven′chẽr-səm), *adj.* adventurous.

ad·ven·tur·ess (əd-ven′chẽr-is), *n.* 1. [Rare], a woman adventurer. 2. an unscrupulous woman who tries to become rich and socially accepted by exploiting her charms, by scheming, etc.

ad·ven·tur·ous (əd-ven′chẽr-əs), *adj.* [ME. *aventurous;* OFr. *aventuros* < *aventure;* see ADVENTURE], 1. fond of adventure; willing to take chances; daring. 2. full of danger; risky.

ad·verb (ad′vẽrb), *n.* [L. *adverbium* < *ad-,* to + *verbum,* a word], 1. any of a class of words used to modify a verb, adjective (or other adverb) by expressing time, place, manner, degree, cause, etc. 2. any phrase or clause similarly used. Abbreviated **adv., ad.**

ad·ver·bi·al (əd-vũr′bi-əl, ad-vũr′byəl), *adj.* [L. *adverbialis;* see ADVERB], 1. of an adverb. 2. having the nature or function of an adverb. 3. added to an adverb base: as, an *adverbial* suffix. Abbreviated **adv.**

ad·ver·bi·al·iz·er (əd-vũr′bi-əl-īz′ẽr, ad-vũr′byəl-īz′ẽr), *n.* a suffix that forms adverbs from other words.

ad·ver·bi·al·ly (əd-vũr′bi-əl-i, ad-vũr′byəl-i), *adv.* as an adverb.

‡**ad ver·bum** (ad vũr′bəm), [L.], to a word; word for word; verbatim.

ad·ver·sar·y (ad′vẽr-ser′i), *n.* [*pl.* ADVERSARIES (-iz)], [ME. & OFr. *adversarie;* L. *adversarius* < *adversus;* see ADVERSE, ADVERT], a person who opposes or fights against another; opponent; enemy. —***SYN.*** see **opponent.**

the Adversary, Satan.

ad·ver·sa·tive (əd-vũr′sə-tiv, ad-vũr′sə-tiv), *adj.* [L. *adversativus* < *adversatus,* pp. of *adversari,* to be opposed to], expressing opposition or antithesis. *n.* an adversative word, such as *but, yet, however.*

ad·verse (əd-vũrs′, ad-vũrs′, ad′vẽrs), *adj.* [ME.; OFr. *avers, advers;* L. *adversus,* turned opposite to, pp. of *advertere;* see ADVERT], 1. hostile; opposed; contrary in direction. 2. unfavorable; harmful. 3. opposite in position. 4. in *botany,* toward the stem.

ad·ver·si·ty (əd-vũr′sə-ti, ad-vũr′sə-ti), *n.* [*pl.* ADVERSITIES (-tiz)], [ME. *adversite;* OFr. *aversite;* L. *adversitas* < *adversus,* turned against, pp. of *advertere;* see ADVERT], 1. misfortune; wretched state; poverty and trouble. 2. an instance of misfortune; calamity.

ad·vert (əd-vũrt′, ad-vũrt′), *v.i.* [L. *advertere; ad-,* to + *vertere,* to turn], to call attention; refer or allude (*to* something).

ad·vert·ence (əd-vũr′t'ns, ad-vũr′t'ns), *n.* [ME.; OFr. *avertance;* L. *advertentia* < ppr. of *advertere;* see ADVERT], attention.

ad·vert·en·cy (əd-vũr′t'n-si, ad-vũr′t'n-si), *n.* advertence.

ad·vert·ent (əd-vũr′t'nt, ad-vũr′t'nt), *adj.* [L. *advertens,* ppr. of *advertere;* see ADVERT], attentive.

ad·ver·tise (ad′vẽr-tīz′, ad′vẽr-tīz′), *v.t.* [ADVERTISED (-tīzd′, -tīzd′), ADVERTISING], [Fr. base *a(d)vertiss-* (cf. ADVERTISEMENT); *avertir, advertir,* to warn, call attention to; L. *advertere;* see ADVERT], 1. to tell people about or praise, as through newspapers, radio, etc., usually so as to get them to buy. 2. [Archaic], to notify or warn. *v.i.* 1. to call the public's attention to things for sale, help wanted, etc., as by printed notices or announcements. 2. to ask for publicly by printed notice, etc. (with *for*): as, *advertise* for a servant. Also spelled **advertize.**

ad·ver·tise·ment (ad′vẽr-tīz′mənt, əd-vũr′tiz-mənt), *n.* [Fr. *avertissement,* advertisement; see ADVERTISE], a public notice or announcement, usually paid for, as of things for sale, needs, etc.: also spelled **advertizement:** abbreviated **ad, ad., adv., advt.**

ad·ver·tis·er (ad′vẽr-tīz′ẽr, ad′vẽr-tīz′ẽr), *n.* a person who advertises: also spelled **advertizer.**

ad·ver·tis·ing (ad′vẽr-tīz′iŋ, ad′vẽr-tīz′iŋ), *n.* 1. printed or spoken matter that advertises. 2. the business of preparing and issuing advertisements. *adj.* 1. that advertises. 2. having to do with advertising. Also spelled **advertizing.** Abbreviated **advtg.**

advertising man, a man whose work or business is advertising: often colloquially abbreviated to **ad man.**

ad·ver·tize (ad′vẽr-tīz′, ad′vẽr-tīz′), *v.t. & v.i.* [ADVERTIZED (-tīzd′, -tīzd′), ADVERTISING], to advertise.

ad·vice (əd-vīs′), *n.* [ME. *avis;* OFr. *avis;* LL. **advisum* < *advisus,* pp. of *advidere; ad-,* at + *videre,* to look], 1. opinion given as to what to do or how to handle a situation; counsel. 2. *usually pl.* information or report: as, diplomatic *advices.*

ad·vis·a·bil·i·ty (əd-vīz′ə-bil′ə-ti), *n.* the quality of being advisable.

ad·vis·a·ble (əd-vīz′ə-b'l), *adj.* to be advised or recommended; prudent and wise; fitting and sensible.

ad·vis·a·bly (əd-vīz′ə-bli), *adv.* in an advisable manner; prudently; wisely.

ad·vise (əd-vīz′), *v.t.* [ADVISED (-vīzd′), ADVISING], [ME. *avisen,* orig., to consider; OFr. *aviser;* LL. *advisare* < L. *ad,* at + *visum,* pp. of *videre,* to look], 1. to give advice to; counsel. 2. to offer as advice; recommend. 3. to notify; inform. *v.i.* 1. to discuss something and get advice; consult (*with* a person). 2. to give advice.

***SYN.*—advise** implies the making of recommendations as to a course of action by someone with actual or supposed knowledge, experience, etc.; **counsel** implies the giving of advice after careful deliberation and suggests that weighty matters are involved; **admonish** suggests earnest, gently reproving advice concerning a fault, error, etc., given by someone fitted to do so by age or position; to **caution** is to give advice that puts one on guard against possible danger, failure, etc.; **warn,** often interchangeable with **caution,** is used when a serious danger or penalty is involved.

ad·vised (əd-vīzd′), *adj.* [pp. of *advise*], thought out; planned; deliberate: now chiefly in *well-advised, ill-advised.*

ad·vis·ed·ly (əd-vīz′id-li), *adv.* with due consideration; deliberately.

ad·vise·ment (əd-vīz′mənt), *n.* [ME. *avisement;* OFr. < *aviser;* see ADVISE], careful consideration.
take under advisement, to consider carefully.

ad·vis·er, ad·vi·sor (əd-vīz′ẽr), *n.* one who advises.
legal advisor, a lawyer.

ad·vi·so·ri·ly (əd-vī′zə-rə-li), *adv.* in an advisory manner or capacity.

ad·vi·so·ry (əd-vī′zə-ri), *adj.* 1. advising or empowered to advise. 2. relating to advice. *n.* [*pl.* ADVISORIES (-iz)], a warning about weather conditions, issued by the Weather Bureau.

ad·vo·ca·cy (ad′və-kə-si), *n.* [OFr. *advocacie;* ML. *advocatia* < *advocatus;* see ADVOCATE], an advocating; speaking or writing in support (*of* something).

ad·vo·cate (ad′və-kit; *also, and for v. always,* ad′və-kāt′), *n.* [ME. & OFr. *avocat;* L. *advocatus,* a counselor < *advocare; ad-,* to + *vocare,* to call], 1. a person who pleads another's cause, as a lawyer: abbreviated **Adv.** 2. a person who speaks or writes in support of something: as, an *advocate* of socialism. *v.t.* [ADVOCATED (-id), ADVOCATING], [< the *n.*], to speak or write in support of; be in favor of. —*SYN.* see **support.**

ad·vo·ca·tion (ad′və-kā′shən), *n.* 1. [Obs.], advocacy. 2. in *Scottish & papal law,* the transfer by a superior court to itself of an action pending in an inferior court.

ad·vo·ca·tor (ad′və-kā′tẽr), *n.* [LL.; see ADVOCATE], a person who advocates.

ad·voc·a·to·ry (əd-vok′ə-tôr′i, ad-vok′ə-tō′ri, ad′və-kāt′ẽr-i), *adj.* [< *advocate* + *-ory*], 1. of an advocate. 2. of advocacy; advocating.

‡ad·vo·ca·tus di·a·bo·li (ad′və-kā′təs dī-ab′ə-lī′), [L.], the devil's advocate.

ad·vow·son (ad-vou′z′n), *n.* [ME. *advowson, avowiesoun;* OFr. *avoeson;* L. *advocatio,* a summoning, calling to; see ADVOCATE], in *English law,* the right to name the holder of a church benefice.

advt., [*pl.* ADVTS.], advertisement.

A·dy·gei Autonomous Region (ä′di-gā′), a division of the R.S.F.S.R., in the northwest Caucasus: area, 1,505 sq. mi.; pop., 254,000; capital, Maikop.

ad·y·na·mi·a (ad′i-nā′mi-ə), *n.* [Mod. L.; Gr. < *a-,* without + *dynamis,* power], lack of vital force as a result of illness; debility.

ad·y·nam·ic (ad′i-nam′ik, ā′dī-nam′ik), *adj.* of or characterized by adynamia; weak.

ad·y·tum (ad′i-təm), *n.* [*pl.* ADYTA (-tə)], [L.; Gr. *adyton,* neut. of *adytos,* not to be entered < *a-,* not + *dyein,* to enter], 1. the innermost room or shrine in certain old temples. 2. a sanctum.

adz, adze (adz), *n.* [ME. *adis, adse;* AS. *adesa,* adz, ax], an axlike tool for dressing wood, etc., with a curved blade at right angles to the handle.

TYPES OF ADZ

Ad·zhar Autonomous Soviet Socialist Republic (äd′zhär), a division of the Georgian S.S.R., in the Transcaucasus: area, 1,080 sq. mi.; pop., 170,000; capital, Batum.

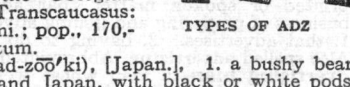

ad·zu·ki bean (ad-zōō′ki), [Japan.], 1. a bushy bean plant of China and Japan, with black or white pods. 2. its small, brownish bean. Also spelled **adsuki.**

ae (ā), *adj.* [< AS. *an,* whence Eng. *one*], [Scot.], one.

Æ, see **Russell, George William.**

æ, 1. a diphthong in some Latin words, equivalent to *ai* in Greek, usually written *ae* or replaced by *e* in modern spelling of derived English words, as in *demon* (*daemon*), *ether* (*aether*), etc., and pronounced (ē, i, or e). 2. an Anglo-Saxon character symbolizing a low front unrounded vowel like that in Modern English *hat, add, rack,* etc. 3. a character in the International Phonetic Alphabet symbolizing this vowel.

Ae., ae., *aetatis,* [L.], aged (a specified number of years); at the age of.

A.E.A., Actors' Equity Association: a branch of the Associated Actors and Artists of America.

Ae·a·cus (ē′ə-kəs), *n.* [L.; Gr. *Aiakos*], in *Greek mythology,* a king of Aegina who after he died became one of the three judges of the dead in the lower world, with Minos and Rhadamanthus.

A.E. and P., Ambassador Extraordinary and Plenipotentiary.

ae·cid·i·um (ē-sid′i-əm), *n.* [*pl.* AECIDIA (-ə)], [Mod. L., dim. < Gr. *aikia,* harm, injury], an aecium.

ae·ci·o·stage (ē′si-ə-stāj′), *n.* [< *aecium* + *stage*], in *botany,* the period in their life cycle during which certain rusts produce aecia.

ae·ci·um (ē′si-əm, ē′shi-əm), *n.* [*pl.* AECIA (-si-ə, -shi-ə)], [Mod. L. < Gr. *aikia,* injury], in *botany,* a cuplike spore fruit produced by certain rusts, in which chains of spores are developed.

a·ë·des (ā-ē′dēz), *n. sing. & pl.* [Mod. L.; Gr. *aēdēs,* unpleasant < *a-,* not + *hēdys,* sweet], 1. a kind of mosquito that can carry the virus of yellow fever. 2. any mosquito of the same genus as this one.

ae·dile (ē′dīl), *n.* [L. *aedilis* < *aedes,* building, temple], in ancient Rome, an official in charge of buildings, roads, sanitation, public games, etc.: also spelled **edile.**

A.E.F., American Expeditionary Force (or Forces).

Ae·ge·an (ē-jē′ən), *n.* a sea between Greece and Asia Minor, joining with the Mediterranean: length, 400 mi.; width, 200 mi. *adj.* in or of the Aegean.

AEGEAN SEA

Aegean civilization (or **culture**), the civilization of the people who lived in the Aegean islands and near-by regions before the ancient Greeks: it flourished in the Bronze Age.

Aegean Islands, a group of islands in the Aegean, including the Dodecanese, Sporades, and Cyclades.

Ae·geus (ē′joos, ē′ji-əs), *n.* [L.; Gr. *Aigeus*], in *Greek legend,* a king of Athens who killed himself when he thought his son Theseus was dead.

Ae·gi·na (ē-jī′nə), *n.* an island off the southeastern coast of Greece: area, 41 sq. mi.; pop., 6,500.

Ae·gir (ē′jir, ā′gir), *n.* [ON.], in *Norse mythology,* the god of the sea.

ae·gis (ē′jis), *n.* [L. < Gr. *aigis,* goatskin < *aix aigos,* goat], 1. in *Greek mythology,* a shield or breastplate used by Zeus and, later, by his daughter Athena; hence, 2. a protection. 3. sponsorship; auspices. Also spelled **egis.**

Ae·gis·thus (ē-jis′thəs), *n.* [L.; Gr. *Aigisthos*], in *Greek legend,* the son of Thyestes and lover of Clytemnestra: he helped her to kill her husband, Agamemnon.

Ae·gos·pot·a·mi (ē′gəs-pot′ə-mī′), *n.* a town in ancient Thrace: in a naval battle (405 B.C.) near this town, the fleet of Sparta under Lysander defeated the Athenian fleet, ending the Peloponnesian War.

Ae·gyp·tus (ē-jip′təs), *n.* in *Greek legend,* a king of Egypt whose fifty sons married the fifty daughters of his brother Danaus: cf. **Danaides.**

Ael·fric (al′frik), *n.* (*Aelfric Grammaticus*), English abbot and writer; lived 955?–1020?

-ae·mi·a (ē′mi-ə), -emia.

Ae·ne·as (i-nē′əs, ē-nē′əs), *n.* [L.; Gr. *Aineias*], in *Greek & Roman legend,* a Trojan, son of Anchises and Venus, and hero of Virgil's *Aeneid:* escaping from ruined Troy, Aeneas wandered for years before coming to Latium.

Ae·ne·id (i-nē′id, ē-nē′id), *n.* [L. *Aeneis, Aeneidos* < *Aeneas*], a Latin epic poem by Virgil, about Aeneas and his adventures.

a·ë·ne·ous (ā-ē′ni-əs), *adj.* [L. *aeneus* < *aes,* copper, bronze], having the color and luster of brass.

Ae·o·li·a (ē-ō′li-ə), *n.* Aeolis.

Ae·o·li·an (ē-ō′li-ən), *adj.* 1. of Aeolis, its people, language, etc. 2. of Aeolus; hence, 3. [often a-], of the wind; carried or produced by the wind. *n.* 1. an inhabitant of Aeolis; member of the Greek tribes that settled in ancient Thessaly, Boeotia, Lesbos, and Asia Minor. 2. a dialect of ancient Greek associated with the reputed descendants of these tribes. Also spelled **Eolian.**

aeolian harp, a box with an opening in it across which strings or wires are stretched so that they make musical sounds when air blows over them.

Ae·ol·ic (ē-ol′ik), *adj.* of Aeolis; Aeolian. *n.* the Aeolian Greek dialect. Also spelled **Eolic.**

Ae·o·lis (ē′ə-lis), *n.* a region in northwestern Asia Minor, settled in ancient times by the Aeolians: also **Aeolia.**

ae·o·lo·trop·ic (ē′ə-lə-trop′ik), *adj.* [< Gr. *aiolos,* varying; + *-tropic*], in *physics,* having different properties in different directions: opposed to *isotropic.*

ae·o·lot·ro·py (ē′ə-lot′rə-pi), *n.* the state or quality of being aeolotropic.

Ae·o·lus (ē′ə-ləs), *n.* [L.; Gr. *Aiolos*], 1. in *Greek mythology,* the god of the winds. 2. a king of Thessaly, the Aeolians' forefather.

ae·on (ē′ən, ē′on), *n.* [LL.; Gr. *aiōn,* an age, lifetime, eternity], an extremely long, indefinite period of time; thousands and thousands of years: also spelled **eon.**

ae·o·ni·an (ē-ō′ni-ən), *adj.* [Gr. *aiōnios;* see AEON], lasting forever; eternal: also spelled **eonian.**

‡ae·quo a·ni·mo (ē′kwō an′ə-mō′), [L.], with calm mind; with equanimity.

aer- (âr, ā′ẽr), aero-: words beginning with *aer-* may also be spelled **aër-.**

aer·ate (ā′ẽr-āt′, âr′āt), *v.t.* [AERATED (-id), AERATING], [*aer-* + *-ate*], 1. to expose to air; cause air to circulate through. 2. to combine oxygen with (the blood) by breathing. 3. to charge (liquid) with gas, as in making soda water.

aer·a·tion (ā'ẽr-ā'shən, âr-ā'shən), *n.* an aerating or being aerated.

aer·a·tor (ā'ẽr-ā'tẽr, âr'ā-tẽr), *n.* 1. a person or thing that aerates. 2. a machine that charges a liquid with gas. 3. a kind of fumigating device.

aer·i- (âr'i, ā'ẽr-i, ā-êr'i), aero-: words beginning with *aeri-*, may also be spelled **aëri-**.

aer·i·al (âr'i-əl, ā-êr'i-əl), *adj.* [L. *aerius* < *aer* (see AIR); + *-al*], 1. of air; in the air. 2. like air; light as air. 3. not substantial; unreal; imaginary. 4. high up. 5. of or for aircraft or flying: as, an *aerial* map, *aerial* mine, etc. 6. in *botany*, growing in the air instead of in soil or water. *n.* (âr'i-əl), in *radio & television*, a wire or set of wires, often high in the air, for sending or receiving the electromagnetic waves; antenna.

aer·i·al·ist (âr'i-əl-ist, ā-êr'i-əl-ist), *n.* an acrobat who performs on a trapeze, high wire, etc.

aerial ladder, a ladder that can be extended for reaching high places, mounted on a fire engine, etc.

aer·i·al·ly (âr'i-əl-i, ā-êr'i-əl-i), *adv.* 1. in an aerial manner. 2. in the air.

aerial railway, an arrangement of overhead cables or rails with cars suspended from them, used to carry people or things across a canyon, river, etc.

aerial torpedo, a bomb shaped like a torpedo, dropped from an airplane.

aer·ie (âr'i, êr'i), *n.* [ME. *aire;* ML. *aeria, eyria;* OFr. *aire;* Pr. *agre;* prob. < L. *ager*, field, but influenced by L. *aer*, air & ME. *ei*, egg], 1. the nest of an eagle or other bird of prey that builds in a high place; hence, 2. a house or stronghold on a high place. 3. the young (of an eagle, hawk, etc.) in the nest. Also spelled **aery, eyrie, eyry.**

aer·if·er·ous (âr-if'ẽr-əs, ā'ẽr-if'ẽr-əs), *adj.* [*aeri-* + *-ferous*], carrying air.

aer·i·fi·ca·tion (âr'ə-fi-kā'shən, ā'ẽr-ə-fi-kā'shən), *n.* an aerifying or being aerified.

aer·i·form (ā-êr'ə-fôrm', âr'ə-fôrm'), *adj.* [*aeri-* + *-form*], 1. having the form of air or gas. 2. like air; insubstantial.

aer·i·fy (ā-êr'ə-fī', âr'ə-fī'), *v.t.* [AERIFIED (-fīd'), AERIFYING], [*aeri-* + *-fy*], 1. to change into air or gas. 2. to put air into; aerate.

aer·o, a·ër·o (âr'ō, ā'ẽr-ō), *adj.* of or for flying or aircraft.

aer·o- (âr'ō, âr'ə, ā'ẽr-ō, ā'ẽr-ə), [< Gr. *aēr*, air], a combining form meaning: 1. *air, of the air*, as in *aerolite*. 2. *of aircraft, connected with flying*, as in *aerobatics*. 3. *gas, of gases*, as in *aerodynamics*. Words beginning with *aero-* may also be spelled **aëro-**.

aer·o·bat·ics (âr'ə-bat'iks, ā'ẽr-ə-bat'iks), *n.pl.* [*aero-* + acro*batics*], 1. spectacular feats done in flying, as loops, rolls, etc. 2. [construed as sing.], the art of doing such feats in flying.

aer·obe (âr'ōb, ā'ẽr-ōb'), *n.* [< *aero-* + Gr. *bios*, life], a microorganism that can live and grow only where free oxygen is present.

aer·o·bic (âr-ō'bik, ā'ẽr-ō'bik), *adj.* 1. able to live or grow only where free oxygen is present. 2. of or produced by aerobes.

aer·o·bi·um (âr-ō'bi-əm, ā'ẽr-ō'bi-əm), *n.* [*pl.* AEROBIA (-ə)], [Mod. L.; see AEROBE], an aerobe.

aer·o·do·net·ics (âr'ō-də-net'iks, ā'ẽr-ō-də-net'iks), *n. pl.* [construed as sing.], [< *aero-* + Gr. *donētos*, agitated < *donein*, to shake; + *-ics*], the branch of aviation that has to do with gliding.

aer·o·drome (âr'ə-drōm', ā'ẽr-ə-drōm'), *n.* an airdrome.

aer·o·dy·nam·ics (âr'ō-dī-nam'iks, ā'ẽr-ō-dī-nam'iks), *n.pl.* [construed as sing.], [*aero-* + *dynamics*], the branch of physics that deals with the forces (resistance, pressure, etc.) exerted by air or other gases in motion.

aer·o·dyne (âr'ə-dīn', ā'ẽr-ə-dīn'), *n.* [*aero-* + *-dyne*], any aircraft that is heavier than air.

aer·o·em·bo·lism (âr'ō-em'bə-liz'm, ā'ẽr-ō-em'bə-liz'm), *n.* [*aero-* + *embolism*], a condition caused by a sudden, considerable lowering of air pressure, as in flying at high altitudes, characterized by the formation of nitrogen bubbles in the blood, acute pain in the joints and lungs, etc.: cf. **bends, decompression sickness.**

aer·o·gram (âr'ə-gram', ā'ẽr-ə-gram'), *n.* [*aero-* + *-gram*], 1. a radiogram. 2. a letter, etc. sent by air mail.

aer·o·graph·ics (âr'ə-graf'iks, ā'ẽr-ə-graf'iks), *n.pl.* [construed as sing.], [< *aerography* + *-ics*], the study of atmospheric phenomena.

aer·og·ra·phy (âr-og'rə-fi, ā'ẽr-og'rə-fi), *n.* [*aero-* + *-graphy*], description of the air or the atmosphere.

aer·o·lite (âr'ə-līt', ā'ẽr-ə-līt'), *n.* [*aero-* + *-lite*], a meteorite of stone.

aer·ol·o·gy (âr-ol'ə-ji, ā'ẽr-ol'ə-ji), *n.* [*aero-* + *-logy*], the study and investigation of the air, or of atmospheric phenomena, especially in relation to flying.

aer·o·ma·rine (âr'ō-mə-rēn', ā'ẽr-ō-mə-rēn'), *adj.* [*aero-* + *marine*], of the navigation of aircraft above the ocean.

aer·o·me·chan·ic (âr'ō-mi-kan'ik, ā'ẽr-ō-mi-kan'ik), *n.* a mechanic whose work is repairing and adjusting aircraft. *adj.* relating to aeromechanics.

aer·o·me·chan·ics (âr'ō-mi-kan'iks, ā'ẽr-ō-mi-kan'iks), *n.pl.* [construed as sing.], [*aero-* + *mechanics*], the science of air or other gases in motion or equilibrium: it has two branches, aerodynamics and aerostatics.

aer·om·e·ter (âr-om'ə-tẽr, ā'ẽr-om'ə-tẽr), *n.* [*aero-* + *-meter*], an instrument for measuring the weight and density of air or other gases.

aer·om·e·try (âr-om'ə-tri, ā'ẽr-om'ə-tri), *n.* [*aero-* + *-metry*], the science of measuring air.

aer·o·naut (âr'ə-nôt', ā'ẽr-ə-nôt'), *n.* [Fr. *aéronaute* < Gr. *aēr*, air + *nautēs*, sailor], the pilot or navigator of a balloon or dirigible.

aer·o·nau·tic (âr'ə-nô'tik, ā'ẽr-ə-nô'tik), *adj.* 1. of aeronautics. 2. of aeronauts.

aer·o·nau·ti·cal (âr'ə-nô'ti-k'l, ā'ẽr-ə-nô'ti-k'l), *adj.* aeronautic.

aer·o·nau·tics (âr'ə-nô'tiks, ā'ẽr-ə-nô'tiks), *n.pl.* [construed as sing.], [*aeronaut* + *-ics*], the science or art of making and flying aircraft; aviation.

aer·o·neu·ro·sis (âr'ō-nyoo-rō'sis, ā'ẽr-ō-nyoo-rō'sis), *n.* [*aero-* + *neurosis*], a nervous condition resulting from the emotional tension of constant flying, characterized by abdominal pains, digestive disturbances, etc.

aer·o·pha·gi·a (âr'ə-fā'ji-ə, ā'ẽr-ə-fā'ji-ə), *n.* [*aero-* + *-phagia*], an abnormal, spasmodic swallowing of air: often a symptom of hysteria.

aer·o·pho·bi·a (âr'ə-fō'bi-ə, ā'ẽr-ə-fō'bi-ə), *n.* [*aero-* + *-phobia*], an abnormal fear of air, especially of drafts.

aer·o·phore (âr'ə-fôr', ā'ẽr-ə-fôr'), *n.* [*aero-* + *-phore*], an apparatus for supplying air or oxygen through a face mask, as to workers in mines, under water, etc.

aer·o·pho·tog·ra·phy (âr'ō-fə-tog'rə-fi, ā'ẽr-ō-fə-tog'rə-fi), *n.* [*aero-* + *photography*], photographing the ground, etc. from an aircraft.

aer·o·phyte (âr'ə-fīt', ā'ẽr-ə-fīt'), *n.* [*aero-* + *-phyte*], a nonparasitic plant that grows on an aerial part of another plant, as many orchids; air plant; epiphyte.

aer·o·plane (âr'ə-plān', ā'ẽr-ə-plān'), *n.* an airplane.

aer·o·pulse (âr'ə-puls', ā'ẽr-ə-puls'), *n.* [*aero-* + *pulse* (throb)], a jet engine in which the high pressure developed in the burning of the fuel closes the air-intake valves of the combustion chamber: when the air is expelled from the jet, the pressure is lowered enough to open the valves for fresh air: also **pulsejet.**

aer·o·scope (âr'ə-skōp', ā'ẽr-ə-skōp'), *n.* [*aero-* + *-scope*], an apparatus for gathering bacteria, dust, etc. from the air, for microscopic examination.

a·er·o·sol (âr'ə-sōl', ā'ẽr-ə-sol'), *n.* [*aero-* + *sol* (solution)], a suspension of colloidal particles in a gas.

aerosol bomb, a container and atomizer for an insecticide.

aer·o·space (âr'ə-spās'), *n.* [*aero-* + *space*], the earth's atmosphere and the space outside it, considered as one continuous field.

aer·o·stat (âr'ə-stat', ā'ẽr-ə-stat'), *n.* [Fr. *aérostat* < Gr. *aēr*, air + *statos*, sustaining], a dirigible, balloon, or other lighter-than-air craft.

aer·o·stat·ic (âr'ə-stat'ik, ā'ẽr-ə-stat'ik), *adj.* [Fr. *aérostatique;* see AERO- & STATIC], 1. of aerostatics. 2. aeronautic. 3. used in aerostats.

aer·o·stat·i·cal (âr'ə-stat'i-k'l, ā'ẽr-ə-stat'i-k'l), *adj.* aerostatic.

aer·o·stat·ics (âr'ə-stat'iks, ā'ẽr-ə-stat'iks), *n.pl.* [construed as sing.], [*aero-* + *statics*], the branch of physics that deals with the equilibrium of air or other gases, and with the equilibrium of solid bodies, such as aerostats, floating in air or other gases.

aer·o·sta·tion (âr'ō-stā'shən, ā'ẽr-ō-stā'shən), *n.* [Fr. *aérostation* < *aérostat;* see AEROSTAT], 1. the art or science of flying lighter-than-air craft. 2. [Archaic], aerostatics.

aer·o·ther·a·peu·tics (âr'ō-ther'ə-pū'tiks, ā'ẽr-ō-ther'ə-pū'tiks), *n.pl.* [construed as sing.], [*aero-* + *therapeutics*], the treatment of disease by the use of air, especially by exposing the patient to changes of atmospheric pressure.

ae·ru·gi·nous (i-rōō'ji-nəs), *adj.* [L. *aeruginosus* < *aerugo* < *aes*, copper], of or like verdigris; bluish-green, like copper rust.

aer·y (âr'i, ā'ẽr-i), *adj.* [L. *aerius* < *aer;* see AIR], [Poetic], airy; of or like air.

aer·y (âr'i, êr'i), *n.* an aerie.

Aes·chi·nes (es'ki-nēz'), *n.* Athenian orator; lived 389–314 B.C.; rival of Demosthenes.

Aes·chy·lus (es'kə-ləs), *n.* Greek writer of tragedies; lived 525–456 B.C.

Aes·cu·la·pi·an (es'kyoo-lā'pi-ən), *adj.* 1. of Aesculapius; hence, 2. medical. *n.* a physician.

Aes·cu·la·pi·us (es'kyoo-lā'pi-əs), *n.* [L.; Gr. *Asklēpios*], in *Roman mythology*, the god of medicine and of healing,

son of Apollo: identified with the Greek Asclepius.
Ae·sir (ā′sir, ē′sir), *n.pl.* [ON., pl. of *ass*, a god; cf. ANSELM], the principal gods of Norse mythology, including Odin, Thor, Balder, Loki, Freya, and Tyr.
Ae·sop (ē′səp, ē′sop), *n.* Greek fable writer; lived c. 620–560 B.C.
aes·the·si·a (es-thē′zhə, es-thē′zhi-ə), *n.* [Mod. L. < Gr. *aisthesis*, perception, sense-impression], the ability to feel sensation: also spelled **esthesia.**
aes·thete (es′thēt), *n.* [Gr. *aisthētēs*, a person who perceives], 1. a person highly sensitive to art and beauty. 2. a person who exaggerates the value of artistic sensitivity or makes a cult of art and beauty; believer in art for art's sake. Also spelled **esthete.**
SYN.—**aesthete,** although applied to one highly sensitive to art and beauty, is often used derogatorily to connote effeteness, decadence, etc.; **dilettante** refers to one who appreciates art as distinguished from one who creates it, but is used disparagingly of one who dabbles superficially in the arts; a **connoisseur** is one who has expert knowledge or a keen discrimination in matters of art and, by extension, in any matters of taste (a *connoisseur* of fine foods); **virtuoso,** in this comparison, denotes a collector or connoisseur of art objects, and is sometimes used derogatorily to suggest faddishness.
aes·thet·ic (es-thet′ik), *adj.* [Gr. *aisthētikos*, sensitive < *aisthanesthai*, to perceive], 1. of aesthetics. 2. of beauty. 3. sensitive to art and beauty; showing good taste; artistic. Also spelled **esthetic.**
aes·thet·i·cal (es-thet′i-k'l), *adj.* aesthetic: also spelled **esthetical.**
aes·thet·i·cal·ly (es-thet′i-k'l-i, es-thet′ik-li), *adv.* 1. in an aesthetic manner. 2. from the point of view of aesthetics. Also spelled **esthetically.**
aes·the·ti·cian (es′thə-tish′ən), *n.* an expert or specialist in aesthetics: also spelled **esthetician.**
aes·thet·i·cism (es-thet′ə-siz'm), *n.* 1. aesthetic doctrine; cult of beauty, art, and good taste. 2. sensitivity to art and beauty. Also spelled **estheticism.**
aes·thet·ics (es-thet′iks), *n.pl.* [construed as sing.], [< *aesthetic*], the study or philosophy of beauty; theory of the fine arts and of people's responses to them: also spelled **esthetics.**
aes·ti·val (es′tə-v'l, es-tī′v'l), *adj.* [Fr.; LL. *aestivalis; L. aestivus* < *aestas*, summer], of summer: also spelled **estival.**
aes·ti·vate (es′tə-vāt′), *v.i.* [AESTIVATED (-id), AESTIVATING], [< L. *aestivatus*, pp. of *aestivare* < *aestas*, summer], 1. to spend the summer. 2. to spend the summer in a dormant condition, as snails: opposed to *hibernate*. Also spelled **estivate.**
aes·ti·va·tion (es′tə-vā′shən), *n.* 1. in *zoology*, the habit or state of aestivating. 2. in *botany*, the arrangement of petals in a flower bud before it opens: see **vernation.** Also spelled **estivation.**
A.-E. Sud., Anglo-Egyptian Sudan.
aet., aetat., *aetatis*, [L.], aged (a specified number of years); at the age of.
ae·ther (ē′thēr), *n.* ether.
ae·the·re·al (i-thêr′i-əl), *adj.* ethereal.
ae·ti·ol·o·gy (ē′ti-ol′ə-ji), *n.* etiology.
Aet·na (et′nə), *n.* Etna, a volcanic mountain in Sicily.
Ae·to·li·a (ē-tō′li-ə), *n.* a region in the western part of ancient Greece.
Ae·to·li·an (ē-tō′li-ən), *adj.* of Aetolia, its people, etc. *n.* a native or inhabitant of Aetolia.
af- (af), ad-: used before *f*, as in *affix*.
Af., 1. Africa. 2. African.
A.F., 1. Air Force. 2. Anglo-French: also **AF., A.-F.**
A.F., a.f., audio frequency.
A.F.A.M., Ancient Free and Accepted Masons.
a·far (ə-fär′), *adv.* [*a-*, on + *far*], [Poetic or Archaic], at or to a distance; from a distance; far away.
a·feard, a·feared (ə-fêrd′), *adj.* [orig. pp. of ME. *aferen*, to frighten; AS. *afæran; a-* + *færan*, to frighten < *fær*, sudden danger; see FEAR], [Archaic or Dial.], frightened; afraid.
a·fe·brile (ā-fē′bril, ā-feb′ril), *adj.* [*a-*, not + *febrile*], having no fever.
af·fa·bil·i·ty (af′ə-bil′ə-ti), *n.* [Fr. *affabilité;* L. *affabilitas;* see AFFABLE], the quality or state of being affable.
af·fa·ble (af′ə-b'l), *adj.* [Fr.; L. *affabilis* < *ad-*, to + *fari*, to speak < base *fa-*, as in *fable*], easy to approach and talk to; pleasant and polite. —*SYN.* see **amiable.**
af·fa·bly (af′ə-bli), *adv.* in an affable manner.
af·fair (ə-fâr′), *n.* [ME. *afere;* OFr. *afaire* < *a faire*, to do < L. *ad*, to + *facere*, to do], 1. a thing to do; business. 2. *pl.* matters of business. 3. any matter, occurrence, or thing. 4. [< *love affair*], an amorous relationship or episode between two people not married to each other; an amour.
‡**af·faire d'a·mour** (à′fâr′ dà′mōōr′), [Fr.], a love affair.
‡**af·faire de coeur** (à′fâr′ də kër′), [Fr., affair of the heart], a love affair.
‡**af·faire d'hon·neur** (à′fâr′ dô′nër′), [Fr., an affair of honor], a duel.
af·fect (ə-fekt′), *v.t.* [< L. *affectus*, pp. of *afficere*, to influence, attack < *ad-*, to + *facere*, to do], 1. to have an effect on; influence; produce a change in. 2. to move or stir the emotions of. *n.* 1. [Obs.], a disposition or tendency. 2. (af′ekt), [G. *affekt* < L. *affectus;* see the *v.*], in *psychology*, *a*) an emotion, feeling, or mood as a factor in behavior. *b*) a stimulus arousing an emotion, feeling, or mood.
SYN.—**affect** implies the producing of an effect strong enough to evoke a reaction; to **influence** is to affect in such a way as to produce a change in action, thought, nature, or behavior (to *influence* legislation); **impress** is used of that which produces a deep or lasting effect on the mind; **touch** and the stronger **move,** as considered here, are both applied to the arousing of emotion, sympathy, etc., but **move** also denotes an influencing so as to effect a change; **sway** emphasizes the influencing of a person so as to turn him from a given course (threats will not *sway* us). See also **assume.**
af·fect (ə-fekt′), *v.t.* [Fr. *affecter;* L. *affectare*, to aim to do, strive after < *afficere;* see AFFECT (to influence)], 1. to like to have, use, wear, be in, etc.: as, she *affects* plaid coats. 2. to make a pretense of being, having, feeling, liking, etc.; feign: as, he *affected* indifference to their teasing.
af·fec·ta·tion (af′ek-tā′shən), *n.* [L. *affectatio* < pp. of *affectare;* see AFFECT (to feign)], 1. an affecting or pretending to like, have, etc.; show or pretense. 2. artificial behavior meant to impress others; mannerism for effect. —*SYN.* see **pose.**
af·fect·ed (ə-fek′tid), *adj.* [pp. of *affect* (to feign)], 1. assumed for effect; artificial. 2. behaving in an artificial way to impress people; full of affectation.
af·fect·ed (ə-fek′tid), *adj.* [pp. of *affect* (to influence)]. 1. attacked by disease; afflicted. 2. influenced; acted upon. 3. emotionally moved or touched. 4. [see AFFECT, *n.*], disposed. 5. in *algebra*, consisting of terms that involve different powers of an unknown quantity.
af·fect·ed·ly (ə-fek′tid-li), *adv.* in an affected manner; with affectation.
af·fect·ing (ə-fek′tiŋ), *adj.* [ppr. of *affect* (to influence)]. emotionally touching; full of pathos. —*SYN.* see **moving.**
af·fec·tion (ə-fek′shən), *n.* [ME. *affecciun;* OFr. *affection;* L. *affectio*, a state of feeling < pp. of *afficere;* see AFFECT (to influence)], 1. a mental state or tendency; disposition. 2. *often pl.* fond or tender feeling; warm liking: usually distinguished from *love*. 3. a disease; ailment. 4. an attribute or property of a thing. —*SYN.* see **disease, love.**
af·fec·tion·al (ə-fek′shən-'l), *adj.* of the affections.
af·fec·tion·ate (ə-fek′shən-it), *adj.* [Latinized from Fr. *affectionné*], full of affection; tender and loving.
af·fec·tive (ə-fek′tiv), *adj.* [Fr. *affectif;* LL. *affectivus* < L. *affectus*], of affects; of feelings; emotional.
af·fec·tiv·i·ty (af′ek-tiv′ə-ti), *n.* [*affective* + *-ity*], in *psychology*, sensitivity to emotional stimuli; tendency to affects, or emotional responses.
af·fer·ent (af′ēr-ənt), *adj.* [L. *afferens*, ppr. of *afferre* < *ad-*, to + *ferre*, to bear], in *physiology*, bringing inward to a central part: as, *afferent* nerves lead to the spinal cord: opposed to *efferent*.
af·fi·ance (ə-fī′əns), *n.* [ME. *affiaunce;* OFr. *afiance* < *afier*, to trust in < ML. *affidare*, to pledge faith < L. *ad*, to + *fidare*, to trust], 1. trust or faith. 2. a plighting of faith; promise of marriage; betrothal. *v.t.* [AFFIANCED (-ənst), AFFIANCING], to pledge, especially in marriage; betroth.
af·fi·anced (ə-fī′ənst), *adj.* [pp. of *affiance*], pledged in marriage; betrothed; engaged.
af·fi·ant (ə-fī′ənt), *n.* [< ppr. of OFr. *afier;* see AFFIANCE], in *law*, a person who makes an affidavit; deponent.
af·fi·da·vit (af′ə-dā′vit), *n.* [ML., he has made oath; perf. tense of *affidare;* see AFFIANCE], in *law*, a written statement made on oath, usually before a notary public or other authorized person.
af·fil·i·ate (ə-fil′i-āt′), *v.t.* [AFFILIATED (-id), AFFILIATING], [< L. *affiliatus*, pp. of *affiliare*, to adopt as a son < *ad-*, to + *filius*, son], 1. to take in as a member or branch. 2. to connect or associate (oneself). 3. to decide legally who is the father of; hence, 4. to trace the source and connections of (a language, etc.). *v.i.* to associate oneself; join. *n.* (ə-fil′i-it), an affiliated individual or organization; member.
af·fil·i·a·tion (ə-fil′i-ā′shən), *n.* [Fr.; ML. *affiliatio;* see AFFILIATE], an affiliating or being affiliated; connection, as with organizations, clubs, etc.
af·fined (ə-fīnd′), *adj.* [< Fr. *affiné*, related; see AFFINITY], 1. joined or connected in some way; related. 2. [Obs.], under obligation; bound.
af·fin·i·tive (ə-fin′ə-tiv), *adj.* having or characterized by affinity; related or connected.
af·fin·i·ty (ə-fin′ə-ti), *n.* [*pl.* AFFINITIES (-tiz)], [L. *affinitas* < *affinis*, adjacent, related by marriage < *ad-*, to + *finis*, end], 1. relationship by marriage: distinguished from *consanguinity*. 2. close relationship; connection. 3. similarity of structure, as of species or languages, implying common origin; family resemblance. 4. a mutual attraction, especially between a man and a woman. 5. a person of the opposite sex who especially attracts one. 6. the force that causes the atoms of certain elements to combine and stay combined.

af·firm (ə-fũrm′), *v.t.* [ME. *affermen;* OFr. *affermer;* L. *affirmare,* to present as fixed < *ad-,* to + *firmare,* to make firm], 1. to say positively; declare firmly; assert to be true. 2. to confirm; ratify. Opposed to *deny.* *v.i.* in *law,* to declare solemnly, but not under oath; make affirmation. —*SYN.* see **assert.**

af·firm·ance (ə-fũr′məns), *n.* [OFr. *affermance* < L. *affirmans,* ppr. of *affirmare;* see AFFIRM], 1. an affirming or declaring. 2. a confirming. 3. in *law,* an upholding by a higher court of a lower court's judgment.

af·firm·ant (ə-fũr′mənt), *adj.* [L. *affirmans,* ppr. of *affirmare;* see AFFIRM], affirming. *n.* 1. a person who affirms or declares. 2. in *law,* a person who declares solemnly, but not under oath.

af·fir·ma·tion (af′ẽr-mā′shən), *n.* [L. *affirmatio* < pp. of *affirmare;* see AFFIRM], 1. an affirming or confirming; ratification. 2. a positive declaration; assertion. 3. in *law,* a solemn declaration, but not under oath: permitted to a person who has conscientious objections to taking oaths.

af·firm·a·tive (ə-fũr′mə-tiv), *adj.* [Fr. *affirmatif;* L. *affirmativus* < *affirmare;* see AFFIRM], affirming; saying that it is true; answering "yes." *n.* 1. a word or expression indicating assent or agreement. 2. the side upholding the proposition being debated.
answer in the affirmative, to answer "yes."

af·firm·a·to·ry (ə-fũr′mə-tôr′i, ə-fũr′mə-tō′ri), *adj.* affirmative.

af·fix (ə-fiks′; *for n.,* af′iks), *v.t.* [AFFIXED or AFFIXT (-fikst′), AFFIXING], [L. *affixus,* pp. of *affigere,* to fasten to < *ad-,* to + *figere,* to fasten], 1. to fasten; attach. 2. to add at the end; append. *n.* [Fr. *affixe* < L. *affixus;* see the *v.*], 1. a thing affixed. 2. in *linguistics,* a prefix, suffix, or infix.

af·fix·a·tion (af′ik-sā′shən), *n.* 1. affixture. 2. in *linguistics,* the adding of affixes to roots or bases in order to vary function, modify meanings, etc.: distinguished from *compounding, composition.*

af·fix·ture (ə-fiks′chẽr), *n.* an affixing or being affixed.

af·fla·tus (ə-flā′təs), *n.* [L.; pp. of *afflare,* to blow on < *ad-,* to + *flare,* to blow], inspiration or powerful impulse, as of an artist, poet, etc.

af·flict (ə-flikt′), *v.t.* [< obs. *afflict,* afflicted; ME. *aflight;* OFr. *afflit, afflict;* L. *afflictus,* pp. of *affligere,* to strike down < *ad-,* to + *fligere,* to strike, hit], to cause pain or suffering to; distress very much.

af·flic·tion (ə-flik′shən), *n.* [ME. *affliccion;* OFr. *affliction;* L. *afflictio*], 1. an afflicted condition; pain; suffering. 2. anything causing pain or distress; calamity.
SYN.—**affliction** implies pain, suffering, or distress imposed by illness, loss, misfortune, etc.; **trial** suggests suffering that tries one's endurance, but in a weaker sense refers to annoyance that tries one's patience; **tribulation** describes severe affliction continuing over a long and trying period; **misfortune** is applied to a circumstance or event involving adverse fortune and to the suffering or distress occasioned by it.

af·flic·tive (ə-flik′tiv), *adj.* [Fr. *afflictif;* see AFFLICT], causing pain or misery.

af·flu·ence (af′loo-əns), *n.* [Fr.; L. *affluentia* < *affluere,* to flow to < *ad-,* to + *fluere,* to flow], 1. a flowing toward; influx. 2. great plenty; abundance. 3. riches; wealth; opulence.

af·flu·ent (af′loo-ənt), *adj.* [Fr. < L. *affluens,* ppr. of *affluere;* see AFFLUENCE], 1. flowing freely. 2. plentiful; abundant. 3. wealthy; rich. *n.* a stream flowing into a river; tributary. —*SYN.* see **rich.**

af·flux (af′luks), *n.* [L. *affluxus,* pp. of *affluere;* see AFFLUENCE], a flow toward a point, as of blood to an organ.

af·ford (ə-fôrd′, ə-fōrd′), *v.t.* [ME. *aforthen;* AS. *geforthian,* to advance < *forthian,* to further], 1. to have the means for; stand the expense of; spare (money, time, etc.) without serious inconvenience: generally preceded by *can* or *be able.* 2. to be able (*to* do something) without risking serious consequences: as, I can *afford* to speak frankly. 3. to give; yield; supply; furnish: as, music *affords* her pleasure.

af·for·est (ə-fôr′ist, ə-for′ist), *v.t.* [ML. *afforestare;* see AD- & FOREST], to turn (land) into forest; plant many trees on.

af·for·est·a·tion (ə-fôr′is-tā′shən, ə-for′is-tā′shən), *n.* an afforesting; planting of a forest.

af·fran·chise (ə-fran′chīz), *v.t.* [AFFRANCHISED (-chīzd′), AFFRANCHISING], [Fr. *affranchir* < *à,* to + *franchir;* see FRANCHISE], to make free; enfranchise.

af·fray (ə-frā′), *n.* [ME. *affrai,* an attack, alarm; OFr. *esfrai* < *esfraer,* to frighten; LL. **exfridare* < L. *ex,* out of + Gmc. base *frith-,* peace], a noisy brawl or quarrel; public fight or riot; breach of the peace. *v.t.* [ME. *affraien;* OFr. *esfraer;* see the *n.*], [Archaic], to frighten.

af·fri·cate (af′ri-kit), *n.* [L. *affricatus,* pp. of *affricare,* to rub against < *ad-,* to + *fricare,* to rub], in *phonetics,* any of the complex sounds produced when slowly released stop consonants are followed immediately by fricatives (spirants) at the same point of articulation: the English affricates are those in *latch* (IPA tʃ) and *judge* (IPA dʒ).

af·fric·a·tion (af′ri-kā′shən), *n.* in *phonetics,* the slow release of stop consonants causing the formation of affricates.

af·fric·a·tive (ə-frik′ə-tiv), *n.* an affricate. *adj.* of or forming an affricate.

af·fright (ə-frīt′), *v.t.* [ME. *afrighten;* AS. *afyrhtan;* see FRIGHT], [Archaic], to frighten; terrify. *n.* [Archaic], 1. a terrifying. 2. a cause of terror. 3. terror; fright.

af·front (ə-frunt′), *v.t.* [ME. *afronten;* OFr. *afronter,* to encounter face to face; ML. *affrontare* < *ad-,* to + *frons,* forehead], 1. to insult openly or purposely; slight. 2. to confront defiantly. *n.* an open or intentional insult; slight. —*SYN.* see **offend.**

af·fron·tive (ə-frun′tiv), *adj.* [Rare or Archaic], affronting; openly insulting.

af·fu·sion (ə-fū′zhən), *n.* [L. *affusio* < *affusus,* pp. of *affundere* < *ad-,* to + *fundere,* to pour], a pouring on or into, as of water in baptism.

Afg., Afghanistan.

Af·ghan (af′gən, af′gan), *n.* 1. a native or inhabitant of Afghanistan. 2. the language of Afghanistan: also called *Pushtu.* 3. any of a breed of hunting hound, originally from the Near East, with silky hair and a long, narrow head. 4. [a-], a crocheted or knitted soft wool blanket or shawl. *adj.* of Afghanistan, its people, language, etc.

Af·ghan·i·stan (af-gan′ə-stan′, af′gan-ə-stan′), *n.* a country in southwestern Asia, between Iran and India: area, 245,000 sq. mi.; pop., 13,150, 000; capital, Kabul.

‡**a·fi·cio·na·do** (ä-fē′thyô-nä′thô; Eng. ä-fē′syə-nä′dō), *n.* [Sp.], a devotee.

a·field (ə-fēld′), *adv.* [*a-,* on + *field*], 1. in, on, or to the field. 2. away (from home); astray.

a·fire (ə-fīr′), *adv. & adj.* [*a-,* on + *fire*], on fire.

A.F.L., American Federation of Labor: also **A.F. of L.**

a·flame (ə-flām′), *adv. & adj.* [*a-,* on + *flame*], in flames; ablaze; in a glow.

AFL-CIO, American Federation of Labor and Congress of Industrial Organizations, merged in 1955.

a·float (ə-flōt′), *adj.* [*a-,* on + *float*], 1. not grounded; clear of the bottom. 2. floating on the surface. 3. on board ship; at sea. 4. flooded: said of a ship's deck, etc. 5. drifting about. 6. current; in circulation: said of a rumor, etc.
keep afloat, 1. to remain floating or unsunk. 2. to remain solvent.

a·flut·ter (ə-flut′ẽr), *adv. & adj.* [*a-,* on + *flutter*], in a flutter.

‡**à fond** (å′ fōn′), [Fr.], 1. to the bottom or foundation. 2. thoroughly; completely.

a·foot (ə-foot′), *adv. & adj.* [*a-,* on + *foot*], 1. on foot. 2. in motion or operation; in progress; astir.

a·fore (ə-fôr′, ə-fōr′), *adv., prep., conj.* [ME. *afore, aforn;* AS. *onforan,* before; influenced by *ætforan;* see A- & FORE], [Archaic & Dial. except in compounds and nautical use], before.

a·fore·men·tioned (ə-fôr′men′shənd, ə-fōr′men′shənd), *adj.* mentioned before or previously.

a·fore·said (ə-fôr′sed′, ə-fōr′sed′), *adj.* spoken of before; mentioned previously.

a·fore·thought (ə-fôr′thôt′, ə-fōr′thôt′), *adj.* thought out beforehand; premeditated.

a·fore·time (ə-fôr′tīm′, ə-fōr′tīm′), *adv.* in times now past; formerly. *adj.* of former times.

a for·ti·o·ri (ā′ fôr′shi-ō′rī, ā′ fōr′shi-ō′rī), [L., for a stronger (reason)], all the more: said of a conclusion that follows with even greater logical necessity than another already accepted in the argument.

a·foul (ə-foul′), *adv. & adj.* [*a-,* on + *foul*], in a collision or a tangle.
run (or **fall**) **afoul of,** to become entangled with; get into trouble with.

Afr-, Afro-.

Afr., 1. Africa. 2. African.

A.-Fr., Anglo-French.

A.F.R.A., American Federation of Radio Artists: a branch of the Associated Actors and Artists of America, an A.F. of L. labor union.

a·fraid (ə-frād′), *adj.* [obs. pp. of *affray;* see AFFRAY], feeling fear; frightened; apprehensive (with *of, that,* or an infinitive): often used colloquially to indicate regretful realization, etc.: as, I'm *afraid* I can't go.
SYN.—**afraid** is applied to a general feeling of fear or disquiet and is the broadest in application of all the words considered here (to be *afraid* of the dark, to be *afraid* to die); **frightened** implies a sudden, usually temporary seizure of fear (the child was *frightened* by the dog); **timid** implies a lack of courage or self-confidence and suggests overcautiousness, shyness, etc. (he is *timid* about investing money); **timorous** and **fearful** suggest a feeling of disquiet and a tendency to worry rather than an alarming fear (*fearful* of making an error); **terrified** suggests a feeling of intense, overwhelming fear (he stood *terrified* as the tiger charged). —*ANT.* brave, bold, self-controlled.

Af·ra·mer·i·can (af'rə-mer'ə-kən), *adj.* & *n.* Afro-American.

Af·ra·sia (af-rā'zhə), *n.* [*Afr-* + *Asia*], northern Africa east of the Sahara, and southwestern Asia, considered together.

Af·ra·sian (af-rā'zhən), *adj.* of Afrasia. *n.* the offspring of an African and an Asiatic.

a·freet (af'rēt), *n.* [Ar. *'ifrīt*], in *Arabic mythology*, a strong, evil demon or jinni: also spelled **afrit.**

a·fresh (ə-fresh'), *adv.* [*a-*, of + *fresh*], again; anew.

Af·ric (af'rik), *adj.* [Poetic], African.

Af·ri·ca (af'ri-kə), *n.* the second largest continent, situated in the Eastern Hemisphere, south of Europe, between the Atlantic and Indian Oceans: area, 11,500,-000 sq. mi.; pop., 261,000,000: abbreviated **Afr., Af.**

Af·ri·can (af'ri-kən), *adj.* 1. of Africa, its peoples, cultures, etc. 2. Negro or Negroid. *n.* 1. a native or inhabitant of Africa. 2. a member of an African race; Negro or Negroid. Abbreviated **Afr., Af.**

African lily, an African plant of the lily family, having straplike leaves and clusters of blue or white, funnel-shaped flowers; agapanthus.

African violet, any of a group of tropical African plants with violet or pinkish flowers.

Af·ri·kaans (af'ri-känz', af'ri-käns'), *n.* [S. Afr. D. < *Afrika*, Africa], the Dutch dialect spoken in South Africa: also called *Cape Dutch, Taal.*

Af·ri·kan·der (af'ri-kan'dẽr), *n.* [S.Afr.D. < D. *Afrikaner*, with *d* after *Hollander*], 1. formerly, an Afrikaner. 2. a breed of cattle, originally from Africa.

Af·ri·ka·ner (af'ri-kä'nẽr), *n.* [D.], a South African of European, especially Dutch, ancestry; Boer.

af·rit (af'rēt), *n.* an afreet.

Af·ro- (af'rō), [L. *Afer*, an African], a combining form meaning: 1. *Africa.* 2. *African:* also **Afr-.**

Af·ro-A·mer·i·can (af'rō-ə-mer'ə-kən), *adj.* of Negro Americans, their culture, etc. *n.* a Negro American.

aft (aft, äft), *adj.* & *adv.* [AS. *æftan;* akin to Goth. *aftana*, from behind < *afta*, behind, farthest back; *af*, off, away + superl. suffix *-ta: aft* is now felt to be the positive of which *after* is the comparative], at, near, or toward the stern (within the ship).

aft., afternoon.

A.F.T., American Federation of Teachers: an AFL-CIO labor union.

af·ter (af'tẽr, äf'tẽr), *adv.* [ME. *after, efter;* AS. *æfter* (*adv.*); akin to OHG. *aftar* & MHG. *after;* see AFT], 1. behind. 2. later; next; afterward. *prep.* 1. behind. 2. in search of. 3. later than. 4. as a result of; on account of: as, *after* what has happened, he won't go. 5. in spite of: as, *after* all we had done, he was still ungrateful. 6. next to in rank or importance; lower in order than. 7. in the manner of: as, a novel *after* Dickens' style. 8. for; in honor of: as, a child named *after* Lincoln. 9. concerning: as, she asked *after* you. In the etymologies of this dictionary, *after* often means "patterned after." *conj.* following the time when; later than. *adj.* 1. next; later. 2. nearer the rear (especially, of a ship); more aft.

af·ter·birth (af'tẽr-bũrth', äf'tẽr-bũrth'), *n.* 1. the placenta and fetal membranes expelled from the womb after childbirth. 2. in *law*, a child born after the father's death or final will.

af·ter·brain (af'tẽr-brān', äf'tẽr-brān'), *n.* the posterior part of the hindbrain; myelencephalon.

af·ter·burn·er (af'tẽr-bũr'nẽr, äf'tẽr-bũr'nẽr), *n.* 1. a device attached to the tail pipe of some jet engines, utilizing hot exhaust gases to burn extra fuel for additional thrust. 2. an auxiliary device, as on internal-combustion engines and incinerators, for burning undesirable gases produced during the original combustion.

af·ter·damp (af'tẽr-damp', äf'tẽr-damp'), *n.* an asphyxiating gas left in a mine after an explosion of firedamp: also called *chokedamp.*

af·ter·deck (af'tẽr-dek', äf'tẽr-dek'), *n.* the part of a ship's deck toward the stern.

af·ter-din·ner (af'tẽr-din'ẽr, äf'tẽr-din'ẽr), *adj.* made, done, or served following dinner.

af·ter·ef·fect (af'tẽr-ə-fekt', äf'tẽr-ə-fekt'), *n.* an effect coming later, or as a secondary result.

af·ter·glow (af'tẽr-glō', äf'tẽr-glō'), *n.* 1. the glow remaining after a light has gone, as in the western sky after sunset. 2. the pleasant feeling one has after an enjoyable experience.

af·ter·im·age (af'tẽr-im'ij, äf'tẽr-im'ij), *n.* in *psychology*, an image or sensation that stays or comes back after the external stimulus has been withdrawn.

af·ter·life (af'tẽr-līf', äf'tẽr-līf'), *n.* 1. a life after death. 2. one's later years.

af·ter·math (af'tẽr-math', äf'tẽr-math'), *n.* [*after* + dial. *math* < AS. *mæth*, cutting of grass < *mawan*, to mow, with *-th* suffix], 1. a second mowing; grass that grows after the earlier mowing. 2. a result or consequence, usually an unpleasant one.

af·ter·most (af'tẽr-mōst', äf'tẽr-mōst'), *adj.* [*after* + *most;* akin in form to AS. *æftemest*, superl. of *æfter*, after], 1. hindmost; last. 2. nearest to the stern.

af·ter·noon (af'tẽr-nōōn', äf'tẽr-nōōn'), *n.* the time from noon to evening. *adj.* of, in, or for the afternoon.

af·ter·pains (af'tẽr-pānz', äf'tẽr-pānz'), *n.pl.* the pains following childbirth.

af·ter·piece (af'tẽr-pēs', äf'tẽr-pēs'), *n.* a short sketch presented after a longer dramatic production.

af·ter·sen·sa·tion (af'tẽr-sen-sā'shən, äf'tẽr-sen-sā'-shən), *n.* in *psychology*, an afterimage of peripheral origin.

af·ter·shaft (af'tẽr-shaft', äf'tẽr-shäft'), *n.* a feather growing from the posterior side of another feather.

af·ter·taste (af'tẽr-tāst', äf'tẽr-tāst'), *n.* 1. a taste staying in the mouth after eating, drinking, or smoking. 2. the feeling remaining after an experience.

af·ter·thought (af'tẽr-thôt', äf'tẽr-thôt'), *n.* 1. reflection after the event; later explanation. 2. a thought coming too late, after the occasion for which it was apt.

af·ter·time (af'tẽr-tīm', äf'tẽr-tīm'), *n.* the time to come; future.

af·ter·ward (af'tẽr-wẽrd, äf'tẽr-wẽrd), *adv.* [AS. *æfterweard;* see AFT & -WARD], later; subsequently.

af·ter·wards (af'tẽr-wẽrdz, äf'tẽr-wẽrdz), *adv.* [*afterward* + adv. genit. *-(e)s*], afterward.

af·ter·world (af'tẽr-wũrld', äf'tẽr-wũrld'), *n.* a world after this one; world supposedly existing after death.

ag- (ag, əg), ad-: used before *g*, as in *aggrade.*

Ag, *argentum*, [L.], in *chemistry*, silver.

Ag., August.

ag., agriculture.

A.G., 1. Adjutant General. 2. Attorney General.

a·ga (ä'gə), *n.* [Turk.], in Turkey and other Moslem countries, a title of respect for important officials, both military and civil: also spelled **agha.**

a·gain (ə-gen', ə-gān'), *adv.* [ME. *agen, ayein;* AS. *ongegn, ongean; on-*, up to, toward + *gegn*, direct: orig. separable prefix meaning "directly up to," hence, "facing, opposite"; see AGAINST, GAINSAY], 1. [Rare], back in response; in return: as, answer *again.* 2. back into a former position or condition; hence, 3. once more; a second time; anew. 4. besides; further. 5. on the other hand; from the contrary standpoint. 6. [Obs.], in the opposite direction; back.

again and again, often; repeatedly.

as much again, twice as much.

a·gainst (ə-genst', ə-gānst'), *prep.* [ME. *ayeynst, ageinest, agaínest*, opposite to, facing, etc. < AS. *ongegn, ongean* (see AGAIN), with adv. genit. *-es* + unhistoric *-t*], 1. in opposition to: as, fight *against* evil, *against* one's will. 2. toward so as to come in contact with or strike: as, throw the ball *against* the wall. 3. opposite to the course or direction of: as, drive *against* the traffic. 4. in contrast with: as, green *against* the gold. 5. next to; adjoining: as, the house *against* the church. 6. in preparation for; for the possibility of: as, we provided *against* a poor crop.

over against, 1. opposite to. 2. as compared with.

A·ga Khan III (ä'gə kän'), (*Aga Sulton Sir Mahomed Shah*), 1877–1957; leader of Ismailian Moslems.

ag·a·ma (ag'ə-mə), *n.* [Mod. L.; Sp.; of W. Ind. origin], 1. a kind of lizard that changes color like the chameleon. 2. any of a number of lizards related to this.

Ag·a·mem·non (ag'ə-mem'nən, ag'ə-mem'non), *n.* [Gr.], in *Greek legend*, king of Mycenae and commander in chief of the Greek army in the Trojan War, killed by his wife Clytemnestra.

a·gam·ic (ə-gam'ik), *adj.* [Gr. *agamos; a-*, not + *gamos*, marriage], in *biology*, 1. asexual; having no sexual union. 2. able to develop without fertilization.

a·gam·i·cal·ly (ə-gam'i-k'l-i), *adv.* in an agamic way.

ag·a·mo·gen·e·sis (ag'ə-mō-jen'ə-sis), *n.* [Mod. L. < Gr. *agamos* (see AGAMIC); + *-genesis*], in *biology*, asexual reproduction, as by budding, fissure, or parthenogenesis.

ag·a·mous (ag'ə-məs), *adj.* [Gr. *agamos;* see AGAMIC], in *biology*, 1. asexual. 2. producing no flowers or seeds, as ferns and mosses.

A·ga·ña (ä-gä'nyä; Eng. ä-gän'yə), *n.* the capital of Guam: pop., 2,000.

ag·a·pan·thus (ag'ə-pan'thəs), *n.* [Mod. L. < Gr. *agapē*, love + *anthos*, a flower], any of a number of related African plants of the lily family, with clusters of white, blue, or purple flowers.

a·gape (ə-gāp'), *adv.* & *adj.* [*a-*, on + *gape*], 1. gaping; with the mouth wide open, as in surprise, wonder, etc. 2. wide open.

ag·a·pe (ä'gä-pā', ag'ə-pē'), *n.* [LL. < Gr. *agapē*, love], 1. a meal that early Christians ate together; love feast. 2. in *Christian theology*, *a*) God's love for man; divine love. *b*) spontaneous, altruistic love.

a·gar (ä'gär, ā'gẽr, ä'gär, ag'ẽr), *n.* [Malay], 1. agar-agar. 2. a substance containing agar-agar.

a·gar-a·gar (ä'gär-ä'gär, ā'gẽr-ā'gẽr, ä'gär-ä'gär, ag'ẽr-ag'ẽr), *n.* [Malay], a gelatinous product made from seaweed, and used as a base for bacterial cultures, as a laxative, etc.

a·gar·ic (ag'ə-rik, ə-gar'ik), *n.* [L. *agaricum*, larch fungus; Gr. *agaricon*, tree fungus < *Agaria*, a Sarmatian town], any agaricaceous fungus, as the common edible mushroom, a corky fungus parasitic on trees, etc.

a·gar·i·ca·ceous (ə-gar'i-kā'shəs), *adj.* [*agaric* + *-aceous*], belonging to the gill fungi family, including most toadstools and mushrooms.

Ag·as·siz, Alexander (ag′ə-si), 1835–1910; son of *Louis;* American naturalist.
Agassiz, Louis (*Jean Louis Rodolphe Agassiz*), 1807–1873; American naturalist, born in Switzerland.
ag·ate (ag′it, ag′ət), *n.* [Fr.; L. *achates;* Gr. *achatēs* < *Achatēs,* Sicilian river], 1. a hard, semiprecious stone with striped or clouded coloring; kind of chalcedony. 2. any of various tools having agate parts, as a burnishing instrument with a tip of agate. 3. a playing marble made of or like this stone. 4. a very small person: from the tiny figures cut in agate seals. 5. in *printing,* a small size of type, 5 1/2 point. This line is in agate.
a gate·ware (ag′it-wâr′), *n.* 1. pots and pans of iron or steel enameled to look like agate. 2. pottery made to look like agate.
Ag·a·tha (ag′ə-thə), [L.; Gr. *Agathē,* lit., good, fem. of *agathos,* good], a feminine name.
A·gath·o·cles (ə-gath′ə-klēz′), *n.* tyrant of ancient Syracuse; lived 361?–289 B.C.
ag·at·ize (ag′ə-tiz′), *v.t.* [AGATIZED (-tīzd′), AGATIZING], [< *agate* + *-ize*], to make into or like agate.
‡à gauche (à′ gōsh′), [Fr.], to the left; on the left.
a·ga·ve (ə-gä′vi), *n.* [Mod. L. < Gr. *Agauē,* a proper name, lit., illustrious, fem. of *agauos,* famous], any of a number of related plants of the amaryllis family, especially the century plant of American deserts, having tall flower stalks that ascend from thick, fleshy leaves: some agaves yield fiber used for rope.
a·gaze (ə-gāz′), *adv. & adj.* [*a-,* on + *gaze*], gazing.
agcy., agency.
age (āj), *n.* [ME.; OFr. *aage;* ML. **aetaticum* < L. *aetus*], 1. the time that a person or a thing has existed since birth or beginning. 2. the lifetime. 3. the time of life when a person is qualified for full legal rights, adult responsibilities, etc. (preceded by *of*): as, a man comes of *age* at twenty-one. 4. a stage of life. 5. the latter part of a normal lifetime; senility; old age. 6. a generation. 7. a historical or geological period; epoch. 8. *often pl.* [Colloq.], a long time. *v.i.* [AGED (ājd), AGING or AGEING], to grow old or mature; show signs of growing old. *v.t.* to make old or mature. —*SYN.* see **period.**
-age (ij, əj), [OFr.; LL. *-aticum,* belonging to, related to], a noun-forming suffix added to verbs (sense 1) and nouns (sense 2) meaning, in general: 1. *that which belongs or relates to the act of,* as in *passage, marriage;* hence, *a) amount of,* as in *drinkage, wastage, b) cost of,* as in *postage, porterage,* and *c) place of,* as in *steerage.* 2. *that which belongs or relates to the state or condition of,* as in *pupilage, savage* [L. *silvaticus*], *voyage* [L. *viaticum*]; hence, *a) collection of,* as in *peerage, baronage, acreage, foliage, rootage,* and *b) place for,* as in *orphanage.* Senses 1 and 2 are often blended in the same word.
a·ged (ā′jid), *adj.* [pp. of *age*], 1. old; grown old; made old. 2. (ājd), of the age of: as, *aged* five years.
the aged (ā′jid), old people.
a·gee (ə-jē′), *adv. & adj.* [*a-,* intens. + *gee* (command to horse)], [British Dial.], on or to one side; askew.
age·less (āj′lis), *adj.* 1. not growing old. 2. eternal.
age·long (āj′lôŋ′, āj′loŋ′), *adj.* 1. lasting long. 2. lasting forever.
a·gen·cy (ā′jən-si), *n.* [*pl.* AGENCIES (-siz)], [L. *agentia* < ppr. of *agere;* see AGENT], 1. action; power. 2. means; instrumentality. 3. the business of any person, firm, etc. empowered to act for another. 4. the business office or district of such a person, firm, etc. Abbreviated **agcy.**
a·gen·da (ə-jen′də), *n.pl.* [*sing.* AGENDUM (-dəm)], [L., neut. pl. of the gerundive of *agere,* to do, act], 1. things to be done. 2. [also construed as sing.], a list of things to be done or dealt with (at a meeting, etc.).
a·gent (ā′jənt), *n.* [L. *agens, agentis,* ppr. of *agere,* to do, act; Gr. *agein,* to drive], 1. a person or thing that performs actions or is able to do so. 2. an active force or substance producing an effect: as, a chemical *agent.* 3. a person, firm, etc. empowered to act for another: abbreviated **agt.** 4. [Colloq.], a traveling salesman.
SYN.—an **agent** is, generally, a person or thing that acts or is capable of acting, or, in this comparison, one who or that which acts, or is empowered to act, for another (the company's *agent*); **factor** now usually denotes an agent for the sale of goods; a **deputy** is a public official to whom certain authority has been delegated by his superior; **proxy** implies the delegation of power to substitute for another in some formal or ceremonial detail (some stockholders vote by *proxy*).
a·gen·tial (ā-jen′shəl), *adj.* 1. of an agent. 2. of an agency. 3. acting as an agent.
a·gen·tive (ā′jən-tiv), *adj.* [*agent* + *-ive,* after *genitive, accusative,* etc.], of or producing a grammatical form denoting the doer of some action. *n.* an agentive affix or form, as the suffix *-ant,* in *servant, defendant.*
‡a·gent pro·vo·ca·teur (à′zhän′ prô′vô′kà′tër′), [Fr.], a person hired to join or become friendly with others, as with members of a labor union, a political party, etc., in order to incite them to do things that will make them or their organization liable to penalty.
age of consent, in *law,* the age of a girl before which sexual intercourse with her, regardless of whether she has consented, is considered rape.
age-old (āj′ōld′), *adj.* ages old; centuries old; ancient.
ag·er·a·tum (aj′ẽr-ā′təm, ə-jer′ə-təm), *n.* [Mod. L.; Gr. *agēraton,* a kind of plant < *a-,* not + *gēras,* old age], any of a number of plants of the thistle or aster family, having small, thick heads of blue or white flowers.
A·ges·i·la·us (ə-jes′i-lā′əs), *n.* Spartan king and general; lived c. 400–360 B.C.
ag·glom·er·ate (ə-glom′ẽr-āt′), *v.t. & v.i.* [AGGLOMERATED (-id), AGGLOMERATING], [L. *agglomeratus,* pp. of *agglomerare* < *ad-,* to + *glomerare,* to form into a ball], to gather into a cluster, mass, or ball. *adj.* (ə-glom′ẽr-it), gathered into a mass or ball; clustered. *n.* (ə-glom′ẽr-it), 1. a jumbled heap, mass, or cluster. 2. in *geology,* a mass of fragments of volcanic rock fused by heat.
ag·glom·er·a·tion (ə-glom′ẽr-ā′shən), *n.* [L. *agglomeratio*], 1. an agglomerating. 2. an agglomerated condition. 3. a jumbled heap, mass, or cluster.
ag·glom·er·a·tive (ə-glom′ẽr-ā′tiv, ə-glom′ẽr-ə-tiv), *adj.* agglomerating; tending to agglomerate.
ag·glu·ti·nant (ə-glo͞o′t′n-ənt), *adj.* [L. *agglutinans,* ppr. of *agglutinare;* see AGGLUTINATE], sticking together; adhesive. *n.* a sticky or adhesive substance.
ag·glu·ti·nate (ə-glo͞o′t′n-it; *for v.,* ə-glo͞o′t′n-āt′), *adj.* [L. *agglutinatus,* pp. of *agglutinare,* to cement to < *ad-,* to + *glutinare* < *gluten,* glue], 1. stuck together, as with glue. 2. in *linguistics,* forming words by agglutination. *v.t. & v.i.* [AGGLUTINATED (-id), AGGLUTINATING], 1. to stick together, as with glue; join by adhesion. 2. in *linguistics,* to form (words) by agglutination. 3. in *medicine & bacteriology,* to clump, as microorganisms, blood cells, etc.
ag·glu·ti·na·tion (ə-glo͞o′t′n-ā′shən), *n.* [L. *agglutinatio;* see AGGLUTINATE], 1. an agglutinating. 2. an agglutinated condition. 3. a mass of agglutinated parts. 4. in *linguistics,* the systematic combining of independent words into compounds without marked change of form or loss of meaning: term now seldom used. 5. in *medicine & bacteriology,* the clumping together of microorganisms, blood cells, etc. suspended in fluid.
ag·glu·ti·na·tive (ə-glo͞o′t′n-ā′tiv, ə-glo͞o′t′n-ə-tiv), *adj.* 1. tending to agglutinate; sticking together. 2. in *linguistics,* characterized by agglutination.
ag·glu·ti·nin (ə-glo͞o′t′n-in), *n.* a substance causing agglutination (of bacteria, blood cells, etc.).
ag·glu·tin·o·gen (ag′loo-tin′ə-jən), *n.* [< *agglutinin* + *-gen*], any antigen which stimulates the production of agglutinins.
ag·gra·da·tion (ag′rə-dā′shən), *n.* an aggrading or being aggraded.
ag·grade (ə-grād′), *v.t.* [AGGRADED (-id), AGGRADING], [*ag-* (see AD-) + *grade*], to build up the grade or slope of (the earth) by deposition of sediment, as in the bank of a stream.
ag·gran·dize (ag′rən-dīz′, ə-gran′dīz′), *v.t.* [AGGRANDIZED (-dīzd′), AGGRANDIZING], [Fr. *agrandir,* to augment < L. *ad,* to + *grandire,* to increase < *grandis,* great], 1. to increase in power, position, riches, etc. (sometimes used reflexively). 2. to make seem greater.
ag·gran·dize·ment (ə-gran′diz-mənt), *n.* [Fr. *agrandissement;* see AGGRANDIZE], an aggrandizing or being aggrandized; increase in power, position, riches, etc.
ag·gra·vate (ag′rə-vāt′), *v.t.* [AGGRAVATED (-id), AGGRAVATING], [< L. *aggravatus,* pp. of *aggravare,* to make heavier < *ad-,* to + *gravis,* heavy], 1. to make worse; make more burdensome, troublesome, etc. 2. [Colloq.], to exasperate; annoy; vex. —*SYN.* see **intensify.**
ag·gra·va·tion (ag′rə-vā′shən), *n.* 1. an aggravating or being aggravated. 2. a thing or circumstance that aggravates. 3. [Colloq.], exasperation; annoyance.
ag·gre·gate (ag′ri-git; *for v.,* ag′ri-gāt′), *adj.* [L. *aggregatus,* pp. of *aggregare,* to lead to a flock, add to < *ad-,* to + *gregare,* to herd < *grex, gregis,* a herd], 1. gathered into a whole or mass; total. 2. in *botany,* clustered. 3. in *geology,* composed of mineral fragments or crystals mixed in one rock. *n.* 1. a total or whole; group or mass of distinct things gathered together. 2. the sand and pebbles used in making concrete. *v.t.* [AGGREGATED (-id), AGGREGATING], 1. to gather into a whole or mass. 2. to amount to; total. —*SYN.* see **sum.**
in the aggregate, taken all together; on the whole.
ag·gre·ga·tion (ag′ri-gā′shən), *n.* 1. an aggregating or being aggregated. 2. a group or mass of distinct things or individuals.
ag·gre·ga·tive (ag′ri-gā′tiv), *adj.* 1. aggregating. 2. tending to aggregation. 3. taken collectively or as a whole.
ag·gre·ga·to·ry (ag′ri-gə-tôr′i, ag′ri-gə-tō′ri), *adj.* 1. relating to an aggregate. 2. aggregated.
ag·gress (ə-gres′), *v.i.* [< L. *aggressus,* pp. of *aggredi,* to

attack, go to < *ad-*, to + *gradi*, to step < *gradus*, a step], to start a quarrel or attack.

ag·gres·sion (ə-gresh'ən), *n.* [Fr.; L. *aggressio;* see AGGRESS], 1. an unprovoked attack or invasion. 2. the practice or habit of being aggressive.

ag·gres·sive (ə-gres'iv), *adj.* 1. aggressing or inclined to aggress; starting fights or quarrels. 2. full of enterprise and initiative; bold and active; pushing.
SYN.—**aggressive** implies a bold and energetic pursuit of one's ends, connoting, in derogatory usage, a ruthless desire to dominate and, in a favorable sense, enterprise, initiative, etc.; **militant** implies a vigorous, unrelenting espousal of a cause, movement, etc. and rarely suggests the furthering of one's own ends; **assertive** emphasizes self-confidence and a persistent determination to express oneself or one's opinions; **pushing** is applied derogatorily to a forwardness of personality that manifests itself in officiousness, rudeness, etc.

ag·gres·sor (ə-gres'ẽr), *n.* [L.], one that aggresses; person, nation, etc. that starts a fight or makes an unprovoked attack.

ag·grieve (ə-grēv'), *v.t.* [AGGRIEVED (-grēvd'), AGGRIEVING], [ME. *agreven;* OFr. *agrever*, to aggravate; L. *aggravare;* see AGGRAVATE], 1. to cause grief or injury to; offend; slight. 2. to injure in one's legal rights. —*SYN.* see **wrong.**

ag·grieved (ə-grēvd'), *adj.* [pp. of *aggrieve*], 1. having a grievance; offended. 2. injured in one's legal rights.

a·gha (ä'gə), *n.* aga.

a·ghast (ə-gast', ə-gäst'), *adj.* [ME. *agast, agasted*, pp. of *agasten*, to terrify < AS. *a* + *gæstan*, to terrify < *gæst, gast*, spirit, demon; cf. GHOST], terrified; horrified; showing sudden dismay or amazement.

ag·ile (aj'əl, aj'il, aj'īl), *adj.* [Fr.; L. *agilis* < *agere*, to do, act], quick and easy of movement; deft and active.
SYN.—**agile** and **nimble** both imply rapidity and lightness of movement, **agile** emphasizing dexterity in the use of the limbs and **nimble**, deftness in the performance of some act; **quick** implies rapidity and promptness, seldom indicating, out of context, the degree of skillfulness; **spry** suggests nimbleness or alacrity, now usually as displayed by vigorous elderly people; **sprightly** implies animation or vivacity and suggests gaiety, lightness, etc. —*ANT.* torpid, sluggish, lethargic.

a·gil·i·ty (ə-jil'ə-ti), *n.* [Fr. *agilité;* L. *agilitas* < *agilis;* see AGILE], the quality or condition of being agile.

Ag·in·court (aj'in-kôrt', aj'in-kōrt'; Fr. å'zhan'ko͞or'), *n.* a town in northern France, near Calais: site of a battle (1415) won by England in the Hundred Years' War with France.

ag·i·o (aj'i-ō', aj'ō), *n.* [*pl.* AGIOS (-ōz', -ōz)], [It. *aggio*, exchange, premium], 1. a fee paid to exchange one kind of money for another, or to exchange depreciated money for money of full value. 2. agiotage.

ag·i·o·tage (aj'i-ə-tij, aj'ə-tij), *n.* [Fr. < *agioter*, to job in stocks < *agio* (It. *aggio*), premium], 1. exchange business. 2. the business of a stockbroker; speculation in stocks.

a·gist (ə-jist'), *v.t.* [OFr. *agister; a-* (L. *ad*), to + *gister*, to assign a lodging < ML. **jacitare* < L. *jacere*, to lie], to feed or pasture (cattle) for a fixed sum.

a·gist·ment (ə-jist'mənt), *n.* 1. an agisting. 2. an agreement to agist. 3. the profit of agisting.

ag·i·ta·ble (aj'ə-tə-b'l), *adj.* that can be agitated.

ag·i·tate (aj'ə-tāt'), *v.t.* [AGITATED (-id), AGITATING], [< L. *agitatus*, pp. of *agitare*, to put in motion < *agere*, to do, move], 1. to move violently; stir up; shake up. 2. to excite; fluster. 3. to keep discussing so as to cause or increase dissatisfaction and produce changes. *v.i.* to act as an agitator; stir people up so as to produce social or political changes. —*SYN.* see **disturb.**

ag·i·tat·ed (aj'ə-tāt'id), *adj.* shaken; perturbed; excited.

ag·i·ta·tion (aj'ə-tā'shən), *n.* [L. *agitatio;* see AGITATE], 1. an agitating or being agitated; violent motion or stirring. 2. emotional disturbance; tremulous excitement. 3. discussion meant to arouse or increase dissatisfaction with things as they are and produce changes; work of an agitator.

‡a·gi·ta·to (ä'jē-tä'tô), *adj. & adv.* [It. < L. *agitatus;* see AGITATE], in *music*, fast and with excitement: a direction to the performer.

ag·i·ta·tor (aj'ə-tā'tẽr), *n.* [L.; see AGITATE], 1. a person or thing that agitates. 2. a person who tries to arouse or increase dissatisfaction with things as they are so as to produce changes: often used in an unfavorable sense. 3. an apparatus for shaking or stirring.

A·gla·ia (ə-glā'ə), *n.* [L.; Gr. *Aglaia*, lit., brightness], in *Greek mythology*, one of the three Graces.

a·gleam (ə-glēm'), *adv. & adj.* [*a-*, on + *gleam*], gleaming.

ag·let (ag'lit), *n.* [ME.; OFr. *aguillette*, dim. of *aiguille* < L. *acula*, dim. of *acus*, a needle, pin], the metal tip of a cord or lace: also **aiglet.**

a·gley (ə-glī', ə-glē'), *adv.* [*a-*, on + *gley*, squint], [Scot.], awry; off to one side.

a·glim·mer (ə-glim'ẽr), *adv. & adj.* in or to a glimmering condition; glimmering.

a·glit·ter (ə-glit'ẽr), *adv. & adj.* [*a-*, on + *glitter*], in a glitter.

a·glow (ə-glō'), *adv. & adj.* [*a-*, on + *glow*], in a glow (of color or emotion).

a·gly (ə-glī'), *adv.* [Scot.], agley.

A.G.M.A., American Guild of Musical Artists: a branch of the Associated Actors and Artists of America, an A.F. of L. labor union.

ag·mi·nate (ag'mə-nit, ag'mə-nāt'), *adj.* [< L. *agmen*, a group, troop + *-ate*], arranged in a cluster or clusters; grouped together.

ag·nail (ag'nāl'), *n.* [AS. *angnægl*, a corn (on the toe or foot); *ang-*, tight, painful + *nægl*, nail (metal): orig. in reference to the nail-head appearance of the excrescence], 1. a sore or swelling around a fingernail or toenail. 2. a hangnail.

ag·nate (ag'nāt), *n.* [L. *agnatus*, pp. of *agnasci*, to be born in addition to < *ad-*, to + *nasci*, to be born], a relative through male descent or on the father's side. *adj.* 1. related through male descent or on the father's side. 2. akin.

ag·nat·ic (ag-nat'ik), *adj.* 1. of agnation. 2. related through males or on the father's side.

ag·na·tion (ag-nā'shən), *n.* [L. *agnatio;* see AGNATE], an agnate relationship.

Ag·nes (ag'nis), [Fr. *Agnès;* L. *Agnes, Hagnes;* Gr. *hagnē*, fem. of *hagnos*, chaste], a feminine name: diminutive, *Aggie.*

Agnes, Saint, 3d century; one of the four great patronesses of the Western Church: her day is January 21.

Ag·ni (ug'ni, ag'ni), *n.* [Sans. *agni*, fire], in *Hindu mythology*, the Vedic god of fire and guardian of man: he is shown as having two faces.

ag·no·men (ag-nō'mən), *n.* [*pl.* AGNOMINA (-nom'ə-nə), AGNOMENS (-mənz)], [L. *ad*, to + *gnomen*, old form of *nomen*, name], 1. in ancient Rome, a name added to the cognomen, especially as an epithet honoring some achievement. 2. a nickname.

ag·nos·tic (ag-nos'tik), *n.* [ult. < Gr. *agnōstos*, unknown, unknowable < *a-*, not + base of *gignōskein*, to know], a person who thinks it is impossible to know whether there is a God or a future life, or anything beyond material phenomena. *adj.* of or characteristic of an agnostic or agnosticism. —*SYN.* see **atheist.**

ag·nos·ti·cal·ly (ag-nos'ti-k'l-i), *adv.* 1. in an agnostic manner. 2. from an agnostic point of view.

ag·nos·ti·cism (ag-nos'tə-siz'm), *n.* the doctrine of an agnostic: distinguished from *atheism.*

Ag·nus De·i (ag'nəs dē'ī), [L., Lamb of God], 1. a representation of Christ as a lamb, often holding a cross or flag. 2. in the *Roman Catholic Church, a)* a little wax disk with a lamb pictured on it, blessed by the Pope. *b)* a prayer in the Mass, beginning *Agnus Dei. c)* its music. 3. the Anglican anthem, beginning "O Lamb of God."

a·go (ə-gō'), *adj.* [ME. *agon, agan*, pp. of *agon*, to depart; AS. *agan*, to pass away], gone by; past: used following the noun. *adv.* in the past: as, long *ago.*

a·gog (ə-gog'), *adv. & adj.* [Fr. *en gogues*, in mirth], in a state of eager anticipation, excitement, or interest.

-a·gogue (ə-gôg', ə-gog'), [< Gr. *agōgos*, leading], a combining form meaning *leading, directing, inciting*, as in *demagogue, mystagogue:* also spelled **-agog.**

a·gon (ä'gōn), *n.* [Gr. *agōn*, assembly, contest < *agein*, to lead], the conflict of characters in a drama.

a·gone (ə-gôn', a-gon'), *adj. & adv.* [ME. *agon;* see AGO], [Archaic], ago; past.

a·gon·ic (ə-gon'ik), *adj.* [Gr. *agōnos* < *a-*, without + *gōnia*, an angle], forming no angle.

agonic line, the imaginary line on the earth's surface on which true north and magnetic north are identical, and a compass needle makes no angle with the meridian.

ag·o·nis·tic (ag'ə-nis'tik), *adj.* [Gr. *agōnistikos*, fit for contest < *agōn;* see AGON], 1. of ancient Greek athletic contests. 2. contesting; combative. 3. strained for effect.

ag·o·nize (ag'ə-niz'), *v.i.* [AGONIZED (-nīzd'), AGONIZING], [Fr. *agonizer;* ML. *agonizare;* Gr. *agōnizesthai*, to contend for a prize < *agōn*, a contest], 1. to make convulsive efforts; struggle. 2. to be in agony; be in great pain. *v.t.* to cause great pain to; torture.

ag·o·niz·ing (ag'ə-nīz'iŋ), *adj.* [ppr. of *agonize*], 1. that agonizes. 2. very painful.

ag·o·ny (ag'ə-ni), *n.* [*pl.* AGONIES (-niz)], [ME. *agonie;* L. *agonia;* Gr. *agōnia*, a contest for victory < *agōn;* see AGON], 1. great mental or physical pain. 2. death pangs. 3. a convulsive struggle. 4. a sudden, strong emotion: as, an *agony* of joy. —*SYN.* see **distress.**

agony column, a newspaper column for personal advertisements, as to missing relatives, etc.

ag·o·ra (ag'ə-rə), *n.* [*pl.* AGORAE (-rē'), AGORAS (-rəz)], [Gr.], 1. in ancient Greece, an assembly; hence, 2. a place of assembly, especially a market place.

ag·o·ra·pho·bi·a (ag'ə-rə-fō'bi-ə), *n.* [*agora* + *-phobia*], a morbid fear of being in open or public places.

a·gou·ti (ə-go͞o'ti), *n.* [*pl.* AGOUTIS, AGOUTIES (-tiz)], [Fr.; Sp. *aguti* < Tupi native name], a rodent related to the guinea pig, found in the West Indies and Central and South America: it is about as big as a rabbit and has grizzled fur: also spelled **agouty.**

agr., 1. agricultural. 2. agriculture. 3. agriculturist.

A·gra (ä'grä, ä'grə), *n.* 1. a province of Uttar Pradesh, India. 2. a city in this province, famous for the Taj Mahal: pop., 376,000 .

a·graffe (ə-graf′), *n.* [Fr. *agraffe, agrappe* < *a-* (L. *ad*), to + *grappe;* LL. *grappa;* Gmc. *krappo,* a hook], 1. a hook and a loop, used as a clasp for armor or clothing. 2. a metal bracket for holding stones together.
A·gram (ä′gräm), *n.* Zagreb, a city in Yugoslavia.
a·graph·i·a (ā-graf′i-ə), *n.* [Mod. L. < Gr. *a-,* without + *graphein,* to write, draw], a brain disorder in which the patient's ability to write is partly or wholly lost.
a·graph·ic (ā-graf′ik), *adj.* of or having agraphia.
a·grar·i·an (ə-grâr′i-ən), *adj.* [L. *agrarius* < *ager,* a field, country], 1. relating to land; of the cultivation or ownership of land. 2. of agriculture. *n.* a person in favor of more equitable division of land.
a·grar·i·an·ism (ə-grâr′i-ən-iz′m), *n.* 1. the doctrine or methods of agrarians. 2. agitation or political movement for more equitable division of land.
a·gree (ə-grē′), *v.i.* [AGREED (-grēd′), AGREEING], [ME. *agreen;* OFr. *agreer,* to receive kindly < OFr. *a gre,* favorably; *a* (L. *ad*), to + *gre,* good will < L. *gratus,* pleasing], 1. to consent or accede (*to* something). 2. to be in harmony or accord. 3. to be of the same opinion; concur (*with* someone). 4. to arrive at a satisfactory understanding (*about* prices, terms, etc.). 5. to be suitable, healthful, etc. (followed by *with*): as, this climate does not *agree* with him. 6. in *grammar,* to have the same number, person, case, or gender. *v.t.* to grant or acknowledge (followed by a noun clause): as, we *agreed* that it was true.
SYN.—**agree** implies a being or going together without conflict and is the general term used in expressing an absence of inconsistencies, inequalities, unfavorable effects, etc.; **conform** emphasizes agreement in form or essential character; **accord** emphasizes fitness for each other of the things that are being considered together; **harmonize** implies a combination or association of different things in a proportionate, orderly, or pleasing arrangement (*harmonizing* colors); **correspond** is applied to that which matches, complements, or is analogous to something else (their Foreign Office *corresponds* to our State Department); **coincide** stresses the identical character of the things considered (their interests *coincide*); **tally** is applied to a thing that corresponds to another thing as a counterpart or duplicate. See also **consent.** —*ANT.* differ.
a·gree·a·bil·i·ty (ə-grē′ə-bil′ə-ti), *n.* the quality or state of being agreeable.
a·gree·a·ble (ə-grē′ə-b'l), *adj.* [ME. & OFr. *agreable* < *agreer;* see AGREE], 1. pleasing; pleasant; charming. 2. willing or ready to consent. 3. conformable. —*SYN.* see **pleasant.**
a·gree·a·bly (ə-grē′ə-bli), *adv.* 1. in an agreeable manner. 2. in conformity with.
a·greed (ə-grēd′), *adj.* [pp. of *agree*], settled or determined by mutual consent: as, pay the *agreed* price.
a·gree·ment (ə-grē′mənt), *n.* [OFr. *agrement;* see AGREE], 1. an agreeing; being in harmony or accord. 2. an understanding or arrangement between two or more people, countries, etc. 3. a contract.
a·gres·tic (ə-gres′tik), *adj.* [< L. *agrestis,* rural; + *-ic*], 1. rural; rustic; hence, 2. crude; uncouth; unpolished.
A·gric·o·la (ə grik′ə-lə), *n.* (*Gnaeus Julius Agricola*), Roman general; lived 37–93 A.D.
ag·ri·cul·tur·al (ag′ri-kul′chẽr-əl), *adj.* of agriculture; connected with farming: abbreviated **agr., agric.**
ag·ri·cul·tur·al·ist (ag′ri-kul′chẽr-əl-ist), *n.* an agriculturist.
ag·ri·cul·ture (ag′ri-kul′chẽr), *n.* [Fr.; L. *agricultura* < *ager,* a field (see ACRE) + *cultura,* cultivation], the science and art of farming; work of cultivating the soil, producing crops, and raising livestock: abbreviated **agr., agric.**
ag·ri·cul·tur·ist (ag′ri-kul′chẽr-ist), *n.* 1. an agricultural expert. 2. a farmer. Abbreviated **agr., agric.**
Ag·ri·gen·tum (ag′ri-jen′təm), *n.* an ancient city in southern Sicily.
ag·ri·mo·ny (ag′rə-mō′ni), *n.* [*pl.* AGRIMONIES (-niz)], [ME. < AS. *agrimonia* & OFr. *aigremoine,* both < L. *agrimonia;* altered < *agremonia;* Gr. *argemōnē*], 1. a plant that has little yellow flowers on spiky stalks, and fruit like burs. 2. any of a number of plants like this.
ag·ri·ol·o·gy (ag′ri-ol′ə-ji), *n.* [< Gr. *agrios,* wild; + *-logy*], the study of the customs of primitive peoples.
A·grip·pa (ə-grip′ə), *n.* (*Marcus Vipsanius Agrippa*), Roman statesman and general; lived 63–12 B.C.; victor over Antony and Cleopatra at Actium (31 B.C.).
Ag·rip·pi·na (ag′ri-pī′nə), *n.* mother of Nero; 15?–59 A.D.: called *the Younger.*
ag·ro- (ag′rō), [Gr. < *agros,* a field], a combining form meaning *field, earth, soil,* as in *agrobiology.*
ag·ro·bi·ol·o·gy (ag′rō-bī-ol′ə-ji), *n.* [< Gr. *agros,* soil; + *biology*], the science of plant growth and nutrition as applied to improvement of crops and control of soil.
a·grol·o·gy (ə-grol′ə-ji), *n.* [< Gr. *agros,* a field; + *-logy*], the science of soils in relation to crops.
ag·ro·nom·ic (ag′rə-nom′ik), *adj.* of agronomy.
ag·ro·nom·i·cal (ag′rə-nom′i-k'l), *adj.* agronomic.
ag·ro·nom·ics (ag′rə-nom′iks), *n.pl.* [construed as sing.], agronomy.
a·gron·o·mist (ə-gron′ə-mist), *n.* a student of or specialist in agronomy.
a·gron·o·my (ə-gron′ə-mi), *n.* [Fr. *agronomie* < Gr. *agronomos,* overseer of the public lands < *agros,* field + *nomos* < *nemein,* to deal out, manage], the management of farm land; art and science of crop production.
ag·ros·tol·o·gy (ag′rə-stol′ə-ji), *n.* [< L. *agrostis;* Gr. *agrōstis,* kind of grass < *agros,* a field; + *-logy*], the branch of botany dealing with grasses.
a·ground (ə-ground′), *adv. & adj.* [*a-,* on + *ground*], on or onto the ground, as a boat in shallow water; on or onto a beach, reef, etc.
agt., agent.
A·guas·ca·lien·tes (ä′gwäs-kä-lyen′tes), *n.* 1. a state of central Mexico: area, 2,499 sq. mi.; pop., 162,000. 2. its capital: pop., 104,000.
a·gue (ā′gū), *n.* [ME.; OFr. *agu, ague* < ML. *febris acuta,* violent fever; see ACUTE], 1. a fever, usually malarial, marked by regularly recurring chills. 2. a chill; fit of shivering.
a·gue·weed (ā′gū-wēd′), *n.* 1. a shrubby plant with flat-topped clusters of white or bluish-purple flowers; boneset. 2. a variety of gentian.
A·gui·nal·do, E·mi·lio (e-mē′lyô ä′gē-näl′dô), 1870?– ; Filipino leader.
a·gu·ish (ā′gū-ish), *adj.* 1. subject to ague. 2. of, causing, or like an ague.
A·gul·has, Cape (ä-gōōl′yäs; Eng. ə-gul′əs), the southernmost point of Africa.
A.G.V.A., American Guild of Variety Artists: a branch of the Associated Actors and Artists of America, an A.F. of L. labor union.
ah (ä, ô, aŋ), *interj.* [natural exclamation, similar to Fr. & L. *ah,* Gr. *a,* ON. *æ,* OHG. *ā,* Sans. *ā*], an exclamation expressing pain, delight, regret, disgust, surprise, etc., according to the manner of expression.
A.H., *anno Hegirae,* [L.], in the year of the Hegira.
a.h., ampere-hour.
a·ha (ä-hä′), *interj.* an exclamation expressing satisfaction, pleasure, triumph, etc., often mixed with irony or mockery.
A·hab (ā′hab), *n.* [Heb., lit., father's brother], in the *Bible,* a wicked king of Israel, led astray by his wife Jezebel: I Kings 16:22.
A·has·u·e·rus (ə-haz′ū-ēr′əs, ə-hazh′oo-ēr′əs), *n.* [of Per. origin], in the *Bible,* either of two kings of the Medes and Persians, especially the one who took Esther as his wife: Esth. 1, Ez. 4:6.
‡à haute voix (á′ ōt′ vwá′), [Fr., in high voice], aloud.
a·head (ə-hed′), *adv. & adj.* [*a-,* on + *head*], 1. in or to the front. 2. forward; onward. 3. in advance.
ahead of, in advance of; before.
be ahead, [Colloq.], 1. to be winning or profiting. 2. to have as a profit, benefit, or advantage.
get ahead, to advance socially, financially, etc.
get ahead of, to outdo or excel.
a·hem (ə-hem′: *conventionalized pronun.*), *interj.* [lengthened from *hem*], a cough or similar noise in the throat, made to get someone's attention, show skepticism, give a warning, fill a pause, etc.
A·hith·o·phel, A·hit·o·phel (ə-hit′ə-fel′), *n.* [Heb. *'achīthōphel,* lit., brother is foolishness], in the *Bible,* a counselor of David, who joined with Absalom in rebellion against him: II Sam. 15–17: also **Achitophel.**
Ah·mad·na·gar, Ah·med·na·gar (ä′məd-nug′ẽr), *n.* a city in Bombay, India: pop., 42,000.
Ah·med·a·bad, Ah·mad·a·bad (ä′məd-ə-bäd′), *n.* a city in western India, in Bombay: pop., 591,000.
a·horse (ə-hôrs′), *adv. & adj.* [*a-,* on + *horse*], on horseback.
a·hoy (ə-hoi′), *interj.* [interj. *a* + *hoy,* var. of *hey*], in *nautical usage,* a call used in hailing a person or a vessel: as, ship *ahoy!*
Ah·ri·man (ä′ri-mən), *n.* [Per. *Ahrīman;* prob. < Avestan *aṅra mainyu,* the evil (lit., hostile) spirit], in the *Zoroastrian religion,* the spirit of evil: see **Ormazd.**
a·hun·gered (ə-huŋ′gẽrd), *adj.* [ME., pp. of *ahungren* < AS. *ofhyngran,* to be hungry], [Archaic], hungry.
A·hu·ra·Maz·da (ä′hoo-rə-maz′də), *n.* Ormazd.
ai (ī), *interj.* an exclamation of pain, sorrow, pity, etc.
a·i (ä′i), *n.* [*pl.* AIS (-iz)], [Tupi *ai, hai* < the animal's cry], a South American sloth with three toes.
A.I.C., American Institute of Chemists.
aid (ād), *v.t. & v.i.* [OFr. *aider* < L. *adjutare,* freq. of *adjuvare,* to sustain, help; *ad-* + *juvare,* to help], to help; assist. *n.* [OFr. *aide* < the *v.*], 1. help; assistance. 2. a helper; assistant. 3. an officer in the army, navy, etc. who is assistant to a superior; aide. 4. in *English history, a*) a tax or subsidy paid to the king. *b*) an exchequer loan. 5. in *medieval law,* a payment in money made by a vassal to his lord. —*SYN.* see **help.**
A·ï·da (ä-ē′də), *n.* the heroine of an Italian opera of that name by Giuseppe Verdi (1871), an Ethiopian princess who becomes a slave in Egypt and dies with her lover when he is shut up in a tomb.

aide (ād), *n.* [Fr.; see AID], an officer in the army, navy, etc. who is a superior.

aide-de-camp, aid-de-camp (ād'də-kamp'; Fr. ed'də-kän'), *n.* [*pl.* AIDES-DE-CAMP, AIDS-DE-CAMP (ādz'-; Fr. ed'-)], [Fr., lit., camp assistant], an officer serving as assistant and confidential secretary to a general, marshal, etc.: abbreviated **A.D.C.**

‡**aide-mé·moire** (ed'me'mwår'), *n.* [Fr.], a memorandum of a discussion, proposed agreement, etc.

Ai·din (ī-dēn'), *n.* Aydin.

aid station, in *military usage,* a station close to the front lines, where the sick and wounded are given emergency medical treatment: also called *dressing station.*

A.I.E.E., American Institute of Electrical Engineers.

ai·glet (ā'glit), *n.* an aglet.

ai·grette, ai·gret (ā'gret, ā-gret'), *n.* [see EGRET], 1. a heron with long, white plumes: usually **egret.** 2. such a plume or a tuft of these plumes, used for a woman's headdress, etc. 3. any ornament resembling this.

ai·guille (ā-gwēl', ā'gwēl), *n.* [Fr., a needle], 1. a peak of rock shaped like a needle. 2. a needlelike instrument for boring.

ai·guil·lette (ā'gwi-let'), *n.* [Fr., dim. of *aiguille,* a needle], a gilt cord hung in loops from the shoulder of certain military uniforms; aglet.

Ai·ken, Conrad (ā'kin), 1889– ; American poet, critic, and novelist.

ail (āl), *v.t.* [ME. *ailen;* AS. *eglan,* to afflict with dread, trouble: connected with AS. *ege,* terror, dread(akin to ON. *agi,* whence Eng. *awe*)], to be the cause of pain to; be the trouble with. *v.i.* to be feeling pain; be ill.

ai·lan·thic (ā-lan'thik), *adj.* of or like an ailanthus.

ai·lan·thus (ā-lan'thəs), *n.* [Mod. L. <Malaccan *ailanto*], any of a number of related trees with pointed leaflets, fine-grained wood, and clusters of small, greenish flowers with an unpleasant odor; tree of heaven.

ailanthus moth, a large, silk-producing moth native to China and cultivated in the eastern United States: its larvae feed on ailanthus leaves.

Ai·leen (ī-lēn', ā-lēn'), a feminine name: see **Helen.**

ai·le·ron (ā'lə-ron'), *n.* [Fr. < *aile,* wing], a movable hinged section of the wing of an airplane, for banking in turns: see **airplane,** illus.

ail·ing (āl'iŋ), *adj.* sickly; ill. —*SYN.* see **sick.**

ail·ment (āl'mənt), *n.* any bodily or mental disorder; illness, especially a mild one. —*SYN.* see **disease.**

aim (ām), *v.i. & v.t.* [ME. *aimen, amen;* OFr. *aesmer; a-* (L. *ad*) + *esmer* < L. *aestimare,* to estimate], 1. to point (a weapon) or direct (a blow, remark, etc.) so as to hit. 2. to direct (one's efforts): as, we *aimed* at full victory; try or purpose (*to* do or be something). *n.* 1. the act of aiming. 2. the direction of a missile, blow, remark, etc. 3. sighting in pointing a weapon. 4. the object to be attained; intention or purpose. 5. [Obs.], a guess or conjecture. —*SYN.* see **intention.**

take aim, to point a weapon; sight along a gun at the target; direct a missile, blow, etc.

A.I.M.E., 1. American Institute of Mining Engineers. 2. Associate of the Institute of Mechanical Engineers.

aim·less (ām'lis), *adj.* having no aim or purpose.

ain (ān), *adj.* [Scot.], own.

ain't (ānt), [early assimilation, with lengthened and raised vowel, of *amn't,* contr. of *am not;* later confused with *a'nt* (*are not*), *i'nt* (*is not*), *ha'nt* (*has not, have not*)], [Colloq.], am not: also a dialectal or substandard contraction for *is not, has not,* and *have not: ain't* was formerly standard for *am not* and is still defended by some authorities as a proper contraction for *am not* in interrogative constructions: as, I'm going too, *ain't* I?

Ain·tab (īn'tåb'), *n.* Gaziantep, a city in Turkey.

Ai·nu (ī'nōō), *n.* [Ainu, lit., man], 1. a member of a primitive, light-skinned race of Japan, now living mostly in Karafuto and Hokkaido. 2. the language of this race. *adj.* of the Ainus, their language, etc.

A·ïr (ä'ir), *n.* a region and native kingdom in French West Africa: area, c. 30,000 sq. mi.: also called *Asben.*

air (âr), *n.* [ME.; OFr. *air, aer;* L. *aer;* Gr. *aēr,* air, mist], 1. the elastic, invisible mixture of gases (nitrogen, oxygen, hydrogen, carbon dioxide, argon, neon, helium, etc.) that surrounds the earth; atmosphere. 2. space above the earth; sky. 3. a movement of air; breeze; wind. 4. an outward appearance; general impression or feeling given by something: as, an *air* of luxury fills the room. 5. a person's bearing, manner, or appearance: as, he has an *air* of dignity. 6. *pl.* affected, superior manners and graces. 7. public expression or publicity: as, give *air* to your opinions. 8. in *music,* a melody or tune; especially, the main melody in a harmonized composition, usually the soprano or treble part. 9. in *radio,* the medium through which signals and broadcasts reach the audience: a figurative use. *adj.* of aircraft, air forces, etc.: as, *air* power. *v.t.* 1. to let air into or through; put where air can dry, cool, freshen, etc. 2. to make known; publicize. *v.i.* to become aired, dried, cooled, etc. —*SYN.* see **melody.**

get the air, [Slang], to be dismissed; be rejected.

give oneself airs, to act in an affected, superior manner.

in the air, 1. current or prevalent. 2. not decided; not settled; still imaginary.

on the air, in *radio,* broadcasting or being broadcast.

put on airs, to act in an affected, superior manner.

take the air, 1. to go out into the fresh air; go outdoors. 2. [Slang], to go out or away; leave. 3. in *radio,* to begin to broadcast.

up in the air, 1. not settled; not decided. 2. [Colloq.], angry; highly excited, upset, agitated, etc.

walk on air, to feel very happy, very lively, or exalted.

air (âr), *adv. & adj.* [Scot. dial. form of *ere* < AS. *ær*], [Scot.], early; before.

air base, a base for aircraft, especially military aircraft, consisting of a landing field, repair facilities, etc.

air bladder, a sac with air or gas in it, found in most fishes and in other animals and some plants: also called *air cell* or, in a fish, *swimming bladder.*

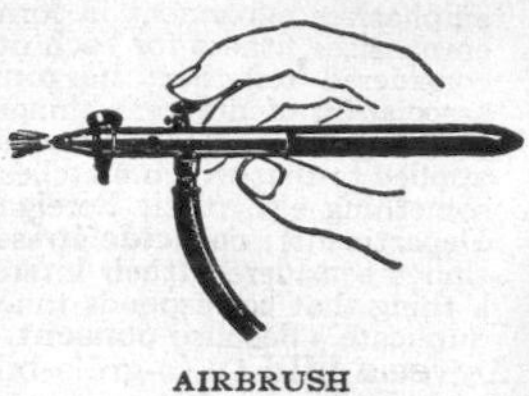

AIR BRAKE

air-borne (âr'bôrn'), *adj.* carried by or through the air: as, *air-borne* bacteria, *air-borne* troops.

air brake, a brake operated by the action of compressed air on a piston, as in a bus or railroad car.

air·bra·sive (âr'brā'siv), *n.* a method of preparing teeth for filling by wearing down the surface with an abrasive substance blown into the cavity by a jet of air.

air·brush (âr'brush'), *n.* a kind of atomizer operated by compressed air and used for spraying on liquid paint: also **air brush.**

AIRBRUSH

air castle, something very agreeable that one imagines but is not likely to do or get; wishful thought; daydream.

air cell, in *anatomy,* a cavity full of air.

air chamber, a cavity or compartment full of air, especially one used in hydraulics to equalize the flow of a fluid.

air coach, a commercial airplane with low passenger rates, corresponding to a railroad day coach.

air cock, a small tap or valve for letting air enter or escape from a pipe, chamber, etc.

air-con·di·tion (âr'kən-dish'ən), *v.t.* to provide with air conditioning.

air-con·di·tioned (âr'kən-dish'ənd), *adj.* having air conditioning.

air conditioning, the process of cleaning the air and controlling its humidity and temperature in buildings, cars, etc.

air-cool (âr'kōōl'), *v.t.* to cool by passing air over, into, or through.

air-cooled (âr'kōōld'), *adj.* cooled by having air passed over, into, or through it: as, an *air-cooled* engine.

Air Corps, *the earlier name for* the aviation branch of the United States Army: see **Army Air Forces.**

air·craft (âr'kraft', âr'kräft'), *n.sing. & pl.* any machine or machines for flying, whether heavier or lighter than air; airplane, dirigible, balloon, helicopter, etc.

aircraft carrier, a ship that carries aircraft, usually small airplanes, and serves as their base: it has a large, flat deck for taking off and landing.

air crew, the crew of an aircraft; in a bomber, the pilot, navigator, radio operator, bombardier, gunners, etc.: distinguished from *ground crew.*

air cushion, 1. a cushion inflated with air. 2. in *mechanics,* a device for lessening shock by means of compressed air.

air cylinder, an air-filled cylinder fitted with a piston, for absorbing or checking the recoil of a gun.

air·drome (âr'drōm'), *n.* [< *air* + Gr. *dromos,* course], [Chiefly British], 1. an airport. 2. an airfield. 3. a hangar. Also **aerodrome.**

air-dry (âr'drī'), *v.t.* [AIR-DRIED (-drīd'), AIR-DRYING], to dry by exposing to the air. *adj.* so dry as to give off no further moisture upon exposure to the air.

Aire·dale (âr'dāl'), *n.* [after *Airedale,* valley of the River *Aire* in Yorkshire, England], any of a breed of large terrier having a hard, wiry, tan coat with black markings.

AIREDALE
(24 in. high at shoulder)

air·field (âr'fēld'), *n.* a field where aircraft can take off and land.

air fleet, a fleet of aircraft, especially one for military purposes.

air-flow (âr'flō'), *adj.* 1. allowing free flow or circulation of air; hence, 2. streamlined.

air flow, a flow of air.

air·foil (âr′foil′), *n.* a part with a flat or curved surface made to be moved through the air so as to keep an aircraft up or control its movements; wing, rudder, etc. of an aircraft.
air force, 1. the aviation branch of the armed forces of a country. 2. the largest unit of this branch.
air gas, dry air charged with vapor from petroleum or some other hydrocarbon, used for lighting or heating.
air gun, a gun operated by means of compressed air.
air hole, 1. a hole that permits passage of air. 2. an unfrozen or open place in the ice on a body of water. 3. an air pocket.
air·i·ly (âr′ə-li), *adv.* in an airy or gay, light manner; jauntily; breezily.
air·i·ness (âr′i-nis), *n.* 1. the quality or state of being airy; being full of fresh air. 2. gay lightness; jauntiness.
air·ing (âr′iŋ), *n.* 1. exposure to the air, especially to outdoor air, for drying, etc. 2. exposure to public knowledge. 3. a walk or ride outdoors.
air jacket, a compartment containing air surrounding some part of a machine, especially for checking the transmission of heat.
air lane, a route for travel by air; airway.
air·less (âr′lis), *adj.* 1. without air; without fresh air. 2. without wind or breeze; still and humid.
air lift, a system of transporting troops, supplies, etc. by aircraft, as when ground routes are blocked.
air-line (âr′līn′), *adj.* 1. of an air line. 2. direct.
air line, 1. the shortest distance between two points on the earth's surface; great-circle route between two places; beeline. 2. a system of air transport. 3. an organization in the business of providing transportation by air. 4. a route for travel by air.
air liner, a large aircraft for carrying passengers.
air lock, 1. an airtight compartment, with adjustable air pressure, between places that do not have the same air pressure, as between the working compartment of a caisson and the outside. 2. a blockage, as in a water pipe, caused by an air bubble.
air mail, 1. mail transported by aircraft. 2. the system of transporting mail by aircraft.
air·man (âr′mən), *n.* [*pl.* AIRMEN (-mən)], 1. an aviator. 2. an enlisted man or woman in the U.S. Air Force.
air mass, in *meteorology,* a large body of air having virtually uniform conditions of temperature and moisture in a horizontal cross section.
Air Medal, a United States military decoration awarded for heroism or meritorious service while participating in an aerial flight: instituted 1942.
air-mind·ed (âr′mīn′did), *adj.* aware of and interested in aviation, aircraft, etc.
air·om·e·ter (âr-om′ə-tẽr), *n.* [*airo-* (for *aero-*) + *-meter*], 1. a gauge for measuring the speed of the movement of air. 2. a gasometer. Also **air meter.**
air passage, 1. a passage or space with air in it, or through which air can pass. 2. a leakage of air. 3. a journey by air. 4. accommodations for such a journey.
air·plane (âr′plān′), *n.* [altered, after *air*, from earlier *aeroplane*], an aircraft that is kept aloft by the aerodynamic forces of air upon its wings and is driven forward by a screw propeller or by other means, as jet propulsion: also **aeroplane:** see TYPES OF AIRPLANE, p. 32.

AIRPLANE

airplane cloth, 1. a strong, plain-weave cloth, originally of linen but later of cotton, used for airplane wings. 2. a similar cotton cloth used for clothes.
airplane spin, in *wrestling,* a hold in which an opponent is lifted up and spun around before being thrown.
air plant, a plant that grows on the trunk or branches of another plant, but not as a parasite, and gets nourishment from the air and the rain; epiphyte.
air pocket, an atmospheric condition that causes an aircraft to make sudden, short drops while in flight.
air·port (âr′pôrt′), *n.* a place where aircraft can land and take off, usually equipped with hangars, facilities for refueling and repair, various accommodations for passengers, etc.

AIRPORT

air pressure, the pressure of atmospheric or compressed air.
air·proof (âr′pro͞of′), *adj.* not penetrable by air. *v.t.* to make airproof.
air pump, a machine for removing or compressing air or for forcing it through something.
air raid, an attack by aircraft, usually bombers.
air-raid shelter (âr′rād′), a cellar, structure, etc. for protection during an air raid.
air-raid warden, a person responsible for various tasks in an air raid, as warning people, directing traffic, etc.
air rifle, a rifle operated by compressed air: it usually shoots small pellets.
air sac, an air-filled space in a bird's body: the air sacs have connections to the lungs.
air·scape (âr′skāp′), *n.* [*air* + land*scape*], a view of the earth from a high position, as from an aircraft.
air shaft, a passage through which fresh air can enter a tunnel, mine, etc.: also **air well.**
air·ship (âr′ship′), *n.* 1. any self-propelled aircraft that is lighter than air and can be steered; dirigible. 2. occasionally, an airplane.
air·sick (âr′sik′), *adj.* sick or nauseated because of traveling by air.
air space, 1. a space with air in it. 2. the amount of breathable air in a room or building. 3. space for maneuvering an aircraft flying in formation.
air speed, the speed of an aircraft determined by its relationship to the air rather than the ground.
air-sprayed (âr′sprād′), *adj.* sprayed by means of compressed air.
air spring, a spring or shock absorber that operates by the elasticity of air.
air·strip (âr′strip′), *n.* an airfield, usually for temporary use, consisting of one or more runways made of prepared metal mats, gravel, etc.
airt (ârt), *n.* [< Gael. *aird*, height, direction], [Scot.], any of the cardinal points of the compass; direction. *v.t.* [Scot.], to guide or direct.
air·tight (âr′tīt′), *adj.* 1. too tight for air or gas to enter or escape; hence, 2. giving no opening for attack: as, an *airtight* alibi.
air valve, a valve by which the entrance or escape of air can be regulated.
air vesicle, in *botany,* a space filled with air, found in many water plants.
air·way (âr′wā′), *n.* 1. an air shaft. 2. an air lane.
the airways, in *radio,* the air; broadcasting.
air·wom·an (âr′woom′ən), *n.* [*pl.* AIRWOMEN (-wim′in)], a woman flyer.
air·wor·thy (âr′wũr′*th*i), *adj.* fit to be flown: said of aircraft.
air·y (âr′i), *adj.* [AIRIER (-i-ẽr), AIRIEST (-i-ist)], 1. in the air; high up. 2. of air. 3. open to the air; breezy. 4. unsubstantial as air; visionary. 5. light as air; delicate; graceful. 6. light-hearted; vivacious; gay. 7. characterized by levity; flippant. 8. [Colloq.], putting on airs; affected.
A·i·sha (ä′i-shä′), *n.* Mohammed's favorite wife; lived 611–678 A.D.: also spelled **Ayesha, Ayeshah.**
aisle (īl), *n.* [ME.; OFr. *aile, ele*, wing (of a building) < L. *ala*, a wing; Eng. *-s-* through confusion with *isle*], 1. a part of a church alongside the nave, choir, or transept, set off by a row of columns, pillars, or piers. 2. a passageway between rows of seats. 3. a narrow passageway or corridor, as between rows of trees, etc.
aisled (īld), *adj.* having an aisle or aisles.
Aisne (ān), *n.* a river in northern France, flowing into the Oise: length, 170 mi.
aitch (āch), *n.* [*pl.* AITCHES (-iz)], [ME. & OFr. *ache*; LL. **accha, aha*; combination of primary vowel (ä) with consonantal symbols intended to exemplify the former quality of the sound], H or h. *adj.* shaped like an H.
aitch·bone (āch′bōn′), *n.* [by faulty separation of ME. *a nache bone;* OFr. *nache*, buttock; L. **natica* < *natis*, buttock], 1. the rump bone. 2. the cut of meat around the rump bone. Also called *edgebone.*
Aix (āks; Fr. eks), *n.* a city in southern France, near Marseilles: pop., 46,000 (1946).
Aix-la-Cha·pelle (āks′lä-sha-pel′; Fr. eks′lä′shȧ′pel′), *n.* Aachen: the French name.
A·jac·cio (ä-yä′chô), *n.* the capital of Corsica: pop., 37,000: birthplace of Napoleon.
a·jar (ə-jär′), *adv. & adj.* [ME. *on char, a-char;* AS. *cyrr*, a turn; see CHORE], slightly open, as a door.
a·jar (ə-jär′), *adv. & adj.* [*a-*, on + *jar*, *v.*], not in harmony.
A·jax (ā′jaks), *n.* [L.; Gr. *Aias*], in Homer's *Iliad*, 1. a strong, brave Greek warrior who killed himself when Achilles' armor was given to Odysseus: called *Ajax Telamon.* 2. one of the swiftest runners among the Greek warriors: called *Ajax the Less.*
Aj·mer (uj-mêr′), *n.* a state of northwestern India: area, 2,400 sq. mi.; pop., 584,000 (est. 1950).
Aj·mer-Mer·wa·ra (uj-mêr′mer-wä′rä), *n.* a former province of northwest central India: since 1950, included in Rajasthan state: area, 2,400 sq. mi.
a k a, also known as: used before an alias, as in police records: as, George Desmond *a k a* George Destry.
Ak·bar (ak′bär), *n.* Mogul emperor of Hindustan (1556–1605); lived 1542–1605.
a·kene (ā-kēn′), *n.* an achene.

TYPES OF AIRPLANE

STRINGFELLOW'S AIRPLANE (1848)

LANGLEY'S AIRPLANE (1903)

WRIGHT BROTHERS' BIPLANE (1903)

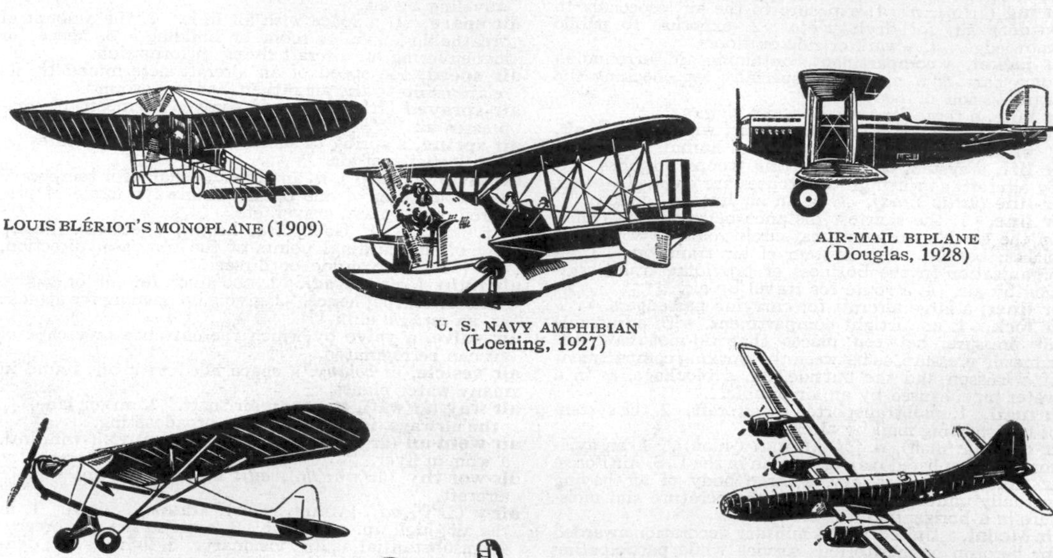

LOUIS BLÉRIOT'S MONOPLANE (1909)

AIR-MAIL BIPLANE
(Douglas, 1928)

U. S. NAVY AMPHIBIAN
(Loening, 1927)

LIGHT MONOPLANE
(Piper Cub, 1940)

MEDIUM BOMBER
(B-25 Mitchell, 1940)

HEAVY BOMBER
(B-29 Superfortress, 1940)

FLYING BOAT
(Martin Mars, 1940)

SINGLE-ENGINE FIGHTER
(P-40 War Hawk, 1940)

TWIN-ENGINE FIGHTER
(P-38 Lightning, 1940)

GLIDER (1942)

HELICOPTER (1944)

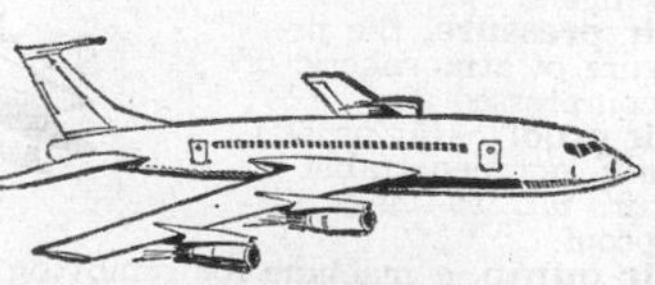

JET-PROPELLED AIRLINER
(Boeing 707, 1959)

A·khe·na·ten, A·khe·na·ton (ä′ke-nä′t′n), *n.* see **Amenhotep** (sense 2).
a·kim·bo (ə-kim′bō), *adv. & adj.* [ME. *in kenebowe*, lit., in keen bow, i.e., in a sharp curve; a folk etym. from ON. *kengboginn*, bow-bent < *keng*, bent + *bogi*, a bow], with hands on hips and elbows bent outward: as, with arms *akimbo*.
a·kin (ə-kin′), *adj.* [*a-*, of + *kin*], 1. of one kin; related. 2. having similar qualities; similar.
A·kins, Zoë (ā′kinz), 1886–1958; American writer.
Ak·kad (ak′ad, äk′äd), *n.* 1. an ancient country north of Babylonia. 2. its chief city. 3. a native or inhabitant of ancient Akkad. 4. any of several Semitic dialects spoken by the Akkads. *adj.* Akkadian. Also spelled **Accad.**
Ak·ka·di·an (ə-kā′di-ən, ə-kä′di-ən), *adj.* 1. of ancient Akkad, its people, or its culture. 2. of the Semitic dialects spoken by the Akkads. *n.* Akkad (in senses 3 & 4).
Ak·ron (ak′rən), *n.* a city in northern Ohio: center of rubber manufacturing: pop., 290,000.
Ak·sum (äk′soom), *n.* an ancient capital of Ethiopia: also spelled **Axum.**
al- (al), [< Ar. *al*], a prefix meaning *the*, used to make a noun definite, as in *algebra, alchemy*.
al- (al, əl), ad-: used before *l*, as in *alliteration*.
-al (əl), [Fr. *-al, -el;* L. *-alis*], 1. an adjective-forming suffix meaning *of, like*, or *suitable for*, as in *comical, hysterical, theatrical*. 2. a suffix of nouns which were originally adjectives, as, *perennial, annual*, or of nouns formed by analogy with these. 3. [ME. *-aile;* OFr. *-aille;* L. *-alia*, neut. pl. of *-alis*], a suffix meaning *the act or process of*, used in nouns formed from verbs, as *avowal*.
-al (al, əl) [< *al*dehyde], in *chemistry*, a suffix signifying *the presence of the aldehydes*, as in *chloral*.
Al, in *chemistry*, aluminum.
al., [L.], 1. *alii*, other persons. 2. *alia*, other things.
A.L., 1. American Legion. 2. American League.
a·la (ā′lə), *n.* [*pl.* ALAE (-lē)], [L., a wing], 1. in *anatomy & zoology*, *a*) a wing. *b*) a winglike structure, as a lobe of the ear. 2. in *botany*, *a*) one of the side petals of a butterfly-shaped corolla. *b*) a thin wing on some seeds.
à la (ä′lä, ä′lə; Fr. à là), [Fr.], 1. to the. 2. in the. 3. at the. 4. in the manner or style of. 5. according to.
Ala., Alabama.
A.L.A., American Library Association.
Al·a·bam·a (al′ə-bam′ə), *n.* 1. a Southern State of the United States: area, 51,609 sq. mi.; pop., 3,267,000; capital, Montgomery: nicknamed *Cotton State:* abbreviated **Ala.** 2. a river flowing through Alabama into Mobile Bay: length, 312 mi.
Al·a·bam·i·an (al′ə-bam′i-ən), *adj.* of Alabama. *n.* a native or inhabitant of Alabama.
al·a·bam·ine (al′ə-bam′ēn, al′ə-bam′in), *n.* [*Alabama* + *-ine*], a name given to chemical element 85, supposedly found in monazite sands in 1931: symbol, Ab: cf. **astatine.**
al·a·bas·ter (al′ə-bas′tẽr), *n.* [ME. & OFr. *alabastre;* L. *alabaster;* Gr. *alabastros* < name of Egypt. town], 1. a translucent, whitish, fine-grained variety of gypsum, used for statues, vases, etc. 2. a semitranslucent, hard variety of calcite sometimes banded like marble. *adj.* of or like alabaster; hard, white, etc.
al·a·bas·trine (al′ə-bas′trin), *adj.* [Gr. *alabastrinos*], of or like alabaster.
‡**à la bonne heure** (à′là′bôn′ẽr′), [Fr., lit., at the good hour], well and good; well done!
à la carte (ä′lə kärt′; Fr. à′là′kàrt′), [Fr.], by the bill of fare; with a separate price for each item on the menu: opposed to *table d'hôte*.
a·lack (ə-lak′), *interj.* [*ah* + *lack*], [Archaic], an exclamation of regret, surprise, dismay, etc.
a·lack·a·day (ə-lak′ə-dā′), *interj.* [for earlier *alack the day*, woe to the day], [Archaic], alack.
‡**à la cré·ole** (à′là′krā′ôl′), [Fr., after the fashion of the Creoles], prepared with tomatoes and highly seasoned.
a·lac·ri·tous (ə-lak′rə-təs), *adj.* showing alacrity.
a·lac·ri·ty (ə-lak′rə-ti), *n.* [Fr. *alacrité;* L. *alacritas*, liveliness < *alacer*, lively], 1. quick willingness; eager readiness. 2. quick, lively action; briskness.
A·la Dagh (ä′lä däkh′), 1. a mountain chain of the Taurus Range, southern Turkey: highest peak, c. 11,000 ft. 2. a mountain of the Elburz Range, northeastern Iran: height, 10,000 ft.
A·lad·din (ə-lad′′n), *n.* a boy in *The Arabian Nights* who found a magic lamp and a magic ring: by rubbing these he could call up a jinni to do whatever he asked.
‡**à la fran·çaise** (à′là′frän′sez′), [Fr.], in the French manner.
A·la·goz (ä′lä-göz′), *n.* a volcano in the Armenian S.S.R.: height, 13,435 ft.
A·lai Mountains (ä-lī′), two mountain ranges in the southern Kirghiz S.S.R.: highest peak, 18,000 ft.
‡**à la jar·di·nière** (à′là′zhàr′dē′nyâr′), [Fr., with garden products], made up with vegetables cut up into cubes.
‡**à la ju·lienne** (à′là′zhü′lyen′), [Fr.; see JULIENNE], cut into thin strips, as fried potatoes, cheese, etc.
à la king (ä′lä kiŋ′, ä′lə kiŋ′), [lit., in kingly style], served in a sauce containing diced mushrooms, pimentos, and green peppers.
‡**à la ly·on·naise** (à′là′lyô′nez′), [Fr., in the manner of *Lyons*, France], fried with sliced onions.
Al·a·man·ni (al′ə-man′ī), *n.pl.* Germanic tribes which invaded and settled in Alsace and part of Switzerland in the early 5th century A.D.: they were conquered by Clovis in 496 A.D.: also spelled **Alemanni.**
Al·a·man·nic (al′ə-man′ik), *adj.* Alemannic.
Al·a·me·da (al′ə-mē′də, al′ə-mā′də), *n.* a city on San Francisco Bay, California: pop., 64,000.
al·a·me·da (al′ə-mā′də), *n.* [Sp. < *álamo*, poplar tree], a walk that is shaded, especially by alamos.
Al·a·mo (al′ə-mō′), *n.* a Franciscan mission at San Antonio, Texas: scene of a siege and massacre of Texans by Mexican troops (1836).
al·a·mo (al′ə-mō′, ä′lə-mō′), *n.* [*pl.* ALAMOS (-mōz′)], [Sp. *álamo*, poplar tree], 1. a poplar tree. 2. a cottonwood tree.
a·la·mode (ä′lə-mōd′, al′ə-mōd′), *adj.* [Fr. *à la mode*], 1. in the fashion; stylish. 2. made or served in a certain style, as pie with ice cream, or beef braised and prepared with vegetables in sauce. Also **à la mode, a la mode.** *n.* a thin, shiny silk.
Al·a·mo·gor·do (al′ə-mə-gôr′dō), *n.* a city in southern New Mexico: pop., 22,000.
‡**à la mort** (à′là′môr′; *often Anglicized to* al′ə-môrt′), [Fr., lit., to the death], 1. very ill, almost to the point of death; hence, 2. dejected; depressed; melancholy. 3. mortally.
Al·an (al′ən), [ML. *Alanus*, of Breton origin], a masculine name: variants, *Allan, Allen*.
Al·an-a-dale (al′ən-ə-dāl′), *n.* Allan-a-dale.
A·land Islands (ô′lənd, ä′lənd), a group of islands at the entrance to the Gulf of Bothnia: area, 572 sq. mi.; pop., 22,000.
à la New·burg (ä′lə nōō′bẽrg, ä′lä nū′bẽrg), [Fr. *à la;* + *Newburg*, after *Newburgh*, Scotland], served in a sauce of creamed egg yolks, wine, and butter.
‡**à la l'an·glaise** (à′län′glez′), [Fr.], in the English manner.
a·lar (ā′lẽr), *adj.* [L. *alaris* < *ala*, a wing], 1. of a wing; of an ala. 2. having wings or alae. 3. winglike; wing-shaped. 4. in *anatomy*, axillary.
A·lar·cón, Pe·dro An·to·ni·o de (pe′drô än-tô′ni-ô de ä′lär-kôn′), 1833–1891; Spanish writer.
Al·a·ric (al′ə-rik), *n.* king of the Visigoths; lived 370?-410 A.D.; conquered Rome (410 A.D.).
a·larm (ə-lärm′), *n.* [ME.; OFr. *alarme;* It. *all'arme*, to arms], 1. a sudden call to arms. 2. a warning of danger. 3. a mechanism designed to warn of danger or of trespassing of any sort: as, a burglar *alarm*. 4. the bell or buzzer of an alarm clock. 5. fear caused by the sudden realization of danger. 6. in *fencing*, a quick stamp on the ground with the advancing foot. *v.t.* 1. to warn of approaching danger. 2. to make suddenly afraid or anxious; frighten. —*SYN.* see **fear, frighten.**
alarm clock, a clock with a bell or buzzer that can be made to sound at whatever time one wishes by setting the mechanism beforehand.
a·larmed (ə-lärmd′), *adj.* [pp. of *alarm*], 1. roused to action or watchfulness. 2. suddenly made afraid or apprehensive; frightened.
a·larm·ing (ə-lär′miŋ), *adj.* [ppr. of *alarm*], that alarms; making suddenly afraid or apprehensive; frightening.
a·larm·ist (ə-lär′mist), *n.* 1. a person who habitually spreads alarming rumors, exaggerated reports of danger, etc. 2. a person easily frightened and likely to anticipate the worst. *adj.* of or like an alarmist.
a·lar·um (ə-lâr′əm, ə-lär′əm), *n.* [Archaic or Poetic], alarm.
a·la·ry (ā′lə-ri, al′ə-ri), *adj.* [L. *alarius* < *ala*, a wing], 1. of a wing or wings; alar. 2. shaped like a wing.
a·las (ə-las′, ə-läs′), *interj.* [ME. < OFr. *a las; a*, ah + *las*, wretched < L. *lassus*, weary], an exclamation expressing sorrow, pity, regret, or apprehensive fear.
A·las·ka (ə-las′kə), *n.* a State of the United States in northwestern North America, separated from Asia by the Bering Strait: bought from Russia in 1867; a Territory from 1912 to 1958: area, 586,400 sq. mi.; pop., 226,000; capital, Juneau: abbreviated **Alas.**
Alaska Highway, a highway built in 1942 by the United States and Canada, extending from British Columbia, Canada to Fairbanks, Alaska, in order to supply American troops in Alaska: length, 1,671 mi.: bought by Canada; popular name, **Alcan Highway.**
A·las·kan (ə-las′kən), *adj.* of Alaska. *n.* a native or inhabitant of Alaska.
Alaska Range, a mountain range in southern Alaska: highest peak, Mt. McKinley, 20,300 ft.
a·late (ā′lāt), *adj.* [L. *alatus* < *ala*, a wing], having wings or winglike attachments.
a·lat·ed (ā′lā-tid), *adj.* alate.

alb (alb), *n.* [ME.; AS., white garment < L. *albus*, white], a long, white linen robe with sleeves tapering to the wrist, worn by a priest at Mass.

ALB

Alb., 1. Albania. 2. Albanian. 3. Albany. 4. Alberta (Canadian province).

al·ba (äl′bə, al′bə), *n.* [Pr., dawn < L. *albus*, white], the conventionalized morning song of Provençal troubadour literature, a lyric in which a lover voices regret at parting from his beloved; aubade.

Al·ba, Duke of (äl′bä), see **Alva,** Duke of.

Alba., Alberta (Canadian province).

al·ba·core (al′bə-kôr′, al′bə-kōr′), *n.* [*pl.* ALBACORES (-kôrz′, -kōrz′), ALBACORE; see PLURAL, II, D, 1], [Port. < Ar. *al*, the + *bukr*, young camel], any of a number of related salt-water fishes of the mackerel family, including the tunny, the bonito, etc.

Al·ba Lon·ga (al′bə lôŋ′gə), an ancient city in Italy, near Rome: supposed birthplace of Romulus and Remus.

Al·ban (ôl′bən, al′bən), [L. *Albanus* < *Alba*, name of several Italian cities], a masculine name.

Alban, Saint, 3d century A.D.; British martyr.

Al·ba·ni·a (al-bā′ni-ə, al-bān′yə), *n.* a country in the western Balkan Peninsula: area, 10,629 sq. mi.; pop., 1,391,000; capital, Tirana; occupied by Italy and Germany (1939–1944): abbreviated **Alb.**

Al·ba·ni·an (al-bā′ni-ən, al-bān′yən), *adj.* of Albania, its people, language, etc. *n.* 1. a native or inhabitant of Albania. 2. the language of the Albanians. Abbreviated **Alb.**

Al·ba·ny (ôl′bə-ni), *n.* 1. the capital of New York, on the Hudson: pop., 130,000. 2. a city in southwestern Georgia: pop., 56,000.

al·ba·ta (al-bā′tə), *n.* [fem. form of pp. of *albare*, to make white < *albus*, white], a silvery alloy of copper, zinc, and nickel.

al·ba·tross (al′bə-trôs′, al′bə-tros′), *n.* [*pl.* ALBATROSSES (-iz), ALBATROSS; see PLURAL, II, D, 1], [altered, prob. after L. *albus*, white < Sp. *alcatraz*, lit., pelican; Port., pelican, orig. bucket; Ar. *al qādūs*, water container < Gr. *kados*, cask, jar; prob. of Sem. origin], any of several large, web-footed birds related to the petrel and found chiefly in the South Seas: they have long, narrow wings and a large, hooked beak in which, like the pelican, they were formerly reputed to carry water.

ALBATROSS (30 in. long)

al·be·it (ôl-bē′it), *conj.* [ME. *al be it*, al(though) it be], although; even though.

Al·be·marle Sound (al′bə-märl′), an arm of the Atlantic, c. 55 mi. long, extending into North Carolina.

Al·bé·niz, Isaac (äl-bā′nith; Sp. äl-bā′nēth), 1860–1909; Spanish composer and pianist.

Al·ber·ich (äl′ber-iH), *n.* [G. < MHG. *alb*, elf + *rich* (OHG. *rihhi*), leader, king, realm], in *German legend*, the king of the dwarfs and leader of the Nibelungs.

Al·bert (al′bẽrt), [Fr.; OHG. *Adalbrecht*, lit., bright through nobility < *adal*, nobility + *beraht*, bright], a masculine name: variants, *Adelbert, Elbert;* feminine, *Alberta, Albertine;* diminutives, *Al, Bert.*

Albert I, 1875–1934; king of the Belgians (1909–1934).

Albert, Prince, 1819–1861; Prince of Saxe-Coburg-Gotha and husband of Queen Victoria of England.

Al·ber·ta (al-bũr′tə), [fem. of *Albert*], a feminine name: variants, *Albertina, Albertine. n.* a province of southwestern Canada: area, 255,285 sq. mi.; pop. 1,123,000: capital, Edmonton: abbreviated **Alta., Alb., Alba.**

Al·ber·ti, Le·on Bat·tis·ta (le-ôn′ bät-tēs′tä äl-ber′tē), 1404–1472; Italian architect; known for his churches.

Al·ber·ti·na (al′bẽr-tē′nə), a feminine name: see **Alberta.**

Al·ber·tine (al′bẽr-tēn′), a feminine name: see **Alberta.**

al·bert·ite (al′bẽr-tīt′), *n.* [after the county of *Albert*, New Brunswick, where it is found], a bituminous, asphaltlike mineral.

Albert Memorial, a monument to Prince Albert of England in Kensington Gardens, London.

Albert Ny·an·za (ni-an′zə, ni-an′zə), a lake in Uganda, Africa: area, 1,640 sq. mi.: also called *Lake Albert.*

Al·ber·tus Mag·nus, Saint (al-bũr′təs mag′nəs), (*Albert von Bollstadt*), 1193?–1280; Bavarian scholastic philosopher: called the *Universal Doctor.*

al·bes·cence (al-bes′′ns), *n.* the quality or condition of being albescent.

al·bes·cent (al-bes′′nt), *adj.* [L. *albescens*, ppr. of *albescere*, to become white < *albus*, white], turning white.

Al·bi·gen·ses (al′bi-jen′sēz), *n.pl.* [ML., after *Albi*, town in southern France], a religious sect that flourished in the south of France c. 1020–1250 A.D. and was finally suppressed for heresy.

Al·bi·gen·si·an (al′bi-jen′si-ən), *adj.* of the Albigenses. *n.* any member of the Albigenses.

al·bin·ic (al-bin′ik), *adj.* of or having albinism.

al·bi·nism (al′bə-niz′m), *n.* lack of normal coloration in a person, animal, or plant; state of being an albino.

al·bi·no (al-bī′nō), *n.* [*pl.* ALBINOS (-nōz)], [Port., lit., whitish < *albo;* L. *albus*, white], 1. a person whose skin, hair, and eyes lack normal coloration: albinos have a white skin, whitish hair, and pink eyes. 2. any animal or plant abnormally lacking in color.

Al·bi·on (al′bi-ən), *n.* [L. < Gaul.; understood as if < L. *albus*, white: the cliffs of southern England are white], [Poetic], England.

al·bite (al′bīt), *n.* [L. *albus*, white; + *-ite*], a sodium-bearing, whitish mineral, $NaAlSi_3O_8$, of the feldspar family, with vitreous luster and good cleavage.

Al·bo·in (al′boin, al′bō-in), *n.* first ruler (565?–573? A.D.) of the kingdom of Lombardy; died 573? A.D.

al·bu·gin·e·ous (al′byoo-jin′i-əs), *adj.* [< L. *albugo*, white spot], of or resembling the white of the eye.

al·bum (al′bəm), *n.* [L., neut. of *albus*, white], 1. a bound or loose-leaf book with blank pages for mounting pictures, clippings, stamps, etc., or collecting autographs. 2. a booklike holder for phonograph records. 3. a set of phonograph records in such a holder. 4. a single, long-playing record containing a number of musical pieces.

al·bu·men (al-bū′mən), *n.* [L. < *albus*, white], 1. the white of an egg. 2. the nutritive protein substance in germinating plant and animal cells. 3. [Rare], an albumin.

al·bu·men·ize (al-bū′mən-īz′), *v.t.* [ALBUMENIZED (-īzd′), ALBUMENIZING], to cover or treat with albumen or an albuminous solution.

al·bu·min (al-bū′min), *n.* [Fr. *albumin;* L. *albumen*, white of egg < *albus*, white], any of a class of complex proteins found in milk, egg, muscle, blood, and in many vegetable tissues and fluids: albumins are soluble in water, coagulated by heat, and consist of carbon, hydrogen, nitrogen, oxygen, and sulfur: formerly called *albumen.*

al·bu·mi·nate (al-bū′mi-nāt′), *n.* a compound of an albumin with an acid or base.

al·bu·mi·noid (al-bū′mi-noid′), *adj.* resembling albumin. *n.* 1. protein. 2. any of the scleroproteins, a group of simple proteins including keratin and collagen, characterized by insolubility.

al·bu·mi·nose (al-bū′mi-nōs′), *adj.* albuminous.

al·bu·mi·nous (al-bū′mi-nəs), *adj.* of, like, or containing albumin or albumen.

al·bu·mi·nu·ri·a (al-bū′mi-nyoor′i-ə), *n.* [*albumin* + *-uria*], the presence of albumin in the urine.

al·bu·mose (al′byoo-mōs′), *n.* [*albumin* + *-ose*], any of a class of chemical compounds derived from albumins by the action of certain enzymes.

Al·bu·quer·que (al′bə-kũr′ki, al′bə-kũr′ki, al′byoo-kũr′ki), *n.* city in central New Mexico: pop., 201,000.

Al·bu·quer·que, Af·fon·so de (ə-fōn′soo də äl′boo-ker′kə), 1453–1515; Portuguese navigator and conqueror in the East Indies.

al·bur·num (al-bũr′nəm), *n.* [L., neut. of *alburnus*, whitish < *albus*, white], the soft, light-colored, young wood between the inner bark and the heartwood of a tree or shrub; sapwood.

BARK
ALBURNUM
HEARTWOOD

ALBURNUM

alc-. Some words beginning *alc-* are also spelled *alk-.*

Al·cae·us (al-sē′əs), *n.* Greek lyric poet; 620–580 B.C.

Al·ca·ic (al-kā′ik), *adj.* [L. *Alcaicus;* Gr. *Alkaikos* <*Alkaios*, Alcaeus], 1. of, characteristic of, or by Alcaeus. 2. of or like his poetry; in either of his two characteristic meters, the *greater Alcaic* and the *lesser. n. usually pl.* verse by Alcaeus or in his metrical patterns: he wrote four-stanza odes, with four lines to a stanza and four feet to a line.

al·caide (al-kād′; Sp. äl-kä′ē-*the*), *n.* [Sp.; Ar. *al qā′īd*, the leader < *qāda*, to lead], 1. a commander or governor of a Spanish fortress. 2. a jailer or warden of a Spanish prison. Also spelled **alcayde.**

al·cal·de (al-kal′di; Sp. äl-käl′de), *n.* [Sp.; Ar. *al-qādi*, the judge < *qada*, to judge], the mayor of a Spanish town, who has judicial powers and functions as well as administrative.

Al·can Highway (al′kan), Alaska Highway.

Al·ca·traz (al′kə-traz′, al′kə-traz′), *n.* a small island in San Francisco Bay: site of a Federal prison.

al·cayde (al-kād′; Sp. äl-kä′ē-*the*), *n.* an alcaide.

al·caz·ar (al-kaz′ẽr, al′kə-zär′; Sp. äl-kä′thär), *n.* [Sp. *alcázar* < Ar. *al-qasr*, the castle], 1. a palace or fortress of the Moors in Spain. 2. [A-], a palace in Seville, Spain, first used by the Moorish rulers and later by the Spanish kings.

Al·ces·tis (al-ses'tis), *n.* [L.; Gr. *Alkēstis*], in *Greek legend*, the wife of Admetus, king of Thessaly, and heroine of a play by Euripides: she offered her life to save that of her husband, but was rescued from Hades by Hercules.

alchem., alchemy.

al·chem·ic (al-kem'ik), *adj.* of or like alchemy.

al·che·mist (al'kə-mist), *n.* a practitioner of alchemy.

al·che·mize (al'kə-mīz'), *v.t.* [ALCHEMIZED (-mīzd'), ALCHEMIZING], to transmute by or as by alchemy.

al·che·my (al'kə-mi), *n.* [OFr. *alchimie;* ML. *alchemia;* Ar. *al-kīmiyā;* ? < Gr. *chymeia* < *cheein*, to pour], 1. the chemistry of the Middle Ages, the chief aims of which were to change the baser metals into gold and to discover the elixir of perpetual youth: abbreviated **alchem.** 2. a method or power of transmutation; seemingly miraculous change of one thing into another.

Al·ci·bi·a·des (al'sə-bī'ə-dēz'), *n.* Athenian politician and general in the Peloponnesian War; lived c. 450–404 B.C.

Al·ci·des (al-sī'dēz), *n.* [L.; Gr. *Alkeidēs*], Hercules.

al·ci·dine (al'si-dīn', al'si-din), *adj.* [Mod. L. *alcidinus* < *Alcidae*, name of the family of birds; see AUK], belonging to a family of diving birds that have a stocky body, short tail and wings, and webbed feet, as the puffins, murres, etc.

Alc·me·ne (alk-mē'ni), *n.* [L.; Gr. *Alkmēnē*], in *Greek mythology*, the mother of Hercules: see **Amphitryon.**

al·co·hol (al'kə-hôl', al'kə-hol'), *n.* [ML. < Ar. *al kohl*, powder of antimony: the change of meaning occurred in European usage], 1. a colorless, volatile, pungent liquid, C_2H_5OH; grain alcohol; ethyl alcohol; ethanol: it can be burnt as fuel, is used in industry and medicine, and is the intoxicating ingredient in whisky, gin, rum, and other fermented or distilled liquors. 2. any intoxicating liquor with this liquid in it. 3. the drinking of such liquors. 4. any of a series of organic compounds the simplest of which are like ethyl alcohol in construction, as methyl alcohol (or wood alcohol), CH_3OH, a very poisonous liquid, and amyl alcohol, $C_5H_{11}OH$, found in fusel oil: all alcohols contain a hydroxyl group and form esters in reactions with organic acids.

al·co·hol·ic (al'kə-hôl'ik, al'kə-hol'ik), *adj.* 1. of alcohol. 2. containing alcohol. 3. caused by alcohol or liquor containing it. 4. suffering from alcoholism. *n.* a person who has chronic alcoholism or is excessively addicted to alcoholic liquor.

al·co·hol·i·cal·ly (al'kə-hôl'i-k'l-i, al'kə-hol'ik-li), *adv.* in an alcoholic manner.

al·co·hol·ic·i·ty (al'kə-hôl-is'ə-ti, al'kə-hol-is'ə-ti), *n.* the quality or state of being alcoholic.

al·co·hol·ism (al'kə-hôl'iz'm, al'kə-hol'iz'm), *n.* 1. a diseased condition caused by habitually drinking too much alcoholic liquor: often **chronic alcoholism.** 2. alcohol poisoning.

al·co·hol·ize (al'kə-hôl-īz', al'kə-hol-īz'), *v.t.* [ALCOHOLIZED (-īzd'), ALCOHOLIZING], 1. to saturate or treat with alcohol. 2. to convert into alcohol.

al·co·hol·om·e·ter (al'kə-hôl-om'ə-tẽr, al'kə-hol-om'ə-tẽr), *n.* [see ALCOHOL & -METER], an instrument for determining the percentage of alcohol in a liquor.

Al·co·ran (al'kō-rän', al'kō-ran'), *n.* [Fr.; Ar. *al qur'ān;* see KORAN], the Koran.

Al·cott, Amos Bron·son (bron'sən ôl'kət), 1799–1888; American philosopher and educational reformer.

Alcott, Louisa May, 1832–1888; daughter of *Amos Bronson;* American novelist.

al·cove (al'kōv), *n.* [Fr.; Sp. *alcoba;* Ar. *al-qobbah; al*, the + *qobbah*, an arch, vault, dome], 1. a recessed section of a room, as a breakfast nook. 2. a secluded bower in a garden; summerhouse.

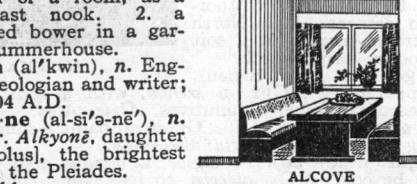

ALCOVE

Al·cuin (al'kwin), *n.* English theologian and writer; 735–804 A.D.

Al·cy·o·ne (al-sī'ə-nē'), *n.* [L.; Gr. *Alkyonē*, daughter of Aeolus], the brightest star in the Pleiades.

Ald., Alderman.

Al·da, Frances (äl'də), (born *Frances Davis*), 1885–1952; American operatic soprano, born in New Zealand.

Al·dan (äl-dän'), *n.* a river in the Yakutsk A.S.S.R., flowing into the Lena River: length, c. 1,300 mi.

Al·deb·a·ran (al-deb'ə-rən), *n.* [Ar. *al-dabarān; al*, the + *dabarān*, following < *dabar*, to follow], a brilliant-red star in the constellation Taurus.

al·de·hyde (al'də-hīd'), *n.* [< *alcohol* + Mod. L. *dehydrogenatum* < L. *de*, without; + *hydrogen*], 1. a colorless, volatile fluid, CH_3CHO, with a strong, unpleasant odor, obtained from alcohol by oxidation. 2. any of a class of such organic compounds.

Al·den, John (ôl'dən), 1599?–1687; Pilgrim settler of Plymouth Colony: character in Longfellow's poem "The Courtship of Miles Standish."

al·der (ôl'dẽr), *n.* [ME. *aler;* AS. *alor;* IE. base **el-* (cf. ELM); prob. akin to **elu-*, yellow], any of a small group of trees and shrubs of the birch family, having toothed leaves and woody cones, and growing in cool, moist soil in temperate climates: the bark is used in dyeing and tanning and the wood for bridges and piles because it resists underwater rot.

al·der·man (ôl'dẽr-mən), *n.* [*pl.* ALDERMEN (-mən)], [AS. *ealdorman; ealdor*, chief, prince < *eald*, old + *man*], 1. in many cities, a municipal officer representing, ordinarily, a certain district or ward: abbreviated **Ald., Aldm.** (as a title). 2. in England and Ireland, one of the senior members of the municipal or borough council. 3. in *Anglo-Saxon history*, the chief officer in a shire.

al·der·man·cy (ôl'dẽr-mən-si), *n.* [*pl.* ALDERMANCIES (-siz)], the position or term of office of an alderman.

al·der·man·ic (ôl'dẽr-man'ik), *adj.* of, like, or fit for an alderman.

Al·der·ney (ôl'dẽr-ni), *n.* 1. one of the Channel Islands of Great Britain: area, 3 sq. mi.; pop., 1,500. 2. [*pl.* ALDERNEYS (-niz)], any of a breed of small dairy cattle originally from this island.

Al·der·shot (ôl'dẽr-shot'), *n.* a town in Hampshire, England: pop., 36,000: site of an army training camp.

Al·dine (ôl'dīn, ôl'dēn), *adj.* [*Ald*us + *-ine*], from the press of Aldus Manutius and his family, who published fine editions of the classics (c. 1494–1597) at Venice and Rome. *n.* an Aldine book, edition, or type.

al·dose (al'dōs), *n.* [*ald*ehyde + *-ose*], in *chemistry*, any sugar containing the aldehyde group.

Al·drich, Thomas Bai·ley (bā'li ôl'drich), 1836–1907; American poet and novelist.

ale (āl), *n.* [ME. *ale;* AS. *ealu;* IE. base **alu-*, bitter; cf. ALUM], a fermented drink made from malt and hops: it is like beer but contains more alcohol and undecomposed sugar.

a·le·a·to·ry (ā'li-ə-tôr'i, ā'li-ə-tō'ri), *adj.* [L. *aleatorius*, of gambling < *aleator*, gambler < *alea*, chance, a dice game], of or depending on chance or luck.

A·lec·to (ə-lek'tō), *n.* [L.; Gr. *Alēktō*], in *Greek mythology*, one of the three Furies.

a·lee (ə-lē'), *adv. & adj.* [*a-*, on + *lee*], on or toward the lee, the side of a ship that is away from the wind.

al·e·gar (al'ə-gẽr, ā'lə-gẽr), *n.* [earlier *alegre; ale* + *egre* (Fr. *aigre*), acrid, keen; cf. EAGER, VINEGAR], a vinegar resulting from the fermentation of ale; sour ale.

ale·house (āl'hous'), *n.* a place where ale is sold and served; saloon; tavern.

A·lek·san·drovsk (ä'lek-sän'drôfsk), *n.* Zaporozhe, a city in the Ukrainian S.S.R.: the former name.

A·le·mán, Mi·guel (mē-gel' ä'le-män'), 1902– ; Mexican statesman; president of Mexico, 1946–1952.

Al·e·man·ni (al'ə-man'ī), *n.pl.* the Alamanni.

Al·e·man·nic (al'ə-man'ik), *n.* the German dialect of the Alamanni: it survives in southern Germany and parts of Switzerland, and constitutes, with Bavarian, Swabian, and Lombard (extinct), High German proper.

A·lem·bert, Jean Le Rond d' (zhän' lə rōn' dà'län'bâr'), 1717–1783; French philosopher, mathematician, and encyclopedist.

a·lem·bic (ə-lem'bik), *n.* [ME. *alambic;* OFr. *alambic;* L. *alambicus;* Ar. *al-anbīq; al*, the + *anbīq*, a still < Gr. *ambix*, a cup], 1. an apparatus made of glass or metal, formerly used for distilling; hence, 2. anything that refines, changes, or purifies.

ALEMBIC

A·len·çon (à'län'sōn'), *n.* 1. a town in northwestern France: pop., 20,000 (1946). 2. (ə-len'sən; Fr. à'län'sōn'), a needle-point lace with a solid floral pattern on a background of fine loops of thread: originally made in Alençon.

a·leph (ä'lif), *n.* [Heb., lit., ox, leader], the first letter of the Hebrew alphabet (א), a neutral vowel: various diacritical marks determine its sound: see **alphabet**, table.

A·lep·po (ə-lep'ō), *n.* a city in northwestern Syria: pop., 320,000 (1943).

a·lert (ə-lũrt'), *adj.* [Fr. *alerte;* It. *all' erta*, on the watch < *alla*, at the + *erta*, a lookout < L. *erigere*, to erect], 1. watchful; vigilantly ready. 2. active; nimble. *n.* 1. an alarm; warning signal. 2. a period of watchfulness, especially before an expected air raid. *v.t.* to warn; warn to be ready: as, the troops were *alerted.* —*SYN.* see **intelligent, watchful.**

on the alert, watchful; vigilant.

-a·les (ā'lēz), [L. pl. of *-alis*], a suffix used in forming the scientific Latin names of orders of plants.

A·les·san·dri·a (ä'les-sän'drē-ä'), *n.* a city in northwestern Italy: pop., 86,000 (est. 1947).

a·leu·rone (ə-lōō'rōn), *n.* [Gr. *aleuron*, wheat meal, flour], in *botany* & *biochemistry*, fine granules of protein present in seeds, and forming an outer layer in cereals.

Al·e·ut (al'i-ōōt'), ***n.*** 1. [*pl.* ALEUTS (-ōōts'), ALEUT], a native of the Aleutian Islands and part of Alaska. 2. the language of these natives.

A·leu·tian (ə-lōō'shən, ə-lū'shən), ***adj.*** 1. of the Aleutian Islands. 2. of the Aleuts, their culture, etc. ***n.*** 1. an Aleut. 2. *pl.* the Aleutian Islands.

Aleutian Islands, a chain of islands extending c. 1,200 miles south-westward from Alaska; pop., 5,600: a part of the State of Alaska.

ALEUTIAN ISLANDS

ale·wife (āl'wīf'), ***n.*** [*pl.* ALEWIVES (-wīvz')], 1. a woman who keeps an alehouse. 2. [? Am. Ind.], an edible North American fish resembling the herring, found in the ocean and in some lakes and streams.

Al·ex·an·der (al'ig-zan'dēr), [L.; Gr. *Alexandros*, lit., defender of men < *alexein*, to defend + *anēr, andros*, man], a masculine name: diminutives, *Aleck, Alex, Sandy;* feminine, *Alexandra, Alexandrina;* equivalents, Fr. *Alexandre*, It. *Alessandro*, Sp. *Alejandro*.

Alexander I, 1. (*Alexander Pavlovich*), 1777–1825; grandson of Catherine the Great; czar of Russia (1801–1825); promoter of the Holy Alliance. 2. 1857–1893; Bulgarian ruler (1879–1886); abdicated. 3. 1876–1903; king of Serbia (1889–1903); assassinated. 4. 1888–1934; son of Peter I of Serbia; king of Yugoslavia (1921–1934). 5. 1893–1920; king of Greece (1917–1920).

Alexander II, (*Alexander Nikolayevich*), 1818–1881; czar of Russia (1855–1881); emancipated the serfs.

Alexander III, 1. (*Orlando Bandinelli*), ?–1181, Pope (1159–1181). 2. 1845–1894; son of *Alexander II;* czar of Russia (1881–1894).

Alexander VI, (*Rodrigo Lanzol y Borgia*), 1431?–1503; Pope (1492–1503); father of Cesare Borgia and Lucrezia Borgia.

Alexander, Sir **Harold Rupert,** 1891– ; British general; governor general of Canada (1946–1952).

Alexander Archipelago, a chain of islands off the southeastern coast of Alaska: largest town, Sitka.

Alexander Nev·ski (nef'ski), 1220?–1263; Russian hero and saint.

Alexander Se·ver·us (si-vêr'əs), 208?–235 A.D.; Roman emperor (222–235 A.D.).

Alexander the Great, 356–323 B.C.; military conqueror; king of Macedonia (336–323 B.C.); helped to spread Greek culture through the East and in Egypt.

Al·ex·an·dra (al'ig-zan'drə), [fem. of *Alexander*], a feminine name: diminutive, *Sandra;* variant, *Alexandrina.* ***n.*** wife of Edward VII of England; lived 1844–1925; queen mother (1910–1925).

Al·ex·an·dret·ta (al'ig-zan-dret'ə), ***n.*** a seaport in southern Turkey: pop., 23,000: Turkish name, *Iskenderun.*

Al·ex·an·dri·a (al'ig-zan'dri-ə), ***n.*** 1. a city in Egypt, on the Mediterranean: pop., 1,513,000: ancient Greek capital of Egypt, founded by Alexander the Great: Arabic name, *El Iskandariya.* 2. a city in northeastern Virginia, near Washington, D.C.: pop., 91,000. 3. a city in central Louisiana: pop., 40,000.

Al·ex·an·dri·an (al'ig-zan'dri-ən), ***adj.*** 1. of Alexander the Great or his rule. 2. of Alexandria, Egypt, or the late Hellenic culture that flourished there. 3. in *prosody*, alexandrine.

Al·ex·an·dri·na (al'ig-zan-drī'nə), a feminine name: see **Alexandra.**

al·ex·an·drine (al'ig-zan'drin), ***n.*** [Fr. *alexandrin:* so called from being used in OFr. poems on *Alexander* the Great], in *prosody*, an iambic line having normally six feet; iambic hexameter. ***adj.*** of an alexandrine or alexandrines.

al·ex·an·drite (al'ig-zan'drīt), ***n.*** [after the Russian Czar *Alexander II*], a variety of chrysoberyl that looks dark green in daylight and deep red under artificial light: it is used in jewelry.

A·le·xan·drou·po·lis (ä'lek-sän-drōō'pô-lēs'), ***n.*** a seaport in Greece, on the Aegean: pop., 17,000; former name, *Dede Agach.*

a·lex·i·a (ə-lek'si-ə), ***n.*** [Mod. L. < Gr. *a-*, without + *lexis*, speech < *legein*, to speak], inability to read, caused by lesions of the brain; word blindness.

a·lex·in (ə-lek'sin), ***n.*** [< Gr. *alexein*, to avert], a substance normally found in the blood and capable of destroying bacteria.

a·lex·i·phar·mic (ə-lek'si-fär'mik), ***adj.*** [Gr. *alexipharmakos* < *alexein*, to ward off + *pharmakon*, a drug, poison], acting as an antidote; counteracting poison. ***n.*** an antidote.

A·lex·is (ə-lek'sis), [Gr., lit., help < *alexein*, to defend], a masculine name. ***n.*** (*Alexis Mikhailovich*), czar of Russia (1645–1676); 1629–1676; father of Peter the Great.

A·lex·i·us I (ə-lek'si-əs), (*Alexius Comnenus*), 1048–1118; emperor of the Byzantine Empire (1081–1118).

al·fal·fa (al-fal'fə), ***n.*** [Sp. < Ar. *al-fachfacha*, very good fodder], a deep-rooted plant of the pea family, with small divided leaves, purple cloverlike flowers, and spiral pods, used extensively in the United States for fodder, pasture, and as a cover crop: also called *lucerne.*

Al·fie·ri, Vit·to·ri·o (vēt-tô'ryô' äl-fyâr'ē), Count, 1749–1803; Italian dramatist and poet.

al·fil·a·ri·a (al-fil'ə-rē'ə), ***n.*** [Sp. Am. < Sp. *alfiler*, a pin; Ar. *al-khilāl*, thorn], a European plant of the geranium family, grown in the United States for fodder.

‡al fi·ne (äl fē'ne), [It.], to the end.

Al·fon·so XIII (al-fon'zō, al-fon'sō; Sp. äl-fôn'sô), 1886–1941; king of Spain (1902–1931); deposed.

al·for·ja (al-fôr'jə; Sp. äl-fôr'hä), ***n.*** [Sp. < Ar. *al-khorj*], 1. a leather or canvas saddlebag used by cowboys; hence, 2. a cheek pouch, as of a chipmunk.

Al·fred (al'frid), [AS. *Ælfred*, lit., elf-counsel, hence, wise counselor < *ælf*, elf + *ræd*, counsel], a masculine name: diminutives, *Al, Alf, Fred;* feminine, *Alfreda.*

Al·fre·da (al-frē'də), a feminine name: see **Alfred.**

Alfred the Great, 849–899 A.D.; king of Wessex (871–899 A.D.) and of England (886–899 A.D.); defeated the Danish invaders; promoted English culture.

al·fres·co (al-fres'kō), ***adv.*** [It.; *al*, for *a il*, in the + *fresco*, fresh, cool], in the open air; outdoors. ***adj.*** outdoor. Also **al fresco.**

Alg., 1. Algerian. 2. Algiers.

alg., algebra.

al·gae (al'jē), ***n.pl.*** [*sing.* ALGA (-gə)], [pl. of L. *alga*, seaweed], a group of plants, one-celled, colonial, or many-celled, containing chlorophyl and having no true root, stem, or leaf: algae are found in water or damp places, and include seaweeds, pond scum, etc.

al·gal (al'gəl), ***adj.*** of or like algae.

al·gar·ro·ba (al'gə-rō'bə), ***n.*** [Sp. < Ar. *al-kharrūbah; al*, the + *kharrūbah*, carob], 1. an evergreen tree bearing large, edible, fleshy pods; carob. 2. its beans or pods: also called *St. John's bread.* 3. the honey mesquite tree. 4. its edible pods.

al·ge·bra (al'jə-brə), ***n.*** [It. < Ar. *al-jebr*, the reunion of broken parts < *al*, the + *jabara*, to reunite], 1. the branch of mathematics that uses positive and negative numbers, letters, and other systematized symbols to express and analyze the relationship between concepts of quantity in terms of formulas, equations, etc.; generalized arithmetic: abbreviated **alg.** 2. a textbook or treatise dealing with this branch of mathematics.

al·ge·bra·ic (al'jə-brā'ik), ***adj.*** 1. of or used in algebra. 2. like or characteristic of algebra.

al·ge·bra·i·cal (al'jə-brā'i-k'l), ***adj.*** algebraic.

al·ge·bra·i·cal·ly (al'jə-brā'i-k'l-i), ***adv.*** 1. by means of algebra. 2. with reference to algebra.

al·ge·bra·ist (al'jə-brā'ist), ***n.*** an expert in algebra.

Al·ge·cir·as (al'ji-sir'əs; Sp. äl'he-thē'räs), ***n.*** a Spanish seaport on the Strait of Gibraltar: pop., 63,000.

Al·ger, Horatio (al'jēr), 1834–1899; American writer of boys' stories.

Al·ger·i·a (al-jêr'i-ə), ***n.*** a country in northern Africa, under French control until 1962: area, 847,552 sq. mi.; pop., 11,240,000; capital, Algiers.

ALGERIA

Al·ger·i·an (al-jêr'i-ən), ***adj.*** of Algeria, its people, etc. ***n.*** a native or inhabitant of Algeria.

Al·ge·rine (al'jə-rēn'), ***adj.*** Algerian. ***n.*** 1. a native of Algeria, especially one of Berber, Arab, or Moorish descent. 2. a North African pirate. 3. a soft woolen, striped cloth.

Al·ger·non (al'jēr-nən), [apparently < OFr. *al grenon*, with a mustache], a masculine name: diminutives, *Algie, Algy.*

-al·gi·a (al'ji-ə, al'jə), [< Gr. *algos*, pain], a suffix meaning *pain*, as in *neuralgia:* also **-algy.**

al·gid (al'jid), ***adj.*** [Fr. *algide;* L. *algidus*, cold < *algere*, to be cold < Gr. *algeein*, to feel pain], cold; chilly.

al·gid·i·ty (al-jid'ə-ti), ***n.*** [*algid* + *-ity*], chilliness; cold.

Al·giers (al-jêrz'), ***n.*** 1. the capital of Algeria; Mediterranean seaport: pop., 884,000: abbreviated **Alg.** 2. a former Barbary State in North Africa: now *Algeria.*

al·goid (al'goid), ***adj.*** [*alga* + *-oid*], like algae.

Al·gol (al'gol), ***n.*** [Ar. *al ghūl*, lit., the ghoul], a bright star in the constellation Perseus and the earliest-known variable star: it is a binary and loses most of its brightness when eclipsed by its dark companion.

al·go·lag·ni·a (al'gə-lag'ni-ə), ***n.*** [Mod. L. < Gr. *algos*, pain + *lagneia*, lust], abnormal sexual pleasure derived from inflicting or suffering pain; masochism or sadism.

al·gol·o·gy (al-gol'ə-ji), ***n.*** [< L. *alga*, seaweed; + *-logy*], the branch of botany that deals with algae.

al·gom·e·ter (al-gom'ə-tēr), ***n.*** [< Gr. *algos*, a pain; + *-meter*], a device for measuring the intensity of pain caused by pressure.

Al·gon·ki·an (al-goŋ′ki-ən), *adj. & n.* 1. Algonquian. 2. in *geology*, late Proterozoic: a term formerly used.

Al·gon·qui·an (al-goŋ′ki-ən, al-goŋ′kwi-ən), *adj.* designating or of a widespread and important family of approximately fifty languages used by a number of North American Indian tribes, including the Arapaho, Cheyenne, Blackfoot, Chippewa, Fox, Shawnee, Ottawa, and others. *n.* 1. this family of languages. 2. a member of any tribe using one of these languages.

Al·gon·quin (al-goŋ′kin, al-goŋ′kwin), *n.* 1. a member of a tribe of Algonquian Indians who lived in the area of the Ottawa River, Canada: now called *Ottawa*. 2. the language of this tribe. 3. Algonquian.

Algonquin Park, a Provincial park in southeastern Ontario, Canada: game preserve: area, 3,900 sq. mi.

al·go·pho·bi·a (al′gə-fō′bi-ə), *n.* [< Gr. *algos*, pain; + *-phobia*], an extreme or abnormal fear of pain.

al·gor (al′gôr), *n.* [L., cold], a chill felt during fever.

al·go·rism (al′gə-riz′m), *n.* [ME. & OFr. *algorisme;* ML. *algorismus*, Arabic system of numerals < Ar. *al-Khowārazmi*, lit., native of Khwarazm (Khiva), mathematician of the 9th c. A.D.], 1. the Arabic system of numerals; decimal system of counting; hence, 2. computing with any kind of numerals.

al·gum (al′gum), *n.* a tree mentioned in the Bible: II Chron. 2:8: see **almug.**

Al·ham·bra (al-ham′brə), *n.* [Sp.; Ar. *al hamrā*, lit., the red (house)], 1. a palace of the Moorish kings, built during the 13th and 14th centuries near Granada, Spain. 2. a city in California, near Los Angeles: pop., 55,000.

ALHAMBRA

Al·ham·bresque (al′ham-bresk′), *adj.* like the Alhambra, especially in richness of ornamentation.

A·li (ä′li, ä-lē′), *n.* fourth caliph of Islam (656–661 A.D.); son-in-law of Mohammed; lived 600–661 A.D.

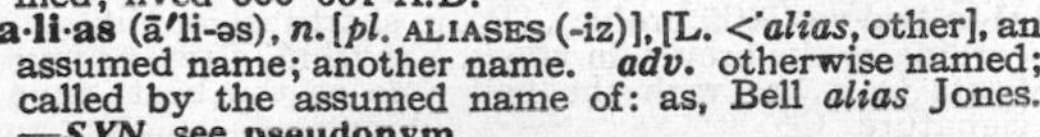

a·li·as (ā′li-əs), *n.* [*pl.* ALIASES (-iz)], [L. < *alias*, other], an assumed name; another name. *adv.* otherwise named; called by the assumed name of: as, Bell *alias* Jones. —*SYN.* see **pseudonym.**

A·li Ba·ba (al′i bab′ə, ä′li bä′bə), in *The Arabian Nights*, a poor woodcutter who found the treasure of the forty thieves in a cave: he made the door of the cave open by saying "Open sesame!"

al·i·bi (al′ə-bī′), *n.* [*pl.* ALIBIS (-bīz′)], [L., contr. < *alius ibi*, elsewhere], 1. in *law*, the plea or fact that an accused person was elsewhere than at the alleged scene of the offense with which he is charged; hence, 2. [Colloq.], any excuse. *v.i.* [Colloq.], to offer an excuse.

al·i·ble (al′ə-b'l), *adj.* [L. *alibilis* < *alere*, to feed, nourish], nourishing.

Al·i·can·te (ä′lē-kän′te; Eng. al′ə-kan′ti), *n.* a city in southeastern Spain: pop., 112,000.

Al·ice (al′is), [L. *Alicia, Alithia;* Gr. *alētheia*, truth], a feminine name: diminutive, *Elsie;* variant, *Alicia.*

Alice blue, [after *Alice* Roosevelt Longworth (1884–), daughter of Theodore Roosevelt], a light blue.

A·li·ci·a (ə-lish′i-ə), a feminine name: see **Alice.**

al·i·dad (al′i-dad′), *n.* an alidade.

al·i·dade (al′i-dād′), *n.* [Fr.; ML. *alhidada;* Ar. *al 'idādah*, a rule], 1. a part of an optical or surveying instrument, consisting of the vernier, indicator, etc. 2. a surveying instrument consisting of a telescope mounted on a rule marked off in degrees, used in topographic mapping.

al·ien (āl′yən, ā′li-ən), *adj.* [ME.; OFr.; L. *alienus* < *alius*, other], belonging to another country or people; foreign; strange. *n.* 1. a foreigner. 2. a foreign-born resident in a country who has not become a naturalized citizen. 3. an outsider. *v.t.* to transfer (land, etc.).
alien to, strange to; not natural to.
SYN.—**alien** is applied to a resident who bears political allegiance to another country; **foreigner,** to a visitor or resident from another country whose language, cultural pattern, etc. are different from one's own; **stranger,** to a person who comes from another region and is unacquainted with local people, customs, etc.; **immigrant,** to a person who comes to a new country to settle there; **émigré,** to one who has left his country to take political refuge in a new land. See also **extrinsic.** —*ANT.* citizen, subject, national.

al·ien·a·ble (āl′yən-ə-b'l, ā′li-ən-ə-b'l), *adj.* capable of being alienated or transferred to a new owner.

al·ien·age (āl′yən-ij, ā′li-ən-ij), *n.* [Fr.; see ALIEN], the legal status of an alien.

al·ien·ate (āl′yən-āt′, ā′li-ən-āt′), *v.t.* [ALIENATED (-id), ALIENATING], [< L. *alienatus*, pp. of *alienare* < *alius*, another], 1. to transfer the ownership of (property) to another. 2. to estrange; make unfriendly: as, his behavior *alienated* his friends. 3. to cause a transference of (affection).

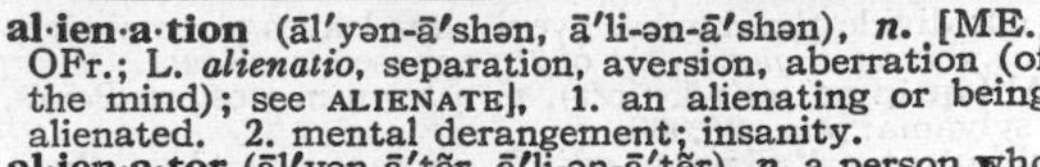

al·ien·a·tion (āl′yən-ā′shən, ā′li-ən-ā′shən), *n.* [ME.; OFr.; L. *alienatio*, separation, aversion, aberration (of the mind); see ALIENATE], 1. an alienating or being alienated. 2. mental derangement; insanity.

al·ien·a·tor (āl′yən-ā′tẽr, ā′li-ən-ā′tẽr), *n.* a person who alienates.

al·ien·ee (āl′yən-ē′, ā′li-ən-ē′), *n.* [see ALIENATE & -EE], a person to whom property is transferred.

al·ien·ism (āl′yən-iz′m, ā′li-ən-iz′m), *n.* 1. the quality or condition of being alien. 2. alienage. 3. the speciality of alienists; psychiatry.

al·ien·ist (āl′yən-ist, ā′li-ən-ist), *n.* [Fr. *aliéniste* < L. *alienatio;* see ALIENATION], a doctor who specializes in mental diseases; psychiatrist: term used in law.

al·ien·or (āl′yən-ẽr, ā′li-ən-ôr′), *n.* [Anglo-Fr. < L. *alienare;* see ALIENATE], a person who transfers the ownership of property.

a·lif (ä′lif), *n.* [Ar.; akin to Heb. *āleph;* see ALEPH], the first letter of the Arabic alphabet (ا).

al·i·form (al′ə-fôrm′, ā′lə-fôrm′), *adj.* [< L. *ala*, a wing; + *-form*], shaped like a wing.

A·li·garh (al′ē-gür′), *n.* a city in India, in Uttar Pradesh: pop., 142,000.

a·light (ə-līt′), *v.i.* [ALIGHTED (-id) or ALIT (-lit′), ALIGHTING], [ME. *alighten;* AS. *alihtan; a-*, out, off + *lihtan*, to dismount, render light < *liht;* see LIGHT (to dismount)], 1. to get down or off; dismount. 2. to come down after flight; descend and settle. 3. to come (*upon*) accidentally.

a·light (ə-līt′), *adj.* [ME. *aliht*, pp. of *alihten*, to light up], 1. lighted; burning. 2. lighted up.

a·lign (ə-līn′), *v.t.* [Fr. *aligner* < *à*, to + *ligne*, line], 1. to bring into a straight line; adjust by line. 2. to bring into agreement, close co-operation, etc.: as, he *aligned* himself with the liberals. *v.i.* to come or fall into line; line up. Also spelled **aline.**

a·lign·ment (ə-līn′mənt), *n.* [Fr. *alignement;* see ALIGN], 1. an aligning or being aligned. 2. arrangement in a straight line. 3. a line or lines formed by aligning. 4. in *engineering*, a ground plan, as of a fieldwork, railroad, etc. Also spelled **alinement.**

THESE LETTERS ARE IN ALIGNMENT.

THESE LETTERS ARE OUT OF ALIGNMENT.

a·like (ə-līk′), *adj.* [ON. *alikr;* also < AS. *gelic* or *onlic;* see LIKE, *adj.*], like one another; showing resemblance; similar: usually a predicate adjective. *adv.* 1. in the same manner; similarly. 2. to the same degree; equally.

al·i·ment (al′ə-mənt), *n.* [L. *alimentum* < *alere*, to nourish], 1. anything that nourishes; food. 2. means of support. *v.t.* (al′ə-ment′), to supply with aliment; nourish.

al·i·men·tal (al′ə-men′t'l), *adj.* of aliment; nourishing.

al·i·men·ta·ry (al′ə-men′tə-ri), *adj.* [L. *alimentarius;* see ALIMENT], 1. connected with food or nutrition. 2. nourishing. 3. furnishing support or sustenance.

alimentary canal (or **tract**), the passage in the body that food goes through: it extends from the mouth through the esophagus, stomach, and intestines to the anus.

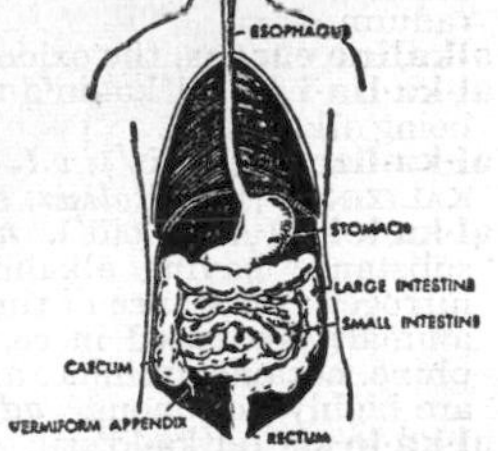

ALIMENTARY CANAL

al·i·men·ta·tion (al′ə-men-tā′shən), *n.* [Fr.; ML. *alimentatio* < L. *alimentum;* see ALIMENT], 1. a nourishing or being nourished. 2. nourishment; nutrition. 3. support; sustenance.

al·i·men·ta·tive (al′ə-men′tə-tiv), *adj.* of alimentation, or nourishment; nutritive.

al·i·mo·ny (al′ə-mō′ni), *n.* [L. *alimonia*, food, support < *alere*, to nourish], 1. means of living. 2. money to live on that a judge orders paid to a woman out of the income of her husband or former husband after a legal separation or divorce, or while legal action on this is pending. 3. like payment to a man by his (former) wife.

A·line (ə-lēn′), a feminine name: see **Adeline.**

a·line (ə-līn′), *v.t. & v.i.*, to align.

a·line·ment (ə-līn′mənt), *n.* alignment.

A·li Pa·sha (ä′li pä-shä′), 1741–1822; Turkish pasha of Janina.

al·i·ped (al′ə-ped′), *adj.* [L. *alipes* < *ala*, wing + *pes, pedis*, foot], wing-footed; having a winglike membrane connected with the feet, as the bat. *n.* an aliped creature.

al·i·phat·ic (al′ə-fat′ik), *adj.* [< Gr. *aleiphar, aleiphatos*, fat, oil], in *chemistry*, of or obtained from fat; fatty: said of certain hydrocarbons.

al·i·quant (al′ə-kwənt), *adj.* [L. *aliquantus*, some, moderate < *alius*, other + *quantus*, how large, how much], in *mathematics*, designating a part of a number that does not divide the number evenly but leaves a remainder: as, 8 is an *aliquant* part of 25: opposed to *aliquot*.

Al·i·quip·pa (al'ə-kwip'ə), *n.* a town in western Pennsylvania: pop., 26,000.

al·i·quot (al'ə-kwət), *adj.* [L., some, several < *alius*, other + *quot*, how many], in *mathematics*, designating a part of a number that divides the number evenly and leaves no remainder: as, 8 is an *aliquot* part of 24: opposed to *aliquant*.

Al·i·son (al'i-sən), [ME. *Alisoun*], a feminine name.

a·lit (ə-lit'), alternative past tense and past participle of **alight.**

a·li·un·de (ā'li-un'di), *adv. & adj.* [L., lit., from another place], in *law*, from some other source: as, evidence clarifying a document but not deriving from the document itself is evidence *aliunde*.

a·live (ə-liv'), *adj.* [ME. *alive, alyfe, on live;* AS. *on life; on*, in + *life*, dat. case of *lif*, life], 1. having life; living. 2. in existence, operation, etc.; unextinguished: as, old hatreds remain *alive*. 3. lively; alert. *Alive* is usually a predicate adjective. —*SYN.* see **living.**

alive to, awake to; aware of; perceiving.

alive with, teeming with; full of (living or moving things): as, a flower *alive with* bees.

look alive! hurry! be alert and quick!

a·liz·a·rin (ə-liz'ə-rin), *n.* [Fr. < *alizari*, Levantine name of madder; prob. < Ar. *al aṣārah*, the juice < *aṣara*, to press], a reddish-yellow crystalline compound, $C_{14}H_8O_4$, produced by oxidizing anthracene and used in preparing dyes: it was originally made from madder.

a·liz·a·rine (ə-liz'ə-rin, ə-liz'ə-rēn'), *n.* alizarin.

al·ka·hest (al'kə-hest'), *n.* [Fr. < ML. *alchahest*], the hypothetical universal solvent sought by the alchemists.

al·ka·les·cence (al'kə-les''ns), *n.* [*alkali* + *-escence*], the process of becoming alkaline.

al·ka·les·cent (al'kə-les''nt), *adj.* [*alkali* + *-escent*], 1. becoming alkaline. 2. somewhat alkaline.

al·ka·li (al'kə-lī'), *n.* [*pl.* ALKALIS, ALKALIES (-līz')], [ME. *alkaly;* OFr. *alcali;* Ar. *al-qalīy; al*, the + *qalīy*, ashes of saltwort < *qalay*, to roast in a pan], 1. any base or hydroxide, as soda, potash, etc., that is soluble in water and can neutralize acids: alkalis have an acrid taste and turn red litmus blue. 2. any soluble mineral salt or mixture of salts found in soils, as in some deserts, and capable of neutralizing acids. *adj.* alkaline.

al·ka·li·fy (al'kə-lə-fī', al-kal'ə-fī'), *v.t. & v.i.* [ALKALIFIED (-fīd'), ALKALIFYING], to make or become alkaline.

alkali metal, any metal, such as sodium, potassium, or lithium, whose hydroxide is an alkali.

al·ka·lim·e·ter (al'kə-lim'ə-tēr), *n.* [*alkali* + *-meter*], an instrument for measuring the amount of alkali in a substance or solution.

al·ka·line (al'kə-līn', al'kə-lin), *adj.* [*alkali* + *-ine*], 1. having the properties of an alkali. 2. of or resembling an alkali. 3. containing an alkali.

al·ka·line-earth metals (al'kə-līn'ũrth'), the group of chemical elements comprising calcium, strontium, barium, and sometimes, beryllium, magnesium, and radium.

alkaline earths, the oxides of the alkaline-earth metals.

al·ka·lin·i·ty (al'kə-lin'ə-ti), *n.* the quality or state of being alkaline.

al·ka·lize (al'kə-līz'), *v.t. & v.i.* [ALKALIZED (-līzd'), ALKALIZING], [Fr. *alcaliser;* see ALKALI], to make alkaline.

al·ka·loid (al'kə-loid'), *n.* [*alkali* + *-oid*], an organic substance having alkaline properties and containing nitrogen; substance of this kind taken from plants and animals, and used in certain drugs, as caffeine, morphine, cocaine, quinine, and strychnine: some alkaloids are highly poisonous. *adj.* like an alkali.

al·ka·lo·sis (al'kə-lō'sis), *n.* [*alkali* + *-osis*], a condition in which the alkali reserve of the body is higher than normal; increased alkalinity of the body fluids.

al·kanes (al'kānz), *n. pl.* [*alkyl* + *methanes*], a series of saturated hydrocarbons of the open-chain type having the general formula C_nH_{2n+2}; methane series.

al·ka·net (al'kə-net'), *n.* [ME.; Sp. *alcaneta*, dim. of *alcana* < Ar. *al ḥinnā*, henna plant], 1. any of a number of related plants whose roots are used to make a red dye; anchusa; bugloss. 2. this dye. 3. any of several other plants whose roots yield a red dye.

al·kan·nin (al-kan'in), *n.* [Mod. L. *Alkanna* < Sp. *alcana* (see ALKANET); + *-in*], a powder made from the root of the alkanet: used in preparing a red dyestuff.

al·kene (al'kēn), *n.* [*alkyl* + *-ene*], any of a series of unsaturated open-chain hydrocarbons containing a double bond and having the general formula C_nH_{2n}: also called *olefin*.

Alk·maar (älk'mär), *n.* a city in the western Netherlands: pop., 38,000 (1947).

Al·ko·ran (al'kō-rän', al'kō-ran'), *n.* the Koran: also spelled **Alcoran.**

al·kyd (al'kid), *adj.* [*alkyl* + *acid*], designating, of, or containing any of several synthetic resins made from phthalic acid, or, more often, phthalic anhydride, and glycerol: these resins are used in paints, etc.

al·kyl (al'kil, al'kēl), *adj.* [*alkali* + *-yl*], in *chemistry*, formed by substituting an element or a group of elements for hydrogen in the molecule of a hydrocarbon: applied only to radicals.

al·kyne (al'kīn), *n.* [< *alkyl* + *-ine*], any of a series of unsaturated open-chain hydrocarbons containing a triple bond and having the general formula C_nH_{2n-2}: also spelled **alkine.**

all (ôl), *adj.* [ME. *al, all;* AS. *all, eall*], 1. the whole extent or quantity of: as, *all* New England, *all* the gold. 2. the entire number of: as, *all* the men went. 3. every one of: as, *all* men must eat. 4. the greatest possible; as much as possible: as, said in *all* sincerity. 5. any; any whatever: as, true beyond *all* question. 6. every: now used only in such phrases as *all manner of men*. 7. alone; only: as, life is not *all* pleasure. *pron.* 1. [construed as pl.], everyone: as, *all* must die. 2. [construed as pl.], every one: as, when he wrote to his friends for help, *all* responded. 3. everything; the whole affair: as, *all* is over between them. 4. every part or bit: as, *all* of it is gone. *n.* 1. everything one has: as, give your *all*. 2. a totality; whole. *adv.* 1. wholly; entirely; altogether; quite: as, *all* worn out, riding *all* through the night. 2. apiece: as, a score of thirty *all*.

above all, before all other things; most of all.

after all, nevertheless; in spite of everything.

all but, 1. all except. 2. nearly; almost.

all in, [Colloq.], very tired; fatigued.

all in all, 1. considering everything. 2. as a whole. 3. everything.

all over, 1. ended. 2. everywhere. 3. [Colloq.], as one characteristically is: as, that's Mary *all over*.

all the (better, worse, etc.), so much the (better, worse, etc.).

all the (farther, closer, etc.), [Colloq. or Dial.], as (far, close, etc.) as.

at all, 1. in the least; to the slightest degree. 2. in any way. 3. under any considerations.

for all, in spite of; despite.

in all, altogether; all being counted.

all- (ôl), a combining form meaning: 1. *wholly, entirely, exclusively*, as in *all-American*. 2. *for every*, as in *all-purpose*. 3. *of everything, of every part*, as in *all-inclusive*.

‡al·la bre·ve (äl'lä bre've), [It., in short fashion, lit., according to the breve], in *music*, a rhythm of two or four beats to a bar with the half note as the beat: time signature, C.

Al·lah (al'ə, ä'lə), *n.* [Ar. *Allāh* < *al*, the + *ilāh*, god], God: so called in the Moslem religion.

Al·la·ha·bad (al'ə-hä-bäd'), *n.* the former capital of the United Provinces, India: pop., 261,000.

‡al·la mar·cia (äl'lä mär'chä), [It.], in *music*, played in the style of a march.

all-A·mer·i·can (ôl'ə-mer'ə-kən), *adj.* 1. made up wholly of Americans. 2. made of American materials only. 3. completely within the United States. 4. representative of the United States as a whole; chosen as the best in the United States. 5. of all the Americas. *n.* 1. an imaginary football or other team made up of college players voted the best of the year in the United States. 2. a player chosen for such team.

Al·lan (al'ən), a masculine name: see **Alan.**

Al·lan-a-dale (al'ən-ə-dāl'), *n.* in *English legend*, a famous member of Robin Hood's band.

al·lan·to·ic (al'ən-tō'ik), *adj.* 1. of or in the allantois. 2. having an allantois.

al·lan·toid (ə-lan'toid), *adj.* [Gr. *allantoeidēs;* see ALLANTOIS], of or like the allantois; sausage-shaped.

al·lan·to·is (ə-lan'tō-is), *n.* [Mod. L. < Gr. *allantoeidēs*, sausage-shaped < *allas*, sausage + *eidos*, form], a membranous pouch in the embryos of mammals, birds, and reptiles, having to do with the formation of the umbilical cord and placenta.

‡al·lar·gan·do (äl'lär-gän'dô), *adj. & adv.* [It.], in *music*, gradually slower and with more power: a direction to the performer.

all-a·round (ôl'ə-round'), *adj.* having many abilities, talents, or uses; not specialized; versatile.

al·lay (ə-lā'), *v.t.* [ALLAYED (-lād'), ALLAYING], [ME. *alaien;* AS. *alecgan; a-*, down + *lecgan*, to lay], 1. to put (fears, etc.) to rest; quiet; calm. 2. to lessen, relieve, or alleviate (pain, grief, etc.). —*SYN.* see **relieve.**

all-clear (ôl'klêr'), *n.* a siren or other signal that an air raid is over.

al·le·ga·tion (al'ə-gā'shən), *n.* [Fr.; L. *allegatio* < *ad-*, to + *legare*, to send on a mission; influenced by *allege*], 1. an alleging. 2. something alleged; assertion. 3. an assertion without proof. 4. in *law*, an assertion which its maker proposes to support with evidence.

al·lege (ə-lej'), *v.t.* [ALLEGED (-lejd'), ALLEGING], [ME. *aleggen*, to produce as evidence; OFr. *eslegier* < ML. **exlitigare;* L. *ex*, out of + *litigare;* see LITIGATE], 1. to assert positively; declare; affirm. 2. to assert or declare without proof: as, Hitler *alleged* that he was saving Europe. 3. to give as a plea, excuse, etc.: as, in his defense he *alleged* temporary insanity.

al·lege·a·ble (ə-lej'ə-b'l), *adj.* that can be alleged.

al·leg·ed·ly (ə-lej'id-li), *adv.* according to allegation.

Al·le·ghe·nies (al'ə-gā'niz), *n.pl.* the Allegheny Mountains.

Al·le·ghe·ny (al'ə-gā'ni), *n.* a river in Pennsylvania,

joining the Monongahela at Pittsburgh to form the Ohio: length, 325 mi.
Allegheny Mountains, a mountain range of the Appalachian system in central Pennsylvania, Maryland, West Virginia, and Virginia.
al·le·giance (ə-lē′jəns), *n.* [ME. < OFr. *a* (L. *ad*), to + *ligeance* < L. *ligare*, to bind; confused with *allege*], 1. the relationship of a vassal to his feudal lord. 2. the duty of being loyal to one's ruler, government, or country. 3. loyalty; devotion, as to a cause, person, etc.
SYN.—**allegiance** refers to the duty of a citizen to his government or a similarly felt obligation to support a cause, leader, etc.; **fidelity** implies strict adherence to an obligation, trust, etc.; **loyalty** suggests a steadfast devotion of an unquestioning kind that one may feel for one's family, friends, or country; **fealty**, now chiefly a literary word, suggests faithfulness that one has sworn to uphold; **homage** implies respect, reverence, or honor rendered to a person because of his rank, achievement, etc. —*ANT.* faithlessness, disaffection.
al·le·gor·ic (al′ə-gôr′ik, al′ə-gor′ik), *adj.* allegorical.
al·le·gor·i·cal (al′ə-gôr′i-k'l, al′ə-gor′i-k'l), *adj.* [< L. *allegoricus;* Gr. *allegorikos;* + *-al*], 1. of or characteristic of allegory. 2. that is or contains an allegory.
al·le·go·rist (al′ə-gôr′ist, al′ə-gō′rist, al′ə-gēr-ist), *n.* a person who uses allegory or writes allegories.
al·le·go·ris·tic (al′ə-gə-ris′tik), *adj.* allegorizing.
al·le·go·rize (al′ə-gə-rīz′), *v.t.* [ALLEGORIZED (-rīzd′), ALLEGORIZING], [Fr. *allégoriser;* L. *allegorizare*], 1. to make into or treat as an allegory. 2. to interpret in an allegorical sense. *v.i.* to make or use allegories.
al·le·go·ry (al′ə-gôr′i, al′ə-gō′ri), *n.* [*pl.* ALLEGORIES (-iz, -riz)], [L. *allegoria;* Gr. *allēgoria*, description of one thing under the image of another < *allos*, other + *agoreuein*, to speak in assembly < *agora*, place of assembly], 1. a story in which people, things, and happenings have another meaning, as in a fable or parable: allegories are used for teaching or explaining. 2. the presenting of ideas by means of such stories; symbolical narration or description.
al·le·gret·to (al′ə-gret′ō), *adj.* & *adv.* [It., dim. of *allegro;* see ALLEGRO], in *music*, moderately fast; faster than *andante* but slower than *allegro:* a direction to the performer. *n.* [*pl.* ALLEGRETTOS (-ōz)], a moderately fast movement or passage.
al·le·gro (ə-lā′grō, ə-leg′rō), *adj.* & *adv.* [It. < L. *alacer*, brisk, sprightly, cheerful], in *music*, fast; faster than *allegretto* but not so fast as *presto:* a direction to the performer. *n.* [*pl.* ALLEGROS (-grōz, -rōz)], a fast movement or passage.
al·lele (ə-lēl′), *n.* an allelomorph.
al·le·lo·morph (ə-lē′lə-môrf′, ə-lel′ə-môrf′), *n.* [< Gr. *allēlōn*, of one another + *morphē*, form], in *genetics*, either of a pair of contrasting characters inherited alternatively according to Mendelian law.
al·le·lu·ia (al′ə-lōō′yə), *interj.* [L.; Gr. *allēlouia;* Heb. *hallēlū-yāh;* see HALLELUJAH], praise ye the Lord! *n.* a song or exclamation of praise; hallelujah.
al·le·mande (al′ə-mand′; Fr. àl′mänd′), *n.* [Fr., lit., German], 1. any of various stately German dances of the 16th, 17th, and 18th centuries, in 2/2 time. 2. the music for this. 3. a piece of music resembling this in rhythm, formerly used as the movement preceding the prelude in a suite.
Al·len (al′ən), a masculine name: see **Alan.**
Al·len, Ethan (al′ən), 1738–1789; American Revolutionary soldier who led the Green Mountain Boys in the capture of Fort Ticonderoga.
Allen, Grant, (*Charles Grant Blairfindie Allen*), 1848–1899; English author and naturalist.
Al·len·by, Edmund Henry Hyn·man (hin′mən al′ən-bi), first Viscount Allenby, 1861–1936; English general; commander in chief of the Egyptian Expeditionary Force (1917–1918).
Al·len·town (al′ən-toun′), *n.* a city in eastern Pennsylvania, on the Lehigh River: pop., 108,000.
al·ler·gen (al′ēr-jən), *n.* [*allergy* + *-gen*], a substance inducing an allergic state or reaction.
al·ler·gen·ic (al′ēr-jen′ik), *adj.* of or acting as an allergen; inducing allergy.
al·ler·gic (ə-lũr′jik), *adj.* 1. of or caused by allergy. 2. having an allergy.
al·ler·gist (al′ēr-jist), *n.* a doctor who specializes in treating allergies.
al·ler·gy (al′ēr-ji), *n.* [*pl.* ALLERGIES (-jiz)], [< Gr. *allos*, other + *ergon*, action, work], a hypersensitivity to a specific substance (such as food, pollen, dust, etc.) or condition (as heat or cold) which in similar amounts are harmless to most people.
al·le·vi·ate (ə-lē′vi-āt′), *v.t.* [ALLEVIATED (-id), ALLEVIATING], [< L. *alleviatus*, pp. of *alleviare* < *allevare* < *ad-*, to + *levis*, light], to make less hard to bear; lighten or relieve (pain, suffering, etc.). —*SYN.* see **relieve.**
al·le·vi·a·tion (ə-lē′vi-ā′shən), *n.* 1. an alleviating or being alleviated. 2. a thing that alleviates.
al·le·vi·a·tive (ə-lē′vi-ā′tiv, ə-lē′vi-ə-tiv), *adj.* alleviating or tending to alleviate. *n.* a thing that alleviates.
al·le·vi·a·tor (ə-lē′vi-ā′tēr), *n.* a person or thing that alleviates.
al·le·vi·a·to·ry (ə-lē′vi-ə-tôr′i, ə-lē′vi-ə-tō′ri), *adj.* alleviative.
al·ley (al′i), *n.* [*pl.* ALLEYS (-iz)], [ME. *aly, ally;* OFr. *alee*, a going, passage < *aler* (Fr. *aller*), to go], 1. a lane in a garden or park. 2. a narrow street or walk between buildings. 3. in *bowling*, *a*) a long, narrow lane, usually of polished wood, along which the balls are rolled. *b*) *usually pl.* a building or hall for bowling. 4. in *tennis*, either of the two narrow lanes opposite each other on the long sides of the court, used in playing doubles.
blind alley, 1. an alley that has no rear outlet; hence, 2. any undertaking, idea, etc. that leads to nothing.
up one's alley, [Slang], suited to one's tastes or abilities.
al·ley (al′i), *n.* [abbrev. of *alabaster*, a material formerly used in making marbles], a large, sometimes white marble used as the shooter in playing marbles; taw.
alley cat, a homeless, mongrel cat that haunts alleys, etc. for food.
al·ley·way (al′i-wā′), *n.* 1. an alley between buildings. 2. any narrow passageway.
all-fired (ôl′fīrd′), *adj.* [altered < *hell-fired*], [Slang], complete; total. *adv.* [Slang], completely; extremely.
All Fools' Day, April 1; April Fools' Day: it is a day when practical jokes are played.
all fours, 1. all four limbs of an animal or human being: as, the cat landed on *all fours.* 2. a card game that has four points for scoring: also called *seven-up.*
be on all fours with, to be exactly alike; be the same as.
go on all fours, 1. to move on all four limbs. 2. to creep or crawl, as a baby. 3. to move along evenly.
all hail, all health: a greeting.
All·hal·low·mas (ôl′hal′ō-məs), *n.* [< *Allhallows* + *mass*], Allhallows.
All·hal·lows (ôl′hal′ōz, ôl′hal′əz), *n.* [< *all* + *hallow* < AS. *halga*, saint], All Saints' Day.
All·hal·low·tide (ôl′hal′ō-tīd′), *n.* [< *Allhallows* + *tide*, *n.*], the time, or season, of Allhallows.
all·heal (ôl′hēl′), *n.* a plant with flat-topped spikes of purple, blue, or white flowers; valerian: also **selfheal.**
al·li·a·ceous (al′i-ā′shəs), *adj.* [< L. *allium*, garlic; + *-aceous*], 1. of a group of strong-smelling bulb plants of the lily family, including the onion, garlic, etc. 2. having the smell or taste of onions or garlic.
Al·li·ance (ə-lī′əns), *n.* a city in eastern Ohio: pop., 28,000.
al·li·ance (ə-lī′əns), *n.* [OFr. *alliance;* L. *alligantia* < *alligare* < *ad-*, to + *ligare*, to bind], 1. an allying or being allied. 2. a union or joining, as of families by marriage. 3. a close association for a common objective, as of nations, political parties, etc. 4. the countries, organizations, or persons forming such a connection. 5. similarity or relationship in characteristics, structure, etc.; affinity.
SYN.—**alliance** refers to any association entered into for mutual benefit; **league**, often interchangeable with **alliance**, stresses formality of organization and definiteness of purpose; **coalition** implies a temporary alliance of opposing parties, etc., as in times of emergency; **confederacy** and **confederation** in political usage refer to a combination of independent states for the joint exercise of certain governmental functions, as defense or customs; **union** implies a close, permanent alliance and suggests complete unity of purpose and interest.
al·lied (ə-līd′; *also, especially in senses 3 & 4,* al′īd), *adj.* [ME. *alied*, pp. of *allien;* see ALLY], 1. united by kinship, treaty, agreement, etc. 2. closely related: as, anatomy and biology are *allied* sciences. 3. [A-], of the Allies of World War I or II. 4. [A-], of England and the United States jointly in World War II: as, the *Allied* High Command. —*SYN.* see **related.**
Al·lier (à′lyā′), *n.* a river in central France, flowing northward into the Loire: length, 250 mi.
Al·lies (al′īz, ə-līz′), *n.pl.* [see ALLY], 1. in World War I, the nations allied by treaty against Germany and the other Central Powers; originally, Great Britain, France, and Russia, later joined by the United States, Italy, Japan, etc. 2. in World War II, the nations associated against the Axis; especially, Great Britain, the Soviet Union, and the United States: sometimes only of the United States and Great Britain: see **United Nations.**
al·li·ga·tor (al′ə-gā′tēr), *n.* [Sp. *el lagarto;* L. *lacerta*, *lacertus*, lizard], 1. a large lizard of the crocodile group, found in the tropical rivers and marshes of the United States and China: its snout is shorter and blunter than the crocodile's. 2. a scaly leather made from an alligator's hide. 3. a machine, tool, etc. with a strong, movable, often toothed jaw.
alligator pear, an avocado.
all-im·por·tant (ôl′im-pôr′t'nt), *adj.* highly important; necessary; essential.
all-in·clu·sive (ôl′in-klōō′siv), *adj.* including everything; comprehensive.

al·lit·er·ate (ə-lit′ẽr-āt′), *v.i.* [ALLITERATED (-id), ALLITERATING], [< *alliteration*], 1. to constitute or have alliteration. 2. to use alliteration. *v.t.* to cause to have alliteration.

al·lit·er·a·tion (ə-lit′ẽr-ā′shən, a′lit-ẽr-ā′shən), *n.* [Fr. *allitération* < L. *ad*, to + *littera*, letter], repetition of an initial sound, usually of a consonant, in two or more words of a phrase, line of poetry, etc., as in "What a *t*ale of *t*error now their *t*urbulency *t*ells!"

al·lit·er·a·tive (ə-lit′ẽr-ā′tiv, ə-lit′ẽr-ə-tiv), *adj.* of, showing, or using alliteration.

al·li·um (al′i-əm), *n.* [L. *alium*, *allium*, garlic], any strong-smelling bulb plant of the lily family, as the onion, garlic, leek, etc.

al·lo- (al′ō, al′ə), [< Gr. *allos*, other], a combining form signifying *variation, departure from the normal, reversal*, as in *allonym, allomorph*.

al·lo·ca·ble (al′ə-kə-b′l), *adj.* that can be allocated.

al·lo·cate (al′ə-kāt′, al′ō-kāt′), *v.t.* [ALLOCATED (-id), ALLOCATING], [< ML. *allocatus*, pp. of *allocare* < L. *ad*, to + *locare*, to place < *locus*, a place], 1. to set apart for a specific purpose: as, they will *allocate* funds for housing. 2. to distribute by a plan; allot; assign. 3. to locate. —*SYN.* see **allot.**

al·lo·ca·tion (al′ə-kā′shən, al′ō-kā′shən), *n.* 1. an allocating or being allocated. 2. a thing allocated.

al·lo·cu·tion (al′ə-kū′shən, al′ō-kū′shən), *n.* [L. *allocutio* < *alloqui*, to speak to < *ad-*, to + *loqui*, to speak], a formal address, especially one warning or advising with authority.

al·lod (al′od), *n.* alodium.

al·lo·di·al (ə-lō′di-əl), *adj. & n.* alodial.

al·lo·di·um (ə-lō′di-əm), *n.* alodium.

al·log·a·mous (ə-log′ə-məs), *adj.* of or caused by allogamy.

al·log·a·my (ə-log′ə-mi), *n.* [< *allo-* + Gr. *gamos*, marriage], fertilization of a flower by the pollen of another; cross-fertilization.

al·lo·graph (al′ə-graf′, al′ə-gräf′), *n.* [*allo-* + *-graph*], a writing, as a signature, made by one person for another: opposed to *autograph*.

al·lom·er·ism (ə-lom′ẽr-iz′m), *n.* [< *allo-* + Gr. *meros*, a part; + *-ism*], variation in chemical make-up without change in crystalline form.

al·lom·er·ous (ə-lom′ẽr-əs), *adj.* of or showing allomerism.

al·lo·morph (al′ə-môrf′), *n.* [*allo-* + *-morph*], 1. in *mineralogy*, *a)* any variety of a substance that has more than one crystalline form but always the same chemical constitution. *b)* a kind of pseudomorph whose constituents have partly or completely changed. 2. in *linguistics*, any of the variant forms of a morpheme as conditioned by position or adjoining sounds.

al·lo·mor·phic (al′ə-môr′fik), *adj.* of or showing allomorphism.

al·lo·mor·phism (al′ə-môr′fiz′m), *n.* the state or quality of being an allomorph or allomorphs (sense 1).

al·lo·nym (al′ə-nim′), *n.* [*allo-* + Gr. *onyma*, name], 1. someone else's name taken by an author. 2. a book that carries such a name.

al·lo·path (al′ə-path′), *n.* 1. a practitioner of allopathy. 2. an advocate of allopathy.

al·lo·path·ic (al′ə-path′ik), *adj.* of or using allopathy.

al·lop·a·thist (ə-lop′ə-thist), *n.* an allopath.

al·lop·a·thy (ə-lop′ə-thi), *n.* [*allo-* + *-pathy*], treatment of disease by remedies that produce effects different from or opposite to those produced by the disease: opposed to *homeopathy*.

al·lo·phane (al′ə-fān′), *n.* [Gr. *allophanēs*, appearing otherwise < *allos*, otherwise + *phainesthai*, to appear], a natural, translucent silicate of aluminum, $Al_2SiO_5 \cdot 5H_2O$, of various colors.

al·lo·phone (al′ə-fōn′), *n.* [*allo-* + *-phone*], in *linguistics*, any of the variant forms of a phoneme as conditioned by position or adjoining sounds.

al·lo·phyl·i·an (al′ə-fil′i-ən), *adj.* [L. *allophylus;* Gr. *allophylos*, alien < *allos*, other + *phylē*, tribe, clan], in *linguistics*, 1. neither Indo-European nor Semitic. 2. speaking allophylian languages.

al·lo·plasm (al′ə-plaz′m), *n.* [*allo-* + *plasm*], in *biology*, a differentiated cell substance, as of flagella and cilia.

al·lot (ə-lot′), *v.t.* [ALLOTTED (-id), ALLOTTING], [OFr. *aloter; a-*, to + *loter* < *lot;* see LOT], 1. to distribute by lot or in shares; apportion. 2. to give or assign (a part or parts of something): as, each speaker is *allotted* five minutes.

SYN.—**allot** and **assign** both imply the giving of a share or portion with no indication of uniform or fixed distribution, **assign** having the extra connotation of authoritativeness (I was *allotted* four seats, to *assign* a task); **apportion** connotes the just, proportionate, often uniform distribution of a fixed number of portions; **allocate** usually implies the allowance of a fixed amount for a specific purpose (to *allocate* $50 for books).

al·lot·ment (ə-lot′mənt), *n.* [Fr. *allotement;* see ALLOT,] 1. an allotting or being allotted. 2. a thing allotted; portion; share. 3. in the *United States armed forces*, a portion of one's pay regularly deducted, as for one's dependents, insurance premiums, etc.

al·lo·trope (al′ə-trōp′), *n.* an allotropic form.

al·lo·trop·ic (al′ə-trop′ik), *adj.* of or having allotropy.

al·lot·ro·pism (ə-lot′rə-piz′m), *n.* allotropy.

al·lot·ro·py (ə-lot′rə-pi), *n.* [< Gr. *allotropos*, of or in another manner < *allos*, other + *tropos*, way, manner], the property that certain chemical elements have of existing in two or more different forms, as carbon in charcoal, diamonds, lampblack, etc.

‡**all' ot·ta·va** (äl′lôt-tä′vä), [It., lit., according to the octave], in *music*, to be played an octave higher or an octave lower, depending on whether the sign or abbreviation (**8, 8va, 8va~~~~**) is above or below the staff.

al·lot·tee (ə-lot′ē′), *n.* [< *allot* + *-ee*], a person to whom something is allotted.

all-out (ôl′out′), *adj.* [Colloq.], complete or wholehearted: as, an *all-out* effort.

all·o·ver (ôl′ō′vẽr), *adj.* 1. over the whole surface. 2. with the pattern repeated over the whole surface: as, *allover* embroidery. *n.* cloth, etc. with such a pattern.

al·low (ə-lou′), *v.t.* [ME. *alowen;* OFr. *alouer;* ML. *allocare* < L. *ad-*, to + *locus*, a place; associated with OFr. *alouer* < L. *allaudare* < *ad*, to + *laudare*, to praise], 1. to permit; let: as, we weren't *allowed* to go. 2. to let have: as, she *allowed* herself no sweets. 3. to let enter; permit the presence of: as, dogs are not *allowed*. 4. to admit (a claim or the like); acknowledge as true or valid. 5. to provide or keep (a certain amount or extra quantity) so as to have enough: as, *allow* an inch for shrinkage. 6. [Dial.], to think; give as one's opinion. —*SYN.* see **let.**

allow for, to make an allowance or allowances for; leave room, time, etc. for.

allow of, 1. to be subject to. 2. to tolerate.

al·low·a·ble (ə-lou′ə-b′l), *adj.* [OFr. *alouable;* see ALLOW], that can be allowed; permissible.

al·low·a·bly (ə-lou′ə-bli), *adv.* in an allowable or allowed manner; with permission.

al·low·ance (ə-lou′əns), *n.* 1. an allowing. 2. something allowed. 3. an amount of money, food, etc. given regularly to a child, dependent, soldier, etc. 4. a reduction in the price of something in consideration of a large order or of turning in a used article, etc. 5. the amount by which something is allowed to be more or less than stated, as to compensate for the weight of the container, inaccuracy of machining, etc. *v.t.* [ALLOWANCED (-ənst), ALLOWANCING], 1. to put on an allowance or a ration. 2. to apportion economically.

make allowance (or **allowances**), to take circumstances, limitations, etc. into consideration.

make allowance (or **allowances**) **for,** 1. to forgive or excuse because of mitigating factors. 2. to leave room, time, etc. for; allow for.

Al·lo·way (al′ə-wā′), *n.* a town in Scotland, near Ayr: birthplace of Robert Burns.

al·low·ed·ly (ə-lou′id-li), *adv.* by allowance or admission; admittedly.

al·loy (al′oi, ə-loi′), *n.* [Fr. *aloi* < OFr. *aleier*, to alloy; see the *v.*], 1. the relative purity of gold or silver. 2. a metal that is a mixture of two or more metals, or of a metal and something else. 3. a less valuable metal mixed with a more valuable one, often to give hardness; hence, 4. something that lowers the value or goodness of another thing when mixed with it. *v.t.* (ə-loi′), [Fr. *aloyer;* OFr. *aleier;* L. *alligare* < *ad-*, to + *ligare*, to bind], 1. to make (a metal) less valuable by mixing with a cheaper metal. 2. to mix (metals). 3. to debase by adding something inferior.

all-pur·pose (ôl′pũr′pəs), *adj.* for every purpose; useful in many ways.

all-right (ôl′rīt′), *adj.* [Slang], 1. honest, honorable, dependable, etc. 2. good; excellent.

all right, 1. satisfactory; adequate. 2. unhurt. 3. correct. 4. yes; very well. 5. certainly.

all-round (ôl′round′), *adj.* all-around.

All Saints' Day, an annual church festival (November 1) in honor of all the saints: also called *Allhallows, Allhallowmas*.

all·seed (ôl′sēd′), *n.* any of various plants having many seeds, as knotweed or goosefoot.

All Souls' Day, in the *Roman Catholic Church*, November 2, a day of services and prayer for the souls in purgatory.

all·spice (ôl′spīs′), *n.* 1. the berry of a West Indian tree of the myrtle family. 2. the spice made from this berry: so named because its flavor seems to combine the tastes of several spices.

all-star (ôl′stär′), *adj.* made up entirely of outstanding or star performers.

al·lude (ə-lōōd′, ə-lūd′), *v.i.* [ALLUDED (-id), ALLUDING], [L. *alludere*, to joke, jest < *ad-*, to + *ludere*, to play], to mention, especially in a casual way; refer indirectly (*to*). —*SYN.* see **refer.**

al·lure (ə-loor′, ə-lyoor′), *v.t. & v.i.* [ALLURED (-loord′, -lyoord′), ALLURING], [OFr. *alurer, aleurer;* see AD- & LURE], to tempt with something desirable; attract; entice; fascinate. *n.* the power to entice or attract; fascination. —*SYN.* see **attract.**

al·lure·ment (ə-loor′mənt, ə-lyoor′mənt), *n.* 1. an alluring. 2. fascination; charm. 3. something that allures.

al·lur·ing (ə-loor′iŋ, ə-lyoor′iŋ), *adj.* [ppr. of *allure*], tempting strongly; highly attractive; charming.
al·lu·sion (ə-lōō′zhən, ə-lū′zhən), *n.* [L. *allusio*, a playing or sporting with < *allusus*, pp. of *alludere*], 1. an alluding. 2. indirect reference; casual mention.
al·lu·sive (ə-lōō′siv, ə-lū′siv), *adj.* 1. containing an allusion. 2. using allusion; full of allusions.
al·lu·vi·al (ə-lōō′vi-əl, ə-lū′vi-əl), *adj.* [L. *alluvius*], 1. of or found in alluvium. 2. made up of alluvium. *n.* alluvial soil.
alluvial cone (or **fan**), a cone-shaped deposit of alluvium made by a swift stream where it runs out into a level plain or meets a slower stream.
al·lu·vi·on (ə-lōō′vi-ən, ə-lū′vi-ən), *n.* [Fr.; L. *alluvio*, an overflowing < *alluere* < *ad-*, to + *luere*, to wash], 1. the washing of water against a shore or bank. 2. a flood. 3. alluvium. 4. in *law*, an increase in land, as by alluvium.
al·lu·vi·um (ə-lōō′vi-əm, ə-lū′vi-əm), *n.* [*pl.* ALLUVIUMS (-əmz), ALLUVIA (-ə)], [L., neut. of *alluvius;* see ALLUVION], sand, clay, etc. deposited by flowing water, especially along a river bed. —*SYN.* see **wash.**
al·ly (ə-lī′; *for n., usually* al′ī), *v.t.* [ALLIED (-līd′), ALLYING], [ME. *alien;* OFr. *alier* < L. *alligare* < *ad-*, to + *ligare*, to bind], 1. to unite or associate for a specific purpose, as families by marriage, nations by treaty, or companies by agreement (with *to* or *with*): generally used reflexively or in the passive. 2. to relate by similarity of structure, certain qualities, etc.: usually in the passive, as, the onion is *allied* to the lily. *v.i.* to become allied. *n.* [*pl.* ALLIES (-īz, -līz′)], 1. a country, person, or group of persons joined with another for a common purpose: see also **Allies.** 2. a plant, animal, or thing closely related in structure, etc. to another. 3. an associate; helper; auxiliary. —*SYN.* see **associate.**
al·lyl (al′il), *n.* [L. *allium*, garlic; + *-yl*], in *chemistry*, the univalent radical C_3H_5, found in oil of garlic, etc.
Al·ma (al′mə), [L., fem. of *almus*, nourishing, bountiful], a feminine name.
al·ma, al·mah (al′mə), *n.* an alme.
Al·ma-A·ta (äl′mə-ä′tə), *n.* the capital of the Kazak S.S.R., Asia: pop., 231,000: former name, *Vyernyi.*
al·ma·gest, Al·ma·gest (al′mə-jest′), *n.* [ME.; OFr. *almageste;* Ar. *al majistī* < *al*, the + Gr. *megistē* (*syntaxis*), greatest (work)], 1. a vast work on astronomy and geography compiled by Claudius Ptolemy c. 150 A.D.; hence, 2. any of several medieval works like this, on astrology, alchemy, etc.
al·ma ma·ter, Al·ma Ma·ter (al′mə mā′tẽr, äl′mə mä′tẽr), [L., fostering mother], 1. the college, university, or school that one attended. 2. its anthem, or hymn.
al·ma·nac (ôl′mə-nak′), *n.* [Sp.; Ar. *al-manākh; al*, the + *manākh*, weather], a yearly calendar of days, weeks, and months, with astronomical data, weather forecasts, tables of useful information, etc.
al·man·dine (al′mən-dēn′, al′mən-din), *n.* [altered < *alabandine;* L. *alabandina*, precious gem < *Alabanda*, city in the interior of Caria], a purplish-red garnet.
al·man·dite (al′mən-dīt′), *n.* almandine.
Al·ma-Tad·e·ma, Sir Lawrence (al′mə-tad′i-mə), 1836–1912; English painter born in Belgium.
al·me, al·meh (al′me), *n.* [Ar. *'alimah*, learned (in music and dancing)], an Egyptian dancing girl.
Al·me·rí·a (äl′me-rē′ä), *n.* a seaport in southeastern Spain, on the Mediterranean: pop., 98,000 (est. 1946).
al·might·i·ly (ôl-mī′t'l-i), *adv.* in an almighty manner.
al·might·i·ness (ôl-mī′ti-nis), *n.* the state or quality of being almighty.
al·might·y (ôl-mī′ti, ôl′mī′ti), *adj.* [ME. *almihtig;* AS. *ealmihtig; eal*, all + *mihtig*, mighty], 1. all-powerful. 2. [Slang], great; extreme. *adv.* [Slang], extremely.
 almighty dollar, [Colloq.], money regarded figuratively as a god, or source of great power.
 the Almighty, God; the Lord.
al·mond (ä′mənd, am′ənd), *n.* [ME. *almande;* OFr. *amande;* L. *amygdala;* Gr. *amygdalē*], 1. the edible, nutlike seed of a fruit resembling the peach. 2. the small, pink-flowered tree that this fruit grows on. 3. anything shaped like an almond. 4. a light-tan color. *adj.* 1. made of almonds. 2. having an almond flavor. 3. almond-shaped. 4. almond-colored.
al·mond-eyed (ä′mənd-īd′, am′ənd-īd′), *adj.* having eyes that look almond-shaped, or oval with pointed ends; slant-eyed.
al·mon·er (al′mən-ẽr, ä′mən-ẽr), *n.* [ME.; OFr. *almosnier;* see ALMS], a person who distributes alms or charity, as for a church, wealthy family, etc.
al·mon·ry (al′mən-ri, ä′mən-ri), *n.* [*pl.* ALMONRIES (-riz)], [OFr. *aumosnerie* < *almosnier;* see ALMONER], a place where alms are given out.
al·most (ôl′mōst, ôl′mōst′), *adv.* [AS. *eallmæst;* see ALL & MOST], very nearly; all but.
alms (ämz), *n.* [*pl.* ALMS], [ME. *almesse;* AS. *ælmesse;* L. *eleemosyna;* Gr. *eleēmosynē*, alms < *eleos*, pity], 1. money, food, clothes, etc. given to poor people. 2. [Obs.], a deed of mercy.
alms·giv·er (ämz′giv′ẽr), *n.* a person who gives alms.
alms·giv·ing (ämz′giv′iŋ), *n.* the giving of alms.
alms·house (ämz′hous′), *n.* a home for people too poor to support themselves; poorhouse.
alms·man (ämz′mən), *n.* [*pl.* ALMSMEN (-mən)], a person, especially a man, supported by alms.
alms·wom·an (ämz′woom′ən), *n.* [*pl.* ALMSWOMEN (-wim′in)], a woman supported by alms.
al·muce (al′mūs), *n.* [ML. *almutia*, a cowl or hood], 1. a headdress resembling a cowl. 2. a kind of tippet, a medieval garment, with a hood and a fur lining.
al·mug (al′mug), *n.* [Heb.], in the *Bible*, a tree, probably sandalwood, from whose wood Solomon made the pillars of the Temple: I Kings 10:12: also **algum.**
al·ni·co (al′ni-kō′), *n.* [*al*uminum + *ni*ckel + *co*balt], an alloy containing aluminum, nickel, cobalt, and iron, used in making magnets.
al·od (al′od), *n.* alodium.
a·lo·di·al (ə-lō′di-əl), *adj.* of an alodium; freehold.
a·lo·di·um (ə-lō′di-əm), *n.* [ML. *allodium, alodium* < OHG. *alōd*, full and free possession < *all*, all + *-ōd*, orig., what fate assigned, hence possessions], in *law*, land owned independently, without any rent, payment in service, etc.; a freehold estate: opposed to *feud.*
al·oe (al′ō), *n.* [*pl.* ALOES (-ōz)], [L.; Gr. *aloē*], 1. any of a large group of plants of the lily family, native to South Africa, with fleshy leaves that are spiny along the edge. 2. *pl.* [construed as sing.], a bitter, laxative drug made from the juice of certain aloe leaves.
al·o·et·ic (al′ō-et′ik), *adj.* [< Gr. *aloē*, aloes], of or containing the drug aloes. *n.* a medicine containing aloes.
a·loft (ə-lôft′, ə-loft′), *adv.* [*a-*, on + *loft;* ME. *loft* < ON. *lopt*, the air], 1. high up; far above the ground. 2. high above the deck of a ship; at the masthead.
a·lo·ha (ə-lō′ə, ä-lō′hä), *n. & interj.* [Haw.], love: a word used as a greeting or farewell.
al·o·in (al′ō-in), *n.* a bitter, crystalline cathartic made from the aloe.
a·lone (ə-lōn′), *adj. & adv.* [< *all* + *one* < AS. *an*, single, alone], 1. apart from anything or anyone else. 2. without any other person. 3. without anything further; with nothing more; only. As an adjective, *alone* generally follows the word it modifies.
 leave alone, 1. to let be by oneself. 2. [Colloq.], not to bother or interfere with.
 let alone, 1. not to bother or interfere with. 2. not to speak of: as, we hadn't a dime, *let alone* a dollar.
 let well enough alone, to be content with things as they are and not try to improve them.
SYN.—**alone,** unqualified, denotes the simple fact of being by oneself or itself; **solitary** conveys the same sense but suggests more strongly the lack of companionship or association (a *solitary* tree in the meadow); **lonely,** and the more poetic **lone,** convey a heightened sense of solitude and gloom (the *lonely* sentinel walks his post); **lonesome** suggests a longing or yearning for companionship, often for a particular person (the child is *lonesome* for his mother). —*ANT.* accompanied.
a·long (ə-lôŋ′, ə-loŋ′), *prep.* [ME. *along, anlong;* AS. *andlang*, along, entire; *and*, over against + *lang*, long], on or beside the length of; over or throughout the length of: as, *along* the wall there is a hedge. *adv.* 1. in a line; lengthwise. 2. progressively forward or onward: as, he walked *along* by himself. 3. together (*with* a person or thing). 4. with one: as, she took her camera *along.*
 all along, all the time; from the very beginning.
 along with, 1. together with. 2. in addition to.
 get along, 1. to go forward. 2. to contrive. 3. to succeed. 4. to agree. 5. [Colloq.], to go away.
a·long (ə-lôŋ′, ə-loŋ′), *adv.* [AS. *gelang*], [Obs. or Dial.], owing to (with *of* or *on*).
a·long·shore (ə-lôŋ′shôr′, ə-loŋ′shôr′), *adv.* along the shore; near or beside the shore.
a·long·side (ə-lôŋ′sīd′, ə-loŋ′sīd′), *adv.* at or by the side; side by side. *prep.* at the side of; side by side with.
 alongside of, at the side of; beside; adjoining.
a·loof (ə-lōōf′), *adv.* [*a-*, on + *loof* < D. *loef*, luff, to windward], at a distance but in view; apart. *adj.* 1. at a distance; removed. 2. distant in sympathy, interest, etc.; reserved and cool: as, her manner was *aloof.*
al·o·pe·ci·a (al′ə-pē′shi-ə, al′ə-pē′si-ə), *n.* [L., baldness, fox mange; Gr. *alōpekia* < *alōpēx*, a fox], baldness.
A·lost (å′lôst′), *n.* a city in west central Belgium: pop., 42,000 (est. 1945): Flemish name, *Aalst.*
a·loud (ə-loud′), *adv.* [*a-*, on + *loud*], 1. loudly. 2. in an audible voice; above a whisper. 3. with the voice: as, reading *aloud.*
a·low (ə-lō′), *adv.* [*a-*, on + *low*], in *nautical usage*, below.
Al·oy·si·us (al′ō-ish′əs, al′ō-is′i-əs), [ML. *Aloisius;* prob. < OFr. *Loeis;* see LOUIS], a masculine name.
alp (alp), *n.* [< L. *Alpes*, the Alps, high mountains; understood as akin to *albus*, white], a high mountain, especially in Switzerland: see **Alps.**
A.L.P., American Labor Party.

al·pac·a (al-pak′ə), *n.* [Sp. *alpaca, alpaco* < Ar. *al*, the + Peruv. *paco*, animal], 1. a kind of llama of Bolivia and Peru. 2. its long, silky wool. 3. a thin cloth woven from this wool, often mixed with other fibers. 4. a glossy, generally black cloth, of cotton and wool.

ALPACA
(40 in. high at shoulder; 60 in. high at head)

al·pen·glow (al′pən-glō′), *n.* [after G. *alpenglühen; alpen*, of the Alps + *glühen*, glow], a reddish-purple glow often seen on mountain tops just before sunrise or after sunset.

al·pen·horn (al′pən-hôrn′), *n.* [G., horn of the Alps], a curved, wooden, powerful-sounding horn, about as long as a man's arm, used by Swiss mountaineers for signaling: also **alphorn.**

al·pen·stock (al′pən-stok′), *n.* [G., lit., alps stick], a strong iron-pointed staff used by mountain climbers.

al·pes·trine (al-pes′trin), *adj.* [L. *alpestris* < *Alpes;* see ALP], 1. of the Alps or any mountainous region. 2. in *botany*, growing at high altitudes; subalpine.

al·pha (al′fə), *n.* [Gr. < Heb. *āleph;* see ALEPH], 1. the first letter of the Greek alphabet (Α, α), corresponding to English *A, a*: see **alphabet**, table. 2. the beginning of anything. 3. the brightest star in a constellation.

alpha and omega, 1. the first and last letters of the Greek alphabet; hence, 2. the beginning and the end.

al·pha·bet (al′fə-bet′), *n.* [L. *alphabetum* < Gr. *alpha* + *beta*, the first two letters of the Greek alphabet], 1. the letters of a language, arranged in the usual order. 2. a system of characters used in writing a language or indicating speech sounds. 3. the first elements or principles, as of a branch of knowledge; rudiments.

al·pha·bet·ic (al′fə-bet′ik), *adj.* alphabetical.

al·pha·bet·i·cal (al′fə-bet′i-k'l), *adj.* 1. of or having to do with the alphabet. 2. in the usual order of the letters of a language, as the entries in this dictionary.

al·pha·bet·ize (al′fə-bə-tīz′), *v.t.* [ALPHABETIZED (-tīzd′), ALPHABETIZING], 1. to arrange in alphabetical order. 2. to express by or provide with an alphabet.

alpha particle, a positively charged particle given off by certain radioactive substances: it consists of two protons and two neutrons, and is converted into an atom of helium by the acquisition of two electrons.

alpha rays, rays of alpha particles: they are less penetrating than beta rays.

alpha test, an intelligence test, originally used by the United States Army in World War I, for examining one's understanding of number and word relations, as well as his general knowledge and judgment.

Al·phe·us (al-fē′əs), *n.* [L.; Gr. *Alpheios*], in *Greek mythology*, a river god who pursued Arethusa until she was changed into a fountain by Artemis.

Al·phon·so (al-fon′zō, al-fon′sō), [Sp. *Alfonso* < OHG. < *adal*, nobility + *funs*, ready], a masculine name.

alp·horn (alp′hôrn′), *n.* an alpenhorn.

al·pho·sis (al-fō′sis), *n.* [Mod. L. < Gr. *alphos*, leprosy], abnormal absence of pigment, as in albinism, etc.

Al·pine (al′pīn, al′pin), *adj.* [L. *alpinus* < *Alpes*, the Alps], 1. of the Alps or their inhabitants. 2. in *ethnology*, designating or of one of the three main divisions of the Caucasian, or white, race. 3. [a-], of or like high mountains. 4. [a-], growing in high altitudes. *n.* a member of the Alpine division of the Caucasian race.

al·pin·ist, Al·pin·ist (al′pin-ist), *n.* a mountain climber.

Alps (alps), *n.pl.* a mountain system in Europe, with ranges in France, Switzerland, Germany, Italy, Austria, and Yugoslavia: highest peak, Mont Blanc.

al·read·y (ôl-red′i), *adv.* by or before the given or implied time; previously: distinguished from *all ready.*

al·right (ôl′rīt′), *adv.* all right: a spelling much used but still generally considered a substandard usage.

Al·sace (al-sās′, al′sas; Fr. ål′zås′), *n.* a former province of northeastern France.

Al·sace-Lor·raine (al′sās′lôr-ān′, al′sas-lə-rān′; Fr. ål′zås′lô′ren′), *n.* a region in northeastern France, consisting of the former provinces of Alsace and Lorraine: seized by Germany in 1871 but restored to France by the Versailles Treaty, and again regained by France in 1944 after German occupation in 1940.

ALSACE-LORRAINE

Al·sa·tian (al-sā′shən), *adj.* [after *Alsatia*, older name for Alsace; ML. *Alisatia* < OHG. *Elisazzo* (G. *Elsass*); prob. < *eli*, foreign + *sazzo*, seat, settlement], 1. of Alsace, its people, etc. 2. of Whitefriars, a district in London. *n.* 1. a native or inhabitant of Alsace. 2. a variety of police dog.

al·sike (al′sīk, ôl′sīk), *n.* [after *Alsike*, Sweden], a European clover with white or pinkish flowers, grown for fodder: also **alsike clover.**

al·si·na·ceous (al′si-nā′shəs), *adj.* [L. *alsine*, luxuriant plant < Gr. *alsinē;* + *-aceous*], of or like chickweed.

Al Si·rat (al si-rät′; Ar. as si-rät′), [Ar., the road], in the *Moslem religion*, 1. the true faith of the Koran. 2. the narrow bridge over hell-fire to Paradise.

al·so (ôl′sō), *adv.* [ME. *al so, al swo;* AS. *eallswa* < *eal*, all + *swa*, so], likewise; too; besides; in addition.

al·so-ran (ôl′sō-ran′), *n.* [Colloq.], a person defeated in a race, competition, election, etc.: a term borrowed from horse racing.

alt (alt), *adj.* [It. *alto;* L. *altus*, high], in *music*, having a high pitch; in the first octave above the treble staff. *n.* 1. a high tone or note, especially one in this octave. 2. this octave.

alt., 1. alternate. 2. alternating. 3. altitude. 4. alto.

Alta., Alberta.

Al·tai·an (al-tā′ən, al-tī′ən), *adj.* Altaic.

Al·ta·ic (al-tā′ik), *adj.* 1. of the Altai Mountains or the peoples inhabiting them. 2. of their languages: see **Ural-Altaic.**

Al·tai Mountains (al-tī′, al-tā′ī), a mountain range in Mongolia, Sinkiang, and south central Siberia: highest peak, c. 15,000 ft.

Al·ta·ir (al-tä′ir), *n.* [Ar. *al tā'ir*, the bird], a star of the first magnitude in the constellation Aquila: see **constellation**, chart.

Al·ta·mi·ra (äl′tä-mē′rä), *n.* a place in northern Spain where there are caves containing prehistoric drawings.

al·tar (ôl′tẽr), *n.* [ME. *alter* < AS. *alter, altare* & OFr. *alter;* both < L. *altare*, high altar < *altus*, high], 1. a place, especially a raised platform, where sacrifices or offerings are made to an ancestor, a god, etc. 2. a table, stand, etc. used for sacred purposes in a place of worship, as the Communion table in Christian churches.
lead to the altar, to marry.

altar boy, a boy or man who helps a priest, vicar, etc. at religious services, especially at Mass.

al·tar·piece (ôl′tẽr-pēs′), *n.* an ornamental carving, painting, etc. above and behind an altar.

alt·az·i·muth (alt-az′i-məth), *n.* [*alt*itude + *azimuth*], an instrument for simultaneously measuring the altitude and azimuth of a star so as to determine precisely its apparent position.

Alt·dorf (ält′dôrf′), *n.* a Swiss town near Lake Lucerne: pop., 4,200: scene of the William Tell legend.

al·ter (ôl′tẽr), *v.t.* [Fr. *altérer;* ML. *alterare* < L. *alter*, other], 1. to change; make different; modify. 2. to resew parts of (a garment) for a better fit. 3. [Dial.], to castrate. *v.i.* to change; become different; vary. —*SYN.* see **change.**

al·ter·a·ble (ôl′tẽr-ə-b'l), *adj.* that can be altered.

al·ter·ant (ôl′tẽr-ənt), *adj.* [ML. *alterans*, ppr. of *alterare;* see ALTER], causing alteration. *n.* 1. a thing that causes alteration. 2. in *dyeing*, a substance used to change a color.

al·ter·a·tion (ôl′tẽr-ā′shən), *n.* [Fr.; ML. *alteratio* < *alter*, other], 1. an altering. 2. the result of this.

al·ter·a·tive (ôl′tẽr-ā′tiv, ôl′tẽr-ə-tiv), *adj.* [ML. *alterativus;* see ALTER], 1. causing alteration; that can cause change. 2. in *medicine*, gradually restoring to health. *n.* an alterative medicine or treatment.

al·ter·cate (ôl′tẽr-kāt′, al′tẽr-kāt′), *v.i.* [ALTERCATED (-id), ALTERCATING], [< L. *altercatus*, pp. of *altercari*, to dispute < *alter*, other], to dispute angrily; quarrel.

al·ter·ca·tion (ôl′tẽr-kā′shən, al′tẽr-kā′shən), *n.* [L. *altercatio;* see ALTERCATE], a quarrel; angry or heated dispute. —*SYN.* see **quarrel.**

altered chord, in *music*, a chord in which one or more tones have been chromatically altered by sharps, flats, or naturals foreign to the key.

al·ter e·go (al′tẽr ē′gō, ôl′tẽr eg′ō), [L., lit., other I], 1. another self; another aspect of oneself. 2. a very close friend or constant companion.

‡**al·ter i·dem** (al′tẽr ī′dem), [L.], another of the same kind; second self.

al·ter·nant (ôl′tẽr-nənt, al-tũr′nənt), *adj.* [L. *alternans*, pp.], alternating; having alternating layers.

al·ter·nate (ôl′tẽr-nit, al′tẽr-nit; *for v.*, ôl′tẽr-nāt′, al′tẽr-nāt′), *adj.* [L. *alternatus*, pp. of *alternare*, to do by turns < *alternus*, one after the other < *alter*, other], 1. occurring by turns; succeeding each other; one and then the other. 2. every other: as, answer *alternate* questions. 3. in *botany*, *a)* growing along the stem singly at various intervals: opposed to *opposite*. *b)* placed at intervals between other

ALTERNATE LEAVES
(of beech)

Table of Alphabets

The sounds of the letters in Arabic, Hebrew, Greek, Russian, and German are shown in parentheses.

ENGLISH Upper and Lower Case	ARABIC		HEBREW		GREEK Print and Script		RUSSIAN Upper and Lower Case		GERMAN Upper and Lower Case	
A a	ا	Alif *1*	א	Aleph *3*	Α α	Alpha (ä)	А а	(ä)	𝔄 𝔞	(ä)
B b	ﺑ ﺒ ب	Be (b)	בּ	Beth (b)	Β β	Beta (b)	Б б	(b)	𝔄̈ 𝔞̈	(e)
C c	ﺗ ﺘ ت	Te (t)	ב	Veth (v) *4*	Γ γ	Gamma (g)	В в	(v)	𝔅 𝔟	(b)
D d	ﺛ ﺜ ث	Se (th)	ג	Gimel (g)	Δ δ	Delta (d)	Г г	(g)	ℭ 𝔠	(k, ts, s)
E e	ﺟ ﺠ ج	Jim (j) *2*	ד	Daleth (d)	Ε ϵ	Epsilon (e)	Д д	(d)	ℭ𝔥 𝔠𝔥	(H, kh)
F f	ﺣ ﺤ ح	He (h) *2*	ה	Heh (h)	Ζ ζ	Zeta (z)	Е е	(ye)	𝔇 𝔡	(d)
G g	ﺧ ﺨ خ	Khe (kh) *2*	ו	Vav (v)	Η η	Eta (ā)	Ж ж	(zh)	𝔈 𝔢	(e, ā)
H h	د	Dal (d)	ז	Zayin (z)	Θ θ	Theta (th)	З з	(z)	𝔉 𝔣	(f)
I i	ذ	Zal (*th*)	ח	Kheth (kh)	Ι ι	Iota (ē)	И и	(i, ē)	𝔊 𝔤	(g, kh)
J j	ر	Re (r)	ט	Teth (t)	Κ κ	Kappa (k)	Й й	(ē) *6*	ℌ 𝔥	(h)
K k	ز	Ze (z)	י	Yod (y)	Λ λ	Lambda (l)	К к	(k)	ℑ 𝔦	(i, ē)
L l	ﺳ ﺴ س	Sin (s) *2*	כּ ךּ	Kaph (k) *5*	Μ μ	Mu (m)	Л л	(l)	𝔍 𝔧	(y)
M m	ﺷ ﺸ ش	Shin (sh) *2*	כ ך	Khaph (kh) *4, 5*	Ν ν	Nu (n)	М м	(m)	𝔎 𝔨	(k)
N n	ﺻ ﺼ ص	Sad (s) *2*	ל	Lamedh (l)	Ξ ξ	Xi (ks)	Н н	(n)	𝔏 𝔩	(l)
O o	ﺿ ﻀ ض	Dad (*th*) *2*	מ ם	Mem (m) *5*	Ο ο	Omicron (o)	О о	(ô, o)	𝔐 𝔪	(m)
P p	ط	Ta (t)	נ ן	Nun (n) *5*	Π π	Pi (p)	П п	(p)	𝔑 𝔫	(n)
Q q	ظ	Za (z)	ס	Samekh (s)	Ρ ρ	Rho (r)	Р р	(r)	𝔒 𝔬	(ō, ô)
R r	ﻋ ﻌ ع	Ain *1, 2*	ע	Ayin *3*	Σ σ ς	Sigma (s) *5*	С с	(s)	𝔒̈ 𝔬̈	(ö)
S s	ﻏ ﻐ غ	Ghain (kh) *2*	פּ ףּ	Peh (p) *5*	Τ τ	Tau (t)	Т т	(t)	𝔓 𝔭	(p)
T t	ﻓ ﻔ ف	Fe (f) *2*	פ ף	Feh (f) *4, 5*	Υ υ	Upsilon (ü, o͞o)	У у	(o͞o)	𝔔(𝔲) 𝔮(𝔲)	(kv)
U u	ﻗ ﻘ ق	Qaf (kä) *2*	צ ץ	Tsadi (ts) *5*	Φ φ	Phi (f)	Ф ф	(f)	ℜ 𝔯	(r)
V v	ﻛ ﻜ ك	Kef (k) *2*	ק	Koph (k)	Χ χ	Chi (H)	Х х	(kh)	𝔖 ſ 𝔰	(s, z) *5*
W w	ﻟ ﻠ ل	Lam (l) *2*	ר	Resh (r)	Ψ ψ	Psi (ps)	Ц ц	(ts)	𝔖𝔠𝔥 ſ𝔠𝔥	(sh)
X x	ﻣ ﻤ م	Mim (m) *2*	שׂ	Sin (s)	Ω ω	Omega (ō)	Ч ч	(ch)	𝔗 𝔱	(t)
Y y	ﻧ ﻨ ن	Nun (n) *2*	שׁ	Shin (sh) *4*			Ш ш	(sh)	𝔘 𝔲	(o͞o)
Z z	ه	He (h)	תּ	Tav (t)			Щ щ	(shch)	𝔘̈ 𝔲̈	(ü)
	و	Waw (w)	ת	Thav (th, s) *4*			Ъ ъ	*7*	𝔙 𝔳	(f)
	ﻳ ﻴ ي	Ye (y) *5*	***Diacritical Marks***				Ы ы	(ē)	𝔚 𝔴	(v)
			◌ֹ (ō, ô) ; ◌ַ (ä)				Ь ь	*8*	𝔛 𝔵	(ks)
			◌ָ (ä) ; ◌ֶ (e)				Э э	(e)	𝔜 𝔶	(ē, ü)
			◌ִ (i, ē) ; ◌ְ (silent)				Ю ю	(ü)	ℨ 𝔷	(ts)
			◌ֻ (o͞o)				Я я	(yä)		

NOTES

1. A neutral letter, silent in the middle of words, but represented by ('), indicating the glottal stop, when used at the beginning of a word.
2. The first form is used at the beginning of a word; the second, in the middle; the third, at the end.
3. A neutral letter, either silent or sounded according to the accompanying diacritical mark.
4. A variant of the preceding character, not counted in the alphabet.
5. The final form is used only as the last letter of a word.
6. Used only as the second vowel in a diphthong.
7. Indicates nonpalatalization of a preceding consonant.
8. Indicates palatalization of a preceding consonant.

parts. *n.* 1. a person selected to take the place of another if necessary; substitute. 2. in *linguistics*, an allomorph. Abbreviated **alt.** *v.t.* [ALTERNATED (-id), ALTERNATING], to do or use by turns; make happen or arrange by turns. *v.i.* 1. to act, happen, etc. by turns; follow successively: as, good times *alternate* with bad. 2. to take turns. 3. to exchange places, etc. regularly. 4. in *electricity*, *a*) to reverse direction regularly and continually, as a current. *b*) to make, or be operated by, such a current. —*SYN.* see **intermittent.**

alternate angles, two angles at opposite ends and on opposite sides of a line crossing two others.

B
C

ALTERNATE ANGLES (B, C)

al·ter·nate·ly (ôl'tẽr-nit-li, al'tẽr-nit-li, ôl-tũr'nit-li, al-tũr'nit-li), *adv.* by turns; in alternate order.

alternating current, an electric current that reverses its direction regularly and continually: abbreviated **A.C., a.c.**

al·ter·na·tion (ôl'tẽr-nā'shən, al'tẽr-nā'shən), *n.* [L. *alternatio;* see ALTERNATE], an alternating; occurrence, position, etc. of things by turns.

alternation of generations, the occurrence of generations in alternate order, first one that reproduces sexually, then one that reproduces asexually, and so on.

al·ter·na·tive (ôl-tũr'nə-tiv, al-tũr'nə-tiv), *adj.* [Fr. *alternatif;* ML. *alternativus;* see ALTERNATE], providing or necessitating a choice between two (or, loosely, more than two) things. *n.* 1. a choice between two or more things. 2. either or any one of the things to be chosen. —*SYN.* see **choice.**

alternative conjunction, a conjunction joining elements which, it implies, are not to be taken together, as *or*, *neither . . . nor*, etc.

al·ter·na·tive·ly (ôl-tũr'nə-tiv-li, al-tũr'nə-tiv-li), *adv.* 1. in an alternative manner; with a choice. 2. as an alternative; on the other hand.

al·ter·na·tor (ôl'tẽr-nā'tẽr, al'tẽr-nā'tẽr), *n.* an electric generator or dynamo producing alternating current.

Alt·geld, John Peter (ôlt'geld), 1847–1902; American statesman; governor of Illinois, 1892–1896.

Al·the·a (al-thē'ə), [L. *Althaea;* Gr. *Althaia*, lit., healer < *althainein*, to heal], a feminine name.

al·the·a, al·thae·a (al-thē'ə), *n.* [L. *althaea;* Gr. *althaia*, wild mallows], a tall shrub of the mallow family, with showy flowers of white, pink, red, or bluish-purple; rose of Sharon.

alt·horn (alt'hôrn'), *n.* [*alt* + *horn*], a brass-wind instrument, the alto saxhorn, often used in place of the French horn: also **alto horn.**

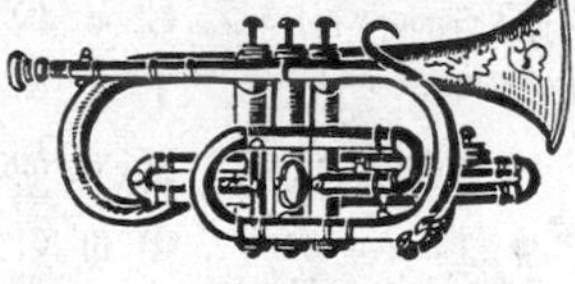

ALTHORN

al·though (ôl-*th*ō'), *conj.* [< *all* + *though*]; in spite of the fact that; granting that; though: now sometimes spelled **altho.**

al·ti·graph (al'tə-graf', al'tə-gräf'), *n.* [*alti-* < L. *altus*, high; + *-graph*], an instrument for recording altitude automatically on a chart: it is essentially an aneroid barometer.

al·tim·e·ter (al-tim'ə-tẽr, al'tə-mē'tẽr), *n.* [*alti-* < L. *altus*, high; + *-meter*], 1. an instrument for measuring the altitude, or height above the ground: in aircraft it is an aneroid barometer with a dial marked in feet or meters. 2. a sextant or quadrant.

al·tim·e·try (al-tim'ə-tri), *n.* [*alti-* < L. *altus*, high; + *-metry*], the science or practice of measuring altitudes, as with an altimeter.

al·ti·scope (al'tə-skōp'), *n.* [*alti-* < L. *altus*, high; + *-scope*], a kind of periscope.

al·ti·tude (al'tə-tōōd', al'tə-tūd'), *n.* [L. *altitudo* < *altus*, high], 1. the height of a thing above a certain level, especially above the earth's surface or sea level. 2. a high place or region. 3. a high degree of authority, rank, etc. 4. in *astronomy*, the angular height of a planet, star, etc. above the horizon. 5. in *geometry*, the perpendicular distance from the base of a figure to its highest point or to the side parallel to the base. Abbreviated **alt.** —*SYN.* see **height.**

al·ti·tu·di·nal (al'tə-tōō'd'n-'l, al'tə-tū'd'n-'l), *adj.* having to do with altitude.

al·to (al'tō), *n.* [*pl.* ALTOS (-tōz)], [It. < L. *altus*, high], in *music*, 1. the range of the lowest female voice (contralto) or the highest male voice. 2. a voice or singer with such a range. 3. an instrument having a similar range, as an althorn. 4. a part for such a voice or instrument. *adj.* 1. singing or playing within this range. 2. for this range. Abbreviated **alt., a.**

alto clef, the C clef on the third line; viola clef.

al·to-cu·mu·lus (al'tō-kū'myoo-ləs), *n.* [*alto-* < L. *altus*, high; + *cumulus*], a formation of high, fleecy clouds in round, white or grayish, partly shaded masses.

al·to·geth·er (ôl'tə-ge*th*'ẽr, ôl'tə-ge*th*'ẽr), *adv.* [ME. *altogedere;* see ALL & TOGETHER], 1. wholly; completely. 2. everything being considered; on the whole. Distinguished from *all together*. *n.* a whole.
in the altogether, [Colloq.], nude.

alto horn, an althorn.

Al·ton (ôl't'n), *n.* a city on the Mississippi, in southwestern Illinois: pop., 43,000.

Al·to·na (äl'tô-nä), *n.* a former city in northern Germany: now part of Hamburg.

Alt·oo·na (al-tōō'nə), *n.* a city in central Pennsylvania: pop., 69,000.

al·to-re·lie·vo (al'tō-ri-lē'vō), *n.* [*pl.* ALTO-RELIEVOS (-vōz)], [It. *alto*, high + *rilievo*, relief; sp. influenced by *relief*], sculpture in which the figures project from a background by half their thickness or more; high relief.

‡**al·to-ri·lie·vo** (äl'tô-rē-lye'vô), *n.* [*pl.* ALTI-RILIEVI (äl'tē-rē-lye'vē)], [It.], alto-relievo.

al·to-stra·tus (al'tō-strā'təs), *n.* [*alto-* < L. *altus*, high; + *stratus*], a formation of gray or bluish sheetlike clouds, like the cirro-stratus but lower and heavier.

al·tri·cial (al-trish'əl), *adj.* [Mod. L. < L. *altricialis* < *altrix*, a nurse], confined to the nest for some time after being hatched: said of certain birds.

al·tru·ism (al'trōō-iz'm), *n.* [Fr. *altruisme* < It. *altrui* or Fr. *autrui*, of or to others; LL. **alterui* < L. *alter*, another], unselfish concern for the welfare of others: opposed to *egoism*.

al·tru·ist (al'trōō-ist), *n.* a person who believes in or practices altruism.

al·tru·is·tic (al'trōō-is'tik), *adj.* of or motivated by altruism; unselfish. —*SYN.* see **philanthropic.**

al·tru·is·ti·cal·ly (al'trōō-is'ti-k'l-i, al'trōō-is'tik-li), *adv.* in an altruistic manner; unselfishly.

al·u·del (al'yoo-del'), *n.* [Fr.; Sp.; Ar. *al uthāl*], a chemical apparatus consisting of a pear-shaped pot with both ends open: condensers for sublimation are made up of aludels placed one above another.

al·u·la (al'yoo-lə), *n.* [*pl.* ALULAE (-lē')], [Mod. L., dim. of *ala*, wing], the bastard wing of a bird: see **bastard wing.**

al·um (al'əm), *n.* [ME.; OFr.; L. *alumen*, alum; for the base, see ALE], 1. a double sulfate of ammonium or a univalent metal (as sodium or potassium) and of a trivalent metal (as aluminum, iron, or chromium): it is used as an astringent, as an emetic, and in the manufacture of baking powders, dyes, and paper; the commonest form is potash alum (potassium aluminum sulfate); $KAl(SO_4)_2 \cdot 12H_2O$. 2. aluminum sulfate: erroneous use.

alum., aluminum.

a·lu·mi·na (ə-lōō'mi-nə), *n.* [Mod. L. < L. *alumen*, *aluminis*, alum], an oxide of aluminum, Al_2O_3, present in bauxite and clay and found as different forms of corundum, including emery, sapphires, rubies, etc.

a·lu·mi·nate (ə-lōō'mi-nāt'), *n.* a salt of aluminum hydroxide reacting as an acid in an alkaline solution.

a·lu·mi·ni·fer·ous (ə-lōō'mi-nif'ẽr-əs), *adj.* [< *aluminum* + *-ferous*], yielding or containing aluminum or alumina.

al·u·min·i·um (al'yoo-min'i-əm), *n.* aluminum: the British term.

a·lu·mi·nize (ə-lōō'mi-nīz'), *v.t.* [ALUMINIZED (-nīzd'), ALUMINIZING], to cover, or treat, with aluminum.

a·lu·mi·no·ther·my (ə-lōō'mi-nō-thũr'mi), *n.* [< *aluminum* + Gr. *thermē*, heat], a metallurgical process in which aluminum reduces another metal from its compounds, simultaneously releasing great heat.

a·lu·mi·nous (ə-lōō'mi-nəs), *adj.* [L. *aluminosus* < *alumen*, alum], of or containing alum, alumina, or aluminum.

a·lu·mi·num (ə-lōō'mi-nəm), *n.* [Mod. L. < L. *alumen*, *aluminis*, alum], one of the chemical elements, a silvery, lightweight, easily worked metal that resists corrosion and is found abundantly, but only in combination: symbol, Al; at. wt., 26.97; at. no., 13. *adj.* of, containing, or made of aluminum. Abbreviated **alum.**

aluminum oxide, alumina.

a·lum·na (ə-lum'nə), *n.* [*pl.* ALUMNAE (-nē)], [L., fem. of *alumnus*], a girl or woman who has attended or been graduated from a school, college, or university.

a·lum·nus (ə-lum'nəs), *n.* [*pl.* ALUMNI (-nī)], [L., a pupil, foster son < *alere*, to nourish], a person, especially a boy or man, who has attended or been graduated from a school, college, or university.

al·um·root (al'əm-rōōt', al'əm-root'), *n.* any of several plants of the saxifrage family, having tiny, bell-shaped flowers and an astringent root.

al·u·nite (al'yoo-nīt'), *n.* [Fr. < *alun;* L. *alumen*, alum], a mineral containing hydrated potassium aluminum sulfate.

Al·va (al'və), a masculine name: see **Alvah.**

Al·va, Duke of (al'və; Sp. äl'vä), (*Fernando Álvarez de Toledo*), 1508?–1583?; Spanish general; suppressed revolt in the Low Countries: also **Alba.**

Al·vah (al'və), [Heb. *'alvāh*, *'alvān;* often associated with L. *albus*, white], a masculine name: variant, *Alvan:* also spelled **Alva.**

Al·van (al'vən), a masculine name: see **Alvah.**

Al·va·ra·do, A·lon·so de (ä-lôn'sô de äl'vä-rä'*th*ô),

1490?–1554; Spanish conquistador in Mexico.
Alvarado, Pe·dro de (pe′thrô), 1495?–1541; Spanish officer with Cortes in the conquest of Mexico.
Álvarez Quintero, Joaquín and **Serafín**, see **Quintero, Joaquín Álvarez** and **Serafín Álvarez.**
al·ve·o·lar (al-vē′ə-lẽr), *adj.* [< *alveolus*], 1. of or like an alveolus or alveoli; socketlike. 2. in *anatomy, a*) relating to the part of the jaws containing the sockets of the teeth. *b*) relating to the air pockets in the lungs. 3. in *phonetics*, formed, as English *t, d, s*, by touching or approaching the upper alveoli with the tongue. *n.* in *phonetics*, a sound articulated by the tongue on or near the upper alveoli; teethridge sound.
al·ve·o·late (al-vē′ə-lit), *adj.* [L. *alveolatus*, hollowed out < *alveus*, cavity], honeycombed; full of small cavities.
al·ve·o·lat·ed (al-vē′ə-lā′tid), *adj.* alveolate.
al·ve·o·lus (al-vē′ə-ləs), *n.* [*pl.* ALVEOLI (-lī′)], [L., dim. of *alveus*, a hollow, cavity], 1. in *anatomy & zoology*, a small cavity or hollow, as a cell of a honeycomb, air cell of a lung, tooth socket, etc. 2. *usually pl.* the ridge of the gums above and behind the upper front teeth; teethridge.
Al·vin (al′vin), [G. *Alwin*, lit., noble friend < OHG. *adal*, nobility + *wini*, friend], a masculine name.
Al·vi·na (al-vī′nə), a feminine name: see **Alvin.**
al·vine (al′vin, al′vīn), *adj.* [< L. *alvus*, belly], of the abdomen or intestines.
al·way (ôl′wā), *adv.* [Archaic or Poetic], always.
al·ways (ôl′wiz, ôl′wāz), *adv.* [< *all* + *way*, with adv. genit. *-s*], 1. at all times; on all occasions; invariably: opposed to *sometimes.* 2. all the time; continually; forever.
a·lys·sum (ə-lis′əm), *n.* [Mod. L.; Gr. *alysson*, madwort < *alyssos*, curing madness < *a-*, without + *lyssa*, madness, rage], 1. any of a number of plants of the mustard family, bearing grayish leaves and white or yellow flowers. 2. a dwarf plant with small spikes of flowers, usually white; sweet alyssum.
am (am; *unstressed*, əm), [AS. *eom, am;* akin to Sans. *asmi; as-*, is + *-mi*, first person pron.; see BE], the first person singular, present indicative, of **be.**
Am, in *chemistry*, americium.
Am., 1. America. 2. American.
AM, A.M., amplitude modulation.
A.M., [L.], 1. *anno mundi*, in the year of the world. 2. *Artium Magister*, master of arts: also **M.A.**
A.M., a.m., *ante meridiem*, [L.], before noon: used to designate the time from midnight to noon.
A.M.A., American Medical Association.
am·a·da·vat (am′ə-də-vat′), *n.* [Ind., after *Ahmadabad*, India, from which it was exported], a small bird of India, often kept for its singing and fighting ability.
Am·a·dis (am′ə-dis), *n.* [Sp., lit., love of God], the hero of several medieval romances in Spanish, French, and English literature.
am·a·dou (am′ə-do͞o′), *n.* [Fr.; Pr.; ? < Port. *amador;* L. *amator*, lover], a spongy material made from certain fungi and used as punk for lighting fires or as a styptic.
a·mah (ä′mə), *n.* [Anglo-Ind. < Port. *ama*], in the Orient, a woman servant or nurse, especially one who nurses or takes care of babies.
a·main (ə-mān′), *adv.* [*a-*, on + *main*, power, strength], [Archaic or Poetic], 1. forcefully; vigorously. 2. at or with great speed. 3. hastily; suddenly.
Am·a·lek·ite (am′ə-lə-kīt′), *n.* [< Heb. *'amālēqī*, an ancient Bedouin tribe said to be descended from Amalek, grandson of Esau; + *-ite*], 1. a member of a Syrian Bedouin tribe. 2. in the *Bible*, a member of a tribe descended from Esau: Gen. 36:12–16.
a·mal·gam (ə-mal′gəm), *n.* [Fr. *amalgame;* ML. *amalgama;* prob. < Ar. *al malgham;* Gr. *malagma*, an emollient < *malassein*, to soften], 1. any alloy of mercury with another metal or other metals: silver amalgam is used as a dental filling. 2. a combination; mixture; blend.
a·mal·gam·a·ble (ə-mal′gəm-ə-b'l), *adj.* that can be amalgamated.
a·mal·gam·ate (ə-mal′gə-māt′), *v.t. & v.i.* [AMALGAMATED (-id), AMALGAMATING], 1. to combine in an amalgam. 2. to unite; mix; combine; consolidate.
a·mal·gam·a·tion (ə-mal′gə-mā′shən), *n.* 1. an amalgamating or being amalgamated. 2. the result of amalgamating; mixture; blend; combination.
a·mal·gam·a·tive (ə-mal′gə-mā′tiv), *adj.* tending to amalgamate.
a·mal·gam·a·tor (ə-mal′gə-mā′tẽr), *n.* 1. a person or thing that amalgamates. 2. a machine for amalgamating silver or certain other metals with mercury and used in separating the metal from the ore.
Am·al·thae·a, Am·al·the·a (am′'l-thē′ə), *n.* [L.; Gr. *Amaltheia*], in *Greek & Roman mythology*, the goat that nursed Zeus (Jupiter): one of its horns was called the *cornucopia*, or *horn of plenty*, because it would become full of whatever its owner wanted.
A·man·da (ə-man′də), [L., lit., worthy to be loved < the gerund stem of *amare*, to love], a feminine name: diminutive, *Mandy.*
am·a·ni·ta (am′ə-nī′tə), *n.* [< Gr. *amanitai*], any of several very poisonous fungi with white spores, as the fly agaric.
a·man·u·en·sis (ə-man′yoo-en′sis), *n.* [*pl.* AMANUENSES (-sēz)], [L.; *a-* (*ab*), from + *manu*, abl. of *manus*, a hand + *-ensis*, relating to], a person who takes dictation or copies something already written; secretary.
am·a·ranth (am′ə-ranth′), *n.* [L. *amarantus;* Gr. *amarantos*, unfading < *a-*, not + *marainein*, to die away], 1. any of a number of related plants, usually with colorful leaves and, in some instances, showy, tassellike heads of flowers, as the love-lies-bleeding, pigweed, tumbleweed, etc. 2. [Poetic], an imaginary flower that never fades or dies. 3. a dark purple; purplish-red.
am·a·ran·thine (am′ə-ran′thin), *adj.* 1. of or like the amaranth. 2. unfading; undying; deathless. 3. deep-purple; purplish-red.
Am·a·ril·lo (am′ə-ril′ō), *n.* a city in northwestern Texas: pop., 138,000.
am·a·ryl·li·da·ceous (am′ə-ril′i-dā′shəs), *adj.* [< Mod. L. *Amaryllidaceae*, name of the family < *amaryllis*], of the amaryllis family of plants, growing chiefly in warm, dry climates.
am·a·ryl·lis (am′ə-ril′is), *n.* [< L. & Gr. *Amaryllis*, a shepherdess' name in poems by Virgil and Theocritus], 1. any of a number of related bulb plants bearing several white, purple, pink, or red lilylike flowers on a single stem, as the belladonna lily. 2. [A-], in ***pastoral poetry***, a shepherdess: a conventional name.
a·mass (ə-mas′), *v.t.* [Fr. *amasser; à*, to + *masser*, to pile up < L. *massa*, a lump or mass], to pile up; collect together; accumulate, especially for oneself.
am·a·teur (am′ə-choor′, am′ə-toor′, am′ə-tyoor′; Fr. à′mà′tẽr′), *n.* [Fr.; L. *amator*, lover < *amare*, to love], 1. a person who does something for the pleasure of it rather than for money; nonprofessional; hence, 2. a person who does something more or less unskillfully. *adj.* 1. of or done by an amateur or amateurs. 2. who is an amateur; made up of amateurs. 3. amateurish.
SYN.—**amateur** refers to one who does something for the pleasure of it rather than for pay and often implies a relative lack of skill; a **dilettante** is an amateur in the arts, but the word is also applied disparagingly to a superficial dabbler in the arts; **novice** and **neophyte** refer to one who is a beginner, hence inexperienced, in some activity, **neophyte** carrying additional connotations of youthful enthusiasm; **tyro** refers to an inexperienced but self-assertive beginner and generally connotes incompetence. —*ANT.* professional, expert.
am·a·teur·ish (am′ə-choor′ish, am′ə-toor′ish, am′ə-tyoor′ish), *adj.* like an amateur; inexpert; unskillful.
am·a·teur·ism (am′ə-choor-iz'm, am′ə-toor′iz'm, am′ə-tyoor′iz'm), *n.* 1. an amateurish method or quality. 2. the rank of an amateur; nonprofessional status.
A·ma·ti (ä-mä′ti), *n.* a violin made by Nicolò Amati or his family.
A·ma·ti, Ni·co·lò or **Ni·co·la** (nē′kô-lô′ ä-mä′tē; nē-kô′lä), 1596–1684; violin maker of Cremona, Italy.
am·a·tive (am′ə-tiv), *adj.* [< L. *amatus*, pp. of *amare*, to love; + *-ive*], of or inclined to love, especially sexual love.
A·ma·to, Pas·qua·le (päs-kwä′le ä-mä′tô), 1879–1942; Italian baritone.
am·a·tol (am′ə-tol′, am′ə-tōl′), *n.* [< *am*monium + *tol*uene], a powerful explosive containing ammonium nitrate and trinitrotoluene (TNT).
am·a·to·ry (am′ə-tôr′i, am′ə-tō′ri), *adj.* [L. *amatorius* < *amare*, to love], of, causing, or showing love, especially sexual love.
am·au·ro·sis (am′ô-rō′sis), *n.* [Gr. *amaurōsis* < *amauros*, dark], partial or total blindness without visible organic change, caused by disease of the optic nerve.
a·maze (ə-māz′), *v.t.* [AMAZED (-māzd′), AMAZING], [ME. *amasen;* AS. *amasian;* see MAZE], 1. to fill with great surprise or sudden wonder; astonish. 2. [Obs.], to bewilder. *n.* [Poetic], amazement. —*SYN.* see **surprise.**
a·maz·ed·ly (ə-māz′id-li), *adv.* in an amazed manner.
a·maze·ment (ə-māz′mənt), *n.* 1. an amazed condition; great surprise or wonder; astonishment. 2. [Obs.], bewilderment.
a·maz·ing (ə-māz′iŋ), *adj.* [ppr. of *amaze*], causing amazement; wonderful; astonishing.
Am·a·zon (am′ə-zon′, am′ə-z'n), *n.* [L.; Gr. *Amazon;* derived by Greek folk etym. < *a-*, without + *mazos*, breast, because of the story that the Amazons cut off one breast to facilitate archery], 1. in *Greek mythology*, a female warrior of a race supposed to have lived in Scythia, near the Black Sea. 2. [a-], a woman or girl soldier; hence, 3. [a-], a large, strong, masculine woman. 4. a river in South America, flowing from the Andes in Peru, across northern Brazil into the Atlantic: length, c. 4,000 mi. 5. a kind of ant that makes slaves of other ants: also **Amazon ant.** 6. a parrot of Central and South America.

Am·a·zo·ni·an (am'ə-zō'ni-ən), *adj.* 1. of, like, or characteristic of an Amazon; hence, 2. warlike and masculine: said of women. 3. of the Amazon River or the country around it.

am·a·zon·ite (am'ə-z'n-īt'), *n.* [after the *Amazon* River], a green semiprecious stone, a kind of microcline: also **Amazon stone.**

Amb., Ambassador.

am·bage (am'bij), *n.* [*pl.* AMBAGES (-iz; L. am-bā'jēz)], [Fr. *ambages* < L. *amb,* around + *agere,* to go], 1. a winding pathway; hence, 2. *usually pl.* a roundabout, indirect way of talking or doing things.

am·ba·gious (am-bā'jəs), *adj.* using ambages; devious.

Am·ba·la (əm-bä'lä), *n.* a city in East Punjab, India: pop., 87,000.

am·ba·ry, am·ba·ri (am-bä'rē), *n.* [Hind. *ambārā*], 1. an East Indian plant. 2. its fiber, used in making rope.

am·bas·sa·dor (am-bas'ə-dēr), *n.* [Fr. *ambassadeur;* It. *ambasciatore;* Pr. *ambaisador* < *ambaisat,* task, mission; ult. base Celt. **ambi-actus,* one sent around, messenger; transmitted via L. (Gaul.) *ambactus,* helper, henchman & Goth. *andbahts,* servant], 1. the highest-ranking representative appointed by one country or government to represent it in another. 2. a special representative: an **ambassador-at-large** is one accredited to no particular country; an **ambassador extraordinary** is one on a special diplomatic mission; an **ambassador plenipotentiary** is one having the power to make treaties. 3. an official messenger or agent with a special mission. Abbreviated **Amb.** Formerly also spelled **embassador.**

am·bas·sa·do·ri·al (am-bas'ə-dôr'i-əl, am-bas'ə-dō'ri-əl), *adj.* relating to an ambassador or ambassadors.

am·bas·sa·dor·ship (am-bas'ə-dēr-ship'), *n.* [*ambassador* + *-ship*], the rank, duties, office, or term of office of an ambassador.

am·bas·sa·dress (am-bas'ə-dris), *n.* 1. a woman ambassador. 2. the wife of an ambassador.

am·ber (am'bēr), *n.* [Fr. *ambre* < Ar. *'anbar,* ambergris], 1. a yellow or brownish-yellow translucent fossil resin found on some seashores and used in jewelry, pipestems, etc.: it is hard, easily polished, and quickly electrified by friction. 2. the color of amber. *adj.* 1. made of or like amber. 2. having the color of amber.

am·ber·gris (am'bēr-grēs', am'bēr-gris), *n.* [Fr. *ambre gris; ambre* (see AMBER) + *gris* < OS. *gris,* gray], a grayish, waxy substance, secreted by sperm whales and found floating in tropical seas: it is used in perfumes.

am·ber·oid (am'bēr-oid'), *n.* a material made to resemble amber, formed of small pieces of amber or some other resin pressed together: also **ambroid.**

am·bi- (am'bi, am'bə), [< L. *ambo,* both], a combining form meaning *both,* as in *ambidextrous.*

am·bi·dex·ter (am'bə-dek'stēr), *adj.* [ML. < L. *ambo,* both + *dexter,* right hand], 1. able to use both hands with equal ease; hence, 2. on both sides (of a dispute) at the same time; deceitful. *n.* 1. a person who can use both hands with equal ease. 2. a deceitful or double-dealing person.

am·bi·dex·ter·i·ty (am'bə-deks-ter'ə-ti), *n.* the quality or state of being ambidextrous.

am·bi·dex·trous (am'bə-dek'strəs), *adj.* [< *ambidexter* + *-ous*], 1. able to use both hands with equal ease. 2. very skillful or versatile. 3. treacherous; deceitful.

am·bi·ence (am'bi-əns), *n.* [Fr. *ambiance*], 1. surroundings; milieu. 2. in art, especially painting, the configuration of secondary designs, themes, etc. enhancing and extending the central design or theme.

am·bi·ent (am'bi-ənt), *adj.* [L. *ambiens,* ppr. of *ambire,* to go around < *ambi-,* around + ppr. of *ire,* to go], surrounding; on all sides.

am·bi·gu·i·ty (am'bi-gū'ə-ti), *n.* [L. *ambiguitas* < *ambiguus*], 1. the quality or state of being ambiguous. 2. [*pl.* AMBIGUITIES (-tiz)], an ambiguous word or remark.

am·big·u·ous (am-big'ū-əs), *adj.* [L. *ambiguus* < *ambigere,* to wander < *ambi-,* about, around + *agere,* to go], 1. having two or more possible meanings. 2. not clear; indefinite; uncertain; vague. —*SYN.* see **obscure.**

am·bit (am'bit), *n.* [L. *ambitus,* a going about, revolution < pp. of *ambire;* see AMBIENT], 1. a circuit or circumference. 2. the limits or scope.

am·bi·tend·en·cy (am'bi-ten'dən-si), *n.* [*ambi-* + *tendency*], in *psychology,* the existence of conflicting tendencies in the same individual.

am·bi·tion (am-bish'ən), *n.* [L. *ambitio,* a going around (to solicit votes) < pp. of *ambire;* see AMBIENT], 1. strong desire to succeed or to achieve something, as fame, power, wealth, etc. 2. the thing so desired.

am·bi·tious (am-bish'əs), *adj.* [L. *ambitiosus,* soliciting the favor of < *ambitio;* see AMBITION], 1. full of or showing ambition. 2. greatly desirous (*of* something); eager for. 3. showing great effort; aspiring.

SYN.—**ambitious** implies a striving for advancement, wealth, fame, etc., and is used with both favorable and unfavorable connotations; **aspiring** suggests a striving to reach some lofty end regarded as somewhat beyond one's normal expectations (an *aspiring* young poet); **enterprising** implies an energetic readiness to take risks or undertake new projects in order to succeed; **emulous** suggests ambition characterized by a competitive desire to equal or surpass another.

am·biv·a·lence (am-biv'ə-ləns), *n.* [*ambi-* + *valence*], simultaneous conflicting feelings toward a person or thing, as love and hate.

am·biv·a·lent (am-biv'ə-lənt), *adj.* of or having ambivalence.

am·bi·ver·sion (am'bi-vũr'shən, am'bi-vũr'zhən), *n.* [*ambi-* + intro*version*], in *psychology,* a condition or character trait midway between introversion and extroversion.

am·bi·vert (am'bi-vẽrt), *n.* one who has ambiversion.

am·ble (am'b'l), *v.i.* [AMBLED (-b'ld), AMBLING], [ME. *amblen;* OFr. *ambler;* L. *ambulare,* to walk], 1. to move smoothly and easily by raising first both legs on one side, then both on the other: said of horses, etc. 2. to go easily and unhurriedly; walk in a leisurely manner. *n.* 1. a horse's ambling gait. 2. a leisurely walking pace.

am·bler (am'blẽr), *n.* a person or animal that ambles.

am·blyg·o·nite (am-blig'ə-nīt'), *n.* [Gr. *amblygonit* < base of *amblygōnios,* wide-angled + *-it* (see -ITE)], a pale-green crystalline mineral, $Li(AlF)PO_4$.

am·bly·o·pi·a (am'bli-ō'pi-ə), *n.* [Mod. L. < Gr. *amblys,* dull + *ōps,* eye], the early stage of amaurosis.

am·bo (am'bō), *n.* [*pl.* AMBOS (-bōz)], [ML.; Gr. *ambōn*], a pulpit or raised reading stand in early Christian churches.

am·bo·cep·tor (am'bə-sep'tẽr), *n.* [< L. *ambo,* both + *receptor,* a taker or receiver], in *bacteriology,* a substance present in the blood during infection, believed to help in the destruction of the disease-causing microorganism by connecting it with another substance in the blood (the *complement*).

Am·boi·na (am-boi'nə), *n.* 1. one of the Molucca Islands, in the Netherlands Indies: area, 384 sq. mi.; pop., 400,000. 2. its capital, a naval base: pop., 17,000.

Amboina wood, the mottled, curled wood of an Asiatic tree, used in making furniture.

Am·boise (än'bwȧz'), *n.* a town in north central France: pop., 5,000: ancient residence of kings.

am·broid (am'broid), *n.* amberoid.

Am·brose (am'brōz), [L. *Ambrosius* < Gr. *ambrosios;* see AMBROSIA], a masculine name.

Ambrose, Saint, 340?–397 A.D.; Bishop of Milan: his day is December 7.

Ambrose Channel, the entrance into New York harbor, across Sandy Hook bar.

am·bro·si·a (am-brō'zhi-ə, am-brō'zhə), *n.* [L.; Gr. < *ambrotos,* immortal < *a-,* not + *brotos,* mortal], 1. in *Greek & Roman mythology,* the food of the gods and immortals. 2. anything that tastes or smells delicious. 3. the ragweed. 4. beebread.

am·bro·si·a·ceous (am-brō'zi-ā'shəs), *adj.* [< Mod. L. *Ambrosiaceae,* the ragweed family < L. *ambrosia;* see AMBROSIA], in *botany,* of the ragweed family.

am·bro·si·al (am-brō'zhi-əl, am-brō'zhəl), *adj.* [L. *ambrosius;* Gr. *ambrosios*], 1. of or fit for the gods; divine. 2. like ambrosia; delicious; fragrant.

Am·bro·si·an (am-brō'zi-ən, am-brō'zhən), *adj.* of, by, or supposedly by Saint Ambrose.

am·bro·si·an (am-brō'zhi-ən, am-brō'zhən), *adj.* ambrosial.

Ambrosian chant, a type of liturgical chant introduced by Saint Ambrose of Milan and characterized by a greater ornamentation of melody than in the Gregorian chant, which superseded it.

am·bro·type (am'brə-tīp', am'brō-tīp'), *n.* [< Gr. *ambrotos,* immortal (see AMBROSIA); + *-type*], an early kind of photograph, consisting of a glass negative backed by a dark surface so as to appear positive.

am·bry (am'bri), *n.* [*pl.* AMBRIES (-briz)], [ME. *ambrie, almarie;* OFr. *almarie, armarie;* L. *armarium,* chest for tools or arms < *arma,* tools, weapons], 1. a cupboard; locker. 2. a niche (in a church) for sacramental vessels, vestments, etc.

ambs·ace (āmz'ās', amz'ās'), *n.* [ME. *ambesas;* OFr. *ambes as;* L. *ambas as; ambas,* both + *as;* see ACE], 1. double aces, the lowest number in throwing dice; hence, 2. the most worthless or least thing possible; bad luck. Also spelled **amesace.**

am·bu·la·cral (am'byoo-lā'krəl), *adj.* of, having the nature of, or located near an ambulacrum.

am·bu·la·crum (am'byoo-lā'krəm), *n.* [*pl.* AMBULACRA (-krə)], [L., lane planted with trees, covered walk < *ambulare,* to walk], in starfishes, sea urchins, and other echinoderms, that part of a ray containing a double row of perforations through which the tube feet are extended and withdrawn.

am·bu·lance (am'byoo-ləns), *n.* [Fr. < *ambulant,* in *hôpital ambulant* < ppr. of L. *ambulare,* to walk, move], 1. a mobile field hospital. 2. a specially equipped automobile or other vehicle for carrying the sick or wounded.

am·bu·lance-chas·er (am'byoo-ləns-chās'ẽr), *n.* [Slang], a lawyer of doubtful reputation who encourages victims of accidents to sue for damages as his clients.

am·bu·lant (am'byoo-lənt), *adj.* [L. *ambulans,* ppr. of *ambulare,* to walk], moving about; walking.

am·bu·late (am'byoo-lāt'), *v.i.* [AMBULATED (-id), AMBULATING], [< L. *ambulatus,* pp. of *ambulare,* to walk], to move about; walk.

am·bu·la·tion (am'byoo-lā'shən), *n.* [L. *ambulatio* <

pp. of *ambulare*, to walk], a moving or walking about.
am·bu·la·tor (am'byoo-lā'tēr), *n.* 1. one who ambulates. 2. a device for measuring distance walked; pedometer.
am·bu·la·to·ry (am'byoo-lə-tôr'i, am'byoo-lə-tō'ri), *adj.* [L. *ambulatorius* < *ambulare*, to walk about], 1. of or for walking. 2. able to walk. 3. moving from one place to another; movable. 4. in *law*, variable; changeable. *n.* [*pl.* AMBULATORIES (-iz, -riz)], any covered or sheltered place for walking. —*SYN.* see **itinerant.**
am·bus·cade (am'bəs-kād'), *n., v.t. & v.i.* [AMBUSCADED (-id), AMBUSCADING], [Fr. *embuscade;* It. *imboscata*, an ambush < ML. *imboscare;* see AMBUSH], ambush.
am·bus·ca·do (am'bəs-kā'dō), *n.* [*pl.* AMBUSCADOS (-dōz)], [Obs.], an ambuscade.
am·bush (am'boosh), *n.* [OFr. *embusche* < *embuschier;* see the *v.*], 1. an arrangement of soldiers or other persons in hiding to make a surprise attack. 2. those who are thus in hiding. 3. the place where they are hiding. 4. a lying in wait to attack. *v.t. & v.i.* [ME. *embusshen;* OFr. *embuschier*, to lay an ambush; ML. *imboscare*, to set an ambush < *in-* + *boscus*, a wood, woodland], 1. to hide for a surprise attack. 2. to attack from hiding; waylay.
am·bush·ment (am'boosh-mənt), *n.* an ambush.
Am·chit·ka (am-chit'kə), *n.* an island in the Aleutians.
A.M.D.G., *ad majorem Dei gloriam*, [L.], to the greater glory of God: Jesuit motto.
A.M.E., African Methodist Episcopal.
a·me·ba (ə-mē'bə), *n.* [*pl.* AMEBAS (-bəz), AMEBAE (-bē)], an amoeba.
a·me·bic (ə-mē'bik), *adj.* amoebic.
a·meer (ə-mêr'), *n.* an amir.
A·me·li·a (ə-mē'li-ə, ə-mēl'yə), [of Gmc. origin; lit., prob., diligent < base of *amal*, work, trouble], a feminine name.
a·mel·io·ra·ble (ə-mēl'yə-rə-b'l), *adj.* that can be ameliorated.
a·mel·io·rant (ə-mēl'yə-rənt), *n.* a thing that ameliorates.
a·mel·io·rate (ə-mēl'yə-rāt'), *v.t.* [AMELIORATED (-id), AMELIORATING], [Fr. *améliorer* < L. *ad*, to + *meliorare*, to better < *melior*, better], to make better; improve. *v.i.* to become better. —*SYN.* see **improve.**
a·mel·io·ra·tion (ə-mēl'yə-rā'shən), *n.* [Fr. *améliora-tion;* see AMELIORATE], betterment; improvement.
a·mel·io·ra·tive (ə-mēl'yə-rā'tiv, ə-mēl'yə-rə-tiv), *adj.* ameliorating; improving.
a·mel·io·ra·tor (ə-mēl'yə-rā'tēr), *n.* a person or thing that ameliorates.
A·men (ä'mən), *n.* [Egypt., lit., hidden one], the ancient Egyptian god of life and reproduction: also spelled **Amon**: see also **Amen-Ra.**
a·men (ā'men', ä'men'), *interj.* [L.; Gr.; Heb. *āmēn*, truly, certainly], may it be so!: used after a prayer or to express approval. *adv.* verily. *n.* a speaking or writing of "amen."
a·me·na·bil·i·ty (ə-mē'nə-bil'ə-ti, ə-men'ə-bil'ə-ti), *n.* the quality or condition of being amenable.
a·me·na·ble (ə-mē'nə-b'l, ə-men'ə-b'l), *adj.* [Anglo-Fr. < Fr. *amener*, to lead; *a-* (L. *ad*), to + *mener* < L. *minare*, to drive < *minari*, to threaten], 1. responsible or answerable. 2. willing to follow advice; open to suggestion; responsive; submissive. 3. that can be tested by (with *to*): as, *amenable* to the laws of physics. —*SYN.* see **obedient.**
a·me·na·bly (ə-mē'nə-bli, ə-men'ə-bli), *adv.* in an amenable manner.
amen corner, those seats to the side of and facing the pulpit of certain churches, especially in some small towns of the United States, where those leading the responsive amens usually sit.
a·mend (ə-mend'), *v.t.* [ME. *amenden;* OFr. *amender* < L. *emendare*, to correct < *ex-*, from + *mendum*, fault, blemish], 1. to improve. 2. to remove the faults of; correct; emend. 3. to change or revise, especially a legislative bill, a law, etc. *v.i.* to improve one's conduct.
a·mend·a·to·ry (ə-men'də-tôr'i, ə-men'də-tō'ri), *adj.* tending or serving to amend; corrective.
‡a·mende ho·no·ra·ble (å'mänd' ô'nô'rå'bl'; Eng. ə-mend' on'ēr-ə-b'l), [Fr.], 1. honorable reparation. 2. a formal and satisfactory apology to an offended person.
a·mend·ment (ə-mend'mənt), *n.* [ME. < OFr. *amende-ment* < *amender;* see AMEND], 1. improvement; betterment. 2. a correction of errors, faults, etc. 3. a revision or change proposed or made in a bill, law, etc. 4. a statement of this.
a·mends (ə-mendz'), *n.pl.* [construed also as sing.], [Fr. *amendes*, pl. of *amende*, a fine; see AMEND], payment made or satisfaction given for injury, insult, loss, etc.: as, he made *amends* for his rudeness.
A·men·ho·tep (ä'mən-hō'tep), *n.* 1. (*Amenophis III*), king of Egypt (1410?–1375? B.C.); died 1375? B.C. 2. (*Amenophis IV*), king of Egypt (1375?–1358? B.C.) and religious reformer; died 1358? B.C.: also called *Akhenaten, Akhenaton, Ikhnaton.*
a·men·i·ty (ə-men'ə-ti, ə-mē'nə-ti), *n.* [*pl.* AMENITIES (-tiz)], [Fr. *aménité;* L. *amoenitas* < *amoenus*, pleasant, delightful], 1. pleasantness; attractiveness. 2. *pl.* attractive or desirable features, as of a place, climate, etc. 3. *pl.* courteous acts; civilities.
a·men·or·rhe·a, a·men·or·rhoe·a (ā-men'ə-rē'ə), *n.* [Mod. L. < Gr. *a-*, not + *mēn*, month + *rheein*. to flow], abnormal absence or suppression of menstruation.
A·men-Ra (ä'mən-rä'), *n.* [Egypt. *Ämen-Rā; Ämen*, lit., hidden one + *Rā*, sun], the ancient Egyptian sun god: also spelled **Amon-Ra.**
‡a men·sa et tho·ro (ā men'sə et thō'rō), [L.], from bed and board: legal phrase used in divorce proceedings.
am·ent (am'ənt, ā'mənt), *n.* [L. *amentum*, thong, strap], a tassellike spike of small, closely clustered, unisexual flowers lacking petals and sepals, as on a willow, birch, or poplar; catkin.
a·ment (ā'mənt, ā'ment), *n.* [L. *amens*, senseless, mad; *a-*, away + *mens*, mind], in *psychology*, a person who has a mental deficiency; feeble-minded person.
am·en·ta·ceous (am'ən-tā'shəs), *adj.* [*ament* (catkin) + *-aceous*], in *botany*, 1. of or like an ament or aments. 2. amentiferous.
a·men·ti·a (ə-men'shə, ā-men'shi-ə), *n.* [L., want of reason < *a-* (*ab*), away, from + *mens*, mind], 1. congenital subnormality of intelligence; feeble-mindedness: distinguished from *dementia*. 2. a type of temporary confusional insanity.
am·en·tif·er·ous (am'ən-tif'ēr-əs), *adj.* [< *ament* (catkin) + *-ferous*], in *botany*, bearing aments.
a·men·tum (ə-men'təm), *n.* [*pl.* AMENTA (-tə)], in *botany*, an ament.
a·merce (ə-mūrs'), *v.t.* [AMERCED (-mūrst'), AMERCING], [ME. *amercen;* OFr. *amercier* < *a merci*, at the mercy of], 1. to punish by imposing a fine. 2. to punish.
a·merce·ment (ə-mūrs'mənt), *n.* [ME. *amerciment;* OFr. *amerciment*, a fine; see AMERCE], 1. punishment, especially by fine. 2. the fine or penalty imposed.
A·mer·i·ca (ə-mer'ə-kə, ə-mer'i-kə), *n.* [after *Amerigo* Vespucci], 1. North America. 2. South America. 3. North America, South America, and Central America considered together. 4. the United States. Abbreviated **A., Am., Amer.**
the Americas, America (sense 3).
A·mer·i·can (ə-mer'ə-kən, ə-mer'i-kən), *adj.* 1. of or in America. 2. of, in, or characteristic of the United States, its people, etc.: as, the *American* language. *n.* 1. a native or inhabitant of America. 2. a citizen of the United States. 3. the English language as spoken in the United States. Abbreviated **Amer., A., Am.**
A·mer·i·ca·na (ə-mer'ə-kā'nə, ə-mer'ə-kan'ə, ə-mer'ə-kä'nə), *n.pl.* [< *America* + *-ana*], a collection of books, papers, objects, facts, data, etc. having to do with America, its people, and its history.
American aloe, a century plant.
American Beauty, a variety of hybrid, perennial red rose.
American cheese, a kind of fairly hard, mild Cheddar cheese, popular in the United States.
American dialects, regional varieties of spoken American English: usually distinguished as Coastal Eastern, General Eastern, General American, Highland Southern, and Plantation Southern.
American eagle, the bald eagle of North America, shown on the coat of arms of the United States.
American English, the English language as spoken and written in the United States: usually distinguished from *British English:* abbreviated **AmnE., AmE.**
American Expeditionary Forces, the United States troops in Europe during World War I: abbreviated **A.E.F.**
American Federation of Labor, a federation of labor unions of the United States and Canada, founded in 1881: merged with the Congress of Industrial Organizations in 1955: abbreviated **A.F.L., A.F. of L.**

AMERICAN EAGLE (30 in. long)

American Indian, an Indian (sense 2).
A·mer·i·can·ism (ə-mer'ə-kən-iz'm), *n.* 1. a custom, characteristic, or belief of or originating in the United States. 2. a word, phrase, or idiom originating in or peculiar to American English. 3. devotion or loyalty to the United States, or to its traditions, customs, etc.
A·mer·i·can·ist (ə-mer'ə-kən-ist), *n.* 1. a person who makes a study of America, its history, geology, etc. 2. an anthropologist specializing in the study of the American Indians and their culture. 3. a person sympathetic toward the United States, its policies, etc.

A·mer·i·can·i·za·tion (ə-mer'ə-kən-i-zā'shən), *n.* an Americanizing or being Americanized.
A·mer·i·can·ize (ə-mer'ə-kən-īz'), *v.t. & v.i.* [AMERICANIZED (-īzd'), AMERICANIZING], to make or become American in character, manners, methods, ideals, etc.; assimilate to United States customs, speech, etc.
American Labor Party, a political party of New York State, founded in 1936.
American Legion, an organization of veterans of World War I or II, founded in 1919.
American leopard, a jaguar.
American Library Association, an organization of librarians and libraries, founded in 1876.
American plan, a system of hotel operation in which the price charged to guests covers room, service, and meals: distinguished from *European plan.*
American Revolution, 1. a sequence of actions by American colonists from 1763 to 1783 protesting British domination and culminating in the Revolutionary War. 2. the Revolutionary War (1775–1783), fought by the American colonies for independence from England.
American Samoa, a possession of the United States since 1899, consisting of six Samoan islands in the South Pacific: area, 76 sq. mi.; pop., 20,000; capital, Pago Pago on Tutuila Island.
American screw gauge, a standard gauge for checking the diameter of wood and machine screws.
American Veterans Committee, an organization of veterans of World War II: abbreviated **AVC, A.V.C.**
American Veterans of World War II, an organization of veterans of World War II: shortened to **Amvets.**
am·er·ic·i·um (am'ēr-ish'i-əm), *n.* [Mod. L. < *America*], a chemical element, one of the transuranium elements produced by atomic fission: symbol, Am; at. wt., 241 (?); at. no., 95.
Amerigo Vespucci, see **Vespucci, Amerigo.**
Am·er·ind (am'ə-rind'), *n.* [*Amer*ican + *Ind*ian], an American Indian or Eskimo.
Am·er·in·di·an (am'ə-rin'di-ən), *n.* an Amerind. *adj.* of the Amerinds or their culture.
Am·er·in·dic (am'ə-rin'dik), *adj.* Amerindian.
Ames (āmz), *n.* a city in central Iowa: pop., 27,000.
ames·ace (āmz'ās'), *n.* ambsace.
am·e·thyst (am'ə-thist), *n.* [ME. *ametist;* OFr. *ametiste;* L. *amethystus;* Gr. *amethystos,* not drunken (the Greeks believed that the amethyst prevented intoxication); *a-*, not + *methystos,* drunken < *methyein,* to be drunken < *methy,* strong drink], 1. a purple or violet variety of quartz, used in jewelry. 2. a purple variety of corundum, used in jewelry: called *Oriental amethyst.* 3. purple; violet. *adj.* purple; violet.
am·e·thys·tine (am'ə-this'tin), *adj.* [L. *amethystinus;* Gr. *amethystinos*], 1. made of amethyst. 2. like amethyst, especially in color.
am·e·tro·pi·a (am'ə-trō'pi-ə), *n.* [Mod. L. < Gr. *ametros,* disproportionate; + *-opia*], any condition of imperfect refraction of the eye, as nearsightedness, farsightedness, or astigmatism.
Am·for·tas (äm-fôr'täs), *n.* [MHG. *Anfortas*], the leader of the knights of the Holy Grail: cf. **Parsifal.**
Am·ha·ra (äm-hä'rä), *n.* a district of northern Ethiopia, formerly a kingdom.
Am·har·ic (am-har'ik, äm-hä'rik), *n.* the Southern Semitic language used officially in Ethiopia.
Am·herst, Jeffrey (am'ērst), Baron, 1717–1797; English general; fought in the French and Indian Wars.
‡**a·mi** (å'mē'), *n.* [*pl.* AMIS (-mē')], [Fr.], a (man or boy) friend.
a·mi·a·bil·i·ty (ā'mi-ə-bil'ə-ti), *n.* the quality or state of being amiable.
a·mi·a·ble (ā'mi-ə-b'l), *adj.* [ME.; OFr. < L. *amicabilis,* friendly < *amicus,* friend; confused with OFr. *amable* < L. *amabilis,* worthy of love; both from L. *amare,* to love], having a pleasant disposition; friendly.
SYN.*—amiable** and **affable** suggest qualities of friendliness, easy temper, etc. that make one likable, **affable** also implying a readiness to be approached, to converse, etc.; a **good-natured** person is one who is disposed to like as well as be liked and is sometimes one easily imposed on; **obliging** implies a ready, often cheerful, desire to be helpful (the *obliging* clerk took my order); **genial** suggests good cheer and sociableness (our *genial* host); **cordial** suggests graciousness and warmth (a *cordial* greeting). —ANT.*** surly, ill-natured.
a·mi·a·bly (ā'mi-ə-bli), *adv.* in an amiable manner.
am·i·an·thus (am'i-an'thəs), *n.* [L. *amiantus,* asbestos; Gr. *amiantos lithos,* lit., unspotted stone, asbestoslike stone < *a-*, not + *miainein,* to stain or spot], a kind of asbestos with long, silky fibers.
am·ic (am'ik), *adj.* of an amide.
am·i·ca·bil·i·ty (am'ik-ə-bil'ə-ti), *n.* the quality or state of being amicable.
am·i·ca·ble (am'i-kə-b'l), *adj.* [L. *amicabilis;* see AMIABLE], friendly; peaceable.
am·i·ca·bly (am'i-kə-bli), *adv.* in an amicable manner.
am·ice (am'is), *n.* [ME. < OFr. *amit* < L. *amictus,* a cloak; confused with OFr. *aumuce* < ML. *almutia,* cowl or hood], 1. an oblong white linen cloth worn about the neck and shoulders by a priest at Mass. 2. a hooded, fur-lined tippet or cape; almuce.
a·mi·cus cu·ri·ae (ə-mī'kəs kyoor'i-ē'), [L., friend of the court], in *law,* a person, either an attorney or a layman, called in to advise the court on some legal matter.
a·mid (ə-mid'), *prep.* [ME. *amidde, on midden;* AS. *on middan; on,* at + *middan,* middle], among; in the middle of: also **amidst.**
am·id (am'id), *n.* an amide.
am·ide (am'īd, am'id), *n.* [*ammonia* + *-ide*], in *chemistry,* 1. any of a group of organic compounds containing the $CO{\cdot}NH_2$ radical (e.g., acetamide) or an acid radical in place of one hydrogen atom of an ammonia molecule (e.g., sulfanilamide). 2. any of the ammono bases in which one hydrogen atom of the ammonia molecule is replaced by a metal (e.g., sodamide).
a·mid·ic (ə-mid'ik), *adj.* of or made from an amide.
am·i·din (am'i-din), *n.* [Fr. *amidon* < L. *amylum,* starch; + *-in*], in *chemistry,* a transparent, water-soluble substance made by heating starch in water.
a·mi·do (ə-mē'dō, am'i-dō'), *adj.* [< *amide*], of an amide or amides.
a·mi·do- (ə-mē'dō, am'i-dō'), [< *amide*], a combining form meaning *having one hydrogen atom in the ammonia molecule replaced by an acid radical.*
a·mi·do·gen (ə-mē'də-jən, ə-mid'ə-jən), *n.* [*amido-* + *-gen*], the hypothetical monovalent radical NH_2.
am·i·dol (am'ə-dōl', am'ə-dol), *n.* [*amido-* + phen*ol*], a colorless crystalline compound, $C_6H_8ON_2{\cdot}HCl$, used as a developer in photography.
a·mid·ship (ə-mid'ship), *adv.* amidships.
a·mid·ships (ə-mid'ships), *adv.* in or toward the middle of a ship; midway between bow and stern.
a·midst (ə-midst'), *prep.* [ME. *amidde,* with adv. genit. *-s* + unhistoric *-t*], amid; among.
‡**a·mie** (å'mē'), *n.* [*pl.* AMIES (-mē')], [Fr., fem. of *ami*], a (woman or girl) friend.
Am·i·ens (am'i-ənz; Fr. å'myan'), *n.* a city in northern France, on the Somme River: pop., 93,000.
‡**a·mi·go** (ä-mē'gô; Eng. ə-mē'gō), *n.* [*pl.* AMIGOS (-gôs; Eng. -gōz)], [Sp.], a friend.
am·in (am'in), *n.* an amine.
a·mine (ə-mēn', am'in), *n.* [*ammonia* + *-ine*], in *chemistry,* a derivative of ammonia in which hydrogen atoms have been replaced by radicals containing hydrogen and carbon atoms (e.g., methylamine, CH_3NH_2).
a·mi·no (am'i-nō', ə-mē'nō), *adj.* [< *amine*], of an amine or amines.
a·mi·no- (am'i-nō', ə-mē'nō), [< *amine*], a combining form meaning *having one hydrogen atom in the ammonia molecule replaced by an alkyl or other nonacid radical.*
amino acids, 1. a group of nitrogenous organic compounds that serve as units of structure of the proteins and are essential to human metabolism. 2. chemical compounds in which a hydrogen atom in the alkyl group attached to the COOH (carboxyl) group of an organic acid is replaced by an NH_2 group.
a·mir (ə-mêr'), *n.* [Ar. *amīr*], in Moslem countries, a ruler or prince: also spelled **ameer.**
Am·ish (am'ish, ä'mish), *n.pl.* [after Jacob *Ammann* (or *Amen*), the founder], Mennonites of a sect founded in the 17th century. *adj.* designating or of this sect.
a·miss (ə-mis'), *adv.* [*a-*, at + *miss*], 1. away from the mark; astray. 2. incorrectly; wrongly. 3. faultily; defectively. *adj.* beside the mark; faulty; deficient: used predicatively.
am·i·to·sis (am'ə-tō'sis), *n.* [Mod. L.; *a-*, not + *mitosis*], in *biology,* direct or simple cell division; cell division in which the nucleus divides without structural change: opposed to *mitosis.*
am·i·tot·ic (am'ə-tot'ik), *adj.* of or by amitosis.
am·i·ty (am'ə-ti), *n.* [*pl.* AMITIES (-tiz)], [Fr. *amitié;* OFr. *amistie;* LL. **amicitas* < L. *amicus,* friendly < *amare,* to love], friendship; friendly, peaceful relations, as between nations, groups, etc.
Am·man (äm'män), *n.* the capital of Jordan: pop., 245,000: in the *Bible,* called *Rabbath Ammon.*
am·me·ter (am'mē'tēr), *n.* [*ampere* + *-meter*], an instrument for measuring the strength of an electric current in terms of amperes.
am·mi·a·ceous (am'i-ā'shəs), *adj.* [L. & Gr. *ammi,* umbelliferous plant; + *-aceous*], belonging to the carrot or parsnip family, a group of plants with hollow stems and generally edible roots.
am·mine (am'ēn), *n.* [*ammonia* + *-ine*], in *chemistry,* 1. a molecule of ammonia (NH_3) as found in certain complex compounds. 2. any of certain complex compounds containing this molecule.
am·mi·no- (ə-mē'nō, am'i-nō'), [< *ammine*], a combining form used in the names of certain chemical compounds, meaning *containing one or more ammines.*
am·mo (am'ō), *n.* [Slang], ammunition.
Am·mon (am'ən), *n.* [L.; Gr. *Ammōn;* Egypt. *Åmen*], 1. Amen, the ancient Egyptian god. 2. in ancient Egypt, *a name for* Zeus or Jupiter.
Am·mon (am'ən), *n.* [Heb. *ʿammōn,* lit., prob. populous], in the *Bible,* a Semitic tribe descended from Lot's son: Gen. 19:38; Deut. 2:19–20.
am·mo·ni·a (ə-mōn'yə, ə-mō'ni-ə), *n.* [< *sal ammoniac*], 1. a colorless, pungent gas, NH_3, composed of nitrogen and hydrogen: its compounds are used as fertilizers, in

medicine, etc. 2. a water solution of this gas: in full, *ammonia water* or *aqua ammoniae.*
am·mo·ni·ac (ə-mō′ni-ak′), *n.* [Fr.; L. *ammoniacum;* Gr. *ammōniakon*, gum resin from a plant said to grow near the temple of Jupiter *Ammon* in Libya], a pungent gum resin obtained from an herb found in Mediterranean countries: it is used as a cement, a stimulant, etc.: also **gum ammoniac.** *adj.* ammoniacal.
am·mo·ni·a·cal (am′ə-nī′ə-k'l), *adj.* of, like, or containing ammonia.
am·mo·ni·ate (ə-mō′ni-āt′), *v.t.* [AMMONIATED (-id), AMMONIATING], to mix or combine with ammonia. *n.* (ə-mō′ni-it), any of several compounds containing ammonia: as, the *ammoniate* of calcium chloride.
am·mon·ic (ə-mon′ik, ə-mō′nik), *adj.* of or from ammonia or ammonium.
am·mon·i·fi·ca·tion (ə-mon′ə-fi-kā′shən), *n.* 1. infusion with ammonia or ammonium compounds. 2. the production of ammonia by bacterial action in the decay of nitrogenous organic matter.
am·mon·i·fy (ə-mon′ə-fī′), *v.t.* [AMMONIFIED (-fīd′), AMMONIFYING], to cause to undergo ammonification. *v.i.* to undergo ammonification.
am·mo·nite (am′ə-nīt′), *n.* [L. *cornu Ammonis*, horn of Ammon < *Jupiter Ammon*, whose statues were represented with ram's horns; see AMMON], the flat, spiral or coiled fossil shell of an extinct mollusk, somewhat resembling a ram's horn.

AMMONITE (5 in.-6 ft.)

am·mo·nite (am′ə-nīt′), *n.* [*ammonia* + *-ite*], a fertilizer produced from animal waste.
am·mo·ni·um (ə-mō′ni-əm), *n.* [Mod. L. < *ammonia*], in *chemistry*, the radical NH_4, present in salts produced by the reaction of ammonia with an acid: its compounds are like those of the alkali metals.
ammonium chloride, a white crystalline compound, NH_4Cl, produced by the reaction of ammonia with hydrochloric acid; sal ammoniac: it is used in dry cells, fertilizers, dyes, etc., and as a flux in soldering.
ammonium hydroxide, an alkali, NH_4OH, formed by dissolving ammonia in water.
ammonium nitrate, a colorless, crystalline salt, NH_4NO_3, used in some explosives.
am·mo·no (am′ə-nō′), *adj.* 1. of or containing ammonia. 2. derived from ammonia: used to describe compounds bearing the same relation to ammonia as certain other compounds bear to water: as, sodium amide, $NaNH_2$, is an *ammono* base corresponding to sodium hydroxide, NaOH.
am·mo·no- (am′ə-nō′), [< *ammonia*], a combining form meaning *of ammonia, containing ammonia.*
am·mu·ni·tion (am′yoo-nish′ən), *n.* [Fr. *amunition*, by faulty separation of *la munition;* L. *munitio* < *munire*, to fortify], 1. bullets, gunpowder, shot, shells, bombs, grenades, rockets, and other projectiles and missiles. 2. any means of attack or defense: as, argument is his *ammunition*. 3. [Archaic], any military supplies.
am·ne·si·a (am-nē′zhi-ə, am-nē′zhə), *n.* [Mod. L.; Gr. *amnēsia*, forgetfulness < *a-*, not + *mnasthai*, to remember], partial or total loss of memory caused by brain injury, or by shock, repression, etc.
am·ne·sic (am-nē′sik, am-nē′zik), *adj.* of amnesia. *n.* a person suffering from amnesia.
am·nes·tic (am-nes′tik), *adj.* [< Gr. *amnēstos*, forgotten (see AMNESTY); + *-ic*], causing amnesia.
am·nes·ty (am′nəs-ti, am′nes-ti), *n.* [*pl.* AMNESTIES (-tiz)], [Fr. *amnestie;* L. *amnestia;* Gr. *amnēstia*, a forgetting < *a-*, not + *mnasthai*, to remember], 1. a general pardon, especially for political offenses against a government. 2. a deliberate overlooking, as of an offense. *v.t.* [AMNESTIED (-tid), AMNESTYING], to grant amnesty to; pardon.
am·ni·on (am′ni-ən), *n.* [*pl.* AMNIONS (-ənz), AMNIA (-ə)], [Gr., dim. of *amnus*, lamb], the innermost membrane of the sac enclosing the embryo of a mammal, reptile, or bird.
am·ni·ot·ic (am′ni-ot′ik), *adj.* of the amnion.
amn't (am″nt), [Colloq.], am not: see also **ain't.**
a·moe·ba (ə-mē′bə), *n.* [*pl.* AMOEBAS (-bəz), AMOEBAE (-bē)], [Mod. L.; Gr. *amoibē*, change < *ameibein*, to change], a microscopic, one-celled animal found in stagnant water or as a parasite in other animals: it moves by making continually changing protrusions of its body, feeds by engulfing bits of food, and multiplies by fission: also spelled **ameba.**

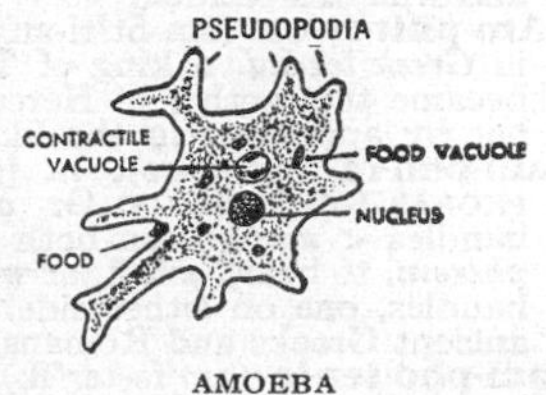

AMOEBA

am·oe·bae·an, am·oe·be·an (am′i-bē′ən), *adj.* [< L. *amoebaeum* (*carmen*); Gr. (*asma*) *amoibaion*, responsive (song) < *amoibē;* see AMOEBA], answering or responding to each other, as the responsive readings of a church service or the successive strophes of a verse dialogue.
a·moe·bic (ə-mē′bik), *adj.* 1. of or like an amoeba or amoebas. 2. caused by amoebas. Also spelled **amebic.**
amoebic dysentery, a form of dysentery caused by a certain kind of amoeba.
a·moe·boid (ə-mē′boid), *adj.* [see -OID], like or characteristic of an amoeba, as in constantly changing shape: also spelled **ameboid.**
a·mok (ə-muk′, ə-mok′), *adj. & adv.* amuck. *n.* among Malayans, the condition of being amuck.
a·mo·le (ə-mō′lā; Sp. ä-mô′le), *n.* [Mex.Sp. < Nahuatl], 1. the roots of any of various plants of the southwestern United States and Mexico, used as a substitute for soap. 2. any of these plants.
A·mon (ä′mən), *n.* the ancient Egyptian sun god: also spelled **Amen.**
a·mong (ə-muŋ′), *prep.* [ME.; AS. *on gemang*, in the company (of); *on*, in + *gemang*, a mingling, crowd, company < *gemengan*, to mingle; see MINGLE], 1. in the company of; surrounded by; included with: as, you are *among* friends. 2. from place to place in: as, he passed *among* the crowd. 3. in the number or class of: as, fairest *among* women. 4. by many; with many: as, popular *among* businessmen. 5. as compared with: as, one *among* thousands. 6. with a portion for each of: as, the estate was divided *among* the relatives. 7. with one another: as, don't quarrel *among* yourselves. 8. by the concerted or joint action of: as, we have, *among* us, made him a success.
a·mongst (ə-muŋst′, ə-muŋkst′), *prep.* [*among* + adv. genit. *-s* + unhistoric *-t*], among.
a·mon·til·la·do (ə-mon′ti-lä′dō; Sp. ä-môn′tē-lyä′dô), *n.* [Sp. < *Montilla*, a town in Spain + *-ado*, -ate], a variety of dry, pale Spanish sherry.
a·mor·al (ā-môr′əl, ā-mor′əl), *adj.* [*a-*, not + *moral*], not concerned with moral standards; not to be judged by criteria of morality; neither moral nor immoral.
A.M.O.R.C., Ancient Mystic Order Rosae Crucis (Rosicrucian Order): see **Rosicrucianism.**
am·o·ret·to (am′ə-ret′ō; It. ä′mô-ret′tô), *n.* [*pl.* AMORETTI (-i; It. -tē)], [It., dim. < *amore* (L. *amor*), love; cf. AMOUR], an infant cupid: especially common in Italian art of the 16th century.
‡am·o·ri·no (ä′mô-rē′nô), *n.* [*pl.* AMORINI (-nē)], [It., dim. < *amore*, love], an amoretto.
am·o·rist (am′ə-rist), *n.* [L. *amor*, love; + *-ist*], a person much occupied with love and love-making.
am·o·rous (am′ə-rəs), *adj.* [ME.; OFr.; LL. *amorosus*, loving < L. *amor*, love < *amare*, to love], 1. fond of loving or of making love. 2. in love; enamored or fond (*of* a person or thing). 3. full of or showing love or sexual desire: as, *amorous* words. 4. of sexual love or love-making.
‡a·mor pa·tri·ae (ā′môr pā′tri-ē′), [L.], love of one's country; patriotism.
a·mor·phism (ə-môr′fiz'm), *n.* the quality or state of being amorphous.
a·mor·phous (ə-môr′fəs), *adj.* [Gr. *amorphos* < *a-*, without + *morphē*, form], 1. without definite form; shapeless. 2. of no definite type; anomalous. 3. unorganized; vague. 4. in *biology*, without definite or specialized structure, as some lower forms of life. 5. in *chemistry & mineralogy*, not crystalline. 6. in *geology*, without stratification or other division.
a·mort (ə-môrt′), *adj.* [< Fr. *à*, to + *mort*, death < L. *mors, mortis*, death], [Archaic], not alive; spiritless.
a·mor·tise (am′ẽr-tīz′, ə-môr′tīz′), *v.t.* [AMORTISED (-tīzd′), AMORTISING], to amortize.
a·mor·tiz·a·ble (am′ẽr-tīz′ə-b'l, ə-môr′tiz-ə-b'l), *adj.* that can be amortized.
a·mor·ti·za·tion, a·mor·ti·sa·tion (am′ẽr-tə-zā′shən, ə-môr′tə-zā′shən), *n.* [ML. *amortizatio;* see AMORTIZE], 1. an amortizing or being amortized. 2. money put aside for amortizing a debt, etc.
a·mor·tize (am′ẽr-tīz′, ə-môr′tīz′), *v.t.* [AMORTIZED (-tīzd′), AMORTIZING], [ME. *amortisen* < OFr. *amortir*, to extinguish, deaden, sell in mortmain (< ML. *amortire*); or < ML. *amortizare;* both ML. forms < L. *ad*, to + *mors*, death], 1. to put money aside at intervals, as in a sinking fund, for gradual payment of (a debt, etc.). 2. in *accounting*, to write off (expenditures) by prorating over a fixed period. 3. in *law*, to transfer or sell (property) in mortmain.
a·mor·tize·ment (ə-môr′tiz-mənt), *n.* amortization.
A·mos (ā′məs), [Heb. *'āmōs*, lit., borne (by God?)], a masculine name. *n.* 1. a Hebrew prophet of the 8th century B.C. 2. a book of the Old Testament containing prophecies attributed to him.
a·mount (ə-mount′), *v.i.* [ME. *amounten*, to ascend, rise; OFr. *amonter* < *amont*, upward; *a-* (L. *ad*), to + *mont* < L. *montem*, acc. sing. of *mons*, mountain],

1. to add up (*to* a sum, quantity, etc.): as, the bill *amounts* to $4.50. 2. to be equal (*to* something) in meaning, value, or effect: as, her criticisms *amount* to nothing. *n.* 1. the sum of two or more quantities; total. 2. a principal plus its interest. 3. the whole meaning, value, or effect. 4. a quantity: as, a fair *amount* of resistance. Abbreviated **amt.** —*SYN.* see **sum.**

a·mour (ə-moor′), *n.* [Fr.; L. *amor*, love], a love affair, especially of an illicit or secret nature.

‡a·mour-pro·pre (à′mōōr′prô′pr′), *n.* [Fr.], self-love; self-esteem.

A·moy (ə-moi′), *n.* 1. an island city in Fukien province, China, in Taiwan Strait: pop., 234,000. 2. the island.

amp., 1. amperage. 2. ampere; amperes.

am·pe·lop·sis (am′pə-lop′sis), *n.* [Mod. L. < Gr. *ampelos*, vine + *opsis*, appearance], any of a group of climbing shrubs of the grape family.

am·per·age (am-pêr′ij, am′pêr′ij), *n.* [< *ampere* + *-age*], the strength of an electric current, measured in amperes: abbreviated **amp.**

am·pere (am′pêr, am-pêr′), *n.* [after A. M. *Ampère*], the standard unit for measuring the strength of an electric current; amount of current sent by one volt through a resistance of one ohm: abbreviated **amp., a.**

Am·père, An·dré Ma·rie (äṅ′drā′ mà′rē′ äṅ′pâr′), 1775–1836; French physicist and mathematician; developed the science of electrodynamics.

am·pere-hour (am′pêr-our′), *n.* the amount of electricity produced in one hour by a current of one ampere: abbreviated **a.h., amp.-hr.**

ampere turn, the amount of magnetomotive force produced by an electric current of one ampere flowing around one turn of a wire coil.

am·per·sand (am′pẽr-sand′, am′pẽr-sand′), *n.* [< *and per se and*, lit., (the sign) & by itself (is) *and*], a sign (& or &), meaning *and*: it represents the *e* of the Latin word *et*, and.

am·phet·a·mine (am-fet′ə-mēn′, am-fet′ə-min), *n.* [*a*lpha-*m*ethyl-beta-*phe*nyl-*et*hyl-*amine*], a drug used as a nasal spray or inhalant, in sinusitis, etc.

am·phi- (am′fi), [< Gr. *amphi*], a prefix meaning: 1. *on both sides, on both ends*, as in *amphistylar*. 2. *around, about*. 3. *of both kinds*, as in *amphibiotic*.

am·phi·ar·thro·sis (am′fi-är-thrō′sis), *n.* [*amphi-* + Gr. *arthrōsis*, a jointing < *arthron*, a joint], a form of jointing in which an elastic cartilage connects the bones and motion is limited.

am·phi·as·ter (am′fi-as′tẽr), *n.* [*amphi-* + *-aster*], in mitosis, the long spindle with asters at either end that forms during the prophase, or first stage.

Am·phib·i·a (am-fib′i-ə), *n.pl.* [Mod. L.; see AMPHIBIOUS], in *zoology*, a class of vertebrates, including frogs, toads, newts, and salamanders, that usually begin life in the water as tadpoles with gills, and later develop lungs: they are cold-blooded and scaleless.

am·phib·i·an (am-fib′i-ən), *adj.* [< Mod. L. *amphibia*; Gr. *amphibia*, neut. pl.; see AMPHIBIOUS], 1. of the Amphibia. 2. amphibious. *n.* 1. any member of the Amphibia. 2. any animal that lives both on land and in water. 3. any plant that lives and grows either on land or in water. 4. a person or thing of double or doubtful nature. 5. any aircraft that can take off from or come down on either land or water. 6. a tank or other vehicle that can travel on either land or water.

AMPHIBIAN PLANE

am·phi·bi·ot·ic (am′fi-bī-ot′ik), *adj.* [< *amphi-* + Gr. *biōtikos*, relating to life < *bios*, life], that lives in water in one stage of development, and on land in another.

am·phib·i·ous (am-fib′i-əs), *adj.* [Gr. *amphibios*, living a double life; *amphi-*, on both sides + *bios*, life], 1. that can operate on both land and water. 2. that can live both on land and in water. 3. having two natures or qualities; of a mixed nature.

am·phi·bole (am′fi-bōl′), *n.* [Fr.; L. *amphibolus*, ambiguous; Gr. *amphibolos* < *amphiballein*, to throw around, be uncertain, doubt; *amphi-*, on both sides + *ballein*, to throw], a mineral composed largely of silica, calcium, and magnesia: its varieties include asbestos and hornblende.

am·phi·bol·ic (am′fi-bol′ik), *adj.* of or like amphibole.

am·phi·bol·ic (am′fi-bol′ik), *adj.* 1. relating to amphibology; ambiguous; doubtful. 2. fluctuating.

am·phib·o·lite (am-fib′ə-lit′), *n.* [< *amphibole* + *-ite*], a rock consisting largely of hornblende.

am·phi·bol·o·gy (am′fi-bol′ə-ji), *n.* [*pl.* AMPHIBOLOGIES (-jiz)], [Fr. *amphibologie*; LL. *amphibologia* (altered after words ending in *-logia*, -logy) < L. *amphibolia*; Gr. *amphibolia*, ambiguity < *amphiballein*; see AMPHIBOLE], 1. double or doubtful meaning; ambiguity, especially from uncertain grammatical construction. 2. an ambiguous phrase, proposition, etc.

am·phib·o·lous (am-fib′ə-ləs), *adj.* [L. *amphibolus*; Gr. *amphibolos*; see AMPHIBOLE], that can have two meanings; ambiguous.

am·phib·o·ly (am-fib′ə-li), *n.* [*pl.* AMPHIBOLIES (-iz)], [OFr. & L. *amphibolia*; see AMPHIBOLOGY], amphibology.

am·phi·brach (am′fi-brak′), *n.* [L. *amphibrachys*; Gr. *amphibrachys*, lit., short before and after; *amphi-*, at both ends + *brachys*, short], a metrical foot consisting of one long syllable between two short ones, or, in English, of one accented syllable between two unaccented ones. Example: Fŏrgŏttĕn, | fŏrgóttĕn, | ŭnwántĕd | hĕ wándĕred.

am·phi·chro·ic (am′fi-krō′ik), *adj.* [< *amphi-* + Gr. *chroa*, color; + *-ic*], in *chemistry*, forming one color when treated with an acid and another when treated with a base, as litmus.

am·phi·coe·lous (am′fi-sē′ləs), *adj.* [Gr. *amphikoilos*, hollowed out all around; *amphi-*, around + *koilos*, hollow], concave on both sides; biconcave.

am·phic·ty·on (am-fik′ti-ən), *n.* [L. (pl.) *Amphictyones*; Gr. *Amphiktyones*; prob. orig. *amphiktiones*, those that dwelt around, next neighbors], a delegate to the council or assembly of an amphictyony.

am·phic·ty·on·ic (am-fik′ti-on′ik), *adj.* [Gr. *amphiktyonikos*], of the amphictyons or an amphictyony.

am·phic·ty·o·ny (am-fik′ti-ə-ni), *n.* [*pl.* AMPHICTYONIES (-niz)], [Gr. *amphiktyonia*; see AMPHICTYON], in ancient Greece, a confederation of states established around a religious shrine or center, as at Delphi.

am·phi·go·ry (am′fi-gôr′i, am′fi-gō′ri), *n.* [*pl.* AMPHIGORIES (-iz, -riz)], [Fr. *amphigouri*], a piece of nonsense verse or prose, as in parody or burlesque.

am·phim·a·cer (am-fim′ə-sẽr), *n.* [< L. *amphimacrus*; Gr. *amphimakros*, lit., long at both ends < *amphi-*, on both ends + *makros*, long], in *Greek & Latin verse*, a metrical foot consisting of one short syllable between two long ones: shown in scansion as –⏑–.

am·phi·mix·is (am′fi-mik′sis), *n.* [Mod. L.; *amphi-* + Gr. *mixis*, a mixing], in *biology*, 1. the uniting of male and female germ cells from two individuals in reproduction. 2. crossbreeding.

Am·phi·on (am-fī′ən), *n.* [L.; Gr. *Amphiōn*], in *Greek mythology*, the son of Zeus and Antiope: with a lyre that Hermes gave him he built a wall around Thebes by charming the stones into place.

am·phi·ox·us (am′fi-ok′səs), *n.* [< *amphi-* + Gr. *oxys*, sharp], the lancelet, a small sea animal.

am·phi·pod (am′fi-pod′), *n.* [*amphi-* + *-pod*], any of several crustaceans with one set of feet for jumping or walking and another set for swimming, as the sand flea, fresh-water shrimp, etc.

am·phi·pro·style (am-fip′rə-stīl′, am′fi-prō′stīl), *adj.* [< L. *amphiprostylos*; see AMPHI- & PROSTYLE], in *architecture*, having rows of columns at the front and back, but none along the sides. *n.* an amphiprostyle temple or other building.

am·phis·bae·na (am′fis-bē′nə), *n.* [L.; Gr. *amphisbaina*; *amphis-*, *amphi-*, at both ends + *baina* < *bainein*, to go], 1. a mythical serpent with a head at each end of its body. 2. a wormlike tropical lizard with a head and tail that look very much alike.

am·phis·ci·ans (am-fish′i-ənz, am-fish′ənz), *n.pl.* [ML. *amphiscii* < Gr. *amphiskios*, pl. *amphiskioi*, casting a shadow both ways < *amphi-*, on both sides + *skia*, shadow], the inhabitants of the Torrid Zone, where a shadow at noon falls to the north or the south, depending on the time of the year.

am·phis·ci·i (am-fish′i-ī′), *n.pl.* amphiscians.

am·phi·sty·lar (am′fi-stī′lẽr), *adj.* [< *amphi-* + Gr. *stylos*, pillar; + *-ar*], having columns at both front and back or on both sides.

am·phi·the·a·ter, am·phi·the·a·tre (am′fə-thē′ə-tẽr, am′fə-thē′ə-tẽr), *n.* [L. *amphitheatrum*; Gr. *amphitheatron*; *amphi-*, around + *theatron*; see THEATER], 1. a round or oval building with an open space (arena) surrounded by rising rows of seats; hence, 2. a scene of contest; arena. 3. a sloping gallery in a theater. 4. a level place surrounded by rising ground; valley of this form.

am·phi·the·ci·um (am′fi-thē′shi-əm, am′fi-thē′si-əm), *n.* [Mod. L. < *amphi-* + Gr. *thēkion*, dim. of *thēkē*, a case, container], in *botany*, the outer layer of cells in the spore case of a moss.

Am·phi·tri·te (am′fi-trī′ti), *n.* [L.; Gr. *Amphitritē*], in *Greek mythology*, one of the Nereids, goddess of the sea and wife of Poseidon.

Am·phit·ry·on (am-fit′ri-ən), *n.* [L.; Gr. *Amphitryōn*], in *Greek legend*, a king of Thebes: his wife, Alcmene, became the mother of Hercules by Zeus, who seduced her by appearing in the likeness of Amphitryon.

am·pho·ra (am′fə-rə), *n.* [*pl.* AMPHORAE (-rē′), AMPHORAS (-rəz)], [L. < Gr. *amphoreus*, a jar with two handles < *amphi-*, on both sides + *phoreus*, bearer < *pherein*, to bear], a tall jar with a narrow neck and two handles, one on either side near the top, used by the ancient Greeks and Romans.

am·pho·ter·ic (am′fə-ter′ik), *adj.* [< Gr. *amphoteros*, both], having both acid and basic properties.

am·ple (am′p'l), *adj.* [Fr.; L. *amplus*], 1. spacious; roomy; large in size, extent, scope, etc. 2. more than enough; abundant. 3. enough; adequate. —*SYN.* see **plentiful.**

am·plex·i·caul (am-plek′si-kôl′), *adj.* [L. *amplexus,* pp. of *amplectari,* to twine around + *caulis,* stem], in *botany,* clasping or encircling a stem, as the base of some leaves.

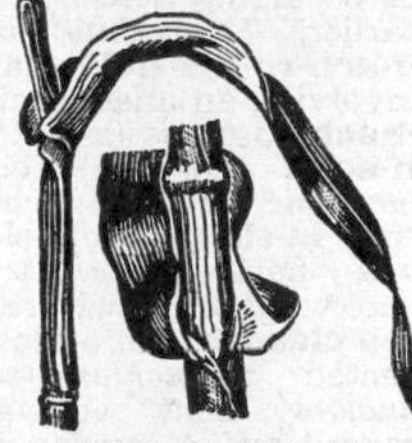
AMPLEXICAUL LEAF (of corn)

am·pli·a·tion (am′pli-ā′shən), *n.* [L. *ampliatio* < *ampliare,* to widen < *amplus,* large, wide], 1. amplification; enlargement. 2. something added; extension.

am·pli·fi·ca·tion (am′plə-fi-kā′shən), *n.* [L. *amplificatio;* see AMPLIFY], 1. an amplifying or being amplified. 2. additional matter, details, etc.: as, the *amplification* of a report. 3. a statement, etc. with something added.

am·pli·fi·ca·to·ry (am-pli′fi-kə-tôr′i, am-pli′fi-kə-tō′ri), *adj.* of, or having the nature of, amplification.

am·pli·fi·er (am′plə-fī′ẽr), *n.* 1. a person or thing that amplifies. 2. in *electricity & radio,* a circuit, electronic tube, apparatus, etc. for increasing the strength of electrical impulses.

am·pli·fy (am′plə-fī′), *v.t.* [AMPLIFIED (-fīd′), AMPLIFYING], [Fr. *amplifier;* L. *amplificare* < *amplus,* large + *facere,* to make], 1. to make larger or stronger; increase or extend (power, authority, etc.). 2. to make more complete, fuller, etc.: as, *amplify* your statement. 3. to exaggerate. 4. to strengthen (electrical impulses) by means of electronic tubes, etc. *v.i.* to speak or write at length or in great detail; expatiate.

am·pli·tude (am′plə-tōōd′, am′plə-tūd′), *n.* [L. *amplitudo* < *amplus,* large], 1. the quality or state of being ample; extent; size. 2. abundance; fullness; copiousness. 3. scope or breadth, as of mind. 4. in *astronomy,* the angular distance of a star from the true east or west point of the horizon, at the moment of its rising or setting. 5. in *mathematics & physics,* the extreme range of a fluctuating quantity, as an alternating current, pendulum, etc., generally measured from the average or mean to the extreme.

amplitude modulation, 1. the changing of the amplitude of the transmitting radio wave in accordance with the sound being broadcast. 2. broadcasting that uses this. Abbreviated **AM, A.M.** Distinguished from *frequency modulation.*

am·ply (am′pli), *adv.* 1. in an ample manner. 2. to an ample degree.

am·poule (am′pōōl), *n.* [Fr.; L *ampulla,* ampulla], a small, sealed glass container for one dose of a sterile medicine to be injected hypodermically.

am·pule (am′pūl), *n.* an ampoule.

am·pul·la (am-pul′ə, am-pool′ə), *n.* [*pl.* AMPULLAS (-əz), AMPULLAE (-ē)], [L.], 1. an almost round bottle with two handles, used by the ancient Greeks and Romans. 2. a container used in churches for holy oil, consecrated wine, etc. 3. in *anatomy,* a sac or dilated part of a tube or canal, as of a milk duct in a mammary gland.

am·pul·la·ceous (am′pə-lā′shəs), *adj.* [L. *ampullaceus* < *ampulla*], shaped like an ampulla or a bladder.

am·pu·tate (am′pyoo-tāt′), *v.t.* [AMPUTATED (-id), AMPUTATING], [L. *amputatus,* pp. of *amputare* < *amb-,* about + *putare,* to prune], to cut off, especially by surgery.

am·pu·ta·tion (am′pyoo-tā′shən), *n.* [L. *amputatio*], an amputating or being amputated.

am·pu·ta·tor (am′pyoo-tā′tẽr), *n.* a person or thing that amputates.

am·pu·tee (am′pyoo-tē′), *n.* [< *amputate* + *-ee*], a person who has had a limb or limbs amputated: one with two limbs amputated is called a *double amputee,* etc.

am·ri·ta (əm-rē′tə), *n.* [< Sans. *amrta,* deathless, hence drink that makes immortal], in *Hindu mythology,* 1. the ambrosial drink granting immortality. 2. the immortality granted by this.

Am·rit·sar (um-rit′sẽr), *n.* a city in northern India, Punjab state: pop., 326,000.

A.M.S., Army Medical Staff.

Am·ster·dam (am′stẽr-dam′), *n.* 1. one of the two capitals of the Netherlands, on the Zuider Zee: pop., 872,000. 2. a city in eastern New York: pop., 29,000.

amt., amount.

am·trac (am′trak), *n.* [*am*phibious + *trac*tor], a small, open, armed amphibious vehicle with tractor treads, used in sea-to-shore operations in World War II.

a·muck (ə-muk′), *adj. & adv.* [Malay *amoq,* engaging furiously in battle], in a frenzy to kill: also **amok.**
 run amuck, 1. to rush about in a frenzy to kill. 2. to lose control of oneself and do or attempt violence.

A·mu Dar·ya (ä-mōō′ där′yä), a river in the Asiatic U.S.S.R., flowing northwestward into Lake Aral: length, 1,500 mi.: ancient name, *Oxus.*

am·u·let (am′yoo-lit), *n.* [Fr. *amulette;* L. *amuletum*], something worn, often around the neck, as a protection against injury or evil; a charm.

A·mund·sen, Ro·ald (rō′äl ä′mən-s′n), 1872–1928; Norwegian explorer; first to reach the South Pole (1911).

A·mur (ä-moor′), *n.* a river in eastern Asia, flowing between Manchuria and the U.S.S.R. into Tartary Strait: length, 2,900 mi.

a·mus·a·ble (ə-mūz′ə-b'l), *adj.* that can be amused.

a·muse (ə-mūz′), *v.t.* [AMUSED (-mūzd′), AMUSING], [Fr. *amuser* < *à* (L. *ad*), to + OFr. *muser,* to gaze at, stare fixedly], 1. to keep agreeably occupied or interested; entertain: as, we *amused* ourselves with games. 2. to make laugh, smile, etc. with pleasure; appeal to the sense of humor of.
 SYN.—**amuse** suggests the agreeable occupation of the mind, especially by something that appeals to the sense of humor (the monkey's antics *amused* him); to **divert** is to take the attention from serious thought or worry to something gay or light; **entertain** implies planned amusement or diversion, often with some intellectual appeal (who will *entertain* at the dinner?); **beguile** suggests the occupation of time with an agreeable activity, largely to dispel boredom or tedium. —*ANT.* bore.

a·mused (ə-mūzd′), *adj.* [pp. of *amuse*], 1. agreeably occupied or interested. 2. caused to laugh, smile, etc. with pleasure. 3. showing amusement.

a·mus·ed·ly (ə-mūz′id-li), *adv.* in an amused manner.

a·muse·ment (ə-mūz′mənt), *n.* 1. an amusing or being amused. 2. something that amuses or entertains.

amusement park, an outdoor place where there are various devices for entertainment, as a merry-go-round, roller coaster, etc., and, generally, booths for the sale of things to eat and drink.

amusement tax, a tax on various forms of entertainment, paid on admissions to theaters, etc.

a·mu·si·a (ā-mū′zi-ə), *n.* [Mod. L. < Gr. *amousos,* unmusical < *a-,* without + *mousa,* music], in *psychology,* a disorder characterized by inability to recognize or reproduce musical sounds.

a·mus·ing (ə-mūz′iŋ), *adj.* [ppr. of *amuse*], 1. entertaining; diverting. 2. causing laughter or mirth. —*SYN.* see **funny.**

a·mu·sive (ə-mū′ziv), *adj.* amusing or tending to amuse.

A·my (ā′mi), [Fr. *Aimée,* lit., beloved < fem. pp. of *aimer,* to love; L. *amare*], a feminine name.

a·myg·da·la (ə-mig′də-lə), *n.* [*pl.* AMYGDALAE (-lē′)], [L. < Gr. *amygdalē,* an almond], 1. [Obs.], an almond. 2. in *anatomy,* a tonsil: so called from its shape.

a·myg·da·la·ceous (ə-mig′də-lā′shəs), *adj.* [L. *amygdalaceus;* see AMYGDALA], belonging to a group of shrubs and trees with soft, fleshy fruit that contains a single hard seed or stone, as the peach, almond, cherry, etc.

a·myg·da·late (ə-mig′də-lit, ə-mig′də-lāt′), *adj.* [< *amygdala* + *ate*], of or like almonds.

am·yg·dal·ic (am′ig-dal′ik), *adj.* 1. of almonds. 2. in *chemistry,* designating or of a crystalline acid, $C_{20}H_{28}O_{13}$, formed by the decomposition of amygdalin.

a·myg·da·lin (ə-mig′də-lin), *n.* [< *amygdala* + *-in*], a crystalline glucoside, $C_{20}H_{27}NO_{11}$, present in bitter almonds.

a·myg·da·line (ə-mig′də-lin, ə-mig′də-līn′), *adj.* [L. *amygdalinus;* see AMYGDALA], 1. of or like an almond or almonds. 2. having to do with the tonsils.

a·myg·da·loid (ə-mig′də-loid′), *adj.* [< *amygdala* + *-oid*], 1. almond-shaped. 2. designating or of a volcanic rock having small bubble holes filled with secondary minerals. *n.* this rock.

am·yl (am′il, ā′mil), *n.* [*amylum* + *-yl*], any of various isomeric forms of the monovalent radical C_5H_{11}, found in certain compounds.

am·yl- (am′il), amylo-.

am·y·la·ceous (am′i-lā′shəs), *adj.* [*amyl-* + *-aceous*], of or like starch.

amyl alcohol, a colorless, sharp-smelling alcohol, $C_5H_{11}OH$, obtained by the fermentation of starchy substances and also present in fusel oil.

am·yl·ase (am′i-lās′), *n.* [*amyl-* + *-ase*], an enzyme that helps change starch into sugar: it is found in saliva, pancreatic juice, etc.

am·yl·ene (am′i-lēn′), *n.* [*amyl-* + *-ene*], any of several isomeric hydrocarbons having the formula C_5H_{10}.

a·myl·ic (ə-mil′ik), *adj.* of amyl.

am·y·lo- (am′i-lō, am′i-lə), [< *amylum*], a combining form meaning: 1. *of starch,* as in *amylogen.* 2. *of amyl.* Also, before a vowel, **amyl-.**

a·myl·o·gen (ə-mil′ə-jən), *n.* [*amylo-* + *-gen*], the water-soluble part of the starch granule.

am·y·loid (am′i-loid′), *adj.* [*amyl-* + *-oid*], like or containing starch. *n.* a starchy food or substance.

am·y·lol·y·sis (am′i-lol′ə-sis), *n.* [*amylo-* + *-lysis*], the changing of starch into soluble substances by the action of enzymes.

am·y·lop·sin (am′i-lop′sin), *n.* [*amylo-* + try*psin*], the amylase in the pancreatic juice.

am·y·lose (am′i-lōs′), *n.* [*amyl-* + *-ose*], any of a group

of complex carbohydrates, as cellulose or starch, which are converted by hydrolysis into two or more simple sugars: now called *polysaccharide:* formula, $(C_6H_{10}O_5)_n$.
am·y·lum (am'i-ləm), *n.* [L.; Gr. *amylon*], starch.
am·y·tal (am'i-tal', am'i-tôl'), *n.* [invented trade-mark based on *amylethyl*], a colorless crystalline compound, $C_{11}H_{18}O_3N_2$, used as a sedative and hypnotic.
an (ən; *stressed*, an), *adj., indefinite article* [weakened variant of *one* < AS. *an*, the numeral one, which lost stress and shortened its vowel as it came into use as a mere particle; the older and fuller form of *a*], 1. one; one sort of. 2. each; any one. 3. to each; in each; for each; per: as, two *an* hour. The chief grammatical function of *an* (*a*) is to contrast with *the*. It connotes a thing not previously noted or recognized; *the* connotes a thing previously noted or recognized. *An* now replaces *a* before all words beginning with a vowel sound or mute *h*, as, *an* orange, *an* honor; older usage also favored *an* before *h* in an unstressed initial syllable, as, *an* hotel, and before the sound (ū, yoo), as, *an* union, *an* eulogy (chiefly British usage). See also **a.**
an, an' (an), *conj.* [< *and;* ME. *an, and*, and, if], 1. [Dial.], and. 2. [Archaic], if.
an- (an), a- (not, without): used before vowels and *h*, as in *anandrous, anhydrite.*
an- (an), ad-: used before *n*.
-an (ən), [Fr. *-ain, -en* < L. *-anus*, of, belonging to; also directly < L.], a suffix used in forming adjectives (and nouns derived from them), from nouns, meaning, in general: 1. *of, belonging to, characteristic of,* as in *diocesan*. 2. *born in, living in,* as in *American*. 3. *believing in, following,* as in *Mohammedan*. Also, after a vowel, **-n.**
an., 1. *anno*, [L.], in the year. 2. anonymous.
A.N., AN., A.-N., Anglo-Norman.
an·a (an'ə), *adv.* [Gr. *ana*, apiece, of each], of each (ingredient referred to): used in doctors' prescriptions.
a·na (ā'nə, ä'nə), *n.* [< *-ana*, anecdotes], a collection of anecdotes, reminiscences, etc.
an·a- (an'ə, ə-na'), [< Gr. *ana*, up, on, again, etc.], a prefix meaning: 1. *up, upward,* as in *anadromous.* 2. *back, backward,* as in *anagram.* 3. *again,* as in *Anabaptist.* 4. *throughout,* as in *analysis.* 5. *according to, similar to,* as in *analogy, anacardiaceous.*
-a·na (ā'nə, an'ə, ä'nə), [neut. pl. of L. *-anus*], a suffix used in forming collective plurals from proper nouns, and meaning *sayings, writings, anecdotes,* or *facts of,* as in *Americana.*
an·a·bae·na (an'ə-bē'nə), *n.* [Mod. L. < Gr. *anabainein;* see ANABASIS], 1. a fresh-water alga, often found in reservoirs, which gives a fishy taste and odor to water. 2. a mass of such algae.
An·a·bap·tist (an'ə-bap'tist), *n.* [Mod. L. < L. *anabaptismus;* Gr. *anabaptismos*, second baptism < *anabaptizein; ana-*, again + *baptizein*, to baptize], a member of a sect that denied the validity of infant baptism and practiced baptism of adults: originated in Switzerland c. 1522. *adj.* of this sect.
an·a·bas (an'ə-bas'), *n.* [Mod. L.; Gr. *anabas* < *anabainein* (see ANABASIS): so named from its habit of climbing], any of a number of related fresh-water fishes of Africa and Asia resembling the perch: they can live for a long time out of water.
A·nab·a·sis (ə-nab'ə-sis), *n.* [*pl.* ANABASES (-sēz')], [Gr. < *anabainein*, to go up; *ana-*, up + *bainein*, to go], 1. the military expedition (401–400 B.C.) of Cyrus the Younger to overthrow his brother, Artaxerxes II. 2. a book about this by the Greek writer Xenophon. 3. [a-], a military expedition.
an·a·bat·ic (an'ə-bat'ik), *adj.* [Gr. *anabatikos;* see ANABASIS], rising; moving upward: said of air currents or winds.
an·a·bi·o·sis (an'ə-bi-ō'sis), *n.* [Mod. L.; Gr. < *anabioein*, to come to life again], a bringing back to life or consciousness; resuscitation.
an·a·bi·ot·ic (an'ə-bi-ot'ik), *adj.* of anabiosis; stimulating; resuscitating.
an·a·bol·ic (an'ə-bol'ik), *adj.* of or promoting anabolism.
a·nab·o·lism (ə-nab'ə-liz'm), *n.* [< Gr. *anabolē*, a rising up; *ana-*, up + *bolē*, a stroke; + *-ism*], the process in a plant or animal by which food is changed into living tissue; constructive metabolism: opposed to *catabolism.*
an·a·branch (an'ə-branch'), *n.* [< *ana*stomosing *branch*], 1. a river branch that re-enters the main stream. 2. a river branch that becomes absorbed by sandy ground.
an·a·can·thous (an'ə-kan'thəs), *adj.* [Gr. *anakanthos; an-*, not + *akanthos*, spiny < *akantha*, thorn], in *botany*, having no spines; without thorns.
an·a·car·di·a·ceous (an'ə-kär'di-ā'shəs), *adj.* [< Mod. L. *anacardium*, genus of the cashew family < Gr. *ana*, similar to + *kardia*, heart: so called from the resemblance of the fruit to a bird's heart], belonging to the cashew family of trees and shrubs, as the pistachio, mango, etc., with small flowers and fruit containing a single hard seed.
a·nach·ro·nism (ə-nak'rə-niz'm), *n.* [Fr. *anachronisme;* L. *anachronismus;* Gr. *anachronismos* < *anachronizein*, to refer to a wrong time < *ana-*, against + *chronos*, time], 1. the representation of something as existing or occurring at other than its proper time, especially earlier. 2. anything out of its proper historical time.
a·nach·ro·nis·tic (ə-nak'rə-nis'tik), *adj.* containing or involving an anachronism.
a·nach·ro·nous (ə-nak'rə-nəs), *adj.* anachronistic.
an·ac·id (an-as'id), *adj.* [*an-*, without + *acid*], in *medicine*, without normal acidity.
a·nac·la·sis (ə-nak'lə-sis), *n.* [Gr. *anaklasis* < *anaklan; ana-*, back + *klan*, to bend], in *anatomy*, a bending backward; recurvature, as of a joint.
an·a·clas·tic (an'ə-klas'tik), *adj.* [Gr. *anaklastos*, reflected < *anaklan* (see ANACLASIS); + *-ic*], 1. in *anatomy*, bent backward; recurved. 2. in *optics*, of, caused by, or causing refraction.
an·a·cli·nal (an'ə-kli'n'l), *adj.* [see ANACLITIC], in *geology*, lying across the dip of the rocks, as a valley.
an·a·clit·ic (an'ə-klit'ik), *adj.* [< Gr. *anaklinein*, to lean upon; *ana-*, on + *klinein*, to lean], 1. leaning; dependent. 2. in *psychoanalysis*, having the libido dependent upon another instinct.
an·a·co·lu·thic (an'ə-kə-lōō'thik, an'ə-kə-lū'thik), *adj.* [Gr. *anakolouthos*], of or using anacoluthon.
an·a·co·lu·thon (an'ə-kə-lōō'thon, an'ə-kə-lū'thon), *n.* [*pl.* ANACOLUTHA (-thə)], [Gr. *anakolouthos*, inconsequent; *an-*, not + *akolouthos*, following], 1. a change from one grammatical construction to another within the same sentence, sometimes as a rhetorical device. 2. a sentence in which this occurs. Example: *Romeo and Juliet*, I, iii. "A man, young lady! lady, such a man as all the world—why, he's a man of wax!"
An·a·con·da (an'ə-kon'də), *n.* a city in western Montana, known for its copper refinery: pop., 12,000.
an·a·con·da (an'ə-kon'də), *n.* [orig., Eng. name for a Ceylonese snake], 1. a very long, heavy South American snake of the boa family. 2. any similar large snake that crushes its victim in its coils.
A·nac·re·on (ə-nak'ri-ən, ə-nak'ri-on'), *n.* Greek lyric poet; 572?–488? B.C.
A·nac·re·on·tic (ə-nak'ri-on'tik), *adj.* 1. of or by Anacreon. 2. like Anacreon's poems. *n.* 1. a poem of this kind. 2. *pl.* verses in the stanza form (abab) and rhythm (– ⏑ | – ⏑ | – ⏑ | – |) much used by Anacreon.
an·a·cru·sis (an'ə-krōō'sis), *n.* [Mod. L.; Gr. *anakrousis* < *anakrouein*, to push back; *ana-*, back + *krouein*, to strike], one or more unaccented syllables added to the beginning of a line of verse which would ordinarily commence with an accented syllable.
an·a·dem (an'ə-dem'), *n.* [L. *anadema;* Gr. *anadēma* < *anadein*, to bind up, wreathe; *ana-*, up + *dein*, to bind], [Poetic], a wreath or garland for the head.
an·a·di·plo·sis (an'ə-di-plō'sis), *n.* [L.; Gr. *anadiplōsis* < *anadiploun*, to double < *ana-*, up, again + *diploos*, double], the repetition of a key word, especially the last one, at the beginning of the next sentence or clause, as "He gave his life; life was all he could give."
a·nad·ro·mous (ə-nad'rə-məs), *adj.* [Gr. *anadromos; ana-*, upward + *dromos*, a running < *dramein*, to run], going up rivers to spawn: said of the salmon, shad, etc.
A·na·dyr Range (ä-nä-dir'), a mountain range in far northeastern Siberia: part of the Stanovoi system.
a·nae·mi·a (ə-nē'mi-ə), *n.* anemia.
a·nae·mic (ə-nē'mik), *adj.* anemic.
an·aer·obe (an-âr'ōb, an-ā'ẽr-ōb'), *n.* [Mod. L. *anaerobium;* see AN- (not) & AEROBE], a microorganism that can live and grow where there is no air or free oxygen: anaerobes get oxygen by the decomposition of compounds containing it.
an·aer·o·bic (an'âr-ō'bik, an-ā'ẽr-ō'bik), *adj.* 1. of or produced by anaerobes. 2. able to live and grow where there is no air or free oxygen, as certain bacteria.
an·aer·o·bi·um (an'âr-ō'bi-əm, an'ā-ẽr-ō'bi-əm), *n.* [*pl.* ANAEROBIA (-ə)], [Mod. L. < Gr. *an-* (see A-, without) + *aero-* (see AERO-) + *bios*, life], an anaerobe.
an·aes·the·si·a (an'əs-thē'zhə, an'əs-thē'zhi-ə), *n.* anesthesia.
an·aes·thet·ic (an'əs-thet'ik), *adj. & n.* anesthetic.
an·aes·the·tist (ə-nes'thə-tist), *n.* an anesthetist.
an·aes·the·tize (ə-nes'thə-tīz'), *v.t.* to anesthetize.
an·a·glyph (an'ə-glif'), *n.* [Gr. *anaglyphē* < *ana-*, up + *glyphein*, to carve out], an ornament carved in low relief.
an·a·go·ge (an'ə-gō'ji), *n.* [Gr. *anagōgē*, a leading up < *ana-*, up + *agein*, to lead, drive], mystical interpretation, as of the Scriptures.
an·a·gog·ic (an'ə-goj'ik), *adj.* [Gr. *anagōgikos*, mystical; see ANAGOGE], 1. of or by anagoge. 2. in *psychology*, relating to the moral or allegorical tendencies of the unconscious: a term used by C. G. Jung.
an·a·gram (an'ə-gram'), *n.* [Mod. L. *anagramma* < Gr. *anagrammatizein*, to transpose letters < *ana-*, back + *gramma*, letter < *graphein*, to write], 1. a word or phrase made from another by rearranging its letters, as *now—won, made—dame.* 2. *pl.* a game of making words by changing or adding letters.
an·a·gram·mat·ic (an'ə-grə-mat'ik), *adj.* of, like, arranged as, or containing an anagram.
an·a·gram·mat·i·cal (an'ə-grə-mat'i-k'l), *adj.* anagrammatic.

an·a·gram·ma·tize (an'ə-gram'ə-tīz'), *v.t.* [ANAGRAMMATIZED (-tīzd'), ANAGRAMMATIZING], to make an anagram of.

An·a·heim (an'ə-hīm'), *n.* a city in southwestern California, near Los Angeles: pop., 104,000.

a·nal (ā'n'l), *adj.* [Mod. L. *analis* < L. *anus*, anus], of or near the anus.

anal., 1. analogous. 2. analogy. 3. analysis.

an·al·cite (an-al'sīt, an'al-sīt'), *n.* [< Gr. *analkēs*, weak; + *-ite*], a kind of mineral, a zeolite found in traprock.

an·a·lec·ta (an'ə-lek'tə), *n.pl.* [L.], analects.

an·a·lects (an'ə-lekts'), *n.pl.* [L. *analecta* < Gr. *analegein*, to collect; *ana-*, up + *legein*, to gather], collected literary excerpts or fragments of writing.
 the Analects, a collection of Confucius' teachings.

an·a·lep·tic (an'ə-lep'tik), *adj.* & *n.* [Gr. *analēptikos*, restorative < *analambanein*, to recover; *ana-*, up + *lambanein*, to take], in *medicine*, restorative.

an·al·ge·si·a (an'al-jē'zi-ə, an'al-jē'si-ə), *n.* [Mod. L.; Gr. *analgēsia; an-*, without + *algēsia*, pain < *algos*, pain], a state of not being able to feel pain.

an·al·ge·sic (an'al-jē'zik, an'al-jē'sik), *adj.* of or causing analgesia. *n.* something that produces analgesia.

analog computer, a computer using coded physical quantities, such as electrical resistance, voltage, etc., to solve problems, especially differential equations, and usually giving the solutions in the form of a graphic display, such as an oscilloscope pattern.

an·a·log·i·cal (an'ə-loj'i-k'l), *adj.* [L. *analogicus*], of, using, or based upon analogy.

a·nal·o·gist (ə-nal'ə-jist), *n.* a person who uses analogy.

a·nal·o·gize (ə-nal'ə-jīz'), *v.i.* [ANALOGIZED (-jīzd'), ANALOGIZING], [Gr. *analogizesthai*, to calculate], to use, or reason by, analogy. *v.t.* to explain by analogy.

a·nal·o·gous (ə-nal'ə-gəs), *adj.* [L. *analogus;* Gr. *analogos;* see ANALOGY], 1. similar or comparable in certain respects. 2. in *biology*, similar in function but not in origin and structure. Abbreviated **anal.**

an·a·logue, an·a·log (an'ə-lôg', an'ə-log'), *n.* [Fr. *analogue* < L. *analogus*; see ANALOGY], 1. a thing or part that is analogous. 2. in *linguistics*, a cognate.

a·nal·o·gy (ə-nal'ə-ji), *n.* [*pl.* ANALOGIES (-jiz)], [Fr. *analogie;* L. *analogia;* Gr. *analogia*, proportion < *analogos*, in due ratio; *ana-*, according to + *logos*, ratio, relation], 1. similarity in some respects between things otherwise unlike; partial resemblance. 2. an explaining of something by comparing it point by point with something else. 3. in *biology*, similarity in function between parts dissimilar in origin and structure: distinguished from *homology*. 4. in *logic*, the inference that certain admitted resemblances imply probable further similarity. 5. in *linguistics*, the process by which new or less familiar words, constructions, or pronunciations conform with the pattern of older or more familiar (and often unrelated) ones: as, *energize* is formed from *energy* by *analogy* with *apologize* from *apology*. Abbreviated **anal.** —*SYN.* see **likeness.**

an·al·pha·bet·ic (an-al'fə-bet'ik, an'al-fə-bet'ik), *adj.* & *n.* illiterate.

an·a·lyse (an'ə-līz'), *v.t.* [ANALYSED (-līzd'), ANALYSING], to analyze.

a·nal·y·sis (ə-nal'ə-sis), *n.* [*pl.* ANALYSES (-sēz')], [Gr., a dissolving, resolution of a whole into parts; *ana-*, up, throughout + *lysis*, a loosing < *lyein*, to loose], 1. a separating or breaking up of any whole into its parts so as to find out their nature, proportion, function, relationship, etc. 2. a statement of the results of this process. 3. in *chemistry*, *a)* the separation of compounds and mixtures into their constituent substances for the purpose of determining the nature (*qualitative analysis*) or the proportion (*quantitative analysis*) of the constituents. *b)* the determination of the nature or proportion of one or more constituents of a substance, whether separated out or not. 4. in *mathematics*, *a)* the solving of problems by means of equations. *b)* examination of the relations of variables, as in differential calculus. 5. psychoanalysis. Abbreviated **anal.**

an·a·lyst (an'ə-list), *n.* [Fr. *analyste*], 1. a person who analyzes: as, a news *analyst*. 2. a psychoanalyst.

an·a·lyt·ic (an'ə-lit'ik), *adj.* [ML. *analyticus;* Gr. *analytikos* < *analytos*, dissoluble; see ANALYSIS], analytical.

an·a·lyt·i·cal (an'ə-lit'i-k'l), *adj.* 1. of analysis or analytics. 2. skilled in or using analysis. 3. that separates into constituent parts. 4. in *grammar*, using two or more words instead of an inflected form, as *more often* instead of *oftener;* expressing the principal grammatical relationships by the use of particles instead of inflections: opposed to *synthetic* or *inflectional*.

an·a·lyt·i·cal·ly (an'ə-lit'i-k'l-i, an'ə-lit'ik-li), *adv.* 1. in an analytical manner. 2. as regards analysis.

analytical psychology, 1. psychology using mainly the introspective method. 2. a type of psychoanalysis originated by C. G. Jung.

analytic geometry, the branch of geometry in which position is indicated by algebraic symbols and solutions are obtained by algebraic analysis.

an·a·lyt·ics (an'ə-lit'iks), *n.pl.* [construed as sing.], 1. the part of logic having to do with analyzing. 2. mathematical analysis.

an·a·lyz·a·ble (an'ə-līz'ə-b'l), *adj.* that can be analyzed.

an·a·lyze (an'ə-līz'), *v.t.* [ANALYZED (-līzd'), ANALYZING], [Fr. *analyser* < *analyse*, analysis; see ANALYSIS], 1. to separate or break up (any whole) into its parts so as to find out their nature, proportion, function, relationship, etc. 2. to examine the constituents or parts of; determine the nature or tendencies of. 3. to psychoanalyze. 4. in *chemistry*, to separate (compounds or mixtures) into their constituent substances in order to determine the nature or the proportion of the constituents. 5. in *grammar*, to resolve (a sentence) into its grammatical elements. 6. in *mathematics*, to solve by means of equations. Also spelled **analyse.**

an·am·ne·sis (an'am-nē'sis), *n.* [Gr. *anamnēsis* < *anamimnēskein; ana-*, again + *mimnēskein*, to call to mind], a remembering, especially of a supposed life before this life.

an·a·mor·pho·scope (an'ə-môr'fə-skōp'), *n.* [*anamorphosis* + *-scope*], a special lens or mirror for making images normal again after distortion by anamorphosis.

an·a·mor·pho·sis (an'ə-môr'fə-sis, an'ə-môr-fō'sis), *n.* [*pl.* ANAMORPHOSES (-sēz')], [Gr. *anamorphōsis*, a forming anew < *ana-*, again + *morphoun*, to form], 1. a distorted image which looks normal when viewed with a special device. 2. the making of such images. 3. in *biology*, a gradual change of form by evolution: distinguished from *metamorphosis*. 4. in *botany*, an abnormal change of form that gives the appearance of a different species.

an·an·drous (an-an'drəs), *adj.* [*an-* + *-androus*], in *botany*, without stamens.

An·a·ni·as (an'ə-nī'əs), *n.* 1. in the *Bible*, a notorious liar who fell dead together with his wife when Peter rebuked him: Acts 5:1–10. 2. [Colloq.], a liar.

an·an·thous (an-an'thəs), *adj.* [*an-* + *-anthous*], in *botany*, lacking flowers.

an·a·pest, an·a·paest (an'ə-pest'), *n.* [L. *anapaestus;* Gr. *anapaistos* < *ana-*, back + *paiein*, to strike], 1. a metrical foot consisting of two short syllables followed by a long one, or two unaccented syllables followed by an accented one. 2. a line of verse made up of such feet. Example: "Ănd thĕ shéen | ŏf thĕir spéars | wăs ăs fóam | ŏn thĕ séa."

an·a·pes·tic, an·a·paes·tic (an'ə-pes'tik), *adj.* of or made up of anapests.

an·a·phase (an'ə-fāz'), *n.* [*ana-*, up + *phase*], in *biology*, the stage in mitosis, after the metaphase and before the telophase, in which the chromosomes move toward the centrosomes.

a·naph·o·ra (ə-naf'ə-rə), *n.* [L.; Gr. < *ana-*, up, back + *pherein*, to carry], 1. the rhetorical device of repeating a word or phrase at the beginning of successive clauses or sentences. 2. in *linguistics*, the device of syntactical cross reference through pronouns, auxiliary verbs, etc.

an·aph·ro·dis·i·ac (an-af'rə-diz'i-ak), *adj.* [*an-* + *aphrodisiac*], that lessens sexual desire. *n.* a drug, etc. for causing a lessening of sexual desire.

an·a·phy·lac·tic (an'ə-fə-lak'tik), *adj.* of anaphylaxis.

an·a·phy·lax·is (an'ə-fə-lak'sis), *n.* [Gr. *ana-*, without + *phylaxis*, watching, guarding], a condition of hypersensitivity to proteins and other substances in which exposure to or injection of the foreign matter results in attacks, sometimes causing collapse and death.

an·a·plas·tic (an'ə-plas'tik), *adj.* 1. in *medicine*, characterized by a reversion to a more primitive, imperfectly developed form: said of cells. 2. in *surgery*, of or by anaplasty.

an·a·plas·ty (an'ə-plas'ti), *n.* [< Gr. *anaplastos*, plastic; + *-y*], plastic surgery.

an·arch (an'ärk), *n.* [< Gr. *anarchos*, without a leader; *an-*, without + *archos*, leader], an anarchist.

an·ar·chic (an-är'kik), *adj.* 1. of, like, or involving anarchy. 2. advocating anarchy. 3. tending to bring about anarchy; lawless.

an·ar·chi·cal (an-är'ki-k'l), *adj.* anarchic.

an·arch·ism (an'ēr-kiz'm), *n.* [< *anarchy* + *-ism*]. 1. the theory that all forms of government interfere unjustly with individual liberty and are therefore undesirable. 2. resistance, sometimes by terrorism, to organized government.

an·arch·ist (an'ēr-kist), *n.* 1. a person who believes in or advocates anarchism. 2. a person who promotes anarchy. *adj.* anarchistic.

an·ar·chis·tic (an'ēr-kis'tik), *adj.* of or like anarchism or anarchists.

an·arch·y (an'ēr-ki), *n.* [*pl.* ANARCHIES (-kiz)], [Gr. *anarchia;* see ANARCH], 1. the complete absence of government and law. 2. political disorder and violence; hence, 3. disorder in any sphere of activity.

an·ar·throus (an-är'thrəs), *adj.* [Gr. *anarthros* < *an-*, without + *arthron*, joint, article], 1. in *Greek grammar*, used without the article. 2. in *zoology*, really or apparently having no joints.

an·a·sar·ca (an'ə-sär'kə), *n.* [Mod. L.; Gr. *ana*, through-out + *sarx*, flesh], generalized edema; generalized dropsy.

An·as·ta·sia (an'ə-stā'shə, an'ə-stā'zhə), [LL., fem. of *Anastasius;* Gr. *Anastasios*, lit., of the resurrection], a feminine name.

An·as·ta·si·us I (an'əs-tā'shi-əs), 430?–518 A.D.; emperor of the Eastern Roman Empire (491–518 A.D.).

Anastasius II, ?–721 A.D.; emperor of the Eastern Roman Empire (713–716 A.D.).

an·as·tig·mat·ic (an'as-tig-mat'ik, an-as'tig-mat'ik), *adj.* [*an-* + *astigmatic*], 1. free from astigmatism. 2. corrected for astigmatism.

anastigmatic lens, in *photography*, a compound lens made up of one converging and one diverging lens so that the astigmatism of one is neutralized by the equal and opposite astigmatism of the other.

a·nas·to·mose (ə-nas'tə-mōz'), *v.t.* & *v.i.* [ANASTOMOSED (-mōzd'), ANASTOMOSING], [Fr. *anastomoser*], to join by anastomosis.

a·nas·to·mo·sis (ə-nas'tə-mō'sis), *n.* [*pl.* ANASTOMOSES (-sēz)], [Mod. L.; Gr. *anastomōsis*, opening < *ana-*, again + *stoma*, mouth], 1. a connection between blood vessels, veins in a leaf, channels of a river, etc. 2. a surgical joining of one hollow or tubular organ to another, as of the severed ends of the intestine after resection.

a·nas·tro·phe (ə-nas'trə-fi), *n.* [Gr. *anastrophē* < *anastrephein; ana-*, back + *strephein*, to turn], reversal of the usual order of the parts of a sentence; inversion. Example: "Came the dawn."

anat., 1. anatomical. 2. anatomist. 3. anatomy.

an·a·tase (an'ə-tāz'), *n.* [Fr. < Gr. *anatasis*, prolongation, extension], octahedrite, a mineral.

a·nath·e·ma (ə-nath'ə-mə), *n.* [*pl.* ANATHEMAS (-məz)], [L.; Gr., thing devoted to evil; previously, anything devoted < *anatithenai*, to set up, dedicate; *ana-*, up + *tithenai*, to place, set], 1. a thing or person accursed or damned; hence, 2. anything greatly detested. 3. a formal curse excommunicating a person from a church or damning something. 4. any strong curse.

a·nath·e·ma·ti·za·tion (ə-nath'ə-mə-ti-zā'shən), *n.* an anathematizing or being anathematized.

a·nath·e·ma·tize (ə-nath'ə-mə-tīz'), *v.t.* & *v.i.* [ANATHEMATIZED (-tīzd'), ANATHEMATIZING], [LL. *anathematizare;* Gr. *anathematizein*, to make accursed; see ANATHEMA], to utter an anathema (against); curse. —*SYN.* see **curse.**

An·a·to·li·a (an'ə-tō'li-ə), *n.* 1. Asia Minor: ancient name. 2. the Asiatic part of modern Turkey.

An·a·to·li·an (an'ə-tō'li-ən), *adj.* 1. of Anatolia or its people. 2. Anatolic. *n.* a native or inhabitant of Anatolia.

An·a·tol·ic (an'ə-tol'ik), *adj.* 1. designating or of a subfamily of Indo-European languages, including the Armenian and extinct Phrygian. 2. Anatolian.

an·a·tom·ic (an'ə-tom'ik), *adj.* [Gr. *anatomikos*, skilled in anatomy; see ANATOMY], anatomical.

an·a·tom·i·cal (an'ə-tom'i-k'l), *adj.* 1. of or connected with anatomy. 2. structural. Abbreviated **anat.**

an·a·tom·i·cal·ly (an'ə-tom'i-k'l-i, an'ə-tom'ik-li), *adv.* 1. with reference to anatomy. 2. from the viewpoint of the science of anatomy.

a·nat·o·mist (ə-nat'ə-mist), *n.* [Fr. *anatomiste*], 1. a person skilled in anatomy. 2. a person who dissects or analyzes. Abbreviated **anat.**

a·nat·o·mize (ə-nat'ə-mīz'), *v.t.* & *v.i.* [ANATOMIZED (-mīzd'), ANATOMIZING], [Fr. *anatomiser;* ML. *anatomizare;* see ANATOMY], 1. to dissect (animal bodies, etc.) in order to examine the structure; hence, 2. to analyze.

a·nat·o·my (ə-nat'ə-mi), *n.* [*pl.* ANATOMIES (-miz)], [Fr. *anatomie;* L. *anatomia;* Gr. *anatomia, anatomē*, a cutting up < *anatemnein; ana-*, up + *temnein*, to cut], 1. the dissecting of a plant or animal in order to determine the position, structure, etc. of its parts. 2. the science of the morphology or structure of plants or animals. 3. a textbook dealing with this science. 4. the structure of an organism or body, or a model of it as dissected. 5. a skeleton. 6. any analysis. Abbreviated **anat.**

a·nat·ro·pous (ə-nat'rə-pəs), *adj.* [Mod. L.; see ANA- & -TROPOUS], in *botany*, inverted early in its development so that the micropyle is turned down toward the funicle: said of an ovule.

a·nat·to (ä-nä'tō), *n.* annatto.

An·ax·ag·o·ras (an'ak-sag'ə-rəs), *n.* Greek philosopher and geometrician who taught in Athens; 500?–428 B.C.; advanced the theory of atoms.

A·nax·i·man·der (a-nak'si-man'dẽr), *n.* Greek philosopher; 611?–547? B.C.

An·ax·im·i·nes (an'ak-sim'i-nēz'), *n.* Greek philosopher: 4th century B.C.

ANC, Army Nurse Corps.

anc., 1. ancient. 2. anciently.

-ance (əns), [Fr. *-ance;* L *-antia, -entia*], a suffix used to form nouns from verbs or from adjectives in *-ant*, and meaning: 1. *a —ing or being —ed*, as in *utterance.* 2. *the quality or state of being —ant*, as in *vigilance.* 3. *a thing that —s*, as in *conveyance.* 4. *a thing that is —ant*, as in *dissonance.* 5. *a thing that is —ed*, as in *inheritance.* A word ending in *-ance* may combine two or more of the above meanings. Also **-ancy, -ence, -ency.**

an·ces·tor (an'ses-tẽr), *n.* [ME. & OFr. *ancestre;* L. *antecessor*, one who goes before < pp. of *antecedere; ante-*, before + *cedere*, to go], 1. any person from whom one is descended; forebear. 2. an early type of animal from which later kinds have evolved. 3. in *law*, the person from whom an estate has been inherited.

an·ces·tral (an-ses'trəl), *adj.* [OFr. *ancestrel*], of or inherited from an ancestor or ancestors.

an·ces·tress (an'ses-tris), *n.* a woman ancestor.

an·ces·try (an'ses-tri), *n.* [*pl.* ANCESTRIES (-triz)], [ME. *ancestrie;* OFr. *ancesserie* < *ancestre;* see ANCESTOR], 1. family descent or lineage. 2. ancestors collectively.

An·chi·ses (an-kī'sēz), *n.* [L.; Gr. *Anchisēs*], in *Roman legend*, the father of Aeneas.

an·chor (aŋ'kẽr), *n.* [AS. *ancor;* L. *ancora;* Gr. *ankyra*, an anchor, hook], 1. a heavy object, usually a shaped iron weight with hooks, lowered into the water by cable or chain to keep a ship from drifting. 2. any device that holds something else secure, keeps it from giving way, etc. 3. anything that gives or seems to give stability or security. *v.t.* to keep from drifting, giving way, etc., by or as by an anchor. *v.i.* to lower the anchor overboard so as to keep from drifting; lie at anchor.

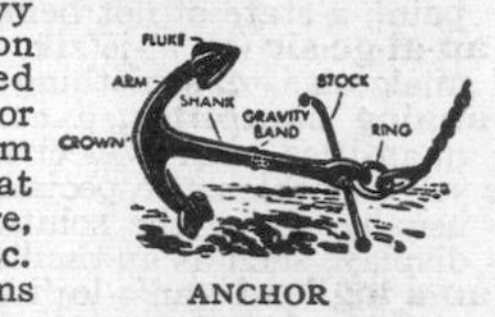

ANCHOR

at anchor, anchored.

cast (or **drop**) **anchor,** 1. to throw or lower the anchor overboard. 2. to stay or settle (in a place).

drag anchor, 1. to drift inshore because of the failure of the anchor to hold. 2. to lose ground; slip or fail.

ride at anchor, to be anchored: said of ships.

weigh anchor, 1. to raise the anchor, hence, 2. to leave; go away.

An·chor·age (aŋ'kẽr-ij), *n.* a city in southern Alaska, on Cook Inlet: pop., 44,000.

an·chor·age (aŋ'kẽr-ij), *n.* [*anchor* + *-age*], 1. money charged for the right to anchor, as in a port. 2. an anchoring or being anchored. 3. a place to anchor. 4. something that can be firmly held on to or relied on.

an·chor·age (aŋ'kẽr-ij), *n.* [< *anchorite*], the dwelling of an anchorite.

an·cho·ress (aŋ'kẽr-is), *n.* a woman anchorite.

an·cho·ret (aŋ'kẽr-it, aŋ'kə-ret'), *n.* an anchorite.

an·cho·ret·ic (aŋ'kə-ret'ik), *adj.* [Gr. *anachōrētikos;* see ANCHORITE], of or like an anchorite; solitary.

an·cho·rite (aŋ'kə-rīt'), *n.* [OFr. *anachorete;* L. *anachoreta;* Gr. *anachōrētēs*, one retired < *anachōrein; ana-*, back + *chōrein*, to retire], 1. a person who lives alone and apart from society for religious meditation. 2. a hermit; recluse.

an·cho·rit·ic (aŋ'kə-rit'ik), *adj.* anchoretic.

anchor man, 1. the end man in a tug of war. 2. the final runner on a relay team. 3. the final performer in any group activity.

an·cho·vy (an'chə-vi, an'chō'vi, an-chō'vi), *n.* [*pl.* ANCHOVIES (-viz), ANCHOVY; see PLURAL, II, D, 1], [Port. & Sp. *anchova;* Basque *anchova, anchua*, anchovy; akin to *anztua*, dry, dried fish], any of several very small fishes of the herring family, found in warm seas: anchovies are usually salted, spiced, and canned in oil, or made into a salty paste.

anchovy pear, 1. a West Indian fruit that tastes like a mango. 2. the tree it grows on.

an·chu·sa (an-kōō'zə, aŋ-kū'sə), *n.* [Mod. L.; L. *anchusa;* Gr. *anchousa*], any of a number of related plants with hairy leaves, small flowers, usually blue, and roots yielding a red dye; alkanet; bugloss.

an·chu·sin (an-kōō'zin, aŋ-kū'sin), *n.* alkannin.

an·chy·lose (aŋ'ki-lōs'), *v.t.* & *v.i.* [ANCHYLOSED (-lōst'), ANCHYLOSING], to ankylose.

an·chy·lo·sis (aŋ'ki-lō'sis), *n.* ankylosis.

‡an·cienne no·blesse (än'syen' nô'bles'), [Fr., old nobility], French nobility before Revolution of 1789.

‡an·cien ré·gime (än'syan' rā'zhēm'), [Fr., old order], the former social and governmental system, especially that in France before the Revolution of 1789.

an·cient (ān'shənt), *adj.* [ME. *ancien;* OFr. *ancien*, ult. < L. *ante*, before], 1. of times long past; belonging to the early history of the world, especially before the end of the Western Roman Empire. 2. having existed a long time; antique; very old. Abbreviated **anc.** *n.* 1. a person who lived in ancient times. 2. an aged person. —*SYN.* see **old.**

the ancients, 1. the people who lived in ancient, especially Graeco-Roman, times. 2. the ancient or classical writers and artists, especially of Graeco-Roman times.

an·cient (ān'shənt), *n.* [confusion of *ensign* with earlier *ancien*, ancient], [Archaic], 1. an ensign. 2. a person who carries an ensign or flag.

ancient history, 1. history from the beginning of re-

corded events to the end of the Roman Empire in the West in 476 A.D. 2. [Colloq.], something of the recent past that is well known or no longer important.
an·cient·ly (ān′shənt-li), ***adv.*** in ancient times.
Ancient of Days, God.
an·cient·ry (ān′shənt-ri), ***n.*** 1. the quality or state of being ancient. 2. ancient times; antiquity.
an·cil·lar·y (an′sə-ler′i), ***adj.*** [L. *ancillaris* < *ancilla*, maidservant], 1. subordinate (often with *to*). 2. helping; auxiliary. ***n.*** a helper; servant.
an·cip·i·tal (an-sip′ə-t′l), ***adj.*** [L. *anceps*, *ancipitis*, two-headed, two-sided < *an-* for *ambi-*, around, on both sides + *caput*, head], in *botany*, two-edged, as the flat stems of certain grasses.
An·cón (aŋ′kon; Sp. äŋ-kôn′), ***n.*** a town in the Canal Zone, near the city of Panama: pop., 1,200.
an·con (aŋ′kon), ***n.*** [*pl.* ANCONES (aŋ-kō′nēz)], [L.; Gr. *ankon*, elbow < *ankos*, a bend], 1. in *anatomy*, the elbow. 2. in *architecture*, a bracketlike projection supporting a cornice; console.
An·co·na (äŋ-kô′nä), ***n.*** a city in central Italy, on the Adriatic: pop., 96,000.
an·co·ne·al (aŋ-kō′ni-əl), ***adj.*** [see ANCON], of the elbow.
-an·cy (ən-si), -ance.
an·cy·los·to·mi·a·sis (an′si-los′tə-mī′ə-sis), ***n.*** [Mod. L. < *ancylostoma*, hookworm genus < Gr. *ankylos*, crooked + *stoma*, the mouth; + *-iasis*], an infestation by hookworms: also **ankylostomiasis**.
and (and; *unstressed*, ənd, ən, ′n), ***conj.*** [ME. *and*, *an*; AS. *and*, *ond*; akin to G. *und*, OHG. *unti*, OS. *endi*, ON. *enn*; the original meaning was "thereupon, then, next"], 1. also; in addition; moreover; as well as. 2. plus; added to: as, 6 *and* 2 makes 8. 3. as a consequence or result: as, he told her *and* she wept. 4. [Obs.], if. 5. [Colloq.], to; in order to: as, try *and* come today.
and., andante.
An·da·lu·sia (an′də-lōō′zhə, an′də-lōō′shə), ***n.*** an old province of southern Spain: see **Spain**, map.
An·da·lu·sian (an′də-lōō′zhən, an′də-lōō′shən), ***adj.*** of Andalusia, its people, etc. ***n.*** 1. a native or inhabitant of Andalusia. 2. Spanish dialect of Andalusia. 3. a Mediterranean variety of chicken like the leghorn.
an·da·lu·site (an′də-lōō′sīt), ***n.*** [< *Andalusia*, where it was discovered], a silicate of aluminum, Al_2SiO_5, found in rhombic crystals of different colors.
An·da·man Islands (an′də-mən), a group of islands in the Bay of Bengal, southwest of Burma: with Nicobar Islands, a state of India. See **Nicobar Islands.**
an·dan·te (an-dan′ti, än-dän′tā), ***adj. & adv.*** [It., ppr. of *andare*, to walk], in *music*, moderately slow; slower than allegretto but faster than larghetto: abbreviated **and.** ***n.*** a moderately slow movement or passage.
an·dan·ti·no (an′dan-tē′nō, än′dän-tē′nō), ***adj. & adv.*** [It., dim. of *andante*], in *music*, slightly faster than andante: the current sense, although the word properly means "a little varied from andante." ***n.*** [*pl.* ANDANTINOS (-nōz)], a movement or passage in this tempo.
An·de·an (an-dē′ən, an′di-ən), ***adj.*** of the Andes Mountains or their inhabitants.
An·der·sen, Hans Christian (an′dẽr-s′n), 1805–1875; Danish novelist and writer of fairy stories.
Andersen-Nexö, Martin, see **Nexö, Martin Andersen.**
An·der·son (an′dẽr-s′n), ***n.*** 1. a city in central Indiana: pop., 49,000. 2. a city in northwestern South Carolina: pop., 41,000.
An·der·son, Marian (an′dẽr-s′n), 1908 ; American contralto.
Anderson, Max·well (maks′wel, maks′wəl), 1888–1959; American playwright.
Anderson, Sher·wood (shũr′wood), 1876–1941; American novelist and short-story writer.
An·der·son·ville (an′dẽr-s′n-vil′), ***n.*** a town in central Georgia: site of a Confederate prison in the Civil War.
an·des·ite (an′di-zīt′), ***n.*** [after the *Andes* Mountains], a very small-grained, dark-gray, often porphyritic rock of volcanic origin, containing phenocrysts of feldspar and darker minerals, but never quartz.
An·des Mountains (an′dēz), a mountain system extending the length of western South America: highest peak, Aconcagua, 23,080 ft.
and·i·ron (and′ī′ẽrn), ***n.*** [ME. *andyron*, *aundiren*, *andyre* < OFr. *andier*; ending confused with Eng. *iron*], either of a pair of metal supports used to hold up logs in a fireplace: also called *firedog*.

ANDIRONS

and/or, either *and* or *or*, according to what is meant: as, personal *and/or* real property.
An·dor·ra (an-dôr′ə, an-dor′ə), ***n.*** 1. a republic in the Pyrenees Mountains, between Spain and France: area, 191 sq. mi.; pop., 7,000. 2. its capital: pop., 2,000.
an·dra·dite (an′drə-dīt′), ***n.*** [after J. B. de *Andrada* (1763?–1838), Braz. geologist], a variety of iron garnet containing calcium, $Ca_3Fe_2Si_3O_{12}$, varying from light green to black in color.
An·drás·sy, Count Gyu·la (dyoo′lä än′dräsh-i), 1823–1890; Hungarian statesman.
An·dré, Major John (än′drā, an′dri), 1751–1780; British army officer hanged as a spy in the American Revolution.
Andrea del Sarto, see **Sarto, Andrea del.**
An·dre·a·nof Islands (än-drā-ä′nôf), a group of the Aleutian Islands.
An·dré·ef, An·dré·ev, see **Andreyev.**
An·drew (an′drōō), [OFr. *Andrieu*; L. *Andreas*; Gr. *Andreas*, lit., manly < *anēr*, *andros*, man], a masculine name: diminutive, *Andy*; equivalents, L. *Andreas*, Fr. *André*, It. *Andrea*, Sp. *Andrés*. ***n.*** one of the twelve apostles; brother of Simon Peter.
An·drewes, Lan·ce·lot (lan′sə-lət an′drōōz), 1555–1626; English theologian; first on the list of divines appointed to make the Authorized Version of the Bible.
Andrew of Crete, Saint, 660–732 A.D.; archbishop of Crete; inventor of the musical canon.
An·drews, Roy Chapman (an′drōōz), 1884–1960; American naturalist, explorer, and author.
An·dre·yev, Le·o·nid Ni·ko·la·ye·vich (le′ô-nēd′ nē-kô-lä-yā′vich än-drā′yef), 1871–1919; Russian novelist and playwright: also spelled **Andreév**, etc.
an·dro- (an′drō, an′drə), [< Gr. *anēr*, *andros*, man, male], a combining form meaning: 1. *man*, *male*, *masculine*, as in *androgynous*. 2. *anther*, *stamen*. Also, before a vowel, **andr-**.
An·dro·cles (an′drə-klēz′), ***n.*** Androclus.
an·dro·clin·i·um (an′drə-klin′i-əm), ***n.*** [< *andro-* + Gr. *klinē*, a bed], the receptacle of a composite flower.
An·dro·clus (an′drə-kləs), ***n.*** [L. *Androclus* or *Androcles*; Gr. *Androklēs*], a Roman slave who, according to legend, escaped death when thrown into the arena with a lion because the lion recognized him as the man who had once extracted a thorn from its foot.
an·droe·ci·um (an-drē′shi-əm, an-drē′si-əm), ***n.*** [*pl.* ANDROECIA (-ə)], [Mod. L. < *andr-* + Gr. *oikos*, house], in *botany*, the stamens and the parts belonging to them, collectively; all the microsporophylls of a flower.
an·dro·gen (an′drə-jən), ***n.*** [*andro-* + *-gen*], a male sex hormone or similar substance that can give rise to masculine characteristics.
an·drog·e·nous (an-droj′ə-nəs), ***adj.*** [*andro-* + *-genous*], 1. in *biology*, producing male offspring. 2. in *botany*, bearing stamens only.
an·dro·gyne (an′drə-jin), ***n.*** [Fr.; L.; Gr. *androgynē*], in *botany*, an androgynous plant.
an·drog·y·nous (an-droj′ə-nəs), ***adj.*** [L. *androgynus*; Gr. *androgynos* < *anēr*, *andros*, man + *gynē*, woman], 1. both male and female in one; hermaphroditic. 2. in *botany*, bearing both staminate and pistillate flowers in the same inflorescence or cluster.
an·drog·y·ny (an-droj′ə-ni), ***n.*** the state of being androgynous; hermaphroditism.
An·drom·a·che (an-drom′ə-ki), ***n.*** [L.; Gr. *Andromachē*], in *Greek legend*, the faithful wife of Hector.
An·drom·e·da (an-drom′i-də), ***n.*** [L.; Gr. *Andromedē*], 1. in *Greek legend*, an Ethiopian princess whom Perseus rescued from a sea monster and then married. 2. in *astronomy*, a northern constellation just south of Cassiopeia: see **constellation**, chart.
An·dros, Sir Edmund (an′drəs), 1637–1714; British governor of American colonies.
An·dros·cog·gin (an′drə-skog′in), ***n.*** a river flowing from New Hampshire through southwestern Maine into the Kennebec River: length, 175 mi.
an·dro·sphinx (an′drə-sfiŋks′), ***n.*** [*andro-* + *sphinx*], a sphinx with the head of a man and the body of a lion.
an·dros·ter·one (an-dros′tẽr-ōn′), ***n.*** [*andro-* + *sterol* + *-one*], a male sex hormone, $C_{19}H_{30}O_2$, found in male urine.
-an·drous (an′drəs), [< Gr. *anēr*, *andros*, man, male], a suffix meaning *having stamens:* used in forming botanical adjectives, as in *monandrous*.
An·dva·ri (än′dwä-ri, änd′vä-ri), ***n.*** in *Norse mythology*, a dwarf from whom Loki stole gold and a magic ring.
ane (ān), ***adj. & pron.*** [AS. *an*, one], [Dial.], one.
-ane (ān), [a modern formation, arbitrarily coined], a suffix denoting a hydrocarbon of the paraffin series, as in *methane*, *ethane*.
a·near (ə-nêr′), ***adv. & prep.*** [Dial. or Poetic], near.
an·ec·dot·age (an′ik-dōt′ij), ***n.*** [< *anecdote* + *-age*], 1. a collection of anecdotes. 2. senility: a humorous usage.
an·ec·do·tal (an′ik-dō′t′l), ***adj.*** 1. of or like an anecdote. 2. full of anecdotes.
an·ec·dote (an′ik-dōt′), ***n.*** [Fr.; ML. *anecdota*; Gr. *anekdota*, neut. pl. of *anekdotos*, unpublished; *an-*, not + *ekdotos* < *ekdidonai*; *ek-*, out + *didonai*, to give],

1. *pl.* originally, little-known, entertaining facts of history or biography; hence, 2. a short, entertaining account of some happening, usually personal or biographical. —*SYN.* see **story.**

an·ec·dot·ic (an'ik-dot'ik), *adj.* 1. anecdotal. 2. fond of telling anecdotes.

an·ec·dot·i·cal (an'ik-dot'i-k'l), *adj.* anecdotic.

an·ec·dot·ist (an'ek-dōt'ist), *n.* a person who tells or collects anecdotes.

a·nele (ə-nēl'), *v.t.* [ANELED (-nēld'), ANELING], [ME. *anelien* < *an-*, on + *ele*, oil < AS. *ele* < L. *oleum*], [Archaic], to anoint, especially in extreme unction.

an·e·lec·tric (an'ə-lek'trik), *adj.* [*an-*, not + *electric*], that cannot become electrified by friction.

a·ne·mi·a (ə-nē'mi-ə), *n.* [Mod. L.; Gr. *anaimia* < *a-*, *an-*, without, not + *haima*, blood], a condition in which there is a reduction of the number of red blood corpuscles or of the total amount of hemoglobin in the blood stream or of both: also spelled **anaemia.**

a·ne·mic (ə-nē'mik), *adj.* of or having anemia: also spelled **anaemic.**

an·e·mo- (an'ə-mə, ə-nem'ə), [< Gr. *anemos*, the wind], a combining form meaning *wind*, as in *anemometer*.

a·nem·o·graph (ə-nem'ə-graf', ə-nem'ə-gräf'), *n.* [*anemo-* + *-graph*], an instrument for recording the velocity or direction of the wind.

an·e·mog·ra·phy (an'ə-mog'rə-fi), *n.* [see ANEMOGRAPH], 1. the science of measuring and recording the velocity and direction of winds. 2. a treatise on winds.

an·e·mol·o·gy (an'ə-mol'ə-ji), *n.* [*anemo-* + *-logy*], the study of winds.

an·e·mom·e·ter (an'ə-mom'ə-tẽr), *n.* [*anemo-* + *-meter*], a gauge for measuring the pressure or velocity of the wind.

an·e·mom·e·try (an'ə-mom'ə-tri), *n.* the act of determining the velocity of the wind by the use of an anemometer.

ANEMOMETER

a·nem·o·ne (ə-nem'ə-nē'), *n.* [Gr. *anemōnē* < *anemos*, wind], 1. any of a number of related plants with cup-shaped flowers, usually of white, purple, or red; windflower. 2. a sea anemone, an invertebrate animal resembling a flower.

an·e·moph·i·lous (an'ə-mof'ə-ləs), *adj.* [*anemo-* + *phil-* + *-ous*], fertilized by the wind, as plants to which pollen is blown.

an·e·moph·i·ly (an'ə-mof'ə-li), *n.* [see ANEMOPHILOUS], pollination by the wind.

SEA ANEMONE (18 in. in diameter)

a·nem·o·scope (ə-nem'ə-skōp'), *n.* [*anemo-* + *-scope*], an instrument for showing or recording the direction of the wind.

an·e·mo·sis (an'ə-mō'sis), *n.* [Mod. L. < Gr. *anemos*, the wind], a crack made in young timber by the wind; wind shake.

a·nenst (ə-nenst'), *prep.* [ME. *anenst*, *anentst*, with unhistoric *-t* < genit. *anentes*, of anent], [Rare], anent.

a·nent (ə-nent'), *prep.* [ME. *anant*, *anent*, *anont* (with unhistoric *-t*) < AS. *on efen*, *onemn*, lit., on even (with), level (with), in line (with)], respecting; as regards; concerning; about.

an·er·gy (an'ẽr-ji), *n.* [Mod. L. *anergia* < Gr. *an-*, without + *ergon*, work], in *medicine*, 1. a loss of strength; lack of energy. 2. a condition in which the body fails to respond to the injection of an antigen.

an·er·oid (an'ẽr-oid'), *adj.* [< Gr. *a-*, without + *nēros*, liquid; + *-oid*], not using liquid. *n.* an aneroid barometer.

aneroid barometer, a barometer with a needle connected to the top of a metal box that contains little or no air, so that a change in atmospheric pressure causes the needle to move by making the elastic top of this box bend in or out.

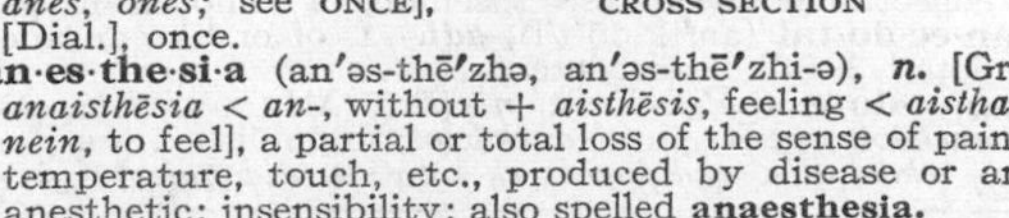

ANEROID BAROMETER, WITH CROSS SECTION

anes (āns), *adv.* [ME. *anes*, *ones*; see ONCE], [Dial.], once.

an·es·the·si·a (an'əs-thē'zhə, an'əs-thē'zhi-ə), *n.* [Gr. *anaisthēsia* < *an-*, without + *aisthēsis*, feeling < *aisthanein*, to feel], a partial or total loss of the sense of pain, temperature, touch, etc., produced by disease or an anesthetic; insensibility: also spelled **anaesthesia.**

an·es·the·si·ol·o·gy (an'əs-thē'zi-ol'ə-ji), *n.* the science of anesthesia and anesthetics.

an·es·thet·ic (an'əs-thet'ik), *adj.* [Gr. *anaisthētos*], 1. relating to, with, or characterized by anesthesia. 2. producing anesthesia. *n.* anything, as a drug, gas, etc., that produces anesthesia. Also spelled **anaesthetic.**

anesthetic to, incapable of feeling or responding to.

an·es·the·tist (ə-nes'thə-tist), *n.* a person trained to administer anesthetics: also spelled **anaesthetist.**

an·es·the·tize (ə-nes'thə-tīz'), *v.t.* [ANESTHETIZED (-tīzd'), ANESTHETIZING], to cause anesthesia in; give anesthetics to; make insensible: also spelled **anaesthetize.**

A·ne·to, Pico de (pē'kô *the* ä-ne'tô), the highest mountain in the Pyrenees, in Spain: height, 11,167 ft.: French name, *Pic de Néthou.*

an·eu·rysm, an·eu·rism (an'yoor-iz'm), *n.* [Mod. L.; Gr. *aneurysma* < *ana-*, up + *eurys*, broad], a sac formed by local enlargement of the wall of an artery, caused by disease or injury.

a·new (ə-nōō', ə-nū'), *adv.* [earlier *of new*], 1. again. 2. in a new manner or way.

an·frac·tu·os·i·ty (an-frak'chōō-os'ə-ti), *n.* 1. the quality or state of being anfractuous. 2. [*pl.* ANFRACTUOSITIES (-tiz)], a winding channel, passage, etc.

an·frac·tu·ous (an-frak'chōō-əs), *adj.* [Fr. *anfractueux;* L. *anfractuosus* < *anfractus*, pp. of *anfringere* < *an-*, *ambi-*, around + *frangere*, to break], winding; roundabout; devious; tortuous.

An·ga·ra (äŋ'gä-rä'), *n.* a river in central Siberia, flowing from Lake Baikal northward and westward to the Yenisei River: length, 1,300 mi.

an·ga·ry (aŋ'gə-ri), *n.* [L., enforced service < Gr. *angaros*, a dispatch bearer], in *international law*, the right of a belligerent to use or destroy a neutral's property if necessary, subject to full indemnification.

an·ge·kok (aŋ'gə-kok'), *n.* [Esk.], an Eskimo medicine man.

an·gel (ān'jəl), *n.* [ME.; OFr. *angele;* L. *angelus;* Gr. *angelos*, messenger], 1. a messenger of God. 2. a supernatural being, either good or bad, to whom is attributed more than human power, intelligence, etc. 3. a guiding spirit or influence: as, one's good *angel.* 4. a conventionalized image of a white-robed figure in human form with wings and a halo. 5. a person regarded as beautiful, good, innocent, etc. 6. a former English gold coin with the archangel Michael and the dragon shown on it, last issued in 1634. 7. [Slang], one who provides the money for producing a play, etc. *v.t.* [Slang], to back financially. —*SYN.* see **sponsor.**

An·ge·la (an'jə-lə), [contr. of *Angelica* < ML. *angelica*, angelic < L. *angelicus;* see ANGELIC], a feminine name: variants, *Angelica, Angelina, Angeline.*

angel cake, a light, spongy, white cake made without shortening or egg yolks: also called *angel food.*

an·gel·fish (ān'jəl-fish'), *n.* [*pl.* ANGELFISH, ANGELFISHES (-iz); see FISH], 1. a kind of shark with winglike pectoral fins. 2. any of a number of bright-colored tropical fishes with spiny fins.

an·gel·ic (an-jel'ik), *adj.* [L. *angelicus;* Gr. *angelikos* < *angelos*, a messenger], 1. of an angel or the angels; spiritual; heavenly. 2. like an angel in beauty, goodness, innocence, etc.

An·gel·i·ca (an-jel'i-kə), a feminine name: see **Angela.**

an·gel·i·ca (an-jel'i-kə), *n.* [ML. (*herba*) *angelica*, lit., the angelic (herb) < *angelicus* (see ANGELIC): so named from its medical uses], any of a number of related plants of the carrot family, with tall stalks, large divided leaves, clusters of white or greenish flowers, and roots and fruit used in flavoring, perfumes, medicine, etc.

an·gel·i·cal (an-jel'i-k'l), *adj.* angelic.

An·gel·i·co, Fra (frä än-jel'i-kō'), (*Giovanni da Fiesole*), 1387–1455; Italian painter of religious subjects.

An·ge·li·na (an'jə-lē'nə, an'jə-lī'nə), a feminine name: see **Angela.**

An·ge·line (an'jə-līn'), a feminine name: see **Angela.**

An·gell, James Row·land (rō'lənd ān'jəl), 1869–1949; American educator and psychologist; president of Yale University (1921–1937).

Angell, Sir **Norman** (born *Ralph Norman Angell Lane*), 1874– ; British author and lecturer; received Nobel peace prize, 1933.

an·gel·ol·o·gy (ān'jəl-ol'ə-ji), *n.* [see ANGEL & -LOGY], the branch of theology dealing with angels.

An·ge·lus, an·ge·lus (an'jə-ləs), *n.* [L.; see ANGEL], in the *Roman Catholic Church,* 1. a prayer said at morning, noon, and night in observance of the Annunciation. 2. the bell rung to announce the time for this prayer.

an·ger (aŋ'gẽr), *n.* [ME. *anger;* ON. *angr*, distress, sorrow < IE. base **angh-*, strait, constricted, seen in L. *angustus*, narrow, tight, *angustia*, tightness, distress; cf. ANGUISH], 1. a feeling that may result from injury, mistreatment, opposition, etc.: it usually shows itself in a desire to hit out at something or someone else; wrath; indignation; rage; ire. 2. [Obs.], pain or trouble. 3. [Dial.], an inflammation of a sore or wound. *v.t.* [ON. *angra*, to distress], 1. to make angry; enrage. 2. [Dial.], to make painfully inflamed.

SYN.—**anger,** the broadest term in this comparison, implies emotional agitation of no specified intensity aroused by great displeasure; **indignation** implies righteous anger aroused by what is considered unjust, mean, or shameful; **rage** suggests a violent outburst of anger in which self-control is lost; **fury** implies an overwhelming rage of a frenzied kind that borders on madness; **ire**, chiefly a literary word, suggests a show of great anger in acts, words, looks, etc.; **wrath** implies deep indignation expressing itself in a desire to punish or get revenge. —*ANT.* pleasure, forbearance.

An·gers (an′jẽrz, aŋ′gẽrz; Fr. än′zhā′), ***n.*** a city in northwestern France: pop., 94,000 (1946).

An·ge·vin (an′jə-vin), ***adj.*** [Fr.], 1. of or from Anjou. 2. of or belonging to the Plantagenet line of English kings (1154–1399). ***n.*** 1. a native or inhabitant of Anjou. 2. a person of the Plantagenet royal line.

An·ge·vine (an′jə-vin, an′jə-vīn′), ***adj. & n.*** Angevin.

an·gi·na (an-jī′nə, an′ji-nə), ***n.*** [L., quinsy; Gr. *anchonē*, a strangling < *anchein*, to squeeze], 1. any inflammatory disease of the throat, especially one characterized by spasmodic suffocation, as croup or quinsy. 2. angina pectoris.

angina pec·to·ris (pek′tə-ris), [L., angina of the breast], a heart disease in which there are spasms of pain in the chest, with feelings of suffocation, usually due to anemia of the heart muscle.

an·gi·o- (an′ji-ō), [< Gr. *angeion*, case, vessel, capsule], a combining form meaning *seedcase, blood vessel, lymph vessel*, as in *angioma, angiosperm.*

an·gi·o·carp (an′ji-ō-kärp′), ***n.*** [*angio-* + *-carp*], any fruit that grows encased in an external covering.

an·gi·ol·o·gy (an′ji-ol′ə-ji), ***n.*** [*angio-* + *-logy*], the study of blood vessels and lymph vessels.

an·gi·o·ma (an′ji-ō′mə), ***n.*** [*pl.* ANGIOMATA (-mə-tə), ANGIOMAS (-məz)], [< *angio-* + *-oma*], a tumor made up mainly of blood vessels and lymph vessels.

an·gi·o·sperm (an′ji-ō-spũrm′), ***n.*** [*angio-* + *-sperm*], any plant that has the seeds enclosed in an ovary: opposed to *gymnosperm.*

Ang·kor (aŋ′kôr), ***n.*** an ancient city in Cambodia, French Indo-China, now in ruins.

Angkor Vat (vat), [Siamese *wat*, temple; Sans. *vāta*, enclosed ground], an ancient Khmer temple in Angkor.

Angl., 1. Anglican. 2. Anglicized.

an·gle (aŋ′g'l), ***n.*** [Fr.; L. *angulus*, a corner, angle; Gr. *ankylos*, bent, crooked], 1. the shape made by two straight lines meeting in a point, or by two plane surfaces meeting along a line. 2. the space between such lines or surfaces. 3. the amount of difference in direction between them, measured in degrees. 4. a sharp or projecting corner. 5. an aspect, as of a problem; point of view: as, consider this from all *angles.* ***v.t. & v.i.*** [ANGLED (-g'ld), ANGLING], 1. to move or bend at an angle or by means of angles. 2. [Colloq.], to give a specific aspect or point of view to (a story, report, etc.). —*SYN.* see **phase.**

an·gle (aŋ′g'l), ***v.i.*** [ANGLED (-g'ld), ANGLING], [< ME. *angel;* AS. *angel, angul*, fishhook, hook; for the base see ANKLE], 1. to fish with a hook and line. 2. to scheme or use tricks so as to get something: as, he *angled* for her attention.

an·gled (aŋ′g'ld), ***adj.*** [pp. of *angle* (to bend)], 1. set at an angle. 2. having an angle or angles.

angle iron, a piece of iron or steel in the form of an angle, especially a right angle, used for joining or reinforcing two beams, girders, etc.

ANGLE IRON

angle of attack, in *aeronautics*, the acute angle between the line of the normal wind direction and the chord of an airfoil.

angle of incidence, 1. the angle made by a light ray with a line perpendicular to the surface on which the ray falls. 2. in *aeronautics*, the angle of attack.

angle of view, in *optics*, the angle subtended by two lines drawn from the corners of the objective to the center of a lens.

angle plate, two plates of metal set at right angles, having slots for the reception of bolts: used in machine set-up work.

an·gle·pod (aŋ′g'l-pod′), ***n.*** a vine of the southern United States, bearing angular pods.

an·gler (aŋ′glẽr), ***n.*** [< *angle* (to fish)], 1. a fisherman who uses hook and line. 2. a person who schemes and uses tricks to get something. 3. a salt-water fish that lives on other fish, attracting them by means of a filament on its head.

An·gles (aŋ′g'lz), ***n.pl.*** [L. *Angli;* AS. *Angle, Engle*, the Angles < *Angel, Angul*, district in Holstein, lit., hook: so named from its shape], a Germanic, Anglo-Frisian people that settled in eastern England in the 5th century A.D.: the name *England* is from *Englaland*, land of the Angles, and *English* is from *Englisc*, of the Angles.

An·gle·sey (aŋ′g'l-si), ***n.*** an island and county of Wales: area, 276 sq. mi.: pop., 49,000.

an·gle·site (aŋ′gli-sīt′), ***n.*** [after *Anglesey*, where it was discovered], a native lead sulfate, $PbSO_4$, occurring in colorless or variously colored orthorhombic crystals.

an·gle·worm (aŋ′g'l-wũrm′), ***n.*** an earthworm: so called because used as fishing bait.

An·gli·a (aŋ′gli-ə), ***n.*** [see ANGLES], England: the ancient Latin name.

An·gli·an (aŋ′gli-ən), ***adj.*** 1. of Anglia; English. 2. of the Angles, their culture, dialect, etc. ***n.*** 1. a member of the Angles. 2. a dialect spoken by the Angles: applied especially to the Anglo-Saxon of Mercia and Northumbria.

An·glic (aŋ′glik), ***n.*** [< *Angle* + *-ic*], a simplified form of the English language for international communication: developed by R. E. Zachrisson (1880–1937), Swedish linguist. ***adj.*** Anglian.

An·gli·can (aŋ′gli-kən), ***adj.*** [L. *Anglicanus* < *Anglicus*, of the Angles, of England], 1. of England, its people, or their culture. 2. of the Church of England or of any other church with the same faith and forms, as the Protestant Episcopal Church. ***n.*** a member of the Church of England or of another church with the same faith and forms. Abbreviated **Angl.**

An·gli·can·ism (aŋ′gli-kən-iz'm), ***n.*** the doctrine and practice of the Church of England.

‡An·gli·ce (aŋ′gli-si), ***adv.*** [ML.; see ANGLES], in English; in the English manner or style: as, she lived in Wien, *Anglice* Vienna.

An·gli·cism (aŋ′glə-siz'm), ***n.*** [L. *Anglicus* (see ANGLICAN); + *-ism*], 1. a word, idiom, or meaning peculiar to English, especially British English; Briticism. 2. a typically English trait, custom, etc. 3. the quality of being English.

An·gli·cist (aŋ′glə-sist), ***n.*** a student of or authority on the English language and literature.

An·gli·ci·za·tion (aŋ′glə-si-zā′shən), ***n.*** 1. an Anglicizing or being Anglicized. 2. the result of Anglicizing.

An·gli·cize (aŋ′glə-sīz′), ***v.t. & v.i.*** [ANGLICIZED (-sīzd′), ANGLICIZING], [< L. *Anglicus* (see ANGLICAN); + *-ize*], to change to English idiom, pronunciation, customs, manner, etc.: abbreviated **Angl.**

An·gli·fy (aŋ′glə-fī′), ***v.t.*** [ANGLIFIED (-fīd′), ANGLIFYING], to Anglicize.

an·gling (aŋ′gliŋ), ***n.*** [< *angle* (to fish)], the act or art of fishing with hook and line.

An·glist (aŋ′glist), ***n.*** an authority on England.

An·glo- (aŋ′glō), [< L. *Anglus*, English; see ANGLES], a combining form meaning: 1. *English*, as in *Anglo-American, Anglophile.* 2. *Anglican*, as in *Anglo-Catholic.*

An·glo-A·mer·i·can (aŋ′glō-ə-mer′ə-kən), ***adj.*** 1. English and American; of or between England and the United States. 2. of Anglo-Americans. ***n.*** an American of English birth or ancestry.

An·glo-Cath·o·lic (aŋ′glō-kath′ə-lik, aŋ′glō-kath′lik), ***n.*** a member of the Church of England who believes that its Catholicism is and should be the same as before the Reformation. ***adj.*** of Anglo-Catholics or their beliefs and practice.

An·glo-E·gyp·tian Sudan (aŋ′glō-i-jip′shən), Sudan (sense 1): the former name.

An·glo-French (aŋ′glō-french′), ***adj.*** 1. English and French; of or between England and France. 2. of Anglo-French. ***n.*** the medieval French spoken in England by the Norman conquerors: see **Norman French.** Abbreviated **Anglo-Fr., A.-Fr., A.F., AF.**

An·glo-In·di·an (aŋ′glō-in′di-ən), ***adj.*** 1. English and Indian; of or between England and India. 2. of Anglo-Indians or their speech. ***n.*** 1. an English citizen living in India. 2. a person of both English and Indian ancestry. 3. the speech of Anglo-Indians, characterized by Anglicization of native words. Abbreviated **Anglo-Ind.**

Anglo-Ir., Anglo-Irish.

Anglo-L., Anglo-Latin.

An·glo·ma·ni·a (aŋ′glō-mā′ni-ə), ***n.*** an exaggerated liking for and imitation of English customs, manners, institutions, etc.

An·glo-Nor·man (aŋ′glō-nôr′mən), ***adj.*** 1. English and Norman. 2. of the Anglo-Normans or their language. ***n.*** 1. a Norman settler in England after the Norman Conquest. 2. the French dialect spoken by such settlers. Abbreviated **Anglo-Norm., A.N., AN., A.-N.**

An·glo-Norse (aŋ′glō-nôrs′), ***n.*** Old Norse as spoken by Scandinavian settlers in eastern and northern England before the Norman Conquest. ***adj.*** of Anglo-Norse. Abbreviated **Anglo-N.**

An·glo·phil (aŋ′glə-fil), ***n. & adj.*** Anglophile.

An·glo·phile (aŋ′glə-fil′, aŋ′glō-fīl′), ***n.*** [*Anglo-* + *-phile*], a person who admires or is extremely fond of England, its people, customs, influence, etc. ***adj.*** of Anglophiles.

An·glo·phobe (aŋ′glə-fōb′, aŋ′glō-fōb′), ***n.*** a person who has Anglophobia. ***adj.*** of Anglophobes.

An·glo·pho·bi·a (aŋ′glə-fō′bi-ə, aŋ′glō-fō′bi-ə), ***n.***

[*Anglo-* + *-phobia*], hatred or fear of England, its people, customs, influence, etc.

An·glo-Sax·on (aŋ′glō-sak′s'n), *n.* [< L. *rex Angul-Saxonum*, king of the Anglo-Saxons (title of Alfred the Great)], 1. a member of the Germanic, Ingwinian peoples (Angles, Saxons, and Jutes) living in England before the Norman Conquest. 2. their West Germanic, Low German language, which they called *Englisc;* Old English. 3. a person of English nationality or descent. *adj.* 1. of the Anglo-Saxons, their language, or culture. 2. of their descendants; English. Abbreviated **AS., A.S., A.-S., Ang.-Sax.**

An·go·la (aŋ-gō′lə), *n.* a Portuguese colony on the southwest coast of Africa: area, 486,079 sq. mi.; pop., 4,833,000; capital, Luanda.

An·go·la (aŋ-gō′lə), *n.* Angora.

An·go·ra (aŋ-gôr′ə, aŋ-gō′rə, aŋ′gə-rə), *n.* [< *Angora* (Ankara), city in Asia Minor], 1. Ankara. 2. a kind of cat with long, silky fur. 3. *a)* a kind of goat raised for its long, silky hair. *b)* this hair (**Angora wool**), used in making mohair, or the cloth made from this hair. 4. *a)* a kind of domestic rabbit (in full, **Angora rabbit**), raised for its long, silky hair. *b)* a soft yarn made from this hair and woven into sweaters, etc.

an·gos·tu·ra (aŋ′gəs-toor′ə, aŋ′gəs-tyoor′ə), *n.* [after *Angostura*, former name of Ciudad Bolivar in Venezuela], a bitter aromatic bark used as a medicinal tonic and as a flavoring in bitters.

an·gri·ly (aŋ′grə-li), *adv.* in an angry manner.

an·gry (aŋ′gri), *adj.* [ANGRIER (-gri-ẽr), ANGRIEST (-gri-ist)], [ME. *angri*, troubled < *anger*], 1. feeling, showing, or resulting from anger: as, an *angry* reply. 2. wild and stormy, as if angry. 3. inflamed and sore, as a cut, wound, etc.

‡**Angst** (äŋst), *n.* [G.], [often a-], a gloomy, often neurotic feeling of generalized anxiety and depression.

ang·strom, Ang·strom (aŋ′strəm), *n.* [after A. J. *Ångström*], one hundred-millionth of a centimeter, a unit used in measuring the length of light waves: symbol, λ: abbreviated **A.** Also **Angstrom unit**: abbreviated **A.U., Å., A.**

Ång·ström, An·ders Jöns (än′ders yöns ôŋ′ström; Eng. aŋ′strəm), 1814–1874; Swedish physicist.

an·guil·li·form (aŋ-gwil′ə-fôrm′), *adj.* [< L. *anguilla*, eel; + *-form*], shaped like an eel.

an·guine (aŋ′gwin), *adj.* [L. *anguinus* < *anguis*, snake], of or like a snake.

an·guish (aŋ′gwish), *n.* [ME. *anguisse;* OFr. *anguisse;* L. *angustia*, tightness, distress < *angere*, to tighten, choke; see ANGER], great mental or physical pain; agony. *v.t.* to make feel such pain. *v.i.* to feel such pain. —*SYN.* see **distress.**

an·guished (aŋ′gwisht), *adj.* [pp. of *anguish*], 1. feeling anguish. 2. showing or resulting from anguish.

an·gu·lar (aŋ′gyoo-lẽr), *adj.* [L. *angularis* < *angulus;* see ANGLE, *n.*], 1. having or forming an angle or angles; having sharp corners. 2. measured by an angle: as, *angular* distance. 3. with prominent bones; gaunt. 4. without ease or grace; stiff: as, an *angular* stride.

an·gu·lar·i·ty (aŋ′gyoo-lar′ə-ti), *n.* 1. the quality or condition of being angular. 2. [*pl.* ANGULARITIES (-tiz)], an angular form or part; sharp corner; angle.

an·gu·late (aŋ′gyoo-lit; *also, and for v. always*, aŋ′gyoo-lāt′), *adj.* [L. *angulatus*, pp. of *angulare*, to make angular < *angulus*; see ANGLE, *n.*], having angles or corners. *v.t.* [ANGULATED (-id), ANGULATING], to make angular. *v.i.* to become angular.

an·gu·la·tion (aŋ′gyoo-lā′shən), *n.* 1. an angulating. 2. an angular form, part, or position.

An·gus (aŋ′gəs), [Gael. *Aonghas* & Ir. *Aonghus* < *aon*, one], a masculine name. *n.* 1. in *Celtic mythology*, the god of love. 2. a county of eastern Scotland: pop., 278,000; county seat, Forfar: formerly called *Forfar.*

An·halt (än′hält), *n.* a former state of central Germany.

An·hwei (än′hwā′), *n.* a province of eastern China: area, 57,440 sq. mi.; pop., 33,560,000.

an·hy·drid (an-hī′drid), *n.* an anhydride.

an·hy·dride (an-hī′drīd, an-hī′drid), *n.* [< Gr. *anhydros* (see ANHYDROUS); + *-ide*], 1. an oxide that reacts with water to form an acid or a base. 2. any compound formed by the removal of the elements of water, usually from an acid.

an·hy·drite (an-hī′drīt), *n.* [< Gr. *anhydros* (see ANHYDROUS); + *-ite*], anhydrous calcium sulfate, $CaSO_4$, a granular, white or light-colored mineral resembling marble.

an·hy·drous (an-hī′drəs), *adj.* [Gr. *anhydros* < *an-*, without + *hydōr*, water], 1. without water. 2. having no water of crystallization; not hydrated.

a·ni (ä′nē), *n.* [*pl.* ANIS (-nēz)], [Sp.; Port. < native name in Brazil], an American bird, generally black, related to the cuckoo.

an·il (an′il), *n.* [Port.; Ar. *al-nīl; al*, the + *nīl*, blue < Sans. *nīla*, dark blue], 1. a West Indian shrub from which indigo is made. 2. indigo.

an·ile (an′īl, ā′nīl, an′il), *adj.* [L. *anilis* < *anus*, old woman], of or like an old woman; infirm; weak.

an·i·lin (an′'l-in), *n. & adj.* aniline.

an·i·line (an′'l-ēn′, an′'l-in, an′'l-in′), *n.* [*anil* + *-ine*], a colorless, poisonous, oily liquid, $C_6H_5NH_2$, a derivative of benzene used in making dyes; phenylamine. *adj.* made from aniline.

aniline dye, 1. any dye made from aniline. 2. any dye like aniline chemically; commonly, any dye produced synthetically from coal-tar products.

a·nil·i·ty (ə-nil′ə-ti), *n.* [L. *anilitas;* see ANILE], 1. the state or quality of being anile. 2. [*pl.* ANILITIES (-tiz)], an anile act, remark, or thought.

anim., animato.

an·i·ma (an′ə-mə), *n.* [L.], life principle; soul.

an·i·mad·ver·sion (an′ə-mad-vũr′zhən, an′ə-mad-vũr′-shən), *n.* [L. *animadversio* < pp. of *animadvertere;* see ANIMADVERT], an unfavorable remark (*on* or *upon* something); adverse criticism; blame.

an·i·mad·vert (an′ə-mad-vũrt′), *v.i.* [L. *animadvertere*, to observe, censure < *animum*, acc. of *animus*, mind + *ad-*, to + *vertere*, to turn], to comment (*on* or *upon*), usually with disapproval; remark critically.

an·i·mal (an′ə-m'l), *n.* [L., living being < *anima*, breath, air, soul], 1. any living organism typically capable of moving about but not of making its own food by photosynthesis: distinguished from *plant.* 2. any such organism other than a human being; especially, any four-footed creature; beast; brute. 3. a brutish, debased, or inhuman person. *adj.* 1. of, like, derived from, or characteristic of an animal or animals. 2. sensual, gross, bestial, etc. —*SYN.* see **carnal.**

the animal, animality: as, it's *the animal* in him.

animal cracker, a small, sweet cracker shaped like an animal.

an·i·mal·cu·la (an′ə-mal′kyoo-lə), *n.* plural of **animalculum.**

an·i·mal·cu·lae (an′ə-mal′kyoo-lē′), *n.pl.* [L. fem. pl., formed by assuming *animalcula* to be fem. sing.], animalcula.

an·i·mal·cule (an′ə-mal′kyool), *n.* [L. *animalculum*, dim. of *animal*], a very small animal, especially one that cannot be seen without a microscope.

an·i·mal·cu·lum (an′ə-mal′kyoo-ləm), *n.* [*pl.* ANIMALCULA (-lə)], [see ANIMALCULE], an animalcule.

animal husbandry, the care and raising of domesticated animals, as cattle, horses, sheep, etc.

an·i·mal·ism (an′ə-m'l-iz'm), *n.* 1. the activity, appetites, nature, etc. of animals. 2. the doctrine that man is a mere animal with no soul or spiritual quality.

an·i·mal·ist (an′ə-m'l-ist), *n.* a believer in animalism.

an·i·mal·i·ty (an′ə-mal′ə-ti), *n.* [*pl.* ANIMALITIES (-tiz)], [Fr. *animalité;* see ANIMAL], 1. animal characteristics or nature. 2. the animal kingdom; animal life.

an·i·mal·ize (an′ə-m'l-īz′), *v.t.* [ANIMALIZED (-īzd′), ANIMALIZING], 1. to change into animal matter. 2. to make (a person) resemble a beast; make sensual; dehumanize.

animal kingdom, animals collectively, as distinguished from plants (vegetable kingdom).

an·i·mal·ly (an′ə-m'l-i), *adv.* physically, as distinguished from mentally or spiritually.

animal magnetism, hypnotism; mesmerism.

animal spirits, healthy, lively vigor; cheerful gaiety.

an·i·mate (an′ə-māt′; *for adj.*, an′ə-mit), *v.t.* [ANIMATED (-id), ANIMATING], [< L. *animatus*, pp. of *animare*, to make alive, fill with breath < *anima*, air, soul], 1. to give life to; bring to life. 2. to make gay, energetic, or spirited. 3. to inspire. 4. to give motion to; put into action: as, the breeze *animated* the leaves. *adj.* 1. living; having life. 2. lively; vigorous; spirited. *SYN.*—**animate** implies a making alive or lively (an *animated* conversation) or an imparting of motion or activity (*animated* cartoons); to **quicken** is to rouse to action that which is lifeless or inert (the rebuff *quickened* his resolution); **exhilarate** implies an enlivening or elevation of the spirits; **stimulate** implies a rousing from inertia, inactivity, or lethargy, as if by goading; **invigorate** means to fill with vigor or energy in a physical sense (an *invigorating* tonic); **vitalize** implies the imparting of vigor or animation in a nonphysical sense (to *vitalize* a dull story). —*ANT.* deaden, depress, enervate. See also **living.**

an·i·mat·ed (an′ə-māt′id), *adj.* [pp. of *animate*], 1. living; alive or seeming alive. 2. showing animation; vigorous; lively; gay. —*SYN.* see **lively, living.**

animated cartoon, a kind of motion picture made by photographing a series of thousands of drawings, each showing a stage of movement slightly changed from the one before, so that the figures in them seem to move when the drawings are shown in rapid succession.

an·i·mat·er (an′ə-māt′ẽr), *n.* an animator.

an·i·ma·tion (an′ə-mā′shən), *n.* [L. *animatio;* see ANIMATE], 1. an animating or being animated. 2. an animate condition; life. 3. vivacity; brisk, lively quality. 4. the preparation of animated cartoons.

‡**a·ni·ma·to** (ä′nē-mä′tô), *adj. & adv.* [It.], in *music*, with animation: abbreviated **anim.**

an·i·ma·tor (an′ə-mā′tẽr), *n.* [L.], 1. a person or thing that animates. 2. a person who draws the changes in movement in animated cartoons.

an·i·mé (an′ə-mā′, an′ə-mi), *n.* [Sp.; prob. < native word], any of various resins; especially, a fossilized copal found in the West Indies and Africa, used in making varnish, etc.

an·i·mism (an'ə-miz'm), *n.* [< L. *anima*, air, soul; + *-ism*], 1. the belief that all life is produced by a spiritual force separate from matter. 2. the belief that natural phenomena and objects, as rocks, trees, the wind, etc. are alive and have souls. 3. the doctrine of the existence of soul as independent of matter. 4. a belief in the existence of spirits, demons, etc.
an·i·mist (an'ə-mist), *n.* a person who believes in animism of any kind.
an·i·mis·tic (an'ə-mis'tik), *adj.* of or characterized by animism.
an·i·mos·i·ty (an'ə-mos'ə-ti), *n.* [*pl.* ANIMOSITIES (-tiz)], [Fr. *animosité;* L. *animositas*, boldness, spirit < *animosus*, spirited < *animus;* see ANIMUS], strong hatred; ill will; open or active hostility. —*SYN.* see **enmity.**
an·i·mus (an'ə-məs), *n.* [L., soul, mind, disposition, passion], 1. an animating force. 2. an intention to do something. 3. a grudge; animosity.
an·i·on (an'ī'ən), *n.* [Gr. *anion*, thing going up, neut. ppr. of *anienai*, to go up < *ana-*, up + *ienai*, to go], a negative ion: in electrolysis, anions go toward the anode.
an·ise (an'is), *n.* [ME. *anis;* Fr. *anis* < L. *anisum;* Gr. *anēson*], 1. a plant of the carrot family, with small, white or yellow flowers. 2. its fragrant seed, used for flavoring and in medicine.
an·i·seed (an'i-sēd'), *n.* the seed of anise.
an·i·sette (an'i-zet', an'i-set'), *n.* [Fr., dim. < *anis;* see ANISE], a sweet, anise-flavored liqueur.
an·i·so- (an-ī'sə), [< Gr. *anisos*, unequal], a combining form meaning *not equal, not alike*, as in *anisomerous.*
an·i·som·er·ous (an'ī-som'ēr-əs), *adj.* [*aniso-* + *-merous*], in *botany*, having an unequal number of parts in the floral whorls.
an·i·so·met·ric (an'ī-sə-met'rik), *adj.* [*an-*, not + *isometric*], not isometric; with asymmetrical parts.
an·i·so·me·tro·pi·a (an-ī'sə-mi-trō'pi-ə), *n.* [*aniso-* + *metr-* + *-opia*], a condition of the eyes in which they have unequal refractive power.
an·i·so·trop·ic (an'ī-sə-trop'ik), *adj.* [*an-*, not + *isotropic*], 1. not isotropic. 2. in *botany*, having unequal responses to external stimuli. 3. in *physics*, having properties, as conductivity, speed of transmission of light, etc., which vary according to the direction in which they are measured.
A·ni·ta (ə-nē'tə), [Sp. dim.; see ANNA], a feminine name: diminutive, *Nita.*
An·jou (an'jōō; Fr. äN'zhōō'), *n.* an old province of western France about the city of Angers: the name has been used by several royal houses, notably by the Plantagenets.

DOMINION OF THE HOUSE OF ANJOU (1145–1205)

An·ka·ra (äŋ'kə-rə, aŋ'kə-rə), *n.* the capital of Turkey: pop., 646,000: also **Angora.**
An·ka·ra·tra Mountains (äŋ'kə-rä'trä), a group of mountains in central Madagascar: highest peak, 8,550 ft.
an·ker·ite (aŋ'kēr-īt'), *n.* [after an Austrian mineralogist], a mineral much like dolomite but with iron largely replacing the magnesia.
ankh (aŋk), *n.* [Egypt., life, soul], a cross with a loop at the top, an ancient Egyptian symbol of life.
An·king (än'kiŋ'), *n.* a city in Anhwei province, China, on the Yangtze River: pop., 121,000.
an·kle (aŋ'k'l), *n.* [ME. *ancle, ancleou;* AS. *ancleow;* akin to OHG. *anklāo;* IE. base **ank-*, to bend, curve], 1. the joint that connects the foot and the leg. 2. the part of the leg between the foot and calf.
an·kle·bone (aŋ'k'l-bōn'), *n.* the bone of the ankle; talus; astragalus.
an·klet (aŋ'klit), *n.* 1. anything worn around the ankle as a fetter, ornament, or support. 2. a short sock worn by girls or women.
an·ky·lose (aŋ'kə-lōs'), *v.t. & v.i.* [ANKYLOSED (-lōst'), ANKYLOSING], [< *ankylosis*], to stiffen or join by ankylosis: also spelled **anchylose.**
an·ky·lo·sis (aŋ'kə-lō'sis), *n.* [Gr. *ankylōsis* < *angkyloun*, to crook, stiffen < *angkylos*, crooked, bent], 1. in *medicine*, a stiffening of a joint, caused by fibrous or bony union. 2. in *zoology*, a joining of bones or fibrous parts into a single part. Also spelled **anchylosis.**
an·ky·los·to·mi·a·sis (aŋ'ki-los'tə-mī'ə-sis), *n.* ancylostomiasis.
an·lace (an'lis, an'ləs), *n.* [ME. *anlace, anlas, anelas;* by metathesis < OFr. *alenaz, alenas, alesnaz* < *alesne*, awl (< Gmc. base **alisna*, awl) + *-az* (< L. *-aceus*)], a broad, tapering medieval dagger.

‡**An·la·ge** (än'lä-gə), *n.* [*pl.* ANLAGEN (-gən)], [G., foundation < *anlegen*, lay out], 1. the basis of a later development. 2. in *biology*, the primordium. Also **anlage.**
Ann (an), a feminine name: see **Anna.**
ann., 1. annual. 2. annuity.
An·na (an'ə), [Fr. *Anne;* L. *Anna;* Gr. *Anna;* Heb. *hannāh*, lit., grace], a feminine name: diminutives, *Annie, Nan, Nancy;* variants, *Ann, Anne, Hannah;* equivalents, Fr. *Anne, Annette, Nannette*, Sp. *Ana.*
an·na (an'ə), *n.* [Hind. *ānā*], a copper coin of India, equal to 1/16 of one rupee.
An·na·bel, An·na·belle (an'ə-bel'), [prob. < *Anna* + L. *bella*, fem. of *bellus*, pretty], a feminine name.
an·na·berg·ite (an'ə-būrg'īt), *n.* [< *Annaberg*, Germany; + *-ite*], a native arsenate of nickel, $Ni_3As_2O_8 \cdot 8H_2O$, occurring in apple-green, crystalline masses.
an·nal·ist (an''l-ist), *n.* a person who writes annals.
an·nals (an''lz), *n.pl.* [*sing.* ANNAL (an''l)], [L. *annalis*, pl. *annales* < *annus*, year], 1. a written account of events year by year in chronological order. 2. historical records or chronicles; history. 3. *sing.* the record of a single year or event. 4. any journal containing reports of discoveries in some field, meetings of a society, etc.
An·nam (ə-nam', an'am), *n.* a former state of French Indochina, now divided between North Vietnam and South Vietnam: see **Vietnam:** also spelled **Anam.**
An·na·mese (an'ə-mēz'), *adj.* 1. of Annam. 2. of the Annamese, their culture, or language. *n.* 1. [*pl.* ANNAMESE], one of a Mongolian people in Annam and Cochin-China; also, a native or inhabitant of Annam. 2. the language of the Annamese.
An·na·mite (an'ə-mīt'), *adj. & n.* Annamese.
An·nap·o·lis (ə-nap''l-is), *n.* the capital of Maryland, on Chesapeake Bay: pop., 23,000: site of the United States Naval Academy.
Ann Ar·bor (an' är'bēr), a city in southeastern Michigan: pop., 67,000.
an·nates (an'its), *n.pl.* [Fr. *annate;* ML. *annata* < L. *annus*, year], in the *Roman Catholic Church*, a payment to the Pope of the first year's revenue from a benefice.
an·nats (an'ats), *n.pl.* annates.
an·nat·to (ə-nä'tō), *n.* [of W. Ind. origin], a dye of reddish yellow made from pulp around the seeds of a certain tropical tree: it is used for coloring butter, etc.
Anne (an), a feminine name: see **Anna.** *n.* daughter of James II; 1665–1714; queen of Great Britain and Ireland (1702–1714); last of the Stuart monarchs.
Anne, Saint, mother of the Virgin Mary.
an·neal (ə-nēl'), *v.t.* [ME. *anelen;* AS. *anælan, onælan*, to burn; *an-, on-*, on + *ælan*, to burn < *al, æl*, fire], 1. to heat (glass, metals, etc.) and then cool slowly to prevent brittleness. 2. to strengthen and temper (the mind, will, etc.). 3. [Archaic], to bake; glaze; fire.
Anne Boleyn, see **Boleyn, Anne.**
an·ne·lid (an''l-id), *n.* [Fr. *annélide* < *annelés*, ringed < L. *annellus*, dim. of *anulus*, a ring], a worm with a body made of joined segments or rings, as an earthworm, leech, etc. *adj.* of such worms or the phylum to which they belong.
Anne of Austria, 1601–1666; wife of Louis XIII of France and regent during minority of Louis XIV.
Anne of Bohemia, 1366–1394; wife of Richard II of England.
Anne of Cleves (klēvz), 1515–1557; fourth wife of Henry VIII of England.
An·nette (an-et', ə-net'), a feminine name: see **Anna.**
an·nex (ə-neks'; *for n.*, an'eks), *v.t.* [Fr. *annexer* < L. *annexus*, pp. of *annectere* < *ad-*, to + *nectere*, to tie, bind], 1. to add on or attach, as a smaller thing to a larger. 2. to incorporate into a country, state, etc. the territory of (another country, state, etc.). 3. to add to as a condition, consequence, etc. 4. [Archaic], to join; connect. *n.* 1. an addition to a building. 2. a near-by building used as an addition to the main building. 3. an added part of a document, record, etc.
an·nex·a·tion (an'ek-sā'shən), *n.* [ML. *annexatio*], 1. an annexing or being annexed. 2. something annexed.
an·nex·a·tion·ist (an'ek-sā'shən-ist), *n.* a person who advocates the annexing of territory by his country.
an·nex·ment (ə-neks'mənt), *n.* something annexed.
An·nie Oak·ley (an'i ōk'li), [after woman rifle expert (1860–1926) whose small targets resembled punched tickets], [Slang], a free ticket; pass.
an·ni·hi·la·ble (ə-nī'ə-lə-b'l), *adj.* that can be annihilated.
an·ni·hi·late (ə-nī'ə-lāt'), *v.t.* [ANNIHILATED (-id), ANNIHILATING], [< L. *annihilatus*, pp. of *annihilare*, to bring to nothing < *ad-*, to + *nihilare* < *nihil*, nothing], to destroy wholly; demolish. —*SYN.* see **destroy.**
an·ni·hi·la·tion (ə-nī'ə-lā'shən), *n.* [Fr.], an annihilating or being annihilated.
an·ni·hi·la·tor (ə-nī'ə-lā'tēr), *n.* a person or thing that annihilates.
An·nis·ton (an'is-tən), *n.* a city in eastern Alabama: pop., 34,000.

an·ni·ver·sa·ry (an'ə-vũr'sẽr-i), *adj.* [L. *anniversarius* < *annus*, year + *versum*, pp. of *vertere*, to turn], 1. recurring at the same date every year; occurring annually. 2. of or connected with an anniversary. *n.* [*pl.* ANNIVERSARIES (-iz)], 1. the yearly return of the monthly date of some event. 2. the celebration of this.

‡**an·no Do·mi·ni** (an'ō dom'ə-nī'), [L.], in the year of the Lord; in the (given) year since the beginning of the Christian era: abbreviated **A.D.**

‡**an·no mun·di** (an'ō mun'dī), [L.], in the year of the world; in the (given) year since the supposed creation of the world: abbreviated **A.M.**

‡**an·no reg·ni** (an'ō reg'nī), [L.], in the year of the reign: abbreviated **a.r.**

an·no·tate (an'ō-tāt'), *v.t.* & *v.i.* [ANNOTATED (-id), ANNOTATING], [< L. *annotatus*, pp. of *annotare* < *ad-*, to + *notare*, to note, mark < *nota*, a mark, sign], to provide critical or explanatory notes for (a literary work, etc.).

an·no·ta·tion (an'ō-tā'shən), *n.* [L. *annotatio*], 1. an annotating or being annotated. 2. a critical or explanatory note or notes.

an·no·ta·tor (an'ō-tā'tẽr), *n.* [L., observer], a person who annotates.

an·nounce (ə-nouns'), *v.t.* [ANNOUNCED (-nounst'), ANNOUNCING], [OFr. *anoncier*; L. *annuntiare*, to make known < *ad-*, to + *nuntiare*, to report < *nuntius*, messenger], 1. to declare publicly; give notice of formally; proclaim. 2. to say. 3. to make known the arrival of. 4. to make known through the senses: as, footsteps *announced* his return. 5. in *radio & television*, to be an announcer for. *v.i.* to act as a radio or television announcer. —*SYN.* see **declare.**

an·nounce·ment (ə-nouns'mənt), *n.* [Fr. *annoncement*; see ANNOUNCE], 1. an announcing or being announced. 2. something announced. 3. a written or printed notice.

an·nounc·er (ə-noun'sẽr), *n.* 1. a person who announces. 2. a person who introduces radio or television programs, identifies the station, etc.

‡**an·no ur·bis con·di·tae** (an'ō ũr'bis kon'di-tē'), [L.], in the (given) year of the founded city: the ancient Roman way of reckoning dates from Rome's founding c. 753 B.C.: abbreviated **A.U.C.**

an·noy (ə-noi'), *v.t.* [ME. *anuien*; OFr. *anoier*, *ennoier*; L. *inodiare* < *in odio*, in aversion, at enmity], 1. to irritate; vex; bother, as by a repeated action, noise, etc. 2. to make angry. 3. to harm; injure; molest.

SYN.—**annoy** implies temporary disturbance of mind caused by something that displeases one or tries one's patience; **vex** implies a more serious source of irritation and greater disturbance, often intense worry; **irk** stresses a wearing down of one's patience by persistent annoyance; **bother** implies minor disturbance of one's peace of mind and may suggest mild perplexity or anxiety; to **tease** is to annoy by persistent, irritating actions, remarks, etc.; **plague** suggests mental torment comparable to the physical suffering caused by an affliction. —*ANT.* comfort, soothe.

an·noy·ance (ə-noi'əns), *n.* 1. an annoying or being annoyed. 2. a thing or person that annoys.

an·noy·ing (ə-noi'iŋ), *adj.* [ppr. of *annoy*], irritating; vexing; bothersome.

an·nu·al (an'yoo-əl), *adj.* [ME.; OFr. *annuel*; L. *annualis*, yearly < *annus*, year], 1. of or measured by a year. 2. that comes once a year; yearly. 3. for a year's time, work, etc.: as, an *annual* wage. 4. alive only one year or season. *n.* 1. a book or magazine published once a year; yearbook. 2. a plant that lives only one year or season: symbol, ○, ⊙, ⏀. Abbreviated **ann.**

an·nu·al·ly (an'yoo-ə-li, an'yool-i), *adv.* [*annual* + *-ly*], each year; every year; yearly.

annual ring, any of the rings of wood seen in cross sections of the stems of most trees and shrubs: each ring shows a year's growth.

an·nu·i·tant (ə-nū'ə-tənt, ə-nōō'ə-tənt), *n.* a person receiving an annuity.

an·nu·i·ty (ə-nū'ə-ti, ə-nōō'ə-ti), *n.* [*pl.* ANNUITIES (-tiz)], [Fr. *annuité*; ML. *annuitas* < L. *annus*, year], 1. a yearly payment of money. 2. the right to receive such a payment. 3. an investment yielding fixed payments during the holder's lifetime or for a stated number of years. Abbreviated **ann.**

an·nul (ə-nul'), *v.t.* [ANNULLED (-nuld'), ANNULLING], [Fr. *annuler* < L. *annullare*, to bring to nothing < *ad-*, to + *nullum*, nothing, neut. of *nullus*, none], to do away with; make of no effect; invalidate; make null and void; cancel. —*SYN.* see **abolish.**

an·nu·lar (an'yoo-lẽr), *adj.* [L. *annularis* < *annulus*, *anulus*, a ring], 1. like or forming a ring. 2. annulate. —*SYN.* see **round.**

annular eclipse, an eclipse in which a ring of sunlight can be seen around the edge of the moon.

annular ligament, in *anatomy*, the ligament surrounding the ankle joint or wrist joint.

an·nu·late (an'yoo-lit, an'yoo-lāt'), *adj.* [L. *annulatus* < *annulus*, a ring], 1. provided with rings; ringed. 2. made up of rings.

an·nu·lat·ed (an'yoo-lā'tid), *adj.* annulate.

an·nu·la·tion (an'yoo-lā'shən), *n.* [< *annulate* + *-ion*], 1. formation of rings. 2. a ring.

an·nu·let (an'yoo-lit), *n.* [L. *annulus*, a ring; + *-et*], 1. a small ring. 2. in *architecture*, a ringlike molding where the shaft of a column joins the capital.

an·nul·ment (ə-nul'mənt), *n.* an annulling or being annulled; invalidation; cancellation.

an·nu·lose (an'yoo-lōs'), *adj.* [< L. *annulus*, a ring; + *-ose*], having rings; ringed.

an·nu·lus (an'yoo-ləs), *n.* [*pl.* ANNULI (-lī'), ANNULUSES (-ləs-iz)], [L.], any ring or ringlike part, mark, or space.

an·num (an'əm), *n.* [L., acc. of *annus*, year], a year.

an·nun·ci·ate (ə-nun'shi-āt', ə-nun'si-āt'), *v.t.* [ANNUNCIATED (-id), ANNUNCIATING], [< L. *annuntiatus*, pp. of *annuntiare*; see ANNOUNCE], to announce.

an·nun·ci·a·tion (ə-nun'si-ā'shən, ə-nun'shi-ā'shən), *n.* [L. *annuntiatio*; see ANNOUNCE], 1. an announcing or being announced. 2. an announcement. 3. [A-], the angel Gabriel's announcement to Mary that she was to give birth to Jesus: Luke 1:26–38. 4. [A-], the church festival on March 25 commemorating this; Lady Day.

an·nun·ci·a·tor (ə-nun'shi-ā'tẽr, ə-nun'si-ā'tẽr), *n.* [L. *annuntiator*], 1. a person or thing that announces. 2. an electric indicator used in hotels, offices, etc. to show the source of calls.

Annunzio, Gabriele D', see **D'Annunzio, Gabriele.**

‡**an·nus mi·ra·bi·lis** (an'əs mi-rab'ə-lis), [L.], year of wonders.

a·no·ci·as·so·ci·a·tion (ə-nō'si-ə-sō'si-ā'shən, ə-nō'si-ə-sō'shi-ā'shən), *n.* [< *a-*, not + L. *nocere*, to harm; + *association*], the prevention of shock in surgery by calming the patient beforehand, and using local anesthetics and sharp dissection, so as to keep pain sensations from reaching the central nervous system.

a·no·ci·a·tion (ə-nō'si-ā'shən, ə-nō'shi-ā'shən), *n.* [contr. of *anociassociation*], anociassociation.

an·ode (an'ōd), *n.* [Gr. *anodos*, a way up < *ana-*, up + *hodos*, way], a positive electrode, as in a battery, radio tube, etc.: see **battery**, illus.

an·od·ic (an-od'ik), *adj.* 1. of or from an anode. 2. in *medicine*, going upward; rising.

an·od·ize (an'ə-dīz'), *v.t.* [ANODIZED (-dīzd'), ANODIZING], [< *anode* + *-ize*], to put a protective oxide film on (a light metal) by an electrolytic process.

an·o·dyne (an'ə-dīn'), *adj.* [L. *anodynus*; Gr. *anōdynos* < *an-*, without + *odynē*, pain], relieving or lessening pain. *n.* [Gr. *anōdynon* < the *adj.*], anything that relieves or lessens pain; anything that soothes.

a·noint (ə-noint'), *v.t.* [ME. *anointen*; OFr. *enoindre*; L. *inungere*; *in-*, on + *ungere*, to smear], 1. to pour or rub oil or ointment on. 2. to put oil on in a ceremony of making sacred or consecrating to high office.

a·noint·ment (ə-noint'mənt), *n.* an anointing or being anointed.

an·o·lyte (an'ə-līt'), *n.* [*an*ode + electro*lyte*], the part of an electric battery, electrolyte, etc. near the anode.

a·nom·a·lism (ə-nom''l-iz'm), *n.* 1. the state of being anomalous. 2. an anomaly.

a·nom·a·lis·tic (ə-nom''l-is'tik), *adj.* 1. tending to be anomalous. 2. of an anomaly.

anomalistic month, the time that the moon takes to go from perigee to perigee.

anomalistic year, the time a planet takes to go from perihelion to perihelion.

a·nom·a·lous (ə-nom'ə-ləs), *adj.* [L. *anomalus*; Gr. *anōmalos* < *an-*, not + *homalos* < *homos*, the same], deviating from the regular arrangement, general rule, or usual method; abnormal. —*SYN.* see **irregular.**

a·nom·a·ly (ə-nom'ə-li), *n.* [*pl.* ANOMALIES (-liz)], [Fr. *anomalie*; L. *anomalia*; Gr. *anōmalia*, inequality; see ANOMALOUS], 1. departure from the regular arrangement, general rule, or usual method; abnormality. 2. anything anomalous. 3. in *astronomy*, a planet's angular distance from its perihelion, measured as if viewed from the sun.

a·non (ə-non'), *adv.* [ME.; AS. *on an*, acc., in one, together, straightway], 1. soon; shortly. 2. at another time. 3. [Archaic], immediately; at once.

ever and anon, now and then; once in a while.

anon., anonymous.

an·o·nym (an'ə-nim), *n.* [Fr. *anonyme* < Gr. *anōnymos*; see ANONYMOUS], 1. a person whose name is not known. 2. a false name; pseudonym.

an·o·nym·i·ty (an'ə-nim'ə-ti), *n.* a being anonymous.

a·non·y·mous (ə-non'ə-məs), *adj.* [Gr. *anōnymos* < *an-*, without + *onyma* < *onoma*, name], 1. with no name known or acknowledged. 2. given, written, etc. by a person whose name is withheld. Abbreviated **anon., an., a.**

a·noph·e·les (ə-nof'ə-lēz'), *n.* [Mod. L.; Gr. *anōphelēs*, harmful; *an-*, without + *ophelēs*, use, help], the mosquito that can carry the malaria parasite and transmit the disease.

ANOPHELES (3/16 in. long)

a·no·rak (ä'nə-räk'), *n.* [Esk. (Greenland) *ânorâq*], a heavy, leather or cloth jacket with a hood, worn in the cold north.

an·or·thite (an-ôr′thīt), *n.* [Gr. *an-*, not + *orthos*, straight; + *-ite*], a lime feldspar, $CaAl_2(SiO_4)_2$, found in basic igneous rocks.

an·or·tho·site (an-ôr′thə-sīt′), *n.* [< Fr. *anorthose* < Gr. *an-*, not + *orthos*, straight; + *-ite*], an igneous rock, made up largely of a soda-lime feldspar.

an·os·mi·a (an-os′mi-ə), *n.* [Mod. L. < Gr. *an-*, without + *osmē*, smell], total or partial loss of the sense of smell.

an·oth·er (ə-nuth′ẽr), *adj.* [ME. *an other; an*, one, an, a + *other*], 1. an additional; one more. 2. a different; not the same. 3. a similar but actually different; some other: as, *another* Caesar. *pron.* 1. one additional. 2. a different one. 3. one of the same kind.

an·ox·e·mi·a (an′ok-sē′mi-ə), *n.* [*an-*, not + *oxygen* + *-emia*], a reduction in the normal amount of oxygen in the blood, as at high altitudes.

an·ox·i·a (an-ok′si-ə), *n.* [*an-*, not + *oxygen* + *-ia*], in *medicine*, a condition in which there is not enough oxygen or tissue oxidation.

ans., answer.

an·sate (an′sāt), *adj.* [L. *ansatus* < *ansa*, a handle], having a handle or handlelike part.

ansate cross, an ankh.

‡An·schluss (än′shloos), *n.* [G., a joining], 1. a union; economic and political union of two countries. 2. the annexation of Austria by Nazi Germany in 1938.

An·sel (an′s'l), [L. *Anselmus*; ? < Gmc. **Anshelm*, God's defender], a masculine name.

An·selm, Saint (an′selm), 1033–1109; archbishop of Canterbury (1093–1109): his day is April 21.

an·ser·ine (an′sẽr-īn′, an′sẽr-in), *adj.* [L. *anserinus* < *anser*, a goose], 1. of or like a goose. 2. stupid; foolish.

an·swer (an′sẽr), *n.* [ME. *andsware*; AS. *andswaru* < *and-*, against + *swerian*, to swear], 1. a reply to a question, argument, letter, etc. 2. any response or retaliation: as, his *answer* was a well-aimed blow. 3. a solution to a problem. 4. in *law*, a defense. 5. in *music*, a repetition of a theme, made by an instrument or voice other than the original one. Abbreviated **ans., an., a.** *v.i.* 1. to reply in words, by an action, etc. 2. to react to a stimulus; respond (with *to*): as, the horse *answered* to its rider's touch. 3. to serve the purpose; be sufficient. 4. to be responsible or liable (*to* a person *for* an action, accusation, etc.). 5. to agree; be in conformity (with *to*): as, he *answers* to the description. *v.t.* 1. to reply to in some way. 2. to fulfill satisfactorily; comply with; be sufficient for; serve: as, the makeshift tent *answered* their purpose. 3. to atone for. 4. to defend oneself against (an accusation, criticism, etc.); refute. 5. to agree with; conform to; suit: as, he *answers* the description.

answer back, [Colloq.], to reply forcefully, rudely, or impertinently; talk back.

SYN.*—answer** implies a saying, writing, or acting in return, as required by the situation or by courtesy (to *answer* a letter, the phone, etc.); **respond** implies an appropriate reaction made voluntarily or spontaneously to that which serves as a stimulus (to *respond* to an appeal); **reply** in its strictest application refers to an answer that satisfies in detail the question asked; **retort** suggests a reply, especially one that is quick or witty, made in retaliation to a charge, criticism, etc.; **rejoin** implies an answer, originally to a reply, now often to an objection. —ANT.*** question, ask, inquire.

an·swer·a·ble (an′sẽr-ə-b'l), *adj.* 1. responsible; accountable. 2. that can be answered. 3. [Archaic], in proportion; corresponding. —***SYN.*** see **responsible.**

ant (ant), *n.* [ME. *amete*; AS. *æmete, æmette*: akin to OHG. *âmeiza* < *â-*, off + *meizen*, Goth. *maitan*, AS. **mætan*, to cut; hence, lit., "the cutter off"], any of a group of black or red insects, generally wingless, that live in colonies.

ANTS A, pupa; B, female (after loss of wings); C, male (with wings); D, worker (3/8 in. long)

an't (ant, änt, ānt), [Chiefly Dial. or British Colloq.], are not: the normal contracted form in varieties of English which have lost final and preconsonantal *r*: also variously heard at different levels of usage as an assimilated form for *am not*, and as a contracted form for *is not, have not*, and *has not*: cf. **ain't.**

ant- (ant), anti-.

-ant (ənt), [Fr. *-ant*; L. *-antem* or *-entem*, acc. ppr. ending], a suffix used in forming: 1. adjectives meaning *—ing*, as in *defiant, radiant*. 2. nouns meaning *a person* or *thing that —s*, as in *occupant, accountant*.

ant., 1. antiquity; antiquities. 2. antonym.

an·ta (an′tə), *n.* [*pl.* ANTAE (-tē)], [L.], in *architecture*, a kind of pier or square column forming the end of a wall on either side of a door or in a corner.

ant·ac·id (ant-as′id), *adj.* [*ant-* + *acid*], that neutralizes acids; counteracting acidity. *n.* an antacid substance, such as sodium bicarbonate.

An·tae·an (an-tē′ən), *adj.* of or like Antaeus.

An·tae·us (an-tē′əs), *n.* [L.; Gr. *Antaios*], in *Greek mythology*, a giant wrestler who was invincible as long as he was touching his mother, the earth.

an·tag·o·nism (an-tag′ə-niz'm), *n.* [Gr. *antagōnisma* < *antagōnizesthai*; see ANTAGONIZE], 1. the state of being in active opposition (*to* or *against* someone or something); hostility. 2. an opposing force, principle, etc. —***SYN.*** see **enmity.**

an·tag·o·nist (an-tag′ə-nist), *n.* [Gr. *antagōnistēs* < *antagōnizesthai*; see ANTAGONIZE], 1. a person who opposes, fights, or competes with another; adversary; opponent. 2. a muscle that counteracts another. —***SYN.*** see **opponent.**

an·tag·o·nis·tic (an-tag′ə-nis′tik), *adj.* 1. showing or in antagonism; opposing; hostile. 2. mutually opposed; counteracting.

an·tag·o·nis·ti·cal·ly (an-tag′ə-nis′ti-k'l-i, an-tag′ə-nis′tik-li), *adv.* in an antagonistic manner.

an·tag·o·nize (an-tag′ə-nīz′), *v.t.* [ANTAGONIZED (-nīzd′), ANTAGONIZING], [Gr. *antagōnizesthai*, to struggle against < *anti-*, against + *agōnizesthai*; see AGONIZE], 1. to contend against; oppose. 2. to incur the dislike of; make an enemy of. *v.i.* to act antagonistically.

An·ta·ki·ya (än′tä-kē′yä), *n.* Antioch: the Arabic name.

ant·al·ka·li (ant-al′kə-lī′), *n.* [*pl.* ANTALKALIES, ANTALKALIS (-līz′)], [*ant-* + *alkali*], a substance that neutralizes an alkali or counteracts alkalinity.

ant·al·ka·line (ant-al′kə-līn′), *adj.* neutralizing an alkali or counteracting alkalinity. *n.* an antalkali.

An·ta·na·na·ri·vo (ån′tå-nä′nå-rē′vō), *n.* Tananarive.

ant·arc·tic (ant-ärk′tik), *adj.* [ME. *antartyk*; OFr. *antartique*; L. *antarcticus*; Gr. *antarktikos*, southern < *anti-*, opposite + *arktos*, a bear; see ARCTIC], of or near the South Pole or the region around it. *n.* 1. the region around the South Pole. 2. the Antarctic Circle.

Ant·arc·ti·ca (ant-ärk′ti-kə), *n.* a region, mainly of ice fields, about the South Pole: area, c. 5,000,000 sq. mi.: claims to parts of it have been made by various countries: sometimes called the *Antarctic Continent*.

Antarctic Archipelago, a group of islands between South America and Antarctica.

Antarctic Circle, antarctic circle, an imaginary circle parallel to the equator, 23°30′ from the South Pole.

ANTARCTIC CIRCLE

Antarctic Ocean, the ocean surrounding Antarctica.

Antarctic Zone, all of the region south of the Antarctic Circle.

An·tar·es (an-târ′ēz), *n.* [Gr. *Antarēs* < *anti-*, like + *Arēs*, Mars: so named because of its color], a large red star, the brightest in the constellation Scorpio: see **constellation,** chart.

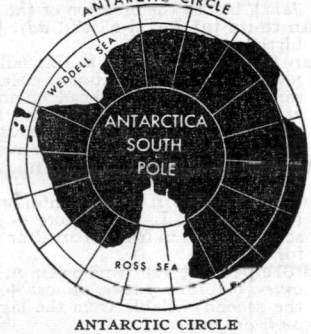

ant bear, 1. a large South American anteater. 2. an aardvark.

an·te (an′ti), *n.* [L., before], 1. in *poker*, the stake that each player must put into the pool before receiving cards or drawing new ones to his hand; hence, 2. [Slang], the amount one must pay as his share. *v.t. & v.i.* [ANTEED or ANTED (-tid), ANTEING], 1. in *poker*, to put in (one's stake). 2. [Slang], to pay (one's share).

ante up, to ante; pay.

an·te- (an′ti, an′tə), [< L. *ante*, before], a prefix meaning: 1. *before, prior to*, as in *antecedent, ante-Victorian*. 2. *before, in front of*, as in *anteroom, antepenult*.

ant·eat·er (ant′ēt′ẽr), *n.* any of several mammals that feed mainly on ants, as the pangolin, aardvark, echidna, etc.: anteaters have a long, sticky tongue and a long snout.

ANTEATER (5 ft. long)

an·te·bel·lum (an′ti-bel′əm), *adj.* [L. *ante bellum*], before the war; specifically, before the American Civil War.

an·te·cede (an′tə-sēd′), *v.t. & v.i.* [ANTECEDED (-id), ANTECEDING], [L. *antecedere*; *ante-*, before + *cedere*, to go], to go before in rank, space, or time; precede.

an·te·ced·ence (an′tə-sēd′'ns), *n.* [L. *antecedentia*; see ANTECEDE], 1. a going before; being prior; priority; precedence. 2. in *astronomy*, retrograde motion.

an·te·ced·en·cy (an′tə-sēd′'n-si), *n.* antecedence.

an·te·ced·ent (an′tə-sēd′'nt), *adj.* [L. *antecedens*, ppr. of *antecedere*; see ANTECEDE], going before; prior; previous; preceding. *n.* 1. any happening or thing prior to another. 2. anything logically preceding. 3. *pl.*

one's ancestry, past life, education, etc. 4. in *grammar*, the word, phrase, or clause to which a pronoun refers. 5. in *logic*, the conditional part of a hypothetical proposition. 6. in *mathematics*, the first term of a ratio; the first or third term of a proportion. —*SYN.* see **cause, previous.**

an·te·ced·ent·ly (an'tə-sēd''nt-li), *adv.* before; as an antecedent.

an·te·ces·sor (an'tə-ses'ẽr), *n.* [L. < pp. of *antecedere;* see ANTECEDE], a predecessor.

an·te·cham·ber (an'ti-chām'bẽr), *n.* [Fr. *antichambre; anti-* (for L. *ante,* before) + *chambre,* chamber], a smaller room leading into a larger or main room.

an·te·choir (an'ti-kwīr'), *n.* a partially or wholly enclosed part of a chapel in front of the choir.

‡an·te Chris·tum (an'ti kris'təm), [L.], before Christ: abbreviated **A.C.**

an·te·date (an'ti-dāt', an'ti-dāt'), *v.t.* 1. to assign too early a date to. 2. to be or happen at an earlier date than; come before in time. 3. to make happen earlier; set an earlier date for. 4. to anticipate. *n.* [Rare], a date given that is earlier than the right one.

an·te·di·lu·vi·an (an'ti-di-lōō'vi-ən), *adj.* [< *ante-* + L. *diluvium,* a flood], 1. of the time before the Flood; hence, 2. very old; old-fashioned or primitive. *n.* an antediluvian person or thing.

an·te·fix (an'ti-fiks'), *n.* [*pl.* ANTEFIXES (-fik'siz)], [L. *antefixus;* see ANTE- & FIX], in *classical architecture,* a small decorative fixture put at the eaves of a roof to hide the ends of the tiles.

an·te·lope (an't'l-ōp'), *n.* [*pl.* ANTELOPES (-ōps'), ANTELOPE; see PLURAL, II, D, 1], [OFr. *antelop;* ML. *antalopus;* Gr. *antholops,* deer], 1. any of a group of swift, cud-chewing, horned, deerlike animals related to oxen and goats. 2. leather made from its hide.

an·te me·rid·i·an (an'ti-mə-rid'i-ən), *adj.* [L. *antemeridianus; ante-,* before + *meridianus,* of midday], before noon.

‡an·te me·ri·di·em (an'ti mə-rid'i-em), [L.], before noon: abbreviated **A.M., AM, a.m.**

an·te-mor·tem (an'ti-môr'təm), *adj.* [L. *ante mortem,* before death], made or done just before one's death.

an·te·mun·dane (an'ti-mun'dān), *adj.* [*ante-* + *mundane*], before the creation of the world.

an·te·na·tal (an'ti-nā't'l), *adj.* [*ante-* + *natal*], before birth; prenatal.

an·ten·na (an-ten'ə), *n.* [L., sail yard], 1. [*pl.* ANTENNAE (-ē), ANTENNAS (-əz)], either of a pair of jointed sense organs on the head of an insect, crab, lobster, etc.; feeler. 2. [*pl.* ANTENNAS (-əz)], in *radio & television,* a wire or set of wires used in sending and receiving the electromagnetic waves; aerial.

an·ten·nule (an-ten'yool), *n.* [< *antenna* + *-ule*], a small antenna (feeler).

an·te·pen·di·um (an'ti-pen'di-əm), *n.* [*pl.* ANTEPENDIA (-ə)], [ML. < L. *ante,* before + *pendere,* to hang], 1. a screen or veil in front of an altar in a church. 2. a cloth for a pulpit.

an·te·pe·nult (an'ti-pē'nəlt), *n.* [L. *antepaenultima* < *ante-,* before + *paene,* almost + fem. of *ultimus,* last], the second syllable from the last in a word, as *-lu-* in *an·te·di·lu·vi·an.*

an·te·pe·nul·ti·mate (an'ti-pi-nul'tə-mit), *adj.* [< *antepenult* (after *ultimate*)], second from the last; third from the end. *n.* 1. anything second from the last. 2. an antepenult.

an·te·ri·or (an-têr'i-ẽr), *adj.* [L., compar. of *ante,* before], 1. front or forward (in space); toward the front: opposed to *posterior.* 2. preceding (in time); previous; earlier.

an·te·ri·or·ly (an-têr'i-ẽr-li), *adv.* before.

an·ter·o- (an'tẽr-ō), [< L. **anterus* (falsely assumed as positive of *anterior;* see ANTERIOR)], a combining form meaning *anterior, front, fore,* as in *anteroparietal.*

an·te·room (an'ti-rōōm', an'ti-room'), *n.* [*ante-* + *room*], a room through which another room is entered; waiting room.

an·ter·o·pa·ri·e·tal (an'tẽr-ō-pə-rī'ə-t'l), *adj.* [*antero-* + *parietal*], of the front part of the side (parietal) plates of the skull.

an·te·type (an'ti-tīp'), *n.* [*ante-* + *type*], an earlier form of something; prototype.

an·te·ver·sion (an'ti-vũr'shən), *n.* [< L. *anteversus,* pp. of *antevertere;* see ANTEVERT], a displacing of a bodily organ, especially the uterus, in which its axis is inclined farther forward than is normal.

an·te·vert (an'ti-vũrt'), *v.t.* [L. *antevertere; ante-,* before + *vertere,* to turn], to cause anteversion of.

An·theil, George (an'tīl), 1900– ; American composer.

ant·he·li·on (ant-hē'li-ən, an-thē'li-ən), *n.* [*pl.* ANTHELIA (-ə), ANTHELIONS (-ənz)], [Mod. L.; Gr. *anthēlion* < *anti-,* against + *hēlios,* sun], a halo around an object's shadow cast by the sun on a cloud or bank of mist at high altitudes or in polar regions.

an·thel·min·tic (an'thel-min'tik), *adj.* [< *anti-* + Gr. *helmins,* worm], killing or ejecting intestinal worms. *n.* an anthelmintic medicine.

an·them (an'thəm), *n.* [ME. *antefne;* AS. *antefn;* ML. *antiphona;* Gr. *antiphōna* < *antiphōnos,* sounding back < *anti-,* over against + *phōnē,* voice], 1. formerly, a religious song sung antiphonally. 2. a religious choral song usually based on words from the Bible. 3. the official national song of a country. 4. any song of praise or joy.

an·the·mi·on (an-thē'mi-ən), *n.* [*pl.* ANTHEMIA (-ə)], [Gr. *anthemion,* a flower], a flat decoration of floral or leaf forms, used in painting and relief sculpture.

an·ther (an'thẽr), *n.* [Fr. *anthère;* L. *anthera,* medicine composed of flowers; Gr. *anthēros,* blooming < *anthein,* to bloom < *anthos,* a flower], the part of a stamen that contains the pollen.

an·ther·id·i·al (an'thẽr-id'i-əl), *adj.* of an antheridium.

an·ther·id·i·um (an'thẽr-id'i-əm), *n.* [*pl.* ANTHERIDIA (-ə)], [Mod. L. < *anther* + Gr. dim. suffix *-idion*], in flowerless and seedless plants (cryptogams), the organ in which the male sex cells are developed.

an·ther·o·zo·id (an'thẽr-ə-zō'id, an'thẽr-ə-zoid'), *n.* [< L. *anthera,* anther + *zooid*], in *botany,* a spermatozoid developing in the antheridium.

an·the·sis (an-thē'sis), *n.* [Gr. *anthēsis* < *anthein;* see ANTHER], the state of full bloom in a flower.

ant hill, a mound of dirt carried by ants from their underground nest and heaped around its entrance.

an·tho- (an'thō, an'thə), [< Gr. *anthos,* a flower], a prefix meaning *a flower, of flowers,* as in *anthocarpous.*

an·tho·car·pous (an'thə-kär'pəs), *adj.* [*antho-* + *-carpous*], designating or of a multiple fruit, as the pineapple or strawberry, formed from the ovaries of several blossoms.

an·tho·cy·an (an'thə-sī'ən), *n.* anthocyanin.

an·tho·cy·a·nin (an'thə-sī'ə-nin), *n.* [< *antho-* + Gr. *kyanos,* blue; + *-in*], a soluble, reddish-blue pigment in flowers and plants.

an·tho·di·um (an-thō'di-əm), *n.* [*pl.* ANTHODIA (-ə)], [Mod. L. < Gr. *anthōdēs,* flowerlike < *anthos,* a flower], the head of a composite flower or plant with tubular, radiating flowers, as the aster.

an·thol·o·gist (an-thol'ə-jist), *n.* a person who compiles an anthology.

an·thol·o·gize (an-thol'ə-jīz'), *v.i.* [ANTHOLOGIZED (-jīzd'), ANTHOLOGIZING], to make anthologies. *v.t.* to make an anthology of.

an·thol·o·gy (an-thol'ə-ji), *n.* [*pl.* ANTHOLOGIES (-jiz)], [L. & Gr. *anthologia,* a flower gathering, garland, collection of short poems < *anthologos* < *anthos,* flower + *legein,* to gather], a collection of poems, stories, etc.

An·tho·ny (an'thə-ni, an'tə-ni), [L. *Antonius,* name of a Roman gens], a masculine name: diminutive, *Tony;* variant, *Antony;* feminine, *Antonia;* equivalents, L. *Antonius,* It. & Sp. *Antonio,* Fr. *Antoine,* G. *Anton.*

Anthony, Saint, 1. (*Anthony the Great*), c. 250–350 A.D.; Egyptian founder of Christian monasticism: his day is January 17. 2. (*Anthony of Padua*), 1195–1231; Franciscan friar of Padua: his day is June 13.

Anthony, Mark, see **Antonius, Marcus.**

An·tho·ny, Susan Brow·nell (brou-nel' an'thə-ni), 1820–1906; American leader of the suffragist movement.

an·tho·phore (an'thə-fôr', an'thə-fōr'), *n.* [< Gr. *anthophoros,* flower-bearing < *anthos,* a flower + *pherein,* to bear], in *botany,* an elongation of the thalamus between the calyx and corolla in some plants, forming a stalklike part on which the pistils and corolla are carried.

ANTHOPHORE

an·tho·tax·y (an'thə-tak'si), *n.* [*antho-* + *-taxy*], the arrangement of flowers in a cluster about the axis of a plant.

-an·thous (an'thəs), [< Gr. *anthos,* a flower], a suffix meaning *having flowers* (of a specified kind or number), as in *monanthous.*

an·tho·zo·an (an'thə-zō'ən), *n.* [< Mod. L. *Anthozoa,* name of the class < *antho-* + Gr. *zōia,* pl. of *zōion,* animal; + *-an*], any of a class of sea organisms, comprising corals, sea anemones, etc. *adj.* of the anthozoans.

an·thra·cene (an'thrə-sēn'), *n.* [< Gr. *anthrax,* coal; + *-ene*], a crystalline hydrocarbon, $C_{14}H_{10}$, obtained by distilling coal tar and used in making alizarin dyes.

an·thra·cite (an'thrə-sīt'), *n.* [Gr. *anthrakitis,* kind of coal < *anthrax,* coal], hard coal, which gives much heat and little smoke.

an·thra·cit·ic (an'thrə-sit'ik), *adj.* of or characteristic of anthracite.

an·thrac·nose (an-thrak'nōs), *n.* [< Gr. *anthrax,* coal, carbuncle + *nosos,* disease], a fungus disease of plants, in which roundish dead spots appear chiefly on leaves or fruit.

an·thra·coid (an'thrə-koid'), *adj.* [< *anthrax* + *-oid*], like anthrax.

an·thra·qui·none (an'thrə-kwi-nōn'), *n.* [< Gr. *anthrax,* coal; + *quinone*], a yellow crystalline ketone, $C_6H_4(CO)_2C_6H_4$, produced from anthracene by oxidation: it is used in the manufacture of certain dyes and dye intermediates.

an·thrax (an'thraks), *n.* [L.; Gr., coal, ulcer, carbuncle],

1. a boil or carbuncle. 2. an infectious, usually fatal disease of cattle, sheep, etc., which can be transmitted to man: it is characterized by malignant pustules. 3. one of these pustules.

an·thro·po- (an′thrə-pō, an′thrə-pə), [< Gr. *anthrōpos*, man], a combining form meaning *man, human*, as in *anthropology:* also, before a vowel, **anthrop-**.

an·thro·po·cen·tric (an′thrə-pə-sen′trik), *adj.* [*anthropo-* + *centric*], that considers man as the central fact, or final aim, of the universe.

an·thro·po·gen·e·sis (an′thrə-pə-jen′ə-sis), *n.* [*anthropo-* + *genesis*], the study of man's origin and development.

an·thro·pog·e·ny (an′thrə-poj′ə-ni), *n.* anthropogenesis.

an·thro·po·ge·og·ra·phy (an′thrə-pō′ji-og′rə-fi), *n.* [*anthropo-* + *geography*], the study of the geographical distribution of man and of his relationship to his physical environment.

an·thro·pog·ra·phy (an′thrə-pog′rə-fi), *n.* [*anthropo-* + *-graphy*], the branch of anthropology that deals with the distribution of man according to his physical characteristics, languages, customs, etc.

an·thro·poid (an′thrə-poid′), *adj.* [*anthrop-* + *-oid*], manlike; resembling man; especially, designating or of any of the most highly developed apes, including the chimpanzee, gorilla, orangutan, and gibbon. *n.* any anthropoid ape.

an·thro·po·log·i·cal (an′thrə-pə-loj′i-k'l), *adj.* of or connected with anthropology.

an·thro·pol·o·gist (an′thrə-pol′ə-jist), *n.* a student of or specialist in anthropology.

an·thro·pol·o·gy (an′thrə-pol′ə-ji), *n.* [*anthropo-* + *-logy*], the study of the races, physical and mental characteristics, distribution, customs, social relationships, etc. of mankind: often restricted to the study of the institutions, myths, etc. of primitive peoples.

an·thro·po·met·ric (an′thrə-pə-met′rik), *adj.* of or connected with anthropometry.

an·thro·po·met·ri·cal (an′thrə-pə-met′ri-k'l), *adj.* anthropometric.

an·thro·pom·e·try (an′thrə-pom′ə-tri), *n.* [*anthropo-* + *-metry*], the part of anthropology having to do with measurement of the human body to determine differences in races, individuals, etc.

an·thro·po·mor·phic (an′thrə-pə-môr′fik), *adj.* [*anthropo-* + *-morphic*], of, characterized by, or like anthropomorphism.

an·thro·po·mor·phism (an′thrə-pə-môr′fiz'm), *n.* [*anthropomorphous* + *-ism*], the attributing of human shape or characteristics to gods, objects, animals, etc.

an·thro·po·mor·phize (an′thrə-pə-môr′fiz), *v.t.* & *v.i.* [ANTHROPOMORPHIZED (-fīzd), ANTHROPOMORPHIZING], to attribute human shape or characteristics to (gods, objects, etc.).

an·thro·po·mor·pho·sis (an′thrə-pə-môr′fə-sis), *n.* [*anthropo-* + meta*morphosis*], a changing into human form.

an·thro·po·mor·phous (an′thrə-pə-môr′fəs), *adj.* [Gr. *anthrōpomorphos* < *anthrōpos*, a man + *morphē*, form, shape], having human shape and appearance.

an·thro·po·nom·ics (an′thrə-pə-nom′iks), *n.pl.* [construed as sing.], anthroponomy.

an·thro·pon·o·my (an′thrə-pon′ə-mi), *n.* [*anthropo-* + *-nomy*], the science dealing with the laws of human development in relation to environment and to other organisms.

an·thro·pop·a·thism (an′thrə-pop′ə-thiz'm), *n.* anthropopathy.

an·thro·pop·a·thy (an′thrə-pop′ə-thi), *n.* [LL. *anthropopathia;* Gr. *anthrōpopatheia*, humanity < *anthrōpos*, man + *pathos*, suffering], the attributing of human feelings and passions to gods or objects.

an·thro·poph·a·gi (an′thrə-pof′ə-jī′), *n.pl.* [*sing.* ANTHROPOPHAGUS (-gəs)], [Gr. *anthrōpophagos* < *anthrōpos*, man + *phagos* < *phagein*, to eat], cannibals.

an·thro·po·phag·ic (an′thrə-pə-faj′ik), *adj.* [see ANTHROPOPHAGI], cannibalistic.

an·thro·poph·a·gite (an′thrə-pof′ə-jit′), *n.* [see ANTHROPOPHAGI], a cannibal.

an·thro·poph·a·gous (an′thrə-pof′ə-gəs), *adj.* [see ANTHROPOPHAGI], cannibalistic; eating human flesh.

an·thro·poph·a·gy (an′thrə-pof′ə-ji), *n.* [see ANTHROPOPHAGI], cannibalism.

an·ti (an′tī, an′ti), *n.* [*pl.* ANTIS (-tīz, -tiz)], [see ANTI-], [Colloq.], a person opposed to some policy, proposal, action, etc. *adj.* [Colloq.], opposed; against.

an·ti- (an′ti; *now often* an′tī), [Gr. *anti-*, *ant-* < *anti*, against], a prefix used in forming adjectives and nouns derived from them. It means: 1. *against, hostile to*, as in *antilabor, anti-imperialist, anti-Semitism*. 2. *that counteracts, that operates against*, as in *antiaircraft*. 3. *that prevents, cures*, or *neutralizes*, as in *antitoxin*. 4. *opposite, reverse*, as in *antiperistalsis*. 5. *rivaling*, as in *antipope*. Also, before a vowel, sometimes **ant-**, as in *antacid*.

an·ti·air·craft (an′ti-âr′kraft, an′ti-âr′kräft), *adj.* used for defense against enemy aircraft: as, an *antiaircraft* gun: abbreviated **A.A.**

an·ti·ar (an′ti-är′), *n.* [Javanese *antjar*], 1. the upas tree of Java. 2. a poison made from its gum resin.

an·ti·ar·in (an′ti-ə-rin), *n.* antiar (the poison).

an·ti·bac·te·ri·al (an′ti-bak-têr′i-əl), *adj.* that checks the growth or effect of bacteria.

an·ti·bi·o·sis (an′ti-bī-ō′sis), *n.* [Mod. L.; *anti-* + Gr. *biōsis*, way of life < *bios*, life], in *biology*, an association between organisms which is harmful to one of them.

an·ti·bi·ot·ic (an′ti-bī-ot′ik), *adj.* 1. of antibiosis. 2. harmful to life; specifically, destroying, or inhibiting the growth of, bacteria. 3. of antibiotics. *n.* any of certain chemical substances produced by various groups of microorganisms, specifically bacteria, fungi, and actinomycetes, and having the capacity, in dilute solutions, to inhibit the growth of or to destroy bacteria and other microorganisms: the antibiotics, including penicillin, streptomycin, tyrothricin, etc., are used in the treatment of various infectious diseases.

an·ti·bod·y (an′ti-bod′i), *n.* [*pl.* ANTIBODIES (-iz)], [*anti-* + *body*], a protein produced in the body in response to contact of the body with an antigen, and having the specific capacity of neutralizing or reacting with the antigen.

an·tic (an′tik), *adj.* [It. *antico* < L. *antiquus;* see ANTIQUE], fantastic and queer; grotesque; ludicrous. *n.* 1. an antic act, gesture, etc.; caper. 2. [Archaic], a clown; fool; buffoon. *v.i.* to do antics.

an·ti·cat·a·lyst (an′ti-kat′'l-ist), *n.* [*anti-* + *catalyst*], a substance that slows down a chemical reaction.

an·ti·cath·ode (an′ti-kath′ōd), *n.* [*anti-* + *cathode*], in an X-ray tube, the piece opposite the cathode, serving as the target for the cathode's discharge.

an·ti·chlor (an′ti-klôr′, an′ti-klōr′), *n.* [*anti-* + *chlor*ine], any substance for removing excess chlorine from textiles or other materials that have been bleached.

an·ti·christ (an′ti-krīst′), *n.* [ME. *anticrist;* OFr. *antecrist;* L. *antichristus;* Gr. *antichristos* < *anti-*, against + *Christos*, Christ], 1. an opponent of or disbeliever in Christ. 2. [A-], in the *Bible*, the great antagonist of Christ, expected to spread universal evil before the end of the world but finally to be conquered at Christ's second coming: I John 2:18. 3. a false Christ.

an·tic·i·pant (an-tis′ə-pənt), *adj.* [L. *anticipans*, ppr. of *anticipare;* see ANTICIPATE], expecting; anticipating (with *of*). *n.* a person who anticipates.

an·tic·i·pate (an-tis′ə-pāt′), *v.t.* [ANTICIPATED (-id), ANTICIPATING], [< L. *anticipatus*, pp. of *anticipare* < *ante-*, before + **capare* < *capere*, to take], 1. to expect; feel beforehand; look forward to. 2. to make happen earlier than due: as, don't *anticipate* calamity by refusing to prepare for it. 3. to prevent; forestall: as, he *anticipated* his opponent's blows. 4. to foresee (a command, wish, etc.) and perform in advance: as, the servant *anticipated* his master's request. 5. to use or enjoy in advance: as, she *anticipated* her legacy. 6. to do something before (someone else). 7. in *business*, to meet (an obligation) before due. —*SYN.* see **expect**.

an·tic·i·pa·tion (an-tis′ə-pā′shən), *n.* [L. *anticipatio*, preconception; see ANTICIPATE], 1. an anticipating or being anticipated. 2. something anticipated. 3. expectation. 4. foreknowledge; presentiment. 5. in *law*, the assignment or taking of income from a trust fund before it is due. 6. in *music*, the beginning of a tone of a chord before the preceding chord has ended.

an·tic·i·pa·tive (an-tis′ə-pā′tiv), *adj.* inclined to anticipate; of or full of anticipation.

an·tic·i·pa·tor (an-tis′ə-pā′tẽr), *n.* a person who anticipates.

an·tic·i·pa·to·ri·ly (an-tis′ə-pə-tôr′ə-li, an-tis′ə-pə-tō′rə-li), *adv.* with anticipation.

an·tic·i·pa·to·ry (an-tis′ə-pə-tôr′i, an-tis′ə-pə-tō′ri), *adj.* anticipating; occurring in advance.

an·ti·clas·tic (an′ti-klas′tik), *adj.* [< *anti-* + Gr. *klastos*, broken < *klaein*, to break; + *-ic*], in *mathematics*, having curvatures opposite each other at a given point; convex in one direction and concave in the other, as a saddle: opposed to *synclastic*.

an·ti·cler·i·cal (an′ti-kler′i-k'l), *adj.* opposed to the clergy or church hierarchy, especially to its influence in public affairs.

an·ti·cler·i·cal·ism (an′ti-kler′i-k'l-iz'm), *n.* opposition to the clergy or church hierarchy, especially to its influence in public affairs.

an·ti·cli·mac·tic (an′ti-klī-mak′tik), *adj.* of, having, or like an anticlimax.

an·ti·cli·max (an′ti-klī′maks), *n.* [*anti-* + *climax*], 1. a sudden drop from the dignified or important in thought or expression to the commonplace or trivial, often for humorous effect. 2. a descent, as in a series of events, which is in ludicrous or disappointing contrast to a preceding rise.

an·ti·cli·nal (an′ti-klī′n'l), *adj.* [< *anti-* + Gr. *klinein*, to

incline; + *-al*], 1. inclined in opposite directions. 2. in *geology*, of or like an anticline.
an·ti·cline (an′ti-klīn′), *n.* [< *anticlinal*, after *incline*, *decline*], in *geology*, a fold of stratified rock from the crest of which the strata slope downward in opposite directions: opposed to *syncline*.
an·ti·cli·no·ri·um (an′ti-kli-nō′ri-əm), *n.* [*pl.* ANTICLINORIA (-ə)], [Mod. L. < *anticline* + Gr. *oros*, mountain], in *geology*, a succession of anticlines and synclines resembling a row of arches.
An·ti·cos·ti (an′ti-kos′ti), *n.* an island at the mouth of the St. Lawrence River, Quebec, Canada: area, c. 3,000 sq. mi.
an·ti·cy·clone (an′ti-sī′klōn), *n.* 1. an atmospheric condition in which the direction of the outward-spiraling winds and the relations of barometric pressure are opposite to those of a cyclone. 2. the area of high pressure in which this condition is centered. 3. an atmospheric disturbance at the edge of this area.
an·ti·cy·clon·ic (an′ti-sī-klon′ik), *adj.* of or connected with an anticyclone.
an·ti·dot·al (an′ti-dō′t'l, an′ti-dō′t'l), *adj.* of, like, or serving as an antidote.
an·ti·dote (an′ti-dōt′), *n.* [L. *antidotum;* Gr. *antidoton* < *anti-*, against + *dotos*, given < *didonai*, to give], 1. a remedy to counteract a poison. 2. anything that tends to counteract an evil.
an·ti·drom·ic (an′ti-drom′ik), *adj.* [< *anti-* + Gr. *dromos*, a course; + *-ic*], in *physiology*, running or conveying in a direction opposite to the normal, as a nerve fiber, etc.
an·ti·en·er·gis·tic (an′ti-en′ẽr-jis′tik), *adj.* resisting applied energy: opposed to *synergistic*.
An·tie·tam (an-tē′təm), *n.* a creek in western Maryland, flowing into the Potomac River: site of a Civil War battle (1862).
an·ti·fe·brile (an′ti-fē′brəl, an′ti-feb′rəl), *adj.* [*anti-* + *febrile*], reducing fever. *n.* an antifebrile drug.
an·ti·fed·er·al·ist (an′ti-fed′ẽr-əl-ist), *n.* 1. a person opposed to federalism. 2. [A-], a person who opposed the adoption of the Constitution of the United States. *adj.* [A-], designating or of a former political party led by Thomas Jefferson which opposed the Federalists.
an·ti·freeze (an′ti-frēz′, an′ti-frēz′), *n.* a substance of low freezing point, as alcohol, used especially in the radiators of water-cooled automobile engines in cold weather to prevent freezing.
an·ti·fric·tion (an′ti-frik′shən), *adj.* reducing friction. *n.* a device, lubricant, etc. for reducing friction.
an·ti·gen (an′tə-jən, an′tə-jin), *n.* [*anti-* + *-gen*], a substance, usually a protein, carbohydrate, or fat-carbohydrate complex, which causes the production of an antibody when introduced directly into the body, as into the blood stream.
An·tig·o·ne (an-tig′ə-nē′), *n.* [L.; Gr. *Antigonē*], in *Greek legend*, the daughter of Oedipus and Jocasta: she defied her uncle, Creon, by performing funeral rites for her brother, Polynices.
An·tig·o·nus I (an-tig′ə-nəs), (*Antigonus Cyclops*), 382–301 B.C.; Macedonian general of Alexander the Great.
An·ti·gua (an-tē′gwə, an-tē′gə), *n.* a British island of the Leeward group in the West Indies: area, 108 sq. mi.; pop., 54,000; chief town, St. John.
an·ti·he·lix (an′ti-hē′liks), *n.* [*pl.* ANTIHELICES (-li-sēz′), ANTIHELIXES (-lik-siz)], the rounded piece of cartilage inside the outer rim (helix) of the ear.
an·ti·his·ta·mine (an′ti-his′tə-mēn′, an′ti-his′tə-min), *n.* any of several drugs used to minimize the action of histamine in certain allergic conditions: it is variously claimed that they relieve the symptoms in asthma, hay fever, the common cold, etc.
an·ti-im·pe·ri·al·ist (an′ti-im-pêr′i-əl-ist), *n.* a person opposed to imperialism.
an·ti·ke·to·gen·e·sis (an′ti-kē′tə-jen′ə-sis), *n.* [Mod. L.; *anti-* + *ketone* + *genesis*], the use of certain substances, as glucose, to prevent ketosis, as in diabetes.
an·ti·knock (an′ti-nok′, an′ti-nok′), *n.* a substance added to the fuel of internal-combustion engines to do away with or reduce noise resulting from too rapid combustion.
an·ti·la·bor (an′ti-lā′bẽr), *adj.* opposed or harmful to labor unions and the interests, gains, etc. of workers.
An·ti-Leb·a·non (an′ti-leb′ə-nən), *n.* a mountain range in Syria, east of the Lebanon mountains.
an·ti·lith·ic (an′ti-lith′ik), *adj.* [*anti-* + *lithic*], in *medicine*, preventing the formation or development of calculi, as of the urinary tract. *n.* an antilithic drug or other substance.
An·til·le·an (an′ti-lē′ən, an-til′i-ən), *adj.* of the Antilles. *n.* a native or inhabitant of the Antilles.
An·til·les (an-til′ēz), *n.pl.* a group of islands in the West Indies: see **Greater Antilles, Lesser Antilles.**
an·ti·log·a·rithm (an′ti-lôg′ə-rith′m, an′ti-log′ə-rith′m), *n.* the number corresponding to a logarithm: as, the *antilogarithm* of 1 is 10.
an·til·o·gy (an-til′ə-ji), *n.* [*pl.* ANTILOGIES (-jiz)], [Gr. *antilogia* < *antilogos; anti-*, against + *logos* < *legein*, to speak], a contradiction in ideas, statements, or terms.
an·ti·ma·cas·sar (an′ti-mə-kas′ẽr), *n.* [*anti-* + *macassar*, an oil formerly used as a hair dressing], a small cover on the back or arms of a chair, sofa, etc. to prevent soiling.
an·ti·ma·lar·i·al (an′ti-mə-lâr′i-əl), *adj.* preventing or relieving malaria. *n.* an antimalarial drug.
an·ti·masque, an·ti·mask (an′ti-mask′, an′ti-mäsk′), *n.* [*anti-* + *masque*], a comic sketch between the acts of a masque, often a burlesque of the masque.
an·ti·mat·ter (an′ti-mat′ẽr), *n.* a form of matter in which the electrical charge or other property of the constituent particles is the reverse of that in usual observed matter.
an·ti·mere (an′ti-mêr′), *n.* [*anti-* + *-mere*], in *zoology*, either of the corresponding parts opposite each other on both sides of an organism's axis.
an·ti·mis·sile (an′ti-mis′'l), *adj.* designed as a defense against ballistic missiles.
an·ti·mo·ni·al (an′tə-mō′ni-əl), *adj.* of or containing antimony. *n.* a medicine, etc. containing antimony.
an·ti·mo·nic (an′tə-mō′nik, an′tə-mon′ik), *adj.* 1. of or containing antimony. 2. in *chemistry*, designating or of compounds of pentavalent antimony.
an·ti·mo·ni·ous (an′tə-mō′ni-əs), *adj.* 1. of or like antimony. 2. in *chemistry*, designating or of compounds of trivalent antimony.
an·ti·mon·soon (an′ti-mon-sōōn′), *n.* the air current above and moving oppositely to a monsoon.
an·ti·mo·ny (an′tə-mō′ni), *n.* [Fr. *antimoine;* ML. *antimonium:* the symbol Sb < L. name, *stibium*], a silvery-white, brittle, metallic chemical element of crystalline structure, found only in combination: used in alloys with other metals to harden them and increase their resistance to chemical action; compounds of antimony are used in medicines and pigments: symbol, Sb; at. wt., 121.76; at. no., 51.
an·ti·mo·nyl (an′ti-mə-nil′), *n.* [< *antimony* + *-yl*], in *chemistry*, the univalent radical SbO, found in certain salts, notably antimonyl potassium tartrate.
antimonyl potassium tartrate, a poisonous, colorless or white crystalline powder, an antimonious tartrate, $KSbOC_4H_4O_6$, used as an emetic and as a mordant in dyeing: also called *tartar emetic*.
an·ti·node (an′ti-nōd′), *n.* in *physics*, the point halfway between two adjacent nodes in a vibrating body.
an·ti·no·mi·an (an′ti-nō′mi-ən), *n.* [< *antinomy* + *-an*], [also A-], a member of a Christian sect which held that faith alone, not obedience to the moral law, is necessary for salvation. *adj.* of this sect or doctrine.
an·ti·no·my (an-tin′ə-mi), *n.* [*pl.* ANTINOMIES (-miz)], [L. *antinomia* < Gr. *antinomia; anti-*, against + *nomia* < *nomos*, law], 1. the opposition of one law, regulation, etc. to another. 2. a contradiction or inconsistency between two apparently reasonable principles or laws.
An·ti·och (an′ti-ok′), *n.* 1. the capital of ancient Syria, in the northwestern part of the country: now a city in southern Turkey: pop., 46,000: Arabic name, *Antakiya*. 2. an ancient city in Pisidia, Asia Minor.
An·ti·o·chus III (an-tī′ə-kəs), 242–187 B.C.; king of Syria (223–187 B.C.): called *the Great*.
Antiochus IV, ?–163 B.C.; king of Syria (175–163 B.C.): called *Antiochus Epiphanes*.
an·ti·par·ti·cle (an′ti-pär′ti-k'l), *n.* any of the constituent particles of antimatter.
‡**an·ti·pas·to** (än′tē-päs′tô), *n.* [It.; *anti-* (L. *ante*), before + *pasto* < L. *pastus*, food < *pascere*, to feed], an appetizer of salted fish, meat, olives, etc.
An·tip·a·ter (an-tip′ə-tẽr), *n.* Macedonian general under Alexander the Great; lived 398?–319 B.C.
an·ti·pa·thet·ic (an′ti-pə-thet′ik), *adj.* [< *antipathy*], 1. having antipathy. 2. opposed or antagonistic in character, tendency, etc.
an·ti·pa·thet·i·cal (an′ti-pə-thet′i-k'l), *adj.* antipathetic.
an·tip·a·thy (an-tip′ə-thi), *n.* [*pl.* ANTIPATHIES (-thiz)], [Gr. *antipatheia; anti-*, against + *patheia* < *pathein*, to suffer, feel], 1. an opposition in character, nature, tendency, etc. 2. a definite dislike; strong repugnance. 3. the object of such dislike. —*SYN.* see **aversion.**
an·ti·pe·ri·od·ic (an′ti-pêr′i-od′ik), *adj.* preventing the periodic return of attacks of disease, as of certain fevers. *n.* an antiperiodic medicine.
an·ti·per·i·stal·sis (an′ti-per′ə-stal′sis), *n.* in *physiology*, backward peristaltic action in which the contents of the intestines are moved upward.
an·ti·per·son·nel (an′ti-pẽr-sə-nel′), *adj.* directed against or intended to destroy people rather than material objects: as, *antipersonnel* mines.
an·ti·phlo·gis·tic (an′ti-flō-jis′tik), *adj.* [*anti-* + *phlogistic*], counteracting inflammation. *n.* an antiphlogistic medicine, diet, etc.
an·ti·phon (an′tə-fon′), *n.* [ML. *antiphona;* Gr. *antiphōna;* see ANTHEM], 1. a hymn, psalm, etc. chanted or sung in responsive, alternating parts. 2. anything composed for responsive chanting or singing. 3. verses chanted or a piece of plainsong sung before or after a psalm, canticle, etc.
an·tiph·o·nal (an-tif′ə-n'l), *adj.* of or like an antiphon; sung or chanted in alternation. *n.* an antiphonary.
an·tiph·o·nar·y (an-tif′ə-ner′i), *n.* [*pl.* ANTIPHONARIES (-iz)], [ML. *antiphonarium;* see ANTIPHON], a collection

of antiphons, especially a book of responsive prayers.
an·ti·phon·ic (an'ti-fon'ik), *adj.* antiphonal.
an·tiph·o·ny (an-tif'ə-ni), *n.* [*pl.* ANTIPHONIES (-niz)], [< Gr. *antiphōnos* (see ANTHEM); + *-y*], 1. the opposition of sounds. 2. harmony produced by this. 3. an antiphon. 4. antiphonal chanting or singing. 5. any response or echo.
an·tiph·ra·sis (an-tif'rə-sis), *n.* [L.; Gr. *antiphrasis* < *anti-*, against + *phrazein*, to speak], the use of words or phrases in a sense opposite to the proper one.
an·tip·o·dal (an-tip'ə-d'l), *adj.* 1. of the antipodes; on the other side of the earth. 2. exactly opposite.
an·ti·pode (an'ti-pōd'), *n.* [sing. of *antipodes*], anything diametrically opposite; exact opposite.
an·tip·o·de·an (an-tip'ə-dē'ən, an'ti-pə-dē'ən), *adj.* 1. antipodal. 2. Australian. *n.* 1. a person who lives on the other side of the earth. 2. an Australian.
an·tip·o·des (an-tip'ə-dēz'), *n.pl.* [L.; Gr. *antipodes*, pl. of *antipous*, with the feet opposite; *anti-*, opposite + *pous, podos*, foot], 1. any two places directly opposite each other on the earth. 2. [construed as pl. or sing.], a place on the other side of the earth: in British usage, New Zealand and Australia are usually meant. 3. two opposite or contrary things. 4. [construed as pl. or sing.], the exact opposite. 5. [A-], a group of islands southeast of New Zealand. 6. [Obs.], the people on the other side of the earth.
an·ti·pope (an'ti-pōp'), *n.* a pope set up against the one chosen by church laws, as in a schism.
an·ti·pro·ton (an'ti-prō'ton), *n.* [*anti-* + *proton*], in *physics*, a nuclear particle of very short duration, with approximately the same mass as the proton but carrying a negative charge.
an·ti·py·ret·ic (an'ti-pī-ret'ik), *adj.* [*anti-* + *pyretic*], reducing fever. *n.* anything that reduces fever.
an·ti·py·rine (an'ti-pī'rēn, an'ti-pī'rin), *n.* [< *antipyretic*], a drug derived from coal tar, used to relieve headaches and neuralgia and to reduce fevers.
antiq., antiqu., 1. antiquarian. 2. antiquity; antiquities.
an·ti·quar·i·an (an'ti-kwâr'i-ən), *adj.* 1. of antiques. 2. of antiquaries. *n.* an antiquary.
an·ti·quar·y (an'ti-kwer'i), *n.* [*pl.* ANTIQUARIES (-iz)], [L. *antiquarius* < *antiquus*; see ANTIQUE], a person who collects or studies antiquities.
an·ti·quate (an'ti-kwāt'), *v.t.* [ANTIQUATED (-id), ANTIQUATING], [< L. *antiquatus*, pp. of *antiquare* < *antiquus*; see ANTIQUE], 1. to make old or obsolete; cause to become old-fashioned. 2. to give an antique appearance or style to.
an·ti·quat·ed (an'ti-kwāt'id), *adj.* 1. old; obsolete. 2. old-fashioned; out-of-date. —*SYN.* see **old.**
an·tique (an-tēk'), *adj.* [Fr. < L. *antiquus*, ancient, old < *ante*, before], 1. of ancient times; ancient; old. 2. out-of-date; antiquated. 3. of ancient Greece or Rome; in the style of classical antiquity. 4. of or in the style of a former period. *n.* 1. anything from ancient times; relic. 2. the ancient style, especially of Greek or Roman sculpture, architecture, etc. 3. a piece of furniture, silverware, etc. made in a former period. 4. in *printing*, a variety of boldface type. **This line is in antique.** *v.t.* [ANTIQUED (-tēkt'), ANTIQUING], to make look antique. —*SYN.* see **old.**
an·tiq·ui·ty (an-tik'wə-ti), *n.* [*pl.* ANTIQUITIES (-tiz)], [Fr. *antiquité*; L. *antiquitas* < *antiquus*; see ANTIQUE], 1. the early period of history, especially before the Middle Ages. 2. the quality of being ancient or old; great age: as, a book of great *antiquity*. 3. the people, especially writers, of ancient times. 4. *usually in pl.* a relic, monument, etc., of the distant past. 5. *usually pl.* ancient manners, customs, etc.
an·ti·ra·chit·ic (an'ti-rə-kit'ik), *adj.* [*anti-* + *rachitic*], that cures or prevents rickets. *n.* a remedy or preventive for rickets.
an·ti·re·mon·strant (an'ti-ri-mon'strənt), *n.* a person opposed to remonstrance or remonstrants; specifically, [A-], any of a group of Dutch Calvinists who opposed the Arminian Remonstrants.
an·tir·rhi·num (an'ti-rī'nəm), *n.* [Mod. L.; Gr. *antirrhinon*, snapdragon < *anti-*, like + *rhis, rhinos*, nose], any of a number of related plants of the figwort family, with small, white, yellow, red, or purplish flowers and narrow leaves; snapdragon.
an·ti·rust (an'ti-rust', an'ti-rust'), *adj.* 1. that prevents rust. 2. that cannot rust. *n.* something that prevents rust.
An·ti·sa·na, Mount (än'tē-sä'nä), a volcanic mountain in north central Ecuador: height, 18,885 ft.
an·ti·scor·bu·tic (an'ti-skôr-bū'tik), *adj.* [*anti-* + *scorbutic*], that cures or prevents scurvy. *n.* a remedy or preventive for scurvy.
antiscorbutic acid, vitamin C: also called *ascorbic acid, cevitamic acid.*
an·ti-Sem·ite (an'ti-sem'īt), *n.* an anti-Semitic person.
an·ti-Se·mit·ic (an'ti-sə-mit'ik), *adj.* 1. having or showing prejudice against Jews; disliking or fearing Jews and Jewish things. 2. discriminating against or persecuting Jews. 3. of or caused by anti-Semitism.
an·ti-Sem·i·tism (an'ti-sem'ə-tiz'm), *n.* 1. prejudice against Jews; dislike or fear of Jews and Jewish things. 2. discrimination against or persecution of Jews.
an·ti·sep·sis (an'ti-sep'sis), *n.* [*anti-* + *sepsis*], 1. the condition of being antiseptic. 2. the use of antiseptics.
an·ti·sep·tic (an'ti-sep'tik), *adj.* [*anti-* + *septic*], 1. preventing infection, decay, etc.; inhibiting the action of microorganisms. 2. using antiseptics. 3. free from infection. *n.* any antiseptic substance, as alcohol, etc.
an·ti·sep·ti·cal·ly (an'ti-sep'ti-k'l-i, an'ti-sep'tik-li), *adv.* by means of antiseptics.
an·ti·sep·ti·cize (an'ti-sep'tə-sīz'), *v.t.* [ANTISEPTICIZED (-sīzd'), ANTISEPTICIZING], to make (something) antiseptic; apply antiseptics to.
an·ti·se·rum (an'ti-sêr'əm), *n.* [*anti-* + *serum*], a serum with antibodies in it.
an·ti·slav·er·y (an'ti-slāv'ēr-i), *adj.* against slavery.
an·ti·so·cial (an'ti-sō'shəl), *adj.* 1. unsociable. 2. against the basic principles of society; against the welfare of the people generally. —*SYN.* see **unsocial.**
an·ti·spas·mod·ic (an'ti-spaz-mod'ik), *adj.* relieving or preventing spasms. *n.* a remedy or preventive for spasms.
An·tis·the·nes (an-tis'thə-nēz'), *n.* Greek Cynic philosopher; lived 444-? B.C.
an·tis·tro·phe (an-tis'trə-fi), *n.* [Gr. *antistrophe* < *antistrephein*, to turn about; *anti-*, against, opposite + *strephein*, to turn], 1. the return movement, left to right, made by the chorus of an ancient Greek play in answering the previous strophe; hence, 2. that part of a choric song performed while making this movement. 3. in a Pindaric ode, the stanza, usually in the same or similar form, which follows the strophe. 4. in poems with contrasting or parallel stanza systems, a stanza of the second system.
an·ti·stroph·ic (an'ti-strof'ik), *adj.* of, or having the nature of, antistrophe.
an·ti·tank (an'ti-taŋk'), *adj.* for use against tanks in war: abbreviated **AT** (no period).
an·tith·e·sis (an-tith'ə-sis), *n.* [*pl.* ANTITHESES (-sēz')], [Gr. < *antitithenai*; *anti-*, against + *tithenai*, to place, set], 1. a contrast or opposition of thoughts, usually in two phrases, clauses, or sentences, as in the sentence "You are going; I am staying." 2. the second part of such an expression. 3. a contrast or opposition. 4. the exact opposite: as, joy is the *antithesis* of sorrow.
an·ti·thet·ic (an'ti-thet'ik), *adj.* [Gr. *antithetikos*], 1. of or containing antithesis. 2. exactly opposite. —*SYN.* see **opposite.**
an·ti·thet·i·cal (an'ti-thet'i-k'l), *adj.* antithetic.
an·ti·tox·ic (an'ti-tok'sik), *adj.* of, containing, or acting as an antitoxin.
an·ti·tox·in (an'ti-tok'sin), *n.* [*anti-* + *toxin*], 1. a substance found in blood serum and formed in the body to act against a specific toxin. 2. a serum containing an antitoxin: taken from the blood of an infected animal, such a serum is injected into a person to prevent a specific disease, as diphtheria, tetanus, etc.
an·ti·trades (an'ti-trādz'), *n.pl.* 1. winds that blow steadily above and opposite to the trade winds. 2. prevailing westerly winds of the temperate zone.
an·tit·ra·gus (an-tit'rə-gəs), *n.* [*pl.* ANTITRAGI (-gī')], the fleshy, cartilaginous protrusion at the rear of the external ear, opposite the tragus.
an·ti·trust (an'ti-trust'), *adj.* against the trusts; opposed to or regulating business monopolies, cartels, etc.
an·ti·type (an'ti-tīp'), *n.*[Gr. *antitypos*; *anti-*, against, corresponding to + *typos*, form, figure], 1. the person or thing represented or foreshadowed by an earlier type or symbol. 2. an opposite type.
an·ti·ven·in (an'ti-ven'in), *n.* [*anti-* + OFr. or ME. *venin* < L. *venenum*, poison (see VENOM)], 1. an antitoxin for venom, as of snakes, formed in the blood by gradually increased injections of the specific venom. 2. a serum containing this antitoxin.
an·ti·war (an'ti-wôr'), *adj.* opposed to war.
ant·ler (ant'lēr), *n.* [ME. *aunteler*; OFr. *antoiller* < L. **anteoculare* < *ante-*, before + *ocularis*, of the eyes], 1. the branched, deciduous horn of any animal of the deer family. 2. any branch of such a horn.
ant·lered (ant'lērd), *adj.* 1. having antlers 2. ornamented with antlers.
ant lion, 1. any of several insects whose larva lies hidden in a pit which it has dug and eats ants, etc. that fall in. 2. its larva.
An·to·fa·gas·ta (än'tô-fä-gäs'tä), *n.* a seaport in northern Chile: pop., 51,000.
An·toi·nette (an'twə-net', an'tə-net'; Fr. än'twà'net'), a feminine name: diminutive, *Nettie, Netty*: see **Antonia.**
Antoinette, Marie, see **Marie Antoinette.**
An·to·ni·a (an-tō'ni-ə), [L., fem. of *Antonius*; see ANTHONY], a feminine name: variant, *Antoinette.*

An·to·ni·nus, Marcus Aurelius (an'tə-nī'nəs), see **Marcus Aurelius.**

An·to·ni·nus Pi·us (an'tə-nī'nəs pī'əs), 86–161 A.D.; Roman emperor (138–161 A.D.).

An·to·ni·us, Mar·cus (mär'kəs an-tō'ni-əs), (*Mark*, or *Marc, Antony* or *Anthony*), 83?–30 B.C.; Roman general and triumvir.

an·to·no·ma·si·a (an'tə-nō-mā'zhə), ***n.*** [L.; Gr. < *antonomazein*, to call by another name < *anti-*, instead of + *onomazein*, to name < *onoma*, name], 1. the use of an epithet or title in place of a name, as in calling a judge *his honor*. 2. the use of a proper name belonging to some other person, place, etc. instead of a common noun, as in calling a traitor a *Quisling*.

An·to·ny (an'tə-ni), 1. a masculine name: see **Anthony.** 2. see **Antonius, Marcus.**

an·to·nym (an'tə-nim'), ***n.*** [Gr. *antōnymia* < *anti-*, opposite + *onoma, onyma*, name], a word whose meaning is opposite to that of another word: as, *sad* is the *antonym* of *happy:* abbreviated **ant.**

an·ton·y·mous (an-ton'i-məs), ***adj.*** of, or having the nature of, an antonym. —***SYN.*** see **opposite.**

an·tre (an'tẽr), ***n.*** [Fr. < L. *antrum* < Gr. *antron*, cave; cf. ANTRUM], [Archaic or Poetic], a cave; cavern.

An·trim (an'trim), ***n.*** a county of Northern Ireland: pop., 197,000; chief city, Belfast.

an·trorse (an-trôrs'), ***adj.*** [Mod. L. *antrorsus* < *antero-* + L. *versus*, turned], in *biology*, upward or forward.

an·trum (an'trəm), ***n.*** [*pl.* ANTRUMS (-trəmz), ANTRA (-trə)], [L.; Gr. *antron*, cave], 1. a cave or cavity. 2. in *anatomy*, a cavity; especially, either of a pair of sinuses in the upper jaw.

An·tung (än'dooŋ'; Eng. an'tooŋ'), ***n.*** a seaport of China, in Manchuria, on the Yalu River: pop., 271,000.

Ant·werp (ant'wẽrp), ***n.*** 1. a province of northern Belgium. 2. its capital: pop., 263,000 (1948).

A·nu·bis (ə-nū'bis, ə-nōō'bis), ***n.*** [L.; Gr. *Anoubis;* Egypt. *Anpu*], in *Egyptian religion*, a god with the head of a jackal, who led the dead to judgment: identified with the Greek Hermes.

ANUBIS

a·nu·cle·ar (ā-nōō'kli-ẽr, ā-nū'kli-ẽr), ***adj.*** [*a-*, not + *nuclear*], in *biology*, without a nucleus or nuclei.

an·u·ran (ə-nū'rən), ***adj.*** [Gr. *an-*, not + *oura*, tail; + *-an*], in *zoology*, belonging to a group of amphibians that includes the frogs and toads. ***n.*** any member of this group.

an·u·rous (ə-nū'rəs), ***adj.*** [see ANURAN], having no tail, as a frog or toad; acaudal.

a·nus (ā'nəs), ***n.*** [*pl.* ANUSES (-iz), ANI (ā'nī)], [L.], the opening at the lower end of the alimentary canal.

an·vil (an'vil), ***n.*** [ME. *anfelt;* AS. *onfilte* < *an-, on-*, on + **filtan*, to hit, beat < IE. base **pel(d)-*, to beat into motion (seen in *impel*); cf. FELT, *n.*], 1. an iron or steel block on which metal objects are hammered into shape. 2. in *anatomy*, the incus, one of the three bones of the middle ear: see **ear,** illus.

ANVIL

anx·i·e·ty (aŋ-zī'ə-ti), ***n.*** [*pl.* ANXIETIES (-tiz)], [L. *anxietas* < *anxius;* see ANXIOUS], 1. a state of being uneasy, apprehensive, or worried about what may happen; misgiving. 2. a thought or thing that causes this. 3. an eager and often slightly worried desire: as, *anxiety* to do well. —***SYN.*** see **care.**

anx·ious (aŋk'shəs, aŋ'shəs), ***adj.*** [L. *anxius* < *angere*, to choke, give pain], 1. having anxiety or anxieties; uneasy; apprehensive. 2. causing anxiety. 3. eagerly wishing. —***SYN.*** see **eager.**

anxious seat, at American revival meetings, a bench near the preacher for those with a troubled conscience who seek salvation.

an·y (en'i), ***adj.*** [ME.; AS. *ænig, anig* < *an*, one; lit., *one* + *-y*], 1. one (no matter which) of more than two: as, *any* boy may go. 2. some (no matter how much, how many, or what kind): as, do you have *any* apples? 3. even one; the least amount or number of: as, I haven't *any* money. 4. every: as, *any* child can tell. ***pron. sing. & pl.*** any person or persons (of more than two); any amount or number. ***adv.*** to any degree or extent; at all: as, is he *any* better this morning?

an·y·bod·y (en'i-bud'i, en'i-bod'i), ***pron.*** 1. any person; anyone. 2. a person of fame, importance, etc.

an·y·how (en'i-hou'), ***adv.*** 1. in any manner or way. 2. at any rate; in any case. 3. haphazardly; carelessly.

an·y·one (en'i-wun'), ***pron.*** any person; anybody.

any one, 1. any single. 2. any single person or thing.

an·y·thing (en'i-thiŋ'), ***pron.*** [ME. *ani thing;* AS. *ænige thinga*, somehow; see ANY & THING], any thing; any event, fact, etc. ***n.*** a thing, no matter of what kind. ***adv.*** in any way; at all.

anything but, by no means; not at all.

an·y·way (en'i-wā'), ***adv.*** 1. in any manner or way. 2. at least; nevertheless. 3. haphazardly; carelessly.

an·y·ways (en'i-wāz'), ***adv.*** 1. in any way; at all. 2. [Colloq.], in any case; anyhow.

an·y·where (en'i-hwâr'), ***adv.*** 1. in any place; to any place. 2. [Colloq.], at all; to any extent.

anywhere from [Colloq.], any amount, rate, time, etc. between (stated limits): as, *anywhere from* five to ten dollars.

get anywhere, [Colloq.], to have any success.

an·y·wise (en'i-wīz'), ***adv.*** [AS. *ænige wisan;* see ANY & WISE, *n.*], in any manner or way; at all.

An·zac (an'zak), ***n.*** [an acrostic formed from the title], a soldier in the Australian and New Zealand Army Corps. ***adj.*** of the Anzacs.

An·zi·o (an'zi-ō', an'tsi-ō'; It. än'tsyô), ***n.*** a port in Italy, south of Rome: pop., 7,000: site of Allied beachhead in the invasion of Italy (January, 1944).

a/o, A/O., account of.

A one (ā' wun'), [orig. a designation of first-class ships, as in Lloyd's Register, *A* indicating the excellent condition of the hull, *1* that of the equipment], [Colloq.], first-class; first-rate; superior: also **A 1, A number 1.**

A·o·ran·gi (ä'ô-räŋ'gi), ***n.*** Mount Cook.

a·o·rist (ā'ə-rist), ***n.*** [Gr. *aoristos*, indefinite < *a-*, without + *horizein*, to define < *horos*, a limit], a past tense of Greek verbs, denoting an action without indicating whether completed, continued, or repeated. ***adj.*** designating or in this tense.

a·o·ris·tic (ā'ə-ris'tik), ***adj.*** 1. of or in the aorist. 2. indefinite.

a·or·ta (ā-ôr'tə), ***n.*** [*pl.* AORTAS (-təz), AORTAE (-tē)], [Mod. L.; Gr. *aortē* < *aeirein*, to raise, heave], the main artery of the body, carrying blood from the left ventricle of the heart to all organs and parts except the lungs: see **heart,** illus.

a·or·tic (ā-ôr'tik), ***adj.*** of the aorta.

a·ou·dad (ä'oo-dad'), ***n.*** [Fr.; Moorish *audad*], a wild North African sheep with large, curved horns and a heavy growth of hair from the throat to the knees.

‡à ou·trance (à'ōō'träns'), [Fr.], to the utmost; to the bitter end; to the death.

ap- (ap, əp), 1. ad-: used before *p*. 2. apo-.

AP, A.P., Ᵽ, Associated Press.

Ap., 1. Apostle. 2. April.

a·pace (ə-pās'), ***adv.*** [ME. *apas;* see A- (on) & PACE], at a fast pace; with speed; swiftly.

A·pach·e (ə-pach'i), ***n.*** [*pl.* APACHES (-iz), APACHE], [prob. < Zuñi *ápachu*, enemy], a member of a tribe of fierce, nomadic Athapascan Indians of northern Mexico and the southwestern United States.

a·pache (ə-päsh', ə-pash'; Fr. à'pàsh'), ***n.*** [*pl.* APACHES (-iz; Fr. à'pàsh'), APACHE], [Fr. < *Apache*], a gangster or thug of Paris. ***adj.*** designating a dance, performed as an exhibition in cabarets, etc., which represents an apache handling his girl in a brutal, masterful way.

Ap·a·lach·ee Bay (ap'ə-lach'i), a bay on the northwestern coast of Florida.

Ap·a·lach·i·co·la (ap'ə-lach'i-kō'lə), ***n.*** a river in Florida, flowing into the Gulf of Mexico: length, 90 mi.

a·pa·nage (ap'ə-nij), ***n.*** appanage.

‡a·pa·re·jo (ä'pä-re'hô), ***n.*** [*pl.* APAREJOS (-hôz)], [Sp.], a kind of packsaddle made of a stuffed leather pad.

A·par·ri (ä-pä'rē), ***n.*** a seaport in the Philippines, on Luzon: pop., 24,000.

a·part (ə-pärt'), ***adv.*** [ME. *apart;* OFr. *a part* < L. *ad*, to, at + *partem*, acc. of *pars*, a part, side], 1. to one side; at a little distance; aside. 2. separately or away in place or time. 3. away from one another. 4. separately or independently in function, use, etc.: as, viewed *apart*. 5. in or to pieces. ***adj.*** separated; not together: used predicatively.

apart from, other than; besides.

take apart, to reduce (a whole) to its parts.

a·part·heid (ə-pärt'hīt), ***n.*** [S. Afr. D., apartness], the policy of strict racial segregation and discrimination against the native Negroes and other colored peoples as practiced in the Union of South Africa.

a·part·ment (ə-pärt'mənt), ***n.*** [Fr. *appartement;* It. *appartamento;* see APART], 1. a room or suite of rooms to live in. 2. a room. 3. *pl.* [British], a suite of rooms to live in. ***adj.*** of, in, or for an apartment or apartments. Abbreviated **apt.**

apartment house, a building in which the rooms are arranged and rented as apartments.

ap·a·tet·ic (ap'ə-tet'ik), ***adj.*** [Gr. *apatētikos*, deceiving < *apatē*, deceit], in *zoology*, resembling the surroundings in color or form.

ap·a·thet·ic (ap'ə-thet'ik), ***adj.*** [< *apathy*, after *pathetic*], 1. feeling no emotion; unmoved. 2. not interested; indifferent; listless. —***SYN.*** see **impassive.**

ap·a·thet·i·cal·ly (ap'ə-thet'i-k'l-i, ap'ə-thet'ik-li), ***adv.*** in an apathetic manner.

ap·a·thy (ap'ə-thi), ***n.*** [*pl.* APATHIES (-thiz)], [Fr.

apathie; L. *apathia;* Gr. *apatheia* < *a-*, without + *pathos*, emotion < *pathein*, to feel], 1. lack of emotion. 2. lack of interest; listless condition; indifference.

ap·a·tite (ap′ə-tīt′), *n.* [< Gr. *apatē*, deceit; + *-ite;* so named from being mistaken for other minerals], a granular mineral, calcium fluophosphate, in varied colors of white, blue, green, brown, etc.

ape (āp), *n.* [ME.; AS. *apa;* akin to G. *affe;* orig. a non-IE. loan word], 1. a chimpanzee, gorilla, orang-utan, or gibbon; large, tailless monkey that can stand and walk in an almost erect position. 2. any monkey. 3. a person who imitates; mimic. *v.t.* [APED (āpt), APING], to imitate; mimic. —*SYN.* see **imitate.**

a·peak (ə-pēk′), *adv.* [*a-*, on + *peak*], in *nautical usage*, in a vertical or nearly vertical position.

A·pel·doorn (ä′pəl-dōrn′), *n.* a city in the central Netherlands: pop., 84,000 (1947).

A·pel·les (ə-pel′ēz), *n.* Greek painter; 4th century B.C.

Ap·en·nines (ap′ə-nīnz′), *n.pl.* a mountain range in central Italy: highest peak, Monte Corno, 9,560 ft.

‡a·per·çu (ä′pâr′sü′), *n.* [*pl.* APERÇUS (-sü′)], [Fr.], 1. a glance. 2. an insight. 3. a digest.

a·pe·ri·ent (ə-pêr′i-ənt), *adj. & n.* [L. *aperiens*, ppr. of *aperire;* see APERTURE], laxative. —*SYN.* see **physic.**

a·pe·ri·od·ic (ā′pêr-i-od′ik), *adj.* [*a-*, not + *periodic*], 1. not periodic; occurring irregularly. 2. in *physics*, without periodic vibrations.

‡a·pé·ri·tif (ä′pā′rē′tēf′), *n.* [Fr. < L. *apertus;* see APERTURE], an alcoholic drink taken before meals to stimulate the appetite.

a·per·i·tive (ə-per′ə-tiv), *adj. & n.* [after Fr. *apéritif;* see APÉRITIF], aperient.

ap·er·ture (ap′ẽr-chẽr), *n.* [L. *apertura* < *apertus*, pp. of *aperire*, to open < *ab-*, from + *perire*, to produce], 1. an opening; hole; gap. 2. the diameter of the opening in a camera, telescope, etc., through which light passes.

ap·er·y (āp′ẽr-i), *n.* [*pl.* APERIES (-iz)], [see APE], 1. an aping; mimicking. 2. an apish act.

a·pet·a·lous (ā-pet′'l-əs), *adj.* [*a-*, without + *petal* + *-ous*], without petals.

a·pex (ā′peks), *n.* [*pl.* APEXES (-pek-siz), APICES (ap′i-sēz′, ā′pi-sēz′)], [L., a point], 1. the highest point of anything; tip; peak; vertex. 2. the tip and contiguous portion of the blade of the tongue. 3. a climax. —*SYN.* see **summit.**

aph- (af), apo-, as in *aphesis.*

a·phaer·e·sis (ə-fer′ə-sis, a-fer′ə-sis), *n.* [L.; Gr. *aphairesis* < *aphairein*, to take away < *apo-*, away + *hairein*, to take], elimination of the first letter or syllable of a word (e.g., *bo* for *hobo*): also spelled **apheresis.**

aph·a·nite (af′ə-nīt′), *n.* [< Gr. *aphanēs*, invisible; + *-ite*], rock so closely grained that its individual crystals cannot be seen by the unaided eye.

a·pha·si·a (ə-fā′zhə, ə-fā′zhi-ə), *n.* [Mod. L.; Gr. *aphasia* < *aphatos*, unuttered; *a-*, not + *phatos* < *phanai*, to speak], a total or partial loss of the power to use or understand words, usually caused by brain disease or injury.

a·pha·si·ac (ə-fā′zi-ak′), *n.* a person who has aphasia.

a·pha·sic (ə-fā′zik), *adj.* of or having aphasia. *n.* an aphasiac.

a·phe·li·on (a-fē′li-ən, ə-fē′li-ən), *n.* [*pl.* APHELIONS (-ənz), APHELIA (-ə)], [< Gr. *apo*, from + *hēlios*, sun], the point farthest from the sun in the orbit of a planet or comet: cf. **perihelion.**

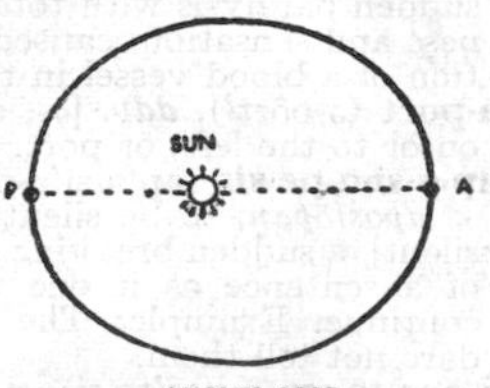

APHELION
Planet at aphelion A and at perihelion P

a·phe·li·ot·ro·pism (ə-fē′li-ot′rə-piz′m), *n.* [*ap-* + *heliotropism*], a tendency of certain plants to turn away from the sun.

a·pher·e·sis (ə-fer′ə-sis, a-fer′ə-sis), *n.* aphaeresis.

aph·e·sis (af′ə-sis), *n.* [Gr., a letting go < *apo*, from + *hienai*, to send], loss of a short unaccented syllable at the beginning of a word (e.g., *squire* for *esquire*): a form of aphaeresis.

a·phet·ic (ə-fet′ik), *adj.* of or characterized by aphesis.

a·phid (ā′fid, af′id), *n.* [Mod. L. *aphis*, pl. *aphides* (Linnaeus)], an insect that lives on plants by sucking their juice; plant louse.

a·phid·i·an (ə-fid′i-ən), *adj.* of aphids. *n.* an aphid.

a·phis (ā′fis, af′is), *n.* [*pl.* APHIDES (af′i-dēz′)], [Mod. L.], an aphid.

a·pho·ni·a (ə-fō′ni-ə), *n.* [Mod. L. < Gr. *aphōnia* < *aphōnos*, voiceless < *a-*, without + *phōnē*, sound, voice < *phanai*, to speak], loss of voice due to organic or psychic causes.

APHID
(winged and wingless phases, magnified)

a·phon·ic (ə-fon′ik), *adj.* [Gr. *aphōnos;* see APHONIA], 1. of or having aphonia. 2. in *phonetics*, not sounded; not pronounced.

aph·o·rism (af′ə-riz′m), *n.* [Fr. *aphorisme;* Gr. *aphorismos*, definition or short, pithy sentence < *aphorizein*, to divide, mark off < *apo-*, from + *horizein*, to bound < *horos*, boundary], 1. a short, concise statement of a principle. 2. a short, pointed sentence expressing a truth or precept; maxim; adage. —*SYN.* see **saying.**

aph·o·rist (af′ə-rist), *n.* a person who uses aphorisms.

aph·o·ris·tic (af′ə-ris′tik), *adj.* 1. of or like an aphorism. 2. full of aphorisms.

aph·o·ris·ti·cal·ly (af′ə-ris′ti-k'l-i), *adv.* in an aphoristic manner; pithily.

aph·o·rize (af′ə-rīz′), *v.i.* [APHORIZED (-rīzd′), APHORIZING], to write or speak in aphorisms.

a·pho·tic (ā-fō′tik), *adj.* [Gr. *aphōs, aphōtos; a-*, not + *phōs, phōtos*, light], without light.

aph·ro·dis·i·ac (af′rə-diz′i-ak′), *adj.* [Gr. *aphrodisiakos* < *Aphroditē*], arousing or increasing sexual desire. *n.* any aphrodisiac drug, food, or other agent.

Aph·ro·di·te (af′rə-dī′ti), *n.* [Gr. *Aphroditē*, the foam-born: said to be so named because supposed to have sprung from the sea (*aphros*, foam)], 1. in *Greek mythology*, the goddess of love and beauty, identified with Venus by the Romans. 2. [a-], a kind of butterfly.

aph·tha (af′thə), *n.* [*pl.* APHTHAE (-thē)], [L.; Gr. *aphtha* < *haptein*, to inflame], 1. thrush, a children's disease in which small, white, inflamed spots appear in the mouth. 2. *pl.* the spots or pustules of this disease.

a·phyl·lous (ə-fil′əs), *adj.* [Gr. *aphyllos* < *a-*, without + *phyllon*, a leaf], lacking leaves, as most cactuses.

A·pi·a (ä-pē′ä, ä′pē-ä′), *n.* a seaport of the Territory of Western Samoa, on Upolu Island.

a·pi·a·ceous (ā′pi-ā′shəs), *adj.* [< Mod. L. *apiaceae*, carrot family < L. *apium*, parsley, celery], of the carrot or parsnip family of plants; ammiaceous.

a·pi·an (ā′pi-ən), *adj.* [L. *apianus* < *apis*, bee], of a bee or bees.

a·pi·ar·i·an (ā′pi-âr′i-ən), *adj.* [< *apiary* + *-an*], having to do with bees or the care of bees. *n.* an apiarist.

a·pi·a·rist (ā′pi-ə-rist), *n.* [< *apiary* + *-ist*], a person who keeps bees.

a·pi·ar·y (ā′pi-er′i), *n.* [*pl.* APIARIES (-iz)], [L. *apiarium*, beehive < *apis*, bee], a place where bees are kept for their honey: it generally consists of a number of hives.

ap·i·cal (ap′i-k'l, ā′pi-k'l), *adj.* [< L. *apex, apicis*, tip, highest point], 1. of, at, or constituting the apex. 2. in *phonetics*, articulated with the apex of the tongue. *n.* a sound so articulated, as *t, d, s, l.*

ap·i·ces (ap′i-sēz′, ā′pi-sēz′), *n.* alternative plural of **apex.**

a·pic·u·late (ə-pik′yoo-lit, ə-pik′yoo-lāt′), *adj.* [LL. *apiculatus, apiculus*, dim. of L. *apex*, point], in *botany*, ending abruptly in a small point, as some leaves.

a·pi·cul·ture (ā′pi-kul′chẽr), *n.* [< L. *apis*, bee; + *culture*], the raising and care of bees; beekeeping.

a·piece (ə-pēs′), *adv.* [*a* + *piece*], to or for each; each.

‡à pied (á′pyā′), [Fr.], on foot; afoot.

a·pi·ol·o·gy (ā′pi-ol′ə-ji), *n.* [< L. *apis*, bee; + *-logy*], the scientific study of bees.

A·pis (ā′pis), *n.* [L. < Gr. < Egypt. *Hapi*], the sacred bull worshiped by the ancient Egyptians because of a supposed connection with the god Ptah.

ap·ish (āp′ish), *adj.* 1. like an ape. 2. stupidly imitative. 3. silly, affected, mischievous, etc.

a·piv·o·rous (ā-piv′ẽr-əs), *adj.* [< L. *apis*, bee; + *-vorous*], feeding on bees, as some birds.

a·pla·cen·tal (ā′plə-sen′t'l, ap′lə-sen′t'l), *adj.* in *zoology*, having no placenta, as the kangaroo.

ap·la·nat·ic (ap′lə-nat′ik), *adj.* [< *a-*, not + Gr. *planatikos*, wandering < *planan*, to stray], in *optics*, corrected for distortion, lack of sharpness, etc.: said of a lens.

ap·lite (ap′līt), *n.* [< Gr. *haploos*, simple; + *-ite*], a light-colored, finely grained granite made up largely of quartz and feldspar.

a·plomb (ə-plom′, ə-plôm′), *n.* [Fr., lit., perpendicularity; *à*, to + *plomb*, the metal lead; see PLUMB], self-possession; assurance; poise. —*SYN.* see **confidence.**

ap·ne·a, ap·noe·a (ap-nē′ə), *n.* [Mod. L. < Gr. *apnoia; a-*, without + *pnoiē, pnoia, pnoē*, wind], 1. temporary stopping of breathing. 2. asphyxia.

ap·o- (ap′ə), [< Gr. *apo*, off, from off], a prefix meaning: 1. *off, from, away from*, as in *apogamy.* 2. *detached*, as in *apocarp.* Also, before a vowel, **ap-.**

A.P.O., APO, Army Post Office.

Apoc., 1. Apocalypse. 2. Apocrypha. 3. Apocryphal.

a·poc·a·lypse (ə-pok′ə-lips′), *n.* [L. *apocalypsis;* Gr. *apokalypsis* < *apokalyptein*, to disclose; *apo-*, from + *kalyptein*, to cover], 1. [A-], the last book of the New Testament; book of Revelation. 2. a prophetic disclosure; revelation.

a·poc·a·lyp·tic (ə-pok′ə-lip′tik), *adj.* 1. of, like, or conveying a revelation. 2. having to do with the Apocalypse.

a·poc·a·lyp·ti·cal (ə-pok'ə-lip'ti-k'l), ***adj.*** apocalyptic.

ap·o·carp (ap'ə-kärp'), ***n.*** [*apo-* + *-carp*], a group of separate or partially joined carpels, as in the flower of the stonecrop, buttercup, etc.

a·po·car·pous (ap'ə-kär'pəs), ***adj.*** [*apo-* + *-carpous*], in *botany*, having separate or partially joined carpels.

ap·o·chro·mat·ic (ap'ə-krō-mat'ik), ***adj.*** [*apo-* + *chromatic*], in *optics*, more highly corrected than a chromatic lens.

a·poc·o·pate (ə-pok'ə-pāt'), ***v.t.*** [APOCOPATED (-id), APOCOPATING], [Mod. L. *apocopatus*, pp. of *apocopare*, to cut off < Gr. *apokopē*; see APOCOPE], to shorten by apocope. ***adj.*** (ə-pok'ə-pit), shortened by apocope.

a·poc·o·pe (ə-pok'ə-pi'), ***n.*** [Gr. *apokopē*, a cutting off < *apokoptein*, to cut off; *apo-*, from + *koptein*, to strike, cut off], the cutting off or dropping of the last sound, letter, or syllable of a word (e.g., *mos'* for *most*).

a·poc·ry·pha (ə-pok'rə-fə), ***n.pl.*** [LL., pl. of *apocryphus*; Gr. *apokryphos*, hidden, obscure < *apokryptein*; *apo-*, away + *kryptein*, to hide], 1. any writings, anecdotes, etc. of doubtful authenticity or authorship. 2. [A-], fourteen books of the Septuagint, regarded by Protestants as not canonical: they are not found in Hebrew and are entirely rejected in Judaism, but eleven of them are fully accepted in the Roman Catholic canon: abbreviated **Apoc.** 3. [A-], various writings falsely attributed to Biblical characters or kept out of the New Testament as not genuine.

a·poc·ry·phal (ə-pok'rə-f'l), ***adj.*** 1. of doubtful authorship or authenticity. 2. not genuine; spurious; counterfeit. 3. [A-], of or like the Apocrypha: abbreviated **Apoc.** —***SYN.*** see **fictitious.**

a·poc·y·na·ceous (ə-pos'ə-nā'shəs), ***adj.*** [< Mod. L. *Apocynaceae*, the dogbane family < Gr. *apokynon*, dogbane < *apo-*, from + *kyōn*, dog], of the dogbane family of plants, which are mainly tropical, with simple leaves and a milky, often poisonous juice.

ap·od (ap'əd), ***adj.*** apodal. ***n.*** an apodal bird, fish, or reptile.

ap·o·dal (ap'ə-d'l), ***adj.*** [Gr. *apous*, *apodos*, footless; *a-*, without + *pous*, foot; + *-al*], in *zoology*, 1. lacking feet. 2. lacking pelvic fins.

ap·o·deic·tic (ap'ə-dīk'tik), ***adj.*** apodictic.

ap·o·deic·ti·cal·ly (ap'ə-dīk'ti-k'l-i), ***adv.*** apodictically.

ap·o·dic·tic (ap'ə-dik'tik), ***adj.*** [L. *apodicticus*; Gr. *apodeiktikos*, proving clearly < *apodeiknynai*, to show by argument; *apo-*, from + *deiknynai*, to show], in *philosophy*, that can clearly be shown or proved; absolutely certain; necessarily true.

ap·o·dic·ti·cal·ly (ap'ə-dik'ti-k'l-i), ***adv.*** in an apodictic manner; by demonstrating conclusively.

a·pod·o·sis (ə-pod'ə-sis), ***n.*** [*pl.* APODOSES (-sēz')], [Gr., a giving back < *apo-*, back + *didonai*, to give], the clause expressing the conclusion or result in a conditional sentence: opposed to *protasis*.

ap·o·gam·ic (ap'ə-gam'ik), ***adj.*** of, or having the nature of, apogamy.

a·pog·a·my (ə-pog'ə-mi), ***n.*** [*apo-* + *-gamy*], the development of a plant without the union of sexual organs or cells; development of a sporophyte from a gametophyte without fertilization; apomixis.

ap·o·gee (ap'ə-jē'), ***n.*** [Fr. *apogée*; L. *apogaeum*; Gr. *apogaion* < *apo-*, from + *gaia*, *gē*, earth], 1. the point farthest from the earth in the orbit of the moon or of a man-made satellite: opposed to *perigee*: abbreviated **apo., apog.** 2. the highest or farthest point.

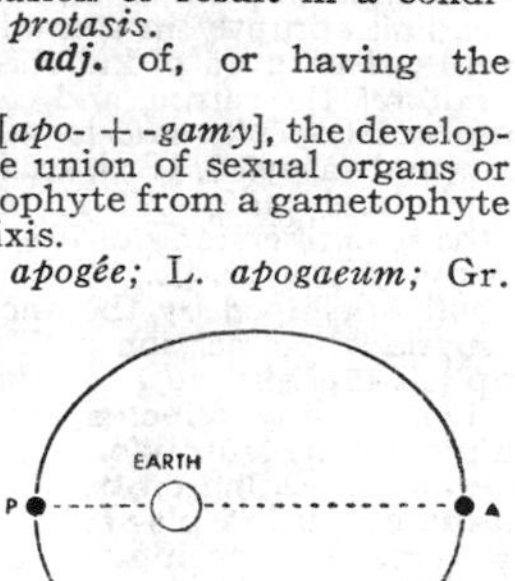

EARTH P A

APOGEE
Moon at apogee A and at perigee P

ap·o·ge·ot·ro·pism (ap'ə-ji-ot'rə-piz'm), ***n.*** [*apo-* + *geotropism*], a tendency to grow or move away from the earth, or from the pull of gravity, found in some roots, leaves, etc.

‡à point (à'pwan'), [Fr., to (the) point], 1. at the opportune moment; just in time. 2. just sufficiently.

A·pol·lo (ə-pol'ō), [L.; Gr. *Apollōn*], 1. in *Greek & Roman mythology*, the god of music, poetry, prophecy, and medicine, later identified with Helios, a sun god: Apollo was represented as the type of manly youth and beauty; hence, 2. any handsome young man.

A·pol·lyon (ə-pol'yən), ***n.*** [Gr. *apollyōn*, destroying, ruining < *apollynai*, *apolluein*, to destroy < *apo-*, from + *lyein*, to loose], 1. the angel of the bottomless pit; the Devil; Satan: Rev. 9:11. 2. an evil spirit subdued by the hero, Christian, of Bunyan's *Pilgrim's Progress*.

a·pol·o·get·ic (ə-pol'ə-jet'ik), ***adj.*** [Fr. *apologétique*; L. *apologeticus*; Gr. *apologētikos*, suitable for defense < *apologeisthai*; see APOLOGY], 1. that apologizes; showing realization of and regret for a fault, wrong, etc.; making conciliatory excuses. 2. defending in writing or speech. ***n.*** a formal defense, often written, of a belief, cause, etc.

a·pol·o·get·i·cal (ə-pol'ə-jet'i-k'l), ***adj.*** apologetic.

a·pol·o·get·ics (ə-pol'ə-jet'iks), ***n.pl.*** [construed as sing.], [see APOLOGETIC], the branch of theology having to do with the defense and proofs of Christianity.

ap·o·lo·gi·a (ap'ə-lō'ji-ə), ***n.*** [L.; Gr.; see APOLOGY], an apology (chiefly in sense 1).

a·pol·o·gist (ə-pol'ə-jist), ***n.*** [Fr. *apologiste*; see APOLOGY], a person who writes or speaks in defense or justification of a doctrine, faith, action, etc.

a·pol·o·gize (ə-pol'ə-jīz'), ***v.i.*** [APOLOGIZED (-jīzd'), APOLOGIZING], 1. to make an apology (*for* something or someone); acknowledge and express regret for a fault, wrong, etc. 2. to make a formal defense in speech or writing.

ap·o·logue (ap'ə-lôg', ap'ə-log'), ***n.*** [Fr.; L. *apologus*; Gr. *apologos*], a short allegorical story with a lesson or moral; fable.

a·pol·o·gy (ə-pol'ə-ji), ***n.*** [*pl.* APOLOGIES (-jiz)], [L. *apologia*; Gr. *apologia*, a speaking in defense < *apo-*, from + *logos*, word], 1. a formal spoken or written defense; argument to show that some idea, religion, etc. is right. 2. an acknowledging and expressing regret for a fault, injury, insult, etc.; asking a person's pardon. 3. a makeshift; inferior article or substitute: as, he is a sorry *apology* for an actor.

ap·o·mix·is (ap'ə-mik'sis), ***n.*** [Mod. L. < Gr. *apo*, from + *mixis*, a mingling], apogamy.

ap·o·mor·phine (ap'ə-môr'fēn, ap'ə-môr'fin), ***n.*** [*apo-* + *morphine*], a crystalline alkaloid, $C_{17}H_{17}NO_2$, produced by synthesis from morphine: used as an emetic.

ap·o·neu·ro·sis (ap'ə-nyoo-rō'sis), ***n.*** [*pl.* APONEUROSES (-sēz)], [Gr. *aponeurōsis* < *apo-*, from + *neuron*, a nerve], a fibrous membrane that covers certain muscles and connects them with tendons.

ap·o·pemp·tic (ap'ə-pemp'tik), ***adj.*** [< Gr. *apopemptikos* < *apopemptein*, to send off], of farewell or leave-taking; valedictory: as, an *apopemptic* song.

a·poph·a·sis (ə-pof'ə-sis), ***n.*** [Mod. L.; Gr. *apophasis*, denial < *apophanai*, to deny], the act of mentioning something by saying that it will not be mentioned. Example: We will not remind you of his many crimes.

ap·o·phthegm (ap'ə-them'), ***n.*** an apothegm.

a·poph·y·ge (ə-pof'ə-jē'), ***n.*** [Gr. *apophygē* < *apopheugein*, to flee away; *apo-*, from + *pheugein*, to flee], in *architecture*, the concave curve where the end of a column spreads into its base or capital.

a·poph·yl·lite (ə-pof'ə-līt', ap'ə-fil'īt), ***n.*** [< *apo-* + Gr. *phyllon*, a leaf; + *-ite*], a mineral, hydrous potassium calcium silicate, found in square, transparent prisms or grayish-white, layerlike masses.

a·poph·y·sis (ə-pof'ə-sis), ***n.*** [*pl.* APOPHYSES (-sēz')], [Mod. L.; Gr. *apophysis*, an offshoot < *apo-*, from + *phyein*, to grow], 1. in *anatomy*, a natural outgrowth or process on a vertebra or other bone. 2. in *botany*, a swelling at the base of the capsule in some mosses.

ap·o·plec·tic (ap'ə-plek'tik), ***adj.*** [Gr. *apoplēktikos* < *apoplēktos*, stricken, disabled by a stroke], 1. of, like, or causing apoplexy. 2. having apoplexy. 3. likely to have apoplexy; liable to apoplexy: as, he was *apoplectic* with rage. ***n.*** a person having or liable to have apoplexy.

ap·o·plec·ti·cal (ap'ə-plek'ti-k'l), ***adj.*** apoplectic.

ap·o·plex·y (ap'ə-plek'si), ***n.*** [OFr. *apoplexie*; L. *apoplexia*; Gr. *apoplēxia* < *apoplēssein*, to strike down, disable by a stroke; *apo-*, from + *plēssein*, to strike], sudden paralysis with total or partial loss of consciousness and sensation, caused by the breaking or obstruction of a blood vessel in the brain.

a·port (ə-pôrt'), ***adv.*** [*a-*, on + *port*], in *nautical usage*, on or to the left, or port, side.

ap·o·si·o·pe·sis (ap'ə-sī'ə-pē'sis), ***n.*** [L.; Gr. *aposiōpēsis* < *aposiōpan*, to be silent; *apo-*, from + *siōpan*, to be silent], a sudden breaking off of a thought in the middle of a sentence as if one were unable or unwilling to continue. Example: The horrors I saw there—but I dare not tell them.

a·pos·ta·sy (ə-pos'tə-si), ***n.*** [*pl.* APOSTASIES (-siz)], [ME. *apostasie*; L. *apostasia*; Gr. *apostasia* < *apo-*, away + *stasis*, a standing], an abandoning of what one believed in, as a faith, political party, principles, etc.

a·pos·tate (ə-pos'tāt, ə-pos'tit), ***n.*** [ME.; OFr.; L. *apostata*; Gr. *apostatēs* < *apostēnai*, to revolt, stand off; *apo-*, from + *stēnai*, to stand], a person guilty of apostasy; renegade. ***adj.*** guilty of apostasy.

a·pos·ta·tize (ə-pos'tə-tīz'), ***v.i.*** [APOSTATIZED (-tīzd'), APOSTATIZING], [ML. *apostatizare* < L. *apostata*; see APOSTATE], to be an apostate; abandon one's faith, political party, etc.

a pos·te·ri·o·ri (ā' pos-têr'i-ō'rī, ā' pos-têr'i-ôr'ī), [L., from what comes later; *a*, from + *posteriori*, abl. of *posterior*, compar. of *posterius*, subsequent, following], 1. from effect to cause, or from particular instances to a generalization; inductively. 2. of such reasoning; inductive. 3. based on observation or experience; empirical. Opposed to *a priori*.

a·pos·til, a·pos·tille (ə-pos'til), ***n.*** [Fr. *apostille*], a note, especially one in the margin.

a·pos·tle, A·pos·tle (ə-pos''l), ***n.*** [ME. *apostel*; AS. *apostol*; L. *apostolus*; Gr. *apostolos*, a person sent forth < *apostellein*; *apo-*, from + *stellein*, to send], 1. [usually A-], any of the twelve disciples sent out by Christ to teach the gospel: originally, Andrew, Bartholomew,

James (the younger, son of Alphaeus), James (the elder) and John (sons of Zebedee), Jude (or Lebbaeus or Thaddaeus), Judas Iscariot, Matthew (or Levi), Philip, Simon the Canaanite, Simon (called Peter), and Thomas (or Didymus). Paul, the "Apostle to the Gentiles," was not among the original twelve. Judas was replaced by Matthias. 2. [usually a-], a person sent out on a special mission or as a preacher. 3. the first Christian missionary in any country or place. 4. any early Christian missionary or leader. 5. an early advocate or leader of a new principle or movement, especially one aimed at reform. 6. any of the twelve administrative officials of the Mormon Church.

Apostles' Creed, an old statement of belief in the basic Christian doctrines, formerly supposed to have been composed by the Twelve Apostles: it begins, "I believe in God the Father Almighty . . . ."

a·pos·to·late (ə-pos′t'l-it, ə-pos′t'l-āt′), ***n.*** [L. *apostolatus* < *apostolus;* see APOSTLE], the office, duties, or period of activity of an apostle.

ap·os·tol·ic (ap′əs-tol′ik), ***adj.*** [L. *apostolicus;* Gr. *apostolikos* < *apostolos;* see APOSTLE], 1. of an apostle. 2. of the Apostles, their teachings, work, or times. 3. according to the Apostles' faith or teaching. 4. [often A-], of the Pope; papal.

ap·os·tol·i·cal (ap′əs-tol′i-k'l), ***adj.*** apostolic.

Apostolic Fathers, 1. a group of early Christians, contemporaries of the apostles, regarded as the fathers of the Christian church. 2. a collection of writings attributed to them.

apostolic see, 1. a see, or bishopric, founded by an apostle. 2. [A- S-], in the *Roman Catholic Church,* the Pope's see, reputedly founded at Rome by Peter.

apostolic succession, the doctrine that the religious authority and mission conferred by Jesus on Saint Peter and the other Apostles have come down through an unbroken succession of bishops (in the *Roman Catholic Church,* bishops of Rome, or Popes).

a·pos·tro·phe (ə-pos′trə-fi), ***n.*** [L.; Gr. *apostrophē,* a turning away from the audience to address one person < *apostrephein; apo-,* from + *strephein,* to turn], words addressed to a person or thing, whether absent or present, generally in an exclamatory tone and as a digression in a speech or literary writing.

a·pos·tro·phe (ə-pos′trə-fi), ***n.*** [Fr.; L. *apostrophus;* Gr. *apostrophos* < same base as prec. *apostrophe*], the sign (') used: 1. to show the omission of a letter or letters from a word (e.g., *it's* for *it is, o'* for *of*). 2. to indicate the possessive case of English nouns and some pronouns (e.g., *Mary's* dress, the *girls'* club, *one's* duty): originally the apostrophe showed the omission of *e* in the inflectional ending of this case. 3. in forming some plurals, as of figures and letters (e.g., five *6's,* dot the *i's*).

ap·os·troph·ic (ap′ə-strof′ik), ***adj.*** of or using rhetorical apostrophe or a grammatical apostrophe.

a·pos·tro·phize (ə-pos′trə-fiz′), ***v.t. & v.i.*** [APOSTROPHIZED (-fizd′), APOSTROPHIZING], to speak or write an apostrophe or apostrophes (to): as, Wordsworth *apostrophized* John Milton in the sonnet beginning "Milton! thou should'st be living at this hour."

apothecaries' measure, a system of liquid measure used in pharmacy. In the United States:

60 minims (♏) = 1 fluid dram (f℥)
8 fluid drams = 1 fluid ounce (f℥)
16 fluid ounces = 1 pint
8 pints = 1 gallon (231 cubic inches)

In Great Britain:

60 minims = 1 fluid dram
8 fluid drams = 1 fluid ounce
20 fluid ounces = 1 pint
8 pints = 1 gallon (277.724 cubic inches)

apothecaries' weight, a system of weights used in pharmacy:

20 grains = 1 scruple
3 scruples = 1 dram
8 drams = 1 ounce
12 ounces = 1 pound

a·poth·e·car·y (ə-poth′ə-ker′i), ***n.*** [*pl.* APOTHECARIES (-iz)], [ME. *apothecarie;* OFr. *apotecaire;* LL. *apothecarius* < L. *apotheca;* Gr. *apothēkē,* storehouse < *apotithenai; apo-,* away + *tithenai,* to put], a person who makes and sells (and formerly also prescribed) drugs and medical preparations; druggist; pharmacist.

ap·o·the·ci·um (ap′ə-thē′shi-əm, ap′ə-thē′si-əm), ***n.*** [*pl.* APOTHECIA (-ə)], [Mod. L.; Gr. **apothēkion,* dim. of *apothēkē;* see APOTHECARY], in *botany,* an open, cuplike structure containing sacs in which sexual spores are developed, as in lichens and certain fungi.

ap·o·thegm (ap′ə-them′), ***n.*** [Fr. *apophthegme;* Gr. *apophthegma,* a terse, pointed saying < *apophthengesthai; apo-,* from + *phthengesthai,* to cry out, utter], a short, terse saying; maxim: also **apophthegm.** Example: "Brevity is the soul of wit."

ap·o·theg·mat·ic (ap′ə-theg-mat′ik), ***adj.*** of, containing, or using apothegms; sententious.

ap·o·them (ap′ə-them′), ***n.*** [*apo-* + Gr. *thema,* that which is placed < *tithenai,* to place], in *mathematics,* the perpendicular from the center of a regular polygon to any one of its sides.

a·poth·e·o·sis (ə-poth′i-ō′sis, ap′ə-thē′ə-sis), ***n.*** [*pl.* APOTHEOSES (-sēz, -sēz′)], [L.; Gr. *apotheōsis* < *apotheoun,* to deify < *apo-,* from + *theos,* a god], 1. the act of making a god of a person; attributing of divinity to a human being; deification. 2. the glorification of a person or thing. 3. a glorified ideal.

a·poth·e·o·size (ə-poth′i-ə-sīz′, ap′ə-thē′ə-sīz′), ***v.t.*** [APOTHEOSIZED (-sīzd′), APOTHEOSIZING], [< *apotheosis* + *-ize*], 1. to make into a god; raise to godhood; deify. 2. to glorify; idealize.

app., 1. appended. 2. appendix. 3. appointed. 4. apprentice.

ap·pal (ə-pôl′), ***v.t.*** [APPALLED (-pôld′), APPALLING], to appall.

Ap·pa·la·chi·an (ap′ə-lā′chi-ən, ap′ə-lach′ən), ***adj.*** of the Appalachian Mountains.

Appalachian Mountains, a mountain system in eastern North America, extending from southern Quebec, Canada, to northern Alabama: length, 1,500 mi.; highest peak, Mount Mitchell, North Carolina, 6,711 ft.

Ap·pa·la·chi·ans (ap′ə-lā′chi-ənz, ap′ə-lach′ənz), ***n.pl.*** the Appalachian Mountains.

Appalachian tea, a plant with clusters of white flowers, variously colored berries, and finely toothed leaves used for tea: also called *withe rod.*

ap·pall (ə-pôl′), ***v.t.*** [ME. *appallen;* OFr. *apallir,* to grow pale < *a-,* to + *pale;* see PALE, PALLID], to horrify; shock; dismay: also spelled **appal.** —***SYN.*** see **dismay.**

ap·pal·ling (ə-pôl′iŋ), ***adj.*** [ppr. of *appall*], horrifying; shocking; causing dismay.

ap·pa·nage, ap·a·nage (ap′ə-nij), ***n.*** [Fr. *apanage* < OFr. *apaner* < L. *ad,* to + *panis,* bread], 1. money, land, etc. given by kings and princes to their younger children as a means of support; hence, 2. a person's rightful extra gain; perquisite. 3. any territory governed by another country; dependency. 4. an accompanying endowment; adjunct.

appar., apparently.

ap·pa·ra·tus (ap′ə-rā′təs, ap′ə-rat′əs), ***n.*** [*pl.* APPARATUS, APPARATUSES (-iz)], [L., a making ready, preparation < *apparare* < *ad-,* to + *parare,* to prepare], 1. the instruments, materials, tools, etc. needed for a specific use, experiment, etc. 2. any set of standards or values for judging, measuring, or testing. 3. the notes, indexes, glossaries, etc. of a scholarly edition, especially of an edition of a text. 4. any complex device or machine. 5. in *physiology,* a set of organs for a specific function: as, the digestive *apparatus.*

ap·par·el (ə-par′əl), ***n.*** [ME. *appareil;* OFr. *apareil,* preparation < *apareiller,* to prepare; *a-,* to + *pareiller,* to put like things together < L. **pariculus,* like, similar; ult. < *par,* equal], 1. clothing; garments; attire. 2. anything that clothes or adorns: as, the white *apparel* of winter. 3. in *nautical usage,* a ship's outfit or furnishings, as rigging, anchor, guns, etc. ***v.t.*** [APPARELED or APPARELLED (-əld), APPARELING or APPARELLING], to clothe; dress.

ap·par·ent (ə-par′ənt, ə-pâr′ənt), ***adj.*** [ME.; OFr. *aparant* < L. *apparens,* ppr. of *apparere;* see APPEAR], 1. visible; readily seen. 2. readily understood; evident; obvious. 3. appearing (but not necessarily) real or true; seeming. See also **heir apparent.** —***SYN.*** see **evident.**

ap·par·ent·ly (ə-par′ənt-li, ə-pâr′ənt-li), ***adv.*** [*apparent* + *-ly*], 1. plainly; clearly; obviously. 2. seemingly; to all appearances. Abbreviated **appar.**

ap·pa·ri·tion (ap′ə-rish′ən), ***n.*** [Fr.; L. *apparitio,* attendants, service < *apparere,* to attend, appear], 1. anything that appears, especially suddenly or unexpectedly; hence, 2. a ghost; phantom. 3. an appearing or becoming apparent.

ap·par·i·tor (ə-par′ə-tẽr, ə-pâr′ə-tẽr), ***n.*** [L. < *apparere;* see APPEAR], 1. formerly, an officer who carried out the orders of a civil court. 2. an officer of a church court who serves summonses, etc.

ap·pas·si·o·na·ta (ə-pä′si-ə-nä′tə), ***adj.*** [It.], in *music,* impassioned.

ap·peal (ə-pēl′), ***v.t.*** [ME. *appelen, apelen;* Fr. *appeler;* L. *appellare,* to accost, apply to, appeal; iterative < *appellere,* to prepare < *ad-,* to + *pellere;* see COMPEL], 1. [Archaic], to accuse. 2. to make an appeal of (a law case, etc.). ***v.i.*** 1. to make or ask for an appeal in a law case. 2. to make an urgent request (*to* a person *for* a decision, opinion, help, sympathy, etc.). 3. to resort; turn. 4. to be attractive, interesting, etc.; arouse a favorable response: as, his argument *appealed* to me. ***n.*** [Fr. *apel;* see the *v.*], 1. a call upon some authority or person for a decision, opinion, etc. 2. an urgent request for help, sympathy, etc. 3. a quality that arouses sympathetic response; interest; attraction. 4. [Archaic], an accusation. 5. in *law, a)* the transference of a case to a higher court for rehearing. *b)* a request for this. *c)* the right to this. *d)* a case thus transferred.

SYN.—**appeal** implies an earnest, sometimes urgent request for something and in legal usage connotes resort to a higher court or authority; **plead**, applied to formal statements in court answering to allegations or charges, carries into general usage the implication of entreaty by argument (he *pleaded* for tolerance); **sue** implies respectful or formal solicitation for relief, a favor, etc.; **petition** implies a formal request, usually in writing and in accordance with established rights; **pray** and **supplicate** suggest humility in entreaty and imply that the request is addressed to God or to a superior authority, **supplicate** in addition suggesting a kneeling or other abjectly prayerful attitude.

ap·peal·a·ble (ə-pēl′ə-b'l), *adj.* 1. that can be appealed against or to. 2. that can be appealed to a higher court.

ap·pear (ə-pêr′), *v.i.* [ME. *aperen;* OFr. *aparoir;* L. *apparere* < *ad-*, to + *parere*, to come forth, be visible], 1. to come into sight. 2. to be in sight. 3. to become understood. 4. to seem; look. 5. to be said in a piece of writing. 6. to present oneself formally in court as attorney, plaintiff, etc. 7. to come before the public: as, he will *appear* in *Hamlet.* 8. to be published.

ap·pear·ance (ə-pêr′əns), *n.* [ME. *apparence;* OFr. *apparence;* L. *apparentia* < ppr. of *apparere;* see APPEAR], 1. an appearing. 2. the look or outward aspect of anything. 3. anything that appears; thing seen. 4. an apparition. 5. a pretense or show: as, he gave the *appearance* of being busy.

keep up appearances, to maintain an outward show of what is proper, decorous, etc.

make an appearance, 1. to put in an appearance. 2. to appear publicly.

put in an appearance, to be present for a short time, as at a party, meeting, etc.

SYN.—**appearance** and **look** refer generally to the outward impression of a thing, but the former often implies mere show or pretense (an *appearance* of honesty), and the latter (often in the plural) refers specifically to physical details (the *look* of an abandoned house, good *looks*); **aspect** also refers to physical details, especially to facial features or expression (a man of handsome *aspect*) or to the distinguishing features at a given time or place (in spring the yard had a refreshing *aspect*); **semblance**, which also refers to the outward impression as contrasted with the inner reality, usually does not imply deception (a *semblance* of order); **guise** is usually used of a deliberately misleading appearance (under the *guise* of patriotism).

ap·peas·a·ble (ə-pēz′ə-b'l), *adj.* that can be appeased.

ap·pease (ə-pēz′), *v.t.* [APPEASED (-pēzd′), APPEASING], [ME. *apaisen;* OFr. *apaisier* < *a-*, to + *pais*, peace < L. *pax, pacis*, peace], 1. to pacify or quiet, especially by giving in to the demands of. 2. to satisfy or relieve: as, water *appeases* thirst. —*SYN.* see **pacify.**

ap·pease·ment (ə-pēz′mənt), *n.* 1. an appeasing or being appeased. 2. the policy of giving in to the demands of a hostile or dangerous power in an attempt to prevent trouble.

‡**ap·pel** (å′pel′), *n.* [Fr., lit., an appeal, call < *appeler;* see APPEAL], in *fencing*, a quick tap with the foot, originally to warn one's opponent of a thrust.

ap·pel·lant (ə-pel′ənt), *adj.* [Fr. < ppr. of *appeler;* see APPEAL], in *law*, relating to appeals; appealing. *n.* a person who appeals, especially to a higher court.

ap·pel·late (ə-pel′it), *adj.* [L. *appellatus*, pp. of *appellare;* see APPEAL], in *law*, 1. appealed to. 2. appellant.

appellate court, a court that has the power to review appeals and reverse the decisions of lower courts.

ap·pel·la·tion (ap′ə-lā′shən), *n.* [L. *appellatio* < pp. of *appellare;* see APPEAL], 1. the act of calling by a name; naming. 2. a name; title; designation.

ap·pel·la·tive (ə-pel′ə-tiv), *adj.* [L. *appellativus* < pp. of *appellare;* see APPEAL], 1. having to do with the giving of names; naming. 2. in *grammar*, relating to a common noun. *n.* 1. a name; title. 2. in *grammar*, a common noun.

ap·pel·lee (ap′ə-lē′), *n.* [Fr. *appelé*, pp. of *appeler;* see APPEAL], in *law*, a person appealed against; defendant in an appeal.

ap·pel·lor (ə-pel′ôr, ap′ə-lôr′), *n.* [Anglo-Fr. *apelour;* OFr. *apeleor;* L. *appellator*, one who appeals < *appellare;* see APPEAL], in *law*, a person who carries an appeal to a higher court.

ap·pend (ə-pend′), *v.t.* [Fr. *appendre;* L. *appendere* < *ad-*, to + *pendere*, to suspend], to attach; affix; add as a supplement or appendix.

ap·pend·age (ə-pen′dij), *n.* [*append* + *-age*], 1. anything appended; adjunct. 2. in *biology*, any subordinate or external organ or part, as a leg, tail, etc.

ap·pend·ant, ap·pend·ent (ə-pen′dənt), *adj.* [Fr., ppr. of *appendre;* see APPEND], 1. attached; added. 2. attendant; consequent. 3. in *law*, belonging to as a subsidiary right. *n.* 1. an appendage. 2. in *law*, a subsidiary right attached to a major one.

ap·pen·dec·to·my (ap′ən-dek′tə-mi), *n.* [*pl.* APPENDECTOMIES (-miz)], [*appendix* + *-ectomy*], the surgical removal of the vermiform appendix.

ap·pen·di·ces (ə-pen′də-sēz′), *n.* alternative plural of **appendix.**

ap·pen·di·ci·tis (ə-pen′də-sī′tis), *n.* [< *appendix* + *-itis*], inflammation of the vermiform appendix.

ap·pen·di·cle (ə-pen′di-k'l), *n.* [L. *appendicula*, dim. of *appendix*], a small appendage or appendix.

ap·pen·dix (ə-pen′diks), *n.* [*pl.* APPENDIXES (-dik-siz), APPENDICES (-də-sēz′)], [L., appendage < *appendere;* see APPEND], 1. additional or supplementary material at the end of a book. 2. in *anatomy*, an outgrowth of an organ; especially, the vermiform appendix, a small, saclike appendage of the large intestine: see **alimentary canal**, illus. Abbreviated **app.**

ap·per·ceive (ap′ẽr-sēv′), *v.t.* [ME. *aperceiven;* OFr. *aperceivre* < L. *ad*, to + *percipere;* see PERCEIVE], 1. to interpret (new ideas, impressions, etc.) by the help of past experience. 2. [Obs.], to perceive.

ap·per·cep·tion (ap′ẽr-sep′shən), *n.* [Fr. *aperception* < *apercevoir*, to perceive < L. *ad*, to + *percipere;* see PERCEIVE], 1. perception. 2. an apperceiving. 3. in *metaphysics*, the mind's being conscious of its consciousness.

ap·per·cep·tive (ap′ẽr-sep′tiv), *adj.* relating to apperception; perceptive.

ap·per·tain (ap′ẽr-tān′), *v.i.* [ME. *appertienen;* OFr. *apertenir;* L. *appertinere* < *ad-*, to + *pertinere;* see PERTAIN], to belong as a function, part, etc.; relate; pertain.

ap·pe·tence (ap′ə-təns), *n.* appetency.

ap·pe·ten·cy (ap′ə-tən-si), *n.* [*pl.* APPETENCIES (-siz)], [L. *appetentia*, a longing after < ppr. of *appetere;* see APPETITE], 1. a strong desire; craving; appetite. 2. an instinctive tendency; propensity. 3. an attraction between things; affinity.

ap·pe·tite (ap′ə-tīt′), *n.* [ME. & OFr. *appetit;* L. *appetitus*, eager desire for < *appetere*, to strive after < *ad-*, to + *petere*, to seek], 1. a desire; craving. 2. a desire for food in general or for some specific food.

ap·pe·tiz·er (ap′ə-tīz′ẽr), *n.* a thing that stimulates the appetite; small portion of tasty food or a drink at the beginning of a meal to stimulate the appetite.

ap·pe·tiz·ing (ap′ə-tīz′iŋ), *adj.* 1. stimulating the appetite. 2. savory; delicious.

Ap·pi·an Way (ap′i-ən), [after the Roman censor *Appius* Claudius Caecus, by whom it was begun c. 312 B.C.], an ancient Roman military road, about 365 miles long, from Rome to Capua to Brindisi.

ap·plaud (ə-plôd′), *v.t. & v.i.* [L. *applaudere* < *ad-*, to + *plaudere*, to clap hands, strike], 1. to show approval (of) by clapping the hands or by cheering, stamping the feet, etc. 2. to praise; approve; commend.

ap·plause (ə-plôz′), *n.* [L. *applausus*, pp. of *applaudere;* see APPLAUD], approval or praise, especially as shown by clapping hands, cheering, etc.

ap·ple (ap′'l), *n.* [ME. *appel;* AS. *æppel*, fruit, apple; also, eyeball, anything round; akin to Crimean Goth. *apel;* the word appears also in OIr. *aball* (W. *afall*), apple tree & L. *Abella*, name of a Campanian town], 1. a round, firm, fleshy, edible fruit with a green, yellow, or red skin and small seeds. 2. the tree it grows on, widely distributed in temperate regions. 3. any of various somewhat similar plants, fruits, or fruitlike growths, as the May apple, love apple, etc.

apple butter, a kind of jam made from apples stewed with spices.

apple cart, a huckster's handcart, usually with two wheels, for selling apples in the street, etc.

upset the (or **one's**) **apple cart**, to disrupt a procedure, spoil one's plans, etc.

apple green, a clear yellowish green.

ap·ple·jack (ap′'l-jak′), *n.* [*apple* + *jack;* see JACK (nickname)], apple brandy; alcoholic drink made from apple cider.

apple of discord, 1. in *Greek mythology*, a golden apple marked "For the most beautiful," claimed by Athena, Hera, and Aphrodite, and awarded by Paris to Aphrodite: in return, she helped him to get the beautiful Helen, thus starting the Trojan War; hence, 2. anything causing trouble, discord, or jealousy.

apple of one's eye, 1. the pupil of one's eye; hence, 2. any thing or person that one cherishes.

ap·ple-pie order (ap′'l-pī′), [Colloq.], neat order; good condition.

apple polisher, [Slang], a person who curries favor by gifts, flattery, etc., as a child bringing his teacher an apple.

ap·ple·sauce (ap′'l-sôs′), *n.* 1. a dessert or relish made of apples cut into pieces, sweetened, and cooked to a pulp in water. 2. [Slang], nonsense; hokum.

Ap·ple·ton (ap′'l-tən), *n.* a city in eastern Wisconsin: pop., 48,000.

Ap·ple·ton layer (ap′'l-tən), [after E. V. *Appleton* (1892–), Eng. scientist], a stratum of electrically charged air in the Heaviside layer.

ap·pli·ance (ə-plī′əns), *n.* 1. [Rare], an applying or being applied. 2. a device or machine, especially for household use. —*SYN.* see **implement.**

ap·pli·ca·bil·i·ty (ap′li-kə-bil′ə-ti), *n.* the quality of being applicable.

ap·pli·ca·ble (ap′li-kə-b'l), *adj.* [< L. *applicare* (see APPLY); + *-able*], that can be applied; appropriate. —*SYN.* see **relevant.**

ap·pli·cant (ap′li-kənt), *n.* [< L. *applicans*, ppr. of *applicare;* see APPLY], a person who applies, as for employment, help, etc.

ap·pli·ca·tion (ap'li-kā'shən), *n.* [Fr.; L. *applicatio,* a binding on, joining to < pp. of *applicare;* see APPLY], 1. an applying or being applied. 2. the act of putting something on: as, the *application* of cosmetics. 3. a putting to use. 4. anything applied, especially a remedy. 5. a way of applying; method of using. 6. a requesting. 7. a request: as, an *application* for employment. 8. a form to be filled out with pertinent data in applying for something, as for employment. 9. continued mental or physical exertion; diligence. 10. relevance: as, this idea has no *application* to the case.

ap·pli·ca·tive (ap'li-kā'tiv), *adj.* applying or capable of being applied, as to some practical use; applicatory.

ap·pli·ca·tor (ap'li-kā'tēr), *n.* [< L. *applicatus* (see APPLICATION); + *-or*], any device for applying or inserting medicine, etc.

ap·pli·ca·to·ry (ap'li-kə-tôr'i, ap'li-ki-tō'ri), *adj.* applying; suitable for practical use.

ap·plied (ə-plīd'), *adj.* [pp. of *apply*], used in actual practice or to work out practical problems: as, *applied* science: distinguished from *pure, abstract, theoretical.*

ap·pli·er (ə-plī'ēr), *n.* a person or thing that applies.

ap·pli·qué (ap'li-kā'), *adj.* [Fr.], applied or fastened on: said of one material attached by sewing, etc. to another. *n.* any decoration or trimming of this kind. *v.t.* [APPLIQUÉD (-kād'), APPLIQUÉING], 1. to decorate with appliqué. 2. to put on as appliqué.

ap·ply (ə-plī'), *v.t.* [APPLIED (-plīd'), APPLYING], [ME. *applien;* OFr. *aplier* < L. *applicare,* to attach to < *ad-,* to + *plicare,* to fold], 1. to put on; place so as to be touching or close: as, *apply* glue to the surface. 2. to use practically or specifically: as, *apply* your knowledge to the problem. 3. to refer to a person or thing with (an epithet or suitable term). 4. to concentrate (one's faculties) on; employ (oneself) diligently: as, he *applied* himself to his work. *v.i.* 1. to make a request (*to* someone *for* something). 2. to be appropriate, suitable, or relevant: as, this principle always *applies.*

ap·pog·gia·tu·ra (ə-poj'ə-too'rə), *n.* [It. < *appoggiare,* to rest, lean; LL. *appodiare,* to support < *ad-,* to + **podiare,* to support < L. *podium;* see PODIUM], in *music,* an ornamental tone preceding another tone; grace note.

APPOGGIATURA

ap·point (ə-point'), *v.t.* [ME. *apointen;* OFr. *apointer,* to arrange, make ready; LL. **appunctare* < L. *ad,* to + *punctum,* a point < *pungere,* to prick], 1. to ordain; prescribe; set (a date, place, etc.): as, he *appointed* a time for the meeting. 2. to name or select for an office, position, etc.: as, I *appoint* him chairman. 3. to furnish and arrange: now usually in *well-appointed,* etc. 4. in *law,* to decide the disposition of (property) by special authority. *v.i.* to make appointments, as to an office, position, etc. —*SYN.* see **furnish.**

ap·point·ee (ə-poin'tē'), *n.* [< Fr. *appointé;* pp. of *appointer;* see APPOINT], a person appointed.

ap·poin·tive (ə-poin'tiv), *adj.* of or filled by appointment: as, an *appointive* position.

ap·point·ment (ə-point'mənt), *n.* [Fr. *appointement*], 1. an appointing or being appointed. 2. a naming or selecting for an office, position, etc. 3. a person thus selected. 4. a position thus filled. 5. an arrangement to meet a person or be in a certain place at a set time; engagement. 6. *pl.* furniture; equipment. 7. in *law,* the disposal of property by special authority.

ap·poin·tor (ə-poin'tēr, ə-poin'tôr), *n.* in *law,* a person given special authority (power of appointment) to dispose of property.

Ap·po·mat·tox (ap'ə-mat'əks), *n.* a town in central Virginia, where General Lee surrendered to General Grant (April 9, 1865), ending the Civil War.

ap·por·tion (ə-pôr'shən, ə-pōr'shən), *v.t.* [OFr. *apportionner;* see AD- & PORTION], to divide and distribute proportionally or according to a plan; portion out; allot. —*SYN.* see **allot.**

ap·por·tion·ment (ə-pôr'shən-mənt, ə-pōr'shən-mənt), *n.* 1. an apportioning or being apportioned. 2. the distribution resulting from this.

ap·pos·a·ble (ə-pōz'ə-b'l), *adj.* that can be apposed: as, the human thumb is *apposable,* for it can move so as to touch the tip of each of the four fingers.

ap·pose (ə-pōz'), *v.t.* [APPOSED (-pōzd'), APPOSING], [Fr. *apposer* < L. *appositus,* pp. of *apponere,* to put near to < *ad-,* to + *ponere,* to put], 1. to put (*to* another thing). 2. to put side by side; place opposite or near.

ap·po·site (ap'ə-zit), *adj.* [L. *appositus;* see APPOSE], appropriate; fitting; relevant; apt. —*SYN.* see **relevant.**

ap·po·si·tion (ap'ə-zish'ən), *n.* [L. *appositio,* a setting before < *appositus;* see APPOSE], 1. an apposing or being apposed; putting side by side. 2. the position resulting from this. 3. in *grammar, a*) the placing of a word or expression beside another so that the second explains and has the same grammatical construction as the first. *b*) the relationship between such words: as, *cousin* is in *apposition* with *Mary* in "Mary, my cousin, is here."

ap·pos·i·tive (ə-poz'ə-tiv), *adj.* of or in apposition. *n.* a word, phrase, or clause in apposition.

ap·prais·a·ble (ə-prāz'ə-b'l), *adj.* that can be appraised.

ap·prais·al (ə-prāz''l), *n.* 1. an appraising or being appraised. 2. an appraised value or price; estimate.

ap·praise (ə-prāz'), *v.t.* [APPRAISED (-prāzd'), APPRAISING], [OFr. *apreiser* < LL. *appretiare* < L. *ad,* to + *pretium,* value; influenced by *praise*], 1. to set a price for; decide the value of. 2. to estimate the quantity of. 3. to judge the quality or worth of. —*SYN.* see **estimate.**

ap·praise·ment (ə-prāz'mənt), *n.* appraisal.

ap·prais·er (ə-prāz'ēr), *n.* 1. a person who appraises. 2. a person given authority to decide the value of goods, property, etc.

ap·pre·ci·a·ble (ə-prē'shi-ə-b'l, ə-prē'shə-b'l), *adj.* [Fr. *appréciable* < *apprécier,* to appreciate < LL. *appretiare;* see APPRAISE], 1. that can be appreciated. 2. enough to be perceived or estimated; noticeable: as, an *appreciable* difference in pay. —*SYN.* see **perceptible.**

ap·pre·ci·a·bly (ə-prē'shi-ə-bli, ə-prē'shə-bli), *adv.* to an appreciable extent; noticeably.

ap·pre·ci·ate (ə-prē'shi-āt'), *v.t.* [APPRECIATED (-id), APPRECIATING], [< LL. *appretiatus,* pp. of *appretiare;* see APPRAISE], 1. to think well of; value; enjoy; esteem. 2. to recognize gratefully. 3. to estimate the quality or worth of. 4. to estimate rightly. 5. to be fully or sensitively aware of; notice with discrimination. 6. to raise the price of: opposed to *depreciate.* *v.i.* to rise in value.

SYN.—**appreciate,** in this comparison, implies sufficient critical judgment to see the value or to enjoy (he *appreciates* good music); to **value** is to rate highly because of worth (I *value* your friendship); to **prize** is to value highly or take great satisfaction in (he *prizes* his Picasso collection); to **treasure** is to regard as precious and implies special care to protect from loss; to **esteem** is to hold in high regard and implies warm attachment or respect (an *esteemed* statesman); to **cherish** is to prize or treasure, but connotes greater affection for or attachment to the thing cherished (she *cherished* her friends). See also **understand.** —*ANT.* despise, disdain.

ap·pre·ci·a·tion (ə-prē'shi-ā'shən), *n.* [Fr. *appréciation* < *apprécier;* see APPRECIABLE], 1. an appreciating. 2. grateful recognition, as of benefits. 3. an estimate, especially a correct one. 4. sensitive awareness; discriminating perception or enjoyment, as of art. 5. a rise in value or price: opposed to *depreciation.*

ap·pre·ci·a·tive (ə-prē'shi-ā'tiv, ə-prē'shi-ə-tiv), *adj.* feeling or showing appreciation.

ap·pre·ci·a·tor (ə-prē'shi-ā'tēr), *n.* a person who appreciates something.

ap·pre·ci·a·to·ry (ə-prē'shi-ə-tôr'i, ə-prē'shi-ə-tō'ri), *adj.* appreciative.

ap·pre·hend (ap'ri-hend'), *v.t.* [Fr. *appréhender;* L. *apprehendere,* to take hold of < *ad-,* to + *prehendere;* see PREHENSILE], 1. to take into custody; arrest. 2. to take hold of mentally; perceive; understand. 3. to anticipate with anxiety; dread. 4. [Obs.], to seize.

ap·pre·hen·si·ble (ap'ri-hen'sə-b'l), *adj.* [L. *apprehensibilis* < pp. of *apprehendere;* see APPREHEND], that can be apprehended.

ap·pre·hen·sion (ap'ri-hen'shən), *n.* [L. *apprehensio* < pp. of *apprehendere;* see APPREHEND], 1. an apprehending or being apprehended; seizing; grasping. 2. arrest. 3. mental grasp; perception; understanding. 4. opinion. 5. *often in pl.* foreboding; fear; dread.

ap·pre·hen·sive (ap'ri-hen'siv), *adj.* [ML. *apprehensivus* < pp. of L. *apprehendere;* see APPREHEND], 1. able to apprehend; quick to understand or learn. 2. having to do with perceiving or understanding. 3. troubled by fears; anxious; uneasy.

ap·pren·tice (ə-pren'tis), *n.* [ME. *aprentis;* OFr. *aprentis* < *aprendre,* to teach < L. *apprehendere;* see APPREHEND], 1. a person under legal agreement to work a specified length of time for a master craftsman in a craft or trade in return for instruction and, formerly, support. 2. any learner or beginner; novice: abbreviated **app.** *v.t.* [APPRENTICED (-tist), APPRENTICING], to place or accept as an apprentice; indenture.

ap·pren·tice·ship (ə-pren'tis-ship'), *n.* [*apprentice* + *-ship*], 1. the state of being an apprentice. 2. the duties or training period of an apprentice. 3. any training or period of training.

ap·pressed (ə-prest', a-prest'), *adj.* [< L. *appressus,* pp. of *apprimere,* var. of *adprimere,* to press to; *ad-,* to + *primere,* to press], in *botany & zoology,* pressed close to or flat against a surface.

ap·prise, ap·prize (ə-prīz'), *v.t.* [APPRISED or APPRIZED (-prīzd'), APPRISING or APPRIZING], [Fr. *appris,* pp. of *apprendre,* to teach, inform < L. *apprehendere;* see APPREHEND], to inform; notify. —*SYN.* see **notify.**

ap·prize, ap·prise (ə-prīz′), *v.t.* [APPRIZED or APPRISED (-prīzd′), APPRIZING or APPRISING], [OFr. *apreisier, apreiser;* see APPRAISE], to appraise.

ap·proach (ə-prōch′), *v.i.* [ME. *aprochen;* OFr. *aprochier;* LL. *appropiare* < L. *ad,* to + *propius,* compar. of *prope,* near], to come or go near or nearer. *v.t.* 1. to come near or nearer to. 2. to come to resemble; approximate. 3. to bring near (*to* something). 4. to make advances, a proposal, or a request to. *n.* 1. a coming near; approximation; resemblance. 2. *often in pl.* an advance or overture (to someone). 3. a way of coming toward or reaching a person or place; access. 4. in *golf,* a stroke after the tee shot, meant to knock the ball onto the putting green.

ap·proach·a·bil·i·ty (ə-prōch′ə-bil′ə-ti), *n.* the quality or state of being approachable.

ap·proach·a·ble (ə-prōch′ə-b'l), *adj.* 1. that can be approached. 2. easily approached; friendly; receptive.

ap·pro·bate (ap′rə-bāt′), *v.t.* [APPROBATED (-id), APPROBATING], [< L. *approbatus,* pp. of *approbare;* see APPROVE], 1. to approve. 2. to sanction.

ap·pro·ba·tion (ap′rə-bā′shən), *n.* [L. *approbatio;* see APPROBATE], 1. approval. 2. sanction.

ap·pro·ba·tive (ap′rə-bā′tiv), *adj.* [Fr. *approbatif* < L. *approbatus*], showing approbation or approval.

ap·pro·ba·to·ry (ə-prō′bə-tôr′i, ə-prō′bə-tō′ri), *adj.* 1. of the nature of approbation. 2. approbative.

ap·pro·pri·a·ble (ə-prō′pri-ə-b'l), *adj.* that can be appropriated.

ap·pro·pri·ate (ə-prō′pri-āt′; *for adj.,* ə-prō′pri-it), *v.t.* [APPROPRIATED (-id), APPROPRIATING], [< L. *appropriatus,* pp. of *appropriare,* to make one's own < *ad-,* to + *proprius,* one's own], 1. to take for one's own or exclusive use; hence, 2. to steal. 3. to set aside for a specific use or certain person: as, the legislature *appropriates* money for the schools. *adj.* suitable; fit; proper. —*SYN.* see **fit.**

ap·pro·pri·a·tion (ə-prō′pri-ā′shən), *n.* 1. an appropriating or being appropriated. 2. a thing appropriated; anything, especially money, set aside for a specific use.

ap·pro·pri·a·tive (ə-prō′pri-ā′tiv), *adj.* inclined to appropriate; appropriating.

ap·pro·pri·a·tor (ə-prō′pri-ā′tēr), *n.* 1. a person who appropriates. 2. the holder of a church benefice.

ap·prov·a·ble (ə-prōōv′ə-b'l), *adj.* 1. that can be approved. 2. deserving approval.

ap·prov·al (ə-prōōv′'l), *n.* 1. an approving or being approved. 2. favorable attitude or opinion. 3. consent; sanction.

on approval, for the customer to examine and decide whether to buy or return.

ap·prove (ə-prōōv′), *v.t.* [APPROVED (-prōōvd′), APPROVING], [ME. *aproven;* OFr. *aprover;* L. *approbare* < *ad-,* to + *probare,* to try, test < *probus,* good], 1. to sanction; consent to; confirm. 2. to be favorable toward; think or declare to be good, satisfactory, etc. 3. to prove or show (often used reflexively). 4. [Obs.], to prove by testing. *v.i.* to give approval; have a favorable opinion (*of* someone or something).

SYN.—**approve,** the most general of the following terms, means simply to regard as good or satisfactory; **endorse** adds the further implication of active support or advocacy (to *endorse* a candidate for office); **sanction** adds the still further implication of positive authorization (a practice *sanctioned* by the charter); **certify** implies official approval because of compliance with the requirements or standards (a *certified* public accountant); **ratify** implies official approval of that which has been done by one's representative (to *ratify* a peace treaty). —*ANT.* disapprove, reject.

ap·prov·er (ə-prōōv′ēr), *n.* 1. a person who approves. 2. [British], an informer.

approx., 1. approximate. 2. approximately.

ap·prox·i·mal (ə-prok′sə-məl), *adj.* [L. *approximare* (see APPROXIMATE); + *-al*], in *anatomy,* adjoining; side by side.

ap·prox·i·mate (ə-prok′sə-mit; *for v.,* ə-prok′sə-māt′), *adj.* [LL. *approximatus,* pp. of *approximare,* to come near < L. *ad,* to + *proximus,* superl. of *prope,* near], 1. near in position; close together. 2. much like; resembling. 3. more or less correct or exact. Abbreviated **approx.** *v.t.* [APPROXIMATED (-id), APPROXIMATING], 1. to come near to; approach or be almost the same as: as, this painting *approximates* reality. 2. to bring near; make approach (*to* something). *v.i.* to come near; be almost the same.

ap·prox·i·mate·ly (ə-prok′sə-mit-li), *adv.* in an approximate manner; nearly; almost: abbreviated **approx.**

ap·prox·i·ma·tion (ə-prok′sə-mā′shən), *n.* 1. an approximating; approaching. 2. anything that approximates; close estimate; near likeness.

ap·pur·te·nance (ə-pûr′t'n-əns), *n.* [ME. *appertenaunce;* Anglo-Fr. *apurtenance;* OFr. *apertenance* < ppr. of L. *appertinere;* see APPERTAIN], 1. anything that appertains; thing added to a more important thing; adjunct. 2. an additional, subordinate right or privilege.

ap·pur·te·nant (ə-pûr′t'n-ənt), *adj.* [< OFr. *apertenant*], appertaining; pertinent. *n.* an appurtenance.

Apr., April.

‡a·près moi le dé·luge (å′pre′ mwå′ lə dā′lüzh′), [Fr.], after me the deluge: a saying attributed to Louis XV of France.

a·pri·cot (ā′pri-kot′, ap′ri-kot′), *n.* [Fr. *abricot;* Port. *albricoque;* Ar. *al-barkūk;* MGr. *praikokion;* L. *praecoquus,* early matured fruit < *prae-,* beforehand + *coquere,* to cook], 1. a small, yellowish-orange, peachlike fruit. 2. the tree that it grows on. 3. a yellowish-orange color.

A·pril (ā′prəl), *n.* [altered, after the L., from ME. *Avril;* OFr. *avrill;* L. *aprilis;* prob. < **apero-,* latter, second; akin to Sans. *aparaḥ,* latter, later, successor, Goth. *afar,* after; original meaning, prob. "second month"], the fourth month of the year, having 30 days: abbreviated **Apr., Apl., Ap., A.**

April fool, a victim of jokes played on April Fools' Day.

April Fools' Day, April 1; All Fools' Day.

a pri·o·ri (ā′ pri-ō′ri, ä′ pri-ôr′i), [L.; *a, ab,* from + *prior,* compar. of *prius,* first], 1. from cause to effect; from a generalization to particular instances; deductively. 2. of such reasoning; deductive. 3. based on theory instead of experience or experiment. 4. before examination or analysis. Opposed to *a posteriori.*

a·pri·or·i·ty (ā′prī-ôr′ə-ti, ā′pri-or′ə-ti), *n.* 1. the quality or fact of being a priori. 2. the use of a priori reasoning.

a·pron (ā′prən, ā′pērn), *n.* [by faulty separation of *a napron;* ME. *napron;* OFr. *naperon* < *nape,* a cloth; L. *mappa,* a cloth, napkin], 1. a garment of cloth, leather, etc. worn over the front part of the body, usually to protect one's clothes. 2. anything like an apron in appearance or use. 3. a waterproof protecting shield in an open vehicle. 4. the hard-surfaced area, often paved, in front of an airplane hangar. 5. the part of a stage in front of the curtain. 6. an endless belt for carrying things. 7. a protective work of planking or other material along a river bank, below a dam, etc. 8. in *geology,* a sheet of sand or gravel lying in front of a glacial moraine. *v.t.* to put an apron on; provide an apron for.

apron string, a string for tying an apron on.

tied to his mother's (or **wife's,** etc.) **apron strings,** dominated by his mother (or wife, etc.).

ap·ro·pos (ap′rə-pō′), *adv.* [Fr. *à propos,* to the purpose < L. *ad,* to + *propositus,* pp. of *proponere;* see PROPOUND], 1. at the right time; opportunely. 2. by the way: used to introduce a remark. *adj.* relevant; apt. —*SYN.* see **relevant.**

apropos of, in connection with; with regard to.

apse (aps), *n.* [L. *apsis, absis;* see APSIS], 1. a semicircular or polygonal projection of a church, generally at the east end and with a domed or vaulted roof: also **apsis.** 2. an apsis.

ap·si·dal (ap′si-d'l), *adj.* of an apse or apsis.

ap·sis (ap′sis), *n.* [*pl.* APSIDES (-si-dēz′)], [L. *apsis, absis,* an arch; Gr. *hapsis,* a fastening < *haptein,* to fasten], 1. an apse. 2. that point in the orbit of the moon, a planet, etc. nearest to (*lower apsis*), or that farthest from (*higher apsis*), the center of attraction: also **apse.**

line of apsides, line that coincides with the major axis of an orbit.

apt (apt), *adj.* [ME. & OFr. *apte;* L. *aptus,* pp. of *apere;* Gr. *haptein,* to fasten], 1. appropriate; fitting; relevant: as, an *apt* statement. 2. tending or inclined; likely: as, eating too fast is *apt* to cause indigestion. 3. quick to learn or understand: as, an *apt* student. 4. [Archaic], ready; prepared. —*SYN.* see **fit, likely, quick.**

apt., [*pl.* APTS.], apartment.

ap·ter·al (ap′tēr-əl), *adj.* [Gr. *apteros* (see APTEROUS); + *-al*], 1. in *architecture,* having columns at one or both ends, but not along the sides. 2. in *zoology,* apterous.

ap·ter·ous (ap′tēr-əs), *adj.* [Gr. *apteros* < *a-,* without + *pteron,* a wing], in *biology,* having no wings or winglike parts.

ap·ter·yg·i·al (ap′tēr-ij′i-əl), *adj.* [< Gr. *apterygos* < *a-,* without + *pteryx,* a wing], in *zoology,* lacking paired fins or limbs.

ap·ter·yx (ap′tēr-iks), *n.* [Gr. *a-,* without + *pteryx,* wing], any of a number of related, nearly extinct, tailless birds of New Zealand, with a long slender bill, undeveloped wings, and hairlike feathers; kiwi.

APTERYX (15 in. long)

ap·ti·tude (ap′tə-tōōd′, ap′tə-tūd′), *n.* [Fr. < LL. *aptitudo* < L. *aptus;* see APT], 1. the quality of being apt or appropriate; fitness. 2. a natural tendency or inclination. 3. an ability; capacity; talent. 4. quickness to learn or understand. —*SYN.* see **talent.**

aptitude test, a test for determining the probability of a person's success in some activity in which he is not yet trained.

Ap·u·le·ius, Lu·ci·us (lōō′shi-əs, lōō′shəs ap′yoo-lē′əs), 2d century A.D.; Roman philosopher and satirist.

A·pu·li·a (ə-pū′li-ə), *n.* a department of southeastern Italy: formerly a province of ancient Rome.
A·pu·re (ä-pōō′re), *n.* a river in Venezuela, flowing into the Orinoco River: length, 300 mi.
A·pu·ri·mac (ä′pōō-rē′mäk), *n.* a river in southern Peru, flowing into the Ucayali River: length, 600 mi.
A·pus (ā′pəs), *n.* [Mod. L., bird of paradise, lit., footless (see APODAL): specimens orig. obtained from the East Indies lacked feet], a southern constellation: also called *Bird of Paradise*: see **constellation**, chart.
a·py·ret·ic (ā′pī-ret′ik, ap′ī-ret′ik), *adj.* [Gr. *apyretos;* see A- & PYRETIC], in *medicine*, without fever.
aq·ua (ak′wə, ä′kwə, ā′kwə), *n.* [*pl.* AQUAS (-wəz, -kwəz), AQUAE (-wē, -kwē)], [L.], 1. water. 2. in *pharmacy*, liquid; solution, especially in water: abbreviated **aq.** *adj.* [< *aquamarine*], bluish-green.
aqua am·mo·ni·ae (ə-mō′ni-ē′), [Mod. L., lit., water of ammonia], a water solution of ammonia; ammonium hydroxide: also **aqua ammonia.**
aq·ua·cade (ak′wə-kād′), *n.* [*aqua* + *-cade;* coined after *motorcade*], an aquatic exhibition or entertainment consisting of swimming, diving, etc., often to music.
aqua for·tis (fôr′tis), [L., strong water], nitric acid.
aq·ua·ma·rine (ak′wə-mə-rēn′), *n.* [L. *aqua marina*, sea water], 1. a transparent, pale bluish-green variety of beryl, used in jewelry. 2. its color. *adj.* bluish-green.
aq·ua·plane (ak′wə-plān′), *n.* [*aqua* + *-plane;* see AIRPLANE], a board on which one rides standing up as it is pulled by a motorboat. *v.i.*[AQUAPLANED (-plānd′), AQUAPLANING], to ride on such a board.

AQUAPLANE

aqua re·gi·a (rē′ji-ə), [L., lit., kingly water], a mixture of nitric and hydrochloric acids: so called because it can dissolve gold and platinum.
aq·ua·relle (ak′wə-rel′), *n.* [Fr. < It. *acquerella*, water color < *acqua;* L. *aqua*, water], a kind of painting in transparent water colors.
a·quar·i·um (ə-kwâr′i-əm), *n.* [*pl.* AQUARIUMS (-əmz), AQUARIA (-ə)], [L., neut. of *aquarius*, of water < *aqua*, water], 1. a tank, usually with glass sides, or a pool, bowl, etc. for keeping live water animals and water plants. 2. a building where such collections are exhibited.
A·quar·i·us (ə-kwâr′i-əs), *n.* [L., the water carrier < *aqua*, water], 1. a large central constellation, supposedly outlining a man pouring water from a container in his right hand: see **constellation**, chart. 2. the eleventh sign of the zodiac (♒), entered by the sun about January 21: see **zodiac**, illus.
a·quat·ic (ə-kwat′ik, ə-kwät′ik), *adj.* [L. *aquaticus* < *aqua*, water], 1. growing or living in or upon water: as, *aquatic* plants. 2. done in or upon the water: as, *aquatic* sports. *n.* an aquatic plant or animal.
a·quat·ics (ə-kwat′iks, ə-kwät′iks), *n.pl.* aquatic performances or sports.
aq·ua·tint (ak′wə-tint′), *n.* [Fr. *aquatinte;* It. *acqua tinta*, dyed in water < L. *aqua*, water + *tintus*, pp. of *tingere*, to dye, tinge], 1. a process by which spaces rather than lines are etched with acid, producing an etching like an ink drawing or a water color. 2. an etching made in this way. *v.t.* to etch in this way.
aq·ua·tone (ak′wə-tōn′), *n.* [*aqua* + *tone*], 1. a process of photoengraving on a sensitized aluminum plate coated with gelatin and celluloid. 2. a print made by this process.
aqua vi·tae (vī′tē), [L., water of life], 1. in *alchemy*, alcohol; hence, 2. brandy or other strong liquor.
aq·ue·duct (ak′wi-dukt′), *n.* [L. *aquaeductus; aquae*, genit. of *aqua*, water + *ductus*, pp. of *ducere*, to lead], 1. a large pipe or conduit made for bringing water from a distant source. 2. any elevated structure built to support such a pipe or conduit. 3. in *anatomy*, a passage or canal.
a·que·ous (ā′kwi-əs, ak′wi-əs), *adj.* [< base of L. *aqua*, water; + *-ous*], 1. of or like water; watery. 2. formed by the action of water, as certain rocks made of sediment. 3. of the aqueous humor.
aqueous humor, a watery fluid in the space between the cornea and the lens of the eye: see **eye**, illus.
Aq·ui·la (ak′wi-lə; *sometimes* ə-kwil′ə), *n.* [L., eagle], a northern constellation in the Milky Way, supposedly outlining an eagle: see **constellation**, chart.
aq·ui·le·gi·a (ak′wi-lē′ji-ə, ā′kwi-lē′ji-ə), *n.* [Mod. L.; ML. *aquileja*], a columbine.
A·qui·le·ia (ä′kwē-le′yä), *n.* an ancient town in Italy, at the northern end of the Adriatic.
aq·ui·line (ak′wə-lin′, ak′wə-lin), *adj.* [L. *aquilinus* < *aquila*, eagle], 1. of or like an eagle. 2. like an eagle's: said especially of a curved or hooked nose.
A·qui·nas, Saint **Thomas** (ə-kwī′nəs), 1225?–1274; Italian scholastic philosopher: cf. **Thomism.**
A·qui·taine (ak′wi-tān′), *n.* a former district of southwestern France: later called *Guyenne.*
Aq·ui·ta·ni·a (ak′wi-tā′ni-ə), *n.* the southwestern division of ancient Gaul, conquered by Julius Caesar in 56 B.C.

AQUITAINE

‡a quo (ā′ kwō′), [L.], from which: opposed to *ad quem.*
ar (är), *n.* an are (unit of measure).
ar-, ad-: used before *r*, as in *arrest.*
-ar (ẽr), [< ME. *-er* < OFr. *-er, -ier, -air* < L. *-aris;* or directly < L. *-aris;* also < L. *-arius*, a suffix of nouns of agency], a suffix used in forming: 1. adjectives, or nouns derived from adjectives, meaning *of, relating to, like, of the nature of*, as in *regular, singular, polar.* 2. nouns denoting *agency*, as in *bursar, vicar.* In some nouns formed after *scholar*, etc., *-ar* is equivalent to *-er.*
Ar., 1. Arabic. 2. Aramaic. 3. *argentum*, [L.], silver.
A.R., 1. Army Regulation. 2. Autonomous Republic.
a.r., *anno regni*, [L.], in the year of the reign.
A·ra (ā′rə), *n.* [L., an altar], a southern constellation: see **constellation**, chart.
Ar·ab (ar′əb), *n.* 1. a native or inhabitant of Arabia. 2. any of a race of Semites, native to Arabia; commonly, a Bedouin: some Arab tribes are now widely scattered and mixed with other races. 3. any of a breed of swift, graceful horses native to Arabia. 4. a waif of the streets; street Arab. *adj.* Arabian.
Arab., 1. Arabian. 2. Arabic.
Ar·a·bel·la (ar′ə-bel′ə), [prob. < Gmc. base *ara*, eagle + *-bella;* influenced in form by L. *bella*, fem. of *bellus*, beautiful], a feminine name: diminutive, *Bella.*
ar·a·besque (ar′ə-besk′), *n.* [Fr.; It. *arabesco* < *Arabo*, Arab: with reference to the designs in Moorish architecture], 1. a complex and elaborate design of intertwined flowers, foliage, geometrical patterns, etc. painted or carved in low relief. 2. in *ballet dancing*, a position in which one leg is extended straight backward and the arms are extended, one forward and one backward. 3. in *music*, a short, brilliant composition in rondo form. *adj.* 1. of or done in arabesque. 2. resembling arabesque; fantastic and elaborate.

ARABESQUE

A·ra·bi·a (ə-rā′bi-ə, ə-rā′byə), *n.* a peninsula in southwestern Asia, largely a desert region: area, 1,000,000 sq. mi.; pop., c. 10,000,000.
Arabia Fe·lix (fē′liks), [L. *felix*, happy, fortunate], 1. the fertile region of Yemen, southwestern Arabia: the ancient Latin name. 2. all of ancient Arabia except the northern parts.
A·ra·bi·an (ə-rā′bi-ən, ə-rā′byən), *adj.* of Arabia or the Arabs. *n.* 1. a native or inhabitant of Arabia; Arab. 2. any of a breed of swift, graceful horses native to Arabia. Abbreviated **Arab.**
Arabian Desert, a desert area of Egypt between the Nile and the Red Sea.
Arabian Nights, a collection of ancient stories from Arabia, India, Persia, etc.: also called *The Arabian Nights' Entertainment, The Thousand and One Nights.*
Arabian Sea, an extension of the Indian Ocean, between India and Arabia.
Ar·a·bic (ar′ə-bik), *adj.* 1. of Arabia. 2. of the Arabs, their language, culture, etc. 3. [a-], designating the gum (*gum arabic*) obtained from certain kinds of acacia. 4. [a-], designating an acid found in gum arabic. *n.* the Semitic language of the Arabs, used in Arabia, Syria, Jordan, Iraq, northern Africa, etc. Abbreviated **Arab., Ar.**
Arabic numerals, the figures **1, 2, 3, 4, 5, 6, 7, 8, 9,** and the **0** (zero).
a·rab·i·nose (ə-rab′ə-nōs′, ar′ə-bə-nōs′), *n.* [*arabic* + *-in* + *-ose*], a pentose sugar, $C_5H_{10}O_5$, obtained especially from certain vegetable gums.
Ar·ab·ist (ar′əb-ist), *n.* an expert in Arabic; student of Arabic linguistics or literature.
ar·a·ble (ar′ə-b′l), *adj.* [Fr.; L. *arabilis* < *arare*, to plow], suitable for plowing. *n.* plow land; arable land.
Arab League, a confederation of the states of Syria, Jordan, Iraq, Saudi Arabia, Lebanon, Egypt, and Yemen, formed in 1945.

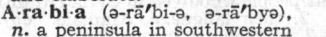

Ar·a·by (ar′a-bi), *n.* [Archaic or Poetic], Arabia.
a·ra·ceous (ə-rā′shəs), *adj.* [*arum* + *-aceous*], of the arum family of plants, chiefly tropical, bearing flowers on a fleshy spike enclosed in a hoodlike leaf.
A·rach·ne (ə-rak′ni), *n.* [L.; Gr. *Arachnē* < *arachnē*, spider], in *Greek mythology*, a girl turned into a spider by Athena for challenging the goddess to a weaving contest.
a·rach·nid (ə-rak′nid), *n.* [Mod. L. *Arachnida*, the arachnids < Gr. *arachnē*, spider], any of a large group of arthropods with four pairs of legs, lunglike sacs or breathing tubes, and a body usually divided into two segments: spiders, scorpions, and mites are arachnids.
a·rach·ni·dan (ə-rak′ni-dən), *adj.* & *n.* arachnid.
a·rach·noid (ə-rak′noid), *adj.* [< Gr. *arachnē*, spider; + *-oid*], 1. in *anatomy*, designating the middle of three membranes covering the brain and the spinal cord. 2. in *botany*, covered with or consisting of soft, fine hairs or fibers. 3. in *zoology*, of an arachnid. *n.* 1. the arachnoid membrane. 2. an arachnid.
A·ra·fu·ra Sea (ä′rä-foo͞′rä), a part of the South Pacific Ocean, between Australia and New Guinea.
Ar·a·gon (ar′ə-gon′, ar′ə-gən), *n.* a northeastern region in Spain, formerly a separate kingdom.

ARAGON (c. 1470 A.D.)

A·ra·gon, Louis (lwē′ á′rá′gōn′), 1895– ; French novelist, poet, and journalist.
Ar·a·go·nese (ar′ə-gə-nēz′), *adj.* of Aragon, its people, language, etc. *n.* 1. [*pl.* ARAGONESE], a native or inhabitant of Aragon. 2. the Spanish dialect spoken in Aragon.
a·rag·o·nite (ə-rag′ə-nīt′, ar′ə-gən-īt′), *n.* [after *Aragon*, region in Spain], a mineral made up of calcium carbonate in orthorhombic crystals, with less distinct cleavage and greater density than calcite.
A·ra·gua·ya (ä′rə-gwä′yə), *n.* a river in central Brazil: length, 1,100 mi.
A·ra·kan Mountains (ä′rä-kän′, ar′ə-kan′), a mountain range in western Burma: highest peak, 10,000 ft.
Ar·al, Lake (âr′əl), an inland body of salt water in the Asiatic U.S.S.R., east of the Caspian Sea: area, 24,400 sq. mi.: also **Aral Sea.**
a·ra·li·a (ə-rā′li-ə), *n.* [Mod. L.], an araliaceous plant.
a·ra·li·a·ceous (ə-rā′li-ā′shəs), *adj.* [< *aralia* + *-aceous*], belonging to the ginseng family of plants, which are usually woody and have flat clusters of small, white or greenish flowers and, often, fragrant leaves.
Ar·am (âr′əm), *n.* ancient Syria: the Hebrew name.
Aram., Aramaic.
Ar·a·mae·an, Ar·a·me·an (ar′ə-mē′ən), *n.* 1. any member of an ancient people who lived in Syria (Aram) and Mesopotamia. 2. their language, Aramaic. *adj.* 1. of these people. 2. of their language.
Ar·a·ma·ic (ar′ə-mā′ik), *n.* a group of northwest Semitic languages spoken in Biblical times, including the language used in Palestine after the captivity and spoken by Jesus and his disciples: abbreviated **Aram., Ar.**
A·rap·a·ho (ə-rap′ə-hō′), *n.* [*pl.* ARAPAHO, ARAPAHOES (-hōz′)], any member of a tribe of Algonquian Indians who lived in the area of the upper Platte and Arkansas Rivers: also spelled **Arapahoe.**
ar·a·pai·ma (ar′ə-pī′mə), *n.* [Port. < a Tupian word], a large, edible fresh-water fish of South America.
Ar·a·rat (ar′ə-rat′), *n.* a mountain in eastern Turkey (formerly Armenia): higher of its two peaks, 16,915 ft.: supposed landing place of Noah's Ark: Gen. 8:4.
a·ra·ro·ba (ä′rə-rō′bə), *n.* [Port. < Braz. native name], 1. a bitter, yellow powder used in medicine: also called *Goa powder*. 2. the Brazilian tree yielding this powder: it has striped wood.
A·rau·can (ə-rô′kən), *n.* 1. the language of the Araucanians. 2. an Araucanian.
Ar·au·ca·ni·an (ar′ô-kā′ni-ən), *n.* a member of a linguistic stock of South American Indians of Chile and the Argentine pampas. *adj.* 1. of the Araucanians. 2. of their language.
ar·au·ca·ri·a (ar′ô-kâ′ri-ə), *n.* [Mod. L. < Sp. *Araucano*, Araucanian tribe], any of a number of related South American or Australian evergreen trees of the pine family.
A·ra·wak (ä′rä-wäk′), *n.* a member of any branch of the Arawakan Indians.
A·ra·wa·kan (ä′rä-wä′kən), *adj.* of a large linguistic family of South American Indian tribes north of the Amazon.
ar·ba·lest, ar·ba·list (är′bə-list), *n.* [ME. *arbelaste*, *arblaste* < AS. *arblast* or OFr. *arbaleste*, *arcbaleste*; L. *arcuballista* < *arcus*, a bow + *ballista*; see BALLISTA], a crossbow consisting of a steel bow set crosswise in a wooden shaft: it propelled arrows, balls, or stones.
Ar·be·la (är-bē′lə), *n.* an ancient Persian city, now in northern Iraq: modern name, *Erbil*.
ar·bi·ter (är′bi-tẽr), *n.* [L., orig., one who goes to a place, a witness, judge < *ad-*, to + *bitere*, *betere*, to come, go], 1. a person selected to judge a dispute; umpire; arbitrator. 2. a person fully authorized to judge or decide. —*SYN.* see **judge.**
‡**ar·bi·ter e·le·gan·ti·ae** (är′bi-tẽr el′ə-gan′shi-ē′), [L.], judge of elegance; authority in questions of good taste.
ar·bi·tra·ble (är′bə-trə-b′l), *adj.* that can be arbitrated; subject to arbitration.
ar·bi·trage (är′bə-trij; *also, for 2,* är′bə-träzh′), *n.* [Fr. < *arbitrer*, to judge < L. *arbitrari*; see ARBITRATE], 1. arbitration. 2. a buying of bills of exchange, stocks, etc. in one market and selling them again at a higher price in another market.
ar·bi·tral (är′bə-trəl), *adj.* [Fr.; L. *arbitralis*; see ARBITER], of arbiters or arbitration.
ar·bit·ra·ment (är-bit′rə-mənt), *n.* [ME. & OFr. *arbitrement* < L. *arbitrari*; see ARBITRATE], 1. arbitration. 2. an arbitrator's verdict or award. 3. the power to judge; right to decide.
ar·bi·trar·i·ly (är′bə-trer′ə-li; *emphatic, often* är′bə-trâr′ə-li), *adv.* in an arbitrary manner.
ar·bi·trar·i·ness (är′bə-trer′i-nis), *n.* the quality or condition of being arbitrary.
ar·bi·trar·y (är′bə-trer′i), *adj.* [L. *arbitrarius* < *arbiter*; see ARBITER], 1. discretionary. 2. based on one's preference, notion, or whim; hence, 3. capricious. 4. absolute; despotic. —*SYN.* see **dictatorial.**
ar·bi·trate (är′bə-trāt′), *v.t.* [ARBITRATED (-id), ARBITRATING], [< L. *arbitratus*, pp. of *arbitrari*, to give a decision < *arbiter*; see ARBITER], 1. to give to an arbitrator to decide; settle by arbitration. 2. to decide (a dispute) as an arbitrator. *v.i.* 1. to act as an arbitrator (*in* a dispute, *between* persons). 2. to submit a dispute to arbitration.
ar·bi·tra·tion (är′bə-trā′shən), *n.* [L. *arbitratio*; see ARBITRATE], an arbitrating or being arbitrated; settlement of a dispute by a person or persons chosen to hear both sides and come to a decision.
ar·bi·tra·tor (är′bə-trā′tẽr), *n.* [L.; see ARBITRATE], 1. a person selected as a judge of a dispute; arbiter. 2. a person fully authorized to judge or decide.
ar·bi·tress (är′bə-tris), *n.* a woman arbiter.
Ar·blay, Madame d' (där′blā; Fr. dár′blā′), see **Burney, Fanny.**
ar·bor (är′bẽr), *n.* [ME. *erber*, *herber*; OFr. *erbier*, *herbier* < L. *herbarium*, place covered with grass, etc. < *herba*, grass, herb], 1. a place shaded by trees or shrubs or, especially, by vines on a latticework; bower. 2. [Obs.], a plot of grass; garden; orchard.
ar·bor (är′bẽr), *n.* [*pl.*, for 1 & 2, ARBORES (-bə-rēz′); for 3, ARBORS (-bẽrz)], [L., a tree, beam], 1. a tree. 2. a family tree. 3. in *metal casting*, the beam or bar in the center of an interior mold or core.
ar·bor (är′bẽr), *n.* [Fr. *arbre*, tree, axis < L. *arbor*, tree, beam], in *mechanics*, 1. a shaft; beam. 2. a spindle; axle. 3. a bar that holds cutting tools. *v.t.* to set in such a bar, shaft, etc.
ar·bo·ra·ceous (är′bə-rā′shəs), *adj.* [*arbor* (tree) + *-aceous*], 1. treelike. 2. wooded.
Arbor Day, in most States of the United States, a day in late April or early May observed by planting trees.
ar·bo·re·al (är-bôr′i-əl, är-bō′ri-əl), *adj.* [L. *arboreus*, of a tree < *arbor*, tree; + *-al*], 1. of or like a tree. 2. living in trees or adapted for living in trees.
ar·bored (är′bẽrd), *adj.* 1. having an arbor, or bower. 2. having trees on both sides or around it.
ar·bo·re·ous (är-bôr′i-əs, är-bō′ri-əs), *adj.* 1. arboreal. 2. full of trees. 3. arborescent.
ar·bo·res·cent (är′bə-res′'nt), *adj.* [L. *arborescens*, ppr. of *arborescere*, to become a tree < *arbor*, tree], treelike in shape or growth; branching.
ar·bo·re·tum (är′bə-rē′təm), *n.* [*pl.* ARBORETUMS (-təmz), ARBORETA (-tə)], [L. < *arbor*, tree], 1. a place where many kinds of trees and shrubs are grown for exhibition or study; hence, 2. a wooded public park.
ar·bo·ri·cul·ture (är′bə-ri-kul′chẽr), *n.* [< L. *arbor*, tree + *cultura*, culture], the scientific cultivation of trees and shrubs.
ar·bor·i·za·tion (är′bẽr-i-zā′shən), *n.* [< *arbor* (tree) + *-ize* + *-ation*], 1. a treelike figure or arrangement. 2. the forming of such a figure or arrangement.
ar·bor·ous (är′bẽr-əs), *adj.* of or made up of trees.
ar·bor·vi·tae (är′bẽr-vī′tē), *n.* [L., tree of life], 1. any of a number of related trees of the pine family, having soft, fragrant, scalelike leaves; thuja. 2. in *anatomy*, the treelike structure of the white substance in a longitudinal section of the cerebellum. Also, especially in sense 2, **arbor vitae.**
ar·bour (är′bẽr), *n.* an arbor (bower): British spelling.
Ar·buth·not, John (är-buth′nət, är′bəth-not′), 1667–1735; English physician and author.
ar·bu·tus (är-bū′təs), *n.* [L., wild strawberry tree], 1. any of a number of related trees and shrubs of the heath family, with dark-green leaves, clusters of white or pinkish flowers, and strawberrylike berries. 2. a related trailing plant with clusters of white or pink flowers; trailing arbutus; Mayflower.
arc (ärk), *n.* [Fr. < L. *arcus*, a bow, arch], 1. a bowlike curved line or object. 2. in *astronomy*, *a*) the apparent curved path of a star or planet. *b*) the angular measure-

ment of this. 3. in *electricity*, the band of sparks or incandescent light between two closely placed electrodes when a current leaps the gap from one to the other. 4. in *geometry*, a part of a curved line, as of a circle. *v.i.* [ARCED or ARCKED (ärkt), ARCING or ARCKING], in *electricity*, to form an arc

Arc, Jeanne d' (zhän' dȧrk'), see **Joan of Arc.**

ARC, A.R.C., American (National) Red Cross.

ar·cade (är-kād'), *n.* [Fr.; ML. *arcata* < L. *arcus*, a bow, arch], 1. a passage having an arched roof; hence, 2. any covered passageway, especially one with shops along the sides. 3. an avenue of trees. 4. in *architecture*, *a)* a line of arches and their supporting columns. *b)* an arched building. *v.t.* [ARCADED (-id), ARCADING], to make into or provide with an arcade.

Ar·ca·di·a (är-kā'di-ə), *n.* 1. an ancient pastoral district of the central Peloponnesus, Greece; hence, 2. any place of rural peace and simplicity.

ARCADIA

Ar·ca·di·an (är-kā'di-ən), *adj.* 1. of Arcadia. 2. like or characteristic of Arcadia; rustic; peaceful and simple. *n.* 1. a native or inhabitant of Arcadia. 2. a person of simple manners and tastes.

Ar·ca·dy (är'kə-di), *n.* [Poetic], Arcadia.

ar·cane (är-kān'), *adj.* [< L. *arcanus*; see ARCANUM], hidden or secret.

ar·ca·num (är-kā'nəm), *n.* [*pl.* ARCANUMS (-nəmz), ARCANA (-nə)], [L., neut. of *arcanus*, shut in, hidden < *arcere*, to shut up < *arca*, chest], 1. a secret; mystery. 2. a secret remedy; elixir.

ar·ca·ture (är'kə-chẽr), *n.* [< ML. *arcata* (see ARCADE); + *-ure*], in *architecture*, 1. a small arcade. 2. a closed or false arcade, as for ornament.

‡arc-bou·tant (ȧr'bōō'tän'), *n.* [*pl.* ARCS-BOUTANTS (ȧr'bōō'tän')], [Fr.], in *architecture*, a flying buttress.

arc furnace, an electric furnace in which the heat comes from an arc between an electrode and the material being heated.

arch (ärch), *n.* [ME.; OFr. *arche*; ML. *arca*; L. *arcus*, a bow, arch], 1. a curved structure, as of masonry, used as a support over an open space, as in a bridge, doorway, etc. 2. any similar structure, as a monument. 3. the form of an arch. 4. anything shaped like an arch. 5. in *anatomy*, an archlike part: as, the dental *arch*, *arch* of the foot, etc. *v.t.* 1. to provide with an arch or arches. 2. to cause to take the form of an arch. *v.i.* 1. to form an arch. 2. to span as an arch.

arch (ärch), *adj.* [< *arch-*, with changed meaning because of use in *archknave*, *archrogue*], 1. main; chief; principal. 2. clever; crafty: as, an *arch* villain. 3. gaily mischievous; pert: as, an *arch* look.

arch- (ärch; *in* archangel *& its derivatives*, ärk), [ME. *arche-*; AS. *arce-*, *erce-*; L. *archi-*, *arch-* < Gr. *archos*, ruler], a prefix meaning *main, chief, principal:* used in forming titles of rank, as *archduke*, *archbishop*.

-arch (ärk), [< Gr. *archos*, ruler], a suffix meaning *ruler*, as in *heptarch*, *matriarch*.

arch., 1. archaic. 2. archery. 3. archipelago. 4. architect. 5. architectural. 6. architecture.

Ar·chae·an (är-kē'ən), *adj.* Archean.

ar·chae·o- (är'ki-ō), [< Gr. *archaios*, ancient < *archē*, the beginning], a combining form meaning *ancient, original*, as in *archaeology*: sometimes spelled **archeo-**.

ar·chae·o·log·i·cal (är'ki-ə-loj'i-k'l), *adj.* of or connected with archaeology: also spelled **archeological.**

ar·chae·ol·o·gist (är'ki-ol'ə-jist), *n.* a student of or specialist in archaeology: also spelled **archeologist.**

ar·chae·ol·o·gy (är'ki-ol'ə-ji), *n.* [*archaeo-* + *-logy*], the scientific study of the life and culture of ancient peoples, as by excavation of ancient cities, relics, artifacts, etc.: also spelled **archeology**: abbreviated **archaeol.**

ar·chae·op·ter·yx (är'ki-op'tẽr-iks), *n.* [Mod. L.; *archaeo-* + Gr. *pteryx*, wing], an extinct reptilelike bird of the Jurassic Period, which had teeth, a lizardlike tail, and well-developed wings.

Ar·chae·o·zo·ic (är'ki-ə-zō'ik), *adj.* Archeozoic.

ar·cha·ic (är-kā'ik), *adj.* [Gr. *archaikos* < *archaios*, old, ancient], 1. belonging to an earlier period; ancient. 2. antiquated; old-fashioned. 3. that has ceased to be used except in poetry, church ritual, etc.: as, *thou* is an *archaic* form of *you*. Abbreviated **arch.** —*SYN.* see **old.**

ar·cha·i·cal·ly (är-kā'i-k'l-i, är-kā'ik-li), *adv.* 1. in an archaic manner. 2. as an archaism.

ar·cha·ism (är'ki-iz'm, är'kā-iz'm), *n.* [Fr. *archaisme* < Gr. *archaismos* < *archaios*; see ARCHAIC], 1. the use or imitation of archaic words, technique, etc. 2. an archaic word, usage, technique, etc.

ar·cha·ist (är'ki-ist, är'kā-ist), *n.* 1. a student of or expert in archaic things or antiquities. 2. a person who is fond of using archaisms in speaking or writing.

ar·cha·is·tic (är'ki-is'tik, är'kā-is'tik), *adj.* 1. using archaisms. 2. characterized by archaism.

ar·cha·ize (är'ki-iz', är'kā-īz'), *v.t.* [ARCHAIZED (-īzd'), ARCHAIZING], to make archaistic or archaic. *v.i.* to use archaisms.

arch·an·gel (ärk'ān'jəl, ärk'ān'jəl), *n.* [< OFr. *archangel* or LL. *archangelus*; Gr. *archangelos* < *archos*, chief, first + *angelos*, messenger, angel], 1. an angel of the highest rank; a chief angel. 2. the plant angelica. 3. [A-], *a)* a region in the R.S.F.S.R., on the Arctic Ocean: pop., 1,278,000. *b)* its capital, a seaport on the White Sea: pop., 256,000: Russian name, *Arkhangelsk*. *c)* a gulf of the White Sea: see **Dvina Bay.**

arch·bish·op (ärch'bish'əp), *n.* [ME. *archebischop*; AS. *arcebiscop*; L. *archiepiscopus*; Gr. *archiepiskopos*; *archi-*, chief + *episkopos*, overseer], a bishop of the highest rank; a chief bishop, who presides over an archbishopric or archdiocese: abbreviated **Abp., abp., Arch.**

arch·bish·op·ric (ärch'bish'əp-rik), *n.* [ME. *archebischopriche*; AS. *arcebiscoprice*; *arcebiscop* (see ARCHBISHOP) + *rice*, jurisdiction], 1. the office, rank, duties, or term of an archbishop. 2. the church district or province over which an archbishop has jurisdiction.

Archd., 1. Archdeacon. 2. Archduke.

arch·dea·con (ärch'dē'k'n), *n.* [AS. *arcediacon*, *archidiacon*; L. *archidiaconus*; Gr. *archidiakonos* < *archos*, chief + *diakonos*, servant, minister], a chief deacon; church official ranking just below a bishop or an archpriest: in the Anglican Church he has supervisory duties under the bishop.

arch·dea·con·ry (ärch'dē'k'n-ri), *n.* [*pl.* ARCHDEACONRIES (-riz)], 1. the office, rank, duties, or jurisdiction of an archdeacon. 2. an archdeacon's residence.

arch·di·o·cese (ärch'dī'ə-sēs', ärch'dī'ə-sis), *n.* [*arch-* + *diocese*], the diocese of an archbishop.

arch·du·cal (ärch'dōō'k'l, ärch'dū'k'l), *adj.* of an archduke or archduchy.

arch·duch·ess (ärch'duch'is), *n.* 1. the wife or widow of an archduke. 2. a princess of the former royal family of Austria.

arch·duch·y (ärch'duch'i), *n.* [*pl.* ARCHDUCHIES (-iz)], the territory ruled by an archduke or archduchess.

arch·duke (ärch'dōōk', ärch'dūk'), *n.* a chief duke, especially a prince of the former Austrian royal family.

Ar·che·an (är-kē'ən), *adj.* [Gr. *archaios*, ancient < *archē*, beginning], in *geology*, ancient; designating or of the oldest known rocks: also spelled **Archaean.**

arched (ärcht), *adj.* [pp. of *arch*], 1. furnished or covered with an arch or arches. 2. having the form or shape of an arch; curved.

ar·che·gone (är'ki-gōn'), *n.* an archegonium.

ar·che·go·ni·al (är'ki-gō'ni-əl), *adj.* of an archegonium.

ar·che·go·ni·ate (är'ki-gō'ni-it), *adj.* having archegonia.

ar·che·go·ni·um (är'ki-gō'ni-əm), *n.* [*pl.* ARCHEGONIA (-ə)], [Mod. L., dim. < Gr. *archegonos*, the first of a race; *arche-* < *archos*, first, chief + *gonos*, offspring], in *botany*, the flask-shaped female reproductive organ in mosses, ferns, etc.

arch·en·e·my (ärch'en'ə-mi), *n.* [*pl.* ARCHENEMIES (-miz)], a chief enemy.
the archenemy, Satan.

ar·chen·ter·on (är-ken'tẽr-on), *n.* [< *archi-* + Gr. *enteron*, intestine], in *zoology*, the cavity at the center of an embryo in the gastrula stage of development, forming a primitive digestive tract.

ar·che·ol·o·gy (är'ki-ol'ə-ji), *n.* archaeology.

Ar·che·o·zo·ic (är'ki-ə-zō'ik), *adj.* [*arch(a)eo-* + *zo-* + *-ic*], designating or of the earliest known geological era, characterized by thick lava flows, mountain formation, and microscopic plant and animal life.
the Archeozoic, the Archeozoic Era or its rocks: see **geology**, chart.

arch·er (ärch'ẽr), *n.* [ME.; OFr. *archier*; L. *arcarius*, bowman < *arcus*, a bow], 1. a person who shoots with a bow and arrows; bowman. 2. [A-], the constellation Sagittarius.

arch·er·y (ärch'ẽr-i), *n.* [ME. & OFr. *archerie* < *archier*; see ARCHER], 1. the practice, art, or technique of shooting with bow and arrow. 2. an archer's bows, arrows, and other equipment. 3. archers collectively. Abbreviated **arch.**

ar·che·spore (är'ki-spôr', är'ki-spōr'), *n.* [Mod. L. *archesporium*; see ARCHI- & SPORE], in *botany*, a cell or group of cells from which the spore mother cells develop.

ar·che·type (är'kə-tip'), *n.* [L. *archetypus*; Gr. *archetypon* < *arche-*, first + *typos*; see TYPE, *n.*], the original pattern, or model, from which all other things of the same kind are made; prototype. —*SYN.* see **model.**

arch·fiend (ärch'fēnd'), *n.* [*arch-* + *fiend*], a chief fiend.
the archfiend, Satan.

ar·chi- (är'ki), [see ARCH-], a prefix meaning: 1. *chief, first*, as in *archidiaconal*. 2. in *biology*, *primitive, original*, as in *archiplasm*.

Ar·chi·bald (är′chi-bôld′), [of Gmc. origin; OHG. *Erchaubald*, prob. nobly bold], a masculine name: diminutives, *Archie, Archy*.

ar·chi·blast (är′ki-blast′), *n.* [*archi-* + *-blast*], in *biology*, 1. egg protoplasm. 2. the outer of the two layers of an embryo in an early stage of development.

ar·chi·carp (är′ki-kärp′), *n.* [*archi-* + *-carp*], in *botany*, the female reproductive organ in an ascomycetous fungus, giving rise to spore sacs (asci) after fertilization: also called *ascogonium*.

ar·chi·di·ac·o·nal (är′ki-dī-ak′ə-n'l), *adj.* [*archi-* + *diaconal*], 1. of an archdeacon. 2. of an archdeaconry.

ar·chi·e·pis·co·pa·cy (är′ki-ə-pis′kə-pə-si), *n.* [*archi-* + *episcopacy*], church rule by archbishops.

ar·chi·e·pis·co·pal (är′ki-ə-pis′kə-p'l), *adj.* [ML. *archiepiscopalis;* see ARCHI- & EPISCOPAL], 1. of an archbishop. 2. of an archbishopric.

ar·chil (är′kil), *n.* [ME. *orchell;* OFr. *orchel, orcheil;* It. *orchello*], 1. any of a number of lichens yielding a purple dye. 2. the dye.

ar·chi·mage (är′ki-māj′), *n.* [< *archi-* + L. *magus* < Gr. *magos;* cf. MAGI], a great magician or wizard.

ar·chi·man·drite (är′ki-man′drīt), *n.* [ML. & LL. *archimandrita;* Late Gr. *archimandritēs* < *archi-*, chief + *mandra*, enclosure, monastery], in the *Orthodox Eastern Church*, the head of a monastery or of a number of monasteries.

Ar·chi·me·de·an (är′ki-mē′di-ən, är′ki-mi-dē′ən), *adj.* [L. *Archimedeus* < *Archimedes*], of, discovered, or invented by Archimedes.

Archimedean (or **Archimedes'**) **screw**, an ancient water-raising device attributed to Archimedes, made up of a spiral tube on a shaft or a large screw in a cylinder, revolved by hand.

ARCHIMEDEAN SCREW

Ar·chi·me·des (är′ki-mē′dēz), *n.* Greek mathematician and physicist; 287?-212 B.C.; discovered principles of the lever and of specific gravity.

ar·chine (är-shēn′) *n.* [Russ.], a Russian unit of linear measure equal to 28 inches: also spelled **arshin**.

arch·ing (är′chiŋ), *adj.* [ppr. of *arch*], forming an arch. *n.* 1. an arched part. 2. a series of arches.

ar·chi·pe·lag·ic (är′kə-pə-laj′ik), *adj.* of or constituting an archipelago.

ar·chi·pel·a·go (är′kə-pel′ə-gō′), *n.* [*pl.* ARCHIPELAGOES, ARCHIPELAGOS (-gōz′)], [It. *arcipelago* < Gr. *archi-*, chief + *pelagos*, sea], 1. [A-], the Aegean Sea; hence, 2. any sea with many islands. 3. such a group of islands. Abbreviated **arch.** See **Malay Archipelago**, map.

ar·chi·plasm (är′kə-plaz'm), *n.* [*archi-* + *-plasm*], 1. the most primitive living matter. 2. archoplasm.

ar·chi·tect (är′kə-tekt′), *n.* [L. *architectus;* Gr. *architektōn; archi-*, chief + *tektōn*, worker], 1. a person whose profession is designing buildings, drawing up plans, and generally supervising the construction; specialist in architecture. 2. any similar designer: as, a naval *architect*. 3. any builder or creator. Abbreviated **arch.**

ar·chi·tec·ton·ic (är′ki-tek-ton′ik), *adj.* [L. *architectonicus;* Gr. *architektonikos* < *architektōn;* see ARCHITECT], 1. of an architect or architecture; constructive. 2. done as though by an architect; showing design. 3. controlling. 4. in *philosophy*, having to do with the systematizing of knowledge. *n.* architectonics.

ar·chi·tec·ton·ics (är′ki-tek-ton′iks), *n.pl.* [construed as sing.], 1. the science of architecture. 2. structural design: as, the *architectonics* of Beethoven's symphonies. 3. in *philosophy*, the science of systematizing knowledge.

ar·chi·tec·tur·al (är′kə-tek′chẽr-əl), *adj.* 1. of or connected with architecture. 2. having the qualities of architecture. Abbreviated **arch.**

ar·chi·tec·tur·al·ly (är′kə-tek′chẽr-əl-i), *adv.* 1. from the standpoint of architecture. 2. in an architectural manner.

ar·chi·tec·ture (är′kə-tek′chẽr), *n.* [Fr.; L. *architectura;* see ARCHITECT], 1. the science, art, or profession of designing and constructing buildings. 2. a building, or buildings collectively. 3. a style of construction: as, Elizabethan *architecture*. 4. design and construction. 5. any framework, system, etc. Abbreviated **arch.**

ar·chi·trave (är′kə-trāv′), *n.* [Fr.; It. < L. *archi-* + *trabs*, a beam], in *architecture*, 1. the lowest part of an entablature, a beam resting directly on the tops of the columns: see **entablature**, illus. 2. the molding around a doorway, window, etc.

ar·chi·val (är′kī-v'l), *adj.* of, in, or containing archives.

ar·chives (är′kīvz), *n.pl.* [Fr., pl. of *archif* < L. *archivum, archium;* Gr. *archeion*, town hall < *ta archeia*, public records < *archē*, the beginning, magistracy], 1. a place where public records, documents, etc. are kept. 2. the public records, documents, etc. kept in such a place.

ar·chi·vist (är′kə-vist), *n.* a person having charge of archives.

ar·chi·volt (är′kə-vōlt′), *n.* [It. *archivolto, arcovolta;* see ARCH, *n.* & VAULT], in *architecture*, 1. the inner curve of an arch or the structural parts of this. 2. an ornamental molding on the wall side of an arch.

arch·ly (ärch′li), *adv.* in an arch manner; gaily and mischievously.

arch·ness (ärch′nis), *n.* the quality of being arch, or gaily mischievous.

ar·chon (är′kon, är′kən), *n.* [Gr. *archōn* < *archein*, to be first, rule], 1. one of the nine chief magistrates of ancient Athens. 2. a ruler.

ar·cho·plasm (är′kə-plaz'm), *n.* [Mod. L. *archoplasma* < Gr. *archōn* (see ARCHON); + *-plasm*], in *biology*, that part of the cell protoplasm which forms the asters, astral rays, and spindles in mitosis.

arch·priest (ärch′prēst′), *n.* [*arch-* + *priest*], 1. formerly, a priest who acted as a bishop's chief assistant; dean. 2. a chief priest; hence, 3. the chief proponent of a school of thought, political theory, etc.

arch·way (ärch′wā′), *n.* a passageway under an arch.

-ar·chy (är-ki, ẽr-ki), [Gr. *-archia* < *archos*, ruler], a suffix meaning *ruling, that which is ruled*, as in *heptarchy, monarchy*.

arcked (ärkt), alternative past tense and past participle of **arc.**

arck·ing (ärk′iŋ), alternative present participle of **arc.**

arc lamp, a lamp in which the light is produced by an arc between electrodes.

arc light, 1. an arc lamp. 2. the light of an arc lamp.

A.R.C.S., 1. Associate of the Royal College of Science. 2. Associate of the Royal College of Surgeons.

arc·tic (ärk′tik; *also, esp. for n. 3,* är′tik), *adj.* [ME. *artic;* OFr. *artique;* L. *arcticus;* Gr. *arktikos*, lit., of the (constellation of the) Bear (Gr. *arktos*), northern, arctic], 1. of, characteristic of, or near the North Pole or the region around it; hence, 2. very cold; frigid. *n.* 1. the region around the North Pole. 2. the Arctic Circle. 3. an overshoe: see **arctics.**

Arctic Circle, arctic circle, an imaginary circle parallel to the equator, 23°30′ from the North Pole.

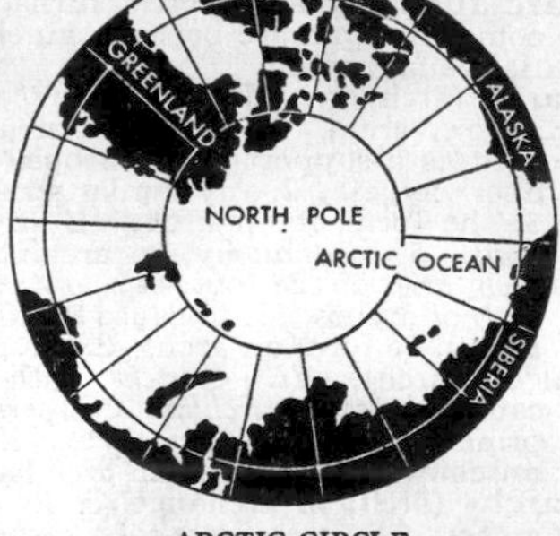

ARCTIC CIRCLE

Arctic Ocean, the ocean around the North Pole, north of the Arctic Circle: area, 5,440,000 sq. mi.

arc·tics (ärk′tiks, är′tiks), *n.pl.* [< *arctic*], warmly lined, waterproof overshoes.

Arctic Zone, all the region north of the Arctic Circle; the North Frigid Zone.

Arc·tu·rus (ärk-toor′əs, ärk-tyoor′-əs), *n.* [L.; Gr. *Arktouros* < *arktos*, a bear + *ouros*, a guard], the brightest star in the constellation Boötes: see **constellation**, chart.

ar·cu·ate (är′kū-it, är′kū-āt′), *adj.* [L. *arcuatus*, pp. of *arcuare*, to arch, bend like a bow < *arcus*, a bow], curved like a bow; arched.

ar·cu·a·tion (är′kū-ā′shən), *n.* [L. *arcuatio;* see ARCUATE], 1. a curving or being curved like a bow. 2. the use of arches in building. 3. a row of arches.

-ard (ẽrd), [OFr.; MHG. *-hart* < *hart*, bold, hardy], a suffix (originally an intensive) used in forming nouns meaning *one who is too ———*, *one who does* (something not admirable) *too much*, as in *sluggard, drunkard:* also **-art**, as in *braggart*.

ar·deb (är′deb), *n.* [colloq. Ar. *ardabb*, for Ar. *al irdabb;* prob. ult. < Gr. *artabē*, a Persian measure], a unit of dry measure used in Egypt and Moslem countries, varying from 1/2 peck to 7 1/2 bushels.

Ar·den (är′d'n), *n.* 1. a wooded district in Warwickshire, England, the site of a former forest made famous by Shakespeare in *As You Like It;* hence, 2. a land of romance.

ar·den·cy (är′d'n-si), *n.* [< *ardent* + *-cy*], a being ardent; ardor.

Ar·dennes (år′den′), *n.* a wooded and partly hilly section in southern Belgium and northeastern France.

ar·dent (är′d'nt), *adj.* [L. *ardens, ardentis*, ppr. of *ardere*, to burn], 1. glowing; beaming. 2. passionate; vehement; eager; intensely enthusiastic. 3. [Obs.], burning; aflame. —*SYN.* see **passionate.**

ardent spirits, strong alcoholic liquor; whisky, gin, etc.

ar·dor (är′dẽr), *n.* [ME.; OFr. *ardour, ardor;* L. *ardor*, a flame, fire < *ardere*, to burn], 1. emotional warmth; passion; eagerness; enthusiasm; zeal. 2. intense heat; fire. —*SYN.* see **passion.**

ar·dour (är′dẽr), *n.* ardor: British spelling.

ar·du·ous (är′jōō-əs), *adj.* [L. *arduus*, steep], 1. difficult to do; requiring exertion; laborious. 2. steep; hard to climb. 3. energetic; working hard. —*SYN.* see **hard.**

TYPES OF ARCHITECTURE

EGYPTIAN (Pyramid)

EGYPTIAN (Temple at Karnak)

ASSYRIAN (Palace near Nineveh)

BYZANTINE (church)

GREEK IONIC
(Erechtheum, Athens)

GREEK DORIC
(Temple of Paestum)

MAYAN
(Temple at Chichén Itzá, Yucatan)

CHINESE
(Pagoda of Sung Yueh Ssu)

CHINESE BUDDHIST
(Drum Tower, Peking)

RUSSIAN
(Cathedral of St. Basil, Moscow)

FRENCH GOTHIC
(Rheims Cathedral)

ENGLISH GOTHIC
(Westminster Abbey)

INDIAN (Taj Mahal)

MODERN (house)

MODERN (house)

are (är), [AS. (Northumbrian) *aron* < verbal base found also in *am* & *art;* see AM], the plural and second person singular, present indicative, of **be:** see also **aren't.**

are (âr), *n.* [Fr. < L. *area;* see AREA], a unit of surface measure in the metric system, equal to 100 square meters or 119.6 square yards: abbreviated **a.**

ar·e·a (âr'i-ə), *n.* [*pl.* AREAS (-əz); *for 6, often* AREAE (-ē')], [L., level piece of ground], 1. originally, a level surface or piece of ground. 2. a part of the earth's surface; region; tract. 3. the total outside surface of anything, as measured in square units. 4. a yard of a building; areaway. 5. scope; range; extent. 6. in *biology,* a limited part of the surface of an organism.

ar·e·a·way (âr'i-ə-wā'), *n.* 1. a sunken yard or court leading into a cellar, for entrance or light and air. 2. a passageway between buildings or parts of a building.

ar·e·ca (ar'i-kə, ə-rē'kə), *n.* [Port.; prob. < Malayalam *aḍekka*], any of a number of related palms with a smooth trunk, white flowers, orange-colored fruit, and large, feathery leaves, as the betel palm.

A·re·ci·bo (ä're-sē'bô), *n.* a seaport in northern Puerto Rico: pop., 29,000.

a·re·na (ə-rē'nə), *n.* [*pl.* ARENAS (-nəz), ARENAE (-nē)], [L. *arena, harena,* sand, sandy place, arena], 1. the central part of an ancient Roman amphitheater, where gladiatorial contests and shows took place. 2. any place like this: as, an *arena* for boxing matches. 3. any sphere of struggle or exertion. 4. in the *theater,* a central stage without a proscenium, surrounded by seats: often used attributively, as in *arena theater* (also called *theater-in-the-round*), *arena staging.*

ar·e·na·ceous (ar'i-nā'shəs), *adj.* [L. *arenaceus;* see ARENA], 1. sandy. 2. growing in sand.

ar·e·nic·o·lous (ar'i-nik'ə-ləs), *adj.* [< L. *arena,* sand + *colere,* to dwell], living in sand, as some burrowing animals.

aren't (ärnt), are not: also occasionally used as a substitute for a contraction of *am not* in interrogative constructions: see also **ain't.**

ar·e·o- (âr'i-ə), [< Gr. *Areos,* genit. of *Arēs,* Mars], a combining form meaning *of Mars,* as in *areology.*

ar·e·o·cen·tric (âr'i-ō-sen'trik), *adj.* in *astronomy,* with the planet Mars regarded as center.

a·re·o·la (ə-rē'ə-lə), *n.* [*pl.* AREOLAE (-lē'), AREOLAS (-ləz)], [L., small open place, dim. of *area;* see AREA], 1. a small space, as between the veins of a leaf or the ribs of an insect's wing. 2. in *anatomy,* a small space around something, as the dark area around a nipple. 3. in *biology,* a small hollow in a surface.

a·re·o·lar (ə-rē'ə-lẽr), *adj.* 1. of or like an areola. 2. consisting of areolae.

ar·e·ole (âr'i-ōl'), *n.* [Fr.], an areola.

ar·e·ol·o·gy (âr'i-ol'ə-ji), *n.* [*areo-* + *-logy*], the study of the planet Mars.

Ar·e·op·a·gite (ar'i-op'ə-jīt', ar'i-op'ə-gīt'), *n.* [L. *Areopagites;* Gr. *Areiopagitēs*], any member of the Areopagus in ancient Athens.

Ar·e·op·a·gus (ar'i-op'ə-gəs), *n.* [L. < Gr. *Areiopagos* < *Areios,* of Ares + *pagos,* hill], 1. the hill of Ares, west of the Acropolis in ancient Athens, where the high court of judges sat; hence, 2. this court. 3. any important law court.

A·re·qui·pa (ä're-kē'pä), *n.* a city in southern Peru: pop., 122,000.

Ar·es (âr'ēz), *n.* [L.; Gr. *Arēs*], in *Greek mythology,* the god of war, son of Zeus and Hera: identified with the Roman god Mars.

a·rête (ə-rāt'; Fr. ȧ'ret'), *n.* [Fr., lit., fish skeleton, awn of wheat, ridge; OFr. *areste;* L. *arista,* awn of grain, fishbone], a sharp, narrow ridge or crest of a mountain.

Ar·e·thu·sa (ar'i-thū'zə, ar'i-thōō'sə), *n.* [L.; Gr. *Arethousa*], 1. in *Greek mythology,* a woodland nymph, changed into a stream by Artemis so that she might escape her pursuer, the river god Alpheus. 2. [a-], a variety of orchid, usually with one long, narrow leaf and one rose-purple flower.

A·re·ti·no, Pie·tro (pye'trô ä're-tē'nô), 1492–1556; Italian satirical writer.

A·rez·zo (ä-ret'tsô), *n.* a city in central Italy: pop., 65,000.

Arg., 1. Argentina. 2. Argentine.

ar·gal (är'g'l), *conj. & adv.* [altered < L. *ergo*], [Archaic], ergo; therefore; hence.

ar·gal (är'g'l), *n.* argol.

ar·gal (är'g'l), *n.* an argali.

ar·ga·la (är'gə-lə), *n.* [Hind. *hargīlā*], 1. a stork of India, the adjutant. 2. an African stork, the marabou.

ar·ga·li (är'gə-li), *n.* [*pl.* ARGALIS (-liz), ARGALI; see PLURAL, II, D, 1], [Mongol.], 1. a wild sheep of Asia, with large, curved horns. 2. any of several other wild sheep, as the American bighorn.

Ar·gand burner (är'gənd), [after Aimé *Argand* (1755–1803), the inventor, a Swiss chemist], an oil burner made up of two concentric tubes separated by a cylindrical wick through which air is passed to increase the rate of combustion.

ar·gent (är'jənt), *n.* [Fr.; L. *argentum;* Gr. *argyros,* silver < *argos,* white], 1. [Archaic or Poetic], silver. 2. [Obs.], silver coin; money. *adj.* of silver; silvery.

ar·gen·tal (är-jen't'l), *adj.* of, like, or containing silver.

ar·gen·te·ous (är-jen'ti-əs), *adj.* [L. *argenteus;* see ARGENT], of or like silver; silvery.

Ar·gen·teuil (ȧr'zhän'tö'i), *n.* a city in northern France, on the Seine: pop., 63,000.

ar·gen·tic (är-jen'tik), *adj.* [< L. *argentum* (see ARGENT); + *-ic*], of or containing silver, with a higher valence than in the corresponding argentous compounds.

ar·gen·tif·er·ous (är'jən-tif'ẽr-əs), *adj.* [< L. *argentum* (see ARGENT); + *-ferous*], containing silver, as ore.

Ar·gen·ti·na (är'jən-tē'nə), *n.* a country in southern South America: area, 1,079,965 sq. mi.; pop., 20,956,000; capital, Buenos Aires: abbreviated **Arg.**

Ar·gen·tine (är'jən-tēn', är'jən-tin'), *adj.* of Argentina, its people, or culture. *n.* a native or inhabitant of Argentina. Abbreviated **Arg.**

the Argentine, Argentina.

ar·gen·tine (är'jən-tin, är'jən-tīn'), *adj.* [Fr. *argentin;* L. *argentinus;* see ARGENT], of or like silver; silvery. *n.* 1. silver. 2. any of several metals like silver.

Ar·gen·tin·e·an (är'jən-tin'i-ən), *n.* an Argentine.

ar·gen·tite (är'jən-tīt'), *n.* [< L. *argentum* (see ARGENT); + *-ite*], native silver sulfide, Ag_2S, a heavy, dark-gray mineral that is an important ore of silver.

ar·gen·tol (är'jən-tōl', är'jən-tol'), *n.* [< L. *argentum* (see ARGENT); + *-ol*], an organic compound of silver, used in powder form as an antiseptic.

ar·gen·tous (är-jen'təs), *adj.* [< L. *argentum* (see ARGENT); + *-ous*], of or containing monovalent silver.

ar·gen·tum (är-jen'təm), *n.* [L.; see ARGENT], silver: symbol, Ag: abbreviated **Ar.**

ar·gil (är'jil), *n.* [Fr. *argile;* L. *argilla;* Gr. *argilla* < *argos,* white], clay, especially that used for pottery.

ar·gil·la·ceous (är'ji-lā'shəs), *adj.* [L. *argillaceus;* see ARGIL], like or containing clay; clayey.

ar·gil·lite (är'ji-līt'), *n.* [L. *argilla* (see ARGIL); + *-ite*], a hardened mudstone showing no slatelike cleavage.

ar·gi·nine (är'jə-nēn', är'jə-nin, är'jə-nīn'), *n.* [< L. *argentum;* + *-ine:* its first discovered salts were silvery], a colorless amino acid, $C_6H_{14}O_2N_4$, necessary in nutrition, obtained from plant and animal proteins by hydrolysis or by the action of bacteria in digestion.

Ar·give (är'jīv; *sometimes* är'gīv), *adj.* 1. of ancient Argos or Argolis. 2. Greek. *n.* 1. a native of Argos or Argolis. 2. any Greek: Homeric name.

Ar·go (är'gō), *n.* [L.; Gr. *Argō*], 1. in *Greek legend,* the ship on which Jason sailed to find the Golden Fleece. 2. a large southern constellation between Canis Major and the Southern Cross.

ar·gol (är'g'l), *n.* [ME. *argoile*], tartar in its natural form as deposited in wine casks: also spelled **argal.**

Ar·go·lis (är'gə-lis), *n.* a district of ancient Greece, on the east coast of the Peloponnesus.

ar·gon (är'gon), *n.* [< Gr. *argon,* neut. of *aergos,* inert; *a-,* without + *ergon,* work], one of the chemical elements, an inert, colorless, odorless gas constituting nearly one per cent of the atmosphere: it is used in incandescent light bulbs, radio tubes, etc.: symbol, A; at. wt., 39.944; at. no., 18.

Ar·go·naut (är'gə-nôt'), *n.* [L. *Argonauta;* Gr. *Argonautēs; Argō,* Jason's ship + *nautēs,* sailor < *naus,* ship], 1. in *Greek legend,* any of the men who sailed with Jason to search for the Golden Fleece. 2. a person who took part in the California gold rush of 1848–49. 3. [a-], in *zoology,* the paper nautilus.

Ar·go·nau·tic (är'gə-nô'tik), *adj.* of the Argonauts.

Ar·gonne (är'gon; Fr. ȧr'gôn'), *n.* a forest in northeastern France.

Ar·gos (är'gos, är'gəs), *n.* a city in eastern Peloponnesus, Greece: pop., 13,500: capital of ancient Argolis.

ar·go·sy (är'gə-si), *n.* [*pl.* ARGOSIES (-siz)], [earlier *ragusy* < It. *Ragusa,* vessel of *Ragusa;* sp. influenced by the *Argo;* see ARGO], [Now Poetic], 1. a large ship, especially a merchant ship. 2. a fleet of such ships.

ar·got (är'gō, är'gət), *n.* [Fr.; orig. (in thieves' jargon), concern with thievery; prob. < *argot* (now *ergot*), a claw, spur], the specialized vocabulary and idioms of those in the same work, way of life, etc., as the secret jargon of criminals: see **slang.** —*SYN.* see **dialect.**

ar·gu·a·ble (är'gū-ə-b'l), *adj.* 1. that can be argued about. 2. that can be supported by argument.

ar·gue (är'gū), *v.i.* [ARGUED (-gūd), ARGUING], [ME. *arguen;* OFr. *arguer;* L. *argutare,* to prattle, prate, freq. of *arguere,* to make clear, prove; OFr. meaning and form influenced by *arguere*], 1. to give reasons (*for* or *against* a proposal, proposition, etc.). 2. to dispute (*with* or *against* a person or *about* a thing). 3. to present objections. *v.t.* 1. to give reasons for and against; discuss; debate. 2. to try to prove by giving reasons; maintain; contend. 3. to give evidence of; indicate: as, his manners *argue* a good upbringing. 4. to persuade (*into* or *out of* an opinion, etc.) by giving reasons. —*SYN.* see **discuss.**

ar·gu·fy (är'gyoo-fī'), *v.t. & v.i.* [ARGUFIED (-fīd'), ARGUFYING], [< *argue* + *-fy*], [Colloq. or Dial.], to argue, especially about something petty or just for the sake of arguing; wrangle.

ar·gu·ment (är'gyoo-mənt), *n.* [Fr.; L. *argumentum,* evidence, proof < *arguere;* see ARGUE], 1. a reason or

reasons offered for or against something. 2. the offering of such reasons; reasoning. 3. discussion in which there is disagreement; dispute; debate. 4. a short statement of subject matter; summary. 5. [Archaic], proof. 6. [Obs.], a topic; theme. 7. in *mathematics*, an independent variable whose value determines that of a function: as, the number is the *argument* of which the logarithm is the function.
***SYN.*—argument** refers to a discussion in which there is disagreement and suggests the use of logic and the bringing forth of facts to support or refute a point; **dispute** basically refers to a contradiction of an assertion and implies vehemence or anger in debate; **controversy** connotes a disagreement of lengthy duration over a matter of some weight or importance (the Darwinian *controversy*).

ar·gu·men·ta·tion (är'gyoo-men-tā'shən), ***n.*** [Fr.; L. *argumentatio* < *argumentare;* see ARGUE], 1. the process of arriving at reasons and conclusions; arguing or reasoning. 2. debate; discussion. 3. writing or speaking that argues: conventionally distinguished from *description, narration, exposition.*

ar·gu·men·ta·tive (är'gyoo-men'tə-tiv), ***adj.*** [Fr. *argumentatif;* see ARGUMENT], 1. of or containing argument; controversial. 2. apt to argue; contentious.

‡ar·gu·men·tum (är'gyoo-men'təm), ***n.*** [L.], an argument: used with Latin phrases, *ad hominem, ad rem,* etc.

Ar·gus (är'gəs), ***n.*** [L.; Gr. *Argos; argos,* bright], 1. in *Greek mythology,* a giant with a hundred eyes, ordered by Hera to watch Io: after he was killed by Hermes, his eyes were put in the tail of the peacock. 2. any alert watchman. 3. an East Indian bird resembling the peacock.

Ar·gus-eyed (är'gəs-īd'), ***adj.*** [see ARGUS], vigilant; keenly observant.

ar·gyle (är'gīl), ***adj.*** [< *Argyll,* Scotland: the pattern is adapted from a clan tartan of *Argyll*], knitted or woven in a pattern of diamond-shaped figures of different colors: as, *argyle* socks.

Ar·gyll (är-gīl'), ***n.*** a county on the west coast of Scotland: pop., 63,000; county seat, Inveraray.

ar·gyr·o·dite (är-jir'ə-dīt'), ***n.*** [Gr. *argyrōdēs,* rich in silver < *argyros,* silver], a lustrous, gray mineral, Ag_8GeS_6, made up of silver, germanium, and sulfur.

ar·gy·rol (är'jə-rôl', är'jə-rol'), ***n.*** [< Gr. *argyros,* silver; + *-ol*], silver vitellin, a compound of silver and a protein, used as a local antiseptic, especially in treating inflamed mucous tissues: a trade-mark (**Argyrol**).

a·ri·a (ä'ri-ə, âr'i-ə), ***n.*** [It. < L. *aer;* see AIR], an air or melody in an opera, cantata, or oratorio, especially for solo voice with instrumental accompaniment.

-a·ri·a (ā'ri-ə, âr'i-ə), [Mod. L. < L. *-arius*], a plural suffix used, especially in botany and zoology, to form nouns designating groups and genera.

Ar·i·ad·ne (ar'i-ad'ni), ***n.*** [L.; Gr. *Ariadnē*], in *Greek legend,* king Minos' daughter, who gave Theseus the thread by which he found his way out of the Minotaur's labyrinth: he took her with him, but later deserted her.

Ar·i·an (âr'i-ən, är'yən), ***n. & adj.*** Aryan.

Ar·i·an (âr'i-ən), ***adj.*** [L. *Arianus* < *Arius*], of Arius or Arianism. ***n.*** a believer in Arianism.

-ar·i·an (âr'i-ən), [L. *-arius,* -ary + *-anus,* -an], a suffix denoting: 1. *age.* 2. *sect.* 3. *social belief.* 4. *occupation.* It is used in forming adjectives and nouns derived from adjectives, as *octogenarian, antiquarian.*

Ar·i·an·ism (âr'i-ən-iz'm), ***n.*** the doctrines of Arius, who taught that Jesus was not of the same substance as God, but only the best of created beings.

A·ri·ca (ä-rē'kä), ***n.*** a department of northern Chile: formerly part of Tacna-Arica: pop., 13,000.

ar·id (ar'id), ***adj.*** [L. *aridus* < *arere,* to be dry], 1. dry; parched. 2. barren; unfertile. 3. uninteresting; lifeless; dull. —***SYN.*** see **dry.**

a·rid·i·ty (ə-rid'ə-ti), ***n.*** 1. the quality or state of being arid; dryness; barrenness. 2. dullness; lifelessness.

Ar·i·el (âr'i-əl), ***n.*** [< L. *ariel;* Gr. *ariēl;* Heb. *'arī'ēl,* lion of God: a name applied to Jerusalem in the Old Testament], 1. the airy spirit who was the servant of Prospero, a character in Shakespeare's play *The Tempest.* 2. a satellite of the planet Uranus.

ar·i·el (âr'i-el'), ***n.*** [Ar. *aryal*], a kind of gazelle of Asia and Africa.

Ar·i·es (âr'ēz, âr'i-ēz'), ***n.*** [L., the Ram], 1. a northern constellation between Pisces and Taurus, supposedly outlining a ram: see **constellation,** chart. 2. the first sign of the zodiac (♈), which the sun enters about March 21: see **zodiac,** illus.

ar·i·et·ta (ar'i-et'ə), ***n.*** [It., dim. of *aria;* see ARIA], a short melody or aria.

ar·i·ette (ar'i-et'), ***n.*** [Fr.; It. *arietta*], an arietta.

a·right (ə-rīt'), ***adv.*** [*a-,* on + *right*], correctly; rightly.

ar·il (ar'il), ***n.*** [Mod. L. *arillus;* ML., dried grape], an additional covering that forms on certain seeds after fertilization, developing from the stalk of the ovule.

ar·il·late (ar'ə-lāt'), ***adj.*** covered with an aril.

ar·il·lode (ar'i-lōd'), ***n.*** [< Mod. L. *arillus* (see ARIL); + *-ode* (like)], a false aril, developing from an opening in the covering of the ovule instead of its stalk.

Ar·i·ma·the·a, Ar·i·ma·thae·a (ar'i-mə-thē'ə), ***n.*** a town in ancient Palestine.

A·rim·i·num (ə-rim'i-nəm), ***n.*** Rimini: ancient name.

ar·i·ose (ar'i-ōs', ar'i-ōs'), ***adj.*** [L. *arioso* < *aria;* see ARIA], songlike; melodic: distinguished from *recitative.*

a·rio·so (ä-ryō'sō), ***adj.*** [It.; see ARIOSE], like an aria; melodious. ***adv.*** in arioso style. ***n.*** an arioso composition.

A·ri·os·to, Lo·do·vi·co (lô'dô-vē'kô ä'ri-ôs'tô), 1474–1533; Italian poet; author of *Orlando Furioso.*

-ar·i·ous (âr'i-əs), [< L. *-arius;* + *-ous*], a suffix meaning *relating to, connected with,* as in *hilarious, vicarious.*

a·rise (ə-rīz'), ***v.i.*** [AROSE (-rōz'), ARISEN (-riz''n), ARISING], [ME. *arisen;* AS. *arisan; a-,* out + *risan,* to rise], 1. to get up, as from bed. 2. to move upward; rise; ascend. 3. to come into being; begin; originate. 4. to result or spring (*from* something). —***SYN.*** see **rise.**

a·ris·ta (ə-ris'tə), ***n.*** [*pl.* ARISTAE (-tē)], [L.], 1. the beardlike part of grain or grasses; awn. 2. a bristlelike process, as on the antennae of certain insects.

Ar·is·tar·chus (ar'is-tär'kəs), ***n.*** Greek astronomer; 3d century B.C.; discovered the precession of the equinoxes.

a·ris·tate (ə-ris'tāt), ***adj.*** [L. *aristatus* < *arista,* beard of grain], in *botany* & *zoology,* having an awn.

Ar·is·ti·des (ar'is-tī'dēz), ***n.*** Athenian statesman and general; lived 530?–468? B.C.: called *the Just.*

Ar·is·tip·pus (ar'is-tip'əs), ***n.*** Greek philosopher; 435?–356? B.C.; founded the Cyrenaic school.

ar·is·toc·ra·cy (ar'ə-stok'rə-si), ***n.*** [*pl.* ARISTOCRACIES (-siz)], [L. *aristocratia;* Gr. *aristokratia* < *aristos,* best + *kratia* < *kratein,* to rule], 1. originally, government by the best citizens. 2. government by a privileged minority or upper class, usually of inherited wealth and social position. 3. a country with this form of government; oligarchy. 4. a privileged ruling class; nobility. 5. those considered the best in some way: as, an *aristocracy* of brains. 6. aristocratic quality or spirit.

a·ris·to·crat (ə-ris'tə-krat', ar'is-tə-krat'), ***n.*** [Fr. *aristocrate* < *aristocratique;* Gr. *aristokratikos;* see ARISTOCRATIC], 1. a member of the aristocracy; nobleman. 2. a person with the tastes, manners, beliefs, prejudices, etc. of the upper class. 3. a person who believes in aristocracy as a form of government.

ar·is·to·crat·ic (ə-ris'tə-krat'ik, ar'is-tə-krat'ik), ***adj.*** [Gr. *aristokratikos* < *aristos,* best + *kratein,* to rule], 1. of, characteristic of, or favoring aristocracy as a form of government. 2. of an aristocracy or upper class. 3. like or characteristic of an aristocrat: used in either a favorable sense (proud, distinguished, etc.) or an unfavorable (snobbish, etc.).

a·ris·to·crat·i·cal·ly (ə-ris'tə-krat'i-k'l-i, ar'is-tə-krat'ik-li), ***adv.*** in an aristocratic manner.

a·ris·to·lo·chi·a·ceous (ə-ris'tə-lō'ki-ā'shəs), ***adj.*** [L. *aristolochia,* a plant useful in childbirth < Gr. *aristolocheia* < *aristos,* best + *locheia,* childbirth; + *-aceous*], belonging to the birthwort family of plants, which tend to climb or twine and have large, irregularly shaped, bad-smelling flowers of striking colors and markings.

Ar·is·toph·a·nes (ar'is-tof'ə-nēz'), ***n.*** Greek writer of satirical comic dramas; lived 448?–380? B.C.

Ar·is·to·te·li·an (ar'is-tə-tē'li-ən, ə-ris'tə-tēl'yən), ***adj.*** of or characteristic of Aristotle or his philospohy. ***n.*** 1. a follower of Aristotle, or of his philosophy or way of thinking. 2. a person who tends to be empirical or practical in his thinking, rather than metaphysical or idealistic: distinguished from *Platonist.*

Aristotelian logic, 1. Aristotle's method of deductive logic, characterized by the syllogism. 2. the formal logic developed from Aristotle's.

Ar·is·tot·le (ar'is-tot''l), ***n.*** Greek philosopher; 384–322 B.C.; pupil of Plato.

a·ris·to·type (ə-ris'tə-tīp'), ***n.*** [< Gr. *aristos,* best; + *-type*], in *photography,* 1. any method of printing that uses paper coated with salts of silver in collodion or gelatin. 2. a print made by such a method.

a·rith·me·tic (ə-rith'mə-tik'), ***n.*** [ME. *arsmetrike, arsmetike;* OFr. *arismetrique* (influenced in form by L. *ars metrica,* the art of measurement); L. *arithmetica;* Gr. (*hē*) *arithmetikē* (*technē*), (the) counting (art) < *arithmētikos,* arithmetical < *arithmein,* to count < *arithmos,* number], 1. the science or art of computing by positive, real numbers. 2. knowledge of or skill in this science: as, my *arithmetic* is poor. 3. a textbook on this science. ***adj.*** (ar'ith-met'ik), arithmetical.

ar·ith·met·i·cal (ar'ith-met'i-k'l), ***adj.*** of, based on, or using arithmetic.

ar·ith·met·i·cal·ly (ar'ith-met'i-k'l-i, ar'ith-met'ik-li), ***adv.*** 1. by means of arithmetic. 2. according to the principles of arithmetic.

a·rith·me·ti·cian (ə-rith'mə-tish'ən, ar'ith-mə-tish'ən), ***n.*** [Fr.; see ARITHMETIC], a person skilled in arithmetic.

arithmetic mean, the average obtained by dividing a sum by the number of its addends.

arithmetic progression, a sequence of terms each of which, after the first, is derived by adding to the preceding one a constant quantity (the *common difference,* or *constant*): 5, 9, 13, 17, etc. are in *arithmetic progression.*

A·ri·us (ə-rī′əs, âr′i-əs), *n.* Greek theologian of Alexandria; lived 280?–336 A.D.: see **Arianism.**

‡**a ri·ve·der·ci** (ä rē′ve-der′chē), [It.], until we meet again; good-by: implies temporary parting.

Ar·i·zo·na (ar′ə-zō′nə), *n.* a Southwestern State of the United States, on the Mexican border: area, 113,909 sq. mi.; pop., 1,302,000; capital, Phoenix: nicknamed *Sunset State:* abbreviated **Ariz.**

Ar·i·zo·nan (ar′ə-zō′nən), *adj.* of Arizona. *n.* a native or inhabitant of Arizona.

Ar·i·zo·ni·an (ar′ə-zō′ni-ən), *adj. & n.* Arizonan.

Ar·ju·na (är′joo-nə), *n.* the hero of the Hindu epic, the Mahabharata.

ark (ärk), *n.* [AS. *arc, earc;* L. *arca* < *arcere,* to shut up, enclose], 1. the ark of the covenant. 2. in the *Bible,* the huge boat in which Noah, his family, and two of every kind of creature survived the Flood: Gen. 6; hence, 3. any boat like this; big, awkward boat. 4. a place of refuge. 5. [Obs. or Dial.], a chest; coffer.

Ar·kan·san (är-kan′zən), *n.* a native or inhabitant of the State of Arkansas.

Ar·kan·sas (är′kən-sô′; *formerly also* är-kan′zəs), *n.* 1. a Southern State of the south central United States: area, 53,102 sq. mi.; pop., 1,786,000; capital, Little Rock: nicknamed *Bear State:* abbreviated **Ark.** 2. (*also* är-kan′zəs), a river flowing southeastward from Colorado into the Mississippi: length, 1,460 mi.

Ar·khan·gelsk (är-khän′gelsk), *n.* Archangel: the Russian name.

ark of the covenant, the chest containing the two stone tablets inscribed with the Ten Commandments, kept in the holiest part of the ancient Jewish Tabernacle: Ex. 25:10.

ar·kose (är′kōs), *n.* [Fr.], a sandstone containing unaltered feldspar, usually formed in mountainous regions from weathered granite.

Ark·wright, Sir Richard (ärk′rīt′), 1732–1792; English inventor of a cotton-spinning machine.

Arl·berg (ärl′berkh), *n.* 1. a mountain pass in western Austria. 2. a tunnel below this pass: length, c. 6 1/2 mi.

Arles (ärlz; Fr. årl), *n.* a city on the Rhone River, southern France: pop., 35,000.

arles (ärlz), *n.pl.* [now often construed as sing.], [ME.; prob. via OFr. < L. **arrhula,* dim. of *arrha,* earnest money], [Scot. or British Dial.], money paid in advance to confirm a pledge; token payment; earnest money.

Ar·ling·ton (är′liŋ-tən), *n.* 1. a town in eastern Massachusetts: pop., 50,000. 2. a city in northeastern Texas, near Fort Worth: pop., 45,000.

Arlington National Cemetery, a national cemetery in Virginia, near Washington, D. C.

Ar·liss, George (är′lis), 1868–1946; English actor.

arm (ärm), *n.* [ME.; AS. *arm, earm;* akin to Goth. *arms,* OHG. *arm;* IE. base **arē,* to join, fit together (+ *-m* suffix), seen also in L. *armus,* upper arm, shoulder blade, Gr. *harmos,* joint, Sans. *īrmá-h,* shoulder joint, etc.], 1. an upper limb of the human body; part between shoulder and hand. 2. anything immediately resembling this; especially, *a)* a branch of a tree. *b)* a branch of a river. *c)* the forelimb of a vertebrate animal. *d)* any limb of an invertebrate animal. 3. anything commonly in contact with the human arm; especially, *a)* a sleeve of a garment. *b)* a support for the arm on a chair, sofa, etc. 4. anything thought of as armlike, especially in being attached or connected to something larger: as, an *arm* of the sea, a yard*arm,* the *arm* of a balance, the *arm* of a phonograph, an *arm* of the government, etc. 5. anything thought of as functioning like an arm: as, the long *arm* of the law.

arm in arm, with arms interlocked, as two persons walking together.

keep at arm's length, to keep at a distance; not permit to become friendly or intimate.

receive (or **welcome**) **with open arms,** to receive with warm cordiality.

arm (ärm), *n.* [ME. & OFr. *armes, pl.;* L. *arma,* implements, weapons; see ARM (limb), sense 3], 1. any weapon: see **arms.** 2. [a merging with *arm* (limb), senses 4 & 5], any combatant branch of the military forces, as the infantry, artillery, etc. *v.t.* [ME. *armen;* OFr. *armer;* L. *armare,* to arm < *arma;* see the *n.*], 1. to provide with weapons, tools, etc. 2. to provide with protective covering; fortify. *v.i.* to equip oneself with weapons, as in preparing for war. —*SYN.* see **furnish.**

Arm., 1. Armenian. 2. Armoric.

Ar.M., *Architecturae Magister,* [L.], Master of Architecture.

ar·ma·da (är-mä′də, är-mā′də), *n.* [Sp., an armed force, L. *armata,* fem. of *armatus,* pp. of *armare;* see ARM, *v.*], 1. a fleet of warships. 2. [A-], the fleet of warships sent against England by Philip II of Spain in 1588: called the *Invincible* (or *Spanish*) *Armada,* it was almost entirely destroyed by the English navy and bad weather. 3. a fleet of warplanes.

ar·ma·dil·lo (är′mə-dil′ō), *n.* [*pl.* ARMADILLOS (-ōz)], [Sp., dim. of *armado* < L. *armatus,* pp. of *armare;* see ARM, *v.*], any of a number of related toothless, burrowing mammals of Texas and Central and South America, having an armorlike covering of bony plates: some armadillos can roll up into a ball when attacked.

ARMADILLO (30 in. long)

Ar·ma·ged·don (är′mə-ged′′n), *n.* [LL. *Armagedon;* Gr. *Armageddōn, Harmagedōn;* ? < Heb. *har,* mountain + *megiddon,* the plain of Megiddo, proverbial scene of decisive battles], 1. in the *Bible,* the place where the last, decisive battle between the forces of good and evil will be fought before the Day of Judgment: Rev. 16:16; hence, 2. any great, decisive battle.

Ar·magh (är-mä′), *n.* 1. a county of Northern Ireland: pop., 114,000. 2. its county seat: pop., 9,300.

ar·ma·ment (är′mə-mənt), *n.* [L. *armamentum,* pl. *armamenta,* implements, ship's tackle < *armare;* see ARM, *v.*], 1. *often pl.* all the military forces and equipment of a nation. 2. all the guns and other military equipment of a warship, warplane, tank, fortification, etc. 3. an arming or being armed for war.

ar·ma·ture (är′mə-chẽr), *n.* [Fr.; L. *armatura,* arms, equipment < *armatus,* pp. of *armare;* all senses from that of "armored, protected"; see ARM, *v.*], 1. armor. 2. an armorlike covering of an animal or plant. 3. flat wire wound around a cable. 4. a soft iron bar placed across the poles of a magnet to keep it from losing magnetic power. 5. the part that revolves in an electric motor or dynamo: it consists of a laminated iron core with wire wound around it: see **dynamo,** illus. 6. the vibrating part in an electric relay or bell. 7. in *sculpture,* a framework for supporting the clay in modeling.

arm·chair (ärm′châr′), *n.* a chair with supports at the sides for one's arms or elbows.

armed (ärmd), *adj.* [pp. of *arm*], provided with arms (weapons), armor, etc.

armed (ärmd), *adj.* [< *arm* (limb)], having arms; having upper limbs: usually in compounds, as *long-armed.*

armed forces, all the military, naval, and air forces of a country or group of countries.

Ar·me·ni·a (är-mē′ni-ə, är-mēn′yə), *n.* 1. a former country in southwestern Asia, south of the Caucasus Mountains. 2. the Armenian Soviet Socialist Republic.

Ar·me·ni·an (är-mē′ni-ən, är-mēn′yən), *adj.* of Armenia, its people, language, etc. *n.* 1. a native or inhabitant of Armenia. 2. the Indo-European, Anatolic language of the Armenians. Abbreviated **Arm., Armen.**

ARMENIA (1919)

Armenian Soviet Socialist Republic, a republic of the U.S.S.R., in the Transcaucasus: area, 11,580 sq. mi.; pop., 1,800,000; capital, Erivan: sometimes called *Armenia,* although made up of only part of the former Armenia.

Ar·men·tières (år′män′tyâr′), *n.* a town in northern France, near the Belgian border: pop., 23,000.

ar·met (är′met), *n.* [Fr.; OFr. *armette,* dim. of *arme;* see ARM (weapon)], a type of round medieval helmet with a movable visor.

arm·ful (ärm′fool′), *n.* [*pl.* ARMFULS (-foolz′)], as much as the arms or one arm can hold.

arm·hole (ärm′hōl′), *n.* an opening for the arm in any garment.

ar·mi·ger (är′mi-jẽr), *n.* [*pl.* ARMIGERI (är-mij′ə-rī′)], [L. < *arma,* arms + *gerere,* to carry], 1. originally, an armorbearer for a knight; squire. 2. a person ranking next to a knight and entitled to a coat of arms.

ar·mil·lar·y (är′mi-ler′i, är-mil′ẽr-i), *adj.* [< L. *armilla,* armlet, bracelet < *armus,* shoulder], 1. of or like a ring or bracelet. 2. made up of circles or rings.

Ar·min (är′min), [L. *Arminius;* of Gmc. origin; prob. < bases *aran,* eagle + *wini,* friend], a masculine name: equivalent, Fr. *Armand:* see **Herman.**

arm·ing (är′miŋ), *n.* 1. the act of one who arms; taking up or supplying weapons. 2. heraldic arms. 3. a part put on something to make it complete or ready for use.

Ar·min·i·an (är-min′i-ən), *adj.* 1. of Jacobus Arminius. 2. of Arminianism. *n.* a believer in Arminianism.

Ar·min·i·an·ism (är-min′i-ən-iz′m), *n.* the doctrines of Jacobus Arminius, which revised the Calvinist views of the freedom of the will and predestination.

Ar·min·i·us (är-min′i-əs), *n.* (G. name, *Hermann*), Teutonic hero; 18? B.C.–21 A.D.

Ar·min·i·us, Ja·co·bus (jə-kō′bəs är-min′i-əs), (*Jacob Harmensen*), 1560–1609; Dutch Protestant theologian.

ar·mip·o·tent (är-mip′ə-tənt), *adj.* [L. *armipotens* < *arma,* arms + *potens;* see POTENT], powerful in battle.

ar·mi·stice (är′mə-stis), *n.* [Fr. < L. *arma,* arms +

stare, to stand still], a temporary stopping of warfare by mutual agreement, as a truce preliminary to the signing of a peace treaty or agreement.

Armistice Day, November 11, the anniversary of the armistice of World War I in 1918: since 1954, celebrated as **Veterans' Day.**

arm·let (ärm′lit), ***n.*** [*arm* (limb) + *-let*], 1. a band worn for ornament around the arm, especially the upper arm. 2. a short, bandlike sleeve. 3. a small arm or inlet of the sea.

ar·moire (är-mwär′), ***n.*** [Fr.; OFr. *armarie;* see AMBRY], a large, usually ornate cupboard, cabinet, or clothes-press.

ar·mor (är′mẽr), ***n.*** [ME. *armure;* OFr. *armure;* L. *armatura* < *armare;* see ARM, *v.*], 1. covering worn to protect the body against weapons. 2. any defensive or protective covering, as on animals or plants, or the metal plate on warships, warplanes, etc. 3. the armored forces of an army; tanks, reconnaissance cars, etc. ***v.t. & v.i.*** to put armor on.

HELMET
BEAVER
GORGET
PAULDRON
LANCE REST
BREASTPLATE
TASSE
GAUNTLET
CUISSE
KNEEPIECE
GREAVE
SOLLERET

ARMOR

ar·mor·bear·er (är′mẽr-bâr′ẽr), ***n.*** a person who carried the armor or weapons of a warrior, as in the Middle Ages.

ar·mor-clad (är′mẽr-klad′), ***adj.*** covered with armor.

ar·mored (är′mẽrd), ***adj.*** [pp. of *armor*], 1. covered with armor. 2. equipped with armored vehicles: as, an *armored* division.

armored cable, an electric cable covered with metal tape for mechanical protection.

armored car, any of various vehicles covered with armor plate, as a truck for carrying money to or from a bank; specifically, in *military usage*, a wheeled motor vehicle with such armor plate, usually carrying a mounted machine gun and used especially as a reconnaissance car.

armored force, a military force consisting of tank units with supporting troops and used primarily as a unit of offense.

ar·mor·er (är′mẽr-ẽr), ***n.*** 1. formerly, a person who made or repaired armor and arms. 2. a maker of firearms. 3. in *military usage*, an enlisted man in charge of the maintenance and repair of the small arms of his unit, warship, etc.

ar·mo·ri·al (är-môr′i-əl, är-mō′ri-əl), ***adj.*** [*armory* + *-al*], of coats of arms; heraldic.

armorial bearings, heraldic devices on a coat of arms.

Ar·mor·ic (är-môr′ik, är-mor′ik), ***adj.*** of Armorica, its people, language, etc. ***n.*** 1. a native or inhabitant of Armorica. 2. the language of Armorica.

Ar·mor·i·ca (är-môr′i-kə, är-mor′i-kə), ***n.*** an ancient region in northwestern France, corresponding to Brittany.

Ar·mor·i·can (är-môr′i-kən, är-mor′i-kən), ***adj. & n.*** Armoric.

armor plate, a protective covering of specially hardened steel plates, as on a warship or tank.

ar·mor-plat·ed (är′mẽr-plāt′id), ***adj.*** covered with armor plate.

ar·mor·y (är′mẽr-i), ***n.*** [*pl.* ARMORIES (-iz)], [altered, by association with *armor*, from OFr. *armoierie*, science of heraldry < *armoier*, to blazon coats of arms < *arme;* see ARM (weapon)], 1. a storehouse for weapons; arsenal. 2. a building housing the drill hall and offices of a unit of the National Guard. 3. a place where firearms are made; armaments factory. 4. [Archaic], armor. 5. [Archaic], armorial bearings. 6. heraldry.

ar·mour (är′mẽr), ***n., v.i. & v.t.*** armor: British spelling.

ar·mour·er (är′mẽr-ẽr), ***n.*** armorer: British spelling.

ar·mour·y (är′mẽr-i), ***n.*** armory: British spelling.

arm·pit (ärm′pit′), ***n.*** the hollow under the arm at the shoulder; axilla.

arms (ärmz), ***n.pl.*** [see ARM (weapon)], 1. weapons. 2. warfare; fighting. 3. heraldic symbols. 4. insignia of countries, corporations, etc.: See also **small arms.**
bear arms, 1. to carry or be equipped with weapons. 2. to serve as a combatant in the armed forces.
carry arms, 1. to carry or be equipped with weapons. 2. to hold a rifle in a vertical position against the right shoulder.
take up arms, 1. to go to war or rise in rebellion. 2. to enter a dispute.
to arms! get ready to fight!
under arms, equipped with weapons; ready for war.
up in arms, 1. prepared to fight. 2. indignant.

ar·mure (är′myoor), ***n.*** [Fr.; see ARMOR], 1. a kind of cloth woven to resemble chain mail. 2. [Obs.], armor.

ar·my (är′mi), ***n.*** [*pl.* ARMIES (-miz)], [ME. & OFr. *armee* < L. *armata*, pp. of *armare;* see ARM, *v.*], 1. a large, organized body of soldiers for waging war, espe-

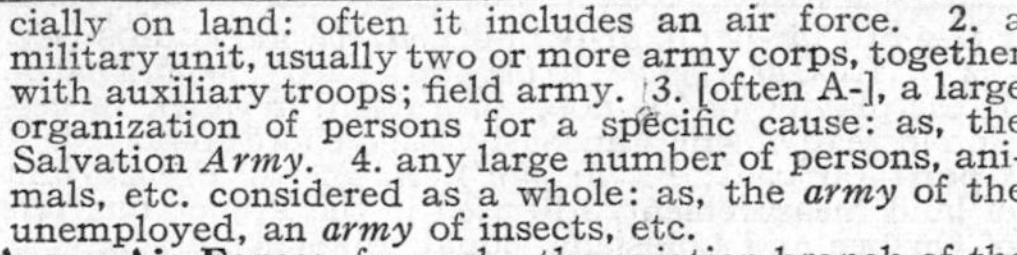

cially on land: often it includes an air force. 2. a military unit, usually two or more army corps, together with auxiliary troops; field army. 3. [often A-], a large organization of persons for a specific cause: as, the Salvation *Army*. 4. any large number of persons, animals, etc. considered as a whole: as, the *army* of the unemployed, an *army* of insects, etc.

Army Air Forces, formerly, the aviation branch of the United States Army: abbreviated **A.A.F.**

army ant, any of a number of ants that travel in large groups searching for food, as the driver ant: also called *foraging ant.*

army corps, a tactical military unit of two or more divisions with auxiliary services, usually commanded by a lieutenant general: abbreviated **A.C.**

army of occupation, an army that goes into a defeated country to enforce peace terms, keep order, etc.

Army of the United States, the United States Army, the Organized Reserves, the National Guard, and Selective Service personnel, collectively: organized temporarily during time of war or other national emergency.

army worm, the yellow and gray larva of a certain moth: so called because it travels in large groups, ruining crops and grass.

Arn·hem (ärn′hem), ***n.*** a city on the Rhine, in the Netherlands: pop., 98,000 (1947).

ar·ni·ca (är′ni-kə), ***n.*** [Mod. L.], 1. any of a number of related plants bearing bright yellow flowers on long stalks with clusters of leaves at the base. 2. a medicine made from one kind of these plants, for treating sprains, bruises, etc.

Ar·no (är′nô), ***n.*** a river in Tuscany, Italy, flowing into the Ligurian Sea: length, 140 mi.

Ar·nold (är′nəld), [G.; OHG. *Aranold;* Gmc. **Arnwald* < bases *aran*, eagle + *wald*, power], a masculine name: equivalents, Fr. *Arnaud*, It. *Arnoldo*, Sp. *Arnaldo*.

Ar·nold, Benedict (är′nəld), 1741–1801; American Revolutionary general who became a traitor.

Arnold, Sir **Edwin,** 1832–1904; English poet and journalist.

Arnold, Henry Har·ley (här′li), 1886–1950; American general in command of air forces, World War II.

Arnold, Matthew, 1822–1888; English poet, critic, and essayist.

Arnold, Thomas, 1795–1842; father of *Matthew;* English educator.

ar·oid (ar′oid), ***adj.*** [< *arum* + *-oid*], of the arum family of plants; araceous. ***n.*** any plant of this family.

a·roi·de·ous (ə-roi′di-əs), ***adj.*** araceous.

a·roint (ə-roint′), ***v.i.*** [? coined by Shakespeare (*Macbeth* I, iii, 6)], [Obs.], begone; avaunt (usually with *thee*): used in the imperative.

a·ro·ma (ə-rō′mə), ***n.*** [ME. & OFr. *aromat;* L. *aromata*, pl. of *aroma;* Gr. *arōma*, sweet spice], 1. a pleasant, often spicy odor; fragrance, as of a plant, cooking, etc. 2. a characteristic quality or atmosphere, as of music, poetry, etc. —***SYN.*** see **smell.**

ar·o·mat·ic (ar′ə-mat′ik), ***adj.*** [ME. *aromatik;* OFr. *aromatique;* L. *aromaticus;* Gr. *aromatikos*, fragrant], 1. of or having an aroma; smelling sweet or spicy; fragrant; pungent. 2. in *chemistry*, of or designating any of a series of benzene ring compounds, many of which have an odor or are derived from materials having an odor. ***n.*** an aromatic plant, chemical, etc.

ar·o·mat·i·cal (ar′ə-mat′i-k'l), ***adj.*** aromatic.

a·ro·ma·tize (ə-rō′mə-tīz′), ***v.t.*** [AROMATIZED (-tīzd′), AROMATIZING], to make aromatic.

A·roos·took (ə-rōōs′took), ***n.*** a river in northern Maine, flowing into the St. John River: length, 140 mi.

a·rose (ə-rōz′), past tense of **arise.**

a·round (ə-round′), ***adv.*** [*a-*, on + *round;* all senses derive from those of "circling, within a circle"], 1. round; especially, *a)* in a circle; along a circular course or circumference. *b)* in or through a course or circuit, as from one place to another. *c)* on all sides; in every direction. *d)* in circumference. *e)* in or to the opposite direction, belief, etc. *f)* in various places. 2. [Colloq.], within a close periphery; near by: as, stay *around*. 3. [Colloq.], to a (specified or understood) place: as, come *around* to see us. ***prep.*** 1. round; especially, *a)* so as to encircle, surround, or envelop; about. *b)* on the circumference, border, or outer part of. *c)* on all sides of; in every direction from. *d)* in various places in or on. *e)* so as to rotate or revolve about (a center or axis). 2. [Colloq.], somewhat close to; about: as, *around* five pounds, *around* 1890. Cf. **round.** See also phrases under **bring, come, get,** etc.
have been around, [Colloq.], to have had wide experience; be sophisticated.

a·rous·al (ə-rouz′'l), ***n.*** an arousing or being aroused.

a·rouse (ə-rouz′), ***v.t.*** [AROUSED (-rouzd′), AROUSING], [*a-* + *rouse*], 1. to stir up, as to anger or action; excite. 2. to wake. ***v.i.*** to become aroused. —***SYN.*** see **incite, stir.**

fat, āpe, bâre, cär; ten, ēven, hêre, ovẽr; is, bīte; lot, gō, hôrn, tōōl, look; oil, out; up, ūse, fũr; get; joy; yet; chin; she; thin, *th*en; zh, leisure; ŋ, ring; ə for *a* in *ago*, *e* in *agent*, *i* in *sanity*, *o* in *comply*, *u* in *focus;* ′ as in *able* (ā′b'l); Fr. bål; ë, Fr. coeur; ö, Fr. feu; Fr. mon; ô, Fr. coq; ü, Fr. duc; H, G. ich; kh, G. doch. See pp. x–xii. ‡ foreign; * hypothetical; < derived from.

ar·peg·gio (är-pej′ō, är-pej′i-ō′), *n.* [*pl.* ARPEGGIOS (-ōz, -ōz′)], [It. < *arpeggiare*, to play on a harp < *arpa*, a harp], 1. the playing of the notes of a chord in quick succession instead of simultaneously. 2. a chord so played.

ar·pent (är′pənt; Fr. ȧr′pän′), *n.* an old French unit of land measurement, still used in the French quarters of Quebec and Louisiana, equal to about an acre.

ar·que·bus (är′kwi-bəs), *n.* [Fr. *arquebuse, harquebuse;* It. *archibuso;* by way of MFr. < D. *haakbuse*, lit., a hook box: so named because of method of support during firing], an early type of portable gun, fired by a matchlock and trigger and supported on a hooked staff or forked rest during firing: also **harquebus.**

arr., 1. arranged. 2. arrangements. 3. arrival.

ar·rack (ar′ək), *n.* [Fr. *arac;* Ar. *'araq*, sweat, palm sap, liquor], in the Orient, strong alcoholic drink, especially that made from rice or molasses.

ar·raign (ə-rān′), *v.t.* [ME. *araynen;* OFr. *arainier, araisnier;* ML. *adrationare* < L. *ad*, to + *ratio*, reason], 1. to bring before a law court to stand trial. 2. to call to account or in question; accuse. —*SYN.* see **accuse.**

ar·raign·ment (ə-rān′mənt), *n.* an arraigning or being arraigned.

Ar·ran (ar′ən), *n.* a Scottish island in the Firth of Clyde: area, 165 sq. mi.; pop., 8,000.

ar·range (ə-rānj′), *v.t.* [ARRANGED (-rānjd′), ARRANGING], [ME. *arayngen;* OFr. *arangier; a-*, to + *rangier*, to set in order < *rang*, rank; see RANGE], 1. to put in order; put in the correct order. 2. to sort systematically; classify. 3. to settle (a dispute); adjust (a claim, difference, etc.). 4. in *music*, to adapt (a composition) to other instruments or voices than those for which it was written, or to a certain band or orchestra. *v.i.* 1. to come to an agreement (*with* a person, *about* a thing). 2. to make plans; provide or prepare (with *for* or an infinitive). 3. in *music*, to write adaptations, especially as a profession.

ar·range·ment (ə-rānj′mənt), *n.* [Fr.; see ARRANGE], 1. an arranging or being arranged. 2. a result or manner of arranging. 3. a combination of parts; hence, 4. loosely, a contrivance; apparatus. 5. *usually in pl.* a preparation; plan: as, *arrangements* have been made for the party: abbreviated **arr.** 6. a settlement or adjustment, as of a dispute, difference, etc. 7. in *music, a)* adaptation of a composition to other instruments or voices than those for which it was originally written, or to the style of a certain band or orchestra. *b)* the composition as thus adapted.

ar·rant (ar′ənt), *adj.* [var. of *errant*], 1. out-and-out; unmitigated; notorious: as, an *arrant* fool. 2. [Obs.], wandering: see **errant.**

ar·ras (ar′əs), *n.* [after *Arras*, city in Artois, France, where it was made], 1. a kind of tapestry. 2. a wall hanging of tapestry.

ar·ray (ə-rā′), *v.t.* [ME. *arraien;* OFr. *arreier;* L. **arredare*, to put in order < *ad-*, to + Gmc. base *raid-* (IE. **reidh-*, to be moving) as in Goth. *raidjan*, AS. *(ge)rædan*, put in order; cf. READY, CURRY, *v.*], 1. to place in order; marshal, as troops. 2. to dress in finery; deck out. *n.* 1. an orderly grouping or arrangement, especially of troops. 2. troops in order; military force. 3. an impressive display of assembled persons or things. 4. clothes; finery.

ar·ray·al (ə-rā′əl), *n.* 1. the act or process of arraying. 2. something arrayed.

ar·rear·age (ə-rêr′ij), *n.* [ME. *arerage;* OFr. *arrerage* < *arere;* see ARREARS], 1. the state of being in arrears. 2. arrears. 3. a thing kept in reserve.

ar·rears (ə-rêrz′), *n.pl.* [< ME. *arere;* OFr. *arere*, backward < L. *ad*, to + *retro*, behind], 1. unpaid and overdue debts. 2. any obligation not met on time; unfinished business, work, etc.

in arrears (or **arrear**), behind in paying a debt, doing one's work, etc.

ar·rest (ə-rest′), *v.t.* [ME. *aresten;* OFr. *arester* < L. *ad*, to + *restare*, to stop, stay back], 1. to stop or check the motion, course, or spread of. 2. to seize or take into custody by authority of the law. 3. to catch and keep (one's attention, sight, etc.). *n.* [ME. & OFr. *arest* < the *v.*], 1. an arresting or being arrested; especially, a taking or being taken into custody by authority of the law. 2. a thing for checking motion.

under arrest, in legal custody, as of the police.

ar·rest·er (ə-res′tẽr), *n.* a person or thing that arrests.

ar·rest·ing (ə-res′tiŋ), *adj.* [ppr. of *arrest*], attracting attention; interesting; striking.

ar·rest·ment (ə-rest′mənt), *n.* [Rare], an arresting or being arrested; arrest.

ar·res·tor (ə-res′tẽr), *n.* a person who arrests.

Ar·rhe·ni·us, Svan·te Au·gust (svän′te ou′gəst är-rā′ni-əs), 1859–1927; Swedish chemist and physicist; first to present theory of ionization; received Nobel prize in chemistry, 1903.

ar·rhyth·mi·a (ə-rith′mi-ə, ə-rith′mi-ə), *n.* [Mod. L.; Gr. *arrhythmia*, lack of rhythm < *a-*, without + *rhythmos*, measure], any irregularity in the rhythm of the heart's beating.

ar·rhyth·mic (ə-rith′mik, ə-rith′mik), *adj.* of or characterized by arrhythmia.

‡**ar·rière-ban** (ȧ′ryâr′bän′), *n.* [Fr.; OFr. *arban, harban* < OHG. *hariban; hari*, army, host + *ban*, command under penalty; sp. altered through popular etym.], 1. in medieval France, a king's calling of his vassals to do their military duty. 2. the vassals so assembled.

‡**ar·rière-pen·sée** (ȧ′ryâr′pän′sā′), *n.* [Fr., lit., a back-thought], an ulterior motive or mental reservation.

Ar Ri·mal (är ri-mäl′), Rub' al Khali, Arabia.

ar·ris (ar′is), *n.* [OFr. *areste;* see ARÊTE], in *architecture*, the edge made by two straight or curved surfaces coming together at an angle, as in a molding.

ar·riv·al (ə-rīv′'l), *n.* [ME. & OFr. *arrivaile* < *arriver;* see ARRIVE], 1. an arriving. 2. a person or thing that arrives or has arrived. Abbreviated **arr.**

ar·rive (ə-rīv′), *v.i.* [ARRIVED (-rīvd′), ARRIVING], [ME. *ariven;* OFr. *ar(r)iver* < L. *ad*, to + *ripa*, shore], 1. to reach one's destination; come to a place. 2. to come: as, the time has *arrived* for action. 3. to attain success, fame, etc.: as, he has *arrived* professionally.

arrive at, 1. to reach by traveling. 2. to reach by work, thinking, development, etc.

‡**ar·ri·ve·der·ci** (ä-rē′ve-der′chē), *interj.* [It.] until we meet again; good-by: implies temporary parting.

ar·ro·ba (är-rō′bä), *n.* [Sp. & Port.; Ar. *al rub'*, the quarter (of the unit of weight *al qinṭar*)], 1. a Spanish unit of weight used in Mexico and some South American countries, equal to 25.36 pounds. 2. a Portuguese unit of weight used in Brazil, equal to 32.39 pounds. 3. a unit of liquid measure used in some Spanish-speaking countries, equal to 17.04 quarts (for wine) or 13.28 quarts (for oil).

ar·ro·gance (ar′ə-gəns), *n.* [ME.; OFr.; L. *arrogantia*], the quality or state of being arrogant; haughtiness.

ar·ro·gan·cy (ar′ə-gən-si), *n.* arrogance.

ar·ro·gant (ar′ə-gənt), *adj.* [ME.; OFr.; L. *arrogans*, ppr. of *arrogare;* see ARROGATE], full of or due to unwarranted pride and self-importance; overbearing; haughty. —*SYN.* see **proud.**

ar·ro·gate (ar′ə-gāt′), *v.t.* [ARROGATED (-id), ARROGATING], [< *arrogatus*, pp. of L. *arrogare*, to claim < *ad-*, to, for + *rogare*, to ask], 1. to claim or seize without right; appropriate (to oneself) arrogantly. 2. to ascribe or attribute without reason.

ar·ro·ga·tion (ar′ə-gā′shən), *n.* 1. an arrogating. 2. an unwarranted claim or assumption.

‡**ar·ron·disse·ment** (ȧ′rōn′dēs′män′), *n.* [*pl.* ARRONDISSEMENTS (-män′)], [Fr. < *arrondir*, to make round], 1. in France, the largest administrative subdivision of a department. 2. a municipal subdivision, as of Paris.

ar·row (ar′ō), *n.* [AS. *earh, arwe;* akin to Goth. *arhwa-;* same word as L. *arcus*, a bow < common IE. base **arqui-*, curved, bowed; original sense of *arrow* was "belonging to the bow"; cf. ARC, ARCHER], 1. a slender shaft, usually pointed at one end and feathered at the other, for shooting from a bow. 2. anything like an arrow in form, speed, purpose, etc. 3. a sign (←) used to indicate direction or position.

ar·row·head (ar′ō-hed′), *n.* 1. the separable, pointed head or tip of an arrow, made formerly of flint or stone, now usually of metal. 2. anything shaped like an arrowhead, as an indicating mark, part of a cuneiform character, etc.: the sign (<) as used throughout this dictionary shows the derivation of one word or word form from another, often in a different language. 3. any of a number of related plants with arrow-shaped leaves and white, cuplike flowers.

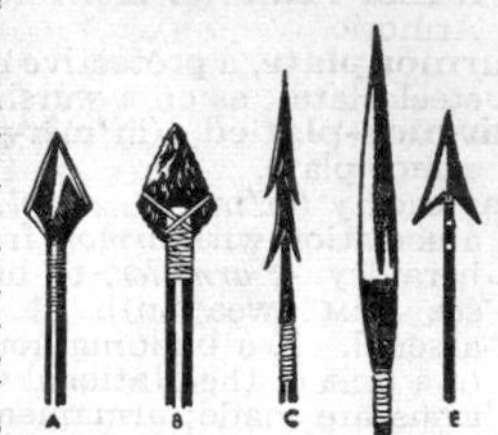

TYPES OF ARROWHEAD
A, modern hunting; B, American Indian; C, South Sea Islands; D, South American Indian; E, ancient Greek

ar·row·root (ar′ō-rōōt′, ar′ō-root′), *n.* [so named from use as antidote for poisoned arrows], 1. a tropical American plant with large leaves, white flowers, and starchy roots. 2. a starch made from its roots.

ar·row·wood (ar′ō-wood′), *n.* any of various trees or shrubs with long, straight stems used by the Indians to make arrows; variety of dogwood; viburnum.

ar·row·y (ar′ō-i, ar′ə-wi), *adj.* 1. having the shape or speed of an arrow. 2. of or full of arrows.

ar·roy·o (ə-roi′ō), *n.* [*pl.* ARROYOS (-ōz)], [Sp.; L. *arrugia*, shaft or pit (in a gold mine)], 1. a dry gully. 2. a rivulet; stream.

Ar·ru Islands (ä′rōō), *n.* Aru Islands.

arse (ärs), *n.* [ME. *ers, ars;* AS. *ears, ærs;* akin to OHG. *ars*, etc.], the buttocks: now a vulgar term.

ar·se·nal (är′s'n-əl, är′snəl), *n.* [It. *arsenale*, a dock; Ar. *dār aṣ-ṣinā'ah*, workshop, lit., house of skill or trade < *al*, the + *ṣinā'ah*, skill, trade], a place for making or storing weapons and other munitions.

ar·se·nate (är′s'n-āt′, är′s'n-it), *n.* [*arsenic* + *-ate*], in *chemistry*, a salt or ester of arsenic acid.

ar·se·nic (är′s'n-ik, är′snik), *n.* [ME. *arsenik;* OFr. *arsenic;* L. *arsenicum;* Gr. *arsenikon*, yellow orpiment

< Ar. *az zirnikh* or Heb. *zarnīq;* ult. < Per. *zar*, gold; associated in Gr. with *arsenikos*, strong, masculine], 1. a silvery-white, brittle, very poisonous chemical element, compounds of which are used in making insecticides, glass, medicines, etc.: symbol, As; at. **wt.**, 74.91; at. no., 33. 2. loosely, arsenic trioxide, As_2O_3 or As_4O_6, a very poisonous compound of arsenic: it is a white powder and has no taste.

ar·sen·ic (är-sen′ik), *adj.* of or containing arsenic, especially arsenic with a valence of five.

arsenic acid, a colorless arsenic compound, H_3AsO_4.

ar·sen·i·cal (är-sen′i-k'l), *adj.* of or containing arsenic. *n.* a preparation that contains arsenic.

ar·se·nide (är′s'n-īd′, är′s'n-id), *n.* in *chemistry*, a compound of arsenic and an element or a radical, in which arsenic has a negative valence of three.

ar·se·ni·ous (är-sē′ni-əs), *adj.* arsenous.

ar·se·nite (är′s'n-īt′), *n.* a salt or ester of arsenous acid.

ar·se·niu·ret·ed, ar·se·niu·ret·ted (är-sē′nyoo-ret′id, är-sen′yoo-ret′id), *adj.* [< *arseniuret*, old name for arsenide < L. *arsenicum*, arsenic; + *-uret*, Mod. L. *-uretum*, formerly used as equivalent to *-ide*], combined with arsenic.

ar·se·no- (är′s'n-ō, är-sen′ə), a combining form meaning *having arsenic as a constituent*, as in *arsenopyrite*.

ar·se·no·py·rite (är′s'n-ō-pī′rīt, är-sen′ə-pī′rīt), *n.* [*arseno-* + *pyrite*], a hard, brittle, silvery-white mineral, iron arsenic sulfide, FeAsS, the main ore of arsenic.

ar·se·nous (är′s'n-əs), *adj.* 1. of or containing arsenic. 2. in *chemistry*, containing arsenic with a valence of three. Also **arsenious.**

‡ars gra·ti·a ar·tis (ärz′ grā′shi-ə är′tis), [L.], art for art's sake.

ar·shin (är-shēn′), *n.* an archine.

ar·sine (är-sēn′, är′sēn), *n.* [*arsenic* + *-ine*], 1. arseniureted hydrogen, AsH_3, a very poisonous, inflammable gas that smells like garlic. 2. any of its derivatives.

ar·sis (är′sis), *n.* [*pl.* ARSES (-sēz)], [L.; Gr. *arsis*, a lifting up, omission < *airein*, to lift, raise up], 1. originally, the unaccented part of a foot of verse. 2. now, the accented part of a foot of verse: this sense resulted from a misunderstanding of the original Greek. 3. in *music*, the unaccented part of a measure; upbeat.

‡ars lon·ga, vi·ta bre·vis (ärz′ lôŋ′gə vī′tə brev′is), [L.], art (is) long, life (is) short.

ar·son (är′s'n), *n.* [OFr. *arson, arsoun* < L. *arsus*, pp. of *ardere*, to burn], the crime of purposely setting fire to another's building or property, or to one's own so as to collect insurance.

ars·phen·a·mine (ärs′fen-ə-mēn′, ärs′fen-am′in), *n.* [*ars*enic + *phen*yl + *amine*], a yellowish arsenical powder used in treating **syphilis** and some other infections; salvarsan.

‡ars po·e·ti·ca (ärz pō-et′i-kə), [L.], the art of poetry.

art (ärt), *n.* [ME. *art, arte;* OFr. *arte;* L. *ars, artis;* IE. base **ar-*, to join, fit together, as in L. *artus*, joint; cf. ARM, ARTICULATE], 1. human ability to make things; creativeness. 2. skill. 3. any specific skill or its application. 4. creative work generally, or its principles; making or doing of things that have form and beauty: art includes painting, sculpture, architecture, music, literature, drama, the dance, etc.: see also **fine arts.** 5. any branch of this, especially painting, drawing, or work in any other graphic or plastic medium. 6. products of creative work; paintings, statues, etc. 7. *usually in pl.* any of certain branches of academic learning, as literature, music, and mathematics: in this sense the *arts* are usually distinguished from the *sciences*. 8. any craft, trade, etc., or its principles: as, the cobbler's *art*. 9. artful behavior; cunning. 10. *usually in pl.* a trick; wile.

SYN.—**art,** the word of widest application in this group, denotes in its broadest sense merely the ability to make something or to execute a plan; **skill** implies expertness or great proficiency in doing something; **artifice** usually stresses mechanical proficiency in executing a plan but implies a relative lack of ingenuity or inventiveness; **craft** implies ingenuity in execution, sometimes even suggesting trickery or deception; in another sense, **craft** is distinguished from **art** in its application to a lesser skill involving little or no creative thought.

art (ärt), archaic second person singular, present indicative, of **be:** used with *thou*.

-art (ẽrt), -ard, as in *braggart*.

art., 1. article. 2. artificial. 3. artillery. 4. artist.

ar·tal (är′täl), *n.* plural of **rotl.**

Ar·ta·xer·xes I (är′tə-zũrk′sēz), 5th century B.C.; son of Xerxes I; king of Persia (464–424 B.C.).

Artaxerxes II, ?–359 B.C.; king of Persia (404–359 B.C.).

ar·te·fact (är′ti-fakt′), *n.* an artifact.

ar·tel (är-tel′), *n.* [Russ. *artel';* It. *artieri, pl.*, workmen, artisans], a group of people working collectively at something and sharing the income and liability; kind of co-operative found especially in the Soviet Union.

Ar·te·mis (är′tə-mis), *n.* [L.; Gr. *Artemis*], in *Greek mythology*, the goddess of the moon, wild animals, and hunting, Apollo's twin sister: identified with the Roman goddess Diana.

ar·te·mis·i·a (är′tə-miz′i-ə, är′tə-mish′i-ə), *n.* [L., mugwort; Gr. *artemisia* < *Artemis;* reason for name unknown], any of a number of related aromatic plants of the composite family, with small, yellow or white flower heads; wormwood.

ar·te·ri·al (är-têr′i-əl), *adj.* [Fr. *artérial* (now *artériel*); see ARTERY], 1. of or like an artery or arteries. 2. designating or of the blood in the arteries, which has undergone oxygenation in the lungs or gills and is brighter red than the blood in the veins. 3. designating or of a main road or channel with many branches.

ar·te·ri·al·i·za·tion (är-têr′i-əl-i-zā′shən), *n.* an arterializing or being arterialized.

ar·te·ri·al·ize (är-têr′i-əl-īz′), *v.t.* [ARTERIALIZED (-īzd′), ARTERIALIZING], to change (venous blood) into arterial blood by oxygenation.

ar·te·ri·o- (är-têr′i-ō), [< Gr. *artēria*, artery], a combining form meaning *artery, of the arteries*, as in *arteriosclerosis*.

ar·te·ri·o·scle·ro·sis (är-têr′i-ō-skli-rō′sis), *n.* [*arterio-* + *sclerosis*], a thickening and hardening of the walls of the arteries, as in old age.

ar·te·ri·o·scle·rot·ic (är-têr′i-ō-skli-rot′ik), *adj.* of or having arteriosclerosis.

ar·ter·y (är′tẽr-i), *n.* [*pl.* ARTERIES (-iz)], [L. *arteria*, windpipe, artery; Gr. *artēria;* prob. < *aeirein*, to raise], 1. any one of the system of branching tubes carrying blood from the heart to all parts of the body: distinguished from *vein*. 2. a main road or channel: as, a railroad *artery*.

ar·te·sian well (är-tē′zhən), [Fr. *artésien*, lit., of Artois (OFr. *Arteis*), France], a well drilled deep until it reaches water, which is then forced up by underground pressure.

ARTESIAN WELL
A, C, E, impermeable strata; B, D, water-bearing strata; W, well

art·ful (ärt′fəl), *adj.* [*art* + *-ful*], 1. artificial; imitative. 2. skillful or clever, especially in getting what one wishes; adroit; ingenious; hence, 3. crafty; deceitful; cunning. 4. [Archaic], showing considerable art or skill.

ar·thral·gi·a (är-thral′jə), *n.* neuralgic pain in a joint or joints.

ar·thral·gic (är-thral′jik), *adj.* of or having arthralgia.

ar·thrit·ic (är-thrit′ik), *adj.* of or having arthritis.

ar·thri·tis (är-thrī′tis), *n.* [Gr. < *arthron*, a joint], inflammation of a joint or joints.

ar·thro- (är′thrō, är′thrə), [< Gr. *arthron*, a joint], a combining form meaning *joint, of the joints*, as in *arthropod:* also, before a vowel, **arthr-.**

ar·thro·mere (är′thrə-mêr′), *n.* [*arthro-* + *-mere*], any body segment of a jointed animal.

ar·thro·pod (är′thrə-pod′), *n.* [*arthro-* + *-pod*], any member of a large group of invertebrate animals with jointed legs and a segmented body: the arthropods include crustaceans, arachnids, insects, and myriapods.

ar·thro·spore (är′thrə-spôr′, är′thrə-spōr′), *n.* [*arthro-* + *spore*], in *botany*, a vegetative resting cell with thick walls, found in certain algae.

Ar·thur (är′thẽr), [ML. *Arthur, Arthurus*], a masculine name: diminutive, *Art;* equivalent, It. *Arturo*. *n.* a real or legendary king of Britain and hero of the Round Table; supposed to have lived 6th c. A.D.

Ar·thur, Chester Alan (är′thẽr), 1830–1886; twenty-first president of the United States (1881–1885).

Ar·thu·ri·an (är-thoor′i-ən är-thyoor′i-ən,), *adj.* of King Arthur or his knights.

ar·ti·choke (är′ti-chōk′), *n.* [It. *articiocco;* Sp. *alcachofa;* Ar. *alkharshuf*], 1. a thistlelike plant. 2. its flower head, cooked as a vegetable. 3. the Jerusalem artichoke, a kind of sunflower, with a tuber that is cooked as a vegetable.

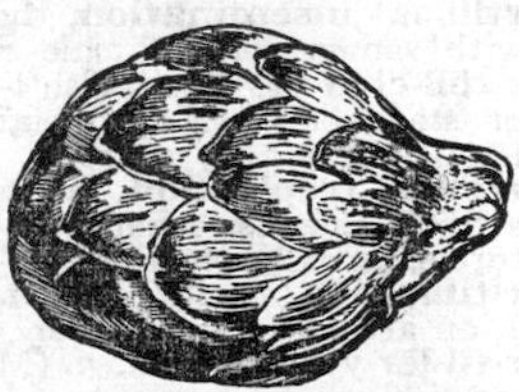

ARTICHOKE

ar·ti·cle (är′ti-k'l), *n.* [ME.; OFr.; L. *articulus*, dim. of *artus*, a joint; see ART (creation)], 1. one of the sections or items of a written document, as of a constitution, treaty, etc. 2. *pl.* the parts of a formal declaration considered as a whole. 3. a complete piece of writing, as a report or essay, that is part of a newspaper, magazine, or book. 4. any one of a group of things: as, an *article* of luggage. 5. a thing for sale; commodity. 6. in *grammar*, any one of the words *a*, *an*, or *the* (and their equivalents in other languages), used as adjectives: *a* and *an* are the *indefinite articles* and *the* is the *definite article*. 7. in *zoology*, any segment of a jointed part. Abbreviated **art.** *v.t.* [ARTICLED

(-k'ld), ARTICLING], 1. to state (a person's offenses, etc.) in articles. 2. to accuse. 3. to bind by the articles of an agreement. *v.i.* to bring charges (*against*).

Articles of Confederation, the constitution of the thirteen original States of the United States: it was adopted in 1781 and replaced in 1788 by the present Constitution.

Articles of War, formerly, the code of laws governing members of the armed forces of the United States: see **Uniform Code of Military Justice.**

ar·tic·u·lar (är-tik'yoo-lẽr), *adj.* [L. *articularis* < *articulus*, a joint, dim. of *artus;* see ARTICLE, ART (creation)], of a joint or joints: as, an *articular* inflammation.

ar·tic·u·late (är-tik'yoo-lit; *for v.*, är-tik'yoo-lāt'), *adj.* [L. *articulatus*, pp. of *articulare*, to separate into joints, utter distinctly < *articulus;* see ARTICULAR], 1. jointed. 2. spoken in distinct syllables or words. 3. expressing oneself clearly. 4. able to speak. 5. well formulated; clearly presented: as, an *articulate* argument. *v.t.* [ARTICULATED (-id), ARTICULATING], 1. to joint; put together by joints. 2. to utter distinctly; pronounce carefully; enunciate. 3. to express clearly. 4. in *phonetics*, to produce (a speech sound or speech sounds) by moving an articulator; phonate. *v.i.* 1. to speak distinctly; pronounce clearly. 2. to be jointed. 3. in *phonetics*, to produce speech sounds.

ar·tic·u·la·tion (är-tik'yoo-lā'shən), *n.* [L. *articulatio;* see ARTICULATE], 1. a jointing or being jointed. 2. the method or manner of this. 3. utterance or enunciation. 4. a spoken sound, especially a consonant. 5. a joint between bones or similar parts. 6. in *botany*, *a)* a joint in a stem or between two separable parts, as a branch and leaf. *b)* a node or space between two nodes. 7. in *phonetics*, a movement of an articulator.

ar·tic·u·la·tor (är-tik'yoo-lā'tẽr), *n.* 1. a person or thing that articulates. 2. in *phonetics*, any organ in the mouth or throat which, when moved, gives or helps to give speech sounds their characteristic acoustic properties: in English, the chief articulators are the lips (especially the lower lip), the apex, front, and back of the tongue, and the glottis; the uvula is a minor articulator (co-articulator).

ar·ti·fact (är'ti-fakt'), *n.* [L. *ars, artis*, skill, art + *factus;* see FACT], 1. any object made by human work. 2. in *histology*, any structure or changed appearance produced artificially or by death. Also spelled **artefact.**

ar·ti·fice (är'tə-fis), *n.* [L. *artificium*, trade or profession < *artifex*, artist, master of a trade < *ars*, art + *facere*, to make], 1. skill; ingenuity. 2. trickery; craft. 3. a clever expedient; artful device. —*SYN.* see **art, trick.**

ar·tif·i·cer (är-tif'ə-sẽr), *n.* [prob. < *artifice* + *-er*], 1. a maker or craftsman, especially a skillful one. 2. a person who devises; inventor. 3. a military mechanic.

ar·ti·fi·cial (är'tə-fish'əl), *adj.* [ME.; OFr.; L. *artificialis* < *artificium;* see ARTIFICE], 1. made by human work or art: opposed to *natural.* 2. made in imitation of something natural; simulated: as, *artificial* teeth. 3. unnatural or affected: as, an *artificial* smile. 4. in *botany*, cultivated; not native. Abbreviated **art.**

SYN.—**artificial** is applied to anything made by human work, especially if in imitation of something natural (*artificial* hair); **synthetic** is applied to a substance that is produced by chemical synthesis and is used as a substitute for a natural substance which it resembles (*synthetic* dyes); **ersatz,** which refers to an artificial substitute, always implies an inferior substance (*ersatz* coffee made of acorns); **counterfeit** and **spurious** are applied to a careful imitation deliberately intended to deceive (*counterfeit* money, a *spurious* signature). —*ANT.* natural.

artificial horizon, an instrument on an aircraft, operated by a gyroscope and containing a liquid level, for indicating the position of the craft with reference to the true horizon.

artificial insemination, the impregnation of a female with semen from a male without sexual intercourse.

ar·ti·fi·ci·al·i·ty (är'tə-fish'i-al'ə-ti), *n.* 1. the quality or state of being artificial. 2. [*pl.* ARTIFICIALITIES (-tiz)], something artificial.

artificial respiration, the maintenance of breathing by artificial means, usually by creating and relaxing pressure externally on the chest cavity at regular intervals.

ar·til·ler·ist (är-til'ẽr-ist), *n.* 1. a student of gunnery. 2. an artilleryman; gunner.

ar·til·ler·y (är-til'ẽr-i), *n.* [ME.; OFr. *artillerie* < *atilier* (sp. influenced by *arte*) < L. **apticulare*, to set aright < *aptus*, suitable; see APT], 1. formerly, apparatus for hurling heavy missiles, as catapults, arbalests, etc. 2. now, guns of large caliber, too heavy to carry; mounted guns (excluding machine guns), as cannon: distinguished from *small arms.* Artillery may be mobile, stationary, or mounted on ships, airplanes, etc. 3. the science of guns; gunnery. Abbreviated **A., art., Arty.**

the artillery, the military branch specializing in the use of heavy mounted guns.

ar·til·ler·y·man (är-til'ẽr-i-mən), *n.* [*pl.* ARTILLERYMEN (-mən)], a soldier in the artillery.

ar·ti·o·dac·tyl (är'ti-ə-dak'til), *adj.* [Gr. *artios*, even + *daktylos*, finger or toe], having an even number of toes or digits, as a camel, hog, etc. *n.* any hoofed mammal having an even number of digits.

ar·ti·san (är'tə-z'n), *n.* [Fr. < It. *artigiano* < LL. **artitianus* < L. *artitus*, pp. of *artire*, to instruct in arts < *ars, artis*, art], a skilled workman or craftsman.

art·ist (är'tist), *n.* [Fr. *artiste;* It. *artista* < L. *ars, artis*, art], 1. a person who works in or is skilled in any of the fine, especially graphic, arts. 2. a person who does anything very well, with a feeling for form, effect, etc.: as, his cook is an *artist.* 3. an artiste. Abbreviated **art.**

ar·tiste (är-tēst'), *n.* [Fr.; see ARTIST], 1. a skilled professional entertainer. 2. a person very skilled in some trade or occupation: often humorous or facetious.

ar·tis·tic (är-tis'tik), *adj.* [Fr. *artistique*], 1. of art or artists. 2. done skillfully; aesthetically satisfying. 3. that appreciates art and beauty; fond of the fine arts.

ar·tis·ti·cal·ly (är-tis'ti-k'l-i, är-tis'tik-li), *adv.* 1. in an artistic manner. 2. from the standpoint of art.

art·ist·ry (är'tis-tri), *n.* 1. the practice or pursuit of art. 2. artistic quality, ability, work, or workmanship.

art·less (ärt'lis), *adj.* 1. lacking skill or art; hence, 2. uncultured; ignorant. 3. not artistic; clumsy; crude. 4. without artificiality; simple; natural. 5. without guile or deceit; ingenuous; innocent. —*SYN.* see **naive.**

Ar·tois (år'twå'), *n.* a former province of northern France.

art·y (är'ti), *adj.* [ARTIER (-ti-ẽr), ARTIEST (-ti-ist)], [Colloq.], pretending to be artistic; ostentatiously artistic.

Arty., Artillery.

Ar·tzy·ba·shev, Mi·kha·il (mi-khä-ēl' är'tsi-bä'shef), 1878–1927; Russian novelist.

A.R.U., American Railway Union.

A·ru·ba (ä-ro͞o'bə), *n.* an island in the Netherlands Antilles, off Venezuela: area, 70 sq. mi.; pop., 55,000.

A·ru Islands (ä'ro͞o), a group of islands in the Netherlands East Indies, southwest of New Guinea: area, 3,326 sq. mi.; pop., 18,000: also spelled **Arru Islands.**

ar·um (âr'əm), *n.* [L.; Gr. *aron*, the wake robin], any of a number of related plants bearing flowers on a fleshy spike surrounded by a hoodlike leaf.

a·run·di·na·ceous (ə-run'di-nā'shəs), *adj.* [L. *arundinaceus* < *arundo*, reed, cave], of or like a reed.

a·rus·pex (ə-rus'peks), *n.* [*pl.* ARUSPICES (-pi-sēz')], a soothsayer: see **haruspex.**

A·ru·wi·mi (ä'roo-wē'mi), *n.* a river in the northern Belgian Congo, flowing into the Congo: length, 800 mi.

A.R.V., American Standard Revised Version (of the Bible), printed in 1901.

-ar·y (er'i; *also, chiefly Brit.*, ẽr-i), 1. [L. *-arius, -aria, -arium*], a suffix meaning *relating to, connected with*, used in forming adjectives and nouns, as *auxiliary, dictionary.* 2. [L. *-aris*], a suffix meaning *relating to, like*, as in *military:* also **-ar**, as in *nuclear.*

Ar·y·an (âr'i-ən, är'yən), *adj.* [Sans. *arya*, lord, master, *ārya*, a tribal name; akin to OPer. *ariya*, a tribal name; orig. applicable only to the Indo-Iranian tribes, but popularized in a wider sense by Max Müller and less reputable authors; not connected with *Eire, Ire*land, *Ir*ish], 1. formerly, designating or of the family of languages that includes Iranian, Sanskrit, and most of the European languages; Indo-European. 2. designating or of the Indic and Iranian branches of the Indo-European family of languages. 3. of the Aryans. *n.* 1. the hypothetical parent language of the Indo-European family. 2. a person belonging to, or supposed to be a descendant of, the prehistoric people who spoke this language. *Aryan* has no validity as a racial term, although it has been so used, notoriously by the Nazis to mean "a Caucasian of non-Jewish descent," etc. The use of the word in connection with race is due to the idea, regarded by most ethnologists as false, that peoples who spoke the same or related languages must have had a common racial origin. Misuse of *Aryan* has led to its replacement in scientific discussion by *Indo-European* (in sense 1 of the *n.* & *adj.*).

Ar·y·an·ize (âr'i-ən-īz', är'yən-īz'), *v.t.* [ARYANIZED (-īzd'), ARYANIZING], 1. to make Aryan. 2. in *Nazi usage*, to rid of (so-called) non-Aryan elements. See **Aryan.**

ar·y·te·noid (ar'i-tē'noid), *adj.* [Gr. *arytainoeidēs*, ladle-shaped < *arytaina*, a ladle, cup + *eidos*, form], 1. designating or of two small cartilages at the back of the larynx, connected with the vocal cords. 2. relating to any of certain muscles in the larynx. *n.* 1. an arytenoid cartilage. 2. an arytenoid muscle.

as (az; *unstressed*, əz), *adv.* [weakened form of *also;* ME. *as, ase;* AS. *alswa, ealswa; al, eall*, all + *swa*, so; lit., wholly so, quite so, just as], 1. to the same amount or degree; equally. Example: I am *as* good as he. 2. for instance; thus: see the use of *as* throughout this dictionary after a definition and before an example of usage. *conj.* 1. to the same amount or degree that. Example: It flew straight *as* an arrow. 2. in the same manner that; according to the way that. Example: Do *as* you are told. 3. at the same time that; while. Example: She arrived *as* I was leaving. 4. because. Example: *As* you object, we won't go. 5. that the consequence was. Example: The question was so obvious *as* to need no reply. 6. though. Example: Tall *as* he was, he couldn't reach the apples. *pron.* 1. a fact that. Example: He is tired, *as* anyone can see. 2. that (preceded by *such* or *the same*). Example: This is the same color *as* yours (is). *prep.* in the role, function, capacity, or sense of. Example: He poses *as* a friend.

as . . . as, a correlative construction used to indicate the equality or sameness of two things: *as large as, as heavy as, as many as,* etc. See also **good, well, much, far,** etc. for certain idiomatic phrases with *as.*

as for, with reference to; concerning.

as if, as it (or one) would if: also **as though.**

as is, [Slang], just as it is; without any changes: said of damaged goods being sold.

as it were, as if it were so; so to speak.

as to, 1. with reference to; concerning. 2. as if to.

as (as), *n.* [*pl.* ASSES (-iz; L. -ēz)], [L., a whole, integer], 1. an ancient Roman unit of weight and measure: as a weight, it was equal to about twelve ounces; as a unit of length, to about twelve inches. 2. an ancient Roman coin of copper alloy.

as- (əs), ad-: used before *s,* as in *assimilate.*

As, in *chemistry,* arsenic.

AS., Anglo-Saxon: also **A.S., A.-S.**

As., 1. Asian. 2. Asiatic.

A·sa (ā′sə), [Heb. *āsā,* lit., healer], a masculine name. *n.* in the *Bible,* a king of Judah, who opposed idolatry: I Kings 15:8–24.

as·a·fet·i·da, as·a·foet·i·da (as′ə-fet′i-də, as-fet′i-də), *n.* [LL. *asa* < Per. *azā,* gum + L. *fetida, foetida;* see FETID], a bad-smelling gum resin obtained from various Asiatic plants of the carrot family: it is used as an antispasmodic.

as·a·rum (as′ə-rəm), *n.* [L., hazelwort, wild spikenard; Gr. *asaron*], any of various related plants with kidney-shaped leaves and brownish flowers; wild ginger.

As·ben (äs′ben′), *n.* Aïr.

as·bes·tine (as-bes′tin), *adj.* [L. *asbestinus;* Gr. *asbestinos*], of, or having the properties of, asbestos.

as·bes·tos, as·bes·tus (as-bes′təs, az-bes′təs), *n.* [ME. *asbeston;* L. *asbestos;* Gr. *asbestos,* inextinguishable; *a-,* not + *sbestos* < *sbennynai,* to extinguish: the name was ? first applied to quicklime and later transferred to the mineral], a grayish mineral, a silicate of calcium and magnesium, which occurs in long, threadlike fibers: because it does not burn and is a nonconductor of electricity, it is used in fireproof curtains, roofing, insulation, etc. *adj.* woven of or containing asbestos.

As·bur·y, Francis (az′ber′i, az′bẽr-i), 1745–1816; first Methodist bishop in America.

As·bur·y Park (az′ber′i, az′bẽr-i), an ocean resort in east central New Jersey: pop., 17,000.

As·ca·ni·us (as-kā′ni-əs), *n.* [L.], in *Roman legend,* the son of Aeneas.

ASCAP, American Society of Composers, Authors, and Publishers.

as·ca·rid (as′kə-rid), *n.* [Gr. *askarides,* pl. of *askaris,* intestinal worm], a nematode worm that is an intestinal parasite, as the roundworm.

as·cend (ə-send′), *v.i.* [ME. *ascenden;* OFr. *ascendre;* L. *ascendere* < *ad-,* to + *scandere,* to climb], 1. to go up; come up; move upward; rise. 2. to proceed from a lower to a higher level or degree, as in rank, pitch, etc. 3. to slope or lead upward. 4. in *astronomy,* to move away from the horizon and toward the zenith. *v.t.* to move upward along; mount; climb.

as·cend·a·ble (ə-sen′də-b'l), *adj.* that can be ascended.

as·cend·ance, as·cend·ence (ə-sen′dəns), *n.* ascendancy.

as·cend·an·cy, as·cend·en·cy (ə-sen′dən-si), *n.* the quality or state of being in the ascendant; domination.

as·cend·ant, as·cen·dent (ə-sen′dənt), *adj.* [L. *ascendens,* ppr.], 1. ascending; rising. 2. controlling; predominant; superior. 3. in *botany,* pointing upward. *n.* 1. in *astrology,* the sign of the zodiac just above the eastern horizon at any given moment; horoscope. 2. a dominating position; ascendancy. 3. [Rare], an ancestor: opposed to *descendant.*

in the ascendant, at or heading toward the height of power, influence, fame, etc.

as·cend·er (ə-sen′dẽr), *n.* 1. a person or thing that ascends. 2. in *typography,* the extension or upward part of any of the tall lower-case letters, as *b, d, k,* etc.; hence, 3. any of these letters.

as·cend·i·ble (ə-sen′də-b'l), *adj.* ascendable.

as·cend·ing (ə-sen′diŋ), *adj.* [ppr. of *ascend*], 1. that ascends. 2. in *botany,* rising or curving upward.

as·cen·sion (ə-sen′shən), *n.* [L. *ascensio,* a rising < pp. of *ascendere;* see ASCEND], 1. an ascending; ascent. 2. [A-], Ascension Day. 3. [A-], a British island in the South Atlantic: area, 34 sq. mi.

the Ascension, in the *Bible,* the bodily ascent of Jesus into heaven on the fortieth day after his resurrection: Acts 1:9.

as·cen·sion·al (ə-sen′shən-'l), *adj.* of ascension or ascent.

Ascension Day, the fortieth day after Easter, celebrating the Ascension: also called *Holy Thursday.*

as·cen·sive (ə-sen′siv), *adj.* [< L. *ascensus,* pp. of *ascendere;* + *-ive*], 1. ascending. 2. causing to ascend.

as·cent (ə-sent′), *n.* [< *ascend,* by analogy with *descent*], 1. an ascending or rising. 2. an advancement, as in rank, popularity, etc. 3. a going up; climbing. 4. a way leading up; upward slope; acclivity. 5. the amount of upward slope or elevation: as, an *ascent* of three degrees. 6. a going back in time or genealogy.

as·cer·tain (as′ẽr-tān′), *v.t.* [ME. *acertainen;* OFr. *acertainer, acertener* < *a-,* to + *certain* < L. *certus,* fixed], 1. to find out with certainty. 2. [Archaic], to make certain to the mind. —*SYN.* see **learn.**

as·cer·tain·ment (as′ẽr-tān′mənt), *n.* an ascertaining or being ascertained.

as·cet·ic (ə-set′ik), *adj.* [Gr. *askētikos,* exercised < *askein,* to exercise], of or characteristic of ascetics or asceticism; self-denying; austere. *n.* 1. a person who leads a life of contemplation and rigorous self-denial for religious purposes. 2. anyone who lives with strict self-discipline and abstinence. —*SYN.* see **severe.**

as·cet·i·cal·ly (ə-set′i-k'l-i, ə-set′ik-li), *adv.* 1. in an ascetic manner. 2. by means of asceticism.

as·cet·i·cism (ə-set′ə-siz'm), *n.* 1. the practices or way of life of an ascetic; systematic self-denial for some ideal. 2. the religious doctrine that one can reach a higher spiritual state by rigorous self-discipline and self-denial.

Asch, Sho·lem (or **Sho·lom**) (shô′ləm äsh′; Eng. shō′ləm ash′), 1880–1957; American playwright, novelist, and short-story writer in Yiddish.

As·cham, Roger (as′kəm), 1515–1568; English scholar and writer; tutor to Queen Elizabeth I.

as·ci (as′ī), *n.* plural of **ascus.**

as·cid·i·an (ə-sid′i-ən), *n.* [Gr. *askidion;* see ASCIDIUM], any of a number of related water animals, usually sac-shaped, with a tough outer covering or tunic; tunicate.

as·cid·i·um (ə-sid′i-əm), *n.* [*pl.* ASCIDIA (-ə)], [Mod. L.; Gr. *askidion,* dim. of *askos,* wineskin, leather bag, bladder], in *botany,* a pitcherlike leaf or structure, as of the pitcher plant or bladderwort.

as·ci·tes (ə-sī′tēz), *n.* [L.; Gr. *askitēs,* kind of dropsy < *askos;* see ASCIDIUM], an accumulation of serous fluid in the abdominal cavity.

as·cle·pi·a·da·ceous (as-klē′pi-ə-dā′shəs), *adj.* [< L. *asclepias,* the common swallowwort (Gr. *asklēpias* < *Asklēpios,* Asclepius); + *-aceous*], belonging to the milkweed family of plants, having milky juice, waxy pollen masses, and pods with tufted seeds.

As·cle·pi·a·de·an (as-klē′pi-ə-dē′ən), *adj.* [< *Asclepiades,* name of Gr. inventor of the verse], designating or of a type of classical verse consisting usually of a spondee, two (or three) choriambs, and an iamb. *n.* an Asclepiadean verse.

As·cle·pi·us (as-klē′pi-əs), *n.* [L.; Gr. *Asklēpios*], in *Greek mythology,* the god of healing and medicine, corresponding to the Romans' Aesculapius.

as·co·carp (as′kə-kärp′), *n.* [< Gr. *askos,* bladder; + *-carp*], in *botany,* a structure shaped like a globe, cup, or disk, containing spore sacs; sac fruit of an ascomycetous fungus.

as·co·go·ni·um (as′kə-gō′ni-əm), *n.* [*pl.* ASCOGONIA (-ə)], [Mod. L.; Gr. *askos,* bladder + *gonos,* offspring < *gignesthai,* to be born], in *botany,* the female gamete, or archicarp, in an ascomycetous fungus.

as·co·my·cete (as′kə-mī-sēt′), *n.* [*pl.* ASCOMYCETES (-sēts′)], [< Mod. L. *Ascomycetes,* a class of fungi < Gr. *askos,* bladder + *mykēs, mykētos,* fungus], an ascomycetous fungus.

as·co·my·ce·tous (as′kə-mī-sē′təs), *adj.* [< Mod. L. *Ascomycetes* (see ASCOMYCETE); + *-ous*], belonging to a class of fungi, including the mildews, yeasts, knot and wart fungi, cup fungi, etc., which reproduce through spores developed in saclike structures (called *asci*).

a·scor·bic acid (ə-skôr′bik), [*a-,* not + *scorbutic* + *-ic*], vitamin C: also called *cevitamic acid.*

as·co·spore (as′kə-spôr′, as′kə-spōr′), *n.* [< Gr. *askos,* bladder; + *spore*], any of the spores in an ascus.

as·cot (as′kət), *n.* 1. [A-], a famous horse-racing meet held annually at Ascot Heath, Berkshire, England: it is a British social event. 2. a kind of necktie or scarf with very broad ends hanging from the knot, one upon the other: supposedly developed for wear at the Ascot.

ASCOT TIE

as·crib·a·ble (ə-skrīb′ə-b'l), *adj.* that can be ascribed.

as·cribe (ə-skrīb′), *v.t.* [ASCRIBED (-skrībd′), ASCRIBING], [ME. *ascriven;* L. *ascribere* < *ad-,* to + *scribere,* to write], 1. to assign (*to* a supposed cause or source); impute; attribute. 2. to regard as belonging (*to* something) as a quality or attribute.

SYN.—**ascribe**, in this comparison, implies assignment to someone of something that may reasonably be deduced (to *ascribe* a motive to someone); **attribute** implies assignment of a quality, factor, or responsibility that may reasonably be regarded as applying (to *attribute* an error to carelessness); **impute** usually implies the assignment of something unfavorable or accusatory (to *impute* evil to someone); **assign** implies the placement of something in a particular category because of some quality, etc. attributed to it (to *assign* a poem to the 17th century); **credit** implies belief in the possession by someone of some quality, etc. (to *credit* one with intelligence); **attach** implies the connection of something with something else as being appropriate to it (different people *attach* different meanings to words).

as·crip·tion (ə-skrip′shən), *n.* [L. *ascriptio* < pp. of *ascribere;* see ASCRIBE], 1. an ascribing or being ascribed. 2. a statement that ascribes; specifically, a prayer or text ascribing glory to God.

as·cus (as′kəs), *n.* [*pl.* ASCI (as′ī)], [Mod. L.; Gr. *askos*, bladder], a spore sac in an ascomycetous fungus.

-ase (ās, āz), [after the ending of *diastase*], a suffix used in forming names of enzymes, usually meaning *that decomposes*, as in *amylase*.

a·sep·sis (ə-sep′sis, ā-sep′sis), *n.* [*a-*, without + *sepsis*], 1. the condition of being aseptic. 2. aseptic treatment or technique.

a·sep·tic (ə-sep′tik, ā-sep′tik), *adj.* [*a-*, not + *septic*], not septic; free from or keeping away disease-producing or putrefying microorganisms: distinguished from *antiseptic*. *n.* an aseptic substance or preparation.

a·sep·ti·cal·ly (ə-sep′ti-k'l-i, ā-sep′tik-li), *adv.* by aseptic means; with the use of aseptics.

a·sex·u·al (ā-sek′shoo-əl, ə-sek′shoo-əl), *adj.* [*a-*, not + *sexual*], 1. having no sex; sexless. 2. in *biology*, designating or of reproduction without the union of male and female germ cells.

a·sex·u·al·i·ty (ā-sek′shoo-al′ə-ti), *n.* the quality or state of being asexual.

As·gard (as′gärd, az′gärd), *n.* [ON. *Āsgarthr; āss*, god + *garthr*, yard, court], in *Norse mythology*, the home of the gods and slain heroes.

As·gar·dhr (äs′gär′thr′), *n.* Asgard.

As·garth (äs′gärth), *n.* Asgard.

ash (ash), *n.* [ME. *asche;* AS. *asce, æsce;* akin to ON. *aske*, Goth. *azgo*], 1. the white or grayish powder left of something after it has been burned. 2. the silvery-gray color of wood ash; pallor. See also **ashes.**

ash (ash), *n.* [ME. *asch, esche;* AS. *æsce;* akin to OHG. *ask*, ON. *askr;* IE. base **os-ko* < **ōsen;* ash tree, seen in L. *ornus*, mountain ash (< **ōsen-os*)], 1. any of a group of timber and shade trees belonging to the olive family, having pinnate leaves, winged fruit, and tough, elastic wood with a straight, close grain. 2. the wood.

a·shamed (ə-shāmd′), *adj.* [pp. of obs. *ashame*, to shame; ME. *aschamien*, to make ashamed; AS. *ascamian, gescamian;* see SHAME], 1. feeling shame, as from doing something bad, wrong, foolish, etc. 2. reluctant because fearing shame beforehand.

SYN.—**ashamed** implies embarrassment, and sometimes guilt, felt because of one's own or another's wrong or foolish behavior (*ashamed* of his tears); **humiliated** implies a sense of being humbled or disgraced (*humiliated* by my failure); **mortified** suggests humiliation so great as to seem almost fatal to one's pride or self-esteem (she was *mortified* by his obscenities); **chagrined** suggests embarrassment coupled with irritation or regret over what might have been prevented (*chagrined* at his error). —*ANT.* proud.

A·shan·ti (ə-shan′ti, ə-shän′ti), *n.* 1. a region in central Ghana: originally a native kingdom, it was a British colony in the Gold Coast from 1901 to 1957: area, 24,379 sq. mi.; pop., 930,000; capital, Kumasi. 2. an inhabitant of this region. 3. the language spoken there.

ash can, 1. a large can for ashes and trash. 2. [Naval Slang], a depth bomb; depth charge.

ash·en (ash′'n), *adj.* 1. of ashes. 2. like ashes, especially in color; pale; pallid. —*SYN.* see **pale.**

ash·en (ash′'n), *adj.* 1. of the ash tree. 2. made of its wood.

ash·es (ash′iz), *n.pl.* [see ASH (powder)], 1. the unburned particles and white or grayish powder remaining after a thing has been burned. 2. the part of the body left after cremation; hence, 3. a dead person; human remains. 4. fine volcanic lava.

Ashe·ville (ash′vil), *n.* a city in western North Carolina: pop., 60,000.

Ash·ke·naz·ic (ash′kə-naz′ik, äsh′kə-nä′zik), *adj.* of the Ashkenazim or their culture.

Ash·ke·naz·im (ash′kə-naz′im, äsh′kə-nä′zim), *n.pl.* [Heb.], 1. the Jews who settled in middle and northern Europe after the Diaspora. 2. their descendants. Distinguished from *Sephardim*.

Ash·kha·bad (äsh′khä-bäd′), *n.* capital of the Turkmen S.S.R.: pop., 170,000.

Ash·land (ash′lənd), *n.* 1. a city on the Ohio River, in northeastern Kentucky: pop., 31,000. 2. a city in north central Ohio: pop., 17,000.

ash·lar, ash·ler (ash′lẽr), *n.* [ME. *ascheler;* OFr. *aiseler;* L. *axillarium* < *axis, assis*, a plank, beam: so called from its resemblance to wooden beams], 1. a square, hewn stone used in building. 2. a thin, dressed, square stone used for facing brick walls, etc. 3. masonry made of either kind of ashlar.

ash·man (ash′man′), *n.* [*pl.* ASHMEN (-men′)], a man who takes away ashes and trash.

a·shore (ə-shôr′, ə-shōr′), *adv. & adj.* [*a-*, on + *shore*], 1. to or on the shore. 2. to or on land.

Ash·ta·bu·la (ash′tə-bū′lə), *n.* a city in northeastern Ohio, near Lake Erie: pop., 25,000.

Ash·ton-un·der-Lyne (ash′tən-un′dẽr-līn′), *n.* a city in western England, near Manchester: pop., 46,000.

Ash·to·reth (ash′tə-rith, ash′tə-reth′), *n.* [*pl.* ASHTAROTH (-rôth′, -roth′)], [Heb.; see APHRODITE], the ancient Phoenician and Syrian goddess of love and fertility: identified with Astarte.

ash tray, a container for smokers' tobacco ashes.

A·shur (ä′shoor), *n.* [Assyr.], in *Assyrian mythology*, the chief deity, god of war and empire: also **Asshur, Assur, Asur.**

A·shur·ba·ni·pal (ä′shoor-bä′ni-päl′), *n.* king of Assyria (669–626 B.C.); lived ?–626 B.C.: also **Assurbanipal.**

Ash Wednesday, the first day of Lent and seventh Wednesday before Easter: so called from the practice of putting ashes on the forehead as a sign of penitence.

ash·y (ash′i), *adj.* [ASHIER (-i-ẽr), ASHIEST (-i-ist)], 1. of, like, or covered with ashes. 2. of ash color; pale; pallid.

A·sia (ā′zhə, ā′shə), *n.* the largest continent: situated in the Eastern Hemisphere and separated from northern Europe by the Ural Mountains: area, 16,990,000 sq. mi.; pop., c. 1,600,000,000.

Asia Minor, a peninsula in western Asia, between the Black Sea and the Mediterranean, including most of Asiatic Turkey: formerly called *Anatolia*.

A·sian (ā′zhən, ā′shən), *adj. & n.* Asiatic.

A·si·at·ic (ā′zhi-at′ik, ā′shi-at′ik), *adj.* of or characteristic of Asia or its people. *n.* a native or inhabitant of Asia. Abbreviated **As.**

Asiatic beetle, a beetle of Japanese origin, harmful to grasses.

Asiatic cholera, an acute, usually fatal, infectious disease characterized by profuse diarrhea, vomiting, intestinal pain, etc.

a·side (ə-sīd′), *adv.* [earlier *on side*], 1. on or to one side. 2. away; on reserve: as, put this *aside* for me. 3. out of the way; out of one's mind: as, lay the proposal *aside* temporarily. 4. apart; notwithstanding: as, joking *aside*, I mean it. *n.* words spoken aside; actor's words supposed to be heard only by the audience, not by the other actors.

aside from, 1. with the exception of. 2. apart from.

as·i·nine (as′ə-nīn′), *adj.* [L. *asininus*, asslike < *asinus*, ass], like an ass, regarded as a stupid animal; stupid; silly; unintelligent. —*SYN.* see **silly.**

as·i·nin·i·ty (as′ə-nin′ə-ti), *n.* 1. the quality or state of being asinine; stupidity. 2. [*pl.* ASININITIES (-tiz)], an asinine act or remark.

A·sir (ä-sir′), *n.* a southwestern district of Saudi Arabia: formerly a principality.

-a·sis (ə-sis), [L.; Gr., ending of nouns derived from verbs with roots ending in *-a-* + fem. suffix *-sis*, denoting state or process], a suffix used in forming names of some diseases, meaning *a condition resembling, a condition characterized by*, as in *elephantiasis, psoriasis*.

ask (ask, äsk), *v.t.* [ME. *askien;* AS. *ascian, acsian;* akin to OHG. *eiscōn*, OS. *ēscon*, to demand, question; IE. base **ais-*, to wish, desire, seek out; seen in Sans. *iṣta-*, (he) desires, etc.], 1. to use words in an effort to find out; seek the answer to (a question); inquire about. 2. to put a question to (a person); inquire of. 3. to request; solicit; beg. 4. to demand or expect: as, they *ask* ten dollars for it. 5. to be in need of or call for (a thing). 6. to invite. 7. [Archaic], to publish (banns); also, to publish the banns of. *v.i.* 1. to make a request (*for* something). 2. to inquire (with *about, after*, or *for*).

SYN.—**ask** and the more formal **inquire** and **query** usually denote no more than the seeking of an answer or information, but **query** also often implies doubt as to the correctness of something (the printer *queried* the spelling of several words); **question** and **interrogate** imply the asking of a series of questions (he *questioned* the witness), **interrogate** adding the further implication of systematic examination (to *interrogate* a prisoner of war); **catechize** is equivalent to **interrogate** but implies the expectation of certain fixed answers, especially with reference to religious doctrine; **quiz**, used especially in schools, implies a thorough questioning to test knowledge of some subject. —*ANT.* answer, tell.

a·skance (ə-skans′), *adv.* [ME. *askaunce;* prob. for **askaunces*], 1. with a sidewise glance; obliquely; hence, 2. with suspicion, disapproval, etc.

a·skant (ə-skant′), *adv.* askance.

a·skew (ə-skū′), *adv.* [*a-*, on + *skew*], to one side; awry; crookedly. *adj.* on one side; awry.

Ask·ja (äsk′yä), *n.* a volcano in Iceland: height, 3,376 ft.

a·slant (ə-slant′), *adv.* [*a-*, on + *slant*], on a slant; slantingly; obliquely. *prep.* slantingly over; obliquely across. *adj.* slanting.

a·sleep (ə-slēp′), *adj.* [*a-*, on + *sleep*], 1. in a condition of sleep; sleeping; hence, 2. inactive; dull; backward.

3. numb: as, her arm is *asleep*. 4. dead. *adv.* into a sleeping condition.

a·slope (ə-slōp′), *adv.* [*a-*, on + *slope*], slopingly; at a slant. *adj.* sloping.

As·ma·ra (äs-mä′rə), *n.* the capital of Eritrea, Africa: pop., 21,600.

As·mo·de·us (az′mō-dē′əs, as′mō-dē′əs), *n.* [L. *Asmodaeus;* Gr. *Asmodaios;* Heb. *ashmadai*], in *Jewish demonology*, an evil spirit; chief demon.

As·nières (ä′nyâr′), *n.* a city in France, near Paris: pop., 72,000 (1946).

a·so·cial (ā-sō′shəl), *adj.* [*a-*, not + *social*], not social; not gregarious; characterized by withdrawal and avoidance of contact with others. —*SYN.* see **unsocial**.

A·so·san (ä′sô-sän′), *n.* a volcano in Kyushu, Japan: height, 5,223 ft.; width of crater, c. 12 mi.

asp (asp), *n.* [ME.; OFr. *aspe;* L. *aspis;* Gr. *aspis*], any of several small, poisonous snakes of Africa, Arabia, and Europe, as the horned viper, common European viper, etc.

asp (asp), *n.* [Poetic], an aspen.

as·par·a·gus (ə-spar′ə-gəs), *n.* [L.; Gr. *aspharagos*, a sprout, asparagus; IE. base **sp(h)er(e)g-* (seen also in *spark*), to spring up, sprout; cf. early Eng. *sperage;* AS. *speragi* < L.], 1. any of a number of related plants with small, scalelike leaves, many flat or needlelike branches, and whitish flowers. 2. the tender shoots of a certain plant of this group, used as a vegetable.

as·par·tic acid (as-pär′tik), [coined after *asparagus*], an amino acid, $C_4H_7O_4N$, occurring in proteins in white prisms or colorless leaflets, used in organic synthesis.

As·pa·si·a (as-pā′zhi-ə, as-pā′shi-ə), *n.* clever, influential Greek woman, mistress of Pericles; 470?–410 B.C.

A.S.P.C.A., American Society for Prevention of Cruelty to Animals.

as·pect (as′pekt), *n.* [ME.; L. *aspectus*, pp. of *aspicere*, to look at < *ad-*, to, at + *spicere, specere*, to look], 1. [Rare], a glance; gaze. 2. the way one appears; looks. 3. the appearance of a thing as seen from a specific point; view. 4. the appearance or interpretation of an idea, problem, etc. as considered from a specific viewpoint. 5. a facing in a given direction. 6. a side facing in a given direction; exposure: as, the eastern *aspect* of the house. 7. in *astrology*, the position of stars in relation to each other or to the observer. 8. in *grammar*, the form that a verb takes to indicate duration or completion of action: e.g., he *was eating* (imperfect aspect); he *ate* (perfect aspect). 9. in *physics*, the position of a plane (flat surface) in relation to a liquid or gaseous substance through which it is moving or which is moving past it. —*SYN.* see **appearance, phase**.

as·pen (as′pən), *n.* [ME. *aspe;* AS. *æspe* + *-en* as in *ashen, beechen; æspe* is akin to OHG. *aspa;* IE. base **ŏsen;* see ASH (tree)], any of several kinds of poplar tree with flattened leafstalks that cause the leaves to flutter in the least breeze. *adj.* of or like an aspen; fluttering; trembling.

as·per (as′pẽr), *n.* [< Fr. *aspre* < Byzantine Gr. *aspron*, said to be < L. *asper*, rough], a former silver coin of Turkey and Egypt (now only a money of account), equal to 1/120 of a piaster.

As·per·ges (ə-spũr′jēz), *n.* [2d pers. sing., fut. indic., of L. *aspergere;* see ASPERSE], in the *Roman Catholic Church*, 1. the sprinkling of altar, clergy, and people with holy water before High Mass. 2. a hymn sung during this ceremony, beginning *Asperges me.*

as·per·gil·lum (as′pẽr-jil′əm), *n.* [*pl.* ASPERGILLA (-ə), ASPERGILLUMS (-əmz)], [ML. < L. *aspergere* (see ASPERSE) + neut. dim. *-illum*], a brush or perforated container for sprinkling holy water.

as·per·gil·lus (as′pẽr-jil′əs), *n.* [*pl.* ASPERGILLI (-ī)], [Mod. L.; see ASPERGILLUM: so named from appearing similar to the aspergillum], in *botany*, any of a number of related fungi bearing chains of spores attached to stalks on the swollen end of a threadlike branch, as the yellow mildew.

as·per·i·ty (as-per′ə-ti), *n.* [*pl.* ASPERITIES (-tiz)], [ME. & OFr. *asprete;* L. *asperitas*, roughness < *asper*, rough], 1. roughness or harshness, as of surface, sound, weather, etc. 2. harshness or sharpness of temper.

as·perse (ə-spũrs′), *v.t.* [ASPERSED (-spũrst′), ASPERSING], [< L. *aspersus*, pp. of *aspergere*, to sprinkle on < *ad-*, to + *spargere*, to sprinkle, strew], 1. [Rare], to strew water on, as in baptizing. 2. to spread false rumors concerning, or damaging charges against; besmirch the reputation of; slander.

as·per·sion (ə-spũr′zhən, ə-spũr′shən), *n.* [L. *aspersio;* see ASPERSE], 1. a sprinkling. 2. a defaming. 3. a damaging or disparaging remark; slander; innuendo.

as·per·so·ri·um (as′pẽr-sôr′i-əm, as′pẽr-sō′ri-əm), *n.* [*pl.* ASPERSORIA (-ə), ASPERSORIUMS (-əmz)], [LL. < L. *aspersus;* see ASPERSE], 1. a basin, font, etc. for holy water. 2. an aspergillum.

as·phalt (as′fôlt, as′falt), *n.* [LL. *asphaltum;* Gr. *asphalton, asphaltos;* prob. of Sem. origin], 1. a brown or black tarlike substance, a variety of bitumen, found in a natural state or obtained by evaporating petroleum. 2. a mixture of this with sand or gravel, for cementing, paving, roofing, etc. *v.t.* to pave, roof, etc. with asphalt.

as·phal·tum (as-fal′təm), *n.* asphalt.

as·pho·del (as′fə-del′), *n.* [L. *asphodelus;* Gr. *asphodelos*, ? a narcissus; see DAFFODIL], 1. any of a number of related plants of the lily family, having fleshy roots, narrow leaves, and white or yellow flowers like lilies. 2. any of a group of plants like these but with leafless flower stems.

as·phyx·i·a (as-fik′si-ə), *n.* [Gr., a stopping of the pulse < *a-*, not + *sphyzein*, to throb], loss of consciousness as a result of too little oxygen and too much carbon dioxide in the blood: suffocation causes asphyxia.

as·phyx·i·ant (as-fik′si-ənt), *adj.* causing or tending to cause asphyxia. *n.* an asphyxiant substance or condition.

as·phyx·i·ate (as-fik′si-āt′), *v.t.* [ASPHYXIATED (-id), ASPHYXIATING], 1. to cause asphyxia in. 2. to suffocate. *v.i.* to undergo asphyxia.

as·phyx·i·a·tion (as-fik′si-ā′shən), *n.* an asphyxiating or being asphyxiated.

as·phyx·i·a·tor (as-fik′si-ā′tẽr), *n.* a person or thing that asphyxiates.

as·pic (as′pik), *n.* [Fr.; OFr. *aspe* (see ASP); final *-ic* in Fr. prob. by association with *aspic* (a kind of lavender), because plant juices were used for treating snake bite], 1. [Poetic], an asp (poisonous snake). 2. a jelly of meat juice, tomato juice, etc. used as a relish or for a mold of meat, seafood, etc.

as·pic (as′pik), *n.* [Fr. *aspic;* Pr. *espic;* L. *spica*, a spike, ear of corn], a kind of lavender, a fragrant plant used in making oil of lavender.

as·pi·dis·tra (as′pi-dis′trə), *n.* [Mod. L. < Gr. *aspis*, a shield + *astron*, a star], any of a number of related plants of the lily family, with dark, inconspicuous flowers and large, stiff, glossy, evergreen leaves.

as·pir·ant (ə-spīr′ənt, as′pə-rənt), *adj.* [L. *aspirans*, ppr. of *aspirare;* see ASPIRE], aspiring. *n.* a person who aspires, as after honors, high position, etc.

as·pi·rate (as′pə-rāt′), *v.t.* [ASPIRATED (-id), ASPIRATING], [< L. *aspiratus*, pp. of *aspirare;* see ASPIRE], 1. to begin (a word) or precede (a sonorous speech sound) by the gradual glottal closure represented by English *h*. 2. to follow (a consonant, especially a stop consonant), with a puff of suddenly released breath: thus, initial *p, t, k* in English are phonetically p^h, t^h, k^h. 3. in *Greek grammar*, to pronounce as a fricative. 4. in *medicine*, to remove (fluid or gas), as from a body cavity, by suction. *n.* (as′pẽr-it), 1. the speech sound represented by English *h* or the Greek rough breathing: it is formed by gradually narrowing the vocal lips (glottis) for *w, r, l*, a following vowel, etc. 2. an expiratory breath puff such as follows initial *p, t, k* in English. 3. loosely, any sound preceded by that of *h* or followed by a puff of breath. 4. in *Greek grammar*, a fricative sound. *adj.* (as′pẽr-it), aspirated.

as·pi·rat·ed (as′pə-rāt′id), *adj.* 1. preceded by or containing the sound of *h*. 2. followed by a puff of breath.

as·pi·ra·tion (as′pə-rā′shən), *n.* [L. *aspiratio*, a blowing or breathing < pp. of *aspirare;* see ASPIRE], 1. act of breathing; breath. 2. an aspiring; strong desire or ambition, as for advancement, honor, etc. 3. the removal by suction of fluid or gas, as from a body cavity. 4. in *phonetics*, *a*) a pronouncing with an aspirate. *b*) an aspirate.

as·pi·ra·tor (as′pə-rā′tẽr), *n.* [see ASPIRATE], 1. any apparatus for moving air, fluids, etc. by suction. 2. an apparatus using suction to remove a fluid or gas from a body cavity.

as·pir·a·to·ry (ə-spīr′ə-tôr′i, ə-spīr′ə-tō′ri), *adj.* [< *aspirate* + *-ory*], of or suited for breathing or suction.

as·pire (ə-spīr′), *v.i.* [ASPIRED (-spīrd′), ASPIRING], [Fr. *aspirer;* L. *aspirare*, to breathe upon, aspire to < *ad-*, to + *spirare*, to breathe], 1. to be ambitious (*to* get or do something); long or seek (often followed by *after*). 2. [Archaic], to rise high; tower.

as·pi·rin (as′pẽr-in, as′prin), *n.* [G. < *acetyl* + *spirsäure*, salicylic acid; + *-in*], 1. a white, crystalline powder, acetylsalicylic acid, $C_9H_8O_4$, used for reducing fever, relieving headaches, etc. 2. a tablet of this.

a·squint (ə-skwint′), *adv.* & *adj.* [prob. < *a*, on + unrecorded AS. cognate of D. *schuinte*, slant; see SQUINT], with a squint; out of the corner of the eye.

As·quith, Herbert Henry (as′kwith), first Earl of Oxford and Asquith, 1852–1928; British statesman; prime minister (1908–1916).

ass (as), *n.* [ME. *asse;* AS. *assa, assen;* Celt. *assan;* L. *asinus*], 1. a donkey: in fables it is shown as obstinate and stupid; hence, 2. a stupid or silly person; fool.

ass (as), *n.* [Slang], arse: vulgar term.

ass., 1. assistant. 2. association. 3. assorted.

as·sa·fet·i·da, as·sa·foet·i·da (as′ə-fet′i-də), *n.* asafetida.

as·sa·gai (as'ə-gī'), *n.* [< Sp. *azagaya* or Port. *azagaia* < Ar. *az-zaghāyah; az,* for *al,* the + *zaghāyah,* spear, of Berber origin], 1. a slender spear or javelin, often with an iron tip, used by some South African tribes. 2. a tree of the dogwood family, having hard wood used to make such spears. *v.t.* to pierce with an assagai. Also spelled **assegai.**

as·sa·i (ə-sä'ē, ə-sī), *n.* [Braz. Port. *assahy* < native name], 1. any of a variety of Brazilian palms having a dark-purple, fleshy fruit. 2. a drink made from this fruit.

as·sail (ə-sāl'), *v.t.* [ME. *assailen;* OFr. *asaillir;* LL. *assilire,* to leap on < L. *ad,* to + *salire,* to leap], 1. to attack physically and violently; assault. 2. to attack with arguments, ridicule, etc. 3. to face (a difficulty, task, etc.) with determination. —*SYN.* see **attack.**

as·sail·ant (ə-sāl'ənt), *n.* [Fr. *assaillant,* ppr. of *assaillir;* see ASSAIL], *n.* a person who assails; attacker.

As·sam (a-sam', as'am), *n.* a state of northeastern India, on the borders of Burma and Tibet: area, 58,739 sq. mi.; pop., 10,418,000 (est. 1950); capital, Shillong.

As·sa·mese (as'ə-mēz'), *adj.* of Assam, its people, language, etc. *n.* 1. [*pl.* ASSAMESE], a native or inhabitant of Assam. 2. the Indo-European, Indic language of the Assamese.

Assam States, a group of individual states in Assam, including Manipur and those of the Khasi Hills.

as·sas·sin (ə-sas'in), *n.* [Fr.; ML. *assassinus;* Ar. *hashshāshīn,* hashish eaters < *hashīsh,* hemp], 1. [A-], a member of a secret band of hashish-eating Moslems who killed Christian leaders during the Crusades; hence, 2. a murderer who strikes suddenly and without warning: now generally used of the hired or delegated killer of some politically important personage.

as·sas·si·nate (ə-sas'ə-nāt'), *v.t.* [ASSASSINATED (-id), ASSASSINATING], [< ML. *assassinatus,* pp. of *assassinare,* to kill < *assassinus;* see ASSASSIN], 1. to murder by surprise attack, as assassins do. 2. to harm or ruin (one's reputation, etc.). —*SYN.* see **kill.**

as·sas·si·na·tion (ə-sas'ə-nā'shən), *n.* an assassinating or being assassinated.

assassin bug, any of a number of related insects having a curved, sucking beak and living chiefly on the blood of other insects.

as·sault (ə-sôlt'), *n.* [ME. *assaut;* OFr. *assaut, assalt* < L. *ad,* to + *saltare,* to leap], 1. a violent attack, either physical or verbal. 2. rape: a euphemism. 3. in *law,* an unlawful threat to harm another physically, or an unsuccessful attempt to do so. 4. in *military science,* *a)* a sudden attack upon a fortified place. *b)* the concluding stage of an attack. *v.t. & v.i.* to make an assault (upon). —*SYN.* see **attack.**

assault and battery, in *law,* the carrying out of threatened physical harm or violence; a beating.

as·say (ə-sā', as'ā), *n.* [ME. *assai;* OFr. *essai;* trial, test < L. *exagium,* a weighing < *ex-,* out + *agere,* to transact, deal], 1. an examination or testing. 2. the analysis of ore, especially gold or silver ore, or of an alloy, etc., to determine the nature and proportion of the ingredients or to test the purity. 3. a substance to be thus tested or analyzed. 4. the result or report of such an analysis. 5. [Obs.], an attempt. *v.t.* (ə-sā'), 1. to make an assay of; test; analyze. 2. [Archaic], to attempt. *v.i.* to be shown by analysis to contain a specified proportion of some precious metal: as, this ore *assays* high in gold. See also **essay.**

as·se·gai (as'ə-gī'), *n. & v.t.* assagai.

as·sem·blage (ə-sem'blij), *n.* [Fr. < *assembler;* see ASSEMBLE], 1. an assembling or being assembled. 2. a group or gathering of persons. 3. a collection of things. 4. a fitting together of parts, as of a machine. 5. a whole that results from such fitting together.

as·sem·ble (ə-sem'b'l), *v.t. & v.i.* [ASSEMBLED (-b'ld), ASSEMBLING], [ME. *assemblen;* OFr. *assembler, asembler;* L. *assimulare* < *ad-,* to + *simul,* together], 1. to gather together into a group; collect. 2. to fit or put together the parts of (a machine, etc.). —*SYN.* see **gather.**

as·sem·bly (ə-sem'bli), *n.* [*pl.* ASSEMBLIES (-bliz)], [ME. *assemble;* OFr. *assemblee* < *assembler;* see ASSEMBLE], 1. an assembling or being assembled. 2. a group of persons gathered together, as for legislation, worship, etc. 3. [A-], in some States of the United States, the lower house of the legislature. 4. a fitting together of parts to make a whole, as in making automobiles, etc. 5. the parts to be thus fitted together. 6. the factory in which such assembling is done. 7. in *military science,* a call, as by bugle or drum, for soldiers to form ranks.

assembly line, in many factories, an arrangement whereby each worker performs a specialized operation on the work as it is passed along from one to another, often on a slowly moving belt or track.

as·sem·bly·man (ə-sem'bli-mən), *n.* [*pl.* ASSEMBLYMEN (-men', -mən)], 1. a member of a legislative assembly. 2. [A-], in some States of the United States, a member of the lower house of the legislature.

assembly plant, a factory in which parts, as of aircraft, are assembled.

as·sent (ə-sent'), *v.i.* [ME. *assenten;* OFr. *assenter;* L. *assentare, assentari* < *assentire* < *ad-,* to + *sentire,* to feel], 1. to consent; comply. 2. to agree; concur. *n.* [ME. < OFr. *assenter;* see the *v.*], 1. consent; acquiescence. 2. agreement; concurrence. —*SYN.* see **consent.**

as·sen·ta·tion (as'en-tā'shən), *n.* [L. *assentatio* < pp. of *assentare;* see ASSENT], immediate and usually flattering or hypocritical assent.

as·sent·er (ə-sen'tẽr), *n.* a person who assents.

as·sen·tor (ə-sen'tẽr), *n.* 1. an assenter. 2. in *English law,* the voter whose endorsement must be added to those of the proposer and seconder for the nomination of a political candidate.

as·sert (ə-sũrt'), *v.t.* [< L. *assertus,* pp. of *asserere,* to join to, claim < *ad-,* to + *serere,* to join, bind], 1. to state positively; declare; affirm. 2. to maintain or defend (rights, claims, etc.).

assert oneself, 1. to insist on one's rights, or on being recognized. 2. to thrust oneself forward.

SYN.—to **assert** is to state positively with great confidence but with no objective proof (he *asserted* that man's nature would never change); to **declare** is to assert openly or formally, often in the face of opposition (they *declared* their independence); **affirm** implies deep conviction in one's statement and the unlikelihood of denial by another (I cannot *affirm* that he was there); **aver** connotes implicit confidence in the truth of one's statement from one's own knowledge of the matter; **avouch** implies firsthand knowledge or authority on the part of the speaker; **warrant,** in this comparison, is colloquial, and implies positiveness by the speaker (I *warrant* he'll be late again). —*ANT.* deny, controvert.

as·sert·er (ə-sũr'tẽr), *n.* a person who asserts.

as·ser·tion (ə-sũr'shən), *n.* [L. *assertio,* formal declaration; see ASSERT], 1. an asserting. 2. something asserted; positive statement; declaration.

as·ser·tive (ə-sũr'tiv), *adj.* 1. characterized by assertion; positive. 2. unduly confident or insistent in stating or claiming. —*SYN.* see **aggressive.**

as·ser·tor (ə-sũr'tẽr), *n.* a person who asserts.

as·ser·to·ry (ə-sũr'tẽr-i), *adj.* that asserts or affirms.

asses' bridge, [transl. of L. *pons asinorum;* see ASS], in *Euclidean geometry,* the proposition that the base angles of an isosceles triangle are equal: so called from the difficulty of learners in grasping it.

as·sess (ə-ses'), *v.t.* [OFr. *assesser* < LL. *assessare,* to impose a tax, set a rate < L. *assessus,* pp. of *assidere,* to sit beside, assist (in office), in LL., to assess < *ad-,* to + *sedere,* to sit], 1. to set an estimated value on (property, etc.) for taxation. 2. to set the amount of (damages, a fine, etc.). 3. to impose a fine, tax, or special payment on (a person or property). 4. to impose (an amount) as a fine, tax, etc.

as·sess·ment (ə-ses'mənt), *n.* 1. an assessing. 2. a way or schedule of assessing. 3. an amount assessed.

as·ses·sor (ə-ses'ẽr), *n.* [ME. & OFr. *assessour;* L. *assessor* < *assessus;* see ASSESS], 1. a person who sets valuations on property or income for taxation. 2. a judge's assistant, chosen for his special knowledge of some field. 3. an adviser to a committee, etc.

as·ses·so·ri·al (as'ə-sôr'i-əl, as'ə-sō'ri-əl), *adj.* of an assessor or assessors.

as·set (as'et), *n.* [OFr. (pl. *assez*), thing assigned, portion (hence equity, asset) < *asseter,* to assign, place, dispose < LL. *asseditare,* to put, place < L. *ad-,* to + freq. of *sedere,* to sit; associated with Anglo-Fr. *assetz,* sufficient (esp. in *aver assetz,* to have enough) < OFr. *asez,* enough < L. *ad satis,* to sufficiency], 1. anything owned that has exchange value. 2. a valuable or desirable thing to have: as, charm is her chief *asset.* 3. *pl.* in *accounting,* all the entries on a balance sheet that shows the entire property or resources of a person or business, as accounts and notes receivable, cash, inventory, equipment, real estate, etc. 4. *pl.* in *law,* property, as of a business, bankrupt, etc., usable to pay debts.

as·sev·er·ate (ə-sev'ə-rāt'), *v.t.* [ASSEVERATED (-id), ASSEVERATING], [< L. *asseveratus,* pp. of *asseverare,* to assert strongly < *ad-,* to + *severus,* earnest, severe], to state seriously or positively; assert.

as·sev·er·a·tion (ə-sev'ə-rā'shən), *n.* [L. *asseveratio*], 1. an asseverating. 2. an emphatic statement.

As·shur (ä'shoor), *n.* Ashur.

as·si·du·i·ty (as'ə-dū'ə-ti), *n.* [L. *assiduitas,* constant presence < *assidere,* to sit by < *ad-,* to + *sedere,* to sit], 1. the quality or condition of being assiduous; diligence. 2. [*pl.* ASSIDUITIES (-tiz)], an instance of this.

as·sid·u·ous (ə-sij'oo-əs), *adj.* [L. *assiduus;* see ASSIDUITY], 1. done with constant and careful attention. 2. diligent; persevering. —*SYN.* see **busy.**

as·sign (ə-sīn'), *v.t.* [ME. *assignen;* OFr. *assigner;* L. *assignare,* to mark out, allot < *ad-,* to + *signare;* see SIGN], 1. to set or fix for a specific purpose; designate: as, *assign* a day for the meeting. 2. to appoint: as, I was *assigned* to watch the road. 3. to give out as a task; allot: as, the teacher *assigned* a new lesson. 4. to ascribe; refer: as, jealousy was *assigned* as the motive for the crime. 5. in *law,* to make over to another; transfer, as a claim, right, property, etc. *v.i.* in *law,* to transfer a claim, property, etc. to another. *n. usually pl.* an assignee. —*SYN.* see **allot, ascribe.**

as·sig·nat (as'ig-nat'; Fr. å'sē'nyå'), *n.* [Fr.; L. *assignatus,* pp. of *assignare;* see ASSIGN], a piece of paper currency issued during the French Revolution with confiscated lands as the security.

as·sig·na·tion (as′ig-nā′shən), *n.* [OFr. *assignacion;* L. *assignatio* < pp. of *assignare;* see ASSIGN], 1. an assigning or being assigned. 2. anything assigned. 3. an appointment to meet, especially one made secretly by lovers; tryst; rendezvous. 4. in *law,* a transference of a claim, right, property, etc.

as·sign·ee (ə-sī′nē′, as′ə-nē′), *n.* [Fr. *assigné;* see ASSIGN,], in *law,* 1. a person to whom a claim, right, property, etc. is transferred; an assign. 2. a person appointed to act for another.

as·sign·er (ə-sīn′ẽr), *n.* a person who assigns.

as·sign·ment (ə-sīn′mənt), *n.* [ME.; OFr. *assignement;* ML. *assignamentum* < *assignare;* see ASSIGN], 1. an assigning or being assigned; appointment; allotment. 2. anything assigned or allotted, as a lesson, task, etc. 3. in *law, a*) a transfer of a claim, right, property, etc. *b*) a paper, as a deed, authorizing this. —*SYN.* see **task.**

as·sign·or (ə-sī′nôr′, as′ə-nôr′), *n.* in *law,* a person who assigns a claim, right, property, etc.

as·sim·i·la·ble (ə-sim′'l-ə-b'l), *adj.* that can be assimilated.

as·sim·i·late (ə-sim″'l-āt′), *v.t.* [ASSIMILATED (-id), ASSIMILATING], [< L. *assimilatus,* pp. of *assimilare* < *ad-,* to + *similare,* to make similar to < *similis,* like], 1. to take up and make part of itself or oneself; absorb and incorporate; digest: as, the body *assimilates* food. 2. to compare or liken. 3. to make like or alike; cause to resemble (with *to*): as, *assimilate* the final sound of a prefix to the initial sound of a word. *v.i.* 1. to become like or alike. 2. to be absorbed and incorporated: as, minority groups often *assimilate* by intermarriage.

as·sim·i·la·tion (ə-sim″'l-ā′shən), *n.* [L. *assimilatio;* see ASSIMILATE], 1. an assimilating or being assimilated. 2. in *phonetics, a*) the process whereby a sound, influenced by a contiguous or neighboring sound, tends to become like it in position and type of articulation: thus, in *cupboard, clapboard,* the *p* has been lost by assimilation to *b. b*) an example of this process. 3. in *physiology,* the change of digested food and other material into part of the living organism.

as·sim·i·la·tion·ism (ə-sim″'l-ā′shən-iz'm), *n.* the policy of absorbing minority groups of different races, religions, etc., especially by intermarriage.

as·sim·i·la·tive (ə-sim″'l-ā′tiv), *adj.* [ML. *assimilativus*], assimilating; of or causing assimilation.

as·sim·i·la·to·ry (ə-sim″'l-ə-tôr′i, ə-sim″'l-ə-tō′ri), *adj.* assimilative.

As·sin·i·boine (ə-sin′ə-boin′), *n.* a river in south central Canada, flowing from southeastern Saskatchewan into the Red River at Winnipeg, Manitoba: length, 450 mi.

As·si·si (ə-sē′zi; It. äs-sē′zē), *n.* a town in central Italy: pop., 22,500: birthplace of St. Francis.

as·sist (ə-sist′), *v.t.* & *v.i.* [Fr. *assister* < L. *assistere* < *ad-,* to + *sistere,* to make stand < *stare,* to stand], to help; aid. *n.* 1. an instance or act of helping. 2. in *baseball,* a play that helps put a batter or runner out. 3. in *ice hockey,* the act of a player who passes the puck to the teammate scoring a goal.—*SYN.* see **help.**

assist at, to be present at; attend.

as·sist·ance (ə-sis′təns), *n.* [Fr.; see ASSIST], help; aid.

as·sist·ant (ə-sis′tənt), *adj.* [Fr. < ppr. of L. *assistere;* see ASSIST], assisting; helping; that serves as a helper. *n.* 1. a person who assists or serves in a subordinate position. 2. a thing that aids. Abbreviated **ass., asst.**

assistant professor, a college teacher ranking above an instructor and below an associate professor.

As·siut (ä-sūt′), *n.* Asyut.

as·size (ə-sīz′), *n.* [ME. & OFr. *assise,* court session < *asseoir* < L. *assidere;* see ASSESS], 1. originally, an assembly or its decree; hence, 2. *pl.* court sessions held periodically in each county of England to try civil and criminal cases. 3. *pl.* the time or place of such sessions. 4. an inquest, the writ instituting it, or the verdict. 5. formerly, a law regulating standards of price, measure, weight, ingredients, etc. for goods to be sold. 6. these standards as usually prescribed.

assn., association.

assoc., 1. associate. 2. associated. 3. association.

as·so·ci·a·ble (ə-sō′shi-ə-b'l, ə-sō′shə-b'l), *adj.* [Fr.], that can be associated, connected, or joined.

as·so·ci·ate (ə-sō′shi-āt′; *for n. & adj., usually* ə-sō′shi-it), *v.t.* [ASSOCIATED (-id), ASSOCIATING], [< L. *associatus,* pp. of *associare,* to join to, unite with < *ad-,* to + *sociare,* to join, unite with < *socius,* companion], 1. to connect; combine; join. 2. to bring (a person) into relationship with oneself or another as companion, partner, friend, etc. 3. to connect in the mind: as, she *associates* rain with grief. *v.i.* 1. to join (*with* another or others) as a companion, partner, friend, etc. 2. to unite as friends, partners, etc.; join for a common purpose; keep company. *n.* 1. a person associated; friend; partner; colleague; fellow worker. 2. a member without full status or privileges, as of a society, institute, etc. 3. anything joined with another thing or things. 4. in some colleges and universities, a title conferred on one who has completed a course shorter than that required for a degree: as, an *associate* in music. *adj.* 1. united or related by the same interests, purposes, etc. 2. having secondary status or privileges: as, an *associate* justice. 3. accompanying; connected. Abbreviated **assoc.**

SYN.—**associate** refers to a person who is frequently in one's company, usually because of some work or project shared in common (business *associates*); **colleague** denotes a fellow worker, especially in one of the professions, and may or may not imply a close, personal relationship (his *colleagues* at the university); **companion** always refers to a person who actually accompanies one and usually implies a close personal relationship (a dinner *companion,* the *companions* of one's youth); **comrade** refers to a close associate and implies a sharing in activities and fortunes (*comrades* in arms); **ally** now usually refers to a government joined with another or others in a common pursuit, especially war; a **confederate** is one who joins with another or others for some common purpose, specifically in some unlawful act; an **accomplice** is one who unites with others, either as a principal or a subordinate, with criminal intent to commit an offense. See also **join.**

Associated Press, a large, privately owned agency for gathering news and distributing it among member newspapers: abbreviated **AP, A.P., Æ** (no period).

associate professor, a college teacher ranking above an assistant professor and below a full professor.

as·so·ci·a·tion (ə-sō′si-ā′shən, ə-sō′shi-ā′shən), *n.* [Fr.; ML. *associatio,* a joining with; see ASSOCIATE], 1. an associating or being associated. 2. the state of being associated; companionship; fellowship; partnership. 3. an organization of persons having common interests, purposes, etc.; society; league: abbreviated **ass., assn., assoc.** 4. a connection between ideas, sensations, etc.; hence, 5. the use of such connections as a literary device or technique. 6. association football.

as·so·ci·a·tion·al (ə-sō′si-ā′shən-'l, ə-sō′shi-ā′shən-'l), *adj.* of or based on association, as of ideas.

association football, soccer: so called from the British controlling body, the National Football Association.

as·so·ci·a·tive (ə-sō′shi-ā′tiv, ə-sō′shi-ə-tiv), *adj.* of, characterized by, or causing association.

as·soil (ə-soil′), *v.t.* [ME. *assoilen* < OFr. *assoil,* pres. indic. form of *assoldre;* L. *absolvere;* see ABSOLVE], [Archaic], 1. to pardon; absolve. 2. to atone for.

as·so·nance (as′ə-nəns), *n.* [Fr.; L. *assonans,* ppr. of *assonare,* to sound to < *ad-,* to + *sonare,* to sound], 1. likeness of sound. 2. a rough similarity. 3. a partial rhyme in which the stressed vowel sounds are alike but the consonant sounds are unlike, as in *late* and *make.*

as·so·nant (as′ə-nənt), *adj.* [Fr.], in *prosody,* having assonance. *n.* a word assonant with another.

as·sort (ə-sôrt′), *v.t.* [OFr. *assorter* < *a-* (L. *ad*), to + *sorte;* see SORT], 1. to separate into classes according to sorts or kinds; classify. 2. to supply (a warehouse, etc.) with an assortment of goods. *v.i.* 1. to be of the same sort; fall into a group or class; hence, 2. to match or harmonize (*with*). 3. to consort or associate (*with*).

as·sort·ed (ə-sôr′tid), *adj.* [pp. of *assort*], 1. in an assortment; various; miscellaneous. 2. classified. 3. matched: as, a poorly *assorted* pair. Abbreviated **ass.**

as·sort·ment (ə-sôrt′mənt), *n.* 1. an assorting or being assorted; classification. 2. an assorted, or miscellaneous, group or collection; variety.

As·souan (äs-wän′), *n.* Aswan.

A.S.S.R., Autonomous Soviet Socialist Republic.

asst., assistant.

as·suage (ə-swāj′), *v.t.* [ASSUAGED (-swājd′), ASSUAGING], [ME. *aswagen;* OFr. *asouagier* < L. *ad,* to + *suavis,* sweet], 1. to lessen (pain, distress, etc.); allay; mitigate. 2. to pacify; calm (passion, anger, etc.). 3. to satisfy or quench (thirst, etc.). —*SYN.* see **relieve.**

as·suage·ment (ə-swāj′mənt), *n.* 1. an assuaging or being assuaged. 2. an assuaging thing.

As·suan (äs-wän′), *n.* Aswan.

as·sua·sive (ə-swā′siv), *adj.* [incorrectly < *assuage,* as if < L. **assuadere;* see SUASION], soothing; allaying.

as·sum·a·ble (ə-sōōm′ə-b'l, ə-sūm′ə-b'l), *adj.* that can be assumed.

as·sume (ə-sōōm′, ə-sūm′), *v.t.* [ASSUMED (-sōōmd′, -sūmd′), ASSUMING], [L. *assumere,* to take up, claim < *ad-,* to + *sumere,* to take], 1. to take or put on (the appearance, form, role, etc. of). 2. to seize; usurp: as, Hitler *assumed* control. 3. to take into association; take on; receive: as, he was *assumed* as a partner. 4. to take upon oneself; undertake. 5. to take for granted; suppose (something) to be a fact. 6. to pretend to have; feign. *v.i.* to be pretentious or presumptuous.

SYN.—**assume** implies the putting on of a false appearance but suggests a harmless or excusable motive (an *assumed* air of bravado); **pretend** and **feign** both imply a profession or display of what is false, the more literary **feign** sometimes suggesting an elaborately contrived situation (to *pretend* not to hear, to *feign* deafness); to **affect** is to make a show of being, having, using, wearing, etc., usually for effect (to *affect* a British accent); **simulate** emphasizes the imitation of typical signs involved in assuming an appearance or characteristic not one's own (to *simulate* interest). See also **presume.**

as·sumed (ə-sōōmd′, ə-sūmd′), *adj.* [pp. of *assume*], 1. pretended; put on; fictitious. 2. taken for granted.

as·sum·ing (ə-sōōm′iŋ, ə-sūm′iŋ), *adj.* [ppr. of *assume*], presumptuous. *n.* presumption.

as·sump·sit (ə-sump′sit), *n.* [L., he has undertaken; 3d pers. sing., perf. indic., of *assumere;* see ASSUME], in *law,* 1. an agreement or promise, written, spoken, or implied, and not under seal. 2. an action to recover damages for the nonfulfillment of such an agreement.

as·sump·tion (ə-sump′shən), *n.* [ME. *assumpcioun;* L. *assumptio* < pp. of *assumere;* see ASSUME], 1. a supposed bodily ascent into heaven. 2. [A-], the ascent of the Virgin Mary into heaven. 3. [A-], the church festival celebrating this (August 15). 4. an assuming or being assumed. 5. anything taken for granted; supposition. 6. presumption.

as·sump·tive (ə-sump′tiv), *adj.* 1. assumed. 2. of, or having the character of, an assumption. 3. assuming; presumptuous.

As·sur (ä′soor), *n.* Ashur.

as·sur·ance (ə-shoor′əns), *n.* [ME. *assuraunce;* OFr. *asseurance;* LL. *assecurantia* < *assecurare;* see ASSURE], 1. an assuring or being assured. 2. sureness; confidence; certainty. 3. anything that inspires confidence, as a promise, positive statement, etc.; guarantee. 4. firmness of mind; self-confidence. 5. impudent forwardness; presumption. 6. [British], insurance. —*SYN.* see **certainty, confidence.**

As·sur·ba·ni·pal (ä′soor-bä′ni-päl′), *n.* Ashurbanipal.

as·sure (ə-shoor′), *v.t.* [ASSURED (-shoord′), ASSURING], [ME. *assuren;* OFr. *asseurer;* LL. *assecurare* < L. *ad,* to + *securus;* see SECURE], 1. to make (a person) sure of something; convince. 2. to give confidence to; reassure: as, the news *assured* us. 3. to declare to or promise confidently: as, I *assure* you I'll be there. 4. to make (a doubtful thing) certain; guarantee. 5. to insure. 6. [Obs.], to make secure.

as·sured (ə-shoord′), *adj.* [pp. of *assure*], 1. sure; guaranteed. 2. confident. 3. insured. *n.* an insured person.

as·sur·ed·ly (ə-shoor′id-li), *adv.* 1. surely; certainly. 2. with confidence.

as·sur·er (ə-shoor′ẽr), *n.* a person or thing that gives assurance; specifically, [British], an underwriter of insurance policies.

as·sur·gent (ə-sũr′jənt), *adj.* [L. *assurgens,* ppr. of *assurgere,* to rise up, swell < *ad-,* to + *surgere,* to rise], 1. rising. 2. in *botany,* rising at an oblique angle, as some stems.

Assyr., Assyrian.

As·syr·i·a (ə-sir′i-ə), *n.* an ancient empire in western Asia in the region of the upper Tigris River: capital, Nineveh: in the seventh century B.C. it extended from India to Egypt and Asia Minor.

ASSYRIA

As·syr·i·an (ə-sir′i-ən), *adj.* 1. of Assyria, its people, language, or culture. 2. designating or of the ancient architecture of Assyria, characterized by low, massive brick walls, carved slabs, and rich ornamentation: see TYPES OF ARCHITECTURE, p. 77. *n.* 1. a native or inhabitant of Assyria. 2. the Semitic language of the Assyrians. Abbreviated **Assyr.**

As·syr·i·ol·o·gy (ə-sir′i-ol′ə-ji), *n.* [< *Assyria* + *-logy*], the study of the civilization of ancient Assyria.

As·tar·te (as-tär′ti), *n.* [L.; Gr. *Astartē* < Sem.; see APHRODITE], in *Phoenician mythology,* the goddess of the moon, fertility, and sexual love: cf. **Ishtar, Ashtoreth.**

a·stat·ic (ā-stat′ik, ə-stat′ik), *adj.* [Gr. *astatos,* unstable; *a-,* not + *statos;* see STATIC], 1. unstable; unsteady. 2. in *physics,* not taking a definite position or direction: as, an *astatic* needle is not affected by the earth's magnetism.

a·stat·i·cal·ly (ā-stat′i-k'l-i, ə-stat′ik-li), *adv.* in an astatic manner.

a·stat·i·cism (ā-stat′ə-siz'm, ə-stat′ə-siz'm), *n.* the quality or state of being astatic.

as·ta·tine (as′tə-tēn′, as′tə-tin), *n.* [< Gr. *astatos,* unstable; + *-ine*], an unstable chemical element formed from bismuth when it is bombarded by alpha particles: symbol, At; at. wt., 211 (?); at. no., 85 (formerly designated as *alabamine*).

as·ter (as′tẽr), *n.* [L.; Gr. *astēr,* star], 1. any of various related plants of the composite family, with spear-shaped leaves and purplish, blue, pink, or white flowers like daisies. 2. the China aster. 3. in *biology,* a structure shaped like a star, formed in the cytoplasm of a cell during mitosis.

as·ter- (as′tẽr), [< Gr. *astēr,* star], a combining form denoting *relationship to a star,* as in *asterism, asteroid:* also **asteri-, astero-.**

-as·ter (as′tẽr), [L. dim. suffix], a suffix denoting: 1. *diminution.* 2. *similarity.* 3. *inferiority* or *worthlessness,* as in *poetaster:* the current sense.

as·ter·a·ceous (as′tẽr-ā′shəs), *adj.* [*aster* + *-aceous*], in *botany,* of the aster or thistle family.

as·te·ri·a·ted (as-têr′i-ā′tid), *adj.* [Gr. *asterios,* starred < *astēr,* star], 1. having radiate form; star-shaped. 2. in *mineralogy,* having asterism.

as·ter·isk (as′tẽr-isk′), *n.* [L. *astericus;* Gr. *asteriskos,* dim. of *astēr,* a star], a starlike sign (*) used in printing to indicate footnote references, omissions, etc.: it is used throughout this dictionary to indicate hypothetical forms of words. *v.t.* to mark with this sign.

as·ter·ism (as′tẽr-iz'm), *n.* [Gr. *asterismos,* a marking with stars < *asterizein,* to mark with stars < *astēr,* a star], 1. in *astronomy, a*) a constellation. *b*) a star cluster. 2. in *mineralogy,* a starlike figure produced in some crystals by reflected or transmitted light. 3. in *printing,* three asterisks placed in triangular form (* * * or * * *) to call special attention to a passage.

a·stern (ə-stũrn′), *adj. & adv.* [*a-,* in + *stern, n.*], 1. behind a ship. 2. at or toward the rear. 3. backward. Distinguished from *aft.*

a·ster·nal (ā-stũr′n'l), *adj.* [*a-,* not + *sternal*], 1. not joined to the sternum. 2. without a sternum.

as·ter·oid (as′tẽr-oid′), *adj.* [Gr. *asteroeidēs* < *astēr,* star + *-eidēs,* -oid], starlike; shaped like a star or starfish. *n.* 1. in *astronomy,* any of the small planets with orbits between those of Mars and Jupiter; planetoid. 2. in *zoology,* a starfish.

as·the·ni·a (as-thē′ni-ə, as′thə-nī′ə), *n.* [L.; Gr. *astheneia,* weakness < *a-,* without + *sthenos,* strength], a lack or loss of bodily strength; bodily weakness.

as·then·ic (as-then′ik), *adj.* [Gr. *asthenikos*], of or having asthenia. *n.* in *psychology,* a person of slender physique.

as·the·no·pi·a (as′thə-nō′pi-ə), *n.* [Mod. L. < Gr. *asthenēs,* weak (see ASTHENIA); + *-opia*], a strained condition of the eyes, often with headache, dizziness, etc.

asth·ma (az′mə, as′mə), *n.* [Gr., a panting, asthma < *azein,* to breathe hard], a chronic disorder characterized by wheezing, coughing, difficulty in breathing, and a suffocating feeling.

asth·mat·ic (az-mat′ik, as-mat′ik), *adj.* [L. *asthmaticus;* Gr. *asthmatikos*], of or having asthma. *n.* a person who has asthma.

asth·mat·i·cal (az-mat′i-k'l, as-mat′i-k'l), *adj.* asthmatic.

as·tig·mat·ic (as′tig-mat′ik), *adj.* 1. of or having astigmatism. 2. correcting astigmatism.

a·stig·ma·tism (ə-stig′mə-tiz'm), *n.* [< Gr. *a-,* without + *stigma, stigmatos,* a mark, puncture; + *-ism*], a structural defect of a lens or the eyes that prevents light rays from an object from meeting in a single focal point, so that indistinct images are formed.

a·stir (ə-stũr′), *adv. & adj.* [*a-,* on + *stir,* movement], 1. in motion; in excited activity. 2. out of bed.

As·to·lat (as′tə-lät′, as′tə-lat′), *n.* an English town in Arthurian legend: some scholars think that it was in the region now called Surrey.

a·stom·a·tous (ā-stom′ə-təs, ā-stō′mə-təs), *adj.* [*a-,* not + *stomat-* + *-ous*], in *biology,* without a stoma; without stomata.

as·ton·ied (ə-ston′id), *adj.* [pp. of ME. *astonien;* see ASTONISH], [Archaic], bewildered; dazed.

as·ton·ish (ə-ston′ish), *v.t.* [ME. *astonien;* OFr. *estoner* < L. **extonare; ex-,* out + *tonare,* to thunder; equiv. to "strike with lightning"], to fill with sudden wonder or surprise; amaze. —*SYN.* see **surprise.**

as·ton·ish·ing (ə-ston′ish-iŋ), *adj.* [ppr. of *astonish*], surprising; amazing.

as·ton·ish·ment (ə-ston′ish-mənt), *n.* 1. an astonishing; sudden surprise; amazement. 2. anything that astonishes.

As·tor, John Jacob (as′tẽr), 1763–1848; American fur merchant and capitalist.

Astor, Viscountess, (*Nancy Langhorne*), 1879– ; first woman member of the British House of Commons, born in America.

As·tor·i·a (as-tôr′i-ə, as-tō′ri-ə), *n.* 1. a seaport in northwestern Oregon, on the Columbia River: pop., 12,000. 2. a section of the Borough of Queens, New York City.

as·tound (ə-stound′), *v.t.* [ME. *astouned, astoned,* pp. of *astonien;* see ASTONISH], to bewilder with sudden surprise; amaze; astonish greatly. —*SYN.* see **surprise.**

astr., 1. astronomer. 2. astronomical. 3. astronomy.

as·tra·chan (as′trə-kən), *n.* 1. astrakhan. 2. [A-], a variety of apple, originally from Russia.

a·strad·dle (ə-strad′'l), *adv. & adj.* [*a-,* on + *straddle*], in a straddling position; astride.

As·trae·a (as-trē′ə), *n.* [L.; Gr. *Astraia*], in *Greek & Roman mythology,* the goddess of justice, who was the last deity to leave the earth after the fabled golden age and became the constellation Virgo: also spelled **Astrea.**

as·tra·gal (as′trə-g'l), *n.* [L. *astragalus;* Gr. *astragalos,* a turning joint, anklebone, vertebra, architectural molding], 1. in *anatomy,* the astragalus. 2. in *architecture,* a small, convex molding, sometimes cut like beading.

as·trag·a·lus (as-trag'ə-ləs), *n.* [*pl.* ASTRAGALI (-lī')], [L.; see ASTRAGAL], 1. in *anatomy*, the anklebone; talus. 2. in *architecture*, an astragal.
As·tra·khan (as'trə-kan'; Russ. äs'trä-khän'y'), *n.* a city on the Volga in the U.S.S.R.: pop., 294,000.
as·tra·khan (as'trə-kən), *n.* 1. the pelt of very young lambs from Astrakhan, with tightly curled wool. 2. a woolly cloth imitating this. Also spelled **astrachan.**
as·tral (as'trəl), *adj.* [L. *astralis* < *astrum* < Gr. *astron*, star < same base as *astēr* and ult. < same IE. base *(ə)*stēr*- as Eng. *star*], 1. of, from, or like the stars. 2. in *biology*, of an aster. 3. in *theosophy*, designating or of an alleged supernatural substance.
astral body, 1. a supposed spirit or ghostlike double of the human body, able to leave it at will. 2. loosely, a star or planet.
astral lamp, an oil lamp made to cast no shadow downward.
a·stray (ə-strā'), *adv. & adj.* [ME. < pp. of OFr. *estraier;* see STRAY], off the right path or way.
As·tre·a (as-trē'ə), *n.* Astraea.
as·trict (ə-strikt'), *v.t.* [< L. *astrictus*, pp. of *astringere;* see ASTRINGE], [Rare], 1. to bind; constrict; limit. 2. to restrict legally or morally.
as·tric·tion (ə-strik'shən), *n.* [L. *astrictio* < pp. of *astringere;* see ASTRINGE], 1. a binding or contracting, as of body tissues. 2. [Obs.], astringency.
as·tric·tive (ə-strik'tiv), *adj. & n.* [< L. *astrictus*, pp. of *astringere* (see ASTRINGE); + *-ive*], astringent.
a·stride (ə-strīd'), *adv. & adj.* [*a-*, on + *stride*], 1. with a leg on either side; astraddle. 2. with legs far apart. *prep.* with a leg on either side of (a horse, etc.).
as·tringe (ə-strinj'), *v.t.* [ASTRINGED (-strinjd'), ASTRINGING], [L. *astringere*, to contract < *ad-*, to + *stringere*, to draw, bind], [Rare], to constrict; compress.
as·trin·gen·cy (ə-strin'jən-si), *n.* an astringent quality.
as·trin·gent (ə-strin'jənt), *adj.* [L. *astringens*, ppr. of *astringere;* see ASTRINGE], 1. that contracts body tissue and blood vessels, checking the flow of blood; styptic. 2. causing to shrink or contract. 3. harsh; severe; stern. *n.* an astringent substance, drug, etc.
as·tro- (as'trō, as'trə), [< Gr. *astron*, a star; see ASTRAL], a combining form meaning: 1. in *astronomy*, *of a star* or *stars*, as in *astrophysics*. 2. in *biology*, *of an aster*, as in *astrosphere*.
astrol., 1. astrologer. 2. astrological. 3. astrology.
as·tro·labe (as'trə-lāb'), *n.* [ME. *astrolabie;* OFr. *astrolabe;* LL. *astrolabium;* Gr. *astrolabon* < *astron*, a star (see ASTRAL) + *lambanein*, to take], an instrument formerly used to find the altitude of a star, etc.: it was replaced by the sextant.
as·trol·o·ger (ə-strol'ə-jēr), *n.* [ME.; L. *astrologus;* Gr. *astrologos*, astronomer; see ASTROLOGY], 1. a person who practices or studies astrology. 2. [Obs.], an astronomer. Abbreviated **astrol.**
as·tro·log·i·cal (as'trə-loj'i-k'l), *adj.* 1. of astrology. 2. [Obs.], astronomical. Abbreviated **astrol.**
as·trol·o·gy (ə-stol'ə-ji), *n.* [ME. *astrologie;* L. & Gr. *astrologia*, astronomy, astrology < *astron*, star (see ASTRAL) + *logia* < *legein*, to speak], 1. a pseudo science claiming to foretell the future by studying the supposed influence of the relative positions of the moon, sun, and stars on human affairs. 2. [Obs.], primitive astronomy. Abbreviated **astrol.**
as·trom·e·try (ə-strom'ə-tri), *n.* [*astro-* + *-metry*], that branch of astronomy dealing with the measurement of planets, stars, etc. and their positions and movements.
astron., 1. astronomer. 2. astronomical. 3. astronomy.
as·tro·naut (as'trə-nôt'), *n.* [< Fr. *astronaute*; cf. ASTRONAUTICS], a person trained to make rocket flights in outer space.
as·tro·nau·tics (as'trə-nô'tiks), *n.pl.* [construed as sing.], [<Fr. *astronautique* (coined 1927); cf. ASTRO- & AERONAUTICS], the science that deals with the problems of travel in outer space, specially to the moon and to other planets.
as·tron·o·mer (ə-stron'ə-mēr), *n.* [ME.], a student of or an authority on astronomy: abbreviated **astr., astron.**
as·tro·nom·ic (as'trə-nom'ik), *adj.* astronomical.
as·tro·nom·i·cal (as'trə-nom'i-k'l), *adj.* 1. of astronomy: abbreviated **astr., astron.** 2. very large, as the numbers or quantities used in astronomy.
astronomical day, the mean solar day, noon to noon.
as·tro·nom·i·cal·ly (as'trə-nom'i-k'l-i, as'trə-nom'ik-li), *adv.* 1. from the viewpoint of astronomy. 2. by means of astronomy. 3. as in astronomy: as, *astronomically* large numbers.
astronomical unit, a unit of length equal to the mean radius of the earth's orbit (c. 93 million miles).
astronomical year, the period in which the earth makes a complete revolution around the sun (365 days, 5 hours, 48 minutes, 45.51 seconds); time from one equinox to the next corresponding equinox; solar year.
as·tron·o·my (ə-stron'ə-mi), *n.* [ME. & OFr. *astronomie;* L. *astronomia;* Gr. *astronomia* < *astron*, star (see ASTRAL) + *nomos*, law, system of laws < *nemein*, to arrange], the science of the stars and other heavenly bodies, dealing with their composition, motion, relative position, size, etc.: abbreviated **astr., astron.**
as·tro·pho·tog·ra·phy (as'trō-fə-tog'rə-fi), *n.* [*astro-* + *photography*], photography as used in investigating astronomical phenomena.
as·tro·phys·i·cal (as'trō-fiz'i-k'l), *adj.* [*astro-* + *physical*], of astrophysics.
as·tro·phys·ics (as'trō-fiz'iks), *n.pl.* [construed as sing.], [*astro-* + *physics*], the science of the physical properties and phenomena of the stars, planets, etc.
as·tro·sphere (as'trə-sfēr'), *n.* [*astro-* + *sphere*], in *biology*, 1. the central body of an aster; centrosphere. 2. all of an aster except the centrosome.
as·tu·cious (as-tōō'shəs, as-tū'shəs), *adj.* [Fr. *astucieux*], astute.
As·tu·ri·an (as-toor'i-ən), *adj.* of Asturias, its people, language, etc. *n.* 1. a native or inhabitant of Asturias. 2. the Spanish dialect of the Asturians.
As·tu·ri·as (as-toor'i-əs; Sp. ä-stōōr'yäs), *n.* an old province of northwestern Spain: see **Spain,** map.
as·tute (ə-stōōt', ə-stūt'), *adj.* [L. *astutus* < *astus*, craft, cunning], shrewd; keen; cunning; crafty; wily. —*SYN.* see **shrewd.**
As·ty·a·nax (ə-stī'ə-naks'), *n.* [L.; Gr. *Astyanax*], in *Greek legend*, the young son of Hector and Andromache: he was killed at Troy by the Greek conquerors.
a·sty·lar (ā-stī'lēr), *adj.* [< *a-*, not + Gr. *stylos*, pillar; + *-ar*], in *architecture*, having no columns or pilasters.
A·sun·ción (ä-sōōn-syôn'), *n.* the capital of Paraguay, on the Paraguay River: pop., 206,000.
a·sun·der (ə-sun'dēr), *adv.* [ME. *a sundir, on sunder;* AS. *on sundran; on*, on + *sunder;* see SUNDER], 1. into parts or pieces. 2. in different directions; apart. *adj.* separated; not close; apart.
A·sur (ä'soor), *n.* Ashur.
As·wan, As·wân (äs-wän'), *n.* a city in southern Egypt, below the first cataract of the Nile: pop., 25,000: a dam on the Nile near Aswan provides irrigation for the surrounding region: also spelled **Assuan, Assouan:** ancient name, *Syene.*
a·syl·lab·ic (ā'si-lab'ik), *adj.* not syllabic.
a·sy·lum (ə-sī'ləm), *n.* [*pl.* ASYLUMS (-ləmz), ASYLA (-lə)], [L.; Gr. *asylon*, asylum < *a-*, without + *sylē*, right of seizure], 1. formerly, a sanctuary, as a temple, where criminals, debtors, etc. were safe from arrest. 2. place of safety; refuge. 3. the protection given by a sanctuary or refuge. 4. an institution for the care of the mentally ill, or of the aged, the poor, etc. —*SYN.* see **shelter.**
a·sym·met·ric (ā'si-met'rik, as'i-met'rik), *adj.* asymmetrical: abbreviated **asym., asymm.**
a·sym·met·ri·cal (ā'si-met'ri-k'l, as'i-met'ri-k'l), *adj.* not symmetrical: abbreviated **asym., asymm.**
a·sym·me·try (ā-sim'i-tri, as-im'i-tri), *n.* [Gr. *asymmetria; a-*, not + *symmetria;* see SYMMETRY], lack of symmetry.
as·ymp·tote (as'im-tōt', as'imp-tōt'), *n.* [Gr. *asymptōtos; a-*, not + *symptōtos*, self-intersecting < *syn-*, together + *piptein*, to fall], in *mathematics*, a straight line always approaching but never meeting a curve; tangent at infinity.

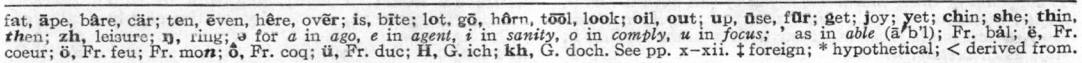

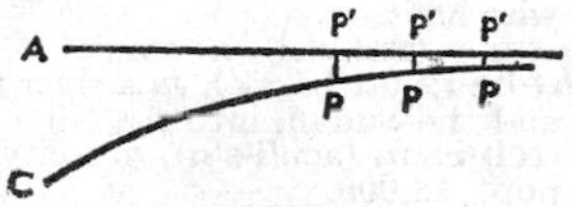

ASYMPTOTE

A, asymptote of curve C (PP' becomes smaller but does not disappear)

as·ymp·tot·ic (as'im-tot'ik, as'imp-tot'ik), *adj.* of, or of the nature of, an asymptote.
as·ymp·tot·i·cal (as'im-tot'i-k'l, as'imp-tot'i-k'l), *adj.* asymptotic.
a·syn·chro·nism (ā-siŋ'krə-niz'm, as-iŋ'krə-niz'm), *n.* [*a-*, not + *synchronism*], lack of synchronism; failure to occur at the same time.
a·syn·chro·nous (ā-siŋ'krə-nəs, as-iŋ'krə-nəs), *adj.* [*a-*, not + *synchronous*], not synchronous.
as·yn·det·ic (as'in-det'ik), *adj.* using asyndeton.
a·syn·de·ton (ə-sin'də-ton'), *n.* [Gr. *asyndeton* < *a-*, not + *syndetos*, united with < *syndein*, to bind together], in *rhetoric*, the practice of leaving out the conjunctions between co-ordinate sentence elements. Example: Smile, shake hands, part.
a·syn·tac·tic (ā'sin-tak'tik), *adj.* [*a-*, not + *syntactic*], not syntactical.
As·yut, As·yût (ä-sūt'), *n.* a city in central Egypt: pop., 121,000: also spelled **Assiut.**
at (at; *unstressed*, ət), *prep.* [ME.; AS. *æt;* akin to Goth., OS., ON. *at* & L. *ad*, at, in, to], 1. on; in; near; by: as, *at* the office, *at* heart. 2. to or toward: as, gaze *at*, throw *at*. 3. through: as, come in *at* the front door. 4. from: as, get the facts *at* their source. 5. attending: as, *at* the party. 6. occupied in; busy with: as, *at* work. 7. in a condition or state of: as, *at* war. 8. in the manner of: as, *at* a trot. 9. because of: as, terrified *at* the sight.

10. according to: as, *at* his discretion. 11. in the amount, degree, number, price, etc. of: as, *at* twenty miles per hour, *at* five cents each. 12. on or close to the age or time of: as, *at* five o'clock, *at* once, *at* sixty-five. Basically, *at* is the preposition of general (usually static) location, answering the question "Where?" It is replaced by *in, on, over, under, near, by* when more precise indications of locality are needed. The meanings of all these are latent in *at* but not emphasized by it.

at-, ad-: used before *t*, as in *attend*.

At, in *chemistry*, astatine.

at., 1. atmosphere. 2. atomic. 3. attorney.

at·a·bal (at'ə-bal'), *n.* [Sp.; Ar. colloq. *aṭ-ṭabl* < *al*, the + *ṭabl*, drum], a kind of kettledrum or tabor used by the Moors: also spelled **attabal**.

A·ta·ba·li·pa (ä'tä-bä'li-pä'), *n.* Atahualpa.

at·a·brin (at'ə-brin), *n.* atabrine.

at·a·brine (at'ə-brin, at'ə-brēn'), *n.* [G. *atebrin; ? < antifebrin;* see ANTI-, FEBRILE, -INE], quinacrine hydrochloride, a synthetic drug used in treating malaria: a trade-mark (**Atabrine**): also **atebrin**.

A·ta·ca·ma Desert (ä'tä-kä'mä), a desert area in northern Chile, containing valuable nitrate deposits.

at·a·ghan (at'ə-gan'), *n.* a Moslem sword: see **yataghan**.

A·ta·hual·pa (ä'tä-wäl'pä), *n.* last Inca king of Peru (1525–1533); lived 1500?–1533: also **Atabalipa**.

At·a·lan·ta (at''l-an'tə), *n.* [L. *Atalanta;* Gr. *Atalantē*], in *Greek legend*, a beautiful, swift-footed maiden who offered to marry any man able to defeat her in a race, death being the penalty for failure: Hippomenes won from her by dropping three golden apples, which she stopped to pick up, along the way.

at·a·man (at'ə-man'), *n.* [Russ. *atamanu* < Pol. *hetman;* see HETMAN], a Cossack chief.

at·a·mas·co lily (at'ə-mas'kō), [Am. Ind. *attamusco*, lit., stained with red], 1. a bulb plant with hollow stems, grassy leaves, and purple-tinged, white, funnel-shaped flowers. 2. any of a number of related plants with pink or yellow flowers.

at·a·rax·i·a (at'ə-rak'si-ə), [Gr. *ataraxia* < *a-*, not + *tarassein*, to disturb], calmness of the mind and emotions; tranquillity.

at·a·rax·ic (at'ə-rak'sik), *n.* [< *ataraxia* + *-ic*], a tranquilizing drug: see **tranquilizer**.

at·a·rax·y (at'ə-rak'si), *n.* ataraxia.

A·ta·turk (ä'tä-tũrk'), *n.* see **Kemal Ataturk, Mustafa**.

a·tav·ic (ə-tav'ik), *adj.* [Fr. *atavique* < L. *atavus;* see ATAVISM], of a remote ancestor.

at·a·vism (at'ə-viz'm), *n.* [Fr. *atavisme* < L. *atavus*, father of a great-grandfather, ancestor < *at-*, beyond + *avus*, grandfather], 1. resemblance to a remote ancestor in some characteristic which nearer ancestors do not have. 2. reversion to a primitive type.

at·a·vist (at'ə-vist), *n.* a person or thing characterized by atavism.

at·a·vis·tic (at'ə-vis'tik), *adj.* 1. of or due to atavism. 2. tending to atavism.

a·tax·i·a (ə-tak'si-ə), *n.* [Gr. *ataxia*, disorder < *ataktos; a-*, not + *taktos* < *tassein*, to arrange], 1. total or partial inability to co-ordinate voluntary bodily movements, especially muscular movements. 2. locomotor ataxia.

a·tax·ic (ə-tak'sik), *adj.* of or due to ataxia. *n.* a person who has ataxia.

a·tax·y (ə-tak'si), *n.* ataxia.

At·ba·ra (ät'bä-rä'), *n.* a river flowing through Ethiopia and the Sudan, into the Nile: length, c. 500 mi.

Atch·i·son (ach'i-s'n), *n.* a city in northeastern Kansas: pop., 13,000.

A·te (ā'ti, ā'tē), *n.* [Gr. *atē*], 1. [a-], in ancient Greek culture, criminal folly or reckless ambition of man beyond his proper sphere, punished by nemesis (retributive justice). 2. the goddess personifying such impulses: later she was considered the avenger of sin.

ate (āt; Brit. et), past tense of **eat**.

-ate, [< L. *-atus*, pp. ending of verbs of 1st conjugation], a suffix used: 1. (āt), to form verbs, originally from stems containing the Latin pp. ending *-atus*, but now from various other stems, and meaning: *a) to become*, as in *evaporate, maturate. b) to cause to become*, as in *invalidate, sublimate. c) to form* or *produce*, as in *ulcerate, salivate. d) to provide* or *treat with*, as in *vaccinate, refrigerate. e) to put in the form of* or *form by means of*, as in *delineate, triangulate. f) to arrange for*, as in *orchestrate. g) to combine, infuse*, or *treat with*, as in *chlorinate, oxygenate.* 2. (it, āt), to form adjectives from nouns, and meaning: *a) of* or *characteristic of*, as in *collegiate, roseate. b) having* or *filled with*, as in *proportionate, passionate. c)* in *botany & zoology, having* or *characterized by*, as in *spatulate, caudate.* 3. (it, āt), to form adjectives from verbs and roughly equivalent to the *-ed* of the English past participle, as *animate (animated), determinate (determined)*.

-ate (āt, it), [L. *-atus*, a noun ending], a noun suffix denoting: 1. *an office, function, official, group of officials*, or *agent*, as in *episcopate, potentate, directorate.* 2. *a person* or *thing that is the object of* (an action), as in *legate, mandate.* 3. [L. *-atum*, neut. of *-atus*], in *chemistry, a salt made from* (an acid with a name ending in *-ic*), as in *acetate, nitrate.*

at·e·brin (at'ə-brin), *n.* in *pharmacy*, atabrine.

at·el·ier (at''l-yā'; Fr. å'tə-lyā'), *n.* [Fr.], a studio or workshop.

‡a tem·po (ä tem'pō), [It.], in *music*, in time: a direction to the performer to return to the rate of speed immediately preceding the movement: abbreviated **a tem.**

Ath·a·bas·can (ath'ə-bas'kən), *adj. & n.* Athapascan.

Ath·a·bas·ka (ath'ə-bas'kə), *n.* 1. a river in Alberta, Canada, flowing northeastward into Lake Athabaska: length, 765 mi. 2. a lake in northern Alberta and Saskatchewan, Canada: area, 3,085 sq. mi.

ath·a·na·si·a (ath'ə-nā'zhi-ə, ath'ə-nā'zhə), *n.* [Gr. < *a-*, not + *thanatos*, death], immortality.

Ath·a·na·sian (ath'ə-nā'zhən), *adj.* of Athanasius. *n.* a follower of Athanasius and his doctrines.

Athanasian Creed, a statement of Christian faith of unknown authorship, formerly attributed to Athanasius: it maintains belief in the Trinity as opposed to Arianism.

Ath·a·na·sius, Saint (ath'ə-nā'shəs, ath'ə-nā'shi-əs), 293?–373 A.D.; Greek church father, patriarch of Alexandria, and opponent of Arianism: his day is May 2.

a·than·a·sy (ə-than'ə-si), *n.* athanasia.

Ath·a·pas·can (ath'ə-pas'kən), *adj.* designating or of the most widely scattered linguistic family of North American Indians, ranging from Alaska to northern Mexico and including the Navajo and Apache tribes. *n.* 1. an Indian of this family. 2. a language of this family, as the Hupa of California: also **Athabascan**.

a·the·ism (ā'thē-iz'm), *n.* [Fr. *athéisme* < Gr. *atheos; a-*, without + *theos*, god], the belief that there is no God.

a·the·ist (ā'thē-ist), *n.* [Fr. *athéiste;* see ATHEISM], a person who believes that there is no God.

SYN.—an **atheist** rejects all religious belief and denies the existence of God; an **agnostic** questions the existence of God, heaven, etc. in the absence of material proof and in unwillingness to accept supernatural revelation; **deist**, a historical term, was applied to 18th-century rationalists who believed in God as a creative, moving force but who otherwise rejected formal religion and its doctrines of revelation, divine authority, etc.; **freethinker**, the current parallel term, similarly implies rejection of the tenets and traditions of formal religion as incompatible with reason; **unbeliever** is a more negative term, simply designating, without further qualification, one who does not accept any religious belief; **infidel** is applied to a person not believing in a certain religion or the prevailing religion. —***ANT.*** theist.

a·the·is·tic (ā'thē-is'tik), *adj.* 1. of atheism or atheists. 2. inclined to atheism; impious.

a·the·is·ti·cal (ā'thē-is'ti-k'l), *adj.* atheistic.

a·the·is·ti·cal·ly (ā'thē-is'ti-k'l-i), *adv.* 1. in an atheistic manner. 2. from an atheistic point of view.

ath·el·ing (ath'əl-iŋ), *n.* [AS. *ætheling* < *æthele*, noble], a nobleman or prince of the Anglo-Saxons.

Ath·el·stan (ath'əl-stan', *ath'*əl-stən), [AS. *Æthelstan*, lit., noble stone], a masculine name. *n.* king of England (924–940 A.D.); lived 895–940 A.D.

A·the·na (ə-thē'nə), *n.* [Gr. *Athēnē*], in *Greek mythology*, the goddess of wisdom, skills, and warfare: identified by the Romans with Minerva.

ath·e·nae·um, ath·e·ne·um (ath'ə-nē'əm), *n.* [< L. *Athenaeum;* Gr. *Athēnaion*], 1. [A-], the temple of Athena at Athens, where writers and scholars met. 2. a Roman school of law, literature, etc. founded by Hadrian. 3. a literary or scientific club. 4. any building or hall used as a library or reading room.

A·the·nai (ä-thē'ne), *n.* Athens: the Greek spelling.

A·the·ne (ə-thē'nē), *n.* Athena.

A·the·ni·an (ə-thē'ni-ən), *adj.* of Athens, its people, or culture. *n.* 1. a native or inhabitant of Athens. 2. a citizen of ancient Athens.

Ath·ens (ath'inz), *n.* 1. a city in Greece, in ancient times the center of Greek culture and now the capital of the country: pop., 565,000: Greek spelling, *Athenai.* 2. a city in northern Georgia: pop., 31,000. 3. any city likened to ancient Athens as a cultural center.

a·ther·man·cy (ā-thũr'mən-si), *n.* the quality of being athermanous.

a·ther·ma·nous (ā-thũr'mə-nəs), *adj.* [Gr. *a-*, not + *therman-* < *thermē*, heat; + *-ous*], impervious to heat rays: opposed to *diathermanous*.

ath·er·o·scle·ro·sis (ath'ẽr-ō-skli-rō'sis), *n.* [< Gr. *athērōma*, a tumor filled with grainy matter < *atherē*, grain; + *sclerosis*], arteriosclerosis in which the inmost wall of the artery undergoes fatty degeneration.

a·thirst (ə-thũrst'), *adj.* [ME. *ofthurst;* AS. *ofthyrsted*, pp. of *ofthyrstan; of-*, intens. + *thyrstan*, to thirst], 1. [Archaic & Poetic], thirsty. 2. eager (*for* a thing).

ath·lete (ath'lēt), *n.* [L. *athleta;* Gr. *athlētēs*, contestant in the games < *athlein*, to contest for a prize < *athlos*, a contest < *athlon*, a prize], a person trained in exercises, games, or contests requiring physical strength, skill, stamina, speed, etc.

athlete's foot, ringworm of the feet, a contagious skin disease caused by a tiny fungus often found in gymnasiums, shower rooms, etc.

athlete's heart, a heart condition in which there is some enlargement, caused by continued physical exertion and strain.

ath·let·ic (ath-let'ik), *adj.* [L. *athleticus;* Gr. *athletikos*],

1. of, like, or proper to athletes or athletics. 2. physically strong, skillful, active, etc.
ath·let·i·cal·ly (ath-let'i-k'l-i, ath-let'ik-li), *adv.* in an athletic manner.
ath·let·i·cism (ath-let'ə-siz'm), *n.* 1. addiction to athletics. 2. an athletic quality.
ath·let·ics (ath-let'iks), *n.pl.* [sometimes construed as sing.], athletic sports, games, exercises, etc.
ath·o·dyd (ath'ō-did), *n.* [contr. < *aero-thermo-dynamic duct*], a ramjet, a type of jet engine.
at-home (at-hōm'), *n.* an informal reception at one's home, usually in the afternoon.
Ath·os, Mount (ath'os, ā'thos), a mountain in northeastern Greece: height, 6,346 ft.
a·thwart (ə-thwôrt'), *prep.* [*a-*, on + *thwart*], 1. across; from one side to the other of. 2. against; in opposition to. 3. in *nautical usage,* across the course or length of. *adv.* 1. obliquely; crosswise. 2. so as to block or thwart.
-at·ic (at'ik), [< Fr. or L.; Fr. *-atique;* L. *-aticus;* Gr. *-atikos* < base ending *-at* + suffix *-ikos,* -ic], a suffix meaning *of, of the kind of:* used in adjectives of Greek and Latin origin, as *lymphatic, chromatic.*
a·tilt (ə-tilt'), *adj. & adv.* [*a-*, on + *tilt*], 1. tilted; in an inclined position. 2. tilting, as with a spear.
a·tin·gle (ə-tiŋ'g'l), *adj.* [*a-*, on + *tingle*], tingling; excited.
-a·tion (ā'shən), [< Fr. or L.; Fr. *-ation;* L. *-ation(em),* suffix formed from pp. type *-at-* of *-are* verbs of 1st conjugation], a suffix used to form nouns from: 1. verbs in *-ate,* as in *translation.* 2. verbs in *-ize,* as in *realization.* 3. verbs of French origin without suffix, as in *causation.* 4. Latin words without a corresponding English verb, as in *constellation.* 5. other (Anglo-Saxon, etc.) verbs, as in *starvation.* It means: 1. *a —ing* or *being —ed,* as in *activation.* 2. *the result of being —ed* or *a thing that is —ed,* as in *compilation.*
-a·tive (ā'tiv, ə-tiv), [< Fr. or L.; Fr. *-atif,* fem. *-ative;* L. *-ativus*], a suffix meaning *of the nature of, relating to:* used in forming adjectives generally from *-ate* verbs, as *demonstrative, correlative.*
Atkins, Tommy, see **Tommy Atkins.**
Atl., Atlantic.
At·lan·ta (at-lan'tə), *n.* the capital of Georgia: **pop.,** 487,000.
At·lan·te·an (at'lan-tē'ən), *adj.* [L. *Atlanteus,* of Atlas, of the Atlantic < *Atlas,* Atlas, Mount Atlas], 1. of or like Atlas. 2. of Atlantis.
at·lan·tes (at-lan'tēz), *n.pl.* [*sing.* ATLAS (at'ləs)], [L.; Gr. *Atlantes,* pl. of *Atlas*], in *architecture,* standing or kneeling figures or half figures of men, used in place of columns to support an entablature.
At·lan·tic (at-lan'tik), *n.* [L. *Atlanticum (mare),* Atlantic (ocean) < *Atlanticus,* of Mount Atlas < *Atlas;* see ATLAS], the ocean touching the American continents to the west and Europe and Africa to the east: area, 31,830,000 sq. mi.; average depth, 12,880 ft. *adj.* designating, of, in, on, or near this ocean. Abbreviated **Atl.**
Atlantic Charter, a declaration of peace aims in World War II, made by Roosevelt and Churchill at a meeting on the Atlantic, August, 1941.
Atlantic City, an ocean resort in southern New Jersey: pop., 60,000.
Atlantic plain, one of the chief physiographic divisions of the United States, including all the plains on the eastern seacoast.
At·lan·tis (at-lan'tis), *n.* [L.; Gr.], a legendary island or continent supposed to have existed in the Atlantic west of Gibraltar and to have sunk into the ocean.
At·las (at'ləs), *n.* [*pl.,* except in sense 7, ATLASES (-iz)], [L.; Gr. < IE. base meaning "to bear"], 1. in *Greek legend, a)* a giant compelled to support the heavens on his shoulders. *b)* in Homer, a god in charge of the pillars of heaven. *c)* a king changed into a mountain; hence, 2. any person who carries a great burden. 3. [a-], a book of maps: Atlas supporting the earth was often pictured on the front page of such books. 4. [a-], a book of tables, charts, illustrations, etc. of a specific subject or subjects: as, an anatomical *atlas.* 5. [a-], a large size of drawing paper. 6. [a-], [< sense 1, *a*], in *anatomy,* the top vertebra of the neck. 7. [a-], [*pl.* ATLANTES (at-lan'tēz)], in *architecture,* any of the atlantes.
atlas grid, a system of parallel and perpendicular lines on an aerial photograph, dividing it into small squares for locating points on the photograph quickly.
Atlas Mountains, a mountain system along the northwestern coast of Africa, chiefly in Morocco and Algeria: highest peak, Tizi-n-Tamjurt, 13,665 ft.
At·li (ät'li), *n.* [ON. < Goth. *Attila;* see ATTILA], in *Norse mythology,* a king of the Huns, killed by his wife, Gudrun, because he had killed her brothers for the treasure of Sigurd.
atm., 1. atmosphere; atmospheres. 2. atmospheric.
at·man (ät'mən), *n.* [Sans., breath, soul, Supreme Spirit], in *Hinduism,* 1. the individual soul or ego. 2. [A-], the universal soul; source of all individual souls.
at·mos·phere (at'məs-fêr'), *n.* [Mod. L. *atmosphaera* < Gr. *atmos,* vapor + *sphaira,* sphere], 1. all the air surrounding the earth. 2. the gaseous mass surrounding any star, planet, etc. 3. the air in any given place. 4. a pervading or surrounding mental or social influence; social environment. 5. the general tone of a work of art: as, a play with a fateful *atmosphere.* 6. [Colloq.], the general effect, often exotic, produced by decoration, furnishings, etc.: as, a restaurant with *atmosphere.* 7. in *physics,* a unit of pressure equal to 14.69 pounds per square inch: abbreviated **at., atm.**
at·mos·pher·ic (at'məs-fer'ik), *adj.* 1. of or in the atmosphere: as, *atmospheric* disturbances. 2. caused, produced, or operated by the atmosphere. 3. of, having, or giving atmosphere or an atmosphere: as, *atmospheric* lighting. Abbreviated **atm.**
at·mos·pher·i·cal (at'məs-fer'i-k'l), *adj.* atmospheric.
at·mos·pher·i·cal·ly (at'məs-fer'i-k'l-i, at'məs-fer'ik-li), *adv.* 1. with regard to atmosphere. 2. by atmospheric pressure or influence.
atmospheric pressure, the pressure due to the weight of the earth's atmosphere, equal at sea level to about 14.69 pounds per square inch: abbreviated **atm. press.**
at·mos·pher·ics (at'məs-fer'iks), *n.pl.* in *radio,* 1. disturbances in reception, produced by natural electric discharges, as in a storm; static. 2. the phenomena producing these disturbances.
at. no., atomic number.
at·oll (at'ôl, at'ol, ə-tol'), *n.* [< Maldive Is. term; ? < Malayalam *aḍal,* uniting], a ring-shaped coral island almost or completely surrounding a lagoon.

ATOLL

at·om (at'əm), *n.* [Fr. *atome;* L. *atomus;* Gr. *atomos,* uncut, indivisible, atom < *a-*, not + *tomos* < *temnein,* to cut], 1. a tiny particle; extremely small bit of anything; jot. 2. in *chemistry* & *physics,* any of the smallest particles of an element that combine with similar particles of other elements to produce compounds: atoms combine to form molecules, and consist of a complex arrangement of electrons revolving about a positively charged nucleus containing protons and neutrons; the fission of a nucleus by bombardment either with neutrons (as in atomic bombs), or with certain other very small particles, releases energy.

ATOM OF HELIUM

at·om·bomb (at'əm-bom'), *n.* an atomic bomb: also **atom bomb.** *v.t.* to attack or destroy with such bombs.
a·tom·ic (ə-tom'ik), *adj.* 1. of an atom or atoms, atomic bombs, the energy in the atom, etc.: abbreviated **at.** 2. separated into atoms. 3. very small; minute.
Atomic Age, the period characterized by the use of atomic energy: regarded as beginning with the creation of the first self-maintaining nuclear chain reaction on December 2, 1942.
a·tom·i·cal·ly (ə-tom'i-k'l-i, ə-tom'ik-li), *adv.* in an atomic way; specifically, *a)* into atoms or very small particles. *b)* by atomic energy.
atomic bomb, an extremely destructive type of bomb, the power of which results from the immense quantity of energy suddenly released when a chain reaction of nuclear fission is set off by neutron bombardment in the atoms of a charge of plutonium or of the uranium isotope with an atomic weight of 235 (U 235): first used in warfare (1945) by the United States against the Japanese cities of Hiroshima and Nagasaki.
atomic cocktail, [Slang], a dose of medicine to be swallowed, containing a radioactive element, used in medical treatment and diagnosis, as of cancer.
atomic energy, the energy released from an atom in nuclear reactions; especially, the energy released in nuclear fission or nuclear fusion.
Atomic Energy Commission, a United States board formed in 1946, for the domestic control of atomic energy.
at·o·mic·i·ty (at'ə-mis'ə-ti), *n.* 1. the condition of being made up of atoms. 2. in *chemistry, a)* the number of atoms in a molecule. *b)* the number of replaceable atoms or groups of atoms in the molecule of a compound. *c)* valence.
atomic number, in *chemistry,* a number representing

the relative position of an element in the periodic table, in which the elements are arranged according to their nuclear charges; number representing the positive charge or number of protons in the nucleus of the atom of an element: abbreviated **at. no.**: isotopes have the same atomic numbers but different atomic weights.

atomic structure, in *physics,* a conventionalized, hypothetical concept of an atom, regarded as consisting of a central, positively charged nucleus and a number of negatively charged electrons revolving about it in various orbits: the number and arrangement of the electrons vary in the different elements.

atomic theory, the theory that all material objects and substances are composed of atoms: see **atom.**

atomic volume, in *chemistry,* the quotient obtained by dividing the atomic weight of an element by its specific gravity: abbreviated **at. vol.**

atomic weight, in *chemistry,* a number representing the weight of one atom of an element as compared with an arbitrarily selected number representing the weight of one atom of another element taken as the standard (usually oxygen at 16): abbreviated **at. wt.**

at·om·ism (at′əm-iz′m), *n.* [*atom* + *-ism*], the theory that the universe is made up of tiny, simple particles that cannot be destroyed or divided.

at·om·ist (at′əm-ist), *n.* a person who believes in atomism. *adj.* of atomism or atomists.

at·om·is·tic (at′əm-is′tik), *adj.* atomist.

at·om·ize (at′əm-īz′), *v.t.* [ATOMIZED (-īzd′), ATOMIZING], 1. to separate into atoms. 2. to reduce (a liquid) to a fine spray. 3. to disintegrate; break into parts.

at·om·iz·er (at′əm-īz′ẽr), *n.* a device for breaking a liquid, especially a medicine or perfume, into very small particles and spraying these out.

ATOMIZER

at·o·my (at′ə-mi), *n.* [*pl.* ATOMIES (-miz)], [by mistaken division of *anatomy* as *an atomy;* prob. due to association with *atom*], [Archaic], a skeleton.

at·o·my (at′ə-mi), *n.* [*pl.* ATOMIES (-miz)], [< L. *atomi,* pl. of *atomus,* atom], 1. an atom; tiny thing. 2. a tiny being; pygmy.

a·ton·al (ā-tōn′'l), *adj.* having atonality; lacking tone.

a·ton·al·ism (ā-tōn′'l-iz'm), *n.* the use or theory of atonality in composing music.

a·to·nal·i·ty (ā′tō-nal′ə-ti), *n.* [*a-,* not + *tonality*], in *music,* lack of tonality through intentional disregard of key.

a·tone (ə-tōn′), *v.i.* [ATONED (-tōnd′), ATONING], [< *atonement*], 1. to make amends or reparation (*for* wrongdoing, a wrongdoer, etc.). 2. [Obs.], to be in agreement. *v.t.* [Obs.], 1. to expiate. 2. to harmonize.

a·tone·ment (ə-tōn′mənt), *n.* [*at* + obs. *onement,* physical union, conjunction < *one* + *-ment*], 1. an atoning. 2. satisfaction given for wrongdoing, injury, etc.; amends; expiation. 3. [A-], in *theology, a*) the effect of Jesus' sufferings and death in redeeming mankind and bringing about the reconciliation of God to man. *b*) this reconciliation.

a·ton·ic (ə-ton′ik, ā-ton′ik), *adj.* [Gr. *atonos;* see ATONY], 1. caused by or characteristic of atony. 2. unaccented: said of a word or syllable. 3. [Rare], in *phonetics,* lenis. *n.* 1. an unaccented syllable or word. 2. [Rare], in *phonetics,* a lenis consonant.

at·o·ny (at′ə-ni), *n.* [Fr. *atonie;* L. *atonia;* Gr. *atonia,* languor < *a-,* not + *tonos,* tone < *teinein,* to stretch], 1. lack of bodily tone; weakness of the body or of a muscle or an organ. 2. in *phonetics,* lack of stress.

a·top (ə-top′), *adj. & adv.* [*a-,* on + *top*], on the top; at the top. *prep.* on the top of.

-a·to·ry (ə-tôr′i, ə-tō′ri), [L. *-atorius; -ator* + *-ius,* -y], an adjective-forming suffix meaning *of, characterized by, produced by,* as in *accusatory, exclamatory.*

at·ra·bil·i·ar (at′rə-bil′yẽr), *adj.* atrabilious.

at·ra·bil·i·ous (at′rə-bil′yəs), *adj.* [< L. *atra bilis,* black bile; after *bilious*], 1. having "black bile"; melancholy; morose. 2. hypochondriac.

a·trem·ble (ə-trem′b'l), *adj.* trembling.

A·treus (ā′trōōs, ā′tri-əs), *n.* [L.; Gr. *Atreus*], in *Greek legend,* a king of Mycenae, son of Pelops and father of Agamemnon and Menelaus: to avenge the treachery of his brother, Thyestes, who seduced his wife and planned his murder, Atreus killed Thyestes' sons and served their flesh to him at a banquet.

a·trip (ə-trip′), *adj.* [*a-,* on + *trip*], in *nautical usage,* raised just off the bottom: said of an anchor.

a·tri·um (ā′tri-əm), *n.* [*pl.* ATRIA (-ə), ATRIUMS (-əmz)], [L.], 1. the central court or main room of an ancient Roman house. 2. a hall or entrance court. 3. in *anatomy, a*) a chamber or cavity, especially an auricle of the heart. *b*) a passage: as, diseases can enter the body through an *atrium* of infection.

a·tro·cious (ə-trō′shəs), *adj.* [< L. *atrox, atrocis,* fierce, cruel < *ater,* black; + *-ious*], 1. very cruel, evil, brutal, etc. 2. [Colloq.], very bad; in bad taste; abominable: as, an *atrocious* dress. —*SYN.* see **outrageous.**

a·troc·i·ty (ə-tros′ə-ti), *n.* [*pl.* ATROCITIES (-tiz)], [Fr. *atrocité;* L. *atrocitas* < *atrox;* see ATROCIOUS], 1. atrocious behavior or condition; brutality, etc. 2. an atrocious act. 3. [Colloq.], a thing in very bad taste; very displeasing thing: as, that picture's an *atrocity.*

a·troph·ic (ə-trof′ik), *adj.* of or caused by atrophy.

at·ro·phy (at′rə-fi), *n.* [Fr. *atrophie;* L. *atrophia;* Gr. *atrophia,* a wasting away < *a-,* not + *trephein,* to nourish], a wasting away, especially of body tissue, an organ, etc., or the failure of an organ or part to grow because of insufficient nutrition. *v.i.* [ATROPHIED (-fid), ATROPHYING], to waste away; fail to grow. *v.t.* to cause atrophy in.

at·ro·pin (at′rə-pin), *n.* atropine.

at·ro·pine (at′rə-pēn′, at′rə-pin), *n.* [< Mod. L. *Atropa,* deadly nightshade < Gr. *Atropos* (see ATROPOS); + *-ine*], a poisonous, crystalline alkaloid obtained from belladonna and similar plants, used to relieve spasms and dilate the pupil of the eye.

at·ro·pism (at′rə-piz'm), *n.* [*atropine* + *-ism*], poisoning resulting from the improper use of atropine.

At·ro·pos (at′rə-pos′), *n.* [L.; Gr. *Atropos,* lit., not to be turned < *a-,* not + *trepein,* to turn], in *Greek mythology,* that one of the three Fates who is represented as cutting the thread of life.

A.T.S., 1. American Temperance Society. 2. American Tract Society. 3. Army Transport Service.

att., attorney.

at·ta·bal (at′ə-bal′), *n.* an atabal.

at·tach (ə-tach′), *v.t.* [ME. *atachen;* OFr. *atachier* < *a-,* to + *tach,* a nail], 1. to fasten by sticking, tying, etc. 2. to make (a person or thing) part of; join (often used reflexively): as, he *attached* himself to us. 3. to connect by ties of affection, attraction, etc. 4. to add (*to*) or affix, as a signature. 5. to ascribe (with *to*): as, I *attach* great significance to the news. 6. to appoint by authority or order. 7. in *law, a*) to take (property, salary, etc.) by writ. *b*) to arrest (a person). 8. in *military usage,* to join (troops, a unit, etc.) temporarily to some other unit. *v.i.* to be fastened or joined; adhere; belong: as, a moral obligation *attaches* to high rank. —*SYN.* see **ascribe, tie.**

at·ta·ché (at′ə-shā′, ə-tash′ā; Fr. à′tà′shā′), *n.* [Fr., pp. of *attacher;* see ATTACH], a member of the diplomatic staff of an ambassador or minister to another country.

attaché case, a slim, flat case, usually of leather, for carrying documents, papers, etc.

at·tach·ment (ə-tach′mənt), *n.* [Fr. *attachement* < *attacher;* see ATTACH], 1. an attaching or being attached. 2. anything that attaches a thing or person to another; hence, 3. affectionate regard; devotion. 4. anything added or attached. 5. an accessory for an electrical appliance, machine, etc. 6. in *law, a*) a taking of a person, property, etc. into custody. *b*) a writ authorizing this. —*SYN.* see **love.**

at·tack (ə-tak′), *v.t.* [Fr. *attaquer;* It. *attaccare;* prob. < same source as *attach*], 1. to use force against in order to harm; start a fight or quarrel with; take the offensive against; assault. 2. to begin a fight against with words; speak or write against. 3. to begin working on energetically; undertake vigorously, as a problem, task, etc. 4. to begin acting upon harmfully: as, the disease *attacked* him suddenly. *v.i.* to make an assault. *n.* 1. an attacking. 2. any hostile offensive action, especially with armed forces; onslaught. 3. an onset or occurrence of a disease. 4. a beginning of any task, undertaking, etc. 5. act or manner of such beginning.

SYN.—**attack** implies vigorous, aggressive action, whether in actual combat or in an undertaking (to *attack* a city, a problem, etc.); **assail** means to attack by repeated blows, thrusts, etc. (*assailed* by reproaches); **assault** implies a sudden, violent attack or onslaught and suggests direct contact and the use of force; **beset** implies an attack or onset from all sides (*beset* with fears); **storm** suggests a rushing, powerful assault that is stormlike in its action and effect; **bombard** means to attack with artillery or bombs, and in figurative use suggests persistent, repetitious action (to *bombard* a speaker with questions). —*ANT.* defend, resist.

at·tain (ə-tān′), *v.t.* [ME. *attainen, atteinen;* OFr. *ataindre, ateindre;* L. *attingere* < *ad-,* to + *tangere,* to touch], 1. to gain through effort; accomplish; achieve. 2. to reach or come to; arrive at: as, he *attained* the age of ninety. —*SYN.* see **reach.**

attain to, to be successful in gaining or reaching.

at·tain·a·bil·i·ty (ə-tān′ə-bil′ə-ti), *n.* the quality of being attainable.

at·tain·a·ble (ə-tān′ə-b'l), *adj.* that can be attained.

at·tain·der (ə-tān′dẽr), *n.* [OFr. *ataindre, ateindre,* to accuse, convict; see ATTAIN], loss of civil rights, inheritance, property, etc. of a person sentenced to death or outlawed.

at·tain·ment (ə-tān′mənt), *n.* 1. an attaining or being attained. 2. anything attained, as an acquired skill.

at·taint (ə-tānt′), *v.t.* [ATTAINTED (-id), ATTAINTING; *archaic* pp. ATTAINT], [ME. *ataynten, atteinten,* to convict < OFr. *ateint,* pp. of *ateindre;* see ATTAIN], 1. to convict of crime punishable by attainder; condemn to attainder. 2. to taint or stain; disgrace; dishonor. 3. [Rare], to infect. 4. [Archaic], to accuse. 5. [Obs.], to prove guilty. *n.* 1. an attainder. 2. a taint; disgrace. 3. [Archaic], a touch or hit in tilting.

at·tain·ture (ə-tān′chẽr), *n.* 1. attainder. 2. dishonor; disgrace.

at·tar (at′ẽr), *n.* [Per. *'atar*, fragrance; Ar. *'iṭr*, perfume], an oil or perfume made from the petals of flowers, especially of roses.

attar of roses, a fragrant oil made from the petals of roses, especially damask roses.

at·tem·per (ə-tem′pẽr), *v.t.* [ME. *attempren;* OFr. *atemprer;* L. *attemperare*, to fit, adjust < *ad-*, to + *temperare*, to control, moderate], 1. to modify or reduce by mixture. 2. to control the temperature of. 3. to moderate (anger, etc.); soothe. 4. to adapt; make suitable (*to*). 5. [Rare], to temper (metals).

at·tempt (ə-tempt′), *v.t.* [OFr. *atempter, attenter;* It. *attentare;* L. *attemptare, attentare*, to try, solicit < *ad-*, to + *temptare, tentare*, to try, attack], 1. to try to do, try to get, etc.; try; endeavor. 2. [Archaic], to tempt. *n.* 1. a try; an endeavor. 2. an attack, as on a person's life. —*SYN.* see **try.**

attempt the life of, to try to kill.

at·tend (ə-tend′), *v.t.* [ME. *attenden;* OFr. *atendre*, to wait, expect; L. *attendere*, to stretch toward, give heed to < *ad-*, to + *tendere*, to stretch], 1. to take care or charge of; wait upon. 2. to accompany; go with. 3. to accompany as a circumstance or result: as, success *attended* his efforts. 4. to be present at: as, he *attends* the movies daily. 5. [Archaic], to await. 6. [Archaic], to listen to; pay attention to. *v.i.* 1. to pay attention; give heed. 2. to be in readiness; wait (with *on* or *upon*). 3. [Obs.], to wait or delay. —*SYN.* see **accompany.**

attend to, 1. to devote or apply oneself to. 2. to take care of; look after.

at·tend·ance (ə-ten′dəns), *n.* [ME.; OFr. *atendance* < *atendre;* see ATTEND], 1. an attending. 2. the persons or number of persons attending a meeting, game, etc.

at·tend·ant (ə-ten′dənt), *adj.* [Fr., ppr. of *attendre;* see ATTEND], 1. attending or serving: as, an *attendant* nurse. 2. being present. 3. accompanying: as, *attendant* difficulties. *n.* 1. a person who attends or serves. 2. a person present. 3. an accompanying thing; concomitant.

at·tent (ə-tent′), *adj.* [L. *attentus*, pp. of *attendere;* see ATTEND], [Archaic], attentive.

at·ten·tion (ə-ten′shən), *n.* [L. *attentio* < pp. of *attendere;* see ATTEND], 1. an attending; giving heed; observing carefully. 2. the ability to give heed or observe carefully. 3. careful observation; heed; notice. 4. thoughtful consideration for others. 5. *usually in pl.* act of consideration, courtesy, or devotion: as, a suitor's *attentions* to a woman. 6. in *military science, a*) the erect, motionless posture of soldiers in readiness for another command. *b*) a command to assume this posture. 7. in *psychology*, a readiness to respond to stimuli.

come to attention, in *military science*, to assume an erect, motionless posture.

stand at attention, in *military science*, to stand erect and motionless.

at·ten·tive (ə-ten′tiv), *adj.* [Fr. *attentif* < *attendre;* see ATTEND], 1. paying attention; observant. 2. considerate, courteous, devoted, etc.: as, an *attentive* husband. —*SYN.* see **thoughtful.**

at·ten·u·a·ble (ə-ten′ū-ə-b'l), *adj.* that can be attenuated.

at·ten·u·ant (ə-ten′ū-ənt), *adj.* [Fr. *atténuant* < ppr. of L. *attenuare;* see ATTENUATE], in *medicine*, diluting or thinning, as liquids. *n.* an attenuant substance.

at·ten·u·ate (ə-ten′ū-āt′), *v.t.* [ATTENUATED (-id), ATTENUATING], [< L. *attenuatus*, pp. of *attenuare*, to make thin < *ad-*, to + *tenuare* < *tenuis*, thin], 1. to make slender or thin. 2. to dilute; rarefy. 3. to lessen or weaken in severity, value, etc. 4. in *bacteriology*, to make (a virus, etc.) less deadly. *v.i.* to become thin, weak, etc. *adj.* (ə-ten′ū-it), attenuated.

at·ten·u·a·tion (ə-ten′ū-ā′shən), *n.* [L. *attenuatio;* see ATTENUATE], an attenuating or being attenuated.

at·ten·u·a·tor (ə-ten′ū-ā′tẽr), *n.* a person or thing that attenuates.

at·test (ə-test′) *v.t.* [Fr. *attester* < L. *attestari* < *ad-*, to + *testari*, to bear witness < *testis*, a witness], 1. to declare to be true or genuine. 2. to certify by oath or signature. 3. to serve as proof of; demonstrate; make clear. 4. to place (a person) on oath. *v.i.* to bear witness; certify (usually with *to*). *n.* attestation.

at·test·ant (ə-tes′tənt), *adj.* [L. *attestans*, ppr. of *attestari;* see ATTEST], attesting. *n.* one who attests.

at·tes·ta·tion (at′es-tā′shən), *n.* [L. *attestatio* < pp. of *attestari;* see ATTEST], 1. an attesting. 2. testimony.

at·test·er, at·test·or (ə-tes′tẽr), *n.* a person who attests.

At·tic (at′ik), *adj.* [L. *Atticus;* Gr. *Attikos*], 1. of Attica. 2. of or characteristic of Athens, its people, culture, etc.; Athenian. 3. classical; simple, restrained, etc.: said of a style. *n.* 1. the Greek dialect of Attica. 2. an Athenian.

at·tic (at′ik), *n.* [Fr. *attique*, an attic < *Attique*, Attic, used as an architectural term for a low story directly below the roof; see ATTIC (of Attica)], in *architecture*, 1. a low wall or story above the cornice of a classical façade. 2. the room or rooms just below the roof of a house; garret.

At·ti·ca (at′i-kə), *n.* a state of ancient Greece: capital, Athens.

ATTICA

Attic faith, unshakable faith.

At·ti·cism, at·ti·cism (at′i-siz'm), *n.* [Gr. *Attikismos* < *Attikos*, Attic], 1. anything typical of Attic Greek; hence, 2. a graceful, restrained phrase.

At·ti·cize, at·ti·cize (at′i-sīz′), *v.t.* [ATTICIZED (-sīzd′), ATTICIZING], [Gr. *Attikizein* < *Attikē*, Attica + *-izein*, -ize], to make conform to the Attic customs, style, idiom, etc. *v.i.* to use Attic dialect or literary style.

Attic salt, Attic wit, graceful, piercing wit.

At·ti·la (at′'l-ə), *n.* [Goth., lit., little father < *atta*, father (like L. & Gr. *atta*, father < baby talk) + *-ila*, dim. suffix: so named by the Goths, who were dominated for a time by the Huns], king of the Huns (433?–453 A.D.); lived 406?–453 A.D.: called *the Scourge of God.*

at·tire (ə-tīr′), *v.t.* [ATTIRED (-tīrd′), ATTIRING], [ME. *atiren;* OFr. *atirier*, to put in order, arrange < *a tire*, in a row, in order; *a* (L. *ad*), to + *tire*, order, row, dress], to clothe; dress up; array. *n.* 1. clothes; finery. 2. in *heraldry*, a stag's antlers.

at·tire·ment (ə-tīr′mənt), *n.* attire.

at·ti·tude (at′ə-tōōd′, at′ə-tūd′), *n.* [Fr.; It. *attitudine*, attitude, aptness; L. *aptitudo* < *aptus;* see APT], 1. a bodily posture showing or meant to show a mental state, emotion, or mood. 2. a manner of acting, feeling, or thinking that shows one's disposition, opinion, etc.: as, she has a friendly *attitude* toward all; hence, 3. one's disposition, opinion, etc. 4. in *aeronautics*, the position of an aircraft in relation to a given point of reference, usually on the ground level. —*SYN.* see **posture.**

strike an attitude, to assume a posture or pose, often an affected or theatrical one.

at·ti·tu·di·nize (at′ə-tōō′d'n-īz′, at′ə-tū′d'n-īz′), *v.i.* [ATTITUDINIZED (-īzd′), ATTITUDINIZING], [It. *attitudine* (see ATTITUDE); + *-ize*], to strike an attitude; pose.

At·tle·bor·o (at′'l-būr′ō), *n.* a city in southeastern Massachusetts: pop., 27,000.

Att·lee, Clement Richard (at′li), first Earl Attlee, 1883– ; English Labor party leader; prime minister (1945–1951).

at·torn (ə-tūrn′), *v.i.* [OFr. *atorner, atourner; a-* (L. *ad*), to + *torner;* see TURN], in *law*, 1. originally, to transfer homage and service from one feudal lord to another. 2. to continue as tenant under a new landlord.

at·tor·ney (ə-tūr′ni), *n.* [*pl.* ATTORNEYS (-niz)], [ME. *aturne;* OFr. *atorné*, one appointed, pp. of *atorner;* see ATTORN], any person legally empowered to act for another; especially, a lawyer: abbreviated **at., att., atty.** —*SYN.* see **lawyer.**

attorney at law, a lawyer.

attorney general, [*pl.* ATTORNEYS GENERAL, ATTORNEY GENERALS], 1. the chief law officer of a national or State government, and legal adviser to the chief executive. 2. [A- G-], the head of the United States Department of Justice: abbreviated **Att. Gen., Atty. Gen., A.G.**

at·tract (ə-trakt′), *v.t.* [< L. *attractus*, pp. of *attrahere*, to draw to < *ad-*, to + *trahere*, to draw], 1. to draw to itself or oneself; make approach or adhere: as, a magnet *attracts* iron filings. 2. to get the admiration, attention, etc. of; allure: as, her beauty *attracted* people. *v.i.* to be attractive.

SYN.—**attract** implies the exertion of a force such as magnetism to draw a person or thing and connotes susceptibility in the thing drawn; **allure** implies attraction by that which seductively offers pleasure, delight, reward, etc.; **charm** suggests the literal or figurative casting of a spell and implies very pleasing qualities in the agent; **fascinate** and **enchant** both also suggest a magical power, **fascinate** stressing irresistibility and **enchant**, the evoking of great admiration; **captivate** implies a capturing of the attention or affection, but suggests a light, passing influence. —*ANT.* repel.

at·tract·er (ə-trak′tẽr), *n.* an attractor.

at·trac·tion (ə-trak′shən), *n.* [L. *attractio;* see ATTRACT], 1. an attracting. 2. power of attracting; hence, 3.

charm; fascination. 4. anything that attracts: as, movies are sometimes called *attractions*. 5. in *physics*, the mutual action by which bodies, particles, etc. tend to draw together or cohere: opposed to *repulsion*.

attraction sphere, in *biology*, the central area of an aster, including the centrosome: also called *centrosphere*.

at·trac·tive (ə-trak′tiv), *adj.* [Fr. *attractif*], 1. that attracts. 2. pleasing, charming, pretty, etc.

at·trac·tor (ə-trak′tẽr), *n.* a person or thing that attracts.

at·tra·hent (at′rə-hənt), *adj.* [L. *attrahens*, ppr. of *attrahere;* see ATTRACT], that attracts or draws.

at·trib·ut·a·ble (ə-trib′yoo-tə-b'l), *adj.* that can be attributed.

at·tri·bute (ə-trib′yoot; *for n.*, at′rə-būt′), *v.t.* [ATTRIBUTED (-id), ATTRIBUTING], [< L. *attributus*, pp. of *attribuere*, to assign < *ad-*, to + *tribuere*, to assign], to set down or think of as belonging to, produced by, or resulting from; assign or ascribe (*to*): as, the play is *attributed* to Shakespeare, he *attributes* his poverty to bad luck. *n.* 1. a characteristic or quality of a thing. 2. an object used in literature or art as a symbol for a person, position, etc.: as, winged feet are the *attribute* of Mercury. 3. in *grammar*, a word or phrase used as an adjective. Abbreviated **attrib.** —***SYN.*** see **ascribe, quality.**

at·tri·bu·tion (at′rə-bū′shən), *n.* [L. *attributio;* see ATTRIBUTE], 1. an attributing or being attributed. 2. anything attributed; an attribute.

at·trib·u·tive (ə-trib′yoo-tiv), *adj.* [Fr. *attributif;* see ATTRIBUTE], 1. attributing. 2. of or like an attribute. 3. in *grammar*, expressing a quality meant to apply to a following substantive: said of adjectives, and distinguished from *predicate* and *predicative*. *n.* an attributive word; modifier: as, in "black cat," *black* is an *attributive*. Abbreviated **attrib.**

at·trite (ə-trīt′), *adj.* [< L. *attritus;* see ATTRITION], [Rare], worn down by friction.

at·tri·tion (ə-trish′ən), *n.* [L. *attritio* < *attritus*, pp. of *atterere*, to wear, rub away < *ad-*, to + *terere*, to rub], 1. a wearing away by friction. 2. the process or state of being gradually worn down. 3. any gradual wearing or weakening: as, a siege is a battle of *attrition*. 4. in *theology*, the lowest degree of repentance, caused by fear of punishment: distinguished from *contrition*.

At·tu (at-to͞o′), *n.* an island in the western Aleutians.

at·tune (ə-to͞on′, ə-tūn′), *v.t.* [ATTUNED (-to͞ond′, -tūnd′), ATTUNING], [< *ad-* + *tune*], 1. to tune. 2. to bring into harmony or agreement.

atty., attorney.

Atty. Gen., Attorney General.

at. vol., atomic volume.

a·twain (ə-twān′), *adv.* [*a-*, on + *twain*], [Archaic or Poetic], in two: as, cut *atwain*.

a·tween (ə-twēn′), *prep. & adv.* [Archaic or Dial.], between.

a·twit·ter (ə-twit′ẽr), *adv. & adj.* [*a-*, on + *twitter*], in a twitter.

at. wt., atomic weight.

a·typ·ic (ā-tip′ik), *adj.* atypical.

a·typ·i·cal (ā-tip′i-k'l), *adj.* [*a-*, not + *typical*], not typical; not characteristic; abnormal.

‡**au** (ō), [Fr., contr. of *à le; à*, to + *le*, masc. form of def. article, the], see **à la.**

Au, *aurum*, [L.], in *chemistry*, gold.

A.U., astronomical unit.

‡**au·bade** (ō′bȧd′), *n.* [Fr. < Sp. *albada* < *alba*, dawn < L. *albus*, white; cf. ALBA], a piece of music suitable for performance at sunrise, or in the morning: the counterpart of *serenade*.

Aube (ōb), *n.* a river in northern France, flowing into the Seine: length, 130 mi.

Au·ber, Da·niel (dȧ′nyel′ ō′bâr′), 1782–1871; French composer.

‡**au·berge** (ō′berzh′), *n.* [Fr.], an inn.

Au·brey (ô′bri), [Fr. *Aubri;* G. *Alberich* < OHG. *alb*, elf + *rihhi*, ruler, control], a masculine name.

Au·burn (ô′bẽrn), *n.* 1. a city in central New York: pop., 35,000. 2. a city in southern Maine: pop., 24,000.

au·burn (ô′bẽrn), *adj. & n.* [ME. *auburne;* OFr. *auborne, alborne;* L. *alburnus* < *albus*, white; meaning influenced by association with ME. *brun;* see BROWN], reddish brown.

Auck·land (ôk′lənd), *n.* a seaport in North Island, New Zealand: pop., 413,000.

‡**au con·traire** (ō′ kōn′trâr′), [Fr.], on the contrary.

‡**au cou·rant** (ō′ ko͞o′rän′), [Fr., lit., with the current], fully informed; well acquainted with current matters; up-to-date.

auc·tion (ôk′shən), *n.* [L. *auctio*, an increasing, public sale < *auctus*, pp. of *augere*, to increase], 1. a public sale where items are sold one by one, each going to the last and highest of a series of competing bidders. 2. auction bridge. 3. the bidding in bridge. *v.t.* to sell at auction; put up at auction. —***SYN.*** see **sell.**

auction off, to sell at auction.

put up at auction, to offer for sale at an auction.

auction bridge, a variety of the game of bridge in which the players bid for the right to say what suit shall be trump or to declare no-trump: see also **contract bridge.**

auc·tion·eer (ôk′shən-êr′), *n.* a person who auctions things, usually as a business. *v.t.* to auction.

aud., auditor.

au·da·cious (ô-dā′shəs), *adj.* [Fr. *audacieux* < L. *audacia*, audacity < *audax*, bold < *audere*, to be bold, to dare], 1. daring; reckless; bold. 2. too daring; presumptuous; insolent; impudent. —***SYN.*** see **brave.**

au·dac·i·ty (ô-das′ə-ti), *n.* [L. *audax;* see AUDACIOUS], 1. bold courage; daring. 2. presumption; insolence; impudence. 3. [*pl.* AUDACITIES (-tiz)], an audacious act or remark. —***SYN.*** see **temerity.**

Au·den, Wys·tan Hugh (wis′tən ô′d'n), 1907– ; English poet in the United States.

au·di·bil·i·ty (ô′də-bil′ə-ti), *n.* the capacity or condition of being audible.

au·di·ble (ô′də-b'l), *adj.* [ML. *audibilis* < L. *audire*, to hear], that can be heard; loud enough to be heard.

au·di·bly (ô′də-bli), *adv.* so as to be audible.

au·di·ence (ô′di-əns, ôd′yəns), *n.* [ME.; OFr.; L. *audientia*, a hearing, listening < *audiens*, ppr. of *audire*, to hear], 1. those assembled to hear and see a concert, play, etc. 2. those who listen to a radio program or view a televised program. 3. those who pay attention to what one writes or says; one's public. 4. the act or state of hearing. 5. an opportunity to have one's ideas heard; a hearing. 6. a formal interview with a person in high position.

audience room, a room for formal interviews.

au·di·ent (ô′di-ənt), *adj.* [L. *audiens* < *audire*, to hear], listening; giving attention.

au·dile (ô′dil), *adj.* [< L. *audire*, to hear; + *-ile*], auditory. *n.* in *psychology*, a person who relies mainly on his sense of hearing or whose imagery is chiefly in terms of sound.

au·di·o (ô′di-ō′), *adj.* [< L. *audire*, to hear], 1. in *electricity*, of frequencies corresponding to sound waves that can normally be heard by the human ear. 2. in *television*, designating or of the sound phase of a broadcast, as distinguished from the *video* (or picture) portion.

au·di·o- (ô′di-ō, ô′di-ə), [see AUDIO], a combining form meaning *relating to hearing*, as in *audiometer:* also **audi-.**

au·di·o-fre·quen·cy (ô′di-ō-frē′kwən-si), *adj.* of the band of audible sound frequencies or corresponding electric current frequencies, about 20 to 20,000 cycles per second.

au·di·o·me·ter (ô′di-om′ə-tẽr), *n.* [*audio-* + *-meter*], an instrument for measuring one's hearing or the intensity of sounds.

au·di·o-vis·u·al aids (ô′di-ō-vizh′o͞o-əl), motion pictures, lantern slides, phonograph records, and other materials except books, used in teaching, illustrating lectures, etc.

au·di·phone (ô′də-fōn′), *n.* [< L. *audire*, to hear; + *-phone*, after *telephone*], a device for the hard of hearing that transmits sound to the auditory nerves through the bones of the head.

au·dit (ô′dit), *n.* [L. *auditus*, a hearing, pp. of *audire*, to hear], 1. a regular examination and checking of accounts or financial records. 2. a settlement or adjustment of accounts. 3. an account thus examined and adjusted. 4. a final statement of account. *v.t. & v.i.* 1. to examine and check (accounts, claims, etc.). 2. to attend (a college class) as a listener receiving no credits.

au·di·tion (ô-dish′ən), *n.* [L. *auditio* < pp. of *audire*, to hear], 1. the act or sense of hearing. 2. a hearing to test the abilities, voice, etc. of an actor, musician, or speaker. *v.t.* to give an audition to. *v.i.* to perform in an audition.

au·di·tive (ô′də-tiv), *adj.* [Rare], auditory.

au·di·tor (ô′də-tẽr), *n.* [L., hearer < *audire*, to hear], 1. a hearer; listener. 2. a person who audits accounts: abbreviated **aud.** 3. a person who audits classes.

au·di·to·ri·ly (ô′də-tôr′ə-li, ô′də-tō′rə-li), *adv.* by means of hearing; through the sense of hearing.

au·di·to·ri·um (ô′də-tôr′i-əm, ô′də-tō′ri-əm), *n.* [*pl.* AUDITORIUMS (-əmz), AUDITORIA (-ə)], [L., neut. of *auditorius;* see AUDITORY], 1. a room where the audience sits in a church, theater, etc. 2. a building or hall for speeches, concerts, etc.

au·di·to·ry (ô′də-tôr′i, ô′də-tō′ri), *adj.* [L. *auditorius* < *auditor;* see AUDITOR], of hearing or the sense of hearing. *n.* [*pl.* AUDITORIES (-iz)], [L. *auditorium*], 1. the hearers of a speech, concert, etc.; audience. 2. an auditorium.

Au·drey (ô′dri), [OFr. < Gmc.; akin to AS. *æthelthryth*, lit., noble might; *æthel*, noble + *thryth*, might, strength, etc.], a feminine name.

Au·du·bon, John James (ô′də-bon′), 1785–1851; American ornithologist, painter, and naturalist.

Au·er, Leopold (ou′ẽr), 1845–1930; Hungarian violinist and teacher.

‡**au fait** (ō′ fe′), [Fr., lit., to the fact], acquainted with the facts; proficient; expert.

‡**Auf·klä·rung** (ouf′klâr′ooŋ), *n.* [G. < *aufklären*, to enlighten; *auf-*, up + *klären*, to clear < *klar*, clear], the Enlightenment, 18th-century philosophical movement.

‡**au fond** (ō' fōn'), [Fr., at the bottom], basically; essentially; at heart.

‡**auf Wie·der·se·hen** (ouf vē'dĕr-zā'ən), [G.], till we see each other again; good-by: implies temporary parting.

Aug., August.

aug., 1. augment. 2. augmentative.

Au·ge·an (ô-jē'ən), *adj.* [< L. *Augeas;* Gr. *Augeias*], 1. in *Greek legend,* of King Augeas or his stable, which held three thousand oxen and remained uncleaned for thirty years until Hercules cleaned it in one day by diverting two rivers through it; hence, 2. filthy.

au·gend (ô'jend, ô-jend'), *n.* [L. *augendum* < *augere,* to increase], a number having another number (the addend) added to it.

au·ger (ô'gẽr), *n.* [by faulty separation of ME. *a nauger, a navegar;* AS. *nafogar,* nave drill < *nafu,* nave (of a wheel) + *gar,* a spear], 1. a tool for boring holes in wood larger than those made by a gimlet. 2. any similar tool, as for boring holes in the earth.

TYPES OF AUGER
A, screw auger; B, ship auger; C, lip-ring auger

aught (ôt), *n.* [ME.; AS. *awiht; a, an,* one + *wiht,* a creature, thing; see WHIT], 1. anything whatever; any little part. 2. [*a naught* (see NAUGHT), wrongly divided *an aught*], a zero. *adv.* to any degree; in any way; at all.

Au·gier, É·mile (ā'mēl' ō'zhyā'), (*Guillaume Victor Émile Augier*), 1820–1889; French playwright.

au·gite (ô'jīt), *n.* [L. *augites;* Gr. *augitēs,* a precious stone < *augē,* bright, shining], a black complex silicate mineral of vitreous luster and granular structure, occurring in igneous rocks; kind of pyroxene.

aug·ment (ôg-ment'; *for n.,* ôg'ment), *v.t.* [Fr. *augmenter;* L. *augmentare* < *augmentum,* an increase < *augere,* to increase], 1. to make greater, as in size, quantity, strength, etc.; enlarge. 2. in *grammar,* to add an augment to. *v.i.* to become greater; increase. *n.* [L. *augmentum*], 1. an increase. 2. in *grammar,* a prefixed vowel or lengthening of the initial vowel to show past time in Greek and Sanskrit verbs: abbreviated **aug.** —*SYN.* see **increase.**

aug·men·ta·tion (ôg'men-tā'shən), *n.* [Fr.; ML. *augmentatio* < pp. of L. *augmentare;* see AUGMENT], 1. an augmenting or being augmented. 2. a thing that augments; addition; increase. 3. in *music,* variation of a theme by doubling the time value of the notes.

aug·ment·a·tive (ôg-men'tə-tiv), *adj.* [Fr. *augmentatif*], 1. augmenting; capable of augmenting. 2. in *grammar,* increasing the force of an idea expressed by a word: as, an *augmentative* prefix. *n.* an augmentative prefix, suffix, word, etc.; intensifier. Examples: *per*durable, eat *up.* Abbreviated **aug., augm.**

aug·ment·ed interval (ôg-men'tid), in *music,* an interval that is a half step greater than the corresponding major interval.

au gra·tin (ō grä't'n, ō gra't'n; Fr. ō' grà'tan'), [Fr., lit., with scrapings], made with a lightly browned crust of bread crumbs or grated cheese.

Augs·burg (ôgz'bẽrg; G. ouks'boorkh), *n.* a city in southern Germany, in Bavaria: pop., 204, 000.

au·gur (ô'gẽr), *n.* [L., orig., a priest at rituals of fertility and increase; prob. < OL. **augos,* **augeris,* increase, growth < *augere,* to increase; meaning influenced by association with *auspex;* see AUSPEX], 1. in ancient Rome, any of certain priests who foretold events by interpreting omens, such as the appearance of the entrails of sacrificial animals, the motions of birds in flight, etc. 2. a fortuneteller; prophet; soothsayer. *v.t. & v.i.* [L. *augurari* < the *n.*], 1. to foretell; prophesy. 2. to be an omen (of).
  augur ill (or **well**), to be a bad (or good) omen.

au·gu·ry (ô'gyẽr-i), *n.* [*pl.* AUGURIES (-iz)], [L. *augurium,* divination < *augur;* see AUGUR], 1. the art or practice of divination; prophecy. 2. a formal ceremony conducted by an augur. 3. an omen; sign; portent; indication.

Au·gust (ô'gəst), *n.* [ME.; L. *Augustus* < *Augustus* Caesar; see AUGUST, *adj.*], the eighth month of the year, having 31 days: abbreviated **Aug., Ag.**

au·gust (ô-gust'), *adj.* [L. *augustus* < *augere,* to increase], 1. inspiring awe and reverence; imposing and magnificent. 2. dignified and majestic, as from high position or rank. —*SYN.* see **grand.**

Au·gus·ta (ô-gus'tə), [L., fem. of *Augustus*], a feminine name. *n.* 1. a city in eastern Georgia: pop., 71,000. 2. the capital of Maine, on the Kennebec River: pop., 22,000.

Au·gus·tan (ô-gus'tən), *adj.* 1. of or characteristic of Augustus Caesar, his reign (27 B.C.–14 A.D.), or his times. 2. of or characteristic of any age having standards or tastes like those of Augustus' age. 3. classical; elegant. 4. of Augsburg: as, Luther's *Augustan* Confession. *n.* a writer living in an Augustan age.

Augustan age, 1. the period of Latin literature during the reign of Augustus Caesar, when elegance and correctness were highly valued. 2. the similar period of English literature during the reign of Queen Anne.

Au·gus·tin (ô-gus'tin), [L. *Augustinus,* dim. of *Augustus*], a masculine name: variants, *Austin, Augustine;* equivalents, Fr. & G. *Augustin,* It. *Agostino.*

Au·gus·tine (ô'gəs-tēn', ô-gus'tin), a masculine name: see **Augustin.**

Augustine, Saint, 1. 354–430 A.D.; Latin church father; bishop of Hippo, in northern Africa; known for *Confessions* and *De Civitate Dei* (*The City of God*): his day is August 28. 2. ?–604 A.D.; Roman monk who went to spread Christianity among the English; first archbishop of Canterbury: his day is May 28.

Au·gus·tin·i·an (ô'gəs-tin'i-ən), *adj.* 1. of Saint Augustine of Hippo or his doctrines. 2. designating or of any of several orders named for him. *n.* 1. a person who believes in Augustinianism. 2. a member of an Augustinian religious order.

Au·gus·tin·i·an·ism (ô'gəs-tin'i-ən-iz'm), *n.* the doctrines of Saint Augustine of Hippo, who taught absolute predestination and the immediate efficacy of grace.

Au·gus·tin·ism (ô-gus'tin-iz'm), *n.* Augustinianism.

Au·gus·tus (ô-gus'təs), [L. < *augustus;* see AUGUST, *adj.*], a masculine name: diminutives, *Gus, Gustus;* feminine, *Augusta;* equivalents, Fr. *Auguste,* G. *August,* It. *Augusto.* *n.* (*Gaius Julius Caesar Octavianus*), grandnephew of Julius Caesar and first emperor of Rome (27 B.C.–14 A.D.); lived 63 B.C.–14 A.D.: also called *Octavian.*

‡**au jus** (ō' zhü'), [Fr., with the juice], served in its natural juice or gravy: said of meat.

auk (ôk), *n.* [dial. *alk* < ON. *alka*], any of a number of related diving birds of northern seas, with a heavy body, webbed feet, a short tail, and short wings used as paddles.

auk·let (ôk'lit), *n.* [*auk* + *-let*], any of several small kinds of auk.

‡**au lait** (ō' le'), [Fr.], with milk.

auld (ôld), *adj.* [Dial. & Scot.], old.

auld lang syne (ôld' laŋ sīn'), [Scot., lit., old long since], old times; the good old days (of one's youth, etc.).

GREAT AUK (30 in. high)

au·lic (ô'lik), *adj.* [Fr. *aulique;* L. *aulicus;* Gr. *aulikos,* princely < *aulē,* a court], of a court; courtly.

Au·lic Council (ô'lik), in the Holy Roman Empire, a personal council of the emperor that served as a supreme court: dissolved in 1806.

‡**au na·tu·rel** (ō' nà'tü'rel'), [Fr.], 1. in the natural state; hence, 2. naked. 3. prepared or served simply: said of food.

aunt (ant, änt), *n.* [OFr. *ante, aunte;* L. *amita,* paternal aunt], 1. the sister of one's mother or father. 2. the wife of one's uncle.

aunt·ie, aunt·y (an'ti, än'ti), *n.* aunt: a familiar or affectionate form.

au·ra (ô'rə), *n.* [*pl.* AURAS (-rəz), AURAE (-rē)], [L.; Gr., air, breeze], 1. an invisible emanation or vapor, as the aroma of flowers. 2. an invisible atmosphere supposedly arising from and surrounding a person or thing: as, he was enveloped in an *aura* of grandeur. 3. in *electricity,* an air current caused by an electric discharge from a sharp metallic point. 4. in *medicine,* a sensation preceding an epileptic seizure or hysterics, as of a wave of cold air rising to the head.

au·ral (ô'rəl), *adj.* of an aura.

au·ral (ô'rəl), *adj.* [< L. *auris,* ear; + *-al*], of or received through the ear or the sense of hearing.

Au·rang·zeb (ôr'əŋ-zeb', ou'rəŋ-zeb'), *n.* sixth and last Mogul emperor of Hindustan; 1658–1707; lived 1618–1707; also spelled **Aurungzeb.**

au·re·ate (ô'ri-it), *adj.* [LL. *aureatus* < L. *aureus* < *aurum,* gold], 1. golden; gilded. 2. splendid; ornate.

Au·re·li·a (ô-rē'li-ə, ô-rēl'yə), [L., lit., golden < *aurum,* gold], a feminine name.

Au·re·li·an (ô-rē'li-ən), *n.* (*Lucius Domitius Aurelianus*), Roman emperor (270–275 A.D.) and militarist; lived 212?–275 A.D.

Aurelius, Marcus, see **Marcus Aurelius.**

au·re·o·la (ô-rē'ə-lə), *n.* an aureole.

au·re·ole (ô'ri-ōl'), *n.* [L. *aureolus,* dim. of *aureus;* see AUREATE], 1. a halo; radiance encircling the head or body, as in religious paintings, etc.: also called *glory.* 2. a band or fringe of light around the sun, etc., as

when seen in a mist or during an eclipse; sun's corona.
au·re·o·my·cin (ô'ri-ō-mī'sin), *n.* [< L. *aureus*, golden (from its color) + Gr. *mykēs*, fungus; + *-in*], an antibiotic drug similar to penicillin, effective against certain viruses and against both Gram-positive and Gram-negative bacteria.
‡au re·voir (ō' rə-vwär'), [Fr. < L. *revidere*, to see again; *re-*, again + *videre*, to see], until we meet again; good-by: implies temporary parting.
au·ri- (ô'ri), [< L. *auris*, ear], a combining form meaning *ear*, as in *auriform*.
au·ric (ô'rik), *adj.* [< L. *aurum*, gold], 1. of or containing gold. 2. in *chemistry*, designating or of compounds in which gold has a valence of three.
au·ri·cle (ô'ri-k'l), *n.* [L. *auricula*, dim. of *auris*, ear], 1. the external part of the ear. 2. either of two upper chambers of the heart, into which the blood flows from the veins: see **heart**, illus. 3. in *botany & zoology*, an earlike part or organ.
au·ric·u·la (ô-rik'yoo-lə), *n.* [*pl.* AURICULAS (-ləz), AURICULAE (-lē')], [see AURICLE], 1. a kind of primrose with leaves shaped like a bear's ear. 2. an auricle.
au·ric·u·lar (ô-rik'yoo-lẽr), *adj.* [ML. *auricularis* < L. *auricula;* see AURICLE], 1. of or near the ear; of the sense of hearing. 2. received by or spoken directly into the ear: as, an *auricular* confession. 3. shaped like an ear. 4. in *anatomy*, of an auricle. *n. usually in pl.* any of the feathers covering the opening of a bird's ear.
au·ric·u·late (ô-rik'yoo-lit), *adj.* [< L. *auricula* (see AURICLE); + *-ate*], 1. having ears. 2. having auricles.
au·rif·er·ous (ô-rif'ẽr-əs), *adj.* [L. *aurifer* < *aurum*, gold + *ferre*, to bear, bring forth], bearing or yielding gold.
au·ri·form (ô'ri-fôrm'), *adj.* [*auri-* + *-form*], ear-shaped.
Au·ri·ga (ô-rī'gə), *n.* [L., *auriga*, charioteer < *aurea*, bridle + *agere*, to drive, guide], a northern constellation between Perseus and Gemini, supposedly outlining a charioteer: see **constellation**, chart.
au·rist (ô'rist), *n.* [< *auri-* + *-ist*], a doctor specializing in ear diseases; otologist.
au·rochs (ô'roks), *n.* [*pl.* AUROCHS], [G. *auerochs* < OHG. *urohso; ur-* (< IE. base **wer-*, damp; cf. URINE) + *ohso*, ox], 1. originally, the wild ox of Europe, now extinct. 2. now, the European bison.
Au·ro·ra (ô-rôr'ə, ô-rō'rə), *n.* [*pl.* in senses 4, 5, and 6, AURORAS (-əz, -rəz), AURORAE (-ē, -rē)], [L.], 1. in *Roman mythology*, the goddess of dawn: identified with the Greek Eos. 2. a city in northeastern Illinois: pop., 64,000. 3. a city in Colorado, near Denver: pop., 49,000. 4. [a-], the dawn. 5. [a-], the beginning or early period of anything. 6. [a-], the aurora australis or aurora borealis.
aurora aus·tra·lis (ô-strā'lis), [L., lit., southern aurora < *auster*, south wind, south], luminous bands or streamers of light sometimes appearing in the night sky of the Southern Hemisphere.
aurora bo·re·a·lis (bôr'i-al'is, bō'ri-ā'lis), [L., lit., northern aurora < *boreas* < Gr. *boreas*, *borras*, north wind, north], luminous bands or streamers of light sometimes appearing in the night sky of the Northern Hemisphere; northern lights.
au·ro·ral (ô-rôr'əl, ô-rō'rəl), *adj.* 1. of or like the dawn; rosy; dawning. 2. of or like the aurora (borealis or australis). 3. bright; radiant.
au·ro·re·an (ô-rôr'i-ən, ô-rō'ri-ən), *adj.* of or like the dawn; auroral.
au·rous (ô'rəs), *adj.* [L. *aureus*, golden < *aurum*, gold], 1. containing gold. 2. in *chemistry*, designating or of compounds in which gold has a valence of one.
au·rum (ô'rəm), *n.* [L.], gold: symbol, Au (no period).
Aus., 1. Austria. 2. Austrian.
Au·schwitz (ou'shvits), *n.* 1. a city in southwestern Poland: pop., 6,700. 2. a Nazi concentration camp in this city: notorious as an extermination center.
aus·cul·tate (ôs'kəl-tāt'), *v.t. & v.i.* [AUSCULTATED (-id), AUSCULTATING], [< pp. of L. *auscultare*, to listen], to examine by auscultation.
aus·cul·ta·tion (ôs'kəl-tā'shən), *n.* [L. *auscultatio*, a listening < *auscultare*, to listen], 1. a listening. 2. a listening, often with the aid of a stethoscope, to sounds in the chest, abdomen, etc. so as to determine the condition of the heart, lungs, etc.
aus·cul·ta·tor (ôs'kəl-tā'tẽr), *n.* one who auscultates.
‡Aus·gleich (ous'glīH'), *n.* [*pl.* AUSGLEICHE (-glī'Hə)], [G.], an agreement by compromise; specifically, the treaty between Austria and Hungary (1867) establishing their union into a dual monarchy.
aus·pex (ôs'peks), *n.* [*pl.* AUSPICES (-pi-sēz')], [L., contr. of *avispex* < *avis*, bird + *spicere*, to see], a Roman priest who found omens in the flight of birds, etc.; augur.
aus·pi·cate (ôs'pi-kāt'), *v.t.* [AUSPICATED (-id), AUSPICATING], [< pp. of *auspicari*, to take the auspices < *auspex;* see AUSPEX], to begin formally or auspiciously; inaugurate.
aus·pice (ôs'pis), *n.* [*pl.* AUSPICES (-iz)], [L. *auspicium*, omen < *auspex;* see AUSPEX], 1. an omen. 2. a watching for omens in the flight of birds; divination. 3. any prophecy, especially when favorable. 4. *usually pl.* patronage; protection.
aus·pi·cial (ôs-pish'əl), *adj.* 1. of augury. 2. auspicious.
aus·pi·cious (ôs-pish'əs), *adj.* [< L. *auspicium;* see AUSPICE], 1. of good omen; favorable; propitious. 2. successful; prosperous. —*SYN.* see **favorable.**
Aus·sie (ôs'i), *n.* [Slang], an Australian, especially one in the armed forces.
Aust., 1. Austria. 2. Austria-Hungary. 3. Austrian.
Aus·ten, Jane (ôs'tin, ôs'tən), 1775–1817; English novelist.
Aus·ter (ôs'tẽr), *n.* [L.], [Poetic], the south wind: a personification.
aus·tere (ô-stêr'), *adj.* [ME.; OFr.; L. *austerus*, harsh; Gr. *austēros*, dry, harsh < *auein*, to dry < *auos*, dry], 1. severe; stern; harsh; rigorous. 2. morally strict; abstinent; ascetic. 3. very simple; lacking ornament. 4. grave; sober: as, an *austere* face. —*SYN.* see **severe.**
aus·ter·i·ty (ô-ster'ə-ti), *n.* [*pl.* AUSTERITIES (-tiz)], [L. *austeritas*], 1. the quality or condition of being austere. 2. *usually in pl.* an austere habit or practice.
Aus·ter·litz (ôs'tẽr-lits'; G. ous'ter-lits'), *n.* a town in Moravia, Czechoslovakia: pop., 4,500: scene of Napoleon's victory (1805) over the Austrian and Russian armies.
Aus·tin (ôs'tin, ôs'tən), a masculine name: see **Augustin.** *n.* the capital of Texas, on the Colorado River: pop., 187,000.
Aus·tin, Alfred (ôs'tin, ôs'tən), 1835–1913; English poet; poet laureate (1896–1913).
Austin, John, 1790–1859; English jurist and author.
Austin, Stephen F., 1793–1836; founder of the first colony in Texas (1822).
aus·tral (ôs'trəl), *adj.* [L. *australis*, southern < *auster*, south wind, the south], 1. southern; southerly. 2. [A-], Australian.
Austral., 1. Australia. 2. Australian. 3. Australasia. 4. Australasian.
Aus·tral·a·sia (ôs'trəl-ā'zhə, ôs'trəl-ā'shə), *n.* 1. the part of the earth including Australia, Tasmania, New Zealand, Malaysia, Melanesia, Micronesia, and Polynesia. 2. Australia, Tasmania, New Zealand, and the British possessions of Melanesia.
Aus·tral·a·sian (ôs'trəl-ā'zhən, ôs'trəl-ā'shən), *adj.* of Australasia or its peoples. *n.* a native or inhabitant of Australasia.

AUSTRALASIA

Aus·tral·ia (ô-strāl'yə), *n.* 1. a continent in the Southern Hemisphere, between the South Pacific and Indian Oceans. 2. a British Commonwealth comprising this continent and Tasmania: area, 2,974,581 sq. mi.; pop., 8,986,000; capital, Canberra: official name, *the Commonwealth of Australia.*
Aus·tral·ian (ô-strāl'yən), *adj.* of Australia, its people, languages, or culture. *n.* a native or inhabitant of Australia.
Australian Alps, a mountain range in southeastern Australia, in Victoria and New South Wales provinces: highest peak, Mount Kosciusko, 7,352 ft.
Australian ballot, a type of ballot listing candidates for election to public office, marked by the voter in privacy so that his vote will be secret: it originated in Australia and is widely used in the United States.
Australian Capital Territory, a federal territory in New South Wales: seat of the Australian government: area, 939 sq. mi.; pop., 45,000: formerly called *Federal Capital Territory.*
Australian crawl, a modified crawl stroke in which alternate arm and leg action causes the swimmer's body to roll slightly as it is propelled forward.
Aus·tra·sia (ô-strā'zhə, ô-strā'shə), *n.* the eastern territory of the Franks from the 5th to the 9th centuries, composed of what is now northeastern France, Belgium, and western Germany.
Aus·tri·a (ôs'tri-ə), *n.* a country in central Europe: area, 32,375 sq. mi.; pop., 7,049,000; capital, Vienna: abbreviated **Aus., Aust.:** German name, *Österreich.*
Aus·tri·a-Hun·ga·ry (ôs'tri-ə-huŋ'gə-ri), *n.* a former monarchy in central Europe: it included territory that became Austria, Czechoslovakia, and Hungary, as well as parts of Poland, Romania, Yugoslavia, and Italy, and was broken up by the Versailles Treaty: area, 240,000 sq. mi.
Aus·tri·an (ôs'tri-ən), *adj.* of Austria, its people, dialect, or culture. *n.* 1. a native

AUSTRIA-HUNGARY

or inhabitant of Austria. 2. the German dialect of Austria. Abbreviated **Aus., Aust.**

Aus·tro- (ôs′trō, ôs′trə), a combining form meaning *Austria*, as in *Austro-Hungarian*.

aus·tro- (ôs′trō, ôs′trə), [< L. *auster*, the south, south wind], a combining form meaning: 1. *south wind*. 2. [A-], *South*. 3. [A-], *Australian*.

Aus·tro-Hun·gar·i·an (ôs′trō-huŋ-gâr′i-ən), *adj.* of Austria-Hungary.

Aus·tro·ne·sia (ôs′trō-nē′zhə, ôs′trō-nē′shə), *n.* [< *Austro-* (south) + Gr. *nēsos*, island; + *-ia*], the islands in the central and south Pacific.

Aus·tro·ne·sian (ôs′trō-nē′zhən, ôs′trō-nē′shən), *adj.* 1. of Austronesia, its people, etc. 2. designating or of a family of languages spoken there, comprising the Indonesian, Melanesian, Micronesian, and Polynesian subfamilies; Malayo-Polynesian. *n.* these languages.

aut- (ôt), auto-.

au·ta·coid (ô′tə-koid′), *n.* [< *aut-* + Gr. *akos*, cure, remedy; + *-oid*], an organic substance, such as a hormone, carried by the blood stream or other body fluids from a part of the body where it is formed to another part on which it has activating effects, like those of drugs: also spelled **autocoid**.

au·tar·chic (ô-tär′kik), *adj.* of or characteristic of an autarchy.

au·tar·chi·cal (ô-tär′ki-k'l), *adj.* autarchic.

au·tarch·y (ô′tär-ki), *n.* [*pl.* AUTARCHIES (-kiz)], [Gr. *autarchia* < *autarchos*, autocrat, absolute ruler < *autos*, self + *archos*, first, ruler], 1. absolute rule; despotism. 2. a country under such rule. 3. loosely, autarky.

au·tar·kic (ô-tär′kik), *adj.* of or characterized by autarky.

au·tar·ky (ô′tär-ki), *n.* [Gr. *autarkeia*, independence, self-sufficiency < *autos*, self + *arkein*, to achieve, endure, suffice], economic self-sufficiency as a national policy; getting along without goods from other countries.

‡aut Cae·sar aut ni·hil (ôt sē′zẽr ôt ni′hil), [L.], 1. either (a) Caesar or nothing; hence, 2. either everything or nothing.

au·te·cious (ô-tē′shəs), *adj.* autoecious.

au·te·cism (ô-tē′siz'm), *n.* autoecism.

auth., 1. author. 2. authoress. 3. authorized.

au·then·tic (ô-then′tik), *adj.* [ME. *autentike*; OFr. *autentique*; L. *authenticus*; Gr. *authentikos*, genuine, authentic < *authentēs*, one who does things himself, murderer < *autos*, self + **hentēs* (used in comp.) < IE. base meaning "to gain, acquire, achieve"], 1. authoritative; trustworthy; reliable: as, an *authentic* news report. 2. genuine; real: as, an *authentic* antique.

SYN.—**authentic** implies authoritativeness and trustworthiness, stressing that the thing considered is in agreement with fact or actuality (an *authentic* report); **genuine** is applied to that which really is what it is represented to be, emphasizing freedom from admixture, adulteration, sham, etc. (*genuine* silk, *genuine* grief); **bona fide** is properly used when a question of good faith is involved; **veritable** implies correspondence with the truth and connotes absolute affirmation (a *veritable* fool). —*ANT.* spurious, counterfeit, sham.

au·then·ti·cal·ly (ô-then′ti-k'l-i, ô-then′tik-li), *adv.* in an authentic manner.

au·then·ti·cate (ô-then′ti-kāt′), *v.t.* [AUTHENTICATED (-id), AUTHENTICATING], [< ML. *authenticatus*, pp. of *authenticare* < L. *authenticus*; see AUTHENTIC], 1. to make authentic or valid. 2. to establish the truth of; verify; prove to be genuine. 3. to prove (a painting, book, etc.) to be the product of a certain person. —*SYN.* see **confirm**.

au·then·ti·ca·tion (ô-then′ti-kā′shən), *n.* an authenticating or being authenticated.

au·then·ti·ca·tor (ô-then′ti-kā′tẽr), *n.* a person or thing that authenticates.

au·then·tic·i·ty (ô′thən-tis′ə-ti), *n.* the quality or state of being authentic; reliability; genuineness.

au·thor (ô′thẽr), *n.* [ME. *autour*; OFr. *auteur*; L. *auctor*, enlarger, originator, author < *augere*, to increase], 1. a person who makes or originates something; creator; instigator. 2. the writer (*of* a book, article, etc.). 3. a person whose profession is writing books, etc. 4. an author's writings. *v.t.* to be the author of.

au·thor·ess (ô′thẽr-is), *n.* [Now Rare], a woman author.

au·tho·ri·al (ô-thôr′i-əl, ô-thō′ri-əl), *adj.* of an author.

au·thor·i·tar·i·an (ə-thôr′ə-târ′i-ən, ə-thor′ə-târ′i-ən), *adj.* [< *authority* + *-arian*], believing in, relating to, or characterized by unquestioning obedience to authority rather than individual freedom of judgment and action. *n.* a person who believes in, advocates, practices, or enforces such obedience.

au·thor·i·tar·i·an·ism (ə-thôr′ə-târ′i-ən-iz′m, ə-thor′ə-târ′i-ən-iz′m), *n.* authoritarian principles; policy or practice of unquestioning obedience to the authority of a dictator or a small dictatorial group.

au·thor·i·ta·tive (ə-thôr′ə-tā′tiv, ə-thor′ə-tā′tiv), *adj.* 1. asserting authority; fond of giving orders; dictatorial. 2. having authority; official. 3. based on competent authority; reliable because coming from recognized experts: as, an *authoritative* dictionary.

au·thor·i·ty (ə-thôr′ə-ti, ə-thor′ə-ti), *n.* [*pl.* AUTHORITIES (-tiz)], [ME. & OFr. *autorite*, *auctorite*; L. *auctoritas* < *auctor*; see AUTHOR], 1. the power or right to give commands, enforce obedience, take action, or make final decisions; jurisdiction. 2. this power as delegated to another; authorization: as, he has my *authority* to do it. 3. power or influence resulting from knowledge, prestige, etc. 4. a person, writing, etc. cited in support of an opinion. 5. *usually in pl.* a government official or other person having the power or right to enforce orders, laws, etc. 6. a person with much knowledge or experience in some field, whose opinion is hence reliable; expert. —*SYN.* see **influence**, **power**.

au·thor·i·za·tion (ô′thẽr-i-zā′shən), *n.* 1. an authorizing or being authorized. 2. legal power or right; sanction.

au·thor·ize (ô′thə-rīz′), *v.t.* [AUTHORIZED (-rīzd′), AUTHORIZING], [ME. *autorizen*; OFr. *autoriser*; ML. *auctorizare* < L. *auctor*; see AUTHOR], 1. to give official approval to or permission for: as, the city *authorized* a housing project. 2. to give power or authority to; commission. 3. to give authority or justification for.

SYN.—**authorize** implies the giving of power or right to act, ranging in application from a specific legal power to discretionary powers in dealings of any kind; to **commission** a person is to authorize as well as instruct him to perform a certain duty, as the execution of an artistic work, or to appoint him to a certain rank or office; **accredit** implies the sending of a person, duly authorized and with the proper credentials, as an ambassador, delegate, etc.; **license** implies the giving of formal legal permission to do some specified thing and often emphasizes regulation (to *license* hunters).

au·thor·ized (ô′thə-rīzd′), *adj.* [pp. of *authorize*], 1. established or justified by authority. 2. having authority: as, my *authorized* agent. Abbreviated **auth.**

Authorized Version, the revised English translation of the Bible published in England in 1611 with the authorization of King James I: abbreviated **Auth. Ver., A.V.**: also called *King James Version*.

au·thor·less (ô′thẽr-lis), *adj.* with the author or authors unknown; anonymous.

au·thor·ship (ô′thẽr-ship′), *n.* [*author* + *-ship*], 1. the profession or occupation of a writer. 2. the origin (of a book, etc.) with reference to its author: as, a story of unknown *authorship*. 3. the source (of an idea, etc.) with reference to its originator.

Auth. Ver., Authorized Version.

au·tism (ô′tiz'm), *n.* [*aut-* + *-ism*], in *psychology*, a state of mind characterized by daydreaming, hallucinations, and disregard of external reality.

au·tis·tic (ô-tis′tik), *adj.* of or having autism.

au·to (ô′tō), *n.* [*pl.* AUTOS (-tōz)], [Colloq.], an automobile. *v.i.* [Colloq.], to go by automobile.

au·to- (ô′tō, ô′tə), [< Gr. *autos*, self], a combining form meaning: 1. *self*, as in *autobiography*, *automobile*: also, before a vowel, **aut-**. 2. [< *automobile*], *self-propelled*, as in *autotruck*.

‡Au·to·bahn (ou′tō-bän′; Eng. ô′tə-bän′), *n.* [*pl.* AUTOBAHNEN (-bä′nən); Eng. AUTOBAHNS (-bänz′)], [G.; *auto* (contr. of *automobil*, automobile) + *bahn*, a course, highway], in Germany, a four-lane highway for fast driving, with a strip of grass, etc. down the middle to separate traffic bound in opposite directions.

au·to·bi·og·ra·pher (ô′tə-bi-og′rə-fẽr, ô′tə-bi-og′rə-fẽr), *n.* a person who writes the story of his life.

au·to·bi·o·graph·ic (ô′tə-bī′ə-graf′ik), *adj.* 1. of or like an autobiography. 2. giving the story of, or based largely on, one's own life: as, an *autobiographic* novel. 3. characteristic of autobiography or autobiographers: as, *autobiographic* touches.

au·to·bi·o·graph·i·cal (ô′tə-bī′ə-graf′i-k'l), *adj.* autobiographic.

au·to·bi·o·graph·i·cal·ly (ô′tə-bī′ə-graf′i-k'l-i, ô′tə-bī′ə-graf′ik-li), *adv.* 1. in an autobiographic manner or form. 2. by means of autobiography.

au·to·bi·og·ra·phy (ô′tə-bi-og′rə-fi, ô′tə-bi-og′rə-fi), *n.* [*pl.* AUTOBIOGRAPHIES (-fiz)], [*auto-* + *bio-* + *-graphy*], 1. the art or practice of writing the story of one's own life. 2. the story of one's own life written by oneself.

au·to·chrome (ô′tə-krōm′), *n.* [< *auto-* + Gr. *chrōma*, color], a kind of photographic plate for taking pictures in color.

au·toch·thon (ô-tok′thən), *n.* [*pl.* AUTOCHTHONS (-thənz), AUTOCHTHONES (-thə-nēz′)], [Gr. *autochthōn*, sprung from the land itself < *autos*, self + *chthōn*, earth, ground], 1. a person who was born where he lives; native. 2. *pl.* the earliest known inhabitants of a place; aborigines. 3. any indigenous animal or plant.

au·toch·thon·ic (ô′tok-thon′ik), *adj.* autochthonous.

au·toch·tho·nous (ô-tok′thə-nəs), *adj.* [*autochthon* + *-ous*], native to a place; indigenous; aboriginal.

au·to·clave (ô′tə-klāv′), *n.* [< Fr.; *auto-* + L. *clavis*, a key], a container for sterilizing, cooking, etc. by superheated steam under pressure. *v.t.* [AUTOCLAVED (-klāvd'), AUTOCLAVING], to sterilize or cook by means of such a device.

au·to·coid (ô'tə-koid'), *n.* an autacoid.

au·toc·ra·cy (ô-tok'rə-si), *n.* [*pl.* AUTOCRACIES (-siz)], [Fr. *autocratie;* Gr. *autokrateia,* absolute power < *autokratēs;* see AUTOCRAT], 1. a kind of government in which one person has supreme power; dictatorship; despotism. 2. a country with this kind of government. 3. unlimited power or authority of one person over others.

au·to·crat (ô'tə-krat'), *n.* [Fr. *autocrate;* Gr. *autokratēs,* absolute ruler < *autos,* self + *kratos,* power, rule], 1. a ruler with supreme power over his people; dictator; despot. 2. anyone having unlimited power over others. 3. any domineering, self-willed person.

au·to·crat·ic (ô'tə-krat'ik), *adj.* of or like an autocrat or autocracy; dictatorial; despotic.

au·to·crat·i·cal (ô'tə-krat'i-k'l), *adj.* autocratic.

au·to-da-fé (ô'tō-də-fā', ou'tō-də-fā'), *n.* [*pl.* AUTOS-DA-FÉ (ô'tōz-, ou'tōz-)], [Port., lit., act of the faith; *auto* (< L. *actus;* see ACT) + *da,* of the + *fé* (< L. *fides,* faith)], 1. in the Inquisition, the ceremony connected with trying and sentencing a heretic. 2. the execution by the secular power of the sentence thus passed; hence, 3. a public burning of a heretic.

‡au·to de fe (ou'tô de fe'), [*pl.* AUTOS DE FE (ou'tôs)], [Sp.], an auto-da-fé.

au·to·dyne (ô'tə-dīn'), *adj.* [*auto-* + *dyne*], designating or of a system of heterodyne radio reception in which a single tube serves both as oscillator and first detector. *n.* 1. an autodyne system. 2. an autodyne receiver.

au·toe·cious (ô-tē'shəs), *adj.* [< *auto-* + Gr. *oikos,* house, dwelling; + *-ous*], in *biology,* passing the entire life cycle on one host, as certain parasites do.

au·toe·cism (ô-tē'siz'm), *n.* the state of being autoecious.

au·to·e·rot·ic (ô'tō-i-rot'ik), *adj.* of or indulging in autoerotism.

au·to·e·rot·i·cism (ô'tō-i-rot'ə-siz'm), *n.* autoerotism.

au·to·er·o·tism (ô'tō-er'ə-tiz'm), *n.* [*auto-* + *erotism:* term coined by Havelock Ellis], 1. sexual sensation arising without external stimulus, direct or indirect, from another person. 2. self-generated sexual activity directed toward oneself, as masturbation.

au·tog·a·mous (ô-tog'ə-məs), *adj.* of or characterized by autogamy.

au·tog·a·my (ô-tog'ə-mi), *n.* [*auto-* + *-gamy*], self-fertilization, as in a flower receiving pollen from its own stamens.

au·to·gen·e·sis (ô'tō-jen'ə-sis), *n.* [*auto-* + *genesis*], spontaneous generation.

au·to·ge·net·ic (ô'tō-jə-net'ik), *adj.* of or resulting from autogenesis.

au·to·ge·net·i·cal·ly (ô'tō-jə-net'i-k'l-i), *adv.* by autogenesis.

au·tog·e·nous (ô-toj'ə-nəs), *adj.* [Gr. *autogenēs* < *autos,* self + *genesis,* origin, birth], 1. self-generated or self-generating. 2. produced in or obtained from oneself: as, an *autogenous* vaccine is one obtained from the patient's body.

au·tog·e·ny (ô-toj'ə-ni), *n.* autogenesis.

au·to·gi·ro (ô'tə-jī'rō), *n.* [*pl.* AUTOGIROS (-rōz)], [< *auto-* + Gr. *gyros,* a circle], a kind of aircraft that moves forward by means of a propeller and is supported in the air mainly by means of another large propeller mounted horizontally above the fuselage and turned by air pressure rather than motor power: also spelled **autogyro:** a trade-mark (**Autogiro**).

au·to·graft (ô'tō-graft', ô'tō-gräft'), *n.* [*auto-* + *graft*], tissue transplanted from one place to another on the same body.

au·to·graph (ô'tə-graf', ô'tə-gräf'), *n.* [L. *autographum,* neut. of *autographus* < Gr. *autographos,* written with one's own hand < *autos,* self + *graphein,* to write], 1. a person's own signature or handwriting. 2. a thing written in one's own handwriting; original manuscript. 3. a copy made by autography. *v.t.* 1. to write (something) with one's own hand. 2. to write one's signature on or in. 3. to reproduce by means of autography.

au·to·graph·ic (ô'tə-graf'ik), *adj.* 1. of, for, or like an autograph or autographs. 2. written in one's own handwriting. 3. of or reproduced by autography (sense 4).

au·to·graph·i·cal (ô'tə-graf'i-k'l), *adj.* autographic.

au·tog·ra·phy (ô-tog'rə-fi), *n.* [< *autograph*], 1. the writing of something with one's own hand. 2. a person's own handwriting. 3. autographs in general. 4. a kind of lithography.

au·to·gy·ro (ô'tə-jī'rō), *n.* an autogiro.

au·to·harp (ô'tō-härp'), *n.* [*auto-* + *harp*], a type of zither for playing chordal accompaniments, fitted with a series of dampers each of which, when depressed, deadens all the strings except those necessary to the required chord.

au·to·hyp·no·sis (ô'tō-hip-nō'sis), *n.* [*auto-* + *hypnosis*], 1. the act of hypnotizing oneself. 2. the hypnosis resulting from this.

au·toi·cous (ô-toi'kəs), *adj.* autoecious.

au·to·in·fec·tion (ô'tō-in-fek'shən), *n.* [*auto-* + *infection*], infection from a source within the organism itself, as from harmful bacteria previously present but heretofore away from vulnerable areas.

au·to·in·oc·u·la·tion (ô'tō-in-ok'yoo-lā'shən), *n.* [*auto-* + *inoculation*], 1. inoculation of a patient with virus from his own body. 2. a spreading of infection from one part to others in the body.

au·to·in·tox·i·ca·tion (ô'tō-in-tok'sə-kā'shən), *n.* [*auto-* + *intoxication*], poisoning by toxic substances generated within the body.

au·to·ist (ô'tō-ist), *n.* a person who drives an automobile; motorist.

au·to·ki·net·ic (ô'tō-ki-net'ik, ô'tō-kī-net'ik), *adj.* [*auto-* + *kinetic*], that moves automatically; self-moving.

au·to·ly·sin (ô'tə-lī'sin), *n.* [*autolysis* + *-in*], a substance that can destroy the cells or tissues of the organism in which it is produced.

au·tol·y·sis (ô-tol'ə-sis), *n.* [*auto-* + *-lysis*], the destruction of cells or tissues by substances within them, as after death or in some diseases.

au·to·lyt·ic (ô'tō-lit'ik), *adj.* of or by autolysis.

au·to·lyze (ô'tə-līz'), *v.t.* & *v.i.* [AUTOLYZED (-līzd'), AUTOLYZING], to affect with or undergo autolysis.

au·to·mat (ô'tə-mat'), *n.* [G. < Gr. *automatos;* see AUTOMATIC], a restaurant in which patrons get food from small compartments with doors opened by putting coins into slots.

au·tom·a·ta (ô-tom'ə-tə), *n.* alternative plural of **automaton.**

au·to·mate (ô'tə-māt'), *v.t.* [AUTOMATED, AUTOMATING], to convert (a factory, etc.) to automation.

au·to·mat·ic (ô'tə-mat'ik), *adj.* [Gr. *automatos,* self-moving, self-thinking < *autos,* self + component < IE. **mntos,* thinking], 1. done without conscious thought or volition, as if mechanically, or from force of habit. 2. moving, operating, etc. by itself; regulating itself: as, *automatic* machinery. *n.* 1. an automatic (or, popularly, semiautomatic) pistol, etc. 2. any automatic machine. —*SYN.* see **spontaneous.**

au·to·mat·i·cal·ly (ô'tə-mat'i-k'l-i, ô'tə-mat'ik-li), *adv.* in an automatic manner; by automatic action.

automatic pilot, a gyropilot.

automatic pistol (or **rifle,** etc.), 1. a pistol, rifle, etc. that uses the force of the explosion of a shell to eject the empty cartridge case and place the next cartridge into the breech so that shots are fired in rapid succession until the trigger is released. 2. in popular usage, a semiautomatic pistol, etc.

automatic tuning, the tuning in of stations on a radio receiver by means of push buttons.

au·to·ma·tion (ô'tə-mā'shən), *n.* [arbitrary coinage, c. 1949], in manufacturing, a system or method in which many or all of the processes of production, movement, and inspection of parts and materials are automatically performed or controlled by self-operating machinery, electronic devices, etc.

au·tom·a·tism (ô-tom'ə-tiz'm), *n.* [*automatic* + *-ism*], 1. the quality or condition of being automatic. 2. automatic action. 3. in *philosophy,* the theory that one's thinking does not control but only accompanies his actions. 4. in *physiology, a)* action independent of outside stimulus. *b)* action not controlled by the will. *c)* the power of such action. 5. in *psychology,* an automatic or unconscious action, as a tic. 6. in *surrealism,* free expression of the unconscious mind without control by the conscious.

au·tom·a·ton (ô-tom'ə-ton', ô-tom'ə-tən), *n.* [*pl.* AUTOMATONS (-tonz', -tənz), AUTOMATA (-tə)], [Gr. *automaton,* neut. of *automatos;* see AUTOMATIC], 1. anything that can move or act of itself. 2. an apparatus with a concealed mechanism that enables it to move or work of itself. 3. a person or animal acting in an automatic or mechanical way.

au·to·mo·bile (ô'tə-mə-bēl', ô'tə-mə-bēl', ô'tə-mō'bēl), *n.* [Fr.; see the *adj.*], a car, usually four-wheeled, propelled by an engine or motor that is part of it, and meant for traveling on streets or roads; motorcar. *v.i.* [AUTOMOBILED (-bēld', -bēld', -bēld), AUTOMOBILING], [Now Rare], to drive or ride in an automobile. *adj.* [*auto-* + *mobile*], 1. (ô'tə-mō'bil), self-moving; self-propelled. 2. of or for an automobile.

au·to·mo·bil·ist (ô'tə-mə-bēl'ist, ô'tə-mō'bil-ist), *n.* [Now Rare], a driver of an automobile; motorist.

au·to·mo·tive (ô'tə-mō'tiv), *adj.* [*auto-* + *-motive*], 1. self-propelling; self-moving. 2. having to do with automobiles.

au·to·nom·ic (ô'tə-nom'ik), *adj.* 1. autonomous. 2. of the autonomic nervous system. 3. in *botany,* resulting from internal causes.

au·to·nom·i·cal (ô'tə-nom'i-k'l), *adj.* autonomic.

autonomic nervous system, the sympathetic and parasympathetic divisions of the nervous system, innervating glands as well as smooth and cardiac muscle: so called because formerly thought to function independently of the central nervous system.

au·ton·o·mist (ô-ton'ə-mist), *n.* a person desiring or advocating autonomy.

au·ton·o·mous (ô-ton′ə-məs), *adj.* [Gr. *autonomos,* independent < *autos,* self + *nomos,* law], 1. of an autonomy. 2. having self-government. 3. in *biology,* functioning independently of other parts. 4. in *botany,* autonomic.

au·ton·o·my (ô-ton′ə-mi), *n.* [Gr. *autonomia*], 1. the quality or condition of being autonomous; self-government. 2. [*pl.* AUTONOMIES (-miz)], any state that governs itself.

au·to·phyte (ô′tə-fīt′), *n.* [*auto-* + *-phyte*], in *botany,* any plant that can make its own food: opposed to *saprophyte.*

au·to·plas·tic (ô′tə-plas′tik), *adj.* 1. of or involving autoplasty. 2. adaptable to the environment.

au·to·plas·ty (ô′tə-plas′ti), *n.* [*auto-* + *-plasty*], the repairing of injuries with tissue from another part of the patient's body.

au·top·sy (ô′top-si, ô′təp-si), *n.* [*pl.* AUTOPSIES (-siz)], [Gr. *autopsia,* a seeing with one's own eyes < *autos,* self + *opsis,* a sight, appearance], 1. [Rare], a personal inspection. 2. an examination and dissection of a dead body to discover the cause of death, damage done by disease, etc.; post-mortem; necropsy.

au·to·some (ô′tə-sōm′), *n.* [*auto-* (self) + chromo*some*], any chromosome other than the sex chromosomes; cf. **heterochromosome.**

au·to·sta·bil·i·ty (ô′tō-stə-bil′ə-ti), *n.* [*auto-* + *stability*], in *mechanics,* 1. stability due to a thing's qualities. 2. stability due to an automatic stabilizing mechanism, as a gyroscope.

au·to·sug·ges·tion (ô′tō-səg-jes′chən), *n.* [*auto-* + *suggestion*], suggestion to oneself arising within oneself and having effects on one's thinking and bodily functions.

au·to·tox·e·mi·a, au·to·tox·ae·mi·a (ô′tō-tok-sē′mi-ə), *n.* [*auto-* + *toxemia*], autointoxication.

au·to·tox·in (ô′tə-tok′sin), *n.* [*auto-* + *toxin*], any toxin or poison produced inside the body.

au·to·trans·form·er (ô′tō-trans-fôr′mẽr), *n.* [*auto-* + *transformer*], in *electricity,* a transformer with part of the winding common to both primary and secondary circuits.

au·to·troph·ic (ô′tə-trof′ik), *adj.* [*auto-* + *trophic*], in *botany,* making its own food: said of a plant in which photosynthesis can occur.

au·to·truck (ô′tō-truk′), *n.* [*auto-* + *truck*], a truck driven by a motor.

au·to·type (ô′tə-tīp′), *n.* [*auto-* + *-type*], 1. any facsimile. 2. in *photography, a)* a process of reproducing in monochrome by a carbon pigment. *b)* a picture thus reproduced.

au·tox·i·da·tion (ô-tok′sə-dā′shən), *n.* [*aut-* + *oxidation*], in *chemistry,* the oxidation of a substance by its exposure to air.

au·tumn (ô′təm), *n.* [ME. *autumpne;* OFr. *autompne;* L. *autumnus, auctumnus;* prob. of Etruscan origin], 1. the season that comes between summer and winter; hence, 2. any period of maturity or of beginning decline. *adj.* of, in, characteristic of, or like autumn. Also called *fall.*

au·tum·nal (ô-tum′n'l), *adj.* [L. *autumnalis*], 1. of, in, or characteristic of autumn. 2. blooming or maturing in autumn. 3. of or in the later period of life.

autumnal equinox, the equinox occurring about September 23.

au·tum·nal·ly (ô-tum′n'l-i), *adv.* in or as in autumn.

autumn crocus, any of various related plants of the lily family, with large, white, pink, or purplish flowers in autumn; colchicum: not related to the true crocus.

au·tun·ite (ô′tən-īt′), *n.* [*Autun,* name of a French city + *-ite*], a yellowish uranium calcium phosphate: it is radioactive and occurs in the form of crystals or scales.

Au·vergne (ō-vûrn′; Fr. ō′ver′ny′), *n.* an old province of central France.

‡**aux** (ō; *before vowel sounds,* ōz), [Fr., contr. of *à les; à,* to + *les,* pl. def. art., the], see **à la.**

aux., auxiliary.

‡**aux armes** (ō′ zȧrm′), [Fr.], to arms!

Aux Cayes (ō′ kā′), Cayes, a seaport in Haiti.

aux·il·ia·ry (ôg-zil′yə-ri, ôg-zil′ə-ri, ôg-zil′i-er′i), *adj.* [L. *auxiliaris,* helpful < *auxilium,* aid < pp. of *augere,* to increase], 1. helping; assisting; giving aid or support. 2. subsidiary. 3. additional; supplementary. *n.* [*pl.* AUXILIARIES (-riz, -iz)], 1. an auxiliary person or thing. 2. *pl.* foreign or allied armed forces aiding those of a country at war. 3. an assisting or supplementary group or organization: as, this club has a women's *auxiliary.* 4. an auxiliary verb. Abbreviated **auxil.**

auxiliary ship, 1. a ship that tends and supplies warships. 2. a naval vessel not used for combat, as a mine layer or hospital ship.

auxiliary verb, a verb that helps form tenses, aspects, moods, or voices of other verbs, as *have, be, may, can, must, do, shall, will.* Examples: *has* and *been* in "He has been working."

aux·in (ôk′sin), *n.* [< Gr. *auxein,* to increase, grow; + *-in*], any of several related substances found in plant sprouts, human urine, etc., which can stimulate cell growth in plant tissues, promote root formation, etc.

aux·o·chrome (ôk′sə-krōm′), *n.* [< Gr. *auxanein,* to increase; + *chrome*], in *chemistry,* any group of atoms, as the -OH radical, which, when added to a chromogen, converts it into a pigment or dye.

Av., Avenue.

av., 1. average. 2. avoirdupois.

A.V., 1. Artillery Volunteers. 2. Authorized Version.

a.v., A/V, ad valorem.

a·vail (ə-vāl′), *v.i. & v.t.* [ME. *availen* < OFr. *a* (L. *ad*), to + *valoir,* to be worth < L. *valere,* to be strong], to be of use, help, worth, or advantage (to), as in accomplishing an end: as, will force alone *avail* us? *n.* use or help; advantage; profit: as, he tried, but to no *avail.*
avail oneself of, to take advantage of (an opportunity, etc.); utilize.

a·vail·a·bil·i·ty (ə-vāl′ə-bil′ə-ti), *n.* 1. the quality or condition of being available. 2. [*pl.* AVAILABILITIES (-tiz)], an available person or thing.

a·vail·a·ble (ə-vāl′ə-b'l), *adj.* 1. that one can avail himself of; that can be used. 2. that can be got, had, or reached; handy; accessible. 3. [Obs.], that can avail. 4. in *law,* valid.

av·a·lanche (av′ə-lanch′, av′ə-länch′), *n.* [Fr. (altered by association with *avaler,* to descend) < *lavanche* < LL. *labina,* slippery place < L. *labes,* a falling down < *labi,* to slip, glide down], 1. a mass of loosened snow, earth, etc. suddenly and swiftly sliding down a mountain and often growing as it descends. 2. anything regarded as like an avalanche: as, an *avalanche* of mail, of blows, etc. *v.i. & v.t.* [AVALANCHED (-lancht′, -länch′), AVALANCHING], to come down (on) like an avalanche.

Av·a·lon, Av·al·lon (av′ə-lon′), *n.* [Fr. < ML. *Avallonis* (*insula*) < Celt.], in *Celtic legend,* the isle of the dead, an island paradise in the west where King Arthur and other heroes supposedly went after death: also **Avilion.**

‡**a·vant-garde** (ȧ′vän′gȧrd′), *n.* [Fr., lit., advance guard], vanguard.

av·a·rice (av′ə-ris), *n.* [ME.; OFr.; L. *avaritia* < *avarus,* greedy < *avere,* to wish, desire], too much desire to get and keep money; greed for riches; cupidity.

av·a·ri·cious (av′ə-rish′əs), *adj.* [Fr. *avaricieux*], having avarice; greedy for riches; grasping and miserly. —*SYN.* see **greedy.**

a·vast (ə-vast′, ə-väst′), *interj.* [< D. *hou'vast, houd vast,* hold fast], in *nautical usage,* stop! cease!

av·a·tar (av′ə-tär′), *n.* [Sans. *avatāra* < *ava-,* down + *tarati,* he goes, passes beyond], 1. in *Hindu religion,* a god's coming down in bodily form to the earth; incarnation. 2. an embodiment; bodily manifestation.

a·vaunt (ə-vônt′, ə-vänt′), *interj.* [ME.; OFr. *avant,* forward; LL. *abante* < L. *ab,* from + *ante,* before], [Archaic], begone! go away!

A.V.C., AVC, American Veterans Committee.

avdp., avoirdupois.

a·ve (ā′vi, ä′vā), *interj.* [L., imperative of *avere,* to be well], 1. hail! 2. farewell! *n.* 1. the salutation *ave.* 2. [A-], the prayer *Ave Maria.* 3. [A-], the time when this prayer is said.

Ave., Avenue.

‡**a·vec plai·sir** (ȧ′vek′ plā′zêr′), [Fr.], with pleasure.

A·vel·la·ne·da (ä-ve′yä-ne′*th*ä, ä-vel′yä-ne′*th*ä), *n.* a city in Argentina, on the Rio de la Plata: suburb of Buenos Aires: pop., 386,000.

A·ve Ma·ri·a (ä′vi mə-rē′ə, ā′vi mə-rī′ə), [L.], 1. "Hail, Mary," the first words of the Latin version of a prayer to the Virgin Mary used in the Roman Catholic Church. 2. this prayer. 3. any of several musical settings of this.

av·e·na·ceous (av′i-nā′shəs), *adj.* [L. *avenaceus* < *avena,* oats], of or like oats or the oat grasses.

a·venge (ə-venj′), *v.t. & v.i.* [AVENGED (-venjd′), AVENGING], [ME. *avengen;* OFr. *avengier; a-* (L. *ad*), to + *vengier* < L. *vindicare,* to claim, punish, avenge], 1. to get revenge for (an injury, etc.). 2. to take vengeance on behalf of, as for a wrong.
SYN.—**avenge** implies the infliction of deserved or just punishment for wrongs or oppressions; **revenge** implies the infliction of punishment as an act of retaliation, usually for an injury against oneself, and connotes personal malice, bitter resentment, etc. as the moving force.

av·ens (av′inz), *n.* [ME. & OFr. *avence*], any of a number of related, usually small plants of the rose family, with white, yellow, red, or purple flowers.

Av·en·tine (av′ən-tīn′, av′ən-tin), *n.* [L. *Aventinus* (*mons*), Aventine (hill)], one of the seven hills on which Rome was built. *adj.* of this hill.

a·ven·tu·rine, a·ven·tu·rin (ə-ven′chẽr-in), *n.* [Fr.; It. (*vetro*) *avventurino,* aventurine (glass): so named from resembling the mineral *avventurina* (< *avventura,* chance), so named from its rarity; see ADVENTURE], 1. a sort of glass flecked with spangles, as from copper filings or bits of chromic oxide. 2. a translucent quartz shot through with sparkling bits of mica, etc.

a·ve·nue (av′ə-nōō′, av′ə-nū′), *n.* [Fr. < *avenir*, to happen, come < L. *advenire; ad-*, to + *venire*, to come], 1. a way of approach or departure. 2. a roadway, pathway, or drive, often bordered with trees. 3. a street, especially a wide one; thoroughfare: abbreviated **Av., Ave.**

a·ver (ə-vũr′), *v.t.* [AVERRED (-vũrd′), AVERRING], [ME. *averren;* OFr. *averrer*, to confirm < L. *ad*, to + *verus*, true], 1. to declare to be true; assert; affirm. 2. in *law*, to prove; justify. —*SYN.* see **assert.**

av·er·age (av′rij, av′ẽr-ij), *n.* [prob. < Fr. *avarie*, damage to ship or goods, mooring charges; It. *avaria* < Ar. *'awar*, damaged goods; order of main sense development (in *n.*), 3 *a*, 3 *c*, 1, 2], 1. the numerical result obtained by dividing the sum of two or more quantities by the number of quantities; an arithmetical mean: abbreviated **av.** 2. an approximation to this; usual or normal kind, amount, quality, rate, etc.: as, his opinion is the *average*. 3. in *marine law*, *a*) a loss incurred by damage to a ship at sea or to its cargo. *b*) an incurring of such loss. *c*) the equitable division of such loss among the interested parties. *d*) a charge arising from such loss. *adj.* 1. constituting a numerical average: as, his *average* speed is high. 2. usual; normal; ordinary. 3. in *marine law*, assessed in accordance with the laws of average. *v.i.* [AVERAGED (-rijd, -ijd), AVERAGING], 1. to be or amount to on an average: as, the children *average* six years of age. 2. to buy or sell more shares, goods, etc. so as to get a better average price. *v.t.* 1. to calculate the average or mean of. 2. to do, take, etc. on an average: as, he *averages* eight hours of work a day. 3. to divide proportionately among more than two: as, they *averaged* the loss among themselves.

average out, [Colloq.], to arrive at an average eventually.

on the average, as an average quantity, rate, etc.: as, he works eight hours a day, *on the average*.

SYN.—**average** refers to the result obtained by dividing a sum by the number of quantities added (the *average* of 7, 9, 17 is 33 ÷ 3 or 11) and in extended use is applied to the usual or ordinary kind, instance, etc.; **mean** commonly designates a figure intermediate between two extremes (the *mean* temperature for a day with a high of 56° and a low of 34° is 45°) and figuratively implies moderation (the golden *mean*); the **median** is the middle number or point in a series arranged in order of size (the *median* grade in the group 50, 55, 85, 88, 92, is 85, the *average* is 76); **norm** implies a standard of average performance for a given group (a child below the *norm* for his age in reading comprehension). See also **normal.**

a·ver·ment (ə-vũr′mənt), *n.* 1. an averring or being averred. 2. something averred; assertion.

A·ver·nus (ə-vũr′nəs), *n.* [L.], 1. a small lake in an extinct volcano near Naples, Italy, at the edge of which the entrance to Hades was anciently said to be. 2. in *Roman mythology*, Hades; hell.

A·ver·ro·ës (ə-ver′ō-ēz′), *n.* (Ar. *ibn-Rushd*), Moslem philosopher and physician; 1126–1198.

Av·er·ro·ism (av′ə-rō′iz′m), *n.* the teachings of Averroës, especially that the soul is mortal.

a·verse (ə-vũrs′), *adj.* [L. *aversus*, pp. of *avertere;* see AVERT], 1. unwilling; set against; reluctant. 2. in *botany*, turned away from the main stem or axis: opposed to *adverse*. —*SYN.* see **reluctant.**

a·ver·sion (ə-vũr′zhən, ə-vũr′shən), *n.* [L. *aversio* < *aversus;* see AVERSE], 1. an averting; turning away. 2. intense or definite dislike; antipathy; repugnance. 3. the object arousing such dislike. 4. reluctance.

SYN.—**aversion** and **antipathy** both imply an ingrained feeling against that which is disagreeable or offensive, **aversion** stressing avoidance or rejection, and **antipathy,** active hostility; **repugnance** emphasizes the emotional resistance or opposition one offers to that which is incompatible with one's ideas, tastes, etc.; **loathing** suggests a feeling of extreme disgust or intolerance; **revulsion** suggests a drawing back or away from in disgust, horror, etc.; **abhorrence** implies a feeling of extreme aversion or repugnance. —*ANT.* attraction, affinity.

a·vert (ə-vũrt′), *v.t.* [L. *avertere*, to turn away; *a-* (*ab-*), from + *vertere*, to turn], 1. to turn away: as, he *averts* his glance from ugly things. 2. to prevent; ward off or avoid: as, to *avert* trouble. —*SYN.* see **prevent.**

A·ves (ā′vēz), *n.pl.* [L., pl. of *avis*, bird], in *zoology*, the class of vertebrates comprising the birds.

A·ves·ta (ə-ves′tə), *n.* [< Per.], the sacred writings of the ancient Zoroastrian religion and of its present-day form among the Parsees.

A·ves·tan (ə-ves′tən), *adj.* 1. of the Avesta. 2. of the Indo-European, Iranian language in which the Avesta was written. *n.* this language, sometimes identified as that of the Medes.

a·vi·an (ā′vi-ən), *adj.* [< L. *avis*, bird], of Aves; of birds.

a·vi·ar·y (ā′vi-er′i), *n.* [*pl.* AVIARIES (-iz)], [L. *aviarium* < *avis*, bird], a large cage for keeping many birds.

a·vi·ate (ā′vi-āt′, av′i-āt′), *v.i.* [AVIATED (-id), AVIATING], [back-formation < *aviation*], to fly in, especially to operate, an aircraft.

a·vi·a·tion (ā′vi-ā′shən, av′i-ā′shən), *n.* [Fr. < L. *avis*, bird], the art or science of flying airplanes; making and operating heavier-than-air craft: abbreviated **avn.**

a·vi·a·tor (ā′vi-ā′tẽr, av′i-ā′tẽr), *n.* [< L. *avis*, bird; + *-ator*], a person who flies airplanes; pilot; airman; flier.

a·vi·a·trix (ā′vi-ā′triks, av′i-ā′triks), *n.* a woman aviator: also **a·vi·a·tress** (ā′vi-ā′tris, av′i-ā′tris).

Av·i·cen·na (av′i-sen′ə), *n.* (Ar. *ibn-Sina*), Moslem physician and philosopher; 980–1037 A.D.

a·vi·cul·ture (ā′vi-kul′chẽr), *n.* [< L. *avis*, bird + *cultura*, culture], the raising and care of birds.

av·id (av′id), *adj.* [L. *avidus* < *avere*, to desire], very eager or greedy. —*SYN.* see **eager.**

av·i·din (av′i-din), *n.* [*avid* + *-in:* so named because of its peculiar biotin-binding capacity], a substance, protein in nature, found in egg white and neutralized in action by biotin, which forms a compound with it.

a·vid·i·ty (ə-vid′ə-ti), *n.* [Fr. *avidité;* L. *aviditas* < *avidus;* see AVID], 1. great eagerness; greed. 2. [Rare], in *chemistry*, *a*) the strength of a base or acid in terms of its dissociation. *b*) degree of affinity.

a·vi·fau·na (ā′vi-fô′nə), *n.* [< L. *avis*, bird; + *fauna*], all the birds of a region.

A·vi·gnon (å′vē′nyôn′), *n.* a city in southern France, on the Rhone River: pop., 60,000 (1946): seat of the papacy (1309–1377).

Ávila Camacho, Manuel, see **Camacho, Manuel Ávila.**

A·vil·ion (ə-vil′yən), *n.* [Fr.], Avalon.

a·vir·u·lent (ā-vir′yoo-lənt, ā-vir′oo-lənt), *adj.* not virulent or no longer virulent, as certain bacteria, etc.

a·vi·so (ə-vī′zō), *n.* [*pl.* AVISOS (-zōz)], [Sp.; LL. *advisum;* see ADVICE], 1. advice; information; notification. 2. a dispatch boat.

a·vi·ta·min·o·sis (ā-vī′tə-min-ō′sis), *n.* [*a-*, without + *vitamin* + *-osis*], a pathological condition caused by not having enough vitamins in one's food.

Av·lo·na (äv-lô′nä), *n.* Valona, a seaport in Albania.

avn., aviation.

av·o·ca·do (av′ə-kä′dō, ä′və-kä′dō), *n.* [*pl.* AVOCADOS (-dōz)], [Mex. Sp. *avogato* < Nahuatl *ahuacatl*], 1. a thick-skinned, pear-shaped tropical fruit, yellowish green to purplish black, with a single large seed and yellow, buttery flesh, used in salads; alligator pear. 2. the tree that it grows on.

AVOCADO

av·o·ca·tion (av′ə-kā′shən), *n.* [L. *avocatio*, a calling away < pp. of *avocare; a-* (*ab-*), away + *vocare*, to call], 1. something one does in addition to his vocation or regular work, and usually for fun; hobby: the current sense. 2. one's regular work; vocation: now generally avoided to prevent confusion with sense 1. 3. [Obs.], the fact of being called away or distracted from something.

a·voc·a·to·ry (ə-vok′ə-tôr′i, ə-vok′ə-tō′ri), *adj.* [< ML. *avocatorius;* see AVOCATION], calling, or summoning, back or away; recalling.

av·o·cet (av′ə-set′), *n.* [Fr. *avocette;* It. *avocetta*], any of a number of related long-legged wading birds with webbed feet and a slender bill that curves upward: also spelled **avoset.**

A·vo·ga·dro, A·me·de·o (ä′me-de′ô ä′vô-gä′drô; Eng. ä′və-gä′drō), Count of Quaregna, 1776–1856; Italian chemist and physicist; known for his work on gases.

A·vo·ga·dro's law (ä′və-gä′drōz), the theory, formulated by Avogadro, that equal volumes of all gases under identical conditions of temperature and pressure contain equal numbers of molecules.

a·void (ə-void′), *v.t.* [ME. *avoiden;* Anglo-Fr. *avoider;* OFr. *esvuidier, évuider*, to empty < *es-* (< L. *ex*), out + *vuidier;* see VOID], 1. to make void; annul, invalidate, or quash (a plea, etc. in law). 2. to keep away from; shun. 3. to get out of; shirk. 4. [Obs.], to void; empty. —*SYN.* see **escape.**

a·void·a·ble (ə-void′ə-b'l), *adj.* that can be avoided, or shunned.

a·void·ance (ə-void′əns), *n.* 1. an avoiding or being avoided. 2. a making void; annulment. 3. a being vacant or becoming vacant, as of a church benefice.

av·oir·du·pois (av′ẽr-də-poiz′, av′ẽr-də-poiz′), *n.* [ME. *aver de poiz;* OFr. *aveir de peis; aveir*, goods (< L. *habere*, to have) + *de* (< L. *de*), from + *peis* (< L. *pensum*), weight], 1. the system of weights based on a pound of 16 ounces, etc.: abbreviated **av., avdp., avoir.:** see **avoirdupois weight.** 2. [Colloq.], heaviness or weight, especially of a person.

avoirdupois weight, an English and American system of weighing in which 16 drams = 1 ounce, 16 ounces = 1 pound, and 2,000 pounds = 1 ton: see also **apothecaries' weight, troy weight.**

A·von (ā′vən, av′ən), *n.* any of three rivers in England, especially the one on which lies Stratford, Shakespeare's birthplace.

av·o·set (av′ə-set′), *n.* an avocet.

‡**à vo·tre san·té** (å′ vô′tr′ sän′tā′), [Fr.], to your health: a toast in drinking.

a·vouch (ə-vouch′), *v.t.* [ME. *avouchen;* OFr. *avochier*, to affirm positively < L. *advocare;* see ADVOCATE], 1. to vouch for; guarantee. 2. to declare the truth of; assert; affirm. 3. to acknowledge openly; avow. *v.i.* to give assurance. —*SYN.* see **assert.**

a·vow (ə-vou′), *v.t.* [ME. *avowen;* OFr. *avouer* < L. *advocare;* see ADVOCATE], 1. to declare openly; admit frankly; confess. 2. to acknowledge (oneself) to be: as, he *avowed* himself a patriot. —*SYN.* see **acknowledge.**

a·vow·al (ə-vou′əl), *n.* [< *avow*], open acknowledgment or declaration; frank admission; confession.

a·vowed (ə-voud′), *adj.* [pp. of *avow*], openly acknowledged; self-confessed; known: as, an *avowed* fascist.

a·vow·ed·ly (ə-vou′id-li), *adv.* by avowal; admittedly.

‡á vues·tra sa·lud (á vwes′trä sä-lōōd′), [Sp.], to your health: a toast in drinking.

a·vul·sion (ə-vul′shən), *n.* [L. *avulsio* < *a-*, from + pp. of *vellere,* to pull], 1. a tearing away; separation by force. 2. a part thus torn. 3. in *law,* the sudden transference of a piece of land from one person's estate to another's without change of ownership, as by a change in the course of a stream.

a·vun·cu·lar (ə-vuŋ′kyoo-lẽr), *adj.* [< L. *avunculus,* maternal uncle, dim. of *avus,* ancestor; + *-ar*], of, like, or in the relationship of, an uncle.

aw (ô), *interj.* a sound of protest, dislike, disgust, etc.

a·wa (ə-wô′, ə-wä′), *adv.* [Scot.], away.

a·wait (ə-wāt′), *v.t.* [ME. *awaiten;* OFr. *awaitier; a-* (L. *ad*), to + *waitier,* to watch], 1. to wait for; expect. 2. to be in store for; be ready for. —*SYN.* see **expect.**

a·wake (ə-wāk′), *v.t.* [AWOKE (-wōk′) or AWAKED (-wākt′), AWAKED or AWOKE, AWAKING; *obs.* pp. AWOKEN, AWAKEN], [a merging of two words: ME. *awaken* < AS. *awacan* (*on-* + *wacan,* to arise, awake) & ME. *awakien* < AS. *awacian* (*on-* + *wacian,* to be awake, watch)], 1. to rouse from sleep; wake; hence, 2. to rouse from inactivity; activize. 3. to call forth (memories, fear, etc.). *v.i.* 1. to come out of sleep; wake. 2. to become active. *adj.* [< obs. pp. *awaken*], 1. not asleep. 2. active; alert.

awake to, 1. to make or become aware of. 2. aware of.

a·wak·en (ə-wāk′ən), *v.t. & v.i.* [ME. *awakenen;* AS. *awæcnian,* to awaken, originate < *on-* + *wæcnian,* to awake, come into being], to awake; wake up; rouse. —*SYN.* see **stir.**

a·wak·en·ing (ə-wāk′ən-iŋ), *n. & adj.* 1. (a) waking up. 2. (an) arousing or reviving, as of impulses, religion, etc.

a·ward (ə-wôrd′), *v.t.* [ME. *awarden;* Anglo-Fr. *awarder;* ONorm.Fr. *eswarder;* OFr. *esgarder; es-* (< L. *ex*) + *garder;* see GUARD], 1. to give, as by legal decision; adjudge: as, the plaintiff was *awarded* his damages. 2. to give as the result of judging or considering; grant: as, we *award* a prize for the best essay. *n.* 1. a decision, as by judges. 2. something awarded; prize. —*SYN.* see **reward.**

a·ware (ə-wâr′), *adj.* [ME.; AS. *gewær* < *wær,* cautious], conscious; knowing; informed; cognizant.

SYN.—**aware** implies having knowledge of something through alertness in observing or in interpreting what one sees, hears, feels, etc. (to be *aware* of a fact); **conscious** implies awareness of a sensation, feeling, fact, condition, etc. and may suggest mere recognition or a focusing of attention (*conscious* of a draft in the room, *conscious* humor); one is **cognizant** of something when one has certain or special knowledge of it through observation or information (*cognizant* of the terms of the will); **sensible** implies awareness of something that is not expressed directly or explicitly (*sensible* of their solemn grief).

a·wash (ə-wäsh′, ə-wôsh′), *adv. & adj.* [*a-*, on + *wash*], 1. just above the surface of the water. 2. floating on the water.

a·way (ə-wā′), *adv.* [ME. *away, aweie;* AS. *aweg* < phr. *on weg* < *on,* on + *weg,* way, in the sense "from this (that) place"], 1. from any given place: as, he ran *away.* 2. far: as, *away* behind. 3. off; aside: as, the land dropped *away.* 4. from one's possession: as, don't give *away* the secret. 5. out of existence: as, the sound faded *away.* 6. at once: as, fire *away.* 7. without stopping; continuously: as, he worked *away* all night. *adj.* 1. not present; absent; gone: as, he is *away.* 2. at a distance: as, a mile *away.* *interj.* 1. begone! 2. let's go!

away with, 1. take away. 2. go or come away. Used generally as an imperative expression without a verb.

do away with, 1. to get rid of; put an end to. 2. to get rid of by killing.

where away? in what direction?: said of something being sighted from a ship.

awe (ô), *n.* [ME. *age, aghe, awe* < ON. *agi;* akin to AS. *ege,* Goth. *agis,* OHG. *egī;* IE. base **agh-*, to be afraid or depressed], 1. a mixed feeling of reverence, fear, and wonder, caused by something majestic, sublime, etc. 2. [Archaic], the power of inspiring fearful reverence. 3. [Obs.], terror. *v.t.* [AWED (ôd), AWING], to inspire awe in; fill with awe.

stand (or **be**) **in awe of,** to respect and fear.

SYN.—**awe** refers to a feeling of fearful or profound respect or wonder inspired by the greatness, superiority, grandeur, etc. of a person or thing and suggests an immobilizing effect; **reverence** is applied to a feeling of deep respect mingled with love for something one holds sacred or inviolable and suggests a display of homage, deference, etc.; **veneration** implies worshipful reverence for a person or thing regarded as hallowed or sacred and specifically suggests acts of religious devotion; **dread,** as it comes into comparison here, suggests extreme fear mixed with awe or reverence (a *dread* of divine retribution).

a·weath·er (ə-weth′ẽr), *adv. & adj.* [*a-*, on + *weather*], in *nautical usage,* in the direction from which the wind is blowing; to windward.

a·weigh (ə-wā′), *adj.* [*a-*, on + *weigh*], in *nautical usage,* clearing the bottom; being weighed: said of an anchor.

awe·less (ô′lis), *adj.* having no awe: also spelled **awless.**

awe·some (ô′səm), *adj.* [*awe* + *-some*], 1. inspiring awe. 2. showing awe; feeling awe.

awe-strick·en (ô′strik′′n), *adj.* awe-struck.

awe-struck (ô′struk′), *adj.* filled with awe.

aw·ful (ô′fool), *adj.* [ME. *awful, agheful;* see AWE & -FUL], 1. inspiring awe. 2. terrifying; appalling. 3. worthy of reverence and solemn respect. 4. (ô′f′l), [Colloq.], *a)* very bad, ugly, disagreeable, unpleasant, etc.: as, an *awful* joke. *b)* great: as, an *awful* bore.

aw·ful·ly (ô′fool-i), *adv.* 1. in a way to inspire awe. 2. (ô′f′l-i, ô′fli), [Colloq.], *a)* very; extremely: as, an *awfully* pretty dress. *b)* very much; extremely.

a·while (ə-hwīl′), *adv.* [AS. *ane hwile,* a while], for a while; for a short time.

awk·ward (ôk′wẽrd), *adj.* [ME. *awkwarde* < ON. *afug* or AS. **afoc,* turned backward + AS. *-weard,* Eng. *-ward*], 1. clumsy; ungainly; bungling: as, an *awkward* person. 2. inconvenient to use; hard to handle; unwieldy: as, an *awkward* tool. 3. inconvenient; uncomfortable; cramped: as, an *awkward* position. 4. embarrassing; inopportune: as, an *awkward* remark. 5. not easy to manage; delicate: as, his attitude made the situation *awkward.*

SYN.—**awkward** implies unfitness for smooth, easy functioning and has the broadest application of the terms here, suggesting ungracefulness, unmanageableness, inconvenience, tactlessness, embarrassment, etc. (an *awkward* implement, step, position, remark, etc.); **clumsy,** emphasizing stiffness or bulkiness, suggests a lack of flexibility or dexterity, unwieldiness, etc. (a *clumsy* build, *clumsy* galoshes); **maladroit** and **inept** both imply tactlessness in social relations, **maladroit** often emphasizing this as a tendency and **inept** stressing inappropriateness of a particular act or remark.—*ANT.* deft, handy, graceful.

awkward age, early adolescence, characterized by rapid growth, awkward behavior, and emotional instability.

awl (ôl), *n.* [ME. *alle, awl, ouel, awel* < AS. *æl, ealle, awel;* akin to OHG. *āla;* IE. base **ē(i)la,* awl, bodkin, pricker, as in Sans. *ārā,* awl], a small, pointed tool for making holes in wood, leather, etc.

A

B

TYPES OF AWL

A, peg awl; B, sewing awl

A.W.L., a.w.l., absent (or absence) with leave.

aw·less (ô′lis), *adj.* aweless.

awl·wort (ôl′wũrt′), *n.* a small water plant of the mustard family, bearing clusters of awl-shaped leaves around the root.

awn (ôn), *n.* [ME. *awne, agun* < ON. *ǫgn* (pl. *agnir*), chaff; akin to AS. *egenu,* Goth. *ahana,* OHG. *agana;* IE. base **ak-*, sharp, pointed (with *-n* suffix); cf. ACUTE], the bristly fibers or beard on a head of barley, oats, etc.

awned (ônd), *adj.* having awns.

awn·ing (ôn′iŋ), *n.* [? < MFr. *auvans,* pl. of *auvent,* cloth shade for store window; + *-ing*], a piece of canvas stretched over a frame before a window, etc. as a protection from the sun or rain.

a·woke (ə-wōk′), alternative past tense and occasional past participle of **awake.**

a·wok·en (ə-wōk′ən), obsolete past participle of **awake.**

A.W.O.L., a.w.o.l., absent (or absence) without leave: often pronounced (ā′wôl′).

a·wry (ə-rī′), *adv. & adj.* [ME. *a wrie;* see A- (on) & WRY], 1. with a twist to a side; not straight; askew. 2. wrong; amiss: as, our plans went *awry.*

ax, axe (aks), *n.* [*pl.* AXES (ak′siz)], [ME.; AS. *eax, æx;* akin to Goth. *aqizi,* ON. *ǫx,* OS. *acus,* OHG. *ahhus;* Gmc. base **aqwizi,* **akusi* < IE. **agw(e)sī* as in L. *ascia,* carpenter's ax], 1. a tool for chopping trees and splitting wood: it has a long wooden handle and a metal head with a blade usually on only one side. 2. any similar tool or weapon, as a battle-ax, headsman's ax, etc. *v.t.* [AXED (akst), AXING], to trim with an ax.

get the ax, 1. [Colloq.], to be executed by beheading. 2. [Slang], to be discharged from one's job.

have an ax to grind, [Colloq.], to have an object of one's own to gain or promote.

ax., 1. axiom 2. axis.

Ax·el (ak′səl), [Sw., supporter ?], a masculine name.
ax·es (ak′sēz), *n.* plural of **axis.**
ax·es (ak′siz), *n.* plural of **ax.**
ax·i·al (ak′si-əl), *adj.* 1. of or like an axis. 2. forming an axis. 3. around or along an axis.
ax·i·al·ly (ak′si-ə-li), *adv.* in the direction or line of the axis.
ax·il (ak′sil), *n.* [< L. *axilla;* see AXILLA], the upper angle between a leaf, twig, etc. and the stem from which it grows.

AXIL

ax·ile (ak′sil, ak′sīl), *adj.* [*axis* + *-ile*], in *botany,* in or of the axis.
ax·il·la (ak-sil′ə), *n.* [*pl.* AXILLAE (-ē), AXILLAS (-əz)], [L., armpit < *ala,* wing], 1. the armpit. 2. in *botany,* an axil.
ax·il·lar (ak′sə-lẽr), *adj.* axillary. *n.* one of the stiff feathers on the underside of a bird's wing where it joins the body.
ax·il·la·ry (ak′sə-ler′i), *adj.* [Fr. *axillaire*], 1. in *anatomy,* of or near the axilla. 2. in *botany,* of, in, or growing from an axil. *n.* in *zoology,* an axillar.
ax·i·ol·o·gy (ak′si-ol′ə-ji), *n.* [< Gr. *axios,* worthy; + *-logy*], the branch of philosophy dealing with the nature of value and the types of value, as in morals, aesthetics, religion, and metaphysics.
ax·i·om (ak′si-əm), *n.* [Fr. *axiome;* L. *axioma;* Gr. *axiōma,* authority, authoritative sentence < *axioun,* to think worthy < *axios,* worthy], 1. a statement universally accepted as true; maxim. 2. an established principle or law of a science, art, etc. 3. in *logic & mathematics,* a statement that needs no proof because its truth is obvious; self-evident proposition: abbreviated **ax.**
ax·i·o·mat·ic (ak′si-ə-mat′ik), *adj.* [Gr. *axiōmatikos*], 1. of or like an axiom; self-evident. 2. full of maxims; aphoristic.
ax·i·o·mat·i·cal·ly (ak′si-ə-mat′i-k'l-i, ak′si-ə-mat′ik-li), *adv.* 1. by using axioms. 2. self-evidently.
ax·is (ak′sis), *n.* [*pl.* AXES (-sēz)], [L., axle, axis], 1. an imaginary or real straight line on which an object supposedly or actually rotates: as, the *axis* of a planet. 2. a straight line around which the parts of a thing, system, etc. are regularly arranged: as, the *axis* of a picture. 3. a main line of motion, development, etc. 4. an alignment between countries, groups, etc. for promoting their purposes: now usually a derogatory term. 5. in *aeronautics,* any of three straight lines, the first running through the center of the fuselage lengthwise, the second at right angles to this and parallel to the horizontal airfoils, and the third perpendicular to the first two at their point of intersection. 6. in *anatomy, a*) the second cervical vertebra. *b*) any of several axial parts, especially the spinal column. 7. in *botany, a*) the main stem of a plant. *b*) the central system of a cluster. 8. in *geometry, a*) a straight line through the center of a plane figure or solid, especially one around which the parts are symmetrically arranged. *b*) a straight line for measurement or reference, as in a graph: see also **abscissa, ordinate.** 9. in *optics, a*) a straight line through the centers of both surfaces of a lens (*optic axis*). *b*) a straight line from the object of vision to the fovea of the eye (*visual axis*). Abbreviated **ax.**

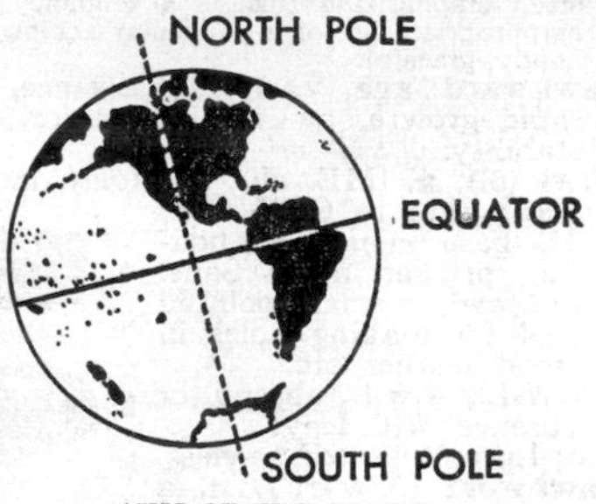

AXIS OF THE EARTH

the Axis, the countries aligned against the United Nations in World War II: originally applied to Nazi Germany and Fascist Italy (Rome-Berlin Axis), later extended to include Japan, etc. (Rome-Berlin-Tokyo Axis).
ax·is (ak′sis), *n.* [L.], a white-spotted deer of India and southern Asia, with slender, sparsely branched antlers: also called *hog deer.*
ax·le (ak′s'l), *n.* [ME. *axel* (only in comp. *axeltre*); see AXLETREE], 1. a rod on or with which a wheel revolves. 2. an axletree. 3. the spindle at either end of an axletree.
ax·le·tree (ak′s'l-trē′), *n.* [ME. *axeltre;* ON. *öxultre; öxull,* axle + *tre,* tree, beam; *axle-* is akin to AS. *eax,* OHG. *ahsa;* IE. base **aĝes-,* **aks-,* thing on which something turns (< **aĝ-,* to drive), seen also in AS. *eaxel,* L. *axis,* axle], the bar connecting two opposite wheels of a carriage, wagon, etc.
ax·man (aks′mən), *n.* [*pl.* AXMEN (-mən)], a person who uses an ax.
Ax·min·ster (aks′min-stẽr), *n.* a type of carpet with a long, soft pile; formerly made by hand in Axminster, England: now generally machine-made.
ax·o·lotl (ak′sə-lot′'l), *n.* [Sp.; Nahuatl, lit., servant of water], any of various salamanders of Mexico and the western United States that mature sexually and breed in the larval stage: used for food in Mexico.

AXOLOTL (8 in. long)

ax·on (ak′son), *n.* [Mod. L.; Gr. *axōn,* axis, axle], that part of a nerve cell through which impulses travel away from the cell body.
ax·one (ak′sōn), *n.* an axon.
ax·seed (aks′sēd′), *n.* [*ax* + *seed:* so named from the shape of the pods], any of a group of European plants of the bean family, now cultivated in the United States, having pinnate leaves and pink or white flowers.
Ax·um (äk′soom), *n.* Aksum.
ay (ā), *adv.* [Archaic], always: also spelled **aye.**
ay (ī), *adv. & n.* yes: also spelled **aye.**
ay (ā), *interj.* a sound expressing sorrow, distress, etc.
A·ya·cu·cho (ä′yä-kōō′chô), *n.* a city in south central Peru: pop., 20,000: site of a battle (1824) which secured for Peru its independence from Spain.
ay·ah (ä′yə), *n.* [Anglo-Ind. < Hindu *āya* < Port. *aia,* governess], a native nursemaid or lady's maid in India.
Ay·din (ī-dēn′), *n.* a city in western Turkey, southwest of Smyrna: pop., 12,000: also spelled **Aidin.**
aye (ā), *adv.* [ME. *ai, ay* < ON. *ei*], [Archaic], always; ever.
aye (ī), *adv.* [? < *aye* (always)], yes; yea. *n.* an affirmative vote or a person voting in the affirmative.
aye-aye (ī′ī′), *n.* [Fr. < Malagasy; origin echoic], a kind of lemur of Madagascar, with shaggy, generally brown fur, large ears, pointed claws, and a long, bushy tail.
Ayesha, Ayeshah, see **Aisha.**
a·yin (ä′yēn, ä′yin), *n.* [Heb. *'ayin*], the sixteenth letter of the Hebrew alphabet (ע), representing originally a voiced velar fricative, but now used only with diacritical marks to indicate vowel sounds: see **alphabet,** table.
Ay·ma·ra (ī′mä-rä′), *n.* 1. [*pl.* AYMARAS (-räz′), AYMARA], a member of a South American Indian tribe living largely in Bolivia and Peru and believed to have been the builders of a great ancient culture, later supplanted by the Incan. 2. their language.
Ay·ma·ran (ī′mä-rän′), *adj.* of the Aymaras or their language. *n.* Aymara, the language.
Ayr (âr, ar), *n.* 1. a county of southwestern Scotland, on the Firth of Clyde: pop., 299,000. 2. its county seat: pop., 41,600.
Ayr·shire (âr′shir, ar′shir), *n.* any of a breed of dairy cattle which are brown or red with white markings, originally from the county of Ayr, Scotland. *adj.* 1. of this breed. 2. of the county of Ayr.
‡a·yun·ta·mien·to (ä-yōōn′tä-myen′tô), *n.* [*pl.* AYUNTAMIENTOS (-tôs)], [Sp.], 1. a municipal government. 2. the place where it is located; city hall or town hall.
A·yu·thi·a (ä-ū′tē-ä; Eng. ä-ū′thē-ə), *n.* a city in central Thailand: former capital: pop., 50,000.
az- (az), azo-.
a·zal·ea (ə-zāl′yə), *n.* [Gr. *azalea,* fem. of *azaleos,* dry: so called because it thrives in dry soil], 1. any of a number of related flowering shrubs resembling the rhododendron: the flowers have various colors and are usually fragrant. 2. the flower of any of these plants.
‡a·zan (ä-zän′), *n.* [< Ar. *ādhan*], the Moslem summons to prayer: it is usually called five times a day by the muezzin, from a minaret on the mosque.
A·za·ña, Ma·nuel (mä-nwel′ ä-thä′nyä), 1880–1940; Spanish statesman; president of the Spanish Republic (1936–1939).
A·za·zel (ə-zā′zəl, az′ə-zel′), *n.* [Heb. *'azāzēl,* lit., removal], in Milton's *Paradise Lost,* one of the angels who rebelled with Satan.
a·zed·a·rach (ə-zed′ə-rak′), *n.* [< Fr. *azédarac* (via Sp.) < Ar. *azādirakht* < Per. *azād dirakht,* lit., aristocratic tree], 1. the chinaberry tree (sense 1). 2. the bark of this tree, used in medicine as a cathartic, emetic, etc.
A·zer·bai·jan, Az·er·bai·dzhan (ä′zẽr-bī-jän′, az′ẽr-bī-jän′), *n.* 1. a province of northwestern Iran: capital, Tabriz. 2. the Azerbaijan Soviet Socialist Republic. See **Iran and Iraq,** map.
A·zer·bai·ja·ni (ä′zẽr-bī-jä′ni, az′ẽr-bī-jä′ni), *n.* [*pl.* AZERBAIJANIS (-niz), AZERBAIJANI], 1. a native or inhabitant of Azerbaijan. 2. one of a Turkic people of Azerbaijan. 3. the Turkic dialect spoken there.
Azerbaijan Soviet Socialist Republic, a republic of the U.S.S.R., on the Caspian Sea, in Transcaucasia: area, 33,200 sq. mi.; pop., 3,210,000; capital, Baku.
A·zil·ian (ə-zil′yən), *adj.* [< Mas d'*Azil,* cavern in the French Pyrenees, where traces were found], denoting or of a stage of prehistoric culture after the Magdalenian and before the Neolithic.

az·i·muth (az'ə-məth), *n.* [ME. *azymuth;* OFr. *azimut* < Ar. *as-sumūt; as* < *al,* the + *sumūt,* pl. of *samt,* way, path], in *astronomy,* etc., distance in angular degrees (or mils, in military usage) in a clockwise direction from the north point or, in the Southern Hemisphere, south point; arc of the horizon measured from such a point to a vertical arc passing from the zenith through the center of a star.

NORTH STAR · AZIMUTH 30° · WEST · EAST · SOUTH

AZIMUTH

az·in (az'in), *n.* an azine.

az·ine (az'ēn, az'in), *n.* [*az-* + *-ine*], any of a group of chemical compounds with a six-membered ring containing one or more nitrogen atoms: the group consists of the diazines, triazines, etc.

az·o (az'ō, ā'zō), *adj.* [< *azote*], in *chemistry,* containing nitrogen.

az·o- (az'ō, ā'zō), [< *azote*], a combining form meaning *nitrogen,* used in forming the names of certain chemical compounds: also, before a vowel, **az-.**

az·o·ben·zene (az'ō-ben'zēn, ā'zō-ben-zēn'), *n.* [*azo-* + *benzene*], an orange-red crystalline compound, $C_{12}H_{10}N_2$, derived from nitrobenzene in an alkaline solution.

azo dyes, in *chemistry,* a large group of dyes containing the divalent radical -N:N-.

a·zo·ic (ə-zō'ik), *adj.* [Gr. *azōos* < *a-,* without + *zōē,* life], 1. without life. 2. [sometimes A-], in *geology,* designating or of the period of time before life appeared on the earth.

az·ole (az'ōl, ə-zōl'), *n.* [*az-* + *-ole*], any of a group of chemical compounds with a five-membered ring containing one or more nitrogen atoms: the group consists of the diazoles, triazoles, etc.

a·zon·ic (ā-zon'ik), *adj.* not restricted to any single zone or region; not local.

A·zores (ə-zôrz', ā'zôrz), *n.pl.* a group of Portuguese islands west of Portugal: area, 922 sq. mi.; pop., 254,000: see **Canary Islands,** map.

az·ote (az'ōt, ə-zōt'), *n.* [Fr.; coined by Lavoisier from Gr. *a-,* not + *zōē,* life, because the gas does not support life], nitrogen.

az·oth (az'oth), *n.* [< Ar. *al zāwūq,* the quicksilver], in *alchemy,* 1. the metal mercury; quicksilver. 2. Paracelsus' universal remedy.

a·zot·ic (ə-zot'ik), *adj.* [Rare], of or containing azote, or nitrogen; nitric.

az·o·tize (az'ə-tīz'), *v.t.* [AZOTIZED (-tīzd'), AZOTIZING], [< *azote* + *-ize*], to nitrogenize.

A·zov, Sea of (ä'zôf, ā'zov), an arm of the Black Sea, southern U.S.S.R.: area, 14,520 sq. mi.

Az·ra·el (az'ri-əl), *n.* [Ar. *'Azrā'īl;* Heb. *'azra'ēl,* lit., help of God], the angel who, according to ancient Jewish and Moslem belief, parts the soul from the body in death.

Az·tec (az'tek), *n.* [of Aztec origin], 1. a member of a people who lived in Mexico and had an advanced civilization before the conquest of Mexico by Cortes in 1519. 2. their language. *adj.* of the Aztecs, their language, culture, etc.

Az·tec·an (az'tek-ən), *adj.* 1. Aztec. 2. Nahuatlan.

az·ure (azh'ēr, ā'zhēr), *adj.* [ME. *azure, asur;* OFr. *azur;* (with omission of initial *l-,* as if *l'azur*) < Ar. *lāzaward* < Per. *lāzhuward,* lapis lazuli], of or like the color of a clear sky; sky-blue; blue. *n.* 1. sky blue or any similar blue color. 2. [Poetic], the blue sky.

az·u·rite (azh'ə-rīt'), *n.* [*azure* + *-ite*], 1. a blue ore of copper, basic copper carbonate, $2CuCO_3 \cdot Cu(OH)_2$. 2. a semiprecious gem made from this ore.

az·y·gous (az'i-gəs), *adj.* [Gr. *azygos,* unmatched < *a-* not + *zygon,* a yoke], not one of a pair; having no mate; odd: as, an *azygous* muscle.

B

B, b (bē), *n.* [*pl.* B's, b's, Bs, bs (bēz)], 1. the second letter of the English alphabet: from the Greek *beta,* a borrowing from the Phoenician: see **alphabet,** table. 2. the sound of B or b, normally a voiced lip stop. 3. a type or impression for B or b. 4. *a symbol for* the second in a sequence or group. *adj.* 1. of B or b. 2. second in a sequence or group.

B (bē), *n.* 1. an object shaped like B. 2. a Roman numeral for 300: with a superior bar (B̄), 300,000. 3. the second party in a given case. 4. a large size of shot. 5. in *chemistry, the symbol for* boron. 6. in *education,* a grade second in quality: as, a *B* in history. 7. in *music,* *a)* the seventh tone or note in the scale of C major, or the second in the scale of A minor. *b)* a key, string, etc. producing this tone. *c)* the scale having B as the keynote. 8. in *physics, a symbol for* magnetic induction. *adj.* 1. shaped like B. 2. secondary; inferior to the best: as, a class *B* motion picture.

B, in *chess,* bishop.

B-, bomber: followed by a number to designate a specific model of United States bombing airplane.

b, in *algebra,* a symbol representing a known quantity or a constant.

B., 1. Bible. 2. Boston. 3. British. 4. Brotherhood. 5. in *medicine,* bacillus.

B., b., 1. bachelor. 2. battery. 3. bay. 4. bicuspid. 5. bolivar. 6. book. 7. born. 8. brother. 9. in *baseball, a)* base. *b)* base hit. *c)* bat. 10. in *music,* bass; basso.

b., in *sports,* 1. bowled. 2. bye.

ba (bä), *n.* in *Egyptian mythology,* the soul, symbolized by a bird with a human head.

Ba, in *chemistry,* barium.

B.A., 1. *Baccalaureus Artium,* [L.], Bachelor of Arts: also **A.B.** 2. British Academy.

baa (bä), *v.i.* & *n.* [echoic], bleat.

B.A.A., Brother Artists Association: a branch of the Associated Actors and Artists of America, an A.F. of L. labor union.

Ba·al (bā'əl, bāl), *n.* [*pl.* BAALIM (-im), BAALS (-əlz, bālz)], [ME.; L.; Heb. *ba'al;* Phoen. *ba'al,* lord, owner 1. among some ancient Semitic peoples, a sun god, or god of fertility and flocks; hence, 2. a false god; idol

Baal·bek (bäl'bek, bāl'bək'), *n.* a town in Lebanon. pop., 4,500: site of ruins of ancient Heliopolis.

Ba·al·ish (bā'əl-ish, bāl'ish), *adj.* 1. of or like Baal. 2. idolatrous.

Ba·al·ism (bā'əl-iz'm, bāl'iz'm), *n.* 1. the worship of Baal; hence, 2. idolatry.

Ba·al·ist (bā'əl-ist, bāl'ist), *n.* 1. a worshiper of Baal; hence, 2. an idolater.

Ba·al·ite (bā'əl-īt', bāl'īt), *n.* a Baalist.

Bab (bäb), *n.* a shortening of *Bāb-ud-Dīn* (literally, Gate of the Faith), a Persian title taken by the founder of Babism.

Bab., Babylonian.

Ba·bar (bä'bẽr), *n.* Baber.

bab·bitt (bab'it), *n.* Babbitt metal. *v.t.* to line with Babbitt metal; put Babbitt metal on.

bab·bitt, Bab·bitt (bab'it), *n.* [after George *Babbitt,* the title character of a satirical novel by Sinclair Lewis (1922)], an uncultivated, conventional businessman; philistine; person characterized by babbittry.

Babbitt, Irving, 1865–1933; American educator, critic, and author.

Babbitt metal, [after Isaac *Babbitt* (1799–1862), Am. inventor], 1. a soft, silver-colored alloy of tin, copper, and antimony, used to reduce friction in bearings, etc. 2. loosely, any antifriction alloy.

bab·bitt·ry, Bab·bitt·ry (bab'it-ri), *n.* the behavior, attitudes, etc. of babbitts as a class, characterized by a striving for business and social success, conventionality, smugness, and a lack of interest in cultural matters; Philistinism.

bab·ble (bab''l), *v.i.* [BABBLED (-'ld), BABBLING], [ME. *bablen* (like Norw. *bable,* Sw. *babbla,* G. *babbeln,* to prattle, L. *balbutire,* to stammer, Sans. *balbuthah,* stammerer), of echoic origin; prob. not of continuous derivation but recoined from common experience], 1. to

B

make incoherent sounds, as a baby does; talk like a child; prattle. 2. to talk unwisely or too much; reveal secrets. 3. to make a continuous low sound: as, the brook *babbles*. ***v.t.*** 1. to say indistinctly or incoherently. 2. to say unwisely or inadvisedly; blab. ***n.*** 1. confused, incoherent talk or vocal sounds. 2. foolish or meaningless talk. 3. a continuous murmur.

babe (bāb), ***n.*** [ME.; like similar forms (W. *baban*, Alb. *bebe*, baby, L. *papa*, Gr. *papa*, G. *papa*, father, MHG. *babe*, old woman, Lith. *boba*, mother) formed in imitation of baby cries], 1. a baby; infant; hence, 2. a naive, gullible, or helpless person. 3. [Slang], a girl or young woman, especially a pretty one.

Ba·bel (bā′b'l, bab′'l), ***n.*** [Heb. *bābel;* Assyr.-Babylonian *Bāb-ilu*, Babylon, lit., gate of God (? transl. of Turanian *Ca-dimirra*, Gate of God)], 1. in the *Bible*, a city in Shinar in which Noah's descendants tried to build a tower intended to reach to heaven: God punished its builders for this presumption and prevented them from finishing by causing them all suddenly to speak in different languages so that they could not understand one another: Gen. 11:1–9; hence, 2. any impossibly high tower or building. 3. an impracticable scheme. 4. [also b-], *a)* a confusion of voices, languages, etc.; tumult. *b)* a place of such confusion.

Bab el Man·deb (bab′ el′ man′deb, bäb′ el′ män′deb), the strait joining the Red Sea and the Gulf of Aden: width, 20 mi.

Ba·ber (bä′bẽr), ***n.*** (*Zahir ud-Din Muhammed*), founder and first emperor of the Mogul dynasty of India; lived 1483–1530: also spelled **Babar, Babur.**

Bab·i (bä′bē), ***n.*** [< *Bab*], 1. Babism. 2. a Babist. ***adj.*** Babist.

ba·bies'-breath (bā′biz-breth′), ***n.*** 1. a fairly tall plant of the pink family, with small, fragrant, white or pink flowers. 2. any of several similar plants, as the wild madder, grape hyacinth, etc. Also **baby's-breath.**

bab·i·ru·sa, bab·i·rous·sa, bab·i·rus·sa (bab′i-rōō′sə, bä′bi-rōō′sə), ***n.*** [Malay *bābī*, hog + *rūsa*, deer], a wild hog of southeast Asia and East India that has a pair of hornlike tusks curving up backward from each jaw.

Bab·ism (bäb′iz'm), ***n.*** [see BAB], a Persian religion founded c. 1844 by the Bab, Mirza Ali Mohammed: it forbids begging, drinking alcoholic liquors, buying and selling slaves, having more than one wife, etc.

Bab·ist (bäb′ist), ***adj.*** of Babism. ***n.*** a believer in Babism.

Bab·ite (bäb′īt), ***adj.* & *n.*** Babist.

ba·boo (bä′bōō), ***n.*** [Hind. *bābū*], 1. a Hindu title equivalent to *Mr.*, *Sir*, or *Esq.* 2. a native clerk in India who can write English. 3. a native of India who has a little English education: derogatory term. Also spelled **babu.**

ba·boon (ba-bōōn′, bə-bōōn′), ***n.*** [ME. *babewyne;* OFr. *babuin*], a fierce ape of Africa and Arabia, having a doglike snout and teeth, a large head with cheek pouches, bare calluses on the rump, and a short tail.

ba·boon·er·y (ba-bōōn′ẽr-i, bə-bōōn′ẽr-i), ***n.*** baboonish behavior.

ba·boon·ish (ba-bōōn′ish, bə-bōōn′ish), ***adj.*** like a baboon; stupid; uncouth.

Ba·bur (bä′bẽr), ***n.*** Baber.

ba·bush·ka (bə-boosh′kə), ***n.*** [Russ., grandmother], a kerchief or scarf worn on the head by a woman or girl.

Ba·bu·yan Islands (bä′bōō-yän′), a small group of islands in the Philippines, off the north coast of Luzon.

ba·by (bā′bi), ***n.*** [*pl.* BABIES (-biz)], [ME. *babi*, dim. of *babe;* see BABE], 1. an infant; very young child. 2. a person who behaves like an infant; helpless or cowardly person. 3. the youngest or smallest in a group. 4. [Slang], a girl or young woman, especially a pretty one. ***adj.*** 1. of or for an infant. 2. extremely young. 3. small of its kind. 4. infantile or childish. ***v.t.*** [BABIED (-bid), BABYING], to treat like a baby; pamper; coddle. —***SYN.*** see **indulge.**

baby beef, meat from a prime heifer or steer fattened for butchering when one to two years old.

baby blue-eyes (blōō′īz′), a California plant with dark-spotted blue flowers.

baby buggy, a light carriage for wheeling a baby about; perambulator.

baby farm, a place where young children can be boarded: the term now generally implies mistreatment and neglect.

baby grand, a small grand piano.

ba·by·hood (bā′bi-hood′), ***n.*** 1. the period or condition of being a baby; infancy. 2. babies collectively.

ba·by·ish (bā′bi-ish), ***adj.*** 1. like a baby; infantile; hence, 2. timid, silly, etc.

Bab·y·lon (bab′'l-ən, bab′i-lon′), ***n.*** [L.; Gr. *Babylōn;* Heb. *bābel;* see BABEL], 1. an ancient city on the Euphrates River, the capital of Babylonia and later of Chaldea, famous for wealth, luxury, and wickedness. 2. any city or place of great wealth, luxury, and vice.

Bab·y·lo·ni·a (bab′'l-ō′ni-ə), ***n.*** [L.; Gr. *Babylōnia* < *Babylōn;* see BABYLON], an ancient empire of southwestern Asia, in the lower valley of the Tigris and Euphrates Rivers: it flourished c. 2700–538 B.C.

Bab·y·lo·ni·an (bab′'l-ō′ni-ən), ***adj.*** 1. of Babylon, its people, etc. 2. of Babylonia. 3. wicked. ***n.*** 1. a native or inhabitant of Babylon or Babylonia. 2. the Semitic language of the Babylonians. Abbreviated **Bab.**

Babylonian Captivity, 1. the exile of the Jews, deported by Nebuchadnezzar into Babylonia in 597 B.C. 2. the period of forced residence of the Popes at Avignon, France (1309–1377): so called after the exile of the Jews.

Bab·y·lo·nish (bab′'l-ō′nish), ***adj.*** Babylonian.

ba·by's-breath (bā′biz-breth′), ***n.*** babies'-breath.

ba·by-sit (bā′bi-sit′), ***v.i.*** to act as a baby sitter.

baby sitter, a person hired to take care of a child or children, as when the parents are away for the evening: also **sitter.**

Ba·car·di (bə-kär′di), ***n.*** [after *Bacardi*, orig. distiller], a variety of Cuban rum. ***adj.*** made with Bacardi rum.

bac·ca·lau·re·ate (bak′ə-lô′ri-it), ***n.*** [ML. *baccalaureatus;* as if < L. *bacca laureus*, laurel berry, but actually < L. **baccalaris* or **baccalarius*, vassal farmer, young man < *bacca*, a cow; cf. BACHELOR], 1. the degree of bachelor of arts, bachelor of science, etc. 2. an address or sermon delivered to a graduating class at commencement: also **baccalaureate sermon.**

bac·ca·rat, bac·ca·ra (bak′ə-rä′, bak′ə-rä′), ***n.*** [Fr.; prob. < *Baccarat*, a town in France], 1. a gambling game played with cards. 2. in this game, the ten, which counts zero.

bac·cate (bak′āt), ***adj.*** [L. *baccatus* < *bacca*, berry], 1. like a berry, as in pulpiness or shape. 2. bearing berries.

Bac·chae (bak′ē), ***n.pl.*** [L.; Gr. *Bakchai* < *Bakchos*, Bacchus], 1. women companions of Bacchus. 2. women worshipers or priestesses of Bacchus.

bac·cha·nal (bak′ə-n'l, bak′ə-nal′), ***n.*** [L., place devoted to Bacchus], 1. a worshiper of Bacchus; bacchant or bacchante; hence, 2. a drunken carouser. 3. *pl.* the Bacchanalia. 4. a dance or song in honor of Bacchus. 5. a drunken party; orgy. ***adj.*** 1. of Bacchus or his worship; bacchanalian. 2. carousing.

Bac·cha·na·li·a (bak′ə-nā′li-ə, bak′ə-nāl′yə), ***n.pl.*** 1. an ancient Roman festival in honor of Bacchus; hence, 2. [b-], a drunken party; orgy.

bac·cha·na·li·an (bak′ə-nā′li-ən, bak′ə-nāl′yən), ***adj.*** 1. of or like bacchanals or the Bacchanalia. 2. noisily drunken; carousing; orgiastic. ***n.*** a drunken carouser.

bac·chant (bak′ənt), ***n.*** [*pl.* BACCHANTS (-ənts), BACCHANTES (bə-kan′tēz)], [< L. *bacchans*, ppr. of *bacchari*, to celebrate the feast of Bacchus], 1. a priest or worshiper of Bacchus; hence, 2. a drunken carouser. ***adj.*** 1. worshiping Bacchus. 2. fond of alcoholic liquor.

bac·chan·te (bə-kan′ti, bə-kant′, bak′ənt), ***n.*** [Fr.; see BACCHANT], 1. a priestess or woman votary of Bacchus; hence, 2. a woman who carouses.

bac·chan·tic (bə-kan′tik), ***adj.*** of or like bacchants or bacchantes.

Bac·chic (bak′ik), ***adj.*** 1. of Bacchus or his worship. 2. [often b-], bacchanalian; drunken; carousing.

Bac·chus (bak′əs), ***n.*** [L.; Gr. *Bakchos*], an ancient Greek and Roman god of wine and revelry: earlier called *Dionysus* by the Greeks.

bac·ci- (bak′si), [< L. *bacca*, berry], a combining form meaning *berry*, as in *baccivorous*.

bac·cif·er·ous (bak-sif′ẽr-əs), ***adj.*** [L. *baccifer* < *bacca*, berry + *ferre*, to bear; + *-ous*], that bears berries.

bac·ci·form (bak′si-fôrm′), ***adj.*** [*bacci-* + *-form*], shaped like a berry.

bac·civ·o·rous (bak-siv′ə-rəs), ***adj.*** [*bacci-* + *-vorous*], eating berries; living on berries.

bach (bach), ***v.i.*** [< *bachelor*], [Slang], to live alone or keep house for oneself, as a bachelor.

Bach, Jo·hann Christian (yō′hän bäkh′), 1735–1782; son of *Johann Sebastian;* German organist and composer.

Bach, Jo·hann Se·bas·tian (yō′hän si-bäs′tyən), 1685–1750; German organist and composer.

Bach, Karl Phil·ipp E·ma·nu·el (kärl fēl′ip ā-mä′nōō-el), 1714–1788; son of *Johann Sebastian;* German composer.

bach·e·lor (bach′ə-lẽr, bach′lẽr), ***n.*** [ME. *bacheler;* OFr. *bacheler, bachelier;* L. **baccalaris* or **baccalarius*, vassal farmer, young fellow < *bacca*, a cow], 1. originally, a young knight holding a farm or farms in vassalage, who served under another's banner. 2 a person who has received the baccalaureate from a college or university: as, a *Bachelor* of Arts: abbreviated **B., b.** 3. an unmarried man. ***adj.*** of or for a bachelor.

bach·e·lor-at-arms (bach′ə-lẽr-ət-ärmz′), ***n.*** a young knight serving under another's banner.

bachelor girl, [Colloq.], an unmarried girl or young woman who works and lives independently.

bach·e·lor·hood (bach′ə-lẽr-hood′, bach′lẽr-hood′), ***n.*** the state or period of being a bachelor; way of life of an unmarried man.

Bachelor of Arts, 1. a degree given by a college or university to a person who has completed a four-year course or its equivalent in the humanities, social sciences, etc. 2. a person who has this degree. Abbreviated **B.A., A.B.**

Bachelor of Science, 1. a degree given by a college or

university to a person who has completed a four-year college course or its equivalent, with a major in science rather than the humanities. 2. a person who has this degree. Abbreviated **B.S., B.Sc.**
bach·e·lor's-but·ton (bach'ə-lẽrz-but''n, bach'lẽrz-but''n), *n.* any of several plants with button-shaped flowers, including the cornflower, knapweed, and tansy.
bach·e·lor·ship (bach'ə-lẽr-ship', bach'lẽr-ship'), *n.* [*bachelor* + *-ship*], bachelorhood.
ba·cil·lar (bə-sil'ẽr, bas''l-ẽr), *adj.* [Mod. L. *bacillarius* < L. *bacillum*, small staff], 1. rod-shaped; bacilliform. 2. consisting of rodlike structures. 3. of, like, characterized by, or caused by bacilli.
bac·il·lar·y (bas''l-er'i, bə-sil'ẽr-i), *adj.* bacillar.
ba·cil·li (bə-sil'ī), *n.* plural of **bacillus.**
ba·cil·li·form (bə-sil'ə-fôrm'), *adj.* rod-shaped; shaped like a bacillus.
ba·cil·lus (bə-sil'əs), *n.* [*pl.* BACILLI (-ī)], [Mod. L. < L. *bacillum*, dim. of *baculus*, a stick], 1. any of a genus of rod-shaped bacteria which occur in chains, produce spores, and are active only in the presence of oxygen: abbreviated **B.** 2. any rod-shaped bacterium: distinguished from *coccus, spirillum:* see **bacteria,** illus. 3. *usually pl.* loosely, any of the bacteria, especially those causing disease.
back (bak), *n.* [ME. *bak;* AS. *bæc*, back; akin to ON. *bak*, OHG. *bahho* < IE. **bheg*, to bend], 1. the part of the body opposite to the front; in man and many other animals, the part to the rear or top, opposite the chest, breast, or belly, and reaching from the base of the neck to the end of the spine; hence, 2. the backbone. 3. a support for the human back: as, the *back* of a chair. 4. the part of a garment or harness associated with the back of a person or an animal. 5. physical strength. 6. the rear or hinder part of anything. 7. the farther or other side of something; reverse. 8. the part of anything opposite the part that is used: as, the *back* of the hand. 9. the part of a tool or weapon opposite the useful edge. 10. the unexposed face of a fabric; wrong side. 11. the part of a book that holds it together; part showing when the book is shelved. 12. in *football*, a player in a position behind the front line; quarterback, halfback, or fullback. *adj.* 1. at the rear; behind. 2. distant. 3. of or for a time in the past: as, *back* pay. 4. in a backward direction; returning; reversed: as, a *back* stroke. 5. in *phonetics*, made at the rear of the mouth; velar; guttural. *adv.* [ME. *bac* < *abac;* AS. *on bæc*, backward], 1. at, to, or toward the rear; backward. 2. to or toward a former position. 3. into or toward a previous condition. 4. to or toward an earlier time. 5. for the purpose of reserve or concealment: as, to hold *back* information. 6. in return or requital: as, to pay one *back*. *v.t.* 1. to cause to move backward, or to the rear (sometimes with *up*). 2. to stand behind; hence, 3. to support; second; approve (often with *up*). 4. to make a wager in support of; bet on. 5. to get on the back of; mount. 6. to provide with a back or backing. 7. to form the back of. 8. to sign on the back; endorse. *v.i.* 1. to move or go backward (often with *up*). 2. to shift counterclockwise: said of the wind; opposed to *veer*. —*SYN.* see **support.**
back and fill, 1. to handle sails so that they repeatedly spill wind and fill with wind. 2. to zigzag. 3. to take first one position and then another; vacillate.
back and forth, to and fro; from side to side.
back down, [Colloq.], to withdraw from a position or attitude; surrender a claim.
back out, [Colloq.], 1. to withdraw from an enterprise. 2. to refuse to keep a promise or engagement.
back water, 1. to row or paddle backward; hence, 2. to withdraw from a position or a claim.
behind one's back, without one's knowledge or consent.
be on one's back, to be ill, unable to help oneself, etc.
get (or **put**) **one's back up,** 1. to make or become angry, as a cat arching its back. 2. to be obstinate.
go back on, [Colloq.], 1. to back out. 2. to be disloyal to; desert; fail.
turn one's back on, 1. to show anger, contempt, etc. toward by turning away from. 2. to ignore the plight of; desert; fail.
with one's back to the wall, in a desperate position, as a fighter cornered and unable to retreat.
back (bak), *n.* [D. *bak;* Fr. *bac*, trough, ferryboat], a shallow vat, tray, or tub used in industry.
back·ache (bak'āk'), *n.* a continuous ache, or pain, in the back.
Back Bay, a wealthy residential district in Boston.
back·bite (bak'bīt'), *v.t. & v.i.* [BACKBIT (-bit'), BACKBITTEN (-bit''n) or BACKBIT, BACKBITING], [see BACK & BITE], to speak maliciously about (an absent person or persons); slander. *n.* a backbiting.
back·board (bak'bôrd', bak'bōrd'), *n.* 1. a board that forms or supports the back of something. 2. in *basketball*, a board or flat surface just behind the basket.
back·bone (bak'bōn'), *n.* [ME. *bakbon, bacbon;* see BACK & BONE], 1. the column of bones along the center of the back of man and many animals, made up of separate bones (vertebrae) connected by muscles and tendons; spine; hence, 2. a main support; stiffening part. 3. courage; determination. —*SYN.* see **fortitude.**
back·boned (bak'bōnd'), *adj.* having a backbone.
back·break·ing (bak'brāk'iŋ), *adj.* requiring great physical exertion; very tiring.
back·chat (bak'chat'), *n.* [Colloq.], back talk.
back·court (bak'kôrt', bak'kōrt'), *n.* the back part of a tennis court, basketball court, etc.
back·cross (bak'krôs'), *v.t. & v.i.* to cross, or breed (a hybrid) with one of its parents. *n.* such a breeding.
back·door (bak'dôr', bak'dōr'), *adj.* 1. of a rear entrance; hence, 2. secret; underhand; surreptitious.
back·drop (bak'drop'), *n.* a curtain hung at the back of a stage, often painted to represent some scene.
backed (bakt), *adj.* having a back or backing: often used in hyphenated compounds meaning *having a* (specified kind of) *back*, as *canvas-backed.*
back·er (bak'ẽr), *n.* 1. a person who backs another person or a project; patron; supporter. 2. a person who bets on a contestant. —*SYN.* see **sponsor.**
back·fall (bak'fôl'), *n.* 1. *a*) a falling back. *b*) that which falls back. 2. in *wrestling*, a fall in which the wrestler lands on his back.
back·field (bak'fēld'), *n.* in *football*, 1. the four players (quarterback, two halfbacks, and fullback) whose regular position is behind the line of scrimmage. 2. their positions regarded as a unit.
back·fire (bak'fīr'), *n.* 1. a fire started to stop an advancing prairie fire or forest fire by creating a burned area in its path. 2. an explosion occurring too soon in a cylinder of a gasoline or oil engine, thereby tending to reverse the motion of the piston. 3. an explosion in an intake or exhaust pipe. 4. an explosion in the back part of a gun. *v.i.* 1. to use or set a backfire. 2. to explode as a backfire. 3. to have an unexpected and unwelcome result; go awry: as, his plan *backfired.*
back·for·ma·tion (bak'fôr-mā'shən), *n.* a word actually formed from, but looking as if it were the base of, another word. Example: *burgle* (from *burglar*).
back·gam·mon (bak'gam'ən, bak'gam'ən), *n.* [prob. *back* + *gammon*, a game], a game played on a special board by two people: each has fifteen pieces, which he moves according to the throw of dice.

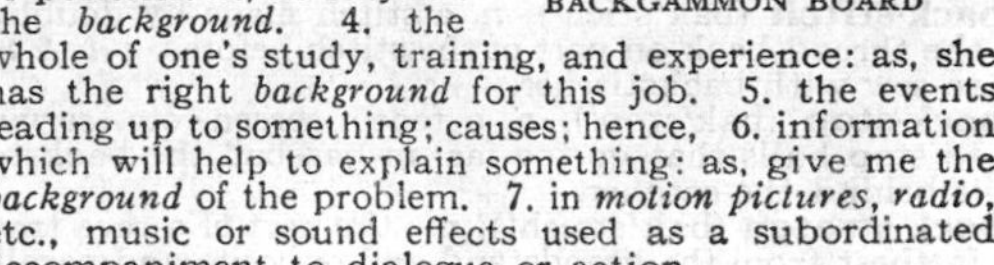
BACKGAMMON BOARD

back·ground (bak'ground'), *n.* 1. the distant part of a landscape, picture, etc. 2. surroundings, especially those behind something and providing harmony or contrast; surrounding area or surface. 3. an unimportant or seemingly unimportant place or position: as, he stays in the *background.* 4. the whole of one's study, training, and experience: as, she has the right *background* for this job. 5. the events leading up to something; causes; hence, 6. information which will help to explain something: as, give me the *background* of the problem. 7. in *motion pictures, radio,* etc., music or sound effects used as a subordinated accompaniment to dialogue or action.
back·hand (bak'hand'), *n.* 1. handwriting that slants backward, up to the left. 2. a method of stroking, as in tennis, with the back of the hand turned forward, the arm being brought forward from across the body. 3. a stroke so made. *adj.* backhanded. *adv.* with a backhanded stroke.

Backhandwriting

back·hand·ed (bak'han'did), *adj.* 1. made or performed with the back of the hand, or with the back of the hand turned forward, as some strokes in tennis. 2. with the letters slanting backward, up to the left. 3. not direct; equivocal; insincere; sarcastic: said of a compliment that contains a rebuke, etc. 4. turned in a direction opposite to the normal: as, a *backhanded* cable. 5. clumsy.
back·house (bak'hous'), *n.* a small building behind the main one; especially, a privy.
back·ing (bak'iŋ), *n.* 1. the

BACKHAND STROKE

act of supporting at the back or strengthening with a back. 2. something placed in back or forming a back for support or strengthening. 3. support or aid given to a person or cause; endorsement. 4. those giving such support or aid. 5. a going backward.

back·lash (bak′lash′), *n.* 1. a quick, sharp recoil. 2. a snarl in a reeled fishing line. 3. in *mechanics*, the jarring reaction of loose or worn parts; play.

back·log (bak′lôg′, bak′log′), *n.* 1. a large log at the back of a fire, as in a fireplace, to support other logs. 2. an accumulation or reserve, as of unfilled orders. *v.i. & v.t.* [BACKLOGGED (-lôgd′, -logd′), BACKLOGGING], to accumulate in reserve.

back number, 1. an old issue of a periodical. 2. [Colloq.], an old-fashioned or passé person or thing.

back order, an order not yet filled: abbreviated **b.o.**

back pay, overdue or retroactive wages.

back·rest (bak′rest′), *n.* a support for or at the back.

back road, a road that is away from the main road; country road, usually in poor condition.

back-scratch·er (bak′skrach′ẽr), *n.* 1. a device for scratching the back. 2. a person who scratches another's back; hence, 3. [Colloq.], a toady.

back seat, 1. a seat at the back; hence, 2. [Colloq.], a secondary or inconspicuous position.

back-seat driver (bak′sēt′), a passenger in an automobile who offers advice and directions for driving.

back·set (bak′set′), *n.* 1. a setback; relapse; reverse. 2. a backward current; eddy.

back·sheesh, back·shish (bak′shēsh′), *n.* baksheesh.

back·side (bak′sīd′), *n.* [ME. *bak side*], 1. the back; hind part. 2. the rump; buttocks.

back·sight (bak′sīt′), *n.* in *surveying*, 1. a sight taken from a located point back to the point from which the location was originally made. 2. a sight taken on a point of known elevation in order to determine the elevation of the instrument.

back·slap·per (bak′slap′ẽr), *n.* [Colloq.], a person who slaps others on the back; effusively friendly, too hearty person.

back·slide (bak′slīd′, bak′slīd′), *v.i.* [BACKSLID (-slid′, -slid′), BACKSLIDDEN (-slid′′n, -slid′′n) or BACKSLID, BACKSLIDING], to slide backward in morals or religious enthusiasm; become less virtuous, less pious, etc.

back·spin (bak′spin′), *n.* the backward rotation of a ball, wheel, etc. that is moving forward.

back·stage (bak′stāj′), *adv.* 1. in the dressing rooms of a theater. 2. at or to the rear of the stage; upstage. *adj.* (bak′stāj′), 1. situated backstage. 2. concealed.

back·stair (bak′stâr′), *adj.* backstairs.

back·stairs (bak′stârz′), *adj.* secret; underhanded; involving intrigue.

back stairs, 1. stairs at the back, used (in large houses or palaces) by servants, secret visitors, etc.; hence, 2. a way or method of intrigue.

back·stay (bak′stā′), *n.* 1. a rope or shroud slanting sharply aft from the top of the mast of a ship to help support the mast: often called *running backstay*: see **shroud,** illus. 2. a rope or shroud extending from the mast to the stern: often called *permanent backstay.* 3. a support for the back.

back·stitch (bak′stich′), *n.* a stitch made by doubling the thread back on part of the stitch before. *v.t. & v.i.* to sew with backstitches.

back·stop (bak′stop′), *n.* a fence, screen, etc. serving to stop balls that go too far: in baseball the backstop is behind the catcher.

back·stretch (bak′strech′), *n.* the part of a race track farthest from the grandstand and opposite and parallel to the homestretch.

back·stroke (bak′strōk′), *n.* 1. a stroke backward; backhanded stroke. 2. a stroke made by a swimmer lying face upward. *v.i.* to perform a backstroke. *v.t.* to hit with a backstroke.

back·swept (bak′swept′), *adj.* formed so as to extend or slope away from the front.

back·sword (bak′sôrd′, bak′sōrd′), *n.* 1. a sword sharpened on only one edge; broadsword. 2. a hilted stick used in saber-fencing practice; singlestick. 3. a person who fences with the backsword.

back talk, [Colloq.], a talking back; saucy or insolent answers or retorts.

back·track (bak′trak′), *v.i.* to return by the same path; retreat.

back·ward (bak′wẽrd), *adv.* [ME. *bacward, bakward,* for *abacward; abac* (< AS. *on bæc,* back) + *-ward* (< AS. *-weard,* toward)], 1. behind; toward the back or rear. 2. with the back or rear foremost. 3. in reverse. 4. in a way contrary to the normal or usual way. 5. toward earlier times; into the past. 6. from a better to a worse state. *adj.* 1. turned or directed toward the rear or in the opposite way. 2. hesitant; not eager; reluctant; bashful; shy. 3. late in developing or growing; retarded; slow; behind time.

back·ward·ness (bak′wẽrd-nis), *n.* 1. the state of being retarded or undeveloped. 2. shyness; bashfulness; reluctance.

back·wards (bak′wẽrdz), *adv.* [*backward* + adv. genit. *-(e)s*], backward.

back·wash (bak′wôsh′, bak′wäsh′), *n.* 1. water moved backward, as by a ship, an oar, etc. 2. a backward current or flow, as of air from an airplane propeller. 3. a reaction or commotion caused by some event.

back·wa·ter (bak′wô′tẽr, bak′wä′tẽr), *n.* 1. water moved backward or held back by a dam, tide, etc. 2. stagnant water in a small stream or inlet; hence, 3. a place or condition regarded as stagnant, backward, etc.: as, he lives in a cultural *backwater.* *adj.* like a backwater; stagnant; backward.

back·wood (bak′wood′), *adj.* backwoods.

back·woods (bak′woodz′, bak′woodz′), *n.pl.* 1. heavily wooded areas far from centers of population. 2. [Colloq.], any remote, thinly populated place. *adj.* in, from, or characteristic of backwoods.

back·woods·man (bak′woodz′mən), *n.* [*pl.* BACKWOODSMEN (-mən)], a man who lives in or comes from the backwoods.

ba·con (bā′kən, bā′k'n), *n.* [ME. & OFr.; OHG. *bahho, bacho,* side of bacon], salted and smoked meat from the back or sides of a hog: see **pork, illus.**

bring home the bacon, [Colloq.], 1. to earn a living. 2. to succeed; win.

Ba·con, Francis (bā′kən, bā′k'n), Baron Verulam, Viscount St. Albans, 1561–1626; English philosopher, essayist, and statesman.

Bacon, Nathaniel, 1647–1676; American colonist born in England; led a rebellion to gain governmental reform.

Bacon, Roger, 1214?–1294; English scientist and philosopher.

Ba·co·ni·an (bā-kō′ni-ən), *adj.* 1. of Francis Bacon, his philosophy, or his style of writing. 2. designating or of the theory that Francis Bacon wrote Shakespeare's works. *n.* 1. a person who believes in the philosophy of Francis Bacon. 2. a person who believes that Francis Bacon wrote the works of Shakespeare.

bact., bacteriology.

bac·te·re·mi·a (bak′tə-rē′mi-ə), *n.* [see BACTERIA & -EMIA], the presence of bacteria in the blood stream.

bac·te·ri- (bak′tə-ri), bacterio-.

bac·te·ri·a (bak-têr′i-ə), *n.pl.* [*sing.* BACTERIUM (-əm)], [Mod. L., pl. of *bacterium* < Gr. *baktērion,* dim. of *baktron,* a staff], typically one-celled microorganisms which have no chlorophyll, multiply by simple division, and can be seen only with a microscope: they occur in three main forms, spherical (cocci), rod-shaped (bacilli), and spiral (spirilla); some bacteria cause diseases such as pneumonia, tuberculosis, and syphilis, but others are necessary for fermentation, nitrogen fixation, etc.

A B C

TYPES OF BACTERIA
A, rod (bacillus); B, spiral (spirillum); C, sphere (coccus)

bac·te·ri·al (bak-têr′i-əl), *adj.* of or produced by bacteria.

bac·te·ri·al·ly (bak-têr′i-əl-i), *adv.* 1. by the action of bacteria. 2. in the manner of bacteria.

bac·te·ri·cid·al (bak-têr′ə-sīd′əl), *adj.* that destroys bacteria.

bac·te·ri·cide (bak-têr′ə-sīd′), *n.* [*bacteri-* + *-cide*], an agent or substance that destroys bacteria.

bac·te·rin (bak′tə-rin), *n.* [< *bacteri-* + *-in*], a vaccine that contains specific bacteria and is injected into a person's body to increase his immunity to them.

bac·te·ri·o- (bak-têr′i-ə), [< *bacterium*], a combining form meaning *of bacteria,* as in *bacteriology:* also **bacteri-.**

bac·te·ri·o·log·i·cal (bak′têr′i-ə-loj′i-k'l, bak-têr′i-ə-loj′i-k'l), *adj.* of or connected with bacteriology.

bac·te·ri·ol·o·gist (bak′têr′i-ol′ə-jist, bak-têr′i-ol′ə-jist), *n.* a student of or specialist in bacteriology.

bac·te·ri·ol·o·gy (bak′têr′i-ol′ə-ji, bak-têr′i-ol′ə-ji), *n.* [*bacterio-* + *-logy*], the science that deals with bacteria: abbreviated **bacteriol., bact.**

bac·te·ri·ol·y·sis (bak′têr′i-ol′ə-sis, bak-têr′i-ol′ə-sis), *n.* [*bacterio-* + *-lysis*], 1. chemical decomposition caused by bacteria. 2. the dissolution or destruction of bacteria.

bac·te·ri·o·lyt·ic (bak-têr′i-ə-lit′ik), *adj.* of, producing, or characterized by bacteriolysis.

bac·te·ri·o·phage (bak-têr′i-ə-fāj′), *n.* [*bacterio-* + *-phage*], a microscopic agent that destroys disease-producing bacteria in a living organism.

bac·te·ri·os·co·py (bak′têr′i-os′kə-pi, bak-têr′i-os′kə-pi), *n.* [*bacterio-* + *-scopy*], the study of bacteria by means of the microscope.

bac·te·ri·o·sta·sis (bak-têr′i-ə-stā′sis), *n.* [Mod. L.; see BACTERIO- & STASIS], prevention of the growth or multiplication of bacteria.

bac·te·ri·o·stat·ic (bak-têr′i-ə-stat′ik), *adj.* [Mod. L.; see BACTERIO- & STATIC], preventing the growth or multiplication of bacteria. *n.* a bacteriostatic substance.

bac·te·ri·um (bak-têr′i-əm), *n.* singular of **bacteria.**

bac·ter·ize (bak′tẽr-īz′), *v.t.* [BACTERIZED (-īzd′), BACTERIZING], to cause a change in by bacterial action.

bac·ter·oid (bak′tēr-oid′), *adj.* resembling bacteria. *n.* a structurally modified form of bacterium, as that forming nodules on the roots of leguminous plants.

Bac·tri·a (bak′tri-ə), *n.* an ancient country in the northeastern part of modern Afghanistan: also **Balkh.**

Bac·tri·an (bak′tri-ən), *adj.* of Bactria. *n.* 1. a native or inhabitant of Bactria. 2. the language of Bactria.

Bactrian camel, a camel with two humps, native to southwestern Asia: it is shorter and hairier than the Arabian camel.

ba·cu·li·form (ba-kū′lə-fôrm′), *adj.* [< L. *baculum,* a stick; + *-form*], shaped like a rod.

bac·u·line (bak′yoo-lin, bak′yoo-lin′), *adj.* [< L. *baculum,* a stick; + *-ine*], having to do with a rod or stick, or with punishment administered with a rod.

bad (bad), *adj.* [WORSE (wũrs), WORST (wũrst)], [ME. *bad, badde,* bad, worthless; ? < AS. *bæddel,* hermaphrodite], 1. not good; not as it should be; defective in quality; below standard; lacking in worth; inadequate. 2. unfit; unskilled. 3. unfavorable; unpleasant; disagreeable: as, *bad* news. 4. rotted; decomposed; spoiled. 5. incorrect; faulty; erroneous: as, *bad* spelling. 6. wicked; immoral. 7. harmful; injurious; dangerous. 8. severe: as, a *bad* storm. 9. ill; in poor health; in pain. 10. bothered; sorry; distressed: as, he feels *bad* about it. 11. offensive; disgusting: as, a *bad* smell. 12. in *law,* defective; not valid; void. *adv.* [Colloq.], badly. *n.* 1. anything that is bad; bad quality or state. 2. wickedness. 3. those who are wicked (preceded by *the*).

go to the bad, [Colloq.], to degenerate; become wicked, shiftless, seedy, etc.

in bad, [Colloq.], 1. in trouble. 2. in disfavor.

not bad, [Colloq.], good; fairly good; not unsatisfactory: also **not half bad, not so bad.**

SYN.—**bad,** in this comparison, is the broadest term, ranging in implication from merely unsatisfactory to utterly depraved; **evil** and **wicked** connote willful violation of a moral code, but **evil** often has ominous or malevolent implications (an *evil* hour) and **wicked** is sometimes weakened in a playful way to mean merely mischievous (*wicked* wit); **ill,** which is slightly weaker than **evil** in its implications of immorality, is now used chiefly in certain idiomatic phrases (*ill*-gotten gains); **naughty** today implies mere mischievousness or disobedience (a *naughty* child). —***ANT.*** good, moral.

bad (bad), 1. archaic past tense of **bid:** see **bid.** 2. obsolete past tense of **bide.**

Ba·da·joz (bä′dä-hôth′), *n.* a city in southern Spain, on the border of Portugal: pop., 64,000 (est. 1946).

bad blood, a feeling of (mutual) enmity.

bade (bad), 1. alternative past tense of **bid:** see **bid.** 2. alternative past tense of **bide.**

bad egg, [Slang], a worthless, dishonest, or vicious person.

Ba·den (bä′d'n), *n.* 1. a division of southwestern Germany: formerly a duchy: area, 5,818 sq. mi.; pop., 1,185,000 (est. 1947); capital, Karlsruhe. 2. a famous health resort there: pop., 34,000 (est. 1947): also **Baden-Baden.**

Ba·den-Pow·ell (bā′dən-pō′əl), first Baron (*Sir Robert Stephenson Smyth*), 1857–1941; British soldier; founder of Boy Scouts and Girl Guides.

badge (baj), *n.* [ME. *bage, bagge*], 1. a distinctive mark or sign worn to show one's rank, belief, membership, etc.; hence, 2. any distinctive sign or symbol. *v.t.* [BADGED (bajd), BADGING], to mark with a badge.

badg·er (baj′ēr), *n.* [*pl.* BADGERS (-ērz), BADGER; see PLURAL, II, D, 1], [16th-c. term for earlier *brock;* ? < obs. n. & personal name *badger,* corn dealer], 1. a burrowing animal with a broad back, thick short legs, and long claws on the forefeet. 2. its fur. 3. a brush of badger's hair. 4. in Australia, *a)* a wombat. *b)* a bandicoot. 5. [B-], [Colloq.], a native or inhabitant of Wisconsin, called the *Badger State.* *v.t.* to torment as if baiting a badger; nag at. —***SYN.*** see **bait.**

BADGER (2 ft. long)

bad·i·nage (bad′'n-ij, bad′i-näzh′), *n.* [Fr. < *badiner,* to jest, make merry < *badin,* fool < Pr. *badar,* to gape < ML. *badare,* to gape, trifle], playful, teasing talk; banter. *v.t.* [BADINAGED (-ijd, -näzhd′), BADINAGING], to banter; tease with playful talk.

bad·lands (bad′landz′), *n.pl.* any section of barren land where rapid erosion has cut the loose, dry soil or soft rocks into strange shapes. —***SYN.*** see **waste.**

Bad Lands, badlands of southwestern South Dakota and northwestern Nebraska.

bad·ly (bad′li), *adv.* 1. in a bad manner; harmfully, unpleasantly, incorrectly, wickedly, etc. 2. [Colloq.], very much; greatly: as, he wants that job *badly.*

bad·min·ton (bad′min-tən), *n.* [after *Badminton,* estate of the Duke of Beaufort], 1. a game in which a feathered cork (shuttlecock) is batted back and forth across a net by players with light rackets (battledores); battledore and shuttlecock. 2. a drink made with claret, soda, and sugar.

Ba·do·glio, Pie·tro (pye′trô bä-dô′lyô), 1871–1956; Italian marshal; premier (1943–1944).

bad-tem·pered (bad′tem′pērd), *adj.* having a bad temper or cranky disposition; irritable.

Bae·de·ker (bā′di-kēr), *n.* 1. any of a series of guidebooks to foreign countries first published in Germany by Karl Baedeker (1801–1859). 2. loosely, any guidebook.

baff (baf), *v.i.* [prob. < OFr. *baffe,* soft blow; via Scot.], in *golf,* to hit the ground with the sole of the club in striking the ball. *n.* such a stroke, lofting the ball.

Baf·fin, William (baf′in), 1584–1622; English explorer.

Baffin Bay, an arm of the Atlantic, between Greenland and Baffin Island: discovered by William Baffin.

Baffin Island, an island in Northwest Territories, Canada, northeast of the mainland: area, 211,000 sq. mi.; pop., 2,000.

baf·fle (baf′'l), *v.t.* [BAFFLED (-'ld), BAFFLING], [16th-c. Scot.; prob. respelling (cf. *duff* for *dough, Affleck* for *Auchinleck*) of obs. Scot. *bauchle*], 1. to frustrate or balk by puzzling or bewildering; confound. 2. to interfere with; hinder; impede. *v.i.* to struggle without result. *n.* 1. a baffling or being baffled. 2. an obstructing device, as a wall or screen to hold back or turn aside the flow of liquids, gases, etc. 3. in *radio,* a mounting for the loudspeaker, designed to improve reproduction of low frequencies. —***SYN.*** see **frustrate.**

baf·fle·ment (baf′'l-mənt), *n.* a baffling or being baffled.

baf·fle·plate (baf′'l-plāt′), *n.* a baffle (sense 2).

baf·fling (baf′liŋ), *adj.* [ppr. of *baffle*], 1. puzzling; bewildering. 2. inscrutable: as, a *baffling* person. 3. obstructing; hindering.

baf·fy (baf′i), *n.* [< Scot. *baff,* a blow; of echoic origin], [Obs.], a golf club with a wooden head and backward-slanting face for giving the ball high loft: now called *spoon* or *number three wood.*

bag (bag), *n.* [ME. *bagge;* ON. *baggi*], 1. a container made of fabric, paper, leather, etc., with an opening at the top that can be closed; sack or pouch. 2. a piece of hand luggage; satchel; suitcase. 3. a woman's small container for money, cosmetics, etc.; handbag; purse. 4. a container for game. 5. its contents; total kill of a day's hunting. 6. a bagful. 7. anything shaped like a bag. 8. the swelling or bagging part of something. 9. an udder or similar pouchlike membrane. 10. a sac inside an animal to hold a secretion, fluid, etc. 11. [Slang], [< *baggage,* 3], a woman. 12. in *baseball,* a base. Abbreviated **bg.** *v.t.* [BAGGED (bagd), BAGGING], 1. to make bulge. 2. to enclose within a bag. 3. to seize; capture. 4. to kill in or as in hunting. 5. [Slang], to obtain or collect. *v.i.* 1. to swell like a full bag. 2. to hang loosely.

bag and baggage, [Colloq.], 1. with all one's possessions. 2. completely; entirely.

be in the bag, [Slang], to have its success assured.

be left holding the bag, [Colloq.], to be left to suffer the bad consequences or the blame for something.

B.Ag., Bachelor of Agriculture.

ba·gasse (bə-gas′), *n.* [Fr. *bagasse, bagace;* Mod. Pr. *bagasso,* refuse from processing of grapes or olives < Gallo-Roman **bacacea* < L. *vinacea,* grapeskin, husk < *vinum,* grapes], the part of sugar cane or sugar beets left after the juice has been taken out: it is used for fuel and in the manufacture of insulation.

bag·a·telle (bag′ə-tel′), *n.* [Fr.; It. *bagatella*], 1. something of little importance or value; trifle. 2. a game somewhat like billiards, played with cues and nine balls on a table having nine holes. 3. a short musical composition, especially for the piano.

Bag·dad (bag′dad, bäg-däd′), *n.* 1. the capital of Iraq, on the Tigris River: pop., 499,000: see **Iran and Iraq,** map. 2. a former caliphate in the region of the Tigris and Euphrates Rivers. Also spelled **Baghdad.**

Bage·hot, Walter (baj′ət), 1826–1877; English economist and political writer.

ba·gel (bā′g'l), *n.* [Yid. < *beigen* (cf. G. *biegen*), to bend, twist], a bread roll made of yeast dough twisted into a small doughnutlike shape, cooked in simmering water, and then baked in the oven.

bag·gage (bag′ij), *n.* [ME. *bagage;* OFr. *bagage* < *bague,* bundle < ML. *baga,* leather bag], 1. the trunks, bags, and other equipment of a traveler; luggage. 2. the supplies and gear of an army. 3. [by transference of sense "army baggage" to "camp follower"; prob. influenced by Fr. *bagasse,* harlot, camp follower; OFr. *baiasse* < ML. **bagassa,* **bacassa,* girl, servant girl], formerly, a prostitute or wanton; hence, 4. a saucy, impudent, or lively girl.

bag·gage·mas·ter (bag′ij-mas′tēr, bag′ij-mäs′tēr), *n.* a person in charge of receiving and dispatching baggage, especially at a railway station.

bag·gie (bäg'i, beg'i), *n.* [dim. of *bag*], [Scot.], 1. a little bag. 2. the belly or stomach.
bag·gi·ly (bag''l-i), *adv.* in a baggy manner.
bag·gi·ness (bag'i-nis), *n.* the state of being baggy.
bag·ging (bag'iŋ), *n.* cloth for making bags; sacking.
bag·gy (bag'i), *adj.* [BAGGIER (-i-ēr), BAGGIEST (-i-ist)], 1. puffed or swelling in a baglike way. 2. hanging loosely; unpressed: as, *baggy* trousers.
Bagh·dad (bag'dad, bäg-däd'), *n.* Bagdad.
bag·man (bag'mən), *n.* [*pl.* BAGMEN (-mən)], [British], a traveling salesman.
bagn·io (ban'yō, bän'yō), *n.* [It. *bagno;* L. *balneum,* bath, bathing place; Gr. *balaneion,* bath; akin to Sans. *galanah,* dripping], 1. a Turkish or Italian bathhouse. 2. in the Orient, a prison for slaves. 3. a house of prostitution; brothel.
bag·pipe (bag'pip'), *n.* *sometimes pl.* a shrill-toned musical instrument with a mouthpiece, finger-operated stops, and a leather bag from which air is forced into reed pipes to produce the sound: now played chiefly in Scotland.

BAGPIPE

B. Agr., Bachelor of Agriculture.
B.Ag.Sc., Bachelor of Agricultural Science.
ba·guette, ba·guet (ba-get'), *n.* [Fr. *baguette,* a rod; It. *bacchetta,* dim. of *bacchio,* a pole, cudgel; L. *baculum,* a walking stick, staff], 1. a thing with the shape of a convex oblong, as a gem, watch, etc. 2. this shape. 3. in *architecture,* a small, convex molding.
Ba·gui·o (bä'gē-ō', bag'i-ō'), *n.* a city in north central Luzon, in the Philippines: pop., 24,100.
bag·wig (bag'wig'), *n.* a wig with the back hair held in a cloth bag or snood: worn in the 18th century.
bag·worm (bag'wûrm'), *n.* the larva of any of various moths, that builds a cocoon like a bag: one variety infests orange trees.
bah (bä, ba), *interj.* an exclamation expressing contempt, scorn, or disgust.
‡**ba·ha·dur** (ba-hô'door, ba-hä'door), *n.* [Hind. *bāhadur,* hero, brave], a Hindu title of respect, used especially of foreign officers and officials.
Ba·ha·i (bə-hä'ē), *n.* [*pl.* BAHAIS (-ēz)], 1. a believer in Bahaism. 2. Bahaism.
Ba·ha·ism (bə-hä'iz'm), *n.* [Ar. *ba-ha,* splendor; + *-ism*], a religious sect developed out of Babism: begun in 1863 by Mirza Husayn Ali.
Ba·ha·ist (bə-hä'ist), *n.* a believer in Bahaism. *adj.* of Bahaism or Bahaists.
Ba·ha·ma Islands (bə-hā'mə, bə-hä'mə), a group of British islands in the West Indies, southeast of Florida and north of Cuba: area, 4,404 sq. mi.; pop., 70,000 (est. 1944); capital, Nassau.
Ba·ha·mas (bə-hā'məz, bə-hä'məz), *n.pl.* the Bahama Islands.
Ba·hí·a (bə-hē'ə; Port. bä-ē'ä), *n.* a seaport in central Brazil: pop., 388,000: also called *São Salvador.*

BAHAMA ISLANDS

Ba·hí·a Blan·ca (bä-ē'ä bläŋ'kä), a city on the coast of central Argentina: pop., 115,000.
Bah·rein Islands (bä-rān'), islands in the Persian Gulf, off the Arabian coast: they constitute a native Arab state under British protection: area, 250 sq. mi.; pop., 120,000; capital, Manama.
baht (bät), *n.* [*pl.* BAHTS (bäts), BAHT], [< Thai], the monetary unit of Thailand, a silver coin equal to about $.40 in 1948.
Bai·kal, Lake (bī-käl'), a lake in the Buryat Mongol A.S.S.R., southern Siberia: area, 13,300 sq. mi.
bail (bāl), *n.* [OFr., power, control, jurisdiction < *bailler,* to keep in custody, deliver < L. *bajulare,* to bear a burden < *bajulus,* porter, carrier], 1. money or credit deposited with the court to get an arrested person temporarily released on the assurance that he will come back for trial, etc. at the proper time. 2. the release thus brought about. 3. the person or persons giving bail. *v.t.* 1. to deliver (goods) in trust for a special purpose. 2. to set (an arrested person) free on bail (often with *out*). 3. to have (an arrested person) set free by giving bail (often with *out*).
go bail for, to furnish bail for.
bail (bāl), *n.* [OFr. *baille,* bucket < LL. **bajula,* vessel; cf. prec. BAIL (money)], a bucket or scoop for dipping up water and removing it from a boat. *v.i. & v.t.* 1. to remove water from (a boat) with or as with a bail. 2. to dip out (water, etc.) with or as with a bail.
bail out, to make a parachute jump from an aircraft.
bail (bāl), *n.* [ME. *beil;* ON. *beygla*], 1. a hoop-shaped support for holding up the cloth of a canopy, etc. 2. a hoop-shaped handle for a bucket, kettle, etc.
bail (bāl), *n.* [ME. < OFr. *baile* < L. *bajulus,* porter, carrier], 1. *pl.* an outer fortification made of stakes; palisades. 2. the outer wall or the outer court of a medieval castle. 3. a bar or pole to keep animals separate in a barn. 4. in *cricket,* either of two pieces of wood laid across the three stumps to form a wicket.
bail·a·ble (bāl'ə-b'l), *adj.* 1. that can be bailed. 2. allowing payment of bail.
bail bond, a bond (money or property) offered or deposited as bail: abbreviated **b.b.**
bail·ee (bāl'ē'), *n.* [*bail* (to deliver in trust) + *-ee*], a person who receives property from another under contract of bailment.
bai·ley (bā'li), *n.* [*pl.* BAILEYS (-iz)], [ME. *baili,* var. of *baile, bail;* see BAIL (fortification)], the outer wall or court of a medieval castle: term still kept in some proper names, as *Old Bailey.*
Bai·ley bridge (bā'li), [after the Eng. inventor, D. C. *Bailey*], in *military engineering,* a portable bridge consisting of a series of prefabricated steel sections in the form of lattices.
bail·ie (bāl'i), *n.* [Scot. < ME. *baili;* OFr. *baili* < L. *bajulus;* see BAILIFF], in Scotland, a municipal official corresponding to an alderman in England.
bail·iff (bāl'if), *n.* [ME. *bailif, baillif;* OFr. *bailif* < L. *bajulus,* porter], 1. a sheriff's assistant, who serves processes, etc. 2. an officer who has charge of prisoners and guards the jurors in a court. 3. in England, an administrative official of a district, with power to collect taxes, serve as a magistrate, etc. 4. an overseer or steward of an estate.
bail·i·wick (bāl'ə-wik'), *n.* [ME. *bailie,* bailiff + *wick;* AS. *wic,* village], 1. the district within which a bailiff has jurisdiction; hence, 2. one's special field of interest or authority.
bail·ment (bāl'mənt), *n.* 1. the providing of bail for an arrested person. 2. the delivering of goods to be held in trust for a specific purpose and returned when that purpose is ended.
bail·or (bāl'ôr', bāl'ēr), *n.* in *law,* a person who delivers property to another under contract of bailment.
bails·man (bālz'mən), *n.* [*pl.* BAILSMEN (-mən)], a person who gives bail for someone.
‡**bain-ma·rie** (ban'ma'rē'), *n.* [*pl.* BAINS-MARIE (ban'-)], [Fr.; L. *balneum Mariae,* lit., bath of Maria; faulty transl. of Gr. *kaminos Marias,* furnace of Maria (an alchemist)], a pan for holding hot water, into which other pans, containing food, etc. are put for heating.
Bai·ram (bī'räm', bī'räm'), *n.* [Turk. *bairâm*], either of two Moslem religious festivals following the fast of Ramadan.
Baird Mountains (bârd), a mountain range in northwestern Alaska.
bairn (bârn), *n.* [ME. *bearn;* AS. *bearn* < *beran,* to bear], [Scot.], a son or daughter; child.
bait (bāt), *v.t.* [ME. *baiten;* ON. *beita,* to make bite; caus. < *bita,* to bite], 1. to set dogs on for sport: as, people formerly *baited* animals for amusement; hence, 2. to torment or goad, especially by insulting or provocative remarks. 3. [Rare], to feed (animals) during a break in a journey. 4. to put food, etc. on (a hook or trap) as a lure for animals or fish. 5. to lure; tempt; entice. *v.i.* to stop for food during a journey. *n.* 1. food, etc. put on a hook or trap as a lure. 2. anything used as a lure; enticement. 3. a stop for rest or food during a journey.
SYN.—to **bait** is to torment or goad and implies malicious delight in the persecution (Jew-*baiting*); to **badger** is to pester so persistently as to bring to a state of frantic confusion; to **hound** is to pursue or attack relentlessly until the victim succumbs (he was *hounded* out of office); **heckle** denotes the persistent questioning and taunting of a public speaker so as to annoy or confuse him; **hector** implies a continual bullying or nagging in order to intimidate or break down resistance; **torment,** in this comparison, suggests continued harassment so as to cause acute suffering (*tormented* by her memories); **ride** is colloquial and implies harassment or teasing by ridiculing, criticizing, etc. (they were *riding* the rookie unmercifully from the dugout).
bait·er (bāt'ēr), *n.* a person who baits; especially, one who torments or goads others.
baize (bāz), *n.* [OFr. *baie,* pl. *baies,* baize < L. *badius,* chestnut-brown], 1. a thick, coarse woolen cloth, now often dyed green, used to cover tables, etc. 2. a drape, table cover, etc. made of this.
Ba·ja Ca·li·for·nia (bä'hä kä'lē-fôr'nyä), Lower California, a peninsula in Mexico: the Mexican name.
bake (bāk), *v.t.* [BAKED (bākt), BAKING], [ME. *baken;* AS. *bacan;* akin to G. *backen;* IE. base **bhogo,* warming, roasting], 1. to cook (food) by dry heat, especially in an oven. 2. to make dry and hard by heat; fire, as glazed stoneware. 3. to expose (oneself) to the rays of the sun, a lamp, etc. 4. [Obs.], to harden or cake. *v.i.* 1. to bake bread, pastry, etc. 2. to become baked; hence, 3. to become dry and hard in the sun: said of soil. *n.* 1. a baking. 2. a product of baking. 3. the amount baked. 4. [Scot.], a cracker.

bake·house (bāk'hous'), *n.* a bakery; especially, that room or part of a bakery containing the ovens.

ba·ke·lite (bā'kə-līt', bāk'līt), *n.* [after L. H. *Baekeland*, Belgian chemist], a synthetic resin made from formaldehyde and phenol, and used for the same purposes as hard rubber, celluloid, etc.: a trade-mark (**Bakelite**).

bak·er (bāk'ẽr), *n.* [ME. *bakere;* AS. *bæcere* < *bacan;* see BAKE], 1. a person whose work or business is baking bread, pastry, etc. 2. a small, portable oven.

Bak·er, George Pierce (pêrs bāk'ẽr), 1866–1935; American professor of the drama.

Baker, Mount, a mountain in the Cascade Range, northwestern Washington: height, 10,750 ft.

Baker, Newton Diehl (dēl), 1871–1937; American statesman and lawyer; secretary of war (1916–1921).

Baker Island, a small island in the Pacific, near the equator.

baker's dozen, thirteen: bakers formerly added an extra roll to the dozen bought, probably as a safeguard against the penalty for giving too few.

Bak·ers·field (bāk'ẽrz-fēld'), *n.* a city in south central California: pop., 57,000.

bak·er·y (bāk'ẽr-i, bāk'ri), *n.* [*pl.* BAKERIES (-iz, -riz)], a place where bread, pastries, etc. are baked or sold.

bak·ing (bāk'iŋ), *n.* 1. cooking by dry heat, in an oven, etc. 2. the amount baked at a single time. 3. a drying or hardening by heat.

baking powder, a leavening agent that raises dough by the gas (carbon dioxide) produced when baking soda and acid react in the presence of water: it usually contains baking soda mixed with either starch or flour and cream of tartar, sodium aluminum sulfate, or primary calcium phosphate.

baking soda, sodium bicarbonate, $NaHCO_3$, used in baking as a leavening agent and in medicine to counteract acidity.

bak·sheesh, bak·shish (bak'shēsh'), *n.* [Hind. & Per. *bakhshīsh* < *bakhshidan,* to give], in Turkey, Egypt, and some other Eastern countries, a tip; gratuity.

Bakst, Le·on Ni·ko·la·e·vich (lā'ôn' ni-kô-lä-yä'vich bäkst'), 1866?–1924; Russian painter.

Ba·ku (bä-ko͞o'), *n.* the capital of the Azerbaijan S.S.R., on the Caspian Sea: it is an oil center: pop., 968,000.

Ba·ku·nin, Mi·kha·il (mi-khä-ēl' bä-ko͞o'nin; Eng. bə-kū'nin), 1814–1876; Russian anarchist; progenitor of nihilism.

Bal., Baluchistan.

bal., 1. balance. 2. balancing.

Ba·laam (bā'ləm), *n.* in the *Bible,* a prophet hired to curse the Israelites: when he beat his donkey, the animal rebuked him: Numb. 22–24.

Bal·a·kla·va (bal'ə-klä'və), *n.* a seaport in the Crimea, U.S.S.R.: pop., 1,300: see **Crimea,** map.

bal·a·lai·ka (bal'ə-lī'kə), *n.* [Russ.], a Russian stringed instrument somewhat like a guitar but with a triangular body.

BALALAIKA

bal·ance (bal'əns), *n.* [ME.; OFr. < L. *bilanx, bilancis,* having two scales < *bis,* twice + *lanx,* a dish, scale], 1. an instrument for weighing, especially one that opposes equal weights, as in two matched scales hanging from either end of a lever supported exactly in the middle; scales. 2. the imaginary scales of fortune or fate, as an emblem of justice or the power to decide; hence, 3. the power to decide human fate, value, etc. 4. a state of equilibrium or equipoise; equality of two things in weight, force, quantity, etc. 5. bodily equilibrium: as, he kept his *balance* on the tightrope. 6. mental or emotional equilibrium. 7. the equilibrium of various elements in a design, painting, musical composition, etc.; harmonious proportion. 8. a weight, force, etc. that counteracts another or causes equilibrium; counterpoise. 9. equality of debits and credits in an account. 10. the excess of credits over debits or of debits over credits. 11. the amount still owed after a partial settlement. 12. a balancing. 13. [B-], the constellation Libra, or the seventh sign of the zodiac. 14. a balance wheel. 15. [Colloq.], whatever is left over; remainder. Abbreviated **bal.** (in senses 10 & 11). *v.t.* [BALANCED (-ənst), BALANCING], 1. to weigh in or as in a balance. 2. to compare as to relative importance, value, etc. 3. to counterpoise or counteract; offset; make up for. 4. to bring into or keep in a state of equilibrium or equipoise; poise; keep steady: as, he *balanced* himself on the stilts. 5. to make or be proportionate to; be equal to in weight, force, etc. 6. to find any difference which may exist between the debit and credit sides of (an account). 7. to equalize the debit and credit sides of (an account). 8. to settle (an account) by paying what is due. 9. in *dancing,* to move toward and then back from (a partner). *v.i.* 1. to be in equilibrium. 2. to be equal in value, weight, etc. 3. to have the credit and debit sides equal to each other. 4. to waver slightly; tilt and return to equilibrium. 5. in *dancing,* to balance partners. —***SYN.*** see **remainder, symmetry.**
in the balance, not yet settled; not yet determined.

balanced diet (or **ration**), a diet with the right amount, proportion, and variety of the foods needed for health.

balanced sentence, a sentence consisting of two parts with corresponding, often identical, structure (e.g., "Bad men excuse their faults; good men will leave them.").

balance of power, 1. a distribution of military and economic power among nations that is sufficiently even to keep any one of them from being too strong or dangerous. 2. the power of a minority to give control to a larger group by allying with it.

balance of trade, the difference in value between all the imports and all the exports of a country.

bal·anc·er (bal'ən-sẽr), *n.* 1. a person or thing that balances. 2. an acrobat. 3. either of the halteres (balancing organs) of a fly, mosquito, etc. 4. in *radio,* a device used with a direction finder to increase its accuracy.

balance sheet, a summarized statement showing the profits, losses, assets, liabilities, net worth, etc. of a business, usually figured at the close of a fiscal period: abbreviated **b.s.**

balance wheel, a wheel that regulates the movement of a mechanism, as in a watch, clock, music box, etc.

bal·a·noid (bal'ə-noid'), *adj.* [Gr. *balanoeidēs* < *balanos,* acorn + *eidēs,* form], acorn-shaped.

bal·as (bal'əs), *n.* [ME.; OFr. *balais;* Ar. *balakhsh* < Per. *Badakhshan,* name of a Persian province where the gem occurs], a pink or orange type of ruby spinel, a semiprecious stone.

bal·a·ta (bal'ə-tə), *n.* [Sp. < Tupi or Galibi *balata*], 1. a West Indian tree, the bully tree. 2. its milky sap, which dries into a rubberlike gum, used in making golf balls, insulated wire, etc.

Ba·la·ton (bä'lä-tôn), *n.* a lake in western Hungary: area, 265 sq. mi.: German name, *Plattensee.*

ba·laus·tine (bə-lôs'tin), *n.* [< L. *balaustium,* flower of the wild pomegranate; Gr. *balaustion*], 1. the wild pomegranate tree. 2. its flower.

Bal·bo·a (bal-bō'ə), *n.* a seaport in the Canal Zone, on the Pacific Ocean: pop., 3,100.

bal·bo·a (bäl-bō'ə), *n.* [Sp., after Vasco de *Balboa*], a silver coin, the monetary unit of Panama, equal in 1944 to about one dollar.

Bal·bo·a, Vas·co Nú·ñez de (väs'kô no͞o'nyeth *th*e bäl-bô'ä; Eng. bal-bō'ə), 1475–1517; Spanish explorer; discovered Pacific Ocean (1513).

bal·brig·gan (bal-brig'ən), *n.* [after *Balbriggan,* Eire], 1. a knitted cotton material used for hosiery, underwear, etc. 2. a similar woolen material. 3. *pl.* garments made of balbriggan. *adj.* made of balbriggan.

bal·co·nied (bal'kə-nid), *adj.* having a balcony.

bal·co·ny (bal'kə-ni), *n.* [*pl.* BALCONIES (-niz)], [It. *balcone* < OHG. *balcho,* a beam], 1. a platform projecting from the wall of a building and enclosed by a railing or balustrade: balconies usually open onto an upper story. 2. in a theater or auditorium, a tier of seats above the main floor and projecting over it.

BALCONY

bald (bôld), *adj.* [ME. *balled;* ? < W. *bal,* white spot, blaze (on animals); influenced by *ball* (sphere)], 1. having white on the head, as some animals and birds. 2. lacking hair on the head. 3. lacking the natural covering. 4. bare; plain; unadorned. 5. frank; blunt; flat; unqualified: as, a *bald* statement. —***SYN.*** see **bare.**

bal·da·chin, bal·da·quin (bal'də-kin, bôl'də-kin), *n.* [< It. or Fr.; Fr. *baldaquin* < It. *baldacchino* < *Baldacco,* Bagdad, where the cloth was manufactured], 1. a rich brocade, formerly made of silk and gold. 2. a canopy of this or other material, carried in church processions or placed over an altar or throne. 3. a marble or stone structure like a canopy, built over an altar.

bald cypress, a tree of the pine family, with small, needlelike leaves shed in the fall.

bald eagle, a large, strong eagle of North America: the adult has a white-feathered head and neck.

Bal·der (bôl'dẽr), *n.* [ON. *Baldr* < *baldor,* bold, hero], in *Norse mythology,* the god of light, peace, virtue, and wisdom, son of Odin and Frigg: he was killed by the trickery of Loki: also spelled **Baldr.**

bal·der·dash (bôl′dẽr-dash′), *n.* [< 16th-c. slang (in sense 2)], 1. nonsense; senseless talk or writing. 2. [Obs.], a senseless mixture of liquors, as of milk and beer.

bald·head (bôld′hed′), *n.* 1. a person who has a bald head. 2. a bird or animal with a patch of white on the top of its head.

bald-head·ed (bôld′hed′id), *adj.* having a bald head.

bald·pate (bôld′pāt′), *n.* 1. a bald-headed person. 2. the American widgeon. *adj.* bald-headed.

bal·dric (bôl′drik), *n.* [ME. *bauderik;* OFr. *baudrei;* prob. < OHG. personal name], a belt worn over one shoulder and across the chest to support a sword, trumpet, etc.

Bald·win (bôld′win), [OFr. *Baldewin, Baudoïn;* MHG. *Baldewin,* lit., bold friend < OHG. *bald* (akin to AS. *beald,* bold) + *wini,* friend], a masculine name. *n.* a moderately tangy, red winter apple.

Baldwin I, 1. 1058–1118; king of Jerusalem (1100–1118). 2. 1171?–1205; leader of the Fourth Crusade (1202–1204); emperor at Constantinople in 1204.

Bald·win, James Mark (bôld′win), 1861–1934; American psychologist.

Baldwin, Stanley, 1867–1947; British statesman; prime minister (1923–1924, 1924–1929, 1935–1937).

bale (bāl), *n.* [ME.; OFr. *bale, balle;* OHG. *balla,* a package, ball], a large package or bundle, especially a standardized quantity of goods, as raw cotton, compressed, bound, and sometimes wrapped: abbreviated **bl.** *v.t.* [BALED (bāld), BALING], to make into a bale or bales. —*SYN.* see **bundle.**

bale (bāl), *n.* [ME. *bale, baelu;* AS. *bealu*], [Poetic], 1. evil; disaster; harm. 2. sorrow; woe.

bale (bāl), *n.* [see BALEFIRE], [Archaic], a balefire.

bale (bāl), *n., v.i. & v.t.* bail (bucket, etc.).

Bal·e·ar·ic Islands (bal′i-ar′ik, bə-lêr′ik), a group of Spanish islands, including Majorca and Minorca, in the Mediterranean, east of Spain: area, 1,935 sq. mi.; pop., 382,000; capital, Palma.

BALEARIC ISLANDS

ba·leen (bə-lēn′), *n.* [ME. *balene, baleyne;* OFr. *baleine;* L. *balaena,* a whale], a stiff, flexible substance growing from the upper jaw of certain whales; whalebone.

BALEEN (hanging in plates from upper jaw of right whale)

bale·fire (bāl′fīr′), *n.* [AS. *bælfyr,* fire of the funeral pyre; *bæl,* great fire (akin to ON. *bal*) + *fyr,* fire], 1. an outdoor fire; bonfire. 2. a beacon fire. 3. [Obs.], a funeral pyre.

bale·ful (bāl′fəl), *adj.* [ME. *baleful, baluful;* AS. *bealufull;* *bealu,* calamity + *-full,* full], 1. deadly; harmful; evil. 2. [Archaic], sorrowful; wretched. —*SYN.* see **sinister.**

Balfe, Michael William (balf), 1808–1870; Irish composer and singer.

Bal·four, Arthur James (bal′foor), first Earl of Balfour, 1848–1930; British statesman; prime minister (1902–1906).

Balfour Declaration, a declaration by the British government (November, 1917) favoring the establishment in Palestine of a Jewish "National Home."

Ba·li (bä′li), *n.* an island of Indonesia, east of Java: area, 2,168 sq. mi.; pop., 1,203,000.

BALI

Ba·li·nese (bä′li-nēz′), *adj.* of Bali, its people, language, or culture. *n.* 1. [*pl.* BALINESE], a native or inhabitant of Bali. 2. the language of the Balinese.

balk (bôk), *n.* [ME. *balke;* AS. *balc, balca,* a bank, ridge; akin to G. *balken;* IE. base **bhel-əĝ,* plank, beam, as in Russ. *bolozno,* thick board], 1. a ridge of unplowed land between furrows. 2. a roughly hewn piece of timber. 3. the tie beam of a house. 4. an obstruction; thwarting; disappointment. 5. a blunder; error. 6. in *baseball,* an uncompleted pitch, entitling the base runners to advance one base. 7. in *billiards,* the area at one end of the table between the balk line and the cushion, from which a player must cue off or resume playing when his ball has left the table. *v.t.* 1. to miss intentionally; let slip. 2. to obstruct; thwart; foil. 3. [Obs.], to make balks in (land). *v.i.* to stop and obstinately refuse to move or act. Also spelled **baulk.** —*SYN.* see **frustrate.**

Bal·kan (bôl′kən), *adj.* 1. of the Balkan Peninsula. 2. of the Balkans, their people, etc. 3. of the Balkan Mountains.

Bal·kan·ize (bôl′kən-īz′), *v.t. & v.i.* [BALKANIZED (-īzd′), BALKANIZING], to break up into small, mutually hostile political units, as the Balkans after World War I.

Balkan Mountains, a mountain range extending across central Bulgaria to the Black Sea.

Balkan Peninsula, a peninsula in southern Europe, east of Italy and west of the Black Sea.

Bal·kans (bôl′kənz), *n.pl.* the countries of the Balkan Peninsula; Yugoslavia, Romania, Bulgaria, Albania, Greece, and European Turkey: also **Balkan States.**

Balkh (bälkh), *n.* Bactria.

Bal·khash, Lake (bäl-khäsh′), a salt lake in the Kazak S.S.R., Asia: area, 7,200 sq. mi.

balk line, 1. *a*) a line marking off the balk on a billiard table. *b*) any of four lines drawn on the table, parallel to the sides and ends: when playing balk-line billiards, a player may not make more than one or two caroms in any space on the cushion side of a balk line without driving a ball out of that space. 2. a line on the take-off run in the high jump, pole vault, etc., the crossing of which by a contestant is counted as one of the specified number of trials allowed.

balk·y (bôk′i), *adj.* [BALKIER (-i-ẽr), BALKIEST (-i-ist)], in the habit of balking. —*SYN.* see **contrary.**

ball (bôl), *n.* [ME. *ball, bal;* ON. *böllr;* akin to OHG. *balla;* IE. base **bhel-,* to swell up], 1. any round object; sphere; globe. 2. a planet or star, especially the earth. 3. a round or egg-shaped object used in various games. 4. any of several such games, especially baseball. 5. a throw or pitch of a ball. 6. the style of delivery of a baseball or other ball. 7. a round, solid missile; cannon ball; kind of bullet. 8. the eyeball. 9. a rounded part of the body: as, the *ball* of the foot. 10. in *baseball,* a pitch that is wide of the plate or goes above the shoulder or below the knee of the batter and is not struck at by him. 11. in *horticulture,* the roots of a plant, bound and packed for shipping. *v.i. & v.t.* to form into a ball.
ball up, [see BOLLIX], [Slang], to muddle; confuse.
be on the ball, [Slang], to be alert; be efficient.
have something on the ball, [Slang], to have ability.
play ball, 1. to begin or resume playing a ball game. 2. to begin or resume any activity. 3. [Colloq.], to co-operate.

ball (bôl), *n.* [Fr. *bal* < *baler,* to dance; L. *ballare;* Gr. *ballizein,* to dance, jump about < *ballein,* to throw], a formal social dance.

Ball, John (bôl), ?–1381; English priest; executed for his part in peasants' revolt (1381), led by Wat Tyler.

bal·lad (bal′əd), *n.* [Fr. *ballade,* dancing song < L. *ballare;* see BALL (dance)], 1. a romantic or sentimental song with the same melody for each stanza. 2. a song or poem that tells a story in short stanzas and simple words, with repetition, refrain, etc.: most old ballads are of unknown authorship and have been handed down orally, usually with additions and changes.

bal·lade (bə-läd′, ba-läd′), *n.* [Fr.; see BALLAD], 1. a verse form that has three stanzas of eight or ten lines each and an envoy of four or five lines: the last line of each stanza and of the envoy is the same, and an intricate rhyme pattern is repeated in each stanza. 2. a short composition of a romantic or narrative nature for piano or orchestra.

bal·lad·eer (bal′ə-dêr′), *n.* a ballad singer.

bal·lad·mon·ger (bal′əd-muŋ′gẽr), *n.* 1. a seller of popular ballads; especially, one who hawks them in the streets. 2. an inferior poet; poetaster.

bal·lad·ry (bal′əd-ri), *n.* 1. ballads in general. 2. the art of composing ballads.

ballad stanza, the four-line stanza commonly used in ballads, generally rhymed *abcb.*

ball and chain, 1. a heavy metal ball on a chain which can be fastened to a prisoner's body to keep him from escaping. 2. [Slang], one's wife or, rarely, husband.

ball-and-sock·et joint (bôl′ən-sok′it), a joint, as that of the hip or shoulder, formed by a ball in a socket, allowing limited movement in any direction.

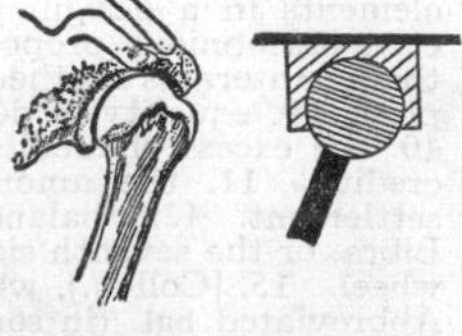
BALL-AND-SOCKET JOINTS

Bal·la·rat (bal′ə-rat′, bal′ə-rat′), *n.* a city in Victoria, Australia: pop., 38,000 (1947).

bal·last (bal′əst), *n.* [LG.; D. *barlast; bar,* bare, waste + *last,* a load], 1. anything heavy carried in a ship or vehicle to give stability or in an aircraft to help control altitude. 2. anything giving stability and firmness to character, human relations, etc. 3. crushed rock or gravel, as that placed between and below the ties of a railroad. *v.t.* 1. to furnish with ballast; stabilize. 2. to fill in (a railroad bed, etc.) with ballast.

ball bearing, 1. a bearing in which friction is reduced because the parts turn upon freely rolling metal balls. 2. a metal ball for such a bearing.

ball cock, a device consisting of a valve connected by a lever with a floating ball which shuts the valve when raised and opens it when lowered, as in flush toilets.

bal·le·ri·na (bal'ə-rē'nə), *n.* [It. < *ballare;* see BALL (dance)], a woman ballet dancer.
bal·let (bal'ā, ba'lā'), *n.* [Fr. *ballette,* dim. of *bal;* see BALL (dance)], 1. an intricate group dance using pantomime and conventionalized movements to tell a story. 2. dancing of this kind. 3. dancers of ballet.
bal·let·o·mane (bal'ət-ə-mān'), *n.* [Fr. coinage; *balleto-* (< It. *balletto,* ballet) + *-mane* < *manie,* lit., mania], a person enthusiastic about the ballet.
ball-flow·er (bôl'flou'ẽr), *n.* in *architecture,* a molding that looks like a ball held in the petals of a flower.
bal·lis·ta (bə-lis'tə), *n.* [*pl.* BALLISTAE (-tē)], [L. *ballista* < Gr. *ballein,* to throw], a device used in ancient warfare to hurl heavy stones and similar missiles.
bal·lis·tic (bə-lis'tik), *adj.* 1. of or connected with ballistics. 2. of the motion and force of projectiles.
bal·lis·ti·cian (bal'is-tish'ən), *n.* an expert in ballistics.
ballistic missile, a long-range missile that is guided by preset mechanisms in the first part of its flight, but is a free-falling object as it approaches its target.
bal·lis·tics (bə-lis'tiks), *n.pl.* [construed as sing.], the science dealing with the motion and impact of projectiles, such as bullets, rockets, bombs, etc.
bal·lo·net (bal'ə-net'), *n.* [Fr. *ballonnet,* dim. of *ballon;* see BALLOON], any of several auxiliary air or gas containers within a balloon or airship, which can be inflated or deflated during flight.
bal·loon (bə-lōōn'), *n.* [Fr. *ballon;* It. *ballone* < *balla,* a ball, globe; OHG. *balla;* see BALL], 1. a large, airtight bag which will rise and float above the earth when filled with hot air or a gas lighter than air, such as hydrogen or helium. 2. a bag of this sort with an attached basket or car for carrying passengers or instruments. 3. a small, inflatable rubber bag, used as a toy. 4. a globular glass container used in distilling. 5. the outline enclosing the words said by a character in a cartoon, as in comic strips. *v.t.* to cause to swell like a balloon; inflate. *v.i.* to travel by balloon. 2. to swell; expand. *adj.* like a balloon; large, round, and soft.
balloon barrage, a line of anchored balloons holding up nets and cables and used as an antiaircraft defense.
bal·loon·ist (bə-lōōn'ist), *n.* 1. a person who goes aloft in balloons. 2. the pilot of an airship.
balloon sail, a large, light sail used on yachts together with or instead of the customary working sails.
balloon tire, a large tire filled with air at a low pressure.
bal·lot (bal'ət), *n.* [It. *ballotta,* dim. of *balla;* see BALLOON], 1. originally a ball, now a ticket, paper, etc., by which a vote is registered. 2. act or method of voting, especially secret voting by the use of ballots or voting machines. 3. the total number of votes cast in an election. 4. a list of people running for office; ticket. *v.i.* to decide by means of the ballot; vote.
ballot box, a box into which voters put their ballots.
bal·lotte·ment (bə-lot'mənt; Fr. bȧ'lôt'män'), *n.* [Fr. < *ballotter,* to toss; prob. < *ballotte;* see BALLOT], 1. a method of determining pregnancy by pushing against the uterus with the finger, through either the abdominal wall or the vagina, so as to feel the impact of the embryo. 2. a similar method of diagnosing floating kidney.
ball·play·er (bôl'plā'ẽr), *n.* a person who plays ball games, especially baseball.
ball point pen, a type of fountain pen having instead of a point a small ball bearing that rolls over an ink reservoir and deposits the ink on the writing surface.
ball·room (bôl'rōōm', bôl'room'), *n.* a large room or hall for dancing.
ballroom dancing, a kind of dancing in which two people dance as partners to a waltz, foxtrot, etc.
ball valve, a valve that works by the action of a ball resting on the inlet hole: pressure of the rising fluid raises the ball and opens the hole; when the pressure is removed, the ball drops and closes the hole.

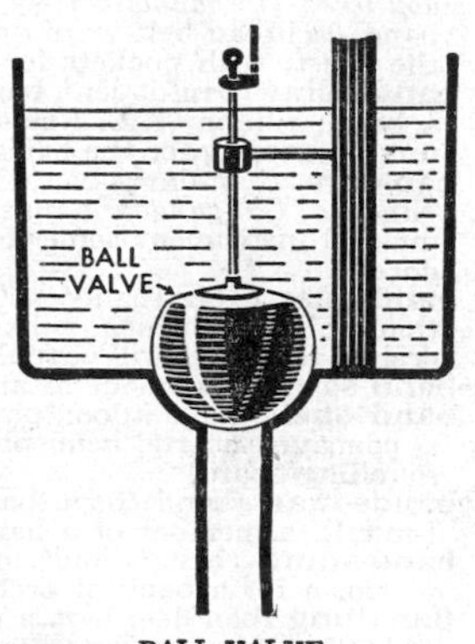

BALL VALVE

bal·ly·hoo (bal'i-hōō'), *n.* [after *Ballyhooly,* village in County Cork, Ireland], [Colloq.], 1. loud talk; noisy uproar. 2. loud, exaggerated, or sensational advertising or propaganda. *v.t.* & *v.i.* (*also* bal'i-hōō'), [BALLYHOOED (-hōōd', -hōōd'), BALLYHOOING], [Colloq.], to advertise or promote by sensational, showy methods.
balm (bäm), *n.* [ME. *baume;* OFr. *basme;* L. *balsamum* < Gr. *balsamon,* balsam], 1. an aromatic gum resin obtained from certain trees and plants and used as medicine; balsam. 2. any fragrant ointment or aromatic oil for healing or anointing. 3. anything healing or soothing, especially to the mind or temper: as, sleep was a *balm* to his troubles. 4. any of various aromatic plants similar to mint. 5. pleasant odor; fragrance.
bal·ma·caan (bal'mə-kan'), *n.* [after *Balmacaan,* Inverness, Scotland], a loose overcoat with raglan sleeves.
balm·i·ly (bäm''l-i), *adv.* in a balmy manner.
balm·i·ness (bäm'i-nis), *n.* the quality or state of being balmy.
balm of Gilead, 1. a small evergreen tree of the myrrh family, native to Asia and Africa. 2. an aromatic ointment prepared from its resin. 3. the American balsam fir. 4. a resin-bearing American poplar.
Bal·mor·al (bal-môr'əl, bal-mor'əl), *n.* [< *Balmoral* Castle, Scotland], 1. a striped or figured woolen petticoat worn beneath a skirt looped up in front. 2. the woolen material used for this. 3. [usually b-], a kind of laced walking shoe. 4. a round, brimless Scottish cap, flat on top.
Bal·mung (bäl'mooŋ), *n.* [G.], Siegfried's sword.
balm·y (bäm'i), *adj.* [BALMIER (-i-ẽr), BALMIEST (-i-ist)], 1. having the qualities of balm; soothing, soft, fragrant, mild, etc. 2. [var. of *barmy*], [British Slang], mildly crazy; idiotic; foolish.
bal·ne·al (bal'ni-əl), *adj.* [< L. *balneum,* bath; + *-al*], of a bath or bathing.
bal·ne·ol·o·gy (bal'ni-ol'ə-ji), *n.* [< L. *balneum,* bath; + *-logy*], the study of the therapeutic use of various sorts of bathing.
ba·lo·ney (bə-lō'ni), *n.* [altered < *bologna,* sausage], 1. bologna. 2. [Slang], nonsense; buncombe. ***interj.*** [Slang], nonsense! Also spelled **boloney.**
bal·sa (bôl'sə, bäl'sə), *n.* [Sp.], 1. a tropical American tree that has a very lightweight wood used for airplane models, rafts, etc. 2. the wood. 3. a raft, especially one made up of a frame resting on cylindrical floats.
bal·sam (bôl'səm), *n.* [AS. < L. *balsamum;* see BALM], 1. any of various oily or gummy, aromatic resins obtained from certain trees and plants, and used in some medicines and perfumes; balm. 2. any of various aromatic, resinous oils or fluids. 3. anything healing or soothing. 4. any impatiens, a kind of plant. 5. any of various plants or trees that yield balsam; especially, the balsam fir.
bal·sa·me·a·ceous (bôl'sə-mi-ā'shəs, bal'sə-mi-ā'shəs), *adj.* [*balsam* + *-aceous*], of a family of plants and trees yielding balsams and resins: see **burseraceous.**
balsam fir, an evergreen timber tree, native to Canada and the northern United States, the source of balsam lumber and turpentine: also called *balm of Gilead, fir pine.*
bal·sam·ic (bôl-sam'ik, bal-sam'ik), *adj.* 1. of or like balsam. 2. containing or yielding balsam. 3. balmy; soothing, healing, fragrant, etc.
bal·sa·mi·na·ceous (bôl'sə-mi-nā'shəs, bal'sə-mi-nā'shəs), *adj.* [Fr. *balsamine* < Gr. *balsaminē,* balsam plant; + *-aceous*], of the balsam family of plants, bearing irregular flowers with a spur or nectar sac formed by one of the sepals.
balsam poplar, a North American poplar whose buds are coated with a fragrant, sticky substance.
balsam spruce, a North American evergreen tree with silvery bark, drooping cones, and blue-green needles.
Balt., Baltic.
Bal·tic (bôl'tik), *adj.* 1. of the Baltic Sea. 2. of the Baltic States. *n.* the western branch of the Balto-Slavic languages, including Lithuanian and Lettish.
Baltic Sea, a sea northeast of Germany and west of Estonia, Latvia, and Lithuania, joining the North Sea: area, 163,000 sq. mi.; average depth, 180 ft.
Baltic States, Lithuania, Latvia, and Estonia: Finland is sometimes included.
Bal·ti·more (bôl'tə-môr', bôl'tə-mōr'), *n.* a seaport in northern Maryland, on Chesapeake Bay: pop., 939,000 (metropolitan area, 1,727,000).
Baltimore, Lord, see **Calvert, George.**
Baltimore oriole, [so named from having the colors of the coat of arms of Lord *Baltimore,* in colonial times proprietor of Maryland], a North American oriole that has an orange body with black on the head, wings, and tail: also called *hangbird, hangnest, golden robin.*
Bal·to- (bôl'tō), a combining form meaning *Baltic.*
Bal·to-Sla·vic (bôl'tō-slä'vik, bôl'tō-slav'ik), *adj.* designating or of a subfamily of Indo-European languages, including the Baltic and Slavic groups.
Ba·lu·chi·stan (bə-lōō'chi-stän', bə-lōō'chi-stan', bə-lōō'ki-stan'), *n.* a former province of western Pakistan, which included a union of native states (the *Baluchistan States*): two divisions of West Pakistan now comprise this area.
bal·us·ter (bal'əs-tẽr), *n.* [Fr. *balustre;* It. *balaustro,* pillar < *balausto;* L. *balaustium;* Gr. *balaustion,* flower of

the wild pomegranate: from the resemblance in shape], any of the small posts that support the upper rail of a railing, as on a staircase.

bal·us·trade (bal'ə-strād'), *n.* [Fr. *balustrade;* It. *balaustrata* < *balaustro;* see BALUSTER], a row of balusters with a rail supported on them.

Bal·zac, Ho·no·ré de (ô'nô'rā' də bál'zák'; Eng. on'ə-rā' də bal'zak), 1799–1850; French novelist.

Bam·berg (bam'bẽrg; G. bäm'berkh), *n.* a city in northern Bavaria, Germany: pop., 54,000.

‡**bam·bi·no** (bäm-bē'nô; Eng. bam-bē'nō), *n.* [*pl.* BAMBINI (-nē)], [It., child, dim. of *bambo,* childish], 1. a child; baby. 2. any image of the infant Jesus.

bam·boo (bam-bōō'), *n.* [Malay *bambu*], 1. any of a number of treelike tropical grasses having a springy, hollow, jointed stem, varying greatly in circumference and sometimes reaching a height of 120 feet: the stems are used for furniture, canes, etc. and the young shoots for food. 2. a stalk or cane of bamboo. *adj.* 1. of bamboo. 2. made of bamboo stems.

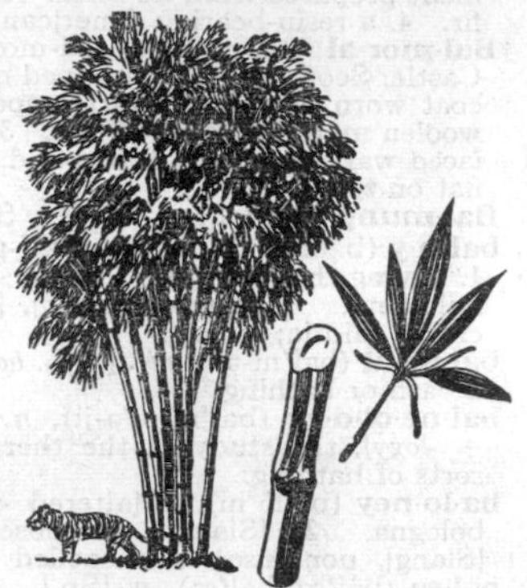

BAMBOO TREE, STEM, LEAF

bam·boo·zle (bam-bōō'z'l), *v.t.* [BAMBOOZLED (-z'ld), BAMBOOZLING], [c. 1700; cant form, with reversed vowels, of *bumbazzle* < *bombace, bombast;* see BOMBAST], [Colloq.], 1. to trick; cheat. 2. to confuse; puzzle.

ban (ban), *v.t.* [BANNED (band), BANNING], [ME. *bannen;* AS. *bannan,* to summon, proclaim; akin to L. *fari,* to speak, Gr. *phanai,* to say; IE. base **bha-*], 1. to prohibit (a thing); forbid. 2. to prohibit (a person) from doing something. 3. [Archaic], to curse; condemn; place under ban. *n.* [ME. < the *v.;* also < OFr. *ban,* decree < OHG. *bann,* prohibition], 1. in medieval times, a proclamation, especially an official call to arms. 2. an excommunication or condemnation by church authorities. 3. a curse. 4. official disapproval intended to prevent something; a prohibition. 5. a sentence or decree of outlawry. 6. (bän), in France, the younger group of army reserves. 7. (bän), formerly, in Prussia, a division of the Landwehr. —*SYN.* see **forbid.**

ban (ban), *n.* [Serbo-Croatian; ult. prob. < Per. *bān,* a lord, master], an overlord; governor: title used among the ancient Hungarians and later among Croatians and Slavonians.

ba·nal (bā'n'l, bə-nal', bə-näl', ban''l), *adj.* [Fr. < *ban;* see BAN (proclamation)], trite; hackneyed; commonplace; trivial. —*SYN.* see **insipid.**

ba·nal·i·ty (bə-nal'ə-ti), *n.* [*pl.* BANALITIES (-tiz)], [Fr. *banalité* < *banal;* see BANAL], 1. a trite or trivial idea, remark, etc.; platitude. 2. triteness; triviality.

ba·nan·a (bə-nan'ə), *n.* [Sp. & Port.], 1. a treelike tropical plant related to the plantains, with long, broad leaves and large clusters of edible fruit. 2. the fruit: it is narrow and somewhat curved, and has a sweet, creamy flesh covered by a yellowish or reddish skin.

BANANA
(9 ft. high)

banana oil, 1. amyl acetate, $CH_3CO_2C_5H_{11}$, a colorless liquid with an odor somewhat like that of bananas: it is used in flavorings, in making lacquers, etc. 2. [Slang], insincere or foolish talk; nonsense.

Ba·nat (bä-nät'), *n.* [< *ban* (an overlord)], an agricultural region formerly in southeastern Hungary, now in southwestern Romania and northeastern Yugoslavia.

Ban·bur·y tarts (ban'ber'i, bam'bẽr-i), [after *Banbury,* Oxfordshire, England, noted for its cakes], small baked pastries filled with mincemeat.

Ban·croft, George (ban'krôft, baŋ'kroft), 1800–1891; American statesman and historian.

band (band), *n.* [ME. < ON. *band;* also (in meaning "thin strip") < Fr. *bande,* flat strip; OFr. *bende;* OHG. *binta* < *bintan,* to bind], 1. something that binds, ties together, or encircles. 2. a strip of wood, metal, rubber, etc. fastened around something to bind or tie it together. 3. a contrasting strip or stripe running across or along the edge of a material, or separating different sorts of material. 4. a narrow strip of cloth used for decoration or to prevent raveling; binding; banding: often in combination, as in *hatband.* 5. a neckband; collar. 6. *usually pl.* two strips hanging in front from the neck, as part of certain academic, legal, or clerical dress. 7. a belt to drive wheels or pulleys in machinery. 8. [Archaic], something that restrains; fetter; bond. 9. in *architecture,* a thin layer or molding. 10. in *mining,* a thin layer of ore or metal. 11. in *radio,* a continuous sequence of broadcasting frequencies within given limits: as, a *band* from 830 to 870 kilocycles. *v.t.* [OFr. *bander* < the *n.*], 1. to put a band on or around; tie with a band. 2. to mark with a band.

band (band), *n.* [Fr. *bande,* a troupe, division; orig., prob., those following the same sign < Goth. *bandwa,* a sign], 1. a group of people gathered or united for a common purpose. 2. a group of musicians playing together, especially upon wind and percussion instruments: as, a brass *band,* a dance *band.* *v.i.* & *v.t.* to gather or unite for a common purpose (usually with *together*). —*SYN.* see **troop.**

band·age (ban'dij), *n.* [Fr. < *bande,* a band, strip], a strip of cloth, especially gauze, or other dressing used to bind or cover an injured part of the body. *v.t.* [BANDAGED (-dijd), BANDAGING], to put a bandage on (an injured part or person).

ban·dan·na, ban·dan·a (ban-dan'ə), *n.* [Hind. *bāndhnū,* method of dyeing], a large, colored handkerchief, usually with a figure or pattern on a bright background.

Ban·da Sea (bän'də), a part of the Pacific between the Moluccas and Timor, in the East Indies.

B and B, a drink made of brandy and benedictine.

band·box (band'boks'), *n.* [so named from being made to hold *bands* (collars)], a light box of wood or pasteboard to hold hats, collars, etc.

ban·deau (ban-dō', ban'dō), *n.* [*pl.* BANDEAUX (-dōz', -dōz)], [Fr., a fillet, diadem], 1. a narrow ribbon, especially one worn around the head to confine the hair. 2. a narrow brassiere.

‡**ban·de·ril·la** (bän'de-rēl'yä), *n.* [Sp., small banner < *bandera,* banner], in *bullfighting,* any of several barbed darts with little streamers attached to them, which the banderillero tries to stick into the neck and shoulders of the bull.

‡**ban·de·ril·le·ro** (bän'de-rē-lye'rô), *n.* [Sp. < *banderilla*], in *bullfighting,* a man whose task is to stick banderillas into the neck and shoulders of the bull.

ban·de·role, ban·de·rol (ban'də-rōl'), *n.* [Fr. *banderole;* It. *banderuola,* dim. of *bandiera,* banner], 1. a narrow flag, especially one attached to a lance or carried at the masthead of a ship; pennant; streamer. 2. a ribbon carrying an inscription or symbol; hence, 3. a replica of such a ribbon, as a picture or scroll. 4. a small flag over a tomb or at a funeral. Also **bannerol.**

ban·di·coot (ban'di-kōōt'), *n.* [< Telugu *pandikokku,* pig rat], 1. a very large rat of India and Ceylon, which destroys gardens and rice fields. 2. any of several ratlike animals of Australia and near-by islands, which carry their young in pouches, and eat insects and vegetables.

ban·dit (ban'dit), *n.* [*pl.* BANDITS (-dits), BANDITTI (ban-dit'i)], [It. *bandito* < *bandire,* to outlaw; ML. *bannire,* to ban; see BAN, *v.*], a robber; brigand; highwayman.

ban·dit·ry (ban'di-tri), *n.* a bandit's work; brigandage.

ban·dit·ti (ban-dit'i), *n.* alternative plural of **bandit.**

Ban·djer·ma·sin (bän'jẽr-mä'sin), *n.* Banjermasin: the Dutch name.

band·mas·ter (band'mas'tẽr, band'mäs'tẽr), *n.* the leader or conductor of a band of musicians.

Ban·doeng (bän'dooŋ), *n.* Bandung: Dutch spelling.

ban·dog (ban'dôg'), *n.* [*band* (something that binds) + *dog*], 1. a dog kept tied up as a watchdog or because he is ferocious. 2. a mastiff or bloodhound.

ban·do·leer, ban·do·lier (ban'də-lêr'), *n.* [Fr. *bandoulière;* It. *bandoliera* < *bandola,* dim. of *banda,* a band], a broad belt worn over one shoulder and across the chest, with pockets for carrying ammunition, etc.

ban·do·line (ban'də-lēn', ban'də-lin), *n.* [Fr. < *bandeau,* a band, ribbon + L. *linere,* to smear], a sticky, perfumed dressing for the hair.

ban·dore (ban-dôr', ban'dôr), *n.* [Sp. *bandurria;* L. *pandura;* Gr. *pandoura,* musical instrument], an ancient musical instrument somewhat like a guitar: also **pandore.**

band-pass filter (band'pas'), in *electricity,* a combination of filters which will pass frequencies within a desired range but will virtually cut out other frequencies.

band saw, a saw made as an endless belt on pulleys.

band shell, an outdoor platform for concerts, having a concave, nearly hemispherical back serving as a sounding board.

bands·man (bandz'mən, banz'mən), *n.* [*pl.* BANDSMEN (-mən)], a member of a band, especially of musicians.

band·stand (band'stand', ban'stand'), *n.* an outdoor platform for a band or orchestra, usually with a roof.

Ban·dung (bän'dooŋ), *n.* a city in western Java: pop., 167,000: Dutch spelling, **Bandoeng.**

band·wag·on (band'wag''n), *n.* a high, elaborately decorated wagon for the band to ride in, as in a parade. **on the bandwagon,** [Colloq.], on the winning or popular side, as in an election.

ban·dy (ban'di), *v.t.* [BANDIED (-did), BANDYING], [Fr.

bander, to bandy at tennis < *bande;* see BAND (a group)], 1. to toss back and forth, as a ball. 2. to pass (gossip, rumor, etc.) about freely and carelessly. 3. to give and take; exchange: as, let's not *bandy* words.

ban·dy (ban'di), *n.* [*pl.* BANDIES (-diz)], [prob. < Fr. *bander*, to bend], 1. a club bent at one end, used to strike a ball; hockey club. 2. a game played with such a club; variety of field hockey. ***adj.*** bent or curved outward; bowed.

ban·dy-leg·ged (ban'di-leg'id, ban'di-legd'), ***adj.*** having bandy legs; bowlegged.

bane (bān), ***n.*** [ME.; AS. *bana*, slayer; akin to Goth. *banja*, stroke, wound; IE. base **bhen*, to strike, wound, as in Sans. *banta*, ill, made sick], 1. [Poetic], deadly harm; ruin. 2. the cause of harm, death, etc. 3. deadly poison: now obsolete except in *ratsbane*, etc.

bane·ber·ry (bān'ber'i, bān'bẽr-i), ***n.*** [*pl.* BANEBERRIES (-iz)], 1. any of a number of related plants with poisonous berries colored white, red, or purplish black, and clusters of small, white flowers. 2. the berry of any of these plants.

bane·ful (bān'fəl), ***adj.*** full of bane; venomous; deadly; ruinous. —***SYN.*** see **pernicious.**

Banff (bamf), ***n.*** 1. a summer resort in Banff National Park. 2. a county of northeastern Scotland: pop., 49,000: also **Banffshire.** 3. its county seat.

Banff National Park, a Canadian national park in the Rocky Mountains, southwestern Alberta: area, 2,585 sq. mi.

Banff·shire (bamf'shir), ***n.*** Banff (sense 2).

bang (baŋ), ***v.t.*** [ON. *banga*, to pound, hammer; akin to G. *bengel*, cudgel], 1. to hit with a resounding blow; strike hard and noisily. 2. to close (a door, etc.) noisily. 3. to handle violently. ***v.i.*** 1. to make a loud noise through concussion or explosion: as, firecrackers *bang.* 2. to move noisily or with a violent impact (*against* something). ***n.*** 1. a hard, noisy blow or impact. 2. a loud, sudden noise, as of hitting or exploding. 3. [Slang], pleasure; enjoyment; stimulation. ***adv.*** 1. hard and noisily. 2. loudly and abruptly. ***interj.*** a sound imitating that of a shot or explosion.

bang up, to do physical damage to.

bang (baŋ), ***v.t.*** [< dial. *bangled*, hanging loosely, flapping < *bangle, v.t.*, freq. of *bang*], to cut (hair) short and straight. ***n.*** 1. a fringe of hair cut in this way. 2. *pl.* banged hair worn across the forehead.

bang (baŋ), ***n.*** bhang.

Ban·ga·lore (baŋ'gə-lôr', baŋ'gə-lōr'), ***n.*** a city in southern India: pop., 779,000: capital of Mysore state.

ban·ga·lore torpedo (baŋ'gə-lôr', baŋ'gə-lōr'), [< *Bangalore*, India], in *military usage*, a piece of metal tubing filled with high explosive, used especially to blast a path through a barbed-wire entanglement or to detonate buried mines.

bang·board (baŋ'bôrd', baŋ'bōrd'), ***n.*** [*bang, v.* + *board*], a large board mounted along one side of a wagon, against which corn huskers toss the ears of corn, causing them to rebound into the wagon.

Bang·ka (bäŋ'kə), ***n.*** an island of Indonesia, east of Sumatra: area, 4,611 sq. mi.; pop., 230,000: also spelled **Banka.**

Bang·kok (baŋ'kok), ***n.*** the capital of Thailand, a seaport in the southern part: pop., 1,328,000.

ban·gle (baŋ'g'l), ***n.*** [Hind. *bangrī*, glass bracelet], a decorative bracelet, armlet, or anklet.

Ban·gor (baŋ'gôr), ***n.*** a city in southern Maine, on the Penobscot River: pop., 39,000.

Bang's disease (baŋz), [after B. L. F. *Bang*, 19th-c. Danish physician], an infectious disease of cattle, caused by a bacterium and often resulting in abortion.

bang-up (baŋ'up'), ***adj.*** [Slang], very good; excellent.

Bang·we·u·lu, Lake (baŋ'wi-ōō'lōō), a lake in Northern Rhodesia, Africa: area, 1,900 sq. mi.

ban·ian (ban'yən), ***n.*** a banyan.

ban·ian (ban'yən), ***n.*** [Port. < Hind. *vaniyo*, trader; Sans. *vaṇij*, merchant], 1. a Hindu merchant of a caste that refuses to eat meat. 2. a loose-fitting gown or shirt worn in India.

ban·ish (ban'ish) ***v.t.*** [ME. *banischen;* OFr. *banir;* ML. *bannire*, to proclaim, banish < *bannum*, a ban], 1. to put out of the country as a punishment; exile. 2. to send away; dismiss. 3. to put out of one's thoughts.

***SYN.*—banish** implies removal from a country (not necessarily one's own) as a formal punishment; **exile** implies compulsion to leave one's own country, either because of a formal decree or through force of circumstance; **expatriate** suggests more strongly voluntary exile and often implies the acquiring of citizenship in another country; to **deport** is to send (an alien) out of the country, either because of unlawful entry or because his presence is regarded as undesirable; to **transport** is to banish (a convict) to a penal colony; **ostracize** today implies forced exclusion from society, as because of disgrace (after his bankruptcy he was *ostracized* by all his friends).

ban·ish·ment (ban'ish-mənt), ***n.*** a banishing or being banished; exile.

ban·is·ter (ban'is-tẽr), ***n.*** [altered < *baluster*], 1. a baluster. 2. *pl.* a balustrade. Also spelled **bannister.**

Ban·jer·ma·sin (bän'jẽr-mä'sin), ***n.*** a seaport on the southern coast of Borneo: pop., 150,000: Dutch name, *Bandjermasin.*

ban·jo (ban'jō), ***n.*** [*pl.* BANJOS, BANJOES (-jōz)], [altered < *bandore*], a stringed musical instrument having a long neck and a circular body covered on top with tightly stretched skin: the strings are plucked with the fingers or a plectrum.

BANJO

ban·jo·ist (ban'jō-ist), ***n.*** a person who plays the banjo.

bank (baŋk), ***n.*** [Fr. *banque;* It. *banca* < OHG. *bank*, a bench (see BANK, a mound): money-changers ‡formerly used a bench or table in transacting their business], 1. an establishment for receiving, keeping, lending, or, sometimes, issuing money and making easier the exchange of funds by checks, notes, etc.: banks make profit by lending money at interest: abbreviated **bk.** 2. the office or building of such an establishment. 3. the fund or pool held by the banker or dealer in some gambling games. 4. in *medicine*, any place for gathering and distributing blood for transfusions or parts of the body for transplantation: as, an eye (i.e., corneal) *bank.* ***v.i.*** 1. to deposit money in or do business with a bank. 2. to operate or manage a bank. 3. to keep the bank, as in some gambling games. ***v.t.*** to deposit (money) in a bank.

bank on, [Colloq.], to depend on; rely on.

bank (baŋk), ***n.*** [ME. *banke* < Anglo-N. **banki* (ON. *bakki*); IE. base **bhong-*, an arching up < **bheg-*, to bend, as in OHG. *bank* & AS. *benc* (see BENCH)], 1. a long mound or heap, as of ground or clouds; ridge. 2. a steep rise or slope, as of a hill. 3. a stretch of rising land at the edge of a body of water, especially a stream. 4. a shoal or shallow place, as in a sea or lake. 5. the sloping of an airplane laterally to avoid slipping sideways on a turn. 6. a cushion of a billiard table. 7. in *mining*, the face or top end of the body of ore. ***v.t.*** 1. to heap dirt around for protection from cold, light, etc.; embank. 2. to arrange (a fire) by covering with ashes, adding fuel, etc. so that it will burn low and keep longer. 3. to heap or pile up so as to form a bank. 4. to give a rising slope to (a curve in a road, etc.). 5. to slope (an airplane) laterally on a turn, with the inside wing low and the outside wing high so as to prevent slipping sideways. 6. in *billiards*, *a*) to stroke (a ball) so that it recoils from a cushion. *b*) to make (a shot) in this way. ***v.i.*** 1. to take the form of a bank or banks. 2. to bank an airplane; fly with lateral slope on a turn. —***SYN.*** see **shoal, shore.**

bank (baŋk), ***n.*** [ME. *banck;* OFr. *banc*, a bench < OHG. *bank* (see BANK, mound)], 1. a bench for rowers in a galley. 2. a row or tier of oars. 3. a row or series of objects; tier. 4. a row of keys in a keyboard or console. 5. in *electricity*, a group of pieces of similar equipment placed near each other and operating in conjunction. ***v.t.*** to arrange in a bank.

Ban·ka (bäŋ'kə), ***n.*** Bangka.

bank·a·ble (baŋk'ə-b'l), ***adj.*** acceptable to a bank.

bank account, money deposited in a bank and subject to withdrawal by the depositor.

bank annuities, British government bonds; consols.

bank bill, 1. a bank note. 2. a bill of exchange issued or accepted by a bank.

bank·book (baŋk'book'), ***n.*** the book in which the account of a depositor in a bank is recorded: also called *passbook.*

bank discount, interest deducted by a bank from a loan when the loan is made: it is equal to the normal interest from the date of the loan to the date of the final payment.

bank draft, a draft or bill of exchange drawn by a bank on another bank: abbreviated **B/D.**

bank·er (baŋk'ẽr), ***n.*** [< *bank* (financial establishment), by analogy with Fr. *banquier*], 1. a person or company that owns or manages a bank. 2. the keeper of the bank in some gambling games.

bank·er (baŋk'ẽr), ***n.*** [< *bank* (a shoal)], a person or ship engaged in cod fishing on the Newfoundland banks.

bank holiday, 1. in Great Britain, any of six legal holidays on which banks are closed. 2. any weekday on which banks are closed.

bank·ing (baŋk'iŋ), ***n.*** the work of a banker; business or study of operating a bank: abbreviated **bkg., bank.**

banking house, a company in the business of banking.

bank night, [Colloq.], an evening when cash prizes are given away at a motion-picture theater.
bank note, a promissory note issued by a bank, payable on demand: it is a form of paper money.
bank paper, 1. bank notes collectively. 2. any bankable notes, bills, etc.
bank rate, a standard rate of discount set by a central bank or banks.
bank·rupt (baŋk′rupt, baŋk′rəpt), ***n.*** [Fr. *banqueroute;* It. *banca rotta; banca,* bench + *rotta,* broken < L. *ruptus,* pp. of *rumpere,* to break], 1. a person legally declared unable to pay his debts: the property of a bankrupt is divided among his creditors or administered for their benefit: abbreviated **bkpt.** 2. loosely, anyone unable to pay his debts. 3. a person who lacks a certain quality: as, a mental *bankrupt.* ***adj.*** 1. that is a bankrupt; unable to pay one's debts; insolvent. 2. lacking in some quality. ***v.t.*** to cause to become bankrupt.
bank·rupt·cy (baŋk′rupt-si, baŋk′rəp-si), ***n.*** [*pl.* BANKRUPTCIES (-siz)], state or instance of being bankrupt.
bank·si·a (baŋk′si-ə), ***n.*** [after Sir Joseph *Banks,* Eng. botanist (1743–1820)], an Australian evergreen with clusters of showy yellow flowers.
Bank·side (baŋk′sīd′), ***n.*** a district along the south bank of the Thames in London: former site of many theaters, including the Shakespearean Globe Theater.
ban·ner (ban′ẽr), ***n.*** [ME. *banere;* OFr. *banere, baniere;* LL. *bandum* < Goth. *bandwa,* a sign], 1. a piece of cloth bearing an emblem, motto, slogan, etc. 2. a flag. 3. a headline extending across a newspaper page. ***adj.*** foremost; leading; excelling.
ban·ner·et, ban·ner·ette (ban′ẽr-et′), ***n.*** a small banner.
ban·ner·et (ban′ẽr-it, ban′ẽr-et′), ***n.*** [ME. & OFr. *baneret,* dim. of *banere,* banner], 1. originally, a knight allowed to lead his men into battle under his own banner. 2. a degree of knighthood above that of knight bachelor: often awarded for bravery in battle.
ban·ner·ol (ban′ẽr-ōl′), ***n.*** a banderole.
ban·nis·ter (ban′is-tẽr), ***n.*** a banister.
ban·nock (ban′ək), ***n.*** [ME. *bannok;* AS. *bannuc;* Gael. *bannach,* a cake], [Scot.], a thick, flat cake made of oatmeal or barley meal baked on a griddle.
Ban·nock·burn (ban′ək-bũrn′, ban′ək-bũrn′), ***n.*** a town in central Scotland: site of a battle (1314) in which Scotland, under Robert Bruce, won its independence from England.
banns (banz), ***n.pl.*** [see BAN (proclamation)], the proclamation, generally made in church on three successive Sundays, of an intended marriage: also spelled **bans.**
ban·quet (baŋ′kwit, ban′kwit), ***n.*** [Fr. < dim. of *banc,* a table], 1. an elaborate meal; feast. 2. a formal dinner, usually with toasts and speeches. ***v.t.*** to honor with or entertain at a banquet. ***v.i.*** to eat sumptuously.
ban·quette (baŋ-ket′), ***n.*** [Fr., dim. of *banc,* a bench], 1. a gunners' platform extending along the inside of a trench or parapet. 2. a raised way; sidewalk. 3. an upholstered bench, especially one along a wall in a restaurant.
Ban·quo (baŋ′kwō, ban′kō), ***n.*** a character in Shakespeare's ***Macbeth:*** the ghost of Banquo disrupts a banquet by appearing only to Macbeth, who had ordered his murder.
ban·shee, ban·shie (ban′shē, ban-shē′), ***n.*** [Ir. *bean sidhe* < *bean,* woman + *sith,* fairy], in *Irish & Scottish folklore,* a female spirit believed to wail outside a house as a warning that a death will occur soon in the family.
ban·tam (ban′təm), ***n.*** [after *Bantam,* province in Java], 1. [B-], any of several breeds of small fowl: the male often is a good fighter. 2. a small but aggressive or pugnacious person. 3. a bantamweight. ***adj.*** like a bantam; small, aggressive, etc.
ban·tam·weight (ban′təm-wāt′), ***n.*** a boxer or wrestler who weighs between 113 and 118 pounds. ***adj.*** of bantamweights.
ban·ter (ban′tẽr), ***v.t.*** [17th-c. slang; prob. influenced by *bandy, v.*], to tease or make fun of in a playful, good-natured way. ***v.i.*** to exchange banter (*with* someone). ***n.*** good-natured teasing, ridicule, or joking.
ban·ter·ing·ly (ban′tẽr-iŋ-li, ban′triŋ-li), ***adv.*** in a bantering manner.
Ban·ting, Sir **Frederick Grant** (ban′tiŋ), 1891–1941; Canadian physician; co-discoverer of insulin; received Nobel prize in medicine, 1923.
bant·ling (bant′liŋ), ***n.*** [altered < G. *bankling,* bastard < *bank,* a bench], a youngster; brat.
Ban·tu (ban′tōō′), ***n.*** [Bantu *ba-ntu,* mankind, men; *ba,* var. of *aba,* pl. personal prefix + *-ntu,* a person], 1. [*pl.* BANTU, BANTUS (-tōōz′)], a member of a large group of Negroid tribes in central and southern Africa. 2. the family of languages of these tribes. ***adj.*** of the Bantu or their languages.
Ban·ville, Thé·o·dore Faul·lain de (tā′ô′dôr′ fō′lan′ də bän′vēl′), 1823–1891; French poet and dramatist.
ban·yan (ban′yən), ***n.*** [so called (orig. by Europeans) in allusion to a tree of this kind at Gambroon (now Bandar Abbas) on the Persian Gulf, under which the *banians* (see BANIAN) had built a pagoda], an East Indian fig tree from whose branches grow shoots that take root and become new trunks: also spelled **banian.**
ban·zai (bän′zä′i, bän′zī′), ***interj.*** [Japan., lit., ten thousand years], a Japanese greeting, battle cry, and cheer, meaning "May you live ten thousand years!"
banzai charge, a suicidal charge by Japanese troops, especially as a diversionary action.
ba·o·bab (bā′ō-bab′, bä′ō-bab′), ***n.*** [prob. E.Afr. native name], a tall tree with a thick trunk, found in Africa and India: fiber from its bark is used for making rope, paper, etc., and the gourdlike fruit has an edible pulp.
bap., bapt., baptized.
bap·tism (bap′tiz′m), ***n.*** [ME. & OFr. *baptesme;* L. *baptisma,* a dipping in < Gr. *baptisma,* immersion < *baptizein,* to plunge, immerse], 1. a baptizing or being baptized; specifically, the ceremony or sacrament of admitting a person into Christianity or a specific Christian church by dipping him in water or sprinkling water on him, as a symbol of washing away sin. 2. any experience or ordeal that initiates, tests, or purifies.
bap·tis·mal (bap-tiz′m'l), ***adj.*** [ML. *baptismalis* < L. *baptismus*], connected with or used in baptism.
baptism of fire, 1. the first time that new troops are under fire or in combat. 2. any experience that tests one's courage, strength, etc. for the first time.
Bap·tist (bap′tist), ***n.*** [ME. *baptiste,* baptizer; OFr.; L. *baptista;* Gr. *baptistēs* < *baptizein,* to plunge, immerse], 1. [b-], originally, a person who baptizes; especially, 2. John the Baptist. 3. a member of a Protestant denomination holding that baptism should be given only to adult believers and by immersion rather than sprinkling: abbreviated **Bap., Bapt.**
bap·tis·ter·y (bap′tis-tri, bap′tis-tẽr-i), ***n.*** [*pl.* BAPTISTERIES (-triz, -iz)], [L. *baptisterium,* place for bathing; Gr. *baptisterion* < *baptizein,* to plunge, immerse], 1. a place, especially in or near a church, used for baptizing. 2. a baptismal font or tank.
bap·tist·ry (bap′tis-tri), ***n.*** [*pl.* BAPTISTRIES (-triz)], a baptistery.
bap·tize (bap-tīz′, bap′tīz), ***v.t.*** [BAPTIZED (-tīzd′, -tīzd), BAPTIZING], [ME. *baptisen;* OFr. *baptiser;* L. *baptizare;* Gr. *baptizein,* to plunge, immerse], 1. to dip (a person) into or sprinkle with water as a symbol of admission into Christianity or a specific Christian church and of washing away sin; administer baptism to. 2. to purify; cleanse; initiate. 3. to give a first name to (a person) as part of the baptismal ceremony; christen.
bar (bär), ***n.*** [ME. & OFr. *barre;* LL. *barra*], 1. any piece of wood, metal, etc. longer than it is wide or thick, often used as a barrier, fastening, lever, etc. 2. an oblong piece or mass of soap, chocolate, metal, etc. 3. a unit of quantity based on such a piece: as, this gun barrel contains four *bars* of copper. 4. a thing that blocks the way or prevents entrance, departure, or further movement: cf. **sand bar.** 5. anything that hinders or prevents: as, illiteracy is a *bar* to success. 6. a strip, stripe, band, or broad line, as of light or color. 7. the part of a law court, enclosed by a railing, where the judges or lawyers sit, or where prisoners are brought to trial. 8. a law court or system of courts; hence, 9. any place of judgment: as, he was condemned at the *bar* of public opinion. 10. lawyers collectively. 11. the legal profession. 12. a counter at which alcoholic drinks and sometimes food are served. 13. an establishment or room with such a counter. 14. the mouthpiece of a horse's bit, or the part of a horse's mouth into which it is fitted. 15. in *heraldry,* a horizontal stripe or stripes on a shield or bearing. 16. in *law, a*) the nullifying of a claim or action. *b*) the process of bringing this about. 17. in *music, a*) a vertical line across a staff, dividing it into measures. *b*) a measure. *c*) two vertical lines across a staff; double bar. 18. in *zoology,* either of the ends of the wall of a horse's hoof, curving into the sole. ***v.t.*** [BARRED (bärd), BARRING], 1. to fasten with or as with a bar. 2. to obstruct by means of a bar or bars; shut off; close. 3. to oppose; prevent. 4. to keep (a person) out of; exclude: as, he was *barred* from the contest. 5. to mark with stripes. 6. in *law,* to prevent or stop (an action) by legal objection. ***prep.*** leaving out; excluding: as, it's the best hotel in town, *bar* none. —***SYN.*** see **hinder, shoal.**
cross the bar, to die.
BAR, B.A.R., Browning automatic rifle.
Bar., Baruch.
bar., 1. barometer. 2. barrel. 3. barrister.
B.Ar., Bachelor of Architecture.
Ba·rab·bas (bə-rab′bəs), ***n.*** in the *Bible,* the prisoner whom the people wanted freed instead of Jesus: Matt. 27:16–21.
bar·a·the·a (bar′ə-thē′ə), ***n.*** [19th c.; ? coined], a soft fabric made of silk and wool or silk and cotton.
barb (bärb), ***n.*** [ME. & OFr. *barbe;* L. *barba* (for **farba*), a beard; see BEARD], 1. a thin, somewhat beardlike growth near the mouth of certain animals. 2. a piece of white linen for covering the throat and sometimes the chin, worn by certain nuns. 3. a sharp point curving or projecting backward from the main point of a fishhook, harpoon, arrow, etc. 4. sharpness; sting: as, the *barb* of his wit made us wince. 5. one of the hairlike branches growing from the shaft of a feather:

see **feather,** illus. 6. in *botany, a*) a hooked hair or bristle. *b*) an awn. ***v.t.*** to provide with a barb or barbs.

barb (bärb), ***n.*** [Fr. *barbe,* Barbary horse; It. *barbero* < *Barbarie;* Ar. *Barbar,* Berbers], 1. a horse of a breed native to Barbary, noted for speed, strength, and gentle behavior. 2. a variety of pigeon.

Bar·ba·di·an (bär-bā′di-ən), ***adj.*** of Barbados. ***n.*** a native or inhabitant of Barbados.

Bar·ba·dos (bär-bā′dōz, bär′bə-dōz′), ***n.*** an island of the West Indies Federation, east of the Windward Islands: area, 166 sq. mi.; pop., 237,000.

Bar·ba·ra (bär′bə-rə, bär′brə), [L., fem. of *barbarus* (see BARBAROUS), lit., foreign, strange], a feminine name: diminutives, *Babs, Bab.*

bar·bar·i·an (bär-bâr′i-ən, bär-bâr′yən), ***n.*** [< L. *barbarus;* see BARBAROUS], 1. originally, anyone not a member of one's own national, cultural, or religious group; alien; foreigner: in the ancient world applied especially to non-Greeks, non-Romans, or non-Christians. 2. a member of a people or group with a civilization regarded as primitive, savage, etc. 3. an insensitive, coarse, or unmannerly person; boor. 4. a savage, cruel person; brute. ***adj.*** of or like a barbarian or barbarians; especially, *a*) uncivilized; rude. *b*) savage; cruel; barbarous.

SYN.—**barbarian** basically refers to a civilization regarded as primitive, usually without further connotation (the Anglo-Saxons were a *barbarian* people); **barbaric** suggests the crudeness and lack of restraint regarded as characteristic of primitive peoples (*barbaric* splendor); **barbarous** connotes the cruelty and brutality regarded as characteristic of primitive peoples (*barbarous* warfare); **savage** implies a more primitive civilization than **barbarian** and connotes even greater fierceness and cruelty (a *savage* inquisition). —***ANT.*** civilized.

bar·bar·ic (bär-bar′ik), ***adj.*** [L. *barbaricus;* Gr. *barbarikos* < *bar aros;* see BARBAROUS], 1. of, like, or characteristic of barbarians; primitive. 2. wild, crude, and unrestrained. —***SYN.*** see **barbarian.**

bar·ba·rism (bär′bə-riz′'m), ***n.*** [L. *barbarismus;* Gr. *barbarismos* < *barbaros;* see BARBAROUS], 1. the use of words and expressions not standard in a language. 2. a word or expression of this sort (e.g., "youse" for "you"): see also **impropriety, solecism.** 3. the state of being primitive or lacking civilization. 4. a barbarous action, custom, etc. 5. brutal behavior; barbarity.

bar·bar·i·ty (bär-bar′ə-ti), ***n.*** [*pl.* BARBARITIES (-tiz)], 1. cruelty; brutality; inhumanity. 2. a cruel or brutal act. 3. a barbaric taste, manner, form, etc. 4. a word or expression that is substandard in usage.

bar·ba·rize (bär′bə-rīz′), ***v.t.*** [BARBARIZED (-rīzd′), BARBARIZING], [Gr. *barbarizein,* to side with the barbarians], to make barbarous; specifically, to corrupt (speech or style) with barbarisms. ***v.i.*** to become barbarous.

Bar·ba·ros·sa (bär′bə-rôs′ə, bär′bə-ros′ə), ***n.*** [It. < *barba,* beard + *rossa,* red: so named from his beard], Frederick I of Germany (1123?–1190).

bar·ba·rous (bär′bə-rəs), ***adj.*** [L. *barbarus;* Gr. *barbaros,* foreign, strange, ignorant; prob. < **barbar,* echoic word used for description of strange tongues], 1. originally, different from one's own language or customs; foreign; alien: in the ancient world, any person or thing that was non-Greek, non-Roman, or non-Christian was called barbarous. 2. characterized by words and phrases that are substandard in usage; also, not classical: said of language. 3. characteristic of barbarians; primitive or lacking in civilization. 4. crude, coarse, rough, etc. 5. cruel; brutal. 6. harsh in sound; raucous. —***SYN.*** see **barbarian.**

Bar·ba·ry (bär′bə-ri), ***n.*** the Moslem region west of Egypt, in North Africa.

Barbary ape, a tailless ape found in northern Africa and on Gibraltar, often trained to do tricks.

Barbary Coast, 1. the coastal region in northern Africa, from Tripoli to Morocco. 2. a district in San Francisco before the earthquake of 1906, known for its saloons, gambling places, and houses of prostitution.

Barbary States, the former countries of Morocco, Algiers, Tunis, and Tripoli in northern Africa: they were centers of piracy in the Mediterranean.

bar·bate (bär′bāt), ***adj.*** [L. *barbatus,* bearded < *barba,* a beard], 1. bearded. 2. in *botany,* having hairlike tufts, or awns, as oats, barley, etc.

bar·be·cue (bär′bə-kū′), ***n.*** [Sp. *barbacoa* < Haitian *barbacoa,* framework of sticks], 1. originally, a raised framework for smoking, drying, or broiling meat. 2. a hog, steer, etc. broiled or roasted whole over an open fire. 3. any meat broiled on a spit over an open fire. 4. an entertainment, usually outdoors, at which such meat is prepared and eaten. 5. a restaurant that makes a specialty of barbecuing. ***v.t.*** [BARBECUED (-kūd′), BARBECUING], 1. to roast or broil (an animal) whole. 2. to prepare (meat or fish) by broiling, cutting into thin slices, and putting into highly seasoned sauce made from the drippings. 3. to prepare (sliced or chopped meat) with barbecue sauce. ***adj.*** 1. barbecued. 2. of barbecued meat.

barbecue sauce, a highly seasoned sauce made chiefly of vinegar, vegetables, sugar, and spices.

barbed (bärbd), ***adj.*** 1. having a barb or barbs. 2. stinging; cutting: as, *barbed* words.

barbed wire, wire with many sharp points all along it: used for making barriers.

bar·bel (bär′b'l), ***n.*** [OFr. < L. *barbula,* dim. of *barbus,* < *barba,* a beard], 1. a threadlike growth hanging from the lips of certain fishes: it is an organ of touch. 2. a large European fresh-water fish with such growths.

bar·bel·late (bär′bə-lāt′, bär′bel′it), ***adj.*** [LL. *barbellus,* irreg. dim. of L. *barba,* beard; + *-ate*], in *botany,* covered with short, hooked bristles or hairs.

bar·ber (bär′bẽr), ***n.*** [ME. *barbour;* OFr. *barbeor;* ult. < L. *barba,* a beard], a person whose work or business is cutting and dressing hair, shaving and trimming beards, etc. ***v.t.*** to cut and dress the hair of; shave; trim the beard of.

barber college, a school for teaching the trade of barbering.

barber pole, a pole with spiral stripes of red and white, used as a symbol of the barber's trade.

bar·ber·ry (bär′ber′i, bär′bẽr-i), ***n.*** [*pl.* BARBERRIES (-iz)], [ME. *barberi;* OFr. *barberis;* ML. *barberis*], 1. any of a number of related spiny shrubs with sour, oblong, red berries and yellow flowers. 2. the berry.

bar·ber·shop (bär′bẽr-shop′), ***n.*** a barber's place of business. ***adj.*** [Colloq.], designating or characterized by the close harmony of male voices, especially in sentimental songs: as, a *barbershop* quartet.

barber's itch, an infectious inflammation of the hair follicles of the face and neck, caused by a fungus: so called because it can be contracted in unsanitary barbershops.

Bar·ber·ton (bär′bẽr-tən), ***n.*** a city in northeastern Ohio, near Akron: pop., 34,000.

bar·bet (bär′bit), ***n.*** [Fr., dim. of *barbe,* a beard], 1. a variety of curly-haired poodle. 2. any of several varieties of tropical birds that have bristles growing from the base of a broad bill.

bar·bette (bär-bet′), ***n.*** [Fr. < *Barbe,* Barbara, patron saint of artillerymen], 1. a platform for guns in a fort, high enough to permit firing over the walls. 2. the armored structure around a gun platform on a warship.

bar·bi·can (bär′bi-kən), ***n.*** [ME.; OFr. *barbicane;* ML. *barbacana;* prob. < Per. *barbar-khānah,* house on a wall], a defensive tower or similar fortification at a gate or bridge leading into a town or castle.

bar·bi·cel (bär′bə-sel′), ***n.*** [Mod. L. *barbicella,* dim. of L. *barba,* a beard], any of the very small projections on the barbules of a feather.

Bar·bi·rol·li, John (bär′bə-rō′li), 1899– ; English orchestra conductor.

bar·bi·tal (bär′bi-tal, bär′bit-əl), ***n.*** [*barbi*turic + *-al*], diethylbarbituric acid, a habit-forming drug in the form of a white powder, used to induce sleep; veronal.

bar·bi·tu·rate (bär′bə-tyoor′it, bär-bich′ẽr-it), ***n.*** [*barbituric* + *-ate*], any salt of barbituric acid, used as a sedative or to deaden pain.

bar·bi·tu·ric (bär′bə-tyoor′ik, bär′bə-toor′ik), ***adj.*** [Mod. L. *Usnea barbata,* lit., bearded moss (ML. *usnea* < Ar. *ushnah,* moss + L. *barbata,* fem. of *barbatus,* bearded < *barba,* beard); + *uric* acid], designating or of a crystalline acid, $CH_2CONHCONHCO$, derivatives of which are used to induce sleep or deaden pain.

Bar·bi·zon (bär′bi-zon′; Fr. bȧr′bē′zôɴ′), ***n.*** a village in northern France, famous as an art center (1830–1870).

Bar·bu·da (bär-bōō′də), ***n.*** an island dependency in the West Indies Federation: area, 62 sq. mi.; pop., 1,000.

bar·bule (bär′būl), ***n.*** [L. *barbula,* dim. of *barba,* a beard], 1. a very small barb; barbel. 2. any of the parts forming the fringe along the barbs of a feather.

Bar·busse, Hen·ri (äɴ′rē′ bȧr′büs′), 1873–1935; French novelist and journalist.

Bar·ca (bär′kə), ***n.*** 1. Cyrenaica, a district in northern Africa. 2. an ancient Carthaginian family of which Hamilcar and Hannibal were members.

bar·ca·role, bar·ca·rolle (bär′kə-rōl′), ***n.*** [Fr. < It. *barcaruola* < *barca,* boat], 1. a song sung by Venetian gondoliers. 2. any piece of music imitating this.

Bar·ce·lo·na (bär′s'l-ō′nə; Sp. bär′the-lô′nä), ***n.*** a city in Spain, on the Mediterranean: pop., 1,446,000.

bard (bärd), ***n.*** [Gael. & Ir. *bardh,* bard], 1. an ancient Celtic poet, composer, and singer: bards sang to the music of the harp. 2. [Poetic], a poet.

bard, barde (bärd), ***n.*** [Fr. *barde;* Sp. or It. *barda,* leather armor for horses < Ar. *barda'ah,* support for a saddle, saddle pad], a piece of armor for a horse. ***v.t.*** to put bards on (a horse).

bard·ic (bär′dik), ***adj.*** of, like, or by a bard.

Bard of Avon, William Shakespeare: so called from his birthplace, Stratford-on-Avon.

bare (bâr), ***adj.*** [ME. *bare, bar;* AS. *bær;* IE. base *bhoso-s; ? < *bhes, to denude], 1. not covered or clothed; naked; stripped. 2. exposed; revealed. 3. threadbare. 4. without equipment or furnishings; empty: as, a *bare* room. 5. simple; plain: as, *bare* facts. 6. mere: as, a *bare* subsistence wage. *v.t.* [BARED (bârd), BARING], to make bare; uncover; strip; expose.

lay bare, to uncover; open to view; expose.

SYN.—**bare,** in this comparison, implies the absence of the conventional or appropriate covering (*bare* legs, *bare*headed); **naked** implies the absence of clothing, either entirely or from some part, and connotes a revealing of the body (a *naked* bosom); **nude,** which is somewhat euphemistic for **naked,** is commonly applied to the undraped human figure in art; **bald** suggests a lack of natural covering, especially of hair on the head; **barren** implies a lack of natural covering, especially vegetation, and connotes destitution and fruitlessness (*barren* lands). See also **strip.** —***ANT.*** covered, clothed.

bare (bâr), [Archaic], alternative past tense of **bear.**

bare·back (bâr′bak′), ***adv.*** **&** ***adj.*** on a horse with no saddle.

bare·faced (bâr′fāst′), ***adj.*** 1. with the face uncovered or unmasked. 2. unconcealed; open. 3. shameless.

bare·foot (bâr′foot′), ***adj.*** **&** ***adv.*** without shoes and stockings.

bare·foot·ed (bâr′foot′id), ***adj.*** barefoot.

ba·rège (bä′rezh′), ***n.*** [Fr. < *Barèges,* town in France], a gauzy cloth of silk and worsted, or cotton and worsted, used for veils, etc.: also **barége.**

bare·hand·ed (bâr′han′did), ***adj.*** **&** ***adv.*** 1. with hands uncovered or unprotected. 2. [Colloq.], in unquestionable guilt; in the act.

bare·head·ed (bâr′hed′id), ***adj.*** **&** ***adv.*** with the head bare; without a hat, etc. on.

Ba·reil·ly, Ba·re·li (bə-rā′li), ***n.*** a city in Uttar Pradesh, India: pop., 208,000.

bare·leg·ged (bâr′leg′id, bâr′legd′), ***adj.*** **&** ***adv.*** with the legs bare; without stockings on.

bare·ly (bâr′li), ***adv.*** 1. openly. 2. without clothing or covering. 3. only just; no more than; scarcely. 4. meagerly; scantily. 5. [Archaic], merely.

Ba·rents Sea (bä′rents), a part of the Arctic Ocean, north of Scandinavia, Finland, and Russia.

bare·sark (bâr′särk′), ***n.*** [altered after *bare* + *sark,* shirt < *berserk*], a frenzied fighter; berserker. ***adv.*** without armor on; with only a shirt on.

bar·fly (bär′flī′), ***n.*** [Slang], a person who spends much time in barrooms.

bar·gain (bär′g'n, bär′gin), ***n.*** [ME. & OFr. *bargaine* < *bargaignier,* to haggle], 1. an agreement to exchange, sell, or buy goods. 2. the terms of such an agreement. 3. such an agreement considered in relation to one of the parties: as, he made a bad *bargain.* 4. any mutual agreement or contract. 5. something offered, bought, or sold at a price favorable to the buyer. ***v.i.*** 1. to discuss or dispute terms for selling, buying, etc.; haggle. 2. to make a bargain, or agreement (*with* someone). ***v.t.*** to trade; barter.

bargain for, 1. to try to get cheaply. 2. to expect; anticipate; count on.

into the bargain, beyond what has been agreed on.

strike a bargain, 1. to agree on terms. 2. to come upon a bargain.

bargain basement, that part of a department store, usually in the basement, where goods are sold at lower prices than in the main part.

bar·gain·er (bär′g'n-ẽr, bär′gin-ẽr), ***n.*** a person who bargains.

bar·gain·or (bär′gin-ôr′, bär′gin-ẽr), ***n.*** in *law,* the person who grants or sells in a bargain and sale.

barge (bärj), ***n.*** [ME.; OFr.; LL. *barga*], 1. a large boat, usually flat-bottomed, for carrying heavy freight on rivers, canals, etc. 2. a large pleasure boat, especially one used for state ceremonies, pageants, etc. 3. the official launch of a flagship. 4. a houseboat. 5. [Slang], any clumsy boat. ***v.t.*** [BARGED (bärjd), BARGING], to carry by barge. ***v.i.*** 1. to move slowly and clumsily. 2. [Colloq.], to enter, especially in a rude, abrupt, clumsy way (with *in* or *into*). 3. [Colloq.], to collide with (with *into*).

barge·board (bärj′bôrd′, bärj′bōrd′), ***n.*** [see BARGE COUPLE], a board, often ornate, attached along the barge couples of a gabled roof, as in Tudor and Gothic architecture.

barge couple, [? < base of Fr. *barge,* slope (of a river), Sp. *barga,* steepest part of a slope, Cym. *bargod,* edge, eaves trough], in *architecture,* 1. either of the pair of outside rafters forming the projection of a gabled roof. 2. two beams fitted together to strengthen a building.

BARGEBOARD

barge course, the overhang of a projecting gable roof.

bar·gee (bär-jē′), ***n.*** [*barge* + *-ee*], [British], a bargeman.

barge·man (bärj′mən), ***n.*** [*pl.* BARGEMEN (-mən)], a man who operates, or works aboard, a barge.

bar·ghest (bär′gest), ***n.*** [? < ON. *bjarg, berg,* mountain + *gastr* or AS. *giest,* stranger; akin to G. *berg geist,* mountain spirit], an imaginary, doglike goblin whose appearance supposedly means death or bad luck.

Bar Harbor, a resort town on Mount Desert Island, Maine: pop., 4,000.

Ba·ri (bä′ri), ***n.*** a city in southeastern Italy, on the Adriatic: pop., 274,000.

bar·ic (bar′ik), ***adj.*** [Rare], of, derived from, or containing barium.

bar·ic (bar′ik), ***adj.*** [< Gr. *barys,* weighty; + *-ic*], in *physics,* of weight or pressure, especially that of the atmosphere; barometric.

ba·ril·la (bə-ril′ə), ***n.*** [Sp. *barrilla,* impure soda], 1. either of two varieties of saltwort native to Spain, Sicily, and the Canary Islands, from which soda ash can be obtained. 2. this soda ash. 3. any soda ash obtained by burning seaweed, etc.

bar·ite (bâr′īt), ***n.*** a white, crystalline mineral composed mainly of barium sulfate; heavy spar: it is the principal source of barium and its compounds, and is used in the manufacture of paint.

bar·i·tone (bar′ə-tōn′), ***n.*** [It. *baritono;* Gr. *barytonos,* deep-toned < *barys,* heavy, deep + *tonos,* tone], 1. a male voice with a range between tenor and bass, from the second A below middle C to the first F above. 2. this range. 3. a man with such a voice. 4. a brass-wind instrument with a similar range. 5. a musical part for a baritone voice. 6. in *Greek grammar,* a word not having the acute accent on the final syllable. ***adj.*** 1. for or having a baritone or similar range. 2. in *Greek grammar,* not having the acute accent on the final syllable. Abbreviated **barit.** Also spelled **barytone.**

bar·i·um (bâr′i-əm), ***n.*** [Mod. L. < Gr. *barys,* heavy], a silver-white, slightly malleable, metallic chemical element, found as a carbonate or sulfate and used in alloys: symbol, Ba; at. wt., 137.36; at. no., 56.

bark (bärk), ***n.*** [ME.; ON. *börkr;* akin to MD. & G. *borke*], 1. the outside covering of trees and some plants: see **alburnum,** illus. 2. such material used in tanning, dyeing, etc. 3. cinchona, a medicinal bark. ***v.t.*** 1. to treat or cure with bark; tan (leather). 2. to take the bark off (a tree or log). 3. [Colloq.], to take the skin off: as, he *barked* his knees. —***SYN.*** see **skin.**

bark (bärk), ***v.i.*** [ME. *beorken;* AS. *beorcan* & ON. *berkja;* echoic; ult. akin to *break*], 1. to make the characteristic sound that a dog makes; make a sharp, abrupt outcry. 2. to make a similar sound: as, the engine *barked.* 3. to speak sharply; snap. 4. [Colloq.], to cough. 5. [Slang], to advertise a show, sale, etc. by shouting in public. ***v.t.*** to say or advertise with a bark or shout. ***n.*** 1. the sharp, abrupt sound made by a dog. 2. any sharp, abrupt noise like this.

bark at the moon, to make futile outcries or protests.

bark up the wrong tree, 1. to attack the wrong thing. 2. to direct one's energies in the wrong direction.

bark (bärk), ***n.*** [Fr. *barque;* It. *barca;* L. *barca,* small boat], 1. [Poetic], any sailing boat, especially a small one. 2. a sailing vessel with its two forward masts square-rigged and its rear mast rigged fore-and-aft. Also spelled **barque.**

bark beetle, any of a group of small beetles whose larvae are bred under the bark of trees, which are damaged as a result.

bar·keep·er (bär′kēp′ẽr), ***n.*** 1. a proprietor or manager of a bar where alcoholic drinks are sold. 2. a bartender. Sometimes shortened to **barkeep.**

bark·en·tine (bär′kən-tēn′), ***n.*** [< *bark* (sailboat) after *brigantine*], a sailing vessel with its foremast square-rigged and its two other masts rigged fore-and-aft: also spelled **barquentine.**

bark·er (bär′kẽr), ***n.*** 1. an animal, person, or thing that makes a barking sound. 2. a person in front of a side show, theater, store, etc. who attracts customers by loud, animated talking.

bark·er (bär′kẽr), ***n.*** 1. a person or machine that takes bark off a tree, etc. 2. a person or machine that prepares bark.

Bark·ley, Al·ben William (al′b'n bärk′li), 1877–1956; vice-president of the United States (1949–1953).

bar·ley (bär′li), ***n.*** [see PLURAL, II, D, 3], [ME. *barlic, berley;* AS. *bærlic, adj.,* of barley < *bere,* barley + *-lic* (modern *-ly*), adj. suffix; IE. base *bhares, as in L. *far,* whence *farina,* meal], 1. a cereal grass with bearded spikes of flowers. 2. its seed or grain, used in making liquors, soups, etc.

bar·ley·corn (bär′li-kôrn′), ***n.*** [ME. *barli-corn*], 1. barley or the grain of barley. 2. formerly, a unit of length equal to 1/3 inch. 3. any strong alcoholic liquor, especially whisky: usually **John Barleycorn,** a humorous personification.

barley sugar, a clear, hard candy made by melting sugar, formerly with a barley extract added.

barley water, a drink made by boiling barley in water, given to invalids, etc.

Bar·low, Joel (bär'lō), 1754–1812; American poet and diplomat.

barm (bärm), *n.* [ME. *berme;* AS. *beorma,* yeast; akin to LG. *barme;* IE. base *bher-, to surge up, seen also in *ferment*], the foamy yeast that appears on the surface of malt liquors as they ferment.

bar·maid (bär'mād'), *n.* a woman who serves alcoholic drinks in a bar.

bar·man (bär'mən), *n.* [*pl.* BARMEN (-mən)], a bar-keeper or bartender.

Bar·me·cide (bar'mə-sīd'), *n.* [Ar.], 1. in *The Arabian Nights,* a ruling prince of Bagdad who pretends to serve a feast to a beggar, but gives him no food; hence, 2. a person who offers imaginary benefits. *adj.* pretended, false, deceptive, or illusory.

Barmecide feast, 1. a pretended feast with no food; hence, 2. any pretended or illusory generosity or hospitality.

‡bar mitz·vah, bar miz·vah (bär mits-vô', bär'mits'-və), [Heb. *bar mitswāh,* son of duty], in *Judaism,* 1. a Jewish boy who has arrived at the age of responsibility, thirteen years. 2. the ceremony celebrating this event.

barm·y (bär'mi), *adj.* [BARMIER (-mi-ẽr), BARMIEST (-mi-ist)], 1. full of barm; yeasty, foamy, or frothy. 2. [British Slang], silly; idiotic: often confused with *balmy.*

barn (bärn), *n.* [ME.; AS. *berexrn; bere,* barley + *ærn,* a building, house], 1. a farm building for sheltering harvested crops, livestock, wagons, etc. 2. a large building for streetcars, etc. 3. [Colloq.], any room or building like a barn in size, temperature, etc.

Bar·na·bas (bär'nə-bəs), [L.; Gr.; Aram. *barnebhū'āh,* lit., son of exhortation], a masculine name: diminutive, *Barney;* variant, *Barnaby.*

Barnabas, Saint, a Levite, born in Cyprus; disciple of Paul and one of the first Christian missionaries.

Bar·na·by (bär'nə-bi), a masculine name: see **Barnabas.**

bar·na·cle (bär'nə-k'l), *n.* [ME. *bernekke, barnakylle, bernake;* (West) Fr. *bernicle, bernacle, bernache;* Bret. *bernic,* kind of shellfish: the goose was popularly thought to grow from the shellfish], 1. a barnacle goose. 2. any of a number of related shell-bearing sea animals that attach themselves to rocks, wharves, ship bottoms, etc.; hence, 3. [Colloq.], a person hard to get rid of.

BARNACLES

bar·na·cled (bär'nə-k'ld), *adj.* covered with barnacles.

barnacle goose, a European wild goose.

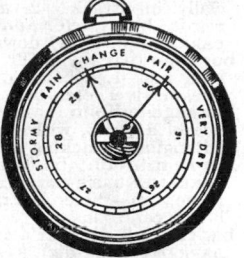

bar·na·cles (bär'nə-k'lz), *n.pl.* [< ME. *bernakile;* OFr. *bernac,* kind of bit], 1. nose pincers for controlling an unruly horse. 2. an instrument of torture resembling such pincers. 3. [British Colloq.], eyeglasses.

Bar·nard (bär'nẽrd), a masculine name: see **Bernard.**

Bar·nard, George Grey (bär'nẽrd), 1863–1938; American sculptor.

Barnard, Henry, 1811–1900; American educational reformer.

Bar·na·ul (bär'nä-ōōl'), *n.* a city in the south central R.S.F.S.R., on the Ob River: pop., 148,000.

barn dance, 1. a party held in a barn, with square dances, etc. 2. any party characterized by rural dancing, dress, music, etc. 3. a country dance resembling the schottische.

barn owl, a kind of owl, usually brown and gray with a spotted white breast, found chiefly in hollow trees and barns.

barn·storm (bärn'stôrm'), *v.i.* [*barn* + *storm, v.*], 1. to go about the country performing plays, giving lectures, etc., using barns or any available places in small towns and rural districts. 2. [from the use of barns as hangars], to tour the country giving short airplane rides, exhibitions of stunt flying, etc.

barn·storm·er (bärn'stôr'mẽr), *n.* 1. a person who barnstorms; hence, 2. a second-rate actor: from the idea that the best actors do not have to barnstorm. 3. a free-lance aviator.

barn swallow, a common swallow with a long, deeply forked tail: it usually nests on rafters in barns.

Bar·num, Phineas Taylor (bär'nəm), 1810–1891; American showman.

barn·yard (bärn'yärd'), *n.* the yard or ground near a barn, often enclosed. *adj.* 1. of a barnyard. 2. like or fit for a barnyard; earthy, smutty, etc.

bar·o- (bar'ō, bar'ə), [< Gr. *baros,* weight], a prefix meaning *of atmospheric pressure,* as in *barograph.*

bar·o·cy·clon·om·e·ter (bar'ō-sī'klə-nom'ə-tẽr), *n.* [< *baro-* + *cyclone* + *-meter*], a barometric instrument used to locate cyclones and follow their movement.

Ba·ro·da (bə-rō'də), *n.* 1. an independent state of India, north of Bombay: area, 8,236 sq. mi.; pop., 2,855,000. 2. its capital: pop., 110,000.

bar·o·gram (bar'ə-gram'), *n.* [*baro-* + *-gram*], the line recorded by a barograph or similar device.

bar·o·graph (bar'ə-graf', bar'ə-gräf'), *n.* [*baro-* + *-graph*], a barometer that automatically records on a revolving cylinder variations in atmospheric pressure.

Ba·ro·ja, Pí·o (pē'ō bä-rō'hä), 1872–1956; Spanish novelist.

ba·rom·e·ter (bə-rom'ə-tẽr), *n.* [*baro-* + *-meter*], 1. an instrument for measuring atmospheric pressure and thus for forecasting the weather or finding height above sea level: abbreviated **bar.** 2. anything that reflects or indicates change: as, breadlines are a *barometer* of unemployment.

BAROMETER

bar·o·met·ric (bar'ə-met'rik), *adj.* 1. of or like a barometer. 2. measured or shown by a barometer: abbreviated **bar.**

bar·o·met·ri·cal (bar'ə-met'ri-k'l), *adj.* barometric.

bar·o·met·ri·cal·ly (bar'ə-met'ri-k'l-i), *adv.* by means of a barometer.

bar·on (bar'ən), *n.* [ME. & OFr. *baron, barun* < base of OHG. *baro,* a man; IE. base *bher-, to carry, bring, as also in *bairn*], 1. in the Middle Ages, a feudal tenant of the king or of any higher-ranking lord; nobleman. 2. a member of the lowest rank of British nobility. 3. this rank or its title: abbreviated **Bn.** 4. a European or Japanese nobleman of like rank. 5. a powerful capitalist; magnate. 6. a double sirloin of beef.

bar·on·age (bar'ən-ij), *n.* [ME.; OFr. < *baron*], 1. the barons as a class; peerage. 2. the rank, title, status, or domain of a baron. 3. the nobility in general. 4. a list or annotated account of the barons.

bar·on·ess (bar'ə-nis), *n.* [ME. & OFr. *baronesse*], 1. a baron's wife, widow, or (in some European countries) daughter. 2. a lady with a barony in her own right. Abbreviated **Bnss.**

bar·on·et (bar'ə-nit, bar'ə-net'), *n.* [dim. of *baron*], 1. a man holding the lowest hereditary British rank, below a baron but above a knight: a baronet has precedence over all knights except Knights of the Garter, is addressed as "Sir," and may add *Bart.* to his name, as, Sir John Doe, Bart. 2. the title that shows this rank: abbreviated **Bt.**

bar·on·et·age (bar'ə-nit-ij), *n.* 1. baronets as a class. 2. a list or annotated account of the baronets.

bar·on·et·cy (bar'ə-nit-si), *n.* [*pl.* BARONETCIES (-siz)], 1. the title, rank, or status of a baronet. 2. the patent giving such rank.

ba·rong (bə-rôŋ', bä-roŋ'), *n.* [native name; prob. akin to Malay *parang;* see PARANG], a heavy sheath knife used by the Moros of the Philippines.

ba·ro·ni·al (bə-rō'ni-əl), *adj.* 1. of a baron or barons. 2. fit for a baron; grand, showy, etc.: as, a *baronial* mansion.

bar·o·ny (bar'ə-ni), *n.* [*pl.* BARONIES (-niz)], [ME. & OFr. *baronie*], 1. a baron's domain. 2. the rank, title, or status of a baron.

ba·roque (bə-rōk'; Fr. bå'rôk'), *adj.* [Fr.; Port. *barroco,* imperfect pearl], 1. irregular in shape: said of pearls. 2. of, characteristic of, or like a style of art and architecture characterized by much ornamentation and curved rather than straight lines. 3. designating or of the period in which this flourished (c. 1550–1750). 4. of the late or decadent baroque period style; rococo; hence, 5. fantastically overdecorated; gaudily ornate. *n.* baroque style, baroque art, etc.

bar·o·scope (bar'ə-skōp'), *n.* [*baro-* + *-scope*], 1. an instrument for indicating changes in atmospheric pressure. 2. an instrument that measures the weight lost by an object in the air and shows that this weight equals that of the air displaced.

Ba·rot·se·land (bə-rot'si-land'), *n.* a region in the western part of Northern Rhodesia, Africa.

ba·rouche (bə-rōōsh'), *n.* [G. *barutsche;* It. *baroccio* < L. *birotus,* having two wheels < *bis,* two + *rota,* a wheel], a four-wheeled carriage with a collapsible hood, two double seats opposite each other, and a box seat in front for the driver.

bar pin, a long, bar-shaped, ornamental brooch, or pin.

barque (bärk), *n.* a bark (sailing vessel).

bar·quen·tine (bär'kən-tēn'), *n.* a barkentine.

bar·rack (bar'ək), *n.* [Fr. *baraque* < It. *barraca* < Sp. *barraca,* cabin, mud hut < *barro,* clay, mud < LL.

*barrum, clay], 1. [Rare], an improvised hut. 2. *pl.* [often construed as sing.], *a*) a building or group of buildings for housing soldiers: abbreviated **bks., Bks., B.K.S.** *b*) a large, plain, often temporary building for housing workmen, etc. *v.t. & v.i.* to house in barracks.

barracks bag, a cloth bag to hold a soldier's equipment and personal possessions.

bar·ra·cu·da (bar'ə-kōō'də), *n.* [*pl.* BARRACUDA, BARRACUDAS (-dəz); see PLURAL, II, D, 2], [Sp.; ? < dial. *barraco*, tooth growing over another], any of various related fierce, edible, pikelike fishes of tropical seas.

bar·rage (bə-räzh'), *n.* [Fr., in *tir de barrage*, artillery fire; see BARRAGE (a barring)], 1. a curtain of artillery fire laid down to keep enemy forces from moving, or to cover or prepare the way for one's own forces, especially in attack. 2. a heavy, prolonged attack of words, blows, etc. *v.t. & v.i.* [BARRAGED (-räzhd'), BARRAGING], to lay down a barrage (against).

bar·rage (bär'ij), *n.* [Fr. < *barrer*, to stop < *barre*; see BAR, *n.*], 1. a barring. 2. a man-made barrier in a stream, river, etc.; dam.

bar·rage balloon (bə-räzh'), an anchored balloon, often one of a series, with cables or nets attached to it for entangling attacking airplanes.

bar·ra·mun·da (bar'ə-mun'də), *n.* [*pl.* BARRAMUNDA, BARRAMUNDAS (-dəz); see PLURAL, II, D, 2], [< native name], an edible Australian fish with both gills and lungs; ceratodus.

bar·ra·mun·di (bar'ə-mun'di), *n.* [*pl.* BARRAMUNDI, BARRAMUNDIS (-diz), BARRAMUNDIES (-diz); see PLURAL, II, D, 2], a barramunda.

bar·ran·ca (bə-raŋ'kə), *n.* [Sp.], a deep ravine.

Bar·ran·quil·la (bä'rän-kēl'yä), *n.* a city in northwestern Columbia: pop., 411,000.

bar·ra·tor, bar·ra·ter (bar'ə-tẽr), *n.* [ME. *baratour*; OFr. *barateor*, swindler < *barater*, to cheat < *barate*, fraud, strife; ON. *baratta*, struggle, quarrel], a person guilty of barratry.

bar·ra·trous (bar'ə-trəs), *adj.* of the nature of barratry; of or tending to barratry.

bar·ra·try (bar'ə-tri), *n.* [Fr. *baraterie*, orig., misuse of office < *barater*; see BARRATOR], 1. the buying or selling of ecclesiastical or civil positions. 2. the habitual bringing about of quarrels or lawsuits. 3. in *maritime law*, negligence or fraud on the part of a ship's officers or crew resulting in loss to the owners.

barred (bärd), *adj.* [pp. of *bar*], 1. having bars or stripes. 2. closed off with bars; hence, 3. not allowed.

barred owl, a variety of large, North American owl with bars of brown feathers across the breast.

bar·rel (bar'əl), *n.* [ME. *barel*; OFr. *baril*; ? < LL. *barra*, a stave, bar; see BAR, *n.*], 1. a large, wooden, cylindrical container with sides that bulge outward and flat ends, made usually of staves bound together with hoops. 2. the capacity or contents of a standard barrel (in the United States, usually 31 1/2 gallons; in Great Britain, 36 imperial gallons; in dry measure, various amounts, as 196 pounds of flour, 200 pounds of pork or fish, etc.): abbreviated **bbl., bl., bar.** 3. a revolving cylinder, wound with a chain or rope: as, the *barrel* of a windlass. 4. any hollow or solid cylinder: as, the *barrel* of a fountain pen. 5. the straight tube of a gun, which directs the projectile. 6. the quill of a feather. 7. the body of a horse, cow, etc. 8. [Colloq.], a great amount: as, a *barrel* of fun. *v.t.* [BARRELED or BARRELLED (-əld), BARRELING or BARRELLING], 1. to put or pack in a barrel or barrels. 2. to store away. *v.i.* [Slang], to go at high speed.

barrel chair, a kind of upholstered chair with an upright, rounded back.

bar·rel-house (bar'əl-hous'), *adj.* in *jazz music*, of or in the unrestrained style of playing associated with a barrel house.

barrel house, formerly, a small, disreputable saloon with a row of racked barrels along the wall.

barrel organ, a mechanical musical instrument having a cylinder studded with pins which open pipe valves or strike metal tongues when the cylinder is revolved, producing a tune; hand organ.

barrel roll, a complete revolution made by an airplane around its longitudinal axis while in flight.

barrel vault, in *architecture*, a semi-cylindrical vault.

bar·ren (bar'ən), *adj.* [ME. *barein, barain*; OFr. *baraigne, brehaigne*], 1. that cannot bear offspring; sterile: as, a *barren* woman. 2. not bearing or pregnant at the regular time: said of animals or plants. 3. without vegetation; unfruitful: as, *barren* soil. 4. unproductive; unprofitable; not worthwhile. 5. lacking richness, interest, etc.; unattractive; boring. 6. empty; lacking; devoid; as, *barren* of creative spirit. *n.* 1. an area of unproductive land. 2. *usually pl.* land with shrubs, brush, etc. and sandy soil. —*SYN.* see **bare, sterile.**

Barren Grounds, a region of bare tundras in Canada, northwest of Hudson Bay: also **Barren Lands.**

bar·ren·ness (bar'ən-nis), *n.* the quality or state of being barren.

Bar·rès, Au·guste Mau·rice (ō'güst' mō'rēs' bå'res'), 1862–1923; French novelist and essayist.

bar·ret (bar'it), *n.* [Fr. *barrette*; It. *berretta*; see BIRETTA], a small, flat cap; biretta.

Barrett, Elizabeth, see **Browning, Elizabeth Barrett.**

bar·rette (bə-ret'), *n.* [Fr., dim. of *barre*; see BAR, *n.*], a small bar or clasp worn by a girl or woman for holding the hair in place.

bar·ri·cade (bar'ə-kād', bar'ə-kād'), *n.* [Fr. < It. *barricata*, pp. of *barricare*, to fortify < *barra*, a bar], 1. a barrier thrown up hastily for defense, as in street fighting. 2. any barrier. *v.t.* (bar'ə-kād'), [BARRICADED (-id), BARRICADING], 1. to keep in or out with a barricade. 2. to put up barricades in; obstruct.

bar·ri·ca·do (bar'i-kā'dō), *n.* [*pl.* BARRICADOES (-dōz)], [Fr. *barricade*; see BARRICADE], a barricade. *v.t.* [BARRICADOED (-dōd), BARRICADOING], to barricade.

Bar·rie, Sir **James Matthew** (bar'i), 1860–1937; Scottish dramatist and novelist.

bar·ri·er (bar'i-ẽr), *n.* [ME. *barrere*; OFr. *barriere* < *barre*; see BAR, *n.*], 1. originally, a fortress, stockade, etc. for defending an entrance or gate. 2. a thing that prevents going ahead or approaching; obstruction, as a fence, wall, etc. 3. anything that holds apart or separates: as, shyness was a *barrier* between them. 4. a boundary or limitation. 5. a customs gate on a country's border. 6. [sometimes B-], the part of the south polar ice sheet that extends into the sea. 7. in *horse racing*, a gate that keeps the horses in line before the start of a race. —*SYN.* see **obstacle.**

barrier beach, a ridge of sand and gravel thrown up along a coast line by the waves.

barrier reef, a long ridge of rock or coral near and parallel to the coast line, usually serving as a breakwater.

the Barrier Reef, the barrier reef along the eastern coast of Australia.

bar·ring (bär'iŋ), *prep.* [ppr. of *bar*], excepting; excluding.

bar·ri·o (bär'ri-ō'), *n.* [Sp. < *barra*; LL. *barra*; see BAR, *n.*], in Spanish-speaking countries, a political subdivision of a city; suburb.

bar·ris·ter (bar'is-tẽr), *n.* [< *bar* (court of justice)], in England, a qualified member of the legal profession who presents and pleads cases in court; counselor-at-law: distinguished from *solicitor*: abbreviated **barr., bar.** —*SYN.* see **lawyer.**

bar·room (bär'rōōm', bär'room'), *n.* a room with a bar or counter at which alcoholic drinks are sold.

Bar·row (bar'ō), *n.* a city in northern Lancashire, England, on the Irish Sea: pop., 64,000: also **Barrow-in-Furness.**

bar·row (bar'ō), *n.* [ME. *barewe*; AS. *bearwe*, basket, barrow < *beran*, to bear], 1. a traylike frame with two handles at each end and sometimes with four legs, used for carrying loads; handbarrow. 2. a wheelbarrow. 3. a handcart. 4. the capacity or contents of a barrow.

bar·row (bar'ō), *n.* [ME. *berg, beoruh*; AS. *beorg*, hill, mound; akin to G. *berg*; IE. base **bhergh*, raised up, high], 1. a heap of earth or rocks marking a grave, especially an ancient one; tumulus. 2. [Dial.], a mountain; hill.

bar·row (bar'ō), *n.* [ME. *barg*; AS. *bearg, bearh*; akin to G. *barg*; IE. base **bher-*, cut], a castrated pig.

Bar·row, Point (bar'ō), a cape at the northernmost point of Alaska.

Bar·row-in-Fur·ness (bar'ō-in-fũr'nes), *n.* Barrow.

Bar·ry, Philip (bar'i), 1896–1949; American dramatist.

Bar·ry·more, Ethel (bar'ə-mōr', bar'i-mōr'), 1879–1959; American actress.

Barrymore, John, 1882–1942; American actor.

Barrymore, Lionel, 1878–1954; American actor.

Barrymore, Maurice, (born *Herbert Blythe*), 1847–1905; father of *Ethel*, *Lionel*, and *John*; American actor, born in England.

bar sinister, in *heraldry*, erroneously, a baton or bend sinister.

Bart., Baronet.

bar·tend·er (bär'ten'dẽr), *n.* a man who mixes and serves alcoholic drinks at a bar.

bar·ter (bär'tẽr), *v.i.* [ME. *bartren*; OFr. *barater*, to barter, trick, cheat < *barate*, a struggle, noise, quarrel < ON. *baratta*; ? influenced by Bret. *barad*, deception, trickery], to trade by exchanging goods or services without using money. *v.t.* to give (goods or services) in return for other goods or services; trade. *n.* 1. the act or practice of bartering. 2. anything bartered. —*SYN.* see **sell.**

barter away, to give or trade for too small a return.

Barth, Karl (bärt), 1886– ; Swiss theologian.

Bar·thol·di, Fré·dé·ric Au·guste (frā'dā'rēk' ō'güst' bår'tôl'dē'), 1834–1904; French sculptor of the Statue of Liberty.

Bar·thol·o·mew (bär-thol'ə-mū'), [OFr. *Barthelemieu*; L. *Bartholomaeus*; Gr. *Bartholomaios* < Aram., lit., son of Talmai], a masculine name: diminutive, *Bart*; equivalents, Fr. *Bartholomé, Barthélemy*, It. *Bartolomeo*, G. *Bartholomäus, Barthel*, Sp. *Bartolomé*.

Bartholomew, Saint, in the *Bible*, one of the twelve apostles: his day is August 24.

bar·ti·zan, bar·ti·san (bär′tə-z'n, bär′tə-zan′), *n.* [revived by Sir Walter Scott from a Scot. form altered < ME. *bretasce;* see BRATTICE], a small, overhanging turret on a tower, battlement, etc., used originally for defense or as a lookout.

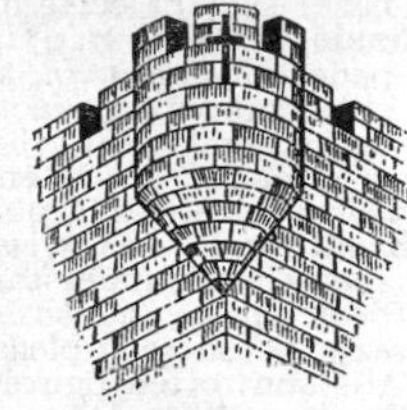

BARTIZAN

Bart·lett, John (bärt′lit), 1820–1905; American publisher who compiled a book of quotations.
Bartlett, Josiah, 1729–1795; American Revolutionary patriot.
Bartlett, Paul Way·land (wā′lənd), 1865–1925; American sculptor.
Bartlett pear, [after E. *Bartlett* of Dorchester, Mass., the distributor], a large, juicy variety of pear.
Bar·tók, Bé·la (bä′lä bär′tôk), 1881–1945; Hungarian composer and compiler of Hungarian folk songs.
Bar·to·lom·me·o, Fra (frä bär′tô-lô-me′ô), 1475–1517; Florentine painter.
Bar·ton, Clara (bär′t'n), 1821–1912; American philanthropist; organizer of the American Red Cross.
Bar·uch (bâr′ək), *n.* [Heb., lit., blessed], 1. in the *Bible,* Jeremiah's scribe: Jer. 32:12–14. 2. a book of the Old Testament Apocrypha attributed to him. Abbreviated **Bar.**
Ba·ruch, Bernard Man·nes (man′əs bə-ro͞ok′), 1870– ; American financier and statesman.
ba·ry·ta (bə-rī′tə), *n.* [< Gr. *barys,* heavy], 1. barium oxide. 2. loosely, barium hydroxide.
ba·ry·tes (bə-rī′tēz), *n.* [< Gr. *barys,* heavy], barium sulfate in native form; barite.
ba·ryt·ic (bə-rit′ik), *adj.* having to do with baryta.
bar·y·tone (bar′ə-tōn′), *adj.* & *n.* baritone.
bar·y·tron (bar′ə-tron′), *n.* [*bary-* + *electron*], a mesotron: also called *meson.*
B.A.S., 1. Bachelor of Agricultural Science. 2. Bachelor of Applied Science. Also **B.A.Sc.**
bas·al (bā′s'l), *adj.* 1. of, at, or forming the base; hence, 2. basic; fundamental; fundamentally important.
basal anesthesia, in *medicine,* anesthesia induced as a preliminary to further and deeper anesthesia.
basal metabolism, the quantity of energy used by any organism at rest; amount of heat produced by the human organism fourteen to eighteen hours after eating and when at rest for thirty to sixty minutes but not asleep: it is measured by the rate (*basal metabolic rate*) at which heat is given off, and is expressed in calories per hour per square meter of skin surface.
ba·salt (bə-sôlt′, bas′ôlt), *n.* [L. *basaltes,* dark, hard marble], 1. a hard, heavy, dark volcanic rock, sometimes found in the form of columns. 2. a kind of glassy, black pottery designed by Josiah Wedgwood.
ba·sal·tic (bə-sôl′tik), *adj.* of or like basalt.
‡bas bleu (bä′ blö′), [Fr.], a bluestocking.
bas·cule (bas′kūl), *n.* [Fr., a seesaw], a device so balanced that when one end is lowered the other end is raised; seesaw or similar apparatus.
bascule bridge, a kind of drawbridge counterweighted so that it can be raised and lowered easily.

BASCULE BRIDGE

base (bās), *n.* [*pl.* BASES (-iz)], [ME.; OFr. *bas;* L. *basis;* see BASIS], 1. the part of a thing that the thing stands or rests on; lowest part or bottom of a thing; foundation. 2. the foundation or most important element, as of a system or set of ideas. 3. anything from which a start is made; basis. 4. a goal, starting place, or safety point in certain games, as baseball: abbreviated **B., b.** (in baseball). 5. the point of attachment of a part of the body: as, the *base* of the thumb. 6. a center of operations or source of supply; headquarters. 7. the bottommost layer or coat, as of paint. 8. in *chemistry,* a substance which forms a salt when it reacts with an acid; in terms of the theory of the dissociation of electrolytes, a compound, such as sodium hydroxide or ammonium hydroxide, which liberates hydroxyl ions in aqueous solutions; in terms of the modern theory of acids and bases, a substance that removes hydrogen ions (protons) from an acid and combines with them in a chemical reaction. 9. in *dyeing,* a substance used for fixing colors. 10. in *geometry,* the line or plane upon which a figure is thought of as resting. 11. in *heraldry,* the lower portion of a shield. 12. in *linguistics,* any morpheme to which prefixes, suffixes, etc. are added; stem; root. 13. in *mathematics,* a constant figure upon which a mathematical table is computed, as in logarithms. *adj.* forming a base. *v.t.* [BASED (bāst), BASING], 1. to make a base or foundation for. 2. to put (a thing) on a base or foundation: often used figuratively, as, he *based* his argument on authority. 3. to establish or found.
get to first base, 1. in *baseball,* to reach first base safely; hence, 2. [Slang], to succeed in the first step of anything.
SYN.—**base,** as compared here, refers to a part or thing at the bottom acting as a support or underlying structure; **basis,** conveying the same idea, is the term preferred for nonphysical things (the *base* of a lamp, the *basis* of a theory); **foundation** stresses solidity in the underlying or supporting thing and often suggests permanence and stability in that which is built on it (the *foundation* of a house); **groundwork,** closely synonymous with **foundation,** is principally applied to nonphysical things (the *groundwork* of a good education).
base (bās), *adj.* [ME. & OFr. *bas;* LL. *bassus,* thick, stumpy, low], 1. deep or low: said of sounds: see **bass.** 2. morally low; low-minded; dishonorable; disgraceful; vile: as, it is *base* to betray a friend. 3. inferior in social position; menial; servile. 4. inferior in quality; coarse, shabby, etc. 5. impure or corrupted; not classical: said of language. 6. comparatively worthless: as, iron is a *base* metal, gold a precious one. 7. debased; counterfeit. 8. [Archaic], short. 9. [Archaic], of servile, humble, or illegitimate birth. 10. [Obs.], low or inferior in place or position. *n.* 1. a deep, low sound; bass tone. 2. a bass voice, bass part, etc.
SYN.—**base** implies a putting of one's own interests ahead of one's obligations, as because of greed or cowardice (*base* motives); **mean** suggests a contemptible pettiness of character or conduct (his *mean* attempts to slander her); **ignoble** suggests a lack of high moral or intellectual qualities (to work for an *ignoble* end); **abject,** in careful discrimination, implies debasement and a contemptible lack of self-respect (an *abject* servant); **sordid** connotes the depressing drabness of that which is mean or base (the *sordid* details of their affair); **vile** suggests disgusting foulness or depravity (*vile* epithets); **low** suggests rather generally coarseness, vulgarity, depravity, etc., specifically in reference to taking grossly unfair advantage (so *low* as to kick a cripple's crutch); **degrading** suggests a lowering or corruption of moral standards (the *degrading* aspects of army life). —*ANT.* noble, moral, virtuous.
base·ball (bās′bôl′), *n.* 1. a game played with a hard, rawhide-covered ball and wooden bat by two opposing teams, properly of nine players each: it is played on a field with four bases forming a diamond-shaped circuit which a runner must complete to score a run. 2. the ball used in this game.
base·board (bās′bôrd′, bās′bōrd′), *n.* 1. a board or molding covering a plaster wall where it meets the floor. 2. any board serving as a base.
base·born (bās′bôrn′), *adj.* 1. born of parents in a low social position; of humble birth or origin. 2. born of parents not married to each other; of illegitimate birth.
base·burn·er, base-burn·er (bās′bũr′nẽr), *n.* any stove or furnace in which more coal is fed automatically from above when that at the base is consumed.
base hit, in *baseball,* a hit by which the batter gets on base without benefit of an opponent's error and without forcing out a runner already on base: abbreviated **B., b.**
base hospital, a military hospital far from the battle front: distinguished from *field hospital.*
Ba·sel (bä′z'l), *n.* a city in northern Switzerland, on the Rhine: pop., 163,000: also **Basle.**
base·less (bās′lis), *adj.* having no basis in fact; unfounded.
base level, 1. in *geology,* the level below which a stream cannot erode its bed; limit of large-scale erosion, determined by projecting sea level inland. 2. in *surveying,* the elevation to which other elevations are referred.
base line, 1. a line serving as a base. 2. in *baseball,* the straight line between any two consecutive bases.
base·ly (bās′li), *adv.* in a base or mean manner.
base·man (bās′mən), *n.* [*pl.* BASEMEN (-mən)], in *baseball,* any of the three infielders stationed at first, second, and third base, respectively.
base·ment (bās′mənt), *n.* [*base, v.* or *n.* + *-ment;* prob. after Fr. (*sou*)*bassement,* basement], 1. the foundation or lower part of a wall or walls; hence, 2. the lowest story of a building or the one just below the main floor, usually wholly or partially lower than the surface of the ground.
base metal, 1. any of the common, nonprecious metals: distinguished from *precious metal.* 2. the metal under a coating or plating. 3. the main metal in an alloy.
base·ness (bās′nis), *n.* 1. the quality or state of being morally base. 2. a base or dishonorable act or trait.
base runner, in *baseball,* any member of the team at bat who is on base.
bas·es (bās′iz), *n.* plural of **base.**
ba·ses (bā′sēz), *n.* plural of **basis.**
bash (bash), *v.t.* [echoic; akin to (? <) ON. **basca,* to strike; see BASK], [Colloq.], to strike with a violent blow; smash (*in*). *n.* [Colloq.], a violent blow.
Ba·shan (bā′shan, bā′shən), *n.* a region east and northeast of the Sea of Galilee, Palestine.

ba·shaw (bə-shô′), *n.* [see PASHA, the usual sp.], 1. a Turkish official. 2. an important or self-important person, especially an official.

bash·ful (bash′fəl), *adj.* [ME. *baschen, baissen*, to abash (see ABASH); + *-ful*], showing social timidity and embarrassment; shy. —*SYN.* see **shy.**

bash·i-ba·zouk (bash′i-bə-zōōk′), *n.* [Turk. *bashi-bozuq; bashi*, headdress + *bozuq*, disorderly, unkempt], a member of the Turkish irregulars, troops notorious in the 19th century for their brutality.

Bash·kir (bȧsh-kêr′), *n.* 1. a member of a Turko-Tartar tribe of Moslems inhabiting the Bashkir A.S.S.R. 2. their language.

Bashkir Autonomous Soviet Socialist Republic, a division of the R.S.F.S.R., west of the South Urals: area, 54,233 sq. mi.; pop., 3,304,000; capital, Ufa.

bas·ic (bās′ik), *adj.* 1. of or at the base; forming a base or basis; fundamental; essential. 2. in *chemistry*, of, having the nature of, or containing a base; alkaline. 3. in *mineralogy*, designating or of a rock having less than 52 per cent silica. 4. designating, of, or resulting from a process of manufacturing steel in which the refractory lining of the furnace is a basic substance, as magnesite, and the basic slag in the charge serves as the refining agent.

bas·i·cal·ly (bās′i-k'l-i, bās′ik-li), *adv.* at basis; at bottom; fundamentally; primarily.

basic dress, a simple, dark dress that can be worn with changes of accessories.

Basic English, [*B*ritish, *A*merican, *S*cientific, *I*nternational, *C*ommercial], a simplified form of the English language for international communication and for first steps into full English, invented by Charles K. Ogden (1889–1957): it consists of a selected vocabulary of 850 essential words and is copyrighted. See list, p. 123.

ba·sic·i·ty (bə-sis′ə-ti), *n.* in *chemistry*, 1. the quality or condition of being a base. 2. the capacity of an acid to react with a base, measured by the number of chemical equivalents of a base with which one gram molecular weight of the acid reacts.

basic slag, a slag of steel manufacture having low silica (and high alkaline) content: also used as a fertilizer.

ba·sid·i·o·my·cete (bə-sid′i-ō′mī-sēt′), *n.* [< *basidium* + *mycete*], in *botany*, a basidiomycetous fungus, as a mushroom, rust, smut, puffball, etc.

ba·sid·i·o·my·ce·tous (bə-sid′i-ō′mī-sē′təs), *adj.* in *botany*, belonging to a group of fungi having basidia.

ba·sid·i·um (bə-sid′i-əm), *n.* [*pl.* BASIDIA (-ə)], [Mod. L. < Gr. *basis*, base + Mod. L. *-idium*, dim. suffix], in *botany*, any of a number of club-shaped cells in certain fungi, bearing a definite number of spores (usually four) on short, slender stalks.

Bas·il (baz′'l, bā′z'l), [L. *Basilius;* Gr. *Basileios*, lit., kingly < *basileus*, king], a masculine name.

bas·il (baz′'l), *n.* [OFr. *basile;* ML. *basilicum;* Gr. *basilikos*, royal < *basileus*, king], any of a group of fragrant plants of the mint family, used as an herb.

Bas·il, Saint (baz′'l), 330?–379? A.D.; Cappadocian church father and bishop of Caesarea.

bas·i·lar (bas′ə-lẽr), *adj.* [Mod. L. *basilaris* < L. *basis;* see BASIS], 1. of or at the base, especially of the skull. 2. fundamental; basic; basal.

bas·i·lar·y (bas′ə-ler′i), *adj.* basilar.

ba·sil·ic (bə-sil′ik), *adj.* [Fr. *basilique;* L. *basilicus;* Gr. *basilikos;* see BASIL], 1. designating or of a large vein of the upper arm, on the inner side of the biceps muscle. 2. of a basilica; basilican. 3. [Obs.], kingly.

ba·sil·i·ca (bə-sil′i-kə), *n.* [*pl.* BASILICAS (-kəz)], [L.; Gr. *basilikē* (*stoa*), royal (portico) < *basilikos;* see BASILIC], 1. originally, a royal palace. 2. in ancient times, a rectangular building with a broad nave ending in an apse, and flanked by colonnaded aisles, used as a courtroom, public hall, etc. 3. an early Christian church shaped like this.

ba·sil·i·cal (bə-sil′i-k'l), *adj.* basilic.

ba·sil·i·can (bə-sil′i-kən), *adj.* of or like a basilica.

bas·i·lisk (bas′ə-lisk′), *n.* [ME.; L. *basiliscus;* Gr. *basiliskos*, dim. of *basileus*, king; hence, king of animals], 1. a mythical lizardlike monster with supposedly fatal breath and glance, fabled to have been hatched by a serpent from a cock's egg: also called *cockatrice.* 2. a tropical American lizard with an erectile crest on its back and tail and an inflatable pouch on its head. 3. an obsolete cannon decorated with metal lizards.

ba·sin (bā′s'n), *n.* [ME. & OFr. *bacin;* LL. *baccinum* < *bacca*, water vessel], 1. a round, wide, shallow container for liquid; bowl. 2. its contents or capacity. 3. a wash bowl or sink. 4. a pond, reservoir, or other large hollow containing water. 5. a bay. 6. the area drained by a river and its branches: called *river basin.* 7. a great hollow in the earth's surface filled by an ocean: called *ocean basin.*

bas·i·net (bas′ə-nit), *n.* [ME.; OFr. *bacinet*, dim. of *bacin;* see BASIN], a light, round steel helmet, often with a visor, used in the Middle Ages: also **basnet.**

ba·si·on (bā′si-ən), *n.* [< Gr. *basis;* see BASE (foundation)], the midpoint of the front border of the foramen magnum.

ba·sip·e·tal (bā-sip′ə-t'l), *adj.* [< *basic* + *petal*], in *botany*, developing from the apex down toward the base: said of certain plant structures.

basis (bā′sis), *n.* [*pl.* BASES (-sēz)], [L.; Gr., a step, pedestal < *bainein*, to go], 1. the base, foundation, or chief supporting factor of anything. 2. the principal constituent of anything. 3. the basic principle or theory, as of a system of knowledge. 4. in *military science*, a starting point; base. —*SYN.* see **base.**

bask (bask, bäsk), *v.i. & v.t.* [coinage due to Shakespeare's misunderstanding of Lydgate; ME. *basken*, to beat, strike (cf. *bash*); only in Gower & Lydgate], to expose (oneself) pleasantly to warmth: as, he *basked* in the sun: often figuratively, as, he *basked* in her favor.

Bas·ker·ville, John (bas′kẽr-vil), 1706–1775; English printer and type designer.

bas·ket (bas′kit, bäs′kit), *n.* [ME. < OCelt. *bascauda*, crock with woven pattern, whence ML. *bascauda;* IE. base **bhasquo-*, a bunch, bundle, as in L. *fascis*, bundle (of rods)], 1. a container made of interwoven cane, rushes, strips of wood, etc. 2. the amount that this holds; basketful: abbreviated **bkt., bskt.** 3. anything used or shaped like a basket. 4. a passenger cabin hung from a balloon. 5. in *basketball*, *a*) the goal, a net shaped like a basket open at the bottom. *b*) a toss of the ball through this net, counted as a score when properly made.

bas·ket·ball (bas′kit-bôl′, bäs′kit-bôl′), *n.* 1. a game played by two opposing teams of five players each, usually in a zoned floor area with a raised goal (basket) at either end through which the ball must be tossed: the game was invented in 1891 by Dr. James A. Naismith of Springfield, Mass. 2. the large, round, inflated, leather-covered ball used in this game.

basket case, a hospital patient who has undergone amputation of both arms and legs: such cases rarely occur, loss of all limbs being usually fatal.

basket hilt, a hilt with a basketlike guard for the hand, as on some swords.

bas·ket·ry (bas′kit-ri, bäs′kit-ri), *n.* 1. the craft of making baskets. 2. baskets collectively; basketware.

basket weave, a weave of fabrics resembling the weave used in basketmaking.

bas·ket·work (bas′kit-wũrk′, bäs′kit-wũrk′), *n.* work that is interlaced or woven like a basket.

basking shark, a large shark with small, weak teeth: often found basking on the surface in northern seas.

Basle (bäl), *n.* Basel.

bas·net (bas′nit), *n.* a basinet.

ba·so·phile (bā′sə-fil′, bā′sə-fil), *n.* [< *basic* + *-phile*], in *biology*, a cell or tissue that is readily stained with basic dyes.

ba·so·phil·ic (bā′sə-fil′ik), *adj.* readily stained with basic dyes: said of cells or tissues.

Basque (bask), *n.* [Fr. < LL. *Vasco*, one of the Basques (*Vascones*)], 1. any member of a certain people living in the western Pyrenees. 2. their language. *adj.* of the Basques, their country, or language.

basque (bask), *n.* [Fr. < Pr. *basto* < ?; altered by association with Fr. *basquine*, kind of petticoat < Sp. *basquina* < *basco, vasco;* see BASQUE (one of the Basques)], a woman's blouse with a tight-fitting waist; tight-fitting bodice or tunic.

Basque Provinces, a region in northern Spain inhabited by Basques.

BASQUE PROVINCES

Bas·ra (bus′rə), *n.* a seaport in southern Iraq: pop., 85,000: also spelled **Busra, Busrah.**

bas-re·lief (bä′ri-lēf′, bä′ri-lēf′, bas′ri-lēf′), *n.* [Fr.; It. *basso-rilievo;* see BASSO & RELIEF], sculpture in which the figures project only a little from the background.

Bas-Rhin (bä′ran′), *n.* a department of France, on the Rhine: formerly Lower Alsace: area, 1,484 sq. mi.; pop., 712,000; capital, Strasbourg.

bass (bās), *n.* [ME. *bas;* see BASE (low); sp. influenced by It. *basso*], 1. the lowest male singing voice. 2. a low, deep sound or tone of or as of such a voice. 3. the lowest part in vocal or instrumental music. 4. a singer or instrument having a very low range; specifically, a bass viol. *adj.* 1. having a very low musical pitch or range. 2. for the bass or basses. 3. able to sing or play bass. Abbreviated **B., b.**

bass (bas), *n.* [*pl.* BASS, BASSES (-iz); see PLURAL, II, D, 2], [ME. < *bars;* AS. *bears, bærs;* IE. base **bhares*, a point: in reference to the dorsal fins], any of various edible perchlike fishes found in fresh or salt water.

bass (bas), *n.* [< ME. *bast;* AS. *bæst*, inner bark of trees], 1. bast. 2. basswood.

bass-bar (bās′bär′), *n.* a strip of wood running lengthwise inside instruments of the viol group to support the pressure of the bridge.

bass clef (bās), *in music*, 1. a sign on a staff indicating that the notes on the staff are below middle C: symbol,

BASIC ENGLISH

OPERATIONS	THINGS						QUALITIES	
100 ETC.	400 General				200 Pictured		100 General	50 Opposites
COME	ACCOUNT	EDUCATION	METAL	SENSE	ANGLE	KNEE	ABLE	AWAKE
GET	ACT	EFFECT	MIDDLE	SERVANT	ANT	KNIFE	ACID	BAD
GIVE	ADDITION	END	MILK	SEX	APPLE	KNOT	ANGRY	BENT
GO	ADJUSTMENT	ERROR	MIND	SHADE	ARCH	LEAF	AUTOMATIC	BITTER
KEEP	ADVERTISEMENT	EVENT	MINE	SHAKE	ARM	LEG	BEAUTIFUL	BLUE
LET	AGREEMENT	EXAMPLE	MINUTE	SHAME	ARMY	LIBRARY	BLACK	CERTAIN
MAKE	AIR	EXCHANGE	MIST	SHOCK	BABY	LINE	BOILING	COLD
PUT	AMOUNT	EXISTENCE	MONEY	SIDE	BAG	LIP	BRIGHT	COMPLETE
SEEM	AMUSEMENT	EXPANSION	MONTH	SIGN	BALL	LOCK	BROKEN	CRUEL
TAKE	ANIMAL	EXPERIENCE	MORNING	SILK	BAND	MAP	BROWN	DARK
BE	ANSWER	EXPERT	MOTHER	SILVER	BASIN	MATCH	CHEAP	DEAD
DO	APPARATUS	FACT	MOTION	SISTER	BASKET	MONKEY	CHEMICAL	DEAR
HAVE	APPROVAL	FALL	MOUNTAIN	SIZE	BATH	MOON	CHIEF	DELICATE
SAY	ARGUMENT	FAMILY	MOVE	SKY	BED	MOUTH	CLEAN	DIFFERENT
SEE	ART	FATHER	MUSIC	SLEEP	BEE	MUSCLE	CLEAR	DIRTY
SEND	ATTACK	FEAR	NAME	SLIP	BELL	NAIL	COMMON	DRY
MAY	ATTEMPT	FEELING	NATION	SLOPE	BERRY	NECK	COMPLEX	FALSE
WILL	ATTENTION	FICTION	NEED	SMASH	BIRD	NEEDLE	CONSCIOUS	FEEBLE
ABOUT	ATTRACTION	FIELD	NEWS	SMELL	BLADE	NERVE	CUT	FEMALE
ACROSS	AUTHORITY	FIGHT	NIGHT	SMILE	BOARD	NET	DEEP	FOOLISH
AFTER	BACK	FIRE	NOISE	SMOKE	BOAT	NOSE	DEPENDENT	FUTURE
AGAINST	BALANCE	FLAME	NOTE	SNEEZE	BONE	NUT	EARLY	GREEN
AMONG	BASE	FLIGHT	NUMBER	SNOW	BOOK	OFFICE	ELASTIC	ILL
AT	BEHAVIOUR	FLOWER	OBSERVATION	SOAP	BOOT	ORANGE	ELECTRIC	LAST
BEFORE	BELIEF	FOLD	OFFER	SOCIETY	BOTTLE	OVEN	EQUAL	LATE
BETWEEN	BIRTH	FOOD	OIL	SON	BOX	PARCEL	FAT	LEFT
BY	BIT	FORCE	OPERATION	SONG	BOY	PEN	FERTILE	LOOSE
DOWN	BITE	FORM	OPINION	SORT	BRAIN	PENCIL	FIRST	LOUD
FROM	BLOOD	FRIEND	ORDER	SOUND	BRAKE	PICTURE	FIXED	LOW
IN	BLOW	FRONT	ORGANIZATION	SOUP	BRANCH	PIG	FLAT	MIXED
OFF	BODY	FRUIT	ORNAMENT	SPACE	BRICK	PIN	FREE	NARROW
ON	BRASS	GLASS	OWNER	STAGE	BRIDGE	PIPE	FREQUENT	OLD
OVER	BREAD	GOLD	PAGE	START	BRUSH	PLANE	FULL	OPPOSITE
THROUGH	BREATH	GOVERNMENT	PAIN	STATEMENT	BUCKET	PLATE	GENERAL	PUBLIC
TO	BROTHER	GRAIN	PAINT	STEAM	BULB	PLOUGH	GOOD	ROUGH
UNDER	BUILDING	GRASS	PAPER	STEEL	BUTTON	POCKET	GREAT	SAD
UP	BURN	GRIP	PART	STEP	CAKE	POT	GREY	SAFE
WITH	BURST	GROUP	PASTE	STITCH	CAMERA	POTATO	HANGING	SECRET
AS	BUSINESS	GROWTH	PAYMENT	STONE	CARD	PRISON	HAPPY	SHORT
FOR	BUTTER	GUIDE	PEACE	STOP	CARRIAGE	PUMP	HARD	SHUT
OF	CANVAS	HARBOUR	PERSON	STORY	CART	RAIL	HEALTHY	SIMPLE
TILL	CARE	HARMONY	PLACE	STRETCH	CAT	RAT	HIGH	SLOW
THAN	CAUSE	HATE	PLANT	STRUCTURE	CHAIN	RECEIPT	HOLLOW	SMALL
A	CHALK	HEARING	PLAY	SUBSTANCE	CHEESE	RING	IMPORTANT	SOFT
THE	CHANCE	HEAT	PLEASURE	SUGAR	CHEST	ROD	KIND	SOLID
ALL	CHANGE	HELP	POINT	SUGGESTION	CHIN	ROOF	LIKE	SPECIAL
ANY	CLOTH	HISTORY	POISON	SUMMER	CHURCH	ROOT	LIVING	STRANGE
EVERY	COAL	HOLE	POLISH	SUPPORT	CIRCLE	SAIL	LONG	THIN
NO	COLOUR	HOPE	PORTER	SURPRISE	CLOCK	SCHOOL	MALE	WHITE
OTHER	COMFORT	HOUR	POSITION	SWIM	CLOUD	SCISSORS	MARRIED	WRONG
SOME	COMMITTEE	HUMOUR	POWDER	SYSTEM	COAT	SCREW	MATERIAL	
SUCH	COMPANY	ICE	POWER	TALK	COLLAR	SEED	MEDICAL	
THAT	COMPARISON	IDEA	PRICE	TASTE	COMB	SHEEP	MILITARY	
THIS	COMPETITION	IMPULSE	PRINT	TAX	CORD	SHELF	NATURAL	
I	CONDITION	INCREASE	PROCESS	TEACHING	COW	SHIP	NECESSARY	
HE	CONNECTION	INDUSTRY	PRODUCE	TENDENCY	CUP	SHIRT	NEW	
YOU	CONTROL	INK	PROFIT	TEST	CURTAIN	SHOE	NORMAL	
WHO	COOK	INSECT	PROPERTY	THEORY	CUSHION	SKIN	OPEN	
AND	COPPER	INSTRUMENT	PROSE	THING	DOG	SKIRT	PARALLEL	
BECAUSE	COPY	INSURANCE	PROTEST	THOUGHT	DOOR	SNAKE	PAST	
BUT	CORK	INTEREST	PULL	THUNDER	DRAIN	SOCK	PHYSICAL	
OR	COTTON	INVENTION	PUNISHMENT	TIME	DRAWER	SPADE	POLITICAL	
IF	COUGH	IRON	PURPOSE	TIN	DRESS	SPONGE	POOR	
THOUGH	COUNTRY	JELLY	PUSH	TOP	DROP	SPOON	POSSIBLE	
WHILE	COVER	JOIN	QUALITY	TOUCH	EAR	SPRING	PRESENT	
HOW	CRACK	JOURNEY	QUESTION	TRADE	EGG	SQUARE	PRIVATE	
WHEN	CREDIT	JUDGE	RAIN	TRANSPORT	ENGINE	STAMP	PROBABLE	
WHERE	CRIME	JUMP	RANGE	TRICK	EYE	STAR	QUICK	
WHY	CRUSH	KICK	RATE	TROUBLE	FACE	STATION	QUIET	
AGAIN	CRY	KISS	RAY	TURN	FARM	STEM	READY	
EVER	CURRENT	KNOWLEDGE	REACTION	TWIST	FEATHER	STICK	RED	
FAR	CURVE	LAND	READING	UNIT	FINGER	STOCKING	REGULAR	
FORWARD	DAMAGE	LANGUAGE	REASON	USE	FISH	STOMACH	RESPONSIBLE	
HERE	DANGER	LAUGH	RECORD	VALUE	FLAG	STORE	RIGHT	
NEAR	DAUGHTER	LAW	REGRET	VERSE	FLOOR	STREET	ROUND	
NOW	DAY	LEAD	RELATION	VESSEL	FLY	SUN	SAME	
OUT	DEATH	LEARNING	RELIGION	VIEW	FOOT	TABLE	SECOND	
STILL	DEBT	LEATHER	REPRESENTATIVE	VOICE	FORK	TAIL	SEPARATE	
THEN	DECISION	LETTER	REQUEST	WALK	FOWL	THREAD	SERIOUS	
THERE	DEGREE	LEVEL	RESPECT	WAR	FRAME	THROAT	SHARP	
TOGETHER	DESIGN	LIFT	REST	WASH	GARDEN	THUMB	SMOOTH	
WELL	DESIRE	LIGHT	REWARD	WASTE	GIRL	TICKET	STICKY	
ALMOST	DESTRUCTION	LIMIT	RHYTHM	WATER	GLOVE	TOE	STIFF	
ENOUGH	DETAIL	LINEN	RICE	WAVE	GOAT	TONGUE	STRAIGHT	
EVEN	DEVELOPMENT	LIQUID	RIVER	WAX	GUN	TOOTH	STRONG	
LITTLE	DIGESTION	LIST	ROAD	WAY	HAIR	TOWN	SUDDEN	
MUCH	DIRECTION	LOOK	ROLL	WEATHER	HAMMER	TRAIN	SWEET	
NOT	DISCOVERY	LOSS	ROOM	WEEK	HAND	TRAY	TALL	
ONLY	DISCUSSION	LOVE	RUB	WEIGHT	HAT	TREE	THICK	
QUITE	DISEASE	MACHINE	RULE	WIND	HEAD	TROUSERS	TIGHT	
SO	DISGUST	MAN	RUN	WINE	HEART	UMBRELLA	TIRED	
VERY	DISTANCE	MANAGER	SALT	WINTER	HOOK	WALL	TRUE	
TOMORROW	DISTRIBUTION	MARK	SAND	WOMAN	HORN	WATCH	VIOLENT	
YESTERDAY	DIVISION	MARKET	SCALE	WOOD	HORSE	WHEEL	WAITING	
NORTH	DOUBT	MASS	SCIENCE	WOOL	HOSPITAL	WHIP	WARM	
SOUTH	DRINK	MEAL	SEA	WORD	HOUSE	WHISTLE	WET	
EAST	DRIVING	MEASURE	SEAT	WORK	ISLAND	WINDOW	WIDE	
WEST	DUST	MEAT	SECRETARY	WOUND	JEWEL	WING	WISE	
PLEASE	EARTH	MEETING	SELECTION	WRITING	KETTLE	WIRE	YELLOW	
YES	EDGE	MEMORY	SELF	YEAR	KEY	WORM	YOUNG	

RULES

ADDITION OF 'S' TO THINGS WHEN THERE IS MORE THAN ONE

ENDINGS IN 'ER', 'ING', 'ED' FROM 300 NAMES OF THINGS

'LY' FORMS FROM QUALITIES

DEGREE WITH 'MORE' AND 'MOST'

QUESTIONS BY CHANGE OF ORDER AND 'DO'.

FORM-CHANGES IN NAMES OF ACTS, AND 'THAT,' 'THIS,' 'I,' 'HE,' 'YOU,' 'WHO,' AS IN NORMAL ENGLISH

MEASURES NUMBERS DAYS, MONTHS AND THE INTERNATIONAL WORDS IN ENGLISH FORM.

ORTHOLOGICAL INSTITUTE
45 GORDON SQUARE
LONDON W.C. 1,
ENGLAND

F: see **clef**, illus. 2. the range so shown. Also called *F clef*, distinguished from *G* (or *treble*) *clef*.
bass drum (bās), the largest and lowest-toned of the double-headed drums.
bas·set (bas′it), *n.* [OFr., short-legged dog, orig., short, dim. of *basse*, fem. of *bas*; see BASE (low)], a kind of hound with a long body, short legs, and long, drooping ears, used in hunting: also **basset hound.**
bas·set (bas′it), *n.* [? < Fr. *basset*, dim. of *basse*; see BASSET (hound)], in *geology* & *mining*, an outcropping. *v.i.* to appear at or emerge above the surface.
Basse-Terre (bäs′ter′), 1. the western part of Guadeloupe. 2. the capital of Guadeloupe: pop., 13,600.
basset horn, a clarinet in F: in size it is between a clarinet proper and a bass clarinet.
bass horn (bās), a tuba.
bas·si·net (bas′ə-net′, bas′ə-net′), *n.* [Fr. *bercelonnette*, dim. of *berceau*, cradle], a large basket used as a baby's bed, often hooded and on wheels.
bas·so (bas′ō; It. bäs′sô), *n.* [*pl.* BASSOS (-ōz); It. BASSI (-sē)], [It. < LL. *bassus*], a bass voice, voice part, or singer. *adj.* bass. Abbreviated **B., b.**
bas·soon (ba-sōōn′, bə-sōōn′), *n.* [Fr. *basson*; It. *bassone* < *basso*; see BASSO], 1. a double-reed bass musical instrument of the wood-wind class, with a long, curved mouthpiece. 2. an organ stop with a deep tone like that of a bassoon.
basso pro·fun·do (prə-fun′dō), [< It. *basso* (see BASSO) + *profondo*, deep; L. *profundus*; see PROFOUND], 1. a very deep bass voice. 2. a man with such a voice.
bas·so-re·lie·vo (bas′ō-ri-lē′vō), *n.* [*pl.* BASSO-RELIEVOS (-vōz)], [It. *basso-rilievo*], bas-relief.
‡**bas·so-ri·lie·vo** (bäs′sô-ri-lye′vô), *n.* [*pl.* BASSI-RILIEVI (bäs′sē-ri-lye′vē)], [It.], bas-relief.

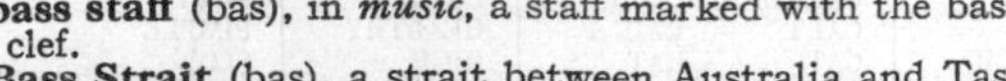

BASSOON

bass staff (bās), in *music*, a staff marked with the bass clef.
Bass Strait (bas), a strait between Australia and Tasmania: width, 80–150 mi.
bass viol (bās), the largest and deepest-toned musical instrument of the viol group, resembling a huge violin: also called *double bass*, *contrabass*, *string bass*.
bass·wood (bas′wood′), *n.* 1. any of a number of related trees with fragrant, yellowish flowers and light, soft, durable wood; linden. 2. its wood. The word is also loosely used of the tulip tree or its wood.
bast (bast), *n.* [ME.; AS. *bæst*], 1. phloem. 2. fiber obtained from phloem, used in making ropes, mats, etc.
bas·tard (bas′tẽrd), *n.* [ME.; OFr. *bastard*, *bastart* < Goth. *bansts*, a stable, barn; + *-ard*], 1. a person born of parents not married to each other; illegitimate child. 2. a counterfeit; sham. 3. anything inferior or varying from standard. *adj.* 1. of illegitimate birth or origin; of uncertain origin. 2. sham; inferior. 3. not standard. The word is widely and vulgarly used as an indiscriminate term of abuse and sometimes of playful affection.
bastard file, a medium file, neither coarse nor fine.
bas·tard·i·za·tion (bas′tẽr-di-zā′shən), *n.* 1. a bastardizing or being bastardized. 2. a corruption; misuse.
bas·tard·ize (bas′tẽr-dīz′), *v.t.* [BASTARDIZED (-dīzd′), BASTARDIZING], 1. to make, declare, or show to be a bastard. 2. to misuse; corrupt: as, he *bastardized* the language. *v.i.* to become inferior.
bas·tard·ly (bas′tẽrd-li), *adj.* like a bastard; of illegitimate or uncertain origin, counterfeit, etc.
bastard type, in *printing*, a type face cast on a body larger or smaller than that which properly belongs to it.
bastard wing, the part of a bird's wing corresponding to the thumb, consisting usually of three quills; alula.
bas·tar·dy (bas′tẽr-di), *n.* [OFr. *bastardie*; see BASTARD], 1. the state of being a bastard; illegitimacy. 2. the begetting of a bastard.
baste (bāst), *v.t.* [BASTED (-id), BASTING], [ME. *bastin*; OFr. *bastir*; OHG. *bastjan*, to sew with bast], to sew with long, loose stitches so as to keep the parts together until properly sewed.
baste (bāst), *v.t.* [BASTED (-id), BASTING], [< OFr. *basser*, to moisten < *bassiner*, to moisten < *bassin*; see BASIN], to moisten (meat) with melted butter, drippings, etc. while roasting.
baste (bāst), *v.t.* [BASTED (-id), BASTING], [ON. *beysta*], 1. to strike; beat. 2. to attack with words; abuse.
bas·tille, bas·tile (bas-tēl′; Fr. bȧs′tē′y′), *n.* [ME. *bastile* (Fr. *bastille*) < OFr. *bastir*, to build; see BASTION], 1. in ancient warfare, a tower or raised, movable structure for defense or attack; small fortress. 2. a prison.
the Bastille, a castlelike fortress in Paris built in 1369 and used as a state prison until stormed and destroyed (1789) in the French Revolution: its destruction is commemorated on Bastille Day, July 14.
bas·ti·nade (bas′tə-nād′), *n.* bastinado.
bas·ti·na·do (bas′tə-nā′dō), *n.* [*pl.* BASTINADOES (-dōz)], [Sp. *bastonada* < *baston*, a stick], 1. a beating or blow with a stick, usually on the bottoms of the feet: an Oriental method of punishment. 2. a rod, stick, or cudgel. *v.t.* [BASTINADOED (-dōd), BASTINADOING], to inflict the bastinado on.
bast·ing (bāst′iŋ), *n.* [see BASTE (to sew)], 1. the act of sewing with loose, temporary stitches. 2. *pl.* loose, temporary stitches. 3. a thread used for basting.
bas·tion (bas′chən, bas′ti-ən), *n.* [Fr.; It. *bastione* < *bastia* < *bastire*, to build < Gmc. *bastjan*, to make with bast, thatch, build < *bast*, bast], 1. a projection from a fortification, arranged to give a wider firing range. 2. any strong defense or bulwark: often used figuratively.
bas·tioned (bas′chənd, bas′ti-ənd), *adj.* having bastions.

BASTION

Bas·togne (bas-tōn′; Fr. bȧs′tôn′y′), *n.* a town in southeastern Belgium: besieged in World War II during German counteroffensive (1944).
Ba·su·to (bə-sōō′tō), *n.* any of a Bantu people living in the region of Basutoland.
Ba·su·to·land (bə-sōō′tō-land′), *n.* a British colony in South Africa: area, 11,716 sq. mi.; pop., 664,000; capital, Maseru.
bat (bat), *n.* [ME. *batte*; AS. *batt*, cudgel < Celt.; influenced in some senses by OFr. *batre*; see BATTER (to beat)], 1. any stout club, stick, or cudgel; hence, 2. a club used in striking the ball in baseball and cricket: abbreviated **B., b.** (in baseball). 3. a tennis racket, ping-pong paddle, etc. 4. the process of batting. 5. a turn or chance at batting. 6. [British], a batsman at cricket. 7. a chunk, wad, or lump, as of clay. 8. *usually pl.* cotton batting, especially of an inferior quality; batt. 9. [Colloq.], a blow or hit; hence, 10. [Colloq.], speed; fast pace. 11. [Slang], a drinking bout; spree. *v.t.* [BATTED (-id), BATTING], to strike with or as with a bat. *v.i.* 1. to use a bat, as in games. 2. to take a turn at batting.
at bat, having a turn at batting, as in baseball.
bat around, [Slang], 1. to travel about. 2. to consider or discuss (an idea, plan, etc.).
go to bat for, [Slang], to intervene on behalf of; defend; advocate.
bat (bat), *n.* [altered < ME. *bakke* < ON.], any of a number of related mouse-like mammals with a furry body and membranous wings, usually seen flying at night.
blind as a bat, entirely blind.
have bats in the belfry, [Slang], to be insane; have crazy notions.

BAT (10 in. across)

bat (bat), *v.t.* [BATTED (-id), BATTING], [var. of obs. *bate* < OFr. *batre*; see BATTER (to beat)], [Colloq.], to wink; blink; flutter.
not bat an eye, [Colloq.], not show surprise; not be taken aback.
bat., 1. battalion. 2. battery.
Ba·taan (bə-tän′, bə-tan′, ba-tan′), *n.* a peninsula west of Manila Bay in the Philippines: famous for the stand made by American soldiers against numerically superior Japanese forces in 1942: see **Philippine Islands,** map.
Ba·tan·gas (bä-täŋ′gäs) *n.* a city on the southern coast of Luzon, in the Philippines: pop., 49,000.
Ba·tan Islands (bä-tän′), the northernmost group of islands in the Philippines: area, 74 sq. mi.
Ba·ta·vi·a (bə-tā′vi-ə; D. bä-tä′vi-ä), *n.* Jakarta, a city in Java: the former, Dutch name.
batch (bach), *n.* [ME. *bacche*, *batche* < AS. *bacan*, to bake], 1. the amount (of bread, etc.) produced at one baking. 2. the amount of material, as dough, needed for one operation. 3. the quantity of anything made in one operation or lot. 4. a number of things or persons taken as a group; lot; set.
bate (bāt), *v.t.* [BATED (-id), BATING], [< *abate*], 1. to abate; reduce; diminish. 2. to hold in. 3. [Archaic], to deprive (*of*). *v.i.* to be or become reduced.
with bated breath, with the breath held in because of fear, excitement, etc.
bate (bāt), *v.t.* & *v.i.* [BATED (-id), BATING], [< ON. *beita*, to cause to bite; cf. Sw. *beta* & G. *beizen*, to soak in lye, of parallel origin], in *tanning*, to soften by soaking in an alkaline solution. *n.* an alkaline solution for softening hides: dung was formerly so used.
ba·teau (ba-tō′), *n.* [*pl.* BATEAUX (-tōz′)], [Fr.; OFr. *batel* < AS. *bat*, boat], a lightweight, flat-bottomed river boat used chiefly in Canada and Louisiana.
bat·fish (bat′fish′), *n.* [*pl.* BATFISH, BATFISHES (-iz); see FISH], [*bat* (mammal) + *fish*], any of various fishes resembling a bat, as the flying gurnard, a sting ray, etc.
bat·fowl (bat′foul′), *v.i.* [*bat* (a club) + *fowl*], to catch birds at night by blinding them with a light, and netting or hitting them when they fly toward it.
Bath (bath, bäth), *n.* 1. a city in southwestern England, known for the hot springs there: pop., 77,000 (est.

1946). 2. a city in southwestern Maine: pop., 11,000.

bath (bath, bäth), *n.* [*pl.* BATHS (bathz, bäthz)], [ME.; AS. *bæth;* akin to G. *bad;* IE. base *bhe-, to warm], 1. a washing or dipping of a thing, especially the body, in water or other liquid, etc.: often used figuratively, as, Europe has had a *bath* of blood. 2. water or other liquid for bathing, or for dipping or soaking anything. 3. a container for such liquid. 4. a bathtub. 5. a bathroom. 6. a building or set of rooms for bathing. 7. *often pl.* a resort where bathing is part of the medical treatment; spa. 8. in *chemistry, a)* a material that acts as a medium for regulating the temperature of things put in or on it. *b)* the container for this. 9. in *metallurgy,* molten metal in a furnace. 10. in *photography,* the solution used in developing and fixing. *v.t. & v.i.* to soak or steep in a bath.

Bath brick, [after *Bath,* England, where first made], a brick-shaped piece of earth containing carbonate of lime or of calcium, used for cleaning polished metal.

Bath chair, a hooded wheelchair of a kind used at Bath, England.

bathe (bāth), *v.t.* [BATHED (bāthd), BATHING], [ME. *bathien, bathen;* AS. *bathian* < *bæth;* see BATH], 1. to put into a liquid; immerse. 2. to give a bath to; wash. 3. to wet; moisten. 4. to cover or envelop as if with liquid: as, the trees are *bathed* in moonlight. *v.i.* 1. to take a bath; bathe oneself. 2. to go into or be in a body of water so as to swim, cool oneself, etc. 3. to soak oneself in some substance or influence, as sunlight. *n.* [British], a bathing in the sea, a pool, etc.; a swim.

bath·er (bāth'ēr), *n.* a person who bathes or swims.

ba·thet·ic (bə-thet'ik), *adj.* [< *bathos,* by analogy with *pathetic*] characterized by bathos.

bath·house (bath'hous', bäth'hous'), *n.* 1. a building equipped for bathing. 2. a building used by bathers for changing clothes.

bath·i·nette (bath'ə-net', bäth'ə-net'), *n.* [< *bath,* after *bassinet*], a portable folding bathtub for babies, made of rubberized cloth, etc.: a trade-mark (**Bathinette**).

bathing cap, a tight-fitting cap of rubber, etc. worn to keep the hair from getting wet in bathing.

bathing suit, a garment designed for swimming.

bath·o- (bath'ō), [Gr. *bathos,* depth], a combining form meaning *depth,* as in *bathometer.*

bath·o·lite (bath'ə-līt'), *n.* a batholith.

bath·o·lith (bath'ə-lith'), *n.* [*batho-* + *-lith*], a large, deep-seated igneous rock intrusion, usually granite, often forming the base of a mountain range, and uncovered only by erosion.

ba·thom·e·ter (bə-thom'ə-tēr), *n.* [*batho-* + *-meter*], an instrument for measuring water depths.

ba·thos (bā'thos), *n.* [Gr. *bathos,* depth], 1. change from the exalted to the trivial in writing or speech; anticlimax. 2. false pathos; sentimentality.—***SYN.*** see **pathos.**

bath·robe (bath'rōb', bäth'rōb'), *n.* a long, loose-fitting coat for wear to and from the bath, in lounging, etc.

bath·room (bath'ro͞om', bäth'room'), *n.* 1. a room to bathe in, etc. 2. a toilet.

Bath·she·ba (bath-shē'bə, bath'shi-bə), *n.* [Heb. *Bathsheba'*, lit., daughter of Sheba, daughter of the oath], in the *Bible,* the mother of Solomon by King David, whom she married after he had sent her first husband, Uriah, to death in battle: II Sam. 11.

bath·tub (bath'tub', bäth'tub'), *n.* 1. originally, any tub used to take a bath in. 2. a bathroom fixture designed for this purpose.

Bath·urst (bath'ērst, bäth'ērst), *n.* 1. the capital of Gambia, in western Africa: pop., 21,000. 2. a city in New South Wales, Australia: pop., 17,000.

bath·y- (bath'i), [< Gr. *bathys,* deep], a combining form meaning *deep, of the sea depths,* as in *bathysphere.*

bath·y·scaph (bath'i-skaf'), *n.* [< *bathy-* + Gr. *skaphē,* boat], a deep-sea diving apparatus for reaching great depths without a cable: it consists of a ballasted, balloonlike hydrostat filled with a fluid lighter than water, and a steel observation cabin.

bath·y·sphere (bath'i-sfêr'), *n.* [*bathy-* + *-sphere*], a round, watertight chamber with windows, in which men can be lowered into the sea depths to observe and study the plants and animals there.

ba·tik (bə-tēk', bä'tēk, bat'ik), *n.* [Malay], 1. a method of dyeing designs on cloth by coating with removable wax the parts not to be dyed. 2. cloth thus decorated. 3. a design thus made. *adj.* of or like batik. *v.t.* to dye or design by means of batik. Also spelled **battik.**

bat·ing (bāt'iŋ), *prep.* [ppr. of *bate* (to abate)], [Archaic], excluding; except for.

ba·tiste (ba-tēst', bə-tēst'), *n.* [Fr.; OFr. *baptiste:* so called from the supposed original maker, *Baptiste* of Cambrai], 1. a fine, thin linen. 2. a light muslin.

bat·man (bat'mən), *n.* [*pl.* BATMEN (-mən)], [*bat,* packsaddle < Fr. *bat;* OFr. *bast;* LL. **bastum* < **bastare,* to carry; Gr. *bastazein,* to lift, carry; + *man*], the servant of an officer in the British army.

ba·ton (ba-ton', bat''n; Fr. bä'tōn), *n.* [Fr. *bâton* < OFr. *baston* < LL. *bastum,* a stick], 1. a staff serving as a symbol of office. 2. a short, narrow, diagonal band on a coat of arms, running from the upper right corner to the lower left (as seen by the observer) to indicate bastardy in the family line: cf. **bend sinister.** 3. a slender stick used by the conductor of an orchestra, choir, etc. for directing. 4. a hollow metal rod, with a knob at one end, twirled in a showy way by a drum major or drum majorette.

Bat·on Rouge (bat''n ro͞ozh'), the capital of Louisiana, on the Mississippi: pop., 152,000.

Ba·tra·chi·a (bə-trā'ki-ə), *n.pl.* [Mod. L. < Gr. *batracheios,* relating to frogs < *batrachos,* frog], 1. amphibians without tails, as frogs and toads. 2. loosely, all amphibians.

ba·tra·chi·an (bə-trā'ki-ən), *adj.* [< *Batrachia*], of or like the Batrachia. *n.* any member of the Batrachia.

bats·man (bats'mən), *n.* [*pl.* BATSMEN (-mən)], in *baseball & cricket,* the batter.

batt (bat), *n.* [see BAT (a club)], *usually pl.* cotton batting.

batt., 1. battalion. 2. battery.

bat·tal·ion (bə-tal'yən), *n.* [Fr. *bataillon;* It. *battaglione* < L. *battalia;* see BATTLE], 1. a large group of soldiers arrayed for battle. 2. a large group somewhat like this: as, a *battalion* of strikers. 3. *pl.* military forces. 4. a tactical unit now usually made up of four infantry companies and a headquarters company, or four artillery batteries and a headquarters battery: three battalions form a regiment. Abbreviated **batt., bat., Bn.**

bat·ten (bat''n), *n.* [Fr. *bâton;* see BATON], 1. a sawed strip of wood, flooring, etc. 2. a strip of wood put over a seam between boards as a fastening or covering. 3. a short, flexible strip of wood inserted in a horizontal pocket at the outer edge of a jib-headed sail to prevent it from cupping. 4. a strip used to fasten canvas over a ship's hatchways. *v.t.* to fasten or supply with or as with battens (often with *down*).

bat·ten (bat''n), *v.i.* [ON. *batna,* to become better, improve; base **bat-* (IE. **bhad-*), good, as in *betre, beztr,* Eng. *better, best*], 1. to grow fat; thrive. 2. to be well fed or wealthy at another's expense. 3. to become fruitful, fertile, or rank. *v.t.* to fatten up; overfeed.

bat·ten (bat''n), *n.* [Fr. *battant*], in a loom, the movable frame that presses into place the threads of a woof.

bat·ter (bat'ēr), *v.t.* [ME. *bateren, batteren* < OFr. *batre, battre* < LL. *battere* < L. *battuere, batuere,* to beat; also, in part, freq. of Eng. *bat,* to strike], 1. to beat or strike with blow after blow; pound. 2. to break to bits by pounding. 3. to injure by pounding, hard wear, or use: as, the furniture was *battered.* *v.i.* to pound noisily. *n.* in *printing,* 1. a broken place on the face of type or of a plate. 2. type thus broken.

bat·ter (bat'ēr), *n.* in *baseball & cricket,* the player whose turn it is to bat; batsman.

bat·ter (bat'ēr), *n.* [ME. *bature;* OFr. *bature;* prob. < *batre;* see BATTER (to beat)], a thin mixture of flour, milk, etc., used in making cakes, waffles, etc.

bat·ter (bat'ēr), *v.t. & v.i.* [< Fr. *abattre,* to beat off, abate, lessen; see BATTER (to beat)], to slope gradually. *n.* the gradual inward slope of a wall due to lessening in its thickness from bottom to top.

bat·ter·ing-ram (bat'ēr-iŋ-ram'), *n.* 1. an ancient military machine having a heavy wooden beam, sometimes with an iron ram's head at its end, for battering down gates, walls, etc. 2. anything used like this to force entrance.

Bat·ter·sea (bat'ēr-si), *n.* a borough of London.

bat·ter·y (bat'ēr-i), *n.* [*pl.* BATTERIES (-iz)], [Fr. *batterie* < *battre;* see BATTER (to beat)], 1. a battering; a beating; a pounding. 2. machinery used in battering. 3. any set of devices arranged, connected, or used together. 4. in *baseball,* the pitcher and the catcher. 5. in *electricity,* a cell or connected group of cells storing an electrical charge and capable of furnishing a current. 6. in *law,* any illegal beating or touching of another person either directly or with an object: see **assault and battery.** 7. in *military science, a)* an emplacement for heavy guns or a fortification equipped with such guns. *b)* a set of heavy guns. *c)* the men who operate such guns: usually the basic unit of field artillery and equivalent to a company. 8. in *music,* the percussion instruments of an orchestra. 9. in the *navy,* the guns, or a set of the guns, of a warship. 10. in *optics,* a series of lenses or prisms. Abbreviated **batt., bat., Btry., B., b.**

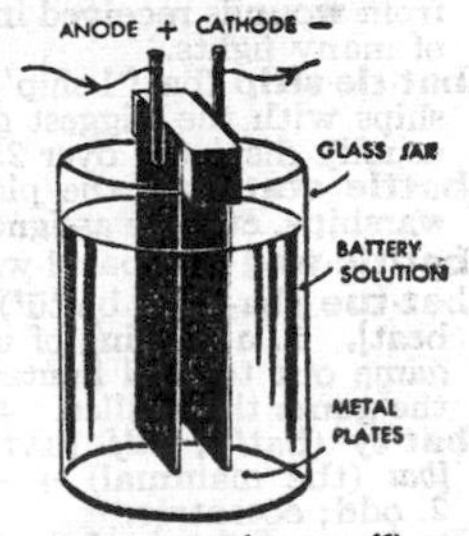

BATTERY (wet cell)

in battery, in firing position after recovery from the recoil of a previous discharge: said of a heavy gun.
the Battery, a part of New York City, at the southern tip of Manhattan.

bat·tik (bat′ik), *n., adj., v.t.* batik.

bat·ting (bat′iŋ), *n.* 1. the action of a person who bats, as in baseball. 2. [see BATT], cotton or wool fiber wadded in sheets.

batting average, 1. a number expressing the average effectiveness of a baseball player's batting, figured by dividing the number of safe hits by the number of times at bat. 2. [Colloq.], the average level of competence or success reached by a person in any activity.

bat·tle (bat′'l), *n.* [ME. & OFr. *bataile;* L. *battalia, battualia,* exercises of gladiators and soldiers in fighting and fencing < *battuere;* see BATTER (to beat)], 1. a fight, especially a large-scale engagement, between armed forces on land, at sea, or in the air. 2. armed fighting; combat or war. 3. any fight or fighting; conflict. *v.t. & v.i.* [BATTLED (-'ld), BATTLING], to fight.
give (or **do**) **battle,** to engage in battle; fight.
SYN.—**battle** denotes a conflict between armed forces in a war and implies a large-scale, prolonged contest over a particular area; **engagement,** the more formal term, stresses the actual meeting of opposing forces, with no restrictive connotation as to duration; a **campaign** is a series of military operations with a particular objective and may involve a number of battles; **encounter** usually suggests a chance meeting of hostile forces; **skirmish** refers to a brief, light encounter between small detachments; **action** stresses the detailed operations of active fighting (killed in *action*); **combat,** the most general of these terms, simply implies armed fighting without further qualification.

bat·tle (bat′'l), *v.t.* [Archaic or Poetic], to build battlements on (a fort, etc.).

battle array, 1. order or formation of troops, etc. for battle. 2. battle equipment.

bat·tle-ax, bat·tle-axe (bat′'l-aks′), *n.* 1. a heavy ax with a wide blade, formerly used as a weapon of war. 2. [Slang], a woman who is harsh, domineering, etc.

Battle Creek, a city in south central Michigan: pop., 44,000.

battle cruiser, a large warship with longer range and greater speed and maneuverability than a battleship but less heavily armored.

battle cry, 1. a shout used by troops in battle. 2. a slogan or motto for any kind of struggle, contest, etc.

bat·tle·dore (bat′'l-dôr′, bat′'l-dōr′), *n.* [ME. *batildore;* ?< Pr. *batedor,* beater], 1. a flat, wooden paddle used to hit a shuttlecock back and forth in the game of battledore and shuttlecock. 2. this game.

battle fatigue, combat fatigue.

bat·tle·field (bat′'l-fēld′), *n.* 1. the place where a battle takes place or took place; site of a battle. 2. any area of conflict.

battle front, the sector where actual combat is taking place between armed forces.

bat·tle·ground (bat′'l-ground′), *n.* a battlefield.

bat·tle·ment (bat′'l-mənt), *n.* [ME. *batelment;* OFr. < *bateiller, batailler,* to fortify with battlements < *bataille,* fortification on a wall or tower < LL. **battacula,* place of battle < *battere;* see BATTER (to beat)], 1. a low wall with open spaces for shooting, built on top of a castle wall, tower, or fort. 2. an architectural decoration like this.

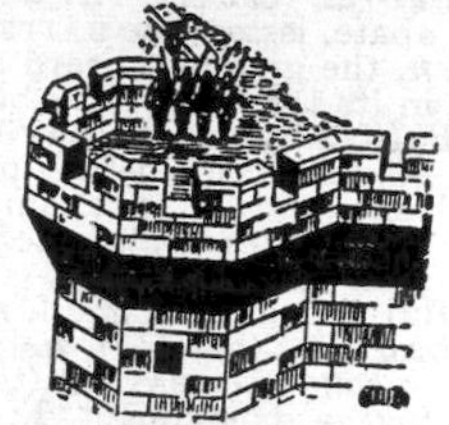
BATTLEMENT

bat·tle·plane (bat′'l-plān′), *n.* any airplane for combat; warplane.

battle royal, [*pl.* BATTLES ROYAL], 1. a fight or bout involving several or many contestants; free-for-all. 2. a long, bitterly fought battle. 3. a heated dispute.

bat·tle-scarred (bat′'l-skärd′), *adj.* 1. having scars from wounds received in combat. 2. having the marks of many fights.

bat·tle·ship (bat′'l-ship′), *n.* any of a class of large warships with the biggest guns and very heavy armor: it usually displaces over 25,000 tons.

battle stations, the places to which soldiers, sailors, warships, etc. are assigned for a battle or an emergency.

bat·tle·wag·on (bat′'l-wag′'n), *n.* [Slang], a battleship.

bat·tue (ba-tōō′, ba-tū′), *n.* [Fr., fem. pp. of *battre,* to beat], 1. a beating of underbrush and woods to drive game out toward hunters. 2. a hunt of this kind. 3. the game thus killed. 4. any mass killing.

bat·ty (bat′i), *adj.* [BATTIER (-i-ẽr), BATTIEST (-i-ist)], [*bat* (the mammal) + *-y*], [Slang], 1. insane; crazy. 2. odd; eccentric.

Ba·tum (bä-tōōm′), *n.* a seaport in the Georgian S.S.R.: pop., 82,000.

bau·ble (bô′b'l), *n.* [ME.; OFr. *babel, baubel, belbel,* a toy; redupl. of *bel* < L. *bellus,* pretty], 1. a showy but worthless thing; trinket; gewgaw. 2. a baby's toy. 3. [Archaic], a jester's baton with an ornament at the end.

Bau·cis (bô′sis), *n.* in *Greek legend,* an old woman, the devoted wife of Philemon: although poor, the old couple showed such genuine hospitality to Zeus and Hermes disguised as mortals that the grateful gods made Baucis a priestess.

bau·de·kin (bô′də-kin), *n.* [ME.; OFr. *baudequin;* ML. *baldakinus* < *Baldacco;* see BALDACHIN], baldachin (kind of brocade).

Bau·de·laire, Pierre Charles (pyâr shârl bō′dlâr′), 1821–1867; French poet and essayist.

baud·kin (bôd′kin), *n.* baudekin.

Bau·douin I (bō′dwan′), 1930– ; son of Leopold III; king of the Belgians (1951–).

bau·drons (bô′drənz), *n.* [Scot.], a cat: an epithet used without an article.

Bau·er, Harold (bou′ẽr), 1873–1951; English pianist.

Bau·haus (bou′hous′), *n.* [G. < *bauen,* to build + *haus,* a house], the architectural school of Walter Gropius, founded in Germany, 1919: it became known for its adaptation of science and technology to art, and for experimental use of metal, glass, etc. in buildings.

baulk (bôk), *n., v.t. & v.i.* balk.

Bau·mé (bō′mā′), *adj.* [after Antoine *Baumé* (1728–1804), Fr. chemist], designating or of a scale used in hydrometers: abbreviated **Bé.**

baum marten (boum), [< G. *baummarder; baum,* tree + *marder,* marten], the brown fur of the European marten.

baux·ite (bôk′sīt, bō′zīt), *n.* [Fr. < *Baux,* town near Arles], the claylike ore from which aluminum is obtained: it consists mainly of hydrated aluminum oxide, but contains some other substances.

Ba·var·i·a (bə-vâr′i-ə), *n.* a division of southern Germany, formerly a duchy, kingdom, and republic: area 30,054 sq. mi.; pop., 9,278,000; capital, Munich: German name, *Bayern.*

Ba·var·i·an (bə-vâr′i-ən), *adj.* of Bavaria, its people, dialect, etc. *n.* 1. a native or inhabitant of Bavaria. 2. the High German dialect of the Bavarians. Abbreviated **Bav., Bavar.**

Bavarian cream, a gelatin dessert made with whipped cream, eggs, and fruit flavoring.

baw·bee (bô′bē′, bô′bē′), *n.* [? < name of a Scot. mintmaster, the laird of *Sillebawby*], [Scot.], a halfpenny or any small coin.

baw·cock (bô′kok′), *n.* [< Fr. *beau,* fine + *coq,* cock (bird)], [Archaic], a good fellow.

bawd (bôd), *n.* [ME. *baude,* lewd person; ? < *baudestrot* < OFr. *baudetrot,* pander < *baud,* gay, bold < OHG. *bald,* bold], 1. a person, now usually a woman, who keeps a brothel; procuress. 2. [Rare], a prostitute.

bawd·i·ly (bô′d'l-i), *adv.* in a bawdy manner.

bawd·i·ness (bô′di-nis), *n.* the quality or state of being bawdy; indecent language or behavior.

bawd·ry (bôd′ri), *n.* [ME. & OFr. *bauderie,* gaiety < *baud*], 1. bawdiness. 2. [Archaic], the occupation of a bawd. 3. [Obs.], adultery or whoredom.

bawd·y (bô′di), *adj.* [BAWDIER (-di-ẽr), BAWDIEST (-di-ist)], characteristic of a bawd; indecent; obscene.

bawd·y·house (bô′di-hous′), *n.* a house of prostitution; brothel.

bawl (bôl), *v.i. & v.t.* [< ON. *baula,* to low like a cow, bellow], 1. to shout or call out noisily; howl; bellow; yell. 2. [Colloq.], to weep noisily. *n.* 1. a bawling; howl; bellow. 2. [Colloq.], a noisy weeping.
bawl out, 1. to shout or call out. 2. [Slang], to give a scolding to; reprimand.

Bax·ter, Richard (bak′stẽr), 1615–1691; English Puritan minister and writer.

bay (bā), *n.* [Fr. *baie;* LL. *baia*], 1. a part of a sea or lake, indenting the shore line; wide inlet: abbreviated **B., b.** 2. any level land area making an indentation, as into a woods, range of hills, etc. *v.t.* to dam (water).

bay (bā), *n.* [ME. *bai;* OFr. *baée* (Fr. *baie*) < *baer, bayer,* to gape, yawn; LL. *badare,* to gape], 1. an opening or alcove marked off by pillars, columns, etc. 2. a part of a building projecting from the main part; wing. 3. a compartment, as in a barn, for storing hay or grain. 4. a place for the sick and wounded on a ship: usually **sick bay.** 5. a recess in the wall line of a building, as for a window. 6. any opening in a wall.

bay (bā), *v.i.* [ME. *baien, abaien;* OFr. *baier, abaier* < L. *ad,* at + LL. *badare,* to gape], 1. to bark excitedly and continually. 2. to bark or howl in long, deep tones. *v.t.* 1. to bark at; howl at. 2. to chase with yelps and barks. 3. to bring to or hold at bay. *n.* 1. a baying. 2. the situation of or as of a hunted animal forced to turn and fight.
at bay, 1. with escape cut off; cornered. 2. held off: as, the bear kept the hunters *at bay.*
bring to bay, to force into a situation that makes escape impossible; corner.

bay (bā), *n.* [OFr. *baie, baye;* L. *baca,* berry], 1. an evergreen tree with glossy, leathery leaves and greenish-yellow flowers; laurel tree. 2. *pl.* a wreath of bay leaves, a classical token of honor given to poets and conquerors; hence, 3. *pl.* honor; fame. 4. any of various trees or shrubs like the laurel.

bay (bā), *adj.* [Fr. *bai;* L. *badius*], reddish-brown: said

especially of horses. *n.* 1. a horse (or other animal) of this color. 2. reddish brown.
ba·ya·dere, ba·ya·deer (bä'yə-dêr'), *n.* [Fr. *bayadère;* Port. *bailadeira,* dancer < *bailar,* dance; see BALLET], 1. a dancing girl, especially one in a temple in India. 2. a fabric or design with crosswise stripes. *adj.* striped crosswise.
bay·ard (bā'ẽrd), *n.* [OFr. *bayard, baiard,* bay horse; see BAY (reddish-brown)], 1. a bay horse. 2. [B-], in medieval romances, a magic horse given to Rinaldo by Charlemagne. 3. any horse: humorous term.
Ba·yard, Seigneur **Pierre Ter·rail de** (pyâr te'rå'y' də bå'yår'; Eng. bā'ẽrd), 1473?–1524; French soldier-hero, known as ***chevalier sans peur et sans reproche*** (the fearless and irreproachable knight).
bay·ber·ry (bā'ber'i, bā'bẽr-i), *n.* [*pl.* BAYBERRIES (-iz)], 1. the fruit of the bay tree. 2. the wax myrtle, a shrub with clusters of gray berries having a waxy coating used in making candles. 3. its fruit. 4. a tropical tree yielding an oil used in bay rum.
Bay City, a city in east central Michigan: pop., 54,000.
Bay·ern (bī'ẽrn), *n.* Bavaria: the German name.
Ba·yeux Tapestry (bā-yōō'; Fr. bå'yö'), an 11th-century tapestry, over 200 feet long and 1 2/3 feet wide, in the museum of Bayeux, northern France, picturing incidents that led to the Norman Conquest: the work is traditionally ascribed to the wife of William the Conqueror.
Bayle, Pierre (pyâr bel), 1647–1706; French rationalist philosopher.
bay leaf, the aromatic leaf of the bay tree, dried and used as a seasoning.
bay·o·net (bā'ə-nit, bā'ə-net', bā'ə-net'), *n.* [Fr. *bayonnette* < *Bayonne,* where the first bayonets were made], 1. a detachable daggerlike blade put on the muzzle end of a rifle, for hand-to-hand fighting. 2. a part like a bayonet in shape or function. *v.t.* [BAYONETED (-id), BAYONETING], to stab, prod, or kill with a bayonet. *v.i.* to use a bayonet.
Ba·yonne (bā-yōn', bā'ōn), *n.* 1. a city in northeastern New Jersey: pop., 74,000. 2. (bå'yôn'), a city in southwestern France: pop., 33,000.
bay·ou (bī'ōō), *n.* [Am. Fr.; prob. < Choctaw *bayuk,* small stream], in some parts of the southern United States, a marshy inlet or outlet of a lake, river, etc.; also, a backwater.
Bay·reuth (bī-roit', bī'roit), *n.* a city in northern Bavaria, Germany, known for the Wagnerian music festivals held there: pop., 59,000.
bay rum, an aromatic liquid formerly obtained from leaves of the bayberry tree, now made of certain oils, water, and alcohol: it is used in medicines and cosmetics.
Bay State, Massachusetts.
bay window, 1. a window or series of windows jutting out from the wall of a building and forming an alcove within, especially one rising from the ground. 2. [Slang], a large, protruding belly.
bay·wood (bā'wood'), *n.* a soft, light kind of mahogany: so called because it comes from the region of the Bay of Campeche.
ba·zaar, ba·zar (bə-zär'), *n.* [Per. *bāzār,* a market], 1. in Oriental countries, a market or street of shops. 2. a shop or department for selling various kinds of goods. 3. a sale of various articles, usually to raise money for a club, church, etc.
Ba·zaine, Fran·çois A·chille (frän'swå' ä'shēl' bå'zen'), 1811–1888; French marshal.
Ba·zin, Re·né Fran·çois (rə-nā' frän'swå' bå'zan'), 1853–1932; French novelist.
ba·zoo·ka (bə-zōō'kə), *n.* [echoic term orig. invented to name a comic musical horn consisting of a length of pipe open at both ends; ? influenced by *bazoo,* loud talk, *kazoo,* noisemaker], a weapon of metal tubing, for aiming and launching electrically fired, armor-piercing rockets: first used in World War II by the United States.

BAZOOKA

B.B.A., Bachelor of Business Administration.
B battery, an electric battery used in the plate circuit and the screen-grid circuit of certain radio tubes: it is usually made up of a number of dry cells in series, supplying voltages of 22 1/2 or multiples of this.
B.B.C., British Broadcasting Corporation.
bbl., [*pl.* BBLS.], barrel; barrels.
BB (shot), (bē'bē'), [a designation of the size], a size of shot measuring .18 of an inch in diameter, fired from an air rifle (*BB gun*).
B.C., 1. Bachelor of Chemistry. 2. Bachelor of Commerce. 3. before Christ. 4. British Columbia.
B.C., b.c., 1. battery commander. 2. bass clarinet.
B.C.E., 1. Bachelor of Chemical Engineering. 2. Bachelor of Civil Engineering.
bch., [*pl.* BCHS.], bunch.
B.C.L., Bachelor of Civil Law.
B.C.S., Bachelor of Chemical Science.
bd., 1. board. 2. bond. 3. bound. 4. bundle.
B/D, 1. bank draft. 2. bills discounted.
B.D., 1. Bachelor of Divinity. 2. bills discounted.
bdel·li·um (del'i-əm), *n.* [L. < Gr. *bdellion*], 1. a myrrhlike gum resin. 2. any tree yielding this. 3. in the *Bible,* a jewel variously interpreted as being a carbuncle (Gen. 2:12), a crystal (Numb. 11:7), or a pearl (rabbinical interpretation).
bd. ft., board foot; board feet.
bdl., [*pl.* BDLS.], bundle.
bds., 1. boards. 2. (bound in) boards. 3. bundles.
be (bē; *unstressed,* bi), *v.i.* [WAS (wuz, wäz, wəz) or WERE (wũr), BEEN (bin, ben, bēn), BEING (bē'iŋ)], [ME. *been, beon;* AS. *beon. Be* is a defective verb with parts from three unrelated stems: 1) the IE. substantive verb, base **es-,* as in Sans. *ásmi, asti,* Goth. *im, ist,* Eng. *am, is;* 2) IE. base **wes-,* stay, remain, as in Sans. *vasati,* lingers, stays, Goth. *wisan, was, wēsum,* remain, be, Eng. *was, were;* 3) IE. base **bheu-,* grow, become, as in Sans. *bhávati,* occurs, is there, L. *fieri* (*fis, fit, fimus*), be, become, occur, Eng. *be*], I. as a substantive verb, *be* means: 1. to exist; live: as, Caesar *is* no more. 2. to happen or occur: as, when will the wedding *be?* 3. to remain or continue: as, will he *be* here long? 4. to come to; belong: as, peace *be* with you. II. as a copula, *be* links its subject to a predicate nominative, adjective, or pronoun so as to express attribution or identity, and, by extension, value, cause, signification, etc.; it is sometimes equivalent to the mathematical sign (=). Examples: Mrs. Siddons *was* an actress, he *is* handsome, that coat *is* fifty dollars, this argument will *be* the death of me, let x *be* y. III. as an auxiliary, *be* is used: 1. with the past participle of a transitive verb to form the passive voice: as, he will *be* whipped. 2. with the past participle of certain intransitive verbs to form the perfect tense: as, Christ *is* risen. 3. with the present participle of another verb to express continuation: as, the player *is* running with the ball. 4. with the present participle or infinitive of another verb to express futurity, possibility, obligation, intention, etc.: as, he *is* going next week, she *is* to wash the dishes. *Be* is conjugated, in the present indicative: (I) *am,* (he, she, it) *is,* (we, you, they) *are;* in the past indicative: (I, he, she, it) *was,* (we, you, they) *were.* Archaic forms are (thou) *art, wert, wast.* The present subjunctive is *be,* the past subjunctive *were.*
be off, go away.
be- (bē, bi), [AS. *bi-, be-* (G. *be-;* Goth. *bi-*); weakened from *be, bi,* about, near], a prefix of various uses and meanings: I. prefixed to verbs: 1. with the general meaning of *around,* as in *besprinkle, beset.* 2. as an intensifier, with the general meanings of *completely, thoroughly, excessively,* as in *bedeck, besmear.* 3. as a deprivative, with the general meaning of *away,* as in *bereave, betake.* 4. as a transitive prefix, with the general meaning of *about,* as in *bethink, bemoan.* II. prefixed to nouns (sometimes adjectives) to form transitive verbs: 1. with the general sense of *make,* as in *besot, bepretty, bedirty.* 2. with the general senses of *furnish with, cover with, affect by,* as in *befriend, bedizen, becloud.* III. prefixed to past participles in *-ed* used as adjectives, with the general senses of *covered with, furnished with, furnished with to excess,* as in *bemedaled, bewhiskered.*
Be, in *chemistry,* beryllium.
Bé., Baumé.
B.E., 1. Bachelor of Education. 2. Bachelor of Engineering. 3. Bank of England. 4. Board of Education.
B.E., B/E, b.e., bill of exchange.
beach (bēch), *n.* [southeastern Eng. dial., orig., pebbles, shingles; AS. type **bæce*], a nearly level stretch of pebbles and sand beside a sea, lake, etc., often washed by high water; sandy shore; strand. *v.t. & v.i.* to ground (a boat) on a beach; drive (a boat) ashore. —*SYN.* see **shore.**
on the beach, 1. not aboard a ship; hence, 2. unemployed.
beach·comb·er (bēch'kōm'ẽr), *n.* 1. a long wave rolling ashore; comber. 2. a man who loafs on beaches or wharves, especially on the South Sea islands, living on what he can beg or find.
beach flea, any of a number of related small, crusty-shelled animals found on sea beaches, which jump like fleas but do not bite.
beach·head (bēch'hed'), *n.* a position established by invading troops on an enemy shore.
beach-la-mar (bēch'lä-mär'), *n.* bêche-de-mer (mixed language).

beach umbrella, a large umbrella used as a sunshade on beaches, in gardens, etc.
beach wagon, a station wagon.
bea·con (bē'kən, bē'k'n), *n.* [ME. *beekne, bekne;* AS. *beacen, becn,* a sign, signal; Gmc. base *baukna < IE. *bhāu, gleam, shine; influenced by *taikna, token], 1. a signal fire. 2. any light for warning or guiding. 3. a lighthouse. 4. a hill, station, or tower from which signals are given. 5. something serving as a signal, summons, etc. 6. a guiding signal given by radio to airplanes; beam. *v.t.* 1. to light up (darkness, etc.). 2. to provide or mark with signals or lights. 3. to guide by or as by beacons. *v.i.* 1. to shine brightly, as a beacon. 2. to serve as a summons or guide.
Bea·cons·field (bē'kənz-fēld'), Earl of, see **Disraeli.**
bead (bēd), *n.* [ME. *bede,* prayer, prayer bead; shortening of *ibede;* AS. *gebed,* prayer < *biddan,* to pray], 1. a small, usually round piece of glass, wood, metal, etc., pierced for stringing. 2. *pl.* a string of beads for counting off prayers; rosary. 3. *pl.* a string of beads; necklace. 4. any small, round object, as the sight at the muzzle end of a gun barrel. 5. a drop or bubble. 6. foam or head on beer, etc. 7. a small quantity of metal, as gold or silver, obtained by refining. 8. in *architecture, a)* a narrow, half-round molding. *b)* a molding composed of small rounded ornaments, like a string of beads. 9. in *chemistry,* a beadlike mass usually formed inside the loop of a platinum wire by the action of a flux, such as borax, upon the oxide or salt of certain metals: used in identifying certain metals in their compounds, since the metal determines the color of the bead. *v.t.* 1. to decorate or string with beads. 2. to string like beads. *v.i.* to form a bead or beads.
 count (or **tell** or **say**) **one's beads,** to say prayers with a rosary.
 draw a bead on, to take careful aim at.
bead·ed (bēd'id), *adj.* 1. decorated with beads. 2. having a bead or beads. 3. formed into or like beads.
bead·house (bēd'hous'), *n.* an almshouse; especially, formerly, one where the inmates were required to pray for its benefactors: also spelled **bedehouse.**
bead·ing (bēd'iŋ), *n.* 1. beadwork. 2. a molding, edge, or pattern resembling a row of beads. 3. a narrow, half-round molding. 4. a narrow trimming, as on a garment. 5. a beadlike openwork. 6. bubbles or froth on beer, wine, etc.
bea·dle (bē'd'l), *n.* [ME. *bedel, budel, bidel;* OFr. *bedel;* Frankish *bidal,* messenger < *bieten,* to bid; in ME. this form replaced the native AS. *bydel,* messenger < *beodan,* to bid], 1. a court messenger. 2. in England, an official who leads university processions, carrying a mace. 3. formerly, a minor parish officer in the Church of England, who kept order in church, etc.; hence, 4. a similar minor official, as in a synagogue.
bea·dle·dom (bē'd'l-dəm), *n.* [*beadle* + *-dom*], fussiness and stupidity of minor officials; petty bureaucracy.
bead·roll (bēd'rōl'), *n.* 1. a list of names; lengthy series. 2. [Archaic], in the *Roman Catholic Church,* a list of the dead for whose souls prayers are to be said.
bead-ru·by (bēd'rōō'bi), *n.* [*pl.* BEAD-RUBIES (-biz)], any of a group of small North American plants with white flowers and red berries shaped like beads.
beads·man (bēdz'mən), *n.* [*pl.* BEADSMEN (-mən)], [ME. *bedeman; bede,* prayer (see BEAD); + *man*], 1. a person who prays for another's soul, especially one hired to do so. 2. a person in a poorhouse. 3. a beggar. Also spelled **bedesman.**
beads·wom·an (bēdz'woom'ən), *n.* [*pl.* BEADSWOMEN (-wim'in)], a woman, especially one in a poorhouse, who prays for a benefactor: also spelled **bedeswoman.**
bead·work (bēd'wŭrk'), *n.* 1. decorative work in beads. 2. beaded molding; beading.
bead·y (bēd'i), *adj.* [BEADIER (-i-ēr), BEADIEST (-i-ist)], 1. small, round, and glittering like a bead. 2. decorated with beads. 3. full of or covered with drops or bubbles.
bea·gle (bē'g'l), *n.* [ME. *begle, begele;* ? < OFr. *begueule,* wide-throat (with reference to its bark)], a small hound with a smooth coat, short legs, and drooping ears.

BEAGLE
(13–15 in. high at shoulder)

beak (bēk), *n.* [ME. *bec, beke;* OFr. *bec;* L. *beccus* < Gaul.], 1. a bird's bill, especially the large, sharp, horny bill of a bird of prey. 2. a beaklike part or thing, as the mouth part of various insects, fishes, etc., or the spout of a pitcher. 3. the metal-covered ram projecting from the prow of an ancient warship. 4. [Slang], the nose, especially if large and hooked. 5. [British Slang], *a)* a magistrate. *b)* a schoolmaster. 6. in *architecture,* the outward-sloping upper surface of the drip of a cornice, by which water is directed away from the wall beneath.
beaked (bēkt, bēk'id), *adj.* 1. having a beak. 2. beaklike; curved, hooked, etc.
beak·er (bēk'ēr), *n.* [ME. *biker;* ON. *bikarr,* a cup; LL. *bicarium,* wine cup < Gr. *bikos,* wine jar], 1. a large or ornate cup; wine cup; goblet. 2. its contents. 3. a jarlike container of glass or metal with a lip for pouring, used by chemists, druggists, etc.
beam (bēm), *n.* [ME.; AS., a tree, piece of wood, column, etc.; akin to G. *baum,* a tree], I. 1. the squared-off trunk of a tree. 2. a long, thick piece of wood, metal, or stone, used in building. 3. one of the two large rollers of a loom. 4. the barlike, horizontal part of a plow, to which the handles, share, etc. are attached. 5. the crossbar of a balance. 6. the balance itself. 7. the shank of an anchor. 8. a long, stiff feather in the wing of a hawk, etc. 9. the main shaft of a deer's antlers. 10. any of the heavy, horizontal crosspieces of a ship. 11. a ship's breadth at its widest. 12. the side of a ship or the direction out sidewise from a ship. 13. [Slang], the width of the hips. 14. in *mechanics,* a lever that is moved back and forth by a piston rod and transmits its motion to the crank, etc. II. [orig. transl. of L. *columna lucis,* column of light], 1. a slender shaft of light or other radiation: also used figuratively. 2. [< the *v.i.*], a radiant look, smile, etc. 3. in *radio, a)* a signal sent continuously in one direction from a landing field, harbor, etc. as a guide for incoming aircraft or ships. *b)* the angle at which a microphone receives or a loud-speaker transmits most effectively. *c)* the maximum effective range of a microphone or loud-speaker. *v.t.* [ME. *beamien* < the *n.,* II], 1. to give out (shafts of light); radiate. 2. to guide or communicate with (aircraft, etc.) by a beam. 3. to direct or aim (a radio signal, program, etc.). *v.i.* 1. to shine brightly; be radiant. 2. to smile warmly.
 off the beam, 1. not following the direction of a guiding beam, as an airplane; hence, 2. [Slang], *a)* going in the wrong direction. *b)* wrong; incorrect.
 on the beam, 1. in the direction of a ship's beam; at right angles to the keel. 2. following the direction of a guiding beam, as an airplane; hence, 3. [Slang], *a)* going in the right direction. *b)* working or functioning well; alert, keen, etc.
beam compass, a compass having adjustable points on a beam or rod, used for drawing large circles.
beamed (bēmd), *adj.* [pp. of *beam*], 1. having beams, especially exposed and sometimes false ones: as, a *beamed* ceiling. 2. in *radio,* directed toward a certain place: as, a *beamed* program.
beam-ends (bēm'endz'), *n.pl.* the ends of a ship's beams.
 on the beam-ends (or **beam's ends**), 1. tipping so far to the side as to be in danger of overturning. 2. at the end of one's resources, money, etc.
beam·ing (bēm'iŋ), *adj.* 1. sending out beams or rays; shining. 2. smiling warmly; happy.
beam·ish (bēm'ish), *adj.* [*beam* + *-ish;* used by Lewis Carroll in a nonsense verse about the Jabberwock (*Through the Looking Glass*), apparently with the sense of *happy, fine,* etc.], beaming; radiant.
beam·y (bēm'i), *adj.* [BEAMIER (-i-ēr), BEAMIEST (-i-ist)], 1. sending out beams of light; radiant; bright. 2. beamlike; broad; massive. 3. having horns or antlers. 4. in *nautical usage,* having a broad beam; of more than adequate width as compared with over-all length.
bean (bēn), *n.* [ME. *beane;* AS. *bean;* akin to ON. *baun,* etc.; IE. base ? *bhabhā, as in L. *faba,* a bean], 1. the edible, smooth, kidney-shaped seed of certain plants of the legume or pea family. 2. a pod with such seeds. 3. a plant bearing such pods. 4. the bean-shaped seed of some other plants. 5. any of these plants. 6. [Slang], head; brain; mind. *v.t.* [Slang], to hit on the head.
bean·bag (bēn'bag'), *n.* 1. a small cloth bag filled with beans, for throwing in certain games. 2. such a game.
bean ball, [Slang], in *baseball,* a pitch deliberately aimed at the batter's head.
bean beetle, a small, tan insect with eight black spots on each wing cover: it is harmful to bean plants.
bean caper, any of a number of related plants having flower buds used in pickling.
bean·o (bēn'ō), *n.* [< the *beans* used as counters, by analogy with *lotto,* etc.], bingo.
bean·pole (bēn'pōl'), *n.* 1. a long stick put upright in the ground for bean plants to grow on. 2. [Colloq.], a tall, lanky person.
bean·stalk (bēn'stôk'), *n.* the main stem of a bean plant.
bean tree, any of various trees bearing podlike fruit, as the catalpa, carob, etc.
bear (bâr), *v.t.* [BORE (bôr, bōr) or *archaic* BARE (bâr), BORNE or BORN (bôrn, bōrn), BEARING: BORN is used only in the sense of *given birth,* in passive forms when *by* does not follow], [ME. *beren;* AS. *beran;* akin to Goth. *bairan,* L. *ferre,* Gr. *pherein,* Sans. *bharati* (he bears)], 1. to carry; transport. 2. to carry with one or on it; show; wear: as, the letter *bore* his signature. 3. to carry and bring forth; give birth to. 4. to support or hold up; sustain. 5. to sustain the burden of;

undergo: as, let him *bear* the expenses. 6. to undergo successfully; withstand; stand; endure: as, they *bore* the torture. 7. to be capable of withstanding; allow; permit of: as, this will *bear* investigation. 8. to carry or conduct (oneself): as, he *bears* himself well. 9. to carry over or hold (a sentiment): as, *bear* a grudge. 10. to move or push as if carrying: as, the crowd *bore* us along. 11. to give, offer, or supply: as, he will *bear* witness. *v.i.* 1. to have the strength to endure or suffer. 2. to be productive: as, the tree *bears* well. 3. to extend, lie, point, or move in a given direction: as, the ship *bore* west. 4. to be oppressive; weigh: as, grief *bears* heavily on her.

bear away, to keep or change a ship's course away from the wind.

bear down, 1. to press or push down; exert pressure; hence, 2. to make a strong effort.

bear down on, 1. to press down on; exert pressure on; hence, 2. to make a strong effort toward accomplishing. 3. to come or go toward; approach, especially another ship from windward.

bear on, 1. to have bearing on or relation to: as, his story *bears on* the crime. 2. to point or be aimed in the direction of.

bear out, to support or confirm.

bear up, to endure, as under a strain; keep up one's spirits.

bear with, to put up patiently with; tolerate.

SYN.—**bear** implies a putting up with something that distresses, annoys, pains, etc., without suggesting the way in which one sustains the imposition; **suffer** suggests passive acceptance of or resignation to that which is painful or unpleasant; **endure** implies a holding up against prolonged pain, distress, etc. and stresses stamina or patience; **tolerate** and the more informal **stand** both imply self-imposed restraint of one's opposition to what is offensive or repugnant; **brook,** a literary word, is usually used in the negative, suggesting determined refusal to put up with what is distasteful. See also **carry.**

bear (bâr), *n.* [*pl.* BEARS (bârz), BEAR; see PLURAL, II, D, 1], [ME. *bere;* AS. *bera,* orig. sense "the brown one"; IE. base **bher-os,* brown, as also in *beaver*], 1. a large, heavy, clumsy mammal with shaggy fur and a very short tail, native to temperate and arctic zones: the commonest varieties are the brown bear, black bear, grizzly bear, and white polar bear. 2. [B-], either of two constellations in the northern hemisphere, the Great Bear (also called *Ursa Major,* etc.) and the Little Bear (also called *Ursa Minor,* etc.): see also **Big Dipper, Little Dipper.** 3. a bearlike person; anyone who is clumsy, rude, etc. 4. in *mechanics,* a press for punching holes. 5. in the *stock exchange,* etc., a speculator who sells and promises to deliver shares, commodities, etc. which he does not yet own, hoping to buy them at a lower price before the date of delivery; manipulator who sells short: opposed to *bull. adj.* of or favorable to such speculators and their manipulations for lowering prices of stocks, etc. *v.t.* [BEARED (bârd), BEARING], to reduce or try to reduce the price of or prices in.

be a bear for punishment, 1. to be able to withstand much rough treatment; be rugged and tough. 2. to show dogged determination in spite of rough treatment, hardship, etc.

bear·a·ble (bâr'ə-b'l), *adj.* that can be borne or endured.

bear·a·bly (bâr'ə-bli), *adv.* in a bearable manner.

bear·bait·ing (bâr'bāt'iŋ), *n.* an old sport in which dogs were made to fight or torment a chained bear.

bear·ber·ry (bâr'ber'i, bâr'bẽr-i), *n.* [*pl.* BEARBERRIES (-iz)], 1. a trailing shrub of the heath family, having small bright-green leaves, white or pinkish flowers, and red berries. 2. a related shrub with black berries. 3. a variety of holly.

bear·cat (bâr'kat'), *n.* 1. an Asiatic variety of civet with a prehensile tail. 2. a panda. 3. [Colloq.], a strong, brave, fierce fighter.

beard (bêrd), *n.* [ME.; AS.; akin to G. *bart,* D. *baard;* IE. base **bhardhā,* as also in L. *barba* (for earlier **farba*)], 1. the hair growing around the lips and on the chin and cheeks, especially of a man; whiskers. 2. this hair, especially on the chin and cheek, when worn long or trimmed in various shapes. 3. any beardlike part, as of certain animals, fishes, birds, etc. 4. a hairy outgrowth on the head of certain grains, grasses, etc.; awn. 5. anything that projects like a beard; barb or hook. *v.t.* 1. to grasp by the beard. 2. to face or oppose courageously; defy. 3. to provide with a beard.

Beard, Charles Austin (bêrd), 1874–1948; American political scientist and historian.

Beard, Daniel Carter, 1850–1941; American author, artist, and naturalist; founder of Boy Scouts in the United States.

beard·ed (bêr'did), *adj.* [pp. of *beard*], 1. having a beard. 2. in *botany,* having an awn or awns.

beard·less (bêrd'lis), *adj.* 1. having no beard. 2. too young to have a beard; hence, 3. young, callow, etc.

Beards·ley, Aubrey Vincent (bêrdz'li), 1872–1898; English artist and illustrator.

beard·tongue (bêrd'tuŋ'), *n.* [so named from the bearded, tonguelike stamen], any of a number of related plants of the figwort family, bearing white, pink, red, blue, or purple flowers; pentstemon.

bear·er (bâr'ẽr), *n.* 1. a person or thing that bears, carries, or supports. 2. a plant or tree that produces fruit or blooms. 3. a person who carries or attends the casket at a funeral; pallbearer. 4. a person having or presenting for payment a check, note, money order, etc. *adj.* made out to the bearer: as, *bearer* bonds.

bear garden, 1. a place for bearbaiting or similar pastimes. 2. any rough, noisy, rowdy place.

bear grass, 1. any of a group of plants of the lily family, with grasslike leaves and small, white flowers. 2. any of various similar plants, as a kind of camass.

bear·ing (bâr'iŋ), *n.* 1. way of carrying and conducting oneself; carriage; manner; mien. 2. anything that bears weight or pressure; a support or supporting part. 3. a producing; birth. 4. ability to produce. 5. anything borne or produced, as crop, fruit, etc. 6. an enduring; endurance. 7. the position of an object, point, etc. with reference to that of something else or to a point on the compass: often used in the plural: as, the ship lost her *bearings.* 8. application; relation; relevant meaning: as, the evidence had no *bearing* on the case. 9. in *architecture,* the part of a lintel or beam that rests on supports. 10. in *heraldry,* any figure on the field. 11. in *mechanics,* any part of a machine in or on which another part revolves, slides, etc.

lose one's bearings, to lose one's way.

SYN.—**bearing,** in this comparison denoting manner of carrying or conducting oneself, refers to characteristic physical and mental posture; **carriage,** also applied to posture, specifically stresses the physical aspects of a person's bearing (an erect *carriage*); **demeanor** refers to behavior as expressing one's attitude or a specified personality trait (a demure *demeanor*); **mien,** a literary word, refers to one's bearing and manner (a man of melancholy *mien*); **deportment** refers to one's behavior with reference to standards of conduct or social conventions; **manner** is applied to customary or distinctive attitude, actions, speech, etc. and, in the plural, refers to behavior conforming with polite conventions.

bearing rein, a short rein for pulling and keeping a horse's head up; checkrein.

bear·ish (bâr'ish), *adj.* 1. bearlike; rude, rough, cross, surly, etc. 2. directed toward or causing a lowering of prices in the stock exchange, etc.

bear-lead·er (bâr'lē'dẽr), *n.* a private teacher or traveling companion for a young man.

Bear River, a river flowing through Utah, Wyoming, and Idaho into Great Salt Lake: length, c. 450 mi.

bear's-breech (bârz'brēch'), *n.* any of a number of related herbs or thistlelike shrubs with long, spiny or lobed leaves and long spikes of white, rose, or purplish flowers; acanthus.

bear's-ear (bârz'êr'), *n.* a variety of primrose with yellow flowers and leaves shaped like a bear's ear.

bear's-foot (bârz'foot'), *n.* a bad-smelling variety of hellebore, with toothed leaves and clusters of five-petaled, cup-shaped flowers.

bear·skin (bâr'skin'), *n.* 1. the pelt, fur, or hide of a bear. 2. a shaggy woolen fabric somewhat like this. 3. anything made from bearskin, as a rug, coat, etc. 4. a tall fur cap worn as part of some uniforms.

bear·wood (bâr'wood'), *n.* a small tree of the western United States, the bark of which is used as a laxative: also called *cascara buckthorn.*

beast (bēst), *n.* [ME. *beeste, beste;* OFr. *beste;* L. *bestia;* prob. < IE. **dwejes-to-,* that which is feared], 1. originally, any animal except man. 2. any large, four-footed animal; quadruped. 3. qualities or impulses like an animal's: as, it's the *beast* in him. 4. a person who is brutal, gross, vile, disgusting, stupid, etc.

beast·li·ness (bēst'li-nis), *n.* 1. the quality or state of being beastly; bestiality. 2. a beastly act. 3. [Colloq.], disagreeable or unpleasant quality.

beast·ly (bēst'li), *adj.* [BEASTLIER (-li-ẽr), BEASTLIEST (-li-ist)], 1. of, like, or characteristic of a beast; bestial, brutal, gross, etc. 2. [Colloq.], disagreeable; disgusting. *adv.* [British], very: as, *beastly* bad news.

beast of burden, any animal used for carrying things.

beast of prey, any animal that hunts and kills other animals for food.

beat (bēt), *v.t.* [BEAT, BEATEN (bēt'n), BEATING], [ME. *beten;* AS. *beatan;* akin to ON. *bauta,* OHG. *bōzzan*], 1. to hit or strike repeatedly; pound. 2. to punish by striking repeatedly and hard; whip; flog; spank. 3. to dash repeatedly against: as, waves *beat* the shore. 4. to make flat or smooth by walking or riding; form by treading: as, we *beat* a path to the road. 5. to shape or flatten by hammering; forge. 6. to mix by stirring or striking repeatedly with a utensil; whip (cream, etc.). 7. to move (wings, etc.) up and down; flap; flail. 8. to hunt through; search: as, the posse *beat* the countryside for the fugitive. 9. to make, force, or drive by or as by hitting or flailing: as, he *beat* his way through the crowd. 10. to get ahead of; outdo; master; defeat. 11. to mark (time or rhythm) by tapping, etc. 12. to sound or signal, as by a drumbeat. 13. [Colloq.], to baffle; puzzle. 14. [Colloq.], to cheat; trick. *v.i.* 1. to strike, hit, or dash repeatedly and, usually, hard. 2. to move or sound rhythmically; throb. 3. to hunt through underbrush, woods, etc. for game. 4. to take beating or stirring: as, this cream doesn't *beat* well. 5. to have a beat or rhythm; pulsate, vibrate, etc.: as, the heart *beats*. 6. to make a sound by being struck, as a drum. 7. [Colloq.], to win. 8. in *nautical usage*, to progress by tacking into the wind. 9. in *radio*, to combine two waves of different frequencies, thus producing additional frequencies equal to the difference between these. *n.* 1. a beating, as of the heart. 2. any of a series of blows or strokes. 3. any of a series of movements or sounds; throb. 4. a habitual path or round of duty: as, a policeman's *beat*. 5. the unit of musical rhythm: as, four *beats* to a measure. 6. the gesture of the hand, baton, etc. used to mark this. 7. [Colloq.], a person or thing that surpasses: as, you never saw the *beat* of it. 8. [Slang], a cheat; dead beat. 9. in *acoustics*, the regularly recurring amplification of sound produced by two simultaneous sounds having different rates of vibration. 10. in *journalism*, a publishing of news before rival newspapers; scoop. 11. in *radio*, one cycle of a frequency formed by beating. *adj.* [alternative pp. of the *v.*], [Slang], 1. tired; exhausted. 2. of or belonging to a group of young people in the United States who reject conventional attitudes, dress, etc. and affect extreme slang speech and an interest in jazz music and some other forms of art expression.

beat about, 1. to hunt or look through or around. 2. in *nautical usage*, to tack into the wind.
beat a retreat, to retreat; withdraw.
beat back, to force to retreat; drive back.
beat down, 1. to put down; suppress. 2. [Colloq.], to force to a lower price.
beat it! [Slang], go away!
beat off, to drive back; repel.
beat up (on), [Slang], to give a beating to; thrash.
on the beat, in tempo.

SYN.—**beat**, the most general word in this comparison, conveys the basic idea of hitting or striking repeatedly, whether with the hands, feet, an implement, etc.; **pound** suggests heavier, more effective blows than **beat** (to *pound* with a hammer); **pommel** implies the beating of a person with the fists and suggests a continuous, indiscriminate rain of damaging blows; **thrash**, originally referring to the beating of grain with a flail, suggests similar broad, swinging strokes, as in striking a person repeatedly with a stick, etc.; **flog** implies a punishing by the infliction of repeated blows with a stick, strap, whip, etc.; **whip**, often used as an equivalent of **flog**, specifically suggests lashing strokes or motions; **maul** implies the infliction of repeated heavy blows such as to bruise or lacerate. All of these terms are used loosely, especially by journalists, in describing a decisive victory in a contest.

‡Be·a·ta Vir·go Ma·ri·a (bē-ā'tə vũr'gō mə-rī'ə), [L.], Blessed Virgin Mary: abbreviated **B.V.M.**

beat·en (bēt''n), *adj.* [alternative pp. of *beat*], 1. struck with repeated blows; whipped. 2. shaped or made thin by hammering. 3. flattened by treading; much traveled: as, a *beaten* path. 4. defeated. 5. tired out. 6. searched through for game. 7. mixed. 8. [Colloq.], puzzled; confused.
off the beaten track (or **path**), unusual, unfamiliar, original, etc.

beat·er (bēt'ẽr), *n.* 1. a person or thing that beats. 2. an implement or utensil for beating. 3. a person who drives game from cover in a hunt.

be·a·tif·ic (bē'ə-tif'ik), *adj.* [L. *beatificus;* see BEATIFY], 1. making blissful or blessed. 2. showing happiness or delight; blissful; joyful: as, a *beatific* smile.

be·a·tif·i·cal·ly (bē'ə-tif'i-k'l-i, bē'ə-tif'ik-li), *adv.* in a beatific manner.

be·at·i·fi·ca·tion (bi-at'ə-fi-kā'shən), *n.* [Fr.], 1. a beatifying or being beatified. 2. in the *Roman Catholic Church*, the process of determining the sanctity of a person who has died and declaring him to be among the blessed in heaven: he is then entitled to public worship and is usually, but not necessarily, canonized.

be·at·i·fy (bi-at'ə-fī'), *v.t.* [BEATIFIED (-fīd'), BEATIFYING], [L. *beatificare* < *beatus*, happy + *facere*, to make], 1. to make blissfully happy; bless. 2. in the *Roman Catholic Church*, to pronounce the beatification of by papal decree.

beat·ing (bēt'iŋ), *n.* 1. the act of a person or thing that beats. 2. a whipping or thrashing. 3. a throbbing; pulsation. 4. a defeat.

be·at·i·tude (bi-at'ə-tōōd', bi-at'ə-tūd'), *n.* [Fr. *béatitude;* L. *beatitudo* < *beatus*, happy, blessed], 1. perfect blessedness or happiness. 2. a blessing.
the Beatitudes, the pronouncements in the Sermon on the Mount, which begin "Blessed are the poor in spirit": Matt. 5:3-12.

beat·nik (bēt'nik), *n.* [*beat, adj. 2.* + Russ. *-nik*, equivalent to Eng. *-er*], [Slang], a member of the beat group.

Be·a·trice (bē'ə-tris), [It.; < L. *beatrix*, she who makes happy < *beatus;* see BEATITUDE], a feminine name: diminutive, *Bea;* variant, *Beatrix*. *n.* 1. (*also* It. be'ä-trē'che), a Florentine woman (*Beatrice Portinari*, 1266–1290) loved by Dante and immortalized in his *Divine Comedy*. 2. the witty heroine of Shakespeare's *Much Ado About Nothing*.

Be·a·trix (bē'ə-triks), a feminine name: diminutive, *Trixie:* see **Beatrice.**

Beat·ty, David (bē'ti), first Earl Beatty, 1871–1936; British admiral; commanded British fleet during World War I.

beau (bō), *n.* [*pl.* BEAUS (bōz), BEAUX (bōz; Fr. bō)], [Fr., a dandy < *beau, bel*, pretty; L. *bellus*, pretty, charming], 1. a man greatly concerned with his personal appearance and with fashion; dandy. 2. the sweetheart or lover of a woman or girl.

Beau Brum·mell (bō brum'əl) 1. (*George Bryan Brummell*), 1778–1840; Englishman famous for his fashionable dress and manners; hence, 2. any dandy or fop.

Beau·fort scale (bō'fẽrt), [after Sir Francis *Beaufort* (1774–1857), Brit. naval officer who invented it in 1805], in *meteorology*, a scale of wind force, ranging from 0 for speeds of less than one mile per hour (a calm) to 12 or higher for speeds of more than 72 miles per hour (hurricane force).

Beaufort Sea, an extension of the Arctic Ocean, north of Alaska and northwest Canada.

‡beau geste (bō' zhest'), [*pl.* BEAUX GESTES (bō' zhest')], [Fr.], 1. a fine or beautiful gesture; hence, 2. an act or offer that seems fine, noble, etc., but is empty.

Beau·har·nais, Jo·sé·phine de (zhō'zā'fēn' də bō'är'-ne'), see **Josephine.**

beau i·de·al (bō' ī-dē'əl), [*pl.* BEAUX or BEAUS (bōz) IDEAL], [Fr.], 1. ideal beauty. 2. the perfect type or conception: as, the *beau ideal* of fashion: a sense due to mistranslation.

Beau·mar·chais, de (də bō'mår'she'), (pseudonym of *Pierre Augustin Caron*), 1732–1799; French dramatist.

beau monde (bō mond; Fr. bō' mōnd'), [Fr., lit., elegant world], fashionable society.

Beau·mont (bō'mont), *n.* a city in southeastern Texas: pop., 119,000.

Beau·mont, Francis (bō'mont), 1584–1616; English dramatist who collaborated with John Fletcher.

Beau·re·gard, Pierre G. T. (pyâr bō'rə-gärd'), 1818–1893; Confederate general in the Civil War.

beau·te·ous (bū'ti-əs), *adj.* beautiful. —*SYN.* see **beautiful.**

beau·ti·cian (bū-tish'ən), *n.* a person who does hairdressing, manicuring, etc. in a beauty shop.

beau·ti·fi·ca·tion (bū'tə-fə-kā'shən), *n.* 1. a beautifying. 2. the fact or state of being beautified.

beau·ti·fi·er (bū'tə-fī'ẽr), *n.* a person or thing that makes (something) beautiful or more beautiful.

beau·ti·ful (bū'tə-fəl), *adj.* having beauty.
the beautiful, 1. that which has beauty; the quality of beauty. 2. those who are beautiful.

SYN.—**beautiful** is applied to that which gives the highest degree of pleasure to the senses or to the mind and suggests that the object of delight approximates one's conception of an ideal; **lovely** refers to that which delights by inspiring affection or warm admiration; **handsome** implies attractiveness by reason of pleasing proportions, symmetry, elegance, etc. and carries connotations of masculinity, dignity, or impressiveness; **pretty** implies a dainty, delicate, or graceful quality in that which pleases and carries connotations of femininity or diminutiveness; **comely** applies to persons only and suggests a wholesome attractiveness of form and features rather than a high degree of beauty; **fair** suggests beauty that is fresh, bright, or flawless and, when applied to persons, is used especially of complexion and features; **good-looking** is closely equivalent to **handsome** or **pretty**, suggesting a pleasing appearance but not expressing the fine distinctions of either word; **beauteous**, equivalent to **beautiful** in poetry and lofty prose, is now often used in humorously disparaging references to beauty. —*ANT.* ugly.

beau·ti·fy (bū'tə-fī'), *v.t.* [BEAUTIFIED (-fīd'), BEAUTIFYING], [*beauty* + *-fy*], to make beautiful or more beautiful. *v.i.* to become beautiful. —*SYN.* see **adorn.**

beau·ty (bū'ti), *n.* [*pl.* BEAUTIES (-tiz)], [ME. & OFr. *bealte, beaute;* LL. **bellitas* < L. *bellus*, pretty, lovely], 1. the quality attributed to whatever pleases or satisfies in certain ways, as by line, color, form, texture, proportion, rhythmic motion, tone, etc., or by behavior, attitude, etc. 2. a thing having this quality. 3. good looks. 4. a very good-looking woman. 5. any very attractive feature.

beauty shop (or **salon** or **parlor**), a place where women go for hairdressing, manicuring, etc.

beauty sleep, [Colloq.], 1. sleep before midnight, popularly thought to be most restful. 2. any extra sleep.

beauty spot, 1. a little piece of black paper, cloth, etc. that a woman sometimes puts on her face or back to emphasize the beauty or whiteness of the skin; patch. 2. a natural mark or mole on the skin. 3. any place noted for its beauty.

beaux (bōz; Fr. bō), *n.* alternative plural of **beau.**

‡beaux-arts (bō'zär'), *n.pl.* [Fr.], the fine arts.

‡beaux-es·prits (bō'zes'prē'), *n.* plural of **bel-esprit.**

bea·ver (bē′vẽr), *n.* [*pl.* BEAVERS (-vẽrz), BEAVER; see PLURAL, II, D, 1], [ME. *bever;* AS. *beofor;* IE. base **bher-os,* brown, in form **bhebhru-s*], 1. an animal that lives on land and in water, and has soft, brown fur, chisellike teeth, webbed hind feet, and a flat, broad tail. 2. its fur. 3. a man's high silk hat, originally made of this fur. 4. a heavy cloth of felted wool, used for overcoats, etc.

BEAVER (2 1/2 ft. long)

bea·ver (bē′vẽr), *n.* [ME. & OFr. *baviere,* beaver of a helmet; orig., bib < *bave,* saliva, foam], 1. in medieval armor, a movable part attached to the helmet or to the breastplate, for protecting the mouth and chin: see **armor,** illus. 2. later, the visor of a helmet.

bea·ver·board (bē′vẽr-bôrd′, bē′vẽr-bōrd′), *n.* artificial board made of fiber, used for walls, partitions, etc.: a trade-mark (**Beaverboard**).

Bea·ver·brook (bē′vẽr-brook′), first Baron (*William Maxwell Aitken*), 1879– ; English statesman and newspaper publisher.

be·bee·rine (bi-bē′rēn, bi-bē′rin), *n.* [*bebeeru* + *-ine*], a drug obtained from bebeeru bark.

be·bee·ru (bi-bē′rōō), *n.* [Sp. *bibiru* < the native name], a large South American evergreen tree.

Be·bel, Au·gust (ou′goost bā′bəl), 1840–1913; German socialist and author.

be-bop (bē′bop′), *n.* [? from sound made on a trumpet], a modification of jazz music, characterized by much improvisation, lack of restraint, deviation from key, and, often, meaningless lyrics.

be·calm (bi-käm′), *v.t.* 1. to make quiet or still; calm. 2. to make (a sailing vessel) motionless from lack of wind.

be·came (bi-kām′), past tense of **become.**

be·cause (bi-kôz′, bə-kuz′), *conj.* [ME. *bi cause; bi,* by + *cause*], for the reason or cause that; on account of the fact that; since: as, I came in *because* it was raining.

because of, by reason of; on account of.

bec·ca·fi·co (bek′ə-fē′kō), *n.* [*pl.* BECCAFICOS (-kōz)], [It. < *beccare,* to peck + *fico,* a fig], any of several small songbirds, eaten as a delicacy in Italy.

bé·cha·mel (bā′shä-mel′), *n.* [Fr. < *Béchamel,* steward to Louis XIV], a white sauce made of cream, butter, flour, etc.

be·chance (bi-chans′, bi-chäns′), *v.t. & v.i.* to happen (to); befall; chance.

be·charm (bi-chärm′), *v.t.* to hold by a charm or spell; fascinate.

‡**bêche-de-mer** (besh′də-mer′), *n.* [Fr., worm of the sea; altered < Port. *bicho do mar,* sea slug], 1. [*pl.* BÊCHES-DE-MER (besh′-)], any of a number of related cucumber-shaped water animals with a leathery skin and a mouth surrounded by branched tentacles; trepang; sea cucumber. 2. a mixed trade language, combining elements from English and Malay, spoken by both natives and whites in island areas of the central western Pacific: also **beach-la-mar.**

Bech·u·a·na (bech′ōō-ä′nə, bek′yū-ä′nə), *n.* 1. [*pl.* BECHUANA, BECHUANAS (-nəz)], a member of a Bantu-speaking people living in Bechuanaland. 2. their language.

Bech·u·a·na·land (bech′ōō-ä′nə-land′, bek′yū-ä′nə-land′), *n.* a British protectorate in South Africa: area, 275,000 sq. mi.; pop., 300,000 (est. 1947).

beck (bek), *n.* [< *beckon*], a gesture of the hand, head, etc., meant to summon. *v.t. & v.i.* [Archaic], to summon by a beck; beckon.

at the beck and call of, at the service of; obedient to the wishes of.

beck (bek), *n.* [ME. *bek;* ON. *bekkr,* a brook; akin to AS. *bæc* & Eng. dial. *bache;* see BEACH], a little stream, especially one with a rocky bottom.

beck·et (bek′it), *n.* [? < OFr. or MD. *becquet*], a contrivance, as a looped rope or large hook and eye, used for fastening loose ropes, oars, spars, etc.

Becket, Thomas à, see **Thomas à Becket.**

becket bend, a kind of knot; sheet bend: see **knot,** illus.

beck·on (bek′'n), *v.i. & v.t.* [ME. *bekken, beknen;* AS. *biecnan, beacnian,* to make signs < *beacen,* a sign; see BEACON], to call or summon by a silent gesture, nod, etc.: often used figuratively: as, the woods *beckon. n.* a summoning gesture.

be·cloud (bi-kloud′), *v.t.* 1. to cloud over; darken. 2. to confuse; muddle.

be·come (bi-kum′), *v.i.* [BECAME (-kām′), BECOME, BECOMING], [ME. *bicumen;* AS. *bicuman, becuman;* see BE- & COME], 1. to come to be: as, in that instant he *became* a man. 2. to grow to be; change or develop into by growth: as, the tadpole *becomes* a frog. 3. [Obs.], to happen. *v.t.* 1. to befit; suit. 2. to be suitable to in appearance: as, that hat *becomes* you.

become of, to happen to; be the fate of.

be·com·ing (bi-kum′iŋ), *adj.* [ppr. of *become*], 1. suitable; appropriate; seemly: as, cursing is not *becoming* to a lady. 2. suitable (to the wearer) in appearance: as, a *becoming* blouse. *n.* the change from nonbeing to being; a coming into existence.

Bec·que·rel, Alex·an·dre Ed·mond (å′lek′san′dr′ ed′mōn′ bek′rel′), 1820–1891; French physicist; father of *Antoine Henri.*

Becquerel, An·toine Cé·sar (än′twån′ sā′zår′), 1788–1878; French physicist; father of *Alexandre Edmond.*

Becquerel, An·toine Hen·ri (än′twån′ än′rē′), 1852–1908; French physicist; discoverer of radioactivity; shared Nobel prize in physics, 1903, with Pierre and Marie Curie.

Becquerel rays, invisible rays that come from radioactive substances, as radium, uranium, thorium, etc.

bed (bed), *n.* [ME.; AS. *bed, bedd;* akin to G. *bett;* IE. base **bhedh,* to bury, as in W. *bedd,* Bret. *béz,* a grave; orig. sense "a sleeping hollow in the ground"; see sense 6], 1. a thing for sleeping or resting on; piece of furniture consisting usually of a bedstead, spring, mattress, and bedding. 2. a bedstead. 3. any place used for sleeping or reclining. 4. such a place regarded as the scene of sexual intercourse or procreation. 5. the grave. 6. a plot of soil where plants are raised. 7. the flowers or vegetables growing in this. 8. the bottom of a river, lake, etc. 9. an enclosing substance, as rock in which shells, minerals, etc. are lodged. 10. any flat surface used as a foundation or support: as, a *bed* of masonry, a railroad *bed.* 11. a pile or heap resembling a bed, especially in softness or shape: as, a *bed* of leaves. 12. a geological layer; stratum: as, a *bed* of coal. *v.t.* [BEDDED (-id), BEDDING], 1. to provide with a sleeping place. 2. to put to bed. 3. to have sexual intercourse with. 4. to fix or place firmly; embed. 5. to plant in a bed or beds of earth. 6. to make (earth) into a bed or beds for plants. 7. to lay out flat like a bed; arrange in layers. *v.i.* 1. to go to bed; rest; sleep. 2. to form in layers; stratify.

be brought to bed (of), to give birth (to a child).

bed and board, 1. sleeping accommodations and meals; facilities for living; hence, 2. home; the married state: as, she has left his *bed and board.*

bed down, to prepare and use a sleeping place.

get up on the wrong side of the bed, to be cross or grouchy.

put to bed, 1. to get (a child, etc.) ready for sleep; put into a bed. 2. to lock (type, plates, etc.) into a form and place on a printing press; hence, 3. [Slang], to continue working on an edition of (a newspaper, etc.) until it is ready for the press.

take to one's bed, to go to bed because of illness, etc.

be·daub (bi-dôb′), *v.t.* 1. to make daubs on; smudge or smear over. 2. to overdecorate; ornament showily.

Be·daux, Charles Eugene (bə-dō′), 1887–1944; American industrial engineer born in France; originator of the Bedaux system, a point system of wage payment.

be·daz·zle (bi-daz′'l), *v.t.* to dazzle thoroughly; bewilder; confuse.

bed·bug (bed′bug′), *n.* a small, wingless, biting insect with a broad, flat, reddish-brown body and an unpleasant odor: it infests beds, upholstered furniture, etc.

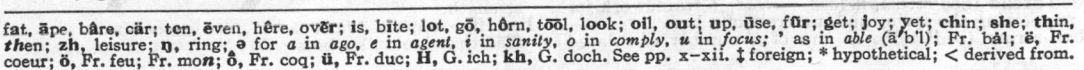

BEDBUG (3/16 in. long)

bed·cham·ber (bed′chām′bẽr), *n.* a bedroom.

bed·clothes (bed′klōz′, bed′klōthz′), *n.pl.* sheets, pillows, blankets, etc.

bed·cov·er (bed′kuv′ẽr), *n.* a cover for a bed; coverlet; bedspread.

bed·der (bed′ẽr), *n.* in *gardening,* a plant used for bedding.

bed·ding (bed′iŋ), *n.* [ME.; AS.], 1. mattresses and bedclothes. 2. straw, hay, etc., used to bed animals. 3. any base or foundation. 4. a putting to bed. 5. a growing of plants in a mass for a showy effect. 6. in *geology,* stratification. *adj.* in *gardening,* suitable for planting in a bed.

Bed·does, Thomas Lov·ell (luv′əl bed′ōz), 1803–1849; English poet and dramatist.

Bede (bēd), *n.* English theologian and historian; 673–735 A.D.; wrote *Ecclesiastical History of the English Nation:* called *the Venerable Bede.*

be·deck (bi-dek′), *v.t.* to cover with decorations; adorn. —*SYN.* see **adorn.**

bede·house (bēd′hous′), *n.* a beadhouse.

be·del, be·dell (bē′d'l), *n.* a beadle: archaic spelling.

bedes·man (bēdz′mən), *n.* a beadsman.

bedes·wom·an (bēdz′woom′ən), *n.* [*pl.* BEDESWOMEN (-wim′in)], a beadswoman.

be·dev·il (bi-dev′'l), *v.t.* [BEDEVILED or BEDEVILLED (-'ld), BEDEVILING or BEDEVILLING], 1. to plague

diabolically; torment. 2. to bewitch. 3. to worry; harass; bewilder. 4. to corrupt; spoil.
be·dev·il·ment (bi-dev'’l-mənt), ***n.*** 1. a bedeviling. 2. the fact or state of being bedeviled.
be·dew (bi-dōō', bi-dū'), ***v.t.*** [ME.], 1. to wet with dew. 2. to make drops of liquid form on.
bed·fast (bed'fast', bed'fäst'), ***adj.*** bedridden.
bed·fel·low (bed'fel'ō), ***n.*** 1. a person who shares one's bed; bedmate. 2. any associate, co-worker, etc.
Bed·ford (bed'fẽrd), ***n.*** 1. Bedfordshire. 2. the county seat of Bedfordshire: pop., 60,000. 3. a city in northeastern Ohio: pop., 15,000.
Bedford cord, [after *Bedford,* England], a heavy wool or cotton cloth resembling corduroy.
Bed·ford·shire (bed'fẽrd-shir), ***n.*** a county of central England: pop., 312,000; county seat, Bedford: also called *Bedford.*
be·dight (bi-dīt'), ***adj.*** [pp. of obs. v. *bedight; be-* + *dight* < ME. *dihten,* to prepare, set in order; AS. *dihtan,* to arrange, dispose, compose, write < L. *dictare;* see DICTATE], [Archaic], bedecked; arrayed.
be·dim (bi-dim'), ***v.t.*** [BEDIMMED (-dimd'), BEDIMMING], to make dim; darken or obscure: said especially of the eyes or the vision.
Bed·i·vere, Sir (bed'ə-vêr'), in ***Arthurian legend,*** the loyal knight who was with the dying King Arthur and saw him go away to Avalon.
be·diz·en (bi-dī'z'n bi-diz'’n,), ***v.t.*** [*be-* + *dizen*], to dress or decorate in a cheap, showy way.
be·diz·en·ment (bi-dī'z'n-mənt, bi-diz'’n-mənt), ***n.*** a bedizening.
bed jacket, a woman's short, loose upper garment, sometimes worn over a nightgown.
bed·lam (bed'ləm), ***n.*** [ME. *Bedlem, Bethlem* < the London hospital of St. Mary of *Bethlehem*], 1. [B-], a famous old London hospital for the mentally ill. 2. any similar hospital. 3. any noisy, confused place or situation. 4. noise and confusion; uproar. ***adj.*** full of noise and confusion.
bed·lam·ite (bed'ləm-īt'), ***n.*** [*bedlam* + *-ite*], a patient in a hospital for the mentally ill; insane person.
bed linen, bed sheets, pillowcases, etc., whether of linen or not.
Bed·ling·ton terrier (bed'liŋ-t'n), [after *Bedlington,* a town in England], a blue or liver-colored, woolly-coated terrier, about 15 or 16 inches high, resembling a small lamb.
Bed·loe's Island (bed'lōz), Liberty Island.
bed·mate (bed'māt'), ***n.*** 1. a person who shares one's bed. 2. one's wife or husband.
bed molding, in *architecture,* a molding below a projecting part, especially between the corona and frieze.
bed of roses, [Colloq.], 1. a life of ease and luxury. 2. an easy situation.
Bed·ou·in (bed'ōō-in), ***n.*** [Fr. *bédouin;* Ar. *badāwin,* desert dwellers], 1. an Arab of any of the nomadic desert tribes of Arabia, Syria, or North Africa. 2. any wanderer or nomad. ***adj.*** of or like the Bedouins.
bed·pan (bed'pan'), ***n.*** 1. a covered pan for holding hot coals, used to warm a bed. 2. a shallow pan serving as a toilet for a person who is ill and has to stay in bed.
bed·plate (bed'plāt'), ***n.*** a plate forming the base, as of a machine or stove.
bed·post (bed'pōst'), ***n.*** any of the vertical supporting posts at the corners of some beds.
be·drag·gle (bi-drag''l), ***v.t.*** [BEDRAGGLED (-'ld), BEDRAGGLING], to make wet, limp, and dirty, as by dragging through mire.
be·drag·gled (bi-drag''ld), ***adj.*** [pp. of *bedraggle*], soiled and wet; unkempt: as, a *bedraggled* dress.
bed·rail (bed'rāl'), ***n.*** a rail along the side of a bed.
bed rest, 1. a resting in bed. 2. a metal or wooden device used to prop patients up in bed.
bed·rid (bed'rid'), ***adj.*** [ME. *bedrede;* AS. *bedreda, bedrida* < *bed* (see BED) + *rida,* rider < *ridan,* to ride], bedridden.
bed·rid·den (bed'rid''n), ***adj.*** [see BEDRID], having to stay in bed, usually for a long period, because of illness, infirmity, etc.
bed·rock (bed'rok'), ***n.*** 1. solid rock beneath the soil and superficial rock; hence, 2. a secure foundation. 3. the very bottom. 4. basic principles.
bed·roll (bed'rōl'), ***n.*** a portable roll of bedding, generally for sleeping outdoors.
bed·room (bed'rōōm', bed'room'), ***n.*** a room to sleep in.
bed·side (bed'sīd'), ***n.*** the side of a bed; space beside a bed: as, the nurse was at his *bedside* constantly. ***adj.*** 1. near a bed: as, a *bedside* table. 2. with a patient or patients: as, a doctor's *bedside* manner.
bed·sore (bed'sôr', bed'sōr'), ***n.*** a sore on the body of a bedridden person, caused by chafing or pressure.
bed·spread (bed'spred'), ***n.*** a cover spread over the blanket on a bed, mainly for ornament.
bed·spring (bed'spriŋ'), ***n.*** 1. a framework of springs placed in a bedstead to support the mattress and make the bed softer. 2. any of these springs.
bed·stead (bed'sted'), ***n.*** [*bed* + *stead*], a framework for supporting the spring and mattress of a bed.
bed·straw (bed'strô'), ***n.*** any of a number of related plants with clusters of small, yellow or white flowers and stalkless leaves: formerly used as straw for beds.
bed·tick (bed'tik'), ***n.*** the cloth case of a mattress, containing the hair, kapok, etc.
bed·time (bed'tīm'), ***n.*** the time when one goes to bed.
bedtime stories, 1. stories told to children at bedtime. 2. pleasant but unconvincing accounts or explanations.
bed·ward (bed'wẽrd), ***adv.*** [*bed* + *-ward*], on the way to bed.
bed·wards (bed'wẽrdz), ***adv.*** bedward.
bed-wet·ting (bed'wet'iŋ), ***n.*** urinating in bed.
bee (bē), ***n.*** [ME. *beo, bee* ; AS. *beo;* akin to OHG. *bia,* OSw. *bī,* etc.], 1. any of a number of related four-winged, hairy insects which feed on the nectar of flowers. 2. a meeting of neighbors, friends, pupils, etc. to work at the same thing or for competition or amusement: as, a sewing *bee,* spelling *bee.*
have a bee in one's bonnet, 1. to be preoccupied or obsessed with one notion. 2. to be not quite sane.

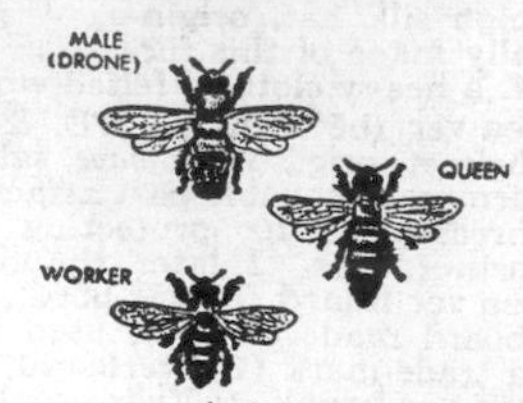

BEES (3/4 in. long)

bee (bē), ***n.*** [ME. *beah;* AS. *beah, beag,* a ring, armlet < *bugan,* to bend, turn], in ***nautical usage,*** 1. a metal ring. 2. a bee block.
bee balm, 1. Oswego tea, a plant with red flowers and a mintlike scent. 2. the garden balm, a plant whose leaves have the odor and flavor of lemons.
Bee·be, Charles William (bē'bi), 1877–1962; American ornithologist, explorer, and author.
bee beetle, a kind of beetle parasitic in beehives.
bee bird, an American flycatcher or kingbird: so called because it lives on insects caught in flight.
bee block, [see BEE (a ring)], a piece of wood on each side of the bowsprit of a ship, used for fastening stays from the mast or foremast.
bee·bread (bē'bred'), ***n.*** a yellowish-brown mixture of pollen and honey, made and eaten by some bees.
beech (bēch), ***n.*** [ME. *becke;* AS. *bece;* umlaut derivative < stem of AS. *boc;* IE. base ****bhāgos,*** as also in L. *fagus,* beech; cf. BOOK], 1. any of a number of related trees with smooth, gray bark, hard wood, dark-green leaves, and edible three-cornered nuts. 2. the wood of any of these trees. ***adj.*** of any of these trees; beechen.
Bee·cham, Sir **Thomas** (bē'chəm), 1879–1961; English orchestral conductor.
beech·drops (bēch'drops'), ***n.*** a wiry plant with brown stems and small clusters of whitish-purple flowers, parasitic on beech roots.
beech·en (bēch'ən), ***adj.*** 1. of the beech tree. 2. made of beechwood.
Bee·cher, Henry Ward (bē'chẽr), 1813–1887; brother of ***Harriet Beecher Stowe;*** American preacher and lecturer.
Beecher, Ly·man (lī'mən), 1775–1863; American clergyman and theologian: father of ***Henry Ward*** and ***Harriet Beecher Stowe.***
beech mast, beechnuts.
beech·nut (bēch'nut'), ***n.*** the nut of the beech tree.
beech·wood (bēch'wood'), ***n.*** the wood of the beech tree.
bee eater, any of a number of related small, brightly colored birds that feed on bees and other insects.
beef (bēf), ***n.*** [*pl.* BEEVES (bēvz), BEEFS (bēfs)], [ME. *beef, boef;* OFr. *boef, buef;* L. *bos, bovis,* ox], 1. a full-grown ox, cow, bull, or steer, especially one bred and fattened for meat. 2. meat from such animals. 3. [Colloq.], human flesh or muscle; hence, 4. [Colloq.], strength; brawn. 5. [Slang], a complaint. ***v.i.*** [Slang], to complain; protest.
beef up, [Slang], to make stronger, more powerful, etc.

BEECHNUTS AND LEAVES

beef cattle, cattle bred and fattened for meat.
beef·eat·er (bēf'ēt'ẽr), ***n.*** 1. a person who eats beef; hence, 2. a large, well-fed, red-faced person. 3. in England, a yeoman of the king's guard. 4. a guard at the Tower of London. 5. [Slang], an Englishman.
beef·i·ness (bēf'i-nis), ***n.*** the state of being beefy; fleshiness; brawn; strength.
bee fly, any of various flies that look like bees.

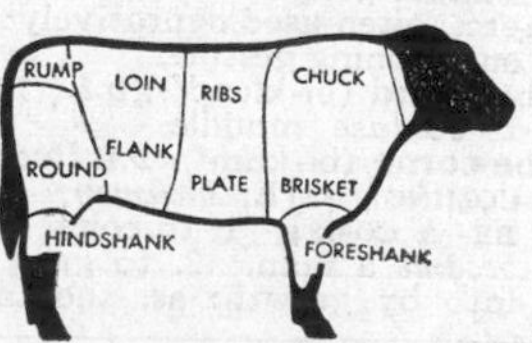

BEEF CUTS

beef·steak (bēf′stāk′), *n.* a slice of beef to be broiled or fried.
beef tea, a drink made from beef extract or by boiling lean strips of beef.
beef·y (bēf′i), *adj.* [BEEFIER (-i-ẽr), BEEFIEST (-i-ist)], beeflike; fleshy and solid; muscular and heavy; brawny.
bee gum, 1. a hollow gum tree used as a hive by bees. 2. a beehive, especially one made from such a tree.
bee·hive (bē′hīv′), *n.* 1. a box or other shelter for a colony of domestic bees, in which they make and store honey; hence, 2. [Colloq.], a place of great activity.
bee·keep·er (bē′kēp′ẽr), *n.* a person who keeps bees for producing honey; apiarist.
bee killer, any of various large flies that kill bees with their piercing beaks; robber fly.
bee·line (bē′līn′), *n.* a straight line or route from one place to another: from the fact that a bee usually flies straight back to its hive after getting pollen.

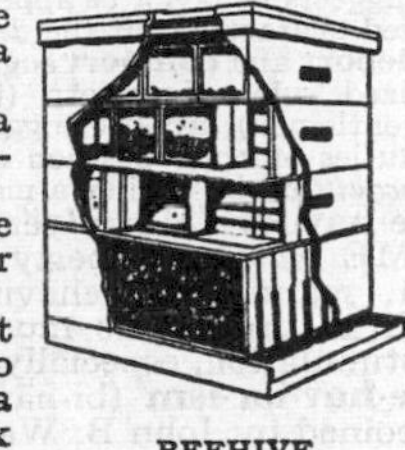
BEEHIVE

make a beeline for, [Colloq.], to go straight toward.
Be·el·ze·bub (bi-el′zi-bub′), *n.* [L.; Gr. *Beelzeboub;* Heb. *ba'alzevūv*, lit., god of insects; *ba'al* (see BAAL) + *zevūv*, a fly], 1. the chief devil; Satan. 2. any devil. 3. in Milton's *Paradise Lost*, Satan's chief lieutenant among the fallen angels.
bee martin, the kingbird: so called because it eats bees.
bee moth, a kind of moth whose larvae, hatched in beehives, eat the wax of the honeycomb.
been (bin; *also, chiefly Brit.*, bēn &, *especially if unstressed*, ben), [ME. *ben;* AS. *beon;* see BE], past participle of **be.**
bee plant, any plant that especially attracts bees, as the white clover, spiderflower, etc.
beer (bêr), *n.* [ME. & AS. *beor;* akin to OHG. *bior*, G. *bier;* only W. Gmc.; ? < Gmc. **beuza*, foaming], 1. a mildly alcoholic drink made from malt, hops, etc. 2. any undistilled, fermented malt beverage, as ale, porter, or stout. 3. any of several soft drinks made from extracts of roots and plants: as, ginger *beer.*
beer and skittles, anything comfortable; pleasure or enjoyment, as that of drinking beer while playing the old game of skittles.
Beer·bohm, Sir **Max** (bêr′bōm′), 1872–1956; English satirist, caricaturist, and critic.
Beer·she·ba (bêr-shē′bə, bē′ẽr-shē′bə), *n.* an ancient city in southwestern Palestine.
beer·y (bêr′i), *adj.* [BEERIER (-i-ẽr), BEERIEST (-i-ist)], 1. of or like beer. 2. resulting from drinking beer; drunken; tipsy; maudlin.
beest·ings (bēs′tiŋz), *n.* [ME. *bestinge;* AS. *bysting* < *beost*, beestings], the first milk of a cow after having a calf: its chemical composition is different from that of later milk: also spelled **biestings.**
bees·wax (bēz′waks′), *n.* a tallowlike substance secreted by honeybees and used by them in making their honeycomb: it is used in candles, polishes, etc. *v.t.* & *v.i.* to polish, etc. with beeswax.
bees·wing (bēz′wiŋ′), *n.* 1. a gauzy film that sometimes forms in old wine. 2. wine that has this.
beet (bēt), *n.* [ME. *bete;* AS. *bete* < L. *beta*], 1. any of a number of related plants with edible leaves and a thick, fleshy, white or red root. 2. the root of any of these plants; some varieties are eaten as a vegetable, and some serve as a source of sugar.
Bee·tho·ven, Lud·wig van (lōōt′viH, lōōd′viH vän bā′tō-vən), 1770–1827; German composer.
bee·tle (bē′t'l), *n.* [ME. *betil;* AS. *bitel, bitela* < *bitan*, to bite], 1. any of a number of related insects with biting mouth parts and hard front wings used to cover the membranous hind wings when these are folded. 2. any insect resembling a beetle.
bee·tle (bē′t'l), *n.* [AS. (Anglian) *betel*, mallet, hammer; akin to MHG. *bôzel*, a cudgel; ult. connected with *beat*], 1. a heavy mallet, usually wooden, for driving wedges, tamping earth, etc. 2. a household mallet or pestle for mashing or beating. 3. a club used in finishing handmade linen. 4. a machine for finishing cloth by beating it over or between rollers. *v.t.* [BEETLED (-'ld), BEETLING], 1. to pound with a beetle. 2. to put a glossy finish on (cloth) by flattening the fibers.
bee·tle (bē′t'l), *v.i.* [BEETLED (-'ld), BEETLING], [prob. < *beetle-browed*], to project or jut; overhang. *adj.* jutting; overhanging.
bee·tle-browed (bē′t'l-broud′), *adj.* [ME. *bitelbrowed;* see BEETLE (insect) & BROW], 1. having bushy or overhanging eyebrows; hence, 2. frowning; scowling.
bee·tle·head (bē′t'l-hed′), *n.* [*beetle* (mallet) + *head*], a stupid person; blockhead.
bee·tling (bēt′liŋ), *adj.* [ppr. of *beetle* (to jut)], projecting; overhanging.
bee tree, 1. a hollow tree used as a hive by bees. 2. the basswood: so called because its flowers have much nectar.
beet sugar, sugar extracted from certain beets.
beeves (bēvz), *n.* alternative plural of **beef.**
bee wolf, the larva of a bee beetle.
bef., before.
B.E.F., British Expeditionary Force.
be·fall (bi-fôl′), *v.i.* [BEFELL (-fel′), BEFALLEN (-fôl′ən), BEFALLING], [ME. *bifallen;* AS. *befeallan*, to fall, fall to as a share or right; *be-* + *feallan*, to fall], 1. to happen; come to pass; occur. 2. [Archaic], to be fitting; also, to pertain. *v.t.* 1. to happen to: as, what *befell* them? 2. [Archaic], *a)* to be fitting to. *b)* to pertain to.
be·fit (bi-fit′), *v.t.* [BEFITTED (-id), BEFITTING], to be suitable or proper for; be suited or becoming to.
be·fit·ting (bi-fit′iŋ), *adj.* [ppr. of *befit*], proper or right; suitable.
be·fog (bi-fôg′, bi-fog′), *v.t.* [BEFOGGED (-fôgd′, -fogd′), BEFOGGING], 1. to cover with or envelop in fog; make foggy; hence, 2. to make hard to see or understand; blur; obscure; confuse.
be·fool (bi-fōōl′), *v.t.* 1. to fool or deceive; trick; dupe. 2. to call (a person) a fool. 3. to treat as a fool.
be·fore (bi-fôr′, bi-fōr′), *adv.* [ME. *beforen, biforen;* AS. *beforan, biforan; be-* + *foran*, before]. 1. ahead; in advance; in front. 2. in the past; up to now; previously. 3. ahead (of a given time); earlier; sooner. *prep.* 1. ahead of in time, space, or order; in advance of. 2. just in front of: as, he paused *before* the door; hence, 3. into the sight, notice, presence, etc. of: as, a thought flashed *before* her mind, he appeared *before* the court. 4. earlier than; prior to. 5. still to be reached, accomplished, etc. by: as, the hardest task was *before* them. 6. in preference to; rather than: as, I'd take that book *before* this. *conj.* 1. in advance of the time that: as, drop in *before* you go. 2. sooner than; rather than: as, I'd die *before* I'd tell. Abbreviated **bef.**
be·fore·hand (bi-fôr′hand′, bi-fōr′hand′), *adv.* & *adj.* ahead of time; early: often implying anticipation or forethought.
be·fore·time (bi-fôr′tīm′, bi-fōr′tīm′), *adv.* [Archaic], formerly.
be·foul (bi-foul′), *v.t.* [ME. *befoulen;* AS. *befylan;* see FOUL], 1. to make filthy; dirty; soil; hence, 2. to cast aspersions on. 3. to entangle or foul.
be·friend (bi-frend′), *v.t.* to act as a friend to; assist.
be·fud·dle (bi-fud′'l), *v.t.* [BEFUDDLED (-'ld), BEFUDDLING], 1. to fuddle; confuse (the mind, etc.); stupefy. 2. to stupefy with alcoholic liquor.
beg (beg), *v.t.* [BEGGED (begd), BEGGING], [ME. *beggin* < Anglo-Fr. *begger;* OFr. *begard*, beggar; MD. *beggaert;* ? < *beggen*, to request urgently], 1. to ask for as charity: as, he *begged* a dime. 2. to ask as a kindness or favor. 3. to ask earnestly; entreat. 4. to request courteously: as, I *beg* your pardon. *v.i.* 1. to ask for alms; be a beggar. 2. to ask humbly; entreat.
beg off, to ask to be released from.
beg the question, 1. to use an argument that assumes as proved the very thing one is trying to prove. 2. loosely, to evade the issue.
go begging, to fail to find a taker; be unwanted.
SYN.—**beg** implies humbleness or earnestness in asking for something and is now often used in polite formulas (I *beg* to differ, I *beg* to report); **solicit** stresses courtesy and formality in requesting something (we *solicit* your aid, he *solicits* our trade); **entreat** implies the use of all the persuasive power at one's command; **beseech** suggests great fervor or passion in the asking and connotes anxiety in the outcome; **implore** is stronger still, suggesting desperation or great distress; **importune** suggests persistence in entreating, often to the point of becoming offensive.
beg (beg; Turk. bāg), *n.* bey.
be·gan (bi-gan′), past tense of **begin.**
be·get (bi-get′), *v.t.* [BEGOT (-got′) or *archaic* BEGAT (-gat′), BEGOTTEN (-got′'n) or BEGOT, BEGETTING], [ME. *begeten*, to obtain; AS. *begitan*, to acquire; see BE- & GET], 1. to be the father or sire of. 2. to bring into being; produce: as, tyranny *begets* rebellion.
be·get·ter (bi-get′ẽr), *n.* a person or thing that begets.
beg·gar (beg′ẽr), *n.* [ME. *beggere;* OFr. *begard;* see BEG], 1. a person who begs or asks charity, especially one who does so for a living; hence, 2. a person who is very poor. 3. a rascal; scoundrel: in this sense, often used humorously. *v.t.* 1. to make a beggar of; make (a person) poor. 2. to make appear poor or useless: as, her beauty *beggars* description.
beg·gar·dom (beg′ẽr-dəm), *n.* 1. beggars collectively. 2. the state of being a beggar.
beg·gar-lice (beg′ẽr-līs′), *n.* [*pl.* BEGGAR-LICE], beggar's-lice.
beg·gar·li·ness (beg′ẽr-li-nis), *n.* [< *beggarly* + *-ness*], 1. extreme poverty. 2. shabbiness. 3. inadequacy.
beg·gar·ly (beg′ẽr-li), *adj.* like or fit for a beggar; very poor, worthless, inadequate, etc.

beg·gar's-lice (beg'ẽrz-līs'), *n.* [*pl.* BEGGAR'S-LICE], 1. any of a number of plants, as the tick trefoil, cleavers, etc., with prickly fruit or seeds that stick to one's clothes. 2. the fruit or seed of any of these plants.

beg·gar's-ticks (beg'ẽrz-tiks'), *n.* [*pl.* BEGGAR'S-TICKS], 1. the prickly, one-seeded fruit, or achene, of a bur marigold. 2. a bur marigold. 3. beggar's-lice.

beg·gar-ticks (beg'ẽr-tiks'), *n.* [*pl.* BEGGAR-TICKS], beggar's-ticks.

beg·gar·weed (beg'ẽr-wēd'), *n.* 1. any of a number of plants that grow in waste land, as some tickseeds and knotweed. 2. a West Indian plant of the pea family, with purple or blue flowers and twisted pods: it is grown for fodder in the southern United States.

beg·gar·y (beg'ẽr-i), *n.* [*pl.* BEGGARIES (-iz)], [ME. *beggerie* < *beggere;* see BEG], 1. extreme poverty. 2. beggardom. 3. a place where beggars live.

Beg·hard (beg'ẽrd, bi-gärd'), *n.* [ML. *beghardus, begardus* < OFr. *begard;* see BEG, *v.*], a member of any of several lay brotherhoods in Belgium, Holland, etc. in the 13th century.

be·gin (bi-gin'), *v.i.* [BEGAN (-gan'), BEGUN (-gun'), BEGINNING], [ME. *biginnan;* AS. *beginnan;* Gmc. base **ginnan*, as in Goth. *du-ginnan*, to commence], 1. to start. 2. to come into being. 3. to be or do in the slightest degree (with an infinitive): as, they don't *begin* to compare. *v.t.* 1. to cause to start; commence. 2. to cause to come into being; originate.

SYN.*—begin**, the most general of these terms, indicates merely a setting into motion of some action, process, or course (to *begin* eating); **commence**, the more formal term, is used with reference to a ceremony or an elaborate course of action (to *commence* a court action); **start** carries the particular implication of leaving a point of departure in any kind of progression (to *start* a journey, the boulder *started* a landslide); **initiate**, in this connection, refers to the carrying out of the first steps in some course or process, with no indication of what is to follow (to *initiate* peace talks); **inaugurate** suggests a formal or ceremonial beginning or opening (to *inaugurate* a new library). —ANT.*** end, finish, conclude.

be·gin·ner (bi-gin'ẽr), *n.* 1. a person who begins anything. 2. a person just beginning to do or learn something; inexperienced, unskilled person; novice.

be·gin·ning (bi-gin'iŋ), *n.* 1. a starting or commencing. 2. the time or place of starting; birth; origin; source: as, English democracy had its *beginning* in the Magna Charta. 3. the first part: as, the *beginning* of this book is dull. 4. *usually pl.* an early stage or example: as, the *beginnings* of scientific agriculture. —***SYN.*** see **origin.**

be·gird (bi-gũrd'), *v.t.* [BEGIRT (-gũrt') or BEGIRDED (-id), BEGIRT, BEGIRDING], [ME. *bigirden;* AS. *begyrdan; be-* + *gyrdan;* see BE- & GIRD], 1. to bind around; gird. 2. to encircle; surround; encompass.

beg·ohm (beg'ōm'), *n.* [billion + megohm], in *electricity*, a unit of resistance equivalent to a billion ohms.

be·gone (bi-gôn', bi-gon'), *interj. & v.i.* (to) be gone; go away; get out: usually in the imperative.

be·go·ni·a (bi-gōn'yə, bi-gō'ni-ə), *n.* [after Michel *Bégon* (1638–1710), Fr. botanist], any of a number of related plants with showy white, pink, or red flowers and ornamental leaves.

be·got (bi-got'), past tense and alternative past participle of **beget.**

be·got·ten (bi-got''n), alternative past participle of **beget.**

be·grime (bi-grīm'), *v.t.* [BEGRIMED (-grīmd'), BEGRIMING], to cover with grime; make dirty; soil.

be·grudge (bi-gruj'), *v.t.* [*be-* + *grudge*], 1. to grumble at. 2. to envy (another) the possession of. 3. to give with ill will or reluctance: as, he *begrudges* her every cent. —***SYN.*** see **envy.**

be·guile (bi-gīl'), *v.t.* [BEGUILED (-gīld'), BEGUILING], 1. to mislead by guile or deceit; deceive. 2. to deprive (*of* or *out of*) by deceit; cheat: as, he was *beguiled* of his money. 3. to pass (time) pleasantly; while away. 4. to charm or delight. —***SYN.*** see **amuse, deceive, lure.**

be·guile·ment (bi-gīl'mənt), *n.* 1. a beguiling. 2. the fact or state of being beguiled.

Beg·uin (beg'in; Fr. bā'gan'), *n.* [OFr. < *begard;* see BEG, *v.*], a Beghard.

Beg·uine (beg'ēn; Fr. bā'gēn'), *n.* [OFr. < *begard;* see BEG, *v.*], 1. a member of any of several lay sisterhoods that began in the Low Countries in the 12th century: they were not restricted by vows. 2. [b-], (bi-gēn'), a native dance of Martinique: its music and rhythm have been popularized in the United States by Negroes.

be·gum (bē'gəm), *n.* [Anglo-Ind. < Hind. *begam*, lady < Turk. *bigim*, princess, fem. of *big*, prince], 1. in India, a Moslem princess or lady of high rank. 2. in England, a wealthy Anglo-Indian woman.

be·gun (bi-gun'), past participle of **begin.**

be·half (bi-haf', bi-häf'), *n.* [ME. *behalf* in phr. *on mi behalfe*, on my side < AS. *be*, by + *healf*, half, side], support, interest, side, etc.

in behalf of, in the interest of; for.

on behalf of, 1. in behalf of. 2. speaking for; representing.

Be·har (bə-här'), *n.* Bihar.

be·have (bi-hāv'), *v.t.* [BEHAVED (-hāvd'), BEHAVING], [see BE- & HAVE], to conduct or manage (oneself), especially in a correct or proper way. *v.i.* 1. to conduct oneself or itself; act in a specified way. 2. to conduct oneself well; do the right things. 3. to act or react.

***SYN.*—behave**, used reflexively (as also the other words in this comparison), implies action in conformity with the required standards of decorum (did the children *behave* themselves?); **conduct** implies the direction or guidance of one's actions in a specified way (he *conducted* himself well at the trial); **demean** suggests behavior or appearance that is indicative of the specified character trait (he *demeaned* himself like a gracious host); **deport** and **comport** suggest behavior in accordance with the fixed rules of society (they always *deport* themselves like gentlemen); **acquit** suggests behavior in accordance with the duties of one's position or with one's obligations (the rookie *acquitted* himself like a major leaguer).

be·hav·ior (bi-hāv'yẽr), *n.* [< *behave* by analogy with ME. *havoir*, property < OFr. *aveir* < *avoir*, to have], 1. manner of behaving; actions; conduct; manners. 2. an organism's muscular or glandular responses to stimulation, especially those that can be observed.

be·hav·ior·ism (bi-hāv'yẽr-iz'm), *n.* [*behavior* + *-ism;* coined by John B. Watson, Am. psychologist, in 1913], the doctrine that observed behavior provides the only valid data of psychology: it rejects the concept of *mind.*

be·hav·ior·ist (bi-hāv'yẽr-ist), *n.* a person, especially a psychologist, who accepts behaviorism. *adj.* of or connected with behaviorism.

be·hav·ior·is·tic (bi-hāv'yẽr-is'tik), *adj.* behaviorist.

be·hav·iour (bi-hāv'yẽr), *n.* behavior: British spelling.

be·head (bi-hed'), *v.t.* [ME. *biheafden;* AS. *beheafdian* < *be-* + *heafod*, the head], to cut off the head of; decapitate.

be·held (bi-held'), past tense and past participle of **behold.**

be·he·moth (bi-hē'məth, bē'ə-məth), *n.* [Heb. *behēmōth*, intens. pl. of *behēmāh*, beast; hence, colossal beast; ? < Egypt. *p-ehe-mau*, water ox], 1. in the *Bible*, a huge animal, assumed to be the hippopotamus: Job 40:15–24; hence, 2. any huge animal.

be·hest (bi-hest'), *n.* [ME. *behest, bihest* < AS. *behæs*, a vow; *be-* + *hæs* (see HEST); *-t* is unhistoric], an order; bidding; command.

be·hind (bi-hīnd'), *adv.* [ME. *bihinden;* AS. *behindan; be-* + *hindan*, behind; see HIND], 1. in the rear: as, he walked *behind.* 2. at an earlier time; in the past: as, my joy lies *behind.* 3. in a former place, condition, etc.: as, the girl he left *behind.* 4. yet to come: as, there is greater news *behind.* 5. below standard; in or into a retarded state: as, he dropped *behind* in his studies. 6. into arrears: as, he fell *behind* in his dues. 7. slow in time; late: as, the train was running *behind.* 8. to or toward the back: as, looking *behind.* ***prep.*** 1. remaining after: as, the dead leave their wealth *behind* them. 2. in the rear of; back of: as, he sat *behind* me. 3. inferior to in position, achievement, etc. 4. later than: as, the train was *behind* schedule. 5. on the other or farther side of; beyond: as, *behind* the hill. 6. supporting or advocating: as, Congress is *behind* the plan. 7. hidden by; not yet revealed about: as, there's something *behind* this news. *adj.* 1. that follows, as in a line: as, the person *behind.* 2. in arrears. Used predicatively. *n.* [Colloq.], the buttocks.

be·hind·hand (bi-hīnd'hand'), *adv. & adj.* 1. behind in paying debts, etc.; in arrears. 2. behind time; slow; late. 3. behind or slow in progress, advancement, etc.

be·hold (bi-hōld'), *v.t.* [BEHELD (-held'), BEHELD or *archaic* BEHOLDEN (-hōl'd'n), BEHOLDING], [ME. *biholden;* AS. *bihealdan*, to hold, keep hold of; *be-* + *healdan;* see HOLD (to grasp)], to hold in view or attention; look at; regard. *interj.* look! see! —***SYN.*** see **see.**

be·hold·en (bi-hōl'd'n), *adj.* [ME., pp. of *bihealden*, to behold], held under obligation, as from gratitude; indebted: as, he is *beholden* to you for your advice.

be·hoof (bi-hōōf'), *n.* [ME.; *bihof*, profit, need, use; AS. *behof*, profit, need; akin to G. *behuf;* base < W. Gmc. **behafjan; be-* + **hafjan;* see HEAVE], behalf, benefit, interest, sake, etc.

be·hoove (bi-hōōv'), *v.t. & v.i.* [BEHOOVED (-hōōvd'), BEHOOVING], [ME. *bihofian;* AS. *behofian*, to have need of < *behof;* see BEHOOF], 1. to be necessary (for): as, it *behooves* me to write him. 2. to be fitting (for) or incumbent (upon): as, it *behooves* a lady to wear black for mourning.

be·hove (bi-hōv', bi-hōōv'), *v.t. & v.i.* [BEHOVED (-hōvd', -hōōvd'), BEHOVING], to behoove.

Beh·ring, E·mil von (ā'mēl fôn bā'riŋ), 1854–1917; German physician; demonstrated practical use of diphtheria toxin; received Nobel prize in medicine, 1901.

Behr·man, Samuel Nathaniel (bâr'mən), 1893– ; American dramatist.

beige (bāzh), *n.* [Fr., orig., natural color of wool < It. *bambagia*, cotton < MGr. *bambax*, cotton], 1. a soft wool fabric, formerly undyed and unbleached. 2. its characteristic sandy color; grayish tan. *adj.* grayish-tan.

be·ing (bē′iŋ), *n.* [see BE], 1. existence; living; life. 2. one's fundamental nature: as, she responds to music with her whole *being*. 3. a creature that lives or exists, or is assumed to do so: as, a human *being*, a divine *being*. 4. [B-], God: usually, *the Supreme Being*. 5. fulfillment of possibilities; essential completeness. 6. in *philosophy*, that which is, is possible, or can be logically conceived. *adj.* at hand; immediate: as, for the time *being*, I'll stay.

Bei·rut (bā′ro͞ot, bā-ro͞ot′), *n.* the capital of Lebanon, on the Mediterranean: pop., 500,000: also spelled **Beyrouth.**

be·jew·el (bi-jo͞o′əl), *v.t.* [BEJEWELED or BEJEWELLED (-əld), BEJEWELING or BEJEWELLING], to cover or decorate with or as with jewels.

Bel (bāl), *n.* [Bab. dial. form of *Baal*], in *Babylonian mythology*, the god of heaven and earth.

bel (bel), *n.* [after Alexander Graham *Bell*, the inventor], in *radio & telegraphy*, a unit for expressing in logarithms the ratios of power.

Bel., 1. Belgian. 2. Belgic. 3. Belgium.

be·la·bor (bi-lā′bēr), *v.t.* 1. to beat severely; hit or whip. 2. to beat with words; attack verbally. 3. [Obs.], to work at or upon.

Be·las·co, David (bə-las′kō), 1854–1931; American playwright, actor, and theatrical manager.

be·lat·ed (bi-lāt′id), *adj.* [< *be-* + *late* + *-ed*], 1. [Archaic], overtaken by night. 2. too late; tardy.

be·lay (bi-lā′), *v.t. & v.i.* [BELAYED (-lād′), BELAYING], [ME. *bileggen;* AS. *belecgan*, to make fast; *be-* + *lecgan*, to lay], 1. in *nautical usage*, to make (a rope) secure by winding around a belaying pin, cleat, etc.; hold fast; hence, 2. [Colloq.], to hold; stop: as, *belay* there!

belaying pin, in *nautical usage*, a removable wooden or metal pin in the rail, around which ropes can be fastened.

bel can·to (bel kän′tō), [It., lit., beautiful song], a style of singing characterized by brilliant vocal display and purity of tone.

belch (belch), *v.i. & v.t.* [ME. *belchen;* AS. *bealcian*, to bring up, emit, give forth, splutter out; akin to D. *balken*, to shout out, bray], 1. to expel (gas) through the mouth from the stomach; eructate. 2. to speak (curses, etc.) violently (*forth*). 3. to vomit. 4. to throw (flame, lava, etc.) forth violently, as under pressure, and often in spasms: as, the volcano *belched* flame. *n.* 1. a belching; eructation. 2. a thing belched.

bel·dam (bel′dəm), *n.* [*bel-* < Fr. *belle* (see BELLE); + *dame*], 1. any old woman. 2. a hideous old woman; hag. 3. [Obs.], a grandmother.

bel·dame (bel′dəm, bel′dām), *n.* a beldam.

be·lea·guer (bi-lē′gēr), *v.t.* [D. *belegeren*, to besiege; *be-* + *legeren*, to camp < *leger* (akin to G. *lager*), a camp], 1. to besiege by encircling, as with an army. 2. to surround, as with denunciations.

Be·lém (be-len′), *n.* a seaport and capital of Pará, Brazil: pop., 303,000: also called *Pará*.

bel·em·nite (bel′əm-nīt′), *n.* [Gr. *belemnon*, a dart, arrow; prob. akin to *ballein*, to throw], 1. the cigar-shaped fossil shell of an extinct kind of cuttlefish: also called *thunderstone*. 2. the animal itself.

‡**bel-es·prit** (bel′es′prē′), *n.* [*pl.* BEAUX-ESPRITS (bō′-zes′prē′)], [Fr., lit., beautiful spirit], a clever, cultivated person.

Bel·fast (bel′fast, bel′fäst, bel-fast′), *n.* a seaport and capital of Northern Ireland, on the North Channel: pop., 440,000.

Bel·fort (bel′fôr′), *n.* a city in eastern France: pop., 36,000.

bel·fry (bel′fri), *n.* [*pl.* BELFRIES (-friz)], [ME. *berfrai;* OFr. *berfroi;* OHG. *bergfrid*, lit., protector of peace < *bergen*, to protect + *frid*, peace], 1. a movable tower used in ancient warfare for attacking walled positions; hence, 2. any tower. 3. a bell tower. 4. the part of a tower or steeple that holds the bell or bells.

Belg., 1. Belgian. 2. Belgium.

bel·ga (bel′gə), *n.* [L., a Belgian], a Belgian unit of currency; money of account equivalent to $.139 when established in 1926.

Bel·gae (bel′jē), *n.pl.* [L.], a former Gallic people of northern France and Belgium.

Bel·gian (bel′jən, bel′ji-ən), *adj.* of Belgium, its people, etc. *n.* a native or inhabitant of Belgium. Abbreviated **Belg., Bel.**

Belgian Congo, a former Belgian colony in central Africa, on the Atlantic: now an independent country (see **Congo**, sense 2).

Belgian hare, a large, reddish-brown domestic rabbit.

Bel·gic (bel′jik), *adj.* [L. *Belgicus* < *Belgae*], 1. of Belgium. 2. of the Netherlands. 3. of the Belgae. *n.* the Gallic language of the Belgae. Abbreviated **Bel.**

Bel·gium (bel′jəm, bel′ji-əm), *n.* a country in western Europe, on the North Sea: area, 11,775 sq. mi.; pop., 9,129,000; capital, Brussels: abbreviated **Belg.**

Bel·grade (bel-grād′, bel′grād), *n.* the capital of Yugoslavia, on the Danube: pop., 520,000: Serbian name, *Beograd*.

Bel·gra·vi·a (bel-grā′vi-ə), *n.* [< *Belgrave*], 1. in Victorian London, a residential area surrounding Belgrave Square, home of the newly rich, upper middle class; hence, 2. this social class, its life, tastes, etc.

Bel·gra·vi·an (bel-grā′vi-ən), *adj.* 1. of Belgravia; hence, 2. fashionable, exclusive, grand, etc. *n.* 1. an inhabitant of Belgravia. 2. a member of the Belgravian social class.

Be·li·al (bē′li-əl, bēl′yəl), *n.* [Heb. *belīya'al*, without value], 1. in the *Old Testament*, wickedness or worthlessness as an evil force; hence, 2. in the *New Testament*, Satan. 3. in Milton's *Paradise Lost*, one of the fallen rebel angels.

be·lie (bi-lī′), *v.t.* [BELIED (-līd′), BELYING (-lī′iŋ)], [ME. *belyen, bileogen;* AS. *beleogan*, to deceive by lying; *be-* + *leogan;* see LIE], 1. to lie about; hence, 2. to disguise or misrepresent: as, his words *belie* his thoughts. 3. to leave unfulfilled; disappoint: as, war *belied* hopes for peace. 4. to show to be mistaken; prove false.

be·lief (bə-lēf′), *n.* [ME. *bileve* < *be-* + *leve* < *ileve*, *leve* < AS. *geleafa*, belief; akin to G. *glaube*], 1. the state of believing; conviction that certain things are true; faith, especially religious faith. 2. trust; confidence: as, I have *belief* in his ability. 3. acceptance of or assent to something as trustworthy, real, etc.: as, a claim beyond *belief*. 4. anything believed or accepted as true. 5. an opinion; expectation; judgment: as, my *belief* is that he'll come. 6. a creed or doctrine.

SYN.—**belief**, the term of broadest application in this comparison, implies mental acceptance of something as true, whether based on reasoning, prejudice, or the authority of the source; **faith** implies complete, blind acceptance of something, especially of something not supported by reason; **trust** implies assurance, often apparently intuitive, in the reliability of someone or something; **confidence** also suggests such assurance, especially when based on reason or the evidence of one's senses; **credence**, unqualified, suggests mere mental acceptance of something, with no indication of either great or little reliance in its truth (to place *credence* in a rumor). See also **opinion.** —*ANT.* doubt, incredulity.

be·liev·a·ble (bə-lēv′ə-b'l), *adj.* that can be believed.

be·lieve (bə-lēv′), *v.t.* [BELIEVED (-lēvd′), BELIEVING], [ME. *bileven* < *be-* + *ileven, leven* < AS. *geliefan*, to believe], 1. to take as true, real, etc. 2. to have confidence in a statement or promise of (another person). 3. to suppose; expect; assume. *v.i.* 1. to have trust or confidence: as, he *believes* in you. 2. to have faith, especially religious faith. 3. to hold views or opinions.

believe in, to have confidence in the truth, existence, efficacy, etc. of: as, he didn't *believe* in fairies.

be·liev·er (bə-lēv′ēr), *n.* 1. a person who believes. 2. a person with any specific religious faith.

be·like (bi-līk′), *adv.* [Archaic], quite likely; probably.

Be·lin·da (bə-lin′də), [L., graceful], a feminine name: diminutive, *Linda*.

Bel·i·sa·ri·us (bel′ə-sâr′i-əs), *n.* general of the Eastern Roman Empire; lived 505?–565 A.D.

Be·li·toeng (be-lē′toŋ), *n.* Billiton: the Dutch name.

be·lit·tle (bi-lit′'l), *v.t.* [BELITTLED (-'ld), BELITTLING], 1. to make (a thing) little or smaller. 2. to make seem little, less important, etc.; speak of as unimportant; speak slightingly of; depreciate. —*SYN.* see **disparage.**

Be·lize (be-lēz′), *n.* a seaport and capital of British Honduras: pop., 33,000.

bell (bel), *n.* [ME. & AS. *belle;* akin to LG. *belle*, ON. *bjalla;* IE. base **bhel-*, to sound], 1. a hollow object, usually cuplike, made of metal or other hard material which rings when struck. 2. such an object rung to mark the hours or the beginning and end of a period of time. 3. the sound made by a bell. 4. anything shaped like a bell, as a flower, the flare of a horn, etc. 5. *pl.* a musical instrument made up of a series of metal bars or hollow tubes that sound like bells. 6. in *nautical usage*, *a*) a bell rung every half hour to mark the periods of the watch, which begin at *one bell* (12:30, 4.30, and 8:30 o'clock) and end at *eight bells* (4:00, 8:00, and 12:00 o'clock). *b*) any of these periods. *v.t.* 1. to attach a bell or bells to. 2. to shape like a bell. *v.i.* to become bell-shaped.

bell (bel), *n., v.i. & v.t.* [ME. *bellen;* AS. *bellan*, to roar; see BELL (cuplike object)], bellow; roar.

Bell, Ac·ton (ak′tən bel), see **Brontë, Anne.**

Bell, Alexander Gra·ham (grā′əm), 1847–1922; American inventor of the telephone, born in Scotland.

Bell, Cur·rer (kũr′ēr), see **Brontë, Charlotte.**

Bell, Ellis, see **Brontë, Emily.**

Bel·la (bel′ə), a feminine name: see **Arabella, Isabella.**

bel·la·don·na (bel′ə-don′ə), *n.* [It. *bella donna*, beautiful lady < L. *bella*, fem. of *bellus*, beautiful + *domina*, lady: so called from use as cosmetic], 1. a poisonous plant with purplish or reddish bell-shaped flowers and black berries; deadly nightshade. 2. a drug obtained

from this plant and used to dilate the pupil of the eye, stimulate the heart, relieve spasms, etc.: cf. **atropine.**
belladonna lily, 1. a kind of amaryllis with large, lilylike, fragrant, rose-colored flowers. 2. the flower.
Bel·la·my, Edward (bel'ə-mi), 1850–1898; American author and political theorist; wrote *Looking Backward.*
bell·bird (bel'bûrd'), *n.* any of various birds that make bell-like sounds.
bell·boy (bel'boi'), *n.* a boy or man employed by a hotel, club, etc. to carry luggage and do errands.
bell buoy, a buoy with a warning bell rung by the motion of the waves.
Belle (bel), [Fr.; see BELLE], a feminine name.
belle (bel), *n.* [Fr., fem. of *beau;* see BEAU], 1. a very attractive woman or girl. 2. the most attractive or most popular woman or girl of a certain place or on a given occasion: as, the *belle* of the ball.
Bel·leau Wood (be'lō'), a forest in France, east of Paris: site of a battle (1918) in World War I.
Bel·leek (bə-lēk'), *n.* [after *Belleek,* County Donegal, Ireland, where it was made], a fine, glossy, often iridescent pottery resembling porcelain: also **Belleek ware.**
Belle Isle, Strait of, a strait between Labrador and Newfoundland: width, 10–15 mi.
Bel·ler·o·phon (bə-ler'ə-fon', bə-ler'ə-fən), *n.* [L.; Gr. *Bellerephōn*], in *Greek mythology,* the hero who killed the monster Chimera, aided by the winged horse Pegasus.
belles-let·tres (bel'let'rə), *n.pl.* [Fr., lit., beautiful letters, fine literature], literature as one of the fine arts; fiction, poetry, drama, etc. as distinguished from technical and scientific writings.
bel·let·rist (bel'let'rist), *n.* a writer of belles-lettres.
bel·le·tris·tic (bel'le-tris'tik), *adj.* of or concerned with belles-lettres.
Belle·ville (bel'vil'), *n.* 1. a city in southwestern Illinois: pop., 37,000. 2. a town in northeastern New Jersey: pop., 35,000.
Bell·flow·er (bel'flou'ẽr), *n.* a city in southwestern California, near Los Angeles: pop., 46,000.
bell·flow·er (bel'flou'ẽr), *n.* any of a number of related plants with showy, bell-shaped flowers, usually of blue, white, or pink; campanula.
bell·hop (bel'hop'), *n.* [Slang], a bellboy.
bel·li·cose (bel'ə-kōs'), *adj.* [L. *bellicosus* < *bellicus,* of war < *bellum,* war; OL. *duellum,* lit., dispute between two < *duo,* two], of a quarrelsome or hostile nature; warlike. —*SYN.* see **belligerent.**
bel·li·cos·i·ty (bel'ə-kos'ə-ti), *n.* the quality or state of being bellicose; hostility; hostile attitude.
bel·lied (bel'id), *adj.* having a belly: used in hyphenated compounds to mean *having a* (specified kind of) *belly:* as, the yellow-*bellied* sapsucker.
bel·lig·er·ence (bə-lij'ẽr-əns), *n.* [< *belligerent*], 1. the state or quality of being belligerent. 2. war.
bel·lig·er·en·cy (bə-lij'ẽr-ən-si), *n.* 1. the state of being a belligerent. 2. belligerence.
bel·lig·er·ent (bə-lij'ẽr-ənt), *adj.* [Fr. *belligérant,* waging war < L. *belligerans,* ppr. of *belligerare,* to wage war < *bellum,* war + *gerere,* to carry on], 1. at war. 2. of war; of fighting. 3. seeking war; warlike. *n.* any person, group, or nation engaged in war or fighting.
SYN.—**belligerent** implies a taking part in war or fighting or in actions that are likely to provoke fighting (*belligerent* nations); **bellicose** implies a warlike or hostile nature, suggesting a readiness to fight (a *bellicose* mood); **pugnacious** and **quarrelsome** both connote aggressiveness and a willingness to initiate a fight, but **quarrelsome** more often suggests pettiness and eagerness to fight for little or no reason (he is *quarrelsome* when drunk); **contentious** suggests an inclination to argue or quarrel, usually with annoying persistence. —*ANT.* peaceful, friendly.
Bel·ling·ham (bel'iŋ-ham'), *n.* a city in northwestern Washington, on Bellingham Bay: pop., 35,000.
Bel·li·ni, Gen·ti·le (jen-tē'le bel-lē'nē; Eng. be-lē'ni), 1429?–1507; son of *Jacopo;* Venetian painter.
Bellini, Gio·van·ni (jō-vän'nē), 1430?–1516; son of *Jacopo;* Venetian painter; teacher of Titian.
Bellini, Ja·co·po (yä-kō'pō), c. 1400–c. 1470; father of *Gentile* and *Giovanni;* Venetian painter.
Bellini, Vin·cen·zo (vēn-chen'tsō), 1801–1835; Italian operatic composer; wrote *Norma.*
bell jar, a bell-shaped container or cover made of glass: also called *bell glass, cloche.*
bell·man (bel'mən), *n.* [*pl.* BELLMEN (-mən)], a town crier.
bell metal, an alloy of copper and tin used in bells.
bell-mouthed (bel'mouthd', bel'moutht'), *adj.* having a flaring mouth or opening like that of a bell.
Bel·loc, Hi·laire (hi-lâr' bel'ok), (*Joseph Hilary Pierre Belloc*), 1870–1953; English author.
Bel·lo Ho·ri·zon·te (be'lō-rē-zōn'tə), a city in southeastern Brazil: pop., 339,000: also **Belo Horizonte.**
Bel·lo·na (bə-lō'nə), *n.* [L. < *bellum;* see BELLICOSE], in *Roman mythology,* the goddess of war, sister of Mars.
bel·low (bel'ō), *v.i.* [ME. *belwen;* AS. (LWS.) *bylgan;* see BELLY], 1. to roar with a powerful, reverberating sound, as a bull, elephant, etc. 2. to make a sound like this. 3. to cry out loudly, as in anger or pain. *v.t.* to utter loudly or powerfully. *n.* 1. the roar of a bull, elephant, etc. 2. any loud, powerful sound like this.
bel·lows (bel'ōz, bel'əz), *n. sing. & pl.* [ME. *beli,* pl. *belwis;* AS. *belg, bælg, bylg;* see BELLY], 1. a device for producing a stream of air under pressure, used for blowing fires, in pipe organs, etc. 2. anything like a bellows, as the folding part of a camera, the lungs, etc.

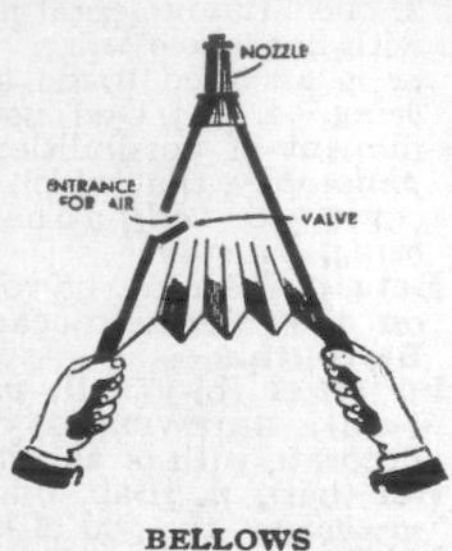

BELLOWS

Bel·lows, George (bel'ōz), (*George Wesley Bellows*), 1882–1925; American painter and lithographer.
bell·weth·er (bel'weth'ẽr), *n.* 1. a male sheep wearing a bell, usually the leader of the flock. 2. a leader, especially of a foolish, sheeplike crowd.
bell·wort (bel'wûrt'), *n.* 1. any of a number of related plants of the lily family, with drooping, yellow, bell-shaped flowers and stemless leaves. 2. a bellflower.
bel·ly (bel'i), *n.* [*pl.* BELLIES (-iz)], [ME. *bely, beli,* belly, stomach; AS. *belg, bælg, bielg,* leather bag, bellows], 1. the lower front part of the human body between the chest and thighs; abdomen. 2. the underside of an animal's body. 3. the abdominal cavity, especially as a center of pain or receptacle of food; hence, 4. the stomach. 5. the capacity of the stomach. 6. the deep interior (of a thing): as, the *belly* of a ship. 7. an enlarged or bulging part or section. 8. any curved surface or area, especially if hollow. 9. the front part or underside of anything: opposed to *back.* 10. the upper plate or front of a musical instrument of the viol group. 11. [Obs.], the womb. *v.t. & v.i.* [BELLIED (-id), BELLYING], to swell out; curve out; bulge.
bel·ly·ache (bel'i-āk'), *n.* [Colloq.], pain in the abdomen. *v.i.* [BELLYACHED (-ākt'), BELLYACHING], [Slang], to complain.
bel·ly·band (bel'i-band'), *n.* 1. a girth or cinch around an animal's belly, for keeping a saddle, harness, or pack in place. 2. a cloth band put around a baby's abdomen to reinforce the weak muscles.
bel·ly·but·ton (bel'i-but''n), *n.* [Colloq.], the navel: also **belly button.**
bel·ly·ful (bel'i-fool'), *n.* 1. enough or more than enough to eat. 2. [Slang], enough or more than enough of anything.
belly laugh, [Slang], 1. a hearty laugh. 2. anything that produces such a laugh, as a line in a play.
Bel·mont (bel'mont), *n.* a town in eastern Massachusetts: pop., 29,000.
Be·lo Ho·ri·zon·te (be'lō-rē-zōn'tə), Bello Horizonte.
Be·loit (bə-loit'), *n.* a city in southern Wisconsin: pop., 33,000.
be·long (bi-lôŋ', bi-loŋ'), *v.i.* [ME. *bilangen* < *be-,* intens. + AS. *langian,* to go along with], to have a proper or suitable place; have the proper qualities to be: as, she *belongs* in the movies.
belong to, 1. to be part of; be related to or connected with. 2. to be owned by; be the possession of. 3. to be associated with; be a member of.
be·long·ing (bi-lôŋ'iŋ, bi-loŋ'iŋ), *n.* 1. a thing or person that belongs to one. 2. *pl.* possessions; property.
Be·lo·rus·sia (bye'lə-rush'ə), *n.* Byelorussia.
Be·lo·stok (bye'lô-stôk'), *n.* Bialystok: Russian name.
be·lov·ed (bi-luv'id, bi-luvd'), *adj.* [ME., pp. of *biluven;* see BE- & LOVE], dearly loved. *n.* a beloved person.
be·low (bi-lō'), *adv. & adj.* [see BE- & LOW], 1. in or to a lower place; beneath. 2. in a lower place on a page. 3. in a following part (of a book, etc.). 4. in hell. 5. on earth. 6. on or to a lower floor or deck. 7. in a lesser rank, function, etc. 8. in *music,* in a lower pitch. *prep.* 1. lower than, as in position, rank, worth, etc. 2. unworthy of; beneath: as, it is *below* her to say that.
Bel·sen (bel'z'n), *n.* a Nazi concentration camp and extermination center, near Hanover, Germany.
Bel·shaz·zar (bel-shaz'ẽr), *n.* [Heb. *bēlshatstsar* < Bab. *bel-sharra-uṣur,* lit., may Bel protect the king], in the *Bible,* the last king of Babylon, who was warned of defeat by the handwriting on the wall: Dan. 5.
belt (belt), *n.* [ME. & AS. *belt;* ult. < L. *balteus,* a belt], 1. a strip or band of leather or other material worn around the waist to hold clothing up, support tools, etc., or as an ornament or sign of rank. 2. any encircling thing like this. 3. a series of armored plates around a ship at the water line. 4. a wide, endless strap or band for transferring motion from one wheel or pulley to another or others, or for carrying things. 5. an area or zone distinguished from others in some way: as, the corn *belt.* 6. an encircling or beltlike road, highway, or route; belt line. 7. [Slang], a blow; cuff. *v.t.* 1. to surround or encircle with or as with a belt; girdle. 2. to fasten or attach with a belt. 3. to strike with a belt; hence, 4. [Slang], to strike with force.
below the belt, 1. unfair; foul. 2. unfairly. Originally said of a blow to the groin in boxing.
tighten one's belt, 1. to endure hunger, privation, etc. as best one can. 2. to live more thriftily.

Bel·tane (bel′tān), *n.* [Scot. < Gael. *Bealltainn*], 1. May 1 (Old Style). 2. the ancient Celtic May Day.
belt·ed (bel′tid), *adj.* [pp. of *belt*], 1. wearing a belt, especially as a mark of distinction: as, a *belted* knight. 2. having or marked by a band or stripe.
belt·ing (bel′tiŋ), *n.* 1. material for making belts. 2. belts collectively. 3. [Slang], a beating.
belt line, a railroad, trolley line, etc. that makes a circuit.
be·lu·ga (bə-lōō′gə), *n.* [*pl.* BELUGA, BELUGAS (-gəz); see PLURAL, II, D, 2], [< Russ. < *byeli*, white], 1. a large, white sturgeon of the Black Sea and the Caspian Sea. 2. a large white dolphin of the arctic seas.
bel·ve·dere (bel′və-dêr′), *n.* [It., beautiful view < L. *bellus*, beautiful, fine + *videre*, to see], 1. a small summerhouse on a height, or an open, roofed gallery in an upper story, built for giving a view of the scenery. 2. [B-], an art gallery in the Vatican: it contains the statue of Apollo called *Apollo Belvedere.*
be·ma (bē′mə), *n.* [*pl.* BEMATA (-mə-tə)], [Gr. *bēma*, platform, lit., a step < base of *bainein*, to go], 1. in ancient Greece, a platform from which a speaker addressed an audience. 2. in the *Orthodox Eastern Church*, a low enclosure surrounding the altar.
be·maul (bi-môl′), *v.t.* to maul severely.
be·mazed (bi-māzd′), *adj.* [ME. *bemased*, pp. of *bemasen; be-* + *masen*, to maze; see MAZE], muddled; dazed.
be·mean (bi-mēn′), *v.t.* [*be-* + *mean* (humble)], to make low or mean; debase.
be·mire (bi-mīr′), *v.t.* 1. to make dirty with or as with mire, mud, etc. 2. to stick or bog down in mud.
be·moan (bi-mōn′), *v.t. & v.i.* [ME. *bimaenen;* AS. *bemænan;* see BE- & MOAN], to moan or wail about (a loss, grief, etc.); lament.
be·mock (bi-mok′), *v.t.* to mock or mock at.
be·muse (bi-mūz′), *v.t.* [*be-* + *muse*], to muddle; confuse; stupefy.
be·mused (bi-mūzd′), *adj* [pp. of *bemuse*], 1. stupefied; confused. 2. plunged in thought; preoccupied.
ben (ben), *n.* [Heb. *bēn*], son (of): as, Rabbi *Ben* Ezra.
ben (ben), *n.* [Scot. < Gael. *beann*, a peak], [Scot. & Irish], a mountain peak: as, *Ben* Nevis.
ben (ben), *n.* [Ar. *bān*, the tree], the seed of an East Indian tree, which yields an oil (*oil of ben*) used in some perfumes.
ben (ben), *adv. & prep.* [Scot.; AS. *binnan* < *be-* + *innan*, in], within. *adj.* inner. *n.* the inner room or parlor.
ben·a·dryl (ben′ə-dril), *n.* a drug used in the treatment of certain allergic conditions, as hives, hay fever, and asthma: a trade-mark (**Benadryl**).
be·name (bi-nām′), *v.t.* [BENAMED (-nāmd′), BENAMED or BENEMPT (-nempt′) or BENEMPTED (-nemp′tid), BENAMING], [Archaic], to give a name to; call.
Be·na·res (bə-nä′riz), *n.* a sacred city of the Hindus in Uttar Pradesh, India, on the Ganges: pop., 574,000.
Be·na·ven·te, Ja·cin·to (hä-thēn′tô be′nä-ven′te), 1866–1954; Spanish dramatist; received Nobel prize in literature, 1922.
Ben·bow, John (ben′bō′), 1653–1702; English admiral.
bench (bench), *n.* [ME. *benche, benk;* AS. *benc;* akin to G. *bank;* sense 2 is a transl. of ML. *banca*, Anglo-Fr. *baunk*], I. 1. a long seat made of wood, stone, etc., often without a back. 2. a worktable. 3. a seat between the two sides of a boat. 4. a terrace along the bank of a body of water, often marking a former shore line. 5. a stand upon which dogs are exhibited at shows. 6. a level, narrow, high area. II. 1. the place where judges sit in a court; hence, 2. [sometimes B-], the status or office of a judge. 3. judges collectively. 4. a law court. *v.t.* 1. to provide with a bench or benches. 2. to place on a bench, especially an official one. 3. to exhibit on a platform at a dog show. 4. in *sports*, to take (a player) out of a game.
on the bench, 1. presiding in a law court; serving in court as a judge. 2. in *sports*, not taking part in the game, as a substitute player.
bench dog, any dog exhibited at a dog show.
bench·er (ben′chẽr), *n.* 1. [Rare], a person who sits on or works at a bench; hence, 2. [often B-], in England, a member of the inner or higher bar who acts as one of the governors of an Inn of Court.
Bench·ley, Robert (bench′li), 1889–1945; American humorist.
bench mark, a surveyor's mark made on a permanent landmark that has a known position and altitude: bench marks are used as reference points in determining other altitudes within a given line of levels.
bench warrant, an order issued by a judge or law court for the arrest of a person charged with contempt of court or a criminal offense: distinguished from *magistrate's warrant.*
bend (bend), *v.t.* [BENT (bent) or *archaic* BENDED (-id), BENDING], [ME. *benden;* AS. *bendan*, to confine with a string (AS. *bend*); hence, to fetter, bend (a bow)], 1. originally, to cause tension in (a bow, etc.), as by drawing with a string; hence, 2. to make (an object) curved or crooked. 3. to turn from a straight line; cause to swerve: as, he *bent* his steps from the path. 4. to make stoop, bow, or give in: as, he *bent* the prisoner's will to his wishes. 5. to turn or direct (one's eyes, attention, energy, etc. *to*). 6. in *nautical usage*, to fasten into position: said of sails and ropes. *v.i.* 1. to turn or be turned from a straight line or from some direction or position; swerve; curve. 2. to yield by curving or crooking, as from pressure. 3. to crook or curve the body from a standing position; stoop; bow (often with *over*). 4. to give in; yield: as, he *bent* to her wishes. 5. to move from a given line or direction; incline away. 6. to direct one's attention, energy, etc. (*to* something). *n.* 1. a bending or being bent. 2. a bent or curving part. 3. in *shipbuilding*, a wale. —*SYN.* see **curve.**
bend (bend), *n.* [ME. < *bend, v.*], 1. any of various knots, as the fisherman's bend, carrick bend, etc., used to tie one rope to another or to something else. 2. in *tanning*, one half of a trimmed hide or butt.
the bends, [Colloq.], cramps that often attack a person who goes too quickly from a place of abnormal atmospheric pressure to one of normal pressure, as in deep-sea diving: also called *caisson disease.*
bend (bend), *n.* [OFr. *bende* < OHG. *binda* < *bindan*, to bind], in *heraldry*, a stripe or band from the upper left to the lower right corner of a coat of arms.
Ben Da·vis (ben dā′vis), a variety of large red winter apple.
Ben Day process (ben dā), [after *Benjamin Day* (1838–1916), New York printer], in *photoengraving*, a process for adding tone or shading in reproducing line drawings, etc., by applying patterns of dots, stipples, or the like from an inked transparent film directly onto a plate before etching or onto a negative before the plate is made: also **Benday process.**
bend·er (ben′dẽr), *n.* 1. a person or thing that bends. 2. [Slang], a drinking bout; spree.
Ben·di·go (ben′di-gō′), *n.* a city in central Victoria, Australia: pop., 40,000.
bend sinister, a band or stripe from the upper right to the lower left corner of a coat of arms: in literature, it has come to signify bastardy in the family line: cf. **bar sinister, baton.**
ben·dy (ben′di), *n.* [Hind. *bhindi*], the okra plant: its pods are used as a vegetable.
ben·e (ben′e), *n.* [native name], a wild hog of New Guinea.
bene (bēn), *n.* [AS. *ben*], [Archaic], a prayer or boon.
be·neath (bi-nēth′), *adv. & adj.* [ME. *bineothen;* AS. *beneothan; be-* + *neothan*, down; see NETHER], 1. in a lower place; below. 2. just below something; underneath. *prep.* 1. below; lower than. 2. directly under; underneath. 3. covered by: as, *beneath* blankets. 4. under the influence of (something powerful, oppressive, etc.): as, living *beneath* a tyranny. 5. inferior to or lower than in rank, quality, etc. 6. unworthy of: as, it is *beneath* him to cheat.
ben·e·dic·i·te (ben′ə-dis′ə-ti), *interj.* [L.], bless you! *n.* 1. the invocation of a blessing, as in asking grace at meals. 2. [B-], the canticle that begins *Benedicite, omnia opera Domini Domino* (Bless the Lord, all ye works of the Lord).
Ben·e·dick (ben′ə-dik′), *n.* 1. in Shakespeare's *Much Ado About Nothing*, a bachelor who finally falls in love with the clever Beatrice. 2. [b-], a benedict.
Ben·e·dict (ben′ə-dikt′), [L. *Benedictus*, lit., blessed; see BENEDICTION], a masculine name: variants, *Bennet, Bennett.*
ben·e·dict (ben′ə-dikt′), *n.* [< *Benedick*], 1. a recently married man, especially one who seemed to be a confirmed bachelor. 2. any married man.
Benedict XIV, 1675–1758; Pope (1740–1758); known as a patron of art and literature.
Benedict XV, 1854–1922; Pope (1914–1922).
Benedict, Saint, 480?–543? A.D.; Italian monk; founded the monastery of Monte Cassino, first seat of the Benedictine order: his day is March 21.
Ben·e·dic·tine (ben′ə-dik′tin, ben′ə-dik′tēn), *adj.* [Fr. *bénédictin*], 1. of Saint Benedict. 2. designating the monastic order based on his teachings, founded c. 529 A.D. 3. of this order or its members. *n.* 1. a Benedictine monk or nun. 2. [b-], (ben′ə-dik′tēn), a liqueur, originally made by Benedictine monks.
Benedictine rule, the rules governing life in Benedictine monasteries.
ben·e·dic·tion (ben′ə-dik′shən), *n.* [L. *benedictio* < *benedicere*, to speak well of; *bene*, well + *dicere*, to speak], 1. a blessing. 2. an invocation of divine blessing, especially at the end of a church service. 3. a giving of thanks; grace. 4. blessedness. 5. [B-], in the *Roman Catholic Church*, a special ritual of blessing.
ben·e·dic·to·ry (ben′ə-dik′tẽr-i), *adj.* [ML. *benedictorius*

< L. *benedictus*, pp. of *benedicere;* see BENEDICTION], of or giving a benediction.

Ben·e·dic·tus (ben'ə-dik'təs), *n.* [L., blessed, pp. of *benedicere;* see BENEDICTION], 1. a short hymn of praise used in the Mass, beginning *Benedictus qui venit in nomine Domini* (Blessed is He that cometh in the name of the Lord): Matt. 21:9. 2. Zacharias' hymn at the birth of his son, John the Baptist: Luke 1:68. 3. music for either of these hymns.

ben·e·fac·tion (ben'ə-fak'shən), *n.* [LL. *benefactio* < L. *benefacere*, to do well; *bene*, well + *facere*, to do], 1. a benefiting, especially as an act of charity. 2. anything given as a benefit. 3. in *metallurgy*, the preliminary conditioning of an ore for refinement.

ben·e·fac·tor (ben'ə-fak'tẽr, ben'ə-fak'tẽr), *n.* [LL. < pp. of *benefacere;* see BENEFACTION], a person who has given help or financial assistance; patron.

ben·e·fac·tress (ben'ə-fak'tris, ben'ə-fak'tris), *n.* a woman benefactor.

be·nef·ic (bə-nef'ik), *adj.* [L. *beneficus* < *benefacere;* see BENEFACTION], kindly; charitable.

ben·e·fice (ben'ə-fis), *n.* [ME.; OFr.; L. *beneficium* < *benefacere;* see BENEFACTION], 1. land held by a feudal tenant for services rendered the owner. 2. an endowed church office providing a living for a vicar, rector, etc. 3. its income. *v.t.* [BENEFICED (-fist), BENEFICING], to provide with a benefice.

be·nef·i·cence (bə-nef'ə-s'ns), *n.* [< Fr. or L.; Fr. *beneficence* < L. *beneficentia* < *benefacere;* see BENEFACTION], 1. a being kind or doing good. 2. a kindly action or gift.

be·nef·i·cent (bə-nef'ə-s'nt), *adj.* 1. showing beneficence; doing good. 2. resulting in benefit.

ben·e·fi·cial (ben'ə-fish'əl), *adj.* [Fr.; LL. *beneficialis* < L. *benefacere;* see BENEFACTION], 1. productive of benefits; advantageous; favorable. 2. receiving benefit. 3. in *law*, for one's own benefit: as, *beneficial* interest.

ben·e·fi·ci·ar·y (ben'ə-fish'ẽr-i, ben'ə-fish'i-er'i), *adj.* [L. *beneficiarius*, of a favor < *benefacere;* see BENEFACTION], of or holding a benefice. *n.* [*pl.* BENEFICIARIES (-iz)], 1. a holder of a benefice. 2. anyone receiving benefit. 3. a person named to receive the income or inheritance from a will, insurance policy, etc.

ben·e·fit (ben'ə-fit), *n.* [ME. *benefet, bienfet;* Anglo-Fr. *benfet;* OFr. *bienfait*, a kindness; L. *benefactum*, meritorious act < *benefacere;* see BENEFACTION], 1. a kindly, charitable act; favor. 2. anything contributing to an improvement in condition; advantage. 3. *often pl.* payments made by an insurance company, public agency, welfare society, etc. 4. any public performance, bazaar, dance, etc. the proceeds of which are to help a certain person, group, or cause. *v.t.* [BENEFITED (-id), BENEFITING], to do good to or for; aid. *v.i.* to receive advantage; profit.

benefit of clergy, 1. the exemption which the medieval clergy had from trial or punishment except in a church court. 2. an administering or sanctioning by the church: as, their marriage was without *benefit of clergy*.

benefit society (or **association**), an organization which, by means of dues, secures for its members certain benefits, such as life insurance, hospitalization, etc.

Be·ne·lux (ben'i-luks), *n.* [< *Be*lgium, *Ne*therlands, *Lux*emburg], in *political science*, Belgium, the Netherlands, and Luxemburg.

be·nempt (bi-nempt'), alternative past participle of **bename.**

be·nempt·ed (bi-nemp'tid), alternative past participle of **bename.**

Be·neš, E·du·ard (e'dōō-ärt be'nesh), 1884–1948; Czechoslovakian statesman; president of Czechoslovakia (1935–1948); served in exile (1938–1945).

Be·nét, Stephen Vincent (be-nā'), 1898–1943; brother of *William Rose;* American poet and writer.

Benét, William Rose, 1886–1950; brother of *Stephen Vincent;* American poet, dramatist, and editor.

‡be·ne va·le (be'ni vā'li), [L.], farewell.

be·nev·o·lence (bə-nev'ə-ləns), *n.* [ME. & OFr. *benivolence;* L. *benevolentia;* see BENEVOLENT], 1. an inclination to do good; kindliness. 2. a kindly, charitable activity; gift; beneficence. 3. a forced loan formerly levied by some English kings on their subjects.

be·nev·o·lent (bə-nev'ə-lənt), *adj.* [OFr. *benivolent;* L. *benevolens; bene*, well + *volens*, ppr. of *volere*, to wish], doing or inclined to do good; kindly; benignant; charitable: opposed to *malevolent*. —*SYN.* see **kind.**

Beng., 1. Bengal. 2. Bengali.

Ben·gal (ben-gôl', beŋ-gôl'), *n.* 1. a former province of British India divided (1948) between Pakistan and India: see **East Bengal, West Bengal.** 2. West Bengal. *adj.* (ben'gôl', beŋ'gôl'), of or from Bengal.

Bengal, Bay of, a part of the Indian Ocean, east of India and west of Burma and the Malay Peninsula.

Ben·ga·lese (ben'gə-lēz', beŋ'gə-lēz'), *adj.* of Bengal, its people, or their language. *n.* [*pl.* BENGALESE], a native of Bengal.

Ben·gal·i (ben-gôl'i, beŋ-gôl'i), *n.* 1. a native of Bengal. 2. the Indo-European, Indic language of Bengal. *adj.* of Bengal, its people, or their language.

ben·ga·line (beŋ'gə-lēn', beŋ'gə-lēn'), *n.* [Fr. < *Bengal*, whence the cloth was imported], a heavy, corded cloth of silk and either wool or cotton.

Bengal light, a firework with a brilliant blue light, often used as a signal.

Ben·ga·si, Ben·gha·zi (ben-gä'zi, beŋ-gä'zi), *n.* a city on the coast of Libya, North Africa: pop., 65,000.

Be·ni (bā'ni), *n.* a river in western Bolivia, joining the Mamoré to form the Madeira: length, 1,000 mi.

be·night·ed (bi-nīt'id), *adj.* [pp. of obs. *benight*], 1. caught or surrounded by darkness or night; hence, 2. intellectually or morally backward; unenlightened.

be·nign (bi-nīn'), *adj.* [ME. & OFr. *benigne;* L. *benignus*, good < *bene*, well + *genus*, type], 1. good-natured; kindly. 2. favorable; beneficial. 3. in *medicine*, doing little or no harm; not malignant. —*SYN.* see **kind.**

be·nig·nan·cy (bi-nig'nən-si), *n.* [< *benignant*], the quality or condition of being benignant.

be·nig·nant (bi-nig'nənt), *adj.* [< *benign*, by analogy with *malignant*], 1. kindly or gracious, especially to inferiors. 2. benign; beneficial.

be·nig·ni·ty (bi-nig'nə-ti), *n.* [*pl.* BENIGNITIES (-tiz)], [ME. & OFr. *benignite;* L. *benignitas;* see BENIGN], 1. benignancy; kindliness. 2. a kind act; favor.

Be·nin (be-nēn'), *n.* 1. a former native kingdom: now a district in Nigeria, Africa: area, 8,627 sq. mi.; pop., 493,000. 2. a river in western Nigeria flowing into the Gulf of Guinea.

ben·i·son (ben'ə-z'n, ben'ə-s'n), *n.* [ME. *beneisun;* OFr. *beneison* < L. *benedictio*], a blessing; benediction.

Ben·ja·min (ben'jə-mən), [Heb. *binyāmīn*, lit., son of the right hand; hence, favorite son], a masculine name: diminutives, *Ben, Benny*. *n.* in the *Bible*, 1. Jacob's youngest son and his favorite. 2. the tribe of Israel descended from him.

ben·ja·min (ben'jə-mən), *n.* [altered < *benjoin;* see BENZOIN], gum benzoin.

Ben·ja·min, Judah Philip (ben'jə-mən), 1811–1884; American statesman and lawyer; secretary of state in the Confederate cabinet (1862–1865).

Ben Lo·mond (lō'mənd), 1. a mountain in Scotland, near Loch Lomond: height, 3,190 ft. 2. a mountain in northeastern Tasmania: height, 5,160 ft.

ben·ne (ben'i), *n.* [Malay *bijen*, seed], the sesame, an East Indian plant whose seeds yield an oil used like olive oil.

ben·net (ben'it), *n.* [ME. *(herbe) beneit* (Fr. *benoîte*); ML. *benedicta;* L. *(herba) benedicta*, blessed (herb) < *benedictus*, pp. of *benedicere;* see BENEDICTION: formerly reputed to protect from the devil], 1. a yellow-flowered plant of the rose family: also **herb bennet.** 2. poison hemlock. 3. common valerian.

Ben·net, Ben·nett (ben'it), a masculine name: see **Benedict.**

Ben·nett, Arnold (ben'it), (*Enoch Arnold Bennett*), 1867–1931; English novelist.

Bennett, James Gordon, 1795–1872; American journalist; founder and editor of the New York *Herald*.

Ben Ne·vis (nē'vis, nev'is), a mountan in west central Scotland: highest peak in Great Britain: height, 4,405 ft.

Ben·ning·ton (ben'iŋ-tən), *n.* a town in Vermont: pop. 8,000: a Revolutionary War battle (1777) was fought near here.

Be·no·ni (bə-nō'nī), *n.* a city in the Transvaal, Union of South Africa: pop., 78,000.

bent (bent), past tense and past participle of **bend.** *adj.* 1. not straight; curved; crooked. 2. strongly inclined or determined (with *on*): as, she is *bent* on going. 3. set in a course; bound: as, travelers westward *bent*. *n.* 1. an inclining; tendency. 2. a mental leaning; propensity: as, a *bent* for music. 3. [Archaic], impetus. —*SYN.* see **inclination.**

to (or at) the top of one's bent, to (or at) the top or limit of one's capacity or ability.

bent (bent), *n.* [ME.; AS. *beonot*, bent, a rush < WGmc. **binut*, as in G. *binse*], 1. [*pl.* BENT], the stiff flower stalk of certain grasses. 2. any of various reedy grasses. 3. any of a number of related grasses, chiefly low-growing and spreading: also **bent grass.** 4. [Archaic], a heath; moor.

Ben·tham, Jeremy (ben'thəm, ben'təm), 1748–1832; English philosopher and political scientist.

Ben·tham·ism (ben'thəm-iz'm, ben'təm-iz'm), *n.* the utilitarian philosophy of Jeremy Bentham, which holds that the greatest happiness of the greatest number should be the ultimate goal of society and of the individual.

Ben·tham·ite (ben'thəm-īt', ben'təm-īt'), *n.* a follower of Jeremy Bentham or advocate of Benthamism.

ben·thic (ben'thik), *adj.* of the benthos; benthonic.

ben·thon·ic (ben-thon'ik), *adj.* of the benthos; benthic.

ben·thos (ben'thos), *n.* [Mod. L.; Gr. *benthos*, depth of the sea], the plants and animals at the bottom of the sea.

Bent·ley, Richard (bent'li), 1662–1742; English clergyman and classical scholar.

Ben·ton, Thomas Hart (ben't'n), 1. 1782–1858; American statesman; instrumental in securing coinage ratio at 16 to 1. 2. 1889– ; American painter.

ben·ton·ite (ben't'n-īt'), *n.* [from Fort *Benton* (after Thomas Hart *Benton*, Am. statesman) in Montana, where it is found], a soft, porous clay formed as a weathering product from volcanic ash.

‡**ben tro·va·to** (ben trô-vä'tô), [It., lit., well found], well thought up; artfully invented.

be·numb (bi-num'), *v.t.* [ME. *binumen*, pp. of *binimen*, to take away; AS. *beniman; be-* + *niman*, to take; *-b* by analogy with *dumb*], 1. to make numb. 2. to deaden the mind, will, or feelings of; stupefy.

benz- (benz), benzo-.

ben·zal·de·hyde (ben-zal'də-hīd'), *n.* [*benz-* + *aldehyde*], a clear, pleasant-smelling liquid, C_6H_5CHO, found in the oil of the bitter almond and used in making dyes, perfumes, flavorings, etc.

ben·ze·drine (ben'zə-drēn', ben'zə-drin, ben-zed'rin), *n.* [*benz-* + eph*edrine*], amphetamine, $C_6H_5CH_2CH(NH_2)CH_3$, a derivative of ephedrine, used as an inhalant to relieve nasal congestion, and as a stimulant of the central nervous system: a trade-mark (**Benzedrine**).

ben·zene (ben'zēn, ben-zēn'), *n.* [*benzoin* + *-ene*], a clear, inflammable liquid, C_6H_6, obtained by scrubbing coal gas with oil and by the fractional distillation of coal tar: it is used as a solvent for fats and in making lacquers, varnishes, many dyes, and other organic compounds: abbreviated **Bz.**: also called *benzol*.

benzene ring (or **nucleus**), a structural unit believed to exist in the molecules of aromatic organic compounds, consisting of a ring of six atoms of carbon: in the molecule of benzene six atoms of hydrogen are believed to be attached to the ring, one to each atom of carbon, but in derivatives of benzene one or more atoms of hydrogen are replaced by atoms of other elements or by groups of atoms.

ben·zi·dine (ben'zi-dēn', ben'zi-din), *n.* [< *benzene*], a white, crystalline organic base, $NH_2C_6H_4C_6H_4NH_2$, used in the manufacture of certain dyes.

ben·zine (ben'zēn, ben-zēn'), *n.* [*benzoin* + *-ine;* orig. applied to *benzene*], a mixture of hydrocarbons, a colorless inflammable liquid, obtained in the fractional distillation of petroleum and used as a motor fuel and as a solvent for fats and oils in dry cleaning, etc.

ben·zo- (ben'zō), [see BENZENE], a combining form meaning *relating to benzene:* also **benz-**.

ben·zo·ate (ben'zō-it, ben'zō-āt'), *n.* [*benzo-* + *-ate*], a salt or ester of benzoic acid.

ben·zo·ic (ben-zō'ik), *adj.* [*benzoin* + *-ic*], of or derived from benzoin.

benzoic acid, a white, crystalline organic acid, C_6H_5COOH, produced commercially from toluene and used as an antiseptic and preservative.

ben·zo·in (ben'zō-in, ben-zō'in, ben'zoin), *n.* [Fr. *benjoin;* Sp. *benjuí;* It. *benzoi* < Ar. *lubān jāwī*, incense of Java; *lu-* dropped because falsely assumed to be the article], 1. the resin from certain styracaceous trees of Sumatra and Java, used in medicine, perfumery, etc. 2. any of a number of related shrubs or trees of the laurel family, as the spicebush or benjamin bush.

ben·zol (ben'zōl, ben'zol), *n.* [*benz-* + *-ol*], benzene: as used in the chemical industry, the term sometimes denotes a mixture distilling below 100° C., 70 per cent of which is benzene.

ben·zo·phe·none (ben'zō-fē'nōn), *n.* [*benzo-* + *phenol* + *-one*], a white, crystalline organic compound, $C_6H_5COC_6H_5$, classified as a ketone: it is produced by the distillation of calcium benzoate and is used as an intermediate compound in the formation of certain other organic compounds.

ben·zo·yl (ben'zō-il), *n.* [*benzo-* + *-yl*], a univalent radical, C_6H_5CO, found in benzoic acid and in certain derivatives of the acid.

ben·zyl (ben'zil), *n.* [*benz-* + *-yl*], a univalent radical, $C_6H_5CH_2$, found in organic compounds derived from toluene.

Be·o·grad (be-ô'gråd), *n.* Belgrade: the Serbian name.

Be·o·wulf (bā'ə-woolf'), *n.* [< ?; prob. understood in AS. as *beo*, bee + *wulf*, wolf, and hence as a kenning for "bear"], the hero of the Anglo-Saxon folk epic of that name, an Anglian poem probably composed c. 700 A.D., distinguished by dramatic projection of character and supple alliterative verse: Beowulf slays Grendel and Grendel's mother, eventually becomes king of his people, and dies after a fight with a dragon that is ravaging his kingdom.

be·paint (bi-pānt'), *v.t.* 1. to cover with paint. 2. to color.

be·queath (bi-kwēth', bi-kwēth'), *v.t.* [BEQUEATHED (-kwēthd', -kwētht'), BEQUEATHING], [ME. *bequethen, bicwethen;* AS. *becwethan*, to declare, give by will; *be-* + *cwethan*, to say; see QUOTH], 1. to leave (property, etc.) to another by last will and testament. 2. to give by inheritance; hand down: as, he *bequeathed* his talent to his son.

be·queath·al (bi-kwēth'əl), *n.* a bequeathing.

be·quest (bi-kwest'), *n.* [ME. *bicweste* < *be-* + AS. *cwiss*, a saying < *cwethan*, to speak (see QUOTH); *-t* is unhistoric], 1. a bequeathing. 2. anything bequeathed.

Bé·ran·ger, Pierre Jean de (pyâr zhän də bā'rän'zhā'), 1780–1857; French lyric poet.

Be·rar (bā-rär'), *n.* formerly, a division of Central Provinces, India: since 1950, part of Madhya Pradesh.

be·rate (bi-rāt'), *v.t.* [BERATED (-id), BERATING], [*be-* + *rate, v.t.*], to scold or rebuke severely. —*SYN.* see **scold.**

Ber·ber (bũr'bẽr), *n.* 1. any of a Moslem people living in northern Africa. 2. their Hamitic language. *adj.* of the Berbers, their culture, or their language.

Ber·ber·a (bũr'bẽr-ä), *n.* a city in Somalia, on the Gulf of Aden: pop., 20,000.

ber·be·ri·da·ceous (bũr'bẽr-i-dā'shəs), *adj.* [< Mod. L. *Berberidaciae*, name of the family; + *-aceous*], of the barberry family of plants.

ber·ber·in (bũr'bẽr-in), *n.* berberine.

ber·ber·ine (bũr'bẽr-ēn', bũr'bẽr-in), *n.* [< LL. *berberis*, barberry; + *-ine*], a bitter, yellow alkaloid, $C_{20}H_{17}NO_4 \cdot 6H_2O$ or $C_{20}H_{19}NO_5 \cdot 6H_2O$, obtained from barberry and other plants: it is used in dyeing and as a drug.

‡**ber·ceuse** (bâr'söz'), *n.* [*pl.* BERCEUSES (bâr'söz')], [Fr. < *bercer*, to rock, lull to sleep], a lullaby.

Berch·tes·ga·den (berH'tes-gä'dən; Eng. berk'təs-gä'd'n), *n.* a village in the Bavarian Alps, southern Germany: Adolf Hitler had a country home there.

Ber·di·chev (ber-dē'chef), *n.* a city in the west central Ukrainian S.S.R.: pop., 53,000.

be·reave (bi-rēv'), *v.t.* [BEREAVED (-rēvd') or BEREFT (-reft'), BEREAVING], [ME. *bireavien;* AS. *bereafian*, to deprive, rob; *be-* + *reafian;* akin to G. *berauben;* see REAVE (to rob)], 1. to deprive or rob, as of life, hope, happiness, etc. 2. to leave destitute or forlorn, as by loss or death. 3. [Obs.], to take away by force.

be·reave·ment (bi-rēv'mənt), *n.* 1. a bereaving. 2. the fact or state of being bereaved. 3. the loss of someone through death.

be·reft (bi-reft'), alternative past tense and past participle of **bereave.** *adj.* 1. deprived. 2. left sad and lonely, as by loss of someone dear.

Ber·e·ni·ce (bẽr-nēs', bũr'nis, ber'ə-ni'si), [L.; Gr. *Berenikē*, lit., victory-bringing], a feminine name: variant, *Bernice*.

Ber·es·ford, Charles William (ber'iz-fẽrd), first Baron Beresford, 1846–1919; British admiral.

Ber·e·si·na (ber'ə-zē'nə; Russ. be-rez'i-nä'), *n.* a river in Byelorussia, flowing into the Dnepr: length, 330 mi.: a famous battle was fought on the Beresina in 1812 during Napoleon's retreat from Moscow.

be·ret (bə-rā', ber'ā), *n.* [Fr. *béret;* Pr. *berret;* LL. *birrettum;* see BIRETTA], 1. a flat, round cap of felt, wool, or other cloth. 2. a biretta.

BERET

berg (bũrg), *n.* [< *iceberg*], an iceberg.

Ber·ga·ma (ber'gə-mä'), *n.* a town in western Turkey, on the site of ancient Pergamum: pop., 22,000.

ber·ga·mot (bũr'gə-mot'), *n.* [Fr. *bergamote;* It. *bergamotta;* Turk. *beg-armūdi*, prince's pear; form influenced by *Bergamo*, name of an Italian city], 1. a kind of pear. 2. a citrus fruit whose thin, yellow rind yields an oil used in some perfumes. 3. this oil. 4. any of several plants of the mint family, as the horsemint.

Ber·gen (ber'gən, bũr'gən), *n.* a seaport in southwestern Norway: pop., 116,000.

Ber·ge·rac, Cy·ra·no de (sir'ə-nō' də ber'jə-rak'; Fr. sē'rä'nō' də bâr'zhə-räk'), 1619–1655; French playwright, author, and soldier, famous for his large nose: he is the hero of a poetic drama of the same name by Edmond Rostand (1897).

Berg·son, Hen·ri (än'rē' bårg'sōn', bãrk'sōn'; Eng. berg's'n), 1859–1941; French philosopher; received Nobel prize in literature, 1927.

Berg·so·ni·an (berg-sō'ni-ən), *adj.* of Henri Bergson or his philosophy. *n.* a believer in Bergson's philosophy.

Berg·son·ism (berg's'n-iz'm), *n.* the philosophy of Bergson, which maintains that there is an original life force carried through all successive generations.

be·rhyme, be·rime (bi-rīm'), *v.t.* 1. to make rhymes about. 2. to satirize in verse.

be·rib·boned (bi-rib'ənd), *adj.* covered with ribbons.

ber·i·ber·i (ber'i-ber'i), *n.* [Singh. *beri*, weakness], a deficiency disease, occurring mainly in Asia, caused by lack of vitamin B_1 in the diet: it is characterized by extreme weakness, paralysis, anemia, and wasting away.

Be·ring, Vi·tus (vē'toos bā'riŋ; Eng. bêr'iŋ, bâr'iŋ), 1680–1741; Danish navigator in the employ of Russia.

Ber·ing Sea (bâr'iŋ, bêr'iŋ), a sea between Siberia and Alaska, connecting with the Pacific and Arctic Oceans: area, 876,000 sq. mi.; average depth, 4,716 ft.

Bering Strait, the strait between Siberia and Alaska: width, 36 mi.: discovered by Vitus Bering (1741).

Berke·le·ian (bẽrk-lē'ən, bärk-lē'ən), *adj.* of George

Berkeley or his philosophy. *n.* a person who believes in Berkeley's philosophy.

Berke·le·ian·ism (bẽrk-lē′ən-iz'm, bärk-lē′ən-iz'm), *n.* the philosophy of George Berkeley, which holds that physical objects exist only in being perceived.

Berke·ley (būrk′li), *n.* a city near San Francisco, California: pop., 111,000.

Berke·ley, George (būrk′li, bärk′li), 1685–1753; Irish philosopher, bishop, and writer.

Berkeley, Sir **William,** 1606–1677; British governor of Virginia (1642–1676).

berke·li·um (būrk′li-əm), *n.* [< University of California at *Berkeley,* where first isolated], a radioactive chemical element produced by bombarding americium with alpha particles having a high energy level: it does not occur naturally on earth: symbol, Bk; at. wt., 243(?); at. no., 97.

Berk·shire (būrk′shir, bärk′shir), *n.* 1. a county of south central England: pop., 403,000; county seat, Reading. 2. (būrk′shir), any of a breed of medium-sized hogs, black with white spots.

Berk·shire Hills (būrk′shir), a range of hills and mountains in western Massachusetts: highest peak, Mt. Greylock, 3,505 ft.

Ber·lin (bẽr-lin′), *n.* 1. a city in eastern Germany, the capital of the German Reich from 1871 to 1945: pop., 3,294,000: in postwar occupation divided into an eastern sector (under a Soviet commandant) and three western sectors (under American, British, and French commandants): the eastern sector is the site of the capital of the German Democratic Republic (East Germany). 2. (būr′lin), a city in northeastern New Hampshire: pop., 18,000.

ber·lin (bẽr-lin′, būr′lin), *n.* [after *Berlin,* Germany, where it was first used], 1. a four-wheeled closed carriage with a footman's platform behind, separate from the body. 2. (bẽr-lin′), a berline. 3. [sometimes B-], a fine, soft, wool yarn: also called *Berlin wool.*

ber·line (bẽr-lin′; Fr. ber′lēn′), *n.* an automobile body with a glass partition between the front seat and the rear seat: also **berlin.**

Ber·li·oz, Louis Hector (ber′li-ōz′; Fr. bâr′lyôz′), 1803–1869; French composer.

berm, berme (būrm), *n.* [Fr. *berme* & D. *berm;* MD. *baerm;* IE. base **bher-,* an edge, point, as also in Eng. *brim* (< IE. **bhre-m*)], 1. a ledge or shoulder, as along the edge of a paved road. 2. a ledge or space between the ditch and the parapet in a fortification.

Ber·me·jo (ber-me′hô), *n.* a river in northern Argentina, flowing into the Paraguay River: length, 1,000 mi.

Ber·mu·da (bẽr-mū′də), *n.* a group of British islands in the Atlantic, east of South Carolina: area, 20 sq. mi.; pop., 44,000; capital, Hamilton.

Bermuda onion, a large onion with a mild flavor, grown in Texas and California as well as in Bermuda.

Bermuda shorts, tailored shorts of wool, cotton, etc., extending to just above the knee, for business or informal wear: often worn with knee-length stockings: also called *walking shorts.*

Ber·mu·di·an (bẽr-mū′di-ən), *adj.* of Bermuda. *n.* a native or inhabitant of Bermuda.

Bern (būrn, bern), *n.* the capital of Switzerland: pop., 163,000: also spelled **Berne.**

Ber·na·dotte, Jean Bap·tiste Jules (zhän bȧ′tēst′ zhül ber′nȧ′dôt′; Eng. būr′nə-dot′), 1764–1844; French marshal under Napoleon; as Charles XIV John, he was king of Sweden and Norway (1818–1844).

Ber·nard (būr′nẽrd, būr′närd, bẽr-närd′), [Fr.; G. *Bernhard,* lit., bold as a bear < OHG. *bero,* bear + *hart,* bold, hard], a masculine name: diminutive, *Bernie;* variant, *Barnard;* equivalent, G. *Bernhard.*

Ber·nard, Claude (klōd′ bâr′nȧr′), 1813–1878; French physiologist.

Ber·nard·ine (būr′nẽr-din, būr′nẽr-dēn′), *adj.* 1. of Saint Bernard of Clairvaux. 2. of the order of Cistercian monks founded by him in 1115. *n.* a monk belonging to this order.

Bernard of Clair·vaux, Saint (klâr′vō′), 1091–1153; French churchman; founder of Cistercian order.

Bernard of Clu·ny, Saint (klōō′ni), 12th century; French Benedictine monk and writer of Latin verse: also called *Bernard of Morlaix* (môr′le′).

Bernard of Men·thon, Saint (män′tôn′), 10th century; French monk who founded several Alpine hospices.

Berne (būrn, bern), *n.* Bern.

Ber·nese Alps (būr′nēz′, būr′nēs′), a range of the Alps, in south central Switzerland: highest peak, Finsteraarhorn, 14,026 ft.

Bern·har·di, Fried·rich von (frēd′riH fôn bern-här′di), 1849–1930; German general.

Bern·hardt, Sarah (būrn′härt′; Fr. bâr′nȧr′), (born *Rosine Bernard*), 1844–1923; French actress.

Ber·nice (bẽr-nēs′, būr′nis), a feminine name: see **Berenice.**

ber·ni·cle goose (būr′ni-k'l, bär′ni-k'l), barnacle goose.

Ber·ni·na (ber-nē′nä), *n.* 1. a mountain pass across the Rhaetian Alps of southeastern Switzerland. 2. the highest peak of the Rhaetian Alps: height, 13,303 ft.

Ber·ni·ni, Gio·van·ni Lo·ren·zo (jô-vän′nē lô-ren′tsô ber-nē′nē), 1598–1680; Italian architect and sculptor.

ber·ret·ta (bə-ret′ə), *n.* a biretta.

Ber·ri (ber′i; Fr. be′rē′), *n.* a former province in central France: also spelled **Berry.**

ber·ried (ber′id), *adj.* 1. bearing berries. 2. like a berry. 3. bearing eggs: said of lobsters, crayfish, etc.

ber·ry (ber′i), *n.* [*pl.* BERRIES (-iz)], [ME. & AS. *berie,* a berry, grape; cf. Goth. *weina-basi,* lit., wineberry; IE., base may be **bhā-,* gleam, shine], 1. any small, juicy, fleshy fruit with seeds, as a strawberry, mulberry, etc. 2. the dry seed or kernel of various plants, as a coffee bean. 3. an egg of a lobster, crayfish, etc. 4. [Slang], a dollar. 5. in *botany,* any fleshy simple fruit with one or more seeds and a skin, as a tomato, cranberry, banana, grape, etc. *v.i.* [BERRIED (-id), BERRYING], 1. to bear berries. 2. to look for berries; pick berries.

‡ber·sa·glie·re (ber′sä-lye′re), *n.* [*pl.* BERSAGLIERI (-rē)], [It.], a rifleman; specifically, [B-], any of a special unit of sharpshooters in the Italian army.

ber·seem (bẽr-sēm′), *n.* [Ar. *barsim;* ult. < *birshīm,* clover], a kind of clover, grown for fodder.

ber·serk (būr′sẽrk, bẽr-sūrk′), *n.* [see BERSERKER], a berserker. *adj. & adv.* in or into a state of violent rage or frenzy.

ber·serk·er (būr′sẽr-kẽr, bẽr-sūr′kẽr), *n.* [ON. *berserkr,* warrior clothed in bearskin < *ber,* a bear + *serkr,* coat], 1. in *Norse legend,* a warrior who worked himself into a frenzy before a battle. 2. a person who acts like a berserker.

berth (būrth), *n.* [< base of *bear* (to carry)], 1. enough space at sea; hence, 2. space for anchoring or tying up. 3. a ship's place of anchorage. 4. a position, place, duty, office, etc. 5. a built-in bed or bunk, as in a ship's cabin or a Pullman car. *v.t.* 1. to put into a berth. 2. to furnish with a berth. *v.i.* to have or occupy a berth.

give a wide berth to, to stay at a prudent distance from.

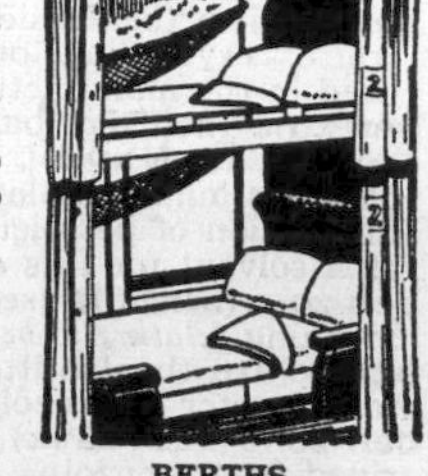
BERTHS

Ber·tha (būr′thə), [G.; OHG. *Berahta, Perahta,* lit., bright one < *beraht,* bright, shining; akin to AS. *beorht, bryht,* bright], a feminine name. *n.* [b-], [Fr. *berthe* < Fr. form of the name], a woman's wide collar, often of lace.

Ber·til·lon, Al·phonse (ȧl′fôns′ bâr′tē′yôn′), 1853–1914; French anthropologist.

Ber·til·lon system (būr′t'l-on′; Fr. bâr′tē′yôn′), [after Alphonse *Bertillon,* its inventor], a system of identifying people through records of body measurements, markings or deformities, coloring, etc.: fingerprinting was later incorporated into the system.

Ber·tram (būr′trəm), [G.; OHG. *Berahtram, Berahthraban* < *beraht,* bright + *hraban, hramn,* raven], a masculine name: diminutive, *Berti;* variant, *Bertrand.*

Ber·trand (būr′trənd), a masculine name: see **Bertram.**

be·ruf·fled (bi-ruf′'ld), *adj.* with ruffles.

Ber·wick (ber′ik), *n.* a county of southeastern Scotland: pop., 24,000; county seat, Duns.

Ber·wyn (būr′win), *n.* a city in northeastern Illinois, near Chicago: pop., 54,000.

Ber·yl (ber′il), [prob. < *beryl,* but said to mean "prophetic, soothsayer"], a feminine name.

ber·yl (ber′il), *n.* [ME. & OFr. *beril;* L. *beryllus;* Gr. *bēryllos,* sea-green gem], beryllium aluminum silicate, $Be_3Al_2(SiO_3)_6$, a very hard, lustrous mineral that is a source of beryllium: emerald and aquamarine are two of several different varieties of beryl.

be·ryl·li·um (bə-ril′i-əm), *n.* [Mod. L. < *beryl*], a hard, rare, metallic chemical element, found only in combination with others: it forms strong, hard alloys with several metals, including copper and nickel: symbol, Be; at. wt., 9.02; at. no., 4: former name, *glucinum.*

Ber·ze·li·us, Baron **Jöns Ja·kob** (yöns yä′kôp ber-sā′li-əs; Eng. bẽr-zē′li-əs), 1779–1848; Swedish chemist; inventor of the modern system of writing chemical symbols and formulas.

Bes (bes), *n.* [Egypt. *besa*], an Egyptian god of pleasure.

Be·san·çon (bə-zän′sôn′), *n.* a city in eastern France: pop., 73,000.

Be·sant, Sir **Walter** (bi-zant′), 1836–1901; English writer.

be·seech (bi-sēch′), *v.t.* [BESOUGHT (-sôt′) or BESEECHED (-sēcht′), BESEECHING], [ME. *bisechen;* AS. *besecan; be-* + *secan,* to seek], 1. to ask earnestly; entreat; implore. 2. to ask for earnestly; solicit eagerly; beg. —*SYN.* see **beg.**

be·seem (bi-sēm′), *v.i.* [ME. *beseme;* see BE- & SEEM], to be suitable or appropriate (to): what appears to be the direct object of the verb (e.g., *him* in "it ill beseems him") is really the indirect object.

be·set (bi-set′), *v.t.* [BESET, BESETTING], [ME. *bisetten;* AS. *besettan; be-* + *settan,* to set], 1. to cover or set thickly with; stud. 2. to attack from all sides; besiege. 3. to surround or hem in. —*SYN.* see **attack.**

be·set·ting (bi-set′iŋ), *adj.* [ppr. of *beset*], constantly harassing or attacking: as, a *besetting* temptation.

be·show (bi-shō′), *n.* [Am. Ind. (Makah) *bishowk*], an edible fish resembling the mackerel, found in the North Pacific.

be·shrew (bi-shrōō′), *v.t.* [ME. *bischrewen* < *be-* + *schrewen*, to curse], [Archaic], to curse: now used only as a literary archaism in mild imprecations: as, *beshrew* you.

be·side (bi-sīd′), *prep.* [ME. *bi siden* < *be-*, by + *side*], 1. by or at the side of; alongside; near; close to. 2. in comparison with: as, *beside* yours my share seems small. 3. in addition to; besides. 4. other than; aside from: as, that's *beside* the point. *adv.* besides; in addition.
 beside oneself, mad, as with fear, rage, etc.

be·sides (bi-sīdz′), *adv.* [ME. < *beside* + adv. genit. -*(e)s*], 1. in addition; as well. 2. except for that mentioned; else. 3. moreover; furthermore. *prep.* 1. in addition to; as well as. 2. other than; except.

be·siege (bi-sēj′), *v.t.* [BESIEGED (-sējd′), BESIEGING], [ME. *bisegen* < *be-* + *segen*, to lay siege to < *sege*, seat, siege; see SIEGE], 1. to hem in with armed forces, especially for a sustained attack; lay siege to. 2. to close in on; crowd around. 3. to overwhelm: as, they *besieged* us with invitations.

be·siege·ment (bi-sēj′mənt), *n.* a besieging or being besieged.

be·smear (bi-smêr′), *v.t.* [AS. *bismierwan*; see BE- & SMEAR], to smear over; bedaub; soil.

be·smirch (bi-smūrch′), *v.t.* [*be-* + *smirch*], to make dirty; soil; stain; sully.

be·som (bē′zəm), *n.* [ME. *besum*, broom, rod; AS. *besema*, rod; in pl., bundle of twigs; akin to G. *besen*; IE. base **bhas-*, **bhes-*, a bundle], 1. a broom, especially one made of twigs tied to a handle. 2. anything that cleanses: used figuratively. 3. the broom (plant).

be·sot (bi-sot′), *v.t.* [BESOTTED (-id), BESOTTING], 1. to make a sot of; stupefy or confuse, as with alcoholic drink or narcotics. 2. to make silly or foolish.

be·sot·ted (bi-sot′id), *adj.* [pp. of *besot*], 1. silly; foolish; infatuated. 2. stupefied, as with liquor.

be·sought (bi-sôt′), alternative past tense and past participle of **beseech**.

be·spake (bi-spāk′), archaic past tense of **bespeak**.

be·span·gle (bi-spaŋ′g'l), *v.t.* to cover with spangles or something like spangles.

be·spat·ter (bi-spat′ẽr), *v.t.* 1. to spatter over, as with mud; dirty by spattering; hence, 2. to blacken (one's reputation, etc.) with false charges; defame.

be·speak (bi-spēk′), *v.t.* [BESPOKE (-spōk′) or *archaic* BESPAKE (-spāk′), BESPOKEN (-spōk′'n) or BESPOKE, BESPEAKING], [ME. *bispeken*; AS. *besp(r)ecan*; see BE- & SPEAK], 1. to speak for in advance; engage beforehand; reserve: as they have *bespoken* a box at the opera. 2. to be indicative of; show: as, his charity *bespeaks* a generous nature. 3. to foreshadow; point to: as, today's events *bespeak* future tragedy. 4. [Archaic or Poetic], to speak to; address.

be·spec·ta·cled (bi-spek′ti-k'ld), *adj.* wearing spectacles; having glasses on.

be·spoke (bi-spōk′), past tense and alternative past participle of **bespeak**. *adj.* [British], 1. ordered in advance. 2. made to special order; custom-made.

be·spo·ken (bi-spōk′'n), alternative past participle of **bespeak**.

be·spread (bi-spred′), *v.t.* [BESPREAD, BESPREADING], to spread over; spread thickly.

be·sprent (bi-sprent′), *adj.* [ME. *bespreynt*, pp. of *besprengen*; AS. *besprengan*; *be-* + *sprengan*, caus. < *springan*, to spring], [Poetic], sprinkled; strewed.

be·sprin·kle (bi-spriŋ′k'l), *v.t.* to sprinkle over (*with* something).

Bess (bes), a feminine name: see **Elizabeth**.

Bes·sa·ra·bi·a (bes′ə-rā′bi-ə), *n.* a district ceded to the U.S.S.R. by Romania in 1940 and made part of the Moldavian S.S.R.

Bes·sa·ra·bi·an (bes′ə-rā′bi-ən), *adj.* of Bessarabia. *n.* a native or inhabitant of Bessarabia.

Bes·se·mer (bes′ə-mẽr), *n.* a city in central Alabama, near Birmingham: pop., 33,000.

Bes·se·mer, Sir Henry (bes′ə-mẽr), 1813–1898; English engineer and inventor; discovered Bessemer process for manufacturing steel.

Bessemer converter, a large steel retort in which Bessemer steel is made.

Bessemer process, [after Sir Henry *Bessemer*], a method of making steel by forcing a blast of air through molten iron to remove carbon and impurities.

BESSARABIA

Bessemer steel, steel made by the Bessemer process.

best (best), *adj.* [superlative of *good*], [ME. *best*, *betst*; AS. *betst*; akin to Goth. *batists*, best; IE. base **bhăd-*, good: though now the superl., *best* has no original connection with *good*], 1. most excellent; of the most excellent sort; surpassing all others. 2. most suitable, most desirable, most favorable, most profitable, etc. 3. largest: as, it took the *best* part of an hour to do this. 4. most healthy; least indisposed: as, he feels *best* in the morning. *adv.* [superlative of *well*], 1. in the most excellent manner; in the most suitable way. 2. in the highest degree; to the greatest extent. *n.* 1. people of the highest worth, ability, or reputation: as, he is among the *best* in his profession. 2. the most excellent thing, condition, circumstance, action, etc. 3. the most one can do; utmost: as, he did his *best*. 4. advantage: as, she got the *best* of her opponent. 5. finest clothes: as, dressed in her *best*. *v.t.* to defeat; excel.
 all for the best, ultimately good or fortunate, despite contrary appearances or misgivings.
 as best one can, as well as one can.
 at best, 1. under the most favorable conditions or interpretation. 2. at most.
 at one's best, in one's best mood, form, health, etc.
 get (or **have**) **the best of**, 1. to outdo. 2. to outwit.
 had best, ought to; would be prudent or wise to.
 make the best of, to utilize or adapt oneself to as well as possible.
 with the best, as ably as the most able.

be·stead (bi-sted′), *adj.* [ME. *bistad*; *bi-*, be- + *stad*, placed; ON. *staddr*, ppr. of *stethja*, to fix, place], situated; placed. *v.t.* to help; avail.

bes·tial (bes′chəl, bes′tyəl), *adj.* [ME.; OFr.; L. *bestialis* < *bestia*, beast], 1. of beasts or lower animals. 2. like a beast in qualities or behavior; brutish or savage; brutal, coarse, vile, etc.

bes·ti·al·i·ty (bes′chi-al′ə-ti, bes′ti-al′ə-ti), *n.* [*pl.* BESTIALITIES (-tiz)], 1. bestial quality, character, or behavior. 2. a bestial act or practice.

bes·tial·ize (bes′chəl-īz′, bes′tyəl-īz′), *v.t.* [BESTIALIZED (-īzd′), BESTIALIZING], to make bestial; brutalize.

bes·ti·ar·y (bes′ti-er′i), *n.* [*pl.* BESTIARIES (-iz)], [ML. *bestiarium* < L. *bestiarius*, relating to beasts < *bestia*, beast], a medieval collection of fables, allegories, and fanciful, often moralistic, stories about animals.

be·stir (bi-stūr′), *v.t.* [BESTIRRED (-stūrd′), BESTIRRING], [ME. *bistirien*; AS. *bestyrian*; see BE- & STIR, *v.*], to stir up; exert or busy (oneself).

best man, the principal attendant of the bridegroom at a wedding.

be·stow (bi-stō′), *v.t.* [ME. *bistowen*; see BE- & STOW], 1. to give or present as a gift (often with *on* or *upon*): as, he *bestows* millions on this charity. 2. to give in marriage. 3. to apply; devote: as, he *bestowed* much time on the project. 4. [Archaic], to put or place, as in storage. 5. [Archaic], to house. —*SYN.* see **give**.

be·stow·al (bi-stō′əl), *n.* a bestowing.

be·stow·ment (bi-stō′mənt), *n.* a bestowing.

be·strad·dle (bi-strad′'l), *v.t.* to straddle; bestride.

be·strew (bi-strōō′), *v.t.* [for prin. pts. see STREW], [ME. *bistrewen*; AS. *bestreowian*; see BE- & STREW], 1. to cover over (a surface); strew. 2. to scatter over or about. 3. to lie scattered over or about: as, papers *bestrewed* the streets.

be·stride (bi-strīd′), *v.t.* [for prin. pts. see STRIDE], [ME. *bestriden*; AS. *bestridan*; see BE- & STRIDE], 1. to sit on, mount, or stand over with a leg on each side. 2. to stride over or across.

be·strow (bi-strō′), *v.t.* [for prin. pts. see STROW], to bestrew.

best-sell·er (best′sel′ẽr), *n.* a book, phonograph record, etc. currently outselling most others.

be·stud (bi-stud′), *v.t.* [BESTUDDED (-id), BESTUDDING], to cover the surface of with or as with studs.

bet (bet), *n.* [prob. by apheresis < *abet*], 1. an agreement between two persons or sides that the one proved wrong about an outcome or fact will do or give a stipulated thing or pay a stipulated sum of money to the other; wager. 2. the terms of such an agreement; thing or sum thus staked. 3. the proposition about which such an agreement is made. 4. the thing or person that something is or may be thus staked on: as, this team is a good *bet*. *v.t.* [BET or BETTED (-id), BETTING], 1. to declare in or as in a bet: as, I *bet* he'll be late. 2. to stake (money, etc.) in a bet. *v.i.* to make a bet or bets (*on*, *against*, *with*); wager.
 bet a person on, to bet with a person about.
 you bet (you)! [Colloq.], certainly! yes indeed!

bet., between.

be·ta (bā′tə, bē′tə), *n.* [L.; Gr. *bēta*; Heb. *bēth*, lit., house; of Phoen. origin], 1. the second letter of the Greek alphabet (Β, β), corresponding to English *B*, *b*: see **alphabet**, table: it is often used to mark the second r series. 2. in *astronomy*, any star that is brightest in a constellation. *adj.* in *chemistry*, g the relative position of the carbon atom, a substituting atom or group of atoms is d in one of two or more isomerous organic ounds.

in (bē′tə-in), *n.* betaine.

a·ine (bē′tə-ēn′, bē′tə-in), *n.* [L. *beta*, beet; + *-ine*], crystalline basic organic compound, $(CH_3)_3NCH_2$-COO, found in the residues from the preparation of beet sugar and in other plant products.

be·take (bi-tāk′), *v.t.* [for prin. pts. see TAKE], [ME. *bitaken;* see BE- & TAKE], 1. to go (used reflexively): as, he *betook* himself to his own kingdom. 2. to apply or devote (oneself): as, *betake* yourself to your studies.

be·ta·naph·thol (bā′tə-naf′thōl, bē′tə-nap′thol), *n.* a colorless, crystalline isomer of naphthol, used in medicine as an antiseptic and parasiticide.

beta particle, one of the electrons forming beta rays.

beta rays, rays given off by radioactive substances, consisting of electrons that move with velocities varying from 30,000 to 180,000 miles per second: see also **alpha rays, gamma rays.**

beta test, a test for determining the intelligence of people who cannot read or write, first used by the United States Army in World War I: also see **alpha test.**

be·ta·tron (bā′tə-tron′) *n.* [*beta* rays + *electron*], a device used to accelerate the velocities of electrons.

be·tel (bē′t'l), *n.* [Port. < Malay *vettilai*], 1. a climbing pepper plant of Asia. 2. its leaf.

Be·tel·geuse, Be·tel·geux (bē′t'l-jōōz′, bet″'l-jooz′), *n.* [Fr. *Bételgeuse;* Ar. *bayt al jauza*, lit., house of the twins], a very large, red, first-magnitude star, largest in the constellation Orion: its diameter (200,000,000 miles) is greater than that of the earth's orbit.

betel nut, the fruit of the betel palm: in the Far East it is chewed together with a little lime and leaves of the betel (pepper) plant.

betel palm, any of a number of related tropical palms with a smooth trunk, a feathery crown of leaves, fragrant white flowers, and orange-colored, nutlike fruit: also called *areca palm.*

bête noire (bāt′ nwär′; Fr. bet′nwȧr′), [Fr., lit., black beast], a person or thing feared, disliked, and avoided.

beth (bāth, beth, bāz), *n.* [Heb. *bēth;* see BETA], the second letter of the Hebrew alphabet (ב), corresponding to English *B, b:* minus the dot (ב) it is often called *veth* and corresponds to English *V, v:* see **alphabet,** table.

Beth·a·ny (beth′ə-ni), *n.* an ancient town near Jerusalem, on the Mount of Olives: see **Judea,** map.

Beth·el (beth′əl), *n.* an ancient village in central Palestine, near Jerusalem: see **Judea,** map.

beth·el (beth′əl), *n.* [Heb. *bēth 'ēl*, house of God], 1. a spot where God is worshiped, marked by a pillar: Gen. 28:17–19. 2. a holy place. 3. a church or other place of worship for seamen. 4. in England, a place of worship for Protestants belonging to any church except the Anglican.

Be·thes·da (bə-thez′də), *n.* [LGr. *Bethesda;* Aram. *bēth 'esda*, lit., house of mercy], 1. in the *Bible*, a pool at Jerusalem, supposed to have healing properties: John 5:2. 2. a chapel or holy place. 3. a town in central Maryland, near Washington, D.C.: pop., 57,000.

be·think (bi-thiŋk′), *v.t.* [BETHOUGHT (-thôt′), BETHINKING], [ME. *bithenchen;* AS. *bethencan; be-* + *thencan;* see THINK], to think of, consider, or recollect (generally used reflexively). *v.i.* [Archaic], to ponder.

Beth·le·hem (beth′li-əm, beth′li-hem′), *n.* 1. an ancient town in Judea: birthplace of Jesus: see **Judea,** map. 2. a town in western Jordan on the same site: pop., 9,100. 3. a city in eastern Pennsylvania: pop., 75,000.

Beth·mann-Holl·weg, The·o·bald von (tā′ô-bält′ fôn bāt′män-hōl′vākh), 1856–1921; chancellor of Germany (1909–1917).

Beth·nal Green (beth′nəl), a borough of London.

be·thought (bi-thôt′), past tense and past participle of **bethink.**

be·tide (bi-tīd′), *v.i.* [BETIDED (-id), BETIDING], [ME. *betiden* < *be-* + AS. *tidan*, to happen < *tid*, time; see TIDE], to happen. *v.t.* to happen to; befall.

be·times (bi-tīmz′), *adv.* [*be-* + *time*, with adv. genit. *-(e)s*], 1. early: as, he awoke *betimes*. 2. promptly; quickly. 3. before it is too late.

‡bê·tise (be′tēz′), *n.* [Fr. < *bête*, beast; LL. *besta;* L. *bestia*], a foolish act, remark, suggestion, etc.; absurdity.

be·to·ken (bi-tō′kən), *v.t.* [ME. *betocnen;* AS. *betacnian; be-* + *tacnian*, to mark < *tacen*, token; see TOKEN], 1. to be a token or sign of; foreshow. 2. to indicate; denote.

‡bé·ton (bā′tōn′), *n.* [Fr., concrete < L. *bitumen;* see BITUMEN], concrete made of gravel, sand, and cement.

bet·o·ny (bet′ə-ni), *n.* [*pl.* BETONIES (-niz)], [AS. *betonice;* LL. *betonica*, altered < L. *vettonica*, after the *Vettones*, an ancient tribe in Gaul], any of a number of related plants of the mint family, having spikes or whorls of white, yellow, red, or purple flowers.

be·tray (bi-trā′), *v.t.* [ME. *betrain, betrayen* < *be-* + *traien*, betray; OFr. *traïr;* L. *tradere*, to hand over, deliver], 1. to help the enemy of (one's country, cause, etc.); be a traitor to. 2. to break faith with; fail to meet the hopes of: as, he *betrayed* my trust in him. 3. to deceive; lead astray; victimize. 4. to seduce and fail to marry. 5. to reveal unknowingly or against one's own wishes: as, his face *betrays* his fear. 6. to reveal or show signs of; indicate: as, the house *betrays* its age. 7. to disclose (secret information, confidential plans, etc.). —*SYN.* see **deceive, reveal.**

be·tray·al (bi-trā′əl), *n.* 1. a betraying. 2. the fact or state of being betrayed.

be·troth (bi-trôth′, bi-trōth′), *v.t.* [BETROTHED (-trôtht′, -trōthd′), BETROTHING], [ME. *bitreouthen, bitrouthen* < *be-* + *treuthe* < AS. *treowth*, truth], 1. to promise in marriage: as, her father has *betrothed* her to his friend. 2. [Archaic], to promise to marry.

be·troth·al (bi-trôth′əl, bi-trō′thəl), *n.* a betrothing or being betrothed; mutual pledge to marry; engagement.

be·trothed (bi-trôtht′, bi-trōthd′), *adj.* [pp. of *betroth*], engaged to be married. *n.* a betrothed person.

Bet·sy (bet′si), a feminine name: see **Elizabeth.**

bet·ted (bet′id), alternative past tense and past participle of **bet.**

bet·ter (bet′ẽr), *adj.* [comparative of *good*], [ME. *bettere, betere;* AS. *betera;* see BEST], 1. more excellent; of a more excellent sort; surpassing another or others. 2. more suitable, more desirable, more favorable, more profitable, etc. 3. larger: as, it cost the *better* part of my pay. 4. improved in health or disposition as compared to an earlier state: as, he has been ill, but now he is *better*. *adv.* [comparative of *well*], 1. in a more excellent manner; in a more suitable way. 2. in a higher degree; to a greater extent; more: as, *better* than a pound. *n.* 1. a person superior in authority, position, etc.: as, obey your *betters*. 2. a more excellent thing, condition, circumstance, action, etc. 3. advantage: as, I got the *better* of my rival. *v.t.* 1. to outdo; surpass. 2. to make better; improve. *v.i.* to become better. —*SYN.* see **improve.**

better off, 1. in a better situation or condition. 2. having more income, wealth, etc.

for the better, leading to a more favorable situation.

get (or **have**) **the better of,** 1. to outdo. 2. to outwit.

go (a person) **one better,** [Slang], to outdo; surpass.

had better, ought to; would be prudent or wise to.

think better of, 1. to think about again and reach a different conclusion; reconsider. 2. to think more highly of.

bet·ter (bet′ẽr), *n.* one who bets: also spelled **bettor.**

better half, [Colloq.], 1. a wife. 2. a husband: occasionally so used.

bet·ter·ment (bet′ẽr-mənt), *n.* 1. a bettering; improvement. 2. in *law*, an improvement that increases the value of property and is more extensive than mere repairs.

Bet·ter·ton, Thomas (bet′ẽr-tən), 1635?–1710; English actor and theatrical manager.

bet·ting (bet′iŋ), *n.* the act or practice of making bets; wagering.

bet·tor (bet′ẽr), *n.* one who bets: also spelled **better.**

Bet·ty (bet′i), a feminine name: see **Elizabeth.**

bet·u·la·ceous (bech′ə-lā′shəs), *adj.* [L. *betula*, birch (< Gaul. *betulla* < **betu-*, bitumen: said by Pliny to be so named because the Celts obtained tar by carbonization of the wood); + *-aceous*], belonging to the birch family of trees, which comprise hornbeams, ironwoods, hazelnuts, and birches.

be·tween (bi-twēn′), *prep.* [ME. *betwenen* & *betwen(e);* AS. *be . . . tweonum* & *be . . . tweon*, orig. as in *be sæm tweonum*, lit., by seas twain < *be*, by + *tweon(um)* < *twegen, twa*, two; see TWAIN], 1. in or through the space that separates (two things). 2. in or of the time, amount, or degree that separates (two things); intermediate to: as, *between* blue and green. 3. separating. 4. connecting; relating: as, a bond *between* friends. 5. along a course that connects; from one to the other of: as, the road runs *between* here and there. 6. by the action of both of: as, *between* them they landed the fish. 7. in the combined possession of: as, the men had fifty dollars *between* them. 8. to the exclusion of all but both of: as, they divided it *between* them. 9. one or the other of: as, choose *between* love and duty. 10. as a consequence of the combined effect of: as, *between* her job and her studies she has no time for fun. *adv.* 1. in an intermediate space, position, or function. 2. in an intermediate time; in the interval. Abbreviated **bet.**

between ourselves, in confidence; as a secret: also **between you and me, between you, me, and the gatepost.**

in between, 1. in an intermediate position. 2. in the midst of; surrounded by.

be·twixt (bi-twikst′), *prep. & adv.* [ME. *bitwix, bitwyx;* AS. *betwix, betweochs* < *be-* + a form related to *twegen, twa*, two], between: now archaic except in the phrase *betwixt and between*, in an intermediate position, neither altogether one nor altogether the other.

Beu·lah (bū′lə), [Heb. *be 'ūlāh*, married], a feminine name. *n.* 1. the land of Israel: Isa. 62:4. 2. in Bunyan's *Pilgrim's Progress*, a country of peace and rest near the end of life's journey: short for *Land of Beulah*.

Bev, bev (bev), *n.* [*pl.* BEV, BEV], [*b*illion *e*lectron-*v*olts], a unit of energy equal to one billion electron-volts.

bev·a·tron (bev'ə-tron') *n.* [< *bev* + *-tron*, as in *cyclotron*], a synchrotron for accelerating protons to an energy level in excess of one billion electron-volts.

bev·el (bev''l), *n.* [prob. < OFr. **bevel*], 1. a tool consisting of a rule with a movable arm, used in measuring or marking angles and in fixing surfaces at an angle: also **bevel square.** 2. an angle other than a right angle. 3. sloping part or surface, as the angled edge of plate glass. *v.t.* [BEVELED or BEVELLED (-'ld), BEVELING or BEVELLING], to cut to an angle other than a right angle. *v.i.* to slope at an angle. *adj.* sloped; beveled.

BEVEL

bevel gear, a gearwheel meshed with another so that their shafts are at an angle of less than 180°.

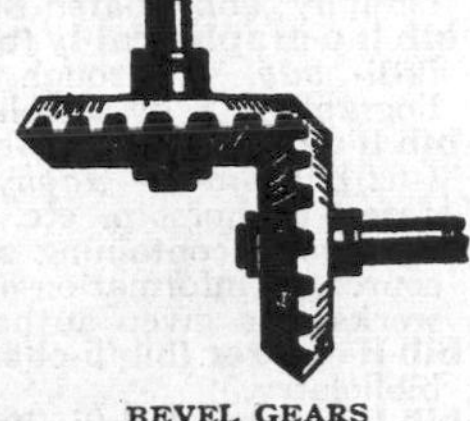

BEVEL GEARS

bev·er·age (bev'rij, bev'ẽr-ij), *n.* [ME.; OFr. *bevrage* < *bevre;* L. *bibere;* see IMBIBE], any drink, as milk, coffee, lemonade, etc.

Bev·er·idge, Albert Jeremiah (bev'ẽr-ij), 1862–1927; American historian and statesman.

Bev·er·idge, Sir **William Henry** (bev'ẽr-ij, bev'rij), 1879–1963; English economist.

Bev·er·ley, Bev·er·ly (bev'ẽr-li), [lit., beaver lea; ME. *bever* (see BEAVER, the animal) + *ley* (see LEA)], a feminine name.

Bev·er·ly (bev'ẽr-li), *n.* a city in northeastern Massachusetts: pop., 36,000.

Beverly Hills, a city in California: pop., 31,000: suburb of Los Angeles.

bev·y (bev'i), *n.* [*pl.* BEVIES (-iz)], [? < OFr. *bevee, buvee,* drink, drinking; ? hence, a drinking group], 1. a group, especially of girls or women. 2. a flock: now chiefly of quail. —*SYN.* see **group.**

be·wail (bi-wāl'), *v.t. & v.i.* [see BE- & WAIL], to wail (over); weep (for); lament; mourn; complain (about).

be·ware (bi-wâr'), *v.i. & v.t.* [BEWARED (-wârd'), BEWARING], [associated with *be* + *ware* (see WARE, WARY); but prob. < AS. *bewarian,* to keep watch, guard; *be-* + *warian,* to watch, be wary], to be wary or careful (of); be on one's guard (against).

be·wil·der (bi-wil'dẽr), *v.t.* [*be-* + *wilder* < AS. *wilde,* wild], 1. to confuse hopelessly; befuddle; puzzle. 2. [Archaic], to cause (a person) to be lost in a wilderness. —*SYN.* see **puzzle.**

be·wil·dered (bi-wil'dẽrd), *adj.* [pp. of *bewilder*], lost in perplexity; completely confused; puzzled.

be·wil·der·ment (bi-wil'dẽr-mənt), *n.* 1. the fact or condition of being bewildered. 2. a confusion; jumble.

be·witch (bi-wich'), *v.t.* [ME. *biwicchen* < *be-* + *wicchen;* AS. *wiccian* < *wicca,* wizard, *wicce,* witch], 1. to use witchcraft or magic on; cast a spell over. 2. to attract and delight irresistibly; enchant; fascinate; charm.

be·witch·er·y (bi-wich'ẽr-i), *n.* bewitchment.

be·witch·ing (bi-wich'iŋ), *adj.* [ppr. of *bewitch*], enchanting; fascinating.

be·witch·ment (bi-wich'mənt), *n.* 1. power to bewitch. 2. a bewitching or being bewitched; spell.

be·wray (bi-rā'), *v.t.* [ME. *biwraien; be-* + AS. *wregan,* to inform], [Archaic], to divulge; reveal; betray.

bey (bā), *n.* [Turk. *bey, beg*], 1. the governor of a minor Turkish district or province. 2. a Turkish title of respect or rank. 3. the native ruler of Tunis.

Beyle, Ma·rie Hen·ri (mȧ'rē' än'rē' bāl'), see **Stendhal.**

Bey·og·lu (bā'ə-lōō', bā'ōkh-lōō'), *n.* the modern section of Istanbul, Turkey: also called *Pera.*

be·yond (bi-yond'), *prep.* [ME. *bigeonden;* AS. *begeondan* < *be-* + *geond,* yonder, across], 1. on or to the far side of; farther on than; past. 2. farther on in time than; later than. 3. outside the reach, possibility, or understanding of: as, *beyond* help, *beyond* belief. 4. more or better than; in addition to; exceeding: as, he says nothing *beyond* what we already know. *adv.* farther out; farther away.

the beyond, 1. whatever is beyond or far away. 2. whatever follows death: often **the great beyond.**

Bey·routh (bā'rōōt, bā-rōōt'), *n.* Beirut.

bez·ant, bez·zant (bez''nt, bə-zant'), *n.* [ME. *besant;* OFr. *besan, besant;* L. *byzantius* (*nummus*), Byzantine (coin) < *Byzantium*], 1. a gold coin issued in Byzantium. 2. any of various gold and silver coins used i[n] Europe c. 450–1450 A.D. 3. in *architecture & heraldry,* a circular figure representing such a coin.

bez antler (bez, bāz), [< OFr. *bes-* < L. *bis,* twice; + *antler*], the second branch from the base of a deer's horn: also called *bay antler.*

bez·el, bez·il (bez''l), *n.* [OFr. *bisel* (Fr. *biseau*), sloping edge, bias], 1. a sloping surface, as the cutting edge of a chisel. 2. the slanting faces of a cut jewel, especially those of the upper half. 3. the groove and flange holding a gem or a watch crystal in place.

Bé·ziers (bā'zyā'), *n.* a city in southern France: pop., 65,000.

be·zique (bə-zēk'), *n.* [Fr. *bésique,* earlier *basseque;* cf. It. *bazzica,* card game], a card game resembling pinochle, but using a double, triple, or quadruple deck of all the cards above the six.

be·zoar (bē'zôr, bē'zōr), *n.* [Fr. *bézoard;* Sp. *bezoar;* Ar. *bāzahr;* Per. *pādzahr; pād,* expelling + *zahr,* poison], a hard mass deposited around a foreign substance, found in the stomach or intestines of some animals and formerly thought to be a remedy for poisoning.

bf, b. f., in *printing,* boldface.

B/F, in *bookkeeping,* brought forward.

B. F., 1. Bachelor of Finance. 2. Bachelor of Forestry.

B.F.A., Bachelor of Fine Arts.

bg., [*pl.* BGS.], bag.

B-girl (bē'gũrl'), *n.* [< *bar girl*], a woman employed by a bar to entice men into buying drinks freely.

Bha·ga·vad-Gi·ta (bug'ə-vəd-gē'tä), *n.* [Sans. *Bhagavadgītā,* Song of the Blessed One], a philosophical dialogue that is a sacred Hindu text, found in the *Mahabharata,* one of the ancient Sanskrit epics.

bhang (baŋ), *n.* [Hind. < Sans. *bhangā,* hemp], 1. the Indian hemp plant. 2. its dried leaves and seed capsules, which have narcotic and intoxicating properties. Also spelled **bang.**

Bha·rat (bur'ut), *n.* Republic of India: Hindi name.

bhees·ty, bhees·tie (bēs'ti), *n.* [Hind. *bhīstī* < Per. *bihishtī,* lit., one from paradise], in India, a water carrier, especially for troops or a household.

Bho·pal, Bho·pol (bō-päl', bō-pôl'), *n.* 1. the capital of Madhya Pradesh, a state of central India: pop., 225,000. 2. a former state of central India.

Bhu·tan (bōō-tän'), *n.* a state in the Himalaya Mountains, bounded by Tibet, Sikkim, and India: area, 18,000 sq. mi.; pop., 640,000.

Bhu·tan·ese (bōō'tən-ēz'), *n.* 1. [*pl.* BHUTANESE], a native or inhabitant of Bhutan. 2. the language of the Bhutanese. *adj.* of Bhutan, its people, or their language.

bi- (bī), [L. *bi-* < *bis,* twice], a prefix used to form adjectives, adverbs, verbs, and nouns, and meaning: 1. *having two,* as in *biangular, bicapsular.* 2. *doubly, on both sides, in two ways* or *directions,* as in *biconvex, bilingual.* 3. *coming, happening,* or *issued every two,* as in *biennial, biweekly.* 4. *coming, happening,* or *issued twice during every,* as in *bimonthly, biyearly:* often replaced by *semi-* or *half-,* to avoid confusion with sense 3. 5. *using two* or *both,* as in *bilabial, bimanual.* 6. *joining two, combining* or *involving two,* as in *bilateral, bipartisan.* 7. in *botany & zoology, twice, doubly, in pairs,* as in *bifurcate, bipinnate.* 8. in *chemistry, a*) *having twice as many atoms or chemical equivalents for a definite weight of the other constituent of the compound,* as in sodium *bicarbonate* ($NaHCO_3$, as distinguished from sodium carbonate, Na_2CO_3). *b*) in organic compounds, *having a combination of two radicals of the same composition,* as in *biphenyl,* $(C_6H_5)_2$: usually replaced by *di-* except in the names of acid salts, as sodium *bisulfate,* etc. Also, before a vowel, **bin-;** before *c* or *s,* **bis-.**

bi- (bī), bio-.

Bi, in *chemistry,* bismuth.

Bia·lik, Cha·im Nach·man (khä'im nȧkh'män byä'lik), 1873–1934; Hebrew poet, translator, and editor, born in Russia.

Bia·lys·tok (byä-lis'tôk), *n.* a city in Poland: pop., 121,000: Russian name, *Belostok.*

Bian·co, Mon·te (môn'te byäŋ'kô), Mont Blanc.

bi·an·gu·lar (bī-aŋ'gyə-lẽr), *adj.* having two angles.

bi·an·nu·al (bī-an'yōō-əl), *adj.* coming twice a year; semiannual: see also **biennial.**

bi·an·nu·al·ly (bī-an'yōō-əl-i), *adv.* twice a year.

bi·an·nu·late (bī-an'yoo-lit, bī-an'yoo-lāt'), *adj.* in *zoology,* having two rings or bands of color, etc.

Biar·ritz (byȧ'rēts'; Eng. bē'ə-rits), *n.* a resort in southwestern France, on the Bay of Biscay: pop., 22,000.

bi·as (bī'əs), *n.* [Fr. *biais,* a slope, slant], 1. a slanting or diagonal line, cut or sewn in cloth. 2. a mental leaning or inclination; partiality; prejudice. 3. in *bowling, a*) the bulge or weight in the side of the ball that causes it to roll in a curve. *b*) this curve or tendency to curve. *c*) the force causing this. 4. in *radio,* the fixed voltage applied to an electrode, usually with the

age as reference. *adj.* slanting; diagonal. , 1. diagonally. 2. awry. *v.t.* [BIASED or əst), BIASING or BIASSING], 1. to cause to have nfluence; prejudice. 2. in *radio*, to apply a (an electrode). —*SYN.* see **prejudice.**
ne bias, diagonally; obliquely; specifically, cut or wed diagonally across the weave: said of cloth.
u·ric·u·lar (bī'ô-rik'yə-lẽr), *adj.* in *anatomy*, 1. bi-uriculate. 2. of the external opening of both ears.
·au·ric·u·late (bī'ô-rik'yə-lit), *adj.* [*bi-* + *auriculate;* see AURICLE], 1. in *anatomy*, having two auricles, as the heart of a mammal, bird, etc. 2. in *botany*, having two earlike parts, as some leaves.
bi·ax·i·al (bī-ak'si-əl), *adj.* having two axes, as some crystals.
bib (bib), *v.t. & v.i.* [BIBBED (bibd), BIBBING], [ME. < *bibben*, to drink; L. *bibere*, to drink], to drink; imbibe; tipple. *n.* 1. an apronlike cloth for tying around a child's neck at meals. 2. the upper part of an apron.
Bib., 1. Bible. 2. Biblical.
bib and tucker, [Colloq.], clothes.
bi·bas·ic (bī-bās'ik), *adj.* [Rare], in *chemistry*, dibasic.
bibb (bib), *n.* [< *bib*, *n.:* so named because in position it resembles a child's bib], 1. a bibcock. 2. a wooden bracket supporting the trestletrees of a ship's mast.
bib·ber (bib'ẽr), *n.* a person who bibs; drinker; toper.
bib·cock (bib'kok'), *n.* [*bib* + *cock:* from the position of the nozzle], a faucet whose nozzle is bent downward.
‡bi·be·lot (bēb'lō'; Eng. bib'lō), *n.* [Fr.; OFr. *beubelot* < *belbel*, a toy; see BAUBLE], a small object whose value lies in its beauty or rarity.
bi-bi·va·lent (bī'bī-vā'lənt, bī-biv'ə-lənt), *adj.* in *chemistry*, separating into two bivalent ions: said of electrolytes.
Bibl., bibl., 1. Biblical. 2. bibliographical.
Bi·ble (bī'b'l), *n.* [ME. & OFr. *bible* < L. *biblia* < Gr. *biblia*, collection of writings, pl. of *biblion*, little book, dim. of *biblos*, papyrus bark < Egypt.], 1. the sacred book of Christianity; Old Testament and New Testament: the Roman Catholic (Douay) Bible also includes much of the Apocrypha. 2. the sacred book of Judaism; Old Testament. 3. any collection or book of writings sacred to a religion: as, the Koran is the Moslem *Bible*. 4. [b-], any book regarded as authoritative or official. Abbreviated **Bib., B.** See also **Authorized Version, Revised Standard Version, Douay Bible, Vulgate, Septuagint, Apocrypha.**

BOOKS OF THE BIBLE

(Names used in the Douay Bible, when different, are in parentheses.)

Old Testament

Genesis	Proverbs
Exodus	Ecclesiastes
Leviticus	Song of Solomon (Canticle of Canticles)
Numbers	Isaiah (Isaias)
Deuteronomy	Jeremiah (Jeremias)
Joshua (Josue)	Lamentations
Judges	Ezekiel (Ezechiel)
Ruth	Daniel
I Samuel (I Kings)	Hosea (Osee)
II Samuel (II Kings)	Joel
I Kings (III Kings)	Amos
II Kings (IV Kings)	Obadiah (Abdias)
I Chronicles (I Paralipomenon)	Jonah (Jonas)
II Chronicles (II Paralipomenon)	Micah (Micheas)
Ezra (I Esdras)	Nahum
Nehemiah (II Esdras)	Habakkuk (Habacuc)
Esther	Zephaniah (Sophonias)
Job	Haggai (Aggeus)
Psalms	Zechariah (Zacharias)
	Malachi (Malachias)

Old Testament Apocrypha

I Esdras (III Esdras)	Additions to Daniel, including the Song of the Three Holy Children, the Story of Susanna, and the Idol Bel and the Dragon
II Esdras (IV Esdras)	Prayer of Manasses
Tobit (Tobias)	I Maccabees (I Machabees)
Judith	II Maccabees (II Machabees)
Additions to Esther	
Wisdom of Solomon	
Ecclesiasticus	
Baruch	

New Testament

atthew	Ephesians	Hebrews
rk	Philippians	James
	Colossians	I Peter
	I Thessalonians	II Peter
ts	II Thessalonians	I John
	I Timothy	II John
ians	II Timothy	III John
ians	Titus	Jude
	Philemon	Revelation (Apocalypse)

oined c. 1925 by H. L. Mencken], those regions of the United States, particularly areas in the South, where fundamentalist beliefs prevail and Christian clergymen are especially influential.
bible paper, a thin, strong, opaque paper used for many Bibles, dictionaries, etc.
Bib·li·cal, bib·li·cal (bib'li-k'l), *adj.* 1. of or in the Bible. 2. in keeping with or according to the Bible. Abbreviated **Bib., Bibl., bibl.**
Bib·li·cist (bib'li-sist), *n.* 1. a person who takes the words of the Bible literally. 2. an expert on the Bible; specialist in Biblical literature.
bib·li·o- (bib'li-ō, bib'li-ə), [< Gr. *biblion*, a book], a combining form meaning: 1. *book, of books*, as in *bibliophile*. 2. *of the Bible.*
bib·li·o·film (bib'li-ə-film'), *n.* a kind of microfilm used especially for reproducing rare or fragile books.
bibliog., bibliography.
bib·li·o·graph (bib'li-ə-graf', bib'li-ə-gräf'), *n.* a bibliographer.
bib·li·og·ra·pher (bib'li-og'rə-fẽr), *n.* [Gr. *bibliographos*, writer of books < *biblion*, a book + *graphos* < *graphein*, to write], an expert in bibliography.
bib·li·o·graph·ic (bib'li-ə-graf'ik), *adj.* bibliographical.
bib·li·o·graph·i·cal (bib'li-ə-graf'i-k'l), *adj.* of bibliography: abbreviated **Bibl., bibl.**
bib·li·o·graph·i·cal·ly (bib'li-ə-graf'i-k'l-i, bib'li-ə-graf'ik-li), *adv.* 1. through the use or in the style of a bibliography. 2. by a bibliographer.
bib·li·og·ra·phy (bib'li-og'rə-fi), *n.* [*pl.* BIBLIOGRAPHIES (-fiz)], [*biblio-* + *-graphy*], 1. the study of the editions, dates, authorship, etc. of books and other writings. 2. a book containing such information. 3. a list of sources of information on a given subject, or of literary works of a given author, publisher, etc.
bib·li·ol·a·ter (bib'li-ol'ə-tẽr), *n.* a person who manifests bibliolatry.
bib·li·ol·a·try (bib'li-ol'ə-tri), *n.* [*biblio-* + *-latry*], excessive reverence or enthusiasm for a literal interpretation of the Bible.
bib·li·o·man·cy (bib'li-ə-man'si), *n.* [*pl.* BIBLIOMANCIES (-siz)], [*biblio-* + *-mancy*], prediction based on a Bible verse or literary passage chosen at random.
bib·li·o·ma·ni·a (bib'li-ə-mā'ni-ə), *n.* [*biblio-* + *mania*], a craze for collecting books, especially rare ones.
bib·li·op·e·gy (bib'li-op'ə-ji), *n.* [< *biblio-* + Gr. *pēgia* < *pēgnynai*, to fasten, bind], the art of bookbinding.
bib·li·o·phil (bib'li-ə-fil'), *n.* a bibliophile.
bib·li·o·phile (bib'li-ə-fīl'), *n.* [*biblio-* + *-phile*], 1. a person who loves or admires books, especially for their style of binding, printing, etc. 2. a collector of books.
bib·li·oph·i·lism (bib'li-of'ə-liz'm), *n.* [< *bibliophile* + *-ism*], love for or collecting of books.
bib·li·o·pole (bib'li-ə-pōl'), *n.* [L. *bibliopola;* Gr. *bibliopōlēs* < *biblion*, a book + *pōlein*, to sell], a bookseller, especially one dealing in rare works.
bib·li·o·pol·ic (bib'li-ə-pol'ik), *adj.* of or characteristic of a bibliopole or bibliopoles.
bib·li·op·o·ly (bib'li-op'ə-li), *n.* [< *bibliopole*], bookselling.
bib·li·o·the·ca (bib'li-ə-thē'kə), *n.* [L.; Gr. *bibliothēkē*, library, bookcase < *biblion*, a book + *thēkē* < *tithenai*, to place], 1. a library; book collection. 2. a bookseller's catalogue. 3. [Obs.], the Bible.
Bib·list (bib'list, bī'blist), *n.* 1. a Biblicist. 2. a person who believes that the Bible presents the only true religious faith.
bib·u·lous (bib'yoo-ləs), *adj.* [L. *bibulus* < *bibere*, to drink], 1. highly absorbent. 2. addicted to alcoholic liquor. 3. drunk.
bi·cam·er·al (bī-kam'ẽr-əl), *adj.* [< *bi-* + L. *camera*, a vault, chamber], made up of or having two legislative chambers: as, Congress is a *bicameral* legislature.
bi·cap·su·lar (bī-kap'syoo-lẽr), *adj.* in *botany*, 1. having two capsules. 2. having a capsule with two cells.
bi·car·bon·ate (bī-kär'bə-nit, bī-kär'bə-nāt'), *n.* [*bi-* + *carbonate*], an acid salt of carbonic acid containing the radical HCO_3.
bicarbonate of soda, sodium bicarbonate; baking soda: abbreviated **bicarb.**
bice (bīs), *n.* [ME. *bis, bys;* OFr. *bis, bise*, dusky, dark], 1. a grayish blue, duller than azure. 2. a grayish-blue pigment made from smalt or azurite. 3. loosely, a green color or pigment.
bi·cen·te·nar·y (bī-sen'tə-ner'i, bī'sen-ten'ẽr-i), *n.* [*pl.* BICENTENARIES (-iz)], [*bi-* + *centenary*], 1. a period of 200 years. 2. a bicentennial. *adj.* 1. of a period of 200 years. 2. of a bicentennial.
bi·cen·ten·ni·al (bī'sen-ten'i-əl), *adj.* [*bi-* + *centennial*], 1. happening once in a period of 200 years. 2. lasting for 200 years. *n.* 1. a 200th year of existence or duration; 200th anniversary. 2. the celebration of this.
bi·ceph·a·lous (bī-sef'ə-ləs), *adj.* [*bi-* + *cephalous*], two-headed.
bi·ceps (bī'seps), *n.* [*pl.* BICEPSES (-iz)], [L. < *bis*, two + *caput*, head], 1. a muscle having two heads, or points of origin; especially, the large muscle in the front of the upper arm or the corresponding muscle at the back of the thigh. 2. loosely, strength or muscular development, especially of the arm.

bi·chlo·ride (bī-klôr′īd, bī-klō′rid), *n.* 1. a binary compound containing two atoms of chlorine for each atom of another element; dichloride. 2. bichloride of mercury.
bichloride of mercury, a poisonous compound, $HgCl_2$, used as a disinfectant: also called *corrosive sublimate.*
bi·chro·mate (bī-krō′māt, bī-krō′mit), *n.* [*bi-* + *chromate*], a dichromate. *v.t.* (bī-krō′māt), [BICHROMATED (-id), BICHROMATING], to treat or mix with a bichromate.
bi·cip·i·tal (bī-sip′ə-t'l), *adj.* [< L. *biceps, bicipitis;* see BICEPS], 1. with two heads or points of origin, as a biceps muscle. 2. of a biceps.
bick·er (bik′ẽr), *v.i.* [ME. *bikeren* < ON. *bikkja* + freq. suffix *-er;* cf. Norw. *bikla,* of same origin, sense, and formation], 1. to have a petty quarrel; wrangle; squabble. 2. to make quick, rippling noises or movements; gurgle; patter. 3. to flicker, twinkle, etc., as a light. *n.* a bickering; petty quarrel.
Bi·col (bi-kōl′), *n.* Bikol.
bi·col·or (bī′kul′ẽr), *adj.* [L. < *bis,* two + *color*], of two colors.
bi·col·ored (bī′kul′ẽrd), *adj.* bicolor.
bi·con·cave (bī-kon′kāv, bī-koŋ′kāv, bī′kon-kāv′), *adj.* concave on both surfaces.
bi·con·vex (bī-kon′veks, bī′kon-veks′), *adj.* convex on both surfaces.
bi·corn (bī′kôrn), *adj.* [L. *bicornis* < *bis,* twice + *cornu,* horn], 1. having two horns. 2. crescent-shaped.
bi·cor·nu·ate (bī-kôr′nū-it), *adj.* bicorn.
bi·cor·po·ral (bī-kôr′pẽr-əl), *adj.* having two bodies or main parts.
bi·cor·po·re·al (bī′kôr-pôr′i-əl, bī′kôr-pō′ri-əl), *adj.* bicorporal.
bi·cron (bī′kron, bik′ron), *n.* [*bi*llion + mi*cron*], one billionth (.000,000,001) of a meter: symbol, $\mu\mu$.
bi·cus·pid (bī-kus′pid), *adj.* [< *bi-* + L. *cuspis,* pointed end], having two points: as, a *bicuspid* tooth. *n.* any of eight adult teeth with two-pointed crowns; premolar tooth. Abbreviated **B., b.**
bi·cus·pi·date (bī-kus′pi-dāt′), *adj.* bicuspid.
bicuspid valve, the valve between the left auricle and the left ventricle of the heart: also called *mitral valve.*
bi·cy·cle (bī′si-k'l), *n.* [Fr. < *bi-* + Gr. *kyklos,* a wheel], a vehicle consisting of a tubular metal frame mounted on two large, wire-spoked wheels, one behind the other, and equipped with handle bars and a saddlelike seat: it is propelled by foot pedals or, if it is a motor bicycle, by a small gasoline motor. *v.i. & v.t.* [BICYCLED (-k'ld), BICYCLING], to ride or travel on a bicycle.
bi·cy·clic (bī-sī′klik, bī-sik′lik), *adj.* of or forming two cycles, circles, etc.
bi·cyc·lic (bī-sik′lik, bī′sik-lik), *adj.* of or like a bicycle.
bi·cy·cli·cal (bī-sī′kli-k'l), *adj.* made up of two cycles; bicyclic.
bi·cy·clist (bī′si-klist), *n.* a person who rides a bicycle.
bi·cyc·u·lar (bī-sik′yoo-lẽr), *adj.* of bicycles; bicyclic.
bid (bid), *v.t.* [BADE (bad) or BID or *archaic* BAD, BIDDEN (bid′'n) or BID, BIDDING], [a fusion of two verbs: ME. *bidden,* to pray, beg, command (AS. *biddan*) & ME. *beden,* to offer, announce, command (AS. *beodan*)], 1. to command or ask: as, do as you are *bidden.* 2. [past tense & pp. BID], to offer or propose (a certain amount) as the price or fee for. 3. to declare; say; tell: as, *bid* defiance to your enemies. 4. [Archaic or Dial.], to invite. 5. [Colloq.], to offer membership to: as, the fraternity may *bid* five new men. 6. [past tense & pp. BID], in *card games,* to state (the number of tricks or points one expects to take) and declare (a suit or no trump). *v.i.* [past tense & pp. BID], to make a bid. *n.* 1. a bidding; offer; proposal. 2. an amount, etc. offered or proposed. 3. an attempt or try (*for* something). 4. [Colloq.], an invitation, especially to become a member. 5. in *cards, a*) a bidding. *b*) the number of tricks or points stated. *c*) a player's turn to bid.
bid fair, to seem likely (to be or do something).
bid in, at an auction, to bid more than the best offer in an attempt to raise the final purchasing price.
bid up, to raise the amount bid, as in an auction or card game.
bid (bid), obsolete past participle of **bide.**
bi·dar·ka (bī-där′kə), *n.* [< Russ. *baidarka,* dim. of *baidara,* canoe, coracle], a sealskin-covered canoe used by Eskimos of Alaska.
bi·dar·kee (bī-där′kē), *n.* a bidarka.
bid·da·ble (bid′ə-b'l), *adj.* 1. obedient; docile. 2. worth bidding on: as, a *biddable* bridge hand.
Bid·de·ford (bid′ə-fẽrd), *n.* a city in southwestern Maine: pop., 19,000.
bid·den (bid′'n), alternative past participle of **bid.** *adj.* invited.
bid·den (bid′'n), obsolete past participle of **bide.**
bid·der (bid′ẽr), *n.* a person who bids, as in a card game or auction.
bid·ding (bid′iŋ), *n.* 1. a command or request. 2. an invitation or summons. 3. the bids or the making of bids in a card game or auction.
at the bidding of, obedient to; at the disposal of.
do the bidding of, to be obedient to; carry out the orders of.
Bid·dle, Francis (bid′'l), 1886– ; American lawyer; attorney-general of the United States (1941–1945).
Biddle, John, 1615–1662; English theologian; founder of English Unitarianism.
Biddle, Nicholas, 1786–1844; American financier.
bid·dy (bid′i), *n.* [*pl.* BIDDIES (-iz)], [< *chickabiddy*], a chicken, especially a hen.
bide (bīd), *v.i.* [BODE (bōd) or BIDED (-id) or BADE (bad), BIDED, BIDING; *obs.* past tense BAD, pp. BID, BIDEN, BIDDEN (bid′'n)], [ME. *biden;* AS. *bidan,* to stay, wait, expect], [Archaic or Dial.], 1. to stay; continue. 2. to dwell; reside. 3. to wait. *v.t.* to endure.
bide one's time, to wait patiently for an opportunity.
bi·den·tate (bī-den′tāt), *adj.* [*bi-* + *dentate*], having two teeth or toothlike parts.
bi·det (bi-dā′), *n.* [Fr., orig., a pony < ?: from straddling stance assumed by user], a low, bowl-shaped, porcelain bathroom fixture equipped with running water, used for bathing the crotch, etc.
bield (bēld), *n. & v.t.* [Scot.], shelter.
Bie·le·feld (bē′lə-felt′), *n.* a city in northwestern Germany: pop., 175,000.
‡**bien en·ten·du** (byan′nän′tän′dü′), [Fr.], 1. well understood. 2. certainly; to be sure.
bi·en·ni·al (bī-en′i-əl), *adj.* [L. *biennalis* < *biennium,* period of two years < *bis,* twice + *annus,* year], 1. happening every two years. 2. lasting or living for two years. *n.* 1. a biennial event or occurrence. 2. in *botany,* a plant that lasts two years, usually producing flowers and seed the second year.
bi·en·ni·al·ly (bī-en′i-əl-i), *adv.* every two years.
‡**bien·ve·nue** (byan′və-nü′), *n.* [Fr., lit., well come], a welcome.
Bien·ville, Jean Bap·tiste de (zhän′ bȧ′tēst′ də byan′-vēl′; Eng. bi-en′vil), 1680–1768; French governor of Louisiana; founder of New Orleans.
bier (bêr), *n.* [ME. *bere;* AS. *bær* < same base as *beran,* to bear], 1. a platform or portable framework on which a coffin or corpse is placed. 2. a coffin.
Bierce, Ambrose (bêrs), 1842–1914?; American writer.
biest·ings (bēs′tiŋz), *n.pl.* beestings.
bi·fa·cial (bī-fā′shəl), *adj.* 1. having two faces or main surfaces. 2. in *botany,* having two unlike opposite surfaces.
bi·far·i·ous (bī-fâr′i-əs), *adj.* [L. *bifarius,* twofold < *bis,* twice + *fari,* to speak], in *botany,* arranged in two rows.
biff (bif), *n. & v.t.* [prob. echoic], [Slang], strike; hit; cuff.
bif·fin (bif′in), *n.* [via Brit. dial. < *beef* + *-ing:* name refers to the color of the apple], any of various deep-red apples for cooking or baking.
bi·fid (bī′fid), *adj.* [L. *bifidus,* forked < *bis,* twice + *findere,* to cleave, divide], divided into two equal parts by a cleft; forked.
bi·fi·lar (bī-fī′lẽr), *adj.* [*bi-* + *filar* < L. *filum,* thread], having or involving the use of two threads, as certain instruments for measuring distances.
bi·flag·el·late (bī-flaj′ə-lāt′), *adj.* [*bi-* + *flagellate*], in *biology,* having two whiplike parts, as certain protozoa.
bi·flex (bī′fleks), *adj.* [< *bi-* + L. *flexus,* pp. of *flectere,* to bend], having two bends or curves.
bi·fo·cal (bī-fō′k'l; *also, esp. for the n.,* bī′fō′k'l), *adj.* adjusted or ground to two different focal lengths. *n.* a lens with one part ground for close focus, as for reading, and the other ground for distant focus.
bi·fo·cals (bī-fō′k'lz, bī′fō′k'lz), *n.pl.* a pair of glasses with bifocal lenses.
bi·fo·li·ate (bī-fō′li-it), *adj.* [*bi-* + *foliate*], having two leaves.
bi·form (bī′fôrm′), *adj.* 1. having two forms. 2. incorporating the features of two forms.
Bif·rost (bēf′rost), *n.* [ON. *bifröst,* lit., the tremulous way; *bif-* < *bifask,* to tremble + *röst,* a distance], in *Norse mythology,* the rainbow bridge from Midgard, the earth, to Asgard, home of the gods.
bi·fur·cate (bī′fẽr-kāt′, bī-fũr′kit), *adj.* [LL. *bifurcatus;* L. *bifurcus* < *bi-* + *furca,* two-pronged fork], having two branches or peaks; forked. *v.t. & v.i.* (bī′fẽr-kāt′, bī-fũr′kāt), [BIFURCATED (-id), BIFURCATING], to divide into two parts or branches, as a road.
bi·fur·ca·tion (bī′fẽr-kā′shən), *n.* 1. a bifurcating; dividing into two parts. 2. the place where this occurs.
big (big), *adj.* [BIGGER (-ẽr), BIGGEST (-ist)], [ME. *big, bigg* < Gmc. base **bugja,* swollen up, thick, big (seen also in Norw. dial. *bugge,* big man & Eng. *bug,* insect); IE. base **bhu-, *bu-,* to blow out, swell out, as in L. *bucca,* swollen cheek], 1. of great size, extent, or capacity; large. 2. full-grown. 3. swollen, pregnant, or filled (*with* something). 4. loud. 5. important; prominent; impressive: as, he does *big* things. 6.

extravagant; pompous: as, *big* talk. 7. magnanimous; noble: as, he has a *big* heart. *Big* is much used in combination to form adjectives (*big*-bodied, *big*-headed, *big*-souled, *big*-talking, etc.). *adv.* [Colloq.], 1. pompously; boastfully; extravagantly: as, he talks *big*. 2. impressively. —*SYN.* see **large.**

big·a·mist (big′ə-mist), *n.* a person who commits bigamy.

big·a·mous (big′ə-məs), *adj.* [LL. *bigamos*], 1. constituting or involving bigamy. 2. guilty of bigamy.

big·a·my (big′ə-mi), *n.* [*pl.* BIGAMIES (-miz)], [ME. & OFr. *bigamie;* LL. *bigamus* < *bis*, twice + Gr. *gamos*, marriage], the criminal offense of marrying a second time while a previous marriage is still legally in effect.

big·a·roon (big′ə-rōōn′), *n.* a bigarreau.

big·ar·reau (big′ə-rō′, big′ə-rō′), *n.* [Fr. < *bigarré*, flecked < *bigarrer*, to fleck], a variety of sweet cherry, heart-shaped and firm-fleshed.

Big Ben, 1. the great bell in the Parliament clock tower in London. 2. the clock itself.

Big Bertha, [Slang], [in allusion to Frau *Bertha* Krupp von Bohlen und Halbach: the Krupp steelworks made most of the German artillery], 1. a very large cannon used by the Germans to bombard Paris in World War I; hence, 2. any very large cannon.

Big Dipper, a dipper-shaped group of stars in the constellation Ursa Major (Great Bear).

Big Five, 1. after World War I, the United States, Great Britain, France, Italy, and Japan. 2. after World War II, the United States, the Soviet Union, Great Britain, China, and France.

big game, 1. large wild animals hunted for sport, as lions, tigers, moose, etc. 2. [Colloq.], the object of any important or dangerous undertaking.

big·gin (big′in), *n.* [Fr. *béguin*, a cap < name of a cap worn by the nuns called *Beguines*], [British], 1. a cap or hood, especially for a child. 2. a white cap worn by a sergeant-at-law.

big·gish (big′ish), *adj.* somewhat big.

big·head (big′hed′), *n.* [Colloq.], conceit; egotism: also **big head.**

big-heart·ed (big′här′tid), *adj.* quick to give or forgive; generous; magnanimous.

big·horn (big′hôrn′), *n.* [*pl.* BIGHORNS (-hôrnz′), BIGHORN; see PLURAL, II, D, 1], a wild sheep with long curved horns, found in the Rocky Mountains.

Big Horn, a river flowing through western Wyoming into the Yellowstone River in Montana: length, 336 mi.

Big Horn Mountains, a range of the Rocky Mountains, in northern Wyoming: highest point, 13,165 ft.

big house, [Slang], penitentiary.

bight (bīt), *n.* [ME.; AS. *byht* < base of AS. *bugan* (cf. BOW); akin to D. & G. *bucht*, a bay; IE. base **bheugh-*, to bend, yield, flee], 1. a bending; corner; hollow; fork. 2. a loop in a rope. 3. a curve in a river, coast line, etc. 4. a bay.

big·no·ni·a (big-nō′ni-ə), *n.* [after the Abbé *Bignon*], any of a number of related climbing evergreen vines with stiff leaves and large clusters of yellowish-red, trumpet-shaped flowers: also called *trumpet flower*.

big·no·ni·a·ceous (big-nō′ni-ā′shəs), *adj.* belonging to the bignonia family of plants, which have large flowers, often trumpet-shaped, and opposite leaves.

big·ot (big′ət), *n.* [OFr.; prob. < Sp. *hombre de bigote*, lit., man with a mustache (*bigote*, mustache, ult. < L. *biga*, span of horses), hence man of spirit, firm character, obstinate person], 1. a person who holds blindly and intolerantly to a particular creed, opinion, etc. 2. a narrow-minded, intolerant person. —*SYN.* see **zealot.**

big·ot·ed (big′ət-id), *adj.* like or characteristic of a bigot; narrow-minded; prejudiced.

big·ot·ry (big′ət-ri), *n.* [*pl.* BIGOTRIES (-riz)], [Fr. *bigoterie*], bigoted behavior, attitude, or act; intolerance.

big shot, [Slang], a person regarded as important or influential; bigwig.

big time, [Slang], 1. vaudeville performed only in the larger cities, paying the actors better and requiring fewer daily appearances; hence, 2. the level regarded as highest or best in any given profession, occupation, etc. 3. a very enjoyable time.

big top, [Colloq.], 1. the roof of a circus tent; hence, 2. a circus.

big tree, the giant sequoia or redwood tree.

big·wig (big′wig′), *n.* [Colloq.], an important and influential person.

Bi·har (bi-här′), *n.* 1. a state of northeastern India: area, 70,368 sq. mi.: pop., 36,548,000 (est. 1950); capital, Patna. 2. a city in this state: pop., 47,000. Also spelled **Behar.**

bi·hour·ly (bī-our′li), *adj.* & *adv.* once every two hours.

bi·jou (bē′zhōō, bi-zhōō′), *n.* [*pl.* BIJOUX (bē′zhōōz, bi-zhōōz′)], [Fr.; prob. < Bret. *bizou*, a ring], 1. a jewel. 2. something small and exquisite; trinket.

bi·jou·te·rie (bē-zhōō′tẽr-i), *n.* [Fr.; see BIJOU], 1. bijoux generally; jewelry. 2. trinkets.

bi·ju·gate (bī′joo-gāt′, bī-jōō′git), *adj.* [*bi-* + *jugate*], having two pairs of leaflets, as some pinnate leaves.

bi·ju·gous (bī′joo-gəs), *adj.* bijugate.

Bi·kan·er (bē′kə-nêr′), *n.* 1. an individual native state in northwestern India: area, 23,181 sq. mi.; pop., 1,293,000. 2. its capital: pop., 127,000.

bike (bīk), *n.*, *v.t.* & *v.i.* [< *bicycle*], [Colloq.], bicycle.

Bi·ki·ni (bi-kē′nē), *n.* 1. an atoll in the Marshall Islands: site of atomic bomb tests in 1946. 2. an extremely brief two-piece bathing suit for women.

Bi·kol (bi-kōl′), *n.* 1. a member of a Christianized Malayan people of southeastern Luzon and neighboring islands. 2. their language. Also spelled **Bicol.**

bi·la·bi·al (bī-lā′bi-əl), *adj.* [*bi-* + *labial*], 1. having two lips; bilabiate. 2. in *phonetics*, made by stopping or constricting the air stream between the lips, as the English consonants *p*, *b*, and *m*, Spanish intervocalic *b*, etc. *n.* a bilabial sound.

bi·la·bi·ate (bī-lā′bi-āt′, bī-lā′bi-it), *adj.* [*bi-* + *labiate*], in *botany*, having two lips, as flowers of the mint family.

bil·an·der (bil′ən-dẽr, bī′lən-dẽr), *n.* [< D. *bijlander*, lit., coaster < *bij*, by + *land*, land], a small, two-masted ship used on the canals and along the coast of the Netherlands, etc.

bi·lat·er·al (bī-lat′ẽr-əl), *adj.* [*bi-* + *lateral*], 1. of, having, or involving two sides, halves, factions, etc. 2. on two or both sides. 3. affecting both sides equally; reciprocal. 4. having bilateral symmetry.

Bil·ba·o (bil-bä′ō), *n.* a seaport in north central Spain: pop., 176,000.

bil·ber·ry (bil′ber′i, bil′bẽr-i), *n.* [*pl.* BILBERRIES (-iz)], [ME. < ON. base of Dan. *böllebær;* cf. G. dial. *boll-beeren*, lit., ball berries], 1. a shrub of the heath family, with small, egg-shaped leaves, rose-colored flowers, and dark-blue berries. 2. its fruit. Also called *whortleberry*.

bil·bo (bil′bō), *n.* [*pl.* BILBOES (-bōz)], [after *Bilbao*, Spain, once famous for its ironworks], 1. *pl.* a long iron bar with shackles that slide back and forth on it, for fettering a prisoner's feet. 2. [Archaic], a sword or rapier.

bile (bīl), *n.* [Fr.; L. *bilis*], 1. the bitter, yellow-brown or greenish fluid secreted by the liver and found in the gall bladder: it is discharged into the duodenum and helps in digestion. 2. bitterness of spirit; choler; bad temper; anger.

bi·lec·tion (bī-lek′shən), *n.* a bolection.

bile·stone (bīl′stōn′), *n.* a gallstone.

bilge (bilj), *n.* [var. of *bulge*], 1. the bulge of a barrel or cask. 2. the rounded, lower part of a ship's hull or hold. 3. stagnant, dirty water that gathers there: also **bilge water.** 4. [Slang], something silly or distasteful; nonsense. *v.t.* & *v.i.* [BILGED (biljd), BILGING], 1. to break open in the bottom or bilge area: said of a vessel. 2. to bulge or swell out.

bilge keel (or **piece**), a beam fastened lengthwise on either side of a ship's bottom to prevent heavy rolling, damage to the bilges, etc.

bilg·y (bil′ji), *adj.* having the appearance or odor of bilge water.

bil·i·ar·y (bil′i-er′i, bil′yẽr-i), *adj.* [Fr. *biliaire*], 1. of or involving the bile. 2. bile-carrying. 3. bilious.

bi·lin·e·ar (bī-lin′i-ẽr), *adj.* [*bi-* + *linear*], of or bounded by two straight lines.

bi·lin·gual (bī-liŋ′gwəl), *adj.* [< L. *bilinguis* < *bis*, two + *lingua*, tongue], 1. of two languages. 2. using or capable of using two languages, often with equal facility.

bi·lin·gual·ism (bī-liŋ′gwəl-iz′m), *n.* the quality of being bilingual.

bil·ious (bil′yəs), *adj.* [Fr. *bilieux;* L. *biliosus* < *bilis*, bile], 1. of the bile. 2 having or resulting from some ailment of the bile or the liver. 3. bad-tempered; cross; bitter.

bi·lit·er·al (bī-lit′ẽr-əl), *adj.* [< *bi-* + L. *litera*, letter], made up of two letters. *n.* any two-letter linguistic element.

-bil·i·ty (bil′ə-ti), -ability: used to form nouns corresponding to adjectives ending in *-ble*, as *responsibility*.

bilk (bilk), *v.t.* [first used in cribbage; ? altered < *balk*], 1. to balk; deceive; swindle; defraud. 2. to get away without paying (a debt, etc.). *n.* 1. a bilking or being bilked. 2. a person who cheats; swindler.

Bill (bil), [< *Will;* see WILLIAM], a masculine nickname: diminutive, *Billy*.

bill (bil), *n.* [ME. *bille;* Anglo-L. *billa*, altered < ML. *bulla*, sealed document; L. *bulla*, knob, bubble], 1. a statement of charges for goods or services. 2. a statement or list, especially of things offered, as a menu or theater program. 3. an advertising poster or handbill. 4. the entertainment offered in a theater. 5. a draft of a law proposed to a lawmaking body. 6. a bill of exchange. 7. any promissory note. 8. a bank note or piece of paper money. 9. [Obs.], a written document, especially one with a seal. 10. in *law*, a written declaration of the charges against a defendant. *v.t.* [ME. *billen* < *bille*], 1. to make out a bill of (items); list. 2. to present a statement of charges to. 3. to advertise or announce by bills or posters. 4. to post bills or placards throughout (a town, etc.). 5. to ship (goods).

fill the bill, [Colloq.], to be satisfactory; meet the requirements.

foot the bill, [Colloq.], to pay the cost.

bill (bil), *n.* [ME. *bill, bile;* AS. *bile;* IE. base **bhei-,* to strike, hit], 1. a bird's beak: see **bird**, illus. 2. a beaklike mouth part, as of a turtle. 3. the point of an anchor fluke. 4. [Colloq.], the peak, or visor, of a cap. *v.i.* 1. to touch bills together. 2. to caress lovingly; be affectionate.

bill and coo, to kiss, talk softly, etc., as in love-making.

bill (bil), *n.* [ME. *bill, bil;* AS. *bill;* IE. base **bhei-;* see BILL (beak)], 1. formerly, a broadsword. 2. an ancient weapon usually consisting of a hook-shaped blade with a spike at the back, on a long, pointed shaft; halberd. 3. a person armed with such a weapon. 4. a billhook.

bill (bil), *n.* [prob. < *bell,* to bellow < AS. *bellan,* to roar, bellow], [Rare], the cry of the bittern.

bill·a·ble (bil'ə-b'l), *adj.* that can be billed; subject to billing.

bill·a·bong (bil'ə-boŋ'), *n.* [Australian native term], in Australia, a backwater channel that forms a lagoon or pool.

bill·board (bil'bôrd', bil'bōrd'), *n.* [*bill* (a list) + *board*], a signboard, usually outdoors, for announcements and advertising posters.

bill·board (bil'bôrd', bil'bōrd'), *n.* [*bill* (a beak) + *board*], a ledge behind the cathead of a ship, on which the fluke of a secured anchor rests.

bil·let (bil'it), *n.* [Fr., dim. of *bille;* see BILL (an account)], 1. a written order to provide quarters or lodging for military personnel. 2. lodging; quarters. 3. a position, job, or situation. 4. [Archaic], a brief document; note. *v.t.* 1. to assign (soldiers, etc.) to lodging by billet. 2. to assign (a person) to a post. 3. to serve a billet on.

bil·let (bil'it), *n.* [ME. & OFr. *billette,* dim. of *bille* < Gaul. **bilia,* tree trunk], 1. a piece of firewood. 2. a wooden club. 3. a small metal bar, often square. 4. in *architecture,* a log-shaped insert in a Norman molding. 5. in *heraldry,* a rectangular bearing. 6. [? < another source], in *saddlery, a)* that part of a belt or strap which fits into a buckle. *b)* a loop for securing the loose end of a buckled strap.

bil·let-doux (bil'i-do͞o'; Fr. bē'ye'do͞o'), *n.* [*pl.* BILLETS-DOUX (bil'i-do͞oz'; Fr. bē'ye'do͞o')], [Fr., lit., sweet letter], a love letter.

bill·fish (bil'fish'), *n.* [*pl.* BILLFISH, BILLFISHES (-iz); see FISH], 1. any of various fishes with long, narrow jaws that resemble a beak, as many gars, the needlefish, the skipper, etc. 2. a sailfish; spearfish.

bill·fold (bil'fōld'), *n.* a folding, pocket-size case, usually of leather, for carrying bank notes and papers; wallet.

bill·head (bil'hed'), *n.* 1. a sheet of paper at the top of which a name and business address are printed, used for statements of charges. 2. a name and business address printed on such a sheet; letterhead.

bill·hook (bil'hook'), *n.* a curved or hooked tool for pruning and cutting.

bil·liard (bil'yẽrd), *adj.* of or for billiards. *n.* a point scored in billiards by causing the cue ball to touch the other two balls; carom.

bil·liards (bil'yẽrdz), *n.* [Fr. *billard,* the game; orig., a stick, cue < *bille;* see BILLET (piece of wood)], 1. a game played with three hard balls on an oblong, felt-covered table that has raised, cushioned edges: a long, tapering stick called a cue is used to hit and move the balls. 2. any of a number of similar games: pool is sometimes called *pocket billiards.*

Bil·lie (bil'i), [fem. dim. of *William*], a feminine name.

bill·ing (bil'iŋ), *n.* 1. the listing of the actors' names on a playbill or theater marquee. 2. the order in which the names are listed.

Bil·lings (bil'iŋz), *n.* a city in southern Montana: pop., 53,000.

Bil·lings, Josh (josh bil'iŋz), see **Shaw, Henry Wheeler.**

bil·lings·gate (bil'iŋz-gāt'), *n.* [after a fish market in London, notorious for the foul language used there], foul, vulgar, abusive talk.

bil·lion (bil'yən), *n.* [Fr. contr. < L. *bis,* twice + *million,* million], 1. in the United States and France, a thousand millions (1,000,000,000). 2. in Great Britain and Germany, a million millions (1,000,000,000,000). 3. a billion (unspecified but understood) monetary units, as dollars, pounds, etc.: as, the firm has made a *billion. adj.* amounting to one billion in number.

bil·lion·aire (bil'yən-âr'), *n.* [*billion* + million*aire*], a person whose wealth comes to at least a billion dollars, pounds, francs, etc.

bil·lionth (bil'yənth), *adj.* 1. coming last in a series of a billion. 2. designating any of the billion equal parts of something. *n.* 1. the last in a series of a billion. 2. any of the billion equal parts of something.

Bil·li·ton (bi-lē'ton), *n.* an island of Indonesia, between Sumatra and Borneo: area, 1,866 sq. mi.; pop., 80,000: Dutch name, *Belitoeng.*

bill of attainder, a legislative bill making certain crimes, especially treason and outlawry, punishable by forfeiture of property and loss of all civil rights: prohibited in the United States by the Constitution.

bill of entry, an account, entered at a customhouse, of incoming and outgoing goods.

bill of exchange, a written order to pay a certain sum of money to the person named or to his account; draft: abbreviated **B/E, B.E., b.e.**

bill of fare, a list of the foods served; menu.

bill of health, a certificate stating whether there is infectious disease aboard a ship or in the port which the ship is leaving: it is given to the captain for him to show at the next port.

clean bill of health, 1. a bill of health certifying the absence of infectious disease; hence, 2. [Colloq.], a good record; favorable recommendation.

bill of lading, 1. originally, a cargo list. 2. a contract issued to a shipper by a transportation agency, listing the goods shipped, acknowledging their receipt, and promising delivery to the person named: abbreviated **B/L, b.l.**

bill of rights, 1. a list of the rights and freedoms assumed to be essential to a group of people. 2. [B- R-], an act of the British Parliament passed in 1689 to prevent a restoration of royal absolutism. 3. [B- R-], the first ten amendments to the Constitution of the United States, which guarantee certain rights to the people, as freedom of speech, assembly, and worship.

bill of sale, a written statement certifying that the ownership of something has been transferred by sale: abbreviated **B/S, b.s.**

bil·lon (bil'ən), *n.* [Fr.], an alloy of gold or silver with a greater proportion of another metal, as copper: used in some coins.

bil·low (bil'ō), *n.* [ON. *bylgja;* cf. BELLY, BELLOWS], 1. a large wave; great swell of water. 2. any large swelling mass or surge, as of smoke, sound, etc. *v.i.* to surge, swell, or rise like or in a billow. —*SYN.* see **wave.**

bil·low·y (bil'ō-i), *adj.* [BILLOWIER (-i-ẽr), BILLOWIEST (-i-ist)], swelling in or as in a billow or billows.

bill·post·er (bil'pōs'tẽr), *n.* a person hired to fasten advertisements or notices on walls, billboards, etc.

bill·stick·er (bil'stik'ẽr), *n.* a billposter.

bil·ly (bil'i), *n.* [*pl.* BILLIES (-iz)], [< *billet* (wooden club)], a club or heavy stick; truncheon, especially one carried by a policeman.

bil·ly (bil'i), *n.* [*pl.* BILLIES (-iz)], [< dial. *billycan*], a can or kettle used in outdoor cooking.

bil·ly- (bil'i), [< the nickname *Billy* < *Willie* < *William;* cf. JACK-], a formative element denoting: 1. *masculinity,* as in *billy goat.* 2. [British Dial.], *intimacy* or *intimate use,* as in *billycan* (dial.), a billy.

bil·ly·cock (bil'i-kok'), *n.* [< 18th c. *bully-cocked,* worn in the style of a bully], [British Colloq.], a type of felt hat with a low, round crown, as a derby.

billy goat, [see BILLY-], [Colloq.] a male goat.

bi·lo·bate (bī-lō'bāt), *adj.* having or divided into two lobes.

bi·lo·bat·ed (bī-lō'bā-tid), *adj.* bilobate.

bi·loc·u·lar (bī-lok'yoo-lẽr), *adj.* [*bi-* + *locular*], in *biology,* having or divided into two cells or chambers.

bi·loc·u·late (bī-lok'yoo-lāt', bī-lok'yoo-lit), *adj.* bilocular.

Bi·lox·i (bi-lok'si), *n.* a town in Mississippi, on the Gulf of Mexico: pop., 44,000.

bil·sted (bil'sted), *n.* [18th c.; early sp. *boilsted* suggests orig. *bilested;* ? < *bile* + dial. *stead,* aid, remedy (with reference to medicinal use of the balsam)], a tree with maplelike leaves and spiny fruit: also called *sweet gum.*

bil·tong (bil'toŋ), *n.* [S.Afr.D.; *bil,* rump (from which it is cut) + *tong,* tongue (from the shape)], sun-dried strips of meat.

bi·mane (bī'mān), *n.* [Fr. < Mod. L. *bimanus*], a bimanous mammal.

bi·ma·nous (bī-mā'nəs, bim'ə-nəs), *adj.* [Mod. L. *bimanus;* L. *bi-,* bi- + *manus,* hand], having two hands.

bi·man·u·al (bī-man'ū-əl), *adj.* [*bi-* + *manual*], using or needing the use of two hands.

bi·men·sal (bī-men's'l), *adj.* [*bi-* + *mensal*], bimonthly.

bi·mes·tri·al (bī-mes'tri-əl), *adj.* [L. *bimestris* < *bi-* + *mensis,* month], 1. lasting two months. 2. bimonthly.

bi·me·tal·lic (bī'mə-tal'ik), *adj.* [Fr. *bimétallique; bi-* + *métallique,* metallic], 1. of, containing, or using two metals. 2. of or based on bimetallism.

bi·met·al·lism (bī-met''l-iz'm), *n.* 1. the use of two metals, usually gold and silver, as the monetary standard, with fixed values in relation to each other. 2. the doctrine, actions, or policies supporting this.

bi·met·al·list (bī-met''l-ist), *n.* a person who believes in or advocates bimetallism.

bi·month·ly (bī-munth'li), *adj. & adv.* 1. once every two months. 2. twice a month; semimonthly: loosely so used. *n.* [*pl.* BIMONTHLIES (-liz)], a publication appearing once every two months.

bi·mo·tored (bī-mō'tẽrd), *adj.* having two motors, as some airplanes.

bin (bin), *n.* [ME. *binne;* AS. *binn,* manger, crib; prob. < Celt.], 1. a receptacle, especially for ashes or trash. 2. a box or enclosed space for storing foods, fuels, etc. *v.t.* [BINNED (bind), BINNING], to put or store in a bin.
bin- (bin), bi-: used before a vowel, as in *binary.*
bi·nal (bī'n'l), *adj.* [Mod. L. *binalis* < L. *bini,* two by two], twofold.
bi·na·ry (bī'nə-ri), *adj.* [L. *binarius* < *bini,* two by two < *bis,* double], 1. made up of two parts; twofold; double. 2. in *chemistry,* composed of two elements or radicals, or of one element and one radical: as, *binary* compounds. *n.* [*pl.* BINARIES (-riz)], 1. a set of two; couple; pair. 2. a binary star.
binary star, two stars revolving around a common center of gravity; double star.
bi·nate (bī'nāt), *adj.* [LL. *binatus* < L. *bini;* see BINARY], in *botany,* composed of or almost divided into two parts: said of a leaf.
bin·au·ral (bin-ô'rəl), *adj.* [*bin-* + *aural*], 1. having two ears. 2. of or involving the use of both ears. 3. (*usually* bī-nô'rəl), designating or of sound reproduction or transmission in which two sources of sound are used to give a stereophonic effect.
bind (bīnd), *v.t.* [BOUND (bound), BINDING], [ME. *binden;* AS. *bindan;* akin to ON. *binda;* IE. base ***bhendh-**, as in L. (*of*)*fend*(*ix*)], 1. to tie together; make fast or tight, as with a rope or band. 2. to hold; make prisoner; restrain. 3. to gird or encircle with (a belt, girdle, etc.); wrap around. 4. to bandage (often with *up*). 5. to make stick together; make coalesce into a mass. 6. to tighten the bowels of; constipate. 7. to strengthen, secure, or ornament the edges of by a band, as of tape. 8. to fasten together and protect with a cover, as a book. 9. to secure (a bargain, pledge, etc.); obligate by duty, love, etc.: as, he is *bound* to help his mother. 10. to put under oath, legal restraint, or contract. 11. to unite or hold, as by a feeling of loyalty. *v.i.* 1. to do the act of binding. 2. to grow tight, hard, or stiff. 3. to stick together. 4. to be obligatory. *n.* 1. anything that binds. 2. a twining stem. 3. in *music,* a line to indicate that the sound of certain notes is to be sustained; slur. —*SYN.* see **tie.**
bind out, to require (a person) to serve under written contract or legal bond.
bind over, to put under legal bond to appear at a specified time and place, as before a law court.
bind·er (bīn'dẽr), *n.* 1. a person who binds. 2. a bookbinder. 3. a thing that binds or holds together. 4. a band, cord, etc. 5. a binding substance, as tar. 6. a cover for holding sheets of paper together. 7. in *agriculture, a*) a device attached to a reaper, for tying grain in bundles. *b*) a machine that both reaps and binds grain. 8. in *law,* a temporary contract, in effect pending execution of the final contract.
bind·er·y (bīn'dẽr-i), *n.* [*pl.* BINDERIES (-iz)], a place where books are bound.
bind·ing (bīn'diŋ), *n.* 1. the action of a person or thing that binds. 2. the state of being bound. 3. a band or bandage. 4. tape used in sewing for strengthening seams, edges, etc. 5. the covers and backing of a book. 6. a band of masonry, brick, etc. 7. a cohesive substance for holding a mixture together. *adj.* 1. that binds. 2. tight; restrictive. 3. that holds one to an agreement, promise, etc.; obligatory.
bin·dle (bin'd'l), *n.* [prob. < *bundle*], [Slang], a bundle of bedding carried by a hobo.
bindle stiff, [Slang], a hobo.
bind·weed (bīnd'wēd'), *n.* any of a number of related plants, usually trailing or twining; convolvulus.
bine (bīn), *n.* [dial. form of *bind*], any climbing, twining stem, as of the hop, woodbine, etc.
Bi·net-Si·mon test (bi-nā' sī'mən; Fr. bē'ne'sē'mōn'), [after Fr. psychologists who devised it, Alfred *Binet* (1857–1911), Théodore *Simon* (1873–)], a Binet test.
Bi·net test (bi-nā'; Fr. bē'ne'), an intelligence test that consists of questions, problems, and things to do, graded in terms of mental age (*Binet age*): see **I.Q.**
binge (binj), *n.* [? < dial. *binge,* to soak], [Slang], a drunken celebration or spree.
Bing·en (biŋ'ən), *n.* a town on the Rhine, in western Germany: pop., 15,000.
Bing·ham·ton (biŋ'əm-tən), *n.* a city in south central New York: pop., 76,000.
bin·go (biŋ'gō), *n.* [? < *bingo,* 18th-c. thieves' cant meaning "brandy," "drinker"; ? formed by analogy with *lotto,* etc., of echoic origin; cf. use as interj.], a gambling game, like lotto, usually with many players.
Binh-Dinh (bin'y'-din'y'; Eng. bin'din'), *n.* a city in South Vietnam: pop., 160,000.
bin·na·cle (bin'ə-k'l), *n.* [formerly *bittacle* < Port. *bitacola,* binnacle < L. *habitaculum,* dwelling place < *habitare,* to inhabit], the case enclosing a ship's compass, usually located near the helm.
bin·o·cle (bin'ə-k'l), *n.* [< L. *bini,* double + *oculus,* an eye], a field glass, telescope, etc. for use with both eyes.
bin·oc·u·lar (bin-nok'yə-lẽr, bi-nok'yə-lẽr), *adj.* [< L. *bini,* double + *ocularis,* of the eyes < *oculus,* an eye], using, or for the use of, both eyes at the same time. *n.* **a binocular instrument.**
bin·oc·u·lars (bī-nok'yə-lẽrz, bi-nok'yə-lẽrz), *n.pl.* 1. field glasses. 2. opera glasses.

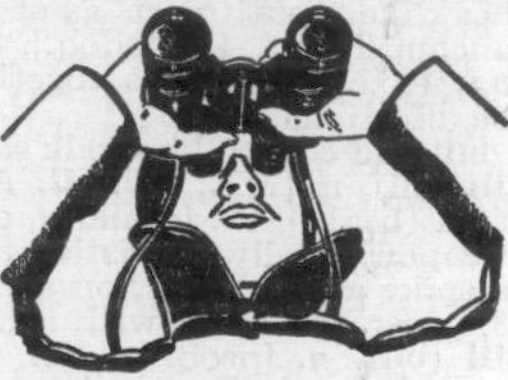
BINOCULARS

bi·no·mi·al (bī-nō'mi-əl), *n.* [LL. *binomius* < *bi-* + Gr. *nomos,* law], 1. a mathematical equation or expression consisting of two terms connected by a plus or minus sign. 2. the scientific name of a plant or animal, consisting of the genus name followed by that of the species. *adj.* 1. having two names. 2. composed of two terms. 3. of binomials.
binomial nomenclature (or **system**), the scientific system of giving a double name to each plant and animal, consisting of the name of the genus followed by that of the species: e.g., ***Ananas sativus*** (pineapple).
binomial theorem, an algebraic short cut for raising a binomial to any power, invented by Sir Isaac Newton. Example: $(a + b)^2 = a^2 + 2ab + b^2$.
bi·nu·cle·ar (bī-nōō'kli-ẽr, bī-nū'kli-ẽr), *adj.* binucleate.
bi·nu·cle·ate (bī-nōō'kli-āt', bī-nū'kli-it), *adj.* of or having two nuclei or centers.
Bin·yon, Laurence (bin'yən), 1869–1943; English poet and art critic.
bi·o- (bī'ō, bī'ə), [Gr. < *bios,* life], a combining form meaning *life, of living things, biological,* as in *biography, biochemistry:* also **bi-.**
bi·o·cat·a·lyst (bī'ō-kat'ə-list), *n.* [*bio-* + *catalyst*], a substance that activates or speeds up a biochemical reaction; coenzyme, vitamin, or hormone.
bi·oc·el·late (bī-os'ə-lāt', bī'ō-sel'it), *adj.* [*bi-* + *ocellate*], in *zoology,* having two simple eyes or eyelike markings.
bi·o·chem·i·cal (bī'ō-kem'i-k'l), *adj.* of or connected with biochemistry.
bi·o·chem·ist (bī'ō-kem'ist), *n.* a student of or specialist in biochemistry.
bi·o·chem·is·try (bī'ō-kem'is-tri), *n.* the branch of chemistry that deals with plants and animals and their life processes; biological chemistry: abbreviated **biochem.**
bi·o·dy·nam·ics (bī'ō-dī-nam'iks), *n.pl.* [construed as sing.], [*bio-* + *dynamics*], the branch of physiology that deals with the life processes of plants and animals: opposed to *biostatics.*
biog., 1. biographer. 2. biographical. 3. biography.
bi·o·gen (bī'ə-jən), *n.* [*bio-* + *-gen*], the hypothetical smallest unit of protoplasm.
bi·o·gen·e·sis (bī'ō-jen'ə-sis), *n.* [*bio-* + *genesis*], 1. the development of living organisms from other living organisms. 2. the theory that living organisms come only from other living organisms, and not from nonliving matter.
bi·o·ge·net·ic (bī'ō-jə-net'ik), *adj.* of or connected with biogenesis.
bi·o·ge·net·i·cal (bī'ō-jə-net'i-k'l), *adj.* biogenetic.
bi·og·e·nous (bī-oj'ə-nəs), *adj.* [*bio-* + *-genous*], 1. produced from or inhabiting living things. 2. producing life.
bi·og·e·ny (bī-oj'ə-ni), *n.* biogenesis.
bi·o·ge·og·ra·phy (bī'ō-jē-og'rə-fi), *n.* the branch of biology that deals with the geographical distribution of plants and animals: abbreviated **biogeog.**
bi·og·ra·pher (bī-og'rə-fẽr, bi-og'rə-fẽr), *n.* a writer of a biography or biographies: abbreviated **biog.**
bi·o·graph·ic (bī'ə-graf'ik), *adj.* biographical.
bi·o·graph·i·cal (bī'ə-graf'i-k'l), *adj.* 1. of or connected with biography. 2. about a person's life. Abbreviated **biog.**
bi·og·ra·phy (bī-og'rə-fi, bi-og'rə-fi), *n.* [Gr. *biographia* < *bios,* life + *graphein,* to write], 1. the histories of individual lives, considered as a branch of literature. 2. [*pl.* BIOGRAPHIES (-fiz)], an account of a person's life, described by another; life story. Abbreviated **biog.**
biol., 1. biological. 2. biologist. 3. biology.
bi·o·log·ic (bī'ə-loj'ik), *adj.* biological.
bi·o·log·i·cal (bī'ə-loj'i-k'l), *adj.* 1. of or connected with biology; of plants and animals. 2. of the nature of living matter. 3. used in or produced by practical biology. Abbreviated **biol.** *n.* a biological product.
bi·o·log·i·cal·ly (bī'ə-loj'i-k'l-i, bī'ə-loj'ik-li), *adv.* 1. from the viewpoint of biology. 2. by means of biology.
biological warfare, the use of disease-spreading microorganisms, toxins, etc. against enemy armed forces or civilians.
bi·ol·o·gist (bī-ol'ə-jist), *n.* a student of or specialist in biology: abbreviated **biol.**
bi·ol·o·gy (bī-ol'ə-ji), *n.* [*bio-* + *-logy*], 1. the science that deals with the origin, history, physical characteristics, habits, etc. of plants and animals: it includes botany, zoology, and their subdivisions: abbreviated **biol.** 2. animal and plant life, as of a given area. 3. biological history, principles, etc.
bi·o·lu·mi·nes·cence (bī'ō-lōō-mə-nes''ns), *n.* [*bio-* + *luminescence*], a giving off of light from living matter, caused by internal oxidation.

bi·ol·y·sis (bī-ol'ə-sis), *n.* [*bio-* + *-lysis*], the destruction of life, as by bacteria or other microorganisms.

bi·o·lyt·ic (bī'ə-lit'ik), *adj.* of or produced by biolysis.

bi·o·met·rics (bī'ə-met'riks), *n.pl.* [construed as sing.], [< *bio-* + *metric*], that branch of biology which deals with its data statistically and by quantitative analysis.

bi·om·e·try (bī-om'ə-tri), *n.* [*bio-* + *-metry*], 1. calculation of the probable human life span. 2. biometrics.

Bi·on (bī'ən), *n.* Greek pastoral poet; c. 3d century B.C.

bi·o·nom·ics (bī'ə-nom'iks), *n.pl.* [construed as sing.], [< *bionomy* + *-ics*], the branch of biology that deals with the adaptation of living things to their environment; ecology.

bi·on·o·my (bī-on'ə-mi), *n.* [*bio-* + Gr. *nomos*, law], 1. the science that deals with the natural laws controlling life processes. 2. bionomics.

bi·o·phys·i·cal (bī'ō-fiz'i-k'l), *adj.* of biophysics.

bi·o·phys·ics (bī'ō-fiz'iks), *n.pl.* [construed as sing.], the branch of physics that deals with living matter.

bi·o·plasm (bī'ō-plaz'm), *n.* living matter; protoplasm.

bi·op·sy (bī'op-si), *n.* [see BIO- & -OPSIS], in medicine, the excision of a piece of living tissue for diagnostic examination by microscope, etc.

bi·o·scope (bī'ə-skōp'), *n.* [*bio-* + *-scope*], a motion-picture projector.

bi·os·co·py (bī-os'kə-pi), *n.* [*bio-* + *-scopy*], in *medicine*, examination to find out whether life is present.

-bi·o·sis (bī-ō'sis, bi-ō'sis), [< Gr. *biōsis*, way of life < *bios*, life], a combining form meaning *a* (specified) *way of living*, as in *symbiosis*.

bi·o·so·cial (bī'ō-sō'shəl), *adj.* of the communal or family relationships of animals, as bees, apes, etc.

bi·o·stat·i·cal (bī'ō-stat'i-k'l), *adj.* of biostatics.

bi·o·stat·ics (bī'ō-stat'iks), *n.pl.* [construed as sing.], [*bio-* + *statics*], the branch of physiology that deals with the relation of structure to function in plants and animals: opposed to *biodynamics*.

bi·o·ta (bī-ō'tə), *n.* [see BIOTIC], the plant and animal life of a region.

bi·o·ther·a·py (bī'ō-ther'ə-pi), *n.* [*bio-* + *therapy*], the treatment of disease by means of substances secreted by or derived from living organisms, as serums, vaccines, bile, penicillin, etc.

bi·ot·ic (bī-ot'ik), *adj.* [Gr. *biōtikos* < *bios*, life], of life; of living things.

bi·ot·i·cal (bī-ot'i-k'l), *adj.* biotic.

bi·o·tin (bī'ə-tin), *n.* [*biotic* + *-in*], a bacterial growth factor, $C_{10}H_{16}O_3N_2S$, found in liver, egg yolk, and yeast; vitamin H: the lack of it may cause dermatitis.

bi·o·tite (bī'ə-tīt'), *n.* [after J. B. *Biot* (1774–1862), Fr. naturalist], a dark-brown or black mineral of the mica family, found in igneous and metamorphic rocks.

bi·o·type (bī'ō-tīp'), *n.* [*bio-* + *-type*], a group of plants or animals with similar hereditary characteristics.

bi·pa·ri·e·tal (bī'pə-rī'ə-t'l), *adj.* of or connected with the prominent rounded part of the two parietal bones.

bi·pa·rous (bip'ə-rəs), *adj.* [*bi-* + *-parous*], 1. bearing two offspring at a birth. 2. in *botany*, dividing into two branches.

bi·par·ti·san (bī-pär'tə-z'n), *adj.* of, having members from, or representing two parties.

bi·par·tite (bī-pär'tīt), *adj.* [L. *bipartitus*, pp. of *bipartire*; *bi-*, two + *partire*, to divide], 1. having two parts. 2. having two corresponding parts: as, a *bipartite* agreement. 3. in *botany*, divided in two nearly to the base, as some leaves.

bi·par·ti·tion (bī'pär-tish'ən), *n.* partition, or division, into two parts.

bi·ped (bī'ped), *n.* [L. *bipes*; *bi-* + *pes*, *pedis*, foot], any animal with only two feet. *adj.* two-footed; bipedal.

bi·pe·dal (bī'pi-d'l, bī'ped-'l, bi'pi-d'l), *adj.* [L. *bipedalis*; see BIPED], having only two feet.

bi·pen·nate (bī-pen'āt), *adj.* [see BI- & PENNATE], having two wings.

bi·pet·al·ous (bī-pet''l-əs), *adj.* having two petals.

bi·phen·yl (bī-fen'il, bī-fē'nil), *n.* [*bi-* + *phenyl*], a white, crystalline hydrocarbon whose molecule consists of a double phenyl group, $C_6H_5 \cdot C_6H_5$.

bi·pin·nate (bī-pin'āt), *adj.* [see BI- & PINNATE], having pinnate leaflets on stems that grow opposite each other on a main stem.

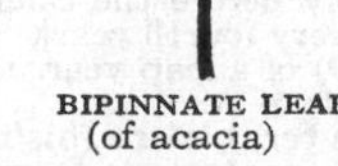

BIPINNATE LEAF
(of acacia)

bi·plane (bī'plān'), *n.* [*bi-* + *plane*], an airplane with two main planes, typically one above the other: see TYPES OF AIRPLANE, p. 32.

bi·pod (bī'pod'), *n.* [*bi-* + *tripod*], a two-legged stand for instruments, weapons, etc.

bi·po·lar (bī-pō'lẽr), *adj.* 1. of or having two poles. 2. of or involving both of the earth's poles or polar regions.

bi·quad·rate (bī-kwod'rit), *n.* [*bi-* + *quadrate*], in *mathematics*, the square of the square; fourth power: also called *quartic*.

bi·quad·rat·ic (bī'-kwod-rat'ik), *adj.* in *mathematics*, of or involving the biquadrate, or fourth power, of a quantity. *n.* 1. a biquadrate. 2. an algebraic equation of the fourth power.

bi·quar·ter·ly (bī-kwôr'tẽr-li), *adj.* happening or appearing twice in every three-month period.

bi·ra·di·al (bī-rā'di-əl), *adj.* in *biology*, having both bilateral and radial symmetry.

birch (bũrch), *n.* [ME. *birche*; AS. *beorc*; akin to G. *birke*; IE. **bhereg-ā* < base **bhereĝ-*, shine, white], 1. any of a number of related trees that generally have slender branches, hard, close-grained wood, and smooth bark easily stripped off in layers. 2. the wood of any of these trees. 3. a birch rod or bunch of twigs used for whipping. *v.t.* to beat with a birch. *adj.* of birch.

birch·en (bũr'chən), *adj.* of birch.

bird (bũrd), *n.* [ME. *brid*; AS. *bridd*, bird, especially a young bird], 1. any of a group of warm-blooded vertebrates with feathers and wings. 2. a small game bird: distinguished from *waterfowl*. 3. a clay pigeon. 4. [Obs.], a young bird or fowl; nestling. 5. [Slang], a person: as, he's a queer *bird*. 6. [Slang], a sound of disapproval made by the lips fluttering. 7. in *badminton*, the round, feather-tipped cork struck with the racket; shuttlecock. *v.i.* to shoot or catch birds.

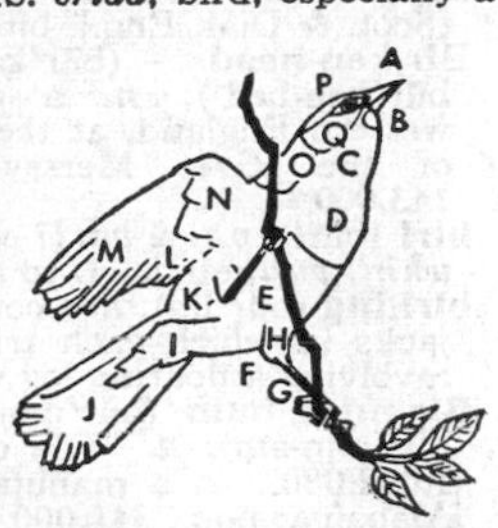

BIRD

A, bill; B, chin; C, throat; D, breast; E, abdomen; F, heel; G, tarsus; H, tibia; I, tail coverts; J, tail feathers; K, flanks; L, secondaries; M, primaries; N, wing coverts; O, nape; P, crown; Q, auriculars

bird in the hand, something sure or definite because already in one's possession: opposed to *bird in the bush*, something unsure, etc.

birds of a feather, people with the same characteristics or tastes.

eat like a bird, to eat very little food.

bird·bath (bũrd'bath', bũrd'bäth'), *n.* a basinlike garden ornament for birds to bathe in.

bird·call (bũrd'kôl'), *n.* 1. the sound or song of a bird. 2. an imitation of this. 3. a device for imitating bird sounds. Also **bird call**.

bird dog, a dog trained for hunting birds, as a pointer.

bird-foot (bũrd'foot'), *n.* bird's-foot.

bird grass, a weed of the buckwheat family, with jointed stems, narrow leaves, and spikes of tiny, greenish flowers; knotgrass.

bird·house (bũrd'hous'), *n.* 1. a small box, often resembling a house, for birds to live in. 2. a building for exhibiting birds.

bird·ie (bũr'di), *n.* 1. any small bird: a child's word. 2. in *golf*, a score of one stroke under par for any hole.

bird·lime (bũrd'līm'), *n.* 1. a sticky substance spread on twigs to catch birds. 2. anything that catches or snares. *v.t.* to spread or catch with birdlime.

bird·man (bũrd'man', bũrd'mən), *n.* [*pl.* BIRDMEN (-men', -mən)], 1. a person whose work deals with birds, as an ornithologist or taxidermist. 2. [Colloq.], an aviator.

bird of ill omen, 1. a bearer of bad news. 2. an unlucky person.

bird of paradise, any of a number of brightly colored birds found in and near New Guinea.

bird of passage, 1. any migratory bird. 2. anyone who travels or roams about constantly.

bird of peace, the dove.

bird of prey, any of a number of flesh-eating birds, as the eagle, hawk, owl, vulture, etc.

bird pepper, a kind of pepper with oblong, red fruit.

bird·seed (bũrd'sēd'), *n.* seed for feeding caged birds.

bird's-eye (bũrdz'ī'), *n.* 1. any of various plants with small, bright flowers, as the bird's-eye primrose, herb Robert, etc. 2. a pattern of small diamond-shaped figures, each with a dot like a bird's eye in the center, woven into cottons and linens. 3. a cotton or linen cloth with such a pattern: used for diapers, napkins, etc. *adj.* 1. seen from above or a distance; general; cursory: as, a *bird's-eye* view. 2. having markings that resemble birds' eyes: as, *bird's-eye* maple.

bird's-foot (bũrdz'foot'), *n.* any of various plants whose leaves or flowers resemble a bird's foot, as the bird's-foot trefoil, bird's-foot fern, etc.: also **bird-foot**.

bird's-foot fern, a kind of fern with small, wiry leaves in groups of three.

bird's-foot trefoil, any of a number of related plants of the pea family, with small, yellow flowers.

bird's-foot violet, a kind of violet bearing large, purple

flowers with dark upper petals and pale lower ones.
bird shot, small shot for shooting birds.
bird·wom·an (bũrd′woom′ən), *n.* [*pl.* BIRDWOMEN (-wim′in)], [Colloq.], a woman aviator; aviatrix.
bi·reme (bī′rēm), *n.* [L. *biremis* < *bi-* + *remus*, oar], a kind of ship used in ancient times, having two rows of oars on each side, one under the other.
bi·ret·ta (bi-ret′ə), *n.* [It. *birretta;* LL. *birrettum*, dim. of L. *birrus*, a hood, cloak; prob. < Celt. base appearing in Cymric *byrr*, MIr. *berr*, short], a square cap with three projections and a tassel on top, worn by Roman Catholic clergy: also spelled **birretta, beretta, berretta.**

BIRETTA

birk (bũrk, birk), *n.* & *adj.* [Scot. & Dial. Eng.], birch.
birk·en (bũr′kən, bir′kən), *adj.* [Scot. & Dial. Eng.], birchen.
Bir·ken·head (bũr′kən-hed′, bũr′kən-hed′), *n.* a city in western England, at the mouth of the River Mersey: pop., 143,000.
birl (bũrl), *v.t.* & *v.i.* [? echoic refashioning of *birr*, after *whirl, purl*, etc.], 1. to revolve rapidly. 2. to whirr.
birl·ing (bũr′liŋ), *n.* a competitive game among lumberjacks in which each tries to keep his balance while revolving a floating log with his feet.
Bir·ming·ham (bũr′miŋ-ham; *also, and for 1 always,* bũr′miŋ-əm), *n.* 1. a city in central England: pop., 1,092,000. 2. a manufacturing city in north central Alabama: pop., 341,000.
Bir·o·bi·jan, Bir·o·bi·dzhan (bêr′ō-bi-jän′), *n.* 1. the Jewish National Autonomous Region, an autonomous region of the R.S.F.S.R. 2. its capital: pop., 41,000.
birr (bũr), *n.* [ME. *bir, byr;* ON. *byrr*, impetus, strong wind], 1. onrush; energy; force. 2. emphatic speech or statement. 3. a vibrant whirring sound. *v.i.* to make or move with a birr.
birth (bũrth), *n.* [ME. *birthe, burde;* AS. *byrde, gebyrde* < *beran*, to bear], 1. the act of bringing forth offspring. 2. a person or thing born or produced. 3. the act of being born; nativity. 4. descent or origin. 5. descent from nobility. 6. the beginning of anything: as, the *birth* of a nation. 7. an inherited or natural inclination to act in certain ways: as, an actor by *birth*.
give birth to, 1. to bring forth (offspring). 2. to be the cause of; originate.
birth control, control of how many children a woman will have and when she will have them; specifically, contraception.
birth·day (bũrth′dā′), *n.* 1. the day of a person's birth or a thing's beginning. 2. the anniversary of this day.
birth·mark (bũrth′märk′), *n.* a skin blemish present at birth.
birth·place (bũrth′plās′), *n.* 1. the place of one's birth: abbreviated **bp., bpl.** 2. the place of a thing's origin.
birth rate, the number of births per year per thousand of population in a given community, area, or group: sometimes other units of time or population are used in giving the birth rate.
birth·right (bũrth′rīt′), *n.* 1. the rights that a person has because he was born in a certain family, nation, etc. 2. the rights of the first-born. —*SYN.* see **heritage.**
birth·root (bũrth′rōōt′, bũrth′root′), *n.* any of a number of related plants of the lily family, with short, thick rootstocks, leaves in groups of three, and three-parted flowers; trillium; birthwort: so called because formerly supposed to be of help in childbirth.
birth·stone (bũrth′stōn′), *n.* a precious or semiprecious gem symbolizing the month of one's birth: the usual list, beginning with that of January, is as follows: garnet, amethyst, bloodstone, diamond, emerald, pearl, ruby, sardonyx, sapphire, opal, topaz, and turquoise.
birth·wort (bũrth′wũrt′), *n.* 1. any of a number of related plants with unusual flower formations and coloring; aristolochia: formerly supposed to be of help in childbirth. 2. the birthroot.
bis (bis), *adv.* [L.; OL. *duis* < base of *duo*, two], twice: used as a direction to repeat, especially in music.
bis- (bis), bi-: used before *c* or *s*, as in *bissextile*.
Bi·sa·yan (bi-sä′yən), *n.* Visayan.
Bi·sa·yas (bi-sä′yäs), *n.pl.* the Visayan Islands.
Bis·cay, Bay of (bis′kā, bis′ki), a part of the Atlantic, north of Spain and west of France.
bis·cuit (bis′kit), *n.* [*pl.* BISCUITS (-kits), BISCUIT], [ME. *besquite, bisqwite;* OFr. *bescoit;* akin to It. *biscotto* < L. *bis*, twice + *coctus*, pp. of *coquere*, to cook], 1. [Chiefly British], *a)* a hard, unraised bread made in crisp wafers. *b)* any of these wafers; cracker or cooky. 2. a quick bread, made light by baking powder, soda, or yeast, and baked in small pieces. 3. any of these pieces. 4. light brown; tan. 5. pottery or porcelain after the first firing and before glazing.
‡bise (bēz), *n.* [Fr.; OHG. *bisa*], a cold north or northeast wind blowing down from the Swiss Alps.
bi·sect (bī-sekt′), *v.t.* [< *bi-* + L. *sectus*, pp. of *secare*, to cut], 1. to cut in two. 2. in *geometry*, to divide into two equal parts. *v.i.* to divide; fork.
bi·sec·tion (bī-sek′shən), *n.* 1. a bisecting or being bisected. 2. a line or point of bisecting. 3. either of two equal sections.
bi·sec·tor (bī-sek′tẽr), *n.* 1. a thing that bisects something. 2. a straight line that bisects an angle or line.
bi·sec·trix (bī-sek′triks), *n.* [*pl.* BISECTRICES (bī′sek-trī′sēz)], in *crystallography*, either of the two lines bisecting the acute and obtuse angles formed by the optic axes in a biaxial crystal.
bi·ser·rate (bi-ser′it, bi-ser′āt), *adj.* 1. in *botany*, having notched teeth along the margin, as some leaves; doubly serrate. 2. in *zoology*, notched on both sides, as some antennae.
bi·sex·u·al (bī-sek′shōō-əl), *adj.* 1. of both sexes. 2. having both male and female organs, as certain animals and plants; hermaphroditic. *n.* 1. a hermaphrodite. 2. a person who is sexually attracted by both sexes.
bish·op (bish′əp), *n.* [ME. *bischop;* AS. *biscop, bisceop;* L. *episcopus;* Gr. *episkopos*, overseer, bishop; *epi-*, upon + *skopos* < *skopein*, to look], 1. a high-ranking clergyman with authority over a church district or diocese: abbreviated **bp.** 2. in the early Christian era, a religious or spiritual overseer. 3. a chessman that can move in a diagonal direction across any number of squares: abbreviated **B.** 4. a sweet drink of spiced wine and fruit juices.
bish·op·ric (bish′əp-rik), *n.* [ME. *bischopriche;* AS. *bisceoprice; bisceop*, bishop + *rice*, jurisdiction, kingdom], 1. the church district controlled by a bishop; diocese. 2. the position, authority, or rank of a bishop.
bish·op's-cap (bish′əps-kap′), *n.* any of a group of small woodland herbs with heart-shaped leaves and white or greenish flowers; miterwort.
Bis·marck (biz′märk), *n.* the capital of North Dakota, on the Missouri River: pop., 28,000.
Bis·marck, Ot·to E·du·ard Le·o·pold von (ôt′ō ā′dōō-ärt lā′ô-pôlt fôn bis′märk; Eng. biz′märk), 1815–1898; Prussian prince and chancellor; unified Germany: called the *Iron Chancellor*.
Bismarck Archipelago, a group of islands northeast of New Guinea: part of the Australian trust territory of New Guinea: area, 19,200 sq. mi.; pop., 157,000.

BISMARCK ARCHIPELAGO

bis·muth (biz′məth), *n.* [G. *bismut, wismut*], a hard, brittle, metallic element that is grayish-white with a tinge of red, used chiefly in making alloys of low melting point: symbol, Bi; at. wt., 209.00; at. no., 83.
bis·muth·al (biz′məth-əl), *adj.* of or containing bismuth.
bis·mu·thic (biz-mū′thik, biz-muth′ik), *adj.* containing bismuth with a valence of five.
bis·muth·ous (biz′məth-əs), *adj.* containing bismuth with a valence of three.
bi·son (bī′s'n, bī′z'n), *n.* [*pl.* BISON], [Fr., L., wild ox < Gmc. **wisunt;* cf. FITCHEW], any of a number of related four-legged mammals with a shaggy mane, short, curved horns, and a humped back, as the American buffalo or the European aurochs.

AMERICAN BISON (10 ft. long)

bisque (bisk), *n.* [Fr.], 1. a rich meat soup made from shellfish, rabbit, fowl, etc. 2. a thick, strained, creamed vegetable soup. 3. an ice cream containing ground macaroons or nuts.
bisque (bisk), *n.* [< *biscuit*], 1. in *ceramics*, biscuit. 2. a red-yellow color.
bisque (bisk), *n.* [Fr.; earlier *biskaye;* ? < *Biscay*], in *tennis, golf, croquet*, etc., a handicap of one point, stroke, turn, etc. per game.
bis·sex·tile (bi-seks′t'l, bi-seks′tīl), *adj.* [L. *bisextilis*, containing an intercalary day < *bisextus* < *bis*, twice + *sextus*, sixth: so called because February 24 (sixth day before the calends of March) was reckoned twice every fourth year], 1. denoting the extra day (February 29) of a leap year. 2. designating or of a leap year. *n.* a leap year.
bis·ter, bis·tre (bis′tẽr), *n.* [Fr. *bistre*], 1. a dark-brown pigment made from soot. 2. dark brown. *adj.* dark-brown.
bis·tort (bis′tôrt), *n.* [Fr. *bistorte;* ML. *bistorta*, lit., twice twisted < L. *bis*, twice + *tortus*, pp. of *torquere*, to twist], a plant with spikes of pink or white flowers; its twisted root is used as an astringent.

bis·tou·ry (bis′too-ri), *n.* [*pl.* BISTOURIES (-riz)], [Fr. *bistouri*], a small, slender surgical knife with a straight or curved blade and a very sharp point.

bis·tro (bis′trō; Fr. bē′strō′), *n.* [Fr. (Parisian) slang, wine seller, wine shop < dial. *bistro*, a shepherd], 1. a small wine shop or restaurant where wine is served. 2. a small night club or bar.

bi·sul·cate (bī-sul′kāt), *adj.* [*bi-* + *sulcate*], 1. having two grooves. 2. in *zoology*, cloven-hoofed.

bi·sul·fate (bī-sul′fāt), *n.* an acid sulfate; compound of an element or radical which, in water solutions, produces hydrogen ions as well as sulfate ions.

bi·sul·fide (bī-sul′fīd, bī-sul′fid), *n.* 1. hydrosulfide. 2. erroneously, a disulfide.

bi·sul·fite (bī-sul′fīt), *n.* an acid sulfite; compound of an element or radical which, in water solutions, produces hydrogen ions as well as sulfite ions.

bi·sym·met·ric (bī′si-met′rik), *adj.* bisymmetrical.

bi·sym·met·ri·cal (bī′si-met′ri-k'l), *adj.* having double symmetry.

bi·sym·me·try (bī-sim′ə-tri), *n.* the quality or condition of being bisymmetrical.

bit (bit) *n.* [ME. *bit, bitt* < AS. *bite*, a bite < *bitan*, to bite], 1. metal mouthpiece on a bridle, acting as a control: see **harness,** illus. 2. anything that curbs or controls. 3. the part of a key that actually turns the lock. 4. the cutting part of any tool, as the blade of a plane. 5. the tool itself: see **brace and bit,** illus. 6. a drilling or boring tool for use in a bitstock, drill press, etc. *v.t.* [BITTED (-id), BITTING], 1. to put a bit into the mouth of (a horse); train to the bit; hence, 2. to check or curb. 3. to make the bit on (a key).
  take (or get) the bit in one's teeth, 1. to get the bit between the teeth, so that it fails to restrain: said of horses; hence, 2. to be beyond control: said of persons.

bit (bit), *n.* [ME. *bite;* AS. *bita*, a piece, morsel, bit < *bitan*, to bite], 1. a small piece or quantity. 2. somewhat: as, he's a *bit* of a bore. 3. [orig. used of a small silver coin worth 1/8 of the Spanish peso (hence, normally 12 1/2 cents); use in multiples of two is due to practice of quartering certain South American dollar coins, each segment (quarter) thus having the value of 25 cents or two bits], [Colloq.], an amount equal to 12 1/2 cents: now usually in *two bits, four bits*, etc. 4. [Colloq.], a short time; moment. 5. a very small role in a play or motion picture. *adj.* very small: as, she has a *bit* part.
  bit by bit, little by little; gradually.
  do one's bit, to do one's share.

bit (bit), past tense and alternative past participle of **bite.**

bi·tar·trate (bī-tär′trāt), *n.* an acid tartrate; compound of an element or radical which, in water solutions, produces hydrogen ions as well as tartrate ions.

bitch (bich), *n.* [ME. *bicche;* AS. *bicce;* akin to ON. *bikkja;* IE. base **bheg-*, to arch, swell out (in reference to pudenda)], 1. the female of the dog, wolf, fox, etc. 2. a bad or bad-tempered woman: used as a strong term of contempt or hostility. *v.i.* [Slang], to complain. *v.t.* [< *botch*], [Slang], to botch; spoil by bungling (usually with *up*).

bitch·y (bich′i), *adj.* of or like a bitch.

bite (bīt), *v.t.* [BIT (bit), BITTEN (bit′'n) or BIT, BITING], [ME. *biten;* AS. *bitan;* akin to Goth. *beitan;* IE. base **bheid-*, to split, crack; cf. FISSURE], 1. to seize, grip, or cut with or as with the teeth. 2. to cut into, as with a sharp weapon. 3. to sting, as a snake. 4. to cause to smart, as cold wind. 5. to grip; press hard into, as a car wheel, ice skate, etc. 6. to eat into; corrode. *v.i.* 1. *a)* to press or snap the teeth (*into, at*, etc.). *b)* to have a tendency to do this. 2. to cause a biting sensation or have a biting effect. 3. to swallow a bait; hence, 4. to be caught, as by a trick. *n.* [< the *v.*], 1. a biting. 2. biting quality; sting: as, there's a *bite* to his words. 3. a wound, bruise, or sting from biting. 4. a mouthful. 5. a tight hold or grip. 6. an edge or surface that grips. 7. [Colloq.], a small lunch; snack. 8. in *dentistry*, the way the upper and lower teeth meet. 9. in *etching*, the corrosion of the metal plate by the acid.
  bite off more than one can chew, to attempt more than one is capable of.
  bite the dust (or **ground**), 1. to fall dead or dying, as in combat. 2. to be humbled or defeated.

Bi·thyn·i·a (bi-thin′i-ə), *n.* an ancient kingdom of northwestern Asia Minor: see **Roman Empire,** map.

bit·ing (bīt′iŋ), *adj.* [ppr. of *bite*], 1. cutting; sharp. 2. sarcastic; sneering. —*SYN.* see **incisive.**

Bi·tolj (bē′tôl′y'), *n.* a city in southern Yugoslavia: pop., 33,000: Turkish name, *Monastir.*

bit player, an actor with a small role.

bit·stock (bit′stok′), *n.* a handle for holding and turning bits; brace.

bitt (bit), *n.* [? < ON. *biti*, a beam], in *nautical usage*, any of the deck posts, often in pairs, around which ropes or cables are wound and held fast. *v.t.* to wind (ropes or cables) around a bitt.

‡**bit·te** (bit′ə; G. bit′e), *interj.* [G., lit., (I) request (of you)], 1. please. 2. I beg your pardon. 3. you're welcome; don't mention it: said in answer to thanks.

bit·ten (bit′'n), past participle of **bite.**

bit·ter (bit′ẽr), *adj.* [ME. *biter;* AS. *biter, bitor, bitter* < base of *bitan*, to bite], 1. having a sharp and disagreeable taste; acrid, as quinine or peach stones. 2. causing or showing sorrow, discomfort, or pain; grievous. 3. sharp and disagreeable; harsh; severe; piercing: as, a *bitter* wind, *bitter* enmity, *bitter* remarks. *adv.* bitterly. *n.* a bitter quality or thing: as, take the *bitter* with the sweet. *v.t. & v.i.* to make or become bitter.

bitter apple, 1. a gourd plant of Europe, Africa, and Asia, bearing round, yellow fruit with a bitter pulp. 2. the fruit, used to make a cathartic. Also called *colocynth.*

bitter cassava, a kind of cassava from whose roots tapioca is made.

bitter end, [merging of archaic *bitter*, turn of cable around a bitt, and *bitter, adj.*, 2: with the anchor cable out to the bitter end, any further misfortune would mean shipwreck], in *nautical usage*, 1. that end of a rope or cable that is wound around a bitt. 2. the inboard end of a rope or cable.
  to the bitter end, 1. until the end, however uncomfortable. 2. until death.

bit·ter-end·er (bit′ẽr-en′dẽr), *n.* [Colloq.], a person who persists beyond reason; one who will not give in.

Bitter Lakes, two lakes forming part of the Suez Canal, on the Isthmus of Suez, Egypt.

bit·tern (bit′ẽrn), *n.* [*pl.* BITTERNS (-ẽrnz), BITTERN; see PLURAL, II, D, 1], [ME. *bitor, botor;* OFr. *butor;* ult. < L. *butio* < echoic base **bu-*], a heronlike wading bird with a booming cry.

bit·tern (bit′ẽrn), *n.* [prob. < *bitter, adj.*], the bitter liquid left after the crystallization of salt from brine.

bit·ter·nut (bit′ẽr-nut′), *n.* a kind of hickory tree bearing small, bitter nuts with a thin shell.

bitter principle, any of various bitter substances found in plants, as lupulin, aloin, etc.

bit·ter·root (bit′ẽr-ro͞ot′, bit′ẽr-root′), *n.* a plant of the Rocky Mountains, with clusters of narrow leaves and white or pink flowers.

Bitter Root Range, a mountain range between Montana and Idaho: length, 400 mi.; highest peak, 10,000 ft.

bit·ters (bit′ẽrz), *n.pl.* a liquor containing bitter herbs, roots, etc. and usually alcohol, used as a medicine and as an ingredient in some cocktails.

bit·ter·sweet (bit′ẽr-swēt′), *n.* 1. a poisonous vine with purple flowers and red berries that taste bitter and sweet. 2. a climbing shrub with clusters of greenish flowers, yellow fruit, and red seeds. 3. bitterness and sweetness combined. *adj.* both bitter and sweet; both painful and pleasant.

bit·ter·weed (bit′ẽr-wēd′), *n.* a kind of ragweed.

bi·tu·men (bi-to͞o′mən, bi-tū′mən, bich′oo-mən), *n.* [L.], 1. originally, mineral pitch. 2. any of several hard or semisolid materials obtained as asphaltic residue in the distillation of coal tar, wood tar, petroleum, etc., or occurring as natural asphalt.

bi·tu·mi·nize (bi-to͞o′mə-nīz′, bi-tū′mə-nīz′), *v.t.* [BITUMINIZED (-nīzd′), BITUMINIZING], to impregnate with, or convert into, bitumen.

bi·tu·mi·nous (bi-to͞o′mə-nəs, bi-tū′mə-nəs), *adj.* [Fr. *bitumineux;* L. *bitumineus* < *bitumen*], 1. of the nature of bitumen. 2. containing or made with bitumen.

bituminous coal, coal that yields pitch or tar when it burns; soft coal.

bi·va·lence (bī-vā′ləns, biv′ə-ləns), *n.* the quality or state of being bivalent.

bi·va·len·cy (bī-vā′lən-si, biv′ə-lən-si), *n.* bivalence.

bi·va·lent (bī-vā′lənt, biv′ə-lənt), *adj.* 1. having two valences. 2. having a valence of two. Also, esp. for 2, **divalent.** 3. in *biology*, double: said of a chromosome formed by two similar chromosomes that lie close together or appear to join completely. *n.* a double chromosome.

bi·valve (bī′valv′), *n.* 1. any mollusk having two valves or shells hinged together, as a mussel, clam, etc. 2. a seed capsule with two valves. *adj.* 1. having two shells hinged together. 2. having two valves.

biv·ou·ac (biv′o͞o-ak′, biv′wak), *n.* [Fr. < OHG. *biwacht*, lit., by-watch; *bi-*, by + *wacht*, a guard], 1. originally, a night guard to avoid surprise attack. 2. a temporary encampment (usually of soldiers) in the open, with or without shelter. *v.i.* [BIVOUACKED (-akt′, -wakt), BIVOUACKING], to encamp in the open.

bi·week·ly (bī-wēk′li), *adj. & adv.* 1. (occurring) once every two weeks. 2. semiweekly. *n.* [*pl.* BIWEEKLIES (-liz)], a publication that appears biweekly.

bi·year·ly (bī-yêr′li), *adj. & adv.* twice a year.

bi·zarre (bi-zär′), *adj.* [Fr. < Sp. or Port. *bizarro*, bold, handsome, knightly < Basque *bizar*, a beard], 1. odd in manner, appearance, etc.; grotesque; queer; eccentric. 2. marked by extreme contrasts and incongruities of color, design, or style. —*SYN.* see **fantastic.**

Bi·zerte (bē'zert'; Eng. bi-zũr'tə), *n.* a town on the coast of Tunisia, near Tunis: pop., 28,000.

Bi·zet, Georges (zhôrzh bē'ze'; Eng. bi-zā'), (born *Alexandre César Léopold Bizet*), 1838–1875; French composer.

B.J., Bachelor of Journalism.

Björn·son, Björn·stjer·ne (byörn'styâr-nə byörn'sôn), 1832–1910; Norwegian poet, dramatist, novelist, and social reformer; received Nobel prize in literature, 1903.

Bk, in *chemistry*, berkelium.

bk., [*pl.* BKS.], 1. bank. 2. block. 3. book.

bkg., banking.

bkkpg., bookkeeping.

bkpt., bankrupt.

bks., Bks., B.K.S., barracks.

bkt., 1. basket; baskets. 2. bracket.

bl., 1. bale; bales. 2. barrel; barrels. 3. black.

B/L, [*pl.* BS/L], bill of lading.

B.L., 1. Bachelor of Laws. 2. Bachelor of Letters.

b.l., 1. bill of lading. 2. breech-loading.

B.L.A., Bachelor of Liberal Arts.

blab (blab), *v.t. & v.i.* [BLABBED (blabd), BLABBING], [ME. *blabbe;* see BLABBER], 1. to give away (secrets). 2. to chatter; prattle. *n.* 1. loose chatter; gossip. 2. a person who blabs.

blab·ber (blab'ẽr), *n.* [< the *v.*], a person who blabs. *v.t. & v.i.* [ME. *blabberen,* freq. of *blab;* akin to ON. *blabbra,* ODan. *blable,* MD. *blabberen,* etc.; echoic], [Obs. or Dial.], to blab; babble.

black (blak), *adj.* [ME. *blak, blakke;* AS. *blæc;* akin to OHG. *blah;* IE. base **bhleg-*, shine, gleam, as in L. *flagrare,* flame, burn, whence *flagrant;* orig. sense, "sooted, smoke-black from flame"], 1. opposite to white: see **color.** 2. dark-complexioned. 3. Negro. 4. totally without light; in complete darkness; dark. 5. soiled; dirty. 6. wearing black clothing. 7. evil; wicked; harmful. 8. disgraceful. 9. sad; dismal; gloomy. 10. sullen; angered. 11. without hope: as, a *black* future. 12. [Colloq.], inveterate; confirmed; deep-dyed: as, a *black* villain. Abbreviated **bl., blk.** *n.* 1. the darkest color. 2. a spot of this color; smut. 3. a dye or paint of this color. 4. dark clothing, as for mourning. 5. a person of dark complexion. 6. a Negro. *v.t. & v.i.* 1. to blacken; soil. 2. to put blacking on (shoes, etc.).
black out, 1. to cover (writing, printing, etc.) with black pencil marks or paint. 2. to cause a blackout in. 3. to lose consciousness, as an aviator in coming out of a power dive.

Black, Hugo La Fayette (lä'fi-et' blak), 1886– ; American jurist; associate justice, United States Supreme Court (1937–).

black alder, a shrub with glossy leaves and bright red berries; winterberry.

black·a·moor (blak'ə-moor'), *n.* [< *black* + *Moor*], 1. a Negro, especially an African Negro. 2. any dark-skinned person.

black-and-blue (blak'ən-blōō'), *adj.* discolored from congestion of blood under the skin; bruised.

black-and-tan (blak'ən-tan'), *n.* any of a breed of small, lean dogs having a smooth, black coat with tan markings: also called *Manchester terrier, rat terrier.*

Black and Tan, a member of the British troops sent to Ireland to help put down disturbances during the Sinn Fein rebellion (1919–1921).

black and white, 1. print; writing: as, put your agreement down in *black and white.* 2. a drawing or picture done in black and white.

black art, black magic.

black·ball (blak'bôl'), *n.* 1. originally, a small, black ball used as a vote against a person or thing. 2. a secret ballot or vote against a person or thing. *v.t.* 1. to vote against; hence, 2. to exclude from social life, etc.; ostracize.

black bass (bas), any of a number of related fresh-water game fishes of North America, having a long body and spiny fins.

black bear, 1. a variety of large American bear. 2. a variety of large bear found in Asia.

Black·beard (blak'bêrd'), *n.* (*Edward Teach*), an English privateer who became a pirate; lived ?–1718.

black·bee·tle (blak'bē't'l), *n.* a cockroach; oriental cockroach: also **black beetle.**

black belt, 1. [often B- B-], that part of the southern United States where Negroes are a majority of the population. 2. any district, as of a city, in which Negroes are a majority. 3. an area of very rich soil in the coastal plain of Alabama and Mississippi.

black·ber·ry (blak'ber'i, blak'bẽr-i), *n.* [*pl.* BLACKBERRIES (-iz)], 1. the small, edible, dark purple or black fruit of any of a number of related brambles of the rose family. 2. a bush or vine bearing this fruit.

blackberry lily, a plant of the iris family, bearing orange-colored flowers with red spots, and fruit like a blackberry.

black bindweed, 1. a European twining vine with long-stemmed leaves and small red berries. 2. a European twining plant now found in America as a tenacious weed.

black·bird (blak'bũrd'), *n.* any of various birds the male of which is almost entirely black, as the purple grackle, cowbird, red-winged blackbird, common English thrush, etc.

black·board (blak'bôrd', blak'bōrd'), *n.* a smooth surface of slate or other dark material on which one can write or draw with chalk.

black book, a book containing names of those blacklisted.
be in one's black book, to be regarded unfavorably by one.

black·boy (blak'boi'), *n.* 1. an Australian plant with long, wiry leaves and long spikes of flowers; grass tree. 2. a blackfellow: patronizing term.

black bread, a dark, coarse bread, usually made of rye flour.

black buck, a long-horned antelope of India that is brownish-black above and white below.

Black·burn (blak'bẽrn), *n.* a city in Lancashire, England: pop., 109,000 (est. 1946).

Blackburn, Mount, a mountain of the Wrangell Range, southeastern Alaska: height, 16,140 ft.

Black Canyon, 1. a canyon between Arizona and Nevada, cut by the Colorado River, near Hoover Dam. 2. a canyon in western Colorado, cut by the Gunnison River: a national monument.

black·cap (blak'kap'), *n.* 1. any of various birds with a black, caplike crown, as the chickadee, a European warbler, etc. 2. the black raspberry.

black·cock (blak'kok'), *n.* [*pl.* BLACKCOCKS (-koks'), BLACKCOCK; see PLURAL, II, D, 1], the male of the black grouse.

black coffee, coffee without cream or sugar.

black country, [often B- C-], a mining and industrial district in the English Midlands around Birmingham: so called because of the prevailing soot and grime.

black·damp (blak'damp'), *n.* chokedamp, a gas found in mines, etc.

Black Death, a deadly disease, probably bubonic plague, which greatly reduced the population of Europe and Asia in the 14th century: so called from the black spots caused on the skin.

black diamonds, coal.

black·en (blak''n), *v.i.* [ME. *blaknen* < *blak,* black], to become black or dark. *v.t.* 1. to make black; darken. 2. to slander; defame; vilify.

black eye, 1. an eye with a very dark iris. 2. a discoloration of the skin or flesh surrounding an eye, resulting from a sharp blow, or contusion. 3. [Colloq.], *a*) shame; dishonor; bad reputation. *b*) a cause or source of this.

black-eyed peas (blak'īd'), the seeds of the cowpea.

black-eyed Su·san (sōō'z'n), 1. a hairy plant bearing yellow, daisylike flowers with a purple-brown, cone-shaped center: also called *yellow daisy.* 2. the bladder ketmie.

black·face (blak'fās'), *adj.* 1. having a black or blackened face. 2. in *printing,* bold-faced. *n.* 1. a Negro in a minstrel show. 2. a person made up as a Negro. 3. make-up used by performers of Negro roles, usually exaggerated for comic effect. 4. in *printing,* boldface.

Black·feet (blak'fēt'), *n.pl.* [*sing.* BLACKFOOT (-foot')], members of three tribes of Algonquian Indians who lived in Montana and Saskatchewan, east of the Rocky Mountains.

black·fel·low (blak'fel'ō), *n.* a member of any dark-skinned native tribe of Australia: patronizing term.

black·fish (blak'fish'), *n.* [*pl.* BLACKFISH, BLACKFISHES (-iz); see FISH], 1. a small, black whale. 2. any of a number of dark fishes, as the sea bass, tautog, etc. 3. an edible, minnowlike, fresh-water fish of Siberia and Alaska.

black flag, the flag of piracy, usually with a white skull and crossbones on a black background; Jolly Roger.

black fly, any of a number of related small, biting flies of North American forests.

Black·foot (blak'foot'), *n.* [*pl.* BLACKFEET (-fēt'); *collectively,* BLACKFOOT], a member of the Blackfeet. *adj.* of the Blackfeet.

Black Forest, a mountainous district, about 100 miles long, in southwestern Germany: German name, *Schwarzwald.*

Black Friar, a Dominican friar.

Black Friday, 1. any Friday in which there is misfortune or disaster. 2. Good Friday: so called because the clergy wear black vestments on that day.

black frost, a severe frost.

black grouse, a large grouse found in Europe and Asia, the male of which is almost entirely black.

black·guard (blag'ẽrd, blag'ärd), *n.* [see GUARD], 1. originally, the lowest servants of a large household, in charge of pots and pans. 2. *a*) a person who uses abusive language. *b*) scoundrel; villain. *adj.* 1. vulgar, low, etc. 2. abusive. *v.t.* to abuse with words; rail at; revile. *v.i.* to behave as a blackguard.

black·guard·ly (blag'ẽrd-li, blag'ärd-li), *adj.* of or

characteristic of a blackguard. *adv.* in the manner of a blackguard.
black gum, a tall tree with crooked branches, greenish-white flowers, and bluish fruit: also called *pepperidge.*
Black Hand, [transl. of Sp. *mano negra:* a symbol like a black hand affixed to threatening letters from the society], 1. originally, a 19th-century anarchist society in Spain. 2. a group of Sicilian immigrant blackmailers who operated in New York in the early 20th century; hence, 3. any similar secret society.
black haw, 1. a kind of viburnum with clusters of white flowers and blue-black berries. 2. the sheepberry.
Black Hawk, 1767–1838; American Indian chief of the Fox and Sac; leader in the Black Hawk War.
black·head (blak′hed′), *n.* 1. a scaup duck: the male has a glossy, black head and neck. 2. a black-tipped plug of dried fatty matter in a pore of the skin; comedo. 3. a disease of turkeys that affects the liver, comb, etc.
black·heart (blak′härt′), *n.* a dark, heart-shaped, sweet cherry with purplish flesh.
black-heart·ed (blak′här′tid), *adj.* wicked; malevolent.
Black Hills, mountains of western South Dakota and northeastern Wyoming: highest point, Harney Peak.
black hole, 1. [B- H-], a small dungeon in a fortress at Calcutta: of 146 Europeans reputedly confined there on the night of June 20, 1756, 123 were said to have died from heat and lack of air; hence, 2. any dungeon.
black horehound, a bad-smelling weed of the mint family, with purple flowers.
black·ing (blak′iŋ), *n.* a black polish for use on stoves, shoes, boots, etc.
black·ish (blak′ish), *adj.* somewhat black.
black·jack (blak′jak′), *n.* [see JACK-], 1. a large mug, formerly made of leather coated with tar. 2. the black flag. 3. a small, leather-covered bludgeon with a flexible handle. 4. a small oak with black bark, common in the eastern United States. 5. a card game in which the object is to get a combination of cards adding to twenty-one. 6. in *mining*, zinc sulfide. Also **black jack.** *v.t.* 1. to hit with a blackjack. 2. to force (a person) to do something by threatening, as if with a blackjack.
black knot, 1. a disease of cherry and plum trees, in which hard, black swellings appear on twigs and branches. 2. the fungus causing this disease.
black lead, a soft, black substance, almost entirely carbon; graphite: it is used in lead pencils, as a polish, etc.
black·leg (blak′leg′), *n.* 1. an infectious disease of cattle and sheep, usually resulting in death. 2. a fungous disease of cabbage and similar plants. 3. [British], a strikebreaker or scab. 4. [Colloq.], a gambler who cheats; crook.
black-let·ter (blak′let′ẽr), *adj.* 1. printed in black letter. 2. unlucky; unfortunate: as, a *black-letter* day.
black letter, 1. a kind of type: in England it is called *Gothic* or *Old English.* **This line is in black letter.** 2. any heavy-faced type.
black-list (blak′list′), *v.t.* to put on a black list.
black list, a list of suspected persons or of those to be punished, refused employment, etc.
black·ly (blak′li), *adv.* [*black* + *-ly*], 1. drearily; gloomily. 2. angrily; menacingly. 3. in a sinister way.
black magic, magic with an evil purpose; sorcery.
black·mail (blak′māl′), *n.* [lit., black rent < ME. *maille*, rent, tribute; OFr. *maille*, a coin], 1. formerly, a tribute paid to freebooters and bandits along the Scottish border to assure safety from looting. 2. payment extorted to prevent disclosure of information that would bring disgrace or ruin if made public. 3. a blackmailing. *v.t.* 1. to get or try to get blackmail from. 2. to coerce (*into* doing something) as by threats.
Black Ma·ri·a (mə-rī′ə), a vehicle, formerly painted black, used to take arrested persons to and from jail; patrol wagon.
black mark, a mark indicating something unfavorable in one's record.
black market, a place or system for selling goods illegally, especially in violation of rationing or price control: cf. **gray market.**
black mass, 1. a religious service or mass at which the clergy are dressed in black. 2. a blasphemous imitation of the mass.
black measles, a severe form of measles with a very dark rash.
black mold, bread mold.
Black Monk, a monk of the Benedictine order: so called from the black dress.
Black·more, Richard Dod·dridge (dod′rij blak′môr, blak′mōr), 1825–1900; English novelist.
Black Mountains, a part of the Appalachian mountain system in western North Carolina: highest peak, Mount Mitchell, 6,711 ft.
Black Muslim, a member of a militant, secret Islamic sect of American Negroes that advocates asceticism, racial separation, and the establishment of exclusive Negro States.
black nightshade, a weedy plant of the nightshade family, with white flowers, poisonous leaves, and black berries that can be poisonous, especially if eaten green: also called *deadly nightshade.*
black oak, 1. a kind of oak with dark leaves or bark. 2. its wood.
black·out (blak′out′), *n.* 1. the extinguishing of all stage lights to end a play or scene. 2. an elimination or concealing of all lights that might be visible to enemy air raiders, etc. at night. 3. a momentary lapse of consciousness, such as an aviator often experiences in coming out of a steep dive. 4. suppression, censorship, concealment, etc., as of news. *adj.* of or for a blackout.
black pepper, 1. a hot seasoning made by grinding the dried, black berries of a kind of pepper plant. 2. the plant.
black·poll (blak′pōl′), *n.* a kind of warbler, the male of which has a black crown: also **blackpoll warbler.**
Black·pool (blak′po͞ol′), *n.* a seaport and resort in northwestern England: pop., 144,000.
Black Prince, Edward, Prince of Wales (1330–1376).
black race, loosely, the Negro division of mankind.
Black Rod, 1. in England, the chief usher (Gentleman Usher of the Black Rod) to the Order of the Garter and the House of Lords: so called from his symbol of office, an ebony rod. 2. a similar official in British colonial parliaments.
black rot, 1. a plant disease that causes fruits and vegetables to discolor and decay. 2. the fungus causing this disease.
black rust, 1. a disease of wheat, rye, barley, etc. 2. the fungus causing this disease.
Black Sea, a sea surrounded by the U.S.S.R., Asia Minor, and the Balkan Peninsula: area, 164,000 sq. mi.; average depth, 3,900 ft.: ancient name, *Euxine Sea.*
black sheep, 1. a sheep with black fleece. 2. a person regarded as undesirable, disgraceful, etc. by other members of his family or group.
black shirt, Black Shirt, a member of the Italian Fascist party or of the German Nazi Elite Guard (*Schutzstaffel*): so called from the black shirt worn as part of the uniform.
black·smith (blak′smith′), *n.* 1. a man who works, repairs, and shapes iron with a forge, anvil, hammer, etc. 2. a man who shoes horses.
black·snake (blak′snāk′), *n.* 1. any of various black or dark-colored snakes, especially one of a harmless variety found in North America. 2. a long, heavy whip of braided leather or rawhide. Also **black snake.**
black spruce, 1. a kind of spruce with dark leaves and soft, light wood. 2. its wood.
Black·stone, Sir **William** (blak′stōn′, blak′stən), 1723–1780; English jurist and legal historian.
black·tail (blak′tāl′), *n.* a mule deer.
black tea, tea fermented and withered before being dried by heating.
black·thorn (blak′thôrn′), *n.* 1. a thorny, white-flowered shrub with purple or black, plumlike fruit; sloe. 2. a cane or stick made of the stem of this shrub. 3. a kind of hawthorn.
black tie, 1. a black bow tie, properly worn with a dinner jacket; hence, 2. a dinner jacket and the proper accessories. Distinguished from *white tie.*
black·top (blak′top′), *n.* a bituminous mixture, usually asphalt, used as a surface for roads, etc. *v.t.* [BLACKTOPPED (-topt), BLACKTOPPING], to cover with blacktop.
black vomit, 1. vomit characteristic of yellow fever, dark because of the blood in it. 2. yellow fever.
Black·wall hitch (blak′wôl′), a kind of knot: see **knot,** illus.
black walnut, 1. a tall walnut tree with edible, oily nuts and hard, heavy, dark-brown wood, much used in making furniture. 2. its wood. 3. its nut.
black·wa·ter fever (blak′wô′tẽr, blak′wot′ẽr), an acute fever due to infection with malignant tertiary malaria.
Black·wells Island (blak′welz′), former name of Welfare Island in the East River, New York City.
black widow, the female of an American variety of spider, having a glossy black body with reddish markings underneath, and a very poisonous bite: so called because it eats its mate.
blad·der (blad′ẽr), *n.* [ME. *bladre, bledder;* AS. *blæddre;* akin to G. *blatter;* IE. base **bhel-*, to swell up, swell out, in the form **bhle-*], 1. a bag of membranous tissue in the bodies of many animals, capable of inflation to receive and contain liquids or gases: the *urinary bladder* in the pelvic cavity holds urine flowing from the kidneys. 2. a thing resembling such a bag: as, a football *bladder.* 3. in *botany*, *a*) an inflated covering of certain fruits. *b*) an air sac, as in some water plants.
bladder campion, a plant of the pink family, with an inflated calyx.
blad·der·nose (blad′ẽr-nōz′), *n.* a variety of seal, the male of which has on its head a hoodlike sac that can be inflated: also called *hooded seal.*

blad·der·nut (blad′ẽr-nut′), *n.* 1. the bladderlike, inflated pod of any of a number of related shrubs or small trees. 2. the plant it grows on.
bladder worm, the tapeworm larva at the stage in which its head and neck are enclosed in a bladderlike sac; cysticercus; hydatid.
blad·der·wort (blad′ẽr-wũrt′), *n.* any of a number of related plants found growing in bogs or floating on water, with small, bladderlike parts on their leaves for catching small organisms as food.
blad·der·y (blad′ẽr-i), *adj.* 1. like a bladder. 2. having a bladder or bladders.
blade (blād), *n.* [ME. *blad, blade* < AS. *blæd,* a leaf; akin to G. *blatt;* IE. base *bhlē-, *bhlō-, to sprout up, leaf, flower, as in L. *flos, floris,* a flower; cf. FLORAL], 1. the leaf of a plant, especially grass. 2. a broad, flat section or surface, as of a knife, bone, propeller, oar, etc. 3. a flat bone: as, the shoulder *blade.* 4. the cutting part of a tool, instrument, or weapon. 5. a sword. 6. a swordsman. 7. a gay, dashing young man. 8. in *botany,* the flat, expanded part of a leaf; lamina. 9. in *phonetics,* the flat part of the tongue, behind the tip. *v.i.* [BLADED (-id), BLADING], to grow with blades.
blade·bone (blād′bōn′), *n.* the shoulder blade; scapula.
Bla·go·vesh·chensk (blä′gô-vyesh′chensk), *n.* a city in the southeastern U.S.S.R., on the Amur River: pop., 59,000.
blah (blä), *n. & interj.* [echoic], [Slang], nonsense.
blain (blān), *n.* [ME. *bleine;* AS. *blegen,* a blister; for IE. base see BALL (sphere)], an inflamed sore or swollen place; pustule or blister.
Blaine, James Gil·les·pie (gi-les′pi blān), 1830–1893; American statesman.
Blake, Robert (blāk), 1599–1657; British admiral.
Blake, William, 1757–1827; English poet and engraver.
blam·a·ble, blame·a·ble (blām′ə-b'l), *adj.* [ME.], that deserves blame; culpable.
blame (blām), *v.t.* [BLAMED (blāmd), BLAMING], [ME. *blamen;* OFr. *blasmer,* to speak evil of; LL. *blasphemare;* Gr. *blasphēmein;* see BLASPHEME], 1. to accuse (a person, etc.) of being at fault; condemn (*for* something); censure. 2. to find fault with (*for* something). 3. to put the responsibility of, as an error, fault, etc. (*on* someone or something). *n.* 1. a blaming; accusation; condemnation; censure. 2. responsibility for a fault or wrong. 3. [Archaic], fault. —*SYN.* see **criticize.**
be to blame, to be blamable; be at fault.
blamed (blāmd), *adj. & adv.* [pp. of *blame*], [Colloq.], a mild expletive, used as a substitute for *damned.*
blame·ful (blām′fəl), *adj.* 1. finding or imputing blame; blaming. 2. blameworthy.
blame·less (blām′lis), *adj.* free from blame.
blame·wor·thy (blām′wũr′*th*i), *adj.* deserving to be blamed.
Blanc, Lou·is (lwē blän), 1811–1882; French socialist.
Blanc, Mont, see **Mont Blanc.**
Blan·ca Peak (blaŋ′kə), the highest peak of the Sangre de Cristo range, southern Colorado: height, 14,390 ft.
blanch (blanch, blänch), *v.t.* [ME. *blanchen;* OFr. *blanchir* < *blanc,* white; see BLANK], 1. to make white; take color from. 2. to make pale. 3. in *cookery,* to remove the skin of by scalding. 4. in *horticulture,* to bleach (endive, celery, etc.) by earthing up or covering so as to keep away light and improve the appearance, flavor, or tenderness. 5. in *metallurgy,* to brighten with acid or by coating with tin. *v.i.* to whiten; turn pale.
blanch (blanch, blänch), *v.t.* [var. of *blench*], to turn aside or head off (a deer, etc.).
Blanche, Blanch (blanch), [Fr. *Blanche,* lit., white, fem. of *blanc;* see BLANK], a feminine name: equivalents, G. & Sp. *Blanca,* It. *Bianca.*
blanc·mange (blə-mänzh′), *n.* [Fr. < *blanc,* white + *manger,* to eat], a sweet, molded, jellylike dessert made of a starchy substance and milk.
bland (bland), *adj.* [L. *blandus,* mild], 1. pleasantly smooth; agreeable; suave: as, he has a *bland* manner. 2. mild; soothing; temperate: as, *bland* medicine. —*SYN.* see **soft, suave.**
blan·dish (blan′dish), *v.t. & v.i.* [ME. *blandissen* < OFr. *blandir,* to flatter; L. *blandiri,* to flatter < *blandus,* mild], to flatter; coax; cajole.
blan·dish·ment (blan′dish-mənt), *n.* 1. a blandishing; flattery; cajolement. 2. a flattering or cajoling act, remark, etc.
blank (blaŋk), *adj.* [ME.; OFr. *blanc,* fem. *blanche;* OHG. *blanch,* white, gleaming; akin to AS. *blanca,* white steed; Gmc. base *blank-, gleaming < IE. base *bhleg-, to shine, gleam; see BLACK, BLINK], 1. [Rare], colorless; white. 2. not written on; not marked; empty: as, a *blank* sheet of paper. 3. having an empty, vacant, or monotonous look or character. 4. without interest or expression: as, *blank* looks. 5. empty of thought; lacking ideas: as, my mind is *blank.* 6. unproductive; barren: as, *blank* years. 7. utter; complete: as, a *blank* denial. 8. lacking certain elements or characteristics. *n.* 1. an empty space, especially one to be filled out in a printed form or document. 2. a printed form or document with such empty spaces. 3. an emptiness; vacant place or time. 4. the center spot of a target; hence, 5. a thing aimed at or pointed at. 6. a lottery or raffle ticket that fails to win. 7. a manufactured article yet to be cut to a pattern or marked with a design. 8. a powder-filled cartridge without a bullet; blank cartridge. 9. a mark, usually a dash (—), indicating an omitted word, especially an oath or curse. *v.t.* 1. to conceal or obscure by covering over (usually with *out*). 2. in *games,* to hold (an opponent) scoreless.
draw a blank, 1. to draw a lottery ticket that fails to win. 2. [Colloq.], to be unsuccessful in any attempt.
blank check, 1. a check form that has not been filled in. 2. a check carrying a signature only and allowing the bearer to fill in any amount; hence, 3. permission to use an unlimited amount of money, authority, etc.
blank endorsement, an endorsement naming no payee, making the endorsed amount payable to the bearer.
blan·ket (blaŋ′kit), *n.* [ME.; OFr. *blanquete;* dim. of *blanc,* white; see BLANK], 1. a large piece of cloth, often soft woolen, used for warmth as a bed cover or a covering for animals. 2. anything used as or resembling a blanket: as, a *blanket* of leaves. *adj.* covering a group of conditions or requirements; including many items: as, a *blanket* insurance policy. *v.t.* 1. to cover with or as with a blanket. 2. to apply uniformly to, as regulations or rates. 3. to overspread; overlie. 4. to cut off the wind of (a sailboat, etc.) by passing close to windward, as in yacht racing. 5. to suppress; hinder; obscure: as, a powerful radio station *blankets* a weaker one.
blan·ke·ty-blank (blaŋ′ki-ti-blaŋk′), *adj. & adv.* [redupl. < *blank, n.,* 9], [Slang], humorous euphemism for damned, etc.
blank·ly (blaŋk′li), *adv.* in a blank manner; especially, *a*) with an empty or vacuous look or expression. *b*) utterly; completely; starkly.
blank verse, 1. [Rare], unrhymed verse. 2. unrhymed verse typically having five iambic feet per line, as in Elizabethan drama.
blare (blâr), *v.t. & v.i.* [BLARED (blârd), BLARING], [ME. *bloryyn, bleren,* to cry noisily < LG.; same base as in *bleat*], 1. to sound loudly with a trumpetlike quality. 2. to announce or exclaim loudly. *n.* 1. a loud, trumpetlike sound. 2. brilliance or glare, as of color.
blar·ney (blär′ni), *n.* [see BLARNEY STONE], flattery. *v.t. & v.i.* [BLARNEYED (-nid), BLARNEYING], to flatter; wheedle; coax.
Blarney stone, a stone in Blarney Castle in the county of Cork, Ireland, said to impart skill in blarney to those who kiss it.
Blas·co-I·bá·ñez, Vi·cen·te (vē-then′te bläs′kô-ē-bä′nyeth), 1867–1928; Spanish novelist.
bla·sé (blä-zā′, blä′zā), *adj.* [Fr., pp. of *blaser,* to satiate], having indulged in pleasure so much as to be somewhat weary of it; satiated and bored.
blas·pheme (blas-fēm′), *v.t.* [BLASPHEMED (-fēmd′), BLASPHEMING], [ME. *blasfemen;* OFr. *blasfemer;* LL. *blasphemare;* Gr. *blasphēmein,* to speak evil of], 1. to speak irreverently or profanely of or to (God or sacred things). 2. to curse or revile. *v.i.* to utter blasphemy.
blas·phe·mous (blas′fi-məs), *adj.* [L. *blasphemus;* Gr. *blasphēmos;* see BLASPHEME], characterized by blasphemy; irreverent; profane.
blas·phe·my (blas′fi-mi), *n.* [*pl.* BLASPHEMIES (-miz)], [ME. *blasfemie;* OFr. *blaspheme;* L. *blasphemia;* Gr. *blasphēmia;* see BLASPHEME], 1. profane or mocking speech, writing, or action concerning God or anything regarded as sacred. 2. contempt for God.
SYN.—**blasphemy,** the strongest of the following terms, refers to any remark deliberately mocking or contemptuous of God; **profanity** extends the concept to irreverent remarks referring to any person or thing regarded as sacred; **swearing** and **cursing,** in this connection, both refer to the utterance of profane oaths and imprecations, the latter, especially, to the calling down of evil upon someone or something.
blast (blast, bläst), *n.* [ME.; AS. *blæst,* puff of wind; akin to OHG. *blast;* see BLAZE (to proclaim)], 1. a gust of wind; strong rush of air. 2. the sound of a sudden rush of air or gas, as through a trumpet. 3. a strong, artificially created jet of air. 4. the steady current of air in a blast furnace. 5. an abrupt and damaging influence; blight. 6. an explosion, as of dynamite. 7. a charge of explosive causing this. *v.i.* to suffer or wither from a blight. *v.t.* 1. to damage or destroy by or as by a blight; wither; shrivel; ruin. 2. to blow up or move with or as with an explosive; explode. —*SYN.* see **wind.**
blast off, [Colloq.], to take off with explosive force and begin its flight: said of a rocket or ballistic missile.
in (or **at**) **full blast,** at full speed or capacity.
-blast (blast), [< Gr. *blastos,* a sprout], a combining form meaning *formative, embryonic,* as in *mesoblast.*
blast·ed (blas′tid, bläs′tid), *adj.* [pp. of *blast*], 1. blighted; withered; destroyed. 2. damned; confounded; accursed: a mild expletive.
blas·te·ma (blas-tē′mə), *n.* [*pl.* BLASTEMATA (-mə-tə)], [Gr. *blastēma,* a bud < *blastanein,* to bud or sprout], the undifferentiated embryonic tissue from which cells, tissues, and organs are developed.

blast furnace, a towerlike furnace for separating metal from the impurities in the ore: a blast of air is forced into the furnace from below to produce the intense heat needed.

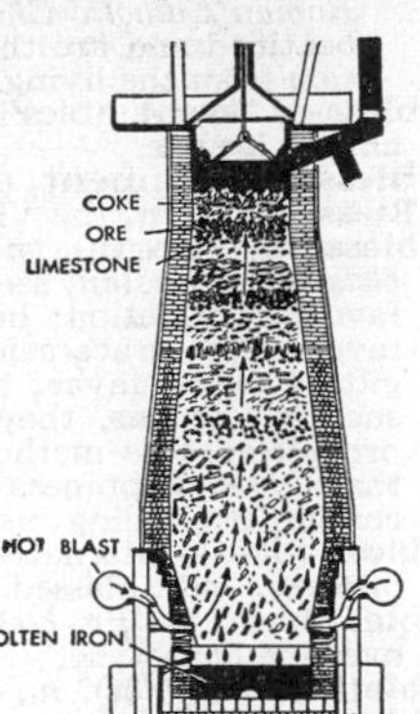

BLAST FURNACE

blas·tie (blas′ti, bläs′ti), *n.* [Scot.], a dwarf.
blast·ment (blast′mənt, bläst′mənt), *n.* [Rare], a blasting, or blight.
blas·to- (blas′tō, blas′tə), [< Gr. *blastos*, a sprout], a combining form indicating *connection with the embryo, relation to germination*, as in *blastoderm, blastogenesis:* also, before a vowel, **blast-.**
blas·to·coele (blas′tə-sēl′), *n.* [*blasto-* + *-coele*], the segmentation cavity of a developing ovum or of the blastula: see **blastula,** illus.
blas·to·cyst (blas′tə-sist), *n.* [*blasto-* + *-cyst*], a blastula.
blas·to·derm (blas′tə-dũrm′), *n.* [*blasto-* + *-derm*], the part of a fertilized ovum that gives rise to the germinal disk from which the embryo develops.
blas·to·disk (blas′tə-disk′), *n.* [*blasto-* + *disk*], in *embryology*, the germinal disk.
blast-off, blast·off (blast′ôf′), *n.* [Colloq.], the launching of a rocket, ballistic missile, etc.
blas·to·gen·e·sis (blas′tə-jen′ə-sis), *n.* [*blasto-* + *-genesis*], 1. reproduction by budding, as in coral. 2. the theory that the germ plasm transmits hereditary characters: opposed to *pangenesis*.
blas·to·mere (blas′tə-mêr′), *n.* [*blasto-* + *-mere*], any of the cells resulting from the first few divisions of the ovum after fertilization.
blas·to·pore (blas′tə-pôr′, blas′tə-pōr′), *n.* [*blasto-* + *-pore*], the opening into the gastrula cavity.
blas·to·sphere (blas′tə-sfêr′), *n.* [*blasto-* + *-sphere*], the blastula.
blas·tu·la (blas′choo-lə), *n.* [Mod. ‡L., dim. < Gr. *blastos*, a germ, sprout], 1. the stage of development at which an embryo consists of one or several layers of cells around a central cavity, forming a hollow sphere. 2. [*pl.* BLASTULAE (-lē′)], an embryo at this stage.

MICROMERES
BLASTOCOELE
MACROMERES
BLASTULA

blas·tu·lar (blas′choo-lẽr), *adj.* of, or having the nature of, a blastula.
blat (blat), *v.i.* [BLATTED (-id), BLATTING], [var. of *bleat*], [Colloq.], to make a sound like that of a sheep or calf; bleat. *v.t.* to blurt out; blab.
bla·tan·cy (blā′t'n-si), *n.* [BLATANCIES (-siz)], a blatant quality or thing.
bla·tant (blā′t'nt), *adj.* [coined by E. Spenser; prob. < L. *blaterare*, to babble, or Eng. dial. *blate*, to bellow], 1. disagreeably loud or boisterous; noisy. 2. too conspicuous; obtrusive. 3. very showy; gaudy; flashy. —*SYN.* see **vociferous.**
blath·er (bla*th*′ẽr), *n.* [ON. *blathr*], foolish talk; nonsense. *v.i. & v.t.* to speak foolishly. Also **blether.**
blath·er·skite (bla*th*′ẽr-skīt′), *n.* [Colloq.], 1. blather. 2. a talkative, foolish person.
blau·bok (blou′bok′), *n.* [*pl.* BLAUBOK, BLAUBOKS (-boks′); see PLURAL, II, D, 2], [D. *blauwbok*, lit., blue buck], a large, bluish-gray antelope of South Africa, now extinct.
Bla·vat·sky, E·le·na Pe·trov·na (i-lē′nə pə-trōv′nə blə-vät′ski), (born *Helena Hahn*), 1831–1891; Russian noblewoman and theosophist.
blaw (blô), *v.t. & v.i.* [British Dial. or Scot.], to blow.
blaze (blāz), *n.* [ME. *blase;* AS. *blæse, blase*, a torch, flame; IE. base **bhles-*, shine], 1. a brilliant mass or burst of flame; fire. 2. any bright light or glare: as, the *blaze* of searchlights. 3. a sudden, spectacular occurrence; outburst: as, a *blaze* of oratory. 4. a brightness; vivid display; flash. 5. *pl.* hell: a euphemism, especially in the phrase *go to blazes!* *v.i.* [BLAZED (blāzd), BLAZING], 1. to burn rapidly or brightly; flame. 2. to give off a strong, vivid light; have a bright color; glare. 3. to be deeply stirred or excited, as with anger. *v.t.* 1. to cause to burn. 2. to shine with (light, etc.).
blaze away, 1. to fire guns; shoot. 2. to speak heatedly.
SYN.—**blaze** suggests a hot, intensely bright, relatively large and steady fire (the *blaze* of a burning house); **flame** generally refers to a single, shimmering, tonguelike emanation of burning gas (the *flame* of a candle); **flicker** suggests an unsteady, fluttering flame, especially one that is dying out (the last *flicker* of his oil lamp); **flare** implies a sudden, bright, unsteady light shooting up into darkness (the *flare* of a torch); **glow** suggests a steady, warm, subdued light without flame or blaze (the *glow* of burning embers); **glare** implies a steady, unpleasantly bright light (the *glare* of a bare electric light bulb).
blaze (blāz), *n.* [prob. D. < *bles*, white spot < ON. *blesi* < same ult. source as *blaze* (flame)], 1. a light-colored spot on an animal's face. 2. a mark made on a tree by cutting off a piece of bark. *v.t.* [BLAZED (blāzd), BLAZING], 1. to make a blaze on (a tree). 2. to indicate (a trail, path, etc.) in this way.
blaze (blāz), *v.t.* [BLAZED (blāzd), BLAZING], [ME. *blasen;* ON. *blasa*, to blow; akin to G. *blasen;* IE. base **bhlē-;* see BLADDER], to make known publicly; spread the news of; proclaim.
blaz·er (blāz′ẽr), *n.* [< *blaze* (fire) + *-er*], 1. a light, brightly colored sports jacket. 2. a dish for use in cooking over coals or an alcohol flame.
blazing star, 1. any of a number of unrelated American plants bearing showy, colorful flowers, as the button snakeroot, torch lily, fairy wand, etc. 2. a person or thing that attracts great attention. 3. [Obs.], a comet.
bla·zon (blā′z'n), *n.* [ME. *blasoun;* OFr. *blason*, a shield, blazon], 1. a coat of arms; heraldic shield, emblem, or banner; hence, 2. a technical description or illustration of a coat of arms. 3. showy display. *v.t.* [< the *n.;* mistakenly associated with *blaze* (proclaim)], 1. to make known far and wide; proclaim (often with *forth, out,* or *abroad*). 2. to describe technically or paint (coats of arms).
bla·zon·ment (blā′z'n-mənt), *n.* 1. a blazoning. 2. a thing blazoned.
bla·zon·ry (blā′z'n-ri), *n.* [*pl.* BLAZONRIES (-riz)], [see BLAZON], 1. the art of properly describing or illustrating coats of arms. 2. emblems or bearings of heraldry; coats of arms; hence, 3. any brilliant display.
bldg., building.
-ble (b'l), -able.
B.L.E., Brotherhood of Locomotive Engineers: a labor union.
blech (blēch), *v.t.* [ME. *blechen;* AS. *blæcan* < *blac*, pale, bleak], 1. to decolorize by means of chemicals or by exposure to the sun's rays. 2. to whiten; blanch. *v.i.* to become white, colorless, or pale. *n.* 1. a bleaching or whitening. 2. any chemical used in bleaching. 3. the degree of whiteness resulting from bleaching.
bleach·er (blēch′ẽr), *n.* a person or thing that bleaches.
bleach·ers (blēch′ẽrz), *n.pl.* [< *bleacher:* in reference to the effects of exposure], seats for spectators at outdoor baseball games, sporting events, etc.: most bleachers are roofless and are made of planks laid lengthwise.
bleach·er·y (blēch′ẽr-i), *n.* [*pl.* BLEACHERIES (-iz)], a place where bleaching is done.
bleaching powder, chloride of lime or any other powder used in bleaching.
bleak (blēk), *adj.* [prob. < ON. *bleikr*, pale; akin to ME. *bleche*, AS. *blac*, pale], 1. exposed to wind and cold; unsheltered; treeless; bare. 2. pale; wan; of sickly color. 3. cold; cutting; harsh. 4. cheerless; gloomy; desolate; depressing.
bleak (blēk), *n.* [*pl.* BLEAK, BLEAKS (blēks); see PLURAL, II, D, 2], [prob. < ON. *bleikja* < *bleikr*, pale], a small, slender European fish of the carp family, with silvery scales used in making artificial pearls.
blear (blêr), *adj.* [ME. *bler-*, in *blereyed;* LG. *bler*, blear], 1. made dim by tears, mucous film, etc.: said of eyes. 2. blurred; dim; indistinct; misty. *v.t.* 1. to dim (the eyes) with tears, film, etc. 2. to obscure (the face) with tears, etc. 3. to blur (a surface or an outline).
blear-eyed (blêr′īd′), *adj.* 1. having blear eyes. 2. dull-witted.
blear·i·ly (blêr′ə-li), *adv.* in a bleary manner.
blear·i·ness (blêr′i-nis), *n.* a bleary quality or state.
blear·y (blêr′i), *adj.* [BLEARIER (-i-ẽr), BLEARIEST (-i-ist)], 1. somewhat blear or blurred. 2. having blear eyes.
bleat (blēt), *v.i.* [ME. *bleten;* AS. *blætan;* IE. base **blē-;* echoic in origin], 1. to make the cry of a sheep, lamb, goat, or calf. 2. to make a sound like this cry; hence, 3. to speak foolishly, whine, etc. *v.t.* to say in a weak, trembling voice. *n.* 1. the cry of a sheep, goat, or calf. 2. any noise like this.
bleb (bleb), *n.* [< ME. *bleb, blob* < sound produced in forming a bubble with the lips], 1. a small swelling on the skin or on plants; blister; vesicle. 2. an air bubble, as in water or glass.
bled (bled), past tense and past participle of **bleed.**
bleed (blēd), *v.i.* [BLED (bled), BLEEDING], [ME. *bleden;* AS. *bledan* < *blod*, blood], 1. to emit blood; lose blood. 2. to suffer wounds or die from loss of blood; hence, 3. to suffer; feel pain, grief, or sympathy. 4. to ooze. 5. to ooze sap, juice, etc., as bruised plants. 6. to run

together, as dyes in wet cloth. 7. to come through a covering coat of paint, as certain stains. 8. in *printing* & *bookbinding*, to have a small part at the edge cut off when the paper is trimmed: said of pictures, designs, etc. ***v.t.*** 1. to draw blood from; leech. 2. to ooze (sap, juice, etc.). 3. to take sap or juice from. 4. to empty of liquid or gas. 5. [Colloq.], to extort money from. 6. in *printing & bookbinding*, to print (a picture, design, etc.) so that a small part at the edge is cut off when the paper is trimmed. ***n.*** the part of a printed picture, design, etc. that overlaps the margin to be trimmed. ***adj.*** having such an overlapping part: as, a *bleed* page.
bleed white, 1. to bleed until all the blood is out. 2. to take all the money or resources from.

bleed·er (blēd'ẽr), ***n.*** 1. a person who draws blood from another. 2. a person who bleeds profusely from even a slight cut; hemophiliac.

bleeding heart, a plant with fernlike leaves and drooping clusters of pink or reddish heart-shaped flowers.

blem·ish (blem'ish), ***v.t.*** [ME. *blemissen*, to wound, spoil; OFr. *blemir, blesmir* < *bleme, blesme*, pale, wan], to mar; slightly impair; injure; sully. ***n.*** 1. a defect or shortcoming; fault. 2. any flaw, as a stain, spot, scar, etc. —***SYN.*** see **defect.**

blench (blench), ***v.t. & v.i.*** [var. of *blanch* (to make white)], to make or become pale; whiten.

blench (blench), ***v.i.*** [ME. *blenchen*, to blench, steal away; AS. *blencan*, to deceive; akin to *blink*], to shy away; shrink back; flinch; quail.

blend (blend), ***v.t.*** [BLENDED (-id) or BLENT (blent), BLENDING], [ME. *blenden;* AS. *blendan* & ON. *blanda*, to mix; IE. base **bhlendh-*, to glimmer indistinctly, as also in *blind, blunder*], 1. to mix or mingle (varieties of tea, tobacco, etc.), especially so as to produce a desired quality. 2. to mix or fuse thoroughly, so as to produce something different in color, taste, etc. from any of its ingredients: as, an artist *blends* paints. ***v.i.*** 1. to mix; merge; unite. 2. to pass gradually or imperceptibly into each other, as colors. 3. to go well together; harmonize. ***n.*** 1. a blending; thorough mixture. 2. the result of blending; a mixture of varieties: as, a *blend* of coffee. —***SYN.*** see **mix.**

blende (blend), ***n.*** [G. *blende* < *blenden*, to blind, dazzle], 1. sphalerite, an ore of zinc or zinc sulfide. 2. any of certain other sulfides, especially metallic sulfides, having a fairly bright luster.

blended whisky, whisky blended with neutral spirits, as of grain or potatoes.

blending inheritance, the blending of characteristics of the parents in the offspring, as in a pink flower that results from the mating of a red flower with a white one.

Blen·heim (blen'əm), ***n.*** a village in Bavaria, Germany: site of a battle (1704) in which the British and their allies under Marlborough defeated the Franco-Bavarian armies: German name, *Blindheim.*

Blenheim spaniel, [after *Blenheim* Palace, seat of the Duke of Marlborough, where the dogs were bred], a variety of toy spaniel that is white with reddish-brown spots.

blen·ni·oid (blen'i-oid'), ***adj.*** of or like a blenny.

blen·ny (blen'i), ***n.*** [*pl.* BLENNIES (-iz), BLENNY; see PLURAL, II, D, 1], [L. *blennius;* Gr. *blennos* < *blenna*, slime, mucus], any of a number of related spiny-finned fishes covered with a slimy substance.

blent (blent), alternative past tense and past participle of **blend.**

bleph·ar·i·tis (blef'ə-rī'tis), ***n.*** [*blephar-* + *-itis*], inflammation of the eyelids.

bleph·a·ro- (blef'ə-rə), [< Gr. *blepharon*, eyelid], a combining form meaning *eyelid, eyelids:* also, before a vowel, **blephar-.**

Blér·i·ot, Louis (bler'i-ō'; Fr. blā'ryō'), 1872–1936; French aviator and inventor of the monoplane.

bles·bok (bles'bok'), ***n.*** [*pl.* BLESBOK, BLESBOKS (-boks'); see PLURAL, II, D, 2], [D.; *bles*, blaze + *bok*, a buck], a South African antelope that has a large, white mark on its face.

bles·buck (bles'buk'), ***n.*** [*pl.* BLESBUCK, BLESBUCKS (-buks'); see PLURAL, II, D, 2], a blesbok.

bless (bles), ***v.t.*** [BLESSED or BLEST (blest), BLESSING], [ME. *blessen, bletsien;* AS. *bletsian, bledsian* < *blod*, blood: rite of consecration by sprinkling the altar with blood], 1. to make holy by a spoken formula or a sign; hallow; consecrate. 2. to set apart for a holy purpose; call holy. 3. to ask divine favor for; hence, 4. to wish well to; feel gratitude toward. 5. to favor or endow (*with*): as, he has been *blessed* with eloquence. 6. to make happy or prosperous; gladden: as, he *blessed* us with his leadership. 7. to think (oneself) happy; congratulate (oneself). 8. to worship; glorify; praise. 9. to make the sign of the cross upon (oneself). 10. to curse: used ironically or euphemistically. 11. [Obs., except in prayers, exclamations, etc.], to keep; guard.
bless me (or **you, him,** etc.)! an exclamation of surprise, pleasure, dismay, etc.

bless·ed (bles'id, blest), ***adj.*** [pp. of *bless*], 1. holy; sacred; consecrated. 2. enjoying great happiness; blissful. 3. of or in eternal bliss; beatified. 4. bringing comfort or joy. 5. confounded; cursed: a mild oath.
the blessed, 1. people who are blessed. 2. in the *Roman Catholic Church*, those dead who have been beatified and are thereby entitled to receive veneration from the living.

bless·ed event (bles'id), the birth of a child: now chiefly jocular.

Blessed Sacrament, the Eucharist.

Blessed Virgin, the Virgin Mary.

bless·ing (bles'iŋ), ***n.*** [ME. *blessinge, bletsing;* AS. *bletsung* < *bletsian;* see BLESS], 1. a statement of divine favor; benediction; hence, 2. an invoking of divine favor. 3. a grace said before or after eating. 4. the gift of divine favor; hence, 5. a wish for prosperity, success, etc.: as, they send us their *blessing.* 6. approval: as, this method has his *blessing.* 7. anything that gives happiness or prevents misfortune. 8. a cursing or scolding: used ironically.

blest (blest), alternative past tense and past participle of **bless.** ***adj.*** blessed.

blet (blet), ***n.*** [Fr. *blet, blette*, overripe, soft], decay in overripe fruit.

bleth·er (bleth'ẽr), ***n., v.i. & v.t.*** blather.

blew (blōō), past tense of **blow.**

B.L.F.E., Brotherhood of Locomotive Firemen and Enginemen: a labor union.

blg., building.

blight (blīt), ***n.*** [17th-c. gardening term; ? < AS. *blieian* or ON. *blīkja* in sense "to turn pale"], 1. any atmospheric or soil condition, parasite, or insect that kills, withers, or checks the growth of plants. 2. any of several plant diseases, as rust, mildew, or smut. 3. anything that destroys, prevents growth, etc. 4. a person or thing that withers the hopes or ambitions of another person. 5. the condition or result of being blighted. ***v.t.*** 1. to cause a blight in or on; wither; hence, 2. to destroy. 3. to disappoint or frustrate. ***v.i.*** to suffer blight.

blight·er (blīt'ẽr), ***n.*** 1. a person or thing that blights. 2. [Slang, chiefly British], *a)* a low or contemptible fellow; rascal. *b)* a fellow; chap.

blight·y, Blight·y (blī'ti), ***n.*** [*pl.* BLIGHTIES (-tiz)], [Hind. *bilāyalī*, foreign country; Ar. *wilāyalī* < *wilāyat*, government < *wālī*, governor], [British Slang], 1. England; home. 2. in World War I, a wound or furlough permitting a soldier to be sent home from the front.

blimp (blimp), ***n.*** [echoic coinage], [Colloq.], a small, nonrigid or semirigid airship.

blind (blīnd), ***adj.*** [ME.; AS.; see BLEND], 1. without the power of sight; sightless; eyeless. 2. of or for sightless persons. 3. lacking insight or understanding. 4. done without adequate directions or knowledge: as, a *blind* search. 5. reckless; unreasonable. 6. out of sight; hard to see; hidden: as, a *blind* intersection. 7. having no opening; blank: as, a *blind* wall. 8. closed at one end: as, a *blind* alley. 9. not controlled by intelligence: as, *blind* destiny. 10. insensible. 11. drunk. 12. illegible; indistinct: as, a *blind* letter. 13. not bearing flowers or fruit, as imperfect plants. 14. in *aeronautics*, by the use of instruments only: as, *blind* flying. 15. in *architecture*, *a)* false. *b)* walled up: as, a *blind* window. 16. in *bookbinding*, without gilding or coloring: as, *blind* tooling. ***v.t.*** 1. to make sightless. 2. to make temporarily unable to see; dazzle. 3. to deprive of the power of insight or judgment. 4. to make dim; obscure. 5. to outshine or eclipse. 6. to hide. ***n.*** 1. anything that obscures or prevents sight. 2. anything that keeps out light, as a window shade or shutter. 3. a place of concealment; ambush. 4. a person or thing used to deceive or mislead; decoy. ***adv.*** 1. blindly. 2. recklessly. 3. in *aeronautics*, by the use of instruments alone: as, he can fly *blind.*
the blind, people who are blind.

blind·age (blīn'dij), ***n.*** [*blind, n.* + *-age*], in *earlier military usage*, a screen or other covering for the concealment and protection of troops, as in trenches.

blind alley, 1. a passage shut off at one end; hence, 2. anything offering no opportunity for progress or advancement.

blind date, [Slang], a social engagement arranged by a third person for a man and a woman who are strangers to each other.

blind·er (blīn'dẽr), ***n.*** either of two leather flaps on a horse's bridle that shut out the side view: see **harness,** illus.

blind·fish (blīnd'fish'), ***n.*** [*pl.* BLINDFISH, BLINDFISHES (-iz); see FISH], any of a number of small fishes with functionless eyes, found in underground streams, waters of caves, etc.

blind·fold (blīnd'fōld'), ***v.t.*** [altered by confusion with *fold* < ME. *blindfeld*, struck blind, pp. of *blindfellen; blind* + *fellen*, to strike; see FELL, *v.*], 1. to cover the eyes of with a cloth or bandage. 2. to hinder the sight of. 3. to delude; mislead. ***n.*** something used to cover the eyes. ***adj.*** 1. having the eyes covered; unable to see. 2. reckless; heedless. ***adv.*** 1. blindly. 2. recklessly; heedlessly.

Blind·heim (blint'hīm), ***n.*** Blenheim.

blind·man's buff (blīnd'manz' buf'), [*blindman* + *buff* < *buffet*], a game in which a blindfolded player has to catch and identify another: a variation of tag.

blind spot, 1. the small area, insensitive to light, in the retina of the eye where the optic nerve enters; hence, 2. a person's lack of sensitivity to a particular thing; a prejudice or ignorance that one has but is often unaware of. 3. an area where radio reception is difficult.

blind staggers, a disease of horses or cattle characterized by staggering.

blind·sto·ry (blīnd'stôr'i, blīnd'stō'ri), *n.* [*pl.* BLINDSTORIES (-iz, -riz)], in *architecture,* 1. a windowless story. 2. in Gothic churches, a gallery (triforium) without windows, above the main arches.

blind tiger, [Slang], a place where alcoholic liquor is sold illegally: also called *blind pig, speakeasy.*

blind·worm (blīnd'wûrm'), *n.* a legless lizard having a dark, snakelike body with greenish or yellow spots or stripes, a small head, very small eyes, and a brittle tail: also called *slowworm.*

blink (bliŋk), *v.i.* [ME. *blenken, blenchen* (see BLENCH), confused with *blinken;* ? < D. *blinken,* to shine, dazzle; see BLANK], 1. to wink rapidly. 2. to flash on and off; twinkle. 3. to look with eyes half-shut, winking, as in a glare. 4. to look (*at*) as if not seeing; disregard; ignore; condone: as, she *blinked* at my mistake. 5. to turn sour: said of milk. *v.t.* 1. to wink (the eyes) rapidly. 2. to cause (eyes, light, etc.) to wink or blink. 3. to close the eyes to (a fact or situation); evade or avoid. 4. to signal (a message) by flashing a light, etc. *n.* [ME. < the *v.*], 1. a twinkle; brief flash; glimmer. 2. a quick look; glimpse. 3. a moment; time that it takes to wink. 4. a winking. 5. a shining reflection on the horizon caused by ice masses at sea. *adj.* habitually winking. —*SYN.* see **wink.**

on the blink, [Slang], not working right; out of order.

blink·ard (bliŋk'ẽrd), *n.* 1. a person who chronically or habitually blinks his eyes. 2. a person who fails to perceive or understand; stupid person.

blink·er (bliŋ'kẽr), *n.* 1. a flap to shut off a horse's side view; blinder. 2. a flashing warning light at crossings. 3. [Slang], an eye. *v.t.* to put blinkers or blinders on.

blink·ers (bliŋ'kẽrz), *n.pl.* [< *blinker*], a sort of goggles.

bliss (blis), *n.* [ME. *blisse;* AS. *bliss, bliths,* joy < *blithe,* joyful], 1. great joy or happiness. 2. spiritual joy; heavenly rapture. 3. any cause of bliss. —*SYN.* see **ecstasy.**

bliss·ful (blis'fəl), *adj.* full of bliss; causing or characterized by great happiness.

blis·ter (blis'tẽr), *n.* [ME. < D. *bluister* or OFr. *blestre* < ON. *blastr;* see BLADDER], 1. a little swelling of the skin, filled with watery matter and caused by burning or rubbing. 2. anything shaped like a blister; hence, 3. a gun turret shield on an airplane. 4. something used or applied to cause a blister. *v.t.* 1. to cause blisters to form on. 2. to beat severely. 3. to lash with words. *v.i.* to have or form a blister or blisters.

blister beetle, 1. a small gray, black, or striped insect from which a substance is obtained that can blister the skin; Spanish fly. 2. any of a number of beetles related to this insect: some are harmful to plants.

blister rust, a disease of pine trees caused by certain fungi: it causes blisters on the bark.

blis·ter·y (blis'tẽr-i), *adj.* characterized by or full of blisters.

blithe (blīth), *adj.* [ME.; AS. < Gmc. *blithia, light, bright (said of the sky); IE. base *bhlei-, to shine, gleam], gay; joyful; cheerful.

blith·er·ing (blith'ẽr-iŋ), *adj.* [*blither,* var. of *blether, blather* + *-ing*], jabbering; talking without sense.

blithe·some (blīth'səm), *adj.* blithe; lighthearted.

B.Litt., *Baccalaureus Lit(t)erarum,* [L.], Bachelor of Letters; Bachelor of Literature: also **B.Lit.**

blitz (blits), *n.* [< *blitzkrieg*], [Colloq.], 1. a destructive attack, usually by aerial bombardment; hence, 2. any sudden, overwhelming attack. *v.t.* 1. to subject to a blitz; overwhelm and destroy. 2. in *gin rummy,* to hold (one's opponent) scoreless.

blitz·krieg (blits'krēg'), *n.* [G. *blitz,* lightning + *krieg,* war], 1. sudden, swift, large-scale offensive warfare intended to win a quick victory. 2. swift, sudden, overwhelming attack.

bliz·zard (bliz'ẽrd), *n.* [dial. *bliz,* violent blow (akin to G. *blitz,* lightning) + *-ard;* current senses first heard in Estherville, Iowa, 1870], 1. originally, an effective shot or blow; hence, 2. a severe snowstorm with high wind. 3. a violent windstorm.

blk., 1. black. 2. block. 3. bulk.

B.LL., *Baccalaureus Legum,* [L.], Bachelor of Laws: also, **LL.B.**

bloat (blōt), *adj.* [ME. *blout,* soft; ON. *blautr;* akin to L. *fluere,* to flow; IE. base *bhlē-, to swell; cf. BLADDER], bloated. *v.t. & v.i.* [prob. < the *adj.*], 1. to swell, as with water or air. 2. to puff up, as with pride. *n.* 1. a bloated person or thing. 2. [Slang], a drunkard. 3. in *veterinary medicine,* a swelling of the abdomen caused by watery foods or eating too fast.

bloat (blōt), *v.t.* [< ME. *blote,* soft with moisture < ON. *blautr,* soaked; see BLOAT (to swell)], to cure or preserve (herring, etc.) by soaking in salt water, smoking, and half-drying. *n.* a bloater.

bloat·ed (blōt'id), *adj.* [pp. of *bloat* (to swell)], 1. swollen; distended; too large. 2. puffed up, as with pride. 3. unhealthily fat from overeating.

bloat·er (blōt'ẽr), *n.* [orig. *bloat herring,* soft herring (as opposed to dried): the curing process has been altered], a fat herring or mackerel that has been bloated, or cured.

blob (blob), *n.* [see BLEB], 1. a small, round drop or mass of a thick, viscous substance or liquid: as, a *blob* of paint. 2. a small mass or splash of color. *v.t.* [BLOBBED (blobd), BLOBBING], to splash or splotch, as with blobs.

bloc (blok), *n.* [Fr.; OFr.; LG. *block,* a lump, solid mass], 1. a group of persons, often of different political loyalties, combined for a common cause or purpose. 2. a group of political or racial units.

Bloch, Ernest (blok; G. blôkh), 1880–1959; American composer born in Switzerland.

block (blok), *n.* [ME. *blok;* OFr. *bloc;* see BLOC], 1. any large, solid piece of wood, stone, or metal, often with flat surfaces. 2. a blocklike stand or platform on which hammering, chopping, etc. is done: as, a butcher's *block,* headman's *block.* 3. an auctioneer's platform. 4. a mold upon which things are shaped, as hats; hence, 5. the shape of a hat. 6. a blockhead. 7. a blocking; obstruction or hindrance. 8. a pulley or system of pulleys in a frame. 9. any solid piece of material used to strengthen or support. 10. a large, hollow building brick. 11. a child's toy brick, usually wooden. 12. a group of buildings regarded as a unit; hence, 13. a city square. 14. one side of a city square. 15. any number of persons or things regarded as a unit; bloc. 16. [Slang], a person's head. 17. in *medicine,* a blocking; interruption of the passage of impulses through a nerve by means of pressure or anesthetics. 18. in *printing,* a piece of engraved wood, etc. with a design or picture. 19. in *psychiatry,* a sudden interruption in speech or thought processes, resulting from deep emotional conflict, repression, etc. 20. in *radio,* the sudden cessation of oscillations of an oscillator, accompanied by a high plate current. 21. in *railroading,* a length of track governed by signals. 22. in *sports,* an interception or thwarting of an opponent's play or movement. 23. in *stamp collecting,* a set of four or more undetached stamps forming a rectangle. Abbreviated **bk., blk.** *v.t.* [Fr. *bloquer* < the *n.*], 1. to impede the passage or progress of; obstruct. 2. to blockade. 3. to create difficulties for; stand in the way of; hinder. 4. to shape or mold on a block; stamp with a block. 5. to form into blocks. 6. to strengthen or support with blocks. 7. in *chemistry,* to render inactive. 8. in *games & sports,* to hinder (an opponent or his play). 9. in *medicine,* to prevent the transmission of impulses in; deaden (a nerve), especially by anesthetizing. 10. in *psychiatry,* to withhold or forget, as the result of a block. 11. in *radio,* to stop (the output of alternating current from an electron tube) by overloading the input. 12. in *railroading,* to run (trains) by the block system. *v.i.* to behave so as to hinder. *adj.* 1. made or taken in the form of blocks: as, *block* coal. 2. block-shaped. 3. set out like or belonging to a city square. 4. in aggregate. 5. in *stenography,* having no indentation in address, heading, or paragraphs. —*SYN.* see **hinder.**

block in (or **out**), to sketch or diagram roughly; plan in outline.

block up, 1. to fill in (with bricks, etc.). 2. to obstruct. 3. to elevate on blocks.

go to the block, 1. to be beheaded. 2. to be up for sale in an auction.

on the block, up for sale or auction.

block·ade (blo-kād'), *n.* [*block* + *-ade*], 1. a shutting off of a place or region by hostile troops or ships in order to prevent passage. 2. any blocking action designed to isolate an enemy and cut off communication and commerce with him. 3. the force that maintains a blockade. 4. any strategic barrier. *v.t.* [BLOCKADED (-id), BLOCKADING], to subject to a blockade.

run the blockade, to go past or through a blockade.

blockade runner, a ship or person that tries to go through or past a blockade.

block·age (blok'ij), *n.* [*block* + *-age*], a blocking or being blocked.

block and tackle, an arrangement of one or more pulley blocks, with rope or cables, for pulling or hoisting large, heavy objects.

block booking, a method of leasing motion pictures by the lot, without letting the exhibitors select only those that they wish to exhibit.

block·bust·er (blok'bus'tẽr), *n.* [Slang], a large bomb that is dropped from an airplane and can demolish an entire city block.

block·head (blok′hed′), *n.* 1. a block of wood shaped like a head, used for shaping or displaying hats or wigs. 2. a stupid or foolish person; nitwit.
block·house (blok′hous′), *n.* 1. a strong wooden fort with a projecting second story and openings in the walls for the defenders to shoot from. 2. any building of squared timber or logs.
blocking condenser, a condenser for preventing the passage of direct current.
block·ish (blok′-ish), *adj.* 1. blocklike; hence, 2. stupid; dull.
Block Island, an island off the coast of Rhode Island: pop., 500.
block lava, lava formed in sharp, angular, rough-surfaced blocks.

BLOCKHOUSE

block letter, in *printing,* 1. a type cut from wood. 2. a style of letter that is simple in form, as sans-serif.
block line, a rope or cable used in a block and tackle.
block plane, a carpenter's plane for cutting across the grain on board ends.
block printing, printing with engraved blocks coated with ink or dyes.
block system, a system of dividing a railroad track into several sections and regulating the trains by automatic signals (**block signals**) so that there is usually no more than one train in one section.
block tin, partially refined tin cast in blocks, used in commerce.
block·y (blok′i), *adj.* [BLOCKIER (-i-ẽr), BLOCKIEST (-i-ist)], 1. having contrasting blocks or patches. 2. stocky; chunky. 3. tending to break apart into large chunks or masses.
Bloem·fon·tain (blōōm′fon-tān′), *n.* the capital of the Orange Free State, Union of South Africa: pop., 109,000.
Blois (blwȧ), *n.* a city in central France, on the Loire River: pop., 27,000.
bloke (blōk), *n.* [word found in Shelta, Irish tinkers' argot], [Slang], 1. a fellow. 2. a contemptible fellow.
blond (blond), *adj.* [Fr., fem. *blonde* < LL. *blondus,* yellow], 1. having a pink-and-white skin, yellow or yellowish-brown hair, and blue or gray eyes. 2. straw-colored; flaxen: said of hair. 3. light-colored: as, *blond* furniture. *n.* 1. a blond man or boy. 2. blonde (lace).
blonde (blond), *adj.* blond. *n.* 1. a blonde woman or girl. 2. a type of silk bobbin lace: so called because of its original resemblance to flaxen hair.
blood (blud), *n.* [ME. *blod, blode;* AS. *blod;* akin to G. *blut;* only in Gmc. in this sense; ? < IE. **bhlō-*, to spring up, well forth], 1. the fluid, usually red, circulating in the heart, arteries, and veins of people and many animals. 2. a similar fluid in lower animals. 3. the spilling of blood; murder. 4. the essence of life; life: often **lifeblood.** 5. the life fluid, sap, or juice of a plant. 6. passion, temperament, or disposition. 7. parental heritage; family line; lineage. 8. racial heritage; race: loosely and unscientifically so used, for blood is not one of the ethnic differentiae. 9. kinship; family relation. 10. descent from nobility. 11. an animal of pure breed or stock. 12. a dandy.
bad blood, anger; hatred.
blood is thicker than water, family ties are stronger than others.
have (someone's) blood on one's head, to be responsible for (someone's) death or misfortune.
in cold blood, 1. with cruelty; unfeelingly. 2. dispassionately; deliberately.
make one's blood boil, to make one angry or resentful.
make one's blood run cold, to frighten or terrify one.
blood bank, 1. a place where whole blood or plasma is typed, processed, and stored for future use. 2. any reserve of blood for use in transfusion.
blood bath, the killing of many people; massacre.
blood brother, 1. a brother by birth. 2. a person bound to one by the ceremony of mingling his blood with one's own.
blood count, a count of the number of red corpuscles and white corpuscles in a given volume of a person's blood.
blood·cur·dling (blud′kũr′dliŋ), *adj.* very frightening; causing terror or horror.
blood·ed (blud′id), *adj.* 1. having (a specific kind of) blood: as, hot-*blooded.* 2. of fine stock or breed; pedigreed; thoroughbred.
blood group, any of several (usually four) groups into which any person's blood is classified with reference to the type of agglutinogen of its corpuscles.
blood·guilt·y (blud′gil′ti), *adj.* guilty of murder or bloodshed.
blood heat, the normal temperature of human blood, 98.6° F.
blood·hound (blud′hound′), *n.* [ME. *blodhound, blodhond;* see BLOOD & HOUND], 1. any of a breed of large, keen-scented dogs with a smooth coat, wrinkled face, and drooping ears: bloodhounds are used to hunt escaped prisoners. 2. a person who pursues keenly or relentlessly; sleuth.

BLOODHOUND (25 in. high)

blood·i·ly (blud′'l-i), *adv.* 1. in a bloody manner. 2. cruelly; savagely.
blood·i·ness (blud′-i-nis), *n.* the state of being bloody.
blood·less (blud′lis), *adj.* 1. without blood. 2. without bloodshed. 3. not having enough blood; anemic or pale. 4. having little energy or vitality. 5. unfeeling; cruel.
blood·let·ting (blud′let′iŋ), *n.* [ME. *blodleting* < *blodleten,* to let blood; AS. *blodlætan; blod,* blood + *lætan,* to set free, let], 1. the opening of a vein to remove blood; bleeding; leeching. 2. bloodshed.
blood·line (blud′lin′), *n.* a direct line of descent; pedigree; strain: usually of animals.
blood·mo·bile (blud′mə-bēl′), *n.* [*blood* + auto*mobile*], a traveling unit equipped for collecting blood from donors for blood banks.
blood money, 1. money paid for killing or helping to bring about the death of someone. 2. money paid as compensation to the next of kin of a murdered person.
blood plasma, the fluid part of blood, as distinguished from the corpuscles, now used in transfusions.
blood poisoning, a diseased condition of the blood due to certain microorganisms, their toxins, or other poisonous matter; septicemia.
blood pressure, the pressure exerted by the blood against the inner walls of the blood vessels, especially the arteries: it varies with health, age, emotional tension, physical exercise, etc.
blood pudding, 1. a dish made of pig's blood, suet, etc.: also called *black pudding.* 2. a kind of sausage that is dark from the blood in it; blood sausage.
blood purge, the killing off of people regarded as disloyal by a political party or government.
blood-red (blud′red′), *adj.* 1. stained red with blood. 2. having the deep-red color of blood.
blood relation, a person related by birth.
blood revenge, a form of revenge in which either the next of kin of a murdered person or some member of his clan must undertake to kill the murderer or a relative of the murderer.
blood·root (blud′rōōt′, blud′root′), *n.* a North American plant of the poppy family, with a white flower, a large, lobed leaf, a fleshy, red root, and red sap.
blood·shed (blud′shed′), *n.* the shedding of blood; killing; slaughter.
blood·shot (blud′shot′), *adj.* [earlier *bloodshotten; blood* + *shotten,* old pp. of *shoot*], suffused or tinged with blood; red and hurting: as, the eyes become *bloodshot* when small blood vessels break in them.
blood·stain (blud′stān′), *n.* a dark discoloration caused by a blot or smear of blood. *v.t.* to discolor with blood.
blood·stained (blud′stānd′), *adj.* 1. soiled or discolored with blood. 2. guilty of murder.
blood·stone (blud′stōn′), *n.* 1. a semiprecious, dark-green variety of quartz spotted with red jasper, used as a gem: the usual birthstone for March: often called *heliotrope.* 2. hematite, a valuable iron ore.
blood stream, the blood flowing through the body.
blood·suck·er (blud′suk′ẽr), *n.* [ME. *blodsoukere*], 1. an animal that sucks blood, especially a leech. 2. a person who extorts or takes from others as much as he can get.
blood test, an examination of a small amount of a person's blood for diagnosis, classification, etc.
blood·thirst·y (blud′thũrs′ti), *adj.* eager for blood; murderous; cruel.
blood type, a blood group.
blood typing, the classification of human blood to determine compatible blood groups for transfusion.
blood vessel, any of the many tubes through which the blood circulates; any artery, vein, or capillary.
blood·wort (blud′wũrt′), *n.* any of various plants with red roots or leaves, as the dock, bloodroot, etc.
blood·y (blud′i), *adj.* [BLOODIER (-i-ẽr), BLOODIEST (-i-ist)], [ME. *blodi;* AS. *blodig*], 1. of, like, or containing blood. 2. covered or stained with blood; bleeding. 3. involving bloodshed. 4. bloodthirsty. 5. having the color of blood. 6. [British Slang], cursed; damned. *adv.* [British Slang], very. *v.t.* [BLOODIED (-id), BLOODYING], to cover or stain with blood.
Bloody Mary, see **Mary I.**
bloom (blōōm), *n.* [ME. *blome;* ON. *blomi,* flowers and foliage on trees; akin to G. *blume,* flower; IE. base **bhlō-*, to spring up, as in L. *flos, floris,* whence ult.

Eng. *flower;* cf. BLOOD], 1. a flower; blossom. 2. the state or time of flowering; hence, 3. a state or time of most health, beauty, vigor, or freshness; prime. 4. a youthful, healthy glow (of cheeks, skin, etc.). 5. the grayish, powdery coating on various fruits, as the plum, grape, etc., and on some leaves. 6. any similar coating, as on new coins. *v.i.* 1. to flower; blossom. 2. to be at one's prime; have health, vigor, beauty, or freshness. 3. to glow with color, health, etc. *v.t.* to make flower; give a bloom to; cause to flourish.

bloom (blōōm), *n.* [AS. *bloma,* lump of metal], 1. a spongy mass of wrought iron ready for further working. 2. a thick bar of iron or steel obtained by rolling or hammering an ingot.

bloom·er (blōōm'ẽr), *n.* [after Amelia Jenks *Bloomer* (1818–1894), American reformer who advocated it], formerly, a costume for women or girls, consisting of a short skirt and loose trousers gathered at the ankles.

bloom·ers (blōōm'ẽrz), *n.pl.* [see BLOOMER], 1. roomy, baggy trousers gathered at the knee, worn by girls and women for athletics. 2. an undergarment somewhat like these.

bloom·er·y (blōōm'ẽr-i), *n.* [*pl.* BLOOMERIES (-iz)], a furnace for making blooms (wrought iron).

Bloom·field (blōōm'fēld'), *n.* a town in New Jersey, near Newark: pop., 52,000.

bloom·ing (blōōm'iŋ), *adj.* [ppr. of *bloom*], 1. flowering; blossoming. 2. thriving; flourishing. 3. [Colloq.], utter; confounded: as, he's a *blooming* fool.

Bloom·ing·ton (blōōm'iŋ-tən), *n.* 1. a city in eastern Minnesota, near Minneapolis and St. Paul: pop., 50,000. 2. a city in central Illinois: pop., 36,000. 3. a city in southern Indiana: pop., 31,000.

bloom·y (blōōm'i), *adj.* [BLOOMIER (-i-ẽr), BLOOMIEST (-i-ist)], 1. blooming; blossomy. 2. having a bloom (powdery coating).

blos·som (blos'əm), *n.* [ME. *blosme;* AS. *blostma, blosma, blostm;* ult. < same IE. base as *bloom*], 1. a flower or bloom, especially of a fruit-bearing plant. 2. a state or time of flowering. *v.i.* 1. to have or open into blossoms; bloom. 2. to begin to thrive or flourish; develop.

blos·som·y (blos'əm-i), *adj.* 1. like a blossom. 2. full of blossoms.

blot (blot), *n.* [ME.; altered < AS. *plott,* spot of ground, clod; prob. after OFr. *blotte, blote,* clod of earth], 1. a spot or stain, especially of ink. 2. an erasure. 3. an unsightly thing, especially one out of place: as, that building is a *blot* on the landscape. 4. a moral stain; disgrace. 5. a disgraceful person. *v.t.* [BLOTTED (-id), BLOTTING], [ME. *blotten* < the *n.;* ? < OFr. *blotter,* to stain], 1. to make blots on; spot; stain; blur. 2. to stain (a reputation); disgrace. 3. to erase or cancel (usually with *out*). 4. to darken or hide entirely; obscure (with *out*). 5. to dry with or as with blotting paper. *v.i.* 1. to make blots. 2. to become blotted. 3. to be absorbent.

blot (blot), *n.* [prob. < MD. *bloot* or Dan. *blot,* naked, uncovered], 1. in *backgammon,* an exposed man; hence, 2. an exposed point; failing.

blotch (bloch), *n.* [extension of *blot* (spot) < OFr. *bloche,* clod of earth, tumor], 1. a discolored or broken-out patch on the skin. 2. any large, irregular blot or stain. *v.t.* to cover or mark with blotches.

blotch·y (bloch'i), *adj.* [BLOTCHIER (-i-ẽr), BLOTCHIEST (-i-ist)], 1. like a blotch. 2. covered with blotches.

blot·ter (blot'ẽr), *n.* 1. a piece of blotting paper. 2. a book for recording events or transactions as they occur: as, a police *blotter* is a record of arrests and charges.

blotting paper, a thick, soft, absorbent paper used to dry a surface that has just been written on in ink.

blot·to (blot'ō), *adj.* [? < *blot* (to absorb)], [Slang], very drunk; unconscious because of drinking too much.

blouse (blous, blouz), *n.* [Fr. (18th c.) workman's or peasant's smock], 1. a loose upper garment worn by certain European peasants and workmen. 2. a loose outer garment extending to the waistline or just below, worn by women and children; kind of shirtwaist. 3. a coat or tunic worn by soldiers, marines, and navy officers. 4. a sailor's jumper. *v.i. & v.t.* [BLOUSED (bloust, blouzd), BLOUSING], to gather in at the waistline; drape.

blow (blō), *v.i.* [BLEW (blōō), BLOWN (blōn), BLOWING], [ME. *blowen;* AS. *blawan;* akin to G. *blähen;* IE. base **bhle-, *bhlo-;* see BLADDER, BLAST], 1. to stir or speed up the motion of air; move, as air: as, the wind *blows.* 2. to send forth air with or as with the mouth; hence, 3. to pant; be breathless. 4. to make or give sound by blowing or being blown. 5. to spout water and air: as, whales *blow.* 6. to be carried by the wind: as, the paper *blew* away. 7. to storm. 8. to lay eggs: said of flies. 9. [Colloq.], to brag; boast. 10. [Slang], to go away; leave. *v.t.* 1. to cause air to come from (a bellows, blower, etc.). 2. to send out (breath) from the mouth. 3. to force air onto, into, or through. 4. to drive by blowing. 5. to give out or spread (news). 6. to sound by blowing. 7. to make (a sound or signal) by blowing. 8. to cool, warm, dry, or soothe by blowing on or toward. 9. to intensify (a fire) by blowing; hence, 10. to inflame. 11. to inflate, as with anger. 12. to shape or form by air or gas. 13. to clean or clear by blowing through. 14. to burst or break by an explosion (usually with *up* or *out*). 15. to cause (a horse) to pant. 16. to lay or deposit eggs in. 17. to melt (a fuse, etc.). 18. [Colloq.], to spend (money) freely. 19. [Colloq.], to treat (*to* something). 20. [Slang], to go away from; leave. *n.* [< the *v.*], 1. a blowing or being blown. 2. a blast or gale. 3. a boast. 4. [Slang], a braggart.

blow hot and cold, [orig. with reference to the scent in hunting], to be favorable toward and then opposed to; vacillate.

blow in, [Slang], 1. to arrive. 2. to spend all (one's money).

blow off, 1. to let steam or hot water out, as from a boiler. 2. [Colloq.], to let one's emotions or thoughts out, as by loud or long talking.

blow out, 1. to put out by blowing. 2. to burst suddenly, as a tire. 3. to come out suddenly or violently, as steam or air. 4. to melt because of too much electric current, as a fuse; hence, 5. to fail, as an electrical apparatus.

blow over, 1. to move away, as rain clouds; hence, 2. to pass over or by; pass from the memory.

blow up, 1. to fill with air or gas. 2. to burst or explode. 3. to arise and become more intense, as a storm. 4. [Colloq.], to scold severely. 5. [Colloq.], to lose one's temper. 6. to enlarge (a photograph).

blow (blō), *n.* [ME. *blaw, blowe;* prob. < *blow, v.i.;* cf. Fr. *soufflet,* box on the ears < *souffler,* to blow], 1. a hit or stroke with the fist or anything else. 2. a sudden attack or forcible effort. 3. any sudden calamity or misfortune; shock.

at a (or **one**) **blow,** by one action; with a single effort.

come to blows, to begin fighting one another.

without striking a blow, with little or no effort.

blow (blō), *v.i.* [BLEW (blōō), BLOWN (blōn), BLOWING], [ME. *blowen;* AS. *blowan;* akin to G. *blühen;* ult. < same IE. base as *bloom & blossom*], to bloom; blossom. *v.t.* 1. to cause to bloom. 2. to put forth (blossoms). *n.* 1. a mass of blossoms. 2. any splendid display.

blow·er (blō'ẽr), *n.* 1. a person who blows. 2. any device for producing a current of air or blowing air into a room, furnace, etc.

blow·fish (blō'fish'), *n.* [*pl.* BLOWFISH, BLOWFISHES (-iz); see FISH], the walleyed pike, a fresh-water fish.

blow·fly (blō'flī'), *n.* [*pl.* BLOWFLIES (-flīz')], [*blow* (see BLOW, *v.i.,* 8) + *fly*], any two-winged fly that lays its eggs in meat, or in the sores or wounds of living animals.

blow·gun (blō'gun'), *n.* 1. a long, tubelike weapon through which darts or pellets are blown. 2. a device using compressed air for spraying paint, oil, etc.

blow-hard (blō'härd'), *n.* [Slang], a person who talks much and foolishly or boastfully.

blow·hole (blō'hōl'), *n.* 1. a hole in the top of the head of whales or certain other animals, used for breathing. 2. a hole through which gas or air can escape. 3. a hole in the ice to which seals, whales, etc. come to get air. 4. a flaw in cast metal caused by an air or gas bubble.

blow·ing (blō'iŋ), *n.* 1. the sound of a blast of air or gas. 2. noisy breathing, as of a horse.

blown (blōn), past participle of **blow** (to send forth air). *adj.* 1. swollen with gas. 2. out of breath, as with effort. 3. flyblown. 4. made by blowing or by using a blowpipe, etc.

blown (blōn), past participle of **blow** (to bloom). *adj.* having bloomed; in full bloom: often **full-blown.**

blow·off (blō'ôf'), *n.* 1. a blowing off of steam, water, etc. 2. an apparatus for doing this. 3. [Slang], a boaster.

blow·out (blō'out'), *n.* 1. the act or result of blowing out. 2. the bursting of a tire. 3. the melting of an electric fuse from too much current. 4. [Slang], a party, banquet, or celebration.

blow·pipe (blō'pīp'), *n.* 1. a tube for forcing air or gas into a flame to intensify and concentrate its heat. 2. a blowtube. 3. a blowgun.

blow·torch (blō'tôrch'), *n.* a small gasoline torch that shoots out a hot flame intensified by a blast of air: it is used to melt metal, remove old paint, etc.

blow·tube (blō'tōōb', blō'tūb'), *n.* 1. a metal tube used in blowing glass. 2. a blowgun.

blow·up (blō'up'), *n.* 1. an explosion. 2. [Colloq.], an angry or hysterical outburst.

blow·y (blō'i), *adj.* [BLOWIER (-i-ẽr), BLOWIEST (-i-ist)], windy.

blowzed (blouzd), *adj.* blowzy.

blowz·y (blouz'i), *adj.* [BLOWZIER (-i-ẽr), BLOWZIEST (-i-ist)], [< obs. *blouze,* ruddy, fat-faced wench], 1. fat, ruddy, and coarse-looking. 2. slovenly; frowzy.

bls., 1. bales. 2. barrels.

B.L.S., Bachelor of Library Science.

blub·ber (blub′ẽr), *n.* [ME. *blubber, blober*, a bubble; prob. of echoic origin; see BLEB], the fat of the whale and other sea mammals, from which an oil is obtained.
blub·ber (blub′ẽr), *v.i.* [ME. *blubren, bloberen*, to bubble up; see BLUBBER (fat)], to weep loudly, like a child. *v.t.* 1. to say while blubbering. 2. to wet, disfigure, or swell with weeping. *n.* loud weeping; blubbering. *adj.* swollen, as from weeping. —*SYN.* see **cry.**
blub·ber·y (blub′ẽr-i), *adj.* 1. of or full of blubber. 2. like blubber in appearance, texture, etc.; fat. 3. swollen or disfigured, as by blubbering, or weeping.
blu·cher (blo͞o′chẽr, blo͞o′kẽr), *n.* [after Field Marshal von *Blücher*], 1. a heavy half boot. 2. a kind of shoe in which the upper laps over the vamp, which is of one piece with the tongue.
Blü·cher, Geb·hard Le·be·recht von (gep′härt lā′bə-reHt fôn blü′Hẽr; Eng. blo͞o′chẽr, blo͞o′kẽr), 1742–1819; Prussian general; helped defeat Napoleon at Waterloo.
bludg·eon (bluj′ən), *n.* [? altered < MFr. *bougeon*, dim. of *bouge*, a club], a short club with a thick, heavy, or loaded end. *v.t. & v.i.* 1. to strike with or as with a bludgeon. 2. to threaten; coerce; bully.
blue (blo͞o), *adj.* [ME. *bleu, blew;* OFr. *bleu;* OHG. *blao*], 1. of the color blue; having the color of the clear sky or the deep sea. 2. [influenced by ME. *blo* < ON. *blā*, livid], livid: said of the skin. 3. gloomy; depressed or depressing. 4. suggestive of the flames of hell; baleful: as, the air was *blue* with oaths. 5. puritanical; rigorous: as, *blue* laws. 6. [Colloq.], indecent; obscene; risqué; suggestive. *n.* 1. the color of the clear sky or the deep sea; any color between green and violet in the spectrum. 2. any blue pigment or dye. 3. bluing. 4. anything colored blue, as the second ring of an archer's target. 5. a person who wears blue in a uniform or as a school color, etc.; hence, 6. a sailor. 7. *pl.* [Slang], a sailor's blue uniform. *v.t.* [BLUED (blo͞od), BLUING or BLUEING], 1. to make blue. 2. to use bluing on or in. *v.i.* to become blue.
once in a blue moon, very seldom; almost never.
out of the blue, as if from the sky; without being expected or foreseen.
the blue, 1. the sky. 2. the sea.
the blues, 1. [short for *blue devils*], [Colloq.], a depressed, unhappy feeling; hence, 2. a type of Negro folk song, characterized by minor harmony, slow jazz rhythm, and melancholy words. 3. any imitation of this.
blue baby, a baby born with cyanosis as a result of a congenital heart lesion or incomplete lung expansion.
Blue·beard (blo͞o′bêrd′), *n.* [Fr. *Barbe bleu*], a character in an old story who married and then murdered one wife after another.
blue·bell (blo͞o′bel′), *n.* any of various plants with blue, bell-shaped flowers, as the wild hyacinth, harebell, etc.
blue·ber·ry (blo͞o′ber′i, blo͞o′bẽr-i), *n.* [*pl.* BLUEBERRIES (-iz)], 1. a small, edible, blue-black berry with tiny seeds. 2. the shrub on which it grows.
blue·bird (blo͞o′bũrd′), *n.* any of a number of related small North American songbirds, the male of which usually has a bluish back and a reddish breast.
blue-black (blo͞o′blak′), *adj.* intensely black; so black as to have a bluish cast in bright light.
blue blood, 1. descent from nobility or royalty. 2. a person of such descent; aristocrat.
blue-blood·ed (blo͞o′blud′id), *adj.* 1. of royal or noble descent; aristocratic. 2. of pure breed.
blue·bon·net (blo͞o′bon′it), *n.* 1. a broad, flat cap of blue woolen, worn in Scotland; hence, 2. its wearer; Scotsman. 3. in *botany*, *a)* a bluebottle. *b)* a blue-flowered lupine. Also **blue bonnet.**
blue·book (blo͞o′book′), *n.* a blue book (senses 3 & 4).
blue book, 1. a British parliamentary publication: so called from its blue cover. 2. the official United States list of governmental officeholders. 3. a book listing people who are socially prominent. 4. a booklet with a blue paper cover, used in many colleges for students to write examination answers in.
blue·bot·tle (blo͞o′bot′'l), *n.* 1. a plant bearing blue, white, pink, or purple flowers with bottle-shaped rays; cornflower; bachelor's-button. 2. a large blowfly with a steel-blue abdomen and a hairy body. 3. any of several similar flies.
blue·cap (blo͞o′kap′), *n.* 1. a kind of bird, the titmouse. 2. a bluebonnet.
blue cheese, a cheese similar to Roquefort, but made of cow's milk.
blue-chip (blo͞o′chip′), *adj.* [after the high-value *blue chips* of poker], 1. designating any high-priced stock with a good record of earnings and price stability. 2. [Colloq.], excellent, valuable, etc.
blue·coat (blo͞o′kōt′), *n.* a policeman.
blue-col·lar (blo͞o′kol′ẽr), *adj.* [from the color of many work shirts], designating or of industrial workers, especially the semiskilled and unskilled.
Blue Cross, (any of) a system of non-profit health-insurance organizations offering hospitalization and, variously, medical benefits to subscribers, especially to groups of employees and their families.
blue-curls (blo͞o′kũrlz′), *n.* 1. any of a number of related plants of the mint family, having narrow leaves and blue flowers with blue or purple fuzz. 2. a purple-flowered selfheal. Also **blue curls.**
blue devils, 1. delirium tremens or its hallucinations. 2. a depressed feeling; the blues.
blue-eyed grass (blo͞o′īd′), any of a group of plants of the iris family, with blue flowers and grasslike leaves.
Blue·field (blo͞o′fēld′), *n.* a city in West Virginia: pop., 19,000.
blue·fish (blo͞o′fish′), *n.* [*pl.* BLUEFISH, BLUEFISHES (-iz); see FISH], 1. a blue-and-silver food fish, common along the Atlantic coast of North America. 2. any of various other fishes, as the bluegill, blue bass, etc.
blue flag, any iris with blue flowers.
blue fox, 1. an arctic fox during the period when its fur has a bluish cast. 2. its fur. 3. the fur of the white fox when dyed blue.
blue·gill (blo͞o′gil′), *n.* a bluish fresh-water sunfish.
blue·grass (blo͞o′gras′, blo͞o′gräs′), *n.* any of several related grasses with bluish-green stems.
Bluegrass Region (or **Country**), a region in central Kentucky where there is much bluegrass: also **the Bluegrass.**
blue-green algae (blo͞o′grēn′), a kind of algae that are typically bluish green.
blue gum, a kind of eucalyptus tree.
blue·hearts (blo͞o′härts′), *n.* [*pl.* BLUEHEARTS], a plant with spikes of blue flowers and hairy leaves.
blue·ing (blo͞o′iŋ), *n.* bluing.
blue·ish (blo͞o′ish), *adj.* bluish.
blue·jack (blo͞o′jak′), *n.* 1. blue vitriol. 2. a small oak tree of the southern United States.
blue·jack·et (blo͞o′jak′it), *n.* an enlisted man in the United States or British navy.
blue·jay (blo͞o′jā′), *n.* any of a number of related noisy, crested birds with a blue back: also **blue jay.**
blue laws, puritanical laws, especially those prohibiting dancing, entertainments, sports, etc. on Sunday.
blue mass, in *pharmacology*, a preparation containing powdered mercury, used in making blue pills.
blue Monday, [? after D. *blaaw maandag:* orig. a minister's term, from the excessive work done on Sunday], [Colloq.], any Monday: so called because considered depressing as the beginning of a week of work contrasted with the pleasures of the weekend.
Blue Mountains, 1. a mountain range of northeastern Oregon and southeastern Washington. 2. a mountain range of Jamaica: highest peak, 7,388 ft.
Blue Nile, a river flowing through northern Ethiopia and the Sudan to join the White Nile.
blue·nose (blo͞o′nōz′), *n.* [Colloq.], 1. a puritanical person. 2. [B-], a Nova Scotian: so called because of the cold climate.
blue-pen·cil (blo͞o′pen′s'l), *v.t.* to edit, cut, or correct (a manuscript, etc.): from the blue marking made by the pencils generally used by editors.
blue peter, [prob. < *blue repeater*, signal flag used in Brit. Navy], a blue signal flag with a white square in the center, used to announce a ship's sailing, etc.
blue pill, in *pharmacology*, a pill of blue mass, used as a laxative.
blue·point (blo͞o′point′), *n.* [< *Blue Point*, Long Island, near which beds of such oysters are located], a small oyster, usually eaten raw.
blue·print (blo͞o′print′), *n.* 1. a photographic reproduction in white on a blue background, as of architectural or engineering plans; hence, 2. any exact or detailed plan or outline. *v.t.* to make a blueprint of.
blue racer, a harmless, long, blue-green North American variety of black snake, that moves rapidly.
blue ribbon, 1. originally, the blue silk ribbon of the British Order of the Garter; hence, 2. first place in a competition; first prize. 3. the badge of certain temperance societies.
blue-rib·bon jury (or **panel**) (blo͞o′rib′ən), [Colloq.], a jury whose members have been carefully selected.
Blue Ridge Mountains, a range of the Appalachians, extending from West Virginia and Maryland to northern Georgia.
blue-sky law (blo͞o′skī′), [Colloq.], [said to be so named from the comment made by a proponent of the first such law that certain business groups were trying to "capitalize the blue skies"], a law regulating the sale of stocks, bonds, etc., for the protection of the public.
blue·stock·ing (blo͞o′stok′iŋ), *n.* [from the unconventional blue worsted stockings worn by the leading figure at literary meetings in 18th-c. London], a learned, bookish, or pedantic woman.
blue·stone (blo͞o′stōn′), *n.* 1. a blue-gray sandstone. 2. blue vitriol.
blue streak, [Colloq.], anything regarded as like a streak of lightning in speed, vividness, etc.
blu·et (blo͞o′it), *n.* [Fr. *bleuet*, dim. of *bleu*, blue], a blue-flowered plant growing in small, rounded tufts.
blue vitriol, crystalline cupric sulfate, $CuSO_4 \cdot 5H_2O$.
blue·weed (blo͞o′wēd′), *n.* a bristly weed with blue flowers and pink buds: also called *viper's bugloss.*
blue-winged teal (blo͞o′wiŋd′), any of a group of small North American ducks found on ponds and

rivers and having bluish markings on the wings.
blue·wood (blōō′wood′), *n.* a shrub of the buckthorn family, found in the southwestern United States.
bluff (bluf), *v.t. & v.i.* [17th c.; prob. < D. *bluffen* or *verbluffen*, to baffle, mislead], 1. to mislead (a person) by a false, bold front. 2. to frighten (a person) by threats that cannot be made good. 3. in *poker*, to try to mislead (other players) by betting or raising the bet while holding poor cards. *n.* 1. a bluffing. 2. a person who bluffs. —*SYN.* see **blunt.**
bluff (bluf), *adj.* [orig. a nautical term < D. *blaf*, flat, broad], 1. having, or ascending steeply with, a broad, flat front. 2. having a rough, frank manner; brusque. *n.* a high, steep, broad-faced bank or cliff.
bluff·er (bluf′ẽr), *n.* a person who bluffs; impostor; liar.
blu·ing (blōō′iŋ), *n.* a blue liquid, powder, etc., generally of indigo, used in rinsing white fabrics to prevent yellowing: also spelled **blueing.**
blu·ish (blōō′ish), *adj.* somewhat blue: also spelled **blueish.**
Blum, Lé·on (lā′ōn′ blüm; Eng. lā′on bloom), 1872–1950; French Socialist leader; premier of France (1936–1937); interim premier (Dec., 1946–Jan., 1947).
blun·der (blun′dẽr), *v.i.* [ME. *blondren, blunderen*, freq. < ON. *blunda*, to shut the eyes; akin to Sw. dial. *blundra*, to do blindly; IE. base **bhlendh-*, to be indistinct, glimmer indistinctly; cf. BLEND], 1. to move clumsily or carelessly; flounder; stumble. 2. to make a foolish mistake; be grossly mistaken. *v.t.* 1. to say stupidly, clumsily, or confusedly; blurt (with *out*). 2. to do clumsily or poorly; bungle. *n.* a foolish or stupid mistake. —*SYN.* see **error.**
blun·der·buss (blun′dẽr-bus′), *n.* [D. *donderbus*, thunder box; altered after *blunder* because of the gun's random action], 1. an obsolete short gun with a broad muzzle. 2. a person who blunders.

BLUNDERBUSS

blunge (blunj), *v.t.* [BLUNGED (blunjd), BLUNGING], [? < *plunge*], in *ceramics*, to mix (clay, etc.) with water.
blung·er (blun′jẽr), *n.* 1. a large wooden spatula for blunging. 2. a blunging apparatus. 3. a person who blunges.
blunt (blunt), *adj.* [ME.; prob. < ON.; for IE. base see BLEND], 1. slow to perceive; dull; obtuse. 2. having a dull edge or point. 3. plain-spoken; bluff. *v.t.* to make dull or insensitive. *v.i.* to become dull or insensitive.
SYN.—**blunt** implies a candor and tactlessness that show little regard for another's feelings ("You're a fool," was his *blunt* reply); **bluff** suggests a coarse heartiness of manner and a good nature that causes the candor to seem inoffensive (a *bluff* old gardener); **brusque** implies apparent rudeness as evidenced by abruptness of speech or behavior (a *brusque* rejection); **curt** suggests a terseness of expression that implies a lack of tact or courtesy (a *curt* dismissal); **gruff** suggests bad temper and roughness of speech and manner, connoting, in addition, a harshness or throatiness in utterance (a *gruff* sergeant). See also **dull.** —*ANT.* suave, tactful.
blur (blũr), *v.t. & v.i.* [BLURRED (blũrd), BLURRING], [16th c.; ? < *blear* + *blot*], 1. to smear; stain; blot; smudge. 2. to make or become hazy or indistinct in outline or shape. 3. to dim. *n.* 1. the state of being blurred or dim. 2. an obscuring stain or blot. 3. a moral stain. 4. anything indistinct to the sight or the mind.
blurb (blũrb), *n.* [arbitrary coinage (c. 1914) by Gelett Burgess, "to sound like a publisher"], [Colloq.], an exaggerated or fulsome advertisement or announcement, as on a book jacket.
blur·ry (blũr′i), *adj.* 1. somewhat blurred; hazy in outline; dim. 2. full of blurs; smeary; stained.
blurt (blũrt), *v.t.* [16th–17th c.; ? < *blow*, *blast*, etc. + *spurt*, *squirt*], to say thoughtlessly, suddenly, or impulsively (with *out*).
blush (blush), *v.i.* [ME. *bluschen, blyschen*, to glow, glance; AS. *blyscan, bliscan*, to shine; cf. *blyse*, torch; IE. base **bhles-*, to shine, gleam, as in *blaze*], 1. to become red in the face from shame, embarrassment, or confusion. 2. to be ashamed (usually with *at* or *for*). 3. to be or become rosy. *v.t.* 1. to reveal by blushing. 2. to redden. *n.* 1. a reddening of the face from shame, etc. 2. a rosy color: as, the *blush* of youth. *adj.* having the color of a blush.
at first blush, [orig. ME. sense], at first sight; without further consideration.
blush·ful (blush′fəl), *adj.* blushing.
blus·ter (blus′tẽr), *v.i.* [ME. *blostren, blustren*, to rush violently < or akin to LG. *blüstern, blistern*], 1. to blow stormily: said of wind. 2. to speak in a noisy, violent, or swaggering manner. 3. to use empty threats. *v.t.* 1. to force by blustering; bully. 2. to say noisily and violently. *n.* 1. stormy noise; noisy commotion. 2. noisy, violent, or swaggering talk.
blus·ter·ous (blus′tẽr-əs), *adj.* blustery.
blus·ter·y (blus′tẽr-i), *adj.* blustering.
blvd., boulevard.
-bly (bli), -ably: used to form adverbs corresponding to adjectives ending in *-ble*, as *possibly.*
BM, [Colloq.], bowel movement.
B.M., 1. *Baccalaureus Medicinae*, [L.], Bachelor of Medicine. 2. *Baccalaureus Musicae*, [L.], Bachelor of Music. 3. British Museum.
B.M.R., basal metabolic rate.
Bn., 1. Baron. 2. Battalion.
B.N., bank note.
B'nai B'rith (b'nā brith, b'nā brēth), [Heb. *benāi berīth*, sons of the covenant], a Jewish fraternity founded in New York in 1843, now international in membership.
Bnss., Baroness.
bo (bō), *n.* [Slang], a hobo.
B/O, in *bookkeeping*, brought over.
B.O., 1. Board of Ordnance. 2. body odor.
b.o., 1. back order. 2. bad order. 3. box office. 4. branch office. 5. broker's order. 6. buyer's option.
bo·a (bō′ə), *n.* [L., a large water serpent], 1. any of a number of large, nonpoisonous, tropical snakes that crush their prey in their coils, as the python, anaconda, etc. 2. a woman's long scarf of fur or feathers, worn around the neck or shoulders.
Bo·ab·dil (bō′əb-dēl′), *n.* (*Mohammed XI*), Moorish king of Granada; lived ?–1533?
boa constrictor, a species of boa, pale brown with dark crossbars, which attains a length of 10–15 feet.
Bo·a·di·ce·a (bō′ə-di-sē′ə), *n.* a British queen who, according to Tacitus, led an attempted revolt against the Romans; ?–62 A.D. also **Boudicca.**
Bo·a·ner·ges (bō′ə-nũr′jēz), *n.pl.* [Gr. *boanerges*; prob. < Aram. form of Heb. *benāi regesh*, sons of wrath; interpreted in Gr. as "sons of thunder"], 1. the Apostles John and James: an epithet used by Jesus: Mark 3:17. 2. [construed as sing.], [*pl.* BOANERGES, BOANERGESSES (-jə-siz)], a loudmouthed vociferous preacher or orator.

BOA CONSTRICTOR

boar (bôr, bōr), *n.* [*pl.* BOARS (bôrz, bōrz), BOAR; see PLURAL, II, D, 1], [ME. *bore, boor*; AS. *bar*; akin to OHG. *bēr*, D. *beer*; only in W. Gmc.], 1. an uncastrated male hog or pig. 2. a wild hog of Europe, Africa, and Asia, with a hairy coat and a long snout.

BOAR (4 ft. long)

board (bôrd, bōrd), *n.* [ME. & AS. *bord*, a plank, flat surface; akin to G. *brett*; IE. base **bherdh-*, to cut], 1. a long, thin, flat piece of sawed wood ready for use; thin plank. 2. a flat piece of wood or similar material, often rectangular, for some special use: as, a parchesi *board*, bulletin *board*, ironing *board*. 3. pasteboard or stiff paper, often used for book covers. 4. a table for meals; hence, 5. the food served at a table. 6. meals provided regularly for pay. 7. a council table. 8. a group of administrators; council: as, a *board* of education. Abbreviated **bd.** *v.t.* 1. to cover or close up with boards (often with *up*). 2. to provide with meals, or room and meals, regularly for pay. 3. to put (a person) where board is supplied. *v.i.* to receive meals, or room and meals, regularly for pay.
across the board, in *horse racing*, to win, place, or show: said of betting.
the boards, the stage (of a theater).
tread the boards, to be an actor in the theater.
board (bôrd, bōrd), *n.* [ME. & AS. *bord*, side of a ship, shield; akin to ON. *borth*, edge, border, ship's side; IE. base **bher-*, to form an edge], 1. the side of a ship, as in *overboard*. 2. a rim, border, or coast, as in *seaboard*. 3. in *nautical usage*, *a)* a tack. *b)* the distance made in a single tack. *v.t.* 1. to come alongside (a ship) especially with hostile purpose. 2. to come over the rail and onto the deck of (a ship); hence, 3. to get on (a train, bus, etc.). 4. to accost. *v.i.* in *nautical usage*, to tack. (Phrases on next page)

go by the board, 1. to fall or be swept overboard; hence, 2. to be got rid of, lost, ruined, etc.
on board, on or in a ship, aircraft, bus, etc.

board·er (bôr′dẽr, bōr′dẽr), *n.* [see BOARD (plank)], a person who gets his meals, or room and meals, regularly for a fixed sum; paying guest.

board·er (bôr′dẽr, bōr′dẽr), *n.* a person who boards a ship, aircraft, etc.; especially, one of the crew detailed to board a hostile ship.

board foot, [*pl.* BOARD FEET], a unit of measure of lumber, equal to a board one foot square and one inch thick: abbreviated **bd. ft.**

board·ing (bôrd′iŋ, bōrd′iŋ), *n.* 1. a structure or covering of boards. 2. boards collectively; light timber.

board·ing (bôrd′iŋ, bōrd′iŋ), *n.* [see BOARD (ship's side)], 1. a coming or going aboard (a ship, train, etc.). 2. an attack on or capture of a ship by boarders.

board·ing·house (bôrd′iŋ-hous′, bōrd′iŋ-hous′), *n.* [see BOARD (plank)], a house where meals, or lodging and meals, can be had for pay: also **boarding house.**

boarding school, a school providing lodging and meals for the pupils.

board measure, measurement of lumber in board feet.

board of health, a government department that supervises public health.

board of trade, 1. an association of businessmen for the protection and furtherance of their business interests. 2. [B- T-], a British governmental department supervising commerce and industry: abbreviated **B.O.T.**

board rule, a measuring stick for finding out quickly how many board feet there are in a quantity of lumber.

board·walk (bôrd′wôk′, bōrd′wôk′), *n.* 1. a walk made of thick boards. 2. a walk placed along a beach or sea front.

boar·fish (bôr′fish′, bōr′fish′), *n.* [*pl.* BOARFISH, BOARFISHES (-iz); see FISH], any of various fishes with a projecting snout like a boar's.

boar·hound (bôr′hound′, bōr′hound′), *n.* a great Dane or other large dog used in hunting wild boar.

boar·ish (bôr′ish, bōr′ish), *adj.* like a boar; swinish.

Bo·as, Franz (frants bō′äs), 1858–1942; American anthropologist, born in Germany.

boast (bōst), *n.* [ME. *bost* < Anglo-Fr.], 1. a bragging; boasting. 2. anything boasted of. *v.i.* [ME. *bosten* < the *n.*], 1. to talk about deeds, abilities, etc., either one's own or another's, in a manner showing too much pride and satisfaction; brag. 2. to be vainly proud; exult. *v.t.* 1. to brag about. 2. to glory in having or doing (something); be proud of.

SYN.—**boast,** the basic term in this list, merely suggests pride or satisfaction, as in one's deeds or abilities (you may well *boast* of your efficiency); **brag** suggests greater ostentation and overstatement (he *bragged* of what he would do in the race); **vaunt,** a formal, literary term, implies greater suavity but more vainglory than either of the preceding (*vaunt* not in your triumph); **swagger** suggests a proclaiming of one's superiority in an insolent or overbearing way; **crow** suggests loud boasting in exultation or triumph (stop *crowing* over your victory).

boast (bōst), *v.t.* [prob. < ME. *boozen* (see BOSS, to emboss) with unhistoric *-t*], to do preliminary shaping on (a statue, etc.) with a broad chisel.

boast·ful (bōst′fəl), *adj.* boasting; inclined to brag.

boat (bōt), *n.* [ME. *boot, bote;* AS. *bat;* akin to G. *boot;* IE. base **bheidh-,* to split: in the sense "hollowed-out tree trunk"; cf. FISSURE], 1. a small, open vessel or water craft propelled by oars, sails, or engine. 2. a large vessel; ship: landsman's term applied especially to river steamers. Abbreviated **bt.** 3. any similar craft: as, a flying *boat.* 4. a boat-shaped dish: as, a gravy *boat.* *v.t.* to lay or carry in the boat: as, *boat* the oars. *v.i.* to go in a boat; row, sail, or cruise.
in the same boat, in the same situation; running similar risks.

boat·bill (bōt′bil′), *n.* a tropical American wading bird of the heron family, with a large bill.

boat·build·ing (bōt′bil′diŋ), *n.* the building of boats.

boat hook, a long pole with a metal hook on one end, for maneuvering boats, logs, or rafts.

boat·house (bōt′hous′), *n.* a building primarily for storing a boat or boats, but often equipped with recreational facilities.

boat·ing (bōt′iŋ), *n.* 1. rowing, sailing, or cruising. 2. boats collectively.

boat·load (bōt′lōd′), *n.* 1. all the freight or passengers that a boat can carry or contain. 2. the load carried by a boat.

boat·man (bōt′mən), *n.* [*pl.* BOATMEN (-mən)], a man who operates, works on, rents, or sells boats.

boats·man (bōts′mən), *n.* [*pl.* BOATSMEN (-mən)], a boatman.

boat·swain (bō′s'n, bōt′swān′), *n.* a ship's warrant officer or petty officer in charge of the deck crew, the rigging, etc.: also **bosun.**

boat train, a train timed to reach or leave a port at the convenience of ship's passengers.

Bo·az (bō′az), *n.* [Heb. *bō'az,* lit., swiftness], in the *Bible,* Ruth's husband: Ruth 4:13.

bob (bob), *n.* [ME. *bobbe,* hanging cluster; senses 8–12 < the *v.*, 13 < *bobsled,* etc.], 1. [British Dial.], a hanging cluster. 2. any knoblike hanging weight or pendant: as, an ear *bob.* 3. a short refrain attached to a song. 4. a short curl or knob of hair. 5. a docked tail, as of a horse. 6. a woman's or girl's short haircut. 7. a suckling calf. 8. a quick, jerky motion, like that of a cork on water. 9. a float on a fishing line. 10. a type of Scottish dance. 11. a quick curtsy. 12. a tap or light blow. 13. a bobsled or bob skate. *v.t.* [BOBBED (bobd), BOBBING], [ME. *bobben,* to knock against; also < *bobbe,* hanging cluster], 1. to knock against; cause to knock against; rap. 2. to make move with a jerky motion. 3. to do jerkily. 4. to cut (hair, a tail, etc.) short; dock. *v.i.* 1. to move or act in a bobbing manner; move suddenly; hence, 2. to dance athletically or awkwardly. 3. to curtsy quickly. 4. to fish with a bob. 5. to try to catch suspended or floating fruit with the teeth (usually with *for*).
bob up, to come up unexpectedly; appear suddenly.

bob (bob), *n.* [*pl.* BOB], [? < *Bob,* nickname for *Robert*], [British Slang], a shilling: as, it costs six *bob.*

bobbed (bobd), *adj.* [pp. of *bob*], 1. having a bob or bobs. 2. in the style or shape of a bob; cut short.

bob·ber·y (bob′ẽr-i), *n.* [*pl.* BOBBERIES (-iz)], [Anglo-Ind. < Hind. *bāp-rē,* O father!, exclamation of sorrow or surprise], a row; hubbub.

bob·bin (bob′in), *n.* [Fr. *bobine*], 1. a reel or spool for thread, yarn, or fine wire, used in spinning, weaving, machine sewing, etc. 2. a small notched pin of wood, bone, or ivory, used in making bobbin lace. 3. a thing like a bobbin.

Bobbin and Joan, a European wild flower of the arum family, the cuckoopint.

bob·bi·net (bob′ə-net′, bob′ə-net′), *n.* [*bobbin* + *net*], a machine-made imitation of bobbin lace.

bobbin lace, a lace whose design is laid out with pins around which thread is drawn and interlaced by means of bobbins.

bob·by (bob′i), *n.* [*pl.* BOBBIES (-iz)], [after Sir Robert (*Bobby*) Peel (1788–1850), who remodeled the London police force], [British Slang], a policeman.

bobby pin, [from use with *bobbed* hair], a small metal hairpin with the ends pressing close together.

bobby socks, [Colloq.], [< *bob,* to cut (hair, etc.) short], ankle socks worn by girls and women.

bobby sox·er (sok′sẽr), [< the *bobby socks* worn by many of them], [Colloq.], a girl in her teens, especially one regarded as conforming to current fads.

bob·cat (bob′kat′), *n.* [*pl.* BOBCATS (-kats′), BOBCAT; see PLURAL, II, D, 1], a wildcat; American lynx.

bob·o·link (bob′'l-iŋk′), *n.* [earlier *Bob Lincoln, bob-lincoln;* echoic, after its call], a migratory songbird of North American fields and meadows.

bob skate, a skate with two runners.

bob·sled (bob′sled′), *n.* 1. a long sled made of two short sleds joined together. 2. either of the sleds thus joined. 3. a long toboggan, equipped with steering apparatus and brakes, often ridden by a four-man team in races. *v.i.* to ride on a bobsled.

bob·sleigh (bob′slā′), *n.* & *v.i.* bobsled.

bob·stay (bob′stā′), *n.* a rope or chain for tying down a bowsprit to keep it from bobbing.

bob·tail (bob′tāl′), *n.* 1. a tail cut short; docked tail. 2. a horse or dog with a bobtail. *adj.* 1. having a bobtail. 2. cut short; abbreviated. *v.t.* 1. to dock the tail of. 2. to cut short; curtail.

bob·white (bob′hwīt′), *n.* [*pl.* BOBWHITES (-hwīts′), BOBWHITE; see PLURAL, II, D, 1], [echoic, after its call], a small North American quail having markings of brown and white on a gray body: sometimes called *partridge.*

bo·cac·cio (bə-kä′chō), *n.* [It. *boccaccio* < *boccaccia,* large mouth < *bocca,* mouth; see BUCCAL], a large-mouthed rockfish, found near California.

Boc·cac·cio, Gio·van·ni (jō-vän′nē bō-kät′chō; Eng. bō-kä′chi-ō), 1313–1375; Italian author; wrote the *Decameron.*

Boc·che·ri·ni, Lu·i·gi (lōō-ē′jē bô′ke-rē′nē), 1743–1805; Italian composer.

Boche, boche (bosh, bôsh, bōsh; Fr. bôsh), *n.* [*pl.* BOCHES (-iz; Fr. bôsh)], [Fr. slang (first used c. 1865) < *caboche,* hard head, head (see CABBAGE, vegetable); orig. in sense of "obstinate young man"; next found in printers' argot as *tête de boche,* hard head, hence—prob. by association with *tête carrée* (*d'Allemand*), lit., squarehead (of a German)—German; later shortened to *boche*], a German, especially a German soldier: hostile term.

Bo·chum (bō′khoom), *n.* a city in the Ruhr Basin, Germany: pop., 245,000 (1946).

bock (bok), *n.* [G. *bockbier,* contr. < *oanbock-, ambock-,* Bavarian dial. pronunciation of *Eimbecker bier* < *Eimbeck,* Hanover, where first brewed], a dark beer usually made in the spring: also **bock beer.**

bode (bōd), *v.t.* [BODED (-id), BODING], [ME. *bodien;* AS. *bodian* < *boda,* messenger], to be an omen of; presage.
bode ill (or **well**), to be a bad (or good) omen.

bode (bōd), alternative past tense of **bide.**

Bo·den·see (bō′dən-zā′), *n.* Lake of Constance: the German name: also called *Lake Boden.*

bod·ice (bod′is), *n.* [altered < *bodies*, pl. of *body*], 1. the close-fitting upper part of a woman's dress. 2. a woman's wide, sleeveless vest tightly laced in front, worn over a blouse or dress.

bod·ied (bod′id), *adj.* [pp. of *body*], 1. having a body, substance, or form. 2. having a specified kind of body: as, able-*bodied*.

bod·i·less (bod′i-lis), *adj.* 1. without a body; disembodied. 2. insubstantial. 3. without a torso.

bod·i·ly (bod′'l-i), *adj.* [ME. *bodilich* < *bodi*, body], 1. physical: opposed to *mental*. 2. of, in, or for the body. *adv.* 1. in person; in the flesh: as, he is *bodily* present. 2. as a single body; in entirety. 3. as a single group.
SYN.—**bodily** refers to the human body as distinct from the mind or spirit (*bodily* ills); **physical**, while often interchangeable with **bodily**, suggests somewhat less directly the anatomy and physiology of the body (*physical* exercise); **corporeal** refers to the material substance of the body and is opposed to *spiritual* (his *corporeal* remains); **corporal** refers to the effect of something upon the body (*corporal* punishment); **somatic** is the scientific word and refers to the body as distinct from the psyche, with no philosophical or poetic overtones (the *somatic* differences between individuals). —*ANT.* mental, psychic, spiritual.

bod·ing (bō′diŋ), *n.* [ME. *bodynge*, *bodunge*; AS. *bodung* < *bodian*, to announce < *boda*, messenger], an omen; foreboding. *adj.* ominous; foreboding.

bod·kin (bod′kin), *n.* [ME. *boidekyn*, *bodekin*; ? < Celt.; cf. W. *bidog*, dagger], 1. a pointed instrument for making holes in cloth. 2. a long, ornamental hairpin. 3. a thick, blunt needle. 4. [Obs.], a dagger or stiletto. 5. in *printing*, a kind of awl for picking out letters from set type.

Bod·le·ian (bod-lē′ən, bod′li-ən), *adj.* [after Sir Thomas *Bodley*, who restored it c. 1600], designating or of the Oxford University library.

Bo·do·ni (bə-dō′nē), *n.* a style of type designed by the Italian printer, Giambattista Bodoni (1740–1813).
This line is in Bodoni.

bod·y (bod′i), *n.* [*pl.* BODIES (-iz)], [ME. *bodi*, *bodig*; AS. *bodig*; orig. sense "cask," as in OHG. *botah*, *botacha* (G. *bottich*), MLG. *boddike*, tub for brewing], 1. the whole physical structure and substance of a man, animal, or plant. 2. the trunk or torso of a man or animal. 3. the stem of a plant. 4. the main or central part of anything. 5. the part of an automobile, truck, etc. that holds the load or passengers; part of a vehicle that is not the chassis. 6. the part of a garment that covers the trunk or upper part of the trunk. 7. a dead person; corpse. 8. the flesh or material substance, as opposed to the spirit. 9. a portion of matter; mass; separate part: as, a *body* of water. 10. a group of people or things regarded as a unit: as, a *body* of soldiers. 11. the majority of a number of people or things. 12. strength or concentration, as of wine; substance or consistency, as of a liquid. 13. sturdiness or durability, as of a fabric. 14. [Colloq.], a human being; person. 15. in *geometry*, a solid. 16. in *law*, something regarded as a person: as, the *body* corporate. 17. in *printing*, the shank of a type. *v.t.* [BODIED (-id), BODYING], 1. to give a body to; furnish with a body; make substantial. 2. to make part of; embody.
body forth, 1. to give shape or form to. 2. to symbolize or represent.
keep body and soul together, to stay alive (in adverse circumstances).
SYN.—**body** refers to the whole physical substance of a person or animal, whether dead or alive; **corpse** and the euphemistic **remains** refer to a dead human body; **carcass** is used of the dead body of an animal or, contemptuously, of a human being; **cadaver** refers primarily to a dead human body used for dissection in medical studies.

body color, 1. a pigment that gives opacity to paint. 2. an opaque coat of paint.

body corporate, in *law*, a corporation.

bod·y·guard (bod′i-gärd′), *n.* a person or persons, usually armed, assigned to guard someone.

body politic, people constituting a political unit with a government; state.

body snatcher, a person who steals corpses from graves.

Boe·o·ti·a (bi-ō′shi-ə, bi-ō′shə), *n.* an ancient Greek state, northwest of Attica: capital, Thebes.

Boe·o·tian (bi-ō′shən), *adj.* of or like Boeotia or its people, who were reputed to be dull and stupid. *n.* 1. a native or inhabitant of Boeotia. 2. a dull, stupid person.

Boer (bōr, bôr, boor), *n.* [D. *boer*, peasant; see BOOR], a descendant of Dutch colonists in South Africa. *adj.* of the Boers.

Boer War, a war (1899–1902) in which Great Britain defeated the Boers of South Africa.

Bo·e·thi·us (bō-ē′thi-əs), *n.* (*Anicius Manlius Severinus Boethius*), Roman philosopher and statesman; 480?–524? A.D.

bog (bog, bôg), *n.* [Ir. *bogach*, a bog < Gael. *bog*, soft, moist], wet, spongy ground; small marsh or swamp. *v.t. & v.i.* [BOGGED (bogd, bôgd), BOGGING], to become stuck or cause to become stuck in or as in a bog; sink in or as in a bog (often with *down*).

bog asphodel, any of several plants of the lily family that grow in bogs and have stiff, narrow leaves and small, yellow flowers.

bo·gey (bō′gi), *n.* [*pl.* BOGEYS (-giz)], 1. a bogy (hobgoblin). 2. [after Colonel *Bogey*, imaginary partner assumed to play a first-rate game], in *golf*, *a*) a set number of strokes for a hole or for the course, used as a standard of skill; par. *b*) one stroke more than par on a hole.

bog·gi·ness (bog′i-nis, bôg′i-nis), *n.* the quality or state of being boggy.

bog·gle (bog′'l), *v.i.* [BOGGLED (-'ld), BOGGLING], [< Scot. *bogle*, specter; prob. < ME. *bugge*, specter (as in *bug*bear); now confused with *bungle*], 1. to be startled; shy away (with *at*). 2. to hesitate or have scruples (with *at*). 3. to give false reasons for not doing something; equivocate; shuffle (with *at*). 4. to bungle. *v.t.* to bungle or botch. *n.* 1. a boggling. 2. a scruple. 3. a botch. 4. [Dial.], a hobgoblin; bogy: also **bogle**.

bog·gy (bog′i, bôg′i), *adj.* [BOGGIER (-i-ẽr), BOGGIEST (-i-ist)], 1. like a bog; marshy. 2. full of bogs.

bo·gie (bō′gi), *n.* [*pl.* BOGIES (-giz)], a bogy (hobgoblin).

bo·gie (bō′gi), *n.* [*pl.* BOGIES (-giz)], [< north Brit. dial.], 1. a low, swiveled undercarriage at either end of a railroad car. 2. one wheel of the several pairs supporting the tread of an armored tank or tractor. 3. [North British Dial.], a low, heavy cart or truck. Also **bogy**.

bo·gle (bō′g'l), *n.* [see BOGGLE], a bogy (hobgoblin).

bog oak, the wood of oak found preserved in peat bogs.

Bo·go·tá (bō′gə-tä′), *n.* the capital of Colombia: **pop.**, 1,329,000.

bog·trot·ter (bog′trot′ẽr, bôg′trot′ẽr), *n.* 1. a person who lives in or wanders among bogs, as certain Irish vagabonds formerly did; hence, 2. an Irishman: contemptuous term.

bo·gus (bō′gəs), *adj.* [orig. (slang), counterfeiter's apparatus], not genuine; spurious; counterfeit. —*SYN.* see **false**.

bogus paper, an imitation Bristol or Manila paper made from wood pulp.

bog·wood (bog′wood′, bôg′wood′), *n.* a black, heavy wood from certain trees preserved in peat bogs.

bo·gy (bō′gi), *n.* [*pl.* BOGIES (-giz)], [see BOGGLE & BUG], 1. an imaginary evil being or spirit; goblin. 2. a bogylike or frightening person or thing; bugbear. Also spelled **bogey, bogie**.

bo·gy (bō′gi), *n.* [*pl.* BOGIES (-giz)], a bogie (undercarriage).

Boh., 1. Bohemia. 2. Bohemian.

bo·hea (bō-hē′), *n.* [< Chin. dial. pron. of *Wu-i*, hills in Fukien, China, where the tea is grown], an inferior variety of black tea: originally, a superior variety.

Bo·he·mi·a (bō-hē′mi-ə), *n.* 1. a region of Czechoslovakia: formerly a kingdom and province of Austria-Hungary: area, 20,102 sq. mi.: Czech name, *Čechy*: abbreviated **Boh.** 2. *a*) Bohemians (sense 4) collectively *b*) a community of such people.

Bo·he·mi·an (bō-hē′mi-ən), *n.* 1. a native or inhabitant of Bohemia. 2. the West Slavic language of the Czechs: also called *Czech*. 3. [from the fact that the gypsies passed through Bohemia to reach western Europe], a gypsy. 4. an artist, dilettante, etc. who lives unconventionally. *adj.* 1. of Bohemia, its people, or their language; Czech. 2. like or characteristic of a Bohemian (sense 4); unconventional, arty, etc. Abbreviated **Boh.** (*n.* 1 & 2, *adj.* 1).

Bohemian Forest, a wooded mountain region between Bavaria and Bohemia: German name, *Böhmerwald*.

Bo·he·mi·an·ism (bō-hē′mi-ən-iz'm), *n.* [< Fr. *Bohémien*, gypsy], the way of life, attitude, or habits of Bohemians (sense 4).

Böh·mer·wald (bö′mẽr-vält′), *n.* the Bohemian Forest: also **Böhmer Wald**: the German name.

Bo·hol (bə-hôl′), *n.* an island in the Philippines, between Cebu and Leyte: area, 1,534 sq. mi ; pop., 603,000.

Bohr, Niels (nēls bōr, bôr), 1885–1962; Danish physicist; received Nobel prize in physics, 1922.

Bohr theory, a theory suggesting that the transfer of electrons from one orbit to another accounts for the absorption and radiation of energy by the hydrogen atom: proposed by Niels Bohr in 1913.

bo·hunk (bō′huŋk), *n.* [prob. < *Bo*hemian + *Hun*garian], [Slang], 1. a person from east central Europe. 2. any unskilled laborer; especially, one from east central Europe. Vulgar term of prejudice and contempt.

Bo·iar·do, Mat·te·o Ma·ri·a (mät-te′ô mä-rē′ä bô-yär′dô), 1434–1494; Italian poet.

boil (boil), *v.i.* [ME. *boilen*, *boylen*; OFr. *boillir*; L. *bullire* < *bulla*, a bubble, stud], 1. to bubble up and vaporize over direct heat. 2. to reach the vaporizing stage. 3. to seethe or churn like boiling liquids. 4. to be agitated, as with rage. 5. to cook by boiling. *v.t.*

1. to heat to the boiling point. 2. to cook, make, or clean by boiling. *n.* the act or state of boiling.
boil away, to evaporate as a result of boiling.
boil down, 1. to lessen in quantity by boiling; hence, 2. to make more terse; condense; summarize.
boil over, 1. to come to a boil and spill over the rim. 2. to lose one's temper; get excited.
SYN.—**boil,** the basic word, refers to the vaporization of a liquid over direct heat or, metaphorically, to great agitation, as with rage (it made my blood *boil*); **seethe** suggests violent boiling with much bubbling and foaming or, in an extended sense, violent excitement (the country *seethed* with rebellion); **simmer** implies a gentle, continuous cooking at or just below the boiling point or, metaphorically, imminence of eruption, as in anger or revolt; **stew** refers to slow, prolonged boiling or, in an extended colloquial sense, unrest caused by worry or anxiety.

boil (boil), *n.* [orig., & still dial., *bile;* ME. *byle, bile;* AS. *byle, byl;* akin to G. *beule;* IE. base **bhu-*, to inflate], an inflamed, painful, pus-filled swelling on the skin, with a hard center: it is caused by infection.

Boi·leau-Des·pré·aux, Ni·co·las (nē'kô'lä' bwá'lō'dā'-prā'ō'), 1636–1711; French critic: usually **Boileau.**

boiled oil, (boild), oil boiled or heated to serve as a dryer in paints, etc.

boiled shirt, [Slang], 1. a man's dress shirt; hence, 2. a pompous man.

boil·er (boil'ẽr), *n.* 1. a container in which things are boiled or heated. 2. a large, strong container in which water is turned to steam for heating or power, as in a steam engine. 3. a tank to hold hot water.

boil·ing point (boil'iŋ), 1. the temperature at which a specified liquid boils: the usual boiling point of water at sea level is 212° F., or 100° C.: abbreviated **b.p.** 2. [Colloq.], the point at which a person loses his temper.

Bois de Bou·logne (bwä də bōō'lō'ny'; Eng. boo-lōn'), a park on the outskirts of Paris.

Boi·se (boi'si, boi'zi), *n.* the capital of Idaho: pop., 34,000.

bois·ter·ous (bois'tẽr-əs), *adj.* [extended form of ME. *boistous, boystous,* rough in quality < Anglo-Fr. *boistous* (OFr. *boisteus*), rough (said of a road)], 1. rough; violent; turbulent. 2. loud and exuberant; noisily good-natured. —*SYN.* see **vociferous.**

Boj·er, Jo·han (yō-hän' boi'ẽr), 1872–1959; Norwegian novelist and playwright.

Bok, Edward William (bok), 1863–1930; American editor and author.

Bo·kha·ra (bô-khä'rä; Eng. bō-kä'rə), *n.* 1. a part of the Uzbek Republic, U.S.S.R.: formerly a state of western Asia. 2. a city in the Uzbek S.S.R.: pop., 69,000. Also **Bukhara.**

Bol., 1. Bolivia. 2. Bolivian.

bo·la (bō'lə), *n.* [Sp., a ball; L. *bulla,* a bubble, ball], a weapon made of a long cord or thong with heavy balls at the end, used for throwing at and entangling cattle, etc.: also **bolas.**

bo·lar (bō'lẽr), *adj.* of or like bole (clay).

bo·las (bō'ləs), *n.* [Sp., pl.], a bola.

bold (bōld), *adj.* [ME. *bold;* AS. *beald, bald;* IE. base **bhel-to,* swollen up, bold < **bhel-* to inflate, swell up], 1. daring; fearless; audacious. 2. very free in behavior or manner; taking liberties; impudent; shameless. 3. steep; abrupt. 4. prominent and clear; striking and sharp: as, he writes a *bold* hand. 5. [Obs.], confident. —*SYN.* see **brave.**
make bold, to be so bold as (to do something); dare.

bold·face (bōld'fās'), *n.* in *printing,* a type with a heavy face: the words listed in this dictionary are in boldface: abbreviated **bf, b.f.**

bold-faced (bōld'fāst'), *adj.* 1. impudent; unabashed; forward. 2. printed in boldface.

bold·ness (bōld'nis), *n.* 1. the quality of being bold. 2. a bold act, remark, etc.

bole (bōl), *n.* [ME. *bol;* ON. *bolr;* IE. base **bhel-*, to swell up; cf. BOLD], a tree trunk.

bole (bōl), *n.* [ME. & OFr. *bol;* ML. *bolus,* clay; Gr. *bōlos,* lump of earth], a variety of easily pulverized, reddish clay.

bo·lec·tion (bō-lek'shən), *n.* [orig. form & etym. unknown], in *architecture,* the part of a molding that projects beyond the surface of a panel: also **bilection.**

bo·le·ro (bō-lâr'ō), *n.* [*pl.* BOLEROS (-ōz)], [Sp.], 1. a Spanish dance done to castanets and lively music in 3/4 time. 2. the music for this dance. 3. a short, open vest, with or without sleeves, worn by men and women.

bo·le·tus (bə-lē'təs), *n.* [L.; Gr. *bōlitēs;* prob. < *bōlos,* a lump], any of a number of related large, fleshy toadstools with spore-bearing tubes or pores on the under-surface of the cap.

Bol·eyn, Anne (bool'in), 1507–1536; second wife of Henry VIII of England; mother of Elizabeth I.

bo·lide (bō'līd, bō'lid), *n.* [Fr. < L. *bolis,* fiery meteor; Gr. *bolis,* missile, arrow], a bright, shooting meteor, especially one that explodes.

Bol·ing·broke (bol'iŋ-brook, bool'iŋ-brook'), first Viscount, (*Henry St. John*), 1678–1751; English political writer and statesman.

bol·i·var (bol'ə-vẽr; Sp. bô-lē'vär), *n.* [*pl.* BOLIVARS (-vẽrz); Sp. BOLIVARES (bô'lē-vä'res)], [after Simón *Bolívar*], the monetary unit of Venezuela, a silver coin equal to about $0.30 in 1950: abbreviated **B., b.**

Bol·í·var, Si·món (bol'ə-vẽr; Am. Sp. sē-môn' bô-lē'vär), 1783–1830; Venezuelan general and revolutionist; helped free South America from Spain: called *the Liberator.*

Bo·liv·i·a (bə-liv'i-ə), *n.* an inland country in west central South America: area, 424,000 sq. mi.; pop., 3,549,000; capitals, La Paz and Sucre: abbreviated **Bol.**

bo·liv·i·a (bə-liv'i-ə), *n.* [< the name of the country], a soft, woolen cloth resembling plush.

Bo·liv·i·an (bə-liv'i-ən), *adj.* of Bolivia or its people. *n.* a native or inhabitant of Bolivia. Abbreviated **Bol.**

bo·li·via·no (bô-lē'vyä'nô), *n.* [*pl.* BOLIVIANOS (-nôs)], [Am. Sp. < *Bolivia*], the monetary unit of Bolivia, equal to about 2.4 cents in 1950.

boll (bōl), *n.* [ME. *bolle;* AS. *bolla;* see BOWL (cup)], the pod of a plant, especially of flax or cotton.

Bol·land, John (bol'ənd), 1596–1665; Flemish Jesuit; editor of *Acta Sanctorum* (*Acts of the Saints*).

bol·lard (bol'ẽrd), *n.* [< LG. *poller, polder* < OFr. *poldre, poltre,* orig., colt, horse; then, supporting beam < ML. *pulletrium* < L. *pullus,* colt; see PULLEY], a strong post on a ship or dock, for holding a hawser fast.

bol·lix (bol'iks), *v.t.* [BOLLIXED (-ikst), BOLLIXING], [euphemistic respelling of nautical slang < ME. *ballokes;* AS. *beallucas,* testicles (dim. of *ball*), used as an extension of *ball, v.i.*], [Slang], to make a muddle of; bungle; botch (usually with *up*).

boll weevil, a small, grayish beetle with a long beak, whose larvae are hatched in the bolls of cotton plants and do much damage to the cotton.

boll·worm (bōl'wũrm'), *n.* a kind of moth larva that feeds on cotton bolls, ears of corn, tomatoes, etc.

bo·lo (bō'lō), *n.* [*pl.* BOLOS (-lōz)], [Sp.], a large, single-edged knife used in the Philippine Islands as a weapon or utensil; machete.

Bo·lo·gna (bô-lô'nyä), *n.* 1. a city in northern Italy: pop., 351,000. 2. [usually b-], (bə-lō'nə, bə-lō'nyə, bə-lō'ni), a highly seasoned, smoked sausage of beef, pork, and veal: also **bologna sausage.**

Bo·lo·gnese (bō'lō-nyēz'), *n.* [*pl.* BOLOGNESE], a native or inhabitant of Bologna. *adj.* of Bologna, its people, or their dialect.

bo·lo·graph (bō'lə-graf', bō'lə-gräf'), *n.* [*bolo-* (see BOLOMETER) + *-graph*], 1. a record of variations registered by a bolometer. 2. a bolometer.

bo·lom·e·ter (bō-lom'ə-tẽr), *n.* [< Gr. *bolē,* ray, lit., something thrown < *ballein,* to throw; + *-meter*], in *physics,* an instrument for measuring and recording the intensity of small amounts of radiant energy: it is also used in radio for detection of ultra-high frequencies.

Bol·she·vik, bol·she·vik (bol'shə-vik', bōl'shə-vik'), *n.* [*pl.* BOLSHEVIKS (-viks'), BOLSHEVIKI (-vē'ki; Russ. bôl'shə-vē-kē')], [Russ. (1903) < *bolshe,* the larger, majority], 1. originally, a member of the majority faction (*Bolsheviki*) of the Social Democratic Party of Russia: the Bolsheviks wrested power from the Kerensky government in 1917, five months after the Czar was overthrown, and formed the Communist Party. 2. a member of a Communist party, especially that of the Soviet Union. 3. loosely, any radical: hostile usage. *adj.* of, characteristic of, or like the Bolsheviks or Bolshevism.

Bol·she·vism, bol·she·vism (bol'shə-viz'm, bōl'shə-viz'm), *n.* the policies and practices of the Bolsheviks.

Bol·she·vist, bol·she·vist (bol'shə-vist, bōl'shə-vist), *n. & adj.* Bolshevik.

Bol·she·vis·tic, bol·she·vis·tic (bol'shə-vis'tik, bōl'shə-vis'tik), *adj.* Bolshevik.

Bol·she·vize, bol·she·vize (bol'shə-vīz', bōl'shə-vīz'), *v.t.* [BOLSHEVIZED (-vīzd'), BOLSHEVIZING], to make Bolshevik; indoctrinate with Bolshevism.

bol·son (bōl'sən; Sp. bôl-sôn'), *n.* [Sp., lit., big purse], a flat desert valley surrounded by mountains and draining into a shallow lake in the center.

bol·ster (bōl'stẽr), *n.* [ME. *bolstre;* AS. *bolster;* for IE. base see BALL (sphere)], 1. a long, narrow cushion or pillow. 2. a soft pad for easing pressure on any part of the body. 3. any bolsterlike object or support. *v.t.* to prop up with or as with a bolster; support so as to keep from falling (often with *up*).

bolt (bōlt), *n.* [ME. & AS.; akin to G. *bolz;* IE. base **bheld,* to knock, strike], 1. a short, heavy arrow with a thick, blunt head, shot from a crossbow; hence, 2. a sudden, unforeseen occurrence, often an unfortunate one. 3. a flash of lightning; thunderbolt. 4. a sliding bar for locking a door, gate, etc. 5. a similar bar in a lock, moved by a key. 6. a metal rod or pin, often threaded and used with a nut to hold parts together. 7. a roll of cloth, paper, etc. of a given length. 8. [< the *v.t.*], a bolting or withdrawal from one's party or group. 9. in *firearms,* a sliding bar that pushes the cartridge into place, closes the breech, and extracts the empty cartridge case after firing. *v.t.* 1. to shoot or discharge (an arrow, etc.). 2. to say suddenly or unexpectedly; blurt. 3. to swallow (food) hurriedly; gulp down. 4. to hold together or fasten with or as with a bolt. 5. to roll (cloth, etc.) into bolts. 6. to withdraw support from or abandon (a party, group, etc.). *v.i.* 1. to go forth suddenly; spring; dart. 2. to start suddenly and run away, as a horse. 3. to swallow food hurriedly. 4. to withdraw support from or abandon a group, political party, etc. 5. in *horticulture*, to produce seed prematurely. *adv.* like an arrow; suddenly.

bolt from the blue, 1. a thunderbolt from a clear sky; hence, 2. a sudden, unforeseen occurrence, often an unfortunate one.

bolt upright, very straight upright; straight as a dart.

shoot one's bolt, to do the most or the best that one can; make a maximum or exhaustive effort.

bolt (bōlt), *v.t.* [ME. *bulten;* OFr. *bulter, buleter*, dissimilated < **bureter* < *bure* (L. **bura*), coarse cloth; akin to It. *burattare* < *buratto*, sieve], 1. to sift (flour, grain, etc.) so as to separate and grade. 2. to inspect and separate, as good from bad; examine closely.

bolt·er (bōl'tẽr), *n.* [< *bolt* (to run away)], 1. a runaway horse. 2. a person who withdraws from his political party or stops supporting its candidates or policies.

bolt·er (bōl'tẽr), *n.* [< *bolt* (to sift)], a device for sifting flour, etc.

bolt·head (bōlt'hed'), *n.* 1. the end of a bolt opposite the threaded end. 2. a long-necked glass flask, used by early chemists.

Bol·ton (bōl't'n), *n.* a city in western England: pop., 164,000 (est. 1946).

bol·to·ni·a (bōl-tō'ni-ə), *n.* [Mod.L., after the Eng. botanist James *Bolton*], any of several plants of the composite family, with white or purplish, asterlike flowers.

bolt·rope (bōlt'rōp'), *n.* [*bolt, n.* + *rope*], a rope sewn into the edge seam of a sail to prevent tearing.

bo·lus (bō'ləs), *n.* [*pl.* BOLUSES (-iz)], [L.; Gr. *bōlos*, a lump], 1. a small, round lump or mass of something. 2. in *veterinary medicine*, a large pill.

bomb (bom), *n.* [Fr. *bombe;* Sp. *bomba* < L. *bombus;* Gr. *bombos*, deep and hollow sound], 1. an explosive, incendiary, or gas-filled container, for dropping, hurling, or setting in place to be exploded by a timing mechanism. 2. a sudden, surprising occurrence, especially an unpleasant one. *v.t. & v.i.* to attack, damage, or destroy (anything) with a bomb or bombs.

bom·ba·ca·ceous (bom-bə-kā'shəs), *adj.* [LL. *bombax* (see BOMBAST); + *-aceous*], belonging to the family of silk-cotton trees, which bear fruit with woolly seeds.

bom·bard (bom-bärd'), *v.t.* [Fr. *bombarder* < *bombarde*, cannon < *bombe;* see BOMB], 1. to attack with or as with artillery or bombs. 2. to keep attacking or pressing with questions, suggestions, etc. 3. to direct a stream of particles, as neutrons, against the atomic nuclei of (an element) to produce nuclear transformations. *n.* (bom'bärd), an early type of cannon, hurling stones or other missiles. —*SYN.* see **attack**.

bom·bard·ier (bom'bẽr-dêr'), *n.* [Fr. < *bombarde;* see BOMBARD], 1. a person who operates the bomb sight and releases the bombs in a bomber. 2. a noncommissioned artillery officer in the British army. 3. [Archaic], an artilleryman. 4. [Archaic], a ship with heavy cannon.

bom·bard·ment (bom-bärd'mənt), *n.* a bombarding or being bombarded.

bom·bar·don (bom'bẽr-dən, bom-bär'dən), *n.* [It. *bombardone* < *bombardo* < L. *bombus;* see BOMB], 1. an early type of bassoon. 2. a bass or contrabass tuba. 3. an organ stop with a bass reed.

bom·ba·sine (bom'bə-zēn', bom'bə-zēn'), *n.* bombazine.

bom·bast (bom'bast), *n.* [OFr. *bombace;* LL. *bombax*, cotton < *bambax*, cotton (with form influenced by L. *bombyx*, silk, silkworm < Gr. *bombyx*) < Late Gr. *bambax;* Gr. *pambax;* Per. *pambak*, cotton], 1. originally, a soft material used for padding; hence, 2. high-sounding but unimportant or silly language; pompous speech.

bom·bas·tic (bom-bas'tik), *adj.* [see BOMBAST], using, characterized by, or fond of high-sounding but unimportant or silly language; pompous; grandiloquent.

SYN.—**bombastic** refers to speech or writing that is pompous and inflated and suggests extravagant verbal padding and little substance; **grandiloquent** suggests an overreaching eloquence and implies the use of grandiose, high-flown language and an oratorical tone; **flowery** language is full of figurative and ornate expressions and high-sounding words; **euphuistic** is applied to an extremely artificial style of writing in which there is a straining for effect at the expense of thought; **turgid** implies such inflation of style as to obscure meaning.

bom·bas·ti·cal·ly (bom-bas'ti-k'l-i, bom-bas'tik-li), *adv.* in a bombastic manner.

Bom·bay (bom-bā'), *n.* 1. a state of western India; formerly a presidency: area, 108,142 sq. mi.; pop., 29,344,000 (est. 1950). 2. its capital, on the Arabian Sea: pop., 1,490,000.

bom·ba·zine (bom'bə-zēn', bom'bə-zēn'), *n.* [Fr. *bombesin;* LL. *bombacinium*, silk texture < L. *bombyx;* see BOMBAST], a twilled cloth of silk with worsted or cotton, often used for mourning: also spelled **bombasine**.

bomb bay, a compartment for the bombs in a bomber, made so that it can be opened when they are to be dropped.

‡**bombe** (bōnb), *n.* [Fr.; see BOMB], a frozen dessert consisting of a melon or a mold with an inner coating of one kind of ice cream and a center of another.

bomb·er (bom'ẽr), *n.* 1. an airplane designed for dropping bombs: see TYPES OF AIRPLANE, p. 32. 2. a person that bombs.

bomb·ing run (bom'iŋ), a flight by a bombing crew over the target for the release of bombs.

bomb·proof (bom'prōōf'), *adj.* capable of withstanding bombardment. *n.* a bombproof shelter, often underground.

bomb rack, a device underneath or within an aircraft for transporting and releasing aerial bombs.

bomb·shell (bom'shel'), *n.* 1. a bomb. 2. any sudden unforeseen occurrence, especially an unpleasant one.

bomb sight, an instrument for aiming bombs dropped from aircraft.

bom·by·cid (bom'bi-sid), *n.* [< L. *bombyx;* see BOMBAST], any of a certain family of moths found chiefly in tropical regions, as the silkworm moth.

Bon (bon; Fr. bōn), *n.* a cape near Tunis, Africa.

Bon (bōn), *n.* [Japan.], a religious festival observed by Japanese Buddhists from July 13 to 16, when the spirits of dead ancestors are supposed to come back.

Bo·na (bō'nä), *n.* Bône.

bo·na·ci (bō'nä-sē'), *n.* [Am. Sp. *bonasi*], any of certain groupers important as food fishes, found near Florida, the West Indies, etc.

bo·na fi·de (bō'nə fī'di, bō'nə fīd'), [L.], in good faith; without dishonesty, fraud, or deceit. —*SYN.* see **authentic**.

‡**bo·na fi·des** (bō'nə fī'dēz), [L.], good faith; honesty.

‡**bon a·mi** (bōn'ȧ'mē'), [Fr.], good friend: said of a man or boy.

bo·nan·za (bō-nan'zə), *n.* [Sp., fair weather at sea, prosperity < L. *bonus*, good], 1. a very rich vein or pocket of ore; hence, 2. [Colloq.], any source of wealth or high profits.

Bo·na·parte (bō'nə-pärt'; Fr. bô'nȧ'pȧrt'), family name of *Napoleon I, Napoleon II, Louis Napoleon*, etc.: also **Buonaparte**.

Bonaparte, Jerome, 1784–1860; brother of Napoleon I; king of Westphalia (1807).

Bonaparte, Joseph, 1768–1844; brother of Napoleon I; king of Naples (1806–1808) and of Spain (1808–1813).

Bonaparte, Louis, 1778–1846; brother of Napoleon I; king of Holland (1806).

Bonaparte, Lu·cien (lü'syan'), 1775–1840; brother of Napoleon I; prince of Canino.

Bo·na·part·ism (bō'nə-pär'tiz'm), *n.* 1. belief in and support of Napoleon Bonaparte and his actions, methods, and doctrines. 2. the methods, doctrines, etc. of any political dictator like Napoleon Bonaparte.

Bo·na·part·ist (bō'nə-pär'tist), *n.* a person who practices or advocates Bonapartism.

Bon·a·ven·tu·ra, Saint (bon'ə-ven-tyoor'ə), (born *Giovanni di Fidanza*), 1221–1274; Italian cardinal, scholar, and writer: called the *Seraphic Doctor*.

bon·bon (bon'bon'; Fr. bōn'bōn'), *n.* [Fr. *bon*, good, emphasized by repetition], a small piece of candy, often with a creamy filling.

‡**bon·bon·nière** (bōn'bô'nyâr'), *n.* [Fr.], a container for bonbons; candy box or dish.

bond (bond), *n.* [ME. *bond, band* < AS. *bindan*, to bind], 1. anything that binds, fastens, or confines. 2. *pl.* fetters; shackles; hence, 3. *pl.* imprisonment; captivity. 4. a uniting force; tie; link. 5. a binding agreement; covenant. 6. a duty or obligation imposed by a contract, promise, etc. 7. a substance or device, as glue, solder, or a chain, which holds things together or unites them. 8. bond paper. 9. in *chemistry*, *a)* a unit of combining capacity equivalent to one atom of hydrogen. *b)* the means or mechanism by which atoms or groups of atoms are combined in molecules. 10. in *commerce*, *a)* an agreement by an agency holding taxable goods that taxes on them will be paid before they are sold. *b)* the condition of goods kept in a warehouse until taxes are paid. *c)* an insurance contract by which a bonding agency guarantees payment of a specified sum to an employer, etc., in the event of a financial loss caused him by the act of a specified employee or by some contingency over which the payee has no control. 11. in *finance*, an interest-bearing certificate issued by a government or business, promising to pay the holder a specified sum on a specified date: it is a common means of raising capital. 12. in *law*, *a)* a written obligation under seal to pay specified sums, or to do or not do specified things. *b)* a person acting as surety for another's action; payer of bail. *c)* an amount paid as surety or bail. 13. in *masonry*, any arrangement of bricks, etc. in a wall, which binds them into a compact whole. Abbreviated **bd.** *v.t.* 1. to connect with or as with a bond; bind. 2. to furnish a bond (sense 12, *a*) and thus become a surety for (another). 3. to place or hold (goods) in or under bond. 4. to issue interest-bearing certificates on; mortgage. 5. to put under bonded debt. 6. to arrange (timbers, bricks, etc.) in a pattern that gives strength. *v.i.* to connect, hold together, or solidify by or as by a bond.

bottled in bond, stored in casks in bonded warehouses for the length of time stated on the label and then bottled there, as some whisky.

bond (bond), *n.* [ME. *bonde;* AS. *bonda, bunda;* see BONDAGE], [Obs.], a serf or slave. *adj.* in bondage; in serfdom; in slavery; unfree.

bond·age (bon′dij), *n.* [ME.; ML. *bondagium* < AS. *bonda, bunda,* husbandman, servant; ON. *bondi* < *buandi* < *bua,* to inhabit, dwell], 1. serfdom; slavery. 2. subjection to some force, compulsion, or influence. —*SYN.* see **servitude.**

bond·ed (bon′did), *adj.* [pp. of *bond*], 1. subject to or secured by a bond or bonds. 2. placed in a warehouse pending payment of taxes.

bonded warehouse, a warehouse, certified by the Department of Internal Revenue and guaranteed by a bonding agency, where goods may be stored until necessary duties or taxes are paid.

bond·hold·er (bond′hōl′dẽr), *n.* an owner of bonds issued by a company, government, or person.

bond·maid (bond′mād′), *n.* a girl or woman bond servant or slave.

bond·man (bond′mən), *n.* [*pl.* BONDMEN (-mən)], 1. a feudal serf. 2. [Archaic], a man or boy slave.

bond paper, 1. rag paper used for bonds. 2. a strong, superior stock of paper with a hard surface, used for letterheads, etc.

bond-ser·vant (bond′sũr′vənt), *n.* 1. a person bound to service without pay. 2. a slave. Also **bond servant.**

bonds·man (bondz′mən, bonz′mən), *n.* [*pl.* BONDSMEN (-mən)], 1. a bondman. 2. a person who takes responsibility for another by furnishing a bond; surety.

bond·wom·an (bond′woom′ən), *n.* [*pl.* BONDWOMEN (-wim′ən)], a woman slave.

Bône (bōn), *n.* a seaport in northern Algeria: pop., 164,000: also **Bona.**

bone (bōn), *n.* [ME. *bone, boon;* AS. *ban,* bone, esp. of a limb; akin to G. *bein,* a leg; only Gmc.], 1. any part or piece of the hard tissue forming the skeleton of most full-grown vertebrate animals, especially a piece between two joints. 2. this hard tissue. 3. *pl.* the skeleton; hence, 4. *pl.* the body, living or dead. 5. a bonelike substance or thing. 6. a thing made of bone or bonelike material. 7. *pl.* flat sticks used as clappers by end men in minstrel shows, for keeping time to music, etc. 8. *pl.* [construed as sing.], an end man in a minstrel show. 9. *pl.* [Colloq.], dice. 10. [Slang], a student who studies hard. *v.t.* [BONED (bōnd), BONING], 1. to remove the bones from. 2. to put whalebone or other stiffening into. 3. to fertilize. *v.i.* [Slang], to apply oneself diligently; especially, to study hard (often with *up*).

feel in one's bones, to think or be certain without any real reason: have a presentiment.

have a bone to pick, to have something to quarrel or complain about.

make no bones about, [Colloq.], 1. to make no attempt to hide; admit freely. 2. to have no objection to or qualms about.

bone ash, a white porous ash prepared by burning bones in the open air and consisting chiefly of calcium phosphate: used as a fertilizer and in making bone china: also **bone earth.**

bone·black (bōn′blak′), *n.* a fine charcoal made by roasting animal bones in closed containers and used as a coloring, in refining sugar, etc.: also **bone black.**

bone china, a kind of china made with clay to which bone ash or calcium phosphate has been added.

boned (bōnd), *adj.* [pp. of *bone*], 1. having (a specific kind of) bone: as, brittle-*boned.* 2. having the bones taken out. 3. having stays of whalebone, etc.

bone-dry (bōn′drī′), *adj.* as dry as bone; very dry.

bone·head (bōn′hed′), *n.* [Slang], a stupid person; fool.

bone·less (bōn′lis), *adj.* without bones; specifically, with the bones removed: as, *boneless* sardines.

bone meal, crushed or finely ground bones, used as feed or fertilizer.

bone of contention, a matter for argument.

bone oil, a thick, black oil obtained by the dry distillation of bones.

bon·er (bōn′ẽr), *n.* [Slang], a stupid or silly blunder. —*SYN.* see **error.**

bone·set (bōn′set′), *n.* a plant of the composite family, with flat clusters of white or bluish-purple flowers: used as a drug to increase perspiration, as a tonic, etc.

bon·fire (bon′fīr′), *n.* [ME. *banfir, banefyre,* lit., bone fire, fire for burning corpses], a fire built out-of-doors.

bon·go (boŋ′gō), *n.* [*pl.* BONGOS (-gōz)], [native African name], a large African antelope, reddish-brown with white stripes.

bon·go (boŋ′gō), *n.* [*pl.* BONGOS (-gōz)], [Am. Sp. < ?], either of a pair of small, joined drums, each of different pitch, played with the hands: in full, **bongo drum.**

Bon·heur, Ro·sa (rō′zȧ′ bô′nẽr′), 1822–1899; French painter of animals.

bon·ho·mie, bon·hom·mie (bon′ə-mē′; Fr. bô′nô′mē′), *n.* [Fr. < *bonhomme; bon,* good + *homme,* man], good nature; pleasant, affable manner.

bon·i·face (bon′ə-fās′), *n.* [after *Boniface,* landlord in Farquhar's comedy, *The Beaux' Stratagem*], a tavern keeper; innkeeper.

Bon·i·face VIII, (bon′ə-fās′), 1235?–1303; Pope (1294–1303).

Boniface, Saint, (born *Winfrid*), 680?–755 A.D.; English monk and missionary in Germany.

bon·i·ness (bōn′i-nis), *n.* bony quality or condition.

Bo·nin Islands (bō′nin), a group of islands in the Pacific, 500 mi. southeast of Honshu: area, 30 sq. mi.; pop., 5,000: Japanese name, *Ogasawara Jima.*

bo·ni·to (bə-nē′tō), *n.* [*pl.* BONITOS, BONITOES (-tōz), BONITO; see PLURAL, II, D, 1], [Sp.], any of several salt-water food fishes of the mackerel family.

‡**bon jour** (bōn′ zhōōr′), [Fr.], good day; good morning.

bon mot (bōn′ mō′), [*pl.* BONS MOTS (bōn′ mōz′; Fr. mō′)], [Fr., lit., good word], a witticism; apt saying.

Bonn (bon), *n.* a city in western Germany, on the Rhine: pop., 147,000; established as capital of (the Federal Republic of) West Germany in 1949.

‡**bonne** (bôn), *n.* [Fr., fem. of *bon,* good; L. *bonus,* fem. *bona,* good], 1. a maidservant. 2. a nursemaid.

‡**bonne a·mie** (bôn′ ȧ′mē′), [Fr., fem. of *bon ami*], good friend: said of a woman or girl.

‡**bonne foi** (bôn′ fwȧ′), [Fr.], good faith; honesty.

bon·net (bon′it), *n.* [ME. *bonet, bonette;* OFr. *bonet;* ML. *abonnis,* kind of cap], 1. a flat, brimless cap, worn by men and boys in Scotland. 2. a brimless hat with a chin ribbon, worn by children and women. 3. a feathered headdress, worn by some American Indians. 4. a protective covering, as an automobile hood or chimney screen. 5. [Colloq.], any hat worn by women or girls. 6. in *nautical usage,* formerly, a strip of canvas fastened by lacing to the bottom of a sail to increase sail area. *v.t.* to put a bonnet on.

‡**bon·net rouge** (bô′nā′ rōōzh′), [*pl.* BONNETS ROUGES (-nā′ rōōzh′)], [Fr., red cap], 1. the red cap, symbol of liberty, worn by the French revolutionists of 1793; hence, 2. a revolutionist or radical.

bon·ni·ly (bon′ə-li), *adv.* in a bonny manner.

bon·ni·ness (bon′i-nis), *n.* a bonny quality or state.

bon·ny, bon·nie (bon′i), *adj.* [BONNIER (-i-ẽr), BONNIEST (-i-ist)], [Fr. *bon,* fem. *bonne;* see BONNE], [now mainly Scot. or Eng. Dial.], 1. beautiful; handsome; pretty. 2. healthy-looking; robust. 3. fine; pleasant.

bon·ny·clab·ber (bon′i-klab′ẽr), *n.* [Ir. *bainne,* milk + *clabar,* clabber < *claba,* thick], thickly curdled milk.

bon·sai (bon-sī′), *n.* [Japan., lit., tray arrangement], 1. the art of dwarfing and shaping trees and shrubs by pruning, controlled fertilization, etc. 2. such a tree or shrub.

‡**bon soir** (bōn′ swȧr′), [Fr.], good evening.

bon·spiel (bon′spēl, bon′spəl), *n.* [prob. < D. *bondspel*], [Scot.], a curling match between two clubs, towns, etc.

bon·te·bok (bon′tə-bok′), *n.* [*pl.* BONTEBOK, BONTEBOKS (-boks′); see PLURAL, II, D, 2], [D.; *bonte,* mottled, variegated + *bok,* buck], a purplish-red antelope of South Africa, white on the face and rump.

‡**bon ton** (bōn′ tōn′), [Fr., lit., good tone], 1. stylishness. 2. good breeding; fine manners. 3. fashionable society.

bo·nus (bō′nus), *n.* [*pl.* BONUSES (-iz)], [L., good], 1. anything given in addition to the customary or required amount; gift of something extra. 2. an extra dividend paid out of accumulated profits. 3. money charged by a State for granting a charter to a corporation. 4. a payment made by a government to discharged members of the armed forces.

SYN.—**bonus** refers to anything given over and above the regular wages, salary, remuneration, etc. (a Christmas *bonus,* a soldier's *bonus*); a **bounty** is a reward given by a government for a specific undertaking considered in the public interest, as the production of certain crops, the destruction of vermin, etc.; **premium,** as compared here, implies a reward or prize offered as an inducement to buy, sell, compete, etc. (a toy given as a *premium* with each package); **dividend** refers to a prorated share in an amount distributed among stockholders, policyholders, etc. from profits or surplus.

‡**bon vi·vant** (bōn′ vē′vän′), [*pl.* BONS VIVANTS (bōn′ vē′vän′)], [Fr.], a person who enjoys good food and other pleasant things.

‡**bon voy·age** (bōn′ vwȧ′yȧzh′), [Fr., lit., good voyage], pleasant journey.

bon·y (bōn′i), *adj.* [BONIER (-i-ẽr), BONIEST (-i-ist)], 1. of or like bone. 2. having many bones. 3. having large or protruding bones; hence, 4. thin; emaciated.

bonze (bonz), *n.* [Fr.; Port. *bonzo;* Japan. *bonzō;* prob. < Chin. *fan seng,* religious person], a Chinese or Japanese Buddhist monk.

boo (bōō), *interj. & n.* [echoic], a sound that one makes to express disapproval, scorn, etc., or to startle. *v.i.* [BOOED (bōōd), BOOING], to make this sound. *v.t.* to shout "boo" at.

boob (bōōb), *n.* [< *booby*], [Slang], a stupid or foolish person.

boo·by (bōō'bi), *n.* [*pl.* BOOBIES (-biz)], [Sp. *bobo*, a labial echoic word parallel with It. *babbo*, father, Eng. *baby*, etc.], 1. a stupid or foolish person; nitwit. 2. a booby gannet. 3. the player who gets the poorest score in a game, or does worst in a contest.

booby gannet, a large, tropical sea bird related to the gannets, with eyes near the base of the bill.

booby hatch, 1. a hatchway leading to storage space under the poop deck of a ship. 2. [Slang], a hospital for the mentally ill.

booby prize, a prize, usually a ridiculous one, given to whoever has done worst in a game, race, etc.

booby trap, 1. any scheme or device for tricking a person unawares. 2. an antipersonnel mine made to be exploded by some action of the intended victim, as by picking up an innocent-looking object to which the detonator is attached.

boo·dle (bōō'd'l), *n.* [? < D. *boedel*, property, estate], [Slang], 1. a crowd; mob; caboodle. 2. counterfeit money. 3. something given as a bribe; graft. 4. the loot taken in a robbery.

boo·gie-woo·gie (boo'gi-woo'gi), *n.* [echoic; ? suggested by the characteristic "walking" bass; ? redupl. of *boogie*, var. of *bogy* (hobgoblin)], 1. a style of jazz piano playing in which repeated bass figures in 8–8 rhythm accompany melodic variations in the treble. 2. any jazz music in this style. *adj.* 1. of such music. 2. in this style.

boo·hoo (bōō'hōō'), *v.i.* [BOOHOOED (-hōōd'), BOOHOOING], [echoic], to weep noisily. *n.* (bōō'hōō'), [*pl.* BOOHOOS (-hōōz')], noisy weeping.

book (book), *n.* [ME. *boke, book;* AS. *boc*, pl. *bec* < same base as Eng. *beech* (see BEECH): prob. so called because runes were first carved on beech], 1. a number of sheets of paper, parchment, etc. with writing or printing on them, fastened together along one edge, usually between protective covers; literary or scientific work, anthology, etc., distinguished by length and form from a magazine, tract, etc. 2. a number of blank sheets fastened together in a similar way. 3. any of the main divisions of some books, as of the Bible, the *Iliad*, etc. 4. a book of blank or ruled sheets or printed forms, for the entry of accounts, records, etc.: as, an account *book;* hence, 5. a record; account. 6. something regarded as a subject for study: as, the *book* of life. 7. *pl.* studies; lessons. 8. the words of an opera or musical play; libretto: distinguished from *score.* 9. a booklike package, as of matches or tickets. 10. a list or record of bets made, usually on horse races. 11. in *bridge*, etc., a specified number of cards or tricks making a set. Abbreviated **bk., B., b.** *v.t.* 1. to record in a book; list. 2. to engage ahead of time, as lectures, rooms, performances, transportation, etc. 3. to record charges against on a police record. *adj.* in, from, or according to a book or books.

bring to book, 1. to force to explain; demand an accounting from. 2. to reprimand.

by the book, according to the rules; in the prescribed or usual way.

close the books, in *bookkeeping*, to make no further entries, balance the books, and draw up statements from them.

in one's bad books, out of favor with one; in one's bad graces.

in one's good books, in one's favor; in one's good graces.

keep books, to keep a record of business transactions.

know like a book, to know well or fully; be very familiar with.

on the books, 1. recorded. 2. listed; enrolled.

the Book, the Bible.

the book, [Colloq.], any set of ideas, rules, etc. regarded as authoritative.

without book, 1. without reading the lines; from memory. 2. without authority.

book·bind·er (book'bīn'dẽr), *n.* a person whose trade or business is bookbinding.

book·bind·er·y (book'bīn'dẽr-i), *n.* a place where bookbinding is done.

book·bind·ing (book'bīn'diŋ), *n.* the art, trade, or business of binding books.

book·case (book'kās'), *n.* a set of shelves or a cabinet for holding books.

book club, 1. a lending library supported by members who pay a fixed price for the privilege of borrowing books. 2. an organization that sells books, usually at reduced prices, to members who undertake to buy a minimum number of them annually.

book end, an ornamental weight or bracket placed at the end of a row of books to keep them upright.

book·ie (book'i), *n.* [Slang], in *horse racing*, a bookmaker.

book·ing (book'iŋ), *n.* an engagement, as for a lecture, performance, etc.

book·ish (book'ish), *adj.* 1. of or connected with books. 2. inclined to read and study; literary; scholarly. 3. having mere book learning. 4. pedantic; stodgy.

book jacket, a detachable cover of paper, etc. for protecting the binding of a book, usually with colored illustrations and designs for advertising or calling attention to the book.

book·keep·er (book'kēp'ẽr), *n.* a person whose profession is bookkeeping.

book·keep·ing (book'kēp'iŋ), *n.* the profession or art of keeping a systematic record of business transactions: abbreviated **bkkpg.**

book-learn·ed (book'lũr'nid), *adj.* having much book learning, as distinguished from practical experience: a somewhat contemptuous term.

book learning, 1. knowledge gained from reading or studying. 2. [Colloq.], formal education.

book·let (book'lit), *n.* a small book, often paper-covered.

book·lore (book'lôr', book'lōr'), *n.* book learning.

book louse, any of a group of wingless insects that destroy old books and papers.

book·mak·er (book'māk'ẽr), *n.* 1. a maker of books; compiler or publisher. 2. a person in the business of taking bets on race horses.

book·man (book'mən), *n.* [*pl.* BOOKMEN (-mən)], 1. a man who is familiar with books; literary or scholarly man. 2. a man whose business is making, publishing, or selling books.

book·mark (book'märk'), *n.* 1. anything put between the pages of a book to make it easy to find the place. 2. a bookplate.

book matches, safety matches made of paper and fastened into a small cardboard folder.

book·mo·bile (book'mə-bēl'), *n.* [*book* + *automobile*], a traveling lending library transported in a truck, trailer, etc. to small towns or rural areas lacking permanent libraries.

book of account, 1. a book to keep accounts in. 2. *pl.* the records needed for auditing the accounts of a business.

Book of Common Prayer, the official book of services and prayers for the Church of England or, with some minor modifications, for the Episcopal Church.

Book of Mormon, the sacred book of the Mormon Church, first published in 1830.

Book of the Dead, in ancient Egypt, a book containing prayers, hymns, and charms meant to help the soul in the afterworld.

book·plate (book'plāt'), *n.* a label with the owner's name or some identifying design or words on it, for pasting in a book.

book·rack (book'rak'), *n.* 1. a rack or shelf for books. 2. a rack for holding a book open before a reader.

book review, an article or talk dealing with the contents, literary worth, etc. of a book, especially a recently published book.

book scorpion, any of a number of related small arachnids resembling a scorpion without a tail, found beneath stones, in old papers and books, etc.

book·sell·er (book'sel'ẽr), *n.* a person whose work or business is selling books.

book·stack (book'stak'), *n.* a series of bookshelves, one over the other, as in a library.

book·stall (book'stôl'), *n.* 1. an establishment, often an outdoor booth or counter, where books are sold. 2. [British], a newsstand.

book·stand (book'stand'), *n.* 1. a stand or counter where books are displayed and sold. 2. a bookstall. 3. a bookrack.

book·store (book'stôr', book'stōr'), *n.* a store where books, and often stationery, office supplies, etc., are sold.

book value, the value of anything, especially of a business as shown on the account books: it often differs from actual value: abbreviated **B/v** (no period).

book·work (book'wũrk'), *n.* work that involves reading or studying.

book·worm (book'wũrm'), *n.* 1. any of a number of insect larvae that harm books by feeding on the binding, paste, etc. 2. a person who spends much time reading or studying.

boom (bōōm), *v.i.* [echoic; ME. *bummen*, to hum; akin to D. *bommen*, G. *bummen*, Eng. *bomb*], to make a deep, hollow, resonant sound. *v.t.* to speak or indicate with such a sound: as, the clock *boomed* the hour. *n.* 1. a booming sound, as of thunder, heavy guns, etc. 2. the resonant cry of certain animals, as the bullfrog.

boom (bōōm), *n.* [D., a tree, beam, pole; same word ult. as Eng. *beam*], 1. a spar extending from a mast to hold the bottom of a sail outstretched. 2. [< use of ship's boom for this purpose], a long beam or pole extending from the upright of a derrick to lift and guide anything lifted. 3. a log or barrier of logs to obstruct navigation. 4. in *lumbering*, *a*) a barrier across a river or around an area of water to prevent floating logs from dispersing. *b*) the area in which logs are thus confined. ***v.t.*** 1. to stretch out (sails) on, with, or as with a boom. 2. to stretch out (sails) so as to take maximum advantage of a wind abaft the beam and hence make speed. ***v.i.*** 1. to sail with or as with studding-sails boomed out. 2. to sail with maximum speed (usually with *along*). 3. to go rapidly along; move with speed or vigor.

boom (bōōm), ***v.i.*** [< 1 & 2 of prec. *v.i.*; later associated with *boom* (noise)], to increase suddenly or grow swiftly; take a favorable turn; flourish: as, business *boomed*. ***v.t.*** 1. to cause to increase suddenly or grow swiftly; make flourish: as, the war *boomed* the aircraft industry. 2. to try to make favorable prospects for; popularize; support: as, they *boomed* him for mayor. ***n.*** 1. a period of business prosperity, industrial expansion, etc.: opposed to *depression*. 2. a sudden favorable turn in business or political prospects. ***adj.*** of, like, or resulting from a boom in business, etc.

boom·er·ang (bōōm'ēr-aŋ), ***n.*** [< Australian native name], 1. a flat, curved stick that can be thrown so that it will return to a point near the thrower: it is used as a weapon by Australian aborigines. 2. something that goes contrary to the expectation of the person using or doing it and results in his disadvantage or harm. ***v.i.*** to act as a boomerang; result in harm to the user or doer.

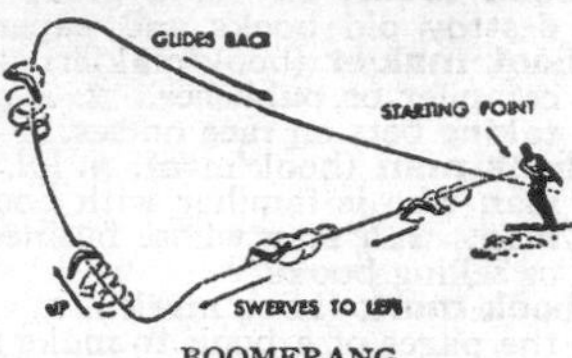

BOOMERANG

Boom·er State (bōōm'ēr), Oklahoma: a nickname.

boon (bōōn), ***n.*** [ON. *bon*, a petition; meaning prob. influenced by *boon*, *adj.*], 1. a welcome benefit; blessing. 2. [Archaic], a favor or request.

boon (bōōn), ***adj.*** [ME. *boon*, *bon*; OFr. *bon*; L. *bonus*, good], 1. [Archaic & Poetic], kind, generous, pleasant, etc. 2. merry; convivial: now only in ***boon companion***.

boon·docks (bōōn'doks'), ***n.pl.*** [orig. World War II military slang < Tag. *bundok*, mountain], [Colloq.], 1. a wild, often wooded area; wilderness. 2. a hinterland (sense 2).

boon·dog·gle (bōōn'dôg''l, bōōn'dog''l), ***v.i.*** [BOONDOGGLED (-'ld), BOONDOGGLING], [orig. dial. n., ornamental leather strap; modern sense c. 1935], [Slang], to do trifling, valueless work. ***n.*** such work.

Boone, Daniel (bōōn), 1734–1820; American frontiersman.

boor (boor), ***n.*** [D. *boer* < *bouwen*, to build, cultivate; cf. G. *bauer*], 1. originally, a peasant or farm worker; hence, 2. a person with the manners and habits attributed to peasants; rude, awkward, ill-mannered person. 3. [B-], a Boer.

boor·ish (boor'ish), ***adj.*** like or characteristic of a boor; rude; awkward; ill-mannered.

boost (bōōst), ***v.t.*** [prob. nautical *bouse*, to haul up with tackle + unhistoric *-t*], [Colloq.], 1. to raise by or as by a push from behind or below; push up. 2. to urge the merits of; speak in favor of. ***n.*** [Colloq.], 1. a push to help propel a person or thing upward or forward. 2. a raising or increase. —***SYN.*** see **lift.**

boost·er (bōōs'tēr), ***n.*** 1. [Colloq.], a person who boosts; enthusiastic supporter. 2. in *electricity*, a device for controlling or varying the electromotive force in a circuit. 3. in *radio*, an amplifier. 4. in *TV*, a device on a receiver to strengthen incoming signals. 5. an auxiliary device to increase power, thrust, etc.; especially, an early stage of a launching rocket for a spacecraft, etc.

booster shot, [Colloq.], a second injection of a vaccine, given at a proper interval after the original, weaker injection to maintain immunity.

boot (bōōt), ***n.*** [ME. & OFr. *bote*; *n.* senses 3 & 4 orig. of boot-shaped parts of horse-drawn vehicles], 1. a protective covering, of leather, rubber, cloth, etc., for wearing on the foot and part or all of the leg: in England, shoes are called boots. 2. a boot-shaped instrument of torture for crushing the foot and leg. 3. the baggage compartment of an automobile. 4. a protective shield or cover for the driver of an open vehicle. 5. a patch for the inner surface of an automobile tire to protect a break or weak spot in the casing. 6. a box that holds the reed in a reed pipe of an organ. 7. a kick. 8. [Slang], a recent recruit to the navy. ***v.t.*** 1. to put boots on. 2. to torture with the boot. 3. to kick. 4. [Slang], to put (a person) out of a place or job; dismiss.

bet your boots, to be certain; rely on it.
die with one's boots on, to die in action.
lick the boots of, to be servile toward; fawn on.
the boot, [Slang], discharge, as from work; dismissal.

boot (bōōt), ***n., v.t. & v.i.*** [ME. *bote*, *boote*; AS. *bot*, advantage, remedy], [Obs.], remedy; profit; benefit.
to boot, besides; in addition.

boot·black (bōōt'blak'), ***n.*** a person whose work is shining shoes or boots.

boot camp, [Colloq.], a station where navy or marine recruits receive basic training.

boot·ed (bōōt'id), ***adj.*** [pp. of *boot*], 1. wearing boots. 2. kicked. 3. [Slang], discharged; dismissed. 4. having horny plates of skin, as the feet of some birds.

boot·ee (bōō-tē'), ***n.*** [*boot* (shoe) + dim. *-ee*], 1. a short boot or light overboot worn by women and children. 2. (bōō'tē) a baby's soft, knitted shoe.

Bo·ö·tes (bō-ō'tēz), ***n.*** [L. < Gr. *boōtēs*, plowman < *bous*, ox], a northern constellation including the bright star Arcturus: see **constellation, chart.**

booth (bōōth, bōōth), ***n.*** [ME. *bothe*; ON. *both*, *buth*, temporary dwelling < *bua*, to dwell], 1. a temporary shed or stall for the sale of goods, as at markets and fairs. 2. a small temporary structure or enclosure for voting at elections. 3. a small permanent structure or enclosure to house a sentry, public telephone, etc. 4. a small, partially enclosed compartment with a table and seats, as in some restaurants.

Booth, Bal·ling·ton (bal'iŋ-tən bōōth), 1859–1940; son of *William*; founder of Volunteers of America.

Booth, Edwin Thomas, 1833–1893; son of *Junius Brutus* and brother of *John Wilkes*; American actor.

Booth, Evangeline Cor·y (kôr'i), 1865–1950; daughter of *William*; general of Salvation Army (1934–1939).

Booth, John Wilkes (wilks), 1838–1865; son of *Junius Brutus*; American actor; assassin of Abraham Lincoln.

Booth, Junius Brutus, 1796–1852; father of *Edwin* and *John Wilkes*; English Shakespearean actor.

Booth, William, 1829–1912; English revivalist; founder of Salvation Army: called *General Booth*.

Boo·thi·a (bōō'thi-ə), ***n.*** 1. a gulf of the Arctic Ocean, near Baffin Island. 2. a peninsula of Northwest Territories, Canada.

boot·jack (bōōt'jak'), ***n.*** [see BOOT & JACK-], a device for helping a person to pull off boots.

Boo·tle (bōō't'l), ***n.*** a seaport in western England, near Liverpool: pop., 83,000.

boot·leg (bōōt'leg'), ***v.t. & v.i.*** [BOOTLEGGED (-legd'), BOOTLEGGING], [in allusion to concealing objects in the leg of a high boot], to make, carry, or sell (liquor, etc.) illegally. ***adj.*** 1. bootlegged. 2. of bootlegging. ***n.*** bootlegged liquor.

boot·leg·ger (bōōt'leg'ēr), ***n.*** a person who bootlegs things, especially alcoholic liquors.

boot·less (bōōt'lis), ***adj.*** [*boot* (profit) + *-less*], without benefit; useless.

boot·lick (bōōt'lik'), ***v.t. & v.i.*** [Slang], to try to gain favor with (someone) by fawning, servility, etc.

boot·lick·er (bōōt'lik'ēr), ***n.*** [Slang], a toady; flatterer.

boots (bōōts), ***n.pl.*** [construed as sing.], [British], a servant who shines shoes, as in a hotel.

boots and saddles, [? confusion of Fr. *boute-selle!*, lit., put saddle!], a cavalry bugle call used as the first signal for mounted drill or other mounted formation.

boot tree, a wooden or metal form put into a boot or shoe to keep its shape; shoe tree.

boo·ty (bōō'ti), ***n.*** [*pl.* BOOTIES (-tiz)], [Fr. *butin* < MLG. *bute*, booty; prob. influenced by *boot* (profit)], 1. equipment or goods taken from the enemy; spoils of war. 2. pillage. 3. any valuable gain; prize. —***SYN.*** see **spoil.**

booze (bōōz), ***v.i.*** [BOOZED (bōōzd), BOOZING], [D. *buizen*; see BOUSE (drink)], [Colloq.], to drink too much alcoholic liquor. ***n.*** [Colloq.], 1. an alcoholic drink; liquor. 2. a drinking spree.

booz·i·ly (bōōz''l-i), ***adv.*** [Colloq.], in a boozy manner.

booz·y (bōōz'i), ***adj.*** [BOOZIER (-zi-ēr), BOOZIEST (-zi-ist)], [Colloq.], drunk, especially habitually so.

bop (bop), ***v.t.*** [echoic], [Slang], to strike; punch. ***n.*** [Slang], a blow.

bop (bop), ***n.*** [clipped form of *be-bop*], a style of jazz, characterized by complex rhythms, experimental harmonic structures, and instrumental virtuosity.

bor., 1. boron. 2. borough.

bo·ra (bō'rə), ***n.*** [It. dial. for *borea*; L. *boreas*, Boreas], a fierce, cold northeasterly wind of the Adriatic Sea.

bo·rac·ic (bō-ras'ik), ***adj.*** [< *borax* + *-ic*], boric.

bo·ra·cite (bôr'ə-sit', bō'rə-sit'), ***n.*** [L. *borax* + *-ite*], a mineral composed of the borate and chloride of magnesium, $Mg_7Cl_2B_{16}O_{30}$, found either in hard, crystalline form or as a soft, white mass.

bor·age (būr'ij, bôr'ij, bor'ij), ***n.*** [ME.; OFr. *borrage*, *bourage*; ML. *borrago*, *burrago*; prob. < *burra*, coarse hair], a plant with blue flowers and hairy leaves and stem, sometimes used in salads.

bo·rag·i·na·ceous (bə-raj'ə-nā'shəs), ***adj.*** of the borage family of plants, chiefly hairy herbs with small flowers and narrow leaves.

bo·rate (bôr'āt, bō'rāt), ***n.*** a salt or ester of boric acid. ***v.t.*** [BORATED (-id), BORATING], to treat or mix with borax or boric acid.

bo·rat·ed (bôr'āt-id, bō'rāt-id), ***adj.*** [pp. of *borate*], treated or mixed with borax or boric acid.

bo·rax (bôr'aks, bō'raks), ***n.*** [ME.; OFr. *boras*, *borax*;

LL. *borax;* Ar. *bauraq, būraq;* Per. *būrah*], a white, crystalline salt, $Na_2B_4O_7$, with an alkaline taste, used as a flux in soldering metals and in the manufacture of glass, enamel, artificial gems, soaps, antiseptics, etc.

Bor·deaux (bôr-dō′), *n.* 1. a seaport in southwestern France, on the Garonne River: pop., 254,000 (1946). 2. white or red wine from near Bordeaux: the red is generally called *claret.*

Bordeaux mixture, a mixture of lime, water, and copper sulfate, used as a spray on trees and plants to kill insects and fungi.

bor·del (bôr′d'l), *n.* [ME.; OFr., dim. of *borde,* cottage, board hut < OHG. *bord,* board], a brothel.

bor·del·lo (bôr-del′ō), *n.* [It. < OFr.], a bordel.

bor·der (bôr′dẽr), *n.* [ME. & OFr. *bordure* < *border,* to border < OHG. *bord,* margin; see BOARD (edge)], 1. an edge or part near an edge; margin; side. 2. a dividing line or territory between two countries, states, etc. 3. a narrow strip along an edge; fringe; edging. 4. an ornamental strip of flowers or shrubs along the edge of a garden, walk, etc. *v.t.* 1. to provide with a border. 2. to extend along the edge of; bound. *adj.* of, forming, or near a border.

border on (or **upon**), 1. to be next to or adjoining. 2. to be like; almost be.

the Border, the district on and near the boundary between Scotland and England.

SYN.—**border** refers to the boundary of a surface and may imply the limiting line itself or the part of the surface immediately adjacent to it; **margin** implies a bordering strip more or less clearly defined by some distinguishing feature (the *margin* of a printed page); **edge** refers to the limiting line itself or the terminating line at the sharp convergence of two surfaces (the *edge* of a box); **rim** is applied to the edge of a circular or curved surface; **brim** refers to the inner rim at the top of a vessel, etc.; **brink** refers to the edge of a steep slope. All of these terms have figurative application (the *border* of good taste, a *margin* of error, an *edge* on one's appetite, the *rim* of consciousness, a mind filled to the *brim,* the *brink* of disaster).

bor·der·er (bôr′dẽr-ẽr), *n.* one living near a border.

bor·der·land (bôr′dẽr-land′), *n.* 1. land constituting or near a border. 2. a vague or undetermined situation, condition, place, etc.

bor·der·line (bôr′dẽr-līn′), *n.* a boundary; dividing line. *adj.* 1. on a boundary; hence, 2. falling between two classifications; indefinite; doubtful.

Border States, the States having Negro slavery and bordering on free territory in the United States before the Civil War; Missouri, Kentucky, Virginia, Maryland, and Delaware.

bor·dure (bôr′jẽr), *n.* [Fr.; see BORDER], a border around the field of a coat of arms.

bore (bôr, bōr), *v.t.* [BORED (bôrd, bōrd), BORING], [ME. *boren, borien;* AS. *borian,* to bore < *bor,* auger; IE. base **bher-,* to cut with a sharp point], 1. to make a hole in or through with a drill, etc. 2. to make (a hole, tunnel, etc.) by drilling, burrowing, digging, etc. 3. to force (one's way), as through a crowd. 4. to weary by being dull, uninteresting, or monotonous. *v.i.* 1. to bore a hole or passage. 2. to be drilled by a tool: as, soft materials *bore* easily. 3. to move forward, as if by boring. *n.* [ME. < the *v.;* also < ON. *bora,* a hole], 1. a hole made by or as by boring. 2. the hole or hollow part of a tube, pipe, or gun. 3. the inside diameter of such a hole; caliber. 4. a tool for boring. 5. a person or thing that wearies by being dull, uninteresting, etc.

bore (bôr, bōr), *n.* [ME. *bare,* a wave, billow; ON. *bara,* a billow], 1. a high, abrupt tidal wave in a narrow channel, having great force; eagre. 2. loosely, any high, swift tidal flow.

bore (bôr, bōr), past tense of **bear.**

bo·re·al (bôr′i-əl, bō′ri-əl), *adj.* [LL. *borealis* < *Boreas*], 1. northern. 2. of the north wind.

Bo·re·as (bôr′i-əs, bō′ri-əs), *n.* [L.; Gr. *Boreas,* north wind; orig., wind from the mountains < IE. base meaning "mountain"; cf. OSlav. *gora,* mountain], 1. in *Greek mythology,* the god of the north wind. 2. the north wind.

bore·dom (bôr′dəm, bōr′dəm), *n.* the condition of being bored or uninterested; ennui.

bor·er (bôr′ẽr, bōr′ẽr), *n.* 1. a tool for boring or drilling. 2. an insect or worm that bores holes in fruit, etc.

bore·some (bôr′səm, bōr′səm), *adj.* boring; tiresome.

Bor·ghe·se (bôr-ge′se), *n.* an important family of Italian nobility from the 16th to the 19th centuries, originally from Siena.

Bor·gia, Ce·sa·re (che′zä-re bôr′jä), 1476?–1507; son of Pope Alexander VI; Italian soldier and cardinal; unified the Papal States.

Borgia, Lu·cre·zia (lōō-kre′tsyä), 1480–1519; daughter of Pope Alexander VI and sister of Cesare Borgia: her reputation as a poisoner, etc. is disputed by some modern authorities.

Bor·glum, Gut·zon (gut′sən bôr′gləm), 1871–1941; American sculptor and painter.

bo·ric (bôr′ik, bō′rik), *adj.* of or containing boron.

boric acid, a white, crystalline compound, H_3BO_3, with the properties of a weak acid, used as a mild antiseptic and in the manufacture of cements, enamels, etc.: also called *boracic acid.*

bo·ride (bôr′īd, bō′rīd), *n.* [*boron* + *-ide*], a compound consisting of boron and one other, more positive, element or radical.

bor·ing (bôr′iŋ, bōr′iŋ), *adj.* [ppr. of *bore*], 1. for making holes. 2. wearying by being dull, uninteresting, etc. *n.* 1. the action of a person or thing that bores. 2. a hole made by boring. 3. *usually in pl.* a chip, flake, etc. made by boring.

Bor·is (bôr′is, bō′ris), [Russ., lit., fight], a masculine name.

Boris III, 1894–1943; king of Bulgaria (1918–1943).

born (bôrn), past participle of **bear** (to give birth): now used only in passive constructions not followed by *by:* abbreviated **B., b.** *adj.* 1. brought into life or existence. 2. by birth or nature: as, a *born* musician.

borne (bôrn), past participle of **bear** (to carry): see **born.**

Bor·ne·o (bôr′ni-ō, bōr′ni-ō), *n.* 1. a large island in the East Indies, southwest of the Philippines, partly in Indonesia and partly belonging to Great Britain: area, 290,285 sq. mi. 2. the southern part of this island: a division of Indonesia: area, 208,285 sq. mi.; pop., 2,900,000 (est. 1948).

bor·ne·ol (bôr′ni-ōl′, bōr′ni-ol′), *n.* [< *Borneo* + *-ol*], a white, crystalline terpene alcohol, $C_{10}H_{18}O$, resembling camphor, found in the trunk of a tree native to Borneo and Sumatra and used in perfumery, as an antiseptic, etc.

Born·holm (bôrn′hôlm), *n.* a Danish island in the Baltic Sea, south of Sweden: area, 227 sq. mi.; pop., 47,000.

born·ite (bôr′nīt), *n.* [after Ignatius von *Born,* Austrian metallurgist], copper iron sulfide, Cu_5FeS_4, a lustrous, bronze-blue ore of copper.

Bor·nu (bôr-nōō′), *n.* a former sultanate: now a part of Nigeria: area, c. 50,000 sq. mi.; pop., c. 4,000,000.

Bo·ro·din, A·lek·san·dr Por·fir·e·vich (ä′lyek-sän′dr′ pôr′fir-ye′vich bô′rô-dēn′; Eng. bôr′ə-din), 1833–1887; Russian composer.

Bor·o·di·no (bôr′ə-dē′nō; Russ. bô′rô-dē′nô), *n.* a Russian village near Moscow: site of a battle (1812) in which the Russians retreated before the French.

bo·ron (bō′ron, bō′ron), *n.* [< *borax*], a nonmetallic, chemical element occurring only in combination, as with sodium and oxygen in borax, and produced in the form either of a brown amorphous powder or very hard, brilliant crystals: its compounds are used in the preparation of boric acid, water softeners, soaps, enamels, glass, pottery, etc.: symbol, B; at. wt., 10.82; at. no., 5: abbreviated **bor.**

bo·ro·sil·i·cate (bôr′ə-sil′ə-kit, bō′rə-sil′ə-kāt′), *n.* any of several salts derived from both boric acid and silicic acid and found in certain minerals, such as tourmaline.

bor·ough (būr′ō), *n.* [ME. *burg, burch;* AS. *burg, burh, buruh,* town, fortified place; akin to *beorgan,* to protect], 1. in the United States, a self-governing, incorporated town. 2. one of the administrative units of New York City. 3. in England, *a*) a town with a municipal corporation and rights to self-government granted by royal charter. *b*) a town that sends one or more representatives to Parliament. Abbreviated **bor.**

bor·row (bor′ō, bôr′ō), *v.t. & v.i.* [ME. *borwen, borgien;* AS. *borgian,* to borrow, lend, receive on pledge < *borh, borg,* a pledge], 1. to take or receive (something) with the understanding that one will return it or its equivalent. 2. to adopt or take over (something) as one's own: as, he *borrowed* my theory. 3. in *arithmetical subtraction,* to take (a unit of ten) from the next higher denomination in the minuend and add it to the next lower: done when the number to be subtracted is the greater. *n.* [Obs.], 1. a guarantee; bail. 2. a person who acts as surety.

borrow trouble, to worry about anything needlessly or before one has to.

Bor·row, George (bor′ō, bôr′ō), 1803–1881; English writer; wrote about gypsy life, as in *Romany Rye.*

Bors, Sir (bôrs), a knight of King Arthur's Round Table, nephew of Sir Lancelot.

borsch (bôrsh; Russ. bôrshch), *n.* [Russ. *borshch*], a Russian beet soup, served usually with sour cream.

borsch (or **borsht**) **circuit,** [humorously so called from the characteristic cuisine], [Slang], summer camps in the Catskills and White Mountains, where entertainment is provided for the guests.

borsht (bôrsht), *n.* borsch.

bort (bôrt), *n.* [? < OFr. *bourt, bourde,* bastard], a dark-colored, poorly crystallized variety of diamond used for industrial purposes as an abrasive.

bortz (bôrts), *n.* bort.

bor·zoi (bôr′zoi), *n.* [Russ., swift], any of a breed of large dog with a narrow head, long legs, and silky coat; Russian wolfhound.

bos·cage (bos′kij), *n.* [ME.; OFr. < OHG. *busk*, forest, thicket; see BUSH (shrub)], a thicket; grove; shrubbery.

bosch·bok (bosh′bok′), *n.* [*pl.* BOSCHBOK, BOSCHBOKS (-boks′); see PLURAL, II, D, 2], [D., *bosch*, bush + *bok*, buck], the bushbuck, a South African antelope.

bosch·vark (bosh′värk′), *n.* [D.; *bosch*, bush + *vark*, pig], a wild hog of South Africa.

Bose, Sir **Ja·ga·dis Chan·dra** (jə-gə-dēs′ chun′drə bōsh; Eng. bōs), 1858–1937; Indian physicist and plant physiologist.

bosh (bosh), *n. & interj.* [Turk., empty, worthless], [Colloq.], nonsense.

bosh (bosh), *n.* [? < G. *böschung*, slope], 1. the lower part of the shaft of a blast furnace, where the walls begin to slope. 2. in *smelting*, a trough for cooling hot metal.

bosh·bok (bosh′bok′), *n.* [*pl.* BOSHBOK, BOSHBOKS (-boks′); see PLURAL, II, D, 2], a boschbok.

bosk (bosk), *n.* [ME. *bosk, boske;* see BUSH (shrub)], a small clump of trees; grove; thicket.

bos·kage (bos′kij), *n.* boscage.

bos·ket (bos′kit), *n.* [Fr. *bosquet;* It. *boschetto*, dim. of *bosco* < ML. *boscus;* see BUSH (shrub)], a small grove; thicket.

bosk·y (bos′ki), *adj.* [< *bosk*], 1. covered with underbrush; wooded. 2. shaded with trees, bushes, etc.

bo's'n (bō′s'n), *n.* a boatswain.

Bos·ni·a (boz′ni-ə), *n.* a part of Yugoslavia: formerly a kingdom in the western Balkan Peninsula.

Bos·ni·a-Her·ze·go·vi·na (boz′ni-ə-her′tsə-gō-vē′nə), *n.* a federated republic of Yugoslavia: area, 19,678 sq. mi.; pop., 2,848,000; capital, Sarajevo.

Bos·ni·an (boz′ni-ən), *adj.* of Bosnia or its people. *n.* a native or inhabitant of Bosnia.

bos·om (booz′əm, bōō′zəm), *n.* [ME.; AS. *bosm;* akin to G. *busen;* only in W.Gmc. languages], 1. the human breast. 2. a thing like this: as, the *bosom* of a hill. 3. the breast regarded as the source of feelings. 4. the enclosing space formed by the breast and arms in embracing. 5. a surface thought of as like this: as, the *bosom* of the river. 6. the interior; midst: as, the *bosom* of one's family. 7. the part of a dress, shirt, etc. that covers the breast. *v.t.* 1. to put into or take to the bosom; embrace; cherish. 2. to conceal in the bosom; hide. *adj.* 1. of the bosom. 2. cherished; intimate: as, a *bosom* companion. —*SYN.* see **breast.**

Bos·pho·rus (bos′fə-rəs), *n.* the Bosporus.

Bos·po·rus (bos′pə-rəs), *n.* the strait between the Sea of Marmara and the Black Sea: length, c. 20 mi.

BOSPORUS

bos·quet (bos′kit), *n.* a bosket.

boss (bôs, bos), *n.* [D. *baas*, a master, orig., uncle], [Colloq.], 1. a person in authority over employees, as *a)* a foreman. *b)* an employer. 2. a person who controls a political machine or organization, usually within a certain place: often **political boss.** *v.t.* [Colloq.], to act as boss of; exercise authority or undue authority over. *adj.* [Colloq.], chief.

boss (bôs, bos), *n.* [ME. & OFr. *boce, boche* (Fr. *bosse*), a hump, swelling; prob. LL. *bocia* (It. *boccia*), a ball], 1. a raised part or protruding ornament on a flat surface. 2. a projecting knob or stud, as on a shield. 3. in *geology*, a protuberant body of igneous rock laid bare by erosion. 4. in *mechanics*, the enlarged part of a shaft. *v.t.* 1. to form raised ornaments on the surface of. 2. to decorate with studs or knobs.

boss (bos, bôs), *n.* [cf. dial. *boss, buss*, calf], a cow or calf.

boss·ism (bôs′iz'm, bos′iz'm), *n.* domination or control by bosses, especially of a political machine or party.

Bos·suet, Jacques Bé·nigne (zhäk bā′nēn′y′ bô′swe′), 1627–1704; French bishop and orator.

boss·y (bôs′i, bos′i), *adj.* [< *boss* (employer)], [Colloq.], domineering.

boss·y (bôs′i, bos′i), *adj.* [< *boss* (raised ornament)], decorated with bosses; studded.

boss·y (bos′i, bôs′i), *n.* [dim. of *boss* (cow)], a cow or calf.

Bos·ton (bôs′t'n, bos′t'n), *n.* the capital of Massachusetts, on Boston Bay: pop., 697,000 (metropolitan area, 2,589,000): abbreviated **B.**

bos·ton (bôs′t n, bos′t'n), *n.* [Fr.], 1. a card game for four players, using two decks of cards: terms used in the game refer to the siege of Boston (1775–1776). 2. a kind of waltz.

Boston brown bread, a dark steamed bread made of corn meal, rye, wheat, etc. and molasses.

Boston bull, a Boston terrier.

Boston cream pie, a cake of two layers with icing and a creamy filling.

Bos·to·ni·an (bôs-tō′ni-ən, bos-tō′ni-ən), *adj.* of Boston. *n.* a native or inhabitant of Boston.

Boston Massacre, an outbreak (1770) in Boston against British troops, in which several citizens were killed.

Boston rocker, a type of 19th-century American rocking chair, having a curved wooden seat and a high back formed of spindles held in place by a broad headpiece.

Boston Tea Party, a protest (1773) against the British duty on tea imported by the American colonies: colonists disguised as Indians boarded British ships in Boston harbor and dumped the tea overboard.

Boston terrier, any of a breed of small dog having a smooth coat of brindle or black with white markings: it originated as a cross between a bulldog and a bull terrier.

BOSTON TERRIER (14–20 in. high)

bo·sun (bō′s'n), *n.* a boatswain.

Bos·well, James (boz′wel, boz′wəl), 1740–1795; Scottish lawyer and writer; biographer of Samuel Johnson.

Bos·worth (boz′wẽrth), *n.* a town in Leicestershire, England: in the battle of Bosworth Field (1485), the Earl of Richmond defeated Richard III and became Henry VII, first Tudor king of England.

bot (bot), *n.* [? < Gael. *botus*, belly worm < *boiteag*, maggot], a botfly larva: also spelled **bott.**

bot., 1. botanical. 2. botanist. 3. botany. 4. bottle.

B.O.T., Board of Trade.

bo·tan·ic (bə-tan′ik), *adj.* botanical.

bo·tan·i·cal (bə-tan′i-k'l), *adj.* [Fr. *botanique;* LL. *botanicus;* Gr. *botanikos* < *botanē*, a plant, herb < *boskein*, to feed, graze; + *-al*], 1. of plants and plant life. 2. of or connected with the science of botany. 3. of vegetable drugs. Abbreviated **bot.** *n.* a vegetable drug prepared from bark, roots, herbs, etc.

botanical garden, a place where collections of living and preserved plants and trees are kept and exhibited.

bo·tan·i·cal·ly (bə-tan′i-k'l-i, bə-tan′ik-li), *adv.* according to botany; from the viewpoint of botany.

bot·a·nist (bot′'n-ist), *n.* [Fr. *botaniste*], a student of or specialist in botany: abbreviated **bot.**

bot·a·nize (bot′'n-īz′), *v.i.* [BOTANIZED (-īzd′), BOTANIZING], 1. to gather plants for botanical study. 2. to study plants, especially in their natural environment. *v.t.* to investigate the plant life of.

bot·a·ny (bot′'n-i), *n.* [< *botanical*], 1. the science that deals with plants, their life, structure, growth, classification, etc.: abbreviated **bot.** 2. the plant life of an area. 3. the life cycle of a plant or plant group. 4. [*pl.* BOTANIES (-iz)], a textbook of botany.

Botany Bay, a bay on the southeastern coast of Australia, near Sydney: site of a former British penal colony.

Botany wool, [< *Botany* Bay, orig. source of export], a kind of merino wool.

botch (boch), *v.t.* [ME. *bocchen*, to repair; prob. < D. *botsen*, to patch], 1. to repair or patch clumsily. 2. to spoil by poor performance; bungle. *n.* 1. a badly patched place or part. 2. a bungling or unskillful piece of work.

botch·y (boch′i), *adj.* botched; badly done.

bot·fly (bot′flī′), *n.* [*pl.* BOTFLIES (-flīz′)], [see BOT], any of a number of related flies resembling small bumblebees: the larvae are parasitic in horses, sheep, etc.

both (bōth), *adj. & pron.* [ME. *bothe, bathe;* ON. *bathir* < Gmc. **ba*, two, both (cf. AS. *ba*, Goth. *bai*) elided onto base of Eng. *the;* see THE], the two: as, *both* birds sang loudly, *both* were small. *conj. & adv.* together; equally; as well; not only; alike: used correlatively with *and*, as, I am *both* tired *and* hungry.

Bo·tha, Lou·is (lōō-ē′ bō′tə), 1862–1919; South African statesman; first premier of the Union of South Africa (1910–1919).

both·er (both′ẽr), *v.t. & v.i.* [earlier *bodder* (in Swift); prob. Anglo-Ir. for *pother*], 1. to annoy; worry; trouble; harass. 2. to bewilder; fluster: as, a big city *bothers* him. 3. to concern or trouble (oneself): as, she *bothers* too much about everything. *n.* 1. a cause or condition of worry, anxiety, or irritation; trouble; fuss. 2. a person who gives trouble. *interj.* a mild expression of annoyance, etc.: as, Oh, *bother!* —*SYN.* see **annoy.**

both·er·a·tion (both′ẽr-ā′shən), *n. & interj.* [Colloq.], bother.

both·er·some (both′ẽr-səm), *adj.* causing bother; annoying; troublesome; irksome.

Both·ni·a, Gulf of (both′ni-ə), an arm of the Baltic Sea, between Finland and Sweden.

Both·well (both′wel, both′wəl), fourth Earl of, (*James Hepburn*), 1536?–1578; third husband of Mary, Queen of Scots.

bo tree (bō), [Singh. *bo* < Pali *bodhi* < *bodhi-taru; bodhi*, wisdom, enlightenment + *taru*, tree], 1. a fig tree of India: also called *pipal*. 2. [B- T-], the sacred tree of Buddhism: Gautama supposedly got heavenly inspiration under a bo tree at Buddh Gaya.

bot·ry·oid (bot′ri-oid′), *adj.* [Gr. *botryoeidēs* < *botrys*,

bunch of grapes + *-eidēs*, -oid], in *botany*, shaped like a bunch of grapes.
bot·ry·oi·dal (bot′ri-oi′d'l), *adj.* botryoid.
bot·ry·o·my·co·sis (bot′ri-ō-mī-kō′sis), *n.* [< Gr. *botrys*, bunch of grapes; + *mycosis*], a disease of horses caused by a micrococcus producing a tumorous growth especially in the shoulder, or at the cut end of the spermatic cord after castration.
bot·ry·ose (bot′ri-ōs′), *adj.* 1. botryoid. 2. bearing flower clusters in which the lower flowers develop first; racemose.
bots (bots), *n.pl.* [construed as sing.], a disease of horses and cattle caused by the presence in the stomach of the larvae of botflies.
bott (bot), *n.* a bot.
Bot·ti·cel·li, San·dro (sän′drō bot′i-chel′i; It. bôt′tē-chel′lē), 1444?–1510; Italian Renaissance painter.
bot·tle (bot′'l), *n.* [ME. *botel;* OFr. *bouteille;* LL. *butticula*, a bottle < *buttis*, a vat]. 1. a container, as for liquids, usually of glass or earthenware, having a narrow neck and no handles. 2. its contents; amount that a bottle holds. Abbreviated **bot.** *v.t.* [BOTTLED (-'ld), BOTTLING], 1. to put into a bottle or bottles. 2. to keep in or as in a bottle; restrain (with *up*).
hit the bottle, [Slang], to drink too much alcoholic liquor.
the bottle, alcoholic liquor: as, a slave to *the bottle*.
bot·tle (bot′'l), *n.* [ME. & OFr. *botel*, dim. of *botte* < MD. *bote*, a bundle], [Obs.], a bundle, as of hay.
bottle green, very dark green.
bot·tle·neck (bot′'l-nek′), *n.* 1. the neck of a bottle. 2. a narrow passage or road. 3. any hindrance to progress: as, a labor shortage is a *bottleneck*.
bot·tle·nose (bot′'l-nōz′), *n.* a variety of dolphin with a bottle-shaped snout; porpoise.
bottle tree, any of various related Australian trees, some of which have a swollen, bottle-shaped trunk.
bot·tom (bot′əm), *n.* [ME. *botom, bothom;* AS. *botm, bodan;* akin to G. *boden*, ground; IE. base **bhudh-men*, ground, soil, as also in L. *fundus*, ground, *profundus*, deep; cf. FUNDAMENT, PROFOUND], 1. the lowest part of anything. 2. the part on which something rests; base. 3. the underside; hence, 4. whichever end is underneath: as, the *bottom* of a barrel. 5. the seat of a chair. 6. the bed or ground beneath a body of water. 7. *often pl.* low land, as along a river; bottom land. 8. the part of a ship's hull normally below water; keel. 9. a ship. 10. fundamental element or quality; basis; cause; origin; source. 11. endurance; stamina. 12. [Colloq.], the buttocks. *adj.* 1. of, at, or on the bottom. 2. lowest; last; undermost; basic. *v.t.* 1. to provide with a bottom, as a chair. 2. to find the meaning of; understand; fathom. 3. to place on a foundation; base; establish (usually with *on* or *upon*). *v.i.* 1. to reach or rest upon the bottom. 2. to be based or established (usually with *on* or *upon*).
at bottom, fundamentally; actually.
be at the bottom of, to be the underlying cause of; be the real reason for.
bet one's bottom dollar, [Slang], 1. to bet one's last dollar; bet everything one has. 2. to be certain.
bottoms up! [Colloq.], drink deep!
get to the bottom of, to find out the meaning of or reason for; solve.
bottom grass, 1. grass that grows on bottom lands. 2. any low-growing grass used to form turf or sod.
bottom heat, heat artificially applied to plants through the soil, as by electricity, steam pipes, fermenting manure, etc.
bottom land, low land through which a river flows: it is rich in alluvial deposits.
bot·tom·less (bot′əm-lis), *adj.* 1. having no bottom. 2. seeming to have no bottom; very deep, endless, etc.
bottomless pit, the underworld; hell.
bot·tom·ry (bot′əm-ri), *n.* [< *bottom*, a ship, after D. *bodomerij*, bottomry], a contract by which a shipowner borrows money for equipment, repairs, or a voyage, pledging the ship as security: if the ship is lost, the debt is canceled.
bot·u·lin (boch′ə-lin), *n.* the toxin causing botulism.
bot·u·li·nus (boch′ə-lī′nəs), *n.* the bacillus producing botulin.
bot·u·lism (boch′ə-liz'm), *n.* [L. *botulus*, sausage; + *-ism:* so named by Ermengem (1896) from German cases involving sausages], poisoning resulting from the toxin produced by a certain bacillus sometimes found in foods improperly canned or preserved: it is characterized by nausea, vomiting, muscular weakness, and, sometimes, disturbances of vision.
Bou·cher, Fran·çois (frän′swȧ′ bōō′shā′), 1703–1770; French genre and landscape painter.
Bou·ci·cault, Dion (bōō′si-kôlt′, bōō′si-kō′), 1820?–1890; British playwright and actor.
bou·clé (bōō-klā′), *n.* [Fr., buckled, curled < *boucle;* see BUCKLE], 1. a kind of yarn having a loose thread that gives the cloth made from it a tufted or knotted texture. 2. cloth made from this yarn.
Bou·dic·ca (bōō-dik′ə), *n.* Boadicea.
bou·doir (bōō′dwär, bōō-dwär′), *n.* [Fr., lit., pouting room < *bouder*, to pout, sulk + *-oir*, as in *parloir*, etc.], a woman's private sitting room or dressing room.
bouf·fant (bōō-fänt′; Fr. bōō′fän′), *adj.* [Fr., ppr. of *bouffer*, to puff out], puffed out; full, as some skirts.
‡bouf·fante (bōō′fänt′), *adj.* [Fr., fem.; see BOUFFANT], bouffant.
‡bouffe (bōōf), *n.* [Fr.; L. *buffa*, a joke], a comic opera: see **opera bouffe.**
bou·gain·vil·lae·a (bōō′gən-vil′i-ə), *n.* [Mod. L., after L. A. de *Bougainville*], any of a number of related plants with small flowers surrounded by large, showy, colored bracts.
Bou·gain·ville (bōō′gan′vēl′), *n.* one of the Solomon Islands: it is part of the Australian trust territory of New Guinea: area, 3,880 sq. mi.; pop., 49,000.
Bou·gain·ville, Lou·is An·toine de (lwē än′twȧn′ də bōō′gan′vēl′), 1729–1811; French explorer.
bough (bou), *n.* [ME. *bouh, bogh;* AS. *boh*, shoulder or arm, hence twig or branch; akin to G. *bug*, shoulder; IE. base **bhāghus-*, elbow and forearm], branch of a tree, especially a large branch.
bough·pot (bou′pot′), *n.* 1. a large container for cut branches or flowers; jardiniere. 2. [British], a bouquet. Also spelled **bowpot.**
bought (bôt), past tense and past participle of **buy.**
bought·en (bôt′'n), *adj.* [Dial.], bought; not homemade: as, *boughten* gloves.
bou·gie (bōō′zhē′, bōō′zhē′), *n.* [Fr., wax candle < *Bugia*, in North Africa, whence wax candles were imported], 1. a wax candle. 2. in *medicine*, a slender instrument introduced into a body canal, especially the urethra or rectum, for stretching or dilating it.
Bou·gue·reau, A·dolphe Wil·liam (ȧ′dôlf′ wēl′yȧm′ bōō′grō′), 1825–1905; French painter.
bouil·la·baisse (bōōl′yə-bās′; Fr. bōō′yȧ′bes′), *n.* [Fr. < Pr. *boulh-abaisso*, lit., boils and settles < *bouli* (Fr. *bouillir*), to boil + *abaissa* (Fr. *abaisser*); see ABASE], a chowder made of two or more kinds of fish and sometimes seasoned with wine.
bouil·lon (bool′yon, bool-yon′, bool′yən; Fr. bōō′yōn′), *n.* [Fr. < *bouillir*, to boil], a clear broth, usually of beef.
bouillon cube, a small cube of concentrated stock for making bouillon.
Boul·der (bōl′dẽr), *n.* a town in northern Colorado: pop., 38,000.
boul·der (bōl′dẽr), *n.* [< *boulder stone;* ME. *bulderstan* < ON.; cf. Sw. *bullersten*, lit., noise stone], any large rock worn and rounded by weather and water: also spelled **bowlder.**
Boulder Canyon, the canyon of the Colorado River, above Boulder (Hoover) Dam.
boulder clay, unstratified material left by a glacier, consisting of boulders and rocks embedded in a hard clay matrix.
Boulder Dam, Hoover Dam: the former name.
bou·le (bōō′lē), *n.* [Gr. *boulē*], 1. an ancient Greek senate, or legislative assembly of elders. 2. [B-], the lower branch of the modern Greek legislative assembly.
boul·e·vard (bool′ə-värd′, bōō′lə-värd′), *n.* [Fr., altered < G. *bollwerk*, bulwark], 1. originally, the top surface of a military rampart or a street laid on a destroyed rampart. 2. now, a broad street, often lined with trees, grass plots, etc.: abbreviated **blvd., boul.**
‡bou·le·ver·se·ment (bōōl′vers′män′), *n.* [Fr.], a confused reversal of things; overthrow; upset; turmoil.
Bou·logne (bōō′lōn′y′; Eng. boo-lōn′), *n.* a city in France, on the English Channel: pop., 34,000: also called *Boulogne-sur-Mer.*
Bou·logne-Bil·lan·court (bōō′lōn′y′-bē′yän′kōōr′), *n.* a city on the Seine, west of Paris: pop., 94,000.
Bou·logne-sur-Mer (bōō′lōn′y′-sür′mâr′), *n.* Boulogne.
boul·ter (bōl′tẽr), *n.* [Corn. dial.; of Celt. origin], a long fishing line with hooks attached along its length.
boun (boun), *v.t.* & *v.i.* [ME. *bounen;* see BOUND (going)], [Archaic], to make ready or betake (oneself).
bounce (bouns), *v.t.* [BOUNCED (bounst), BOUNCING], [ME. *bunsen, bounsen*, to thump < D. *bonzen* or LG. *bunsen*, to thump, strike], 1. to bump or thump: as, he *bounced* the crate down the steps. 2. to cause to bound or rebound, as a ball. 3. [Slang], to put (a person) out by force. 4. [Slang], to discharge from employment. *v.i.* 1. to bound or rebound, as a ball. 2. to move suddenly; spring; jump. 3. to move in a sudden or noisy rush: as, she *bounced* into the room. 4. [Slang], to be returned to the payee by a bank as a worthless check, because of insufficient funds in the drawer's account. *n.* 1. a bound; rebound; leap; jump. 2. capacity for bouncing: as, the ball has lost its *bounce*. 3. a loud or heavy thump. 4. [British], impudence; bluster. 5. [Slang], great energy; spirit; dash.
get the bounce, [Slang], to be dismissed or discharged.

bounc·er (boun′sẽr), *n.* [see BOUNCE], 1. anything very big. 2. [Rare], a braggart or liar. 3. [Slang], anyone hired to remove very disorderly people from a night club, restaurant, etc.
bounc·ing (boun′siŋ), *adj.* [ppr. of *bounce*], 1. big; heavy; buxom. 2. healthy; strong; lusty.
bouncing Bet (or **Bess**), a kind of soapwort with dense clusters of white or pinkish flowers.
bound (bound), *v.i.* [Fr. *bondir*, to leap, make a noise, orig., to echo back; LL. **bombitare*, to buzz, hum < L. *bombus*, a humming, buzzing], 1. to move with a leap or series of leaps. 2. to spring back from a surface after striking it, as a ball; bounce; rebound. *v.t.* to cause to bound or bounce. *n.* 1. a jump; leap. 2. a springing back from a surface after striking it; bounce. —*SYN.* see **skip.**
bound (bound), past tense and past participle of **bind.** *adj.* 1. confined by binding; tied. 2. closely connected or related. 3. certain; destined: as, he's *bound* to lose. 4. under compulsion; obliged: as, he is legally *bound* to do it. 5. constipated. 6. provided with a binding or cover, as a book: abbreviated **bd.** 7. [Colloq.], determined; resolved: as, despite risk, he was *bound* to go.
bound up in (or **with**), 1. deeply devoted to. 2. implicated or involved in.
bound (bound), *adj.* [< ME. *bounen*, to prepare < *bun*, ready < ON. *buinn*, pp. of *bua*, to prepare, with unhistoric *-d*, after prec. *bound*], going; headed (often with *for* or *to*): as, *bound* for home.
bound (bound), *n.* [ME. *bounde;* OFr. *bunne, bodne, bonde;* LL. *bodina, butina*], 1. a boundary; limit. 2. *pl.* an area near, alongside, or enclosed by a boundary. *v.t.* 1. to provide with bounds; limit; confine. 2. to be a limit or boundary to. 3. to name the boundaries of (a state, etc.). *v.i.* to have a boundary (*on* another country, etc.). —*SYN.* see **limit.**
out of bounds, 1. beyond the boundaries or limits, as of a playing field. 2. prohibited; forbidden.
-bound (bound), a combining form used in hyphenated compounds, meaning *going,* or *headed in* (a specified direction) or *to* (a specified place), as in *south-bound.*
bound·a·ry (boun′də-ri), *n.* [*pl.* BOUNDARIES (-riz)], [< *bound, n.*], anything marking a limit; bound; border.
bound·en (boun′dən), *adj.* [old pp. of *bind*], 1. obligated; indebted; obliged. 2. binding; obligatory: as, one's *bounden* duty.
bound·er (boun′dẽr), *n.* [*bound* (to leap) + *-er*], [Colloq.], an ill-mannered, rude, pushing person.
bound·less (bound′lis), *adj.* having no bounds; unlimited; infinite; vast.
boun·te·ous (boun′ti-əs), *adj.* [ME. *bountevous;* OFr. *bontif, bontive;* see BOUNTY; mod. spelling as if < *bounty*], 1. giving without restraint; generous. 2. abundant; plentiful; ample.
boun·ti·ful (boun′ti-fəl), *adj.* [see BOUNTY], 1. giving without restraint; generous. 2. abundant; plentiful.
boun·ty (boun′ti), *n.* [*pl.* BOUNTIES (-tiz)], [ME. *bounte;* OFr. *bonte;* L. *bonitas*, goodness < *bonus*, good], 1. lack of restraint in giving; generosity. 2. something given freely; generous gift. 3. a reward, premium, or allowance, especially one given by a government for killing certain animals, raising certain crops, etc. —*SYN.* see **bonus.**
bou·quet (bō-kā′, bōō-kā′), *n.* [Fr., a plume, nosegay, older *bosquet;* OFr. *boschet;* see BOSKET], 1. a bunch of flowers. 2. (bōō-kā′), aroma; fragrance, especially of a wine or brandy. —*SYN.* see **scent.**
Bour·bon (boor′bən), *n.* 1. the ruling family of France (1589–1793; 1814–1830); of Spain (1700–1808; 1814–1833; 1874–1931); of Naples (1735–1805; 1815–1860); and of Parma (1748–1859). 2. a political and social reactionary. 3. Réunion, a French island: the former name.
bour·bon (boor′bən, bũr′bən), *n.* [< *Bourbon* County, Kentucky, where it has been produced], a whisky made from corn, sometimes with added rye or malt. *adj.* designating, of, or made with such whisky.
Bour·bon·ism (boor′bən-iz′m), *n.* advocacy or support of conservative government, like that of the Bourbons; extreme political and social reaction.
bour·don (boor′d′n), *n.* [Fr. < LL. *burdo;* origin echoic], 1. a bass stop on the organ, usually of the sixteen-foot pipes. 2. the drone of a bagpipe.
bourg (boorg; Fr. bo͞or), *n.* [Fr. < OHG. *burg*, town], 1. a medieval town or village; especially one near a castle. 2. a market town.
bour·geois (boor-zhwä′, boor′zhwä; Fr. bo͞or′zhwȧ′), *n.* [*pl.* BOURGEOIS], [Fr.; OFr. *burgeis* < *bourg;* see BOURG], 1. originally, a freeman of a medieval town. 2. a shopkeeper. 3. a member of the bourgeoisie. 4. a person with the characteristic traits or viewpoint of the bourgeoisie. 5. *pl.* the bourgeoisie. *adj.* of or characteristic of a bourgeois or the bourgeoisie; middle-class: used variously to mean commonplace, conventional, respectable, thrifty, smug, greedy, etc.
bour·geois (bẽr-jois′), *n.* [after a French type founder, *Bourgeois*], a size of type, 9 point. This line is in bourgeois.
bour·geoise (boor-zhwäz′; Fr. bo͞or′zhwȧz′), *n.* [*pl.* BOURGEOISES (-zhwäz′; Fr. -zhwȧz′)], feminine of **bourgeois.**
bour·geoi·sie (boor′zhwä-zē′; Fr. bo͞or′zhwȧ′zē′), *n.* [construed as sing. or pl.], [Fr. < *bourgeois;* see BOURGEOIS], 1. the social class between the aristocracy or very wealthy and the working class, or proletariat; middle class. 2. in *Marxist doctrine*, capitalists as a social class antithetical to the proletariat.
bour·geon (bũr′jən), *n., v.t. & v.i.* burgeon.
Bourges (bo͞orzh), *n.* a city in central France: pop., 51,000 (1946).
Bour·get, Paul (pôl bo͞or′zhā′), 1852–1935; French poet, critic, and novelist.
Bour·gogne (bo͞or′gôn′y′), *n.* Burgundy: French name.
bourn, bourne (bôrn, bōrn, boorn), *n.* [ME. *burne;* AS. *burne, burna*, a stream], a brook or stream: also **burn.**
bourn, bourne (bôrn, bōrn, boorn), *n.* [Fr. *borne;* OFr. *bonne, bodne;* LL. *bodina, bonna*, boundary, limit], 1. a goal; objective. 2. [Poetic], loosely, a domain. 3. [Archaic], a limit; boundary.
Bourne·mouth (bôrn′məth, bōrn′məth, boorn′məth), *n.* a resort city in England, on the English Channel: pop., 122,000.
‡bour·rée (bo͞o′rā′), *n.* [Fr. < *bourrir*, to beat wings, whir; OFr. *burir*, to dart forth < OHG. dial. *burjan*], 1. a lively French or Spanish dance similar to a gavotte. 2. music for this dance or in a similar rapid tempo.
bourse (boors), *n.* [Fr., a purse, exchange; OFr. *borse;* LL. *bursa*, a purse, bag; Gr. *bursa*, a hide], 1. a central place where merchants transact business; stock exchange. 2. [B-], the stock exchange of Paris or any of a number of other European cities.
bouse (bo͞oz, bouz), *n.* [ME. *bous;* MD. *buse*, a drink, cup], 1. any drink. 2. alcoholic liquor. 3. a drinking spree. 4. [Colloq.], bad liquor. *v.t. & v.i.* [BOUSED (bo͞ozd, bouzd), BOUSING], [ME. *bousen;* MD. *busen* < the *n.* or < MHG. *bus*, bloating fullness], to drink; carouse. Also spelled **bowse.** See **booze.**
bouse (bous, bouz), *v.t. & v.i.* [BOUSED (bousd, bouzd), BOUSING], [< D.; see BOOST], in *nautical usage*, to pull up by means of a tackle; hoist.
bou·stro·phe·don (bo͞o′strə-fē′d′n), *n.* [Gr. *boustrophēdon*, lit., turning like oxen in plowing < *bous*, ox + *strephein*, to turn], an ancient form of writing in which the lines run, as in plowing, alternately left to right and right to left.
bous·y (bo͞oz′i, bouz′i), *adj.* [see BOUSE (drink)], drunk.
bout (bout), *n.* [for earlier *bought*, apparently a pp. form of ME. *bowen*, AS. *bugan*, to bend, but prob. suggested by LG. *bucht;* meaning influenced by *'bout* < *about*], 1. a going and coming back again, as across a field in plowing; turn. 2. a struggle; contest or match: as, a boxing *bout.* 3. a period of time spent in some activity; spell or term: as, a *bout* of floor scrubbing.
bou·ton·niere, bou·ton·nière (bo͞o′t′n-yer′), *n.* [Fr. *boutonnière*, a buttonhole], a flower or flowers worn in the buttonhole, as of a lapel.
bo·vid (bō′vid), *adj.* [< L. *Bovidae*, name of the family < *bos, bovis*, ox], of the ox family of ruminants, having, characteristically, a pair of hollow, unbranched horns, and including cattle, sheep, goats, antelopes, etc.
bo·vine (bō′vin, bō′vīn), *adj.* [LL. *bovinus* < L. *bos, bovis*, ox], 1. of an ox; of a cow. 2. oxlike or cowlike; hence, 3. slow, patient, stupid, stolid, etc. *n.* an ox, cow, or similar animal.
bow (bou), *v.i.* [ME. *bowen, bouwen;* AS. *bugan*, to bend; akin to G. *biegen;* IE. base **bheugh-*, to bend; the n. is 17th c.], 1. [Dial.], to bend; stoop. 2. to bend the head or body in respect, agreement, recognition, etc. 3. to yield or submit, as to authority. 4. to express assent, greeting, etc. by bowing. *v.t.* 1. [Dial.], to bend. 2. to bend (the head or body) in respect, agreement, recognition, etc. 3. to indicate (agreement, thanks, etc.) by bowing. 4. to weigh down; overwhelm; crush (often with *down*): as, the load *bowed* him down. *n.* a bending of the head or body, as in greeting, etc.
bow and scrape, to be too polite and ingratiating.
make one's bow, 1. to make a formal entrance. 2. to retire formally, as from the stage or public life.
take a bow, to acknowledge an introduction, applause, etc.
bow (bō), *n.* [ME. *bowe, boge;* AS. *boga* < *bugan;* see BOW (to bend)], 1. anything curved or bent, as a rain*bow*, ox*bow*, etc. 2. a curve; bend. 3. a device for shooting arrows: it is a flexible, curved strip of wood, metal, etc. with a cord connecting the two ends. 4. *pl.* bowmen; archers. 5. a slender stick, originally curved, strung along its length with horsehairs and drawn across the strings of a violin, etc. to play it. 6. a bowknot. *adj.* bow-shaped; curved; bent. *v.t. & v.i.* 1. to bend or curve in the shape of a bow. 2. in *music*, to play (a violin, etc.) with a bow.

BOW AND ARROW

bow (bou), *n.* [16th c. < LG. or

Scand.; cf. LG. *būg*, D. *boeg*, Sw. *bog*, shoulder, shoulders of a ship, bows; ult. < same base as *bough*], 1. the front part of a ship, boat, or airship; prow. 2. the oarsman nearest the bow. *adj.* of or near the bow; fore: opposed to *stern*.

bows on, head first.

bows under, making difficult progress; overwhelmed.

bow compass (bō), a pair of drawing compasses whose legs are joined by a flexible steel band instead of a hinge, the angle between being adjusted by a screw.

Bow·ditch, Nathaniel (bou'dich), 1773–1838; American navigator, mathematician, and astronomer.

bowd·ler·ize (boud'lẽr-iz'), *v.t.* [BOWDLERIZED (-īzd'), BOWDLERIZING], [after Dr. Thomas *Bowdler*, who in 1818 published an expurgated edition of Shakespeare], to remove supposedly offensive passages from (a book, etc.); expurgate.

bow·el (bou'əl, boul), *n.* [ME. *bouel, boel;* OFr. *boel, buele;* LL. *botellus*, intestine; L. *botellus*, dim. of *botulus*, sausage], 1. an intestine, especially of a human being; gut; entrail. 2. *pl.* the interior or inner part: as, the *bowels* of the mountain. 3. *pl.* [Archaic], the inside of the body, regarded as the source of pity, tenderness, etc.; hence, tender emotions. *v.t.* [BOWELED or BOWELLED (-əld, bould), BOWELING or BOWELLING], to disembowel.

move one's bowels, to pass waste matter from the large intestine; defecate.

bowel movement, 1. the passing of waste matter from the large intestine. 2. the waste matter thus passed; feces.

bow·er (bou'ẽr), *n.* [ME. *boure;* AS. *bur*, room, hut, dwelling (cf. *buan*, to dwell, stay, live); akin to G. *bauer*, bird cage; IE. base **bheu-*, to grow, be, live, as also in L. *fui*, to be; cf. FUTURE], 1. a place enclosed by overhanging boughs of trees; shaded retreat. 2. [Poetic], a cottage; rural residence or abode. 3. [Archaic], a bedchamber; boudoir. *v.t.* to form into a bower; enclose with boughs, etc.

bow·er (bou'ẽr), *n.* [G. *bauer*, peasant: so called from the figure sometimes used as the jack in a deck of cards], either of the two highest cards in certain games: the jack of trumps (*right bower*) or the jack of the other suit having the same color as the trump (*left bower*): if a joker is used, it is called the *best bower*.

bow·er (bou'ẽr), *n.* [< *bow* (prow)], the heaviest anchor of a ship, normally carried at the bow.

bow·er·bird (bou'ẽr-bũrd'), *n.* any of certain Australian birds related to the crow: the male builds a bower or decorates a piece of ground to attract the female.

bow·er·y (bou'ẽr-i), *adj.* 1. like a bower; leafy and shady. 2. full of bowers.

bow·er·y (bou'ẽr-i), *n.* [*pl.* BOWERIES (-iz)], [D. *bouwerij*, farm < *bouer*, farmer], 1. a farm or plantation of an early Dutch settler of New York. 2. [B-], a street in New York City, or the district around this street, characterized by cheap hotels, saloons, etc.

bow·fin (bō'fin'), *n.* a fresh-water fish with a rounded tail fin and a long, narrow fin on its back; mudfish.

bow hand (bō), 1. the hand that holds the bow in archery, usually the left hand. 2. the hand that holds the bow of a violin, etc. in playing, usually the right hand.

bow·head (bō'hed'), *n.* a kind of whale with a very large, arched head that yields whalebone; right whale.

bow·ie knife (bō'i, bōō'i), [after Colonel James *Bowie* (d. 1836), its inventor], a steel hunting knife about fifteen inches long, with a single edge: it is usually carried in a sheath.

BOWIE KNIFE

bow·ing (bō'iŋ), *n.* the manner or technique of using the bow in playing a violin, etc.

bow·knot (bō'not', bō'not'), *n.* a knot having either one loop and one end or two loops and two ends: it is untied by pulling the end or ends: see **knot,** illus.

bowl (bōl), *n.* [ME. *bolle;* AS. *bolla;* akin to G. *bolle;* IE. base **bhel-*, to swell out, inflate; sp. influenced by *bowl* (ball)], 1. a hollow, rounded, cup-shaped container or dish, open at the top. 2. a large drinking cup; hence, 3. any intoxicating drink. 4. convivial drinking. 5. a thing or part like a bowl: as, the *bowl* of a spoon. 6. an amphitheater; stadium. 7. the capacity or contents of a bowl.

bowl (bōl), *n.* [ME. *bowle, boule;* OFr. *boule;* L. *bulla*, a bubble, stud], 1. a heavy ball rolled on a level surface in bowling, especially that used in the game of bowls. 2. a turn or delivery of the ball in bowling or bowls. 3. a roller, drum, or wheel, as in some machines. *v.i.* 1. to participate in bowling; play the game of bowls. 2. to throw a bowl, usually underhand, so as to make it roll. 3. to move swiftly and smoothly (usually with *along*): as, the car *bowled* steadily along. 4. in *cricket*, to deliver a ball to the batsman. *v.t.* 1. to throw so as to make roll; roll. 2. to cause to move along swiftly and smoothly, as on wheels. 3. in *cricket*, to put out (a batsman) by bowling the bails off the wicket (with *out*).

bowl over, 1. to knock over with something rolled; hence, 2. [Colloq.], to astonish and confuse; stagger.

bowl·der (bōl'dẽr), *n.* a boulder.

bow·leg (bō'leg'), *n.* 1. a leg with outward curvature. 2. the condition or degree of such curvature.

bow·leg·ged (bō'leg'id, bō'legd'), *adj.* having bowlegs.

bowl·er (bōl'ẽr), *n.* a person who bowls.

bowl·er (bōl'ẽr), *n.* [< *bowl* (ball), because of its shape], [British], a derby hat.

bow·line (bō'lin, bō'lin'), *n.* [ME. *boweline, bouline;* prob. < ON. *boglina;* see BOW (prow of a ship) & LINE], 1. a rope running forward from the middle of a square sail's weather edge to the bow, used to keep the sail taut when the ship is sailing into the wind. 2. a bowline knot.

on a bowline, with sails set so as to go as nearly against the wind as possible; close-hauled.

bowline knot, a knot used to tie off a loop: see **knot,** illus.

bowl·ing (bōl'iŋ), *n.* 1. a game in which a heavy ball is bowled along a wooden lane (bowling alley) in an attempt to knock over ten wooden pins set upright at the far end; tenpins. 2. the game of bowls. 3. the playing of either of these games. *adj.* of or for bowling.

bowling alley, 1. a long, narrow, enclosed wooden lane used in bowling: the player rolls a ball down it so as to knock down the pins placed upright at the far end. 2. *often pl.* a building for bowling.

bowling green, a smooth, level lawn for playing the game of bowls.

bowls (bōlz), *n.* 1. an old game played on a smooth lawn (bowling green) with a weighted wooden ball (bowl) which is rolled in an attempt to make it stop near another, stationary ball (jack). 2. ninepins or tenpins. 3. skittles.

bow·man (bō'mən), *n.* [*pl.* BOWMEN (-mən)], a man armed with bow and arrows; archer.

bow·man (bou'mən), *n.* [*pl.* BOWMEN (-mən)], the oarsman nearest the bow of a boat.

bown, bowne (boun), *v.t. & v.i.* to boun.

bow pen (bō), a bow compass equipped with a pen.

bow·pot (bou'pot'), *n.* a boughpot.

bowse (bōōz, bouz), *n., v.t. & v.i.* [BOWSED (bōōzd, bouzd), BOWSING], bouse (drink).

bow·shot (bō'shot'), *n.* the distance that an arrow can travel when shot from a bow.

bow·sprit (bou'sprit', bō'sprit'), *n.* [ME. *bouspret;* prob. < D. *boegspriet; boeg*, bow of a ship + *spriet*, sprit], a large, tapered pole or plank extending forward from the bow of a sailing vessel: the foremost stays are fastened to it.

bow·string (bō'striŋ'), *n.* 1. a cord stretched from one end of a bow to the other, which the archer pulls back to get the tension needed for shooting the arrow. 2. any strong, light cord. *v.t.* to strangle with a bowstring; garrote.

bowstring hemp, any of a group of plants of the lily family, with stiff, thick leaves that yield a fiber used in making bowstrings.

bow tie (bō), a necktie tied in a small bowknot.

bow window (bō), a bay window built in a curve.

bow·wow (bou'wou'), *n.* [echoic], a sound imitating a dog's bark. *v.i.* to make this sound; bark.

bow·yer (bō'yẽr), *n.* [*bow* (the weapon) + *-yer*], 1. a person who makes or deals in bows. 2. [Rare], a bowman.

box (boks), *n.* [ME. & AS., small lidded receptacle; ML. *buxis;* LL. *buxus;* Gr. *pyxis*, box of boxwood < *pyxos*, boxwood], 1. any of many kinds of containers, usually with lids, and of various sizes, shapes, and materials; case; carton. 2. the contents or capacity of a box. 3. a gift, especially a Christmas present, in a box. 4. formerly, the tool box on a coach or carriage, on which the driver sat; hence, 5. the driver's seat in a vehicle. 6. a boxlike thing. 7. a small, enclosed group of seats, as in a theater, stadium, etc. 8. a small booth or shelter for men on outdoor duty. 9. a small country house used by sportsmen: as, a grouse *box*. 10. a horse stall. 11. a space or section for a certain person or group: as, a press *box*, jury *box*. 12. a short, newspaper article enclosed in borders. 13. in *baseball*, *a)* the place where a player must stand while at bat. *b)* the place where the pitcher stands. 14. in *mechanics*, a protective casing for a part: as, a journal *box*. Abbreviated **bx.** *v.t.* 1. to provide with a box. 2. to put into a box, etc., as for storage or shipment. 3. to boxhaul. *adj.* 1. shaped or made like a box. 2. packaged in a box.

box in, 1. to box up. 2. to block (another racer) so as to prevent him from getting ahead.

box the compass, 1. to name the thirty-two points of the compass in order: from the fact that compasses were kept in boxes. 2. to make a complete circuit, returning to the starting point.

box up, to keep in; surround or confine.

box (boks), *n.* [ME.; ? playful use of *box* (container) in sense "gift"], a blow struck with the hand or fist, especially on the ear or the side of the head. *v.t.* 1. to strike with the hand or fist; cuff, especially on the ear. 2. to fight by boxing with. *v.i.* 1. to fight with the fists. 2. to be a boxer.

box (boks), *n.* [ME. & AS.; L. *buxus*; Gr. *pyxos*], 1. any of a number of related evergreen shrubs or small trees with small, leathery leaves and inconspicuous flowers. 2. the hard, close-grained wood of this plant.

box·ber·ry (boks'ber'i, boks'bēr-i), *n.* [*pl.* BOXBERRIES (-iz)], 1. a creeping evergreen plant with small flowers and red fruit; wintergreen. 2. a trailing plant with pinkish-white flowers and red berries; partridgeberry.

box calf, a type of tanned calf leather characterized by square markings.

box camera, a relatively inexpensive camera shaped like a box and having a fixed focus and, generally, a single shutter speed.

box·car (boks'kär'), *n.* 1. a fully enclosed railroad freight car. 2. *pl.* [Slang], in *dice,* a throw of twelve.

box coat, 1. a type of heavy overcoat, formerly worn by coachmen. 2. an outer coat that fits somewhat loosely and hangs straight from the shoulders.

box elder, a kind of maple tree that grows rapidly and drops its leaves early.

Box·er (bok'sēr), *n.* [< *box* (a blow); Eng. transl. of Chin. phrase *I-He-Chuan,* "righteous-uniting-band," misunderstood as "righteous-uniting-fists"], a member of a Chinese society that led an unsuccessful uprising (the *Boxer Rebellion,* 1900) against foreign powers and foreigners in China, as a result of which China was forced to make economic and territorial concessions.

box·er (bok'sēr), *n.* [< *box* (a blow)], 1. a man who boxes; pugilist; prize fighter. 2. any of a breed of medium-sized dog with a sturdy body and a smooth fawn or brindle coat: it is related to the bulldog.

box·ful (boks'fəl), *n.* the contents or capacity of a box.

box·haul (boks'hôl'), *v.t.* 1. to change (the course of a ship) by veering around sharply instead of tacking normally; tack by sternway. 2. to haul (the yards) so as to meet slight shifts in wind direction.

box·ing (bok'siŋ), *n.* [< *box* (to hit)], the art, science, or occupation of fighting with the fists, especially in special padded mittens.

box·ing (bok'siŋ), *n.* 1. the act or process of packing a box or boxes. 2. a boxlike covering or casing. 3. material used for boxes.

Boxing Day, in England, the first weekday after Christmas, a legal holiday marked by the presentation of Christmas boxes to employees, postmen, etc.

boxing gloves, padded leather mittens worn for boxing.

box kite, a kite with an oblong, box-shaped framework, covered with paper or fabric except at the ends and the middle.

box office, a place where admission tickets are sold, as in a theater: abbreviated **b.o.**

good box office, [Slang], having appeal for the audience; likely to be popular.

box pleat (or **plait**), a double pleat with the under edges folded toward each other.

box score, a statistical summary of a baseball game, showing the number of hits, runs, errors, etc.: it is printed in boxlike form.

box seat, a seat in a box at a theater, stadium, etc.

box spring, a bedspring consisting of a boxlike, cloth-enclosed frame containing rows of coil springs.

box stall, a large, enclosed, more or less square stall, as for a horse or cow.

box·thorn (boks'thôrn'), *n.* any of a group of shrubs of the nightshade family, with small, inconspicuous flowers and red or orange-red berries.

box·wood (boks'wood'), *n.* 1. the hard, close-grained wood of the box shrub or tree, used in fine woodwork. 2. the plant.

boy (boi), *n.* [ME. *boie;* akin to & prob. < East Fris. *boi*], 1. a male child from birth to the age of physical maturity; lad; youth. 2. any man; fellow: familiar term. 3. a male domestic worker or servant: term applied especially by Caucasians to native workers in India, Africa, etc. 4. a bellboy, messenger boy, etc. 5. [Colloq.], a son: as, he's my *boy.* *interj.* [Slang], an exclamation of pleasure, surprise, etc.: often **oh, boy!**

bo·yar (bō-yär', boi'ēr), *n.* [Russ. *boyarin,* pl. *boyare,* grandee], 1. a member of the privileged aristocracy in Czarist Russia, ranking just below the ruling princes: the rank was abolished by Peter I. 2. formerly, a member of the privileged aristocracy in Romania.

bo·yard (bō-yärd', boi'ērd), *n.* a boyar.

boy·cott (boi'kot'), *v.t.* [after Captain *Boycott,* land agent ostracized by his neighbors during the Land League agitation in Ireland in 1880], 1. to join together in refusing to deal with, so as to punish, cause to do something, etc. 2. to refuse to buy, sell, or use: as, they *boycotted* the newspaper. *n.* a boycotting.

Boyd (boid), [Celt., yellow], a masculine name.

boy friend, [Colloq.], a boy or man who is a friend, escort, or sweetheart of a girl or woman.

boy·hood (boi'hood), *n.* [see -HOOD], 1. the time or state of being a boy. 2. boys collectively.

boy·ish (boi'ish), *adj.* of, fit for, like, or characteristic of a boy or boyhood.

Boyle, Robert (boil), 1627–1691; English physicist and chemist; first to distinguish between chemical elements and compounds.

Boyne (boin), *n.* a river in eastern Ireland: length, 70 mi.: site of a battle (1690) in which William III of England defeated James II, who had been deposed.

boy scout, 1. a member of the Boy Scouts. 2. [Slang], a man regarded as being very naive or idealistic: disparaging term.

Boy Scouts, a world-wide boys' organization that stresses outdoor life and service to others: founded in England, 1908, by Sir Robert S. S. Baden-Powell.

boy·sen·ber·ry (boi's'n-ber'i, boi'z'n-ber'i), *n.* [*pl.* BOYSENBERRIES (-iz)], [after Rudolph *Boysen,* Am. horticulturist who developed it], a berry, dark red or almost black when ripe, resulting from crossing varieties of raspberry, loganberry, and blackberry.

Boz (boz), see **Dickens, Charles.**

Boz·za·ris, Mar·kos (mär'kôs bôt-sä'ris), 1788?–1823; Greek soldier and patriot.

bp., 1. birthplace: also **bpl.** 2. bishop.

B.P., [L.], 1. *Baccalaureus Pharmaciae,* Bachelor of Pharmacy. 2. *Baccalaureus Philosophiae,* Bachelor of Philosophy.

b.p., B/P, 1. bill of parcels. 2. bills payable.

b.p., 1. below proof. 2. boiling point.

B.P.D.P.A., Brotherhood of Painters, Decorators, and Paperhangers of America: an A.F. of L. labor union.

B.P.E., Bachelor of Physical Education.

B picture, [Slang], a motion picture made quickly and inexpensively.

B.P.O.E., Benevolent and Protective Order of Elks.

Br, in *chemistry,* bromine.

Br., 1. Breton. 2. Britain. 3. British.

br., 1. branch. 2. brig. 3. bronze. 4. brother.

b.r., B/R, bills receivable.

bra (brä), *n.* [< *brassiere*], a brassiere.

Bra·bant (brə-bant', brä'bənt), *n.* 1. a region in the southern Netherlands and northern Belgium: formerly a duchy of the Netherlands. 2. a province of central Belgium: capital, Brussels.

brab·ble (brab''l), *v.i.* [BRABBLED (-'ld), BRABBLING], [? < D. *brabbelen,* to stammer], [Dial.], to quarrel noisily over trifles; squabble. *n.* quarrelsome chatter.

brace (brās), *v.t.* [BRACED (brāst), BRACING], [ME. *bracen;* OFr. *bracer,* to brace, embrace < L. *brachia,* pl. of *brachium,* an arm], 1. to tie or bind on firmly. 2. to tighten, especially by stretching. 3. to strengthen or make firm by supporting the weight of, resisting the pressure of, etc.; prop up. 4. to equip with braces. 5. to make ready for an impact, shock, etc. 6. to give vigor or energy to; stimulate; invigorate. 7. [Slang], to ask a loan from. *n.* [OFr. *brace,* armful, fathom < L. *brachia*], 1. two of a kind; a couple; pair. 2. a device that keeps something firmly in place; thing that clasps or connects; fastener. 3. *pl.* [British], suspenders. 4. a device for setting up or maintaining tension, as a guy wire. 5. either of the signs { }, used to connect or enclose words, lines, or staves of music. 6. a device, as a beam, used to strengthen by supporting the weight of, resisting the strain or pressure of, etc.; prop. 7. *a*) any of various splints or devices for supporting a weak or deformed part of the body. *b*) a dental device consisting of a wire arrangement worn on the teeth to force irregularly aligned teeth to grow into proper occlusion. 8. a tool for holding and rotating a drilling bit. —*SYN.* see **pair.**

brace up, [Colloq.], to brace oneself; call forth one's courage, resolution, etc.

brace (brās), *n.* [Fr. *bras* (*de vergue*), brace (of a yard) < L. *brachium,* an arm], in *nautical usage,* a rope passed through a block at the end of a yard, by which the yard is swung from the deck.

brace and bit, a tool for boring, consisting of a removable drill (bit) in a rotating handle (brace).

brace·let (brās'lit), *n.* [Fr., dim. of OFr. *bracel, brachel* < L. *brachiale,* armlet < *brachium,* an arm], 1. an ornamental band or chain worn about the wrist or arm. 2. [Colloq.], a handcuff.

brac·er (brās'ēr), *n.* [ME.; OFr. *brasseure* < *brasse,* arms < L. *brachia,* pl. of *brachium,* an arm], a protective band worn about the wrist or arm in archery or fencing.

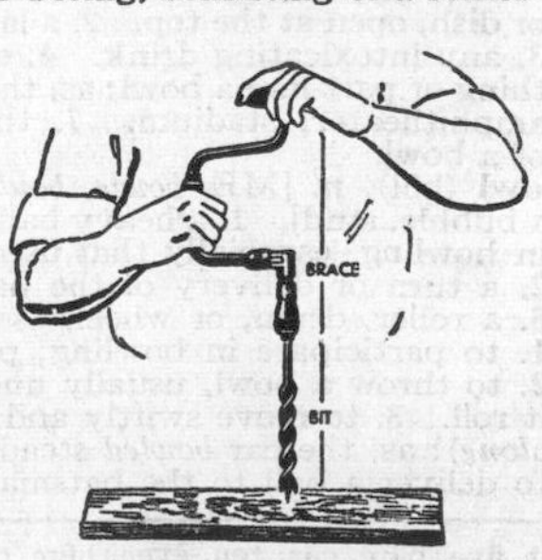

BRACE AND BIT

brac·er (brās'ẽr), *n.* 1. a person or thing that braces. 2. [Slang], a drink taken as a stimulant.

brach (brach), *n.* [ME. & OFr. *brache;* OHG. *braccho, bracco,* dog that hunts by scent], [Archaic], a female hound; bitch.

brach·et (brach'it), *n.* [OFr., dim. of *brache*], a brach.

bra·chi- (brā'ki, brak'i), brachio-.

bra·chi·al (brā'ki-əl, brak'i-əl), *adj.* [L. *brachialis* < *brachium,* an arm], 1. of the arm. 2. armlike. 3. of an armlike part.

bra·chi·al·gi·a (brā'ki-al'ji-ə, brak'i-al'ji-ə), *n.* [*brachi-* + *-algia*], pain in the arm or arms.

bra·chi·ate (brā'ki-it, brak'i-it), *adj.* [*brachi-* + *-ate*], having pairs of opposite branches arranged alternately on the stem or trunk, as in the maple.

bra·chi·o- (brā'ki-ō, brak'i-ə), [< L. *brachium;* Gr. *brachiōn,* an arm], a combining form meaning *arm, connected with an arm* or *the arms,* as in *brachiopod:* also **brachi-**.

bra·chi·o·pod (brā'ki-ə-pod', brak'i-ə-pod'), *n.* [*brachio-* + *-pod*], any of a number of related small, soft-bodied sea animals with upper and lower shells and two armlike parts, one on each side of the mouth.

bra·chi·um (brā'ki-əm, brak'i-əm), *n.* [*pl.* BRACHIA (-ə)], [L.], 1. the part of the arm that extends from shoulder to elbow. 2. in *biology,* any armlike part or process. 3. in *zoology,* a limb corresponding to the human arm.

brach·y- (brak'i), [< Gr. *brachys,* short], a combining form meaning *short,* as in *brachycephalic.*

brach·y·ce·phal·ic (brak'i-sə-fal'ik), *adj.* [*brachy-* + *-cephalic*], having a relatively short or broad skull; having a skull whose width is 80 per cent or more of its length: opposed to *dolichocephalic:* see also **cephalic index.**

brach·y·ceph·a·lous (brak'i-sef'ə-ləs), *adj.* brachycephalic.

brach·y·ceph·a·ly (brak'i-sef'ə-li), *n.* the condition of being brachycephalic.

brach·y·dac·tyl·ic (brak'i-dak-til'ik), *adj.* [*brachy-* + *dactyl* + *-ic*], having abnormally short fingers or toes.

bra·chyl·o·gy (brə-kil'ə-ji), *n.* [*brachy-* + *-logy*], 1. conciseness of speech; brevity. 2. [*pl.* BRACHYLOGIES (-jiz)], an abridged expression.

brach·y·u·ran (brak'i-yoor'ən), *adj.* [< *brachy-* + Gr. *oura,* a tail], designating or of any of a group of crustaceans having five pairs of legs, stalked eyes, and a short tail, and comprising the common crabs. *n.* a brachyuran crustacean; crab.

brach·y·u·rous (brak'i-yoor'əs), *adj.* brachyuran.

brac·ing (brās'iŋ), *adj.* [ppr. of *brace*], invigorating; stimulating; refreshing. *n.* 1. a device that braces. 2. braces; suspenders.

brack·en (brak'ən), *n.* [ME. *braken* < ON; cf. Sw. *brakan,* Dan. *bregne,* fern], 1. any of a number of large, coarse ferns, as the brake. 2. a growth of such ferns.

brack·et (brak'it), *n.* [earlier *bragget* < Fr. *braguette,* dim. of *brague,* kind of mortise < L. *brace,* sing. of *bracae,* breeches < Gallic *braca,* pants], 1. a support projecting from a wall, etc. 2. any angle-shaped support, especially one in the form of a right triangle. 3. a wall shelf or shelves held up by brackets. 4. a gas or electric wall fixture. 5. either of the signs [ ], used to enclose a word, figure, etc., often so as to show that it is inserted: abbreviated **bkt.** 6. a list or group contained within brackets or braces; hence, 7. a classification: as, there are several income *brackets.* 8. in *military usage,* the interval between the ranges of two rounds of artillery fire, one over and the other short of the target, used to find the correct range. *v.t.* 1. to provide or support with brackets. 2. to enclose within or mark with brackets. 3. to group or classify together. 4. in *military usage,* to fire both beyond and short of (a target) so as to find the correct range.

BRACKETS

brack·et·ing (brak'it-iŋ), *n.* 1. a series of brackets. 2. the use of brackets.

brack·ish (brak'ish), *adj.* [earlier Scot. *brack* < MD. *brac, brack;* + *-ish;* cf. MD. *brackwater*], 1. mixed with salt; briny; hence, 2. distasteful; nauseous.

bract (brakt), *n.* [L. *bractea,* thin metal plate], a modified leaf, usually small and scalelike, sometimes large and brightly colored, growing at the base of a flower or on its stalk.

brac·te·al (brak'ti-əl), *adj.* of, or having the nature of, a bract.

brac·te·ate (brak'ti-it), *adj.* having bracts.

brac·te·o·late (brak'ti-ə-lāt'), *adj.* having bractlets.

brac·te·ole (brak'ti-ōl'), *n.* a bractlet.

bract·let (brakt'lit), *n.* a small or secondary bract at the base of a flower.

brad (brad), *n.* [ME. *brad, brod;* ON. *broddr,* a spike], a thin wire nail with a small or off-center head.

brad·awl (brad'ôl'), *n.* a straight awl with a chisel edge, used for making holes to put brads into.

brad·ded (brad'id), *adj.* fastened with brads.

Brad·dock, Edward (brad'ək), 1695–1755; commander of British forces in the French and Indian War.

Brad·ford (brad'fẽrd), *n.* 1. a city in Yorkshire, northern England: pop., 289,000. 2. a city in northern Pennsylvania: pop., 15,000.

Brad·ford, Gamaliel (brad'fẽrd), 1863–1932; American essayist and biographer.

Bradford, William, 1590–1657; second governor of Plymouth Colony.

Brad·ley, Omar Nelson (brad'li), 1893– ; American general.

Brad·street, Anne (brad'strēt'), 1612?–1672; American colonial poet.

brad·y- (brad'i), [< Gr. *bradys,* slow], a combining form meaning *slow, delayed, tardy,* as in *bradycardia.*

Bra·dy, Mat·hew B. (math'ū brā'di), 1823?–1896; American photographer, best known for his photographs of Lincoln and the Civil War.

brad·y·car·di·a (brad'i-kär'di-ə), *n.* [< *brady-* + Gr. *kardia,* heart], abnormally slow beating of the heart.

brae (brā), *n.* [ME. *bra, bro;* ON. *bra,* eyelid, brow, river bank], [Scot.], a sloping bank; hillside.

brag (brag), *v.t. & v.i.* [BRAGGED (bragd), BRAGGING], [ME. *braggen;* prob. < OFr. *braguer,* to flaunt, brag; ? < source of *bray*], to boast. *n.* 1. a boast; boasting. 2. a person or thing boasted of. 3. a boaster; braggart. 4. an old card game, much like poker. *adj.* [Archaic], 1. spirited. 2. worthy of a boast. —***SYN.*** see **boast.**

Bra·ge (brä'gə), *n.* Bragi.

Bragg, Brax·ton (braks'tən brag), 1817–1876; Confederate general; military adviser of Jefferson Davis.

Bragg, Sir **William Henry,** 1862–1942; British physicist; received Nobel prize in physics, 1915.

Bragg, William Lawrence, 1890– ; son of *William Henry;* British physicist; shared Nobel prize with his father, 1915.

brag·ga·do·ci·o (brag'ə-dō'shi-ō'), *n.* [*pl.* BRAGGADOCIOS (-ōz')], [*brag* + It. ending; coined by Spenser], 1. a braggart. 2. noisy boasting or bragging.

brag·gart (brag'ẽrt), *n.* [Fr. *bragard* < OFr. *braguer;* see BRAG], an offensively boastful person. *adj.* bragging; boastful.

brag·ger (brag'ẽr), *n.* a person who brags.

Bra·gi (brä'gē), *n.* in *Norse mythology,* the god of poetry and eloquence, son of Odin and Frigga.

Bra·he, Ty·cho (tü'kō brä'ə), 1546–1601; Danish astronomer.

Brah·ma (brä'mə), *n.* [Hind. < Sans. *brahman,* worship, prayer], in *Hindu theology,* 1. the supreme and eternal essence or spirit of the universe. 2. the chief member of the trinity (Brahma, Vishnu, and Siva) and creator of the universe. 3. (brā'mə), a breed of domestic cattle developed from the zebu of India and having a large hump over the shoulders: also **Brahman.**

Brah·ma, brah·ma (brä'mə, brā'mə), *n.* [< *Brahmaputra*], any of an Asiatic breed of large domestic fowls with feathered legs and small tail and wings.

Brah·man (brä'mən), *n.* [*pl.* BRAHMANS (-mənz)], [Hind. < Sans. *brāhmana* < *brahman,* worship, prayer], a member of the priestly Hindu caste, which is the highest. *adj.* Brahmanic.

Brah·ma·ni, Brah·ma·nee (brä'mə-nē'), *n.* a woman of the Brahman caste.

Brah·man·ic (brä-man'ik), *adj.* of Brahmans or Brahmanism.

Brah·man·i·cal (brä-man'i-k'l), *adj.* Brahmanic.

Brah·man·ism (brä'mən-iz'm), *n.* 1. the religious doctrines and system of the Brahmans. 2. the former Hindu caste system.

Brah·ma·pu·tra (brä'mə-pōō'trə), *n.* a river flowing through Tibet and India into the Bay of Bengal: length, 1,700 mi.

Brah·min (brä'min), *n.* 1. a Brahman. 2. a cultured person from a long-established upper-class family, especially one regarded as haughty or conservative.

Brah·min·ic (brä-min'ik), *adj.* of or characteristic of a Brahmin or Brahmins.

Brah·min·i·cal (brä-min'i-k'l), *adj.* Brahminic.

Brah·min·ism (brä'min-iz'm), *n.* 1. Brahmanism. 2. the characteristic spirit, attitude, etc. of Brahmins.

Brahms, Jo·han·nes (yō-hä'nəs brämz'; G. bräms'), 1833–1897; German composer.

braid (brād), *v.t.* [ME. *breiden, braiden;* AS. *bregdan,* to move quickly, jerk, pull, twist; see UPBRAID], 1. to interweave three or more strands of (hair, straw, etc.). 2. to tie up (the hair) in a ribbon or band. 3. to trim or bind with braid. *n.* 1. a band or strip formed by braiding. 2. a strip of braided hair. 3. a woven band of cloth, tape, ribbon, etc., used to bind or decorate clothing. 4. a ribbon or band for tying up the hair.

braid·ing (brād′iŋ), *n.* 1. braids collectively. 2. trimming with or of braid.
brail (brāl), *n.* [ME.; OFr. *braiel, brayel,* a cincture, belt for trousers < *braie;* L. *braca,* pl. *bracae,* breeches], one of the ropes used to gather in sails before furling. *v.t.* to haul in with brails (usually with *up*).
Bră·i·la (brə-ē′lä), *n.* a city in eastern Romania, on the Danube: pop., 97,000 (est. 1945).
Braille, braille (brāl), *n.* [after Louis *Braille*], 1. a system of printing and writing for the blind, in which letters, numerals, and punctuation are made of raised dots distinguishable by the fingers. 2. the characters used in this system. *v.t.* [BRAILLED (brāld), BRAILLING], to print or write in such characters.
Braille, Louis (brāl; Fr. brä′y′), 1809–1852; Frenchman who invented Braille in 1829.
brain (brān), *n.* [ME.; AS. *brægen, bregn;* akin to OFris. *brein,* MLG. *bregen;* IE. base **mreghno-,* skull], 1. the mass of nerve tissue in the cranium of vertebrate animals: it is the main part of the nervous system, and is made up of gray matter (the outer cortex of nerve cells) and white matter (the inner mass of nerve fibers); the human brain comprises the cerebrum, the cerebellum, the pons, and the medulla oblongata. 2. a corresponding organ in invertebrate animals. 3. *often pl.* intelligence; mental ability. *v.t.* to dash out the brains of.

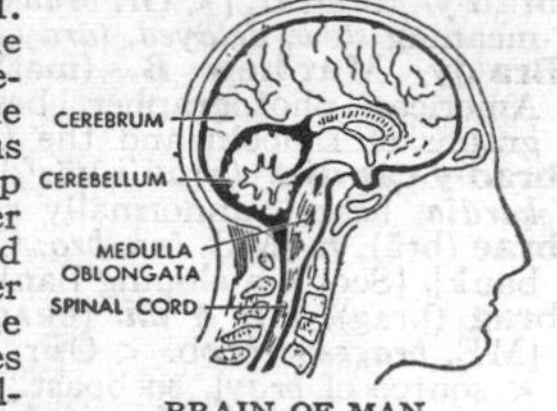

BRAIN OF MAN

beat one's brains, to try hard to remember, understand, or solve something.
have on the brain, to be obsessed by.
brain cell, any nerve cell of the brain.
brain child, [Colloq.], an idea, plan, etc. regarded as produced by a person's mental labor.
brain fever, encephalitis.
brain·less (brān′lis), *adj.* 1. having no brain. 2. foolish; stupid.
brain·pan (brān′pan′), *n.* the part of the skull containing the brain; cranium.
brain·sick (brān′sik′), *adj.* having or caused by a mental disorder.
brain storm, 1. a series of sudden, violent cerebral disturbances. 2. [Colloq.], a sudden inspiration, idea, or plan: humorous term.
brain·storm·ing (brān′stôrm′iŋ), *n.* the unrestrained offering of ideas or suggestions by all members of a group meeting as in a business planning conference.
brain trust, [Slang], a group of advisers with expert or special knowledge: term applied originally to the advisers surrounding President Franklin D. Roosevelt during his first administration.
brain·wash (brān′wôsh′, brān′wăsh′), *v.t.* [journalese (c. 1951); < *brain* + *wash*], [Colloq.], to indoctrinate so intensively and thoroughly as to effect a radical transformation of beliefs and mental attitudes.
brain wave, 1. [Colloq.], a sudden inspiration; brain storm. 2. in *physiology,* rhythmic electric impulses given off by nerve centers in the brain and spinal cord during sleep.
brain·y (brān′i), *adj.* [BRAINIER (-i-ẽr), BRAINIEST (-i-ist)], [Colloq.], intelligent; mentally acute.
braise (brāz), *v.t.* [BRAISED (brāzd), BRAISING], [Fr. *braiser* < *braise,* live coals < Gmc. *brasa,* glowing coals], to cook (meat) by browning in fat and then simmering in a covered pan with a little liquid.
brake (brāk), *n.* [ME.; prob. taken as sing. of *bracken*], a large, coarse fern; bracken.
brake (brāk), *n.* [ME. < MLG. *brake* or OD. *braeke,* flax brake < *breken,* to break; senses 3–7 variously influenced by OFr. *brac,* form of *bras,* an arm & Eng. *break, v.t.*], 1. a device for beating or crushing flax or hemp so that the fiber can be separated. 2. a device for kneading dough. 3. a rack; former instrument of torture. 4. a restraining frame for a horse's foot while it is being shod. 5. a heavy harrow. 6. a handle or lever on a machine: as, a pump *brake.* 7. any device for slowing or stopping the motion of a vehicle or machine, as by causing a block or band to press against a moving part: many brakes are operated by compressed air, hydraulic pressure, or electromagnetic force. *v.t.* [BRAKED (brākt), BRAKING], 1. to break up (flax, clods of earth, etc.) into smaller pieces. 2. to knead (dough, etc.). 3. to slow down or stop with or as with a brake. *v.i.* 1. to operate a brake or brakes. 2. to be slowed down or stopped by a brake.
brake (brāk), *n.* [prob. < MLG. *brake,* stumps, broken branches; akin to *breken,* to break], a clump or area of brushwood, briars, etc.; thicket.
brake (brāk), *n.* a break (carriage).
brake (brāk), archaic past tense of **break.**
brake·age (brāk′ij), *n.* 1. the action or application of a brake. 2. braking capacity.
brake band, a band that serves as a braking force by creating friction when applied to the drum of a brake, as in an automobile.
brake drum, the metal cylinder, as on the hub of a wheel, to which the brake band is applied in braking.
brake horsepower, the actual horsepower of an engine, measured by a brake attached to the driving shaft and recorded on a dynamometer.
brake lining, a material woven of cotton, asbestos, fine copper wire, etc. and fastened to the brake band to create the friction necessary for braking.
brake·man (brāk′mən), *n.* [*pl.* BRAKEMEN (mən)], an operator of brakes or assistant to the conductor on a railroad train.
brake shoe, a block curved to fit the shape of a wheel and forced against it to act as a brake: see **hydraulic brake,** illus.
brakes·man (brāks′mən), *n.* [*pl.* BRAKESMEN (-mən)], [British], a brakeman.
Bra·man·te, Do·na·to d'A·gno·lo (dô-nä′tô dä′nyô-lô brä-män′te), 1444–1514; Italian architect.
bram·ble (bram′b'l), *n.* [ME. *brembel;* AS. *bræmbel,* earlier *bræmel* < *brom,* broom; cf. G. *brombeere,* blackberry; IE. base **bher-,* point, sharp edge], 1. any of a number of related shrubs of the rose family, as the raspberry, dewberry, blackberry, etc.: they are usually prickly. 2. any prickly shrub.
bram·bling (bram′bliŋ), *n.* [earlier *bramline;* prob. < ME. *brame,* bramble], a bright-colored finch found in Europe and Asia.
bram·bly (bram′bli), *adj.* 1. full of or covered with brambles. 2. like brambles; prickly.
Bran (bran), *n.* [? < Ir. *bran,* raven], 1. a mythical king of Britain. 2. in *Celtic mythology,* a god of the underworld.
bran (bran), *n.* [ME. *bran, bren;* OFr. *bren*], the skin or husk of grains of wheat, rye, oats, etc. separated from the flour, as by sifting.
branch (branch, bränch), *n.* [ME. *branche;* OFr. *branche, brance;* LL. *branca,* a claw, paw], 1. any woody extension growing from the trunk, main stem, or bough of a tree, bush, or shrub, especially an offshoot from a main limb; bough; limb; twig. 2. anything like a branch; ramification. 3. a tributary stream running out of or into a larger stream. 4. any stream smaller than a creek; brook, rivulet, etc. 5. any part or extension coming out from a main body or system in a branchlike way; offshoot. 6. a member, division, or part of something: as, chemistry is a *branch* of learning. 7. a division of a family. 8. a separately located unit of a business: as, a suburban *branch* of a department store. Abbreviated **br.** *v.i.* 1. to put forth branches; spread in or divide into branches; ramify. 2. to come out from the trunk, stem, or main part as a branch. *v.t.* 1. to separate into branches. 2. to embroider with a pattern of flowers, foliage, etc.
branch off, 1. to separate into branches; fork. 2. to go off in another direction; diverge.
branch out, 1. to put forth branches. 2. to extend the scope of interests, activities, etc.
bran·chi·ae (braŋ′ki-ē′), *n.pl.* [*sing.* BRANCHIA (-ə)], [L., pl. of *branchia;* Gr. *branchia,* pl. of *branchion,* a gill], in *zoology,* gills.
bran·chi·al (braŋ′ki-əl), *adj.* of or like branchiae.
bran·chi·ate (braŋ′ki-it), *adj.* having branchiae.
bran·chi·o- (braŋ′ki-ə), [< Gr. *branchia,* gills], a combining form meaning *gills,* as in *branchiopod.*
bran·chi·o·pod (braŋ′ki-ə-pod′), *n.* [*branchio-* + *-pod*], any of a group of related crustaceans with many pairs of flattened, leaflike limbs.
brand (brand), *n.* [ME.; AS. *brand, brond,* a flame, torch, sword < *biernan, brinnan, v.i.,* to burn; see BURN], 1. a stick that is burning or partially burned. 2. a mark made on the skin with a hot iron, formerly used to punish and identify criminals, now used on cattle to show ownership. 3. the iron thus used. 4. a mark of disgrace; stigma. 5. a mark or label of identification, grade, etc. on merchandise; trade-mark; hence, 6. the kind or make of a commodity: as, a *brand* of cigarettes. 7. a fungous disease of plants that makes the leaves look burnt. 8. any fungus causing this disease. 9. [Archaic & Poetic], a sword. *v.t.* 1. to mark with or as with a brand. 2. to put a mark of disgrace on; stigmatize.
Bran·deis, Louis Dem·bitz (dem′bits bran′dīs), 1856–1941; American jurist; associate justice, Supreme Court (1916–1939).
Bran·den·burg (bran′dən-bũrg′; G. brän′dən-boorkh′), *n.* 1. a province of Prussia: formerly a kingdom: area, 15,072 sq. mi.; pop., 2,516,000 (1946); capital, Berlin. 2. a city west of Berlin: pop., 64,000.
Bran·des, Ge·org Mor·ris (gi-org′ mor′is brän′dəs), (b. *Georg Morris Cohen*), 1842–1927; Danish literary critic.
brand goose, a brant.
bran·died (bran′did), *adj.* [pp. of *brandy*], 1. treated or flavored with brandy. 2. containing brandy.
bran·dish (bran′dish), *v.t.* [ME. *brandischen;* OFr. *brandir* < OHG. *brand,* sword; cf. BRAND], to wave or shake menacingly, as a sword; flourish. *n.* a menacing shake or wave.

brand·ling (brand′liŋ), *n.* [*brand, n.* + *-ling*], a small, red or yellowish worm, used for fish bait.

brand-new (brand′nōō′, brand′nū′), *adj.* [orig., fresh from the fire; see BRAND], 1. entirely new; recently made; not secondhand. 2. loosely, recently acquired.

bran·dy (bran′di), *n.* [*pl.* BRANDIES (-diz)], [earlier *brandywine, brandewine;* D. *brandewijn,* lit., burnt wine: so called from being distilled], 1. an alcoholic liquor distilled from wine. 2. a similar liquor distilled from fruit juice. *v.t.* [BRANDIED (-did), BRANDYING], to flavor, treat, or mix with brandy.

Bran·dy·wine (bran′di-wīn′), *n.* a creek in southeastern Pennsylvania and Delaware: site of a battle (1777) in which the British under Howe defeated the Americans.

branks (braŋks), *n.pl.* [Norm.Fr. *branques;* OFr. *branches;* see BRANCH], an iron curb for the tongue, held in place by a frame around the head: formerly used to punish noisy, quarrelsome women.

bran-new (bran′nōō′, bran′nū′), *adj.* brand-new.

bran·ny (bran′i), *adj.* of, like, or containing bran.

brant (brant), *n.* [*pl.* BRANTS (brants), BRANT; see PLURAL, II, D, 1], [? < *brand,* because of burnt color of the bird], any of a number of related small, dark wild geese of Europe and North America.

Brant, Joseph (brant), (born *Thayendanegea*), 1742–1807; Mohawk Indian chief who served as an officer with the British army in the American Revolution.

bran·tail (bran′tāl′), *n.* [< *brandtail*], a small bird with a red tail; European redstart.

brash (brash), *adj.* [orig., dial. & Scot.; prob. < *break* + *dash, crash, rash,* etc.], 1. brittle or fragile, as some wood. 2. rash; too hasty. 3. insolent; impudent. *n.* 1. pyrosis, a temporary stomach disorder with acid belching: usually **water brash.** 2. a sudden shower of rain.

brash (brash), *n.* [Fr. *brèche* < OHG. *brecha,* fragment < *brehhan,* to break], 1. broken pieces or fragments, as of rock or ice. 2. the debris of hedge or tree prunings.

bra·sier (brā′zhẽr), *n.* a brazier.

Bra·sil (brä-sēl′), *n.* Brazil: Spanish and Portuguese name.

bra·sil·e·in (brə-zil′i-in), *n.* brazilein.

Bra·síl·i·a (brä-sēl′yə, brə-sil′i-ə), *n.* the capital of Brazil, in the east central part: pop., 120,000.

bras·il·in (braz′′l-in), *n.* brazilin.

Bra·şov (brä-shôv′), *n.* a city in central Romania: pop., 127,000: German name, *Kronstadt.*

brass (bras, bräs), *n.* [*pl.* BRASSES (-iz); see PLURAL, II, D, 3], [ME. *bras;* AS. *bræs,* alloy of tin and copper, bronze; prob. akin to Celt. *brace;* see BRASSAGE], 1. a yellowish metal that is essentially an alloy of copper and zinc. 2. *pl.* things made of brass, as ornaments, implements, etc. 3. *pl.* brass-wind musical instruments. 4. an inscribed plate of brass. 5. hardness. 6. [Colloq.], bold impudence. 7. [Slang], money. 8. [Slang], military officers of high rank: see **brass hat.** 9. in *machinery,* the lining or bushing of a bearing. *adj.* made of or containing brass. *v.t.* to coat with brass.

brass·age (bras′ij, bräs′ij), *n.* [Fr. < *brasser,* to stir, orig., to brew; OFr. *bracier* < Gaul. *brace,* grain used for preparation of malt], a charge made by a government for the expense of coining: the face value of a coin is the worth of the bullion plus brassage.

bras·sard (bras′ärd, brə-särd′), *n.* [Fr. < *bras,* an arm], 1. armor for the arm from elbow to shoulder. 2. an arm band with a badge or emblem, worn as a sign of distinction.

brass·art (bras′ẽrt), *n.* [var. of *brassard*], a brassard.

brass band, a band in which the instruments played are mainly brasses.

brass hat, [Slang], 1. a staff officer in the British army: so called from the gold braid on his cap; hence, 2. any military officer of high rank.

bras·si·ca·ceous (bras′i-kā′shəs), *adj.* [< L. *brassica,* cabbage; + *-aceous*], belonging to the mustard family of plants, including the turnip, cabbage, and broccoli.

brass·ie (bras′i, bräs′i), *n.* [< *brass:* so called because orig. made with a brass plate on the bottom of the head], a golf club with a wooden head and a loft between that of a driver and a spoon, used for long fairway play: also spelled **brassy, brassey:** see **golf club,** illus.

bras·siere, bras·sière (brə-zêr′, bras′i-er′), *n.* [Fr. < *bras,* an arm], an undergarment worn by women to support the breasts or give a desired contour to the bust.

brass·i·ly (bras′′l-i, bräs′′l-i), *adv.* in a brassy manner.

brass·i·ness (bras′i-nis, bräs′i-nis), *n.* the quality or condition of being brassy.

brass knuckles, linked metal rings or a metal bar with holes for the fingers, worn for rough fighting.

brass tacks, [Colloq.], basic facts; really important matters.

get (or **come**) **down to brass tacks,** [Colloq.], to discuss basic facts or really important matters.

brass·ware (bras′wâr′, bräs′wâr′), *n.* articles made of brass.

brass-wind (bras′wind′, bräs′wind′), *adj.* of the brass winds.

brass winds (windz), musical instruments made of coiled metal tubes, through which tones are made by blowing into a cup-shaped mouthpiece.

brass·y (bras′i, bräs′i), *adj.* [BRASSIER (-i-ẽr), BRASSIEST (-i-ist)], 1. of or decorated with brass. 2. like brass. 3. cheap and showy. 4. impudent; insolent. 5. loud; blaring. *n.* [*pl.* BRASSIES (-iz)], a brassie.

brat (brat), *n.* [ME.; AS. *bratt,* a cloak; Gael. *bratt,* a cloak, cloth, rag: present sense from the rough, shabby clothes worn by poor children], a child, especially an impudent, unruly child: scornful or playful term.

Bra·ti·sla·va (brä′ti-slä′və), *n.* a city in southern Czechoslovakia, on the Danube: pop., 247,000: German name, *Pressburg;* Hungarian name, *Pozsony.*

brat·tice (brat′is), *n.* [ME. *bretasce,* parapet; OFr. *bretesche,* wooden tower; prob. < OHG. *bret,* a board], 1. formerly, a temporary breastwork or parapet put up during a siege. 2. in *mining, a*) a partition, as for ventilation. *b*) a cloth impregnated with creosote for ventilation. *v.t.* [BRATTICED (-ist), BRATTICING], to furnish with a brattice.

brat·tle (brat′′l), *v.i.* [BRATTLED (-′ld), BRATTLING], [echoic], [Scot.], 1. to rattle or clatter. 2. to scamper noisily. *n.* [Scot.], a rattling noise.

Braun·schweig (broun′shvīkh), *n.* Brunswick: the German name.

bra·va·do (brə-vä′dō, brə-vā′dō), *n.* [*pl.* BRAVADOES, BRAVADOS (-dōz)], [Sp. < *bravo,* brave], pretended courage or defiant confidence when there is really little or none.

brave (brāv), *adj.* [Fr.; It. *bravo,* brave, bold, orig., wild, savage < L. *barbarus;* see BARBAROUS], 1. not afraid; having courage. 2. showing to good effect; having a fine appearance. 3. [Archaic], fine; superior. *n.* 1. any brave man. 2. [< 17th-c. N. Am. Fr.], a North American Indian warrior. 3. [Archaic], a bully. *v.t.* [Fr. *braver* < the *adj.*], [BRAVED (brāvd), BRAVING], 1. to defy; dare. 2. to meet or undergo with courage. 3. [Obs.], to make brave. *v.i.* [Obs.], to boast.

SYN.—**brave** implies fearlessness in meeting danger or difficulty and has the broadest application of the words considered here; **courageous** suggests constant readiness to deal with things fearlessly by reason of a stout-hearted temperament or a resolute spirit; **bold** stresses a daring temperament, whether displayed courageously, presumptuously, or defiantly; **audacious** suggests an imprudent or reckless boldness; **valiant** emphasizes a heroic quality in the courage or fortitude shown; **intrepid** implies absolute fearlessness and especially suggests dauntlessness in facing the new or unknown; **plucky** emphasizes gameness in fighting against something when one is at a decided disadvantage. —***ANT.*** craven, cowardly.

brav·er·y (brāv′ẽr-i), *n.* [*pl.* BRAVERIES (-iz)], [Fr. *braverie,* gallantry, splendor < *brave*], 1. courage; valor. 2. fine appearance, show, or dress; showiness.

‡bra·vis·si·mo (brä-vēs′sē-mō′), *interj.* [It., superl. of *bravo*], very well done! splendid!

bra·vo (brä′vō), *interj.* [It.; see BRAVE, *adj.*], well done! very good! excellent! *n.* [*pl.* BRAVOS (-vōz)], a shout of "bravo!"

bra·vo (brä′vō, brā′vō), *n.* [*pl.* BRAVOES, BRAVOS (-vōz); It. BRAVI (brä′vē)], [It.; see BRAVE, *adj.*], a hired killer; assassin; desperado.

bra·vu·ra (brə-vyoor′ə; It. brä-vōō′rä), *n.* [It., bravery, spirit < *bravo,* brave], 1. a bold attempt or display of daring; dash. 2. in *music, a*) a brilliant passage or piece that displays the performer's skill and technique. *b*) brilliant technique in performance.

braw (brô, brä), *adj.* [< *brave, adj.*], [Scot.], 1. finely dressed. 2. fine; excellent.

brawl (brôl), *v.i.* [ME. *brallen, braulen,* to cry out, quarrel < OFr. *brailler,* to shout < *braire,* to bray; for the vowel, see MAUL], 1. to create a disturbance by quarreling or fighting. 2. to move or flow noisily over rapids, falls, etc.: said of water. *n.* 1. a noisy quarrel or fight; row; uproar. 2. [Slang], a noisy party.

brawl (brôl), *n.* [Fr. *branle* < *branler,* to sway, toss about, swing < Gmc. *brand,* sword; see BRAND], 1. an old French country dance. 2. the music for this.

brawn (brôn), *n.* [ME. *braun;* OFr. *braon,* fleshy or muscular part, buttock < OHG. *brato,* eatable flesh, OLG. *brado,* calf (of leg), whence ML. *brado,* ham], 1. muscle; strong, well-developed muscles. 2. muscular strength. 3. cooked and pickled boar's flesh. 4. headcheese.

brawn·i·ness (brôn′i-nis), *n.* the quality or state of being brawny.

brawn·y (brôn′i), *adj.* [BRAWNIER (-i-ẽr), BRAWNIEST (-i-ist)], [< *brawn*], strong; muscular.

brax·y (brak′si), *n.* [< ?; prob. akin to AS. *broc,* disease, sickness], any of various intestinal disorders of sheep, especially one resembling anthrax. *adj.* having braxy.

bray (brā), *v.i.* [ME. *braien;* OFr. *braire;* LL. *bragire,* to cry out], to make a loud, harsh sound, as a donkey. *v.t.* to utter loudly and harshly. *n.* 1. the loud, harsh cry that a donkey makes. 2. a sound like this.
bray (brā), *v.t.* [ME. *braien;* OFr. *breier,* to pound, pulverize; prob. < OHG. *brekan,* to break], 1. to crush or pound into a powder, as in a mortar. 2. to spread thin, as ink.
bray·er (brā′ẽr), *n.* [see BRAY (to crush)], in *printing,* a roller used for spreading ink.
Braz., 1. Brazil. 2. Brazilian.
‡**bra·za** (brä′thä, brä′sä), *n.* [Sp. < *brazo* (L. *brachium*), an arm], a Spanish measure of length equal to 5.48 feet in Spain and 5.68 feet in Argentina.
braze (brāz), *v.t.* [BRAZED (brāzd), BRAZING], [Fr. *braser,* to solder; OFr. *brazer,* to burn; prob. < Gmc. *brasa,* glowing coals], to solder with a metal having a high melting point, especially with an alloy of zinc and copper.
braze (brāz), *v.t.* [BRAZED (brāzd), BRAZING], [AS. *bræsian* < *bræs;* see BRASS], 1. to make, coat, or decorate with brass or a brasslike substance. 2. to make hard like brass.
bra·zen (brā′z'n), *adj.* [ME. *brasen;* AS. *bræsen* < *bræs;* see BRASS], 1. of brass. 2. like brass in color or other qualities. 3. having no shame. 4. having the ringing sound of brass; harsh and piercing. *v.t.* to make impudent or bold and shameless.
brazen out (or **through**), to behave as if unashamed of.
bra·zen-faced (brā′z'n-fāst′), *adj.* having, or uttered with, a brazen expression; impudent; shameless.
bra·zier (brā′zhẽr), *n.* [Fr. *brasier;* see BRAISE], a metal container to hold burning coals or charcoal.
bra·zier (brā′zhẽr), *n.* [ME. *brasiere* < *bras;* see BRASS], a person who does brasswork.
Bra·zil (brə-zil′), *n.* a country in central and northeastern South America, on the Atlantic: area, 3,275,510 sq. mi.; pop., 66,302,000; capital, Brasília: abbreviated **Braz.**
bra·zil (brə-zil′), *n.* [ME. *brasile;* Sp. & Port. *brasil;* prob. (because of color) < Gmc. *brasa;* see BRAISE], 1. brazilwood. 2. a red dye from this wood.
bra·zil·e·in (brə-zil′i-in), *n.* [< *brazil* + *-in*], a bright-red compound, $C_{16}H_{12}O_5$, obtained by oxidizing brazilin and used as a dye: also spelled **brasilein.**
Bra·zil·ian (brə-zil′yən), *adj.* of Brazil, its people, or culture. *n.* a native or inhabitant of Brazil. Abbreviated **Braz.**
braz·i·lin (braz′'l-in), *n.* [*brazil* + *-in*], a bright-yellow compound, $C_{16}H_{14}O_5$, obtained from brazilwood in the form of a crystalline powder: also spelled **brasilin.**
Brazil nut, the edible, oily, three-sided seed, or nut, of the Brazil-nut tree.
Bra·zil-nut tree (brə-zil′nut′), a very tall tree of tropical America, bearing round, hard-shelled fruit with edible seeds.
bra·zil·wood (brə-zil′wood′), *n.* [see BRAZIL (wood)], the reddish wood of certain trees of South America and the East and West Indies, yielding a red dye.
Bra·zos (brä′zos, brā′zos), *n.* a river in Texas, flowing into the Gulf of Mexico: length, 870 mi.
Braz·za·ville (brȧ′zȧ′vēl′), *n.* the capital of the Congo (sense 3), on the Congo River: pop., 100,000.
B.R.C.A., Brotherhood of Railway Carmen of America: an AFL-CIO labor union.
B.R.C.S., British Red Cross Society.
BrE., British English.
breach (brēch), *n.* [ME. *breche;* AS. *bryce* < *brecan,* to break; influenced by OFr. *breche* < OHG. *brecha* < *brehhan,* to break], 1. a breaking or being broken. 2. a failure to observe the terms, as of a law, promise, etc. 3. an opening made by breaking something; gap. 4. a breaking of waves over or upon a ship, sea wall, etc. 5. waves that do this. 6. a break or interruption in friendly relations. 7. a hernia. *v.t.* to make a breach in; break open or through.
breach of faith, a failure to keep faith; breaking of a promise.
breach of promise, a breaking of a promise, especially a promise to marry.
breach of the peace, any unnecessary disturbance of the public peace.
breach of trust, in *law,* a violation of duty by a person holding property in trust.
bread (bred), *n.* [ME. *breed, brede;* AS. *bread,* crumb, morsel; akin to G. *brot;* IE. base **bhreu, bhrū-,* to swell up, ferment (cf. BREW); the AS. meanings suggest folk etym. < *breotan,* to break up], 1. a food made by mixing flour or ground grain with water, milk, etc. and then baking the mixture, usually after kneading it. 2. food generally, regarded as a source of life. 3. a livelihood; a living: as, he earns his *bread.* 4. anything resembling bread. *v.t.* to cover with bread crumbs before cooking.
bread and butter, 1. bread with butter on it; hence, 2. means of subsistence; livelihood.
break bread, 1. to eat. 2. to partake of the sacrament or attend Communion.
cast one's bread upon the waters, to be generous or do good deeds without expecting something in return.
know which side one's bread is buttered on, to know what is to one's economic interest.
take the bread out of (a person's) mouth, to deprive (a person) of his means of living.
bread-and-but·ter (bred′'n-but′ẽr), *adj.* 1. youthful; immature. 2. commonplace; everyday. 3. prompted by necessity. 4. for the purpose of thanking, as a letter sent to one's host after a visit.
bread·bas·ket (bred′bas′kit, bred′bäs′kit), *n.* 1. a region that supplies much grain. 2. [Slang], the stomach or abdomen. 3. [Slang], an aerial bomb made up of both explosives and incendiaries.
bread·board (bred′bôrd′, bred′bōrd′), *n.* 1. a board on which dough is kneaded, shaped, or rolled. 2. a board on which bread is sliced.
bread box, a box in which bread, pastry, etc. is put to help keep it fresh.
bread·fruit (bred′frōōt′), *n.* 1. a large, round fruit with starchy, whitish pulp, breadlike when baked. 2. the tree that bears it, found on South Pacific islands.
bread line, a line of people waiting to be given food as government relief or private charity.
bread mold, a kind of fungus that grows on decaying bread: also called *black mold.*
bread·nut (bred′nut′), *n.* the seeded fruit of a tree resembling the breadfruit.
bread·root (bred′rōōt′, bred′root′), *n.* 1. the thick, starchy, edible root of a hairy plant of the pea family. 2. the plant.
bread·stuff (bred′stuf′), *n.* 1. ground grain or flour for making bread. 2. bread.
breadth (bredth), *n.* [ME. *brǽde, brede;* AS. *brædu* < *brad,* broad; *-th* by analogy with *length*], 1. how broad a thing is; distance from side to side; width: abbreviated **B., b.** 2. a piece of a given and regular width: as, a *breadth* of linoleum. 3. spaciousness; magnitude; scope; extent. 4. lack of narrowness or of restriction: as, he has true *breadth* of understanding.
breadth·ways (bredth′wāz′), *adv.* in the direction of the breadth.
breadth·wise (bredth′wīz′), *adv.* breadthways.
bread·win·ner (bred′win′ẽr), *n.* a person who supports his dependents by his earnings.
break (brāk), *v.t.* [BROKE (brōk) or *archaic* BRAKE (brāk), BROKEN (brō′k'n) or *archaic* BROKE, BREAKING], [ME. *breken;* AS. *brecan;* akin to G. *brechen;* IE. base **bhreg;* cf. FRACTURE, FRAGILE], 1. to cause to come apart by force; separate into pieces by shattering; crack; smash; burst. 2. to cut open the surface of (soil, the skin, etc.). 3. to bring to an end by force; overwhelm: as, the strike was *broken.* 4. to make unusable or inoperative by cracking or disrupting. 5. to tame or make obedient with or as with force. 6. to lower in rank or grade; demote. 7. to reduce to poverty or bankruptcy. 8. to surpass (a record). 9. to fail to follow the terms of; violate: as, he *broke* his agreement. 10. to escape from suddenly: as, they cannot *break* prison. 11. to destroy or disrupt the order or completeness of; make irregular: as, the troops *broke* formation and ran. 12. to interrupt (a journey, electric circuit, etc.). 13. to reduce the effect of by interrupting (a fall, the wind, etc.). 14. to cut through or penetrate (silence, darkness, etc.). 15. to make known; tell; disclose. 16. to begin; open; start. 17. to exchange (a bill or coin) for smaller units. *v.i.* 1. to divide into separate pieces; come apart; burst. 2. to scatter; disperse: as, let's *break* and run. 3. to quarrel; stop associating (often with *up* or *with*). 4. to become unusable or inoperative; break down; weaken. 5. to become poverty-stricken or bankrupt. 6. to change suddenly: as, his voice *broke.* 7. to move away suddenly; burst forth; escape. 8. to begin suddenly to utter, perform, etc. (with *into, forth in,* or *out in*): as, he *broke* into song. 9. to come into being, evidence, or general knowledge: as, day was *breaking,* the story *broke.* 10. to appear suddenly above water, as a periscope, fish, etc. 11. to fall apart slowly; disintegrate. 12. to change into a diphthong: said of vowels. 13. to curve near the plate: said of a pitched baseball. 14. [Colloq.], to happen in a certain way: as, things were *breaking* badly. *n.* 1. a breaking; breach; fracture. 2. a breaking in, out, or forth. 3. the result of a breaking; broken place; separation; crack. 4. a beginning to appear: as, the *break* of day. 5. an interruption or discontinuing of regularity. 6. the result of this; an interval; pause; omission. 7. *pl.* a series of dots used as punctuation; suspension points. Example: Came the dawn . . . . 8. a sudden change or deviation. 9. a lowering or drop, as of prices. 10. an imperfection; flaw. 11. an unbroken series or sequence, as of points in billiards. 12. [Colloq.], an improper or untimely action or remark. 13. [Slang], a chance piece of luck, especially of good luck. 14. in *music, a)* the point where one register changes to another. *b)* this change. *c)* a transitional or ornamental phrase played during the pause between regular divisions of a jazz melody.
break away, 1. to go suddenly; get away; escape. 2. to start too soon, as in a race.

break down, 1. to go out of working order. 2. to give way to tears or emotion. 3. to have a physical or nervous collapse. 4. to crush or overcome (opposition, etc.). 5. to separate into parts; analyze.

break in, 1. to enter forcibly or unexpectedly. 2. to interrupt. 3. to adapt for a specific purpose; train.

break in on (or **upon**), 1. to intrude on. 2. to interrupt.

break into, 1. to enter forcibly. 2. to interrupt. 3. to begin suddenly to utter, perform, etc.

break of, to make give up (a habit).

break off, 1. to stop abruptly, as in talking. 2. to stop being friendly or intimate.

break out, 1. to begin suddenly. 2. to escape. 3. to become covered with pimples or a rash. 4. to loosen a ship's anchor from the bottom before weighing.

break up, 1. to separate; disperse. 2. to take apart; dismantle and scrap. 3. to put a stop to. 4. [Colloq.], to distress; upset; grieve.

break with, 1. to stop being friendly or intimate with. 2. to stop conforming to.

SYN.*—break,** the most general of these terms, expresses their basic idea of separating into pieces as a result of impact, stress, etc.; **smash** and **crash** add connotations of suddenness, violence, and noise; **crush** suggests a crumpling or pulverizing pressure; **shatter,** sudden fragmentation and a scattering of pieces; **crack,** incomplete separation of parts or a sharp, snapping noise in breaking; **split,** separation lengthwise, as along the direction of grain or layers; **fracture,** the breaking of a hard or rigid substance, as bone or rock; **splinter,** the splitting of wood, etc. into long thin, sharp pieces. All of these terms are used figuratively to imply great force or damage (to ***break one's heart, ***smash*** one's hopes, ***crush*** the opposition, ***shatter*** one's nerves, etc.).

break (brāk), *n.* [prob. < *break* (to break a horse)], a large, four-wheeled carriage for six or more passengers: also spelled **brake.**

break·a·ble (brāk'ə-b'l), ***adj.*** that can be broken. ***n.*** a thing easily broken; fragile article.

break·age (brāk'ij), *n.* [see -AGE], 1. a breaking or being broken; break. 2. things or quantity broken. 3. loss or damage due to breaking. 4. the sum allowed for such loss or damage.

break·bone fever (brāk'bōn'), dengue.

break·down (brāk'doun'), *n.* 1. a breaking down; failure to work, as of machinery. 2. a failure of health; physical collapse: as, he had a nervous *breakdown.* 3. decomposition. 4. an analysis. 5. a lively, shuffling dance originated by American Negroes. ***adj.*** in *electricity*, causing the failure of an insulator: said of an excessive voltage.

break·er (brāk'ẽr), *n.* 1. a person or thing that breaks. 2. a device for breaking up rock, coal, etc. 3. a wave that breaks into foam. —***SYN.*** see **wave.**

break·er (brāk'ẽr), *n.* [Sp. *barrica*], a small keg for water, often carried in boats.

break·fast (brek'fəst), *n.* [*break* + *fast, n.*], the first meal of the day. ***v.i.*** to eat breakfast. ***v.t.*** to give breakfast to.

breakfast food, any prepared cereal for eating at breakfast.

break-front (brāk'frunt'), ***adj.*** having a break front. ***n.*** a large cabinet with a break front.

break front, a front, as of a cabinet, with the continuity of the main surface broken.

break·neck (brāk'nek'), ***adj.*** that may cause a broken neck; dangerous to life and limb: as, *breakneck* speed.

break of day, dawn; daybreak.

break·through (brāk'thro͞o'), *n.* the act, result, or place of breaking through against resistance, as in warfare.

break·up (brāk'up'), *n.* 1. a breaking up; dispersion. 2. a disintegration or decay. 3. a collapse. 4. a stopping or ending.

break·wa·ter (brāk'wô'tẽr, brāk'wot'ẽr), *n.* a barrier to break the impact of waves, as before a harbor.

bream (brēm), *n.* [*pl.* BREAM, BREAMS (brēmz); see PLURAL, II, D, 2], [ME. *breme;* OFr. *bresme* < OHG. *brahsima;* IE. base **bherek-*, to shine, gleam], 1. a European fresh-water fish related to the carp. 2. any of various salt-water fishes, as the sea bream. 3. any of a number of fresh-water sunfishes.

bream (brēm), ***v.t.*** [D. *brem*, furze; see BRAMBLE], to clean (a ship's bottom), originally with burning furze.

breast (brest), *n.* [ME. *breest, brest;* AS. *breost;* akin to G. *brust;* IE. base **bhreus*, to swell, sprout], 1. either of two milk-secreting glands protruding from the upper, front part of a woman's body. 2. a corresponding gland in a female primate. 3. a corresponding undeveloped gland in the male. 4. figuratively, a source of nourishment. 5. the upper, front part of the body, between the shoulders, neck, and abdomen. 6. the part of a garment, etc. that is over the breast. 7. the breast regarded as the source of emotions; hence, 8. one's feelings. 9. anything like the breast: as, the *breast* of the sea. 10. in *mining*, the face of an excavation or tunnel. ***v.t.*** 1. to oppose the breast to; face. 2. to face firmly; oppose; contend with. 3. to move forward against.

make a clean breast of, to confess (guilt, etc.) fully.

***SYN.*—breast** refers to the front part of the human torso from the shoulders to the abdomen, or it designates either of the female mammary glands; **bosom** refers to the entire human breast but, except in euphemistic applications (a big-*bosomed* matron), is now more common in figurative usage where it implies the human breast as a source of feeling, a protective, loving enclosure, etc. (the *bosom* of his family); **bust,** as considered here, almost always implies the female breasts and is the conventional term in referring to silhouette, form, etc., as in garment fitting, beauty contests, etc.

breast·bone (brest'bōn'), *n.* a thin, flat bone extending down the front of the chest and attached to the ends of the upper ribs by cartilages; sternum.

Breas·ted, James Henry (bres'tid), 1865–1935; American Egyptologist and historian.

breast-feed (brest'fēd'), ***v.t.*** [BREAST-FED (-fed'), BREAST-FEEDING], to feed (a baby) milk from the breast; suckle; nurse.

breast·pin (brest'pin'), *n.* an ornamental pin or brooch worn on a dress, near the throat.

breast·plate (brest'plāt'), *n.* 1. a piece of armor for the breast: see **armor,** illus. 2. in ancient times, an embroidered cloth set with twelve jewels representing the twelve tribes of Israel, worn on the breast by a Jewish high priest. 3. a strap across the breast of a saddled horse. 4. the abdominal part of a turtle's shell; plastron.

breast stroke, 1. a stroke in which the swimmer faces the water and brings both arms outward and sideways from a position close to the chest, at the same time drawing up the legs and then extending them quickly backward. 2. a variation of this in which the arms are stretched forward and brought back to the sides.

breast·work (brest'wũrk'), *n.* a low, quickly constructed barrier to protect gunners.

breath (breth), *n.* [ME. *breth;* AS. *bræth*, odor, exhalation; akin to G. *brodem*, vapor; IE. base **bher-*, to boil up, foam up (of water, etc.), as also in L. *fer-mentum;* cf. BARM, FERMENT], 1. air or vapor given off from anything. 2. air carrying fragrance; odor. 3. air taken into and let out of the lungs. 4. breathing; respiration. 5. the capacity to breathe; power to breathe easily. 6. life; spirit. 7. a puff or whiff, as of air; slight breeze. 8. something produced by a breath, as moisture on a mirror. 9. a whisper; murmur; word or words. 10. the time taken by a single respiration; a moment. 11. a slight pause or rest. 12. in *phonetics*, a voiceless exhalation of air producing a hiss or puff, as in pronouncing *s* or *p*.

below one's breath, in a whisper or murmur.

catch one's breath, 1. to gasp or pant. 2. to pause or rest so as to regain a normal rhythm of breathing.

in the same breath, almost simultaneously.

out of breath, breathless from or as from exertion.

save one's breath, to refrain from talking: said when talk would be useless.

under one's breath, in a whisper or murmur.

breath·a·ble (brēth'ə-b'l), ***adj.*** that can be breathed; fit to be breathed.

breathe (brēth), ***v.i.* & *v.t.*** [BREATHED (brēthd), BREATHING], [ME. *brethen* < *breth;* see BREATH], 1. to take (air) into the lungs and let it out again; alternately inhale and exhale. 2. to inhale. 3. to exhale. 4. to live. 5. to give out (an odor). 6. to give out or come out from or as from the lungs: as, he *breathed* confidence into his followers. 7. to blow softly. 8. to speak or sing softly; whisper; murmur. 9. to give or take time to breathe; rest: as, *breathe* your horse. 10. to pant (with *hard*) or cause to pant, as from exertion. 11. in *phonetics*, to speak without voicing.

breathe again (or **freely**), to have a feeling of relief or reassurance.

breathe one's last, to die.

not breathe a word, to say nothing; keep a secret.

breathed (bretht; *also, for 2,* brēthd), ***adj.*** [pp. of *breathe*], 1. having a (specified kind of) breath: usually in hyphenated compounds, as, *foul-breathed.* 2. in *phonetics*, voiceless.

breath·er (brēth'ẽr), *n.* 1. a person who breathes in a certain way: as, a mouth *breather.* 2. [Colloq.], a thing that causes panting or increased breathing, as brisk exercise. 3. [Colloq.], a rest to regain one's breath.

breath·ing (brēth'iŋ), ***adj.*** [ppr. of *breathe*], 1. that breathes; living; alive. 2. lifelike. ***n.*** 1. respiration. 2. a single respiration. 3. the time taken by a single respiration; a moment. 4. a light breeze. 5. aspiration; yearning. 6. utterance. 7. the sound of the letter *h* in English; an aspirate. 8. a mark to show an *h* sound, as before some initial vowels in Greek.

breathing space, 1. enough space or time to breathe freely. 2. a chance to rest or consider a situation.

breath·less (breth′lis), *adj.* 1. without breath. 2. no longer breathing; dead. 3. out of breath; panting or gasping. 4. holding the breath or unable to breathe normally because of excitement, eagerness, fear, etc. 5. having no breeze; stifling.
breath-tak·ing (breth′tāk′iŋ), *adj.* 1. that takes one's breath away; hence, 2. very exciting; thrilling.
breath·y (breth′i), *adj.* characterized by an excessive and audible emission of breath: said of the voice, speech, a speaker, etc.
B. Rec., b. rec., bills receivable.
brec·ci·a (brech′i-ə, bresh′i-ə), *n.* [It., a breach, fragments of stone; see BRASH], a rock consisting of sharp-cornered bits, often of glacial or volcanic origin, cemented together by sand, clay, or lime.
Brecht, Ber·tolt (ber′tôlt breHt; Eng., brekt), 1898–1956; German dramatist.
Breck·in·ridge, John Cabell (brek′in-rij), 1821–1875; American statesman; vice-president of the United States (1857–1861); Confederate secretary of war.
Breck·nock·shire (brek′nək-shir′), *n.* a county of Wales: area, 733 sq. mi.; pop., 56,000.
bred (bred), past tense and past participle of **breed.**
Bre·da (brā-dä′), *n.* a city in the Netherlands: pop., 109,000.
brede (brēd), *n.* [var. of *braid* (band)], [Archaic], a braid; design or piece of embroidery.
bree (brē), *n.* [ME. *bre;* AS. *briw*], [Scot.], broth.
breech (brēch), *n.* [ME. *breech, breche;* AS. *brec,* pl. of *broc;* akin to G. *bruch;* IE. base, either **bhrāg-*, to smell (cf. FRAGRANT), or **bhrăg-*, to make a crackling noise], 1. the buttocks; rump. 2. the under or back part of a thing, as of a pulley. 3. the part of a gun behind the barrel. *v.t.* (brēch, brich), 1. to clothe with breeches. 2. to provide with a breech, as a gun.
breech·block (brēch′blok′), *n.* the steel part of a breech-loading gun which when open permits loading and when closed receives the force of the combustion.
breech·cloth (brēch′klôth′, brēch′kloth′), *n.* a cloth worn to cover the buttocks; loincloth.
breech·clout (brēch′klout′), *n.* a breechcloth.
breech delivery, the delivery of a fetus presenting itself with its breech at the head of the birth canal.
breech·es (brich′iz), *n.pl.* [see BREECH], 1. trousers reaching to the knees. 2. [Colloq.], any trousers.
breeches buoy, a device for rescuing people at sea, consisting of a pair of short canvas breeches suspended from a life preserver that is run along a rope from ship to shore or to another ship.
breech·ing (brich′iŋ, brēch′iŋ), *n.* 1. a harness strap put around a horse's hindquarters to help him hold back on a down grade. 2. the parts of a gun that make up the breech.
breech·less (brēch′lis), *adj.* 1. without a breech. 2. without breeches.
breech·load·er (brēch′lōd′ẽr), *n.* any breech-loading gun.

BREECHES BUOY

breech-load·ing (brēch′lōd′iŋ), *adj.* loading at the breech instead of the muzzle, as many guns.
breed (brēd), *v.t.* [BRED (bred), BREEDING], [ME. *breden;* AS. *bredan,* to produce or cherish offspring < *brod,* fetus, hatching, brood; see BROOD; cf. FOOD, FEED], 1. to bring forth (offspring) from the womb; hatch from the egg; hence, 2. to be the source of; produce: as, ignorance *breeds* prejudice. 3. to cause to reproduce; raise: as, he *breeds* dogs. 4. to rear; train: as, he *bred* his son to the medical profession. *v.i.* 1. to be produced; originate: as, crime *breeds* in slums. 2. to bring forth offspring; reproduce. *n.* 1. a race or stock, especially one with certain inherited characteristics: as, there are many *breeds* of dog. 2. a kind; sort; type: as, men of the same *breed.*
breed·er (brēd′ẽr), *n.* 1. an animal or plant that produces offspring. 2. a person who breeds animals or plants. 3. a cause; source; originator.
breeder reactor, a nuclear reactor that, in addition to generating atomic energy, creates additional fuel by producing more fissionable material than it consumes.
breed·ing (brēd′iŋ), *n.* [see BREED], 1. the producing of young. 2. the rearing of young; upbringing. 3. good upbringing; good manners and intelligent social behavior: as, tolerance is a sign of *breeding.* 4. the producing of plants and animals, especially for the purpose of improving the stock.
Breed's Hill, a hill near Bunker Hill in Boston, where the Battle of Bunker Hill was actually fought.
breeks (brēks), *n.pl.* [Dial.], breeches.
breeze (brēz), *n.* [16th-c. nautical term *brize* < Sp. & Port. *briza,* northeast wind; cf. It. *brezza,* cold wind from the north], 1. a light current of air; wind, especially a gentle wind. 2. [Colloq.], commotion or disturbance. 3. in *meteorology,* any wind ranging in speed from 4 to 31 miles per hour: designated as light (4–7 mph), gentle (8–12 mph), moderate (13–18 mph), fresh (19–24 mph), and strong (25–31 mph). *v.i.* 1. to blow: as, it's beginning to *breeze.* 2. [Slang], to move or go briskly or jauntily. —*SYN.* see **wind.**
breeze (brēz), *n.* [Fr. *braise,* live coals, embers; see BRAZE (to solder)], a substance left when coke or charcoal is burned, used as a filler for concrete, etc.
breeze·way (brēz′wā), *n.* a covered passageway between a house and garage, sometimes enclosed on the sides.
breez·i·ly (brēz′′l-i), *adv.* in a breezy manner; briskly; jauntily.
breez·i·ness (brēz′i-nis), *n.* a breezy quality or state.
breez·y (brēz′i), *adj.* [BREEZIER (-i-ẽr), BREEZIEST (-i-ist)], 1. having a breeze or breezes; breeze-swept. 2. brisk; lively; carefree: as, he has a *breezy* manner.
Bre·genz (brā′gents), *n.* a city in western Austria, on Lake Constance: pop., 21,000.
breg·ma (breg′mə), *n.* [*pl.* BREGMATA (-mə-tə)], [Gr. *bregma*], the part of the skull where the frontal bone and side bones come together.
breg·mat·ic (breg-mat′ik), *adj.* of the bregma.
Bre·men (brā′mən, brem′ən), *n.* a port in northern Germany, on the Weser River: pop., 563,000.
Brem·er·ha·ven (brem′ẽr-hä′v′n; G. brā′mẽr-hä′fən), *n.* a seaport at the mouth of the Weser River in northern Germany: pop., 141,000.
Brem·er·ton (brem′ẽr-tən), *n.* a city in western Washington, on Puget Sound: pop., 30,000.
Bren·da (bren′də), [prob. fem. of *Brand* < G. *brand* or ON. *brandr,* a sword; see BRAND], a feminine name.
Bren gun (bren), [< *Br*no, Czechoslovakia, where first made + *En*field, England, where manufactured for the Brit. army], a light, fast, gas-operated machine gun used by the British army in World War II.
Bren·ner Pass (bren′ẽr), a mountain pass across the Alps at the border between Austria and Italy: height, 4,470 ft.

BRENNER PASS

brent (brent), *n.* a brant.
br'er (brũr), [S. Dial.], brother: used before a name.
Bre·scia (bre′shä), *n.* a city in northern Italy: pop., 147,000.
Bres·lau (bres′lô; G. bres′lou), *n.* a city in southwestern Poland, on the Oder River: formerly in Germany: pop., 429,000: Polish name, *Wrocław.*
Brest (brest), *n.* a city on the northwestern coast of France: pop., 111,000.
Brest-Li·tovsk (brest′li-tôfsk′), *n.* a city in the Byelorussian S.S.R.: pop., 73,000: under the terms of a treaty signed there by the Soviet Union and the Central Powers in 1918 the Soviet Union lost much territory, including the Ukraine, Poland, the Baltic Provinces, Finland, etc. Now called *Brest.*
Bre·tagne (brə′tån′y′), *n.* Brittany: the French name.
breth·ren (breth′rin, breth′rən), *n.pl.* [ME. *bretheren,* pl. of *brother*], [Archaic], brothers: now used only of fellow members of a fraternity, religious group, etc.
Bret·on (bret′′n), *adj.* [ult. same word as *Briton*], of Brittany, its people, or their language. *n.* 1. a native or inhabitant of Brittany. 2. the Celtic language of the Bretons: abbreviated **Bret., Br.** 3. a kind of hat with the brim turned upward all around, worn by girls and women: from the hat worn by Breton peasants.
Breton lace, a delicate lace with a design of heavy thread embroidered on net.
Bret·ton Woods (bret′′n), a village in the White Mountains of New Hampshire: an international conference was held there in 1944 to seek means for improving the world economic and monetary situation.
Breu·ghel, Jan (yän broo′g'l), 1568–1625; son of *Pieter;* Flemish painter: also spelled **Brueghel, Bruegel.**
Breughel, Pie·ter (pyā′tẽr), 1520?–1569; Flemish painter of peasant life: also spelled **Brueghel, Bruegel.**
breve (brēv), *n.* [It. < L. *brevis,* short], 1. a letter of authority, as from a pope. 2. a curved mark (˘) put over a vowel or syllable to show that it is short. 3. in *law,* a writ or brief. 4. in *music, a)* a note equal to two whole notes. *b)* the sign for this (|⊖|).
bre·vet (brə-vet′, brev′it), *n.* [ME.; OFr., a note, dim. of *bref,* a letter], in *military usage,* a commission promoting an officer to a higher rank without higher pay. *adj.* held or given by brevet. *v.t.* [BREVETTED or BREVETED (-id), BREVETTING or BREVETING], to give a brevet to. Abbreviated **brev., bvt.**
bre·vet·cy (brə-vet′si), *n.* [*pl.* BREVETCIES (-siz)], any rank conferred by brevet; honorary rank.
brev·i- (brev′i), [< L. *brevis,* short], a combining form meaning *short.*
bre·vi·ar·y (brē′vi-er′i, brev′i-er′i), *n.* [*pl.* BREVIARIES (-iz)], [L. *breviarium,* abridgment < *brevis,* short], a

book containing the daily offices and prayers of the Roman Catholic Church or the Orthodox Eastern Church.

bre·vier (brə-vêr′), *n.* [OFr. < L. *breviarium:* so called from use in printing breviaries], a size of type, 8 point. This line is in brevier.

brev·i·ros·trate (brev′i-ros′trāt), *adj.* [*brevi-* + *rostrate*], having a short beak or bill: said of a bird.

brev·i·ty (brev′ə-ti), *n.* [*pl.* BREVITIES (-tiz)], [L. *brevitas* < *brevis*, short], 1. the quality of being brief; shortness of time. 2. the quality of being concise; terseness.

brew (brōō), *v.t.* [ME. *brewen;* AS. *breowan;* akin to G. *brauen;* IE. base **bhreu, bhrū-*, to swell up, ferment, as also in *bread*], 1. to make (beer, ale, etc.) from malt and hops by steeping, boiling, and fermenting. 2. to make (tea, punch, etc.) by steeping, boiling, or mixing. 3. to plot; contrive. *v.i.* 1. to brew beer, ale, etc. 2. to begin to form, as a storm; gather. *n.* 1. a beverage brewed. 2. an amount brewed.

brew·age (brōō′ij), *n.* [*brew* + *-age*], 1. anything brewed; malt liquor. 2. brewing.

brew·er (brōō′ẽr), *n.* a person whose work or business is brewing beer, ale, etc.

brew·er·y (brōō′ẽr-i), *n.* [*pl.* BREWERIES (-iz)], an establishment where beer, ale, etc. are brewed.

brew·ing (brōō′iŋ), *n.* 1. the preparation of a brew. 2. a brew; amount of brew made at any one time.

brew·is (brōō′is), *n.* [ME. *brewes, brouwis;* OFr. *brouet, broues*, beef broth, dim. of *bro*, broth; Gmc. base **brod*, bread; cf. BREAD], [Dial.], 1. beef broth. 2. bread soaked in beef broth.

Brew·ster, William (brōō′stẽr), 1567?–1644; English settler of Plymouth Colony.

Bri·an (brī′ən), [Celt., strong], a masculine name: also spelled **Bryan.**

Brian Bo·ram·he (brēn bô-rō′, bô-rōō′), Brian Boru.

Bri·an Bo·ru (brī′ən bô-rō′, bô-rōō′), (Ir. *Brian Boramhe*), 926–1014 A.D.; king and hero of Ireland.

Bri·and, A·ris·tide (ȧ′rē′stēd′ brē′äN′), 1862–1932; French statesman; premier of France (1909–1911; 1921–1922; 1925–1926; 1929).

bri·ar (brī′ẽr), *n.* brier.

Bri·ar·e·an (brī-er′i-ən), *adj.* 1. of Briareus. 2. like Briareus; many-handed.

Bri·ar·e·us (brī-er′i-əs), *n.* [L.; Gr. *Briareōs* < *briaros*, strong], in *Greek mythology*, a hundred-handed giant who fought with the Olympians against the Titans.

bri·ar·root (brī′ẽr-rōōt′, brī′ẽr-root′), *n.* brierroot.

bri·ar·wood (brī′ẽr-wood′), *n.* brierwood.

bri·ar·y (brī′ẽr-i), *adj.* briery.

brib·a·ble (brīb′ə-b′l), *adj.* that can be bribed.

bribe (brīb), *n.* [ME.; OFr., morsel of bread given to beggars < *briber*, to beg], 1. anything, especially money, given or promised to induce a person to do something illegal or wrong. 2. anything given or promised to induce a person to do something against his wishes. *v.t.* [BRIBED (brībd), BRIBING], 1. to offer or give a bribe to. 2. to get or influence by bribing. *v.i.* to give a bribe or bribes.

brib·er·y (brīb′ẽr-i), *n.* [*pl.* BRIBERIES (-iz)], [ME. & OFr. *briberie*, theft, robbery; see BRIBE], the giving, offering, or taking of bribes.

bric-a-brac, bric-à-brac (brik′ə-brak′), *n.* [Fr. *bric-à-brac* < phr. *à bric et à brac*, by hook or crook], 1. small, rare, or artistic objects placed about a room for ornament. 2. knickknacks.

brick (brik), *n.* [16th c. < OFr. *brique, briche*, a fragment; akin to MD., MLG. *breken* & AS. *brecan*, to break (see BREAK)], 1. a substance made from clay molded into oblong blocks and baked by sun or fire, used in building, paving, etc. 2. one of these blocks, usually 2 1/2 x 4 x 8 inches. 3. bricks collectively. 4. anything shaped like a brick. 5. [Colloq.], a fine fellow. *adj.* 1. built or paved with brick. 2. like brick: as, *brick* red. *v.t.* 1. to build or pave with brick. 2. to close or wall in with brick (with *up* or *in*).

make bricks without straw, to do something without the necessary materials.

brick·bat (brik′bat′), *n.* 1. a piece of brick, especially one used as a missile; hence, 2. an unfavorable remark.

brick cheese, a semihard, elastic American cheese with a strong, sweetish taste, shaped like a brick and containing many small holes.

brick·kiln (brik′kil′, brik′kiln′), *n.* a furnace or oven for baking bricks.

brick·lay·er (brik′lā′ẽr), *n.* a person whose work is bricklaying.

brick·lay·ing (brik′lā′iŋ), *n.* the act or work of building or paving with bricks.

brick-red (brik′red′, brik′red′), *adj.* of the color brick red.

brick red, a yellowish or brownish red.

brick·work (brik′wũrk′), *n.* 1. anything built of bricks. 2. bricklaying.

brick·y (brik′i), *adj.* 1. made of or full of bricks. 2. like a brick, especially in color.

brick·yard (brik′yärd′), *n.* a place where bricks are made or sold.

bri·cole (bri-kōl′, brik′′l), *n.* [Fr.; akin to *break*], 1. a medieval catapult. 2. an indirect or oblique stroke. 3. a harness for men, used for dragging heavy guns through passages where horses cannot be used.

brid·al (brīd′′l), *n.* [ME. *brydale;* AS. *brydealo*, bridal, bride-ale, bride feast; *bryd*, bride + *ealo*, ale], a wedding. *adj.* 1. of a bride. 2. of a wedding.

Bri·dal·veil (brī′d′l-vāl′), *n.* a waterfall in Yosemite National Park, California: height, 620 ft.

bridal wreath, a kind of spiraea, a shrub with dark, glossy leaves and small, white flowers.

bride (brīd), *n.* [ME. *bride, bryde;* AS. *bryd;* akin to G. *braut*, betrothed, fiancée; prob. < base of *bread, brew*, as *lord, lady* < *loaf*], a woman who has just been married or is about to be married.

bride (brīd), *n.* [Fr.; OFr. *bridle;* ME. *bridel;* see BRIDLE], in lacemaking and other needlework, a loop or tie that connects parts of a pattern.

bride·groom (brīd′grōōm′, brīd′groom′), *n.* [ME. *bridegome;* AS. *brydguma*, suitor < *bryd*, bride + *guma* (akin to L. *homo*), man; the modern *-groom* is due to folk etym.], a man who has just been married or is about to be married.

brides·maid (brīdz′mād′), *n.* one of the women attending the bride just before and during a wedding.

bride·well (brīd′wel, brīd′wəl), *n.* [after a former house of correction in London, orig. a royal palace, named from the near-by *St. Bride's* (*Bridget's*) *Well*], a prison for minor offenses; jail; house of correction.

bridge (brij), *n.* [ME. *brigge, brugge;* AS. *brycg, bricg;* IE. base **bhrū, bhrēu-*, log, beam, stick, hence wooden causeway], 1. a structure built over a river, railroad, highway, etc. to provide a way across for vehicles or pedestrians. 2. a thing like a bridge. 3. the bony part of the nose. 4. the curved bow of a pair of glasses fitting over the nose. 5. the thin, removable arch over which the strings are stretched on some musical instruments: see **violin,** illus. 6. a reef or ridge in a channel. 7. a platform above the main deck of a ship, from which it is controlled, as by the commanding officer. 8. a dividing partition for keeping fuel in place in a furnace or boiler. 9. in *billiards & pool*, a cue rest, a notched piece of wood at the end of a rod. 10. in *dancing*, a bending backward to touch the floor. 11. in *dentistry*, a fixed or removable mounting for false teeth, attached to a real tooth or teeth. 12. in *electricity*, a device used primarily in measuring resistances, frequencies, etc., by comparing the effect of the unknown element with that of a known or standard element in the circuit. 13. in *music*, a connecting passage between two subjects, as in a composition in sonata form: also **bridge passage.** *v.t.* [BRIDGED (brijd), BRIDGING], 1. to build a bridge on or over. 2. to make a passage over; span; get across.

burn one's bridges, to cut off all of one's ways to retreat.

bridge (brij), *n.* [earlier (1886) *biritch*, "Russian whist," altered after *bridge;* game and name possibly of Russ. origin], a card game similar to whist: see **auction bridge, contract bridge.**

bridge·board (brij′bôrd′, brij′bōrd′), *n.* any of the notched boards holding the steps of a wooden staircase.

bridge·head (brij′hed′), *n.* [after Fr. *tête de pont*], a fortified place or position established by an attacking force on the enemy's side of a bridge, river, or gap.

Bridge of Sighs, 1. a covered passageway between the Doges' Palace and the prisons in Venice. 2. a passageway formerly joining the Tombs prison and the criminal court in New York City.

Bridge·port (brij′pôrt′, brij′pōrt′), *n.* a city in Connecticut, on Long Island Sound: pop., 157,000.

Bridg·es, Robert (brij′əz), 1844–1930; English poet and physician; poet laureate (1913–1930).

Bridg·et (brij′it), [Ir. *Brighid*, lit., strong, lofty; akin to Sans. *bṛhatī*, high, powerful], a feminine name: diminutive, *Biddy;* equivalents, Fr. & G. *Brigitte.*

Bridget, Saint, 1303?–1373; Swedish nun; founder of the Order of the Most Holy Saviour.

Bridge·town (brij′toun), *n.* the principal city of Barbados, in the West Indies Federation: pop., 19,000.

bridge·work (brij′wũrk′), *n.* 1. the building of bridges. 2. a fixed or removable mounting for a false tooth or teeth, fastened to a real tooth or teeth. 3. the making of such mountings.

bridg·ing (brij′iŋ), *n.* braces used between timbers, as of a floor, for reinforcement and distribution of strain.

bri·dle (brī′d′l), *n.* [ME. *bridel;* AS. *bridel, bridels*, earlier *brigdels* < *bregdan*, to pull, turn; see BRAID], 1. a head harness for guiding a horse: it consists of headstall, bit, and reins. 2. a thing like a horse's bridle. 3. anything that controls or restrains. *v.t.*

[BRIDLED (-d'ld), BRIDLING], 1. to put a bridle on. 2. to curb or control with or as with a bridle. *v.i.* 1. to raise one's head high with the chin drawn in as an expression of anger, scorn, pride, etc.; hence, 2. to become angry, scornful, etc.: as, he *bridled* at the idea that his work was clumsy. —*SYN.* see **restrain.**

bridle hand, the hand in which the reins are usually held; left hand.

bridle path, a path for horseback riding.

bri·dle-wise (brī'd'l-wīz'), *adj.* trained to obey the pressure of the reins on the neck instead of the pull on the bit.

bri·doon (bri-dōōn'), *n.* [Fr. *bridon* < *bride,* a bridle, check], the snaffle bit and reins of a military bridle, used with or without curbs.

Brie cheese (brē), [after *Brie,* France, where first made], 1. a soft, white cheese imported from France. 2. an American cheese resembling this.

brief (brēf), *adj.* [OFr. *bref, brief;* L. *brevis*], 1. of short duration. 2. short in length. 3. terse; concise. 4. curt. *n.* [ME. *bref;* OFr. *bref, brief;* L. *breve,* summary, short catalogue < the *adj.*], 1. a summary. 2. a short catalogue of the main points of a law case for use in court by counsel. 3. in the *Roman Catholic Church,* a papal letter less formal than a bull. *v.t.* 1. to summarize. 2. [British], to furnish with a legal brief; hence, 3. [British], to hire as counsel. 4. in *military usage,* to give (a person) all the pertinent facts about a planned operation: as, the pilots were *briefed* before each flight. 5. [Colloq.], to tell about.

hold a brief for, to argue in behalf of or in defense of.

in brief, in short; in a few words.

SYN.—**brief** and **short** are opposites of *long* in their application to duration (a *brief* or *short* interval), although **brief** often emphasizes compactness, conciseness, etc. (a *brief* review) and **short** often implies incompleteness or curtailment (a *short* measure, to make *short* work of it); **short** is usually used where linear extent is referred to (a *short* man). See also **abridgment.**—*ANT.* long, prolonged.

brief case, a flat case or bag, usually of leather, for carrying papers, books, etc.

brief·less (brēf'lis), *adj.* 1. without a brief; hence, 2. without clients: said of a lawyer.

brief of title, in *law,* an abstract, or summary, of all the legal documents, records, and court proceedings affecting the title to a piece of property.

briefs (brēfs), *n.pl.* [see BRIEF], legless undershorts.

bri·er (brī'ẽr), *n.* [ME. *brere* (with vowel change as in *friar,* ME. *frere*); AS. *brer, brær* < same IE. base as *broom*], 1. any prickly or thorny bush, as a bramble, wild rose, etc. 2. a growth of such bushes. 3. a twig of a brier. Also spelled **briar.**

bri·er (brī'ẽr), *n.* [Fr. *bruyère,* white heath], 1. the tree heath, bearing a root from which tobacco pipes are made. 2. this root. 3. a pipe made from this root. Also spelled **briar.**

bri·er·root (brī'ẽr-rōōt', brī'ẽr-root'), *n.* brierwood: also spelled **briarroot.**

bri·er·wood (brī'ẽr-wood'), *n.* 1. the root wood, especially the root burl, of the brier (white heath). 2. a tobacco pipe made of this. Also spelled **briarwood.**

bri·er·y (brī'ẽr-i), *adj.* full of briers; prickly: also spelled **briary.**

Bri·eux, Eu·gène (ö'zhen' brē'ö'), 1858–1932; French dramatist.

brig (brig), *n.* [< *brigantine*], a two-masted ship with square sails: abbreviated **br.**

brig (brig), *n.* [< ?], 1. the prison on a United States warship. 2. [Military Slang], the guardhouse.

Brig., 1. Brigade. 2. Brigadier.

bri·gade (bri-gād'), *n.* [Fr.; It. *brigata,* troop, company < *brigare,* to contend < LL. *briga,* strife, quarrel], 1. a large unit of soldiers. 2. formerly, a unit of the United States Army comprising two or more regiments and commanded by a brigadier general. 3. any group of people organized to do a particular thing or acting under an authority: as, a fire *brigade.* *v.t.* [BRIGADED (-id), BRIGADING], 1. to gather into a brigade. 2. to sort into groups; classify.

brig·a·dier (brig'ə-dêr'), *n.* [Fr. < *brigade;* see BRIGADE], 1. a person commanding a brigade. 2. in the United States armed forces, a brigadier general. 3. in the British armed forces, an officer temporarily commanding a brigade. Abbreviated **Brig.** (as a title). 4. in the French army, a cavalry corporal.

brigadier general, [*pl.* BRIGADIER GENERALS], a military officer ranking above a colonel and below a major general: now normally an assistant divisional commander: abbreviated **Brig. Gen., B.G.** (as a title).

brig·and (brig'ənd), *n.* [Fr.; It. *brigante* < *brigare;* see BRIGADE], a bandit, usually one of a roving band.

brig·and·age (brig'ən-dij), *n.* [Fr. < *brigand*], 1. organized plundering. 2. brigands collectively.

brig·an·dine (brig'ən-dēn', brig'ən-dīn'), *n.* [Fr.; It. *brigantina* < *brigare;* see BRIGADE], a flexible coat of armor made of small metal scales or rings sewed onto leather or linen.

brig·an·tine (brig'ən-tēn', brig'ən-tīn'), *n.* [Fr. *brigantin;* It. *brigantino,* brigantine, pirate vessel; see BRIGAND], a two-masted ship with the mainmast fore-and-aft-rigged and the foremast square-rigged; hermaphrodite brig.

Brig. Gen., Brigadier General.

bright (brīt), *adj.* [ME. *briht;* AS. *bryht,* earlier *beorht;* akin to OHG. *beraht,* Goth. *bairhts,* shining, gleaming; IE. base **bherĕg-,* to gleam, white; cf. BIRCH], 1. shining; giving light; full of light. 2. brilliant in color or sound; vivid; clear. 3. lively; vivacious; cheerful. 4. mentally quick; clever. 5. reflecting happiness or hope. 6. famous; illustrious. 7. favorable; auspicious. *adv.* in a bright manner. *n.* [Poetic], brightness; splendor.

SYN.—**bright,** the most general term here, implies the giving forth or reflecting of light, or a being filled with light (a *bright* day, star, shield, etc.); **radiant** emphasizes the actual or apparent emission of rays of light; **shining** implies a steady, continuous brightness (the *shining* sun); **brilliant** implies intense or flashing brightness (*brilliant* sunlight, diamonds, etc.); **luminous** is applied to objects that are full of light or give off reflected or phosphorescent light; **lustrous** is applied to objects whose surfaces gleam by reflected light and emphasizes gloss or sheen (*lustrous* silk). See also **intelligent.**—*ANT.* dull, dim, dark.

Bright, John (brīt), 1811–1889; English statesman, political economist, and orator.

bright·en (brīt''n), *v.t. & v.i.* [ME. *brihten;* AS. *brihtan, beorhtan* < *beorht*], 1. to make or become bright or brighter. 2. to make or become happy or happier; gladden; cheer up.

bright·ness (brīt'nis), *n.* 1. the quality or condition of being bright. 2. the luminous aspect of a color (as distinct from its hue) by which it is regarded as approaching the maximum luminosity of pure white or the lack of luminosity of pure black.

Brigh·ton (brī't'n), *n.* a resort city on the southern coast of England: pop., 146,000.

Bright's disease, [after Dr. Richard *Bright* (1789–1858), London physician who first diagnosed it], a kidney inflammation characterized by the presence of albumin in the urine; nephritis.

Brig·id, Saint (brij'id, brē'id), 453–523 A.D.; Irish abbess and patron saint: also **Bridget,** sometimes confused with Saint Bridget of Sweden.

brill (bril), *n.* [*pl.* BRILL, BRILLS (brilz); see PLURAL, II, D, 2], [? < Corn. *brilli,* mackerel], an edible European flatfish related to the turbot.

Brill, Abraham Ar·den (är'd'n bril), 1874–1948; American psychoanalyst born in Austria.

Bril·lat-Sa·va·rin, An·thelme (än'telm' brē'yȧ'sȧ'vȧ'ran'), 1755–1826; French expert on foods and cooking.

bril·liance (bril'yəns), *n.* [< *brilliant*], 1. great brightness or radiance. 2. intensity or vividness, as of a color or musical tone. 3. splendor; magnificence. 4. keen intelligence; quickness of mind.

bril·lian·cy (bril'yən-si), *n.* brilliance.

bril·liant (bril'yənt), *adj.* [Fr. *brillant,* sparkling, ppr. of *briller,* to sparkle, glitter < It. *brillare,* sparkle, whirl], 1. shining brightly; sparkling. 2. vivid. 3. splendid; magnificent. 4. very able; keenly intelligent; talented. *n.* 1. a gem, especially a diamond, cut in a certain way with many facets to increase its sparkle. 2. this way of cutting a gem. 3. in *printing,* the smallest size of type in common use, 3 1/2 point. This line is in brilliant.—*SYN.* see **bright, intelligent.**

bril·lian·tine (bril'yən-tēn', bril'yən-tēn'), *n.* [Fr. *brillantine;* see BRILLIANT & -INE], 1. an oily liquid that gives gloss to the hair. 2. a glossy cloth made of mohair and cotton.

brim (brim), *n.* [ME.; AS. *brim, brymm,* sea, surf, edge of the sea; IE. base **bher-,* point, edge; cf. BROOM], 1. the topmost edge of a cup, glass, bowl, etc. 2. a rim or edge around a body of water. 3. the water at such an edge. 4. the projecting rim or edge of anything: as, the *brim* of a hat. *v.t.* [BRIMMED (brimd), BRIMMING], to fill to the brim. *v.i.* to be full to the brim. —*SYN.* see **border.**

brim·ful, brim·full (brim'fool', brim'fool'), *adj.* full to the brim.

brim·mer (brim'ẽr), *n.* a cup, glass, or bowl filled to the brim; bumper.

brim·stone (brim'stōn'), *n.* [ME. *brimston, brinston, bernston* < *brinnen, brennen,* to burn + *ston,* a stone], sulfur.

Brin·di·si (brin'də-zi; It. brēn'dē-zē), *n.* a city in southeastern Italy: pop., 42,000: naval base on the Adriatic: ancient name, *Brundisium.*

brin·dle (brin'd'l), *n.* [< *brindled*], 1. a brindled color. 2. a brindled animal. *adj.* brindled.

brin·dled (brin'd'ld), *adj.* [< earlier *brinded,* after *kindled,* etc.; prob. < ME. *brended* < *brennen,* to burn], streaked or spotted with a darker color: said especially of a gray or tawny cow, dog, etc.

brine (brīn), *n.* [ME.; AS. *bryne;* akin to D. *brijn;* IE. base **bhrēi-,* to cut; orig. sense "cutting, sharp"], 1. water full of salt; any heavily saturated salt solution; hence, 2. any large body of salt water, as the ocean. *v.t.* [BRINED (brīnd), BRINING], to put into brine, as in pickling.

Bri·nell test (bri-nel'), [after Swed. metallurgist, J. A.

Brinell], a test for determining the relative hardness of a metal by measuring the diameter of the indentation made when a hardened steel ball is forced into the metal under a given pressure.

bring (briŋ), ***v.t.*** [BROUGHT (brôt), BRINGING], [ME. *bringen;* AS. *bringan;* akin to G. *bringen;* base only in Gmc. & Celt.], 1. to cause (a person or thing) to come along together with oneself; take along (*to* a place or person); fetch. 2. to cause to come about; make happen: as, fascism *brought* disaster. 3. to cause to have: as, rest *brings* one health. 4. to lead, persuade, or influence along a course of action or belief. 5. to cost or sell for: as, used cars *brought* a good price in June. 6. in *law, a*) to present in a law court: as, *bring* charges. *b*) to advance (evidence, etc.).

bring about, to cause; make happen; accomplish.

bring around (or **round**), 1. to cause to change an opinion; convince; persuade. 2. to put or coax into a good humor. 3. [Colloq.], to bring back to consciousness or health. 4. [Colloq.], to bring on a visit.

bring down, 1. to cause to come down or fall; hence, 2. to wound or kill. 3. to cause to lessen.

bring forth, 1. to give birth to; produce (fruit, flowers, etc.). 2. to make manifest; disclose.

bring forward, 1. to introduce; show. 2. in *bookkeeping*, to carry over.

bring in, 1. to import. 2. to produce, as income or revenue. 3. to give (a verdict or report).

bring off, to accomplish.

bring on, 1. to cause; cause to begin or happen. 2. to aid in advancing.

bring out, 1. to expose; reveal; make clear. 2. to bring (a play, person, etc.) before the public; publish (a book, magazine, etc.). 3. to cause to appear. 4. to introduce (a girl) formally to society.

bring over, 1. to cause to change an opinion; convince; persuade. 2. to bring on a visit.

bring to, 1. to revive (a person who is unconscious, drunk, etc.). 2. to cause (a ship) to stop.

bring up, 1. to take care of during infancy and childhood; rear. 2. to introduce, as into discussion. 3. to cough up. 4. to vomit. 5. to stop abruptly.

SYN.—**bring** (in strict usage) implies a carrying or conducting to and **take,** similar action away from, a specified or implied place (*bring* the book to me; I will *take* it back to the library); **fetch** implies a going after something, getting it, and bringing it back.

bring·ing-up (briŋ′iŋ-up′), ***n.*** 1. care during infancy and childhood; rearing. 2. education, especially in how to behave. Also **upbringing.**

brink (briŋk), ***n.*** [ME. < Anglo-N. form of ON. *brekka*, hillside], the edge, especially at the top of any steep place; verge: often used figuratively, as, he is on the *brink* of disaster. —***SYN.*** see **border.**

brink·man·ship (briŋk′mən-ship′), ***n.*** [*brink* + *-manship*, as in *statesmanship*], the policy of pursuing a course of action to the brink of catastrophe.

brin·y (brin′i), ***adj.*** [BRINIER (-i-ẽr), BRINIEST (-i-ist)], of or like brine; very salty.

‡**bri·o** (brē′ō), ***n.*** [It.], animation; vivacity; zest.

bri·oche (brē′ōsh, brē′osh; Fr. brē′ôsh′), ***n.*** [*pl.* BRIOCHES (-iz; Fr. brē′ôsh′)], [Fr.], a light roll made with butter, eggs, and yeast.

bri·o·lette (brē′ə-let′), ***n.*** [Fr. < *brillant*, a brilliant], a teardrop diamond cut in triangular facets: see **gem,** illus.

bri·o·ny (brī′ə-ni), ***n.*** [*pl.* BRIONIES (-niz)], a bryony.

bri·quette, bri·quet (bri-ket′), ***n.*** [Fr. *briquette*, dim. of *brique*, brick], a brick made of compressed coal dust, etc., used for fuel or kindling.

‡**bri·sance** (brē′zäns′), ***n.*** [Fr., lit., breaking, ppr. of *briser*, to break; OFr. *bruiser;* see BRUISE], the shattering effect of the sudden release of energy, as in an explosion of nitroglycerine or in nuclear fission.

Bris·bane (briz′bān, briz′bən), ***n.*** a seaport and the capital of Queensland, on the eastern coast of Australia: pop., 622,000.

Bri·se·is (brī-sē′is), ***n.*** [L.; Gr. *Brisēis*], in *Greek legend*, a pretty woman whose seizure by Agamemnon from Achilles, her captor, led to a quarrel between the men.

brisk (brisk), ***adj.*** [prob. < Fr. *brusque;* see BRUSQUE], 1. quick in manner or movement; keen and energetic. 2. keen; sharp; invigorating: as, the air was *brisk* and cold. —***SYN.*** see **active.**

bris·ket (bris′kit), ***n.*** [ME. *brusket;* prob. < OFr. *bruschet, brischet*, of Gmc. origin; cf. Dan. *bryske;* same IE. base as in *breast*], 1. the breast of an animal. 2. meat cut from this part: see **beef,** illus.

bris·ling (bris′liŋ), ***n.*** [Norm. dial. < older Dan. *bretling* < LG. *bretling*, lit., the broad one], a small, edible European fish resembling a sardine.

bris·tle (bris″l), ***n.*** [ME. *brustle, bristele* < AS. *byrst;* akin to G. *borste*, bristles; IE. base *bhares, *bhores-, point, sharp], 1. any short, stiff, prickly hair of an animal or plant. 2. any of the hairs of a hog or some other animals, used for brushes. 3. any of the hairs of a brush. ***v.i.*** [BRISTLED (-′ld), BRISTLING], 1. to be or become stiff and erect, like bristles. 2. to have one's hair stand up. 3. to stiffen with fear, anger, etc.; become ready for a fight. 4. to be thick with or as with bristles. ***v.t.*** 1. to cause to stand up like bristles. 2. to put bristles on or in. 3. to make bristly.

bris·tle·tail (bris″l-tāl′), ***n.*** any of several wingless insects with bristlelike parts at the posterior end.

bris·tly (bris′li), ***adj.*** [BRISTLIER (-li-ẽr), BRISTLIEST (-li-ist)], 1. having bristles; rough with bristles. 2. bristlelike; stiff and short; prickly.

Bris·tol (bris′t′l), ***n.*** 1. a seaport in southwestern England, on the Avon River: pop., 437,000. 2. a city in central Connecticut: pop., 45,000.

Bristol board (or **paper**), [after *Bristol*, England], a fine, smooth pasteboard, usually not glazed.

Bristol Channel, an arm of the Atlantic, between Wales and southwestern England: length, 85 mi.

brit (brit), ***n.pl.*** [*sing.* BRIT], [Corn. < OCelt. *brith*, varicolored; akin to Corn. *bruit*, speckled], 1. the young of the herring and some other fishes. 2. the small sea animals eaten by the whalebone whale.

Brit., 1. Britain. 2. Britannia. 3. British.

Brit·ain (brit″n, brit′ən), ***n.*** England, Wales, and Scotland: see **Great Britain:** abbreviated **Brit., Br.**

Bri·tan·ni·a (bri-tan′i-ə, bri-tan′yə), ***n.*** [L.], 1. Britain: the ancient Latin name: see **Roman Empire,** map. 2. Great Britain, including Ireland and the Dominions. 3. the British Empire. Abbreviated **Brit.** 4. [Poetic], the female figure symbolizing Britain or the British Empire. 5. [b-], Britannia metal.

Britannia metal, britannia metal, an alloy of tin, copper, and antimony, used in making tableware.

Bri·tan·nic (bri-tan′ik), ***adj.*** [L. *Britannicus* < *Britannia*], of Britain or Great Britain; British.

Brit·i·cism (brit′ə-siz′m), ***n.*** a word, phrase, or idiom peculiar to or characteristic of British English: as, *petrol* is a *Briticism* for *gasoline*.

Brit·ish (brit′ish), ***adj.*** [AS. *Brittisc, Brettisc* < *Bret, Bryt*, pl. *Brettas*, name of the Celt. inhabitants of Britain (cf. BRETON, BRETAGNE); of Celt. origin], 1. of Great Britain or its people. 2. of the British Commonwealth of Nations. ***n.*** 1. the language of the ancient Britons; Cymric. 2. British English. Abbreviated **Brit., Br., B.**

the British, the people of Great Britain: sometimes broadly applied to all the people of the British Commonwealth of Nations.

British America, 1. the British possessions in or adjacent to the Americas. 2. Canada: more properly, *British North America*.

British Columbia, a province of southwestern Canada: area, 366,255 sq. mi.; pop., 1,659,000; capital, Victoria: abbreviated **B.C.**

British Commonwealth of Nations, 1. the British Empire; political aggregate comprising: (1) the United Kingdom (Great Britain and Northern Ireland); the Channel Islands; the Isle of Man; the British colonies, protectorates, and dependencies; and (2) Canada, Australia, New Zealand, India, Pakistan, Ceylon, Malaysia, Ghana, Nigeria, Sierra Leone, Tanganyika, Uganda, Jamaica, Trinidad and Tobago, and Cyprus: area, 11,299,000 sq. mi.; pop., 727,919,000; capital, London. 2. occasionally, the United Kingdom and the Dominions.

British East Africa, a group of British territories in eastern Africa, including Kenya and the protectorate of Zanzibar: abbreviated **B.E.A.**

British Empire, 1. the British Commonwealth of Nations. 2. occasionally, the United Kingdom (Great Britain and Northern Ireland) and its dependencies.

British English, the English language as spoken and written in England: abbreviated **BrE.:** usually distinguished from *American English*.

Brit·ish·er (brit′ish-ẽr), ***n.*** a native of Great Britain, especially an Englishman: sometimes broadly applied to any British subject.

British Guiana, a British colony in northern South America, on the Atlantic: area, 83,000 sq. mi.; pop., 590,000; capital, Georgetown.

British Honduras, a British colony in Central America, on the Caribbean: area, 8,867 sq. mi; pop., 90,000; capital, Belize: abbreviated **Br. Hond.**

British India, the part of India formerly under British rule: see **India.**

British Isles, Great Britain, Ireland, the Isle of Man, and the Channel Islands.

Brit·ish·ism (brit′ish-iz′m), ***n.*** a Briticism.

British Malaya, British territories in the Malay Peninsula and the Malay Archipelago: the former name.

British Museum, a famous museum in London, containing art treasures, one of the largest libraries in the world, a department of natural history, etc.

British North America, Canada.

British Somaliland, a former British protectorate in eastern Africa: merged with Italian Somaliland to form the independent republic of Somalia.

British thermal unit, a unit of heat equal to 252 calories; quantity of heat required to raise the temperature of one pound of water from 62° F. to 63° F.: abbreviated **B.T.U., Btu, B.t.u.**

British West Africa, the former British possessions in western Africa.

British West Indies, the British possessions in the West Indies, including the West Indies Federation, the Bahamas, and Bermuda: abbreviated **B.W.I.**

Brit. Mus., British Museum.

Brit·on (brit'′n, brit'ən), *n.* [ME. & OFr. *Briton;* L. *Brito, Britto;* of Celt. origin; see BRITISH], 1. a native or inhabitant of Great Britain or the British Commonwealth of Nations. 2. a member of an early Celtic people living in the southern part of Britain at the time of the Roman invasion.

brits·ka (brits'kə), *n.* [Pol. *bryczka,* dim. of *bryka,* freight wagon], a long, spacious carriage with a folding top: also spelled **britzka, britzska.**

Brit·ta·ny (brit''n-i), *n.* a former province on the northwestern coast of France: French name, *Bretagne.*

BRITTANY

brit·tle (brit''l), *adj.* [ME. *britel, brutel* < AS. *breotan,* to break to pieces], easily broken or shattered; crisp. *n.* a crisp, breakable candy: as, peanut *brittle.* —*SYN.* see **fragile.**

Br·no (bŭr'nô), *n.* a city in central Czechoslovakia: pop., 306,000.

bro., [*pl.* BROS.], brother.

broach (brōch), *n.* [ME. *broche,* a pin, peg, spit; OFr. *broche, broc;* LL. *brocca,* a spike < L. *broccus,* with projecting teeth], 1. a sharp-pointed rod for holding roasting meat; spit; skewer. 2. a tapered bit pulled or pushed through a hole to make the hole larger or of a certain shape. 3. a mason's narrow chisel. 4. a hole made by a broach. 5. a brooch. *v.t.* 1. to make a hole in so as to let out liquid. 2. to start a discussion of; bring up; introduce. —*SYN.* see **utter.**

broad (brôd), *adj.* [ME. *brod;* AS. *brad;* akin to G. *breit*], 1. wide; of large extent from side to side. 2. having great extent or expanse; spacious. 3. extending about; clear; open: as, *broad* daylight. 4. open to the sight; obvious: as, a *broad* purpose. 5. strongly marked: said of dialects or accents. 6. outspoken; unreserved: as, a *broad* statement; hence, 7. ribald: as, a *broad* joke. 8. all-inclusive; tolerant; liberal: as, he takes a *broad* view of the matter. 9. extensive; general: as, in a *broad* sense that's true. 10. main; essential: as, in *broad* outline. 11. spoken with the tongue held flat and low in the mouth and the oral passage wide open, as *a* in *father*: the current phonetic term is *open.* *adv.* in a broad manner; widely. *n.* 1. the broad part of anything. 2. [Slang], a woman or girl: a vulgar term. *SYN.*—**broad** and **wide** both are applied to extent from side to side of surfaces having height or length, **wide** being preferred when the distance between limits is stressed (two feet *wide,* a *wide* **aperture**), and **broad,** when the full extent of surface is considered (*broad* hips, *broad* plains); **deep,** in this connection, refers to extent backward, as from the front, an opening, etc.; (a *deep* lot, a *deep* cave). —*ANT.* narrow.

broad arrow, 1. an arrow with a broad head. 2. an identification mark that the British government puts on its property and on prisoners' uniforms.

BROAD ARROW

broad·ax, broad·axe (brôd'aks'), *n.* an ax with a broad blade, used as a weapon or for cutting timber.

broad bean, a plant bearing large, thick, broad pods with flat seeds, used chiefly for fodder.

broad·bill (brôd'bil'), *n.* any of various birds with a broad bill, as the scaup and shoveler ducks, spoonbill, etc.

broad·brim (brôd'brim'), *n.* 1. a hat with a very broad brim, like that worn by Quakers; hence, 2. [often B-], [Colloq.], a Quaker; Friend.

broad·cast (brôd'kast', brôd'käst'), *v.t.* [BROADCAST or, *in radio,* BROADCASTED (-id), BROADCASTING], 1. to scatter (something) over a broad area. 2. to spread (information, etc.); inform many people of. 3. to transmit widely by radio. *v.i.* to broadcast radio programs. *adj.* 1. widely scattered. 2. of or for radio broadcasting. *n.* 1. a sowing by broadcasting. 2. a radio program. *adv.* far and wide.

broad·cast·er (brôd'kas'tẽr, brôd'käs'tẽr), *n.* 1. a person, organization, etc. that prepares, makes, or transmits radio broadcasts. 2. equipment for radio broadcasting; transmitter.

broadcasting station, 1. an organization for broadcasting radio programs: it is often part of a network. 2. the studios, offices, etc. of such an organization.

Broad-Church (brôd'chũrch'), *adj.* in the *Church of England,* 1. designating a group (*Broad Church*) with liberal views as to doctrine and communion. 2. of this group or its views.

broad·cloth (brôd'klôth', brôd'kloth'), *n.* 1. a fine, smooth woolen cloth: so called because it originally came in widths over a yard. 2. a fine, smooth cotton or silk cloth, used for shirts, etc.

broad·en (brôd''n), *v.t. & v.i.* to make or become broad or broader; widen; expand.

broad-gauge (brôd'gāj'), *adj.* 1. for or having a broad gauge. 2. [Colloq.], broad-minded.

broad gauge, 1. a width (between the rails) of more than 56 1/2 inches (standard gauge). 2. a railroad having such a gauge. 3. a locomotive or car for such a railroad.

broad-gauged (brôd'gājd'), *adj.* broad-gauge.

broad·ish (brôd'ish), *adj.* somewhat broad.

broad jump, a jump for distance rather than height, made either from a stationary position (*standing broad jump*) or with a running start (*running broad jump*).

broad·leaf (brôd'lēf'), *n.* any of various tobaccos with broad leaves used for making cigars.

broad·loom (brôd'lōōm'), *adj.* woven on a wide loom: said of rugs and carpets.

broad-mind·ed (brôd'mīn'did), *adj.* tolerant of other people's opinions and behavior; not bigoted; liberal.

Broads, The (brôdz), a low, level district in Suffolk and Norfolk, England, characterized by marshes, lakes, etc.

broad seal, the public seal of a state or nation.

broad·sheet (brôd'shēt'), *n.* a broadside (sense 6).

broad·side (brôd'sīd'), *n.* 1. the entire side of a ship above the water line. 2. all the guns that can be fired from one side of a ship. 3. their simultaneous fire. 4. a vigorous, effective attack in words, especially in a newspaper. 5. the broad surface of any large object. 6. a large sheet of paper printed on one side, as with advertising or a political message. 7. [Colloq.], violent abuse. *adv.* with the length turned (*to* an object): as, the ship came *broadside* to the dock.

broad·sword (brôd'sôrd', brôd'sōrd'), *n.* a sword with a broad blade, for slashing rather than thrusting.

broad·tail (brôd'tāl'), *n.* 1. a thick-tailed sheep of Asia Minor; karakul. 2. the flat, wavy pelt of its lamb; astrakhan.

Broad·way (brôd'wā'), *n.* 1. a street that runs northward through New York City, known for its brightly lighted theater section, night clubs, etc.; hence, 2. the New York commercial theater or entertainment industry, or its life, world, etc.

Brob·ding·nag (brob'diŋ-nag'), *n.* in Swift's *Gulliver's Travels,* the land of the giants, where Gulliver becomes a pet of the court: often misspelled **Brobdignag.**

Brob·ding·nag·i·an (brob'diŋ-nag'i-ən), *adj.* 1. of Brobdingnag. 2. like the giants of that place; gigantic; huge. *n.* a giant.

bro·cade (brō-kād'), *n.* [Sp. *brocado* < pp. of LL. *brocare,* to embroider, stitch; see BROACH], a rich cloth with a raised design woven into it, as of silk, velvet, gold, or silver. *v.t.* [BROCADED (-id), BROCADING], to weave a raised design into (cloth).

bro·cad·ed (brō-kād'id), *adj.* 1. woven like or into brocade. 2. decorated or covered with brocade.

broc·a·tel, broc·a·telle (brok'ə-tel'), *n.* [Fr. *brocatelle;* It. *broccatello,* dim. of *broccato,* brocaded; see BROCADE], a heavy, figured cloth like brocade, usually of silk and linen, used in upholstery.

broc·co·li (brok'ə-li), *n.* [It., pl. of *broccolo,* a sprout, cabbage sprout, dim. of *brocco,* LL. *brocca;* see BROACH], 1. a kind of cauliflower. 2. a related vegetable with small, loose, white or green heads; sprouting broccoli.

bro·ché (brō-shā'), *adj.* [Fr. < *brocher,* to stitch, brocade < *broche;* see BROACH], woven with a raised design.

bro·chette (brō-shet'), *n.* [Fr., dim. of *broche;* see BROACH], a small skewer.

bro·chure (brō-shoor', brō-shyoor'), *n.* [Fr. < *brocher,* to stitch; see BROACH], a pamphlet.

brock (brok), *n.* [AS. & Gael. *broc*], a badger.

Brock·en (brok'ən), *n.* a mountain in the Harz Mountains, Germany: scene of the Walpurgis Night in German folklore: height, 3,745 ft.

brock·et (brok'it), *n.* [ME. *broket;* Fr. *brocart, broquart,* yearling (of roe deer); OFr. *broc,* a spit, tine of a stag's horn; see BROACH], 1. a male deer two years old. 2. a small South American deer with short, unbranched horns.

Brock·ton (brok'tən), *n.* an industrial city in eastern Massachusetts: pop., 73,000.

bro·gan (brō'gən), *n.* [Ir., dim. of *brōg*], a brogue (shoe).

brogue (brōg), *n.* [prob. < Ir. *barrōg,* a hold, grip (especially on the tongue)], the pronunciation or accent peculiar to a dialect, especially that of English as spoken by the Irish.

brogue (brōg), *n.* [Gael. & Ir. *brōg*, a shoe], 1. a coarse shoe of untanned leather, formerly worn in Ireland. 2. a man's heavy, comfortable oxford shoe, usually with decorative perforations.

brogue (brōg), *n.* [apparently < *brogger* (Anglo-Fr. *brogour*), var. of *broker*], [Scot.], a trick; deception.

broi·der (broi'dẽr), *v.t.* [altered (after *broid*, old var. of *braid*) < *brouder, broudre* < Fr. *broder;* OFr. *brosder* < Gmc. **bruzdan*, to embroider], [Archaic], to embroider.

broi·der·y (broi'dẽr-i), *n.* [ME. *broiderie, brouderi;* Fr. *broderie;* see BROIDER], [Archaic], embroidery.

broil (broil), *v.t.* [ME. *broilen;* OFr. *bruillir*, to broil, roast < *bruir*, to burn; prob. < Gmc. **brojan*, to brew], 1. to cook by exposing to direct heat. 2. to expose directly to intense heat. *v.i.* 1. to cook by broiling. 2. to be exposed directly to great heat. 3. to become heated or angry. *n.* 1. a broiling; great heat. 2. anything broiled.

broil (broil), *n.* [Fr. *brouiller*, to mix, confuse, quarrel; OFr. *broouiler*, to dirty; prob. < Gmc. **brod-*, broth], a noisy quarrel; brawl. *v.i.* to take part in a broil.

broil·er (broil'ẽr), *n.* 1. a pan, gridiron, etc. for broiling. 2. the part of a stove designed for broiling. 3. a chicken suitable for broiling.

bro·kage (brō'kij), *n.* [ME. *brocage;* see BROKER], the business or fee of a broker, especially a marriage broker.

broke (brōk), past tense and archaic past participle of **break**. *adj.* [Slang], 1. having little or no money; penniless. 2. bankrupt.
  go broke, [Slang], 1. to lose all or most of one's money or property; become penniless. 2. to become bankrupt.

bro·ken (brō'kən), [ME.; AS. *brocen* < *brecan*, to break; see BREAK], past participle of **break**. *adj.* 1. splintered, fractured, burst, etc. 2. violated: as, a *broken* promise. 3. weak or weakened. 4. subdued in feelings. 5. bankrupt. 6. interrupted; discontinuous. 7. faltering: as, she wept and told her story in *broken* tones. 8. imperfectly spoken, especially with reference to grammar and syntax: as, he speaks *broken* English. 9. tamed; subdued and trained. 10. [Colloq.], demoted. For phrases, see **break**.

bro·ken-down (brō'kən-doun'), *adj.* 1. shattered, as in health. 2. ruined; useless.

bro·ken·heart·ed (brō'kən-här'tid), *adj.* crushed by grief or despair; heartbroken.

broken wind, in *veterinary medicine*, the heaves.

bro·ken-wind·ed (brō'kən-win'did), *adj.* gasping with or as with the heaves.

bro·ker (brō'kẽr), *n.* [ME. *brokour, brocour;* Anglo-Fr. *brocour;* ONorm.Fr. *broceor* < OFr. *brokier, brochier*, to broach, tap; orig. sense "wine dealer"], 1. a person paid a fee or commission for acting as an agent in making contracts or sales. 2. a stockbroker.

bro·ker·age (brō'kẽr-ij), *n.* [*broker* + *-age*], 1. the business or office of a broker. 2. a broker's fee.

bro·ma (brō'mə), *n.* [Gr. *brōma*, food < *bibrōskein*, to eat], 1. cocoa from which the oil has been removed. 2. in *medicine*, any solid food that is chewed.

bro·mal (brō'mal), *n.* [G.; *brom*, bromine + *al*kohol, alcohol], an oily, colorless, sharp-smelling liquid, CBr_3COH, obtained by passing bromine through alcohol.

bro·mate (brō'māt), *n.* [*bromine* + *-ate*], a salt of bromic acid. *v.t.* [BROMATED (-id), BROMATING], in *pharmacy*, 1. to treat (a substance) with bromine. 2. to combine with bromine.

Brom·berg (brom'bẽrg; G. brôm'berH), *n.* a city in northwestern Poland: pop., 220,000: Polish name, *Bydgoszcz*.

brome (brōm), *n.* [L. *bromos;* Gr. *bromos*, oats], any of a large group of related grasses, mostly weeds, with flat leaves and drooping spikes of flowers: also **brome grass**.

bro·me·li·a·ceous (brō-mē'li-ā'shəs), *adj.* [Mod.L. *Bromelia*, name of the family of plants (after Swed. botanist Olaf *Bromel*); + *-aceous*], of the pineapple family of plants, which generally have stiff leaves and spikes or heads of bright flowers.

Brom·field, Louis (brom'fēld), 1896?–1956; American novelist.

bro·mic (brō'mik), *adj.* [*bromine* + *-ic*], of or containing bromine, especially bromine with a valence of five.

bromic acid, an acid, $HBrO_3$, of which bromates are salts: it cannot be prepared in the pure state, and is found only in dilute aqueous solutions.

bro·mid (brō'mid), *n.* bromide.

bro·mide (brō'mīd, brō'mid), *n.* [*bromine* + *-ide*], 1. a compound of bromine with another element or radical. 2. potassium bromide, KBr, used in medicine as a sedative. 3. a trite saying or statement. 4. [Slang], a person who says trite things. —*SYN.* see **platitude**.

bromide paper, in *photography*, sensitized paper coated with a gelatin bromide emulsion, used in printing.

bro·mid·ic (brō-mid'ik), *adj.* [see BROMIDE], using or containing a trite remark or remarks.

bro·min (brō'min), *n.* bromine.

bro·mi·nate (brō'mi-nāt'), *v.t.* [BROMINATED (-id), BROMINATING], in *chemistry*, to combine with bromine.

bro·mine (brō'mēn, brō'min), *n.* [Fr. *brome* < Gr. *orōmos*, stench; + *-ine*], a chemical element, usually in the form of a reddish-brown, corrosive liquid volatilizing to form a vapor that has an unpleasant odor and is very irritating to mucous membranes: used in making dyes, in photography, and, in the form of certain compounds, in antiknock motor fuel: symbol, Br; at. wt., 79.916; at. no., 35.

bro·mism (brō'miz'm), *n.* in *medicine*, a condition caused by overuse of bromine or its compounds.

bro·mize (brō'mīz), *v.t.* [BROMIZED (-mīzd), BROMIZING], in *chemistry*, to treat with bromine or a bromide.

bron·chi (broŋ'kī), *n.* plural of **bronchus**.

bron·chi·a (broŋ'ki-ə), *n.pl.* [LL. < Gr. *bronchia*], bronchial tubes smaller than the bronchi but larger than the bronchioles.

bron·chi·al (broŋ'ki-əl), *adj.* of the bronchi, the bronchia, or the bronchioles.

bronchial tubes, the bronchi and the tubes branching from them.

bron·chi·ole (broŋ'ki-ōl'), *n.* [dim. of *bronchia*, after Mod.L. diminutives ending in *-iola*], any of the small subdivisions of the bronchia.

bron·chit·ic (broŋ-kit'ik), *adj.* of, connected with, or having bronchitis.

bron·chi·tis (broŋ-kī'tis), *n.* [*bronch-* + *-itis*], an inflammation, acute or chronic, of the mucous lining of the bronchial tubes.

bron·cho (broŋ'kō), *n.* [*pl.* BRONCHOS (-kōz)], a bronco.

bron·cho- (broŋ'kō, broŋ'kə), [< Gr. *bronchos*, windpipe], a combining form meaning *having to do with the bronchi*, as in *bronchoscope*: also, before a vowel, **bronch-**.

bron·cho·bust·er (broŋ'kō-bus'tẽr), *n.* a broncobuster.

bron·cho·pneu·mo·ni·a (broŋ'kō-nōō-mō'nyə, broŋ'kō-nū-mō'ni-ə), *n.* inflammation of the bronchia accompanied by inflamed, pus-forming patches in the near-by lobules of the lungs: it is generally a secondary disease following an infection of the upper respiratory tract.

bron·cho·scope (broŋ'kə-skōp'), *n.* [*broncho-* + *-scope*], a slender, tubular instrument with a small electric light, for examining or treating the inside of the windpipe or the bronchi, or for removing foreign bodies from them.

bron·chus (broŋ'kəs), *n.* [*pl.* BRONCHI (-kī)], [Mod. L. < Gr. *bronchos*, windpipe], either of the two main branches of the trachea, or windpipe: see **lung**, illus.

bron·co (broŋ'kō), *n.* [*pl.* BRONCOS (-kōz)], [Sp., rough, rude, crabbed, morose], a small horse or pony, usually wild or partially tamed, of the western United States: also spelled **broncho**.

bron·co·bust·er (broŋ'kō-bus'tẽr), *n.* [Slang], 1. a person who tames broncos. 2. a cowboy. Also spelled **bronchobuster**.

Bron·të, Anne (bron'ti), (pseudonym *Acton Bell*), 1820–1849; sister of *Charlotte;* English novelist.

Brontë, Charlotte, (*Mrs. Arthur B. Nicholls;* pseudonym *Currer Bell*), 1816–1855; English novelist; wrote *Jane Eyre*.

Brontë, Emily Jane, (pseudonym *Ellis Bell*), 1818–1848; sister of *Charlotte;* English novelist; wrote *Wuthering Heights*.

bron·to- (bron'tō, bron'tə), [< Gr. *brontē*, thunder], a combining form meaning: 1. *thunder*, as in *brontograph*. 2. in *paleontology*, *hugeness*, as in *brontosaurus*. Also, before a vowel, **bront-**.

bron·to·sau·rus (bron'tə-sô'rəs), *n.* [*bronto-* + Gr. *sauros*, lizard], a huge, extinct American dinosaur of the Jurassic Period, which had a long, slender neck, a small head, and a thick, tapering tail.

BRONTOSAURUS

Bronx (broŋks), *n.* 1. a borough of New York City, between the Hudson and East rivers: pop., 1,425,000. 2. a cocktail made with gin, vermouth, and orange juice.

Bronx cheer, [Slang], a noisy vibration of the lips to show derision or scorn.

bronze (bronz), *n.* [Fr.; It. *bronzo* & ML. *brundium;* supposedly < It. town *Brindisi*, L. *Brundisium*], 1. an alloy of copper and tin. 2. anything, as a work of art, made of bronze. 3. a reddish-brown color like that of bronze: abbreviated **br.** *adj.* of or like bronze. *v.t.*

fat, āpe, bâre, cär; ten, ēven, hêre, ovẽr; is, bīte; lot, gō, hôrn, tōōl, look; oil, out; up, ūse, fũr; get; joy; yet; chin; she; thin, *th*en; zh, leisure; ŋ, ring; ə for *a* in *ago*, *e* in *agent*, *i* in *sanity*, *o* in *comply*, *u* in *focus;* ' as in *able* (ā'b'l); Fr. bål; ë, Fr. coeur; ö, Fr. feu; Fr. mo*n*; ô, Fr. coq; ü, Fr. duc; H, G. ich; kh, G. doch. See pp. x–xii. ‡ foreign; * hypothetical; < derived from.

[BRONZED (bronzd), BRONZING], [Fr. *bronzer* < the *n.*], to make look like bronze; give a bronze color to. *v.i.* to tan darkly: said of persons.

Bronze Age, a period of civilization characterized by bronze tools and weapons, usually regarded as between the Stone Age and the Iron Age.

Bronze Star, a United States Army military decoration awarded for heroic or meritorious achievement not involving participation in aerial flight: instituted in 1942.

bronz·y (bron'zi), *adj.* resembling bronze, especially in color.

broo (brōō; Scot. brü), *n.* [? < OFr. *breu*], [Scot. & N. Eng. Dial.], broth.

brooch (brōch, brōōch), *n.* [ME. *broche;* see BROACH], a large ornamental pin with a clasp, worn usually at the bosom or neck of a woman's dress.

brood (brōōd), *n.* [ME. & AS. *brod;* akin to G. *brut,* a hatching, IE. base **bhrē-*, to warm, heat < **bher-*, to well up, ferment; cf. FERMENT], 1. the offspring of animals, especially of birds or fowl. 2. a group of birds or fowl hatched at one time and cared for together; hence, 3. the children in a family. 4. a breed or kind: as, a *brood* of ideas. *v.t.* 1. to sit on and hatch (eggs). 2. to hover over or protect (offspring, etc.) with or as with wings. *v.i.* 1. to brood eggs or offspring. 2. to think deeply about something, usually with unhappiness, anxiety, etc.

brood on (or **over**), 1. to hover over; hang low over. 2. to think about constantly, usually with unhappiness, anxiety, etc.

brood·er (brōōd'ẽr), *n.* 1. a person or animal that broods. 2. a heated shelter for raising young fowl.

brood·y (brōōd'i), *adj.* [BROODIER (-i-ẽr), BROODIEST (-i-ist)], 1. ready to brood: said of chickens. 2. inclined to brood, or dwell on one's own thoughts.

brook (brook), *n.* [ME. *broc;* AS. *broc;* prob. < base of *break,* in the sense of "a stream bursting forth"], a small stream, usually not so large as a river.

brook (brook), *v.t.* [ME. *bruken,* to use, enjoy; AS. *brucan,* to use], to put up with; endure: usually in the negative: as, I cannot *brook* his insolence. —***SYN.*** see **bear.**

Brooke, Rupert (brook), 1887–1915; English poet.

Brook Farm, a farm near West Roxbury, Massachusetts, where a group of American writers and scholars experimented in setting up a model communist community from 1841 to 1847.

brook·let (brook'lit), *n.* a little brook.

brook·lime (brook'līm'), *n.* [ME. *broc-lemok, broc-leomeke; broc,* brook + *leomeke,* brooklime < AS. *hleomoc*], any of several veronicas that grow in wet places.

Brook·line (brook'līn), *n.* a town in Massachusetts: suburb of Boston: pop., 54,000.

Brook·lyn (brook'lin), *n.* a borough of New York City, on western Long Island: pop., 2,627,000.

Brooklyn Bridge, a bridge in New York City between Brooklyn and Manhattan: length, 5,989 ft.

Brooks, Phillips (brooks), 1835–1893; American clergyman and writer.

Brooks, Van Wyck (van wīk), 1886–1963; American critic, translator, and historian.

Brooks Range (brooks), a range of mountains extending across northern Alaska: highest peak, c. 5,000 ft.

brook trout, the speckled trout of eastern North America.

brook·weed (brook'wēd'), *n.* either of two plants related to the primrose, one European and the other North American, that grow in moist places and have small white flowers.

broom (brōōm, broom), *n.* [ME. & AS. *brom,* brushwood; akin to OHG. *brāma,* thorny bush, bramblebush (see BRAMBLE); IE. base **bher-*, point, edge, thorn], 1. any of a group of shrubs of the pea family, with small leaves, slender branches, and flowers of yellow, purple, or white. 2. a brush with a long handle, used for sweeping: brooms were originally made of twigs of broom. *v.t.* to use a broom on; sweep.

broom·corn (brōōm'kôrn', broom'kôrn'), *n.* a variety of grass resembling corn: the long, stiff stems of the flower clusters are used in brooms and brushes.

broom·rape (brōōm'rāp', broom'rāp'), *n.* [*broom* + *rape* (the vegetable); used as transl. of ML. *rapum genistae,* lit., broom tuber], any of a number of related leafless plants with yellow, purplish, or reddish-brown flowers: they are parasitic on the roots of other plants.

broom·stick (brōōm'stik', broom'stik'), *n.* the handle of a broom.

bros., brothers.

broth (brôth, broth), *n.* [ME. & AS.; akin to OHG. *brod;* ult. < base of *brew*], water in which meat and, sometimes, vegetables or cereals have been boiled; thin, watery soup.

broth·el (brôth'əl, broth'əl, broth'əl), *n.* [ME., wretched person < AS. *breothan,* to waste away, go to ruin; confused with *bordel*], a house of prostitution.

broth·er (bruth'ẽr), *n.* [*pl.* BROTHERS; *archaic* BRETHREN (breth'rən) is still used in senses 6 & 7], [ME.; AS. *brothor;* akin to Goth. *brothar,* L. *frater,* OIr. *brāthir,* Sans. *bhrātar;* IE. base **brāter*], 1. a man or boy related to one by having the same parents: sometimes also used of animals. 2. a man or boy related to one by having one parent in common; half brother. 3. a stepbrother. 4. a foster brother. 5. a friend who is like a brother. 6. a lay member of a men's religious order. 7. a fellow member of the same race, creed, profession, or organization. Abbreviated **bro., br., B., b.** *v.t.* to treat or address as a brother.

broth·er·hood (bruth'ẽr-hood'), *n.* [ME. *brotherhede;* see BROTHER & -HOOD], 1. the state or quality of being a brother; bond between brothers. 2. an association of men united in a common interest, work, creed, etc., as a fraternity or religious order: abbreviated **B.**

broth·er-in-law (bruth'ẽr-in-lô'), *n.* [*pl.* BROTHERS-IN-LAW], 1. the brother of one's husband or wife. 2. the husband of one's sister. 3. occasionally, the husband of the sister of one's wife or husband.

Brother Jonathan, [said to be from Washington's frequent jocular reference to *Jonathan* Trumbull, governor of Connecticut], [Colloq.], 1. the United States. 2. its people.

broth·er·li·ness (bruth'ẽr-li-nis), *n.* the quality of being brotherly.

broth·er·ly (bruth'ẽr-li), *adj.* 1. of or like a brother. 2. friendly, kind, loyal, etc. *adv.* as a brother should.

brougham (brōōm, brōō'əm, brō'əm), *n.* [after Lord *Brougham* (1778–1868)], 1. a closed, four-wheeled carriage with the driver's seat outside. 2. an electrically powered automobile, between a coupe and a sedan in size. 3. a gasoline-powered limousine with the driver's seat unenclosed.

BROUGHAM

brought (brôt), [AS. *broht-*, p.t., *(ge)broht,* pp.; akin to OFris. *brohte, (ge)broht,* OHG. *brahta, (ge)braht,* Goth. *brahta* (pp. does not appear); anomalously used (as in OFris., OHG., Goth.) with strong inf. *bringan* (see BRING), but actually forms of *brengan,* to bring, produce a caus. v. < W. Gmc. **brangjan* < **brang* (p.t. of **bringan*) + *-jan,* caus. suffix; the expected strong forms **brang,* **(ge)brungen* do not appear], past tense and past participle of **bring.**

Broun, Hey·wood (hā'wood brōōn), (born *Matthew Heywood Campbell Broun*), 1888–1939; American journalist.

Brou·wer, A·dri·aen (ä'dri-än brou'wẽr), 1606?–1638; Flemish painter.

brow (brou), *n.* [ME. *browe, bruwe;* AS. *bru;* akin to ON. *brūn;* IE. base **bhru,* eyebrow, as in Sans. *bhrū-h*], 1. the eyebrow. 2. the forehead. 3. a person's facial expression: as, an angry *brow.* 4. the edge of a cliff; projecting upper part or top of a hill.

brow·beat (brou'bēt'), *v.t.* [BROWBEAT, BROWBEATEN (-bēt''n), BROWBEATING], to intimidate with harsh, stern looks and words; bully.

brown (broun), *adj.* [ME. *brown, broun, brun;* AS. *brun;* akin to G. *braun;* IE. base **bhrou-no-* < **bhero-s,* **bheru-s;* see BEAR (animal)], 1. having the color of chocolate or coffee, a combination of red, black, and yellow. 2. tanned by or as by the sun; dark-skinned. *n.* 1. brown color. 2. any pigment or dye that makes things brown. Abbreviated **br.** *v.t. & v.i.* to make or become brown, especially by exposure to sunlight or heat.

brown out, to cause a brownout in.

do up brown, [Slang], to do completely; do perfectly.

Brown, Charles Brock·den (brok'dən broun), 1771–1810; American novelist.

Brown, John, 1800–1859; American abolitionist; led raid on government arsenal at Harper's Ferry (1859) to establish a stronghold for escaped slaves; hanged for treason: called *Old Brown of Osawatomie.*

brown algae, kind of algae in which the green chlorophyll is somewhat obscured by brown pigmentation.

brown bear, a bear with brown fur, found in Europe, North America, etc.

brown betty, a baked apple pudding made with butter, spices, sugar, and bread crumbs.

brown bread, 1. any bread made of dark flour. 2. a dark, sweetened, steamed bread.

brown coal, lignite, a dark-brown coal, usually with a woody texture.

Browne, Charles Far·rar (fär'ẽr broun), see **Ward, Artemus.**

Browne, Sir **Thomas,** 1605–1682; English physician and author.

Brown·i·an movement (broun'i-ən), [after Robert *Brown* (1773–1858), who first demonstrated it], the constant zigzag movement of colloidal dispersions in a liquid medium, caused by collision with molecules of the liquid.

brown·ie (broun′i), *n.* [dim. of *brown:* from its supposed color], 1. a small, helpful elf or goblin in stories, who does housework and other good deeds for people at night. 2. [B-], a girl scout between the ages of eight and eleven. 3. a flat, moist chocolate cake with nuts in it, generally cut into small bars.

Brown·ing, Elizabeth Bar·rett (bar′it broun′iŋ), 1806–1861; wife of *Robert;* English poet.

Browning, John Moses, 1855–1926; American inventor of automatic firearms.

Browning, Robert, 1812–1889; English poet; husband of *Elizabeth Barrett.*

brown·ish (broun′ish), *adj.* somewhat brown.

brown·out (broun′out′), *n.* a partial elimination or dimming of lights in a city to prevent observation by enemy air raiders at night or to save fuel.

brown rice, unpolished grains of rice.

brown rot, 1. a disease of stone fruits and pome fruits, marked by blight of flowers and twigs, rotting, etc. 2. any fungus causing this disease.

brown shirt, 1. [often B- S-], a person who belonged to the Nazi *Sturmabteilung* (S.A.) in Germany or to some similar organization in other countries: so called from the uniform; hence, 2. a Nazi; Hitlerite.

brown·stone (broun′stōn′), *n.* a reddish-brown sandstone, used for building.

brownstone front, 1. a façade of brownstone; hence, 2. a house with such a façade.

brown study, [orig., somber thought < early sense of *brown,* somber, gloomy], a condition of being deeply absorbed in thought; reverie.

brown sugar, sugar that is wholly or partly unrefined.

Browns·ville (brounz′vil), *n.* 1. a seaport in Texas, at the mouth of the Rio Grande: pop., 48,000. 2. a town in northwestern Florida, near Pensacola: pop., 38,000.

Brown Swiss, a hardy breed of dairy cattle, first raised in Switzerland.

brown·tail (broun′tāl′), *n.* a white moth with a tuft of reddish-brown hairs at the posterior end: its hairy larvae are harmful to trees.

brown thrasher, a songbird related to the mockingbird, brownish-red above and whitish below.

browse (brouz), *n.* [OFr. *brouz,* pl. of *broust,* a bud or shoot < OS. *brustian,* to sprout], twigs, leaves, and young shoots of trees or shrubs, which animals feed on. ***v.t.*** [BROWSED (brouzd), BROWSING], [OFr. *brouster* < the *n.*], 1. to feed on or nibble at. 2. to graze on. ***v.i.*** 1. to feed on or nibble at leaves, twigs, etc. 2. to glance through a book, library, etc. in a leisurely way.

B.R.T., Brotherhood of Railroad Trainmen: a labor union.

Bruce (brōōs), [Scot. < Fr. *Brieux,* locality in France], a masculine name.

Bruce, Robert the, 1274–1329; king of Scotland (1306–1329); won independence of Scotland from England.

Bruce, Stanley Melbourne, 1883– ; Australian statesman; prime minister (1923–1929).

bru·cel·lo·sis (brōō′sə-lō′sis), *n.* [after Sir David *Bruce* (1855–1931), Scot. physician; + *-osis*], undulant fever.

bruc·in (brōōs′in), *n.* brucine.

bruc·ine (brōōs′ēn, brōōs′in), *n.* [after James *Bruce* (1730–1794), Scot. traveler], a bitter, poisonous, white alkaloid, $C_{23}H_{26}N_2O_4$, found in seeds of nux vomica and several other related plants.

Bruck·ner, An·ton (än′tōn brook′nẽr), 1824–1896; Austrian organist and composer.

Bruegel, Jan, etc., see **Breughel, Jan,** etc..

Bru·ges (brōō′jəz, brōōzh; Fr. brüzh), *n.* a city in northwestern Belgium: pop., 53,000.

Brug·ge (broog′ə), *n.* Bruges: the Flemish name.

bru·in (brōō′in), *n.* [D., brown], a bear, especially a brown bear: name used in fairy tales.

bruise (brōōz), *v.t.* [BRUISED (brōōzd), BRUISING], [ME. *brusen;* merging of AS. *brysan,* to crush, pound & OFr. *bruser, bruiser,* to break, shatter], 1. to injure the surface of (the skin) without breaking it but causing discoloration; hence, 2. to injure the surface or outside of. 3. to crush with or as with mortar and pestle. 4. to hurt slightly, as feelings. ***v.i.*** to be or become bruised. ***n.*** 1. a discoloration of the skin caused by a blow. 2. an injury to the outside of fruit, plants, etc.

bruis·er (brōōz′ẽr), *n.* [< *bruise;* sense 1 is 18th c.], 1. a professional boxer, especially one who is strong and hits hard. 2. a strong, pugnacious man; bully.

bruit (brōōt), *n.* [Fr., noise, uproar, rumor < *bruire,* to rumble, roar; prob. < L. *rugire,* to roar; ? influenced by LL. *bragire,* to cry out], [Archaic], 1. clamor. 2. rumor. ***v.t.*** to spread a report of; rumor.

‡Bru·maire (brü′mâr′), *n.* [Fr. < *brume,* fog, mist < L. *bruma;* see BRUMAL], the second month (October 22–November 20) of the French Revolutionary Calendar, adopted by the First Republic in 1793.

bru·mal (brōō′m'l), *adj.* [L. *brumalis* < *bruma,* winter, shortest day of the year < **brevima* < *brevissima,* superl. of *brevis,* short], of winter; wintry.

brume (brōōm), *n.* [Fr. < L. *bruma;* see BRUMAL], mist; fog; vapor.

brum·ma·gem (brum′ə-jəm), *adj.* [after *Birmingham,* formerly *Bromwycham,* England, where cheap jewelry and gift toys were manufactured], [Colloq.], not genuine; cheap and gaudy. ***n.*** [Colloq.], anything cheap and gaudy, especially imitation jewelry.

Brummell, George Bryan, see **Beau Brummell.**

bru·mous (brōō′məs), *adj.* [< L. *bruma;* + *-ous;* see BRUMAL], foggy; misty.

brunch (brunch), *n.* [*b*reakfast + l*unch*], [Colloq.], a combined breakfast and lunch.

Brun·dis·i·um (brun-diz′i-əm), *n.* Brindisi: the ancient name.

Bru·nei (broo-nī′), *n.* 1. a sultanate in British Borneo, on the northern coast of Borneo: area, 2,226 sq. mi.; pop., 80,000. 2. its capital: pop., 16,000.

Bru·nel·les·chi, Fi·lip·po (fē-lēp′pô brōō′ne-les′kē), 1377?–1446; Florentine architect.

bru·net (brōō-net′), *adj.* [Fr.; OFr. *brunet, brunette,* dim. of *brun,* brown; OHG. *brun*], 1. having a dark or olive color. 2. having black or dark-brown hair and eyes, and a dark complexion. ***n.*** a man or boy with such hair, eyes, and complexion.

bru·nette (brōō-net′), *adj.* [Fr., fem. of *brunet*], brunet. ***n.*** a woman or girl with black or dark-brown hair and eyes, and a dark complexion.

Brun·hild (brōōn′hild; G. brōōn′hilt), *n.* [< OHG. *brunna,* armor + *hilti* (or OS. *hild*), fight; hence, fighter in armor], in the *Nibelungenlied,* a queen of Iceland whom Gunther, king of Burgundy, gets as his bride with the help of Siegfried's magic: see **Brünnhilde, Brynhild.**

Brünn (brün), *n.* Brno, a city in Czechoslavakia: the German name.

Brünn·hil·de (brün-hil′də; Eng. broon-hil′də), *n.* [G., var. of *Brunhild;* form < G. *brünne* (< OHG. *brunna*) + *Hilde,* fem. given name (< OHG. *hilti*)], in Richard Wagner's *Die Walküre,* a Valkyrie whom Siegfried releases from enchantment: see **Brunhild, Brynhild.**

Bru·no (brōō′nō), [OHG. < *brun,* brown], a masculine name.

Bru·no, Gior·da·no (jôr-dä′nô brōō′nô), 1548? 1600; Italian philosopher; championed Copernican theories of astronomy; burned at the stake by the Inquisition.

Bruno of Cologne, Saint, 1030?–1101; founder of the Carthusian order of monks: his day is October 6.

Bruns·wick (brunz′wik), *n.* 1. a former division of central Germany: earlier, a duchy. 2. a city in central Germany: pop., 246,000. German name, *Braunschweig.*

brunt (brunt), *n.* [ME. *brunt, bront* < ON. *bruncer,* heat; akin to *brenna,* to burn], 1. shock (of an attack); impact (of a blow). 2. the main part of the shock or impact: as, he bore the *brunt* of the argument.

Bru·sa (brōō′sä), *n.* Bursa.

brush (brush), *n.* [ME. *brusshe;* OFr. *broce, brosse,* bush, brushwood; LL. **brustia, bruscia;* ? < OHG. *brusta, burst,* a bristle], 1. a device having bristles, hairs, or wires fastened into a back of some sort, with or without a handle attached: brushes are used for cleaning, polishing, painting, smoothing the hair, etc. 2. brushwork. 3. any bushy tail, especially that of a fox. 4. the act of brushing. 5. a motion that barely touches; light touch in passing. 6. in *electricity,* a piece, plate, rod, or bundle of carbon, copper, etc. used as a conductor between an outside circuit and a revolving part, as in a motor. ***v.t.*** [ME. *bruschen* < *brusshe;* or ? < OFr. *brosser,* to beat underbrush for game < *brosse,* a brush, thicket], 1. to use a brush on; clean, polish, paint, smooth, etc. with a brush. 2. to go over lightly, as with a brush. 3. to touch or graze in passing. 4. to remove by or as by brushing. ***v.i.*** to move so as to push lightly aside, skim, or graze past something.
  brush aside (or **away**), 1. to sweep out of the way. 2. to dismiss from consideration.
  brush off, to dismiss; get rid of.
  brush up, 1. to make neat or presentable; clean up. 2. to refresh one's memory.

brush (brush), *n.* [ME. *brusche;* OFr. *brosse;* see prec. BRUSH], 1. brushwood. 2. sparsely settled country, covered with brush.

brush (brush), *v.i.* [ME. *bruschen,* rush], to go fast; hurry. ***n.*** a short, quick fight or quarrel; skirmish.

brush discharge, a visible, brushlike electric discharge, as in the air surrounding a wire at high potential; corona.

brush-off (brush′ôf′), *n.* [Slang], dismissal.
  give the brush-off, [Slang], to dismiss; get rid of in an abrupt way.

brush·wood (brush′wood′), *n.* 1. chopped-off tree branches. 2. low, woody growth; underbrush; brush.

brush·work (brush′wũrk′), *n.* 1. work done with a brush; painting. 2. a characteristic way of putting on paint with a brush: as, Renoir's *brushwork.*

brush·y (brush′i), *adj.* [BRUSHIER (-i-ẽr), BRUSHIEST (-i-ist)], brushlike; rough and bristly; bushy.
brush·y (brush′i), *adj.* [BRUSHIER (-i-ẽr), BRUSHIEST (-i-ist)], thick with bushes or shrubs; covered with underbrush.
brusque (brusk, broosk), *adj.* [Fr. < It. *brusco;* prob. < ML. *bruscus,* brushwood; ult. < L. *ruscus,* butcher's-broom], abrupt, blunt, or short in manner or speech; curt. —*SYN.* see **blunt.**
‡**brus·que·rie** (brüs′kə-rē′), *n.* [Fr.], brusqueness.
Brus·sels (brus′′lz), *n.* the capital of Belgium: pop., with suburbs, 1,001,000: French name, *Bruxelles.*
Brussels carpet, [after *Brussels,* Belgium, where it was made], a patterned carpeting made of small loops of colored woolen yarn in a linen warp.
Brussels lace, a machine-made lace with an appliquéd design.
Brussels sprouts, 1. a kind of cabbage with a tuft of leaves at the top and a stem covered with edible, small, cabbagelike buds or heads. 2. the heads of this plant.

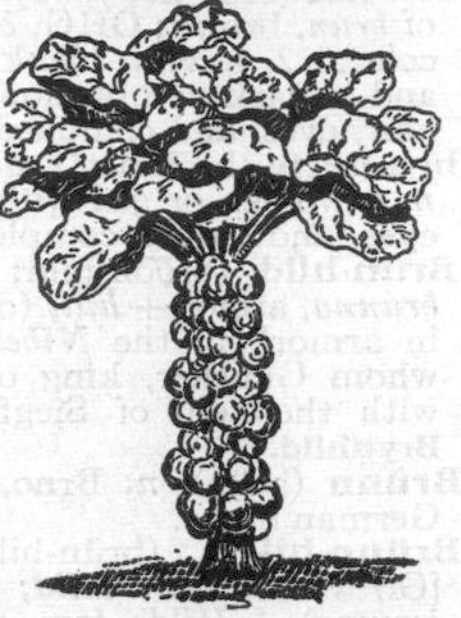
BRUSSELS SPROUTS

‡**brut** (brüt), *adj.* [Fr.; see BRUTE], 1. dry: said of wines. 2. with the minimum (1 per cent or less) of liqueur added: said of champagne.
bru·tal (brōō′t'l), *adj.* [LL. *brutalis*], like a brute; savage, cruel, coarse, rude, etc. —*SYN.* see **cruel.**
bru·tal·i·ty (brōō-tal′ə-ti), *n.* 1. the condition or quality of being brutal. 2. [*pl.* BRUTALITIES (-tiz)], a brutal act.
bru·tal·ize (brōō′t'l-īz′), *v.t.* & *v.i.* [BRUTALIZED (-īzd′), BRUTALIZING], to make or become brutal.
brute (brōōt), *adj.* [Fr. *brut,* fem. *brute* < L. *brutus,* senseless, irrational], 1. lacking the ability to reason: as, a *brute* beast. 2. not conscious; insensate: as, the *brute* force of nature. 3. of or like an animal; hence, 4. brutal; cruel; gross; sensual; stupid. *n.* 1. an animal. 2. the animal impulses in man; sensuality: as, it's the *brute* in him that makes him act like that. 3. a person who is brutal or very stupid, gross, sensual, etc.
bru·ti·fy (brōō′tə-fī′), *v.t.* & *v.i.* [BRUTIFIED (-fīd′), BRUTIFYING], to brutalize.
brut·ish (brōōt′ish), *adj.* of or like a brute; savage, gross, stupid, etc.
Bru·tus (brōō′təs), *n.* (*Marcus Junius Brutus*), Roman statesman; 85?–42 B.C.; one of the conspirators who murdered Julius Caesar.
Bru·xelles (brü′sel′), *n.* Brussels: the French name.
Bry·an (brī′ən), a masculine name: see **Brian.**
Bry·an, William Jen·nings (jen′iŋz brī′ən), 1860–1925; American statesman, orator, and reformer; Democratic presidential nominee (1896; 1900; 1908); secretary of state (1913–1915).
Bry·ansk (bri-änsk′; Russ. bryänsk), *n.* a city in western R.S.F.S.R.: pop., 201,000.
Bry·ant, William Cul·len (kul′′n brī′ənt), 1794–1878; American poet and journalist.
Bryce, James (brīs), Viscount Bryce, 1838–1922; British jurist, statesman, and historian.
Bryce Canyon National Park (brīs), a national park in southwestern Utah: area, 56 sq. mi.
Bryn·hild (brin′hild, brün′hild), *n.* [ON. *Brynhildr* < *brynja,* coat of mail, armor + *hildr,* fight], in *Norse legend,* a Valkyrie awakened from an enchanted sleep by Sigurd: when she is deceived by him into marrying Gunnar, she brings about Sigurd's death and then kills herself: see **Brunhild, Brünnhilde.**
bry·ol·o·gy (brī-ol′ə-ji), *n.* [< Gr. *bryon,* moss, lichen; + *-logy*], the branch of botany dealing with mosses and liverworts (bryophytes).
bry·o·ny (brī′ə-ni), *n.* [*pl.* BRYONIES (-niz)], [L. *bryonia;* Gr. *bryōnia* < *bryein,* to swell], any of a number of related vines of the gourd family, with large, fleshy roots, five-lobed leaves, and clusters of greenish-white flowers.
bry·o·phyte (brī′ə-fīt′), *n.* [< Gr. *bryon,* moss; + *-phyte*], any moss or liverwort.
bry·o·phyt·ic (brī′ə-fit′ik), *adj.* of a bryophyte.
bry·o·zo·an (brī′ə-zō′ən), *adj.* [< Gr. *bryon,* moss + *zōē,* life], belonging to a group of minute water animals that usually form fixed, branching, mosslike colonies, reproducing by budding. *n.* any animal of this group.
Bryth·on (brith′ən), *n.* [W. < Celt. base of L. *Brito, Britto;* see BRITON, BRITISH], a Briton of Cornwall, Wales, or ancient Cumbria.
Bry·thon·ic (bri-thon′ik), *adj.* of the Brythons or their language. *n.* the Celtic language of the Brythons: Brythonic and Goidelic (Gaelic) are the two great divisions of Celtic.
Brzesć nad Bu·giem (bzheshch näd boo′gyem), Brest-Litovsk, city in Byelorussian S. S. R.: Polish name.
B/s, 1. bags. 2. bales.
B.S., 1. Bachelor of Science. 2. Bachelor of Surgery.
b.s., balance sheet.
b.s., B/S, bill of sale.
B.S.A., Boy Scouts of America.
B.Sc., *Baccalaureus Scientiae,* [L.], Bachelor of Science.
B.S.C.P., Brotherhood of Sleeping Car Porters: an A.F. of L. labor union.
B.S.Ed., Bachelor of Science in Education.
bskt., basket.
Bs/L, bills of lading.
Bt., Baronet.
B.T., B. Th., *Baccalaureus Theologiae,* [L.], Bachelor of Theology.
Btry., Battery.
B.T.U., Btu, B.t.u., British thermal unit (or units).
bu., 1. bureau. 2. bushel; bushels: also **bsh.**
bub (bub), *n.* [? < G. *bube,* boy], [Colloq.], brother; boy; little fellow: used in direct address.
bu·bal, bu·bale (bū′b'l), *n.* a bubalis.
bu·ba·line (bū′bə-lin′, bū′bə-lin), *adj.* [L. *bubalinus* < *bubalus;* Gr. *boubalos;* see BUBALIS], of a group of large, horned antelopes, including the hartebeests, etc.
bu·ba·lis (bū′bə-lis), *n.* [Mod.L.; Gr. *boubalis* < *boubalos;* see BUFFALO], a large African antelope.
bub·ble (bub′′l), *n.* [ME. *burble, burbelle, bubel* < the *v.*], 1. a film of liquid enveloping air or gas: as, soap *bubbles.* 2. a space filled with air or gas in a liquid or solid, as in carbonated water, glass, etc. 3. any idea or scheme that is plausible at first but quickly shows itself to be flimsy and worthless. 4. the act, process, or sound of bubbling. *v.i.* [BUBBLED (-'ld), BUBBLING], [ME. *burblen, bobelen;* prob. echoic], 1. to make bubbles; rise in bubbles; boil; foam. 2. to make a boiling or gurgling sound. *v.t.* 1. to form bubbles in; make bubble. 2. [Archaic], to cheat; swindle.
bubble over, 1. to overflow, as boiling liquid. 2. to be unable to keep back one's excitement, zest, etc.
bubble bath, 1. a bath perfumed and softened by a solution, crystals, or powder that forms surface bubbles. 2. such a solution, etc.
bubble gum, a kind of chewing gum that can be blown into large bubbles.
bub·bler (bub′lẽr), *n.* a drinking fountain in which water comes up out of a vent so that it can be drunk without a cup.
bub·bly (bub′li), *adj.* 1. containing or full of bubbles. 2. giving off bubbles.
bu·bo (bū′bō), *n.* [*pl.* BUBOES (-bōz)], [LL. < Gr. *boubōn,* groin, swollen gland], an inflamed swelling of a lymph gland, especially in the armpit or groin.
bu·bon·ic (bū-bon′ik), *adj.* of, characterized by, or having buboes.
bubonic plague, a contagious disease, usually fatal, characterized by buboes, chills and fever, prostration, and delirium: fleas from infected rats are the carriers.
bu·bon·o·cele (bū-bon′ə-sēl′), *n.* [Gr. *boubōn,* groin; + *-cele*], an incomplete or partial inguinal hernia forming a swelling in the groin.
Bu·ca·ra·man·ga (bōō-kä′rä-mäŋ′gä), *n.* a city in northern Colombia: pop., 185,000.
buc·cal (buk′′l), *adj.* [L. *bucca,* cheek, mouth cavity; + *-al*], 1. of the cheek or cheeks. 2. of the mouth or mouth cavity.
buc·ca·neer (buk′ə-nêr′), *n.* [Fr. *boucanier,* user of a *boucan* (Braz.), grill for roasting meat; orig. applied to Fr. hunters of wild oxen in Haiti], a pirate,or sea robber, especially one who raided along the Spanish coasts of America in the 17th and 18th centuries.
buc·ci·na·tor (buk′si-nā′tẽr), *n.* [L. < pp. of *buccinare,* to blow a trumpet < *buccina,* a trumpet], the thin, flat muscle in the cheek which retracts the corners of the mouth.
bu·cen·taur (bū-sen′tôr), *n.* [< Gr. *bous,* ox + *kentauros,* centaur], 1. a mythological creature, half bull and half man. 2. [It. *bucentoro;* prob. < prec.: from the figurehead], a state barge of ancient Venice.
Bu·ceph·a·lus (bū-sef′ə-ləs), *n.* [L., lit., ox-headed < Gr. *bous,* ox + *kephalē,* a head], the war horse of Alexander the Great.
Bu·ce·reș·ti (boo-koo-resht′), *n.* Bucharest: the Romanian name.
Buch·an, Sir **John** (buk′ən), first Baron Tweedsmuir, 1875–1940; Scottish novelist and historian; governor general of Canada (1935–1940).
Bu·chan·an, James (bū-kan′ən), 1791–1868; fifteenth president of the United States (1857–1861).
Bu·cha·rest (bū′kə-rest′, bōō′kə-rest′), *n.* the capital of Romania: pop., 1,279,000.
Buch·en·wald (bōōkh′ən-vält′; *often Anglicized to* book′′n-wôld′), *n.* a Nazi concentration camp near Weimar, Germany: notorious as a "medical experimentation" center and extermination camp.
Buch·man·ism (buk′mən-iz′m), *n.* [after Frank N. D. *Buchman* (1878–1961), American evangelist, the founder], a religious movement that advocates a return to the faith and practices of primitive Christianity, personal confession, etc.: often called *Oxford Group Movement.*
Buch·man·ite (buk′mən-īt′), *n.* a follower of Buchmanism.

buck (buk), *n.* [ME. *bucke, buk;* AS. *bucca, buc,* he-goat, male deer; akin to G. *bock,* male deer, ram, he-goat; IE. base **bhūĝo-,* as also in Arm. *buc,* lamb], 1. [*pl.* BUCKS (buks), BUCK; see PLURAL, II, D, 1], a male deer, goat, rabbit, etc.: the female is a doe. 2. the act of bucking. 3. a dandy. 4. [Colloq.], a young male: used contemptuously or patronizingly of a young male Negro or Indian. 5. [Slang], a dollar. *v.i.* 1. to jump upward quickly and descend with back and forelegs stiff, in an attempt to throw off a rider: said of a horse, mule, etc. 2. to plunge forward with lowered head, as a goat. 3. [Colloq.], to resist something as if plunging against it. 4. [Colloq.], to move jerkily, as a car. *v.t.* 1. to charge against, especially with the head down, as in football. 2. to dislodge or throw by bucking. 3. [Colloq.], to resist. *adj.* male.

buck for, [Military Slang], to work hard for (a promotion, etc.).

buck up, [Colloq.], to cheer up; brace up; renew one's courage, confidence, etc.

buck (buk), *n.* [D. *zaagbok,* sawbuck; *zaag,* saw + *bok;* see BUCK (male deer)], 1. a sawbuck; sawhorse. 2. a somewhat similar gymnastic apparatus with a padded, leather-covered top, for vaulting over, etc.

buck (buk), *v.t.* [ME. *bouken* < MLG. & MD.; cf. LG. *büken,* G. *bauchen*], [Archaic or Dial.], to bleach, soak, or wash (clothes) in lye or soapsuds. *n.* [Archaic or Dial.], 1. lye or soapsuds for washing clothes. 2. clothes washed in this.

buck (buk), *n.* in *poker,* a counter, etc. placed before a player to remind him that the next turn to deal is his or of his obligation, after he has won a jackpot, to order a new jackpot on his next turn to deal.

pass the buck, [Colloq.], to evade blame, responsibility, etc. by passing it to someone else.

Buck, Pearl (buk), 1892– ; American novelist; received Nobel prize in literature, 1938.

buck and wing, a complicated, fast tap dance.

buck·a·roo (buk'ə-rōō', buk'ə-rōō'), *n.* [*pl.* BUCKAROOS (-rōōz', -rōōz')], [altered < Sp. *vaquero*], a cowboy.

buck·ay·ro (buk-ā'rō), *n.* a buckaroo.

buck bean, [after D. *boksboon,* lit., goat's bean], a bog plant with white or pink flowers and leaves made up of three leaflets.

buck·board (buk'bôrd', buk'bōrd'), *n.* [< *buck* (to move jerkily)], a four-wheeled, open carriage with the seat carried on a flooring of long, flexible boards whose ends rest directly on the axles.

BUCKBOARD

buck·een (buk-ēn'), *n.* [< *buck* (a dandy)], in Ireland, a young man who pretends to be aristocratic or wealthy.

buck·er (buk'ẽr), *n.* a horse, mule, etc. that bucks.

buck·et (buk'it), *n.* [ME. *boket,* dim. of AS. *buc,* pitcher, bucket], 1. a deep, rounded, flat-bottomed container hung from a curved handle, for holding or carrying water, coal, etc.; pail. 2. a bucketful. 3. a thing like a bucket, as a dredge scoop. *v.t. & v.i.* 1. to carry, draw, or lift (water, etc.) in a bucket or buckets. 2. [Colloq.], to ride (a horse) at a fast pace.

kick the bucket, [? < obs. *bucket,* beam on which a slaughtered pig was hung], [Slang], to die.

buck·et·ful (buk'it-fool'), *n.* the amount that a bucket can contain; contents of a full bucket.

bucket seat, a single seat with a rounded back, as in some automobiles and airplanes, often made so that it can be tipped forward.

bucket shop, an establishment ostensibly accepting orders to buy and sell stocks, bonds, and commodities but actually engaged in gambling on the rise and fall of their prices, or in betting secretly against its customers, speculating with funds entrusted to it, etc.

buck·eye (buk'ī'), *n.* [*buck* (male deer) + *eye:* from the appearance of the seed], 1. any of several kinds of horse chestnut with large, showy clusters of flowers, large leaves, and burs containing nuts. 2. the brown, glossy seed or nut of such a tree. 3. [B-], [Colloq.], a native or inhabitant of Ohio, called the *Buckeye State.*

BUCKEYE

buck fever, [Colloq.], nervous excitement of beginning hunters when they first see game.

buck·hound (buk'hound'), *n.* a dog somewhat like a greyhound, used for hunting deer.

Buck·ing·ham (buk'iŋ-əm), Duke of, see **Villiers, George.**

Buckingham Palace, the official residence in London of British sovereigns.

Buck·ing·ham·shire (buk'iŋ-əm-shir'), *n.* a county in south central England: pop., 349,000 (est. 1945); county seat, Aylesbury.

buck·ish (buk'ish), *adj.* of or like a buck, or dandy; foppish.

buck·le (buk''l), *n.* [ME. *bocle,* a buckle, boss of a shield; OFr. *bocle, bucle,* boss of a shield, ring; LL. *bucula, buccula,* beaver, shield; L. *buccula,* cheek strap of a helmet, beaver, lit., little cheek, dim. of *bucca,* cheek; cf. BUD (a swelling)], 1. a clasp or catch for fastening the ends of a strap, belt, etc. 2. a clasplike ornament for shoes, the hair, etc. *v.t.* [BUCKLED (-'ld), BUCKLING], 1. to fasten or join with a buckle. 2. to bring together; join. *v.i.* 1. to be fastened or joined by a buckle. 2. to engage in a struggle; grapple.

buckle down, to apply oneself energetically; work hard.

buck·le (buk''l), *v.t. & v.i.* [BUCKLED (-'ld), BUCKLING], [D. *bukken,* to bow; influenced by Fr. *boucler,* to bulge], to bend, warp, or crumple: as, the steel girders *buckled* in the fire. *n.* a distortion caused by buckling; bend, bulge, kink, etc.

buckle under, [Colloq.], to give in; yield; submit.

Buck·le, Henry Thomas (buk''l), 1821–1862; English historian.

buck·ler (buk'lẽr), *n.* [OFr. *bocler:* so named from the *bocle,* or boss, in its center; see BUCKLE (a clasp)], 1. a small, round shield held in the hand or worn on the arm. 2. a person or thing serving as a protection or defense. *v.t.* to protect by shielding; defend.

buck·o (buk'ō), *n.* [*pl.* BUCKOES (-ōz)], [< *buck* (he-goat)], a bully.

buck private, [Slang], an enlisted man of the lowest grade in the army.

buck·ra (buk'rə), *n.* [< Nigerian *mbākara,* a master], a white man: term originating in Africa, also used in the West Indies, etc.

buck·ram (buk'rəm), *n.* [ME. *bokeram;* OFr. *bouqueran, bouquerant;* ? < *Bokhara,* in Asia Minor], 1. a coarse cotton, hemp, or linen cloth stiffened with glue or a gluelike substance, for use in bookbinding, etc. 2. stiffness or formality. *adj.* 1. of or like buckram. 2. stiff; formal. *v.t.* to stiffen with buckram.

buck·saw (buk'sô'), *n.* [*buck* (sawbuck) + *saw*], a wood-cutting saw set in a frame, held with both hands when used.

BUCKSAW

buck·shot (buk'shot'), *n.* a large lead shot for shooting deer and other large game.

buck·skin (buk'skin'), *n.* 1. the skin of a buck. 2. a soft, strong, yellowish-gray leather made from the skins of deer or sheep. 3. a yellowish-gray horse. 4. *pl.* trousers or shoes made of buckskin. 5. [B-], an American soldier of the American Revolution. *adj.* made of buckskin.

buck·thorn (buk'thôrn'), *n.* [*buck* (male deer) + *thorn*], 1. any of a number of related trees or shrubs with small greenish or white flowers and thorny branches. 2. a spiny tree of the sapodilla family, found in the southern United States.

buck·tooth (buk'tōōth'), *n.* [*pl.* BUCKTEETH (-tēth')], [*buck* (male deer) + *tooth*], a projecting tooth.

buck·toothed (buk'tōōtht', buk'toothd'), *adj.* having buckteeth.

buck·wheat (buk'hwēt'), *n.* [*buck,* beech < ME. & AS. *boc;* + *wheat:* from the resemblance of the seeds to beechnuts], 1. a plant with fragrant, white flowers, grown for its triangular seeds. 2. the seed of this plant from which a dark flour is made. 3. this flour.

buckwheat cake, a pancake made of buckwheat flour.

bu·col·ic (bū-kol'ik), *adj.* [L. *bucolicus;* Gr. *boukolikos* < *boukolos,* herdsman < *bous,* ox], 1. of shepherds; pastoral. 2. of the countryside; rural; rustic. *n.* 1. a pastoral poem. 2. a rustic; countrified person: humorously so called. —***SYN.*** see **rural.**

Bu·co·vi·na (bōō'kə-vē'nə), *n.* a division of northern Romania, part of which was ceded to the U.S.S.R. in 1940: also spelled **Bukovina.**

bud (bud), *n.* [ME. *budde,* bud, beetle; AS. *budda,* beetle; akin to MLG. *botte,* MHG. *butte,* G. *(hage)butte;* IE. base **bu, *bhu,* to inflate, swell up, as also in L. *bucca,* cheek (cf. BUCCAL)], 1. a small swelling or projection on a plant, from which a shoot, cluster of leaves, or flower develops; hence, 2. any undeveloped or immature person or thing. 3. a swelling or projection on the body of some lower animals that develops into a new individual. *v.i.* [BUDDED (-id), BUDDING], [< the *n.*], 1. to put forth buds. 2. to begin to develop; hence, 3. to be young, undeveloped, promising, etc. *v.t.* 1. to put forth as a bud or buds. 2. to cause to bud. 3. to insert a bud of (a plant) into the bark of another sort of plant.

in (the) bud, 1. in the time of budding. 2. in a budding condition.

nip in the bud, to check at the earliest stage.

bud (bud), *n.* [Slang], buddy; fellow: used in addressing a man or boy.

Bu·da·pest (bōō'də-pest', bū'də-pest'), *n.* the capital of Hungary, on the Danube: pop., 1,850,000.

Bud·dha (bood'ə), *n.* [Sans., the enlightened one; pp. of *budh*, to awake, know], Gautama Siddhartha, a religious philosopher and teacher who lived in India 563?–483? B.C. and was the founder of Buddhism: the name is a title applied by Buddhists to someone regarded as embodying divine wisdom and virtue, and has also been given to other religious leaders of Asia.

Bud·dhism (bood'iz'm), *n.* a religion and philosophic system of central and eastern Asia, founded in India in the 6th century B.C. by Buddha: it teaches that right living, right thinking, and self-denial will enable the soul to reach Nirvana, a divine state of release from earthly and bodily pain, sorrow, and desire.

Bud·dhist (bood'ist), *n.* a believer in Buddhism. *adj.* of Buddha or Buddhism.

bud·dle (bud''l, bood''l), *n.* [< dial. *buddle*, to wash ore], in *mining*, a shallow, inclined trough or drain for washing ore.

bud·dle·ia (bud-lē'ə, bud'li-ə), *n.* [Mod.L. < Adam *Buddle*, Eng. botanist], any of a number of related shrubs or trees growing in warm climates and bearing clusters of small purplish, yellow, or white flowers.

bud·dy (bud'i), *n.* [*pl.* BUDDIES (-iz)], [c. 1852; ? < Brit. dial. *butty*, companion, with weakening of stop consonant], [Colloq.], 1. a comrade; companion. 2. a fellow soldier. 3. little boy: so used in direct address.

budge (buj), *v.t. & v.i.* [BUDGED (bujd), BUDGING], [Fr. *bouger*, to move < LL. *bullicare*, to boil < L. *bullire*, to bubble < *bulla*, a bubble, knob], to move slightly: as, the boy can't *budge* the heavy door.

budge (buj), *n.* [ME. *bougee, bouge, bulge*, a bag, swelling; OFr. *bulge, bilge*, a bag; L. *bulga*, leather bag; see BULGE], a kind of fur; lambskin with the wool worn outward. *adj.* 1. lined or trimmed with budge, as formerly a scholar's gown; hence, 2. solemn; pompous.

budg·er·i·gar (buj'ēr-i-gär'), *n.* [native name], an Australian parakeet having a greenish-yellow body, marked with bright blue on the cheeks and tail feathers, and wings striped with brown.

budg·et (buj'it), *n.* [ME. *bougette;* OFr. *bougette*, dim. of *bouge;* see BUDGE (lambskin)], 1. a bag or pouch with its contents; hence, 2. a collection of items; stock. 3. a plan or schedule adjusting expenses during a certain period to the estimated or fixed income for that period. 4. the cost or estimated cost of living, operating, etc. *v.t.* 1. to put on a budget; plan according to a budget. 2. to plan for; schedule: as, *budget* your time.

budg·et·ar·y (buj'i-ter'i), *adj.* of a budget.

budget plan, an installment plan.

budg·ie (buj'i), *n.* [Colloq.], a budgerigar.

Bud·weis (boot'vis), *n.* a city in southwestern Czechoslovakia: pop., 64,000.

Bu·ell, Don Car·los (don kär'lōs bū'əl), 1818–1898; Union general in the Civil War.

Bue·na Park (bwe'nə), a city in southwestern California, near Los Angeles: pop., 46,000.

‡bue·nas no·ches (bwe'näs nô'ches), [Sp.], good night.

Bue·na Vis·ta (bwe'nä vēs'tä; Eng. bū'nə vis'tə), a village in northwestern Mexico: site of a battle (1847) in which United States forces defeated the Mexicans.

‡bue·no (bwe'nô), *interj.* [Sp.], good; correct; very well.

Bue·nos Ai·res (bwā'nōs ī'rās, bō'nəs âr'ēz; Sp. bwe'nôs ī'res), 1. a province in Argentina: pop., 5,334,000. 2. the capital of Argentina, on the La Plata River: pop., 3,845,000. 3. a lake in southern Argentina and Chile: length, 75 mi.

‡bue·nos di·as (bwe'nôs dē'äs), [Sp.], good day; good morning.

buff (buf), *n.* [earlier *buffe*, buffalo < Fr. *buffle;* see BUFFALO], 1. a heavy, soft, brownish-yellow leather made from the skin of the buffalo or ox. 2. a military coat made of this leather. 3. a stick or spindle covered with leather, used for cleaning or shining. 4. a buffing wheel. 5. a dull brownish yellow. 6. [Colloq.], the bare skin. 7. [Colloq.], a devotee; fan: as, a jazz *buff*. *adj.* 1. made of buff. 2. of the color buff. *v.t.* 1. to clean or shine with a buff. 2. to make smooth or soft like buff. —*SYN.* see **polish.**

buff (buf), *n.* [ME. & OFr. *buffe;* see BUFFET (a blow)], a blow: now only in *blindman's buff*. *v.t.* to lessen the force of. *v.i.* to serve as a buffer.

Buf·fa·lo (buf''l-ō'), *n.* a city in New York, on Lake Erie: pop., 533,000.

buf·fa·lo (buf''l-ō'), *n.* [*pl.* BUFFALOES, BUFFALOS (-ōz'), BUFFALO; see PLURAL, II, D, 1], [Port. *bufalo;* L. *bufalus, bubalus*, wild ox; Gr. *boubalos*, a variety of African stag < *bous*, ox], 1. any of various wild oxen, sometimes domesticated, as the water buffalo of India, Cape buffalo of Africa, etc. 2. popularly but unscientifically, the American bison. 3. a robe made of buffalo skin. 4. a buffalo fish. *v.t.* [Slang], to intimidate; overawe; bamboozle: as, she's got him *buffaloed.*

BUFFALO

buffalo berry, 1. the tart, red or yellow berry of either of two shrubs of the oleaster family. 2. either of these shrubs.

Buffalo Bill, see **Cody, William Frederick.**

buffalo bird, any of several birds that perch on buffalo and cattle to eat the insects on them; cowbird.

buffalo bug, a small, black beetle with white spots.

buffalo fish, any of several large, humpbacked fresh-water fishes of the sucker family.

buffalo grass, a short prairie grass with fine leaves.

buffalo moth, the hairy larva of the carpet beetle, harmful to furs and woolens.

buffalo robe, a robe made of the skin of the bison.

buff·er (buf'ēr), *n.* [*buff* (to lessen force) + *-er*], 1. a device using padding, springs, hydraulic pressure, etc. to lessen or absorb the shock of collision or impact. 2. any person or thing that serves to lessen shock.

buf·fer (buf'ēr), *n.* [*buff* (to polish) + *-er*], 1. a person who buffs. 2. a buffing wheel or stick.

buffer state, a small country situated between two large, antagonistic powers and regarded as lessening the possibility of conflict between these.

buf·fet (buf'it), *n.* [ME.; OFr. < *buffe*, a blow; prob. echoic], a blow, usually with the hand or fist: often used figuratively, as, the *buffets* of fate. *v.t.* 1. to hit with the hand or fist; punch; slap. 2. to beat back: as, the waves *buffeted* the boat. *v.i.* 1. to struggle; fight. 2. to force a way by struggling or hitting.

buf·fet (bə-fā', boo-fā'; Brit. buf'it), *n.* [Fr.; OFr. *buffet*, display bench; cf. It. *buffetto*], 1. a piece of furniture with drawers and cupboards for dishes, table linen, silver, etc. 2. (boo-fā', boo'fā), a counter or table where refreshments are served, or a restaurant with such a counter or table.

buf·fet supper (or **lunch**) (boo-fā'), a meal at which guests help themselves to food from a buffet or table.

buff·ing wheel (buf'iŋ), a wheel covered with leather, cloth, etc., for buffing, or polishing, metal.

buf·fle·head (buf''l-hed'), *n.* [obs. *buffle*, buffalo, fool (< Fr., buffalo < It. *bufalo*); + *head*], a small North American duck, black on top and white underneath.

‡buf·fo (bōōf'fô; Eng. bōō'fō), *n.* [*pl.* BUFFI (-fē)], [It., comic; see BUFFOON], an opera singer, generally a bass, who plays a comic role. *adj.* comic.

Buf·fon, Comte **Georges Lou·is Le·clerc de** (zhôrzh lwē lə-kler' də bü'fôn'), 1707–1788; French naturalist.

buf·foon (bu-fōōn'), *n.* [Fr. *bouffon;* It. *buffone*, jester; *buffare*, to jest; ult. base, IE. **bu*, **bhu*, to swell up (as the cheeks); cf. BUD (a swelling)], a person who tries to amuse by jokes and tricks; clown; prankster.

buf·foon·er·y (bu-fōōn'ēr-i), *n.* [*pl.* BUFFOONERIES (-iz)], the jokes and tricks of a buffoon; clowning.

Bug (boog, bug), *n.* 1. a river in the Ukraine, flowing southeastward into the Black Sea: length, 500 mi. 2. a river in eastern Europe, flowing northwestward into the Vistula: length, 450 mi.: part of it forms the boundary between Poland and the U.S.S.R.

bug (bug), *n.* [ME. *bugge*, confused form of AS. *budda*, beetle; see BUD (a swelling)], 1. any crawling insect with sucking mouth parts and forewings thickened toward the base, as a water bug, squash bug, etc. 2. any insect or similar animal. 3. a bedbug. 4. [Colloq.], any microscopic organism, especially one causing disease; germ. 5. [Slang], a tiny microphone hidden to record conversation secretly. 6. [Slang], a defect, as in a machine. 7. [Slang], a person who is fond of or addicted to a specified thing: often used in combination, as, a *shutterbug* pursues photography as a hobby. *v.t.* [BUGGED (bugd), BUGGING], [Slang], 1. to hide a microphone in (a room, etc.), as for recording conversation secretly. 2. to annoy, anger, etc.

bug (bug), *n.* [ME. *bugge* < W. *bwg, bwgan*], [Obs.], a bugbear; hobgoblin.

bug·a·boo (bug'ə-bōō'), *n.* [*pl.* BUGABOOS (-bōōz')], [*bug* (hobgoblin) + *boo*], a bugbear.

bug·bane (bug'bān'), *n.* any of a number of related tall plants with long spikes of white flowers, some with an unpleasant odor, supposed to be disagreeable to insects.

bug·bear (bug'bâr'), *n.* [*bug* (hobgoblin) + *bear* (the animal)], 1. an imaginary hobgoblin or terror described to frighten children into good conduct. 2. anything

causing seemingly needless or excessive fear or anxiety.
bug-eyed (bug'īd'), *adj.* [Slang], with eyes bulging.
bug·ger (bug'ẽr), *n.* [Fr. *bougre* < ML. *Bulgarus*, lit., a Bulgarian; orig., 11th-c. Bulgarian heretic], 1. a sodomite. 2. a contemptible person. 3. a fellow; chap: used humorously or affectionately. *v.t.* to commit sodomy with.
bug·ger·y (bug'ẽr-i), *n.* [OFr. *bougrerie* < *bougre;* see BUGGER], sodomy: legal term in England.
bug·gy (bug'i), *n.* [*pl.* BUGGIES (-iz)], [18th c.; also *bougée*, pp. of Fr. *bouger*, to move (see BUDGE): prob. facetious in origin], 1. a light carriage with two or four wheels and one seat, usually drawn by one horse. 2. a small perambulator or carriage for a baby; baby buggy.
bug·gy (bug'i), *adj.* [BUGGIER (-i-ẽr), BUGGIEST (-i-ist)], infested or swarming with bugs.
bug·house (bug'hous'), *n.* [Slang], a hospital for the mentally ill; insane asylum. *adj.* [Slang], insane; crazy.
bu·gle (bū'g'l), *n.* [ME.; OFr., wild ox; L. *buculus*, heifer, young ox, dim. of *bos*, ox], 1. a hunting horn. 2. a wind instrument like a trumpet but smaller, and usually without keys or valves, used chiefly for military calls and signals. *v.i. & v.t.* [BUGLED (-g'ld), BUGLING], to blow on a bugle; call or signal by or as by blowing a bugle.
bu·gle (bū'g'l), *n.* [? < *bugle* (horn): from the appearance], a long glass bead, generally black and tubular, for trimming dresses, etc. *adj.* trimmed with bugles.
bu·gle (bū'g'l), *n.* [ME. *bugil, bugle;* OFr. *bugle;* LL. *bugula*], any of a number of plants of the mint family, with spikes of blue, rose, purple, or white flowers.
bu·gled (bū'g'ld), *adj.* trimmed with bugles (beads).
bu·gler (bū'glẽr), *n.* 1. a person who plays a bugle. 2. a soldier, boy scout, etc. designated to blow signals on a bugle: abbreviated **Bglr.** (as a title).
bu·gle·weed (bū'g'l-wēd'), *n.* any of a number of plants of the mint family, with tiny, bell-shaped flowers of white or blue.
bu·gloss (bū'glos, bū'glôs), *n.* [Fr. *buglosse;* L. *buglossa;* Gr. *bouglōssos*, oxtongue < *bous*, ox + *glōssa*, tongue], any of a number of related plants with small, blue or white flowers and hairy stems and leaves; anchusa.
bugs (bugz), *adj.* [Slang], crazy; insane.
bug·seed (bug'sēd'), *n.* [so named from appearance of the seeds], a fleshy plant of the goosefoot family, with flat, oval seeds.
buhl (bōōl), *n.* [after André Charles *Boulle* (1642–1732), Fr. woodworker], 1. decoration of furniture with designs of tortoise shell, colored metals, etc. inlaid in wood. 2. furniture thus decorated.
buhr (bũr), *n.* 1. buhrstone. 2. a knob of siliceous rock in calcareous or softer formations. Also spelled **burr.**
buhr·stone (bũr'stōn'), *n.* [*buhr*, var. of *burr* + *stone*], 1. a hard siliceous rock used to make grinding stones. 2. a stone made of this. Also spelled **burrstone.**
build (bild), *v.t.* [BUILT (bilt) or *archaic* BUILDED (-id), BUILDING], [ME. *bilden, bylden;* AS. *byldan*, to build < base of *bold*, a house], 1. to make by putting together materials, parts, etc.; construct; erect. 2. to make a basis for; establish: as, *build* your theory on facts. 3. to create. *v.i.* 1. to put up a building; have a house, etc. built: as, when are you going to *build?* 2. to be in the business of building houses, etc. 3. to develop a plan, etc. (with *on* or *upon*). 4. in *card games*, to form a sequence according to suit, number, etc. *n.* the manner or form of construction: as, he has a stocky *build.*
build up, 1. to construct gradually; form by degrees. 2. to make strong or healthy. 3. to erect buildings in; fill up.
build·er (bil'dẽr), *n.* 1. a person or animal that builds. 2. a person in the business of building houses, etc. 3. an ingredient or substance that makes soap work better.
build·er's knot (bil'dẽrz), a clove hitch: see **knot**, illus.
build·ing (bil'diŋ), *n.* 1. anything that is built, as a house, factory, etc.; structure: abbreviated **bldg., blg.** 2. the act, process, art, work, or business of putting materials or parts together to make houses, ships, etc.
SYN.—**building** is the general term applied to a fixed construction with walls and a roof, as a house, factory, institution, etc.; **edifice** implies a large or stately building and is sometimes used figuratively (the *edifice* of democracy); **structure** also suggests an imposing building, but has special application when the manner or material of construction is being stressed (a steel *structure*); **pile** is applied in poetry and lofty prose to a very large building or mass of buildings.
building and loan association, an organization that helps its members to build or buy homes, either by investing their savings or by loans.
build-up (bild'up'), *n.* [Slang], favorable publicity or praise, especially when systematic and intended to make something popular, well-known, etc.
built (bilt), past tense and past participle of **build.**
built-in (bilt'in'), *adj.* made as part of the structure; not movable or detachable: as, a *built-in* bathtub.
Bu·kha·ra (bōō-khä'rä; Eng. boo-kä'rə), *n.* Bokhara.
Bu·kha·rin, Ni·ko·lai I·van·o·vich (ni-kô-lī' i-vän'ô-vich bōō-khä'rin), 1888–1938; Russian Communist leader and editor; convicted of treason and executed.
Bu·ko·vi·na (bōō'kə-vē'nə), *n.* Bucovina.
Bul (bool), *n.* [Heb.], Cheshvan: early Hebrew name.
bul., bulletin.
Bu·la·wa·yo (boo'lə-wä'yō), *n.* a city in southwestern Southern Rhodesia: pop., 49,000.
bulb (bulb), *n.* [L. *bulbus;* Gr. *bolbos;* ult. < same IE. base as *bud* (a swelling)], 1. an underground bud that sends down roots and consists of a very short stem covered with leafy scales or layers, as in a lily, onion, hyacinth, etc. 2. a corm, tuber, or rhizome resembling a bulb, as in a crocus, dahlia, etc. 3. any plant that grows from a bulb. 4. anything shaped like a bulb; rounded thing or enlarged part: as, an incandescent light *bulb*, the *bulb* of a syringe. 5. in *anatomy*, *a)* an enlargement on some tissues and organs, as at the root of a hair. *b)* the medulla oblongata.
bul·ba·ceous (bul-bā'shəs), *adj.* [L. *bulbaceus*], in *botany*, 1. of or like a bulb. 2. having or growing from a bulb.
bulb·ar (bul'bẽr), *adj.* of a bulb.
bulbed (bulbd), *adj.* having a bulb or bulbs.
bulb·if·er·ous (bul-bif'ẽr-əs), *adj.* producing bulbs.
bul·bil (bul'bil), *n.* [< L. *bulbillus, falsely assumed to be dim. of *bulbus;* see BULB], a small bulb or fleshy bud on a flower stalk, as in some onions, or in the axil of a leaf, as in a tiger lily.
bulb·ous (bul'bəs), *adj.* [L. *bulbosus*], 1. of, shaped like, or having a bulb or bulbs. 2. growing from a bulb.
bul·bul (bool'bool), *n.* [Per.; prob. echoic], 1. a kind of songbird, perhaps a nightingale, of Persia. 2. any of various small, bright-colored birds related to the thrush, found in Asia and Africa.
Bul·finch, Charles (bool'finch'), 1763–1844; American architect.
Bulfinch, Thomas, 1796–1867; American writer and mythologist; son of *Charles.*
Bul·gan·in, Ni·ko·lai A·le·ksan·dro·vich (nē'kô-lī' ä'lyek-sän'drô-vich bōōl-gä'nin), 1895– ; premier of the Soviet Union (1955–1958).
Bul·gar (bul'gẽr, bul'gär, bool'gär), *n. & adj.* Bulgarian.
Bul·gar·i·a (bul-gâr'i-ə, bool-gâr'i-ə), *n.* a country in the Balkans, on the Black Sea: area, 42,796 sq. mi.; pop., 7,614,000; capital, Sofia: abbreviated **Bulg.**
Bul·gar·i·an (bul-gâr'i-ən, bool-gâr'i-ən), *adj.* of Bulgaria, its people, or their language. *n.* 1. a native or inhabitant of Bulgaria. 2. the Slavic language of the Bulgarians. Abbreviated **Bulg.**
bulge (bulj), *n.* [ME.; OFr. *boulge*, a swelling, bag < L. *bulga*, leather bag; ult. < same IE. base as *bud* (a swelling)], an outward swelling; protuberance. *v.i. & v.t.* [BULGED (buljd), BULGING], to swell or bend outward; protrude. —*SYN.* see **projection.**
Bulge, Battle of the (bulj), the last major German counteroffensive of World War II (December 16, 1944–January, 1945), an unsuccessful attempt to push the Allies back through Belgium to Paris.
bulg·er (bul'jẽr), *n.* a golf club with a very convex wooden face.
bulg·y (bul'ji), *adj.* having a bulge or bulges.
bu·lim·i·a (bū-lim'i-ə), *n.* [Gr. *boulimia* < *bous*, ox + *limos*, hunger], in *medicine*, a continuous, immoderate hunger.
bu·lim·ic (bū-lim'ik), *adj.* having bulimia.
bulk (bulk), *n.* [ME. *bulke, bolke*, a heap; ON. *bulki*, a heap, ship's cargo; IE. base *bhel-, to swell up; cf. BOLE], 1. size, mass, or volume, especially if great. 2. the main mass or body of something; largest part or portion: as, he invested the *bulk* of his fortune. 3. a ship's hold or cargo. Abbreviated **blk.** *v.i.* 1. to form into a mass. 2. to increase in size, importance, etc. 3. to have size or importance: as, this factor *bulks* large in our minds. *v.t.* to make (something) form into a mass. *adj.* 1. total; aggregate. 2. not packaged.
break bulk, to make (a package, shipment, etc.) incomplete by removing a part: abbreviated **b.b.**
in bulk, 1. not packaged. 2. in large amounts; in great volume.
SYN.—**bulk, mass,** and **volume** all refer to a quantity of matter or collection of units forming a body or whole, **bulk** implying a body of great size, weight, or numbers (the lumbering *bulk* of a hippopotamus, the *bulk* of humanity), **mass,** an aggregate, multitude, or expanse forming a cohesive, unified, or solid body (an egg-shaped *mass*, a *mass* of color, the *mass* of workers), and **volume,** a moving or flowing mass, often of a fluctuating nature (*volumes* of smoke, the *volume* of production).
bulk (bulk), *n.* [ME. *balk, bolk;* ON. *balkr*, partition, wall], [Archaic], a projecting framework or stall built as the front of a shop.
bulk·head (bulk'hed'), *n.* [*bulk* (framework) + *head*], 1. an upright partition separating parts of a ship, airplane, etc. for protection against fire, leakage, etc. 2. a

wall or embankment for holding back earth, fire, water, etc. 3. a boxlike structure built over an opening, as a stairway, elevator shaft, etc.
bulk·i·ness (bul′ki-nis), *n.* a bulky quality or state.
bulk·y (bul′ki), *adj.* [BULKIER (-ki-ẽr), BULKIEST (-ki-ist)], 1. of great bulk; large; massive. 2. awkwardly large; big and clumsy.
bull (bool), *n.* [ME. *bule, bole;* AS. *bula,* a steer; akin to G. *bulle;* IE. base **bhel-,* to swell up; cf. PHALLUS], 1. the male of any bovine animal, as the ox, buffalo, etc. 2. the male of certain other large animals, as the elephant, elk, moose, walrus, whale, etc. 3. a person who buys stocks or securities and tries to raise, or anticipates a rise in, their market price, in order to sell at a profit. 4. a very large, noisy, or strong person. 5. [B-], *a)* the constellation Taurus. *b)* the corresponding sign of the zodiac: see **zodiac,** illus. 6. [Slang], a policeman. 7. [Slang], foolish, empty, or insincere talk; nonsense. *v.t.* to try to raise the price of (stocks) or prices in (a stock market). *v.i.* to go up in price, as stocks. *adj.* 1. male. 2. like a bull in size, strength, etc. 3. rising in price: as, a *bull* market.
shoot the bull, [Slang], 1. to talk nonsense. 2. to talk.
take the bull by the horns, to face and deal boldly with a danger or difficulty.
bull (bool), *n.* [ME. & OFr. *bulle;* It. *bulla;* LL. *bulla;* L. *bulla,* a knob, seal; cf. BULLETIN], 1. a seal affixed to a document, especially to one from the Pope. 2. an official document, edict, or decree from the Pope.
bull (bool), *n.* [Early Mod. Eng., a jest; ME. *bul,* a lie; OFr. *boule,* a lie, bragging statement; L. *bulla,* a bubble], an absurd and illogical mistake in statement.
bull- (bool), [< *bull* (ox); cf. JACK-], a combining form meaning: 1. *of a bull* or *bulls,* as in *bullfight.* 2. *like a bull* or *bull's,* as in *bullhead.* 3. *large* or *male,* as in *bullfrog, bullfinch.*
bull., bulletin.
Bull, John (bool), [first used by Arbuthnot (1712)], England, the English people, etc.: a personification.
Bull, O·le (ō′lə bōōl′), 1810–1880; Norwegian violinist.
bul·la (bool′ə, bul′ə), *n.* [*pl.* BULLAE (-ē)], [LL.; see BULL (papal document)], 1. a round lead seal attached to an official document from the Pope. 2. in *medicine,* a large blister or vesicle.
bull·ace (bool′is), *n.* [ME. *bolace;* OFr. *beloce;* ML. **bullucea,* small plum], 1. a purple wild plum, larger than the sloe. 2. the tree it grows on.
bul·late (bool′it, bul′it), *adj.* [L. *bullatus* < *bulla,* a bubble], in *botany,* blistered or puckered in appearance, as a leaf of savoy cabbage.
bull·bait·ing (bool′bāt′iŋ), *n.* the tormenting of bulls by dogs, formerly a popular sport in England.
bull·bat (bool′bat′), *n.* [*bull-* + *bat*], a nighthawk.
bull brier, a kind of vine of the greenbrier group: so called from its large thorns.
bull·dog (bool′dôg′, bool′dog′), *n.* [*bull-* + *dog*], 1. a short-haired, square-jawed, heavily built dog that has great courage and a strong, stubborn grip. 2. a short-barreled revolver of large caliber. 3. a heat-resisting material used as lining in puddling furnaces. 4. [British], *a)* a sheriff's officer. *b)* a university attendant employed to enforce the rules of behavior for students. *adj.* like or characteristic of a bulldog; courageous, stubborn, etc. *v.t.* to throw (a steer) by taking hold of its horns and twisting its neck.

BULLDOG

bulldog edition, the early edition of a morning newspaper, chiefly for out-of-town distribution.
bull·doze (bool′dōz′), *v.t.* [BULLDOZED (-dōzd′), BULLDOZING], [? < *bull*-whip + *dose,* hence, lit., to give a dose of the whip: orig. in reference to intimidation of Negroes seeking to vote], [Colloq.], to force or frighten by threatening; intimidate; bully.
bull·doz·er (bool′dōz′ẽr), *n.* [orig. used of Louisiana vigilantes; see BULLDOZE], 1. a person who bulldozes. 2. a tractor with a large, shovellike blade on the front for pushing or moving earth, debris, etc. 3. the blade alone.

BULLDOZER

bul·let (bool′it), *n.* [Fr. *boulette,* dim. of *boule,* a ball], 1. a small piece of lead, steel, or other metal formed into a ball or cone-shaped missile with a round or pointed end, to be shot from a firearm: bullets are now usually set in a metal casing. 2. loosely, a bullet with its casing; cartridge.
bul·let-head·ed (bool′it-hed′id), *adj.* round-headed.
bul·le·tin (bool′ə-t′n, bool′ə-tin), *n.* [It. *bulletino, bulleta,* dim. of LL. *bulla;* see BULL (papal edict)], 1. a brief official statement about a matter of public concern. 2. a brief statement of the latest news, as in a newspaper or radio broadcast. 3. a regular publication, as of an organization, society, etc. Abbreviated **bul., bull.** *v.t.* to announce or publish in a bulletin.
bulletin board, a board or wall area on which bulletins or notices are put up.
bul·let·proof (bool′it-prōōf′), *adj.* that bullets cannot pierce. *v.t.* to make bulletproof.
bull fiddle, [Slang], a bass viol.
bull·fight (bool′fīt′), *n.* an entertainment in which a bull is first provoked by men on horseback and afoot, who stick lances and darts into it, and is then maneuvered into position for the kill by the matador, who must run his sword skillfully down into its neck: popular in Spain and Spanish America.
bull·fight·er (bool′fīt′ẽr), *n.* a participant in a bullfight, especially a matador.
bull·fight·ing (bool′fīt′iŋ), *n.* 1. the performance of a bullfight. 2. the art or profession of a bullfighter.
bull·finch (bool′finch′), *n.* [*bull-* + *finch*], any of a number of small, variously colored songbirds of Europe and Asia, with a short, rounded beak: they are related to the grosbeaks.
bull·finch (bool′finch′), *n.* [? < *bull fence*], a hedge with a ditch on one side, too high for a horse and rider to jump.

BULLFIGHTER

bull·frog (bool′frôg′, bool′frog′), *n.* [see BULL-], a large North American frog that has a deep, loud croak.
bull·head (bool′hed′), *n.* [see BULL-], 1. any of various fishes with a large head, as some kinds of catfish, the miller's thumb, sculpin, etc. 2. a bullheaded person.
bull·head·ed (bool′hed′id), *adj..* 1. having a head shaped like a bull's. 2. blindly stubborn; headstrong.
bul·lion (bool′yən), *n.* [D. *bulioen;* Fr. *billon,* small coin, alloy of copper with silver < *bille,* a stick, bar < Gallic **bilia,* tree trunk], 1. gold and silver regarded as raw material. 2. ingots of gold or silver, as before coinage.
bul·lion (bool′yən), *n.* [Fr. *bouillon* < L. *bulla,* a bubble], a heavy fringe or lace of twisted gold or silver thread.
bull·ish (bool′ish), *adj.* 1. of or like a bull. 2. rising or making rise in price on the stock exchange.
Bul·litt, William Christian (bool′it), 1891– ; American diplomat.
Bull Moose, a member of the Progressive Party led by Theodore Roosevelt in the presidential campaign of 1912: so called from the symbol of the party.
bull·necked (bool′nekt′), *adj.* having a short, thick neck.
bull nose, a contagious disease of pigs, caused by a bacillus and characterized by a swelling of the snout and a sloughing off of the infected tissues.
bull·ock (bool′ək), *n.* [ME. *bulloke;* AS. *bulluc*], 1. a castrated bull; ox; steer. 2. [Obs.], a young bull.
bull pen, 1. a fenced enclosure for bulls. 2. [Colloq.], *a)* a large room or enclosure in a penitentiary, where prisoners are herded during riots. *b)* a barred enclosure in a jail, where prisoners are kept together temporarily, as between their arrest and the placing of charges. 3. in *baseball,* an area alongside the playing field, where relief pitchers practice and warm up.
bull·pout (bool′pout′), *n.* the common bullhead or horned pout.
bull ring, an enclosed arena for bullfighting.
bull-roar·er (bool′rôr′ẽr), *n.* a flat piece of wood at the end of a string, which makes a roaring noise when whirled: used in religious ceremonies of some tribes.
Bull Run, a stream in northeastern Virginia: site of two Civil War battles (1861 and 1862), in which Union forces were defeated.
bull session, [cf. BULL, *n.* 7], [Colloq.], an informal discussion or conversation among a small group.
bull's-eye (boolz′ī′), *n.* [cf. Fr. *oeil de boeuf,* Dan. *koöie,* cow eye, Sw. *oxoga,* ox eye, all applied to small, round windows], 1. a thick, circular glass in a roof, ship's deck, etc., for admitting light. 2. any circular opening for light or air. 3. the circular central mark of a target. 4. a shot that hits this. 5. a direct hit. 6. a successful act. 7. a convex lens for concentrating light. 8. a lantern with such a lens. 9. a hard, round candy. 10. in *nautical usage,* a small wooden pulley.
bull snake, a gopher snake.
bull terrier, any of a breed of strong, lean, active dog

with a smooth, white coat: it is a cross between the bulldog and the terrier.

bull-tongue (bool'tuŋ'), *v.t. & v.i.* to plow with a bull tongue.

bull tongue [so called from its shape], a simple, heavy plow, usually with a single shovel, used especially in cotton growing.

bull-whip (bool'hwip'), *n.* [*bull-* + *whip*], a long, heavy whip, formerly used by cattle drivers and teamsters.

bul·ly (bool'i), *n.* [*pl.* BULLIES (-iz)], [orig., sweetheart; D. *boel*, lover, brother < MHG. *buole* (G. *buhle*), lover; later influenced by *bull* (ox)], 1. a person who hurts, frightens, threatens, or tyrannizes over those who are smaller or weaker. 2. a pimp. 3. [Archaic], a hired cutthroat or thug. 4. [Archaic], a fine fellow. *v.t.* [BULLIED (-id), BULLYING], to act the bully toward; force (a person) into doing something by threatening loudly; browbeat; bulldoze. *v.i.* to be a bully. *adj.* 1. gallant; dashing: as, my *bully* boy. 2. [Colloq.], fine; very good. *interj.* [Colloq.], good! well done!

bul·ly (bool'i), *n.* [Fr. *bouilli*, boiled beef < *bouillir*, to boil], canned or corned beef: also **bully beef.**

bul·ly·rag (bool'i-rag'), *v.t.* [see BULLY, *v.t.* & RAG, *v.t.*], [BULLYRAGGED (-ragd'), BULLYRAGGING], to frighten or abuse by bluster and threats.

bully tree, [altered < *balata tree*], any of several tropical trees of the sapodilla family, especially the balata.

Bü·low, Prince Bern·hard von (bern'härt fôn bü'lō), 1849–1929; German statesman; chancellor (1900–1909).

bul·rush (bool'rush'), *n.* [ME. *bulryshe, bolroyshe* < AS. *bol*, bole of a tree + *risc*, a rush], 1. any of a number of related tall plants of the sedge family, with grasslike leaves and spikelets of flowers, found in water and wet land. 2. [British], the cattail. 3. in the *Bible*, the papyrus.

bul·wark (bool'wẽrk), *n.* [ME., D. & MHG. *bolwerk*, a rampart; see BOULEVARD], 1. an earthwork or defensive wall; fortified rampart. 2. a breakwater. 3. a defense; protection. 4. *usually pl.* the part of a ship's side above the deck. *v.t.* 1. to provide bulwarks for. 2. to be a bulwark to.

Bul·wer-Lyt·ton, Edward George Earle (bool'wẽr-lit'ən), first Baron Lytton, 1803–1873; English dramatist and novelist; father of *Edward Robert.*

Bulwer-Lytton, Edward Robert, first Earl of Lytton, see **Meredith, Owen.**

bum (bum), *n.* [< *bummer;* prob. < G. *bummler*, loafer, habitually tardy person < *bummeln*, to go slowly, waste time], 1. [Colloq.], a loafer; idler; vagrant: sometimes used jokingly. 2. [Slang], a dissolute or worthless person. 3. [Slang], a spree. *v.i.* [BUMMED (bumd), BUMMING], 1. [Colloq.], to loaf; idle away time in a somewhat dissolute way. 2. [Colloq.], to live by begging or sponging on people. 3. [Slang], to drink heavily. *v.t.* [Slang], to get by begging or sponging on people. *adj.* [BUMMER (-ẽr), BUMMEST (-ist)], [Slang], inferior or poor in quality. —*SYN.* see **vagrant.**

give (a person) the bum's rush, [Slang], to eject (a person) forcibly.

on the bum, [Colloq.], 1. living the life of a vagrant. 2. out of repair; broken.

bum (bum), *n.* [ME. *bom;* prob. < *botem*, bottom; cf. D. dial. *boem* < *bodem*, & obs. *bummery* for *bottomry*], [British Slang], the buttocks.

bum·bail·iff (bum'bāl'if), *n.* [*bum* (buttocks) + *bailiff:* ? because the officer was often close behind], [British], a bailiff or sheriff's officer: used contemptuously.

bum·ble·bee (bum'b'l-bē'), *n.* [ME. *bumblen*, to buzz (echoic); + *bee*], any of a number of related large, hairy, yellow-and-black bees that make a loud, humming sound in flight.

bum·bling (bum'bliŋ), *adj.* [ppr. of *bumble*, to buzz (see BUMBLEBEE) or of *bumble*, to blunder, bustle about; prob. influenced by Mr. *Bumble*, officious beadle in Dickens' *Oliver Twist*], noisily and blunderingly self-important.

bum·boat (bum'bōt'), *n.* [*bum* (buttocks) + *boat;* orig., (17th c.) sailors' slang for *garbage boat*], a boat used in peddling provisions, etc. to ships.

bum·kin (bum'kin), *n.* a bumpkin (beam).

bump (bump), *v.t.* [echoic], 1. to hit or knock against; collide lightly with. 2. [Slang], to take the place of; displace, as from a job, airplane seat, etc. *v.i.* 1. to hit or collide with a bump (often with *into* or *against*). 2. to move with bumps or jolts. *n.* 1. a blow; light collision; jolt. 2. a swelling or lump, especially one caused by a blow. 3. a natural high place on the skull, supposed by phrenologists to indicate a specific mental faculty: as, the *bump* of wit.

bump off, 1. to bump so as to cause to fall off (a table, etc.); hence, 2. [Slang], to murder; kill.

bump·er (bump'ẽr), *n.* a metal bar fastened to the front or back of an automobile to give some protection if the car bumps into something.

bump·er (bump'ẽr), *n.* [< *bump*, influenced by Fr. *bombé*, bulging, *bombarde*, large drinking vessel, etc.], 1. a cup or glass filled to the brim. 2. [Colloq.], anything unusually large of its kind. *v.t.* 1. to fill to the brim. 2. to drink a toast to. *adj.* [Colloq.], unusually large or abundant: as, a *bumper* crop.

bump·i·ly (bump''l-i), *adv.* in a bumpy manner.

bump·i·ness (bump'i-nis), *n.* the quality or state of being bumpy.

bump·kin (bump'kin), *n.* [prob. < D. *boomkin*, short tree; dim. of *boom*, a tree], 1. a short, projecting beam or spar on a ship, as at the stern of a yacht for securing a permanent backstay; boom: also spelled **bumkin.** 2. [? in allusion to the characteristic short, blocky build], an awkward or loutish person from the country; clumsy yokel.

bump·tious (bump'shəs), *adj.* [prob. < *bump*, by analogy with *fractious*, etc.], disagreeably conceited, arrogant, or pushing.

bump·y (bump'i), *adj.* [BUMPIER (-i-ẽr), BUMPIEST (-i-ist)], full of bumps; rough; jolting.

bun (bun), *n.* [ME. *bunne*, small loaf; ? < OFr. *bon*, good], 1. a small roll, usually somewhat sweetened and often spiced or enriched with raisins, etc. 2. hair worn in a roll or knot on a woman's head or neck. Also spelled **bunn.**

bu·na (bōō'nə, bū'nə), *n.* [G. < *bu*tadien, butadiene + *Na*, (symbol for) sodium], synthetic rubber made by polymerizing butadiene: a trade-mark (**Buna**).

bunch (bunch), *n.* [ME. *bunche, bonch*, a hump; akin to MLG. *bunk*, D. *bonk*, Norw. *bunka*, a hump, heap, bunch], 1. a cluster or tuft of things growing together: as, a *bunch* of grapes. 2. a collection of things of the same kind fastened or grouped together, or regarded as belonging together: as, a *bunch* of keys. Abbreviated **bch.** 3. [Rare], a hump. 4. [Colloq.], a group (of people). *v.t. & v.i.* 1. to form or collect into a bunch or bunches; gather together in one place. 2. to gather into loose folds or wads, as a dress, skirt, etc.

bunch·ber·ry (bunch'be'ri, bunch'bẽr-i), *n.* [*pl.* BUNCHBERRIES (-iz)], a shrub with tiny, greenish flowers and tight clusters of red berries; dwarf dogwood.

Bunche, Ralph Johnson (bunch), 1904–; American educator and United Nations statesman; received Nobel peace prize, 1950.

bunch·flow·er (bunch'flou'ẽr), *n.* a plant of the lily family, with a cluster of greenish or white flowers on a tall stalk and a cluster of narrow leaves at the base.

bunch grass, any of various grasses that grow in tufts.

bunch·y (bun'chi), *adj.* [BUNCHIER (-chi-ẽr), BUNCHIEST (-chi-ist)], 1. growing in bunches. 2. like or having a bunch or bunches.

bun·co (buŋ'kō), *n.* [*pl.* BUNCOS (-kōz)], [< Sp. *banca*, card game (c. 1875)], [Colloq.], a swindle, especially one carried out with confederates, as at a card game, lottery, etc.; confidence game. *v.t.* [Colloq.], to swindle; cheat. Also spelled **bunko.**

bun·combe (buŋ'kəm), *n.* [< *Buncombe* county, North Carolina: from the fact that the representative to Congress (1819–1821) from the district including this county continually felt bound to "make a speech for Buncombe"], [Colloq.], 1. talk that is empty, insincere, or merely for effect. 2. anything said or done merely for effect; humbug. Also spelled **bunkum.**

‡Bund (boont; Eng. boond), *n.* [*pl.* BUNDE (bün'də); Eng. BUNDS (boondz)], [G. < root of *binden*, to bind], 1. a league; confederation. 2. a league of North German states established in 1867. 3. an organized group of people, especially one for political purposes. 4. the German-American Bund, a former pro-Nazi organization in the United States.

bund (bund), *n.* [Anglo-Ind.; Hind. *band*, embankment, dike < Per.], in the Orient, an embankment or quay.

Bun·del·khand (bun'dəl-kund', boon'dəl-khund'), *n.* a former agency of British India, in east central India: area, 10,081 sq. mi.

Bun·des·rat, Bun·des·rath (boon'dəs-rät'), *n.* [G., genit. of *bund* (see BUND, league) + *rat, rath*, council], 1. formerly, the federal council of the German Empire. 2. the federal council of Switzerland.

bun·dle (bun'd'l), *n.* [ME. *bundel;* MD. *bondel, bundel* < base of *bind*], 1. a number of things tied, wrapped, or otherwise held together: abbreviated **bd., bdl.** 2. a package; parcel. 3. a bunch; collection; group. 4. in *botany*, any of the bunches of specialized cells that conduct fluids in higher plants. *v.t.* [BUNDLED (-d'ld), BUNDLING], 1. to make into a bundle; wrap or tie together. 2. to put or send hastily or without ceremony (with *away, off, out,* or *into*). *v.i.* 1. to move or go hastily; bustle. 2. to lie in the same bed with one's sweetheart without undressing: formerly a courting custom, especially in New England.

bundle up, to put on plenty of warm clothing.

SYN.—**bundle** refers to a number of things bound together for convenience in carrying, storing, etc. and does not in itself carry connotations as to size, compactness, etc. (a *bundle* of discarded clothing); **bale** implies a standardized or uniform quantity of goods, as raw cotton, hay, etc., compressed into a rectangular mass and tightly bound; **parcel** and **package** are applied to something wrapped or boxed for transportation, sale, etc. and imply moderateness of size and a compact or orderly arrangement; **pack** is applied to package of a standard amount (a *pack* of cigarettes) or to a compact bundle carried on the back of a person or animal.

bung (buŋ), *n.* [ME. *bunge;* MD. *bonghe*], 1. a cork or other stopper for the hole in the side or end of a barrel, cask, or keg. 2. a bunghole. *v.t.* 1. to close (a bunghole) with a stopper. 2. to stop up; close. 3. [prob. influenced by *bang*], [Slang], to bruise or damage, as in a fight (with *up*).

bun·ga·low (buŋ'gə-lō'), *n.* [Anglo-Ind.; Hind. *bānglā*, thatched house, lit., belonging to Bengal], 1. in India, a low, one-storied house, usually with a wide, sweeping porch or veranda. 2. a small house or cottage, usually of one story or one and a half stories.

bung·hole (buŋ'hōl'), *n.* the hole in the side or end of a barrel, cask, or keg through which liquid can be poured in or drawn out.

bun·gle (buŋ'g'l), *v.t.* [BUNGLED (-g'ld), BUNGLING], [echoic; akin to Sw. *bangla*, to work ineffectually], to spoil by clumsy work; botch. *v.i.* to do or make things badly or clumsily. *n.* 1. a bungling, or clumsy, act. 2. a bungled piece of work.

Bu·nin, I·van A·lek·se·ye·vich (ē-vän' ä'lyeks-yā'ye-vich bōō'nēn), 1870–1953; Russian novelist and poet; received Nobel prize in literature, 1933.

bun·ion (bun'yən), *n.* [17th-c. Fr. *bouillon*, lump on horse's foot (< L. *bulla*, a bubble), influenced by ME. *bunny*, a lump (< OFr. *bugne, beugne*, a swelling)], an inflammation and swelling of the bursa at the base of the big toe, with a thickening of the skin.

bunk (buŋk), *n.* [D. *bank*, a bench], 1. a shelflike bed or berth built into or against a wall, as in a ship. 2. any narrow bed or cot. *v.i.* 1. to sleep in a bunk. 2. [Colloq.], to go to bed or sleep, especially in a makeshift manner.

bunk (buŋk), *n.* [< *bunkum, buncombe*], [Slang], buncombe; nonsense; twaddle.

bunk·er (buŋ'kēr), *n.* [Scot.; extension of *bank* (a bench); orig. a seat], 1. a large bin or tank, as for a ship's coal or fuel oil. 2. a unit of a modern underground steel-and-concrete fortification system. 3. a sand trap or mound of earth serving as a hazard or obstacle on a golf course. *v.t.* 1. to supply (a ship) with fuel. 2. in *golf*, to hit (a ball) into a bunker.

Bun·ker Hill (buŋ'kēr), a hill in Boston, Massachusetts: the Battle of Bunker Hill (1775), in which American colonial troops were defeated by the British, was actually fought on near-by Breed's Hill.

bunk·mate (buŋk'māt'), *n.* a person who shares the same bunk or occupies an adjoining bunk.

bun·ko (buŋ'kō), *n.* [*pl.* BUNKOS (-kōz)], *& v.t.* [BUNKOED (-kōd), BUNKOING], bunco.

bun·kum (buŋ'kəm), *n.* buncombe.

bunn (bun), *n.* a bun.

bun·ny (bun'i), *n.* [*pl.* BUNNIES (-iz)], [dim. of *bun*], a rabbit: pet name used by children.

Bun·sen, Robert Wil·helm (vil'helm boon'zən; Eng. bun's'n), 1811–1899; German chemist; discovered rubidium and cesium; invented Bunsen burner, etc.

Bunsen burner, [see prec. entry], a small gas burner that produces a hot, blue flame, used in chemistry laboratories, etc.: it consists of a hollow metal tube with adjustable holes at the bottom for admitting air to be mixed with the gas.

bunt (bunt), *v.t. & v.i.* [? < base of Bret. *bounta*, to butt, via Corn.], 1. [British Dial.], to strike or butt with or as with horns. 2. in *baseball*, to bat (a pitched ball) lightly so that it does not go beyond the infield: usually done as a sacrifice play. *n.* 1. a shove. 2. in *baseball*, *a)* the act of bunting, especially to advance a runner on base at a sacrifice. *b)* a hit made by bunting.

bunt (bunt), *n.* [< earlier dial., a puffball], 1. disease of wheat in which the grains are destroyed. 2. the smut fungus causing this disease.

bunt (bunt), *n.* [? < MLG. & MD. *bunt*, a binding bundle; akin to Eng. *bund*], 1. the sagging part of a fish net. 2. the bellying part of a square sail.

bun·tine (bun'tin), *n.* bunting (cloth).

bunt·ing (bun'tiŋ), *n.* [? < ME. *bunten*, to sift; hence, cloth used for sifting], 1. a thin cloth used in making flags, etc. 2. flags collectively. 3. strips of cloth in patriotic colors, used as holiday decorations for halls, automobiles, etc. 4. a baby's garment of soft, warm cloth made into a kind of hooded blanket that can be closed so that only the face is exposed.

bunt·ing (bun'tiŋ), *n.* [ME. *bounting, bunting*, pet name applied to bird < ME. *Bunetun*, OFr. *Bonneton*, double dim. of *bon*, good; see ROBIN], any of various small birds of the finch family, having a short, stout bill.

bunt·line (bunt'lin, bunt'līn), *n.* [ME. *bunt*, middle part of a sail + *line*, a rope], one of the ropes attached to the foot rope of a square sail to prevent the sail from bellying when drawn up to be furled.

Bun·yan, John (bun'yən), 1628–1688; English author and preacher; wrote *Pilgrim's Progress.*

Bunyan, Paul, see **Paul Bunyan.**

Buo·na·parte (bô'nə-pärt'; It. bwô'nä-pär'te), *n.* Bonaparte: Italian form of the name.

Buo·nar·ro·ti, Michelangelo (bwô'när-rô'tē), see **Michelangelo.**

buoy (boi, bōō'i), *n.* [OFr. *boye, buie* or MD. *boei;* L. *boia*, fetter (by which the float was anchored)], 1. a floating object anchored in a lake, river, etc. to warn of rocks, shoals, etc. or to mark a channel: there are various kinds of buoy, some with bells or lights. 2. an air-filled or cork device to keep a person afloat; life buoy: it may be in the form of a jacket, belt, or ring. *v.t.* [Sp. *boyar*, to float], 1. to mark or provide with a buoy. 2. to keep afloat in a liquid; hence, 3. to lift or hold up in mind or spirits; encourage.
 buoy up, 1. to keep afloat. 2. to lift or hold up in mind or spirits; encourage. 3. to raise to the surface of a liquid.

TYPES OF BUOY

A, can; B, nun; C, whistle; D bell; E, lighted whistle; F, lighted bell; G, spar; H, lighted with mooring

buoy·age (boi'ij, bōō'i-ij), *n.* 1. a system of or provision for buoys. 2. buoys collectively.

buoy·an·cy (boi'ən-si, bōō'yən-si), *n.* [< *buoyant*], 1. the ability or tendency to float or rise in liquid or air. 2. the power to keep something afloat; upward pressure on a floating object. 3. lightness or resilience of spirit; gaiety; cheerfulness.

buoy·ant (boi'ənt, bōō'yənt), *adj.* [? < Sp. *boyante* < *boyar*, to float], having or showing buoyancy.

bu·pres·tid (bū-pres'tid), *n.* [L. *bupresilis;* Gr. *bouprēstis*, venomous beetle which, on being eaten with fodder, caused cattle to swell up and die < *bous*, ox + *prēsthein*, to inflate], any of a number of related beetles that have long, flat bodies, usually bright-colored: the larvae are harmful to woody plants and to cattle.

bur (bũr), *n.* [ME. *burre;* < ON.; cf. Dan. *borre*, bur, burdock], 1. the rough, prickly seedcase or fruit of certain plants, as of the sticktight, cocklebur, etc. 2. a weed or other plant with burs; hence, 3. a person who clings like a bur. 4. a burr. *v.t.* [BURRED (bũrd), BURRING], 1. to remove burs from. 2. to burr.

Bur., Burma.

bur., bureau.

bu·ran (bōō-rän'), *n.* [Turk.], a strong windstorm of the steppes of Russia and Siberia, accompanied in winter with driving snow and in summer with hot dust.

Bur·bage, Richard (bũr'bij), 1567?–1619; English actor; associate of Shakespeare.

Bur·bank (bũr'baŋk), *n.* a city in California, near Los Angeles: pop., 90,000.

Bur·bank, Luther (bũr'baŋk), 1849–1926; American horticulturist; bred new varieties of vegetables, fruits, and flowers.

bur·ble (bũr'b'l), *v.i.* [BURBLED (-b'ld), BURBLING], [ME. *burbelen*, to bubble; echoic], to make a gurgling or bubbling sound.

bur·bot (bũr'bət), *n.* [*pl.* BURBOT, BURBOTS (-bəts); see PLURAL, II, D, 2], [Fr. *bourbotte*, altered, after *bourbe*, mud, mire < *barbote* < *barbe;* L. *barba*, a beard], a fresh-water fish of the cod family, having a spotted body with a broad, flat head and chin barbels.

burd (bũrd), *n.* [ME. *burde, bird, berde*, dial. var., by metathesis < AS. *bryd*, bride; see BRIDE], [Obs.], a lady; young lady.

bur·den (bũr'd'n), *n.* [ME. *burden, birden, birthen;* AS. *byrthen* < base of *beran*, to bear; see BEAR, BIRTH], 1. anything carried or endured; load (of material things or duty, work, sorrow, etc.). 2. a very heavy load; whatever is hard to bear. 3. the carrying of loads: as, a beast of *burden*. 4. the carrying capacity of a ship, or the weight of its cargo. *v.t.* to make bear a burden; load; weigh down; oppress. Also **burthen.**

bur·den (bũr'd'n), *n.* [ME. *burdoun*, bass in music, refrain; OFr. *bourdon*, a humming, buzzing; ML. *burdo, burdonis*, a drone, humming sound; echoic], 1. a bass accompaniment in music. 2. a chorus or refrain of a song. 3. the drone of a bagpipe. 4. a repeated, central idea; theme: as, the *burden* of a speech.

burden of proof, the obligation to prove a statement.

bur·den·some (bũr'd'n-səm), *adj.* hard to bear; heavy; oppressive; troublesome. —*SYN.* see **onerous.**

bur·dock (bũr′dok′), *n.* [*bur* (seedcase) + *dock* (plant)], any of a number of related plants of the composite family, with burs, large leaves, and a strong smell.

bu·reau (byoo′rō), *n.* [*pl.* BUREAUS, BUREAUX (-rōz)], [Fr., writing table or desk, office < OFr. *burel*, coarse cloth (as covering this) < LL. **bura*, coarse woolen; prob. < L. *burra*, coarse hair], 1. [British], a writing table or desk, with drawers for papers, etc. 2. a chest of drawers, with or without a mirror, for clothing, etc. 3. an office, especially one for a specific part of a business: as, an information *bureau*. 4. a government department, or a subdivision of a government department. Abbreviated **bur., bu.**

bu·reau·cra·cy (byoo-rok′rə-si, byoo-rō′krə-si), *n.* [*pl.* BUREAUCRACIES (-siz)], [Fr. *bureaucratie* < *bureau* + Gr. *kratia* < *kratein*, to be strong], 1. the administration of government through departments and subdivisions managed by sets of officials following an inflexible routine. 2. the officials collectively. 3. governmental officialism or inflexible routine: see also **red tape.** 4. the concentration of authority in administrative bureaus.

bu·reau·crat (byoo′rə-krat′), *n.* [< *bureaucracy*], 1. an official in a bureaucracy; hence, 2. an official who follows and insists on an inflexible routine, proper forms, rules, etc.

bu·reau·crat·ic (byoo′rə-krat′ik), *adj.* 1. of or characterized by bureaucracy. 2. of, like, or characteristic of a bureaucrat or bureaucrats.

bu·reau·crat·i·cal·ly (byoo′rə-krat′i-k′l-i), *adv.* in a bureaucratic manner.

Bureau of Internal Revenue, the bureau of the United States Department of the Treasury in charge of collecting Federal taxes.

Bureau of Standards, the bureau of the United States Department of Commerce in charge of testing weights, measures, materials, etc.

bu·rette, bu·ret (byoo-ret′), *n.* [Fr., dim. of OFr. *buire*, flagon < *buire*, to drink], a graduated glass tube with a stopcock at the bottom, used by chemists, etc. for measuring small quantities of liquid or gas.

BURETTE

burg (bũrg), *n.* [earlier var. of *borough;* colloq. use < *-burg* in place names], 1. originally, a fortified or walled town. 2. [Colloq.], a city, town, or village. Also **burh.**

-burg (bũrg), a suffix meaning *burg* or *borough*, as in *Vicksburg, Johannesburg:* also **-burgh,** as in *Pittsburgh.*

burg·age (bũr′gij), *n.* [ME.; OFr. *burgage, bourgage;* ML. *burgagium* < *burgus* < OHG. *burg*, borough; see BOROUGH], in *law*, a former system of tenure or lease of land, especially in towns, from an overlord for a yearly rental.

bur·gee (bũr′jē), *n.* [< OFr. *burgeis*, owner (of a vessel); see BOURGEOIS (shopkeeper)], an identifying flag on a ship, triangular or swallow-tailed in shape.

bur·geon (bũr′jən), *v.i. & v.t.* [ME. *burjounen;* OFr. *burjoner* < *burjon*, a bud], to put forth (buds, etc.); sprout. *n.* a bud; sprout.

-burg·er (bũr′gẽr), [< ham*burger*], [Slang], a combining form meaning *sandwich of ground meat* (*and*), as in *steakburger, cheeseburger*, etc.

bur·gess (bũr′jis), *n.* [ME. & OFr. *burgeis;* see BOURGEOIS (shopkeeper)], 1. a citizen or freeman of a borough. 2. in England, a member of Parliament representing a borough, corporate town, or university. 3. a member of the House of Burgesses, the lower house of the legislature of Maryland or Virginia before the American Revolution.

Bur·gess, Ge·lett (jə-let′ bũr′jis), (*Frank Gelett Burgess*), 1866–1951; American humorist and illustrator.

burgh (bũrg; Scot. bur′ō, bur′ə), *n.* [ME.; Scot. var. of *borough*], 1. [British], a borough. 2. in Scotland, an incorporated or chartered town. Also **burh.**

-burgh (bũrg; Scot. bur′ə), -burg.

burgh·er (bũr′gẽr), *n.* [D. *burger*, citizen < *burg*, **town**], a freeman of a burgh; citizen of a town.

Burgh·ley, Baron (bũr′li), see **Cecil, William.**

bur·glar (bũr′glẽr), *n.* [OFr. *burglour;* Anglo-L. *burglator;* LL. *burgulator;* ? < Gmc. *burg*, a dwelling + L. *latro* (OFr. *lere*), robber], a person who commits burglary.

bur·glar·i·ous (bẽr-glâr′i-əs), *adj.* of, involving, constituting, or inclined to burglary.

bur·glar·ize (bũr′glə-rīz′), *v.t.* [BURGLARIZED (-rīzd′), BURGLARIZING], [Colloq.], to commit burglary in or upon.

bur·glar·proof (bũr′glẽr-pro͞of′), *adj.* constructed so as to be safe against burglary.

bur·gla·ry (bũr′glə-ri), *n.* [*pl.* BURGLARIES (-riz)], [< *burglar*], 1. the act of breaking into a house at night to commit theft or other felony. 2. the act of breaking into any building at any time to commit theft or other felony. 3. loosely, theft; robbery. —*SYN.* see **theft.**

bur·gle (bũr′g'l), *v.i. & v.t.* [BURGLED (-g'ld), BURGLING], [< *burglar*], [Colloq. & Humorous], to burglarize or commit burglary.

bur·go·mas·ter (bũr′gə-mas′tẽr, bũr′gə-mäs′tẽr), *n.* [D. *burgemeester* < *burg*, town, city + *meester*, a master], 1. the mayor or head magistrate of a city or town in the Netherlands, Flanders, Austria, or Germany. 2. a large arctic gull; ice gull.

bur·go·net (bũr′gə-net′), *n.* [Fr. *bourguignotte*, orig., fem. of *Bourguignot*, Burgundian < *Bourgogne*, Burgundy], a lightweight helmet or cap made of steel, worn in the 16th century.

bur·goo (bũr′go͞o, bẽr-go͞o′), *n.* [18th-c. nautical slang; early sp. also *burgoût*], 1. a thick oatmeal porridge or gruel. 2. [Dial.], *a*) a highly seasoned soup of meat and vegetables. *b*) a barbecue, or feast, at which this is served.

Bur·gos (bo͝or′gôs), *n.* a city in north central Spain: pop., 78,000 (est. 1947).

Bur·goyne, John (bẽr-goin′, bũr′goin), 1722–1792; British general in American Revolution; defeated in the battle of Saratoga (1777): called *Gentleman Johnny.*

bur·grave (bũr′grāv), *n.* [G. *burggraf; burg* (see BOROUGH) + *graf*, a count; see MARGRAVE], in *German history*, the lord of a burg and its environs, originally appointed, later hereditary.

Bur·gun·di·an (bẽr-gun′di-ən), *adj.* of Burgundy, its people, etc. *n.* a native or inhabitant of Burgundy.

Bur·gun·dy (bũr′gən-di), *n.* 1. a former duchy, kingdom, and province of eastern France: French name, *Bourgogne.* 2. [*pl.* BURGUNDIES (-diz)], a kind of wine, either red or white, originally made there.

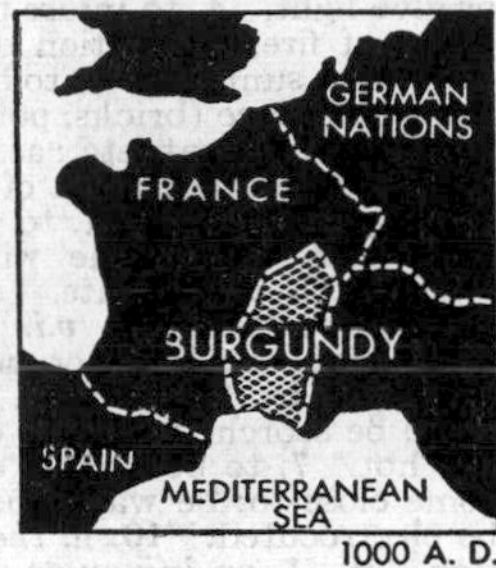

BURGUNDY

burh (boorkh), *n.* a burg or burgh.

bur·i·al (ber′i-əl), *n.* [ME. *buryel, biriel*, false sing. < *berieles, buriles;* AS. *byrgels*, tomb < *byrgan*, to bury], a burying; putting of a dead body into a grave, tomb, the sea, etc.; interment. *adj.* of or connected with burial.

burial ground, a place for burial; cemetery; graveyard.

bur·i·er (ber′i-ẽr), *n.* a person or thing that buries.

bu·rin (byoo′rin), *n.* [Fr.; It. *burino, borino* < OHG. *boro*, borer], 1. a pointed cutting tool used by engravers or marble workers. 2. the style of an engraver's work.

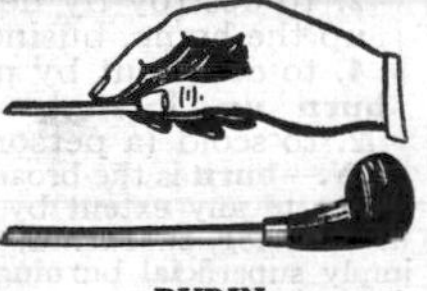
BURIN

burke (bũrk), *v.t.* [BURKED (bũrkt), BURKING], [after William *Burke*, executed for the act, in Edinburgh, 1829], 1. originally, to murder by suffocating, etc., so as to leave the body unmarked and fit to be sold for dissection; hence, 2. to get rid of quietly; suppress, as a parliamentary bill, discussion, etc.

Burke, Edmund (bũrk), 1729–1797; English statesman and orator; attacked the French Revolution.

burl (bũrl), *n.* [ME. *burle;* OFr. *bourle*, flocks or ends of threads < *bourre* < L. *burra*, coarse hair], 1. a knot in wool, thread, yarn, or cloth that gives a nubby appearance to cloth. 2. a kind of knot on some tree trunks. 3. veneer made from wood with burls in it. *v.t.* to finish (cloth) by taking out the burls, loose threads, etc.

bur·lap (bũr′lap), *n.* [17th c. *borelappe*(*s*); prob. < D.; cf. D. *boer*, farmer & *boenlap*, rubbing cloth; *lap* is akin to Eng. *lap* (to fold)], a coarse cloth made of jute, flax, or hemp, used for making bags, as a wall covering, etc.

bur·laps (bũr′laps), *n.pl.* [construed as sing.], burlap.

burled (bũrld), *adj.* having burls.

Bur·leigh, Baron (bũr′li), Burghley: see **Cecil, William.**

bur·lesque (bẽr-lesk′), *n.* [Fr. < It. *burlesco* < *burla*, a jest, mockery], 1. any broadly comic or satirical imitation of something; derisive caricature; parody. 2. (*also, facetiously,* bũr′li-kū′), a sort of vaudeville characterized by low comedy and display of nudity. *adj.* 1. derisively or comically imitating; parodying. 2. of or connected with the kind of vaudeville called burlesque. *v.t. & v.i.* [BURLESQUED (-leskt′), BURLESQUING], to imitate derisively or comically; parody. —*SYN.* see **caricature.**

bur·ley, Bur·ley (bũr′li), *n.* [? < a proper name], a tobacco grown in Kentucky and surrounding States: it is thin-leaved and usually light-colored after curing.

bur·li·ness (bũr′li-nis), *n.* the quality of being burly.

Bur·lin·game, An·son (an′s'n bũr′lin-gām′, bũr′liŋ-gām′), 1820–1870; American diplomat.

Bur·ling·ton (bũr′liŋ-tən), *n.* 1. a city in northwestern Vermont, on Lake Champlain: pop., 36,000. 2. a city in north central North Carolina: pop., 33,000. 3. a city in southeastern Iowa, on the Mississippi: pop., 32,000.

bur·ly (bũr′li), *adj.* [BURLIER (-li-ẽr), BURLIEST (-li-ist)], [*burlich, burli*, northern forms of ME. *borelich;* prob. < ON.; akin to OHG. *burlîh*, lofty, exalted; cf. (rare) AS. *borlice*, very], big and strong; heavy and muscular.

Bur·ma (bũr′mə), *n.* a country in southeastern Asia, on the Bay of Bengal: formerly a British colony: area, 261,610 sq. mi.; pop., 20,662,000; capital, Rangoon: abbreviated **Bur.**

Bur·man (bũr′mən), *n.* [*pl.* BURMANS (-mənz)], *& adj.* Burmese.

bur marigold, any of various weedy plants of the composite family, with yellow flowers and burs; sticktight.

Burma Road, the road from Lashio, northern Burma, to Yünnan and Chungking, China: used as an Allied supply route in World War II.

Bur·mese (bẽr-mēz′), *adj.* of Burma, its people, or their language. *n.* [*pl.* BURMESE], 1. a native or inhabitant of Burma. 2. the language of the Burmese.

burn (bũrn), *v.t.* [BURNED (bũrnd) or BURNT (bũrnt), BURNING], [ME. *bernen, brennen;* AS. *bærnan, bernan, v.t., biernan, brinnan, v.i.;* akin to G. *brennen;* IE. **bhre-n-wō* < base **bhreu-*, to boil forth, well out, as also in *burn* (stream)], 1. to destroy by fire. 2. to put to death by fire. 3. to set on fire; cause to blaze, shine, or give light. 4. to injure by fire or something with the effect of fire, as friction or acid; scorch, singe, scald, etc. 5. to sunburn. 6. to brand. 7. to cauterize. 8. to harden or glaze (bricks, pottery, etc.) by fire; fire. 9. to cause by fire, heat, etc.: as, he *burned* a hole in his coat. 10. to cause a sensation of heat in: as, the horseradish *burned* his throat. 11. to use (candles, lights, heaters, etc.). 12. to inflame with anger, desire, etc. 13. [Slang], to electrocute. 14. in *chemistry*, to make undergo combustion. *v.i.* 1. to be on fire; flame; blaze. 2. to give out light or heat; shine; glow. 3. to be destroyed by fire or heat. 4. to be injured by fire or heat; be scorched, singed, etc. 5. to die by fire. 6. to feel hot. 7. to be excited or inflamed. 8. [Colloq.], to come close to; be warm: used in games. 9. [Slang], to be electrocuted. 10. in *chemistry*, to undergo combustion. *n.* 1. an injury or damage caused by fire, heat, wind, etc. 2. a mark made by branding. 3. a sunburn.

burn down, to burn to the ground.

burn oneself out, to exhaust oneself by too much work or dissipation.

burn out, 1. to cease burning through lack of fuel. 2. to destroy by heat from friction, etc. 3. to burn up the home, business establishment, or property of. 4. to drive out by means of fire.

burn up, [Slang], 1. to make or become angry. 2. to scold (a person) severely.

SYN.—**burn** is the broadest term in this comparison, denoting injury to any extent by fire, intense heat, friction, acid, etc. (a *burnt* log, sun*burned*, wind*burned*); **scorch** and **singe** both imply superficial burning, **scorch** emphasizing discoloration or damaging of texture (to *scorch* a shirt in ironing), and **singe**, the burning off, often intentional, of bristles, feathers, the ends of hair, etc.; **sear** implies the burning of animal tissue and is applied specifically to the quick browning of the outside of roasts, etc. in cooking to seal in the juices; **char** implies a reduction by burning to charcoal or carbon. All of these terms have figurative applications (a *burning* desire, a *scorching* tirade, a *singed* reputation, a soul-*searing* experience, *charred* hopes).

burn (bũrn), *n.* [ME. *burne;* AS. *burna, brunna;* akin to G. *brunnen;* see BURN, *v.*], [Scot.], a little stream.

Burne-Jones, Sir **Edward Co·ley** (kō′li bũrn′jōnz′), 1833–1898; English painter and designer.

burn·er (bũr′nẽr), *n.* 1. the part of a stove, furnace, lamp, etc. from which the flame comes. 2. an apparatus for burning; furnace, stove, etc.: as, an oil *burner*. 3. a person whose work consists in burning something.

bur·net (bũr′nit), *n.* [ME.; OFr. *burnete* < *brunette;* see BRUNET], any of various plants of the rose family, with white, red, purple, or greenish flower heads or spikes.

Bur·nett, Frances Hodg·son (hoj′sən bũr-net′), 1849–1924; American novelist, born in England.

Bur·ney, Fanny (bũr′ni), (*Frances Burney; Madame d'Arblay*), 1752–1840; English novelist and diarist.

burn·ing (bũrn′iŋ), *adj.* 1. that burns. 2. of the utmost seriousness or importance: as, a *burning* issue.

burning bush, 1. a large shrub or tree with inconspicuous flowers and red fruit; wahoo. 2. a strong-smelling, bushy plant with loose spires of white flowers that give off an inflammable vapor; fraxinella.

burning glass, a convex lens for focusing the sun's rays so as to produce heat or set fire to something.

bur·nish (bũr′nish), *v.t. & v.i.* [ME. *burnissen;* OFr. *burnir, brunir*, to make brown < *brun;* see BRUNET], to make or become shiny by rubbing; polish. *n.* gloss; polish. —***SYN.*** see **polish.**

bur·nish·er (bũr′nish-ẽr), *n.* 1. a person who burnishes. 2. a burnishing tool.

Burn·ley (bũrn′li), *n.* a city in eastern Lancashire, England: pop., 81,000.

bur·noose, bur·nous (bẽr-nōōs′, bũr′nōōs), *n.* [Fr. *burnous;* Ar. *burnus;* ? < Gr. *birros*, a cloak], a long cloak with a hood, worn by Arabs and Moors.

Burns, Robert (bũrnz), 1759–1796; Scottish poet.

Burn·side, Ambrose Everett (bũrn′sīd′), 1824–1881; Union general in the Civil War.

burn·sides (bũrn′sīdz′), *n.pl.* [after A. E. *Burnside*], heavy growth of hair on the cheeks; side whiskers.

burnt (bũrnt), alternative past tense and past participle of **burn.**

burnt offering, an animal, food, etc. burned at an altar as an offering or sacrifice to a god.

burnt sienna, 1. a dark brown. 2. paint of this color.

burnt umber, 1. a reddish brown. 2. paint of this color.

bur oak, 1. a North American oak tree bearing acorns in prickly cups. 2. its hard wood.

burp (bũrp), *n. & v.i.* [echoic], [Slang], belch.

burr (bũr), *n.* 1. a prickly seedcase; bur. 2. a plant with burs. 3. a person who clings like a bur. 4. a rough edge or ridge left on metal or other material by cutting or drilling. 5. a washer on the small end of a rivet. 6. a dentist's drill. *v.t.* to form a rough edge on. Usually spelled **bur,** for *n.* 1, 2, 3.

burr (bũr), *n.* [prob. echoic], 1. the trilling of *r*, with uvula or tongue; hence, 2. any rough pronunciation: as, a Scottish *burr*. 3. a whirring sound. *v.i.* 1. to speak with a burr. 2. to make a whirring sound. *v.t.* to pronounce with a burr.

burr (bũr), *n.* 1. buhr. 2. buhrstone. Also spelled **bur.**

Burr, Aaron (bũr), 1756–1836; American statesman; vice-president of the United States (1801–1805); killed Alexander Hamilton in a duel.

bur reed, any of a number of related plants with narrow leaves and rounded, burlike fruit.

bur·ring machine (bũr′iŋ), a machine for turning edges on metal cylinders or disks.

burring reamer, 1. a tapered reamer for removing burrs caused by cutting metal. 2. a tool for countersinking.

bur·ro (bũr′ō, boor′ō), *n.* [*pl.* BURROS (-ōz)], [Sp. < *burrico;* L. *burricus*, small horse], a donkey.

Bur·roughs, John (bũr′ōz, bũr′əz), 1837–1921; American naturalist and author.

bur·row (bũr′ō), *n.* [ME. *burg, bureh;* see BOROUGH], 1. a hole or tunnel dug in the ground by an animal. 2. any similar passage or hole for shelter, refuge, etc. *v.i.* 1. to make a burrow or burrows. 2. to live or hide in or as in a burrow. 3. to search, as if by digging. 4. to dig. *v.t.* 1. to make burrows in (the ground). 2. to make by burrowing. 3. to hide in or as in a burrow.

burrowing owl, a ground owl of North and South America having long legs and a small head: it makes its nest in burrows dug in the ground.

burr·stone (bũr′stōn′), *n.* buhrstone.

bur·ry (bũr′i), *adj.* [BURRIER (-i-ẽr), BURRIEST (-i-ist)], 1. full of burs. 2. like a bur or burs; prickly.

bur·ry (bũr′i), *adj.* [BURRIER (-i-ẽr), BURRIEST (-i-ist)], having a burr or burrs.

Bur·sa (bōōr′sä), *n.* a city in northwestern Turkey: pop., 131,000: also called **Brusa.**

bur·sa (bũr′sə), *n.* [*pl.* BURSAE (-sē), BURSAS (-səz)], [LL., a purse, bag; Gr. *bursa*, a hide], in *anatomy*, a sac or pouchlike cavity, especially between joints.

bur·sal (bũr′s'l), *adj.* 1. having to do with public revenue and disbursement; fiscal. 2. of or functioning as a bursa.

bur·sar (bũr′sẽr), *n.* [LL. *bursarius*, treasurer < *bursa;* see BURSA], 1. a college treasurer or similar official in charge of the college funds. 2. in Scotland, a university student who has a scholarship.

bur·sar·i·al (bẽr-sâr′i-əl), *adj.* of a bursar or bursary.

bur·sa·ry (bũr′sə-ri), *n.* [*pl.* BURSARIES (-riz)], [ML. *bursaria* < LL. *bursarius;* see BURSAR], 1. a treasury, especially of a college. 2. in Scotland, a university scholarship.

‡Bur·schen·schaft (boor′shən-shäft′), *n.* [*pl.* BURSCHENSCHAFTEN (-shäf′tən)], [G. < *bursch*, student, young fellow], any of various social fraternities at German universities.

burse (bũrs), *n.* [Fr. *bourse;* see BOURSE], 1. a purse. 2. in Scotland, *a*) a university scholarship fund. *b*) a scholarship. 3. in the *Roman Catholic Church*, a flat, silk case for carrying chalice linen to and from the altar.

bur·seed (bũr′sēd′), *n.* a weedy plant with spikes of flowers and bristly fruit.

bur·ser·a·ceous (bũr′sẽr-ā′shəs), *adj.* [Mod. L. *bersera* (< Joachim *Burser*, G. botanist), the generic type of the family; + *-aceous*], designating or of a family of tropical trees and shrubs that yield balsams and resins.

bur·si·form (bũr′sə-fôrm′), *adj.* [< ML. *bursa*, pouch + *-form*], in *anatomy & zoology*, shaped like a bursa, or sac; pouchlike.

bur·si·tis (bẽr-sī′tis), *n.* [< *bursa* + *-itis*], inflammation of a bursa.

burst (būrst), *v.i.* [BURST, BURSTING], [ME. *berstan, brestan;* AS. *berstan;* akin to G. *bersten;* IE. base **bhres,* to burst, break, crack], 1. to come apart suddenly and violently, as under internal pressure; fly into pieces; break open or out; explode. 2. to give sudden expression in some way: as, she *burst* into tears. 3. to enter, come forth, appear, etc. suddenly and violently: as, he *burst* into the room. 4. to be full beyond normal capacity; be blown up to the bursting point; bulge. *v.t.* 1. to puncture or rupture with sudden violence; make explode. 2. to make (a thing) swell or fill up to the bursting point. *n.* [ME. *burst, brist,* a damage, defect, injury; AS. *byrst,* loss], 1. a bursting; outbreak; explosion. 2. the result of a bursting; break; breach. 3. a sudden activity or spurt: as, a *burst* of speed. 4. the series of shots fired from an automatic firearm by a single pull on the trigger.
burst a blood vessel, 1. to have a vein or artery burst. 2. [Colloq.], to become very excited.

bur·then (būr'*th*ən), *n. & v.t.* [Archaic], burden.

bur·ton (būr't'n), *n.* [prob. < the name *Burton* or *Barton*], a kind of tackle used with single or double pulley blocks for setting up or tightening rigging, or moving heavy articles.

Bur·ton, Harold Hitz (hits būr't'n), 1888– ; associate justice, United States Supreme Court (1945–1958).

Burton, Sir **Richard Francis,** 1821–1890; English explorer and writer.

Burton, Robert, 1577–1640; English scholar and clergyman; wrote *The Anatomy of Melancholy.*

Bu·run·di (boo-roon'di), *n.* a country in east central Africa, east of Congo (sense 2): formerly part of the UN trust territory of Ruanda-Urundi: area, 10,745 sq. mi.; pop., 2,234,000; capital, Usumbura.

bur·weed (būr'wēd'), *n.* any of various plants with burs, as the burdock, bur marigold, cocklebur, etc.

bur·y (ber'i), *v.t.* [BURIED (-id), BURYING], [ME. *buryen, birien, berien;* AS. *byrgan;* akin to AS. *beorgan,* G. *bergen,* to put in safety, preserve, conceal; IE. base **bhergh,* to save, preserve], 1. to put (a dead body) into the earth, a tomb, the sea, etc., usually in a ceremonial manner; inter. 2. to have or perform funeral services for. 3. to cover for, or as if for, concealment. 4. to put away, as from one's life, social life, the memory, etc.: as, we *buried* our friendship. 5. to sink; immerse: as, he *buries* himself in his work. —*SYN.* see **hide.**

Bur·yat (boor-yät'), *adj.* of the Buryat A.S.S.R., its people, or their language. *n.* 1. [*pl.* BURYAT, BURYATS (-yäts')], a member of one of the Mongolian tribes living in south central Siberia. 2. the language of the Buryats.

Buryat Autonomous Soviet Socialist Republic, a division of the R.S.F.S.R. in south central Siberia, north of the Mongolian Republic: area, 127,020 sq. mi.

burying ground, a cemetery; graveyard.

bus (bus), *n.* [*pl.* BUSES, BUSSES (-iz)], [< *omnibus*], 1. a large motor coach that can carry many passengers, generally following a regular route; omnibus. 2. [Colloq.], an automobile.

bus., business.

bus boy, a waiter's assistant who sets and clears tables, brings water, etc.

bus·by (buz'bi), *n.* [*pl.* BUSBIES (-biz)], [18th c., a large wig; prob. < the name *Busby*], a tall fur hat, worn by hussars, artillerymen, and engineers in the British Army.

BUSBY

bush (boosh), *n.* [ME. *bussh, bosch, bosk,* a bush, thicket; ON. *buskr;* prob. < ML. *boscus;* ? < Frank. *busk,* forest, thicket], 1. a low-spreading, woody plant, generally smaller than a tree; shrub. 2. a thick growth of bushes; thicket; undergrowth. 3. a thick tail or anything else resembling a bush. 4. [< Colonial D. *bosch,* bush], shrubby woodland; wild or uncleared country. *v.i.* 1. to grow thickly; spread in a bushlike way. 2. to have the shape of a bush. *v.t.* to decorate, support, etc. with bushes.
beat around the bush, to talk around a subject without getting to the point; speak indirectly or hintingly.
be bushed, [Colloq.], to be very tired; be fatigued.

bush (boosh), *n.* [D. *bos,* a box; see BOX (container)], a bushing (metal lining). *v.t.* to put a bushing in.

bush bean, a low, bushy variety of bean plant.

bush·buck (boosh'buk'), *n.* [*pl.* BUSHBUCK, BUSHBUCKS (-buks'); see PLURAL, II, D, 2], a small, striped antelope of South Africa.

bush cranberry, a shrub or tree of the honeysuckle family, with clusters of white flowers and red, cranberrylike fruit; cranberry tree.

bush·el (boosh'əl), *n.* [ME. *busshel, buschel;* OFr. *buissel, boissel, boisse,* grain measure < Gallic **bostia,* amount one can hold in one hand], 1. a unit of dry measure for grain, fruit, etc., equal to 4 pecks or 8 gallons: abbreviated **bu., bsh.** 2. any container with a capacity of one bushel. 3. a weight taken as the equivalent of one bushel. 4. loosely, any large quantity.

bush·el (boosh'əl), *v.t. & v.i.* [BUSHELED OR BUSHELLED (-əld), BUSHELING OR BUSHELLING], [? < G. *bosseln,* to patch up, repair], in *tailoring,* to alter or mend.

bush·el·bas·ket (boosh'əl-bas'kət, boosh'əl-bäs'kət), *n.* a rounded basket with a capacity of one bushel.

bush·el·er, bush·el·ler (boosh'əl-ēr), *n.* [see BUSHEL (to mend)], a person who alters or mends men's clothing.

bush·el·man (boosh'əl-mən), *n.* [*pl.* BUSHELMEN (-mən)], a busheler; tailor.

bush·ham·mer (boosh'ham'ēr), *n.* [prob. < G. *bosshammer* < *bossen,* to beat, dress (stone) + *hammer,* hammer], a hammer whose face is cut up into projecting points, used for dressing stone.

bu·shi·do, Bu·shi·do (bōō'shē-dō'), *n.* [Japan., way of the warrior], the code of conduct for the samurai of feudal Japan, emphasizing loyalty, courage, and plain living, and preferring suicide (hara-kiri) to dishonor.

bush·i·ness (boosh'i-nis), *n.* a bushy quality or state.

bush·ing (boosh'iŋ), *n.* [< *bush* (bushing)], 1. a removable metal lining, for reducing the effect of friction on moving parts or for decreasing the diameter of a hole. 2. in *electricity,* a similar insulating lining or part.

bush league, [Slang], in *baseball,* a small or second-rate minor league.

bush leaguer, [Slang], 1. a baseball player in a bush league; hence, 2. an unimportant or second-rate performer in any sphere of activity.

Bush·man (boosh'mən), *n.* [*pl.* BUSHMEN (-mən)], [transl. of D. *boschjesman* < *bosch* (see BUSH, 4) + *man,* man], 1. a member of a nomadic people living in the region of the Kalahari Desert in southwestern Africa. 2. their language: it is regarded as forming, with Hottentot, a separate linguistic family.

bush·man (boosh'mən), *n.* [*pl.* BUSHMEN (-mən)], 1. a person who lives in the Australian bush. 2. a backwoodsman.

bush·mas·ter (boosh'mas'tēr, boosh'mäs'tēr), *n.* a large, poisonous snake of Central and South America.

bush·rang·er (boosh'rān'jēr), *n.* [see BUSH (wild country) & RANGE, *v.*], 1. a person who lives as a wanderer in the bush. 2. in Australia, a person, especially a highwayman, who makes the bush his hide-out.

bush·whack·er (boosh'hwak'ēr), *n.* [< D. *boschwachter,* forest watcher, woodsman; now associated with *whack*], 1. a person accustomed to beating or cutting his way through bushes; backwoodsman. 2. a guerrilla fighter, especially one on the Confederate side in the Civil War: so called by the Northern soldiers. 3. a sickle or scythe for cutting underbrush.

bush·whack·ing (boosh'hwak'iŋ), *n.* [see BUSHWHACKER], 1. the act of cutting or beating one's way through underbrush. 2. guerrilla fighting.

bush·y (boosh'i), *adj.* [BUSHIER (-i-ēr), BUSHIEST (-i-ist)], 1. covered or overgrown with bushes. 2. bushlike; thick and spreading: as, a *bushy* tail.

bus·i·ly (biz''l-i, biz'i-li), *adv.* in a busy manner.

busi·ness (biz'nis), *n.* [ME. *bisinesse, besinesse;* AS. *bisignes* < *bisgian;* see BUSY], 1. one's work; occupation; profession. 2. rightful concern or responsibility: as, it was not his *business* to remake the world. 3. a matter or affair. 4. the buying and selling of commodities and services; commerce; trade. 5. a commercial or industrial establishment; store, factory, etc. 6. commercial practice or policy: as it is poor *business* to insult the customers. 7. action in a drama, especially for a particular effect, to take up a pause in dialogue, etc. 8. [Obs.], (biz'i-nis), the quality or state of being busy. *adj.* of or for business. Abbreviated **bus.**
business is business, sentiment, friendship, etc. cannot be allowed to interfere with profit-making.
have no business, to have no right (to do something).
mean business, [Colloq.], to be in earnest.
SYN.—**business,** in this comparison, refers generally to the buying and selling of commodities and services and connotes a profit motive; **commerce** and **trade** both refer to the distribution or exchange of commodities, especially as this involves their transportation, but **commerce** generally implies such activity on a large scale between cities, countries, etc.; **industry** refers chiefly to the large-scale manufacture of commodities.

business college (or **school**), a school offering instruction in stenography, bookkeeping, office routine, etc.

business cycle, the continual alternation between periods of prosperity (booms) and periods of depression (slumps) as characteristic of business and industry.

busi·ness·like (biz'nis-līk'), *adj.* having the qualities needed in business; efficient, methodical, etc.

busi·ness·man (biz'nis-man'), *n.* [*pl.* BUSINESSMEN (-men')], a man in business, especially as an owner or executive.

busi·ness·wom·an (biz′nis-woom′ən), *n.* [*pl.* BUSINESSWOMEN (-wim′in)], a woman in business, especially as an owner or executive.

busk (busk), *n.* [Fr. *busc;* It. *busco,* torso, truss], a piece of stiffening material for corsets, as whalebone, etc.

busk (busk), *v.t.* [ME. *busken,* to prepare, adorn; ON. *buask,* to make oneself ready < *bua,* to prepare + *sik,* reflexive pron.], [Scot.], 1. to make ready. 2. to outfit.

bus·kin (bus′kin), *n.* [? < OFr. *broissequin* < MD. *broseken,* small leather boot; ? altered after *buckskin* (shoe)], 1. a boot reaching to the calf or knee, worn long ago. 2. the high, thick-soled, laced boot worn by actors in ancient Greek and Roman tragedy: distinguished from *sock.* 3. tragic drama; tragedy.

BUSKINS

bus·kined (bus′kind), *adj.* 1. wearing buskins. 2. acting in tragedy; tragic.

bus·man (bus′mən), *n.* [*pl.* BUSMEN (-mən)], the driver or conductor of a bus.

bus·man's holiday, a holiday in which one's recreation is very similar to one's daily work.

Bu·so·ni, Fer·ruc·cio Ben·ve·nu·to (fe-rōōt′chô ben′-ve-nōō′tô bōō-zō′nē), 1866–1924; Italian composer.

Bus·ra, Bus·rah (bus′rə), *n.* Basra.

buss (bus), *n., v.t. & v.i.* [? akin to G. (dial.) *bus,* kiss, or W. & Gael. *bus,* kiss, lip], [Archaic or Dial.], kiss, especially in a rough or playful manner.

bus·ses (bus′iz), *n.* alternative plural of **bus.**

bust (bust), *n.* [Fr. *buste;* It. *busto*], 1. a piece of sculpture representing the head, shoulders, and upper chest of a human body. 2. the bosom, especially of a woman. —*SYN.* see **breast.**

bust (bust), *v.t. & v.i.* [orig., dial. var. of *burst*], [Slang], 1. to burst; break. 2. to make or become bankrupt. 3. to demote or become demoted. 4. to tame: said of broncos, etc. 5. to hit or punch. *n.* [Slang], 1. a failure. 2. a blow or punch. 3. a spree.

bus·tard (bus′tẽrd), *n.* [OFr. *bistard, oustard;* Pr. *austarda;* L. *avis tarda,* lit., slow bird], a large, heavy, long-legged game bird of Europe, Asia, and Africa, related to the crane and the plover.

bust·er (bus′tẽr), *n.* [see BUST (to burst)], [Slang], 1. something very large, noteworthy, or extraordinary. 2. a person who breaks up (trusts, etc.). 3. a spree. 4. [B-], little boy: used in direct address.

bus·tic (bus′tik), *n.* [? altered < native name], a tree of the sapodilla family, found in southern Florida.

bus·tle (bus′'l), *v.i. & v.t.* [BUSTLED (-'ld), BUSTLING], [for earlier *buskle* < ME. *busken;* see BUSK, *v.*], to hurry busily, fussily, and noisily. *n.* a bustling; commotion.

bus·tle (bus′'l), *n.* [late 18th c. < G. *buschel,* a bunch, pad], 1. a framework or padding worn over the hips by women to fill out the skirt. 2. a large bow or gathered material worn over the back of the skirt below the waist.

BUSTLE

bus·y (biz′i), *adj.* [BUSIER (-i-ẽr), BUSIEST (-i-ist)], [ME. *busi, bisie;* AS. *bisig, bysig,* occupied, diligent; akin to D. *bezig;* seen only in LG. & Eng.], 1. active; at work; not idle. 2. full of activity; constantly moving. 3. being used: said especially of a telephone. 4. meddlesome. *v.t.* [BUSIED (-id), BUSYING], [ME. *busien;* AS. *bysigan, bisgian,* to occupy, employ, trouble < *bisgu,* occupation, labor, affliction], to make or keep busy: often used reflexively.

SYN.—**busy,** suggests active employment in some task or activity, either temporarily or habitually (I'm *busy* just now); **industrious** suggests habitual devotion to one's work or activity (an *industrious* salesclerk); **diligent** implies unremitting attention, usually to a particular task, and connotes enjoyment in the task itself (a *diligent* student of music); **assiduous** suggests painstaking, persevering preoccupation with some task (*assiduous* study); **sedulous** implies unremitting devotion to a task until the goal is reached (a *sedulous* investigation of the crime). —*ANT.* idle, lazy, indolent.

bus·y·bod·y (biz′i-bod′i), *n.* [*pl.* BUSYBODIES (-iz)], a person who concerns himself with other people's affairs; inquisitive meddler; a gossip.

bus·y·ness (biz′i-nis), *n.* [Rare], the quality or condition of being busy.

but (but; *unstressed,* bət), *prep.* [ME. *but, bote, bute, buten;* AS. *butan, buton,* without, outside < *be,* by + *utan,* out, from without < *ut,* out; *butan* is primarily an adv.], 1. except; with the exception of; save: as, nobody came *but* me. 2. otherwise than; other than: as, we cannot choose *but* stay. *conj.* I. *co-ordinating, in either a simple or compound sentence:* 1. with the exception that; only: as, nobody came *but* I (came). 2. yet; still; however: as, he is a villain, *but* he has some virtues. 3. on the contrary: as, I am old, *but* you are young. II. *subordinating, in a complex sentence:* 1. unless; if not: as, it never rains *but* it pours. 2. that: as, I don't question *but* you're correct. 3. that . . . not: as, I never think of summer *but* I think of childhood. 4. otherwise than; other than; more than: as, I cannot *but* try. 5. who . . . not; which . . . not: as, not a man *but* felt it. 6. than: as, there was nothing else to do *but* (to) go. *adv.* I. *in simple sentences or clauses where it was originally a conjunction:* 1. only: as, if I had *but* known. 2. merely; no more than; not otherwise than: as, he is *but* a child. 3. just: as, I heard it *but* now. 4. [Dial.], without; outside. II. *introducing a sentence:* on the other hand; yet. *But* always functions as an adversative correlator; it is often indistinguishable, therefore, as any one of the preceding parts of speech.
  all but, very nearly; almost.
  but for, if it were not for.

but (but), *adj.* [AS. *butan,* outside, without], [Scot.], outside; outer. *n.* [Scot.], the outer room, especially the kitchen, of a cottage.
  but and ben, 1. the outer and inner parts of a dwelling; hence, 2. the whole house.

but (but), *n.* a butt (fish).

bu·ta·di·ene (bū′tə-dī′ēn, bū′tə-dī-ēn′), *n.* [*butane* + *di-* + *-ene*], a hydrocarbon, $CH_2=CH—CH=CH_2$, obtained from petroleum or alcohol and used, after polymerization, to make buna, a synthetic rubber.

bu·tane (bū′tān, bū-tān′), *n.* [L. *butyrum* (see BUTTER); + *-ane*], either of two hydrocarbons (normal butane, isobutane) in the methane series, having the same formula, C_4H_{10}, but different structures, according to the way each carbon atom links with the other three.

bu·ta·none (bū′tə-nōn′), *n.* [*butane* + *-one*], a highly inflammable liquid, $CH_3COCH_2CH_3$, that is a by-product of acetone, used as a solvent.

butch·er (booch′ẽr), *n.* [ME. *bocher;* OFr. *bochier, bouchier,* one who kills and sells he-goats; OFr. *boc,* he-goat; see BUCK (male deer)], 1. a person whose work is killing animals or dressing their carcasses for meat. 2. a person who sells meat. 3. anyone who kills as if slaughtering animals. 4. a person who sells candy, magazines, etc. in railroad cars or theaters; candy butcher. *v.t.* 1. to kill or dress (animals) for meat. 2. to kill (people, game, etc.) brutally, senselessly, or in large numbers; slaughter. 3. to mess up; botch.

butch·er·bird (booch′ẽr-bũrd′), *n.* a shrike which, after killing prey, hangs it on thorns.

butcher knife, a large, sharp knife for cutting meat, etc.

butch·er·ly (booch′ẽr-li), *adj. & adv.* 1. like a butcher. 2. with bloody cruelty or savagery.

butch·er's-broom (booch′ẽrz-brōōm′, booch′ẽrz-broom′), *n.* [said to be so named because once used by butchers for sweeping their shops], a plant with glossy, leaflike branches, clusters of small white flowers, and large, red berries.

butcher shop, a store where meat, poultry, etc. are sold.

butch·er·y (booch′ẽr-i), *n.* [*pl.* BUTCHERIES (-iz)], [ME. *bocherie;* OFr. *boucherie;* see BUTCHER], 1. a place where animals are killed for meat; slaughterhouse. 2. a butcher shop. 3. the act or result of butchering. 4. the work or business of butchering. 5. brutal bloodshed or slaughter. —*SYN.* see **slaughter.**

Bute (būt), *n.* 1. a Scottish island in the Firth of Clyde: area, 46 sq. mi. 2. a county of Scotland, including this island, Arran, and other islands in the Firth of Clyde: area, 218 sq. mi.; pop., 15,000; county seat, Rothesay.

bu·tene (bū′tēn), *n.* [< *butyl* + *-ene*], one of the three hydrocarbons of the butylene series having the general formula, C_4H_8.

Bute·shire (būt′shir), *n.* Bute (county).

But·ler (but′lẽr), *n.* a city in western Pennsylvania: pop., 21,000.

but·ler (but′lẽr), *n.* [ME. *boteler;* OFr. *bouteillier,* cup-bearer < *bouteille;* see BOTTLE (container)], a manservant, now usually the head servant of a household, in charge of wines, pantry, table silver, etc.

But·ler, Benjamin Franklin (but′lẽr), 1818–1893; American lawyer and politician; Union general in the Civil War.

Butler, Nicholas Murray, 1862–1947; American educator; president of Columbia University (1902–1946); received Nobel peace prize, 1931.

Butler, Pierce, 1866–1939; American jurist; associate justice, United States Supreme Court (1923–1939).

Butler, Samuel, 1. 1612–1680; English poet. 2. 1835–1902; English novelist.

butler's pantry, a serving pantry between the kitchen and the dining room.

but·ler·y (but′lẽr-i), *n.* [*pl.* BUTLERIES (-iz)], [reformed < *butler* + *-y;* orig., ME. *botelerie* < OFr. *bouteillerie;* cf. BOTTLE], the butler's pantry; buttery.

butt (but), *n.* [several bases, not clearly discernible in the various meanings, seem to have been confused in Eng. or Fr.: ME. *but, butte,* thick end, ? akin to ON. *būtr,* block of wood, D. *bot,* stumpy, stocky, or ? < OFr. *bout,* end < *buter* (see BUTT, to strike with head); ME. *but,* target, boundary < Fr. *but,* mark, aim, goal

< *abuter*, to reach one's goal, arrive, aim (see ABUT) or ? < ON. *būtr*], 1. the thick end of anything. 2. the remaining end of anything; stub; stump. 3. the stub of a partially smoked cigarette or cigar. 4. [? influenced by Fr. *butte*, mound < OFr. *buter*], a mound of earth below or behind a target, for receiving fired rounds. 5. a target. 6. *pl.* a target range. 7. an object of ridicule or criticism. 8. [Slang], a cigarette. 9. [Slang], the buttocks. 10. in the *leather business*, the part of a hide or pelt that covered the animal's back and sides. *v.t. & v.i.* to join end to end.

butt (but), *v.t.* [ME. *butten*, to drive, thrust; OFr. *buter*, to thrust against < Frank. *botan*, to thrust against; OHG. *bōzan*, to beat], 1. to strike or push with the head or horns; ram with the head. 2. to strike or bump against. 3. to abut on. 4. to make abut (*on, upon*, or *against*). *v.i.* 1. to make a butting motion. 2. to move or drive headfirst. 3. to stick out; project. 4. to abut. *n.* [ME.; prob. < OFr. *buter*, or < the *v.*], 1. a butting; thrust with the head. 2. a thrust in fencing.

butt in, [Slang], 1. to interfere; meddle. 2. to intrude.

butt into, [Slang], to interfere or meddle in.

butt (but), *n.* [Fr. *boute, botte;* It. *botte;* LL. *bottis*, cask], 1. a large barrel or cask for wine or beer. 2. a measure of liquid capacity equal to 126 gallons or two hogsheads.

butt (but), *n.* [ME. *butte, but* (also in tur*bot*, hali*but*); prob. < MLG. *butte* (whence Sw. *butta*, D. *bot*, G. *butte*) < MLG. *butte, adj.*, lumpy], any of various flatfishes, as the halibut, turbot, etc.: also spelled **but.**

Butte (būt), *n.* a city in southwestern Montana: pop., 28,000.

butte (būt), *n.* [Fr., mound < OFr. *buter;* see BUTT (to hit)], a steep hill standing alone in a plain; small mesa.

but·ter (but'ẽr), *n.* [ME. *butere;* AS. *butere;* L. *butyrum;* Gr. *boutyron* < *bous*, ox, cow + *tyros*, cheese], 1. the thick, yellowish product that results from churning the fatty part of milk. 2. any of various substances somewhat like butter; specifically, *a*) any of certain other spreads for bread: as, apple *butter*, peach *butter*. *b*) any of certain vegetable oils having a solid consistency at ordinary temperatures: as, cacao *butter*. *c*) any of certain metallic chlorides: as, *butter* of antimony. 3. [Colloq.], flattery. *v.t.* 1. to spread with butter. 2. [Colloq.], to flatter (often with *up*).

know which side one's bread is buttered on, to be prudently aware of what one's material security or comfort depends on.

look as if butter would not melt in one's mouth, to look innocent or demure.

but·ter-and-eggs (but'ẽr-'n-egz'), *n.* any of various plants bearing flowers in two tones of yellow, as the toadflax, a kind of narcissus, etc.

but·ter·ball (but'ẽr-bôl'), *n.* 1. a bufflehead. 2. [Colloq.], a fat person.

butter bean, 1. a kind of bean plant with yellow pods; wax bean. 2. the lima bean: so called in the southern United States.

but·ter·bur (but'ẽr-bũr'), *n.* any of several related plants with clusters of white or purplish flowers: so called because the large, round or kidney-shaped leaves are sometimes used to wrap up butter.

but·ter·cup (but'ẽr-kup'), *n.* 1. any of a number of plants of the crowfoot family, with yellow, cup-shaped flowers. 2. its flower.

but·ter·fat (but'ẽr-fat'), *n.* the fatty part of milk, from which butter is made.

but·ter·fin·gers (but'ẽr-fiŋ'gẽrz), *n.* [Colloq.], a person who fails to hold things, as if his fingers were buttery.

but·ter·fish (but'ẽr-fish'), *n.* [*pl.* BUTTERFISH, BUTTERFISHES (-iz); see FISH], any of various fishes with a slippery coating, as the gunnel, dollarfish, etc.

but·ter·fly (but'ẽr-flī'), *n.* [*pl.* BUTTERFLIES (-flīz')], [ME. *buterflige, buterflie;* AS. *buttorfleoge*], 1. any of a group of insects having a sucking mouth part, slender body, and four broad, membranous wings covered with tiny scales, usually bright-colored. 2. a person, especially a woman, thought of as like a butterfly in being brightly dressed, frivolous, fickle, etc.

BUTTERFLIES

A, swallowtail (3 1/4 in. wide); B, New Guinea golden (2 1/4 in. wide)

butterfly damper, a butterfly valve.

butterfly fish, any of various fishes resembling butterflies in coloring or in having winglike fins, as the ocellated blenny, certain small tropical fishes, etc.

butterfly table, a small drop-leaf table with leaf supports shaped like a butterfly's wings.

butterfly valve, a damper or throttle valve for a pipe, consisting of two hinged plates that somewhat resemble the wings of a butterfly.

butterfly weed, a milkweed with showy, orange-colored flowers and a fleshy root used in medicine as a cathartic, for increasing perspiration, etc.

but·ter·ine (but'ə-rēn', but'ə-rin), *n.* 1. an imitation butter; butter substitute. 2. such a substance with a little butter mixed into it.

butter knife, a small, dull-edged knife for cutting or spreading butter.

but·ter·milk (but'ẽr-milk'), *n.* 1. the sour liquid left after the butterfat in milk has been made into butter. 2. artificially curdled milk.

but·ter·nut (but'ẽr-nut'), *n.* 1. the edible, oily, hard-shelled nut of the North American white walnut tree. 2. this tree. 3. the souari nut, fruit of a South American tree. 4. *pl.* brown homespun overalls. 5. a Confederate soldier in the Civil War: so called from their brown homespun clothes.

but·ter·scotch (but'ẽr-skoch'), *n.* a hard, sticky candy made by melting brown sugar and butter together. *adj.* made of, or having the flavor of, butterscotch.

but·ter·weed (but'ẽr-wēd'), *n.* any of various plants with yellow flowers, as a kind of ragwort, etc.

but·ter·wort (but'ẽr-wũrt'), *n.* any of a number of small plants of the bladderwort family, with flat, sticky leaves on which insects are caught.

but·ter·y (but'ri, but'ẽr-i), *n.* [*pl.* BUTTERIES (-riz, -iz)], [ME. *boterie*, ale cellar, pantry; OFr. *boterie*, storage room for casks; see BUTT (cask)], 1. a storeroom for whisky, wine, etc. 2. a pantry.

but·ter·y (but'ẽr-i), *adj.* 1. like butter. 2. containing or spread with butter.

but·ting (but'iŋ), *n.* [< ME. *but*, boundary; see BUTT (thick end)], a boundary or limit.

butt joint, in *engineering*, any joint made by putting plates or bars together end to end: it is sometimes strengthened with an additional plate or plates.

BUTT JOINTS

but·tock (but'ək), *n.* [ME. *buttok, bottok* < *but* (see BUTT, thick end) + dim. *-ock*], 1. either of the two fleshy, rounded parts at the back of the hips; either half of the rump. 2. *pl.* the rump. 3. *sometimes pl.* the rounded part of a ship's stern above the water line.

but·ton (but''n), *n.* [ME. *boton, botoun;* OFr. *boton*, a button, bud < *boter, buter;* see BUTT (to strike with head)], 1. any small disk, knob etc. used as a fastening or ornament, as on a garment. 2. anything small and shaped like a button. 3. a small emblem of membership, distinction, etc., generally worn in the lapel. 4. a small knob. 5. a small knob for operating a doorbell, electric lamp, etc. 6. a guard on the tip of a fencing foil. 7. a small, immature mushroom. 8. [Slang], the point of the jaw. *v.t. & v.i.* to fasten with or as with a button or buttons.

but·ton·ball (but''n-bôl'), *n.* a buttonwood.

but·ton·bush (but''n-boosh'), *n.* any of a number of shrubs of the madder family, with dense, round clusters of small, white flowers.

but·ton·hole (but''n-hōl'), *n.* a hole or slit in a garment, etc. into which a button is inserted. *v.t.* 1. to make buttonholes in. 2. to make with a buttonhole stitch. 3. to hold (a person) by or as by a buttonhole; detain in conversation.

buttonhole stitch, a closely worked loop stitch making a reinforced edge, as around a buttonhole.

but·ton·hook (but''n-hook'), *n.* a small hook for pulling buttons through buttonholes, as in some shoes.

but·ton·mold (but''n-mōld'), *n.* a small disk of wood, metal, etc. which is made into a button by covering with cloth or leather.

BUTTONHOLE STITCH

but·tons (but''nz), *n.pl.* [construed as sing.], [Colloq.], a bellboy, hotel page, etc.

button snakeroot, any of a number of plants of the composite family, with narrow leaves and, usually, a globe-shaped tuber and purple flowers.

button tree, 1. any of a number of related trees or shrubs of tropical America, with buttonlike fruit. 2. a buttonwood.

but·ton·wood (but''n-wood'), *n.* 1. a kind of plane tree with buttonlike, hanging fruit; sycamore. 2. its wood.

but·ton·y (but''n-i), *adj.* 1. of or like a button. 2. having or decorated with many buttons.

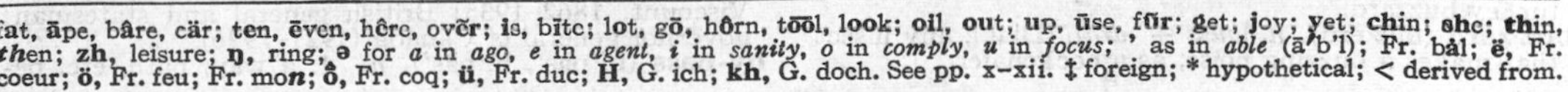

but·tress (but′ris), *n.* [ME. *buttrace;* OFr. *bouterez* < *buter;* see BUTT (to strike with head)], 1. a structure, generally of brick or stone, built against a wall to support or reinforce it. 2. anything like a buttress; support; prop. *v.t.* 1. to support or reinforce with a buttress. 2. to prop up; bolster.

BUTTRESS

butts and bounds, in *law,* the boundaries of a piece of land.
butt shaft, a blunt or unbarbed arrow.
butt weld, a welded butt joint.
bu·tyl (bū′til), *n.* [L. *butyrum* (see BUTTER); + *-yl*], any of the four organic radicals (normal butyl, secondary butyl, tertiary butyl, isobutyl) combined from the same elements in the same proportion by weight and having a valence of one, but differing in properties and structure; C_4H_9.
butyl alcohol, an alcohol, C_4H_9OH, formed by the combination of hydroxyl with butyl: there are four types, corresponding to the four types of butyl.
bu·tyl·ene (bū′t'l-ēn′), *n.* [*butyl* + *-ene*], any of the three hydrocarbons of the ethylene series having the same formula, C_4H_8, but differing properties and structures.
butyl (rubber), a synthetic rubber prepared as the copolymer of butylene with isoprene, etc., and vulcanized to form a substance that is especially impermeable to gases: a trade-mark **(Butyl).**
bu·tyn (bū′tin), *n.* a colorless crystalline substance, $(C_{18}H_{30}N_2)_2H_2SO_4$, used as an anesthetic, especially for surface anesthesia of mucous membranes and in the eye: a trade-mark **(Butyn).**
bu·tyr·a·ceous (bū′tēr-ā′shəs), *adj.* [L. *butyrum* (see BUTTER); + *-aceous*], of, like, or producing butter.
bu·tyr·ate (bū′tēr-āt′), *n.* [*butyric* + *-ate*], a salt or ester of butyric acid.
bu·tyr·ic (bū-tir′ik), *adj.* [L. *butyrum* (see BUTTER); + *-ic*], of or obtained from butter.
butyric acid, a colorless, bad-smelling acid, $C_3H_7CO_2H$, found in rancid butter, perspiration, etc.
bu·tyr·in (bū′tə-rin), *n.* [*butyric* + *-in*], a glyceryl ester of butyric acid.
bux·om (buk′səm), *adj.* [ME. *buhsum, buxum,* flexible, obedient < base of *bugan,* to bow, bend + *-sum,* -some], 1. healthy, comely, plump, jolly, etc.: said of a woman or girl. 2. [Archaic], flexible; pliant; hence, 3. [Archaic], obedient; obliging.
buy (bī), *v.t.* [BOUGHT (bôt), BUYING], [ME. *bien, buggen, biggen;* AS. *bycgan, bicgan;* prob. IE. base **bheug(h)-,* to bend, as in AS. *bugan* (see BOW, to bend); orig. sense "to compromise in bartering"], 1. to get by paying or agreeing to pay money; purchase. 2. to get by an exchange or sacrifice: as, he would *buy* fame with health. 3. to be the means of purchasing: as, all that money can *buy.* 4. to bribe. *v.i.* to buy things; be a buyer. *n.* 1. a buying. 2. anything bought or buyable. 3. [Colloq.], something bought or buyable that is worth the price.
  bad buy, [Colloq.], something bought or buyable that is not worth the price.
  buy in, 1. to gather a stock of by buying. 2. to buy back at a higher price than any other bidder: said of the owner of something being sold at an auction. 3. [Slang], to pay money so as to become a participant, member, etc.
  buy into, [Slang], to pay money so as to get shares of, membership in, etc.
  buy off, to bribe.
  buy out, to buy all the stock, business rights, etc. of.
  buy up, to buy all of or all that is available of.
  good buy, [Colloq.], something bought or buyable that is worth the price.
buy·a·ble (bī′ə-b'l), *adj.* that can be bought.
buy·er (bī′ēr), *n.* 1. a person who buys; consumer. 2. an employee whose work is to buy goods for a business firm, store, etc.
buy·er's strike (bī′ērz), an organized boycott (by consumers) of certain goods or merchants in an attempt to bring down prices.
buzz (buz), *v.i.* [echoic], 1. to make a sound like that of a prolonged *z;* hum like a bee. 2. to talk excitedly or incessantly, especially in low tones. 3. to gossip. 4. to move with a buzzing sound. *v.t.* 1. to utter or tell (gossip, rumors, etc.) in a buzzing manner. 2. to make (wings, etc.) buzz. 3. to fly an airplane low over (a building, etc.). 4. to signal (someone) with a buzzer. 5. [Colloq.], to telephone. *n.* 1. a sound like that of a prolonged *z* or a bee's hum; buzzing. 2. a confused sound, as of many excited voices.
  buzz about (or **around**), to scurry about.
  give (a person) a buzz, [Slang], to telephone (a person).
buz·zard (buz′ērd), *n.* [ME. *busard, bosarde;* OFr. *busart, buzart;* L. *buteo,* kind of hawk], 1. any of various hawks that are slow and heavy in flight. 2. the turkey buzzard.
buz·zard (buz′ērd), *n.* [*buzz* + *-ard*], [Dial.], any insect that makes a buzzing noise, as a cockchafer.
Buz·zards Bay (buz′ērdz), an arm of the Atlantic, on the southeastern coast of Massachusetts.
buzz bomb, [Colloq.], a self-propelled bomb characterized by a loud buzzing sound in flight, used by Nazi Germany in World War II: also called *V-1.*
buz·zer (buz′ēr), *n.* an apparatus, especially an electrical device, that makes a buzzing noise as a signal.
buzz saw, a circular saw rotated by machinery.
buzz·wig (buz′wig′), *n.* 1. a large, bushy wig. 2. a person wearing such a wig; hence, 3. a very important person.
B.V., *Beata Virgo,* [L.], Blessed Virgin.
B.V.M., *Beata Virgo Maria,* [L.], Blessed Virgin Mary.
bvt., 1. brevet. 2. brevetted.
B.W.I., British West Indies.
bx., [*pl.* BXS.], box; boxes.
by (bī), *prep.* [ME. *by, bi, be;* AS. *be* (unstressed), *bi* (stressed); cf. BY-, BE-; orig. adv. of place, meaning "beside, near," but already highly specialized prep. in AS.], 1. *expressing relation in space:* near; at; beside: as, stand *by* the door. 2. *expressing relation in time:* *a*) in or during: as, he travels *by* night. *b*) for a fixed time: as, she works *by* the hour. *c*) not later than: as, be back *by* ten o'clock. 3. *expressing direction of movement:* *a*) through: as, we went *by* way of New York. *b*) past; beyond: as, he walked right *by* me. *c*) toward: as, the region lies north *by* west of this point. 4. *expressing direction of effort:* in behalf of: as, he did well *by* his children. 5. *expressing means or agency:* through the means, work, or operations of: as, things made *by* human labor, poems *by* Dryden. 6. *expressing manner or mode:* *a*) according to: as, he fights *by* the book. *b*) in: as, it grows dark *by* degrees. 7. *expressing permission, sanction, etc.:* with the authority or sanction of: as, yes, *by* heaven; 8. *expressing measure or extent:* *a*) in or to the amount or degree of: as, apples *by* the peck. *b*) and in another dimension: as, two *by* four. *adv.* 1. close at hand; near: as, stand *by.* 2. away; aside: as, we have put money *by.* 3. close in passing; past: as, the car sped *by.* *adj.* & *n.* bye.
  by and by, after a while.
  by and large, on the whole; considering everything.
  by the by, incidentally; by the way.
by- (bī), [< *by*], a prefix meaning: 1. *close by, near,* as in *bystander.* 2. *side,* as in *bystreet.* 3. *on the side, secondary, incidental to the main,* as in *by-product.* Also spelled **bye-.**
by-and-by (bī′'n-bī′), *n.* future time.
by-bid·der (bī′bid′ēr), *n.* one engaged in by-bidding.
by-bid·ding (bī′bid′iŋ), *n.* bidding by prearrangement with the auctioneer or owner so as to raise the price of the thing being sold at auction.
by-blow (bī′blō′), *n.* a child born out of wedlock: also spelled **bye-blow.**
Byd·goszcz, Byd·goshch (bid′gôshch), *n.* Bromberg: the Polish name.
bye (bī), *n.* [see BY], 1. a run made on a passed ball in the game of cricket. 2. in sports tournaments in which competitors are paired, the position of the odd man, who advances automatically to the next round without having to play. 3. in *golf,* any hole or holes left unplayed at the end of a match. Abbreviated **b.** *adj.* aside from the main consideration; incidental. Also spelled **by.**
  by the bye, incidentally; by the way.
bye-bye (bī′bī′), *n.* & *interj.* good-by: a child's word.
by-e·lec·tion (bī′i-lek′shən), *n.* a special election held in the interval between regular elections, generally to fill a vacancy.
Bye·lo·rus·sia (bye′lə-rush′ə), *n.* 1. the western part of European Russia. 2. the Byelorussian Soviet Socialist Republic. Also spelled **Belorussia.**
Bye·lo·rus·sian (bye′lə-rush′ən), *adj.* of Byelorussia, its people, or their dialect. *n.* 1. a native or inhabitant of Byelorussia. 2. the dialect of Russian spoken in Byelorussia.
Byelorussian Soviet Socialist Republic, a republic of the U.S.S.R., in western European Russia: area, 89,300 sq. mi.; pop., 5,568,000; capital, Minsk: also called *White Russian Soviet Socialist Republic.*
Bye·lo·stok (bye′lô-stok′), *n.* Bialystok: also spelled **Belostok.**
bye-low (bī′lō′), *adv.* & *interj.* hush: used in lullabies.
by·gone (bī′gôn′, bī′gon′), *adj.* past; gone by. *n.* anything that is gone or past.
  let bygones be bygones, to let past offenses or disagreements be forgotten.
by·law (bī′lô′), *n.* [*by-* < ME. *by, bi,* town (< ON. *bȳr,* village < *būa,* to dwell); + *law;* meaning influenced by *by,* prep.], 1. a law of local application adopted by an organization or assembly. 2. a secondary law or rule.
by-line (bī′līn′), *n.* a line printed above a newspaper or magazine article, telling who wrote it.
by·name (bī′nām′), *n.* 1. a second name; surname. 2. a nickname.
Byng, Julian Hed·worth George (hed′wērth biŋ), first Viscount, 1862–1935; British general and statesman; governor general of Canada (1921–1926).
by-pass (bī′pas′, bī′päs′), *n.* 1. a way, path, etc. be-

tween two points that avoids or is auxiliary to the main way; detour. 2. a pipe or channel providing such a way for gas or liquid, as that leading to the pilot light in a gas stove. 3. in *electricity*, a shunt. ***v.t.*** 1. to go around instead of through. 2. to furnish with a by-pass.

by-pass condenser, in *radio*, a low-impedance condenser which provides an alternate path for alternating current while not passing any direct current.

by-passed (bī′past′, bī′päst′), ***adj.*** [pp. of *by-pass*], avoided by means of a by-pass.

by·past (bī′past′, bī′päst′), ***adj.*** past; bygone.

by·path, by-path (bī′path′, bī′päth′), ***n.*** a side path; private or little-used path.

by·play (bī′plā′), ***n.*** action, gestures, etc. going on aside and apart from the main action or conversation, as in a play.

by-prod·uct (bī′prod′əkt), ***n.*** anything produced in the course of making another thing; secondary or incidental product or result.

Byrd, Richard Evelyn (bûrd), 1888–1957; American naval officer, flyer, and explorer; explored Antarctica (1928, 1933, 1939, 1947, 1955).

Byrd, William, 1540?–1623; English composer.

byre (bīr), ***n.*** [AS., a hut; akin to *bower*], a cow barn.

Byrnes, James Francis (bûrnz), 1879– ; American jurist and statesman; secretary of state (1945–1947).

byr·nie (bûr′ni), ***n.*** [ME. *brunie, burne;* ON. *brynja;* akin to *byrne*, Goth. *brunjō;* prob. < Gaul. form of base appearing in OIr. *bruinne*, OCym. *broun*, breast; hence, orig., breast protector], a coat of chain mail.

by·road (bī′rōd′), ***n.*** a road that is not a main road; side road.

By·ron (bī′rən), [Fr. *Biron*, orig. a family name < *Biron*, district in Périgord, France], a masculine name.

By·ron, George Gordon (bī′rən), sixth Baron Byron, 1788–1824; English poet.

By·ron·ic (bī-ron′ik), ***adj.*** 1. of Byron or his writings. 2. like or characteristic of Byron or his writings; romantic, proud, cynical, ironic, etc.

bys·sus (bis′əs), ***n.*** [*pl.* BYSSES (-iz), BYSSI (-ī)], [L.; Gr. *byssos*, fine linen or cotton], 1. a fine, yellow flax grown in ancient times. 2. a linen cloth made of this or of cotton or silk, used as a mummy wrapping in ancient Egypt. 3. in *zoology*, a tuft of filaments in certain mollusks, serving to attach them to an object.

by·stand·er (bī′stan′dẽr), ***n.*** a person who stands near but does not participate; mere or chance onlooker.

by·street (bī′strēt′), ***n.*** a side street, off a main street.

by-talk (bī′tôk′), ***n.*** incidental or irrelevant talk; small talk.

by·way (bī′wā′), ***n.*** a side path or road; private or little-traveled way.

by·word (bī′wûrd′), ***n.*** [ME. & AS. *biword; bi* (see BY) + *word*], 1. a familiar saying; proverb. 2. a person or thing proverbial as being contemptible or ridiculous. 3. a byname.

by-work (bī′wûrk′), ***n.*** work done aside from one's regular work during one's leisure time.

Byz., Byzantine.

By·zan·tine (bi-zan′tin, biz′'n-tēn′, biz′'n-tīn′), ***adj.*** [L. *Byzantinus*], 1. of or like Byzantium or the Byzantine Empire, its culture, etc. 2. designating or of a style of architecture developed in Byzantium and eastern Europe between the 4th and 15th centuries: it is characterized by domes over square areas, round arches, elaborate mosaics, etc.: see TYPES OF ARCHITECTURE, p. 77. ***n.*** a native or inhabitant of Byzantium.

Byzantine Empire, the eastern division of the later Roman Empire (395–1453 A.D.): capital, Byzantium (Constantinople): also called *Eastern Empire.*

BYZANTINE EMPIRE

By·zan·ti·um (bi-zan′shi-əm, bi-zan′ti-əm), ***n.*** an ancient city on the Bosporus, made the capital of the Roman Empire in 330 A.D.: Istanbul (Constantinople) was built on its site.

Bz., benzene.

C

C, c (sē), ***n.*** [*pl.* C's, c's, Cs, cs (sēz)], 1. the third letter of the English alphabet: from the Greek *gamma*, a borrowing from the Phoenician: see **alphabet,** table. 2. a sound of C or c: in English, the sound is (k) before original back vowels (a, o, u), before all consonants but *h*, and at the end of words; it is (s) before original front vowels (e, i, y), and in words ending in *-ce* or their derivatives; *ch* and medial *-ci-* have come to symbolize (ch), IPA [tʃ], and (sh), IPA [ʃ], as in *church, vicious.* 3. a type or impression for C or c. 4. *a symbol for* the third in a sequence or group. ***adj.*** 1. of C or c. 2. third in a sequence or group.

C (sē), ***n.*** 1. an object shaped like C. 2. a Roman numeral for 100: with a superior bar (C̄), 100,000. 3. in *chemistry, the symbol for* carbon. 4. in *education*, a grade third in quality: as, a *C* in biology. 5. in *mathematics, a symbol for* constant. 6. in *music, a)* the first tone or note in the scale of C major, or the third in the scale of A minor. *b)* a key, string, etc. producing this tone. *c)* the scale having C as the keynote. *d)* the sign for 4/4 time. *e)* contralto. 7. in *physics, the symbol for* coulomb. 8. in *phonetics, a)* the voiceless, palatal stop of the International Phonetic Alphabet. *b)* with or without an inverted superior caret [č], a common linguistic symbol for the voiceless affricate (ch), IPA [tʃ]. ***adj.*** shaped like C.

C-, cargo transport: followed by a number to designate a specific model of United States Army airplane designed to carry cargo or troops.

C., 1. Catholic. 2. Celtic. 3. Chancellor. 4. Congress. 5. Conservative. 6. Corps. 7. Court.

C., c., 1. candle. 2. capacity. 3. carbon. 4. carton. 5. case. 6. cathode. 7. cent; cents. 8. centigrade. 9. centime. 10. centimeter. 11. century. 12. [*pl.* cc.], chapter. 13. chief. 14. church. 15. circa. 16. cirrus. 17. congius. 18. copper. 19. copy. 20. copyright. 21. corps. 22. cost. 23. cubic. 24. hundredweight.

c., 1. catcher. 2. child. 3. city. 4. cloudy. 5. center.

Ca, in *chemistry*, calcium.

ca., 1. cathode. 2. centiare; centiares. 3. circa.

C.A., 1. Central America. 2. Coast Artillery. 3. Confederate Army. 4. Court of Appeal.

C.A., c.a., 1. chartered accountant. 2. chief accountant. 3. commercial agent. 4. consular agent. 5. controller of accounts.

C/A, 1. capital accountant. 2. credit account. 3. current account.

CAA, Civil Aeronautics Authority.

Caa·ba (kä′bə, kä′ə-bə), ***n.*** Kaaba, a Moslem shrine at Mecca.

cab (kab), ***n.*** [< *cabriolet*], 1. an automobile or horse-drawn carriage for public hire; taxicab. 2. the place in a locomotive, motor truck, crane, derrick, steam shovel, etc. where the operator sits.

cab (kab), ***n.*** [Heb. *qab*, hollow vessel < *qābab*, to hollow out], a Hebrew dry measure, equal to about two quarts: also spelled **kab.**

CAB, Civil Aeronautics Board.

ca·bal (kə-bal′), ***n.*** [Fr., intrigue, club, society; popularized in Eng. from the initials of the ministers of Charles II (1671); ML. *cabbala;* see CABALA], 1. a small group of persons joined in a secret design or scheme; junto. 2. the intrigues of such a group; plot. ***v.i.*** [CABALLED (-bald′), CABALLING], to form or join in a cabal; plot; intrigue. —***SYN.*** see **plot.**

cab·a·la (kab′ə-lə, kə-bä′lə), ***n.*** [ML. *cabbala;* Heb. *qabbālāh*, received lore, mysterious doctrine < *qābal*, to receive, take], 1. an occult religious philosophy developed by certain Jewish rabbis, based on a mystical interpretation of the Scriptures. 2. occultism; mystical

or secret doctrine. Also spelled **cabbala, kabala.**
ca·bal·ic (kə-bal′ik), *adj.* cabalistic.
cab·a·lism (kab′ə-liz'm), *n.* occult doctrine.
cab·a·list (kab′ə-list), *n.* 1. a person who believes in the cabala. 2. a mystic.
cab·a·lis·tic (kab′ə-lis′tik), *adj.* 1. of the cabala. 2. secret; mystic.
cab·a·lis·ti·cal (kab′ə-lis′ti-k'l), *adj.* cabalistic.
ca·bal·le·ro (kab′əl-yâr′ō; Sp. kä′bä-lye′rô), *n.* [*pl.* CABALLEROS (-ōz; Sp. -rôs)], [Sp. < *caballo;* L. *caballus,* a horse; see CAVALIER], 1. a Spanish gentleman, cavalier, or knight. 2. in the southwestern United States, *a*) a horseman. *b*) a lady's escort or admirer.
ca·ba·na (kə-bä′nə, kə-ban′ə; Sp. kä-bä′nyä), *n.* [Sp. *cabaña;* LL. *capanna,* hut], 1. a cabin, cottage, or hut. 2. a small shelter used as a bathhouse. Also **cabaña.**
‡ca·bane (kȧ′bȧn′), *n.* [Fr., cabin], an arrangement of struts supporting the wings of an airplane.
cab·a·ret (kab′ə-rā′ kab′ə-rā′), *n.* [Fr., pothouse, poor tavern < Norm. dial.; MD. borrowings *camaret, cabaret* suggest OFr. **cabaneret,* little hut; see CABIN], 1. a restaurant or barroom with dancing and singing as entertainment; hence, 2. entertainment of this type.
cab·bage (kab′ij), *n.* [ME. *cabache;* OFr. *caboche;* dial. It. *kapocco,* the head < L. *caput,* the head], 1. a common vegetable of the mustard family, with thick leaves compressed into a round head on a short, stout stalk. 2. a bud at the end of the branch on some palm trees: also called *palm cabbage.* *v.i.* [CABBAGED (-ijd), CABBAGING], to form a cabbagelike head.
cab·bage (kab′ij), *v.t.* & *v.i.* [CABBAGED (-ijd), CABBAGING], [prob. < Fr. *cabasser,* to put into a basket, steal < *cabas,* basket; LL. **capacium,* reed basket], to steal. *n.* [prob. < the *v.*], cloth appropriated by a tailor when cutting out clothes.
cabbage palm, any of several palms with terminal buds used as a vegetable; palmetto.
cabbage palmetto, a palm tree with fan-shaped leaves, of the southern United States: also called *fan palm.*
cabbage tree, any of several trees, as the fan or cabbage palms, growing in tropical America and Australia: the buds are eaten as vegetables.
cab·ba·la (kab′ə-lə, kə-bä′lə), *n.* cabala.
cab·by (kab′i), *n.* [*pl.* CABBIES (-iz)], [Colloq.], a cabman.
Cab·ell, James Branch (branch kab′'l), 1879–1958; American novelist, essayist, and critic.
ca·ber (kā′bẽr), *n.* [Gael. *cabar*], a pole, especially one thrown in a Gaelic game to test muscular strength.
cab·ette (kab-et′), *n.* a woman taxicab driver.
Ca·be·za de Va·ca, Ál·var Nú·ñez (äl′vär nōō′nyeth kä-be′thä *the* väkä), 1490?-1557?; Spanish explorer and colonial governor in the Americas.
cab·e·zon (kab′ə-zon′; Sp. kä′be-sôn′), *n.* [Sp. < *cabeza,* a head], any of several fishes; especially, a large fish of the sculpin family found off the coast of California.
cab·in (kab′in), *n.* [ME. *caban;* OFr. *caban, cabane;* Pr. *cabana;* LL. *capanna,* hut], 1. a small, roughly constructed house; cottage. 2. an officer's quarters, originally in a deckhouse of a ship; hence, 3. any enclosed office, bedroom, or living quarters on a ship, or quarters under the cabin trunk of a smaller vessel. 4. an enclosed space for passengers in an aircraft. *v.t.* to confine in or as in a cabin; cramp.
cabin boy, a boy whose work is to serve and run errands for the officers and passengers aboard a ship.
cabin class, a class of accommodations in a passenger ship, formerly the best (*first class*), now the second-best (lower than *first class* and higher than *tourist class*).
cabin cruiser, a powerboat with a cabin and the necessary equipment for living on board: also **cruiser.**
cab·i·net (kab′ə-nit), *n.* [Fr., dim. of *cabine* < Eng. *cabin*], 1. a case with drawers or shelves to hold small art objects, jewels, etc. 2. a case for foods, medicines, supplies, etc. 3. formerly, a private council room; hence, 4. a meeting held in such a room. 5. [often C-], a body of official advisers to the chief executive of a nation, usually the heads of the various governmental departments. 6. [Archaic], a small room. 7. [Obs.], a small cabin. *adj.* 1. of a cabinet, or private room. 2. private; secret; confidential. 3. suitable for a cabinet; valuable or beautiful enough to keep in a case or a private room. 4. of a political cabinet.
cab·i·net·mak·er (kab′ə-nit-māk′ẽr), *n.* a workman who makes fine furniture or woodwork.
cab·i·net·work (kab′ə-nit-wũrk′), *n.* fine woodwork.
ca·ble (kā′b'l), *n.* [ME. *cable, cabel;* OFr. *cable;* LL. *capulum,* a cable, rope < L. *capere,* to take hold], 1. a thick, heavy rope, now often of wire; hence, 2. the anchor chain of a ship; chain cable: anchor cables were formerly of rope. 3. a cable's length. 4. a bundle of insulated wires through which an electric current can be passed: telegraph or telephone cables are often laid under the ground or on the ocean floor. 5. a cablegram. *v.t.* [CABLED (-b'ld), CABLING], 1. to fasten with a cable. 2. to furnish with a cable or cables. 3. to transmit by means of a cable under the sea. 4. to send a cablegram to. *v.i.* to send a cablegram.

CABLE

Ca·ble, George Washington (kā′b'l), 1844–1925; American author.
cable car, a car drawn by a moving cable, as across a canyon, up a steeply inclined street, etc.
ca·ble·gram (kā′b'l-gram′), *n.* [*cable* + *-gram*], a message sent across the sea by telegraphic cable.
ca·ble-laid (kā′b'l-lād′), *adj.* made of three plain-laid ropes twisted together counter-clockwise, each containing three strands.
cable railway, a street railway on which the cars are pulled by a continuously moving underground cable to which they are attached by a grip that can be released to halt the car.
cable's length, a unit of nautical measure equal to 720 feet (120 fathoms) or, in the British navy, 608 feet (1/10 of a nautical mile).
ca·blet (kā′blit), *n.* [< *cable* + *-et*], a cable-laid rope whose circumference is less than ten inches.
cab·man (kab′mən), *n.* [*pl.* CABMEN (-mən)], a driver of a cab.
ca·bobs (kə-bobz′), *n.pl.* [Ar. *kabāb*], 1. in the Orient, pieces of meat roasted on a skewer and highly seasoned. 2. in India, roast meat. Also spelled **kabobs.**
ca·bo·chon (kab′ə-shon′; Fr. kȧ′bô′shôn′), *n.* [Fr. < *caboche,* the head; see CABBAGE (vegetable)], 1. any precious stone cut in convex shape, polished but not faceted. 2. the style in which such a stone is prepared: often **en cabochon.**
ca·boo·dle (kə-bōō′d'l), *n.* [< *kit, kith,* family, relations + *boodle* < D. *boedel,* property, possessions], [Slang], lot; number; group: as, the whole *caboodle.*
ca·boose (kə-bōōs′), *n.* [MD. *kabuys, kambuis,* earlier *kaban huis,* cabin house, ship's galley; see CABIN, CABARET], 1. a ship's galley or kitchen. 2. the trainmen's car on a freight train, usually at the rear.
Cab·ot, John (kab′ət), (It. *Giovanni Caboto*), 1450–1498; Italian navigator in the service of England; discovered coast of North America (1497).
Cabot, Sebastian, 1474?–1557; British cartographer and explorer, born in Italy; son of *John.*
ca·bril·la (kə-bril′ə, kä-brē′yä), *n.* [Sp., prawn, dim. of *cabra,* goat], any of various edible, perchlike fishes of Florida and the West Indies, as the groupers.
cab·ri·ole (kab′ri-ōl′), *n.* [Fr.; see CABRIOLET], in *furniture,* a leg that curves outward and then tapers inward down to a clawlike foot grasping a ball: characteristic of Queen Anne and Chippendale furniture.
cab·ri·o·let (kab′ri-ə-lā′, kab′ri-ə-let′), *n.* [Fr., dim. of *cabriole,* a leap, caper; It. *capriola* < L. *capreolus,* wild goat < *caper,* he-goat], 1. a light two-wheeled carriage, usually with a hood that folds, drawn by one horse. 2. an automobile somewhat like a coupe, with a folding top.

CABRIOLET

cab·stand (kab′stand′), *n.* a place where cabs are stationed for hire.
C.A.C., Coast Artillery Corps.
ca' canny, see **canny.**
ca·ca·o (kə-kā′ō, kə-kä′ō), *n.* [*pl.* CACAOS (-ōz)], [Sp. < Mex. *cacauatl,* cacao seed], 1. a small evergreen tree grown in tropical America for its seeds. 2. the seed, from which cocoa and chocolate are made: also **cacao bean.**
cacao butter, a yellowish fat obtained from cacao seeds, used in cosmetics, pharmacy, etc.: also **cocoa butter.**
cach·a·lot (kash′ə-lot′, kash′ə-lō′), *n.* [Fr.; Sp. *cachalote;* ? < Port. *cachola,* big head, fat head; cf. Catalan *capgros,* fat head, hence sperm whale], the sperm whale.
cache (kash), *n.* [Fr. < *cacher,* to conceal; L. *coacticare,* to store up, collect], 1. a place in which stores of food, supplies, etc. are hidden. 2. a place for hiding anything. 3. anything stored or hidden in such a place. *v.t.* & *v.i.* [CACHED (kasht), CACHING], to hide or store (things) in a cache. —*SYN.* see **hide.**
ca·chet (ka-shā′, kash′ā), *n.* [Fr. < *cacher,* to hide], 1. originally, a seal or stamp on an official letter, indicating the confidential nature of the contents; hence, 2. a mark by which quality or authenticity can be distinguished. 3. a mark stamped or imprinted on mail. 4. a kind of capsule, etc. for enclosing disagreeable medicine.
ca·chex·i·a (kə-kek′si-ə), *n.* [Fr. *cachexie;* Gr. *kachexia,* bad habit of body < *kakos,* bad + *hexis,* habit, state < *echein,* to have], general poor health, with weakness and malnutrition: applied sometimes to mental health.
ca·chex·y (kə-kek′si), *n.* cachexia.
cach·in·nate (kak′ə-nāt′), *v.i.* [CACHINNATED (-id), CACHINNATING], [< L. *cachinnatus,* pp. of *cachinnare;* of echoic origin], to laugh loudly or too much.
cach·in·na·tion (kak′ə-nā′shən), *n.* [L. *cachinnatio;* see CACHINNATE], loud or unrestrained laughter.
ca·chou (kə-shōō′, ka-shōō′), *n.* [Fr.; Malay *kachu*], 1.

catechu. 2. a lozenge for sweetening the breath.
ca·chu·cha (kä-chōō′chä), *n.* [Sp.], 1. a Spanish dance in 3/4 time, like the bolero. 2. music for this.
ca·cique (kə-sēk′), *n.* [Sp. < a Haitian word meaning "lord," "prince"], 1. in Latin America and the West Indies, a native chief. 2. any of several kinds of tropical American oriole. 3. in the Philippines, an owner of much land. Also spelled **cassique.**
cack·le (kak′'l), *v.i.* [CACKLED (-'ld), CACKLING], [ME. *cakelen;* D. *kakeln;* IE. base **koko*, as in L. *cacillare*, G. *gackern;* of echoic origin; cf. COCK (rooster)], 1. to make the characteristic sound of a hen or goose. 2. to laugh or talk in a shrill, noisy manner; prattle. *v.t.* to say or utter in a cackling manner. *n.* 1. the act or sound of cackling. 2. silly talk; chatter. 3. shrill, noisy, broken laughter.
cac·o- (kak′ə, kak′ō), [< Gr. *kakos*, bad, evil], a combining form meaning *bad, poor, harsh,* as in *cacography, cacophony:* also, before a vowel, **cac**: opposed to *eu-*.
cac·o·de·mon, cac·o·dae·mon (kak′ə-dē′mən), *n.* [*caco-*, bad, evil + *demon*, after Gr. *kakodaimōn*], an evil spirit or devil.
cac·o·dyl (kak′ə-dil, kak′ə-dēl′), *n.* [< Gr. *kakōdēs*, bad-smelling < *kakos*, bad + *ozein*, to smell; + *-yl*], in *chemistry,* 1. the radical $As(CH_3)_2$, composed of arsenic and methyl: its compounds are poisonous and bad-smelling. 2. a poisonous, colorless liquid, $As_2(CH_3)_4$, with a bad smell: it is a polymer of this radical.
cac·o·e·thes, cac·o·ë·thes (kak′ō-ē′thēz), *n.* [L. < Gr. *kakoēthēs* < *kakos*, bad + *ēthos*, habit, custom], 1. a bad habit. 2. an itch (to do something); mania.
cac·o·gen·ics (kak′ə-jen′iks), *n.pl.* [construed as sing.], [*caco-* + *eugenics*], dysgenics.
cac·o·graph·ic (kak′ə-graf′ik), *adj.* of or characterized by cacography.
ca·cog·ra·phy (ka-kog′rə-fi), *n.* [*caco-* + *-graphy*], 1. bad handwriting. 2. incorrect spelling.
ca·col·o·gy (kə-kol′ə-ji), *n.* [*caco-* + *-logy*], substandard pronunciation or diction.
cac·o·mis·tle (kak′ə-mis′'l), *n.* [Sp. < native Mex. ‡ *tlacomiztli*], a slender, long-tailed, raccoonlike animal of the United States and Mexico.
cac·o·mix·le (kak′ə-mis′'l, kak′ə-mik′s'l), *n.* a cacomistle.
ca·coph·o·nous (kə-kof′ə-nəs), *adj.* [*caco-* + *phon-* + *-ous*], discordant.
ca·coph·o·ny (kə-kof′ə-ni), *n.* [*pl.* CACOPHONIES (-niz)], [Gr. *kakophōnia* < *kakophōnos*, harsh-sounding < *kakos*, bad, evil + *phōnē*, voice], harsh, jarring sound; discord.
cac·ta·ceous (kak-tā′shəs), *adj.* [< Mod. L. *Cactaceae*, cactus family; see CACTUS], of the cactus family.
cac·tus (kak′təs), *n.* [*pl.* CACTUSES (-iz), CACTI (-tī)], [L. < Gr. *kaktos*, prickly], any of various plants with fleshy stems, branches bearing spines or scales instead of leaves, and, sometimes, showy flowers: cactuses grow in hot, arid parts of North and South America.
ca·cu·mi·nal (kə-kū′mə-n'l), *adj.* [< L. *cacumen*, top + *-al*], in *phonetics,* pronounced with the tip of the tongue turned backward and upward against or toward the hard palate, as Swedish *d* or *t* following an *r;* retroflex; cerebral. *n.* a cacuminal consonant.

CACTUS
(prickly pear)

cad (kad), *n.* [< Fr. *cadet;* see CADET], a man or boy whose behavior is not gentlemanly; ill-mannered fellow: word originally applied to servants, then to town boys, by students at British universities and public schools.
ca·das·ter (kə-das′tẽr), *n.* a cadastre.
ca·das·tral (kə-das′trəl), *adj.* of a cadastre.
ca·das·tre (kə-das′tẽr), *n.* [Fr.; Pr.; prob. < L. *catasta*, scaffold, place for public burning of martyrs; Gr. *katastasis*, a bringing forward, settled method or system], a public record of the extent, value, and ownership of land for purposes of taxation.
ca·dav·er (kə-dav′ẽr, kə-dā′vẽr), *n.* [L. < *cadere*, to fall], a dead body, especially of a person; corpse, as for dissection. —*SYN.* see **body.**
ca·dav·er·ic (kə-dav′ẽr-ik), *adj.* of or like a cadaver.
ca·dav·er·ine (kə-dav′ẽr-in, kə-dav′ə-rēn′), *n.* [*cadaver* + *-ine*], a colorless, bad-smelling, liquid ptomaine, $C_5H_{14}N_2$, produced by the hydrolysis of proteins, as in putrefying flesh.
ca·dav·er·ous (kə-dav′ẽr-əs), *adj.* [L. *cadaverosus*, corpselike; see CADAVER], of, like, or suggestive of a cadaver; especially, pale, ghastly, or gaunt and haggard.
cad·dice (kad′is), *n.* caddis (material or worm).
cad·die (kad′i), *n.* [Scot. form of Fr. *cadet;* see CADET], 1. originally, an errand boy; hence, 2. in *golf,* a person who attends the player, carrying his clubs, etc. *v.i.* [CADDIED (-id), CADDYING], to act as a caddie. Also spelled **caddy.**
cad·dis (kad′is), *n.* [ME. & OFr. *cadas*, floss silk; confused with Fr. *cadis*, coarse serge], 1. a coarse woolen material; worsted yarn. 2. a worsted ribbon.
cad·dis (kad′is), *n.* a caddis worm.
caddis fly, [? < OFr. *cadas*, floss silk (with reference to the cocoon)], a small, mothlike fly: the larvae live in fresh water in cocoons covered with sand, gravel, etc.
cad·dish (kad′ish), *adj.* like or characteristic of a cad; ill-mannered.
caddis worm, the wormlike larva of the caddis fly, used as bait by anglers.
Cad·do (kad′ō), *n.* [*pl.* CADDO, CADDOES (-ōz)], a member of a confederacy of North American Indians formerly living in Louisiana, Arkansas, and eastern Texas, of Caddoan linguistic stock.
Cad·do·an (kad′ō-ən), *adj.* designating or of a family of North American Indian languages spoken by the Caddo and other tribes in southwestern Arkansas and near-by parts of Louisiana, Texas, and Oklahoma, by the Pawnee in Nebraska and Kansas, and by some other tribes in North Dakota. *n.* this family of languages.
cad·dy (kad′i), *n.* [*pl.* CADDIES (-iz)], [< earlier *catty* < Malay *kati*, weight equivalent to a little more than a pound], a small container used for tea.
cad·dy (kad′i), *n.* [*pl.* CADDIES (-iz)] & *v.i.* [CADDIED (-id), CADDYING], caddie.
cade (kād), *n.* [Fr.; Pr. < L. dial. *catanus*], a large, bushy European juniper whose wood yields a thick, brown oil used in medicine.
-cade (kād), [< *cavalcade*], a suffix meaning *procession, parade,* as in *aquacade, motorcade.*
ca·delle (kə-del′), *n.* [Fr.; Pr. *cadello;* L. *catella*, fem. of *catellus*, puppy, whelp], the larva or adult of a small beetle harmful to grain.
ca·dence (kā′d'ns), *n.* [ME.; ult. < L. *cadens*, ppr. of *cadere*, to fall], 1. fall of the voice in speaking. 2. flow of rhythm. 3. measured movement, as in dancing or marching, or the beat of such movement. 4. inflection or modulation in tone. 5. in *music,* *a*) the harmonic ending, final trill, etc. of a phrase or movement. *b*) a cadenza.
ca·denced (kā′d'nst), *adj.* having cadence; rhythmical.
ca·den·cy (kā′d'n-si), *n.* [*pl.* CADENCIES (-siz)], 1. cadence. 2. descent of a younger son or of the younger branch of a family.
ca·dent (kā′d'nt), *adj.* 1. [Obs.], falling. 2. having cadence; cadenced.
ca·den·za (kə-den′zə; It. kä-dent′sä), *n.* [It.; see CADENCE], 1. an elaborate, often improvised musical passage played by an unaccompanied instrument in a concerto, usually toward the end of the first movement. 2. any brilliant flourish put into an aria or a solo passage.
Ca·det (kə-det′), *n.* [Russ. *Kadet* < *K. Dti*, used as pl. of *K.D.*, the initials of the party's name], a member of the Constitutional Democrats, a right-wing political party in Czarist Russia.
ca·det (kə-det′), *n.* [Fr. form of Gascon *capdet*, lit., little chief, Gascon noble's younger son < L. *caput*, head + dim. suffix *-et*], 1. a younger son or brother in a gentleman's family; hence, 2. formerly, a younger son who became a gentleman volunteer in the army to offset his lack of patrimony; hence, 3. a student in training to become an officer in the armed forces: as, an air-force *cadet.* 4. a student at a military school.
ca·det·cy (kə-det′si), *n.* [*pl.* CADETCIES (-siz)], a cadetship.
ca·det·ship (kə-det′ship), *n.* [*cadet* + *-ship*], 1. the position or rank of a cadet. 2. the period of time during which one is a cadet.
cadet teacher, 1. an upperclass college student who does practice teaching. 2. a public school teacher assigned to a regular position but without its customary benefits, such as pension, etc., and paid at a daily rate.
cadge (kaj), *v.t.* & *v.i.* [CADGED (kajd), CADGING], [ME. *caggen;* prob. var. of *cacchen*, to catch; cf. GRUDGE], [Dial.], 1. to peddle. 2. [Colloq.], to beg or get by begging.
cadg·y (kaj′i), *adj.* [< *cadge* + *-y*], [Scot. & British Dial.], 1. lustful; lewd; wanton. 2. merry; cheerful.
ca·di (kä′di, kā′di), *n.* [Ar. *qādi*], a minor Moslem magistrate or judge.
Ca·dil·lac, Sieur **An·toine de la Mothe** (äɴ′twäɴ′ də lä môt′ kȧ′dē′yȧk′; Eng. kad′'l-ak′), 1656?–1730; French explorer and colonial governor in America.
Cá·diz (kā′diz; Sp. kä′thēth), *n.* a city in southwestern Spain, on the Atlantic: pop., 76,000.
Cad·man, Charles Wake·field (wāk′fēld′ kad′mən), 1881–1946; American composer.
Cad·me·an (kad-mē′ən), *adj.* of, like, or like that of Cadmus.

Cadmean victory, a victory won at great sacrifice and destructive to the victors: see **Cadmus.**
cad·mic (kad′mik), *adj.* of, derived from, or containing cadmium.
cad·mi·um (kad′mi-əm), *n.* [Mod. L.; named by Strohmeyer (1817); L. *cadmia,* zinc ore, calamine < *Cadmus*], a blue-white, malleable, ductile, metallic chemical element occurring as a sulfide or carbonate in zinc ores: it is used in some alloys, electroplating, pigment, etc.: symbol, Cd; at. wt., 112.41; at. no., 48.
cadmium sulfide, a pigment, CdS, varying from lemon yellow (*cadmium yellow*) to yellowish orange (*cadmium orange*).
Cad·mus (kad′məs), *n.* in *Greek legend,* a Phoenician prince who founded Thebes and killed a dragon sacred to Mars: from the dragon's teeth, which he sowed in the earth, armed men sprang up and proceeded to fight one another until only five were left, who then helped Cadmus build the city.
ca·dre (kad′ri; Fr. kä′dr′), *n.* [Fr. *cadre,* a frame; It. *quadro;* L. *quadrum,* a square], 1. a framework. 2. a nucleus around which an expanded organization, as a military unit, can be built. 3. staff officers.
ca·du·ce·an (kə-dōō′si-ən, kə-dū′si-ən), *adj.* of the caduceus.
ca·du·ce·us (kə-dōō′si-əs, kə-dū′si-əs), *n.* [*pl.* CADUCEI (-ī′)], [L.], 1. the staff of an ancient herald; especially, the winged staff with two serpents twined about it, carried by Mercury. 2. Mercury's staff as a symbol of the medical profession.

CADUCEUS

ca·du·ci·ty (kə-dōō′sə-ti, kə-dū′sə-ti), *n.* [Fr. *caducité* < *caduc,* falling; L. *caducus;* see CADUCOUS], 1. the quality or state of being perishable. 2. senility.
ca·du·cous (kə-dōō′kəs, kə-dū′kəs), *adj.* [L. *caducus,* falling < *cadere,* to fall], 1. dropping off. 2. fleeting; unenduring. 3. in *botany,* falling off early, as some leaves.
cae·cal (sē′k′l), *adj.* of the caecum.
cae·cil·i·an (sē-sil′i-ən), *n.* [< L. *caecilia,* variety of lizard], any of a group of legless, tropical amphibians resembling worms.
cae·cum (sē′kəm), *n.* [*pl.* CAECA (-kə)], [L. < *intestinum caecum,* blind intestine < *caecus,* blind], 1. the pouch which is the beginning of the large intestine: see **alimentary canal,** illus. 2. in *zoology,* a cavity open at one end. Also spelled **cecum.**
Caed·mon (kad′mən), *n.* first English poet whose name is known; fl. 670 A.D.
Cae·li·an (sē′li-ən), *n.* [< L. *Caelius Mons,* Caelian hill, named after the Tuscan *Caeles Vibenna*], one of the seven hills on which Rome was built.
Caen (kän), *n.* a city in northern France, on the Orne River: pop., 68,000.
cae·no·gen·e·sis (sē′nə-jen′ə-sis, sen′ə-jen′ə-sis), *n.* cenogenesis.
Caer·le·on (kär-lē′ən), *n.* [W. *Caerlleon;* OW. *Cair Legion,* for L. *Castra legionum,* lit., camp of the legions, whence AS. *Legaceaster,* orig. name of Chester], in *Arthurian legend,* a city where King Arthur held court.
Caer·nar·von (kär-när′vən), *n.* 1. Caernarvonshire. 2. the county seat of Caernarvonshire: pop., 9,000.
Caer·nar·von·shire (kär-när′vən-shir′), *n.* a county of northwestern Wales: pop., 124,000; county seat, Caernarvon: also **Carnarvon.**
caes·al·pin·i·a·ceous (sez′al-pin′i-ā′shəs), *adj.* [< Mod. L. *caesalpinaceae,* senna family; after Andrea *Cesalpino,* It. botanist], of the senna family of tropical plants, which have finely cut leaves, showy flowers, and pods that are usually flat.
Cae·sar (sē′zẽr), *n.* [L., the hairy one; cf. CZAR, KAISER], 1. Julius Caesar's family name. 2. the title of the emperor of Rome from Augustus to Hadrian, or of the emperor of the Holy Roman Empire. 3. an emperor or dictator.
Caesar, Julius, (*Gaius Julius Caesar*), 100?–44 B.C.; Roman statesman and general; as dictator, extended and unified the Roman empire.
Caes·a·re·a (ses′ə-rē′ə, sez′ə-rē′ə), *n.* 1. the ancient capital of the Roman province of Palestine, located in the northwest part on the Mediterranean. 2. Kayseri, a city in Turkey: the ancient name.
Cae·sar·e·an, Cae·sar·i·an (si-zâr′i-ən), *adj.* of Julius Caesar or the Caesars.
Caesarean operation (or **section**), a surgical operation for delivering a baby by cutting through the mother's abdominal and uterine walls: so called because Julius Caesar was supposedly born in this manner.
Cae·sar·ism, cae·sar·ism (sē′zẽr-iz′m), *n.* absolutism in government; autocracy; imperialism.
cae·si·um (sē′zi-əm), *n.* cesium.
caes·pi·tose (ses′pi-tōs′), *adj.* cespitose.
cae·su·ra (si-zhoor′ə, si-zyoor′ə), *n.* [*pl.* CAESURAS (-əz), CAESURAE (-ē)], [L., a cutting, felling < *caedere,* to cut], 1. a break or pause in a line of verse: in Greek and Latin verse, the caesura falls within the metrical foot; in English verse, it is usually about the middle of the line: shown in scanning by the sign ‖, as, "Loveliest of trees, ‖ the cherry now." 2. a pause showing rhythmic division of a melody.
cae·su·ral (si-zhoor′əl, si-zyoor′əl), *adj.* of a caesura.
C.A.F., c.a.f., 1. cost and freight. 2. cost, assurance, and freight.
ca·fé (kə-fā′, ka-fā′), *n.* [Fr., coffee, coffeehouse; see COFFEE], 1. a coffeehouse or restaurant. 2. coffee. 3. a restaurant serving alcoholic drinks and sometimes providing entertainment.
‡**ca·fé au lait** (kȧ′fā′ ō′lā′), [Fr.], 1. coffee with milk. 2. pale brown.
‡**ca·fé noir** (kȧ′fā′ nwȧr′), [Fr.], black coffee.
café society, 1. a well-publicized set of habitual frequenters of cafés or night clubs in New York City; hence, 2. any similar set elsewhere.
caf·e·te·ri·a (kaf′ə-têr′i-ə), *n.* [Am. Sp., coffee store], a restaurant in which food is displayed on counters and patrons serve themselves.
caf·fe·ine, caf·fe·in (kaf′i-in, kaf′ēn′), *n.* [Fr. *caféine* < *café,* coffee], the alkaloid $C_8H_{10}N_4O_2$, present in coffee, tea, and kola: it is a stimulant to the heart and central nervous system: the methyl derivative of theobromine.
caf·tan (kaf′tən, käf-tän′), *n.* [Turk. *qaftān*], a long-sleeved robe with a girdle, worn in eastern Mediterranean countries: also spelled **kaftan.**

CAFTAN

cage (kāj), *n.* [ME.; OFr.; L. *cavea,* hollow place, cage], 1. a box or enclosed structure made of wires, bars, etc. for confining birds or animals. 2. a fenced-in area for confining prisoners of war. 3. any openwork structure or frame. 4. an elevator car. 5. [Archaic], a jail. 6. in *baseball,* a partially enclosed backstop used for batting practice, etc. 7. in *basketball,* the basket. 8. in *hockey,* the network frame used as a goal. *v.t.* [CAGED (kājd), CAGING], to put in a cage; confine.
cage·ling (kāj′liŋ), *n.* a bird kept in a cage.
cag·er (kāj′ẽr), *n.* [Colloq.], a basketball player.
cage·y (kāj′i), *adj.* [prob. < *cage,* a jail], [Slang], sly; tricky; cunning: also spelled **cagy.**
Ca·glia·ri (kä′lyä-rē′), *n.* a city on the coast of southern Sardinia: pop., 143,000.
Ca·glia·ri, Pa·o·lo (pä′ô-lô kä′lyä-rē′), see **Veronese, Paolo.**
Ca·glio·stro, Count **A·les·san·dro di** (ä′les-sän′drô dē kä-lyôs′trô), (born *Guiseppe Balsamo*), 1743–1795; Sicilian alchemist and impostor.
‡**Ca·gou·lard** (kȧ′gōō′lär′), *n.* [Fr. < *cagoule,* monk's cloak], a member of a secret French fascist society, whose plot to overthrow the republic was revealed in 1937.
‡**ca·hier** (kȧ′yā′; Eng. kə-hêr′), *n.* [Fr.; OFr. *quair;* see QUIRE], 1. a book of loose leaves held together; notebook; hence, 2. a report.
ca·hoots (kə-hōōts′), *n.pl.* [? < *cohort* or < Fr. *cahute,* a cabin], [Slang], partnership.
go cahoots, [Slang], to share alike.
in cahoots, [Slang], in partnership: usually applied to shady dealing.
Cai·a·phas (kā′ə-fəs, kī′ə-fəs), *n.* [Gr. *Kaiaphas*], in the *Bible,* the high priest who presided at the trial that led to the condemnation of Jesus: Matt. 26:57–66.
Cai·cos Islands (kī′kōs), see **Turks and Caicos Islands.**
Cai·jan (kā′jən), *n.* Cajun.
cai·man (kā′mən), *n.* a cayman.
Cain (kān), *n.* [Heb. *qayin,* lit., smith, craftsman], 1. in the *Bible,* the oldest son of Adam and Eve: he killed his brother Abel: Gen. 4; hence, 2. a murderer.
raise Cain, [Slang], 1. to create a great commotion. 2. to cause much trouble.
Caine, Hall (kān), (Sir *Thomas Henry Hall Caine*), 1853–1931; English novelist.
Cai·no·zo·ic (kī′nə-zō′ik, kā′nə-zō′ik), *adj.* Cenozoic.
ca·ique, ca·ïque (kä-ēk′), *n.* [Fr.; It. *caicco;* Turk. *qayiq*], 1. a light rowboat used on the Bosporus. 2. a sailboat used especially in the eastern Mediterranean.
‡**ça i·ra** (sȧ′ ē′rȧ′), [Fr.], it will go (on): the refrain of a popular song of the French Revolution.
caird (kârd), *n.* [< Scot. Gael. *ceard,* a tinker], [Scot.], a wandering tinker, vagrant, gypsy, etc.
Caird, Edward (kârd), 1835–1908; Scottish philosopher and theologian.
Caird Coast (kârd), a region in Antarctica, east of the Weddell Sea: part of Falkland Islands Dependency.
cairn (kârn), *n.* [Scot. < Gael. *carn*], a conical heap of stones built as a monument or landmark.
cairn·gorm (kârn′gôrm′), *n.* [name of Scot. mountain and mountain range; Gael. *carngorm,* blue cairn], a yellow or brown variety of quartz, used as a gem: also **Cairngorm stone.**
cairn terrier, [said to be so named from burrowing in or around cairns], a small, shaggy Scottish terrier.
Cai·ro (kī′rō), *n.* 1. the capital of the United Arab Republic, in Egypt on the Nile: pop., 3,035,000. 2. (kâr′ō), a city in southern Illinois: pop., 9,000.

cais·son (kā′sən), *n.* [Fr. < *caisse*, chest, box], 1. a box of explosives to be fired as a mine. 2. a chest for holding ammunition. 3. a two-wheeled wagon for transporting ammunition. 4. a watertight box inside which men can do construction work under water. 5. a watertight box for raising and floating sunken ships, etc.: after the box is sunk and attached, the water is forced out of it so that it floats and raises the ship. 6. a hollow, boat-shaped box, used as a floodgate at a dock or basin.

CAISSON

caisson disease, decompression sickness.

Caith·ness (kāth′nes, kāth-nes′), *n.* a county of northern Scotland: pop., 25,700; county seat, Wick.

cai·tiff (kā′tif), *n.* [ME.; OFr. *caitif*, a captive, wretched man; L. *captivus* < *capere*, to take], a mean, evil, or cowardly person. *adj.* evil; mean; cowardly.

caj·e·put (kaj′ə-pət), *n.* 1. a cajuput. 2. a California laurel.

ca·jole (kə-jōl′), *v.t. & v.i.* [CAJOLED (-jōld′), CAJOLING], [Fr. *cajoler*; ? < OFr. *cageoler*, to use decoy songbirds to lure wild birds into a cage; see CAGE], to coax with false words, flattery, etc.; wheedle. —*SYN.* see **coax.**

ca·jole·ment (kə-jōl′mənt), *n.* a cajoling.

ca·jol·er·y (kə-jōl′ẽr-i), *n.* [*pl.* CAJOLERIES (-iz)], [Fr. *cajolerie*], a cajoling, or coaxing, wheedling, etc.

Ca·jun (kā′jən), *n.* [< *Acadian*], 1. a native of Louisiana supposed to have had Acadian French ancestors: sometimes used contemptuously. 2. the dialect of the Cajuns. Also spelled **Caijan.**

caj·u·put (kaj′ə-pət), *n.* [Malay *kāyūputih*; *kāyū*, tree + *putih*, white], an East Indian tree of the myrtle family, yielding a greenish oil used externally in some skin diseases: also spelled **cajeput.**

cake (kāk), *n.* [ME. *kake* < ON.; akin to Norw., Sw., Ice. *kaka*, Dan. *kage*, OHG. *kuocho*, cake, AS. *coecil*, *cecil*, little cake; IE. base **gag*, **gog*, something round, lump of something; not connected with *cook* & L. *coquere*], 1. a small, flat mass of baked or fried dough or batter. 2. a mixture of flour, eggs, milk, sugar, etc. baked and often covered with icing. 3. a small, flat mass of fish, vegetables, etc. fried on both sides. 4. a compactly shaped, solid mass, as of soap, ice, etc. *v.t. & v.i.* [CAKED (kākt), CAKING], to form into a hard mass. **take the cake,** [Slang], 1. to win the prize. 2. to excel.

cake flour, finely ground and well sifted wheat flour for baking.

cakes and ale, the good things of life; worldly pleasures.

cake·walk (kāk′wôk′), *n.* 1. an elaborate step or walk formerly performed by Negroes in the South competing for the prize of a cake. 2. a strutting dance developed from this. *v.i.* to perform a cakewalk.

Cal., 1. California. 2. large caloric; large calories.

cal., 1. calendar. 2. caliber. 3. small calorie(s).

cal·a·bar (kal′ə-bẽr), *n.* calaber.

Cal·a·bar bean (kal′ə-bär′, kal′ə-bär′), [prob. after *Calabar*, name of a river, town, and district in Southern Nigeria], the poisonous brown seed of an African climbing plant, used in medicine for various nervous disorders, to contract the pupil of the eye, etc.

cal·a·bash (kal′ə-bash′), *n.* [Fr. *calebasse*; Pr. *calabasso*, *carabasso*; ? < Per. *kharbuz*, melon], 1. a tropical American tree of the bignonia family. 2. its gourdlike fruit. 3. the dried, hollow shell of a gourd or calabash, used as a bowl, pipe, etc. 4. any of various gourds.

cal·a·ber (kal′ə-bẽr), *n.* [< Fr. *Calabre*, Calabria], 1. a gray Siberian squirrel. 2. its fur. Also spelled **calabar.**

cal·a·boose (kal′ə-bōōs′, kal′ə-bōōs′), *n.* [Sp. *calabozo*], [Slang], a prison; jail.

Ca·la·bri·a (kə-lā′bri-ə; It. kä-lä′bryä), *n.* a department of southwestern Italy, opposite Sicily.

ca·la·di·um (kə-lā′di-əm), *n.* [Mod. L. < Malay *kalādi*, kind of plant], a tropical American plant of the arum family, with large, brilliantly colored leaves.

Cal·ais (kal′ā, kal′is; Fr. kȧ′le′), *n.* a city in France, on the English Channel, opposite Dover: pop., 50,000 (1946).

Ca·lak·mul (kä′läk-mōōl′), *n.* a ruined Mayan city in Campeche state, Mexico.

cal·a·man·co (kal′ə-maŋ′kō), *n.* [Sp. *calamaco*, *calamanco*], 1. a glossy woolen cloth with checks on one side only. 2. clothing made of this.

cal·a·man·der (kal′ə-man′dẽr, kal′ə-man′dẽr), *n.* [< *Coromandel*, name of E. Indian coast around Madras, with interchange of *r* and *l*; cf. Fr. *calambar*], the hard wood of any of certain East Indian trees related to the ebony: it is striped hazel-brown and black and is used in making furniture: also **calamander wood.**

cal·a·mar·y (kal′ə-mâr′i, kal′ə-mẽr-i), *n.* [*pl.* CALAMARIES (-iz)], [L. *calamarius*, of a writing reed < *calamus*, a reed, pen; see CALAMUS], a squid with a pen-shaped skeleton.

cal·a·mine (kal′ə-mīn′, kal′ə-min), *n.* [Fr.; ML. *calamina* < L. *cadmia*, calamine; see CADMIUM], 1. hydrous zinc silicate, $(ZnOH)_2SiO_3$, a zinc ore. 2. [British], native zinc carbonate, $ZnCO_3$: also called *smithsonite*. Variously used in skin ointments and lotions.

cal·a·mint (kal′ə-mint′), *n.* [ME. *calament*; OFr. *calament*; ML. *calamentum*; L. *calaminthe*; Gr. *kalaminthē*], a variety of mint: also **calamint balm.**

cal·a·mite (kal′ə-mīt′), *n.* [< Mod. L. *Calamites*, genus of fossil plants < Gr. *kalamitēs*, reedlike < *kalamos*, a reed], any of a number of related fossil plants like the horsetail, found in coal deposits.

ca·lam·i·tous (kə-lam′ə-təs), *adj.* [Fr. *calamiteux*], causing calamity; bringing calamity with it.

ca·lam·i·ty (kə-lam′ə-ti), *n.* [*pl.* CALAMITIES (-tiz)], [Fr. *calamité*; L. *calamitas*; IE. base **qel(a)*, to strike, smash, as in L. *incolumis*, safe, unharmed], 1. misery. 2. any extreme misfortune; disaster. —*SYN.* see **disaster.**

cal·a·mus (kal′ə-məs), *n.* [*pl.* CALAMI (-mī′)], [ME.; L.; Gr. *kalamos*, a stalk, reed, stubble], 1. a plant with long, narrow leaves; sweet flag. 2. its root. 3. a palm tree whose stems form canes. 4. the quill of a feather.

ca·lash (kə-lash′), *n.* [Fr. *calèche*; G. *kalesche*; Czech *kolésa*; prob. < *kolo*, a wheel], 1. a light, low-wheeled carriage, usually with a folding top: also spelled **calèche.** 2. a folding top of a carriage. 3. a folding hood or bonnet, worn by women in the 18th century.

cal·a·thus (kal′ə-thəs), *n.* [*pl.* CALATHI (-thī′)], [L.; Gr. *kalathos*], in ancient Greece, a basket for fruits: it was a symbol of abundance.

cal·a·ver·ite (kal′ə-vâr′īt), *n.* [< *Calaveras* County, California, where first discovered + *-ite*], a native telluride of gold, $AuTe_2$, containing some silver.

calc- (kalk), [G. *kalk*, lime < L. *calx*, lime], a combining form meaning *calcareous*, as in *calcspar*.

cal·ca·ne·um (kal-kā′ni-əm), *n.* [L. < *calx*, the heel], a calcaneus.

cal·ca·ne·us (kal-kā′ni-əs), *n.* [LL.; see CALCANEUM], the heel bone; one of the tarsal bones.

cal·car (kal′kär), *n.* [*pl.* CALCARIA (-kâr′i-ə)], [L. < *calx*, the heel], 1. in *botany*, a hollow projection at the base of a petal. 2. in *zoology*, a protuberance on a bird's wing or leg. Also called *spur*.

cal·ca·rate (kal′kə-rāt′, kal′kə-rit), *adj.* having calcars.

cal·car·e·ous (kal-kâr′i-əs), *adj.* [L. *calcarius* < *calx*, lime], of, like, or containing calcium carbonate, calcium, or lime.

cal·ca·rif·er·ous (kal′kə-rif′ẽr-əs), *adj.* [< L. *calcar*, spur; + *-ferous*], in *botany* & *zoology*, bearing a spur or spurs.

cal·ce·i·form (kal′si-ə-fôrm′, kal-sē′ə-fôrm′), *adj.* [< L. *calceus*, a shoe; + *-form*], shaped like a slipper.

cal·ce·o·la·ri·a (kal′si-ə-lā′ri-ə, kal′si-ə-lâr′i-ə), *n.* [Mod. L. < L. *calceolarius*, one who makes shoes < *calceolus*, dim. of *calceus*, a shoe < *calx*, the heel], any of a group of South American plants of the figwort family, bearing showy, slipper-shaped flowers.

cal·ce·o·late (kal′si-ə-lāt′), *adj.* [< L. *calceolus*, slipper, dim. of *calceus*, shoe; + *-ate*], in *botany*, shaped like a slipper: said of the blossoms of certain plants.

cal·ces (kal′sēz), *n.* alternative plural of **calx.**

Cal·chas (kal′kəs), *n.* [L.; Gr. *Kalchas*], in *Greek legend*, a priest of Apollo who accompanied the Greeks during the Trojan War.

cal·ci- (kal′si), [< L. *calx*, *calcis*, lime], a combining form meaning *calcium* or *lime*, as in *calciferous*, *calcify*.

cal·cic (kal′sik), *adj.* from or having calcium or lime.

cal·cif·er·ol (kal-sif′ẽr-ōl′, kal-sif′ẽr-ol′), *n.* [*calciferous* + ergost*erol*], vitamin D_2: it is a crystalline alcohol, $C_{28}H_{43}OH$.

cal·cif·er·ous (kal-sif′ẽr-əs), *adj.* [*calci-* + *-ferous*], producing or containing calcite.

cal·cif·ic (kal-sif′ik), *adj.* [< *calcify* + *-ic*], calciferous.

cal·ci·fi·ca·tion (kal′sə-fi-kā′shən), *n.* 1. a calcifying; deposition of calcium salts in the tissues. 2. a calcified substance or structure.

cal·ci·fy (kal′sə-fī′), *v.t. & v.i.* [CALCIFIED (-fīd′), CALCIFYING], [*calci-* + *-fy*], to change into a hard, stony substance by the deposit of lime.

cal·ci·mine (kal′sə-mīn′, kal′sə-min), *n.* [< L. *calx*, *calcis*, lime], a white or colored liquid used as a wash for plastered ceilings or walls. *v.t.* [CALCIMINED (-mīnd′, -mind), CALCIMINING], to cover with calcimine. Also spelled **kalsomine.**

cal·ci·na·tion (kal′sə-nā′shən), *n.* [ME.; Fr.; ML. *calcinatio*], 1. a calcining. 2. a calcined substance.

cal·cin·a·to·ry (kal-sin′ə-tôr′i, kal′sin-ə-tō′ri), *adj.* for calcining. *n.* a furnace or vessel for calcining.

cal·cine (kal′sīn, kal′sin), *v.t. & v.i.* [CALCINED (-sīnd′, -sind), CALCINING], [Fr. *calciner*; ML. *calcinare*],

1. to change to calx or powder by heat. 2. to burn to ashes or powder. 3. to oxidize.

cal·cite (kal′sīt′), *n.* [< L. *calx, calcis,* lime; + *-ite*], calcium carbonate, $CaCO_3$, with hexagonal crystallization, a mineral found in the form of limestone, chalk, and marble: distinguished from *aragonite.*

cal·ci·um (kal′si-əm), *n.* [Mod. L. < L. *calx, calcis,* lime], a soft, silver-white metallic chemical element found in limestone, marble, chalk, etc., always in combination: symbol, Ca; at. wt., 40.08; at. no., 20.

calcium arsenate, a white compound, $Ca_3(AsO_4)_2$, used as an insecticide in the form of a spray or dust.

calcium carbide, a dark-gray crystalline compound, CaC_2, used in making acetylene and calcium cyanamide.

calcium carbonate, a white powder or colorless, crystalline compound, $CaCO_3$, found mainly in limestone, marble, and chalk, as calcite, aragonite, etc., and in bones, teeth, shells, and plant ash: used in making lime.

calcium chloride, a white, crystalline compound, $CaCl_2$, used in making ice, as a dehydrating agent, etc.

calcium cyanamide, a white, crystalline compound, $CaCN_2$, used as a fertilizer: also called *lime nitrogen.*

calcium hydroxide, a white, crystalline compound, $Ca(OH)_2$, prepared by the action of water on calcium oxide, used in making alkalies, bleaching powder, plaster, etc.: also called *slaked lime.*

calcium light, a brilliant white light produced when a very hot flame is played on a piece of lime; limelight.

calcium oxide, a white, soft, caustic solid, CaO, prepared by heating calcium carbonate; quicklime.

calcium phosphate, any of a number of phosphates of calcium found in bones, teeth, and other animal tissues and used in medicine and in the manufacture of enamels, glass, cleaning agents, etc.

cal·cog·ra·phy (kal-kog′rə-fi), *n.* [< *calci-* + *-graphy*], the art of drawing with crayons.

calc-sin·ter (kalk′sin′tẽr), *n.* [G. *kalksinter; kalk,* lime + *sinter,* slag], travertine.

calc·spar, calc-spar (kalk′spär′), *n.* [*calc-* + *spar* (mineral) after G. *kalkspar,* calcspar], calcite.

calc-tu·fa (kalk′tōō′fə), *n.* in *mineralogy,* porous lime carbonate deposited by the waters of calcareous springs; calcareous tufa.

cal·cu·la·bil·i·ty (kal′kyoo-lə-bil′ə-ti), *n.* the quality or state of being calculable.

cal·cu·la·ble (kal′kyoo-lə-b′l), *adj.* that can be calculated.

cal·cu·late (kal′kyoo-lāt′), *v.t.* [CALCULATED (-id), CALCULATING], [< L. *calculatus,* pp. of *calculare,* to reckon < *calculus,* pebble used in doing arithmetic; dim. of *calx,* limestone], 1. to determine by arithmetic; compute; reckon. 2. to ascertain or determine by reasoning; estimate. 3. to plan; intend: used in the passive. 4. [Colloq.], to think; suppose. *v.i.* 1. to do arithmetic; make a computation. 2. to rely or depend (*on*).

SYN.—**calculate** refers to the mathematical determination of a quantity, amount, etc. and implies the use of higher mathematics (to *calculate* distances in astronomy); **compute** suggests simpler mathematics and implies a determinable, hence precise, result (to *compute* the volume of a cylinder); **estimate** implies the judging, usually in advance, of a quantity, cost, etc. and connotes an approximate result (to *estimate* the cost of building a house); **reckon,** an informal substitute for **compute,** suggests the use of simple arithmetic such as can be performed mentally (to *reckon* the days before elections).

cal·cu·lat·ing (kal′kyoo-lā′tiŋ), *adj.* [ppr. of *calculate*], 1. scheming; cunning. 2. shrewd; cautious.

calculating machine, a machine for doing rapid addition, subtraction, multiplication, and division.

cal·cu·la·tion (kal′kyoo-lā′shən), *n.* [L. *calculatio*], 1. a calculating. 2. something deduced by calculating; inference; plan. 3. forethought; prudence.

cal·cu·la·tive (kal′kyoo-lā′tiv), *adj.* 1. having to do with calculation. 2. calculating or tending to calculate.

cal·cu·la·tor (kal′kyoo-lā′tẽr), *n.* [L.], 1. a person who calculates. 2. a book of tables for calculating. 3. a calculating machine.

cal·cu·li (kal′kyoo-lī′), *n.* alternative plural of **calculus.**

cal·cu·lous (kal′kyoo-ləs), *adj.* [L. *calculosus*], in *medicine,* caused by or having a calculus or calculi.

cal·cu·lus (kal′kyoo-ləs), *n.* [*pl.* CALCULI (-lī′), CALCULUSES (-iz)], [L.; see CALCULATE], 1. an abnormal stony mass or deposit in the body. 2. in *higher mathematics, a)* a method of calculation. *b)* the use of symbols. *c)* a method of analysis: see **differential calculus, integral calculus.** *d)* a textbook of calculus. *e)* a school course or class in calculus.

Cal·cut·ta (kal-kut′ə), *n.* a seaport in northeastern India, on the Hooghly River: capital of West Bengal province: pop., 1,261,000.

cal·dar·i·um (kal-dâr′i-əm), *n.* [*pl.* CALDARIA (-ə)], [L.], in ancient Roman baths, a room for taking hot baths.

‡cal·de·ra (käl-de′rä; Eng. kal-dē′rə), *n.* [Sp. < L. *caldaria,* warm bath, pot < *calidus,* warm], a broad, craterlike basin of a volcano, formed by an explosion or by collapse of the cone.

Cal·de·rón de la Bar·ca, Pe·dro (pe′*th*rô käl′de-rôn′ de lä bär′kä; Eng. kôl′dẽr-ən), 1600–1681; Spanish poet and playwright.

cal·dron (kôl′drən), *n.* [ME. *caldron, caudron;* OFr. *caudron, chaudron;* L. *caldaria;* see CALDERA], a large kettle or boiler: also spelled **cauldron.**

Cald·well, Ers·kine (ũr′skin kôld′wel, kôld′wəl), 1903– ; American writer.

Ca·leb (kā′ləb), [Heb. *kālēb,* lit., dog; hence, faithful], a masculine name. *n.* in the *Bible,* one of the only two men who survived the forty years' wanderings of the Israelites after the exodus from Egypt: he and Joshua, because of their righteousness, were permitted to enter Canaan: Num. 26:65; Deut. 1:36.

‡ca·lèche (kå′lesh′), *n.* [Fr.; see CALASH], 1. in Quebec, a two-wheeled carriage with a folding top. 2. a calash.

Cal·e·do·ni·a (kal′ə-dō′ni-ə, kal′ə-dōn′yə), *n.* [L.], [Obs. or Poetic], Scotland.

Cal·e·do·ni·an (kal′ə-dō′ni-ən, kal′ə-dōn′yən), *adj.* 1. of ancient Caledonia; hence, 2. Scottish: humorous or poetic term. *n.* a native or inhabitant of ancient Caledonia or Scotland.

Caledonian Canal, a canal in northern Scotland, extending from the North Atlantic to the North Sea: length, 60 1/2 mi.

cal·e·fa·cient (kal′ə-fā′shənt), *adj.* [L. *calefaciens,* ppr. of *calefacere* < *calere,* to be warm + *facere,* to make], making warm; heating. *n.* a remedy that warms.

cal·e·fac·tion (kal′ə-fak′shən), *n.* [L. *calefactio* < *calefacere;* see CALEFACIENT], 1. a heating. 2. the state of being made warm.

cal·e·fac·to·ry (kal′ə-fak′tə-ri), *adj.* [L. *calefactorius* < *calefacere;* see CALEFACIENT], producing heat; giving warmth. *n.* [*pl.* CALEFACTORIES (-riz)], 1. a heated room in a monastery. 2. a warming pan.

cal·en·dar (kal′ən-dẽr), *n.* [ME.; L. *calendarium,* account book < *calendae, kalendae,* calends], 1. a system of determining the beginning, length, and divisions of a year. 2. a table, register, etc. that shows the days, weeks, and months of a given year. 3. a register; list; schedule, as of pending court cases. Abbreviated **cal.** *v.t.* 1. to enter in a calendar. 2. to schedule.

calendar day, the twenty-four hours from one midnight to the next midnight.

calendar month, any of the twelve divisions of a year.

calendar year, the period of time from January 1 through December 31: distinguished from *fiscal year.* There are 365 days in a regular year, 366 in a leap year.

cal·en·der (kal′ən-dẽr), *n.* [Fr. *calendre;* LL. *calendra;* L. *cylindrus;* Gr. *kylindros,* roller, cylinder], 1. a machine with rollers between which paper or cloth is run to give it a smooth or glossy finish. 2. [for *calenderer*], an operator of such a machine. *v.t.* [Fr. *calendrer* < the *n.*], to press (paper, cloth, etc.) in a calender.

cal·en·der (kal′ən-dẽr), *n.* [Per. *qalandar*], a member of an order of wandering dervishes among the Sufis.

cal·ends (kal′əndz), *n.pl.* [ME. *kalendes;* AS. *calend,* month; L. *calendae, kalendae,* the first of the month < *calare,* to announce solemnly; Gr. *kalein,* to proclaim], the first day of each month in the ancient Roman calendar: also spelled **kalends.**

ca·len·du·la (kə-len′jə-lə), *n.* [Mod. L. < L. *calendae,* calends: prob. because the plants flower in most months of the year], 1. any of various related plants of the daisy family, with yellow or orange flowers, as the pot marigold. 2. the dried florets of such a plant, used as a remedy for wounds, etc.

cal·en·ture (kal′ən-choor′, kal′ən-chẽr), *n.* [Fr.; Sp. *calentura* < *calentar,* to heat < L. *calens,* ppr. of *calere,* to be warm, glow], a tropical fever with delirium.

‡ca·le·sa (kä-le′sä), *n.* [Sp.], a kind of calash; cab.

ca·les·cence (kə-les′′ns), *n.* a calescent condition.

ca·les·cent (kə-les′′nt), *adj.* [L. *calescens,* ppr. of *calescere,* to grow warm < *calere,* to be warm or hot], increasing in warmth; getting hot.

calf (kaf, käf), *n.* [*pl.* CALVES (kavz, kävz)], [ME.; AS. *cealf* & ON. *kalfr;* IE. base **gelebh,* to swell out; hence, swelling, fetus, offspring; cf. CALF (leg), CHILD], 1. a young cow or bull. 2. the young of some other large animals, as the elephant, whale, hippopotamus, seal, etc.; hence, 3. a large piece of ice broken off from an iceberg or coast glacier. 4. a small island lying near a larger one. 5. leather from the hide of a calf; calfskin: abbreviated **cf.** (in *bookbinding*). 6. [Colloq.], an awkward, callow, or silly young person.

kill the fatted calf, to make a feast of celebration or welcome.

calf (kaf, käf), *n.* [*pl.* CALVES (kavz, kävz)], [ME.; ON. *kalfi;* IE. base **gelebh;* see CALF (animal)], the fleshy back part of the leg between the knee and the ankle.

calf love, [Colloq.], the immature love that boys and girls may feel for each other; puppy love.

calf·skin (kaf′skin′, käf′skin′), *n.* 1. the skin of a calf. 2. leather made from this.

Cal·ga·ry (kal′gə-ri), *n.* a city in southern Alberta, Canada: pop., 129,000.

Cal·houn, John Cald·well (kôld′wel kal-hōōn′), 1782–1850; American statesman; vice-president of the United States (1825–1832).

Ca·li (kä′li), *n.* a city in southwestern Colombia: pop., 136,000 (1945).

Cal·i·ban (kal′ə-ban′), *n.* [form. of *canibal,* cannibal, with interchanged *n* & *l*; *canibal* occurs in Hakluyt's *Voyages* (1598)], a deformed, savage creature, the slave of Prospero in Shakespeare's *The Tempest*.

cal·i·ber (kal'ə-bẽr), *n.* [Fr. & Sp. *calibre* < *calibo*; prob. < Ar. *qālib*, a mold, last], 1. the size of a bullet or shell as measured by its diameter. 2. the diameter of the bore of a gun. 3. the diameter of a cylindrical body or of its hollowed interior. Abbreviated **cal.** 4. quality; ability. Also spelled **calibre.**

cal·i·brate (kal'ə-brāt'), *v.t.* [CALIBRATED (-id), CALIBRATING], 1. to determine the caliber of. 2. to fix, check, or correct the graduations of (a measuring instrument, as a thermometer).

cal·i·bra·tion (kal'ə-brā'shən), *n.* a calibrating or being calibrated.

cal·i·bra·tor (kal'ə-brā'tẽr), *n.* a person or thing that calibrates.

cal·i·ces (kal'i-sēz'), *n.* plural of **calix.**

‡**ca·li·che** (kä-lē'che), *n.* [Sp. Am. < Sp. *caliche*], 1. impure sodium nitrate, $NaNO_3$, found in Chile. 2. crusted calcium carbonate formed on certain soils in dry regions.

cal·i·cle (kal'i-k'l), *n.* [L. *caliculus*, dim. of *calix*, a cup], in *zoology*, a small, cuplike cavity in coral; calyculus.

cal·i·co (kal'ə-kō'), *n.* [*pl.* CALICOES, CALICOS (-kōz')], [< *Calicut*, India, where it was first obtained], 1. originally, a cotton cloth from India. 2. any of several kinds of cotton cloth: in England, it is unprinted and uncolored, in the United States, coarse and usually printed. *adj.* 1. of calico. 2. like calico; spotted.

cal·i·co·back (kal'ə-kō-bak'), *n.* a calico bug.

calico bass, a small, fresh-water food fish related to the sunfishes, found in the central and eastern United States.

calico bug, a black beetle with red, orange, and yellow markings, destructive to cabbage, radishes, etc.

calico bush (or **flower** or **tree**), the mountain laurel, an evergreen bush of the eastern United States.

Cal·i·cut (kal'ə-kut'), *n.* a city on the western coast of Madras state, southern India: pop., 159,000.

ca·lif (kā'lif, kal'if), *n.* a caliph.

cal·if·ate (kal'ə-fāt', kal'ə-fit), *n.* caliphate.

Cal·i·for·ni·a (kal'ə-fôr'nyə, kal'ə-fôr'ni-ə), *n.* a Western State of the United States, on the Pacific Coast: area, 158,693 sq. mi.; pop., 15,717,000; capital, Sacramento: abbreviated **Calif., Cal.**

California, Gulf of, an arm of the Pacific, between Lower California and the Mexican mainland.

Cal·i·for·ni·an (kal'ə-fôr'nyən, kal'ə-fôr'ni-ən), *adj.* of California. *n.* a native or inhabitant of California.

California orange, an orange, especially a navel orange, grown in California.

California poppy, a variety of poppy with small flowers varying in color from pale cream to deep orange.

cal·i·for·ni·um (kal'ə-fôr'ni-əm), *n.* [< University of *California* + *-ium*], a radioactive chemical element produced by the atomic bombardment of curium: symbol, Cf; at. wt., 244(?); at. no., 98.

ca·lig·i·nous (kə-lij'ə-nəs), *adj.* [L. *caliginosus* < *caligo*, darkness, gloom], dark; obscure.

Ca·lig·u·la (kə-lig'yoo-lə), *n.* (*Gaius Caesar*), Roman emperor (37–41 A.D.); lived 12–41 A.D.

cal·i·pash (kal'ə-pash', kal'ə-pash'), *n.* [W. Ind.; prob. < Sp. *carapacho* < *caparacho*, a shell], a greenish, jellylike, edible substance under the upper shell of a turtle.

cal·i·pee (kal'ə-pē', kal'ə-pē'), *n.* [var. of *calipash*], a yellowish, jellylike, edible substance inside the lower shell of a turtle.

cal·i·per (kal'ə-pẽr), *n.* [var. of *caliber*], 1. *usually pl.* an instrument consisting of a pair of movable curved legs fastened together at one end with a screw or rivet, used to measure the thickness or diameter of something: there are *inside calipers* and *outside calipers*. 2. a caliper rule. *v.t.* & *v.i.* to measure with calipers. Also spelled **calliper.**

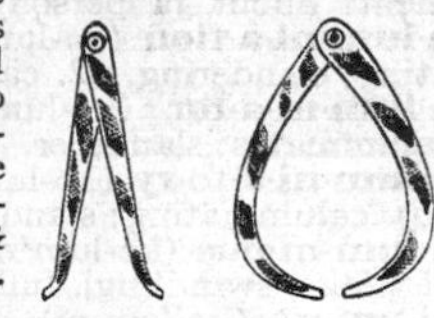

CALIPERS

caliper rule, a graduated rule with one sliding jaw and one that is stationary.

ca·liph (kā'lif, kal'if), *n.* [ME. *caliphe*; OFr. *calife*; Ar. *khalīfa*, caliph, successor < *khalafa*, to succeed], in a Moslem state, supreme ruler; successor: the title taken by Mohammed's successors as secular and religious heads of Islam: also spelled **calif, kalif, kaliph, khalif.**

cal·iph·ate (kal'ə-fāt', kal'ə-fit), *n.* 1. the office, reign, or rank of a caliph. 2. the land ruled by a caliph.

cal·i·say·a bark (kal'ə-sā'ə), [Sp. *calisaya*: said to be from the name of the Peruvian Indian who informed the Spaniards of the uses of the bark], the bark of a kind of cinchona, from which quinine is obtained.

cal·is·then·ic (kal'əs-then'ik), *adj.* relating to calisthenics: also spelled **callisthenic.**

cal·is·then·i·cal (kal'əs-then'i-k'l), *adj.* calisthenic.

cal·is·then·ics (kal'əs-then'iks), *n.pl.* [< Gr. *kallos*, beauty + *sthenos*, strength], 1. athletic exercises; simple gymnastics. 2. [construed as sing.], the art of developing bodily strength and gracefulness by such exercises. Also spelled **callisthenics.**

ca·lix (kā'liks), *n.* [*pl.* CALICES (kal'i-sēz')], [L.], a cup; chalice.

calk (kôk), *v.t.* [ME. *cauken*, to tread; OFr. *cauquer*, to tread, tread in; L. *calcare*, to tread < *calx*, a heel], 1. to make (a boat, etc.) watertight by filling the seams or cracks with oakum, tar, etc. 2. to stop up (cracks of windows, pipes, etc.) with a filler. 3. to make (a joint of overlapping plates) tight by hammering the edge of one plate into the side of the other. Also spelled **caulk.**

calk (kôk), *n.* [ME. *calke*; AS. *calc*, shoe, hoof; L. *calx*, a heel], 1. the part of a horseshoe that projects downward to prevent slipping. 2. a metal plate fastened to the heel or sole of a shoe to give it longer wear or to prevent slipping. *v.t.* 1. to fasten calks on. 2. to cut (a horse's leg) with a calk.

calk·er (kôk'ẽr), *n.* 1. a person who calks boats, ships, etc. 2. a tool used in calking. Also spelled **caulker.**

calk·er (kôk'ẽr), *n.* a calk on a shoe.

call (kôl), *v.t.* [ME. *callen*; Late AS. *ceallian* < ON. *kalla*; akin to OHG. *kallōn*; IE. base **gal-*, to scream, shriek, as in MIr. *gall*, swan], 1. to say in a loud tone; shout; announce. 2. to summon. 3. to convoke judicially or officially, as a court or legislative body (often with *together*). 4. to name; apply a name to. 5. to summon to a specific duty, profession, etc.: as, he was *called* to the army. 6. to address an invocation or appeal to. 7. to awaken (a person). 8. to give a signal to. 9. to telephone. 10. to estimate or consider as being. 11. to utter imitative sounds in order to attract (an animal or bird). 12. to stop; call a halt to (a baseball game, etc.). 13. to demand or order payment of (a loan or a bond issue). 14. in *games*, to tell the aim, etc. of (a shot) before making it. 15. in *poker*, to require a show of cards by equaling the bet of (another player). *v.i.* 1. to speak in a loud tone; shout. 2. to visit for a short while. 3. to telephone. 4. in *poker*, to require a show of cards by equaling the bet of another player. *n.* 1. a calling. 2. a loud utterance. 3. a summons; invitation. 4. a signaling; signal. 5. a demand: as, a *call* for low-priced books. 6. a sound uttered to attract an animal or bird. 7. the distinctive cry or sound of an animal or bird. 8. religious duty or vocation regarded as divinely inspired. 9. need; occasion: as, **no** *call* for laughter. 10. an order or demand for payment. 11. a brief visit, especially a formal or professional visit.

call back, 1. to ask or command to come back. 2. to retract. 3. to telephone again or in return.

call down, 1. to invoke. 2. [Slang], to scold; rebuke.

call for, 1. to demand. 2. to come and get; stop for.

call forth, to bring into action or existence.

call in, 1. to summon for help or consultation. 2. to take out of circulation, as coin or bonds. 3. to ask for payment of.

call into question, to raise a question about.

call off, 1. to order away; divert. 2. to read aloud in order from a list. 3. [Colloq.], to cancel a scheduled event.

call on (or **upon**), 1. to visit briefly. 2. to ask (a person) to speak, do something, etc.

call out, 1. to speak aloud; shout. 2. to summon. 3. to challenge.

call up, 1. to recall. 2. to summon, especially for military duty. 3. to telephone.

on call, 1. available when called for or summoned. 2. payable when demanded.

within call, close enough to be called or spoken to.

SYN.—**call,** in this comparison, is the basic word signifying to request the presence of someone at some place (he *called* the waiter over); **summon,** the more formal term, implies authority or peremptoriness in the request (to *summon* a witness); **convoke** and **convene** refer to the summoning of a group to assemble as for deliberation or legislation, but **convoke** implies greater authority or formality (to *convene* a class, to *convoke* a congress); **invite** suggests a courteous request for someone's presence, especially as a guest or participant, and usually suggests that the decision to come rests with the invited.

cal·la (kal'ə), *n.* [< Gr. *kallaia*, wattles of a cock], 1. a plant of the arum family, with a large, white leaf surrounding a yellow flower spike. 2. its flower. Also **calla lily.**

call·a·ble (kôl'ə-b'l), *adj.* that can be called; specifically, *a*) that must be paid upon demand, as a loan. *b*) that must be presented for payment upon notice, as a bond.

cal·lant (kä'lənt), *n.* [D. *kalant*, fellow, customer; dial. Fr. *caland*, for Fr. *chaland*, customer], [Scot.], a young fellow; boy: also **callan** (kä'lən).

Cal·la·o (kä-yä'ô), *n.* a seaport in Peru, near Lima: pop., 129,000.

call·board (kôl'bôrd', kôl'bōrd'), *n.* in the *theater*, a bulletin board backstage for posting instructions, time of rehearsals, etc.

call·boy (kôl′boi′), *n.* 1. a boy who calls actors when it is time for them to go on the stage. 2. a bellboy.

call·er (kôl′ẽr), *n.* 1. a person or thing that calls. 2. a person who makes a short visit. —*SYN.* see **visitor**.

cal·ler (kal′ẽr, kä′lẽr), *adj.* [MScot.; var. of *calver*, fresh], [Scot.], 1. fresh; not decayed or tainted: said of food. 2. fresh and cool; refreshing: said of the weather, a breeze, etc.

Cal·les, Plu·tar·co E·li·as (plo͞o-tär′kô e-lē′äs kä′yes), 1877–1945; Mexican statesman and militarist; president of Mexico (1924–1928).

call girl, [Slang], a prostitute sent out to a man who telephones for an appointment.

cal·li·graph·ic (kal′ə-graf′ik), *adj.* of calligraphy.

cal·lig·ra·phy (kə-lig′rə-fi), *n.* [Gr. *kalligraphia* < *kalligraphos* < *kallos*, beauty + *graphein*, to write], 1. beautiful handwriting. 2. handwriting.

call·ing (kôl′iŋ), *n.* 1. the action of one that calls. 2. a vocation; occupation; trade; profession.

calling card, a small card with one's name and, sometimes, one's address on it, used in making visits, etc.

Cal·li·o·pe (kə-lī′ə-pē′), *n.* [L. < Gr. *Kalliopē*, the beautiful-voiced < *kallos*, beauty + *ops*, *opos*, voice], 1. in *Greek mythology*, the Muse of eloquence and epic poetry. 2. [c-], (*usually* kal′i-ōp′), a musical instrument with a series of steam whistles, played like an organ.

cal·li·op·sis (kal′i-op′sis), *n.* [Mod. L. < Gr. *kalli-* (< *kallos*, beauty) + *opsis*, appearance], the coreopsis.

cal·li·per (kal′ə-pẽr), *n.* & *v.t.* caliper.

cal·li·pyg·i·an (kal′ə-pij′i-ən), *adj.* [Gr. *kallipygos* < *kallos*, beauty + *pygē*, buttocks], having shapely buttocks.

cal·lis·then·ic (kal′əs-then′ik), *adj.* calisthenic.

cal·lis·then·ics (kal′əs-then′iks), *n.pl.* calisthenics.

Cal·lis·to (kə-lis′tō), *n.* [L.; Gr. *Kallistō*], in *Greek & Roman mythology*, a nymph who, because she was loved by Zeus (Jupiter), was changed into a bear by Hera (Juno): Zeus placed her among the stars as the constellation of the Bear.

call letters, the letters, and sometimes the numbers, that identify a radio sending station, whether on land or on a ship.

call loan, a loan that must be repaid on demand.

call money, money borrowed as a call loan.

call number, a number used in libraries to show the department to which a book belongs and its location on the shelves.

cal·los·i·ty (kə-los′ə-ti, ka-los′ə-ti), *n.* [*callo(u)s* + *-ity*], 1. the quality or state of being callous or hardened. 2. [*pl.* CALLOSITIES (-tiz)], a hardened, thickened place on the skin of an animal or the bark of a tree; callus. 3. the quality of being hardhearted.

cal·lous (kal′əs), *adj.* [L. *callosus* < *callum*, hard skin], 1. having a callus or calluses; thick-skinned. 2. unfeeling; insensitive. *v.t.* & *v.i.* to make or become callous.

cal·low (kal′ō), *adj.* [ME. *calowe;* AS. *calu*, bare, bald; akin to G. *kahl*, bald; IE. base ***gal-**, bald, naked, as in Russ. *golová*, head], 1. unfledged; without feathers. 2. undeveloped; inexperienced; immature.

call rate, the rate of interest on call loans.

call slip, in libraries, a form on which the patron lists the title and call number of a desired book.

call to quarters, in *military usage*, a signal by bugle or drums a short time before taps notifying soldiers to retire to their quarters.

cal·lus (kal′əs), *n.* [*pl.* CALLUSES (-iz)], [L. < *callum* hard skin], 1. a hardened, thickened place on the skin. 2. a hard substance formed around the ends of a broken bone that helps them to knit. 3. a growth that forms over a cut or wounded area on a plant stem; callosity. *v.i.* to develop a callus.

calm (käm), *n.* [ME. & Fr. *calme;* It. *calma;* LL. *cauma*, heat of the sun; Gr. *kauma*, heat < *kaiein*, to burn: prob. < the period of rest, at midday], 1. lack of wind or motion; stillness; tranquillity; serenity. 2. in *meteorology*, a condition in which the air movement is less than one mile per hour. *adj.* undisturbed; unruffled; tranquil; still. *v.t.* & *v.i.* to make or become calm (often with *down*).

SYN.—**calm**, basically applied to the weather, suggests a total absence of agitation or disturbance (a *calm* sea, mind, answer); **tranquil** implies a more intrinsic or permanent peace and quiet than **calm** (they lead a *tranquil* life); **serene** suggests an exalted tranquillity (he died with a *serene* smile on his lips); **placid** implies an undisturbed or unruffled calm and is sometimes used in jocular disparagement to suggest dull equanimity (she's as *placid* as a cow); **peaceful** suggests a lack of turbulence or disorder (a *peaceful* gathering).—*ANT.* stormy, agitated, excited.

cal·ma·tive (kal′mə-tiv, käm′ə-tiv), *adj.* calming; soothing; sedative. *n.* a calmative medicine.

calm·y (kä′mi), *adj.* [Poetic or Archaic], calm.

cal·o·mel (kal′ə-m′l, kal′ə-mel′), *n.* [Fr. < Gr. *kalos*, beautiful + *melas*, black], mercurous chloride, HgCl, a white, tasteless powder, used as a cathartic, for intestinal worms, etc.

ca·lor·ic (kə-lôr′ik, kə-lor′ik), *n.* [Fr. *calorique* < L. *calor*, heat], 1. a substance or principle formerly thought to exist, to which the phenomena of burning and oxidation were attributed. 2. heat. *adj.* of heat.

cal·o·ric·i·ty (kal′ə-ris′ə-ti), *n.* [*caloric* + *-ity*], the ability of living animals to develop body heat and maintain a relatively constant temperature.

cal·o·rie (kal′ə-ri), *n.* [Fr. < L. *calor*, heat], 1. the amount of heat needed to raise the temperature of one gram of water one degree centigrade: called *small calorie:* abbreviated **cal.** 2. [usually C-], the amount of heat needed to raise the temperature of one kilogram of water one degree centigrade: called *large calorie, great calorie:* used as the unit for measuring the energy produced by food when oxidized in the body: abbreviated **Cal.** Also spelled **calory.**

cal·o·rif·ic (kal′ə-rif′ik), *adj.* [Fr. *calorifique;* L. *calorificus* < *calor*, heat + *facere*, to make, produce], producing heat.

cal·o·rim·e·ter (kal′ə-rim′ə-tẽr), *n.* [< L. *calor*, heat + *-meter*], an apparatus for measuring amounts of heat, as in chemical combination, friction, etc.

cal·o·ri·met·ric (kal′ə-ri-met′rik, kə-lôr′i-met′rik), *adj.* of calorimetry.

cal·o·ri·met·ri·cal (kal′ə-ri-met′ri-k′l, kə-lôr′i-met′ri-k′l), *adj.* calorimetric.

cal·o·rim·e·try (kal′ə-rim′ə-tri), *n.* [< L. *calor*, heat + *-metry*], the process of measuring the quantity of heat.

cal·o·rize (kal′ə-rīz′), *v.t.* [CALORIZED (-rīzd′), CALORIZING], [L. *calor*, heat + *-ize*], to coat or alloy (a metal) with aluminum by heating in a closed retort containing an aluminum mixture.

cal·o·ry (kal′ə-ri), *n.* [*pl.* CALORIES (-riz)], a calorie.

ca·lotte (kə-lot′), *n.* [Fr.; It. *calotta;* Gr. *kalyptra*, kind of hood < *kalyptein*, to cover], 1. a small, brimless cap: also spelled **calot.** 2. a skullcap worn by Roman Catholic clergymen. 3. a hoodlike crest on the heads of certain birds.

cal·o·yer (kal′ə-yẽr, kə-loi′ẽr), *n.* [Fr.; It. *caloiero;* Gr. *kalogēros*, monk < *kalos*, beautiful + *gēros*, *gēras*, old age], a monk of the Eastern Orthodox Church.

cal·pac, cal·pack (kal′pak), *n.* [Turk. *qālpāk*], a large cap made of felt or sheepskin, worn in some parts of the Near East: also spelled **kalpak.**

Cal·pur·ni·a (kal-pũr′ni-ə), *n.* [L.], in Shakespeare's *Julius Caesar*, Caesar's wife.

cal·trop, cal·trap (kal′trəp), *n.* [ME. *caltrap*, *calketrappe;* AS. *calcatrippe*, *coltetræppe*, star thistle, caltrop; ONorm. Fr. *cauketrape;* see CALK, *n.* & TRAP], 1. an iron device with four sharp spikes, placed on the ground to hinder advancing enemy cavalry. 2. a similar device with hollow spikes that puncture pneumatic tires passing over them. 3. any of a number of plants with pointed flowers or fruits, as the star thistle, water chestnut, etc.

cal·u·met (kal′yoo-met′, kal′yoo-met′), *n.* [Fr., reed pipe, dim. of OFr. *chalemel;* LL. *calamellus*, dim. of L. *calamus*, a reed], a long-stemmed tobacco pipe, smoked by North American Indians as a token of peace.

CALUMET

ca·lum·ni·ate (kə-lum′ni-āt′), *v.t.* & *v.i.* [CALUMNIATED (-id), CALUMNIATING], [< L. *calumniatus*, pp. of *calumniari*, to slander < *calumnia;* see CALUMNY], to spread false and harmful statements about (a person); slander.

ca·lum·ni·a·tion (kə-lum′ni-ā′shən), *n.* 1. a calumniating; slandering. 2. calumny.

ca·lum·ni·a·tor (kə-lum′ni-ā′tẽr), *n.* a person who calumniates; slanderer.

ca·lum·ni·a·to·ry (kə-lum′ni-ə-tôr′i, kə-lum′ni-ə-tō′ri), *adj.* calumniating; slanderous; defamatory.

ca·lum·ni·ous (kə-lum′ni-əs), *adj.* [L. *calumniosus*, full of tricks, swindling], full of calumnies; slanderous.

cal·um·ny (kal′əm-ni), *n.* [*pl.* CALUMNIES (-niz)], [Fr. *calomnie;* L. *calumnia*, trickery, slander < *calvire*, to deceive], 1. a false and malicious statement meant to hurt someone's reputation. 2. slander.

cal·var·i·a (kal-vâr′i-ə), *n.* [L.; cf. CALVARY], the upper, domed part of the skull.

Cal·va·ry (kal′və-ri), *n.* [LL. *Calvaria;* L. *calvaria*, skull; used to translate Gr. *kranion*, skull (cf. CRANIUM), which was used by the Evangelists to translate Aram. *gūlgūlthā*, Golgotha, lit., skull: so named prob. from the shape of the place], 1. in the *Bible*, the place near Jerusalem where the crucifixion of Jesus took place: Luke 23:33, Matt. 27:33. 2. [c-], [*pl.* CALVARIES (-riz)], a representation of the crucifixion of Jesus.

calve (kav, käv), *v.i.* & *v.t.* [CALVED (kavd, kävd), CALVING], [ME. *calfen*, *caulfen;* AS. *cealfian* < *cealf;* see CALF (animal)], 1. to give birth to (a calf). 2. to release (a mass of ice): said of an iceberg or a glacier.

Cal·vé, Em·ma (em′må′ kål′vā′), (born *Emma de Roquer*), 1862?–1942; French operatic soprano.

Cal·vert, George (kal′vẽrt), first Baron Baltimore, 1580?–1632; English statesman; founder of Maryland.
calves (kavz, kävz), *n.* plural of **calf.**
Cal·vin (kal′vin), [Mod. L. *Calvinus;* Fr. *Cauvin, Chauvin;* prob. < L. *calvus,* bald], a masculine name.
Cal·vin, John, (kal′vin), (born *Jean Chauvin* or *Caulvin*), 1509–1564; French Protestant reformer.
Cal·vin·ism (kal′vin-iz′m), *n.* the religious system of John Calvin and his followers, which emphasizes the doctrines of predestination and salvation solely by God's grace.
Cal·vin·ist (kal′vin-ist), *n.* 1. a follower of John Calvin; believer in Calvinism; hence, 2. a dogmatist. *adj.* of or like Calvin, Calvinism, or Calvinists.
Cal·vin·is·tic (kal′və-nis′tik), *adj.* 1. of Calvinism or Calvinists. 2. like a Calvinist; dogmatic.
Cal·vin·is·ti·cal (kal′və-nis′ti-k'l), *adj.* Calvinistic.
cal·vi·ti·es (kal-vish′i-ēz′), *n.* [L. < *calvus,* bald], baldness.
calx (kalks), *n.* [*pl.* CALXES (-iz), CALCES (kal′sēz)], [L., small stone, lime], the ashy powder left after a metal or mineral has been calcined.
cal·y·ces (kal′ə-sēz′, kā′lə-sēz′), *n.* alternative plural of **calyx.**
ca·lyc·i·nal (kə-lis′ə-n'l), *adj.* calycine.
cal·y·cine (kal′i-sin, kal′i-sīn′), *adj.* of or like a calyx.
cal·y·cle (kal′i-k'l), *n.* [see CALYCULUS], 1. in *botany,* a secondary calyx, usually consisting of small leaves below and around the main calyx. 2. in *zoology,* a calyculus.
ca·lyc·u·lus (kə-lik′yoo-ləs), *n.* [*pl.* CALYCULI (-lī′)], [L., dim. of *calyx,* a bud, pod, calyx], in *anatomy* & *zoology,* a small, cuplike part, as a taste bud.
Cal·y·don (kal′ə-don′), *n.* an ancient Greek city in Aetolia.
Cal·y·do·ni·an (kal′ə-dō′ni-ən, kal′ə-dōn′yən), *adj.* of Calydon.
Calydonian boar, in *Greek mythology,* a boar sent by Artemis to scourge the fields of Calydon: it was finally killed by Meleager.
Ca·lyp·so (kə-lip′sō), *n.* [L. < Gr. *Kalypsō*], 1. in Homer's *Odyssey,* a sea nymph who did not let Odysseus (Ulysses) leave her island for seven years. 2. [c-], any of a number of related orchids found in bogs, bearing on each stem a single white flower with purple or yellow markings. 3. [c-], the flower.
ca·lyp·so (kə-lip′sō), *adj.* [? < *Calypso*], designating or of songs improvised and sung by natives of Trinidad: they are lively ballads, often on political, sexual, or humorous themes, characterized by wrenched syllabic stress, loose rhyme, and journalistic language. *n.* a calypso song or calypso music.
ca·lyp·tra (kə-lip′trə), *n.* [Mod. L.; Gr. *kalyptra,* covering for the head, veil], 1. the remains of the female sex organ, or archegonium, of a moss, forming the caplike covering of the spore case. 2. any similar covering of a fruit or flower.
ca·lyp·tro·gen (kə-lip′trə-jən), *n.* [< Mod. L. *calyptra* (< Gr. *kalyptra*), veil; + *-gen*], in *botany,* the outer layer of cells from which the root cap is developed.
ca·lyx (kā′liks, kal′iks), *n.* [*pl.* CALYXES (-iz), CALYCES (kal′ə-sēz′, kā′lə-sēz′)], [L., outer covering, pod], the outer whorl of leaves, or sepals, at the base of a flower.
cam (kam) *n.* [ME. & AS. *camb,* comb, crest; influenced by D. *cam* in this sense; cf. G. *kammrad,* lit., comb wheel, cogwheel], a moving piece of machinery, such as a wheel, projection on a wheel, etc., which gives an eccentric, alternating, or otherwise irregular motion to a wheel, roller, shaft, etc., or receives such motion from it.

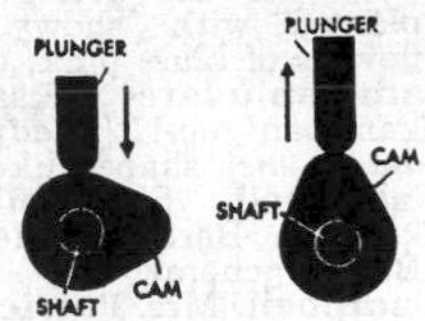

CAM

Cam., Cambridge.
Ca·ma·cho, Ma·nuel Á·vi·la (mä-nwel′ ä′vē-lä′ kä-mä′chô), 1897–1955; Mexican statesman; president of Mexico (1940–1946).
Ca·ma·güey (kä′mä-gwā′), *n.* a city in central Cuba: pop., 128,000.
ca·ma·ra·de·rie (kä′mə-rä′dẽr-i, kä′mə-rä′də-rē′), *n.* [Fr. < *camarade;* see COMRADE], loyalty and good spirit among comrades; comradeship.
cam·a·ril·la (kam′ə-ril′ə; Sp. kä′mä-rēl′yä), *n.* [Sp., dim. of *camara,* chamber < L. *camera, camara,* a vault, arched roof], 1. a small meeting room; private chamber; hence, 2. any of various notorious groups of confidential advisers to former Spanish monarchs. 3. a group of secret or confidential advisers to anyone in authority; cabal; clique.
cam·ass, cam·as (kam′as), *n.* [Chinook *quamash,* bulb], a plant of the lily family, native to the western United States, with sweet, edible bulbs: also **quamash.**
Camb., Cambridge.
cam·ber (kam′bẽr), *n.* [Fr. *cambre* < *cambrer,* to arch, vault < OFr. *chambre,* bent; L. *camur,* bent, crooked], 1. a slight convex curve of a surface, as of a road. 2. a piece of timber arched in the middle. 3. in *aeronautics,* the slight arch in the surface of a wing or other airfoil. *v.t. & v.i.* [Fr. *cambrer*], to arch slightly; curve convexly.
Cam·ber·well (kam′bẽr-wel′), *n.* a borough of London.
cam·bist (kam′bist), *n.* [Fr. *cambiste;* It. *cambista* < *cambiare,* to exchange; LL. *cambiare;* prob. of Celt. origin], 1. a person who deals in bills of exchange. 2. a book that gives the rates of foreign exchange and equivalents of measures, weights, etc.
cam·bi·um (kam′bi-əm), *n.* [LL., change], the layer of tissue between the bark and wood in woody plants, from which new wood and bark develop.
Cam·bo·di·a (kam-bō′di-ə, kam-bō′dyə), *n.* a kingdom in the southern part of the Indochinese peninsula, on the Gulf of Siam: area, 66,606 sq. mi.; pop., 4,845,000; capital, Pnom-Penh.
cam·bo·gi·a (kam-bō′ji-ə), *n.* [< *Cambodia;* see GAMBOGE], gamboge, a yellow gum resin.
Cam·brai (kän′bre′), *n.* a city in northern France: pop., 25,000.
Cam·bri·a (kam′bri-ə), *n.* [ML.; var. of ML. *Cumbria* < base of OCelt. *Combroges,* lit., co-landers, whence Celt. *Cymry,* Britons of the West, Welshmen], [Poetic], Wales.
Cam·bri·an (kam′bri-ən), *adj.* 1. of Cambria; Welsh. 2. designating or of the first geological period in the Paleozoic Era, marked by the appearance of the first simple marine animal and plant life, as shown by fossils found in Wales and Cumberland. *n.* a native or inhabitant of Cambria; Welshman.
the Cambrian, the Cambrian Period or its rocks: see **geology,** chart.
Cambrian Mountains, a mountain range in Wales.
cam·bric (kām′brik), *n.* [< *Kamerik,* Fl. name of *Cambrai,* France < L. *Camaracum,* name of the town], 1. a very fine, thin linen. 2. a cotton cloth like this.
cambric tea, a hot drink of weak tea, milk, and sugar.
Cam·bridge (kām′brij), *n.* 1. a city in Cambridgeshire, England: pop., 93,000: home of Cambridge University. 2. Cambridgeshire. 3. a city in eastern Massachusetts, across the Charles River from Boston: pop., 108,000. Abbreviated **Cam., Camb.** (in senses 1 & 3).
Cam·bridge·shire (kām′brij-shir′), *n.* a county of east central England: pop., 167,000; county seat, Cambridge.
Cam·by·ses II (kam-bī′sēz), ?–522 B.C.; son of Cyrus the Great; last Median king of Persia.
Cam·den (kam′dən), *n.* a city in New Jersey, on the Delaware River, opposite Philadelphia: pop., 117,000.
came (kām), past tense of **come.**
came (kām), *n.* [MD. *kaam*], a grooved lead bar used to fasten together panes of glass, tile, etc.
cam·el (kam′'l), *n.* [ME. < AS. or OFr.; L. *camelus;* Gr. *kamēlos;* Heb. *gāmāl*], 1. a large, domesticated, four-footed animal with a humped back, long neck, and large, cushioned feet: because it can store water in its body, the camel is used in Asian and African deserts; the Arabian camel, or dromedary, has one hump, the Bactrian camel has two humps. 2. a watertight cylinder used to raise sunken ships, wrecks, etc.: see **caisson** (sense 5).
cam·el·eer (kam′'l-êr′), *n.* a person who drives a camel.
cam·el-hair (kam′'l-hâr′), *adj.* camel's-hair
ca·mel·li·a (kə-mēl′yə, kə-mel′i-ə), *n.* [< *Camelli,* It. form of the name of G. J. *Kamel* (d. 1706), Moravian Jesuit missionary to the Far East], 1. any of a number of evergreen trees or shrubs of the tea family, native to Asia, with shiny, dark-green leaves and white or red, rose-shaped flowers. 2. the flower.
ca·mel·o·pard (kə-mel′ə-pärd′, kam′'l-ə-pärd′), *n.* [LL. *camelopardus;* L. *camelopardalus;* Gr. *kamēlopardalis* < *kamēlos,* camel + *pardalis,* pard, leopard: so called from neck (like a camel's) and spots (like a pard's)], 1. a giraffe. 2. [C-], a northern constellation between Ursa Major and Cassiopeia.
Cam·e·lot (kam′ə-lot′), *n.* the legendary English town where King Arthur had his court and Round Table.
cam·el's-hair (kam′'lz-hâr′), *adj.* made of camel's hair or a similar material. Also **camel-hair.**
camel's hair, 1. the hair of the camel. 2. cloth made of this hair, sometimes mixed with wool or other fiber: it is usually light tan and very soft.
camel's-hair brush, an artist's small brush: it is made of hair from a squirrel's tail.
Cam·em·bert cheese (kam′əm-ber′), [< district near *Camembert,* France], a soft, creamy kind of cheese.
Ca·me·nae (kə-mē′nē), *n.pl.* in *Roman mythology,* nymphs having prophetic powers who inhabited springs and fountains: later identified with the Greek Muses.
cam·e·o (kam′i-ō′, kam′yō), *n.* [*pl.* CAMEOS (-ōz′, -yōz)], [It. *cammeo* & OFr. *camaieu* < ML. *camaeus;* cf. Sp. *camafeo,* Port. *camafeio;* ? < L. **camateum,* wrought], 1. a gem having two layers, with a figure carved in one layer so that it is raised on a background of the other.

2. a carving made in this way: opposed to *intaglio.*
cam·er·a (kam′ẽr-ə), *n.* [L. *camera, camara,* a vault; Gr. *kamara,* vaulted chamber], 1. a chamber; specifically, the private office of a judge. 2. a camera obscura. 3. [< *camera obscura*], a device for taking photographs, consisting of a closed box, or something like it, containing a sensitized plate or film on which an image is formed when light enters the box through a lens or hole. 4. in *television,* that part of the transmitter which consists of a lens and a special cathode-ray tube containing a plate on which the image to be televised is projected for transformation into a flow of electrons.

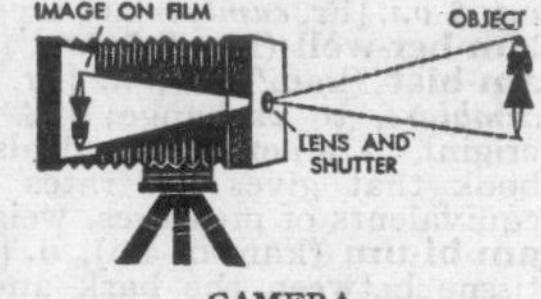

CAMERA

in camera, 1. in a judge's private office. 2. privately.
cam·er·al (kam′ẽr-′l), *adj.* [G. *kameral* < ML. *cameralis;* see CAMERA], 1. of a chamber. 2. of a council that manages public business.
camera lu·ci·da (lo͞o′si-də, lū′si-də), [L., light chamber; see CAMERA & LUCID], an apparatus containing a prism or an arrangement of mirrors for reflecting an object on a surface so that its outline may be traced: often used with a microscope.
cam·er·a·man (kam′ẽr-ə-man′), *n.* [*pl.* CAMERAMEN (-men′)], an operator of a camera, especially of a motion-picture camera.
camera ob·scu·ra (ob-skyoor′ə, ob-skū′rə), [L., dark chamber; see CAMERA & OBSCURE], a camera consisting of a dark chamber with a lens or opening through which an image is projected in natural colors onto an opposite surface: used in drawing, exhibits, etc.
cam·er·len·go (kam′ẽr-leŋ′gō), *n.* a camerlingo.
cam·er·lin·go (kam′ẽr-liŋ′gō), *n.* [It., chamberlain < L. *camera,* chamber; see CAMERA], in the *Roman Catholic Church,* a cardinal who has charge of the papal treasury and accounts; papal chamberlain.
Cam·er·on, Richard (kam′ẽr-ən), ?–1680; a Scottish Covenanter whose followers founded the Reformed Presyterian Church (1743).
Cam·er·o·ni·an (kam′ẽr-ō′ni-ən), *adj.* of Richard Cameron, his beliefs, or his followers. *n.* a follower of Cameron; member of Reformed Presbyterian Church.
Cam·e·roon (kam′ə-ro͞on′), *n.* Cameroun.
Cam·e·roons (kam′ə-ro͞onz′), *n.* a former British trust territory in western Africa: see **Cameroun** and **Nigeria.**
Ca·me·roun (kam-ro͞on′; Fr. kȧ′m′-ro͞on′), *n.* 1. a country in west central Africa, on the Gulf of Guinea: the southern section of Cameroons joined Cameroun by plebescite in 1961: area, 183,576 sq. mi.; pop., 4,096,000; capital, Yaoundé. 2. a mountain in Cameroun: height, 13,349 ft. Also **Cameroon.**
cam gear, a gear not centered on the shaft, used where discontinuous action is required.
Ca·mil·la (kə-mil′ə), a feminine name: see **Camille.**
Ca·mille (kə-mēl′), [Fr. < L. *camilla,* virgin of unblemished character], a feminine name: variant, *Camilla.*
ca·mion (kam′i-ən; Fr. kȧ′myōn′), *n.* [Fr.], 1. a dray. 2. a wagon or truck, especially for transporting heavy artillery.
cam·i·sade (kam′i-sād′), *n.* [Archaic], a camisado.
cam·i·sa·do (kam′i-sā′dō), *n.* [Sp. *camisada* < *camisa;* see CHEMISE], [Archaic], an attack at night, originally one in which shirts were worn over armor for identification.
ca·mise (kə-mēs′), *n.* [Ar. *qamis;* LL. *camisa;* see CHEMISE], a loose-fitting shirt; smock; dressing gown.
cam·i·sole (kam′ə-sōl′), *n.* [Fr. < Sp. *camisola,* dim. of *camisa;* see CHEMISE], 1. formerly, a kind of jacket for men. 2. a woman's loose underwaist or corset cover. 3. a woman's loose jacket worn as a dressing gown. 4. a kind of strait jacket.
cam·let (kam′lit), *n.* [Fr. *camelot;* LL. *camelotum;* ? < Ar. *khamlat* < *khaml,* pile, plush], 1. an Oriental cloth made of camel's hair and silk. 2. a similar fabric of silk and wool. 3. clothing made of either of these fabrics.
Cam·maerts, É·mile (ā′mēl′ käm′ȧrts), 1878– ; Belgian poet in England.
Cam·o·ëns, Luiz Vaz de (kam′ō-enz′), see **Camões.**
Ca·mões, Lu·iz Vaz de (lo͞o-ēsh′ vȧzh də kə-moinsh′), 1524–1580; Portuguese epic poet.
cam·o·mile (kam′ə-mīl′), *n.* [OFr. *camamille;* L. *chamomilla;* Gr. *chamaimēlon,* earth apple; *chamai,* ground + *mēlon,* apple], any of several plants of the aster family, with scented leaves and daisylike flowers: the dried leaves, flowers, and buds of one variety are used in medicine: also spelled **chamomile.**
Ca·mor·ra (kə-mor′ə; It. kä-môr′rä), *n.* [It., assault with violence], 1. an Italian secret society organized by criminal elements in Naples, c. 1820, which became politically powerful and later notorious for terror, blackmail, and violence. 2. [c-], any secret society like this.
Ca·mor·rist (kə-mor′ist), *n.* 1. a member of the Camorra. 2. [c-], a member of a secret society.
cam·ou·flage (kam′ə-fläzh′), *n.* [Fr. < *camoufler,* to disguise: ? < *camouflet,* puff of smoke, smoke bomb; cf. Fr. *moufler,* to muffle, cover up], 1. the process of disguising or changing the appearance of troops, ships, guns, etc. by paint, nets, leaves, etc. to conceal them from the enemy. 2. a disguise of this sort. 3. any device used to conceal; deception. *v.t. & v.i.* [CAMOUFLAGED (-fläzhd′), CAMOUFLAGING], to conceal (a thing or person) by changing the appearance; disguise.
cam·ou·fleur (kam′ə-flūr′; Fr. kȧ′mo͞o′flėr′), *n.* [Fr. < *camoufler;* see CAMOUFLAGE], an expert in camouflage.
camp (kamp), *n.* [Fr.; It. *campo;* L. *campus,* a field], 1. *a)* a place where tents, huts, or other temporary shelters are put up, as for soldiers. *b)* the soldiers in such a place; hence, 2. *a)* a group of people who support or advance a common opinion, cause, etc. *b)* the position taken by such a group. 3. a group of tents, huts, etc. used for temporary lodging. 4. a tent, cabin, or the like, used for outings or vacations. 5. a place in the country for vacationers or children, with facilities for recreation, as swimming, riding, etc., often organized and supervised. 6. military life. 7. the people living in a camp. 8. camping. *v.i.* 1. to set up a camp; encamp. 2. to live in a camp; stay temporarily in a camp. 3. to live as if in a camp, without conveniences or comforts. *v.t.* 1. to put into camp. 2. to provide with accommodations.
break camp, to dismantle a camp; pack up camping equipment and go away.
camp out, to live in or as in a camp, tent, etc., without conveniences or comforts.
in the same camp, in agreement; having the same ideas.
Camp, Walter Chauncey (kamp), 1859–1925; American football authority and coach.
cam·pa·gna (käm-pä′nyə; It. käm-pä′nyä), *n.* [It.; see CAMPAIGN], 1. a level plain. 2. [C-], the plain around Rome.
cam·paign (kam-pān′), *n.* [Fr. *campaigne, campagne,* open country suited to military maneuvers; hence, military expedition; It. *campagna;* LL. *campania,* level country; L. *campus,* a field], 1. a series of military operations with a particular objective. 2. a series of organized, planned actions for a particular purpose, as for electing a candidate. *v.i.* to participate in, or go on, a campaign. —*SYN.* see **battle.**
cam·paign·er (kam-pān′ẽr), *n.* a person who campaigns or has served in many campaigns.
Cam·pa·ni·a (kam-pā′ni-ə; It. käm-pä′nyä), *n.* a department of southwestern Italy: chief city, Naples.
cam·pa·ni·le (kam′pə-nē′li), *n.* [*pl.* CAMPANILES (-liz), CAMPANILI (-lē)], [It. < LL. *campana,* a bell], a bell tower, usually near a church.
cam·pa·nol·o·gy (kam′pə-nol′ə-ji), *n.* [< LL. *campana,* a bell; + *-logy*], 1. the study of bells. 2. the art of bell ringing.
cam·pan·u·la (kam-pan′yoo-lə), *n.* [Mod. L., dim. of LL. *campana,* a bell], any campanulaceous plant, as the Canterbury bell, harebell, etc.
cam·pan·u·la·ceous (kam-pan′yoo-lā′shəs), *adj.* [< *campanula* + *-aceous*], of the bellflower family of plants, with showy, bell-shaped flowers of blue, pink, or white.
cam·pan·u·late (kam-pan′yoo-lit, kam-pan′yoo-lāt′), *adj.* [< *campanula* + *-ate*], shaped like a bell.
Camp·bell, Sir **Colin** (kam′b′l, kam′′l), Baron Clyde, 1792–1863; British general.

CAMPANILE

Campbell, Mrs. **Patrick,** (*Beatrice Stella Tanner Campbell*), 1867–1940; English actress.
Campbell, Thomas, 1777–1844; Scottish poet.
Camp·bell-Ban·ner·man, Sir **Henry** (kam′b′l-ban′ẽr-mən, kam′′l-ban′ẽr-mən), 1836–1908; British statesman; prime minister (1905–1908).
Camp·bell·ite (kam′′l-īt′, kam′b′l-īt′), *n.* a member of the Disciples of Christ, a religious denomination founded by Alexander Campbell (1788–1866) of Virginia: they do not use *Campbellite* of themselves.
camp chair, a lightweight folding chair.
camp·craft (kamp′kraft′, kamp′kräft′), *n.* the art or practice of camping outdoors.
cam·pea·chy wood (kam-pē′chi), [after *Campeche,* Mexico], logwood.
Cam·pe·che (kam-pē′chi; Sp. käm-pe′che), *n.* 1. a state of Mexico, on the Yucatan peninsula: area, 19,670 sq. mi.; pop., 150,000. 2. its capital: pop., 31,000.
Campeche, Gulf of, a part of the Gulf of Mexico, off southern Mexico.
camp·fire (kamp′fīr′), *n.* 1. an outdoor fire at a camp. 2. a gathering around such a fire for social purposes.
campfire girl, a member of the Camp Fire Girls of America.
Camp Fire Girls of America, an organization of girls between the ages of ten and eighteen, founded in

1910 for the purpose of building character and health by co-operation, outdoor activities, etc.

camp follower, 1. a civilian who goes along with an army to sell goods or services. 2. a prostitute with an army. 3. the wife of a serviceman who follows him in his transfers from post to post.

camp·ground (kamp′ground′), *n.* 1. a place where a camp is set up. 2. a place where a camp meeting or religious revival is held.

cam·phene (kam′fēn, kam-fēn′), *n.* [*camph*or + *-ene*], a colorless, crystalline compound, $C_{10}H_{16}$, prepared synthetically from pinene and used like camphor.

cam·phol (kam′fōl, kam′fol), *n.* [*camph*or + *-ol*], a compound like camphor; borneol.

cam·phor (kam′fẽr), *n.* [ME. *camfere;* Fr. *camphre;* LL. *canfora, camphora;* Ar. *kāfūr;* Malay *kāpūr*, chalk], 1. a volatile, crystalline substance, $C_{10}H_{16}O$, with a strong characteristic odor, derived chiefly from the wood of the camphor tree: used to protect fabrics from moths, in manufacturing celluloid, and in medicine as an irritant and stimulant. 2. any of several derivatives of terpenes.

cam·phor·ate (kam′fẽr-āt′), *v.t.* [CAMPHORATED (-id), CAMPHORATING], to put camphor in or on.

camphorated oil, a solution of camphor in cottonseed oil, used as a liniment.

camphor ball, a small ball of camphor or naphthalene for protecting fabrics from moths; moth ball.

cam·phor·ic (kam-fôr′ik, kam-for′ik), *adj.* of or containing camphor.

camphor ice, an ointment made of white wax, camphor, spermaceti, and castor oil.

camphor tree, a large laurel tree, native to the Far East and Oceania, which yields camphor.

Cam·pi·nas (kəm-pē′nəs; Sp. käm-pē′näs), *n.* a city in southeastern Brazil: pop., 102,000.

cam·pi·on (kam′pi-ən), *n.* [prob. < Anglo-Fr. **cam-pagnon*, Norm. *compagnon* < *campagne;* see CAMPAIGN, CHAMPAIGN], any of various plants of the pink family, with red or white flowers.

Cam·pi·on, Thomas (kam′pi-ən), 1567–1620; English poet and composer of songs.

camp meeting, a religious gathering held outdoors or in a tent, etc., usually lasting several days.

cam·po (kam′pō, käm′pō), *n.* [Port.; Sp.; L. *campus*, field, plain; cf. CAMPUS], 1. [*pl.* CAMPOS (-pōz)], a level, grassy plain in South America, often with scattered plants and small trees. 2. [*pl.* CAMPI (-pi)], a small square, or open place, in a town.

Cam·po·bel·lo (kam′pō-bel′ō), *n.* an island in the Bay of Fundy: a part of New Brunswick.

camp·o·ree (kam′pə-rē′), *n.* [*camp* + jamb*oree*], a gathering or assembly of boy scouts on the regional or district level: distinguished from *jamboree*.

camp·stool (kamp′stōōl′), *n.* a light folding stool.

cam·pus (kam′pəs), *n.* [*pl.* CAMPUSES (-iz)], [L., a field], 1. an open place or field used by the ancient Romans for military exercises, public assemblies, etc. 2. the grounds of a school or college. *adj.* 1. on or of the campus. 2. of the student body: as, *campus* activities.

cam·shaft (kam′shaft′), *n.* a shaft of which a cam is an essential part, or to which a cam is fastened.

Ca·mus, Al·bert (äl′bâr′kä′mü′), 1913–1960; French writer, born in Algeria: won Nobel prize in literature, 1957.

can (kan; *as an auxiliary, usually* kən, k′n), *v.i.* [past tense COULD (kood)], [ME.; AS. *can, cann*, 1st and 3d pers. sing., pres. indic., of *cunnan*, to know, have power to, be able; common Gmc. < IE. base **genē-*, **genō-*, seen also in Eng. *know*, L. *gnosco*, etc.; orig. meaning "to be able mentally or spiritually," as distinguished from *may*, "to be able physically"], 1. to know how to. 2. to be able to. 3. to have the right to. 4. [Colloq.], to be permitted to; may. *Can* is used both as an auxiliary verb and as a substitution verb, and is followed by an infinitive without *to*.

can but, can only.

SYN.—**can,** in formal usage, denotes ability, either physical or mental (he *can* walk, I *can* understand you); **may** denotes possibility (I *may* go tomorrow) or, in formal usage, permission (you *may* have another cooky); in informal and colloquial usage, **can** is most frequently used to express permission, especially in interrogative and negative statements (*can't* I go?, you *cannot!*).

can (kan), *n.* [ME. & AS. *canne*, a cup, container; IE. base **gan(dh)*, container], 1. a container, usually made of metal, for liquids. 2. a container made of tinned iron or other metal, in which liquids, foods, etc. are sealed for preservation. 3. the contents of a can; canful. 4. [Slang], *a)* prison. *b)* buttocks. *c)* toilet. *v.t.* [CANNED (kand), CANNING], 1. to put into a can; put up in airtight cans or jars for preservation. 2. [Slang], to make a phonograph record of. 3. [Slang], to dismiss; discharge. 4. [Slang], to dispense with.

Can., 1. Canada. 2. Canadian.

can., 1. canon. 2. canto.

Ca·naan (kā′nən), *n.* [via L. & Gr. < Heb. *kena′n*], the Promised Land of the Israelites, a region roughly corresponding to modern Palestine.

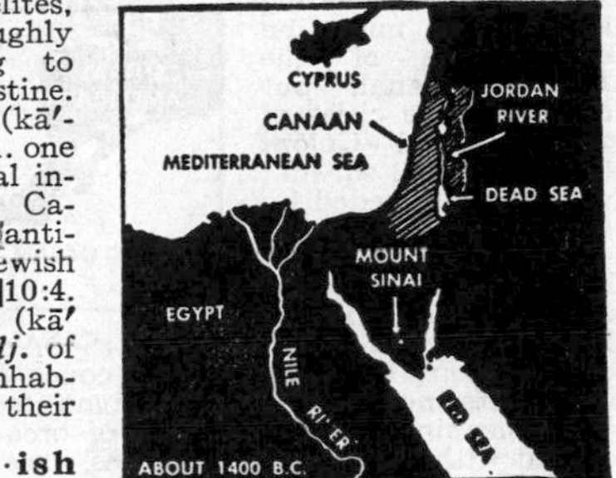

CANAAN

Ca·naan·ite (kā′nən-īt′), *n.* 1. one of the original inhabitants of Canaan. 2. an anti-Roman Jewish zealot: Matt. 10:4.

Ca·naan·it·ic (kā′nən-it′ik), *adj.* of Canaan, its inhabitants, or their language.

Ca·naan·it·ish (kā′nən-īt′ish), *adj.* 1. Canaanitic. 2. like or characteristic of a Canaanite or Canaanites.

Canad., Canadian.

Can·a·da (kan′ə-də), *n.* a country in northern North America: a member of the British Commonwealth of Nations: area, 3,852,000 sq. mi.; pop., 16,081,000; capital, Ottawa: abbreviated **Can.** *adj.* 1. of or from Canada. 2. of, from, or connected with the northern parts of North America.

Canada balsam, a thick, yellow, resinous fluid from the balsam fir tree, used as a transparent cement in microscopy.

Canada goose, the largest variety of wild goose of Canada and the northern United States: it is brownish-gray, with black head and neck and a white patch on each side of the face.

Canada jay, a North American jay with gray and black feathers and no crest.

Canada lily, a wild lily with small, funnel-shaped, orange-yellow or reddish flowers.

Canada lynx, a North American lynx, related to but larger than the bobcat.

Canada thistle, a prickly weed with purplish flowers, wavy leaves, and creeping roots.

Ca·na·di·an (kə-nā′di-ən), *adj.* of Canada, its people, or culture. *n.* a native or inhabitant of Canada. Abbreviated **Canad., Can.**

Canadian bacon, cured, smoked pork taken from the loin in a boneless strip and having a hamlike flavor.

Canadian French, French as spoken by French Canadians, mainly in Quebec and the Maritime Provinces.

Canadian River, a river in Oklahoma, flowing eastward into the Arkansas River: length, 906 mi.

Canadian Shield, an area of about 2,000,000 square miles of pre-Cambrian rock formation, largely granite, gneiss, marble, and other igneous and metamorphic rock, found in Canada near the Great Lakes: it has large deposits of copper, gold, and iron ore.

ca·naille (kə-nāl′; Fr. kȧ′nä′y′), *n.* [Fr., a mob, pack of dogs; It. *canaglia* < L. *canis*, a dog], the mob; rabble.

ca·nal (kə-nal′), *n.* [Fr.; L. *canalis*, a channel < *canna*, a pipe, reed], 1. an artificial waterway for transportation or irrigation. 2. a river artificially improved by locks, levees, etc. to permit navigation. 3. any of the long, narrow markings on the planet Mars. 4. in *anatomy & zoology*, a tube or duct. *v.t.* [CANALLED or CANALED (-nald′), CANALLING or CANALING], to build a canal through or across.

ca·nal·boat (kə-nal′bōt′), *n.* a freight-carrying boat, usually long and narrow, used on canals: also **canal boat.**

can·a·lic·u·lar (kan′ə-lik′yoo-lẽr), *adj.* [Mod. L. *canalicularis* < L. *canaliculus*], of, having, or like a canaliculus.

can·a·lic·u·late (kan′ə-lik′yoo-lit, kan′ə-lik′yoo-lāt′), *adj.* [Mod. L. *canaliculatus;* see CANALICULUS], in *botany & zoology*, having a groove or grooves.

can·a·lic·u·lat·ed (kan′ə-lik′yoo-lā′tid), *adj.* canaliculate.

can·a·lic·u·lus (kan′ə-lik′yoo-ləs), *n.* [*pl.* CANALICULI (-lī′)], [L., dim. of *canalis*, a channel, pipe], in *anatomy, botany & zoology*, a very small groove, as in bone.

ca·nal·i·za·tion (kə-nal′ə-zā′shən, kan′'l-i-zā′shən), *n.* 1. a canalizing. 2. a system or network of canals or channels. 3. the formation of canals in the body tissues, effected naturally or artificially, as sometimes to drain wounds. 4. direction (*of* thought, etc.) into a specific channel or channels.

ca·nal·ize (kə-nal′īz, kan′'l-īz′), *v.t.* [CANALIZED (-īzd, -īzd′), CANALIZING], 1. to make a canal through. 2. to change into or make like a canal. 3. to direct into a specific channel or channels. 4. to give an outlet to.

canal rays, in *physics*, rays consisting of positive ions passing through openings in the cathode of a vacuum tube.

Canal Zone, a military reservation of the United States, consisting of a strip of land extending about five miles on either side of the Panama Canal, but excluding the cities of Panama and Colón: land area, 362 sq. mi.; pop., 42,000: ceded by Panama (1904) as a perpetual lease: abbreviated **C.Z.**

CANAL ZONE

ca·na·pé (kan'ə-pi; Fr. kȧ'nȧ'pā'), *n.* [Fr., orig., canopy of netting over a couch or bed to keep off insects; now, the couch or divan itself, whence the Eng. meaning], a toasted slice of bread or a cracker spread with spiced meat, sardines, cheese, etc., served as an appetizer, often with drinks.

Ca·na·ra (kän'ə-rə; Eng. kə-nä'rə), *n.* Kanara, India.

ca·nard (kə-närd'; Fr. kȧ'när'), *n.* [Fr., a duck, hence a hoax; ? transl. of G. *ente* in this sense], 1. an absurd or exaggerated report spread as a hoax; false statement or rumor. 2. an obsolete kind of airplane.

Can·a·rese (kän'ə-rēz'), *adj.* & *n.* Kanarese.

ca·nar·y (kə-nâr'i), *n.* [*pl.* CANARIES (-iz)], [Fr. *canarie;* Sp. *canario* < L. *Canaria* (*insula*), Canary (island) < L. *canis*, a dog: so called from its large dogs], 1. a lively old Spanish dance. 2. a canary bird. 3. a sweet wine like madeira, originally made in the Canary Islands. 4. canary yellow. *adj.* of the color canary yellow.

canary bird, a small, yellow songbird of the finch family, native to the Canary Islands, Madeira, and the Azores.

canary grass, a grass native to the Canary Islands whose seed (*canary seed*) is used as a bird food.

Canary Islands, a group of islands off northwestern Africa, forming two provinces of Spain: area, 2,807 sq. mi.; pop., 944,000.

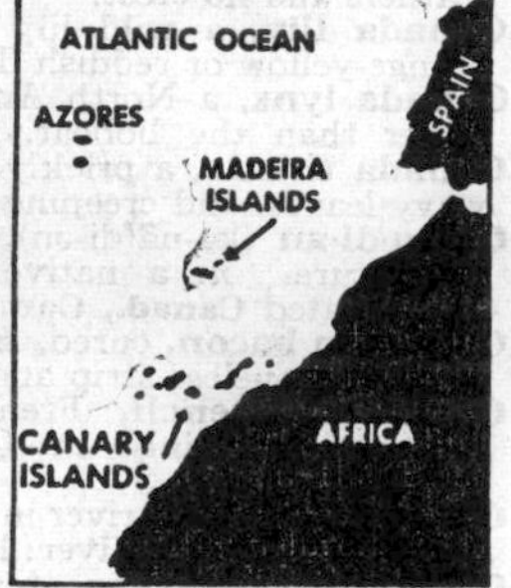

CANARY ISLANDS

canary seed, grass seed used as food for birds.

canary yellow, a light yellow.

ca·nas·ta (kə-nas'tə), *n.* [Sp., basket], a card game using a double deck of cards.

Ca·na·ver·al, Cape (kə-nav'ẽr-əl), a cape on the eastern coast of Florida: U.S. proving ground and launching site for guided missiles, rockets, and spacecraft.

Can·ber·ra (kan'bẽr-ə), *n.* the capital of Australia, in the Australian Capital Territory, on the Murrumbidgee River: pop., 53,000.

Can·by, Henry Sei·del (sī'd'l kan'bi), 1878–1961; American writer, teacher, and editor.

can·can (kan'kan'; Fr. kän'kän'), *n.* [Fr., tittle-tattle, scandal, hence scandalous dance; prob. < L. *quam-quam*, though, conj. introducing qualifications, etc.], a gay, wild dance, with much high kicking.

can·cel (kan's'l), *v.t.* [CANCELED or CANCELLED (-s'ld), CANCELING or CANCELLING], [Fr. *canceller;* L. *cancellare*, to make resemble a lattice, strike out wr ting by drawing lines across < *cancelli*, lattice, grating, pl. of *cancellus*, dim. of *cancer*, crossed bars, lattice], 1. to cross out; strike out with lines or marks. 2. to annul; make invalid. 3. to do away with; abolish. 4. to neutralize; balance (often with *out*). 5. in *mathematics*, to strike out (common factors) by drawing a line through them. 6. in *printing*, to delete or omit. *v.i.* to balance (with *out*). *n.* 1. the deletion or omission of matter in type or in print. 2. *a*) the matter deleted or omitted. *b*) the replacement for this. Abbreviated **canc.**

can·cel·er, can·cel·ler (kan's'l-ẽr), *n.* a person or thing that cancels.

can·cel·late (kan'sə-lāt'), *adj.* in *anatomy*, cancellous.

can·cel·la·tion (kan's'l-ā'shən), *n.* 1. a canceling or being canceled. 2. something canceled. 3. the mark showing that something is canceled. Abbreviated **canc.**

can·cel·lous (kan'sə-ləs), *adj.* [< L. *cancelli;* see CANCEL], in *anatomy*, having a latticelike structure: said of the spongy part of bones.

can·cer (kan'sẽr), *n.* [L., a crab; later, malignant tumor; dissimilation from *carcro; IE. base *qa-, hard, as in Sans. *karkata*, a crab; see CANKER], 1. a malignant new growth anywhere in the body of a person or animal; malignant tumor: cancers tend to spread and ulcerate. 2. anything bad or harmful that spreads and destroys. 3. [C-], a northern constellation between Gemini and Leo, supposedly resembling a crab in shape. 4. [C-], the fourth sign of the zodiac (♋), entered by the sun at the summer solstice, about June 22: see **zodiac,** illus.

can·cer·ous (kan'sẽr-əs), *adj.* of, like, or having cancer.

can·croid (kaŋ'kroid), *adj.* [< L. *cancer, cancri* (see CANCER); + *-oid*], 1. like a crab. 2. like cancer.

can·de·la·brum (kan'd'l-ä'brəm, kan'd'l-ab'rəm), *n.* [*pl.* CANDELABRA (-brə), CANDELABRUMS (-brəmz)], [L. < *candela*, a candle, torch], a large, branched candlestick: also **candelabra** [*pl.* CANDELABRAS].

can·dent (kan'd'nt), *adj.* [L. *candens*, ppr. of *candere*, to shine, glisten], glowing with heat; white-hot.

can·des·cence (kan-des''ns), *n.* incandescence.

can·des·cent (kan-des''nt), *adj.* [L. *candescens*, ppr. of *candescere*, inceptive form of *candere*, to shine], glowing; incandescent.

Can·di·a (kan'di-ə), *n.* 1. Crete. 2. a city in Crete: pop., 64,000: also called *Herakleion.*

can·did (kan'did), *adj.* [L. *candidus*, white, pure, sincere < *candere*, to glow, shine], 1. not prejudiced; unbiased; impartial. 2. honest; outspoken. —*SYN.* see **frank.**

can·di·da·cy (kan'də-də-si), *n.* [*pl.* CANDIDACIES (-siz)], the fact, state, or term of being a candidate.

can·di·date (kan'də-dāt', kan'də-dit), *n.* [L. *candidatus*, white-robed < *candidus*, white: those who sought office in Rome wore white gowns], 1. a person who seeks, or has been proposed for, an office, an award, etc. 2. a person apparently destined to come to a certain end.

can·di·da·ture (kan'də-dā'chẽr, kan'də-də-chẽr), *n.* candidacy.

candid camera, any small camera with a fast lens, used to take informal pictures of unposed subjects.

can·died (kan'did), *adj.* [pp. of *candy*], 1. cooked in or with sugar. 2. wholly or partly crystallized into sugar. 3. sugary; sweetened; made pleasant.

Can·di·ot (kan'di-ot'), *adj.* of Candia; Cretan. *n.* a Cretan.

Can·di·ote (kan'di-ōt'), *adj.* & *n.* Candiot.

can·dle (kan'd'l), *n.* [ME. *candel, candele;* AS. *candel;* L. *candela*, a light, torch < *candere*, to shine, be bright], 1. a cylindrical mass of tallow or wax with a wick through its center, which gives light when burned. 2. anything like a candle in form or use. 3. a unit of luminous intensity, based on a standard candle: abbreviated **C., c.**: see also **international candle.** *v.t.* [CANDLED (-d'ld), CANDLING], to examine (eggs) by holding in front of a light, originally that of a candle: light shining through the egg shows how fresh it is, whether it has been fertilized, etc.

(a game) not worth the candle, 1. with stakes not sufficient to pay for the lights; hence, 2. (a thing) not worth doing.

burn the candle at both ends, to work or play too much so that one's energy is quickly dissipated.

not hold a candle to, not be nearly so good as.

can·dle·ber·ry (kan'd'l-ber'i), *n.* [*pl.* CANDLEBERRIES (-iz)], 1. the fruit of the candlenut or of the wax myrtle tree. 2. either of these trees.

can·dle·fish (kan'd'l-fish'), *n.* [*pl.* CANDLEFISH, CANDLEFISHES (-iz); see FISH], a small, oily, edible fish related to the smelt, found in the North Pacific.

can·dle-foot (kan'd'l-foot'), *n.* a foot-candle.

can·dle·hold·er (kan'd'l-hōl'dẽr), *n.* a candlestick.

can·dle·light (kan'd'l-līt'), *n.* 1. the light given by a candle or candles. 2. the time for lighting candles; twilight; evening.

Can·dle·mas (kan'd'l-məs), *n.* [ME. *candelmasse;* AS. *candelmæsse; candel*, a candle + *mæsse*, a mass], a church feast, February 2, commemorating the purification of the Virgin Mary: candles for sacred uses are blessed on this day: also **Candlemas Day.**

can·dle·nut (kan'd'l-nut'), *n.* 1. the fruit of a tree growing in the Pacific Islands: the natives burn the fruit as candles. 2. the tree. Also called **candleberry.**

can·dle·pin (kan'd'l-pin'), *n.* a pin shaped like a candle, used in a game of tenpins called *candlepins.*

candle power, 1. the luminous intensity or illuminating capacity of a standard candle. 2. luminous intensity or illuminating capacity, as of a lamp, measured in candles. Abbreviated **c.p.**

can·dler (kan'dlẽr), *n.* a person who candles eggs.

can·dle·stick (kan'd'l-stik'), *n.* a cupped or spiked holder for a candle or candles.

can·dle·wick (kan'd'l-wik'), *n.* the wick of a candle.

candlewick bedspread, a bedspread, usually of cotton, with a pattern of tufts of thick cotton yarn somewhat resembling frayed candlewicks.

can·dle·wood (kan'd'l-wood'), *n.* [so called prob. because of the bright flame that the wood produces], 1. any of a number of related spiny desert plants with slender stems and clusters of brightly colored flowers. 2. the wood of these plants. 3. any resinous wood cut for kindling or used for torches, etc.

can·dor (kan'dẽr), *n.* [L., whiteness, radiance, openness < *candere*, to be white, shine], 1. the quality of being open-minded or fair; impartiality. 2. honesty in expressing oneself; sincerity; frankness. 3. [Obs.], purity. 4. [Obs.], kindliness.

can·dour (kan'dẽr), *n.* candor: British spelling.

can·dy (kan'di), *n.* [*pl.* CANDIES (-diz)], [< *sugar candy;* Fr. *sucre candi;* It. *zucchero candi;* Ar. *qandi;* Per. *qand*, cane sugar; prob. < Sans. *khanda*, piece (of sugar)], 1. crystallized sugar made by boiling and evaporating cane sugar, sirup, etc. 2. a solid confection of sugar or sirup, flavored, colored, and often enriched with nuts or fruits. *v.t.* [CANDIED (-did), CANDYING], [Fr. *candir;* It. *candire* < *candi;* see the *n.*], 1. to preserve by cooking with sugar. 2. to crystallize into sugar. 3. to cover with or as with crystallized sugar. 4. to sweeten; make pleasant. *v.i.* to become candied (in senses 2 & 3).

candy pull, a party, or social gathering, especially of young people, at which the guests entertain themselves by making taffy or similar candy.

can·dy·tuft (kan'di-tuft'), *n.* [< *Candia,* ancient name of Crete], any of several plants of the mustard family, with clusters of white, pink, or purplish flowers.

cane (kān), *n.* [ME. & OFr. *cane, canne;* It. *canna;* L. *canna,* a reed, cane; Gr. *kanna;* cf. Assyr. *qanu,* Heb. *qaneh,* tube, reed], 1. the slender, hollow, jointed, usually flexible stem of any of certain plants, as bamboo, rattan, etc. 2. any plant with such a stem. 3. the stem of a small fruit plant, as the blackberry, raspberry, etc. 4. a stem used as a walking stick or for beating. 5. any walking stick. 6. a stick used for beating. 7. sugar cane. 8. split rattan, used in making chair seats, wickerwork, etc. *v.t.* [CANED (kānd), CANING], 1. to beat with a cane. 2. to make or furnish (chairs, etc.) with cane.

Ca·ne·a (kä-nē'ä; Gr. hän-yä'), *n.* a seaport in northwestern Crete: pop., 27,000: Greek name, *Khania.*

cane·brake (kān'brāk'), *n.* [*cane* + *brake* (thicket)], a dense growth of cane plants.

ca·nel·la (kə-nel'ə), *n.* [ML., dim. of L. *canna;* see CANE], the fragrant inner bark of certain tropical American trees, used as a spice and a tonic.

can·e·phor (kan'ə-fôr'), *n.* a canephoros.

ca·neph·o·ros (kə-nef'ə-ros'), *n.* [*pl.* CANEPHOROI (-roi')], [via L. < Gr. *kanēphoros* < *kaneon,* a rush basket + *pherein,* to bear], 1. in ancient Greece, a basket bearer; specifically, any of the girls who carried on their heads baskets holding the sacred things used at feasts. 2. in *architecture,* a representation of this, sometimes used as a caryatid.

ca·nes·cent (kə-nes''nt), *adj.* [L. *canescens,* ppr. of *canescere,* to become white < *canere,* to be white < *canus,* white, hoary], becoming white; whitening.

cane sugar, the sugar from sugar cane; sucrose.

can·field (kan'fēld'), *n.* [after Richard A. *Canfield,* Am. who invented the game], in *card games,* a form of solitaire used for gambling.

Canfield, Dorothy, see **Fisher, Dorothy Canfield.**

cangue (kaŋ), *n.* [Fr.; Port. *canga,* a yoke < Annamite *gong*], a large board frame used to confine the neck and hands: an old Chinese punishment for petty crime.

Ca·nic·u·la (kə-nik'yoo-lə), *n.* [L., dim. of *canis,* a dog], Sirius, the Dog Star.

ca·nic·u·lar (kə-nik'yoo-lēr), *adj.* [L. *canicularis* < *canicula,* dim. of *canis,* a dog], 1. of Sirius, the Dog Star. 2. of Procyon, a star in the constellation of Canis Minor. 3. measured by the rising of either of these stars. 4. of the dog days in July and August.

ca·nine (kā'nin), *adj.* [L. *caninus* < *canis,* a dog], 1. of or like a dog. 2. of the family of animals that includes dogs, wolves, jackals, and foxes. 3. of a canine tooth. *n.* 1. a dog. 2. a canine tooth.

canine tooth, one of the four sharp-pointed teeth between the incisors and bicuspids: also called *cuspid* or, in the upper jaw, *eyetooth:* see **tooth,** illus.

Ca·nis Ma·jor (kā'nis mā'jēr), [L., the Greater Dog], a southern constellation southeast of Orion, containing the Dog Star, Sirius: see **constellation,** chart.

Canis Mi·nor (mī'nēr), [L., the Lesser Dog], a northern constellation east of Orion, near Gemini, containing the bright star Procyon: see **constellation,** chart.

can·is·ter (kan'is-tēr), *n.* [L. *canistrum,* wicker basket; Gr. *kanistron* < *kanna,* a reed], 1. a box or can for coffee, tea, tobacco, etc. 2. canister shot. 3. the part of a gas mask that contains the chemicals for filtering the air to be breathed.

canister shot, an old-fashioned kind of ammunition for a cannon, consisting of lead or iron shot packed in a container that scattered its contents from the gun muzzle when fired: also called *case shot.*

can·ker (kaŋ'kēr), *n.* [ME. *cancre, canker, cankir* < AS. *cancer* & OFr. *cancre, chancre;* L. *cancer;* see CANCER], 1. an ulcerlike sore that spreads, usually in the mouth. 2. a cankerworm. 3. a disease of plants that causes decay of bark and wood. 4. anything causing decay or rot. *v.t.* 1. to attack, infect, or consume with canker. 2. to cause to decay or rot. *v.i.* to be attacked by canker; become infected with canker.

can·ker·ous (kaŋ'kēr-əs), *adj.* 1. of, having, or like a canker or cankers. 2. causing canker. 3. corrupting.

can·ker·worm (kaŋ'kēr-wũrm'), *n.* any of several larvae or measuring worms that feed on the leaves of fruit and shade trees.

can·na (kan'ə), *n.* [L., a reed, cane], 1. any of a number of related tropical plants of the banana family, with thick roots, large leaves, and brilliant flowers. 2. the flower of any of these plants.

can·na·bin (kan'ə-bin), *n.* a poisonous, white crystalline resin extracted from cannabis and believed to be its active narcotic principle.

can·na·bis (kan'ə-bis), *n.* [L., hemp < same IE. base as AS. *hænep,* whence Eng. *hemp*], 1. an Asiatic plant yielding hemp and hashish. 2. hashish.

Can·nae (kan'ē), *n.* 1. an ancient city in southeastern Italy: in a famous battle fought near Cannae in 216 B.C. Hannibal defeated the Romans by tactics of encirclement and annihilation now classical in military science. 2. any such tactical battle.

canned (kand), *adj.* [pp. of *can* (to put in cans)], 1. preserved in cans or jars. 2. [Slang], discharged from a position. 3. [Slang], put on a phonograph record: said of music, speeches, etc.

can·nel coal (kan''l), [< *candle coal*], a variety of bituminous coal that burns with a bright flame and has a high volatile content: often shortened to **cannel.**

can·ner (kan'ēr), *n.* a person whose work or business is canning foods.

can·ner·y (kan'ēr-i), *n.* [*pl.* CANNERIES (-iz)], a factory where foods are canned.

Cannes (kanz, kan; Fr. kàn), *n.* a resort on the Riviera, southeastern France: pop., 46,000 (1946).

can·ni·bal (kan'ə-b'l), *n.* [Sp. *canibal,* a savage, cannibal; altered < *Caribal,* native of the Caribbean, Carib (term used by Columbus), as if from L. *canis,* a dog], 1. a person who eats human flesh. 2. an animal that eats other animals of its own kind. *adj.* of or resembling cannibals; having the habits of cannibals.

can·ni·bal·ism (kan'ə-b'l-iz'm), *n.* the act or habit of eating others of one's own kind.

can·ni·bal·is·tic (kan'ə-b'l-is'tik), *adj.* of, like, or characteristic of cannibals or cannibalism.

can·ni·bal·is·ti·cal·ly (kan'ə-b'l-is'ti-k'l-i, kan'ə-b'l-is'tik-li), *adv.* in a cannibalistic manner.

can·ni·bal·ize (kan'ə-b'l-īz'), *v.t.* & *v.i.* [CANNIBALIZED (-īzd'), CANNIBALIZING], to salvage the useful parts of (destroyed or worn-out military equipment).

can·ni·kin (kan'ə-kin), *n.* [< *can* + *-kin*], 1. a small can; cup. 2. a wooden bucket or pail.

can·ni·ly (kan''l-i), *adv.* in a canny manner.

can·ni·ness (kan'i-nis), *n.* the quality of being canny.

can·ning (kan'iŋ), *n.* the act or process of putting foods in cans or jars for preservation.

Can·ning, George (kan'iŋ), 1770–1827; British statesman; prime minister (1827).

can·non (kan'ən), *n.* [*pl.* CANNONS (-ənz), CANNON; see PLURAL, II, D, 4], [Fr. *canon;* It. *cannone;* L. *canna;* see CANE; in *n.* 7 & *v.* 2, altered < *carom*], 1. a large, mounted piece of artillery too heavy to be carried by a soldier. 2. any large gun with a relatively short barrel, as a howitzer. 3. a miniature gun like a cannon. 4. a cannon bit. 5. a part on a bell by which it is hung. 6. the cannon bone. 7. [British], in *billiards,* a carom. 8. in *mechanics,* a hollow tube within which a shaft revolves independently of the outer tube. *v.t.* 1. to attack with cannon. 2. [British], to cause to carom. *v.i.* 1. to fire cannon. 2. [British], to make a carom.

Can·non, Joseph Gur·ney (gũr'ni kan'ən), 1836–1926; American politician; member of House of Representatives (1873–1891; 1893–1913; 1915–1923).

can·non·ade (kan'ən-ād'), *n.* [Fr. *canonnade* < *canon,* a cannon], 1. a continuous firing of artillery. 2. an attack with artillery. *v.t.* [CANNONADED (-id), CANNONADING], to attack or fire at with artillery. *v.i.* to fire artillery.

cannon ball, a heavy ball of iron or other metal, formerly used as a projectile in cannon.

cannon bit a smooth, round bit for a horse: also **canon bit.**

cannon bone, the bone between hock or knee and fetlock in four-legged, hoofed animals.

cannon cracker, a large firecracker that explodes with a loud noise.

can·non·eer (kan'ən-êr'), *n.* [Fr. *canonnier* < *canon,* a cannon], an artilleryman; gunner.

cannon fodder, soldiers, sailors, etc. thought of as being expended, i.e., killed or maimed, in war.

can·non·ry (kan'ən-ri), *n.* [*pl.* CANNONRIES (-riz)], 1. cannon collectively; artillery. 2. cannon fire.

cannon shot, 1. a shot from a cannon. 2. projectiles for firing from a cannon. 3. the range of fire of a cannon.

can·not (kan'ot, ka-not', kan'ət), can not.

cannot but, must; have no choice but to.

can·nu·la (kan'yoo-lə), *n.* [*pl.* CANNULAE (-lē')], [L. dim. of *canna;* see CANE], a tube for insertion into body cavities, usually for drainage.

can·nu·lar (kan'yoo-lēr), *adj.* tubular.

can·nu·late (kan'yoo-lit, kan'yoo-lāt'), *adj.* cannular.

can·ny (kan'i), *adj.* [CANNIER (-i-ēr), CANNIEST (-i-ist)], [< *can* (to know, be able)], [Scot.], 1. careful; cautious; wary. 2. thrifty. 3. shrewd. 4. careful in action; gentle. *adv.* [Scot.], in a canny manner.

ca' canny (kä, kô), 1. [Scot.], call "canny"; hence,

go warily. 2. [British], cautious; slow; hesitating: as, *ca' canny* business methods.

ca·noe (kə-nōō'), *n.* [earlier *canoa;* Sp. *canoa* < the Carib name], a narrow, light boat moved with paddles. *v.i.* [CANOED (-nōōd'), CANOEING], 1. to paddle a canoe. 2. to go in a canoe. *v.t.* to transport by canoe.

can·oe·ist (kə-nōō'ist), *n.* a person who paddles a canoe; especially, one skilled in doing so.

can·on (kan'ən), *n.* [ME.; AS., a rule; LL. < L., measuring line, rule; Gr. *kanōn* < *kanē, kannē,* a reed, rod], 1. a law or body of laws of a church: as, the Roman Catholic *canon,* Anglican *canon,* etc. 2. any law or decree. 3. a standard used in judging something; criterion. 4. a list of books of the Bible officially accepted by the church as genuine. 5. [C-], a part of the Mass that follows the Sanctus or offertory. 6. a list of saints recognized by the Roman Catholic Church. 7. an official list or catalogue. 8. in *music,* a round; composition in which there are exact repetitions of a preceding part in the same or related keys. 9. in *printing,* a large size of type, 48 point. —*SYN.* see **law.**

can·on (kan'ən), *n.* [ME. *canon, canoun;* AS. *canonic;* L. *canonicus* < *canon;* see CANON (law)], 1. a member of a clerical group living according to a canon, or rule. 2. a clergyman serving in a cathedral or collegiate church.

cañ·on (kan'yən; Sp. kä-nyôn'), *n.* a canyon.

can·on·ess (kan'ən-is), *n.* 1. a woman member of a religious group living according to a canon, or rule, but not under an everlasting vow such as a nun takes. 2. a woman holding a canonry.

ca·non·i·cal (kə-non'i-k'l), *adj.* [LL. *canonicalis;* L. *canonicus* < *canon;* see CANON (law)], 1. of, according to, or ordered by church law. 2. authoritative; accepted. 3. belonging to the canon of the Bible.

canonical hour, any of the seven periods of the day assigned to prayer and worship: they are matins (with lauds), prime, tierce, sext, nones, vespers, and complin.

ca·non·i·cals (kə-non'i-k'lz), *n.pl.* the clothes that a clergyman must wear when conducting church services.

ca·non·i·cate (kə-non'i-kāt', kə-non'i-kit), *n.* the benefice or position of a canon; canonry.

can·on·ic·i·ty (kan'ən-is'ə-ti), *n.* [< L. *canonicus* (see CANONICAL); + *-ity*], 1. the right to be included in the Biblical canon. 2. the quality of being genuine. 3. conformity to church law.

can·on·ist (kan'ən-ist), *n.* 1. an expert in canon law. 2. a skilled composer of musical canons.

can·on·is·tic (kan'ən-is'tik), *adj.* of a canonist.

can·on·is·ti·cal (kan'ən-is'ti-k'l), *adj.* canonistic.

can·on·i·za·tion (kan'ən-ə-zā'shən), *n.* 1. a canonizing. 2. the fact or state of being canonized.

can·on·ize (kan'ən-īz'), *v.t.* [CANONIZED (-īzd'), CANONIZING], [LL. *canonizare* < L. *canon,* canon], 1. to declare (a dead person) a saint; add to the list of saints; hence, 2. to glorify. 3. to put in the Biblical canon. 4. to give church sanction or authorization to.

canon law, 1. the laws governing the ecclesiastical affairs of a Christian church. 2. the laws (called *Corpus Juris Canonici*) formerly governing the Roman Catholic Church: see **Codex Juris Canonici.**

can·on·ry (kan'ən-ri), *n.* [*pl.* CANONRIES (-riz)], 1. the benefice or position of a canon. 2. canons collectively.

can·on·ship (kan'ən-ship'), *n.* [*canon* + *-ship*], the position or term of office of a canon.

ca·no·pic urn (kə-nō'pik), [< L. *Canopicus,* of Canopus; see CANOPUS], an urn used in ancient Egypt to preserve and bury the internal organs of the dead.

Ca·no·pus (kə-nō'pəs), *n.* [L.; Gr. *Kanōpos, Kanōbos*], 1. the brightest star in southern skies, in the constellation Argo: see **constellation,** chart. 2. an ancient seacoast city in Lower Egypt, east of Alexandria.

can·o·py (kan'ə-pi), *n.* [*pl.* CANOPIES (-piz)], [ME. *canope;* OFr. *conopé;* ML. *canopeum;* L. *conopeum;* Gr. *kōnōpeion,* couch with mosquito curtains; dim. of *kōnōps,* gnat; cf. CANAPÉ], 1. a drapery, awning, or other rooflike covering fastened above a bed, throne, etc., or on poles over a person or sacred thing. 2. a high covering; overhanging shelter: as, the *canopy* of the sky. 3. in *architecture,* a rooflike projection over a door, pulpit, etc. *v.t.* [CANOPIED (-pid), CANOPYING], to place or form a canopy over; cover.

ca·no·rous (kə-nôr'əs, kə-nō'rəs), *adj.* [L. < *canor,* a tune < *canere,* to sing], songlike; melodious; musical.

Ca·nos·sa (kä-nôs'sä), *n.* an ancient town in northern Italy: scene of penance (1077) of Henry IV of Germany, Holy Roman Emperor, before Pope Gregory VII.
go to Canossa, to do penance.

Ca·no·va, An·to·nio (än-tô'nyô kä-nô'vä), 1757–1822; Italian sculptor.

Can·so, Cape (kan'sō), the northeastern tip of the mainland of Nova Scotia.

canst (kanst; *unstressed* kənst), archaic second person singular, present indicative, of **can:** used with *thou.*

cant (kant), *n.* [ONorm. Fr., singing < L. *cantus,* pp. of *canere,* to sing], 1. whining, singsong speech, especially as used by beggars. 2. the secret slang of beggars, thieves, etc.; argot. 3. the special words and phrases used by those in a certain sect, occupation, etc.; jargon. 4. insincere or almost meaningless talk used merely from convention or habit. 5. religious phraseology used hypocritically; insincere, pious talk. *v.i.* [< the *n.*], to use cant; speak in cant (in all senses of the *n.*). *adj.* 1. used only by a certain group: said of words or phrases. 2. trite; platitudinous. 3. hypocritical; insincere: said of words or phrases. —*SYN.* see **dialect.**

cant (kant), *n.* [OFr. *cant,* a corner, edge, angle; LL. *cantus,* a side, corner; L. *cantus, canthus,* tire of a wheel; prob. < Cym. *cant,* tire of a wheel, edge], 1. a corner or outside angle, as of a building. 2. a sloping or slanting surface; beveled edge. 3. a sudden movement, toss, or pitch that causes tilting, turning, or overturning. 4. the tilt, turn, or slant of direction or position thus caused. *v.t.* 1. to give a sloping edge to; bevel. 2. to tilt or overturn. 3. to throw off or out by tilting. 4. to throw with a jerk; pitch; toss. *v.i.* 1. to tilt or turn over. 2. to slant. 3. in *nautical usage,* to turn; change direction. *adj.* 1. with oblique sides or corners. 2. slanting.

can't (kant, känt), cannot.

Cant., 1. Canterbury. 2. Canticles. 3. Cantonese.

Cantab., Cantabrigian.

can·ta·bi·le (kän-tä'bi-lā'), *adj. & adv.* [It. < *cantare,* to sing; L. *cantare,* freq. of *canere,* to sing], in *music,* in an easy, flowing manner; songlike. *n.* music in this style. Abbreviated **cantab.**

Can·ta·brig·i·an (kan'tə-brij'i-ən), *adj.* [< L. *Cantabrigia,* Cambridge], 1. of Cambridge, England. 2. of the University of Cambridge. *n.* 1. a native or inhabitant of Cambridge, England. 2. a student or graduate of the University of Cambridge.

can·ta·le·ver (kan't'l-ev'ẽr, kan't'l-ē'vẽr), *n.* cantilever.

can·ta·loupe, can·ta·loup (kan'tə-lōp'), *n.* [Fr. *cantaloup;* It. *cantalupo* < *Cantalupo,* near Rome, where the melon was first grown in Europe], 1. a melon with a hard, ribbed rind and sweet, juicy, orange-colored flesh. 2. loosely, any muskmelon.

can·tan·ker·ous (kan-taŋ'kẽr-əs), *adj.* [prob. < ME. *contekous* < *contac, contek,* strife, quarrel; formed by analogy with *rancorous, cankerous*], bad-tempered; quarrelsome; contentious; perverse.

can·ta·ta (kən-tä'tə, kan-tä'tə), *n.* [It. < pp. of *cantare;* see CANTABILE], a musical composition consisting of vocal solos, choruses, etc., used as a setting for a story to be sung but not acted.

‡**can·ta·tri·ce** (It. kän'tä-trē'che; Fr. kȧn'tȧ'trēs'), *n.* [*pl.* It. CANTATRICI (-chē); Fr. CANTATRICES (-trēs')], [Fr. & It.; L. *cantatrix,* fem. of *cantator,* singer < pp. of *cantare,* to sing], a woman professional singer.

can·teen (kan-tēn'), *n.* [Fr. *cantine* < It. *cantina,* wine cellar, a vault < *canto,* an angle, corner; see CANT (an angle, edge)], 1. a military shop where soldiers can buy refreshments and provisions; post exchange; hence, 2. a place outside a military camp where refreshment and entertainment are provided for members of the armed forces. 3. a recreation center for teen-agers. 4. a small flask for carrying drinking water. 5. formerly, a military kit containing cooking equipment.

canteen cup, in *military usage,* a drinking cup of metal or plastic shaped as a carrying case for a canteen.

can·ter (kan'tẽr), *n.* [contr. < *Canterbury gallop:* from the slow pace at which the pilgrims rode to Canterbury], an easy gallop. *v.i. & v.t.* to ride at an easy gallop.

Can·ter·bur·y (kan'tẽr-ber'i, kan'tẽr-bẽr-i), *n.* a city in Kent, the ecclesiastical center of England and site of a famous cathedral: pop., 30,000: abbreviated **Cant.**

Canterbury bell, any of a number of campanulas with bell-shaped flowers of white, pink, or blue.

Canterbury Tales, an unfinished literary work (1387–1400) by Chaucer, consisting of a prologue, connecting passages, and twenty-four stories told to one another by a company of pilgrims on their way to Thomas à Becket's shrine at Canterbury: it is largely in verse.

can·thar·i·des (kan-thar'ə-dēz'), *n.pl.* [*sing.* CANTHARIS (kan'thə-ris)], [L. pl. of *cantharis,* kind of beetle, Spanish fly < Gr. *kantharis,* blistering beetle], in *pharmacy,* a preparation of powdered, dried Spanish flies, used internally as a diuretic or genitourinary stimulant, and externally as a skin irritant.

can·tha·ris (kan'thə-ris), *n.* [*pl.* CANTHARIDES (kan-thar'ə-dēz')], the Spanish fly: see **cantharides.**

cant hook, [see CANT (an angle, tilt)], a pole with a movable hooked arm at or near one end, for catching hold of logs and turning them over.

can·thus (kan'thəs), *n.* [*pl.* CANTHI (-thī)], [Mod. L.; Gr. *kanthos*], the corner on either side of the eye, where the eyelids meet.

can·ti·cle (kan'ti-k'l), *n.* [ME.; L. *canticulum,* dim. of *canticum,* song < *cantus,* a singing; pp. of *canere,* to sing], 1. a song or chant. 2. a hymn whose words are taken directly from the Bible, used in certain church services.

CANT HOOK

Can·ti·cles (kan'ti-k'lz), ***n.pl.*** a book of the Old Testament: also called *The Song of Solomon, Song of Songs,* and (in the Douay Bible) *Canticle of Canticles:* abbreviated **Cant.**

Can·ti·gny (kän'tē'nyē'), ***n.*** a village in northeastern France: site of first major battle (1918) involving United States troops in World War I.

can·ti·le·ver (kan't'l-ev'ẽr, kan't'l-ē'vẽr), ***n.*** [as if < *cant* (an angle) + *lever,* ? in obs. sense "bar, beam"; earlier *candiliver, cantinglivre* suggest Sp. **can de llevar,* lit., raising-dog, hence supporting bracket; cf. Sp. *can de levantar,* of similar sense], 1. a bracket or block projecting from a wall to support a balcony, cornice, etc. 2. a projecting beam or structure anchored at one end to a pier and extending over a space to be bridged: it is usually joined to a similar structure extending from an opposite pier. Also spelled **cantalever.**

cantilever bridge, a bridge whose span is formed by the projecting ends of two cantilevers, the opposite ends of which are supported on piers.

CANTILEVER BRIDGE

can·ti·na (kan-tē'nə; Sp. kän-tē'nä), ***n.*** [Sp.; cf. CANTEEN], in the southwestern United States, a place where liquor is sold; saloon.

can·tle (kan't'l), ***n.*** [ME., a bit, piece cut off; OFr., a corner, piece; LL. *cantellus,* dim. of *cantus;* see CANT (angle)], 1. a piece, especially when cut off or out; slice. 2. the upward-curving rear part of a saddle.

can·to (kan'tō), ***n.*** [*pl.* CANTOS (-tōz)], [It.; L. *cantus,* song; pp. of *canere,* to sing], 1. any of the main divisions of a long poem, corresponding to the chapters of a book. 2. [Obs.], a song or ballad. Abbreviated **can.**

Can·ton (kan-ton'), ***n.*** 1. a port of southeastern China; capital of Kwangtung province: pop., 1,599,000: Chinese name, *Kwangchow.* 2. the Pearl River in China, between Canton and the sea. 3. (kan'tən, kan't'n), a city in northeastern Ohio: pop., 114,000.

can·ton (kan'tən, kan-ton'), ***n.*** [Fr.; It. *cantone* < LL. *canto,* a corner, edge, region < L. *cantus;* see CANT (an angle, edge)], 1. one of the political divisions of a country or territory; district: the Swiss Republic is divided into cantons. 2. in *heraldry,* a small, square section of an escutcheon, usually in the upper right, or dexter, corner. ***v.t.*** 1. (kan'ton, kan-ton'), to divide into districts or parts. 2. (kan-ton', kan-tōn'), to assign quarters to (troops, etc.); quarter.

can·ton·al (kan'tən-'l), ***adj.*** of a canton or cantons.

Can·ton crepe (kan'tən), a soft, crinkled silk fabric, like crepe de Chine but heavier.

Can·ton·ese (kan'tən-ēz'), ***adj.*** 1. of Canton, China or its people. 2. of the Chinese dialect spoken in and around Canton. ***n.*** 1. [*pl.* CANTONESE], a native or inhabitant of Canton. 2. the Chinese dialect spoken by the Cantonese. Abbreviated **Cant.**

Can·ton flannel (kan'tən), a soft, warm cotton cloth with fleecy nap on one side, used for baby clothes, etc.: also called *cotton flannel, flannelette.*

can·ton·ment (kan-ton'mənt, kan'tən-mənt, kan-tōn'mənt), ***n.*** [Fr. *cantonnement;* see CANTON (district)], 1. the assignment of troops to temporary quarters, especially winter or training quarters; hence, 2. the quarters assigned. 3. in India, a military post.

can·tor (kan'tẽr, kan'tôr), ***n.*** [L., singer < pp. of *canere,* to sing], 1. a church choir leader; precentor. 2. a singer of liturgical solos in a synagogue.

can·trip (kan'trip), ***n.*** [< earlier Scot. *cast cantrapes,* to tell fortunes], [Scot.], 1. a magic spell. 2. a prank.

can·tus (kan'təs), ***n.*** [*pl.* CANTUS], [L.; see CANTO], 1. a song; melody; especially, the principal part, usually the soprano, of a polyphonic work. 2. an ecclesiastical style of music.

‡can·tus fir·mus (kan'təs fũr'məs), [ML., lit., firm song], 1. a liturgical chant or plain song: see **plain song.** 2. a simple melody serving as the main theme of a contrapuntal work.

cant·y (kän'ti), ***adj.*** [< LG. *kantig,* cheery, hearty < *kant,* ready], [Scot. & British Dial.], lively; cheery.

Ca·nuck (kə-nuk'), ***n.*** [< *Canada;* prob. after *Chinook*], [Slang], 1. a Canadian. 2. a French-Canadian.

Ca·nute II (kə-nōōt', kə-nūt'), 994?–1035 A.D.; king of England (1016–1035) and of Denmark (1018–1035): also **Cnut, Knut.**

can·vas (kan'vəs), ***n.*** [ME. & OFr. *canevas;* It. *canavaccio;* LL. *canabacius,* hempen cloth; L. *cannabis,* hemp], 1. a coarse cloth of unbleached hemp, cotton, or flax: a closely woven, heavy canvas is used for tents, sails, etc., and a loosely woven kind for needlework. 2. a sail or set of sails. 3. *a)* a piece of canvas on which an oil painting is made. *b)* such a painting. 4. a tent or tents, especially circus tents. ***adj.*** made of canvas.

under canvas, 1. in tents, especially army or circus tents. 2. with sails unfurled. 3. by means of sails.

under light canvas, with all additional sails (studding sails, spinnaker, etc.) set.

can·vas·back (kan'vəs-bak'), ***n.*** [*pl.* CANVASBACKS (-baks'), CANVASBACK; see PLURAL, II, D, 1], [< the grayish, canvaslike appearance of the back], a North American wild duck.

can·vass (kan'vəs), ***v.t.*** [< *canvas:* prob. because canvas was used for sifting], 1. to examine or discuss in detail; look over carefully. 2. to go through (places) or among (people) asking for (votes, opinions, orders, etc.). ***v.i.*** to try to get votes, orders, etc.; solicit. ***n.*** 1. an examination or discussion of something. 2. the soliciting of votes, orders, etc., especially in trying to find out the probable outcome of an election, sales campaign, etc.

can·yon (kan'yən), ***n.*** [Sp. *cañón* < *caña,* a tube, funnel; L. *canna,* a reed, cane], a long, narrow valley between high cliffs, usually with a stream flowing through it: also spelled **cañon.**

‡can·zo·ne (kän-tsô'ne), ***n.*** [*pl.* CANZONI (-nē)], [It. < L. *cantio, cantionis,* a singing < pp. of *canere,* to sing], a lyric poem of Provençal or early Italian origin, often set to music: it is somewhat like a madrigal.

can·zo·net (kan'zə-net'), ***n.*** [It. *canzonetta,* dim. of *canzone;* see CANZONE], a short, sprightly song.

caou·tchouc (kōō'chook, kou-chook'), ***n.*** [Fr. < native Carib (Tupi) name, *cahuchu*], 1. crude rubber obtained from latex; India rubber. 2. pure rubber.

Cap (kap), ***n.*** [Slang], captain: a term of address.

cap (kap), ***n.*** [ME. *cappe;* AS. *cæppe,* a cap, cape, hood; LL. *cappa, capa,* a cape, hooded cloak], 1. any close-fitting head covering, brimless or with only a front visor, and made of wool or cotton, as a boy's cap or overseas cap, or of muslin or lace, as a nurse's or baby's cap. 2. a special covering for the head, worn as a mark of occupation, rank, academic degree, etc. (e.g., a cardinal's cap, fool's cap, mortarboard, etc.). 3. a caplike part or thing; cover; top or top part, as the cap-shaped part of a mushroom, a metal jar cover, the cover over a camera lens, a kneecap, the metal reinforcements on shoe toes, a mountain top, the capital of a column, etc. 4. a percussion cap; hence, 5. a little paper percussion cap for toy guns. 6. a size of writing paper (14 x 17 inches): legal cap is slightly smaller: see **foolscap.** ***v.t.*** [CAPPED (kapt), CAPPING], 1. to put a cap on. 2. to cover (the top or end of): as, snow *capped* the hills. 3. to provide something equal to, better than, or corresponding to; match or surpass.

cap the climax, to exceed the limit; be or do more than could be expected or believed.

set one's cap for, [Colloq.], to try to win (a man) as a husband or lover.

cap., 1. [*pl.* CAPS.], capital. 2. capitalize. 3. *capitulum,* [L.], chapter. 4. captain.

ca·pa·bil·i·ty (kā'pə-bil'ə-ti), ***n.*** [*pl.* CAPABILITIES (-tiz)], 1. the quality of being capable; practical ability or mental capacity. 2. the capacity of being used or developed. 3. *pl.* abilities, features, etc. not yet developed or utilized.

ca·pa·ble (kā'pə-b'l), ***adj.*** [Fr.; LL. *capabilis* < L. *capere,* to take, seize], 1. having ability; able; skilled; competent. 2. [Archaic], having capacity; capacious. —***SYN.*** see **able.**

capable of, 1. susceptible of; admitting of; open to. 2. having the ability or qualities necessary for.

ca·pa·bly (kā'pə-bli), ***adv.*** in a capable manner.

ca·pa·cious (kə-pā'shəs), ***adj.*** [< L. *capax, capacis* < *capere,* to take, hold, contain; + *-ous*], able to contain a great deal; roomy; spacious.

ca·pac·i·tance (kə-pas'ə-təns), ***n.*** [*contr.* < *capacity reactance*], in *electricity,* that property of a condenser which determines how much charge can be stored in it for a given potential difference across its terminals.

ca·pac·i·tate (kə-pas'ə-tāt'), ***v.t.*** [CAPACITATED (-id), CAPACITATING], [< *capacity* + *-ate*], to prepare, fit, or qualify (*for* something).

ca·pac·i·tive (kə-pas'ə-tiv), ***adj.*** of electrical capacitance.

capacitive coupling, in *radio,* the coupling of two circuits by means of a condenser or other capacitance.

ca·pac·i·tor (kə-pas'ə-tẽr), ***n.*** in *electricity,* a condenser.

ca·pac·i·ty (kə-pas'ə-ti), ***n.*** [*pl.* CAPACITIES (-tiz)], [L. *capacitas* < *capax;* see CAPACIOUS], 1. the ability to contain, absorb, or receive and hold. 2. all that can be contained; maximum amount of holding space; content or volume: as, the theater was filled to *capacity.* 3. the power of receiving and holding knowledge, impressions, etc.; mental ability. 4. the ability or qualifications (*for,* or *to* do, something); aptitude. 5. the quality of being adapted (*for* something) or susceptible (*of* something); capability. 6. a condition of being qualified or authorized; position, function, status, etc.: as, he acts in the *capacity* of an adviser. 7. in *electricity,* capacitance: abbreviated **c., C., cy., K., k.** 8. in *law,* legal authority or competency. —***SYN.*** see **function.**

cap and bells, a fool's cap with little bells on it, worn by court jesters.

cap and gown, a costume consisting of a flat cap (called *mortarboard*) and a long, dark-colored robe, worn at some academic ceremonies, as commencement, by teachers, students receiving degrees, etc.: often used to symbolize the academic life.

cap-a-pie, cap-à-pie (kap'ə-pē'), *adv.* [OFr. *de cap a pie; cap*, head < L. *caput; pié*, foot < L. *pes*], from head to foot; entirely.

ca·par·i·son (kə-par'ə-s'n), *n.* [earlier Fr. *caparasson* (now *caparaçon*); Sp. *caparazon* < LL. *cappa, capa*, cape, hooded cloak], 1. an ornamented covering for a horse; trappings. 2. clothing, equipment, and ornaments; outfit. *v.t.* 1. to cover (a horse) with trappings. 2. to adorn with rich clothing; deck out; outfit.

cape (kāp), *n.* [16th-c. *Spanish cape* < Sp. *capa*, orig., a hood, via Fr. *cape*, hooded cloak; see CAPE (headland)], a sleeveless garment fastened at the neck and hanging over the back and shoulders, worn separately or attached to a dress or cloak.

cape (kāp), *n.* [Fr. *cap;* It. *capo* < L. *caput*, the head], a piece of land projecting into a body of water; promontory; headland.
the Cape, 1. the Cape of Good Hope. 2. Cape Colony. 3. Cape Cod.

cape (kāp), *n.* capeskin.

Cape Bret·on Island (brit'ən, bret'ən), an island constituting the northeastern part of Nova Scotia, Canada: area, 3,120 sq. mi.; pop., 133,000.

Cape Cod, Cape Charles, Cape Hatteras, etc., see **Cod, Charles, Hatteras,** etc.

Cape Cod Bay, a part of Massachusetts Bay, formed by Cape Cod.

Cape Cod Canal, a ship canal joining Buzzards Bay and Cape Cod Bay.

Cape Colony, Cape of Good Hope province: the former name: abbreviated **C.C.**

Cape Dutch, Afrikaans, the Dutch dialect spoken in South Africa.

Ča·pek, Ka·rel (chä'pek), 1890–1938; Czech novelist and playwright.

cap·e·lin (kap'ə-lin), *n.* [*pl.* CAPELIN, CAPELINS (-linz); see PLURAL, II, D, 2], [Fr. *caplan, capelan*], a variety of smelt found in North Atlantic waters, used as food and especially as bait for cod fishing: also **caplin.**

Ca·pel·la (kə-pel'ə), *n.* [L., a kid, dim. of *caper*, goat, or *capra*, she-goat], a yellow, first-magnitude star, the brightest in the constellation Auriga: see **constellation,** chart.

Cape Province, Cape of Good Hope province.

ca·per (kā'pēr), *v.i.* [< *capriole*], to skip or jump about in a gay, playful manner; frisk; gambol. *n.* 1. a gay, playful jump or leap. 2. a wild, foolish action; prank.
cut a caper (or **capers**), 1. to caper. 2. to frolic about; play silly tricks.

ca·per (kā'pēr), *n.* [ME. & OFr. *caperis;* L. *capparis;* Gr. *kapparis*], 1. a prickly, trailing Mediterranean bush. 2. *pl.* its green flower buds, pickled and used to flavor sauces, etc.

cap·er·cail·lie (kap'ẽr-kāl'yi), *n.* [< Gael. *capull* (? < L. *caballus*, a horse) *coille*, lit., horse of the woods], the largest species of European grouse: also called *cock of the woods.*

cap·er·cail·zie (kap'ẽr-kāl'yi, kap'ẽr-kāl'zi), *n.* a capercaillie.

Ca·per·na·um (kə-pũr'ni-əm), *n.* an ancient city in Palestine, on the Sea of Galilee.

cape·skin (kāp'skin'), *n.* [orig. made from the skin of goats from the *Cape* of Good Hope], leather made from the skin of certain goats, used especially for gloves.

Ca·pet, Hugh (kā'pit, kap'it), 940?–996 A.D.; king of France (987–996 A.D.).

Ca·pe·tian (kə-pē'shən), *adj.* designating or of the French dynasty (987–1328 A.D.) founded by Hugh Capet.

Cape Town, seaport and capital of Cape of Good Hope province: pop., 344,000: seat of the legislature of the Union of South Africa: also **Cape·town** (kāp'toun'), *n.*

Cape Verde Islands (vũrd), a group of Portuguese islands, 320 mi. west of Cape Verde: area, 1,557 sq. mi.; pop., 165,000; capital, Praia.

Cape York Peninsula, a large peninsula in northeastern Australia, part of Queensland.

cap·ful (kap'fool'), *n.* [*pl.* CAPFULS (-foolz')], as much as a cap can hold.

caph (käf, kôf), *n.* kaph, the eleventh letter of the Hebrew alphabet.

ca·pi·as (kā'pi-əs, kap'i-əs), *n.* [L., 2d pers. sing., pres. subj., of *capere*, to take], in *law*, a writ directing an officer to arrest the person named.

cap·il·la·ceous (kap''l-ā'shəs), *adj.* [L. *capillaceus*, hair-like < *capillus*, hair], 1. having hairlike filaments. 2. like a hair or thread.

cap·il·lar·i·ty (kap''l-ar'ə-ti), *n.* [Fr. *capillarité* < L. *capillaris;* see CAPILLARY], 1. the property of exerting or having capillary attraction or repulsion. 2. capillary attraction or repulsion.

cap·il·lar·y (kap''l-er'i), *adj.* [L. *capillaris* < *capillus*, hair; ? < a dim. form of *caput*, the head], 1. of or like a hair, especially in being very slender. 2. having a very small bore. 3. in or of capillaries. *n.* [*pl.* CAPILLARIES (-iz)], 1. a tube with a very small bore: also **capillary tube.** 2. any of the tiny blood vessels connecting the arteries with the veins.

capillary action, capillary attraction or repulsion.

capillary attraction (or **repulsion**), a force that is the resultant of adhesion, cohesion, and surface tension in liquids which are in contact with solids, as in a capillary tube: when the cohesive force is greater, the surface of the liquid tends to rise in the tube (resulting in apparent attraction); when the adhesive force is greater, the surface tends to be depressed in the tube (resulting in apparent repulsion).

capillary tube, a capillary (sense 1).

‡cap·i·ta (kap'i-tə), *n.* plural of **caput.**

cap·i·tal (kap'ə-t'l), *adj.* [ME.; OFr.; L. *capitalis*, of the head < *caput*, the head; see CHIEF], 1. involving or punishable by death (originally by decapitation): as, a *capital* offense. 2. chief; principal; of primary importance. 3. of most political importance, as being the seat of government: as, a *capital* city. 4. of or having to do with capital. 5. first-rate; excellent. See also **capital letter.** *n.* 1. a capital letter: see also **small capital.** 2. a city or town that is the official seat of government of a state, nation, etc. Abbreviated **cap.** 3. wealth (money or property) owned or used in business by a person, corporation, etc. 4. an accumulated stock of such wealth. 5. wealth, in whatever form, used or capable of being used to produce more wealth; hence, 6. any source of profit or benefit; assets; resources: as, energy and education are his only *capital.* 7. [often C-], capitalists collectively: distinguished from *labor.* 8. in *accounting, a*) the net worth of a business; amount by which the assets exceed the liabilities. *b*) the face value of all the stock issued or authorized by a corporation. —*SYN.* see **chief.**
make capital of, to take advantage of, as for personal profit or power; make the most of; exploit.

cap·i·tal (kap'ə-t'l), *n.* [ME.; OFr. *chapitel;* L. *capitellum*, dim. of *caput*, the head], the top part of a column or pilaster.

CAPITAL

capital account, 1. an account of the total capital invested in fixed assets by the owners of a business, including real estate, machinery, etc., but excluding current or operating expenses. 2. in *accounting*, a summary of the assets and liabilities of a business on any given date.

capital expenditure, money spent for expanding and improving a business: it does not include operating expenses.

capital gains, profit resulting from the sale of capital investments, as stocks, etc.

capital goods, commodities for use in production, as raw materials, machinery, buildings, etc.; producers' goods: distinguished from *consumers' goods.*

cap·i·tal·ism (kap'ə-t'l-iz'm), *n.* 1. the economic system in which all or most of the means of production and distribution, as land, factories, railroads, etc., are privately owned and operated for profit, originally under fully competitive conditions: it has been generally characterized by a tendency toward concentration of wealth, and, in its later phase, by the growth of great corporations, increased governmental control, etc. 2. the principles, methods, interests, power, influence, etc. of capitalists, especially of those with large holdings. 3. the state of being a capitalist.

cap·i·tal·ist (kap'ə-t'l-ist), *n.* 1. a person who has capital; owner of wealth used in business. 2. an upholder of capitalism. 3. loosely, a wealthy person. *adj.* capitalistic.

cap·i·tal·is·tic (kap'ə-t'l-is'tik), *adj.* 1. of or characteristic of capitalists or capitalism. 2. upholding, preferring, or practicing capitalism.

cap·i·tal·is·ti·cal·ly (kap'ə-t'l-is'ti-k'l-i, kap'ə-t'l-is'tik-li), *adv.* 1. in a capitalistic manner. 2. toward capitalism: as, he is *capitalistically* inclined.

cap·i·tal·i·za·tion (kap'ə-t'l-i-zā'shən, kap'ə-t'l-ī-zā'shən), *n.* 1. *a*) a capitalizing or being capitalized. *b*) the amount or sum resulting from this. 2. the total capital funds of a corporation, represented by stocks, bonds, etc. 3. in *accounting, a*) the total invested in a business by the owner or owners. *b*) the total corporate liability. *c*) the total reached after adding liabilities.

cap·i·tal·ize (kap'ə-t'l-īz'), *v.t.* [CAPITALIZED (-īzd'), CAPITALIZING], 1. to use as capital; convert into capital. 2. to use to one's advantage or profit (often with *on*). 3. to calculate the present value of (a periodical payment, annuity, income, etc.); convert (an income, etc.) into one payment or sum equivalent to the computed present value. 4. to establish the capital stock of (a business firm) at a certain figure. 5. to convert (floating debt) into stock or shares. 6. to supply capital to or for (an enterprise). 7. to print or write (a word or words) in capital letters. 8. to begin (a word) with a capital letter. 9. in *accounting*, to set up (expenditures) as assets. Abbreviated **cap.** (in senses 6 & 7).

capital letter, any letter written or printed in a form larger than, and often different from, that of the corresponding small letter, as A, B, C, etc.; upper-case letter.

capital levy, a tax levied on all capital, whether individual or corporate, other than income.

cap·i·tal·ly (kap'ə-t'l-i), *adv.* [see CAPITAL, *adj.*], in an excellent or admirable manner; very well.

capital punishment, execution as punishment for a crime; death penalty.

capital ship, any armored vessel, other than an aircraft carrier, of over 10,000 tons displacement and with 8-inch guns or larger; battleship or battle cruiser.

capital stock, 1. the capital of a corporation, divided into negotiable shares. 2. the face value of all such shares. Abbreviated **C.S., c.s.**

capital surplus, any surplus of a business firm not derived from direct earnings or profits.

cap·i·tate (kap'ə-tāt'), *adj.* [L. *capitatus*, having a head < *caput*, the head], 1. enlarged at the head or tip. 2. head-shaped, as some flowers.

cap·i·ta·tion (kap'ə-tā'shən), *n.* [LL. *capitatio* < L. *caput*, the head], 1. the act of counting heads or individuals. 2. a tax or fee of so much per head; payment per capita.

Cap·i·tol (kap'ə-t'l), *n.* [ME. & OFr. *capitolie;* L. *Capitolium*, temple of Jupiter in Rome < *caput*, the head], 1. the temple of Jupiter on the Capitoline Hill in Rome. 2. the hill itself. 3. the building in which the United States Congress meets, at Washington, D. C. 4. [usually c-], the building in which a State legislature meets.

Cap·i·to·line (kap'ə-t'l-īn'), *n.* one of the seven hills on which Rome was built. *adj.* 1. of this hill. 2. of the temple of Jupiter which stood there.

ca·pit·u·lar (kə-pich'ə-lẽr), *adj.* [ML. *capitularis* < L. *capitulum*, chapter, dim. of *caput*, the head], of a chapter, especially that of a religious order, or similar body. *n.* [< the *adj.*; also, shortened form of *capitulary*], 1. a member of a chapter. 2. a capitulary (sense 2).

ca·pit·u·lar·y (kə-pich'ə-ler'i), *adj.* [ML. *capitularius* < *capitularis;* see CAPITULAR], capitular. *n.* [*pl.* CAPITULARIES (-iz)], 1. a capitular (sense 1). 2. *pl.* ordinances, especially those made formerly by Frankish kings or those made now by cathedral chapters.

ca·pit·u·late (kə-pich'ə-lāt'), *v.i.* [CAPITULATED (-id), CAPITULATING], [< ML. *capitulatus*, pp. of *capitulare*, to draw up in heads or chapters, arrange conditions < L. *capitulum;* see CAPITULAR], 1. to give up (*to* an enemy) on prearranged conditions; surrender conditionally. 2. to give up; stop resisting. —*SYN.* see **yield.**

ca·pit·u·la·tion (kə-pich'ə-lā'shən), *n.* [Fr.; see CAPITULATE], 1. a statement of the main parts of a subject. 2. a capitulating; conditional surrender. 3. a document containing terms of surrender, conditions of office, articles of concession, etc.; treaty; covenant; convention. 4. *pl.* such terms, conditions, concessions, etc.

ca·pit·u·lum (kə-pich'ə-ləm), *n.* [*pl.* CAPITULA (-lə)], [L., dim. of *caput*, the head], 1. in *anatomy & zoology*, a knoblike part, as at the end of a bone in a joint. 2. in *botany*, a close, thick cluster of flowers all attached directly to the same stem, as a clover bloom.

cap·lin (kap'lin), *n.* a capelin.

Cap'n (kap''n, kap''m), *n.* [Dial.], Captain.

ca·pon (kā'pon, kā'pən), *n.* [ME.; AS. *capun;* L. *capo;* Gr. *kapōn* < *koptein*, to cut], a castrated rooster, especially one fattened for eating.

cap·o·ral (kap'ə-ral'), *n.* [Fr. < *tabac du caporal*, lit., corporal's tobacco: so named because better than *tabac du soldat* (soldier's tobacco); It. *caporale;* see CORPORAL], a kind of tobacco.

Cap·o·ret·to (kap'ə-ret'ō), *n.* a town in Yugoslavia (before 1947, in Italy): pop., 6,300: scene of a severe Italian defeat (1917) in World War I.

ca·pote (kə-pōt'), *n.* [Fr., dim. of *cape;* see CAPE], 1. a long cloak, usually with a hood. 2. a woman's bonnet tying under the chin. 3. a movable hood or top for a vehicle.

ca·pouch (kə-po͞osh', kə-po͞och'), *n.* a capuche.

Cap·pa·do·ci·a (kap'ə-dō'shi-ə, kap'ə-dō'shə), *n.* an ancient kingdom and Roman province in south central Asia Minor: see **Roman Empire,** map.

cap·pa·ri·da·ceous (kap'ə-ri-dā'shəs), *adj.* [< L. *capparis* (see CAPER, the plant); + *-aceous*], belonging to a family of chiefly tropical plants, of which the caper is typical.

cap·per (kap'ẽr), *n.* a person or device that caps or makes caps.

cap·re·o·late (kap'ri-ə-lāt', kə-prē'ə-lit), *adj.* [< L. *capreolus*, a wild goat, tendril; + *-ate*], in *botany*, having tendrils.

Ca·pri (kä'pri; *occas.* kə-prē'), *n.* an island in the Bay of Naples: area, 4 sq. mi.; pop., 8,000.

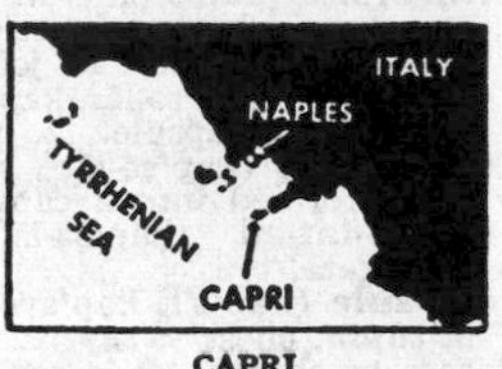

CAPRI

‡ca·pric·ci·o (kə-prē'chi-ō; It. kä-prēt'chô), *n.* [*pl.* CAPRICCIOS (-ōz); It. CAPRICCI (-chē)], [It.; see CAPRICE], 1. a prank; whim; caprice. 2. a musical composition of irregular form, usually lively and whimsical in spirit.

‡ca·pric·ci·o·so (kə-prē'-chi-ō'sō; It. kä-prēt-chô'sô), *adj. & adv.* [It.; see CAPRICE], in *music*, in a light, free, whimsical style: a direction to the performer.

ca·price (kə-prēs'), *n.* [Fr.; It. *capriccio*, a shivering, whim, caprice < *capo* (< L. *caput*, the head) + *riccio*, curl, frizzled, lit., hedgehog (< L. *ericius;* see URCHIN); hence, orig., head with bristling hair, horripilation; meaning influenced by association with It. *capriola* (see CAPRIOLE) & *capra* < L. *capra*, she-goat], 1. a sudden turn of mind, emotion, or action, caused by a whim or impulse; freakish notion; vagary. 2. a capricious quality. 3. in *music*, a capriccio.

SYN.—**caprice** refers to a sudden, impulsive, apparently unmotivated turn of mind or emotion (discharged at the *caprice* of a foreman); **whim** and **whimsy** both refer to an idle, quaint, or curious notion, but **whim** more often suggests willfulness and **whimsy** fancifulness (pursuing a *whim* he wrote a poem full of *whimsy*); **vagary** suggests a highly unusual or extravagant notion (the *vagaries* of fashion in women's clothes); **crotchet** implies great eccentricity and connotes stubbornness in opposition to prevailing thought, usually on some insignificant point (his *crotchets* concerning diet).

ca·pri·cious (kə-prish'əs), *adj.* [Fr. *capricieux;* It. *capriccioso;* see CAPRICE], 1. subject to caprices; inclined to change abruptly and without reason; erratic; flighty; unpredictable. 2. [Obs.], fantastic; playful. —*SYN.* see **inconstant.**

Cap·ri·corn (kap'ri-kôrn'), *n.* [ME.; OFr.; L. *capricornus* < *caper*, goat + *cornu*, a horn], 1. a southern constellation between Sagittarius and Aquarius, supposedly resembling a goat in shape: see **constellation,** chart. 2. the tenth sign of the zodiac (♑), entered by the sun at the winter solstice, about December 22: see **zodiac,** illus.

cap·ri·fig (kap'rə-fig'), *n.* [< L. *caprificus*, wild fig; L. *caper*, goat + *ficus*, fig], the wild fig, growing mainly in southern Europe and the Near East.

cap·ri·fo·li·a·ceous (kap'ri-fō'li-ā'shəs), *adj.* [< ML. *caprifolium*, honeysuckle < L. *caper*, goat + *folium*, leaf; + *-aceous*], the honeysuckle family of plants.

cap·ri·ole (kap'ri-ōl'), *n.* [Fr.; It. *capriola* < *capriolare*, to leap like a goat < *capriuolo*, doe, roe; L. *capreolus*, wild goat < *caper*, goat; cf. CABRIOLET], 1. a caper; leap. 2. an upward leap made by a horse without going forward. *v.i.* [CAPRIOLED (-ōld'), CAPRIOLING], to make a capriole.

ca·pro·ic acid (kə-prō'ik), [*capro-* (for L. *caper*, goat) + *-ic:* so named from its smell], a colorless, liquid fatty acid, $C_6H_{12}O_2$, found in butter and other animal fats and used in the manufacture of esters.

caps., capitals (capital letters).

cap·sa·i·cin (kap-sā'ə-sin), *n.* [L. *capsa*, a box; + *-ic* + *-in*], a bitter, strongly irritant, white crystalline alkaloid, $C_{18}H_{27}O_3N$, extracted from capsicum.

cap screw, a bolt with a long thread and, usually, a square head, used with or without a nut for securing cylinder covers, etc.

cap·si·cum (kap'si-kəm), *n.* [LL.; prob. < L. *capsa*, a box: so named from the shape of the seed pods], 1. any of a number of tropical plants with many-seeded pungent pods called *chilies* or *peppers*. 2. these pods prepared as condiments or, in medicine, as a gastric stimulant: they are used whole, cut up, or dried and powdered as in cayenne pepper.

cap·size (kap-sīz'), *v.t. & v.i.* [CAPSIZED (-sīzd'), CAPSIZING], [18th-c. nautical slang; ? repatterned (after dial. *cap*, to overtop + *side*) < Sp. *cabezar*, lit., to sink by the head (< *cabo, cabeza*, the head); cf. early *capacise*], to overturn; upset: said especially of a boat. —*SYN.* see **upset.**

cap·stan (kap'stən), *n.* [Fr. & Pr. *cabestan* < L. *capistrum*, halter, muzzle < *capere*, to take, hold], an apparatus, used mainly on ships, for hauling in cables and hawsers: it consists of a large, spool-shaped cylinder with the cable or hawser wound around it, revolving on an inner shafting; upright windlass.

CAPSTAN

capstan bar, any of the poles

inserted in a capstan and used as levers to turn it.

cap·stone (kap'stōn'), *n.* 1. the uppermost stone of a structure. 2. any of a series of flat slabs placed on top of a wall to protect its joints.

cap·su·lar (kap'sə-lẽr, kap'syoo-lẽr), *adj.* 1. having the nature of a capsule. 2. of or in a capsule.

cap·su·late (kap'sə-lāt', kap'syoo-lāt'), *adj.* contained in or formed into a capsule.

cap·su·lat·ed (kap'sə-lā'tid, kap'syoo-lā'tid), *adj.* capsulate.

cap·sule (kap's'l, kap'syool), *n.* [Fr.; L. *capsula*, dim. of *capsa*, chest < *capere*, to take, contain], 1. a small case or sheath. 2. a cap or seal for a bottle or tube, made of metal, rubber, etc. 3. a small, soluble gelatin container for enclosing a dose of medicine. 4. a closed compartment designed to hold and protect men, instruments, etc., as in an aircraft or spacecraft. 5. in *anatomy*, any sac or membrane enclosing a part. 6. in *botany*, a case, pod, or fruit, containing seeds, spores, or carpels: it usually bursts when ripe. 7. in *chemistry*, a shallow dish or tray for evaporating liquids. *adj.* in a concise or condensed form: as, a *capsule* biography.

cap·tain (kap't'n, kap'tin), *n.* [ME. *capitain, captein*; OFr. *capitaine*; LL. *capitaneus*, of the head < L. *caput*, the head; cf. CHIEFTAIN], 1. a chief or leader: as, *captains* of industry. 2. the head of a group or division; specifically, *a*) an army officer commanding a troop, company, battery, etc., and ranking above a first lieutenant and below a major. *b*) a navy officer ranking below a commodore and above a commander: he corresponds in rank and pay to an army colonel. *c*) the commander or master of a ship. *d*) a superintendent or foreman, as in mining, industry, etc. *e*) the leader of a team or crew, as in sports. *f*) a precinct commander in a police or fire department. *g*) the district leader of a political party. Abbreviated **Capt.** (as a title), **cap.** 3. a great military commander. *v.t.* to be captain of; lead.

cap·tain·cy (kap't'n-si, kap'tin-si), *n.* [*pl.* CAPTAINCIES (-siz)], the rank, commission, or status of a captain.

cap·tain·ship (kap't'n-ship', kap'tin-ship'), *n.* [*captain* + *-ship*], 1. a captaincy. 2. leadership.

cap·tion (kap'shən), *n.* [L. *captio* < pp. of *capere*, to seize, take], 1. [Rare], seizure. 2. in *law*, *a*) [British], legal arrest. *b*) a part of a legal instrument, such as an indictment, showing where, when, and by what authority it was executed. *c*) a heading showing the names of the parties, court, and docket number in a pleading or deposition. 3. a heading; title or subtitle, as of a picture. *v.t.* to supply a caption for.

cap·tious (kap'shəs), *adj.* [L. *captiosus* < *captio*; see CAPTION], 1. made for the sake of argument or fault-finding, as a question, objection, etc.; sophistical; tricky. 2. fond of catching others in mistakes; quick to find fault; quibbling; carping. —*SYN.* see **critical.**

cap·ti·vate (kap'tə-vāt'), *v.t.* [CAPTIVATED (-id), CAPTIVATING], [< L. *captivatus*, pp. of *captivare*, to take captive < *captivus*; see CAPTIVE], 1. originally, to take or hold captive; capture. 2. to capture the attention or affection of, as by beauty, excellence, etc.; charm; fascinate. —*SYN.* see **attract.**

cap·ti·va·tion (kap'tə-vā'shən), *n.* 1. a captivating or being captivated. 2. the ability to captivate; charm.

cap·ti·va·tor (kap'tə-vā'tẽr), *n.* a person or thing that captivates.

cap·tive (kap'tiv), *n.* [L. *captivus* < *captus*, pp. of *capere*, to take; cf. CAITIFF], 1. a person held in confinement or subjection; prisoner. 2. a person who is captivated. *adj.* 1. taken or held prisoner. 2. captivated. 3. of captives or captivity.

captive audience, any group of people forced against their will to listen to something, as passengers on a bus equipped with a radio loudspeaker.

captive balloon, a balloon held in place in the air by a rope or ropes leading to the ground.

cap·tiv·i·ty (kap-tiv'ə-ti), *n.* [*pl.* CAPTIVITIES (-tiz)], [Fr. *captivité*; L. *captivitas*], the condition of being a captive; imprisonment; bondage.

cap·tor (kap'tẽr), *n.* [L.], a person who captures.

cap·ture (kap'chẽr), *n.* [Fr.; L. *captura* < pp. of *capere*, to take], 1. a taking or being taken by force, surprise, etc.; seizure. 2. that which is thus taken or seized; prey; booty. *v.t.* [CAPTURED (-chẽrd), CAPTURING], to take or seize by force, surprise, etc. —*SYN.* see **catch.**

Cap·u·a (kap'ū-ə; It. kä'pwä), *n.* 1. an ancient city in Italy, near Naples. 2. a modern town located on part of the original site: pop., 14,000.

ca·puche (kə-po͞osh', kə-po͞och'), *n.* [Fr.; It. *capuccio*; LL. *capuccium*, *caputium*, cowl < *capa*, *cappa*, cape, hood], the long, pointed hood worn by the Capuchins: also spelled **capouch.**

Cap·u·chin (kap'yoo-chin', kap'yoo-shin'), *n.* [Fr. *capucin*, monk who wears a cowl < *capuce*, It. *cappuccio*, a cowl; see CAPUCHE], 1. a monk of a certain Franciscan order whose members all wear the capuche. 2. [c-], a woman's cloak with a hood. 3. [c-], a South American monkey with a whitish face and a hoodlike crown of black hair.

Cap·u·let (kap'yoo-let', kap'yoo-lit), the family name of Juliet in Shakespeare's *Romeo and Juliet.*

‡**ca·put** (kā'pət, kap'ət), *n.* [*pl.* CAPITA (kap'i-tə)], [L.], a head or headlike structure.

cap·y·ba·ra (kap'i-bä'rə), *n.* [Sp. *capibara* < the Braz. native name], a tailless, partially web-footed animal that lives in and around lakes and streams in South America: it is the largest extant rodent, over 48 inches in length and 24 inches in height.

car (kär), *n.* [ME. & ONorm. Fr. *carre*; LL. *carrum*; L. *carrus*, orig., two-wheeled Celtic war chariot < Gaul. *carros* (OIr. *carr*); IE. **krsos* < base **kers-*, to run, as in L. *currere*, to run (see COURSE); cf. CHARIOT], 1. any vehicle on wheels. 2. [Poetic], a chariot. 3. a vehicle that moves on tracks, as a streetcar. 4. an automobile: also **motorcar.** 5. an elevator cage. 6. the part of a balloon for carrying crew and equipment.

car., carat; carats.

ca·ra·ba·o (kä'rə-bä'ō), *n.* [*pl.* CARABAOS (-ōz), CARABAO; see PLURAL, II, D, 1], [Sp. < Malay *karbau*], in the Philippines, a water buffalo.

car·a·bin (kar'ə-bin), *n.* a carbine.

car·a·bine (kar'ə-bīn'), *n.* a carbine.

car·a·bi·neer, car·a·bi·nier (kar'ə-bə-nêr'), *n.* [Fr. *carabinier*], a cavalryman armed with a carbine.

‡**ca·ra·bi·nie·ri** (kä'rä-bē-nye'rē), *n.pl.* [*sing.* CARABINIERE (-re)], [It. < Fr. *carabinier*, carabineer], the Italian police.

car·a·cal (kar'ə-kal'), *n.* [Fr.; Turk. *qarah-qulaq* < *qara*, black + *qulaq*, ear], 1. a reddish-brown lynx of southwestern Asia, with black-tipped ears. 2. its fur.

Car·a·cal·la (kar'ə-kal'ə), *n.* (*Marcus Aurelius Antoninus*), Roman emperor (211–217 A.D.); lived 188–217.

ca·ra·ca·ra (kä'rə-kä'rə), *n.* [Sp. *caracará* < Braz. native name], any of several large, vulturelike hawks of South America.

Ca·ra·cas (kə-rä'kəs; Sp. kä-rä'käs), *n.* the capital of Venezuela: pop., 739,000.

car·ack (kar'ək), *n.* a carrack; galleon.

car·a·cole (kar'ə-kōl'), *n.* [Fr.; It. *caracollo*; Sp. *caracol*, shell of a snail, winding staircase, caracole], in *horsemanship*, a half turn to the right or left. *v.i.* [CARACOLED (-kōld'), CARACOLING], [Fr. *caracoler* < the *n.*], to make a caracole; move in caracoles.

Ca·rac·ta·cus (kə-rak'tə-kəs), *n.* British chieftain who led in resisting the Roman invasion (c. 43–47 A.D.).

car·a·cul (kar'ə-kəl), *n.* [see KARAKUL], 1. a sheep of central Asia. 2. the loosely curled fur made from the hide of its newborn lambs. Also spelled **karakul.**

ca·rafe (kə-raf', kə-räf'), *n.* [Fr. < Sp. *garrafa* or It. *caraffa*; prob. < Ar. *gharafa*, to draw water], a water bottle of glass or crystal; decanter.

car·a·mel (kar'ə-m'l, kar'ə-mel', kär'm'l), *n.* [Fr.; OFr. *calamele*; ? < LL. *calamellus*, tube (dim. of L. *calamus*, a reed, cane), confused with ML. *canna mellis*, sugar cane; L. *canna*, cane + *mel*, *mellis*, honey], 1. burnt sugar used to color or flavor food. 2. a chewy candy made from sugar, milk, etc.

car·a·mel·ize (kar'ə-m'l-īz', kär'm'l-īz'), *v.t. & v.i.* [CARAMELIZED (-īzd'), CARAMELIZING], to turn into caramel.

ca·ran·goid (kə-raŋ'goid), *adj.* [< Mod. L. *Caranx*, *Carangis*, name of the family (< Sp. *caranga*, *carangue*); + *-oid*], of or like a family of fishes characterized by spiny fins, narrow bodies, and widely forked tails, including the pompano, yellowtail, cavalla, **etc.** *n.* a fish of this family.

car·a·pace (kar'ə-pās'), *n.* [Fr.; Sp. *carapacho*; see CALIPASH], the bonelike covering over all or part of the back of certain animals, as the upper shell of the turtle, armadillo, crab, etc.

car·at (kar'ət), *n.* [Fr.; It. *carato*; Ar. *qīrāt*, pod, husk, weight of 4 grains; Gr. *keration*, little horn, carob seed, carat; dim. of *keras*, a horn], 1. a unit of weight for precious stones and pearls, equal to about 3.086 grains troy or .2 of a gram. 2. one 24th part (of pure gold): 20-*carat* gold is 20 parts pure gold and 4 parts alloy. Abbreviated **car., kt.** Also spelled **karat.**

car·a·van (kar'ə-van'), *n.* [Fr. *caravane*; OFr. *karouan*; Per. *kārwān*, caravan], 1. a company of travelers, especially of merchants or pilgrims traveling together for safety, as through a desert. 2. a number of vehicles traveling together. 3. a large covered vehicle for passengers, circus animals, gypsies, etc.; van.

car·a·van·sa·ry (kar'ə-van'sə-ri), *n.* [*pl.* CARAVANSARIES (-riz)], [Fr. *caravansérai*; Per. *kārwānsarāi*, *kārwān*, caravan + *sarāi*, palace, mansion, inn], 1. in the Orient, a sort of inn with a large central court, where caravans stop for the night. 2. a large inn.

car·a·van·se·rai (kar'ə-van'sə-rī', kar'ə-van'sə-rā'), *n.* a caravansary.

car·a·vel, car·a·velle (kar'ə-vel'), *n.* [Fr. *caravelle*; Sp. *caravela*, *carabela*, dim. of *caraba*, small vessel; LL. *carabus* < Gr. *karabos*, kind of light ship, beetle, crayfish], any of several kinds of fast, small sailing ships, especially one with a narrow, high poop and lateen sails, used by the Spaniards and Portuguese in the 16th century: also spelled **carvel.**

car·a·way (kar'ə-wā'), *n.* [ME. *carawai* < Sp. *alcarahueya*; Ar. *al-karawiyā* < Gr. *karon*, caraway], 1. a plant with spicy, strong-smelling seeds. 2. the seeds,

used as a flavoring for bread, cakes, confections, and cheese, and as a carminative.
carb- (kärb), carbo-.
car·bam·ic (kär-bam′ik), *adj.* [*carb-* + *amido* + *-ic*], designating or of the simple amino acid, $NH_2 \cdot COOH$.
car·ba·zole (kär′bə-zōl′), *n.* [*carb-* + *az-* + *-ole*], a white, crystalline substance, $C_{12}H_9N$, occurring in crude anthracene: certain dyes are made from it.
car·bide (kär′bīd, kär′bid), *n.* [*carb-* + *-ide*], a compound of an element, usually a metal, with carbon; especially, calcium carbide.
car·bine (kär′bīn; *in military usage, now often* kär′bēn), *n.* [Fr. *carabine* < *carabin*, mounted rifleman < *escarrabin*, corpse bearer < *scarabée*, a beetle], 1. a rifle with a short barrel, chiefly for use by cavalry: also spelled **carabin, carabine.** 2. in the *United States Army*, a light, semiautomatic, .30-caliber rifle of relatively great fire power and limited range.
car·bi·neer (kär′bə-nêr′), *n.* a carabineer.
car·bi·nol (kär′bə-nōl′, kär′bə-nol′), *n.* [*carbin* (name used by Kolbe for the methyl radical) + *-ol*], methanol (wood alcohol), or any alcohol derived from it, as diethyl carbinol, $(CH_3 \cdot CH_2)_2CHOH$.
car·bo- (kär′bō, kär′bə), a combining form meaning *carbon*, as in *carbohydrate:* also, before a vowel, **carb-**.
car·bo·hy·drate (kär′bə-hī′drāt), *n.* [*carbo-* + *hydrate*], any of certain organic compounds composed of carbon, hydrogen, and oxygen, including the sugars, starches, and celluloses.
car·bo·lat·ed (kär′bə-lā′tid), *adj.* containing or treated with carbolic acid.
car·bol·ic (kär-bol′ik), *adj.* [< L. *carbo*, coal + *oleum*, oil; + *-ic*], designating or of a poisonous acid, C_6H_6O, obtained from coal or coal tar by distillation, and used, in various solutions, as an antiseptic, disinfectant, etc.: also called *phenol.*
car·bo·lize (kär′bə-līz′), *v.t.* [CARBOLIZED (-līzd′), CARBOLIZING], 1. to treat or sterilize with carbolic acid. 2. to add carbolic acid to.
car·bo·loy (kär′bə-loi′), *n.* [*carb*ide + *o* + *alloy*], tungsten carbide, an extremely hard alloy used in the machine-tool industry for its high abrasive quality: a trade-mark (**Carboloy**).
car·bon (kär′bən), *n.* [Fr. *carbone* < L. *carbo, carbonis*, coal], 1. a nonmetallic chemical element found in many inorganic compounds and all organic compounds: diamond and graphite are pure carbon; carbon is also present, with other substances, in coal, coke, charcoal, soot, etc.: a radioactive isotope of carbon (**carbon 14**) is used in dating archaeological specimens, fossils, etc. and in biochemical research: symbol, C; at. wt., 12.01; at. no., 6: abbreviated **C., c.** 2. a sheet of carbon paper. 3. a carbon copy. 4. in *electricity, a*) a stick of carbon used in an arc lamp. *b*) a carbon plate or rod used in a battery. *adj.* 1. of, containing, or treated with carbon. 2. like carbon.
car·bo·na·ceous (kär′bə-nā′shəs), *adj.* 1. of, consisting of, or containing carbon. 2. containing or like coal.
car·bo·na·do (kär′bə-nā′dō), *n.* [*pl.* CARBONADOES, CARBONADOS (-dōz)], [Sp. *carbonada* < *carbon*, charcoal < L. *carbo*, coal], 1. a piece of meat, often fish or fowl, scored and broiled. 2. a massive form of diamond characterized by opacity and dark color, used for drills: also called *black diamond. v.t.* [CARBONADOED (-dōd), CARBONADOING], 1. to score and then broil (meat). 2. to cut gashes in; slash; hack.
‡**Car·bo·na·ri** (kär′bô-nä′rē), *n.pl.* [*sing.* CARBONARO (-rô], [It., pl. of *carbonaro*, charcoal burner (< L. *carbonarius* < *carbo*, coal): said to be so named from meeting among the charcoal burners and using their jargon], an Italian revolutionary group organized about 1811 to establish a united republican Italy.
car·bon·a·ta·tion (kär′bən-i-tā′shən), *n.* carbonation (sense 1): the preferred form in chemistry.
car·bon·ate (kär′bən-it, kär′bə-nāt′), *n.* [Fr.; see CARBON & -ATE], a salt or ester of carbonic acid. *v.t.* (kär′bə-nāt′), [CARBONATED (-id), CARBONATING], 1. to burn to carbon; carbonize. 2. to charge with carbon dioxide. 3. in *chemistry*, to change into a carbonate.
car·bon·a·tion (kär′bə-nā′shən), *n.* 1. the saturation of water with carbon dioxide, as in the manufacture of soda water: cf. **carbonatation.** 2. the removal of lime, as in sugar refining, by precipitating it with carbon dioxide. 3. carbonization.
carbon bisulfide, carbon disulfide.
carbon copy, 1. a copy, as of a letter, made with carbon paper: abbreviated **cc, C.C., c.c.** 2. [Colloq.], any person or thing very much like another.
Car·bon·dale (kär′bən-dāl′), *n.* a mining town in northeastern Pennsylvania: pop., 15,000.
carbon dioxide, a colorless, odorless gas, CO_2, somewhat heavier than air, that passes out of the lungs in respiration: in photosynthesis, carbon dioxide and water are absorbed by plants, which synthesize certain carbohydrates and release oxygen into the air.
carbon disulfide, a heavy, volatile, colorless liquid, CS_2, highly inflammable and poisonous, used as a solvent, preservative, insecticide, etc.
car·bon·ic (kär-bon′ik), *adj.* 1. of or containing carbon. 2. obtained from carbon.
carbonic acid, a weak, colorless acid, H_2CO_3, formed by the solution of carbon dioxide in water and existing only in solution.
car·bon·ic-ac·id gas (kär-bon′ik-as′id), carbon dioxide.
car·bon·if·er·ous (kär′bə-nif′ẽr-əs), *adj.* [< *carbon* + *-ferous*], 1. producing or containing carbon or coal. 2. [C-], designating or of a great coal-making period of the Paleozoic Era: the warm, damp climate produced great forests, which later formed rich coal seams.
the Carboniferous, 1. the Carboniferous Period. 2. the rock and coal strata formed during this period. See **geology**, chart.
car·bon·i·za·tion (kär′bən-i-zā′shən, kär′bən-ī-zā′shən), *n.* a carbonizing or being carbonized.
car·bon·ize (kär′bə-nīz′), *v.t.* [CARBONIZED (-nīzd′), CARBONIZING], 1. to change into carbon, as by partial burning. 2. to treat, cover, or combine with carbon.
carbon monoxide, a colorless, odorless, highly poisonous gas, CO, produced by the incomplete combustion of any carbonaceous material: it burns with a pale-blue flame.
carbon paper, 1. very thin paper coated on one side with a carbon preparation or similar dark-colored substance: it is placed between two sheets of paper so that the pressure of writing, drawing, etc. on the upper sheet makes a copy on the lower. 2. paper used in the carbon process.
carbon process, a method of printing light-resisting photographs on paper coated with gelatin and pigment.
carbon tetrachloride, a noninflammable, colorless liquid, CCl_4, used in fire extinguishers, as a solvent for fats (in cleaning mixtures), etc.
car·bon·yl (kär′bən-il′), *n.* [*carbon* + *-yl*], in *chemistry*, 1. the bivalent radical CO. 2. any of a series of metal compounds containing this radical.
carbonyl chloride, a colorless, volatile, highly poisonous gas, $COCl_2$, prepared by the reaction of carbon monoxide and chlorine in the presence of activated carbon: also called *phosgene.*
car·bon·yl·ic (kär′bə-nil′ik), *adj.* of or containing carbonyl.
car·bo·run·dum (kär′bə-run′dəm), *n.* [*carb*on + *corundum*], a very hard abrasive substance, a compound of carbon and silicon, SiC, made into grindstones, etc.: a trade-mark (**Carborundum**).
car·box·yl (kär-bok′sil), *n.* [< *carb-* + *oxygen* + *-yl*], the univalent radical CO_2H, occurring in the fatty acids and most other organic acids.
car·box·yl·ic (kär′bok-sil′ik), *adj.* of or containing carboxyl.
car·boy (kär′boi), *n.* [< Per. *qarābah*, large bottle], a large glass bottle enclosed for protection in basketwork or in a wooden crate: used especially as a container for corrosive liquids.
car·bun·cle (kär′buŋ-k'l), *n.* [ME.; OFr. *carbuncle, charboucle;* L. *carbunculus*, a little coal, gem < *carbo*, coal], 1. any of certain deep-red gems, especially a garnet with a smooth, convex surface. 2. a painful, localized, pus-bearing inflammation of the tissue beneath the skin, more severe than a boil and having several openings. 3. any pimple.
car·bun·cu·lar (kär-buŋ′kyoo-lẽr), *adj.* 1. of, or having the nature of, a carbuncle. 2. having carbuncles.
car·bu·ret (kär′bə-rāt′, kär′byoo-ret′), *v.t.* [CARBURETED or CARBURETTED (-id), CARBURETING or CARBURETTING], [*carb-* + *-uret* (< Fr. *-ure*, as in *sulfure*)], 1. to combine chemically with carbon. 2. to mix or charge (gas or air) with volatile compounds of carbon in order to increase the potential heat energy.
car·bu·ret·ant (kär′bə-rāt″'nt, kär′byoo-ret″'nt), *n.* a substance, as gasoline or benzene, added to air or gas to carburet it.
car·bu·re·tion (kär′bə-rā′shən, kär′byoo-resh′ən), *n.* a carbureting or being carbureted.
car·bu·re·tor, car·bu·ret·tor (kär′bə-rā′tẽr, kär′byoo-ret′ẽr), *n.* an apparatus for carbureting air or gas; especially, a device in which air is mixed with gasoline spray to make an explosive mixture in an internal-combustion engine.
car·bu·ri·za·tion (kär′bẽr-i-zā′shən, kär′byoo-ri-zā′shən), *n.* a carburizing or being carburized.
car·bu·rize (kär′bə-rīz′, kär′byoo-rīz′), *v.t.* [CARBURIZED (-rīzd′), CARBURIZING], [< Fr. *carbure*, carbide, hydrocarbon; + *-ize*], to treat or combine with carbon; especially, to treat (iron) by heating in contact with carbon in making case-hardened steel.
car·byl·a·mine (kär′bil-ə-mēn′, kär′bil-am′in), *n.* [< *carbyl*], any of a group of organic cyanides, containing the radical NC.
car·ca·jou (kär′kə-jōō′, kär′kə-zhōō′), *n.* [Canad. Fr. <

native Ind. name], 1. the wolverine. 2. loosely, the cougar, Canada lynx, or American badger.

car·ca·net (kär′kə-net′), *n.* [dim. of Fr. *carcan*, iron collar, as on pillories; ML. *carcannum* < OHG. *kwerka*, throat], [Archaic], an ornamental collar, band, or necklace, usually of gold and often jeweled.

car·cass, car·case (kär′kəs), *n.* [ME. *carkeis, carcais;* OFr. *carcois, charquois;* also < Fr. *carcasse;* It. *carcassa* < same (unknown) source], 1. the dead body of any animal. 2. the body, living or dead, of a human being: scornful or humorous usage. 3. the worthless remains of something, especially its outer shell or semblance. 4. the framework, skeleton, or base structure, as of a ship, building, tire, etc. —*SYN.* see **body.**

Car·cas·sonne (kȧr′kȧ′sôn′), *n.* a city in southern France: pop., 38,000 (1946).

car·cin·o·gen (kär-sin′ə-jən, kär′sin-ə-jen′), *n.* [*carcinoma* + *-gen*], any substance that produces cancer.

car·ci·no·ma (kär′sə-nō′mə), *n.* [*pl.* CARCINOMAS (-məz), CARCINOMATA (-mə-tə)], [L.; Gr. *karkinōma*, cancer < *karkinoun*, to affect with a cancer < *karkinos*, a crab, cancer], any of several kinds of epithelial cancer.

car·ci·no·ma·to·sis (kär′sə-nō′mə-tō′sis), *n.* [see CARCINOMATOUS & -OSIS], a condition in which cancers are spread extensively throughout the body.

car·ci·nom·a·tous (kär′sə-nom′ə-təs, kär′sə-nō′mə-təs), *adj.* [see CARCINOMA], of, having the nature of, or affected by cancer.

card (kärd), *n.* [ME. *carde;* OFr. *carte;* LL. *carta, charta*, a card, paper; L. *charta*, leaf of paper, tablet; Gr. *chartēs*, leaf of paper, layer of papyrus], 1. a flat, stiff piece of thick paper or thin pasteboard, usually rectangular; especially, *a)* one of a pack of small, specially marked cards used in playing various games; playing card: see also **cards.** *b)* the dial of a compass; compass card. *c)* a post card. *d)* a calling card. *e)* a written, printed, or engraved announcement or invitation: as, a wedding *card.* *f)* a card bearing a message or greeting, and, sometimes, appropriate pictures, etc., for some occasion: as, a birthday *card.* *g)* a card to advertise or announce an event, product, etc.: as, a window *card.* *h)* the printed program or record form for sporting events, etc.: as, a race *card;* hence, 2. an event or attraction as described in a printed program: as, a drawing *card.* 3. [Colloq.], a person who attracts attention by his wit, eccentricity, etc. *v.t.* 1. to provide with a card. 2. to put on a card. 3. to list on cards for filing, cataloguing, etc.

card up one's sleeve, a plan or resource kept secret or held in reserve.

in (or **on**) **the cards,** likely to occur; probable or possible: from the use of cards in fortune-telling.

put (or **lay**) **one's cards on the table,** to reveal frankly one's intentions, schemes, resources, etc.

speak by the card, to be precise or assured in speech, as if referring to points on a compass card.

card (kärd), *n.* [ME. & Fr. *carde;* Pr. *carda* < *cardar*, to card < LL. **caritare* < L. *carere*, to card (akin to Eng. *sheer*); sp. affected by association with LL. *cardus*, a card, thistle < L. *carduus*, thistle], a metal comb or wire brush for raising the nap on cloth or disentangling the fibers of wool, cotton, flax, etc. *v.t.* to use such a comb or brush on, as in preparing wool for spinning.

Card., Cardinal.

car·da·mom, car·da·mum (kär′də-məm), *n.* [L. *cardamomum;* Gr. *kardamōmon* < *kardamon*, cress + *amōmon*, spice plant], 1. an Asiatic herb of the ginger family. 2. its seed capsule or seed, used in medicine and as a spice.

car·da·mon (kär′də-mən), *n.* cardamom.

card·board (kärd′bôrd′, kärd′bōrd′), *n.* a material made of paper pulp but thicker and stiffer than paper; pasteboard: it is used for making cards, boxes, etc.

card·case (kärd′kās′), *n.* a pocket case, usually of leather, in which to carry calling cards.

Cár·de·nas (kär′di-näs′; Sp. kär′*the*-näs′), *n.* a seaport on the northwestern coast of Cuba: pop., 41,000.

Cár·de·nas, Lá·za·ro (lä′sä-rô′ kär′de-näs′; Eng. kär′di-näs′), 1895– ; Mexican general and statesman; president of Mexico (1934–1940).

card·er (kär′dẽr), *n.* a person or machine that cards wool, cotton, etc.

card file, a collection of cards containing data or records, arranged systematically, as in alphabetical order, in boxes or drawers: also called *card catalogue.*

car·di·ac (kär′di-ak′), *adj.* [Fr. *cardiaque;* L. *cardiacus;* Gr. *kardiakos* < *kardia*, the heart], 1. of or near the heart. 2. relating to the upper part of the stomach. *n.* a medicine that stimulates cardiac action.

car·di·a·cal (kär-dī′ə-k'l), *adj.* cardiac.

car·di·al·gi·a (kär′di-al′ji-ə), *n.* [Mod. L.; Gr. *kardialgia* < *kardia*, heart + *algos*, pain: so named because mistakenly thought to be located in the heart], a feeling of pain or discomfort in the esophagus or stomach, resulting from certain digestive disorders; heartburn.

Car·diff (kär′dif), *n.* a city in Wales, on the Bristol Channel: pop., 236,000 (est. 1946).

Car·di·gan (kär′di-gən), *n.* 1. Cardiganshire. 2. the county seat of Cardiganshire: pop., 3,000.

car·di·gan (kär′di-gən), *n.* [after 7th Earl of *Cardigan* (1797–1868)], a knitted woolen jacket; sweater that opens down the front: also **cardigan jacket** (or **sweater**).

Car·di·gan Bay (kär′di-gən), a part of St. George's Channel, off the west coast of Wales.

Car·di·gan·shire (kär′di-gən-shir′), *n.* a county of southern Wales: pop., 55,000; county seat, Cardigan: also **Cardigan.**

car·di·nal (kär′d'n-əl, kär′di-n'l), *adj.* [ME.; OFr.; L. *cardinalis* < *cardo*, hinge, that on which something turns or depends], 1. on which something hinges or depends; fundamental; principal; chief. 2. bright-red, like the robe of a cardinal. *n.* [ME.; Fr.; It. *cardinale;* LL. *cardinalis*, a cardinal < the L. *adj.*], 1. one of the seventy Roman Catholic officials appointed by the Pope to his council: they elect a new pope from among themselves: abbreviated **Card.** (as a title). 2. bright red. 3. a woman's short cloak, originally red and usually hooded. 4. the cardinal bird. 5. a cardinal number.

car·di·nal·ate (kär′d'n-əl-āt′, kär′di-n'l-āt′), *n.* [Fr. *cardinalat;* LL. *cardinalatus*], 1. the position or rank of a cardinal. 2. the Pope's council of cardinals.

cardinal bird, a bright-red American songbird, related to the finch: also **cardinal, cardinal grosbeak.**

cardinal flower, 1. the bright-red flower of a North American plant that grows in damp, shady places or in shallow water. 2. this plant.

cardinal number (or **numeral**), any number used in counting or showing how many (e. g., two, forty, 627, etc.): distinguished from *ordinal number* (e.g., second, fortieth, 627th, etc.).

cardinal points, the four principal points of the compass; north, south, east, and west.

car·di·nal·ship (kär′d'n-əl-ship′, kär′di-n'l-ship′), *n.* [*cardinal* + *-ship*], 1. the state of being a cardinal. 2. the position, rank, or term of office of a cardinal.

cardinal virtues, in *theology*, the basic virtues; prudence, justice, fortitude, and temperance.

card index, a card file.

card·ing (kär′diŋ), *n.* 1. the combing and disentangling of fibers of wool, cotton, etc., to prepare them for spinning. 2. carded fibers.

car·di·o- (kär′di-ō, kär′di-ə), [< Gr. *kardia*, the heart], a combining form meaning *of the heart*, as in *cardiograph:* also, before a vowel, **cardi-.**

car·di·o·gram (kär′di-ə-gram′), *n.* [*cardio-* + *-gram*], a record of the heart's action, traced by a cardiograph.

car·di·o·graph (kär′di-ə-graf′, kär′di-ə-gräf′), *n.* [*cardio-* + *-graph*], an instrument for making a graph of the heart's action.

car·di·og·ra·phy (kär′di-og′rə-fi), *n.* the use of a cardiograph; recording the action of the heart.

car·di·oid (kär′di-oid′), *adj.* [Gr. *kardioeidēs*, heart-shaped < *kardia*, the heart + *eidos*, shape], heart-shaped. *n.* in *mathematics*, a curve more or less in the shape of a heart, traced by a point on the circumference of a circle that rolls around the circumference of another equal circle.

car·di·ol·o·gy (kär′di-ol′ə-ji), *n.* [*cardio-* + *-logy*], the study of the heart, its functions, and its diseases.

car·di·tis (kär-dī′tis), *n.* [Mod. L. < Gr. *kardia*, the heart; + *-itis*], inflammation of the heart.

car·doon (kär-dōōn′), *n.* [Fr. *cardon* < *carde;* see CHARD], a plant with edible stalks, resembling the thistle and related to the artichoke.

Car·do·zo, Benjamin Nathan (kär-dō′zō), 1870–1938; American jurist and author; associate justice, United States Supreme Court (1932–1938).

cards (kärdz), *n.pl.* 1. a game or games played with a deck of cards, as bridge, rummy, poker, pinochle, etc. 2. the playing of such games; card playing.

card·sharp (kärd′shärp′), *n.* a professional swindler at cards.

card·sharp·er (kärd′shär′pẽr), *n.* a cardsharp.

card table, a table for card playing; especially, a small, square table with folding legs.

car·du·a·ceous (kär′jōō-ā′shəs), *adj.* [< L. *carduus*, thistle; + *-aceous*], of a family of thistlelike plants (called *thistle family* or *aster family*) with heavy heads of purple, tubular flowers.

Car·duc·ci, Gio·suè (jô-swe′ kär-dōōt′chē), 1835–1907; Italian poet; received Nobel prize in literature, 1906.

CARE (kâr), Co-operative for American Remittances to Europe, Inc.

care (kâr), *n.* [ME.; AS. *caru, cearu*, sorrow; akin to Goth. *kara* & G. *kar-* in *karfreitag*, Good Friday; IE. base **ĝar-*, to cry out, scream, as also in L. *garrulus* (cf. GARRULOUS)], 1. *a)* [Obs.], grief; mental pain; hence, *b)* worry; anxiety. 2. close attention; watchfulness; heed. 3. a liking or regard (*for*); inclination (*to* do something). 4. charge; protection; custody. 5. something to worry about, watch over, or attend to. *v.i.* [CARED (kârd), CARING], 1. to be worried or concerned; mind: generally with conditional clauses and often in the negative, as, our parents don't *care* if we go swimming. 2. to wish or like (*to* do something): as, I don't *care* to answer.

care for, 1. to love or like. 2. to wish for; want. 3. to take charge of; look after; provide for.

care of, in the charge of; at the address of: abbreviated **c/o, c.o.** (on mail).
have a care, to be careful; be cautious: also **take care.**
take care of, 1. to have charge of; be responsible for; look after; attend to. 2. to provide for; protect against trouble, want, etc.
SYN.—**care** suggests a weighing down of the mind, as by dread, apprehension, or great responsibility (worn out by the *cares* of the day); **concern** suggests mental uneasiness over someone or something in which one has an affectionate interest (I feel *concern* for their welfare); **solicitude** implies thoughtfulness, often excessive apprehension, for the welfare, safety, or comfort of another (she stroked his head with great *solicitude*); **worry** suggests mental distress or agitation over some problem (his chief *worry* was that he might fail); **anxiety** suggests a restless, uneasy feeling with less mental activity than **worry**, often over some indefinite but anticipated evil (he viewed the world situation with *anxiety*).—*ANT.* unconcern, indifference.

ca·reen (kə-rēn′), *v.t.* [Fr. *carener*, to careen < *carène, carine;* It. *carena;* L. *carina*, keel of a ship], 1. to cause (a ship) to lean or lie on one side for calking, cleaning, or repairing. 2. to calk, clean, or repair (a ship in this position). 3. to cause to lean sideways; tip; tilt. *v.i.* 1. to lean sideways, as a ship under press of sail. 2. to lurch or toss from side to side. *n.* a careening.

ca·reer (kə-rêr′), *n.* [Early Mod. Eng. *careere, carreer;* Fr. *carrière*, road, racecourse; It. *carriera* < *carro;* see CAR], 1. originally, a racing course; hence, 2. a swift course, as of the sun through the sky; hence, 3. full speed. 4. one's progress through life. 5. one's advancement or achievement in a particular vocation; hence, 6. a lifework; profession; occupation. *v.i.* to run or move at full speed; rush wildly.
in full career, at full speed.

ca·reer·ism (kə-rêr′iz'm), *n.* the behavior of a careerist; exclusive or selfish devotion to professional ambitions.

ca·reer·ist (kə-rêr′ist), *n.* [*career* + *-ist*], a person interested chiefly in achieving his own professional ambitions, to the neglect of other things.

career woman, [Colloq.], a woman who follows a professional or business career, often to the exclusion of marriage.

care·free (kâr′frē′), *adj.* free from anxiety, worry, etc.

care·ful (kâr′fəl), *adj.* [ME.; AS. *cearful, carful;* see CARE & -FUL], 1. caring (*for*) or taking care (*of*). 2. watchful; cautious; wary; dealing thoughtfully or cautiously (*with*). 3. accurately or thoroughly done or made; painstaking: as, a *careful* analysis. 4. [Archaic], feeling or causing sorrow, worry, etc.; anxious.
SYN.—**careful** implies close attention to or great concern for whatever is one's work or responsibility, and usually connotes thoroughness, a guarding against error or injury, etc.; **meticulous** implies extreme, sometimes finical, carefulness about details; **scrupulous** implies a conscientious adherence to what is considered right, true, accurate, etc.; **circumspect** implies a careful consideration of all circumstances to avoid error or unfavorable consequences; **cautious** implies a careful guarding against possible dangers or risks; **prudent** implies the exercise of both caution and circumspection, suggesting careful management in economic and practical matters; **discreet** implies the exercise of discernment and judgment in the guidance of one's speech and action and suggests careful restraint; **wary** implies a cautiousness that is prompted by suspicion.—*ANT.* careless, negligent, lax.

care·less (kâr′lis), *adj.* [ME. *careles, kareles;* AS. *cearleas;* see CARE & -LESS], 1. carefree; untroubled. 2. not paying enough attention; not thinking before one acts or speaks; not painstaking; unwary; neglectful; reckless; heedless; inconsiderate. 3. done or made without enough attention, precision, etc.; negligent; not thorough. 4. artless; unstudied: as, a *careless* grace.
careless of, indifferent to; regardless of; untroubled by.

ca·ress (kə-res′), *v.t.* [CARESSED or *archaic* CAREST (-rest′), CARESSING], [Fr. *caresser;* It. *carezzare;* ult. < L. *carus*, dear], 1. to touch, stroke, or pat lovingly or gently; also, to embrace or kiss: often used figuratively, as of a voice, music, etc. 2. to flatter; cajole. *n.* an affectionate touch or gesture, as a kiss, embrace, etc.
SYN.—**caress** refers to a display of affection by gentle stroking or patting; **fondle** implies a more demonstrative show of love or affection, as by hugging, kissing, etc.; **pet**, as applied generally, implies treatment with special affection and indulgence, including patting, fondling, etc., but informally, along with the slang term **neck**, it refers to indulgence, especially by young couples, in hugging, kissing, and amorous caresses; **cuddle** implies affectionate handling, as of a small child by its mother, by pressing or drawing close within the arms; **dandle** implies a playful affection displayed toward a child by moving him up and down lightly on the knee.

ca·res·sive (kə-res′iv), *adj.* caressing; like a caress.

ca·rest (kə-rest′), archaic past tense and past participle of **caress.**

car·et (kar′it, kâr′it), *n.* [L., there is lacking < pp. of *carere*, to want], a mark (∧) used in writing or correcting proof, to show where something is to be added.

care·tak·er (kâr′tāk′ẽr), *n.* a person whose work is to take care of some thing, place, or person; custodian.

Ca·rew, Thomas (kə-rōō′, kâr′ōō), 1595?–1645?; English poet.

care·worn (kâr′wôrn′, kâr′wōrn′), *adj.* worn out by, or showing the effects of, grief and worry; haggard.

car·fare (kär′fâr′), *n.* the price of a ride on a streetcar, bus, etc.

car·go (kär′gō), *n.* [*pl.* CARGOES, CARGOS (-gōz)], [Sp. *cargo, carga*, burden, load < *cargar*, to load, impose taxes; see CHARGE], 1. the load of commodities carried by a ship; freight. 2. load.

Car·i·a (kâr′i-ə), *n.* an ancient country in southwestern Asia Minor.

Car·ib (kar′ib), *n.* [see CANNIBAL], 1. a member of a tribe of Indians who inhabited the southern West Indies and the northern coast of South America. 2. a family of related South and Central American languages.

Car·ib·be·an (kar′ə-bē′ən, kə-rib′i-ən), *adj.* 1. of the Caribs, their language, culture, etc. 2. of the Caribbean Sea, its islands, etc. *n.* a Carib. Abbreviated **Carib.**

Caribbean Sea, a part of the Atlantic, bounded by the West Indies, Central America, and South America: area, c.750,000 sq. mi.

Car·i·bees (kar′ə-bēz′), *n.pl.* the Lesser Antilles.

Car·i·boo Mountains (kar′ə-bōō′), a mountain range in east central British Columbia, Canada.

car·i·bou (kar′ə-bōō′), *n.* [*pl.* CARIBOUS (-bōōz′), CARIBOU; see PLURAL, II, D, 1], [Canad. Fr.; prob. < Algonquian *khalibou, kaleboo*], any of several varieties of North American reindeer.

car·i·ca·ture (kar′i-kə-chẽr, kar′i-kə-choor′), *n.* [Fr.; It. *caricatura*, satirical picture, lit., an overloading < *caricare*, to load, exaggerate; LL. *carricare*, to load; see CHARGE], 1. the deliberately distorted picturing or imitating of a person, literary style, etc. by exaggerating features or mannerisms for satirical effect. 2. a picture, literary work, performance, etc. in which this is done. 3. a bad likeness; poor imitation; something so distorted, ugly, or inferior as to seem a ludicrous imitation. *v.t.* [CARICATURED (-chẽrd, -choord′), CARICATURING], to portray or imitate in or as in a caricature.
SYN.—**caricature** refers to an imitation or representation of a person or thing, in drawing, writing, or performance, that ludicrously exaggerates its distinguishing features; **burlesque** implies the handling of a serious subject lightly or flippantly, or of a trifling subject with mock seriousness; a **parody** ridicules a written work or writer by imitating the style closely, especially so as to point up its peculiarities or affectations, and by distorting the content nonsensically or changing it to something absurdly incongruous; **travesty,** in contrast, implies that the subject matter is retained, but that the style and language are changed so as to give a grotesquely absurd effect; **satire** refers to a literary composition in which follies, vices, stupidities, and abuses in life are held up to ridicule and contempt; **lampoon** refers to a piece of strongly satirical writing that uses broad humor in attacking and ridiculing the faults and weaknesses of an individual.

car·i·ca·tur·ist (kar′i-kə-chẽr-ist, kar′i-kə-choor′ist), *n.* a person who makes caricatures or is skilled in caricature.

car·ies (kâr′ēz, kâr′i-ēz′), *n.* [L., decay; akin to Gr. *kēr*, death, destruction, Sans. *śṛnāti*, he breaks, crushes, Avestan *sari-*, fragment], decay of teeth or bones, or, sometimes, of tissue.

car·il·lon (kar′ə-lon′, kə-ril′yən; Fr. kȧ′rē′yôn′), *n.* [Fr., chime of bells (orig. composed of four) < ML. **quadrilio*, set of four < L. *quattuor*, four], 1. a set of stationary bells, each producing one tone of the chromatic scale, sounded by means of a keyboard or by a clockwork mechanism. 2. a melody played on such bells. 3. an organ stop producing a sound like that of such bells. *v.i.* to play a carillon.

car·il·lon·neur (kar′ə-lə-nũr′; Fr. kȧ′rē′yô′nẽr′), *n.* [Fr.], a carillon player.

Ca·ri·na (kə-rī′nə), *n.* [L. *carina*, keel], a southern constellation, a subdivision of the constellation Argo, containing the bright star Canopus.

ca·ri·na (kə-rī′nə), *n.* [*pl.* CARINAE (-nē)], [L., a keel; cf. CAREEN], in *biology*, a structure or part resembling a keel or ridge.

ca·ri·nal (kə-rī′n'l), *adj.* of a carina.

car·i·nate (kar′i-nāt′), *adj.* [L. *carinatus* < *carina*, a keel], having a ridge down the middle; keel-shaped.

car·i·nat·ed (kar′i-nā′tid), *adj.* carinate.

Ca·rin·thi·a (kə-rin′thi-ə), *n.* a province of southern Austria: pop., 461,000.

car·i·o·ca (kar′i-ō′kə), *n.* [Braz. Port., native of Rio de Janeiro, where the dance originated], 1. a variety of South American dance. 2. music for this.

car·i·ole (kar′i-ōl′), *n.* [Fr. *carriole;* It. *carriola*, dim. of *carro;* see CAR], 1. a small carriage drawn by one horse. 2. a light, covered cart. Also spelled **carriole.**

car·i·os·i·ty (kâr′i-os′ə-ti), *n.* the quality or state of being carious; decay.

car·i·ous (kâr′i-əs), *adj.* [L. *cariosus*], 1. having caries; decayed. 2. corroded.

cark·ing (kär′kiŋ), *adj.* [ppr. of obs. *cark*, to make or be anxious; ME. *carken;* OFr. *carkier;* LL. *carcare* > *carricare*, to load; see CHARGE], [Archaic or Poetic], oppressive; troublesome; annoying: as, *carking* care.

Carl (kärl), a masculine name: see **Charles.**

carl, carle (kärl), *n.* [ME.; AS. *carl*, a man < ON. *karl*, a man, churl; cf. CHURL], 1. [Archaic or Obs.], a peasant, bondman, or villein. 2. [Scot. or Archaic], an ill-bred fellow; churl. 3. [Scot.], a sturdy fellow.

car·line (kär′lin), *n.* [ON. *kerling*, wife, old woman < *karl*, man, male + fem. suffix], [Scot.], 1. a woman; especially, an old woman. 2. a hag; witch.

car·ling (kär′liŋ), *n.* [Fr. *carlingue;* prob. < ON. *kerling;* see CARLINE], any of the pieces of timber running fore and aft between two of the transverse beams supporting the deck of a ship.

Car·lisle (kär-līl′, kẽr-līl′, kär′līl), *n.* a city in northwestern England: pop., 64,000 (est. 1946).

Car·lism (kär′liz′m), *n.* the principles, activities, or claims of Carlists.

Car·list (kär′list), *n.* [< *Carlos* or ML. *Carolus*, Charles], 1. a supporter of Don Carlos or of his heirs. 2. a supporter of Charles X, king of France (1824–1830).

car·load (kär′lōd′), *n.* 1. a load that fills or can fill a car. 2. the minimum weight of a carload lot. Abbreviated **c.l.**

carload lot, a freight shipment large enough to be shipped at a special rate (called *carload rate*).

Car·los, Don (don kär′ləs; Sp. dôn kär′lôs), 1788–1855; Spanish prince, second son of Charles IV; pretender to the Spanish crown (1833).

Car·lot·ta (kär-lot′ə), a feminine name: see **Charlotte.**

Car·lo·vin·gi·an (kär′lə-vin′ji-ən), *adj. & n.* Carolingian.

Carls·bad (kärlz′bad; G. kärls′bät′), *n.* Karlsbad, a town in Czechoslovakia.

Carls·bad Caverns (kärlz′bad), a national park in southeastern New Mexico, containing large caverns filled with stalagmites and stalactites: area, 77 sq. mi.

Carl·son, Ev·ans For·dyce (ev′ənz fôr′dīs kärl′s′n), 1896–1947; United States Marine Corps general in World War II.

Car·lyle, Thomas (kär-līl′), 1795–1881; Scottish historian, philosopher, and essayist.

car·ma·gnole (kär′mən-yōl′; Fr. kȧr′mȧ′nyôl′), *n.* [Fr., altered (after *Carmagnola*, town in Piedmont, occupied by the revolutionaries in 1792) < older *carmignole*, kind of cap (dial. *carmignola*, jacket); prob. ult. < L. *carminare*, to card wool < *carmen*, a card < *carere;* see CARD (to comb)], 1. the short jacket with wide lapels and metal buttons adopted by French revolutionaries (1792) as part of their costume. 2. this costume, including wide black trousers, a red cap, and a tricolored girdle. 3. a soldier of the French Revolution. 4. a lively song and round dance popular during the French Revolution.

car·man (kär′mən), *n.* [*pl.* CARMEN (-mən, -men′)], 1. a streetcar conductor or motorman. 2. [Obs.], a man who drives a wagon or cart; especially, one hired to haul goods; carter.

Car·man, William Bliss (blis kär′mən), 1861–1929; Canadian poet and essayist.

Car·mar·then (kär-mär′*th*ən), *n.* 1. Carmarthenshire. 2. the county seat of Carmarthenshire: pop., 11,000.

Car·mar·then·shire (kär-mär′*th*ən-shir′), *n.* a county of southern Wales: pop., 179,000; county seat, Carmarthen.

Car·mel, Mount (kär′m'l), a mountain in northwestern Palestine: height, 1,800 ft: see **Samaria,** map.

Car·mel·ite (kär′m'l-īt′), *n.* [Fr.; L. *Carmelites*], 1. a mendicant friar of the order of Our Lady of Mount Carmel, founded in Syria about 1160: also called *White Friar*. 2. a nun of this order. *adj.* of this order.

car·min·a·tive (kär-min′ə-tiv, kär′mi-nā′tiv), *adj.* [< L. *carminatus*, pp. of *carminare*, to card, cleanse < *carere*, to card; + *-ive*], expelling gas from the stomach and intestines. *n.* a carminative medicine.

car·mine (kär′min, kär′mīn), *n.* [Fr. *carmin;* ML. *carminus* < *carmesinus*, purple, crimson < Ar. *qirmiz*, crimson; form influenced by L. *minium*, cinnabar red], 1. a red or purplish-red pigment obtained mainly from cochineal. 2. its color. *adj.* red or purplish-red; crimson.

car·nage (kär′nij), *n.* [Fr.; It. *carnaggio* < LL. *carnaticum*, tribute of animals < L. *caro;* see CARNAL], 1. bloody and extensive slaughter, especially in battle; massacre; bloodshed. 2. [Fr.; Pr. *carnatge*, flesh, carrion < *carn*, flesh < L. *caro*], dead bodies, especially on a battlefield. —***SYN.*** see **slaughter.**

car·nal (kär′n'l), *adj.* [ME.; OFr.; L. *carnalis* < *caro, carnis*, flesh], 1. in or of the flesh; bodily; material or worldly, not spiritual; hence, 2. sensual; sexual.

have carnal knowledge of, to have sexual intercourse with.

SYN.—**carnal** implies relation to the body or flesh as the seat of basic physical appetites, now especially sexual appetites, and usually stresses absence of intellectual or moral influence (*carnal* lust); **fleshly,** expressing less censure, stresses these appetites and their gratification as natural to the flesh (*fleshly* frailty); **sensual** stresses relation to or preoccupation with gratifying the bodily senses and usually implies grossness or lewdness (*sensual* lips); **animal** is applied to the physical nature of man as distinguished from his intellectual and spiritual nature, and now rarely carries a derogatory implication (*animal* spirits).

car·nal·i·ty (kär-nal′ə-ti), *n.* [*pl.* CARNALITIES (-tiz)], a carnal condition, nature, act, or manner; sensuality.

car·nall·ite (kär′n'l-īt′), *n.* [after Rudolf von *Carnall* (1804–1874), G. mineralogist], a hydrous chloride of magnesium and potassium, $MgCl_2 \cdot KCl \cdot 6H_2O$.

Car·nar·von (kär-när′vən), *n.* Caernarvonshire.

car·nas·si·al (kär-nas′i-əl), *adj.* [< Fr. *carnassier*, carnivorous < Pr. *carnasa*, bad flesh < *carn;* see CARNAGE], designating or of the last premolar on either side of the upper jaw and the first molar on either side of the lower jaw in flesh-eating animals. *n.* a carnassial tooth.

Car·nat·ic (kär-nat′ik), *n.* a region in southern India: part of Madras state.

car·na·tion (kär-nā′shən), *n.* [Fr. < L. *carnatio*, fleshiness < *caro, carnis*, flesh], 1. formerly, flesh color or rosy pink; now, deep red. 2. any of the cultivated varieties of the clove pink. 3. its fragrant flower of pink, white, or red. 4. *pl.* those parts of a painting that represent flesh.

car·nau·ba (kär-nou′bə), *n.* [Port. < Braz. (Tupi) native name], a Brazilian palm that yields a wax used to make candles; wax palm.

Car·ne·gie, Andrew (kär-nā′gi, kär′nə-gi), 1835–1919; American industrialist and philanthropist, born in Scotland.

car·nel·ian (kär-nēl′yən), *n.* [altered (after L. *caro, carnis*, flesh: because of its color) < *cornelian*], a red variety of chalcedony, used in jewelry: formerly called *cornelian*.

car·ni·fy (kär′nə-fī′), *v.t.* [CARNIFIED (-fīd′), CARNIFYING], [L. *carnificare* < *caro, carnis*, flesh + *facere*, to make], to form into flesh. *v.i.* 1. to form or become flesh. 2. to become fleshlike.

car·ni·val (kär′nə-v'l), *n.* [< Fr. or It.; Fr. *carnaval;* It. *carnevale;* LL. *carnelevarium* < **carnem levare*, to remove meat (see CARNAL & LEVER); associated by folk etym. with ML. *carne vale*, "Flesh, farewell!" < L. *caro* + *vale*, farewell < *valere*, to be strong], 1. the period of feasting and revelry just before Lent: Mardi gras is the last day of this festival. 2. a reveling or time of revelry; festivity; merrymaking. 3. an entertainment with side shows, rides, games, and refreshments, usually operated as a commercial enterprise, sometimes by a social or charitable organization.

Car·niv·o·ra (kär-niv′ə-rə), *n.pl.* [Mod. L., neut. pl. < L. *carnivorus;* see CARNIVOROUS], in *zoology*, an order of flesh-eating mammals, including the dog, wolf, cat, lion, tiger, bear, seal, etc.

car·ni·vore (kär′nə-vôr′, kär′nə-vōr′), *n.* [Fr.], 1. a carnivorous animal: opposed to *herbivore*. 2. a plant that eats insects.

car·niv·o·rous (kär-niv′ə-rəs), *adj.* [L. *carnivorus* < *caro, carnis*, flesh + *vorare*, to devour, eat], 1. flesh-eating: opposed to *herbivorous*. 2. of the Carnivora.

Car·not, Ma·rie Fran·çois Sa·di (mȧ′rē′ frän′swȧ′ sȧ′dē′ kȧr′nō′), 1837–1894; French statesman; president of France (1887–1894).

Carnot, Ni·co·las Lé·o·nard Sa·di (nē′kō′lä′ lā′ô′nȧr′ sȧ′dē′), 1796–1832; French physicist.

car·no·tite (kär′nə-tīt′), *n.* [after the Fr. official, A. *Carnot*], a radioactive mineral containing hydrous potassium uranium vanadate.

car·ob (kar′əb), *n.* [Fr. *carobe, caroube;* It. *carrubo;* Ar. *kharrūbah*, bean pod], 1. an evergreen tree of the Mediterranean area. 2. its long, edible, fleshy seed pod, used especially as fodder: often called *locust, locust pod, St. John's bread*.

CAROB
A, branch; B, fruit

ca·roche (kə-rōch′, kə-rōsh′), *n.* [MFr. *carroche;* It. *carroccia* < ML. **carrautium* < *carracutium* < L. *carrus;* see CAR], in the 17th century, a coach or carriage used for state occasions.

Car·ol (kar′əl), 1. a feminine name: see **Caroline.** 2. [ML. *Carolus;* see CHARLES], a masculine name.

car·ol (kar′əl), *n.* [ME. *carol, carole*, round dance, joyous song or lyric; OFr. *carole*, kind of dance, Christmas song; ML. *choraula*, a dance to the flute < L. *choraules;* Gr. *choraulēs*, flute player who accompanied the choral dance < *choros*, dance + *aulein*, to play on the flute < *aulos*, flute], a song of joy or praise, especially in honor of the Nativity; Christmas song. *v.i.* [CAROLED or CAROLLED (-əld), CAROLING or CAROLLING], to sing in joy; sing; warble. *v.t.* 1. to sing (a tune, etc.). 2. to praise or celebrate in song.

Car·ol II (kar′əl), 1893–1953; king of Romania (1930–1940); abdicated.

Car·o·le·an (kar′ə-lē′ən), *adj.* of Charles I or Charles II of England, or their period; Carolinian.
Car·o·li·na (kar′ə-lī′nə), *n.* an American colony on the Atlantic coast, first settled in 1653: it was divided into North Carolina and South Carolina in 1729.
the Carolinas, North Carolina and South Carolina.
Car·o·line (kar′ə-lin′, kar′ə-lin), [Fr.; It. *Carolina,* fem. < ML. or L. *Carolus;* see CHARLES], a feminine name: variant, *Carol;* diminutive, *Carrie:* also spelled **Carolyn.** *adj.* (kar′ə-lin′), Carolinian (senses 1 & 2).
Caroline Islands, a chain of about 550 small coral islands in Micronesia: area, 380 sq. mi.; pop., 55,000: formerly a Japanese mandate; after World War II under United States trusteeship.
Car·o·lin·gi·an (kar′ə-lin′ji-ən), *adj.* [< ML. *Carolus* (see CHARLES) + Gmc. *-ing,* patronymic suffix], designating or of the second Frankish dynasty, founded (751 A.D.) by Pepin the Short, son of Charles Martel. *n.* a member of this dynasty. Also called *Carlovingian.*
Car·o·lin·i·an (kar′ə-lin′i-ən), *adj.* [< ML. *Carolus;* see CHARLES], 1. of Charlemagne or his period. 2. of Charles I or Charles II of England, or the period in which they lived. 3. [< *Carolina*], of North Carolina or South Carolina. *n.* a native or inhabitant of North Carolina or South Carolina.
car·o·lus (kar′ə-ləs), *n.* [*pl.* CAROLUSES (-iz), CAROLI (-lī′)], [Mod. L., Charles], any of various coins issued during the reign of any of the kings named Charles; especially, a gold coin issued under Charles I of England, worth originally about twenty shillings.
Car·o·lyn (kar′ə-lin), a feminine name: see **Caroline.**
car·om (kar′əm), *n.* [< Fr. *carambole;* Sp. *carambola,* red ball at billiards], 1. in *billiards,* any shot in which the cue ball hits two other balls, either of which may be hit before the other. 2. in *curling,* etc., a shot like this. 3. a hitting and rebounding. *v.i.* 1. to make a carom. 2. to hit and rebound. Also spelled **carrom.**
car·oms (kar′əmz), *n.pl.* [construed as sing.], a game for two or four players, played with 24 round counters on a large, square board with corner pockets.
car·o·tene (kar′ə-tēn′), *n.* [< L. *carota,* carrot; + *-ene*], a red or orange-colored compound, $C_{40}H_{56}$, found in carrots and certain other vegetables, and changed into vitamin A in the body: also spelled **carotin.**
ca·rot·e·noid (kə-rot′ə-noid′), *n.* [< *carotene* + *-oid*], any of several red and yellow pigments related to carotene. *adj.* 1. of or like carotene. 2. of the carotenoids. Also spelled **carotinoid.**
ca·rot·id (kə-rot′id), *adj.* [Gr. *karōtis,* pl. *karōtides,* the two great arteries of the neck < *karoun,* to plunge into sleep or stupor: so called because compression of these causes unconsciousness], designating, of, or near either of the two principal arteries, one on each side of the neck, which convey the blood from the aorta to the head. *n.* a carotid artery.
ca·rot·id·al (kə-rot′i-d′l), *adj.* [cf. -AL], [Obs.], carotid.
car·o·tin (kar′ə-tin), *n.* carotene.
ca·rot·i·noid (kə-rot′i-noid′), *n. & adj.* [*carotin* + *-oid*], carotenoid.
ca·rous·al (kə-rouz′′l), *n.* [< *carouse;* sometimes confused with *carrousel*], a carousing; hilarious drinking party.
ca·rouse (kə-rouz′), *v.i.* [CAROUSED (-rouzd′), CAROUSING], [OFr. *carous* < G. *gar aus,* quite out < *gar austrinken,* to drink quite out: in reference to swallowing all of one's drink], to drink much alcoholic liquor; drink heartily and heavily; participate in a hilarious drinking party or parties. *n.* 1. a carousing; hilarious drinking party. 2. [Obs.], a glassful drunk all at once, especially as a toast.
car·ou·sel (kar′ə-zel′, kar′oo-sel′), *n.* a carrousel.
carp (kärp), *n.* [*pl.* CARP, CARPS; see PLURAL, II, D, 2], [ME. & OFr. *carpe;* LL. *carpa;* prob. < Slavic, with basic sense "rough, scabby"; cf. Russ. *korop*], 1. any of a group of edible fresh-water fishes living in ponds or other tranquil waters. 2. any of various other similar or related fishes, as the goldfish, dace, etc.
carp (kärp), *v.i.* [ME. *carpen;* ON. *karpa,* to brag; prob. influenced by L. *carpere,* to pluck, hence slander], to talk (*on* or *about* something) in a peevish, grumbling, or accusing way; find fault pettily or unfairly; cavil (*at*).
-carp (kärp), [< Gr. *karpos,* fruit], a terminal combining form meaning *fruit,* as in *endocarp, pericarp.*
carp., carpentry.
car·pal (kär′p'l), *adj.* [Mod. L. *carpalis*], of the carpus. *n.* a bone of the carpus; carpale.
car·pa·le (kär-pā′li), *n.* [*pl.* CARPALIA (-li-ə)], [Mod. L., neut. of *carpalis*], a bone of the carpus; carpal.
Car·pa·thi·an Mountains (kär-pā′thi-ən), mountain ranges extending 800 miles between Poland and Czechoslovakia and into central Romania: highest peak, 8,737 ft.
Car·pa·thi·ans (kär-pā′thi-ənz), *n.pl.* the Carpathian Mountains.
Car·pa·tho-U·kraine (kär-pā′thō-ū-krān′), *n.* a region in the Ukrainian S.S.R.: area, c. 4,870 sq. mi.: formerly a province of Czechoslovakia called *Ruthenia.*
‡**car·pe di·em** (kär′pi dī′em), [L., lit., seize the day], seize present opportunities; make the most of today.
car·pel (kär′p'l), *n.* [Mod. L. dim. < Gr. *karpos,* fruit], 1. a simple pistil, regarded as a modified leaf. 2. any of the two or more carpels that unite to form a compound pistil.
car·pel·lar·y (kär′p'l-er′i), *adj.* of or having carpels.
car·pel·late (kär′p'l-āt′), *adj.* having carpels.

CARPEL

Car·pen·tar·i·a, Gulf of (kär′pən-târ′i-ə), a gulf on the northern coast of Australia: length, 480 mi.; width, 420 mi.
car·pen·ter (kär′pən-tẽr), *n.* [ME.; ONorm. Fr. *carpentier;* LL. *carpentarius,* a carpenter, wagon maker < L. *carpentum,* two-wheeled carriage, cart], a workman who builds and repairs wooden articles or the wooden parts of buildings, etc. *v.i.* to do a carpenter's work. *v.t.* to make or repair by or as if by carpentry.
Car·pen·ter, John Al·den (ôl′d'n kär′pən-tẽr), 1876–1951; American composer.
carpenter bee, any of several kinds of solitary bees that bore long tunnels in timber and lay eggs in these.
car·pen·try (kär′pən-tri), *n.* [ME. & OFr. *carpenterie*], the work or trade of a carpenter: abbreviated **carp.**
car·pet (kär′pit), *n.* [ME. *carpette;* OFr. *carpite,* a carpet, kind of cloth; LL. *carpita, carpeta,* thick woolen cloth < pp. of L. *carpere,* to card, pluck], 1. a thick, heavy fabric of wool, jute, etc. for covering a floor, originally woven or felted, now often piled like a rug. 2. a strip, or several joined strips, of such fabric, used for covering a floor, stairs, etc. 3. any covering resembling or suggesting a carpet. *v.t.* to cover with or as with a carpet.
on the carpet, 1. under consideration. 2. in the position of, or into a place for, being reprimanded.
car·pet·bag (kär′pit-bag′), *n.* an old-fashioned variety of traveling bag, made of carpeting.
car·pet·bag·ger (kär′pit-bag′ẽr), *n.* 1. any of the Northern politicians or adventurers who went South to take advantage of unsettled conditions after the Civil War: contemptuous term, referring to the fact that such men usually carried all their belongings in a single carpetbag. 2. any wandering or irresponsible politician, promoter, etc. 3. in England, a candidate for or member of Parliament who does not actually live in the district he represents, or who moved there for political reasons.
carpet beetle (or **bug**), a black beetle whose larvae feed on furs and woolens, especially carpets.
car·pet·ing (kär′pit-iŋ), *n.* carpets or carpet fabric.
carpet knight, a knight or soldier who has never been in combat and lives in comfort: disparaging term.
carpet sweeper, a hand-operated device for sweeping carpets and rugs: when it is pushed over the floor, a revolving brush picks up dirt.
car·pet·weed (kär′pit-wēd′), *n.* a weed that grows close to the ground, forming a mat.
car·pi (kär′pī), *n.* plural of **carpus.**
-car·pic (kär′pik), -carpous.
carp·ing (kär′piŋ), *adj.* [ppr. of *carp*], tending to find fault; captious; caviling. —*SYN.* see **critical.**
car·po- (kär′pō, kär′pə), [< Gr. *karpos,* fruit], a combining form meaning *fruit* or *seeds,* as in *carpology.*
car·po·go·ni·um (kär′pə-gō′ni-əm), *n.* [*pl.* CARPOGONIA (-ə)], [*carpo-* + *-gonium* < Gr. *gignesthai,* to be born], in botany, the female reproductive organ in plants that do not have flowers or seeds, as ferns, algae, etc.
car·pol·o·gy (kär-pol′ə-ji), *n.* [*carpo-* + *-logy*], the study of the structure of fruits and seeds.
car·poph·a·gous (kär-pof′ə-gəs), *adj.* [Gr. *karpophagos* < *karpos,* fruit + *phagein,* to eat], fruit-eating.
car·po·phore (kär′pə-fôr′, kär′pə-fōr′), *n.* [*carpo-* + *-phore*], in *botany,* the lengthened axis to which the carpels are attached.
car·port (kär′pôrt′, kär′pōrt′), *n.* a shelterfo r an automobile, consisting of a roof extended from the side of a building, sometimes with an additional wall.
car·po·spore (kär′pə-spôr′, kär′pə-spōr′), *n.* in *botany,* a spore developed from the fertilized carpogonium in the red algae.
-car·pous (kär′pəs), [< Gr. *karpos,* fruit], a terminal combining form meaning *fruited; having* (a certain number of) *fruits* or (a certain kind of) *fruit,* as in *monocarpous, apocarpous.*
car·pus (kär′pəs), *n.* [*pl.* CARPI (-pī)], [Mod. L. < Gr. *karpos,* wrist], 1. the wrist. 2. the wrist bones: see **skeleton,** illus.

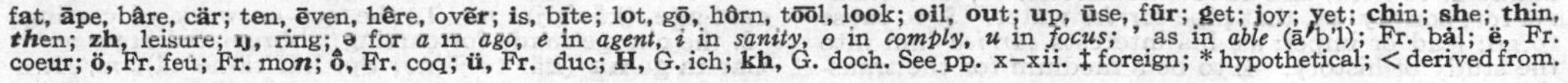
fat, āpe, bâre, cär; ten, ēven, hêre, ovẽr; is, bīte; lot, gō, hôrn, tōōl, look; oil, out; up, ūse, fũr; get; joy; yet; chin; she; thin, *th*en; zh, leisure; ŋ, ring; ə for *a* in *ago, e* in *agent, i* in *sanity, o* in *comply, u* in *focus;* ′ as in *able* (ā′b'l); Fr. bál; ë, Fr. coeur; ö, Fr. feu; Fr. mon; ô, Fr. coq; ü, Fr. duc; H, G. ich; kh, G. doch. See pp. x–xii. ‡ foreign; * hypothetical; < derived from.

car·rack (kar′ək), *n.* [OFr. *carraque, caraque;* Sp. *carraca;* Ar. *qarāqir*, pl. of *qurqūr*, merchant ship < Gr. *kerkouros*, light vessel with a long stern < *kerkos*, tail + *oura*, tail, rear], a galleon: also spelled **carack**.

car·ra·geen, car·ra·gheen (kar′ə-gēn′), *n.* [< *Carrageen*, near Waterford, Ireland], a purplish, edible seaweed: when dried, also called *Irish moss*.

Car·ran·za, Ve·nus·tia·no (ve′nōō-styä′nô kär-rän′sä; Eng. kə-ran′zə), 1859–1920; Mexican statesman; president of Mexico (1915–1920).

Car·ra·ra (kə-rä′rə; It. kär-rä′rä), *n.* a city in northwestern Italy: pop., 59,000: a fine white marble is found near by.

Car·rel, Alexis (kar′əl, kə-rel′), 1873–1944; French surgeon and biologist in America (1905–1939); received Nobel prize in medicine, 1912.

car·rel, car·rell (kar′əl), *n.* [var. of *carol, n.*, in obs. sense "small study in a cloister"], a small enclosure or space in the stack room of a library, designed for study or reading by individual patrons.

car·riage (kar′ij), *n.* [ME. *cariage*, baggage, transport; ONorm. Fr. *cariage*, a cart, carriage < *carier;* see CARRY], 1. a carrying; transportation; conveyance. 2. (kar′i-ij), the cost of carrying; transportation charge. 3. a carrying out (*of* affairs, etc.) or way of carrying out; management. 4. manner of carrying the head and body; posture; poise; bearing. 5. conduct; behavior. 6. a four-wheeled passenger vehicle, usually horse-drawn and often private. 7. a wheeled frame or support for something heavy: as, a gun *carriage*. 8. a moving part (of a machine) for supporting and shifting something: as, the *carriage* of a typewriter. —***SYN.*** see **bearing**.

carriage dog, a coach dog; Dalmatian.

carriage trade, the wealthy customers or patrons of a theater, store, etc.: so called because they arrived, formerly, in private carriages.

car·rick bend (kar′ik), a kind of knot for joining two ropes: see **knot**, illus.

carrick bitt, in *nautical usage*, either of the two posts supporting a windlass.

Car·rie (kar′i), a feminine name: see **Caroline**.

car·ri·er (kar′i-ẽr), *n.* [ME. *cariare* < *carien;* see CARRY], 1. a person or thing that carries: as, a mail *carrier*. 2. a person, company, etc. in the business of transporting goods or passengers. 3. a messenger or porter. 4. a carrier pigeon. 5. a container, support, or course in or on which something is carried or conducted, as a mechanical part or device, a water conduit, etc. 6. a person, animal, or thing that carries and transmits disease germs; especially, a person who is immune to the germs he carries. 7. in *chemistry*, a catalytic agent that causes an element or radical to be transferred from one compound to another. 8. in *electricity & radio*, the steady transmitted wave whose amplitude, frequency, or phase is modulated by the signal. 9. in *naval usage*, an aircraft carrier.

carrier pigeon, a pigeon trained to fly over great distances back to a home point, carrying a written message fastened to its leg; homing pigeon.

car·ri·ole (kar′i-ōl′, kar′i-ôl′), *n.* a cariole.

car·ri·on (kar′i-ən), *n.* [ME. *caroin, carion;* ONorm. Fr. *caroigne;* LL. **caronia*, carcass < L. *caro*, flesh], the decaying flesh of a dead body: sometimes used figuratively. *adj.* 1. of carrion. 2. feeding on carrion. 3. like carrion; decaying, rotten, filthy, etc.

carrion crow, 1. the common crow of Europe. 2. the black vulture.

Car·roll, Lewis (kar′əl), (pseudonym of *Charles Lutwidge Dodgson*), 1832–1898; English writer and mathematician.

car·rom (kar′əm) *n.* & *v.i.* carom.

‡**car·ro·ma·ta** (kär′ô-mä′tä), *n.* [Sp. *carromato* < *carro* (< LL. *carrum;* see CAR)], a long, narrow, two-wheeled cart used in the Philippines for handling goods.

car·ron·ade (kar′ə-nād′), *n.* [< *Carron*, Scotland, where it was first made], an obsolete type of short, light cannon of large bore, for use at close range.

car·ron oil (kar′ən), [< *Carron* ironworks (see CARRONADE), where it was used], a liniment, half linseed oil and half lime water, for treating burns.

car·rot (kar′ət), *n.* [Fr. *carotte;* L. *carota;* Gr. *karōton*, carrot], 1. a plant of the celery family, with a fleshy, orange-red root. 2. the root, eaten as a vegetable.

car·rot·y (kar′ət-i), *adj.* 1. orange-red, like carrots: as, *carroty* hair. 2. red-haired.

car·rou·sel (kar′ə-zel′, kar′oo-sel′), *n.* [Fr.; It. dial. *carozello*, kind of tournament involving various exercises, races, tilting at a ring, or the like < *carrozza*, stately carriage < *carro;* see CAR], a merry-go-round: also spelled **carousel**.

car·ry (kar′i), *v.t.* [CARRIED (-id), CARRYING], [ME. *carien;* ONorm. Fr. *carier* < *car;* L. *carrus*, car, cart], I. 1. to take from one place to another; transport, especially in a vehicle: as, *carry* a package, *carry* the mail. 2. to hold, and direct the motion of; be a channel for; convey: as, that pipe *carries* water. 3. to cause to go; lead or impel: as, his interests *carried* him into the study of history. 4. to be a medium for the transmission of: as, the air *carries* sounds. 5. to transfer or extend: as, *carry* a fence over a certain distance, *carry* personal quarrels into politics; hence, 6. to transfer (a figure, entry, account, etc.) from one column, page, time, etc. to the next in order. 7. to capture (a fortress, etc.); hence, 8. to win over, lead, or influence (an audience, class, etc.). 9. to gain support or victory for (a cause, point, etc.); win (an election, argument, etc.). 10. [Archaic or Southern Dial.], to accompany; escort. 11. in *golf*, to go past or beyond (an object or expanse) or cover (a distance) with one stroke. II. 1. to hold or support (something) while moving: as, she is *carrying* the child in her arms. 2. to bear the weight of or responsibility for. 3. to be pregnant with. 4. to bring with it; involve; imply: as, his statement *carries* conviction. 5. to keep with one; have: as, he *carries* a watch. 6. to hold or poise (oneself, one's weight, etc.) in a specified way; hence, 7. to behave (oneself). 8. in *commerce*, *a*) to keep in stock; deal in: as, the shop will *carry* leather goods. *b*) to keep on one's account books, etc. 9. in *farming*, *a*) to bear as a crop; produce. *b*) to support (livestock). 10. in *hunting*, to keep and follow (a scent). 11. in *music*, to bear or sustain (a melody or part), as in singing. *v.i.* 1. to act as a bearer, conductor, etc. 2. to have or cover a range: as, that shot *carried* to the next hill, his voice doesn't *carry* well. 3. to hold the head, etc. in a specified way, as a horse. *n.* [*pl.* CARRIES (-iz)], 1. the range of, or distance covered by, a gun, golf ball, etc. 2. a portage between two navigable bodies of water. 3. a carrying.

carry all before one, to be irresistible; be completely successful.

carry away, to excite great or unreasoning emotion or enthusiasm in.

carry forward, 1. to proceed or progress with. 2. in *bookkeeping*, to transfer from one column, page, book, or account to another.

carry off, 1. to kill: as, the disease *carried off* thousands. 2. to win (a prize, etc.). 3. to handle (a situation), especially with success.

carry on, 1. to do; engage in; conduct. 2. to go on with; continue as before. 3. [Colloq.], to behave in a wild, silly, or childish way.

carry out, 1. to put (plans, instructions, etc.) into practice. 2. to get done; bring to completion; accomplish.

carry over, 1. to have or be remaining. 2. to transfer or extend to another place or later time. 3. to postpone or allow to postpone; continue.

carry through, 1. to get done; bring to completion; accomplish. 2. to keep (a person) going, through trouble or difficulty; sustain.

SYN.—**carry** means to take something from one place to another and implies a person as the agent or the use of a vehicle or other medium; **bear** emphasizes the support of the weight or the importance of that which is carried (*borne* on a sedan chair, to *bear* good tidings); **convey**, often simply a formal equivalent of **carry**, is preferred where continuous movement is involved (a *conveyer* belt) or where passage through a channel or medium is implied (words *convey* ideas); **transport** is applied to the movement of goods or people from one place to another, especially over long distances; **transmit** stresses causal agency in connection with the sending or conducting of things (the telegrapher *transmitted* the message).

car·ry·all (kar′i-ôl′), *n.* [< *cariole*], 1. a light, covered carriage drawn by one horse and having seats for several people. 2. an enclosed automobile having two long seats placed lengthwise and facing each other.

car·ry·all (kar′i-ôl′), *n.* a large bag, basket, etc.

carrying charge, interest charged by brokers, merchants, etc. on the balance owed on a purchase.

car·ry·ings-on (kar′i-iŋz-on′), *n.pl.* [Colloq.], wild, silly, or childish behavior.

car·ry-o·ver (kar′i-ō′vẽr), *n.* 1. something carried over; extension; remainder. 2. a remainder, as of crops, goods, etc., held for future sale. 3. an amount carried forward in an account.

car·sick (kär′sik′), *adj.* nauseated from riding in a streetcar, railroad car, automobile, etc.

Car·son, Kit (kit kär′s'n), (*Christopher Carson*), 1809–1868; American frontiersman.

Car·son City (kär′s'n), the capital of Nevada, near Lake Tahoe: pop., 5,000.

Car·stensz, Mount (kär′stənz), a mountain in the Nassau range, Netherlands New Guinea: height, 16,-404 ft.

cart (kärt), *n.* [ME.; ON. *kartr;* akin to AS. *cræt;* orig., body of a cart made of wickerwork, hamper; IE. base **ger-*, to twist, plait; cf. CRADLE], 1. a small, strong two-wheeled vehicle, drawn by horses or oxen. 2. a light, uncovered wagon or carriage. 3. a small, wheeled vehicle, drawn or pushed by hand. *v.t.* & *v.i.* to carry or deliver (something) in a cart or other vehicle.

put the cart before the horse, to do things backwards; say or arrange things in reverse order.

cart·age (kär′tij), *n.* 1. the act or work of carting. 2. the charge made for carting: abbreviated **ctge.**

Car·ta·ge·na (kär′tə-jē′nə; Sp. kär′tä-he′nä), *n.* 1. a city on the southeastern coast of Spain: pop., 117,000 (est. 1946). 2. a city in Colombia, on the Caribbean: pop., 102,000 (1945).

carte (kärt), *n.* [Fr., a card], 1. a bill of fare: see **à la carte.** 2. [Scot.], *a*) a playing card. *b*) *pl.* a card game or games. 3. [Archaic], a chart or map.

carte (kärt), *n.* [Fr. *quarte*, lit., a fourth; see QUART], in *fencing*, a position of thrust or parry in which the hand is turned palm up: also spelled **quart, quarte.**

Carte, Richard D'Oy·ly (doi'li kärt'), 1844–1901; English producer of Gilbert and Sullivan operas.

carte blanche (kärt' blänsh'; Fr. kȧrt' bläɴsh'), [*pl.* CARTES BLANCHES (kärts' blänsh'; Fr. kȧrt' bläɴsh')], [Fr., white card, i. e., paper bearing only a person's signature and hence allowing the bearer to fill in any conditions he wishes], 1. full authority. 2. freedom to do as one thinks best.

carte de vi·site (kȧrt' də vē'zēt'), [Fr.], 1. a visiting card. 2. a photograph of a person, mounted on a card the size of a visiting card.

car·tel (kär-tel', kär't'l), *n.* [Fr.; It. *cartello*, dim. of *carta;* L. *charta*, piece of paper or papyrus, writing; see CARD (stiff paper)], 1. a written challenge, as to a duel. 2. a written agreement between nations at war, especially as to the exchange of prisoners. 3. [G. *kartell* < Fr. *cartel*], an association of industrialists, business firms, etc. for establishing a national or international monopoly by price fixing, ownership of controlling stock, etc.; trust: see also **monopoly.** 4. [often C-], a political bloc in certain European countries. —***SYN.*** see **monopoly.**

cart·er (kär'tẽr), *n.* a man whose work or trade is driving a cart.

Car·ter, Mrs. **Leslie** (kär'tẽr), (*Louise Carter*), 1862–1937; American actress.

Carter, Nick (nik), 1. a detective in a popular series of dime novels of the late 19th century. 2. the pseudonym of the several authors who wrote this series.

Car·ter·et, John (kär'tẽr-it), first Earl Granville, 1690–1763; English statesman.

Car·te·sian (kär-tē'zhən), *adj.* [< Renatus *Cartesius*, Latinized form of René *Descartes*], of Descartes, his ideas, or his methods. *n.* a follower of Descartes' ideas or methods.

Car·te·sian·ism (kär-tē'zhən-iz'm), *n.* the philosophical and mathematical ideas and methods of Descartes.

Car·thage (kär'thij), *n.* an ancient city and state in northern Africa, founded by the Phoenicians near the present site of Tunis, and destroyed by the Romans (146 B.C.): see **Punic Wars.**

CARTHAGE

Car·tha·gin·i·an (kär'thə-jin'i-ən), *adj.* of Carthage, its people, or culture. *n.* a native or inhabitant of Carthage.

cart horse, a large, strong horse for drawing heavily loaded carts; work horse.

Car·thu·sian (kär-thōō'zhən, kär-thū'zhən), *n.* [ML. *Cartusianus* < L. name of *Chartreux*, France], a monk or nun of a very strict order founded at Chartreuse, France in 1086, by Saint Bruno. *adj.* of or connected with the Carthusians.

Car·tier, Jacques (zhäk kȧr'tyā'), 1491?–1557?; French navigator; discovered St. Lawrence River.

car·ti·lage (kär't'l-ij), *n.* [Fr.; L. *cartilago;* akin to *cratis*, wickerwork; IE. base **quert-*, **querāt-*, to twist together, plait; cf. CRATE], 1. a tough, elastic, whitish animal tissue; gristle: the skeletons of embryos and young animals are composed largely of cartilage, most of which later turns to bone. 2. any part of the body consisting of cartilage.

car·ti·lag·i·nous (kär't'l-aj'ə-nəs), *adj.* [L. *cartilaginosus*], 1. of or resembling cartilage; gristly. 2. having a skeleton made up mainly of cartilage.

cart·load (kärt'lōd'), *n.* 1. as much as a cart holds or can hold. 2. [Colloq.], a large quantity.

car·to·gram (kär'tə-gram'), *n.* [Fr. *cartogramme;* see CARD (stiff paper) & -GRAM], a map showing geographical statistics by means of lines, dots, shaded areas, etc.

car·tog·ra·pher (kär-tog'rə-fẽr), *n.* [see CARTOGRAPHY], a person whose work is making charts or maps.

car·to·graph·ic (kär'tə-graf'ik), *adj.* of cartography; having to do with maps or their makers.

car·to·graph·i·cal·ly (kär'tə-graf'i-k'l-i, kär'tə-graf'ik-li), *adv.* 1. according to cartography. 2. by means of maps or charts.

car·tog·ra·phy (kär-tog'rə-fi), *n.* [< L. *carta, charta;* see CARD (stiff paper), CHART; + *-graphy*], the art or work of making maps or charts: abbreviated **cartog.**

car·ton (kär't'n), *n.* [Fr.; It. *cartone* < *carta;* see CARD (stiff paper)], 1. a cardboard box, especially a large one. 2. a full carton or its contents: abbreviated **C., c.** 3. in *target shooting*, *a*) the white disk within the bull's-eye. *b*) a shot that hits this disk.

car·toon (kär-tōōn'), *n.* [Fr. *carton* < It. *cartone*, both in sense 2; see CARTON], 1. a drawing, as in a newspaper or magazine, caricaturing or symbolizing, often satirically, some action, situation, or person of topical interest. 2. a full-size preliminary sketch, on strong paper, of a design or picture to be copied in a fresco, tapestry, etc. 3. a comic strip. 4. an animated cartoon. *v.t.* to draw a cartoon of. *v.i.* to draw cartoons.

car·toon·ist (kär-tōōn'ist), *n.* a person who draws cartoons.

car·touche, car·touch (kär-tōōsh'), *n.* [Fr.; It. *cartoccio*, cartridge, roll of paper < *carta*, paper; see CARD (stiff paper)], 1. a scroll-like ornament or tablet. 2. on Egyptian monuments, an oval figure containing the name or title of a ruler or deity. 3. formerly, a cartridge or cartridge box. 4. in some fireworks, a case holding the combustible materials.

car·tridge (kär'trij), *n.* [altered < *cartouche*], 1. a cylindrical case of cardboard, metal, or other material, containing the charge, and usually the projectile, for a firearm. 2. any somewhat similar small container, as for recharging a siphon, refilling a razor, etc. 3. a protected roll of camera film. 4. a replaceable unit in the pickup of an electric phonograph, containing the stylus, or needle. Abbreviated **ctg.**

CARTRIDGE

cartridge belt, a belt for carrying cartridges and equipment, as a water canteen, compass, etc.

cartridge clip, a metal container for cartridges, inserted in certain types of firearms.

car·tu·lar·y (kär'choo-ler'i), *n.* [*pl.* CARTULARIES (-iz)], a chartulary.

cart wheel, 1. the wheel of a cart. 2. a kind of handspring performed sidewise. 3. [Slang], a large coin, especially a silver dollar.

Cart·wright, Edmund (kärt'rīt'), 1743–1823; English clergyman and inventor of the power loom, etc.

Cartwright, John, 1740–1824; brother of *Edmund;* English political reformer.

car·un·cle (kar'əŋ-k'l, kə-ruŋ'k'l), *n.* [Fr. *caroncule;* L. *caruncula*, dim. of *caro*, flesh], 1. an outgrowth of flesh, as the comb and wattles of a fowl. 2. in *botany*, a swelling at or near the hilum of a seed.

ca·run·cu·lar (kə-ruŋ'kyoo-lẽr), *adj.* of or like a caruncle.

ca·run·cu·late (kə-ruŋ'kyoo-lit), *adj.* having a caruncle or caruncles.

ca·run·cu·lous (kə-ruŋ'kyoo-ləs), *adj.* caruncle.

Ca·ru·so, En·ri·co (en-rē'kô, kä-rōō'zô; Eng. kə-rōō'sō), 1873–1921; Italian operatic tenor in America.

car·va·crol (kär'və-krōl', kär'və-krol'), *n.* [< Fr. *carvi*, caraway + L. *acer, acris*, sharp; + *-ol*], a thick oily substance, $C_{10}H_{13}OH$, extracted from oil of mint and other essential oils, used as an antiseptic and anesthetic.

carve (kärv), *v.t.* [CARVED (kärvd), CARVING; *archaic* pp. CARVEN (kär'vən)], [ME. *kerven;* AS. *ceorfan;* akin to G. *kerben*, to notch; IE. base **gerbh-*, to scratch, split, seen also in Gr. *graphein*, to draw, write; cf. GRAPH], 1. to make (an object, design, etc.) by or as by cutting: as, *carve* a design on wood, *carve* a career. 2. to shape or decorate by cutting; decorate the surface of with cut figures, etc.: as, the chest is finely *carved.* 3. to divide by cutting; slice: as, *carve* the meat. *v.i.* 1. to carve statues or designs. 2. to carve meat.

car·vel (kär'v'l), *n.* a caravel.

car·vel-built (kär'v'l-bilt'), *adj.* in *shipbuilding*, with the hull planks laid edge to edge to form a smooth surface: distinguished from *clinker-built.*

car·ven (kär'vən), archaic past participle of **carve.** *adj.* [Archaic or Poetic], carved.

carv·er (kär'vẽr), *n.* 1. a person who cuts meat at the table. 2. a person who carves figures out of wood, etc.; sculptor. 3. a carving knife.

Car·ver, George Washington (kär'vẽr), 1864–1943; American botanist and chemist.

Carver, John, 1576?–1621; first governor of Plymouth Colony.

carv·ing (kär'viŋ), *n.* 1. the work or art of a person who carves. 2. carved work, as a design or statue.

carving fork, a fork with a metal guard to protect the hand, used to hold meat being carved.

carving knife, a large knife for carving meat.

Car·y, Alice (kâr'i), 1820–1871; American poet.

Cary, Phoebe, 1824–1871; American poet; sister of *Alice.*

car·y·at·id (kar'i-at'id), *n.* [*pl.* CARYATIDS (-idz), CARYATIDES (-i-dēz')], [< L. pl. *caryatides;* Gr. *karyatides*, priestesses of the temple of Diana at Karyai, in Laconia], a supporting column that has the form of a draped female figure.

CARYATID

car·y·o- (kar'i-ō, kar'i-ə), karyo-.

car·y·o·phyl·la·ceous (kar'i-ə-fi-lā'shəs), *adj.* [< Mod. L. *caryophyllacea*, name of the family < *caryophyllus*, dianthus < Gr. *karyophyllon*, clove tree < *karyon*, nut, seed + *phyllon*, a leaf], 1. of the pink family, a group of plants with bright-colored flowers, opposite or whorled leaves, and stems usually swollen at the joints. 2. having five petals with long claws in a tubelike calyx.

car·y·op·sis (kar'i-op'sis), *n.* [*pl.* CARYOPSES (-sēz), CARYOPSIDES (-si-dēz')], [Mod. L. < *cary-* (see KARY-) + *-opsis*], a small, dry, one-seeded fruit that remains joined with the seed in a single grain, as in barley, wheat, etc.

car·y·o·tin (kar'i-ō'tin), *n.* karyotin; chromatin.

ca·sa·ba (kə-sä'bə), *n.* [< *Kassaba*, town near Smyrna, Asia Minor, whence the melon came], any of several kinds of muskmelon, with a yellow rind and sweet white flesh: also **casaba melon, cassaba**: often called *winter melon.*

Ca·sa·blan·ca (kas'ə-blaŋ'kə, kä'sä-bläŋ'kə), *n.* a seaport in French Morocco, on the Atlantic: pop., 257,000.

Ca·sa Gran·de (kä'sä grän'dā), the main structure of a series of prehistoric ruins in southern Arizona, now constituting a national monument.

Ca·sals, Pa·blo (pä'blô kä-säls'), 1876– ; Spanish cellist and composer in France.

Ca·sa·no·va, Gio·van·ni Ja·co·po (jô-vän'nē yä'kô-pô kä'sä-nô'vä; Eng. kaz'ə-nō'və), 1725–1798; Italian adventurer; known for his *Memoirs.*

Ca·sau·bon, I·saac (ē'zȧk' kȧ'zō'bōn'; Eng. kə-sô'bən), 1559–1614; French theologian and writer.

Cas·bah (käz'bä), *n.* Kasbah, a section of Algiers.

cas·ca·bel (kas'kə-bel'), *n.* [Sp., a small bell, rattle, rattlesnake], a knob behind the base ring or breech of some muzzle-loading cannons.

cas·cade (kas-kād'), *n.* [Fr.; It. *cascata* < *cascare*, to fall < pp. of L. *cadere*, to fall], 1. a small, steep waterfall, especially one of a series. 2. a thing like this; rippling or showering fall, as of sparks, lace, drapery, etc. *v.t. & v.i.* [CASCADED (-id), CASCADING], to fall, or cause to fall, in a cascade.

Cascade Range, a mountain range in western Oregon, Washington, and British Columbia: highest peak, Mt. Rainier, 14,408 ft.

cas·car·a (kas-kâr'ə), *n.* [Sp. *cáscara*, bark; prob. < *casca*, bark, husk, shell < *cascar;* see CASK], 1. a buckthorn growing on the Pacific coast: also called *bearwood, cascara buckthorn.* 2. cascara sagrada.

cascara sa·gra·da (sə-grā'də), [Sp., lit., sacred bark], 1. a mild laxative made from the bark of the cascara (buckthorn). 2. the bark.

cas·ca·ril·la (kas'kə-ril'ə), *n.* [Sp., dim. of *cáscara;* see CASCARA], 1. a West Indian shrub of the spurge family. 2. its aromatic bark, used as a tonic: usually **cascarilla bark.**

Cas·co Bay (kas'kō), a bay on the southwestern coast of Maine, off Portland.

case (kās), *n.* [ME. *cas, case;* OFr. *cas*, an event, chance; L. *casus*, a falling, accident; pp. of *cadere*, to fall], 1. an example, instance, or occurrence: as, a *case* of measles. 2. a person in whom a disease occurs; patient. 3. a state of affairs; set of circumstances; situation; condition: as, state the *case* briefly. 4. a statement of the facts or circumstances, as in a law court, especially the argument of one side: as, the *case* for the defendant was presented by his lawyer. 5. convincing arguments or evidence; just cause or grounds for a statement or action: as, he has no *case.* 6. a legal action or investigation, especially one studied or cited as a precedent. 7. a question or problem: as, this child is a difficult *case.* 8. [Slang], a peculiar person; queer type: as, he's a *case!* 9. [so named because Latin cases were thought of as "falling away" from the nominative; cf. ACCIDENCE], in *grammar, a*) a form taken by a noun, pronoun, or adjective to show its relation to neighboring words. *b*) any such relation, whether expressed by inflection or otherwise. *c*) such forms or relations collectively. *v.t.* [CASED (kāst), CASING], [Slang], to examine carefully; look over: as, he *cased* the house before robbing it. —*SYN.* see **instance.**

in any case, regardless of what happened or may happen; anyhow.

in case, if; in the event that.

in case of, in the event of; if there is; in order to be prepared for.

in no case, by no means; not under any circumstances.

case (kās), *n.* [ME. *case;* ONorm. Fr. *casse;* L. *capsa*, a box, chest < *capere*, to take, contain, hold], 1. a container, as a box, crate, chest, sheath, folder, etc. 2. a protective cover or covering part: as, a watch *case.* 3. a full box or its contents: as, a *case* of beer: abbreviated **C., c., cs.** 4. a set or pair: as, a *case* of pistols. 5. a frame for a window, door, or stairs. 6. in *printing*, one of the shallow compartmented trays in which type is kept: the *upper case* is used for capitals and special characters, the *lower case* for small letters, figures, etc. *v.t.* [CASED (kāst), CASING], 1. to put in a container. 2. to cover or enclose. 3. to fuse (glass) with an overlay of another color.

ca·se·ase (kā'si-ās'), *n.* [*case*in + *-ase*], an enzyme made from bacterial cultures, which dissolves casein and albumin: used in the process of ripening cheese.

ca·se·ate (kā'si-āt'), *v.i.* [CASEATED (-id), CASEATING], in *medicine*, to undergo caseation.

ca·se·a·tion (kā'si-ā'shən), *n.* [< L. *caseatus*, mixed with cheese < *caseus*, cheese], 1. the precipitation of casein to form cheese. 2. in *medicine*, a degenerative process in which tissue changes into a dry, crumbly, cheeselike substance.

ca·se·fy (kā'sə-fī'), *v.t. & v.i.* [CASEFIED (-fīd'), CASEFYING], [< L. *caseus*, cheese; + *-fy*], to make or become cheeselike.

case·hard·en (kās'här'd'n), *v.t.* 1. in *metallurgy*, to form a hard, thin surface on (iron or steel); hence, 2. to make callous or unfeeling.

case history, collected information about an individual or group, for use especially in sociological, medical, or psychiatric studies.

ca·se·in (kā'si-in, kā'sēn), *n.* [< L. *caseus*, cheese; + *-in*], a phosphoprotein that is one of the chief constituents of milk and the basis of cheese.

ca·se·in·o·gen (kā'si-in'ə-jen', kā-sē'nə-jən), *n.* [< *casein* + *-gen*], that protein of milk which produces casein when acted upon by rennin.

case knife, 1. a knife kept in a case; sheath knife. 2. a table knife.

case law, law based on previous judicial decisions, or precedents: distinguished from *statute law.*

case·mate (kās'māt'), *n.* [Fr.; It. *casamatta* < Gr. *chasmate*, pl. of *chasma* (see CHASM); confused with It. *casa*, a house, and *matto*, foolish, dull, dim, dark], a shellproof or armored enclosure with openings for guns, as in a fortress wall or on a warship.

case·mat·ed (kās'mā'tid), *adj.* fortified with or as with a casemate or casemates.

case·ment (kās'mənt), *n.* [< OFr. *encassement*, a frame; see CASE (box)], 1. a hinged window frame that opens outward: a *casement window* often has two such frames, opening like French doors. 2. a casing; covering.

Case·ment, Sir **Roger David** (kās'mənt), 1864–1916; Irish nationalist; hanged by the British as a traitor in World War I.

case·ment·ed (kās'mən-tid), *adj.* 1. having a casement or casements. 2. encased; covered.

ca·se·ose (kā'si-ōs'), *n.* [*case*in + *-ose*], a soluble protein derivative formed during the digestion of casein.

ca·se·ous (kā'si-əs), *adj.* [< L. *caseus*, cheese], of or like cheese.

ca·sern, ca·serne (kə-zũrn'), *n.* [Fr. *caserne;* Pr. *cazerna*, small hut < LL. *quaterna*, four each; *quattuor*, four], *usually in pl.* any of a series of troop barracks near the battlements of a fortified town.

case shot, a quantity of small projectiles enclosed in a single case, as a shrapnel shell, for firing from a gun.

case system, a method of training law students by analyzing and discussing selected cases and decisions rather than by systematic study of textbooks on law.

case work, social work in which the worker investigates a case of personal or family maladjustment, and gives advice and guidance.

case·worm (kās'wũrm'), *n.* any of various insect larvae that build protective cases about their bodies; especially, the caddis worm.

cash (kash), *n.* [Fr. *casse, caisse*, a box, case, money box, cash; Pr. *caissa*, It. *cassa*, a box; L. *capsa*, a box, chest < *capere*, to take, contain], 1. money that a person actually has, including money on deposit; especially, ready money. 2. bills and coins; currency. 3. money, a check, etc., paid at the time of purchase: as, he paid *cash* for the house. *v.t.* to give or get cash for: as, *cash* a check. *adj.* of, for, requiring, made with, or using cash: as, a *cash* sale.

cash in, 1. to turn into cash; get money for. 2. [Slang], to die.

cash in on, 1. to make a profit from. 2. to make profitable use of.

cash (kash), *n.* [*pl.* CASH], [Port. *caixa* < Tamil *kāsu*], 1. any of several East Indian or Chinese coins of small value. 2. a Chinese copper-alloy coin based on the tael: it has a square perforation in the center so that it can be carried on a string.

cash·a (kash'ə), *n.* [? < *cashmere*], soft cloth made of wool and cashmere, used for dresses, coats, etc.

cash-and-car·ry (kash'ən-kar'i), *adj.* 1. with cash payments and no deliveries. 2. operated on a cash-and-carry system.

ca·shaw (kə-shô'), *n.* the cushaw.

cash·book (kash'book'), *n.* a book in which all receipts and payments of money are originally entered.

cash discount, a discount from the purchase price allowed to the purchaser if he pays within a specified period.

cash·ew (kash′o͞o, kə-sho͞o′), *n.* [altered < Fr. *acajou, cajou;* Port. *acajou* < native Braz. (Tupi) name], 1. a tropical evergreen tree bearing kidney-shaped nutlike seeds, each at the end of an edible, pear-shaped receptacle. 2. the nutlike seed.

cash·ier (ka-shêr′), *n.* [Fr. *caissier* < *caisse;* see CASH (ready money)], a person in charge of the cash receipts and payments of a bank, store, restaurant, etc.

cash·ier (ka-shêr′), *v.t.* [D. *kasseren;* Fr. *casser,* to break < LL. *cassare,* to nullify, destroy < *cassus,* empty, futile & L. *quassare;* see QUASH], 1. to dismiss from a position of command, trust, etc., especially with disgrace; discharge. 2. to discard or reject.

cashier's check, a check drawn by a bank on its own funds and signed by the cashier: abbreviated **C.C., c.c.**

Cash·mere (kash-mêr′), *n.* Kashmir.

cash·mere (kash′mêr), *n.* [< *Kashmir,* India], 1. a fine carded wool obtained from goats of Kashmir and Tibet. 2. a soft, twilled cloth made of this or similar wool. 3. a cashmere shawl.

cash on delivery, payment in cash when a purchase or shipment is delivered: abbreviated **C.O.D., c.o.d.**

ca·shoo (kə-sho͞o′), *n.* catechu.

cash register, a device consisting essentially of an adding machine, usually combined with a money drawer, used by merchants, cashiers, etc.: the amount received for each sale is visibly recorded and automatically added to previous receipts.

cas·i·mere, cas·i·mire (kas′ə-mêr′), *n.* cassimere.

cas·ing (kās′iŋ), *n.* 1. the act or process of encasing. 2. a covering or protective outside part; specifically, *a*) a cleaned intestine, as of cattle, used as a sausage container. *b*) the shoe of an automobile tire. 3. a frame, as of a window or door.

ca·si·no (kə-sē′nō), *n.* [*pl.* CASINOS (-nōz), CASINI (-nē)], [It., dim. of *casa;* L. *casa,* a house, cottage], 1. in Italy, a small country house; summerhouse. 2. a public room or building for musical or theatrical performances, dancing, gambling, etc. 3. cassino.

cask (kask, käsk), *n.* [Sp. *casco,* potsherd, cask, hull, helmet < *cascar,* to break < L. *quassare;* see QUASH], 1. a barrel of any size, especially one for liquids. 2. a full cask or its contents; barrelful. Abbreviated **csk.**

cas·ket (kas′kit, käs′kit), *n.* [prob. < OFr. *cassette,* dim. of *casse* (see CASE, box); *-k* by analogy with *cask*], 1. a small box or chest, as for valuables. 2. a coffin, especially a costly one. *v.t.* to put into a casket.

Cas·lon, William (kaz′lən), 1692–1766; English typefounder.

Cas·par, Cas·per (kas′pẽr), [G. *Kaspar;* see JASPER], a masculine name.

Cas·per (kas′pẽr), *n.* a city in eastern Wyoming: pop., 39,000.

Cas·pi·an (kas′pi-ən), *adj.* of or near the Caspian Sea.

Caspian Sea, an inland sea between the Caucasus and Asia: total area, 169,000 sq. mi.

CASPIAN SEA

casque (kask), *n.* [Fr.; see CASK], a helmet.

casqued (kaskt), *adj.* wearing a casque, or helmet.

Cass, Lewis (kas), 1782–1866; American statesman; governor of Michigan Territory (1813–1831); secretary of state (1857–1860).

cas·sa·ba (kə-sä′bə), *n.* a casaba.

Cas·san·dra (kə-san′drə), *n.* [L.; Gr. *Kassandra*], 1. in *Greek legend,* the daughter of Priam and Hecuba: to win her love, Apollo gave her prophetic power, but later, when thwarted, he decreed that her prophecies should never be believed; hence, 2. a person whose warnings of misfortune are disregarded.

cas·sa·tion (ka-sā′shən), *n.* [Fr. < *casser;* see CASHIER, *v.*], abrogation or annulment, as of a court decision, an election, etc.

Cas·satt, Mary (kə-sat′), 1845–1926; American painter.

cas·sa·va (kə-sä′və), *n.* [Fr. *cassave;* Sp. *casabe* < Haitian *kasabi*], 1. any of a number of tropical plants with edible starchy roots: also called *manioc.* 2. a starch extracted from cassava roots, used in making bread and tapioca. 3. bread made from this starch.

Cas·sel (kas′'l; G. käs′əl), *n.* Kassel, a city in Germany.

cas·se·role (kas′ə-rōl′), *n.* [Fr., dim. of *casse,* a bowl, basin; Pr. *casa,* melting pan; LL. *cattia;* ? < Gr. *kyathion,* dim. of *kyathos,* a bowl, pan], 1. a covered earthenware or glass baking dish in which food can be cooked and then served. 2. a mold of rice, mashed potatoes, etc., baked with a filling of vegetables, meats, etc. 3. in *chemistry,* a deep porcelain saucepan with a handle, used for heating or evaporating a substance.

cas·sia (kash′ə), *n.* [L.; Gr. *kasia, kassia,* kind of cinnamon < Heb. *qĕtsīʻāh* < *qātsa,* to strip off bark], 1. cassia bark. 2. a tree that it comes from. 3. any of a group of herbs, shrubs, and trees of the pea family, common in tropical countries: the pods (*cassia pods*) of some of these plants have a mildly laxative pulp (*cassia pulp*); from others the cathartic drug **senna** is extracted. 4. cassia pods. 5. cassia pulp.

cassia bark, the bark of certain tropical evergreen trees, used in adulterating cinnamon: also called *Chinese cinnamon.*

cas·si·mere (kas′ə-mêr′), *n.* [< *Kashmir;* cf. CASHMERE (wool)], a thin, twilled woolen cloth, used for men's suits: also spelled **casimere, casimire.**

Cas·si·no (kə-sē′nō; It. käs-sē′nô), *n.* a town in Italy, between Naples and Rome: pop., 20,000: scene of heavy fighting in World War II.

cas·si·no (kə-sē′nō), *n.* [see CASINO], a type of card game for two to four players: also spelled **casino.**

Cas·si·o·pe·ia (kas′i-ə-pē′ə), *n.* [L.; Gr. *Kassiopeia*], 1. in *Greek legend,* the wife of Cepheus and mother of Andromeda. 2. a northern constellation between Andromeda and Cepheus: see **constellation,** chart.

Cassiopeia's Chair, the five brightest stars in the constellation Cassiopeia: their outline suggests the shape of a chair.

cas·sique (kə-sēk′), *n.* a cacique.

cas·sit·er·ite (kə-sit′ə-rīt′), *n.* [Gr. *kassiteros*], native tin dioxide, SnO_2, the chief ore of tin: it is brown or black and very hard and heavy.

Cas·si·us (kash′əs, kash′i-əs, kas′i-əs), *n.* (*Gaius Cassius Longinus*), Roman general and chief assassin of Julius Caesar; died 42 B.C.

cas·sock (kas′ək), *n.* [Fr. *casaque;* It. *casacca,* long coat; ? < base of LL. *casubla;* see CHASUBLE], 1. a long, close-fitting vestment, generally black, worn as an outer garment or under the surplice by clergymen, choristers, etc.; hence, 2. the position of a clergyman. 3. a clergyman.

cas·so·war·y (kas′ə-wer′i), *n.* [*pl.* CASSOWARIES (-iz)], [Malay *kasuārī*], a large bird of Australia and New Guinea, able to run fast but unable to fly: it is like the ostrich but smaller, and has a brightly colored neck and head.

cast (kast, käst), *v.t.* [CAST, CASTING], [ME. *casten;* ON. *kasta* < Gmc. base **kas-;* IE. base prob. **g-es-* (< *aĝ-,* to put in motion + *-es* augment), seen also in L. *gestare,* to bear, carry (cf. GESTURE)], 1. to put, deposit, or propel with haste or violence; throw; fling; hurl; hence, 2. to deposit (a ballot or vote). 3. to cause to fall or turn; project; direct: as, this evidence may *cast* some light on the crime. 4. to throw out or drop (a net, anchor, etc.) at the end of a rope or cable. 5. to throw out (a fly, etc.) at the end of a fishing line. 6. to draw (lots) or shake (dice) out of a container. 7. to drop (offspring) or bring forth (young), especially prematurely. 8. to throw off; shed; slough: as, the snake *casts* its skin. 9. to throw down; defeat (a wrestler). 10. to add up (accounts), originally by means of counters. 11. to calculate (a horoscope, tides, etc.). 12. to arrange in some system; formulate; distribute. 13. *a*) to form (molten metal, etc.) into a particular shape by pouring or pressing into a mold. *b*) to make by such a method. 14. to choose and assign actors for (a play or its parts); select (an actor) for a certain role or as a character. 15. to twist; turn; warp. 16. in *printing,* to stereotype or electrotype. *v.i.* 1. to throw dice. 2. to throw out a fly, etc. at the end of a fishing line. 3. to vomit. 4. to turn; veer; warp. 5. to add up figures; calculate. 6. to calculate horoscopes, tides, etc.; hence, 7. to make a forecast, diagnosis, estimate, etc.; conjecture. 8. to consider; deliberate; plan. 9. in *hunting,* to scatter in all directions in search for a lost scent. *n.* 1. a casting; throwing; throw; also, way of casting or distance thrown; specifically, *a*) a throw of dice; also, the number thus thrown; hence, *b*) a stroke of fortune. *c*) a turn of the eye; glance; look. *d*) a throw of a fishing line, net, etc. *e*) an overthrow, as in wrestling. *f*) an adding up; calculation; hence, *g*) a conjecture; forecast. *h*) a sample or sign, as of one's abilities, views, etc. 2. a quantity or thing cast in a certain way; specifically, *a*) something thrown up, off, or out, as bait on a line, a pair (of hawks), produce, vomit, excrement, etc. *b*) something formed in a mold, as a statue, etc.; also, the mold. *c*) a plaster form for immobilizing a broken arm, leg, etc. *d*) the set of actors in a play. 3. the form or direction in which a thing is cast; specifically, *a*) an arrangement. *b*) an appearance or stamp, as of features. *c*) kind; quality. *d*) a tinge; shade. *e*) a turn or twist to one side;

tendency; bent. *f*) a slight error of focus (*in*, *to*, or *of* the eye). 4. in *hunting*, a scattering of the hounds to find a lost scent. 5. in *medicine*, a plastic substance formed in the cavities of some diseased organs: as, renal *casts*. —*SYN*. see **throw**.

cast about, 1. to search; look (*for*). 2. to make plans; devise.

cast aside, to discard; abandon.

cast away, 1. to discard; abandon. 2. shipwrecked.

cast back, 1. to refer to something past. 2. to resemble some distant ancestor.

cast down, 1. to turn downward. 2. to sadden; depress; discourage.

cast off, 1. to discard; abandon; disown. 2. to free. 3. to free a ship from a dock, quay, etc., as by releasing the lines. 4. in *knitting*, to make the last row of stitches.

cast on, in *knitting*, to make the first row of stitches.

cast one's ballot, to vote.

cast out, to force to get out or go away; expel.

cast up, 1. to throw up; vomit. 2. to turn upward. 3. to add up; total.

Cas·ta·li·a (kas-tā′li-ə), *n.* [L.; Gr. *Kastalia*], a spring on Mount Parnassus, sacred to Apollo and the Muses: its waters were considered a source of poetic inspiration.

Cas·ta·li·an (kas-tā′li-ən, kas-tāl′yən), *adj.* 1. of Castalia; hence, 2. poetic.

Cas·ta·lie, Cas·ta·ly (kas′tə-li), *n.* Castalia.

cas·ta·nets (kas′tə-nets′, kas′tə-nets′), *n.pl.* [Fr. *castagnette* (*sing.*); Sp. *castañeta* < L. *castanea*, chestnut: so named from the shape], small, hollowed pieces of hard wood or ivory, used in pairs to beat time to music, especially in Spanish dances: they are held in the hand by a connecting cord or ribbon over the thumb, and clapped against each other with the fingers.

CASTANETS

cast·a·way (kast′ə-wā′, käst′ə-wā′), *n.* [ME. in theological sense "reprobate"], 1. a person or thing cast out or off; especially, an outcast. 2. a shipwrecked person. *adj.* 1. thrown away; discarded. 2. shipwrecked; stranded; cast adrift.

caste (kast, käst), *n.* [Fr.; Port. *casta*, breed, race, caste < L. *castus*, pure, chaste], 1. any of the distinct, hereditary Hindu social classes, each formerly excluded from social dealings with the others. 2. any exclusive social or occupational class or group. 3. rigid class distinction based on birth, wealth, etc., operating as a social system or principle.

lose caste, to lose social status or position.

cas·tel·lan (kas′tə-lən), *n.* [ME. & ONorm. Fr. *castellain*; ML. *castellanus*, keeper of a castle; L., inhabitant of a castle (orig., of a castle) < L. *castellum*; see CASTLE], the warden or governor of a castle.

cas·tel·lat·ed (kas′tə-lā′tid), *adj.* [LL. *castellatus* < L. *castellum*; see CASTLE], 1. built with turrets and battlements, like a castle. 2. having many castles, as a district, river, etc.

cast·er (kas′tẽr, käs′tẽr), *n.* 1. a person or thing that casts. 2. a small bottle or other container for serving vinegar, mustard, salt, or other condiments at the table. 3. a stand for holding several such containers. 4. any of a set of small swiveled wheels for supporting and moving furniture or other heavy articles. Also spelled **castor** (in senses 2, 3, 4).

cas·ti·gate (kas′tə-gāt′), *v.t.* [CASTIGATED (-id), CASTIGATING], [< L. *castigatus*, pp. of *castigare*, to purify, chastise < *castus*, pure], to correct or subdue by punishing; chastise; rebuke. —*SYN.* see **punish.**

cas·ti·ga·tion (kas′tə-gā′shən), *n.* [ME.; L. *castigatio*; see CASTIGATE], severe punishment, criticism, or rebuke.

cas·ti·ga·tor (kas′tə-gā′tẽr), *n.* [L.], a person who castigates.

Cas·ti·glio·ne, Conte **Bal·das·sa·re** (bäl′däs-sä′re käs′tē-lyô′ne), 1478–1529; Italian writer and diplomat.

Cas·tile (kas-tēl′), *n.* a former kingdom of central Spain: see **Spain,** map.

Cas·tile soap, cas·tile soap (kas′tēl, kas-tēl′), [< *Castile*, Spain, where first made], a fine, hard soap prepared from olive oil and sodium hydroxide.

Cas·til·i·an (kas-til′yən, kas-til′i-ən), *adj.* of Castile, its people, language, or culture. *n.* 1. a native or inhabitant of Castile. 2. the Castilian form of Spanish, now the standard form of the language.

Cas·til·la la Nue·va (käs-tēl′yä lä nwe′vä), a former province of central Spain: English name, *New Castile.*

Cas·til·la la Vie·ja (käs-tēl′yä lä vye′hä), a former province of central Spain: English name, *Old Castile.*

cast·ing (kas′tiŋ, käs′tiŋ), *n.* 1. the action of a person or thing that casts (in various senses). 2. a thing formed by pouring or pressing a liquid or plastic substance into a mold to harden; especially, a metal piece so formed. 3. in *zoology*, anything thrown off or ejected, as vomit, feathers, dirt thrown up by worms, etc.

casting vote (or **voice**), the deciding vote cast by the presiding officer when the voting on both sides is equal.

cast-i·ron (kast′ī′ẽrn, käst′ī′ẽrn), *adj.* 1. made of cast iron. 2. very hard, rigid, strong, healthy, etc.

cast iron, a hard, unmalleable pig iron made by casting: it contains between 6 and 8 per cent impurities, including a high proportion of carbon, and is very fluid and fusible when molten.

cas·tle (kas′'l, käs′'l), *n.* [ME. *castle, castel*, a castle < AS. & ONorm. Fr.; AS. *castel*, village; ONorm. Fr. *castel*; both < L. *castellum*, dim. of *castrum*, fort], 1. a large building or group of buildings fortified with thick walls, battlements, and, often, a moat: castles were the strongholds of noblemen in the Middle Ages. 2. any massive dwelling that resembles or suggests such a stronghold. 3. a small tower, especially one on an elephant's back or on the deck of a ship. 4. in *chess*, either of the two corner pieces shaped like a castle tower: it can move only in a vertical or horizontal direction: also called *rook*. *v.t.* [CASTLED (-'ld), CASTLING], 1. to put into, or furnish with, a castle. 2. in *chess*, to move (a king) two squares to either side and then, in the same move, set the castle in the square skipped by the king: permitted only when neither piece has been moved before and the spaces between them are not occupied. *v.i.* in *chess*, 1. to castle a king. 2. to be castled.

cas·tled (kas′'ld, käs′'ld), *adj.* 1. having a castle or castles. 2. castellated.

castle in Spain, castle in the air, anything imagined and desired but not likely to be realized; daydream.

Cas·tle·reagh, Viscount (kas′'l-rā′, käs′'l-rā′), (*Robert Stewart*), second Marquis of Londonderry, 1769–1822; British statesman.

cast·off (kast′ôf′, käst′ôf′), *adj.* thrown away; discarded; abandoned; disowned. *n.* 1. a person or thing cast off. 2. in *nautical usage*, a casting off.

Cas·tor (kas′tẽr, käs′tẽr), *n.* [L.; Gr. *Kastōr*], 1. in *Greek & Roman legend*, the mortal twin of Pollux: see **Dioscuri.** 2. one of the two bright stars in the constellation Gemini: the brighter star is Pollux.

cas·tor (kas′tẽr, käs′tẽr), *n.* [Fr.; L.; Gr. *kastōr*, beaver], 1. [Rare], a beaver. 2. castoreum. 3. a hat of beaver or rabbit fur.

cas·tor (kas′tẽr, käs′tẽr), *n.* a caster (in senses 2, 3, 4).

castor bean, 1. the beanlike seed of the castor-oil plant. 2. the plant.

cas·to·re·um (kas-tôr′i-əm, kas-tō′ri-əm), *n.* [L.; Gr. *kastorion*], a strong-smelling, oily substance obtained from the sexual glands of a beaver, used as a stimulant in medicine, and in making perfumes: also **castor.**

castor oil, a colorless or yellowish oil from castor beans, used as a cathartic and as a lubricant.

cas·tor-oil plant (kas′tẽr-oil′, käs′tẽr-oil′), a tropical plant of the spurge family, with large, beanlike seeds from which castor oil is extracted.

cas·tra·me·ta·tion (kas′trə-mi-tā′shən), *n.* [Fr. *castramétation* < L. *castrametari*, to pitch a camp; *castra*, a camp + *metari*, to measure off], the laying out or planning of a military camp.

cas·trate (kas′trāt), *v.t.* [CASTRATED (-id), CASTRATING], [< L. *castratus*, pp. of *castrare*, to castrate, prune; akin to Sans. *śastrám*, a knife], 1. to remove the testicles of; emasculate; geld; hence, 2. to deprive of essential vigor or significance by mutilating, expurgating, etc.

cas·tra·tion (kas-trā′shən), *n.* [L. *castratio*], 1. a castrating or being castrated.

Cas·tro, Fi·del (fē-del′ käs′trô; Eng. kas′trō) (*Fidel Castor Ruz*), 1926– ; Cuban revolutionary leader; prime minister of Cuba (1959–).

cast steel, steel formed by casting, as distinguished from rolling or forging.

cas·u·al (kazh′o͞o-əl), *adj.* [Fr. *casuel*; Sp. *casual*; LL. *casualis*, by chance < L. *casus*, chance, event; cf. CASE (example)], 1. happening or governed by chance; specifically, *a*) not planned; random; incidental: as, a *casual* visit. *b*) acting or arriving without plan or method; aimless; unpredictable. *c*) working or arriving without regularity; occasional: as, a *casual* worker is one without regular employment. *d*) careless; cursory. *e*) nonchalant; indifferent. 2. of, for, affected by, or resulting from accidents: as, the *casual* ward in a hospital. 3. designating clothing, as sportswear, designed for informal occasions. *n.* 1. a person who does something or is in some place only occasionally or temporarily; especially, a casual worker or occasional recipient of charity. 2. in *military usage*, a person temporarily attached to a unit, awaiting a permanent assignment. —*SYN.* see **accidental, random.**

cas·u·al·ty (kazh′o͞o-əl-ti, kazh′ool-ti), *n.* [*pl.* CASUALTIES (-tiz)], [ME. *casuelte*; Fr. *casualité*; LL. *casualitas*; see CASUAL], 1. an accident, especially an unfortunate or fatal one. 2. in *military usage*, *a*) a member of the armed forces who is lost to active service, especially through being killed, wounded, or captured. *b*) *pl.* losses of personnel resulting from death, injury, etc. 3. anyone hurt or killed in an accident.

cas·u·ist (kazh′o͞o-ist), *n.* [Fr. *casuiste* < L. *casus*, a case, fall], a person who studies or decides questions of right and wrong in conduct; expert in casuistry:

often used disparagingly of one who quibbles, rationalizes, or reasons falsely.

cas·u·is·tic (kazh'ōō-is'tik), *adj.* 1. having to do with questions of right and wrong in conduct. 2. of or for casuists. 3. quibbling; sophistical; specious.

cas·u·is·ti·cal (kazh'ōō-is'ti-k'l), *adj.* casuistic.

cas·u·ist·ry (kazh'ōō-is-tri), *n.* [*pl.* CASUISTRIES (-triz)], [< *casuist*], the solving of special cases of right and wrong in conduct by applying general principles of ethics, and deciding how far circumstances alter cases: often used disparagingly of subtle but evasive reasoning in questions of duty.

‡ca·sus (kā'səs), *n.* [L., lit., a falling, fall], a happening; event; case, as in law.

‡ca·sus bel·li (kā'səs bel'ī), [L.], an event or events provoking war, or used as a pretext for making war.

cat (kat), *n.* [*pl.* CATS (kats), CAT; see PLURAL, II, D, 1], [ME.; AS. *catte, cat;* akin to G. *katze* < LL. *cattus*, etc., all via Celt.; prob. IE. base **qat-*, to bear young, seen in L. *catulus*, offspring, esp. of cats and dogs], 1. a small, lithe, soft-furred animal, domesticated since ancient times and often kept as a pet or for killing mice. 2. any of various flesh-eating mammals related to this, as the lion, tiger, cougar, leopard, etc. 3. a person regarded as like a cat in some way; especially, a woman who makes spiteful remarks. 4. a cat-o'-nine-tails. 5. a double (six-legged) tripod: so called because it always rests on three of its legs no matter how placed. 6. a catfish. 7. [Military Slang], a caterpillar tractor. 8. in *games, a)* the tapering stick or bat used in playing tipcat. *b)* this game. 9. in *military history*, a movable shelter used in besieging. 10. in *nautical usage, a)* a cathead. *b)* tackle for hoisting an anchor to the cathead. *c)* a catboat. *v.t.* [CATTED (-id), CATTING], 1. to hoist (an anchor) to the cathead. 2. to flog with a cat-o'-nine-tails.

let the cat out of the bag, to let a secret be found out.

cat., 1. catalogue. 2. catechism.

cat·a- (kat'ə), [Gr. *kata-* (*kat-* before a vowel, *kath-* before an aspirate) < *kata*, down], a prefix meaning: 1. *down, downward*, as in *catabolism*. 2. *away, completely*, as in *catalysis*. 3. *against*, as in *catapult*. 4. *through, throughout*, as in *cataphoresis*. 5. *backward, in regression*, as in *cataplasia*. Also, before a vowel, **cat-**, and, before an aspirate, **cath-**. Also spelled **kata-**.

cat·a·bol·ic (kat'ə-bol'ik), *adj.* of or caused by catabolism.

ca·tab·o·lism (kə-tab'ə-liz'm), *n.* [< *cata-* + Gr. *bolē*, a throw < *ballein*, to throw; + *-ism*], the process in a plant or animal by which living tissue is changed into waste products of a simpler chemical composition; destructive metabolism: also spelled **katabolism**: opposed to *anabolism*.

ca·tab·o·lite (kə-tab'ə-līt'), *n.* a waste product of catabolism.

cat·a·caus·tic (kat'ə-kôs'tik), *adj.* [coined < Gr. *kata-*, back + *kaustikos*, caustic], designating or of a caustic curve or surface formed by reflection. *n.* a catacaustic curve or surface. Opposed to *diacaustic*.

cat·a·chre·sis (kat'ə-krē'sis), *n.* [*pl.* CATACHRESES (-sēz)], [L. < Gr. *katachrēsis*, misuse of a word < *katachrēsthai; kata-*, against + *chrēsthai*, to use], 1. incorrect use of a word or words, as by misapplication of terminology or by strained or mixed metaphor. 2. a change in the form of a word resulting from a misunderstanding of its etymology.

cat·a·chres·tic (kat'ə-kres'tik), *adj.* [Gr. *katachrestikos*], of the nature of catachresis.

cat·a·cli·nal (kat'ə-klī'n'l), *adj.* [< Gr. *kataklinein*, to slope, incline; *kata-*, down + *klinein*, to bend], in *geology*, descending in the same direction as the dip of rock strata.

cat·a·clysm (kat'ə-kliz'm), *n.* [L. *cataclysmos;* Gr. *katalysmos* < *kataklyzein; kata-*, down + *klyzein*, to wash], 1. a great flood; deluge: also used figuratively, as, *cataclysms* of blood. 2. any great upheaval that causes sudden and violent changes, as an earthquake, war, etc. —*SYN.* see **disaster**.

cat·a·clys·mal (kat'ə-kliz'm'l), *adj.* cataclysmic.

cataclysmal theory, the theory that the shaping of the earth's crust was caused by sudden and violent upheavals rather than by slow action of air, water, etc.

cat·a·clys·mic (kat'ə-kliz'mik), *adj.* 1. of or caused by a cataclysm. 2. having the nature or effect of a cataclysm.

cat·a·comb (kat'ə-kōm'), *n.* [It. *catacomba;* LL. *catacumba*, sepulchral vault (orig., area along the Appian Way, where graves were located), formed by dissimilation < L. *cata tumbas*, at the graves; *cata* (< Gr. *kata*, down), by + *tumbas*, pl. of L. *tumba*, tomb], *usually in pl.* any of a series of vaults or galleries in an underground burial place.

the Catacombs, the underground cemeteries in or around Rome, some of which were used as a refuge by the early Christians.

ca·tad·ro·mous (kə-tad'rə-məs), *adj.* [< *cata-* + Gr. *dromos*, running; + *-ous*], going back to or toward the sea to spawn: said of certain fresh-water fishes.

cat·a·falque (kat'ə-falk'), *n.* [Fr.; It. *catafalco*, funeral canopy, stage; LL. **catafalcum*, scaffold < *cata-*, by, down (< Gr. *kata*, down) + **falicum* < L. *fala*, scaffolding, wooden tower], a temporary wooden framework, usually draped, used to support the coffin in which a dead person lies in state during an elaborate funeral.

Cat·a·lan (kat''l-an', kat''l-ən), *adj.* of Catalonia, its people, or their language. *n.* 1. a native or inhabitant of Catalonia. 2. the Romance language of Catalonia, closely akin to Provençal: it is spoken also in parts of southwestern France, Valencia, western Sardinia, and the Balearic Islands. Abbreviated **Catal.**

cat·a·lase (kat'ə-lās'), *n.* [*catalysis* + *-ase*], an enzyme that can decompose hydrogen peroxide into water and free oxygen.

cat·a·lec·tic (kat'ə-lek'tik), *adj.* [LL. *catalecticus;* Gr. *katalēktikos* < *kata-*, down + *lēgein*, to leave off, cease], in *prosody*, lacking a syllable in the last foot.

cat·a·lep·sis (kat'ə-lep'sis), *n.* catalepsy.

cat·a·lep·sy (kat'ə-lep'si), *n.* [LL. *catalepsis;* Gr. *katalēpsis*, a seizing, grasping < *katalambanein; kata-*, down + *lambanein*, to take, seize], a condition in which consciousness and feeling are suddenly and temporarily lost, and the muscles become rigid: it may occur in epilepsy, schizophrenia, etc.

cat·a·lep·tic (kat'ə-lep'tik), *adj.* [L. *catalepticus;* Gr. *kataleptikos*], of or having catalepsy. *n.* a person subject to catalepsy.

Cat·a·li·na (kat''l-ē'nə), *n.* Santa Catalina, an island off southern California: also **Catalina Island.**

cat·a·lo (kat'ə-lō'), *n.* [*pl.* CATALOES, CATALOS (-lōz')], [*cat*tle + buff*alo*], an animal developed from crossing the American buffalo, or bison, with domestic cattle: also spelled **cattalo.**

cat·a·log (kat''l-ôg', kat''l-og'), *n., v.t. & v.i.* catalogue.

cat·a·logue (kat''l-ôg', kat''l-og'), *n.* [Fr.; LL. *catalogus;* Gr. *katalogos*, a list, register < *katalegein*, to reckon, count up; *kata-*, down, completely + *legein*, to say, count], a complete list; especially, *a)* a card file arranged alphabetically, as of all the books in a library. *b)* a book or pamphlet, often illustrated, listing titles, articles, etc., as of things exhibited or for sale: abbreviated **cat.** *v.t. & v.i.* [CATALOGUED (-ôgd', -ogd'), CATALOGUING], to enter or arrange (items) in a catalogue. —*SYN.* see **list.**

cat·a·logu·er (kat''l-ôg'ẽr, kat''l-og'ẽr), *n.* a person who catalogues.

‡ca·ta·logue rai·son·né (kå'tå'lôg' re'zô'nā'), [Fr., lit., reasoned catalogue], a catalogue arranged by subjects; classified list, often with explanatory notes.

cat·a·logu·ist (kat''l-ôg'ist, kat''l-og'ist), *n.* a cataloguer.

Cat·a·lo·ni·a (kat''l-ō'ni-ə), *n.* an old province of northeastern Spain: Spanish name *Cataluña.*

Cat·a·lo·ni·an (kat'ə-lō'ni-ən), *adj.* Catalan.

ca·tal·pa (kə-tal'pə), *n.* [Mod. L. < Am. Ind. (Creek) *katuhlpa*, lit., head with wings; so named because of its flowers], any of a group of hardy trees with large, heart-shaped leaves, showy clusters of trumpet-shaped flowers, slender pods, and air-borne seeds.

Ca·ta·lu·ña (kä'tä-lōō'nyä), *n.* Catalonia.

ca·tal·y·sis (kə-tal'ə-sis), *n.* [*pl.* CATALYSES (-sēz')], [Gr. *katalysis*, dissolution < *kata-*, down + *lyein*, to loose], the causing or speeding up of a chemical reaction by the addition of some substance which itself undergoes no permanent chemical change thereby: also spelled **katalysis.**

cat·a·lyst (kat''l-ist), *n.* any substance serving as the agent in catalysis; catalyzer.

cat·a·lyt·ic (kat''l-it'ik), *adj.* of, in, or causing catalysis. *n.* a catalyst.

cat·a·lyze (kat''l-īz'), *v.t.* [CATALYZED (-īzd'), CATALYZING], to change by catalysis.

cat·a·ma·ran (kat'ə-mə-ran'), *n.* [Tamil *kaṭṭumaram; kaṭṭu*, tie + *maram*, log, tree], 1. a narrow log raft or float propelled by sails or paddles. 2. a boat with two parallel hulls, built in the style of such a float.

cat·a·me·ni·a (kat'ə-mē'ni-ə), *n.pl.* [Gr. *katamēnia*, neut. pl. of *katamēnios*, monthly < *kata-*, according to + *mēn*, month], menstruation; menstrual discharge.

cat·a·me·ni·al (kat'ə-mē'ni-əl), *adj.* menstrual.

cat·a·mite (kat'ə-mīt'), *n.* [L. *Catamitus*, altered < *Ganymedes* < Gr. *Ganymēdēs*, Ganymede], a boy used in pederasty.

cat·a·mount (kat'ə-mount'), *n.* [*cat* + *a*, of + *mount*], 1. a catamountain. 2. a puma; cougar. 3. a lynx.

cat·a·moun·tain (kat'ə-moun't'n), *n.* [see CATAMOUNT], any of several wild animals of the cat family, especially a leopard or a European wildcat: also **cat-o'-mountain.**

Ca·ta·nia (kä-tä'nyä; Eng. kə-tān'yə), *n.* a city on the eastern coast of Sicily: pop., 274,000 (1947).

cat·a·pho·re·sis (kat'ə-fə-rē'sis, kat'ə-for'i-sis), *n.*

[Mod. L. < *cata-* + Gr. *phorēsis*, a bearing < *pherein*, to bear, carry], in *physical chemistry*, the movement, under the influence of an electrical field, of electrically charged particles suspended in a fluid: also called *electrophoresis*.

cat·a·phyll (kat′ə-fil′), *n.* [< *cata-* + *phyl*], in *botany*, any rudimentary leaf, as a bud scale, preceding the true foliage leaves.

cat·a·pla·si·a (kat′ə-plā′zhi-ə, kat′ə-plā′zi-ə), *n.* [*pl.* CATAPLASIAE (-ē′)], [Mod. L.; see CATA- & PLASIA], in *biology*, a change in cells or tissues, characterized by reversion to an earlier stage.

cat·a·plasm (kat′ə-plaz′m), *n.* [Fr. *cataplasm* < Gr. *kataplasma*], a poultice, often medicated.

cat·a·pult (kat′ə-pult′), *n.* [L. *catapulta*; Gr. *katapeltēs* < *kata-*, down + *pallein*, to toss, hurl], 1. an ancient military contrivance for throwing or shooting stones, spears, etc. 2. a slingshot. 3. a device for launching an airplane from the deck of a ship. *v.t.* to shoot from or as from a catapult; hurl.

CATAPULT

cat·a·ract (kat′ə-rakt′), *n.* [ME., portcullis, whence sense 3; L. *cataracta*; Gr. *kataraktēs*, waterfall, portcullis < *katarrēgnymi* < *kata-*, down + *rēgnymi*, to break], 1. a large waterfall. 2. any downpour like a cataract; deluge. 3. in *medicine*, *a*) an eye disease in which the crystalline lens or its capsule becomes opaque, causing partial or total blindness. *b*) the opaque area.

ca·tarrh (kə-tär′), *n.* [Fr. *catarrhe*; L. *catarrhus*; Gr. *katarrhoos* < *katarrhein*, to flow down < *kata-*, down + *rhein*, to flow], inflammation of a mucous membrane, especially of the nose or throat, causing an increased flow of mucus.

ca·tarrh·al (kə-tär′əl), *adj.* of, like, with, or from catarrh.

ca·tarrh·ous (kə-tär′əs), *adj.* catarrhal.

ca·tas·ta·sis (kə-tas′tə-sis), *n.* [*pl.* CATASTASES (-sēz′)], [Gr. *katastasis*, an arranging, setting forth < *kathistanai* < *kata-*, down + *histanai*, to set up, cause to stand], 1. in *ancient drama*, the heightened part of the action, leading directly to the catastrophe. 2. in *rhetoric*, the narrative part of a speech; exordium.

ca·tas·tro·phe (kə-tas′trə-fi), *n.* [L. *catastropha*; Gr. *katastrophē*, an overthrowing < *katastrephein*, to overturn; *kata-*, down + *strephein*, to turn], 1. the culminating event of a drama, especially of a tragedy, by which the plot is resolved; denouement; hence, 2. a disastrous overthrow or ruin. 3. any great and sudden calamity, disaster, or misfortune. 4. any event that disturbs or overthrows the existing order of things. 5. in *geology*, a cataclysm. —***SYN.*** see **disaster.**

cat·a·stroph·ic (kat′ə-strof′ik), *adj.* of, like, or caused by a catastrophe; disastrous; calamitous.

ca·tas·tro·phism (kə-tas′trə-fiz′m), *n.* the theory that geological changes have been caused in general by sudden upheavals rather than by gradual changes.

cat·a·to·ni·a (kat′ə-tō′ni-ə), *n.* [< *cata-* + Gr. *tonos*, tension], in *psychiatry*, any of various schizophrenic syndromes characterized by phases of stupor, often alternating with phases of excitement and marked muscular rigidity, and often accompanied with stereotypy of posture or activity.

cat·a·ton·ic (kat′ə-ton′ik), *adj.* of or having catatonia. *n.* a catatonic person.

Ca·taw·ba (kə-tô′bə), *n.* [after the *Catawba* (< *Kahtahba*, Indian tribe), a river in South Carolina, where the grape was first raised], 1. a reddish variety of grape. 2. a wine made from this grape.

cat·bird (kat′bũrd′), *n.* a slate-gray North American songbird with a black crown and tail: it makes a mewing sound like that of a cat.

cat·boat (kat′bōt′), *n.* a sailboat with a single sail, a mast set well forward in the bow, and, usually, a centerboard.

cat brier, any of several plants with prickly stems, oval leaves, and black berries; kind of smilax.

cat·call (kat′kôl′), *n.* a shrill noise or whistle expressing derision or disapproval, as of speakers, actors, etc. *v.t.* to deride or show disapproval of with catcalls. *v.i.* to make catcalls.

catch (kach), *v.t.* [CAUGHT (kôt), CATCHING], [ME. *catchen*, *cachen*; ONorm. Fr. *cacher*, *cachier*; LL. *captiare* < L. *captare*, to try to seize < pp. of *capere*, to take], 1. to seize and hold, as after a chase; capture. 2. to seize or take by or as by a trap, snare, etc.; hence, 3. to deceive; ensnare. 4. to come upon suddenly; surprise; discover. 5. to strike suddenly; hit: as, the blow *caught* him in the abdomen. 6. to overtake or get to in time; be in time for: as, he *caught* the train. 7. to intercept the motion or action of; lay hold of; grab: as, he *caught* a fast ball. 8. to take or get: as, *catch* his eye, *catch* a glimpse of her. 9. to take or get passively; incur or contract without effort or intention, as by exposure: as, he *caught* cold. 10. to take in; understand; apprehend. 11. to captivate; charm. 12. in *baseball*, to act as catcher for (a specified pitcher). *v.i.* 1. to become caught; become held, fastened, or entangled: as, her sleeve *caught* on a nail. 2. to take hold or spread, as fire. 3. to take fire; burn. 4. to take and keep hold, as a lock. 5. to act as a catcher. *n.* 1. the act of catching. 2. the thing that catches. 3. the person or thing caught. 4. the amount caught. 5. a person or thing worth catching, especially as a husband or wife: as, that bachelor is a good *catch*. 6. a snatch, scrap, or fragment: as, *catches* of old tunes. 7. a break in the voice, caused by emotion. 8. a simple game of throwing and catching a ball. 9. [Colloq.], a hidden qualification; tricky condition: as, what's the *catch* in his offer? 10. in *music*, a round for three or more unaccompanied voices. 11. in *sports*, a catching of a ball in a specified manner. *adj.* 1. tricky. 2. attracting attention; meant to arouse interest.

catch as catch can, with any hold or approach: originally said of a style of wrestling.

catch at, 1. to try to catch. 2. to reach for eagerly; seize desperately.

catch it, [Colloq.], to receive a scolding or other punishment.

catch on, [Colloq.], 1. to grasp the meaning; understand. 2. to become fashionable, popular, etc.

catch up, 1. to take or lift up suddenly; seize; snatch. 2. to show to be in error. 3. to heckle. 4. to come up and not be behind; overtake. 5. to fasten in loops.

SYN.—**catch,** the most general term here, refers to a seizing or taking of a person or thing, whether by skill or cunning, and usually implies pursuit; **capture** implies a greater measure of resistance or elusiveness than **catch** and therefore stresses seizure by force or stratagem (to *capture* an outlaw); **nab,** an informal word, specifically implies a sudden or quick taking into custody (the police *nabbed* the thief); **trap** and **snare** both imply the literal or figurative use of a device for catching a person or animal and suggests a situation from which escape is difficult or impossible (to *trap* a bear, *snared* by her womanly wiles).

catch·all (kach′ôl′), *n.* a container for various sorts of things: as, most attics are *catchalls*.

catch basin, a sievelike device at the entrance to a sewer to stop matter that could block up the sewer.

catch crop, a supplementary crop grown at a time when the ground would ordinarily lie fallow, as between the plantings of two principal crops.

catch·er (kach′ẽr), *n.* 1. a person or thing that catches. 2. in *baseball*, the player who stands behind home plate and catches pitched balls not hit away by the batter: abbreviated **c.**

catch·ing (kach′iŋ), *adj.* [ppr. of *catch*], 1. contagious; infectious. 2. attractive; catchy.

catch·ment (kach′mənt), *n.* 1. a catching. 2. a reservoir or other basin for catching. 3. anything caught in or as in a catchment.

catchment area (or **basin**), the area draining into a catchment.

catch·pen·ny (kach′pen′i), *adj.* made merely to sell; cheap and flashy; worthless. *n.* [*pl.* CATCHPENNIES (-iz)], a catchpenny commodity.

catch phrase, a phrase that catches or is meant to catch the popular attention.

catch·pole, catch·poll (kach′pōl′), *n.* [ME. *cacchepol* & Late AS. *cæcepol*, taxgatherer < ONorm. Fr. form of OFr. *chacepol*, lit., chicken-chaser; ML. *cacepullus*, *chassepullus* < **cacere*, **chacere*, to chase, catch (LL. *captiare*; see CATCH) + **pollus*, fowl (L. *pullus*; see PULLET): taxgatherers allegedly took poultry in lieu of unpaid taxes], formerly, a sheriff's officer whose usual duty was to arrest nonpaying debtors.

catch stitch, a stitch that catches up the one before it so as to give the appearance of a herringbone pattern.

catch·up (kach′əp, kech′əp), *n.* ketchup; catsup.

catch·weight (kach′wāt′), *n.* in certain sports or competitions, as horse racing, the weight of a contestant as it happens to be, as distinguished from weight fixed by rule or agreement.

catch·word (kach′wũrd′), *n.* 1. originally, the first word of the following page, printed in the lower right-hand corner of each page so as to catch the reader's eye. 2. a word placed so that it will catch attention, as the first or last word of a page in a dictionary, etc., printed at the top of the page as a guide. 3. an actor's cue. 4. a word or phrase repeated so often that it becomes a slogan, as "the century of the common man."

catch·y (kach′i), *adj.* [CATCHIER (-i-ẽr), CATCHIEST (-i-ist)], 1. catching attention; arousing interest. 2. easily caught up and remembered: as, a *catchy* tune. 3. tricky; deceiving. 4. spasmodic; fitful.

cate (kāt), *n.* [< earlier *acate*; ME. *achat*; OFr. *acat*, *achat*, a purchase, thing bought < *acater*, *achater*; see CATER], [Archaic], choice food; a delicacy, or dainty.

cat·e·che·sis (kat′ə-kē′sis), *n.* [*pl.* CATECHESES (-sēz)], [L.; Gr. *katēchēsis* < *katēchein*; see CATECHETICAL], oral

instruction, especially for catechumens, by the method of question and answer.
cat·e·chet·ic (kat'ə-ket'ik), *adj.* catechetical.
cat·e·chet·i·cal (kat'ə-ket'i-k'l), *adj.* [Gr. *katēchētikos* < *katēchētēs*, instructor < *katēchein*, to instruct, teach by word of mouth < *kata-*, thoroughly + *ēchein*, to sound], 1. of, like, or conforming to catechesis or a catechism. 2. consisting of, or teaching by the method of, questions and answers.
cat·e·chin (kat'ə-chin, kat'ə-kin), *n.* [< *catechu* + *-in*], a yellow, powdery, acid compound, $C_{15}H_{14}O_6$, used in tanning, textile printing, etc.
cat·e·chism (kat'ə-kiz'm), *n.* [L. *catechismus;* Gr. *katēchismos* < *katēchizein*, to catechize], 1. a handbook of questions and answers for teaching the principles of a religion. 2. any similar handbook for teaching the fundamentals of a subject. 3. a formal series of questions; close questioning. 4. [Obs.], catechesis.
cat·e·chist (kat'ə-kist), *n.* a person who catechizes.
cat·e·chis·tic (kat'ə-kis'tik), *adj.* of a catechist or catechism.
cat·e·chis·ti·cal (kat'ə-kis'ti-k'l), *adj.* catechistic.
cat·e·chi·za·tion (kat'ə-ki-zā'shən), *n.* a catechizing or being catechized.
cat·e·chize (kat'ə-kīz'), *v.t.* [CATECHIZED (-kīzd'), CATECHIZING], [L. *catechizare;* Gr. *katēchizein;* see CATECHETICAL], 1. to teach by the method of question and answer. 2. to question searchingly or fully. Also spelled **catechise.** —*SYN.* see **ask.**
cat·e·chol (kat'ə-chōl', kat'ə-kōl'), *n.* [< *catechu* + *-ol*], a colorless crystalline compound, $C_6H_6O_2$, used as an antiseptic and in photography as a developer.
cat·e·chu (kat'ə-chōō'), *n.* [< Malay *kāchū*], a hard, brown substance obtained from an Oriental acacia and other Asiatic trees and shrubs, used as an astringent in medicine, and for dyeing, tanning, etc.: also **cashoo.**
cat·e·chu·men (kat'ə-kū'mən), *n.* [L. *catechumenus;* Gr. *katēchoumenos*, person instructed; ppr. of *katēchein*, to instruct], 1. a person, especially an adult, receiving instruction in the fundamentals of Christianity after conversion. 2. a person receiving instruction in the fundamentals of any subject.
cat·e·gor·i·cal (kat'ə-gôr'i-k'l, kat'ə-gor'i-k'l), *adj.* [LL. *categoricus;* see CATEGORY & -ICAL], 1. unqualified; unconditional; absolute; positive; direct; explicit: said of a statement, theory, etc. 2. of, as, or in a category.
categorical imperative, the Kantian doctrine that one's behavior should be governed by principles which one would have govern the behavior of all people.
cat·e·go·ry (kat'ə-gôr'i, kat'ə-gō'ri), *n.* [*pl.* CATEGORIES (-iz, -riz)], [L. *categoria;* Gr. *katēgoria* < *katēgorein*, to accuse, assert, predicate < *kata-*, down, against + *agoreuein*, to declaim, address an assembly < *agora*, assembly], 1. a class or division in a scheme of classification. 2. in *logic*, any of the various basic concepts into which all knowledge can be classified.
ca·te·na (kə-tē'nə), *n.* [*pl.* CATENAE (-nē)], [L.; see CHAIN], a linked series; chain.
cat·e·nar·i·an (kat''n-âr'i-ən), *adj.* of a catenary or a chain.
cat·e·nar·y (kat''n-er'i, kə-tē'nə-ri), *n.* [*pl.* CATENARIES (-iz, -riz)], [L. *catenarius* < *catena;* see CHAIN], the curve made by a flexible chain or cord when it is suspended between two points at the same level. *adj.* 1. designating such a curve. 2. of a catena.
cat·e·nate (kat''n-āt'), *v.t.* [CATENATED (-id), CATENATING], [< LL. *catenatus*, pp. of *catenare* < L. *catena;* see CHAIN], to form into a chain or linked series; link.
cat·e·na·tion (kat''n-ā'shən), *n.* 1. a catenating; linking. 2. a series of things linked together.
ca·ter (kā'tẽr), *v.i.* [< obs. *cater*, buyer; ME. *catour*, *achatour;* OFr. *acator*, *achatour* < *acater*, *achater*, to buy, provide < LL. *accaptare* < L. *ad-*, to + *captare* (intens. of *capere*, to take), to strive, seize], 1. to provide food; serve as a caterer. 2. to provide whatever is needed or desired, especially as a means of pleasure (with *to* or *for*). *v.t.* to serve as caterer for (a banquet, dinner, wedding, etc.).
cat·er·an (kat'ẽr-ən), *n.* [Scot. *catherein;* Gael. *ceathairne*, common people], a Scottish Highlands robber.
cat·er-cor·ner (kat'ẽr-kôr'nẽr), *adj.* & *adv.* cater-cornered.
cat·er-cor·nered (kat'ẽr-kôr'nẽrd), *adj.* [< Fr. *quatre*, four; + *cornered*], diagonal. *adv.* diagonally.
ca·ter-cous·in (kā'tẽr-kuz''n), *n.* [obs. *cater*, four (< Fr. *quatre*) + *cousin;* hence, orig., fourth-cousin, quarter-cousin], [Archaic], a close friend.
ca·ter·er (kā'tẽr-ẽr), *n.* one who caters; one whose work is providing food and service for parties, etc.
cat·er·pil·lar (kat'ẽr-pil'ẽr), *n.* [ME. *catirpel;* ONorm. Fr. *catepilose* (OFr. *chatepelose*), lit., hairy cat < L. *catta*, cat + *pilosus* < *pilus*, hair], 1. the wormlike larva of various insects, especially of a butterfly or moth. 2. a caterpillar tractor. *adj* having an endless-track drive: as, a *caterpillar* grader.
caterpillar tractor, a tractor equipped on each side with a continuous roller belt over cogged wheels, for moving over rough ground: a trade-mark (**Caterpillar Tractor**).

CATERPILLAR TRACTOR

cat·er·waul (kat'ẽr-wôl'), *v.i.* [ME. *caterwrawen*, *caterwawen* < *cater* (cf. G., D. *cater*, male cat) + *wrawlen*, *wawlen*, *v.;* prob. echoic], to make a shrill, howling sound like that of a cat at rutting time; screech; wail; scream. *n.* such a sound.
cat-eyed (kat'īd'), *adj.* able to see well in dim light, as a cat.
cat·fall (kat'fôl'), *n.* in *nautical usage*, a cable or chain for raising the anchor to the cathead.
cat·fish (kat'fish'), *n.* [*pl.* CATFISH, CATFISHES (-iz); see FISH], any of a large group of scaleless fishes with long feelers (called *barbels*), somewhat like a cat's whiskers, about the mouth.
cat·gut (kat'gut'), *n.* [*cat* + *gut;* parallel with D. *kattedarm; cat* prob. refers to noise made by cats], a tough string or thread made from the dried intestines of sheep, horses, etc. and used for surgical sutures, for stringing tennis rackets and musical instruments, etc.
Cath., 1. Catholic. 2. [also c-], cathedral.
Cath·a·rine (kath'rin, kath'ẽr-in), a feminine name: see **Catherine.**
ca·thar·sis (kə-thär'sis), *n.* [Gr. *katharsis*, purification < *kathairein*, to purify < *katharos*, pure], 1. purgation, especially of the bowels. 2. the purifying or relieving of the emotions by art: an Aristotelian concept, applied originally to the effects of tragic drama. 3. in *psychiatry*, the alleviation of fears, problems, and complexes by bringing them to consciousness and giving them expression. Also spelled **katharsis.**
ca·thar·tic (kə-thär'tik), *adj.* [Gr. *kathartikos*], having to do with catharsis; purging. *n.* [L. *catharticum;* Gr. *kathartikon*], a medicine for stimulating evacuation of the bowels; laxative, as castor oil. —*SYN.* see **physic.**
ca·thar·ti·cal (kə-thär'ti-k'l), *adj.* cathartic.
Ca·thay (kə-thā', ka-thā'), *n.* [ML. *Cataya*, of Tatar origin], [Poetic or Archaic], China.
cat·head (kat'hed'), *n.* a projecting beam of iron or wood near the bow of a ship, to which the anchor is hoisted and fastened.
ca·the·dra (kə-thē'drə, kath'i-drə), *n.* [L.; Gr. *kathedra*, a seat, bench < *kata-*, down + *hedra*, a seat < *hezesthai*, to sit], 1. the throne of a bishop in a cathedral. 2. the episcopal see; hence, 3. any seat of high authority.
ex cathedra, from or with official authority.
ca·the·dral (kə-thē'drəl), *n.* [LL. *cathedralis* (supply *ecclesia*, church) < L. *cathedra;* see CATHEDRA], 1. the main church of a bishop's see, containing the cathedra: abbreviated **Cath., cath.** 2. loosely, any large, imposing church. *adj.* 1. of, like, or containing a cathedra. 2. official; authoritative. 3. of or like a cathedral.
Cath·er, Wil·la Si·bert (wil'ə sī'bẽrt kath'ẽr), 1876–1947; American novelist.
Cath·er·ine (kath'rin, kath'ẽr-in), [Fr.; L. *Catharina*, *Ecaterina;* Gr. *Aikaterinē;* form and meaning influenced by *katharos*, pure, unsullied], a feminine name: diminutives, *Cathy, Kate, Kit, Kitty;* equivalents, It. *Caterina*, Ir. *Kathleen*, Russ. *Ekaterina*, Scand. *Karen*, Sp. *Catalina, Catarina;* also spelled **Catharine, Katharine, Katherine, Kathryn.**
Catherine I, 1684?–1727; wife of Peter the Great; empress of Russia (1725–1727).
Catherine II, 1729–1796; German-born empress of Russia (1762–1796): called *Catherine the Great.*
Catherine, Saint, 1. ?–307 A.D.; Christian martyr of Alexandria. 2. 1347–1380; Christian mystic of Siena.
Catherine de Medici, 1519–1589; daughter of *Lorenzo;* queen of France and mother of three kings of France, Francis II, Charles IX, and Henry III.
Catherine of Aragon, 1485–1536; first wife of Henry VIII of England.
cath·e·ter (kath'ə-tẽr), *n.* [L.; Gr. *kathetēr* < *kathienai*, to let down, thrust in < *kata-*, down + *hienai*, to send], a slender tube of metal or rubber, inserted into a body cavity for distending the passage or drawing off fluid, especially urine from the bladder.
cath·e·ter·ize (kath'ə-tẽr-īz'), *v.t.* [CATHETERIZED (-īzd'), CATHETERIZING], to insert a catheter into.
ca·thex·is (kə-thek'sis), *n.* [< Gr. *kathexis*, a holding, transl. of G. *besetzung*, as used by Freud], in *psychoanalysis*, concentration of the psychic energy on some particular person, thing, or idea.
cath·ode (kath'ōd), *n.* [< Gr. *kathodos*, going down < *kata-*, down + *hodos*, way], a negatively charged electrode, as of a vacuum tube, electrolytic cell, etc.: abbreviated **C., c., ca.:** also spelled **kathode:** see **battery,** illus.
cathode rays, streams of electrons projected from the

surface of a cathode: cathode rays produce X rays when they strike solids.

cath·ode-ray tube (kath'ōd-rā'), a vacuum tube in which cathode rays are produced.

ca·thod·ic (kə-thod'ik), *adj.* of or projected from a cathode.

cath·o·lic (kath'ə-lik, kath'lik), *adj.* [L. *catholicus*, universal, general; Gr. *katholikos* < *kata-*, down, completely + *holos*, whole], 1. universal; all-inclusive; of general interest or value; hence, 2. having broad sympathies or understanding; liberal. 3. of the universal Christian church; of the Christian church as a whole. 4. [C-], of the Western (Roman) Christian Church as distinguished from the Eastern (Orthodox) Christian Church; hence, 5. [C-], of the Christian church headed by the Pope; Roman Catholic. 6. [C-], of any of the orthodox Christian churches, including the Roman, Greek Orthodox, and Anglo-Catholic, as distinguished from the Reformed or Protestant churches. *n.* 1. a member of the universal Christian church. 2. [C-], a member of any of the Catholic churches, especially the Roman Catholic. Abbreviated **Cath.**, **C.**

ca·thol·i·cal·ly (kə-thol'i-k'l-i, kə-thol'ik-li), *adv.* in a catholic manner; universally.

Catholic Church, the Roman Catholic Church.

Ca·thol·i·cism (kə-thol'ə-siz'm), *n.* 1. the doctrine, faith, practice, and organization of a Catholic church, especially of the Roman Catholic Church. 2. [c-], catholicity.

cath·o·lic·i·ty (kath'ə-lis'ə-ti), *n.* 1. the quality or state of being catholic, as in taste, sympathy, understanding, etc.; liberality, as of ideas. 2. universality; comprehensive quality. 3. [C-], Catholicism.

ca·thol·i·cize (kə-thol'ə-sīz'), *v.t.* & *v.i.* [CATHOLICIZED (-sīzd'), CATHOLICIZING], 1. to make or become catholic. 2. [C-], to convert or be converted to Catholicism.

ca·thol·i·con (kə-thol'ə-kən), *n.* [Gr. *katholikon*, neut. of *katholikos*; see CATHOLIC], 1. a medicine to cure all diseases; panacea. 2. anything all-inclusive.

Cat·i·line (kat''l-īn'), *n.* (*Lucius Sergius Catilina*), Roman politician and conspirator; 108?–62 B.C.

cat·i·on (kat'ī'ən), *n.* [coined by Faraday < Gr. *kata*, downward + *ion*, neut. ppr. of *ienai*, to go], a positively charged ion: cations move toward the cathode in an electrolyzed solution: also spelled **kation**.

cat·kin (kat'kin), *n.* [dim. of *cat:* from resemblance to a cat's tail], a tassellike spike of closely clustered, small, unisexual flowers without petals, as on a willow, birch, or poplar: also called *ament*.

cat·like (kat'līk'), *adj.* like a cat or cat's; noiseless, stealthy, etc.

cat·ling (kat'liŋ), *n.* [*cat* + *-ling*, dim. suffix], 1. [Rare], a kitten. 2. [Rare], fine catgut. 3. a long, straight, double-edged surgical knife, used in amputating.

cat·mint (kat'mint'), *n.* catnip.

cat nap, a short, light sleep; doze.

cat·nip (kat'nip), *n.* [*cat* + *nip*, dial. for *nep*, catnip], a plant of the mint family, with downy leaves and spikes of bluish flowers: cats like its odor.

Ca·to (kā'tō), *n.* 1. (*Marcus Porcius Cato*), Roman consul, famous for devotion to Roman ideals; 234–149 B.C.: called *the Elder*. 2. (*Marcus Porcius Cato Uticensis*), great-grandson of *Cato the Elder;* 95–46 B.C.; Roman statesman and philosopher: called *the Younger*.

cat-o'-moun·tain (kat'ə-moun't'n), *n.* a catamountain.

cat-o'-nine-tails (kat'ə-nīn'tālz'), *n.* [*pl.* CAT-O'-NINE-TAILS], 1. a whip made of nine knotted cords attached to a handle, formerly used for flogging. 2. the cattail.

ca·top·tric (kə-top'trik), *adj.* [< Gr. *katoptrikos* < *katoptron*, a mirror < *kata-* (see CATA-) + *ops*, the eye, face], of reflected light or mirrors. *n.* catoptrics.

ca·top·tri·cal (kə-top'tri-k'l), *adj.* catoptric.

ca·top·trics (kə-top'triks), *n.pl.* [construed as sing.], [see CATOPTRIC], the branch of optics dealing with the reflection of light.

cat rig, a rig consisting of a single large sail on a mast well forward in the bow; rig of a catboat.

cat·rigged (kat'rigd'), *adj.* having a cat rig.

cat's cradle, a child's game played with a string looped over the fingers and, sometimes, transferred to the hand of another player so as to form designs.

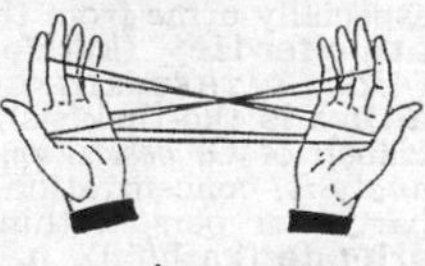
CAT'S CRADLE

cat's-eye (kats'ī'), *n.* 1. a semiprecious quartz gem that reflects light in a way suggestive of the eye of a cat. 2. a small reflector device on road signs, bicycles, etc., used to indicate their presence at night.

Cats·kill Mountains (kats'kil'), a group of mountains in southern New York: resort area: highest peak, Slide Mountain, 4,204 ft.
  the Catskills, the Catskill Mountains.

cat's-paw (kats'pô'), *n.* 1. a person used by another to do dangerous, distasteful, or unlawful work; dupe; tool. 2. a light breeze that ripples the surface of water. 3. a hitch in the loop of a rope that forms a second loop: it is used to hook a tackle: see **knot**, illus.

cat·stick (kat'stik'), *n.* a stick used in playing tipcat or trapball: also called *catty*.

cat·sup (kat'səp, kech'əp), *n.* [var. of *ketchup*], a sauce for meat, fish, etc.; especially, a thick sauce (*tomato catsup*) made of tomatoes flavored with onion, salt, sugar, and spice: also **ketchup**, **catchup**.

Catt, Carrie Chapman (kat), 1859–1947; American leader in the agitation for women's right to vote.

cat·tail (kat'tāl'), *n.* 1. a tall marsh plant with long, flat, reedlike leaves and long, brown, fuzzy, cylindrical flower spikes. 2. a catkin.

cat·ta·lo (kat'ə-lō'), *n.* [*pl.* CATTALOES, CATTALOS (-lōz')], a catalo.

Cat·te·gat (kat'i-gat'), *n.* Kattegat.

cat·ti·ness (kat'i-nis), *n.* a catty quality; meanness.

cat·tish (kat'ish), *adj.* 1. like a cat; feline. 2. catty.

cat·tle (kat''l), *n.* [ME. *catel, katel;* ONorm. Fr. *catel* (OFr. *chatel*); LL. *captale, capitale*, property, goods, stock; L. *capitalis*, principal, chief < *caput*, the head; orig. sense in var. *chattel;* cf. CAPITAL], 1. farm animals collectively; livestock. 2. domesticated bovine animals collectively; cows, bulls, steers, or oxen: the term is usually not applied to calves and heifers. 3. people in the mass: contemptuous term.

cat·tle·man (kat''l-mən), *n.* [*pl.* CATTLEMEN (-mən)], a man who tends cattle or raises them for the market.

cat·ty (kat'i), *adj.* [CATTIER (-i-ẽr), CATTIEST (-i-ist)], 1. of cats. 2. like a cat. 3. spiteful; mean; subtly malicious. *n.* 1. tipcat. 2. a cat (sense 8); catstick.

cat·ty (kat'i), *n.* [*pl.* CATTIES (-iz)], [Malay *kātī;* see CADDY (box)], a unit of weight used in China, Thailand, the Netherlands Indies, Japan, Rangoon, the Philippine Islands, and the Straits Settlements: it varies from place to place, but is generally equal to about 1 1/3 pounds avoirdupois.

Ca·tul·lus (kə-tul'əs), *n.* (*Gaius Valerius Catullus*), Roman lyric poet; 84?–54? B.C.

cat·walk (kat'wôk'), *n.* 1. originally, a narrow bridge connecting the elevated midship section of a ship with the bow or stern. 2. a narrow pathway or platform, as along a bridge or over an engine room.

cat whisker, in *radio*, a thin wire that makes contact with the crystal in a crystal detector.

Cau·ca (kou'kä), *n.* a river in Colombia, flowing northward into the Magdalena River: length, 600 mi.

Cau·ca·sia (kô-kā'zhə, kô-kā'shə), *n.* a region of the U.S.S.R., on either side of the Caucasus, between the Black Sea and the Caspian: also called *the Caucusus*.

Cau·ca·sian (kô-kā'zhən, kô-kash'ən), *adj.* 1. of the Caucasus, its people, or their culture. 2. [so named in 1795 by the G. anthropologist Johann Blumenbach, who erroneously thought that the original home of the hypothetical Indo-Europeans was the Caucasus; although the following senses are now not scientific and often tinged with racism, the word is used in this dictionary in default of a better], designating or of one of the main ethnic divisions of the human race: it includes the Mediterranean, Alpine, and Nordic subdivisions, and is loosely called the *white race*. 3. designating or of all languages in the area of the Caucasus which are neither Indo-European nor Turkic. *n.* 1. a native of the Caucasus. 2. a member of the Caucasian division of mankind: loosely called *white person*. 3. the Caucasian languages; Circassian, Georgian, etc.

Cau·cas·ic (kô-kas'ik), *adj.* Caucasian.

Cau·ca·sus (kô'kə-səs), *n.* 1. a mountain range in southeastern Europe, between the Black Sea and the Caspian: highest peak, Mt. Elbrus. 2. Caucasia.

cau·cus (kô'kəs), *n.* [prob. < Algonquian *cau-cau-a-su*, adviser], 1. a meeting of leaders or members of a party or faction to decide questions of policy, candidates, campaign plans, etc. 2. a controlling organization within a British political party. *v.i.* to hold a caucus.

cau·dad (kô'dad), *adv.* in *anatomy* & *zoology*, toward the tail or the caudal part of the body; posteriorly: opposed to *cephalad*.

cau·dal (kô'd'l), *adj.* [< L. *cauda*, tail], 1. of or like a tail. 2. at or near the tail.

cau·date (kô'dāt), *adj.* [< L. *cauda*, tail], having a tail or taillike part.

cau·dat·ed (kô'dā-tid), *adj.* caudate.

cau·dex (kô'deks), *n.* [*pl.* CAUDICES (-di-sēz'), CAUDEXES (-dek-siz)], [L., stem of a tree], 1. the base of a perennial plant. 2. the axis or stem of a woody plant, especially of a palm or tree fern.

‡cau·dil·lo (kou-dē'lyô, kou-dē'yô; Eng. kô-dēl'yō), *n.* [Sp. < Ar.], leader; commander: title (*El Caudillo*) of Francisco Franco, fascist head of Spain (1939–).

Cau·dine Forks (kô'dīn), two mountain passes in Campania, Italy.

cau·dle (kô'd'l), *n.* [ME. & OFr. *caudel* < L. *calidus*, *caldus*, warm], a warm drink for invalids; especially, a spiced and sugared gruel with wine or ale added.

caught (kôt), [ME. *cahte, cauhte* (for normal *cacched*) through identification of *cacchen*, *v.* with *lacchen* (AS. *laeccan*), p.t. *lahte, lauhte;* cf. CATCH], past tense and past participle of **catch**.

caul (kôl), *n.* [ME. *calle, kalle;* OFr. *cale,* kind of cap < *calotte;* see CALOTTE], 1. the membrane enclosing a fetus, or a part of this membrane sometimes enveloping the head of a child at birth: formerly believed to bring good luck. 2. the part of the peritoneum that extends from the stomach to the large intestine: also called *great omentum.*

cauld (kôld, kôd), *adj.* [Northumbrian AS. *cald*], [Scot. & North Eng. Dial.], cold.

caul·dron (kôl'drən), *n.* a caldron.

cau·les·cent (kô-les''nt), *adj.* [< L. *caulis,* a stem; + *-escent*], in *botany,* having an obvious stem above the ground.

cau·li·cle (kô'li-k'l), *n.* [L. *cauliculus,* dim. of *caulis,* a stalk, stem], in *botany,* a small or rudimentary stem, as in an embryo.

cau·li·flow·er (kô'lə-flou'ẽr), *n.* [earlier *cole florye* (see COLE) < Fr. *chou flori* (now *chou-fleur*), cauliflower; mod. sp. after L. *caulis,* a cabbage], 1. a plant with a compact white head of fleshy stalks bearing small flowers and buds: it is a variety of cabbage. 2. the head of this plant, used as a vegetable.

cauliflower ear, an ear permanently deformed as a result of being injured in boxing, etc.

cau·line (kô'lin, kô'lin), *adj.* [< *caulis*], in *botany,* of or growing on a stem, especially the upper part of a stem.

cau·lis (kô'lis), *n.* [*pl.* CAULES (-lēz)], [L. < Gr. *kaulos*], in *botany,* the main stem or stalk of a plant.

caulk (kôk), *v.t.* to stop up (a crack or joint), as with tar, oakum, etc.: see **calk.**

caulk·er (kôk'ẽr), *n.* 1. a person who caulks boats, ships, etc. 2. a tool used in caulking. Also spelled **calker.**

caus., causative.

caus·a·ble (kôz'ə-b'l), *adj.* that can be caused.

caus·al (kôz''l), *adj.* [L. *causalis*], 1. of a cause or causes. 2. like or constituting a cause. 3. relating to cause and effect. 4. expressing a cause or reason. *n.* in *grammar,* a causal connective, as *since, therefore, for.*

cau·sal·gi·a (kô-zal'ji-ə, kô-zal'jə), *n.* [Mod. L. < Gr. *kausos,* fever, heat + *algos,* pain], neuralgia characterized by a burning sensation.

cau·sal·i·ty (kô-zal'ə-ti), *n.* [*pl.* CAUSALITIES (-tiz)], 1. causal quality or agency. 2. the interrelation of cause and effect; principle that nothing can exist or happen without a cause.

caus·al·ly (kôz''l-i), *adv.* 1. as a cause. 2. by the operation of cause and effect.

cau·sa·tion (kô-zā'shən), *n.* 1. a causing or being caused. 2. a causal agency; anything producing an effect. 3. causality.

caus·a·tive (kôz'ə-tiv), *adj.* [L. *causativus*], 1. producing an effect; causing. 2. expressing causation, as certain verbs: *fell* is a *causative* verb meaning "to cause to fall": abbreviated **caus.** *n.* a causative word or form.

caus·a·tive·ly (kôz'ə-tiv-li), *adv.* 1. as a cause or causative. 2. by causality.

cause (kôz), *n.* [ME.; OFr.; L. *causa,* a cause, reason, judicial process, lawsuit], 1. anything producing an effect or result. 2. a person or thing acting voluntarily or involuntarily as the agent that brings about an effect or result: as, a woman was the *cause* of his downfall. 3. a reason, motive, or ground for producing or trying to produce a given effect. 4. reason enough: as, *cause* for divorce. 5. any activity or movement that a number of people are interested in and support: as, slum clearance is a good *cause.* 6. in *law,* a case to be decided by the court; lawsuit. *v.t.* [CAUSED (kôzd), CAUSING], to be the cause of; bring about; make happen; effect; induce; produce.

make common cause with, to work together with toward the same objective; join forces with.

***SYN.*—cause,** in its distinctive sense, refers to a situation, event, or agent that produces an effect or result (carelessness is often a *cause* of accident); **reason** implies the mental activity of a rational being in explaining or justifying some act or thought (she had a *reason* for laughing); a **motive** is an impulse, emotion, or desire that leads to action (the *motive* for a crime); an **antecedent** is an event or thing that is the predecessor of, and is responsible for, a later event or thing (war always has its *antecedents*); a **determinant** is a cause that helps to determine the character of an effect or result (ambition was a *determinant* in his success).

‡cause cé·lèbre (kōz' sā'leb'r'), [Fr.], a celebrated law case, trial, or controversy.

cause·less (kôz'lis), *adj.* 1. having no apparent cause. 2. without adequate reason or motive; groundless.

cau·se·rie (kō'zə-rē'; Fr. kōz'rē'), *n.* [Fr. < *causer,* to chat; Pr. *causar,* to quarrel; LL. *causare,* to complain < L. *causari,* to plead, dispute, debate < *causa;* see CAUSE], 1. an informal talk or discussion; chat. 2. a short piece of writing in a conversational style.

cause·way (kôz'wā'), *n.* [< *causey* + *way*], 1. a raised way or road, as across wet ground. 2. a paved way or road; highway. *v.t.* to make a causeway over or through; furnish with a causeway.

cau·sey (kô'zi), *n.* [*pl.* CAUSEYS (-ziz)], [ME. *cauce;* ONorm. Fr. *caucie* < LL. *calciare,* to make a road < L. *calx, calcis,* lime], [British Dial.], a causeway.

caus·tic (kôs'tik), *adj.* [L. *causticus;* Gr. *kaustikos* < *kaustos,* burning < *kaiein,* to burn], 1. that can burn, eat away, or destroy living tissue by chemical action; corrosive. 2. cutting; biting; stinging; sardonic; sarcastic. 3. designating or of the curved radial surface, or a plane curve in this surface, formed by the reflection or refraction of rays from a curved solid surface. *n.* [L. *causticum* < the *adj.*], 1. any caustic substance. 2. a caustic surface or curve. —***SYN.*** see **sarcastic.**

caus·ti·cal·ly (kôs'ti-k'l-i, kôs'tik-li), *adv.* in a caustic manner.

caus·tic·i·ty (kôs-tis'ə-ti), *n.* caustic quality.

caustic potash, potassium hydroxide, KOH.

caustic soda, sodium hydroxide, NaOH.

cau·ter·ant (kô'tẽr-ənt), *adj.* cauterizing. *n.* a substance or instrument that cauterizes.

cau·ter·i·za·tion (kô'tẽr-ə-zā'shən), *n.* a cauterizing or being cauterized.

cau·ter·ize (kô'tẽr-īz'), *v.t.* [CAUTERIZED (-īzd'), CAUTERIZING], [LL. *cauterizare* < Gr. *kautēriazein* < *kautērion, kautēr,* burning or branding iron < *kaiein,* to burn], to burn with a hot iron or needle, or with a caustic substance, so as to destroy dead tissue, prevent the spread of infection, etc.

cau·ter·y (kô'tẽr-i), *n.* [*pl.* CAUTERIES (-iz)], [L. *cauterium;* Gr. *kautērion*], 1. an instrument or substance for cauterizing. 2. a cauterizing.

cau·tion (kô'shən), *n.* [L. *cautio* < same base as *cavere,* to be on one's guard, take care], 1. a warning; admonition. 2. a word, sign, etc. by which warning is given. 3. the act or practice of prudence; wariness; being cautious. 4. [Colloq.], an extraordinary person or thing. *v.t.* to warn; admonish. —***SYN.*** see **advise.**

cau·tion·ar·y (kô'shən-er'i), *adj.* urging caution; warning; admonishing.

cau·tious (kô'shəs), *adj.* full of caution; careful to avoid danger; circumspect; wary. —***SYN.*** see **careful.**

cav., 1. cavalier. 2. cavalry.

cav·al·cade (kav''l-kād', kav''l-kād'), *n.* [Fr.; It. *cavalcata* < *cavalcare,* to ride < *cavallo,* horse], a parade or ceremonial procession, as of horsemen, carriages, etc.

cav·a·le·ro (kav'ə-lā'rō), *n.* [Sp. *caballero* < LL. *caballarius;* see CAVALIER], a cavalier: also **cavaliero.**

cav·a·lier (kav'ə-lêr'), *n.* [Fr.; It. *cavaliere* < LL. *caballarius* < L. *caballus,* a horse], 1. an armed horseman; knight. 2. a gallant or courteous gentleman, especially one serving as a lady's escort. Abbreviated **cav.** 3. [C-], a partisan of Charles I of England in his struggles with Parliament (1641–1649); Royalist: opposed to *Roundhead.* *adj.* 1. free and easy; gay; offhand. 2. haughty; arrogant; supercilious. 3. [C-], of the Cavaliers.

cav·a·lier·ly (kav'ə-lêr'li), *adv.* in a cavalier manner. *adj.* like or characteristic of a cavalier; arrogant.

cav·a·lie·ro (kav'ə-lyâ'rō), *n.* a cavalero.

ca·val·la (kə-val'ə), *n.* [*pl.* CAVALLA, CAVALLAS (-əz); see PLURAL, II, D, 2], [Port. < *cavallo,* a horse; L. *caballus,* a horse: all the fishes mentioned below are sometimes called *horse mackerel* in England], 1. the cero, a fish like the mackerel. 2. any of several fishes of the carangoid group, especially an edible fish found off the coasts of tropical America.

ca·val·ly (kə-val'i), *n.* [*pl.* CAVALLY, CAVALLIES (-iz); see PLURAL, II, D, 2], a cavalla.

cav·al·ry (kav''l-ri), *n.* [*pl.* CAVALRIES (-riz)]. [Fr. *cavalerie;* It. *cavalleria* < *cavaliere;* see CAVALIER], combat troops mounted originally on horses but now often on motorized armored vehicles: distinguished from *infantry:* abbreviated **cav.**

cav·al·ry·man (kav''l-ri-mən), *n.* [*pl.* CAVALRYMEN (-mən)], a member of the cavalry.

cav·a·ti·na (kav'ə-tē'nə; It. kä'vä-tē'nä), *n.* [It., dim. of *cavata,* a separate air], 1. a short, simple solo song or melody that is part of a larger composition, such as an opera or oratorio. 2. loosely, any instrumental composition of lyric quality.

cave (kāv), *n.* [ME.; Fr.; L. *cava* < *cavus,* hollow], 1. a hollow place inside the earth, usually an opening, as in a hillside, extending back horizontally; cavern. 2. [British Slang], *a)* secession from a political party over an issue. *b)* those seceding. *v.t.* [CAVED (kāvd), CAVING], [< the *n.*], to hollow out; make a hollow in. *v.i.* [Colloq.], to cave in.

cave in, 1. to collapse; fall or sink in or down. 2. to make collapse; cause to fall or sink in or down. 3. [Colloq.], to give way; give in; submit; yield.

ca·ve·at (kā'vi-at'), *n.* [L., let him beware; 3d pers. sing., pres. subj., of *cavere,* to beware, take heed], 1. in *law,* a notice that an interested party (called the *caveator*) files with the proper legal authorities directing them to stop or refrain from an action until he can be heard. 2. a warning.

‡**ca·ve·at emp·tor** (kā′vi-at′ emp′tôr), [L.], let the buyer beware (i.e., one buys at his own risk).

ca·ve·a·tor (kā′vi-ā′tẽr), *n.* a person who files a caveat.

‡**ca·ve ca·nem** (kā′vi kā′nem), [L.], beware the dog.

cave-in (kāv′in′), *n.* 1. a caving in. 2. a place where the ground, etc., has caved in.

Cav·ell, Edith Louisa (kav′'l), 1865–1915; English nurse in Belgium in World War I; executed by Germans for helping Allied soldiers to escape from occupied Belgium.

cave man, a prehistoric human being of the Stone Age who lived in caves; cave dweller: sometimes applied to men who are rough and crudely direct, especially toward women.

cav·en·dish (kav′ən-dish), *n.* [said to be after the Am. exporter], leaf tobacco softened, mixed with molasses, and pressed into plugs or cakes.

Cav·en·dish, Henry (kav′ən-dish), 1731–1810; English chemist and physicist.

cav·ern (kav′ẽrn), *n.* [Fr. *caverne;* L. *caverna* < *cavus,* hollow], a cave, especially a large cave. *v.t.* 1. to enclose in or as in a cavern. 2. to hollow out.

cav·ern·ous (kav′ẽr-nəs), *adj.* [L. *cavernosus*], 1. full of caverns or cavities. 2. of a cavern. 3. deep and hollow in sound. 4. deep-set, as eyes.

ca·vet·to (kə-vet′ō; It. kä-vet′tô), *n.* [*pl.* CAVETTI (-i; It. -tē), CAVETTOS (-ōz)], [It., dim. of *cavo,* hollow; L. *cavus*], a concave molding used in architecture: see **molding,** illus.

cav·i·ar, cav·i·are (kav′i-är′, kav′i-är′, kä′vi-är′), *n.* [Fr.; It. *caviale* < Turk. *khāvyār*], a salty relish prepared from the eggs of sturgeon, salmon, or certain other fish.

caviar to the general, a thing appealing only to a highly cultivated taste: *Hamlet* II, ii.

cav·i·corn (kav′i-kôrn′), *adj.* [< L. *cavus,* hollow + *cornu,* a horn], in *zoology,* having hollow horns.

cav·il (kav′'l), *v.i.* [CAVILED or CAVILLED (-'ld), CAVILING or CAVILLING], [OFr. *caviller;* L. *cavillari* < *cavilla,* a jest, quibbling], to object unnecessarily or frivolously; resort to trivial faultfinding; carp; quibble (with *at* or *about*). *v.t.* to cavil at. *n.* a trivial objection; quibble.

cav·il·er, cav·il·ler (kav′'l-ẽr), *n.* a person who cavils.

cav·i·ta·tion (kav′ə-tā′shən), *n.* [< L. *cavitas,* a hollow, cavity; + *-ation*], the formation of partial vacuums in a flowing liquid as a result of the separation of its parts.

Ca·vi·te (kä-vē′te), *n.* a seaport on Manila Bay, in the Philippines: pop., 38,000: see **Philippine Islands,** map.

cav·i·ty (kav′ə-ti), *n.* [*pl.* CAVITIES (-tiz)], [Fr. *cavité;* LL. *cavitas* < L. *cavus,* hollow], 1. a hole; hollow place. 2. a natural hollow place within the body: as, the abdominal *cavity.* 3. a hollow place in a tooth, usually caused by decay. —*SYN.* see **hole.**

ca·vort (kə-vôrt′), *v.i.* [Americanism; earlier *cauvaut, cavault;* ? blend of *curvet* (Southern pronun.) & *gavotte*], to prance; leap about; caper: as, the horse *cavorted.*

Ca·vour, Ca·mil·lo Ben·so di (kä-mēl′lô ben′sô dē kä-vōōr′), Count of Cavour, 1810–1861; Italian statesman; premier (1852–1859; 1860–1861); helped unify Italy.

ca·vy (kā′vi), *n.* [*pl.* CAVIES (-viz)], [< Mod. L. *Cavia,* name of the genus < the native name in Fr. Guiana, *cabiai*], any of several short-tailed South American rodents, as the guinea pig.

caw (kô), *n.* [echoic], the harsh, strident sound that a crow or raven makes. *v.i.* to make this sound.

Cawn·pore (kôn-pôr′, kôn-pōr′, kôn-poor′), *n.* a city in northern India, on the Ganges: pop., 705,000: also spelled **Cawnpur.**

Cax·ton (kak′stən), *n.* 1. any book printed by William Caxton. 2. black-letter type like that used by Caxton.

Caxton, William, 1422?–1491; the first English printer.

cay (kā, kē), *n.* [Sp. *cayo;* see KEY (reef)], a coral reef or sand bank off a mainland.

Cay·enne (kī-en′, kā-en′), *n.* the capital of French Guiana: pop., 13,400.

cay·enne (kī-en′, kā-en′), *n.* [< native Braz. *kynnha;* popularly associated with *Cayenne*], 1. a very hot red pepper made from the dried seeds or fruit of a pepper plant, especially of the capsicum: also **cayenne pepper.** 2. the fruit of a capsicum.

Cayes (kā), *n.* a seaport on the southwestern coast of Haiti: pop., 12,000: also **Aux Cayes.**

cay·man (kā′mən), *n.* [*pl.* CAYMANS (-mənz)], [Sp. *caiman* < Carib native name], any of several large alligators of South and Central America.

Cay·man Islands (kī-män′), three islands of Jamaica, south of Cuba: area, 100 sq. mi.; pop., 7,600.

Ca·yu·ga (kā-ū′gə, kī-ū′gə), *n.* [*pl.* CAYUGA, CAYUGAS, (-gəz)], [Am. Ind.], a member of a tribe of Iroquoian Indians who lived around Cayuga Lake and Seneca Lake, in New York: see **Five Nations.**

Cayuga Lake, a lake in western New York: length, 38 mi.; width, 1 to 3 1/2 mi.

Cay·use (kī-ūs′), *n.* [Am. Ind.], 1. a member of a tribe of Oregonian Indians who lived in the Blue Mountains section of northeastern Oregon. 2. [c-], an Indian pony.

Cb, in *chemistry,* columbium.

C battery, in *radio,* a battery that sets the grid of a vacuum tube at some desired potential.

C.B.S., CBS, Columbia Broadcasting System.

cc., chapters.

cc., c.c., cubic centimeter; cubic centimeters.

C.C., c.c., 1. carbon copy. 2. cashier's check. 3. chief clerk. 4. circuit court. 5. city council. 6. civil court. 7. company commander. 8. county clerk. 9. county commissioner. 10. county council. 11. county court.

C.C.A., 1. Chief Clerk of the Admiralty. 2. Circuit Court of Appeals. 3. County Court of Appeals.

CCC, 1. Civilian Conservation Corps. 2. Commodity Credit Corporation.

C clef, in *music,* a sign on a staff (or), indicating that C is the note on the third line (*alto clef*) or on the fourth line (*tenor clef*): distinguished from *treble clef* and *bass clef:* see **clef,** illus.

ccm, centimeters.

Cd, in *chemistry,* cadmium.

cd., cord; cords.

c.d., cash discount.

Ce, in *chemistry,* cerium.

C.E., 1. Chemical Engineer. 2. Chief Engineer. 3. Church of England. 4. Civil Engineer.

Ce·a·rá (se′ä-rä′), *n.* Fortaleza, a city in Brazil.

cease (sēs), *v.t. & v.i.* [CEASED (sēst), CEASING], [ME. *cesen, cessen;* OFr. *cesser;* L. *cessare,* to loiter, cease, give way < pp. of *cedere,* to go away, yield, withdraw], to end; stop; discontinue. *n.* [OFr. *ces* < *v.*], a ceasing: seldom used except in *without cease.* —*SYN.* see **stop.**

cease·less (sēs′lis), *adj.* unceasing; continual.

Ce·bu (se-bōō′), *n.* 1. an island in the Philippines, between Negros and Leyte: area, 1,703 sq. mi.; pop., 947,000. 2. its chief city: pop., 201,000. 3. a province consisting of this island and adjacent small islands: pop., 1,350,000. See **Philippine Islands,** map.

Cech·y (che′hi), *n.* Bohemia: the Czech name.

Ce·cil (sē′s'l, ses′'l), [L. *Caecilius,* name of a Roman gens; prob. < *caecus,* blind, devoid of light; hence, lit., dim-sighted, blind], a masculine name: feminine, *Cecilia, Cecily.*

Cec·il, William (ses′'l, sis′'l), first Baron Burghley, 1520–1598; English statesman; adviser to Elizabeth I.

Ce·cile (sə-sēl′, ses′'l), a feminine name: see **Cecilia.**

Ce·cil·ia (si-sil′yə, si-sēl′yə), [L. *Caecilia,* fem. of *Caecilius;* see CECIL], a feminine name: diminutives, *Cis, Cissie;* Fr. *Cécile;* variants, *Cecily, Cicely, Sheila.*

Cecilia, Saint, ?–230? A.D.; Roman martyr; patron saint of music: her day is November 22.

Cec·i·ly (ses′'l-i), a feminine name: see **Cecilia.**

Ce·cro·pi·a moth (si-krō′pi-ə), [< Mod. L. *Cecropia,* name of a genus of mulberry trees < *Cecrops;* see CECROPS], a large silkworm moth of the United States, having wide wings, each with a crescent-shaped spot of white edged in red.

Ce·crops (sē′krops), *n.* [Gr. *Kekrops*], in *Greek legend,* the first king of Attica and founder of Athens, represented as half man, half dragon.

ce·cum (sē′kəm), *n.* [*pl.* CECA (-kə)], caecum.

ce·dar (sē′dẽr), *n.* [ME. & OFr. *cedre;* L. *cedrus;* Gr. *kedros*], 1. any of a group of wide-spreading evergreen trees having clusters of needlelike leaves, cones, and durable wood with a characteristic fragrance. 2. any of various trees like this, as certain kinds of juniper, thuja, etc. 3. the wood of any of these. *adj.* of cedar.

ce·dar·bird (sē′dẽr-bũrd′), *n.* the cedar waxwing.

cedar chest, a large box made of cedar, in which woolens, furs, etc. are stored for protection against damage by moths.

ce·darn (sē′dẽrn), *adj.* [Poetic], of cedar or cedars.

Cedar Rapids, a city in east central Iowa: pop., 92,000.

cedar waxwing, a brownish-gray, crested American bird with red, waxlike tips on its secondary wing feathers: also **cedarbird.**

cede (sēd), *v.t.* [CEDED (-id), CEDING], [Fr. *céder* < L. *cedere,* to yield], 1. to give up; transfer the title or ownership of. 2. to admit; grant, as a point in debate.

ce·dil·la (si-dil′ə), *n.* [Fr. *cédille;* Sp. *cedilla,* dim. of *zeda;* Gr. *zēta,* the Greek name of the letter *z:* so called because *z* was written after *c* to give the sound of the letter *s*], a hooklike mark put under *c* in some French words (e.g., *garçon*) to show that it is to be sounded like a voiceless *s* [IPA s] or, formerly, in some Spanish words (e.g., *direcçion*) to show that it is to be sounded like voiceless *th* [IPA θ].

Ced·ric (sed′rik, sē′drik), [? < Celt. base meaning "war chief"], a masculine name.

ced·u·la (sej′oo-lə; Sp. the′thōō-lä′), *n.* [Sp. *cédula;* LL. *scedula;* see SCHEDULE], 1. in Spanish-speaking countries, a certificate or permit. 2. in the Philippines, a certificate of personal registration. 3. the tax for this.

cee (sē), *n.* C; c. *adj.* shaped like C.

C.E.F., Canadian Expeditionary Force (or Forces).

ce·i·ba (sā′i-bä′; Sp. the′ē-bä), *n.* [Sp. < native (Arawakan) name in South America], 1. a tropical tree whose seed pods contain kapok; silk-cotton tree. 2. (*also* sī′bə), kapok; silk-cotton.

ceil (sēl), *v.t.* [Fr. *ciel,* canopy, roof < L. *caelum,* heaven, hence ceiling; prob. influenced by OFr. *cieller;* L. *caelare,* to carve], 1. to build a ceiling in or over. 2. to cover (the ceiling or walls of a room), as with plaster. 3. to cover the ceiling or walls of (a room).

ceil·ing (sēl′iŋ), *n.* [< *ceil*], 1. the inside top part or covering of a room, opposite the floor. 2. any overhanging expanse seen from below. 3. an upper limit set on anything: as, a *ceiling* on prices. 4. in *aeronautics, a)* the upper limit of visibility. *b)* the highest that an aircraft can go under certain conditions.

hit the ceiling, [Slang], to become suddenly very angry; lose one's temper.

cel·an·dine (sel′ən-dīn′), *n.* [ME. *celidoine, celydon;* OFr. *celidoine;* L. *chelidonia;* Gr. *chelidonion,* swallowwort < *chelidōn,* a swallow], 1. a weedy plant of the poppy family, with deeply divided leaves and yellow flowers and juice. 2. the pilewort.

Cel·a·nese (sel′ə-nēz′, sel′ə-nēs′), *n.* [coined < *cel*lulose *a*cetate + *-ese* by Dr. Henri Dreyfus, Eng. pioneer in the development of the fiber], rayon made of cellulose acetate: a trade-mark.

-cele (sēl), [< Gr. *kēlē*], 1. a combining form meaning *tumor* or *swelling.* 2. -coele.

Cel·e·bes (sel′ə-bēz′, sə-lē′bēz; D. se-lā′bes), *n.* 1. an island of Indonesia, east of Borneo: area, 65,663 sq. mi. 2. a province of Indonesia, consisting of this island and several small adjacent islands: area, 72,986 sq. mi.; pop., 5,930,000. Abbreviated **Cel.**

cel·e·brant (sel′ə-brənt), *n.* [< L. *celebrans,* ppr. of *celebrare;* see CELEBRATE], 1. a person who performs a religious rite. 2. the priest officiating at Mass.

cel·e·brate (sel′ə-brāt′), *v.t.* [CELEBRATED (-id), CELEBRATING], [< L. *celebratus,* pp. of *celebrare,* to frequent, go in great numbers, honor < *celeber,* frequented, populous], 1. to perform (a ritual, etc.) publicly and formally; solemnize. 2. to commemorate (an anniversary, holiday, etc.) with ceremony or festivity. 3. to proclaim. 4. to honor or praise publicly. *v.i.* 1. to observe a holiday, anniversary, etc. with festivities. 2. to perform a religious ceremony. 3. [Colloq.], to have a convivial good time.

***SYN.*—celebrate** implies the marking of an occasion or event, especially a joyous one, with ceremony or festivity (let's *celebrate* his promotion); to **commemorate** is to honor the memory of some person or event by a ceremony (to *commemorate* Armistice Day); **solemnize** suggests the use of formal, grave ritual in signalizing an event, especially a religious ceremony (to *solemnize* a marriage); **observe** and the less formal **keep** suggest the respectful marking of a day or occasion in the prescribed or appropriate manner (to *observe,* or *keep,* a religious holiday).

cel·e·brat·ed (sel′ə-brāt′id), *adj.* [pp. of *celebrate*], famous; renowned; well-publicized. —***SYN.*** see **famous.**

cel·e·bra·tion (sel′ə-brā′shən), *n.* [L. *celebratio*], 1. a celebrating; formal commemoration. 2. that which is done to celebrate.

cel·e·bra·tor (sel′ə-brā′tēr), *n.* a person who celebrates.

ce·leb·ri·ty (sə-leb′rə-ti), *n.* [*pl.* CELEBRITIES (-tiz)], [L. *celebritas,* multitude, fame < *celeber,* frequented, populous, famous], 1. fame; renown; wide recognition. 2. a famous or well-publicized person.

ce·ler·i·ty (sə-ler′ə-ti), *n.* [Fr. *célérité;* L. *celeritas* < *celer,* swift, quick], swiftness; quickness; speed.

cel·er·y (sel′ēr-i), *n.* [Fr. *céleri;* It. *seleri;* L. *selinon;* Gr. *selinon,* parsley], a plant whose crisp, blanched stalks are eaten as a vegetable.

celery salt, a seasoning made of celery seed and salt.

ce·les·ta (sə-les′tə), *n.* [Fr. *célesta;* see CELESTIAL], a small keyboard instrument whose bell-like tones are produced by the striking of hammers against small metal plates.

CELESTA

Ce·leste (sə-lest′), [Fr. *Céleste* < L. *caelestis;* see CELESTIAL], a feminine name: variants, *Celestine, Celia.*

ce·les·tial (sə-les′chəl), *adj.* [ME.; OFr.; L. *caelestis* < *caelum,* heaven], 1. of the heavens; of the sky. 2. of heaven; heavenly; divine. 3. [C-], Chinese. *n.* 1. any being regarded as living in heaven. 2. [usually C-], a Chinese.

Celestial City, in Bunyan's *Pilgrim's Progress* (1678), the heavenly New Jerusalem toward which Christian makes his pilgrimage.

Celestial Empire, China or the old Chinese Empire: translation of a former Chinese name for China.

celestial globe, a globe representing the celestial sphere, with all the stars, planets, etc. placed in their proper relative positions.

celestial navigation, a determination of position and course, as at sea or in an airplane, by observing the sun, moon, and stars.

celestial pole, either of the two points in the celestial sphere where the earth's axis of rotation, if extended, would intersect.

celestial sphere, 1. the infinite sphere of the heavens hypothecated from the half visible from a point on the earth. 2. the rounded ceiling of a planetarium, upon which is projected a chart of the stars, planets, etc.

Ce·les·tine (sə-les′tēn, sə-les′tin), [Fr. *Célestine;* L. *Caelestina,* lit., heavenly], a feminine name: see **Celeste.**

cel·es·tine (sel′əs-tin, sel′əs-tīn′), *n.* [< L. *caelestis,* celestial; + *-ine:* from its blue color], celestite.

Cel·es·tine V, Saint (sel′əs-tīn′, sə-les′tēn, sə-les′tin), 1215?–1296; Italian Benedictine monk; pope 1294.

cel·es·tite (sel′əs-tīt′), *n.* [altered (by J. D. Dana, Am. mineralogist) < *celestine*], in *mineralogy,* strontium sulfate, $SrSO_4$, which occurs usually in white, crystalline form, but is sometimes blue: most strontium compounds are produced from it.

Cel·ia (sēl′yə, sē′li-ə), a feminine name: see **Celeste.**

ce·li·ac (sē′li-ak′), *adj.* coeliac.

cel·i·ba·cy (sel′ə-bə-si), *n.* [as if < L. **caelibatia;* see CELIBATE], the state of being unmarried, especially that of a person under a vow; single life.

cel·i·bate (sel′ə-bit, sel′ə-bāt′), *n.* [L. *caelibatus* < *caelebs,* unmarried < IE. **qaiwelo-,* alone, whole (akin to **qai-lo,* hale, whole, and hence akin to Goth. *hails,* healthy, OHG. *heil,* healthy, whole, AS. *hal,* Eng. *whole*) + **lib(h)-,* living (akin to Goth. *liban,* Eng. *live*)], 1. an unmarried person. 2. a person who has taken a vow to remain unmarried. *adj.* 1. unmarried; single. 2. bound by a vow to remain unmarried.

cell (sel), *n.* [ME & OFr. *celle;* L. *cella,* small room, hut; IE. base **kel-,* to conceal (in the earth), hence akin to Goth. *halja,* Eng. *hell,* OHG. & OS. *halla,* AS. *heall,* hall], 1. a small convent or monastery attached to a larger one. 2. a hermit's hut. 3. a small room; cubicle, as in a convent or prison. 4. a very small hollow, cavity, or compartment, as of a honeycomb. 5. any very small natural cavity in the body. 6. the space of an insect's wing enclosed by the veins. 7. in *biology,* a very small unit of protoplasm, usually with a nucleus and an enclosing membrane: all plants and animals are made up of one or more cells. 8. in *botany, a)* any compartment of an ovary. *b)* a pollen sac or spore sac. 9. in *electricity, a)* a receptacle containing electrodes and an electrolyte, used either for generating electricity by chemical reactions or for decomposing compounds by electrolysis. *b)* any compartment of a storage battery: see **storage battery,** illus. 10. in *sociology,* any of the smallest organizational units of a group whose purpose is to propagandize, effect reforms, etc.

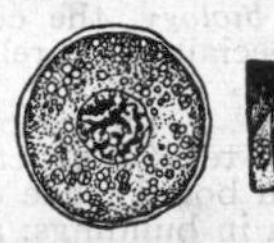

ORGANIC CELLS
Various types of animal cells showing nuclei

cel·la (sel′ə), *n.* [*pl.* CELLAE (-ē)], [L.; see CELL], the inner part of an ancient Greek or Roman temple.

cel·lar (sel′ēr), *n.* [ME. *celler;* OFr. *celier;* L. *cellarium,* pantry, storeroom < *cella;* see CELL], 1. a room or group of rooms below the ground level and usually under a building, often used for storing fuel, provisions, etc. 2. a cellar for wines. 3. a stock of wines: as, he keeps a good *cellar.* *v.t.* to store in a cellar.

cel·lar·age (sel′ēr-ij), *n.* 1. space of or in a cellar. 2. cellars collectively. 3. the fee for storage in a cellar.

cel·lar·er (sel′ēr-ēr), *n.* a person in charge of a cellar or provisions, as in a monastery.

cel·lar·et (sel′ēr-et′), *n.* [*cellar* + *-et*], a cabinet for bottles of wine, liquor, glasses, etc.

Cel·li·ni, Ben·ve·nu·to (ben′ve-nōō′tô chel-lē′nē; Eng. chə-lē′ni), 1500–1571; Italian metalworker and sculptor; known for his autobiography.

cel·list, ′cel·list (chel′ist), *n.* a person who plays the cello; violoncellist.

cel·lo, ′cel·lo (chel′ō), *n.* [*pl.* CELLOS or ′CELLOS (-ōz), CELLI or ′CELLI (-ē)], [< *violoncello*], an instrument of the violin family, between the viola and the double bass in size and pitch; violoncello.

cel·loi·din (se-loi′din), *n.* [*cell* + *-oid* + *-in*], a concentrated solution of pyroxylin used in microscopy for embedding specimens that are to be cut into thin cross sections.

cel·lo·phane (sel′ə-fān′), *n.* [< *cellulose* + Gr. *phanein,* to appear, seem], a thin, transparent material made from cellulose, used as moistureproof wrapping for foods, tobacco, etc., or to make packages look more attractive: formerly a trade-mark (**Cellophane**).

CELLO

cel·lu·lar (sel′yoo-lẽr), *adj.* 1. of or like a cell. 2. consisting of or containing cells.

cel·lu·late (sel′yoo-lāt′), *adj.* cellular. *v.t.* [CELLULATED (-id), CELLULATING], to make cellular; form into cells.

cel·lu·lat·ed (sel′yoo-lāt′id), *adj.* cellular.

cel·lule (sel′ūl), *n.* [L. *cellula*, dim. of *cella;* see CELL], a very small cell.

cel·lu·li·tis (sel′yoo-lī′tis), *n.* [Mod. L. < L. *cellula* (see CELLULE); + *-itis*], an inflammation of a cellular tissue, especially of subcutaneous tissue.

cel·lu·loid (sel′yoo-loid′, sel′ə-loid′), *n.* [*cellulose* + *-oid*], a thin, inflammable substance made from pyroxylin and camphor, used for photographic films, toilet articles, etc.: a trade-mark (**Celluloid**).

cel·lu·lose (sel′yoo-lōs′), *n.* [Fr. < L. *cellula*, dim.; see CELL], the chief substance composing the cell walls or woody part of plants, a carbohydrate of unknown molecular structure but having the composition represented by the empirical formula $(C_6H_{10}O_5)_x$: it is used in the manufacture of paper, rayon, explosives, etc.

cellulose acetate, any of several compounds produced by the action of acetic acid or acetic anhydride upon cellulose in the presence of concentrated sulfuric acid: used in making artificial silks, photographic films, etc.

cellulose nitrate, any ester of nitric acid and cellulose produced by the action of nitric acid upon wood, cotton, or some other form of cellulose in the presence of concentrated sulfuric acid: used in making guncotton, plastics, lacquers, etc.

cel·lu·lous (sel′yoo-ləs), *adj.* 1. full of cells. 2. consisting of cells.

cell wall, in *biology*, the covering or separating wall of a cell; especially, the relatively rigid covering of a plant cell.

ce·lom (sē′ləm), *n.* the coelom.

cel·o·tex (sel′ə-teks′), *n.* [cf. CELLULOSE & TEXTURE], a composition board made of sugar-cane residue, used for insulation in buildings: a trade-mark (**Celotex**).

Cel·si·us (thermometer), (sel′si-əs), [after Anders *Celsius* (1701–1744), Swed. astronomer, the inventor], centigrade (thermometer): abbreviated **Cels., C.**

Celt (selt, kelt), *n.* [Fr. *Celte*, orig., Breton; hence, analogous to Breton; L. *Celta*, pl. *Celtae* (Gr. *Keltoi*) the Gauls], 1. a Celtic-speaking person: the Bretons, Irish, Welsh, and Highland Scots are Celts. 2. one of an ancient people in central and western Europe, reputedly including the Gauls and Britons. Also **Kelt.**

celt (selt), *n.* [< LL. **celtis* inferred < Vulgate *vel celte sculpantur in silice* (Job 19:24); prob. ghost-word (*certe* in other mss.) adopted as genuine by archaeologists c. 1700], a prehistoric tool of stone or bronze, resembling a chisel or ax head.

Cel·tic (sel′tik, kel′tik), *adj.* of the Celts, their languages, culture, characteristics, etc.: existence of a distinct Celtic race is often loosely assumed. *n.* a family of Indo-European languages structurally akin to ancient Gaulish, now spoken in the western British Isles and in Brittany: from the contrasted velar and labial developments of Indo-European **qw-*, it is subdivided into *Goidelic* (represented by Erse, Scottish Gaelic, and Manx) and *Brythonic* (represented by Breton, Cornish, and Welsh). Abbreviated **C., Celt.** Also **Keltic.**

Cel·ti·cism (sel′tə-siz′m), *n.* 1. a Celtic custom. 2. a Celtic idiom, as in Irish English. 3. fondness for Celtic customs.

ce·ment (sə-ment′), *n.* [ME. *ciment;* OFr. *cement, ciment;* L. *caementum*, rough stone, chippings < **caedimentum* < *caedere*, to cut], 1. a substance made of powdered lime and clay, mixed with water and used to fasten stones or bricks together, or as paving: the mixture (mortar) hardens like stone when it dries. 2. any soft substance that fastens things together firmly when it hardens, as paste or glue. 3. a cementlike substance used in filling cavities, as in teeth. 4. anything that joins together or unites; bond. 5. the bony outer crust of the root of a tooth. 6. in *metallurgy*, a dust or powder, as of charcoal or sand, or a finely divided metal, used in cementation. *v.t.* 1. to join or unite with or as with cement. 2. to spread or cover with cement. *v.i.* to become cemented; stick.

ce·men·ta·tion (sē′mən-tā′shən, sem′ən-tā′shən), *n.* 1. a cementing or being cemented. 2. the process by which a solid surrounded by a metallurgic cement is heated intensely and made to combine chemically with the cement to produce a new product, as in making porcelain from green glass.

ce·ment·ite (sə-men′tīt), *n.* [*cement* + *-ite*], the carbide of iron, Fe_3C, occurring in steel, cast iron, and most other alloys of iron and carbon.

ce·men·tum (sə-men′təm), *n.* [L.; cf. CEMENT], the hard, bony tissue forming the outer layer of the root of a tooth: also **cement.**

cem·e·ter·y (sem′ə-ter′i), *n.* [*pl.* CEMETERIES (-iz)], [LL. *caemeterium;* Gr. *koimētērion*, sleeping place < *koiman*, to put to sleep], a place for the burial of the dead; graveyard.

cen., 1. central. 2. century.

-cene (sēn), [< Gr. *kainos*, recent], a combining form meaning *recent, new,* or especially, *designating a* (specified) *epoch in the Cenozoic Era of geological time,* as *Miocene.*

ce·nes·the·sia (sē′nes-thē′zhə, sen′es-thē′zhi-ə), *n.* coenesthesia.

ce·nes·the·sis (sē′nes-thē′sis, sen′es-thē′sis), *n.* coenesthesis.

Ce·nis, Mont (mōn′ sə-nē′), an Alpine peak between France and Italy: height, 6,835 ft.: near it are a railway tunnel, 8 mi. long, and a famous mountain pass.

ce·no- (sē′nō, sen′ə), coeno-.

cen·o·bite (sen′ə-bīt′, sē′nə-bīt′), *n.* [LL. *coenobita* < *coenobium;* Gr. *koinobion*, convent. neut. of *koinobios* < *koinos*, common + *bios*, life], a member of a religious order living in a convent or monastery: opposed to *anchorite:* also spelled **coenobite.**

ce·no·bit·ic (sen′ə-bit′ik, sē′nə-bit′ik), *adj.* of or like a cenobite: living the life of a cenobite; not anchoritic: also spelled **coenobitic.**

ce·no·bit·ism (sen′ə-bit-iz′m, sē′nə-bit-iz′m), *n.* 1. the condition of being a cenobite. 2. the system or practice of cenobites. Also spelled **coenobitism.**

ce·no·gen·e·sis (sē′nə-jen′ə-sis, sen′ə-jen′ə-sis), *n.* [< Gr. *kainos*, new; + *-genesis*], that form of the development of an individual plant or animal which does not repeat the evolutional history of its group: opposed to *palingenesis:* also spelled **caenogenesis.**

cen·o·taph (sen′ə-taf′), *n.* [Fr. *cénotaphe;* L. *cenotaphium;* Gr. *kenotaphion* < *kenos*, empty + *taphos*, a tomb], a monument or empty tomb honoring a dead person whose body is somewhere else.

Ce·no·zo·ic (sē′nə-zō′ik, sen′ə-zō′ik), *adj.* [< Gr. *kainos*, new, recent + *zōē*, life; + *-ic*], designating or of the geological era following the Mesozoic and including the present: it began about 60 million years ago and is characterized by the appearance and development of the mammals: also **Cainozoic.**
the Cenozoic, the Cenozoic Era or its rocks: see **geology,** chart.

cense (sens), *v.t.* [CENSED (senst), CENSING], [< *incense*], 1. to perfume (a room, person, etc.) by burning incense. 2. to burn incense to (a god).

cen·ser (sen′sẽr), *n.* [ME.; OFr. *censier* < *encensier* < *encens;* see INCENSE, *n.*], an ornamented container in which incense is burned; thurible.

cen·sor (sen′sẽr), *n.* [L. < *censere*, to tax, value, judge], 1. one of two Roman magistrates appointed to take the census and, later, to supervise public morals; hence, 2. any supervisor of public morals; person who tells people how to behave. 3. a person whose task is to examine literature, motion pictures, etc., and to remove or prohibit anything considered unsuitable. 4. an official or military officer who reads publications, mail, etc. to remove any information that might be useful to the enemy. 5. any faultfinder or adverse critic; censurer. 6. in *psychoanalysis*, censorship. *v.t.* to examine, review, expurgate, or change (literature, mail, etc.) as a censor; subject to censorship.

cen·so·ri·al (sen-sôr′i-əl, sen-sō′ri-əl), *adj.* of, like, or characteristic of a censor.

cen·so·ri·ous (sen-sôr′i-əs, sen-sō′ri-əs), *adj.* [L. *censorius;* see CENSOR], inclined to find fault; critical.

cen·sor·ship (sen′sẽr-ship′), *n.* [*censor* + *-ship*], 1. a censoring. 2. a system of censoring. 3. the work or position of a censor. 4. in *psychoanalysis*, the agency that prevents unpleasant ideas, memories, etc. from entering the consciousness in their original form.

cen·sur·a·ble (sen′shẽr-ə-b′l), *adj.* deserving censure; blameworthy.

cen·sure (sen′shẽr), *n.* [L. *censura* < *censor;* see CENSOR], 1. a blaming; condemnation; adverse opinion or judgment. 2. [Archaic], a judicial sentence, especially by church law. *v.t.* [CENSURED (-shẽrd), CENSURING], to blame; condemn as wrong; criticize adversely; express disapproval of. —***SYN.*** see **criticize.**

cen·sus (sen′səs), *n.* [L.; pp. of *censere*, to enroll, tax, assess], 1. in *Roman history*, the act of counting the people and evaluating their property for taxation; hence, 2. any official count of population and recording of economic status, age, sex, etc.

cent (sent), *n.* [Fr., a hundred; L. *centum* < IE. **kṃtom;* hence akin to Goth., OS., AS. & OHG. *hund;* see HUNDRED], 1. a hundred: only in *per cent*, etc. 2. a 100th part of a dollar or of certain other monetary units. 3. a coin having the value of a 100th part of a dollar; penny: symbol, ¢. Abbreviated **c., ct., C.**

cent., 1. centigrade. 2. centime. 3. centimeter. 4. central. 5. centum. 6. century.

cen·tal (sen′t′l), *n.* [< L. *centum* (see CENT); prob. after *quintal*], a unit of weight equal to 100 pounds avoirdupois; hundredweight.

cen·tare (sen′târ; Fr. sän′tår′), *n.* a centiare.

cen·taur (sen′tôr), *n.* [L. *Centaurus;* Gr. *Kentauros*], 1. in *Greek mythology*, a monster with a man's head, trunk, and arms, and a horse's body and legs: the centaurs were supposed to have been the offspring of Ixion. 2. [C-], Centaurus.

Cen·tau·rus (sen-tôr′əs), *n.* [L.; see CENTAUR], a southern constellation between Hydra and the Southern Cross: its brightest star, *alpha Centauri*, is nearer the earth than any other known star: see **constellation**, chart.

cen·tau·ry (sen'tô-ri), *n.* [*pl.* CENTAURIES (-riz)], [ME. *centaurie;* ML. *centauria;* L. *centaureum;* Gr. *kentaurion, kentaureion* < *Kentauros*, centaur: so named because the centaur Chiron is said to have discovered medicinal properties of the plant], any of a group of small plants of the gentian family, some of medicinal value, with flat clusters of red or rose flowers.

cen·ta·vo (sen-tä'vō), *n.* [*pl.* CENTAVOS (-vōz; Sp. -vôs)], [Sp., a hundredth < L. *centum*, a hundred], 1. a small coin of the Philippines, Mexico, and certain South American countries, made of bronze or copper and nickel: it is usually equal to 1/100 peso. 2. a coin of Portugal and Brazil equal to 1/100 escudo.

cen·te·nar·i·an (sen'tə-nâr'i-ən), *adj.* [< *centenary*], 1. of 100 years; of a centenary. 2. of a centenarian; at least 100 years old. *n.* a person at least 100 years old.

cen·te·nar·y (sen'tə-ner'i, sen-ten'ə-ri), *n.* [*pl.* CENTENARIES (-iz, -riz)], [L. *centenarius* < *centum*, a hundred], 1. a century; period of 100 years. 2. a centennial. *adj.* 1. relating to a century; of a period of 100 years. 2. of a centennial.

cen·ten·ni·al (sen-ten'i-əl), *adj.* [< L. *centum*, a hundred + *annus*, year], 1. of 100 years. 2. happening once in a period of 100 years. 3. 100 years old. 4. lasting 100 years. 5. of a 100th anniversary. *n.* 1. a 100th year of existence or duration; 100th anniversary. 2. the celebration of this.

cen·ten·ni·al·ly (sen-ten'i-əl-i), *adv.* once in every 100-year period.

cen·ter (sen'tẽr), *n.* [ME.; OFr. *centre;* L. *centrum;* Gr. *kentron*, sharp point, goad, spur, point around which a circle is described < *kentein*, to prick, goad], 1. a point equally distant from all points on the circumference of a circle or surface of a sphere. 2. the point around which anything revolves; pivot. 3. a place considered as the middle or central point of activity; headquarters. 4. the approximate middle point, place, or part of anything. 5. a thing at the middle point. 6. the ring around the bull's-eye of a target, or a shot that hits this. 7. a point or place that actions, forces, people, etc. go to or come from; focal point: as, Broadway is the theatrical *center* for the whole country. 8. in *biology*, a group of cells having a common function. 9. in *football, basketball, hockey*, etc., a player assigned to the center of a floor, field, or line: the center often puts the ball or puck into play. 10. in *mechanics*, one of two tapered or conical pins or rods, as on a lathe, for holding a revolving object in position. 11. in *military usage*, that part of an army situated between the flanks. 12. [often C-], in *politics*, a position, party, or group between left (radicals and liberals) and right (conservatives and reactionaries): so called from the position of the seats occupied in some European legislatures. Abbreviated **ctr.** *v.i.* to be at a center; be centered. *v.t.* 1. to place in, at, near, or toward the center. 2. to draw to one place; gather to a point. 3. to furnish with a center. 4. in *football*, to pass (the ball) from the line to a player in the backfield. Also spelled **centre.** —*SYN.* see **middle.**

center bit, in *mechanics*, a bit with a sharp, projecting center point and cutting wings on either side.

cen·ter·board (sen'tẽr-bôrd', sen'tẽr-bōrd'), *n.* a movable, keellike board or metal plate lowered through a slot in the floor of a sailboat to prevent drifting.

center field, in *baseball*, the middle part of the outfield.

cen·ter·fire (sen'tẽr-fīr'), *adj.* 1. designating a cartridge with the primer set in the center of the base. 2. designating or of a firearm taking a centerfire cartridge. Cf. **rimfire.**

cen·ter·ing (sen'tẽr-iŋ, sen'triŋ), *n.* 1. a placing at, aiming at, or drawing toward a center. 2. the temporary support of an arch or vault during construction.

center of gravity, that point in a thing around which its weight is evenly distributed or balanced; center of mass; point of equilibrium: abbreviated **C.G., c.g.**

center of mass, the point in a body, or in a system of bodies, so situated that any plane drawn through it divides the body or system into parts having exactly equal masses: for bodies near the earth, this coincides with, and is used as a synonym for, *center of gravity.*

cen·ter·piece (sen'tẽr-pēs'), *n.* an ornament, bowl of flowers, etc. for the center of a table.

cen·tes·i·mal (sen-tes'ə-m'l), *adj.* [< L. *centesimus* < *centum*, a hundred], 1. hundredth. 2. of or divided into hundredths.

cen·tes·i·mo (sen-tes'ə-mō'; Sp. & It. sen-tes'ē-mô'), *n.* [*pl.* CENTESIMOS (-mōz'; Sp. -môs'); It. CENTESIMI (-mē')], [It. & Sp. < L. *centesimus;* see CENTESIMAL], a coin equal to 100th part of an Italian lira, Uruguayan peso, or Panamanian balboa.

cen·ti- (sen'ti), [L. < *centum;* see CENT], a combining form meaning: 1. *hundred* or *hundredfold*, as in *centipede*. 2. *a 100th part of*, as in *centigram.*

cen·ti·are (sen'ti-âr'), *n.* [Fr.; see CENTI- & ARE (unit of area)], a 100th part of an are; unit of land measure, equal to one square meter: abbreviated **ca.**

cen·ti·grade (sen'tə-grād'), *adj.* [Fr. < L. *centum*, a hundred + *gradus*, a degree], 1. consisting of or divided into 100 degrees. 2. of or by the centigrade thermometer. Abbreviated **C., c., cent.**

centigrade thermometer, a thermometer on which, under laboratory conditions, 0° is the freezing point and 100° is the boiling point of water; Celsius thermometer: abbreviated **C.**

cen·ti·gram, cen·ti·gramme (sen'tə-gram'), *n.* [Fr. *centigramme;* see CENTI- & GRAM], a unit of weight, equal to 1/100 gram: abbreviated **cg., cgm.** (*sing.* & *pl.*).

cen·ti·li·ter, cen·ti·li·tre (sen'tə-lē'tẽr), *n.* [Fr. *centilitre;* see CENTI- & LITER], a unit of capacity, equal to 1/100 liter (.6102 cubic inch): abbreviated **cl.**

cen·time (sän'tēm; Fr. sän'tēm'), *n.* [Fr.; OFr. *centisme*, the hundredth < L. *centesimus;* see CENTESIMAL], 1. the 100th part of a franc. 2. a coin of this value. Abbreviated **c., C., cent.**

cen·ti·me·ter, cen·ti·me·tre (sen'tə-mē'tẽr), *n.* [Fr. *centimètre;* see CENTI- & METER], a unit of measure, equal to 1/100 meter (.3937 inch): abbreviated **cm., c., C., cent.**

cen·ti·me·ter-gram-sec·ond (sen'tə-mē'tẽr-gram'sek'-ənd), *adj.* in *physics*, designating or of a system of measurement in which the centimeter, gram, and second are used as the units of length, mass, and time, respectively: abbreviated **C.G.S., cgs, c.g.s.**

cen·ti·mo (sen'tə-mō'), *n.* [*pl.* CENTIMOS (-mōz')], [see CENTIME], the 100th part of a Spanish peseta, a Venezuelan bolivar, or a Costa Rican colon.

cen·ti·pede (sen'tə-pēd'), *n.* [Fr.; L. *centipeda* < *centum*, a hundred + *pes, pedis*, a foot], any of a group of related wormlike animals with a pair of legs for each body segment: the front pair are modified into poison fangs.

cen·ti·stere (sen'tə-stêr'), *n.* [Fr. *centistère;* see CENTI- & STERE], a unit of volume, equal to 1/100 cubic meter.

cent mark (or **sign**), the symbol ¢, meaning *cent* or *cents:* it is placed after the numeral (e.g., 40¢).

cent·ner (cent'nẽr), *n.* [G. *centner, zentner;* L. *centenarius*, consisting of a hundred < *centeni*, a hundred each < *centum;* see CENT], 1. a European commercial weight equal to 50 kilograms (110.23 pounds). 2. a metric weight equal to 100 kilograms (220.46 pounds). 3. the cental; 100 pounds. 4. in *assaying*, one dram.

cen·to (sen'tō), *n.* [*pl.* CENTOS (-tōz)], [L., garment of several pieces, patchwork; akin to Gr. *kentrōn*, cloak of rags, Sans. *kanthā*, patched garment, OHG. *hadara*, rag, patch], 1. a literary or musical work made up of passages from other compositions. 2. anything made up of badly matched parts. 3. [Obs.], a patchwork.

cen·tra (sen'trə), *n.* alternative plural of **centrum.**

cen·tral (sen'trəl), *adj.* [L. *centralis*], 1. in, at, or near the center. 2. of or forming the center. 3. from the center. 4. equally distant or accessible from various points. 5. main; principal; chief; basic. 6. in *anatomy & physiology*, *a)* denoting that part of the nervous system consisting of the brain and spinal cord (of a vertebrate). *b)* of the centrum of a vertebra. 7. in *phonetics*, pronounced with the tongue in center position; mixed: said of vowels. Abbreviated **cen., cent.** *n.* 1. a telephone exchange, especially the main one; hence, 2. [sometimes C-], a telephone operator.

Central African Republic, a country in central Africa, north of the Congo Republics: it is a member of the French Community: area, 241,700 sq. mi.; pop., 1,193,000; capital, Bangui: formerly, *Ubangi-Shari.*

Central America, the part of North America between Mexico and South America: area, 226,881 sq. mi.; pop., 11,538,000. Abbreviated **C.A.**

CENTRAL AMERICA

Central Ameri·can, 1. of Central America, its people, etc. 2. a native or inhabitant of Central America.

Central Falls, a city in northeastern Rhode Island, on the Blackstone River: pop., 20,000.

cen·tral·ism (sen'trəl-iz'm), *n.* the principle or system of centralizing power or authority.

cen·tral·ist (sen'trəl-ist), *n.* a person who believes in centralism. *adj.* of or believing in centralism.

cen·tral·i·ty (sen-tral'ə-ti), *n.* 1. the quality, state, or fact of being central; center position. 2. the tendency to remain at or near the center.

cen·tral·i·za·tion (sen'trəl-ə-zā'shən), *n.* 1. a centralizing or being centralized. 2. a concentration of power or authority; systematization under one control.

cen·tral·ize (sen'trə-līz'), *v.t.* [CENTRALIZED (-īzd'), CENTRALIZING], 1. to make central; bring to or focus on a center; gather together. 2. to organize or systematize under one control. *v.i.* to become centralized.

cen·tral·ly (sen'trəl-i), *adv.* 1. in, at, or near the center; from a center. 2. with reference to the center.

Central Park, a public park in the center of Manhattan, New York City: area, 840 acres.

Central Powers, in World War I, Germany and Austria-Hungary: their allies, Turkey and Bulgaria, are sometimes included under this term.

Central Provinces and Be·rar (bā-rär'), Madhya Pradesh: the former name.

Central Standard Time, one of the four standard times in the United States, corresponding to the mean local time of the 90th meridian west of Greenwich, England: it is six hours behind Greenwich time and one hour behind Eastern Standard Time: abbreviated **C.S.T.**

cent·re (sen'tẽr), *n., v.t. & v.i.* [CENTRED (-tẽrd), CENTRING], center: chiefly British spelling.

cen·tri- (sen'tri), centro-, as in *centripetal.*

cen·tric (sen'trik), *adj.* [Gr. *kentrikos* < *kentron;* see CENTER], 1. in, at, or near the center; central. 2. of or having a center. 3. in *physiology,* of a nerve center.

cen·tri·cal (sen'tri-k'l), *adj.* centric.

cen·tric·i·ty (sen-tris'ə-ti), *n.* the state or quality of being centric.

cen·trif·u·gal (sen-trif'yoo-g'l), *adj.* [Mod. L. *centrifugus* (coined by Newton < *centri-* + L. *fugere,* to flee); + *-al*], 1. moving or tending to move away from the center. 2. using or acted on by centrifugal force. 3. in *botany,* developing from the center outward, as certain flower clusters. 4. in *physiology,* conveying away from a center; efferent. *n.* a machine that uses or causes centrifugal movement, as a milk separator.

centrifugal force, the force tending to make rotating bodies move away from the center of rotation: it is due to inertia.

cen·trif·u·gal·ize (sen-trif'yoo-g'l-īz'), *v.t.* [CENTRIFUGALIZED (-īzd'), CENTRIFUGALIZING], to subject to the action of a centrifuge; separate by whirling in a centrifuge.

cen·tri·fuge (sen'trə-fūj'), *n.* [Fr. < Mod. L. *centrifugus*], a machine using centrifugal force to separate particles of varying density, as cream from milk. *v.t.* [CENTRIFUGED (-fūjd'), CENTRIFUGING], to centrifugalize.

cen·trip·e·tal (sen-trip'ə-t'l), *adj.* [Mod. L. *centripetus* (coined by Newton < *centri-* + L. *petere,* to seek, move toward); + *-al*], 1. moving or tending to move toward the center. 2. using or acted on by centripetal force. 3. in *botany,* developing inward toward the center, as certain flower clusters. 4. in *physiology,* conveying toward a center; afferent.

centripetal force, the force tending to make rotating bodies move toward the center of rotation.

cen·trist (sen'trist), *n.* [Fr. *centriste* < *centre*], a person whose political position is neither leftist nor rightist; member of the center, as in some European legislatures.

cen·tro- (sen'trō, sen'trə), [< L. *centrum,* center; Gr. *kentron,* a horn, point, center], a combining form meaning *center,* as in *centrosome:* also **centri-** or, before a vowel, **centr-.**

cen·tro·bar·ic (sen'trə-bar'ik), *adj.* [< *centro-* + Gr. *baros,* weight], having to do with the center of gravity.

cen·troid (sen'troid), *n.* center of mass.

cen·tro·some (sen'trə-sōm'), *n.* [*centro-* + *-some* (body)], a very small body near or, sometimes, in the nucleus in most animal cells and some plant cells: in mitosis it divides into two parts, toward each of which a group of the divided chromosomes moves.

cen·tro·som·ic (sen'trə-som'ik), *adj.* of a centrosome.

cen·tro·sphere (sen'trə-sfêr'), *n.* [*centro-* + *sphere*], 1. in *biology,* the central mass of protoplasm about the centrosome; central mass of an aster. 2. in *geology,* the central part of the earth.

cen·trum (sen'trəm), *n.* [*pl.* CENTRUMS (-trəmz), CENTRA (-trə)], [L.], 1. a center. 2. in *anatomy,* the body of a vertebra.

cen·tu·ple (sen'too-p'l, sen-tōō'p'l, sen-tū'p'l), *adj.* [Fr. < L. *centuplus;* see CENT & DOUBLE], a hundred times as much or as many; hundredfold. *v.t.* [CENTUPLED (-p'ld), CENTUPLING], to make centuple; increase a hundredfold.

cen·tu·pli·cate (sen-tōō'plə-kāt', sen-tū'plə-kāt'; *for adj. & n., usually* sen-tōō'plə-kit, sen-tū'plə-kit), *v.t.* [CENTUPLICATED (-id), CENTUPLICATING], to increase a hundredfold; centuple. *adj.* hundredfold; centuple. *n.* a centuple quantity.

cen·tu·ri·al (sen-tyoor'i-əl, sen-toor'i-əl), *adj.* [L. *centurialis*], having to do with a century (in all senses).

cen·tu·ri·on (sen-tyoor'i-ən, sen-toor'i-ən), *n.* [L. *centurio* < *centuria;* see CENTURY], the commanding officer of an ancient Roman military unit originally made up of 100 men.

cen·tu·ry (sen'chə-ri), *n.* [*pl.* CENTURIES (-riz)], [L. *centuria* < *centum,* a hundred; see CENT], 1. a series or group of 100 persons or things. 2. any period of 100 years, as from 1620 to 1720. 3. any period of 100 years reckoned from a certain time, especially from the beginning of the Christian Era: as, 1801 A.D. through 1900 A.D. is the 19th *century* A.D., 400 B.C. through 301 B.C. is the 4th *century* B.C. 4. an ancient Roman military unit, originally made up of 100 men. 5. a subdivision of the ancient Romans for voting purposes. Abbreviated **C., c., cen., cent.** (in senses 2 & 3).

century plant, a tropical American agave having fleshy leaves and a tall stalk with greenish flowers: so called because mistakenly thought to bloom only once a century.

ceorl (cheôrl, kyûrl), *n.* [AS.; see CHURL], in early English history, a freeman of the lowest class, ranking above a slave and below a thane.

ceph·al- (sef'əl), cephalo-.

ceph·al·ad (sef'ə-lad'), *adv.* [*cephal-* + L. *ad,* to], in *anatomy & zoology,* toward the head, or anterior part of the body: opposed to *caudad.*

ce·phal·ic (sə-fal'ik, se-fal'ik), *adj.* [L. *cephalicus;* Gr. *kephalikos* < *kephalē,* the head], 1. of the head, skull, or cranium. 2. in, on, near, or toward the head.

-ce·phal·ic (sə-fal'ik), a combining form meaning *head* or *skull,* as in *dolichocephalic.*

cephalic index, a measure of the human skull computed by dividing its maximum breadth by its maximum length and multiplying by 100: if an individual's index is 80 or more, he is short-headed (*brachycephalic);* if less than 80, he is long-headed (*dolichocephalic*). Sometimes an intermediate category (*mesocephalic*) is recognized, indexes of 81 or more then being criteria of brachycephaly, and those under 76 of dolichocephaly.

ceph·a·li·za·tion (sef'ə-li-zā'shən), *n.* [< *cephal-* + *-ize* + *-ation*], 1. the increasing importance of the head or anterior end in the development of animal life. 2. the concentration of important organs or functions in or near the head.

ceph·a·lo- (sef'ə-lō, sef'ə-lə), [< Gr. *kephalē,* the head], a combining form meaning ***the head, skull,*** or ***brain,*** as in *cephalopod:* also, before a vowel, **cephal-.**

ceph·a·lo·chor·date (sef'ə-lə-kôr'dāt), *adj.* [< Mod. L. *Cephalochordata,* name of the subphylum; see CEPHALO- & CHORDATA], of a group of small, fishlike animals, including the amphioxus and lancelet, that have a permanent notochord extending from the anterior to the posterior end. *n.* any animal of this group.

ceph·a·lom·e·ter (sef'ə-lom'ə-tẽr), *n.* [*cephalo-* + *-meter*], an instrument for measuring the head or skull; craniometer.

ceph·a·lom·e·try (sef'ə-lom'ə-tri), *n.* [*cephalo-* + *-metry*], the science of measuring heads.

Ceph·a·lo·ni·a (sef'ə-lō'ni-ə, sef'ə-lōn'yə), *n.* one of the Ionian Islands, off western Greece: area, 277 sq. mi.; pop., 66,000: Greek name, *Kephallenia.*

ceph·a·lo·pod (sef'ə-lə-pod'), *n.* [*cephalo-* + *-pod*], any of the highest class of mollusks, having a distinct head with two large eyes, a beak, and muscular tentacles about the mouth, often with suckers on them: the octopus, squid, and cuttlefish are typical.

ceph·a·lo·tho·rax (sef'ə-lə-thôr'aks, sef'ə-lə-thō'raks), *n.* the head and thorax regarded as a single part, in certain crustaceans and arachnids.

ceph·a·lous (sef'ə-ləs), *adj.* [*cephal-* + *-ous*], having a head.

-ceph·a·lous (sef'ə-ləs), [< Gr. *kephalē*], a combining form meaning *-headed,* as in *microcephalous.*

Ceph·e·id variable (sef'i-id), [< *Cepheus* + *-id*], in *astronomy,* any of a class of stars whose light periodically varies in brightness.

Ce·pheus (sē'fūs, sē'fi-əs), *n.* [L.; Gr. *Kēpheus*], 1. in *Greek legend,* the husband of Cassiopeia and father of Andromeda: he was placed among the stars after his death. 2. a northern constellation near Cassiopeia: see **constellation,** chart.

ce·ra·ceous (si-rā'shəs), *adj.* [< L. *cera,* wax < Gr. *kēros,* wax], waxy; waxlike.

Ce·ram (si-ram'; D. sā'räm), *n.* one of the Molucca Islands, in the Netherlands Indies: area, 6,621 sq. mi.; pop., 83,000: also called *Serang.*

ce·ram·ic (sə-ram'ik), *adj.* [Gr. *keramikos* < *keramos,* potter's clay, pottery], 1. of pottery, earthenware, tile, porcelain, etc. 2. of ceramics. Also **keramic.**

ce·ram·ics (sə-ram'iks), *n.pl.* [< *ceramic*], [construed as sing. in senses 1 & 3], 1. the art or work of making pottery, earthenware, tile, porcelain, etc. 2. objects made of these materials. 3. a course of study in pottery or pottery making. Also **keramics.**

cer·a·mist (ser'ə-mist), *n.* an expert in ceramics; ceramic artist.

ce·rar·gy·rite (sə-rär'jə-rīt'), *n.* [< Gr. *keras,* a horn + *argyros,* silver; + *-ite*], silver chloride, AgCl, a native ore of silver; horn silver.

ce·ras·tes (sə-ras'tēz), *n.* [L.; Gr. *kerastēs,* horned (serpent) < *keras,* a horn], a poisonous African snake with a hornlike spine above each eye; horned viper.

ce·rate (sêr'āt), *n.* [L. *ceratus,* pp. of *cerare,* to wax < *cera,* wax < Gr. *kēros,* wax], a thick ointment consisting

of a fat, as oil, lard, etc., mixed with wax, resin, and other ingredients.
ce·rat·ed (sêr'ā-tid), *adj.* [L. *ceratus;* see CERATE], 1. covered with wax; waxed. 2. having a cere.
cer·a·tin (ser'ə-tin), *n.* keratin.
cer·a·to- (ser'ə-tō, ser'ə-tə), [< Gr. *keras, keratos,* a horn], a combining form meaning *horn, hornlike:* also, before a vowel, **cerat-**, as in *ceratodus.*
ce·rat·o·dus (si-rat'ə-dəs, ser'ə-tō'dəs), *n.* [Mod. L.; see CERATO- & -ODUS], a large Australian fish with gills and lungs; barramunda.
cer·a·toid (ser'ə-toid'), *adj.* [Gr. *keratoeides;* see CERATO- & -OID], like a horn in shape or hardness; horny.
Cer·be·re·an (sẽr-bêr'i-ən), *adj.* of or like Cerberus.
Cer·ber·us (sũr'bẽr-əs), *n.* [L.; Gr. *Kerberos*], in *Greek & Roman mythology,* the three-headed dog guarding the gate of Hades.
cer·ca·ri·a (sẽr-kâr'i-ə), *n.* [*pl.* CERCARIAE (-ē')], [Mod. L. < Gr. *kerkos,* tail], the larva of a trematode worm at the stage in which it has the form of a tadpole.
cere (sêr), *n.* [Fr. *cire;* L. *cera,* wax < Gr. *kēros,* wax], a soft, waxlike membrane at the base of the beak of some birds, as the parrot, eagle, etc. *v.t.* [CERED (sêrd), CERING], to wrap in a cerecloth.
ce·re·al (sêr'i-əl), *adj.* [< L. *Cerealis,* of Ceres, goddess of agriculture], of grain or the grasses producing grain. *n.* 1. any grain used for food, as wheat, oats, etc. 2. any grass producing such grain. 3. food made from grain, especially breakfast food, as oatmeal, etc.
cer·e·bel·lar (ser'ə-bel'ẽr), *adj.* of the cerebellum.
cer·e·bel·lum (ser'ə-bel'əm), *n.* [*pl.* CEREBELLUMS (-əmz), CEREBELLA (-ə)], [L., dim. of *cerebrum,* the brain], the section of the brain behind and below the cerebrum: it is regarded as the co-ordinating center for muscular movement: see **brain**, illus.
cer·e·bral (ser'ə-brəl, sə-rē'brəl), *adj.* [Fr. *cérébral* < L. *cerebrum,* the brain], 1. of the brain or the cerebrum. 2. of, appealing to, or conceived by the intellect rather than the emotions.
cerebral palsy, paralysis due to a lesion of the brain, usually one suffered at birth, and characterized chiefly by spasms: see **spastic.**
cer·e·brate (ser'ə-brāt'), *v.i.* [CEREBRATED (-id), CEREBRATING], [< L. *cerebrum,* the brain; + *-ate*], to use one's brain; think.
cer·e·bra·tion (ser'ə-brā'shən), *n.* brain action, conscious or unconscious; cerebrating; thinking.
cer·e·bric (ser'ə-brik, sə-rē'brik), *adj.* [< *cerebrum* + *-ic*], of or derived from the brain.
cer·e·bri·tis (ser'ə-brī'tis), *n.* an inflammation of the cerebrum.
cer·e·bro- (ser'ə-brō, ser'ə-brə), [< L. *cerebrum,* the brain], a combining form meaning: 1. *the brain* or *cerebrum,* as in *cerebritis.* 2. *the brain and* or *cerebrum and,* as in *cerebrospinal.* Also, before a vowel, **cerebr-**.
cer·e·bro·spi·nal (ser'ə-brō-spī'n'l), *adj.* 1. of or affecting the brain and the spinal cord. 2. designating that part of the nervous system comprising the brain and the spinal cord together with their cranial and spinal nerves: distinguished from *autonomic.*
cer·e·brum (ser'ə-brəm, sə-rē'brəm), *n.* [*pl.* CEREBRUMS (-brəmz), CEREBRA (-brə)], [L.], the upper, main part of the brain of vertebrate animals, consisting of two equal hemispheres: in man it is the largest part of the brain and is believed to control conscious and voluntary processes: see **brain**, illus.
cere·cloth (sêr'klôth'), *n.* [formerly *cered cloth;* see CERE], 1. cloth treated with wax or a similar substance. 2. such a cloth used to wrap a dead person for burial.
cere·ment (sêr'mənt), *n.* [Fr. *cirement;* see CERE], 1. a cerecloth; shroud. 2. *usually pl.* any burial clothes.
cer·e·mo·ni·al (ser'ə-mō'ni-əl, ser'ə-mō'nyəl), *adj.* of or consisting of ceremony; ritual; formal. *n.* 1. an established system of rites or formal actions connected with an occasion, as in religion; ritual. 2. a rite.
cer·e·mo·ni·ous (ser'ə-mō'ni-əs, ser'ə-mō'nyəs), *adj.* [Fr. *cérémonieux*], 1. ceremonial. 2. full of ceremony. 3. characterized by ceremony or formality; very polite.
cer·e·mo·ny (ser'ə-mō'ni), *n.* [*pl.* CEREMONIES (-niz)], [L. *caerimonia,* awe, reverent rite, ceremony], 1. a formal act or set of formal acts established by custom or authority as proper to a special occasion, such as a wedding, religious rite, etc. 2. the service or function at which such acts are used. 3. a conventional social act. 4. behavior that follows rigid etiquette. 5. formality or formalities. 6. empty or meaningless formality.
stand on ceremony, to behave with or insist on formality.
SYN.—**ceremony** refers to a formal, usually solemn, act established as proper to some religious or state occasion (the *ceremony* of launching a ship); **rite** refers to the prescribed form for a religious practice (burial *rites*); **ritual** refers to rites or ceremonies collectively, especially to the rites of a particular religion (the *ritual* of the Peruvian snake worshipers); **formality** suggests a conventional, often meaningless, act or custom, usually one associated with social activity (the *formalities* of polite conversation).
Ce·res (sêr'ēz), *n.* [L.], 1. in *Roman mythology,* the goddess of agriculture, daughter of Ops and Saturn: identified with the Greek Demeter. 2. a small planet with its orbit between Mars and Saturn: it was the first asteroid discovered.
ce·re·us (sêr'i-əs), *n.* [L., wax taper < *cera,* wax: so named from the shape of certain varieties], any of several sorts of American cactus, including a number of night-blooming varieties.
ce·ri·a (sêr'i-ə), *n.* [< *cerium*], cerium dioxide, CeO_2, a white compound.
ce·ric (sêr'ik, ser'ik), *adj.* of or containing cerium, especially with a valence of plus four.
cer·if, cer·iph (ser'if), *n.* a serif: British spelling.
ce·rif·er·ous (sə-rif'ẽr-əs), *adj.* [< L. *cera,* wax; + *-ferous*], producing wax.
Ce·ri·go (che'rē-gô'), *n.* one of the Ionian Islands, south of Greece: area, 110 sq. mi.; pop., 9,000: Greek name, *Kythera,* English (Latin) name, *Cythera.*
ce·rise (sə-rēz', sə-rēs'), *n. & adj.* [Fr.; see CHERRY], bright red; cherry red.
ce·rite (sêr'īt), *n.* [< *cerium* + *-ite*], a native hydrous silicate of cerium and other closely related metals.
ce·ri·um (sêr'i-əm), *n.* [named (1803) after the asteroid *Ceres,* then recently discovered], a gray, metallic chemical element of the rare-earth group: symbol, Ce; at. wt., 140.13; at. no., 58.
cerium metals, a series of closely related metals belonging to the rare-earth group and having atomic numbers from 57 to 62; lanthanum, cerium, praseodymium, neodymium, illinium, and samarium.
Cer·nă·u·ţi (cher'nə-oots'), *n.* Chernovtsy.
cer·nu·ous (sũr'nū-əs), *adj.* [L. *cernuus,* stooping], bending or hanging downward, as a flower or bud.
ce·ro (sêr'ō), *n.* [*pl.* CERO, CEROS (-ōz); see PLURAL, II, D, 2], [Sp. *sierra;* L. *serra,* a saw], either of two large food fishes resembling the mackerel.
ce·ro- (sêr'ə, ser'ə), [< L. *cera;* Gr. *kēros,* wax], a combining form meaning *wax:* also, before a vowel, **cer-**.
ce·ro·plas·tic (sêr'ə-plas'tik), *adj.* [Gr. *kēroplastikos* < *kēros,* wax + *plassein,* to mold], 1. having to do with wax modeling. 2. modeled in wax.
ce·ro·plas·tics (sêr'ə-plas'tiks), *n.pl.* [construed as sing.], the art of modeling in wax.
ce·rot·ic (sə-rot'ik), *adj.* [< L. *cerotum,* a wax salve, pomatum < Gr. *kērōton* < *kēros,* wax], designating or of either of two fatty acids, $C_{26}H_{52}O_2$ or $C_{27}H_{54}O_2$, esters of which are found in beeswax and other waxes and oils.
ce·ro·type (sêr'ə-tīp', ser'ə-tīp'), *n.* [*cero-* + *-type*], the process of engraving on a wax-covered metal plate from which a printing surface is prepared by electrotyping.
ce·rous (sêr'əs), *adj.* of or containing cerium with a valence of three.
ce·rous (sêr'əs), *adj.* in *zoology,* like a cere.
Cer·ro de Pas·co (ser'rô de päs'kô), a town in the mountains of west central Peru: pop., 15,700.
cert., 1. certificate. 2. certified.
cer·tain (sũr't'n, sũr'tin), *adj.* [ME. *certein;* Fr. *certain;* L. *certus,* determined, fixed, settled; pp. of *cernere,* to distinguish, decide, resolve], 1. fixed; settled; determined. 2. sure (to happen, etc.); inevitable. 3. not to be doubted; unquestionable: as, the evidence is *certain.* 4. reliable; dependable: as, this is a *certain* cure for the disease. 5. controlled; unerring: as, his aim was *certain.* 6. assured; sure; positive; without doubt: as, I am *certain* of his innocence. 7. not further described or more specifically named but sometimes assumed to be known: as, a *certain* person. 8. some; appreciable: as, to a *certain* extent. —*SYN.* see **sure.**
for certain, as a certainty; without doubt.
cer·tain·ly (sũr't'n-li, sũr'tin-li), *adv.* surely; beyond a doubt.
cer·tain·ty (sũr't'n-ti, sũr'tin-ti), *n.* [ME. *certeinte;* OFr. *certaineté*], 1. the quality, state, or fact of being certain: as, he lived in the *certainty* of death. 2. [*pl.* CERTAINTIES (-tiz)], anything certain; definite fact.
of a certainty, [Archaic], without a doubt; certainly.
SYN.—**certainty** suggests a firm, settled belief or positiveness in the truth of something; **certitude** is sometimes distinguished from the preceding as implying an absence of objective proof, hence suggesting unassailable blind faith; **assurance** suggests confidence, but not necessarily positiveness, usually in something that is yet to happen (I have *assurance* of his support in the coming elections); **conviction** suggests a being convinced because of satisfactory reasons or proof and sometimes implies earlier doubt.—*ANT.* doubt, skepticism.
cer·tes (sũr'tēz), *adv.* [ME.; OFr., in the phrase *a certes* < L. *certus;* see CERTAIN], [Archaic], certainly; verily.
cer·ti·fi·a·ble (sũr'tə-fī'ə-b'l), *adj.* that can be certified.
cer·tif·i·cate (sẽr-tif'ə-kit), *n.* [Fr. *certificat;* ML. *certificatus,* pp. of *certificare,* to certify < L. *certus,* certain + *facere,* to make], a written or printed state-

ment testifying to a fact, qualification, or promise: abbreviated **cert.**, **certif.**, **ct.**, **ctf.** *v.t.* (sẽr-tif′ə-kāt′), [CERTIFICATED (-id), CERTIFICATING], to attest or authorize by a certificate; issue a certificate to.
certificate of deposit, a certificate from a bank stating that a specified person has a specified sum of money on deposit.
certificate of disability discharge, a discharge from the United States Army because of physical unfitness for further service: abbreviated **CDD** (no period).
certificate of incorporation, a legal document stating the name and purpose of a proposed corporation, the names of its incorporators, its stock structure, etc.
certificate of origin, a certificate submitted by an exporter to those countries requiring it, listing goods to be imported and stating their place of origin.
certificate of stock, a certificate issued by a corporation showing that a specified person owns a specified amount of capital stock in the corporation, and is subject to the rights and liabilities of a stockholder.
cer·ti·fi·ca·tion (sũr′tə-fi-kā′shən), *n.* [Fr.], 1. a certifying or being certified. 2. a certified statement.
cer·ti·fied (sũr′tə-fīd′), *adj.* [pp. of *certify*], 1. vouched for; guaranteed. 2. having a certificate. Abbreviated **cert.**
certified check, a check that a bank guarantees to be good.
certified milk, milk guaranteed to have been produced according to certain regulations of an authorized medical milk commission, but not pasteurized.
certified public accountant, an accountant who has received a certificate stating that he has met the requirements of State law: abbreviated **C.P.A.**
cer·ti·fi·er (sũr′tə-fī′ẽr), *n.* a person who certifies.
cer·ti·fy (sũr′tə-fī′), *v.t.* [CERTIFIED (-fīd′), CERTIFYING], [ME. *certifien;* OFr. *certifier;* ML. *certificare;* see CERTIFICATE], 1. to declare (a thing) true, accurate, certain, etc. by formal statement, often in writing; verify; attest; hence, 2. to declare officially insane; send to an asylum or similar institution. 3. to guarantee the quality or worth of; vouch for: as, the bank must *certify* your check. 4. to safeguard (mail) by having the recipient sign for it, after payment of a fee by the sender. Certified mail cannot be insured for indemnification. 5. [Archaic], to assure; make certain. *v.i.* to testify (*to*). —***SYN.*** see **approve.**
cer·ti·o·ra·ri (sũr shi-ə-râr′i, sũr′shi-ə-rā′rī), *n.* [LL., to be made more certain: a word in the writ], in *law,* a writ from a higher court to a lower one, requesting the record of a case for review.
cer·ti·tude (sũr′tə-tōōd′, sũr′tə-tūd′), *n.* [Late ME.; LL. *certitudo*], certainty; assurance. —***SYN.*** see **certainty.**
ce·ru·le·an (sə-rōō′li-ən), *adj.* [L. *caeruleus,* prob. < *caelulum,* dim. of *caelum,* heaven], sky-blue; azure.
ce·ru·men (sə-rōō′mən), *n.* [< L. *cera,* wax, after *albumen*], a yellowish, waxlike substance secreted by glands in the canal of the external ear; earwax.
ce·ruse (sêr′ōōs, sə-rōōs′), *n.* [Fr. *céruse;* L. *cerussa;* ? < Gr. **kēroessa,* waxlike < *kēros,* wax], 1. white lead, $2PbCO_3 \cdot Pb(OH)_2$. 2. a cosmetic containing this.
ce·rus·site (ser′ə-sīt′), *n.* [< L. *cerussa* (see CERUSE); + *-ite*], native lead carbonate, $PbCO_3$, found in crystalline or massive form.
Cer·van·tes, Mi·guel de (mē-gel′ *the* ther-vän′tes; Eng. sẽr-van′tēz), 1547–1616; Spanish satirical novelist and dramatist; author of *Don Quixote.*
cer·vi·cal (sũr′vi-k′l), *adj.* [< L. *cervix, cervicis,* the neck], in *anatomy,* of the neck or cervix.
cer·vi·ces (sẽr-vī′sēz, sũr′və-sēz′), *n.* alternative plural of **cervix.**
cer·vi·ci·tis (sũr′vi-sī′tis), *n.* [see -ITIS], inflammation of the cervix of the uterus.
cer·vi·co- (sũr′vi-kō), [< L. *cervix, cervicis,* the neck], a combining form meaning *cervical* or *cervical and,* as in *cervicodorsal:* also, before a vowel, **cervic-.**
cer·vi·co·dor·sal (sũr′vi-kō-dôr′s′l), *adj.* [*cervico-* + *dorsal*], in *anatomy,* of the neck and the back.
Cer·vin, Mont (mōn′ ser′van′), the Matterhorn, a mountain in the Alps: the French name.
cer·vine (sũr′vīn, sũr′vin), *adj.* [L. *cervinus* < *cervus,* deer], 1. of a deer or the deer family. 2. like a deer.
cer·vix (sũr′viks), *n.* [*pl.* CERVICES (sẽr-vī′sēz, sũr′və-sēz′), CERVIXES (sũr′vik-siz)], [L., the neck], 1. the neck, especially the back of the neck. 2. a necklike part, as of the uterus, urinary bladder, etc.
Ce·sar·e·an, Ce·sar·i·an (si-zâr′i-ən), *adj.* & *n.* Caesarean.
ce·si·um (sē′zi-əm), *n.* [neut. of L. *caesius,* bluish-gray], a soft, bluish-gray, ductile, metallic chemical element, the most electropositive of all the elements: used in photoelectric cells: symbol, Cs; at. wt., 132.91; at. no., 55: also spelled **caesium.**
ces·pi·tose (ses′pi-tōs′), *adj.* [< L. *caespes,* turf, grassy field], of or like turf; growing in clumps; matted.
cess (ses), *n.* [prob. < *assess*], in Ireland, an assessment; tax: now used only in *bad cess to,* meaning "bad luck to."
ces·sa·tion (se-sā′shən), *n.* [L. *cessatio* < pp. of *cessare,* to cease], a ceasing; stop; pause.
ces·sion (sesh′ən), *n.* [Fr. < L. *cessio* < *cessus,* pp. of *cedere,* to yield], a ceding; giving up (of rights, property, etc.) to another; surrendering.
ces·sion·ar·y (sesh′ən-er′i), *n.* [*pl.* CESSIONARIES (-iz)], the person to whom a cession is made; assignee.
cess·pit (ses′pit′), *n.* [*cess-* (< *cesspool*) + *pit*], a pit for garbage, excrement, etc.
cess·pool (ses′pōōl′), *n.* [< It. *cesso,* privy (< L. *secessus,* place of retirement, privy, drain; see SECEDE) or dial. *cess,* bog, drainage place (prob. < *recess*)], 1. a pool or deep hole in the ground to receive drainage or sewage from the sinks, toilets, etc. of a house. 2. a filthy, smelly place.
‡**c'est-à-dire** (se′tà′dêr′), [Fr.], that is to say; namely.
‡**c'est la guerre** (se′là′gâr′), [Fr.], that's war; such is war.
ces·tode (ses′tōd), *n.* [< Gr. *kestos,* a girdle], any of a group of related parasitic worms with ribbonlike bodies and no mouth or intestinal canal, as the tapeworm. *adj.* of these worms.
ces·toid (ses′toid), *adj.* & *n.* cestode.
ces·tus (ses′təs), *n.* [L. *caestus, cestus;* Gr. *kestos,* a girdle], 1. a girdle; belt. 2. in *Greek & Roman mythology,* a girdle belonging to Aphrodite (Venus), which gave whoever wore it the power to excite love.
ces·tus (ses′təs), *n.* [L. *caestus* < *caedere,* to strike, beat], a contrivance made of leather straps, sometimes weighted with lead or iron, worn on the hand by boxers in ancient Rome.

CESTUS

ce·su·ra (si-zhoor′ə, si-zyoor′ə), *n.* [*pl.* CESURAS (-əz), CESURAE (-ē)], a caesura.
ce·ta·cean (si-tā′shən), *adj.* [< L. *cetus,* large sea animal, whale; Gr. *kētos*], of a group of hairless, fishlike water mammals with paddlelike forelimbs: whales, porpoises, and dolphins are cetaceans. *n.* any such animal.
ce·ta·ceous (si-tā′shəs), *adj.* cetacean.
ce·tane (sē′tān), *n.* [< L. *cetus,* whale; + *-ane*], a saturated hydrocarbon of the methane series, $C_{16}H_{34}$, found as a colorless oil in petroleum.
cetane number, a number representing the ignition properties of Diesel engine fuel oils, determined by the percentage of cetane that must be mixed with *a*-methylnaphthalene to produce the ignition quality of the fuel being tested: the higher the number, the better the ignition quality.
‡**ce·te·ris pa·ri·bus** (set′ẽr-is par′i-bəs), [L.], other things being equal: abbreviated **cet. par.**
Ce·tin·je (tse′ti-nye′), *n.* a town in southern Yugoslavia, formerly the capital of Montenegro: pop., 9,100.
Ce·tus (sē′təs), *n.* [L., the whale], an equatorial constellation south of Pisces: see **constellation,** chart.
Ceu·ta (sū′tə, sōō′tə; Sp. the-ōō′tä), *n.* a Spanish seaport in Africa, opposite Gibraltar: pop., 63,000.
Cé·vennes (sā′ven′), *n.* 1. a mountain range in south central France: highest peak, Mézenc, 5,754 ft. 2. a former district of France, in northeastern Languedoc.
ce·vi·tam·ic acid (sē′vī-tam′ik, sē′vi-tam′ik), [< *C* + *vitamin* + *-ic*], vitamin C: also called *ascorbic acid, antiscorbutic acid.*
Cey·lon (si-lon′), *n.* a country on an island off the southern tip of India: it is a member of the British Commonwealth of Nations: area, 25,332 sq. mi.; pop., 9,172,000; capital, Colombo: abbreviated **Cey.**

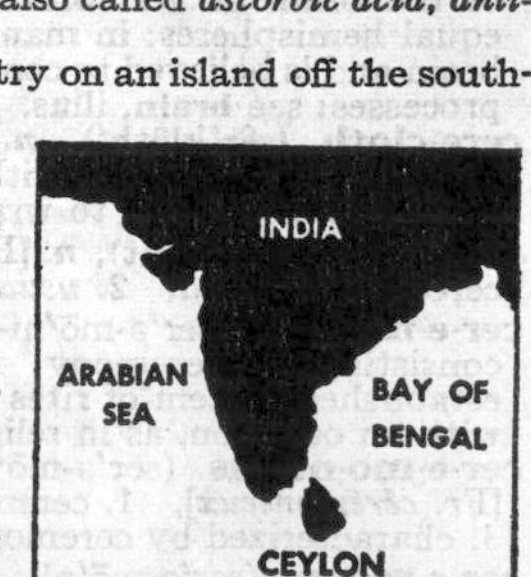

CEYLON

Cey·lo·nese (sē′lə-nēz′), *adj.* of Ceylon, its people, or culture. *n.* [*pl.* CEYLONESE], a native or inhabitant of Ceylon.
Ceylon moss, an East Indian seaweed from which agar-agar is made.
Cé·zanne, Paul (pôl sā′zän′), 1839–1906; French postimpressionist painter.
cf., 1. *confer,* [L.], compare. 2. in *baseball,* center field; center fielder. 3. in *bookbinding,* calf.
Cf, in *chemistry,* californium.
c/f, in *bookkeeping,* carried forward.
C.F., c.f., cost and freight.
C.F.I., c.f.i., cost, freight, and insurance.
c.f.m., cubic feet a minute.
c.f.s., cubic feet a second.
cg., centigram; centigrams.
C.G., Coast Guard.
C.G., c.g., 1. captain of the guard. 2. center of gravity. 3. commanding general. 4. consul general.
cgm., centigram.
C.G.S., cgs, c.g.s., centimeter-gram-second.
Ch., 1. Chaldean. 2. Chaldee. 3. China. 4. Chinese.

Ch., ch., 1. chancery. 2. chaplain. 3. check. 4. chief. 5. child; children. 6. church.
ch., [*pl.* CHS.], chapter.
c.h., 1. courthouse. 2. customhouse.
chab·a·zite (chab′ə-zīt′), *n.* [Fr. *chabazie*, missp. of Gr. *chalazie*, vocative of *chalaza*, hailstone], in *mineralogy*, a form of zeolite occurring in colorless to flesh-colored rhombohedral crystals.
Cha·blis (shå′blē′; Eng. shab′li), *n.* a very dry, white Burgundy wine from the region of Chablis, France.
cha·bouk, cha·buk (chä′book), *n.* [Hind. *chābuk*, a whip < Per.], a long horsewhip, used in Eastern countries for flogging people.
chac·ma (chak′mə), *n.* [< the Hottentot name], a large, blackish-gray baboon of South Africa.
Cha·co (chä′kō), *n.* a region in South America between the Pilcomayo River and Paraguay River, in dispute until 1938, when it was divided between Bolivia and Paraguay: area, 100,000 sq. mi.: see also **Gran Chaco.**

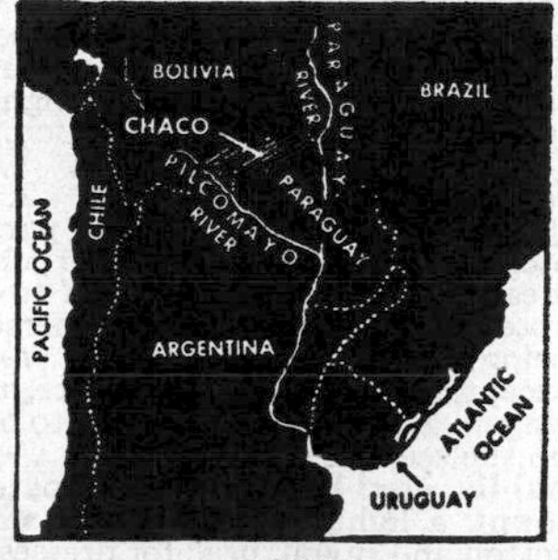

CHACO

‡cha·conne (shå′kōn′), *n.* [Fr.; Sp. *chacona*], 1. a slow, stately dance of the 18th century, similar to the passacaglia and derived from an early Spanish dance. 2. music for this dance, in 3/4 time. 3. a similar movement in various musical compositions.
‡cha·cun à son goût (shå′kun′nå′ sōn′ gōō′), [Fr.], everyone to his own taste.
Chad (chad, chäd), *n.* 1. a country in central Africa: a former French colony, it is now a member of the French Community: area, 495,750 sq. mi.; pop., 2,576,000; capital, Fort-Lamy. 2. a lake between Chad and Nigeria: area, 6,500 sq. mi. French spelling, **Tchad.**
Chad·wick, George White·field (hwīt′fēld′ chad′wik), 1854–1931; American composer.
Chaer·o·ne·a (ker′ə-nē′ə), *n.* an ancient Greek city in Boeotia, on the Attic border.
chae·ta (kē′tə), *n.* [*pl.* CHAETAE (-tē)], [Mod. L.; Gr. *chaitē*, hair], a bristle, bristlelike part, or spine; seta.
chae·to- (kē′tō, kē′tə), [< Gr. *chaitē*, hair], a combining form meaning *hair* or *bristles*: also **chaet-.**
chae·toph·o·rous (ki-tof′ẽr-əs), *adj.* [*chaeto-* + *-phorous*], in *zoology*, bearing bristles.
chae·to·pod (kē′tə-pod′), *n.* [*chaeto-* + *-pod*], in *zoology*, any of a class of annelids whose body segments have unjointed appendages bearing bristles.
chafe (chāf), *v.t.* [CHAFED (chāft), CHAFING], [ME. *chaufen;* OFr. *chaufer*, to warm; L. *calefacere*, to make warm < *calere*, to be warm + *facere*, to make], 1. to rub so as to stimulate or make warm. 2. to wear away by rubbing. 3. to irritate or make sore by rubbing. 4. to annoy; irritate: as, the delay *chafed* her. *v.i.* 1. to rub (often with *on* or *against*). 2. to be or become angry or irritable. *n.* 1. a chafing. 2. an injury or irritation caused by rubbing. 3. annoyance; vexation.
chafe at the bit, to be impatient; become angry or irritable because of delay: originally said of horses.
chaf·er (chāf′ẽr), *n.* [ME.; AS. *ceafor;* akin to G. *käfer;* prob. "devourer" < base **caf-* (as in AS. *ceafl;* see JOWL) < IE. **ĝeph-*, jaw, to eat up, devour], any of a group of related beetles that feed on plants, as the cockchafer, scarab, rose bug, etc.
chaff (chaf, chäf), *n.* [ME. *chaf;* AS. *ceaf;* akin to MD. *caf* (G. dial. *kaf*); ? < same IE. base as in *chafer, jowl*], 1. threshed or winnowed husks of wheat or other grain. 2. fine-cut hay or straw, used for fodder. 3. anything worthless. 4. light talk; banter; good-natured teasing. *v.t. & v.i.* to tease or ridicule in a good-natured manner.
chaf·fer (chaf′ẽr), *n.* [ME. *chaffare, cheapfare*, merchandise, trade < *cheap*, AS. *ceap, cep*, a purchase, bargain; + *fare*, AS. *faru*, a journey, success], 1. a haggling over price; bargaining. 2. [Obs.], buying and selling. *v.i.* 1. to haggle over price; bargain. 2. to chat idly. *v.t.* 1. to bandy (words). 2. [Obs.], to buy or sell.
chaf·finch (chaf′inch), *n.* [AS. *ceaffinc;* see CHAFF & FINCH: so called because it eats chaff], a small European songbird, often kept in a cage as a pet.
chaff·y (chaf′i, chäf′i), *adj.* [CHAFFIER (-i-ẽr), CHAFFIEST (-i-ist)], 1. full of chaff. 2. like chaff; worthless.
chaf·ing dish (chāf′iŋ), [see CHAFE], a pan with a heating apparatus beneath it, to cook food at the table or to keep food hot.
Cha·gall, Marc (märk shä-gäl′), 1887– ; Russian painter in France and elsewhere.
Cha·gres (chä′gres), *n.* a river in Panama and the Canal Zone: a dam on this river forms Gatun Lake.
cha·grin (shə-grin′), *n.* [Fr. grief, sorrow, vexation; ? < Norm. *chagreiner*, to become gloomy (said of the weather); OFr. *graignier*, to sorrow < *grain*, sorrow < OHG. *gram*, sorrow, trouble], a feeling of disappointment, humiliation, embarrassment, etc. caused by failure or discomfiture of some kind; mortification. *v.t.* [CHAGRINED (-grind′), CHAGRINING], [Fr. *chagriner*], to cause to feel chagrin; discomfit: chiefly in the passive.
Cha·har (chä′här), *n.* a former province of Inner Mongolia.
Chaikovsky, Pëtr Ilich, see **Tchaikovsky, Pëtr Ilich.**
chain (chān), *n.* [ME. *chaine, cheine;* OFr. *chaine, chaene* < L. *catena*, a chain], 1. a flexible series of joined links, usually of metal. 2. *pl.* bonds; fetters; hence, 3. *pl.* captivity; bondage. 4. any chainlike ornament. 5. a chainlike measuring instrument, or its measure of length: as, a surveyor's *chain* (66 feet long), an engineer's *chain* (100 feet long): abbreviated **chn.** 6. a connected series of things or events. 7. in *bacteriology*, four or more cells joined end to end. 8. in *chemistry*, a linkage of atoms in a molecule: see **open chain, closed chain.** *v.t.* 1. to fasten or shackle with chains. 2. to restrain; bind. 3. to imprison; confine; keep in bondage. —*SYN.* see **series.**
chain gang, a gang of prisoners chained together, as when working.
chain letter, a letter to be circulated among many people by being copied and passed from one to another after it has been read.
chain lightning, lightning that zigzags rapidly across the sky.
chain mail, flexible armor made of joined metal links.
chain·man (chān′mən), *n.* [*pl.* CHAINMEN (-mən)], 1. a man whose work is to carry or take care of metal chains. 2. either of the two workers needed to use a surveyor's chain.
chain measure, a system of linear measurement used in surveying:

7.92 inches	=	1 link
100 links (66 ft.)	=	1 chain
10 chains	=	1 furlong
80 chains	=	1 mile

chain pump, a pump consisting of an endless chain of cups conveyed over a wheel or drum.
chain reaction, 1. a series of chemical reactions in which the products of each reaction activate additional molecules of the reactants, thus causing new reactions: it can be started by light, an electric spark, sodium vapor, bombardment with alpha particles from radium, etc.; hence, 2. any sequence of events, each of which results in, or has an effect on, the following.
chain shot, cannon shot consisting of two balls or half balls connected by a chain, formerly used in naval warfare to destroy masts, sails, etc.
chain·stitch (chān′stich′), *v.t.* to ornament, crochet, or sew with chain stitches.
chain stitch, a fancy stitch in which the loops are connected in a chainlike way, as in crocheting.
chain store, any of a group of retail stores owned and controlled by one company, usually with the same merchandise and policy.
chain·work (chān′wũrk′), *n.* any product or handiwork in which parts are linked together, as in sewing with a chain stitch.
chair (châr), *n.* [ME. *chaire, chaere;* OFr. *chaiere* < L. *cathedra;* see CATHEDRA], 1. a seat for one person: it usually has four legs and a back. 2. a seat of authority or dignity; hence, 3. an office or position of authority, as a judgeship, professorship, or chairmanship. 4. a person who presides over a meeting; chairman. 5. a covered chair carried on poles; sedan. 6. *a)* the electric chair. *b)* execution by the electric chair. *v.t.* 1. to place in a chair; seat. 2. to place in authority; choose as chairman. 3. [British], to carry (a person) in public triumph on, or as though on, a chair.
take the chair, 1. to preside as chairman; hence, 2. to open a meeting.
chair car, a railroad car with individual chairs; parlor car: distinguished from *coach, sleeping car*, etc.
chair·man (châr′mən), *n.* [*pl.* CHAIRMEN (-mən)], 1. a person who presides at a meeting or heads a committee, board, etc.: abbreviated **chm., chmn.** 2. a man whose work is to carry or wheel people in a chair.
chair·man·ship (châr′mən-ship′), *n.* [*chairman* + *-ship*], 1. the office or position of chairman. 2. the term of office of a chairman.
chair·wom·an (châr′woom′ən), *n.* [*pl.* CHAIRWOMEN (-wim′in)], a woman who presides at a meeting or heads a committee, board, etc.
chaise (shāz), *n.* [Fr., Parisian var. of *chaire*, orig. in sense "sedan chair"; see CHAIR], any of several kinds of lightweight carriage, some with a collapsible top, having two or four wheels and drawn by one or two horses.

chaise longue (shāz′lôŋg′; Fr. shez′lōng′), [*pl.* CHAISE LONGUES (lôŋgz′; Fr. lōng′)], [Fr., lit., long chair], a couchlike chair with a support for the back of the sitter and a seat long enough to support his outstretched legs.

Chal., 1. Chaldaic. 2. Chaldean. 3. Chaldee.

cha·la·za (kə-lā′zə), *n.* [*pl.* CHALAZAS (-zəs), CHALAZAE (-zē)], [Mod. L.; Gr. *chalaza*, hailstone, hard lump, pimple], either of the whitish spiral bands extending from the yolk to the lining membrane at each end of a bird's egg: see **egg,** illus.

chal·can·thite (kal-kan′thīt), *n.* [< L. *chalcanthum* < Gr. *kalkanthon*, vitriol (< *kalkos*, copper + *anthos*, flower); + *-ite*], blue vitriol, a crystalline copper sulfate.

Chal·ce·don (kal′si-dən, kal′si-don′), *n.* an ancient city in Asia Minor.

chal·ced·o·ny (kal-sed′'n-i, kal′sə-dō′ni), *n.* [*pl.* CHALCEDONIES (-iz, -niz)], [L. *chalcedonius;* Gr. *chalkēdōn;* prob. after *Chalkēdōn*, Chalcedon], a kind of quartz that has the luster of wax and is variously colored, usually grayish or milky: it comprises onyx, agate, sard, cat's-eye, jasper, carnelian, and chrysoprase.

chal·cid (kal′sid), *n.* [< Mod. L. *Chalcis*, name of the typical genus of the family Chalcididae < Gr. *chalkos*, copper: so named because of their metallic color], any of a large group of very small insects, either four-winged or wingless, whose larvae are parasitic on the eggs, larvae, or pupae of other insects: also **chalcid fly.** *adj.* of these insects.

Chal·cid·i·ce (kal-sid′ə-sē′), *n.* a peninsula in northeastern Greece: Greek name, *Khalkidike.*

chal·co- (kal′kō, kal′kə), [< Gr. *chalkos*, copper, brass], a combining form meaning *copper* or *brass*, as in *chalcocite.*

chal·co·cite (kal′kə-sīt′), *n.* [see CHALCO-], native cuprous sulfide, Cu_2S, a dark-colored mineral with a metallic luster: it is an important copper ore.

chal·co·graph·ic (kal′kə-graf′ik), *adj.* of, or having the nature of, chalcography.

chal·cog·ra·phy (kal-kog′rə-fi), *n.* [*chalco-* + *-graphy*], the art of engraving on copper or brass.

chal·co·py·rite (kal′kə-pī′rīt, kal′kə-pir′īt), *n.* [*chalco-* + *pyrite*], a yellow sulfide of copper and iron, $CuFeS_2$, an important copper ore; copper pyrites.

Chald., 1. Chaldaic. 2. Chaldean. 3. Chaldee.

Chal·da·ic (kal-dā′ik), *adj. & n.* Chaldean: abbreviated **Chal., Chald.**

Chal·de·a (kal-dē′ə), *n.* an ancient region in southwestern Asia, on the Euphrates River and the Persian Gulf.

CHALDEA

Chal·de·an (kal-dē′ən), *adj.* [L. *Chaldaeus;* Gr. *Chaldaios*], 1. of Chaldea, its people, their language, or culture: astrology and magic flourished in Chaldea; hence, 2. having to do with astrology or occult lore. *n.* 1. a native or inhabitant of Chaldea; member of a Semitic people related to the Babylonians. 2. an astrologer or sorcerer. 3. the Semitic language of the Chaldeans. Abbreviated **Ch., Chal., Chald.**

Chal·dee (kal-dē′, kal′dē), *adj. & n.* 1. Chaldean: abbreviated **Ch., Chal., Chald.** 2. formerly and erroneously, Biblical Aramaic.

chal·dron (chôl′drən), *n.* [prob. < OFr. *chauderon;* see CALDRON], a unit of dry measure variously equal to 32, 36, or more bushels, formerly used in England for measuring coal, coke, lime, etc.

cha·let (sha-lā′, shal′i; Fr. shȧ′le′), *n.* [Swiss Fr.; ? < dim. of L. *casa*, a house, cabin], 1. a herdsman's hut or cabin in the Swiss Alps. 2. a Swiss cottage with overhanging eaves. 3. any house built in this style.

Cha·lia·pin, Fe·o·dor I·va·no·vitch (fyô′dôr ē-vä′nô-vich′ shȧ-lyä′pin; Eng. shä′li-ä′pin), 1873–1938; Russian operatic basso.

chal·ice (chal′is), *n.* [ME. & OFr. *chalice, calice;* L. *calix*, a cup], 1. a cup; goblet. 2. the cup for the wine of Holy Communion. 3. a cup-shaped flower.

chal·iced (chal′ist), *adj.* 1. held in a chalice. 2. cup-shaped: said of a flower.

chalk (chôk), *n.* [ME.; AS. *cealc;* L. *calx, calcis*, limestone, chalk], 1. a white, gray, or yellowish limestone that is soft and easily pulverized: it is composed mainly of small sea shells. 2. chalklike substance. 3. a piece of chalk, often colored, used for writing on a blackboard, etc. 4. a score; tally; reckoning, as of credit. *adj.* made or drawn with chalk: as, a *chalk* drawing. *v.t.* 1. to treat with chalk; lime or fertilize (soil). 2. to rub or smear with chalk; hence, 3. to make pale. 4. to write, draw, or mark with chalk.
chalk out, 1. to mark out. 2. to outline; plan.
chalk up, 1. to make a record of. 2. to score. 3. to charge or credit to (an account).
walk a chalk line, [Colloq.], to behave with strict propriety or obedience.

chalk·i·ness (chôk′i-nis), *n.* the quality of being chalky.

chalk·stone (chôk′stōn′), *n.* [ME. *chalcston*], 1. a lump or mass of chalk. 2. a hard lump or mass formed in the tissue and joints of a person with gout; tophus.

chalk talk, a lecture accompanied with explanatory diagrams, etc. drawn in chalk on a blackboard.

chalk·y (chôk′i), *adj.* [CHALKIER (-i-ẽr), CHALKIEST (-i-ist)], 1. of, containing, or covered with chalk. 2. like chalk in color or texture.

chal·lenge (chal′ənj, chal′inj), *n.* [ME. *chalenge;* OFr. *chalenge, chalonge, calenge, calonge*, accusation, claim, dispute < L. *calumnia*, false accusation], 1. a demand for identification: as, a sentry gave the *challenge.* 2. a calling into question: as, a *challenge* of the premises of an argument. 3. a call to take part in a fight, contest, etc.; defiance. 4. a demand; claim upon. 5. an exception to a vote or to someone's right to vote. 6. in *law*, a formal objection or exception. *v.t.* [CHALLENGED (-ənjd, -injd), CHALLENGING], 1. to make a challenge to (a person); call to account. 2. to make objection to; question. 3. to call to take part in a fight, contest, etc.; defy; dare. 4. to call for; claim; demand: as, this idea *challenges* attention. 5. to take exception to (a vote) as not being valid or (a person at the polls) as not being legally qualified to vote. 6. in *law*, to take formal exception to. *v.i.* 1. to make, utter, or issue a challenge. 2. in *hunting*, to begin to bark or bay on picking up the scent: said of hounds.

chal·lis, chal·lie (shal′i), *n.* [? patois form of *Calais*, Fr. town], a lightweight fabric of wool, wool mixture, or cotton and rayon, used for dresses: it is usually printed.

chal·one (kal′ōn), *n.* [Gr. *chalōn*, ppr. of *chalein*, to slacken], an internal secretion that reduces, restrains, or arrests the activity of various organs of the body.

Châ·lons-sur-Marne (shȧ′lōn′ sür′mȧrn′), *n.* a city in northeastern France: pop., 31,000 (1946): scene of a battle (451 A.D.), in which the Romans and Visigoths defeated the Huns led by Attila.

Cha·lon-sur-Saône (shȧ′lōn′sür′sōn′), *n.* a city in east central France: pop., 33,000 (1946).

chal·u·meau (shal′yoo-mō′; Fr. shȧ′lü′mō′), *n.* [Fr.; OFr. *chalemel* < L. *calemellus*, dim. of *calamus*, reed], 1. *a)* an obsolete double-reed wind instrument of the oboe family. *b)* an obsolete single-reed wind instrument, forerunner of the clarinet. 2. the lowest register of the modern clarinet.

cha·lutz (khä-lōōts′), *n.* [*pl.* CHALUTZIM (-lōōt-sēm′)], a halutz.

cha·lyb·e·ate (kə-lib′i-āt, kə-lib′i-it), *adj.* [< L. *chalybs;* Gr. *chalyps, chalybos*, steel < *Chalybes*, name of a people in Pontus, noted for their steel], 1. containing salts of iron. 2. tasting like iron. *n.* a chalybeate liquid or medicine.

cham (kam), *n.* [Archaic], a khan; Tatar ruler.

cha·made (shə-mäd′), *n.* [Fr.; Port. *chamada* < *chamar* < L. *clamare*, to cry out, shout], [Archaic], in *military usage*, a signal for a parley or retreat, sounded on a drum or trumpet.

cham·ber (chām′bẽr), *n.* [ME. *chambre;* OFr. *chambre, cambre;* LL. *camera*, a chamber, room; see CAMERA], 1. a room in a house, especially a bedroom. 2. *pl.* [British], a suite of rooms used by one person. 3. *pl.* a judge's office located near the courtroom. 4. an assembly hall. 5. a legislative or judicial body or division: as, the *Chamber* of Deputies. 6. a council: as, a *chamber* of commerce. 7. an enclosed space in the body of a plant or animal. 8. the part of a gun that holds the charge. 9. a chamber pot. 10. [Archaic], a chamberlain's office. *v.t.* to provide a chamber or chambers for; put into a chamber. *v.i.* [Obs.], to live in a chamber.

chamber concert, a concert of chamber music.

cham·bered (chām′bẽrd), *adj.* having a chamber or chambers; having compartments.

cham·ber·lain (chām′bẽr-lin), *n.* [ME. *chamberling, chamberlein;* OFr. *chambarlan, chamberlenc;* OHG. *chamarlinc* < *chamara, kamara* (L. *camera*) + dim. suffix *-linc;* see CAMERA & -LING], 1. an officer in charge of the household of a ruler or lord; steward. 2. a high official in certain royal courts. 3. a treasurer. 4. [Archaic], the bedchamber attendant of a ruler or lord.

Cham·ber·lain, Sir **Austen** (chām′bẽr-lin), (*Joseph Austen Chamberlain*), 1863–1937; son of *Joseph;* British statesman; received Nobel peace prize, 1925.

Chamberlain, Joseph, 1836–1914; father of *Austen* and *Neville;* British statesman.

Chamberlain, Neville, (*Arthur Neville Chamberlain*), 1869–1940; son of *Joseph;* British statesman; prime minister (1937–1940).

cham·ber·maid (chām′bẽr-mād′), *n.* a woman whose work is taking care of the bedrooms, as in hotels.

chamber music, music suitable for performance in a room or small hall, as trios, quartets, and quintets.

chamber of commerce, an association established to defend and further the business interests of its community.

chamber pot, a portable container kept in a bedroom and used as a toilet.
cham·bray (sham′brā), *n.* [Fr., after *Cambrai*, town in France; cf. CAMBRIC], a variety of gingham made by weaving white cotton threads across a colored warp: used for dresses, shirts, etc.
cha·me·le·on (kə-mē′li-ən, kə-mēl′yən), *n.* [L. *chamaeleon;* Gr. *chamaileōn; chamai*, on the ground + *leōn*, lion], 1. any of various lizards that can change the color of their skin; hence, 2. a changeable or fickle person.

CHAMELEON (6 in. long)

cha·me·le·on·ic (kə-mē′li-on′ik), *adj.* like a chameleon; changeable; fickle.
cham·fer (cham′fẽr), *n.* [Fr. *chanfrein* < OFr. *chanfraindre* < *chant fraindre;* L. *canthum frangere;* see CANT (an angle, edge) & FRAGILE], 1. the flat surface created by slicing off the square edge or corner of a block of wood, stone, etc. 2. a groove or fluting, as in wood. *v.t.* 1. to cut a chamfer on; bevel. 2. to make a groove or fluting in.
cham·frain (cham′frin), *n.* a chamfron.
cham·fron (cham′frən), *n.* [Fr. *chanfrein;* OFr. *chaufrain, chanfrain*, snaffle, chamfron < *chafresner*, to fasten rein or bridle on a horse < L. *caput*, the head + *frenum*, a bridle, reins], the headpiece of the armor worn by war horses in medieval times.
cham·ois (sham′i), *n.* [*pl.* CHAMOIS], [Fr. < LL. *camox, camoce*], 1. a small, goatlike antelope of the mountains of Europe and southwestern Asia, having straight horns with the tips bent backward. 2. a soft leather made from the skin of sheep, deer, goats, etc., originally from the skin of the chamois: also spelled **shammy, chammy.** *adj.* 1. made of chamois. 2. fawn-colored. *v.t.* [CHAMOISED (-id), CHAMOISING (-i-iŋ)], 1. to prepare like a chamois skin. 2. to dry or polish with a chamois skin.

CHAMOIS (2 ft. high)

cham·o·mile (kam′ə-mīl′), *n.* camomile.
Cha·mo·nix (sham′ə-ni; Fr. shȧ′mô′nē′), *n.* a valley north of Mt. Blanc, in eastern France.
Cha·mor·ro (chä-môr′rō), *n.* 1. [*pl.* CHAMORROS (-rōz)], a member of one of the native tribes of Guam and the Marianas Islands. 2. the Indonesian language spoken by the Chamorros.
Cha·mou·ni (shȧ′mōō′nē′), *n.* Chamonix.
champ (champ), *v.t.* & *v.i.* [earlier *cham;* prob. echoic], 1. to chew hard and noisily; munch. 2. to bite down on hard or restlessly: as, the horse *champed* at the bit. *n.* a champing; noisy chewing.
champ (champ), *n.* [Slang], a champion.
cham·pac (cham′pak, chum′puk), *n.* [Hind. *campak* < Sans. *campaka*], an Indian tree of the magnolia family, with fragrant, yellow flowers: also spelled **champak.**
Cham·pagne (shän′pȧn′y′; Eng. sham-pān′), *n.* a former province of northeastern France.
cham·pagne (sham-pān′), *n.* 1. originally, any of various wines, effervescent or still, white or red, produced in Champagne, France. 2. now, any effervescent white wine: regarded as a symbol of luxurious living. 3. the typical color of such wine; pale, tawny yellow or greenish yellow. *adj.* 1. of this color. 2. of or for this wine.

CHAMPAGNE

Cham·paign (sham-pān′), *n.* a city in east central Illinois: pop., 50,000.
cham·paign (sham-pān′), *n.* [OFr. *champaigne* (Fr. *campagne*); LL. *campania* < L. *campus*, a field], 1. a broad expanse of plain. 2. flat, open country. *adj.* 1. flat and open, as champaign. 2. having to do with flat and open country.
cham·pak (cham′pak, chum′puk), *n.* the champac.
cham·per·tous (cham′pẽr-təs), *adj.* in *law*, of the nature of, or having to do with, champerty.
cham·per·ty (cham′pẽr-ti), *n.* [*pl.* CHAMPERTIES (-tiz)], [Fr. *champart*, field share < L. *campi pars; campi*, genit. of *campus*, a field + *pars*, a part], in *law*, an illegal act by which a person not concerned in a lawsuit makes a bargain with the litigants to help maintain the costs of the suit in return for a share of any proceeds.
cham·pi·gnon (sham-pin′yən; Fr. shän′pē′nyōn′), *n.* [Fr. (with altered suffix) < LL. *campania;* see CHAMPAIGN], the common edible mushroom.
cham·pi·on (cham′pi-ən), *n.* [ME.; OFr.; LL. *campio*, gladiator < L. *campus*, a field, place for games], 1. a valiant fighter. 2. a person who fights for another or for a cause; defender; protector; supporter: as, a *champion* of the oppressed. 3. a winner of first place or first prize in a competition. *adj.* winning or capable of winning first place; excelling over all others. *v.t.* 1. to fight for; defend; support. 2. [Obs.], to challenge.
cham·pi·on·ship (cham′pi-ən-ship′), *n.* [*champion* + *-ship*], 1. a championing; defending or supporting. 2. the position or title of a champion. 3. the period of time that a champion keeps his title.
Cham·plain, Lake (sham-plān′), a lake between northern New York and Vermont: length, 125 mi.
Cham·plain, Samuel de (də sham-plān′; Fr. shän′-plan′), 1567?–1635; French explorer; first governor of Canada.
Cham·pol·lion, Jean Fran·çois (zhän frän′swȧ′ shän′-pô′lyōn′), 1790–1832; French Egyptologist.
‡**Champs É·ly·sées** (shän′zā′lē′zā′), [Fr., lit., Elysian fields], a famous and fashionable avenue in Paris.
Chan., Chanc., 1. Chancellor. 2. Chancery.
chance (chans, chäns), *n.* [ME. *chance, chaunce;* OFr. *cheance;* LL. *cadentia*, that which falls out; L. *cadens*, ppr. of *cadere*, to fall], 1. the way things happen or turn out. 2. apparent absence of cause or design; fortuity; luck: often personified. 3. a happening; fortuitous event; accidental circumstance. 4. a risk or gamble. 5. a share in a lottery. 6. an opportunity: as, you'll have a *chance* to go. 7. a possibility or probability: as, there is a *chance* that he will live. 8. [Archaic], a mishap; mischance. *adj.* happening by chance; accidental: as, a *chance* encounter. *v.i.* [CHANCED (chanst, chänst), CHANCING], to come about by chance; happen: as, it *chanced* that he lost. *v.t.* to leave to chance; risk. —*SYN.* see **happen, random.**
by chance, 1. possibly; perchance. 2. accidentally.
chance on (or **upon**), to find or meet by chance.
on the chance, relying on the possibility.
chance·ful (chans′fəl, chäns′fəl), *adj.* 1. eventful. 2. [Archaic], dependent on chance. 3. [Archaic], risky.
chan·cel (chan′s′l, chän′s′l), *n.* [ME.; OFr. *chancel, cancel;* LL. *cancellus;* L. *cancelli, pl.*, lattices, crossbars], the part of a church around the altar, usually at the east end, reserved for the use of the clergy and the choir: it is sometimes set off by a railing or lattice.
chan·cel·ler·y (chan′sə-lẽr-i, chän′sə-lẽr-i), *n.* [*pl.* CHANCELLERIES (-iz)], [ME. *chancelerie;* OFr. *chancellerie*], 1. the rank or position of a chancellor; chancellorship. 2. a chancellor's office or the building that houses it. 3. the office of an embassy, consulate, etc.
chan·cel·lor (chan′sə-lẽr, chän′sə-lẽr), *n.* [ME. & OFr. *chanceler;* LL. *cancellarius*, keeper of the barrier, secretary: so called from the lattice behind which he worked; see CHANCEL], 1. a high official, as a secretary to a king. 2. the chief secretary of an embassy, consulate, etc. 3. a high official secretary in the British government, sometimes with judicial powers. 4. the title of the head or president in some universities. 5. the prime minister in certain countries: as, Bismarck was *chancellor* of Germany. 6. a chief judge of a court of chancery or equity in some States of the United States. Abbreviated **Chan., Chanc., C.** (as a title).
Chancellor of the Exchequer, the highest minister of finance in the British government, and a member of the Cabinet.
chan·cel·lor·ship (chan′sə-lẽr-ship′, chän′sə-lẽr-ship′), *n.* [*chancellor* + *-ship*], the position or term of office of a chancellor.
Chan·cel·lors·ville (chan′sə-lẽrz-vil′), *n.* a town in Spotsylvania County, Virginia: site of a Confederate victory (1863).
chance-med·ley (chans′med′li, chäns′med′li), *n.* [lit., mixed chance; see CHANCE & MEDDLE], 1. accidental homicide; unpremeditated manslaughter, as in self-defense. 2. haphazard action.
chan·cer·y (chan′sẽr-i, chän′sẽr-i), *n.* [*pl.* CHANCERIES (-iz)], [ME. *chancerie, chauncerie* < *chancelerie;* OFr. *chancellerie;* LL. *cancellaria*, chancery court, office of a *cancellarius;* see CHANCELLOR], 1. a division of the High Court of Justice in England and Wales, presided

over by the Lord High Chancellor of England. 2. a court of equity. 3. the laws, practice, and proceedings of a court of equity; equity. 4. a court of record; office of public archives. 5. a chancellery. Abbreviated **Chan., Chanc., Ch., ch.**

in chancery, 1. in process of litigation in a court of equity. 2. in an awkward or helpless situation. 3. in *wrestling,* with the head held firmly between an opponent's arm and his chest.

chan·cre (shaŋ'kẽr), *n.* [Fr.; see CANCER], a venereal sore or ulcer; primary lesion of syphilis.

chan·croid (shaŋ'kroid), *n.* [< *chancre* + *-oid*], a nonsyphilitic venereal ulcer, usually on or about the genitals, caused by a bacterium: also called *soft chancre.*

chanc·y (chan'si, chän'si), *adj.* [CHANCIER (-si-ẽr), CHANCIEST (-si-ist)], [< *chance, n.*], 1. [Scot.], lucky. 2. [Colloq.], risky; uncertain.

Chan·dar·na·gar (chun'dẽr-nug'ẽr), *n.* Chandernagor.

chan·de·lier (shan'də-lêr'), *n.* [Fr.; OFr. *chandelabre* < L.; see CANDELABRUM], a fixture with branches for several candles, electric bulbs, etc., usually hanging from a ceiling.

chan·delle (shän'del'), *n.* [Fr., lit., candle, in various popular phrases], a quick, simultaneous climb and turn made by an airplane in flight.

Chan·der·na·gor (chun'dẽr-nə-gôr'), *n.* a former dependency of French India, north of Calcutta: since 1950, a part of India: area, c. 4 sq. mi.; pop., 36,300.

chan·dler (chan'dlẽr, chän'dlẽr), *n.* [ME. *candeler, chaundeler;* OFr. *chandelier* < *chandoile,* candle; L. *candela,* a candle], 1. a maker or seller of candles. 2. a retailer of supplies and groceries: as, a ship *chandler* sells provisions for ships.

chan·dler·y (chan'dlẽr-i, chän'dlẽr-i), *n.* [*pl.* CHANDLERIES (-iz)], 1. a warehouse or storeroom for candles and other small wares. 2. the merchandise, business, or warehouse of a chandler.

Chang·chow (chaŋ'chou'; Chin. chäŋ'jō'), *n.* a city in Fukien province, southeastern China: pop., 100,000: also called *Lungki.*

Chang·chun (chäŋ'choon'), *n.* a city in Kirin province, Manchuria: pop. 630,000: see **Hsinking.**

change (chānj), *v.t.* [CHANGED (chānjd), CHANGING], [ME. *changen;* OFr. *changier;* LL. *cambiare* < L. *cambire,* to exchange, barter < Celt. < derivative base **kmb* (to barter, exchange) of IE. **kamb,* to bend, crook (whence OIr. *camm,* W. *cam,* Bret. *kamm,* crooked)], 1. to put or take (a thing) in place of something else; substitute: as, he *changed* his clothes. 2. to give and receive reciprocally; exchange: as, they *changed* places. 3. to cause to become different; alter; convert: as, success *changed* him. 4. to give or receive the equivalent of (a coin or banknote) in currency of other, especially lower, denominations. 5. to substitute a fresh covering, as a diaper, on. *v.i.* 1. to become different; alter; vary: as, the scene *changes.* 2. to pass from one phase to another, as the moon. 3. to leave one train, bus, etc. and board another. 4. to put on other clothes. 5. to make an exchange. *n.* 1. a changing or being changed; substitution, alteration, or variation. 2. variety. 3. something that is or may be substituted; something of the same kind but new or fresh. 4. another set of clothes; fresh outfit to replace what one is wearing. 5. money given to a purchaser as the difference between the price of what he is buying and the larger amount of money that he has given in payment. 6. an equivalent sum in smaller denominations, given for money of larger denominations. 7. small coins. 8. a place where merchants meet to do business; exchange: sometimes erroneously, **'change.** 9. *usually pl.* in *bell ringing,* any pattern or order in which the bells are rung. 10. in *music,* modulation; shift of key.

change trains (or **busses,** etc.), to leave one train (or bus, etc.) and board another.

ring the changes, 1. to ring a set of bells with all possible variations. 2. to do or say a thing in many and various ways.

***SYN.*—change** denotes a making or becoming distinctly different and implies either a radical transmutation of character or replacement with something else (I'll *change* my shoes); **alter** implies a partial change, as in appearance, so that the identity is preserved (to *alter* a garment); **vary** suggests irregular or intermittent change (to *vary* one's reading); **modify** implies minor change, often so as to limit or moderate (to *modify* the language of a report); **transform** implies a change in form and now, usually, in nature or function (to *transform* matter into energy); **convert** suggests more strongly change to suit a new function (to *convert* a dining room into a bedroom).

change·a·bil·i·ty (chān'jə-bil'ə-ti), *n.* the quality or state of being changeable.

change·a·ble (chān'jə-b'l), *adj.* [ME.], 1. that can change or be changed; liable or tending to change; variable; alterable. 2. having a changing appearance or color, as some silk when looked at from different angles.

change·ful (chānj'fəl), *adj.* full of change; inconstant.

change·less (chānj'lis), *adj.* unchanging; immutable.

change·ling (chānj'liŋ), *n.* [*change* + *-ling*], 1. a child secretly put in the place of another. 2. any ugly, queer, idiotic, or bad-tempered child, superstitiously explained away as being a substitute left by the fairies for a child stolen by them. 3. [Archaic], a changeable person; turncoat. 4. [Archaic], a feeble-minded person; idiot.

change of life, the time in a woman's life at which menstruation permanently ceases; menopause.

change o·ver (chānj'ō'vẽr), *n.* a complete change, as in goods produced, methods of production, equipment, etc.

change ringing, the ringing of a series of unrepeated changes on bells.

Chang·sha (chäŋ'shä'), *n.* the capital of Hunan province, China: pop., 312,000.

Chang·teh (chäŋ'te'; Chin. chäŋ'du'), *n.* a city on the Yüan Kiang River, Hunan, China: pop., 300,000.

chan·nel (chan''l), *n.* [ME.; OFr. *chanel, canel;* see CANAL], 1. the bed of a running stream, river, etc. 2. the deeper part of a stream, harbor, etc. 3. a body of water joining two larger bodies of water. 4. a tubelike passage for liquids. 5. any means of passage; course through which something moves or passes. 6. the proper or official course of transmission of communications, as in the army: as, the soldier made his request through *channels.* 7. a long groove or furrow. 8. a long, grooved bar of rolled metal; channel bar, channel iron, etc. 9. a frequency band assigned to a single transmitting station, as in radio, television, telegraphy, etc.: the width and position of the band differ for each type of transmission. *v.t.* [CHANNELED, CHANNELED (-'ld), CHANNELING, CHANNELLING], 1. to make a channel or channels in. 2. to put grooves, or fluting, in (a pillar, column, etc.). 3. to send through a channel.

chan·nel (chan''l), *n.* [orig., *chain wale*], formerly, any of several metal ledges on the sides of a ship to secure the rigging and keep the ropes free of the gunwales.

channel bar (or **iron),** a rolled metal bar whose section is shaped thus ⊔.

Channel Islands, a group of British islands in the English Channel, off the coast of Normandy, including Alderney, Jersey, and Guernsey: area, 75 sq. mi.; pop., 96,000 (est. 1947): abbreviated **C.I.**

Chan·ning, William Ellery (chan'iŋ), 1780–1842; American clergyman, author, and philanthropist.

‡chan·son (shän'sōn'; Eng. shan'sən, shan'son), *n.* [*pl.* CHANSONS (-sōn'; Eng. -sənz, -sonz)], [Fr.], a song.

‡chan·son de geste (shän'sōn' də zhest'), [Fr., song of heroic acts], an Old French epic tale in verse, especially of the type of the *Chanson de Roland* (*Song of Roland*), c. 1100: typically written in ten-syllable lines characterized by assonance and arranged in *laisses* (irregular stanzas), these poems fall into cycles organized around Charlemagne (*geste du roi*), William of Orange (*geste de Guillaume*), and the Northern traitors (*geste de Doon de Mayence*).

chant (chant, chänt), *n.* [Fr.; L. *cantus,* song < the *v.*], 1. a song; melody. 2. a simple song in which a number of syllables or words are sung in a monotone. 3. words, as of a canticle or psalm, to be sung in this way. 4. a monotonous tone of voice; singsong mode of speaking; intonation. *v.i.* [ME. *chanten;* OFr. *chanter, canter;* L. *cantare* < pp. of *canere,* to sing], 1. to say something monotonously or repetitiously. 2. to sing a chant; intone. 3. [Poetic], to sing; warble. *v.t.* 1. to sing. 2. to celebrate in song. 3. to say monotonously. 4. to sing or recite in the manner of a chant; intone.

‡chan·tage (shän'tȧzh'; Eng. chan'tij), *n.* [Fr.; cf. slang *faire chanter,* to make pay, lit., make sing], blackmail.

chant·er (chan'tẽr, chän'tẽr), *n.* 1. one who chants. 2. a priest or chorister who sings in the chantry. 3. in a bagpipe, the pipe that produces the melody.

chan·te·relle (shan'tə-rel', chan'tə-rel'), *n.* [Fr., dim. < L. *cantharus,* drinking cup; Gr. *kantharos*], a yellow, edible mushroom that smells somewhat like a plum.

‡chan·teuse (shän'töz'), *n.* [Fr.; see CHANT], a woman singer.

chan·tey (shan'ti; *popularly,* chan'ti), *n.* [*pl.* CHANTEYS (-tiz)], [< Fr. *chantez,* imperative of *chanter;* see CHANT], a song that sailors sing in rhythm with their motions while working: chanteys include *capstan chanteys* and *halyard* (i.e., hauling) *chanteys:* also **chanty, shantey.**

chan·ti·cleer (chan'ti-klêr'), *n.* [ME. *chaunticlere;* OFr. *Chante-cler,* name of the rooster in "Reynard the Fox"; see CHANT & CLEAR], a rooster: used as a proper name.

Chan·til·ly (shan-til'i; Fr. shän'tē'yē'), *n.* a town in northern France: famous for lace made there.

chant·ress (chan'tris, chän'tris), *n.* a woman chanter or singer.

chan·try (chan'tri, chän'tri), *n.* [*pl.* CHANTRIES (-triz)], [ME. & OFr. *chanterie;* see CHANT], 1. an endowment to pay for the saying of Masses and prayers in behalf of a specified person's soul. 2. a chapel or altar endowed for the same purpose; small chapel attached to a church.

chant·y (shan'ti; *popularly,* chan'ti), *n.* [*pl.* CHANTIES (-tiz)], a chantey.

Cha·nu·kah (khä'noo-kä), *n.* [Heb.], Hanukkah: see **Jewish holidays.**

Chao·an (chou'än'), *n.* a city in Kwangtung province, China: pop., 300,000: also called *Chaochow.*

Chao·chow (chou'jō'), *n.* Chaoan.

cha·os (kā′os), *n.* [L.; Gr. *chaos*, abyss < *chainein*, to gape; cf. CHASM], 1. the disorder of formless matter and infinite space, supposed to have existed before the ordered universe. 2. any great confusion or disorder. 3. [Archaic], an abyss; chasm. —*SYN.* see **confusion.**

cha·ot·ic (kā-ot′ik), *adj.* in a condition of chaos; in a completely confused or disordered condition.

cha·ot·i·cal·ly (kā-ot′i-k'l-i, kā-ot′ik-li), *adv.* in a chaotic manner or condition.

chap (chap, chop), *n.* [ME. *chaft;* ON. *kjaptr*], 1. a jaw. 2. a cheek: also **chop.**

chap (chap), *n.* [< *chapman*, in sense "one to be dealt with"], [Colloq.], a man or boy; fellow.

chap (chap), *v.t. & v.i.* [CHAPPED or CHAPT (chapt), CHAPPING], [ME. *chappen*, var. of *choppen* (see CHOP, to cut), specialized in sense], to split; crack open; roughen: as, her skin *chaps* easily. *n.* a chapped place in the skin.

chap., 1. chaplain. 2. chapter.

‡**cha·pa·ra·jos** (chä′pä-rä′hôs), *n.pl.* [Mex. Sp.], leather trousers worn over ordinary trousers by cowboys to protect their legs: also called *chaps.*

‡**cha·pa·re·jos** (chä′pä-re′hôs), *n.pl.* chaparajos.

chap·ar·ral (chap′ə-ral′), *n.* [Sp. < *chaparro*, evergreen oak; ? < Basque *tšapar*], a thicket of shrubs, thorny bushes, etc., originally, of evergreen oaks.

chaparral cock, a brownish, long-tailed bird related to the cuckoo; road runner: the female is called *chaparral hen.*

chaparral pea, a thorny shrub of the pea family, growing in chaparrals along the western coast of the United States.

chap·book (chap′book′), *n.* [*chap* < *chapman* + *book:* from the fact that chapmen sold such books in the streets], a small book or pamphlet of poems, ballads, religious tracts, etc.

chape (chāp), *n.* [Fr.; LL. *cappa*, cape, hooded cloak], 1. a metal plate or mounting on a scabbard or sheath, especially a protection for the point. 2. the piece that fastens a buckle to a strap.

cha·peau (sha-pō′; Fr. shȧ′pō′), *n.* [*pl.* CHAPEAUX (-pōz′; Fr. -pō′), CHAPEAUS (-pōz′)], [Fr.; OFr. *chapel* < LL. *capellus*, dim. of *cappa;* see CAP], a hat.

‡**cha·peau bras** (shȧ′pō′ brȧ′), [Fr. *chapeau*, hat + *bras*, the arm: from the fact that it could be carried under the arm], a collapsible three-cornered hat worn by men in the 18th century.

chap·el (chap′'l), *n.* [ME. & OFr. *chapelle, chapele* < LL. *capella*, dim. of *cappa*, a cope, cape; orig., sanctuary in which the *cappa* or cope of St. Martin was preserved; then, any sanctuary], 1. a place of Christian worship subordinate to and smaller than a church. 2. a private place of worship, as in a hospital or school. 3. a room or recess in a church, set apart for special services and having its own altar. 4. a service in a chapel, or any religious service, as at a school. 5. the singers of a private chapel, collectively. 6. in Great Britain, any place of worship for those who are not members of an established church.

chap·er·on, chap·er·one (shap′ə-rōn′), *n.* [Fr., hood, coping < *chape*, a cope (cf. CHAPE): sense development, "protection," hence, "protector"], a person, especially an older or married woman, who accompanies young unmarried people in public or is present at their parties, dances, etc. for the sake of propriety or good form. *v.t.* [CHAPERONED (-rōnd′), CHAPERONING], to act as chaperon to. —*SYN.* see **accompany.**

chap·er·on·age (shap′ə-rōn′ij), *n.* the duties or supervision of a chaperon.

chap·fall·en (chap′fôl′ən, chop′fôl′ən), *adj.* [*chap* (jaw) + *fallen*], disheartened; depressed; humiliated: also **chopfallen.**

chap·i·ter (chap′i-tēr), *n.* [Fr. *chapitre;* see CHAPTER], in *architecture*, the capital of a column.

chap·lain (chap′lin), *n.* [ME. *chapelein;* OFr. *chapelain;* LL. *capellanus*, orig., custodian of St. Martin's cloak; see CHAPEL], 1. a clergyman attached to a chapel, as of a royal court, prison, etc. 2. a clergyman or layman appointed to perform religious functions in a public institution, club, etc. 3. a minister, priest, or rabbi serving in a religious capacity with the armed forces. Abbreviated **Ch., ch., chap.**

chap·lain·cy (chap′lin-si), *n.* [*pl.* CHAPLAINCIES (-siz)], the position or term of office of a chaplain.

chap·lain·ship (chap′lin-ship′), *n.* [*chaplain* + *-ship*], a chaplaincy.

chap·let (chap′lit), *n.* [ME. & OFr. *chapelet*, dim. of *chapel*, headdress, cap, dim. < LL. *cappa;* see CAP, CAPE], 1. a wreath or garland for the head. 2. a string of prayer beads one third the length of a rosary. 3. the prayers told with such beads. 4. any string of beads; necklace. 5. in *architecture*, a small convex molding somewhat resembling a string of beads.

chap·let·ed (chap′lit-id), *adj.* [see CHAPLET], having a wreath or garland on the head.

Chap·lin, Charles Spencer (chap′lin), 1889– ; American motion-picture actor and producer, born in England.

chap·man (chap′mən), *n.* [*pl.* CHAPMEN (-mən)], [ME. *chapman, chepman;* AS. *ceapman*, trader; *ceap*, trade, a bargain (cf. CHEAP); + *man;* ult. same as G. *kaufmann*], 1. [British], a peddler; hawker. 2. [Archaic], a trader; dealer.

Chap·man, George (chap′mən), 1559?–1634; English poet and playwright; translator of Homer.

chaps (chaps), *n.pl.* [Colloq.], chaparajos.

chaps (chaps, chops), *n.pl.* [see CHAP (a jaw or cheek), *sing.*], chops (jaws).

chap·ter (chap′tēr), *n.* [ME. *chapiter;* OFr. *chapitre, chapitle;* L. *capitulum*, head, chapter of a book, dim. of *caput*, the head], 1. any of the main divisions of a book or other writing. 2. a thing like a chapter; part; episode; section. 3. [from meeting at which a *chapter* of monastic rule, etc. was read], a group of canons headed by a dean, or any similar church division. 4. a meeting of such a group. 5. a local division of a club, fraternity, or similar organization. Abbreviated **ch., chap., C., c.** *v.t.* to divide (a book, etc.) into chapters.

chapter and verse, 1. the exact Scriptural reference; hence, 2. authority (for a statement, belief, etc.).

chapter house, 1. the building in which the chapter of a cathedral meets. 2. the house of a chapter of a fraternity or sorority.

Cha·pul·te·pec (chä-po͞ol′te-pek′; Eng. chə-pul′tə-pek′), *n.* a fortress near Mexico City, captured (September, 1847) by General Winfield Scott in the Mexican War.

‡**cha·que·ta** (chä-ke′tä), *n.* [Sp.], a heavy jacket worn by cowboys.

char (chär), *v.t & v.i.* [CHARRED (chärd), CHARRING], [back-formation < *charcoal*], 1. to reduce to charcoal by burning; burn up. 2. to scorch. *n.* anything charred; cinders; charcoal. —*SYN.* see **burn.**

char (chär), *n. & v.i.* [CHARRED (chärd), CHARRING], chare.

char (chär), *n.* [*pl.* CHARS (chärz), CHAR; see PLURAL, II, D, 1], [< Gael. *ceara*, red < *cear*, blood], a kind of trout with small scales and a red belly: also spelled **charr.**

char·a·banc, char-à-banc (shar′ə-baŋk′, shar′ə-baŋ′; Fr. shȧ′rȧ′bän′), *n.* [*pl.* CHARABANCS, CHAR-À-BANCS (-baŋks′, -baŋz′; Fr. -bän′)], [Fr. *char-à-banc*, lit., car with bench], a large excursion bus with transverse seats facing forward.

char·a·cin (kar′ə-sin), *n.* [< Mod. L. *characinidae*, the name of the family < Gr. *karax*, a kind of fish], any of a large group of strong-jawed, fresh-water fish of Africa and South America.

char·ac·ter (kar′ik-tēr, kar′ək-tēr), *n.* [ME. *caracter, carecter;* OFr. *caracter;* L. *character*, an engraving instrument; Gr. *charaktēr* < *charattein*, to engrave], 1. a distinctive mark. 2. any conventional mark, sign, or symbol used in writing and printing, as +, −, 7, 0, X, Y, Z, etc. 3. style of printing or handwriting. 4. a mystic symbol; code; cipher. 5. a distinctive trait, quality, or attribute. 6. essential quality; nature; kind or sort. 7. an individual's pattern of behavior or personality; moral constitution. 8. moral strength; self-discipline, fortitude, etc. 9. reputation. 10. good reputation: as, left without a shred of *character*. 11. a description of the traits or qualities of a person or type; character sketch. 12. a statement about the behavior, qualities, etc. of a person; recommendation. 13. status; position: as, he spoke in the *character* of lawyer. 14. a personage: as, he was a great *character* in his day. 15. a person in a play, story, novel, etc. 16. [Colloq.], a person conspicuously different from others; queer or eccentric person. *v.t.* 1. to write, print, or inscribe. 2. [Archaic], to represent; also, to characterize. —*SYN.* see **disposition, quality.**

in character, consistent with the role or general character; appropriate.

out of character, not consistent with the role or general character; inappropriate.

character actor, an actor usually cast in the role of a person with pronounced or eccentric characteristics.

char·ac·ter·is·tic (kar′ik-tēr-is′tik), *adj.* [Gr. *charaktēristikos;* see CHARACTER], of or constituting the character; in character; typical; distinctive; special: as, the *characteristic* odor of cabbage. *n.* 1. a distinguishing trait, feature, or quality; peculiarity. 2. the whole number, or integral part, of a logarithm, as distinguished from the fractional remainder, or mantissa: as, 4 is the *characteristic* of the logarithm 4.7193.

SYN.—**characteristic** suggests the indication of a quality that is peculiar to, and helps identify, something or someone (the *characteristic* taste of honey); **individual** and **distinctive** refer to, or suggest the possession of, a quality or qualities that distinguish something from others of its class or kind, **distinctive** often implying a meritorious difference (an *individual*, or *distinctive*, literary style).

char·ac·ter·is·ti·cal·ly (kar′ik-tēr-is′ti-k'l-i, kar′ik-tēr-

is′tik-li), *adv.* in a characteristic manner; typically.
char·ac·ter·i·za·tion (kar′ik-tẽr-ə-zā′shən, kar′ik-trə-zā′shən), *n.* 1. a characterizing; description of characteristics. 2. the delineation of character or creation of characters in a play, story, etc., especially by imitating or describing actions, utterances, and gestures.
char·ac·ter·ize (kar′ik-tẽr-īz′), *v.t.* [CHARACTERIZED (-īzd′), CHARACTERIZING], [LL. *characterizare;* Gr. *charactērizein;* see CHARACTER], 1. to describe the particular qualities, features, or traits of. 2. to be the distinctive character of; mark: as, a miser is *characterized* by greed. 3. to give character to.
character sketch, 1. a short essay describing a person or type of person. 2. in the *theater*, a performance depicting a person of pronounced or unusual characteristics.
char·ac·ter·y (kar′ik-tẽr-i, kar′ik-tri), *n.* [*pl.* CHARACTERIES (-iz, -triz)], [see CHARACTER], 1. the symbols or a system of symbols used to express thoughts. 2. the expression of thought by such symbols.
cha·rade (shə-rād′; *chiefly Brit.* shə-räd′), *n.* [Fr.; Pr. *charrada* < *charrar*, to gossip, chatter; prob. echoic], a game in which a word or phrase to be guessed is acted out in pantomime, syllable by syllable or as a whole.
char·coal (chär′kōl′), *n.* [ME. *char cole;* prob. < *charren* (cf. CHARE, CHORE), to turn + *cole*, coal; hence, lit., wood turned to coal], 1. a black form of carbon produced by partially burning or oxidizing wood or other organic matter in large kilns or retorts from which air is excluded: used as a fuel, filter, gas absorbent, etc. 2. a pencil or crayon made of this substance. 3. a drawing made with such a pencil or crayon. *v.t.* to write or draw with charcoal.
charcoal burner, 1. a device in which charcoal is burned. 2. a person whose work is producing charcoal.
Char·cot, Jean Mar·tin (zhäṅ′ mȧr′taṅ′ shȧr′kō′), 1825–1893; French physician who specialized in diseases of the nervous system.
chard (chärd), *n.* [earlier *card;* Fr. *carde;* L. *carduus*, thistle, artichoke; sp. influenced by Fr. *chardon*, artichoke], 1. the leafstalks of the artichoke, blanched for use as a vegetable. 2. a kind of beet whose large leaves and thick stalks are used as food: also **Swiss chard.**
Char·din, Jean Bap·tiste Si·mé·on (zhäṅ bȧ′tēst′ sē′mā′ôṅ′ shȧr′daṅ′), 1699–1779; French painter.
chare (châr), *n.* [ME. *cher, cherre;* AS. *cerr, cierr, cyrr*, a turn, job, piece of work < *cierran*, to turn; cf. CHORE], an odd job; household task; chore. *v.i.* [CHARED (chârd), CHARING], 1. to do odd jobs or chores. 2. to be a charwoman; do housework for pay. Also spelled **char.**
charge (chärj), *v.t.* [CHARGED (chärjd), CHARGING], [ME. *chargen;* OFr. *chargier, carchier;* LL. *carricare*, to load a wagon, cart < L. *carrus*, car, wagon; cf. CAR], I. 1. to put a load on or in; load or fill to usual capacity. 2. to load (a gun). 3. to fill (a substance) with another substance: as, the air was *charged* with steam. 4. to add carbon dioxide to (water, etc.). 5. to add an electrical charge to (a battery, etc.); replenish. II. 1. to load a burden on; give as a task, duty, etc. to: as, the law *charges* each person with individual responsibility. 2. to give a command to; instruct: as, a soldier is *charged* to obey. 3. to put blame on; censure; accuse: as, he *charged* her with negligence. 4. *a*) to put liability on (a person). *b*) to make liable for (a purchase, error etc.). 5. to ask as a price: as, we *charge* a dime for this service. 6. to put down as a debt or charge against a person's name or account: as, *charge* the cost to me. III. 1. to put full weight on; bear down on; attack vigorously. 2. to bring (a gun) to bear on; level; direct. 3. in *heraldry*, to place a bearing on. *v.i.* 1. to crouch or squat when a command is given: said of dogs. 2. to ask payment (*for*): as, we *charge* for this service. 3. to attack vigorously. *n.* I. 1. a load; burden. 2. the maximum or necessary quantity, as of electricity, fuel, etc., that a container or apparatus is built to accommodate. II. 1. responsibility or duty (*of*): as, take *charge* of finances. 2. care, safekeeping, or custody (*of*); hence, 3. a person or thing entrusted to someone's care: as, he became a public *charge.* 4. instruction; command; injunction: as, the jury received its *charge* from the judge. 5. accusation; indictment: as, *charges* of cruelty. III. 1. cost; price; expense: abbreviated **chg.** 2. a debt. IV. 1. an attack with maximum weight and speed; onslaught; onset; hence, 2. the signal for this. 3. in *heraldry*, a bearing. —*SYN.* see **accuse, command.**
  charge off, 1. to treat or regard as a loss. 2. to set down as belonging; ascribe.
  in charge, 1. having the responsibility, control, or supervision. 2. [British], under arrest.
  in charge of, 1. having the responsibility, control, or supervision of. 2. under the control or supervision of; in the custody of.
char·gé (shär-zhā′; Fr. shȧr′zhā′), *n.* a chargé d'affaires.
charge·a·ble (chär′jə-b′l), *adj.* 1. that can be charged. 2. that may become a public charge.
charge account, a business arrangement by which a customer may buy things and pay for them within a specified future period.
char·gé d'af·faires (shär-zhā′ da-fâr′; Fr. shȧr′zhā′dȧ′-fâr′), [*pl.* CHARGÉS D'AFFAIRES (shär-zhāz′ da-fâr′; Fr. shȧr′zhā′dȧ′fâr′)], [Fr., lit., entrusted with business], 1. a government official who temporarily takes the place of a minister, ambassador, or other diplomat. 2. an official of lower rank than an ambassador or minister, sent as a diplomatic representative to a smaller or less important country than his own.
charg·er (chär′jẽr), *n.* 1. a person or thing that charges. 2. a war horse. 3. an apparatus used to charge storage batteries.
charg·er (chär′jẽr), *n.* [ME. *chargeour*], [Archaic], a large, flat dish; platter.
Cha·ri (shȧ′rē′), *n.* the Shari, a river in French Equatorial Africa: the French name.
char·i·ly (châr′ə-li), *adv.* in a chary manner; cautiously.
char·i·ness (châr′i-nis), *n.* 1. the quality of being chary; being cautious. 2. frugality.
Char·ing Cross (châr′iŋ), a section of London, on the southeastern side of Trafalgar Square.
char·i·ot (char′i-ət), *n.* [ME.; OFr., dim. of *char, car;* see CAR], 1. a horse-drawn, two-wheeled cart used in ancient times for war, racing, triumphal parades, etc. 2. [Archaic], a light, four-wheeled carriage, used for pleasure or on some state occasions. *v.t.* & *v.i.* to drive or ride in a chariot.

CHARIOT

char·i·ot·eer (char′i-ə-têr′), *n.* [ME. *charieter;* OFr. *charetier, charioteur*], 1. a chariot driver. 2. [C-], Auriga, a northern constellation.
char·is·mat·ic (kar′iz-mat′ik), *adj.* [< Gr. *charisma*, divine gift], supposedly having some divinely inspired power, as to prophesy, perform miracles, etc.
char·i·ta·ble (char′ə-tə-b′l), *adj.* [ME.; OFr.; see CHARITY], 1. kind and generous in giving money or other help to those in need. 2. of or for charity. 3. kindly in judging others; lenient. —*SYN.* see **philanthropic.**
char·i·ta·bly (char′ə-tə-bli), *adv.* in a charitable manner.
char·i·ty (char′ə-ti), *n.* [*pl.* CHARITIES (-tiz)], [OFr. *charite* < L. *caritas*, dearness, affection, high regard < *carus*, dear], 1. in *Christianity*, the love of God for man or of man for his fellow men. 2. an act of good will or affection. 3. the feeling of good will; benevolence. 4. the quality of being kind or lenient in judging others. 5. a giving of money or other help to those in need; benefaction. 6. an institution, organization, or fund for giving help to those in need. —*SYN.* see **mercy.**
cha·ri·va·ri (shə-riv′ə-rē′, shä′ri-vä′ri, shiv′ə-ri), *n.* [Fr.], a mock serenade, as to newlyweds, made by blowing toy horns, beating on pans, etc.: also **shivaree.**
chark (chärk), *n.* charcoal or coke. *v.t.* [back-formation < *charcoal*], to change into charcoal or coke by burning.
char·kha, char·ka (chũr′kə, chär′kə), *n.* [Hind.], in India, a spinning wheel, used especially for cotton.
char·la·dy (chär′lā′di), *n.* [*pl.* CHARLADIES (-diz)], [British], a charwoman.
char·la·tan (shär′lə-t′n), *n.* [Fr. < It. *ciarlatano*, a quack < *cerretano*, one who cries out in the market place < LL. *cerretanus*, seller of papal indulgences at *Cerreto;* sp. influenced by *ciarlare*, to prate], a person who pretends to have knowledge or ability that he does not have; impostor; mountebank. —*SYN.* see **quack.**
char·la·tan·ism (shär′lə-t′n-iz′m), *n.* [Fr. *charlatanisme*], the methods of a charlatan; quackery.
char·la·tan·ry (shär′lə-t′n-ri), *n.* [*pl.* CHARLATANRIES (-riz)], 1. charlatanism. 2. an act of charlatanism.
Char·le·magne (shär′lə-mān′), *n.* (*Charles I*), king of the Franks (768–814 A.D.); emperor of the West (800–814 A.D.); lived 742–814 A.D.; established Holy Roman Empire: called *Charles the Great.*
Charles (chärlz), [Fr. < L. *Carolus* (< Gmc. *Karl*) or directly < OHG. *Karl;* lit., full-grown; akin to AS. *ceorl* (Eng. *churl*)], a masculine name: diminutives, *Charley, Charlie;* variant, *Carl;* feminine, *Charlotte, Caroline;* equivalents, L. *Carolus*, G. *Carl, Karl*, It. *Carlo*, Sp. *Carlos*, D. *Karel.*
Charles I, 1. (*Charles Stuart*), 1600–1649; son of James I; king of England (1625–1649); convicted of treason and beheaded. 2. (*Charles Francis Joseph*), 1887–1922; nephew of Francis Ferdinand; emperor of Austria and king of Hungary (1916–1918). 3. Charlemagne. 4. see **Charles II,** 1.
Charles II, 1. 823–877 A.D.; king of France, as Charles I (840–877 A.D.); Holy Roman emperor (875–877 A.D.): called *the Bald.* 2. 1630–1685; son of Charles I; king of England (1660–1685).
Charles V, 1. 1337–1380; father of Charles VI; king of France (1364–1380): called *the Wise.* 2. 1500–1558; Holy Roman emperor (1519–1556) and king of Spain (1516–1556).
Charles VI, 1368–1422; king of France (1380–1422): called *the Mad, the Beloved.*
Charles VII, (*Charles Albert; Charles of Bavaria*), 1697–1745; Holy Roman emperor (1742–1745).
Charles, Cape, a cape in southeastern Virginia, at the north entrance to Chesapeake Bay.
Charles Edward Stuart, 1720–1788; grandson of

James II; English prince: called *The Young Pretender, Bonnie Prince Charlie.*
Charles Martel, see **Martel, Charles.**
Charles River, a river in eastern Massachusetts, flowing into Boston harbor: length, 47 mi.
Charles's Wain (chärl'ziz), [AS. *Carles wægn*, wagon of *Carl* (Charlemagne): so named because of confusion between Charlemagne and King Arthur (L. *Arcturus*), who were associated in popular legend; orig., the wain of *Arcturus* (star in the constellation Boötes)], 1. the Big Dipper. 2. occasionally, Ursa Major.
Charles·ton (chärlz'tən), *n.* 1. a seaport in South Carolina: pop., 66,000. 2. the capital of West Virginia: pop., 86,000. 3. [< name of the seaport], a lively dance in 4/4 time, characterized by a twisting step: it was popular during the 1920's.
Charles·town (chärlz'toun'), *n.* a section of Boston: site of Bunker Hill.
char·ley horse (chär'li), [ballplayers' slang, c. 1888; prob. with reference to a lame racehorse], [Colloq.], a cramp in the leg or arm muscles caused by strain.
char·lock (chär'lək), *n.* [AS. *cerlic, cyrlic*], a weed of the mustard family, with yellow flowers; wild mustard.
Char·lotte (shär'lət), [Fr., fem. of *Charlot*, dim. of *Charles*], a feminine name: diminutives, *Lotta, Lottie, Lotty;* equivalent, It. *Carlotta.* *n.* a city in southern North Carolina: pop., 202,000.
char·lotte (shär'lət), *n.* [Fr. < the fem. name], a pudding or dessert made of fruit, gelatin, etc. in a mold of bread, cake, or graham-cracker crumbs.
Char·lot·te A·ma·li·e (shär-lot'ə ä-mä'li-ə), the capital of the Virgin Islands of the United States, on St. Thomas Island: pop., 13,000: formerly called *St. Thomas.*
Char·lot·ten·burg (shär-lot''n-bürg'; G. shär-lôt'ən-boorH'), *n.* a residential section of Berlin: pop., 208,000: once a city of Brandenburg, Prussia.
charlotte russe (ro͞os), [Fr., lit., Russian charlotte], a dessert made of whipped cream or custard in a mold of sponge cake.
Char·lottes·ville (shär'ləts-vil'), *n.* a city in central Virginia: pop., 29,000.
Char·lotte·town (shär'lət-toun'), *n.* the capital of Prince Edward Island, Canada: pop., 19,000.
charm (chärm), *n.* [ME. & OFr. *charme;* L. *carmen*, song, verse, charm], 1. originally, a chanted word, phrase, or verse assumed to have magic power to help or hurt; incantation. 2. any object assumed to have such power, as an amulet or talisman; hence, 3. a trinket worn on a bracelet, necklace, watch chain, etc. 4. any action or gesture assumed to have magic power. 5. the ability to fascinate, allure, or please greatly. *v.t.* 1. to act on as though by magic. 2. to attract or please greatly; enchant; allure; fascinate; delight. *v.i.* to be charming; please greatly. —*SYN.* see **attract.**
charmed life, a life seemingly protected from harm as though by magic: *Macbeth* V, viii.
charm·er (chär'mẽr), *n.* [see CHARM], 1. a delightful or fascinating person: usually said of a woman. 2. an enchanter: as, a snake *charmer.*
‡**char·meuse** (shär'möz'), *n.* [Fr., fem. of *charmeur;* charmer], a soft, lightweight silk cloth with a finish like that of satin.
charm·ing (chärm'iŋ), *adj.* [ppr. of *charm*], 1. attractive; fascinating; delightful. 2. using a charm or charms.
char·nel (chär'n'l), *n.* [ME.; OFr. *charnel, carnel;* LL. *carnale*, graveyard; neut. of *carnalis*, of flesh < L. *caro, carnis*, flesh], a charnel house. *adj.* 1. of or serving as a charnel. 2. like or fit for a charnel; deathlike.
charnel house, 1. originally, a tomb; hence, 2. any place where there are corpses, bones, etc.
Cha·ron (kâr'ən), *n.* [L.; Gr. *Charōn*], 1. in *Greek mythology*, the boatman who ferried dead souls across the river Styx to Hades; hence, 2. a ferryman: humorous usage.
char·pai (chär'pī'), *n.* a charpoy.
Char·pen·tier, Gus·tave (güs'tåv' shår'pän'tyā'), 1860–1956; French composer; wrote the opera *Louise.*
char·poy (chär'poi'), *n.* [Hind. *cārpāī; cār*, four + *pāī*, foot], in India, a bedstead or cot.
char·qued (chär'kid), *adj.* jerked: said of beef.
char·qui (chär'ki), *n.* [Sp. *charqui, charqué* < Peruv. *charqui*, dried meat], jerked or dried beef.
charr (chär), *n.* [*pl.* CHARRS (chärz), CHAR; see PLURAL, II, D, 1], a char (fish).
char·ry (chär'i), *adj.* [CHARRIER (-i-ẽr), CHARRIEST (-i-ist)], like charcoal.
chart (chärt), *n.* [Fr. *charte;* L. *charta;* see CARD (paper)], 1. a map of a body of water, showing coast lines, depths, tides, currents, a ship's course, etc. 2. a simple outline map on which information can be plotted or written. 3. a sheet giving information in the form of diagrams, tables, and illustrations; also, a graph. 4. such a diagram, table, etc. *v.t.* 1. to make a chart of; map; outline. 2. to plot (a course) on, or by reference to, a chart or charts. 3. to show by, on, or as by, a chart.
char·ter (chär'tẽr), *n.* [ME. *chartre, chartere;* OFr. *chartre, cartre;* L. *chartula*, dim. of *charta;* see CARD (stiff paper)], 1. a franchise or written grant of specified rights made by a government or ruler to a person, business corporation, etc. 2. a declaration or document setting forth the aims and principles of a group, as of nations, united in an undertaking; specifically, [C-], the Charter of the United Nations. 3. permission from a society for the organization of a local chapter or lodge. 4. a special privilege or exemption. 5. *a)* the hire or lease of a ship, bus, airplane, etc. *b)* the agreement (called *charter party*) governing this. *v.t.* 1. to grant a charter to. 2. to hire or lease by charter or charter party. 3. to hire for exclusive use. —*SYN.* see **hire.**
char·ter·age (chär'tẽr-ij), *n.* a chartering; grant of a charter.
char·tered accountant (chär'tẽrd), in Great Britain, a member of an Institute of Chartered Accountants: abbreviated **C.A., c.a.**
char·ter·er (chär'tẽr-ẽr), *n.* a person who charters a ship or ships.
Char·ter·house (chär'tẽr-hous'), *n.* [altered (by folk etym.) < Anglo-Fr. *chartouse* (Fr. *chartreuse*), Carthusian monastery], 1. a Carthusian monastery. 2. a London hospital founded (1611) on the site of a Carthusian monastery. 3. the school into which this hospital was later converted. 4. the modern boarding school (called *public school* in England) at Godalming, Surrey, which inherits the tradition of the former school.
charter member, any of the founders or original members of an organization, especially of one with a charter.
Charter of the United Nations, the document establishing the United Nations and outlining its principles, functions, and organization, adopted at an international conference in San Francisco (1945).
charter party, [Fr. *charte partie*, divided deed: so named because half was kept by each party to the transaction], 1. an agreement between a shipowner and a carrier, merchant, etc. for the commercial lease of a ship or space on a ship, especially as recorded in a document. 2. the hiring or leasing of a vessel or space in a vessel by such agreement. 3. [Colloq.], a party, as of amateur fishermen, etc., which hires or charters a vessel for sport fishing, cruising, etc.
Chart·ism (chär'tiz'm), *n.* 1. a movement for democratic social and political reform in England (1836–1848) based on principles set forth in the People's Charter (1838). 2. the principles of this movement.
Chart·ist (chär'tist), *n.* a person who supported Chartism. *adj.* of Chartism or Chartists.
chart·less (chärt'lis), *adj.* 1. without a chart; unguided. 2. not mapped: as, a *chartless* sea.
char·tog·ra·pher (kär-tog'rə-fẽr), *n.* a cartographer.
char·to·graph·ic (kär'tə-graf'ik), *adj.* cartographic.
char·tog·ra·phy (kär-tog'rə-fi), *n.* cartography.
Char·tres (shär'tr'), *n.* a city in northern France: pop., 24,000: site of a 13th-century Gothic cathedral.
char·treuse (shär-tröz'), *n.* [after *La Grande Chartreuse*, Carthusian monastery in France], 1. a yellow, pale-green, or white liqueur made by the Carthusian monks. 2. pale, yellowish green. *adj.* of this color.
char·tu·lar·y (kär'choo-ler'i), *n.* [*pl.* CHARTULARIES (-iz)], [ML. *chartularium* < L. *chartula*, dim. of *charta;* see CARD (paper)], a list of charters; book containing duplicates of all charters issued: also **cartulary.**
char·wom·an (chär'woom'ən), *n.* [*pl.* CHARWOMEN (-wim'in)], [see CHARE, CHORE], a woman who does cleaning or scrubbing, as in office buildings.
char·y (châr'i), *adj.* [CHARIER (-i-ẽr), CHARIEST (-i-ist)], [AS. *cearig*, sorrowful < *caru, cearu*, care; change of sense after *care*], 1. careful; cautious: as, a burnt child is *chary* of fire. 2. shy: as, he was *chary* of strangers. 3. frugal; stingy: as, he was *chary* of his hospitality.
Cha·ryb·dis (kə-rib'dis), *n.* [L.; Gr. *Charybdis*], a whirlpool off the coast of Sicily, opposite the rock Scylla.
between Scylla and Charybdis, faced with a choice of two dangers.
chase (chās), *v.t.* [CHASED (chāst), CHASING], [ME. *chacen, cacchen;* OFr. *chacier, cachier;* see CATCH], 1. to follow quickly or persistently in order to catch or harm. 2. to run after; follow; pursue. 3. to make run away; drive. 4. to hunt. *v.i.* 1. to go in pursuit; follow along: as, *chase* after him. 2. [Colloq.], to go hurriedly; rush: as, I *chased* around town looking for you. *n.* 1. a chasing; pursuit. 2. the hunting of game for sport. 3. anything hunted; quarry. 4. hunters collectively. 5. in Great Britain, *a)* an unenclosed game preserve: distinguished from *park.* *b)* a license to hunt over a specified area or to keep animals there as game.
give chase, to chase; pursue.
chase (chās), *n.* [OFr. *chasse*, a frame, shrine < *casse*, a box, chest < L. *capsa*, a box, chest], 1. a groove; furrow. 2. the bore of a gun barrel. 3. a hollowed-out groove for drainpipes, in a wall, etc. 4. a rectangular

metal frame in which pages or columns of type are locked. *v.t.* [CHASED (chāst), CHASING], to make a groove or furrow in; indent.

chase (chās), *v.t.* [CHASED (chāst), CHASING], [< *enchase* < Fr. *enchâsser*, to enshrine < *châsse*, shrine; see CHASE (a groove)], to ornament (metal) by engraving, embossing, cutting, etc.

Chase, Sal·mon Port·land (sal′mən pôrt′lənd chās), 1808–1873; American statesman and jurist; chief justice, United States Supreme Court (1864–1873).

Chase, Samuel, 1741–1811; American statesman; associate justice, United States Supreme Court (1796–1811); signer of Declaration of Independence.

Chase, Stuart, 1888– ; American economist and author.

chas·er (chās′ẽr), *n.* [< *chase* (to pursue)], 1. a person or thing that chases; pursuer. 2. a hunter. 3. a gun on the stern or bow of a ship, used during pursuit of or by another ship. 4. a small, fast airplane or ship used to ward off and pursue an enemy craft. 5. a steeplechaser. 6. [Colloq.], a mild drink, as water or a carbonated beverage, taken after or with whisky, rum, etc.

chas·er (chās′ẽr), *n.* [< *chase* (to engrave)], 1. a person who engraves or embosses metal. 2. a tool for engraving. 3. a tool for threading screws.

chasm (kaz′m), *n.* [L. *chasma;* Gr. *chasma*, yawning hollow, gulf < *chainein*, to yawn, gape; cf. CHAOS], 1. a deep crack in the earth's surface; abyss; crevasse; narrow gorge. 2. any break or gap; hiatus. 3. a wide divergence of feelings, sentiments, interests, etc. between people or groups; rift.

chas·mal (kaz′m′l), *adj.* of or like a chasm; abysmal.

chas·sé (sha-sā′), *n.* [Fr.; lit., a chasing; pp. of *chasser*, to chase; cf. SASHAY], 1. originally, a dance step in which one foot rapidly followed the other during the execution of a glide; hence, 2. a forward or sideways gliding step accompanied by one or two rapid linking steps. *v.i.* [CHASSÉD (-sād′), CHASSÉING], 1. to make such a step or steps; dance with such steps. 2. to walk as if in a series of such steps.

chasse·pot (shȧs′pō′), *n.* [after the Fr. inventor, A. A. *Chassepot* (1833–1905)], a breech-loading rifle used by the French army after 1866.

chas·seur (sha-sũr′; Fr. shȧ′sẽr′), *n.* [Fr. < *chasser*, to hunt, chase; see CHASE (to pursue)], 1. a hunter; huntsman. 2. a soldier, especially one of certain French light infantry or cavalry troops, trained and equipped for rapid action. 3. a uniformed attendant or servant.

Chas·sid·ic (ka-sid′ik, khä-sē′dik), *adj.* of or characteristic of the Chassidim: also **Hasidic.**

Chas·sid·im (kas′i-dim; Heb. khä-sē′dim), *n.pl.* [*sing.* CHASSID (kas′id; Heb. khä′sid)], the members of a sect of Jewish mystics that originated in Poland in the 18th century: also **Hasidim.**

chas·sis (shas′i, shas′is, chas′i), *n.* [*pl.* CHASSIS (shas′iz)], [Fr. *châssis;* see CHASE (groove)], 1. a frame on which the carriage of a gun moves back and forth. 2. the lower frame, including the wheels and engine parts, of a motor vehicle. 3. the frame supporting the body of an airplane. 4. in *radio*, *a*) the framework to which the parts of a radio set, amplifier, etc. are attached. *b*) the assembled frame and parts. 5. [Slang], the body.

chaste (chāst), *adj.* [ME.; OFr. *chaste, caste* < L. *castus*, pure, chaste], 1. not indulging in unlawful sexual activity; virtuous: said especially of women. 2. not indecent; modest. 3. restrained and simple in style; not ornate; not extreme.

SYN.—**chaste** and **virtuous,** in this connection, imply moral excellence manifested by forbearance from acts or thoughts that do not accord with virginity or strict marital fidelity; **pure** implies chastity through innocence and an absence of seductive influences rather than through self-restraint; **modest** and **decent** are both applied to propriety in behavior, dress, bearing, or speech as exhibiting morality or purity. Generally, the terms in this comparison are applied more frequently to women than to men.—*ANT.* immoral, lewd, wanton.

chas·ten (chās′'n), *v.t.* [ME. *chastien;* OFr. *chastier* < L. *castigare*, to punish, chastise < *castus*, pure + *agere*, to lead, drive], 1. to punish in order to correct or make better; chastise. 2. to restrain from excess; subdue. —*SYN.* see **punish.**

chas·tise (chas-tīz′), *v.t.* [CHASTISED (-tīzd′), CHASTISING], [ME. *chastisen*, extended form of *chastien;* see CHASTEN], 1. to punish in order to correct, usually by beating. 2. [Archaic], to chasten. —*SYN.* see **punish.**

chas·tise·ment (chas′tiz-mənt, chas-tīz′mənt), *n.* a chastising; punishment, especially by beating.

chas·ti·ty (chas′tə-ti), *n.* [ME. *chastite, chastete;* OFr. *chastete, chasteit;* L. *castitas;* see CHASTE], 1. abstention from unlawful sexual activity: said especially of women. 2. sexual continence; celibacy or virginity: as, monks take a vow of *chastity*. 3. decency; modesty. 4. simplicity of style; lack of ornateness or excess.

chastity belt, a securely fastened, beltlike device of metal, leather, etc. worn by women in the Middle Ages to prevent sexual intercourse during the absence of their husbands.

chas·u·ble (chaz′yoo-b'l, chas′yoo-b'l), *n.* [OFr.; LL. *casubula, casubla, casula*, hooded garment; prob. < L. *casa*, a hut, cottage], a sleeveless outer vestment worn over the alb by priests at Mass.

chat (chat), *v.i.* [CHATTED (-id), CHATTING], [< *chatter*], to talk or converse in a light, easy, informal manner. *n.* 1. light, easy, informal talk or conversation. 2. small talk; chit-chat; chatter. 3. any of several birds with a chattering call, as the stonechat, wheatear, etc.

chat (chat), *n.* [Fr., a cat], 1. an ament or catkin, as of a willow. 2. a samara, as of a maple. 3. a spike, as of plantain.

châ·teau (sha-tō′; Fr. shȧ′tō′), *n.* [*pl.* CHÂTEAUX (-tōz′; Fr. -tō′)], [Fr. < OFr. *chastel, castel* < L. *castellum*, a castle; see CASTLE], 1. a French feudal castle. 2. a large country house, especially one in France.

Cha·teau·bri·and, Vicomte **Fran·çois Re·né de** (frän′swȧ′ rə-nā′ də shȧ′tō′brē′än′), 1768–1848; French political writer and novelist.

Châ·teau-Thier·ry (shȧ′tō′tye′rē′), *n.* a town in northern France, on the Marne River, where American and French troops defeated the Germans (June–July, 1918).

Château wine, any of certain wines made from grapes grown at some particular château in France, especially in the region of Bordeaux: each wine is designated by the name of its château, as *Château Ausone.*

chat·e·lain (shat′'l-ān′; Fr. shä′tlan′), *n.* [Fr. *châtelain;* see CASTELLAN], the keeper of a castle; castellan.

chat·e·laine (shat′'l-ān′, shä′tlen′), *n.* [Fr., fem. of *châtelain;* see CASTELLAN], 1. the lady of a castle; mistress of a château. 2. a woman's ornamental clasp worn at the waist, with keys, purses, watches, etc. fastened to it on a chain: so called from the keys carried by a medieval chatelaine. 3. a decorative chain suspended between two clasps or pins and worn as an ornament on women's clothing.

Chat·ham (chat′əm), *n.* a city in Kent, England: pop., 40,000 (est. 1946).

Chat·ham (chat′əm), first Earl of, see **Pitt, William.**

Chatham Islands, a group of islands forming a part of New Zealand: they are about 500 miles east of South Island: area, 372 sq. mi.; pop., 560.

cha·toy·ant (shə-toi′ənt), *adj.* [Fr., ppr. of *chatoyer*, to change luster like the eye of a cat < *chat*, a cat], having a changeable color or luster: as, *chatoyant* silk. *n.* a gem or polished stone, as the cat's-eye, with such luster.

Chat·ta·hoo·chee (chat′ə-hōō′chi), *n.* a river in western Georgia, flowing southward into the Apalachicola River: length, 500 mi.

Chat·ta·noo·ga (chat′ə-nōō′gə), *n.* a city in southeastern Tennessee, on the Tennessee River: pop., 130,000: site of a battle (November 24–25, 1863) in which Union troops drove the Confederates out of Tennessee.

chat·tel (chat′'l), *n.* [ME. *chatel, catel;* OFr. *chatel;* LL. *captale, capitale;* see CATTLE], 1. an article of personal or movable property as distinguished from real property: furniture, automobiles, livestock, farm equipment, etc. are chattels. 2. [Archaic], a slave.

chattel mortgage, a mortgage on personal property.

chat·ter (chat′ẽr), *v.i.* [Early ME. *cheateren;* echoic and freq.; cf. CHITTER], 1. to make short, indistinct sounds in rapid succession: said of birds, apes, etc. 2. to talk fast, incessantly, and foolishly. 3. to click together rapidly, as the teeth do from fright or cold. 4. to rattle or vibrate: as, an improperly adjusted tool *chatters.* *v.t.* to utter with a chattering sound. *n.* 1. short, indistinct sounds in rapid succession. 2. rapid, foolish talk.

chat·ter·box (chat′ẽr-boks′), *n.* a person who talks incessantly.

chat·ter·er (chat′ẽr-ẽr), *n.* 1. a person who chatters. 2. any of various birds, as the cotinga, waxwing, etc.

chatter mark, 1. a mark left by a tool that chatters. 2. one of a series of small, curved abrasions on the surface of a glaciated rock, resulting from the vibrations of the glacier passing over.

Chat·ter·ton, Thomas (chat′ẽr-tən), 1752–1770; English poet: called *the marvelous boy.*

chat·ti·ly (chat′'l-i), *adv.* in a chatty manner.

chat·ti·ness (chat′i-nis), *n.* the quality of being chatty.

chat·ty (chat′i), *adj.* [CHATTIER (-i-ẽr), CHATTIEST (-i-ist)], 1. fond of chatting. 2. light, familiar, and informal: said of talk.

Chau·cer, Geoffrey (chô′sẽr), 1340?–1400; English poet; wrote the *Canterbury Tales*, etc.

Chau·ce·ri·an (chô-sêr′i-ən), *adj.* of or characteristic of Chaucer or his writings. *n.* a scholar specializing in the life and works of Chaucer.

chauf·fer (chôf′ẽr, shôf′ẽr), *n.* [var. of *chafer* (see CHAFE, to heat), altered after Fr. *chauffoir* < *chauffer*, to heat, warm], a small, portable stove or heater.

chauf·feur (shō′fẽr, shō-fũr′), *n.* [Fr., lit., stoker < *chauffer*, to heat; see CHAFE], a person whose work is to drive an automobile for someone else; driver. *v.t.* to act as chauffeur to; drive (a person) in an automobile.

chaul·moo·gra (chôl-mōō′grə), *n.* [Beng. *cāulmugrā*, East Indian tree], an East Indian tree whose seeds yield a nonvolatile oil used in medicine, especially to treat leprosy.

Chau·mont (shō′mōn′), *n.* a city in eastern France: pop., 17,000 (1946).

Chaun·cey (chôn′si, chän′si), [said to be akin to *chan-*

cellor; prob. < OFr. *cheaunce* (see CHANCE) in the sense "luck"], a masculine name.

chaunt (chônt), ***n., v.t. & v.i.*** [Archaic], chant.

‡**chausses** (shōs; *formerly Anglicized to* chou′siz), ***n.pl.*** in medieval times, a one-piece, tight-fitting garment for the legs and feet; especially, such a garment of mail forming part of a knight's armor.

Chaus·son, Er·nest (er′nest′ shō′sōn′), 1855–1899; French composer.

‡**chaus·sure** (shō′sür′), ***n.*** [Fr. < *chausser*, to shoe; L. *calceare* < *calceus*, shoe < *calx*, the heel], an article of footwear; shoe, boot, slipper, etc.

Chau·tau·qua (shə-tô′kwə), ***n.*** [< Am. Ind. (Seneca) name, said to be < base meaning "child", supposedly so named because when the Senecas first came to the lake they encountered a storm so severe that a child was swept into the lake and drowned], 1. a lake in southwestern New York: length, 18 mi.; width, 1 to 3 mi. 2. a village on this lake. 3. [c-], [< the summer schools inaugurated at Chautauqua in 1874], an assembly lasting several days, for educational and recreational purposes: the program includes lectures, concerts, etc.

chau·vin·ism (shō′vin-iz′m), ***n.*** [Fr. *chauvinisme* < Nicolas *Chauvin*, soldier of Napoleon I, notorious for his bellicose attachment to the lost imperial cause], 1. militant, unreasoning, and boastful devotion to one's country; fanatical patriotism; jingoism. 2. unreasoning devotion to one's race, sex, etc., with contempt for other races, the opposite sex, etc.: as, male *chauvinism.*

chau·vin·ist (shō′vin-ist), ***n.*** [see CHAUVINISM], 1. a person whose patriotism is unreasoning and fanatical; jingo. 2. a person unreasonably devoted to his own race, sex, etc. and contemptuous of other races, the opposite sex, etc. ***adj.*** chauvinistic.

chau·vin·is·tic (shō′vi-nis′tik), ***adj.*** of or characteristic of chauvinism or chauvinists.

chau·vin·is·ti·cal·ly (shō′vi-nis′ti-k'l-i, shō′vi-nis′tik-li), ***adv.*** in the manner of a chauvinist.

Chavannes, Puvis de, see **Puvis de Chavannes.**

chaw (chô), ***n., v.t. & v.i.*** [Colloq.], chew: now substandard or humorous.

chay (chā, chī), ***n.*** [Malayalam *cāyavēr*], 1. the root of an East Indian plant of the madder family, from which a red dye is obtained. 2. the plant.

chaz·an, chaz·zan (khä′z'n, khä-zän′), ***n.*** [Mod. Heb. *ḥazzān, ḥāzān*], a Jewish cantor.

Ch. E., Chemical Engineer.

cheap (chēp), ***adj.*** [< *good cheap*, good bargain; ME. *chep, cep;* AS. *ceap, cep*, a purchase, price, bargain], 1. low in price or cost; not expensive. 2. charging low prices: as, *cheap* jobbers. 3. worth more than the price. 4. costing little labor or trouble; easily got. 5. of little or no value; virtually worthless. 6. held in little esteem; common: as, don't make yourself *cheap.* 7. in *economics,* lowered in exchange value or buying power: as, *cheap* money is often a result of inflation. ***adv.*** cheaply. ***n.*** [AS. *ceap;* akin to Dan. *kjob* (ON. *kaup*) as in *Kjöbnhavn* (Copenhagen); see the *adj.*], 1. a market: now only in place names, as *Cheapside.* 2. [Obs.], a bargain: as, I bought it for *cheap.*

feel cheap, [Slang], to feel embarrassed, ashamed, or somewhat contemptible.

SYN.—**cheap** and **inexpensive** both mean low in cost or price, but **inexpensive** simply suggests value comparable to the price and **cheap,** in this sense, stresses a bargain; **cheap** may also imply inferior quality or value, tawdriness, contemptibleness, etc. (*cheap* jewelry, to feel *cheap*).—***ANT.*** costly, expensive, dear.

cheap·en (chēp′'n), ***v.t.*** [ME. *cheapien, chepen;* AS. *ceapian*, to trade, buy; akin to G. *kaufen;* pres. meaning < *cheap, adj.*], 1. to make cheap or cheaper. 2. to depreciate, belittle, or bring into contempt. 3. [Archaic] to bargain for. ***v.i.*** to become cheap or cheaper.

cheap·ly (chēp′li), ***adv.*** 1. at a low cost; with little expense. 2. in a cheap manner.

Cheap·side (chēp′sīd′), ***n.*** [see CHEAP], a street in London: in the Middle Ages it was a market place.

cheap skate, [Slang], a person unwilling to spend money; miserly, ungenerous person.

cheat (chēt), ***n.*** [ME. *chete* < *eschete;* see ESCHEAT], 1. a fraud; swindle; deception; sham. 2. a person who defrauds, deceives, or tricks others; swindler. 3. a grass closely resembling wheat: also called *chess.* ***v.t.*** 1. to deceive by trickery; defraud; swindle. 2. to fool; beguile. 3. to foil; elude; escape: as, *cheat* death. ***v.i.*** to practice fraud or deception; behave dishonestly or unfaithfully.

cheat on, [Slang], to be sexually unfaithful to.

SYN.—**cheat,** the most general term in this comparison, implies dishonesty or deception in dealing with someone, to obtain some advantage or gain; **defraud,** chiefly a legal term, stresses the use of deliberate deception in criminally depriving a person of his rights, property, etc.; **swindle** stresses the winning of a person's confidence in order to cheat or defraud him of money, etc.; **trick** implies a deluding by means of a ruse, stratagem, etc., but does not always suggest fraudulence or a harmful motive; **dupe** stresses credulity in the person who is tricked or fooled; **hoax** implies a trick skillfully carried off simply to demonstrate the gullibility of the victim.

che·bec (chi-bek′), ***n.*** [echoic of the bird's note], a small flycatcher found in eastern North America: also called *least flycatcher.*

Chech·en-In·gush Autonomous Soviet Socialist Republic (che′chen′iŋ′goosh), a former division of the R.S.F.S.R., in the Caucasus: area, 6,060 sq. mi.; pop., 733,000; abolished in 1945.

check (chek), ***n.*** [ME. *chek, chekke;* OFr. *eschek, eschec, eschac*, a check at chess, repulse, defeat; ML. *scaccus, scahus* < Per. *shāh*, king, principal piece in a game of chess; sense development: king in danger—defeat (hence, stoppage)—a try to repulse or defeat—a trial or test—scrutiny, verification], 1. a sudden stop; abrupt halt. 2. any restraint or control put upon action. 3. a person or thing that restrains or controls. 4. a supervision of accuracy, efficiency, etc.: as, the foreman kept a *check* on his department. 5. a test of accuracy; comparison or standard of comparison; verification; examination. 6. a mark (√) to show approval or verification of something, or to call attention to it. 7. an identification ticket or metal piece showing ownership to secure against loss: as, a hat *check*, a baggage *check.* 8. a piece of paper stating one's bill at a restaurant or bar. 9. a gambling chip. 10. a written order to a bank to pay the amount of money stated: abbreviated **Ch., ch., ck.:** also spelled **cheque.** 11. a pattern of small squares like that of a chessboard. 12. one of the small squares of such a pattern. 13. a cloth with such a pattern. 14. a small split, crack, or chink. 15. in *chess,* the condition of a player's king that is in danger and must be put into a safe position. ***interj.*** 1. [Colloq.], agreed! correct! right! 2. in *chess,* a call meaning that the opponent's king must be taken out of check. ***v.t.*** 1. to stop suddenly; halt abruptly. 2. to restrain; control; curb; hold back. 3. to retard the growth of. 4. to rebuff; repulse; rebuke. 5. to test, measure, verify, or control by investigation, comparison, or examination: as, *check* the accounts. 6. to mark with a check (√). 7. to mark with a crisscross pattern. 8. to deposit temporarily: as, *check* your hat and coat. 9. to make chinks or cracks in. 10. in *agriculture,* to plant in checkrows. 11. in *chess,* to place (an opponent's king) in check. ***v.i.*** 1. to agree with one another item for item: as, the accounts *check.* 2. to write a check; draw a check on a bank account. 3. to crack in small checks: as, paint *checks* when applied to hardwood without sufficient filler. 4. to stop or pause to pick up the scent: said of hunting dogs. 5. in *chess,* to place an opponent's king in check. 6. in *falconry,* to turn away from the right game and follow other and worse game (with *at*). ***adj.*** 1. used to check or verify: as, a *check* experiment. 2. having a crisscross pattern; checked. —***SYN.*** see **restrain.**

check in, to register at a hotel, convention, etc.

check off, to mark as verified, examined, etc.

check out, 1. to settle one's bill and leave a hotel, etc. 2. to add up the prices of purchases and collect the total: said of a cashier, as in a supermarket. 3. [Slang], to die.

check up on, to examine the record, character, etc. of.

in check, in restraint; under control.

check·book (chek′book′), ***n.*** a book containing detachable blank checks, issued to a depositor by a bank.

checked (chekt), ***adj.*** [pp. of *check*], having a pattern of squares: as, a *checked* tablecloth.

check·er (chek′ẽr), ***n.*** [ME. *cheker*, chessboard < *escheker;* OFr. *eschequier* < *eschec;* see CHECK], 1. a small square like those of a chessboard. 2. a pattern of such squares. 3. one of the flat, round pieces used in playing checkers or backgammon. 4. [Archaic], a chessboard. 5. *pl.* in *architecture,* stones arranged like the squares of a chessboard. 6. in *botany, a)* either of two European varieties of service tree resembling the mountain ash, but having a larger, spotted fruit: also **checker tree.** *b) pl.* the fruit of either of these trees. ***v.t.*** [< OFr. *eschequier*], 1. to mark off in squares; arrange in the pattern of a chessboard. 2. to break the uniformity of; make different by color and shading.

check·er (chek′ẽr), ***n.*** 1. a person who examines or verifies. 2. a person who checks hats, luggage, etc. 3. a cashier, as in a supermarket.

check·er·ber·ry (chek′ẽr-ber′i), ***n.*** [*pl.* CHECKERBERRIES (-iz)], 1. the edible, red, berrylike fruit of the wintergreen. 2. the wintergreen. 3. the partridgeberry.

check·er·bloom (chek′ẽr-blōōm′), ***n.*** a plant of the mallow family, with pinkish flowers.

check·er·board (chek′ẽr-bôrd′, chek′ẽr-bōrd′), ***n.*** a board marked off into 64 squares of two alternating colors, used in the games of checkers and chess.

check·ered (chek′ẽrd), ***adj.*** 1. having a pattern of colored squares like those of a checkerboard. 2. varied by the use of color and shading; hence, 3. varied; diversified; full of ups and downs: as, a *checkered* career.

check·ers (chek'ẽrz), *n. pl.* [construed as sing.], a game played on a checkerboard by two players, each with 12 pieces to move; draughts.

check·hook (chek'hook'), *n.* a saddle hook through which the checkrein of a horse's harness is fastened.

checking account, a bank account against which the depositor can draw checks at any time, without presenting a passbook: distinguished from *savings account.*

check list, a list of things to be checked off.

check·mate (chek'māt'), *n.* [ME. *chek mat;* OFr. *eschec mat;* through Ar. < Per. *shāh māt*, lit., the king is dead; *shāh*, king + *māt*, he is dead], 1. *a)* a move in chess that checks the opponent's king so that it cannot be put into safety, thus ending the game. *b)* the position of the king resulting from this; hence, 2. hopeless jeopardy or defeat. *interj.* in *chess*, a call to indicate a checkmate. *v.t.* [CHECKMATED (-id), CHECKMATING], 1. to place in checkmate; mate. 2. to place in hopeless jeopardy; defeat completely; frustrate. Also **mate.**

check·off (chek'ôf'), *n.* an arrangement by which dues of trade-union members are withheld from wages and turned over to the union by the employer.

check-out, check·out (chek'out'), *n.* a store counter where a cashier checks out purchases.

check·rein (chek'rān'), *n.* 1. a short rein attached to the bridle and looped over the checkhook to keep a horse from lowering its head. 2. a short branch rein connecting the driving rein of one of a team of horses to the bit of another. Also called *check line.*

check·room (chek'rōōm', chek'room'), *n.* [see CHECK, *v.*], a room in which hats, coats, baggage, parcels, etc. may be left until called for.

check·row (chek'rō'), *n.* any of several rows planted in squares so that a cultivator can operate between them. *v.t.* to plant (corn, grain, etc.) in checkrows.

check·up (chek'up'), *n.* an examination; investigation.

Ched·dar (ched'ẽr), *n.* [< *Cheddar*, Somersetshire, England, where it was made], a variety of hard, smooth cheese: also **Cheddar cheese.**

chedd·ite (ched'īt, shed'īt), *n.* [< *Chedde*, France, where it was made], an explosive for blasting, consisting of potassium chlorate or perchlorate mixed with a nitro compound and an oily substance, as castor oil.

cheek (chēk), *n.* [ME. *cheke;* AS. *ceace*, jaw, jawbone (as still in *cheek by jowl);* akin to D. *kaak*, LG. *kâke*, jaw; only W. Gmc.; sense 4 < phrases like *have the cheek* (*to do something*)], 1. either side of the face between the nose and the ear, below the eye. 2. a thing suggesting this in shape or position. 3. *usually in pl.* either of two sides of a thing, as the sides of a door jamb, the sidepieces of a gun, the jaws of a vise, or the projections on the sides of a ship's mast which support the trestletrees. 4. [Colloq.], sauciness; insolence; effrontery; impudence. *v.t.* [Colloq.], to speak saucily to; be insolent toward. —*SYN.* see **temerity.**

cheek by jowl, 1. close together. 2. familiar; close.

tongue in cheek, without sincerity; with the real meaning different from the ostensible one.

cheek·bone (chēk'bōn'), *n.* the bone of the upper cheek, just below the eye.

cheek·i·ly (chēk''l-i), *adv.* [see CHEEKY], [Colloq.], saucily; impudently.

cheek·i·ness (chēk'i-nis), *n.* [Colloq.], the quality or state of being cheeky; sauciness; impudence.

cheek pouch, a pouchlike swelling in the cheek of certain rodents, monkeys, etc., used for holding food.

cheek strap, one of the side straps of a bridle, connecting the headband with the bit.

cheek·y (chēk'i), *adj.* [CHEEKIER (-i-ẽr), CHEEKIEST (-i-ist)], [*cheek* + *-y*], [Colloq.], saucy; impudent.

cheep (chēp), *n.* [echoic], a short, faint, shrill sound like that of a young bird; peep; chirp. *v.t. & v.i.* to make, or utter with, such a sound.

cheer (chêr), *n.* [ME. *chere*, the face, demeanor, welcome; OFr. *chere, chiere* < LL. *cara*, the face; Gr. *kara*, the head; modern senses < phr. *good cheer* (Fr. *bonne chère*)], 1. a mood; disposition; state of mind or of feeling. 2. gaiety; gladness; joy; encouragement; comfort. 3. food or entertainment that makes one happy. 4. anything that makes one happy; encouragement. 5. a glad, excited shout used to urge on, welcome, approve, congratulate, etc. 6. [Archaic], facial expression. *v.t.* 1. to fill with joy, good spirits, and hope; gladden; comfort. 2. to urge, incite, or encourage by cheers. 3. to salute with cheers. *v.i.* 1. to be or become glad, happy, or optimistic; feel encouraged; take heart: as, her heart *cheered* at the news. 2. to shout cheers.

be of good cheer, 1. to have a cheerful countenance or manner; hence, 2. to be cheerful.

cheer up, to make or become glad; brighten up.

with good cheer, in a cordial manner.

cheer·ful (chêr'fəl), *adj.* 1. full of cheer; glad; gay; joyful. 2. filling with cheer; bright and attractive: as, a *cheerful* room. 3. willing; hearty: as, a *cheerful* helper. —*SYN.* see **happy.**

cheer·i·ly (chêr'ə-li), *adv.* in a cheery manner.

cheer·i·ness (chêr'i-nis), *n.* a cheery quality or state.

cheer·i·o (chêr'i-ō'), *interj. & n.* [*pl.* CHEERIOS (-ōz')], [British Colloq.], 1. hello. 2. good-by.

cheer·less (chêr'lis), *adj.* not cheerful; without cheer; unhappy; joyless; dreary: as, a *cheerless* prospect.

cheer·ly (chêr'li), *adv.* 1. [Archaic], cheerily. 2. in *nautical usage*, quickly; briskly.

cheer·y (chêr'i), *adj.* [CHEERIER (-i-ẽr), CHEERIEST (-i-ist)], cheerful; gay; lively; pleasant; bright.

cheese (chēz), *n.* [ME. *chese;* AS. *ciese, cyse;* akin to G. *käse;* ult. < L. *caseus* < **cāso-*, curdled, coagulated; IE. base **qwat(h)*, to bubble up, ferment, become soured], 1. a food made from the curds of milk pressed together to form a solid. 2. a shaped mass of this. 3. a thing like cheese in shape or consistency: as, damson *cheese.* 4. the wrinkled, flat, green fruit of the common mallow.

cheese it! [altered < *cease it*], [Slang], stop (whatever one is doing)! run!

cheese (chēz), *n.* [prob. < Urdu *chīz*, thing], [Slang], the important thing: as, he's the big *cheese.*

cheese·cake (chēz'kāk'), *n.* 1. a kind of cake made of sweetened curds, eggs, milk, sugar, etc. 2. [Slang], display of the figure, especially the legs, of a pretty girl, as in some newspaper photographs.

cheese·cloth (chēz'klôth'), *n.* [from its use for wrapping cheese], a thin, cotton cloth with a loose weave.

cheese·mon·ger (chēz'muŋ'gẽr), *n.* a dealer in cheese.

cheese·par·ing (chēz'pâr'iŋ), *n.* 1. a paring of cheese rind. 2. anything as worthless as such a paring. 3. stinginess.

chees·i·ness (chēz'i-nis), *n.* the quality of being cheesy.

chees·y (chēz'i), *adj.* [CHEESIER (-i-ẽr), CHEESIEST (-i-ist)], 1. like cheese in consistency or flavor. 2. [Slang], inferior; poor; inadequate.

chee·tah (chē'tə), *n.* [Hind. *chītā*, leopard < Sans. *citra*, variegated, spotted], a leopardlike animal of Africa and southern Asia, with a small head, long legs, and a black-spotted, tawny coat: it can be trained to hunt: also spelled **chetah.**

chef (shef), *n.* [Fr. < *chef de cuisine;* see CHIEF], 1. a head cook. 2. any cook.

‡chef-d'oeu·vre (she'dë'vr'), *n.* [*pl.* CHEFS-D'OEUVRE (she'dë'vr')], [Fr., principal work], a masterpiece, as in art or literature.

Che·foo (chē'fōō'), *n.* a city on the coast of Shantung province, China: pop., 227,000.

chei·ro- (kī'rō, kī'rə), chiro-.

Che·ka (chā'kä), *n.* [< Russ. names of initial letters of *Chrezvychainaya Kommissia*, the extraordinary commission], a commission in the Soviet Union which acted as secret police against counterrevolutionists (1917–1921): see also **Gay-Pay-Oo, MVD.**

Che·khov, An·ton Pa·vlo·vich (ån-tôn' på-vlô'vich chekh'ôf; Eng. chek'ôf), 1860–1904; Russian novelist, dramatist, and short-story writer: also spelled **Chekov, Chekoff, Tchekhov.**

Che·kiang (che'kyaŋ'; Chin. ju'jyäŋ'), *n.* a province of China, on the East China Sea: area, 39,750 sq. mi.; pop., 22,866,000; capital, Hangchow.

che·la (kē'lə), *n.* [*pl.* CHELAE (-lē)], [Mod. L.; Gr. *chēlē*, claw], a pincerlike claw of a crab, lobster, scorpion, etc.

che·la (chā'lä), *n.* [Hind. *celā*, slave, servant < Sans. *ceṭaka*], in India, a novice or disciple.

che·late (kē'lāt), *adj.* resembling or having pincerlike claws (called *chelae*).

che·lif·er·ous (ki-lif'ẽr-əs), *adj.* in *zoology*, bearing chelae, or claws.

che·li·form (kē'lə-fôrm'), *adj.* having the form of a chela, or pincerlike claw.

Chel·le·an (shel'i-ən), *adj.* [Fr. *chelléen* < *Chelles*, France, where the tools were found], designating or of that division of the Paleolithic Age during which certain flint tools were used.

Chelm·no (khelm'nô), *n.* a Nazi concentration camp in central Poland: notorious as an extermination center.

che·loid (kē'loid), *n.* a keloid.

che·lo·ni·an (ki-lō'ni-ən), *adj.* [< LL. *chelonia;* Gr. *chelonē*], of turtles or tortoises. *n.* a turtle or tortoise.

Chel·sea (chel'si), *n.* 1. a city in Massachusetts: suburb of Boston: pop., 34,000. 2. a borough of London: pop., 51,000.

Chel·ten·ham (chelt'nəm, chelt''n-əm), *n.* a city in Gloucestershire, England: pop., 69,000.

Chel·ya·binsk (chel-yä'binsk), *n.* 1. a region of the R.S.F.S.R., in western Siberia, east of the Ural Mountains: pop., 2,982,000. 2. its capital: pop., 688,000.

Chel·yus·kin, Cape (chel-yoos'kin), the northernmost point of Asia, in central Siberia.

chem., 1. chemical. 2. chemist. 3. chemistry.

chem·ic (kem'ik), *adj.* [Archaic], 1. of alchemy; alchemical. 2. chemical. *n.* [Obs.], a chemist.

chem·i·cal (kem'i-k'l), *adj.* [*chemic* + *-al*], 1. of chemistry: as, a *chemical* reaction. 2. made by or used in chemistry. 3. operated by the use of chemicals. 4. trained in the science of chemistry. Abbreviated **chem.** *n.* any substance used in or obtained by a chemical process or processes.

chemical engineering, the science or profession of applying chemistry to industrial uses.

chem·i·cal·ly (kem′i-k'l-i, kem′ik-li), *adv.* 1. according to the principles of chemistry. 2. by chemical means.
chemical warfare, warfare by means of chemicals and chemical devices other than explosives, as gases, flame throwers, incendiary bombs, smoke screens, etc.
‡**che·min de fer** (shə-man′ də fâr′), [Fr., road of iron], 1. a railroad. 2. a kind of baccarat, a gambling game.
che·mise (shə-mēz′), *n.* [Fr.; LL. *camisia*, shirt, tunic < Gaul.; akin to AS. *hemethe*, shirt (G. *hemd*); IE. base **kem-*, to cover, cloak], an undergarment somewhat like a loose, short slip or long undershirt, worn by women.
chem·i·sette (shem′i-zet′), *n.* [Fr., dim. of *chemise*], 1. a short, sleeveless bodice formerly worn as an undergarment by women. 2. a detachable shirt front formerly worn by women to fill in the neckline of a dress.
chem·ism (kem′iz'm), *n.* [Fr. *chemisme;* see CHEMIST], [Rare], chemical force, action, or affinity.
chem·ist (kem′ist), *n.* [Fr. *chemiste* < LL. *alchimista;* see ALCHEMY], 1. a student of or specialist in chemistry: abbreviated **chem.** 2. [British], a druggist. 3. [Obs.], an alchemist.
chem·is·try (kem′is-tri), *n.* [*pl.* CHEMISTRIES (-triz)], [< *chemist*], 1. the science dealing with the composition and properties of substances, and with the reactions by which substances are produced from or converted into other substances: abbreviated **chem.** 2. the application of this to a specified subject or field of activity. 3. the chemical properties, composition, reactions, and uses of a substance. 4. any process of synthesis or analysis similar to that used in chemistry: as, the main trait of wit is its *chemistry* of incongruities.
Chem·nitz (kem′nits), *n.* a city in Saxony, Germany: pop., 335,000.
chem·o- (kem′ō), a combining form meaning: *having to do with chemicals, of chemical reactions*, as in *chemotherapy:* also, before a vowel, **chem-.**
chem·o·syn·the·sis (kem′ō-sin′thə-sis), *n.* the synthesis by plants of organic chemical compounds with energy derived from other chemical reactions, as from oxidation by bacteria.
chem·o·tax·is (kem′ō-tak′sis), *n.* the property of certain living cells and organisms by which they are attracted to or repelled from chemical substances.
chem·o·ther·a·peu·tics (kem′ō-ther′ə-pū′tiks), *n.pl.* [construed as sing.], chemotherapy.
chem·o·ther·a·pist (kem′ō-ther′ə-pist), *n.* a doctor of internal medicine who uses chemotherapy.
chem·o·ther·a·py (kem′ō-ther′ə-pi), *n.* [*chemo-* + *therapy*], the treatment of infection by the systemic administration of chemicals, such as the sulfonamides.
chem·ot·ro·pism (kem-ot′rə-piz'm), *n.* [see CHEMO- & TROPISM], the tendency of certain plants or other organisms to turn or bend under the influence of chemical substances.
Che·mul·pho, Che·mul·po (che′mool-pō′), *n.* a seaport in western Korea: pop., 109,000: Japanese name, *Jinsen.*
chem·ur·gic (kem-ũr′jik), *adj.* of or produced by chemurgy.
chem·ur·gy (kem′ẽr-ji), *n.* [*chem*ist + *-urgy*], the branch of chemistry dealing with the utilization of farm products in the manufacture of new products not classed as food or clothing (e.g., soy beans as a base for plastics).
Che·nab (chi-nab′), *n.* a river in Punjab, India, flowing into the Sutlej River: length, 600 mi.
Cheng·teh (cheŋ′te′; Chin. chuŋ′du′), *n.* Jehol, a city in Manchuria.
Cheng·tu (cheŋ′to͞o′; Chin. chuŋ′do͞o′), *n.* the capital of Szechwan province, China: pop., 441,000.
che·nille (shə-nēl′), *n.* [Fr., caterpillar < L. *canicula*, dim. of *canis*, a dog: from the supposed resemblance of the material to caterpillars], 1. a tufted, velvety cord used for trimming, embroidery, etc. 2. a fabric filled or woven with chenille, used for rugs, bedspreads, etc.
che·no·pod (kē′nə-pod′, ken′ə-pod′), *n.* a chenopodiaceous plant.
che·no·po·di·a·ceous (kē′nə-pō′di-ā′shəs, ken′ə-pō′di-ā′shəs), *adj.* [< Mod. L. *Chenopodium* (< Gr. *chēnos*, a goose; + *-podium*), name of the genus; + *-aceous*], of the goosefoot family of plants, including spinach, beets, etc.
Che·ops (kē′ops), *n.* (*Khufu*), king of Egypt; fl. 2900 B.C.; builder of the Great Pyramid near Gizeh.
cheque (chek), *n.* a (bank) check: British spelling.
cheq·uer (chek′ẽr), *n.* & *v.t.* checker: British spelling.
cheq·uers (chek′ẽrz), *n. pl.* [construed as sing.], checkers: British spelling.
Cher (sher), *n.* a river in central France, flowing into the Loire River: length, 220 mi.
Cher·bourg (sher′boorg; Fr. sher′bo͞or′), *n.* a seaport in France, on the English Channel: pop., 40,000 (1946).
‡**cher·chez la femme** (sher′shā′ lȧ fȧm′), [Fr.], look for the woman: used, often facetiously, to imply that a woman is the cause of the trouble.
cher·ish (cher′ish), *v.t.* [ME. *cherischen, cherisen* < OFr. *cheris-* < *cherir* < *cher*, dear; L. *carus;* cf. CHARITY], 1. to hold dear; value highly. 2. to take good care of; treat tenderly; foster; nurture. 3. to hold in the mind; cling to: as, he *cherishes* fame. —***SYN.*** see **appreciate.**
Cher·kessk Autonomous Region (cher-kesk′), a division of the R.S.F.S.R., in the Caucasus: area, 1,273 sq. mi.; pop., 97,200; capital, Sulimov.
Cher·nov·tsy (cher-nôf′tsi), *n.* a city in the Ukrainian S.S.R., formerly in Romania: pop., 110,000: German name, *Czernowitz;* Romanian name, *Cernăuţi.*
cher·no·zem (cher′nə-zem′), *n.* [Russ. < *chernyi*, black + *zemlya*, earth, soil], rich, black topsoil, with a lower layer of lime, found characteristically in the grasslands of central European Russia.
Cher·o·kee (cher′ə-kē′, cher′ə-kē′), *n.* [*pl.* CHEROKEE, CHEROKEES (-kēz′, -kēz′)], [< Am. Ind. (Muskhogean); lit., prob. "cave people"], a member of a tribe of Iroquoian Indians whose original home was in the southeastern United States: they now live in the Southwest.
Cherokee rose, an evergreen climbing rose with fragrant, large, white flowers and glossy leaves.
che·root (shə-ro͞ot′), *n.* [Fr. *cheroute;* Tamil *shuruttu*, a roll], a cigar with both ends cut square.
cher·ry (cher′i), *n.* [*pl.* CHERRIES (-iz)], [ME. *cheri;* OFr. *cerise* < LL. *ceresia, cerasia* < Gr. *kerasion*, cherry, fruit of the *kerasos*, cherry tree; *-s* dropped because OFr. *cerise* was assumed to be pl.], 1. a small, fleshy fruit containing a smooth, hard seed: cherries are bright red, reddish black, or yellowish. 2. the tree that it grows on. 3. the wood of this tree. 4. a bright red. *adj.* 1. bright-red; cherry-colored. 2. made of cherry wood. 3. made with or from cherries: as, *cherry* pie. 4. having a flavor more or less like that of cherries.
cherry stone, 1. the pit of a cherry. 2. a small quahog, a variety of clam.
cher·so·nese (kũr′sə-nēz′), *n.* [L. *chersonesus, cherronesus;* Gr. *chersonēsos* < *chersos*, dry land + *nēsos*, island], a peninsula.
chert (chũrt), *n.* [apparently Brit. western dial. form of *sherd, shard*, from nature of the rock; cf. Early Mod. Eng. *shard* for *chard*], 1. a dull-colored, flintlike quartz often found in limestone. 2. any of certain similar rocks composed of hydrated silica and containing impurities.
chert·y (chũr′ti), *adj.* [CHERTIER (-ti-ẽr), CHERTIEST (-ti-ist)], like or containing chert; flinty.
cher·ub (cher′əb), *n.* [*pl.* CHERUBS (-əbz); also, for 1, 2, 3, CHERUBIM (-ə-bim, -yoo-bim) and, in the Vulgate, CHERUBIN (-ə-bin, -yoo-bin)], [LL. *cherub;* Heb. *kerūbh*], 1. a winged heavenly being described in Ezekiel 1: 5–11. 2. any of the second order of angels, usually ranked just below the seraphim and described as excelling in knowledge. 3. a representation of one of the cherubim as a winged angel clothed in red, as in early art, or a chubby, rosy-faced child with wings, as in later art; hence, 4. a person, especially a child, with a sweet, innocent face. 5. an innocent or lovely child.
che·ru·bic (chə-ro͞o′bik), *adj.* 1. of or resembling a cherub; angelic. 2. innocent and sweet. 3. chubby, rosy-faced, etc.
che·ru·bi·cal·ly (chə-ro͞o′bi-k'l-i, chə-ro͞o′bik-li), *adv.* in a cherubic manner; angelically.
cher·u·bim (cher′ə-bim, cher′yoo-bim), *n.* alternative plural and, formerly, alternative singular of **cherub** (in senses 1, 2, 3).
cher·u·bin (cher′ə-bin, cher′yoo-bin), *n.* occasional plural and, formerly, singular of **cherub** (in senses 1, 2, 3), as in the Vulgate.
Che·ru·bi·ni, Ma·ri·a Lu·i·gi (mä-rē′ä lo͞o-ē′jē ke′ro͞o-bē′nē), 1760–1842; Italian composer.
cher·vil (chũr′vil), *n.* [AS. *cerfelle, cærfille;* L. *chaerephyllum, caerefolium;* Gr. *chairephyllon* < *chairein*, to be happy, rejoice + *phyllon*, leaf], 1. a plant of the carrot family, with parsleylike leaves used for flavoring salads, soups, etc. 2. any of various related plants, as sweet cicely.
cher·vo·nets (cher-vô′nits), *n.* [*pl.* CHERVONTSI (-vôn′-tsi)], [Russ.], 1. the former monetary unit of the Soviet Union, equal to 10 gold rubles: replaced March 1, 1936 by the gold ruble. 2. a gold coin of this value. Also spelled **tchervonetz.**
Ches·a·peake Bay (ches′ə-pēk′), an arm of the Atlantic, projecting into Virginia and Maryland: length, 200 mi.
Chesh·ire (chesh′ir, chesh′ẽr), *n.* a county of western England: pop., 1,088,000; county seat, Chester: also called *Chester.*
Cheshire cat, a proverbial grinning cat from Cheshire, England: the one described in Lewis Carroll's *Alice's Adventures in Wonderland* (1856) gradually faded away until only a fixed grin remained.
Chesh·van (khesh′vən), *n.* [Heb.], the second month of the Jewish year: see **Jewish calendar.**
ches·key (ches′ki), *n.* [< Czech *český, adj.*, Czech], [Slang], 1. a person of Czech extraction. 2. the Czech language.
chess (ches), *n.* [ME. *ches, chesse;* OFr. *esches*, pl. of *eschec;* see CHECK], a game of skill played on a chess-

board by two players, each with 16 chessmen to move in different ways: the game progresses by alternate moves until one player wins by checkmating his opponent's king or until neither can do so and a stalemate results.

chess (ches), *n.* [var. of *chase* (a groove), from effect of color in wheat field], 1. any of several varieties of brome grass, especially a weedy kind found among wheat. 2. the darnel.

chess·board (ches′bôrd′, ches′bōrd′), *n.* a board marked off into 64 squares of two alternating colors, used in the games of chess and checkers.

chess·man (ches′man′, ches′mən), *n.* [*pl.* CHESSMEN (-men′, -mən)], [altered < ME. *chess-meyne*, lit., chess retinue; *meyne* (obs. Eng. *meiny*) < OFr. *meyné*], any of the pieces used in the game of chess: each player has 1 king, 1 queen, 2 rooks (or castles), 2 knights, 2 bishops, and 8 pawns.

chest (chest), *n.* [ME. *chest, chist;* AS. *cist*, a coffin; akin to G. *kiste;* L. *cista;* Gr. *kiste*, a box, orig. woven container, basket], 1. a box with a lid and, sometimes, a lock: as, a tool *chest*, treasure *chest*. 2. the place where money, as of a club, is kept; treasury; hence, 3. a fund; public fund: as, the community *chest*. 4. a box for the safe shipping of tea, opium, etc. 5. the capacity of such a box. 6. a sealed container for gas, steam, etc. 7. a piece of furniture with drawers; bureau. 8. the part of the body enclosed by the ribs and breastbone; thorax.

get (something) off one's chest, [Colloq.], to unburden oneself of (some trouble, annoyance, etc.) by talking about it.

ches·ted (ches′tid), *adj.* having a (specified kind of) chest (thorax): as, hollow-*chested*, pigeon-*chested*, etc.

Ches·ter (ches′tẽr), [AS. *ceaster*, walled town; L. *castra*, a camp], a masculine name. *n.* 1. the county seat of Cheshire, England: pop., 60,000. 2. Cheshire. 3. a city in Pennsylvania, near Philadelphia, on the Delaware: pop., 64,000.

ches·ter·field (ches′tẽr-fēld′), *n.* [after a 19th-c. Earl of *Chesterfield*], 1. a single-breasted topcoat, usually with a fly front and a velvet collar. 2. a kind of sofa, heavily stuffed and with upright ends.

Ches·ter·field (ches′tẽr-fēld′), fourth Earl of, (*Philip Dormer Stanhope*), 1694–1773; English statesman, and writer on manners.

Ches·ter·field·i·an (ches′tẽr-fēl′di-ən), *adj.* of, like, or characteristic of the fourth Earl of Chesterfield; suave, urbane, elegant, etc.

Ches·ter·ton, Gilbert Keith (ches′tẽr-tən), 1874–1936; English essayist, novelist, poet, and critic.

Chester White, [after *Chester* County, Pa., where the breed is said to have originated], a variety of large, white hog.

chest·nut (ches′nət, ches′nut′), *n.* [< *chesten-nut;* ME. *chesten, chesteine, chasteine;* OFr. *chastaigne* (Fr. *châtaigne*); L. *castanea;* Gr. *kastanea*], 1. the smooth-shelled, sweet, edible nut of any of a group of trees of the beech family. 2. the tree that it grows on. 3. the wood of this tree. 4. the horse chestnut. 5. reddish brown. 6. a reddish-brown horse. 7. the hard callus on the inner side of a horse's foreleg. 8. [Colloq.], an old, worn-out joke or phrase; cliché; also, a very familiar story, plot, or piece of music. *adj.* reddish-brown.

CHESTNUT
A, leaves and flowers; B, bur; C, nut

pull someone's chestnuts out of the fire, [from story of the monkey and the cat: cf. CAT'S-PAW], to be persuaded or duped into doing a dangerous, painful, hard, or unpleasant thing for someone else.

chest of drawers, an article of furniture, as for a bedroom, consisting of a frame containing a set of drawers for keeping clothing, etc.: usually distinguished from *dresser* or *bureau* by its lack of attached mirror.

chest-on-chest (chest′on-chest′), *n.* a chest of drawers fitted onto another, somewhat larger one, generally resting on short feet.

chest·y (ches′ti), *adj.* [CHESTIER (-ti-ẽr), CHESTIEST (-i-ist)], [Colloq.], 1. having a large chest (thorax) or lung capacity. 2. boastful, proud, or conceited.

che·tah (chē′tə), *n.* a cheetah.

cheth (kheth, khes), *n.* kheth.

Chet·nik (chet′nik), *n.* [Serb.], a Serbian nationalist guerrilla fighter in World War II.

che·val-de-frise (shə-val′də-frēz′), *n.* [*pl.* CHEVAUX-DE-FRISE (shə-vō′də-frēz′)], [Fr., lit., Frisian horse; *cheval*, a horse (pl. *chevaux*) + *de*, of + *Frise*, Friesland: so called because first used by Netherlanders, who lacked cavalry, against Spaniards], 1. a piece of wood with projecting spikes, formerly used to hinder enemy horsemen. 2. a row of spikes or jagged glass set into the masonry on top of a wall to prevent escape or trespassing.

che·val glass (shə-val′), [Fr. *cheval*, horse, hence frame (cf. SAWHORSE); + *glass*], a full-length mirror mounted on swivels in a frame.

chev·a·lier (shev′ə-lêr′), *n.* [ME. & OFr. *chevaler;* LL. *caballarius;* see CAVALIER], 1. a member of the lowest rank of the French Legion of Honor. 2. a chivalrous man; gallant; cavalier. 3. [Archaic], a knight. 4. in *French history*, a noble of the lowest rank.

Chev·i·ot (chev′i-ət, chē′vi-ət), *n.* [after the *Cheviot* Hills], 1. any of a breed of sheep with short, close-set wool. 2. (shev′i-ət), [usually c-], *a)* a close-napped wool fabric in a twill weave, formerly made from the wool of this sheep. *b)* a cotton cloth resembling this.

Chev·i·ot Hills (chev′i-ət, chē′vi-ət), a range of hills forming the border between England and Scotland: highest peak, Cheviot, 2,677 ft.

chev·ron (shev′rən), *n.* [Fr., rafter (∧), hence heraldic chevron (∧), hence chevron (∧ or ∨) < LL. *capro*, rafter; L. *capra* (Fr. *chèvre*), em. of *caper*, goat], a V-shaped bar or bars worn on one or both of the sleeves of a military or police uniform, etc., to show rank or service.

CHEVRONS

chev·ro·tain (shev′rə-tān′, shev′rə-tin), *n.* [Fr. < OFr. *chevrot*, dim. of *chèvre*, she-goat; L. *capra*, fem. of *caper*, goat], any of a number of related small, hornless animals of Asia and Africa, resembling the deer.

chev·y (chev′i), *n.* [*pl.* CHEVIES (-iz)], [< hunting cry *chivy*, in the ballad of *Chevy Chase* < *Cheviot*], [British], 1. a hunting cry. 2. a hunt; chase. *v.t. & v.i.* [CHEVIED (-id), CHEVYING], [British], 1. to hunt; chase; run about. 2. to fret; worry.

chew (chōō, chū), *v.t. & v.i.* [ME. *chewen;* AS. *ceowan*, to bite, chew; akin to G. *kauen;* IE. base **gjeu-*, **gieu-*, as also in L. *gingiva*, a gum, whence Eng. *gingival*], 1. to bite and grind or crush with the teeth; masticate. 2. to consider; cogitate. *n.* 1. the act of chewing. 2. something chewed or for chewing.

chewing gum, a flavored and sweetened preparation, as of chicle, used for chewing.

che·wink (chi-wiŋk′), *n.* [echoic of its note], a kind of finch with red eyes; red-eyed towhee.

chew·y (chōō′i), *adj.* [CHEWIER (-i-ẽr), CHEWIEST (-i-ist)], that needs much chewing: as, *chewy* candy.

Chey·enne (shī-en′), *n.* [Am. Ind. (Sioux) *Shahiyena* < *shâia*, to use a foreign tongue], 1. [*pl.* CHEYENNE, CHEYENNES (-enz′)], a member of a tribe of Algonquian Indians who migrated from Minnesota to the headwaters of the Platte River. 2. (*locally*, shī-an′), the capital of Wyoming: pop., 44,000. 3. a river in Wyoming and South Dakota, flowing into the Missouri: length, 500 mi.

‡chez (shā), *prep.* [Fr.], by; at; at the home of.

chg. [*pl.* CHGS.], charge.

chi (kī, kē; Gr. Hē), *n.* [Gr.], the 22d letter of the Greek alphabet (Χ, χ), transliterated into English by *ch* and generally pronounced as *K:* see **alphabet,** table.

Chi·an (kī′ən), *adj.* of Chios. *n.* a native or inhabitant of Chios.

Chiang Kai-shek (chi-äŋ′ kī′shek′, chyäŋ, jyäŋ), (born *Chiang Chung-cheng*), 1886– ; Chinese general; head of Nationalist government on Taiwan (1950–).

Chi·an·ti (ki-an′ti, ki-än′ti), *n.* [It.], a dry, red wine, originally made in Tuscany in the region of the Chianti mountains.

Chi·a·pas (chi-ä′päs), *n.* a state of southern Mexico: area, 28,729 sq. mi.; pop., 1,106,000; capital, Tuxtla.

chi·a·ro-o·scu·ro (ki-är′ō-ə-skyoor′ō), *n.* [*pl.* CHIARO-OSCUROS (-ōz)], chiaroscuro.

chi·a·ro·scu·rist (ki-är′ə-skyoor′ist), *n.* an artist or photographer using or skilled in using chiaroscuro.

chi·a·ro·scu·ro (ki-är′ə-skyoor′ō), *n.* [*pl.* CHIAROSCUROS (-ōz)], [It., lit., clear dark < L. *clarus*, clear + *obscurus*, dark], 1. a style of painting, drawing, etc. using only light and shade, in order to achieve the effect of a third dimension. 2. the effect achieved by such a style. 3. the way that an artist uses light and shade. 4. a painting, etc. in which chiaroscuro is used.

chi·as·ma (ki-az′mə), *n.* [*pl.* CHIASMATA (-tə)], [Mod. L. < Gr. *chiasma*, a crosspiece < *chiasmos*, placing crosswise < *chiazein*, to mark with a *chi* (χ)], 1. a crossing or intersection of the optic nerves on the ventral surface of the brain. 2. any crosswise fusion.

chi·as·mal (kī-az′m'l), *adj.* of or characterized by chiasma.

chi·as·ma·typ·y (kī-az′mə-tī′pi), *n.* [< *chiasma* + *type* + *-y*], in *genetics*, a supposed twisting of homologous chromosomes about each other during one stage of meiosis, resulting in a possible interchange of genes, or factors, by the chromosomes.

chi·as·mus (kī-az′məs), *n.* [*pl.* CHIASMI (-mī)], [Mod. L.; Gr. *chiasmos;* see CHIASMA], an inversion of the second of two parallel phrases, clauses, etc., as in the sentence "She went to Paris; to New York went he."

chiaus (chous, choush), *n.* [Turk. *chāwush*], in Turkey, a messenger, emissary, sergeant, etc.

Chib·cha (chib′chə), *n.* 1. a member of a tribe of Chibchan Indians who lived in eastern Colombia and had a highly developed civilization. 2. their language.
Chib·chan (chib′chən), *adj.* designating or of a linguistic group of South and Central American Indians.
chi·bouk, chi·bouque (chi-bōōk′, chi-book′), *n.* [Fr. *chibouque;* Turk. *chibūq*], a tobacco pipe with a long stem and a clay bowl.
chic (shēk, shik), *n.* [Fr. < MHG. *schic,* manner, or *schicken,* form, appearance < *schicken,* to arrange, prepare], smart elegance of style and manner: said especially of women or their clothes. *adj.* [CHICQUER (shēk′ẽr, shik′ẽr), CHICQUEST (shēk′ist, shik′ist)], smartly stylish; clever and fashionable.
Chi·ca·go (shə-kä′gō, shi-kô′gō), *n.* a city in northeastern Illinois, on Lake Michigan: pop., 3,550,000 (metropolitan area, 6,221,000).
Chicago Heights, a city in northeastern Illinois, near Chicago: pop., 34,000.
‡**chi·ca·lo·te** (chē′kä-lō′te), *n.* [Sp., name used for various thorny plants < Nahuatl *chicalotl* < *chicaloyo,* thorny], a plant of the poppy family, with large, white or purple flowers and prickly leaves; prickly poppy: found in Mexico and the southwestern United States.
chi·cane (shi-kān′), *n.* [Fr.; the southern Fr. meaning, "kind of golf," suggests the basic sense "cheating at a game" and derivation < Per. *chaugan,* crooked stick, via Ar. & MGr. in the sense "polo stick"; ? akin to or influenced by MHG. *schicken* (see CHIC)], 1. chicanery. 2. in *bridge,* a hand without trumps. *v.i.* [CHICANED (-kānd′), CHICANING], to use chicanery. *v.t.* 1. to trick. 2. to get by chicanery.
chi·can·er·y (shi-kān′ẽr-i), *n.* [*pl.* CHICANERIES (-iz)], [Fr. *chicanerie;* see CHICANE], 1. trickery, especially legal trickery; sophistry; quibbling. 2. a trick or quibble. —*SYN.* see **deception.**
chic·co·ry (chik′ẽr-i), *n.* [*pl.* CHICCORIES (-iz)], chicory.
Chi·chen It·za (chē-chen′ ēt-sä′), the site of important Mayan ruins in central Yucatan, Mexico.
chick (chik), *n.* [< *chicken*], 1. a young chicken. 2. a young bird. 3. a child: term of endearment.
chick·a·dee (chik′ə-dē′, chik′ə-dē′), *n.* [echoic of its note], any of a number of small birds of the titmouse family, with black, gray, and white feathers.
Chick·a·mau·ga (chik′ə-mô′gə), *n.* a creek in northwestern Georgia, flowing into the Tennessee River: scene of a Union defeat (1863) in the Civil War.
chick·a·ree (chik′ə-rē′), *n.* [echoic of its cry], the red squirrel, smallest of the tree squirrels.
Chick·a·saw (chik′ə-sô′), *n.* [*pl.* CHICKASAW, CHICKASAWS (-sôz′)], a member of a tribe of Muskhogean Indians who lived in northern Mississippi and part of Tennessee.
chick·en (chik′in, chik′ən), *n.* [ME. *chiken;* AS. *cycen* (< **kukin*), lit., little cock < base of AS. *cocc* (see COCK) + dim. suffix; akin to MLG. *kûken* (D. *kuiken, kieken*)], 1. a young hen or rooster. 2. any hen or rooster; domestic fowl. 3. the edible flesh of the chicken. 4. a young bird of some other species. 5. a young or inexperienced person. *adj.* 1. made of chicken: as, a *chicken* croquette. 2. small and tender: as, *chicken* lobster. 3. [< *chicken* excrement (euphemism)], *a*) [Military Slang], characterized by unnecessary discipline, pettiness, etc. *b*) [Slang], timid; cowardly.
count one's chickens before they are hatched, to count on something that may not materialize.
chicken breast, a chest condition in which the breastbone is abnormally prominent, as in rickets: also called *pigeon breast.*
chicken cholera, a contagious bacterial disease of fowls, characterized by severe diarrhea.
chicken feed, 1. food for chickens. 2. [Slang], small coins; negligible amount of money.
chicken hawk, any of various hawks that prey or are reputed to prey on chickens and other barnyard fowl; especially, the North American Cooper's hawk.
chick·en-heart·ed (chik′in-här′tid, chik′ən-här′tid), *adj.* cowardly; timid.
chick·en-liv·ered (chik′in-liv′ẽrd, chik′ən-liv′ẽrd), *adj.* cowardly; timid.
chicken pox, an acute, infectious virus disease, usually of young children, characterized by slight fever and a skin eruption: also called *varicella.*
chick-pea (chik′pē′), *n.* [for *chich pea;* Fr. *chiche* < L. *cicer,* pea], 1. a bushy plant of the pea family, with short, hairy pods. 2. the edible pea of this plant.
chick·weed (chik′wēd′), *n.* [for *chicken weed*], any of various weeds with seeds and leaves that birds eat.
chic·le (chik′'l, chē′k'l), *n.* [Sp.; Nahuatl *chictli*], a gumlike substance made from the milky juice of a tropical American sapodilla tree, used in making chewing gum.
chi·co (chē′kō), *n.* [*pl.* CHICOS (-kōz)], [< Sp. *chicalote;* see CHICALOTE], a spiny shrub with fleshy leaves, found in the western United States; greasewood.
Chic·o·pee (chik′ə-pē′), *n.* a city in southwestern Massachusetts, near Springfield: pop., 62,000.
chic·o·ry (chik′ə-ri), *n.* [*pl.* CHICORIES (-riz)], [earlier *cicory;* Fr. *cichorée;* OFr. *cichoree;* L. *cichorium;* Gr. *kichora, kichoreion,* chicory, endive, succory], 1. a plant with blue flowers, a thick root, and leaves used for salad. 2. its root, roasted and ground for mixing with coffee or for use as a coffee substitute: also **succory.**
chide (chīd), *v.t. & v.i.* [CHIDED (chīd′id) or CHID (chid), CHIDED or CHID or CHIDDEN (chid′'n), CHIDING], [ME. *chiden;* AS. *cidan, v.i.;* not found outside AS.], to scold; upbraid; blame; reprove; rebuke.
chief (chēf), *n.* [ME. & OFr. *chef, chief,* leader < L. *caput,* the head], 1. the head or top part of anything. 2. the head of any group or organization; leader; person of highest title or authority: as, the *chief* of a clan, *chief* of a bureau, etc.: abbreviated **C., c., Ch., ch.** 3. [Archaic], the most valuable or main part of anything. 4. in *heraldry,* the upper third of a shield. 5. [usually C-], in *nautical usage,* a chief engineer or chief officer. *adj.* 1. foremost; highest, as in rank or office; at the head. 2. main; principal; leading; most important, most eminent, etc. *adv.* [Archaic], chiefly.
in chief, 1. in the chief position; of highest title or authority: as, editor *in chief.* 2. chiefly. 3. [< L. *in capite*], in *feudal law,* holding or held directly by contract with the chief or king.
SYN.—**chief** is applied to the person or thing that is first in rank, authority, importance, etc., and usually connotes subordination of all others (his *chief* problem was getting a job); **principal** is applied to the person who directs or controls others (a *principal* clerk) or to the thing or person having precedence over all others by reason of size, position, importance, etc. (the *principal* products of Cuba); **main,** in strict usage, is applied to the thing, often part of a system or an extensive whole, that is pre-eminent in size, power, importance, etc. (the *main* line of a railroad); **leading** stresses capacity for guiding, conducting, or drawing others (a *leading* light, question, etc.); **foremost** suggests a being first by having moved ahead to that position (the *foremost* statesman of our time); **capital** is applied to that which is ranked at the head of its kind or class because of its importance or its special significance (the *capital* city).—*ANT.* subordinate, subservient.
chief justice, the presiding judge of a court made up of several judges: abbreviated **C.J.** (as a title).
chief·ly (chēf′li), *adv.* 1. most of all; first of all. 2. mostly; mainly; especially. *adj.* of or like a chief.
chief of staff, the head member of the staff officers of a division or higher unit in the armed forces: abbreviated **C. of S.** (as a title).
chief petty officer, a noncommissioned officer of the highest rank of petty officers in the navy: abbreviated **C.P.O.** (as a title).
chief·tain (chēf′tin, chēf′tən), *n.* [ME. *chevetain;* OFr. *chevetaine;* LL. *capitanus* < L. *caput,* the head; cf. CAPTAIN], 1. a chief of a clan or tribe. 2. any leader of a group.
chief·tain·cy (chēf′tin-si, chēf′tən-si), *n.* [*pl.* CHIEFTAINCIES (-siz)], the rank or position of a chieftain.
chief·tain·ship (chēf′tin-ship′, chēf′tən-ship′), *n.* [*chieftain* + *-ship*], a chieftaincy.
chield (chēld), *n.* [Scot.], a young man; youth; fellow.
chif·fon (shi-fon′, shif′ən), *n.* [Fr., dim. of *chiffe,* a rag, piece of cloth], 1. *pl.* ribbons, laces, and other finery used as accessories to a woman's dress. 2. a sheer silk cloth used for women's dresses, blouses, etc. *adj.* 1. made of chiffon. 2. light and fluffy from being whipped: as, a lemon *chiffon* pie filling.
chif·fo·nier, chif·fon·nier (shif′ə-nêr′), *n.* [Fr., orig., chest of drawers (now, ragpicker) < *chiffon*], a narrow, high bureau or chest of drawers, sometimes with a mirror attached.
chig·ger (chig′ẽr), *n.* [< *chigoe*], 1. the tiny, red larva of certain mites found especially in the southern United States and the tropics: its bite causes severe itching: also called *redbug.* 2. a kind of flea; chigoe.
chi·gnon (shēn′yon; Fr. shē′nyōn′), *n.* [Fr., var. of *chainon,* link; OFr. *chaeignon,* chain, nape (of the neck) < L. *catena;* see CHAIN], a knot or coil of hair sometimes worn at the back of the neck by women.
chig·oe (chig′ō), *n.* [*pl.* CHIGOES (-ōz)], [Fr. *chique;* of W. Ind. origin], 1. a sand flea of South America and the West Indies: the female burrows into the skin, causing sores. 2. the larva of certain mites; chigger.
Chih·li (chē′lē′; Chin. ju′lē′), *n.* Hopei, a province in China: the former name.
Chi·hua·hua (chi-wä′wä), *n.* 1. a state of northern Mexico: area, 94,822 sq. mi.; pop., 1,044,000. 2. its capital: pop., 128,000. 3. any of a breed of very small dog with large, pointed ears, originally from Mexico.
chil·blain (chil′blān′), *n.* [*chill* + *blain* < AS. *blegen,* a sore], a painful swelling or inflamed sore on the feet or hands, caused by exposure to cold.
chil·blained (chil′blānd′), *adj.* having chilblains.
child (chīld), *n.* [*pl.* CHILDREN (chil′drən)], [ME. *childe,* pl. *childre* (now dial. *childer; children* is double pl.); AS. *cild,* pl. *cild, cildru;* akin to Goth. *kilthei,* womb; IE.

*qel-t, a swelling up < base *qel-, rounded; sense development: rounded—swelling—womb—fetus—offspring; cf. CALF (animal)], 1. an infant; baby. 2. an unborn offspring. 3. a boy or girl in the period before puberty. 4. a son or daughter. 5. a descendant. 6. a person like a child in interests, judgment, etc., or regarded as a child; immature or childish adult. 7. a person regarded as the product of a specified place, time, etc.: as, a *child* of the Renaissance. 8. a thing that springs from a specified source; product: as, a *child* of one's imagination. Abbreviated **ch.**, **c.**, **Ch.** (in senses 3, 4, 5).

with child, pregnant.

child·bear·ing (chīld'bâr'iŋ), *n.* the act or process of giving birth to children; parturition.

child·bed (chīld'bed'), *n.* the state of a woman who is giving birth to a child.

child·birth (chīld'bũrth'), *n.* 1. the act of giving birth to a child. 2. birth rate.

childe (chīld), *n.* [var. of *child*], [Archaic], a young man of noble birth: also spelled **child**.

Chil·der·mas (chil'dẽr-məs), *n.* [ME. *childermasse;* AS. *cildramæsse, cildamæsse* < *cildra*, of infants + *mæsse*, mass], [Obs.], December 28, the day commemorating the slaughter of the children by Herod: Matt. 2:16: also called *Holy Innocents' Day*.

child·hood (chīld'hood'), *n.* [ME. *childhod, childhede;* AS. *cildhad;* see CHILD & -HOOD], 1. the time during which one is a child; period from infancy to puberty. 2. the state of being a child.

child·ing (chīl'diŋ), *adj.* [< ME. *childen*, to bear a child], [Archaic], 1. bearing a child or children; pregnant. 2. bearing a cluster of newer blossoms around an older blossom.

child·ish (chīl'dish), *adj.* [ME.; AS. *cildisc;* see CHILD & -ISH], 1. of, like, or characteristic of a child. 2. immature; silly; not fit for an adult. —***SYN.*** see **childlike**.

child labor, the regular, full-time employment of children under a legally defined age in factories, stores, offices, etc.: in the United States, the minimum legal age, as defined by the Fair Labor Standard Acts of 1938, is 16 (in hazardous occupations, 18), but this standard is not observed by all States.

child·less (chīld'lis), *adj.* having no child.

child·like (chīld'līk'), *adj.* 1. belonging or suitable to a child. 2. like or characteristic of a child; innocent, trusting, etc.

SYN.—**childlike** and **childish** are both applied to persons of any age in referring to characteristics or qualities considered typical of a child, **childlike** suggesting the favorable qualities such as innocence, guilelessness, trustfulness, etc. and **childish**, the unfavorable, as immaturity, foolishness, petulance, etc.

child·ly (chīld'li), *adj.* [Rare], childlike; childish.

child psychology, the branch of psychology that deals with the behavior and mental processes of children.

chil·dren (chil'drən), *n.* [mod. double pl. < archaic pl. *childer*, after *brethren*], plural of **child**.

children of Israel, the Jews; Hebrews.

Children's Crusade, either of two ill-fated crusades for the recovery of Jerusalem from the Saracens, undertaken in 1212 by thousands of French and German children: in the first, those who reached the Mediterranean were sold into slavery; the survivors of the second turned back after crossing the Alps.

child's play, any very simple task.

Chi·le (chil'i; Sp. chē'le), *n.* a country on the southwestern coast of South America: area, 286,396; pop., 7,627,000; capital, Santiago.

chil·e (chil'i), *n.* chili.

Chil·e·an (chil'i-ən), *adj.* of Chile, its people, or culture. *n.* 1. a native or inhabitant of Chile. 2. Spanish as spoken in Chile.

chil·e con car·ne (chil'i kon kär'ni), [Sp., lit., red pepper with meat], a highly seasoned Mexican dish made usually of red peppers, spices, beans, and meat: also spelled **chili con carne**.

Chile saltpeter, sodium nitrate, found in Chile and Peru.

chil·i (chil'i), *n.* [*pl.* CHILIES (-iz)], [Sp. < native Mex. name], 1. the dried pod of red pepper, a very hot seasoning. 2. the tropical American plant that bears this pod. 3. chile con carne. Also spelled **chile, chilli**.

chil·i·ad (kil'i-ad'), *n.* [L. *chilias;* Gr. *chilias, chiliados*, the number 1,000 < *chilioi*, a thousand], 1. a thousand; 1,000 (things). 2. 1,000 years.

chil·i·arch (kil'i-ärk'), *n.* [< Gr. *chiliarchēs* < *chilioi*, a thousand + *archos*, leader], in ancient Greece, the military commander of 1,000 men.

chil·i·asm (kil'i-az'm), *n.* [Gr. *chiliasmos* < *chilias;* see CHILIAD], the belief that Christ in person will return and rule on earth during the millennium.

chil·i·ast (kil'i-ast'), *n.* [Gr. *chiliastēs*], a believer in chiliasm.

chili con carne, chile con carne.

chili powder, a powder made of dried chili pods, used as a condiment.

chili sauce, a tomato sauce spiced with chilies, used on meat, etc.

chill (chil), *n.* [ME. *chile, chele* < AS. *ciele*, coldness; Gmc. base ***kal-**, to be cold (cf. COLD); akin to L. *gel-* in *gelidus*, whence Eng. *gelid;* see COOL], 1. a bodily coldness with shivering. 2. a moderate coldness. 3. a checking of enthusiasm. 4. a sudden fear, apprehension, or discouragement. 5. coolness of manner; unfriendliness. 6. in *metallurgy*, a cooled iron mold placed in contact with that part of a casting which is to be cooled rapidly and thus hardened. *adj.* 1. uncomfortably cool; moderately cold. 2. depressing; deadening. 3. cool in manner; unfriendly. *v.i.* 1. to become cool. 2. to become cold; feel cold. 3. in *metallurgy*, to become hardened on the surface by rapid cooling. *v.t.* 1. to make cool. 2. to cause a chill in. 3. to check (enthusiasm, etc.). 4. to depress; dispirit. 5. in *metallurgy*, to harden (metal) by rapid cooling.

chil·li (chil'i), *n.* [*pl.* CHILLIES (-iz)], chili.

Chil·li·coth·e (chil'ə-koth'i), *n.* a city in south central Ohio: pop., 25,000.

chill·i·ly (chil'ə-li), *adv.* in a chilly manner.

chill·i·ness (chil'i-nis), *n.* the state or quality of being chilly.

Chil·lon (shə-lon', shil'ən; Fr. shē'yōn'), *n.* an ancient castle near Lake Geneva in Switzerland, famous in literature for its use as a political prison.

chil·ly (chil'i), *adj.* [CHILLIER (-i-ẽr), CHILLIEST (-i-ist)], 1. moderately cold; uncomfortably cool. 2. chilling; making cold. 3. cool in manner; unfriendly. 4. depressing; dispiriting.

chi·lo- (kī'lō, ki'lə), [< Gr. *cheilos*, lip], a combining form meaning *lip:* also, before a vowel, **chil-**.

chi·lo·plas·ty (kī'lə-plas'ti), *n.* [*chilo-* + *-plasty*], repair of some defect of the lip by plastic surgery.

chi·lo·pod (kī'lə-pod'), *n.* [< Mod. L. *chilopoda;* see CHILO- & -POD], a centipede.

Chil·tern hundreds (chil'tẽrn), [from tract of crown lands containing the Chiltern Hills], in Great Britain, an ancient, now purely nominal, office of profit held from the crown: members of Parliament wishing to resign their seats are temporarily appointed to this office, thus automatically disqualifying themselves as members of Parliament.

chi·mae·ra (kə-mêr'ə, kī-mêr'ə), *n.* [L.], 1. a chimera. 2. any of a group of fishes related to the sharks, with a smooth skin, tapering body, and slender tail.

chim·ar (chim'ẽr), *n.* a chimer (robe).

chimb (chīm), *n.* a chime (rim).

Chim·bo·ra·zo (chim'bə-rā'zō, chim'bə-rä'zō; Sp. chēm'bô-rä'sô), *n.* a volcanic mountain in the Andes, in central Ecuador: height, 20,702 ft.

chime (chīm), *n.* [ME. *chimbe, chymbe;* OFr. *chimbe, chimble, cimble;* L. *cymbalum;* Gr. *kymbalon*, cymbal, bell], 1. a contrivance for striking a bell or set of bells. 2. *usually pl.* a set of bells tuned to the musical scale. 3. a single bell rung by a hammer, as in a clock or doorbell. 4. *usually pl.* the musical sounds or harmony produced by striking a bell or set of bells. 5. harmony; agreement. *v.i.* [CHIMED (chīmd), CHIMING], 1. to ring out when struck; sound as a chime. 2. to sound in harmony, as bells. 3. to recite in cadence or singsong. 4. to harmonize; agree. *v.t.* 1. to ring, play, or strike (a bell, set of bells, etc.); make musical sounds on (bells). 2. to give (the time) by striking bells.

chime in, 1. to join in or interrupt, as a conversation. 2. to be in accord; agree.

chime (chīm), *n.* [ME. *chimbe;* AS. *cimb-* in *cimbiren*, edge iron, *cimbing*, a joining, *cimbstan*, base, pedestal; akin to D. *kim*, G. *kimme*, an edge], the extended rim at each end of a cask or barrel: also spelled **chimb**.

chim·er (chim'ẽr, shim'ẽr), *n.* [ML. *chimera* < MFr. *chamarre* < Sp. *zamarra* < Ar. *sammūr*, sable], a loose, sleeveless robe to which lawn sleeves are attached, worn by Anglican bishops.

chi·me·ra (kə-mêr'ə, kī-mêr'ə), *n.* [L. *chimaera;* Gr. *chimaira*, goat, fabulous monster], 1. [C-], in *Greek mythology*, a fire-breathing monster, represented as having a lion's head, a goat's body, and a serpent's tail. 2. any similar fabulous monster. 3. an impossible or foolish fancy. Also spelled **chimaera**.

chi·mere (chi-mêr', shi-mêr'), *n.* a chimer (robe).

chi·mer·ic (kə-mêr'ik, kī-mer'ik), *adj.* chimerical.

chi·mer·i·cal (kə-mêr'i-k'l, kī-mer'i-k'l), *adj.* [<*chimera* + *-ical*], 1. imaginary; fantastic; unreal. 2. absurd; impossible. 3. indulging in unrealistic fancies; visionary.

chim·ney (chim'ni), *n.* [*pl.* CHIMNEYS (-niz)], [ME. *chemene, chimenee*, orig., fireplace (as in *chimney corner*); OFr. *cheminee;* LL. *caminata*, fireplace; L. *caminus*, furnace, flue; Gr. *kaminos*, oven, fireplace], 1. the passage through which smoke or fumes from a fire escape; flue. 2. a structure containing the flue and extending above the roof of a building. 3. a glass tube for a lamp, placed around the flame to keep it steady. 4. a deep, narrow fissure in a cliff, by which it can be climbed. 5. something like a chimney, as the vent of a volcano. 6. [Chiefly British], a smokestack.

chimney corner, 1. the corner or side of an open fireplace; fireside. 2. a place near the fire.

chimney piece, 1. the mantel of a fireplace; mantelpiece. 2. [Archaic], a decoration put over a fireplace.

chimney pot, a pipe fitted to the top of a chimney to carry the smoke away and increase the draft.

chimney swallow, 1. the chimney swift. 2. the European barn swallow.
chimney sweep, a person who cleans the soot from chimneys.
chimney swift, a sooty-brown North American bird resembling the swallow: so called from its habit of making a nest in an unused chimney.
chim·pan·zee (chim′pan-zē′, chim-pan′zi), *n.* [Fr. *chimpanzé* < Angola (West Africa) Bantu *kampenzi*], an anthropoid ape of Africa, with black hair and large, outstanding ears: it is smaller and less fierce than a gorilla, and is noted for its intelligence.

CHIMPANZEE (4 1/2 ft. standing)

chin (chin), *n.* [ME.; AS. *cin;* akin to G. *kinn,* chin, Goth. *kinnus,* cheek, jawbone; IE. base **g(h)enu-s,* jawbone, seen also in L. *gena,* cheek, Gr. *genus,* chin, jawbone], the part of the face below the lower lip; projecting part of the lower jaw. *v.t.* [CHINNED (chind), CHINNING], in *gymnastics,* to pull (oneself) up, when hanging by the hands from a horizontal bar, until the chin is level with the bar. *v.i.* [Slang], to chatter; talk volubly.
Chin., 1. China. 2. Chinese.
Chi·na (chī′nə), *n.* a country in eastern Asia: area 3,760,000 sq. mi.; pop., 700,000,000; Peking is the capital of the People's Republic of China (*Communist China,* established in 1949): the Kuomintang government (*National Republic of China*) in 1961 controlled only Taiwan and near-by islands: abbreviated **Ch., Chin.** See also **Taiwan.**
chi·na (chī′nə), *n.* 1. a fine porcelain made of clay specially baked, originally imported from China. 2. dishes, ornaments, etc. made of this porcelain. 3. any earthenware dishes or crockery. Also **chinaware.**
China aster, a garden flower with large blooms of various colors, especially lavender and pink, originally native to China and Japan.
china bark, [altered (after *China*) < Sp. *quina* < Peruv. (Quechuan) native name], 1. cinchona bark. 2. the bark of a cascarilla bush grown in Brazil.
chi·na·ber·ry (chī′nə-ber′i), *n.* [*pl.* CHINABERRIES (-iz)], 1. the yellow, berrylike fruit of the China tree. 2. the orange-brown fruit of a tree that grows in dry areas of Mexico, the southwestern United States, and the West Indies; soapberry: it contains saponin and is used by natives as soap. 3. either of these trees.
Chi·na·man (chī′nə-mən), *n.* [*pl.* CHINAMEN (-mən)], 1. originally, a dealer in Chinese imports. 2. a Chinese: contemptuous or patronizing term.
China Sea, a part of the Pacific, east of China, divided into the East China Sea and the South China Sea.
Chi·na·town (chī′nə-toun′), *n.* the Chinese quarter of any city outside of China.
China tree, a tall, graceful tree native to Asia, widely cultivated as a shade tree.
chi·na·ware (chī′nə-wâr′), *n.* china.
chin·ca·pin (chiŋ′kə-pin), *n.* a chinquapin.
chinch (chinch), *n.* [Sp. *chinche;* L. *cimex,* bug], 1. a bedbug. 2. a chinch bug.
chinch bug, a small, white-winged, black bug that damages grain plants by sucking out the juices, especially in dry weather.
chin·chil·la (chin-chil′ə), *n.* [Sp. dim., altered after *chinche* (see CHINCH) < Peruv. (Quechuan) *sinchi,* strong], 1. a small rodent found in the Andes, South America. 2. the expensive, soft, pale-gray fur of this animal. 3. a heavy cloth of wool, or wool and cotton, with a tufted, napped surface, used for making overcoats.

CHINCHILLA (15 in. long)

chin·cough (chin′kôf′), *n.* [earlier *chink cough* understood as *chin cough; chink* akin to LG. & D. *kinken,* to wheeze, cough], whooping cough.
Chin·dwin (chin′dwin′), *n.* a tributary of the Irrawaddy River in Burma: length, 550 mi.
chine (chīn), *n.* [ME.; OFr. *eschine* (Fr. *échine*) < OHG. *scina,* shin bone; see SHIN], 1. the backbone; spine. 2. a cut of meat containing part of the backbone. 3. a ridge.
chine (chīn), *n.* [ME.; AS. *cinu,* fissure; akin to *cinan* (Goth. *keinan*), to burst open; IE. base **ĝei-,* **ĝi-,* to germinate, burst into bloom], [British], a rocky ravine or deep fissure in a cliff: term used on the Hampshire coast and the Isle of Wight.
chine (chīn), *n.* a chime (rim of a cask).
Chi·nese (chi-nēz′), *n.* [OFr. *Chineis* (Fr. *Chinois*)], 1. [*pl.* CHINESE], a native of China or a descendant of the people of China. 2. the standard language of the Chinese, based on Peking speech; Mandarin. 3. any of the various languages of the Chinese. 4. a group of Sino-Tibetan languages comprising Mandarin and most of the other languages of China. *adj.* of China, its people, language, or culture. Abbreviated **Chin., Ch.**
Chinese cabbage, a vegetable with long, narrow, blanched leaves growing in loose, cylindrical heads and tasting somewhat like cabbage, to which it is related.
Chinese Empire, China from the founding of its first dynasty, about 2200 B.C., to the revolution of 1911.
Chinese lantern, a lantern of brightly colored paper, used for outdoor parties, etc., and made so that it can be folded up.
Chinese puzzle, 1. an intricate puzzle; hence, 2. anything intricate and hard to solve.
Chinese red, any of various shades of red, as chrome red or, especially, a brilliant orange-red.
Chinese Revolution, a revolution (1911) in which forces led by Sun Yat-sen overthrew the Manchu dynasty and set up the Chinese republic.
Chinese Turkestan, Sinkiang province, China.
Chinese Wall, a stone wall (20–30 ft. high, 15–20 ft. thick, over 1,400 mi. long) between Mongolia and China proper: it was begun by the Chinese as a defense against invaders over 2,000 years ago and completed c. 1600.
Chinese white, a dense white pigment made of zinc oxide or barium sulfate.
Chinese windlass, a windlass with a barrel consisting of two parts of different diameters; differential windlass.
Chinese wood oil, tung oil.
Ching·hai (chiŋ′hī′), *n.* a province of northwestern China, northeast of Tibet: area, 258,000 sq. mi.; pop., 11,677,000; capital, Sining: also called *Koko Nor.*
Chin Hills (chin), a district of northwestern Burma.
Chink (chiŋk), *n.* [Slang], a Chinese: vulgar term indicating a contemptuous or patronizing attitude.
chink (chiŋk), *n.* [ME. *chine* with unhistoric *-k;* AS. *cinu,* fissure; see CHINE (ravine)], a narrow opening; crack; fissure; slit. *v.t.* 1. to form chinks in. 2. to close up the chinks in.
chink (chiŋk), *n.* [echoic], a sharp, clinking sound, as of coins striking together. *v.t. & v.i.* to make or cause to make this sound.
chin·ka·pin (chiŋ′kə-pin), *n.* a chinquapin.
Chin·kiang (chin′kyaŋ′; Chin. jun′jyäŋ′), *n.* a city in Kiangsu province, China: pop., 217,000.
chi·no (chē′nō), *n.* a strong, twilled cotton cloth used for work clothes, uniforms, etc.
Chi·no- (chī′nō), a combining form meaning *Chinese, Chinese and,* as in *Chino-Soviet.*
Chi·nook (chi-no͞ok′, chi-nook′), *n.* [after the Penute tribal name], 1. any of various Penutian Indian tribes formerly inhabiting the Columbia River valley. 2. their language: also **Chinuk.** 3. Chinook jargon. 4. [c-], *a)* a warm, moist southwest wind blowing from the sea onto the coast of Oregon and Washington in winter and spring. *b)* a dry wind blowing down the eastern slope of the Rocky Mountains at recurring intervals.
Chi·nook·an (chi-no͞o′kən, chi-nook′ən), *adj.* of the Chinooks, their culture, language, etc. *n.* a Chinook.
Chinook jargon, a pidgin language consisting of extremely simplified Chinook intermixed with vocabulary elements from English, French, and neighboring American Indian languages: it was formerly used for communication between the northwest Indians and early American fur traders, etc.
chinook salmon, a variety of Pacific salmon; quinnat salmon.
chin·qua·pin (chiŋ′kə-pin), *n.* [of Am. Ind. origin], 1. the dwarf chestnut tree. 2. a related evergreen tree (called the *Giant Chinquapin*) growing in California and Oregon. 3. the edible nut of either of these trees. Also spelled **chincapin, chinkapin.**
chintz (chints), *n.* [earlier *chints,* pl. of *chint;* Hind. *chhīnt,* chintz; Sans. *chitra,* spotted, bright], a cotton cloth printed in various colors and usually glazed.
Chi·os (kī′os), *n.* 1. a Greek island off the western coast of Asia Minor: area, 350 sq. mi.; pop., 67,000. 2. its capital: pop., 24,000. Greek name, *Khios.*
chip (chip), *v.t.* [CHIPPED (chipt), CHIPPING], [ME. *chippen;* AS. **cippian* (cf. *cipp,* log); akin to D. & G. *kippen,* to cut], 1. to cut or chop with an ax or other sharp tool. 2. to break, cut, or slice off small fragments or thin slices from. 3. to shape by cutting or chopping. *v.i.* 1. to break off into small pieces. 2. in *golf,* to make a chip shot. *n.* [ME. *chippe* < the *v.*], 1. a small, thin piece of wood, stone, etc., cut or broken off. 2. a place

where a small piece has been chipped off: as, a *chip* on the edge of a plate. 3. wood or Cuban palm leaf split and woven into bonnets, hats, etc. 4. a fragment of dried dung used as fuel. 5. a worthless thing. 6. one of the small, round disks often used in poker and other gambling games instead of money; counter. 7. *pl. a)* thin slices or shavings of food: as, potato *chips. b)* [British], French fried potatoes. 8. in *golf*, a chip shot.

chip in [Colloq.], 1. to contribute (money, help, etc.). 2. to put chips or money in as one's stake in a card game.

chip off the old block, a person much like his father in appearance or characteristics.

chip on one's shoulder, [Colloq.], an inclination to fight or quarrel.

in the chips, [Slang], having money; wealthy; affluent.

chip (chip), *n.* [prob. < ON. *kippr*, a pull, jerk < *kippa*, to jerk], in *wrestling*, a trick throw.

chip·muck (chip′muk), *n.* a chipmunk.

chip·munk (chip′muŋk), *n.* [of Am. Ind. origin], a small North American squirrel with striped markings on its back: also called *ground squirrel.*

chipped beef, dried or smoked beef sliced into shavings, usually served with a cream sauce.

Chip·pen·dale (chip′ən-dāl′), *adj.* designating or of furniture made by, or in the style of, Thomas Chippendale (1718?–1779), an English cabinetmaker: it is characterized by graceful lines and, often, rococo ornamentation.

chip·per (chip′ẽr), *adj.* [altered form of north Brit. *kipper;* prob. akin to ON. *kjappi*, he-goat, D. *kipp* (*kjap*), quick, lively], [Colloq.], in good spirits; lively.

chip·per (chip′ẽr), *n.* a person or thing that chips; especially, a tool for chipping.

chip·per (chip′ẽr), *v.i.* [echoic metathesis of *chirrup*], 1. to chirp or twitter: said of birds. 2. [Colloq.], to chatter or prattle; babble.

Chip·pe·wa (chip′ə-wä′, chip′ə-wə, chip′ə-wā′), *n.* 1. [*pl.* CHIPPEWA, CHIPPEWAS (-wäz′, -wəz, -wāz′)], [var. of *Ojibway*], a member of a tribe of Algonquian Indians who lived in an area between western Lake Erie and North Dakota. 2. the Central Algonquian language of this tribe. *adj.* of this tribe. Also called *Ojibway, Ojibwa.*

Chip·pe·way (chip′ə-wā′), *n. & adj.* Chippewa.

chipping sparrow, [< *chip*, echoic word for its cry], a small sparrow with a reddish-brown crown, native to eastern and central North America.

chip·py (chip′i), *n.* [*pl.* CHIPPIES (-iz)], 1. a chipping sparrow. 2. a chipmunk. 3. [Slang], *a)* a promiscuous young woman. *b)* a prostitute.

chip shot, in *golf*, a short, lofting stroke, used when the ball is near the green.

chirk (chũrk), *v.t. & v.i.* [ME. *chirken*, to twitter; var. of *charken;* AS. *cearcian*, to creak, gnash; cf. CHIRP], [Colloq.], to make or become cheerful (with *up*). *adj.* [Colloq.], lively; cheerful.

chirm (chũrm), *n.* [AS. < the *v.*], [Dial. or Rare], a twittering, warbling, or humming sound, as of birds, insects, a distant crowd, etc. *v.i.* [ME. *chirmen*, to cry out; AS. *cirman;* akin to D. *kermen*, to mourn], [Dial. or Rare], to make this sound; twitter, hum, etc.

chi·ro- (kī′rō, kī′rə), [< Gr. *cheir*, the hand], a combining form meaning *hand*, as in *chiromancy*: also **cheiro-**.

chi·rog·ra·pher (kī-rog′rə-fẽr), *n.* an expert in chirography; penman.

chi·ro·graph·ic (kī′rə-graf′ik), *adj.* of chirography.

chi·rog·ra·phy (kī-rog′rə-fi), *n.* [*chiro-* + *-graphy*], handwriting; penmanship.

chi·ro·man·cer (kī′rə-man′sẽr), *n.* a person who practices chiromancy.

chi·ro·man·cy (kī′rə-man′si), *n.* [*chiro-* + *-mancy*], palmistry.

Chi·ron (kī′ron), *n.* [L.; Gr. *Cheirōn*], in *Greek mythology*, the wisest of all Centaurs, famous for his knowledge of medicine: he taught Aesculapius, Achilles, and Hercules.

chi·rop·o·dist (kī-rop′ə-dist, ki-rop′ə-dist), *n.* [*chiro-* + *-pod* + *-ist*], 1. formerly, a person who treated diseases of the hands and feet. 2. a person who treats foot ailments, removes corns, etc.

chi·rop·o·dy (kī-rop′ə-di, ki-rop′ə-di), *n.* the occupation of a chiropodist.

chi·ro·prac·tic (kī′rə-prak′tik), *n.* [< *chiro-* + Gr. *praktikos*, practical], 1. a method of treating disease by manipulation of the joints of the body, especially the spinal column. 2. a chiropractor. *adj.* having to do with this method of treatment.

chi·ro·prac·tor (kī′rə-prak′tẽr), *n.* a person who treats disease by the chiropractic method.

chi·rop·ter (kī-rop′tẽr), *n.* [< *chiro-* + Gr. *pteron*, a wing, feather], a bat (animal).

chi·rop·ter·an (kī-rop′tẽr-ən), *adj.* of or characteristic of the chiropters. *n.* a chiropter; bat.

chirp (chũrp), *v.i.* [ME. *chirpen*, echoic var. of *chirken;* see CHIRK], 1. to make a short, shrill sound, as certain birds or insects do. 2. to speak in a lively, shrill fashion. *v.t.* to utter in a sharp, shrill tone. *n.* a short, shrill sound.

chirr (chũr), *n.* [echoic], a shrill, trilled sound, as of certain insects or birds. *v.i. & v.t.* to make, or utter with, such a sound.

chir·rup (chir′əp), *v.i.* [< *chirp*], 1. to chirp repeatedly. 2. to make a series of sharp, short sounds, as in urging a horse on. *n.* a chirruping sound.

chi·rur·geon (kī-rũr′jən), *n.* [altered, after L. forms < ME. *cirurgian;* OFr. *cirurgien* < *cirurgie;* see SURGERY], [Archaic], a surgeon.

chi·rur·ger·y (kī-rũr′jẽr-i), *n.* [see CHIRURGEON], [Archaic], surgery.

chi·rur·gi·cal (kī-rũr′ji-k′l), *adj.* [< L. *chirurgicus* (< Gr. *cheirourgikos;* see SURGERY); + *-al*], [Archaic], of surgeons or surgery.

chis·el (chiz′′l), *n.* [ME.; OFr. *cisel;* LL. *cisellum* < L. *caesus*, pp. of *caedere*, to cut], a sharp-edged tool for cutting or shaping wood, stone, or metal. *v.i. & v.t.* [CHISELED or CHISELLED (-′ld), CHISELING or CHISELLING], 1. to cut or engrave with a chisel. 2. [Colloq.], to cheat; swindle; also, to get (something) by cheating or swindling.

chis·eled, chis·elled (chiz′′ld), *adj.* [pp. of *chisel*], 1. cut or shaped with a chisel. 2. finely wrought, as if shaped by a chisel; well-formed.

chis·e·ler, chis·el·ler (chiz′′l-ẽr, chiz′lẽr), *n.* 1. a person who uses a chisel. 2. [Colloq.], one who cheats; swindler.

CHISEL

Chi·shi·ma (chē′shē-mä′), *n.* the Kurile Islands of Japan: the Japanese name.

Chis·holm Trail (chiz′əm), a cattle trail extending from San Antonio, Texas, north to Abilene, Kansas: important until c. 1880.

Chi·şi·nâ·u (kē-shē-nu′oo), *n.* Kishinev, the capital of the Moldavian S.S.R.: the Romanian name.

chit (chit), *n.* [ME. *chitte*, var. of *kitte* for *kitten;* sense shows merging with dial. *chit* (< AS. *cith*), shoot, sprout; cf. LAD], 1. a child. 2. a pert, saucy girl.

chit (chit), *n.* [< *chitty;* Hind *ciṭṭhi*, letter, note; Sans. *citra*, speckled, spotted; cf. CHINTZ], 1. [Chiefly British], a short note or letter; memorandum. 2. a voucher of a small sum owed for drink, food, etc.

Chi·ta (chi-tä′), *n.* 1. a territory of the U.S.S.R., in southeastern Siberia: pop., 1,159,000. 2. its capital: pop., 103,000.

chit·chat (chit′chat′), *n.* [redupl. of *chat*], 1. light, familiar, informal talk; chat; small talk. 2. gossip.

chi·tin (kī′tin), *n.* [Fr. *chitine;* Gr. *chitōn;* see CHITON], a horny substance secreted by the upper layers of the skin and forming the hard outer covering of insects, crustaceans, etc.

chi·tin·ous (kī′ti-nəs), *adj.* of or like chitin.

chi·ton (kī′t′n, kī′ton), *n.* [Gr., garment, tunic, coat of mail < Sem.; cf. Heb. *ketōneth*, coat, garment], 1. a loose garment of varying length, similar to a tunic, worn by both men and women in ancient Greece. 2. a small, edible mollusk enclosed in a chitinous shell made up of eight arched, overlapping plates.

chit·ter (chit′ẽr), *v.i.* [ME. *chiteren;* see CHATTER], 1. to twitter. 2. [British Dial.], to shiver with cold.

chit·ter·lings (chit′ẽr-liŋz), *n. pl.* [ME. *chiterling* (orig. also with human applications); base *chit-* (dial. *chid-*); akin to MLG. *kūt*, soft parts of the body, LG. *küte*, animal intestines (D. *kuit*, fish roe), and ult. to G. *kutteln*, tripes, chitterlings, AS. *cyt-* in *cyt-wer*, rounded fish basket; IE. base **geu-*, to bend, curve, be rounded, as also in *cod, cud*], 1. the small intestines of pigs, used for food. 2. *sing.* [Obs.], a frill or ruff.

chiv·al·ric (shiv′′l-rik, shi-val′rik), *adj.* 1. of chivalry. 2. chivalrous.

chiv·al·rous (shiv′′l-rəs), *adj.* [ME. *chevalrous;* OFr. *chevalereus;* see CHIVALRY], 1. having the attributes of an ideal knight; gallant, courteous, honorable, etc. 2. of chivalry; chivalric. —*SYN.* see **civil.**

chiv·al·ry (shiv′′l-ri), *n.* [ME. & OFr. *chevalerie* < *chevaler*, a knight; doublet of *cavalry;* see CAVALIER, CHEVALIER], 1. a group of knights or gallant gentlemen. 2. the medieval system of knighthood. 3. the qualifications of a knight, such as courage, nobility, fairness, courtesy, respect for women, protection of the poor, etc. 4. the demonstration of any of the knightly qualities. 5. [Obs.], the rank or position of a knight.

chive (chīv), *n.* [ME. & OFr. *cive;* L. *cepa*, onion], a hardy plant of the onion family, with small, slender, hollow leaves used to flavor soups, stews, salads, etc.

chiv·y, chiv·vy (chiv′i), *n., v.t. & v.i.* chevy.

Chka·lov (chkä′lôf), *n.* 1. a region of the R.S.F.S.R., in eastern European Russia: pop., 1,677,000. 2. its capital, on the Ural River: pop., 173,000: formerly called *Orenburg.*

chlam·y·date (klam′ə-dāt′), *adj.* [Gr. *chlamyd-*, base of *chlamys*, mantle; + *-ate*], in *zoology*, having a mantle: said of certain mollusks.

chla·mys (klā'mis, klam'is), ***n.*** [*pl.* CHLAMYSES (-iz), CHLAMYDES (klam'i-dēz')], [L.; Gr. *chlamys*], a short mantle clasped at the shoulder, worn by men in ancient Greece.

CHLAMYS

Chlo·e, Chlo·ë (klō'i), [L.; Gr. *Chloē*, blooming, verdant], a feminine name: see also **Daphnis and Chloe.**

chlor- (klôr, klōr), chloro-.

chlo·ral (klôr'əl, klō'rəl), ***n.*** [*chlor-* + *al*cohol], 1. a thin, oily, colorless liquid, CCl_3CHO, with a pungent odor, prepared by the action of chlorine on alcohol. 2. chloral hydrate.

chloral hydrate, a colorless, crystalline compound, $CCl_3 \cdot CH(OH)_2$, used chiefly as a sedative.

chlo·ra·mine (klôr'ə-mēn', klōr-am'in), ***n.*** [*chlor-* + *amine*], a colorless, pungent liquid, NH_2Cl, obtained by the action of ammonia on some hypochlorite.

chlo·rate (klôr'it, klō'rāt), ***n.*** [*chlor-* + *-ate*], a salt of chloric acid.

chlor·dane (klôr'dān, klōr'dān), ***n.*** [*chlor-* + *in*dane, a derivative of indene], a chlorinated, highly poisonous volatile oil, $C_{10}H_6Cl_8$, used as an insecticide.

chlo·ric (klôr'ik, klō'rik), ***adj.*** [*chlor-* + *-ic*], 1. of or containing chlorine with a higher valence than that in corresponding chlorous compounds. 2. designating or of a colorless acid, $HClO_3$, whose salts are chlorates.

chlo·rid (klôr'id, klō'rid), ***n.*** chloride.

chlo·ride (klôr'īd, klō'rid), ***n.*** [*chlor-* + *-ide*], a compound in which chlorine is combined with another element or radical (e.g., a salt of hydrochloric acid).

chloride of lime, calcium chloride, $CaOCl_2$, a white powder obtained by treating slaked lime with chlorine, used for disinfecting and bleaching.

chlo·rin·ate (klôr'ə-nāt', klō'rə-nāt'), ***v.t.*** [CHLORINATED (-id), CHLORINATING], to treat or combine (a substance) with chlorine; especially, to pass chlorine into (water or sewage) for purification.

chlo·rin·a·tion (klôr'ə-nā'shən, klō'rə-nā'shən), ***n.*** a chlorinating.

chlo·rine (klôr'ēn, klôr'in, klō'rēn, klō'rin), ***n.*** [*chlor-* + *-ine*], a greenish-yellow, poisonous, gaseous chemical element with a disagreeable odor, used in the preparation of bleaching agents, in water purification, in various industrial processes, as a lung irritant in chemical warfare, etc.: symbol, Cl; at. wt., 35.457; at. no., 17.

chlo·rite (klôr'īt, klō'rīt), ***n.*** [*chlor-* + *-ite*], a salt of chlorous acid.

chlo·rite (klôr'īt, klō'rīt), ***n.*** [L. *chloritis;* Gr. *chlōritis* < *chlōros*, pale green], a bright-green, complex silicate mineral, similar in structure to the micas.

chlo·ro- (klôr'ō, klôr'ə, klō'rō, klō'rə), [< Gr. *chlōros*, pale green], a combining form meaning: 1. *green*, as in *chlorophyll, chlorosis.* 2. *chlorine, having chlorine as an ingredient*, as in *chloroform.* Also, before a vowel, **chlor-.**

chlo·ro·form (klôr'ə-fôrm', klō'rə-fôrm'), ***n.*** [Fr. *chloroforme;* see CHLORO- & FORMYL], a sweetish, colorless, volatile liquid, $CHCl_3$, used as an anesthetic and solvent. ***v.t.*** 1. to anesthetize with chloroform. 2. to kill with chloroform.

chlo·ro·my·ce·tin (klôr'ə-mī-sē'tin, klō'rə-mī-sē'tin) ***n.*** [*chloro-* + *-mycete* + *-in*], a synthesized antibiotic drug used against certain viruses, rickettsiae, and bacteria.

chlo·ro·phyll, chlo·ro·phyl (klôr'ə-fil', klō'rə-fil'), ***n.*** [Fr. *chlorophylle* < Gr. *chlōros*, green + *phyllon*, a leaf], the green coloring matter of plants: in the presence of sunlight it converts carbon dioxide and water into carbohydrates: it is used as a dye and in medicine.

chlo·ro·phyl·lose (klôr'ə-fil'ōs, klō'rə-fil'ōs), ***adj.*** 1. of or like chlorophyll. 2. having chlorophyll.

chlo·ro·phyl·lous (klôr'ə-fil'əs, klō'rə-fil'əs), ***adj.*** chlorophyllose.

chlo·ro·pic·rin (klôr'ə-pik'rin, klō'rə-pik'rin), ***n.*** [< *chloro-* + *picric* + *-in*], a colorless liquid, CCl_3NO_2, prepared by treating chloroform with concentrated nitric acid, and used in chemical warfare as a gas to cause vomiting: also called *nitrochloroform.*

chlo·ro·plast (klôr'ə-plast', klō'rə-plast'), ***n.*** [*chloro-* + *-plast*], an oval, chlorophyll-bearing body found outside the nucleus in a cell.

chlo·ro·prene (klôr'ə-prēn', klō'rə-prēn'), ***n.*** [*chloro-* + iso*prene*], a colorless liquid, C_4H_5Cl, made from acetylene: it can be polymerized to form a synthetic rubber.

chlo·ro·quine (klôr'ə-kwin, klō'rə-kwin), ***n.*** [< *chloro-* + *quinoline*], a synthetic antimalarial drug.

chlo·ro·sis (klə-rō'sis), ***n.*** [Mod. L.; see CHLORO- & -OSIS], 1. an abnormal condition of plants in which the green parts lose their color or turn yellow. 2. a kind of anemia sometimes affecting girls at puberty and causing the skin to turn a greenish color; greensickness.

chlo·ro·thi·a·zide (klôr'ə-thī'ə-zīd', klō'rə-thī'ə-zīd'), ***n.*** a synthetic drug used in treating hypertension and heart failure by removing extra salt and water through the kidneys.

chlo·rous (klôr'əs, klō'rəs), ***adj.*** [*chlor-* + *-ous*], 1. of or containing chlorine with a lower valence than that in corresponding chloric compounds. 2. designating or of an acid, $HClO_2$, whose salts are chlorites.

chlor·pic·rin (klôr-pik'rin, klōr-pik'rin), ***n.*** chloropicrin.

chlor·prom·a·zine (klôr-prom'ə-zēn', klōr-prom'ə-zēn'), ***n.*** a synthetic drug, $C_{17}H_{19}N_2SCl$, used as a sedative and, experimentally, to control anxiety and agitation in certain kinds of mental illness.

chm., chmn., chairman.

Choate, Rufus (chōt), 1799–1859; American jurist.

chock (chok), ***n.*** [ONorm. Fr. *choque, chouque*, a stump, block], 1. a block or wedge placed under a wheel, barrel, etc., to prevent motion. 2. in *nautical usage*, a block with two hornlike projections curving inward, through which a rope may be run. ***v.t.*** 1. to provide or wedge fast with a chock or chocks. 2. to place (a vessel) on chocks. ***adv.*** completely, so as to be tight or full: as, a bin *chock* full of potatoes.

chock·a·block (chok'ə-blok'), ***adj.*** [see CHOCK & BLOCK], 1. pulled so tight as to have the blocks touching: said of a hoisting tackle. 2. crowded; squeezed together. ***adv.*** tightly together.

chock-full (chok'fool'), ***adj.*** [ME. *chokkefulle;* felt as *chock* (a lump) + *full;* but ? < ME. *chokken*, to ram in, or ME. *choke* (< ON. *kjālki*), jaw-bone], as full as possible; filled to capacity: also **choke-full, chuck-full.**

choc·o·late (chôk'lit, chok'lit, chôk'ə-lit, chok'ə-lit), ***n.*** [Fr., *chocolat;* Sp. & Port. *chocolate;* Mex. *chocolatl*], 1. a paste, powder, sirup, or bar made from cacao seeds that have been ground and roasted. 2. a drink made of chocolate, hot milk or water, and sugar. 3. a candy made of or coated with chocolate. 4. reddish brown. ***adj.*** 1. made of or with chocolate. 2. reddish-brown.

Choc·taw (chok'tô), ***n.*** 1. [*pl.* CHOCTAW, CHOCTAWS (-tôz)], a member of a tribe of Muskhogean Indians who lived in southern Mississippi, Alabama, Georgia, and Louisiana. 2. the language of this tribe. ***adj.*** of this tribe or their language.

choice (chois), ***n.*** [ME. *chois, choise;* OFr. *chois*, choice < *choisir*, to choose < OHG. *cheosan, kiosan*, to choose, test; cf. CHOOSE], 1. a choosing; selection. 2. the right or power to choose; option. 3. a person or thing chosen: as, he was my *choice* for leader. 4. the best or most preferable part. 5. a variety from which to choose. 6. a supply that is well chosen. 7. an alternative. 8. care in choosing. ***adj.*** 1. of special excellence; select; superior. 2. carefully chosen. 3. [Dial.], fastidious.

***SYN.*—choice** implies the chance, right, or power to choose, usually by the free exercise of one's judgment (a bachelor by *choice*); **option** suggests the privilege of choosing as granted by a person or group in authority that normally exercises the power (local *option* on liquor sales); **alternative,** in strict usage, limits a choice to one of two possibilities (the *alternative* of paying a fine or serving 30 days); **preference** suggests the determining of choice by predisposition or partiality (a *preference* for striped ties); **selection** implies a wide choice and the exercise of careful discrimination (*selections* from the modern French poets).

choir (kwīr), ***n.*** [ME. *quere* (with South Eastern dial. vowel change, as in *brier, friar*, and erroneous French-Latin sp.); OFr. *cuer*, a choir; L. *chorus;* see CHORUS], 1. a group of singers in a church. 2. the part of a church where they sing. 3. any group of singers or dancers. ***v.t. & v.i.*** [Poetic], to sing in chorus. Also spelled **quire.**

choir·boy (kwīr'boi'), ***n.*** a boy who sings in a choir.

choir loft, the gallery occupied by the choir in a church.

choir·mas·ter (kwīr'mas'tẽr, kwīr'mäs'tẽr), ***n.*** the conductor of a choir.

Choi·seul (shwȧ'zöl'), ***n.*** one of the Solomon Islands, in the South Pacific: area, 1,500 sq. mi.; pop., 4,000.

choke (chōk), ***v.t.*** [CHOKED (chōkt), CHOKING], [ME. *cheken, choken;* AS. *aceocian, v.t.*, to choke; prob. < base of AS. *ceace*, jawbone (cf. CHEEK), hence, lit., "to clutch with the jaws"], 1. to prevent from breathing by blocking the windpipe or squeezing the throat of; strangle; suffocate; smother; stifle. 2. to block up; obstruct by clogging. 3. to hinder the growth or action of. 4. to fill up. 5. to cut off the air from the carburetor of (a gasoline engine) in order to make a richer gasoline mixture. ***v.i.*** 1. to be suffocated; have difficulty in breathing. 2. to be blocked up; be obstructed. ***n.*** 1. a choking; strangulation. 2. a sound of choking. 3. the valve that shuts off air in the carburetor of a gasoline engine. 4. a constriction, as in a chokebore.

choke back, to hold back (feelings, sobs, etc.).
choke down, to swallow with difficulty.
choke off, to bring to an end; end the growth of.
choke up, 1. to bring up by choking. 2. to block up; clog. 3. to fill too full. 4. [Colloq.], to be speechless, as from strong emotion. 5. [Colloq.], to be unable to function efficiently in a crisis because of tenseness.

choke·ber·ry (chōk'ber'i), *n.* [*pl.* CHOKEBERRIES (-iz)], 1. the astringent berrylike fruit of certain North American shrubs of the rose family. 2. a shrub bearing it.

choke·bore (chōk'bôr', chōk'bōr'), *n.* 1. a shotgun bore that tapers toward the muzzle to keep the shot closely bunched. 2. a gun with such a bore.

choke·cher·ry (chōk'cher'i), *n.* [*pl.* CHOKECHERRIES (-iz)], 1. either of two wild cherry trees of North America. 2. the astringent fruit of either of these.

choke coil, a coil of wire with a core of iron or air, used for control of the alternating current in an electric circuit: it permits the passage of the direct-current component but has such a high reactance that little alternating current goes through: also **choking coil.**

choke·damp (chōk'damp'), *n.* a suffocating gas, chiefly carbon dioxide, found in mines and wells.

choke-full (chōk'fool'), *adj.* chock-full.

chok·er (chōk'ēr), *n.* 1. a person or thing that chokes. 2. a necklace that fits closely around the neck. 3. a narrow fur piece worn around the neck or on the shoulders. 4. [Colloq.], a wide necktie or collar worn tight around the neck.

chok·ing (chōk'iŋ), *adj.* 1. that chokes; causing or tending to cause suffocating or difficulty in breathing: as, a *choking* gas. 2. strained or indistinct with emotion, as if about to choke: as, a *choking* voice.

chok·y (chōk'i), *adj.* [CHOKIER (-i-ēr), CHOKIEST (-i-ist)], 1. inclined to choke. 2. suffocating; stifling. Also spelled **chokey.**

chol- (kol), cholo-.

chol·e- (kol'i), cholo-.

chol·e·cyst (kol'i-sist'), *n.* [Mod. L. *cholecystis* < Gr. *cholē*, bile + *kystis*, bladder], the gall bladder.

chol·er (kol'ēr), *n.* [altered (after L. forms) < ME. *colere, colre;* OFr. *colere;* L. *cholera*, jaundice; Gr. *cholera*, cholera, nausea < *cholē*, gall, bile; IE. base **ĝhel-*, **ĝhlō-*, to gleam, yellow, green; hence akin to Eng. *gall, yellow, gold*], 1. [Obs.], bile: in medieval times it was considered one of the four humors of the body, and the source of anger and irritability. 2. anger; wrath.

chol·er·a (kol'ēr-ə), *n.* [L.; Gr. *cholera;* see CHOLER], 1. any of several intestinal diseases; especially, *a)* cholera morbus. *b)* Asiatic cholera, an infectious disease characterized by violent diarrhea and vomiting, muscular cramps, and collapse. 2. [Obs.], bile; choler.

cholera in·fan·tum (in-fan'təm), [L. lit., cholera of infants], an intestinal disease of infants, characterized by vomiting and diarrhea: it occurs usually in the summer.

cholera mor·bus (môr'bəs), [L., lit., cholera disease], a noninfectious, rarely fatal cholera, with diarrhea and cramps: it is usually caused by contaminated foods: also called *sporadic cholera, bilious cholera.*

cholera nos·tras (nos'tras), [L., lit., cholera of our country, native cholera], cholera morbus.

chol·er·ic (kol'ēr-ik), *adj.* [ME. *colerik*, having choler as the predominant humor, hence of bilious temperament; OFr. *colerique;* L. *cholericus;* Gr. *cholerikos;* see CHOLER], 1. easily angered; quick-tempered. 2. [Obs.], bilious; causing biliousness. —*SYN.* see **irritable.**

cho·les·ter·ol (kə-les'tə-rōl'), *n.* [< *chole-* + Gr. *stereos*, solid, stiff; + *-ol*], a crystalline fatty alcohol, $C_{27}H_{45}OH$, found especially in animal fats, blood, nerve tissue, and bile: some gallstones are almost pure cholesterol.

cho·line (kō'lēn, kol'in), *n.* [*chol-* + *-ine*], a viscous liquid ptomaine, $C_5H_{15}O_2N$, found in many animal and vegetable tissues: a vitamin of the B complex.

chol·la (chōl'yä), *n.* [Sp., lit., skull, head], a spiny cactus with cylindrical stems, growing in the southwestern United States.

chol·o- (kol'ō, kol'ə), [< Gr. *cholē, cholos*, bile; see CHOLER], a combining form meaning *bile, gall*, as in *cholelith:* also **chol-, chole-.**

chol·o·lith (kol'ə-lith'), *n.* [*cholo-* + *-lith*], a gallstone.

Cho·lon (shô'lôn'), *n.* a city in South Viet-Nam: pop., 145,000.

chon·dri·o·some (kon'dri-ə-sōm'), *n.* [< Gr. *chondrion*, little cartilage; + *-some*], in *biology*, any of various very small structures found in different forms in the cytoplasm of cells.

chon·dro- (kon'drō, kon'drə), [< Gr. *chondros*, a grain, cartilage], a combining form meaning *of cartilage:* also, before a vowel, **chondr-,** as in *chondroma.*

chon·dro·ma (kon-drō'mə), *n.* [*pl.* CHONDROMAS (-məz), CHONDROMATA (-mə-tə)], [*chondr-* + *-oma*], a cartilaginous tumor.

choose (chōōz), *v.t.* [CHOSE (chōz), CHOSEN (chō'z'n) or *obs.* CHOSE, CHOOSING], [ME. *chesen, chosen, chousen;* AS. *ceosan;* akin to G. *kiesen*, to select; Gmc. basic sense, "to test by tasting"; IE. base **ĝeus-*, to relish, enjoy by tasting, as also in L. *gustare*, to taste; cf. DISGUST, GUSTO], 1. to take as a choice; pick out by preference from all available; select. 2. to prefer; decide; think proper (with an infinitive object). 3. [Colloq.], to desire; want. *v.i.* to make a choice; select.
cannot choose but, cannot do otherwise than; be compelled (with an infinitive).
SYN.—**choose** implies the exercise of judgment in settling upon a thing or course from among those offered; **select,** and the more informal **pick,** imply a choosing by careful discrimination from a large number available, **pick** sometimes connoting random selection (*pick* a number from 1 to 10); **elect** implies formal action in officially choosing a person or thing; **prefer** implies preconceived partiality for one thing over another but does not always connote the actual getting of what one chooses.—*ANT.* reject.

choos·y (chōōz'i), *adj.* [Colloq.], inclined to be particular in choosing; fussy.

chop (chop), *v.t.* [CHOPPED (chopt), CHOPPING], [ME. *choppen, chappen;* prob. < merging of northern OFr. *choper* (OFr. *coper*, Fr. *couper*), to cut, with MD. *cappen* (D. *kappen*), to chop off], 1. to cut by blows with an ax or other sharp tool; hew. 2. to cut into small bits; mince. 3. to cut short. *v.i.* 1. to make quick, cutting strokes with a sharp tool. 2. to do something with a quick, sharp, or jerky motion. *n.* 1. the act of chopping. 2. a short, sharp blow or stroke. 3. a piece chopped off. 4. a slice of lamb, pork, veal, etc.: chops are cut from the rib, loin, or shoulder. 5. a chapped place in the skin. 6. a short, broken movement of waves.

chop (chop), *n.* [var. of *chap* (jaw)], 1. a jaw. 2. a cheek. See **chops.**

chop (chop), *v.t.* [CHOPPED (chopt), CHOPPING], [Late ME. *choppen*, var. of *chappen*, to barter; AS. *ceapian*, to bargain; see CHEAP], [Obs.], to exchange. *v.i.* 1. to change; shift or veer suddenly, as the wind. 2. [Obs.], to answer back. *n.* an exchange.

chop (chop), *n.* [Hind. *chhāp*], 1. an official seal, stamp, permit, or license in India and China. 2. in China, a brand on or of goods. 3. [Slang], quality; grade; brand: *first chop* means "first rate."

chop-chop (chop'chop'), *adv. & interj.* [Pid. Eng.], quickly; at once.

chop·fal·len (chop'fôl'ən, chop'fôln'), *adj.* chapfallen.

chop·house (chop'hous'), *n.* a restaurant that specializes in chops and steaks.

chop·house (chop'hous'), *n.* [see CHOP (a seal)], a Chinese customhouse.

chop·in (chop'in), *n.* a chopine.

Cho·pin, Fré·dé·ric Fran·çois (frā'dā'rēk' frän'swå' shō'pan'; Eng. shō'pan), 1810–1849; Polish pianist and composer in France.

cho·pine (chō-pēn', chop'in), *n.* [OFr. & Sp. *chapin;* prob. < *chapa*, small leather strip], a woman's shoe with a thick, high sole, worn in the 17th and 18th centuries; kind of patten.

chop·per (chop'ēr), *n.* 1. a person who chops. 2. a tool or machine for chopping, as an ax or cleaver.

chop·py (chop'i), *adj.* [CHOPPIER (-i-ēr), CHOPPIEST (-i-ist)], [< *chop* (to change)], changing constantly and abruptly, as the wind.

chop·py (chop'i), *adj.* [CHOPPIER (-i-ēr), CHOPPIEST (-i-ist)], [< *chop, v. & n.* (cut)], 1. rough with short, broken waves, as the sea. 2. with sharp, abrupt movements; jerky. 3. full of cracks; chapped.

chops (chops), *n. pl.* [see CHAP (jaw)], 1. the jaws. 2. the mouth and lower cheeks. 3. the entrance or mouth of something, as of a channel. Also **chaps.**

chop·sticks (chop'stiks'), *n. pl.* [Pid. Eng. for Chin. *k'wai-tsze*, the quick ones; see CHOP-CHOP], 1. two small sticks of wood or ivory, held together in one hand and used by the Chinese and Japanese to lift food to the mouth. 2. [Colloq.], a short, choppy melody played on the piano with one finger of each hand.

chop stroke, in *tennis*, a stroke made with a cutting or slicing motion.

chop su·ey (chop' sōō'i), [altered < Chin. *tsa-sui*, lit., various pieces], a Chinese-American dish consisting of meat, bean sprouts, celery, mushrooms, etc. cooked together in a sauce and served with rice.

cho·rag·ic (kō-raj'ik, kō-rā'jik), *adj.* of a choragus.

cho·ra·gus (kō-rā'gəs), *n.* [*pl.* CHORAGI (-jī)], [L.; Gr. *chorēgos* < *choros*, chorus + *agein*, to lead], 1. the leader of the chorus in an ancient Greek play. 2. the leader of a chorus, choir, or band.

cho·ral (kôr'əl, kō'rəl), *adj.* [Fr.], of, for, sung by, or recited by a choir or chorus.

cho·ral, cho·rale (kô-ral', kə-ral', kôr'əl), *n.* [< G. *choral* (*gesang*), choral (song), hymn], a simple hymn tune sung by the choir and congregation, often in unison.

chord (kôrd), *n.* [Eng. *cord;* sp. revised after L. *chorda;* Gr. *chordē*, string of a musical instrument], 1. [Poetic], the string of a musical instrument. 2. figuratively, a responsive emotional element: as, his speech struck a sympathetic *chord.* 3. in *aeronautics*, *a)* a straight line extending directly across an airfoil from the leading to the trailing edge. *b)* the length of such a line. 4. in *anatomy*, a structure, such as a tendon, resembling a cord. 5. in *engineering*, a principal horizontal member in a rigid framework, as of a bridge. 6. in *geometry*, a straight line join-

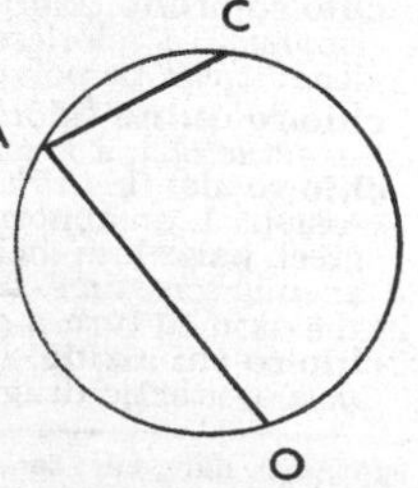

CHORDS (AC, AO)

ing any two points on an arc, curve, or circumference.
chord (kôrd), *n.* [mistakenly altered (after L. *chorda;* see CHORD, a string) < *cord*, contr. < *accord*], in *music*, a combination of three or more tones sounded together in harmony. *v.i. & v.t.* to harmonize.
chor·date (kôr'dāt), *n.* [L. *chorda* (see CHORD, a string); + *-ate*], any animal having at some stage of its development a notochord, gill slits, and a dorsal tubular nerve cord: all the vertebrates, including man, are chordates. *adj.* 1. having a notochord. 2. of a chordate or chordates.
chore (chôr, chōr), *n.* [ME. *cher, cherre;* see CHARE], 1. *usually in pl.* a small routine task, as of a housekeeper or farmer; odd job. 2. a hard or unpleasant task. —*SYN.* see **task.**
cho·re·a (kô-rē'ə, kō-rē'ə), *n.* [L., a dance in a ring; Gr. *choreia,* choral dance], a nervous disease in which there are irregular, jerking movements caused by involuntary muscular contractions: also called *St. Vitus's Dance.*
cho·reg·ra·phy (kə-reg'rə-fi), *n.* choreography.
chor·e·og·raph·er (kô'ri-og'rə-fẽr, kō'ri-og'rə-fẽr), *n.* [< *choreography*], a person who designs or arranges the movements of a dance, especially a ballet.
chor·e·og·ra·phy (kô'ri-og'rə-fi, kō'ri-og'rə-fi), *n.* [Gr. *choreia,* dance; + *-graphy*], 1. dancing, especially ballet dancing. 2. the arrangement or the written notation of the movements of a dance, especially a ballet. 3. the art of devising dances, especially ballets.
cho·ri·amb (kôr'i-amb', kō'ri-amb'), *n.* [L. *choriambus;* Gr. *choriambos* < *choreios,* trochee, lit., pertaining to a chorus + *iambos,* iamb], a metrical foot of four syllables, the first and last long, the middle two short, as in Greek and Latin verse, or the first and last stressed and the middle two unstressed, as in English verse; trochee and iamb combined.
cho·ri·am·bus (kôr'i-am'bəs, kō'ri-am'bəs), *n.* [*pl.* CHORIAMBI (-bī), CHORIAMBUSES (-iz)], a choriamb.
cho·ric (kôr'ik, kō'rik), *adj.* of, for, or in the manner of, a chorus, especially in an ancient Greek play.
cho·rine (kôr'ēn, kō'rin), *n.* [*chorus* + *-ine*], [Colloq.], a girl who sings or dances in a chorus at a theater, cabaret, etc.; chorus girl.
cho·ri·oid (kôr'i-oid', kō'ri-oid'), *adj. & n.* choroid.
cho·ri·on (kôr'i-on', kō'ri-on'), *n.* [Gr. *chorion,* leather, skin], the outermost of the two membranes that completely envelop a fetus.
chor·is·ter (kôr'is-tẽr, kor'is-tẽr), *n.* [< ME. *querister* (mod. sp. mistakenly altered after *chorus*); OFr. *cueristre, cueriste;* see CHOIR], 1. a member of a choir; especially, a boy who sings in a choir. 2. the leader of a choir.
cho·ro·graph·ic (kôr'ə-graf'ik, kō'rə-graf'ik), *adj.* of, by, or according to chorography.
cho·rog·ra·phy (kô-rog'rə-fi, kō-rog'rə-fi), *n.* [< Gr. *chōros,* a place; + *-graphy*], 1. the art of mapping or describing a region or district. 2. such a map or description.
cho·roid (kôr'oid, kō'roid), *adj.* [Gr. *choroeidēs,* contr. < *chorioeidēs* < *chorion,* leather, skin + *eidos,* form], designating or of the chorion or certain other vascular membranes in the body. *n.* the dark, vascular membrane that forms the middle coat of the eye, between the sclera and the retina: see **eye,** illus. Also **chorioid.**
chor·tle (chôr't'l), *v.i. & v.t.* [CHORTLED (-t'ld), CHORTLING], [coined by Lewis Carroll, in *Through the Looking Glass;* prob. < *chuckle* + *snort*], to make or utter with a gleeful chuckling or snorting sound. *n.* such a sound.
cho·rus (kôr'əs, kō'rəs), *n.* [L.; Gr. *choros,* a dance in a ring, chorus], 1. in Greek drama, a company of performers whose singing, dancing, and narration provided explanation and elaboration of the main action. 2. in Elizabethan drama, a person who recites the prologue and epilogue. 3. a group of dancers and singers performing together in a modern musical show, theatrical performance, opera, etc. 4. the part of a drama, song, etc. performed by a chorus. 5. a number of people singing or speaking something together simultaneously. 6. a simultaneous utterance by many: as, a *chorus* of protest. 7. that which is thus uttered. 8. music written for group singing. 9. that part of a musical composition in which the company joins the solo singer; hence, 10. the refrain of a song, following the verse. *v.t. & v.i.* to sing or recite all together and simultaneously; utter in unison.
in chorus, all together and simultaneously; in unison.
chorus girl (or **boy**), a woman (or man) singing or dancing in the chorus of a musical comedy, etc.
chose (chōz), past tense and obsolete past participle of **choose.**
chose (shōz), *n.* [Fr., thing, matter; L. *causa,* matter, affair], in *law,* a piece of personal property; chattel.
Cho·sen (chō'sen'), *n.* Korea: the Japanese name.
cho·sen (chō'z'n), past participle of **choose.** *adj.* 1. picked out by preference; selected; choice. 2. in *theology,* elect; favored by God.
Chou (jō), *n.* a Chinese dynasty (1122?–249 B.C.).
Chou En-lai (jō' en'lī'), 1898– ; Chinese Communist leader.
chough (chuf), *n.* [ME. *choughe;* akin to MD. *cauw* (D. *kauw*), OHG. *kaha,* etc.; IE. base **gou-,* to cry, scream, as also in AS. *ciegan,* to call out], a European bird of the crow family, with red legs and beak and glossy black feathers.
chouse (chous), *n.* [earlier *chiaus;* Turk. *chāwush,* messenger, interpreter: present meaning said to have been adopted because in 1609 a Turk. interpreter swindled several London merchants], 1. [Obs.], a swindler; cheat. 2. [Obs.], a dupe. 3. [Colloq.], a swindle. *v.t.* [CHOUSED (choust), CHOUSING], [Colloq.], to cheat; swindle.
chow (chou), *n.* [prob. < *chowchow*], 1. any of a Chinese breed of medium-sized dog with a compact, muscular body, a thick coat of brown or black, and a blue-black tongue. 2. [Slang], food.

CHOW (20 in. high)

chow·chow (chou'chou'), *n.* [Pid. Eng. < Chin.], 1. chopped pickles in a highly seasoned mustard sauce. 2. a chow. *adj.* mixed; assorted.
chow·der (chou'dẽr), *n.* [Fr. *chaudière,* a pot; LL. *caldaria;* see CALDRON], a dish consisting of fresh fish, clams, etc. stewed with vegetables, often in milk.
chow mein (chou'mān'), [Chin. *ch'ao,* to fry + *mien,* flour], a Chinese-American dish consisting of a thick stew of meat, onions, celery, bean sprouts, etc., served with fried noodles.
CHQ, Corps Headquarters.
Chr., 1. Christ. 2. Christian.
chres·tom·a·thy (kres-tom'ə-thi), *n.* [*pl.* CHRESTOMATHIES (-thiz)], [Gr. *chrēstomatheia* < *chrēstos,* useful + *mathein,* to learn], a collection of passages from literature, used in studying a language or as literary specimens.
Chré·tien de Troyes (krā'tyan' də trwä'), (also *Chrestien de Troyes*), 1140?–1191; French poet.
chrism (kriz'm), *n.* [ME. *crisme;* AS. *crisma;* LL. *chrisma,* an anointing, unction; Gr. *chrisma,* unguent < *chriein,* to rub, anoint], 1. consecrated oil used in baptism and other sacraments in certain churches. 2. a sacramental anointing with such oil.
chris·mal (kriz'm'l), *adj.* relating to chrism.
chris·ma·to·ry (kriz'mə-tôr'i, kriz'mə-tō'ri), *n.* [*pl.* CHRISMATORIES (-iz, -riz)], [ML. *chrismatorium* < LL. *chrisma*], a container or receptacle for the chrism.
chris·om (kriz'əm), *n.* [var. of *chrism;* orig., cloth to keep chrism off the face], 1. a white robe or cloth put on a baby at baptism as a symbol of innocence: it was used as a shroud if the baby died within a month of birth. 2. [Archaic], *a)* a baby in its chrisom; hence, *b)* an innocent baby; infant.
Christ (krīst), *n.* [ME. & AS. *Crist;* L. *Christus;* Gr. *Christos,* lit., the Anointed < *chriein,* to anoint], 1. the Messiah whose appearance is prophesied in the Old Testament. 2. Jesus of Nazareth, regarded by Christians as the realization of the Messianic prophecy: originally a title (*Jesus the Christ*), later used as part of the name (*Jesus Christ*). Abbreviated **Chr.**
Christ (krist, kris), [see CHRIST, *n.*], a masculine name.
Chris·ta·bel (kris'tə-bel'), [< L. *Christus* (see CHRIST) + *bella,* fem. of *bellus,* handsome], a feminine name.
Christ·church (krīst'chũrch'), *n.* a city on the eastern coast of South Island, New Zealand: pop., 159,000 (est. 1947).
christ·cross (kris'krôs', kris'kros'), *n.* [< *Christ's cross*], 1. [Archaic], the figure of a cross (✠) formerly placed before the alphabet in hornbooks, etc.; also, the mark of the cross (×) used as a signature by a person who cannot write. 2. [British Dial.], the alphabet. See **crisscross.**
chris·ten (kris''n), *v.t.* [ME. *christenien;* AS. *cristnian;* see CHRISTIAN], 1. to take into a Christian church by baptism; baptize. 2. to give a name to at baptism. 3. to give a name to. 4. [Colloq.], to make use of for the first time.
Chris·ten·dom (kris''n-dəm), *n.* [ME. & AS. *cristendom,* Christianity; see CHRISTIAN & -DOM], 1. Christians collectively. 2. those parts of the world where most of the inhabitants profess the Christian faith.
chris·ten·ing (kris''n-iŋ, kris'niŋ), *n.* [ME. *cristninge;* see CHRISTEN], the act or ceremony of baptizing and giving a name to an infant; baptism.
Christ·hood (krīst'hood'), *n.* [see -HOOD], the state or fact of being the Christ.
Chris·tian (kris'chən), a masculine name: diminutives, *Chris, Christie:* feminine, *Christiana, Christina, Christine. n.* [ME. & AS. *cristen, cristena;* L. *christianus;* Gr. *christianos,* a Christian < *Christos* (see CHRIST); mod. sp. restored < L.], 1. a person professing belief

in Jesus as the Christ, or in the religion based on the teachings of Jesus: abbreviated **Chr.** 2. the main character in Bunyan's *Pilgrim's Progress* (1678), a refugee fleeing the City of Destruction to seek Zion, the City of God. 3. [Colloq.], a decent, respectable person. ***adj.*** 1. of Jesus Christ. 2. of the teachings of Jesus Christ. 3. of or professing the religion based on these teachings: abbreviated **Chr.** 4. having the qualities demonstrated and taught by Jesus Christ, as love, kindness, etc. 5. of or representing Christians or Christianity. 6. [Colloq.], human, decent, etc.

Christian X, 1870–1947; king of Denmark (1912–1947).

Chris·ti·an·a (kris'ti-an'ə), [L., fem. of *Christianus;* see CHRISTIAN], a feminine name: variants, *Christina, Christine;* diminutives, *Chrissie, Tina, Xina.*

Christian Brothers, a Roman Catholic lay order that undertakes the teaching of youth.

Christian Era, the era beginning with the year formerly thought to be that of the birth of Jesus Christ (born probably c. 4–6 B.C.): *A.D.* marks dates in this era, *B.C.* marks dates before it.

Chris·tia·ni·a (kris-tyä'ni-ä), ***n.*** Oslo, the capital of Norway: the former name.

Chris·tian·ism (kris'chən-iz'm), ***n.*** [Rare], the religious system or principles of Christians.

Chris·ti·an·i·ty (kris'chi-an'ə-ti), ***n.*** [ME. *cristianite, cristiente;* OFr. *crestiente;* L. *christianitas* < *Christianus;* see CHRISTIAN], 1. Christians collectively; Christendom. 2. the Christian religion; doctrines taught by Jesus Christ. 3. a particular Christian religious system: as, Eastern *Christianity.* 4. the state of being a Christian. 5. Christian character, practices, etc.

Chris·ti·an·ize (kris'chən-īz'), ***v.t.*** [CHRISTIANIZED (-īzd'), CHRISTIANIZING], [LL. *christianizare;* Gr. *christianizein,* to profess Christianity], 1. to convert to Christianity. 2. to cause to conform with Christian character or precepts. ***v.i.*** to adopt Christianity.

Chris·tian·like (kris'chən-līk'), ***adj.*** having the qualities or habits of a Christian.

Chris·tian·ly (kris'chən-li), ***adj. & adv.*** like, characteristic of, or in the manner of, a Christian.

Christian name, the baptismal name, as distinguished from the surname or family name; given name.

Christian Science, a religion and system of healing founded by Mary Baker Eddy in 1866, based on an interpretation of the Scriptures as upholding the idea that disease, sin, etc. are caused by mental error and may be eliminated by spiritual treatment without medical aid: abbreviated **C.S.:** official name, **Church of Christ, Scientist.**

Christian Scientist, a person who believes in Christian Science: abbreviated **C.S.**

Chris·ti·na (kris-tē'nə), a feminine name: see **Christiana.**

Chris·tine (kris-tēn'), a feminine name: see **Christiana.**

Christ·less (krīst'lis), ***adj.*** without faith in Jesus Christ; unchristian.

Christ·like (krīst'līk'), ***adj.*** like Jesus Christ, especially in character or spirit; like that of Jesus.

Christ·li·ness (krīst'li-nis), ***n.*** the state of being Christlike.

Christ·ly (krīst'li), ***adj.*** of Jesus Christ; Christlike.

Christ·mas (kris'məs), ***n.*** [AS. *Cristesmæsse;* see CHRIST & MASS (rite)], the yearly celebration, December 25, of the birth of Jesus Christ.

Christmas Day, December 25.

Christmas Eve, the evening before Christmas Day.

Christmas Island, 1. an island in the Indian Ocean, south of Java: area, 62 sq. mi.; pop., 1,100: part of the colony of Singapore. 2. a British island in the Pacific, near the equator: area, 235 sq. mi.; pop., 50.

Christ·mas·tide (kris'məs-tīd'), ***n.*** [*Christmas* + *tide, n.*], Christmas time; time from Christmas Eve through New Year's Day or to Epiphany (January 6).

Christmas tree, an evergreen tree hung with ornaments and lights, set up at Christmas time.

Chris·tophe, Hen·ri (än'rē' krēs'tôf'), 1767–1820; king of Haiti (1811–1820).

Chris·to·pher (kris'tə-fẽr), [ME. *Christofre;* L. *Christophorus;* Gr. *Christophoros,* lit., bearing Christ; *Christos* (see CHRIST) + *pherein,* to bear], a masculine name: diminutives, *Chris, Kit.*

Christopher, Saint, 3d century A.D.; Christian martyr of Asia Minor: his day is July 25.

Christ's-thorn (krīsts'thôrn'), ***n.*** any of several spiny shrubs or trees of southern Europe and the Near East, supposed to have been used for Christ's crown of thorns.

Chris·ty, Howard Chan·dler (chan'dlẽr kris'ti), 1873–1952; American painter and illustrator.

chro·ma (krō'mə), ***n.*** [Gr. *chrōma,* a color], the purity of a color, determined by its degree of freedom from white or gray; color intensity.

chro·mate (krō'māt), ***n.*** [< *chromium* + *-ate*], a salt of chromic acid.

chro·mat·ic (krō-mat'ik), ***adj.*** [L. *chromaticus;* Gr. *chrōmatikos,* suited for color < *chrōma, chrōmatos,* a color], 1. of or containing color or colors. 2. in *biology,* readily stained. 3. in *music, a)* using or progressing by half tones: as, a *chromatic* scale. *b)* producing all the tones of such a scale: as, a *chromatic* instrument. ***n.*** in *music,* a tone modified by an accidental.

chromatic aberration, a property of lenses that causes the various colors in a beam of light to be focused at different points, thus causing a spectrum to appear.

chro·mat·i·cal·ly (krō-mat'i-k'l-i, krō-mat'ik-li), ***adv.*** 1. in a chromatic manner. 2. in a chromatic scale.

chro·mat·ics (krō-mat'iks), ***n. pl.*** [construed as sing.], the scientific study of colors.

chromatic scale, the musical scale made up of thirteen successive half tones to the octave.

chro·ma·tin (krō'mə-tin), ***n.*** [< Gr. *chrōma, chrōmatos,* a color; + *-in*], a granular protoplasmic substance in the nucleus of animal and plant cells that readily takes a deep stain: chromatin contains the genes.

chro·ma·tism (krō'mə-tiz'm), ***n.*** [Gr. *chrōmatismos;* see CHROMATIC], 1. any abnormal coloring in parts of a plant ordinarily green. 2. chromatic aberration.

chro·ma·to- (krō'mə-tō, krō'mə-tə), [< Gr. *chrōma, chrōmatos,* a color], a combining form meaning: 1. *color* or *pigmentation,* as in *chromatology.* 2. *chromatin,* as in *chromatolysis.* Also, before a vowel, **chromat-.**

chro·ma·tol·o·gy (krō'mə-tol'ə-ji), ***n.*** [*chromato-* + *-logy*], 1. chromatics. 2. a treatise on colors.

chro·ma·tol·y·sis (krō'mə-tol'ə-sis), ***n.*** [*chromato-* + *-lysis*], in *medicine,* the breakdown and dissolution of the chromatin in the cell nucleus.

chro·ma·to·phore (krō'mə-tə-fôr', krō'mə-tə-fōr'), ***n.*** [*chromato-* + *-phore*], a color-producing cell in a plant or animal; pigment cell.

chrome (krōm), ***n.*** [Fr. < Gr. *chrōma,* a color: so called because of the bright-colored compounds], 1. chromium. 2. chrome yellow. 3. chrome steel. ***v.t.*** [CHROMED (krōmd), CHROMING], to plate with chromium.

-chrome (krōm), [< Gr. *chrōma;* see CHROME], a suffix meaning: 1. *color, coloring agent,* as in *urochrome.* 2. *chromium,* as in *ferrochrome.*

chrome alum, an alum of which one of the components is chromium: especially, potassium chrome alum, $KCr(SO_4)_2 \cdot 12H_2O$, used in tanning and dyeing.

chrome green, 1. chromic oxide, Cr_2O_3, used as a green pigment. 2. in commercial use, a green pigment made by mixing chrome yellow and Prussian blue.

chrome iron, chromite (mineral): also **chrome iron ore.**

chrome leather, leather tanned with chromium salts.

chrome red, any of various red pigments made from basic lead chromate.

chrome steel, a very strong, hard alloy steel that contains chromium.

chrome yellow, neutral chromate of lead, $PbCrO_4$, used as a yellow pigment.

chro·mic (krō'mik), ***adj.*** designating or of chromium compounds in which the valence of chromium is higher than in the corresponding chromous compounds.

chromic acid, an acid, H_2CrO_4, whose salts are chromates.

chro·mite (krō'mīt), ***n.*** 1. a black mineral, $FeCr_2O_4$, with a metallic luster and an uneven fracture: it is the chief ore of chromium. 2. a salt of chromous acid.

chro·mi·um (krō'mi-əm), ***n.*** [Latinized < Fr. *chrome;* see CHROME], a white, crystalline, very hard, metallic chemical element with a high resistance to corrosion: used in chromium electroplating, in alloy steel, and in alloys containing nickel, copper, manganese, and other metals: symbol, Cr; at. wt., 52.01; at. no., 24.

chromium steel, chrome steel.

chro·mo (krō'mō), ***n.*** [*pl.* CHROMOS (-mōz)], a chromolithograph.

chro·mo- (krō'mō, krō'mə), [< Gr. *chrōma,* a color], a combining form meaning *color, colored, pigment, pigmentation,* as in *chromosome, chromolithograph:* also, before a vowel, **chrom-.**

chro·mo·gen (krō'mə-jən), ***n.*** [*chromo-* + *-gen*], any substance that can become a pigment or coloring matter, as a substance in organic fluids that forms colored compounds when oxidized, or a compound, not itself a dye, that can become a dye.

chro·mo·gen·ic (krō'mə-jen'ik), ***adj.*** 1. of a chromogen or chromogens. 2. producing a color or pigment, as certain bacteria.

chro·mo·lith·o·graph (krō'mō-lith'ə-graf', krō'mō-lith'ə-gräf'), ***n.*** [*chromo-* + *lithograph*], a colored picture printed from a series of stone or zinc plates, the impression from each plate being in a different color: usually **chromo.**

chro·mo·li·thog·ra·pher (krō'mō-li-thog'rə-fẽr), ***n.*** a person who makes chromolithographs.

chro·mo·lith·o·graph·ic (krō'mō-lith'ə-graf'ik), ***adj.*** of chromolithography or chromolithographs.

chro·mo·li·thog·ra·phy (krō'mō-li-thog'rə-fi), ***n.*** the art or process of making chromolithographs.

chro·mo·mere (krō'mə-mêr'), ***n.*** [*chromo-* + *-mere*], any of the granules of chromatin composing a chromosome.

chro·mo·phore (krō'mə-fôr', krō'mə-fōr'), ***n.*** [*chromo-* + *-phore*], any chemical group, as the azo group, that produces color in a compound and unites with certain other groups to form dyes.

chro·mo·pho·to·graph (krō'mō-fō'tə-graf', krō'mō-fō'-

tə-gräf′), *n.* a photograph in which the original colors of the subject are reproduced.
chro·mo·pho·tog·raph·y (krō′mō-fə-tog′rə-fi), *n.* the art or science of making chromophotographs.
chro·mo·plasm (krō′mə-plaz′m), *n.* [*chromo-* + *-plasm*], chromatin.
chro·mo·plast (krō′mə-plast′), *n.* [*chromo-* + *-plast*], 1. in *biology*, any pigmented body found in the cell outside the nucleus. 2. in *botany*, a granule containing a pigment other than green.
chro·mo·so·mal (krō′mə-sō′m'l), *adj.* of a chromosome or chromosomes.
chro·mo·some (krō′mə-sōm′), *n.* [*chromo-* + *-some* (body)], any of the microscopic rod-shaped bodies into which the chromatin separates during mitosis: they carry the genes that convey hereditary characteristics, and are constant in number for each species.
chro·mo·sphere (krō′mə-sfêr′), *n.* [*chromo-* + *-sphere*], 1. the reddish layer of incandescent gases around the sun, visible at a total eclipse. 2. a similar layer surrounding a star.
chro·mo·spher·ic (krō′mə-sfer′ik), *adj.* of, or having the nature of, a chromosphere.
chro·mous (krō′məs), *adj.* designating or of chromium compounds in which the valence of chromium is lower than in the corresponding chromic compounds.
chro·myl (krō′mil, krō′mēl), *n.* [*chrom-* + *-yl*], in *chemistry*, the divalent radical CrO_2.
chron- (kron), chrono-.
Chron., Chronicles.
chron., 1. chronological. 2. chronology.
chro·nax·i·a (krō-nak′si-ə), *n.* [*chron-* + Gr. *axia*, value], the minimum time necessary to excite a tissue, such as muscle or nerve tissue, with an electric current of twice the minimum potential for stimulation: used as an index of tissue excitability.
chro·nax·ie, chro·nax·y (krō′nak-si), *n.* chronaxia.
chron·ic (kron′ik), *adj.* [Fr. *chronique;* L. *chronicus;* Gr. *chronikos*, of time < *chronos*, time], 1. lasting a long time; also, recurring: said of a disease, and distinguished from *acute*. 2. having had an ailment or habit for a long time. 3. perpetual; habitual; constant.
SYN.—**chronic** suggests long duration or frequent recurrence and is used especially of diseases or habits that resist all efforts to eradicate them (*chronic* sinusitis); **inveterate** implies firm establishment as a result of continued indulgence over a long period of time (an *inveterate* liar); **confirmed** suggests fixedness in some condition or practice, often from a deep-seated aversion to change (a *confirmed* bachelor); **hardened** implies fixed tendencies and a callous indifference to emotional or moral considerations (a *hardened* criminal).
chron·i·cal·ly (kron′i-k'l-i, kron′ik-li), *adv.* in a chronic manner; persistently; habitually; continually.
chron·i·cle (kron′i-k'l), *n.* [ME. *cronicle;* Anglo-Fr. *cronicle* < OFr. *chronique;* L. *chronica;* Gr. *chronika*, annals, pl. of *chronikos;* see CHRONIC], 1. a historical record according to date; register of facts or events arranged in the order in which they happened. 2. a narrative; history. *v.t.* [CHRONICLED (-k'ld), CHRONICLING], to tell or write the story or history of; put into a chronicle; recount; record.
chronicle play, a historical play of or like a type that flourished in the Elizabethan period, characterized by free treatment of the facts of history.
chron·i·cler (kron′i-klẽr), *n.* a writer of a chronicle or chronicles; historian.
Chron·i·cles (kron′i-k'lz), *n. pl.* two books of the Old Testament, I and II Chronicles: abbreviated **Chron.**
chro·no- (kro′nō, kro′nə), [Gr. < *chronos*, time], a combining form meaning *time*, as in *chronology:* also, before a vowel, **chron-.**
chron·o·gram (kron′ə-gram′), *n.* [*chrono-* + *-gram*], 1. an inscription in which certain letters, more prominent than the others, express a date in Roman numerals when put together in order. Example: **M**er**C**y **M**i**X**ed with **L**o**V**e **I**n h**I**m-MCMXLVII=1947. 2. the measured record of a chronograph.
chron·o·graph (kron′ə-graf′, kron′ə-gräf′), *n.* [*chrono-* + *-graph*], an instrument for measuring and recording short durations of time.
chron·o·graph·ic (kron′ə-graf′ik), *adj.* of a chronograph.
chro·nol·o·ger (krə-nol′ə-jẽr), *n.* a chronologist.
chron·o·log·ic (kron′ə-loj′ik), *adj.* chronological.
chron·o·log·i·cal (kron′ə-loj′i-k'l), *adj.* [< *chronology* + *-ical*], 1. arranged in the order of occurrence. 2. containing or relating to an account of events in the order of their occurrence. Abbreviated **chron., chronol.**
chron·o·log·i·cal·ly (kron′ə-loj′i-k'l-i, kron′ə-loj′ik-li), *adv.* in or according to the order of occurrence.
chro·nol·o·gist (krə-nol′ə-jist), *n.* an expert in chronology; chronologer.
chro·nol·o·gy (krə-nol′ə-ji), *n.* [*pl.* CHRONOLOGIES (-jiz)], [*chrono-* + *-logy*], 1. the science of measuring time in fixed periods, and of dating events accurately and arranging them in the order of occurrence. 2. the arrangement of events, dates, etc. in the order of occurrence. 3. a list or table of dates in their proper sequence. Abbreviated **chron., chronol.**
chro·nom·e·ter (krə-nom′ə-tẽr), *n.* [*chrono-* + *-meter*], an instrument for measuring time precisely; especially, a highly accurate kind of clock or watch, used on ships to determine longitude.
chron·o·met·ric (kron′ə-met′rik), *adj.* of a chronometer or chronometry.
chron·o·met·ri·cal·ly (kron′ə-met′ri-k'l-i), *adv.* as determined by a chronometer.
chro·nom·e·try (krə-nom′ə-tri), *n.* [*chrono-* + *-metry*], scientific measurement of time; measurement of time by periods.
chron·o·scope (kron′ə-skōp′), *n.* [*chrono-* + *-scope*], an instrument for measuring very small intervals of time.
-chro·ous (krə-əs, krō-əs), [Gr. *-chroos* < *chrōs, chroos*, color], a terminal combining form meaning *colored*, as in *xanthochroous.*
chrys·a·lid (kris′'l-id), *n.* a chrysalis. *adj.* of a chrysalis.
chrys·a·lis (kris′'l-is), *n.* [*pl.* CHRYSALISES (-iz), CHRYSALIDES (kri-sal′ə-dēz′)], [L. *chrysallis;* Gr. *chrysallis*, golden-colored chrysalis of a butterfly < *chrysos*, gold; of Sem. origin; cf. Phoen.-Heb. *hārūz*, gold, Aram. *hara'*, yellow], 1. the form of an insect when between the larval stage and the adult stage and in a case or cocoon; pupa. 2. the case or cocoon. 3. anything in a formative or undeveloped stage.
chrys·an·the·mum (kris-an′thə-məm), *n.* [L.; Gr. *chrysanthemon*, marigold, lit., golden flower < *chrysos*, gold + *anthemon*, a flower], 1. any of a number of plants of the composite family cultivated for their showy, ball-shaped flowers, which bloom in late summer and fall and have a characteristic odor and a variety of colors, most commonly yellow, white, or red. 2. the flower.
chrys·a·ro·bin (kris′ə-rō′bin), *n.* [< Gr. *chrysos*, gold; + *araroba* + *-in*], a yellow, crystalline substance, $C_{15}H_{12}O_3$, derived from Goa powder and used in the treatment of various skin disorders.
Chry·se·is (krī-sē′is), *n.* [L.; Gr. *Chryseïs*], in Homer's *Iliad*, the beautiful daughter of Chryses, priest of Apollo: seized by the Greeks during the Trojan War and given to Agamemnon, she was returned to her father only after Apollo caused a plague to fall on the Greek camp.
chrys·el·e·phan·tine (kris′el-ə-fan′tin), *adj.* [Gr. *chryselephantinos* < *chrysos* (see CHRYSALIS) + *elephantinos* (see ELEPHANT)], made of, or overlaid with, gold and ivory, as the statue of the Olympian Zeus by Phidias.
chry·so- (kri′sō, kri′sə), [< Gr. *chrysos;* see CHRYSALIS], a combining form meaning *golden, yellow*, as in *chrysoberyl:* also, before a vowel, **chrys-.**
chrys·o·ber·yl (kris′ə-ber′il), *n.* [*chryso-* + *beryl*], beryllium aluminate, $BeAl_2O_4$, a yellowish or greenish mineral used as a semiprecious stone.
chrys·o·lite (kris′'l-īt′), *n.* [ME. & OFr. *crisolite;* L. *chrysolithos;* Gr. *chrysolithos*, topaz; see CHRYSO- & -LITE], a green or yellow silicate of magnesium and iron, of vitreous luster and granular structure; olivine: called *peridot* when used as a semiprecious stone.
chrys·o·prase (kris′ə-prāz′), *n.* [ME. & OFr. *crisopace;* L. *chrysoprasus;* Gr. *chrysoprasos* < *chrysos*, gold + *prason*, leek: so called from the color], a light-green quartz, a variety of chalcedony sometimes used as a semiprecious stone.
Chrys·os·tom, Saint **John** (kris′əs-təm, kris-os′təm), 345?–407 A.D.; Greek church father, born in Antioch: his day is January 27.
chrys·o·tile (kris′ə-til), *n.* [< *chryso-* + Gr. *tilos*, fiber], in *mineralogy*, a fibrous variety of serpentine.
chs., chapters.
chtho·ni·an (thō′ni-ən), *adj.* [Gr. *chthonios*, in the earth < *chthon*, the earth], of the gods or spirits of the underworld: applied to such Greek gods as distinguished from those of Olympus.
chub (chub), *n.* [*pl.* CHUBS (chubz), CHUB; see PLURAL, II, D, 1], [Late ME. *chubbe* < unrecorded AS. **cyb(b)* or < MLG. via northern OFr.; Gmc. base **kubb-*, anything rounded, as in Fl. *kobbe*, rounded head of hair, Norw. *kobbe*, seal, *kubbe*, block of wood; IE. base **geu-*, to curve, bend; cf. COD], 1. any of several fresh-water fishes related to the carp. 2. any of a number of unrelated fishes, as the large-mouthed black bass.
chub·bi·ness (chub′i-nis), *n.* the state of being chubby.
chub·by (chub′i), *adj.* [CHUBBIER (-i-ẽr), CHUBBIEST (-i-ist)], [< *chub*], round and plump: as, *chubby* cheeks.
chuck (chuk), *v.t.* [? < Fr. *choquer*, to shock, strike against], 1. to tap or squeeze gently, especially under the chin, as a playful or affectionate gesture. 2. to throw with a quick, short movement; throw; toss; hence, 3. [Colloq.], to discard; get rid of. *n.* 1. a light tap or squeeze under the chin. 2. a toss; throw. 3. [cf. *v.*, 2 & 3], [Slang], food.

chuck (chuk), *n.* [prob. var. of *chock*], 1. a cut of beef including the parts around the neck and the shoulder blade: see **beef**, illus. 2. a clamplike device, as on a lathe, by which the tool or work to be turned is held.

DRILL CHUCK

chuck (chuk), *v.i.* [echoic], to make a clucking noise like that of a hen. *n.* a hen's cluck.
chuck-a-luck (chuk'ə-luk'), *n.* [< *chuck* (to throw) + *luck*], a gambling game in which players bet on the throws of three dice.
chuck-full (chuk'fool'), *adj.* chock-full.
chuck·le (chuk''l), *v.i.* [CHUCKLED (-'ld), CHUCKLING], [prob. < *chuck* (hen's call) + freq. suffix *-le*], 1. to laugh softly in a low tone, as in mild amusement or satisfaction. 2. to cluck, as a hen. *n.* a soft, low-toned laugh. —*SYN.* see **laugh.**
chuck·le (chuk''l), *adj.* [? < *chuck, chock* (a block)], clumsy and stupid. *n.* a clumsy, stupid person.
chuck·le·head (chuk''l-hed'), *n.* [prob. < *chuck, chock* (a block)], [Colloq.], a stupid person; blockhead; dolt.
chuck·le·head·ed (chuk''l-hed'id), *adj.* [see CHUCKLEHEAD], [Colloq.], stupid.
chuck wagon, [*chuck* (a throw, food) + *wagon*], [Slang], a portable kitchen cart for serving food to lumbermen, ranch hands, etc.
chuck-will's-widow (chuk'wilz'wid'ō), *n.* [echoic of its cry], a bird of the goatsucker family.
chud·dah (chud'ə), *n.* a chuddar.
chud·dar, chud·der (chud'ẽr), *n.* [Hind. *cadar*], a large, square cloth worn by women in India as a shawl.
Chud·sko·e (chood-skô'ye), *n.* Peipus, a lake between the Estonian S.S.R. and the Leningrad region, U.S.S.R.: the Russian name.
chuff (chuf), *n.* [ME. *chuffe, choffe*], a boor; churl.
chug (chug), *n.* [echoic], a loud, abrupt, explosive sound, as that made by the exhaust from an engine. *v.i.* [CHUGGED (chugd), CHUGGING], 1. to make such sounds. 2. to move while making such sounds: as, the train *chugged* along.
Chu-Kiang (chōō'jyäŋ'; Eng. chōō'kyäŋ'), *n.* the Pearl River in China: the Chinese name.
chuk·ker, chuk·kar (chuk'ẽr), *n.* [Hind. *cakar* < Sans. *cakra*, wheel], one of the periods of play into which a polo match is divided: a chukker lasts 7 1/2 minutes.
chum (chum), *n.* [late 17th-c. slang; prob. altered sp. of *cham*, clipped form of *chamber* (then pronounced chäm'bẽr, chôm'bẽr) in *chamber fellow, chamber mate;* cf. 17th-c. clipped forms *mob* (*mob*ile vulgus), *cit* (*cit*izen), etc.], [Colloq.], 1. originally, a roommate. 2. an intimate friend. *v.i.* [CHUMMED (chumd), CHUMMING], [Colloq.], 1. originally, to share the same room. 2. to be intimate friends.
chum (chum), *n.* [? < Brit. dial. *cham*, var. of *champ*, to pound, mash up], bait, usually prepared from oily fish, cut up into small pieces and scattered in the water to attract fish to the lines.
chum·mi·ly (chum''l-i), *adv.* in a chummy manner.
chum·my (chum'i), *adj.* [CHUMMIER (-i-ẽr), CHUMMIEST (-i-ist)], [see CHUM (roommate)], [Colloq.], intimate; friendly.
chump (chump), *n.* [? < *chuck* (a block), *chunk* + *lump*], 1. a heavy block of wood. 2. a thick, blunt end. 3. [Colloq.], a stupid or silly person; blockhead; fool. 4. [Slang], the head.
off one's chump, [British Slang], insane; crazy.
Chung·king (chooŋ'kiŋ'; Chin. jooŋ'chiŋ'), *n.* a city in Szechwan province, China, on the Yangtze River: pop., 1,000,000 (est. 1947).
chunk (chuŋk), *n.* [prob. var. of *chuck* (a block)], [Colloq.], 1. a short, thick piece, as of meat, wood, etc. 2. a fair portion. 3. a stocky person or animal.
chunk·i·ness (chuŋ'ki-nis), *n.* the state or quality of being chunky.
chunk·y (chuŋk'i), *adj.* [CHUNKIER (-i-ẽr), CHUNKIEST (-i-ist)], [< *chunk*], [Colloq.], 1. short and thick. 2. stocky; thickset.
church (chũrch), *n.* [ME. *chireche, chirche, kirke;* AS. *cirice, cyrice;* Late Gr. *kyriakon*, house of the Lord < *kyriakē* (*dōma*), Lord's (house) < *kyriakos*, belong to the Lord < *kyrios*, a master, ruler < *kyros*, supreme power], 1. a building set apart or consecrated for public worship, especially one for Christian worship: abbreviated **ch., c.** 2. public worship; religious service. 3. all Christians. 4. [usually C-], a particular sect, denomination, or division of Christians: as, the Methodist *Church, Church* of England: abbreviated **Ch., C.** 5. the ecclesiastical government of a particular religious group, or its power, as opposed to secular government. 6. the profession of the clergy; clerical profession. 7. a group of worshippers. *v.t.* to conduct a church service for; especially, to say prayers over (a woman) after childbirth. *adj.* 1. having to do with organized Christian worship. 2. of or connected with a church.
church·go·er (chũrch'gō'ẽr), *n.* a person who attends church, especially one who does so regularly.
church·go·ing (church'gō'iŋ), *n. & adj.* attending church regularly.
Church·ill (chũrch'il, chũrch''l), *n.* 1. a river flowing through Saskatchewan and Manitoba, Canada, into Hudson Bay: length, 1,000 mi. 2. a seaport at the mouth of this river.
Church·ill, John (chũrch'il, chũrch''l), see **Marlborough,** Duke of.
Churchill, Randolph Henry Spencer, 1849–1895; British statesman.
Churchill, Win·ston (win'st'n), 1. 1871–1947; American journalist and novelist. 2. (*Sir Winston Leonard Spencer Churchill*), 1874– ; son of *Randolph;* British statesman; first lord of the admiralty (1911–1915; 1939–1940); prime minister (1940–1945; 1951–1955); received Nobel prize in literature, 1953.
church·less (chũrch'lis), *adj.* 1. having no church: as, a *churchless* village. 2. attending no church.
church·like (chũrch'līk'), *adj.* like or fit for a church.
church·li·ness (church'li-nis), *n.* the quality or state of being churchly.
church·ly (chũrch'li), *adj.* of or fit for a church.
church·man (chũrch'mən), *n.* [*pl.* CHURCHMEN (-mən)], 1. an ecclesiastic; clergyman; priest. 2. a member of a church, especially of an established church.
Church of Christ, Scientist, the official name of the Christian Science Church.
Church of England, the episcopal church of England; Anglican Church: it was established during the Reformation when the authority of the king replaced that of the Pope, and is supported by the government: abbreviated **Ch. of Eng., C.E., C. of E.**
Church of Jesus Christ of Latter-day Saints, the official name of the Mormon Church.
Church of Rome, the Roman Catholic Church.
church text, in *printing*, Old English type.
church·ward (chũrch'wẽrd), *adv.* toward the church.
church·ward·en (chũrch'wôr'd'n), *n.* [ME. *chirchewardein;* AS. *ciricweard;* see CHURCH & WARDEN], 1. in the *Anglican Church & Protestant Episcopal Church,* a lay officer chosen annually in every parish to attend to the secular affairs of the church and (in England) to act as legal representative of the parish. 2. [British Colloq.], a clay tobacco pipe with a long stem.
church·wom·an (chũrch'woom'ən), *n.* [*pl.* CHURCHWOMEN (-wim'in)], 1. a woman member of a church. 2. a woman active in church affairs.
church·yard (chũrch'yärd'), *n.* the yard or ground adjoining a church, often used as a place of burial.
churl (chũrl), *n.* [ME. *cherl; cherle;* AS. *ceorl*, peasant, freeman, husband; akin to G. *kerl*, fellow, manservant, varlet; IE. base **ĝer-*, **ĝere-*, to become ripe, grow old (cf. CORN, CARL); cf. sense development of *villain*], 1. originally, in England, a member of the lowest order of freemen. 2. a peasant; rustic. 3. a surly, ill-bred person; boor. 4. a miserly person; niggard.
churl·ish (chũr'lish), *adj.* 1. originally, of a churl or churls; rustic; hence, 2. like a churl; surly; boorish. 3. miserly. 4. hard to control; intractable.
churn (chũrn), *n.* [ME. *cherne, chirne;* AS. *cyrin*, for **ciern* (akin to G. dial. *kirn, kern*) < Gmc. base of *corn, kernel*, with reference to grainy appearance of churned cream; cf. CORN], 1. a container or contrivance in which milk or cream is beaten, stirred, and shaken to form butter. 2. a violent stirring; agitation. *v.t.* [ME. *chirnen* < the *n.*], 1. to stir, beat, and shake (milk or cream) in a churn. 2. to make (butter) in a churn. 3. to stir up vigorously; shake violently: as, he *churned* the water until it was foamy. *v.i.* 1. to use a churn in making butter. 2. to move as if churned; seethe.
churn·ing (chũrn'iŋ), *n.* 1. the act of a person who churns. 2. the quantity of butter churned at one time.
churr (chũr), *n., v.i. & v.t.* chirr.
chute (shōōt), *n.* [Fr., a fall; LL. **caduta* < L. *cadere*, to fall], 1. a waterfall or rapids. 2. an inclined trough or passage down which various things may slide or be sent: as, a coal *chute*, laundry *chute*.
chute, 'chute (shōōt), *n.* [Colloq.], a parachute.
Chu Teh (jōō' du'), 1888?– ; Chinese Communist general and leader.
chut·ney (chut'ni), *n.* [*pl.* CHUTNEYS (-niz)], [Hind. *chatnī*], a spicy relish made of fruits, spices, and herbs: also spelled **chutnee.**
Chu·vash (chōō'väsh), *n.* 1. [*pl.* CHUVASH], a member of a Turkic-speaking Bulgarian people living chiefly in the Chuvash A.S.S.R. 2. their language.
Chuvash Autonomous Soviet Socialist Republic, a division of the R.S.F.S.R., in the region of the middle Volga: area, 6,909 sq. mi.; pop., 1,111,000.
chy·la·ceous (kī-lā'shəs), *adj.* of, or having the properties of, chyle.
chyle (kīl), *n.* [L. *chylus;* Gr. *chylos*, juice, humor, chyle < *cheein*, to pour], a milky fluid composed of lymph and emulsified fats: it is formed from chyme in the small intestine, is absorbed by the lacteals, and is passed into the blood through the thoracic duct.
chy·lous (kī'ləs), *adj.* of or like chyle.
chyme (kīm), *n.* [LL. *chymus;* Gr. *chymos*, juice < *cheein*, to pour], the thick, semifluid mass resulting from

gastric digestion of food: it passes from the stomach into the small intestine, where the chyle is formed from it.

chym·ist (kim′ist), *n.* [Obs.], a chemist.

chy·mous (kī′məs), *adj.* of or like chyme.

C.I., Channel Islands.

Cia., *Compañia*, [Sp.], Company.

CIA, C.I.A., Central Intelligence Agency.

Cia·no, Count **Ga·le·az·zo** (gä′le-ät′tsô chä′nô), 1903–1943; son-in-law of Benito Mussolini; Fascist foreign minister of Italy (1936–1943); executed.

Cib·ber, Col·ley (kol′i sib′ẽr), 1671–1757; English actor and playwright; poet laureate (1730).

ci·bo·ri·um (si-bôr′i-əm, si-bō′ri-əm), *n.* [*pl.* CIBORIA (-ə)], [ML.; L., a cup < Gr. *kibōrion*, seed vessel of the Egyptian water lily, hence (either from the material or the shape) a cup], 1. a canopy of wood, stone, etc. that rests on four columns, especially one covering an altar. 2. a covered cup for holding the consecrated wafers of the Eucharist.

C.I.C., Commander in Chief.

ci·ca·da (si-kā′də, si-kä′də), *n.* [*pl.* CICADAS (-dəz), CICADAE (-dē)], [L.], a large flylike insect with transparent wings; seventeen-year locust: the male makes a loud, shrill sound by vibrating a special sound organ on its undersurface.

ci·ca·la (si-kä′lə), *n.* [It. < L. *cicada*], a cicada.

cic·a·trice (sik′ə-tris), *n.* [ME.; Fr.], a cicatrix.

cic·a·tri·cial (sik′ə-trish′əl), *adj.* of or like a cicatrix.

cic·a·tri·cle (sik′ə-trik″l), *n.* 1. in *botany*, a cicatrix. 2. in *embryology*, the protoplasmic disc in the yolk of an egg from which the embryo develops.

ci·cat·ri·cose (si-kat′ri-kōs , sik′ə-tri-kōs′), *adj.* in *botany*, marked by cicatrices.

cic·a·trix (sik′ə-triks), *n.* [*pl.* CICATRICES (sik′ə-trī′sēz)], [L., a scar], 1. in *medicine*, the contracted fibrous tissue at the place where a wound has healed; scar. 2. in *botany*, *a*) the scar left on a stem where a branch, leaf, etc. was once attached. *b*) the mark left where a wound has healed on a tree or plant. *c*) the scarlike mark on a seed showing where it was attached to the pod; hilum.

cic·a·tri·za·tion (sik′ə-tri-zā′shən, sik′ə-trī-zā′shən), *n.* a cicatrizing.

cic·a·trize (sik′ə trīz′), *v.t.* & *v.i.* [CICATRIZED (-trīzd′), CICATRIZING], [LL. *cicatrizare;* see CICATRIX], to heal with the formation of a scar.

Cic·e·ly (sis″l-i), a feminine name: see **Cecily**.

cic·e·ly (sis″l-i), *n.* [*pl.* CICELIES (-iz)], [L. *seselis;* Gr. *seselis*], a plant of the parsley family, with fernlike leaves and umbrellalike clusters of white flowers.

Cic·er·o (sis′ə-rō′), *n.* 1. (*Marcus Tullius Cicero*), Roman statesman, orator, and Stoic philosopher; 106–43 B.C.: abbreviated **Cic.** 2. a city in northeastern Illinois, near Chicago: pop., 69,000.

ci·ce·ro·ne (sis′ə-rō′ni, chich′ə-rō′ni; It. chē′che-rô′ne), *n.* [*pl.* CICERONES (-niz), It. CICERONI (-nē)], [It. < L. *Cicero*, the orator: so called from the usual loquacity of guides], a guide who explains the history and chief features of a place to sight-seers.

Cic·e·ro·ni·an (sis′ə-rō′ni-ən), *adj.* of or like Cicero or his polished literary style; hence, eloquent.

cich·lid (sik′lid), *n.* [< Mod. L. *Cichlidae*, name of the family < Gr. *kichle*, thrush, also sea fish], any of a family of spiny fresh-water fishes related to the American sunfishes. *adj.* of this family.

ci·cho·ri·a·ceous (si-kō′ri-ā′shəs), *adj.* [< Mod. L. *Cichoriaceae*, name of the family < L. *cichorium;* see CHICORY], of a family of shrubs or herbs (the chicory family) including the dandelion, lettuce, endive, etc.

‡ci·cis·be·o (chē′chēz-be′ô; Eng. si-sis′bi-ō′), *n.* [*pl.* CICISBEI (-ē; Eng. -ē′)], [It.], the recognized lover of a married woman.

Cid, the (sid; Sp. thēth), [Sp. < Ar. *sayyid*, a lord], (born *Rodrigo*, or *Ruy, Díaz de Bivar*), 1040?–1099; Spanish hero and soldier of fortune, prominent in Spanish literature: subject of a play by Corneille.

-cid·al (sīd″l), [see -CIDE], a suffix meaning: 1. *of a killer or killing*, as in *homicidal*. 2. *that can kill*, as in *fungicidal*.

-cide (sīd), [< Fr. or L.; Fr. *-cide;* L. *-cida* < *caedere*, to cut down, strike mortally, kill], a suffix meaning *killer* or *killing*, as in *regicide, homicide*.

ci·der (sī′dẽr), *n.* [ME. *cidre, cyder;* OFr. *sidre, cidere;* L. *sicera;* Gr. *sikera;* Heb. *shēkar*, sweet fermented liquor], the juice pressed from apples or, formerly, from other fruits, as cherries, used as a beverage or for making vinegar: *sweet cider* is unfermented juice, *hard cider* is fermented juice.

cider press, a machine that presses the juice out of apples, for making cider.

‡ci-de·vant (sē′də-vän′), *adj.* [Fr., heretofore: applied in the Revolution to former nobles], former; recent.

Cie., cie., *compagnie*, [Fr.], company.

Cien·fue·gos (syen-fwe′gōs), *n.* a seaport on the southern coast of Cuba: pop., 58,000.

C.I.F., c.i.f., cost, insurance, and freight.

ci·gar (si-gär′), *n.* [Sp. *cigarro* said to be < *cigarra*, cicada: from resemblance to the insect's body; in 18th c., also *seegar*], a compact roll of tobacco leaves, often tapered at the ends, used for smoking.

cig·a·rette, cig·a·ret (sig′ə-ret′, sig′ə-ret′), *n.* [Fr. dim. of *cigare*, cigar], 1. a small cylinder of finely cut smoking tobacco rolled in thin paper or, rarely, in a tobacco leaf. 2. a similar cylinder filled with a drug or herb, as with cubeb, which is smoked to relieve asthma.

cigarette holder, a slender tube with a mouthpiece at one end and a hole at the other for holding a cigarette to be smoked.

cil·i·a (sil′i-ə), *n. pl.* [sing. CILIUM (-əm)], [L., pl. of *cilium*, eyelid], 1. the eyelashes. 2. in *biology*, hairlike outgrowths of certain cells, capable of vibratory movement. 3. in *botany*, small hairlike processes extending from certain plant cells, often forming a fringe or hairy surface, as on the underside of some leaves.

cil·i·ar·y (sil′i-er′i), *adj.* 1. of, like, or having cilia. 2. relating to the eyelashes. 3. relating to certain fine structures of the eyeball.

cil·i·ate (sil′i-it, sil′i-āt′), *adj.* in *botany* & *zoology*, having cilia. *n.* any of a class of microscopic protozoans characterized by cilia covering the body.

cil·i·at·ed (sil′i-ā′tid), *adj.* [LL. *ciliatus*], ciliate.

cil·ice (sil′is), *n.* [Fr. (also AS. *cilic*); L. *cilicium;* Gr. *kilikion*, garment of goat's hair < *Kilikia*, Cilicia (1), noted for its goats], 1. a very coarse cloth woven of hair; haircloth. 2. a garment made of this; hair shirt.

Ci·li·ci·a (si-lish′ə, si-lish′i-ə), *n.* 1. an ancient country and Roman province in southeastern Asia Minor, north of Cyprus: see **Roman Empire, map.** 2. a region along the coast of southern Turkey.

Ci·li·cian Gates (si-lish′ən, si-lish′i-ən), a pass in the Taurus Mountains, southeastern Asia Minor.

cil·i·o·late (sil′i-ə-lit, sil′i-ə-lāt′), *adj.* in *botany* & *zoology*, having very small cilia.

cil·i·um (sil′i-əm), *n.* singular of **cilia**.

Ci·ma·bu·e, Gio·van·ni (jô-vän′nē chē′mä-bōō′e), 1240?–1302?; Florentine painter.

Cim·ar·ron (sim′ə-rōn′, sim′ə-rōn′, sim′ə-ron′), *n.* a river flowing eastward from northeastern New Mexico into the Arkansas River, Oklahoma: length, 600 mi.

Cim·bri (sim′bri), *n. pl.* [L. < Gmc.; akin to Gr. *Kimbroi*], a Germanic people, supposed to have originated in Jutland, who invaded Gaul and northern Italy at the end of the 2d century B.C. and were finally defeated by the Romans near Vercellae (101 B.C.): the first Germanic invaders of Italy.

ci·mex (sī′meks), *n.* [*pl.* CIMICES (sim′ə-sēz′)], [L., a bug], a bedbug.

Cim·me·ri·an (si-mêr′i-ən), *n.* [< L. *Cimmerius*, pertaining to the *Cimmerii*, Cimmerians < Gr. *Kimmerioi*], any of a mythical people whose land was described by Homer as a region of perpetual mist and darkness. *adj.* dark; gloomy.

Ci·mon (sī′mən), *n.* Athenian statesman and general; lived 507–449 B.C.

C. in C., Commander in Chief.

cinch (sinch), *n.* [Sp. *cincha;* L. *cingulum*, a girdle < *cingere*, to surround, encircle], 1. a saddle or pack girth. 2. [Colloq.], a sure grip. 3. [Slang], a thing easy to do; sure thing. *v.t.* 1. to tighten a saddle girth on. 2. [Slang], *a*) to get a firm hold on. *b*) to make sure of.

cin·cho·na (sin-kō′nə), *n.* [after the Countess del *Chinchon*, wife of a Peruv. viceroy of the 17th c., who was cured of a fever by the use of the bark], 1. a tropical tree of South America, Asia, and the East Indies, from the bark of which quinine, quinidine, and other valuable medicinal alkaloids are obtained. 2. the bitter bark of this tree.

cin·chon·ic (sin-kon′ik), *adj.* of cinchona.

cin·chon·i·dine (sin-kon′ə-dēn′, sin-kon′ə-din), *n.* an alkaloid, $C_{19}H_{22}ON_2$, used in the treatment of malaria and to reduce fever.

cin·cho·nine (sin′kə-nēn′, sin′kə-nin), *n.* an alkaloid, $C_{19}H_{22}ON_2$, extracted from cinchona, closely related to quinine.

cin·cho·nism (sin′kə-niz′m), *n.* a pathological condition resulting from excessive use of cinchona bark or its derivatives, as quinine: it is characterized by headache, ringing in the ears, and deafness.

cin·cho·nize (sin′kə-nīz′), *v.t.* [CINCHONIZED (-nīzd′), CINCHONIZING], to treat with cinchona, quinine, etc.

Cin·cin·nat·i (sin′sə-nat′i, sin′sə-nat′ə), *n.* a city in southwestern Ohio, on the Ohio River: pop., 503,000.

Cin·cin·na·tus (sin′sə-nat′əs), *n.* (*Lucius Quincius Cincinnatus*), Roman statesman and general; lived 519?–439? B.C.; dictator of Rome (458, 439 B.C.).

cinc·ture (siŋk′chẽr), *n.* [L. *cinctura*, a girdle < *cingere*, to surround, gird], 1. an encircling; enclosure. 2. a belt or girdle. 3. a projecting ring or molding at the bottom and top of a pillar, immediately above the base or below the capital. *v.t.* [CINCTURED (-chẽrd), CINCTURING], to encircle with or as with a cincture.

cin·der (sin′dẽr), *n.* [ME. *sinder, cinder;* AS. *sinder,* dross of iron, slag; akin to G. *sinter,* dross of iron, stalactite, *sintern,* to trickle, coagulate; IE. base **sendhro-*, coagulating fluid, seen also in Czech *sádra* (< IE. **sēndhrā*), gypsum], 1. slag, as from the reduction of metallic ores. 2. volcanic slag. 3. any matter, as coal or wood, burned but not reduced to ashes. 4. a minute piece of such matter. 5. a coal that is still burning but not flaming. 6. *pl.* the ashes from coal or wood. ***v.t.*** to burn to a cinder or cinders.

Cin·der·el·la (sin′dẽr-el′ə), *n.* [*cinder* + dim. suffix, *-ella;* cf. Fr. *Cendrillon* (< *cendre,* ashes) & G. *Aschenbrödel,* lit., scullion (< *asche,* ashes + *brodeln,* to boil)], 1. the title character of a fairy tale, who is treated as a household drudge by her stepsisters and stepmother but attends a court ball through the intervention of her fairy godmother and eventually marries a prince. 2. a girl whose beauty or merit is for the time unrecognized.

cinder track, a racing track covered with fine cinders.

cin·der·y (sin′dẽr-i), ***adj.*** of, like, or containing cinders.

cin·e·ma (sin′ə-mə), *n.* [< *cinematograph*], 1. a motion picture. 2. a motion-picture theater.

the cinema, 1. the art or business of motion pictures. 2. motion pictures collectively.

Cin·e·ma·Scope (sin′ə-mə-skōp′), *n.* see **wide-angle.**

cin·e·mat·ic (sin′ə-mat′ik), ***adj.*** of motion pictures.

cin·e·mat·i·cal·ly (sin′ə-mat′i-k′l-i, sin′ə-mat′ik-li), ***adv.*** 1. in a cinematic manner. 2. from the viewpoint of the cinema.

cin·e·mat·ics (sin′ə-mat′iks), *n. pl.* 1. [construed as sing.], the art of motion pictures. 2. the artistic principles which can be observed in a motion picture or motion pictures.

cin·e·ma·tize (sin′ə-mə-tīz′), ***v.t. & v.i.*** [CINEMATIZED (-tīzd′), CINEMATIZING], to cinematograph.

cin·e·mat·o·graph (sin′ə-mat′ə-graf′, sin′ə-mat′ə-gräf′), *n.* [Fr. *cinématographe* < Gr. *kinēma, kinēmatos,* motion + *graphein,* to write], 1. [British], a motion-picture projector. 2. a camera for taking motion pictures. ***v.t. & v.i.*** to take motion pictures (of); cinematize.

cin·e·ma·tog·ra·pher (sin′ə-mə-tog′rə-fẽr), *n.* a person who films or produces motion pictures.

cin·e·mat·o·graph·ic (sin′ə-mat′ə-graf′ik), ***adj.*** of a cinematograph.

cin·e·ma·tog·ra·phy (sin′ə-mə-tog′rə-fi), *n.* the art of making motion pictures.

cin·e·ol (sin′i-ōl′, sin′i-ol′), *n.* cineole.

cin·e·ole (sin′i-ōl′), *n.* [< Mod. L. *oleum cinae* (oil of wormwood), with transposition of constituents], a liquid substance, $C_{10}H_{18}O$, with a camphorlike odor, present in turpentine and many essential oils.

Cin·e·ra·ma (sin′ə-ram′ə), *n.* see **wide-angle.**

cin·e·rar·i·a (sin′ə-râr′i-ə), *n.* [Mod. L. < L. *cinerarius,* pertaining to ashes < *cinis,* ashes: so named from the ash-colored down on the leaves], a short-stemmed plant with velvety, heart-shaped leaves, and daisylike flowers in shades of purple, red, pink, blue, or white.

cin·e·rar·i·um (sin′ə-râr′i-əm), *n.* [*pl.* CINERARIA (-ə)], [L. < *cinis,* ashes], a place to keep the ashes of cremated bodies.

cin·er·ar·y (sin′ə-rer′i), ***adj.*** [L. *cinerarius* < *cinis,* ashes], 1. of or for the ashes of the cremated dead. 2. of or for ashes.

cin·er·a·tor (sin′ə-rā′tẽr), *n.* [*cinerarium* + *-ator*], a furnace for cremation; crematory.

ci·ne·re·ous (si-nêr′i-əs), ***adj.*** [L. *cinerosus* < *cinis,* ashes], 1. like ashes. 2. of the color of ashes; ash-gray.

cin·er·i·tious (sin′ẽr-ish′əs), ***adj.*** cinereous.

Cin·ga·lese (siŋ′gə-lēz′), ***n. & adj.*** Singhalese.

cin·gu·late (siŋ′gyoo-lit, siŋ′gyoo-lāt′), ***adj.*** having a cingulum.

cin·gu·lat·ed (siŋ′gyoo-lā′tid), ***adj.*** cingulate.

cin·gu·lum (siŋ′gyoo-ləm), *n.* [*pl.* CINGULA (-lə)], [L. < *cingere,* to encircle, gird], 1. a girdle; belt. 2. in *zoology,* a band or girdle, as of color.

cin·na·bar (sin′ə-bär′), *n.* [ME. *cynoper;* OFr. *cinabre, cenobre* < L. *cinnabaris;* Gr. *kinnabari;* Ar. *zinjafr;* Per. *zinjifrah;* confused in OFr. with *sinoble, sinople,* red color < L. *sinopis,* kind of red ochre < *Sinopis* (*terra*), (earth) of Sinope (Gr. *Sinōpē*), Greek colony], 1. mercuric sulfide, HgS, a heavy, bright-red mineral, the principal ore of mercury. 2. artificial mercuric sulfide, used as a red pigment. 3. vermilion; brilliant red.

cin·nam·ic (si-nam′ik, sin′ə-mik), ***adj.*** 1. of or derived from cinnamon. 2. designating a white, crystalline, organic acid, $C_6H_5 \cdot CH{:}CH \cdot COOH$, produced from benzaldehyde: the corresponding aldehyde gives oil of cinnamon its characteristic flavor and odor.

cin·na·mon (sin′ə-mən), *n.* [ME. *cinamome;* OFr. *cinnamone;* L. *cinnamomum;* Gr. *kinnamōmon;* Heb. *qinnāmōn,* cinnamon], 1. the yellowish-brown spice made from the dried inner bark of a tree or shrub of the laurel family native to the East Indies. 2. this bark. 3. any tree or shrub from which this bark is obtained. 4. yellowish brown. ***adj.*** 1. yellowish-brown. 2. made or flavored with cinnamon.

cinnamon bear, a brown variety of the American black bear.

cinnamon stone, essonite, a variety of garnet.

cinque (siŋk), *n.* [ME. *cink;* OFr. *cinc* (Fr. *cinq*); L. *quinque,* five; akin to Gr. *pente,* Sans. *pañca;* see FIVE], 1. a five on dice or playing cards. 2. a throw in dice in which a five turns up.

cin·que·cen·tist (chiŋ′kwə-chen′tist), *n.* an Italian artist or writer of the cinquecento.

cin·que·cen·to (chiŋ′kwə-chen′tō), *n.* [< It. *mil cinque cento;* cf. CINQUE], 1. the 16th century in Italian art and literature. 2. the style of Italian art of this period.

cinque·foil (siŋk′foil′), *n.* [It. *cinquefoglie;* L. *quinquefolium;* see CINQUE & FOIL], 1. a plant of the rose family with yellow flowers and leaves composed of five leaflets. 2. in *architecture,* a circular design made up of five converging arcs.

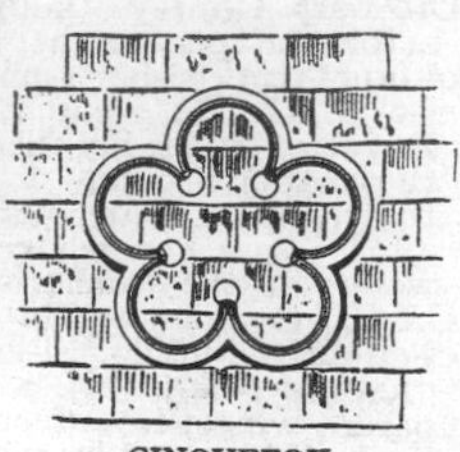
CINQUEFOIL

Cinque Ports (siŋk), [ME. *sink pors;* see CINQUE], a group of towns on the south-east coast of England which formerly provided ships and men to the British navy, for which they received special privileges: to the original five towns (Hastings, Romney, Hythe, Dover, and Sandwich) were later added Winchelsea and Rye.

C.I.O., CIO, Congress of Industrial Organizations: see **AFL-CIO.**

ci·on (sī′ən), *n.* [OFr.; see SCION], a shoot or bud of a plant, especially one for planting or grafting: also spelled **scion.**

Ci·pan·go (si-paŋ′gō), *n.* [Poetic], Japan: name used by Marco Polo.

ci·pher (sī′fẽr), *n.* [ME. *ciphre;* OFr. *cyfre;* LL. *cifra* < Ar. *ṣifr, ṣefr,* a cipher, nothing < *ṣafara,* to be empty], 1. a naught; zero; 0. 2. a person or thing without importance or value; nonentity. 3. secret writing meant to be understood only by those who have the key to it; code. 4. the key to such a code. 5. an intricate weaving together of letters, as the initials of a name; monogram. 6. any Arabic numeral. ***v.i.*** 1. to solve arithmetical problems. 2. to use secret writing. ***v.t.*** 1. to solve by arithmetic. 2. to express in secret writing. Also spelled **cypher.**

cip·o·lin (sip′ə-lin), *n.* [Fr. < It. *cipollino,* lit., little onion (ult. < L. *cepa,* onion): from its structure], a variety of Italian marble with alternating layers or streaks of color, especially of white and green.

cir., circ., 1. circa. 2. circular. 3. circulation. 4. circumference.

cir·ca (sũr′kə), ***prep.*** [L.], about: used to indicate an appoximate date, figure, etc., as, *circa* 1650: abbreviated **c., ca., cir., circ., C.**

Cir·cas·si·a (sẽr-kash′i-ə, sẽr-kash′ə), *n.* region of the U.S.S.R., north of the Caucasus Mountains, on the shores of the Black Sea.

Cir·cas·si·an (sẽr-kash′i-ən, sẽr-kash′ən), *n.* 1. a member of a group of Caucasian tribes of Circassia. 2. an inhabitant of Circassia. 3. the non-Indo-European, North Caucasian language of the Circassians. ***adj.*** of Circassia, its people, or their language.

Cir·ce (sũr′si), *n.* [L.; Gr. *Kirkē*], in Homer's *Odyssey,* an enchantress who turned men into swine.

Cir·ce·an, Cir·cae·an (sẽr-sē′ən), ***adj.*** of or like Circe; dangerously bewitching.

cir·ci·nate (sũr′s′n-āt′), ***adj.*** [L. *circinatus,* pp. of *circinare,* to make round < *circinus* < Gr. *kirkinos,* a circle], rolled into a coil on its axis with the apex in the center, as the new fronds of a fern.

cir·cle (sũr′k′l), *n.* [ME. *cercle, sercle;* OFr. *cercle;* L. *circulus,* a circle, dim. of *circus;* Gr. *kirkos,* a ring], 1. a plane figure bounded by a single curved line every point of which is equally distant from the point at the center of the figure. 2. the line bounding such a figure; circumference. 3. anything shaped like a circle, as the orb of a heavenly body or a halo around it, a ring, crown, etc. 4. the orbit of a planet. 5. a semicircular tier of seats in a theater: as, the dress *circle.* 6. a cycle; period; complete or recurring series, usually ending as it began. 7. a group of people bound together by common interests; group; coterie. 8. a territorial division. 9. range; extent; scope, as of influence or interest. 10. an imaginary circle on the surface of the earth: the *great circle* is a circle with its plane passing through the center of the earth; the *Arctic Circle* is a parallel of latitude. 11. in *logic,* a fault in reasoning in which the premise and conclusion are each in turn used to prove the other. ***v.t.*** [CIRCLED (-k′ld), CIRCLING], 1. to form a circle around; encompass; surround. 2. to move around, as in a circle. ***v.i.*** to go around in a circle; revolve. —***SYN.*** see **coterie.**

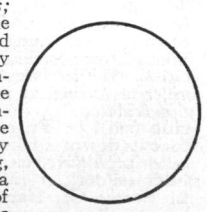

CIRCLE

cir·cler (sũr′klẽr), *n.* a person or thing that circles.

cir·clet (sũr′klit), *n.* [dim. of *circle*], 1. a small circle. 2. a circular band worn as an ornament on the finger, arm, neck, or head.

cir·cuit (sũr′kit), *n.* [OFr. < L. *circuitus*, a going round, circuit < *circumire; circum-*, around + *ire*, to go], 1. the line or the length of the line forming the boundaries of an area. 2. the area bounded. 3. a going around something; revolving; course or journey around: as, the moon's *circuit* of the earth. 4. the regular journey of a person performing his duties, as of an itinerant preacher or a judge holding court at designated places. 5. the district periodically traveled through in the performance of duties, as the territory under the jurisdiction of certain judges. 6. a number of associated theaters at which plays, films, etc. are shown in turn. 7. in *electricity*, a complete or partial path over which current may flow. 8. in *radio*, a hookup. *v.i.* to go in a circuit. *v.t.* to make a circuit of. —*SYN.* see **circumference.**

circuit binding, a bookbinding with flexible edges projecting beyond the leaves to protect them.

circuit breaker, a device that automatically interrupts the flow of an electric current, as when the current becomes excessive.

circuit edges, the projecting edges of a circuit binding.

cir·cu·i·tous (sẽr-kū′i-təs), *adj.* [LL. *circuitosus* < L. *circuitus;* see CIRCUIT], roundabout; indirect; devious.

circuit rider, a Methodist minister who travels from station to station in his circuit to preach.

cir·cuit·ry (sũr′kit-ri), *n.* [< *circuit* + *-ry*], the scheme or system of an electric circuit or circuits, or the elements comprising such a circuit.

cir·cu·i·ty (sẽr-kū′i-ti), *n.* [OFr. *circuité* < L. *circuitus*], the quality or state of being circuitous.

cir·cu·lar (sũr′kyoo-lẽr), *adj.* [L. *circularis*], 1. in the shape of a circle; round. 2. relating to a circle. Abbreviated **cir., circ.** 3. moving in a circle. 4. roundabout; circuitous. 5. intended for circulation among a number of people. *n.* an advertisement, letter, etc., usually prepared in quantities, intended for circulation. —*SYN.* see **round.**

cir·cu·lar·i·ty (sũr′kyoo-lar′ə-ti), *n.* [*pl.* CIRCULARITIES (-tiz)], circular form.

cir·cu·lar·ize (sũr′kyoo-lẽr-īz′), *v.t.* [CIRCULARIZED (-īzd′), CIRCULARIZING], 1. to make circular; make round. 2. to send circulars to.

circular measure, a system for measuring circles:
1 circle = 360 degrees, or 4 quadrants
1 quadrant = 90 degrees
1 degree = 60 minutes
1 minute = 60 seconds

circular mil, a unit of measurement for the thickness of wires, equal to the area of a circle with a diameter of one mil.

circular saw, a saw in the form of a disk with a toothed edge, rotated at high speed by a motor.

cir·cu·late (sur′kyoo-lāt′), *v.i.* [CIRCULATED (-id), CIRCULATING], [< L. *circulatus*, pp. of *circulari*, to form a circle], 1. to move in a circle, circuit, or course and return to the same point, as the blood. 2. to move around; go from person to person or from place to place, as money, rumor, etc. 3. to be distributed to a circle of readers. 4. in *mathematics*, to have an infinitely recurring series of digits: said of a decimal (e.g., .421421-421. . .). *v.t.* to cause to move around from one person or place to another; place in circulation.

circulating library, a library from which books can be borrowed, sometimes for a small daily fee.

circulating medium, any medium of exchange that can be passed without endorsement, as coin; currency.

cir·cu·la·tion (sũr′kyoo-lā′shən), *n.* [L. *circulatio;* see CIRCULATE], 1. a moving around from place to place, as water through pipes. 2. the movement of the blood in the veins and arteries throughout the body. 3. the flow of sap in a plant. 4. the passing of something, as money, news, etc., from person to person or place to place. 5. the distribution of newspapers, magazines, etc. among readers. 6. the extent to which something is circulated, as the average number of copies of a magazine sold in a given period: abbreviated **cir., circ.**

cir·cu·la·tive (sũr′kyoo-lā′tiv), *adj.* 1. circulating or tending to circulate. 2. causing circulation.

cir·cu·la·tor (sũr′kyoo-lā′tẽr), *n.* [L.], 1. a person or thing that circulates something. 2. a circulating decimal: see **circulate** (sense 4).

cir·cu·la·to·ry (sũr′kyoo-lə-tôr′i, sũr′kyoo-lə-tō′ri), *adj.* [L. *circulatorius*], relating to circulation, as of the blood.

cir·cum- (sũr′kəm, sẽr-kum′), [< L. *circum*, around, about], a prefix meaning *around, about, surrounding, on all sides*, as in *circumnavigate, circumscribe, circumstance.*

cir·cum·am·bi·ence (sũr′kəm-am′bi-əns), *n.* [see CIRCUMAMBIENT], a surrounding or encircling.

cir·cum·am·bi·en·cy (sũr′kəm-am′bi-ən-si), *n.* 1. the quality or condition or being circumambient. 2. surroundings; environment.

cir·cum·am·bi·ent (sũr′kəm-am′bi-ənt), *adj.* [*circum-* + *ambient*], enclosing on all sides; surrounding.

cir·cum·am·bu·late (sũr′kəm-am′byoo-lāt′), *v.t. & v.i.* [CIRCUMAMBULATED (-id), CIRCUMAMBULATING], [LL. *circumambulatus*, pp. of *circumambulare* < L. *circum-*, about + *ambulare;* see AMBULATE], to walk around.

cir·cum·am·bu·la·to·ry (sũr′kəm-am′byoo-lə-tôr′i, sũr′kəm-am′byoo-lə-tō′ri), *adj.* circumambulating; roundabout.

cir·cum·bend·i·bus (sũr′kəm-ben′di-bəs), *n.* [jocular formation < L. *circum*, about + Eng. *bend* + L. *-ibus*, ending of L. abl. pl.], a roundabout way; circumlocution.

cir·cum·cise (sũr′kəm-sīz′), *v.t.* [CIRCUMCISED (-sīzd′), CIRCUMCISING], [ME. *circumcisen;* OFr. *circonciser* < L. *circumcisus*, pp. of *circumcidere*, to cut around < *circum-*, around + *caedere*, to cut], 1. to cut off all or part of the foreskin of; also, in certain primitive rituals, to cut off the labia minora of. 2. in the *Bible*, to purify; cleanse from sin.

cir·cum·ci·sion (sũr′kəm-sizh′ən), *n.* [L. *circumcisio*], 1. a circumcising, either as a religious rite of the Jews, Moslems, etc., or as a hygienic measure. 2. in the *Bible*, a cleansing from sin. 3. [C-], the festival on January 1 commemorating the circumcision of Jesus.

cir·cum·fer·ence (sẽr-kum′fẽr-əns), *n.* [ME.; L. *circumferentia* < *circumferens*, ppr. of *circumferre; circum-*, around + *ferre*, to carry], 1. the line bounding a circle or other rounded surface. 2. the measurement of this line; distance around. Abbreviated **cir., circ.**

SYN.—**circumference** refers to the line bounding a circle or any approximately circular or elliptical area; **perimeter** extends the meaning to a line bounding any area, as a triangle, square, or polygon; **periphery**, in its literal sense identical with **perimeter**, is more frequently used of the edge of a concrete object or in an extended metaphorical sense (the *periphery* of understanding); **circuit** now usually refers to a traveling around a periphery (the moon's *circuit* of the earth).

cir·cum·fer·en·tial (sẽr-kum′fẽr-en′shəl), *adj.* of, at, or close to the circumference.

cir·cum·flex (sũr′kəm-fleks′), *n.* [L. *circumflexus*, pp. of *circumflectere; circum-*, around + *flectere*, to bend], a mark (ˆ, ⌒, ˜) used over a vowel in certain languages, as French, or in phonetic keys to indicate some tone or quality of the pronunciation: also **circumflex accent.** *adj.* 1. of or marked by a circumflex. 2. curved; bending or twisting around. *v.t.* 1. to curve; bend or twist around. 2. to pronounce or write with a circumflex.

cir·cum·flex·ion (sũr′kəm-flek′shən), *n.* [LL. *circumflexis;* see CIRCUMFLEX], a bending or winding around.

cir·cum·flu·ent (sẽr-kum′floo-ənt), *adj.* [L. *circumfluens*, ppr. of *circumfluere*, to flow around; *circum-*, around + *fluere*, to flow], flowing around; surrounding; encompassing.

cir·cum·flu·ous (sẽr-kum′floo-əs), *adj.* [L. *circumfluus* < *circumfluere*], 1. circumfluent. 2. surrounded by water.

cir·cum·fuse (sũr′kəm-fūz′), *v.t.* [CIRCUMFUSED (-fūzd′), CIRCUMFUSING], [L. *circumfusus*, pp. of *circumfundere; circum-*, around + *fundere*, to pour], 1. to pour or spread (a fluid) around. 2. to surround (*with* a fluid); bathe or suffuse (*in*).

cir·cum·fu·sion (sũr′kəm-fū′zhən), *n.* a circumfusing or being circumfused.

cir·cum·lo·cu·tion (sũr′kəm-lō-kū′shən), *n.* [L. *circumlocutio;* see CIRCUM- & LOCUTION], 1. a roundabout, indirect, or lengthy way of expressing something; periphrasis. 2. an instance of this.

cir·cum·loc·u·to·ry (sũr′kəm-lok′yoo-tôr′i, sũr′kəm-lok′yoo-tō′ri), *adj.* characterized by circumlocution.

cir·cum·nav·i·gate (sũr′kəm-nav′ə-gāt′), *v.t.* [< L. *circumnavigatus*, pp. of *circumnavigare;* see CIRCUM- & NAVIGATE], to sail around (the earth, etc.).

cir·cum·nav·i·ga·tion (sũr′kəm-nav′ə-gā′shən), *n.* a circumnavigating.

cir·cum·nav·i·ga·tor (sũr′kəm-nav′ə-gā′tẽr), *n.* a person who circumnavigates.

cir·cum·nu·ta·tion (sũr′kəm-nyoo-tā′shən), *n.* [*circum-* + *nutation*], the irregular spiral or elliptical rotation of the apex of a growing stem, root, or shoot, caused by differences in the rate of growth of the opposite sides.

cir·cum·po·lar (sũr′kəm-pō′lẽr), *adj.* [*circum-* + *polar*], 1. surrounding or near either pole of the earth. 2. in *astronomy*, moving around either of the heavenly poles: said of stars always above the horizon.

cir·cum·ro·tate (sũr′kəm-rō′tāt), *v.i.* [CIRCUMROTATED (-id), CIRCUMROTATING], to turn like a wheel; rotate.

cir·cum·scis·sile (sũr′kəm-sis′il), *adj.* [*circum-* + *scissile*], in *botany*, opening or splitting by a transverse fissure around the circumference, leaving an upper and lower half: said of certain seed pods or capsules.

cir·cum·scribe (sũr′kəm-skrīb′), *v.t.* [CIRCUMSCRIBED (-skrībd′), CIRCUMSCRIBING], [ME. *circumscriven;* L. *circumscribere; circum-*, around + *scribere*, to write, draw], 1. to trace a line around; encircle; encompass. 2. to limit; confine. 3. in *geometry*, *a)* to draw a figure around (another figure) so as to touch it at as many points as possible: as, *circumscribe* a triangle with a circle. *b*) to be thus drawn around: as, the hexagon *circumscribed* the square. —*SYN.* see **limit.**

cir·cum·scrip·tion (sũr′kəm-skrip′shən), ***n.*** [L. *circumscriptio* < pp. of *circumscribere*], 1. a circumscribing or being circumscribed. 2. a boundary or outline. 3. a limitation or restriction. 4. a surrounding substance. 5. a circumscribed space. 6. an inscription around a coin, medal, etc.

cir·cum·spect (sũr′kəm-spekt′), ***adj.*** [L. *circumspectus*, pp. of *circumspicere*, to look about < *circum-*, around + *specere*, to look], carefully attentive to all circumstances that may relate to an action, judgment, conduct, etc.; cautious; careful. —*SYN.* see **careful.**

cir·cum·spec·tion (sũr′kəm-spek′shən), ***n.*** [L. *circumspectio;* see CIRCUMSPECT], careful attention to all circumstances relating to an action, judgment, etc.; circumspect action or conduct; prudence; caution.

cir·cum·stance (sũr′kəm-stans′), ***n.*** [ME.; OFr. *circumstance, circonstance;* L. *circumstantia*, a standing around, condition < *circumstare; circum-*, around + *stare*, to stand], 1. a fact or event accompanying another fact or event, either incidentally or as an essential condition or determining factor: as, if you knew all the *circumstances* you would judge me differently. 2. *pl.* conditions surrounding and affecting a person, especially financial conditions: as, they are in comfortable *circumstances*. 3. ceremony; show: as, pomp and *circumstance*. 4. accompanying or surrounding detail, especially fullness of detail: as, the story was told with great *circumstance*. ***v.t.*** [CIRCUMSTANCED (-stanst′), CIRCUMSTANCING], to place in certain circumstances. —*SYN.* see **occurrence.**

under no circumstances, never; under no conditions.
under the circumstances, conditions being what they are or were.

cir·cum·stanced (sũr′kəm-stanst′), ***adj.*** 1. being in a specified circumstance, or condition; situated. 2. supported by certain circumstances, or facts.

cir·cum·stan·tial (sũr′kəm-stan′shəl), ***adj.*** 1. having to do with, or depending on, circumstances. 2. incidental; not of primary importance. 3. full of details; complete.

circumstantial evidence, in *law*, proof of certain attendant circumstances which is used as evidence to infer the proof of a fact: as, proof of possession of stolen property is *circumstantial evidence* in a case of theft.

cir·cum·stan·ti·al·i·ty (sũr′kəm-stan′shi-al′ə-ti), ***n.*** 1. the quality of being circumstantial. 2. particularity; detail.

cir·cum·stan·ti·ate (sũr′kəm-stan′shi-āt′), ***v.t.*** [CIRCUMSTANTIATED (-id), CIRCUMSTANTIATING], to verify in every particular; give detailed proof or support of.

cir·cum·stan·ti·a·tion (sũr′kəm-stan′shi-ā′shən), ***n.*** a circumstantiating or being circumstantiated.

cir·cum·val·late (sũr′kəm-val′āt), ***v.t.*** [CIRCUMVALLATED (-id), CIRCUMVALLATING], [< L. *circumvallatus*, pp. of *circumvallare; circum-*, around + *vallare* < *vallum*, a wall, rampart], to surround with a wall or trench, as for defense. ***adj.*** surrounded by a wall, trench, etc.

cir·cum·vent (sũr′kəm-vent′), ***v.t.*** [< L. *circumventus*, pp. of *circumvenire; circum-*, around + *venire*, to come], 1. to go around; surround. 2. to surround by trickery or craft; hence, 3. to catch in a trap. 4. to gain superiority over; outwit. 5. to prevent from happening.

cir·cum·ven·tion (sũr′kəm-ven′shən), ***n.*** [L. *circumventio*], a circumventing or being circumvented.

cir·cum·ven·tive (sũr′kəm-ven′tiv), ***adj.*** circumventing.

cir·cum·vo·lu·tion (sũr′kəm-və-lōō′shən), ***n.*** [LL. *circumvolutio* < L. *circumvolutus*, pp. of *circumvolvere; circum-*, around + *volvere*, to turn], 1. a rolling, turning around, or coiling. 2. the state of being rolled around, folded, or coiled. 3. a fold or twist. 4. a circuitous course or form.

cir·cum·volve (sũr′kəm-volv′), ***v.t. & v.i.*** [CIRCUMVOLVED (-volvd′), CIRCUMVOLVING], [L. *circumvolvere; circum-*, around + *volvere*, to roll], to revolve.

cir·cus (sũr′kəs), ***n.*** [L., a circle, ring, racecourse; Gr. *kirkos*, a circle], 1. in ancient Rome, an oval or oblong arena with tiers of seats around it, used for games, chariot races, etc. 2. a similar arena, usually enclosed in a tent, for a show of acrobats, wild animals, clowns, etc. 3. a traveling show of this sort. 4. the performance of such a show. 5. [British], a circular open place where many streets come together: as, Piccadilly *Circus*. 6. [Colloq.], any riotously entertaining person, thing, etc.

Cir·cus Max·i·mus (sũr′kəs mak′si-məs), [L., lit., largest racecourse], a large amphitheater built in Rome c. 329 B.C., used for chariot races, games, etc.

Cir·e·na·i·ca (sir′ə-nā′i-kə), ***n.*** a district of northeastern Libya: area, 212,000 sq. mi.; pop., 165,000: also spelled **Cyrenaica.**

cirque (sũrk), ***n.*** [Fr.; L. *circus;* see CIRCUS], 1. a circular space or arrangement. 2. [Poetic], a circle; ring. 3. [Archaic], a circus. 4. in *geology*, a natural amphitheater; steep, hollow excavation in a mountain, made by erosion, etc.

cir·rate (sir′āt), ***adj.*** [L. *cirratus* < *cirrus*, a curl], in *biology*, having cirri.

cir·rho·sis (si-rō′sis), ***n.*** [LL. < Gr. *kirrhos*, tawny: so named by R. T. H. Laënnec (1781–1826) because of the orange-yellow appearance of the diseased liver], a degenerative disease in an organ of the body, especially the liver, marked by excess formation of connective tissue and the subsequent contraction of the organ.

cir·rhot·ic (si-rot′ik), ***adj.*** of, caused by, or having cirrhosis.

cir·ri (sir′ī), ***n.*** plural of **cirrus.**

cir·ri- (sir′i), [< L. *cirrus*], a combining form meaning *curl, ringlet*, as in *cirriped:* also **cirro-, cirrhi-, cirrho-.**

cir·ri·ped (sir′i-ped′), ***n.*** [< Mod. L. *Cirripedia*, name of the order < *cirri-* + L. *pes, pedis*, foot], a kind of crustacean, as a barnacle, having curl-shaped appendages and attaching itself parasitically, in its adult stage, to other organisms, rocks, the bottoms of ships, etc. ***adj.*** of a cirriped or the cirripeds.

cir·ro- (sir′ō), cirri-: also spelled **cirrho-**

cir·ro-cu·mu·lus (sir′ō-kū′myoo-ləs), ***n.*** a formation of small, white, fleecy clouds in groups or rows: mean height, 27,000 ft.: also called *mackerel sky.*

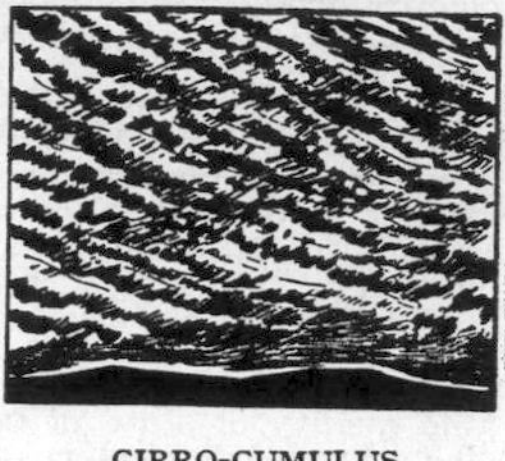

CIRRO-CUMULUS

cir·rose (sir′ōs), ***adj.*** [< L. *cirrus*, a curl; + *-ose*], 1. having a cirrus or cirri. 2. resembling cirri.

cir·ro-stra·tus (sir′ō-strā′təs), ***n.*** a high, thin, delicate formation of clouds, often resembling a tangled web: mean height, 32,000 ft.

cir·rous (sir′əs), ***adj.*** cirrose.

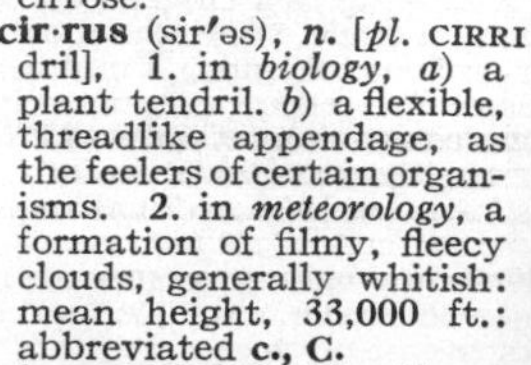

cir·rus (sir′əs), ***n.*** [*pl.* CIRRI (-ī)], [L., a lock, curl, tendril], 1. in *biology*, *a*) a plant tendril. *b*) a flexible, threadlike appendage, as the feelers of certain organisms. 2. in *meteorology*, a formation of filmy, fleecy clouds, generally whitish: mean height, 33,000 ft.: abbreviated **c., C.**

CIRRUS

cir·so- (sũr′sō), [Gr. *kirso-, kirs-* < *kirsos*, enlargement of a vein], a combining form meaning *an enlarged vein:* also, before a vowel, **cirs-.**

cir·soid (sũr′soid), ***adj.*** [orig. < Gr. *kirsoeidēs*, but often thought of as Eng. *cirso-* + *-id*], like a varix, or enlarged blood vessel; varicose.

cis- (sis), [< L. *cis*, on this side], a prefix meaning: 1. *on this side of*, as in *cisalpine*. 2. *subsequent to.*

cis·al·pine (sis-al′pīn, sis-al′pin), ***adj.*** [L. *cisalpinus;* see CIS- & ALPINE], on this (the southern) side of the Alps: from the viewpoint of Rome.

cis·at·lan·tic (sis′ət-lan′tik), ***adj.*** on this (the speaker's) side of the Atlantic.

Cis·cau·ca·sia (sis′kô-kā′zhə, sis′kô-kā′shə), ***n.*** the part of Caucasia north of the Caucasus.

cis·co (sis′kō), ***n.*** [*pl.* CISCOES, CISCOS (-kōz)], [< Canad. Fr. *ciscovette* for *siskowet, siskowit* < Algonquian], any of a number of whitefishes and herrings found in the Great Lakes.

cis·mon·tane (sis-mon′tān), ***adj.*** on this side of the mountains, especially of the Alps.

cis·pa·dane (sis′pə-dān′, sis-pā′dān), ***adj.*** [*cis-* + L. *Padanus*, Po River], on this (the southern) side of the Po River: from the viewpoint of Rome.

cis·soid (sis′oid), ***n.*** [Gr. *kissoeidēs*, ivylike < *kissos*, ivy + *eidos*, form], in *mathematics*, a curve converging into an apex. ***adj.*** designating the angle formed by the concave sides of two intersecting curves: opposed to *sistroid.*

cist (sist; *also, for 1*, kist), ***n.*** [L. *cista;* Gr. *kistē* (cf. CHEST); sense 1 via W. *kist faen*, lit., stone coffin], 1. a primitive tomb made of stone slabs or hollowed out of rock: also **kist.** 2. in ancient Greece, a box or chest containing sacred utensils.

cis·ta·ceous (sis-tā′shəs), ***adj.*** [Mod. L. *cistus* (< Gr. *kistos*, rockrose); + *-aceous*], belonging to the rockrose family of shrubs or woody herbs.

Cis·ter·cian (sis-tũr′shən, sis-tũr′shi-ən), ***n.*** [Fr. *Cistercien* < ML. *Cistercium* (now *Cîteaux*, France), original convent of the order], a monk of the Cistercian Order. ***adj.*** of the Cistercians.

Cistercian Order, a monastic order, a stricter branch of the Benedictine Order, established in 1098 at Cîteaux, France.

cis·tern (sis′tẽrn), ***n.*** [ME. & OFr. *cisterne;* L. *cisterna*, reservoir for water < *cista* (Gr. *kistē*), a chest, box; cf. CHEST], 1. a large receptacle for storing water; especially, a tank in which rain water is collected for use. 2. in *anatomy*, a sac or cavity containing a natural fluid of the body.

cis·ter·na (sis-tũr′nə), ***n.*** [L.; cf. CISTERN], in *anatomy*, a cistern; specifically, any of the enlarged spaces below the arachnoid.
cit., 1. citation. 2. cited. 3. citizen.
cit·a·ble (sit′ə-b'l), ***adj.*** that can or may be cited: also spelled **citeable.**
cit·a·del (sit′ə-d'l, sit′ə-del′), ***n.*** [Fr. *citadelle;* It. *cittadella,* dim. of *cittade,* city < L. *civitas,* citizenship, state], 1. a fortress on a commanding height for defense of a city. 2. a fortified place; stronghold. 3. a refuge; place of retreat. 4. the heavily armored central structure of a warship, on which the guns are mounted.
ci·ta·tion (sī-tā′shən), ***n.*** [ME. *citacion;* OFr. *citation;* L. *citatio,* a summoning < pp. of *citare;* see CITE], 1. a summons to appear before a court of law. 2. a citing; quoting. 3. a passage cited; quotation. 4. honorable mention in an official report for bravery or meritorious service in the armed forces. 5. a reference to a legal statute, a previous law case, a written authority, etc. Abbreviated **cit.**
ci·ta·to·ry (sī′tə-tôr′i, sī′tə-tō′ri), ***adj.*** of a citation.
cite (sīt), ***v.t.*** [CITED (-id), CITING], [Fr. *citer,* to summon; L. *citare,* to arouse, summon < *ciere,* to put into motion, rouse], 1. to summon to appear before a court of law. 2. to summon; stir to action. 3. to quote (a passage, book, speech, writer, etc.). 4. to refer to or mention by way of example, proof, explanation, etc. 5. to mention in an official report for bravery or meritorious service in the armed forces.
cith·a·ra (sith′ə-rə), ***n.*** [L.; Gr. *kithara*], an ancient musical instrument somewhat resembling a lyre: precursor of the zither.

CITHARA

cith·er (sith′ẽr), ***n.*** [Fr. *cithare* < L. *cithara*], 1. a cithara. 2. loosely, a cithern or zither.
cith·ern (sith′ẽrn), ***n.*** [< Fr. *cithare* (see CITHER); prob. influenced by ME. *giterne* (see GITTERN)], a stringed musical instrument of the 16th century, somewhat resembling a guitar: also **cittern.**
cit·ied (sit′id), ***adj.*** 1. having a city or cities on it: as, the *citied* earth. 2. like a city.
cit·i·fied (sit′i-fīd′), ***adj.*** having the manners, dress, etc. attributed to city people.
cit·i·zen (sit′ə-z'n), ***n.*** [ME. & Anglo-Fr. *citizein,* altered (after *denizen,* etc.) < OFr. *citeain* (Fr. *citoyen*) < *cite;* see CITY; sense 3 influenced by use of Fr. *citoyen* during the French Revolution], 1. formerly, a native or inhabitant, especially a freeman or burgess, of a town or city; hence, 2. loosely, a native, inhabitant, or denizen of any place. 3. a member of a state or nation, especially one with a republican form of government, who owes allegiance to it by birth or naturalization and is entitled to full civil rights: as, this British subject is now an American *citizen;* abbreviated **cit.** 4. a civilian, as distinguished from a person in military service, a policeman, etc.
citizen of the world, a person who feels at home in various countries; cosmopolitan person.
SYN.—**citizen** refers to a member of a state or nation, especially one with a republican government, who owes it allegiance and is entitled to full civil rights either by birth or naturalization; **subject** is the term used when the government is headed by a monarch or other sovereign; **national** is applied to a person residing away from the country of which he is, or once was, a citizen or subject, and is especially used of one another by fellow countrymen living abroad; **native** refers to one who was born in the country under question and is applied specifically to an original or indigenous inhabitant of the region. —***ANT.*** alien.
cit·i·zen·ess (sit′ə-z'n-is), ***n.*** [orig. transl. of Fr. *citoyenne* (Revolutionary term)], a woman citizen.
cit·i·zen·ry (sit′ə-z'n-ri), ***n.*** citizens collectively.
cit·i·zen·ship (sit′ə-z'n-ship′), ***n.*** [*citizen* + *-ship*], 1. the status or condition of a citizen. 2. the duties, rights, and privileges of this status.
citizenship papers, the document stating that a naturalized person has been formally declared a citizen.
Cit·lal·te·petl (sēt′läl-tā′pet'l), ***n.*** Orizaba, a mountain in Mexico.
cit·ole (sit′ōl, si-tōl′), ***n.*** [ME.; OFr.; orig. dim. < L. *cithara;* cf. ZITHER, CITHERN], a cithern.
‡ci·toy·en (sē′twȧ′yaṅ′), ***n.*** [*pl.* CITOYENS (-yaṅ′)], [Fr. (fem., *citoyenne*)], a citizen.
cit·ra- (sit′rə), [L. *citra,* on this side of < *citer,* hither], [Rare], a combining form meaning *on this side of, cis-,* as in *citramontane.*
cit·ral (sit′rəl), ***n.*** [*citron* + *al*dehyde], a liquid aldehyde, C_9H_{15}·CHO, with a pleasant odor, found in oil of lemon, oil of lime, etc.
cit·rate (sit′rāt, sit′rit, sī′trāt), ***n.*** [< *citrus* + *-ate*], a salt or ester of citric acid.
cit·re·ous (sit′ri-əs), ***adj.*** [L. *citreus;* see CITRUS], lemon-yellow.
cit·ric (sit′rik), ***adj.*** [< *citrus* + *-ic*], 1. of or from citrons, lemons, oranges, or similar fruits. 2. designating or of an acid, $C_6H_8O_7$, obtained from such fruits, used in making flavoring extracts, dyes, citrates, etc.
cit·rin (sit′rin), ***n.*** [< *citrus* + *-in*], vitamin P, found in lemon juice and paprika.
cit·rine (sit′rin), ***adj.*** [< *citrus* + *-ine*], lemon-yellow. ***n.*** 1. lemon yellow. 2. a yellow, semiprecious variety of quartz resembling topaz.
cit·ron (sit′rən), ***n.*** [Fr., lemon (cf. *cédrat,* citron tree, citron); It. *citrone* < L. *citrus* (**citrum*); Gr. *kitron;* see CITRUS], 1. a yellow, thick-skinned fruit resembling a lime or lemon but larger and less acid. 2. the semitropical tree or shrub bearing this fruit. 3. the candied rind of this fruit, used as a confection, in fruitcake, etc. 4. the citron melon.
cit·ron·el·la (sit′rə-nel′ə), ***n.*** [Mod. L. < *citron;* see CITRON], 1. a volatile, sharp-smelling oil used in perfume, soap, etc. and to keep insects away: also **citronella oil.** 2. the southern Asiatic grass from which this oil is derived.
citron melon, a kind of watermelon with hard, white flesh.
citron wood, 1. the wood of the citron tree. 2. the hard, fragrant wood of the sandarac tree.
cit·rous (sit′rəs), ***adj.*** 1. of fleshy fruits with a thick rind and acid flesh, as oranges, lemons, limes, grapefruit, and citrons. 2. of the trees that bear these fruits; citrus.
cit·rus (sit′rəs), ***n.*** [L., citron tree; akin to Gr. *kitron* (? to Gr. *kedros,* cedar); ? of Oriental (Medish) origin; cf. CITRON], 1. any of a group of trees and shrubs that bear oranges, lemons, limes, or other such fruit. 2. any such fruit. ***adj.*** of these trees and shrubs.
Cit·tà del Va·ti·ca·no (chēt-tä′ del vä′tē-kä′nô), Vatican City: the Italian name.
cit·tern (sit′ẽrn), ***n.*** a cithern.
cit·y (sit′i), ***n.*** [*pl.* CITIES (-iz)], [ME. & OFr. *cite, citet;* L. *civitas* (< *civis,* citizen), orig., citizenship, community of citizens, hence one of the Gaulish states, chief town in such a state], 1. a large, important town. 2. in the United States, an incorporated municipality whose boundaries and powers of self-government are defined by a charter from the State in which it is located: abbreviated **c.** 3. in Canada, a municipality of the highest rank. 4. in Great Britain, a borough or town with a royal charter, usually a town that has been or is an episcopal see. 5. all the people of a city. 6. in ancient Greece, a city-state. ***adj.*** of or in a city.
the City, the financial and commercial district of Greater London.
cit·y-born (sit′i-bôrn′), ***adj.*** born in a city.
cit·y-bred (sit′i-bred′), ***adj.*** raised in a city.
city chicken, strips of pork or veal wound on a skewer, breaded, and fried.
city editor, a newspaper editor who handles local news and distributes assignments to reporters.
city father, any of the important officials of a city; councilman, alderman, etc.
cit·y·fied (sit′i-fīd′), ***adj.*** citified.
city hall, 1. a building which houses the offices of a municipal government; hence, 2. the municipal government, especially as represented by the administration in power.
city manager, an administrator appointed by a city council or similar body to act as manager of the city.
City of David, 1. Jerusalem: so called because David captured it and established his capital there: II Sam. 5:6. 2. Bethlehem: so called because David was born there: I Sam. 16:1.
City of God, heaven.
City of Seven Hills, Rome.
cit·y-state (sit′i-stāt′), ***n.*** a state made up of an independent city and the territory directly controlled by it, as in ancient Greece.
Ciu·dad Bo·lí·var (sū-*thäth′* bô-lē′vär), a city in northeastern Venezuela, on the Orinoco River: pop., 56,000.
Ciu·dad Juá·rez (sū-*thäth′* hwä′res), a city in Mexico, across the Rio Grande from El Paso, Texas: pop., 49,000.
Ciu·dad Tru·jil·lo (sū-*thäth′*trōō-hē′yô), Santo Domingo, the capital of the Dominican Republic: former name.
civ., 1. civil. 2. civilian.
civ·et (siv′it), ***n.*** [Fr. *civette;* It. *zibetto;* Ar. *zabād*], 1. a thick, yellowish, fatty secretion with a musklike scent, obtained from glands in the anal pouch of the civet cat: it is used in making some perfumes. 2. the civet cat. 3. its fur.
civet cat, any of several varieties of a catlike, flesh-eating animal of Africa, India, Malaysia, and southern China, with spotted, yellowish fur: valued for its civet.

civ·ic (siv′ik), ***adj.*** [L. *civicus*, civil < *civis*, citizen], 1. of a city. 2. of citizens. 3. of citizenship.
civ·ics (siv′iks), ***n.pl.*** [construed as sing.], the branch of political science that deals with civic affairs and the duties and rights of citizenship.
civ·il (siv′'l, siv′il), ***adj.*** [Fr.; L. *civilis* < *civis*, citizen], 1. of a citizen or citizens. 2. of a community of citizens, their government, or their interrelations: as, *civil* affairs, *civil* service, *civil* war. 3. suitable for a city dweller; not rustic or countrified; hence, 4. polite; urbane. 5. civilized. 6. not military, naval, or ecclesiastical: as, *civil* law, *civil* marriage. 7. designating legally recognized divisions of time: as, a *civil* year. 8. [sometimes C-], of or according to Roman civil law or modern civil law. 9. in *law*, relating to the private rights of individuals and to legal actions involving these: distinguished from *criminal*, *political*. Abbreviated **civ.**
SYN.—**civil** implies merely a refraining from rudeness (keep a *civil* tongue in your head); **polite** suggests a more positive observance of etiquette in social behavior (it is not *polite* to interrupt); **courteous** suggests a still more positive and sincere consideration of others that springs from an inherent thoughtfulness (he is always *courteous* to strangers); **chivalrous** implies disinterested devotion to the cause of the weak, especially to helping women (he was quite *chivalrous* in her defense); **gallant** suggests a dashing display of courtesy, especially to women (her *gallant* lover).—***ANT.*** rude.
civil death, in *law*, deprivation of all civil rights as a result of being convicted of treason or, sometimes, of being declared an outlaw.
civil disobedience, passive resistance.
civil engineer, a specialist in civil engineering: abbreviated **C.E.** (as a title).
civil engineering, the branch of engineering dealing with the design and construction of highways, bridges, waterworks, harbors, etc.
ci·vil·ian (sə-vil′yən), ***n.*** [ME.; OFr. *civilien* < L. *civilis;* see CIVIL], 1. any person not in military or naval service. 2. a specialist in civil or Roman law. ***adj.*** of civilians; nonmilitary. Abbreviated **civ.**
ci·vil·i·ty (sə-vil′ə-ti), ***n.*** [*pl.* CIVILITIES (-tiz)], [ME. & OFr. *civilite;* L. *civilitas* (< *civilis*, civil), politics, hence politic behavior, politeness], 1. courtesy; politeness; consideration. 2. a polite act or utterance.
civ·i·liz·a·ble (siv′ə-līz′ə-b'l), ***adj.*** that can be civilized.
civ·i·li·za·tion (siv′'l-i-zā′shən, siv′'l-ī-zā′shən), ***n.*** 1. the process of civilizing or becoming civilized. 2. the condition of being civilized; social organization of a high order, marked by advances in the arts, sciences, etc. 3. the total culture of a people, nation, period, etc.: as, the *civilization* of the Occident differs from that of the Orient. 4. the countries and peoples considered to have reached a high stage of social and cultural development.
civ·i·lize (siv′'l-īz′), ***v.t.*** [CIVILIZED (-īzd′), CIVILIZING], [Fr. *civiliser* < L. *civilis;* see CIVIL: lit. etym. sense, "to citify"], 1. to bring out of a condition of savagery or barbarism; instruct in the ways of an advanced society. 2. to better the habits or manners of; refine.
civ·i·lized (siv′'l-īzd′), ***adj.*** [pp. of *civilize*], 1. advanced in social organization and the arts and sciences. 2. of people or countries thus advanced. 3. cultured and courteous; refined.
civil law, 1. Roman law, especially the part that applied to Roman citizens. 2. the body of law having to do with private rights: it developed from Roman law.
civil liberties, liberties guaranteed to the individual by law; rights of thinking, speaking, and acting as one likes without interference or restraint except in the interests of the public welfare.
civil list, in Great Britain and other monarchies, the annual appropriation fixed by the legislature for the personal and household expenses of the royal family.
civ·il·ly (siv′'l-i), ***adv.*** 1. with civility; politely. 2. by civil law.
civil marriage, a marriage performed by a justice of the peace, judge, or similar official, not by a clergyman.
civil rights, those rights guaranteed to the individual by the 13th and 14th Amendments to the Constitution of the United States and by certain other acts of Congress; especially, exemption from involuntary servitude and equal treatment of all people with respect to the enjoyment of life, liberty, and property and to the protection of law.
civil servant, [Chiefly British], a member of the civil service: in British usage, **Civil Servant.**
civil service, [orig. applied to the civilian staff of the British East India Company], 1. all those employed in government administration except in the army, navy, legislature, or judiciary. 2. any government service in which a position is secured through competitive public examination. 3. official regulations for such government service: as, he came under *civil service*. In British usage, **Civil Service.** Abbreviated **C.S., c.s.**
civil war, war between geographical sections or political factions of the same nation.
the Civil War, the war between the North (the Union) and the South (the Confederacy) in the United States (1861–1865).
civil year, a calendar year: cf. **astronomical year.**
civ·ism (siv′iz'm), ***n.*** [Fr. *civisme* < L. *civis*, citizen], the principles and ideals of good citizenship: term of the French Revolution.
civ·vies, civ·ies (siv′iz), ***n.pl.*** [Slang], civilian clothes, as distinguished from military uniform; mufti.
ck., [*pl.* CKS.], 1. cask. 2. check.
Cl, in *chemistry*, chlorine.
cl., 1. centiliter; centiliters. 2. claim. 3. class. 4. clause. 5. clearance. 6. clerk. 7. cloth.
c.l., 1. carload. 2. carload lots. 3. civil law.
clab·ber (klab′ẽr), ***n.*** [Ir. *clabar*], thick, sour milk; curdled milk; bonnyclabber. ***v.i. & v.t.*** to curdle.
clach·an (klåkh′ən), ***n.*** [Scot. Gael; prob. < *clach*, stone], [Scot. or Irish], a hamlet, especially in the Highlands of Scotland.
clack (klak), ***v.i.*** [ME. *clacken;* echoic; cf. CLAQUE, CLATTER], 1. to make an abrupt, sharp sound, as by striking two hard substances together. 2. to chatter; prate; blab. 3. to make a clucking, cackling sound, as a hen. ***v.t.*** 1. to cause to make an abrupt, sharp sound. 2. to blab. ***n.*** 1. an abrupt, sharp sound. 2. something that makes this sound. 3. chatter.
Clack·man·nan (klak-man′ən), ***n.*** 1. a county of Scotland, on the Firth of Forth: pop., 35,000 (est. 1946). 2. its county seat: pop., 2,600.
clack valve, a valve, often hinged at one side, which closes with a clacking sound.
clad (klad), occasional past tense and past participle of **clothe.** ***adj.*** clothed; dressed.
clad·o·phyll (klad′ə-fil), ***n.*** [< Gr. *klados*, a branch, shoot + *phyllon*, leaf], in *botany*, a branch with the shape and appearance of a leaf.
claim (klām), ***v.t.*** [ME. *claimen;* OFr. *claimer, clamer*, to call, cry out, claim; L. *clamare*, to cry out], 1. to demand as rightfully belonging or due to one; ask for on the basis of right or authority; assert one's right to, as a title, accomplishment, etc. that should be recognized: as, he *claimed* the record in the high jump. 2. to call for; require; deserve: as, this problem *claims* our attention. 3. to state as a fact; assert; maintain: a frequent and valid sense, despite objections. ***v.i.*** to assert or put forward a claim. ***n.*** 1. a demand for something rightfully or allegedly due; assertion of one's right to something. 2. a right or title to something: abbreviated **cl.** 3. something claimed, as a piece of land staked out by a settler or miner. 4. a statement of something as a fact; assertion. —***SYN.*** see **demand.**
lay claim to, to assert one's right or title to.
claim·ant (klām′ənt), ***n.*** [orig. law term < *claim* + *-ant*, after *defendant*, etc.], a person who makes a claim.
claiming race, a horse race in which each entering horse must be made available for purchase at a fixed price by anyone entering another horse in the meet.
Claire (klâr), a feminine name: see **Clara.**
clair·voy·ance (klâr-voi′əns), ***n.*** [Fr. < *clairvoyant*], 1. the ability to perceive things that are not in sight or that cannot be seen, attributed to some people. 2. keen perception; great insight.
clair·voy·ant (klâr-voi′ənt), ***adj.*** [Fr. (fem. *clairvoyante*), lit., seeing clearly < *clair*, clear + *voyant*, seeing, ppr. of *voir*, to see], 1. of clairvoyance. 2. apparently having clairvoyance. ***n.*** a clairvoyant person.
clam (klam), ***n.*** [*pl.* CLAMS (klamz), CLAM; see PLURAL, II, D, 1], [< *clamshell* < *clam* (a clamp): so called because of the action of the shells], 1. any of a large variety of hard-shelled bivalve mollusks, some of which live in the shallows of the sea, others in fresh water. 2. the soft, edible part of such a mollusk. ***v.i.*** [CLAMMED (klamd), CLAMMING], to dig, or go digging, for clams.
clam (klam), ***n.*** [Late ME. *clam;* AS. *clamm*, bond, fetter; akin to G. *klamm*, a cramp, fetter; IE. base **glem-* < **gel-;* see CLIMB], a clamp; vise.
clam (klam), ***n.*** [back-formation < *clammy*], clamminess.
cla·mant (klā′mənt), ***adj.*** [L. *clamans, clamantis*, ppr. of *clamare*, to cry out], 1. clamorous; noisy. 2. demanding attention; urgent.
clam·a·to·ri·al (klam′ə-tôr′i-əl, klam′ə-tō′ri-əl), ***adj.*** [< Mod. L. *Clamatores*, name of the suborder (< L. *clamatores*, pl. of *clamator*, bawler < *clamare*, to cry out); + *-ial*], belonging to the flycatcher family of birds.
clam·bake (klam′bāk′), ***n.*** 1. a picnic at which steamed or baked clams and other foods are served. 2. the steaming or baking of clams, usually on heated stones and with layers of other food, as corn, fish, etc., under a covering of seaweed.
clam·ber (klam′bẽr), ***v.i. & v.t.*** [ME. *clamberen, clameren;* akin to G. *klammern* in *sich klammern*, to hook oneself on, cling firmly < Gmc. base of *clamp, clump;* ult. < IE. **gel-;* see CLIMB], to climb by using both hands and feet; climb with difficulty or in a clumsy manner. ***n.*** a clambering; clumsy or hard climb.
clam·mi·ly (klam′'l-i), ***adv.*** in a clammy manner.
clam·mi·ness (klam′i-nis), ***n.*** the quality or condition of being clammy.
clam·my (klam′i), ***adj.*** [CLAMMIER (-i-ẽr), CLAMMIEST (-i-ist)], [ME. *clammy, claymy;* AS. types **clamig* (< *clam*, clay) & **clæmig* (< *clæman*, to smear < *clam*, clay); IE. base **glei-;* see CLAY], moist, cold, and slightly clinging to the touch.

clam·or (klam'ẽr), *n.* [ME. & OFr. *clamour;* L. *clamor* < *clamare,* to cry out], 1. a loud outcry; uproar. 2. a continual, vehement expression of the general feeling or opinion; noisy demand or complaint. 3. a loud, sustained noise. *v.i.* to make a clamor; cry out, demand, or complain noisily. *v.t.* to express or effect with clamor. —*SYN.* see **noise.**

clam·or·ous (klam'ẽr-əs), *adj.* [ML. *clamorosus;* see CLAMOR], 1. noisy; loud and confused. 2. loudly demanding or complaining. —*SYN.* see **vociferous.**

clam·our (klam'ẽr), *n., v.i. & v.t.* clamor: British spelling.

clamp (klamp), *n.* [ME. < LG. *klampe;* IE. base as in *climb, clamber*], any of various devices for clasping or fastening things together, or for bracing or strengthening parts; especially, an appliance with two parts that can be brought together, usually by screws, to grip and hold something. *v.t.* to fasten, strengthen, or brace with a clamp or clamps.

clamp down (on), [Colloq.], to become more strict (with).

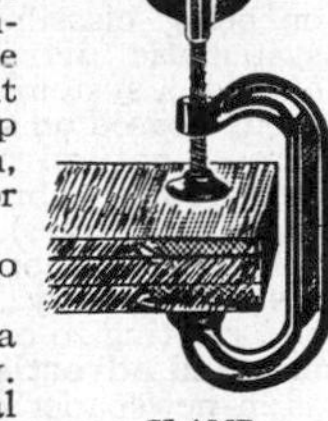

CLAMP

clamp (klamp), *n.* [var. of *clump*], a heavy tread. *v.i.* to tread heavily.

clamp·er (klam'pẽr), *n.* a metal plate with spikes, fastened to the sole of a shoe to prevent slipping on ice.

clam·shell (klam'shel'), *n.* 1. the shell of a clam. 2. a dredging bucket, hinged like the shell of a clam.

clan (klan), *n.* [Gael. & Ir. *clann, cland,* offspring, children, tribe < L. *planta,* offshoot], 1. an early form of social group, as in the Scottish Highlands, composed of several families claiming descent from a common ancestor, bearing the same family name, and following the same chieftain. 2. in certain primitive societies, a tribal division, usually exogamous, of matrilineal or patrilineal descent from a common ancestor. 3. a group of people with interests in common; clique; set.

clan·des·tine (klan-des'tin), *adj.* [Fr. *clandestin;* L. *clandestinus,* secret, hidden < *clam,* secret], secret or hidden, especially for some illicit purpose; surreptitious; furtive; underhand. —*SYN.* see **secret.**

clang (klaŋ), *v.i. & v.t.* [prob. echoic, like L. *clangere,* OHG. *klank,* Gr. *klangē,* but associated with L. *clangere*], 1. to make or cause to make a loud, sharp, ringing sound, as by striking metal. 2. to strike together with this sound. *n.* [< the *v.*], 1. this sound. 2. the loud, harsh sound made by some birds, as cranes.

clan·gor (klaŋ'gẽr, klaŋ'ẽr), *n.* [L. < *clangere*], 1. a clang. 2. a persistent clanging. *v.i.* to clang.

clan·gor·ous (klaŋ'gẽr-əs, klaŋ'ẽr-əs), *adj.* clanging.

clan·gour (klaŋ'gẽr, klaŋ'ẽr), *n.* clangor: British spelling.

clank (klaŋk), *n.* [? < *clang* + *clink;* or < D. *klank;* origin echoic], a sharp, metallic sound, not as resonant as a clang and shorter in duration. *v.i. & v.t.* to make or cause to make this sound.

clan·nish (klan'ish), *adj.* 1. of a clan. 2. tending to associate closely, to the exclusion of others; cliquish.

clans·man (klanz'mən), *n.* [*pl.* CLANSMEN (-mən)], a member of a clan.

clap (klap), *v.i.* [CLAPPED or *archaic* CLAPT (klapt), CLAPPING], [ME. *clappen;* AS. *clæppan,* to throb, beat, clap; akin to ON. *klapp,* OHG. *klapf,* clap, crack, blow; cf. CLATTER], 1. to make a sudden, explosive sound, as of two flat surfaces being struck together. 2. to strike the hands together with the palms turned toward each other, usually as a sign of pleasure or approval. *v.t.* 1. to strike together briskly and loudly: as, he *clapped* his hands. 2. to show pleasure at or approval of by clapping the hands. 3. to strike with an open hand, as in hearty greeting or encouragement. 4. to put, move, set, bring to, etc. swiftly and effectively: as, he was *clapped* into jail. *n.* 1. a sudden, explosive sound, as of two flat surfaces being struck together: as, a *clap* of thunder. 2. the act of striking the hands together, as in applauding. 3. a sharp blow; slap. 4. a sudden movement or stroke.

clap eyes on, [Colloq.], to look at; catch sight of; see.

clap (klap), *n.* [OFr. *clapoir,* brothel, orig., a rabbit hole], gonorrhea (often with *the*): a vulgarism.

clap·board (klab'ẽrd, klap'bôrd', klap'bōrd'), *n.* [partial transl. of G. *klapholz* or LG. *klapholt* < *klappen,* to fit + *holz, holt,* wood, board], 1. a thin, narrow board with one edge thicker than the other, used for covering the outer walls of frame houses. 2. in Great Britain, a small size of board for making wainscoting and barrel staves. *v.t.* to cover with clapboards.

clap·per (klap'ẽr), *n.* 1. a person who claps. 2. a thing that makes a clapping sound, as the tongue of a bell or, facetiously, that of a person.

clap·per·claw (klap'ẽr-klô'), *v.t.* [prob. < *clapper* + *claw*], [Archaic or Dial.], 1. to claw or scratch with the hand and nails. 2. to revile or scold.

clapt (klapt), archaic past tense and past participle of **clap.**

clap·trap (klap'trap'), *n.* [*clap* (applause) + *trap*], showy, insincere, empty talk, expression, etc., intended only to get applause or notice. *adj.* showy and cheap.

claque (klak), *n.* [Fr. < *claquer,* to clap; echoic], 1. a group of people paid to go to a play, opera, etc. and applaud. 2. a group of admiring or fawning followers.

clar., clarinet.

Clar·a (klâr'ə), [< L. *clara,* fem. of *clarus,* clear, bright], a feminine name: variants, *Clare, Clarice, Clarissa;* equivalent, Fr. *Claire.*

clar·a·bel·la (klar'ə-bel'ə), *n.* [Mod. L. < L. *clarus,* clear + *bellus,* delightful], an 8-foot organ stop producing a soft, velvety tone.

Clare (klâr), 1. a masculine name: see **Clarence.** 2. a feminine name: see **Clara.**

Clar·ence (klar'əns), [< name of Eng. dukedom of *Clarence* < *Clare,* town in Suffolk; formed as if < L. *clarens,* ppr. of *clarere,* to make illustrious < *clarus,* clear, illustrious], a masculine name: variant, *Clare.*

clar·ence (klar'əns), *n.* [< the Duke of *Clarence,* later William IV], a closed, four-wheeled carriage with seats for four inside and a seat for the driver outside.

Clar·en·don (klar'ən-dən), first Earl of, (*Edward Hyde*), 1609–1674; English statesman and historian; lord chancellor of England (1658–1667).

clar·en·don (klar'ən-dən), *n.* [< *Clarendon* Press, Oxford, England], a style of type with narrow letters of thick, heavy lines. **This line is in 5-point clarendon.**

Clare of Assisi, Saint, 1194–1253; Italian nun; founder of the order of Poor Clares: her day is August 12.

clar·et (klar'ət), *n.* [ME.; OFr. (*vin*) *claret,* clear (wine); dim. of *cler,* clear < L. *clarus;* see CLEAR], 1. a dry red wine; especially, red Bordeaux. 2. purplish red: also **claret red.** *adj.* purplish-red.

claret cup, an iced drink of claret, lemon juice, brandy, sugar, and soda.

Clar·i·bel (klar'ə-bel'), [< L. *clarus,* clear, bright + *bellus,* pretty, fair], a feminine name.

Clar·ice (klar'is, klə-rēs'), [Fr. *Clarisse*], a feminine name: see **Clara.**

clar·i·fi·ca·tion (klar'ə-fi-kā'shən), *n.* [Fr. < LL. *clarificatio*], a clarifying or being clarified.

clar·i·fi·er (klar'ə-fi'ẽr), *n.* 1. a person or thing that clarifies; especially, a substance used to clarify wine. 2. a large metal pan in which sugar is clarified.

clar·i·fy (klar'ə-fi'), *v.t. & v.i.* [CLARIFIED (-fid'), CLARIFYING], [ME. *clarifien;* OFr. *clarifier;* L. *clarificare* < *clarus,* clear, bright + *facere,* to make], 1. to make or become clear and free from impurities: said of liquids, etc. 2. to make or become easier to understand: as, you must *clarify* your meaning.

clar·i·net (klar'ə-net', klar'ə-net'), *n.* [Fr. *clarinette,* dim. of *clarine,* little bell; LL. *clario;* see CLARION], a single-reed, wood-wind instrument with a long wooden or metal tube and a flaring bell, played by means of holes and keys: it is made in various keys, and has a range of about 3 1/2 octaves: abbreviated **clar.**

clar·i·net·ist, clar·i·net·tist (klar'ə-net'ist), *n.* a person who plays the clarinet.

CLARINET

clar·i·on (klar'i-ən), *n.* [ME. *clarioun;* OFr. *clarion;* LL. *clario,* a trumpet < L. *clarus,* clear], 1. a kind of trumpet producing clear, sharp, shrill tones. 2. [Poetic], the sound of a clarion, or a sound like this. *adj.* clear, sharp, and shrill: as, a *clarion* call. *v.t.* to announce forcefully or loudly.

clar·i·o·net (klar'i-ə-net'), *n.* a clarinet.

Cla·ris·sa (klə-ris'ə), [It.], a feminine name: see **Clara.**

clar·i·ty (klar'ə-ti), *n.* [ME. *claretee;* OFr. *clarte;* L. *claritas* < *clarus,* clear], clearness (in various senses).

Clark, George Rogers (klärk), 1752–1818; American frontiersman and Revolutionary hero.

Clark, William, 1770–1838; brother of *George Rogers;* American explorer; co-leader of the Lewis and Clark expedition (1804–1806).

Clarks·burg (klärks'bẽrg), *n.* a city in northern West Virginia: pop., 28,000.

cla·ro (klä'rō), *adj.* [Sp. < L. *clarus,* clear], light-colored and mild: said of cigars. *n.* such a cigar.

clart (klärt), *v.t.* [Scot. & British Dial.], to smear or bedaub with sticky dirt.

clar·y (klâr'i), *n.* [*pl.* CLARIES (-iz)], [Fr. *sclarée;* ML. *sclarea*], 1. a plant of the sage family, used as a pot-herb. 2. an ornamental variety of this plant.

clash (klash), *v.i.* [echoic], 1. to collide or strike together with a loud, harsh, metallic noise. 2. to conflict; disagree; fail to harmonize. *v.t.* to strike together, bring together, shut, etc. with a loud, harsh, metallic noise. *n.* 1. a loud, harsh noise, as of two metallic objects colliding. 2. conflict; disagreement.

clasp (klasp, kläsp), *n.* [ME. *claspe, clapse* (base form *claps-); akin to MIr. *glass* (< **glabsā*), clasp & AS. *clyppian* (cf. CLIP), to embrace; IE. **gelebh* (cf. CALF) < base **gel-*, (see CLIMB): the basic sense is prob. 2], 1. a fastening, as a hook, buckle, or catch, to hold two things or parts together. 2. a holding; grasping; embrace. 3. a grip of the hand. *v.t.* [CLASPED or *archaic* CLASPT (klaspt, kläspt), CLASPING], [ME. *claspen* < the *n.*], 1. to fasten with a clasp. 2. to hold tightly with the arms or hands; grasp firmly; embrace. 3. to grip with the hand. 4. to entwine about; cling to.

clasp knife, a large pocketknife with a blade or blades that fold into the handle; especially, such a knife with blades which, when open, can be secured by a catch.

claspt (klaspt, kläspt), archaic past tense and past participle of **clasp.**

class (klas, kläs), *n.* [Fr. *classe;* L. *classis,* class or division of the Roman people; Gr. *klēsis,* a calling, summons < *kalein,* to call], 1. a number of people or things grouped together because of certain likenesses or common traits; kind; sort: as, an inferior *class* of novels. 2. a group of people considered as a unit according to economic, occupational, or social status; especially, a social rank or caste: as, the working *class,* the middle *class.* 3. high social rank or caste. 4. the division of society into ranks or castes. 5. a group of students taught together according to standing, subject, etc. 6. a meeting of such a group. 7. a group of students graduating together: as, the *class* of 1950. 8. a division or grouping according to grade or quality. 9. grade or quality. 10. conscripted troops, or men liable to conscription, all of whom were born in the same year: as, they called up the *class* of 1931. 11. in *biology,* a group of animals or plants having a common basic structure and ranking below a *phylum* and above an *order.* Abbreviated **cl.** 12. [Slang], excellence, especially of style, appearance, etc. *v.t.* to put in a class; classify. *v.i.* to be classed.

in a class by itself (or **oneself**), unique.

the classes, the upper classes in the social order: opposed to *the masses.*

class., 1. classic. 2. classical. 3. classification. 4. classified.

class book, 1. a book in which a teacher records grades, absences, etc. 2. a book published by members of a class in a school or college, containing pictures of students and teachers, an account of student activities, etc.

class-con·scious (klas'kon'shəs, kläs'kon'shəs), *adj.* having or showing class consciousness.

class consciousness, an awareness of belonging to or constituting a class in the social order, with definite economic interests; sense of class solidarity.

class day, the day on which special ceremonies are conducted at a school or college before the graduation of the senior class.

clas·sic (klas'ik), *adj.* [L. *classicus,* relating to the classes of the Roman people, especially to the highest class; hence, superior < *classis,* a class], 1. of the highest class; most representative of the excellence of its kind; having recognized worth. 2. in accordance with established principles of excellence in the arts and sciences. 3. of the art, literature, and culture of the ancient Greeks and Romans, or their writers, artists, etc. 4. like or characteristic of the literary and artistic standards, principles, and methods of the ancient Greeks and Romans; hence, 5. balanced, formal, objective, austere, regular, simple, etc.: a term variously interpreted, generally opposed to *romantic.* Abbreviated **class.** 6. [Colloq.], famous as traditional or typical. *n.* 1. a writer, artist, etc. generally recognized as excellent. 2. a literary or artistic work generally recognized as of the highest excellence. 3. [Rare], a classicist. 4. [Colloq.], a famous traditional or typical event: as, this football game is a *classic.* 5. [Slang], a woman's suit, dress, etc. made in a traditional style.

the classics, the literature or language of the ancient Greeks and Romans.

clas·si·cal (klas'i-k'l), *adj.* 1. classic (senses 1, 3, 4, 5). 2. learned in and devoted to Greek and Roman culture, literature, etc. 3. designating or of music that conforms to certain established standards of form, complexity, musical literacy, etc.: as, symphonies, concertos, sonatas, etc. are called *classical* music: variously distinguished from *popular, romantic, modern.* 4. designating or of a course of study that is standard and traditionally authoritative, not new and experimental: as, *classical* political science. Abbreviated **class.**

clas·si·cal·ism (klas'i-k'l-iz'm), *n.* classicism.

clas·si·cal·i·ty (klas'ə-kal'ə-ti), *n.* 1. the quality of being classical. 2. classical scholarship. 3. anything that has a classical quality.

clas·si·cal·ly (klas'i-k'l-i, klas'ik-li), *adv.* in a classical manner or style.

clas·si·cism (klas'ə-siz'm), *n.* [*classic* + *-ism*], 1. the aesthetic principles and methods regarded as characteristic of ancient Greece and Rome; objectivity, formality, balance, simplicity, dignity, restraint, etc.: generally contrasted with *romanticism.* 2. adherence to these principles or to principles derived from them. 3. knowledge of the literature and art of ancient Greece and Rome; classical scholarship. 4. a Greek or Latin idiom or expression.

clas·si·cist (klas'ə-sist), *n.* 1. an advocate of the principles of classicism. 2. a student of or specialist in ancient Greek and Roman literature. 3. one who advocates the teaching of Greek and Latin in the schools.

clas·si·cize (klas'ə-sīz'), *v.t.* [CLASSICIZED (-sīzd'), CLASSICIZING], to make classic. *v.i.* to use or affect a classic style or form.

clas·si·fi·a·ble (klas'ə-fī'ə-b'l), *adj.* that can be classified.

clas·si·fi·ca·tion (klas'ə-fi-kā'shən), *n.* 1. a classifying or being classified; arrangement according to some systematic division into classes or groups. 2. in *biology,* a system of arranging all living organisms into groups based on some factor common to each, as structure or natural relationship: the categories now used are, from the broadest to the narrowest, *phylum* (in botany, *division*), *class, order, family, genus, species,* and *variety.* Abbreviated **class.**

clas·si·fi·ca·to·ry (klas'ə-fi-kā'tēr-i, klə-sif'ə-kə-tôr'i), *adj.* relating to or using classification.

classified advertising, advertising printed in small type, as in newspaper columns, according to subject, under such listings as *help wanted, lost and found,* etc.

clas·si·fi·er (klas'ə-fī'ēr), *n.* a person who classifies.

clas·si·fy (klas'ə-fī'), *v.t.* [CLASSIFIED (-fīd'), CLASSIFYING], [< L. *classis* (see CLASS); + *-fy*], 1. to arrange or group in classes according to some system or principle. 2. to declare (governmental documents, reports, etc.) to be secret or restricted and, hence, available only to authorized persons.

clas·sis (klas'is), *n.* [*pl.* CLASSES (-ēz)], [L.; see CLASS], 1. a church court or governing group consisting of the pastors and elders from the churches in the district. 2. the jurisdiction of such a body.

class·mate (klas'māt', kläs'māt'), *n.* a member of the same class at a school or college.

class·room (klas'rōōm', kläs'room'), *n.* a room for recitations, etc. of a class in a school or college.

class struggle, in *Marxism,* the constant economic and political struggle held to exist between social classes regarded as exploiting and those regarded as exploited; specifically, in capitalist countries, the struggle between capitalists (bourgeoisie) and workers (proletariat).

class·y (klas'i), *adj.* (CLASSIER (-i-ēr), CLASSIEST (-i-ist)], [Slang], first-class, especially in style or manner; elegant; fine.

clas·tic (klas'tik), *adj.* [Gr. *klastos,* broken < *klaein,* to break; + *-ic*], 1. designating an anatomical model with removable sections to show internal structure. 2. in *geology,* consisting of fragments of older rocks.

clath·rate (klath'rāt), *adj.* [< L. *clathri,* lattice (< Gr. *klēthra*); + *-ate*], in *botany,* resembling latticework; reticulated.

clat·ter (klat'ēr), *v.i.* [ME. *clateren;* AS. **clatrian* (inferred < AS. *clatrung,* clattering noise) or < MD. *kleteren,* to rattle; akin to G. *klattern;* Gmc. echoic base **klat-* + freq. suffix; IE. base **gal-,* to cry out, sound loudly], 1. to make, or move with, a rapid succession of loud, sharp noises, as dishes rattling. 2. to chatter noisily. *v.t.* to cause to clatter. *n.* [ME. *clater* < the *v.*], 1. a rapid succession of loud, sharp noises. 2. a tumult; hubbub. 3. noisy chatter.

Claude (klôd), [Fr.; L. *Claudius,* name of a Roman gens; prob. < *claudus,* lame], a masculine name: feminine, *Claudia.*

Clau·di·a (klô'di-ə), [L.], a feminine name: see **Claude.**

clau·di·cant (klô'di-kənt), *adj.* [< L. *claudicans,* ppr. of *claudicare,* to limp < *claudus,* lame], limping; lame.

clau·di·ca·tion (klô'di-kā'shən), *n.* [< L. *claudicare,* to limp; see CLAUDICANT], the act of limping; limp.

Clau·di·us (klô'di-əs), *n.* 1. (*Tiberius Claudius Drusus Nero Germanicus*), Roman emperor (41–54 A.D.); lived 10–54 A.D. 2. (*Marcus Aurelius Claudius*), Roman emperor (268–270 A.D.); lived 214–270 A.D.

claus·al (klôz''l), *adj.* of or constituting a clause.

clause (klôz), *n.* [ME.; OFr.; LL. *clausa* < L. *clausus,* pp. of *claudere,* to close], 1. a group of words containing a subject and verb, usually forming part of a compound or complex sentence: a dependent (subordinate) clause functions as a noun, adjective, or adverb; an independent (principal) clause states the main predication. In English, the most obvious formal difference between a clause and a sentence is that the latter begins with silence and ends with an ending pitch, the former begins or ends with a suspension pitch: clauses may be joined by parataxis (The house is secluded; you will like it), by modified parataxis (The house is secluded, and you will like it), and by hypotaxis (Because the house is secluded, you will like it). 2. a particular article, stipulation, or provision in a formal or legal document. Abbreviated **cl.**

Clau·se·witz, Karl von (kärl fôn klou'zə-vits), 1780–1831; Prussian army officer; writer on military science.

claus·tral (klôs'trəl), *adj.* [ML. *claustralis* < *claustrum,* place that is shut up, orig., that by which a thing is closed, bolt, bar < L. *claudere;* see CLOSE, *v.*], cloistral.

claus·tro·pho·bi·a (klôs'trə-fō'bi-ə), ***n.*** [< L. *claustrum* (see CLAUSTRAL); + *-phobia*], an abnormal fear of being in an enclosed or confined place.

cla·vate (klā'vāt), ***adj.*** [< L. *clava,* a club; + *-ate*], club-shaped.

clave (klāv), archaic past tense of **cleave.**

clav·i·chord (klav'ə-kôrd'), ***n.*** [LL. *clavichordium* < L. *clavis,* a key + *chorda,* a string], a stringed musical instrument with a keyboard, from which the piano developed: it somewhat resembles the harpsichord, except that when the keys are pressed, the strings are struck by little hammers rather than plucked.

CLAVICHORD

clav·i·cle (klav'ə-k'l), ***n.*** [Fr. *clavicule;* L. *clavicula,* dim. of *clavis,* a key], a small bone connecting the breastbone with the shoulder blade; collarbone: see **skeleton,** illus.

clav·i·corn (klav'ə-kôrn'), ***adj.*** [< Mod. L. *Clavicornia,* name of the group < L. *clava,* a club + *cornu,* a horn], of a large group of beetles with club-shaped feelers.

clav·i·cor·nate (klav'ə-kôr'nāt), ***adj.*** in *zoology,* having club-shaped feelers.

cla·vic·u·lar (klə-vik'yoo-lẽr), ***adj.*** of the clavicle.

cla·vi·er (klav'i-ẽr; *also, and for 2 always,* klə-vêr'), ***n.*** [Fr., keyboard < L. *clavis,* a key], 1. the keyboard of an organ, piano, etc. 2. any stringed instrument that has a keyboard; now, usually, a piano. 3. a dummy keyboard used in practicing.

clav·i·form (klav'ə-fôrm'), ***adj.*** [< L. *clava,* a club; + *-form*], club-shaped.

claw (klô), ***n.*** [ME. *clawe, clau;* AS. *clawu,* a claw, hoof < the base (Gmc. **klawjan*) of AS. *clawian,* to scratch; akin to G. *klaue* (Gmc. **klewa*); IE. base **g(e)l-eu* (cf. CLEW) < **gel-;* see CLIMB], 1. a sharp, hooked or curved nail on the foot of an animal or bird. 2. a foot with such nails at its end. 3. the pincers (chela) of a lobster, crab, scorpion, etc. 4. anything resembling or regarded as a claw: as, the *claw* of a hammer. ***v.t. & v.i.*** to scratch, clutch, pull, or tear with or as with claws.

claw hammer, 1. a hammer with one end of the head forked and curved like a claw, used for pulling nails: see **hammer,** illus. 2. [Colloq.], a swallowtail coat.

claw hatchet, a hatchet with one end of the head forked: see **hatchet,** illus.

clay (klā), ***n.*** [ME. *claye, clai;* AS. *clæg;* akin to G. & MLG. *klei;* IE. base **glei-,* to stick together, seen also in L. *glus* (cf. GLUE) & Eng. *clammy*], 1. a firm, plastic, fine-grained earth, chiefly aluminum silicate: it is produced by the deposit of fine rock particles in water, and used in the manufacture of bricks, pottery, and other ceramics. 2. *a*) earth, especially as a symbol of the material of the human body. *b*) the human body.

Clay, Henry (klā), 1777–1852; American statesman.

clay·ey (klā'i), ***adj.*** [CLAYIER (-i-ẽr), CLAYIEST (-i-ist)], 1. of, containing, or full of clay. 2. like clay.

clay·ish (klā'ish), ***adj.*** of the nature of clay; like clay.

clay·more (klā'môr', klā'mōr'), ***n.*** [Gael. *claidheamh-mor* < *claidheamh,* sword + *mor,* great], a large, two-edged broadsword formerly used by Scottish Highlanders.

clay pigeon, a disk of clay, etc. tossed into the air from the trap as a target in trap shooting.

clay stone, 1. a rounded mass of limestone formed in a clay deposit. 2. a kind of rock containing clay.

clay·to·ni·a (klā-tō'ni-ə), ***n.*** [after the Am. botanist John *Clayton* (1693–1773)], any of a group of spring-flowering North American herbs of the purslane family, with white and rose-colored flowers.

-cle (k'l), [< L. dim. suffix, *-culus*], a suffix added to nouns to form the diminutive, as in *particle, ventricle.*

clean (klēn), ***adj.*** [ME. *clene;* AS. *clæne,* clean, pure; akin to OHG. *kleini,* gleaming, bright, fine (whence G. *klein,* small, *kleinod,* gem); IE. base **gel-,* **g(e)lēi-,* gleam brightly, be gay], 1. free from dirt or impurities; unsoiled; unstained. 2. recently laundered. 3. morally pure; sinless. 4. habitually avoiding filth. 5. shapely; well-formed. 6. clever; deft. 7. having no obstructions, flaws, or roughnesses; clear; regular. 8. entire; complete; thorough. 9. lacking completely; having no more of, as money. 10. free from writing: said of paper, etc. 11. legible; having few corrections: as, *clean* copy for the printer. 12. producing little immediate fallout: said of nuclear weapons. 13. in the *Bible, a*) free or freed from ceremonial defilement. *b*) fit for food: said of certain animals. ***adv.*** [AS. *clæne*], 1. in a clean manner. 2. completely; wholly. ***v.t.*** 1. to make clean. 2. to remove (dirt, impurities, etc.) in making clean. 3. to prepare (fish, fowl, etc.) for cooking. ***v.i.*** 1. to be made clean. 2. to perform the act of cleaning.

clean out, 1. to empty so as to make clean. 2. to empty. 3. [Colloq.], to take away or use up the money, resources, etc. of.

clean up, 1. to make clean, neat, or orderly. 2. to make oneself clean and neat; get washed, combed, etc. 3. [Colloq.], to dispose of completely; finish. 4. [Slang], to make much money or profit.

clean up on, [Slang], to defeat; beat.

come clean, [Slang], to confess; tell the truth.

with clean hands, without guilt.

SYN.*—clean,** the broader term, denotes generally the removal of dirt or impurities, as by washing, brushing, etc.; **cleanse** suggests more specifically the use of chemicals, purgatives, etc. and is often used metaphorically to imply purification (to *cleanse* one's mind of evil thoughts).—ANT.*** soil, dirty.

clean-cut (klēn'kut'), ***adj.*** 1. clearly and sharply outlined. 2. well-formed. 3. distinct; clear. 4. good-looking, trim, neat, etc.: as, a *clean-cut* young fellow.

clean·er (klēn'ẽr), ***n.*** 1. a person whose work is cleaning up rooms, buildings, etc. 2. a person who owns, operates, or works in a dry-cleaning establishment. 3. a tool or device for cleaning. 4. a preparation for removing stains, grease, or other dirt.

clean-hand·ed (klēn'han'did), ***adj.*** blameless; innocent.

clean·li·ly (klen'li-li), ***adv.*** in a cleanly manner.

clean-limbed (klēn'limd'), ***adj.*** having shapely limbs.

clean·li·ness (klen'li-nis), ***n.*** the state or habit of being clean.

clean·ly (klen'li), ***adj.*** [CLEANLIER (-li-ẽr), CLEANLIEST (-li-ist)], [ME. *clenlich;* AS. *clænlic* < *clæne;* see CLEAN], 1. clean; having clean habits. 2. always kept clean.

clean·ly (klēn'li), ***adv.*** in a clean manner.

clean·ness (klēn'nis), ***n.*** [ME. *clennesse;* AS. *clænnes*], the quality or condition of being clean.

cleanse (klenz), ***v.t.*** [CLEANSED (klenzd), CLEANSING], [ME. *clensien, clensen;* AS. *clænsian* < *clæne;* see CLEAN], 1. to make clean. 2. to free from guilt; make pure. 3. to purge. ***SYN.*** see **clean.**

cleans·er (klenz'ẽr), ***n.*** any preparation for cleansing.

clean-shav·en (klēn'shāv''n), ***adj.*** having all the hairs shaved off.

Cle·an·thes (kli-an'thēz), ***n.*** Greek Stoic philosopher of the 3d century B.C.

clean·up (klēn'up'), ***n.*** 1. a cleaning up. 2. elimination of crime, vice, graft, etc.: as, the new mayor planned a *cleanup* of the city. 3. [Slang], profit; gain.

clear (klêr), ***adj.*** [ME. *clere, cler;* OFr. *cler, clier;* L. *clarus,* orig., clear-sounding, hence clear, bright; IE. base **kel-,* to cry out, sound loudly, seen also in L. *nomenclator* (for **nomen-calator*), lit., name caller (cf. NOMENCLATURE), & in AS. *hlowan,* to bellow (cf. LOW, to moo)], 1. bright; light; free from clouds or mist: as, a *clear* day. 2. free from cloudiness, muddiness, blemish, etc.; transparent; not turbid: as, a *clear* crystal. 3. free from dimness or blur; easily seen; sharply defined; distinct: as, a *clear* outline. 4. perceptive; logical; orderly: as, a *clear* mind. 5. free from confusion or ambiguity; not obscure; easily understood: as, the meaning is *clear.* 6. obvious; unmistakable: as, a *clear* case of neglect. 7. certain; positive: as, I am *clear* on the matter. 8. ringing; resonant: said of sounds. 9. capable of being heard or understood: said of voices. 10. free from guilt; innocent: as, a *clear* conscience. 11. free from charges or deductions; net: as, he earned a *clear* $10,000. 12. free from qualification; absolute; complete. 13. free from contact or connection. 14. free from impediment or obstruction; open. 15. freed or emptied of freight or cargo. 16. free from debt. 17. free from a legal charge or suspicion of guilt. ***adv.*** 1. in a clear manner; so as to be clear. 2. [Colloq.], all the way: used as an intensive: as, *clear* through the town. ***v.t.*** 1. to make clear or bright. 2. to free from impurities, blemishes, cloudiness, muddiness, etc. 3. to free from obscurity or ambiguity; make intelligible, plain, or lucid. 4. to rid of obstructions, entanglements, or obstacles; open: as, he *cleared* a path through the snow. 5. to remove; get rid of. 6. to unload; empty: as, they *cleared* the freighter of cargo. 7. to free (a person or thing) *of* or *from* something. 8. to free from a legal charge or a suspicion of guilt; prove the innocence of; acquit. 9. to pass or leap over, by, etc. 10. to pass without contact: as, the tug *cleared* the bridge. 11. to discharge (a debt) by paying it. 12. to free (a ship or cargo) by satisfying harbor and customs requirements. 13. to make (a given amount) as profit or earnings not subject to charges or deductions; net. 14. to make (the sight) clear or sharp. 15. to rid (the throat) of phlegm by hawking or coughing. 16. to rid (the voice) of hoarseness in this manner. 17. in *banking,* to pass (a check, etc.) through a clearinghouse. ***v.i.*** 1. to become clear, unclouded, etc. (often with *up*). 2. to satisfy harbor and customs requirements in discharging a cargo or leaving a port (often with *in* or *out*): said of a ship. 3. in *banking,* to exchange checks and other banking

paper, and balance accounts, through a clearinghouse. *n.* 1. a clear space. 2. clearance.
clear away, 1. to take away so as to leave a cleared space. 2. to go away; go out of sight.
clear off, 1. to clear away. 2. to remove something from in order to make clear.
clear out, 1. to clear by emptying. 2. [Colloq.], to go away; depart.
clear the air (or **atmosphere**), to get rid of emotional tensions, misunderstandings, etc.
clear (the decks) for action, 1. to clear the decks of a ship in preparation for a fight; hence, 2. to get ready for any action.
clear up, 1. to make or become clear. 2. to make orderly. 3. to become unclouded, sunny, etc. after being cloudy or stormy. 4. to explain.
in the clear, 1. free from enclosing or limiting obstructions. 2. [Colloq.], free from suspicion, guilt, etc.
SYN.—**clear** suggests freedom from cloudiness, haziness, muddiness, etc., either literally or figuratively (a *clear* liquid, *clear* logic); **transparent** suggests such clearness that objects on the other side (or by extension, meanings, etc.) may be seen distinctly (plate glass is *transparent*); **translucent** implies the admission of light, but so diffused that objects on the other side cannot be clearly distinguished (stained glass is *translucent*); **pellucid** suggests the sparkling clearness of crystal (a slab of *pellucid* ice, *pellucid* writing). See also **evident.** —***ANT.*** opaque, cloudy, turbid.

clear·ance (klêr′əns), *n.* 1. a making clear (in several senses). 2. the clear space between a passing object and the sides or roof of its passageway, as on a bridge, in a tunnel, etc. 3. the distance separating moving objects or mechanical parts. 4. in *banking,* the adjustment of debits and credits, exchange of checks, etc. in a clearinghouse. 5. in *nautical usage, a)* a certificate from the collector of customs authorizing a ship to enter or leave port: also called *clearance papers. b)* the act or process of meeting the requirements for getting this certificate. Abbreviated **cl.** (in senses 2 & 4).

clearance sale, a sale to get rid of old merchandise and make room for new.

Cle·ar·chus (kli-är′kəs), *n.* Spartan general; executed (401 B.C.).

clear-cut (klêr′kut′), *adj.* 1. clearly and sharply outlined. 2. distinct; plain.

clear·eyed (klêr′īd′), *adj.* 1. having clear eyes or vision; hence, 2. perceptive; thinking clearly.

clear·head·ed (klêr′hed′id), *adj.* having a clear mind.

clear·ing (klêr′iŋ), *n.* 1. a making clear or being cleared. 2. a plot of land cleared of trees. 3. in *banking, a)* the exchanging of checks, etc. and balancing of accounts between banks. *b)* the procedure for doing this. *c) pl.* the amount of the balances thus settled.

clear·ing·house (klêr′iŋ-hous′), *n.* an office maintained by a group of banks as a center for exchanging checks drawn against one another, balancing accounts, etc.: abbreviated **C.H.**

clear·ly (klêr′li), *adv.* in a clear manner.

clear·ness (klêr′nis), *n.* the quality or condition of being clear.

clear-sighted (klêr′sīt′id), *adj.* 1. seeing clearly. 2. perceiving, understanding, or thinking clearly.

clear·starch (klêr′stärch′), *v.t. & v.i.* to stiffen (laundry) with a colorless solution of starch.

clear·sto·ry (klêr′stôr′i, klêr′stō′ri), *n.* [*pl.* CLEARSTORIES (-iz, -riz)], a clerestory.

clear·wing (klêr′wiŋ′), *n.* a kind of moth with transparent, scaleless wings.

cleat (klēt), *n.* [ME. *clete;* AS. **cleat* (W.Gmc. **klaut*), a lump; akin to D. *kloot,* G. *klotz,* lump (W.Gmc. **klōt*), & AS. *clott* (cf. CLOT); IE. base **gel-;* see **CLIMB**], 1. a piece of wood or metal, often wedge-shaped, fastened to something to strengthen it or give secure footing: cleats are used on gangways, under shelves, on the soles or heels of shoes, etc. 2. in *nautical usage,* a small piece of wood or metal with projecting ends on which a rope can be fastened. *v.t.* to fasten to or with a cleat.

cleav·a·ble (klēv′ə-b'l), *adj.* [see CLEAVE (to split)], that can be cleft or split.

cleav·age (klēv′ij), *n.* 1. a cleaving; splitting; dividing. 2. the manner in which a thing splits. 3. a cleft; fissure; division. 4. in *biology, a)* cell division, especially the series of mitotic cell divisions that transform the fertilized ovum into the blastula, the earliest embryonic stage. *b)* any single division in this series. 5. in *mineralogy,* the tendency of some minerals to break in definite planes, producing smooth surfaces.

cleave (klēv), *v.t.* [CLEFT (kleft) or CLEAVED (klēvd) or CLOVE (klōv), CLEFT or CLEAVED or CLOVEN (klō′v'n), CLEAVING; *archaic* p.t. CLAVE (klāv), *poetic* pp. CLOVE], [ME. *cleven; cliven;* AS. *cleofan;* akin to G. *klieben;* IE. base **gleubh-,* to cut, slice, as also in L. *glubere,* to flay], 1. to divide by a blow, as of an ax; split; hew apart. 2. to pierce. 3. to sever; disunite. *v.i.* 1. to split; separate; fall apart. 2. to make one's way by cutting, as through underbrush.

cleave (klēv), *v.i.* [CLEAVED (klēvd), CLEAVING; *archaic* p.t. CLAVE (klāv), CLOVE (klōv)], [ME. *cleven, cliven, clevien;* AS. *cleofian, clifian,* to adhere, akin to G. *kleben;* IE. base **gleibh-* < **glei-;* CLAY], 1. to adhere; cling. 2. to be faithful (*to*). —***SYN.*** see **stick.**

cleav·er (klēv′ẽr), *n.* [< *cleave* (to split)], a heavy, sharp-edged cutting tool used by butchers.

CLEAVER

cleav·ers (klēv′ẽrz), *n.* [*pl.* CLEAVERS], [< *cleave* (to cling)], any of various plants with stalkless leaves arranged in whorls, clusters of small flowers of white or yellow, and prickly stems; goose grass.

cleek (klēk), *n.* [Scot. < obs. v. *cleek,* to clutch, snatch; ME. *clechen,* to seize < *cleche,* a claw, fingernail; akin to *clutch*], 1. a large hook. 2. in *golf,* formerly, an iron-headed club with a narrow, slightly sloped face; now, a wooden-headed club with a small head, having slightly more loft than a spoon.

clef (klef), *n.* [Fr.; OFr. *cle, clef;* L. *clavis,* a key], a symbol used in music to indicate the pitch of the notes on the staff: there are three clefs, G (treble), F (bass), and C (tenor or alto).

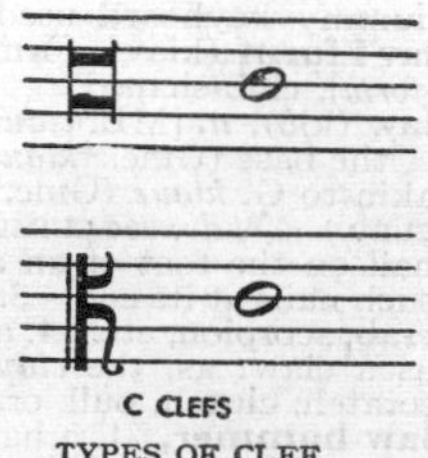

TYPES OF CLEF

cleft (kleft), *n.* [ME. *clyft, clift* < AS. **clyft* < *cleofan;* see CLEAVE (to divide)], an opening made by cleaving; crack; crevice; split; fissure.

cleft (kleft), alternative past tense and past participle of **cleave** (to split). *adj.* 1. split; divided. 2. in *botany,* divided by one or more narrow fissures extending more than halfway to the midrib: said of leaves.

cleft palate, a cleft from front to back along the middle of the palate or roof of the mouth, caused by the failure of the two parts of the palate to join in prenatal development.

Cleis·the·nes (klīs′thi-nēz′), *n.* Athenian statesman; fl. c. 510 B.C.

cleis·to·gam·ic (klīs′tə-gam′ik), *adj.* cleistogamous.

cleis·tog·a·mous (klīs-tog′ə-məs), *adj.* [< Gr. *kleistos,* closed; + *-gamous*], having small, closed, self-pollinating flowers.

cleis·tog·a·my (klīs-tog′ə-mi), *n.* [< Gr. *kleistos,* closed; + *-gamy*], self-pollination of certain closed flowers.

clem·a·tis (klem′ə-tis), *n.* [L. < Gr. *klēmatis,* brushwood, clematis < *klēma,* vine, twig], any of a group of perennial herbs and woody vines of the crowfoot family, with bright-colored flowers of varying size and form.

Cle·men·ceau, Georges (zhôrzh′ klā′män′sō′; Eng. klem′ən-sō′), 1841–1929; French statesman; premier of France (1906–1909; 1917–1920): called *the Tiger.*

clem·en·cy (klem′ən-si), *n.* [*pl.* CLEMENCIES (-siz)], [L. *clementia* < *clemens,* merciful], 1. forbearance, leniency, or mercy, as toward an offender or enemy. 2. a merciful or lenient act. 3. mildness, as of weather. —***SYN.*** see **mercy.**

Clem·ens, Samuel Lang·horne (laŋ′hôrn′ klem′ənz), see **Twain, Mark.**

Clem·ent (klem′ənt), [L. *Clemens* < *clemens,* mild, gentle], a masculine name: diminutive, *Clem;* feminine, *Clementine.*

clem·ent (klem′ənt), *adj.* [L. *clemens*], 1. forbearing; lenient; merciful. 2. mild: said of weather or climate.

Clement I, Saint, 30?–100? A.D.; Pope (90?–99? A.D.); first of the Apostolic Fathers.

Clement VII, (born *Giulio de' Medici*), 1478–1534; Pope (1523–1534); excommunicated Henry VIII.

Clem·en·ti·na (klem′ən-tē′nə), [It.], a feminine name: see **Clementine.**

Clem·en·tine (klem′ən-tēn′, klem′ən-tīn′), [Fr. < L. *Clemens;* see CLEMENT], a feminine name.

Clement of Alexandria, (*Titus Flavius Clemens*), 150?–220? A.D.; Greek Christian theologian.

clench (klench), *v.t.* [ME. *clenchen;* AS. *-clencan* (in *beclencan*), lit., to make cling, caus. of AS. *clingan* (cf. CLING); akin to OHG. *klenken,* to tie, bind & G. *klinke,* door latch; IE. base **gleng(h)* < **gel-;* see CLIMB], 1. to clinch, as a nail. 2. to bring together tightly; close firmly, as the teeth or fist. 3. to grip tightly. *n.* 1. a firm grip. 2. a device that clenches.

cle·o·me (kli-ō′mi), *n.* [Mod. L.], any of a large group of woody, mostly tropical, plants of the caper family, with white, green, or purple flowers having feathery petals and long stamens.

Cle·om·e·nes (kli-om'ə-nēz'), *n.* the name of three Spartan kings of the 6th to the 3d centuries B.C.; especially, *Cleomenes III*, who attempted to institute sweeping social reforms; died 219? B.C.
Cle·on (klē'on), *n.* Athenian politician and general; lived ?–422 B.C.
Cle·o·pa·tra (klē'ə-pā'trə, klē'ə-pat'rə, klē'ō-pä'trə), *n.* queen of Egypt (51–49 B.C.; 48–30 B.C.); mistress of Julius Caesar and Mark Antony; lived 69–30 B.C.
Cleopatra's Needle, 1. an ancient Egyptian obelisk now in Central Park, New York City. 2. another such obelisk on the Thames Embankment, London.
clepe (klēp), *v.t.* [ME. *clepen;* AS. *cleopian, clipian*], 1. [Obs.], to call or address (a person). 2. [Archaic], to call by name; name: generally in the archaic past participle, *yclept, ycleped.*
clep·sy·dra (klep'si-drə), *n.* [*pl.* CLEPSYDRAS (-drəz), CLEPSYDRAE (-drē')], [L.; Gr. *klepsydra,* water clock < *kleptein,* to steal + *hydōr,* water], a device for measuring time by marking the gradual flow of a liquid through a small opening; water clock.
clep·to·ma·ni·a (klep'tə-mā'ni-ə), *n.* kleptomania.
clere·sto·ry (klêr'stôr'i, klêr'stō'ri), *n.* [*pl.* CLERESTORIES (-iz, -riz)], [*clere* (for *clear*) + *story* (floor)], 1. the wall of a church rising above the roofs of the flanking aisles and containing windows for lighting the central part of the structure. 2. any similar windowed wall. Also spelled **clearstory.**
cler·gy (klũr'ji), *n.* [*pl.* CLERGIES (-jiz)], [ME. & OFr. *clergie,* office or dignity of a clergyman; LL. *clericus;* see CLERK], men ordained for religious service, as ministers, priests, etc., collectively.
cler·gy·man (klũr'ji-mən), *n.* [*pl.* CLERGYMEN (-mən)], a member of the clergy; minister, priest, etc.
cler·ic (kler'ik), *n.* [LL. *clericus;* see CLERK], a clergyman. *adj.* relating to a clergyman or the clergy.
cler·i·cal (kler'i-k'l), *adj.* [*cleric* + *-al*], 1. relating to a clergyman or the clergy. 2. relating to a clerk or clerks; of office work, such as keeping records, copying, filing, etc. 3. favoring the influence of the clergy in political matters: often in a derogatory sense. *n.* 1. a clergyman. 2. a person who believes in advancing the political power of the clergy: often in a derogatory sense.
cler·i·cal·ism (kler'i-k'l-iz'm), *n.* 1. political influence or power of the clergy. 2. policies or principles favoring this. Generally a derogatory term.
cler·i·cal·ist (kler'i-k'l-ist), *n.* a person in favor of clericalism.
cler·i·cals (kler'i-k'lz), *n.pl.* clergymen's garments.
cler·i·sy (kler'ə-si), *n.* [ML. *clericia;* cf. CLERGY], learned people as a class; intellectuals collectively.
clerk (klũrk; Brit. klärk), *n.* [ME. *clerke, clerk* < OFr. & AS.; OFr. *clerc,* AS. *cleric, clerc;* both < LL. *clericus;* Gr. *klērikos,* clergyman, priest < *klēros,* clergy, lit., a lot, or that which is chosen by lot], 1. a layman who has certain minor duties in a church. 2. an office worker who keeps accounts and records, does filing and copying, etc.: in public service, other duties, responsibilities, etc. may be involved, as in the case of a city *clerk* or a *clerk* of courts. 3. a person employed in selling goods in a store; salesman or saleswoman. Abbreviated **clk., cl.** 4. [Archaic], a clergyman. 5. [Archaic], anyone able to read and write; literate person; scholar. *v.i.* to work or be employed as a clerk.
clerk·ly (klũrk'li), *adj.* [CLERKLIER (-li-ẽr), CLERKLIEST (-li-ist)], 1. of, like, or characteristic of a clerk. 2. [Archaic], scholarly. *adv.* in a clerkly manner.
Clerk-Max·well, James (klärk'maks'wəl), 1831–1879; Scottish physicist.
clerk·ship (klũrk'ship), *n.* [see -SHIP], the work or position of a clerk.
Cler·mont-Fer·rand (kler'mōn'fe'rän'), *n.* a city in central France: pop., 113,000.
cleve·ite (klēv'īt, klā'vi-īt'), *n.* [after P. T. *Cleve* (1840–1905), Swed. chemist], a radioactive crystalline mineral: it is a variety of uraninite, found in Norway.
Cleve·land (klēv'lənd), *n.* a city in northeastern Ohio, on Lake Erie: pop., 876,000 (metropolitan area, 1,797,000).
Cleve·land, Gro·ver (grō'vẽr klēv'lənd), (*Stephen Grover Cleveland*), 1837–1908; American lawyer and statesman; twenty-second and twenty-fourth president of the United States (1885–1889; 1893–1897).
Cleveland Heights, a city in northeastern Ohio: a suburb of Cleveland: pop., 62,000.
clev·er (klev'ẽr), *adj.* [East Anglian ME. & Early Mod. Eng. *cliver,* replacing earlier *deliver* in literary Eng.; if not dial. (fisherman's) loan word < cognate E. Fris. *clüfer,* prob. < AS. *clifian,* to cleave (hence, discern; cf. SKILL), either directly or via ME. *cliver,* claw, hand (also < AS. *clifian*) in the sense, "adroit with the hand"; for the latter sense development, cf. ADROIT, DEXTEROUS], 1. skillful in doing something; adroit; dexterous; talented. 2. intelligent; able to learn. 3. ingenious; quick-witted; bright. 4. showing ingenuity or intelligence: as, a *clever* book. 5. [Dial.], amiable; good-natured. 6. [Dial. or Slang], handsome, nice, etc.
***SYN.*—clever,** in this comparison, implies quick-wittedness or adroitness, as in contriving the solution to a problem (a *clever* reply); **cunning** suggests great skill or ingenuity, but often implies deception or craftiness (*cunning* as a fox); **ingenious** stresses inventive skill, as in origination or fabrication (an *ingenious* explanation); **shrewd** suggests cleverness accompanied by practicality (a *shrewd* understanding of the situation), sometimes verging on craftiness (a *shrewd* politician). See also **intelligent.**
clev·is (klev'is), *n.* [prob. akin to *cleave* (to cling)], a U-shaped piece of iron with holes in the ends through which a pin is run to attach one thing to another, as a whippletree to the tongue of a wagon.

CLEVIS

clew (kloo), *n.* [ME. *clewe;* AS. *cleowen;* akin to D. *klüwen* & dissimilated G. *knäuel;* IE. base **g(e)l-eu-* (cf. CLAW), seen also in Sans. *glāu-h,* ball], 1. a ball of thread or yarn: in Greek legend, a thread was used by Theseus as a guide out of the labyrinth; hence, 2. something that leads out of a maze, perplexity, etc., or helps to solve a problem: in this sense generally spelled **clue.** 3. in *nautical usage, a*) either of the two lower corners of a square sail. *b*) the lower corner aft of a fore-and-aft sail. *c*) a metal loop fastened in the corner of a sail. *d*) a combination of lines by which a hammock is hung. *v.t.* 1. to wind up into a ball (usually with *up*). 2. to indicate by or as by a clew (with *out*). 3. to trace, as by a clew. Also spelled **clue.**
  clew down, to lower (a sail) by the clews.
  clew up, to raise (a sail) by the clews.
clew lines, the system of ropes and pulleys connecting the clew of a sail with the yard or mast, used in raising or lowering the sail.
cli·ché (klē-shā'), *n.* [Fr. < *clicher,* to stereotype < G. *klitsch,* clump, claylike mass; hence, orig., to pattern in clay], 1. a stereotype printing plate. 2. an expression or idea that has become trite. —***SYN.*** see **platitude.**
Cli·chy (klē'shē'), *n.* a city in France: a suburb of Paris: pop., 56,000.
click (klik), *n.* [echoic; cf. D. *klikken,* Fr. *cliquer, cliqueter*], 1. a slight, sharp sound like that of a door latch snapping into place. 2. a mechanical device, as a catch or pawl, that clicks into position. 3. in *phonetics,* any of a class of sounds, common in some African languages, made by drawing the breath into the mouth and clicking the tongue. *v.i.* 1. to make a click. 2. [Slang], *a*) to be suddenly clear or comprehensible. *b*) to be a success. *v.t.* to cause to click.
click beetle, a kind of beetle that makes a clicking sound when it rights itself after being on its back.
cli·ent (klī'ənt), *n.* [ME.; Fr. < L. *cliens,* follower, retainer; IE. base **klei-,* to lean, incline, as in L. *clinare* (cf. INCLINE); basic sense, "one leaning on another (for protection)"], 1. in ancient Rome, a plebeian who was dependent on a patrician patron. 2. a dependent; person under the patronage of another. 3. a person or company in its relationship to a lawyer, accountant, etc. engaged to act in its behalf. 4. loosely, a customer.
cli·ent·age (klī'ən-tij), *n.* clientele.
cli·en·tele (klī'ən-tel'), *n.* [Fr. < L. *clientela,* relation of patron and client, patronage; see CLIENT], 1. the clients of a lawyer, doctor, etc., or the habitual customers of a store, hotel, amusement place, etc. 2. the number of such clients or customers.
cliff (klif), *n.* [ME. & AS. *clif;* akin to AS. *clipian,* to adhere; basic sense, "slippery, smooth rock"; for IE. base, see CLEAVE (to cling), CLAY], a high, steep rock or face of rock, especially one on a coast.
cliff dweller, a member of a race of ancient American Indians of the Southwest, who lived in hollows or caves of cliffs: they were ancestors of the Pueblo Indians.
Clif·ford (klif'ẽrd), [< *cliff* + *ford;* hence, lit., ford at the cliff], a masculine name: diminutive, *Cliff.*
cliff swallow, a North American swallow that builds its gourdlike nest of mud, grass, and feathers against a cliff or under the eaves of a building.
cliff·y (klif'i), *adj.* having many cliffs; craggy.
Clif·ton (klif'tən), [< *cliff* + *-ton* (town); hence, lit., town at a cliff], a masculine name. *n.* a city in northeastern New Jersey: pop., 82,000.
cli·mac·ter·ic (klī-mak'tẽr-ik, klī'mak-ter'ik), *n.* [L. *climactericus;* Gr. *klimaktērikos* < *klimaktēr,* step of a staircase, round of a ladder < *klimax,* ladder], 1. a period in the life of a person when an important change in health or bodily function occurs, especially the period of the menopause in women. 2. any crucial period or event. *adj.* of or resembling a climacteric; crucial.
  the grand climacteric, the 63d year of a person's life, when especially radical changes are supposed to occur.

cli·mac·ter·i·cal (klī'mak-ter'i-k'l), *adj.* climacteric.
cli·mac·tic (klī-mak'tik), *adj.* of, constituting, or in the order of a climax.
cli·mac·ti·cal (klī-mak'ti-k'l), *adj.* climactic.
cli·mate (klī'mit), *n.* [ME. & OFr. *climat;* L. *clima;* Gr. *klima,* region, zone], 1. the prevailing or average weather conditions of a place, as determined by the temperature and meteorological changes over a period of years: distinguished from *weather.* 2. any prevailing conditions affecting life, activity, etc. 3. a region considered with reference to the kind of weather prevailing there: as, he went south to a warmer *climate.*
cli·mat·ic (klī-mat'ik), *adj.* of climate.
cli·mat·i·cal·ly (klī-mat'i-k'l-i, klī-mat'ik-li), *adv.* with regard to climate.
cli·ma·to·log·ic (klī'mə-tə-loj'ik), *adj.* of climatology.
cli·ma·tol·o·gy (klī'mə-tol'ə-ji), *n.* the science dealing with climate and climatic phenomena.
cli·max (klī'maks), *n.* [L. < Gr. *klimax,* ladder], 1. a series of ideas or events arranged or occurring progressively so that the most forceful is last. 2. the final, culminating element in such a series: in dramatic structure, it is the decisive turning point of the action. 3. the highest point, as of interest, excitement, etc.; culmination. *v.i. & v.t.* to reach, or bring to, a climax. —*SYN.* see **summit.**
climb (klīm), *v.i. & v.t.* [CLIMBED (klīmd) or *archaic* CLOMB (klōm), CLIMBING], [ME. *climben;* AS. *climban;* akin to G. *klimmen;* IE. base **glembh-* (cf. CLAMBER) < **gel-,* to make round, ball up, clench, as the fist; basic sense, "to cling to, grip"], 1. to move up, especially by using the hands and feet; ascend; mount. 2. to ascend gradually or laboriously: as, he *climbed* to power in ten years. 3. in *botany,* to grow upward on (a wall, etc.) by winding around or adhering with tendrils. *n.* 1. a climbing; rise; ascent. 2. a thing or place to be climbed.
climb down, to move down, especially by using the hands and feet; descend: sometimes used figuratively in reference to abandoning an extreme or untenable opinion, attitude, etc.
climb·er (klīm'ẽr), *n.* 1. a person or thing that climbs. 2. a metal spike fastened to a shoe to aid in climbing telephone poles, etc.; climbing iron. 3. [Colloq.], a person who constantly tries to advance himself socially or in business. 4. in *botany,* a plant or vine that grows upward by twining about a support, as with tendrils.
climb indicator, an instrument for indicating the rate of ascent or descent of an aircraft: it is operated by changes in the atmospheric pressure at different levels.
climbing fish, any of a group of fresh-water fish of the East Indies that can live out of water for some time, travel on the ground, and are said to climb trees.
climbing irons, metal spikes fastened to a shoe to aid in climbing telephone poles, etc.
clime (klīm), *n.* [L. *clima;* see CLIMATE], [Poetic], a country; region; realm; climate.
cli·nan·dri·um (kli-nan'dri-əm), *n.* [*pl.* CLINANDRIA (-ə)], [Mod. L. < Gr. *klinē,* bed + *anēr,* man], a cavity in the top of the column of an orchid, containing the anther.
clinch (klinch), *v.t.* [ME. *clenchen;* var. of *clench* with vowel raised by nasalization], 1. to fasten (a nail, bolt, etc. that has been driven through something) by bending or flattening the projecting end. 2. to fasten firmly together by this means. 3. to settle (an argument, bargain, etc.) definitely; close conclusively. *v.i.* 1. to clinch a nail, bolt, etc. 2. in *boxing,* to grip the opponent's body with the arms so as to hinder his punching; hence, 3. [Slang], to embrace. *n.* 1. a fastening or fastening together. 2. a fastening in which the nail, bolt, etc. is clinched. 3. a clinched nail, bolt, etc. 4. the part clinched. 5. in *boxing,* an act of clinching; hence, 6. [Slang], an embrace. 7. in *nautical usage,* a kind of knot or noose in a rope; clench: see **knot,** illus.
clinch·er (klin'chẽr), *n.* 1. a person who clinches. 2. a tool for clinching nails. 3. [Colloq.], a point that is conclusive or decisive, as in an argument.
cling (kliŋ), *v.i.* [CLUNG (kluŋ), CLINGING], [ME. *clingen;* AS. *clingan,* to adhere, stick together; akin to MHG. *klingan,* to climb; IE. base **gleng(h)-* < **gel-;* see CLIMB], 1. to adhere; stick; hold fast by or as by embracing or entwining. 2. to be or stay near, as if holding fast. —*SYN.* see **stick.**
cling·fish (kliŋ'fish'), *n.* [*pl.* CLINGFISH, CLINGFISHES (-iz); see FISH], any of a group of small, tropical marine fishes having a sucking disc on the ventral surface near the head, with which they cling to rocks.
clinging vine, a woman inclined to be helpless and dependent in her relationship with a man.
Cling·mans Dome (kliŋ'mənz), a peak of the Great Smoky Mountains, on the boundary between North Carolina and Tennessee: height, 6,642 ft.
cling·stone (kliŋ'stōn'), *adj.* having a stone that clings to the fleshy part: said of some peaches. *n.* a peach of this sort.
cling·y (kliŋ'i), *adj.* tending to cling; sticking; tenacious.
clin·ic (klin'ik), *n.* [L. *clinicus,* bed-ridden person, physician who attends patients sick in bed < Gr. *klinikos,* of the bed < *klinē,* a bed], 1. the teaching of medicine by examining and treating patients in the presence of students. 2. a class getting such teaching. 3. a place where patients are studied or treated by physicians specializing in various ailments and practicing as a group: as, a cancer *clinic.* 4. the dispensary or outpatient department of a hospital or medical school, where patients are treated free or for a small fee. 5. an organization or institution that offers some kind of advice or treatment: as, a domestic-relations *clinic.*
clin·i·cal (klin'i-k'l), *adj.* 1. of or connected with a clinic or a sickbed. 2. having to do with medical study or practice based on actual treatment and observation of patients, as distinguished from experimental or laboratory study; hence, 3. purely scientific; dispassionately curious: as, she regarded his death with *clinical* detachment. 4. in *ecclesiastical usage,* administered on a sickbed or deathbed.
clin·i·cal·ly (klin'i-k'l-i, klin'ik-li), *adv.* by or according to clinical procedure.
clinical thermometer, a thermometer with which the body temperature is measured.
cli·ni·cian (kli-nish'ən), *n.* an expert in clinical medicine.
clink (kliŋk), *v.i. & v.t.* [ME. *clinken;* origin echoic], to make or cause to make a slight, sharp sound, as of glasses striking together. *n.* 1. such a sound. 2. [so named from the sound of the fetters], [Colloq.], a jail; prison.
clink·er (kliŋk'ẽr), *n.* [D. *klinker,* vitrified brick that clinks when struck; earlier *klinckaerd* < *klinken,* to ring], 1. a very hard brick. 2. a brick with a surface made glassy by heat and fusion. 3. a mass of fused bricks. 4. a hard mass of fused stony matter formed in a furnace from impurities in the coal or in the kiln.
clink·er-built (kliŋk'ẽr-bilt'), *adj.* [*clinker* < *clink,* dial. var. of *clinch*], built with overlapping boards or plates, as in shipbuilding.
clink·stone (kliŋk'stōn'), *n.* in *mineralogy,* any of various varieties of phonolite that make a clinking, metallic sound when struck.
cli·no- (klī'nō, klī'nə), [< Gr. *klino-* < *klinein,* to bend, slope], a combining form meaning *slope, slant,* as in *clinometer:* also, before a vowel, **clin-.**
cli·nom·e·ter (klī-nom'ə-tẽr), *n.* [*clino-* + *-meter*], an instrument for measuring the angle of slope or inclination, as of an embankment.
cli·no·met·ric (klī'nə-met'rik), *adj.* [*clino-* + *-metric*], 1. of or measured by a clinometer. 2. in *mineralogy,* of oblique crystalline structures.
cli·no·met·ri·cal (klī'nə-met'ri-k'l), *adj.* clinometric.
clin·quant (kliŋ'kənt), *adj.* [Fr., ppr. of earlier Fr. *clinquer,* to clink, glitter; prob. < MD. *klinken;* cf. CLINK], glittering or adorned with or, especially, as with gold or silver; tinseled. *n.* imitation gold leaf; tinsel.
Clin·ton (klin'tən), [Eng. place name; ? < Anglo-N. *klint,* hill + AS. *tun,* enclosure, village; see TOWN], a masculine name. *n.* a city in eastern Iowa, on the Mississippi: pop., 34,000.
Clin·ton, De·Witt (də-wit' klin'tən), 1769–1828; nephew of *George;* American statesman; governor of New York (1817–1821; 1825–1828).
Clinton, George, 1739–1812; American statesman; vice-president of the United States (1805–1812).
Clinton, Sir **Henry,** 1738?–1795; British general; commander in chief of British forces in North America (1778–1781).
clin·to·ni·a (klin-tō'ni-ə), *n.* [Mod. L., after DeWitt *Clinton*], any of a group of hardy herbs with broad leaves, white or yellow flowers, and blue berries.
Cli·o (klī'ō), *n.* [L.; Gr. *Kleiō* < *kleiein,* to celebrate < *kleos,* fame, glory], in *Greek mythology,* the Muse of history.
clip (klip), *v.t.* [CLIPPED (klipt), CLIPPING], [ME. *clippen;* ON. *klippa*], 1. to cut or cut off with shears or scissors. 2. to cut short. 3. to cut the hair of. 4. to cut off the edge of (coins, etc.). 5. [Colloq.], to hit or punch with a quick, sharp blow. 6. [Slang], to cheat; swindle; rob. *v.i.* 1. to cut something. 2. to cut out newspaper or magazine clippings. 3. [Colloq.], to move rapidly. *n.* 1. a clipping; shearing. 2. a thing clipped. 3. the amount of wool clipped from sheep at one time or in one season. 4. [Colloq.], a quick, sharp blow, punch, or stroke. 5. [Colloq.], rapid motion or pace.
clip (klip), *v.i. & v.t.* [CLIPPED or *archaic* CLIPT (klipt), CLIPPING], [ME. *clippen;* AS. *clyppan,* to embrace; akin to OFris. *kleppa,* to embrace; IE. base **g(e)leb(h)-,* etc. < **gel-;* see CLASP], 1. to grip tightly; fasten. 2. [Archaic & Dial.], to hug; embrace closely. 3. in *football,* to throw oneself from behind across the lower part of the leg or legs of (an opponent who is not carrying the ball), so as to cause him to fall: an illegal act. *n.* 1. anything that clips or fastens. 2. a cartridge clip. 3. [Obs.], an embrace. 4. in *football,* the act of clipping.
clip-fed (klip'fed'), *adj.* automatically loaded from a cartridge clip: said of certain repeating firearms.
clipped form (or **word**), a shortened form of a word, as *mob* (for *mobile*), *chum* (for *chamber fellow*), etc.

clip·per (klip′ẽr), *n.* [*clip* (to cut) + *-er;* senses 3 & 4 possibly influenced by D. *klepper*, orig., swift horse < LG. *kleppen*, to sound like hoof beats], 1. a person who cuts, shears, etc. 2. a tool for cutting or shearing, as a shears for trimming hedges. 3. [for sense, cf. CUTTER], *a*) a sharp-bowed, narrow-beamed sailing ship (c. 1830–1854) built for great speed. *b*) a modified form of this with less speed and greater cargo capacity; hence, 4. a horse, sled, automobile, airplane, etc. regarded as especially fast.

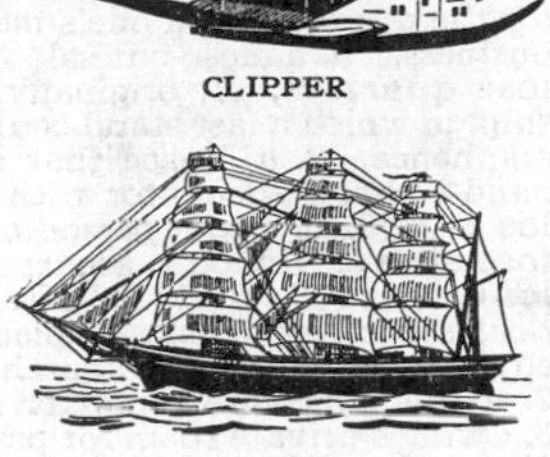
CLIPPER

CLIPPER SHIP

clip·per-built (klip′ẽr-bilt′), *adj.* built with long, smooth lines for speed: said of ships.
clip·pers (klip′ẽrz), *n. pl.* [< *clipper*], a barber's tool for clipping hair.
clip·ping (klip′iŋ), *n.* [< *clip* (to cut)], 1. a piece cut out or off of something. 2. an item cut out of a newspaper, etc. *adj.* 1. cutting. 2. swiftly moving.
clipt (klipt), archaic past tense and past participle of **clip** (to embrace).
clique (klēk, klik), *n.* [Fr. < *cliquer*, to make a noise; see CLAQUE, CLICK], a small, exclusive circle of people; snobbish or narrow coterie. *v.i.* [CLIQUED (klēkt, klikt), CLIQUING], [Colloq.], to gather in, or act as, a clique. —*SYN.* see **coterie.**
cli·quish (klē′kish, klik′ish), *adj.* 1. like a clique. 2. inclined to form a clique or cliques.
cli·quy, cli·quey (klē′ki, klik′i), *adj.* cliquish.
cli·to·ris (klī′tə-ris, klit′ə-ris), *n.* [LL. < Gr. *kleitoris* < *kleiein*, to close, hide], a small, sensitive, erectile organ at the upper end of the external female genital organ: it corresponds to the penis of the male.
Clive (klīv), [< *cliff*], a masculine name.
Clive, Robert (klīv), Baron Clive of Plassey, 1725–1774; British general and statesman; founded empire of British India.
clk., 1. clerk. 2. clock.
clo·a·ca (klō-ā′kə), *n.* [*pl.* CLOACAE (-sē)], [L. < *cluere*, to cleanse], 1. a sewer. 2. a toilet bowl; water closet; privy. 3. in *zoology*, the cavity into which both the intestinal and the genito-urinary tracts empty in reptiles, birds, amphibians, and many fishes.
clo·a·cal (klō-ā′k'l), *adj.* of a cloaca.
cloak (klōk), *n.* [ME. & OFr. *cloke*, a cloak; LL. *cloca*, a bell, cloak: so called from its bell-like appearance; see CLOCK (timepiece)], 1. a loose, usually sleeveless outer garment. 2. something that covers or conceals; disguise. *v.t.* 1. to cover with or as with a cloak. 2. to conceal; hide.
cloak-and-dag·ger (klōk′ən-dag′ẽr), *adj.* of or characteristic of the activities of spies and undercover agents, especially as extravagantly depicted in fiction.
cloak·room (klōk′rōōm′, klōk′room′), *n.* a room where hats, coats, umbrellas, etc. can be left temporarily.
clob·ber (klob′ẽr), *v.t.* [? freq. of *club, v.t.*], [Slang], 1. to beat or hit repeatedly; maul. 2. to defeat decisively.
cloche (klōsh; Fr. klôsh), *n.* [Fr.; LL. *clocca*, a bell; see CLOCK (timepiece)], 1. a bell-shaped glass jar used to cover delicate plants. 2. a closefitting, bell-shaped hat for women.
clock (klok), *n.* [ME. *clocke, clok*, orig., clock with bells; MD. *klocke;* LL. *clocca*, hand bell; prob. < Celt. (cf. OIr. *clocc*, W. *cloch*, bell); akin to G. *glocke* (cf. GLOCKENSPIEL); same echoic base (< IE. **qel-*, to sound) as in AS. *cloccian*, to make a noise (whence Eng. *cluck*); cf. CLOAK], a device for measuring time, usually by means of pointers moving over a dial: unlike a watch, a clock is not worn or carried about in the pocket: abbreviated **clk.** *v.t.* to measure or record the time of (a race, runner, etc.) with a stop watch.
clock (klok), *n.* [prob. < *clock* (timepiece) because of its original bell shape], a woven or embroidered ornament on the side of a stocking, going up from the ankle. *v.t.* to put such an ornament on.
clock·like (klok′līk′), *adj.* with the precision or regularity of a clock.
clock·wise (klok′wīz′), *adv.* & *adj.* [*clock* (timepiece) + *-wise*], in the direction in which the hands of a clock rotate.
clock·work (klok′wũrk′), *n.* 1. the mechanism of a clock. 2. any similar mechanism, consisting of springs and geared wheels, as in some mechanical toys.
like clockwork, very regularly, precisely, and evenly.
clod (klod), *n.* [ME. *clodde, clotte;* AS. *clott, clod-* (in compounds), round mass; var. (with specialized senses) of *clot*], 1. a lump, especially a lump of earth, clay, loam, etc. 2. earth; soil. 3. a dull, stupid fellow; dolt. 4. the part of the neck of beef nearest the shoulder.
clod·dish (klod′ish), *adj.* like a clod; dull; awkward.
clod·dy (klod′i), *adj.* full of clods.
clod·hop·per (klod′hop′ẽr), *n.* [*clod* + *hopper;* ? after *grasshopper*, or like *bogtrotter*], 1. a plowman. 2. an awkward, clumsy fellow; boor. 3. a coarse, heavy shoe, such as is worn by a plowman.
clod·pate (klod′pāt′), *n.* [*clod* + *pate*], a blockhead; clumsy, stupid fellow.
clod·poll, clod·pole (klod′pōl′), *n.* a clodpate.
clog (klog), *n.* [ME. *clogge*, a lump of wood; ? < ON (non-nasal) form of the base (IE. **glegh-*) in *clinch, clutch;* cf. Sw. *klunga*, a lump, mass; influenced as *v.i.* by dial. *clag* (to make sticky)], 1. a weight fastened to the leg of an animal to hinder motion. 2. anything that hinders or obstructs; hindrance. 3. a heavy shoe, usually with a wooden sole: light clogs are used in clog dancing. 4. a clog dance. *v.t.* [CLOGGED (klogd), CLOGGING], 1. to hinder; impede. 2. to obstruct (a passage, etc.); block up. *v.i.* 1. to become clogged or blocked up. 2. to become thick or sticky, so as to clog. 3. to do a clog dance.
clog almanac, a primitive calendar consisting of a block of wood on which notches were cut to record the passage of time.
clog dance, a dance in which clogs are worn to beat out the rhythm.
clog·gy (klog′i), *adj.* tending to clog.
cloi·son·né (kloi′zə-nā′), *adj.* [Fr., lit., partitioned < *cloison*, partition < LL. **clausione* < L. *clausus;* see CLOISTER], denoting a kind of enamel work in which the surface decoration is set in hollows formed by thin strips of wire welded to a metal plate in a complex pattern. *n.* cloisonné enamel.
clois·ter (klois′tẽr), *n.* [ME. *cloistre, cloister;* OFr. *cloistre;* L. *claustrum*, that which closes, bolt, place shut in < pp. of *claudere*, to close], 1. a place of religious seclusion; monastery or nunnery. 2. monastic life. 3. any place where one may lead a secluded life. 4. an arched way or covered walk along the inside wall or walls of a monastery, convent, church, or college building, with a columned opening along one side leading to a courtyard or garden. *v.t.* 1. to confine in or as in a cloister. 2. to furnish or surround with a cloister.

CLOISTER

SYN.—**cloister** is the general term for a place of religious seclusion, for either men or women, and emphasizes in connotation retirement from the world; **convent**, once a general term synonymous with **cloister**, is now usually restricted to such a place for women (nuns), formerly called a **nunnery**; **monastery** usually refers to a cloister for men (monks); an **abbey** is a cloister ruled by an abbot or abbess; a **priory** is a cloister ruled by a prior or prioress and is sometimes a subordinate branch of an abbey.
clois·tered (klois′tẽrd), *adj.* [pp. of *cloister*], 1. secluded; retired from the world. 2. furnished with cloisters.
clois·tral (klois′trəl), *adj.* 1. of, like, or fit for a cloister. 2. confined in a cloister. 3. as if confined in a cloister; secluded; retired.
cloke (klōk), *n.* & *v.t.* [CLOKED (klōkt), CLOKING], [Archaic], cloak.
clomb (klōm), archaic past tense and past participle of **climb.**
clon (klon, klōn), *n.* a clone.
clone (klōn), *n.* [< Gr. *klōn*, a twig], in *botany*, a group of plants all of whose members are directly descended from a single individual, as by grafting or budding.
clon·ic (klon′ik), *adj.* of clonus.
clo·nic·i·ty (klə-nis′ə-ti), *n.* a clonic condition.
clo·nus, clo·nos (klō′nəs), *n.* [Mod. L.; Gr. *klonos*, turmoil], a series of spasms of a muscle or group of muscles.
close (klōs), *adj.* [ME. *clos;* OFr. *clos*, pp. of *clore*, to close (see CLOSE, *v.*); senses under II from notion "with spaces or intervals closed up"], I. *denoting the fact or state of being closed or of confinement, in various senses* 1. shut; not open. 2. enclosed or enclosing; shut in. 3. confined or confining; narrow: as, *close* quarters. 4. in strict confinement; carefully guarded: as, a *close* secret. 5. shut away from observation; hidden; secluded. 6. secretive; reserved; reticent. 7. stingy; niggardly; miserly; close-fisted. 8. confined to specific groups; not open to the public; restricted. 9. confined in circulation; oppressive; humid: said of weather, atmosphere, etc. 10. hard to get; scarce; not easily available: as, credit is *close*. 11. in *phonetics*, uttered with the tongue relatively near the palate: said of certain vowels, as (ē). II. *denoting nearness, proximity, in various senses* 1. with little space between; near

together; with the intervening space closing or closed up. 2. having parts or elements near together; compact; dense: as, *close* marching order, *close* weave. 3. fitting tightly: as, a *close* coat. 4. near, proximate, or down to the surface on which something grows: as, a *close* shave. 5. very near in interests, affection, etc.; intimate; familiar: as, a *close* friend. 6. in strict agreement with an original or model: as a *close* translation. 7. strict; thorough; careful: as, *close* attention. 8. compactly expressed; concise: as, a *close* argument. 9. nearly equal or alike: as, a *close* resemblance. 10. nearly equal in balance, outcome, etc.: as, a *close* contest. ***adv.*** in a close manner; very near; closely.

close to the wind, 1. in *nautical usage,* heading as closely as possible in the direction from which the wind blows. 2. barely avoiding what is unlawful.

SYN.—**close** suggests something whose parts or elements are near together with little space between (*close*-order drill); **dense** suggests such a crowding together of elements or parts as to form an almost impervious mass (a *dense* fog); **compact** suggests close and firm packing, especially within a small space, and usually implies neatness and order in the arrangement of parts (a *compact* bundle); **thick,** in this connection, suggests a great number of parts massed tightly together (*thick* fur). See also **familiar, stingy.**—***ANT.*** open, dispersed.

close (klōz), ***v.t.*** [CLOSED (klōzd), CLOSING[1], [ME. *closen* < OFr. *clos-*, stem of *clore* < L. *claudere,* to close, block up; akin to L. *clavis* < IE. base **glēu-*, **glāu-*, hook, forked limb, hindrance; hence akin to G. *schliessen,* to close, lock, and Eng. dial. *slot,* a bolt, bar], 1. to shut. 2. to fill up or stop (an opening). 3. to bring to a finish; discontinue; conclude. 4. to bring or bind together; unite. ***v.i.*** 1. to become shut; shut itself. 2. to come to an end. 3. to come close, in order to attack; grapple. 4. to come together. 5. to agree. ***n.*** an end; finish.

close down, to shut or stop entirely.

close in, to draw near from various directions, cutting off escape on all sides; surround.

close out, to dispose of (goods) by sale, as in ending a business.

close round, to encircle; surround.

close up, 1. to draw nearer together. 2. to shut or stop up entirely. 3. to heal, as a wound does.

SYN.—**close** suggests a coming or bringing to a stop, as if by shutting something regarded as previously open (nominations are now *closed*); **end** suggests the stopping of some process, whether or not it has been satisfactorily completed (let's *end* this argument at once); to **conclude** is to bring or come to a formal termination, often by arriving at some decision (to *conclude* negotiations); **finish** emphasizes the bringing to a desired end of that which one has set out to do, especially by adding perfecting touches (to *finish* a painting); **complete,** in its distinctive sense, suggests a finishing by filling in the missing or defective parts (the award will *complete* his happiness); to **terminate** is to bring or come to an end regarded as a limit or boundary (to *terminate* a friendship).—***ANT.*** begin, start, commence.

close (klōs), ***n.*** [ME. & OFr. *clos;* L. *clausum;* neut. pp. of *claudere;* see CLOSE, *v.*], 1. an enclosed place. 2. enclosed grounds around or beside a building: as, a cathedral *close.* 3. [British], an entry or passage.

close call (klōs), [Colloq.], a narrow escape from danger.

close corporation (klōs), a corporation in which a few persons hold all of the stock, which is rarely or never placed on the market: also **closed corporation.**

closed chain, the structural form of the molecule of certain chemical compounds, represented in models and formulas as a ring of atoms.

closed circuit, in *television,* a system for transmitting a telecast over cables, rather than through space, to a limited number of receivers connected to a circuit.

closed gentian, a North American plant with dark-blue, closed, tubular flowers, blooming in the fall.

closed primary, a direct primary election in which only the members of a given political party, as determined by enrollment, previous voting record, etc., may vote for candidates of that party.

closed season, any of various annual periods during which it is illegal to kill or capture certain game or fish.

closed shop, 1. a factory, business, etc. operating under a contractual arrangement between a labor union and the employer by which only members of the union may be employed. 2. this arrangement.

close·fist·ed (klōs'fis'tid), ***adj.*** stingy; miserly; close.

close·fit·ting (klōs'fit'iŋ), ***adj.*** fitting tightly enough to show the contours of the body.

close-grained (klōs'grānd'), ***adj.*** having a fine, compact grain or texture, as certain woods.

close harmony, in *music,* harmony consisting primarily of chords having all four tones within the compass of an octave.

close-hauled (klōs'hôld'), ***adj.*** having the sails adjusted (hauled close) for heading as nearly as possible in the direction from which the wind is blowing.

close-lipped (klōs'lipt'), ***adj.*** close-mouthed.

close·ly (klōs'li), ***adv.*** 1. in a close manner; narrowly, tightly, intently, etc. 2. to a close extent.

close-mouthed (klōs'mouthd', klōs'moutht'), ***adj.*** not talking much; telling little; taciturn; reticent.

close·ness (klōs'nis), ***n.*** the condition of being close.

close-or·der drill (klōs'ôr'dẽr), a series of military exercises in marching, maneuvering, the ceremonial handling of arms, etc., in which the troops are arranged in compact units at close intervals and distances.

close-out, close·out (klōz'out'), ***adj.*** designating a sale for the disposal of all one's merchandise, as in ending a business. ***n.*** a close-out sale.

close quarters, 1. originally, an enclosed space on a ship, in which a last stand could be made against boarders; hence, 2. *a*) space that is narrow or crowded. *b*) hand-to-hand encounter with an enemy.

clos·er (klōz'ẽr), ***n.*** a person or thing that closes.

close shave, [Colloq.], a narrow escape from danger.

clos·et (kloz'it), ***n.*** [ME.; OFr., small enclosure, dim. of *clos;* see CLOSE (enclosed place)], 1. a small room or cupboard for clothes, household supplies, linens, etc. 2. a small, private room for reading, meditation, etc. 3. a king's private room for prayer or consultation. 4. a water closet; toilet. ***adj.*** 1. private; concealed. 2. designed or adapted only for private or secluded use: as, *closet* drama is written only to be read, not acted. ***v.t.*** to shut up in a private room for confidential discussion: usually reflexive, as, the treasurer *closeted* himself with the accountants for an hour.

close-up (klōs'up'), ***n.*** 1. in *motion pictures & television,* a picture, as of a character, made with the camera at very close range. 2. a close view.

clo·sure (klō'zhẽr), ***n.*** [ME.; OFr.; L. *clausura,* a closing < pp. of *claudere,* to close], 1. a closing or being closed. 2. a finish; end; conclusion. 3. anything that closes or shuts. 4. the parliamentary procedure by which debate is closed and the measure under discussion brought up for an immediate vote. ***v.t.*** [CLOSURED (-zhẽrd), CLOSURING], to apply closure to (a debate, bill, etc.).

clot (klot), ***n.*** [ME. *clot, clotte;* AS. *clott,* round mass < Gmc. **klutto-* (hence akin to D. *kloot,* ball, G. *klotz,* a block) < IE. **gel-;* see CLIMB; cf. CLOD], a thick, coagulated mass or semisolid lump: as, a blood *clot.* ***v.t. & v.i.*** [CLOTTED (-id), CLOTTING], to become or cause to become a clot or clots; coagulate.

cloth (klôth, kloth), ***n.*** [*pl.* CLOTHS (klôthz, klothz *in the sense* "pieces of cloth"; klôths, kloths *in the sense* "kinds of cloth"); *in the sense* "wearing apparel," CLOTHES (klōz, klōthz), now rarely identified with the sing., is the accepted usage], [ME. *cloth;* AS. *clath,* cloth, hence garment; akin to AS. *-clithan,* to stick, *clitha,* poultice, G. *kleid,* garment; Gmc. **klaith-*, prob. "made to stick (by fulling)" < IE. base **glei-*, to stick, adhere, as also in *clay, glue:* prob. sense development, piece of cloth—garment—garment material], 1. a woven, knitted, or pressed fabric of fibrous material, as cotton, wool, silk, hair, synthetic fibers, etc., used for wearing apparel, household furnishings, etc.: abbreviated **cl.** 2. a piece of such fabric for a specific use: as, table*cloth,* wash*cloth,* loin*cloth.* 3. the usual or identifying dress of any profession; hence, 4. the profession itself, especially the profession of a clergyman. 5. [Obs.], apparel; dress. 6. in *nautical usage,* canvas; sail. ***adj.*** made of cloth.

the cloth, the clergy.

clothe (klōth), ***v.t.*** [CLOTHED (klōthd), or CLAD (klad), CLOTHING], [ME. *clothen;* AS. *clathian* < *clath;* see CLOTH], 1. to put clothes on; dress. 2. to provide with clothes. 3. to cover over as if with a garment; provide; equip; invest: as, *clothed* in the dignity of his office.

clothes (klōz, klōthz), ***n. pl.*** [ME. *clathes, clothes;* AS. *clathas,* clothes, pl. of *clath;* see CLOTH], 1. covering for the body; articles, usually of cloth, designed to cover, protect, or adorn the body; wearing apparel; garments; dress; attire; raiment. 2. bedclothes.

clothes·horse (klōz'hôrs'), ***n.*** 1. a frame on which to hang clothes, etc. for airing or drying. 2. [Slang], a person regarded as paying too much attention to his clothes, or as having little talent except for dressing well.

clothes·line (klōz'līn'), ***n.*** a rope or wire on which clothes are hung for drying or airing.

clothes moth, any of various moths that lay their eggs in woolen clothes, etc. upon which the hatched larvae feed.

clothes·pin (klōz'pin'), ***n.*** a small clip, as a forked peg of wood or plastic, for fastening clothes on a line.

clothes pole, a pole for supporting a clothesline.

clothes·press (klōz'pres'), ***n.*** a closet, wardrobe, or chest in which to keep clothes: also **clothes press.**

clothes tree, an upright pole with branching hooks or pegs near the top to hold coats and hats.

cloth·ier (klōth'yẽr), ***n.*** [ME. *clothere,* clothworker < *clath;* see CLOTH], 1. a person who makes or sells clothes. 2. a dealer in cloth.

Clo·thil·da (klō-til'də), [Fr. < G. *Klothilde* < OHG. **klod,* **chlod,* famous (akin to AS. *hlud,* loud, Gr. *chlytos,* famous, Celt. *klu,* fame, L. *cluere,* to be esteemed) + *Hilde* (see HILDA); lit., famous in battle], a feminine name: also spelled **Clotilda.**

cloth·ing (klōth'iŋ), ***n.*** [ME. (akin to G. *kleidung*) < AS. *clath;* see CLOTH], 1. clothes; garments; wearing apparel. 2. a covering.

Clo·tho (klō'thō), ***n.*** [L.; Gr. *Klōthō* < *klōthein,* to spin], in *Greek mythology,* one of the three Fates, spinner of the thread of human life.

cloth yard, 1. the yard used in measuring cloth, equal to 3 feet (36 inches). 2. the arrow used with the longbow: so called from its length.
Clo·til·da (klō-til′də), a feminine name: see **Clothilda.**
clot·ty (klot′i), *adj.* containing clots; tending to clot.
clo·ture (klō′chẽr), *n.* & *v.t.* [CLOTURED (-chẽrd), CLOTURING], [Fr. *clôture;* OFr. *closture;* LL. **claustura* (altered after *claustrum;* see CLAUSTRAL) < L. *clausura;* see CLOSURE], closure: applied to parliamentary debate.
cloud (kloud), *n.* [ME. *cloude, clude,* orig., mass of rock, hence mass of anything, mass of cloud; AS. *clud,* mass of rock (cf. CLOD); IE. **g(e)l-eu-t* < **gel-;* see CLIMB], 1. a visible mass of vapor, especially one suspended in the sky: see **cirrus, cumulus, stratus,** illus. 2. a mass of smoke, dust, steam, etc. 3. a great number of things close together and in motion: as, a *cloud* of locusts. 4. an appearance of murkiness or dimness, as in a liquid or mirror. 5. a dark marking, as in marble. 6. anything that darkens, obscures, or makes gloomy. *v.t.* 1. to cover or make dark with clouds. 2. to darken; obscure; threaten. 3. to make gloomy or troubled. 4. to cast slurs on; sully (a reputation, etc.). *v.i.* 1. to become cloudy. 2. to become gloomy or troubled.
in the clouds, 1. high up in the sky; hence, 2. fanciful; impractical. 3. in a reverie or daydream.
under a cloud, 1. under suspicion of wrongdoing. 2. in a depressed or troubled state of mind.
cloud·ber·ry (kloud′ber′i), *n.* [*pl.* CLOUDBERRIES (-iz)], a wild raspberry: the fruit is yellowish-red.
cloud·burst (kloud′bũrst′), *n.* a sudden, unusually heavy rain; violent downpour.
cloud-capped (kloud′kapt′), *adj.* having clouds around the top: as, a *cloud-capped* mountain.
cloud chamber, an enclosed chamber supersaturated with water vapor for revealing the presence of moving charged particles by their ionization of the vapor.
cloud·i·ly (kloud′'l-i), *adv.* in a cloudy manner.
cloud·i·ness (kloud′i-nis), *n.* the condition or quality of being cloudy.
cloud·land (kloud′land′), *n.* region of dreams, myth, or imagination; visionary realm.
cloud·less (kloud′lis), *adj.* free from clouds; clear; bright.
cloud·let (kloud′lit), *n.* a small cloud.
cloud rack, a drifting mass of clouds.
cloud·y (kloud′i), *adj.* [CLOUDIER (-i-ẽr), CLOUDIEST (-i-ist)], 1. covered with clouds; overcast: abbreviated c. 2. of or like clouds. 3. variegated or streaked, as marble. 4. opaque; not transparent: said of liquids. 5. obscure; not distinct; dim. 6. frowning; troubled.
clough (kluf, klou), *n.* [ME.; AS. **cloh* < **klanh* < base of *cling;* akin to OHG. *clāh-* in *Clāh-uelde* & G. *klinge,* narrow gorge], a narrow ravine or gorge.
Clough, Arthur Hugh (kluf), 1819–1861; English poet and educator.
clout (klout), *n.* [ME. *cloute;* AS. *clut* (akin to MLG. *klūt,* clod of earth), orig., lump of something, hence piece of cloth, patch; base as in *clot, climb*], 1. [Archaic or Dial.], a piece of cloth or leather for patching. 2. [Colloq.], a blow, with or as with the hand; rap. 3. [Slang], a long, powerful hit in baseball. 4. in *archery, a)* a target of white cloth on a frame. *b)* a shot that strikes the target. *v.t.* [ME. *clutien* < the *n.*], 1. [Archaic or Dial.], to patch or mend coarsely. 2. [Colloq.], to strike, as with the hand; knock; hit.
clove (klōv), *n.* [ME. *clou;* OFr. *clou* (*de girofle*), lit., nail (of clove); L. *clavus,* nail: so called from its shape], 1. the dried flower bud of a tropical evergreen tree, originally native to the East Indies. 2. a pungent, fragrant spice obtained from these buds. 3. the tree.
clove (klōv), *n.* [AS. *clufu,* akin to *cleofan,* to split, divide; see CLEAVE], a segment of a bulb, as of garlic.
clove (klōv), 1. archaic past tense of **cleave** (to cling). 2. alternative past tense and poetic past participle of **cleave** (to split).
clove hitch, a kind of knot for fastening a rope around a spar, pole, or another rope: see **knot,** illus.
clo·ven (klō′v'n), alternative past participle of **cleave** (to split). *adj.* divided; split.
cloven foot, a cloven hoof.
clo·ven-foot·ed (klō′v'n-foot′id), *adj.* 1. having cloven feet; hence, 2. satanic; devilish.
cloven hoof, a hoof divided by a cleft, as in the ox, deer, and sheep: used as a symbol of the Devil, who is usually pictured with such hoofs.
clo·ven-hoofed (klō′v'n-hooft′, klō′v'n-hōōft′), *adj.* 1. having cloven hoofs; hence, 2. satanic; devilish.
clove pink, a variety of pink, a plant with small flowers having a clovelike scent.
clo·ver (klō′vẽr), *n.* [ME.; AS. *clafre, clæfre;* akin to MLG. *klāver, klēver,* D. *klaver* < Gmc. **klaibriōn;* base **klai-,* to adhere < IE. **glei-,* to stick, adhere (cf. CLAY, GLUE): so called from the sticky sap], 1. any of a number of species of low-growing herbs with leaves in three parts and small flowers in dense heads, as *red clover,* used for forage, and *white clover,* common in lawn seed mixtures. 2. any similar leguminous plant of the same or different family, as *sweet clover.*
in clover, 1. originally, in good pasture; hence, 2. living a luxurious life that is free from work and care.
clo·ver·leaf (klō′vẽr-lēf′), *n.* [*pl.* CLOVERLEAVES (-lēvz′)], a multiple highway intersection in the form of a four-leaf clover, which, by means of curving ramps from one level to another, permits traffic to move or turn in any of four directions without interference.

CLOVERLEAF

clo·ver-leaf (klō′vẽr-lēf′), *adj.* in the shape or pattern of a leaf of clover.
Clo·vis I (klō′vis), 466?–511 A.D.; founder of Frankish monarchy; king of the Franks (481–511 A.D.)
clown (kloun), *n.* [Late ME. *cloun, cloyn* < LG. source; cf. D. *kleun, kloen,* orig., a lump, hence lumpish fellow & N.Fris. *klönne,* lout; same base & development as *clod*], 1. originally, a peasant; rustic; hence, 2. a clumsy, rude person; boor. 3. a man whose work is entertaining in a circus or vaudeville by antics, jokes, tricks, etc.; jester; buffoon. *v.i.* 1. to perform as a clown. 2. to play practical jokes, act silly, etc.
clown·er·y (kloun′ẽr-i), *n.* [*pl.* CLOWNERIES (-iz)], the actions or behavior of a clown; clowning.
clown·ish (kloun′ish), *adj.* 1. of, like, or characteristic of a clown. 2. clumsy; rude; boorish.
cloy (kloi), *v.t.* [< *accloy;* ME. *acloien,* to lame a horse with a nail, spike a gun, hence stop up; OFr. *encloyer* < *clou,* a nail; L. *clavus,* a nail], to surfeit by too much of anything, especially anything too sweet, rich, etc. —***SYN.*** see **satiate.**
club (klub), *n.* [ME. *clubbe;* ON. *klubba, klumba,* mass of something, clump; IE. base **gel-* (see CLIMB); sense 3 (17th c.) < basic meaning, as in *clump of trees* or < early use of club carried round as invitation to a gathering (cf. ON. *kolfr,* cudgel, obs. G. *schlegel,* mallet, in same sense)], 1. a heavy stick, usually thinner at one end, used as a weapon. 2. a variously shaped stick or bat used in certain games, as golf, hockey, polo, etc. 3. a group of people associated for a common purpose, usually in an organization that meets regularly. 4. the room, building, or facilities used by such a group. 5. [transl. of Sp. *basto* or It. *bastone,* club, truncheon, figure used on Spanish cards], any of a suit of playing cards characterized by a black trefoil or clover-leaf figure (♣). 6. *pl.* this suit of cards. *v.t.* [CLUBBED (klubd), CLUBBING], 1. to beat or strike with or as with a club. 2. to give or combine (something) for a common purpose; pool (resources, etc.). 3. to use (a rifle) as a club by holding it so as to hit with the butt end. *v.i.* to unite or combine for a common purpose (usually with *together*).
club·ba·ble, club·a·ble (klub′ə-b'l), *adj.* [Colloq.], suited to membership in a club; hence, sociable.
club car, a railroad car with lounge chairs and, usually, a bar.
club·foot (klub′foot′), *n.* 1. a congenital deformity of the foot, characterized by a misshapen or twisted, often clublike, appearance: also called *talipes.* 2. [*pl.* CLUBFEET (-fēt′)], a foot so deformed.
club-foot·ed (klub′foot′id), *adj.* having clubfoot.
club grass, cattail, a tall, reedy marsh plant.
club·hand (klub′hand′), *n.* 1. a deformity of the hand analogous to clubfoot. 2. a hand so deformed.
club·haul (klub′hôl′), *v.t.* [< nautical *club* (to move with anchor adrift) + *haul*], to tack (a vessel in a precarious situation) by dropping the lee anchor as soon as the wind is out of the sails and maneuvering the vessel's head to the wind: the cable is cut when the ship swings off from the wind onto the new tack.
club·house (klub′hous′), *n.* a building occupied by a club.
club·man (klub′mən, klub′man′), *n.* [*pl.* CLUBMEN (-mən, -men′)], a man who is a member of a club or clubs, especially, one who spends much time at club social affairs, night clubs, etc.
club moss, any of a group of flowerless, evergreen plants that grow along the ground like creeping vines: they reproduce by spores borne in club-shaped cases.
club·room (klub′rōōm′, klub′room′), *n.* a room used by a club as a meeting place, for social affairs, etc.
club root, a disease of plants of the cabbage family, caused by a slime mold and characterized by swellings of the roots.
club sandwich, a sandwich of two or more layers, often toasted, containing chicken, bacon, lettuce, mayonnaise, tomatoes, etc.
club steak, a small beefsteak cut from the loin tip.

club·wom·an (klub'woom'ən), *n.* [*pl.* CLUBWOMEN (-wim'in)], a woman member of a club or clubs.
cluck (kluk), *v.i.* [ME. *clokken;* AS. *cloccian;* see CLOCK (timepiece)], to make the sound of a hen calling her chickens or brooding. *v.t.* 1. to call (chickens) by making this sound. 2. to utter with such a sound: as, she *clucked* her disapproval. *n.* 1. the sound made by a hen calling her chickens or when brooding. 2. a sound resembling or imitating this.
clue (kloo), *n.* & *v.t.* clew: usual spelling of *n.*, sense 2.
Cluj (kloozh), *n.* a city in Transylvania: pop., 111,000 (est. 1945): German name, *Klausenberg.*
clum·ber (klum'bẽr), *n.* [< *Clumber*, estate of the Duke of Newcastle], a short-legged spaniel with a heavy body and a thick coat of straight, white hair marked with yellow or orange: also **clumber spaniel.**
clump (klump), *n.* [D. *klomp* or LG. *klump;* akin to ON. *klumba;* see CLUB], 1. a lump; mass. 2. a mass of bacteria. 3. a cluster, as of shrubs or trees. 4. the sound of heavy footsteps. *v.i.* 1. to tramp heavily. 2. to form clumps. *v.t.* 1. to plant in a clump; group together in a cluster. 2. to cause to form clumps.
clump·ish (klump'ish), *adj.* [*clump* + *-ish*], heavy and clumsy.
clump·y (klump'i), *adj.* [CLUMPIER (-i-ẽr), CLUMPIEST (-i-ist)], 1. full of clumps. 2. like clumps. 3. clumpish.
clum·si·ly (klum'zə-li), *adv.* in a clumsy manner.
clum·si·ness (klum'zi-nis), *n.* the state or quality of being clumsy.
clum·sy (klum'zi), *adj.* [CLUMSIER (-zi-ẽr), CLUMSIEST (-zi-ist)], [ME. *clumsid*, numb with cold, pp. of *clumsen*, to benumb < ON.; cf. Sw. dial. *klummsen*, to benumb with the cold; Norw. *klumsa*, to make speechless; base and basic sense as in *clam* (a clamp)], 1. awkward; lacking grace or skill. 2. ill-constructed; awkwardly shaped or made. 3. badly contrived; inelegant: said of style. —*SYN.* see **awkward.**
clung (kluŋ), past tense and past participle of **cling.**
Clu·ny (klü'nē'), *n.* a village in east central France: pop., 3,000.
Clu·ny lace (kloo'ni), [after *Cluny*, France], a heavy bobbin lace with an open design, made of linen or cotton thread.
clu·pe·id (kloo'pi-id), *n.* [< Mod. L. *Clupea*, name of the genus < L. *clupea*, kind of small river fish], any of a family of soft-finned fishes, as herring, sardines, etc. *adj.* of this family of fishes.
clu·pe·oid (kloo'pi-oid'), *adj.* [< Mod. L. *Clupea* (see CLUPEID); + *-oid*], of or like the fish of the herring family. *n.* any fish of the herring family.
clus·ter (klus'tẽr), *n.* [ME.; AS. *clyster, cluster* (akin to north G. dial. *kluster*) with *clys-, clus-* for Gmc. **klut*, base of *clot*], 1. a number of things of the same sort gathered together or growing together; bunch. 2. a number of persons, animals, or things grouped together. *v.i.* & *v.t.* to gather or grow in a cluster or clusters.
clutch (kluch), *v.t.* [ME. *clucchen, clicchen;* AS. *clyccan;* to clench, influenced in sense by ME. *cloke*, a claw; IE. base **glek-* (< **gel-;* cf. CLIMB), as in Ir. *glac*, hand, *glaccaim*, I seize], 1. to grasp, seize, or snatch with a hand or claw. 2. to grasp or hold eagerly or tightly. *v.i.* to snatch or seize (with *at*). *n.* [ME. *clucche* < the *v.*], 1. a claw or hand in the act of seizing. 2. *usually pl.* power; control. 3. a grasp; grip; seizure. 4. a mechanical device, as in an automobile, for engaging and disengaging the motor or engine. 5. the lever or pedal by which this device is operated. 6. a device for gripping and holding, as in a crane. 7. [Slang], a critical situation or emergency: as, he's dependable in the *clutch.* —*SYN.* see **take.**
clutch (kluch), *v.t.* [dial. < ME. *cleken* (< ON. *klekja*), to hatch; prob. IE. base **glag-*, **glak-*, milk (hence newborn, etc.), as also in L. *lac, lactis*, Gr. *gála, gálakt-*, milk; cf. LACTIC, GALAXY], to hatch (chickens). *n.* 1. a nest of eggs. 2. a brood of chicks.
clut·ter (klut'ẽr), *n.* [var. of *clotter* < *clot;* see CLOT]. 1. a jumble; confusion; disorder. 2. [var. of *clatter*], a clatter. *v.t.* to put into disorder; litter; jumble (often with *up*). *v.i.* 1. to make a clatter. 2. to bustle.
Clyde (klīd), a masculine name. *n.* a river in southern Scotland, flowing into the Firth of Clyde: length, 106 mi.
Clyde, Firth of, the estuary of the Clyde in southwestern Scotland: length, 64 mi.
Clyde·bank (klīd'baŋk'), *n.* a city in southwestern Scotland, on the Clyde: pop., 35,000 (est. 1946).
Clydes·dale (klīdz'dāl'), *n.* [after *Clydesdale*, the valley of the River Clyde, Scotland where the breed originated], any of a breed of heavy, strong draft horse.
Clydesdale terrier, a small Scottish terrier of a breed developed from the Skye terrier.
clyp·e·ate (klip'i-āt'), *adj.* [L. *clypeatus*, pp. of *clypeare*, to arm with a shield < *clypeus*, a shield], in *biology*, 1. shaped like a round shield. 2. having a shieldlike process.
clyp·e·at·ed (klip'i-ā'tid), *adj.* clypeate.
clyp·e·i·form (klip'i-ə-fôrm'), *adj.* [L. *clypeus*, a shield; + *-form*], shield-shaped.
clyp·e·us (klip'i-əs), *n.* [*pl.* CLYPEI (-ī')], [L. *clipeus, clypeus*, a shield], a plate or shieldlike process on the head of certain insects.
clys·ter (klis'tẽr), *n.* [< Fr. or L.; Fr. *clystère;* L. *clyster;* Gr. *klystēr* < *klyzein*, to wash], an enema.
Cly·tem·nes·tra, Cly·taem·nes·tra (klī'təm-nes'trə), *n.* in *Greek legend*, the wife of Agamemnon: with the aid of her lover Aegisthus she murdered her husband when he came back from the Trojan War, and was consequently herself killed by their son Orestes.
Cm, in *chemistry*, curium.
cm., centimeter; centimeters.
c.m., 1. church missionary. 2. common meter. 3. corresponding member. 4. court-martial.
C.M.G., Companion of the Order of St. Michael and St. George.
cml., commercial.
C/N, 1. circular note. 2. credit note.
Cni·dus (nī'dəs), *n.* an ancient town in southwestern Asia Minor.
Cnos·sus (nos'əs), *n.* Knossos, an ancient city in Crete.
Cnut II (kə-noot', knoot), see **Canute II.**
co- (kō), 1. a shortened form of *com-*, meaning: *a) together, with*, as in *co-operation*. *b) joint*, as in *co-owner*. *c) equally*, as in *coextensive*. 2. a prefix formed from *complement*, meaning *complement of*, as in *cosine*.
-co (kō), [< *co.*, abbrev. of *company*], a suffix used in forming the trade names of many business firms, commercial products, etc.
Co, in *chemistry*, cobalt.
C/O, cash order.
Co., co., [*pl.* cos.], 1. company. 2. county.
C.O., 1. Commanding Officer. 2. Conscientious Objector.
c/o, c.o., 1. care of. 2. carried over.
coach (kōch), *n.* [Fr. *coche;* G. *kutsche;* Hung. *kocsi*, lit., of Kócs, after *Kócs*, Hungary, where the coach was invented and first used], 1. a large, covered, four-wheeled carriage with seats for passengers inside and an open, raised seat in front for the driver; stagecoach; four-in-hand. 2. [railroad adaptation < *stagecoaching*], a railroad passenger car furnishing the lowest-priced seating accommodations: distinguished from *chair car*, etc. 3. a bus. 4. an enclosed automobile, usually a two-door sedan. 5. [orig., university slang; prob. < notion "driving"], a private tutor who prepares a student in a subject or for an examination. 6. a person who instructs and trains athletes, competing teams, dramatic groups, etc. 7. in *baseball*, a member of the team at bat stationed near first or third base to advise the base runners. *v.t.* 1. to carry in a coach. 2. to instruct (a person) in a subject, or prepare (a person) for an examination, by private tutoring. 3. to instruct and train (athletes, actors, etc.). 4. in *baseball*, to advise (base runners) in their movements. *v.i.* 1. to ride in a coach. 2. to act as a coach.
coach-and-four (kōch'ən-fôr'), *n.* a coach drawn by four horses.
coach dog, a large, lean, short-haired dog with a black and white coat; Dalmatian: so called because formerly trained to run beside a carriage.
coach·er (kōch'ẽr), *n.* 1. a person who coaches. 2. a horse used or trained to draw a coach.
coach·man (kōch'mən), *n.* [*pl.* COACHMEN (-mən)], 1. the driver of a coach or carriage. 2. [said to be so named < a famous coachman-angler], an artificial fly used in angling: it has a peacock-green body, brown hackles, and white wings.
co·ac·tion (kō-ak'shən), *n.* [ML. *coactio*, compulsion < L. *coactare*, to constrain, force, freq. of *cogere;* see COGENT], coercion; force; compulsion.
co·ac·tive (kō-ak'tiv), *adj.* [< L. *coactus*, pp. of *cogere;* see COGENT], coercing; forcing.
co·ac·tive (kō-ak'tiv), *adj.* [*coact*, to act together (< *co-* + *act*) + *-ive*], acting or occurring together.
co·ad·ju·tant (kō-aj'ə-tənt), *adj.* [*coadjutor* + *-ant*], helping each other; co-operating. *n.* an assistant.
co·ad·ju·tor (kō-aj'ə-tẽr, kō'ə-joo'tẽr), *n.* [ME.; OFr. *coadjuteur;* L. *coadjutor; co-*, together + *adjutor* < *adjuvare*, to help; *ad-*, to + *juvare*, to assist], 1. an assistant; helper. 2. a person, often another bishop, appointed to assist a bishop. Abbreviated **coad.**
co·ad·u·nate (kō-aj'yoo-nit, kō-aj'yoo-nāt'), *adj.* [LL. *coadunatus*, pp. of *coadunare*, to unite, join < L. *co-*, together + *adunare*, to join < *ad-*, to + *unare*, to unite < *unus;* see ONE], 1. united; joined together. 2. in *botany* & *zoology*, grown together.
co·ad·ven·ture (kō'əd-ven'chẽr), *v.i.* to adventure together. *n.* a joint adventure.
co·ag·u·la·ble (kō-ag'yoo-lə-b'l), *adj.* that can be coagulated.
co·ag·u·lant (kō-ag'yoo-lənt), *n.* [L. *coagulans*, ppr. of *coagulare*], a substance that brings about coagulation.
co·ag·u·late (kō-ag'yoo-lāt'), *v.t.* [COAGULATED (-id), COAGULATING], [< L. *coagulatus*, pp. of *coagulare*, to cause a fluid to curdle < *coagulum;* see COAGULUM], to cause (a liquid) to become a soft, semisolid mass; curdle; clot. *v.i.* to become coagulated.
co·ag·u·la·tion (kō-ag'yoo-lā'shən), *n.* 1. a coagulating or being coagulated. 2. a coagulated mass.

co·ag·u·la·tive (kō-ag′yoo-lā′tiv), ***adj.*** tending to cause coagulation or become coagulated.

co·ag·u·la·tor (kō-ag′yoo-lā′tẽr), ***n.*** a substance that causes coagulation.

co·ag·u·lin (kō-ag′yoo-lin), ***n.*** any of various coagulating substances formed in animal tissue by the injection of proteid serums; precipitin.

co·ag·u·lum (kō-ag′yoo-ləm), ***n.*** [*pl.* COAGULA (-lə)], [L. *coagulum*, means of coagulation, rennet < *co-*, together + *agere*, to move, put in motion], a clot, curd, or coagulated albuminoid substance.

Co·a·hui·la (kô′ä-wē′lä), ***n.*** a state of northern Mexico: area, 58,062 sq. mi.; pop., 551,000; capital, Saltillo.

coal (kōl), ***n.*** [ME. *cole, col;* AS. *col*, a live coal; akin to G. *kohle*, charcoal; IE. base **geu-*, to glow, as also in Ir. *gúal*, charcoal; sense development: live coal—charcoal—the mineral (orig. called *sea coal, stone coal*)], 1. a black, combustible, mineral solid resulting from the partial decomposition of vegetable matter away from air and under varying degrees of high temperature and great pressure over a period of millions of years: used as a fuel and in the production of coke, coal gas, water gas, and many coal-tar compounds: see **anthracite, bituminous coal, lignite.** 2. a piece of this substance. 3. a piece of glowing or charred wood, coal, or similar substance; ember. 4. charcoal. ***v.t.*** 1. to reduce (a substance) to charcoal by burning. 2. to provide with coal. ***v.i.*** to take in a supply of coal.
haul (or **rake, drag, call**) **over the coals,** to criticize sharply; censure; scold.
heap coals of fire on (**a person's**) **head,** to cause (a person) to feel remorse by returning good for evil.

coal·bin (kōl′bin′), ***n.*** a bin or locker for storing coal.

coal car, a railroad car designed for transporting coal, as from a mine.

coal·er (kōl′ẽr), ***n.*** 1. a ship, railroad, freight car, etc. that transports or supplies coal. 2. a person who sells or supplies coal.

co·a·lesce (kō′ə-les′), ***v.i.*** [COALESCED (-lest′), COALESCING], [L. *coalescere; co-*, together + *alescere*, to grow up], 1. to grow together, as the halves of a broken bone. 2. to unite or merge into a single body, group, or mass. —***SYN.*** see **mix.**

co·a·les·cence (kō′ə-les′'ns), ***n.*** [< L. *coalescens*, ppr. of *coalescere*], 1. a coalescing; growing together. 2. a coalesced condition; merger; combination.

co·a·les·cent (kō′ə-les′'nt), ***adj.*** coalescing; uniting.

coal field, a region where there are coal strata.

coal·fish (kōl′fish′), ***n.*** [*pl.* COALFISH, COALFISHES (-iz); see FISH], a dark-colored fish belonging to the cod family: also called *black pollack.*

coal gas, 1. a gas produced by the destructive distillation of bituminous coal: used for lighting and heating. 2. a poisonous gas given off by burning coal.

coal heaver, a man whose work is carrying or shoveling coal.

coal hod, a kind of bucket for carrying coal; scuttle.

coaling station, a place, as a port or station, where ships or trains take on coal.

co·a·li·tion (kō′ə-lish′ən), ***n.*** [LL. *coalitio* < L. *coalitus*, fellowship < *coalescere;* see COALESCE], 1. a combination; union. 2. a temporary alliance of factions, parties, etc., for some specific purpose, as of political parties in times of national emergency. —***SYN.*** see **alliance.**

co·a·li·tion·ist (kō′ə-lish′ən-ist), ***n.*** a person who advocates or supports a political coalition.

coal measures, 1. coal beds. 2. in *geology*, coal-bearing strata formed just after the Devonian strata and lying above them.

coal mine, a mine or pit from which coal is dug.

coal oil, 1. kerosene or any other oil obtained by fractional distillation of petroleum. 2. crude petroleum.

coal pit, 1. a coal mine. 2. a pit where charcoal is made.

coal·sack (kōl′sak′), ***n.*** in *astronomy*, 1. any black area in the Milky Way. 2. [C-], such an area near the Southern Cross.

coal scuttle, a bucketlike container for holding and carrying coal.

coal tar, a black, thick, opaque liquid obtained by the destructive distillation of bituminous coal: many synthetic compounds have been developed from it, including dyes, medicines, explosives, and perfumes.

coal·y (kōl′i), ***adj.*** [COALIER (-i-ẽr), COALIEST (-i-ist)], 1. full of coal. 2. of or like coal; especially, black.

coam·ing (kōm′iŋ), ***n.*** [17th c.; early spellings suggest identity with *comb* (phonetically spelled) in sense "indented edge"; ? after D. *kam*, comb], 1. a raised border around a roof opening, well, etc. 2. a raised border around a hatch on a ship, to keep out water.

co·ap·ta·tion (kō′ap-tā′shən), ***n.*** [LL. *coaptatio*, an accurate joining together < *coaptare*, to fit, adjust < L. *co-*, together + *aptare*, to fit, adapt, freq. of *apere*, to fasten, bind, join: coined by Augustine to translate Gr. *harmonia* (see HARMONY)], the joining or adjusting of parts to each other, as of the ends of a broken bone.

co·arc·tate (kō-ärk′tāt), ***adj.*** [< L. *coarctatus*, pp. of *coarctare*, to press together < *co-*, together + *arctare, artare*, to press together < *arctus, artus*, fitted, narrow < *artus*, a joint, limb; sp. affected by association with *arcere*, to shut up, enclose], in *biology*, 1. closely connected. 2. having the thorax and abdomen separated only by a constriction.

coarse (kôrs, kōrs), ***adj.*** [specialized var. of *course* in sense of "ordinary, usual," as in *of course*], 1. common; of inferior or poor quality. 2. consisting of rather large elements or particles; not fine in texture: as, *coarse* sand. 3. rough; harsh: as, *coarse* cloth. 4. lacking in refinement; vulgar; indelicate; crude: as, a *coarse* joke.
SYN.—**coarse,** in this comparison, implies such a lack of refinement in manners or speech as to be offensive to one's esthetic or moral sense (*coarse* laughter); **gross** suggests a brutish crudeness or roughness (*gross* table manners); **indelicate** suggests a verging on impropriety or immodesty (an *indelicate* remark); **vulgar,** in this connection, emphasizes a lack of proper training, culture, or good taste (the *vulgar* ostentation of her home); **obscene** is used of that which is offensive to decency or modesty and implies lewdness (*obscene* gestures); **ribald** suggests such mild indecency or lewdness as might bring laughter from those who are not too squeamish (*ribald* jokes).—***ANT.*** refined.

coarse-grained (kôrs′grānd′, kōrs′grānd′), ***adj.*** 1. having a coarse or rough texture. 2. lacking in refinement or delicacy; gross; crude.

coars·en (kôr′s'n, kōr′s'n), ***v.t. & v.i.*** to make or become coarse.

coast (kōst), ***n.*** [ME. *coste*, coast; OFr. *coste*, a rib, hill, shore, coast; L. *costa*, a rib, side], 1. land alongside the sea; seashore. 2. [Obs.], the frontier or borderland of a country. 3. [< Canad. Fr., hillside, slope], an incline down which a slide is taken; hence, 4. a slide or ride, as on a sled going down an incline by the force of gravity. ***v.i.*** 1. to sail near or along the coast; hence, 2. to make short voyages from port to port. 3. to go down an incline on a sled; hence, 4. to continue in motion on momentum or by the force of gravity after propelling power has stopped. 5. to behave aimlessly; not make any serious effort. ***v.t.*** to sail along or near the coast of. —***SYN.*** see **shore.**
the Coast, [Colloq.], in the United States, the Pacific coast.
the coast is clear, there is no apparent danger or hindrance.

coast·al (kōs′t'l), ***adj.*** of, at, near, or along a coast.

Coastal Eastern, American English as typically spoken in the New England coastal area, roughly between the Connecticut River and the Atlantic coast: it exists with various regional differences and levels of sophistication, but has, in general, the following peculiarities of pronunciation: 1) use of a low back rounded vowel (ô, IPA [ɔ]) in such words as *hot, rock, college*, containing ME. ŏ; 2) use of a low central or low back unrounded vowel (á or ä, IPA [a] or [ɑ]), in such words as *pass, staff, path, far, calf, aunt*, containing ME. *ă* + *s, f, th* or ME. *au;* 3) use of the same vowel in such words as *sorrow, horror, brought, daughter*, containing ME. *ŏ* + *r* or ME. *ou;* 4) loss of final and preconsonantal *r* in such words as *sir, bird, farm;* 5) insertion (by many speakers) of unhistoric *r*, as in ***any idea(r) of it, propaganda(r) office, clo(r)th.*** Coastal Eastern acquired great prestige in the 19th century from use in dictionaries and at the Eastern universities; it is the variety of American English closest in type and origins to Received Standard British.

coastal plain, level land extending along a coast.

coast artillery, that branch of the armed forces assigned to protect the harbors and coast lines of the nation, and generally armed with artillery and antiaircraft guns of the largest caliber: distinguished from *field artillery:* abbreviated **C.A.**

coast·er (kōs′tẽr), ***n.*** 1. a person or thing that coasts. 2. a ship that carries cargo or passengers from port to port along a coast. 3. a sled or wagon for coasting. 4. [< obs. sense of *coast*, v.i., "to pass close to or around"], formerly, a small tray on wheels for passing a wine decanter, etc. around a table. 5. a small round tray placed under a glass or bottle to protect a table or other surface. 6. an amusement railway that runs on a specially constructed framework with sharp dips and curves; roller coaster.

coaster brake, a brake in the hub of the rear wheel of a bicycle, operated by reversing the pressure on the pedals: it also releases the wheel from the driving mechanism to permit free coasting.

coast guard, 1. a group of men employed by a government to defend its coasts, prevent smuggling, aid vessels in distress, maintain lighthouses, etc. 2. [C- G-], such a group in the United States: normally under the control of the Treasury Department, in time of war it is placed under the control of the navy. 3. a member of a coast guard. Abbreviated **C.G.**

coast·ing trade (kōs′tiŋ), trade carried on along a coast from port to port, especially within one country.

coast·land (kōst′land′), *n.* land along a coast.

coast line, the contour or outline of a coast.

Coast Range, mountain ranges along the Pacific coast from southern Alaska to southern California.

coast·ward (kōst′wẽrd), *adj. & adv.* toward the coast.

coast·wards (kōst′wẽrdz), *adv.* coastward.

coast·ways (kōst′wāz′), *adv.* coastwise.

coast·wise (kōst′wīz′), *adv. & adj.* along the coast.

coat (kōt), *n.* [ME. *cote, coote;* OFr. *cote,* a coat; LL. *cota, cotta,* a tunic; prob. < Gmc.; cf. Frank. *kotta,* coarse cloth, OS. *kot,* coarse outer garment (OHG. *kozzo,* whence G. *kotze,* shaggy overcoat, etc.)], 1. a sleeved outer garment opening down the front and extending usually just below the hips, worn as part of a suit or as a jacket. 2. a similar garment of varying length, worn out of doors over one's usual clothing. 3. a natural outer covering of an animal, as of skin, fur, wool, etc. 4. the outer covering of a plant or of an animal structure or tissue. 5. a layer of some substance, as paint, over a surface. 6. [Dial.], a petticoat or skirt. 7. [Obs.], customary garb showing one's position, class, etc. *v.t.* 1. to provide or cover with a coat. 2. to cover with a layer of something.

coated paper, a paper whose surface has been treated so that it will take half-tone impressions or color printing.

coat·ee (kōt′ē′), *n.* a short, close-fitting coat, usually with a short skirt or tails.

co·a·ti (kō-ä′ti), *n.* [*pl.* COATIS (-tiz)], [Tupi < *cua,* a cincture + *tim,* the nose: so called from appearance of its snout], a small, flesh-eating animal of Central and South America, like the raccoon but with a long flexible snout.

co·a·ti-mon·di, co·a·ti-mun·di (kō-ä′ti-mun′di), *n.* [Tupi; *coati* (see COATI) + *mondi,* solitary], a coati.

coat·ing (kōt′iŋ), *n.* 1. something covering or spread over a surface: as, a *coating* of enamel. 2. cloth for making coats.

coat of arms, [after Fr. *cotte d'armes,* light garment worn over armor, and generally blazoned with the heraldic arms of the wearer], 1. a shield marked with the insignia or designs (heraldic bearings) of a person, family, institution, etc. 2. a representation of such a shield.

COAT OF ARMS

coat of mail, [*pl.* COATS OF MAIL], [after Fr. *cotte de mailles,* lit., coat of meshes], a suit of armor made of interlinked metal rings or overlapping plates.

coat·tail (kōt′tāl′), *n.* 1. the back part of a coat below the waist. 2. one half of the skirt of a coat that is divided in the back. 3. either of the two long, tapering skirts on the back of a man's dress coat.

co·au·thor (kō-ô′thẽr), *n.* a joint author; collaborator.

coax (kōks), *v.t.* [orig. slang, "to make a coax of" < obs. slang *coax, cox, cokes,* a fool, ninny], 1. to induce or try to induce to do something; persuade by soothing words, agreeable manner, flattery, etc.; wheedle. 2. to get by coaxing. *v.i.* to use persuasion, flattery, etc.

SYN.—**coax** suggests repeated attempts to persuade someone to do something and implies the use of soothing words, an insinuating manner, etc.; **cajole** suggests the use of flattery or other blandishments; **wheedle** implies even more strongly the use of subtle flattery, seduction, or even deceit in gaining one's end.

co·ax·al (kō-ak′s′l), *adj.* coaxial.

co·ax·i·al (kō-ak′si-əl), *adj.* [< *co-* + *axis* + *-al*], 1. having a common axis. 2. designating a compound loudspeaker consisting of a smaller unit mounted within and connected with a larger one on a common axis: the smaller unit reproduces the higher frequencies, beyond the range of the larger.

coaxial cable, a cable for sending telephone, telegraph, and television impulses: it consists of an insulated conductor tube surrounding a central core of conducting material.

cob (kob), *n.* [ME.; prob. < LG. and akin to AS. *copp,* top (cf. CUP); Gmc. base **kubb,* something rounded, lump < IE. base **geu-;* see COD (a bag)], 1. a lump or small mass, as of coal. 2. the central, kernel-bearing part of an ear of corn; corncob; hence, 3. a corncob pipe. 4. a male swan. 5. a short, thickset horse.

cob (kob), *n.* [akin to E.Fris. *kobbe;* prob. < same base as *cob* (a lump) with reference to curved beak], the black-backed sea gull: also spelled **cobb.**

co·balt (kō′bôlt), *n.* [G. *kobalt* < *kobold,* goblin, demon of the mines: term applied to cobalt by miners from ignorance of its value or because it was troublesome], a hard, lustrous, steel-gray, ductile metallic chemical element, found in various ores: it is used in the preparation of alloys; its compounds are used in the production of inks, paints, and varnishes: symbol, Co; at. wt., 58.94; at. no., 27.

cobalt blue, 1. a dark-blue pigment made from cobalt. 2. dark blue.

co·bal·tic (kō-bôl′tik), *adj.* 1. of cobalt. 2. designating or of compounds in which cobalt has a valence of three.

co·balt·ine (kō′bôl-tēn′, kō′bôl-tin), *n.* cobaltite.

co·bal·tite (kō-bôl′tīt, kō′bôl-tīt′), *n.* cobalt sulfarsenide, CoAsS, a silver-white mineral.

co·bal·tous (kō-bôl′təs), *adj.* 1. having the nature of cobalt. 2. designating or of compounds in which cobalt has a valence of two.

cobb (kob), *n.* a cob (gull).

Cobb, Irvin Shrews·bur·y (shrōōz′bẽr-i), 1876–1944; American humorist and short-story writer.

Cob·bett, William (kob′it), (pseudonym *Peter Porcupine*), 1763–1835; English journalist and reformer.

cob·ble (kob′'l), *v.t.* [COBBLED (-'ld), COBBLING], [ME.; form suggests *cob* (a lump) + *-le,* freq. suffix, in sense "to lump together"], 1. to mend or patch (shoes, etc.). 2. to mend or put together clumsily.

cob·ble (kob′'l), *n.* [prob. < *cob* (a lump)], 1. a cobblestone. 2. *pl.* cob coal. *v.t.* [COBBLED (-'ld), COBBLING], to pave with cobblestones.

cob·bler (kob′lẽr), *n.* [of U.S. origin; ? < Hudson Valley *cobble,* stony hill (? < D. dial. *kobel, kovel,* rounded hill; see COB, a lump) < heaped up appearance], 1. an iced drink containing wine, citrus fruit, and sugar. 2. a deep-dish fruit pie with no bottom crust and a thick top crust of biscuit dough.

cob·bler (kob′lẽr), *n.* [ME. *cobelere;* see COBBLE (to mend)], 1. a person whose work is mending shoes. 2. a clumsy, bungling workman.

cob·ble·stone (kob′'l-stōn′), *n.* [ME. *cobil ston;* see COBBLE, *n.* & STONE], a rounded stone formerly much used for paving streets.

cob coal, [cf. *cob* (a lump)], coal in rounded lumps from about the size of a baseball to that of a basketball.

Cob·den, Richard (kob′dən), 1804–1865; English political economist and statesman; advocator of free trade.

co·bel·lig·er·ent (kō′bə-lij′ẽr-ənt), *n.* a nation associated but not allied with another or other nations in waging war: as, Italy became a *co-belligerent* of the Allies after the overthrow of the Fascist government.

Cóbh (kōv), *n.* a seaport in southern Ireland: pop., 7,000: formerly called *Queenstown.*

Cob·ham, John Old·cas·tle, Lord (ōld′kas″'l kob′əm), ?–1417; English leader of a Lollard conspiracy; hanged for heresy and treason.

co·ble (kō′b'l, kob′'l), *n.* [ME.; AS. (Northumbrian) *cuopl;* prob. < Celt.; cf. W. *ceubal,* Bret. *caubal* & LL. *caupulus* (? < Celt.), small ship], 1. in northeast England, a small fishing boat with a lug sail, deep stem, large rudder, and flattish stern: it was formerly much used in piloting. 2. in Scotland, a short, flat-bottomed rowboat.

Co·blenz (kō′blents), *n.* a city in Germany, on the Rhine: pop., 58,000: German spelling, **Koblenz.**

cob·nut (kob′nut′), *n.* [see COB (a lump)], 1. a kind of hazelnut. 2. the tree that it grows on.

co·bra (kō′brə), *n.* [< Port. *cobra* (*de capello*), serpent (of the hood); L. *colubra,* a snake], 1. a very poisonous snake of Asia and Africa, having around its neck loose skin which is expanded into a hood when the snake is excited. 2. leather made of the skin of this snake.

COBRA (4–17 ft. long)

cobra de ca·pel·lo (dē kə-pel′ō), [*pl.* COBRAS DE CAPELLO], [see COBRA], a varicolored cobra found especially in India.

cob·web (kob′web′), *n.* [ME. *copweb* < *coppe,* spider (AS. *-coppe,* in *atorcoppe; ator,* poison + *-coppe,* spider); + *web*], 1. a web spun by a spider. 2. a single thread of such a web, or the substance that it is made of. 3. anything flimsy, gauzy, or ensnaring like the web of a spider. *v.t.* [COBWEBBED (-webd′), COBWEBBING], to cover with or as with cobwebs.

cob·web·by (kob′web′i), *adj.* 1. of or like a cobweb or cobwebs. 2. covered with cobwebs.

co·ca (kō′kə), *n.* [Peruv. *cuca*], 1. a tropical shrub of South America and the West Indies whose dried leaves are the source of cocaine and certain other alkaloids. 2. its dried leaves.

co·caine, co·cain (kō-kān′, kō′kān), *n.* [< *coca* + *-ine*], a crystalline alkaloid obtained from dried coca leaves: it is a narcotic and local anesthetic.

co·cain·ism (kō-kān′iz′m), *n.* a diseased condition resulting from excessive or habitual use of cocaine.

co·cain·ize (kō-kān′īz), *v.t.* [COCAINIZED (-īzd), COCAINIZING], to anesthetize with cocaine.

-coc·cal (kok′'l), a combining form meaning *of* or

produced by a (specified kind of) *coccus*, as in *staphylococcal*.
coc·ci (kok′sī), ***n.*** plural of **coccus**.
-coc·cic (kok′sik), a combining form equivalent to *-coccal*, as in *staphylococcic*.
coc·cid (kok′sid), ***n.*** [< Mod. L. *Coccidae*, name of the family < Gr. ***kokkos***, berry], any insect of the family of scale insects.
coc·cid·i·o·sis (kok-sid′i-ō′sis), ***n.*** [Mod. L. < *coccidium*, little berry; + *-osis*], any of various diseases of domestic animals, birds, and, rarely, man, caused by a class of protozoans living as parasites in the intestines.
coc·cif·er·ous (kok-sif′ẽr-əs), ***adj.*** [< L. *cocci*, pl. of *coccus* (see COCCUS); + *-ferous*], producing berries.
coc·coid (kok′oid), ***adj.*** like a coccus.
-coc·coid (kok′oid), a combining form meaning *like a* (specified kind of) *coccus*, as in *staphylococcoid*.
coc·cus (kok′əs), ***n.*** [*pl.* COCCI (kok′sī)], [Mod. L.; Gr. ***kokkos***, a kernel, seed, berry], 1. a bacterium having a spherical or oval shape: see **bacteria,** illus. 2. in *botany*, any of the carpels into which compound fruits split when ripe: it contains a single seed.
-coc·cus (kok′əs), *coccus* used as a terminal combining form in names of various bacteria, as in *gonococcus*.
coc·cyg·e·al (kok-sij′i-əl), ***adj.*** [LL. *coccygeus* < L. *coccyx* (see COCCYX); + *-al*], of the coccyx.
coc·cyx (kok′siks), ***n.*** [*pl.* COCCYGES (kok-sī′jēz)], [L., cuckoo < Gr. ***kokkyx, kokkygos***, cuckoo: so called because shaped like a cuckoo's beak], a small, triangular bone at the lower end of the vertebral column, formed by the fusion of four rudimentary vertebrae and articulating with the sacrum: see **skeleton,** illus.
Co·cha·bam·ba (kō′chä-bäm′bä), ***n.*** a city in central Bolivia: pop., 100,000 (1946): it is 8,394 ft. above sea level.
Co·chin (kō′chin′), ***n.*** 1. a former native state of southwestern India: since 1950, a part of the state of Travancore and Cochin. 2. [also c-], (kō′chin, koch′in), [< *Cochin-China*, place of origin], any of a breed of very large domestic fowl with buff, black, white, or penciled gray plumage and thickly feathered legs.
Co·chin-Chi·na (kō′chin-chī′nə), ***n.*** a former state of southern French Indo-China, on the South China Sea: it is now part of South Viet-Nam: area, 26,476 sq. mi.; pop., 4,616,000; capital, Saïgon: French name, *Cochinchine:* see Viet-Nam.
Co·chin·chine (kô′shan′shēn′), ***n.*** Cochin-China.
coch·i·neal (koch′ə-nēl′, koch′ə-nēl′), ***n.*** [Fr. *cochenille;* It. *coccineglia* < L. *coccinus, coccineus*, scarlet-colored < *coccum*, a berry; see COCCUS], a red dye made from the dried bodies of the females of a scale insect that attacks cacti of tropical and subtropical America.
coch·le·a (kok′li-ə), ***n.*** [*pl.* COCHLEAE (-ē′)], [L. *coclea, cochlea;* Gr. *kochlias*, snail, snail shell < *kochlos*, shellfish], the spiral-shaped part of the internal ear, containing the auditory nerve endings: see **ear,** illus.
coch·le·ar (kok′li-ẽr), ***adj.*** of the cochlea.
coch·le·ate (kok′li-āt′), ***adj.*** [L. *cochleatus*, spiral-shaped; see COCHLEA], shaped like the shell of a snail.
coch·le·at·ed (kok′li-ā′tid), ***adj.*** cochleate.
cock (kok), ***n.*** [ME. *cock, cok;* AS. *coc, cocc;* echoic; senses 6 & 7 from fancied resemblance; senses 9 & 10 < the *v.*], 1. the male of the chicken; rooster. 2. a male bird. 3. the sound made by a rooster, especially at sunrise; crow. 4. a weather vane in the shape of a rooster; weathercock. 5. a leader; chief; head person. 6. a faucet or valve for regulating the flow of a liquid or gas. 7. the hammer of a firearm. 8. the position of such a hammer when set for firing. 9. a tilting or turning upward, as of the eye. 10. a jaunty, erect position: as, the *cock* of a hat. ***v.t.*** 1. to tilt; set (a hat, etc.) jauntily on one side. 2. to raise stiffly: as, a dog *cocks* his ears. 3. to turn (the eye or ear) toward something. 4. to set the hammer of (a gun) in firing position. ***v.i.*** to assume an erect or tilted position.
cock (kok), ***n.*** [ME. *cokke* < Anglo-N.; cf. ON. ***kǫkkr***, Dan. *kok*, a heap; akin to dial. G. *kocke*], a small, cone-shaped pile, as of hay. ***v.t.*** to pile (hay, etc.) in cocks.
cock·ade (kok-ād′), ***n.*** [Fr. *cocarde* < *coq*, a cock: from resemblance to its comb], a rosette, knot of ribbon, or similar device, worn on the hat as a badge.
cock·ad·ed (kok-ā′did), ***adj.*** wearing, or decorated with, a cockade.
cock-a-doo·dle-doo (kok′ə-dōō′d′l-dōō′), ***n.*** [echoic], 1. the shrill sound made by a rooster; crow. 2. a rooster; cock.
cock-a-hoop (kok′ə-hōōp′), ***adj.*** [Fr. *coq à huppe*, cock with a crest], 1. elated; exultant. 2. boastful; conceited.
Cock·aigne (kok-ān′), ***n.*** [ME. *cokaygne;* OFr. (*pais de*) *cocaigne*, (land of) sugar cake < MLG. *kokenje*, sugar cake, cooky < *koke*, cake; akin to Eng. *cake*, G. *kuchen*, cake], an imaginary land of luxurious and idle living.
cock·a·lo·rum (kok′ə-lôr′əm, kok′ə-lō′rəm), ***n.*** [pseudo L. extension of *cock* (male bird); ? influenced by D. *kockeloeren*, to crow], 1. a small rooster; bantam; hence, 2. a little man with an exaggerated idea of his own importance.
cock-and-bull story (kok′'n-bool′), [for earlier *cock-alane*, Fr. *coq à l'âne*], an absurd, improbable story.
cock·a·teel, cock·a·tiel (kok′ə-tēl′), ***n.*** [D. *kaketielje*, prob. dim. of *kaketoe;* see COCKATOO], a small parrot native to Australia.
cock·a·too (kok′ə-tōō′, kok′ə-tōō′), ***n.*** [*pl.* COCKATOOS (-tōōz′, -tōōz′)], [D. *kaketoe;* Malay. ***kakatua;*** prob. echoic in origin; sp. influenced by *cock* (male bird)], a large, bright-colored parrot of Australia, the East Indies, and the Philippines, often with a high crest.
cock·a·trice (kok′ə-tris), ***n.*** [ME. *cocatrice;* OFr. *cocatrice, cocatris*, altered < *LL. ***calcatrix*** < *calcare*, to tread < *calx*, the heel; translating Gr. notion that it tracked crocodiles and ate their eggs], 1. a fabulous serpent supposedly hatched from a cock's egg and having power to kill by a look. 2. in the *Bible*, an unidentified deadly serpent.
cock·boat (kok′bōt′), ***n.*** [ME. *cokboot, cogbote; cok* < OFr. *coque, cogue* < or akin to MD. *kogghe*, Dan. *kog* (whence ME. *cogge*, small boat); all ult. < L. *concha* (see CONCH)], a small boat, especially one used as a ship's tender.
cock·chaf·er (kok′chāf′ẽr), ***n.*** [*cock*, for Scot. *clock*, a beetle + *chafer* < AS. *ceafor, ceafer*, cockchafer], a large European beetle whose grubs live in the soil for three years feeding on the roots of plants.
cock·crow (kok′krō′), ***n.*** the time when roosters begin to crow; early morning; dawn.
cock·crow·ing (kok′krō′iŋ), ***n.*** cockcrow.
cocked hat, 1. a three-cornered hat with a turned-up brim. 2. a hat pointed in front and in back and with the crown rising to a point.
knock into a cocked hat, [Slang], to damage beyond recognition; ruin.
cock·er (kok′ẽr), ***n.*** a cocker spaniel.
cock·er (kok′ẽr), ***v.t.*** [earlier also *cockle;* akin to Dan. *kokre*, to call as a cock to hens, Norw. *kokla*, to crow, fuss over, pamper; akin to earlier D. *kokelen*, to pamper; prob. < ON.], to coddle; pamper.
cock·er·el (kok′ẽr-əl, kok′rəl), ***n.*** [dim. of *cock* (male bird)], a young rooster, not above a year old.
cocker spaniel, [so called from its use in hunting woodcock], any of a breed of small spaniels with a compact body, short legs, long, silky hair, and long, drooping ears.

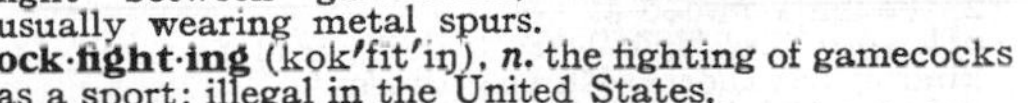

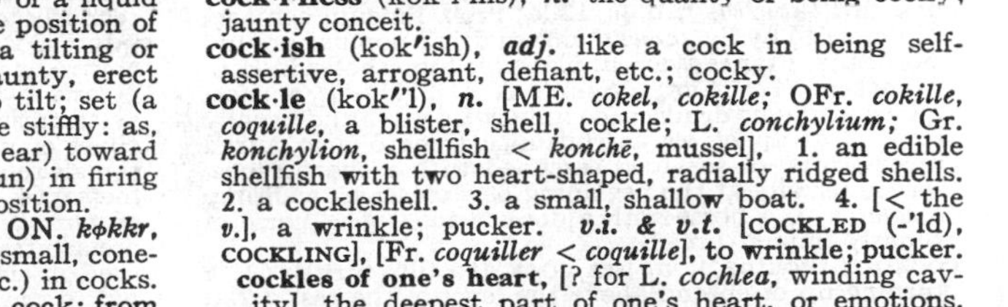

COCKER SPANIEL
(11 in. high)

cock·eye (kok′ī′), ***n.*** [*cock* (to turn on one side) + *eye*], a squinting eye.
cock·eyed (kok′īd′), ***adj.*** [see COCK (to tilt, turn)], 1. cross-eyed. 2. [Slang], crooked; lopsided; awry. 3. [Slang], fantastically absurd. 4. [Slang], drunk.
cock·fight (kok′fīt′), ***n.*** a fight between gamecocks, usually wearing metal spurs.
cock·fight·ing (kok′fīt′iŋ), ***n.*** the fighting of gamecocks as a sport: illegal in the United States.
cock·horse (kok′hôrs′), ***n.*** [16th c., toy horse], a hobbyhorse; rocking horse.
cock·i·ly (kok′ə-li), ***adv.*** in a cocky manner.
cock·i·ness (kok′i-nis), ***n.*** the quality of being cocky; jaunty conceit.
cock·ish (kok′ish), ***adj.*** like a cock in being self-assertive, arrogant, defiant, etc.; cocky.
cock·le (kok′'l), ***n.*** [ME. *cokel, cokille;* OFr. *cokille, coquille*, a blister, shell, cockle; L. ***conchylium;*** Gr. *konchylion*, shellfish < *konchē*, mussel], 1. an edible shellfish with two heart-shaped, radially ridged shells. 2. a cockleshell. 3. a small, shallow boat. 4. [< the *v.*], a wrinkle; pucker. ***v.i. & v.t.*** [COCKLED (-'ld), COCKLING], [Fr. *coquiller* < *coquille*], to wrinkle; pucker.
cockles of one's heart, [? for L. *cochlea*, winding cavity], the deepest part of one's heart, or emotions.
cock·le (kok′'l), ***n.*** [ME. *cockie, cockel;* AS. *coccel*, tares], any of various weeds found in grain fields, as the corn cockle, darnel, etc.
cock·le·boat (kok′'l-bōt′), ***n.*** a small, shallow, lightweight boat; cockboat.
cock·le·bur (kok′'l-bũr′), ***n.*** 1. a ragweed plant bearing burs. 2. the common burdock.
cock·le·shell (kok′'l-shel′), ***n.*** 1. the shell of a cockle. 2. loosely, a scallop shell, etc. 3. a cockleboat.
cock·loft (kok′lôft′, kok′loft′), ***n.*** [orig., lit. or fig., a loft where cocks roost], a small loft or attic; garret.
cock·ney (kok′ni), ***n.*** [*pl.* COCKNEYS (-niz)], [ME. *cokenei*, spoiled child, simpleton, effeminate town dweller; understood as *coken-ey*, lit., cock's egg < *coken* (AS. *cocena*, genit. pl.), of cocks + *-ey* (AS. *æg*), egg, with reference to the small size of eggs allegedly laid by

cocks; development of the word prob. merged the above with OFr. *acoquinei*, idle, spoiled (< *coquin*, rascal) & ? with an original *coken ey*, lit., cooked egg], 1. a native of the East End of London, England, traditionally one born within sound of the bells of St. Mary-le-Bow (Bow Bells) and speaking a characteristic dialect. 2. this dialect, characterized by extreme diphthongization of original vowels, loss of initial *h*, and use of an intrusive *r*. 3. loosely, any native or inhabitant of London: a humorous or disparaging usage. *adj.* 1. of or like cockneys or their dialect. 2. loosely, of Londoners or of London.

cock·ney·dom (kok′ni-dəm), *n.* 1. the district where cockneys live. 2. cockneys collectively.

cock·ney·ese (kok′ni-ēz′), *n.* the characteristic dialect of cockneys.

cock·ney·fy (kok′ni-fī′), *v.t.* [COCKNEYFIED (-fīd′), COCKNEYFYING], to give a cockney quality to (one's speech, manner, etc.).

cock·ney·ism (kok′ni-iz′m), *n.* an idiom, pronunciation, etc. characteristic of cockneys.

cock of the walk, the most important person in any group.

cock·pit (kok′pit′), *n.* 1. an enclosed space for cockfighting; hence, 2. a place where there have been many battles: as, Belgium is the *cockpit* of Europe. 3. any space thought to resemble a typical cockpit; specifically, *a*) in small decked vessels, a sunken space toward the stern used by the steersman, etc.; hence, *b*) in some small airplanes, the space where the pilot and, sometimes, one or two passengers sit: see **airplane,** illus. *c*) formerly, the quarters of junior officers on the after part of the lowest deck of a warship, used as a station for the wounded in battle. *d*) [Obs.], the pit of a theater.

cock·roach (kok′rōch′), *n.* [Sp. *cucaracha*, wood louse, cockroach; confused with *roach*], a straight-winged insect with a flat, yellowish-brown or black body, slender legs, and long feelers: it is a common kitchen pest, especially in warm, damp places.

COCKROACH (1 1/2 in. long)

cocks·comb (koks′kōm′), *n.* 1. the red, fleshy growth on the head of a rooster. 2. a jester's cap somewhat resembling this. 3. the points on such a cap. 4. a plant of the amaranth family, with red or yellow flower heads supposedly like a rooster's crest: some varieties have feathery heads. 5. [Obs.], a coxcomb.

cocks·head (koks′hed′), *n.* a European plant of the pea family, with spiny pods.

cock·shut (kok′shut′), *n.* [Obs. or British Dial.], evening twilight.

cock·shy (kok′shī′), *n.* [*pl.* COCKSHIES (-shīz′)], [*cock* (male bird) + *shy* (throw): from old game of throwing objects at a cock tied to a stake], 1. a throw at a mark. 2. the mark aimed at.

cock·spur (kok′spũr′), *n.* 1. the spur of a rooster. 2. a kind of hawthorn with long thorns.

cock·sure (kok′shoor′), *adj.* [*cock* (with reference to masculine aggressiveness) + *sure*], 1. absolutely sure. 2. sure or self-confident to an offensive degree.

cock·swain (kok′s'n, kok′swān′), *n.* a coxswain.

cock·tail (kok′tāl′), *n.* [c. 1806; prob. fanciful coinage; ? influenced by Fr. *coquetel*, mixed drink popular around Bordeaux, France; various plausible hypotheses in H.L. Mencken, *Am. Lang., Suppl. I*, p. 257], 1. a short mixed alcoholic drink made in various ways and usually iced. 2. an appetizer, as fruit juice, tomato juice, mixed diced fruits, or sea food seasoned with a sharp sauce, served usually at the beginning of a meal: as, a shrimp *cocktail*. 3. a horse with a docked tail. 4. a horse of slightly impure breed.

cock·up (kok′up′), *n.* [see COCK (to tilt, turn)], 1. a turning up of an end above the level of the rest. 2. a hat or cap turned up in front.

cock·y (kok′i), *adj.* [COCKIER (-i-ẽr), COCKIEST (-i-ist)], [< *cock* (male bird)], [Colloq.], jauntily conceited; self-confident in a swaggering way.

co·co (kō′kō), *n.* [*pl.* COCOS (-kōz)], [Sp.; Port. < L. *coccum*, a seed, kernel; Gr. *kokkos*, a berry], 1. the coconut palm tree. 2. its fruit; coconut. *adj.* made of the fiber from coconut husks. Also, by confusion, **cocoa.**

co·coa (kō′kō), *n.* [Sp. & Port. *cacao;* Mex. *cacauatl*, cocoa seed], 1. powder made from cacao seeds that have been roasted and ground. 2. a drink made by adding sugar and hot water or milk to this powder. 3. reddish-yellow brown.

cocoa butter, a yellowish-white fat prepared from cacao seeds: used in pharmacy and in making cosmetics.

co·coa·nut (kō′kə-nut′), *n.* a coconut.

co·con·scious·ness (kō-kon′shəs-nis), *n.* in *psychology*, mental states which, though the individual is not aware of them, can account for certain mental phenomena, as slips of the tongue.

co·co·nut (kō′kə-nut′), *n.* the fruit of the coconut palm, consisting of a thick, fibrous, brown, oval husk under which there is a thin, hard shell enclosing a layer of edible white meat: the hollow center is filled with a sweet, milky fluid called *coconut milk:* also *cocoanut.*

COCONUT
A, tree; B, cross section of fruit

coconut oil, oil obtained from the dried meat of coconuts, used for making soap, etc.

coconut palm (or **tree**), a tall palm tree that bears coconuts, growing throughout the tropics: the nuts provide food and drink, and the foliage is used as thatch.

co·coon (kə-kōōn′), *n.* [Fr. *cocon;* It. *coccone;* LL. *coco*, a hull, shell < L. *coccum;* see COCO], 1. the silky case which the larvae of certain insects spin about themselves to shelter them during the pupa stage. 2. any protective cover like this.

COCOONS
A, Promethea; B, caddis fly

coco palm, a coconut palm.

Co·cos Islands (kō′kōs), a group of coral islands in the Indian Ocean, south of Sumatra: area, 5 sq. mi.; pop., 700: a territory belonging to Australia: also called *Keeling Islands.*

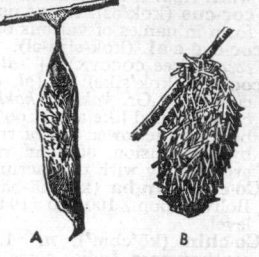

co·cotte (kō′kot′, kə-kot′), *n.* [Fr.; orig., hen < *coq*, cock], a woman who is sexually promiscuous.

Coc·teau, Jean (zhän kôk′tō′), 1889– ; French novelist, playwright, and poet.

Co·cy·tus (kō-sī′təs), *n.* [L.; Gr. *Kōkytos*, lit., a shrieking, wailing < *kōkyein*, to wail], in *Greek mythology*, the river of wailing, a tributary of the Acheron in Hades.

cod (kod), *n.* [*pl.* COD, CODS (kodz); see PLURAL, II, D, 2], [ME.; prob. < *cod* (a bag), in reference to shape], a fish with firm flesh and soft fins, found in the North Atlantic, especially off the banks of Newfoundland and the coast of Norway: it is an important food fish and the source of cod-liver oil.

cod (kod), *n.* [ME.; AS. *codd;* akin to ON. *koddi*, cushion; IE. base *geu- (< *geud, *gud), to curve, arch, as also in L. *guttur*, throat; cf. GUTTURAL], 1. [Archaic], a bag. 2. [Dial.], a pod; husk. 3. [Obs.], the scrotum.

Cod., cod., [*pl.* CODD.], codex.

C.O.D., c.o.d., 1. collect on delivery. 2. [British], cash on delivery.

Cod, Cape (kod), a peninsula in southeastern Massachusetts.

co·da (kō′də), *n.* [It.; L. *cauda*, a tail], in *music*, a final passage, which brings a composition or movement to a definite, formal close.

cod·dle (kod′'l), *v.t.* [CODDLED (-'ld), CODDLING], [? < *caudle*], 1. to cook gently, as an egg, by heating in water not quite at boiling temperature. 2. to treat tenderly, as an invalid or a baby; pamper.

code (kōd), *n.* [Fr.; L. *codex*, tree trunk, wooden tablet covered with wax for writing; earlier *caudex*], 1. a body of laws of a nation, state, city, or organization, arranged systematically for easy reference. 2. any set of principles or rules of conduct: as, a moral *code.* 3. a set of signals representing letters or numerals, used in sending messages, as by telegraph, flags, heliograph, etc. 4. a system of secret writing in which letters, figures, etc. are arbitrarily given certain meanings. 5. the symbols used in such a system. *v.t.* [CODED (-id), CODING], to put in the form, or symbols, of a code.

co·dec·li·na·tion (kō′dek-lə-nā′shən), *n.* in *astronomy*, the complement of the angle of declination: also called *polar distance.*

co·de·fend·ant (kō′di-fen′dənt), *n.* a joint defendant.

co·de·ia (kō-dē′yə), *n.* codeine.

co·de·in (kō′di-in), *n.* codeine.

co·de·ine (kō′di-ēn′, kō′dēn), *n.* [< Gr. *kodeia*, poppy head; + *-ine*], an alkaloid, $C_{18}H_{21}O_3N \cdot H_2O$, derived from opium and resembling morphine, but milder in its action and less habit-forming: used for the relief of pain and as a sedative.

‡**Code Na·po·lé·on** (kôd′ nȧ′pô′lā-ôn′), [Fr.], the Napoleonic code, the body of French civil law enacted under the direction of Napoleon in 1804: it has served as the model for the civil codes of many nations.

co·dex (kō′deks), *n.* [*pl.* CODICES (-də-sēz′, kod′ə-sēz′)], [L.; see CODE], 1. [Archaic], a code; volume of statutes. 2. a manuscript volume, especially of the Scriptures or of a classic text: abbreviated **Cod., cod.**

Codex Ju·ris Ca·no·ni·ci (joor′is kə-non′i-sī′), [L.,

Code of Canon Law], the laws governing the Roman Catholic Church since 1918: superseded the *Corpus Juris Canonici*.
cod·fish (kod′fish′), *n.* [*pl.* CODFISH, CODFISHES; see FISH], the cod.
codg·er (koj′ẽr), *n.* [prob. var. of *cadger*], [Colloq.], a queer person; peculiar fellow: usually preceded by *old*.
co·di·ces (kō′də-sēz′, kod′ə-sēz′), *n.* plural of **codex.**
cod·i·cil (kod′ə-s'l, kod′ə-sil′), *n.* [L. *codicillus*, dim. of *codex;* see CODE], 1. in *law*, an addition to a will, to change or explain some provisions or to add new ones. 2. an appendix or supplement.
cod·i·cil·la·ry (kod′ə-sil′ə-ri), *adj.* of, or having the nature of, a codicil.
cod·i·fi·ca·tion (kod′ə-fi-kā′shən, kō′də-fi-kā′shən), *n.* a codifying or being codified, as of laws.
cod·i·fy (kod′ə-fī′, kō′də-fī′), *v.t.* [CODIFIED (-fīd′), CODIFYING], [< *code* + *-fy*], to arrange (laws, etc.) systematically.
cod·lin (kod′lin), *n.* a codling (apple).
cod·ling (kod′liŋ), *n.* [*pl.* CODLING, CODLINGS (-liŋz); see PLURAL, II, D, 2], [*cod* (fish) + *-ling*], 1. a young cod. 2. any of certain fishes allied to the cod.
cod·ling (kod′liŋ), *n.* [earlier *querdling*, altered (as if with suffix *-ling*) < Anglo-Fr. *querdelyon* < Fr. *coeur de lion*, lit., heart of lion], 1. a variety of elongated apple. 2. an unripe apple. 3. a small, inferior apple.
codling (or **codlin**) **moth,** a small moth whose larva bores into and destroys apples, pears, and quinces.
cod-liv·er oil (kod′liv′ẽr), oil obtained from the livers of the cod and allied fish: it contains various vitamins and is used in medicine to increase the number of red corpuscles in the blood, thus increasing resistance to various diseases.
cod·piece (kod′pēs′), *n.* [*cod* (scrotum) + *piece*], [Archaic], a bag or flap appended to the front of the tight breeches worn by men in the 15th and 16th centuries.
Co·dy, William Frederick (kō′di), 1846–1917; American plainsman, army scout, and circus manager: called *Buffalo Bill*.
co·ed, co-ed (kō′ed′), *n.* [Colloq.], a girl attending a coeducational college.
co·ed·u·ca·tion (kō′ej-oo-kā′shən), *n.* [*co-* + *education*], the educational system in which students of both sexes attend classes together.
co·ed·u·ca·tion·al (kō′ej-oo-kā′shən'l), *adj.* 1. relating to coeducation. 2. having students of both sexes attend classes together: as, a *coeducational* college.
co·ef·fi·cient (kō′ə-fish′ənt), *adj.* [LL. *coefficiens*, ppr. of *coefficere;* see CO- & EFFECT], co-operating. *n.* 1. a factor that contributes to produce a result. 2. in *mathematics*, a number or algebraic symbol prefixed as a multiplier to a variable or unknown quantity: as, *6* is a *coefficient* in *6ab*, *x* is a *coefficient* in $x(y + z)$. 3. in *physics*, a number, constant for a given substance, used as a multiplier in measuring the change in some property of the substance under given conditions: as, the *coefficient* of expansion. Abbreviated **coef., coeff.**
coe·la·canth (sē′lə-kanth′), *n.* [< Gr. *koilos*, hollow + *akantha*, spine], any of a family of primitive fishes, possibly ancestors to land animals: it was formerly believed to be long extinct, but several living specimens have been found in recent times.
-coele (sēl), [< Gr. *koilia*, body cavity], a combining form meaning *cavity, chamber of the body, chamber of an organ*, as in *blastocoele:* also **-cele.**
coe·len·ter·ate (si-len′tẽr-āt′), *n.* [< Mod. L. *Coelenterata*, name of the phylum < *coelenteron;* see COELENTERON], any of a large group of invertebrate salt-water animals, including the hydra, jellyfishes, sea anemones, etc., in which the characteristic structure is a large central cavity. *adj.* of this group of invertebrates.
coe·len·ter·on (si-len′tẽr-on′), *n.* [*pl.* COELENTERA (-ə)], [Mod. L. < Gr. *koilos*, hollow + *enteron*, intestine], the internal cavity of a coelenterate.
coe·li·ac (sē′li-ak′), *adj.* [L. *coeliacus;* Gr. *koiliakos* < *koilia*, the belly < *koilos*, hollow], of or in the cavity of the abdomen: also spelled **celiac.**
coe·lom (sē′ləm), *n.* [Gr. *koiloma* < *koilos*, hollow], the embryonic cavity of nearly all multicellular animals, from which the main cavities of the body develop.
coe·lome (sē′lōm), *n.* a coelom.
co·empt (kō-empt′), *v.t.* to gain control of by coemption.
co·emp·tion (kō-emp′shən), *n.* [L. *coemptio* < *coemere*, to buy up; *co-*, together + *emere*, to buy], the buying up of the entire supply of a commodity in order to gain a monopoly, control prices, etc.
coe·nes·the·si·a (sē′nes-thē′zhə, sen′es-thē′zhi-a), *n.* coenesthesis.
coe·nes·the·sis (sē′nes-thē′sis, sen′es-thē′sis), *n.* [Mod. L. < Gr. *koinos*, common + *aisthēsis*, feeling], in *psychology*, the mass of undifferentiated sensations that make one aware of the body and its condition, as in the feeling of health, illness, discomfort, etc.
coe·no- (sē′nə, sen′ə), [< Gr. *koinos*, common], a combining form meaning *common*, as in *coenocyte:* also, before a vowel, **coen-.**
coe·no·bite (sē′nə-bīt′, sen′ə-bīt′), *n.* a cenobite.
coe·no·cyte (sē′nə-sīt′, sen′ə-sīt′), *n.* [*coeno-* + *-cyte*], an organism consisting of several protoplasmic units contained within one cell wall.
coe·nu·rus (si-nyoor′əs), *n.* [Mod. L. < *coen-* + *-urus*], the larva of a tapeworm that attacks the brains of sheep, causing any of various diseases, as the staggers.
co·en·zyme (kō-en′zīm), *n.* a substance that occurs with an enzyme and activates it.
co·e·qual (kō-ē′kwəl), *adj. & n.* equal.
co·erce (kō-ũrs′), *v.t.* [COERCED (-ũrst′), COERCING], [L. *coercere*, to surround, restrain < *co-*, together + *arcere*, to confine], 1. to restrain or constrain by force, especially by legal authority; curb. 2. to force; compel. 3. to effect by force; enforce. —***SYN.*** see **force.**
co·er·ci·ble (kō-ũr′sə-b'l), *adj.* that can be coerced.
co·er·cion (kō-ũr′shən), *n.* [L. *coercio*], 1. a coercing or the power to coerce. 2. government by force.
co·er·cive (kō-ũr′siv), *adj.* of or characterized by coercion; tending to coerce.
co·es·sen·tial (kō′ə-sen′shəl), *adj.* having one and the same essence or nature.
co·e·ta·ne·ous (kō′i-tā′ni-əs), *adj.* [LL. *coaetaneus* < L. *co-*, with + *aetas*, age], contemporary; coeval.
co·e·ter·nal (kō′i-tũr′n'l), *adj.* equally eternal; existing together eternally.
co·e·ter·ni·ty (kō′i-tũr′nə-ti), *n.* in *theology*, the existence together of eternal beings or things.
Coeur de Li·on (kũr′ də lē′ən; Fr. kër′ də lyōn′), [Fr., lit., heart of a lion], see **Richard I.**
co·e·val (kō-ē′v'l), *adj.* [< LL. *coaevus* < L. *co-*, together + *aevum*, age], of the same age or period; contemporary. *n.* a contemporary. —***SYN.*** see **contemporary.**
co·ex·ec·u·tor (kō′ig-zek′yoo-tẽr), *n.* a person acting as executor jointly with another.
co·ex·ist (kō′ig-zist′), *v.i.* to exist together, at the same time, or in the same place.
co·ex·ist·ence (kō′ig-zis′təns), *n.* existence together, at the same time, or in the same place.
co·ex·ist·ent (kō′ig-zis′tənt), *adj.* having coexistence.
co·ex·tend (kō′ik-stend′), *v.t. & v.i.* to extend equally in space or time.
co·ex·ten·sion (kō′ik-sten′shən), *n.* a coextending or being coextended.
co·ex·ten·sive (kō′ik-sten′siv), *adj.* having the same extent in time or space; extending equally.
cof·fee (kôf′i, kof′i), *n.* [see PLURAL, II, D, 3], [It. *caffè;* Turk. *qahveh;* Ar. *qahwah*, drink made from berries, coffee], 1. an aromatic drink made from the roasted and ground beanlike seeds of a tall tropical plant of the madder family. 2. the seeds, green, roasted, or ground, used in making the drink: they are found in the red berries of the shrub. 3. the shrub itself. 4. the color of coffee containing milk or cream; brown. *adj.* having the flavor or color of coffee.

COFFEE
plant (5–10 ft. high); branch; berry

coffee bean, the seed of the coffee plant.
cof·fee·ber·ry (kôf′i-ber′i, kof′i-ber′i), *n.* [*pl.* COFFEEBERRIES (-iz)], 1. the fruit of the coffee plant. 2. the coffee bean.
coffee break, a brief respite from work when coffee or other refreshment is usually taken.
cof·fee·cake (kôf′i-kāk′, kof′i-kāk′), *n.* a kind of cake or roll, often containing nuts, raisins, etc. or coated with sugar or icing, to be eaten with coffee or the like.
coffee cream, sweet cream with a lower butterfat content than whipping cream.
cof·fee·house (kôf′i-hous′, kof′i-hous′), *n.* a place of public entertainment where coffee and other refreshments are served: in the 17th and 18th centuries coffeehouses were gathering places of literary men, etc.
coffee mill, a machine for grinding roasted coffee beans.
coffee nut, 1. the Kentucky coffee tree, a large tree of the pea family. 2. the fruit of this tree.
cof·fee·pot (kôf′i-pot′, kof′i-pot′), *n.* a container, usually with a lid, in which coffee is made or served.
cof·fee·room (kôf′i-rōōm′, kof′i-room′), *n.* coffee shop.
coffee shop, a restaurant, as in a hotel, where coffee, light refreshments, and now usually meals, are served.
coffee table, a small, low table, usually in a living room, for serving refreshments.

coffee tree, 1. the tree that produces the coffee bean. 2. the Kentucky coffee tree.

cof·fer (kôf′ẽr, kof′ẽr), *n.* [ME. *cofer, cofre;* OFr. *cofre,* a chest; L. *cophinus;* see COFFIN], 1. a chest or strongbox in which money or valuables are kept. 2. *pl.* a treasury; funds. 3. a decorative sunken panel in a vault, dome, ceiling, etc. 4. a cofferdam. 5. a lock for a barge or ship in a canal, river, dock, etc. *v.t.* 1. to enclose in a coffer. 2. to furnish with decorative sunken panels.

cof·fer·dam (kôf′ẽr-dam′, kof′ẽr-dam′), *n.* [*coffer* + *dam* (barrier)], 1. a watertight temporary structure in a river, lake, etc., for keeping the water from an enclosed area that has been pumped dry so that bridge foundations, dams, etc. may be constructed. 2. a watertight box or chamber attached to the side of a ship so that repairs can be made below the water line.

cof·fin (kôf′in, kof′in), *n.* [ME. *cofin, coffin,* a basket, receptacle; OFr. *cofin,* basket, coffer; L. *cophinus;* Gr. *kophinos,* a basket], 1. a case or box to put a dead person into for burial. 2. the hollow part of a horse's hoof. *v.t.* 1. to put into a coffin. 2. to confine tightly.

Cof·fin, Robert Peter Tristram (kôf′in, kof′in), 1892–1955; American poet and novelist.

coffin bone, the foot bone inside the hoof of a horse or other similar animal.

coffin corner, [radio slang, prob. with reference to the grave of the defending team's hopes], in *football,* any of the corners of the playing field formed by a goal line and side line: punts are often directed to a coffin corner so that the ball will roll out of bounds near the opponent's goal line.

coffin nail, [Slang], a cigarette.

cof·fle (kof′'l), *n.* [Ar. *qāfilah,* caravan], animals or slaves fastened together one after another, or driven along together. *v.t.* [COFFLED (-'ld), COFFLING], to fasten together in or as in a coffle.

C. of S., Chief of Staff.

cog (kog), *n.* [ME. *cog, cogge* < Scand.; cf. Norw. *kug,* Sw. *kugge,* a cog, tooth; Gael., Ir. *cog,* a cog], 1. one of a series of teeth on the rim of a wheel, for transmitting or receiving motion by fitting between the teeth of another wheel; gear tooth. 2. a wheel with such teeth on its rim. 3. [Colloq.], a person regarded as a minor part of the entire machinery of an activity, business, etc.
slip a cog, to make an error.

cog (kog), *n.* [altered (after *cog,* gear tooth) < earlier *cock,* to secure; prob. ult. < It. *cocca,* a notch], a projection on a beam that fits into a corresponding groove or notch in another beam, making a joint. *v.t. & v.i.* [COGGED (kogd), COGGING], to join by a cog or cogs.

cog (kog), *n.* [ME. *cogge;* see COCKBOAT], 1. formerly, a broadly built boat with a blunt bow and stern. 2. a small boat; cockboat.

cog (kog), *v.t. & v.i.* [COGGED (kogd), COGGING], [prob. slang extension of *cog* (gear tooth)], 1. to manipulate (dice) in a fraudulent manner. 2. to cheat; swindle. *n.* [Obs.], 1. a cogging at dice. 2. a deception; trick.

cog., cognate.

co·gen·cy (kō′jən-si), *n.* 1. the quality or condition of being cogent; power to convince. 2. [*pl.* COGENCIES (-siz)], a cogent statement.

co·gent (kō′jənt), *adj.* [L. *cogens,* ppr. of *cogere,* to collect < *co-,* together + *agere,* to drive], having a powerful appeal to the mind; compelling; convincing. —*SYN.* see **valid.**

cogged (kogd), *adj.* having cogs (gear teeth) or cogwheels.

cog·i·ta·ble (koj′ə-tə-b'l), *adj.* [L. *cogitabilis* < *cogitare;* see COGITATE], thinkable.

cog·i·tate (koj′ə-tāt′), *v.i.* [COGITATED (-id), COGITATING], [< L. *cogitatus,* pp. of *cogitare* < **coagitare;* see CO- & AGITATE], to think seriously; ponder; meditate. *v.t.* to think about; consider. —*SYN.* see **think.**

cog·i·ta·tion (koj′ə-tā′shən), *n.* [ME. & OFr. *cogitaciun;* L. *cogitatio;* see COGITATE], thought; meditation.

cog·i·ta·tive (koj′ə-tā′tiv), *adj.* 1. capable of thinking. 2. tending to cogitate; thoughtful; meditative.

cog·i·ta·tor (koj′ə-tā′tẽr), *n.* a person who cogitates.

‡co·gi·to er·go sum (koj′i-tō′ ũr′gō sum′), [L.], I think, therefore I exist: the basic tenet of the philosophy of Descartes.

co·gnac (kō′nyak, kon′yak), *n.* [Fr.], 1. a French brandy distilled from wine in the area of Cognac, France. 2. loosely, any French brandy or any brandy.

cog·nate (kog′nāt), *adj.* [L. *cognatus,* related by birth; *co-,* together + *gnatus,* pp. of *gnasci,* older form of *nasci,* to be born], 1. related by family; having the same ancestor. 2. related through the same origin; derived from a common original form: as, English ***apple*** and German ***apfel*** are *cognate* words, English and Flemish are *cognate* languages. 3. having the same nature or quality. *n.* 1. a person related to another by common ancestry. 2. a cognate word, language, or thing. Abbreviated **cog.** —*SYN.* see **related.**

cog·na·tion (kog-nā′shən), *n.* [see COGNATE], relationship by descent from the same ancestor or source.

cog·ni·tion (kog-nish′ən), *n.* [L. *cognito,* knowledge < *cognitus,* pp. of *cognoscere,* to know; *co-,* together + *gnoscere,* older form of *noscere,* to know], 1. the process of knowing or perceiving; perception. 2. anything that is known or perceived.

cog·ni·tive (kog′nə-tiv), *adj.* having to do with cognition.

cog·ni·za·ble (kog′ni-zə-b'l, kon′i-zə-b'l), *adj.* [< *cognize,* to take cognizance of (see RECOGNIZE) + *-able*], 1. that can be recognized, known, or perceived. 2. in *law,* within the jurisdiction of a court.

cog·ni·zance (kog′ni-zəns, kon′i-zəns), *n.* [ME. *cognisaunce, conoissance;* OFr. *cognoisance, connoissance,* knowledge < *conoissant,* ppr. of *conoistre,* to know; L. *cognoscere;* see COGNITION], 1. the fact of being aware; perception; knowledge. 2. notice; heed. 3. the range of knowledge possible through observation. 4. in *heraldry,* the distinguishing crest or other device by which the bearer is recognized. 5. in *law, a)* the hearing of a case in court. *b)* jurisdiction; right or power of dealing with a matter judicially.
take cognizance of, to notice; recognize officially.

cog·ni·zant (kog′ni-zənt, kon′i-zənt), *adj.* having cognizance (*of* something); informed. —*SYN.* see **aware.**

cog·nize (kog′nīz′), *v.t.* [COGNIZED (-nīzd′), COGNIZING], to take cognizance of; notice, perceive, or recognize.

cog·no·men (kog-nō′mən), *n.* [*pl.* COGNOMENS (-mənz), COGNOMINA (-nom′ə-nə)], [L. < *co-,* with + *nomen,* name (see NAME); sp. influenced by association with **gnomen* < Gr. *gnōma,* mark, token; akin to L. *gnoscere;* see COGNITION], 1. the third or family name of an ancient Roman, as *Cicero* in *Marcus Tullius Cicero.* 2. a family name; surname; last name. 3. any name; especially, a nickname.

cog·nom·i·nal (kog-nom′i-n'l), *adj.* 1. of a cognomen. 2. having the same cognomen.

‡co·gno·scen·te (kô′nyô-shen′te), *n.* [*pl.* COGNOSCENTI (-tē)], [It. *cognoscente, conoscente;* orig. ppr. of *conoscere,* to know < L. *cognoscere;* see COGNITION], a connoisseur.

cog·nos·ci·ble (kog-nos′ə-b'l), *adj.* [LL. *cognoscibilis* < L. *cognoscere;* see COGNITION], that can be known or perceived.

cog·no·vit (kog-nō′vit), *n.* [short for L. *cognovit actionem,* lit., he has acknowledged the action], in *law,* a written acknowledgment of his liability made by a defendant in a civil suit to avoid the expense of contending.

co·gon (kə-gōn′), *n.* [Sp. *cogón* < native (Tagalog) name], a tall, coarse grass growing in the Philippines and near-by lands, used as thatching.

cog·wheel (kog′hwēl′), *n.* a wheel with a rim notched into teeth, which mesh with those of another wheel to transmit or receive motion.

COGWHEELS

co·hab·it (kō-hab′it), *v.i.* [LL. *cohabitare;* L. *co-,* together + *habitare,* to dwell], 1. to live together as husband and wife: the word usually implies sexual intercourse, and is applied especially to those not legally married. 2. [Archaic], to live together.

co·hab·it·ant (kō-hab′ə-tənt), *n.* [< L. *cohabitans,* ppr. of *cohabitare;* see COHABIT], a person who lives together with another or others.

co·hab·i·ta·tion (kō-hab′ə-tā′shən), *n.* the act, fact, or state of cohabiting.

Co·han, George Michael (kō-han′), 1878–1942; American actor, playwright, producer, and composer of popular songs.

co·heir (kō-âr′), *n.* a person who inherits jointly with another or others.

co·heir·ess (kō-âr′is), *n.* a girl or woman coheir.

co·here (kō-hêr′), *v.i.* [COHERED (-hêrd′), COHERING], [L. *cohaerere; co-,* together + *haerere,* to stick], 1. to stick together, as parts of a mass. 2. to be connected naturally or logically, as by a common principle; be in accord. —*SYN.* see **stick.**

co·her·ence (kō-hêr′əns), *n.* [Fr.; LL. *cohaerentia* < *cohaerens,* ppr. of *cohaerere;* see COHERE], 1. a sticking together; cohesion. 2. the quality of being logically integrated, consistent, and intelligible; congruity: as, his story lacked *coherence.*

co·her·en·cy (kō-hêr′ən-si), *n.* coherence.

co·her·ent (kō-hêr′ənt), *adj.* [Fr.], 1. sticking together; having cohesion. 2. having coherence; logically connected; consistent; clearly articulated and intelligible.

co·her·er (kō-hêr′ẽr), *n.* [see COHERE], in *radio,* a kind of detector formerly used before the general adoption of the vacuum tube.

co·he·sion (kō-hē′zhən), *n.* [Fr. < L. *cohaesus,* pp. of *cohaerere*], 1. the act or condition of cohering; tendency to stick together. 2. in *physics,* the force by which the molecules of a substance are held together: distinguished from *adhesion.*

co·he·sive (kō-hē′siv), *adj.* sticking together; causing or characterized by cohesion.

co·ho·bate (kō′hō-bāt′), *v.t.* [COHOBATED (-id), COHOBATING], [< ML. *cohobare;* said to be < Ar. *ka'aba,* to repeat (an action)], in *chemistry,* formerly, to redistill, often several times, by pouring the distillate back upon the residue in the retort or upon some matter like this, in an attempt to obtain greater purity.

Co·hoes (kō-hōz′), *n.* a city in New York, on the Hudson: pop., 20,000.
co·hort (kō′hôrt), *n.* [Fr. *cohorte* < L. *cohors*, enclosure; enclosed company; hence, retinue, crowd], 1. an ancient Roman military unit, one tenth of a legion: a cohort consisted of 300–600 men. 2. a band of soldiers. 3. a group; band. 4. now, often, an associate or colleague: as, the mayor came with one of his *cohorts*.
co·hosh (kō′hosh, kə-hosh′), *n.* [< Am. Ind. (Algonquian) native name], any of a number of American herbs of the crowfoot family: some are used in medicine.
co·hune (kə-hōōn′), *n.* [< Central Am. Ind. name *cóhuṅ*], a species of palm with feathery leaves, growing in Central and South America: its wood is used for building and its nuts yield an oil.
coif (koif), *n.* [ME. & OFr. *coife;* LL. *cofea*, a cap, hood; ? < Gr. *kyphellon*, all-enclosing cover or ? < *skyphion*, skull], 1. a cap that fits the head closely. 2. formerly, in England, a white cap worn by lawyers, particularly by sergeants-at-law. 3. the rank of sergeant-at-law. 4. a thick skullcap, as of leather, formerly worn under a hood of mail. *v.t.* to cover with or as with a coif.
‡coif·feur (kwȧ′fẽr′; Eng. kwä-fūr′), *n.* [Fr. < *coiffer* < *coiffe;* see COIF], a hairdresser.
coif·fure (kwä-fyoor′; Fr. kwȧ′für′), *n.* [Fr.; see COIFFEUR], 1. a headdress. 2. a style of arranging the hair.
coign, coigne (koin), *n.* [var. of *coin, quoin*], a projecting corner.
coign of vantage, an advantageous position for observation or action.
coil (koil), *v.t.* [OFr. *coillir*, to gather, pick; L. *colligere*, to gather together < *com-*, together + *legere*, to gather], to wind or gather (rope, etc.) around into a circular or spiral form. *v.i.* 1. to wind around and around. 2. to move in a winding course. *n.* 1. anything wound or gathered into a series of rings or spirals. 2. such a series of rings or spirals. 3. a single turn of a coiled figure. 4. a series of connected pipes in rows or coils. 5. in *electricity*, *a)* a spiral of wire. *b)* any device consisting essentially of such a spiral.
coil (koil), *n.* [Early Mod. Eng. < OFr. *acueil*, collision, etc.], [Archaic], commotion; turmoil.
coin (koin), *n.* [ME. *coyn, coin;* OFr. *coin, coigne*, a wedge, stamp, die, corner; L. *cuneus*, a wedge], 1. a cornerstone; wedge; quoin; coign. 2. a piece of metal with a distinctive stamp, and of a fixed value and weight, issued by a government and used as money. 3. such pieces collectively. 4. [Slang], money. *v.t.* 1. *a)* to make (coins) by stamping metal. *b)* to make (metal) into coins. 2. to make up; devise; invent, as a new word or phrase. *v.i.* to make coins.
coin money, [Colloq.], to make, or earn, money rapidly; be very successful financially.
pay (a person) back in his own coin, to treat (a person) in the same way as he treated oneself or others.
coin·age (koin′ij), *n.* [OFr. *coignaige* < *coigne*], 1. the act or process of coining. 2. a thing or things coined; coins; metal money. 3. a system of money or metal currency. 4. the right to coin money. 5. an invented word or expression: as, *radar* is a recent *coinage*.
co·in·cide (kō′in-sīd′), *v.i.* [COINCIDED (-id), COINCIDING], [Fr. *coincider;* ML. *coincidere;* L. *co-*, together + *incidere*, to fall upon < *in-*, upon, in + *cadere*, to fall], 1. to take up the same place in space; be exactly alike in shape, position, and area. 2. to occur at the same time; take up the same period of time. 3. to agree; be identical: as, our interests *coincide*. —*SYN.* see **agree.**
co·in·ci·dence (kō-in′sə-dəns), *n.* [Fr. < ML. *coincidens*, ppr.], 1. the fact or condition of coinciding. 2. an accidental and remarkable occurrence of events, ideas, etc. at the same time, in a way that sometimes suggests a causal relationship.
co·in·ci·dent (kō-in′sə-dənt), *adj.* [Fr.; ML. *coincidens*, ppr.], 1. coinciding; occurring at the same time. 2. taking up the same position in space at the same time. 3. in exact agreement; identical: as, his hobby is *coincident* with his vocation.
co·in·ci·den·tal (kō-in′sə-den′t′l), *adj.* characterized by coincidence.
coin·er (koin′ẽr), *n.* 1. a maker of coins; especially, a counterfeiter. 2. an inventor or originator.
co·in·her·i·tor (kō′in-her′ə-tẽr), *n.* a person who inherits jointly with another or others.
coin silver, in *metallurgy*, silver of standard fineness for making coins.
co·in·sur·ance (kō′in-shoor′əns), *n.* insurance on commercial property in which two or more insurers (*coinsurers*) carry the risk in proportion to the coverage of the full property value which each has issued: sometimes the insured stands as a coinsurer in assuming part of the risk.
coir (koir), *n.* [Port. *cairo;* Malayalam *kayar*, a rope, cord < Tamil *kayaru*, to be twisted], the prepared fiber of the husks of coconuts, used to make rope, etc.
cois·trel (kois′trəl), *n.* [prob. < OFr. *coustillier*, groom, with interchange of *l* and *r*], [Archaic], 1. a groom in charge of a knight's horses. 2. a knave; varlet.
co·i·tion (kō-ish′ən), *n.* [L. *coitio* < *coitus*, pp. of *coire; co-*, together + *ire*, to go], sexual intercourse.
co·i·tus (kō′i-təs), *n.* [L.], sexual intercourse.
coke (kōk), *n.* [north Eng. dial; prob. < ME. *colke*, a core < IE. base **gel-g̑*, rounded, ball-like, etc.], coal from which most of the gases have been removed by heating: it burns with intense heat and little smoke, and is used as an industrial fuel. *v.t. & v.i.* [COKED (kōkt), COKING], to change into coke.
coke (kōk), *n.* [Slang], 1. cocaine. 2. a variety of soft drink containing no cocaine: a trade-mark (**Coke**). *v.t.* [COKED (kōkt), COKING], [Slang], to affect with cocaine: usually in the passive, with *up*.
Coke, Sir Edward (kook), 1552–1634; English jurist and statesman; lord chief justice of England.
coke oven, an oven in which coke is made.
col (kol), *n.* [Fr., the neck < L. *collum*, the neck], a gap between peaks in a mountain range, used as a pass.
col- (kol), com-: used before *l*.
Col., 1. Colombia. 2. Colonel. 3. Colorado: officially, **Colo.** 4. Colossians.
col., 1. collected. 2. collector. 3. college. 4. colonial. 5. colony. 6. color. 7. colored. 8. column.
co·la (kō′lə), *n.* [Latinized form of W. Afr. name], the kola, an African tree whose nuts contain caffeine.
co·la (kō′lə), *n.* 1. alternative plural of **colon** (intestine). 2. plural of **colon** (in *prosody*).
col·an·der (kul′ən-dẽr, kol′ən-dẽr), *n.* [prob. < L. *colare*, to strain (< *colum*, strainer), as also in Sp. *colador* (ML. *colator*), strainer], a pan with a perforated bottom to drain off liquids, as in washing vegetables.
co·lat·i·tude (kō-lat′ə-tōōd′, kō-lat′ə-tūd′), *n.* in *astronomy*, the complement of the latitude.
Col·bert, Jean Bap·tiste (zhän bȧ′tēst′ kôl′bâr′), 1619–1683; French statesman and financier.
col·can·non (kəl-kan′ən, kôl′kan-ən), *n.* [Ir. *cāl ceannain* < *cāl*, cabbage + *ceannan*, white-headed], an Irish dish made of potatoes, cabbage, and onions boiled together and mashed.
Col·ches·ter (kōl′ches′tẽr, kōl′chis-tẽr), *n.* a city on the southeastern coast of England: pop., 64,000.
col·chi·cine (kol′chi-sēn′, kol′ki-sin), *n.* [*colchic*um + *-ine*], a poisonous, yellow crystalline alkaloid, $C_{22}H_{25}O_6N$, extracted from colchicum.
col·chi·cum (kol′chi-kəm, kol′ki-kəm), *n.* [L.; Gr. *kolchikon*, plant with a poisonous root; prob. < *Kolchis*, Colchis, a country in Asia famous as the home of Medea, sorceress and poisoner in ancient legend], 1. any of a group of plants of the lily family, with crocuslike flowers blooming in the fall: also called *autumn crocus, meadow saffron*. 2. its seeds or fleshy, underground stem, sometimes used in treating rheumatism and gout.
Col·chis (kol′kis), *n.* an ancient country in Transcaucasia, on the eastern shore of the Black Sea: the legendary Golden Fleece was in Colchis.
col·co·thar (kol′kə-thẽr), *n.* [ML.; prob. via Sp. *colcotar* < Ar. *qulquṭār* < Gr. *chalkanthos*, solution of blue vitriol (copper sulfate) < *chalkos*, copper + *anthos*, flower], a brownish-red oxide of iron, obtained by heating ferrous sulfate: it is used as a pigment, polishing agent, etc.
cold (kōld), *adj.* [ME.; AS. (Anglian) *cald* < Gmc. base **kali* (cf. CHILL); akin to G. *kalt*, L. *gelidus* (cf. GELID); for IE. base, see COOL], 1. of a temperature much lower than that of the human body; very chilly; frigid. 2. lacking heat; having lost heat; of less heat than is required: as, this soup is *cold*. 3. dead. 4. feeling chilled. 5. without warmth of feeling; without enthusiasm; indifferent: as, a *cold* personality. 6. not cordial; unfriendly: as, a *cold* reception. 7. chilling; gloomy; dispiriting: as, they had a *cold* realization of their plight. 8. calm; detached; objective: as, *cold* logic. 9. designating colors that suggest cold, as tones of blue, green, or gray. 10. still far from what is being sought: said of the seeker. 11. [Slang], completely mastered: as, the actor had his lines down *cold*. 12. [Slang], insensible: as, the boxer was knocked *cold*. 13. in *hunting*, faint; not strong: said of a scent. *n.* 1. absence of heat; lack of warmth: often thought of as an active force. 2. the sensation produced by a loss or absence of heat. 3. an acute inflammation of the mucous membranes of the respiratory passages, especially of the nose and throat, caused by a virus and characterized by sneezing, coughing, etc.; coryza.
catch cold, to become ill with a cold: also **take cold.**
cold comfort, little or no comfort at all.
have cold feet, [Colloq.], to be timid.
in the cold, ignored; neglected; not participating.
throw cold water on, to be unenthusiastic about or toward; discourage.
cold-blood·ed (kōld′blud′id), *adj.* 1. having blood that varies in temperature, approximating that of the surrounding air, land, or water: as, fishes and reptiles are *cold-blooded* animals. 2. easily affected by cold: as,

sluggish circulation makes one *cold-blooded.* 3. callous; cruel; hard-hearted.
cold chisel, a hardened and tempered steel chisel without a handle, for cutting or chipping cold metal.
cold cream, a creamy, soothing preparation for softening and cleansing the skin.
cold-draw (kōld′drô′), *v.t.* to draw or shape (unheated metal) through a die.
cold frame, an unheated, boxlike, glass structure for protecting young plants.
cold front, in *meteorology,* the forward line of a cold air mass advancing into a warmer air mass.
cold-heart·ed (kōld′här′tid), *adj.* not sympathetic; unfeeling; unkind.
cold light, light not accompanied by the heat of combustion or incandescence, as phosphorescent light.
cold-pack (kōld′pak′), *v.t.* 1. to apply a cold pack to. 2. to can by cold pack.
cold pack, 1. cold, wet blankets or sheets wrapped around a patient's body as a means of treatment. 2. a process of canning foodstuffs in which the raw products are placed in jars first and then subjected to heat.
cold-short (kōld′shôrt′), *adj.* [prob. < Sw. *kallskör* < *kall,* cold + *skör,* brittle], in *metallurgy,* brittle when not at a red heat.
cold-shoul·der (kōld′shōl′dẽr), *v.t.* [Colloq.], to slight; snub; rebuff.
cold shoulder, [Colloq.], deliberate indifference or neglect; slight; rebuff; snub: as, she gave her former friend the *cold shoulder.*
cold snap, a sudden, brief spell of cold weather.
cold sore, a sore consisting of little blisters that often appear about the mouth during a cold or fever; fever blister: see **herpes.**
cold steel, a weapon of steel, as a knife or bayonet.
cold storage, storage of perishable foods, etc. in a very cold place, especially in a refrigerating chamber.
cold sweat, perspiration accompanied by a cold, clammy feeling, as during fear or shock.
cold war, sharp conflict in diplomacy, economics, etc. between states, regarded as potentially leading to actual war.
cold wave, 1. a period of weather colder than is normal. 2. a permanent wave in which the hair is set with a liquid preparation instead of heat.
cole (kōl), *n.* [ME. *cole, col;* AS. *caul, cawl;* L. *caulis, colis,* a cabbage], any of various plants of the mustard family, to which cabbage belongs; especially, rape.
co·lec·to·my (kə-lek′tə-mi), *n.* [see COLON & -ECTOMY], the surgical removal of all or part of the colon.
cole·man·ite (kōl′mən-īt′), *n.* [after William T. *Coleman* (1824–1893), Am. manufacturer of borax], a white or colorless crystalline substance, $Ca_2B_6O_{11}·5H_2O$, a hydrous borate of calcium.
co·le·op·ter (kō′li-op′tẽr, kol′i-op′tẽr), *n.* any coleopterous insect.
co·le·op·ter·an (kō′li-op′tẽr-ən, kol′i-op′tẽr-ən), *n.* a coleopter.
co·le·op·ter·on (kō′li-op′tẽr-on′, kol′i-op′tẽr-on′), *n.* [*pl.* COLEOPTERA (-ə)], [Mod. L.], a coleopter.
co·le·op·ter·ous (kō′li-op′tẽr-əs, kol′i-op′tẽr-əs), *adj.* [Mod. L. *Coleoptera,* name of the order (< Gr. *koleopteros,* sheath-winged < *koleos,* sheath + *pteron,* wing); + *-ous*], belonging to a group of insects, including beetles and weevils, with the front wings modified to form a horny covering for the hind wings, which are functional.
co·le·o·rhi·za (kō′li-ə-rī′zə, kol′i-ə-rī′zə), *n.* [*pl.* COLEORHIZAE (-zē)], [Mod. L. < Gr. *koleos,* a sheath + *rhiza,* a root], a sheath surrounding the early root of certain seedlings, through which the roots emerge.
Cole·ridge, Samuel Taylor (kōl′rij, kō′lə-rij), 1772–1834; English poet and critic.
Cole·ridge-Tay·lor, Samuel (kōl′rij-tā′lẽr), 1875–1912; English composer.
cole·slaw (kōl′slô′), *n.* [< D. *kool,* a cabbage < L. *caulis* (see COLE) + D. *sla* for *salade,* salad], a salad made of shredded raw cabbage, often mixed with salad dressing and seasoning: also **cole slaw.**
co·le·us (kō′li-əs), *n.* [Mod. L. < Gr. *koleos,* a sheath: so named because of the way in which the stamens are joined], any of a group of plants of the mint family native to Africa and the East Indies, grown for their showy, bright-colored leaves.
cole·wort (kōl′wũrt′), *n.* [*cole* + *wort*], 1. cole. 2. any cabbage whose leaves do not form a compact head.
Col·fax, Schuy·ler (skī′lẽr kōl′faks), 1823–1885; vice-president of the United States (1869–1873).
col·ic (kol′ik), *n.* [Fr. *colique;* L. *colicus,* pertaining to colic, sick with colic; Gr. *kōlikos* < *kōlon, kolon,* colon: from being seated in the colon and parts adjacent], acute abdominal pain caused by various abnormal conditions in the bowels. *adj.* 1. of colic. 2. of the colon (part of the large intestine).
col·ick·y (kol′ik-i), *adj.* 1. of or like colic. 2. having or subject to colic. 3. liable to cause colic.
col·ic·root (kol′ik-rōōt′, kol′ik-root′), *n.* 1. a bitter herb of the lily family with white or yellow flowers. 2. any of a number of other plants supposed to cure colic.
col·ic·weed (kol′ik-wēd′), *n.* any of several North American plants, as the Dutchman's-breeches.
Co·li·gny, Gas·pard de (gås′pår′ də kô′lē′nyē′), 1519–1572; French admiral and Protestant leader.
Co·li·ma (kō-lē′mä), *n.* 1. a state of southern Mexico, on the Pacific: area, 2,009 sq. mi.; pop., 79,000. 2. its capital: pop., 23,000. 3. a volcanic mountain in this state, near the coast: height, 14,219 ft.
Col·in (kol′in, kō′lin), [lit., a dove; prob. < St. *Columba,* patron saint of Corn. parishes], a masculine name.
col·in (kol′in), *n.* [Sp. *colin;* Mex. *çolin; c-* for *ç-* by error], 1. the masked bobwhite. 2. any bird of the bobwhite family.
col·i·se·um (kol′ə-sē′əm), *n.* [Mod. L. < L. *colosseum,* neut. of *colosseus,* colossal, huge], 1. [C-], the Colosseum. 2. a large building or stadium for sports events and other public entertainments.
co·li·tis (kō-lī′tis), *n.* [Mod. L. < Gr. *kolon,* colon, large intestine; + *-itis*], inflammation of the mucous membrane of the large intestine.
coll., 1. colleague. 2. collect. 3. collection. 4. collective. 5. collector. 6. college. 7. colloquial.
col·lab·o·rate (kə-lab′ə-rāt′), *v.i.* [COLLABORATED (-id), COLLABORATING], [< L. *collaboratus,* pp. of *collaborare,* to work together < *com-,* with + *laborare,* to work], 1. to work together: especially in reference to literary, artistic, or scientific work. 2. to co-operate with the enemy; be a collaborationist.
col·lab·o·ra·tion (kə-lab′ə-rā′shən), *n.* [< *collaborate*], 1. the act of working together, as in writing a book: abbreviated **collab.** 2. co-operation with the enemy.
col·lab·o·ra·tion·ist (kə-lab′ə-rā′shən-ist), *n.* a person who co-operates with an enemy invader of his country.
col·lab·o·ra·tive (kə-lab′ə-rā′tiv, kə-lab′ə-rə-tiv), *adj.* 1. collaborating or tending to collaborate. 2. resulting from collaboration.
col·lab·o·ra·tor (kə-lab′ə-rā′tẽr), *n.* [Fr. *collaborateur;* see COLLABORATE], a person who works with another or others, as in writing a book: abbreviated **collab.**
col·lage (kə-läzh′; Fr. kô′läzh′), *n.* [Fr., a pasting, paper hanging], 1. a kind of surrealist art in which bits of flat objects, as newspaper, cloth, pressed flowers, etc., are pasted together in incongruous relationship for their symbolic or suggestive effect. 2. a picture so made.
col·la·gen (kol′ə-jen′), *n.* [< Gr. *kolla,* glue; + *-gen*], a gelatinous substance found in connective tissue, bone, and cartilage.
col·lapse (kə-laps′), *v.i.* [COLLAPSED (-lapst′), COLLAPSING], [< L. *collapsus,* pp. of *collabi* < *com-,* together + *labi,* to fall], 1. to fall in or together, as when supports or sides fail to hold; cave in; shrink together suddenly. 2. to break down suddenly; fail; vanish: as, the enemy's defense *collapsed.* 3. to break down or fail suddenly in health. 4. to fold or come together compactly. 5. to fall down, as from a blow or strain. *v.t.* to cause to collapse. *n.* 1. a falling in or together; sudden caving in or shrinking together. 2. a failure or breakdown, as of a business enterprise. 3. a sudden breakdown in health; state of extreme physical depression and prostration with failure of circulation, often preceding death.
col·laps·i·bil·i·ty (kə-lap′sə-bil′ə-ti), *n.* the quality or condition of being collapsible.
col·laps·i·ble (kə-lap′sə-b'l), *adj.* [< *collapse* + *-ible*], made so that it can be folded up compactly.
col·lar (kol′ẽr), *n.* [ME. *coler;* OFr. *coler, colier;* L. *collare,* band or chain for the neck < *collum,* the neck], 1. the part of a dress, blouse, coat, shirt, etc. that encircles the neck. 2. a cloth band or folded-over piece attached to the neck of a shirt, blouse, dress, etc. 3. an ornamental band, chain, or circlet worn around the neck. 4. a band of leather or metal for a dog's neck. 5. a leather-covered roll for the neck of a horse or other draft animal; part of the harness against which the animal strains in pulling a weight: see **harness,** illus. 6. a ring or flange, as on rods, shafts, or pipes, to prevent sideward motion, connect parts, etc. 7. a distinctive band, as of a different color, marking, or texture, around the neck of an animal, bird, etc. 8. the foam that forms on the top of a glass of beer. *v.t.* 1. to put a collar on. 2. to seize by the collar; capture. 3. [Colloq.], to stop and talk to: as, she *collared* him in the hall.
col·lar·bone (kol′ẽr-bōn′), *n.* a flat, slender bone joining the breastbone to the shoulder blade; clavicle.
collar button, a small button, sometimes detachable, for fastening a shirt collar.
col·lard (kol′ẽrd), *n.* [contr. < *cole wort*], a kind of kale whose coarse leaves are borne in tufts.
col·lar·et, col·lar·ette (kol′ẽr-et′), *n.* [Fr. *collarette,* dim.], a small collar or cape of linen, lace, fur, etc.
col·late (ko-lāt′, kol′āt), *v.t.* [COLLATED (-id), COLLATING], [< L. *collatus,* pp. of *conferre,* to bring together; *com-,* together + *ferre,* to carry], 1. to compare (texts, etc.) carefully. 2. to examine (the sheets of a book to be bound) to see that the pages, plates, etc. are in proper order. 3. to appoint (a clergyman) to a benefice. 4. in *library usage,* to examine (a book) page by page to see that none are missing. —*SYN.* see **compare.**
col·lat·er·al (kə-lat′ẽr-əl), *adj.* [ME.; LL. *collateralis* < L. *com-,* together + *lateralis,* lateral < *latus,* a side],

1. side by side; parallel. 2. accompanying; concomitant. 3. of a similar but subordinate nature; secondary. 4. of corresponding value or importance. 5. descended from the same ancestors but in a different line: as, Franklin D. Roosevelt and Theodore Roosevelt were *collateral* relatives. 6. designating or of security given as a pledge for the fulfillment of an obligation; hence, secured or guaranteed by property, as stocks, bonds, etc.: as, a *collateral* loan: abbreviated **collat.** ***n.*** 1. a collateral relative. 2. anything, such as stocks or bonds, that secures or guarantees the discharge of an obligation: it is returned to the debtor when the obligation is fulfilled.

col·la·tion (ko-lā'shən, kə-lā'shən), ***n.*** [ME. *collacioun;* OFr. *collacion,* discourse; L. *collatio, conlatio,* a bringing together, collection < *collatus*], 1. the act, process, or result of collating. 2. a conference or consultation, as the customary gathering of Benedictine monks at the close of the day, when they listen to a reading from a religious book and discuss it. 3. a light meal: originally such a meal was served in a monastery during the reading of a collation (sense 2). 4. the appointment of a clergyman to a benefice. 5. in *library usage,* the technical description of a book, including the number of pages, illustrations, etc.

col·la·tive (ko-lā'tiv, kə-lā'tiv), ***adj.*** [L. *collativus,* brought together < *collatus;* see COLLATE], 1. having the power to confer or bestow. 2. bestowed or held by collation.

col·league (kol'ēg), ***n.*** [Fr. *collègue;* L. *collega,* one chosen at the same time with another, partner in office < *com-,* with + base **leg-* (to pick, choose) of *legare,* to appoint as deputy, send as ambassador; cf. LEGATE], a fellow worker in the same profession; associate in office: abbreviated **coll.** —***SYN.*** see **associate.**

col·lect (kə-lekt'), ***v.t.*** [OFr. *collecter* < L. *collectus;* see COLLECT, *n.*], 1. to gather together; assemble. 2. to gather (stamps, books, etc.) for a hobby. 3. to call for and receive payment for (rent, taxes, bills, etc.). 4. to regain control of (oneself or one's wits); summon up (one's faculties or powers). ***v.i.*** 1. to gather; assemble. 2. to accumulate. 3. to collect payments, etc.: as, the landlord *collects* on the first of the month. ***adj. & adv.*** with payment to be made by the receiver: as, he telephoned *collect:* abbreviated **coll.** —***SYN.*** see **gather.**

col·lect (kol'ekt), ***n.*** [ME. & OFr. *collecte;* LL. *collecta,* a gathering together of ideas from the day's reading; L. *collecta,* a gathering, contribution of money < *collectus,* pp. of *colligere* < *com-,* together + *legere,* to gather], a short prayer suitable to the time or occasion, used in certain church services.

col·lect·a·ble (kə-lek'tə-b'l), ***adj.*** that can be collected.

col·lec·ta·ne·a (kol'ek-tā'ni-ə), ***n. pl.*** [neut. pl. of L. *collectaneus,* gathered together < *collectus;* see COLLECT, *n.*], a collection of writings of one or more authors; anthology.

col·lect·ed (kə-lek'tid), ***adj.*** [pp. of *collect*], 1. gathered together; assembled. 2. in control of oneself; calm and self-possessed; undisturbed; composed. —***SYN.*** see **cool.**

col·lect·i·ble (kə-lek'tə-b'l), ***adj.*** that can be collected.

col·lec·tion (kə-lek'shən), ***n.*** [L. *collectio*], 1. the act or process of collecting. 2. things collected: as, a *collection* of stamps. 3. something that has gathered into a mass or pile; accumulation: as, a *collection* of dust. 4. money collected, as for church use: abbreviated **coll.**

col·lec·tive (kə-lek'tiv), ***adj.*** [L. *collectivus*], 1. formed by collecting; gathered into a whole. 2. of, as, or characteristic of a group; of or characteristic of individuals acting together; common to several or many: as, the *collective* effort of the students. 3. designating or of any enterprise in which people work collectively: as, there are *collective* farms in the Soviet Union. 4. in *grammar,* designating a noun which in the singular form denotes a collection of individuals (e.g., *army, orchestra, crowd*): it is treated as singular when the collection is thought of as a whole and as plural when the individual members are thought of as acting separately: abbreviated **coll., collect.** ***n.*** 1. any collective enterprise. 2. the people who work together in such an enterprise. 3. in *grammar,* a collective noun: abbreviated **coll., collect.**

collective bargaining, negotiation between organized workers and their employer or employers for reaching an agreement on wages, hours, and working conditions.

collective fruit, a fruit formed by a fused cluster of the ovaries of several flowers, as the mulberry.

col·lec·tive·ly (kə-lek'tiv-li), ***adv.*** 1. in a collective manner; with all participating. 2. as a whole; as a group.

collective security, a system of international security in which the participating nations agree to take joint action against a nation that attacks any one of them.

col·lec·tiv·ism (kə-lek'tiv-iz'm), ***n.*** [Fr. *collectivisme* (c. 1880); see COLLECTIVE & -ISM], the ownership and control of the means of production and distribution by the people as a whole; socialism.

col·lec·tiv·ist (kə-lek'tiv-ist), ***n.*** an advocate of collectivism. ***adj.*** of collectivism or collectivists.

col·lec·tiv·is·tic (kə-lek'tiv-is'tik), ***adj.*** of collectivism or collectivists.

col·lec·tiv·i·ty (kol'ek-tiv'ə-ti), ***n.*** 1. the quality or state of being collective. 2. a collective whole. 3. the people as a whole. 4. collectivism.

col·lec·tiv·ize (kə-lek'tiv-īz'), ***v.t.*** [COLLECTIVIZED (-īzd'), COLLECTIVIZING], 1. to establish collectivism in. 2. to transfer from private to public ownership.

col·lec·tor (kə-lek'tẽr), ***n.*** [LL.], 1. a person or thing that collects. 2. a person whose work is to collect money due: abbreviated **coll., col.**

col·lec·tor·ship (kə-lek'tẽr-ship'), ***n.*** [see -SHIP], 1. the office of collector. 2. the district assigned to a collector.

Col·leen (kol'ēn, kə-lēn'), [Ir.; see COLLEEN, *n.*], a feminine name.

col·leen (kol'ēn, kə-lēn'), ***n.*** [Ir. *cailin,* dim. of *caile,* girl], [Irish], a girl.

col·lege (kol'ij), ***n.*** [L. *collegium,* community, society, guild, fraternity < *collega;* see COLLEAGUE], 1. an association of individuals having certain powers, rights, and duties, and engaged in some common pursuit: as, the electoral *college.* 2. [orig. with reference to the university communities of Oxford & Cambridge], an institution of higher education that grants degrees at the completion of courses of study; university. 3. any of the schools of a university offering instruction and granting degrees in any of several specialized courses of study, as liberal arts, architecture, education, business administration, etc. 4. that division of a university which offers a general four-year course leading to the bachelor's degree: distinguished from the graduate and professional schools. 5. a school offering specialized instruction in some profession or occupation: as, business *college, college* of chiropody. 6. the building or group of buildings of a college. Abbreviated **col., coll.**

College of Cardinals, the cardinals of the Roman Catholic Church, serving as a privy council to the Pope: it administers the Holy See in the absence of the Pope and elects his successor.

col·leg·er (kol'ij-ẽr), ***n.*** a member of, or student at, a college; specifically, a student at Eton College in England supported by endowment of the college.

college widow, a young, unmarried woman in a college town who has had social engagements with male students at the college over a number of years.

col·le·gi·al (kə-lē'ji-əl), ***adj.*** [L. *collegialis* < *collegium*], of, or having the nature of, a college (esp. sense 1).

col·le·gi·an (kə-lē'jən, kə-lē'ji-ən), ***n.*** [ML. *collegianus*], a college student; member of a college.

col·le·gi·ate (kə-lē'jit, kə-lē'ji-it), ***adj.*** [< LL. *collegiatus,* member of a college], 1. of the nature of a college. 2. of or like a college. 3. of, like, or characteristic of college students. Abbreviated **col., coll.**

collegiate church, 1. a church with a chapter (college) of canons although it is not a bishop's see. 2. in Scotland, a church with two or more ministers serving together jointly. 3. in the United States, a church associated with others under a joint body of pastors. 4. such an association of churches.

col·len·chy·ma (kə-leŋ'kə-mə), ***n.*** [< Gr. *kolla,* glue + *enchyma,* a steeping, infusion], in *botany,* a layer of elastic plant tissue consisting of elongated cells thickened at the angles.

col·let (kol'it), ***n.*** [Fr., dim. of *col,* the neck < L. *collum,* the neck], 1. a metal band or ring, such as is used in a watch to hold the end of the spring. 2. the part of a ring in which the stone is set. ***v.t.*** to set in, or furnish with, a collet.

col·lide (kə-līd'), ***v.i.*** [COLLIDED (-id), COLLIDING], [L. *collidere* < *com-,* together + *laedere,* to strike, injure], 1. to come into violent contact; strike violently against each other; crash. 2. to conflict; clash.

col·lie (kol'i), ***n.*** [said to be < *coaly,* coal-black < the color of some of the breed; early use of name *Colle* for dogs suggests dim. of name *Colin*], any of a breed of large, long-haired Scottish sheep dog with a long, narrow head and pointed nose.

COLLIE
(24 in. high at shoulder)

col·lied (kol'id), ***adj.*** [*colly* + *-ed*], made black, as with soot.

col·lier (kol'yẽr), ***n.*** [ME. *colyer, colier* < *col,* coal; + *-ier*], 1. a coal miner. 2. a ship for carrying coal. 3. any of its crew.

col·lier·y (kol'yẽr-i), ***n.*** [*pl.* COLLIERIES (-iz)], [*collier* + *-y*], a coal mine and its buildings, equipment, etc.

col·li·gate (kol'ə-gāt'), ***v.t.*** [COLLIGATED (-id), COLLIGATING], [< L. *colligatus,* pp. of *colligare,* to bind

together < *com-*, together + *ligare*, to bind], 1. to bind together. 2. in *logic*, to relate (isolated facts) by some reasonable explanation, especially so as to evolve a general principle.
col·li·ga·tion (kol'ə-gā'shən), *n.* [L. *colligatio*], a colligating or being colligated.
col·li·mate (kol'ə-māt'), *v.t.* [COLLIMATED (-id), COLLIMATING], [< *collimare*, false reading of L. *collineare*, to direct in a straight line < *com-*, with + *lineare*, to make straight < *linea*, a line], 1. to make parallel, as light rays. 2. to adjust the line of sight of (a telescope, etc.).
col·li·ma·tion (kol'ə-mā'shən), *n.* a collimating or being collimated.
col·li·ma·tor (kol'ə-mā'tẽr), *n.* [see COLLIMATE], 1. a small telescope with cross hairs at its focus, fixed to another telescope, surveying instrument, etc. for adjusting the line of sight. 2. the tube of a spectroscope that receives the light and casts it upon the prism in parallel rays: see **spectroscope**, illus. 3. the lens used in this.
col·lin·e·ar (kə-lin'i-ẽr), *adj.* [*col-* + *linear*], in the same straight line.
Col·lins (kol'inz), *n.* [supposedly after its inventor, a bartender named Tom *Collins*], any of several mixed drinks made with lemon or lime juice, sugar, carbonated water, ice, and either gin (*Tom Collins*), rum (*Rum Collins*), or whisky (*John Collins*).
Col·lins, Michael (kol'inz), 1890–1922; Irish soldier and Sinn Fein leader; assassinated.
Collins, Wil·kie (wil'ki), (*William Wilkie Collins*), 1824–1889; English novelist.
Collins, William, 1721–1759; English lyric poet.
col·lin·si·a (kə-lin'si-ə, kə-lin'zi-ə), *n.* [Mod. L., after the Am. botanist Zaccheus *Collins* (1764–1831)], any of a group of hardy, low-growing plants of the figwort family, with flowers arranged in whorls.
col·li·sion (kə-lizh'ən) *n.* [LL. *collisio* < pp. of L. *collidere*], 1. a colliding; sudden, violent contact between moving bodies, as motor vehicles, trains, or ships. 2. a clash of opinions, interests, etc.; conflict.
col·lo·cate (kol'ō-kāt'), *v.t.* [COLLOCATED (-id), COLLOCATING], [< L. *collocatus*, pp. of *collocare*, to place together < *com-*, together + *locare;* see LOCATE], 1. to arrange. 2. to place side by side.
col·lo·ca·tion (kol'ō-kā'shən), *n.* [L. *collocatio*], a collocating or being collocated; arrangement, as of words.
col·lo·di·on (kə-lō'di-ən), *n.* [< Gr. *kollōdēs*, gluelike < *kolla*, glue + *eidos*, form], a highly inflammable, colorless or pale-yellow, viscous solution of nitrated cellulose in a mixture of alcohol and ether: it dries quickly, forming a tough, elastic film, and is used as a protective coating for wounds, photographic plates, etc.
col·logue (kə-lōg'), *v.i.* [COLLOGUED (-lōgd'), COLLOGUING], [< Fr. *colloque*, conference < L. *colloquium* (see COLLOQUY); sp. altered after obs. *colleague*, to conspire], [Dial.], to discuss secretly; confer privately.
col·loid (kol'oid), *n.* [< Gr. *kolla*, glue; + *-oid*], 1. a gelatinous substance made up of very small, insoluble, nondiffusible particles larger than molecules but small enough so that they remain suspended in a fluid medium without settling to the bottom: a colloid does not affect the freezing point, boiling point, or vapor tension of the medium in which it is suspended. 2. the hormonal material secreted by the thyroid gland: it is a protein containing iodine. 3. a clear, structureless material appearing in various body tissues under abnormal conditions: also called *hyalin*. *adj.* colloidal.
col·loi·dal (kə-loi'd'l), *adj.* 1. of, like, or containing a colloid. 2. of the nature, or in the form, of a colloid.
col·lop (kol'əp), *n.* [ME. *colhoppe*, *coloppe*, cooked dish, bacon and eggs < ON.; cf. OSw. *kol-huppadher*, cooked on coal (Sw. *glöd-hoppad;* cf. GLEDE) < *kol*, coal], 1. a small piece or slice of anything, especially of meat. 2. [Archaic], a fold of flesh on the body.
colloq., 1. colloquial. 2. colloquialism. 3. colloquially.
col·lo·qui·al (kə-lō'kwi-əl), *adj.* [< L. *colloquium* (see COLLOQUY); + *-al*], 1. having to do with conversation; conversational. 2. belonging to the words, phrases, and idioms characteristic of conversation and informal writing; informal: the label [Colloq.] is used throughout this dictionary in this sense, and does not indicate substandard or illiterate usage: abbreviated **colloq., coll.**
col·lo·qui·al·ism (kə-lō'kwi-əl-iz'm), *n.* 1. colloquial quality, style, or usage. 2. a colloquial word or expression. Abbreviated **colloq., coll.**
col·lo·quist (kol'ə-kwist), *n.* a participant in a colloquy.
col·lo·quy (kol'ə-kwi), *n.* [*pl.* COLLOQUIES (-kwiz)], [L. *colloquium*, conversation < *com-*, together + *loqui*, to speak], 1. a conversation, especially a somewhat formal one; conference. 2. a literary work written in dialogue or conversation form: as, the *Colloquies* of Erasmus.
col·lo·type (kol'ə-tīp'), *n.* [Gr. *kolla*, glue; + *-type*], 1. a photographic plate made from gelatin film in such a way that inked reproductions can be printed from it. 2. the process by which such a plate is made. 3. the printed reproduction.
col·lude (kə-lōōd', kə-lūd'), *v.i.* [COLLUDED (-id), COLLUDING], [L. *colludere* < *com-*, with + *ludere*, to play], to act in collusion; conspire for fraudulent purposes.
col·lu·nar·i·um (kol'yoo-nâr'i-əm), *n.* [L.], in *medicine*, any solution to be applied to the nasal passages, as nose drops or a nasal douche.
col·lu·sion (kə-lōō'zhən, kə-lū'zhən), *n.* [L. *collusio* < *collusus*, pp. of *colludere;* see COLLUDE], a secret agreement for fraudulent or illegal purpose; conspiracy.
col·lu·sive (kə-lōō'siv, kə-lū'siv), *adj.* characterized by or involving collusion; fraudulent.
col·ly (kol'i), *v.t.* [COLLIED (-id), COLLYING], [< ME. *col;* see COAL], [Dial.], to blacken, as with soot or grime. *n.* [Dial.], soot; grime.
col·lyr·i·um (kə-lir'i-əm), *n.* [*pl.* COLLYRIA (-ə), COLLYRIUMS (-əmz)], [L.; Gr. *kollyrion*, eye salve], any medicated preparation for the eyes; eyewash.
col·ly·wob·bles (kol'i-wob''lz), *n. pl.* [prob. < *colic* + *wobble*], [Colloq.], pain in the abdomen.
Col·mar (kōl'mär; Fr. kôl'mȧr'), *n.* a city in northeastern France, near the Rhine: pop., 46,000.
co·lo- (kō'lō, kol'ō), [< Gr. *kolon*, the colon], a combining form meaning *the colon*, as in *colostomy:* also, before a vowel, **col-**.
Colo., Colorado.
col·o·cynth (kol'ə-sinth'), *n.* [L. *colocynthis;* Gr. *kolokynthis*], 1. a vine of the gourd family that grows in Mediterranean regions. 2. its bitter fruit. 3. a cathartic prepared from this fruit. Also called *bitter apple.*
Co·logne (kə-lōn'; Fr. kô'lôn'y'), *n.* a city in western Germany, on the Rhine: pop., 760,000: German name, *Köln.*
co·logne (kə-lōn'), *n.* [short for *Cologne water* or *eau de Cologne:* so named because manufactured in Cologne], a fragrant liquid made of alcohol and various aromatic oils, used like perfume: also called *eau de Cologne.*
Co·lom·bi·a (kə-lum'bi-ə; Sp. kô-lôm'byä), *n.* a country in northwestern South America, on the Pacific Ocean and the Caribbean Sea: area, 439,829 sq. mi.; pop., 14,132,000; capital, Bogotá: abbreviated **Col.**
Co·lom·bi·an (kə-lum'bi-ən), *adj.* of Colombia, its people, etc. *n.* a native or inhabitant of Colombia.
Co·lom·bo (kə-lum'bō), *n.* the capital of Ceylon, on the west coast: pop., 426,000.
Co·lón (kō-lōn', kō-lon'; Sp. kô-lôn'), *n.* a seaport in Panama, at the entrance to the Panama Canal, on the Caribbean: pop., 58,000.
co·lon (kō'lən), *n.* [L.; Gr. *kōlon*, member, limb, part of a verse], 1. a mark of punctuation (:) used before an extended quotation, explanation, example, series, etc., and after the salutation of a formal letter. 2. [*pl.* COLA (-lə)], in *Greek prosody*, a section of a period (sense 12), consisting of a group of two to six feet forming a rhythmic unit with a principal accent.
co·lon (kō'lən), *n.* [*pl.* COLONS (-lənz), COLA (-lə)], [L.; Gr. *kolon*], that part of the large intestine extending from the caecum to the rectum.
co·lon (kō-lōn'; Sp. kô-lôn'), *n.* [*pl.* COLONS (-lōnz'), Sp. COLONES (-lô'nes)], [Am. Sp. *colón* < Sp. *Colón*, Columbus], 1. the monetary unit of Costa Rica, valued at about **$0.178 in 1946.** 2. the monetary unit of El Salvador, valued at about **$0.40 in 1946.**
Colón Archipelago, the Galápagos Islands.
colo·nel (kũr'n'l), *n.* [earlier *coronel;* Fr. *colonel, coronel;* It. *colonello* < *colonna*, (military) column; L. *columna*, a column; Fr. & Eng. sp. modified after L. & It., but older pronun. kept in Eng.], an army officer ranking just above a lieutenant colonel and below a brigadier general, and corresponding to a captain in the navy; the usual commanding officer of a regiment in the army or of a group in the air force: abbreviated **Col.**
colo·nel·cy (kũr'n'l-si), *n.* [*pl.* COLONELCIES (-siz)], the rank or commission of a colonel.
co·lo·ni·al (kə-lō'ni-əl), *adj.* 1. of or living in a colony or colonies. 2. of or characteristic of the thirteen British colonies that became the United States. Abbreviated **col.** *n.* an inhabitant of a colony.
co·lo·ni·al·ism (kə-lō'ni-əl-iz'm), *n.* the system in which a country maintains foreign colonies for their economic exploitation.
co·lon·ic (kə-lon'ik), *adj.* of the colon (intestine).
col·o·nist (kol'ə-nist), *n.* 1. one of the original settlers or founders of a colony. 2. an inhabitant of a colony.
col·o·ni·za·tion (kol'ə-ni-zā'shən, kol'ə-nī-zā'shən), *n.* a colonizing or being colonized; establishment of a colony or colonies.
col·o·nize (kol'ə-nīz'), *v.t.* [COLONIZED (-nīzd'), COLONIZING], 1. to found or establish a colony or colonies in. 2. to settle (persons) in a colony. *v.i.* 1. to found or establish a colony or colonies. 2. to settle in a colony.
col·on·nade (kol'ə-nād'), *n.* [Fr.; It. *colonnato* < L. *columna*, column], in *architecture*, a series of columns set at regular intervals.
col·on·nad·ed (kol'ə-nā'did), *adj.* furnished with a colonnade.
col·o·ny (kol'ə-ni), *n.* [*pl.* COLONIES (-niz)], [Fr. *colonie;* L. *colonia* < *colonus*, farmer < *colere*, to cultivate]. 1. a group of people who settle in a distant land but remain under the political jurisdiction of their native land. 2. the region thus settled. 3. a territory distant from the state having jurisdiction or nominal control over it: abbreviated **col.** 4. [C-], *pl.* the thirteen British colonies in North America that won their independence in the

Revolutionary War and became the United States: they were Virginia, New York, Massachusetts, Connecticut, Rhode Island, New Hampshire, Maryland, New Jersey, North Carolina, South Carolina, Pennsylvania, Delaware, and Georgia. 5. a community of people of the same nationality or pursuits concentrated in a particular district or place: as, the Hungarian *colony* of Cleveland, an artist's *colony*. 6. such a district or place. 7. in *bacteriology*, a group of similar bacteria growing in or on a culture medium. 8. in *biology*, a group of similar plants or animals living or growing together.

Col·o·phon (kol′ə-fon′), *n.* an ancient Ionian city.

col·o·phon (kol′ə-fon′, kol′ə-fən), *n.* [LL.; Gr. *kolophōn*, summit, top, end, finishing stroke], 1. an inscription at the end of a book, giving facts about its production: much of this information is now usually on the title page. 2. an emblematic or ornamental device, the publisher's trade-mark, put on the last page or title page of a book.

col·o·pho·ny (kol′ə-fō′ni, kə-lof′ə-ni), *n.* [L. *colophonia* (*resina*); Gr. *kolophōnia* (*rhētinē*), lit., Colophonian (resin) < *Colophon*], rosin.

col·o·quin·ti·da (kol′ə-kwin′ti-də), *n.* [ML. < Gr. *kolokynthida*, inflected form of *kolokynthis*], colocynth.

col·or (kul′ẽr), *n.* [ME. *color, colour;* OFr. *colour;* L. *color;* OL. *colos*, orig., a covering < *celare*, to cover, hide], 1. the sensation resulting from stimulation of the retina of the eye by light waves of certain lengths. 2. the property of reflecting light waves of a particular length: the *primary colors* of the spectrum are red, orange, yellow, green, blue, indigo, and violet. 3. any coloring matter; dye; pigment; paint: in *painting*, etc. red, yellow, and blue are the *primary colors*, which, when mixed in various ways, produce the *secondary colors* (green, orange, purple, etc.); black, white, and gray are often called colors (*achromatic colors*), although black is caused by the complete absorption of light rays, white by the reflection of all the rays that produce color, and gray by an imperfect absorption of all these rays (i.e., a mixture of black and white pigments): abbreviated **col.** 4. any color other than black, white, and gray; chromatic color: as, she likes *colors* better than black or white. 5. color of the face, especially healthy rosiness. 6. the color of a person's skin. 7. the color of the skin of a Negro or other person not classified as Caucasian. 8. *pl.* a colored badge, ribbon, costume, etc. that identifies the wearer or shows his connection with something or someone. 9. *pl.* a flag or banner of a country, regiment, etc. 10. *pl.* the side that a person is on; one's position or opinion: as, stick to your *colors*. 11. outward appearance; semblance; aspect. 12. appearance of truth, likelihood, validity, or right; justification: as, the circumstances gave *color* to his contention. 13. kind; sort. 14. vivid and picturesque quality or character: as, there is *color* in his writing. 15. in *art*, the way of using color. 16. in *mining*, a bit of gold. 17. in *music*, timbre, as of a voice or instrument: also **tone color.** 18. in *phonetics*, the degree of openness of a vowel: the dark vowels are the more open ones. ***v.t.*** 1. to give color to; impregnate or cover with color; paint; stain; dye. 2. to change the color of. 3. to give fair or reasonable appearance to; make plausible. 4. to alter or influence to some degree, especially by distortion or exaggeration: as, his experience *colored* his views. ***v.i.*** 1. to become colored. 2. to change color, as ripening fruit. 3. to blush or flush.

call to the colors, 1. call or order to serve in the armed forces of one's country. 2. a bugle signal calling troops to the daily ceremony of raising the flag in the morning or taking it down in the evening.

change color, 1. to become pale. 2. to blush or flush.

lose color, to become pale.

serve with the colors, to serve in the armed forces of one's country.

show one's colors, 1. to reveal one's true self. 2. to make one's opinions, position, etc., known.

under color of, under the pretext or guise of.

with flying colors, with great success.

SYN.—**color** is the general term, for which see the definition above; **shade** refers to any of the gradations of a color with reference to its degree of darkness (a light *shade* of green); **hue,** often equivalent to **color,** is used specifically to indicate a modification of a basic color (orange of a reddish *hue*); **tint** refers to a gradation of a color with reference to its degree of whiteness and suggests a paleness or delicacy of color (pastel *tints*); **tinge** suggests the presence of a small amount of color, usually diffused throughout (white *tinged* with blue).

col·or·a·ble (kul′ẽr-ə-b′l), *adj.* 1. capable of being colored. 2. apparently valid or plausible, but actually specious; deceptive.

Col·o·rad·an (kol′ə-rad′ən, kol′ə-rä′dən), *adj.* of Colorado. *n.* a native or inhabitant of Colorado.

Col·o·rad·o (kol′ə-rad′ō, kol′ə-rä′dō), *n.* 1. a Western State of the United States: area, 104,247 sq. mi.; pop., 1,754,000; capital, Denver: nicknamed ***Centennial State:*** abbreviated **Colo., Col.** 2. a river flowing from Colorado through Utah and Arizona into the Gulf of California: length, 1,360 mi. 3. a river in Texas, flowing into the Gulf of Mexico: length, 840 mi. 4. a desert in southeastern California: area, 2,000 sq. mi.

col·o·rad·o (kol′ə-rad′ō, kol′ə-rä′dō), *adj.* [Sp., red, lit., colored, pp. of *colorar* < L. *colorare* < *color;* see COLOR], of medium strength and color: said of cigars.

Colorado beetle, a black-and-yellow beetle that destroys potatoes: also called *potato bug.*

Colorado Springs, a city in central Colorado: pop., 70,000: site of the United States Air Force Academy.

col·or·a·tion (kul′ẽr-ā′shən), *n.* coloring: as, some animals have protective *coloration.*

col·o·ra·tu·ra (kul′ẽr-ə-tyoor′ə, kol′ẽr-ə-toor′ə), *n.* [It. < L. *coloratus*, pp. of *colorare;* see COLOR], in *music*, 1. brilliant ornamental runs, trills, etc., used to display a singer's skill. 2. music containing such ornaments. 3. a coloratura soprano. *adj.* characterized by coloratura. *adv.* in a coloratura manner.

coloratura soprano, 1. a high soprano voice capable of singing coloratura. 2. a singer with such a voice.

col·or·a·ture (kul′ẽr-ə-choor′, kol′ẽr-ə-choor′), *n.* coloratura.

col·or-bear·er (kul′ẽr-bâr′ẽr), *n.* a person who carries the colors (flag); standard-bearer.

col·or-blind (kul′ẽr-blīnd′), *adj.* unable to distinguish or perceive certain colors or any colors.

color blindness, the condition of being color-blind.

col·ored (kul′ẽrd), *adj.* [pp. of *color*], 1. having color. 2. of a (specified) color. 3. of a race other than the Caucasian; specifically, Negro: abbreviated **cld.** 4. altered, influenced, distorted, or exaggerated to some degree: as, his remarks were *colored* by prejudice.

color filter, a screen of colored glass, etc., used in photography to control the color or light effects.

col·or·ful (kul′ẽr-fəl), *adj.* 1. full of color. 2. full of contrast or variety; picturesque, vivid, etc.

color guard, the persons carrying and escorting the colors (flag).

col·or·if·ic (kul′ẽr-if′ik), *adj.* [Fr. *colorifique;* see COLOR & -FIC], 1. producing or imparting color. 2. of color.

col·or·im·e·ter (kul′ẽr-im′ə-tẽr), *n.* [< *color* + *-meter*], an instrument for determining color or measuring its intensity by comparison with a standard.

col·or·i·met·ric (kul′ẽr-i-met′rik), *adj.* of colorimetry.

col·or·i·met·ri·cal·ly (kul′ẽr-i-met′ri-k′l-i, kul′ẽr-i-met′rik-li), *adv.* as measured or analyzed by a colorimeter.

col·or·im·e·try (kul′ẽr-im′ə-tri), *n.* the analysis or measurement of color by means of a colorimeter.

col·or·ing (kul′ẽr-iŋ), *n.* 1. the act or art of applying colors. 2. anything applied to impart color; pigment, dye, stain, etc.: often called *coloring matter*. 3. appearance with reference to color. 4. specious or false appearance.

col·or·ist (kul′ẽr-ist), *n.* 1. a person who uses colors. 2. an artist skillful in using colors.

col·or·less (kul′ẽr-lis), *adj.* 1. without color. 2. lacking variety or interest; not vivid; dull.

color line, the barrier of social, political, and economic restrictions imposed on Negroes or other colored races.

draw the color line, to accept and keep the color line.

color sergeant, a sergeant whose special duty is to carry or attend to the colors (flag) of his regiment or battalion in the field.

Co·los·sae (kə-los′ē), *n.* a city in ancient Phrygia.

co·los·sal (kə-los′'l), *adj.* like a colossus in size; huge; gigantic: used loosely, as in the motion-picture industry, to denote approval. —***SYN.*** see **enormous.**

Col·os·se·um (kol′ə-sē′əm), *n.* [L., neut. of *colosseus*, gigantic < *colossus;* see COLOSSUS], 1. an amphitheater at Rome, begun by Vespasian in 75 A.D. and completed about five years later: a great part of it is still standing. 2. [c-], a coliseum.

COLOSSEUM

Co·los·sian (kə-losh′ən), *adj.* of Colossae. *n.* a native or inhabitant of Colossae.

Co·los·sians (kə-losh′ənz), *n. pl.* [construed as sing.], the Epistle to the Colossians, a book of the New Testament which was a message from the Apostle Paul to the Christians of Colossae: abbreviated **Col.**

co·los·sus (kə-los′əs), *n.* [*pl.* COLOSSI (-ī), COLOSSUSES (-iz)], [L., Gr. *kolossos*], 1. a gigantic statue; especially, [C-], that of Apollo set at the entrance to the harbor of Rhodes c. 280 B.C. and considered among the seven wonders of the ancient world. 2. any huge or important person or thing.

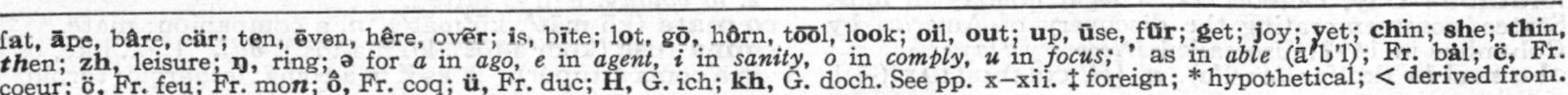

co·los·to·my (kə-los′tə-mi), *n.* [*colo-* + *-stomy*], the surgical operation of forming an artificial anal opening in the colon.
co·los·trum (kə-los′trəm), *n.* [L., beestings], the fluid secreted by the mammary glands for several days just before and after childbirth.
col·our (kul′ẽr), *n. & v.* color: British spelling.
-co·lous (kə-ləs), [< base of L. *colere*, to cultivate, inhabit; + *-ous*], a combining form meaning *growing* (or *living*) *in* or *among*, as in *arenicolous*.
col·pi·tis (kol-pī′tis), *n.* [< Gr. *kolpos*, womb; + *-itis*], inflammation of the vagina; vaginitis.
col·por·tage (kol′pôr′tij), *n.* [Fr.], the work of a colporteur.
col·por·teur (kol′pôr′tẽr), *n.* [Fr., peddler; altered after *col*, the neck < OFr. *comporter;* L. *comportare*, to bear together, collect; *com-*, together + *portare*, to carry], a person who goes from place to place distributing Bibles, religious tracts, etc.
colt (kōlt), *n.* [ME.; AS.; akin to Norw. dial. *kult*, a lump, swelling, half-grown boy; IE. **gel-d*, **gle-d;* same base and same development as *calf*], 1. a young horse, donkey, zebra, etc.; specifically, a young, male horse; hence, 2. a young, inexperienced person. 3. in *nautical usage*, a rope knotted at the end, formerly used for flogging.
Colt, Samuel (kōlt), 1814–1862; American inventor of a type of revolver.
col·ter (kōl′tẽr), *n.* [ME. *colter*, *culter* < OFr. *coltre* or AS. *culter;* both < L. *culter*, plowshare, knife], an edged blade or disk on a plow, for making vertical cuts in the soil: also spelled **coulter.**
colt·ish (kōl′tish), *adj.* of or like a colt; frisky.
colts·foot (kōlts′foot′), *n.* [*pl.* COLTSFOOTS (-foots′)], [so called from shape of the leaves], a plant of the composite family, with small, yellow flowers and large, heart-shaped leaves, used medicinally.
col·u·brine (kol′yoo-brīn′, kol′yoo-brin), *adj.* [L. *colubrinus* < *coluber*, serpent], 1. of, characteristic of, or like a snake. 2. of any of a large group of nonpoisonous snakes.
co·lu·go (kə-lōō′gō), *n.* an East Indian tree-dwelling mammal having a fold of skin on each side that enables it to make long, sailing leaps; flying lemur.
Col·um, Pad·raic (päd′rik kol′əm; Ir. pôth′rig), 1881– ; Irish poet and playwright in the United States.
Co·lum·ba, Saint (kə-lum′bə), 521–597 A.D.; Irish missionary who converted Scotland to Christianity: his day is June 9: called *Apostle of Caledonia.*
col·um·ba·ri·um (kol′əm-bâr′i-əm), *n.* [*pl.* COLUMBARIA (-ə)], [L., lit., dovecote < *columba*, dove; akin to Gr. *kolymbos*, diver (kind of sea bird), OPr. *golimban*, blue < IE. base **qel-*, **qal-*, dark, dark spot: hence named from color], 1. a vault with niches for urns that contain the ashes of cremated bodies. 2. any of these niches. 3. a columbary.
col·um·bar·y (kol′əm-ber′i), *n.* [*pl.* COLUMBARIES (-iz)], [L. *columbarium;* see COLUMBARIUM], a house for pigeons or doves; dovecote.
Co·lum·bi·a (kə-lum′bi-ə, kə-lum′byə), *n.* [< Christopher *Columbus*], 1. [Poetic], the United States: feminine symbol. 2. the capital of South Carolina, on the Congaree River: pop., 97,000. 3. a river rising in British Columbia and flowing between Washington and Oregon to the Pacific: length, 1,214 mi. 4. a city in central Missouri: pop., 37,000.
Co·lum·bi·an (kə-lum′bi-ən, kə-lum′byən), *adj.* 1. of Columbia. 2. of Christopher Columbus. *n.* [c-], a size of type, 16 point.
co·lum·bic (kə-lum′bik), *adj.* designating or of compounds containing columbium with a valence of five.
Col·um·bine (kol′əm-bīn′), *n.* [It. *Colombina* < L. *columbina*, fem. of *columbinus*, dovelike; see COLUMBARIUM], daughter of Pantaloon and sweetheart of Harlequin, a stock character in early Italian comedy and in pantomime.
col·um·bine (kol′əm-bīn′), *n.* [Fr.; ML. *columbina* < L. *columbinus*, dovelike (see COLUMBARIUM): so named because the flower is thought to resemble a group of pigeons], a plant of the crowfoot family, with showy, spurred flowers of various colors. *adj.* [ME.; Fr. *columbin;* L. *columbinus;* see the *n.*], of or like a dove.
co·lum·bite (kə-lum′bīt), *n.* [*columbium* + *-ite*], a black mineral, $Fe(CbO_3)_2$, a compound of columbium and iron.
co·lum·bi·um (kə-lum′bi-əm), *n.* [Mod. L. < *Columbia* (the United States)], niobium: the former name.
co·lum·bous (kə-lum′bəs), *adj.* designating or of compounds containing columbium with a valence of three.
Co·lum·bus (kə-lum′bəs), *n.* 1. the capital of Ohio, in the central part of the State: pop., 471,000. 2. a city in western Georgia: pop., 117,000.
Co·lum·bus, Christopher (kə-lum′bəs), 1446?–1506; Italian explorer in the service of Spain; discovered America (1492).
Columbus Day, October 12, a legal holiday in most States, commemorating the discovery of America by Columbus in 1492: also called *Discovery Day.*
col·u·mel·la (kol′yoo-mel′ə), *n.* [*pl.* COLUMELLAE (-ē)], [L., dim. of *columen;* see COLUMN], any of a number of columnlike structures in plants and animals, as a small bone in the middle ear of amphibians, reptiles, etc.
col·u·mel·li·form (kol′yoo-mel′ə-fôrm′), *adj.* having the form, or shape, of a columella.
col·umn (kol′əm), *n.* [ME. *columne;* OFr. *colomne;* L. *columna*, collateral form of *columen*, column, pillar, projecting object; akin to Gr. *kolophōn*, peak, AS. *holm*, island, wave < IE. base **qel-*, to project], 1. a slender upright structure, generally consisting of a cylindrical shaft, a base, and a capital; pillar: it is usually a supporting or ornamental member in a building. 2. anything like a column in shape or function: as, a *column* of water, the spinal *column*. 3. one of two or more vertical sections of printed matter lying side by side on a page and separated by a rule or blank space. 4. a feature article appearing daily or at intervals in a newspaper or magazine and written by a special writer or devoted to a certain subject. 5. in *military & naval usage*, a formation in which the elements, as troops or ships, are placed one behind another.

CAPITAL
SHAFT
BASE
COLUMN

co·lum·nar (kə-lum′nẽr), *adj.* [L. *columnaris*], 1. like a column. 2. formed in or composed of columns. 3. written or printed in columns.
col·umned (kol′əmd), *adj.* 1. having columns. 2. columnar.
co·lum·ni·a·tion (kə-lum′ni-ā′shən), *n.* the architectural use or arrangement of columns.
col·um·nist (kol′əm-nist, kol′əm-ist), *n.* a person who writes or conducts a column in a newspaper, etc.
co·lure (kə-lyoor′, kō′lyoor), *n.* [< L. *coluri* (pl. of *colurus*) < Gr. *kolouroi*, the colures, lit., dock-tailed (ones), pl. of *kolouros* < *kolos*, docked + *oura*, tail: so named because the "tail" (i.e., the lower part) is always cut off from view by the horizon (in Greece and in comparable latitudes)], in *astronomy*, either of two imaginary circles of the celestial sphere intersecting each other at right angles at the poles: one passes through the ecliptic at the solstice, the other at the equinox.
Col·vin, Sir **Sidney** (kol′vin), 1845–1927; English writer on literature and art.
co·ly (kō′li), *n.* [*pl.* COLIES (-liz)], [LL. *colius;* Gr. *kolios*, green woodpecker], any of a group of small African birds with long tails and crested heads.
col·za (kol′zə), *n.* [Fr.; D. *koolzaad; kool*, a cabbage + *zaad*, a seed], 1. cole or coleseed; especially, rapeseed, which yields an oil burned in lamps. 2. this oil: also called *colza oil, rape oil.*
com- (kom, kəm), [L. *com-* < *cum* (OL. *com*), with], a prefix used to mean: 1. *with, together*, as in *combine*, *compact*. 2. *intensification*, as in *command*. As a result of assimilation in Latin, *com-* appears as *col-* before *l*, *cor-* before *r*, *con-* before *c, d, g, j, n, q, s, t, v*, and *co-* before *h, w*, and all vowels.
Com., 1. Commander. 2. Commission. 3. Commissioner. 4. Committee. 5. Commodore. 6. Communist.
com., 1. comedy. 2. comma. 3. commentary. 4. commerce. 5. commercial. 6. common. 7. commonly. 8. commune. 9. communication. 10. community.
co·ma (kō′mə), *n.* [*pl.* COMAS (-məz)], [Mod. L.; Gr. *kōma*, deep sleep < *koiman*, to put to sleep], a state of deep and prolonged unconsciousness; stupor: it is often caused by injury or disease.
co·ma (kō′mə), *n.* [*pl.* COMAE (-mē)], [L., hair of the head, foliage; Gr. *komē*, hair], 1. in *astronomy*, a globular, cloudlike mass around the nucleus of a comet: the nucleus and coma together form the comet's head. 2. in *botany*, *a*) a bunch of branches. *b*) a terminal cluster of bracts on a flowering stem, as in pineapples. *c*) a tuft of hairs at the end of a seed. 3. in *photography*, a blur caused by the spherical aberration of oblique rays of light passing through a lens.
Co·ma Ber·e·ni·ces (kō′mə ber′ə-nī′sēz), [L.], a constellation in the northern hemisphere, north of Virgo.
Co·man·che (kō-man′chi), *n.* [Mex. Sp., of unc. meaning], 1. a member of a tribe of Shoshonean Indians who formerly ranged from the Platte River to the Mexican border. 2. their Uto-Aztec language: also called *Shoshone-Comanche*. *adj.* of this tribe, their language, or culture.
Co·man·che·an (kō-man′chi-ən), *adj.* [< *Comanche* County, Texas], designating or of a geologic epoch between the Jurassic and Cretaceous Periods or its series of rocks, as typified by those found in the region of the Gulf of Mexico.
the Comanchean, the Comanchean Epoch or its series of rocks.
co·mate (kō′māt), *adj.* [L. *comatus*, hairy], 1. in *astronomy*, surrounded by a coma (globular, cloudlike mass). 2. in *botany*, hairy; tufted.
co·mate (kō-māt′, kō′māt′), *n.* a companion; mate.
com·a·tose (kom′ə-tōs′, kō′mə-tōs′), *adj.* 1. of, like, or in a coma (stupor). 2. as if in a coma; lethargic; torpid.

co·mat·u·la (kō-mat′yoo-lə), *n.* [*pl.* COMATULAE (-lē′)], [Mod. L. < L., fem. of *comatulus*], a comatulid.

co·mat·u·lid (kō-mat′yoo-lid), *n.* [< Mod. L. *Comatulidae*, name of the family < L. *comatulus*, having hair neatly curled, dim. of *comatus*, having long hair, pp. of *comare*, to have hair < *coma*, hair < Gr. *komē*], a free-swimming animal related to the starfish.

comb (kōm), *n.* [ME.; AS. *camb*, comb, lit., toothed object; akin to G. *kamm* (OHG. *kamb*); IE. base **gembh-*, to bite, as in Sans. *jámbha-ḥ*, tooth], 1. a thin strip of bone, plastic, metal, etc. with teeth, which is passed through the hair to arrange or clean it, or is set in the hair to hold it in place or as an ornament. 2. an instrument for currying horses; currycomb. 3. a thing like a comb in form or function, as an instrument used in cleaning and straightening wool, flax, etc. 4. the red, fleshy outgrowth on the top of the head of certain fowls, as on that of a rooster. 5. a thing somewhat like a rooster's comb in position or appearance, as the crest of a helmet or of a wave. 6. a honeycomb. *v.t.* 1. to clean, straighten out, or arrange with a comb. 2. to search thoroughly; look everywhere in: as, we've *combed* the house for that book. *v.i.* to roll over; break: said of waves.

comb (ko͞om, kōm), *n.* a coomb.

comb., combination.

com·bat (kom′bat, kum′bat; *also, for v.*, kəm-bat′), *v.i.* [COMBATED or COMBATTED (-id), COMBATING or COMBATTING], [Fr. *combattre* < L. *com-*, together + LL. *battere* < L. *battuere*, to beat, fight], to fight; battle; contend; struggle. *v.t.* to fight against; oppose by force. *n.* [Fr. < the *v.*], 1. armed fighting; battle. 2. struggle; conflict; strife. *adj.* in *military usage*, of or for combat. —*SYN.* see **battle.**

com·bat·ant (kom′bə-tənt, kum′bə-tənt), *adj.* [OFr. (Fr. *combattant*); ppr. of *combatre;* see COMBAT], 1. fighting. 2. ready or eager to fight. *n.* 1. a person who combats; fighter. 2. in *military usage*, a member of the armed forces who takes part in actual fighting.

combat fatigue, a psychoneurotic condition characterized by anxiety, irritability, depression, etc., often occurring after extreme exertion and lack of sleep in armed combat: also called *battle fatigue.*

combat infantryman's badge, a badge awarded to United States infantrymen of World War II for exemplary conduct in a combat action of a major operation.

com·ba·tive (kəm-bat′iv, kom′bə-tiv, kum′bə-tiv), *adj.* [*combat* + *-ive*], fond of fighting or opposing; ready or eager to fight; pugnacious.

combe (ko͞om, kōm), *n.* a coomb.

comb·er (kōm′ẽr), *n.* 1. a person or thing that combs; especially, a worker or machine that combs wool, flax, etc. 2. a large wave that rolls over or breaks on a beach, reef, etc.

com·bi·na·tion (kom′bə-nā′shən), *n.* [OFr.; LL. *combinatio*, a joining two by two < LL. *combinatus*, pp. of *combinare*], 1. a combining or being combined. 2. a thing made by combining. 3. an association of people for a common purpose. 4. the series of numbers or letters used in opening a combination lock. 5. the mechanism operating such a lock. 6. a one-piece undergarment combining an undershirt and drawers. 7. in *chemistry*, a uniting of substances to form a compound. 8. in *mathematics*, any of the various groupings into which a number of units, as numbers or letters, may be arranged without regard to order: dual combinations of 1, 2, 3, and 4 are 12, 13, 14, 23, 24, 34. Abbreviated **comb.**

com·bi·na·tion·al (kom′bə-nā′shən-'l), *adj.* of a combination.

combination last, a style of shoe last in which an unusually narrow heel is combined with a fore part of standard dimensions.

combination lock, a lock operated by a dial that is turned to a specified series of numbers or letters to work the mechanism that opens it.

com·bi·na·tive (kom′bə-nā′tiv, kəm-bīn′ə-tiv), *adj.* 1. of or characterized by combination. 2. having the ability to combine. 3. resulting from combination.

com·bine (kəm-bīn′), *v.t. & v.i.* [COMBINED (-bīnd′), COMBINING], [ME. *combinen*; LL. *combinare*, to unite < L. *com-*, together + *bini*, two by two < base of *bis*; see BI-, TWO], 1. to come or bring into union; unite; join. 2. to unite to form a chemical compound. *n.* (kom′bin), 1. a machine for harvesting and threshing grain. 2. an association of persons, corporations, etc., for commercial or political purposes. —*SYN.* see **join.**

comb·ings (kōm′iŋz), *n.pl.* loose hair, wool, etc. removed in combing.

combining form, a word or word base used as an element in word formation, as *jack-* in *jackknife*, *tele-* in *telephone:* the word bases used in English word formation are often from Greek and Latin, which used a special form of the word (the *stem*) for combining purposes.

comb jelly, a ctenophore.

com·bo (kom′bō), *n.* [*pl.* COMBOS (-bōz)], [Colloq.], a combination; specifically, a small jazz ensemble.

com·bust (kəm-bust′), *adj.* [ME.; OFr.; L. *combustus*, pp. of *comburere*, to burn up], in *astrology*, so close to the sun as to be obscured or, apparently, extinguished by its light: said of a star or planet.

com·bus·ti·bil·i·ty (kəm-bus′tə-bil′ə-ti), *n.* the quality or state of being combustible.

com·bus·ti·ble (kəm-bus′tə-b'l), *adj.* [Fr.; see COMBUSTION], 1. capable of taking fire; that can be easily burned up; inflammable. 2. easily aroused; excitable; fiery. *n.* an inflammable substance.

com·bus·tion (kəm-bus′chən), *n.* [Fr.; LL. *combustio* < L. *combustus*, pp. of *comburere* (for **com-urere*), to burn up < *com-*, intens. + *urere*, to singe, burn], 1. the act or process of burning. 2. rapid oxidation accompanied by heat and, usually, light. 3. slow oxidation accompanied by relatively little heat and no light. 4. violent excitement or agitation; tumult.

combustion tube, a tube of heat-resistant glass in which a substance can be reduced by combustion, as in a furnace.

comdg., commanding.

Comdr., Commander.

Comdt., Commandant.

come (kum), *v.i.* [CAME (kām), COME, COMING], [ME. *comen, commen;* AS. *cuman;* akin to Goth. *qiman*, G. *kommen;* IE. base **quem-*, **qwā-*, to come, go, as also in L. *venio* (< **qwemjō*), I come], 1. to move from a place thought of as "there" to or into a place thought of as "here": *a*) in the second person, with relation to the speaker: as, *come* to me, will you *come* to the dance tonight? *b*) in the first person, with relation to the person addressed: as, I will *come* to see you. *c*) in the third person, with relation to the person or thing approached: as, he *came* to her and wept, he *came* into the room. 2. to reach by moving toward; hence, 3. to arrive or appear: as, help will *come.* 4. to extend; reach: as, the bus line *comes* near the hotel. 5. to happen; take place; occur: as, success *came* to him early in life. 6. to exist in a certain place or order: as, after 9 *comes* 10. 7. to be born; become actual; evolve; develop: as, peace will *come* in time. 8. to be derived or descended: as, he *comes* from an old family. 9. to be caused; result: as, illness may *come* from a poor diet. 10. to enter into a certain state or condition: as, this word has *come* into use. 11. to become; get to be: as, my shoe *came* loose. 12. to be obtainable or available: as, this dress *comes* in four sizes. 13. to amount: as, the bill *comes* to $5.68. 14. [Colloq.], to have a sexual orgasm. *interj.* look! see here! stop!: used to express irritation, impatience, remonstrance, etc.

come about, 1. to happen; occur. 2. to turn about. 3. in *nautical usage*, to change to another tack.

come across, 1. to meet by accident; find by chance. 2. [Slang], to give, do, or say what is wanted.

come and get it! [Colloq.], the meal is ready!: a summons to eat.

come around (or **round**), 1. to revive; recover. 2. to make a turn or change in direction. 3. to influence, outwit, or gain favor with by cajoling, flattering, etc. 4. [Colloq.], to concede or yield, as to a demand. 5. [Colloq.], to come to visit.

come at, 1. to reach; attain. 2. to approach angrily or swiftly, as in attacking.

come back, 1. to return. 2. [Colloq.], to return to a previous state or position, as of health or success. 3. [Slang], to answer back; retort.

come between, to cause estrangement between; divide.

come by, to get; acquire; gain.

come down, 1. to suffer loss in status, wealth, etc. 2. to be handed down, as from a past generation.

come down on (or **upon**), 1. to attack swiftly. 2. [Colloq.], to scold; upbraid; criticize harshly.

come forward, to offer one's services; volunteer.

come in, 1. to enter. 2. to arrive. 3. to begin to be used; come into fashion.

come in for, [Colloq.], to get; acquire.

come into, 1. to enter into; join. 2. to get; acquire. 3. to inherit.

come off, 1. to become unfastened or detached. 2. to happen; occur. 3. [Colloq.], to end up; come out.

come on, 1. to make progress; become better. 2. to meet by accident; find. 3. to attack. 4. in the *theater*, to make an entrance.

come on! [Colloq.], 1. get started! hurry! 2. stop behaving in this way! Often used as a cajoling expression equivalent to *please.*

come out, 1. to be disclosed; become evident. 2. to be offered for public inspection, sale, etc. 3. to be formally introduced to society; make a debut. 4. to end up: as, he *came out* third in the race.

come out with, 1. to disclose. 2. to say; utter; publish. 3. to offer for public inspection, sale, etc.

come over, to happen to; occur to; seize: as, these feelings often *come over* me.

come through, 1. to wear through. 2. to complete something successfully. 3. [Slang], to do or give what is wanted.

come to, 1. to recover consciousness. 2. to amount to. 3. in *nautical usage, a)* to bring the ship's head nearer the wind. *b)* to anchor.

come under, 1. to pass under the control of; be under the authority of. 2. to fall into (a specified category).

come up, to arise, as in discussion.

come upon, 1. to meet by accident. 2. to attack.

come up to, 1. to reach or extend to. 2. to equal.

come up with, 1. to overtake. 2. to propose; suggest.

how come? [Colloq.], how does it come that? how is it that? why?

come-at-a·ble (kum-at′ə-b'l), *adj.* [Colloq.], that can easily be reached, obtained, etc.; accessible or attainable.

come·back (kum′bak′), *n.* 1. [Colloq.], a return to a previous state or position, as of power, success, etc. 2. [Slang], a witty answer; retort. 3. [Slang], ground for action or complaint; recourse.

co·me·di·an (kə-mē′di-ən), *n.* [Fr. *comédien;* see COMEDY], 1. an actor who plays comic parts. 2. an entertainer who tells jokes, sings comic songs, etc. 3. a writer of comedy. 4. a person who amuses or tries to amuse others by clowning, telling jokes, etc.

co·me·di·enne (kə-mē′di-en′), *n.* [Fr., fem. of *comédien,* comedian], 1. an actress in comedy; actress who plays comic parts. 2. a woman entertainer who tells jokes, sings comic songs, etc.

com·e·do (kom′i-dō′), *n.* [*pl.* COMEDONES (kom′i-dō′-nēz), COMEDOS (-dōz′)], [L., glutton < *comedere,* to eat up, devour; *com-,* intens. + *edere,* to eat], a plug of dirt and fatty matter in a skin duct; blackhead.

come·down (kum′doun′), *n.* a loss of status, wealth, etc.; downfall.

com·e·dy (kom′ə-di), *n.* [*pl.* COMEDIES (-diz)], [ME. *commedy;* OFr. *comedie;* L. *comoedia;* Gr. *kōmōidia* < *kōmos,* banquet, festival + *aeidein,* to sing], 1. originally, any play or other literary composition with a nontragic ending. 2. any of various types of play or motion picture with more or less humorous treatment of characters and situation, and a nontragic ending: see **farce, comedy of manners, high comedy.** 3. the art, technique, or theory of writing, producing, or acting such plays or motion pictures. 4. comedies collectively. 5. the branch of the drama having to do with comedies. 6. something amusing, as an incident or event. 7. a work of literature having a theme suitable for comedy or certain characteristics of comedy. Abbreviated **com.**

cut the comedy, [Slang], to stop joking; stop acting foolishly.

comedy of manners, a type of comedy depicting and satirizing the manners and customs of fashionable society.

come·li·ness (kum′li-nis), *n.* a comely quality.

come·ly (kum′li), *adj.* [COMELIER (-li-ẽr), COMELIEST (-li-ist)], [ME. *cumlie, comly;* AS. *cymlic* < *cyme,* lit., feeble, brittle; hence, delicate, lovely (akin to G. *kaum,* scarcely, MHG. *kume,* weak) + *-lic* (see -LY); IE. base **gow-,* to cry out, as in OHG. *kumen,* to wail], 1. of pleasing appearance; attractive. 2. seemly; decorous; proper; suitable. —*SYN.* see **beautiful.**

Co·me·ni·us, John Amos (kō-mē′ni-əs), (*Jan Amos Komensky*), 1592–1670; Moravian educator and bishop.

come-on (kum′on′), *n.* [Slang], 1. a confidence man. 2. an inviting look or gesture. 3. something offered as an inducement.

com·er (kum′ẽr), *n.* 1. a person who comes: as, the contest is open to all *comers.* 2. [Slang], a person or thing that shows promise of being a success.

co·mes·ti·ble (kə-mes′tə-b'l), *adj.* [Fr. < L. *comestus, comesus,* pp. of *comedere,* to eat; *com-,* intens. + *edere,* to eat], eatable; edible. *n. usually in pl.* food.

com·et (kom′it), *n.* [ME. *comete;* AS. *cometa;* L. *cometa;* Gr. *komētēs* < *komē,* lit., hair of the head; fig., tail of a comet], a heavenly body having a starlike nucleus with a luminous mass around it, and, usually, a long, luminous tail: comets follow an elliptical or parabolic orbit around the sun.

COMET

com·et·ar·y (kom′ə-ter′i), *adj.* of or like a comet.

comet finder (or **seeker**), a low-power telescope with a large field of view, used in looking for comets.

co·meth·er (kō-meth′ẽr), *n.* [dial. contr. < *come hither*], [Anglo-Irish Dial.], 1. an affair; circumstance. 2. friendship; friendly relationship.

put the comether on, to use persuasion on; beguile.

come·up·pance (kum′up′ns), *n.* [< *come* + *up* + *-ance*], [Slang], deserved punishment; retribution.

com·fit (kum′fit, kom′fit), *n.* [ME. *comfyt;* OFr. *confit,* orig., pp. of *confire,* to preserve; L. *conficere;* see CONFECT], a candy; candied fruit; sweetmeat. *v.t.* [Obs.], to preserve with sugar; make into a candy.

com·fort (kum′fẽrt), *v.t.* [ME. *conforten, cumforten;* OFr. *conforter,* to comfort; LL. *confortare,* to make strong < L. *com-,* intens. + *fortis,* strong], 1. to soothe in distress or sorrow; ease the misery or grief of; bring consolation or hope to. 2. [Archaic except in *law*], to help; aid. *n.* 1. aid; encouragement: now only in *aid and comfort.* 2. relief from distress, grief, etc. 3. a person or thing that comforts. 4. a state of ease and quiet enjoyment, free from worry, pain, etc. 5. anything that makes life easy or comfortable. 6. a quilted bed covering: also called *comforter.*

SYN.—**comfort** suggests the lessening of misery or grief by cheering, calming, or inspiring with hope; **console** suggests less positive relief but implies a moderation of the sense of loss or disappointment (to *console* someone on the death of a parent); **solace** suggests the relieving of melancholy, boredom, loneliness, etc. (he *solaced* himself by playing the flute); **relieve** suggests the mitigation, often temporary, of misery or discomfort so as to make it bearable (to *relieve* the poor); **soothe** implies the calming or allaying of pain or distress (she *soothed* the child with a lullaby).—*ANT.* afflict, distress.

com·fort·a·ble (kum′fẽr-tə-b'l; *now often* kumf′tẽr-b'l), *adj.* [ME.; OFr. *confortable*], 1. providing comfort: as, *comfortable* shoes. 2. in a state of comfort; at ease in body or mind; contented: as, he felt *comfortable* after his bath and dinner. 3. [Colloq.], sufficient to satisfy; adequate: as, a *comfortable* salary. *n.* a quilted bed covering: also called *comforter.*

SYN.—**comfortable** implies the absence of disturbing, painful, or distressing features and, in a positive sense, stresses ease, contentment, freedom from care, etc. (a *comfortable* climate); **cozy** suggests such comfort as might be derived from shelter against storm, cold, hardship, etc. (a *cozy* nook by the fire); **snug** is used of something that is small and compact, but just large enough to provide ease and comfort, and often carries additional connotations of coziness (a *snug* apartment); **restful** is applied to that which promotes relaxation, freedom from care, etc. (*restful* music).—*ANT.* miserable.

com·fort·a·bly (kum′fẽr-tə-bli; *now often* kumf′tẽr-bli), *adv.* in a comfortable manner.

com·fort·er (kum′fẽr-tẽr), *n.* [Anglo-Fr. *confortour;* OFr. *conforteor*], 1. a person or thing that comforts. 2. a quilted bed covering. 3. a long woolen scarf.

the Comforter, in *theology,* the Holy Spirit.

com·fort·ing (kum′fẽrt-iŋ), *adj.* [ppr. of *comfort*], encouraging; heartening; consoling.

com·fort·less (kum′fẽrt-lis), *adj.* 1. lacking comfort or comforts. 2. providing no comfort.

comfort station, a public toilet or rest-room.

com·frey (kum′fri), *n.* [*pl.* COMFREYS (-friz)], [ME. & OFr. *confirie;* prob. < LL. *confervia,* comfrey < L. *confervere,* to heal, grow together, orig., to seethe, boil together < *com-,* with + *fervere,* to boil, be hot: prob. so named from use in medicine to congeal wounds], any of a group of European plants of the borage family, with rough, hairy leaves.

com·ic (kom′ik), *adj.* [L. *comicus;* Gr. *kōmikos*], 1. of comedy. 2. amusing or intended to be amusing; humorous; funny. 3. of comic strips or cartoons. *n.* 1. a comedian. 2. the humorous part of art or life. 3. *usually in pl.* [Colloq.], a comic cartoon or strip of cartoons. —*SYN.* see **funny.**

com·i·cal (kom′i-k'l), *adj.* 1. causing amusement; humorous; funny; droll. 2. [Obs.], of or fit for comedy. —*SYN.* see **funny.**

com·i·cal·i·ty (kom′i-kal′ə-ti), *n.* a comical quality.

comic book, a paper booklet of extended comic strips, sometimes of a sensational or violent nature.

comic opera, opera with humorous situations, a story that ends happily, and, usually, some spoken dialogue.

comic strip, a series of cartoons, as in a newspaper, usually telling a humorous or adventurous story.

Co·mines, Phi·lippe de (fē′lēp′ də kô′mēn′), 1445?–1509?; French historian and courtier: also spelled **Commines.**

Com·in·form (kom′in-fôrm′), *n.* [< *Communist Information;* cf. COMINTERN], the Communist Information Bureau, established in October, 1947, by the Communist Parties of Bulgaria, Czechoslovakia, France, Hungary, Italy, Poland, Romania, the Soviet Union, and, originally, Yugoslavia to exchange information and co-ordinate activities: dissolved in 1956.

com·ing (kum′iŋ), *adj.* [ppr. of *come*], 1. approaching. 2. immediately following: as, the *coming* Tuesday. 3. [Colloq.], showing promise of being successful or famous: as, a *coming* young actor. *n.* arrival; approach; advent.

the coming thing, [Colloq.], something that seems certain to become popular, fashionable, or important.

Com·in·tern (kom′in-tũrn′, kom′in-tũrn′), *n.* [< *Communist International*], the international organization of Communist parties, founded in Moscow in 1919 and officially dissolved in 1943: also called *Communist International, Third International.*

co·mi·ti·a (kə-mish′i-ə), *n.* [L., pl. of *comitium,* place where the comitia convened < *com-,* together + pp. stem of *ire,* to go], in ancient Rome, an assembly of citizens for electing officials, passing laws, etc.

com·i·ty (kom′ə-ti), *n.* [*pl.* COMITIES (-tiz)], [L. *comitas* < *comis*, polite, kind; earlier *cosmis;* prob. < *co-*, with + **smi-s* < base **smei-*, to smile; akin to L. *mirus*, wonderful and Eng. *smile*], politeness; civility; courtesy.

comity of nations, 1. the courtesy and respect of peaceful nations for each other's laws and institutions. 2. loosely, the nations practicing such courtesy, etc.

comm., 1. commander. 2. commentary. 3. commerce. 4. commission. 5. committee. 6. commonwealth. 7. communication.

com·ma (kom′ə), *n.* [L.; Gr. *komma*, clause in a sentence, that which is struck or cut off < *koptein*, to cut off], 1. a mark of punctuation (,) used to indicate a slight separation of sentence elements: commas are used to set off nonrestrictive or parenthetical elements, quotations, items in a series, etc. 2. a slight pause.

comma bacillus, the bacillus causing Asiatic cholera.

com·mand (kə-mand′, kə-mänd′), *v.t.* [ME. *commanden;* OFr. *commander;* LL. *commandare;* L. *com-*, intens. + *mandare*, to commit, entrust], 1. to give an order or orders to; direct with authority. 2. to have authority or jurisdiction over; control. 3. to be able to have and use: as, he *commands* a large vocabulary. 4. to deserve and get; require as due, proper, or becoming: as, his knowledge *commands* respect. 5. to control (a position); overlook: as, the fort *commands* the entire valley. *v.i.* to exercise power or authority; be in control; act as a commander. *n.* 1. a commanding. 2. an order; direction; mandate. 3. authority to command. 4. power to control or dominate by position. 5. range of view. 6. ability to have and use; mastery. 7. a military or naval force, or a district, under someone's authority or jurisdiction: abbreviated **comd.** 8. the post where the person in command is stationed.

SYN.—**command,** when it refers to a giving of orders, implies the formal exercise of absolute authority, as by a sovereign, military leader, etc.; **order** often stresses peremptoriness, sometimes suggesting an arbitrary exercise of authority (I *ordered* him out of the house); **direct** and **instruct** are both used in connection with supervision, as in business relations, **instruct** perhaps more often stressing explicitness of details in the directions given; **enjoin** suggests a directing with urgent admonition (he *enjoined* them to secrecy) and sometimes implies the legal prohibiting of an action; **charge** implies the imposition of a task as a duty, trust, or responsibility. See also **power.**

com·man·dant (kom′ən-dant′, kom′ən-dänt′), *n.* [Fr.; ppr. of *commander*], a commanding officer: generally a title of the commander of a district, fort, etc.: abbreviated **Comdt.** (as a title).

com·man·deer (kom′ən-dêr′), *v.t.* [D. *kommandeeren*, to command, (esp. S. Afr.) to commandeer; Fr. *commander;* see COMMAND], 1. to force into military service. 2. to seize (property) for military or governmental use. 3. [Colloq.], to take forcibly.

com·mand·er (kə-man′dẽr, kə-män′dẽr), *n.* [ME. *comaundour;* OFr. *comandeor* < *commander*], 1. a person who commands; leader. 2. the officer in charge of a military unit: a functional title, not a rank. 3. a high ranking member of an order of knighthood, or of a fraternal order. 4. in the *United States Navy*, an officer ranking just above a lieutenant commander and just below a captain, and corresponding to a lieutenant colonel in the army: abbreviated **Comdr., Com.** (as a title), **comm.**

commander in chief, [*pl.* COMMANDERS IN CHIEF], 1. the supreme commander of the armed forces of a nation: in the United States the President is the commander in chief: abbreviated **C.I.C., C. in C.** (as a title). 2. an officer in command of all armed forces in a certain theater of war.

com·man·der·ship (kə-man′dẽr-ship′, kə-män′dẽr-ship′), *n.* [see -SHIP], the rank or position of a commander.

com·mand·er·y (kə-man′dẽr-i, kə-män′dẽr-i), *n.* [*pl.* COMMANDERIES (-iz)], [Fr. *commanderie;* ML. *commendaria* (< *commenda*, commendation, an entrusting < L. *commendare;* see COMMEND), benefice entrusted to someone; sp. influenced by association with *command*], 1. the estate administered by a commander of an order of knights. 2. the rank of a commander in an order of knights. 3. a branch in certain fraternal orders.

com·mand·ing (kə-man′diŋ, kə-män′diŋ), *adj.* [ppr. of *command*], 1. in command: abbreviated **cmdg.** 2. controlling; dominating. 3. impressive. 4. controlling or dominating by position: as, a *commanding* hilltop.

com·mand·ment (kə-mand′mənt, kə-mänd′mənt), *n.* [ME. & OFr. *comandement*], 1. a command; order; mandate; precept; law. 2. any of the Ten Commandments, laws described in the Bible as given by God to Moses on Mount Sinai: Ex. 20:2–17, Deut. 5:6–21.

com·man·do (kə-man′dō, kə-män′dō), *n.* [*pl.* COMMANDOS, COMMANDOES (-dōz)], [D.; Port., lit., party commanded < *commandar*, to govern, command; LL. *commandare;* see COMMAND], 1. originally, in South Africa, a force of Boer troops. 2. a raid or expedition made by such troops. 3. in World War II, a small raiding force trained to operate inside territory held by the enemy. 4. a member of such a group.

command performance, a performance, as of a play, put on for royalty, etc. by command or request.

command post, the field headquarters of an army unit, from which the commander directs operations: abbreviated **C.P.**

com·meas·ur·a·ble (kə-mezh′ẽr-ə-b′l), *adj.* equal in measure or size; commensurate.

com·meas·ure (kə-mezh′ẽr), *v.t.* to equal in measure.

‡**comme il faut** (kô′mēl′fō′), [Fr.], as it should be; proper; fitting.

com·mem·o·rate (kə-mem′ẽr-āt′), *v.t.* [COMMEMORATED (-id), COMMEMORATING], [< L. *commemoratus*, pp. of *commemorare*, to call to mind; *com-*, intens. + *memorare*, to remind; see MEMORY], 1. to honor the memory of by a ceremony, etc. 2. to preserve the memory of; serve as a memorial to. —*SYN.* see **celebrate.**

com·mem·o·ra·tion (kə-mem′ẽr-ā′shən), *n.* [L. *commemoratio*], 1. a commemorating. 2. a celebration in memory of someone or something.

in commemoration of, in honor of the memory of.

com·mem·o·ra·tive (kə-mem′ẽr-ā′tiv, kə-mem′ẽr-ə-tiv), *adj.* serving to commemorate. *n.* anything that commemorates.

com·mem·o·ra·tor (kə-mem′ẽr-ā′tẽr), *n.* a person who commemorates.

com·mem·o·ra·to·ry (kə-mem′ẽr-ə-tôr′i, kə-mem′ẽr-ə-tō′ri), *adj.* commemorative.

com·mence (kə-mens′), *v.i.* & *v.t.* [COMMENCED (-menst′), COMMENCING], [OFr. *comencer;* LL. **cominitiare;* L. *com-*, together + *initiare*, to begin], to begin; start; originate. —*SYN.* see **begin.**

com·mence·ment (kə-mens′mənt), *n.* [ME.; OFr.], 1. a commencing; beginning; start. 2. the time of commencing or beginning. 3. the day when degrees or diplomas are conferred at a school or college. 4. the ceremonies in connection with this.

com·mend (kə-mend′), *v.t.* [ME. *commenden;* L. *commendare*, to entrust to, commend < *com-*, intens. + *mandare*, to put in one's hands, commit to one's charge; see MANDATE], 1. to put in the care of another; entrust. 2. to mention as worthy of regard; recommend. 3. to praise. 4. [Archaic], to recall (a person) to the mind of another; transmit the regards of.

com·mend·a·ble (kə-men′də-b′l), *adj.* deserving to be commended; praiseworthy.

com·mend·a·bly (kə-men′də-bli), *adv.* in a commendable manner.

com·men·dam (kə-men′dam), *n.* [< ML. *dare in commendam*, to give in trust; see COMMANDERY], 1. formerly, the temporary holding of a benefice, with the right to its revenues, by a layman in the absence of an incumbent: he was said to hold the benefice *in commendam*. 2. a benefice held in this way.

com·men·da·tion (kom′ən-dā′shən), *n.* [ME. *commendacion;* OFr. *commentation;* L. *commendatio*], 1. a putting in the care of another; entrusting. 2. recommendation. 3. approval; praise. 4. *usually in pl.* [Archaic], a greeting or remembrance, as to a friend.

com·mend·a·to·ry (kə-men′də-tôr′i, kə-men′də-tō′ri), *adj.* [LL. *commendatorius*], 1. serving to commend; expressing praise or approval. 2. recommending. 3. in *ecclesiastical usage*, holding a benefice in commendam.

com·men·sal (kə-men′səl), *n.* [Fr.; ML. *commensalis* < L. *com-*, with + *mensa*, table], 1. a person who eats at the same table; companion at meals. 2. an animal or plant that lives on, in, or with another, sharing its food but neither parasitic on it nor injured by it. *adj.* designating, of, characteristic of, or like a commensal.

com·men·sal·ism (kə-men′səl-iz′m), *n.* the state of being commensal.

com·men·sal·i·ty (com′en-sal′ə-ti), *n.* commensalism.

com·men·su·ra·bil·i·ty (kə-men′shoor-ə-bil′ə-ti, kə-men′sẽr-ə-bil′ə-ti), *n.* the quality or state of being commensurable.

com·men·su·ra·ble (kə-men′shoor-ə-b′l, kə-men′sẽr-ə-b′l), *adj.* [LL. *commensurabilis* < L. *com-*, together + *mensurare*, to measure < *mensura*, measurement], 1. measurable by the same standard or measure. 2. proportionable; fitly proportioned. —*SYN.* see **proportionate.**

com·men·su·ra·bly (kə-men′shoor-ə-bli, kə-men′sẽr-ə-bli), *adv.* [see COMMENSURABLE], proportionately.

com·men·su·rate (kə-men′shoor-it, kə-men′sẽr-it), *adj.* [*com-* + LL. *mensuratus*, pp. of *mensurare*, to measure < L. *mensura*, measurement], 1. equal in measure or size; coextensive. 2. proportionate; corresponding in measure. 3. measurable by the same standard or measure; commensurable. —*SYN.* see **proportionate.**

com·men·su·ra·tion (kə-men′shoo-rā′shən, kə-men′sə-rā′shən), *n.* the state of being commensurate.

com·ment (kom′ent), *n.* [OFr.; L. *commentum*, invention, falsehood < *commentus*, pp. of *comminisci*, to contrive, devise < *com-*, intens. + base of *meminisse*, to remember < *mens*, the mind], 1. a note in explanation, criticism, or illustration of something written or said; annotation. 2. a remark, as in observation or criticism. 3. talk; chatter; gossip. ***v.i.*** (*less often*, kə-ment′), [Fr. *commenter;* LL. *commentare* < L. *commentari*, to consider thoroughly], to make a comment or comments (*on* or *upon*); make remarks. ***v.t.*** [Archaic], to make comments on; annotate. —***SYN.*** see **remark.**

com·men·tar·i·al (kom′ən-târ′i-əl), ***adj.*** of, or having the nature of, a commentary.

com·men·tar·y (kom′ən-ter′i), ***n.*** [*pl.* COMMENTARIES (-iz)], [L. *commentarius*, notebook, annotation < *commentari;* see COMMENT], 1. a series of explanatory notes or annotations. 2. a series of remarks or observations. 3. a comment. 4. a memoir; historical narrative based on personal experience: as, Caesar's *Commentaries*. Abbreviated **com., comm.** —***SYN.*** see **remark.**

com·men·ta·tor (kom′ən-tā′tẽr), ***n.*** [L., inventor, contriver; see COMMENT], 1. a person who writes a series of explanatory notes or annotations. 2. a person whose profession is reporting, analyzing, and evaluating events, trends, etc.: as, a news *commentator*.

com·merce (kom′ẽrs), ***n.*** [Fr.; L. *commercium* < *com-*, together + *merx, mercis*, merchandise], 1. the buying and selling of goods, especially when done on a large scale between cities, countries, etc.; business dealings; trade: abbreviated **com., comm.** 2. social intercourse. 3. [Rare], sexual intercourse. ***v.i.*** (kə-mũrs′), [COMMERCED (-mũrst′), COMMERCING], to have personal dealings (*with*). —***SYN.*** see **business.**

com·mer·cial (kə-mũr′shəl), ***adj.*** 1. of or connected with commerce. 2. designating unrefined products bought and sold in large quantities for industrial uses: as, *commercial* sulfuric acid. 3. made or done primarily for sale or profit. Abbreviated **com., cml.** ***n.*** in *radio & television*, a paid advertisement.

commercial art, art for commercial purposes, chiefly for advertising.

commercial college, a college or school offering instruction in business or commerce; business college.

com·mer·cial·ism (kə-mũr′shəl-iz′m), ***n.*** 1. the practices and spirit of commerce or business. 2. a business practice, custom, or idiom.

com·mer·cial·i·za·tion (kə-mũr′shəl-i-zā′shən, kə-mũr′shəl-ī-zā′shən), ***n.*** a commercializing or being commercialized.

com·mer·cial·ize (kə-mũr′shəl-īz′), ***v.t.*** [COMMERCIALIZED (-īzd′), COMMERCIALIZING], 1. to put on a business basis; apply commercial methods to. 2. to make the profit motive dominant in; make or do mainly for profit. 3. to put on the market; make a commodity of.

com·mer·cial·ly (kə-mũr′shəl-i), ***adv.*** 1. in a commercial manner. 2. from the viewpoint of business.

commercial paper, checks, promissory notes, bills of exchange, and other negotiable paper used in business.

commercial traveler, [British], a traveling salesman.

com·mi·nate (kom′ə-nāt′), ***v.t. & v.i.*** [COMMINATED (-id), COMMINATING], [< L. *comminatus*, pp. of *comminari*, to threaten; *com-*, intens. + *minari*, to threaten], 1. to threaten, especially with anathema. 2. to curse or ban solemnly; anathematize.

com·mi·na·tion (kom′ə-nā′shən), ***n.*** [L. *comminatio;* see COMMINATE], 1. a threat or denunciation. 2. in the *Anglican Church*, a recital of divine threats against sinners.

com·min·a·to·ry (kə-min′ə-tôr′i, kom′in-ə-tō′ri), ***adj.*** [see COMMINATE], threatening; denunciatory.

Commines, see **Comines, Philippe de.**

com·min·gle (kə-miŋ′g'l), ***v.t. & v.i.*** to mingle together; intermix; blend.

com·mi·nute (kom′ə-nūt′, kom′ə-no͞ot′), ***v.t.*** [COMMINUTED (-id), COMMINUTING], [< L. *comminutus*, pp. of *comminuere*, to make small; *com-*, intens. + *minuere*, to make small; cf. MINOR], to reduce to small, fine particles; make into powder; pulverize.

com·mi·nu·tion (kom′ə-nū′shən, kom′ə-no͞o′shən), ***n.*** a comminuting or being comminuted; pulverization.

com·mis·er·a·ble (kə-miz′ẽr-ə-b'l), ***adj.*** worthy of commiseration; pitiable.

com·mis·er·ate (kə-miz′ẽr-āt′), ***v.t.*** [COMMISERATED (-id), COMMISERATING], [< L. *commiseratus*, pp. of *commiserari*, to pity; *com-*, intens. + *miserari*, to pity; cf. MISERY], to feel or show sorrow or pity for; sympathize with in distress. ***v.i.*** to condole (*with*).

com·mis·er·a·tion (kə-miz′ẽr-ā′shən), ***n.*** [L. *commiseratio*, part of an oration meant to arouse pity], pity; compassion; a commiserating. —***SYN.*** see **pity.**

com·mis·er·a·tive (kə-miz′ẽr-ā′tiv, kə-miz′ẽr-ə-tiv), ***adj.*** commiserating.

com·mis·sar (kom′ə-sär′, kom′ə-sär′), ***n.*** [Fr. *commissaire;* LL. *commissarius;* see COMMISSARY], 1. a commissioner. 2. [Russ. *komissar*], formerly, the head of any of the commissariats in the republics of the Soviet Union: now officially called *minister*.

com·mis·sar·i·al (kom′ə-sâr′i-əl), ***adj.*** of a commissary.

com·mis·sar·i·at (kom′ə-sâr′i-ət), ***n.*** [Fr. < *commissaire;* see COMMISSAR], 1. those branches of an army which provide food and supplies for the troops. 2. food supply. 3. the office of a commissar. 4. a department headed by a commissar. 5. [Russ. *komissariat*], formerly, any of the government departments in the republics of the Soviet Union: now officially called *ministry*. 6. a group of commissars.

com·mis·sar·y (kom′ə-ser′i), ***n.*** [*pl.* COMMISSARIES (-iz)], [ME. *commissarie;* LL. *commissarius* < *commissus*, pp. of *committere;* see COMMIT], 1. a person to whom some duty is given by authority; representative; deputy; specifically, *a*) in France, a police official. *b*) a person representing a bishop in a part of his diocese. *c*) in the Soviet Union, a commissar. 2. formerly, *a*) an army officer in charge of providing soldiers with food and other supplies. *b*) the buildings and personnel in his charge. 3. a store in a lumber camp, army camp, etc., where food and supplies can be obtained.

com·mis·sion (kə-mish′ən), ***n.*** [ME.; OFr.; LL. *commissio*, delegation of business to anyone < L. *commissus*, pp. of *committere;* see COMMIT], 1. an authorization to perform certain duties or tasks, or to take on certain powers. 2. a document giving such authorization. 3. authority to act for another. 4. a thing that a person is authorized to do for another. 5. the state of being authorized to perform certain duties or tasks. 6. a group of people chosen to perform specified duties. 7. a committing; doing. 8. the thing done. 9. a percentage of the money taken in on sales, given as pay to a salesclerk or agent, usually in addition to salary or wages. 10. in *military usage*, *a*) an official certificate conferring rank; specifically, a document issued by the President, making one a commissioned officer in the United States armed forces. *b*) the rank thus granted. Abbreviated **Com.** (in a title), **comm.** ***v.t.*** 1. to give a commission to. 2. to authorize; empower. 3. in *nautical usage*, to put (a vessel) into service. —***SYN.*** see **authorize.**

in commission, 1. in use. 2. in fit condition for use.

out of commission, 1. not in use. 2. not in fit condition for use.

com·mis·sion·aire (kə-mish′ən-âr′), ***n.*** [Fr.], a person commissioned to do errands or small tasks, as a porter, doorkeeper, messenger, etc.

com·mis·sioned (kə-mish′ənd), ***adj.*** [pp. of *commission*], holding rank in the armed forces by a commission from the proper authority: the lowest rank of commissioned officer in the United States Army is second lieutenant, in the Navy, ensign.

com·mis·sion·er (kə-mish′ən-ẽr), ***n.*** 1. a person authorized to do certain things by a commission or warrant. 2. a member of a commission. 3. an official in charge of a governmental department: as, a *commissioner* of highways. 4. one of a group chosen to govern a local political unit. Abbreviated **Com., Comr.** (as a title), **comm.**

com·mis·sion·er·ship (kə-mish′ən-ẽr-ship′), ***n.*** [see -SHIP], the office or position of a commissioner.

commission house, a stockbroker's office that buys and sells stock for customers on a commission basis.

commission merchant, a person who buys or sells goods for others and is paid a commission by them.

commission plan, a form of city government in which all legislative and administrative powers are in the hands of an elected commission (usually five or six members) instead of a mayor and council.

com·mis·su·ral (kə-mish′yoo-rəl, kom′i-syoor′əl), ***adj.*** of, or of the nature of, a commissure.

com·mis·sure (kom′ə-shoor′), ***n.*** [Fr.; L. *commissura* < *commissus*, pp. of *committere;* see COMMIT], 1. a line of union between two parts; joint; seam. 2. in *anatomy*, a band of fibers joining symmetrical parts, as of the right and left sides of the brain and spinal cord.

com·mit (kə-mit′), ***v.t.*** [COMMITTED (-id), COMMITTING], [ME. *committen;* L. *committere*, to bring together, commit; *com-*, together + *mittere*, to send], 1. to give in charge or trust; deliver for safekeeping; consign: as, we *commit* his fame to posterity. 2. to put officially in custody or confinement: as, he was *committed* to prison. 3. to do or perpetrate, as an offense or crime. 4. to pledge; bind; engage: as, *committed* to fight for slum clearance. 5. to refer (a bill, etc.) to a committee.

commit to memory, to memorize; learn by heart.

commit to paper (or **writing**), to write down; record.

SYN.—**commit,** the basic term here, implies the delivery of a person or thing into the charge or keeping of another; **entrust** implies committal based on trust and confidence; **confide** stresses the private nature of information entrusted to another and usually connotes intimacy of relationship; **consign** suggests formal action in transferring something to another's possession or control; **relegate** implies a consigning to a specific class, sphere, place, etc., especially one of inferiority, and usually suggests the literal or figurative removal of something undesirable.

com·mit·ment (kə-mit′mənt), ***n.*** 1. a committing or being committed. 2. official consignment of a person to prison, to an institution for the mentally ill, etc. 3. a court order authorizing such consignment. 4. a pledge or promise. 5. a financial liability undertaken; agreement to buy or sell securities, etc.

com·mit·ta·ble (kə-mit′ə-b'l), ***adj.*** 1. that can be committed. 2. liable to be committed to prison, to an institution for the mentally ill, etc. 3. making a person liable to such commitment: said of offenses.

com·mit·tal (kə-mit′'l), *n.* commitment.

com·mit·tee (kə-mit′i), *n.* [Anglo-Fr. *committé* for Fr. *commis*, pp. of *commettre*, to commit; L. *committere;* see COMMIT], 1. a group of people chosen, as from the members of a legislature or club, to consider some matter or to function in a certain capacity. 2. in *law*, a person to whom someone or something is given in charge. Abbreviated **Com.** (in a title), **comm.**

in committee, under consideration by a committee, as a resolution or bill.

com·mit·tee·man (kə-mit′i-mən), *n.* [*pl.* COMMITTEEMEN (-mən)], a member of a committee.

committee of the whole, a committee comprising all the members present of a legislative body, etc. to permit operating under rules of order different from those used in a regular session.

com·mit·tee·wom·an (kə-mit′i-woom′ən), *n.* [*pl.* COMMITTEEWOMEN (-wim′in)], a woman member of a committee.

com·mix (kə-miks′, ko-miks′), *v.t.* & *v.i.* [back-formation < *commixt;* L. *commixtus;* see COMMIXTURE], [Archaic or Poetic], to mix together; blend.

com·mix·ture (kə-miks′chẽr, ko-miks′chẽr), *n.* [L. *commixtura* < *commixtus*, pp. of *commiscere*, to mix together; *com-*, together + *miscere;* see MIX], a mixture.

com·mode (kə-mōd′), *n.* [Fr., chest of drawers < *commode*, convenient, suitable; L. *commodus*, suitable; see COM- & MODE], 1. a high headdress worn by women around 1700. 2. a chest of drawers. 3. a movable washstand. 4. a piece of furniture containing a chamber pot. 5. a toilet: euphemistic term.

com·mo·di·ous (kə-mō′di-əs), *adj.* [ME., convenient; OFr. *commodieux;* LL. *commodiosus* < *commodus*, suitable; see COM- & MODE], spacious; roomy.

com·mod·i·ty (kə-mod′ə-ti), *n.* [*pl.* COMMODITIES (-tiz)], [Fr. *commodité*, comfort, convenience; L. *commoditas*, fitness, adaptation < *commodus*, suitable; see COM- & MODE], 1. any useful thing. 2. anything bought and sold; any article of commerce.

commodity money, a proposed system of currency whose unit (*commodity dollar*) would have a fluctuating gold value determined at regular intervals on the basis of an official index of commodity prices.

com·mo·dore (kom′ə-dôr′, kom′ə-dōr′), *n.* [earlier *commadore, commandore;* prob., with Sp. or Port. influence, < Fr. *commandeur;* see COMMANDER], 1. in the *United States Navy*, an officer ranking just above a captain and just below a rear admiral: the rank was abolished in 1899 but temporarily restored in World War II. 2. in the *British Navy*, a captain temporarily heading a squadron or division of a fleet: the title is unofficial and carries no rating. 3. a courtesy title given to the president of a yacht club, the senior captain of a merchant fleet, etc. Abbreviated **Com.** (as a title).

Com·mo·dus (kom′ō-dəs), *n.* (*Lucius Aelius Aurelius Commodus*), emperor of Rome (180–192 A.D.); lived 161–192 A.D.

com·mon (kom′ən), *adj.* [ME. *commun;* OFr. *comun;* L. *communis* (OL. *commoinos*), shared by all or many; exactly akin to AS. *gemæne*, public, general (cf. MEAN, common); < *com-*, with + *munus*, obligatory services, duties, etc.; IE. base **mei-*, to barter, exchange; cf. IMMUNE], 1. belonging equally to, or shared by, every one or all: as, the five of us have *common* interests. 2. belonging to the community at large; public. 3. of, from, by, or to all. 4. general; prevalent; widespread. 5. familiar; usual; met with frequently. 6. ordinary; undistinguished. 7. having no rank: as, a *common* soldier. 8. below ordinary; hence, 9. not refined; vulgar; low; coarse. 10. in *grammar*, *a*) designating a noun that refers to any of a group or class, as *book, apple, street:* opposed to *proper*. *b*) designating gender that is either masculine or feminine: as, *child* is of *common* gender. 11. in *mathematics*, belonging equally to two or more quantities: as, a *common* denominator. Abbreviated **com.** *n.* 1. *pl.* [Obs. in sing.], the people; the common people. 2. *sometimes pl.* land owned or used by all the inhabitants of a place; tract of open public land: as, Boston *Commons*. 3. [sometimes C-], in *ecclesiastical usage*, a service suitable for any of a class of festivals. 4. in *law*, the right that a person has, in common with the owner or others, in the land or waters of another.

in common, equally with, or shared by, all concerned.

***SYN.*—common** refers to that which is met with most frequently or is shared by all or most individuals in a group, body, etc., and may imply prevalence, usualness, or, in a depreciatory sense, inferiority (a *common* belief, a *common* hussy); **general** implies connection with all or nearly all of a kind, class, or group and stresses extensiveness (*general* unrest among the people); **ordinary** implies accordance with the regular or customary pattern, stressing commonplaceness and lack of special distinction (an *ordinary* workday); **familiar** applies to that which is widely known and readily recognized (a *familiar* feeling); **popular** and, in this connection, **vulgar** imply widespread currency, acceptance, or favor among the general public or the common people (a *popular* song, *Vulgar* Latin). See also **mutual.**—*ANT.* unusual, exceptional.

com·mon·a·ble (kom′ən-ə-b'l), *adj.* [see COMMON, *n.*, 2], 1. allowed to pasture on land owned by the village, town, etc. 2. held in common.

com·mon·age (kom′ən-ij), *n.* [see COMMON, *n.*, 2 & -AGE], 1. the right to pasture cattle, sheep, etc. on land owned by the village, town, etc. 2. the state of land owned in common. 3. the land so owned. 4. the common people; commonalty.

com·mon·al·ty (kom′ən-əl-ti), *n.* [*pl.* COMMONALTIES (-tiz)], [ME. *comonalte;* OFr. *communalte;* see COMMUNAL], 1. the common people; people not of the upper classes. 2. people in general. 3. a body corporate or its membership.

common carrier, a person or company in the business of transporting passengers or goods for a fee: so called because it undertakes to serve all without discrimination.

common denominator, a common multiple of the denominators of two or more fractions: as, 10 is a *common denominator* of 1/2 and 3/5.

common divisor, a number or quantity that divides two or more numbers or quantities without a remainder; factor common to two or more numbers: as, 6 is a *common divisor* of 6, 12, and 36.

com·mon·er (kom′ən-ẽr), *n.* [ME. *comuner* < *comun;* see COMMON], 1. a person not of the nobility; member of the common people. 2. [Rare], a member of the British House of Commons. 3. at Oxford University, a student who does not have a fellowship or scholarship, and therefore pays for his food (called *commons*).

common fraction, a fraction with the numerator separated from the denominator by a diagonal or horizontal line, as 5/11 or $\frac{3}{4}$.

common law, the unwritten law of a country based on custom, usage, and the decisions of law courts, as contrasted with *statute law:* abbreviated **c.l.**: it is now largely codified by legislative definition.

com·mon-law marriage (kom′ən-lô′), in *law*, a marriage not solemnized by religious or civil ceremony but effected by agreement to live together as husband and wife: authorized by statute in some States.

common logarithm, in *mathematics*, a logarithm having 10 for its base.

com·mon·ly (kom′ən-li), *adv.* in a common manner; usually; ordinarily: abbreviated **com.**

common man, one of the common people.

Common Market, an association formed in 1958 by Belgium, France, West Germany, Italy, Luxemburg, and the Netherlands, to effect a closer economic union, especially by means of mutual tariff concessions: official name, **European Economic Community.**

common measure, in *music*, common time.

common multiple, in *mathematics*, a multiple of each of two or more quantities: as, 12 is a *common multiple* of 2, 3, 4, and 6.

common people, the people of the world, of a country, etc. who are not of the upper classes; masses.

com·mon·place (kom′ən-plās′), *n.* [lit. transl. of L. *locus communis;* Gr. *koinos topos*, general topic], 1. originally, a passage marked for reference, or a collection of such passages in a book called a *commonplace book;* hence, 2. a trite remark; truism; platitude. 3. anything common or ordinary: as, the airplane is now a *commonplace*. *adj.* ordinary; neither new nor interesting; obvious and trite. —*SYN.* see **platitude, trite.**

common pleas, in *law*, civil suits between private parties.

com·mons (kom′ənz), *n.pl.* [see COMMON], 1. the common people; people not of the upper classes; commonalty. 2. [construed as sing.], provisions or food provided for meals in common for all members of a group; especially, 3. such food provided by a college at a fixed charge; hence, 4. a room, building, table, or tables where such food is served. 5. any dining room at a college or similar institution.

the Commons, the House of Commons; lower house of Parliament in Great Britain or Canada.

common school, a public elementary school.

com·mon-sense (kom′ən-sens′), *adj.* having or showing common sense; sound and practical; sensible.

common sense, 1. originally, the faculty which supposedly united and interpreted impressions of the five senses; hence, 2. practical judgment or intelligence; ordinary good sense.

common stock, ordinary capital stock in a company, without a definite dividend rate or the privileges of preferred stock, but usually giving its owner a vote at shareholders' meetings in proportion to his holdings.

common time, in *music*, a rhythm of two beats to the measure or any multiple of this; especially, 4/4 time: also called *common measure*.

com·mon·weal (kom′ən-wēl′), *n.* 1. the public good; the general welfare. 2. [Archaic], a commonwealth. Also **common weal.**

com·mon·wealth (kom′ən-welth′), *n.* [see COMMON & WEALTH], 1. the people of a nation or state; body politic; hence, 2. a nation or state in which there is self-government; democracy or republic: abbreviated **comm.** 3. [C-], any of the dominions in the British Commonwealth of Nations; especially, Australia (official title, *Commonwealth of Australia*). 4. loosely, any State of the United States: strictly, Kentucky, Maryland, Massachusetts, Pennsylvania, or Virginia, which are so termed by charter. 5. [Obs.], the general welfare; commonweal.

the Commonwealth, the government in England under the Cromwells and, later, Parliament from 1649–1660.

Commonwealth of the Philippines, see **Philippine Islands.**

com·mo·tion (kə-mō′shən), *n.* [L. *commotio* < *commotus,* pp. of *commovere,* to move, disturb; *com-,* together + *movere,* to move; see MOTION, MOVE], violent motion; turmoil; agitation; confusion; disturbance.

com·move (kə-mōōv′), *v.t.* [ME. *commoeven;* OFr. *commoveir;* L. *commovere; com-,* intens. + *movere;* see MOVE], to move strongly; agitate; disturb; excite.

com·mu·nal (kom′yoo-n'l, kə-mū′n'l), *adj.* [Fr.; L. *communalis*], 1. of a commune or communes. 2. of a community; belonging to the community; public.

com·mu·nal·ism (kom′yoo-n'l-iz'm, kə-mū′n'l-iz'm), *n.* [Fr. *communalisme*], a theory or system of government in which communes or local communities have virtual autonomy within a federated state.

com·mu·nal·ist (kom′yoo-n'l-ist, kə-mū′n'l-ist), *n.* a person who advocates communalism or lives under it.

com·mu·nal·is·tic (kom′yoo-n'l-is′tik, kə-mū′n'l-is′tik), *adj.* of or characterized by communalism.

com·mu·nal·ize (kom′yoo-n'l-īz′, kə-mū′n'l-īz′), *v.t.* [COMMUNALIZED (-īzd′), COMMUNALIZING], to make communal; make (something) the property of the entire community.

Com·mu·nard (kom′yoo-närd′), *n.* [Fr.], a person who supported or took part in the Commune of Paris (1871).

com·mune (kə-mūn′), *v.i.* [COMMUNED (-mūnd′), COMMUNING], [ME. *communen;* OFr. *comuner,* to make common, share < *comun* (see COMMON); also < OFr. *communier,* to administer the sacrament; L. *communicare,* to partake, communicate (see COMMUNICATE)], 1. to hold intimate converse. 2. to receive Holy Communion. *n.* (kom′ūn), intimate converse; communion.

commune with oneself, to think; ponder.

com·mune (kom′ūn), *n.* [Fr.; L. *communia,* pl. of *commune,* lit., that which is common < *communis;* see COMMON], 1. the common people. 2. a community. 3. the smallest administrative district of local government in France, Belgium, and some other countries in Europe: abbreviated **com.**

the Commune, 1. the revolutionary government of Paris from 1792 to 1794. 2. the revolutionary government established in Paris on March 18, 1871, at the close of the Franco-Prussian War, and suppressed by the Versailles government on May 28, 1871.

com·mu·ni·ca·bil·i·ty (kə-mū′ni-kə-bil′ə-ti), *n.* the quality of being communicable.

com·mu·ni·ca·ble (kə-mū′ni-kə-b'l), *adj.* [Fr.], 1. that can be communicated: said of thoughts, etc. 2. that can be transmitted: said of a disease, etc. 3. [Archaic], talkative.

com·mu·ni·cant (kə-mū′ni-kənt), *n.* [< L. *communicans,* ppr. of *communicare*], 1. a person who receives Holy Communion or belongs to a church that celebrates this sacrament: as, a *communicant* of the Catholic Church. 2. a person who communicates information. *adj.* communicating.

com·mu·ni·cate (kə-mū′nə-kāt′), *v.t.* [COMMUNICATED (-id), COMMUNICATING], [< L. *communicatus,* pp. of *communicare,* to impart, share, lit., to make common < *communis;* see COMMON], 1. to impart; pass along; transmit. 2. to make known; give (information, messages, etc.). *v.i.* 1. to receive Holy Communion. 2. to give, or give and receive, information, signals, or messages in any way, as by talk, gestures, writing, etc. 3. to be connected: as, the living room *communicates* with the dining room.

com·mu·ni·ca·tion (kə-mū′nə-kā′shən), *n.* [Fr.; L. *communicatio;* see COMMUNICATE], 1. a transmitting. 2. a giving, or giving and receiving, of information, signals, or messages by talk, gestures, writing, etc. 3. the information, message, etc. 4. a means of communicating; specifically, *a*) *pl.* a system for sending and receiving messages, as by telephone, telegraph, radio, etc. *b*) *pl.* a system for moving troops and matériel. *c*) a passage or way for getting from one place to another. 5. the science and art of communicating as a branch of study. Abbreviated **com., comm.**

communications zone, in *military usage,* the area between the zone of the interior and the combat zone, serving as a center for communications, supply, evacuation of wounded, troop replacements, etc.

com·mu·ni·ca·tive (kə-mū′nə-kā′tiv, kə-mū′ni-kə-tiv), *adj.* 1. giving information readily; talkative. 2. of communication.

com·mu·ni·ca·tor (kə-mū′nə-kā′tẽr), *n.* [L., a person who participates], a person or thing that communicates.

com·mu·ni·ca·to·ry (kə-mū′ni-kə-tôr′i, kə-mū′ni-kə-tō′ri), *adj.* [Rare], of communication or tending to communicate.

com·mun·ion (kə-mūn′yən), *n.* [ME.; OFr.; L. *communio* < *communis;* see COMMON], 1. a sharing; possession in common; participation. 2. a communing; sharing one's thoughts and emotions with another or others; intimate converse. 3. an intimate spiritual relationship. 4. a group of people professing the same religious faith and practicing the same rites. 5. [C-], a sharing in, or celebrating of, the Eucharist (*Holy Communion*).

com·mun·ion·ist (kə-mūn′yən-ist), *n.* 1. a person who believes in a definite theory about Holy Communion. 2. a person who receives Holy Communion.

com·mu·ni·qué (kə-mū′nə-kā′, kə-mū′nə-kā′), *n.* [Fr. < *communiquer,* to communicate < L. *communicare,* lit., to make common], an official communication or bulletin, as of military operations for a certain period.

com·mu·nism (kom′yoo-niz'm), *n.* [Fr. *communisme* < L. *communis;* see COMMON], 1. *a*) an economic theory or system of the ownership of all property by the community as a whole. *b*) a theory or system of the ownership of all means of production (and distribution) by the community or society, with all members of the community or society sharing in the work and the products; specifically, such a system as practiced in the Soviet Union since 1917, and later in China, Poland, Czechoslovakia, and other communist countries, theoretically based on the doctrines of Marx, Engels, Lenin, and, latterly, Stalin, characterized by state planning and control of the economy, ruthless suppression of all opposition political parties and all deviation within the Party, and the suppression of individual liberties under a dictatorship; since 1940 expansionist by military action and subversion in Estonia, Latvia, Lithuania, Czechoslovakia, etc. 2. [often C-], *a*) a political movement for establishing such a system. *b*) the doctrines, methods, etc. of the Communist parties. 3. loosely, communalism.

com·mu·nist (kom′yoo-nist), *n.* [Fr. *communiste*], 1. an advocate or supporter of communism. 2. [C-], a member of a Communist party. *adj.* 1. of, characteristic of, or like communism or communists. 2. advocating or supporting communism. Abbreviated **Com.**

com·mu·nis·tic (kom′yoo-nis′tik), *adj.* communist.

com·mu·nis·ti·cal·ly (kom′yoo-nis′ti-k'l-i, kom′yoo-nis′tik-li), *adv.* 1. in a communistic manner. 2. toward communism: as, *communistically* inclined.

Communist International, the Comintern.

Communist Manifesto, a document written in 1848 by Karl Marx and Friedrich Engels, summarizing their theory and program of communism.

Communist Party, a political party based on the principles of communism as developed by Marx, Engels, Lenin, and Stalin: dedicated to the establishment of international communism: abbreviated **C.P.**

com·mu·ni·tar·i·an (kə-mū′nə-târ′i-ən), *n.* a member or advocate of a communistic community.

com·mu·ni·ty (kə-mū′nə-ti), *n.* [*pl.* COMMUNITIES (-tiz)], [ME. *comunete;* OFr. *communité;* L. *communitas,* community, fellowship < *communis;* see COMMON], 1. the people living in the same district, city, etc., under the same laws. 2. the district, city, etc. where they live. 3. a group of animals or plants living together in the same environment. Abbreviated **com.** 4. a group of people living together and having interests, work, etc. in common: as, a college *community.* 5. society; the public. 6. ownership or participation in common: as, *community* of social life. 7. similarity; likeness.

community center, a meeting place where people living in the same community may carry on cultural, recreational, or social activities.

community chest (or **fund**), a fund collected annually in many cities and towns by private contributions and used for various sorts of social welfare work.

community singing, singing by all those present at a gathering.

com·mu·ni·za·tion (kom′yoo-ni-zā′shən, kom′yoo-nī-zā′shən), *n.* a communizing or being communized.

com·mu·nize (kom′yoo-nīz′), *v.t.* [COMMUNIZED (-nīzd′), COMMUNIZING], 1. to subject to communal ownership and control. 2. to cause to become communistic.

com·mut·a·bil·i·ty (kə-mūt′ə-bil′ə-ti), *n.* the quality of being commutable.

com·mut·a·ble (kə-mūt′ə-b'l), *adj.* [L. *commutabilis*], that can be commuted; interchangeable.

com·mu·tate (kom′yoo-tāt′), *v.t.* [COMMUTATED (-id), COMMUTATING], [back-formation < *commutation*], to change the direction of (an electric current); especially, to change (alternating current) to direct current.

com·mu·ta·tion (kom′yoo-tā′shən), *n.* [Fr.; L. *commutatio,* a changing < *commutatus,* pp. of *commutare;* see COMMUTE], 1. an exchange; substitution. 2. the substitution of one kind of payment for another. 3.

the payment made in such substitution. 4. daily or regular travel by train, etc. between an outlying district and one's place of work in the city; use of a commutation ticket. 5. in *electricity*, change of the direction of a current by a commutator. 6. in *law*, a change of a sentence or punishment to one that is less severe.

commutation ticket, a ticket entitling the holder to travel back and forth, as on a railroad, a specified number of times or during a specified period: it gives transportation at a fixed, reduced rate.

com·mu·ta·tive (kə-mū'tə-tiv, kom'yoo-tā'tiv), ***adj.*** of commutation; involving substitution.

commutative law, in *logic*, a law stating that the order in which the elements of certain operations are given is immaterial, as in arithmetic, 6 times 9 is the same as 9 times 6.

com·mu·ta·tor (kom'yoo-tā'tẽr), ***n.*** [< L. *commutatus*, pp. of *commutare* (see COMMUTE); + *-or*], 1. a device for changing the direction of an electric current, especially for changing alternating current to direct current. 2. in a dynamo or motor, a revolving part that collects the current from, or distributes it to, the brushes: see **dynamo,** illus.

com·mute (kə-mūt'), ***v.t.*** [COMMUTED (-id), COMMUTING], [L. *commutare*, to change; *com-*, intens. + *mutare*, to change], 1. to exchange; substitute. 2. to change (an obligation, sentence, punishment, etc.) to one that is less severe. 3. in *electricity*, to commutate. ***v.i.*** 1. to be a substitute. 2. to substitute payment in a lump sum, often reduced, for payment in installments. 3. to travel as a commuter; use a commutation ticket.

com·mut·er (kə-mūt'ẽr), ***n.*** a person who travels daily or regularly by train, etc. between an outlying district and his place of work in the city.

com·mu·tu·al (kə-mū'choo-əl), ***adj.*** mutual.

Com·ne·nus (kom-nē'nəs), ***n.*** [*pl.* COMNENI (-nī)], a member of a ruling family of the Byzantine Empire (1057–1059; 1081–1185), which included Alexius I.

Co·mo (kō'mō), ***n.*** 1. a lake in northern Italy; area, 56 sq. mi. 2. a city on this lake: pop., 82,000.

Co·mores (kô'môr'), ***n.pl.*** the Comoro Islands: the French name.

Com·o·rin, Cape (kom'ə-rin), a cape at the southernmost tip of India.

Com·o·ro Islands (kom'ə-rō'), a group of French islands in the Indian Ocean, between Mozambique and Madagascar: area, 790 sq. mi.; pop., 183,000.

co·mose (kō'mōs), ***adj.*** [L. *comosus* < *coma*, hair], in *botany*, having a coma (tuft of hairs); hairy.

comp., 1. companion. 2. comparative. 3. compare. 4. compiled. 5. compiler. 6. composer. 7. composition. 8. compositor. 9. compound. 10. compounded.

com·pact (kəm-pakt'; *also for adj., and for n. always,* kom'pakt'), ***adj.*** [L. *compactus*, concentrated, pp. of *compingere*, to fasten together < *com-*, with, together + *pangere*, to fix, fasten], 1. closely and firmly packed; dense; solid. 2. taking little space; arranged neatly in a small space. 3. brief; terse. 4. composed (*of*). 5. designating or of a model of automobile that is smaller, lighter, and more economical than other models in the manufacturer's line. ***v.t.*** 1. to pack or join firmly together. 2. to make by joining or putting together. 3. to condense. ***n.*** 1. a small case containing a mirror, face powder, and, sometimes, rouge. 2. a compact car. 3. [L. *compactum* < *compactus*, pp. of *compacisci*, to agree together < same base as *compingere*], an agreement between two or more individuals, states, etc.; covenant. —***SYN.*** see **close.**

‡**com·pa·gnie** (kōn'pá'nyē'), ***n.*** [Fr.], company.

‡**com·pa·ñí·a** (kôm'pä-nyē'ä), ***n.*** [Sp.], company.

com·pan·ion (kəm-pan'yən), ***n.*** [ME. *compainoun;* OFr. *compaignon;* LL. **companio*, lit., bread fellow, messmate < L. *com-*, with + *panis*, bread; cf. LORD], 1. a person who associates with or accompanies another or others; associate; comrade. 2. a person employed to live or travel with another: abbreviated **comp.** 3. [C-], a member of the lowest rank in an order of knighthood. 4. a thing that matches another in sort, color, etc.; one of a set of things. ***v.t.*** to accompany; be with as a companion. —***SYN.*** see **associate.**

com·pan·ion (kəm-pan'yən), ***n.*** [D. *kampagne*, quarterdeck < OFr. *compagne*, steward's room in a galley; It. (*camera della*) *compagna*, (room of the) company, crew; see COMPANY], in *nautical usage*, 1. the covering at the head of a companionway. 2. a companionway.

com·pan·ion·a·bil·i·ty (kəm-pan'yən-ə-bil'ə-ti), ***n.*** the quality of being companionable.

com·pan·ion·a·ble (kəm-pan'yən-ə-b'l), ***adj.*** having the qualities of a good companion; sociable; friendly.

com·pan·ion·a·bly (kəm-pan'yən-ə-bli), ***adv.*** in a companionable manner; sociably.

com·pan·ion·ate (kəm-pan'yən-it), ***adj.*** of or characteristic of companions.

companionate marriage, marriage in which the couple would not have children until they are sure that they wish to stay married: divorce by mutual consent would be permitted before children are born.

companion ladder, a ladder or stairs in a companionway.

com·pan·ion·ship (kəm-pan'yən-ship'), ***n.*** [*companion* (comrade) + *-ship*], 1. the relationship of companions; fellowship. 2. a group of companions. 3. [C-], the lowest rank in an order of knighthood.

com·pan·ion·way (kəm-pan'yən-wā'), ***n.*** [*companion* (of a ship) + *way*], 1. the stairway leading from the deck of a ship to the cabins or space below. 2. the space taken up by this stairway.

com·pa·ny (kum'pə-ni), ***n.*** [*pl.* COMPANIES (-niz)], [ME. & OFr. *compaignie;* LL. **compania*, lit., group sharing bread; see COMPANION (comrade)], 1. companionship; society. 2. a group of people. 3. a group of people who have gathered for social purposes. 4. a habitual associate or associates: as, people are judged by the *company* they keep. 5. a group of people who have associated for some purpose: as, a *company* of entertainers, a business *company*. 6. the partners whose names are not given in the title of a firm: as, John Smith and *Company;* abbreviated **Co., co.** 7. [Colloq.], a guest or guests; visitor or visitors. 8. in *military usage*, a body of troops, the lowest administrative unit, normally under the command of a captain and usually a subdivision of a regiment: equivalent to *battery* (artillery), *flight* (air forces), *troop* (cavalry). 9. in *nautical usage*, the whole crew of a ship, including officers. ***v.t.*** [COMPANIED (-nid), COMPANYING], [Archaic], to accompany; go with as a companion. ***v.i.*** [Archaic], to keep company. —***SYN.*** see **troop.**

bear company, to accompany.

keep company, 1. to associate (*with*). 2. to go together; associate habitually: said especially of a couple intending to get married.

part company, 1. to stop associating (*with*). 2. to separate and go in different directions.

company officer, in *military usage*, any commissioned officer below the rank of major.

company union, an organization of workers in one company, factory, or business establishment, not affiliated with any group of labor unions: the term generally implies control by the employers.

compar., comparative.

com·pa·ra·bil·i·ty (kom'pẽr-ə-bil'ə-ti), ***n.*** the quality or state of being comparable.

com·pa·ra·ble (kom'pẽr-ə-b'l), ***adj.*** [L. *comparabilis*], 1. that can be compared; having characteristics in common. 2. worthy of comparison.

com·pa·ra·bly (kom'pẽr-ə-bli), ***adv.*** 1. in a comparable manner. 2. to a comparable degree.

com·par·a·tive (kəm-par'ə-tiv), ***adj.*** [L. *comparativus*], 1. that compares; involving comparison as a method, especially in a branch of study: as, *comparative* anatomy deals with the anatomical similarities and differences in man and the lower animals. 2. estimated by comparison with something else; relative: as, *comparative* happiness. 3. in *grammar*, designating the second degree of comparison of adjectives and adverbs; expressing a greater degree of a quality than that expressed in the positive degree. ***n.*** in *grammar*, 1. the comparative degree: as, *prettier* and *more beautiful* are the *comparatives* of *pretty* and *beautiful*. 2. an adjective or adverb in the comparative degree. Abbreviated **comp., compar.**

comparative linguistics, the branch of linguistics which discovers and describes genetic relationships between languages.

com·par·a·tive·ly (kəm-par'ə-tiv-li), ***adv.*** 1. in a comparative manner. 2. by comparison; relatively.

com·pa·ra·tor (kom'pə-rā'tẽr), ***n.*** any of various instruments for comparing some measurement or other aspect of something, as length, brightness, etc., with that of a fixed standard.

com·pare (kəm-pâr'), ***v.t.*** [COMPARED (-pârd'), COMPARING], [Fr. *comparer;* L. *comparare* < *com-*, with + *par*, equal; cf. COMPEER], 1. to regard as similar; liken (*to*). 2. to examine in order to observe or discover similarities or differences (often followed by *with*): abbreviated **cp., comp.** (see also **cf.**). 3. in *grammar*, to form the positive, comparative, and superlative degrees of (an adjective or adverb). ***v.i.*** to be worthy of comparison (*with*); be regarded as similar or equal. ***n.*** [Poetic], comparison.

beyond (or **past** or **without**) **compare,** without equal; incomparably good, bad, great, etc.

SYN.—**compare** refers to a literal or figurative putting together in order to note points of resemblance and difference, and implies the weighing of parallel features for relative values (to *compare* Shakespeare with Schiller); **contrast** implies a comparing for the purpose of emphasizing differences (to *contrast* farm life with city life); **collate** implies detailed, critical comparison, specifically of different versions of the same text.

com·par·i·son (kəm-par'ə-s'n), ***n.*** [ME.; OFr. *comparaisun;* L. *comparatio* < pp. of *comparare*], 1. a comparing or being compared; estimation of similarities and differences. 2. the quality of being capable or worthy of comparison; similarity; likeness. 3. in *grammar*, the modification of an adjective or adverb to show the three degrees (positive, comparative, and superlative), as *long, longer, longest; good, better, best; slowly, more slowly, most slowly*. 4. in *rhetoric*, a figure of speech, as a simile, by which things are compared.

in comparison with, compared with.

no comparison between, no basis for comparison between: implying great superiority of one person or thing to another.

com·part (kəm-pärt'), ***v.t.*** [< OFr. or L.; OFr. *compartir;* L. *compartiri* < *com-*, intens. + *partiri, partire;* see PART, *v.*], to divide into parts; subdivide; partition.

com·part·ment (kəm-pärt'mənt), ***n.*** [Fr. *compartiment;* It. *compartimento* < L. *com-*, with + *partiri*, to divide < *pars*, a part], 1. any of the divisions into which a space is partitioned off. 2. a small, private section of a railroad car with sleeping accommodations.

com·pass (kum'pəs), ***v.t.*** [ME. *compassen, cumpassen;* OFr. *compasser*, to go around; LL. **compassare* < L. *com-*, together + *passus*, a step], 1. to go round; make a circuit of. 2. to surround completely; form a circle around. 3. to grasp mentally; understand; comprehend. 4. to achieve; accomplish; gain: as, he was unable to *compass* his ends. 5. [< the *n.*, 1], to plan; plot; contrive (something harmful). 6. [Obs.], to curve. ***n.*** [ME. *compas, cumpas*, a circle, compass; OFr. *compas*, a circle; prob. < the *v.*], 1. *often pl.* an instrument consisting of two pointed legs connected at one end by a pivot, used for drawing arcs or circles and taking measurements. 2. a boundary; circumference. 3. an enclosed area; hence, 4. range; extent; reach; scope. 5. any of various instruments for showing direction, especially one consisting of a magnetic needle swinging freely on a pivot and pointing to the magnetic north. 6. [Archaic], a circuit; course. 7. in *music*, the range of a voice or instrument, from its lowest to its highest tone. ***adj.*** round; circular or semicircular. —***SYN.*** see **range.**

DRAWING COMPASS

MARINER'S COMPASS

com·pass·a·ble (kum'pəs-ə-b'l), ***adj.*** that can be compassed; attainable.

compass card, the circular card over which the needle of a compass swings, marked with the points of direction and, often, the degrees of the circle.

com·pass·es (kum'pəs-iz), ***n. pl.*** a compass (sense 1).

com·pas·sion (kəm-pash'ən), ***n.*** [ME.; OFr.; LL. *compassio*, sympathy < **compassus*, pp. of *compati*, to feel pity; L. *com-*, together + *pati*, to suffer], sorrow for the sufferings or trouble of another or others, with the urge to help; pity; deep sympathy. —***SYN.*** see **pity.**

com·pas·sion·ate (kəm-pash'ən-it), ***adj.*** feeling or showing compassion; pitying; sympathizing deeply. ***v.t.*** (kəm-pash'ən-āt'), [COMPASSIONATED (-id), COMPASSIONATING], to pity. —***SYN.*** see **tender.**

compass plant, any of various North American plants, including the rosinweed, with large leaves lying in a north-and-south direction.

compass saw, a handsaw with a narrow, tapering blade for cutting curves.

com·pat·i·bil·i·ty (kəm-pat'ə-bil'ə-ti), ***n.*** [Fr. *compatibilité*], the quality of being compatible.

com·pat·i·ble (kəm-pat'ə-b'l), ***adj.*** [Fr.; LL. *compatibilis* < *compati*; see COMPASSION], capable of living together harmoniously or getting along well together; in agreement; congruous (often followed by *with*).

com·pat·i·bly (kəm-pat'ə-bli), ***adv.*** in a compatible manner.

com·pa·tri·ot (kəm-pā'tri-ət, kəm-pat'ri-ət), ***n.*** [Fr. *compatriote;* LL. *compatriota* < L. *com-*, with + LL. *patriota;* see PATRIOT], a fellow countryman. ***adj.*** of the same country.

com·pa·tri·ot·ism (kəm-pā'tri-ət-iz'm, kəm-pat'ri-ət-iz'm), ***n.*** the fact or state of being compatriots.

com·peer (kəm-pêr', kom'pêr), ***n.*** [ME. *compeer, comper;* OFr. *compair;* L. *compar*, equal; *com-*, with + *par*, equal; cf. COMPARE], 1. a person of the same rank or status; equal; peer. 2. a companion; comrade.

com·pel (kəm-pel'), ***v.t.*** [COMPELLED (-peld'), COMPELLING], [ME. *compellen;* OFr. *compellir;* L. *compellere; com-*, together + *pellere*, to drive; cf. COMPULSION], 1. to force; constrain. 2. to get or bring about by force. 3. to gather or drive together by force, as a flock. 4. to cause to yield; overpower. —***SYN.*** see **force.**

com·pel·la·tion (kom'pə-lā'shən), ***n.*** [L. *compellatio* < *compellare*, to accost, address], 1. an addressing or calling upon by a name or title. 2. the name or title so used; appellation.

com·pend (kom'pend), ***n.*** a compendium.

com·pen·di·ous (kəm-pen'di-əs), ***adj.*** [L. *compendiosus*, short; see COMPENDIUM], containing all the essentials in a brief form; concise and comprehensive.

com·pen·di·um (kəm-pen'di-əm), ***n.*** [*pl.* COMPENDIUMS (-əmz), COMPENDIA (-ə)], [L., a weighing together, abridgment < *compendere*, to weigh together; *com-*, together + *pendere*, to weigh], a summary or abstract containing the essential information in a brief form; concise, comprehensive treatise.

com·pen·sa·ble (kəm-pen'sə-b'l), ***adj.*** [Fr.; see COMPENSATE], entitling to compensation, as an injury.

com·pen·sate (kom'pən-sāt'), ***v.t.*** [COMPENSATED (-id), COMPENSATING], [< L. *compensatus*, pp. of *compensare*, to weigh together, weigh one thing against another; *com-*, with + *pensare*, freq. of *pendere*, to weigh], 1. to make up for; be a counterbalance to in weight, force, etc. 2. to make equivalent return to; recompense; pay: as, the government *compensated* the owners for the land taken from them. 3. in *mechanics*, to counteract or make allowance for (a variation). 4. in *psychology*, to disguise (an undesired trait) by exaggerating a desired or socially approved one. ***v.i.*** to make compensation; make amends. —***SYN.*** see **pay.**

com·pen·sa·tion (kom'pən-sā'shən), ***n.*** [L. *compensatio*], 1. a compensating or being compensated. 2. an instance or means of this. 3. anything given as an equivalent, or to make amends for a loss, damage, etc.; recompense; remuneration; pay. 4. in *biology*, the counterbalancing of a defect in the structure or function of a part by a greater activity or development of another or other parts. 5. in *psychology*, an attempt to disguise an undesired trait by exaggerating a desired or socially approved trait.

com·pen·sa·tion·al (kom'pən-sā'shən-'l), ***adj.*** of or as compensation.

compensation balance, a balance wheel in a watch or clock, for counteracting variations in temperature.

com·pen·sa·tive (kom'pən-sā'tiv, kəm-pen'sə-tiv), ***adj.*** compensating or serving to compensate.

com·pen·sa·tor (kom'pən-sā'tẽr), ***n.*** 1. a person or thing that compensates. 2. any of various mechanical or electrical devices used to equalize, counteract, or correct deviations in speed, direction, flow, etc.

com·pen·sa·to·ry (kəm-pen'sə-tôr'i, kəm-pen'sə-tō'ri), ***adj.*** compensating or serving to compensate.

com·pete (kəm-pēt'), ***v.i.*** [COMPETED (-id), COMPETING], [L. *competere*, to strive together for, be qualified; *com-*, together + *petere*, to seek], 1. to enter into or be in rivalry; strive in opposition; contend; vie. 2. to enter or participate (*in* a contest, athletic meet, etc.).

com·pe·tence (kom'pə-təns), ***n.*** [Fr. *compétence;* L. *competentia*, a meeting, agreement < *competens*, ppr. of *competere;* see COMPETE], 1. sufficient means for one's needs or for a comfortable existence. 2. ability; skill; fitness. 3. in *law*, legal qualification, power, or jurisdiction.

com·pe·ten·cy (kom'pə-tən-si), ***n.*** competence.

com·pe·tent (kom'pə-tənt), ***adj.*** [Fr. *compétent;* L. *competens*, ppr. of *competere;* see COMPETE], 1. well qualified; capable; fit: as, a *competent* doctor. 2. sufficient; adequate: as, a *competent* understanding of law. 3. permissible or properly belonging (with *to*). 4. in *law*, legally qualified, authorized, or fit. —***SYN.*** see **able.**

com·pe·ti·tion (kom'pə-tish'ən), ***n.*** [L. *competitio*], 1. a competing; rivalry. 2. a contest; match. 3. official participation in organized sport. 4. opposition, or effective opposition, in a contest or match. 5. business rivalry; competing for customers or markets.

SYN.—**competition** denotes a striving for the same object, position, prize, etc., usually in accordance with certain fixed rules; **rivalry** implies keen competition between opponents more or less evenly matched, and, unqualified, it often suggests unfriendliness or even hostility; **emulation** implies endeavor to equal or surpass in achievement, character, etc. another, usually one greatly admired.

com·pet·i·tive (kəm-pet'ə-tiv), ***adj.*** of or involving competition; based on or determined by competition.

com·pet·i·tor (kəm-pet'ə-tẽr), ***n.*** [L.], a person who competes, as a business rival.

com·pet·i·to·ry (kəm-pet'ə-tôr'i, kəm-pet'ə-tō'ri), ***adj.*** competitive.

Com·piègne (kōn'pyen'y'), ***n.*** a town in northern France: armistices between the Allies and Germany (1918) and France and Germany (1940) signed here.

com·pi·la·tion (kom'p'l-ā'shən, kom'pi-lā'shən), ***n.*** [Fr.; L. *compilatio*, a pillaging; hence collection of documents < *compilatus*, pp. of *compilare*], 1. a compiling. 2. something compiled, as a book, report, etc.

com·pile (kəm-pīl'), ***v.t.*** [COMPILED (-pīld'), COMPILING], [ME. *compilen;* OFr. *compiler;* L. *compilare*, to snatch together, plunder; *com-*, together + *pilare*, to compress, ram down], 1. to gather and put together (literary materials, facts, etc.) in an orderly form. 2. to compose (a book, etc.) by putting together materials gathered from various sources.

com·pla·cence (kəm-plā's'ns), ***n.*** complacency.

com·pla·cen·cy (kəm-plā's'n-si), ***n.*** [L. *complacens*, ppr.

of *complacere*, to be very pleasing; *com-*, with + *placere*, to please], 1. quiet satisfaction; contentment. 2. self-satisfaction; smugness.

com·pla·cent (kəm-plā's'nt), ***adj.*** [L. *complacens;* see COMPLACENCY], 1. self-satisfied; smug. 2. complaisant.

com·plain (kəm-plān'), ***v.i.*** [ME. *compleinen;* OFr. *complaindre;* LL. *complangere*, orig., to beat the breast; L. *com-*, with + *plangere*, to strike], 1. to express pain, dissatisfaction, etc. 2. to find fault; declare annoyance. 3. to make an accusation; bring a formal charge.

com·plain·ant (kəm-plān'ənt), ***n.*** [Anglo-Fr., ppr.], 1. a person who complains. 2. in *law*, a person who files a charge or makes the complaint in court; plaintiff.

com·plaint (kəm-plānt'), ***n.*** [ME. & OFr. *complainte* < *complaindre*], 1. a complaining; utterance of pain, discomfort, dissatisfaction, etc.; finding fault. 2. a subject or cause for complaining; grievance; hence, 3. an illness; ailment. 4. in *law*, a formal charge or accusation.

com·plai·sance (kəm-plā'z'ns, kəm-plā's'ns, kom'pli-zans'), ***n.*** [Fr. < *complaire;* L. *complacere;* see COMPLACENCY], 1. willingness to please; disposition to be obliging and agreeable; politeness; courtesy; compliance. 2. an act or instance of this.

com·plai·sant (kəm-plā'z'nt, kəm-plā's'nt, kom'pli-zant'), ***adj.*** [Fr., ppr. of *complaire;* see COMPLAISANCE], willing to please; obliging; polite; compliant.

com·plect (kəm-plekt'), ***v.t.*** [L. *complecti;* see COMPLEX], to twine together; interweave.

com·plect·ed (kəm-plek'tid), ***adj.*** [altered < *complexioned*], [Dial. or Colloq.], complexioned.

com·ple·ment (kom'plə-mənt), ***n.*** [L. *complementum*, that which fills up or completes < *complere;* see COMPLETE], 1. that which completes or brings to perfection. 2. the amount or number needed to fill or complete. 3. an entirety; complete set. 4. something added to complete a whole; either of two parts that complete each other. 5. in *grammar*, a word or group of words completing a predication. Examples: *president* in *elect him president* (*objective complement*), *pretty* in *she was pretty* (*predicate complement*). 6. in *immunology*, a protein in the blood or lymph acting with immune bodies to destroy bacteria. 7. in *mathematics*, the number of degrees that must be added to a given angle or arc to make it equal 90 degrees. 8. in *music*, the difference between a given interval and the complete octave. 9. in *nautical usage*, the full crew of officers and men assigned to a ship. ***v.t.*** (kom'plə-ment'), to make complete; be a complement to.

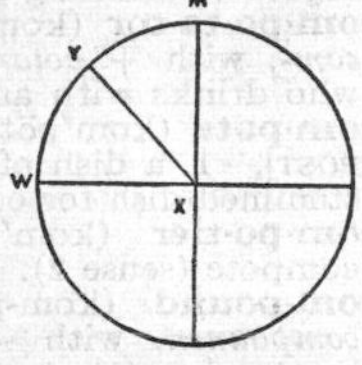

COMPLEMENT
arc YM, complement of arc WY; angle YXM, complement of angle WXY

com·ple·men·tal (kom'plə-men't'l), ***adj.*** complementary.

com·ple·men·ta·ry (kom'plə-men'tēr-i), ***adj.*** 1. acting as a complement; completing. 2. mutually making up what is lacking.

complementary angle, the angle that is the complement of another, specified angle.

complementary colors, any two colors of the spectrum that combine to form white or whitish light: if a disk colored half yellow and half blue is rotated rapidly, it looks white or gray.

com·plete (kəm-plēt'), ***adj.*** [ME. *compleet;* OFr. *complet;* L. *completus*, pp. of *complere*, to fill up, complete; *com-*, intens. + *plere*, to fill], 1. lacking none of the parts; full; whole; entire. 2. ended; finished; concluded. 3. thorough; perfect. 4. [Archaic], accomplished; skilled; consummate. ***v.t.*** [COMPLETED (-id), COMPLETING], 1. to end; finish; conclude. 2. to make entire, thorough, or perfect.

SYN.*—complete** implies inclusion of all that is needed for the integrity, perfection, or fulfillment of something (a *complete* set, *complete* control); **full** implies the inclusion of all that is needed (a *full* dozen) or all that can be held, achieved, etc. (in *full* bloom); **total** implies an adding together of everything without exception (*total* number) and is, in general applications, equivalent to **complete** (*total* abstinence); **whole** and **entire** imply unbroken unity, stressing that not a single part, individual, instance, etc. has been omitted or diminished (the *whole* student body, one's *entire* attention); **intact** is applied to that which remains whole after passing through an experience that might have impaired it (the tornado left the barn *intact*). See also **close.**—ANT.*** partial, defective.

com·plete·ly (kəm-plēt'li), ***adv.*** entirely; wholly; thoroughly; fully; altogether.

com·ple·tion (kəm-plē'shən), ***n.*** [LL. *completio*], 1. a completing; finishing. 2. the state of being completed.

com·plex (kəm-pleks'; *also, and for n. always,* kom'pleks), ***adj.*** [LL., closely connected; L. *complexus*, lit., a weaving or twining together, pp. of *complecti*, to encircle, embrace < *com-*, with + *plectere*, to weave, braid], 1. consisting of two or more related parts. 2. involved; complicated; intricate; not simple. ***n.*** 1. a complex whole. 2. in *psychoanalysis*, *a)* a group of emotional attitudes associated with a particular object, activity, etc. and remaining partly unconscious but strongly influencing the individual's behavior. *b)* popularly, an exaggerated dislike or fear; obsession.

SYN.*—complex** refers to that which is made up of many elaborately interrelated or interconnected parts, so that much study or knowledge is needed to understand or operate it (a *complex* mechanism); **complicated** is applied to that which is highly complex and hence very difficult to analyze, solve, or understand (a *complicated* problem); **intricate** specifically suggests a perplexingly elaborate interweaving of parts that is difficult to follow (an *intricate* maze); **involved**, in this connection, is applied to situations, ideas, etc. whose parts are thought of as intertwining in complicated, often disordered, fashion (an *involved* argument).—ANT.*** simple.

complex fraction, a fraction with a fraction in its numerator or denominator, or in both, as, $\frac{1\,{}^3/_8}{6\,{}^1/_4}$: also called *compound fraction.*

com·plex·ion (kəm-plek'shən), ***n.*** [ME. *complexioun;* OFr. *complexion*, combination of humors, hence constitution, temperament; L. *complexio*, combination, connection < *complexus;* see COMPLEX], 1. originally, the combination of the four humors, or the qualities of cold, heat, dryness, and moisture, in certain proportions believed to determine the temperament and constitution of the body; hence, 2. the temperament or constitution. 3. the color, texture, and general appearance of the skin, especially of the face. 4. general appearance; character; nature; aspect.

com·plex·ioned (kəm-plek'shənd), ***adj.*** having a (specified) complexion: used in hyphenated compounds, as, *light-complexioned.*

com·plex·i·ty (kəm-plek'sə-ti), ***n.*** 1. the condition or quality of being complex. 2. [*pl.* COMPLEXITIES (-tiz)], anything complex or intricate; complication.

complex sentence, a sentence consisting of a main clause and one or more subordinate clauses (e.g., I would go home if I didn't have to work.).

com·pli·a·ble (kəm-plī'ə-b'l), ***adj.*** compliant.

com·pli·a·bly (kəm-plī'ə-bli), ***adv.*** in a compliable manner; in compliance.

com·pli·ance (kəm-plī'əns), ***n.*** 1. a complying, or giving in to a request, wish, demand, etc.; acquiescence. 2. a tendency to give in to others.
in compliance with, in accordance with.

com·pli·an·cy (kəm-plī'ən-si), ***n.*** compliance.

com·pli·ant (kəm-plī'ənt), ***adj.*** complying or tending to comply; yielding; submissive. —***SYN.*** see **obedient.**

com·pli·ca·cy (kom'plə-kə-si), ***n.*** 1. the condition or quality of being complicated. 2. [*pl.* COMPLICACIES (-siz)], anything complicated; complication.

com·pli·cate (kom'plə-kāt'), ***v.t. & v.i.*** [COMPLICATED (-id), COMPLICATING], [< L. *complicatus*, pp. of *complicare*, to fold together; *com-*, together + *plicare*, to fold, weave], 1. to make or become intricate, difficult, or involved. 2. to twist together. ***adj.*** (kom'plə-kit), 1. [Archaic], complicated. 2. in *biology*, folded lengthwise, as some leaves or insect's wings.

com·pli·cat·ed (kom'plə-kāt'id), ***adj.*** made up of parts intricately involved or combined; hard to untangle, solve, understand, analyze, etc. —***SYN.*** see **complex.**

com·pli·ca·tion (kom'plə-kā'shən), ***n.*** [L. *complicatio*, a folding together, multiplication], 1. a complicating. 2. a complicated condition or structure; complex, involved, or confused relationship of parts. 3. a complicating factor, as in the plot of a story or play. 4. in *medicine*, a disease or abnormal condition that occurs during another disease.

com·plice (kom'plis), ***n.*** [Fr.; L. *complex*, a participant, confederate < *complicare;* see COMPLICATE], [Archaic], an accomplice; associate.

com·plic·i·ty (kəm-plis'ə-ti), ***n.*** [*pl.* COMPLICITIES (-tiz)], [Fr. *complicité* < L. *complex*, *complicis;* see COMPLEX], 1. partnership in wrongdoing; fact or state of being an accomplice. 2. complexity.

com·pli·er (kəm-plī'ēr), ***n.*** a person who complies.

com·pli·ment (kom'plə-mənt), ***n.*** [Fr.; It. *complimento;* L. *complementum*, lit., completion, "filling up" (of an act of courtesy); see COMPLEMENT], 1. a formal act or expression of courtesy or respect. 2. something said in admiration or praise. 3. *pl.* courteous greetings; respects: as, please accept this free offer with our *compliments.* 4. [Archaic & Dial.], a gift given for services. ***v.t.*** (kom'plə-ment'), 1. to pay a compliment or compliments to; congratulate. 2. to present something to (a person) as an act of politeness or respect.

com·pli·men·ta·ry (kom'plə-men'tēr-i), ***adj.*** 1. paying or containing a compliment; expressing courtesy, respect, admiration, or praise. 2. given free as a courtesy or in return for a favor: as, a *complimentary* ticket.

com·plin (kom'plin), ***n.*** [ME. *complin*, *compli;* OFr. *complie;* LL. *completa*, complin < fem. of L. *completus;* see COMPLETE], in *ecclesiastical usage*, 1. the last service of the day, generally just after vespers. 2. the hour when this is held; last of the seven canonical hours.

com·pline (kom′plin, kom′plīn), *n.* complin.

com·plot (kom′plot), *n.* [Fr.; OFr. *complot, complote,* agreement (earlier, a crowd, pressing together) < **comploter* < **compeloter,* to form into a ball < *com-*, together + *pelote,* a ball, ult. < L. *pila,* a ball], a plotting together; conspiracy. *v.t. & v.i.* (kəm-plot′), [Fr. *comploter* < the *n.*], to plot together; conspire.

com·ply (kəm-plī′), *v.i.* [COMPLIED (-plīd′), COMPLYING], [It. *complire;* Sp. *cumplir, complir;* L. *complere;* see COMPLETE], 1. to act in accordance with a request, demand, order, rule, etc.: as, they *complied* with the command. 2. [Obs.], to be formally polite.

com·po (kom′pō), *n.* [*pl.* COMPOS (-pōz)], [< *compo*-sition], any of various composite substances, such as mortar or plaster, made by combining ingredients.

com·po·nent (kəm-pō′nənt), *adj.* [L. *componens,* ppr. of *componere,* to put together, compose; *com-*, together + *ponere,* to put, place], serving as one of the parts of a whole; constituent. *n.* 1. a part; constituent; ingredient. 2. in *mechanics,* one of the elements into which a vector quantity, as force, velocity, etc., may be resolved on analysis. —*SYN.* see **element.**

com·po·ny (kəm-pō′ni), *adj.* [< OFr. *componné;* prob. < L. *componere,* to compose, comprise], in *heraldry,* consisting of a single row of squares of two alternate tinctures, generally a metal, as gold, and some color.

com·port (kəm-pôrt′, kəm-pōrt′), *v.t.* [Fr. *comporter,* to allow, admit of; L. *comportare,* to bring together; *com-*, together + *portare,* to bring, carry], to behave or conduct (oneself) in a specified manner. *v.i.* to agree, harmonize, or accord (*with*). *n.* [Obs.], comportment. —*SYN.* see **behave.**

com·port·ment (kəm-pôrt′mənt, kəm-pōrt′mənt), *n.* [Fr. *comportement;* see COMPORT], behavior; deportment.

com·pose (kəm-pōz′), *v.t.* [COMPOSED (-pōzd′), COMPOSING], [Fr. *composer; com-*, with + *poser,* to place; meaning influenced by L. *componere;* see COMPOSITE], 1. to form in combination; make up; constitute: as, mortar is *composed* of lime, sand, and water. 2. to put together; put in proper order or form; hence, 3. to create (an original musical or literary work). 4. to adjust; settle; reconcile: as, their differences were *composed* peaceably. 5. to put (oneself, one's mind, etc.) in a state of tranquillity or repose; calm; allay. 6. in *printing,* to set (type or matter to be printed). *v.i.* 1. to create musical or literary works. 2. to set type.

com·posed (kəm-pōzd′), *adj.* [pp. of *compose*], calm; tranquil; undisturbed; self-possessed. —*SYN.* see **cool.**

com·pos·ed·ly (kəm-pōz′id-li), *adv.* in a composed manner; calmly.

com·pos·er (kəm-pōz′ẽr), *n.* a person who composes, especially one who composes music: abbreviated **comp.**

composing room, a room in which typesetting is done.

composing stick, in *printing,* a metal tray held in one hand by a compositor, in which he arranges the type into words.

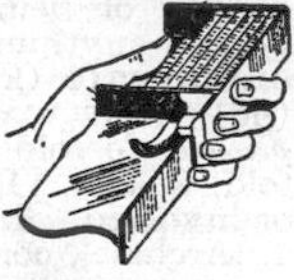

COMPOSING STICK

com·pos·ite (kəm-poz′it), *adj.* [L. *compositus,* pp. of *componere,* to put together; *com-*, together + *ponere,* to put], 1. formed of distinct parts; compound. 2. [C-], in *architecture,* designating one of the classic orders, which combines the scroll-like ornaments of the Ionic capital with the capital of the Corinthian. 3. in *botany,* of a large group of plants having flower heads that consist of a large number of small flowers in clusters surrounded by small leaves: the daisy, aster, dandelion, and sunflower belong to this group. *n.* 1. a thing of distinct parts; compound. 2. in *botany,* a composite plant.

COMPOSITE CAPITAL

composite number, a number that can be divided without a remainder by some number other than itself or 1: distinguished from *prime number.*

composite photograph, a photograph made by superimposing one or more photographs on another, either on a single negative or on one print from several negatives.

COMPOSITE FLOWER (of wild sunflower)

com·po·si·tion (kom′pə-zish′ən), *n.* [ME.; OFr.; L. *compositio,* a putting together, proper arrangement of words < *compositus;* see COMPOSITE], 1. a composing; putting together of a whole by the combination of parts. 2. the putting together of words; art of writing prose or poetry. 3. the creation of musical works. 4. the make-up of a thing; aggregate of ingredients and manner of their combination; constitution. 5. that which is composed. 6. a mixture of various ingredients. 7. a work of music, literature, or art. 8. an exercise in writing done as schoolwork. 9. an arrangement of the parts of a work of art so as to form a unified, harmonious whole. 10. an agreement; settlement, often by compromise. 11. in *law,* a settlement by which a potential bankrupt agrees to pay his creditors part of their claim. 12. in *linguistics,* the device or process of forming compounds from separate words: often distinguished from *affixation.* 13. in *printing,* typesetting. Abbreviated **comp.**

composition of forces, in *mechanics,* the process of finding a force (the *resultant*) whose effect will equal that of two or more given forces (the *components*).

com·pos·i·tor (kəm-poz′i-tẽr), *n.* [L., arranger, disposer; see COMPOSITE], a person who sets type; typesetter.

com·pos·i·to·ri·al (kəm-poz′i-tôr′i-əl, kəm-poz′i-tō′ri-əl), *adj.* having to do with compositors or composers.

com·pos men·tis (kom′pəs men′tis), [L.], in *law,* of sound mind; sane.

com·post (kom′pōst), *n.* [OFr. *composte, compote,* condiment, pickle < L. *compositus;* see COMPOSITE], 1. a composition; compound. 2. a mixture of decomposing vegetable refuse, manure, etc. for fertilizing the soil.

com·po·sure (kəm-pō′zhẽr), *n.* [see COMPOSE], calmness; tranquillity; self-possession. —*SYN.* see **equanimity.**

com·po·ta·tion (kom′pō-tā′shən), *n.* [L. *compotatio* < *com-*, with + *potatus,* pp. of *potare,* to drink], a drinking together; drinking bout.

com·po·ta·tor (kom′pō-tā′tẽr), *n.* [LL. < *compotare; com-*, with + *potare,* to drink; cf. POTION], a person who drinks with another; fellow tippler.

com·pote (kom′pōt; Fr. kōn′pôt′), *n.* [Fr.; see COMPOST], 1. a dish of stewed fruits in sirup. 2. a long-stemmed dish for candy, fruit, etc.

com·po·tier (kom′pə-têr′; Fr. kōn′pô′tyā′), *n.* a compote (sense 2).

com·pound (kom-pound′, kəm-pound′), *v.t.* [ME. *compounen,* with *-d* after *expound;* OFr. *componre, compondre,* to arrange, direct; L. *componere,* to put together; *com-*, together + *ponere,* to put, place], 1. to mix; combine. 2. to make by combining parts or elements. 3. to settle by mutual agreement; compromise. 4. to settle (a debt) by a compromise payment of less than the total claim. 5. to compute (interest) on the sum of the principal and the accumulated interest which has accrued at regular intervals: as, interest *compounded* semiannually. 6. in *pharmacy,* to mix (substances) according to prescription. *v.i.* 1. to agree. 2. to compromise with a creditor. *adj.* (kom′pound, kom-pound′), [< ME. pp.], made up of two or more parts or elements. *n.* (kom′pound), 1. a thing formed by the mixture or combination of two or more parts or elements. 2. a substance containing two or more elements combined in fixed proportions: distinguished from *mixture* in that the constituents of a compound lose their individual characteristics and the compound has new characteristics. 3. a word composed of two or more other words (*free morphemes*), whether hyphenated or not: English compounds are distinguished from phrases by reduced stress on one of the elements (e.g., *black′-bird′, black′ bird′*) and by reduced pause between the elements (*internal open juncture*); many words conventionally written as phrases are actually compounds and may be treated as such (e.g., *ice′ cream′, ice′cream′, push′ but′ton, push′but′ton*). Abbreviated **comp., cpd.**

compound a felony (or **crime**), [< *v.t.,* 3], to agree, for payment, not to inform about or prosecute for a felony (or crime): it is an illegal act.

com·pound (kom′pound), *n.* [Malay *kampuṅ,* enclosure], 1. in the Orient, an enclosed space with a building or group of buildings in it, especially if occupied by foreigners. 2. any similar enclosed space, as for the temporary confinement of prisoners of war.

compound engine, an engine in which the steam is expanded under progressively lower pressures from cylinder to cylinder, to avoid excessive loss of steam by condensation.

compound eye, an eye made up of numerous simple eyes (*ocelli*), as in insects and crustaceans.

compound flower, the flower head of a composite plant.

compound fraction, a complex fraction.

compound fracture, a fracture in which the broken bone has pierced the skin.

compound interest, interest paid on both the principal and the accumulated unpaid interest: distinguished from *simple interest.*

compound interval, in *music,* any interval greater than an octave.

compound leaf, a leaf divided into two or more leaflets with a common leafstalk.

compound number, a quantity expressed in two or more sorts of related units (e.g., 4 ft., 7 in.; 1 lb., 3 oz.).

compound sentence, a sentence consisting of two or more independent, co-ordinate clauses (e.g., I came, I saw, I conquered.).

com·pra·dor, com·pra·dore (kom′prə-dôr′, kom′prə-dôr′), *n.* [Port. *comprador*, buyer], in China and some other Eastern countries, a native agent for a foreign business, who has charge over the native workers, etc.

com·pre·hend (kom′pri-hend′), *v.t.* [ME. *comprehenden;* L. *comprehendere; com-*, with + *prehendere* or *prendere*, to catch hold of, seize; see PREHENSILE], 1. to grasp mentally; understand. 2. to include; take in; comprise. 3. to include by implication; imply. —*SYN.* see **include, understand.**

com·pre·hen·si·bil·i·ty (kom′pri-hen′sə-bil′ə-ti), *n.* the quality or fact of being comprehensible.

com·pre·hen·si·ble (kom′pri-hen′sə-b'l), *adj.* [L. *comprehensibilis*], that can be comprehended; intelligible.

com·pre·hen·si·bly (kom′pri-hen′sə-bli), *adv.* in a comprehensible manner; within comprehension.

com·pre·hen·sion (kom′pri-hen′shən), *n.* [L. *comprehensio* < *comprehensus*, pp. of *comprehendere;* see COMPREHEND], 1. an including; comprising; inclusiveness. 2. the act of or capacity for understanding.

com·pre·hen·sive (kom′pri-hen′siv), *adj.* [LL. *comprehensivus*], 1. including much; inclusive: as, a *comprehensive* survey. 2. able to comprehend well.

com·press (kəm-pres′; *for n.*, kom′pres), *v.t.* [OFr. *compresser;* LL. *compressare* < L. *compressus*, pp. of *comprimere*, to press together, squeeze < *com-*, together + *premere*, to press], to press together; make more compact by or as by pressure. *n.* 1. a pad of folded cloth applied to a part of the body to exert pressure. 2. such a pad medicated or dipped in hot or cold water and used to lessen soreness or inflammation. 3. a machine for pressing cotton into bales. —*SYN.* see **contract.**

com·pressed (kəm-prest′), *adj.* [pp. of *compress*], 1. pressed together; made more compact by pressure. 2. in *botany*, flattened lengthwise, as the stalk of an aspen leaf. 3. in *zoology*, flattened from side to side, as the body of the flounder or other flatfish.

compressed air, air reduced in volume by pressure, held in a container: the force with which it expands when released is used to operate various mechanisms.

com·press·i·bil·i·ty (kəm-pres′ə-bil′ə-ti), *n.* the quality or state of being compressible.

com·press·i·ble (kəm-pres′ə-b'l), *adj.* that can be compressed.

com·pres·sion (kəm-presh′ən), *n.* [Fr.; L. *compressio*], 1. a compressing or being compressed. 2. in *mechanics*, the compressing, or the degree of compressing, of a working fluid in an engine, as of steam in the cylinder of a steam engine after the exhaust valve is closed, or of gas in an internal-combustion engine just before ignition.

com·pres·sive (kəm-pres′iv), *adj.* compressing or tending to compress.

com·pres·sor (kəm-pres′ẽr), *n.* [L.], 1. a person or thing that compresses. 2. a muscle that compresses a part. 3. a machine for compressing air, gas, etc. 4. a surgical instrument for compressing a part of the body.

com·pres·sure (kəm-presh′ẽr), *n.* compression.

com·pris·a·ble, com·priz·a·ble (kəm-prīz′ə-b'l), *adj.* that can be comprised.

com·pris·al, com·priz·al (kəm-prīz′'l), *n.* 1. a comprising. 2. a summary; abstract.

com·prise (kəm-prīz′), *v.t.* [COMPRISED (-prīzd′), COMPRISING], [< Fr. *compris*, pp. of *comprendre;* see COMPREHEND], 1. to include; contain. 2. to consist of; be composed of. Also spelled **comprize.** —*SYN.* see **include.**

com·pro·mise (kom′prə-mīz′), *n.* [Fr. *compromis;* LL. *compromissum*, a compromise, mutual promise < L. *compromissus*, pp. of *compromittere*, to make a mutual promise, abide by the decision of an arbiter; *com-*, together + *promittere*, to promise; see PROMISE], 1. a settlement in which each side gives up some demands or makes concessions. 2. an adjustment of opposing principles, systems, etc., in which part of each is given up. 3. the result of such an adjustment or settlement. 4. something midway between different things. 5. a laying open to danger, suspicion, or disrepute: as, a *compromise* of one's good name. *v.t.* [COMPROMISED (-mīzd′), COMPROMISING], 1. to settle or adjust by concessions on both sides. 2. to lay open to danger, suspicion, or disrepute; endanger the interests of. 3. to surrender or give up (one's interests, principles, etc.). *v.i.* to make a compromise or compromises.

com·pro·mis·er (kom′prə-mīz′ẽr), *n.* a person who compromises or believes in compromise.

comp·tom·e·ter (komp-tom′ə-tẽr), *n.* [*compto-* < Fr. *compter;* L. *computare* (see COMPUTE); + *-meter*], a machine for doing addition, subtraction, division, etc. mechanically: a trade-mark (**Comptometer**).

Comp·ton (komp′tən), *n.* a city in southwestern California, near Los Angeles: pop., 72,000.

Comp·ton, Arthur Hol·ly (hol′i komp′tən), 1892–1962; American physicist.

Compton, Karl Tay·lor (tā′lẽr), 1887–1954; brother of *Arthur Holly;* American physicist.

comp·trol·ler (kən-trōl′ẽr), *n.* [< *controller*, by association with Fr. *compte*, an account], an official in charge of expenditures; controller.

comp·trol·ler·ship (kən-trōl′ẽr-ship′), *n.* [see -SHIP], the position or tenure of office of a comptroller.

com·pul·sion (kəm-pul′shən), *n.* [Fr.; LL. *compulsio* < L. *compulsus*, pp. of *compellere*], 1. a compelling. 2. the fact or state of being compelled; force; coercion; constraint. 3. in *psychopathology*, an irresistible impulse to perform some irrational act.

com·pul·sive (kəm-pul′siv), *adj.* having to do with compulsion; compelling.

com·pul·so·ri·ly (kəm-pul′sẽr-i-li), *adv.* in a compulsory manner.

com·pul·so·ri·ness (kəm-pul′sẽr-i-nis), *n.* the quality of being compulsory.

com·pul·so·ry (kəm-pul′sẽr-i), *adj.* [LL. *compulsorius* < L. *compulsus;* see COMPULSION], 1. compelled; obligatory; required. 2. compelling; coercive.

com·punc·tion (kəm-puŋk′shən), *n.* [ME. *compunccion;* OFr. *compunction;* LL. *compunctio*, a sticking, pricking, hence the pricking of conscience < L. *compunctus*, pp. of *compungere*, to prick, sting; *com-*, intens. + *pungere*, to prick], 1. a sharp feeling of uneasiness brought on by a sense of guilt; twinge of conscience; remorse; scruple. 2. a feeling of slight regret for some wrong done and of pity for the one wronged. —*SYN.* see **penitence, qualm.**

com·punc·tious (kəm-puŋk′shəs), *adj.* 1. of or causing compunction. 2. having compunction.

com·pur·ga·tion (kom′pẽr-gā′shən), *n.* [LL. *compurgatio*, a purifying < L. *compurgatus*, pp. of *compurgare*, to purge, purify; *com-*, intens. + *purgare*, to purge, purify; cf. PURGE], in *law*, formerly, the act of clearing an accused person by the oaths of a certain number of others testifying to their belief in his innocence.

com·pur·ga·tor (kom′pẽr-gā′tẽr), *n.* [see COMPURGATION], in *law*, formerly, one of those who swore to the innocence of an accused person in order to clear him.

com·put·a·bil·i·ty (kəm-pūt′ə-bil′ə-ti), *n.* the quality of being computable.

com·put·a·ble (kəm-pūt′ə-b'l, kom′pyoo-tə-b'l), *adj.* that can be computed.

com·pu·ta·tion (kom′pyoo-tā′shən), *n.* [L. *computatio*], 1. a computing; calculation. 2. a method of computing. 3. a result obtained in computing; computed amount.

com·pute (kəm-pūt′), *v.t.* & *v.i.* [COMPUTED (-id), COMPUTING], [Fr. *computer;* L. *computare; com-*, with + *putare*, to reckon], to determine (a number, amount, etc.) by reckoning; calculate. *n.* computation: chiefly in *beyond compute.* —*SYN.* see **calculate.**

com·put·er (kəm-pū′tẽr), *n.* a person who computes or a device used for computing; specifically, an electronic machine which, by means of stored instructions and information, performs rapid, often complex calculations or compiles, correlates, and selects data: see also **analog computer, digital computer.**

com·rade (kom′rad, kom′rid), *n.* [Fr. *camarade;* Sp. *camarada*, chamberful, chamber mate < L. *camera;* see CHAMBER, CAMERA], 1. a friend; close companion. 2. a person who has interests or concerns in common with others and shares in their activities; partner; associate; fellow: used as a form of address, as in the Communist party; hence, 3. [C-], [Colloq.], a member of the Communist party. —*SYN.* see **associate.**

comrade in arms, a fellow soldier.

com·rade·ship (kom′rad-ship′, kom′rid-ship′), *n.* [see -SHIP], 1. the state of being a comrade. 2. the relation of comrades; friendship; companionship.

Com·stock·er·y (kom′stok′ẽr-i), *n.* [after Anthony *Comstock* (1844–1915), head of the N. Y. Society for Suppression of Vice: prob. coined by G. B. Shaw], zealous suppression of plays, books, etc. considered offensive or dangerous to public morals.

‡**comte** (kōnt), *n.* [Fr.], count (a title).

Comte, Au·guste (ō′güst′ kōnt; Eng. kônt), 1798–1857; French philosopher; exponent of positivism.

Com·ti·an (kom′ti-ən, kôn′ti-ən), *adj.* of Auguste Comte or his positivist philosophy.

Comt·ism (kom′tiz'm, kôn′tiz'm), *n.* the philosophy of Auguste Comte; positivism.

Comt·ist (kom′tist, kôn′tist), *n.* a believer in Comtism.

Co·mus (kō′məs), *n.* [L.; Gr. *komos*, festival; cf. COMEDY], 1. in *Greek & Roman mythology*, a young god of festivity and revelry. 2. a masque (1634) by John Milton, praising chastity.

con (kon), *adv.* [contr. < L. *contra*, against], against; in opposition: as, they argued the matter pro and *con.* *n.* an argument, reason, vote, person, etc. in opposition.

con (kon), *v.t.* [CONNED (kond), CONNING], [ME. *cunnen*, to be able (see CAN, to be able)], to peruse carefully; study; fix in the memory.

con (kon), *v.t.* [CONNED (kond), CONNING], [earlier *cond* < ME. *conduen*, to conduct; OFr. *conduire;* L. *conducere;* see CONDUCT], to direct the course of (a vessel).

n. 1. the station of the person who cons. 2. the act of conning. Also spelled **conn.**

con (kon), *adj.* [Slang], confidence: as, a *con* man. *v.t.* [CONNED (kond), CONNING], [Slang], to swindle (a victim) by first gaining his confidence.

con- (kon), com-: used before all consonants except the cluster *gn*, the lip sounds *p*, *b*, *m*, and the glides *l*, *r*, *h*.

Con., 1. Consul. 2. Conformist.

con., 1. concerto. 2. conclusion. 3. connection. 4. consol. 5. consolidate. 6. consul. 7. *contra*, [L.], against.

Co·na·kry (kô'nȧ'krē'), *n.* seaport and capital of Guinea, Africa: pop., 35,000.

‡**con a·mo·re** (kôn' ä-mô're; Eng. kon' ə-môr'i), [It.], 1. with love; tenderly: a direction to the performer in music. 2. with enthusiasm.

Conan (kō'nən), [< Celt. base meaning "wisdom"], a masculine name.

Co·nant, James Bryant (kō'nənt), 1893– ; American chemist and educator.

co·na·tion (kō-nā'shən), *n.* [L. *conatio*, an attempt < pp. of *conari*, to undertake, attempt], in *psychology*, the act or faculty of striving or making an effort.

con·a·tive (kon'ə-tiv, kō'nə-tiv), *adj.* 1. having to do with conation. 2. in *linguistics*, expressing endeavor or effort, especially as an aspect of the action of verbs. Example: Ar. *qātala*, he has tried to kill (as contrasted with *qatala*, he has killed).

co·na·tus (kō-nā'təs), *n.* [*pl.* CONATUS (-təs)], [L. < *conari*, to try, attempt], 1. an effort or attempt; endeavor. 2. a natural active force, as of plants or animals, analogous to human effort.

‡**con bri·o** (kôn brē'ô), [It.], with spirit; spiritedly: a direction to the performer in music.

conc., 1. concentrate. 2. concentrated. 3. concentration. 4. concerning.

con·cat·e·nate (kon-kat''n-āt'), *adj.* [LL. *concatenatus*, pp. of *concatenare*, to link together < L. *com-*, together + *catenare* < *catena*, a chain], linked together; connected. *v.t.* [CONCATENATED (-id), CONCATENATING], to link together or join, as in a chain.

con·cat·e·na·tion (kon'kat-'n-ā'shən), *n.* [LL. *concatenatio*; see CONCATENATE], 1. a linking together or being linked together in a series. 2. a connected series of things or events regarded as causally or dependently related.

con·cave (kon-kāv', kən-kāv', kon'kāv), *adj.* [Fr.; L. *concavus*, hollow < *com-*, intens. + *cavus*, hollow], hollow and curved like a section of the inside of a sphere. *n.* (kon'kāv, koŋ'-kāv), [OFr. < the *adj.*], a concave surface, line, object, etc. *v.t.* (kon-kāv', kən-kāv'), [CONCAVED (-kāvd'), CONCAVING], to make concave.

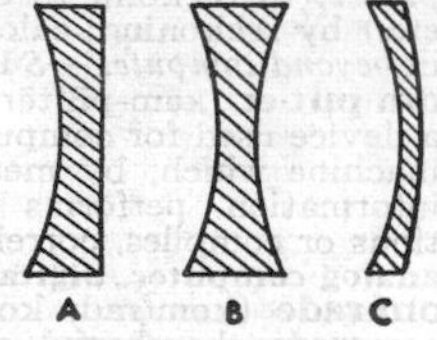

CONCAVE LENSES
A, plano-concave; B, concavo-concave; C, concavo-convex

con·cav·i·ty (kon-kav'ə-ti, kən-kav'ə-ti), *n.* [Fr. *concavité*; LL. *concavitas*], 1. the quality or condition of being concave. 2. [*pl.* CONCAVITIES (-tiz)], a concave surface or object.

con·ca·vo-con·cave (kon-kā'vō-kon-kāv'), *adj.* concave on both sides, as some lenses: see **concave**, illus.

con·ca·vo-con·vex (kon-kā'vō-kon-veks'), *adj.* 1. having one concave side and one convex side. 2. in *optics*, designating a lens whose concave face has a greater degree of curvature than its convex face, so that the lens is thinnest in the middle: see **concave**, illus.

con·ceal (kən-sēl'), *v.t.* [ME. *concelen*; OFr. *conceler*; L. *concelare*, to hide < *com-*, together + *celare*, to hide], 1. to put out of sight; hide; secrete. 2. to keep (information, etc.) from another's knowledge; keep secret. —*SYN.* see **hide.**

con·ceal·ment (kən-sēl'mənt), *n.* 1. a concealing or being concealed. 2. a place or means of hiding.

con·cede (kən-sēd'), *v.t.* [CONCEDED (-id), CONCEDING], [L. *concedere* < *com-*, with + *cedere*, to go, cede, grant], 1. to yield, as in argument; admit the truth of; acknowledge. 2. to admit the justice of; grant as a right: as, he *conceded* the victory. *v.i.* to make a concession.

con·ceit (kən-sēt'), *n.* [ME. *conceite* < *conceiven*; see CONCEIVE], 1. originally, *a*) an idea; thought; concept. *b*) personal opinion; hence, 2. an exaggerated opinion of oneself, one's merits, etc.; vanity. 3. [< It. *concetto*, of same ult. origin], *a*) an affectation in style or in expression of ideas; fanciful or witty expression or notion; startling or strained figure of speech. *b*) the use of such figures in writing or speaking. 4. imagination. *v.t.* 1. [Obs.], to think or imagine. 2. [Dial.], to think well of; take a fancy to. —*SYN.* see **pride.**
out of conceit with, no longer satisfied or pleased with.

con·ceit·ed (kən-sēt'id), *adj.* [see CONCEIT], 1. having an exaggerated opinion of oneself, one's merits, etc.; vain. 2. [Dial.], full of whims and fanciful notions.

con·ceiv·a·bil·i·ty (kən-sēv'ə-bil'ə-ti), *n.* the quality of being conceivable.

con·ceiv·a·ble (kən-sēv'ə-b'l), *adj.* that can be conceived; that can be understood, imagined, or believed.

con·ceiv·a·bly (kən-sēv'ə-bli), *adv.* as far as can be conceived mentally.

con·ceive (kən-sēv'), *v.t.* [CONCEIVED (-sēvd'), CONCEIVING], [ME. *conceiven*; OFr. *conceivre*, *conciver*; L. *concipere*, to take in, receive < *com-*, together + *capere*, to take], 1. to become pregnant with. 2. to form or develop in the mind; imagine. 3. to understand; apprehend. 4. to express; represent in words. *v.i.* 1. to become pregnant. 2. to think; form an idea (*of*).

con·cent (kən-sent'), *n.* [L. *concentus* < *concinere*, to sing together, < *com-*, with + *canere*, to sing], [Rare], 1. harmony of sounds or voices; musical concord; hence, 2. agreement; accord.

con·cen·ter (kon-sen'tẽr), *v.t.* [Fr. *concentrer* < L. *com-*, together + *centrum*, center], to bring to a common center; focus; concentrate. *v.i.* to come together to or at a common center; converge.

con·cen·trate (kon's'n-trāt', kon'sen-trāt'), *v.t.* [CONCENTRATED (-id), CONCENTRATING], [< *concenter* + *-ate*], 1. to bring to, or direct toward, a common center. 2. to collect or focus (one's thoughts, efforts, etc.). 3. to increase the strength or density of. 4. to mass (troops) in a place. *v.i.* 1. to come to or toward a common center. 2. to direct one's thoughts or efforts; fix one's attention (*on* or *upon*). 3. to increase in strength or density. *n.* a substance that has been concentrated. *adj.* concentrated. Abbreviated **conc.**

con·cen·tra·tion (kon's'n-trā'shən, kon'sen-trā'shən), *n.* 1. a concentrating or being concentrated. 2. close or fixed attention. 3. the strength or density, as of a solution: abbreviated **conc.**

concentration camp, 1. a place where troops are massed, as before distribution. 2. a place in which enemy aliens or prisoners of war are kept under guard. 3. a place of confinement for those considered dangerous to the regime: used especially in Nazi Germany for antifascists, Jews, etc.

con·cen·tra·tive (kon's'n-trā'tiv, kən-sen'trə-tiv), *adj.* concentrating or tending to concentrate.

con·cen·tra·tor (kon's'n-trā'tẽr, kon'sen-trā'tẽr), *n.* 1. a person who concentrates. 2. any of various devices for concentrating solutions, ores, etc.

con·cen·tre (kon-sen'tẽr), *v.t.* & *v.i.* concenter: British spelling.

con·cen·tric (kən-sen'trik), *adj.* [ME. *concentrik*; OFr. *concentrique*; ML. *concentricus* < L. *com-*, together + *centrum*, center], having a center in common, as circles.

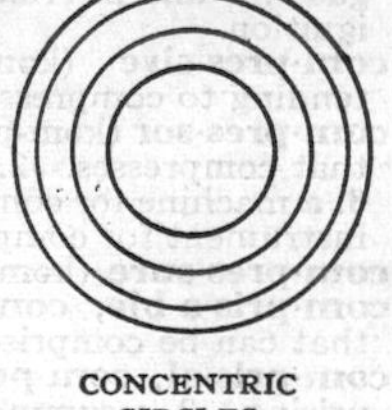
CONCENTRIC CIRCLES

con·cen·tri·cal (kən-sen'tri-k'l), *adj.* concentric.

con·cen·tri·cal·ly (kən-sen'tri-k'l-i, kən-sen'trik-li), *adv.* in a concentric manner; with a center in common.

con·cen·tric·i·ty (kon'sen-tris'ə-ti), *n.* the condition of being concentric.

Con·cep·ción (kôn-sep'syôn'; Eng. kən-sep'si-ōn'), *n.* a city in central Chile: pop., 83,000 (est. 1947).

con·cept (kon'sept), *n.* [L. *conceptus*; see CONCEIVE], an idea, especially a generalized idea of a class of objects; a thought; general notion. —*SYN.* see **idea.**

con·cep·ta·cle (kən-sep'tə-k'l), *n.* [L. *conceptaculum*, receptacle < pp. of *concipere*; see CONCEIVE], in *botany*, a sac opening outward and containing reproductive cells, found in certain primitive plants.

con·cep·tion (kən-sep'shən), *n.* [ME. *concepcioun*; OFr. *conception* < L. *conceptio*, a comprehending, conception < *conceptus*; see CONCEIVE], 1. a conceiving or being conceived in the womb. 2. that which is so conceived; embryo; fetus; hence, 3. the beginning of some process, chain of events, etc. 4. the act, process, or power of conceiving mentally; formulation of ideas. 5. a mental impression or image; general notion; concept. 6. an original idea, design, plan, etc. —*SYN.* see **idea.**

con·cep·tive (kən-sep'tiv), *adj.* [L. *conceptivus*], having the power of conception: generally in reference to the mind.

con·cep·tu·al (kən-sep'chōō-əl), *adj.* [ML. *conceptualis*], of conception or concepts.

con·cep·tu·al·ism (kən-sep'chōō-əl-iz'm), *n.* [*conceptual* + *-ism*], in *philosophy*, the doctrine that universals exist as realities in the mind only and that the mind can form an image corresponding to the general term for a particular concept: distinguished from *realism* and *nominalism*.

con·cep·tu·al·ist (kən-sep'chōō-əl-ist), *n.* a person who believes in conceptualism. *adj.* of conceptualism or conceptualists.

con·cern (kən-sũrn'), *v.t.* [Fr. *concerner*; ML. *concernere*, to perceive, have regard to, fig. use of LL. *concernere*, to sift, mix, as in a sieve < L. *com-*, with + *cernere*, to sift, hence perceive, comprehend], 1. to have a relation to or bearing on; be of interest or importance

to: as, this *concerns* all of us. 2. to involve or interest (used in the passive). 3. to cause to feel uneasy or anxious. *n.* 1. a matter of interest or importance to one; that which relates to or affects one; affair; matter; business. 2. interest in or regard for a person or thing. 3. relation; reference. 4. solicitude; worry; anxiety: as, you need feel no *concern* over your health. 5. a business establishment; company; firm. —*SYN.* see **care.**
as concerns, in regard to; with reference to; about.
concern oneself, 1. to busy oneself (*with, about, over, in* something); take an interest; hence, 2. to be worried, anxious, or uneasy.

con·cerned (kən-sũrnd′), *adj.* 1. involved or interested (*in* some matter). 2. uneasy or anxious.

con·cern·ing (kən-sũr′niŋ), *prep.* [see CONCERN], relating to; having to do with; in regard to; with reference to; about.

con·cern·ment (kən-sũrn′mənt), *n.* [*concern* + *-ment*], 1. an affair; matter; business. 2. relation; reference. 3. importance; interest; consequence. 4. participation; involvement. 5. worry; solicitude; anxiety.

con·cert (kən-sũrt′; *for n. & adj.* kon′sẽrt), *v.t. & v.i.* [Fr. *concerter;* It. *concertare;* L. *concertare,* to contend, contest < *com-,* with + *certare,* to contend, strive; meanings influenced by *consort* & L. *conserere,* to join together], to arrange or settle by mutual understanding; contrive or plan together; devise. *n.* [Fr.; It. *concerto,* agreement, union < *concertare*], 1. mutual agreement; concord; harmony of action. 2. musical consonance. 3. a performance of vocal or instrumental music, usually one in which a number of musicians participate. *adj.* of or for concerts.
in concert, in unison; in agreement; together.

con·cert·ed (kən-sũr′tid), *adj.* [pp. of *concert*], 1. mutually arranged, planned, or agreed upon; combined. 2. in *music,* arranged in parts for voices or instruments.

concert grand (piano), the largest size of grand piano, for concert performance.

con·cer·ti·na (kon′sẽr-tē′nə), *n.* [*concert* + *-ina:* coined by Sir Charles Wheatstone (1802–1875), Eng. physicist who invented it], a small musical instrument of the accordion type, with bellows and keys.

CONCERTINA

‡con·cer·ti·no (kôn′cher-tē′nô), *n.* [It. dim.], a brief concerto.

con·cert·mas·ter (kon′sẽrt-mas′tẽr, kon′sẽrt-mäs′tẽr), *n.* [after G. *konzertmeister*], the leader of the first violin section of a symphony orchestra, who plays the solo passages and often serves as assistant to the conductor.

con·cert·meis·ter (kon′sẽrt-mīs′tẽr; G. kôn-tsert′mīs′-tẽr), *n.* [G., older form of *konzertmeister; concert* (< Fr.; see CONCERT) + *meister,* master (< OHG. *meistar* < L. *magister;* see MASTER)], a concertmaster.

con·cer·to (kən-cher′tō; It. kôn-cher′tô), *n.* [*pl.* CONCERTOS (-tōz); It. CONCERTI (-tē)], [It.; see CONCERT], 1. formerly, a musical composition with the several distinct movements of an orchestral suite, but played by a small group of solo instruments with a larger orchestral ensemble. 2. a composition for one, or two or three, solo instruments and an orchestra: it is based on the sonata form and has, usually, three movements. Abbreviated **con.**

concerto gros·so (grō′sō), [It., lit., big concerto; *grosso,* large < LL. *grossus,* thick], a concerto for a small group of solo instruments and a full orchestra.

concert pitch, in *music,* a pitch, slightly higher than the usual pitch, to which concert instruments are tuned in order to compensate acoustically for the relatively high room temperature of crowded concert halls.

con·ces·sion (kən-sesh′ən), *n.* [Fr.; L. *concessio* < *concessus,* pp. of *concedere*], 1. a conceding; granting; giving in; yielding. 2. a thing conceded or granted; acknowledgment, as of an argument or claim. 3. a privilege granted by a government, company, etc.; especially, *a*) the right to use land. *b*) the right to sell food, check hats and coats, etc., as at a park, theater, etc. 4. the land, trading rights, etc. so granted.

con·ces·sion·aire (kən-sesh′ən-âr′), *n.* [Fr. *concessionnaire*], the holder of a concession granted by a government, company, etc.

con·ces·sion·ar·y (kən-sesh′ən-er′i), *adj.* of a concession. *n.* [*pl.* CONCESSIONARIES (-iz)], a concessionaire.

con·ces·sion·er (kən-sesh′ən-ẽr), *n.* a concessionaire.

con·ces·sive (kən-ses′iv), *adj.* [LL. *concessivus*], 1. having the character of concession; conceding or tending to concede. 2. in *grammar,* expressing concession: as, *though* is a *concessive* conjunction.

conch (koŋk, konch), *n.* [*pl.* CONCHS (koŋks), CONCHES (kon′chiz)], [L. *concha;* Gr. *konchē,* mussel, shell], 1. the spiral, one-piece shell of certain sea mollusks. 2. in *Roman mythology,* such a shell used as a trumpet by the Tritons. 3. a concha.

CONCH

con·cha (koŋ′kə), *n.* [*pl.* CONCHAE (-kē)], [L.; see CONCH], 1. in *anatomy,* any of several structures resembling a shell in form, as a thin, bony projection inside the nasal cavity, the largest hollow of the external ear, or the whole external ear. 2. in *architecture,* *a*) the half dome covering an apse. *b*) the apse.

con·chif·er·ous (koŋ-kif′ẽr-əs), *adj.* [L. *concha* (see CONCH); + *-ferous*], having or bearing a shell.

Con·cho·bar (koŋ′kō-wẽr, kon′oor), *n.* in *Irish legend,* a king of Ulster, the guardian and intended husband of Deirdre: see **Deirdre.**

con·choi·dal (koŋ-koi′d'l), *adj.* [< Gr. *konchē,* a shell; + *-oid* + *-al*], in *mineralogy,* having convexities or concavities like those of a bivalve shell in cross section.

con·chol·o·gist (koŋ-kol′ə-jist), *n.* a student of or a specialist in conchology; collector of shells.

con·chol·o·gy (koŋ-kol′ə-ji), *n.* [< Gr. *konchē,* a shell; + *-logy*], the branch of zoology that deals with mollusks and shells.

con·chy (kon′chi, kon′shi), *n.* [*pl.* CONCHIES (-chiz, -shiz)], [Slang], a conscientious objector.

con·ci·erge (kon′si-ũrzh′; Fr. kōn′syârzh′), *n.* [Fr.; ML. *consergius;* ? < LL. **conservius* < L. *com-,* with + *servus,* slave], 1. a doorkeeper. 2. a caretaker, as of an apartment house; custodian; janitor.

con·cil·i·a·ble (kən-sil′i-ə-b'l), *adj.* that can be conciliated.

con·cil·i·ate (kən-sil′i-āt′), *v.t.* [CONCILIATED (-id), CONCILIATING], [< L. *conciliatus,* pp. of *conciliare,* to call or bring together, win over < *concilium,* a meeting, assembly; see COUNCIL], 1. to win over; soothe the anger of; make friendly; placate. 2. to gain (regard, favor, good will, esteem, etc.) by friendly acts. 3. [Archaic], to reconcile; make consistent. —*SYN.* see **pacify.**

con·cil·i·a·tion (kən-sil′i-ā′shən), *n.* a conciliating or being conciliated.

con·cil·i·a·tive (kən-sil′i-ā′tiv), *adj.* conciliatory.

con·cil·i·a·tor (kən-sil′i-ā′tẽr), *n.* one who conciliates.

con·cil·i·a·to·ry (kən-sil′i-ə-tôr′i, kən-sil′i-ə-tō′ri), *adj.* tending to conciliate or reconcile.

con·cin·ni·ty (kən-sin′ə-ti), *n.* [*pl.* CONCINNITIES (-tiz)], [L. *concinnitas* < *concinnus,* skillfully joined, beautiful < **con-cid-nos,* cut together (so as to fit) < *com-,* with + base of *caedere,* to cut], a skillful arrangement of parts; harmony; elegance, especially of literary style.

con·cise (kən-sīs′), *adj.* [L. *concisus,* cut off, brief; pp. of *concidere,* to cut off < *com-,* intens. + *caedere,* to cut], brief and to the point; terse; succinct.
SYN.—**concise** implies the stating of much in few words, by removing all superfluous elaborations (a *concise* summary); **terse** adds to this the connotation of polished smoothness (a *terse* style); **laconic,** on the other hand, suggests brevity to the point of curtness or ambiguity ("You'll see," was his *laconic* reply); **succinct** implies clarity but compactness in the briefest possible number of words (he spoke in *succinct* phrases); **pithy** suggests forcefulness and wit resulting from compactness (*pithy* axioms).—*ANT.* redundant, prolix.

con·ci·sion (kən-sizh′ən), *n.* [L. *concisio*], 1. originally, a cutting off; schism; division; faction. 2. conciseness.

con·clave (kon′klāv, koŋ′klāv), *n.* [ME.; OFr.; L., a room, closet < *com-,* with + *clavis,* a key], 1. in the *Roman Catholic Church,* *a*) the rooms in which the cardinals meet in private to elect a pope. *b*) the meeting of the cardinals for this purpose. *c*) the cardinals collectively. 2. any private meeting.

con·clav·ist (kon′klāv-ist, koŋ′klāv-ist), *n.* either of two persons, a secretary and a servant, attending a cardinal in conclave.

con·clude (kən-kloo͞d′, kən-klūd′), *v.t.* [CONCLUDED (-id), CONCLUDING], [ME. *concluden,* to conclude; L. *concludere,* to shut up closely, enclose < *com-,* together + *claudere,* to shut], 1. to bring to a close; end; finish. 2. to bring to decision by reasoning; infer; deduce. 3. to decide; determine. 4. to settle; come to an agreement about: as, the nations must *conclude* the peace treaty. *v.i.* 1. to come to a close; end; finish. 2. to come to an agreement. —*SYN.* see **close, decide, infer.**

con·clu·sion (kən-kloo͞′zhən, kən-klū′zhən), *n.* [ME.; OFr.; L. *conclusio,* a closing, conclusion < pp. of *concludere;* see CONCLUDE], 1. the end or last part; as, *a*) the last division of a discourse, often containing a summary of what went before. *b*) the last part of a chain of reasoning; judgment, decision, or opinion formed after investigation or thought. *c)* the third and last part of a syllogism; inference. *d)* the last of a chain of events; outcome. 2. a concluding; final arrangement (*of* a peace treaty, etc.). 3. in *law*, *a)* the formal closing of a plea. *b)* a binding act. Abbreviated **con.**

in conclusion, lastly; in closing.

try conclusions with, to engage in an argument, a contest, etc. with.

con·clu·sive (kən-kloo͞′siv, kən-klū′siv), *adj.* [LL. *conclusivus* < pp. of L. *concludere;* see CONCLUDE], that settles a question; decisive; final.

con·coct (kon-kokt′, kən-kokt′), *v.t.* [< L. *concoctus,* pp. of *concoquere,* to boil together, prepare < *com-*, together + *coquere,* to cook], 1. to make by combining various ingredients; compound. 2. to devise; plan.

con·coc·tion (kon-kok′shən, kən-kok′shən), *n.* [L. *concoctio*], 1. a concocting. 2. something concocted.

con·com·i·tance (kon-kom′ə-təns, kən-kom′ə-təns), *n.* [LL. *concomitantia* < L. *concomitans,* ppr. of *concomitari,* to attend < *com-*, together + *comitari,* to accompany < *comes,* companion], the fact of being concomitant; accompaniment; existence in association.

con·com·i·tan·cy (kon-kom′ə-tən-si, kən-kom′ə-tən-si), *n.* concomitance.

con·com·i·tant (kon-kom′ə-tənt, kən-kom′ə-tənt), *adj.* [< L. *concomitans;* see CONCOMITANCE], accompanying; attendant. *n.* an accompanying or attendant condition, circumstance, or thing.

con·com·i·tant·ly (kon-kom′ə-tənt-li, kən-kom′ə-tənt-li), *adv.* together with; in accompaniment.

Con·cord (koŋ′kẽrd, kon′kôrd), *n.* 1. the capital of New Hampshire, on the Merrimack River: pop., 29,000. 2. a town in eastern Massachusetts: pop., 13,000: site of an early battle of the American Revolution (April 19, 1775). 3. a city in western California, near Oakland: pop., 36,000. 4. a Concord grape.

con·cord (kon′kôrd, koŋ′kôrd), *n.* [Fr. *concorde;* L. *concordia,* agreement, union < *concors, concordis,* of the same mind < *com-*, together + *cor, cordis,* heart], 1. agreement; harmony; accordance. 2. friendly and peaceful relations, as between nations. 3. a treaty establishing this. 4. in *grammar,* agreement between words in regard to forms showing person, gender, number, and case. 5. in *music,* a combination of simultaneous and harmonious tones: opposed to *discord.*

con·cord·ance (kon-kôr′d′ns, kən-kôr′d′ns), *n.* [ME. *concordaunce;* OFr. *concordance;* LL. *concordantia* < L. *concordans,* ppr. of *concordare,* to agree < *concors;* see CONCORD], 1. agreement; consonance; harmony; accord. 2. an alphabetical list of all the important words of a book or author, with references to the passages in which they occur.

con·cord·ant (kon-kôr′d′nt, kən-kôr′d′nt), *adj.* [Fr.; L. *concordans,* ppr. of *concordare;* see CONCORDANCE], agreeing; consonant; harmonious.

con·cor·dat (kon-kôr′dat), *n.* [Fr.; ML. *concordatum,* agreement < L. *concordatus,* pp. of *concordare,* to agree; see CONCORDANCE], 1. a compact; formal agreement; covenant. 2. an agreement between the Pope and a government on church matters.

Concord coach, a type of stagecoach used by early settlers of the western United States.

Concord grape, a large, dark-blue grape native to North America.

con·course (kon′kôrs, koŋ′kôrs), *n.* [Fr. *concours* < L. *concursus,* a running together < *concurrere;* see CONCUR], 1. a moving, running, or flowing together. 2. a crowd; throng; gathering. 3. a place where crowds gather. 4. an open space, as in a park or railroad station. 5. a broad thoroughfare or boulevard.

con·cres·cence (kon-kres′′ns), *n.* [L. *concrescentia* < *concrescere,* to grow together < *com-*, together + *crescere,* to grow], in *biology,* a growing together of parts; uniting of cells, etc.

con·crete (kon-krēt′, kon′krēt), *adj.* [L. *concretus,* pp. of *concrescere;* see CONCRESCENCE], 1. formed into a solid mass; coalesced. 2. having a material, perceptible existence; of, belonging to, or characterized by things or events that can be perceived by the senses; real; actual. 3. referring to a particular; specific, not general or abstract. 4. made of concrete. 5. in *grammar,* designating a thing or class of things that can be perceived by the senses: opposed to *abstract.* *n.* (kon′krēt, kon-krēt′), 1. anything concrete. 2. a hard, compact substance made of sand, gravel, cement, and water, used in the construction of bridges, dams, buildings, etc. *v.t.* [CONCRETED (-id), CONCRETING], 1. (kon-krēt′), to form into a mass; solidify. 2. (kon′krēt), to make of, or cover with, concrete (cement). *v.i.* to solidify.

concrete number, a number telling how many or how much of a specific thing (e.g., *seven* apples, *four* miles).

con·cre·tion (kon-krē′shən), *n.* [L. *concretio;* see CONCRETE], 1. a solidifying or being solidified. 2. a solidified mass; specifically, *a)* in *geology,* an inclusion in sedimentary rock, usually rounded, resulting from the formation of succeeding layers of mineral matter about some nucleus, as a fossil or grain of sand. *b)* in *medicine,* a solidified mass, usually inorganic, deposited in a tissue or cavity of the body; calculus.

con·cre·tion·ar·y (kon-krē′shən-er′i), *adj.* 1. of or formed by concretion. 2. containing concretions.

con·cre·tive (kon-krē′tiv), *adj.* producing or tending to concretion.

con·cret·ize (kon′kri-tīz′), *v.t.* [CONCRETIZED (-tīzd′), CONCRETIZING], to make (something) concrete; make specific; give definite form to.

con·cu·bi·nage (kon-kū′bə-nij), *n.* [Fr.], 1. the cohabitation of a man and a concubine. 2. the state of being a concubine.

con·cu·bi·nar·y (kon-kū′bə-ner′i), *adj.* [ML. *concubinarius*], of, living in, or born from concubinage. *n.* [*pl.* CONCUBINARIES (-iz)], a person living in concubinage.

con·cu·bine (koŋ′kyoo-bīn′, kon′kyoo-bīn′), *n.* [ME.; OFr. masc. *concubin,* fem. *concubine;* L. masc. *concubinus,* fem. *concubina* < *concumbere,* to lie with < *com-*, with + *cubare,* to lie down], 1. a woman who lives with a man although not legally married to him. 2. in certain polygamous societies, a secondary wife; wife of inferior social and legal status: the children of such a union are generally regarded as legitimate.

con·cu·pis·cence (kon-kū′pə-s′ns), *n.* [ME.; OFr.; LL. *concupiscentia* < L. *concupiscens,* ppr. of *concupiscere,* to desire eagerly < *com-*, together + *cupiscere,* to wish, desire < *cupere,* to desire], strong or abnormal desire or appetite; especially, sexual desire; lust.

con·cu·pis·cent (kon-kū′pə-s′nt), *adj.* [L. *concupiscens;* see CONCUPISCENCE], strongly desirous; especially, sexually desirous; lustful.

con·cur (kən-kũr′), *v.i.* [CONCURRED (-kũrd′), CONCURRING], [L. *concurrere,* to run together < *com-*, together + *currere,* to run], 1. to occur at the same time; happen together; coincide. 2. to combine in having an effect; act together: as, several circumstances *concurred* to bring about this result. 3. to agree; be in accord; have the same opinion. —*SYN.* see **consent.**

con·cur·rence (kən-kũr′əns), *n.* [< L. *concurrens,* ppr. of *concurrere;* see CONCUR], 1. a happening together in time or place. 2. a combining to produce or bring about something. 3. agreement; accord. 4. in *geometry, a)* the point where three or more lines meet. *b)* the junction of lines or surfaces. 5. in *law,* a joint right or claim.

con·cur·ren·cy (kən-kũr′ən-si), *n.* [*pl.* CONCURRENCIES (-siz)], concurrence.

con·cur·rent (kən-kũr′ənt), *adj.* [< L. *concurrens;* see CONCURRENCE], 1. occurring at the same time; existing together. 2. meeting in or going toward the same point; converging. 3. acting together; co-operating. 4. in agreement; harmonious. 5. in *law,* having equal jurisdiction or authority. *n.* anything concurrent, as a circumstance or contributory cause.

con·cur·rent·ly (kən-kũr′ənt-li), *adv.* at the same time; simultaneously; conjunctively.

concurrent resolution, a resolution passed by one branch of a bicameral legislature and concurred in by the other, indicating the opinion of the legislature on some matter: it does not have the force of law and, hence, does not require the signature of the chief executive: distinguished from *joint resolution.*

con·cus·sion (kən-kush′ən), *n.* [L. *concussio* < pp. of *concutere,* to shake violently, shake together < *com-*, together + *quatere,* to shake], 1. a violent shaking; agitation; shock, as from impact. 2. in *medicine,* a condition of impaired functioning of some organ, especially the brain, as a result of a violent blow or impact.

con·cus·sive (kən-kus′iv), *adj.* 1. of concussion. 2. tending to cause concussion.

cond., 1. conducted. 2. conductivity. 3. conductor.

Con·dé, Prince **de** (də kōn′dā′), (*Louis II de Bourbon; duc d'Enghien*), 1621–1686; French general: called *the Great Condé.*

con·demn (kən-dem′), *v.t.* [OFr. *condemner;* L. *condemnare* < *com-*, intens. + *damnare,* to harm, condemn; cf. DAMN], 1. to pass an adverse judgment on; disapprove of strongly; censure. 2. to prove (a person) guilty of wrongdoing; declare to be guilty; convict. 3. to give a judicial decision against; inflict a penalty upon; doom. 4. to declare (property) forfeited or legally appropriated for public use. 5. to declare unfit for use or service: as, the ramshackle building was *condemned* by the housing authorities. 6. to declare (a sick person) incurable.

con·dem·na·ble (kən-dem′nə-b′l), *adj.* deserving to be condemned; blamable; culpable.

con·dem·na·tion (kon′dem-nā′shən), *n.* [L. *condemnatio* < pp. of *condemnare*], 1. a condemning or being condemned. 2. a cause for condemning.

con·dem·na·to·ry (kən-dem′nə-tôr′i, kən-dem′nə-tō′-ri), *adj.* condemning; expressing condemnation, explicitly or implicitly.

con·demn·er (kən-dem′ẽr), *n.* a person who condemns.

con·den·sa·bil·i·ty (kən-den′sə-bil′ə-ti), *n.* the quality of being condensable.

con·den·sa·ble (kən-den′sə-b′l), *adj.* that can be condensed.

con·den·sate (kən-den′sāt), *v.t. & v.i.* [CONDENSATED (-id), CONDENSATING], [Rare], to condense. *adj.* [Archaic], condensed. *n.* a product of condensation.

con·den·sa·tion (kon′den-sā′shən), *n.* [LL. *condensatio*],

1. a condensing or being condensed. 2. anything condensed; product of condensation.

con·dense (kən-dens′), *v.t.* [CONDENSED (-denst′), CONDENSING], [Fr. *condenser;* L. *condensare* < *condensus*, very dense < *com-*, intens. + *densus*], 1. to make more dense or compact; compress; reduce the volume of. 2. to express in fewer words; make concise. 3. to concentrate; intensify: said of light rays. 4. to change (a substance) to a denser form, as from a gas to a liquid. *v.i.* 1. to become more dense or compact. 2. to pass into a denser form, as a vapor into a liquid. 3. in *chemistry*, to join with other atoms in the same or different molecules, so as to form a new, more complex compound: said of an atom or atoms. —*SYN.* see **contract.**

condensed milk, a thick, sweetened milk made by evaporating part of the water from cow's milk and adding sugar: distinguished from *evaporated milk.*

condensed type, in *printing*, a type face of narrower width than the standard type for the series.

con·dens·er (kən-den′sẽr), *n.* a person or thing that condenses; specifically, *a*) an apparatus for converting gases or vapors to a liquid state. *b*) a lens or series of lenses for concentrating light rays on an object or area. *c*) in *electricity*, a device consisting of two or more conductor plates separated from one another by a dielectric and used for receiving and storing an electric charge.

con·den·si·bil·i·ty (kən-den′sə-bil′ə-ti), *n.* condensability.

con·den·si·ble (kən-den′sə-b'l), *adj.* condensable.

con·de·scend (kon′di-send′), *v.i.* [ME. *condescenden;* OFr. *condescendre;* LL. *condescendere*, let oneself down, condescend < *com-*, together + *descendere;* see DESCEND], 1. to descend voluntarily to the level, regarded as lower, of the person or persons that one is dealing with; be gracious or affable to inferiors; deign. 2. to deal with others in a patronizing manner. 3. to lower or degrade oneself: as, he *condescended* to accept a bribe. 4. [Obs.], to make concessions; agree; assent. —*SYN.* see **stoop.**

con·de·scend·ence (kon′di-sen′dəns), *n.* 1. condescension. 2. [Scot.], a listing of particulars.

con·de·scend·ing (kon′di-sen′diŋ), *adj.* showing condescension; especially, patronizing.

con·de·scen·sion (kon′di-sen′shən), *n.* [LL. *condescensio* < pp. of *condescendere*], act or instance of condescending; patronizing manner or behavior.

con·dign (kən-dīn′), *adj.* [L. *condignus*, very worthy < *com-*, intens. + *dignus*, worthy], deserved; suitable; adequate: used especially with reference to punishment for wrongdoing.

Con·dil·lac, É·tienne Bon·not de (ā′tyen′ bô′nō′ də kōn′dē′yåk′), 1715–1780; French philosopher.

con·di·ment (kon′də-mənt), *n.* [Fr.; L. *condimentum*, a spice, seasoning < *condire*, to pickle], a seasoning or relish for food, as pepper, mustard, sauces, etc.

con·dis·ci·ple (kon′di-sī′p'l), *n.* [L. *condiscipulus*], 1. a fellow disciple. 2. a fellow student.

con·di·tion (kən-dish′ən), *n.* [ME. & OFr. *condicion;* L. *condicio*, agreement, stipulation, condition, situation < *condicere*, to speak with, agree < *com-*, together + *dicere*, to speak], 1. anything called for as a requirement before the performance, completion, or effectiveness of something else; provision; stipulation: as, this contract imposes several *conditions.* 2. anything essential to the existence or occurrence of something else; prerequisite: as, health is a *condition* of happiness. 3. anything that modifies or restricts the nature, existence, or occurrence of something else; external circumstance or factor: as, *conditions* were favorable for business. 4. manner or state of being: as, the patient is in a critical *condition.* 5. proper or healthy state: as, athletes must train to be in *condition.* 6. social position; rank; station. 7. in *education*, *a*) the requirement imposed on a student that he make up deficiencies in a certain subject in order to pass it. *b*) the grade or mark stating this requirement. 8. in *grammar*, a clause expressing a condition, as one beginning with *if.* 9. in *law*, a clause in a contract, will, etc., that revokes, suspends, or modifies one or more of its stipulations on certain contingencies. 10. in *logic*, a proposition on which the truth of another proposition depends. *v.i.* to negotiate about conditions; make conditions. *v.t.* 1. to stipulate; make terms concerning. 2. to subject to a condition or conditions; impose a condition on. 3. to be a condition of. 4. to bring into proper or fit condition. 5. in *education*, to require (a student) to make up deficiencies in a course in order to pass it. 6. in *psychology*, to develop a conditioned reflex or behavior pattern in (a person or animal); hence, 7. loosely, to accustom (a person) to. —*SYN.* see **state.**

on condition that, provided that; if.

con·di·tion·al (kən-dish′ən-'l), *adj.* 1. containing, implying, or dependent on a condition or conditions; qualified; not absolute: as, a *conditional* award. 2. expressing a condition: as, a *conditional* clause.

con·di·tion·al·i·ty (kən-dish′ən-al′ə-ti), *n.* the quality or state of being conditional.

con·di·tion·al·ly (kən-dish′ən-'l-i), *adv.* with or under a condition or conditions.

con·di·tioned (kən-dish′ənd), *adj.* 1. in a (specified) condition. 2. subject to conditions; depending on certain conditions. 3. in a fit or proper condition. 4. having developed a conditioned reflex or behavior pattern. 5. loosely, accustomed (*to*).

conditioned reflex, a reflex in which the response (e.g., secretion of saliva in a dog) is occasioned by a secondary stimulus (e.g., the ringing of a bell) repeatedly associated with the primary stimulus (e.g., the sight of meat): also **conditioned response.**

con·do·la·to·ry (kən-dōl′ə-tôr′i, kən-dō′lə-tō′ri), *adj.* expressing condolence.

con·dole (kən-dōl′), *v.i.* [CONDOLED (-dōld′), CONDOLING], [LL. *condolere;* L. *com-*, with + *dolere*, to grieve], to express sympathy; mourn in sympathy; commiserate.

con·do·lence (kən-dō′ləns; *rarely*, kon′də-ləns), *n.* [< LL. *condolens;* see CONDOLE], expression of sympathy with another in grief. —*SYN.* see **pity.**

‡**con do·lo·re** (kôn dô-lô′re), [It.], with grief; sadly: a direction to the performer in music.

con·dom (kon′dəm, kun′dəm), *n.* [? altered < *Conton*, name of 18th-c. Eng. doctor, the reputed inventor], a thin protective sheath, generally of rubber, used to prevent venereal infection or as a contraceptive.

con·do·min·i·um (kon′də-min′i-əm), *n.* [Mod. L.; see COM- & DOMINIUM], 1. joint sovereignty; joint rule of a country or region by two or more states. 2. the territory so governed. 3. an arrangement under which a tenant in an apartment building holds full title to his suite.

con·do·na·tion (kon′dō-nā′shən), *n.* [L. *condonatio*, a giving away, pardoning < pp. of *condonare*], 1. a condoning; forgiving by overlooking; specifically, 2. in *law*, an expressed or implied forgiving by a husband or wife of the other's adultery.

con·done (kən-dōn′), *v.t.* [CONDONED (-dōnd′), CONDONING], [L. *condonare* < *com-*, intens. + *donare*, to give], to forgive, pardon, or overlook (an offense).

con·dor (kon′dẽr), *n.* [Sp. *cóndor* < Peruv. (Quechua) *cuntur*], 1. a large vulture of the South American Andes, with black plumage, bare head and neck, and a ruff of downy white feathers at the base of the neck. 2. a similar vulture found in California. 3. (Sp. kôn′dôr), [*pl.* CONDORES (kôn-dô′res)], any of various gold coins with the figure of a condor stamped on them, used in several South American countries.

CONDOR (4 ft. long; 9 ft. wingspread)

Con·dor·cet, Marquis de (də kōn′dôr′se′), (*Marie Jean de Caritat*), 1743–1794; French mathematician and Girondist.

‡**con·dot·tie·re** (kôn′dôt-tye′re), *n.* [*pl.* CONDOTTIERI (-rē)], [It. < *condotto*, one hired < L. *conductus*, pl. *conducti*, hirelings, mercenary soldiers < pp. of *conducere*, to hire, employ, lead together (see CONDUCE); associated in It. with *condotta*, leadership, captaincy < L. pp. of *conducere* in sense of "lead"], in Europe from the 14th to the 16th centuries, a captain of a band of adventurers, hired to lead his mercenaries in battle.

con·duce (kən-dōōs′, kən-dūs′), *v.i.* [CONDUCED (-dōōst′, -dūst′), CONDUCING], [L. *conducere*, to lead or bring together, conduce < *com-*, together + *ducere*, to lead], to tend; contribute; lead (*to* or *toward*).

con·du·cive (kən-dōō′siv, kən-dū′siv), *adj.* conducing; tending; helpful; contributive (*to*).

con·duct (kon′dukt; *for v.*, kən-dukt′), *n.* [< L. *conductus*, pp. of *conducere;* see CONDUCE], 1. a leading; guidance. 2. management; handling. 3. behavior; deportment; way that one acts. 4. [Obs.], an escort; convoy. *v.t.* 1. to lead; escort. 2. to manage; control; direct; carry on. 3. to direct (an orchestra, etc.). 4. to behave (oneself). 5. to be a channel for; convey; transmit: as, this wire *conducts* electricity. *v.i.* 1. to lead. 2. to act as a conductor.

SYN.—**conduct,** in this comparison, implies a supervising by using one's executive skill, knowledge, wisdom, etc. (to *conduct* a sales campaign); **direct** implies less supervision of actual details, but stresses the issuance of general orders or instructions (to *direct* the construction of a dam); **manage** implies supervision that involves the personal handling of all details (to *manage* a department); **control** implies firm direction by regulation or restraint and often connotes complete domination (the school board *controls* the system). See also **behave.**

con·duct·ance (kən-duk′təns), *n.* the ability of a substance to conduct electricity, measured by the ratio of the current to the applied electromotive force: also called *reciprocal of resistance:* abbreviated G., g.

con·duct·i·bil·i·ty (kən-duk′tə-bil′ə-ti), *n.* capacity for conducting (electricity, heat, etc.).

con·duct·i·ble (kən-duk′tə-b'l), ***adj.*** 1. that can conduct (electricity, heat, etc.). 2. that can be conducted.

con·duc·tion (kən-duk′shən), ***n.*** [L. *conductio;* see CONDUCT], 1. a conveying, as of liquid through a channel. 2. in *physics, a)* transmission (of electricity, heat, etc.) by the passage of energy from particle to particle. *b)* conductivity. See also **convection, radiation.**

con·duc·tive (kən-duk′tiv), ***adj.*** 1. having conductivity. 2. having to do with conduction.

con·duc·tiv·i·ty (kon′duk-tiv′ə-ti), ***n.*** 1. the property of conducting or transmitting heat, electricity, etc. 2. in *electricity,* the quantity of electricity that will flow through a unit cube of a given substance in a unit of time; reciprocal of resistivity. Abbreviated **cond.**

con·duc·tor (kən-duk′tẽr), ***n.*** [L.], 1. a person who conducts; leader; guide; manager. 2. the director of an orchestra or other musical group. 3. the person who has charge of the passengers and collects fares on a streetcar, bus, or train. 4. a thing or substance that conducts electricity, heat, etc. Abbreviated **cond.**

con·duc·tress (kən-duk′tris), ***n.*** a woman conductor.

con·duit (kon′dit, kon′doo-it), ***n.*** [ME. & OFr. < L. *conductus,* pp. of *conducere;* see CONDUCE], 1. a pipe or channel for conveying fluids. 2. a tube or protected trough for electric wires. 3. [Archaic], a fountain.

con·du·pli·cate (kon-dōō′plə-kit, kon-dū′plə-kit), ***adj.*** [L. *conduplicatus,* pp. of *conduplicare* < *com-,* with + *duplicare;* see DUPLICATE], folded lengthwise along the middle, as certain leaves and petals in the bud.

con·dy·lar (kon′di-lẽr), ***adj.*** of a condyle or condyles.

con·dyle (kon′dil), ***n.*** [Fr.; L. *condylus,* knuckle of a joint; Gr. *kondylos,* joint], a rounded process at the end of a bone, forming a ball-and-socket joint with the hollow part of another bone.

con·dy·loid (kon′di-loid′), ***adj.*** of or like a condyle.

con·dy·lo·ma (kon′di-lō′mə), ***n.*** [*pl.* CONDYLOMATA (-tə)], [Mod. L.; Gr. *kondylōma* < *kondylos;* see CONDYLE], a wartlike, inflammatory growth on the skin, occurring near the anus or genital organs, especially in the secondary stage of syphilis.

cone (kōn), ***n.*** [Fr.; L. *conus;* Gr. *kōnos,* a wedge, peak, cone], 1. in *geometry, a)* a solid with a circle for its base and a curved surface tapering evenly to an apex so that any point on this surface is in a straight line between the circumference of the base and the apex. *b)* a solid described by the hypotenuse of a right triangle rotated about either of its legs as an axis. *c)* a surface described by a moving straight line passing through a fixed point (called the *vertex*) and tracing any fixed curve, as a circle, ellipse, etc., at another point. 2. any object or mass shaped like a cone, as a crisp shell of pastry for holding a scoop of ice cream, the peak of a volcano, any of various machine parts, etc. 3. in *botany,* the fruit of evergreen trees, consisting of a woody axis on which are arranged stiff, leaflike scales containing ovules or pollen; strobile. ***v.t.*** [CONED (kōnd), CONING], to shape like a cone or a conical segment.

GEOMETRICAL CONE

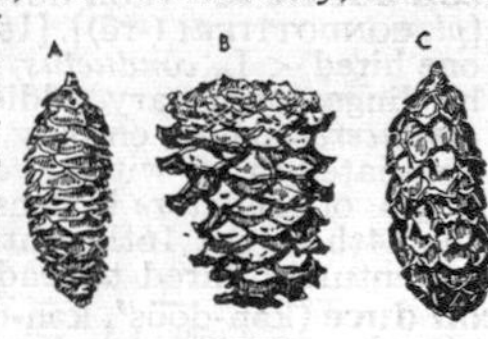

CONES
A, white spruce; B, western yellow pine; C, airplane spruce

cone·flow·er (kōn′flou′ẽr), ***n.*** any of a group of flowers, mostly yellow, with petals radiating from a cone-shaped axis, as the black-eyed Susan.

Con·el·rad (kon′'l-rad′), ***n.*** [*con*trol of *el*ectromagnetic *rad*iation], a system of shifting radiobroadcasting frequencies in the event of an enemy air attack so as to prevent the location of cities by means of radio beams.

cone·nose (kōn′nōz′), ***n.*** any of several varieties of blood-sucking insects with conelike sucking organs, found in the southern and southwestern United States.

Con·es·to·ga wagon (kon′ə-stō′gə), [after *Conestoga,* Lancaster County, Pennsylvania, where the wagons were manufactured], a broad-wheeled covered wagon used by American pioneers crossing the prairies.

co·ney (kō′ni, kun′i), ***n.*** [*pl.* CONEYS (-niz, -iz)], a cony.

Co·ney Island (kō′ni), an island in Brooklyn, New York, at the southwest end of Long Island, famous for its beach and amusement park.

conf., 1. [L.], *confer.* 2. conference. 3. confessor.

con·fab (kon′fab), ***n.*** [Colloq.], a confabulation.

con·fab·u·late (kən-fab′yoo-lāt′), ***v.i.*** [CONFABULATED (-id), CONFABULATING], [< L. *confabulatus,* pp. of *confabulari,* to talk together < *com-,* together + *fabulari,* to converse, chat; see FABLE], to talk together in an informal, familiar way; chat.

con·fab·u·la·tion (kən-fab′yoo-lā′shən), ***n.*** [L. *confabulatio*], a talking together in an informal way; chat.

con·far·re·a·tion (kon-far′i-ā′shən), ***n.*** [L. *confarreatio* < *confarrare,* to marry < *farreum,* spelt cake < *farreus,* spelt < *far,* kind of grain; cf. FARINA, FARINACEOUS], in ancient Rome, the most solemn form of marriage among the patricians, marked by the offering of a cake of spelt as a sacrifice to Jupiter.

con·fect (kən-fekt′), ***v.t.*** [< L. *confectus,* pp. of *conficere,* to prepare < *com-,* with + *facere,* to make, do], to prepare or make, especially by mixing or combining.

con·fec·tion (kən-fek′shən), ***n.*** [ME. *confeccioun;* OFr. *confeccion, confection;* L. *confectio*], 1. a confecting. 2. a bonbon, candy, ice cream, etc. 3. a sweetened compound of drugs; electuary. 4. a fancy, stylish article of women's clothing. ***v.t.*** to prepare as a confection.

con·fec·tion·ar·y (kən-fek′shən-er′i), ***adj.*** 1. of or like a confection. 2. of a confectioner or his work. ***n.*** [*pl.* CONFECTIONARIES (-iz)], 1. a confectionery (sense 3). 2. a confection; candy, etc.

con·fec·tion·er (kən-fek′shən-ẽr), ***n.*** a person whose work or business is making or selling confectionery.

confectioners' sugar, sugar ground into a very fine powder so that it will dissolve more readily.

con·fec·tion·er·y (kən-fek′shən-er′i), ***n.*** [*pl.* CONFECTIONERIES (-iz)], 1. candies, ice cream, and other confections. 2. the business or work of a confectioner. 3. a confectioner's shop or place of business; candy store: sometimes spelled **confectionary.**

con·fed·er·a·cy (kən-fed′ẽr-ə-si), ***n.*** [*pl.* CONFEDERACIES (-siz)], [ME. & OFr. *confederacie* < LL. *confoederatus;* see CONFEDERATE], 1. people, groups, nations, or states united for some common purpose. 2. a league or alliance formed by such a union; federation. 3. people united for an unlawful purpose; conspiracy. —***SYN.*** see **alliance.**

the Confederacy, the group of Southern States that seceded from the United States in 1860 and 1861; Alabama, Arkansas, Florida, Georgia, Louisiana, Mississippi, North Carolina, South Carolina, Tennessee, Texas, and Virginia: also called *Confederate States of America, Southern Confederacy.*

con·fed·er·ate (kən-fed′ẽr-it), ***adj.*** [LL. *confoederatus,* pp. of *confoederare,* to unite by a league < L. *com-,* together + *foederare,* to establish by a league < *foedus,* a league; see FEDERAL], 1. united in a confederacy; joined in an alliance or league. 2. [C-], of the Confederacy. ***n.*** 1. a person, group, nation, or state united with another or others for some common purpose; ally; associate. 2. an associate in an unlawful act or plot; accomplice; co-conspirator. 3. [C-], any Southerner who supported or fought for the Confederacy. ***v.t. & v.i.*** (kən-fed′ẽr-āt′), [CONFEDERATED (-id), CONFEDERATING], to unite in a confederacy; join together; ally. Abbreviated **Confed.** —***SYN.*** see **associate.**

Confederate States of America, the Confederacy.

con·fed·er·a·tion (kən-fed′ẽr-ā′shən), ***n.*** [LL. *confoederatio;* see CONFEDERATE], 1. a uniting or being united in a league or alliance. 2. nations or states joined in a league or union for a special purpose that is not merely temporary. —***SYN.*** see **alliance.**

the Confederation, the union of the American States (1781–1789) under the Articles of Confederation.

con·fed·er·a·tive (kən-fed′ẽr-ā′tiv, kən-fed′ẽr-ə-tiv), ***adj.*** of confederates or a confederation.

con·fer (kən-fũr′), ***v.t.*** [CONFERRED (-fũrd′), CONFERRING], [L. *conferre,* to bring together, compare, confer < *com-,* together + *ferre,* to bring, bear], to give; bestow. ***v.i.*** to have a conference; compare and exchange ideas; meet for discussion; converse. —***SYN.*** see **give.**

‡**con·fer** (kən-fũr′), ***v.t.*** [L., imperative of *conferre;* see CONFER (to converse)], compare: abbreviated **cf., conf.**

con·fer·ee (kon′fẽr-ē′), ***n.*** 1. a participant in a conference. 2. a person on whom an honor, privilege, favor, etc., is conferred. Also spelled **conferree.**

con·fer·ence (kon′fẽr-əns), ***n.*** [Fr. *conférence;* ML. *conferentia* < L. *conferens,* ppr. of *conferre;* see CONFER (to converse)], 1. a conversing or consulting on a serious matter. 2. a formal meeting of a number of people for discussion or consultation. 3. a meeting at which committees from the two branches of a legislature reconcile the differences between bills passed by both branches. 4. [C-], an assembly of ministers of either the Methodist Church or the Mennonite Church for legislating on church matters. 5. an association of religious bodies, schools, athletic teams, etc., for some common purpose.

con·fer·en·tial (kon′fẽr-en′shəl), ***adj.*** of a conference.

con·fer·ment (kən-fũr′mənt), ***n.*** a conferring of an honor, favor, privilege, etc.; bestowal.

con·fer·ra·ble(kən-fũr′ə-b'l), ***adj.*** that can be conferred.

con·fer·ree (kon′fẽr-ē′), ***n.*** a conferee.

con·fer·rer (kən-fũr′ẽr), ***n.*** a person or agency that confers something; giver.

con·fer·va (kən-fũr′və), ***n.*** [*pl.* CONFERVAE (-vē), CONFERVAS (-vəz)], [L., kind of water plant < *confervere,* to seethe, boil together, heal < *com-,* with + *fervere* (see FERVENT): so named from its reputed healing qualities], any of a group of green, fresh-water algae.

con·fer·val (kən-fũr′vəl), ***adj.*** of or like a conferva. ***n.*** a conferva or allied alga.

con·fer·void (kon-fũr′void), ***adj.*** like a conferva. ***n.*** a conferva.

con·fess (kən-fes′), ***v.t.*** [ME. *confessen;* OFr. *confesser;* LL. *confessare* < L. *confessus,* pp. of *confiteri* < *com-,* together + *fateri,* to acknowledge], 1. to admit or acknowledge (a fault, crime, opinion, etc.). 2. to declare one's faith in. 3. [Poetic], to manifest; attest. 4. in *ecclesiastical usage,* *a*) to tell (one's sins) to a priest in penitence in order to receive absolution. *b*) to hear the confession of (a person): said of a priest. ***v.i.*** 1. to admit or acknowledge one's faults or crimes; own up to one's guilt. 2. in *ecclesiastical usage, a*) to tell one's sins in order to receive absolution. *b*) to hear a person tell his sins; serve as a confessor. —***SYN.*** see **acknowledge.**

confess to, to admit; acknowledge; admit having.
stand confessed as, to be revealed or admitted as.

con·fess·ed·ly (kən-fes′id-li), ***adv.*** by confession; avowedly; admittedly.

con·fes·sion (kən-fesh′ən), ***n.*** [ME. *confessioun;* OFr. *confession;* L. *confessio*], 1. a confessing; acknowledgment; admission. 2. something confessed. 3. an admission of guilt, as by a person charged with a crime. 4. the confessing of sins to a priest in order to receive absolution. 5. a form used in public worship, expressing a general acknowledgment of sin. 6. declaration of faith; creed; hence, 7. a group of people adhering to a certain creed; church; sect; denomination. 8. the tomb or shrine of a martyr or confessor.

con·fes·sion·al (kən-fesh′ən-′l), ***n.*** [Fr.; see CONFESSION], 1. a small, enclosed place in a church, where a priest hears confessions. 2. the confession of sins to a priest. ***adj.*** 1. of, like, or for confession. 2. of creeds.

con·fes·sion·ar·y (kən-fesh′ən-er′i), ***adj.*** & ***n.*** [*pl.* CONFESSIONARIES (-iz)], [Rare], confessional.

confession of faith, 1. a declaration of belief. 2. a declaration of the beliefs or doctrines of a religion; creed.

con·fes·sor (kən-fes′ẽr), ***n.*** [L.], 1. a person who confesses. 2. a person who professes his religious faith in spite of persecution: as, Edward the *Confessor:* distinguished from *martyr.* 3. a priest authorized to hear confessions and give absolution: abbreviated **conf.** Also spelled **confesser.**

con·fet·ti (kən-fet′i), ***n.pl.*** [*sing.* CONFETTO (-tō)], [It., pl. of *confetto,* sweetmeat; see COMFIT], 1. candies, or plaster imitations of candies, formerly scattered about at carnivals or other celebrations. 2. [construed as sing.], bits of colored paper now used in this way.

con·fi·dant (kon′fə-dant′, kon′fə-dant′), ***n.*** [Fr. *confident* (fem. *confidente*); It. *confidente* < L. *confidens,* ppr. of *confidere;* see CONFIDE], a close, trusted friend, to whom one confides intimate affairs, secrets, etc.

con·fi·dante (kon′fə-dant′, kon′fə-dant′), ***n.*** a confidant who is a woman.

con·fide (kən-fīd′), ***v.i.*** [CONFIDED (-id), CONFIDING], [L. *confidere* < *com-,* intens. + *fidere,* to trust], to trust (*in* someone); share secrets or discuss private affairs. ***v.t.*** 1. to tell or talk about as a secret: as, she *confided* her difficulties to her friend. 2. to entrust (a duty, object, person, etc. *to* someone); give into the keeping of a trusted person. —***SYN.*** see **commit.**

con·fi·dence (kon′fə-dəns), ***n.*** [L. *confidentia* < *confidens,* ppr. of *confidere;* see CONFIDE], 1. firm belief; trust; reliance. 2. assurance; a being or feeling certain. 3. belief in one's own abilities; self-confidence. 4. someone or something to be trusted. 5. a relationship as confidant: as, take me into your *confidence.* 6. the belief that another will keep a secret; assurance of secrecy: as, told in strict *confidence.* 7. something told as a secret.

SYN.—**confidence,** in this comparison, implies belief in one's own abilities or, especially in the form **self-confidence,** reliance on one's own powers (he has *confidence* he will win); **assurance,** in this connection, suggests an even stronger belief in one's ability, but in an unfavorable sense, it may connote (as does **confidence**) conceited or arrogant self-sufficiency; **self-possession** suggests that presence of mind which results from the ability to control one's feelings and behavior; **aplomb** refers, usually in a favorable sense, to an evident assurance of manner manifesting self-possession (he stood his ground with admirable *aplomb*). See also **belief, certainty.**—***ANT.*** diffidence, shyness.

confidence game, a swindle effected by gaining the confidence of the victim.

confidence man, a swindler who tries to gain the confidence of his victim in order to defraud him.

con·fi·dent (kon′fə-dənt), ***adj.*** 1. full of confidence; expressing confidence; specifically, *a*) assured; certain: as, we are *confident* of victory. *b*) sure of oneself; self-confident; bold: as, a *confident* manner. 2. [Archaic], confiding. ***n.*** a confidant. —***SYN.*** see **sure.**

con·fi·den·tial (kon′fə-den′shəl), ***adj.*** 1. told in confidence; imparted in secret. 2. of or showing confidence. 3. entrusted with private or secret matters: as, a *confidential* agent. —***SYN.*** see **familiar.**

confidential communication, a statement made in confidence to one's attorney, physician, clergyman, husband, or wife, who cannot then be compelled to divulge this in a court of law.

con·fid·ing (kən-fīd′iŋ), ***adj.*** [ppr. of *confide*], trustful or inclined to trust.

con·fig·u·ra·tion (kən-fig′yoo-rā′shən), ***n.*** [L. *configuratio* < *configurare,* to form after < *com-,* together + *figurare;* see FIGURE], 1. arrangement of parts; form or figure as determined by the disposition of parts; contour; outline. 2. [after G. *gestalt*], in *Gestalt psychology,* an integrated whole with independent properties and functions over and above the sum of the properties and functions of its parts. —***SYN.*** see **form.**

con·fig·u·ra·tion·ism (kən-fig′yoo-rā′shən-iz′m), ***n.*** Gestalt psychology.

con·fin·a·ble, con·fine·a·ble (kən-fīn′ə-b′l), ***adj.*** that can be confined.

con·fine (kon′fīn′; *for v.,* kən-fīn′), ***n.*** [Fr. & OFr. *confins, pl.,* a border, boundary; L. *confinium,* boundary, limit < *confinis,* bordering on < *com-,* with + *finis,* an end, limit], 1. *usually in pl.* a boundary or bounded region; border; limit. 2. [Poetic], confinement. 3. [Obs.], a place of confinement. ***v.i.*** [CONFINED (-fīnd′), CONFINING], [Fr. *confiner* < the *n.*], [Rare], to border (*on*) or be contiguous (*with* or *to* another region). ***v.t.*** 1. to keep within limits; restrict: as, please *confine* your remarks to the facts. 2. to keep shut up, as in prison, in bed because of illness, indoors, etc. —***SYN.*** see **limit.**

be confined, to be undergoing childbirth.

con·fine·ment (kən-fīn′mənt), ***n.*** a confining or being confined; specifically, *a*) imprisonment. *b*) limitation; restriction; restraint. *c*) childbirth; lying-in.

con·firm (kən-fũrm′), ***v.t.*** [ME. *confermen;* OFr. *confermer;* L. *confirmare* < *com-,* intens. + *firmare,* to strengthen < *firmus*], 1. to make firm; strengthen; establish; encourage. 2. to make valid by formal approval; ratify. 3. to prove the truth, validity, or authenticity of; verify. 4. in *ecclesiastical usage,* to admit (a person of a certain age) to full membership in a church by a ceremony in which he reaffirms the vows made for him when he was a child.

SYN.—to **confirm** is to establish as true that which was doubtful or uncertain (to *confirm* a rumor); **substantiate** suggests the producing of evidence that proves or tends to prove the validity of a previous assertion or claim (the census figures *substantiate* his charge); **corroborate** suggests the strengthening of one statement or testimony by another (the witnesses *corroborated* her version of the event); to **verify** is to prove to be true or correct by investigation, comparison with a standard, or reference to ascertainable facts (to *verify* an account); **authenticate** implies proof of genuineness by an authority or expert (to *authenticate* a painting); **validate** implies official confirmation of the validity of something (to *validate* a will).—***ANT.*** contradict, disprove.

con·fir·mand (kon′fẽr-mand′), ***n.*** in *ecclesiastical usage,* a person who is to be confirmed.

con·fir·ma·tion (kon′fẽr-mā′shən), ***n.*** [ME. & OFr. *confirmacion;* L. *confirmatio* < pp. of *confirmare*], 1. a confirming or being confirmed; corroboration; ratification; verification. 2. something that confirms or proves. 3. a religious ceremony in which a person of a certain age is admitted to full membership in a church.

con·firm·a·tive (kən-fũr′mə-tiv), ***adj.*** confirming or tending to confirm.

con·firm·a·to·ry (kən-fũr′mə-tôr′i, kən-fũr′mə-tō′ri), ***adj.*** confirming or serving to confirm.

con·firmed (kən-fũrmd′), ***adj.*** [pp. of *confirm*], 1. firmly established, as in a habit or condition; habitual: as, a *confirmed* bachelor. 2. chronic, as a disease. 3. corroborated; proved. 4. having gone through the religious ceremony of confirmation. —***SYN.*** see **chronic.**

con·firm·or (kon′fẽr-môr′, kən-fũr′mẽr), ***n.*** a person who ratifies another's legal title.

con·fis·ca·ble (kən-fis′kə-b′l), ***adj.*** liable to be confiscated or forfeited.

con·fis·cate (kon′fis-kāt′), ***v.t.*** [CONFISCATED (-id), CONFISCATING], [< L. *confiscatus,* pp. of *confiscare,* to lay up in a chest, seize for the public treasury, confiscate < *com-,* together + *fiscus,* wicker basket, money basket or chest, public treasury], 1. to seize (private property) for the public treasury, usually as a penalty. 2. to seize by or as by authority; appropriate. ***adj.*** 1. confiscated. 2. having property confiscated.

con·fis·ca·tion (kon′fis-kā′shən), ***n.*** [L. *confiscatio* < pp. of *confiscare*], 1. a confiscating or being confiscated. 2. something confiscated.

con·fis·ca·tor (kon′fis-kā′tẽr), ***n.*** [L., treasurer], a person who confiscates.

con·fis·ca·to·ry (kən-fis′kə-tôr′i, kən-fis′kə-tō′ri), ***adj.*** 1. of, constituting, or effecting confiscation: as, a *confiscatory* tax. 2. confiscating.

con·fit·e·or (kən-fit′i-ôr′), ***n.*** [L., I confess (see CONFESS)], a formal prayer in which sins are confessed.

con·fi·ture (kon′fi-choor′), ***n.*** [ME.; Late OFr. < *confit,* comfit < *confire,* to preserve; L. *conficere;* cf. COMFIT], a confection, sweetmeat, or preserve.

con·fla·grant (kən-flā′grənt), ***adj.*** [L. *conflagrans,* ppr. of *conflagrare;* see CONFLAGRATION], burning; ablaze.

con·fla·gra·tion (kon′flə-grā′shən), ***n.*** [L. *conflagratio* < pp. of *conflagrare,* to burn < *com-,* intens. + *flagrare,* to burn], a big, destructive fire.

con·fla·tion (kən-flā'shən), *n.* [LL. *conflatio* < L. *conflare*, to blow together < *com-*, together + *flare*, to blow], a combining, as of two variant readings into a single text.

con·flict (kən-flikt'; *for n.*, kon'flikt), *v.i.* [< L. *conflictus*, pp. of *confligere*, to strike together < *com-*, together + *fligere*, to strike], 1. originally, to fight; battle; contend. 2. to clash; be antagonistic, incompatible, or contradictory; be in opposition: as, his interests *conflict* with mine. *n.* 1. a fight; battle; struggle. 2. sharp disagreement or opposition, as of interests, ideas, etc.; clash. 3. emotional disturbance resulting from a clash of impulses in a person.
SYN.—**conflict** refers to a sharp disagreement or collision in interests, ideas, etc. and emphasizes the process rather than the end (the *conflict* over slavery); **fight,** a rather general word for any contest, struggle, or quarrel, stresses physical or hand-to-hand combat; **struggle** implies great effort or violent exertion, physical or otherwise (the *struggle* for existence); **contention** most frequently applies to heated verbal strife, or dispute (religious *contention* broke out); **contest** refers to a struggle, either friendly or hostile, for supremacy in some matter (athletic *contests*, a *contest* of wits).—*ANT.* accord, harmony.

con·flic·tion (kən-flik'shən), *n.* [L. *conflictio* < *conflictus*], a conflicting; being in a conflict.

con·flic·tive (kən-flik'tiv), *adj.* conflicting.

con·flu·ence (kon'flōō-əns), *n.* [LL. *confluentia* < L. *confluens*, ppr. of *confluere* < *com-*, together + *fluere*, to flow], 1. a flowing together, especially of two or more streams. 2. the place of, or a stream formed by, this. 3. a flocking together; hence, 4. a crowd; throng.

con·flu·ent (kon'flōō-ənt), *adj.* [L. *confluens*, *confluentis;* see CONFLUENCE], 1. flowing or running together so as to form one: as, *confluent* streams. 2. in *medicine*, running together so as to form a merged mass, as sores, pimples, etc. *n.* 1. a stream uniting with another; hence, 2. loosely, a tributary.

con·flux (kon'fluks), *n.* [< L. *confluxus*, pp. of *confluere;* see CONFLUENCE], confluence.

con·fo·cal (kon-fō'k'l), *adj.* in *mathematics*, having the same focus or foci.

con·form (kən-fôrm'), *v.t.* [ME. *conformen;* OFr. *conformer;* L. *conformare*, to fashion, form < *com-*, together + *formare;* see FORM], 1. to give the same form to; make similar: as, he *conformed* his ideas to ours. 2. to bring into harmony or agreement; adapt: often used reflexively. *v.i.* 1. to have the same form; be or become similar. 2. to be in accord or agreement: as, the novel *conformed* to my notion of a good story. 3. to act in accordance with rules, customs, etc. 4. in *English history*, to accept and adhere to the usages of the Established Church. —*SYN.* see **adapt, agree.**

con·form·a·bil·i·ty (kən-fôr'mə-bil'ə-ti), *n.* the quality or state of being conformable.

con·form·a·ble (kən-fôr'mə-b'l), *adj.* 1. that conforms; specifically, *a*) similar. *b*) in harmony or agreement. *c*) adapted; suited; corresponding. 2. quick to conform; obedient; submissive; compliant. 3. in *geology*, uninterruptedly parallel: said of contiguous strata.

con·form·a·bly (kən-fôr'mə-bli), *adv.* so as to conform; in accordance.

con·form·ance (kən-fôr'məns), *n.* conformity.

con·for·ma·tion (kon'fôr-mā'shən), *n.* [L. *conformatio* < pp. of *conformare*], 1. [Rare], a conforming or being conformed; adaptation. 2. a completed or symmetrical formation and arrangement of the parts of a thing. 3. the structure or form of a thing as determined by the arrangement of its parts.

con·form·ist (kən-fôrm'ist), *n.* 1. a person who conforms. 2. in *English history*, a person accepting and adhering to the usages of the Established Church: opposed to *nonconformist, dissenter:* abbreviated **Con.**

con·form·i·ty (kən-fôr'mə-ti), *n.* [*pl.* CONFORMITIES (-tiz)], [Fr. *conformité* < *conformer;* see CONFORM], 1. the condition or fact of being in harmony or agreement; correspondence; congruity; similarity. 2. action in accordance with rules, customs, etc. 3. in *English history*, acceptance of and adherence to the usages of the Established Church.

con·found (kən-found', kon-found'), *v.t.* [ME. *confonden;* OFr. *confondre, confundre;* L. *confundere*, to pour or mingle together, confuse, confound < *com-*, together + *fundere*, to pour], 1. to mix up or lump together indiscriminately; confuse. 2. to cause to become confused; bewilder. 3. [Archaic], to defeat; destroy; make to no avail. 4. [Archaic], to make feel ashamed; abash; embarrass. 5. (*usually* kon'found'), to damn: used as a mild oath. —*SYN.* see **puzzle.**

con·found·ed (kən-foun'did; *also, for 2 & 3* kon'foun'did), *adj.* [pp. of *confound*], 1. confused; bewildered. 2. damned: a mild oath. 3. detestable; abominable.

con·fra·ter·ni·ty (kon'frə-tũr'nə-ti), *n.* [*pl.* CONFRATERNITIES (-tiz)], [LL. *confraternitas;* see COM- & FRATERNITY], 1. brotherhood. 2. a group of men associated for some purpose or in a profession.

con·frere (kon'frâr; Fr. kōn'frâr'), *n.* [Fr. *confrère;* see COM- & FRÈRE], colleague; associate; fellow member; fellow worker, as in a profession.

con·front (kən-frunt'), *v.t.* [Fr. *confronter;* ML. *confrontare* < L. *com-*, together + *frons*, forehead; see FRONT], 1. to face; stand or meet face to face. 2. to face boldly, defiantly, or antagonistically. 3. to bring (a person) face to face (*with*): as, he *confronted* the accused with the evidence. 4. to compare.

Con·fu·cian (kən-fū'shən), *adj.* of Confucius, his teachings, or his followers. *n.* a Confucianist.

Con·fu·cian·ism (kən-fū'shən-iz'm), *n.* the ethical teachings formulated by Confucius and introduced into the Chinese religion, emphasizing devotion to parents, family, and friends, ancestor worship, and the maintenance of justice and peace.

Con·fu·cian·ist (kən-fū'shən-ist), *n.* an adherent of Confucianism. *adj.* of Confucianism or Confucianists.

Con·fu·cius (kən-fū'shəs), *n.* (*Kung Fu-tse*), Chinese philosopher and teacher; 557?–479 B.C.

con·fuse (kən-fūz') *v.t.* [CONFUSED (-fūzd'), CONFUSING], [< ME. & OFr. *confus*, confused; L. *confusus*, pp. of *confundere;* see CONFOUND], 1. to mix up; jumble together; put into disorder. 2. to mix up mentally; specifically, *a*) to bewilder; perplex. *b*) to embarrass; disconcert; abash. *c*) to fail to distinguish between; mistake the identity of. —*SYN.* see **puzzle.**

con·fus·ed·ly (kən-fūz'id-li, kən-fūzd'li), *adv.* in a confused manner.

con·fu·sion (kən-fū'zhən), *n.* [ME.; OFr.; L. *confusio*], a confusing or being confused; specifically, *a*) disorder. *b*) bewilderment. *c*) embarrassment. *d*) failure to distinguish between things.
covered with confusion, greatly embarrassed.
SYN.—**confusion** suggests an indiscriminate mixing or throwing together of things so that it is difficult to distinguish the individual elements or parts (the hall was a *confusion* of languages); **disorder** and **disarray** imply a disturbance of the proper order or arrangement of parts (the room was **in** *disorder*, her clothes were in *disarray*); **chaos** implies total and apparently irremediable lack of organization (the troops are in a state of *chaos*); **jumble** suggests a confused mixture of dissimilar things (his drawer was a *jumble* of clothing, books, etc.); **muddle** implies a snarled confusion resulting from mismanagement or incompetency (they've made a *muddle* of the negotiations).—*ANT.* order, system.

con·fu·sion·al (kən-fū'zhən-'l), *adj.* characterized by confusion.

con·fu·ta·tion (kon'fyoo-tā'shən), *n.* [L. *confutatio* < pp. of *confutare*], 1. a confuting. 2. an argument, evidence, etc. that confutes.

con·fut·a·tive (kən-fū'tə-tiv), *adj.* confuting or tending to confute.

con·fute (kən-fūt'), *v.t.* [CONFUTED (-id), CONFUTING], [L. *confutare* < *com-*, intens. + **futare;* IE. base **bhaut-*, **bhut-*, to strike], 1. to prove (a person) to be in error; overcome by argument or proof. 2. to prove (a statement, argument, etc.) to be false or invalid. 3. to make useless; confound. —*SYN.* see **disprove.**

Cong., 1. Congregational. 2. Congregationalist. 3. Congress. 4. Congressional.

cong., congius.

con·ga (koŋ'gə), *n.* [Am. Sp.], 1. a modern ballroom dance of Latin-American origin, in which the dancers form a winding line. 2. the music for this dance, in 4/4 syncopated time, with a heavy accent on the fourth beat of every measure. *v.i.* to dance the conga.

con·gé (kon'zhā; Fr. kōn'zhā'), *n.* [Fr., leave, departure; OFr. *congié;* L. *commeatus*, a going to and fro < *commeare*, to come and go; *com-*, intens. + *meare*, to go], 1. a curt dismissal: as, he gave me my *congé*. 2. a formal leave-taking or farewell. 3. [Archaic], a bow, especially at leave-taking. 4. in *architecture*, a kind of molding: see **molding**, illus.

con·geal (kən-jēl'), *v.t. & v.i.* [ME. *congelen;* OFr. *congeler;* L. *congelare* < *com-*, together + *gelare*, to freeze; cf. GELID], 1. to solidify or thicken by cooling or freezing. 2. to thicken; coagulate; jell.

con·geal·ment (kən-jēl'mənt), *n.* a congealing.

con·gee (kon'jē), *n.* [ME. *conge;* OFr. *congie* (Fr. *congé*) < L. *commeare*, to come and go, leave; cf. PERMEATE], [Now Rare], congé. *v.i.* [Now Rare], to take formal leave; especially, to bow in leaving.

con·ge·la·tion (kon'jə-lā'shən), *n.* [ME.; OFr.; L. *congelatio* < *congelatus*, pp. of *congelare*], 1. a congealing or being congealed. 2. something congealed.

con·gen·er (kon'ji-nẽr), *n.* [L., of the same race or kind < *com-*, together + *genus, generis*, race, kind], a person or thing of the same kind, class, race, or genus.

con·ge·ner·ic (kon'ji-ner'ik), *adj.* [*congener* + *-ic*], belonging to the same kind, class, race, or genus.

con·gen·er·ous (kən-jen'ẽr-əs), *adj.* congeneric.

con·gen·ial (kən-jēn'yəl), *adj.* [see COM- & GENIAL], 1. kindred; compatible: as, *congenial* tastes. 2. having the same tastes and temperament; friendly; sympathetic: as, *congenial* friends. 3. suited to one's needs or disposition; agreeable: as, *congenial* surroundings.

con·ge·ni·al·i·ty (kən-jē'ni-al'ə-ti), *n.* the quality or condition of being congenial.

con·gen·i·tal (kən-jen'ə-t'l), *adj.* [< L. *congenitus*, born together with < *com-*, together + *genitus*, pp. of *gignere*, to bear], existing as such at birth; resulting from one's heredity or prenatal environment: as, a *congenital* disease, a *congenital* idiot. —*SYN.* see **innate.**

con·gen·i·tal·ly (kən-jen'ə-t'l-i), *adv.* from birth; as a result of congenital factors.

con·ger (koŋ'gẽr), *n.* [ME.; OFr. *congre;* LL. *congrus,* for L. *conger;* Gr. *gongros,* conger], a variety of large, edible, salt-water eel: also **conger eel.**

con·ge·ri·es (kon-jêr'ēz, kon-jêr'i-ēz'), *n.* [*pl.* CONGERIES], [L. < *congerere;* see CONGEST], a collection of things or parts massed together; heap; pile.

con·gest (kən-jest'), *v.t.* [< L. *congestus,* pp. of *congerere,* to bring together, pile up < *com-,* together + *gerere,* to carry, perform], 1. to cause too much blood to accumulate in (a part of the body). 2. to overcrowd; fill to excess: as, the shopping district was *congested.* *v.i.* to become congested.

con·ges·tion (kən-jes'chən), *n.* 1. an excessive accumulation of blood in a part of the body. 2. a congesting or congested condition, as of population or traffic.

con·ges·tive (kən-jes'tiv), *adj.* of or with congestion; causing or resulting from congestion.

con·gi·us (kon'ji-əs), *n.* [*pl.* CONGII (-i')], [L. < Gr. *konchos;* akin to *konchē,* conch], 1. an ancient Roman liquid measure equal to a little less than seven pints. 2. in *pharmacy,* a gallon. Abbreviated **cong., C., c.**

con·glo·bate (kon-glō'bāt, koŋ'glō-bāt'), *v.t. & v.i.* [CONGLOBATED (-id), CONGLOBATING], [L. *conglobatus,* pp. of *conglobare;* see CONGLOBE], to form or collect into a ball or rounded mass. *adj.* formed into a ball or rounded mass.

con·globe (kon-glōb'), *v.t. & v.i.* [CONGLOBED (-glōbd'), CONGLOBING], [L. *conglobare* < *com-,* with + *globare,* to make into a ball < *globus;* see GLOBE], to conglobate.

con·glom·er·ate (kən-glom'ẽr-āt'; *for adj. & n.,* kən-glom'ẽr-it), *v.t. & v.i.* [CONGLOMERATED (-id), CONGLOMERATING], [< L. *conglomeratus,* pp. of *conglomerare,* to roll together, wind up < *com-,* together + *glomerare,* to gather into a ball < *glomus,* a ball; akin to *globus* (see GLOBE)], to form or collect into a ball or rounded mass. *adj.* 1. formed or collected into a ball or rounded mass; clustered. 2. made up of separate parts or substances collected together into a single mass. 3. in *geology,* made up of rock fragments or pebbles cemented together in a mass of hardened clay and sand. *n.* 1. a conglomerate mass; cluster. 2. in *geology,* a conglomerate rock.

con·glom·er·at·ic (kən-glom'ẽr-at'ik), *adj.* in *geology,* conglomerate.

con·glom·er·a·tion (kən-glom'ẽr-ā'shən), *n.* 1. a conglomerating or being conglomerated. 2. a collection, mixture, or mass of miscellaneous things.

con·glom·er·it·ic (kən-glom'ẽr-it'ik), *adj.* in *geology,* conglomerate.

con·glu·ti·nate (kən-glōō'tə-nāt'), *adj.* [L. *conglutinatus,* pp. of *conglutinare,* to glue together < *com-,* together + *glutinare,* to glue < *gluten,* glue], glued together; stuck together; adhering. *v.t. & v.i.* [CONGLUTINATED (-id), CONGLUTINATING], to stick together; unite by or as by adhesion.

con·glu·ti·na·tion (kən-glōō'tə-nā'shən), *n.* [L. *conglutinatio*], a conglutinating.

Con·go (koŋ'gō), *n.* 1. a river in Africa, flowing through the Congo (sense 2) into the Atlantic: length, 3,000 mi. 2. a country in central Africa, on the Atlantic: area, 905,378 sq. mi.; pop., 13,984,000; capital, Léopoldville: formerly, *Belgian Congo.* 3. a country in west central Africa, northwest of Congo (sense 2): formerly a territory (called *Middle Congo*) in French Equatorial Africa, it is now a member of the French Community: area, 134,750 sq. mi.; pop., 795,000; capital, Brazzaville.

con·go (koŋ'gō), *n.* congou.

Congo dye (or **color**), any of certain azo dyes, derived mainly from benzidine.

Congo red, a sodium salt of a complex organic acid, used for dyeing wool and cotton and as an acid-base indicator: it becomes blue in an acid solution and remains red in an alkaline or neutral solution.

congo snake, an eellike amphibious animal with two pairs of small, weak legs, found in the swamps of the southeastern United States: also called *congo eel.*

con·gou (koŋ'gōō), *n.* [Chin. *kung-fu,* labor; Amoy *kang-hu-tē,* lit., labor tea, tea on which work has been done], a variety of black Chinese tea.

con·grat·u·lant (kən-grach'ə-lənt), *adj.* congratulating; expressing congratulations. *n.* a congratulator.

con·grat·u·late (kən-grach'ə-lāt'), *v.t.* [CONGRATULATED (-id), CONGRATULATING], [< L. *congratulatus,* pp. of *congratulari,* to wish joy < *com-,* together + *gratulari,* to show joy, wish joy < *gratus,* agreeable], 1. to rejoice with and express one's happiness to (a person who has been fortunate, successful, etc.); felicitate: as, we *congratulated* the boy on winning the race. 2. [Obs.], to rejoice at; celebrate. 3. [Obs.], to greet; hail.

con·grat·u·la·tion (kən-grach'ə-lā'shən), *n.* 1. a congratulating. 2. *pl.* expressions of pleasure and good wishes on the occasion of another's fortune or success.

con·grat·u·la·tor (kən-grach'ə-lā'tẽr), *n.* a person who congratulates.

con·grat·u·la·to·ry (kən-grach'ə-lə-tôr'i, kən-grach'ə-lə-tō'ri), *adj.* expressing congratulations.

con·gre·gate (koŋ'grə-gāt'), *v.t. & v.i.* [CONGREGATED (-id), CONGREGATING], [< L. *congregatus,* pp. of *congregare,* to congregate < *com-,* together + *gregare,* to collect into a flock, gather < *grex, gregis,* a flock], to gather into a mass or crowd; collect; assemble. *adj* (*usually* koŋ'grə-git), 1. collected; assembled. 2. collective.

con·gre·ga·tion (koŋ'grə-gā'shən), *n.* [Fr. *congrégation;* L. *congregatio*], 1. a congregating or being congregated. 2. a gathering of people or things; assemblage. 3. an assembly of people for religious worship or teaching. 4. the members of a particular place of worship. 5. a settlement, town, or parish in the colonies of early New England where Congregationalism was established. 6. in the *Old Testament,* the Jews. 7. in the *Roman Catholic Church,* *a*) a religious community or order not necessarily under solemn vows but bound by a common rule. *b*) a committee of cardinals in charge of some department of church affairs.

con·gre·ga·tion·al (koŋ'grə-gā'shən-'l), *adj.* 1. of or like a congregation. 2. [C-], of Congregationalism or Congregationalists: abbreviated **Cong.**

con·gre·ga·tion·al·ism (koŋ'grə-gā'shən-'l-iz'm), *n.* 1. a form of church organization in which each church and congregation is self-governing. 2. [C-], the faith and form of organization of a Protestant denomination in which each member church is self-governing.

Con·gre·ga·tion·al·ist (koŋ'grə-gā'shən-'l-ist), *n.* a person who believes in Congregationalism or belongs to a Congregational church. *adj.* of Congregationalism or Congregationalists. Abbreviated **Cong.**

con·gre·ga·tive (koŋ'grə-gā'tiv), *adj.* congregating or tending to congregate.

con·gress (koŋ'grəs), *n.* [L. *congressus,* a meeting, interview, hostile encounter; pp. of *congredi,* to come together < *com-,* together + *gradi,* to step, walk < *gradus,* a step], 1. a coming together; meeting. 2. sexual intercourse. 3. social intercourse. 4. an assembly or conference. 5. a formal assembly of representatives from various nations, churches, etc., to discuss problems. 6. any of various legislatures, especially the national legislature of a republic. 7. [C-], *a*) the legislature of the United States, consisting of the Senate and the House of Representatives. *b*) a session of this legislature. *c*) the body of Senators and Representatives serving together for any two-year term. Abbreviated **Cong., C.**

congress boot, a high shoe with a strip of elastic material inserted in each side.

con·gres·sion·al (kən-gresh'ən-'l), *adj.* [< L. *congressio,* a coming together (see CONGRESS); + *-al*], 1. of a congress. 2. [C-], of Congress: abbreviated **Cong.**

Congressional district, any of the districts into which a State is divided for electing Congressmen.

con·gres·sion·al·ist (kən-gresh'ən-'l-ist), *n.* a supporter of a congress.

Congressional Medal of Honor, the highest United States military decoration, awarded by Congress for gallantry at the risk of life above and beyond the call of duty: instituted 1862: also called *Medal of Honor.*

Congressional Record, a daily publication of the proceedings of Congress, including a complete stenographic report of all remarks and debate.

con·gress·man (koŋ'grəs-mən), *n.* [*pl.* CONGRESSMEN (-mən)], a member of Congress, especially of the House of Representatives.

Congress of Industrial Organizations, a group of affiliated labor unions in the United States and Canada, founded 1938: abbreviated **CIO, C.I.O.** See **AFL-CIO.**

Congress of Vienna, a conference of the major European powers held at Vienna in 1814–1815, at the end of the Napoleonic Wars: its purpose was to restore monarchies and readjust territories throughout Europe.

con·gress·wom·an (koŋ'grəs-woom'ən), *n.* [*pl.* CONGRESSWOMEN (-wim'in)], a woman member of Congress, especially of the House of Representatives.

Con·greve, William (kon'grēv, koŋ'grēv), 1670–1729; English dramatist; wrote comedies of manners.

Congreve match, [after Sir William *Congreve* (1772–1828), the inventor], an early kind of friction match.

Congreve rocket, [see CONGREVE MATCH], a kind of rocket formerly used as a weapon of war.

con·gru·ence (koŋ'grōō-əns), *n.* [L. *congruentia;* see CONGRUENT], 1. agreement; correspondence; harmony. 2. correspondence to what is right, proper, or reasonable; suitability; appropriateness. 3. in *English grammar,* concord. 4. in *mathematics,* the relation between two numbers each of which, when divided by a third (called the *modulus*), leaves the same remainder.

con·gru·en·cy (koŋ'grōō-ən-si), *n.* congruence.

con·gru·ent (koŋ'grōō-ənt), *adj.* [L. *congruens,* ppr. of *congruere,* to come together, correspond, agree < *com-,* with + base appearing in *ruere*, to fall violently, go to ruin; IE. base **ghrēu-*, to collapse, topple], 1. agreeing; corresponding; harmonious. 2. in *English grammar*, showing concord. 3. in *geometry*, of the same shape and size: congruent figures, if placed one upon another, coincide exactly in all their parts. 4. in *mathematics*, in congruence: as, *congruent* numbers.

con·gru·i·ty (kən-grōō'ə-ti), *n.* [*pl.* CONGRUITIES (-tiz)], [ME. & OFr. *congruite*], 1. the condition, quality, or fact of being congruous; specifically, *a*) agreement; harmony. *b*) fitness; appropriateness. 2. in *geometry*, exact coincidence: said of two or more figures.

con·gru·ous (koŋ'grōō-əs), *adj.* [L. *congruus*], 1. congruent. 2. corresponding to what is right, proper, or reasonable; fitting; suitable; appropriate.

con·ic (kon'ik), *adj.* [Gr. *kōnikos* < *kōnos*, a peak, cone], conical. *n.* a conic section.

con·i·cal (kon'i-k'l), *adj.* 1. of a cone. 2. resembling or shaped like a cone.

conic projection, a type of map projection formed by projecting the surface of the earth on the surface of a cone and unrolling this to a plane surface on which the parallels of latitude are then concentric circles and the meridians equally spaced radii.

con·ics (kon'iks), *n.pl.* [construed as sing.], the branch of geometry dealing with conic sections.

conic section, in *geometry*, a curve, as an ellipse, parabola, or hyperbola, produced by the intersection of a plane with a right circular cone.

conic sections, the branch of geometry dealing with ellipses, parabolas, and hyperbolas.

co·nid·i·a (kō-nid'i-ə), *n.* plural of **conidium.**

co·nid·i·al (kō-nid'i-əl), *adj.* 1. of or like conidia. 2. producing conidia.

co·nid·i·an (kō-nid'i-ən), *adj.* conidial.

co·nid·i·o·phore (kō-nid'i-ə-fôr', kō-nid'i-ə-fōr'), *n.* [< *conidium* + *-phore*], a specialized, threadlike part that bears conidia, found in certain fungi.

co·nid·i·um (kō-nid'i-əm), *n.* [*pl.* CONIDIA (-ə)], [Mod. L. < Gr. *konis*, dust], a small asexual spore occurring in certain fungi.

co·ni·fer (kō'nə-fẽr, kon'ə-fẽr), *n.* [< L. *conus*, a cone + *ferre*, to bear], any of a large group of cone-bearing trees and shrubs, mostly evergreens, as the pine, spruce, fir, cedar, yew, etc.

co·nif·er·ous (kō-nif'ẽr-əs), *adj.* 1. bearing cones. 2. of conifers.

co·ni·ine (kō'ni-ēn', kō'ni-in), conine.

co·nin (kō'nin), *n.* conine.

co·nine (kō'nēn), *n.* [see CONIUM], a very poisonous, oily alkaloid, $C_8H_{17}N$, extracted from the poison hemlock.

co·ni·um (kō'ni-əm), *n.* [L.; Gr. *kōneion*, hemlock], any of the hemlocks, poisonous plants of the carrot family.

conj., 1. conjugation. 2. conjunction. 3. conjunctive.

con·jec·tur·a·ble (kən-jek'chẽr-ə-b'l), *adj.* that can be conjectured.

con·jec·tur·al (kən-jek'chẽr-əl), *adj.* 1. based on or involving conjecture. 2. inclined to make conjectures.

con·jec·ture (kən-jek'chẽr), *n.* [ME. *coniecture* < L. *conjectura*, a putting together, guess, inference < *conjectus*, pp. of *conjicere*, to throw or bring together, guess < *com-*, together + *jacere*, to throw], 1. guesswork; inferring, theorizing, or predicting from incomplete or uncertain evidence: as, this critic is too fond of *conjecture*. 2. a guess; inference, theory, or prediction based on guesswork. *v.t.* [CONJECTURED (-chẽrd), CONJECTURING], to guess; arrive at, propose, or predict by conjecture. *v.i.* to make a conjecture. —***SYN.*** see **guess.**

con·join (kən-join'), *v.t. & v.i.* [ME. *conjoignen*; OFr. *conjoindre*; L. *conjungere* < *com-*, together + *jungere*, to join], to join together; unite; connect; combine.

con·joint (kən-joint'), *adj.* [ME.; OFr., pp. of *conjoindre*; see CONJOIN], 1. joined together; united; combined; associated. 2. of or involving two or more in association; joint.

con·joint·ly (kən-joint'li), *adv.* jointly; in association.

con·ju·gal (kon'joo-gəl), *adj.* [Fr.; L. *conjugalis* < *conjunx, conjux*, husband or wife < *com-*, together + base akin to L. *jugum* (see YOKE), *jungere* (see JOIN)], of marriage or the relation between husband and wife; matrimonial; connubial.

con·ju·gal·i·ty (kon'joo-gal'ə-ti), *n.* [see CONJUGAL], the state of marriage.

con·ju·gate (kon'joo-git; *also, and for v. always*, kon'joo-gāt'), *adj.* [L. *conjugatus*, pp. of *conjugare*, to join together < *com-*, together + *jugare*, to join < *jugum*, a yoke (see YOKE)], 1. joined together, especially in a pair; coupled. 2. in *botany*, growing in pairs, as leaflets on the axis of some leaves. 3. in *grammar*, derived from the same base and, usually, related in meaning: said of words. 4. in *mathematics*, reciprocally related and interchangeable as to properties, as two points, lines, quantities, etc. *n.* 1. a conjugate word. 2. a conjugate point, line, quantity, etc. *v.t.* [CONJUGATED (-id), CONJUGATING], 1. to join together; unite; couple. 2. in *grammar*, to inflect (a verb) systematically, giving its different forms according to voice, mood, tense, number, and person. *v.i.* 1. [Rare], to unite sexually. 2. in *biology*, to unite in conjugation. 3. in *grammar*, *a*) to conjugate a verb. *b*) to be conjugated.

con·ju·ga·tion (kon'joo-gā'shən), *n.* [L. *conjugatio*], 1. a conjugating or being conjugated; union. 2. in *biology*, the fusion of two gametes or one-celled organisms for reproduction. 3. in *grammar*, *a*) a methodical presentation or arrangement of the inflectional forms of a verb; paradigm. *b*) a class of verbs with similar inflectional forms. Abbreviated **conj.** (in senses 2 & 3).

con·ju·ga·tion·al (kon'joo-gā'shən-'l), *adj.* of conjugation.

con·ju·ga·tive (kon'joo-gā'tiv), *adj.* 1. of conjugation. 2. conjugating or tending to conjugate.

con·ju·ga·tor (kon'joo-gā'tẽr), *n.* [L., one who writes], a person or thing that conjugates.

con·junct (kən-juŋkt', kon'juŋkt), *adj.* [L. *conjunctus*, pp. of *conjungere*; see CONJOIN], [Archaic], joined together; united; joint; associated.

con·junc·tion (kən-juŋk'shən), *n.* [ME. *conjunccion*; OFr. *conjunction*; L. *conjunctio* < pp. of *conjungere*; see CONJOIN], 1. a joining together or being joined together; union; association; combination: as, carelessness, in *conjunction* with laziness, made her a poor worker. 2. coincidence: as, the *conjunction* of events. 3. in *astrology & astronomy*, *a*) the apparent closeness of two or more heavenly bodies. *b*) the condition of being in the same celestial longitude: as, planets in *conjunction*. 4. in *grammar*, an uninflected word used to connect words, phrases, clauses, or sentences; connective: conjunctions may be co-ordinating (e.g., ***and, but, or***), subordinating (e.g., ***if, when, as, because, though,*** etc.), or correlative (***either . . . or, both . . . and,*** etc.). Abbreviated **conj.** (in senses 3 & 4).

con·junc·ti·va (kon'juŋk-tī'və), *n.* [*pl.* CONJUNCTIVAS (-vəz), CONJUNCTIVAE (-vē)], [Mod. L., in *membrana conjunctiva*, connecting membranes; see CONJUNCTIVE], the mucous membrane lining the inner surface of the eyelids and covering the front part of the eyeball.

con·junc·ti·val (kon'juŋk-tī'v'l), *adj.* of the conjunctiva.

con·junc·tive (kən-juŋk'tiv), *adj.* [LL. *conjunctivus* < pp. of L. *conjungere*; see CONJOIN], 1. serving to join together; connective. 2. united; combined; joint. 3. in *grammar*, *a*) used as a conjunction: as, a *conjunctive* adverb. *b*) connecting both the meaning and the construction of sentence elements: as, ***and*** and ***moreover*** are *conjunctive*. *c*) always used in conjunction with the verb: said of unstressed forms of personal, reflexive, or reciprocal pronouns in some Romance languages (e.g., *il* in French *il me faut*). *n.* in *grammar*, a conjunctive word, especially a conjunction. Abbreviated **conj.**

con·junc·tive·ly (kən-juŋk'tiv-li), *adv.* 1. by a conjunction. 2. jointly; together.

con·junc·ti·vi·tis (kən-juŋk'tə-vī'tis), *n.* [Mod. L. < *conjunctiva* + *-itis*], inflammation of the conjunctiva.

con·junc·ture (kən-juŋk'chẽr), *n.* [Fr. *conjoncture*, after It. *congiuntura* < L. *conjunctus*, pp. of *conjungere*; see CONJOIN], 1. a joining together or being joined together. 2. a concurrence or combination, especially of events or circumstances. 3. a critical situation; crisis.

con·ju·ra·tion (kon'joo-rā'shən), *n.* 1. a conjuring; invocation. 2. a magic spell; incantation. 3. magic; sorcery. 4. [Archaic], a solemn entreaty to a deity.

con·jure (kən-joor' *for 1 in v.i. & v.t.*; kun'jẽr, kon'jẽr *for 2 & 3 in v.i. & v.t.*), *v.i.* [CONJURED (-joord', -jẽrd), CONJURING], [ME. *conjuren*; OFr. *conjurer*; L. *conjurare*, to swear together, conspire < *com-*, together + *jurare*, to swear], 1. originally, to be sworn in a conspiracy. 2. to summon a demon, spirit, etc. by an oath or magic spell. 3. to practice magic or legerdemain. *v.t.* 1. to call upon, appeal to, or entreat solemnly, especially by some oath: as, I *conjure* you in the name of God to help me. 2. to summon (a devil, etc.) by an oath or magic spell. 3. to cause to be, appear, come (*up*), or go (*away*, etc.) by or as by magic: as, the music *conjured* my troubles away.

con·jur·er, con·jur·or (kən-joor'ẽr *for 1*; kun'jẽr-ẽr, kon'jẽr-ẽr *for 2 & 3*), *n.* [see CONJURE], 1. a person who solemnly entreats or appeals to someone. 2. a magician; sorcerer. 3. a person skilled in legerdemain.

conk (koŋk), *n.* [< *conch*], [Slang], 1. [British], the nose. 2. the head. 3. a blow on the head. *v.t.* [Slang], to hit on the head.

conk out, [Slang], to fail suddenly in operation, as a motor.

con man, [Slang], a confidence man; swindler.

‡con mo·to (kôn mô'tô), [It.], in *music*, with animated movement: a direction to the performer.

conn (kon), *v.t. & n.* con (nautical term).

Conn., Connecticut.

Con·nacht (kon'əkht, kon'ət), *n.* Connaught.

con·nate (kon'āt), *adj.* [LL. *connatus*, pp. of *connasci*, to be born at the same time < L. *com-*, together + *nasci*, to be born], 1. inborn; innate; congenital. 2. coexisting since birth or the beginning. 3. having the same origin or agreeing in nature; cognate. 4. in *biology*, congenitally or firmly united.

con·na·tion (kə-nā'shən), *n.* the condition of being connate; union from birth.

con·nat·u·ral (kə-nach′ẽr-əl), *adj.* 1. innate; natural. 2. related in nature; cognate.
Con·naught (kon′ôt), *n.* a province of western Ireland: area, 6,610 sq. mi.; pop., 446,000: Irish name, *Connacht.*
con·nect (kə-nekt′), *v.t.* [L. *connectere,* to bind together < *com-,* together + *nectere,* to fasten], 1. to join or fasten (two things together, or one thing *with* or *to* another); link; couple. 2. to show or think of as related; associate: as, we *connect* orange blossoms with weddings. 3. to provide with a circuit for communicating by telephone: as, the operator will *connect* you with Cleveland. 4. in *electricity,* to plug into a circuit; hook up. *v.i.* 1. to join or be joined. 2. to meet so that passengers can transfer promptly: said of trains, busses, etc. 3. to be properly related; fit in. 4. [Slang], to reach the thing aimed at; have or get a desired effect: as, that right to the jaw *connected.* —*SYN.* see **join.**
con·nect·ed (kə-nek′tid), *adj.* [pp. of *connect*], 1. joined together; fastened. 2. joined in proper order; coherent, as ideas, parts of a story, etc. 3. related; affiliated; associated; having something to do (*with*).
con·nect·ed·ly (kə-nek′tid-li), *adv.* in a connected manner; logically; coherently.
con·nec·ter (kə-nek′tẽr), *n.* a connector.
Con·nect·i·cut (kə-net′i-kət), *n.* 1. a New England State of the United States: area, 5,009 sq. mi.; pop., 2,535,000; capital, Hartford: one of the thirteen original States: abbreviated **Conn.** 2. a river flowing from northern New Hampshire into Long Island Sound: length, 400 mi.
connecting rod, a rod connecting two or more moving parts of a machine; especially, a rod connecting the crankshaft and pistons of an automobile.
con·nec·tion (kə-nek′shən), *n.* [L. *connexio* < *connexus,* pp. of *connectere;* see CONNECT], 1. a joining or being joined; coupling; union. 2. a part or thing that joins; means of joining. 3. a relation; association; specifically, *a*) the relation between things that depend on, involve, or follow each other. *b*) the logical linking together of words or ideas; coherence. *c*) the relation of a word, sentence, etc. to the surrounding text as it affects and influences the meaning; context. *d*) relation by family ties, business, etc. 4. *usually in pl. a*) a relative, especially by marriage. *b*) a business associate, acquaintance, etc., especially an influential one: as, he has powerful *connections.* 5. *usually in pl.* the act, fact, or means of meeting busses, trains, etc., or transferring from one to another, at points along a route. 6. a group of people associated together in politics, business, worship, etc. 7. a religious sect or denomination: usually **connexion.** 8. in *electricity,* a circuit. 9. in *telephony & telegraphy,* a line of communication from one point to another. Abbreviated **con.**
in connection with, 1. together with; in conjunction with. 2. with reference to.
con·nec·tion·al (kə-nek′shən-'l), *adj.* of or acting as a connection.
con·nec·tive (kə-nek′tiv), *adj.* connecting or serving to connect. *n.* something that connects; especially, a word that connects phrases, clauses, or other words, as a conjunction or relative pronoun.
connective tissue, tissue found throughout the body, serving to bind together and support other tissues and organs: it is made up of various kinds of fibrils contained in a matrix of intercellular material.
con·nec·tiv·i·ty (kon′ek-tiv′ə-ti), *n.* the quality or condition of being connective.
con·nect·or (kə-nek′tẽr), *n.* a person or thing that connects: also spelled **connecter.**
Con·nel·ly, Marc (märk kon′'l-i), (*Marcus Cook Connelly*), 1890– ; American playwright.
con·nex·ion (kə-nek′shən), *n.* connection: British spelling.
conn·ing tower (kon′iŋ), [ppr. of *con, conn* (to direct)], 1. an armored pilothouse on the deck of a warship, used as an observation and control station. 2. in submarines, a low observation tower serving also as an entrance to the interior.

CONNING TOWER OF SUBMARINE

con·nip·tion (kə-nip′shən), *n.* [arbitrary pseudo-Latin coinage], [Colloq.], a fit of anger, hysteria, etc.; tantrum: also **conniption fit.**
con·niv·ance (kə-nīv′əns), *n.* [Fr. *connivence;* L. *conniventia* < ppr. of *connivere*], a conniving; passive co-operation, as by consent or pretended ignorance, especially in wrongdoing.
con·niv·an·cy (kə-nīv′ən-si), *n.* [Rare], connivance.
con·nive (kə-nīv′), *v.i.* [CONNIVED (-nīvd′), CONNIVING], [< Fr. or L.; Fr. *conniver;* L. *connivere,* to close the eyes, wink, connive < *com-,* intens. + base akin to L. *nictare,* to wink, blink, Goth. *hneiwan,* to bend, bow, AS. *hnigian,* to bow down (the head)], 1. to pretend not to look (*at* crime, deceit, etc.), thus giving tacit consent or co-operation; pretend ignorance of another's wrongdoing. 2. to co-operate secretly (*with* someone), especially in wrongdoing; conspire.
con·niv·ent (kə-nīv′ənt), *adj.* [L. *connivens,* ppr. of *connivere;* see CONNIVE], in *biology,* with the ends inclined toward each other, as wings, anthers, etc.
con·nois·seur (kon′ə-sũr′), *n.* [Fr. *connaisseur* (formerly *connoisseur*); OFr. *conoisseor,* a judge, one well versed in anything < *conoistre* < L. *cognoscere,* to know; see COGNITION], a person who has expert knowledge and keen discrimination in some field, especially in the fine arts or in matters of taste. —*SYN.* see **aesthete.**
con·no·ta·tion (kon′ə-tā′shən), *n.* [ML. *connotatio* < pp. of *connotare*], 1. the act or process of connoting. 2. [< use by John Stuart Mill], something connoted; idea suggested by or associated with a word, phrase, etc. in addition to its explicit meaning, or denotation: as, *politician* has different *connotations* from *statesman.* 3. in *logic,* the sum of all the attributes thought of as essential to the meaning of a term.
con·not·a·tive (kon′ə-tā′tiv, kə-nō′tə-tiv), *adj.* connoting or involving connotation.
con·note (kə-nōt′), *v.t.* [CONNOTED (-id), CONNOTING], [ML. *connotare* < L. *com-,* together + *notare,* to mark; see NOTE], 1. to suggest or convey (associations, overtones, etc.) in addition to the explicit, or denoted, meaning: as, the word *mother* means "female parent," but it generally *connotes* love, care, tenderness, etc. 2. to imply or involve.
con·nu·bi·al (kə-nōō′bi-əl, kə-nū′bi-əl), *adj.* [L. *connubialis* < *connubium,* marriage < *com-,* together + *nubere,* to marry; see NUBILE], 1. of marriage or the state of being married; conjugal. 2. married.
con·nu·bi·al·i·ty (kə-nōō′bi-al′ə-ti, kə-nū′bi-al′ə-ti), *n.* [*pl.* CONNUBIALITIES (-tiz)], 1. marriage. 2. a thing characteristic of marriage.
co·noid (kō′noid), *adj.* [Gr. *kōnoeidēs;* see CONE & -OID], cone-shaped. *n.* 1. a cone-shaped thing. 2. in *geometry,* a solid described by a conic section revolving about its axis.
co·noi·dal (kō-noid′'l), *adj.* of or shaped like a cone or conoid.
‡**co·no·scen·te** (kô′nô-shen′te), *n.* [*pl.* CONOSCENTI (-tē)], [It.], a cognoscente.
con·quer (koŋ′kẽr), *v.t.* [ME. *conqueren;* OFr. *conquerre* (Fr. *conquérir*); LL. *conquaerere,* to search for, procure < L. *com-,* intens. + *quaerere,* to seek, acquire, hence lit., to get what one seeks], 1. to get possession or control of by or as by winning a war. 2. to overcome by physical, mental, or moral force; defeat; get the better of. *v.i.* to win; be victorious.
SYN.—**conquer** implies gaining mastery over someone or something by physical, mental, or moral force (to *conquer* bad habits); **vanquish** implies a thorough overpowering or frustrating, often in a single conflict or battle (a *vanquished* army); to **defeat** is to get the better of, often only for the time being (the *defeated* troops rallied and counterattacked); **overcome** implies the overpowering of an antagonist or the surmounting of difficulties; to **subdue** is to defeat so as to break the spirit of resistance; to **subjugate** is to bring under complete subjection; **overthrow** implies a victory in which a prevailing power is dislodged by force; to **rout** is to defeat so overwhelmingly that the enemy is put to disorderly flight.
con·quer·or (koŋ′kẽr-ẽr), *n.* [ME. *conquerour;* OFr. *conquereor*], a person who conquers; victor.
the Conqueror, William, Duke of Normandy, who became William I of England when he won the Battle of Hastings in 1066: often **William the Conqueror.**
con·quest (koŋ′kwest, kon′kwest), *n.* [ME. & OFr. *conqueste* < pp. of OFr. *conquerre*], 1. act or process of conquering. 2. something conquered, as a country, a people, booty, etc. 3. *a*) a winning of someone's affection or favor. *b*) a person whose affection or favor has been won. —*SYN.* see **victory.**
the (Norman) Conquest, the conquering of England by the Normans under William the Conqueror in 1066.
con·qui·an (koŋ′ki-ən), *n.* a card game like rummy, for two players.
con·quis·ta·dor (kon-kwis′tə-dôr′), *n.* [*pl.* CONQUISTADORS, CONQUISTADORES (-dôrz′)], [Sp., conqueror < *conquistar* < pp. of LL. *conquaerere;* see CONQUER], any of the Spanish conquerors of Mexico, Peru, or other parts of America in the 16th century.
Con·rad (kon′rad), [G. *Konrad* or Fr. *Conrade;* both < OHG. *Kuonrat, Chuonrat,* lit., bold or wise counselor < *kuon,* bold, wise (akin to AS. *cene,* Eng. *keen*) + *rat,*

counsel < *ratan*, to advise (akin to AS. *rædan;* see READ)], a masculine name.
Con·rad, Joseph (kon′rad), (born *Teodor Jozef Konrad Korzeniowski*), 1857–1924; English novelist, born in Poland.
cons., 1. consecrated. 2. consolidated. 3. consonant. 4. constitutional. 5. construction.
cons., Cons., 1. constable. 2. constitution. 3. consul.
con·san·guine (kon-saŋ′gwin), ***adj.*** consanguineous.
con·san·guin·e·ous (kon′saŋ-gwin′i-əs), ***adj.*** [L. *consanguineus,* of the same blood; see COM- & SANGUINE], 1. having the same ancestor. 2. of blood relationship.
con·san·guin·i·ty (kon′saŋ-gwin′ə-ti), ***n.*** [Fr. *consanguinité;* L. *consanguinitas;* see CONSANGUINEOUS], 1. relationship by descent from the same ancestor; blood relationship. 2. close relationship; affinity.
con·science (kon′shəns), ***n.*** [Fr. < L. *conscientia,* consciousness, knowledge, feeling, sense, moral sense < ppr. of *conscire* < *com-,* with + *scire,* to know; replacing ME. *inwit,* knowledge within], a knowledge or feeling of right and wrong, with a compulsion to do right; moral judgment that prohibits or opposes the violation of a previously recognized ethical principle.
in all conscience, 1. in reason or fairness. 2. certainly.
on one's conscience, causing one to feel guilty: said of a thing that one has done and recognized as wrong.
conscience clause, a clause (in a law) that exempts persons whose religious or conscientious scruples forbid compliance.
con·science·less (kon′shəns-lis), ***adj.*** without conscience or ethical principles; unscrupulous.
conscience money, money that one pays to relieve his conscience, as if to compensate for some previous dishonesty or evasion of responsibility.
con·science-strick·en (kon′shəns-strik′ən), ***adj.*** feeling guilty or bad because of having done something wrong.
con·sci·en·tious (kon′shi-en′shəs, kon′si-en′shəs), ***adj.*** [Fr. *conscientieux;* ML. *conscientiosus* < L. *conscientia;* see CONSCIENCE], governed by, or made or done according to, what one knows is right; scrupulous; honest.
conscientious objector, a person who objects to warfare because he believes that it is wrong to kill; especially, a member of any of various religious sects whose tenets prohibit military service: abbreviated **c.o.**
con·scion·a·ble (kon′shən-ə-b'l), ***adj.*** [< *conscience* + *-able*], [Rare], that agrees with one's ideas of right and wrong; just.
con·scious (kon′shəs), ***adj.*** [L. *conscius,* knowing, aware < *conscire;* see CONSCIENCE], 1. having a feeling or knowledge (*of* one's sensations, feelings, etc., or external things); knowing or feeling (*that* something is or was happening or existing); aware; cognizant. 2. able to feel and think; awake. 3. aware of oneself as a thinking being; knowing what one is doing and why. 4. painfully aware of oneself; self-conscious; embarrassed. 5. accompanied by an awareness of what one is thinking, feeling, and doing; intentional: as, *conscious* humor. 6. known to or felt by oneself: as, *conscious* guilt. —***SYN.*** see **aware.**
the conscious, in *psychology,* that part of a person's mental activity of which he is fully aware at any given time: see also **the unconscious.**
con·scious·ness (kon′shəs-nis), ***n.*** 1. the state of being conscious; awareness, especially of what is happening around one. 2. the totality of one's thoughts, feelings, and impressions; mind.
con·script (kən-skript′ *for v.;* kon′skript *for adj. & n.*), ***v.t.*** [< the *adj.*], 1. to enroll for compulsory service in the armed forces; draft. 2. to force (labor, capital, etc.) into service for the government. ***adj.*** [L. *conscriptus,* pp. of *conscribere,* to enroll < *com-,* with + *scribere,* to write], conscripted. ***n.*** a conscripted person; draftee.
con·script fathers (kon′skript), 1. the senators of ancient Rome. 2. legislators of any nation, state, etc.
con·scrip·tion (kən-skrip′shən), ***n.*** [Fr. *conscripcion* (1789); L. *conscriptio,* something drawn up in writing; see CONSCRIPT], 1. a compulsory enrollment of men or, sometimes, women in the armed forces. 2. a forcing of labor, capital, etc. into government service.
con·se·crate (kon′sə-krāt′), ***v.t.*** [CONSECRATED (-id), CONSECRATING], [< the *adj.*], 1. *a*) to set apart as holy; devote to religious use; make or declare sacred: as, the bishop *consecrated* the bread and wine. *b*) to make (someone) a bishop, ruler, etc. by a religious ceremony. 2. to devote; dedicate: as, he *consecrated* his life to art. 3. to cause to be revered or honored; hallow. ***adj.*** [L. *consecratus,* pp. of *consecrare* < *com-,* together + *sacrare;* see SACRED], consecrated. —***SYN.*** see **devote.**
con·se·cra·tion (kon′sə-krā′shən), ***n.*** [ME. *consecracioun;* OFr. *consecration;* L. *consecratio*], 1. a consecrating or being consecrated. 2. a ceremony for this.
con·se·cra·tor (kon′sə-krā′tẽr), ***n.*** [LL.], a person or thing that consecrates.
con·se·cra·to·ry (kon′sə-krə-tôr′i, kon′sə-krə-tō′ri), ***adj.*** of or for consecration.
con·se·cu·tion (kon′sə-kū′shən), ***n.*** [L. *consecutio;* see CONSECUTIVE], 1. logical sequence; chain of reasoning. 2. sequence; succession.
con·sec·u·tive (kən-sek′yoo-tiv), ***adj.*** [Fr. *consécutif* < pp. of L. *consequi;* see CONSEQUENCE], 1. following in order, without interruption; successive: as, four *consecutive* weeks. 2. proceeding from one part or idea to the next in logical order, as a story, reasoning, etc. 3. in *grammar,* stating a result, as a clause.
con·sen·su·al (kən-sen′shōō-əl), ***adj.*** [< *consensus* + *-al*], 1. in *law,* existing by mutual consent, as a contract. 2. in *physiology,* acting in sympathetic response to voluntary movement: said of involuntary movement.
con·sen·sus (kən-sen′səs), ***n.*** [L. < pp. of *consentire;* see CONSENT], 1. agreement, especially in opinion; hence, 2. general opinion.
con·sent (kən-sent′), ***v.i.*** [ME. *consenten;* OFr. *consentir;* L. *consentire* < *com-,* with + *sentire,* to feel (see SENSE)], 1. to agree (*to* do something); give permission, approval, or assent (*to* something proposed or requested). 2. [Archaic], to agree in opinion. ***n.*** 1. permission; approval; acquiescence. 2. agreement in opinion, sentiment, etc.; as, by common *consent.*
SYN.**—consent** implies compliance with something proposed or requested, stressing this as an act of the will; to **assent** is to express acceptance of or adherence to an opinion or proposition; **agree** implies accord reached by settling differences of opinion or overcoming resistance; **concur** implies agreement arrived at formally on a specific matter, often with regard to a line of action; to **accede** is to yield one's assent to a proposal; **acquiesce** implies tacit agreement or restraint of opposition in accepting something about which one has reservations.—***ANT.*** dissent, refuse, deny.
con·sen·ta·ne·ous (kon′sen-tā′ni-əs), ***adj.*** [L. *consentaneus;* see CONSENT], 1. agreeing; suited; consistent. 2. unanimous.
con·sen·tient (kən-sen′shənt), ***adj.*** [L. *consentiens,* ppr. of *consentire;* see CONSENT], united in opinion; agreeing.
con·se·quence (kon′si-kwens′, kon′si-kwəns), ***n.*** [Fr. *conséquence;* L. *consequentia* < *consequens,* ppr. of *consequi,* to follow after < *com-,* with + *sequi,* to follow], 1. a result; effect. 2. a logical result or conclusion; inference. 3. logical sequence. 4. the relation of effect to cause. 5. importance as a cause or influence: as, a matter of slight *consequence.* 6. importance in rank; influence: as, a person of *consequence.* —***SYN.*** see **effect, importance.**
in consequence, as a result; consequently; therefore.
in consequence of, as a result or effect of; because of.
take the consequences, to accept the results of one's actions.
con·se·quent (kon′si-kwent′, kon′si-kwənt), ***adj.*** [OFr.; L. *consequens;* see CONSEQUENCE], 1. following as a result; resulting. 2. following as a logical inference or conclusion. 3. proceeding in logical sequence. ***n.*** 1. anything that follows something else. 2. a result; outcome. 3. in *logic, a*) the second term of a conditional proposition. *b*) an inference. 4. in *mathematics,* the second term of a ratio: distinguished from *antecedent.*
consequent on (or **upon**), 1. following as a result of. 2. inferred from.
con·se·quen·tial (kon′si-kwen′shəl), ***adj.*** [< L. *consequentia* (see CONSEQUENCE); + *-al*], 1. following as an effect or inference. 2. feeling and acting important; pompous. 3. [Rare], important.
con·se·quent·ly (kon′si-kwent′li, kon′si-kwənt-li), ***adv.*** as a result; by logical inference; therefore.
con·serv·a·ble (kən-sũr′və-b'l), ***adj.*** [LL. *conservabilis*], that can be conserved.
con·serv·an·cy (kən-sũr′vən-si), ***n.*** 1. conservation. 2. [British], a commission authorized to supervise a forest, river, or port.
con·ser·va·tion (kon′sẽr-vā′shən), ***n.*** [L. *conservatio* < pp. of *conservare*], 1. a conserving; protection from loss, waste, etc.; preservation. 2. the official care and protection of natural resources, as forests. 3. a forest, fishery, etc., or a part of one, under official supervision.
con·ser·va·tion·ist (kon′sẽr-vā′shən-ist), ***n.*** a person who advocates conservation of the natural resources of a country or region.
conservation of energy, the principle that energy is never consumed but only changes form, and that the total energy in a physical system, such as the universe, cannot be increased or diminished.
con·serv·a·tism (kən-sũr′və-tiz'm), ***n.*** the principles and practices of a conservative person or party; tendency to oppose change in institutions and methods.
con·ser·va·tive (kən-sũr′və-tiv), ***adj.*** [OFr. *conservatif* < pp. of L. *conservare*], 1. conserving or tending to conserve; preservative. 2. tending to preserve established traditions or institutions and to resist or oppose any changes in these: as, a *conservative* political party, *conservative* art. 3. of or characteristic of a conservative: as, *conservative* views. 4. [C-], designating or of the major right-wing political party of Great Britain or the similar one in Canada: abbreviated **C.** 5. moderate; prudent; safe: as, a *conservative* estimate. ***n.*** 1. a preservative. 2. a conservative person. 3. [C-], a member of the Conservative party of Great Britain or Canada: abbreviated **C.**
con·ser·va·toire (kən-sũr′və-twär′, kən-sũr′və-twär′), ***n.*** [Fr. < It. *conservatorio,* institution for "conserving"

foundlings by musical education < ML. *conservatorius*; see CONSERVE], a school for teaching music, art, declamation, etc.; conservatory.

con·ser·va·tor (kon'sẽr-vā'tẽr, kən-sũr'və-tẽr), ***n.*** [L. < pp. of *conservare;* see CONSERVE], a protector; guardian.

con·ser·va·to·ry (kən-sũr'və-tô'ri, kən-sũr'və-tō'ri), ***adj.*** [ML. *conservatorius* < pp. of L. *conservare;* see CONSERVE], preserving or tending to preserve. ***n.*** [*pl.* CONSERVATORIES (-iz, -riz)], 1. a room enclosed in glass, for growing and showing flowers and other plants; greenhouse, especially of a private home, museum, etc. 2. a school for teaching music, art, declamation, etc.; conservatoire.

con·serve (kən-sũrv'; *for n., usually* kon'sũrv), ***v.t.*** [CONSERVED (-sũrvd'), CONSERVING], [ME. *conserven;* OFr. *conserver;* L. *conservare,* to keep, preserve < *com-*, with + *servare;* see SERVE], 1. to keep from being damaged, lost, or wasted: as, *conserve* your energy. 2. to make (fruit) into preserves. ***n. often in pl.*** a kind of jam made of two or more fruits, often with nuts or raisins added.

con·sid·er (kən-sid'ẽr), ***v.t.*** [OFr. *considerer;* L. *considerare,* to look at closely, observe < *com-*, with + *sidus, sideris,* a star; cf. DESIRE], 1. originally, to look at carefully; regard attentively; examine. 2. to think about in order to understand or decide; ponder: as, let's *consider* the problem. 3. to have or keep in mind; take into account: as, her behavior is not hard to understand if you *consider* her background. 4. to have regard for (others, their feelings, etc.); show consideration for. 5. to regard as; believe or think to be: as, money is generally *considered* important. 6. to believe after thought: as, we *consider* that the plaintiff is not guilty. 7. to think of as acceptable or possible: as, would you *consider* going with us? ***v.i.*** to think carefully or seriously; reflect.

***SYN.*—consider** basically denotes a directing of the mind to something in order to understand it or to make a decision about it; **study** implies more intense concentration of the mind and methodical attention to details; **contemplate** implies a deep, continued mental viewing of a thing, sometimes suggesting the use of intuitive powers in envisioning something or dwelling upon it; **weigh** suggests a balancing of contradictory information, conflicting opinions, or possible eventualities, in reaching a decision; **reflect**, suggesting a turning of one's thoughts back to something, implies quiet, earnest consideration.

con·sid·er·a·ble (kən-sid'ẽr-ə-b'l), ***adj.*** [Fr. *considérable;* L. *considerabilis*], 1. worth considering; important; noteworthy. 2. much or large: as, *considerable* success.

con·sid·er·a·bly (kən-sid'ẽr-ə-bli), ***adv.*** to a considerable degree; a great deal; much.

con·sid·er·ate (kən-sid'ẽr-it), ***adj.*** [< L. *consideratus,* pp. of *considerare;* see CONSIDER], having or showing regard for others and their feelings; thoughtful. —***SYN.*** see **thoughtful.**

con·sid·er·a·tion (kən-sid'ə-rā'shən), ***n.*** [L. *consideratio* < pp. of *considerare*], 1. act of considering; careful hought or attention: deliberation or meditation. 2. thoughtful or sympathetic regard or respect, as for others. 3. something that is, or should be, considered, as in making a decision. 4. a thought or opinion produced by considering; reflection. 5. appreciative regard; esteem. 6. claim to regard; importance. **7. a** recompense, as for a service rendered; fee; compensation. 8. in *law*, something of value given or done in exchange for something of value given or done by another, in order to make a binding contract.

in consideration of, 1. because of. 2. in return for.

on no consideration, not for any reason; never.

take into consideration, to keep in mind; make allowance for; take into account.

under consideration, in mind; being thought over or discussed.

con·sid·ered (kən-sid'ẽrd), ***adj.*** [pp. of *consider*], 1. arrived at after careful thought; thought out. 2. respected; esteemed.

con·sid·er·ing (kən-sid'ẽr-iŋ), ***prep.*** [ppr. of *consider*], in view of; taking into account; making allowance for. ***adv.*** [Colloq.], taking all the circumstances into account; all things considered.

con·sign (kən-sīn'), ***v.t.*** [orig., to mark with the sign of the cross, hence dedicate, confirm, sign; Fr. *consigner;* L. *consignare,* to seal, attest, register < *com-*, together + *signare,* to sign, mark < *signum,* a mark, sign], 1. to hand over; give up or deliver: as, they *consigned* him to jail. 2. to put in the charge of; entrust: as, *consign* the orphan to her uncle's care. 3. to assign; give over or set apart (*to* a purpose, a person's use, etc.). 4. to send or deliver, as goods to be sold. —***SYN.*** see **commit.**

con·sig·na·tion (kon'sig-nā'shən), ***n.*** [Fr.; L. *consignatio*], a consigning or being consigned; consignment.

con·sign·ee (kon'sī-nē', kon'si-nē'), ***n.*** a person or agent to whom something, especially goods, is consigned.

con·sign·er (kən-sīn'ẽr), ***n.*** a consignor.

con·sign·ment (kən-sīn'mənt), ***n.*** 1. a consigning or being consigned, especially of goods to an agent. 2. something consigned; especially, a shipment of goods sent to an agent for sale or safekeeping.

on consignment, shipped or turned over to an agent for sale, with the understanding that payment to the shipper will follow sale.

con·sign·or (kən-sīn'ẽr, kon'sī-nôr'), ***n.*** a person or business firm that consigns goods to an agent.

con·sist (kən-sist'), ***v.i.*** [L. *consistere,* to stand together, stand still < *com-*, together + *sistere,* to stand, cause to stand; caus. of *stare,* to stand], 1. to be made up, formed, or composed (*of* certain material or parts): as, water *consists* of hydrogen and oxygen. 2. to be contained, comprised, or inherent (*in* something) as a cause, effect, or characteristic: as, wisdom does not *consist* only in knowing many facts. 3. to exist in harmony (*with*); be congruous or consistent (*with*). 4. [Archaic], to hold together or be held together; exist (usually *by* some means or agent).

con·sist·ence (kən-sis'təns), ***n.*** consistency.

con·sist·en·cy (kən-sis'tən-si), ***n.*** [*pl.* CONSISTENCIES (-siz)], [see CONSISTENT], 1. the condition of holding together; firmness or thickness, as of a liquid. 2. amount or degree of firmness or thickness: as, this oil is of the wrong *consistency.* 3. agreement; harmony; logical connection: as, these accounts show no *consistency.* 4. agreement with what has already been done, agreed on, or expressed; conformity with previous practice.

con·sis·tent (kən-sis'tənt), ***adj.*** [L. *consistens,* ppr. of *consistere;* see CONSIST], 1. [Rare], holding together; firm or coherent: as, *consistent* soil. 2. agreeing; in harmony; in accord; compatible: as, overeating is not *consistent* with good health. 3. holding to the same principles or practice: as, *consistent* behavior.

con·sis·to·ri·al (kon'sis-tôr'i-əl, kon'sis-tō'ri-əl), ***adj.*** of a consistory or government by consistories.

con·sis·to·ri·an (kon'sis-tôr'i-ən, kon'sis-tō'ri-ən), ***adj.*** consistorial.

con·sis·to·ry (kən-sis'tə-ri), ***n.*** [*pl.* CONSISTORIES (-riz)], [ME. & ONorm. Fr. *consistorie;* L. *consistorium,* place of assembly, council < *consistere;* see CONSIST], 1. originally, a meeting place for a council or court. 2. a church council or court, as the papal senate, a bishop's diocesan court, a council of deacons or presbyters, etc. 3. a session of such a body.

con·so·ci·ate (kən-sō'shi-it; *also, and for v. always,* kən-sō'shi-āt'), ***adj.*** [L. *consociatus,* pp. of *consociare,* to share with, join < *com-*, with + *sociare,* to join; see SOCIAL], associated; united. ***n.*** an associate; partner. ***v.i. & v.i.*** [CONSOCIATED (-id), CONSOCIATING], to join together; unite in association.

con·sol (kon'sol, kən-sol'), ***n.*** singular of **consols:** abbreviated **con.**

con·sol·a·ble (kən-sōl'ə-b'l), ***adj.*** that can be consoled.

con·so·la·tion (kon'sə-lā'shən), ***n.*** [L. *consolatio* < pp. of *consolari*], 1. a consoling or being consoled; comfort; solace. 2. a person or thing that consoles.

consolation prize, a prize given to a person who does well but does not win, or who wins in a match for those previously defeated.

con·sol·a·to·ry (kən-sol'ə-tôr'i, kən-sol'ə-tō'ri), ***adj.*** [L. *consolatorius* < pp. of *consolari*], consoling or tending to console; comforting.

con·sole (kən-sōl'), ***v.t.*** [CONSOLED (-sōld'), CONSOLING], [Fr. *consoler;* L. *consolari* < *com-*, with + *solari,* to solace, comfort], to comfort; cheer (a person) up, especially by making up for a loss or disappointment. —***SYN.*** see **comfort.**

con·sole (kon'sōl), ***n.*** [Fr. < the *v.* in sense "help, support"; see CONSOLE, *v.*], 1. an ornamental bracket for supporting a shelf, bust, cornice, etc. 2. a console table. 3. the desklike frame containing the keys, stops, pedals, and other controls of an organ: it is often situated at a distance from the pipes, which are connected to it by an electric cable; hence, 4. a radio or phonograph cabinet meant to stand on the floor.

CONSOLE

console table, 1. formerly, a table supported by ornamental wall brackets, or consoles; hence, 2. a small table with legs curved or carved to resemble consoles, placed against a wall.

con·sol·i·date (kən-sol'ə-dāt'), ***v.t. & v.i.*** [CONSOLIDATED (-id), CONSOLIDATING], [< L. *consolidatus,* pp. of *consolidare* < *com-*, together + *solidare,* to make solid < *solidus,* solid], 1. to combine into one; merge; unite. 2. to make or become solid, strong, or stable: as, the troops *consolidated* their position. Abbreviated **con.** *adj.* consolidated. —*SYN.* see **join.**

Consolidated Fund, a British national fund, created by consolidating various revenues and used to pay interest on the public debt, grants to the royal family, and other charges.

consolidated school, a school attended by pupils from several adjoining districts.

con·sol·i·da·tion (kən-sol'ə-dā'shən), *n.* a consolidating or being consolidated; specifically, *a)* solidification; strengthening. *b)* combination; merger.

con·sol·i·da·tor (kən-sol'ə-dā'tẽr), *n.* a person or thing that consolidates.

con·sol·ing (kən-sōl'iŋ), *adj.* that consoles; comforting.

con·sols (kon'solz, kən-solz'), *n.pl.* [< *consolidated annuities*], British government stock, established in 1751 by consolidating various government securities, and paying 2½ per cent interest (originally 3 per cent).

con·som·mé (kon'sə-mā'; Fr. kōn'sô'mā'), *n.* [Fr., pp. of *consommer* in sense "consumed in the soup"; L. *consummare;* see CONSUMMATE, CONSUME], a clear soup made by boiling meat and, sometimes, grains or vegetables, in water.

con·so·nance (kon'sə-nəns), *n.* [OFr.; L. *consonantia* < *consonans*, ppr. of *consonare*, to sound together with < *com-*, with + *sonare* < *sonus*, a sound], 1. harmony; agreement; congruity. 2. a pleasing combination of simultaneous musical sounds; harmony of tones.

con·so·nan·cy (kon'sə-nən-si), *n.* consonance.

con·so·nant (kon'sə-nənt), *adj.* [Fr. < L. *consonans*, ppr. of *consonare;* see CONSONANCE], 1. in harmony or agreement; in accord. 2. harmonious in tone: opposed to *dissonant.* 3. having rhyme or assonance. 4. consonantal. *n.* 1. any speech sound produced by stopping and releasing the air stream (p, t, k, b, d, g), or stopping it at one point while it escapes at another (m, n, ŋ, l, r), or forcing it through a loosely closed or very narrow passage (f, v, s, z, sh[ʃ], zh[ʒ], th[θ], *th*[ð], H[ç], kh[X], h, w, y[j]), or by a combination of these means (ch[tʃ], j[dʒ]).* 2. loosely, a letter representing such a sound (k, s, etc.) or combination of such sounds (x = ks or gz). Distinguished from *vowel.* 3. in *linguistics, a)* any phoneme, especially one produced as described above, that functions in a word or syllable as a less audible sound, introducing, connecting, or following the more audible sounds (called *sonants*); hence, *b)* any sound, in any language, that does not function as a syllabic. Abbreviated **cons.**

*Symbols are those used in this dictionary to indicate pronunciation; IPA symbols, when different from these, are included in brackets.

con·so·nan·tal (kon'sə-nan't'l), *adj.* 1. having the nature or function of a consonant. 2. of or having a consonant or consonants.

con·sort (kon'sôrt; *for v.*, kən-sôrt'), *n.* [Late ME.; OFr.; L. *consors, consortis*, partner, neighbor < *com-*, with + *sors*, a lot, share; cf. SORT], 1. originally, a partner; companion; hence, 2. a wife or husband; spouse, especially of a reigning king or queen. 3. a ship that travels along with another. 4. [Obs.], *a)* [OFr. *consorte;* L. *consortium*, community of goods < *consors*], association; fellowship; company. *b)* agreement; accord. *c)* [altered < *concert*], harmony of sounds. *v.i.* 1. to keep company; associate. 2. to be in harmony or agreement; be in accord. *v.t.* 1. to associate; join: usually reflexive. 2. [Obs.], *a)* to be or go with; accompany; escort. *b)* to espouse. *c)* to sound in harmony.

con·sor·ti·um (kən-sôr'shi-əm), *n.* [*pl.* CONSORTIA (-ə)], [L., community of goods; see CONSORT], 1. a partnership. 2. an agreement or association of the banking interests of two or more nations, as for giving joint financial aid to another nation.

con·spec·tus (kən-spek'təs), *n.* [L., a view, range of sight; pp. of *conspicere;* see CONSPICUOUS], 1. a general view; survey. 2. a summary; outline; synopsis; digest.

con·spic·u·ous (kən-spik'ū-əs), *adj.* [L. *conspicuus*, open to view < *conspicere*, to look at, observe < *com-*, intens. + *specere*, to behold, see], 1. easy to see or perceive; obvious: as, a *conspicuous* billboard. 2. attracting attention by being unexpected, unusual, or outstanding; remarkable; striking: as, she was *conspicuous* for her beauty. —*SYN.* see **noticeable.**

con·spir·a·cy (kən-spir'ə-si), *n.* [*pl.* CONSPIRACIES (-siz)], [ME. & OFr. *conspiracie* < L. *conspirare;* see CONSPIRE], 1. a planning and acting together secretly, especially for an unlawful or harmful purpose, such as murder or treason. 2. the plan agreed on; plot. 3. the group taking part in such a plan. 4. a combining or working together: as, the *conspiracy* of events. —*SYN.* see **plot.**

con·spir·a·tor (kən-spir'ə-tẽr), *n.* [ME. & Anglo-Fr. *conspiratour;* LL. *conspirator* < pp. of L. *conspirare;* see CONSPIRE], a person who takes part in a conspiracy.

con·spir·a·to·ri·al (kən-spir'ə-tôr'i-əl, kən-spir'ə-tō'ri-əl), *adj.* 1. of or characteristic of a conspirator or conspiracy. 2. conspiring or fond of conspiracy.

con·spire (kən-spīr'), *v.i.* [CONSPIRED (-spīrd'), CONSPIRING], [ME. *conspiren;* OFr. *conspirer;* L. *conspirare*, to breathe together, agree in thought, unite < *com-*, together + *spirare*, to breathe], 1. to plan and act together secretly, especially in order to commit a crime. 2. to combine or work together for any purpose or effect: as, events *conspired* to ruin him. *v.t.* [Rare], to plan for, especially in secret.

‡**con spi·ri·to** (kôn spē'rē-tô'), [It.], in *music*, with spirit; with vigor: a direction to the performer.

const., Const., 1. constable. 2. constant. 3. constitution.

con·sta·ble (kon'stə-b'l, kun'stə-b'l), *n.* [ME. & OFr. *conestable;* LL. *comes stabuli*, lit., count of the stable, hence chief groom < L. *comes*, companion, fellow + *stabulum*, a stable], 1. in the Middle Ages, the highest ranking official of a royal household, court, etc. 2. the warden or keeper of a royal fortress or castle. 3. a policeman. Abbreviated **const., Const., cons., Cons.**

Con·sta·ble, John (kun'stə-b'l), 1776–1837; English landscape painter.

con·sta·ble·ship (kon'stə-b'l-ship', kun'stə-b'l-ship'), *n.* [*constable* + *-ship*], the position or term of office of a constable.

con·stab·u·lar (kən-stab'yoo-lẽr), *adj.* constabulary.

con·stab·u·lar·y (kən-stab'yoo-ler'i), *n.* [*pl.* CONSTABULARIES (-iz)], [< ML. *constabularius;* see CONSTABLE], 1. the territory under the jurisdiction of a constable. 2. the constables of a district, collectively. 3. a police force characterized by a military organization but distinct from the regular army; state police. 4. the police: humorous usage. *adj.* of constables or a constabulary.

Con·stance (kon'stəns), [Fr.; L. *Constantia*, lit., constancy], a feminine name: diminutive, *Connie.*

Constance, Lake of, a lake bounded by Switzerland, Germany, and Austria: length, 46 mi.; area, 205 sq. mi.: German name, *Bodensee.*

con·stan·cy (kon'stən-si), *n.* [ME. & OFr. *constance;* L. *constantia* < *constans*, ppr. of *constare* < *com-*, together + *stare*, to stand], the state or quality of being unchanging; specifically, *a)* being firm in mind or purpose; resoluteness. *b)* being steady in affections or loyalties; faithfulness. *c)* being uniform in nature, value, extent, etc.; regularity; stability.

con·stant (kon'stənt), *adj.* [Fr. < L. *constans;* see CONSTANCY], 1. not changing; remaining the same; specifically, *a)* remaining firm in purpose; resolute. *b)* remaining steady in affections or loyalties; faithful. *c)* remaining uniform in nature, value, extent, etc.; regular; stable. 2. going on all the time; continual; persistent: as, *constant* interruptions. *n.* 1. anything that does not change or vary. 2. in *mathematics* & *physics*, a quantity or factor that does not vary throughout a discussion or investigation: opposed to *variable:* symbol, C: abbreviated **const., Const.** —*SYN.* see **continual, faithful.**

Con·stant, Jean Jo·seph Ben·ja·min (zhän zhô'zef' ban'zhå'man' kōn'stän'), 1845–1902; French painter.

Con·stan·ta (kôn-stån'tsä), *n.* a seaport in southeastern Romania: pop., 61,000.

con·stant·an (kon'stən-tan'), *n.* [coined < *constant*], an alloy of copper (60%) and nickel (40%), used for electrical resistance heating and thermocouples.

con·stant·in (kon'stən-tin), *n.* constantan.

Con·stan·tine (kon'stən-tēn', kon'stən-tīn'), [L. *Constantinus* < *constans;* see CONSTANCY], a masculine name. *n.* (kon'stən-tēn'; Fr. kōn'stän'tēn'), a city in northern Algeria: pop., 107,000.

Constantine I, 1. 280?–337 A.D.; first Christian emperor of Rome (306–337 A.D.): called *the Great.* 2. 1868–1923; son of George I; king of Greece (1913–1917; 1920–1922); abdicated, 1917; recalled by plebiscite, 1920; abdicated, 1922.

Con·stan·ti·no·ple (kon'stan-tə-nō'p'l), *n.* Istanbul, a city in Turkey: the former name.

con·stant·ly (kon'stənt-li), *adv.* [*constant* + *-ly*], 1. always; all the time. 2. repeatedly; very often.

con·stel·late (kon'stə-lāt'), *v.i.* & *v.t.* [CONSTELLATED (-id), CONSTELLATING], [LL. *constellatus*], to unite in or as in a constellation; cluster.

con·stel·la·tion (kon'stə-lā'shən), *n.* [ME. & OFr. *constellacion;* LL. *constellatio* < *constellatus*, set with stars < L. *com-*, with + pp. of *stellare*, to shine < *stella*, a star; see STELLAR], 1. a number of fixed stars arbitrarily considered as a group, usually named after some mythological being that they supposedly resemble in outline: see charts on following pages. 2. the part of the heavens occupied by such a group. 3. any brilliant cluster or gathering: as, a *constellation* of beautiful women. 4. in *astrology*, *a)* the grouping of the planets at any particular time, especially at a person's birth. *b)* one's disposition or fate as supposedly influenced by such grouping. 5. in *psychology*, a group of related thoughts regarded as clustered about one central idea.

con·ster (kon'stẽr), *v.t.* & *v.i.* [Obs. or Dial.], to construe.

con·ster·nate (kon'stẽr-nāt'), *v.t.* [CONSTERNATED (-id), CONSTERNATING], [L. *consternatus*, pp. of *consternare;* see CONSTERNATION], to paralyze with fright or horror; dismay.

con·ster·na·tion (kon'stẽr-nā'shən), *n.* [< Fr. or L.;

Fr. *consternation;* L. *consternatio* < *consternare,* to terrify < *com-,* intens. + base akin to L. *sternax,* headstrong, restive < IE. base **ster-;* akin to ON. *starr,* rigid, stiff], paralyzing amazement or terror; dismay.

con·sti·pate (kon′stə-pāt′), ***v.t.*** [CONSTIPATED (-id), CONSTIPATING], [< L. *constipatus,* pp. of *constipare,* to press or crowd together < *com-,* together + *stipare,* to cram, pack], 1. to cause constipation in. 2. [Obs.], to pack together; compress; condense.

con·sti·pat·ed (kon′stə-pāt′id), ***adj.*** [pp. of *constipate*], having constipation; costive.

con·sti·pa·tion (kon′stə-pā′shən), ***n.*** [L. *constipatio;* see CONSTIPATE], 1. a condition in which the emptying of waste matter from the bowels is infrequent and difficult. 2. [Obs.], compression; condensation.

con·stit·u·en·cy (kən-stich′ōō-ən-si), ***n.*** [*pl.* CONSTITUENCIES (-siz)], [< *constituent* + *-cy*], 1. the voters or, loosely, the residents in a district, regarded as a group. 2. the district of such a group of voters, etc. 3. a group of clients, supporters, etc.

con·stit·u·ent (kən-stich′ōō-ənt), ***adj.*** [< L. *constituens,* ppr. of *constituere;* see CONSTITUTE], 1. necessary in the formation of the whole; component: as, a *constituent* part. 2. that can or does appoint or vote for a representative. 3. authorized to make or revise a political constitution: as, a *constituent* assembly. ***n.*** 1. a person who helps appoint another as his representative, especially by voting in an election. 2. a necessary part or element; component. 3. in *linguistics,* an element of a construction: in "they painted signs" the main elements *they* and *painted signs* are called *immediate constituents;* the further indivisible elements *they, paint, -ed, sign,* and *-s* are called *ultimate constituents.* —***SYN.*** see **element.**

con·sti·tute (kon′stə-tōōt′, kon′stə-tūt′), ***v.t.*** [CONSTITUTED (-id), CONSTITUTING], [< L. *constitutus,* pp. of *constituere,* to set up, establish < *com-,* together + *statuere,* to set], 1. to set up (a law, government, institution, etc.); establish. 2. to set up (an assembly, proceeding, etc.) in a legal or official form. 3. to set up as; appoint; ordain: as, the students *constituted* him their spokesman. 4. to make up; form; compose; be the components or elements of: as, twelve people *constitute* a jury. 5. to form of elements, material, etc.

con·sti·tu·tion (kon′stə-tōō′shən, kon′stə-tū′shən), ***n.*** [ME. *constitucion;* OFr. *constitution;* L. *constitutio* < pp. of *constituere;* see CONSTITUTE], 1. a setting up; establishment. 2. an appointing. 3. a making up; composition. 4. the way in which a thing is made up; structure; organization; make-up. 5. the way in which a person is made up; physical or mental make-up: as, a man of strong *constitution.* 6. the way in which a government, state, society, etc. is organized. 7. the system of fundamental laws and principles of a government, state, society, corporation, etc., written or unwritten. 8. a document or set of documents in which these laws and principles are written down. 9. [C-], the Constitution of the United States: it consists of seven articles and twenty-three amendments, and has been the supreme law of the Federal government since its adoption in 1789. Abbreviated **const., Const., cons., Cons.**

con·sti·tu·tion·al (kon′stə-tōō′shən-'l, kon′stə-tū′shən-'l), ***adj.*** 1. of or in the constitution of a person or thing; basic; essential. 2. for improving a person's constitution; good for one's health. 3. of, in, authorized by, subject to, dependent on, or in accordance with the constitution of a government, state, society, etc.: as, *constitutional* rights, *constitutional* rule. 4. upholding the constitution. ***n.*** [Colloq.], a walk or other exercise taken for one's health. Abbreviated **cons.**

Constitutional Convention, the convention held in May, 1787, at Philadelphia, to draw up the Constitution of the United States: it was attended by representatives of all States except Rhode Island.

con·sti·tu·tion·al·ism (kon′stə-tōō′shən-'l-iz'm, kon′stə-tū′shən-'l-iz'm), ***n.*** 1. government according to a constitution. 2. adherence to constitutional principles or government.

con·sti·tu·tion·al·ist (kon′stə-tōō′shən-'l-ist, kon′stə-tū′shən-'l-ist), ***n.*** 1. a person who believes in government by constitution. 2. an advocate of a particular constitution. 3. a specialist in the study of constitutions and constitutionalism.

con·sti·tu·tion·al·i·ty (kon′stə-tōō′shən-al′ə-ti, kon′stə-tū′shən-al′ə-ti), ***n.*** the quality or condition of being constitutional; especially, accordance with the constitution of a country or state.

con·sti·tu·tion·al·ly (kon′stə-tōō′shən-'l-i, kon′stə-tū′shən-'l-i), ***adv.*** 1. in composition, physique, or temperament; by nature: as, he is *constitutionally* frail. 2. in accordance with the (or a) constitution: as, social change can often be brought about *constitutionally.*

constitutional monarchy, a monarchy in which the powers of the sovereign are limited by a constitution.

con·sti·tu·tive (kon′stə-tōō′tiv, kon′stə-tū′tiv), ***adj.*** [< *constitute* + *-ive*], 1. having power to establish, appoint, or enact. 2. making a thing what it is; basic. 3. forming a part (*of*); constituent; component.

constr., 1. construction. 2. construed.

con·strain (kən-strān′), ***v.t.*** [ME. *constreinen;* OFr. *constreindre, constraindre;* L. *constringere,* to bind together, draw together < *com-,* together + *stringere,* to draw tight], 1. to force into, or hold in, close bounds; confine; restrain; compress. 2. to force; compel; oblige: as, he was *constrained* to agree. 3. to get or produce by force or strain, as a person's consent, an unnatural laugh, etc. —***SYN.*** see **force.**

con·strained (kən-strānd′), ***adj.*** [pp. of *constrain*], 1. compelled; forced; obliged. 2. forced and unnatural.

con·strain·ed·ly (kən-strān′id-li), ***adv.*** in a constrained manner.

con·straint (kən-strānt′), ***n.*** [ME. & OFr. *constreinte;* see CONSTRAIN], 1. confinement; restriction. 2. force; compulsion; coercion. 3. repression of natural feelings or behavior; forced, unnatural, awkward quality of manner. 4. a constraining or being constrained. 5. something that constrains.

con·strict (kən-strikt′), ***v.t.*** [< L. *constrictus,* pp. of *constringere;* see CONSTRAIN], to make smaller or narrower, especially at one place, by binding, squeezing, or shrinking; contract; compress.

con·stric·tion (kən-strik′shən), ***n.*** [L. *constrictio*], 1. a constricting or being constricted; compression; contraction. 2. a feeling of tightness or pressure, as in the chest. 3. something that constricts. 4. a constricted part.

con·stric·tive (kən-strik′tiv), ***adj.*** [L. *constrictivus*], 1. constricting or tending to constrict. 2. of or characterized by constriction.

con·stric·tor (kən-strik′tẽr), ***n.*** something that constricts; specifically, *a*) a muscle that contracts a cavity or opening, or compresses an organ. *b*) a snake that kills by coiling around its prey and squeezing.

con·stringe (kən-strinj′), ***v.t.*** [CONSTRINGED (-strinjd′), CONSTRINGING], [L. *constringere;* see CONSTRAIN], to draw together; contract; compress.

con·strin·gen·cy (kən-strin′jən-si), ***n.*** 1. the quality of being constringent. 2. a constringing.

con·strin·gent (kən-strin′jənt), ***adj.*** [L. *constringens,* ppr. of *constringere;* see CONSTRAIN], causing constriction.

con·stru·a·ble (kən-strōō′ə-b'l), ***adj.*** that can be construed.

con·struct (kən-strukt′), ***v.t.*** [< L. *constructus,* pp. of *construere* < *com-,* together + *struere,* to pile up, build], to put together systematically; build, frame, or devise (a bridge, theory, triangle, etc.). ***n.*** (kon′strukt), 1. something built or put together systematically. 2. an idea or perception resulting from the orderly arrangement of facts, impressions, etc. 3. in *linguistics,* any larger unit of discourse built up of phrases; syntactical construction. —***SYN.*** see **make.**

con·struc·tion (kən-struk′shən), ***n.*** [ME. *construccion;* OFr. *construction;* L. *constructio;* see CONSTRUCT], 1. the act or process of constructing. 2. the way in which something is constructed; manner or method of building. 3. something constructed; structure; building. 4. an explanation or interpretation: as, don't put the wrong *construction* on my statement. 5. the arrangement and relation of words in a clause, sentence, etc.: as, *Jesus wept* is an actor-action *construction.* Abbreviated **constr., cons.**

con·struc·tion·al (kən-struk′shən-'l), ***adj.*** of or in construction.

con·struc·tion·ist (kən-struk′shən-ist), ***n.*** [see CONSTRUCTION, 4], a person who interprets, or believes in interpreting, a law, document, etc. in a specified way.

con·struc·tive (kən-struk′tiv), ***adj.*** [ML. *constructivus*], 1. able or helping to construct; leading to improvements or advances; formative; positive: as, a *constructive* thinker. 2. of construction or structure. 3. not directly expressed but inferred or deduced on the basis of interpretation and implications: as, *constructive* crime.

con·struc·tiv·ism (kən-struk′tiv-iz'm), ***n.*** a movement in painting, sculpture, architecture, etc., especially in Russia during the 1920's, characterized by abstract and geometric design and massive structural form.

con·struc·tor (kən-struk′tẽr), ***n.*** a person who constructs or directs construction; builder.

con·strue (kən-strōō′), ***v.t.*** [CONSTRUED (-strōōd′), CONSTRUING], [ME. *construen;* L. *construere;* see CONSTRUCT], 1. to analyze (a clause, etc.) so as to show its grammatical construction and meaning; hence, 2. to translate. 3. to explain or deduce the meaning of; interpret: as, her sudden departure was *construed* as an insult. 4. to infer or deduce. 5. in *grammar,* to combine in syntax: as, the verb *let,* unlike *permit,* is *construed* with an infinitive omitting the *to.* ***v.i.*** 1. to analyze sentence structure. 2. to be construable, as a sentence. 3. to translate something. 4. to make deductions; judge by inference. —***SYN.*** see **explain.**

con·sub·stan·tial (kon′səb-stan′shəl), ***adj.*** [LL. *consub-*

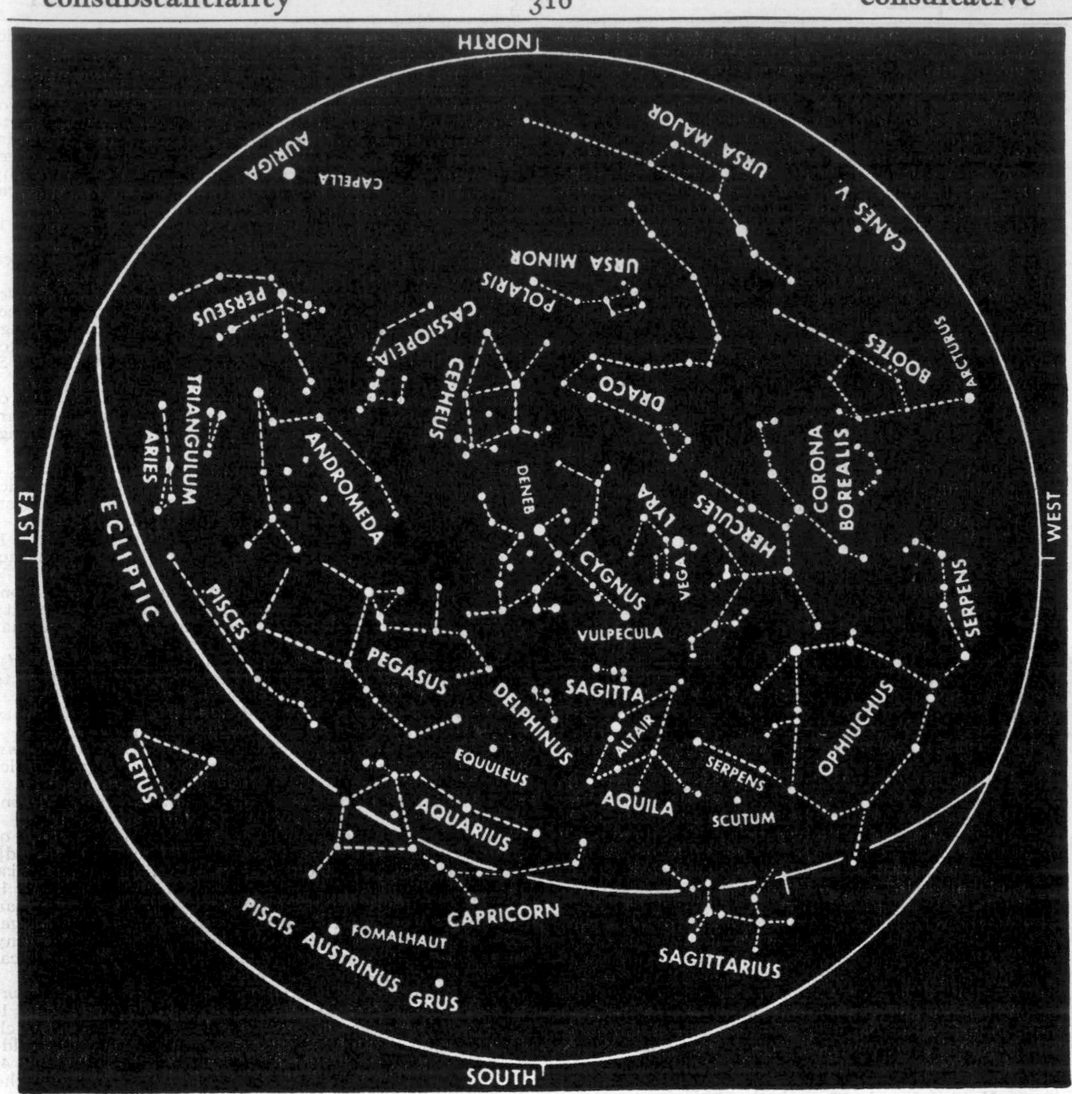

CONSTELLATIONS (northern hemisphere)

stantialis; see COM- & SUBSTANTIAL], having the same substance or essential nature: term used especially in Christian theology in reference to the Trinity.

con·sub·stan·ti·al·i·ty (kon′səb-stan′shi-al′ə-ti), *n.* the state or fact of being consubstantial.

con·sub·stan·ti·ate (kon′səb-stan′shi-āt′), *v.t.* [< ML. *consubstantiatus*, pp. of *consubstantiare* < L. *com-*, with + *substantia;* see SUBSTANCE], 1. to unite in one common substance or nature. 2. to regard as thus united. *v.i.* 1. to hold the doctrine of consubstantiation. 2. to become united in one common substance.

con·sub·stan·ti·a·tion (kon′səb-stan′shi-ā′shən), *n.* [ML. *consubstantiatio* < *consubstantiare* (see CONSUBSTANTIATE), after *transubstantiatio;* see TRANSUBSTANTIATION], in *theology*, the doctrine that the substance of the bread and wine of the Eucharist exists, after consecration, side by side with the substance of the body and blood of Christ but is not changed into it: distinguished from *transubstantiation.*

con·sue·tude (kon′swi-tōōd′, kon′swi-tūd′), *n.* [OFr.; L. *consuetudo;* see CUSTOM], custom; habit; usage.

con·sue·tu·di·nar·y (kon′swi-tōō′d′n-er′i, kon′swi-tū′d′n-er′i), *adj.* [LL. *consuetudinarius* < L. *consuetudo;* see CUSTOM], customary.

con·sul (kon′s′l), *n.* [ME.; OFr.; L. < *consulere*, to deliberate, take counsel; hence akin to *counsel, consult*], 1. either of the two chief magistrates of the ancient Roman republic. 2. one of the three highest officials of the French republic (1799–1804): Napoleon Bonaparte was First Consul. 3. a person appointed by his government to live in a certain city in some foreign country and look after his country's citizens and business interests there. Abbreviated **cons., Cons., con., Con.**

con·su·lar (kon′s′l-ẽr, kon′syoo-lẽr), *adj.* [L. *consularis*], 1. of a consul or consulate. 2. functioning as a consul.

consular agent, an official who does the work of a consul at a place that is commercially unimportant.

con·su·late (kon′s′l-it, kon′syoo-lit), *n.* [L. *consulatus*], 1. the position, powers, and functions of a consul. 2. the office or residence of a consul. 3. the term of office of a consul; consulship. 4. government by consuls. **the Consulate**, [Fr. *Consulat*], the consular government of France from 1799 to 1804.

consul general, [*pl.* CONSULS GENERAL, CONSUL GENERALS], a consul stationed in a principal commercial city, who supervises other consuls within his district.

con·sul·ship (kon′s′l-ship′), *n.* [*consul* + *-ship*], 1. the position, powers, and functions of a consul. 2. the term of office of a consul.

con·sult (kən-sult′), *v.i.* [Fr. *consulter;* L. *consultare* < pp. of *consulere*, to deliberate, consider, ask advice; orig., prob., to call together, as in *consulere senatum*, to gather the senate, then to ask (the senate) for advice, consult < *com-*, with + base akin to Goth. *saljan*, to produce, offer & Eng. *sell*], to talk things over; confer or converse in order to decide or plan something. *v.t.* 1. to seek information or instruction from; ask the advice of; refer to: as, in matters of health, *consult* your doctor. 2. to keep in mind while acting or deciding; consider; show regard for: as, *consult* your own wishes in the matter. 3. [Obs.], *a)* to confer about. *b)* to plan for. *n.* [Obs.], a consultation.

con·sult·ant (kən-sul′t′nt), *n.* [< Fr. or L.; Fr. *consultant* < L. *consultans*, ppr. of *consultare*], 1. a person who consults another person. 2. a person who gives professional or technical advice, as a doctor, lawyer, engineer, editor, etc.

con·sul·ta·tion (kon′s′l-tā′shən), *n.* 1. a consulting. 2. a meeting to discuss, decide, or plan something.

con·sult·a·tive (kən-sul′tə-tiv), *adj.* relating to consul-

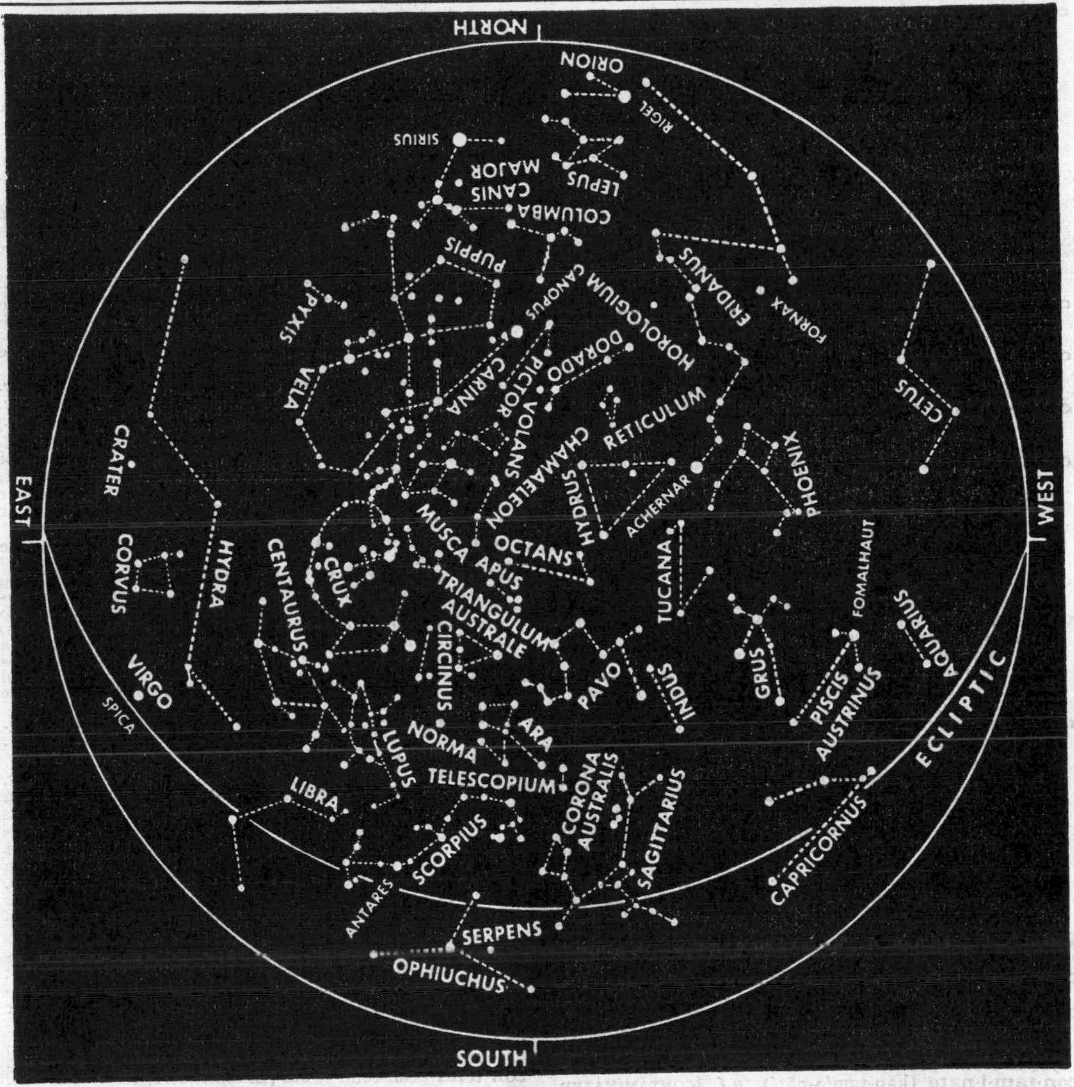

CONSTELLATIONS (southern hemisphere)

tation; advisory: as, his function was *consultative*.

con·sult·a·to·ry (kən-sul′tə-tôr′i, kən-sul′tə-tō′ri) *adj.* [L. *consultatorius*], consultative.

con·sult·ing (kən-sul′tiŋ), *adj.* [ppr. of *consult*], consulted for professional or technical advice in special cases; advisory: as, a *consulting* engineer.

con·sum·a·ble (kən-sōōm′ə-b'l, kən-sūm′ə-b'l), *adj.* that can be consumed. *n.* a consumable commodity.

con·sume (kən-sōōm′, kən-sūm′), ***v.t.*** [CONSUMED (-sōōmd′, -sūmd′), CONSUMING], [ME. *consumen; OFr. consumer;* L. *consumere,* to use up, eat, waste, destroy < *com-,* together + *sumere,* to take < *sub-,* under + *emere,* to buy, take; cf. CONSOMMÉ], 1. to destroy, as by fire; do away with. 2. to use up; spend wastefully; squander (time, energy, money, etc.). 3. to drink or eat up; devour. ***v.i.*** to waste away; perish.

consumed with, filled with (grief, curiosity, etc.); absorbed or carried away by.

con·sum·ed·ly (kən-sōōm′id-li, kən-sūm′id-li), *adv.* extremely or excessively.

con·sum·er (kən-sōōm′ẽr, kən-sūm′ẽr), *n.* [see CONSUME], 1. a person or thing that destroys, uses up, or wastes something. 2. in *economics,* a person who uses goods or services to satisfy his needs rather than to resell them or produce other goods with them: opposed to *producer.*

consumers' goods, in *economics,* goods, such as food, clothing, etc., for satisfying people's needs rather than for producing other goods or services: opposed to *producers' goods.*

con·sum·mate (kən-sum′it; *for v.,* kon′sə-māt′), *adj.* [L. *consummatus,* pp. of *consummare,* to sum up, finish < *com-,* together + *summa,* a sum], complete; perfect; supreme: as, a *consummate* liar. ***v.t.*** [CONSUMMATED (-id), CONSUMMATING], 1. to bring to completion or fulfillment; finish; accomplish. 2. to make (marriage) actual by sexual intercourse.

con·sum·ma·tion (kon′sə-mā′shən), *n.* [OFr. *consommation, consumation;* L. *consummatio*], 1. a consummating or being consummated; completion; fulfillment. 2. an end; conclusion; outcome.

con·sum·ma·tive (kon′sə-mā′tiv), *adj.* consummating or helping to consummate; completing.

con·sum·ma·tor (kon′sə-mā′tẽr), *n.* a person or thing that consummates.

con·sump·tion (kən-sump′shən), *n.* [L. *consumptio* < *consumptus,* pp. of *consumere*], 1. a consuming or being consumed; destruction, waste, or using up of something. 2. a disease that causes the body or part of the body to waste away; especially, tuberculosis of the lungs. 3. in *economics, a*) the using up of goods or services: opposed to *production. b*) the amount used up.

con·sump·tive (kən-sump′tiv), *adj.* [ME. *consumpt* < L. *consumptus;* see CONSUME], 1. consuming or tending to consume; destructive; wasteful. 2. in *economics,* of or for consumers' goods. 3. in *medicine, a*) of tuberculosis of the lungs. *b*) having or inclined to have tuberculosis of the lungs; tuberculous. *n.* a person who has tuberculosis of the lungs.

Cont., Continental.

cont., 1. containing. 2. contents. 3. continent. 4. continue. 5. continued. 6. contra. 7. contract.

con·tact (kon′takt), ***n.*** [L. *contactus*, pp. of *contingere*, to touch, seize < *com-*, together + *tangere*, to touch < IE. base **tag-*, to touch; hence akin to Goth. *tekan*, to touch, AS. *thaccian*, to pat, stroke gently], 1. the act of touching or meeting: as, some shells explode only by *contact* with other objects. 2. the state of being in touch or association (*with*): as, you will come into *contact* with many new ideas. 3. connection: as, he made some valuable *contacts* at the convention, the pilot of the airplane tried to make *contact* with his base. 4. in *electricity*, *a*) a connection or point of connection between two conductors in a circuit. *b*) a device for making such a connection. ***v.t.*** 1. to place in contact. 2. to come into contact with; get in touch with: now widely used in this sense despite objections. ***v.i.*** to be in contact; come into contact. ***interj.*** ready!: a signal in aviation that everything is set for the engine to be started.

contact flying, flying an airplane at a low altitude, so that the course can be determined by observing objects on the ground, as streams, buildings, etc.

contact lenses, small, thin lenses of glass or plastic worn next to the eyeballs, with the edges under the eyelids, sometimes used instead of ordinary eyeglasses.

contact potential, an electromotive force resulting from the contact of two plates of dissimilar metals and equal to the difference in their potentials.

con·ta·gion (kən-tā′jən), ***n.*** [L. *contagio*, a touching < *contingere;* see CONTACT], 1. the spreading of disease from one individual to another by direct or indirect contact. 2. any disease thus spread; contagious disease. 3. a means or medium by which disease is spread; hence, 4. a poison. 5. the spreading of an emotion, idea, custom, etc. from person to person until many are affected: as, the *contagion* of gaiety. 6. a bad influence that tends to spread; corruption: as, racial hatred is a *contagion*.

con·ta·gious (kən-tā′jəs), ***adj.*** [ME.; OFr. *contagieus;* LL. *contagiosus*], 1. spread by direct or indirect contact; communicable: said of diseases. 2. carrying, or liable to transmit, the causative agent of a contagious disease. 3. spreading or tending to spread from person to person: as, *contagious* laughter.

con·tain (kən-tān′), ***v.t.*** [ME. *conteinen;* OFr. *contenir;* L. *continere*, to hold, keep together < *com-*, together + *tenere*, to hold], 1. to have in it; hold; enclose or include. 2. to have the capacity for holding. 3. to be equal or equivalent to: as, a gallon *contains* four quarts. 4. to hold back or within fixed limits. 5. to control or restrain (one's feelings, oneself, etc.). 6. to be divisible by, especially without a remainder: as, 10 *contains* 5 and 2.

SYN.**—contain,** in strict usage, signifies an enclosing within or including as a component, part, or fraction, and **hold,** the capacity for containing (the bottle *contains* two ounces of liquid, but it *holds* a pint); to **accommodate** is to hold comfortably without crowding (an elevator built to *accommodate* twelve people).

con·tain·er (kən-tān′ẽr), ***n.*** a thing that contains or can contain something; box, crate, can, jar, etc.

con·tain·ment (kən-tān′mənt), ***n.*** a containing or being contained; specifically, the policy of attempting to prevent the influence of an opposing nation or political system from spreading.

con·tam·i·nate (kən-tam′ə-nāt′), ***v.t.*** [CONTAMINATED (-id), CONTAMINATING], [< L. *contaminatus*, pp. of *contaminare*, to defile < *contamen*, contact, contagion < *com-*, together + base of *tangere*, to touch; cf. CONTACT], to make impure, unclean, or corrupt by contact; pollute; defile; sully; taint: said of something dirty, diseased, wicked, etc.

SYN.**—contaminate** suggests a coming into contact with something so as to make it impure, unclean, or corrupt (fumes were *contaminating* the air); **taint** emphasizes effect over cause and implies that some measure of decay or corruption has taken place (*tainted* food); **pollute** implies complete befoulment, decay, or corruption through contamination; **defile** implies pollution or desecration of that which should be held sacred.

con·tam·i·na·tion (kən-tam′ə-nā′shən), ***n.*** [L. *contaminatio*], 1. a contaminating or being contaminated. 2. something that contaminates.

con·tam·i·na·tive (kən-tam′ə-nā′tiv), ***adj.*** contaminating or tending to contaminate.

con·tam·i·na·tor (kən-tam′ə-nā′tẽr), ***n.*** a person or thing that contaminates.

contd., continued.

conte (kōnt; Fr. kōnt), ***n.*** [*pl.* CONTES (kōnts; Fr. kōnt)], [Fr. < *conter;* see COUNT, *v.*], 1. formerly, any short fictional tale of adventure. 2. a short story; tale.

con·temn (kən-tem′), ***v.t.*** [OFr. *contemner;* L. *contemnere* < *com-*, intens. + *temnere*, to scorn], to treat or think of with contempt; scorn. —***SYN.*** see **despise.**

con·temn·er (kən-tem′ẽr, kən-tem′nẽr), ***n.*** a person who contemns.

con·tem·nor (kən-tem′nẽr), ***n.*** a person who contemns.

contemp., contemporary.

con·tem·pla·ble (kən-tem′plə-b'l), ***adj.*** that can be contemplated.

con·tem·plate (kon′təm-plāt′), ***v.t.*** [CONTEMPLATED (-id), CONTEMPLATING], [< L. *contemplatus*, pp. of *contemplari*, to gaze attentively, observe; lit., to mark out an augural temple < *com-*, with + *templum*, temple], 1. to look at intently; gaze at. 2. to think about intently; study; consider. 3. to look forward to; expect or intend. ***v.i.*** to meditate; muse. —***SYN.*** see **consider.**

con·tem·pla·tion (kon′təm-plā′shən), ***n.*** [ME. & OFr. *contemplacion;* L. *contemplatio;* see CONTEMPLATE], 1. the act of looking at something intently. 2. the act of thinking about something intently; study; consideration. 3. a looking forward; expectation or intention.

con·tem·pla·tive (kon′təm-plā′tiv, kən-tem′plə-tiv), ***adj.*** of or inclined to contemplation; thoughtful; meditative. —***SYN.*** see **pensive.**

con·tem·pla·tor (kon′təm-plā′tẽr), ***n.*** [L.], a person who contemplates.

con·tem·po·ra·ne·i·ty (kən-tem′pẽr-ə-nē′ə-ti), ***n.*** the condition or quality of being contemporaneous.

con·tem·po·ra·ne·ous (kən-tem′pə-rā′ni-əs), ***adj.*** [L. *contemporaneus* < *com-*, with + *tempus, temporis*, time], existing or happening in the same period of time. —***SYN.*** see **contemporary.**

contemporaneous with, existing or happening at the same time as.

con·tem·po·ra·ne·ous·ly (kən-tem′pə-rā′ni-əs-li), ***adv.*** in or during the same period of time; at the same time.

con·tem·po·rar·y (kən-tem′pə-rer′i), ***adj.*** [< L. *com-*, with + *temporarius*, of time < *tempus, temporis*, time], 1. living or happening in the same period of time. 2. of about the same age. ***n.*** [*pl.* CONTEMPORARIES (-iz)], 1. a person living in the same period of history as another or others. 2. a person or thing of about the same age or date of origin, publication, etc. Abbreviated **contemp.**

contemporary with, living or happening at the same time as.

SYN.**—contemporary** and **contemporaneous** both mean existing or happening at the same period of time, **contemporary** (often applied to the present) referring more often to persons or their works, and **contemporaneous,** to events; **coeval** implies extension over the same period of time when a remote time or very long duration is involved; **synchronous** implies exact correspondence in time of occurrence or rate of movement; **simultaneous** implies occurrence at the same point or brief interval of time.

con·tem·po·rize (kən-tem′pə-rīz′), ***v.t. & v.i.*** [CONTEMPORIZED (-rīzd′), CONTEMPORIZING], to make or be contemporary; synchronize.

con·tempt (kən-tempt′), ***n.*** [ME.; OFr.; L. *contemptus*, scorn; pp. of *contemnere;* see CONTEMN], 1. the feeling or actions of a person toward something he considers low, worthless, or beneath notice; scorn. 2. the condition of being despised. 3. in *law*, the punishable act of showing disrespect for the authority or dignity of a court (or legislature), as by disobedience, unruliness, etc.: in full, **contempt of court** (or **congress,** etc.).

con·tempt·i·bil·i·ty (kən-temp′tə-bil′ə-ti), ***n.*** the quality of being contemptible.

con·tempt·i·ble (kən-temp′tə-b'l), ***adj.*** [L. *contemptibilis;* see -IBLE], 1. deserving of contempt or scorn; worthless; despicable. 2. [Obs.], contemptuous.

con·tempt·i·bly (kən-temp′tə-bli), ***adv.*** in a manner, or to an extent, that deserves and arouses contempt.

con·temp·tu·ous (kən-temp′choo-əs), ***adj.*** [< L. *contemptus;* + *-ous*], showing contempt; scornful; disdainful.

con·tend (kən-tend′), ***v.i.*** [L. *contendere*, to stretch out, strive after < *com-*, together + *tendere*, to stretch, extend], 1. to strive in combat or opposition; fight; struggle: as, Napoleon's troops *contended* with the armies of Europe at Waterloo. 2. to strive in debate or controversy; argue; dispute. 3. to strive in competition; compete; vie: as, he will *contend* for the prize. ***v.t.*** to hold to be a fact; assert: as, we *contend* that he is guilty.

con·tent (kən-tent′), ***adj.*** [ME.; OFr.; L. *contentus*, pp. of *continere;* see CONTAIN], 1. happy enough with what one has or is; not desiring something more or different; satisfied. 2. willing: used in the British House of Lords as an affirmative vote. ***v.t.*** to satisfy; make content: often used reflexively, as, *content* yourself with reading about it. ***n.*** 1. contentment. 2. [British], a vote of *aye;* affirmative vote. —***SYN.*** see **satisfy.**

con·tent (kon′tent; *also, for 1a,* kən-tent′), ***n.*** [L. *contentum;* neut. pp. of *continere;* see CONTAIN], 1. *usually pl.* *a*) all that is contained in something; everything inside: as, the *contents* of a jar, trunk, etc. *b*) all that is contained or expressed in a writing or speech: as, a table of *contents* is a list of chapters, topics, etc. in a book. Abbreviated **cont.** 2. the main substance or meaning: as, the *content* of a poem is distinguished from its form. 3. holding power; capacity. 4. volume or area. 5. the amount (of a specified substance) contained: as, cast iron has a high carbon *content*.

con·tent·ed (kən-ten′tid), ***adj.*** [pp. of *content*], not desiring something more or different; satisfied.

con·ten·tion (kən-ten′shən), ***n.*** [Fr.; L. *contentio* < pp. of *contendere;* see CONTEND], 1. verbal strife; argument; controversy; dispute; quarrel. 2. a statement or point that one argues for as true or valid. 3. strife; struggle; contest. —***SYN.*** see **conflict, discord.**

con·ten·tious (kən-ten′shəs), ***adj.*** [Fr. *contentieux;* L. *contentiosus;* see CONTENTION], 1. argumentative; quarrelsome. 2. of, involving, or characterized by dispute; controversial. —***SYN.*** see **belligerent.**

con·tent·ment (kən-tent′mənt), *n.* [Fr. *contentement*], 1. the state, quality, or fact of being contented. 2. [Archaic], a satisfying or being satisfied.

con·ter·mi·nal (kən-tũr′mi-n'l), *adj.* conterminous.

con·ter·mi·nous (kən-tũr′mi-nəs), *adj.* [L. *conterminus*, bordering upon < *com-*, together + *terminus*, an end], 1. having a common boundary at some point; contiguous. 2. having the same boundaries or limits.

con·test (kən-test′; *for n.*, kon′test), *v.t.* [Fr. *contester*, to contest; L. *contestari*, to call to witness, bring action < *com-*, together + *testari*, to bear witness < *testis*, a witness], 1. to try to disprove or invalidate (something), as by argument or legal action; dispute: as, he will *contest* his father's will. 2. to fight for (ground, a military position, etc.); struggle to win or keep. *v.i.* to contend; struggle (*with* or *against*). *n.* 1. strife; struggle; conflict; fight. 2. verbal strife; controversy; dispute. 3. any race, game, debate, etc. in which there is a struggle to be the winner. —*SYN.* see **conflict.**

con·test·ant (kən-tes′tənt), *n.* [Fr.], a person who contests or competes in a contest.

con·tes·ta·tion (kon′tes-tā′shən), *n.* [< Fr. & L.; Fr. *contestation;* L. *contestatio* < *contestari*], a contesting; conflict; dispute.

con·text (kon′tekst), *n.* [L. *contextus;* pp. of *contexere*, to weave together < *com-*, together + *texere*, to weave], 1. the parts of a sentence, paragraph, discourse, etc. that occur just before and after a specified word or passage, and determine its exact meaning: as, it is unfair to quote this remark out of its *context*. 2. the whole situation, background, or environment relevant to some happening or personality.

con·tex·tu·al (kən-teks′choo-əl, kon-teks′choo-əl), *adj.* of, connected with, or depending on the context.

con·tex·tu·al·ly (kən-teks′choo-əl-i, kon-teks′choo-əl-i), *adv.* according to, or by referring to, the context.

con·tex·ture (kən-teks′chẽr, kon-teks′chẽr), *n.* [Fr. < L. *contextus;* see CONTEXT], 1. a weaving together; fabrication. 2. an interwoven mass; fabric. 3. the way in which a thing is put together; structure; composition.

contg., containing.

con·ti·gu·i·ty (kon′ti-gū′ə-ti), *n.* [*pl.* CONTIGUITIES (-tiz)], [Fr. *contiguité;* ML. *contiguitas*], 1. nearness or contact. 2. [Rare], continuous mass or unbroken series.

con·tig·u·ous (kən-tig′ū-əs), *adj.* [L. *contiguus*, bordering upon < base of *contingere*, to touch upon, border upon; see CONTINGENT], 1. in physical contact; touching. 2. near; adjoining. —*SYN.* see **adjacent.**

con·tig·u·ous·ly (kən-tig′ū-əs-li), *adv.* in such a way as to be contiguous.

contin., 1. continued. 2. *continuetur*, [L.], let it be continued.

con·ti·nence (kon′tə-nəns), *n.* [ME.; OFr.; L. *continentia* < ppr. of *continere;* see CONTAIN], 1. self-restraint; moderation. 2. self-restraint in sexual activity; especially, complete abstinence.

con·ti·nen·cy (kon′tə-nən-si), *n.* continence.

con·ti·nent (kon′tə-nənt), *adj.* [ME.; OFr. < L. *continens*, ppr. of *continere;* see CONTAIN], 1. self-restrained; temperate. 2. characterized by self-restraint, especially by complete abstinence, in sexual activity. *n.* 1. [Rare], a thing that retains or contains something. 2. a large and extensive land mass; mainland, as distinguished from outlying islands: now rare except in *the Continent.* 3. any of the six largest land masses of the earth, conventionally regarded (with or without outlying islands) as units; Africa, Asia, Australia, Europe, North America, and South America: Antarctica is sometimes regarded as the seventh continent: abbreviated **cont.**

the Continent, the mainland of Europe; all of Europe except the British Isles.

con·ti·nen·tal (kon′tə-nen′t'l), *adj.* 1. of a continent. 2. [sometimes C-], of or characteristic of the Continent; European. 3. [C-], of the American colonies at the time of the American Revolution, or of the States just after this. *n.* 1. [usually C-], a person living on the Continent; European. 2. [C-], a soldier of the American army during the Revolutionary period. 3. a piece of paper money issued by the Continental Congress: it became almost worthless before the end of the war, hence the phrase *not worth a continental*, worthless.

Continental Congress, either of two assemblies of representatives from the American colonies during the Revolutionary period: the first was held in 1774 to express grievances against British colonial policy; the second convened in 1775, created the Continental army, issued the Declaration of Independence (1776) and the Articles of Confederation (1778), and operated as the legislative body of the United States for several years.

Continental Divide, the ridge of the Rocky Mountains that separates rivers flowing toward the Atlantic from those flowing toward the Pacific.

continental shelf, the submerged shelf of land that slopes gradually from the exposed edge of a continent for a variable distance to the point where the steep descent to the ocean bottom begins.

con·tin·gence (kən-tin′jəns), *n.* contingency.

con·tin·gen·cy (kən-tin′jən-si), *n.* [*pl.* CONTINGENCIES (-siz)], [< L. *contingens*], 1. the quality or condition of being contingent. 2. dependence on chance or uncertain conditions; uncertainty of occurrence. 3. something whose occurrence depends on chance or uncertain conditions; possible, accidental, or chance event: as, be prepared for any *contingency.* 4. something incidental to another thing. —*SYN.* see **emergency.**

con·tin·gent (kən-tin′jənt), *adj.* [L. *contingens*, ppr. of *contingere*, to touch, meet, happen < *com-*, together + *tangere*, to touch; see CONTACT], 1. that may or may not happen; possible. 2. happening by chance; accidental; fortuitous. 3. dependent (*on* or *upon* something uncertain); conditional. 4. [Archaic], touching; tangential. 5. in *logic*, true only with certain conditions or contexts; not always or necessarily true. *n.* 1. an accidental or chance happening. 2. a share, proportion, or quota, as of troops, ships, laborers, delegates, etc. 3. a group or body forming part of a larger one.

contingent fee, a fee of a lawyer or agent the amount or payment of which depends upon the outcome of a particular litigation or transaction.

con·tin·u·a·ble (kən-tin′ū-ə-b'l), *adj.* that can be continued.

con·tin·u·al (kən-tin′ū-əl), *adj.* [ME. *continuele;* OFr. *continuel* < L. *continuus;* see CONTINUE], 1. happening over and over again; repeated often; going on in rapid succession. 2. continuous; going on uninterruptedly.

SYN.—**continual** applies to that which recurs repeatedly or goes on unceasingly over a long period of time (*continual* arguments); **continuous** applies to that which extends without interruption in either space or time (a *continuous* expanse); **constant** stresses uniformity, steadiness, or regularity in occurrence or recurrence (the *constant* beat of the heart); **incessant** implies unceasing or uninterrupted activity (*incessant* chatter); **perpetual** applies to that which lasts or persists for an indefinitely long time (a *perpetual* nuisance); **eternal** stresses endlessness or timelessness (the *eternal* verities). —*ANT.* intermittent, interrupted.

con·tin·u·al·ly (kən-tin′ū-əl-i), *adv.* [ME. *continuelliche;* see CONTINUAL & -LY], 1. again and again; repeatedly and often. 2. all the time; without interruption.

con·tin·u·ance (kən-tin′ū-əns), *n.* [ME.; OFr.; see CONTINUE], 1. a keeping up, going on, going on with, or lasting (*of* an action, process, or state). 2. the time during which an action, process, or state lasts; duration. 3. a remaining (*in* a place, position, or state); stay. 4. an unbroken succession. 5. a continuation; sequel. 6. in *law*, the postponement or adjournment of proceedings to a later date.

con·tin·u·ant (kən-tin′ū-ənt), *n.* [< L. *continuans*, ppr.; see CONTINUE], a speech sound that can be prolonged as long as the breath lasts, with no change in the quality of the sound: continuants are called *fricatives* (s, f, th [IPA θ], etc.), *nasals* (m, n, ŋ), *liquids* (l, r), or *vowels;* distinguished from *stop.*

con·tin·u·a·tion (kən-tin′ū-ā′shən), *n.* [OFr.; L. *continuatio* < pp. of *continuere;* see CONTINUE], 1. a keeping up or going on without interruption; prolonged and unbroken existence or maintenance. 2. a taking up or beginning again after an interruption; resumption. 3. a part or thing added to make something reach further or last longer; extension; supplement; sequel.

continuation school, a school offering instruction in elementary and vocational subjects to adults who wish to continue their education: classes are held mainly in the evening.

con·tin·u·a·tive (kən-tin′ū-ā′tiv), *adj.* [L. *continuativus*], 1. continuing something. 2. in *grammar*, expressing continuation, or sequel, as the subordinate clause in the sentence "I gave the check to the teller, who cashed it for me."

con·tin·u·a·tor (kən-tin′ū-ā′tẽr), *n.* a person who continues something, as a literary work started by another.

con·tin·ue (kən-tin′ū), *v.i.* [CONTINUED (-ūd), CONTINUING], [ME. *continuen;* OFr. *continuer;* L. *continuare*, to join, unite, make continuous < *continuus*, continuous < *continere;* see CONTAIN], 1. to remain in existence or effect; last; endure: as, the war *continued* for five years. 2. to go on in a specified condition or course of action: as, we *continued* to let him have his way, she *continued* ailing. 3. to remain in the same place or position; stay: as, the chairman *continued* in office for another year. 4. to keep on; persist; persevere: as, we *continued* to demand our rights. 5. to go on again after an interruption; resume: as, after a sip of water, the speaker *continued.* *v.t.* 1. to go on with; carry on; keep up; persist in. 2. to carry further; extend. 3. to go on with (an activity, story, etc.) again after an interruption; resume. 4. to cause to remain; keep; retain: as, the people *continued* Roosevelt in office for four terms. 5. in *law*, to postpone or adjourn to a later date.

SYN.*—continue** implies a going on in a specified condition or course and stresses uninterrupted existence rather than duration; **last** stresses duration, either for the specified time, or, if unqualified, for a time beyond that which is usual; **endure** implies continued resistance to destructive influences or forces; **abide** is applied to that which remains stable and steadfast, especially in contrast to that which is changing and transitory; **persist** implies continued existence beyond the expected or normal time.—ANT.*** stop, cease.

continued fraction, a fraction whose denominator contains a fraction whose denominator contains a fraction, and so forth (e.g., $\cfrac{5}{6+\cfrac{3}{8+\cfrac{4}{5+\ .\ .\ .}}}$).

continued proportion, a series of three or more quantities with the same ratio between each two adjacent terms (e.g., 3,6,12,24).

continued story, a story, usually a novel, published in installments in a magazine or newspaper; serial.

con·tin·u·er (kən-tin'ū-ẽr), ***n.*** a person or thing that continues.

con·ti·nu·i·ty (kon'tə-nōō'ə-ti, kon'tə-nū'ə-ti), ***n.*** [*pl.* CONTINUITIES (-tiz)], [Fr. *continuité; L. continuitas*], 1. the state or quality of being continuous. 2. a continuous series or succession; unbroken, coherent whole. 3. a written plan detailing the succession and connection of scenes in a motion picture. 4. in *radio*, *a)* a series of comments or announcements connecting the parts of a program. *b)* the script of a program.

con·tin·u·ous (kən-tin'ū-əs), ***adj.*** [L. *continuus;* see CONTINUE], going on or extending without interruption or break; unbroken; connected. —***SYN.*** see **continual.**

con·tin·u·um (kən-tin'ū-əm), ***n.*** [*pl.* CONTINUA (-ə)], [L., neut. of *continuus*], a continuous whole, quantity, or series; thing whose parts cannot be separated or separately discerned.

con·to (kon'tō), ***n.*** [*pl.* CONTOS (-tōz)], [Port., lit., million < L. *computus;* see COUNT (enumeration)], a money of account in Brazil and Portugal, formerly equal to 1,000,000 reis, now equal to 1,000 cruzeiros in Brazil and 1,000 escudos in Portugal.

con·tort (kən-tôrt'), ***v.t.*** [< L. *contortus*, pp. of *contorquere*, to whirl, twist < *com-*, together + *torquere*, to twist], to force out of shape by or as by twisting, bending, wrenching, etc.; distort: as, a face *contorted* with anger. —***SYN.*** see **deform.**

con·tor·tion (kən-tôr'shən), ***n.*** 1. a contorting or being contorted; distortion, especially of the face or body. 2. a contorted condition, position, or shape.

con·tor·tion·ist (kən-tôr'shən-ist), ***n.*** a person who can contort his body into unnatural positions.

con·tor·tive (kən-tôr'tiv), ***adj.*** of or characterized by contortion.

con·tour (kon'toor), ***n.*** [Fr.; It. *contorno* < LL. *contornare*, to go around < L. *com-*, intens. + *tornare*, to turn < *turnus*, a lathe < Gr. *tornos*, tool to make a circle with], 1. the outline of a figure, mass, land, etc. 2. the representation of such an outline. ***v.t.*** 1. to make an outline of; represent in contour. 2. to construct (a road, etc.) in accordance with natural contours. ***adj.*** characterized by furrows along the natural contour lines so as to avoid erosion: as, *contour* farming. —***SYN.*** see **outline.**

contour feathers, feathers that form the surface plumage of a bird and determine the outer contour, apart from wings, tail, etc.

contour interval, the difference in elevation represented by each of the contour lines on a map.

contour line, 1. an imaginary line connecting all points of the same elevation on a part of the earth's surface. 2. a line on a map, representing this line.

contour map, a map showing the physical features of an area of land by means of contour lines.

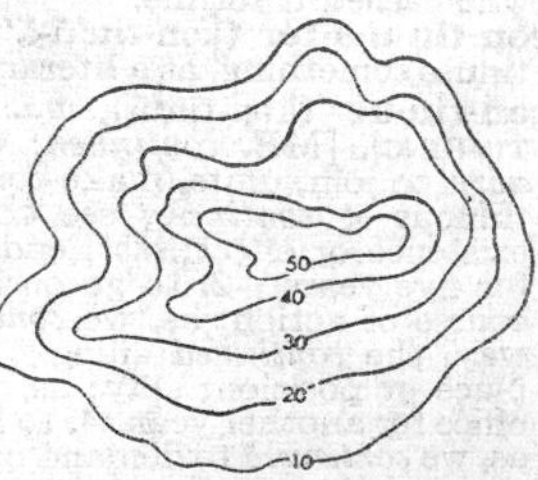

CONTOUR MAP

contr., 1. contract. 2. contracted. 3. contraction. 4. contralto. 5. contrary. 6. contrasted. 7. control. 8. controller.

con·tra (kon'trə), ***adv.*** [L.], to the contrary; contrariwise. ***n.*** something contrary or opposite: abbreviated **cont.**

con·tra- (kon'trə), [< L. *contra*, against], a prefix meaning *against, opposite, opposed to, contrary*, as in *contradict, contraceptive.*

con·tra·band (kon'trə-band'), ***n.*** [Sp. *contrabanda*, a smuggling; It. *contrabando* < *contra-*, against + *bando* < LL. *bandum, bannum* (see BAN, proclamation): first used in 16th c., in reference to illicit trade with Sp. colonies], 1. unlawful or prohibited trade. 2. goods forbidden by law to be imported and exported; smuggled merchandise. 3. contraband of war. 4. during the Civil War, a Negro slave who fled to or was smuggled behind the Union lines or remained in territory captured by the Union Army. ***adj.*** forbidden by law to be imported or exported.

con·tra·band·ist (kon'trə-ban'dist), ***n.*** a person who trades in contraband goods; smuggler.

contraband of war, goods essential to warfare, as ammunition, weapons, etc., which, according to international law, may rightfully be intercepted and seized by either belligerent when shipped to the other one by a neutral country.

con·tra·bass (kon'trə-bās'), ***adj.*** [see CONTRABASSO], having its pitch an octave lower than the normal bass; double-bass. ***n.*** an instrument or voice having the lowest bass tone; specifically, the largest and deepest-toned instrument of the viol class; double bass.

CONTRABASS

con·tra·bass·ist (kon'trə-bā'sist), ***n.*** a person who plays the contrabass.

con·tra·bas·so (kon'trə-bäs'ō), ***n.*** [It. < L. *contra*, opposite + *basso* < *bassus*, low], a contrabass.

con·tra·bas·soon (kon'trə-bə-sōōn'), ***n.*** the double bassoon, which is larger than the regular bassoon and an octave lower in pitch.

con·tra·cep·tion (kon'trə-sep'shən), ***n.*** [*contra-* + *conception*], artificial prevention of the fertilization of the human ovum: often called *birth control.*

con·tra·cep·tive (kon'trə-sep'tiv), ***adj.*** of or used for contraception. ***n.*** any contraceptive device.

con·tra·clock·wise (kon'trə-klok'wīz), ***adj. & adv.*** counterclockwise.

con·tract (kon'trakt; *for v.t. 1 sometimes, and, for rest of v. always,* kən-trakt'), ***n.*** [OFr. < L. *contractus*, a drawing together; pp. of *contrahere*, to draw together, make a bargain < *com-*, together + *trahere*, to draw], 1. an agreement between two or more people to do something; compact; covenant. 2. an agreement, usually written, enforceable by law. 3. a formal agreement of marriage or betrothal. 4. a document containing the terms of an agreement. 5. in *bridge*, *a)* the verbal agreement made by the highest bidder to make a number of tricks. *b)* the number of tricks that he bids. *c)* contract bridge. Abbreviated **contr., cont.** ***v.t.*** [< L. *contractus*], 1. to enter upon, or undertake, by contract. 2. [Rare], to betroth. 3. to get; acquire; incur: as, he *contracted* the disease. 4. to reduce in size; draw together; narrow; shrink: as, cold *contracts* metals. 5. in *grammar*, to shorten (a word or phrase) by the omission of a letter or part, as in *I'm, e'er, can't.* ***v.i.*** 1. to make a contract; agree formally: as, we *contracted* for a new car. 2. to become reduced in size or bulk; draw together; shrink; narrow.

SYN.*—contract** implies a drawing together of surfaces or parts and a resultant decrease in size, bulk, or extent; to **shrink** is to contract so as to be short of the normal or required length, amount, extent, etc. (my shirts have *shrunk*); **condense** suggests reduction of something into a more compact or more dense form without loss of essential content (*condensed* milk); to **compress** is to press or squeeze into a more compact, orderly form (a lifetime's work *compressed* into one volume); **deflate** implies a reduction in size or bulk by the removal of air, gas, or in extended use, anything insubstantial (to *deflate* a balloon, one's ego, etc.).—ANT.*** expand, inflate.

contract bridge, a form of auction bridge in which only the number of tricks named in the contract may be counted toward a game, additional tricks being counted as honors.

con·tract·ed (kən-trak'tid), ***adj.*** [pp. of *contract*], 1. reduced in size or bulk; drawn together; narrowed; shortened; shrunken: abbreviated **contr.** 2. narrowed in mental scope; narrow-minded; illiberal. 3. acquired.

con·tract·i·bil·i·ty (kən-trak'tə-bil'i-ti), ***n.*** the quality of being contractible.

con·tract·i·ble (kən-trak'tə-b'l), ***adj.*** that can be contracted.

con·trac·tile (kən-trak't'l, kən-trak'til), ***adj.*** 1. having the power of contracting. 2. producing contraction.

con·trac·til·i·ty (kon'trak-til'ə-ti), ***n.*** [Fr. *contractilité;* see CONTRACTILE], the ability to contract, or shrink.

con·trac·tion (kən-trak'shən), ***n.*** [Fr.; L. *contractio*], 1. a contracting or being contracted. 2. the drawing up and thickening of a muscle fiber or a muscle in action. 3. in *grammar*, *a)* the shortening of a word or phrase by the omission of one or more letters or sounds (e.g., *aren't* for *are not, dep't* for *department*). *b)* a word form resulting from this: abbreviated **contr.**

con·trac·tive (kən-trak'tiv), ***adj.*** 1. having the power of contracting. 2. producing or tending to produce contraction. 3. of contraction.

con·trac·tor (kon'trak-tẽr; *also, and for 3 usually,* kən-trak'tẽr), ***n.*** [LL.], 1. one of the parties to a contract. 2. a person who contracts to supply certain materials or do certain work for a stipulated sum;

especially, one whose business is contracting to erect buildings. 3. a thing that contracts, narrows, or shortens; especially, a muscle that contracts.
con·trac·tu·al (kən-trak′chōō-əl), ***adj.*** of, or having the nature of, a contract.
con·tra·dance (kon′trə-dans′, kon′trə-däns′), ***n.*** a contredanse.
con·tra·dict (kon′trə-dikt′), ***v.t.*** [< L. *contradictus*, pp. of *contradicere; contra-*, against + *dicere*, to speak], 1. *a*) to assert the opposite of (what someone else has said). *b*) to deny the statement of (a person). 2. to declare (a statement, report, etc.) to be false or incorrect; deny. 3. to be contrary to; go against. ***v.i.*** to speak in denial; oppose verbally. —***SYN.*** see **deny**.
con·tra·dic·tion (kon′trə-dik′shən), ***n.*** [OFr.; L. *contradictio*], 1. a contradicting or being contradicted. 2. a statement in opposition to another; denial. 3. a condition in which things tend to be contrary to each other; inconsistency; discrepancy. 4. a statement that contradicts itself. 5. a person or thing containing or composed of contradictory elements.
con·tra·dic·tious (kon′trə-dik′shəs), ***adj.*** 1. inclined to contradict; contentious. 2. [Archaic], *a*) contradictory. *b*) self-contradictory.
con·tra·dic·tive (kon′trə-dik′tiv), ***adj.*** contradictory.
con·tra·dic·tor (kon′trə-dik′tẽr), ***n.*** a person or thing that contradicts: also spelled **contradicter**.
con·tra·dic·to·ri·ly (kon′trə-dik′tẽr-ə-li), ***adv.*** in a contradictory manner.
con·tra·dic·to·ri·ness (kon′trə-dik′tẽr-i-nis), ***n.*** the quality of being contradictory.
con·tra·dic·to·ry (kon′trə-dik′tẽr-i), ***adj.*** [L. *contradictorius*], 1. involving a contradiction; inconsistent or mutually inconsistent; contrary. 2. inclined to contradict or deny.
con·tra·dis·tinc·tion (kon′trə-dis-tiŋk′shən), ***n.*** distinction by contrast: usually in the phrase *in contradistinction to*, as, we have a representative democracy *in contradistinction to* the simple, direct form of the New England town meeting.
con·tra·dis·tinc·tive (kon′trə-dis-tiŋk′tiv), ***adj.*** characterized by contradistinction.
con·tra·dis·tin·guish (kon′trə-dis-tiŋ′gwish), ***v.t.*** to distinguish (one thing from another) by contrasting.
con·tra·in·di·cant (kon′trə-in′də-kənt), ***n.*** a contraindication.
con·tra·in·di·cate (kon′trə-in′də-kāt′), ***v.t.*** in *medicine*, to make (the indicated, or expected, treatment) inadvisable: said of a symptom or condition of disease.
con·tra·in·di·ca·tion (kon′trə-in′də-kā′shən), ***n.*** in *medicine*, any condition of disease which makes the indicated medication or treatment inadvisable.
con·tral·to (kən-tral′tō), ***n.*** [*pl.* CONTRALTOS (-tōz), CONTRALTI (-ti)], [It.; see CONTRA- & ALTO], 1. the part sung by the lowest female voice or, formerly, the highest male voice. 2. a female voice of the lowest range. 3. a woman or girl who sings in this range. ***adj.*** of or for a contralto. Symbol, C (no period). Abbreviated **contr.**
con·tra·po·si·tion (kon′trə-pə-zish′ən), ***n.*** 1. a placing opposite or over against. 2. a position directly opposite; antithesis.
con·trap·tion (kən-trap′shən), ***n.*** [? formed on *contrive* & words ending in *-ption* (e.g., *deception*)], [Colloq.], a contrivance; gadget; makeshift: often used humorously or contemptuously.
con·tra·pun·tal (kon′trə-pun′t'l), ***adj.*** [It. *contrapunto* (see COUNTERPOINT); + *-al*], 1. of or characterized by counterpoint. 2. according to the principles of counterpoint.
con·tra·pun·tist (kon′trə-pun′tist), ***n.*** an expert in the principles and art of counterpoint.
con·tra·ri·e·ty (kon′trə-rī′ə-ti), ***n.*** [ME. & OFr. *contrarieté*; LL. *contrarietas* < L. *contrarius*], 1. the condition or quality of being contrary. 2. [*pl.* CONTRARIETIES (-tiz)], anything that is contrary; inconsistency or discrepancy.
con·tra·ri·ly (kon′trer-ə-li, kən-trâr′ə-li), ***adv.*** in a contrary manner.
con·tra·ri·ness (kən-trâr′i-nis, kon′trer-i-nis), ***n.*** [see CONTRARY & -NESS], the quality of being contrary.
con·trar·i·ous (kən-trâr′i-əs), ***adj.*** [ME.; ML. *contrariosus* < L. *contrarius*], [Rare or Obs.], contrary, or opposed; especially, *a*) perverse. *b*) adverse.
con·tra·ri·wise (kon′trer-i-wiz′; *for 3, often* kən-trâr′i-wiz′), ***adv.*** [< *contrary* + *-wise*], 1. on the contrary; from the opposite point of view. 2. in the opposite way; in a reversed order, relation, direction, etc. 3. perversely.
con·tra·ry (kon′trer-i; *for 4, often* kən-trâr′i), ***adj.*** [ME. *contrarie;* OFr. *contraire;* L. *contrarius*, opposite, opposed < *contra*, against], 1. opposed; altogether different. 2. opposite in nature, order, direction, etc. 3. unfavorable: as, *contrary* weather. 4. inclined to oppose; perverse; obstinate. ***n.*** [*pl.* CONTRARIES (-iz)], the opposite; thing that is the opposite of another. ***adv.*** in opposition; counter. Abbreviated **contr.**
by contraries, contrary to what is expected.
on the contrary, as opposed to what has been said.
to the contrary, to the opposite effect.
SYN.—**contrary**, in this comparison, implies a habitual disinclination to accept orders, advice, etc.; **perverse** implies an unreasonable obstinacy in deviating from what is considered right or acceptable; **restive** is applied to persons who are impatient under restraint or discipline and hence are hard to control or keep in order; **balky** implies a stopping short and stubbornly refusing to go on. See also **opposite**.
contrary motion, in *music*, the simultaneous rising in pitch of one voice part and the descending of another.
con·trast (kən-trast′; *for n.*, kon′trast), ***v.t.*** [Fr. *contraster;* It. & LL. *contrastare*, to stand opposed to, withstand; L. *contra*, against + *stare*, to stand], to compare so as to point out the differences; set off against one another. ***v.i.*** to show differences on comparison; form a contrast. ***n.*** [Fr. *contraste;* It. *contrasto* < the *v.*], 1. a contrasting or being contrasted. 2. a difference, especially a striking difference, between things being compared. 3. a person or thing showing differences when compared with another. 4. the effect of a striking difference, as in color or tone, of adjacent parts of a painting, photograph, etc. —***SYN.*** see **compare**.
con·trast·y (kən-tras′ti), ***adj.*** in *photography*, characterized by sharp contrasts or gradations of tone, as between light and dark areas, resulting from overdevelopment or underexposure of the negative.
con·tra·val·la·tion (kon′trə-və-lā′shən), ***n.*** [Fr. *contrevallation* < L. *contra*, counter + *vallatio*, entrenchment < *vallum*, rampart], a fortification set up to protect a besieging force from attack by the defenders of the besieged place or by a relieving force from the outside.
con·tra·vene (kon′trə-vēn′), ***v.t.*** [CONTRAVENED (-vēnd′), CONTRAVENING], [Fr. *contrevenir;* LL. *contravenire;* L. *contra*, against + *venire*, to come], 1. to go against; oppose; conflict with; infringe; violate: as, intolerance *contravenes* the basic principles of Americanism. 2. to disagree with in argument; contradict.
con·tra·ven·tion (kon′trə-ven′shən), ***n.*** [Fr. < pp. of LL. *contravenire;* see CONTRAVENE], 1. a conflicting or opposing; infringement; violation. 2. contradiction.
con·tra·yer·va (kon′trə-yũr′və), ***n.*** [Sp. *contrayerba*, lit., counter herb, hence antidote < *contra-*, against + *yerba* < L. *herba*, herb], a plant of the mulberry family, found in tropical America: the fragrant root is used in medicine as a stimulant and tonic.
‡**con·tre·coup** (kōn′tr′-kōō′), ***n.*** [Fr.; *contre* (L. *contra*), against + *coup*, a blow], an injury, as to the brain, resulting from a blow but produced in a part opposite to or distant from the part that received the blow: also **counterstroke**.
‡**con·tre·danse** (kōn′trə-däns′), ***n.*** [Fr., altered < Eng. *country-dance* through confusion of *country* with Fr. *contre*, against, opposite], 1. a dance in which the partners form two facing lines; country-dance. 2. music for this dance. Also **contradance**.
con·tre·temps (kōn′trə-tän′; *sometimes Anglicized to various hybrid forms, as*, kon′trə-tän′, kōn′trə-tän′), ***n.*** [*pl.* CONTRETEMPS (-tän′)], [Fr. < L. *contra*, against + *tempus*, time], an inopportune happening causing confusion or embarrassment; awkward mishap.
con·trib·ut·a·ble (kən-trib′yoo-tə-b'l), ***adj.*** that can contribute or be contributed.
con·trib·ute (kən-trib′yoot), ***v.t. & v.i.*** [CONTRIBUTED (-id), CONTRIBUTING], [< L. *contributus*, pp. of *contribuere;* see COM- & TRIBUTE], 1. to give or provide jointly with others; give to a common fund. 2. to write and give or sell (an article, story, poem, etc.) to a magazine, newspaper, etc. 3. to give or furnish (knowledge, etc.).
contribute to, to have a share in bringing about (a result); be partly responsible for.
con·tri·bu·tion (kon′trə-bū′shən), ***n.*** [Fr.; L. *contributio*], 1. a contributing. 2. money, aid, etc. contributed. 3. a levy or tax for a special purpose, as for supporting an army in the field. 4. something written for, and given or sold to, a magazine, newspaper, etc.
con·trib·u·tive (kən-trib′yoo-tiv), ***adj.*** contributing; having a share in bringing about a result.
con·trib·u·tor (kən-trib′yoo-tẽr), ***n.*** [Anglo-Fr. *contributour*], 1. a person who contributes money, aid, etc. 2. a person who gives or sells his writings to a magazine, newspaper, etc. Abbreviated **contrib.**
con·trib·u·to·ry (kən-trib′yoo-tôr′i, kən-trib′yoo-tō′ri), ***adj.*** 1. contributing; having a share in bringing about a result. 2. involving, or having the nature of, a contribution. ***n.*** [*pl.* CONTRIBUTORIES (-iz, -riz)], 1. a person or thing that contributes. 2. in *law*, a member liable to help make up a deficiency in the assets of a company being dissolved.
con·trite (kən-trīt′, kon′trīt), ***adj.*** [OFr.; L. *contritus*, pp. of *conterere*, to grind < *com-*, together + *terere*, to rub], 1. crushed in spirit by a feeling of remorse or

guilt. 2. showing or resulting from remorse or guilt.

con·tri·tion (kən-trish′ən), *n.* [ME. *contricion;* OFr. *contriciun;* L. *contritio*], a feeling of remorse for sins or guilt; earnest repentance. —*SYN.* see **penitence.**

con·triv·a·ble (kən-trīv′ə-b'l), *adj.* that can be contrived.

con·triv·ance (kən-trīv′əns), *n.* 1. the act, way, or power of contriving. 2. something contrived, as an invention, mechanical device, plan, etc.

con·trive (kən-trīv′), *v.t.* [CONTRIVED (-trīvd′), CONTRIVING], [ME. *contreven, controven;* OFr. *controver*, to find out, contrive; *con-*, intens. + *trover*, to find; cf. *trove* in TREASURE-TROVE], 1. to devise; scheme; plan: as, we must *contrive* a way to deal with the problem. 2. to invent; design; fabricate: as, they have *contrived* an automatic dishwasher. 3. to bring about, as by a scheme; manage: as, he *contrived* to get in. *v.i.* to make a contrivance; form plans.

con·trol (kən-trōl′), *v.t.* [CONTROLLED (-trōld′), CONTROLLING], [Fr. *contrôler*, earlier *contreroler* < *contrerole* < ML. *contrarotulum*, a counter, register < L. *contra*, against + *rotulus;* see ROLL], 1. originally, to check or verify (payments, etc.) by comparison with a duplicate register; hence, 2. to regulate (financial affairs). 3. to verify, as an experiment, by comparison with a standard, or by other experiments. 4. to exercise authority over; direct; command; hence, 5. to curb; restrain; hold back: as, *control* your grief. *n.* [Fr. *contrôle;* OFr. *contrerole*], 1. authority to direct or regulate. 2. a holding back; restraint; curb. 3. a means of restraint; check. 4. a standard of comparison for verifying or checking the findings of an experiment. 5. *often in pl.* an instrument or apparatus to regulate a mechanism: as, the *controls* of an airplane. 6. in *spiritualism*, a spirit supposed to direct the actions and speech of the medium. Abbreviated **contr.** —*SYN.* see **conduct, power.**

control experiment, an experiment in which the variable factors are controlled so as to make it possible to observe the results of varying one factor at a time.

con·trol·la·bil·i·ty (kən-trōl′ə-bil′ə-ti), *n.* the quality or state of being controllable.

con·trol·la·ble (kən-trōl′ə-b'l), *adj.* that can be controlled; that can be regulated or restrained.

con·trol·ler (kən-trōl′ẽr), *n.* [Anglo-Fr. *contrerollour;* OFr. *contreroller* < *contrerole;* see CONTROL], 1. a person in charge of expenditures or finances; especially, a government official so employed: also spelled **comptroller.** 2. a person who controls; one who governs, manages, or restrains. 3. a device for controlling the speed, power, etc. of a machine. Abbreviated **contr.**

con·trol·ler·ship (kən-trōl′ẽr-ship′), *n.* [*controller* + *-ship*], the position or term of office of a controller.

control stick, the lever by which the pilot moves the ailerons and the elevators of an airplane to control its flight.

con·tro·ver·sial (kon′trə-vũr′shəl), *adj.* [L. *controversialis*], 1. subject to controversy; debatable. 2. of controversy. 3. liking to take part in controversy; disputatious.

con·tro·ver·sial·ist (kon′trə-vũr′shəl-ist), *n.* a person who takes part in controversy or likes to do so.

con·tro·ver·sy (kon′trə-vũr′si), *n.* [*pl.* CONTROVERSIES (-siz)], [L. *controversia* < *controversus*, turned in an opposite direction < *contra*, against + *versus*, pp. of *vertere*, to turn], 1. a discussion of a question in which opposing opinions clash; debate; disputation. 2. a quarrel; dispute. —*SYN.* see **argument.**

con·tro·vert (kon′trə-vũrt′, kon′trə-vũrt′), *v.t.* [< *controversy*, after words ending in *-vert* (e.g., *divert, revert*)], 1. to argue against; contradict; deny; dispute. 2. to argue about; debate; discuss. —*SYN.* see **disprove.**

con·tro·vert·i·ble (kon′trə-vũr′tə-b'l), *adj.* that can be controverted; disputable; debatable.

con·tro·vert·i·bly (kon′trə-vũr′tə-bli), *adv.* in a controvertible manner.

con·tu·ma·cious (kon′too-mā′shəs, kon′tyoo-mā′shəs), *adj.* [< L. *contumax* (see CONTUMACY); + *-ous*], obstinately resisting authority; insubordinate; disobedient.

con·tu·ma·cy (kon′too-mə-si, kon′tyoo-mə-si), *n.* [*pl.* CONTUMACIES (-siz)], [L. *contumacia* < *contumax*, haughty, stubborn < *com-*, intens. + *tumere*, to swell up], stubborn refusal to submit to authority, especially that of a law court; insubordination; disobedience.

con·tu·me·li·ous (kon′too-mē′li-əs, kon′tyoo-mē′li-əs), *adj.* [OFr. *contumelieus;* L. *contumeliosus* < *contumelia;* see CONTUMELY], haughtily contemptuous; insulting.

con·tu·me·ly (kon′too-mə-li, kon′tyoo-mə-li, kən-tōō′-mə-li, kon′too-mē′li), *n.* [*pl.* CONTUMELIES (-liz)], [ME. & OFr. *contumelie;* L. *contumelia*, a reproach, abuse; see CONTUMACY], 1. haughty and contemptuous rudeness; insulting and humiliating treatment or language; scornful insolence. 2. an instance of this; scornful insult.

con·tuse (kən-tōōz′, kən-tūz′), *v.t.* [CONTUSED (-tōōzd′, -tūzd′), CONTUSING], [< L. *contusus*, pp. of *contundere*, to beat, break to pieces < *com-*, intens. + *tundere*, to beat], to injure or bruise without breaking the skin.

con·tu·sion (kən-tōō′zhən, kən-tū′zhən), *n.* [L. *contusio;* see CONTUSE], 1. a bruising or being bruised. 2. a bruise; injury in which the skin is not broken.

co·nun·drum (kə-nun′drəm), *n.* [16th-c. university L. slang for pedant, pedantic whim, word play, etc.; early sp. *quonundrum*], 1. a riddle whose answer is a pun. Example: "What's the difference between a bird with one wing and one with two?" *Answer:* "It's a matter of a pinion." 2. any puzzling question or problem. —*SYN.* see **mystery.**

con·va·lesce (kon′və-les′), *v.i.* [CONVALESCED (-lest′), CONVALESCING], [L. *convalescere*, to begin to grow strong < *com-*, intens. + *valescere*, to grow strong < *valere*, to be strong], to recover from illness; regain strength and health; get better.

con·va·les·cence (kon′və-les′'ns), *n.* [Fr.; L. *convalescens*, ppr. of *convalescere;* see CONVALESCE], 1. gradual recovery after illness. 2. the period of such recovery.

con·va·les·cent (kon′və-les′'nt), *adj.* [< L. *convalescens*], 1. gradually recovering health after illness. 2. of convalescence: as, a *convalescent* diet. *n.* a person who is convalescing.

con·val·lar·i·a·ceous (kon′və-lâr′i-ā′shəs), *adj.* [Mod. L. *Convallaria*, lily-of-the-valley genus (< L. *convallis*, valley < *com-*, intens. + *vallis*, valley); + *-aceous*], of a group of bulbless plants with pulpy fruits, as the asparagus.

con·vec·tion (kən-vek′shən), *n.* [L. *convectio* < pp. of *convehere*, to bring together < *com-*, together + *vehere*, to carry, bear], 1. a transmitting or conveying. 2. in *physics*, the transmission of heat or electricity by the mass movement of the heated or electrified particles, as in air, gas, or liquid currents.

con·vec·tion·al (kən-vek′shən-'l), *adj.* of convection.

con·vec·tive (kən-vek′tiv), *adj.* 1. conveying. 2. of, or having the nature of, convection.

con·vec·tor (kən-vek′tẽr), *n.* a medium of convection.

‡**con·ve·nance** (kōn′v'-näns′; Eng. kon′və-näns′), *n.* [*pl.* CONVENANCES (-näns′; Eng. -iz)], [Fr., fitness, propriety < *convenir*, to be in accord, fit; L. *convenire;* see CONVENE], 1. conventional social usage. 2. *pl.* the conventionalities.

con·vene (kən-vēn′), *v.i.* [CONVENED (-vēnd′), CONVENING], [Fr. *convenir;* L. *convenire* < *com-*, together + *venire*, to come], to meet together; assemble, usually for a common purpose. *v.t.* 1. to cause to meet together. 2. to summon before a court of law. —*SYN.* see **call.**

con·ven·er (kən-vēn′ẽr), *n.* 1. a person who convenes with others. 2. a person appointed to call a group together for meetings.

con·ven·ience (kən-vēn′yəns), *n.* [L. *convenientia* < *convenire;* see CONVENE], 1. the quality of being convenient; fitness; serviceableness. 2. personal well-being; comfort. 3. a condition personally favorable or suitable; advantage. 4. anything that adds to one's comfort or makes work less difficult and complicated; useful, handy device, article, etc.

at one's convenience, at a time, or in a place or manner, suitable to one; as one wishes.

con·ven·ien·cy (kən-vēn′yən-si), *n.* convenience.

con·ven·ient (kən-vēn′yənt), *adj.* [ME.; L. *conveniens*, ppr. of *convenire;* see CONVENE], 1. favorable to one's comfort; easy to do, use, or get to; causing little trouble, work, etc.; handy. 2. [Obs.], appropriate.

convenient to, [Colloq.], easily accessible to; near.

con·vent (kon′vənt, kon′vent), *n.* [ME. & OFr.; ML. *conventus*, convent, religious house; L. *conventus*, pp. of *convenire;* see CONVENE], 1. a community of nuns or, sometimes, monks, living under strict religious vows. 2. the building or buildings occupied by such a group; nunnery or, sometimes, monastery. —*SYN.* see **cloister.**

con·ven·ti·cle (kən-ven′ti-k'l), *n.* [ME. *conventicul;* OFr. *conventicule;* L. *conventiculum*, dim. of *conventus*, assembly < pp. of *convenire;* see CONVENE], 1. a religious assembly, especially an illegal or secret one. 2. a place where such an assembly meets. 3. in *English history*, a prohibited meeting of any religious sect that disputed the authority of the Church of England, as of certain Protestants in the 16th and 17th centuries.

con·ven·tion (kən-ven′shən), *n.* [L. *conventio* < pp. of *convenire;* see CONVENE], 1. a convening or being convened. 2. an assembly, often periodical, of members or delegates, as of a political or religious group, commercial organization, professional association, fraternal society, etc. 3. the members or delegates at such an assembly. 4. originally, an agreement as reached by such an assembly; hence, 5. *a)* an agreement between persons, nations, etc. *b)* general agreement on the usages and practices of social life. *c)* custom; usage.

con·ven·tion·al (kən-ven′shən-'l), *adj.* [LL. *conventionalis*], 1. having to do with a convention. 2. of, sanctioned by, or growing out of custom or usage; customary. 3. depending on or conforming to formal or accepted standards or rules rather than nature; not natural, original, or spontaneous: as, *conventional* behavior. 4. stylized; conventionalized. 5. in *law*, contractual; agreed; stipulated.

con·ven·tion·al·ism (kən-ven′shən-'l-iz'm), *n.* 1. adherence to conventional forms or usages. 2. a conventional idea, usage, or verbal expression; formality.

con·ven·tion·al·ist (kən-ven′shən-'l-ist), *n.* a person

who adheres to conventional forms or usages.
con·ven·tion·al·i·ty (kən-ven′shən-al′ə-ti), *n.* [*pl.* CONVENTIONALITIES (-tiz)], 1. the quality, fact, or condition of being conventional; conventional character. 2. conventional behavior or act. 3. a conventional form, usage, or rule: as, the *conventionalities* require that a man wear a necktie with a business suit.
con·ven·tion·al·ize (kən-ven′shən-'l-īz′), *v.t.* [CONVENTIONALIZED (-īzd′), CONVENTIONALIZING], 1. to make conventional. 2. in *art,* to treat in a conventional manner; depict according to the usual patterns.
con·ven·tu·al (kən-ven′cho͞o-əl), *adj.* [ML. *conventualis*], of, like, or characteristic of, a convent. *n.* 1. a member of a convent. 2. [C-], a member of that branch of the Franciscan order which believes in accumulating and holding property in common.
con·verge (kən-vūrj′), *v.i.* [CONVERGED (-vūrjd′), CONVERGING], [LL. *convergere* < L. *com-*, together + *vergere*, to turn, bend], 1. to tend to come together at a point. 2. to move, turn, or be directed toward each other or toward the same place. Opposed to *diverge.* *v.t.* to cause to converge.
con·ver·gence (kən-vūr′jəns), *n.* [< *convergent*], 1. the act, fact, or condition of converging. 2. *a*) the degree of converging. *b*) the point at which things converge. 3. in *biology,* the formation of similarities in unrelated organisms living in the same environment.
con·ver·gen·cy (kən-vūr′jən-si), *n.* [*pl.* CONVERGENCIES (-siz)], convergence.
con·ver·gent (kən-vūr′jənt), *adj.* [L. *convergens*, ppr. of *convergere*], converging or tending to converge.
converging lens, a lens that increases the convergence or decreases the divergence of a beam of light passing through it.

CONVERGENT LINES (at point A)

con·vers·a·ble (kən-vūr′sə-b'l), *adj.* [Fr.; ML. *conversabilis*], 1. easy to talk to; affable. 2. inclined to converse; liking to talk. 3. of or fit for conversation.
con·vers·a·bly (kən-vūr′sə-bli), *adv.* in a conversable manner.
con·ver·sance (kon′vẽr-s'ns, kən-vūr′s'ns), *n.* familiarity or acquaintance (*with*).
con·ver·san·cy (kon′vẽr-s'n-si, kən-vūr′s'n-si), *n.* conversance.
con·ver·sant (kon′vẽr-s'nt, kən-vūr′s'nt), *adj.* [ME.; OFr.; L. *conversans*, ppr. of *conversari;* see CONVERSE, *v.*], familiar or acquainted (*with*), especially as a result of study or experience.
con·ver·sa·tion (kon′vẽr-sā′shən), *n.* [ME. *conversacion;* OFr.; L. *conversatio* < pp. of *conversari;* see CONVERSE, *v.*], 1. a talking together; informal or familiar talk; verbal exchange of ideas, information, etc. 2. social intercourse. 3. sexual intercourse: now only in the legal phrase *criminal conversation,* i.e., adultery as grounds for divorce. 4. knowledge or familiarity based on study or use. 5. [Archaic], manner of living.
con·ver·sa·tion·al (kon′vẽr-sā′shən-'l), *adj.* 1. of or for conversation. 2. fond of or adept at conversation.
con·ver·sa·tion·al·ist (kon′vẽr-sā′shən-'l-ist), *n.* a person who is inclined to take part in conversation or likes to do so, especially one skilled at conversation.
con·ver·sa·tion·al·ly (kon′vẽr-sā′shən-'l-i), *adv.* 1. in a conversational manner. 2. in conversation.
con·ver·sa·tion·ist (kon′vẽr-sā′shən-ist), *n.* a conversationalist.
conversation piece, 1. a type of genre painting in which a group of people, usually of the upper classes, are shown in an appropriate setting: it was popular in the 18th century. 2. an article of furniture, bric-a-brac, etc. that arouses comment or special interest in a room.
‡**con·ver·sa·zi·o·ne** (kôn′ver-sä-tsyô′ne; Eng. kon′vẽr-sät′si-ō′ni), *n.* [*pl.* CONVERSAZIONI (-nē); Eng. CONVERSAZIONES (-niz)], [It., lit., conversation], a social gathering for conversation about literature, the arts, etc.
con·verse (kən-vūrs′; *for n.,* kon′vẽrs), *v.i.* [CONVERSED (-vūrst′), CONVERSING], [ME. *conversen;* OFr. *converser;* L. *conversari,* to live with, keep company with, medial form of *conversare,* to turn around, freq. of *convertere;* see CONVERT], 1. to hold a conversation; talk. 2. [Archaic], to consort; have social intercourse. *n.* 1. familiar talk; conversation. 2. social intercourse or communion. —*SYN.* see **speak.**
con·verse (kən-vūrs′; *also, and for n. always,* kon′vẽrs), *adj.* [L. *conversus,* pp. of *convertere;* see CONVERT], reversed in position, order, action, etc.; opposite; contrary; turned about. *n.* 1. a thing reversed in position, order, action, etc.; the opposite. 2. in *logic,* a proposition produced by conversion.
con·verse·ly (kən-vūrs′li, kon′vẽrs-li), *adv.* contrarily; on the contrary; if or when reversed: as, some are well but unhappy; *conversely,* others are happy but ill.
con·ver·sion (kən-vūr′zhən, kən-vūr′shən), *n.* [OFr.; L. *conversio* < pp. of *convertere*], 1. a converting or being converted. 2. a change from lack of faith to religious belief; adoption of a religion, especially Christianity. 3. a change from one belief, religion, doctrine, opinion, etc. to another. 4. in *finance,* a change of a security, currency, etc. from one form to another. 5. in *law,* *a*) unlawful appropriation and use of another's property. *b*) the exchange of property from real property to personal, or the reverse. 6. in *logic,* the producing of a new proposition by transposing the subject and predicate of the original proposition. 7. in *mathematics,* a change in the form of a quantity or an expression without a change in the value.
con·ver·sion·al (kən-vūr′zhən-'l, kən-vūr′shən-'l), *adj.* of conversion.
con·ver·sion·ar·y (kən-vūr′zhən-er′i, kən-vūr′shən-er′i), *adj.* of conversion.
con·vert (kən-vūrt′; *for n.,* kon′vẽrt), *v.t.* [ME. *converten;* OFr. *convertir;* L. *convertere* < *com-*, together + *vertere,* to turn], 1. to change; transform; turn; transmute: as, *convert* grain into flour. 2. to change from one religion, doctrine, opinion, course, or action to another. 3. to exchange for something equal in value. 4. in *finance,* to change (a security, currency, etc.) from one form into an equivalent of another form. 5. in *football,* to score (an extra point) after a touchdown, as by kicking a field goal with a place kick. 6. in *law,* *a*) to appropriate and use (another's property) unlawfully. *b*) to change (property) from real to personal, or the reverse. 7. in *logic,* to change (a proposition) by transposing the subject and predicate. *v.i.* to be converted. *n.* a person converted, as to a religion. —*SYN.* see **change, transform.**
con·vert·er (kən-vūr′tẽr), *n.* 1. a person or thing that converts. 2. a furnace for converting pig iron into steel in the Bessemer process. 3. a device for transforming electrical energy, as from direct to alternating current. Also spelled **convertor.**
con·vert·i·bil·i·ty (kən-vūr′tə-bil′ə-ti), *n.* the quality or condition of being convertible.
con·vert·i·ble (kən-vūr′tə-b'l), *adj.* [OFr.; LL. *convertibilis*], that can be converted. *n.* 1. a thing that can be converted. 2. an automobile with a top of canvas, etc. that can be folded back.
con·vert·i·bly (kən-vūr′tə-bli), *adv.* in a convertible manner.
con·vert·ite (kon′vẽr-tīt′), *n.* [Archaic], 1. a convert. 2. a reformed prostitute; magdalen.
con·vex (kon-veks′, kən-veks′, kon′veks), *adj.* [L. *convexus,* vaulted, arched; pp. of *convehere,* to bring together < *com-*, together + *vehere,* to bring], having a surface that curves outward, like the surface of a sphere: opposed to *concave.* *n.* (kon′-veks), a convex surface, body, lens, etc.
con·vex·i·ty (kən-vek′sə-ti), *n.* [Fr. *convexité;* L. *convexitas*], 1. the state or quality of being convex. 2. [*pl.* CONVEXITIES (-tiz)], a convex surface, body, lens, etc.

A B C
CONVEX LENSES
A, plano-convex; B, convexo-concave; C, convexo-convex

con·vex·o-con·cave (kən-vek′sō-kon-kāv′), *adj.* 1. having one convex side and one concave side. 2. in *optics,* designating a lens whose convex face has a greater degree of curvature than its concave face, so that the lens is thickest in the middle: see **convex,** illus.
con·vex·o-con·vex (kən-vek′sō-kon-veks′), *adj.* convex on both sides, as some lenses: see **convex,** illus.
con·vex·o-plane (kən-vek′sō-plān′), *adj.* plano-convex.
con·vey (kən-vā′), *v.t.* [ME. *conveien;* ONorm. Fr. *conveier* (OFr. *convoier*), to escort, convoy; LL. **conviare,* to accompany on the way < L. *com-*, together + *via,* way], 1. to take from one place to another; transport; carry. 2. to serve as a channel or medium for; transmit. 3. to make known; communicate; represent in words. 4. to transfer, as property or title to property, from one person to another. —*SYN.* see **carry.**
con·vey·ance (kən-vā′əns), *n.* 1. a conveying; transportation; transmission. 2. means of conveying; carrying device, especially a vehicle. 3. the transfer of the ownership of real property from one person to another. 4. the document by which this is effected; deed.
con·vey·anc·er (kən-vā′ən-sẽr), *n.* [< *conveyance* + *-er*], a lawyer who draws up deeds, etc. transferring the ownership of real property from one person to another.
con·vey·anc·ing (kən-vā′ən-siŋ), *n.* the business of a conveyancer.
con·vey·er, con·vey·or (kən-vā′ẽr), *n.* a person or thing that conveys; especially, a mechanical contrivance, as a continuous chain or belt (*conveyer belt*), for conveying something from one place to another.
con·vict (kən-vikt′; *for n.,* kon′vikt), *v.t.* [ME. *convicten* < L. *convictus,* pp. of *convincere;* see CONVINCE],

1. to prove (a person) guilty: as, the evidence *convicts* him of theft. 2. to find or declare (a person) guilty of an offense charged: as, the jury *convicted* him of theft. 3. to bring to a realization of one's guilt: as, he was *convicted* by his own conscience. *n.* 1. a person found guilty of a crime and sentenced by a law court. 2. a person serving a sentence of confinement, as in a penitentiary.

con·vic·tion (kən-vik′shən), *n.* [LL. *convictio*, demonstration], 1. a convicting or being convicted. 2. a convincing or being convinced. 3. strong belief. —*SYN.* see **certainty, opinion.**

con·vic·tive (kən-vik′tiv), *adj.* having power to convince or convict.

con·vince (kən-vins′), *v.t.* [CONVINCED (-vinst′), CONVINCING], [L. *convincere*, to overcome, convict of error < *com-*, intens. + *vincere*, to conquer], 1. originally, to overcome or convict. 2. to overcome the doubts of; persuade by argument or evidence; cause to feel certain.

con·vin·ci·ble (kən-vin′sə-b'l), *adj.* that can be convinced.

con·vinc·ing (kən-vin′siŋ), *adj.* [ppr. of *convince*], persuading by argument or evidence; causing to feel certain. —*SYN.* see **valid.**

con·viv·i·al (kən-viv′i-əl), *adj.* [L. *convivialis* < *convivium*, a feast < *convivere*, to carouse together < *com-*, together + *vivere*, to live], 1. having to do with a feast; festive. 2. fond of eating, drinking, and good company; sociable; jovial.

con·viv·i·al·ist (kən-viv′i-əl-ist), *n.* a person inclined to conviviality.

con·viv·i·al·i·ty (kən-viv′i-al′ə-ti), *n.* 1. the quality or condition of being convivial; festivity; sociability. 2. [*pl.* CONVIVIALITIES (-tiz)], a convivial act or remark.

con·vo·ca·tion (kon′və-kā′shən), *n.* [L. *convocatio*], 1. a convoking; calling together; assembling by summons. 2. a group of people called together by summons; especially, an ecclesiastical or academic assembly.

con·vo·ca·tion·al (kon′və-kā′shən-'l), *adj.* of a convocation.

con·vo·ca·tor (kon′və-kā′tẽr), *n.* [ML.], 1. a person who orders a convocation. 2. a participant in a convocation.

con·voke (kən-vōk′), *v.t.* [CONVOKED (-vōkt′), CONVOKING], [Fr. *convoquer;* L. *convocare*, to call together < *com-*, together + *vocare*, to call], to call together; summon to assemble; convene. —*SYN.* see **call.**

con·vo·lute (kon′və-lōōt′, kon′və-lūt′), *adj.* [L. *convolutus*, pp. of *convolere;* see CONVOLVE], rolled up in the form of a spiral with the coils falling one upon the other; coiled. *v.t. & v.i.* [CONVOLUTED (-id), CONVOLUTING], to wind around; coil.

con·vo·lut·ed (kon′və-lōōt′id, kon′və-lūt′id), *adj.* [pp. of *convolute*], coiled; twisted; spiraled.

con·vo·lu·tion (kon′və-lōō′shən, kon′və-lū′shən), *n.* [ML. *convolutio* < L. *convolutus*, pp. of *convolvere;* see CONVOLVE], 1. a twisting, coiling, or winding together. 2. a convoluted condition. 3. a fold, twist, or coil of something convoluted. 4. any of the irregular folds or ridges on the surface of the brain.

con·volve (kən-volv′), *v.t.* [CONVOLVED (-volvd′), CONVOLVING], [L. *convolvere*, to roll together < *com-*, together + *volvere*, to roll, turn], to roll, coil, or twist together. *v.i.* to revolve together; intertwine.

con·vol·vu·la·ceous (kən-vol′vyoo-lā′shəs), *adj.* [< Mod. L. *Convolvulaceae*, name of the family < L. *convolvulus;* see CONVOLVULUS], of the morning-glory family of twining, trailing, or erect plants with large, showy, funnel-shaped flowers.

con·vol·vu·lus (kən-vol′vyoo-ləs), *n.* [*pl.* CONVOLVULUSES (-iz), CONVOLVULI (-lī′)], [L., bindweed < *convolvere;* see CONVOLVE], any of a number of trailing, twining, or erect plants with trumpet-shaped flowers, as the bindweed or morning-glory.

con·voy (kon′voi; *also, for v.*, kən-voi′), *v.t.* [Fr. *convoyer;* OFr. *convoier;* LL. *conviare;* see CONVEY], to go with in order to protect by either sea or land; escort. *n.* 1. a convoying or being convoyed. 2. a protecting escort, as ships or troops. 3. ships, troops, etc. being convoyed. —*SYN.* see **accompany.**

con·vulse (kən-vuls′), *v.t.* [CONVULSED (-vulst′), CONVULSING], [< L. *convulsus*, pp. of *convellere*, to tear up, wrench away < *com-*, together + *vellere*, to pluck, pull], 1. to shake or disturb violently; agitate. 2. to throw into convulsions; cause spasms in. 3. to cause to shake with laughter, rage, grief, etc.

con·vul·sion (kən-vul′shən), *n.* [L. *convulsio* < *convulsus;* see CONVULSE], 1. *usually in pl.* a violent, involuntary contraction or spasm of the muscles. 2. a violent fit of laughter. 3. any violent agitation or disturbance, as a social upheaval or an earthquake.

con·vul·sion·ar·y (kən-vul′shən-er′i), *adj.* 1. of or having convulsions. 2. having to do with a convulsionary. *n.* [*pl.* CONVULSIONARIES (-iz)], a person who has convulsions in a religious frenzy.

con·vul·sive (kən-vul′siv), *adj.* 1. having the nature of a convulsion. 2. having or characterized by a convulsion or convulsions. 3. producing convulsions.

co·ny (kō′ni; *orig.* kun′i), *n.* [*pl.* CONIES (-niz)], [ME. *coning;* OFr. *connin, conil* < L. *cuniculus*, rabbit], 1. a rabbit. 2. rabbit fur. 3. a small animal mentioned in the Bible, probably the hyrax or daman. 4. the pika, a small rodent of Asia and western North America. 5. [Archaic], a gullible person; dupe. Also spelled **coney.**

Co·o (kô′ô), *n.* Kos: the Italian name.

coo (kōō), *v.i.* [echoic], 1. to make the soft, murmuring sound of pigeons or doves or a sound like this; hence, 2. to speak gently and lovingly: now only in the phrase *bill and coo.* *v.t.* to express gently and lovingly; utter with a coo. *n.* 1. the sound made by pigeons or doves. 2. any sound like this. *interj.* [British], an expression of surprise, disappointment, irritation, etc.

Cooch Be·har (kōōch′ bə-här′), a former state of northeastern India: now part of West Bengal.

coo·ee (kōō′i, kōō′ē), *n.* [of native echoic origin] a long, shrill call made by Australian aborigines and bushmen to attract attention. *v.i.* [COOEED (-id, -ēd), COOEEING], to call *cooee.* Also spelled **cooey.**

cook (kook), *n.* [ME. & AS. *coc;* LL. *cocus;* L. *coquus* < *coquere*, to cook], a person who prepares meals. *v.t.* [ME. *coken* < *coc;* see the *n.*], 1. to prepare (food) for eating by subjecting to heat, as by boiling, baking, frying, etc. 2. [Colloq.], to tamper with; falsify. *v.i.* 1. to be a cook; act as cook. 2. to undergo cooking; be cooked. 3. [Slang], to spoil; ruin.

cook up, [Colloq.], 1. to concoct; devise. 2. to devise fraudulently.

Cook, James (kook), 1728–1779; English naval officer and explorer; explored Australia, New Zealand, Antarctica, etc.: called *Captain Cook.*

Cook, Mount, a mountain of the Southern Alps, New Zealand: height, 12,349 ft.: also called *Aorangi.*

cook·book (kook′book′), *n.* a book containing recipes and other information for the preparation of food.

cook·er (kook′ẽr), *n.* 1. a stove for cooking. 2. a container in which food is cooked.

cook·er·y (kook′ẽr-i), *n.* [*pl.* COOKERIES (-iz)], [ME. *cokerie*], the art, practice, or work of cooking.

cook·house (kook′hous′), *n.* a place for cooking, as a ship's galley.

cook·ie (kook′i), *n.* a cooky.

Cook Islands, a group of Polynesian islands, belonging to New Zealand: area, 140 sq. mi.: pop., 18,000.

cook·out (kook′out′), *n.* a meal prepared on an outdoor grill, etc. and eaten outdoors, as at a picnic.

cook·stove (kook′stōv′), *n.* a stove for cooking.

Cook Strait, the strait that divides North and South Islands, New Zealand.

cook·y (kook′i), *n.* [*pl.* COOKIES (-iz)], [prob. D. *koekje*, dim. of *koek*, a cake; akin to G. *kuchen*], 1. a small, sweet cake, usually flat. 2. [Scot.], a bun.

cool (kōōl), *adj.* [ME. *cole;* AS. *col;* akin to G. *kühl;* IE. base **gel-*, cold, to freeze, as also in L. *gelu*, cold, frost; cf. COLD, CHILL], 1. moderately cold; neither warm nor very cold. 2. tending to reduce discomfort in warm or hot weather: as, *cool* clothes. 3. not excited; dispassionate; composed; collected: as, he remained *cool* in the emergency. 4. showing dislike or indifference; not cordial. 5. calmly impudent or bold. 6. blue, green, or gray: as, *cool* colors. 7. [Colloq.], without exaggeration: as, he lost a *cool* thousand on the deal. 8. [Slang], very good, pleasing, etc.; excellent. *adv.* in a cool manner. *n.* a cool place, time, thing, part, etc.: as, the *cool* of the evening. *v.i.* [ME. *colien;* AS. *colian*, to cool], to become cool. *v.t.* to make cool.

cool one's heels, [Colloq.], to wait long and tediously.

SYN.—**cool,** in this comparison, implies freedom from the heat of emotion or excitement, suggesting a calm, dispassionate attitude or a controlled alertness in difficult circumstances; **composed** suggests readiness to meet a trying situation through self-possession or the disciplining of one's emotions; **collected** stresses a being in full command of one's faculties or emotions in a distracting situation; **unruffled** suggests the maintenance of poise or composure in the face of something that might agitate or embarrass one; **nonchalant** stresses a cool lack of concern or casual indifference.—*ANT.* excited, agitated.

cool·ant (kōōl′ənt), *n.* a substance used for cooling, as a circulating fluid in an engine, or a lubricant.

cool·er (kōōl′ẽr), *n.* 1. a device or container for cooling things or keeping them cool. 2. anything that cools, as a refreshing drink. 3. [Slang], jail.

cool-head·ed (kōōl′hed′id), *adj.* mentally calm; not easily flustered; imperturbable.

Coo·lidge, Calvin (kōō′lij), (*John Calvin Coolidge*), 1872–1933; thirtieth president of the United States (1923–1929).

coo·lie (kōō′li), *n.* [Hind. *qūlī*, hired servant; ? < *kulī*, aboriginal tribe of Gujarat], 1. in the Orient, an unskilled native laborer. 2. a person doing heavy labor for little pay, especially one transported from the Orient.

cool·ing-off period (kōōl′iŋ-ôf′), a period of time required to pass before strike action may begin.

cool·ish (kōōl′ish), *adj.* somewhat cool.

coo·ly (kōō′li), *n.* [*pl.* COOLIES (-liz)], a coolie.

coomb (koom), *n.* [ME.; AS. *cumb* < Celt. (cf. W. *cwmm*, Bret. *comb*, valley); IE. base **qum-b-* < **qeu-*, to curve, bend], [Dial.], a deep, narrow valley; ravine: also spelled **combe, comb.**

coon (kōōn), *n.* [< *raccoon;* racial sense < misapplication of E. Hogan's song "All *Coons* Look Alike to Me" (1896)], [Colloq.], 1. a raccoon. 2. a Negro: vulgar term of prejudice and contempt.
coon·can (kōōn'kan'), *n.* [var. of *conquian*], a card game like rummy, for two players.
coon's age, [fanciful & emphatic < *raccoon;* for sense cf. *a dog's age*], [Colloq.], an indefinitely long time.
coon·tie (kōōn'ti), *n.* [Am. Ind. (Seminole) *kunti,* coontie flour, starch], any of several tropical American plants of the cycad family, somewhat resembling ferns or palms, with large, dark-green, feathery leaves and underground trunks and roots that yield a starch.
coop (kōōp), *n.* [ME. *cupe,* basket, pen; akin to MD., MLG. *kūpe;* ult. < L. *cupa,* tub, cask; prob. via AS. **cupa,* by-form of *cypa,* basket, cask; IE. base **qeu-p;* see HIVE], 1. a small cage or pen for poultry, etc. 2. a place of confinement. *v.t.* to confine in or as in a coop (usually with *up* or *in*).
fly the coop, [Slang], to escape.
co-op, co·öp (kō-op', kō'op'), *n.* [Colloq.], a co-operative society, store, rooming house, etc.
co-op., coöp., coop., co-operative.
coop·er (kōōp'ẽr, koop'ẽr), *n.* [ME. *coupare;* MD. *cuper;* ML. *cuparius* < L. *cupa,* a cask], a person whose work is making or repairing barrels and casks. *v.t.* & *v.i.* to make or repair (barrels and casks).
Coop·er, James Fen·i·more (fen'ə-môr' kōōp'ẽr, koop'ẽr), 1789–1851; American novelist.
Cooper, Peter, 1791–1883; American inventor, reformer, industrialist, and philanthropist.
coop·er·age (kōōp'ẽr-ij, koop'ẽr-ij), *n.* [see -AGE], 1. the workshop of a cooper. 2. the work of a cooper. 3. the price for such work.
co-op·er·ate (kō-op'ẽr-āt'), *v.i.* [CO-OPERATED (-id), CO-OPERATING], [< LL. *cooperatus,* pp. of *cooperari,* to work together; L. *co-,* with + *operari,* to work < *opus, operis,* work], 1. to act or work together with another or others for a common purpose. 2. to combine in producing an effect: said of things. 3. to practice economic co-operation. Also **coöperate, cooperate.**
co-op·er·a·tion, co·öp·er·a·tion, co·op·er·a·tion (kō-op'ẽr-ā'shən), *n.* [LL. *cooperatio*], 1. a co-operating; joint effort or operation. 2. the association of a number of people in an enterprise, as an industry, credit union, consumers' organization, etc., the benefits or profits of which are shared by all the members.
co-op·er·a·tive, co·öp·er·a·tive, co·op·er·a·tive (kō-op'ẽr-ā'tiv, kō-op'rə-tiv), *adj.* 1. co-operating or inclined to co-operate. 2. designating or of an organization, as for the production or marketing of goods, owned collectively by members who share in its benefits. *n.* such an organization. Abbreviated **co-op., coöp., coop.**
co-op·er·a·tor, co·öp·er·a·tor, co·op·er·a·tor (kō-op'ẽr-ā'tẽr), *n.* [LL.], 1. a person who co-operates. 2. a member of a co-operative organization.
coop·er·y (kōōp'ẽr-i), *n.* [*pl.* COOPERIES (-iz)], the work, shop, or product of a cooper.
co-opt, co·öpt (kō-opt'), *v.t.* [L. *cooptare,* to choose, elect; *co-,* with + *optare,* to choose], to add (a person) to a board, committee, etc. by vote of those already members.
co-op·ta·tion, co·öp·ta·tion (kō'op-tā'shən), *n.* a co-opting or being co-opted.
co-op·ta·tive, co·öp·ta·tive (kō-op'tə-tiv), *adj.* co-opting.
co-or·di·nal, co·ör·di·nal (kō-ôr'də-n'l), *adj.* [*co-* + *ordinal*], 1. of the same order. 2. in *mathematics,* having or defined by (a stated number of) co-ordinates.
co-or·di·nate (kō-ôr'də-nit; *also, and for v. always,* kō-ôr'də-nāt'), *adj.* [ML. *coordinatus,* pp. of *coordinare,* to set in equal rank, arrange; L. *co-,* with + *ordinare,* to arrange < *ordo,* order], 1. of the same order or importance; equal in rank: as, a compound sentence has two or more *co-ordinate* clauses. 2. of or involving co-ordination or co-ordinates. *n.* 1. a co-ordinate person or thing. 2. in *mathematics,* any magnitude of a system of two or more magnitudes used to define the position of a point, line, curve, or plane. *v.t.* [CO-ORDINATED (-id), CO-ORDINATING], 1. to make co-ordinate. 2. to bring into proper order or relation; harmonize; adjust. *v.i.* to become co-ordinate; function harmoniously. Also **coördinate, coordinate.**
co-ordinating conjunction, a conjunction that connects co-ordinate words, phrases, or clauses (e.g., *and, but, for, or, nor, yet*).
co-or·di·na·tion, co·ör·di·na·tion, co·or·di·na·tion (kō-ôr'də-nā'shən), *n.* 1. a co-ordinating or being co-ordinated. 2. the state or relation of being co-ordinate; harmonious adjustment or functioning, as of muscles in producing complex movements.
co-or·di·na·tive, co·ör·di·na·tive, co·or·di·na·tive (kō-ôr'də-nā'tiv, kō-ôr'də-nə-tiv), *adj.* co-ordinating.
co-or·di·na·tor, co·ör·di·na·tor, co·or·di·na·tor (kō-ôr'də-nā'tẽr), *n.* a person or thing that co-ordinates.
Coorg (kōōrg), *n.* a state of southwestern India: area, 1,593 sq. mi.; pop., 169,000; capital, Mercara.
Coos (kōōs), *n.* [< native name], any of several Penutian languages.
coot (kōōt), *n.* [*pl.,* for 1 & 2, COOTS (kōōts), COOT; see PLURAL, II, D, 1], [ME. *coote;* MD. *koet*], 1. a web-footed water bird of the rail family, grayish-black with a white area on its head. 2. the scoter, a northern sea duck. 3. [Colloq.], a foolish person; simpleton.
coot·ie (kōōt'i), *n.* [Brit. World War I army slang; said to be seaman's term < Polynesian *kutu,* parasitic insect; ? associated with Brit. dial. *coot,* anything worthless], [Slang], a louse.
cop (kop), *n.* [ME. *coppe;* AS. *copp;* akin to G. *koppe,* crest (of birds); IE. base **geu-,* to curve, bend; cf. CUD, CUP], 1. the top, as of a hill, or the crest, as of a bird's head. 2. a cone-shaped roll of thread or yarn coiled round a spindle.
cop (kop), *v.t.* [COPPED (kopt), COPPING], [< north Brit. dial. form of obs. *cap,* to seize; prob. < OFr. *caper* < L. *capere,* to take], [Slang], to seize; steal. *n.* [Slang], a policeman.
Cop., 1. Copernican. 2. Coptic.
cop., 1. copper. 2. copyrighted.
co·pai·ba (kō-pā'bə, kō-pī'bə), *n.* [Sp. & Port. < Braz. (Tupi) native name], an aromatic resin obtained from certain South American plants, used in medicine.
co·pal (kō'p'l, kō'pal), *n.* [Sp. < Nahuatl *copalli,* resin], a hard resin obtained from various tropical trees, used in varnishes.
co·palm (kō'päm'), *n.* [? < *copal* + *palm* (because of the palmate leaves of the sweet gum tree)], 1. a yellowish, aromatic resin obtained from the sweet gum tree. 2. the tree.
co·par·ce·nar·y (kō-pär's'n-er'i), *n.* [*pl.* COPARCENARIES (-iz)], [*co-* + *parcenary*], 1. in *law,* joint heirship; partnership in inheritance. 2. joint partnership or ownership. *adj.* of coparcenary or coparceners.
co·par·ce·ner (kō-pär's'n-ẽr), *n.* [*co-* + *parcener*], in *law,* a person who shares jointly with another or others in the inheritance of an estate.
co·par·ce·ny (kō-pär's'n-i), *n.* coparcenary.
co·part·ner (kō-pärt'nẽr), *n.* a person joined with another or others in any enterprise; fellow; partner.
co·part·ner·ship (kō-pärt'nẽr-ship'), *n.* partnership.
co·pa·set·ic (kō'pə-set'ik), *adj.* [Slang], copesetic.
cope (kōp), *v.i.* [COPED (kōpt), COPING], [ME. *coupen;* OFr. *couper, coper,* to slash, strike < *coup,* a blow], 1. to fight or contend (*with*) successfully or on equal terms; be a match for. 2. [Archaic], to meet, encounter, or have to do (*with*). *v.t.* 1. [Archaic], to meet, as in contest; encounter. 2. [Obs.], to requite. 3. [British Colloq.], to cope with.
cope (kōp), *n.* [ME.; OFr. *cape* < L. *cappa;* see CAPE (a cloak)], 1. a large, capelike vestment worn by priests at certain ceremonies. 2. anything that covers like a cope, as a canopy, a vault, or the sky. 3. a coping. *v.t.* [COPED (kōpt), COPING], to cover or provide with a cope, coping, or something similar.
co·peck (kō'pek), *n.* a kopeck, a small Russian coin.
Co·pen·ha·gen (kō'pən-hā'gən), *n.* the capital of Denmark, on the east coast of Zealand Island: pop., 927,000 (1946): Danish name, *København.*
copenhagen blue, [after *Copenhagen*], a dull, light blue.
co·pe·pod (kō'pə-pod'), *n.* [< Gr. *kōpē,* oar; + *-pod*], any of a group of very small crustaceans living in both the sea and fresh water.
Co·per·ni·can (kō-pũr'ni-kən), *adj.* of Copernicus or his astronomical system: abbreviated **Cop.**
Copernican system, the theory of Copernicus that the planets revolve around the sun and that the turning of the earth on its axis accounts for the apparent rising and setting of the stars: basis of modern astronomy.
Co·per·ni·cus, Nic·o·la·us (nik'ə-lā'əs kō-pũr'ni-kəs), 1473–1543; Polish astronomer: see preceding entry.
co·pe·set·ic, co·pe·set·tic (kō'pə-set'ik), *adj.* [arbitrary formation], [Slang], good; satisfactory; excellent.
cope·stone (kōp'stōn'), *n.* 1. the top stone of a wall or building; stone in or for a coping; hence, 2. culmination; finishing stroke.
cop·i·er (kop'i-ẽr), *n.* 1. a person who copies; imitator. 2. a copyist; transcriber.
co·pi·lot (kō'pī'lət), *n.* the assistant pilot of an aircraft.
cop·ing (kōp'iŋ), *n.* [< fig. use of *cope* (a cloak)], the top layer of a masonry wall, usually sloped to carry off water.
coping saw, a saw with a narrow blade in a U-shaped frame, for cutting curved outlines.
co·pi·ous (kō'pi-əs), *adj.* [ME.; L. *copiosus* < *copia,* abundance < *co-,* together + *opes,* wealth], 1. abundant. 2. wordy; profuse or diffuse. —*SYN.* see **plentiful.**
co·pla·nar (kō-plā'nẽr), *adj.* in *mathematics,* in the same plane: said of figures.
Cop·land, Aaron (kōp'lənd), 1900– ; American musician and composer.

Cop·ley, John Sin·gle·ton (siŋ'g'l-tən kop'li), 1738–1815; American painter.
co·pol·y·mer (kō-pol'i-mẽr), *n.* in *chemistry*, a compound produced by copolymerization.
co·pol·y·mer·i·za·tion (kō-pol'i-mẽr-i-zā'shən), *n.* a process resembling polymerization but in which unlike molecules are arranged in alternate sequence in a chain.
co·pol·y·mer·ize (kō-pol'i-mẽr-īz'), *v.t. & v.i.* to subject to or undergo copolymerization.
Cop·pée, Fran·çois É·dou·ard Jo·a·chim (frän'swȧ' ā'dwȧr' zhō'ȧ'kēm' kô'pā'), 1842–1908; French poet and novelist.
cop·per (kop'ẽr), *n.* [see PLURAL, II, D, 3], [ME. *coper;* AS. *copor;* LL. *cuper, cuprum,* contr. of *cyprium* in *Cyprium aes,* Cyprian brass < Gr. *Kyprios,* Cyprus, where the best copper was produced], 1. a reddish-brown, malleable, ductile, metallic element that is an excellent conductor of electricity and heat: symbol, Cu; at. wt., 63.54; at. no., 29: abbreviated **C., c., cop.** 2. a thing made of this metal. 3. a small coin of copper or bronze, as a penny. 4. a large container or boiler, now often made of iron. 5. the color of copper; reddish brown. *adj.* 1. of copper. 2. copper-colored; reddish-brown. *v.t.* to cover with copper.
cop·per (kop'ẽr), *n.* [prob. < *cop* (to seize)], [Slang], a policeman.
cop·per·ah (kop'ẽr-ə), *n.* copra.
cop·per·as (kop'ẽr-əs), *n.* [ME. *coperose;* OFr. *couperose;* ML. *cuperosa, cuprosa;* prob. short for *aqua cuprosa,* lit., copper water; see COPPER], ferrous sulfate, $FeSO_4 \cdot 7H_2O$, a green, crystalline compound used in dyeing, the making of ink, etc.
cop·per·head (kop'ẽr-hed'), *n.* 1. a poisonous snake with a copper-colored head, found in North America: it is related to the rattlesnake but has no rattles. 2. [C-], a Northerner who sympathized with the South at the time of the Civil War: contemptuous and hostile term used in the North.

COPPERHEAD (24 in. long)

Cop·per·mine (kop'ẽr-mīn'), *n.* a river in central Northwest Territories, Canada, flowing into the Arctic Ocean: length, 510 mi.
cop·per·plate (kop'ẽr-plāt'), *n.* 1. a flat piece of copper etched or engraved for printing. 2. a print or engraving made from this. 3. copperplate printing or engraving.
copper pyrites, copper-iron sulfide, $CuFeS_2$; chalcopyrite.
cop·per·smith (kop'ẽr-smith'), *n.* a man whose work is making utensils and similar things out of copper.
copper sulfate, a blue, crystalline substance, $CuSO_4 \cdot 5H_2O$, which effloresces and turns white when heated; cupric sulfate; blue vitriol: used in making pigments, germicides, electric batteries, etc.
cop·per·y (kop'ẽr-i), *adj.* 1. of or containing copper. 2. resembling copper, as in color.
cop·pice (kop'is), *n.* [OFr. *copeis* < *coper, couper,* to cut; see COPE (to fight)], a thicket of small trees or shrubbery; copse.
co·pra (kop'rə), *n.* [Port.; Malayalam *koppara;* Hind. *khoprā*], dried coconut meat, the source of coconut oil: also **coprah, coppra, copperah.**
cop·re·mi·a (kop-rē'mi-ə), *n.* [*copr-* + *-emia*], blood poisoning resulting from the absorption of fecal matter: also spelled **copraemia.**
cop·ro- (kop'rō, kop'rə), [< Gr. *kopros,* dung], a combining form meaning *dung, excrement, feces,* as in *coprolite:* also, before a vowel, **copr-.**
cop·ro·lite (kop'rə-līt'), *n.* [*copro-* + *-lite*], fossilized excrement of animals.
cop·rol·o·gy (kop-rol'ə-ji), *n.* [*copro-* + *-logy*], the study or treatment of pornography in art and literature.
co·proph·a·gous (kop-rof'ə-gəs), *adj.* [*copro-* + *-phagous*], feeding on dung, as some beetles.
cop·ro·phil·i·a (kop'rə-fil'i-ə), *n.* [*copro-* + *-philia*], *n.* 1. in *psychology,* attraction to feces. 2. preoccupation with obscenity; fondness for pornography.
copse (kops), *n.* [< *coppice*], a coppice.
Copt (kopt), *n.* [Mod. L. *Coptus;* see COPTIC], 1. a native of Egypt descended from the ancient inhabitants of that country. 2. a member of the Coptic Church.
Cop·tic (kop'tik), *adj.* [Mod. L. *Copticus* < L. *Coptus,* earlier *Cophtus* < Ar. *Quft, Qift,* the Copts; Coptic *Gyptios, Kyptaios* < Gr. *Aigyptios,* Egyptian], 1. of the Copts, their language, culture, etc. 2. of the Coptic Church. *n.* the ancient Hamitic language of the Copts, now used only in the ritual of the Coptic Church; New Egyptian. Abbreviated **Cop.**
Coptic Church, the native Christian church of Egypt and, at one time, of Ethiopia.
cop·u·la (kop'yoo-lə), *n.* [*pl.* COPULAS (-ləz)], [L., a band, link (earlier **co-apula*) < *co-,* together + *apere,* to join], 1. something that connects or links together. 2. a bone, cartilage, ligament, etc. connecting parts of the body. 3. in *grammar,* a weakened verbal form, especially a form of *be* or any similar verb, as *seem, appear,* etc., which links a subject with a predicate complement. 4. in *logic,* the connecting link between the subject and predicate of a proposition.
cop·u·lar (kop'yoo-lẽr), *adj.* of, or having the nature of, a copula.
cop·u·late (kop'yoo-lāt'; *for adj.,* kop'yoo-lit), *v.i.* [COPULATED (-id), COPULATING], [< L. *copulatus,* pp. of *copulare,* to unite, couple < *copula;* see COPULA], to unite in sexual intercourse. *adj.* [Obs.], coupled; linked.
cop·u·la·tion (kop'yoo-lā'shən), *n.* [Fr.; L. *copulatio;* see COPULATE], 1. a joining together; coupling. 2. the state of being coupled. 3. the act of copulating.
cop·u·la·tive (kop'yoo-lā'tiv, kop'yoo-lə-tiv), *adj.* [Fr. *copulatif;* LL. *copulativus* < L. *copulatus;* see COPULATE], 1. joining together; coupling. 2. involving or comprising connected words or clauses. 3. having the nature of a copula: as, a *copulative* verb. 4. of or for copulating. *n.* a copulative word.
cop·y (kop'i), *n.* [*pl.* COPIES (-iz)], [ME. & OFr. *copie,* abundance, full transcript; ML. *copia,* copious transcript; L. *copia,* plenty; see COPIOUS], 1. a thing made just like another; imitation of an original; full reproduction or transcription. 2. any of a number of books, magazines, engravings, etc. having the same composition or printed matter: as, he has two *copies* of *Tom Jones.* 3. a model or pattern, as of penmanship, to be imitated or reproduced. 4. a manuscript to be set in type. Abbreviated **c., C.** 5. anything that can provide subject matter for a novelist, journalist, etc. *v.t. & v.i.* [COPIED (-id), COPYING], 1. to make a copy or copies of (a piece of writing, etc.); reproduce; transcribe. 2. to make or do something in imitation of (some thing or person); imitate.
SYN.—**copy,** the broadest of these terms, refers to any imitation, often only approximate, of an original (a carbon *copy*); **reproduction** implies a close imitation of the original, often, however, with differences, as of material, size, or quality (a *reproduction* of a painting); a **facsimile** is an exact reproduction in appearance, sometimes, however, differing in scale (a photostated *facsimile* of a document); a **duplicate** is a double, or counterpart, of something, serving all the purposes of the original (all the books of a single printing are *duplicates*); a **replica** is an exact reproduction of a work of art, in strict usage, one made by the original artist. See also **imitate.**
cop·y·book (kop'i-book'), *n.* a book containing models of handwriting for pupils to imitate. *adj.* ordinary; trite; commonplace: as, *copybook* maxims.
copy boy, a boy who runs errands and carries copy from the writers to the editor in a newspaper office.
cop·y·cat (kop'i-kat'), *n.* a person who habitually imitates or mimics: a child's term.
copy desk, the desk in a newspaper office where copy is edited and headlines are written.
cop·y·hold (kop'i-hōld'), *n.* in *English law,* tenure of property proved by a written transcript or record in the rolls of a manorial court.
cop·y·hold·er (kop'i-hōl'dẽr), *n.* 1. a person who reads the manuscript to a proofreader. 2. in *English law,* a person who owns land by copyhold.
cop·y·ist (kop'i-ist), *n.* 1. a person who makes written copies; transcriber. 2. a person who imitates; copier.
cop·y·read·er (kop'i-rē'dẽr), *n.* a person whose work is editing and correcting articles and stories written by others, as in a newspaper office.
cop·y·right (kop'i-rīt'), *n.* [*copy* + *right*], the exclusive right to the publication, production, or sale of the rights to a literary, dramatic, musical, or artistic work, or to the use of a manufacturing or merchandising label, granted by law for a definite period of years to an author, composer, artist, distributor, etc.: in the United States the period of copyright is 28 years, with the optional privilege of one renewal for another 28 years: abbreviated **c., C.** *v.t.* to protect (a book, etc.) by copyright. *adj.* protected by copyright.
cop·y·writ·er (kop'i-rīt'ẽr), *n.* a writer of copy, especially for advertisements.
coque·li·cot (kōk'li-kō'), *n.* [Fr.], 1. the corn poppy. 2. the orange-red color of this flower.
Co·que·lin, Be·noît Cons·tant (bə-nwȧ' kōn'stän' kôk'lan'), 1841–1909; French actor.
co·quet (kō-ket'), *v.i.* [COQUETTED (-id), COQUETTING], [Fr. *coqueter,* to coquet, flirt, lit., to strut like a rooster < *coquet,* dim. of *coc,* a rooster; see COCK], 1. to flirt; try to attract attention or admiration: usually said of a woman. 2. to trifle (*with* an idea, etc.); dally. Also spelled **coquette.** —*SYN.* see **trifle.**
co·quet·ry (kō'kə-tri, kō-ket'ri), *n.* [*pl.* COQUETRIES (-triz, -riz)], [Fr. *coqueterie* < *coqueter;* see COQUET], the behavior or act of a coquette; flirting.
co·quette (kō-ket'), *n.* [Fr. *coquette,* fem. of *coquet,* male flirt; see COQUET], a girl or woman who tries to get men's attention and admiration merely from vanity; flirt. *v.i.* [COQUETTED (-id), COQUETTING], to coquet.
co·quet·tish (kō-ket'ish), *adj.* of, like, or characteristic of a coquette; showing coquetry.
co·quil·la nut (kə-kēl'yə, kə-kē'yə), [Sp. *coquillo* or Port. *coquilho,* dim. of *coco,* coconut], the fruit of a Brazilian palm tree: it has a hard, brown, ivorylike shell used by turners and carvers.

co·qui·na (kə-kē′nə), *n.* [Sp., shellfish, cockle, dim. < dial. form of L. *concha;* see CONCH], a soft, whitish limestone made up of broken sea shells and corals: it is used as a building material in Florida and the West Indies.

co·qui·to (kə-kē′tō), *n.* [*pl.* COQUITOS (-tōz)], [Sp., dim. of *coco*, coco palm], a palm tree of Chile whose sweet sap and seeds are used for food: also **coquito palm.**

cor- (kôr), *com-:* used before *r*, as in *corrupt*.

Cor., 1. Corinthians. 2. Coroner.

cor., 1. corner. 2. coroner. 3. corpus. 4. correct. 5. corrected. 6. correction. 7. correlative. 8. correspondence. 9. correspondent. 10. corresponding. 11. in *music*, cornet.

Cor·a (kôr′ə, kō′rə), [L.; Gr. *Korē*, lit., maiden, name of Proserpine], a feminine name.

cor·a·ci·i·form (kôr′ə-sī′ə-fôrm′), *adj.* [< Mod. L. *Coracii*, name of the suborder < Gr. *korax*, raven; + *-form*], of a kind of tree-dwelling birds that neither perch nor sing, as kingfishers, hornbills, etc.; of nonpasserine birds.

cor·a·cle (kôr′ə-k′l, kor′ə-k′l), *n.* [< W. *corwgl* < *corwg*, carcass, boat], a short but broad boat made of a waterproof material stretched over a wicker or wooden frame.

cor·a·coid (kôr′ə-koid′, kor′ə-koid′), *adj.* [L. *coracoides* < Gr. *korakoeidēs*, like a raven < *korax*, raven + *eidos*, form], 1. designating or of a rudimentary bony process in mammals that extends from the shoulder blade toward the breastbone. 2. designating or of a bone in birds and reptiles that extends from the shoulder blade to the breastbone. *n.* this bony process or bone.

cor·al (kôr′əl, kor′əl), *n.* [ME.; OFr.; L. *corallum, coralium;* Gr. *korallion;* prob. < Heb. *gōrāl*, pebble or Ar. *garal*, small stone], 1. a hard substance made up of the skeletons of certain marine animals (called *polyps*): reefs, shelves, and atolls of coral are found in tropical seas. 2. any of a number of such animals living in large colonies: their skeletons form a stony mass. 3. a piece of coral, especially the red kind used in jewelry. 4. the ovaries of the lobster. 5. a teething toy for babies, made of coral. 6. coral red. *adj.* 1. made of coral. 2. coral-red.

CORAL

cor·al·lif·er·ous (kôr′ə-lif′ẽr-əs, kor′ə-lif′ẽr-əs), *adj.* [see -FEROUS], containing or producing coral.

cor·al·line (kôr′ə-lin, kor′ə-lin′), *n.* [Mod. L. *corallina* < the *adj.*], 1. any animal related to or resembling the corals. 2. any of various algae or seaweeds that produce limestone. *adj.* [LL. *corallinus*, coral-red], 1. consisting of coral or corallines. 2. resembling coral, especially in color.

cor·al·loid (kôr′ə-loid′, kor′ə-loid′), *adj.* [see -OID], resembling coral in appearance and form. *n.* any organism resembling or related to coral.

cor·al·loi·dal (kôr′ə-loid″'l, kor′ə-loid″'l), *adj.* coralloid.

cor·al-red (kôr′əl-red′, kor′əl-red′), *adj.* yellowish-red.

coral red, yellowish red.

coral reef, a reef built up by the action of ocean waves which deposit the limestone skeletons of certain types of coral living in warm tropical waters.

cor·al·root (kôr′əl-ro͞ot′, kor′əl-root′), *n.* any of a group of brownish orchids with branched, corallike rootstocks and no leaves: also **coral-root, coral root.**

Coral Sea, a part of the Pacific, northeast of Australia: American forces defeated the Japanese in a naval and air battle fought there (1942) during World War II.

CORAL SEA

coral snake, a small, poisonous snake with coral-red, yellow, and black bands around its body, found in the southeastern United States and subtropical America.

co·ran·to (kə-ran′tō), *n.* [altered < *courante* after It. & Sp. words ending in *-o*], the courante, a lively dance.

cor·ban (kôr′bən, kôr-bän′), *n.* [Heb. *qorbān*, lit., that which is brought near, oblation], in *Hebrew antiquity*, an offering to God, especially one given in performance of a vow.

cor·beil (kôr′bel), *n.* [Fr. *corbeille* < LL. *corbicula*, dim. of L. *corbis*, a basket], a sculptured basket of fruit, flowers, etc., used in architectural design.

cor·bel (kôr′b'l), *n.* [ME.; OFr., dim. of *corb*, raven; L. *corvus*, raven: so called from its beaked shape], 1. a bracket of stone, wood, or metal projecting from the side of a wall and serving to support a cornice, the spring of an arch, a balustrade, etc. 2. a short timber placed lengthwise under a beam or girder. *v.t.* [CORBELED or CORBELLED (-b'ld), CORBELING or CORBELLING], to provide or support with a corbel or corbels.

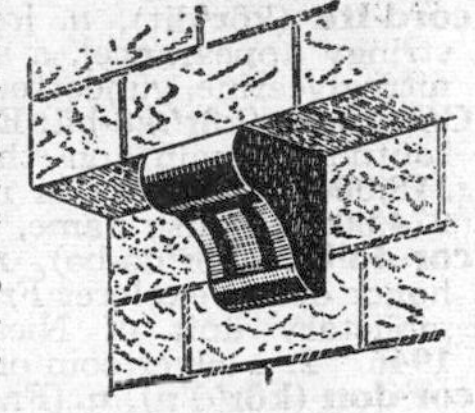

CORBEL

cor·bel·ing, cor·bel·ling (kôr′b'l-iŋ), *n.* 1. the fashioning of corbels; corbel work. 2. a series of corbels.

Cor·bett, James J. (kôr′bit), 1866–1933; American prize fighter; world heavyweight champion (1892–1897).

cor·bie (kôr′bi), *n.* [*pl.* CORBIES (-biz)], [Scot.], [< OFr. *corb;* see CORBEL], a crow or raven: also **corbie crow.**

corbie gable, a gable with corbiesteps.

cor·bie·step (kôr′bi-step′), *n.* [*corbie* + *step*], one of a series of steps forming the roofs of certain gabled houses.

cor·by (kôr′bi), *n.* [*pl.* CORBIES (-biz)], a corbie.

Cor·co·va·do (kôr′kō-vä′*th*oo), *n.* 1. a mountain in Brazil, near Rio de Janeiro: height, 2,309 ft. 2. an arm of the Pacific, off the southern coast of Chile.

Cor·cy·ra (kôr-sī′rə), *n.* Corfu: the ancient name.

cord (kôrd), *n.* [ME. & OFr. *corde;* L. *chorda;* Gr. *chordē*, catgut, chord, cord], 1. thick string or thin rope. 2. any force acting as a tie or bond. 3. [from use of cord in measuring], a measure of wood cut for fuel (128 cubic feet, as arranged in a pile 8 feet long, 4 feet high, and 4 feet wide): abbreviated **cd.** 4. a rib on the surface of a fabric. 5. cloth with a ribbed surface; corduroy. 6. *pl.* corduroy trousers. 7. in *anatomy*, any part resembling a cord: as, the spinal *cord*, vocal *cords*, umbilical *cord:* also **chord.** 8. in *electricity*, a small, flexible insulated cable fitted with a plug or plugs. *v.t.* 1. to fasten, connect, or provide with a cord or cords. 2. to stack (wood) in cords.

cord·age (kôr′dij), *n.* [Fr.; see CORD & -AGE], 1. cords and ropes collectively, especially the ropes in a ship's rigging. 2. the amount of wood, measured in cords, in a given area.

cor·date (kôr′dāt), *adj.* [L. *cordatus* < *cor, cordis*, heart], heart-shaped: as, *cordate* leaves: see **leaf**, illus.

Cor·day, Charlotte (kôr′dā′), (*Marie Anne Charlotte Corday D'Armont*), 1768–1793; French Revolutionary patriot; assassin of Marat.

cord·ed (kôr′did), *adj.* [pp. of *cord*], 1. fastened or tied with cords. 2. made of cords. 3. having a ribbed or twilled surface, as corduroy. 4. stacked in cords, as wood.

Cor·del·ia (kôr-dēl′yə), [said to be < Celt. *Creirydd lydd*, lit., daughter of the sea], a feminine name. *n.* in Shakespeare's *King Lear*, the youngest of Lear's three daughters, and the only one faithful to him.

Cor·de·lier (kôr′də-lêr′), *n.* [Fr. < *cordelle*, dim. of *corde* (see CORD): so named from the knotted cord worn as girdle], 1. a member of the Franciscan religious order. 2. [after the Church of the *Cordeliers*, Paris, where the meetings were held], a member of a radical political club in France during the French Revolution.

cor·delle (kôr-del′), *n.* [Fr., dim. of *corde*, rope; see CORD], a towing rope, especially as formerly used on Mississippi flatboats and keelboats. *v.t.* [CORDELLED (-deld′), CORDELLING], to tow with or as with a cordelle.

cor·dial (kôr′jəl; Brit. kôrd′yəl), *adj.* [Fr.; ML. *cordialis* < L. *cor, cordis*, heart], 1. stimulating the heart; invigorating; reviving. 2. hearty; sincere; deeply felt; warm and genuine. *n.* 1. a medicine, food, or drink that stimulates the heart. 2. an aromatic, sirupy, alcoholic drink; liqueur. —*SYN.* see **amiable.**

cor·dial·i·ty (kôr′ji-al′ə-ti, kôr-jal′ə-ti; Brit. kôr′di-al′ə-ti), *n.* 1. cordial quality; warm, friendly feeling. 2. [*pl.* CORDIALITIES (-tiz)], a cordial act or remark.

cor·di·er·ite (kôr′di-ə-rīt′), *n.* [after P. L. A. *Cordier* (1777–1861), Fr. geologist], iolite.

cord·i·form (kôr′də-fôrm′), *adj.* [< L. *cor, cordis*, heart; + *-form*], heart-shaped.

cor·dil·le·ra (kôr-dil′ẽr-ə, kôr′dil-yâr′ə), *n.* [Sp. < *cordilla*, dim. of *cuerda*, rope, cord < L. *chorda;* see CORD], a ridge or chain of mountains; especially, the principal mountain range of a continent.

Cor·dil·le·ran (kôr-dil′ẽr-ən, kôr′dil-yâr′ən), *adj.* 1. of the Cordilleras. 2. [c-], of a cordillera or cordilleras.

Cor·dil·le·ras (kôr-dil′ẽr-əz, kôr′dil-yâr′əz), *n. pl.* 1. the mountain system in western North America, including the Rocky Mountains, the Coast Range, the Sierra Nevada, the Sierra Madre, etc. 2. the mountain system in western South America, composed of the Andes. 3. these systems regarded as a unit, extending from Alaska to Cape Horn.

cord·ing (kôrd′iŋ), *n.* 1. the ribbed surface of corded cloth. 2. cordage.
cord·ite (kôr′dīt), *n.* [*cord* + *-ite:* so called from its stringy appearance], a smokeless explosive containing nitroglycerine, guncotton, petroleum jelly, and acetone.
Cór·do·ba (kôr′*thô*-bä; Eng. kôr′də-və), *n.* 1. a city in southern Spain, on the Guadalquivir River: pop., 118,000. 2. a city in north central Argentina: pop., 274,000. English name, *Cordova.*
cor·do·ba (kôr′də-bə), *n.* [Sp. *córdoba:* so named in honor of the explorer Francisco F. de *Córdoba*], 1. the monetary unit of Nicaragua, worth about 20¢ in 1946. 2. a silver coin of this value.
cor·don (kôr′d'n), *n.* [Fr., dim. of *corde;* see CORD], 1. a line or circle of people, forts, ships, etc. stationed around an area to guard it. 2. a cord, ribbon, or braid worn as a decoration or badge. 3. a projecting band of stone on the surface of a wall.
‡**cor·don bleu** (kôr′dōn′ blö′), [Fr.], 1. the blue ribbon formerly worn as an emblem by Knights of the Order of the Holy Ghost, the highest order of knighthood in France under the Bourbon monarchy. 2. a very high distinction. 3. a person entitled to wear the cordon bleu; hence, 4. any person highly distinguished in his field.
‡**cor·don sa·ni·taire** (kôr′dōn′ sȧ′nē′târ′), [Fr.], 1. a sanitary cordon; guarded line between affected and unaffected areas, to prevent any movement between them of people, goods, etc., by which disease might be spread; hence, 2. a belt of countries serving to isolate another country and lessen its influence.
Cor·do·va (kôr′də-və, kôr-dō′və), *n.* Córdoba.
Cor·do·van (kôr′də-vən, kôr-dō′vən), *adj.* [< Sp. *cordobán* < *Córdoba,* Spain], 1. of Córdoba. 2. [c-], made of cordovan. *n.* 1. a native or inhabitant of Córdoba. 2. [c-], a soft, colored leather, usually of sheepskin or split horsehide, originally made at Córdoba, Spain. 3. [c-], *pl.* shoes made of this leather.
cor·du·roy (kôr′də-roi′, kôr′də-roi′), *n.* [usually assumed to be < Fr. *corde du roi,* cord of the king (see CORD & ROYAL); but prob. < *cord* + obs. *duroy,* a coarse fabric formerly produced in England; hence, corded duroy], 1. a heavy cotton fabric with a piled, velvety surface, ribbed vertically. 2. *pl.* trousers or, sometimes, a suit made of this fabric. *adj.* 1. made of corduroy. 2. ribbed like corduroy. *v.t.* to build (a road) of logs put down crosswise.
corduroy road, a road built of logs put down crosswise, as across a marsh.
cord·wain (kôrd′wān), *n.* [ME. *corduwane, corduan;* OFr. *cordouan;* Sp. *cordobán;* see CORDOVAN], [Archaic], cordovan leather.
cord·wain·er (kôrd′wān-ẽr), *n.* [ME. *cordwaner, corduaner;* OFr. *cordouanier*], 1. [Archaic], a leatherworker who made things of cordovan. 2. a shoemaker.
cord·wood (kôrd′wood′), *n.* 1. wood cut and stacked in cords or sold by the cord. 2. wood cut in lengths of 4 feet.
core (kôr, kōr), *n.* [ME.; OFr. *cor, coer;* prob. < L. *cor,* heart], 1. the hard central or innermost part of an apple, pear, quince, etc., which contains the seeds. 2. the central or innermost part of anything; hence, 3. the most important part; essence or pith of a matter. 4. in *electricity,* a mass of ferromagnetic material placed inside a wire coil and serving to increase the external magnetic field. 5. in *founding,* that part of a mold which forms the interior of a hollow casting. *v.t.* [CORED (kôrd), CORING], to remove the core of.
Co·re·a (kə-rē′ə, kô-rē′ə, kō-rē′ə), *n.* Korea.
co·re·la·tion (kō′ri-lā′shən), *n.* correlation.
co·re·li·gion·ist (kō′ri-lij′ən-ist), *n.* 1. a person professing the same religion. 2. a member of the same religious denomination.
co·re·op·sis (kôr′i-op′sis, kō′ri-op′sis), *n.* [Mod. L. < Gr. *koris,* bug + *opsis,* appearance: so named from the shape of the seed], 1. any of a group of plants of the composite family, with daisylike flowers of yellow, orange, red, or brownish purple. 2. the flower.
cor·er (kôr′ẽr, kōr′ẽr), *n.* an instrument for removing the cores of apples, etc.
co·re·spond·en·cy (kō′ri-spon′dən-si), *n.* the state of being a corespondent.
co·re·spond·ent (kō′ri-spon′dənt), *n.* [*co-* + *respondent*], in *law,* a person charged with having committed adultery with the wife or husband from whom a divorce is being sought.
corf (kôrf), *n.* [*pl.* CORVES (kôrvz)], [MD.; L. *corbis,* a basket], [British], formerly, a wicker basket, now a small wooden or iron wagon or truck used for carrying coal, ore, etc. in mines.
Cor·fu (kôr′fū; It. kôr-fōō′), *n.* 1. one of the Ionian Islands west of Greece: area, 227 sq. mi.; pop., 106,000. 2. its chief city and port: pop., 32,000. Greek name, *Kerkyra;* ancient name, *Corcyra.*
co·ri·a·ceous (kō′ri-ā′shəs, kor′i-ā′shəs), *adj.* [LL. *coriaceus* < L. *corium,* leather], of or like leather; leathery; tough.
co·ri·an·der (kôr′i-an′dẽr, kō′ri-an′dẽr), *n.* [Fr. *coriandre;* L. *coriandrum* < Gr. *koriannon, koriandron* < *koris,* bug, bedbug: so named from its odor], 1. a European plant of the carrot family. 2. its strong-smelling, seedlike fruit, used in flavoring food and liqueurs, and, in medicine, as a tonic for the stomach.
Co·rinne (kə-rin′, kô-rēn′), [Fr.; L. *Corinna;* Gr. *Korinna,* dim. of *Korē;* see CORA], a feminine name.
Cor·inth (kôr′inth, kor′inth), *n.* an ancient city in southern Greece, famous for its luxury, commerce, and art.
Corinth, Gulf of, an arm of the Ionian Sea, between the Peloponnesus and the mainland of Greece: also called *Gulf of Lepanto.*
Corinth, Isthmus of, a narrow strip of land joining the Peloponnesus and the mainland of Greece: see **Greece,** map.
Co·rin·thi·an (kə-rin′thi-ən), *adj.* 1. of Corinth, its people, or culture. 2. dissolute and given to luxury, as the people of Corinth were reputed to be. 3. in the style of the art of Corinth; elaborately graceful. 4. designating or relating to the most elaborate of the three orders (Doric, Ionic, Corinthian) of Greek architecture, distinguished by a slender, fluted column and a bell-shaped capital decorated with a design of acanthus leaves. *n.* 1. a native or inhabitant of Corinth: often with reference to dissoluteness; hence, 2. a wealthy man about town. 3. a gentleman amateur in sports, especially boxing, horse racing, and cricket. 4. an amateur yachtsman.

CORINTHIAN CAPITAL

Co·rin·thi·ans (kə-rin′thi-ənz), *n. pl.* [construed as sing.], either of the Epistles to the Corinthians, two books of the New Testament which were messages from the Apostle Paul to the Christians of Corinth: abbreviated **Cor.**
Cor·i·o·la·nus (kôr′i-ə-lā′nəs, kor′i-ə-lā′nəs), *n.* a tragedy (c. 1608) by Shakespeare, based on the story of Gnaius Marcius Coriolanus, a Roman general of the 5th century B.C.
co·ri·um (kôr′i-əm, kō′ri-əm), *n.* [*pl.* CORIA (-ə)], [L., skin, hide], the layer of skin that lies beneath the epidermis and contains its blood and nerve supply; dermis; derma: see **skin,** illus.
Cork (kôrk), *n.* 1. a county on the southern coast of Ireland: pop., 356,000. 2. a city in this county: pop., 80,800.
cork (kôrk), *n.* [ME.; Sp. *al-corque,* corkwood slippers; Ar. *alcorque;* ? < L. *quercus,* oak], 1. the light, thick, elastic outer bark of an oak tree (called the *cork oak*) that grows in the Mediterranean area, especially in Spain and Portugal: the bark is stripped off in large plates every 12 to 15 years and is used for various purposes. 2. a piece of cork or something made of cork, especially a stopper for a bottle, cask, etc. 3. a stopper of similar shape made of glass, rubber, metal, etc. 4. the outer bark of the stems of woody plants. *adj.* made of cork. *v.t.* 1. to stop or seal with a cork. 2. to hold back; check. 3. to blacken with burnt cork.
cork·age (kôr′kij), *n.* [*cork* + *-age*], a charge made at a tavern, restaurant, hotel, etc. for every bottle of wine or liquor uncorked and served, especially for bottles bought elsewhere and brought in by guests.
cork cambium, [see CORK, 4], in *botany,* the tissue between the bark and the wood, from which the protective outer bark is formed; phellogen.
corked (kôrkt), *adj.* [pp. of *cork*], 1. stopped with a cork: as, a *corked* bottle. 2. blackened with burnt cork. 3. having the taste and smell of the cork: said of wine, etc. which has been bottled with unsound cork.
cork·er (kôr′kẽr), *n.* [slang senses < corking a bottle], 1. a worker or device that corks bottles. 2. [Slang], a remarkable person or thing. 3. [Slang], an argument, statement, or circumstance that appears conclusive. 4. [Slang], a preposterous lie.
cork·ing (kôr′kiŋ), *adj. & interj.* [< *cork*], [Slang], very good; excellent.
cork·screw (kôrk′skrōō′), *n.* a device for pulling corks out of bottles, usually a spiral-shaped piece of steel with a point at one end and a handle at the other. *adj.* like a corkscrew in shape; spiral; helical. *v.i & v.t.* to move in a winding or spiral course; zigzag.
cork·wood (kôrk′wood′), *n.* 1. any of several trees whose wood is very light and porous. 2. the wood.
cork·y (kôr′ki), *adj.* [CORKIER (-ki-ẽr), CORKIEST (-ki-ist)], 1. of cork. 2. like cork or a cork.
corm (kôrm), *n.* [< Gr. *kormos,* trunk of a tree with branches lopped off < *keirein,* to cut off], the short, fleshy, underground stem of certain plants, as the crocus or gladiolus: it resembles a bulb and is covered with several scalelike leaves.
cor·mo·phyte (kôr′mə-fīt′), *n.* [*cormo-* (< Gr. *kormos;* see CORM) + *-phyte*], any plant with a stem and root.
cor·mo·phyt·ic (kôr′mə-fit′ik), *adj.* of, or having the nature of, a cormophyte.
cor·mo·rant (kôr′mə-rənt), *n.* [ME. *cormoraunt, cormaran,* earlier *cormarenc;* OFr. *cormareng* < *corp marenc;* L. *corvus marinus; corvus,* raven + *marinus* <

mare, the sea], 1. a large, voracious sea bird with webbed toes and a pouch of skin under its beak, into which it puts fish. 2. a greedy person; glutton. *adj.* greedy; gluttonous.

corn (kôrn), *n.* [see PLURAL, II, D, 3], [ME.; AS. *corn*, a seed, grain (cf. KERNEL, PEPPERCORN); akin to G. *korn* (Goth *kaúrn*); IE. base *ĝer-, *ĝerē-, to be ripe, seen also in L. *granum* (< *gerə-nom); cf. GRAIN, CHURL], 1. a small, hard seed or seedlike fruit, especially the seed of any cereal plant; kernel. 2. *a*) a kind of grain that grows in kernels on large ears; maize. *b*) its ears. Also, and originally, called *Indian corn.* 3. in England, wheat. 4. in Scotland and Ireland, oats. 5. [British], the seeds or kernels of all such cereal plants; grain. 6. [British], any plant or plants producing grain. 7. [Colloq.], corn whisky. 8. [Slang], ideas, humor, music, etc. regarded as old-fashioned, trite, banal, or sentimental. *v.t.* 1. to form into grains. 2. to preserve or pickle (meat, etc.) in brine, or with salt in grains, or corns. 3. to feed (animals) grain.

corn (kôrn), *n.* [ME.; OFr. < L. *cornu*, a horn], a horny thickening of the skin, especially on the toes, caused by pressure or friction.

-corn (kôrn), [< L. *cornu*, a horn], a terminal combining form meaning *horn*, as in *Capricorn, unicorn.*

Corn., 1. Cornish. 2. Cornwall.

cor·na·ceous (kôr-nā'shəs), *adj.* [< Mod. L. *Cornaceae*, name of the order < *cornus;* see CORNEL], of a large group of shrubs and herbs of the dogwood family.

Corn Belt, the region in the Middle West where much corn is raised: it extends from central Ohio to central Kansas and Nebraska.

corn borer, a moth larva that feeds on corn, etc.

corn bread, bread made of corn meal.

corn·cake (kôrn'kāk'), *n.* johnnycake.

corn·cob (kôrn'kob'), *n.* 1. the woody core of an ear of corn, on which the kernels grow in rows. 2. a corncob pipe.

corncob pipe, a tobacco pipe with a bowl made of a hollowed piece of dried corncob.

corn cockle, a tall weed of the pink family, with flat, purple-red flowers, which often grows in grainfields.

corn color, light yellow.

corn crake, a brown, short-billed European bird of the rail family, often found in grainfields.

corn·crib (kôrn'krib'), *n.* a small, ventilated structure for storing corn.

corn·dodg·er (kôrn'doj'ẽr), *n.* 1. a bread made of corn meal baked or fried hard in small pones. 2. such a pone. Also **corn-dodger, corn dodger.**

cor·ne·a (kôr'ni-ə), *n.* [L., fem. sing. of *corneus*, horny < *cornu*, a horn], the transparent tissue forming the outer coat of the eyeball and covering the iris and pupil: see **eye,** illus.

cor·ne·al (kôr'ni-əl), *adj.* of the cornea.

corn·ear worm (kôrn'êr'), a certain moth larva that feeds on corn, cotton, etc.; bollworm.

corned (kôrnd), *adj.* [< *corn, v.*], preserved with salt or brine: as, *corned* beef.

Cor·neille, Pierre (pyâr kôr'nā'y'; Eng. kôr-nā'), 1606–1684; French dramatist and poet.

cor·nel (kôr'n'l, kôr'nel), *n.* [OFr. *cornille, corneille;* L. *cornicula*, dim. < *cornum, cornus*, cornel tree; akin to Gr. *kranos*, cornel tree], any of a group of shrubs and small trees with very hard wood, including both the European and the American dogwood.

Cor·nel·ia (kôr-nēl'yə), [L., fem. of *Cornelius*], a feminine name. *n.* the mother of Tiberius and Gaius Gracchus (*the Gracchi*), leaders of the democratic party in ancient Rome; lived 2d century B.C.

cor·nel·ian (kôr-nēl'yən, kẽr-nēl'yən), *n.* [ME. & OFr. *corneline*, dim. < OFr. *corneola;* prob. (because of similarity of color) < L. *cornum;* see CORNEL], carnelian.

Cor·nel·ius (kôr-nēl'yəs), [L., name of a Roman gens], a masculine name: feminine, *Cornelia.*

Cor·ne·li·us, Pe·ter von (pā'tẽr fôn kôr-nā'li-oos), 1783–1867; German painter.

Cor·nell, Ezra (kôr-nel'), 1807–1874; American capitalist and philanthropist.

Cornell, Katharine, 1898– ; American actress.

cor·ne·ous (kôr'ni-əs), *adj.* [L. *corneus* < *cornu*, a horn], horny; hornlike.

cor·ner (kôr'nẽr), *n.* [ME. *corner, cornier;* OFr. *corniere;* LL. *cornerium* < *cornu*, a horn, projecting point], 1. the point or place where lines or surfaces join and form an angle. 2. the space between lines or surfaces at the point of their junction; angle: as, the *corner* of a room. 3. the place where two streets meet. Abbreviated **cor.** 4. a piece used to form, mark, guard, or ornament a corner. 5. a remote, secret, or secluded place: as, look in every nook and *corner*. 6. region; quarter; part: as, the four *corners* of the earth. 7. an awkward position, from which escape is difficult: as, he was driven into a *corner;* hence, 8. a speculative monopoly produced by buying up all or most of the available supply of some stock or commodity so as to be able to raise the price. *v.t.* 1. to furnish with corners. 2. to put into a corner. 3. to drive or force into a corner, or into an awkward position from which escape is difficult; hence, 4. to form a corner in (some stock or commodity). *v.i.* 1. to form a corner. 2. to be situated on or at a corner. *adj.* 1. at or on a corner: as, a *corner* store. 2. used in a corner. —*SYN.* see **monopoly.**

cut corners, 1. to take a direct route by going across corners. 2. to cut down expenses, time or labor required, etc.

the (four) corners of the earth, 1. the farthest parts of the earth; hence, 2. everywhere.

turn the corner, to get safely past the critical point.

cor·nered (kôr'nẽrd), *adj.* [pp. of *corner*], 1. having corners. 2. forced into an awkward position from which escape is difficult.

cor·ner·stone (kôr'nẽr-stōn'), *n.* [ME.], 1. a stone at the corner of a building. 2. such a stone, often inscribed, laid at a ceremony formally beginning the erection of a building. 3. the basic, essential, or most important part; foundation.

cor·ner·ways (kôr'nẽr-wāz'), *adv.* cornerwise.

cor·ner·wise (kôr'nẽr-wīz'), *adv.* [*corner* + *-wise*], 1. with the corner to the front; so as to form a corner. 2. from one corner to an opposite corner; diagonally.

cor·net (kôr-net' *for 1;* kôr'nit, kôr-net' *for 2, 3, 4*), *n.* [ME.; OFr., dim. of *corn*, a horn < L. *cornu*, a horn], 1. a brass-wind musical instrument of the trumpet class, having three valves worked by pistons: abbreviated **cor.** 2. a piece of paper twisted like a cone, for holding sugar, candy, etc. 3. the spreading, white headdress that a Sister of Charity wears. 4. formerly, a British cavalry officer of the lowest rank, who carried his troop's flag.

CORNET

cor·net-à-pis·tons (kôr'nit-ə-pis'tənz; Fr. kôr'ne'à'-pēs'tōn'), *n.* [*pl.* CORNETS-À-PISTONS (kôr'nets-; Fr. kôr'ne'zà'pēs'tōn')], a cornet (musical instrument).

cor·net·cy (kôr'nit-si), *n.* [*pl.* CORNETCIES (-siz)], [Obs.], the rank or commission of a cornet (cavalry officer).

cor·net·tist, cor·net·ist (kôr-net'ist), *n.* a cornet player.

corn·fed (kôrn'fed'), *adj.* 1. fed on corn. 2. [Slang], countrified; healthy and strong but unsophisticated.

corn·field (kôrn'fēld'), *n.* a field in which corn is grown.

corn-flour (kôrn'flou'ẽr, kôrn'flour'), *n.* 1. flour made from corn (maize). 2. [British], flour made from some other grain: see **corn.**

corn·flow·er (kôrn'flou'ẽr), *n.* 1. the bachelor's-button. 2. the corn cockle.

corn·husk (kôrn'husk'), *n.* a husk of an ear of corn.

corn·husk·ing (kôrn'hus'kiŋ), *n.* 1. the husking of corn. 2. a gathering of friends and neighbors for husking corn; husking bee: it is generally a festive event, followed by dancing, etc.

cor·nice (kôr'nis), *n.* [Fr.; It.; prob. < L. *coronis*, curved line, flourish with a pen at the end of a book; Gr. *korōnis*, a wreath, garland], 1. a horizontal molding projecting along the top of a wall, building, etc. 2. the top part of an entablature: see **entablature,** illus. 3. an ornamental band for covering a curtain rod. *v.t.* [CORNICED (-nist), CORNICING], to top with a cornice or something like a cornice.

cor·nic·u·late (kôr-nik'yoo-lāt', kôr-nik'yoo-lit), *adj.* [L. *corniculatus* < *corniculus*, dim. of *cornu*, a horn], having horns or hornlike projections; horned.

Cor·nish (kôr'nish), *adj.* of Cornwall, its people, or culture. *n.* the Brythonic Celtic language spoken by the people of Cornwall until c. 1800, closely related to Breton and Welsh.

Cor·nish·man (kôr'nish-mən), *n.* [*pl.* CORNISHMEN (-mən)], a native or inhabitant of Cornwall.

Corn Laws, in England, certain laws imposing heavy duties on the importation of wheat, repealed in 1846.

corn lily, any of a number of related bulb plants native to South Africa, with slender, grasslike leaves and spikes of showy, funnel-shaped flowers.

corn meal, 1. meal made from corn. 2. meal made from some other grain, as, in Scotland, oats: see **corn.**

corn picker, a machine for picking ears of corn from standing stalks and removing the husks.

corn pit, that part of a produce exchange where trading in corn futures goes on.

corn pone, a kind of corn bread usually made without milk or eggs.

corn poppy, a red, black-spotted poppy often found in cornfields of Europe and Asia.

corn rose, 1. the corn poppy. 2. the corn cockle.

corn salad, a European plant whose leaves are used in salads.

corn shock, a stack of cut cornstalks set up in a field to dry.

corn silk, a tassel of silky fibers growing at the end of an ear of corn, serving to receive pollen.

corn sirup, a sweet sirup made from cornstarch.

corn smut, 1. a fungus disease of corn, marked by large, black swellings on the ear and tassel. 2. the fungus causing this disease.

corn·stalk (kôrn′stôk′), *n.* a stalk of corn.

corn·starch (kôrn′stärch′), *n.* a fine, starchy flour made from Indian corn, used in making puddings, etc.

corn sugar, a dextrose made from cornstarch.

cor·nu (kôr′nū), *n.* [*pl.* CORNUA (-ə)], [L.], 1. a horn. 2. a thing shaped like a horn.

cor·nu·co·pi·a (kôr′nə-kō′pi-ə, kôr′nyoo-kō′pi-ə), *n.* [L. *cornu copiae,* horn of plenty], 1. in *Greek mythology,* the horn of the goat that suckled Zeus. 2. a horn of plenty; a representation, in painting, sculpture, etc., of a horn overflowing with fruits, flowers, and grain; hence, 3. an overflowing fullness; abundance. 4. a cone-shaped paper container for nuts, candy, etc.

CORNUCOPIA

cor·nus (kôr′nəs), *n.* [L.], a cornel.

cor·nut·ed (kôr-nū′tid), *adj.* [< L. *cornutus,* horned < *cornu,* a horn], [Archaic], cuckolded.

Corn·wall (kôrn′wôl, kôrn′wəl), *n.* a county of southwestern England: pop., 318,000; county seat, Bodmin: abbreviated **Corn.**

Corn·wal·lis, Charles (kôrn-wôl′is, kôrn-wol′is), first Marquis Cornwallis, 1738–1805; British general and statesman; commanded British forces during the American Revolution.

corn whisky, whisky made from corn (maize).

corn·y (kôr′ni), *adj.* [CORNIER (-ni-ẽr), CORNIEST (-ni-ist)], 1. of or producing corn. 2. [Slang], countrified; unsophisticated. 3. [Slang], old-fashioned, trite, banal, sentimental, etc.

corn·y (kôr′ni), *adj.* [CORNIER (-ni-ẽr), CORNIEST (-ni-ist)], having or relating to corns on the feet.

cor·o·dy (kôr′ə-di, kor′ə-di), *n.* [*pl.* CORODIES (-diz)], [ME.; ML. *corrodium,* var. of *corredium,* outfit, provision], in *old law,* 1. an allowance of food, etc. for one's maintenance. 2. the right to this.

co·rol·la (kə-rol′ə), *n.* [L., dim. of *corona,* a crown, wreath], the petals, or inner leaves, of a flower.

cor·ol·la·ceous (kôr′ə-lā′shəs, kor′ə-lā′shəs), *adj.* 1. having a corolla. 2. like a corolla.

cor·ol·lar·y (kôr′ə-ler′i, kor′ə-ler′i; Brit. kə-rol′ẽr-i), *n.* [*pl.* COROLLARIES (-iz)], [L. *corollarium,* orig., money paid for a garland, hence gift, gratuity < *corolla;* see COROLLA], 1. a proposition that follows from another that has been proved. 2. an inference or deduction. 3. anything that follows as a normal result: as, improved public health is a *corollary* of slum clearance. Abbreviated **corol., coroll.**

cor·ol·late (kôr′ə-lāt′, kor′ə-lāt′), *adj.* having or like a corolla.

cor·ol·lat·ed (kôr′ə-lā′tid, kor′ə-lā′tid), *adj.* corollate.

Cor·o·man·del Coast (kôr′ə-man′dəl, kor′ə-man′dəl), a coastal region in southeastern India, extending inland to the Eastern Ghats.

co·ro·na (kə-rō′nə), *n.* [*pl.* CORONAS (-nəz), CORONAE (-nē)], [L., a crown; Gr. *korōnē,* anything curved or bent, wreath], 1. a crown or something resembling a crown. 2. a circular chandelier hanging from a church ceiling. 3. a type of cigar characterized by a long, nontapering body, rounded off bluntly at the ends. 4. in *anatomy,* *a*) a crownlike part. *b*) the upper part of a tooth, of a skull, etc. 5. in *architecture,* the top projection of a cornice. 6. in *astronomy,* *a*) a circle of light around the sun or moon. *b*) the halo around the sun, seen only during a total eclipse. 7. in *botany,* the cuplike part on the inner side of the corolla of certain flowers, as the daffodil, milkweed, etc. 8. in *electricity,* a sometimes visible electric discharge resulting from a partial electric breakdown in a gas, as in the air surrounding a wire at high potential.

CORONA OF SUN

Corona Aus·tra·lis (ôs-trā′lis), [L., Southern Crown], a southern constellation near Sagittarius: also called the *Southern Crown:* see **constellation,** chart.

Corona Bo·re·a·lis (bôr′i-al′is, bō′ri-ā′lis), [L., Northern Crown], a northern constellation between Hercules and Boötes, consisting of a semicircular group of stars: also called the *Northern Crown:* see **constellation,** chart.

cor·o·nach (kôr′ə-nəkh, kor′ə-nəkh), *n.* [Ir. *coranach* & Scot. Gael. *corranach* < *comh-,* together + *ranach,* out-cry], 1. [Scot.], a dirge, sung or played on bagpipes. 2. [Irish], a wailing lament for the dead.

Co·ro·na·do, Fran·cis·co Vás·quez de (frän-thēs′kô väs′keth de kô′rô-nä′*th*ô; Eng. kôr′ə-nä′dō), 1510–1554; Spanish explorer of southwestern North America.

cor·o·nal (kôr′ə-n′l, kor′ə-n′l), *n.* [ME. < LL. *coronalis* < L. *corona;* see CORONA], 1. a circlet for the head; diadem; crown; coronet. 2. a wreath; garland. *adj.* (kə-rō′n′l, kôr′ə-n′l, kor′ə-n′l), 1. of a crown, coronet, or halo. 2. in *anatomy,* *a*) of the corona of the skull. *b*) designating, of, or lying in the direction of, the suture between the frontal and parietal bones of the skull.

coronal suture, in *anatomy,* a suture that extends across the skull between the frontal bone and the parietal bones.

cor·o·nar·y (kôr′ə-ner′i, kor′ə-ner′i), *adj.* [L. *coronarius;* see CORONA], 1. of, or in the form of, a crown. 2. in *anatomy,* *a*) like a crown; encircling. *b*) designating or relating to either of two arteries branching from the aorta and supplying blood directly to the heart tissues. *n.* a coronary thrombosis.

coronary thrombosis, the formation of a clot in a branch of either of the coronary arteries, resulting in obstruction of that artery.

cor·o·na·tion (kôr′ə-nā′shən, kor′ə-nā′shən), *n.* [ME. & OFr. *coronacion* < L. *coronatus,* pp. of *coronare,* to crown < *corona;* see CORONA], the act or ceremony of crowning a sovereign.

cor·o·ner (kôr′ə-nẽr, kor′ə-nẽr), *n.* [ME., officer of the crown; Anglo-Fr. *corouner* < *coroune, corone,* a crown; L. *corona;* see CORONA], a public officer whose chief duty is to determine by inquest before a jury the causes of any deaths not obviously due to natural causes: abbreviated **Cor.** (as a title), **cor.**

coroner's jury, a group of people summoned to witness a coroner's inquest and submit a verdict as to the cause of the death investigated.

cor·o·net (kôr′ə-net′, kor′ə-nit), *n.* [OFr. *coronete,* dim. of *corone;* L. *corona;* see CORONA], 1. a small crown worn by princes and others of high rank. 2. an ornamental band of precious metal, jewels, or flowers, worn around the head.

coronet braid, braided hair worn in the manner of a coronet.

cor·o·net·ed, cor·o·net·ted (kôr′ə-net′id, kor′ə-net′id), *adj.* wearing or entitled to wear a coronet.

Co·rot, Jean Bap·tiste Ca·mille (zhän bȧ′tēst′ kȧ′mē′y′ kô′rō′; Eng. kə-rō′), 1796–1875; French landscape painter.

Corp., Corporal.

corp., corpn., corporation.

cor·po·ra (kôr′pẽr-ə), *n.* plural of **corpus.**

CORONET

cor·po·ral (kôr′pẽr-əl), *n.* [< Fr. *caporal;* It. *caporale,* a corporal < *capo,* the head; L. *caput,* the head; sp. affected by association with *corps* or *corporal, adj.*], 1. in the *United States armed forces,* the lowest-ranking noncommissioned officer, just below a sergeant: in the Army, it is the fourth grade of enlisted man (formerly *sergeant*); in the Marine Corps and Air Force, it is the fifth grade. 2. in the *British armed forces,* *a*) the lowest-ranking noncommissioned officer in the Army. *b*) a naval petty officer who assists the master-at-arms. Abbreviated **Corp., Cpl.** (as a title).

cor·po·ral (kôr′pẽr-əl), *adj.* [L. *corporalis* < *corpus, corporis,* body], 1. of the body; bodily. 2. personal. 3. [Archaic], corporeal. —*SYN.* see **bodily.**

cor·po·ral (kôr′pẽr-əl), *n.* [OFr.; ML. *corporale, corporalis* (*palla*), body (cloth); see CORPORAL, *adj.*], in *ecclesiastical usage,* a white linen cloth covering the altar where the bread and wine are placed during the sacrament of the Lord's Supper; Communion cloth.

cor·po·ral·cy (kôr′pẽr-əl-si), *n.* [*pl.* CORPORALCIES (-siz)], the rank of a corporal.

cor·po·ra·le (kôr′pə-rā′lē), *n.* a corporal (cloth).

cor·po·ral·i·ty (kôr′pə-ral′ə-ti), *n.* [LL. *corporalitas;* see CORPORAL, *adj.*], the state or quality of being material or having a body; bodily existence or substance.

cor·po·ral·ly (kôr′pẽr-əl-i), *adv.* in, by, or with the body; bodily.

corporal punishment, punishment inflicted directly on the body, as flogging: now distinguished from capital punishment, imprisonment, etc.

cor·po·rate (kôr′pẽr-it), *adj.* [L. *corporatus,* pp. of *corporare,* to make into a body < *corpus, corporis,* body], 1. united; combined. 2. having the nature of, or acting by means of, a corporation; incorporated. 3. of a corporation: as, *corporate* property. 4. shared by all members of a unified group; common; joint: as, *corporate* responsibility.

cor·po·rate·ly (kôr′pẽr-it-li), *adv.* 1. in a corporate manner or capacity; as a unit or body. 2. [Obs.], bodily.

cor·po·ra·tion (kôr′pə-rā′shən), *n.* [LL. *corporatio,* assumption of a body, incarnation < pp. of L. *corporare;* see CORPORATE], 1. a group of people who get a charter granting them as a body certain of the legal powers, rights, privileges, and liabilities of an individual, distinct from those of the individuals making up the group: a corporation can buy, sell, and inherit property. 2. a group of people, as the mayor and aldermen of an incorporated town, legally authorized to act as an individual. 3. any of the political and economic bodies forming a corporative state, each being composed of the employers and employees in a certain sphere, as agriculture, industry, finance, etc. Abbreviated **corp.**, **corpn.** 4. [prob. from association with *corpulent*, etc.], [Colloq.], a large and prominent abdomen.

cor·por·a·tist (kôr′pẽr-ə-tist), ***adj.*** of or characteristic of a corporative state or its corporations.

cor·po·ra·tive (kôr′pə-rā′tiv, kôr′pẽr-ə-tiv), ***adj.*** [LL. *corporativus*], of or connected with a corporation.

corporative (or **corporate**) **state,** a government, as theoretically in Italy under Fascism (1924–1943), in which political and economic power is vested in an organization of corporations (sense 3).

cor·po·ra·tor (kôr′pə-rā′tẽr), ***n.*** a member of a corporation.

cor·po·re·al (kôr-pôr′i-əl, kôr-pō′ri-əl), ***adj.*** [< L. *corporeus* < *corpus, corporis*, body], 1. of, for, or having the nature of, the body; bodily. 2. of a material nature; physical; perceptible by the senses; tangible. —***SYN.*** see **bodily, material.**

cor·po·re·al·i·ty (kôr-pôr′i-al′ə-ti, kôr-pō′ri-al′ə-ti), ***n.*** the state of being corporeal; bodily existence.

cor·po·re·al·ly (kôr-pô′ri-əl-i, kôr-pō′ri-əl-i), ***adv.*** in a corporeal manner or form; bodily.

cor·po·re·i·ty (kôr′pə-rē′ə-ti), ***n.*** [ML. *corporeitas* < L. *corporeus*], 1. the state or quality of being corporeal; bodily existence. 2. material or bodily substance.

cor·po·sant (kôr′pə-zant′), ***n.*** [Port. *corpo santo*, holy body < L. *corpus sanctum* or *corpus sancti*, body of a saint], a glowing ball of electrical discharge sometimes seen on church steeples or at the ends of a ship's masts, etc. during a storm: also called *St. Elmo's fire.*

corps (kôr, kōr), ***n.*** [*pl.* CORPS (kôrz, kōrz)], [Fr.; OFr. *corps, cors*, body; L. *corpus*, body; cf. CORPSE], 1. a body of people associated under common direction: as, a diplomatic *corps*. 2. in *military usage*, *a)* a separate branch of the armed forces having some specialized function: as, the Signal *Corps*, the Marine *Corps*. *b)* a tactical subdivision of an army, normally headed by a lieutenant general and composed of two or more divisions, plus auxiliary service troops: abbreviated **C.**

corps area, formerly, any of the nine geographical divisions of the United States, formed on the basis of population, for purposes of military administration and training: now called *service command.*

‡**corps de bal·let** (kôr′ də bȧ′le′; Eng. kôr′ də bal-ā′), [Fr.], a troupe or company of ballet dancers.

corpse (kôrps), ***n.*** [earlier sp. *corps* (kôrs); ME. & OFr. *cors, corps;* see CORPS], 1. a dead body, usually of a person. 2. [Obs.], a body, living or dead. —***SYN.*** see **body.**

corps·man (kôr′mən, kōr′mən), ***n.*** [*pl.* CORPSMEN (-mən)], 1. an enlisted man of the United States Army Medical Corps assigned to a combat area to give first aid and remove the wounded. 2. an enlisted pharmacist in the United States Navy.

cor·pu·lence (kôr′pyoo-ləns), ***n.*** [Fr.; L. *corpulentia;* see CORPULENT], fleshiness of body; obesity.

cor·pu·len·cy (kôr′pyoo-lən-si), ***n.*** corpulence.

cor·pu·lent (kôr′pyoo-lənt), ***adj.*** [Fr.; L. *corpulentus* < *corpus*, body], fat; fleshy; stout; obese.

cor·pus (kôr′pəs), ***n.*** [*pl.* CORPORA (-pẽr-ə)], [L.], 1. a human or animal body, especially a dead one: now used humorously. 2. a complete or comprehensive collection, as of laws or writings of a specified type: as, the *corpus* of civil law. 3. the main body or substance of anything. 4. the principal, as distinguished from the interest or income, of an estate, investment, etc. 5. in *anatomy*, the main part of an organ; solid and relatively homogeneous part. Abbreviated **cor.** (in senses 2, 4, 5).

cor·pus cal·lo·sum (kôr′pəs kə-lō′səm), [*pl.* CORPORA CALLOSA (-pẽr-ə -sə)], [Mod. L., lit., callous body], a mass of white, transverse fibers connecting the cerebral hemispheres in the higher mammals: see **brain,** illus.

Cor·pus Chris·ti (kôr′pəs kris′ti; *also, for 1,* kôr′pəs kris′tī), [L., Body of Christ], 1. in the *Roman Catholic Church*, a festival celebrated on the Thursday after Trinity Sunday, in honor of the Eucharist. 2. a city on the coast of southeastern Texas: pop., 168,000.

cor·pus·cle (kôr′pəs-'l, kôr′pus-'l), ***n.*** [L. *corpusculum*, dim. of *corpus*, body], 1. a very small particle. 2. in *anatomy*, a protoplasmic particle with a special function; especially, any of the red cells (*erythrocytes*) or white cells (*leucocytes*) that float in the blood, lymph, etc. of vertebrates: red corpuscles contain hemoglobin, which carries oxygen to the body tissues, and certain white corpuscles sometimes kill harmful microorganisms.

cor·pus·cu·lar (kôr-pus′kyoo-lẽr), ***adj.*** of, consisting of, or characteristic of corpuscles.

cor·pus·cule (kôr-pus′kūl), ***n.*** a corpuscle.

corpus de·lic·ti (di-lik′tī), [L., lit., body of the crime], 1. the facts constituting or proving a crime: the corpus delicti in a murder case is not the body of the victim, but the fact that death has occurred and that it is the result of murder. 2. loosely, the body of the victim in a murder case.

corpus ju·ris (joor′is), [L., a body of law], a collection of all the laws of a nation or district.

Corpus Juris Ca·no·ni·ci (kə-non′ə-sī′), [L., lit., body of canon law], the decrees and canons of the Roman Catholic Church up to 1918.

Corpus Juris Ci·vi·lis (si-vī′lis), [L., lit., body of civil law], the body of Civil, or Roman, law, compiled and issued during the reign of Justinian (528–534 A.D.): it has been the basis of most European law.

cor·pus lu·te·um (kôr′pəs lōō′ti-əm, lū′ti-əm), [*pl.* CORPORA LUTEA (-pẽr-ə -ə)], [Mod. L., lit., luteous body], 1. in *anatomy*, a mass of yellow tissue formed in the ovary by a ruptured Graafian follicle that has discharged its ovum: if the ovum is fertilized, this tissue secretes a necessary hormone. 2. a preparation containing this hormone, used in ovarian therapy.

cor·pus stri·a·tum (kôr′pəs strī-ā′təm), [*pl.* CORPORA STRIATA (-pẽr-ə -tə)], [Mod. L., lit., striated body], in *anatomy*, either of two striated ganglia in front of the thalamus in each half of the brain.

corr., 1. corrected. 2. correspond. 3. correspondence. 4. correspondent. 5. corresponding. 6. corrupt. 7. corrupted. 8. corruption.

cor·ral (kə-ral′), ***n.*** [Sp. < *corro*, a circle, ring < L. *currere*, to run], 1. an enclosure for holding or capturing horses, cattle, and other animals; pen; stockade. 2. an enclosure surrounded by wagons, for defense against attack. ***v.t.*** [CORRALLED (-rald′), CORRALLING], 1. to drive into or confine in a corral. 2. to surround or capture; round up. 3. to arrange (wagons) in the form of a corral. 4. [Slang], to take possession of; lay hold of.

cor·ra·sion (kə-rā′zhən), ***n.*** [< L. *corrasus*, pp. of *corradere*, to scrape together < *com-*, together + *radere*, to scrape], erosion by the abrasive action of running water containing sand, pebbles, and other debris.

cor·rect (kə-rekt′), ***v.t.*** [ME. *correcten* < L. *correctus*, pp. of *corrigere* < *com-*, together + *regere*, to lead straight, direct], 1. to make right; change from wrong to right; remove errors from. 2. to point out or mark the errors or faults of. 3. to make conform with a standard. 4. to scold or punish for the purpose of overcoming faults. 5. to cure, remove, or counteract (a fault, disease, etc.). ***adj.*** 1. conforming with or adhering to a conventional standard; proper: as, *correct* behavior. 2. conforming with fact or logic; true; accurate; right; free from errors: abbreviated **cor.**

SYN.—**correct** connotes little more than absence of error (a *correct* answer) or adherence to conventionality (*correct* behavior); **accurate** implies a positive exercise of care to obtain conformity with fact or truth (an *accurate* account of the events); **exact** stresses perfect conformity with fact, truth, or some standard (the *exact* time, an *exact* quotation); **precise** suggests minute accuracy of detail and often connotes a finicky or overly fastidious attitude (*precise* in all his habits). See also **punish.**—***ANT.*** wrong, false.

correcting plate, a thin lens for correcting incoming light rays in certain reflecting telescopes.

cor·rec·tion (kə-rek′shən), ***n.*** [ME. *correccion;* OFr. *correction;* L. *correctio* < *correctus*], 1. a correcting or being corrected. 2. something in place of a mistake; change from wrong to right, or from abnormal to normal; emendation; rectification; improvement. 3. an amount added or taken away in correcting. 4. punishment or scolding to correct faults. Abbreviated **cor.**

cor·rec·tion·al (kə-rek′shən-'l), ***adj.*** 1. of correction. 2. correcting or tending to correct.

cor·rect·i·tude (kə-rek′tə-tōōd′, kə-rek′tə-tūd′), ***n.*** [< *correct*, after *rectitude*], the quality of being correct, especially in conduct; propriety.

cor·rec·tive (kə-rek′tiv), ***adj.*** [Fr. *correctif*], tending or intended to correct or improve; remedial. ***n.*** something corrective; remedy.

cor·rec·tor (kə-rek′tẽr), ***n.*** [L.], a person or thing that corrects.

Cor·reg·gio (kôr-red′jô; Eng. kə-rej′ō, kə-rej′i-ō′), ***n.*** (*Antonio Allegri da Correggio*), Italian painter; lived 1494–1534.

Cor·reg·i·dor (kə-reg′ə-dôr′), ***n.*** a small, fortified island in the Philippines, at the entrance to Manila Bay: surrendered to Japan, but recaptured by United States forces, in World War II: see **Philippine Islands,** map.

correl., correlative.

cor·re·late (kôr′ə-lāt′, kor′ə-lāt′), ***n.*** [*cor-* + *relate*], either of two closely related things, especially if one implies the other. ***adj.*** closely and naturally related. ***v.i.*** [CORRELATED (-id), CORRELATING], to be mutually related (*to* or *with*). ***v.t.*** to bring (a thing) into mutual relation (*with* another thing); calculate or show the reciprocal relation between (two things): as, *correlate* the findings of psychology with those of sociology.

cor·re·la·tion (kôr′ə-lā′shən, kor′ə-lā′shən), ***n.*** [Mod. L. *correlatio;* see COM- & RELATION], 1. a close or mutual relation: as, the *correlation* between illiteracy and prejudice. 2. the degree of relative correspondence, as between two sets of data: as, a *correlation* of 75 per cent. 3. a correlating or being correlated.

cor·rel·a·tive (kə-rel′ə-tiv), ***adj.*** [*cor-* + *relative*], 1. having or involving a mutual relation; reciprocally dependent. 2. in *grammar,* expressing mutual relation and used in pairs: as, *both . . . and* and *neither . . . nor* are *correlative* conjunctions. ***n.*** 1. a thing closely related to something else; correlate. 2. a correlative word: also called *correlator.* Abbreviated **correl., cor.**

cor·rel·a·tiv·i·ty (kə-rel′ə-tiv′ə-ti), ***n.*** 1. the state of being correlative. 2. the degree of correlation.

cor·re·spond (kôr′ə-spond′, kor′ə-spond′), ***v.i.*** [Fr. *correspondre;* ML. *correspondere* < L. *com-,* together + *respondere,* to answer], 1. to be in agreement (*with* something); be congruent (*to* something); suit; match. 2. to be similar, analogous, or equal (*to* something). 3. to communicate (*with* someone) by exchanging letters, usually habitually. Abbreviated **corr., cor.** —***SYN.*** see **agree.**

cor·re·spond·ence (kôr′ə-spon′dəns, kor′ə-spon′dəns), ***n.*** [ML. *correspondentia* < ppr. of *correspondere;* see CORRESPOND], 1. agreement; conformity. 2. similarity; analogy. 3. communication by exchange of letters; letter writing. 4. letters or the quantity of letters normally received or written. Abbreviated **corr., cor.**

correspondence course, a series of lessons and examinations in a course given by a correspondence school.

correspondence school, a school that gives instruction by mail, sending lessons and examinations to a student periodically, and correcting and grading the answers returned by him.

cor·re·spond·en·cy (kôr′ə-spon′dən-si, kor′ə-spon′dən-si), ***n.*** [*pl.* CORRESPONDENCIES (-siz)], correspondence.

cor·re·spond·ent (kôr′ə-spon′dənt, kor′ə-spon′dənt), ***adj.*** [< ML. *correspondens,* ppr. of *correspondere;* see CORRESPOND], corresponding; agreeing; matching; analogous. ***n.*** 1. a thing that corresponds; correlate. 2. a person who exchanges letters with another, or who writes to a magazine, newspaper, etc. 3. a person hired by a magazine or newspaper to furnish news, articles, etc. of a certain type or from a certain place. 4. a person or firm acting for, or having regular commerce with, another at a distance. Abbreviated **corr., cor.**

cor·re·spond·ing (kôr′ə-spon′diŋ, kor′ə-spon′diŋ), ***adj.*** [ppr. of *correspond*], 1. agreeing; equivalent. 2. similar; analogous. 3. exchanging, or communicating by, letters; handling correspondence: as, a *corresponding* secretary. Abbreviated **corresp., corr., cor.**

cor·re·spon·sive (kôr′ə-spon′siv, kor′ə-spon′siv), ***adj.*** [Archaic], answering mutually; corresponding.

cor·ri·dor (kôr′ə-dẽr, kor′ə-dẽr; *occas.* kôr′ə-dôr′), ***n.*** [Fr.; It. *corridore,* a gallery, corridor, runner < *correre,* to run; L. *currere,* to run], 1. a long passageway or hall, especially one on which several rooms open. 2. a strip of land forming a passageway between two otherwise separated parts of a country, or between an inland country and a seaport.

cor·rie (kôr′i, kor′i), ***n.*** [< Scot. Gael. *coire,* cauldron], [Scot.], a round hollow in a hillside.

Cor·rie·dale (kôr′i-dāl′, kor′i-dāl′), ***n.*** [< *Corriedale,* New Zealand], a breed of rather large, white-faced sheep, originally developed in New Zealand: they produce good wool and mutton lambs.

Cor·ri·en·tes (kor′ri-en′tes), ***n.*** a city in northern Argentina, on the Paraná River: pop., 67,000.

cor·ri·gen·dum (kôr′i-jen′dəm, kor′i-jen′dəm), ***n.*** [*pl.* CORRIGENDA (-də)], [L., gerundive of *corrigere;* see CORRECT], 1. an error to be corrected, especially one in a manuscript or book. 2. *pl.* a list of such errors with their corrections.

cor·ri·gi·bil·i·ty (kôr′i-jə-bil′ə-ti, kor′i-jə-bil′ə-ti), ***n.*** the quality of being corrigible.

cor·ri·gi·ble (kôr′i-jə-b′l, kor′i-jə-b′l), ***adj.*** [Fr.; L. *corrigibilis* < *corrigere;* see CORRECT], 1. that can be corrected, improved, or reformed. 2. submitting to correction or punishment; willing to be reformed.

cor·ri·gi·bly (kôr′i-jə-bli, kor′i-jə-bli), ***adv.*** in a corrigible manner.

cor·ri·val (kə-rī′v′l), ***n.*** [Fr.; L. *corrivalis* < *com-,* with + *rivalis,* rival], a rival; competitor. ***adj.*** competing; rivaling. ***v.t.*** to rival.

cor·rob·o·rant (kə-rob′ə-rənt), ***adj.*** [L. *corroborans,* ppr. of *corroborare*], 1. corroborating. 2. invigorating: said of medicines or tonics. ***n.*** 1. a medicine that strengthens; tonic. 2. a fact that corroborates.

cor·rob·o·rate (kə-rob′ə-rāt′), ***v.t.*** [CORROBORATED (-id), CORROBORATING], [< L. *corroboratus,* pp. of *corroborare,* to strengthen < *com-,* intens. + *roborare* < *robur,* strength], 1. to strengthen. 2. to make more certain; confirm; support: as, the evidence *corroborates* the reporter's story. —***SYN.*** see **confirm.**

cor·rob·o·ra·tion (kə-rob′ə-rā′shən), ***n.*** [Fr.], 1. a corroborating or being corroborated; confirmation by further evidence. 2. anything that corroborates.

cor·rob·o·ra·tive (kə-rob′ə-rā′tiv, kə-rob′ẽr-ə-tiv), ***adj.*** corroborating or tending to corroborate; confirmatory.

cor·rob·o·ra·tor (kə-rob′ə-rā′tẽr), ***n.*** a person or thing that corroborates.

cor·rob·o·ra·to·ry (kə-rob′ẽr-ə-tôr′i, kə-rob′ẽr-ə-tō′ri), ***adj.*** corroborative.

cor·rob·o·ree, cor·rob·o·ri (kə-rob′ẽr-i), ***n.*** [< native *korobra,* dance], 1. a dance festival held at night by Australian aborigines to celebrate tribal victories and similar events. 2. in Australia, *a*) a large or noisy festivity. *b*) an uproar; tumult.

cor·rode (kə-rōd′), ***v.t.*** [CORRODED (-id), CORRODING], [Fr. *corroder;* L. *corrodere,* to gnaw to pieces < *com-,* intens. + *rodere,* to gnaw], to eat into or wear away gradually, as if by gnawing; rust; consume; destroy: said of the action of chemicals, and often used figuratively. ***v.i.*** to become corroded.

cor·rod·i·ble (kə-rōd′ə-b′l), ***adj.*** that can be corroded.

cor·ro·sion (kə-rō′zhən), ***n.*** [Fr.; LL. *corrosio* < pp. of L. *corrodere*], 1. a corroding or being corroded. 2. a substance, as rust, formed by corroding.

cor·ro·sive (kə-rō′siv), ***adj.*** [OFr. *corrosif*], corroding or causing corrosion: often used figuratively. ***n.*** something causing corrosion.

corrosive sublimate, mercuric chloride, a poisonous, white, crystalline salt, $HgCl_2$.

cor·ru·gate (kôr′ə-gāt′, kor′yoo-gāt′), ***v.t. & v.i.*** [CORRUGATED (-id), CORRUGATING], [< L. *corrugatus,* pp. of *corrugare,* to wrinkle < *com-,* intens. + *rugare,* to wrinkle], to shape or contract into folds, or into parallel grooves and ridges; make wrinkles in; furrow. ***adj.*** (kôr′ə-git, kor′yoo-git), corrugated.

cor·ru·gat·ed (kôr′ə-gāt′id, kor′yoo-gāt′id), ***adj.*** [see CORRUGATE], folded or shaped into parallel ridges and furrows so as to form a wavy surface.

corrugated iron, sheet iron or steel, usually galvanized, corrugated to give it added strength in construction.

corrugated paper, paper or pasteboard corrugated so as to be resilient, used for wrapping or packing.

cor·ru·ga·tion (kôr′ə-gā′shən, kor′yoo-gā′shən), ***n.*** 1. a corrugating or being corrugated. 2. any of a series of parallel folds, ridges, wrinkles, or furrows.

cor·rupt (kə-rupt′), ***adj.*** [ME.; OFr. < L. *corruptus,* pp. of *corrumpere,* to destroy, spoil, bribe < *com-,* together + *rumpere,* to break in pieces], 1. originally, changed from a sound condition to an unsound one; spoiled; contaminated; rotten; hence, 2. deteriorated from the normal or standard; specifically, *a*) morally unsound or debased; perverted; evil; depraved. *b*) taking bribes. *c*) containing alterations, foreign admixtures, or errors: said of languages, texts, etc. Abbreviated **corr.** ***v.t. & v.i.*** to make or become corrupt (in various senses). —***SYN.*** see **debase.**

cor·rupt·i·bil·i·ty (kə-rup′tə-bil′ə-ti), ***n.*** the quality or state of being corruptible.

cor·rupt·i·ble (kə-rup′tə-b′l), ***adj.*** that can be corrupted; specifically, *a*) that can be bribed. *b*) liable to decay or destruction.

cor·rup·tion (kə-rup′shən), ***n.*** [ME. *corrupcion;* OFr. *corruption;* L. *corruptio* < *corruptus;* see CORRUPT], 1. a changing or being changed for the worse; making, becoming, or being corrupt. 2. evil or wicked behavior; depravity. 3. bribery. 4. decay; rottenness. 5. a thing or influence that corrupts. Abbreviated **corr.**

cor·rup·tion·ist (kə-rup′shən-ist), ***n.*** a person who engages in or upholds corrupt practices, such as bribery, especially in public life.

cor·rup·tive (kə-rup′tiv), ***adj.*** tending to corrupt or produce corruption.

corrupt practices acts, laws in the United States limiting contributions to and expenditures in election campaigns, illegalizing certain methods of influencing voters, etc.

cor·sage (kôr-säzh′), ***n.*** [Fr. < OFr. *cors;* see CORPS & -AGE], 1. the bodice of a dress. 2. a small bouquet for a woman to wear, usually at the waist or shoulder.

cor·sair (kôr′sâr), ***n.*** [Fr. *corsaire;* ML. *cursarius* < *cursus, cursa,* a raid; L. *cursus,* a run, course < *currere,* to run], 1. a privateer, especially of Barbary; hence, 2. a pirate. 3. a pirate ship.

Corse (kôrs), ***n.*** Corsica: the French name.

corse (kôrs), ***n.*** [Archaic & Poetic], a corpse; dead body.

corse·let (kôrs′lit), ***n.*** [Fr., dim. of OFr. *cors;* see CORPS, CORSET], 1. armor for the body, worn in medieval times: also spelled **corslet.** 2. (kôr′s′l-et′), a woman's lightweight corset, usually without stays.

cor·set (kôr′sit), ***n.*** [Fr., dim. of OFr. *cors;* see CORPS], 1. *sometimes pl.* a close-fitting undergarment, often tightened with laces and reinforced with stays, worn, chiefly by women, to give support or a desired figure to the body from the hips to the breast. 2. [Archaic], a bodice. ***v.t.*** to dress in a corset; fit a corset on.

Cor·si·ca (kôr′si-kə), ***n.*** a French island in the Mediterranean, north of Sardinia: area, 3,367 sq. mi.; pop., 323,000; capital, Ajaccio; French name, *Corse.*

Cor·si·can (kôr′si-kən), ***adj.*** of Corsica, its people, or their dialect. ***n.*** 1. a native or inhabitant of Corsica. 2. the Italian dialect spoken by Corsicans.

cors·let (kôrs′lit), ***n.*** a corselet (armor).

cor·tege (kôr-tāzh′, kôr-tezh′), ***n.*** [Fr. *cortège;* It. *cor-*

teggio, retinue < *corte;* L. *cohors;* see COURT], 1. a number of followers or attendants; retinue. 2. a ceremonial procession.
‡**cor·tège** (kôr′tezh′), *n.* [Fr.], a cortege.
Cor·tes (kôr′tiz; Sp. kôr′tes; Port. kôr′tesh), *n.* [Sp. & Port., pl. of *corte;* L. *cohors;* see COURT], 1. the legislature of Spain before the seizure of power by Franco. 2. the legislature of Portugal. Both have two houses.
Cor·tés (or **Cor·tez**), **Her·nan·do** (er-nän′dô kôr-tes′; Eng. kôr′tez), 1485–1547; Spanish soldier and explorer; conqueror of Mexico.
cor·tex (kôr′teks), *n.* [*pl.* CORTICES (-ti-sēz′)], [L., bark of a tree], 1. in *anatomy*, the outer part or external layers of an internal organ, as of the kidney; especially, the layer of gray matter over most of the brain. 2. in *botany*, the bark or rind.
cor·ti·cal (kôr′ti-k′l), *adj.* [< L. *cortex, corticis*, bark of a tree; + *-al*], 1. of a cortex. 2. consisting of cortex. 3. involving, or in some way caused by, the brain cortex.
cor·ti·cate (kôr′ti-kit, kôr′ti-kāt′), *adj.* [LL. *corticatus* < L. *cortex*, bark of a tree], 1. having a cortex. 2. covered with bark or a barklike substance.
cor·ti·cat·ed (kôr′ti-kā′tid), *adj.* corticate.
cor·ti·ces (kôr′ti-sēz′), *n.* plural of **cortex.**
cor·ti·cose (kôr′ti-kōs′), *adj.* [L. *corticosus*], in *botany*, corticate.
cor·ti·cous (kôr′ti-kəs), *adj.* corticose.
cor·tin (kôr′tin), *n.* [*cortex* + *-in*], the hormone secreted by the adrenal cortex.
cor·ti·sone (kôr′tə-sōn′, kôr′tə-zōn′), *n.* [< *cortico-sterone*], an adrenal-gland hormone extracted from ox bile or prepared synthetically from certain tropical plants, used experimentally in the treatment of rheumatoid arthritis and certain other diseases.
Co·ru·ña, La (lä kô-rōō′nyä), Corunna.
co·run·dum (kə-run′dəm), *n.* [Tamil *kurundam;* Sans. *kuruvinda*, ruby], a common mineral, aluminum oxide, Al_2O_3, second only to the diamond in hardness: a dark, granular variety is used for grinding and polishing; pure, transparent varieties are the ruby, sapphire, Oriental amethyst, and Oriental topaz.
Co·run·na (kō-run′ə), *n.* a city on the northwestern coast of Spain: pop., 80,000: Spanish name, *La Coruña*.
co·rus·cant (kə-rus′kənt), *adj.* [L. *coruscans*, ppr. of *coruscare*], coruscating.
cor·us·cate (kôr′əs-kāt′, kor′əs-kāt′), *v.i.* [CORUSCATED (-id), CORUSCATING], [< L. *coruscatus*, pp. of *coruscare*, to move quickly, glitter < *coruscus*, vibrating, shimmering; akin to Gr. *skairein*, to leap, skip & OHG. *horsc*, rapid], to emit flashes of light; glitter; sparkle.
cor·us·ca·tion (kôr′əs-kā′shən, kor′əs-kā′shən), *n.* [L. *coruscatio* < pp. of *coruscare*], 1. a coruscating; sparkling; glittering. 2. a flash or gleam of light. 3. a sudden brilliant display, as of wit.
‡**cor·vée** (kôr′vā′; Eng. kôr-vā′), *n.* [Fr.; OFr. *corovee*, pp. of *corrover*, to call together; rendering of ML. & LL. *corrogata* < L. *corrogata* (*opera*), collected (works) < pp. of *corrogare*, to bring together (by entreaty), collect < *com-*, intens. + *rogare*, to ask], 1. the enforced and unpaid labor of a peasant for his feudal lord. 2. forced labor exacted by a government, as for the construction of public works.
corves (kôrvz), *n.* plural of **corf.**
cor·vette, cor·vet (kôr-vet′), *n.* [Fr.; Port. *corveta;* L. *corbita* (*navis*), cargo (ship) < *corbis*, basket; prob. misunderstood in Port. as dim. < L. *corvus*, crow, raven], 1. formerly, a sailing warship larger than a sloop and smaller than a frigate, usually having one tier of guns. 2. a small warship of about 1,000 tons, used for antisubmarine and convoy duty.
cor·vine (kôr′vīn, kôr′vin), *adj.* [L. *corvinus* < *corvus*, a raven], of or like a crow or raven.
Cor·vus (kôr′vəs), *n.* [L., Raven], a small southern constellation near Virgo: see **constellation**, chart.
Cor·y·ate, Thomas (kôr′i-ət), 1576?–1617; English wit and writer on his travels: also spelled **Coryat.**
Cor·y·bant (kôr′ə-bant′, kor′ə-bant′), *n.* [*pl.* CORYBANTS (-bants′), CORYBANTES (kôr′ə-ban′tēz, kor′ə-ban′tēz)], [Fr. *Corybante;* L. *Corybas*, pl. *Corybantes;* Gr. *Korybas*], 1. in *Greek mythology*, *a)* one of the attendants who followed the Phrygian goddess Cybele with dancing and revelry in her nightly wanderings. *b)* a priest in the worship of Cybele. 2. [c-], a reveler.
Cor·y·ban·tian (kôr′ə-ban′shən, kor′ə-ban′shən), *adj.* Corybantic.
Cor·y·ban·tic (kôr′ə-ban′tik, kor′ə-ban′tik), *adj.* 1. of the Corybants. 2. [c-], like the Corybants or their orgies; wild and frenzied.
co·ryd·a·lis (kə-rid′ə-lis), *n.* [Mod. L.; Gr. *korydallis*, crested lark < *korys*, helmet], any of a group of plants with yellow, rose, blue, or purple flowers resembling those of the bleeding heart.
Cor·y·don (kôr′ə-d′n, kor′ə-don′), *n.* [L.; Gr. *Korydōn*], 1. a shepherd: traditional name used in pastoral poems; hence, 2. a young country fellow.

cor·ymb (kôr′imb, kor′im), *n.* [L. *corymbus*, cluster of fruit or flowers; Gr. *korymbos*], a broad, flat cluster of flowers in which the outer stems are long and those toward the center progressively shorter, as in the cherry.

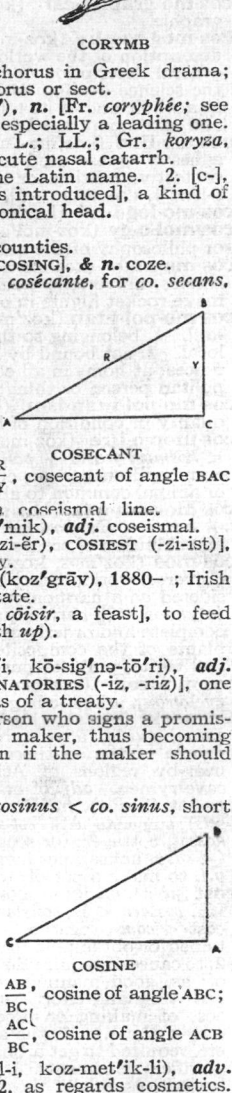

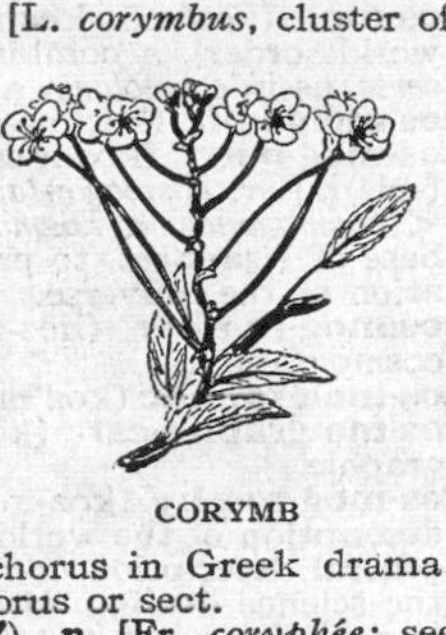
CORYMB

co·rym·bose (kə-rim′bōs), *adj.* 1. of or like a corymb. 2. growing in corymbs.
co·rym·bous (kə-rim′bəs), *adj.* corymbose.
cor·y·phae·us (kôr′ə-fē′əs, kor′ə-fē′əs), *n.* [*pl.* CORYPHAEI (-ī)], [L.; Gr. *koryphaios* < *koryphē*, head, top < *kory-*, head], 1. the leader of the chorus in Greek drama; hence, 2. a leader, as of a chorus or sect.
cor·y·phee (kôr′ə-fā′, kor′ə-fā′), *n.* [Fr. *coryphée;* see CORYPHAEUS], a ballet dancer, especially a leading one.
co·ry·za (kə-rī′zə), *n.* [Mod. L.; LL.; Gr. *koryza*, catarrh], a cold in the head; acute nasal catarrh.
Cos (kos, kôs), *n.* 1. Kos: the Latin name. 2. [c-], [< *Cos*, where the variety was introduced], a kind of lettuce with a cylindrical or conical head.
cos, cosine.
Cos., cos., 1. companies. 2. counties.
cose (kōz), *v.i.* [COSED (kōzd), COSING], & *n.* coze.
co·se·cant (kō-sē′kənt), *n.* [Fr. *cosécante*, for *co. secans*, short for Mod. L. *complementi secans*, lit., secant of the complement], in *trigonometry*, the secant of the complement of an angle or arc: abbreviated **cosec, csc** (no period).

COSECANT
$\frac{R}{Y}$, cosecant of angle BAC

co·seis·mal (kō-sīz′m′l, kō-sīs′m′l), *adj.* [*co-* + *seismal*], of or designating points, or lines connecting such points, simultaneously affected by an earthquake shock. *n.* a coseismal line.
co·seis·mic (kō-sīz′mik, kō-sīs′mik), *adj.* coseismal.
co·sey (kō′zi), *adj.* [COSIER (-zi-ēr), COSIEST (-zi-ist)], & *n.* [*pl.* COSEYS (-ziz)], cozy.
Cos·grave, William Thomas (koz′grāv), 1880– ; Irish statesman in the Irish Free State.
cosh·er (kosh′ēr), *v.t.* [< Ir. *cōisir*, a feast], to feed richly; pamper (sometimes with *up*).
co·sie (kō′zi), *adj.* cozy.
co·sig·na·to·ry (kō-sig′nə-tôr′i, kō-sig′nə-tō′ri), *adj.* signing jointly. *n.* [*pl.* COSIGNATORIES (-iz, -riz)], one of two or more joint signers, as of a treaty.
co-sign·er (kō′sīn′ēr), *n.* a person who signs a promissory note in addition to the maker, thus becoming responsible for the obligation if the maker should default: also called *co-maker*.
co·si·ly (kō′z′l-i), *adv.* cozily.
co·sine (kō′sīn′), *n.* [Mod. L. *cosinus* < *co. sinus*, short for *complementi sinus*, lit., sine of the complement], in *trigonometry*, the sine of the complement of an angle or arc: abbreviated **cos** (no period).

COSINE
$\frac{AB}{BC}$, cosine of angle ABC;
$\frac{AC}{BC}$, cosine of angle ACB

cos·met·ic (koz-met′ik), *adj.* [Gr. *kosmētikos*, skilled in arranging < *kosmein*, to arrange, adorn < *kosmos*, order], beautifying or designed to beautify the complexion, hair, etc. *n.* any such preparation for application to the skin, hair, etc., as rouge and powder.
cos·met·i·cal·ly (koz-met′i-k′l-i, koz-met′ik-li), *adv.* 1. by means of cosmetics. 2. as regards cosmetics.
cos·me·ti·cian (koz′mə-tish′ən), *n.* a person whose work is making, selling, or applying cosmetics.
cos·me·tol·o·gy (koz′mə-tol′ə-ji), *n.* the study of cosmetics and their use.
cos·mic (koz′mik), *adj.* [Gr. *kosmikos* < *kosmos*, universe, order], 1. of the cosmos; relating to the universe as a whole. 2. of the universe exclusive of the earth: as, *cosmic* dust. 3. vast; grandiose. 4. [Rare], orderly: opposed to *chaotic*.
cos·mi·cal·ly (koz′mi-k′l-i, koz′mik-li), *adv.* 1. in relation to, or according to the principles of, the cosmos. 2. on a grandiose scale.
cosmic, dust, small particles, probably meteoric fragments, falling from interstellar space to the earth.
cosmic rays, rays of extremely short wave length and great penetrating power, which bombard the earth from beyond its atmosphere: also called *ultragamma rays*.
cos·mism (koz′miz′m), *n.* the philosophy of the evolution of the universe; theory that the cosmos can be scientifically explained as a self-existent system.

cos·mo- (koz'mō, koz'mə), [< Gr. *kosmos*, universe, world, order], a combining form meaning *world, universe*, as in *cosmology:* also, before a vowel, **cosm-**.
cos·mo·gon·ic (koz'mə-gon'ik), *adj.* of cosmogony.
cos·mog·o·ny (koz-mog'ə-ni), *n.* [*pl.* COSMOGONIES (-niz)], [Gr. *kosmogonia*, creation or origin of the world < *kosmogonos* < *kosmos*, universe, order + *-gonos* < base of *gignesthai*, to produce], 1. the origin or generation of the universe. 2. a theory or account of this.
cos·mog·ra·pher (koz-mog'rə-fẽr), *n.* an expert in cosmography.
cos·mo·graph·ic (koz'mə-graf'ik), *adj.* of cosmography.
cos·mo·graph·i·cal (koz'mə-graf'i-k'l), *adj.* cosmographic.
cos·mog·ra·phy (koz-mog'rə-fi), *n.* [Gr. *kosmographia*, description of the world; see COSMOS & -GRAPHY], 1. a general description or representation of the world. 2. the science dealing with the structure of the universe as a whole and of its related parts: geology, geography, and astronomy are branches of cosmography.
cos·mo·line (koz'mə-lēn'), *n.* [*cos*metic + *-ol* + *-ine*], a heavy grease used in cosmetics and especially as a protective coating for firearms, etc. *v.t.* [COSMOLINED (-lēnd'), COSMOLINING], to coat with cosmoline.
cos·mo·log·i·cal (koz'mə-loj'i-k'l), *adj.* of cosmology.
cos·mol·o·gy (koz-mol'ə-ji), *n.* [*cosmo-* + *-logy*], theory or philosophy of the nature of the universe.
cos·mo·naut (koz'mə-nôt'), *n.* [< Russ.; ult. < Gr. *kosmos*, universe + *nautēs*, sailor], a person trained to make rocket flights in outer space; astronaut.
cos·mo·pol·i·tan (koz'mə-pol'ə-t'n), *adj.* [*cosmopolite* + *-an*], 1. belonging to the whole world; not national or local. 2. not bound by local or national habits or prejudices; at home in all countries or places. *n.* a cosmopolitan person or thing; cosmopolite.
cos·mo·pol·i·tan·ism (koz'mə-pol'ə-t'n-iz'm), *n.* the quality or condition of being a cosmopolitan.
cos·mop·o·lite (koz-mop'ə-līt'), *n.* [Gr. *kosmopolitēs* < *kosmos*, world + *politēs*, citizen < *polis*, city], 1. a cosmopolitan person; citizen of the world. 2. a plant or animal common to all or most parts of the world.
cos·mo·ram·a (koz'mə-ram'ə, koz'mə-rä'mə), *n.* [*cosmo-* + *-rama* < Gr. *horama*, a view, sight < *horan*, to see], an exhibition of scenes of various parts of the world.
cos·mos (koz'məs, koz'mos), *n.* [Mod. L.; Gr. *kosmos*, universe, world, order, harmony], 1. the universe considered as a harmonious and orderly system: opposed to *chaos*. 2. harmony; order; organization. 3. any complete and orderly system. 4. any of a group of tall plants of the composite family, with feathery leaves and white, pink, or purple flowers.
cos·mo·tron (koz'mə-tron'), *n.* [<*cosm*ic ray + *cyclotron*], a high-energy proton accelerator.
Cos·sack (kos'ak, kos'ək), *n.* [Russ. *kozak;* Turk. *qazaq, quzāq*, adventurer, guerrilla], a member of a people of the southern Soviet Union in Europe and near-by regions of Asia, famous as horsemen and cavalrymen. *adj.* of or characteristic of the Cossacks.
cos·set (kos'it), *n.* [Domesday Bk. form *cozez* (for *cotsets*) suggests AS. *cot-sæta*, cot dweller; akin to G. *kossat*, cottager; for sense, cf. G. *hauslamm*, It. *casiccio* (< *casa*, house), pet lamb], 1. a pet lamb. 2. any pet. *v.t.* to make a pet of; fondle; pamper.
cost (kôst), *v.i.* [COST, COSTING], [ME. *costen;* OFr. *coster;* LL. *costare* < L. *constare*, to stand together, stand at, cost < *com-*, together + *stare*, to stand], 1. to be obtained or obtainable for (a certain price); be priced at. 2. to cause or require the expenditure, loss, or experience of: as, good manners *cost* very little, but good work *costs* time and effort. *v.t.* in *business*, to estimate the cost of making or producing. *n.* [ME.; OFr. *coust*, *cost* < the *v.*], 1. the amount of money, time, labor, etc. required to get a thing; price; expenditure. 2. loss; sacrifice; detriment. 3. *pl.* in *law*, *a*) the expenses of a lawsuit, especially those assessed by the court against the losing party. *b*) fees paid to an attorney or counsel. **at all costs**, regardless of the cost or difficulty involved; by any means required: also **at any cost**.
cos·ta (kos'tə), *n.* [*pl.* COSTAE (-tē)], [L., a rib], a rib or riblike part.
cost accounting, in *accounting*, 1. a system of records of production costs. 2. the keeping of such records.
cos·tal (kos't'l), *adj.* [Fr.; ML. *costalis* < L. *costa*, a rib], of or near a rib or the ribs.
co-star (kō'stär'), *n.* [see CO- & STAR], any featured actor or actress given equal prominence with another or others in a motion picture, play, etc. *v.t.* & *v.i.* (kō'-stär'), to present as or be a co-star.
cos·tard (kos'tẽrd, kôs'tẽrd), *n.* [Early Mod. Eng., ribbed apple < Fr. *coste*, a rib + *-ard;* cf. COSTERMONGER], 1. a variety of large apple native to England. 2. [Archaic & Humorous], a person's head.
Cos·ta Ri·ca (kos'tə rē'kə, kôs'tə rē'kə), a country in Central America, northwest of Panama: area, 23,000 sq. mi.; pop., 1,173,000; capital, San José: abbreviated **C.R.**: see **Central America**, map.
Cos·ta Ri·can (kos'tə rē'kən, kôs'tə rē'kən), 1. of Costa Rica, its people, or culture. 2. a native or inhabitant of Costa Rica.

cos·tate (kos'tāt), *adj.* [L. *costatus* < *costa*, a rib], having ribs or riblike ridges.
Cos·tel·lo, John A. (kos'tə-lō'), 1891– ; prime minister of Ireland (1948–1951; 1954–1957).
cos·ter (kos'tẽr, kôs'tẽr), *n.* a costermonger.
cos·ter·mon·ger (kos'tẽr-muŋ'gẽr, kôs'tẽr-muŋ'gẽr), *n.* [Early Mod. Eng. *costardmonger*, apple dealer; *costard* + *monger*], [British], a person who sells fruit, vegetables, etc. from a cart or street stand.
cos·tive (kos'tiv, kôs'tiv), *adj.* [OFr. *costivé* < L. *constipatus;* see CONSTIPATE], constipated.
cost·li·ness (kôst'li-nis), *n.* the quality or state of being costly.
cost·ly (kôst'li), *adj.* [COSTLIER (-li-ẽr), COSTLIEST (-li-ist)], [*cost* + *-ly*], 1. costing much; expensive; dear. 2. very valuable; magnificent; sumptuous. 3. [Archaic], spending lavishly; extravagant.
SYN.—**costly** refers to something that costs much and usually implies richness, magnificence, rareness, etc. (*costly* gems): it is often applied to that which it would cost much in money or effort to correct or replace (a *costly* error); **expensive** implies a price in excess of the article's worth or of the purchaser's ability to pay for it (an *expensive* hat); **dear** implies an exorbitant price or one considerably beyond the normal or fair price (meat is so *dear* these days); **valuable**, in this connection, implies such great value as to bring a high price (a *valuable* collection); **invaluable** suggests value so great that it cannot be appraised in monetary terms (*invaluable* aid). —*ANT.* cheap.
cost·mar·y (kost'mâr'i, kôst'mâr'i), *n.* [ME. *costmarye* < *cost* (< L. *costus* < Gr. *kostos*, costus root, an aromatic plant); + (St.) *Mary*], a kind of chrysanthemum with many small flowers and sweet-smelling leaves.
cos·to- (kos'tō), [< L. *costa*, a rib], in *anatomy, surgery,* & *zoology*, a combining form meaning: 1. *a rib, ribs.* 2. *of the ribs and.* Also, before a vowel, **cost-**.
cost of living, the average cost of the necessities of life, such as food, shelter, clothes, medical expenses, etc.
cost-plus (kôst'plus'), *n.* the cost of production plus a certain rate of profit: used as the basis for payment in many government contracts for war supplies, etc.
cos·trel (kos'trəl), *n.* [ME.; OFr. *costerel*, dim. of *costier*, something at the side < L. *costa*, a rib, side: so named from being carried at the side], [Archaic or Dial.], a large bottle or flask with a loop or loops by which it can be hung from the shoulders or waist.
cos·tume (kos'tōōm, kos'tūm), *n.* [18th-c. art term; Fr.; OIt. *costuma;* L. *consuetudo*, custom; for sense, cf. HABIT], 1. a style of dress; dress in general, including accessories, style of the hair, etc. 2. the style of dress typical of a certain country, period, people, etc., often worn at a masquerade or in a play. 3. a complete set of outer clothes considered as a unit and worn for a particular purpose: as, a riding *costume*. *v.t.* (kos-tōōm', kos-tūm'), [COSTUMED (-tōōmd', -tūmd'), COSTUMING], to provide with a costume; put a costume on; dress.
cos·tum·er (kos-tōōm'ẽr, kos-tūm'ẽr), *n.* a person whose work or business is making, selling, or renting costumes, as for masquerades, theaters, etc.
cos·tum·i·er (kos-tōōm'i-ẽr, kos-tūm'i-ẽr; Fr. kôs'tü'-myā'), *n.* [Fr.], a costumer.
co·sy (kō'zi), *adj.* [COSIER (-zi-ẽr), COSIEST (-zi-ist)], & *n.* [*pl.* COSIES (-ziz)], cozy.
Co·sy·ra (kō-sī'rə), *n.* Pantelleria: the ancient name.
cot (kot), *n.* [orig., military term < Hind. *khāṭ* < Sans. *khaṭvā*], a narrow bed, especially one made of canvas on a frame that can be folded up.
cot (kot), *n.* [ME.; AS., cottage, hut, lit., covered place; akin to MD. *kote*, ON. *kot;* IE. base *geu-, to curve, bend, arch, as also in L. *guttur*, throat; cf. GUTTURAL], 1. [Poetic], a cottage; small house. 2. a small shelter; cote. 3. a covering or sheath, as for a hurt finger.
co·tan·gent (kō-tan'jənt), *n.* [Mod. L. *cotangens* < *co. tangens*, short for *complementi tangens*, lit., tangent of the complement], in *trigonometry*, the tangent of the complement of an angle or arc: abbreviated **cot**, **ctn** (no period).
co·tan·gen·tial (kō'tan-jen'shəl), *adj.* of, or having the nature of, a cotangent.

COTANGENT
$\frac{X}{Y}$, cotangent of angle BAC

cote (kōt), *n.* [ME. *cote, cot;* see COT (cottage)], 1. a small shelter or shed for birds, chickens, sheep, etc. 2. [Dial.], a cottage.
Côte d'A·zur (kōt' dà'zür'), the southeastern coast of France, along the Riviera.
co·tem·po·ra·ne·ous (kō-tem'pə-rā'ni-əs), *adj.* contemporaneous.
co·tem·po·rar·y (kō-tem'pə-rer'i), *adj.* & *n.* contemporary.
co·ten·ant (kō-ten'ənt), *n.* one of two or more tenants who share a place; joint tenant.
co·te·rie (kō'tẽr-i, kō'tə-rē'), *n.* [Fr., orig., organization of peasants holding land from a feudal lord < *cote*, hut < MD. *kote;* akin to AS. *cot*, cottage; cf. COT (cottage)], a group of people who often gather for social purposes; social circle or set; clique.
SYN.—a **coterie** is a small, intimate, somewhat select group

of people associated for social or other reasons (a literary *coterie*); **circle** suggests any group of people having in common some particular interest or pursuit (in music *circles*); **set** refers to a group, usually larger and, hence, less exclusive than a **coterie,** having a common background, interests, etc. (the sporting *set*); **clique** refers to a small, highly exclusive group, often within a larger one, and implies snobbery, selfishness, or, sometimes, intrigue (a *clique* of obscurantist poets).

co·ter·mi·nous (kō-tũr'mə-nəs), ***adj.*** conterminous.

co·thurn (kō'thẽrn, kō-thũrn'), ***n.*** a cothurnus.

co·thur·nus (kō-thũr'nəs), ***n.*** [*pl.* COTHURNI (-nī)], [L.; Gr. *kothornos*], 1. a high, thick-soled boot or buskin worn by actors in ancient Greek and Roman tragedies; hence, 2. tragedy or a lofty, tragic style in drama.

co·tid·al (kō-tīd''l), ***adj.*** indicating the coincidence in time or extent of tides: as, *cotidal* lines on a map.

co·til·lion (kō-til'yən, kə-til'yən), ***n.*** [Fr. *cotillon*, a petticoat, hence dance < OFr. *cote*, a coat], 1. a brisk, lively dance of the 19th century, characterized by many intricate figures and variations and the continual changing of partners. 2. the music for this dance.

co·til·lon (kō-til'yən, kə-til'yən; Fr. kô'tē'yōn'), ***n.*** a cotillion.

Co·to·pax·i (kō'tə-pak'si; Sp. kô'tô-pä'hē), ***n.*** a volcanic mountain in the Andes, in northern Ecuador: height, 19,498 ft.

cot·quean (kot'kwēn'), ***n.*** [*cot* (cottage) + *quean*], [Archaic], 1. a vulgar, scolding woman. 2. a man who does housework or other work regarded as women's.

Cots·wold (kots'wōld, kots'wəld), ***n.*** any of a breed of sheep with long wool, originally from the Cotswolds.

Cots·wolds (kots'wōldz, kots'wəldz), ***n. pl.*** a range of Jurassic hills in Gloucestershire, southwestern England: also **Cotswold Hills.**

cot·ta (kot'ə), ***n.*** [ML. < Gmc. **cott*, woolen coat, cloak; see COAT], a short surplice worn in some churches.

cot·tage (kot'ij), ***n.*** [ME.; Anglo-Fr. *cotage* < OFr. *cote;* see COT (cottage), COTERIE], 1. a small house, usually of one story. 2. a house at a resort or in the country, used for vacations or as a summer home.

cottage cheese, a soft, white cheese made by straining and seasoning the curds of sour milk.

cottage pudding, cake without icing, covered with a sweet sauce.

cot·tag·er (kot'ij-ẽr), ***n.*** 1. a person who lives in a cottage. 2. [British], a farm laborer.

cot·ter, cot·tar (kot'ẽr), ***n.*** [ML. *cotarius* < *cota;* of Gmc. origin; see COT (cottage)], 1. a cottager. 2. [Scot.], a tenant farmer. 3. [Irish], a cottier.

cot·ter (kot'ẽr), ***n.*** [Early Mod. Eng. (also *cotterel*); apparently < LG.; cf. MLG. *kote*, claw, joint, die, MD. *cotel* (D. *keutel*), cone, skittle, joint, in technical senses], 1. a bolt or wedge put through a slot to hold together parts of machinery. 2. a cotter pin.

cotter pin, a split pin used as a cotter, fastened in place by spreading apart its ends after it is inserted.

COTTER PIN

Cot·ti·an Alps (kot'i-ən), the part of the Alps between France and Italy: highest peak, Viso, 12,601 ft.

cot·ti·er (kot'i-ẽr), ***n.*** [ME. & OFr. *cotier* < *cote;* see COT (cottage), COTERIE], 1. in Great Britain and Ireland, a farmer who lives in a cottage: also **cotter, cottar.** 2. [Archaic], in Ireland, a peasant renting a small piece of land under a system (called *cottier tenure*) of renting land to the highest bidder.

cot·ton (kot''n), ***n.*** [ME. *coton;* OSp. *coton* < Ar. *quṭun, quṭn*], 1. the soft, white, fibrous matter around the seeds of various shrubs or woody herbs of the mallow family. 2. a plant or plants producing this material. 3. the crop of such plants. 4. thread or cloth made of cotton. 5. a downy, cottonlike substance growing on other plants. ***adj.*** of cotton.

cotton (up) to, [?< notion of cotton mixing well with wool, etc.], [Colloq.], 1. to agree with; be in harmony with. 2. to become friends with; associate with. 3. to begin to like; become attached to by liking.

COTTON PLANT
(3–4 ft. high)

cotton batting, thin, pressed layers of fluffy, absorbent cotton, used for surgical dressing, etc.

Cotton Belt, the region in the southern part of the United States where much cotton is grown: it extends from the eastern coast through Texas.

cotton cake, a mass of compressed cottonseed from which the oil has been extracted, used as feed.

cotton flannel, a strong cotton cloth with a long, fleecy nap: also called *Canton flannel.*

cotton gin, [see GIN (snare)], a machine for separating cotton fibers from the seeds.

cotton grass, any of a group of grasslike plants of the sedge family, with flower heads resembling cotton.

cotton mill, a factory for making cotton thread or cloth.

cot·ton·mouth (kot''n-mouth'), ***n.*** a large, poisonous snake with a thick body and a whitish mouth, found in the southern United States; water moccasin.

cotton picker, 1. a person or machine that picks cotton. 2. a machine for cleaning raw cotton.

cotton press, a machine for pressing cotton into bales.

cot·ton·seed (kot''n-sēd'), ***n.*** the seed of the cotton plant: also **cotton-seed, cotton seed.**

cottonseed meal, hulled cottonseed ground up after the oil has been removed, used as fertilizer and fodder.

cottonseed oil, an oil pressed from cottonseed, used to make shortening, soap, etc.

cotton stainer, a small, red bug that harms cotton fibers by giving them an indelible red or yellow stain.

cot·ton·tail (kot''n-tāl'), ***n.*** a common American rabbit with a short, fluffy tail that is white underneath.

cot·ton·weed (kot''n-wēd'), ***n.*** any of various plants with white, cottony hairs, as the cudweed.

cot·ton·wood (kot''n-wood'), ***n.*** 1. any of several poplars that have seeds thickly covered with cottony or silky hairs. 2. the wood of any of these trees.

cotton wool, natural or raw cotton; cotton batting.

cot·ton·y (kot''n-i), ***adj.*** 1. of or consisting of cotton. 2. like cotton; downy; fluffy.

cot·y·le·don (kot''l-ē'd'n), ***n.*** [L., kind of plant, navelwort; Gr. *kotylēdōn* < *kotylē*, a hollow, cavity], a seed leaf; earliest leaf or one of the earliest leaves growing out of a seed.

cot·y·le·don·ous (kot''l-ē'd'n-əs), ***adj.*** of, like, or having cotyledons.

couch (kouch), ***n.*** [ME. & OFr. *couche*, a bed, lair; see the *v.*], 1. an article of furniture on which one may sit or lie down; sofa; divan. 2. any resting place. 3. [Chiefly Poetic], a bed; place for sleeping. 4. [Obs.], an animal's lair or den. 5. in *brewing*, a layer of grain spread to germinate. ***v.t.*** [ME. *couchen;* OFr. *coucher, colchier*, to lie down; L. *collocare*, to place together, lay < *com-*, together + *locare*, to place], 1. to lay on or as on a couch. 2. to lower or bring down; especially, to lower (a spear, lance, etc.) to an attacking position. 3. to put in words; state. 4. to embroider with thread laid flat. 5. [Archaic], to put in a layer. 6. [Obs.], to hide. 7. in *brewing*, to spread (grain) in a thin layer to germinate. 8. in *surgery*, formerly, to remove (a cataract) by using a needle to push down the crystalline lens of the eye. ***v.i.*** 1. to lie down on a bed; recline. 2. to lie in hiding; wait in ambush to attack. 3. to be in a pile, as leaves.

couch·ant (kouch'ənt), ***adj.*** [Fr. *couchant*, ppr. of *coucher;* see COUCH], 1. lying down: said especially of animals. 2. in *heraldry*, lying down or crouching, but keeping the head up: as, a lion *couchant.*

couch grass, [var. of *quitch grass*], any of several coarse grasses that spread rapidly by creeping stems.

couch·ing (kouch'iŋ), ***n.*** [see COUCH, *v.t.*, 4], a kind of embroidery done by laying threads flat on the surface to be embroidered and fastening them with fine stitches so as to form a design.

Cou·é, É·mile (ā'mēl' kwā'; Eng. kōō-ā'), 1857–1926; French psychologist; advocated autosuggestion.

cou·gar (kōō'gẽr), ***n.*** [*pl.* COUGARS (-gẽrz); COUGAR; see PLURAL, II, D, 1], [Fr., earlier *cuguacuarana*, apparently for Tupi *suçuarana*, lit., false deer < *suusú*, deer + *rana*, false: so named from its color], a tawny-brown animal of the cat family, with a long, slender body and a long tail, found from Canada to Patagonia: also called *puma, mountain lion, panther.*

cough (kôf), ***v.i.*** [ME. *coughen;* AS. **cohhian*, inferred from intens. *cohhetan;* akin to MD. *cuchen*, to cough, G. *keuchen*, to gasp for air; same echoic base as *chink-* in *chincough;* development of ME. *-gh* as in *duff, laugh*], to expel air suddenly and noisily from the lungs through the glottis, either as the result of an involuntary muscular spasm in the throat or to clear the air passages. ***v.t.*** 1. to expel by coughing. 2. to express or utter by coughing. ***n.*** 1. a coughing. 2. a diseased state of the lungs or throat, causing frequent coughing.

cough up, 1. to bring up or eject (phlegm, etc.) by coughing. 2. [Slang], to hand over (money, etc.).

cough drop, a small medicated tablet, often sweetened and flavored, for the relief of coughs, hoarseness, etc.

could (kood), 1. past tense of **can.** 2. an auxiliary with present or future sense, generally equivalent to *can* in meaning and use, expressing especially a shade of doubt or a smaller degree of ability or possibility (e.g., it *could* be so) or permission (e.g., *could* I go?).

couldn't (kood''nt), could not.

couldst (koodst), [Archaic or Poetic], second person singular, past indicative, of **can**: used with *thou.*
cou·lee (kōō′li), *n.* [Fr. *coulée* < *couler*, to flow], 1. a stream of molten lava or a sheet of solidified lava. 2. a deep gulch or ravine, usually dry in summer.
‡**cou·lée** (kōō′lā′), *n.* [Fr.], a coulee.
cou·lisse (kōō-lēs′), *n.* [Fr. < *couler*, to glide, flow < L. *colare*, to strain, filter], 1. a grooved timber in which a sluice gate, etc. slides. 2. in the *theater*, *a)* any of the side scenes of the stage. *b)* the space between two side scenes on either side of the stage.
‡**cou·loir** (kōō′lwär′), *n.* [Fr. < *couler;* see COULISSE], a deep mountain gorge or gully.
cou·lomb (kōō-lom′), *n.* [after Charles Augustin de *Coulomb* (1736–1806), Fr. physicist], a unit for measuring the quantity of an electric current; amount of electricity provided by a current of one ampere flowing for one second: symbol, C (no period).
coul·ter (kōl′tẽr), *n.* a colter.
Coul·ter, John Merle (mũrl kōl′tẽr), 1851–1928; American botanist.
cou·ma·rin (kōō′mə-rin), *n.* [Fr. *coumarine* < *coumaron*, tonka bean; Sp. *cumarú* or Port. *cumaru*, both < Tupi *cumaru*], a white, vanilla-flavored, crystalline substance obtained from the tonka bean and certain plants or made synthetically: used as a flavoring in baking, in perfumes, etc.
coun·cil (koun′s'l), *n.* [ME. *counceil, conceil, concilie;* OFr. *cuncile, concile;* L. *concilium*, group of people, meeting < **concaliom* < *com-*, with + base of *calare*, to call together; akin to Gr. *kaleein*, to summon, call, AS. *hlowan*, to low, bellow; see LOW (to bellow)], 1. a group of people called together for consultation, discussion, advice, etc. 2. a group of people chosen as an administrative, advisory, or legislative assembly. 3. the legislative body of a city or town. 4. an assembly of church officials to discuss points of doctrine, etc. 5. a body of delegates from labor unions in a city, town, etc. 6. the discussion or deliberation in a council.
Council Bluffs, a city in southwestern Iowa, on the Missouri: pop., 56,000.
coun·cil·man (koun′s'l-mən), *n.* [*pl.* COUNCILMEN (-mən)], a member of a council, especially of the governing body of a city or town.
coun·cil-man·ag·er plan (koun′s'l-man′ə-jẽr), a system of municipal government in which the chief administrative official is a manager chosen by the city council.
council of war, 1. a conference of leading military or naval officers to discuss important military affairs in connection with a campaign. 2. any conference to discuss plans for action.
coun·ci·lor, coun·cil·lor (koun′s'l-ẽr), *n.* [< *counselor*, by confusion with *council*], a member of a council.
coun·sel (koun′s'l), *n.* [ME. *counseil;* OFr. *cunseil, counseil;* L. *consilium* < *com-*, with, together + base **sel-*, take, grasp; akin to AS. *sellan*, to sell, deliver to; cf. SELL], 1. mutual exchanging of ideas, opinions, etc.; discussion and deliberation. 2. *a)* advice resulting from such an exchange. *b)* any advice. 3. a plan; resolution. 4. a person or persons giving advice about legal matters; lawyer or group of lawyers. 5. [Archaic], wisdom; shrewd judgment. 6. [Obs.], a confidential idea, plan, etc.; secret. *v.t.* [COUNSELED or COUNSELLED (-s'ld), COUNSELING or COUNSELLING], 1. to give advice to; advise. 2. to recommend; urge the acceptance of (an action, plan, etc.). *v.i.* to give or take advice. —*SYN.* see **advise, lawyer.**
keep one's own counsel, to be silent; not tell one's ideas, plans, etc.
take counsel, to discuss and deliberate; exchange advice, opinions, etc.
coun·se·lor, coun·sel·lor (koun′s'l-ẽr), *n.* [ME. *counseilere, counseiller;* OFr. *consellier;* L. *consiliarium*, counselor, adviser < *consilium;* see COUNSEL], 1. a person who counsels; adviser. 2. a legal adviser, as of an embassy or legation. 3. a lawyer, especially one who conducts cases in court: in full, **counselor-at-law.** 4. a person in charge of a group of children at a camp. —*SYN.* see **lawyer.**
count (kount), *v.t.* [ME. *counten;* OFr. *conter, cunter* (Fr. *compter*); L. *computare;* see COMPUTE], 1. to name numbers in regular order to (a certain number): as, he *counted* five. 2. to name, one by one, by units or groups, to reach a total; add: as, *count* the money. 3. to check by numbering off; inventory. 4. to take account of; include. 5. to consider; believe to be: as, he *counts* himself fortunate. 6. [Archaic], to ascribe; attribute. *v.i.* 1. to name numbers or things in order. 2. to be included in counting; be taken into account. 3. to have importance, weight, etc.; be worth consideration: as, his foolish opinions don't *count.* 4. in *music*, to keep time by counting. *n.* 1. a counting; adding or numbering. 2. the number reached by counting; total number or quantity. 3. a reckoning; accounting. 4. [Archaic], regard; notice; account. 5. in *boxing*, ten seconds counted to give a boxer who has been knocked down time to rise before he loses the match. 6. in *law*, any of the charges in an indictment, each of which gives a reason and is sufficient for prosecution. —*SYN.* see **rely.**
count for, to be worth.
count in, to include.
count off, to separate into equal divisions by counting.
count on (or **upon**), to rely or depend on.
count out, 1. to disregard; omit. 2. [British], to end a sitting of (Parliament) when the members present are not enough for a quorum. 3. [Colloq.], to keep (a candidate) from office by counting the ballots incorrectly. 4. in *boxing*, to declare (a boxer) defeated when he has remained down for a count of ten.
count (kount), *n.* [OFr. *cunte, conte;* L. *comes, comitis*, companion < *com-*, with + *ire*, to go], a nobleman in European countries, having a rank equivalent to that of an English earl: abbreviated **Ct.** (as a title).
count·down, count-down (kount′doun′), *n.* the schedule of preliminary operations in the firing of a rocket, the detonation of a nuclear explosion, etc.: it is counted off into units of time going down to zero.
coun·te·nance (koun′tə-nəns), *n.* [ME. & OFr. *contenance;* L. *continentia*, lit., way one holds oneself, hence bearing, demeanor, countenance < *continere* < *com-*, together + *tenere*, to hold; cf. CONTINENCE], 1. the expression of the face. 2. the face; facial features; visage. 3. a look of approval on the face; hence, 4. approval; support. 5. composure; calm control. *v.t.* [COUNTENANCED (-nənst), COUNTENANCING], to approve; give support to. —*SYN.* see **face.**
in countenance, calm; composed.
put out of countenance, to cause to lose composure; make feel embarrassed and uneasy; disconcert.
count·er (koun′tẽr), *n.* [ME. *countour;* in senses 1 & 2 < OFr. *conteor;* L. *computator* < *computare;* in senses 3, 4, 5 < OFr. *contouer*, counting room, table of a bank; ML. *computatorium* < L. *computare;* see COUNT, *v.*], 1. a person or thing that counts; computer. 2. an indicator on a machine, for keeping count of turns, strokes, etc. of the machine or its parts. 3. a small device of metal, wood, etc., used for keeping count, especially for keeping score in some games. 4. an imitation coin. 5. a long board or table in a store, behind which the seller stands and on which goods are displayed, wrapped, etc.; also, a similar table in a restaurant, etc.
over the counter, in an office instead of through the stock exchange: said of sales of stock.
under the counter, in a surreptitious manner: said of merchandise sold illegally, especially at prices higher than those established by governmental regulation.
coun·ter (koun′tẽr), *adv.* [Fr. *contre;* L. *contra*, against, opposite], in a contrary direction, manner, etc.; opposite to. *adj.* contrary; opposed. *n.* 1. the opposite; contrary. 2. the part of a horse's breast between the shoulders and under the neck. 3. a stiff leather piece around the heel of a shoe. 4. the part of a ship's stern between the water line and the arched or curved part. 5. a depression between the raised parts of a type face: see **type,** illus. 6. in *boxing*, *a)* a blow given while parrying an opponent's blow. *b)* the act of giving such a blow. 7. in *fencing*, a circular parry of the foil. *v.t. & v.i.* 1. to act, do, move, etc. counter to (a person or thing); oppose. 2. in *boxing*, to attack or strike one's opponent while parrying (his blow).
coun·ter (koun′tẽr), *n. & v.t.* [Archaic], encounter.
coun·ter- (koun′tẽr), [Fr. *contre-;* L. *contra-*, against], a combining form meaning: 1. *opposite, contrary to*, as in *counterclockwise.* 2. *in retaliation*, as in *counterplot.* 3. *opposed to but like, complementary*, as in *counterpart.*
coun·ter·act (koun′tẽr-akt′), *v.t.* to act directly against; check, neutralize, or mitigate the effect of with opposing action.
coun·ter·ac·tion (koun′tẽr-ak′shən), *n.* an action that opposes, checks, etc. another action.
coun·ter·ac·tive (koun′tẽr-ak′tiv), *adj.* counteracting or tending to counteract. *n.* anything that counteracts.
coun·ter·at·tack (koun′tẽr-ə-tak′; *for v., usually* koun′tẽr-ə-tak′), *n.* an attack made in opposition to, or in reprisal for, another attack. *v.t. & v.i.* to attack in reprisal, or so as to offset the enemy's attack.
coun·ter·at·trac·tion (koun′tẽr-ə-trak′shən), *n.* an attraction opposed to or rivaling another attraction.
coun·ter·bal·ance (koun′tẽr-bal′əns; *for v.*, koun′tẽr-bal′əns), *n.* 1. a weight used to balance another weight; counterpoise. 2. any force or influence that balances or offsets another force or influence. *v.t.* to be a counterbalance to; offset.
coun·ter·blast (koun′tẽr-blast′, koun′tẽr-bläst′), *n.* 1. an opposing or answering blast. 2. an expression of strong opposition to someone or something.
coun·ter·blow (koun′tẽr-blō′), *n.* a blow given in return.
coun·ter·change (koun′tẽr-chānj′), *v.t.* 1. to transpose; interchange. 2. to checker; variegate.
coun·ter·charge (koun′tẽr-chärj′; *for v., usually* koun′tẽr-chärj′), *n.* 1. a charge in answer to another charge or against the accuser. 2. an attack in return. *v.t.* 1. to attack in return. 2. to charge or accuse in return.
coun·ter·check (koun′tẽr-chek′; *for v., usually* koun′tẽr-chek′), *n.* 1. anything that checks, restrains, etc. 2. a check upon a check; double check to make certain. *v.t.* 1. to check or restrain by a counteraction. 2. to check again; confirm by a second check.

counter check, a bank check kept on the counter for the use of depositors in making a withdrawal.
coun·ter·claim (koun′tẽr-klām′; *for v., usually* koun′-tẽr-klām′), *n.* an opposing claim; claim, as against the plaintiff in a lawsuit, to offset another claim. *v.t. & v.i.* to present as, or make, a counterclaim.
coun·ter·claim·ant (koun′tẽr-klām′ənt), *n.* a person who makes a counterclaim.
coun·ter·clock·wise (koun′tẽr-klok′wīz′), *adj. & adv.* in a direction opposite to that in which the hands of a clock move.
coun·ter·cur·rent (koun′tẽr-kũr′ənt), *n.* a current running in the opposite direction; opposing current.
coun·ter·dem·on·stra·tion (koun′tẽr-dem′ən-strā′-shən), *n.* a demonstration to oppose or counter the effect of another demonstration.
coun·ter·es·pi·on·age (koun′tẽr-es′pi-ə-nij), *n.* actions to prevent or thwart enemy espionage.
coun·ter·feit (koun′tẽr-fit), *adj.* [ME. *countrefete;* OFr. *contrefait,* pp. of *contrefaire,* to make in opposition, imitate; *contre-,* counter + *faire* < L. *facere,* to make], 1. made in imitation of something genuine with intention to deceive or defraud; forged: as, *counterfeit* money. 2. pretended; sham; feigned; dissembled: as, *counterfeit* sorrow. *n.* 1. an imitation made to deceive. 2. [Archaic], an impostor; cheat. 3. [Archaic], a copy or likeness, as in painting, sculpture, etc. *v.t. & v.i.* 1. to make an imitation of (money, pictures, etc.), usually with intention to deceive or defraud. 2. to pretend. 3. to resemble or make resemble. —*SYN.* see **artificial, false.**
coun·ter·feit·er (koun′tẽr-fit′ẽr), *n.* a person who counterfeits, especially one who counterfeits money.
coun·ter·foil (koun′tẽr-foil′), *n.* [*counter-* + *foil* (a leaf)], the part of a check, postal money order, receipt, etc. kept by the issuer as a record of the transaction.
coun·ter·in·tel·li·gence (koun′tẽr-in-tel′ə-jəns), *n.* counterespionage, censorship, etc. to keep the enemy from getting information that may be of value to him.
coun·ter·ir·ri·tant (koun′tẽr-ir′ə-tənt), *n.* anything used to produce a slight irritation, as of an area of the skin, to relieve more serious irritation elsewhere.
coun·ter·jump·er (koun′tẽr-jump′ẽr), *n.* [Colloq.], a person who works behind the counter of a shop; salesman or saleswoman in a store: contemptuous term.
coun·ter·man (koun′tẽr-mən), *n.* [*pl.* COUNTERMEN (-mən)], a man whose work is serving customers at the counter of a lunchroom or cafeteria.
coun·ter·mand (koun′tẽr-mand′, koun′tẽr-mänd′; *also, and for n. always,* koun′tẽr-mand′, koun′tẽr-mänd′), *v.t.* [Fr. *contremand* < L. *contra,* opposite + *mandare,* to command], 1. to cancel or revoke (a command or order). 2. to call back or order back by a contrary order. *n.* a command or order canceling another; contrary order.
coun·ter·march (koun′tẽr-märch′; *for v., usually* koun′tẽr-märch′), *n.* 1. a march back or in the opposite direction. 2. a marching movement in which a file or column reverses its direction, the individuals remaining in the same order and position: used especially by marching bands. *v.i. & v.t.* to march back; perform, or cause to perform, a countermarch.
coun·ter·meas·ure (koun′tẽr-mezh′ẽr), *n.* a measure, or action, taken in opposition or retaliation.
coun·ter·mine (koun′tẽr-mīn′; *for v., usually* koun′-tẽr-mīn′), *n.* [< *counter* + *mine* after Fr. *contremine* & It. *contramina;* for *v.,* cf. Fr. *contreminer,* It. *contraminare*], 1. a tunnel dug underground and filled with a charge of explosive to destroy an enemy tunnel. 2. a charge of explosive sunk under water to destroy enemy submarine mines. 3. a plot to defeat another plot. *v.i. & v.t.* 1. to intercept (an enemy mine) with a countermine. 2. to defeat (a plot) with another plot.
coun·ter·move (koun′tẽr-mōōv′; *for v.,* koun′tẽr-mōōv′), *n.* a move made in opposition or retaliation. *v.i. & v.t.* to move in opposition or retaliation.
coun·ter·of·fen·sive (koun′tẽr-ə-fen′siv, koun′tẽr-ə-fen′siv), *n.* an attack in force by troops who have been defending a position.
coun·ter·pane (koun′tẽr-pān′), *n.* [altered (after *pane,* cloth, coverlet < Fr. *pan;* L. *pannus,* piece of cloth) < *counterpoint,* coverlet < OFr. *contrepointe, contre pointe,* earlier *cuilte pointe* < L. *culcita puncta,* lit., pricked (i.e., embroidered) quilt; *culcita* (see QUILT) + *puncta* (see POINT)], a bedspread; coverlet.
coun·ter·part (koun′tẽr-pärt′), *n.* [*counter-* + *part*], 1. a person or thing that corresponds to or closely resembles another. 2. a thing which, when added to another, completes or complements it: as, woman is the *counterpart* of man. 3. [Obs.], a copy; duplicate.
coun·ter·plot (koun′tẽr-plot′), *n.* a plot to defeat another plot. *v.t. & v.i.* (*also* koun′tẽr-plot′), to plot against (a plot); defeat (a plot) with another plot.
coun·ter·point (koun′tẽr-point′), *n.* [Fr. *contrepoint;* It. *contrappunto,* lit., pointed against, orig. said of a plain song having accompaniment; see COUNTER- & POINT, *n.*], 1. a melody accompanying another melody note for note. 2. the art of adding a related but independent melody or melodies to a basic melody, in accordance with the fixed rules of harmony, to make a harmonic whole. 3. this kind of composition. Abbreviated **cpt.**
coun·ter·poise (koun′tẽr-poiz′), *n.* [ME. *countrepeis;* ONorm. Fr. *countrepeis* (OFr. *contrepois*); see COUNTER, *adv.* & POISE, *n.*], 1. a weight that balances another. 2. a force, influence, etc. that balances or neutralizes another. 3. a state of balance or equilibrium. *v.t.* to counterbalance; be a counterpoise to.
coun·ter·poi·son (koun′tẽr-poi′z'n), *n.* 1. [Obs.], a substance that counteracts a poison; antidote; specifically. 2. a poison that counteracts another poison.
coun·ter·prop·a·gan·da (koun′tẽr-prop′ə-gan′də), *n.* propaganda to counteract enemy propaganda.
coun·ter·ref·or·ma·tion (koun′tẽr-ref′ẽr-mā′shən), *n.* a reform movement to oppose a previous one.
Counter Reformation, the reform movement in the Roman Catholic Church in the 16th century, following the Protestant Reformation and in answer to it.
coun·ter·rev·o·lu·tion (koun′tẽr-rev′ə-lōō′shən), *n.* 1. a political movement or revolution against a government or social system set up by a previous revolution. 2. a movement to combat revolutionary tendencies.
coun·ter·rev·o·lu·tion·ar·y (koun′tẽr-rev′ə-lōō′shən-er′i), *adj.* of, advocating, or promoting a counterrevolution. *n.* a person who advocates or takes part in a counterrevolution.
coun·ter·scarp (koun′tẽr-skärp′), *n.* [Fr. *contrescarpe;* see COUNTER- & SCARP], the outer slope or wall of a ditch, moat, etc. in a fortification.
coun·ter·shaft (koun′tẽr-shaft′, koun′tẽr-shäft′), *n.* an intermediate shaft that transmits motion from the main shaft of a machine to a working part.
coun·ter·sign (koun′tẽr-sīn′; *also, for v.,* koun′tẽr-sīn′), *n.* 1. a signature added to a previously signed piece of writing in order to authenticate or confirm it. 2. a secret sign or signal in answer to another, as in a secret society. 3. in *military usage,* a secret word or signal, usually changed daily, which must be given to a guard or sentry by someone wishing to pass; password. *v.t.* to authenticate or confirm (a previously signed piece of writing) by signing.
coun·ter·sig·na·ture (koun′tẽr-sig′nə-chẽr), *n.* a signature made in countersigning.
coun·ter·sink (koun′tẽr-siŋk′; *also, for v.,* koun′tẽr-siŋk′), *v.t.* [COUNTERSUNK (-suŋk′, -suŋk′), COUNTERSINKING], 1. to enlarge the top part of (a hole in metal, wood, etc.) so that the head of a bolt, screw, etc. will fit flush with or below the surface. 2. to sink (the head of a bolt, screw, etc.) into such a hole. *n.* 1. a tool for countersinking holes. 2. a countersunk hole.
coun·ter·state·ment (koun′tẽr-stāt′mənt), *n.* a statement made in denial or refutation of another statement.
coun·ter·stroke (koun′tẽr-strōk′), *n.* 1. a stroke given in return. 2. a contrecoup.
coun·ter·tend·en·cy (koun′tẽr-ten′dən-si), *n.* [*pl.* COUNTERTENDENCIES (-siz)], an opposing tendency.
coun·ter·ten·or (koun′tẽr-ten′ẽr), *n.* [OFr. *contreteneur;* see COUNTER- & TENOR], 1. a part for a male voice higher in pitch than the tenor. 2. a male voice of this kind. 3. a singer who has such a voice.
coun·ter·thrust (koun′tẽr-thrust′), *n.* a thrust to counter another thrust.
coun·ter·type (koun′tẽr-tīp′), *n.* 1. an opposite type. 2. a parallel type.
coun·ter·vail (koun′tẽr-vāl′, koun′tẽr-vāl′), *v.t.* [ME. *countrevailen;* OFr. *contrevaloir* < *contre* (see COUNTER, *adv.*) + *valoir,* to avail < L. *valere,* to be strong], 1. to have or use equal force against. 2. to make up for; compensate. 3. to counteract; be successful, useful, etc. against; avail against. *v.i.* to avail (*against*).
coun·ter·weigh (koun′tẽr-wā′), *v.t.* to counterbalance.
coun·ter·weight (koun′tẽr-wāt′), *n.* a weight equal to another; counterbalance. *v.t.* to counterweigh.
counter word, any word freely used as a general term of approval or disapproval without reference to its more exact meaning (e.g., *swell, nice, terrible, lousy, colossal*).
coun·ter·work (koun′tẽr-wũrk′; *for v.,* koun′tẽr-wũrk′), *n.* 1. anything done or made to oppose something else. 2. a fortification to oppose an enemy fortification. *v.t. & v.i.* to work against (someone or something).
count·ess (koun′tis), *n.* [ME. *contesse;* OFr. *cuntesse;* see COUNT (nobleman) & -ESS], 1. the wife or widow of a count or earl. 2. a noblewoman whose rank is equal to that of a count or earl.
count·ing·house (koun′tiŋ-hous′), *n.* a building or office in which a business firm keeps records, handles correspondence, etc.: also called *counting room.*
count·less (kount′lis), *adj.* too many to count; innumerable; myriad.
count palatine, 1. in *German history,* formerly, a count granted certain powers from the emperor in his own

territory. 2. in *English history*, formerly, a count or earl with supreme power in his county.
coun·tri·fied (kun′tri-fīd′), *adj.* [*country* + *-fy* + *-ed*], 1. rural; rustic. 2. having the appearance, actions, etc. attributed to country people. Also spelled **countryfied.**
coun·try (kun′tri), *n.* [*pl.* COUNTRIES (-triz)], [ME. *contre, cuntre;* OFr. *contrée, cuntré;* LL. *contrata*, region, country, that which is beyond or over against (cf. G. *gegend*, district < *gegen*, against) < L. *contra*, opposite, over against], 1. a tract of land; area; region: as, wooded *country.* 2. a land; whole territory of a nation or state. 3. the people of a nation or state. 4. the land of a person's birth or citizenship. 5. land with few houses; rural region: contrasted with *city, town.* 6. any field of activity or sphere of knowledge: as, this subject is strange *country* to me. 7. in *law*, a jury: in reference to the fact that the jury was originally a group of men from the vicinity; jury trial was called *trial by the country.* *adj.* 1. of, in, or from a rural district. 2. like or characteristic of the country; rustic. 3. [Dial.], of one's own country; native.
go to the country, in Great Britain, to dissolve a parliament that has shown by vote that it disagrees with the cabinet, and call for the election of a new House of Commons.
country club, a club in the outskirts of a city or town, equipped with a clubhouse, golf course, etc.
country cousin, a person not used to city life and confused by it.
coun·try-dance (kun′tri-dans′, kun′tri-däns′), *n.* a folk dance, especially one in which the partners form two lines facing each other.
coun·try·fied (kun′tri-fīd′), *adj.* countrified.
coun·try·folk (kun′tri-fōk′), *n.* people living in the country; rural people.
country gentleman, a man of some wealth who lives on a country estate.
country house, a house on a country estate; home of a country gentleman.
coun·try·man (kun′tri-mən), *n.* [*pl.* COUNTRYMEN (-mən)], 1. a man who lives in the country; rustic. 2. a man of one's own country; compatriot.
coun·try·seat (kun′tri-sēt′), *n.* a mansion in the country; rural estate of a landowner.
coun·try·side (kun′tri-sīd′), *n.* 1. a rural region; district of the country. 2. its inhabitants.
coun·try-wide (kun′tri-wīd′), *adj.* extending through an entire country or nation: as, a *country-wide* search.
coun·try·wom·an (kun′tri-woom′ən), *n.* [*pl.* COUNTRYWOMEN (-wim′in)], 1. a woman living in the country. 2. a woman of one's own country; woman compatriot.
coun·ty (koun′ti), *n.* [*pl.* COUNTIES (-tiz)], [ME. *conte;* OFr. *conté, cunté* (Fr. *comté*); LL. *comitatus*, office or jurisdiction of a count or earl < L. *comes;* see COUNT (nobleman)], 1. a small administrative district of a country; especially, *a)* a local administrative subdivision of a State, which in turn is divided into townships. *b)* [British], a shire considered as an administrative, judicial, and political district. Abbreviated **Co., co.** 2. the people living in a county. 3. [Obs.], *a)* the region governed by a count or earl. *b)* [OFr. *cunte;* see COUNT (nobleman)], a count or earl. *adj.* of a county.
county farm, a farm maintained by a county as a home for people without means of support.
county palatine, the land held by a count palatine.
county seat, a town or city that is the center of a county government.
coup (kōō), *n.* [*pl.* COUPS (kōōz; Fr. kōō)], [Fr.; LL. **colpus, colapus;* L. *colaphus*, a cuff, box on the ear; Gr. *kolaphos*], 1. literally, a blow. 2. a sudden, successful move or action; brilliant stroke; clever stratagem.
‡**coup de grâce** (kōō′ də gräs′), [Fr., lit., stroke of mercy], 1. the blow, shot, etc. that brings death to a sufferer; death blow; hence, 2. a finishing stroke.
‡**coup de main** (kōō′ də man′), [Fr., lit., stroke of hand], a surprise attack or movement, as in war.
‡**coup d'é·tat** (kōō′ dā′tà′), [Fr., lit., stroke of state], a sudden, forceful stroke in politics; especially, the sudden, forcible overthrow of a government.
‡**coup de thé·â·tre** (kōō′ də tā′ä′tr′), [Fr., lit., stroke of theater], 1. a surprising or startling turn in a drama. 2. an action for sensational effect; theatrical action.
‡**coup d'oeil** (kōō′ dë′y′), [Fr., lit., stroke of eye], a rapid glance; quick view or survey.
coupe (kōōp; *orig. but now less often*, kōō-pā′), *n.* [see COUPÉ], a closed, two-door automobile that seats two to six people: also **coupé.**
cou·pé (kōō-pā′), *n.* [Fr.; pp. of *couper*, to cut], 1. a closed carriage seating two passengers, with a seat outside for the driver. 2. in European railway cars, a half-compartment at the end, with seats on only one side. 3. a coupe: now the less common form of the word.

COUPÉ

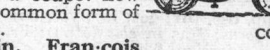

Cou·pe·rin, Fran·çois (frän′swȧ′ kōō′pran′), 1668–1733; French composer.
Cou·pe·rus, Lou·is (lōō-ē′ kōō-pā′rəs), 1863–1923; Dutch writer.
cou·ple (kup′'l), *n.* [ME.; OFr. *cople;* L. *copula*, a band, link; see COPULA], 1. anything joining two things together; bond; link; connection. 2. two things of the same sort that are joined together or associated; pair. 3. a man and woman who are engaged, married, or joined as partners in dances, games, etc. 4. [Colloq.], a few; several: as, I've a *couple* of things to do. 5. in *electricity*, two metals in contact with each other to form a galvanic or thermoelectric current; voltaic couple. 6. in *mechanics*, two equal forces producing rotation by moving in parallel but opposite directions. *v.t.* [COUPLED (-'ld), COUPLING], [ME. *couplen;* OFr. *cupler, copler;* L. *copulare* < *copula*], 1. to join together; link; connect. 2. to join in marriage. 3. in *electricity*, to join (two electric currents) magnetically or by direct connection. *v.i.* 1. to unite in a pair or pairs; pair. 2. to unite in sexual intercourse; copulate. —***SYN.*** see **pair.**
cou·pler (kup′lẽr), *n.* 1. a person who couples. 2. a thing that couples; specifically, *a)* a pneumatic device for coupling two railroad cars. *b)* in an organ, a device connecting two keyboards or keys an octave apart so that they can be played together.
cou·plet (kup′lit), *n.* [Fr., dim. of *couple;* see COUPLE], 1. two successive lines of poetry, especially two of the same length that rhyme. 2. [Rare], a couple; pair.
cou·pling (kup′liŋ), *n.* [see COUPLE, *v.*], 1. a joining together; pairing. 2. a mechanical device for joining parts together. 3. a device for joining two railroad cars together. 4. the part of the body of a dog, horse, etc. between the forequarters and hindquarters. 5. a method or device for joining two electric circuits for the transference of energy from one to the other.

COUPLING OF SHAFT

cou·pon (kōō′pon, kū′pon), *n.* [Fr., remnant, coupon < *couper*, to cut], 1. a detachable printed statement on a bond, specifying the interest due: the holder can present it for payment at the proper time. 2. a part of a ticket or a certificate given with packaged goods, entitling the buyer to a specified right, as an entertainment, redemption for cash or gifts, etc. 3. a part of a printed advertisement that can be used to order goods, samples, etc.
cour·age (kũr′ij), *n.* [ME. *corage;* OFr. *corage, curage*, heart, spirit < L. *cor*, heart], 1. the attitude or response of facing and dealing with anything recognized as dangerous, difficult, or painful, instead of withdrawing from it; quality of being fearless or brave; valor; pluck. 2. [Obs.], mind; purpose; disposition; spirit; temper.
the courage of one's convictions, the courage to do what one thinks is right.
cou·ra·geous (kə-rā′jəs), *adj.* having or showing courage; brave. —***SYN.*** see **brave.**
cou·rant (kōō-ränt′), *n.* a courante.
cou·rante (kōō-ränt′; Fr. kōō′ränt′), *n.* [Fr. < *courant*, ppr. of *courir*, to run, glide; L. *currere*, to run], 1. an old, lively French dance with gliding or running steps. 2. the music for this dance.
Cour·bet, Gus·tave (güs′tàv′ kōōr′be′), 1819–1877; French painter.
cou·ri·er (koor′i-ẽr, kũr′i-ẽr), *n.* [ME. *corour* (OFr. *coreor*, LL. *curritor*); also ME. *courier* (OFr. *coureur*, OPr. *corrieu*); both < L. *currere*, to run], 1. a messenger, usually one sent in haste with important or urgent messages. 2. a person hired to accompany travelers and take care of hotel accommodations, luggage, etc.
cour·lan (koor′lən; Fr. kōōr′län′), *n.* [Fr. < Galibi *kurliri*, echoic of the cry], a tropical American bird resembling the rail.
Cour·land (kōōr′lənd), *n.* Kurland.
course (kôrs, kōrs), *n.* [ME. *cours*, course, running; also Fr. *cours;* both < OFr. *curs, cours* < L. *cursus*, pp. of *currere*, to run; also Fr. *course* < It. *corsa* < *correre* < L. *currere*], 1. an onward movement; going from one point to another; progress. 2. the progress or duration of time: as, in the *course* of a week. 3. a way, path, or channel of movement: as, a race *course*, golf *course*. 4. the direction taken: as, his *course* was due south. 5. a regular mode or manner of action or behavior; way of doing: as, the law must take its *course*. 6. a number of like things in some regular order; series. 7. regular or natural order or development: as, the *course* of true love. 8. a part of a meal served at one time: as, the main *course* was roast beef. 9. a charge or encounter of knights contesting in a tournament. 10. in *architecture*, a continuous layer of bricks, shingles, stones, wood, etc. on the face or roof of a building. 11. in *education*, *a)* a complete, progressive series of studies necessary for graduation, for a degree, etc. *b)* any of the studies; unit of instruction in a subject, made up of recitations, lectures, etc.: as, the psychology *course* was interesting. 12. in *nautical usage*, *a)* one of the sails on the lowest yard of a square-rigged ship. *b)* the point of the compass toward which a ship sails. *v.t.* [COURSED (kôrst, kōrst),

COURSING], 1. to run or chase after; pursue. 2. to cause to chase, as hounds in a hunt. 3. to run through or over; traverse. *v.i.* 1. to run, chase, or race. 2. to hunt with hounds.

a matter of course, a regular or natural thing.

in due course, in the usual or proper sequence (of events).

in the course of, in the progress or process of; during.

of course, 1. in the regular order of things; as was to be expected; naturally. 2. certainly; without doubt.

cours·er (kôr′sẽr, kōr′sẽr), *n.* [ME.; OFr. *corsier;* LL. **cursarius* < L. *cursorius*, of running < *cursus;* see COURSE], [Poetic], a graceful, spirited horse; war horse.

cours·er (kôr′sẽr, kōr′sẽr), *n.* [< L. *cursorius;* see prec.], any of various Asian and African birds related to the plover, known for their swift running.

cours·er (kôr′sẽr, kōr′sẽr), *n.* 1. a person or thing that courses. 2. a dog for coursing.

cours·ing (kôr′siŋ, kōr′siŋ), *n.* 1. the action of a person or thing that courses. 2. hunting with hounds trained to follow game by sight rather than scent.

court (kôrt, kōrt), *n.* [ME. & OFr. *curt, cort;* L. *cors, cortis*, contr. of *cohors, cohortis*, enclosed place; see COHORT], 1. an uncovered space wholly or partly surrounded by buildings or walls; courtyard. 2. a special section or area of a museum, somewhat like such a space but roofed, as with a skylight. 3. a short street, often closed at one end. 4. a specially prepared area for playing any of several ball games, as basketball, handball, tennis, etc. 5. a part of such an area. 6. formerly, a mansion or manor with a large, uncovered entrance area: now used occasionally in proper names, as, Hampton *Court*. 7. a royal palace. 8. the family, advisers, and attendants of a sovereign, considered as a group. 9. a sovereign and his councilors, ministers, etc. as a governing body. 10. any formal gathering, reception, etc. held by a sovereign. 11. respectful or flattering attention paid to someone in order to get something. 12. courtship; wooing. 13. in *law*, *a*) a person or persons appointed to try cases, make investigations, etc.; judge or judges; law court. *b*) a building or hall where trials are held, official investigations made, etc. *c*) a judicial assembly. *d*) a regular session of the assembly. Abbreviated **C., c.** *v.t.* 1. to pay respectful or flattering attention to (a person) in order to get something. 2. to try to get the love of; woo. 3. to try to get; seek: as, you must *court* an opportunity. *v.i.* to carry on a courtship; woo. *adj.* of or fit for a court.

out of court, 1. without a trial. 2. not important enough for consideration or examination.

pay court to, 1. to pay respectful or flattering attention to (a person) in order to get something. 2. to try to get the love of; woo.

court card, [altered < *coat card* by influence of *court, n.*, 8], [British], any king, queen, or jack in a deck of playing cards; face card.

cour·te·ous (kũr′ti-əs), *adj.* [ME. *cortais, corteis, corteous;* OFr. *curteis, corteis* (Fr. *courtois*) < *curt;* see COURT, *n.*, 8 & -OUS], polite and gracious; considerate toward others; well-mannered. —*SYN.* see **civil.**

cour·te·san, cour·te·zan (kôr′tə-z′n, kōr′tə-z′n, kũr′tə-z′n), *n.* [Fr. *courtisane;* It. *cortigiana*, a prostitute, orig., court lady < *corte;* see COURT], a prostitute.

cour·te·sy (kũr′tə-si), *n.* [*pl.* COURTESIES (-siz)], [ME. *cortaisie, corteisie;* OFr. *curteisie, curtoisie;* see COURTEOUS], 1. courteous behavior; gracious politeness. 2. a polite or considerate act or remark. 3. favor; approval: opposed to legal right, as, a title of *courtesy*. 4. (kũrt′si), a curtsy.

courtesy title, a title of address not legally valid but given by custom, as to the children of British dukes.

court hand, a kind of handwriting formerly used in English legal documents; Gothic handwriting.

court·house (kôrt′hous′, kōrt′hous′), *n.* 1. a building in which law courts are held. 2. a building that houses the offices of a county government. Abbreviated **c.h.**

cour·ti·er (kôr′ti-ẽr, kôr′tyẽr, kōr′ti-ẽr), *n.* [ME. *curteour* < OFr. *cortoier*, to frequent the court; see COURT], 1. an attendant at a royal court. 2. a person who uses flattery like that ascribed to courtiers to get something or to win favor.

court·li·ness (kôrt′li-nis, kōrt′li-nis), *n.* the quality of being courtly.

court·ly (kôrt′li, kōrt′li), *adj.* [COURTLIER (-li-ẽr), COURTLIEST (-li-ist)], 1. suitable for a king's court; dignified, polite, elegant, etc.: as, *courtly* manners. 2. flattering, especially in a servile way. *adv.* in a courtly manner.

court-mar·tial (kôrt′mär′shəl, kōrt′mär′shəl), *n.* [*pl.* COURTS-MARTIAL], 1. a court of military or naval personnel for the trial of offenses against military law, or of army or navy personnel: in the United States Army, the three kinds, employed according to the seriousness of the offense, are *summary, special*, and *general*. 2. [*pl.* now often COURT-MARTIALS], a trial by a court-martial. Abbreviated **c.m.** *v.t.* [COURT-MARTIALED or COURT-MARTIALLED (-shəld), COURT-MARTIALING or COURT-MARTIALLING], to try by a court-martial.

Court of St. James, the British royal court.

court plaster, [so called because formerly used by court ladies for small black patches on the face or back], cloth covered with isinglass or some other adhesive material, for protecting minor cuts and scratches in the skin.

Cour·trai (ko͞or′trā′), *n.* a city in northwestern Belgium: pop., 40,000 (est. 1945).

court·room (kôrt′ro͞om′, kōrt′room′), *n.* a room in which a law court is held.

court·ship (kôrt′ship, kōrt′ship), *n.* [*court* + *-ship*], the act, process, or period of courting a woman.

court tennis, see **tennis.**

court·yard (kôrt′yärd′, kōrt′yärd′), *n.* a space enclosed by walls, adjoining or in a castle or other large building.

cous·in (kuz′′n), *n.* [ME. *cosin;* OFr. *cosin, cusin;* L. *consobrinus*, orig., child of a mother's sister, also cousin, relation < *com-*, with + *sobrinus*, cousin on the mother's side < **sororinus* < *soror*, sister; see SORORITY], 1. originally, a collateral relative more distant than a brother or sister, descended from a common ancestor. 2. the son or daughter of one's uncle or aunt: also called *cousin-german, first* (or *full* or *own*) *cousin:* you are a *first cousin* to the child of your uncle or aunt; you are a *second cousin* to the children of your parents' first cousins; you are a *first cousin once removed* (sometimes called *second cousin*) to the children of your first cousins. 3. loosely, any relative by blood or marriage. 4. a person of a nation thought of as related to another nation: as, the English and Australians are sometimes called *cousins*. 5. a title of address used by a sovereign to another sovereign or to a nobleman. 6. [Obs.], in *law*, the next of kin, except parent or child. 7. [Slang], a rival or competitor who unwittingly or unintentionally advances one's interests.

cous·in-ger·man (kuz′′n-jũr′mən), *n.* [*pl.* COUSINS-GERMAN], [Fr. *cousin germain;* see GERMAN (closely related)], a first cousin; child of one's uncle or aunt.

cous·in·ly (kuz′′n-li), *adj.* of, like, characteristic of, or fit for a cousin. *adv.* in a cousinly manner.

cous·in·ry (kuz′′n-ri), *n.* [*pl.* COUSINRIES (-riz)], cousins or other relatives, collectively.

cous·in·ship (kuz′′n-ship′), *n.* [*cousin* + *-ship*], the relationship of cousins.

‡**cou·teau** (ko͞o′tō′), *n.* [*pl.* COUTEAUX (-tō′)], [Fr.], 1. a large knife carried as a weapon. 2. a two-edged dagger.

couth (ko͞oth), obsolete past tense and past participle of **can** (to be able). *adj.* [cf. UNCOUTH], [Archaic], known.

‡**cou·tu·rier** (ko͞o′tü′ryā′), *n.* [Fr.], a man dressmaker.

‡**cou·tu·rière** (ko͞o′tü′ryâr′), *n.* [Fr.], a woman dressmaker.

cou·vade (ko͞o-väd′), *n.* [Fr. < *couver*, to hatch; OFr. *cover;* see COVEY], a custom of some primitive tribes, in which the father goes to bed as if for childbearing when his wife is having a baby.

co·va·lence (kō-vā′ləns), *n.* 1. the number of pairs of electrons that an atom can share with its neighboring atoms. 2. the bond formed by shared pairs of electrons between two atoms.

cove (kōv), *n.* [ME.; AS. *cofa*, cave, cell, etc.; akin to ON. *kofi*, G. *koben*, poor room, pigsty; for IE. base see COD, COOMB; base sense "hole as dwelling"], 1. a sheltered nook or recess, as in cliffs. 2. a small bay or inlet. 3. a strip of open land extending into the woods. 4. in *architecture*, *a*) a concave molding, especially one next to a ceiling. *b*) a concave arch or vault. *v.t. & v.i.* [COVED (kōvd), COVING], to arch over or slope inward.

cove (kōv), *n.* [Gypsy *covo*, that man], [British Slang], a boy or man; chap; fellow.

cov·e·nant (kuv′ə-nənt), *n.* [ME.; OFr. *covenant*, later *couvenant*, agreement, ppr. of *covenir* < L. *convenire;* see CONVENE], 1. a binding and solemn agreement made by two or more individuals, parties, etc. to do or keep from doing a specified thing; compact. 2. an agreement among members of a church to hold to points of doctrine, faith, etc. 3. [C-], an agreement of Presbyterians in Scotland in 1638 to oppose episcopacy: also called *National Covenant*. 4. [C-], an agreement between the parliaments of Scotland and England in 1643 to extend and preserve Presbyterianism in England: also called *Solemn League and Covenant*. 5. [C-], the Covenant of the League of Nations. 6. in *law*, *a*) a formal, sealed contract. *b*) a clause of such a contract. *c*) a suit for damages for violation of such a contract. 7. in *theology*, the promises made by God to man, as recorded in the Bible. *v.i. & v.t.* to promise by or in a covenant.

cov·e·nant·er (kuv′ə-nən-tẽr), *n.* 1. a person who enters into a covenant. 2. [C-], (*also* kuv′ə-nan′tẽr), a person who supported either of the Scottish Presbyterian Covenants (1638, 1643).

Covenant of the League of Nations, the first section of the Treaty of Versailles (1919): it was the constitution of the League of Nations.

cov·e·nan·tor (kuv′ə-nən-tẽr), *n.* in *law*, the person or persons who have promised to carry out the duties, obligations, etc. set down in a covenant.

Cov·ent Garden (kuv′ənt, kov′ənt), 1. a London market area. 2. a theater in this area, first built in 1731.

Cov·en·try (kov′ən-tri, kuv′ən-tri), *n.* 1. a city in Warwickshire, central England: pop., 286,000. 2. [prob. 17th-c. Cavalier phr.: the town was strongly Roundhead], a state of banishment or exclusion from society; ostracism.

send to Coventry, to ostracize; refuse to speak to or deal with socially.

cov·er (kuv′ẽr), *v.t.* [ME. *coveren; OFr. covrir, couvrir* < L. *cooperire; co-*, intens. + *operire*, to hide], 1. to place something on, over, or in front of, so as to hide or protect; overlay with or as with a covering. 2. to extend over; lie upon: as, snow *covered* the highway. 3. to copulate with (a female). 4. to clothe. 5. to coat, sprinkle, etc. thickly: as, he was *covered* with mud. 6. to sit on (eggs); brood; incubate. 7. to conceal; hide; screen. 8. to protect; keep from harm or injury by shielding. 9. to allow; provide for: as, the law *covers* such cases. 10. to protect financially; provide enough money or security for: as, he will *cover* the loss with insurance. 11. to accept (a bet); stake the equivalent of (an opponent's stake) in a wager. 12. to travel over; go through: as, he *covered* the distance in ten minutes. 13. to include; deal with: as, the book *covers* the subject thoroughly. 14. to bring upon (oneself) by one's actions: as, he *covered* himself with glory. 15. to point a firearm at; put or keep within the range and in the aim of a gun, etc. 16. in *card games*, to put a higher card on (a previously played card). 17. in *journalism*, to get news, pictures, etc. of: as, the reporter *covered* the train wreck. 18. in *military usage*, to stand or move behind (a man or men) in order to observe and protect from enemy action. 19. in *sports*, to watch, guard, or defend (an opponent or area); be responsible for. ***v.i.*** 1. to overspread, as a liquid. 2. to put on a cap, hat, etc. *n.* 1. anything that covers, as a bookbinding, lid, top, etc. 2. a shelter for protection, as from gunfire. 3. a hiding place for game, as a thicket, underbrush, etc. 4. [after Fr. *couvert*], a tablecloth and setting for a meal, especially for one person. 5. a cover charge. 6. a pretense. 7. an envelope with a newly issued stamp, which has passed through a post office on the date of issue: valued by stamp collectors because of its dated postal markings.

break cover, to come out of hiding.

cover up, 1. to cover entirely; envelop; wrap. 2. to conceal; be secretive.

take cover, to seek protective shelter or concealment.

under cover, 1. in secret. 2. by pretense. 3. hidden.

cov·er·age (kuv′ẽr-ij), *n.* [see -AGE], 1. the amount, extent, etc. covered by something. 2. in *insurance*, all the risks covered by an insurance policy. 3. in *journalism*, the extent to which a news story is covered.

cov·er·all (kuv′ẽr-ôl′), *n. usually pl.* a one-piece, loose-fitting garment with sleeves, worn by mechanics, etc.

cover charge, [see COVER, *n.*, 4], a charge added to the cost of food and drink at a night club or restaurant.

cover crop, a crop, as rye, vetch, or red clover, grown to protect soil from erosion and loss by leaching.

Cov·er·dale, Miles (kuv′ẽr-dāl′), 1488?–1569; English translator of the Bible.

cov·ered (kuv′ẽrd), *adj.* [pp. of *cover*], 1. having a cover or covering. 2. having a cover on. 3. having a hat, cap, etc. on the head.

covered wagon, a large wagon with an arched cover of canvas, used by American pioneers: also called *schooner*, *prairie schooner*.

cover girl, [Colloq.], a pretty girl whose picture is often put on magazine covers, etc.

cover glass, a thin glass disk or square used to cover a specimen mounted on a slide for examination under a microscope.

cov·er·ing (kuv′ẽr-iŋ), *n.* anything that covers.

covering letter, a letter sent with a package, another letter, etc., as an explanation or introduction.

cov·er·let (kuv′ẽr-lit), *n.* [ME. & Anglo-Fr. *coverlit*, bed covering < OFr. *couvrir*, to cover + *lit* < L. *lectus*, a bed], 1. a bedspread; counterpane. 2. any covering.

Cov·er·ley, Sir Roger de (də kuv′ẽr-li), 1. an idealized country gentleman of the early 18th century in a series of sketches in the *Spectator* by Addison and Steele. 2. an old English country dance.

cov·er·lid (kuv′ẽr-lid), *n.* a coverlet.

cov·er-point (kuv′ẽr-point′), *n.* in *cricket & lacrosse*, the position, or the player in this position, near and assisting a certain other position called *point*.

co·versed sine (kō′vẽrst), [*co-* (as in *cosine*) + *versed sine*], in *trigonometry*, the versed sine of the complement of an angle or arc: abbreviated **covers** (no period).

cov·ert (kuv′ẽrt), *adj.* [ME.; OFr., later *couvert*, pp. of *couvrir;* see COVER], 1. concealed; hidden; disguised; veiled; surreptitious: as, a *covert* threat. 2. in *law*, protected by a husband: said of a married woman. *n.* 1. a covered or protected place; shelter. 2. in *hunting*, a hiding place for game, as a thicket, underbrush, etc. 3. in *zoology*, one of the small feathers that cover the bases of the larger feathers of a bird's wing and tail. —***SYN.*** see **secret.**

covert cloth, a smooth, twilled cloth of wool with cotton, rayon, or silk: used for suits, topcoats, etc.

covert coat, a short topcoat of covert cloth.

cov·er·ture (kuv′ẽr-chẽr), *n.* [ME.; OFr. < LL. **coopertura* < L. *cooperire;* see COVER], 1. a covering; refuge. 2. a concealment; disguise. 3. in *law*, the status of a married woman.

cov·et (kuv′it), *v.t. & v.i.* [ME. *cuveiter;* OFr. *cuveiter, coveitier* < LL. **cupiditare* < L. *cupiditas;* see CUPIDITY], to desire ardently (especially, something that another person has); crave; long for. —***SYN.*** see **envy.**

cov·et·ous (kuv′i-təs), *adj.* [ME. *cuveitus, coveitous*], tending to covet; greedy; avaricious. —***SYN.*** see **greedy.**

cov·ey (kuv′i), *n.* [*pl.* COVEYS (-iz)], [ME. *cove;* OFr. *covée*, a brood < *cover*, to sit on, hatch; L. *cubare*, to lie down], 1. a small flock or brood of birds, especially partridges or quail. 2. a small group of people; bevy. —***SYN.*** see **group.**

cov·in (kuv′in), *n.* [OFr.; LL. *convenium* < L. *convenire;* see CONVENE], 1. [Archaic], deceit. 2. [Obs.], a secret agreement. 3. in *law*, a conspiracy of two or more people to defraud or swindle another or others.

cov·ing (kōv′iŋ), *n.* a cove or coves (*n.* 4*a*).

Cov·ing·ton (kuv′iŋ-tən), *n.* a city in northern Kentucky, on the Ohio River: pop., 60,000.

cow (kou), *n.* [*pl.* cows (kouz); *archaic or poetic*, KINE (kīn)], [ME. *cou, cow*, pl. *kye* (southern double pl. *kyn*); AS. *cu*, pl. *cy;* akin to G. *kuh* (common Gmc.); IE. base **gwou-*, one of the ox species, as also in L. *bos, bovis* (cf. BOVINE), Arm. *kov*, Sans. *gāuḥ*, etc.], 1. a familiar farm animal domesticated for its milk; mature female of any animal of the ox family. 2. the female of certain other animals, as the buffalo, elephant, whale, etc. The male of such animals is called a **bull.**

cow (kou), *v.t.* [< ON. *kūga*, to subdue; akin to *cop, cuff* (hit); meaning influenced by *cow, n., coward*], to frighten; make timid; overawe.

cow·age (kou′ij), *n.* cowhage.

cow·ard (kou′ẽrd), *n.* [ME. *couard;* OFr. *couard, cuard*, coward, lit., with tail between the legs < *coue, coe*, tail; L. *cauda*, tail], a person who lacks courage; one easily or excessively frightened by something recognized as dangerous, difficult, or painful. *adj.* cowardly.

Cow·ard, Noel (kou′ẽrd), 1899– ; English playwright, actor, and composer.

cow·ard·ice (kou′ẽr-dis), *n.* [ME. *cowardise;* OFr. *couardise* < *couard;* see COWARD], lack of courage; being easily or excessively frightened by something recognized as dangerous, difficult, or painful.

cow·ard·li·ness (kou′ẽrd-li-nis), *n.* cowardice.

cow·ard·ly (kou′ẽrd-li), *adj.* having or showing a lack of courage; of, characteristic of, or fit for a coward. ***adv.*** in the manner of a coward.

SYN.—**cowardly,** the general term, suggests a reprehensible lack of courage in the face of danger or pain (a *cowardly* deserter); **craven** implies abject or fainthearted fear (a *craven* fear for one's life); **pusillanimous** implies an ignoble, contemptible lack of courage or endurance (*pusillanimous* submission); **dastardly** connotes a sneaking, malicious cowardice that is manifested in a despicable act (a *dastardly* informer). —***ANT.*** brave.

cow·bane (kou′bān′), *n.* [*cow, n.* + *bane*], any of several plants of the carrot family, with poisonous roots and clusters of small, white flowers; water hemlock.

cow·bell (kou′bel′), *n.* a bell hung from a cow's neck to tinkle when she moves and thus indicate where she is.

cow·ber·ry (kou′ber′i, kou′bẽr-i), *n.* [*pl.* COWBERRIES (-iz)], 1. a shrub with white or pink flowers and dark-red berries. 2. a plant of the rose family, with purple flowers. 3. the fruit of either of these plants.

cow·bind (kou′bīnd′), *n.* a vine with large, fleshy roots, greenish-white flowers, and red berries; white bryony.

cow·bird (kou′bũrd′), *n.* any of a number of small blackbirds often seen near cattle; cow blackbird; cow bunting: cowbirds often lay eggs in other birds' nests.

cow·boy (kou′boi′), *n.* 1. a ranch worker who rides horseback much of the time on his job of herding and tending cattle: also, and in the western States usually, **cowhand.** 2. a conventionalized character in novels, motion-pictures, etc., typically an adventurous Westerner who rides horseback, carries pistols, sings ballads, etc.

cow·catch·er (kou′kach′ẽr), *n.* a metal frame on the front of a locomotive or streetcar to remove obstructions from the tracks.

cow·er (kou′ẽr), *v.i.* [ME. *couren;* prob. < ON.; cf. Dan. *kūre*, Sw. *kura*, to squat; akin to G. *kauern;* IE. base **geu-*, to curve, bend], 1. to crouch or huddle up, as from fear or cold. 2. to shrink and tremble, as from someone's anger, threats, or blows; cringe.

Cowes (kouz), *n.* a resort town and yachting center on the Isle of Wight: pop., 18,000.

cow·fish (kou′fish′), *n.* [*pl.* COWFISH, COWFISHES (-iz); see FISH], 1. any of various marine mammals that feed

on plants, as the manatee, sea cow, or dugong. 2. any of the smaller marine mammals of the whale family, as the grampus. 3. a trunkfish.
cow·girl (kou'gûrl'), *n.* a girl who helps to herd cattle, etc. on a ranch.
cow·hage (kou'ij), *n.* [altered after *cow, n.* < Hind. *kāvāc* < Sans. *kapikacchu* < *kapi*, monkey + *kacchu*, itch], a tropical vine of the pea family, bearing pods with fine barbed hairs on their surface, which easily penetrate animal or human skin, causing intense itching: also spelled **cowage.**
cow·hand (kou'hand'), *n.* a cowboy: also **cow hand.**
cow·herd (kou'hûrd'), *n.* a person whose work is herding or tending cattle at pasture.
cow·hide (kou'hīd'), *n.* 1. the hide of a cow. 2. leather made from it. 3. a whip made of this, often a braided whip. *v.t.* [COWHIDED (-id), COWHIDING], to lash with a cowhide; flog.
cow killer, a wasp of the southern United States that looks like a large ant: so called from the notion that its sting can kill cattle.
cowl (koul), *n.* [ME. *cowle;* AS. *cugele, cugle;* LL. *cuculla*, monk's hood < L. *cucullus*, hood of a cloak; akin to MHG. *kugel*], 1. a monk's hood. 2. a monk's cloak with a hood. 3. something shaped like a cowl; especially, *a)* a hood-shaped, revolving metal cover for the top of a chimney, to increase the draft. *b)* the top part at the front of an automobile body, to which the windshield and dashboard are fastened. *c)* a cowling. *v.t.* to put a cowl on; cover with a cowl or something like it.

MONK'S COWL

cowl (koul), *n.* [ME. *coul, cuvel;* OFr. *cuvel;* L. *cupella*, dim. of *cupa*, vat, cask], [Archaic], a large, two-handled tub for carrying water, usually borne on a pole (*cowlstaff*).
cowled (kould; *poetic* kou'lid), *adj.* 1. wearing or having a cowl. 2. hood-shaped; hooded.
Cow·ley, Abraham (kou'li, kōō'li), 1618–1667; English poet and essayist.
cow·lick (kou'lik'), *n.* [from the notion that the hair looks as if it had been licked by a cow], a tuft of hair that cannot easily be made to lie flat on the head.
cowl·ing (koul'iŋ), *n.* [see COWL (hood)], a detachable metal covering for an airplane engine.
cowl·staff (koul'staf', koul'stäf'), *n.* [*cowl* (tub) + *staff*], [Archaic], a pole run through the handles of a large tub so that it can be carried between two persons.
cow·man (kou'mən), *n.* [*pl.* COWMEN (-mən)], a man who owns or operates a cattle ranch.
co-work·er (kō-wũr'kẽr), *n.* a person who works with another or others; fellow worker.

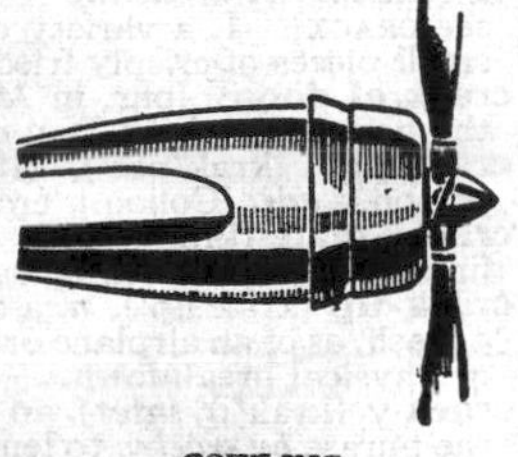
COWLING

cow parsley, a plant with many-lobed leaves and large, flattened clusters of white or purple flowers.
cow parsnip, any of several plants of the carrot family, with flattened clusters of white or purple flowers.
cow·pea (kou'pē'), *n.* 1. a trailing or shrublike vine with very long pods, grown as fertilizer or food for animals. 2. the edible seed of this plant.
Cow·per, William (kōō'pẽr; *now occas.* kou'pẽr), 1731– 1800; English poet.
Cow·per's glands (kou'pẽrz, kōō'pẽrz), [after William *Cowper*, Eng. anatomist (1666–1709)], a pair of small glands with ducts opening into the urethra, found in various male mammals: during sexual excitement they secrete a mucous substance.
cow pilot, a tropical fish with bands of bright green and black around its body, found near coral reefs in the West Indies; pintano.
cow pony, a pony used in herding cattle.
cow·pox (kou'poks'), *n.* a contagious disease of cows that causes pustules on the udders; vaccinia: people inoculated with a vaccine containing the virus of cowpox are temporarily immune to smallpox.
cow·punch·er (kou'pun'chẽr), *n.* [so named from prodding animals in herding], [Colloq.], a cowboy.
cow·rie, cow·ry (kou'ri), *n.* [*pl.* COWRIES (-riz)], [Hind. *kauṛī* < Sans. *kaparda*], the shell of a certain sea animal, used as money in parts of Africa and southern Asia.
cow shark, a large shark of European and West Indian waters.
cow·shed (kou'shed'), *n.* a shelter for cows.
cow·slip (kou'slip'), *n.* 1. the marsh marigold, a swamp plant with yellow flowers. 2. a wild plant of the primrose family, with yellow flowers; English primrose.
cox (koks), *n.* [*pl.* COXES (kok'siz)], [Colloq.], a coxswain. *v.t. & v.i.* to act as coxswain to (a boat).
cox·a (kok'sə), *n.* [*pl.* COXAE (-sē)], [L., hip, angle], 1. the hip or hip joint. 2. the first segment of the leg of an insect or other arthropod.
cox·al (kok's'l), *adj.* of a coxa or coxae.
cox·al·gi·a (kok-sal'ji-ə), *n.* [Mod. L.; see COXA & -ALGIA], a pain in, or disease of, the hip or hip joint.
cox·al·gy (kok'sal'ji), *n.* coxalgia.
cox·comb (koks'kōm'), *n.* [for *cock's comb*], 1. a cap topped with a notched strip of red cloth like a cock's comb, formerly worn by jesters. 2. the strip of red cloth in such a cap. 3. a silly, vain, pretentious, conceited fellow; fop; dandy. 4. a cockscomb.
cox·comb·i·cal (koks-kom'i-k'l, koks-kō'mi-k'l), *adj.* of, characteristic of, or like a coxcomb; foppish.
cox·comb·ry (koks'kōm'ri), *n.* [*pl.* COXCOMBRIES (-iz)], [see COXCOMB], silly conceit or vanity; foppery.
cox·swain (kok's'n, kok'swān'), *n.* [*cock* (cockboat) + *swain*], the person who steers a boat or racing shell: also spelled **cockswain.**
coy (koi), *adj.* [ME., still, quiet; OFr. *coi*, earlier *quei;* LL. *quetus;* L. *quietus;* see QUIET], 1. shy; bashful; demure; retiring. 2. pretending to be shy, often in a coquettish manner. 3. [Obs.], *a)* disdainful. *b)* quiet. *v.i.* [Archaic], to behave in a coy manner. *v.t.* [Obs.], 1. to quiet; soothe. 2. to caress; pet.
coy·ote (kī'ōt, kī-ō'ti, kī-ōt'), *n.* [*pl.* COYOTES (-ōts, -tiz, -ōts'), COYOTE; see PLURAL, II, D, 1], [Am. Sp.; Nahuatl *coyotl*], a small wolf of the western prairies of North America; prairie wolf.
co·yo·til·lo (kō'yə-tēl'yō, kī'ə-tēl'yō), *n.* [Am. Sp. dim. < Nahuatl *coyotl*, coyote], a thorny, poisonous plant found in Mexico and the southwestern United States.

COYOTE (4 ft. long)

coy·pu (koi'pōō), *n.* [*pl.* COYPUS (-pōōz), COYPU; see PLURAL, II, D, 1], [Sp. *coipu* < Araucan *coypu*], a large water rodent of South America whose fur (called *nutria*) is like that of the beaver.
coz (kuz), *n.* [Colloq.], cousin.
coze (kōz), *v.i.* [COZED (kōzd), COZING], [prob. < Fr. *causer*, to chat < LL. *causare*, to complain; L. *causari*, to plead, debate < *causa;* see CAUSE], to have a friendly talk; chat. *n.* a friendly talk.
coz·en (kuz''n), *v.t. & v.i.* [Fr. *cousiner* (< *cousin;* see COUSIN), lit., to act as a cousin, hence to deceive through pretense of relationship], to cheat; defraud; deceive.
coz·en·age (kuz''n-ij), *n.* [*cozen* + *-age*], a cozening; trickery; fraud.
co·zey (kō'zi), *adj.* cozy.
co·zi·ly (kō'z'l-i), *adv.* in a cozy manner.
co·zi·ness (kō'zi-nis), *n.* the quality or condition of being cozy.
co·zy (kō'zi), *adj.* [COZIER (-zi-ẽr), COZIEST (-zi-ist)], [Scot.; prob. < N.; cf. Norw. *kose sig*, to make oneself comfortable, *kosa*, lit., to wipe lightly, hence to stroke, flatter; akin to D. *keuzelen*, to flatter verbally], warm and comfortable; snug: also spelled **cosy, cozey, cosey, cozie, cosie.** *n.* [*pl.* COZIES (-siz)], a knitted or padded cover placed over a teapot to keep the contents hot: also spelled **cosy, cosey.** —*SYN.* see **comfortable.**
cp., compare.
C.P., 1. Chief Patriarch. 2. Command Post. 3. Common Pleas. 4. Common Prayer. 5. Communist Party.
c.p., 1. candle power. 2. chemically pure. 3. circular pitch.
C.P.A., c.p.a., 1. Certified Public Accountant. 2. Chartered Public Accountant.
cpd., compound.
C.P.H., Certificate in Public Health.
Cpl., Corporal.
C.P.O., Chief Petty Officer.
cpt., in *music*, counterpoint.
CQ, 1. a signal used by radio amateurs, inviting others to enter into communication. 2. charge of quarters.
Cr, in *chemistry*, chromium.
cr., [*pl.*, for 1 & 2, CRS.], 1. credit. 2. creditor. 3. creek. 4. crown; crowns.
C.R., Costa Rica.
crab (krab), *n.* [ME. *crabbe;* AS. *crabba*, lit., the scratcher; akin to LG. *krabben*, to scratch, *krabbe*, crab; the OHG. form *krebiz* (G. *krebs*) was borrowed in Fr. *écrevisse* (whence *crayfish*); IE. base **gerbh-*, **grebh-*, to scratch, seen also in *carve*], 1. a shellfish with four pairs of legs, one pair of pincers, and a short, broad

abdomen folded under its thorax. 2. any of several similar animals. 3. a crab louse. 4. any of various machines for hoisting heavy weights. 5. [C-], Cancer, the constellation and fourth sign of the Zodiac. 6. *pl.* the lowest throw of a pair of dice, two aces. 7. in *aviation*, the apparent sidewise motion of an airplane with respect to the ground when headed into a cross wind. *v.i.* [CRABBED (krabd), CRABBING], to fish for crabs; catch crabs. *v.t.* in *aviation*, to head (an airplane) into a cross wind in order to counteract drift, thus causing apparent sidewise motion with respect to the ground.

catch a crab, in *rowing*, to unbalance the boat by failing to clear the water on the recovery stroke, or by missing the water in making a stroke.

crab (krab), *n.* [ME. *crabbe* & MScot. *scrabbe;* merging of *crab* (shellfish) in lit. sense "scratcher," hence "unpleasant thing, morose person" (so used in LG.) with Anglo-N. word akin to ON. *scrapa* (Eng. *scrape*); cf. Sw. dial. *scrabba*, wild apple, Dan. *skrab* (ON. *skrap*, Eng. *scrap*), worthless trash], 1. a crab apple. 2. a person who has a sour temper or is always complaining. *adj.* of a crab apple or the tree that it grows on. *v.t. & v.i.* [CRABBED (krabd), CRABBING], [Colloq.], to complain about or find fault with (a person or thing).

crab one's act (the deal, etc.), [Colloq.], to ruin or frustrate one's scheme (the deal, etc.).

crab apple, 1. any of several varieties of small, very sour apple, growing wild or cultivated, used for making jellies and preserves. 2. a tree bearing crab apples. Also **crab.**

Crabb, George (krab), 1778–1851; English author and philologist.

Crabbe, George (krab), 1754–1832; English poet.

crab·bed (krab'id), *adj.* [< *crab* (apple)], 1. peevish; morose; ill-tempered; cross. 2. hard to understand because intricate or complicated. 3. hard to read or make out because cramped or irregular: as, *crabbed* handwriting.

crab·ber (krab'ẽr), *n.* 1. a person whose work is catching crabs. 2. the boat used in this occupation. 3. [< *crab* (apple)], [Colloq.], a person who constantly complains or finds fault.

crab·by (krab'i), *adj.* [CRABBIER (-i-ẽr), CRABBIEST (-i-ist)], [< *crab* (apple)], peevish; morose; ill-tempered.

crab grass, a coarse grass that spreads quickly because of its freely rooting stems.

crab louse, a louse that infests the pubic regions of the body: it somewhat resembles a crab in shape.

crab spider, any of various spiders that move sideways like crabs.

crab·stick (crab'stik'), *n.* 1. a stick, cane, or club made of the wood of the crab tree or some other wood. 2. a crabbed, ill-tempered person.

crab tree, a tree bearing crab apples.

crack (krak), *v.i.* [ME. *cracken;* AS. *cracian, cearcian,* to resound; akin to G. *krachen;* IE. base **ger-*, to cry hoarsely, as also in Sans. *garjati*, (it) roars, snarls], 1. to make a sudden, sharp noise in breaking. 2. to make a noise like this. 3. to break or split, usually without complete separation of parts. 4. to become harsh or rasping, as the voice when hoarse. 5. to change suddenly from one register to another, as the voice of a boy in adolescence. 6. [Dial.], to talk boastfully; brag. 7. [Dial.], to chat. 8. [Slang], to break down: as, will he *crack* under the strain? 9. [Slang], to joke, gibe, or make sharp remarks. *v.t.* 1. to cause to make a sharp, sudden noise. 2. to break, or cause a narrow split in, by a sharp, sudden blow, or by sustained or sudden pressure, heat, etc. 3. to damage or impair. 4. to cause (the voice) to crack. 5. to subject (petroleum) to the process of cracking. 6. [Colloq.], to hit with a sudden, sharp noise; strike with the fist, open hand, etc. 7. [Colloq.], to find the solution of: as, the police have finally *cracked* that murder case. 8. [Slang], to break open or into: as, the thief *cracked* the safe. 9. [Slang], to make (a joke or jokes). *n.* 1. a sudden, sharp noise, as of something breaking; explosive sound: as, the *crack* of a whip. 2. a break, usually without complete separation of parts; partial fracture; flaw. 3. a narrow opening as between boards; chink; fissure; crevice. 4. the cracking of the voice, as in hoarseness or during adolescence. 5. [Dial.], chatty talk; gossip. 6. [Archaic], a boasting or boast. 7. [Colloq.], a sharp, resonant blow. 8. [Colloq.], the duration of a crack; an instant. 9. [Thieves' Slang], a burglar or burglary. 10. [Slang], an attempt; try. 11. [Slang], a joke, gibe, or sharp remark. *adj.* [Colloq.], excelling in skill or performance; excellent; first-rate. —***SYN.*** see **break.**

crack a book, [Slang], to open and read or study a book, especially a textbook.

crack a smile, [Slang], to break into a smile.

crack down (on), [Colloq.], to become strict or stricter (with).

cracked up to be, [Colloq.], alleged or believed to be.

crack up, [Colloq.], 1. to crash, as in an airplane. 2. to break down physically or mentally.

crack wise, [Slang], to wisecrack.

crack·a·jack (krak'ə-jak'), *adj. & n.* [Slang], crackerjack.

crack·brain (krak'brān'), *n.* a crackbrained person.

crack·brained (krak'brānd'), *adj.* so senseless or unreasonable as to seem insane; crazy.

cracked (krakt), *adj.* 1. broken or fractured without complete separation into parts; having a crack or cracks. 2. harsh or strident: said of a voice. 3. [Colloq.], crackbrained.

crack·er (krak'ẽr), *n.* 1. a person or device that cracks. 2. a firecracker. 3. a little paper roll containing candy, etc., which explodes when the ends are pulled; cracker bonbon: used as a favor at parties. 4. a thin, crisp wafer of unleavened dough: sometimes called *biscuit.* 5. an impoverished white person in the rural sections of the South, especially in Georgia and Florida: contemptuous term.

crack·er-bar·rel (krak'ẽr-bar'əl), *adj.* [< the large barrel of soda crackers formerly found in general stores], [Colloq.], designating, like, or characteristic of the informal discussions on all subjects by persons gathered at a country store: as, a *cracker-barrel* philosopher.

crack·er·jack (krak'ẽr-jak'), *adj.* [late 19th-c. slang; extension of *crack, adj.* + *Jack* (nickname)], [Slang], excellent; first-rate, as in skill or ability. *n.* [Slang], 1. anything excellent. 2. a person of recognized excellence or skill. Also **crackajack.**

crack·ing (krak'iŋ), *n.* [< *crack, v.*], the process of breaking down hydrocarbons by heat and pressure into lighter hydrocarbons of lower molecular weight: by this method the complex hydrocarbons of the heavier fractions of petroleum can be broken down into the simpler hydrocarbons of gasoline.

crack·le (krak''l), *v.i.* [CRACKLED (-'ld), CRACKLING], [freq. of *crack, v.*], to make a succession of slight, sharp, sudden sounds, as of dry wood burning. *v.t.* to crush or break with such sounds. *n.* 1. a succession of such sounds. 2. the finely cracked surface found on some pottery, porcelain, and glassware. 3. ware having such a surface; crackleware.

crack·le·ware (krak''l-wâr'), *n.* pottery or porcelain with a finely cracked surface.

crack·ling (krak'liŋ), *n.* [see CRACKLE], 1. the producing of a succession of slight, sharp, sudden sounds. 2. the browned, crisp rind of roast pork. 3. *pl.* the crisp part remaining after the lard has been removed from hog fat by frying.

crack·ly (krak'li), *adj.* crackling or inclined to crackle.

crack·nel (krak'n'l), *n.* [ME. *crakenelle;* altered < Fr. *craquelin;* D. *krakeling* < *kraken;* akin to Eng. *crack;* see CRACK], 1. a variety of hard, crisp biscuit. 2. *pl.* small pieces of crisply fried fat pork. 3. *pl.* cracklings.

crack of doom, [phr. in *Macbeth*, IV, i], the signal for the beginning of the Day of Judgment.

crack·pot (krak'pot'), *n.* [Colloq.], a crackbrained person. *adj.* [Colloq.], crackbrained.

cracks·man (kraks'mən), *n.* [*pl.* CRACKSMEN (-mən)], [in reference to cracking safes, etc.], [Slang], a burglar.

crack-up (krak'up'), *n.* a cracking up; specifically, *a)* a crash, as of an airplane or moving vehicle. *b)* a mental or physical breakdown.

crack·y (krak'i), *interj.* an exclamation used, usually in the phrase *by cracky*, to lend emphasis to a remark.

Cra·cow (krak'ou, krā'kō), *n.* a city in southwestern Poland, on the Vistula River: pop., 300,000 (1946): Polish name, *Kraków.*

-cra·cy (krə-si), [Fr. or ML.; Fr. *-cracie;* ML. *-cratia;* Gr. *-kratia*, rule < *kratos*, rule, power], a terminal combining form meaning *a* (specified) *type of government, rule by*, as in *autocracy, theocracy.*

cra·dle (krā'd'l), *n.* [ME. *cradel;* AS. *cradol* < **kradula*, little basket; akin to OHG. *kratto* (< **kraddan*), basket; IE base **ger-*, to twist, turn; cf. CART], 1. a baby's small bed, usually on rockers; hence, 2. the earliest period of one's life; infancy. 3. the place of a thing's beginning or early development. 4. [Poetic], a place of rest: as, rocked in the *cradle* of the deep. 5. a framework of bars, cords, rods, etc., for support or protection. 6. a flat, wheeled frame for a mechanic to lie on when working under an automobile. 7. a wooden or metal framework to support a boat, ship, aircraft, etc. while it is being built, repaired, or lifted. 8. the supporting part of a cradle telephone. 9. in *agriculture*, *a)* a frame fastened to a scythe so that the grain can be laid evenly as it is cut. *b)* a scythe fitted with such a frame. 10. in *mining*, a boxlike device on rockers, for washing the gold out of gold-bearing sand. *v.t.* [CRADLED (-d'ld), CRADLING], 1. to place, rock, or hold in or as in a cradle. 2. to take care of in infancy; nurture. 3. to cut (grain) with a cradle scythe. 4. to set, support, or lift in or on a cradle. 5. in

MINER'S CRADLE

mining, to wash (gold-bearing sand) in a cradle. *v.i.* 1. to lie in or as in a cradle. 2. to cut grain with a cradle scythe.
rob the cradle, to take as one's wife, husband, sweetheart, etc. a person much younger than oneself.

cradle scythe, [see CRADLE, *n.*, 9], a scythe with a frame fastened to it for laying the cut grain evenly.

cra·dle·song (krā′d'l-sôŋ′), *n.* a lullaby.

cradle telephone, a telephone in which the mouthpiece and receiver form a unit, which lies on the connecting switch between U-shaped supports when the telephone is not in use.

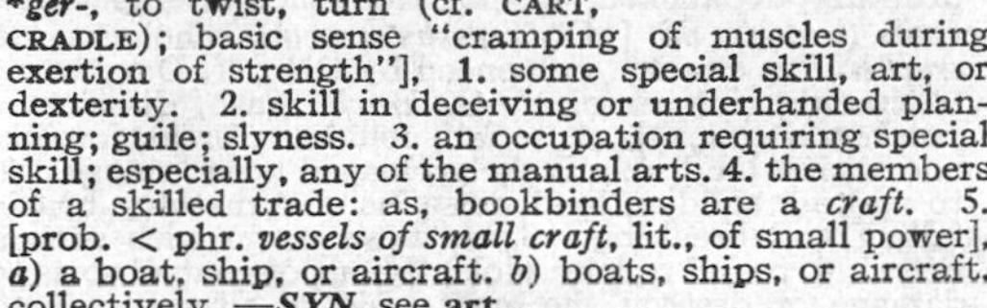
CRADLE SCYTHE

craft (kraft, kräft), *n.* [ME. *crafte;* AS. *cræfte,* strength, power; akin to G. *kraft,* strength, force; sense "skill" only in Eng.; IE. base **ger-*, to twist, turn (cf. CART, CRADLE); basic sense "cramping of muscles during exertion of strength"], 1. some special skill, art, or dexterity. 2. skill in deceiving or underhanded planning; guile; slyness. 3. an occupation requiring special skill; especially, any of the manual arts. 4. the members of a skilled trade: as, bookbinders are a *craft.* 5. [prob. < phr. *vessels of small craft,* lit., of small power], *a)* a boat, ship, or aircraft. *b)* boats, ships, or aircraft, collectively. —*SYN.* see **art.**

-craft (kraft, kräft), [< *craft*], a terminal combining form meaning *the work, skill,* or *practice of,* as in *handicraft, witchcraft.*

craft·i·ly (kraf′t'l-i, kräf′t'l-i), *adv.* in a crafty manner.

craft·i·ness (kraf′ti-nis, kräf′ti-nis), *n.* the quality of being crafty; cunning.

crafts·man (krafts′mən, kräfts′mən), *n.* [*pl.* CRAFTSMEN (-mən)], [*craft's* + *man*], 1. a skilled workman; worker in a skilled trade; artisan. 2. an artist: sometimes said of one skilled in the mechanics of his art, but lacking higher excellence.

crafts·man·ship (krafts′mən-ship′, kräfts′mən-ship′), *n.* [see -SHIP], the skill, art, or work of a craftsman.

craft union, a labor union to which only workers in a certain trade, craft, or occupation can belong: distinguished from *industrial* (or *vertical*) *union:* also called *horizontal union.*

craft·y (kraf′ti, kräf′ti), *adj.* [CRAFTIER (-ti-ẽr), CRAFTIEST (-ti-ist)], [see CRAFT], subtly deceitful; sly; cunning; artful: as, a *crafty* rascal. —*SYN.* see **sly.**

crag (krag), *n.* [northern ME. < Celt.; cf. W. *craig,* Ir. *carraig,* Gael. *creag*], a steep, rugged rock that rises above others or projects from a rock mass.

crag (krag), *n.* [< ON. *kragi* or MLG. *krage;* cf. CRAW], ‡[Scot. & North Eng. Dial.], the neck, throat, or craw.

crag·ged (krag′id), *adj.* craggy.

crag·gi·ness (krag′i-nis), *n.* the quality or state of being craggy.

crag·gy (krag′i), *adj.* [CRAGGIER (-i-ẽr), CRAGGIEST (-i-ist)], having many crags; steep and rugged; rough.

crags·man (kragz′mən), *n.* [*pl.* CRAGSMEN (-mən)], an expert climber of crags.

Craig·av·on (krāg-av′ən), first Viscount, (*James Craig*), 1871–1940; Irish statesman; first prime minister of Northern Ireland (1921–1940).

Crai·gie, Sir **William A.** (krā′gi), 1867–1957; British lexicographer.

Craik, Dinah Maria (krāk), (born *Dinah Maria Mulock*), 1826–1887; English novelist.

Cra·io·va (krä-yô′vä), *n.* a city in southwestern Romania: pop., 75,000 (est. 1945).

crake (krāk), *n.* [*pl.* CRAKES (krāks), CRAKE; see PLURAL, II, D, 1], [ME.; prob. < AS. *cracian,* to resound (cf. CRACK); northern Brit. sense, "crow" < ON. *krāka,* of same ult. origin; cf. CROAK], any of several birds of the rail family, with long legs and a short bill; especially, the land rail, or corn crake.

cram (kram), *v.t.* [CRAMMED (kramd), CRAMMING], [ME. *crammen;* AS. *crammian,* to squeeze in, stuff; akin to MHG. *krammen,* grip with claws; IE. base **grem-*, to press, compress (as in L. *gremium,* lap, bosom) < **ger-*, to hold, seize], 1. to fill (a space, etc.) beyond normal capacity by pressing or squeezing; pack full or too full. 2. to stuff; force: as, he *crammed* the papers into a drawer. 3. to stuff or fill to excess with food. 4. [Colloq.], to prepare (a person) or review (a subject) for an examination by stuffing the mind, usually in a hurried, intensive way. *v.i.* 1. to eat too much or too quickly. 2. [Colloq.], to stuff the mind full of a subject, as in preparation for an examination, usually in a hurried or intensive way. *n.* 1. [Colloq.], a crammed condition; crush. 2. [Colloq.], *a)* the act of cramming information. *b)* the information crammed.

Cram, Ralph Adams (kram), 1863–1942; American architect.

cram·bo (kram′bō), *n.* [< L. *crambe,* cabbage (as in *crambe repetita,* lit., cabbage repeatedly served, hence repeated story, old tale); Gr. *krambē*], 1. a game in which players find rhymes for words given by each other; hence, 2. a rhyme or rhyming: contemptuous term for inferior poetry.

cram·mer (kram′ẽr), *n.* a person or thing that crams.

cram·oi·sy, cram·oi·sie (kram′oi-zi, kram′ə-zi), *adj.* [Fr. *cramoisi;* It. *cremesi;* Ar. *qirmizi,* scarlet-hued], [Archaic], crimson. *n.* [Archaic], crimson cloth.

cramp (kramp), *n.* [ME. *crampe, craumpe* < OFr. *crampe,* bent, twisted < OLG.; cf. MD., MLG. *krampe,* lit., bent in; for ult. base see CRAM], 1. a sudden, painful, involuntary contraction of a muscle or muscles from chill, strain, etc. 2. partial local paralysis, as from excessive use of muscles. 3. *usually in pl.* intestinal griping and pain. *v.t.* 1. to affect with a cramp. 2. to cause to be affected with a cramp.

cramp (kramp), *n.* [MD. or MLG. *krampe,* lit., bent in, hence anything bent in; see CRAMP (muscular contraction)], 1. a metal bar with both ends bent, for holding together blocks of stone, timbers, etc. 2. a clamp. 3. anything that confines or hampers. 4. a cramped condition or part. *v.t.* 1. to fasten with or as with a cramp. 2. to confine; hamper; restrain. 3. to steer. *adj.* 1. confined; restricted; narrowed. 2. hard to read or understand; crabbed, as some handwriting.
cramp one's style, [Slang], to hamper one's usual skill, confidence, etc. in doing something.

cramp·fish (kramp′fish′), *n.* [*pl.* CRAMPFISH, CRAMPFISHES (-iz); see FISH], a kind of fish that can produce an electric current: also called *electric ray, torpedo fish.*

cramp iron, a cramp, or metal bar with both ends bent, for holding stones, etc. firmly together, as in a building.

cram·pon (kram′pən), *n.* [Fr. < Frank. *krampo,* iron hook], 1. either of a pair of iron hooks for raising heavy weights; grappling iron. 2. *usually in pl.* a spiked iron plate used on shoes to prevent slipping; climbing iron.

cram·poon (kram-pōōn′), *n.* a crampon.

cran·ber·ry (kran′ber′i, kran′bẽr-i), *n.* [*pl.* CRANBERRIES (-iz)], [for D. *kranebere,* G. *kranbeere,* lit., crane berry; name used by early D. & G. settlers in U.S., replacing earlier Brit. *fen berry,* etc.], 1. a firm, sour, edible, red berry, the fruit of a trailing evergreen shrub that grows in bogs or marshes. 2. the shrub.

cranberry tree, a shrub or small tree of the honeysuckle family, bearing clusters of white flowers followed by red fruit resembling the cranberry; bush cranberry.

crane (krān), *n.* [*pl.*, for 1 & 2, CRANES (krānz), CRANE; see PLURAL, II, D, 1], [ME. *crane, crone;* AS. *cran;* akin to D. *kraan,* G. *kranich* (with velar suffix); IE. **gr-on* < base **ger-*, to cry hoarsely (cf. CRACK), as also in W. & Bret. *garan,* crane], 1. a large wading bird with very long legs and neck, and a long, straight bill. 2. popularly, any of various herons and storks. 3. any of various machines for lifting or moving heavy weights by means of a movable projecting arm or a horizontal beam that travels over a factory yard, etc. 4. any device with a swinging arm fixed on a vertical axis: as, a fireplace *crane* is used for holding a kettle. *v.t. & v.i.* [CRANED (krānd), CRANING], 1. to raise or move by or as by a crane. 2. to stretch (the neck) as a crane does, as in straining to see something beyond an obstacle or in the distance.

CRANE (4 ft. tall)

Crane, Hart (krān), (*Harold Hart Crane*), 1899–1932; American poet.

Crane, Stephen, 1871–1900; American novelist, poet, and journalist.

CRANE (sense 3)

crane fly, any of various two-winged, slender flies with very long legs: they look like large mosquitoes.

crane's-bill, cranes·bill (krānz′bil′), *n.* [from the long, slender formation of the carpels], a geranium, especially the wild geranium.

cra·ni·al (krā′ni-əl), *adj.* of or from the cranium.

cranial index, in *craniometry,* the ratio of the greatest breadth of the skull to its greatest length from front to back, multiplied by 100.

cranial nerve, a peripheral nerve connected directly with the brain: there are twelve pairs of such nerves in man, including the olfactory, optic, trigeminal, facial, and auditory nerves.

fat, āpe, bâre, cär; ten, ēven, hêre, ovẽr; is, bīte; lot, gō, hôrn, tōōl, look; oil, out; up, ūse, fũr; get; joy; yet; chin; she; thin, *th*en; zh, leisure; ŋ, ring; ə for *a* in *ago,* *e* in *agent,* *i* in *sanity,* *o* in *comply,* *u* in *focus;* ′ as in *able* (ā′b'l); Fr. bál; ë, Fr. coeur; ö, Fr. feu; Fr. mo*n*; ô, Fr. coq; ü, Fr. duc; H, G. ich; kh, G. doch. See pp. x–xii. ‡ foreign; * hypothetical; < derived from.

cra·ni·ate (krā'ni-it), *adj.* having a skull or cranium, as fishes, reptiles, birds, and mammals. *n.* a craniate animal.

cra·ni·o- (krā'ni-ō, krā'ni-ə), [Gr. *kranio-* < *kranion*, skull], a combining form meaning *of the head, cranial*, as in *craniology*.

cra·ni·ol·o·gy (krā'ni-ol'ə-ji), *n.* [*cranio-* + *-logy*], the scientific study of skulls, especially human skulls, and their characteristics, including differences in size, shape, etc.: abbreviated **craniol.**

cra·ni·om·e·ter (krā'ni-om'ə-tẽr), *n.* [*cranio-* + *-meter*], an instrument for measuring skulls.

cra·ni·om·e·try (krā'ni-om'ə-tri), *n.* [*cranio-* + *-metry*], the science of measuring skulls; cranial measurement: abbreviated **craniom.**

cra·ni·ot·o·my (krā'ni-ot'ə-mi), *n.* [*pl.* CRANIOTOMIES (-miz)], [*cranio-* + *-tomy*], the surgical operation of opening the skull, as for brain operations.

cra·ni·um (krā'ni-əm), *n.* [*pl.* CRANIUMS (-əmz), CRANIA (-ə)], [Mod. L.; Gr. *kranion*], 1. the skull. 2. the bones forming the enclosure of the brain, excluding the lower jaw; brainpan.

crank (kraŋk), *n.* [ME., yarn reel; AS. *cranc* in *cranc-stæf*, yarn comb (also in *crencestre*, woman weaver), but later influenced by LG.; closely akin to *cringe, crinkle;* basic sense "something twisted, something used to twist" (cf. G. *krank*, ill, lit., twisted by illness); IE. base **ger-*, to twist, turn], 1. a part, as a handle, connected at right angles to a shaft of a machine in order to transmit motion. 2. a whimsical or unusual turn of speech or thought; whim; caprice. 3. a queer action or idea. 4. [Colloq.], a person given to queer actions, ideas, manners, etc.; an eccentric. 5. [Colloq.], an irritable, complaining person; cranky person. *v.t.* 1. to form into the shape of a crank. 2. to provide with a crank. 3. to start or operate by a crank. *v.i.* 1. to turn a crank, as in starting an engine or operating a device. 2. [Obs.], to wind; twist; zigzag.

crank (kraŋk), *adj.* [earlier *crank sided;* D. or Fris. *krengd*, laid over (< *krengan*, to push over, lit., make cringe); assimilated in form to *crank* (handle)], 1. in *nautical usage*, liable to lurch or capsize. 2. shaky; unsteady.

crank·case (kraŋk'kās'), *n.* the metal casing that encloses the crankshaft of an internal-combustion engine.

crank·i·ly (kraŋ'kə-li), *adv.* in a cranky manner.

crank·i·ness (kraŋ'ki-nis), *n.* the quality or state of being cranky.

cran·kle (kraŋ'k'l), *v.i.* [CRANKLED (-k'ld), CRANKLING], [freq. of *crank*, *v.*], to move in a zigzag course. *n.* a bend; twist.

crank·ous (kraŋk'əs), *adj.* [Scot.], cranky; irritable.

crank·pin (kraŋk'pin'), *n.* a cylindrical bar attaching a connecting rod to a crank: also **crank pin**: see **crank-shaft**, illus.

crank·shaft (kraŋk'shaft', kraŋk'shäft'), *n.* a shaft turning a crank or turned by a crank: in a gasoline engine the movement of the pistons is transmitted to the crankshaft by cranks.

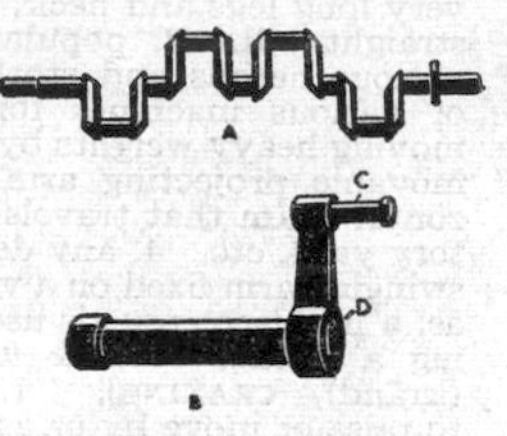

TYPES OF CRANKSHAFT
A, crankshaft for 4-cylinder automobile; B, simple crankshaft; C, crankpin; D, journal

crank·y (kraŋ'ki), *adj.* [CRANKIER (-ki-ẽr), CRANKIEST (-ki-ist)], [see CRANK, *adj.* & CRANK, *n.*], 1. out of order; out of gear; shaky; loose. 2. ill-tempered; irritable; cross. 3. queer; eccentric. 4. in *nautical usage*, unsteady; liable to lurch or capsize. —*SYN.* see **irritable.**

Cran·mer, Thomas (kran'mẽr), 1489–1556; English churchman; archbishop of Canterbury.

cran·nied (kran'id), *adj.* full of crannies or chinks.

cran·nog (kran'əg), *n.* [Ir. < *crann*, a tree, mast, beam], an ancient Irish or Scottish lake dwelling, built on an artificial island or shallows.

cran·noge (kran'ij), *n.* a crannog: erroneous form.

cran·ny (kran'i), *n.* [*pl.* CRANNIES (-iz)], [ME. *crani;* OFr. *cran, cren*, a notch; OIt. *crena*, a groove; LL. *crena*, a notch, groove], a small, narrow opening; fissure; crevice; chink or crack, as in a wall.

Cran·ston (kran'stən), *n.* a city in Rhode Island, near Providence: pop., 67,000.

crap (krap), *n.* [see CRAPS], 1. craps. 2. any throw that causes the thrower to lose at craps.
  crap out, to lose at craps by throwing a two, three, or twelve on the first throw or a seven after the point has been established.

crape (krāp), *n.* [Fr. *crêpe;* see CREPE], 1. a thin, crinkled cloth of silk, rayon, cotton, or wool; crepe. 2. a piece of black crape as a sign of mourning, often in the form of a band worn around the arm.

crape·hang·er (krāp'haŋ'ẽr), *n.* [Slang], a person with a gloomy outlook on things; pessimist.

crap·pie (krap'i), *n.* [*pl.* CRAPPIES (-iz), CRAPPIE; see PLURAL, II, D, 1], [< ?], a small North American sunfish found in sluggish streams and ponds through the eastern and central United States: also **croppie.**

craps (kraps), *n. pl.* [construed as sing.], [Fr. *crabs, craps* < Eng. *crabs*, lowest throw at hazard, two aces], a gambling game played with two dice: a first throw of seven or eleven wins, and a first throw of two, three, or twelve loses; any other first throw, to win, must be repeated before a seven appears.

crap·shoot·er (krap'sho͞ot'ẽr), *n.* a gambler at craps.

crap·u·lence (krap'yoo-ləns), *n.* [< *crapulent*], 1. sickness caused by excess in drinking or eating. 2. gross intemperance, especially in drinking; debauchery.

crap·u·lent (krap'yoo-lənt), *adj.* [LL. *crapulentus* < L. *crapula;* see CRAPULOUS], of, suffering from, or characterized by excess or gross intemperance in drinking or eating.

crap·u·lous (krap'yoo-ləs), *adj.* [LL. *crapulosus* < L. *crapula*, drunkenness < Gr. *kraipalē*, drunken headache], 1. characterized by intemperance, especially in drinking; debauched. 2. sick from such intemperance.

crash (krash), *v.i.* [ME. *crasshyn;* prob. echoic var. of *cracken* (see CRACK), influenced by ON.; cf. Dan. *krase*, to crackle (for sense, cf. G. *krach*, crash, disaster < *krachen*, to crack)], 1. to fall, collide, or break forcibly and with a loud, relatively prolonged noise; smash. 2. to make a sudden, loud noise, as of something brittle falling and breaking. 3. to move or go with such a noise. 4. to fall or land violently out of control so as to damage or destroy the craft: said of aircraft. 5. to collapse; come to sudden ruin; fail: as, their business *crashed*. *v.t.* 1. to cause (a car, airplane, etc.) to crash. 2. to force or impel with a crashing noise (with *in, out, through*, etc.). 3. [Colloq.], to get into (a party, theater, etc.) without an invitation, ticket, etc. *n.* 1. a loud, sudden noise, as of something brittle falling and breaking. 2. a crashing, as of a car or an airplane. 3. a sudden fall, collapse, or ruin, especially of business or a business enterprise. *adj.* [Colloq.], characterized by the use of all possible resources, effort, and speed: as, a *crash* program to build highways. —*SYN.* see **break.**

crash (krash), *n.* [earlier *crasko, crasho*, "Russian linen," prob. a trade contraction of Russ. *krashenina*, colored linen], a coarse cotton or linen cloth with a plain, loose weave, used for towels, curtains, etc.

Crash·aw, Richard (krash'ô), 1613?–1649; English religious poet.

crash dive, a sudden submergence of a submarine to escape from a threatened attack.

crass (kras), *adj.* [L. *crassus*, thick, gross, fat; prob. < IE. **qrăt-tos*, balled together; akin to L. *cratis* (see CRATE), Eng. *hurdle*], 1. [Rare], gross; coarse; thick. 2. grossly stupid, dull, or obtuse.

cras·si·tude (kras'ə-to͞od', kras'ə-tūd'), *n.* [L. *crassitudo* < *crassus;* see CRASS], 1. gross stupidity or ignorance. 2. grossness.

cras·su·la·ceous (kras'yoo-lā'shəs), *adj.* [Mod. L. *Crassula*, name of the genus; + *-aceous*], of a family of juicy plants including the stonecrop, houseleek, etc.

Cras·sus (kras'əs), *n.* 1. (*Lucius Licinius Crassus*), Roman orator and statesman; 140–91 B.C. 2. (*Marcus Licinius Crassus*), Roman statesman; 115?–53 B.C.

-crat (krat), [Fr. *-crate;* Gr. *-kratēs* < *kratos*, rule, power], a terminal combining form meaning ***participant in*** or ***supporter of*** (a specified kind of) ***government*** or ***ruling body***, as in *democrat, aristocrat.*

cratch (krach), *n.* [ME. *crecche* < OFr. *creche, cresche*, crib; see CRÈCHE], [Dial.], a bin or rack for fodder.

crate (krāt), *n.* [L. *cratis;* IE. base **qerăt-* (see CRASS); akin to Eng. *hurdle*], 1. a large basket or hamper of wickerwork, or a box or case made of slats of wood, for packing things to be shipped or stored. 2. its contents. 3. [Slang], an old, decrepit automobile or airplane. *v.t.* [CRATED (-id), CRATING], to pack or enclose in a crate.

cra·ter (krā'tẽr), *n.* [L., mixing bowl, mouth of a volcano; Gr. *kratēr* < *kerannynai*, to mix], 1. in ancient Greece, a kind of bowl or jar. 2. the bowl-shaped cavity at the mouth of a volcano. 3. a pit resembling this, as one made by an exploding bomb. 4. [C-], in *astronomy*, a southern constellation: see **constellation**, chart.

Crater Lake, a lake in the crater of an extinct volcano in Crater Lake National Park: width, 4 mi.; length, 6 mi.; depth, 2,000 ft.

Crater Lake National Park, a national park in southwestern Oregon: area, 251 sq. mi.

Crater Mound, a huge, circular depression in central Arizona, believed to have been made by a meteorite: depth, 600 ft.; diameter, 3/4 mi.

craunch (kränch, krônch), *v.t.* & *v.i.* [earlier form of *crunch*, affected by and ? echoic extension of *crash;* early form *scranch, scraunch*, if orig., may be < MD. *schranzen*, to split up, crush], to crunch. *n.* a crunching.

cra·vat (krə-vat'), *n.* [Fr. *cravate* < *Cravate*, Croat, Croatian < G. *krawat*, dial. form of *Kroat* < Croatian *hrvat:* so applied in Fr. in reference to scarves worn by Croatian soldiers], 1. a neckcloth or scarf. 2. a necktie.

crave (krāv), *v.t.* [CRAVED (krāvd), CRAVING], [ME.

crafien, craven; AS. *crafian,* lit., to demand as right < base of *cræft,* strength, might; see CRAFT], 1. to ask for earnestly or humbly; beg. 2. to long for eagerly; desire intensely. 3. to be in great need of. ***v.i.*** to have an eager longing or intense desire (*for*). —***SYN.*** see **desire.**

cra·ven (krā'vən), ***adj.*** [ME. & OFr. *cravant;* L. *crepans,* ppr. of *crepare,* to rattle, crack, creak; ult. akin to ON. *hrafn,* raven], cowardly; abjectly afraid. ***n.*** a coward; poltroon. —***SYN.*** see **cowardly.**

cry craven, to surrender; give up.

crav·en·ette (krav'ə-net', krā'və-net'), ***n.*** [after *Craven* Street, London], 1. a finish for making certain fabrics waterproof. 2. a fabric with this finish. A trade-mark (**Cravenette**).

crav·ing (krāv'iŋ), ***n.*** [see CRAVE], intense and prolonged desire; yearning, as for food, drink, etc.

craw (krô), ***n.*** [ME. *crawe;* AS. **craga;* akin to MLG. *krage,* throat, food pipe, G. *kragen,* throat; IE. base **gwer-,* to swallow up, as also in L. *vorare,* to swallow; see DEVOUR], 1. the crop of a bird or insect; hence, 2. the stomach of any animal.

to stick in the (or **one's**) **craw,** to be unacceptable or displeasing to one.

craw·fish (krô'fish'), ***n.*** [*pl.* CRAWFISH, CRAWFISHES (-iz); see FISH], [var. of *crayfish: crawfish* is form preferred in the U. S., except among zoologists], a crayfish. ***v.i.*** [Colloq.], to withdraw from a position; back down.

Craw·ford, Francis Marion (krô'fērd), 1854–1909; American novelist.

crawl (krôl), ***v.i.*** [ME. *craulen* < ON. *krafla;* akin to G. *krabbeln;* freq. formation on Gmc. base **krab-, *kreb-,* to scratch; for IE. base see CRAB], 1. to move slowly by dragging the body along the ground, as a worm. 2. to go on hands and knees; creep. 3. to move or go slowly or feebly. 4. to swarm or teem with crawling things. 5. to feel as if insects were crawling on the skin. 6. to move or act in an abjectly servile manner. ***n.*** 1. the act of crawling; slow movement. 2. a swimming stroke in which one lies face downward, with the mouth and nose under water except when turned briefly sideward for breathing, and uses alternate overarm movements and a continuous up-and-down kick.

SYN.—**crawl,** in its strict usage, suggests movement by dragging the prone body along the ground (a snake *crawls*), and, figuratively, connotes abjectness or servility; **creep** suggests movement, often furtive, on all fours (a baby *creeps*), and, figuratively, connotes slow, stealthy, or insinuating progress.

crawl (krôl), ***n.*** [W.Ind.D. *kraal* < Sp. *corral;* see CORRAL], an enclosure made in shallow water by setting stakes vertically, used for confining fish, turtles, etc.

craw·ly (krôl'i), ***adj.*** [CRAWLIER (-i-ēr), CRAWLIEST (-i-ist)], [Colloq.], creepy.

cray·fish (krā'fish'), ***n.*** [*pl.* CRAYFISH, CRAYFISHES (-iz); see FISH], [altered, after *fish* < ME. *crevis, crevice;* OFr. *crevice* (Fr. *écrevisse*); OHG. *krebiz* (akin to *krabbo,* crab & AS. *crabba;* see CRAB)], 1. a small, fresh-water crustacean somewhat resembling a little lobster. 2. a sea shellfish resembling a lobster but without the large pincers: also called *spiny lobster.*

cray·on (krā'ən, krā'on), ***n.*** [Fr., pencil < *craie,* chalk < L. *creta,* chalk, white earth < *Creta,* Crete, where it was found], 1. a small stick of chalk, waxy material, charcoal, etc., used for drawing, coloring, or writing: it may be white or colored. 2. a drawing made with a crayon or crayons. ***v.t.*** to draw with a crayon or crayons.

craze (krāz), ***v.t.*** [CRAZED (krāzd), CRAZING], [ME. *crasen,* to crack, break; either directly < ON. or aphetic for *acrasen* < OFr. *acraser* (Fr. *écraser*) < ON.; cf. D. *krase,* to crackle, Sw. *krasa,* to break up; see CRASH, *v.*], 1. to cause to become mentally ill; make insane. 2. to produce a crackled surface or small cracks in the glaze of (pottery, porcelain, etc.). ***v.i.*** 1. to become mentally ill. 2. to become finely cracked, as the glaze of pottery. ***n.*** 1. an exaggerated enthusiasm; mania. 2. something that is temporarily the fashion; fad. 3. a little crack in the glaze or enamel, as of pottery. —***SYN.*** see **fashion.**

crazed (krāzd), ***adj.*** 1. demented; insane; crazy. 2. having little cracks in the glaze, as some pottery.

cra·zi·ly (krā'z'l-i), ***adv.*** in a crazy manner.

cra·zi·ness (krā'zi-nis), ***n.*** the quality or state of being crazy.

cra·zy (krā'zi), ***adj.*** [CRAZIER (-zi-ēr), CRAZIEST (-zi-ist)], [< *craze*], 1. unsound; cracked; flawed; shaky; rickety; hence, 2. unsound of mind; mentally unbalanced or deranged; psychopathic; insane. 3. of or fit for an insane person. 4. temporarily unbalanced, as with great excitement, rage, etc. 5. [Colloq.], very enthusiastic; very eager: as, she's *crazy* about the movies.

like crazy, [Colloq.], with furious energy, speed, etc.

crazy bone, the funny bone.

crazy quilt, a quilt made of pieces of cloth of various colors and irregular shapes and sizes.

cra·zy·weed (krā'zi-wēd'), ***n.*** the locoweed.

creak (krēk), ***v.i.*** & ***v.t.*** [ME. *creken,* to make a sound like geese, crows, etc.; echoic var. of *craken,* ‡ *croken* with development in sense as the vowel altered its quality; see CROAK], to make, cause to make, or move with a harsh, shrill, grating, or squeaking sound, as rusted hinges. ***n.*** such a sound.

creak·i·ly (krēk'ə-li), ***adv.*** in a creaky manner with a creaking sound.

creak·i·ness (krēk'i-nis), ***n.*** a creaky quality or state.

creak·y (krēk'i), ***adj.*** [CREAKIER (-i-ēr), CREAKIEST (-i-ist)], 1. apt to creak. 2. creaking.

cream (krēm), ***n.*** [ME. *creme;* OFr. *cresme;* LL. *chrisma;* see CHRISM], 1. the oily, yellowish part of milk, which rises to the top. 2. any of various foods made of cream or having a creamy consistency: as, ice *cream.* 3. a cosmetic or emulsion with a creamy consistency. 4. a thick liqueur. 5. the best or finest part of anything. 6. the color of cream; yellowish white. ***adj.*** 1. containing cream; made of cream. 2. having the consistency of cream; creamy. 3. cream-colored. ***v.i.*** 1. to form into cream or a foamy substance. 2. to form a foam or scum on top. ***v.t.*** 1. to remove the cream from. 2. to remove the best part of. 3. to add cream to. 4. to cook with cream or a cream sauce. 5. to beat into a creamy consistency; make into a creamy mixture. 6. to let (milk) form cream. 7. to separate as cream.

cream of, creamed purée of: as, *cream of* tomato soup.

cream cheese, a soft, white cheese made of cream or of milk enriched with cream.

cream-col·ored (krēm'kul'ērd), ***adj.*** yellowish-white.

cream·cups (krēm'kups'), ***n.*** [*pl.* CREAMCUPS], a plant of the poppy family, with small, creamy flowers.

cream·er (krēm'ēr), ***n.*** 1. a small pitcher for cream. 2. a device for separating cream from milk. 3. a refrigerator in which milk is put to form cream. 4. a person or thing that creams.

cream·er·y (krēm'ēr-i), ***n.*** [*pl.* CREAMERIES (-iz)], [Fr. *crèmerie;* see CREAM], 1. a place where milk and cream are pasteurized, separated, and bottled, and butter and cheese are made. 2. a shop where dairy products are sold. 3. a place where milk is put for creaming.

cream·i·ness (krēm'i-nis), ***n.*** the quality or state of being creamy.

cream of tartar, a white, acid, crystalline substance, $KHC_4H_4O_6$, used in medicine and cooking: also called *potassium bitartrate, potassium acid tartrate.*

cream puff, a round shell of pastry filled with whipped cream or custard.

cream sauce, a sauce made of butter and flour cooked together with milk or cream.

cream·y (krēm'i), ***adj.*** [CREAMIER (-i-ēr), CREAMIEST (-i-ist)], 1. full of cream; containing cream. 2. like cream in consistency or color.

crease (krēs), ***n.*** [earlier *creaste,* lit., ridge (as of mountains) < OFr. *creste;* see CREST], 1. a line or mark made by folding and pressing cloth, paper, etc.; ridge, as that pressed into men's trousers. 2. a fold; wrinkle: as, her dress was full of *creases.* 3. in *cricket,* any of the lines that mark off an area on the ground showing the station of the batsman or of the bowler. 4. in *hockey,* a rectangular area marked off by lines in front of the goal cage, which cannot be entered by attacking players except under certain special conditions. ***v.t.*** [CREASED (krēst), CREASING], 1. to fold and make a crease in. 2. to wrinkle; muss. 3. *a)* originally, to put a shot through the ridge of a horse's neck. *b)* to graze and injure slightly with a bullet. ***v.i.*** to become creased.

crease (krēs), ***n.*** a creese.

creas·y (krēs'i), ***adj.*** full of creases.

cre·ate (krē-āt', kri-āt'), ***v.t.*** [CREATED (-id), CREATING], [< L. *creatus,* pp. of *creare,* to create; IE. base **kerē-,* to grow, cause to grow], 1. to cause to come into existence; bring into being; make; originate. 2. to cause; produce; bring about; give rise to: as, an adverse public opinion was *created.* 3. to invest with a new rank, function, etc. 4. to portray (a character) effectively for the first time: said of an actor. ***adj.*** [Archaic], created.

cre·a·tin (krē'ə-tin), ***n.*** creatine.

cre·a·tine (krē'ə-tēn', krē'ə-tin), ***n.*** [< Gr. *kreas,* flesh; + *-ine*], a white, crystalline substance, an alkaloid or amino acid, $C_4H_9N_3O_2$, present chiefly in the muscle tissue of vertebrates.

cre·a·tion (krē-ā'shən, kri-ā'shən), ***n.*** [ME. *creacion* < OFr. or L.; OFr. *creation* < L. *creatio*], 1. a creating or being created. 2. the universe and everything in it; all the world. 3. anything created; especially, something original created by the imagination; invention.

the Creation, in *theology,* God's creating of the world.

cre·a·tion·ism (krē-ā'shən-iz'm, kri-ā'shən-iz'm), ***n.*** in *theology,* 1. the doctrine that God creates a new soul for every human being born. 2. the doctrine that ascribes the origin of matter and of distinct species of animals and plants to acts of creation by God.

cre·a·tion·ist (krē-ā'shən-ist, kri-ā'shən-ist), ***n.*** a person who believes in creationism.

cre·a·tive (krē-ā′tiv, kri-ā′tiv), *adj.* 1. creating or able to create. 2. productive (*of*); inventive.
cre·a·tor (krē-ā′tẽr, kri-ā′tẽr), *n.* [ME. & Anglo-Fr. *creatour;* L. *creator*], 1. a person or, sometimes, a thing that creates. 2. [C-], God; the Supreme Being.
crea·tur·al (krē′chẽr-əl), *adj.* of, or having the nature of, a creature or creatures.
crea·ture (krē′chẽr), *n.* [ME.; OFr.; L. *creatura*], 1. anything created, animate or inanimate. 2. an animate or living being; especially, *a*) a cow, horse, or other animal. *b*) a human being: often used in a patronizing, contemptuous, commiserating, or endearing sense. 3. a person completely dominated by, dependent on, or owing his success, position, etc. to, another.
the creature, whisky or other intoxicating liquor: humorous usage.
creature comfort, anything providing bodily comfort, as food, clothing, or shelter.
crea·ture·ly (krē′chẽr-li), *adj.* creatural.
crèche (krāsh, kresh), *n.* [Fr. < Frank. **kripja* (G. *krippe*), crib; cf. CRATCH, CRIB], 1. a miniature representation of the stable in which Jesus was born, with figures of the infant Jesus, Mary, Joseph, the Magi, etc. 2. a hospital for foundlings. 3. a public nursery where mothers who work can leave their children during the day; day nursery.
Cré·cy (krā′sē′; Eng. kres′i), *n.* a town in northern France: scene of an English victory (1346) over the French: English name, *Cressy.*
cre·dence (krē′d'ns), *n.* [ME.; OFr.; ML. *credentia* < L. *credens,* ppr. of *credere;* see CREED], 1. belief, especially in the reports or testimony of another: as, give no *credence* to rumors. 2. credential: as, a letter of *credence.* 3. in *ecclesiastical usage,* a small table at the side of the communion table, on which the bread and wine are placed before consecration. —*SYN.* see **belief.**
cre·den·da (kri-den′də), *n.pl.* [*sing.* CREDENDUM (-dəm)], [L., pl. of gerundive of *credere;* see CREED], doctrines to be believed; matters of faith.
cre·dent (krē′d'nt), *adj.* 1. believing; giving credence. 2. [Obs.], credible.
cre·den·tial (kri-den′shəl), *adj.* [ML. *credentia* (see CREDENCE); + *-al*], [Rare], entitling to credit, confidence, etc.; accrediting. *n.* 1. that which entitles to credit, confidence, etc. 2. *usually in pl.* a letter or certificate given to a person to show that he has a right to confidence or to the exercise of a certain position or authority.
cre·den·za (kri-den′zə; It. kre-den′tsä), *n.* [*pl.* CREDENZAS (-zəz); It. CREDENZE (-tse)], [It., a credence (sense 3)], a type of buffet, or sideboard.
cred·i·bil·i·ty (kred′ə-bil′ə-ti), *n.* [L. *credibilitas*], the quality or state of being credible.
cred·i·ble (kred′ə-b'l), *adj.* [L. *credibilis* < *credere;* see CREED], that can be believed; worthy of belief or trust; trustworthy; reliable. —*SYN.* see **plausible.**
cred·i·bly (kred′ə-bli), *adv.* in a credible manner.
cred·it (kred′it), *n.* [Fr. *crédit;* It. *credito;* L. *creditus,* pp. of *credere;* see CREED], 1. belief; confidence; trust; faith. 2. the quality of being credible or trustworthy. 3. the favorable estimate of a person's character; reputation; good name. 4. praise or approval to which a person or thing is entitled; commendation: as, he deserves *credit* for telling the truth. 5. a person or thing bringing approval or honor: as, he is a *credit* to the team. 6. *usually pl.* acknowledgment of work done, as in the preparation of a motion picture. 7. the amount of money remaining in a person's account in a bank, etc. 8. in *accounting,* *a*) the acknowledgment of payment on a debt by entry of the amount in an account. *b*) the right-hand side of an account, where such amounts are entered. *c*) an entry on this side. *d*) the sum of such entries. 9. in *business,* *a*) trust in one's integrity in money matters and in one's ability to meet payments when due. *b*) the time allowed for payment. 10. in *education,* *a*) the certification of a student's successful completion of a unit or course of study. *b*) a unit of work so certified. *v.t.* 1. to believe; trust; have confidence or faith in. 2. to bring approval or honor to. 3. to give deserved commendation for. 4. to give credit in a bank account, etc. 5. in *accounting,* to enter on the credit side. 6. in *education,* to enter a credit or credits on the record of (a student). Abbreviated **cr.** —*SYN.* see **ascribe.**
credit one with, to believe that one has; ascribe to one.
credit to one, to believe that one has.
do credit to, to bring approval or honor to.
give credit to, 1. to believe; have confidence or trust in. 2. to commend.
give one credit for, 1. to commend one for. 2. to believe that one has.
on credit, with the agreement that payment will be made at a future date.
to one's credit, bringing approval or honor to one.
cred·it·a·ble (kred′it-ə-b'l), *adj.* bringing approval or honor; deserving commendation; praiseworthy.
cred·it·a·bly (kred′it-ə-bli), *adv.* in a creditable manner.
credit line, an acknowledgment of work done or a contribution made, as in a newspaper or motion picture.
cred·i·tor (kred′i-tẽr), *n.* [Fr. *créditeur;* L. *creditor;* see CREDIT], 1. a person to whom another or others are indebted. 2. in *bookkeeping,* *a*) the credit side of an account. *b*) any entry on this side: abbreviated **cr.**
credit standing, reputation for paying bills, etc.
credit union, a co-operative association for pooling savings of members and making loans to them at a low rate of interest.
cre·do (krē′dō, krā′dō), *n.* [*pl.* CREDOS (-dōz)], [L., I believe; see CREED], 1. a creed. 2. [usually C-], *a*) the Apostles' Creed or the Nicene Creed, both of which begin with *credo.* *b*) the music for either of these.
cre·du·li·ty (krə-dōō′lə-ti, krə-dū′lə-ti), *n.* [*pl.* CREDULITIES (-tiz)], [L. *credulitas* < *credulus;* see CREDULOUS], a tendency to believe too readily; lack of doubt or skepticism.
cred·u·lous (krej′oo-ləs), *adj.* [L. *credulus* < *credere;* see CREED], tending to believe too readily; easily convinced.
Cree (krē), *n.* [*pl.* CREE, CREES (krēz)], [< Am. Ind. (Algonquian) name], 1. a member of a tribe of Algonquian Indians who lived in an area extending from the southern end of Hudson Bay to northern Alberta, Canada. 2. the language of this tribe.
creed (krēd), *n.* [ME. *crede;* AS. *creda;* L. *credo,* lit., I believe (< *credere,* to trust, believe; prob. < IE. base **kred-,* heart + **dhē,* to place, do): so used from being first word of the Apostles' and Nicene Creeds], 1. a brief statement of religious belief; confession of faith. 2. a specific statement of this kind, accepted as authoritative by a church; especially, the Apostles' Creed, the Nicene Creed, or the Athanasian Creed. 3. a statement of belief, principles, or opinions on any subject.
the Creed, the Apostles' Creed.
Creek (krēk), *n.* [? < *creek* (with reference to the many creeks in the tribal territory)], 1. an American Indian of any of several tribes, mainly Muskhogean, now living in Oklahoma. 2. an Indian of the Creek Confederacy or the Creek Nation. 3. the Muskhogean language of the Creeks.
creek (krēk, krik), *n.* [ME. (rare) *creke* (whence mod. pronun. *krēk*), (common) *crike* (whence pronun. *krik*) < ON. *kriki,* a winding, hence winding inlet; akin to D. *kreek,* bay; IE. base as in *crank* (handle)], 1. a small stream, somewhat larger than a brook. 2. a narrow inlet or bay. Abbreviated **cr.**
Creek Confederacy, a former tribal league of Muskhogean Indians in Georgia and Alabama.
Creek Nation, a former semiautonomous league of Indian tribes set up by the Creeks in the Indian Territory.
creel (krēl), *n.* [ME. *crelle;* MFr. *crille,* dial. var. of *grille;* see GRILL], 1. a wicker basket for holding fish: creels are often worn on the back by fishermen. 2. a basketlike cage for trapping fish, shellfish, etc. 3. in *spinning,* a frame for holding the bobbins.
creep (krēp), *v.i.* [CREPT (krept), CREEPING], [ME. *crepen;* AS. *creopan,* to creep, lit., go bent down; akin to Sw. *krypa;* IE. base **ger-,* to twist, turn; cf. CRIPPLE], 1. to move along with the body close to the ground, as on hands and knees. 2. to move slowly. 3. to move stealthily, timidly, or furtively. 4. to come on gradually and almost unnoticed (often with *up*). 5. to cringe; fawn. 6. to grow along the ground or a wall, as some plants. 7. to feel as if insects were creeping on one's skin. 8. to slip slightly out of position. *n.* 1. the act of creeping. 2. a creeping movement. 3. [Slang], a person who inspires a mild feeling of fear or repugnance. —*SYN.* see **crawl.**
make one's flesh creep, to cause one to feel fear, repugnance, etc. as if insects were creeping on one's skin.
the creeps, [Colloq.], a feeling of fear, repugnance, etc. as if insects were creeping on one's skin.
creep·er (krēp′ẽr), *n.* 1. a person, animal, or thing that creeps. 2. any plant whose stem puts out tendrils or rootlets by which it can creep along a surface as it grows. 3. any of various small birds that creep on trees and bushes looking for insects, larvae, etc. to eat, as the American brown creeper, certain warblers, etc. 4. a device with metal hooks for dragging the bottom of a lake, pond, etc.; grapnel. 5. *usually pl.* a metal plate with spikes, fastened to a shoe to prevent slipping. 6. any device for carrying material to or from a machine, or from one part of a machine to another. 7. *pl.* a baby's one-piece garment, combining pants and waist.
creep·ie (krēp′i, krip′i), *n.* [< *creep, v.*], [British Dial.], a low stool.
creep·i·ness (krēp′i-nis), *n.* a creepy quality or state.
creeping bent grass, any of a large group of low-growing grasses, including some lawn and pasture varieties, that root along the stem.
creep·y (krēp′i), *adj.* [CREEPIER (-i-ẽr), CREEPIEST (-i-ist)], 1. creeping; moving slowly. 2. having a feeling of fear, horror, or repugnance, as if insects were creeping on one's skin. 3. tending to produce such a feeling.
creese (krēs), *n.* [Malay *kris*], a dagger with a wavy blade, used by Malays: also spelled **crease, cris, kris.**
creesh (krēsh), *n.* & *v.t.* [< OFr. *cresse, craisse, n.* < L. *crassa,* fem. of *crassus;* see CRASS], [Scot.], grease.
Cre·feld (krā′felt), *n.* Krefeld-Ürdingen, Germany.

cre·mate (krē′māt, kri-māt′), *v.t.* [CREMATED (-id), CREMATING], [< L. *crematus*, pp. of *cremare*, to burn; IE. base **ker-*, to burn; akin to L. *carbo*, coal], 1. to burn up; consume by fire. 2. to burn (a dead body) to ashes.
cre·ma·tion (kri-mā′shən), *n.* [L. *crematio*], the act or process of cremating; burning a dead body to ashes.
cre·ma·tion·ist (kri-mā′shən-ist), *n.* a person who advocates cremation in preference to burial.
cre·ma·tor (krē′mā-tẽr, kri-mā′tẽr), *n.* [LL.], 1. a person who cremates. 2. a furnace for cremating dead bodies. 3. an incinerator for garbage, trash, etc.
cre·ma·to·ri·um (krē′mə-tôr′i-əm, krem′ə-tō′ri-əm), *n.* [Mod. L.], [Chiefly British], a crematory.
cre·ma·to·ry (krē′mə-tôr′i, krem′ə-tō′ri), *n.* [*pl.* CREMATORIES (-iz, -riz)], [Mod. L. *crematorium*], 1. a furnace for cremating dead bodies. 2. a building with such a furnace in it. *adj.* of or for cremation.
‡**crème** (krem), *n.* [Fr.], 1. cream. 2. a thick liqueur.
crème de ca·ca·o (krem′ də kə-kā′ō, kə-kä′ō), [Fr., lit., cream of cocoa], a sweet liqueur with a chocolate flavor.
‡**crème de la crème** (krem′ də lȧ′ krem′), [Fr., lit., cream of the cream], the very best (of something).
crème de menthe (krem′ də mänt′), [Fr., lit., cream of mint], a sweet, greenish liqueur flavored with mint.
Cre·mo·na (kri-mō′nə; It. kre-mô′nä), *n.* 1. a city in northern Italy, on the Po River: pop., 70,000 (1947). 2. any of the famous violins formerly made in Cremona, especially by Nicola Amati (1596–1684) or a member of his family, his pupil Antonio Stradivari (1644–1737), or Guiseppe Guarneri (1683–1745).
cre·nate (krē′nāt), *adj.* [Mod. L. *crenatus* < LL. *crena*, a notch, groove], in *botany*, having a notched or scalloped edge, as certain leaves: see **leaf**, illus.
cre·nat·ed (krē′nā-tid), *adj.* crenate.
cre·na·tion (kri-nā′shən), *n.* 1. the condition of being crenate. 2. a crenate formation.
cren·a·ture (kren′ə-chẽr, krē′nə-chẽr), *n.* 1. a rounded projection on the margin of a leaf, etc. 2. a notch between such projections.
cre·nel (kren′′l), *n.* [OFr., dim. < LL. *crena*, a notch, groove], an indentation or loophole in the top of a battlement or wall; embrasure: also **crenelle.** *v.t.* [CRENELED or CRENELLED (-′ld), CRENELING or CRENELLING], to crenelate.
cren·el·ate, cren·el·late (kren′′l-āt′), *v.t.* [CRENELATED or CRENELLATED (-id), CRENELATING or CRENELLATING], [Fr. *créneler* (< OFr. *crenel*; see CRENEL); + *-ate*], to furnish with battlements or crenels.
cren·el·a·tion, cren·el·la·tion (kren′′l-ā′shən), *n.* 1. a crenelating or being crenelated. 2. a battlement; crenelated structure.
cre·nelle (kri-nel′), *n.* a crenel.
cren·u·late (kren′yoo-lit, kren′yoo-lāt′), *adj.* [Mod. L. *crenulatus* < *crenula*, dim. < LL. *crena*, a notch, groove], having tiny notches or scallops, as some leaves or shells.
cren·u·lat·ed (kren′yoo-lā′tid), *adj.* crenulate.
cren·u·la·tion (kren′yoo-lā′shən), *n.* [see CRENULATE], 1. a tiny notch or scallop. 2. the condition of having tiny notches or scallops.
cre·o·dont (krē′ə-dont′), *n.* [< Mod. L. *Creodonta*, *pl.* < Gr. *kreas*, flesh + *odous*, tooth], any of a group of primitive, flesh-eating mammals with small brains.
Cre·ole (krē′ōl), *n.* [Fr. *créole* < Port. *crioulo* & Sp. *criollo*, native (of a tropic dependency); assumed to be for Sp. *criadillo*, nurseling, dim. of *criado*, lit., created < *criar;* L. *creare*, to create, produce; cf. CREATE], 1. originally, a native, especially of the West Indies, Central America, tropical South America, the Gulf States, or Mauritius, of nonnative descent; hence, 2. a person of French or Spanish descent born in the Americas. 3. [c-], a person of Negro descent born in the Americas: usually **creole Negro.** 4. a person descended from or culturally related to the original French settlers of Louisiana and New Orleans; hence, 5. French as spoken by such people: distinguished from *Cajun.* 6. loosely, anyone from Louisiana. 7. a person descended from or culturally related to original Spanish settlers in the Gulf States, especially Texas. 8. [c-], loosely, a person of mixed Creole and Negro stock. 9. [< Sp. *criollo*], in parts of tropical South America, the child of a white father and a mestiza mother. *adj.* 1. designating, of, or characteristic of, a Creole or Creoles. 2. [c-], designating, of, or characteristic of, a creole or creoles. 3. of Creole.
cre·ol·ized language (krē′ə-līzd′), [< *Creole*], the form of mixed language (e.g., Gullah) that develops when speakers of mutually unintelligible languages remain in persistent, long-lasting, and thorough contact with each other: distinguished from *pidgin languages.*
Cre·on (krē′on), *n.* [Gr. *Kreōn*], in *Greek legend*, the King of Thebes who had his niece Antigone buried alive because she disobeyed him by performing funeral rites over the body of her brother Polynices.
cre·o·sol (krē′ə-sōl′, krē′ə-sol′), *n.* [*creosote* + *-ol*], a colorless, pungent, oily liquid, $C_8H_{10}O_2$, obtained from beechwood tar and the resin guaiacum: it is used as an antiseptic.
cre·o·sote (krē′ə-sōt′), *n.* [< Gr. *kreas* (genit. *kreōs*), flesh + *sōzein*, to save, preserve], a transparent, oily liquid with a pungent odor, obtained by the distillation of wood tar or coal tar: it is used as an antiseptic and as a preservative for wood. *v.t.* [CREOSOTED (-id), CREOSOTING], to treat (wood, etc.) with creosote.
creosote bush, an evergreen shrub with a pungent odor, found in northern Mexico and the southwestern United States.
crepe, crêpe (krāp), *n.* [Fr. *crêpe* < L. *crispa;* see CRISP], 1. a thin, crinkled cloth of silk, rayon, cotton, wool, etc.; crape. 2. a piece of black crepe as a sign of mourning, often in the form of a band worn around the arm: usually spelled **crape.** 3. thin paper crinkled like crepe: also **crepe paper.**
crepe de Chine (krāp′ də shēn′), [Fr., lit., crepe of China], a soft, rather thin silk crepe, used for women's blouses, etc.
crêpes su·zette (krep′ soo-zet′), [Fr.; *crêpe*, pancake, crepe (see CREPE) + *Suzette*, dim. of *Suzanne*], very thin pancakes rolled up and sprinkled with sugar, sometimes served with a flaming brandy sauce.
crep·i·tant (krep′ə-tənt), *adj.* [L. *crepitans*, ppr. of *crepitare;* see CREPITATE], crackling; rattling.
crep·i·tate (krep′ə-tāt′), *v.i.* [CREPITATED (-id), CREPITATING], [L. *crepitare*, freq. of *crepare;* see CRAVEN], to make slight, sharp, and repeated crackling sounds; crackle; rattle.
crep·i·ta·tion (krep′ə-tā′shən), *n.* a crepitating.
crept (krept), past tense and past participle of **creep.**
cre·pus·cle (kri-pus′′l), *n.* [L. *crepusculum* < *creper*, dark], twilight; dusk.
cre·pus·cu·lar (kri-pus′kyoo-lẽr), *adj.* [see prec.], 1. of or like twilight; dim; glimmering; obscure. 2. appearing, flying, or becoming active at twilight or just before sunrise: as, *crepuscular* insects.
cre·pus·cule (kri-pus′kūl), *n.* [Fr. *crépuscule*], crepuscle.
cre·scen·do (krə-shen′dō, krə-sen′dō), *adj. & adv.* [It. < *crescere;* see CRESCENT], in *music*, gradually increasing in loudness or intensity: abbreviated **cresc., cres.** or indicated by the sign <. *n.* [*pl.* CRESCENDOS (-dōz)], in *music*, 1. a gradual increase in loudness or intensity. 2. a passage played crescendo.
cres·cent (kres′′nt), *n.* [Latinized sp. (cf. L. *crescens*) of ME. *cressant;* OFr. *creissant*, ppr. of *creistre*, to increase; L. *crescere*, to come forth, grow; akin to *creare;* see CREATE], 1. the moon in its first or last quarter, when it appears to have one concave edge and one convex edge. 2. the shape of the moon in either of these phases. 3. anything shaped more or less like this, as a curved row of houses. 4. the emblem of Turkey; hence, 5. *a)* Turkish power. *b)* Moslem power. *adj.* 1. [Poetic], increasing; growing. 2. shaped like the moon in its first or last quarter.
cres·cive (kres′iv), *adj.* [L. *crescere* (see CRESCENT); + *-ive*], [Rare], growing; increasing.
cre·sol (krē′sōl, krē′sol), *n.* [*creosote* + *-ol*], any of three isomeric, colorless, oily liquids or solids with the formula C_7H_8O, prepared by the fractional distillation of coal tar and used in the preparation of disinfectants, fumigating compounds, and dyestuffs.
cress (kres), *n.* [ME. *cres, cerse;* AS. *cresse, cerse*, lit., creeper; akin to G. *kresse*, cress, OHG. *kresan*, to creep; IE. base as in *creep*], any of various plants of the mustard family, as water cress, the pungent leaves of which are used in salads and as garnishes.
cres·set (kres′it), *n.* [ME.; OFr. *cresset, craisset* < *craisse;* see GREASE], a metal container for burning oil, wood, etc., fastened to a pole, wall, etc., and used as a torch or lantern.
Cres·si·da (kres′i-də), *n.* in *medieval legend*, a Trojan woman who was unfaithful to her lover, Troilus: the legend is the source of Shakespeare's *Troilus and Cressida:* also spelled **Criseyde** (in Chaucer).
Cres·sy (kres′i), *n.* Crécy: the English name.
crest (krest), *n.* [ME. & OFr. *creste*, orig., a ridge; L. *crista;* IE. base **ker-*, highest part of the body, head, horn; akin to ON. *hrista*, to shake], 1. any process or growth on the head of an animal, as a comb or feathered tuft on the heads of certain fowls and birds. 2. a plume of feathers, or an emblem or decoration, formerly worn on a helmet; hence, 3. a helmet. 4. a heraldic device placed above the shield in a coat of arms, and used separately on seals, silverware, note paper, etc. 5. the top of anything, or the line or surface along the top; summit; ridge: as, the *crest* of a wave, a mountain *crest.* 6. *a)* the ridge of the neck of a horse, lion, etc. *b)* the mane growing on this. 7. a projecting ridge along a bone. 8. [Archaic], courage or pride. *v.t.* 1. to provide or decorate with a crest. 2. to lie at the top of; crown. 3. to reach the crest of. *v.i.* to form a crest, as a wave.
crest·ed (kres′tid), *adj.* having a crest.

crested flycatcher, any of various crested birds that catch insects in flight.
crest·fall·en (krest′fôl″n), *adj.* 1. with drooping crest or bowed head; hence, 2. dejected; disheartened.
crest·ing (kres′tiŋ), *n.* an ornamental ridging on a wall, roof, etc.
cre·syl·ic (kri-sil′ik), *adj.* [< *cresol* + *-yl* + *-ic*], of or from cresol or creosote.
cre·ta·ceous (kri-tā′shəs), *adj.* [L. *cretaceus* < *creta;* see CRAYON], 1. containing, composed of, or having the nature of, chalk. 2. [C-], designating or of the third geological period, following the Jurassic, in the Mesozoic Era: it is marked by the dying out of toothed birds and dinosaurs, the development of early mammals and flowering plants, and the deposit of chalk beds.
the Cretaceous, the Cretaceous Period or its rocks: see **geology,** chart.
Cre·tan (krē′t′n), *adj.* of Crete, its people, or culture. *n.* a native or inhabitant of Crete.
Crete (krēt), *n.* Greek island in eastern Mediterranean: area, 3,199 sq. mi.; pop., 386,000: also called *Candia.*
cre·tin (krē′tin), *n.* [Fr. *crétin,* dial. form of *chrétien;* lit., Christian, hence human being (in contrast to brutes) < L. *Christianus;* see CHRISTIAN; sense development as in *silly*], a person suffering from cretinism.
cre·tin·ism (krē′tin-iz′m, krē′t′n-iz′m), *n.* [Fr. *crétinisme;* see CRETIN], a congenital deficiency of thyroid secretion with resulting deformity and idiocy.
cre·tin·ous (krē′tin-əs, krē′t′n-əs), *adj.* 1. of or like a cretin. 2. having cretinism.
cre·tonne (kri-ton′, krē′ton), *n.* [Fr. < *Creton,* village in Normandy], a heavy, unglazed cotton or linen cloth with patterns printed in colors on one or both sides: used for curtains, chair covers, etc.
Cre·ü·sa (krē-ōō′sə), *n.* in *Greek legend,* 1. the bride of Jason, killed by the sorcery of the jealous Medea. 2. the wife of Aeneas and daughter of Priam, lost in the flight from captured Troy.
cre·vasse (krə-vas′), *n.* [Fr.; see CREVICE], 1. a deep crack; fissure, especially in a glacier. 2. a break in the levee of a river, dike, etc. *v.t.* [CREVASSED (-vast′), CREVASSING], to make a crevasse or crevasses in.
crev·ice (krev′is), *n.* [ME. & OFr. *crevace;* LL. **crepacia, crepatia,* a crack < L. *crepare;* see CRAVEN], a narrow opening caused by a crack or split; fissure; cleft; chink.
crev·iced (krev′ist), *adj.* containing a crevice or crevices.
crew (krōō), *n.* [OFr. *creue,* increase, growth < pp. of *creistre* (Fr. *croître*), to grow < L. *crescere* (see CRESCENT); prob. in part < OFr. *accrue, accreue;* see ACCRUE], 1. a group of people associating together; company. 2. a group of people working together, usually under the direction of a foreman or leader: as, a road *crew,* gun *crew.* 3. all the men working on a ship, aircraft, etc. 4. all of a ship's personnel except the officers. 5. a group; set; crowd; gang; mob: as, the arrested men were a dangerous *crew.* 6. a rowing team, usually of eight men. 7. the sport of rowing in races (at colleges, etc.).
crew (krōō), alternative past tense of **crow** (sense 1).
crew cut, a style of man's haircut in which the hair is cropped close to the head.
crew·el (krōō′əl), *n.* [Late ME. *crule;* prob. via MLG. or MD. < IE. **greu-* (extension of **ger-,* to twist, turn, bend), as in MLG. *krouel* (G. *kräuel*), bent-pronged fork; cf. CRULLER], a loosely twisted, worsted yarn used in fancywork and embroidery.
crew·el·work (krōō′əl-wũrk′), *n.* work done with crewels; embroidery with a design worked in worsted on a cloth background.
crib (krib), *n.* [ME. *cribbe;* AS. *cribb* (also *cryb*), ox stall, couch; akin to G. *krippe;* basic sense "what is woven or plaited, basket"; IE. **ger-bh,* determined form of **ger-,* to turn, twist, plait; cf. CRATCH, CRÈCHE; senses of "steal," etc. < thieves' slang < orig. sense "to basket"; *n.* 4 from Biblical application of sense 1], 1. a rack, trough, or box for fodder; manger. 2. a stall for cattle, oxen, etc. 3. a small, crude house or room. 4. a small bed for a baby, with high sides and ends to keep him from falling out. 5. a framework of wooden or metal bars for support or strengthening, as in a mine. 6. a wooden framework or enclosure for storing grain, salt, etc. 7. [Colloq.], the act of passing off another's ideas or writings as one's own; plagiarism. 8. [Colloq.], *a)* a literal translation of a literary work in a foreign language, used in doing schoolwork, often dishonestly. *b)* notes or similar aids dishonestly used in doing schoolwork. 9. in *cribbage,* the discarded cards used by the dealer in scoring his points. *v.t.* [CRIBBED (kribd), CRIBBING], 1. to shut up in or as in a crib; confine. 2. to furnish with a crib or cribs. 3. [Colloq.], to pass off (another's ideas or writings) as one's own; plagiarize. 4. [Colloq.], to steal. *v.i.* [Colloq.], to do schoolwork dishonestly by using a crib.
crib·bage (krib′ij), *n.* [< *crib* + *-age*], a card game for two, three, or four players, in which the object is to form various combinations that count for points: the score is kept on a small board with rows of holes into which pegs are inserted.
crib·ber (krib′ẽr), *n.* 1. a person who cribs. 2. a horse characterized by crib biting.
crib·bing (krib′iŋ), *n.* [see CRIB], 1. the action of one that cribs. 2. something cribbed. 3. a framework of timber lining a shaft in a mine. 4. crib biting.
crib-bite (krib′bīt′), *v.t.* [for prin. pts. see BITE], to practice crib biting, as some horses.
crib biting, a habit that some horses have of biting the feeding trough and at the same time swallowing air.
crib·ri·form (krib′ri-fôrm′), *adj.* [< L. *cribrum,* sieve; + *-form*], perforated like a sieve.
crib·work (krib′wũrk′), *n.* the framework of a crib, consisting of layers of beams, logs, etc. built up one above another, each layer having its beams or logs at right angles to those of the layer immediately below.
crick (krik), *n.* [Late ME. *crykke;* prob. < ON.; basic sense prob. "twist"; cf. CREEK, CROOK], a painful muscle spasm or cramp in the neck, back, etc. *v.t.* to cause a crick in.
crick·et (krik′it), *n.* [ME. *criket;* OFr. *criquet* < *criquer,* to creak; of echoic origin; cf. D. *krekel,* Fr. *cri-cri*], any of a large group of leaping insects related to the locusts and grasshoppers but usually having long antennae: the males produce a characteristic chirping noise by rubbing parts of the forewings together.

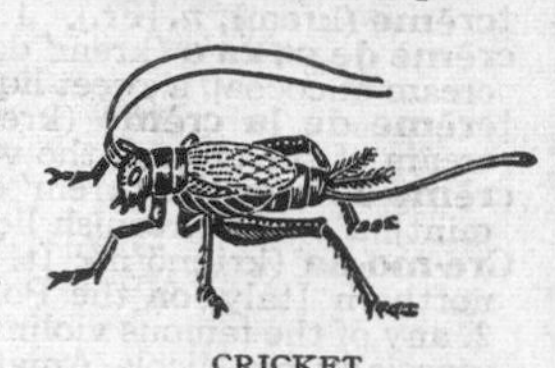
CRICKET

crick·et (krik′it), *n.* [OFr. *criquet,* a stake or bat in a ball game; prob. dim. of MD. *cricke,* a stick, staff; akin to Eng. *crutch*], 1. an outdoor game played by two teams of eleven men each, in which a ball, bats, and wickets are used: one of the most popular sports in England. 2. [Colloq.], fair play; sportsmanship. *v.i.* to play cricket.
crick·et (krik′it), *n.* [< ?], a wooden footstool.
crick·et·er (krik′it-ẽr), *n.* a person who plays cricket.
cri·coid (krī′koid), *adj.* [< Gr. *krikos,* ring; + *-oid*], designating or of the ring-shaped cartilage forming the lower part of the larynx.
cried (krīd), past tense and past participle of **cry.**
cri·er (krī′ẽr), *n.* 1. a person who cries. 2. a person who shouts out announcements of news, court orders, etc.: as, town *criers* were formerly common in New England. 3. a person who shouts out announcements about his wares.
Crile, George Washington (krīl), 1864–1943; American surgeon.
crime (krīm), *n.* [ME. & OFr.; L. *crimen,* verdict, object of reproach, offense; IE. base *(*s*)*qrei-,* extension of **ker-,* echoic for hoarse, rough sounds (hence, orig., cry for help, cry of the offended one); akin to AS. *hream,* outcry, lamentation, Eng. *scream*], 1. an act committed in violation of a law prohibiting it, or omitted in violation of a law ordering it: crimes are variously punishable by death, imprisonment, or the imposition of certain fines or restrictions. 2. extreme violation of the law; wrongdoing of a criminal nature, as felony or treason, which affects the whole public and not just the rights of an individual: distinguished from *misdemeanor.* 3. an offense against morality; sin. 4. the acts of criminals; habitual violation of the law.
Cri·me·a (krī-mē′ə, kri-mē′ə), *n.* a peninsula in Soviet Russia, extending into the Black Sea.
Cri·me·an (krī-mē′ən, kri-mē′ən), *adj.* of the Crimea.
Crimean Autonomous Soviet Socialist Republic, a former division of the R.S.F.S.R., in the Crimea: area, 10,036 sq. mi.; pop., 1,184,000: abolished in 1945; incorporated into Ukrainian S. S. R. in 1954.

CRIMEA

Crimean War, a war (1854–1856) over the domination of southeastern Europe, in which England, France, Turkey, and Sardinia defeated Russia.
crim·i·nal (krim′ə-n′l), *adj.* [< Fr. or LL.; Fr. *criminel;* LL. *criminalis* < L. *crimen;* see CRIME], 1. having the nature of crime; wrong; immoral. 2. involving or relating to crime. 3. guilty of crime. *n.* a person guilty of, or legally convicted of, a crime. Abbreviated **crim.**
criminal conversation, adultery: abbreviated **crim. con.**
crim·i·nal·i·ty (krim′ə-nal′ə-ti), *n.* 1. the quality, state, or fact of being criminal, or of being guilty of crime. 2. [*pl.* CRIMINALITIES (-tiz)], a criminal action.
crim·i·nal·ly (krim′ə-n′l-i), *adv.* 1. in a criminal manner. 2. according to criminal law.
crim·i·nate (krim′ə-nāt′), *v.t.* [CRIMINATED (-id),

CRIMINATING], [< L. *criminatus*, pp. of *criminari* < *crimen;* see CRIME], 1. to accuse of a crime or crimes. 2. to give proof of the guilt of; incriminate. 3. to condemn; censure.
crim·i·na·tion (krim'ə-nā'shən), *n.* the act of criminating; accusation.
crim·i·na·tive (krim'ə-nā'tiv), *adj.* criminatory.
crim·i·na·to·ry (krim'ə-nə-tôr'i, krim'ə-nə-tō'ri), *adj.* criminating or involving crimination; accusatory.
crim·i·no·log·i·cal (krim'ə-nə-loj'i-k'l), *adj.* of criminology.
crim·in·o·log·i·cal·ly (krim'ə-nə-loj'i-k'l-i), *adv.* by or according to criminology.
crim·i·nol·o·gist (krim'ə-nol'ə-jist), *n.* an expert in criminology.
crim·i·nol·o·gy (krim'ə-nol'ə-ji), *n.* [< L. *crimen, criminis* (see CRIME); + *-logy*], the scientific study and investigation of crime and criminals.
crim·mer (krim'ẽr), *n.* krimmer, a kind of fur.
crimp (krimp), *v.t.* [< MD. *crimpen*, to draw together, contract, wrinkle; akin to *cramp, v.*], 1. to press into narrow, regular folds; pleat. 2. to make (hair, etc.) wavy or curly. 3. to gash (the flesh of a fish, etc.) so as to make the muscles contract and stay firm in cooking. 4. to mold (leather for shoe uppers) into shape. *n.* 1. a crimping. 2. anything crimped; pleat or series of pleats. 3. *usually pl.* crimped hair.
put a crimp in, [Slang], to obstruct; hinder.
crimp (krimp), *n.* [< *crimp* (to pleat); prob. via 17th-c. game of cards], a person who gets men to serve as sailors or soldiers by force or trickery. *v.t.* to get (men) to serve as sailors or soldiers by force or trickery.
crim·ple (krim'p'l), *v.t. & v.i.* [CRIMPLED (-p'ld), CRIMPLING], [prob. freq. of *crimp* (to pleat)], to wrinkle; crinkle; crumple.
crimp·y (krimp'i), *adj.* [CRIMPIER (-i-ẽr), CRIMPIEST (-i-ist)], [< *crimp* (pleat)], having small folds; curly; wavy; frizzly: as, *crimpy* hair.
crim·son (krim'z'n), *n.* [ME. *crimosine;* prob. via OSp. *cremesin* < Ar. *qirmiz*, kermes, cochineal insect < Sans. *kṛmi*, worm, insect], 1. deep red. 2. deep-red coloring matter. *adj.* 1. deep-red. 2. bloody. *v.t. & v.i.* to make or become crimson.
crimson clover, a plant of the pea family, with dark-red flower heads: used in scientific farming to enrich the soil for crop rotation.
cringe (krinj), *v.i.* [CRINGED (krinjd), CRINGING], [ME. *crengen* (with nasalized vowel as in *hinge*), caus. < AS. *cringan*, to fall (in battle, etc.), lit., to bend over in death agony; IE. base as in *crank* (handle)], 1. to draw back, bend, crouch, etc., as when afraid; shrink from something dangerous or painful; cower. 2. to act in a timid, servile manner; fawn. *n.* a cringing.
crin·gle (kriŋ'g'l), *n.* [< D. or LG. *kringel*, dim. of *kring*, a circle; IE. base as in *crank* (handle)], a small ring or loop of rope or metal on the edge of a sail, through which a rope may be run for fastening the sail.
cri·nite (krī'nīt), *adj.* [L. *crinitus*, pp. of *crinire*, to provide with hair < *crinis*, hair; akin to L. *crista* (see CREST)], 1. hairy. 2. having a hairy or hairlike tail.
cri·nite (krī'nīt, krin'īt), *n.* [*crinoid* + *-ite*], a fossil crinoid.
crin·kle (kriŋ'k'l), *v.i. & v.t.* [CRINKLED (-k'ld), CRINKLING], [ME. *crenklen, crynklen* < AS. *crincan*, var. of *cringan* (cf. CRINGE) + *-le*, freq. suffix], 1. to be or cause to be undulated; wrinkle; ripple. 2. to rustle, as paper when crushed. *n.* an undulation; wrinkle; ripple.
crin·kle·root (kriŋ'k'l-ro͞ot', kriŋ'k'l-root'), *n.* a plant with small, white or lilac-colored flowers and a white, tuberous, strong-smelling rootstock.
crin·kly (kriŋ'kli), *adj.* [CRINKLIER (-kli-ẽr), CRINKLIEST (-kli-ist)], full of crinkles; wrinkled; ripply; wavy.
crin·kum-cran·kum (kriŋ'kəm-kraŋ'kəm), *n.* [redupl. of *crank*], [Colloq.], 1. anything full of twists and turns, as an elaborate ornamentation. 2. a whimsy.
cri·noid (krī'noid, krin'oid), *adj.* [Gr. *krinoeidēs*, lily-like < *krinon*, lily + *-eidēs*, -oid], 1. lily-shaped; hence, 2. designating or of a large group of small marine animals somewhat flowerlike in form and generally anchored by a stalk opposite the mouth. *n.* an animal of this kind: also called *sea lily*.
crin·o·line (krin''l-in, krin''l-ēn'), *n.* [Fr. < L. *crinis*, hair (Fr. *crin*, horsehair) + *linum*, thread], 1. a coarse, stiff cloth of cotton or silk, used as a lining for stiffening garments: it was formerly made of horsehair and linen. 2. a petticoat of this cloth, worn under a skirt to make it bulge out widely from the waist. 3. a hoop skirt.
cri·num (krī'nəm), *n.* [Mod. L.; Gr. *krinon*, lily], any of a large group of bulbous plants of the amaryllis family, with thick, straplike leaves and large, tubular flowers of white, pink, or red.
cri·o·sphinx (krī'ə-sfiŋks'), *n.* [< Gr. *krios*, ram + *sphinx*, sphinx], a sphinx with a ram's head.
crip·ple (krip''l), *n.* [ME. *cripel, crippel;* AS. (rare) *crypel* (akin to G. *kruppel*) < base of *creopan;* cf. CREEP], a person or animal that is lame or otherwise disabled as a result of injury, disease, or a condition existing from birth. *v.t.* [CRIPPLED (-'ld), CRIPPLING], 1. to make a cripple of; lame. 2. to disable, damage, or impair. —*SYN.* see **maim.**
Cripps, Sir Staf·ford (staf'ẽrd krips), (*Richard Stafford Cripps*), 1889–1952; English statesman and diplomat.
cris (krēs), *n.* a creese.
Cri·sey·de (kri-sā'də), *n.* Cressida: so spelled by Chaucer.
cri·sis (krī'sis), *n.* [*pl.* CRISES (-sēz)], [L.; Gr. *krisis* < *krinein*, to separate; akin to L. *cernere*, to separate, Goth. *hrains*, pure], 1. the turning point in the course of a disease, when it becomes clear whether the patient will recover or die. 2. a turning point in the course of anything; decisive or crucial time, stage, or event. 3. a crucial situation; situation whose outcome decides whether possible bad consequences will follow: as, an economic *crisis*. —*SYN.* see **emergency.**
crisp (krisp), *adj.* [AS.; L. *crispus*, curly, waving, tremulous; akin to MHG. *rispen, rispeln*, to curl], 1. brittle; easily broken, snapped, or crumbled: as, *crisp* bacon. 2. sharp and clear: as, a *crisp* analysis. 3. lively; animated: as, *crisp* dialogue. 4. bracing; fresh and invigorating: as, *crisp* air. 5. closely curled and wiry: as, *crisp* hair. 6. rippled; wavy; wrinkled. *v.t. & v.i.* to make or become crisp. —*SYN.* see **fragile.**
cris·pate (kris'pāt), *adj.* [L. *crispatus*, pp. of *crispare;* see CRISP, *v.*], crisped; curled.
cris·pat·ed (kris'pā-tid), *adj.* crispate.
cris·pa·tion (kris-pā'shən), *n.* [< L. *crispare* (see CRISP); + *-ation*], 1. a curling or being curled. 2. a slight, involuntary contraction of the muscles or skin.
crisp·er (kris'pẽr), *n.* a person or thing that crisps; especially, a curling iron for the hair.
Cris·pi, Fran·ces·co (frän-ches'kô krēs'pē), 1819–1901; Italian statesman; premier of Italy (1887–1891; 1893–1896).
Cris·pin (kris'pin), [L. *Crispinus* < *crispus*, curled; hence, lit., curly], a masculine name.
Crispin, Saint, 3d century A.D.; Roman Christian martyr; patron saint of shoemakers.
crisp·y (kris'pi), *adj.* [CRISPIER (-pi-ẽr), CRISPIEST (-pi-ist)], crisp.
cris·sal (kris'əl), *adj.* [*crissum* + *-al*], of the crissum.
criss·cross (kris'krôs'), *n.* [earlier *Christ-cross*], 1. a mark made of two crossed lines (X), often used as a signature by people who cannot write their names. 2. a pattern made of crossed lines. *adj.* crossing; crossed; marked by crossings. *v.t.* to mark or cover with crossing lines. *v.i.* to move crosswise. *adv.* 1. crosswise. 2. awry.
cris·sum (kris'əm), *n.* [*pl.* CRISSA (-ə)], [Mod. L. < L. *crissare*, to move the haunches], 1. the area under the tail of a bird, around the cloacal opening. 2. the feathers covering this area.
cris·tate (kris'tāt), *adj.* [L. *cristatus* < *crista;* see CREST], crested, as some birds.
cris·tat·ed (kris'tā-tid), *adj.* cristate.
Cris·tó·bal (kris-tō'b'l; Sp. krēs-tô'bäl), *n.* a seaport in the Panama Canal Zone, at the Caribbean end of the Panama Canal, near Colón: pop., 800.
crit., 1. critical. 2. criticism. 3. criticized.
cri·te·ri·on (krī-têr'i-ən), *n.* [*pl.* CRITERIA (-ə), CRITERIONS (-ənz)], [< Gr. *kritērion*, means of judging < *kritēs*, judge; cf. CRITIC], a standard, rule, or test by which a judgment of something can be formed. —*SYN.* see **standard.**
crit·ic (krit'ik), *n.* [< Fr. & L.; Fr. *critique;* L. *criticus;* Gr. *kritikos*, a critic, orig., critical, able to discern; akin to *krinein*, to discern, separate; see CRISIS], 1. a person who forms and expresses judgments of people or things. 2. a person who forms and expresses judgments of the qualities and comparative worth of books, music, paintings, sculpture, plays, motion pictures, etc., especially one who writes such judgments professionally. 3. a person who indulges in faultfinding and censure.
crit·i·cal (krit'i-k'l), *adj.* [*critic* + *-al*], 1. tending to find fault; censorious. 2. characterized by careful analysis: as, a sound *critical* estimate of the problem. 3. of critics or criticism. 4. of or forming a crisis; decisive. 5. dangerous or risky; causing anxiety: as, a *critical* situation in international relations. 6. of the crisis of a disease. 7. designating or of important products or raw materials subject to increased production and restricted distribution under strict control, as in wartime. 8. in *mathematics & physics*, designating a point, etc. at which a change in character, property, or condition is effected: abbreviated **crit.**
SYN.—**critical**, in its strictest use, implies an attempt at objective judging so as to determine both merits and faults (a *critical* review), but it often (and **hypercritical**, always) connotes emphasis on the faults or shortcomings; **faultfinding** implies a habitual or unreasonable emphasis on faults or defects; **captious** suggests a characteristic tendency to find fault with, or argue about, even the pettiest details (a *captious*

critic); **caviling** stresses the raising of quibbling objections on the most trivial points (a *caviling* grammarian); **carping** suggests a peevish or perverse finding of faults, with the implication that they are deserving of blame. See also **acute.**

critical angle, 1. in *optics*, the smallest possible angle of incidence at which light rays are totally reflected. 2. in *aeronautics*, that angle of attack at which the flow of air around an airfoil suddenly changes, with similar changes in lift and drag: see **angle of attack.**

critical constants, the critical temperature, pressure, density, and volume of a substance.

critical point, the stage in temperature and pressure at which the liquid and vapor phases of a substance are indistinguishable from each other.

critical pressure, the vapor tension of a liquid at the critical temperature.

critical state, that condition of a substance in which the liquid state and the vapor state have equal density.

critical temperature, that temperature of a gas above which it cannot be liquefied by pressure alone, regardless of the amount applied.

crit·ic·as·ter (krit'ik-as'tẽr), *n.* [*critic* + *-aster*], an incompetent, inferior critic.

crit·i·cise (krit'ə-sīz'), *v.i.* & *v.t.* [CRITICISED (-sīzd'), CRITICISING], to criticize: British spelling.

crit·i·cism (krit'ə-siz'm), *n.* [*critic* + *-ism*], 1. the act of making judgments; analysis of qualities and evaluation of comparative worth; especially, the definition and judgment of literary or artistic work. 2. a review, article, etc. expressing such analysis and judgment: abbreviated **crit.** 3. a finding fault; censuring; disapproval. 4. the art, principles, or methods of a critic or critics. 5. scientific investigation of literary documents to discover their origin, history, or original form: usually called *textual criticism.*

crit·i·cize (krit'ə-sīz'), *v.i.* & *v.t.* [CRITICIZED (-sīzd'), CRITICIZING], 1. to analyze and judge as a critic. 2. to judge disapprovingly; censure.

SYN.*—criticize,** in this comparison, is the general term for finding fault with or disapproving of a person or thing; **reprehend** suggests sharp or severe disapproval, generally of faults, errors, etc. rather than of persons; **blame** stresses the fixing of responsibility for an error, fault, etc.; **censure** implies the expression of severe criticism or disapproval by a person in authority or in a position to pass judgment; **condemn** and **denounce** both imply an emphatic pronouncement of blame or guilt, **condemn** suggesting the rendering of a judicial decision, and **denounce,** public accusation against persons or their acts.—ANT.*** praise.

cri·tique (kri-tēk'), *n.* [Fr. < Gr. *kritikē* (*technē*), critical (art) < *kritikos;* see CRITIC], 1. an essay or article containing a careful analysis of a literary or artistic work; review. 2. the art of criticizing; criticism.

crit·ter, crit·tur (krit'ẽr), *n.* [Dial.], a creature; specifically, *a*) a domestic animal, especially a cow, steer, etc. *b*) a bear, wolf, etc. *c*) a human being: usually depreciatory or humorous.

the critter, alcoholic liquor: humorous usage.

croak (krōk), *v.i.* [ME. *croken;* AS. **cracian*, inferred < *cræcettan*, to make sounds like a raven; ult. echoic; cf. CROW], 1. to make a deep, hoarse sound in the throat: as, frogs and ravens *croak.* 2. to talk dismally; foretell evil or misfortune; grumble. 3. [Slang], to die. *v.t.* 1. to utter in deep, hoarse tones. 2. [Slang], to kill. *n.* a croaking sound.

croak·er (krōk'ẽr), *n.* 1. an animal that croaks. 2. any of various fishes that make croaking or grunting sounds. 3. a person who talks dismally or foretells evil.

croak·y (krōk'i), *adj.* [CROAKIER (-i-ẽr), CROAKIEST (-i-ist)], croaking or inclined to croak.

Cro·at (krō'at, krō'ət), *n.* 1. a native or inhabitant of Croatia. 2. the Slavic language of the Croats.

Cro·a·tia (krō-ā'shə), *n.* an ancient kingdom: now a federated republic of Yugoslavia, in the northwestern part: capital, Zagreb.

Cro·a·tian (krō-ā'shən), *adj.* of Croatia, its people, language, or culture. *n.* 1. a Croat. 2. the South Slavic language of the Croats; Serbo-Croatian.

Cro·ce, Be·ne·det·to (be'ne-det'tô krô'che; Eng. krō'chi), 1866–1952; Italian philosopher and critic.

cro·ce·in (krō'si-in), *n.* [< L. *croceus*, saffron-colored (< *crocus;* see CROCUS); + *-in*], a red azo dye.

cro·ce·ine (krō'si-in, krō'si-ēn'), *n.* crocein.

cro·chet (krō-shā'), *n.* [Fr., small hook; see CROTCHET], a kind of knitting done with one hooked needle. *v.t.* & *v.i.* [CROCHETED (-shād'), CROCHETING], to knit with such a needle.

cro·cid·o·lite (krə-sid'ə-līt'), *n.* [< Gr. *krokis, krokidos*, var. of *krokys*, nap on woolen cloth; + *-lite*], a fibrous blue or bluish-green silicate of iron and sodium.

crock (krok), *n.* [ME. *crokke;* AS. *crocc, crocca;* akin to G. *krug;* prob. < IE. base **ger-*, to turn, twist; cf. CRIB], 1. an earthenware pot or jar. 2. a broken piece of earthenware.

crock (krok), *n.* [Brit. dial.; prob. < *crock* (pot, jar), with reference to sooted outside surface], [Dial.], soot; smut. *v.t.* [Dial.], to soil with soot or smut.

crock·er·y (krok'ẽr-i), *n.* [< *crock* (pot, jar)], earthenware; pots, jars, dishes, etc. made of baked clay.

crock·et (krok'it), *n.* [ME. *croket;* ONorm. Fr. *croquet* (OFr. *crochet*); see CROTCHET], a carved ornament, usually in the form of curved leaves or flowers, decorating the angles of roofs, gables, cornices, etc., especially in Gothic architecture.

Crock·ett, David (krok'it), (called *Davy Crockett*) 1786–1836; American frontiersman and politician, killed in the defense of the Alamo.

croc·o·dile (krok'ə-dīl'), *n.* [ME. *cocodril, cokadrill;* OFr. *cocodrille;* ML. *cocodrillus;* altered < L. *crocodilus;* Gr. *krokodilos* < *krokē*, pebble, gravel + *drilos*, worm], 1. any of a group of large, lizardlike reptiles living in the water and on the muddy banks of tropical streams: crocodiles have a thick, horny skin composed of scales and plates, a long tail, and a long, narrow, triangular head with massive jaws and cone-shaped teeth. 2. loosely, any crocodilian. 3. [C-], the Limpopo, a river in southeastern Africa.

crocodile bird, a small African bird like the plover, which feeds on the insect parasites of the crocodile.

crocodile tears, insincere tears or a hypocritical show of grief: from an old belief that crocodiles shed tears while eating their prey.

croc·o·dil·i·an (krok'ə-dil'i-ən), *adj.* 1. of or like a crocodile. 2. of a group of reptiles including the crocodile, alligator, cayman, and gavial. *n.* any reptile of this group.

cro·co·i·site (krō-kō'ə-sīt'), *n.* crocoite.

cro·co·ite (krō'kō-īt'), *n.* [< Gr. *krokos*, saffron (see CROCUS); + *-ite*], native chromate of lead, $PbCrO_4$, a red or orange mineral.

cro·cus (krō'kəs), *n.* [*pl.* CROCUSES (-iz), CROCI (-sī)], [L.; Gr. *krokos*, saffron; of Sem. origin; cf. Heb. *karkōm*, Ar. *kurkum*, Aram. *kūrkāmā*, saffron, crocus], 1. any of a large group of plants of the iris family, with a bulblike stem, grasslike leaves, and a yellow, purple, or white flower: it is among the earliest flowers to bloom in the spring. 2. an orange-yellow color; saffron. 3. powdered iron oxide used for polishing.

Croe·sus (krē'səs), *n.* 1. a fabulously rich Lydian king of the 6th century B.C.; hence, 2. a very rich man.

croft (krôft), *n.* [ME.; AS.; akin to MLG. *kroft, krocht*, little hill, field among dunes; Gmc. **krufta*, lit., that which bends; IE. base **ger-*, to turn, bend, twist; cf. CRANK (handle)], [British], 1. a small enclosed field. 2. a small farm, especially one worked by a renter.

croft·er (krôf'tẽr), *n.* [Scot.], a person who rents a croft and works it; peasant farmer.

‡**croix de guerre** (krwä' də gâr'), [Fr., cross of war], a French military decoration awarded for bravery in action.

Cro-Ma·gnon (krō-mag'non; Fr. krō'mà'nyōn'), *adj.* [after the *Cro-Magnon* cave near Dordogne, France, where remains were discovered], belonging to a prehistoric race of men who lived on the European continent, distinguished by their height and erect stature, and their use of stone and bone implements. *n.* a member of this race.

crom·lech (krom'lek), *n.* [W. < *crom*, bent, crooked + *llech*, flat stone], 1. a prehistoric tomb or monument consisting of a large, flat stone laid across upright stones; dolmen. 2. an ancient monument of monoliths, arranged in a circle and surrounding a mound.

Cromp·ton, Samuel (kromp'tən), 1753–1827; English inventor of the spinning mule.

Crom·well, Oliver (krom'wəl, krom'wel), 1599–1658; English general and statesman; lord protector of England (1653–1658): called *Ironsides.*

Cromwell, Richard, 1626–1712; son of *Oliver;* English statesman; lord protector of England (1658–1659).

Cromwell, Thomas, Earl of Essex, 1485?–1540; English statesman.

crone (krōn), *n.* [ME.; revived by Scott, etc.; prob. OFr. (Picardish) *carogne* (cf. CARRION) either directly or via MD. *kronje* in sense "old ewe"], a withered old woman.

Cro·nos (krō'nos), *n.* Cronus.

Cro·nus (krō'nəs), *n.* [L.; Gr. *Kronos*], in *Greek mythology*, a Titan, son of Uranus and Gaea, who overthrew his father to become ruler of the universe and was himself overthrown by his son Zeus: identified by the Romans with Saturn.

cro·ny (krō'ni), *n.* [*pl.* CRONIES (-niz)], [< Gr. *chronios*, lit., contemporary (Brit. university slang) < *chronos*, time], a familiar friend; close companion.

crook (krook), *n.* [ME. *croc, croke* < ON. *krōkr*, var. of *krākr*, a bending, hook, bay, etc.; IE. base as in *crank* (handle)], 1. a hook; hooked, bent, or curved thing or part. 2. a shepherd's staff. 3. a bishop's staff; crosier. 4. a bending or being bent. 5. a bend or curve. 6. [Colloq.], a swindler; thief. *v.t.* & *v.i.* [CROOKED (krookt), CROOKING], to bend or curve.

crook·back (krook'bak'), *n.* [Rare], a hunchback.

crook·ed (krook'id *for 2 & 3;* krookt *for 1*), *adj.* 1. having a crook. 2. not straight; bent; curved; askew. 3. not straightforward; dishonest; swindling.

Crookes space (krooks), [after Sir William *Crookes* (1832–1919), Eng. chemist and physicist], the dark space that appears around the cathode of a vacuum tube when the pressure is low.

Crookes tube, a vacuum tube in which gases are rarefied to a high degree: used by Sir William Crookes in the study of electrical discharge in a gas at low pressure.

crook·neck (krook′nek′), ***n.*** either of two varieties of squash with a long, tapering, curved neck.

croon (kro͞on), ***v.i. & v.t.*** [ME. (northern dial.) < MLG.; cf. MLG. *kronen*, to growl, MD. *krōnen*, to lament, sing softly], 1. to sing or hum in a low, gentle tone. 2. to sing (popular songs) in a soft, sentimental manner. ***n.*** a low, gentle singing, humming, or murmuring.

croon·er (kro͞on′ẽr), ***n.*** a person who croons; especially, a man who sings popular songs in a soft, sentimental manner.

crop (krop), ***n.*** [ME. *croppe;* AS. *cropp*, a bunch, cluster, flower, ear of corn, crop of bird, hence kidney, pebble; akin to G. *kropf*, a swelling, crop of bird; basic sense "something swelling out or swollen"; IE. **gr-eu-b-*, curving out < base **ger-*, to bend, curve, twist, as also in *croup* (rump), *group*], 1. a saclike enlargement of a bird's gullet, with thick muscular walls in which food is softened for digestion; craw. 2. any agricultural product, growing or harvested, as wheat, cotton, fruit, etc. 3. the yield of any product in one season or place. 4. a group or collection appearing together: as, a new *crop* of students, a *crop* of suggestions. 5. the entire tanned hide of an animal. 6. the handle or butt of a whip. 7. a whip with a looped lash and a short stock, used in horseback riding. 8. [< the *v.*], the act or result of cropping; especially, *a)* hair cut close to the head. *b)* this style of haircut. *c)* an earmark made by clipping. ***v.t.*** [CROPPED or *occas.* CROPT (kropt), CROPPING], 1. to cut off the tops or ends of; bite off: as, sheep *crop* grass. 2. to reap. 3. to cause crops to grow on or in. 4. to cut (hair, etc.) short. ***v.i.*** 1. to bear a crop or crops. 2. to plant or grow a crop.

crop out (or **up**), 1. to appear unexpectedly. 2. to appear at the surface.

crop-eared (krop′ẽrd′), ***adj.*** 1. having the ears cropped. 2. having the hair cut short, so that the ears show.

crop·per (krop′ẽr), ***n.*** 1. a person or thing that crops. 2. a machine for cutting or shearing. 3. a person whose work is shearing the nap from cloth. 4. a farmer who works another's land and receives a share of the crop as wages; sharecropper. 5. [? < phr. *neck and crop*], [Colloq.], a heavy or headlong fall; hence, 6. [Colloq.], a failure; disastrous occurrence.

come a cropper, [Colloq.], 1. to fall heavily or headlong. 2. to come to ruin; fail.

crop·pie (krop′i), ***n.*** [*pl.* CROPPIES (-iz), CROPPIE; see PLURAL, II, D, 1], a crappie.

crop rotation, a system of growing successive crops that have different food requirements, to prevent soil depletion, break up a disease cycle, etc.

cropt (kropt), occasional past tense and past participle of **crop.**

cro·quet (krō-kā′), ***n.*** [Fr., dial. form of *crochet;* see CROTCHET], 1. an outdoor game in which the players use long-handled mallets to drive a wooden ball through a series of hoops placed in the ground. 2. the act of croqueting. ***v.t.*** [CROQUETED (-kād′), CROQUETING], in *croquet*, to drive away (an opponent's ball) by hitting one's own which has been placed in contact with it.

cro·quette (krō-ket′), ***n.*** [Fr. < *croquer*, to crunch], a small, rounded or cone-shaped mass of chopped meat, fish, or vegetables, fried in deep fat until browned.

cro·qui·gnole (krō′kə-nōl′, krō′kin-yōl′), ***n.*** [Fr., fillip < *croquer*, Norm. form of *crocher*, to hook up, crook < *croc*, a hook], a method of making the hair wavy by winding strands of it around metal rods and applying heat by either chemical or electrical means.

crore (krôr, krōr), ***n.*** [< Hind. *karōr, krōr;* Sans. *koṭi*, top, highest money], in India, one hundred lacs, or ten millions (of rupees).

cro·sier (krō′zhẽr), ***n.*** [ME. *crocer, croyser;* OFr. *crocier, crossier*, bearer of a staff < *croce, crosse*, bishop's staff < LL. **croccia* < Frank. **krukja*, crutch, bishop's staff (akin to Eng. *crutch*); prob. affected by association with OFr. *croc*, hook, hooked staff (< ON. *krōkr;* see CROOK)], the staff carried by or before a bishop or abbot as a symbol of his function as a pastor: also spelled **crozier.**

cross (krôs), ***n.*** [< ME. *cros* & *crois; cros* < AS. *cros* < ON. *kross* < OIr. *cros* < L. *crux, crucis*, a cross < IE. base **(s)qreu -q-*, extension of **(s)qreu-;* hence akin to L. *curvus* (see CURVE); ME. *crois* < OFr. *crois, cruis* < L. *crux*], 1. an upright post, beam, or stick with another one fastened horizontally across it near the top, on which convicted persons were executed in ancient times. 2. a representation or figure of a cross, used as a badge, ornament, etc.: as, the Distinguished Service *Cross.* 3. a monument in the form of a cross, or with a cross on it, marking a crossroad, boundary, etc. 4. a staff with a cross at the top, carried before an archbishop as a sign of his authority. 5. a representation of a cross, in any of various recognized forms, as a symbol of the crucifixion of Jesus, and hence of the Christian religion. 6. any trouble, misfortune, or affliction that tries one's patience or virtue; also, anything that thwarts or frustrates. 7. any design, mark, or object made by lines or surfaces that intersect one another. 8. such a mark (X) made as a signature, as by a person who cannot write his name. 9. a heraldic emblem in the form of a cross. 10. the figure of a cross used as an insigne of orders of knighthood, orders of merit, or medals of honor. 11. a crossing, or mixing, of varieties, breeds, or races; hybridization. 12. the result of such mixing; hybrid. 13. [C-], in *astronomy*, *a)* the Northern Cross. *b)* the Southern Cross. ***v.t.*** 1. to make the sign of the cross over or upon. 2. to place across or crosswise: as, *cross* your fingers. 3. to lie or cut across; intersect: as, Broadway *crosses* Seventh Avenue at Times Square. 4. to draw or put a line or lines across. 5. to pass over; go from one side to the other of; go across: as, he *crossed* the ocean. 6. to carry (troops, etc.) across. 7. to extend or reach across: as, the bridge *crosses* a river. 8. to meet (each other) in passing. 9. to thwart; oppose; go counter to: as, no one likes to be *crossed.* 10. to interbreed (animals or plants); hybridize; cross-fertilize. ***v.i.*** 1. to lie across; intersect. 2. to go or extend from one side to the other. 3. to meet in passing. 4. to interbreed; hybridize; cross-fertilize. ***adj.*** 1. lying or passing across; transverse; crossing or crossed. 2. contrary; opposed; counter. 3. ill-tempered; cranky; easily annoyed. 4. involving reciprocation. 5. of mixed variety, breed, or race; hybrid; crossbred. —***SYN.*** see **irritable.**

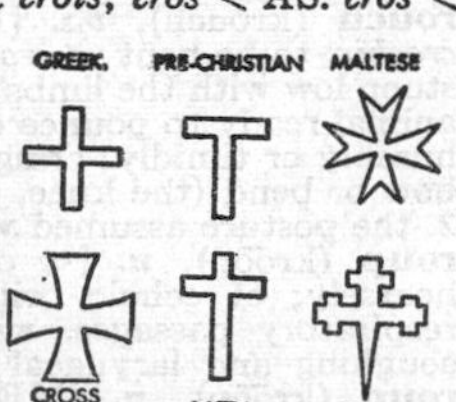

TYPES OF CROSS

cross off (or **out**), to cancel by or as by drawing crosses over or lines across.

cross oneself, to outline the form of a cross by moving the hand from the forehead to the breast and then from one shoulder to another: a religious gesture.

cross one's fingers, to cross one finger over another of the same hand: superstitiously believed to bring good luck or mitigate the wrong of telling a half-truth.

cross one's heart, to make the sign of the cross over one's heart as a token that one is telling the truth.

cross one's mind, to suggest itself to one.

cross one's palm, 1. to make a cross on one's hand with a coin, specifically in paying a fortune teller; hence, 2. to pay one money, especially as a bribe.

cross one's path, to meet one.

cross over, to pass over from one chromosome to another that is homologous: said of chromatin material in a gene or factor.

take the cross, to become a crusader.

the Cross, 1. the cross on which Jesus was put to death; hence, 2. the suffering and death of Jesus. 3. Christianity or Christendom.

cross- (krôs), *cross* used as a combining form in forming words containing any of the various senses of the word, as *crossbow, crossbred, crossbreed.*

cross·bar (krôs′bär′), ***n.*** a bar, line, or stripe placed crosswise, as a bar between goal posts on a football field. ***v.t.*** to furnish or mark with crossbars.

cross·beam (krôs′bēm′), ***n.*** a beam placed across another or from one wall to another; transverse beam.

cross·bed·ded (krôs′bed′id), ***adj.*** in *geology*, having irregular laminations oblique to the main beds of stratified rock.

cross·bill (krôs′bil′), ***n.*** any of several kinds of finch having a bill with curving points that cross.

cross·birth (krôs′bũrth′), ***n.*** in *obstetrics*, any abnormal presentation of the fetus requiring manual turning in the uterus.

cross·bones (krôs′bōnz′), ***n.*** a representation of two thighbones placed across each other, usually under that of a skull, used as a symbol of death or danger, as on a pirate flag or a bottle of poison.

cross·bow (krôs′bō′), ***n.*** a medieval weapon consisting of a bow set transversely on a wooden stock: the stock is grooved to direct an arrow or stone and notched to hold the bowstring, which is drawn up by a small windlass and released by a trigger.

CROSSBOW

cross·bow·man (krôs′bō′mən), ***n.*** [*pl.* CROSSBOWMEN (-mən)], a man armed with a crossbow.

cross·bred (krôs′bred′, krôs′bred′), ***adj.*** produced by the union of different varieties, breeds, or races. ***n.*** a crossbred plant or animal; hybrid; mongrel.

cross·breed (krôs′brēd′, krôs′brēd′), ***v.t. & v.i.*** [CROSSBRED (-bred′, -bred′), CROSSBREEDING], to hybridize;

interbreed; cross. *n.* (krôs′brēd′), an individual or breed produced by the crossing of different varieties or, more rarely, species; hybrid.

cross bun, a hot cross bun.

cross-coun·try (krôs′kun′tri), *adj.* across open country or fields, not by roads.

cross·cut (krôs′kut′), *adj.* 1. made or used for cutting across. 2. cut across. *n.* 1. a cut across. 2. a crosscut saw. 3. a direct path oblique to the main path; short cut. 4. in *mining,* a cutting made across a vein: see **mine,** illus. *v.t. & v.i.* to cut across.

crosscut saw, a saw for cutting wood across the grain.

crosse (krôs), *n.* [Fr.; see LACROSSE], the long-handled, pouched racket used in playing lacrosse: also called *lacrosse stick.*

cross-ex·am·i·na·tion (krôs′ig-zam′ə-nā′shən), *n.* a cross-examining or being cross-examined.

cross-ex·am·ine (krôs′ig-zam′in), *v.t. & v.i.* 1. to question closely. 2. in *law,* to question (a witness already questioned by the opposing side) in order to determine the validity of previous statements.

cross-eye (krôs′ī′), *n.* an abnormal condition in which the eyes are turned toward each other; convergent strabismus.

cross-eyed (krôs′īd′), *adj.* having cross-eye.

cross-fer·ti·li·za·tion (krôs′fũr′t′l-ə-zā′shən), *n.* a cross-fertilizing or being cross-fertilized.

cross-fer·ti·lize (kros′fũr′t′l-īz′), *v.t. & v.i.* 1. to fertilize or be fertilized by pollen from another flower. 2. to fertilize or be fertilized by a sperm (or male gamete) from another individual.

cross fire, in *military usage,* fire directed at a single objective from two or more positions so that the lines of fire cross at or near the objective.

cross fox, 1. a fox marked with a dark cross along the spine and shoulders. 2. the yellowish, black-marked fur of this fox.

cross-grained (krôs′grānd′), *adj.* 1. having an irregular or transverse grain: said of wood. 2. cantankerous; contrary; perverse.

cross hairs, crossed lines, as of fine hair or cobweb, mounted on the front lens of a telescopic gunsight, surveyor's level, etc. to assist in precise aiming or centering of the instrument.

cross·hatch (krôs′hach′), *v.t. & v.i.* to shade (an engraving or drawing) with two sets of parallel lines that cross each other.

cross·head (krôs′hed′), *n.* 1. a bar across the end of a piston rod. 2. one of the headings inserted at intervals in a newspaper article, describing the part of the article that follows.

cross·ing (krôs′iŋ), *n.* [see CROSS], 1. the act of passing across, thwarting, interbreeding, etc. 2. an intersection, as of lines, streets, etc. 3. a place where a street, river, etc. may be crossed. 4. the place in a cruciform church where the transept crosses the nave.

cross·jack (krôs′jak′), *n.* [see CROSS- & JACK], a square sail fastened to the lower yard of a mizzenmast.

cross-leg·ged (krôs′leg′id, krôs′legd′), *adj.* having one leg crossed over another, as in sitting, or having the ankles crossed and the knees apart.

cross·let (krôs′lit), *n.* [Anglo-Fr. *croiselette,* dim. of OFr. *crois;* see CROSS], in *heraldry,* a small cross.

cross-link (krôs′liŋk′), *n.* a crosswise connecting part; specifically, an atom or group connecting parallel chains in a complex molecule. *v.t.* to join crosswise.

cros·sop·te·ryg·i·an (kro-sop′tə-rij′i-ən), *n.* [< Mod. L. *Crossopterygii,* name of the group, lit., fringe fins; + *-an*], any of a group of fishes, extinct except for one species, regarded as the ancestors of amphibians and land vertebrates in general.

cross·o·ver (krôs′ō′vẽr), *n.* 1. a connecting track by which a railroad train can be switched from one line to another. 2. in *biology, a)* a crossing over: see phrase under **cross.** *b)* a character resulting from this.

cross·patch (krôs′pach′), *n.* [*cross-* + dial. *patch,* fool, childish person], [Colloq.], a cross, bad-tempered person.

cross·piece (krôs′pēs′), *n.* a piece lying across something else.

cross-pol·li·nate (krôs′pol′ə-nāt′), *v.t. & v.i.* to subject or be subjected to cross-pollination.

cross-pol·li·na·tion (krôs′pol′ə-nā′shən), *n.* the transfer of pollen from the anther of one flower to the stigma of another, as by action of the wind or insects.

cross-pur·pose (krôs′pũr′pəs), *n.* 1. a contrary or conflicting purpose. 2. *pl.* a game of questions and answers.

at cross-purposes, having, or acting under, a misunderstanding as to each other's purposes.

cross-ques·tion (krôs′kwes′chən), *v.t.* to cross-examine. *n.* a question asked in cross-examination.

cross-re·fer (krôs′ri-fũr′), *v.t.* to refer from one part to another. *v.i.* to make a cross reference.

cross reference, a reference from one part of a book, catalogue, index, etc. to another part, for additional information.

cross relation, in *music,* a relationship between two successive tones in different voices that ordinarily occurs in one voice: also called *false relation.*

cross·road (krôs′rōd′), *n.* 1. a road that crosses another road. 2. a road that connects two or more main roads. 3. *usually pl.* the place where two or more roads intersect: often regarded metaphorically as the gathering point of the near-by rural inhabitants.

at the crossroads, at the point where one must choose between different courses of action.

cross·ruff (krôs′ruf′), *n.* [*cross* + *ruff* (card game)], in *card games,* a play in which each of two partners in turn leads a suit that the other will be able to trump.

cross section, 1. a cutting through something, especially at right angles to its axis. 2. a piece so cut off. 3. a representative part or selection serving to demonstrate the qualities of the whole. 4. in *surveying,* a vertical section of the ground surface taken at right angles to a survey line.

cross-stitch (krôs′stich′), *n.* 1. a stitch made by crossing two stitches diagonally in the form of an **X.** 2. needlework made with this stitch. *v.t. & v.i.* to sew or embroider with this stitch.

cross street, 1. a street that crosses another street. 2. a street that connects two or more main streets.

cross talk, in *radio & telephony,* interference in one channel from another or others.

cross·tie (crôs′tī′), *n.* a beam, post, rod, etc. placed crosswise to give support or strength; specifically, any of the transverse timbers supporting the rails of a railroad track.

cross-town (krôs′toun′), *adj.* going across the main avenues or transportation lines of a city or town: as, a *cross-town* bus route is needed.

cross·trees (krôs′trēz′), *n. pl.* two short, horizontal bars across a ship's masthead, which spread the rigging that supports the mast.

cross·walk (krôs′wôk′), *n.* a lane marked off for pedestrians to use in crossing a street.

cross·way (krôs′wā′), *n.* a crossroad.

cross·ways (krôs′wāz′), *adv.* crosswise.

cross wind, a wind blowing at right angles to the line of flight of an aircraft, the course of a ship, or any given course or direction.

cross·wise (krôs′wīz′), *adv.* 1. in the form of a cross. 2. across; athwart. 3. in a contrary manner.

cross·word puzzle (krôs′wũrd′), an arrangement of numbered squares to be filled in with words, a letter to each square, so that a letter appearing in a word placed horizontally is usually also part of a word placed vertically: numbered definitions, etc. are given as clues for the words to be entered in the corresponding squares.

crotch (kroch), *n.* [Fr. *croche,* a hook < *croc;* see CROSIER], 1. a pole forked on top. 2. a place where two branches or limbs fork from a tree. 3. the place where the legs fork from the human body.

crotched (krocht), *adj.* having a crotch; forked.

crotch·et (kroch′it), *n.* [ME. & OFr. *crochet,* dim. < *croc,* hook; see CROSIER], 1. a small hook. 2. a hooklike part or process. 3. a hooklike device or hooked instrument. 4. [< sense "hooked, twisted"], a peculiar whim; stubborn notion. 5. in *music,* a quarter note (♩). —*SYN.* see **caprice.**

crotch·et·i·ness (kroch′ə-ti-nis), *n.* the quality or state of being crotchety.

crotch·et·y (kroch′ə-ti), *adj.* 1. full of peculiar whims or stubborn notions; cantankerous; eccentric. 2. having the nature of a crotchet.

cro·ton (krō′t′n), *n.* [Mod. L.; Gr. *krotōn,* a tick, castor-oil tree or (in pl.) its seeds: so named from the appearance of the seeds], any of a large group of tropical shrubs, trees, and herbs: two species yield croton oil and cascarilla, important medicinal products.

croton bug, Croton bug [< *Croton* aqueduct (a part of the water-supply system of New York City): so named from becoming numerous in the city after the opening of the aqueduct], a small, winged cockroach.

cro·ton·ic acid (krō-ton′ik, krō-tō′nik), [*croton* + *-ic*], a colorless crystalline compound, $C_3H_5 \cdot COOH$, used in organic synthesis.

croton oil, a thick, bitter oil obtained from croton seeds: it is used externally as a counterirritant and internally as a strong cathartic.

crouch (krouch), *v.i.* [ME. *cruchen, crouchen;* OFr. *crochir,* to be bent < *croc,* a hook; see CROSIER], 1. to stoop low with the limbs drawn close to the body, as an animal ready to pounce or cowering in fear. 2. to bow humbly or timidly; cringe in a servile manner. *v.t.* to bow or bend (the knee, etc.) low. *n.* 1. a crouching. 2. the posture assumed when crouching.

croup (kroo͞p), *n.* [< obs. or dial. *croup,* to speak hoarsely; of echoic origin], an inflammation of the respiratory passages, with labored breathing, hoarse coughing and laryngeal spasm.

croup (kroo͞p), *n.* [ME. & OFr. *croupe* < Frank. **kruppa;* see CROP], the rump of a horse, etc.

crou·pi·er (kroo͞′pi-ẽr; Fr. kroo͞′pyā′), *n.* [Fr., orig., one who rides on the croup, hence an inferior assistant; see CROUP (rump)], 1. a person in charge of a gambling table, who rakes in and pays out the money. 2. a person acting as assistant chairman at a public dinner.

croup·ous (kroo͞p′əs), *adj.* croupy.

croup·y (kroo͞p′i), *adj.* 1. having the disease of croup.

2. having the characteristic harsh breathing and hoarseness of croup. 3. of or like croup.

crouse (krōōs), *adj.* [ME. *crous;* prob. < a LG. source], [Scot. & North Eng. Dial.], lively; pert; bold; brisk.

crou·ton (krōō-ton′, krōō′ton; Fr. krōō′tōn′), *n.* [Fr. *croûton* < *croûte,* a crust; L. *crusta;* see CRUST], one of the small, crisp pieces of toasted or fried bread often served in soup.

Crow (krō), *n.* [transl., via Fr. *gens de corbeaux,* of their native name, *Absaroke,* crow people], 1. [*pl.* CROWS (krōz), CROW], a member of a tribe of Siouan Indians who lived in the upper basins of the Yellowstone and Big Horn Rivers. 2. their Siouan language.

crow (krō), *n.* [ME. *crowe;* AS. *crawa* (akin to G. *krähe*); ult. < base of *crawan;* see CROW, *v.*], 1. any of several species of large, nonmigrating birds with glossy, black plumage and a typical harsh call: the raven, rook, and jackdaw are all crows. 2. [C-], the southern constellation Corvus. 3. a crowbar.
as the crow flies, in a straight, direct line.
eat crow, [Colloq.], to undergo the humiliation of having to retract a statement, admit an error, etc.

crow (krō), *v.i.* [CROWED (krōd) or, for 1, CREW (krōō), CROWED, CROWING], [ME. *crowen;* AS. *crawan;* akin to G. *krähen;* orig. echoic], 1. to make the shrill cry of a rooster. 2. to utter a cry of pleasure or victory. 3. to exult; boast in triumph: as, stop *crowing* over your victory. 4. to make a sound expressive of well-being or pleasure: said of a baby. *n.* 1. the shrill cry of a rooster. 2. a baby's sound expressive of well-being or pleasure. —*SYN.* see **boast.**

crow·bar (krō′bär′), *n.* [from the end's resembling a crow's beak], a long metal bar, usually with a chisellike point at one end, used as a lever for prying, etc.

crow·ber·ry (krō′ber′i, krō′bẽr-i), *n.* [*pl.* CROWBERRIES (-iz)], [apparently transl. of G. *krähenbeeri*], 1. a hardy, evergreen shrub found in northern regions. 2. its black, edible berry. 3. a variety of large cranberry.

crow blackbird, any of a number of North American birds resembling the crow, including the purple grackle.

crowd (kroud), *v.i.* [ME. *crouden;* AS. *crudan,* to press, drive; akin to MHG. *kroten,* to oppress; IE. base **greut-,* to compel, press, seen also in Ir. *gruth,* curdled milk; cf. CURD], 1. to press; push; shove. 2. to press forward; push one's way (*forward, into, through,* etc.). 3. to gather closely together, pressing upon one another; throng. *v.t.* 1. to press; push; shove. 2. to press or force closely together; cram. 3. to fill too full; occupy to excess, as by pressing or thronging. 4. [Colloq.], to put (a person) under pressure or stress. 5. [Colloq.], to press urgently for payment; dun. 6. in *basketball,* to guard (an opponent) closely to prevent his getting the ball. *n.* 1. a large number of people or things gathered closely together. 2. the common people; the masses; the people. 3. [Colloq.], a group of people having something in common; set; clique.
crowd (on) sail, to put up more sails in order to increase the ship's speed.
SYN.—**crowd** is applied to an assembly of persons or things in close proximity or densely packed together and may suggest lack of order, loss of personal identity, etc. (*crowds* lined the street); **throng** specifically suggests a moving press of people (*throngs* of celebrators at Times Square); **multitude** stresses greatness of number in referring to persons or things assembled or considered together (a *multitude* arrayed against him); **swarm** suggests a large, continuously moving group (a *swarm* of sight-seers); **mob,** properly applied to a disorderly or lawless crowd, is an abusive term when used to describe the masses or any specific group of people; **host** specifically suggests a large organized body marshaled together but may be used generally of any sizable group considered collectively (he has a *host* of friends); **horde** specifically refers to any large predatory band (a *horde* of office seekers).

crowd (kroud), *n.* [ME. *crowde, crouth;* W. *crwth;* akin to Gael. *cruinn,* curved, round], an obsolete Celtic musical instrument played with a bow: it was somewhat like a violin but had a shallow, broad body and six or, earlier, three strings.

crowd·ed (kroud′id), *adj.* [pp. of *crowd*], 1. filled with people or things; packed. 2. packed too full. 3. close together; inconveniently lacking room.

crow·foot (krō′foot′), *n.* [*pl.,* for 1 & 2, CROWFOOTS (-foots′); for 3, 4, 5, CROWFEET (-fēt′)], 1. any of a number of plants of the buttercup family, characterized by simple or variously lobed leaves somewhat resembling a crow's foot. 2. any of several other plants with leaves or other parts somewhat resembling a crow's foot, as the plantain. 3. in *electricity,* a zinc electrode shaped somewhat like a crow's foot. 4. in *military usage,* a device with several sharp metal points, placed on the ground to hinder enemy cavalry; caltrop. 5. in *nautical usage,* an arrangement of small cords run through a block pulley to suspend an awning, etc.

crown (kroun), *n.* [ME. *croune, corune;* OFr. *corone;* L. *corona,* a garland, crown; Gr. *korōnē,* curved object, wreath; IE. base *(*s*)*qer,* to turn, bend; hence akin to L. *curvus* (see CURVE)], 1. a garland or wreath worn on the head as an ornament or sign of honor, victory, etc.; hence, 2. a reward; honor. 3. a circlet or head covering, usually heavily jeweled and ornamented, worn by a monarch as an emblem of sovereignty. 4. the position, power, or dominion of a monarch; ruling power in a monarchy. 5. the monarch. 6. anything serving to adorn or honor like a crown. 7. a thing like a crown in shape, position, etc. 8. originally, any coin stamped with the figure of a crown. 9. a silver coin of Great Britain equal to five shillings: abbreviated **cr.** 10. any of various coins whose name means *crown,* as the *krona, krone,* etc. 11. the top part of the skull or head. 12. the top part of a hat. 13. the summit or highest point, as of a mountain, arch, etc. 14. the highest quality, point of development, state, etc. of anything. 15. the enamel-covered part of a tooth, projecting beyond the gum line. 16. an artificial substitute, usually of porcelain or gold, for the crown of a tooth. 17. the lowest point of an anchor, between the arms: see **anchor,** illus. 18. in *botany, a*) a corona. *b*) the point at or just below the surface of the ground where the stem and the root join. *c*) the leafy head of a tree. 19. in *zoology, a*) the crest of an animal. *b*) the flowerlike part of certain sea animals. *v.t.* 1. to put a crown on. 2. to make (a person) a monarch; enthrone. 3. to give honor, dignity, etc. to. 4. to top; surmount (often followed by *with*). 5. to be the crown, highest part, or chief ornament of. 6. to bring to completion; put the finishing touch on. 7. [Slang], to hit (a person) on the head. 8. in *checkers,* to make a king of.
the Crown, 1. the position, power, or dominion of a monarch. 2. the monarch as head of the state.

crown cap, a cork-lined metal stopper whose edges are crimped over the mouth of the bottle.

crown colony, a British colony directly under the control of the home government.

crown·er (krou′nẽr, krōō′nẽr), *n.* [British Dial.], a coroner.

crown glass, 1. window glass made in flat, circular plates by blowing and whirling, with a small knot in the center left by the blower's rod. 2. a very clear optical glass.

crown graft, a plant graft in which the shoot or twig is inserted at the crown of the main stem or trunk.

crown land, land owned by the crown, the income from which goes to the reigning monarch.

crown lens, a lens made of crown glass; specifically, the convex member of an achromatic lens.

crown·piece (kroun′pēs′), *n.* 1. a piece forming the crown or top. 2. the strap of a horse's bridle that goes over the head back of the ears.

Crown Point, a town in New York, on lower Lake Champlain: pop., 1,700: captured from the British (1775) in the American Revolution.

crown prince, the heir apparent to a throne; a monarch's oldest living son.

crown princess, the wife of a crown prince.

crown saw, a saw in the form of a hollow cylinder with teeth on the bottom edge, used to cut circular holes or pieces.

crown wheel, a gear wheel with teeth set in the rim perpendicularly to its plane.

crown·work (kroun′wũrk′), *n.* 1. a fortification consisting of two or more fronts for protecting an advantageous position. 2. in *dentistry, a*) the making or insertion of an artificial crown. *b*) an artificial crown or crowns collectively.

crow's-foot (krōz′foot′), *n.* [*pl.* CROW'S-FEET (-fēt′)], 1. *usually in pl.* one of the wrinkles that often develop at the outer corners of the eyes of adults. 2. a three-pointed, stitched design put on a garment, as at the end of a seam. 3. in *military usage,* a device with several sharp metal points, placed on the ground to hinder enemy cavalry; caltrop.

crow's-nest (krōz′nest′), *n.* 1. a small, sheltered platform close to the top of a ship's mast, used by the lookout. 2. any platform like this.

Croy·don (kroi′d'n), *n.* a city in Surrey, England, near London: pop., 249,000.

croze (krōz), *n.* [prob. < OFr. *croz,* a groove], the groove at either end of the inside of a barrel or cask, in which the head is fixed.

cro·zier (krō′zhẽr), *n.* a crosier.

crs., 1. credits. 2. creditors.

cru·ces (krōō′sēz), *n.* alternative plural of **crux.**

cru·cial (krōō′shəl), *adj.* [Fr. < L. *crux, crucis;* see CROSS], 1. of supreme importance; decisive; critical: as, a *crucial* deci-

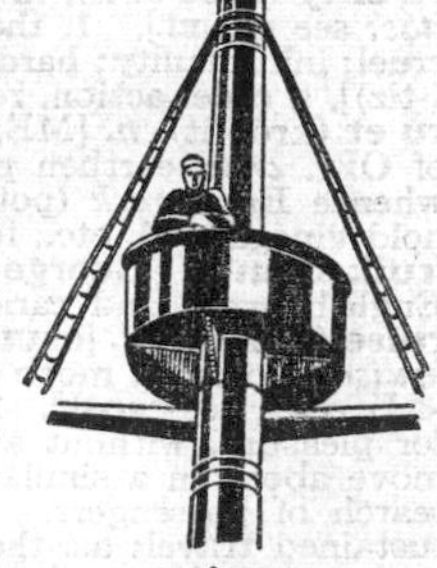
CROW'S-NEST

sion. 2. extremely trying; severe; difficult. 3. in *anatomy*, having the form of a cross. —*SYN.* see **acute.**

cru·ci·ate (krōō′shi-it, krōō′shi-āt′), *adj.* [< Mod. L. *cruciatus* (in L., pp. of *cruciare*, to crucify) < L. *crux, crucis;* see CROSS], 1. in *botany*, having cross-shaped leaves or petals. 2. in *zoology*, crossing: said of wings.

cru·ci·ble (krōō′sə-b'l), *n.* [ML. *crucibulum*, lamp, cresset, melting pot, crucible; prob. < MHG. *kruse*, earthen pot (akin to Eng. *cruse*) + L. suffix *-ibulum* (as in *thuribulum*, censer), but often associated with L. *crux, crucis* (see CROSS) as if lamp burning before cross], 1. a container made of graphite, porcelain, platinum, or other substance that can resist great heat, for melting and calcining ores, metals, etc. 2. the hollow at the bottom of an ore furnace, where the molten metal collects. 3. a severe test; hard trial.

crucible steel, a high-grade steel made by melting blister steel or by fusing flux, wrought iron, and carbon in crucibles: used for making knives, tools, etc.

cru·ci·fer (krōō′sə-fẽr), *n.* [LL., cross-bearer (used in reference to Jesus) < L. *crux, crucis* (see CROSS) + *ferre*, to bear], 1. a person who carries a cross, as in a church procession. 2. in *botany*, any plant of the mustard family, including the mustards, cabbages, cresses, etc., with flowers having four parts that form a cross.

cru·cif·er·ous (krōō-sif′ẽr-əs), *adj.* [< L. *crux, crucis* (see CROSS); + *-ferous*], 1. bearing a cross. 2. in *botany*, of the mustard family.

cru·ci·fix (krōō′sə-fiks′), *n.* [ME. < OFr. or L.; OFr. *crucefix;* L. *crucifixus*, lit., fixed to the cross < *crux* (see CROSS) + *fixus* (see FIX)], 1. a religious symbol consisting of a cross with the figure of Jesus crucified on it. 2. the cross as a religious symbol.

cru·ci·fix·ion (krōō′sə-fik′shən), *n.* 1. a crucifying or being crucified. 2. [C-], the crucifying of Jesus, or a representation of this in painting, statuary, etc.

cru·ci·form (krōō′sə-fôrm′), *adj.* [< L. *crux, crucis* (see CROSS); + *-form*], cross-shaped.

cru·ci·fy (krōō′sə-fī′), *v.t.* [CRUCIFIED (-fīd′), CRUCIFYING], [ME. *crucifien;* OFr. *crucifier;* LL. **crucificare*, for L. *crucifigere* < *crux, crucis* (see CROSS) + *figere* (see FIX)], 1. to put to death by suspending from a cross, with the hands and feet nailed or bound to it. 2. to mortify; subdue. 3. to torment; torture.

crud (krud, krood, krōōd), *v.t. & v.i.* [Dial.], to coagulate: see **curd.**

crud (krud), *n.* [said to be < W. *cryd*, fever, plague; ? < *crud*, metathesis of *curd*], [Military Slang], an imaginary disease: used as a general term for any vague disorder or ailment.

crude (krōōd), *adj.* [L. *crudus*, bleeding, raw, rough; akin to L. *cruor*, blood, Bret. *criz*, raw, uncooked, hard; IE. base **greu-*, congealed, thickened (blood), bloody], 1. in a raw or natural condition; not refined; not prepared, as by heating or other processes. 2. not ripe; immature. 3. lacking finish, grace, tact, taste, etc.; uncultured: as, a *crude* fellow. 4. not carefully made; rough: as, *crude* woodwork. 5. unadorned; bare: as, *crude* reality.

cru·di·ty (krōō′də-ti), *n.* [< Fr. or L.; Fr. *crudité;* L. *cruditas*], 1. the condition or quality of being crude. 2. [*pl.* CRUDITIES (-tiz)], a crude action, remark, etc.

cru·el (krōō′əl), *adj.* [ME. & OFr.; L. *crudelis* < *crudus;* see CRUDE], 1. disposed to inflict pain and suffering; delighting in another's suffering; without mercy or pity. 2. causing, or of a kind to cause, pain, distress, etc.
SYN.—**cruel** implies indifference to the suffering of others or a disposition to inflict it on others (*cruel* fate); **brutal** implies an animallike or savage cruelty that is altogether unfeeling (a *brutal* prison guard); **inhuman** stresses the complete absence of those qualities expected of a civilized human being, such as compassion, mercy, or benevolence; **pitiless** implies a callous refusal to be moved or influenced by the suffering of those one has wronged; **ruthless** implies a cruel and relentless disregard for the rights or welfare of others, while in pursuit of a goal. —*ANT.* humane, kind.

cru·el·ty (krōō′əl-ti), *n.* [ME. & OFr. *cruelte;* L. *crudelitas;* see CRUEL], 1. the quality or condition of being cruel; inhumanity; hardheartedness. 2. [*pl.* CRUELTIES (-tiz)], a cruel action, remark, etc.

cru·et (krōō′it), *n.* [ME. *cruet, crouet* < Anglo-Fr. dim. of OFr. *crue*, earthen pot < Gmc. **kruka* (G. *krug*), whence Eng. *crock* (pot, jar)], a small glass bottle to hold vinegar, oil, etc., for the table.

Cruik·shank, George (krook′shaŋk), 1792–1878; English artist and caricaturist.

cruise (krōōz), *v.i.* [CRUISED (krōōzd), CRUISING], [< D. *kruisen*, to cross, move crosswise, cruise < *kruis*, cross < L. *crux;* see CROSS], 1. to sail from place to place, as for pleasure, without a set destination; hence, 2. to move about in a similar manner: as, a taxi *cruises* in search of passengers. 3. to move at a speed fit for sustained travel: as, the airplane *cruised* at 270 miles an hour. *v.t.* to sail or journey over or about. *n.* a sailing from place to place; cruising voyage, especially a sea voyage.

cruis·er (krōōz′ẽr), *n.* 1. anything that cruises, as a powerboat, airplane, police car, etc. 2. any of several types of fast and maneuverable warship somewhat smaller than a battleship and having less armor and fire power. 3. a powerboat with a cabin and the necessary equipment for living on board.

cruis·ing (krōōz′iŋ), *adj.* designating or at the most efficient, though not the highest, speed of an airplane.

crul·ler (krul′ẽr), *n.* [D. < *krullen*, to curl (see CURL)], a small cake made of sweetened dough enriched with eggs, shaped in twisted strips and fried brown in deep fat; kind of doughnut.

crumb (krum), *n.* [ME.; AS. *cruma*, lit., scraping from bread crust; akin to G. *krume;* IE. **gr-eu*, to scratch, scrape with the fingers (as in G. *krauen*, to scratch) < base **ger-*, to turn, twist], 1. a very small piece broken off something; small particle or bit, especially of bread, cake, etc. 2. any bit or scrap: as, *crumbs* of knowledge. 3. the soft, inner part of bread: distinguished from *crust*. *v.t.* 1. to crumble. 2. in *cookery*, to cover or thicken with crumbs. 3. [Colloq.], to clear (a table, etc.) of crumbs. *v.i.* to come apart in crumbs.

crum·ble (krum′b'l), *v.t.* [CRUMBLED (-b'ld), CRUMBLING], [freq. of *crumb, v.*], to break into crumbs or small pieces. *v.i.* to fall to pieces; disintegrate; decay. *n.* [Rare], a substance that is crumbling.

crum·bli·ness (krum′bli-nis), *n.* the quality of being crumbly.

crum·bly (krum′bli), *adj.* [CRUMBLIER (-bli-ẽr), CRUMBLIEST (-bli-ist)], apt to crumble; easily crumbled.

crum·by (krum′i), *adj.* [CRUMBIER (-i-ẽr), CRUMBIEST (-i-ist)], 1. full of crumbs. 2. soft.

crum·mie, crum·my (krum′i, kroom′i), *n.* [via dial. < AS. *crump, crumb*, crooked (akin to G. *krumm* & D. *krom*); + *-y*], [Scot. & British Dial.], a cow with crooked horns: sometimes used as an epithet for any cow.

crum·my (krum′i), *adj.* [CRUMMIER (-i-ẽr), CRUMMIEST (-i-ist)], [understood as *crumb* + *-y*, with basic notion "brittle, friable, hence worthless"], [Slang], of poor quality, character, or appearance; inferior, shabby, contemptible, etc.

crump (krump, kroomp), *v.t. & v.i.* [echoic], to explode with a crunching sound: said of shells, etc. *n.* a crumping. *adj.* [< the *v.*], [Dial.], brittle; crisp.

crum·pet (krum′pit), *n.* [prob. < ME. *crompid* (cake), pp. of *crompen*, to curl up (cf. G. *krummen*) < AS. *crump*, bent, crooked; see CRIMP], an unsweetened batter cake baked on a griddle, somewhat like a pancake: it is usually toasted and buttered before serving.

crum·ple (krum′p'l), *v.t.* [CRUMPLED (-p'ld), CRUMPLING], [< dial. *crump*, to curl up (cf. CRUMPET) + *-le*, freq. suffix or < ME. *crympelen* (earlier formation < the same elements)], to crush together into creases or wrinkles. *v.i.* 1. to become crumpled. 2. [Colloq.], to collapse; break down. *n.* a crease or wrinkle.

crunch (krunch) *v.i. & v.t.* [earlier *craunch;* of echoic origin], 1. to bite or chew with a noisy, crackling sound. 2. to press, grind, or tread with a noisy, crushing sound. *n.* 1. a crunching. 2. a crunching sound.

crunch·y (krun′chi), *adj.* [CRUNCHIER (-chi-ẽr), CRUNCHIEST (-chi-ist)], making a crunching sound.

cru·or (krōō′ôr), *n.* [L., blood (which flows from a wound); see CRUDE], coagulated blood; gore.

crup·per (krup′ẽr, kroop′ẽr), *n.* [ME. *cropere;* OFr. *cropiere* < *crope, crupe*, rump < Frank. **kruppr;* akin to Eng. *crop*], 1. a leather strap attached to a harness or saddle and passed under a horse's tail: see **harness,** illus. 2. the rump of a horse; croup.

cru·ral (kroor′əl), *adj.* [L. *cruralis* < *crus, cruris;* see CRUS], in *anatomy*, of the leg or crus.

crus (krus), *n.* [*pl.* CRURA (kroor′ə)], [L., leg, shank; akin to Arm. *srun-k*‘, calf (of the leg)], 1. the part of a leg or hind limb between the knee and the ankle; shank. 2. any anatomical structure resembling a leg or (in the plural) a pair of legs, as the cerebral peduncles.

cru·sade (krōō-sād′), *n.* [< Sp. *cruzada*, altered after Fr. *croisade;* both < ML. *cruciata* < pp. of *cruciare*, to mark with a cross < L. *crux;* see CROSS], 1. [sometimes C-], any of the military expeditions which Christians undertook from the end of the 11th to the end of the 13th century to recover the Holy Land from the Moslems. 2. any war or expedition having a religious object and sanctioned by the church. 3. vigorous, concerted action for some cause or idea, or against some abuse. *v.i.* [CRUSADED (-id), CRUSADING], to engage in a crusade.

cru·sad·er (krōō-sād′ẽr), *n.* 1. a participant in medieval crusades. 2. a person engaged in any crusade.

cru·sa·do (krōō-sā′dō), *n.* [*pl.* CRUSADOES, CRUSADOS (-dōz)], [Port. *cruzado;* see CRUSADE], an obsolete Portuguese coin with the figure of a cross on it.

cruse (krōōz, krōōs), *n.* [ME. < MD. *cruyse* or ON. *krūs;* akin to G. *krause*, pot with lid; ? < IE. **gr-eu-s* (cf. G. *kraus*, wrinkled) in sense "twisted, plaited" (with reference to an original basketwork covering) < base **ger-*, to twist, turn], [Archaic], a small container for water, oil, honey, etc.

crush (krush), *v.t.* [ME. *crushen;* OFr. *cruisir, croisir*, to gnash (teeth), crash, break; of Gmc. origin; cf. OSw. *krysta*, Goth. *kriustan*], 1. to press between two opposing forces so as to break or injure; put out of shape or condition by pressure; squeeze together; crumple. 2. to press, grind, or pound into small particles or into powder. 3. to subdue; overwhelm; suppress. 4. to extract by pressing or squeezing. *v.i.* to be or become crushed. *n.* 1. a crushing; severe pressure. 2. a crowded mass, especially of people. 3. [Colloq.], an infatuation. —*SYN.* see **break.**

Cru·soe, Robinson (krōō′sō), the hero of Daniel Defoe's novel *Robinson Crusoe* (1719), who is stranded on an island as the result of a shipwreck.

crust (krust), *n.* [ME. < OFr. or L.; OFr. *crouste;* L. *crusta;* IE. base **greu-*, congealed, thickened (blood), as also in Gr. *kryos*, frost (cf. CRYO-), L. *crudus*, bleeding (cf. CRUDE)], 1. the hard, crisp, outer part of bread. 2. a piece of bread that is mostly this. 3. any dry, hard piece of bread. 4. the pastry shell of a pie. 5. any hard shell, covering, or surface layer, as of snow, soil, etc. 6. a hard deposit formed by wine on the inside surface of a bottle. 7. [Slang], audacity; insolence; forwardness. 8. in *geology*, the outer part of the earth. 9. in *medicine*, a dry, hard outer layer of blood, pus, or other bodily secretion; scab. *v.t. & v.i.* 1. to cover or become covered with a crust. 2. to form or harden into a crust.

Crus·ta·ce·a (krus-tā′shə, krus-tā′shi-ə), *n.pl.* [Mod. L. < *crustaceus*, having a crust, hard shell < L. *crusta*; see CRUST], in *zoology*, a class of invertebrates, including shrimps, crabs, barnacles, and lobsters, that usually live in the water and breathe through gills: they have a hard outer shell and jointed appendages and bodies.

crus·ta·cean (krus-tā′shən), *adj.* of the Crustacea. *n.* any member of the Crustacea.

crus·ta·ceous (krus-tā′shəs), *adj.* [Mod. L. *crustaceus;* see CRUSTACEA], 1. of or like a crust. 2. having a hard crust or shell. 3. in *zoology*, crustacean.

crus·tal (krus′t'l), *adj.* of a crust; especially, of the earth's crust.

crust·ed (krus′tid), *adj.* 1. having a crust. 2. designating wine that has deposited a crust. 3. antiquated.

crust·i·ly (krus′t'l-i), *adv.* in a crusty manner.

crust·i·ness (krus′ti-nis), *n.* the quality or condition of being crusty.

crust·y (krus′ti), *adj.* [CRUSTIER (-ti-ẽr), CRUSTIEST (-ti-ist)], 1. having a crust. 2. hard as a crust; hence, 3. bad-tempered; harsh; surly.

crutch (kruch), *n.* [ME. *crucche;* AS. *crycc*, staff; akin to G. *krücke;* IE. base **ger-*, to twist, turn, bend, as in *crank* (handle) or G. *kriechen*, to cringe, crawl, lit., bend over], 1. any of various devices held in the hand and used by lame people as an aid in walking; usually, a staff with a crosspiece on top that fits under the armpit: crutches are often used in pairs. 2. figuratively, a prop or support. 3. any device that resembles a crutch, as a forked leg rest on a sidesaddle. 4. the crotch of the human body. 5. in *nautical usage*, a forked support for a spar when the sail is furled. *v.t.* to support with or as with a crutch or crutches; prop.

crutched (krucht), *adj.* [ME. *crouched* < *crouch*, a cross < AS. *cruc* < L. *crux;* see CROSS], bearing the sign of the cross: as, the *Crutched* Friars were an early order of English monks who wore crosses on their robes.

crux (kruks), *n.* [*pl.* CRUXES (kruk′siz), CRUCES (krōō′sēz)], [L., a cross; see CROSS], 1. in *heraldry*, a cross. 2. a difficult problem; puzzling thing. 3. a crucial point; critical moment. 4. the essential or most important point. 5. [C-], in *astronomy*, the Southern Cross, a constellation: see **constellation**, chart.

‡**crux an·sa·ta** (kruks′ an-sā′tə), [L., lit., cross with a handle; *crux* (see CROSS) + fem. of *ansatus* < *ansa*, a handle], the ankh, an ancient Egyptian cross.

cru·zei·ro (krōō-zā′rō; Port. krōō-zā′roo), *n.* [Port. < *cruz*, a cross < L. *crux* (see CROSS)], the gold monetary unit of Brazil, equal to 5 1/2 cents in 1950.

cry (krī), *v.i.* [CRIED (krīd), CRYING], [ME. *crien;* OFr. *crier;* L. *quiritare*, to raise a plaintive cry, wail, shriek; prob. of echoic origin (cf. L. *quirritare*, to squeak like a pig), but associated in ancient folk etym. with L. *Quirites*, Roman citizens (as if meaning "to call the *Quirites*," implore their help)], 1. to make a loud vocal sound or shout, as in pain, anger, fright, sorrow, pleading, warning, etc. 2. to express sorrow, pain, fear, etc. by sobbing or shedding tears; weep. 3. to utter its characteristic call: said of an animal. *v.t.* 1. to beg; plead for; implore; beseech: as, the beaten knight *cried* quarter. 2. to utter loudly; shout; exclaim. 3. to proclaim; announce publicly; advertise by calling out that one is selling, buying, repairing, etc. 4. to bring into a specified condition by crying: as, she *cried* herself asleep. *n.* [*pl.* CRIES (krīz)], [ME. & OFr. *cri* < the *v.*], 1. a loud vocal sound expressing pain, anger, fright, etc. 2. any loud utterance; shout. 3. the calling out of an announcement; proclamation. 4. the word or words uttered. 5. an entreaty; urgent appeal. 6. a popular report; rumor. 7. clamor of the people; public outcry. 8. a watchword; rallying call; battle cry; slogan. 9. a sobbing and shedding of tears; fit of weeping. 10. the characteristic vocal sound of an animal. 11. the baying of hounds in the chase; hence, 12. a pack of hounds.
a far cry, 1. a long way. 2. a thing much different.
cry down, to belittle; disparage.
cry for, 1. to plead for. 2. to need greatly.
cry off, to withdraw from an agreement or undertaking; refuse to do something undertaken.
cry one's eyes (or **heart**) **out,** to weep bitterly.
cry out, 1. to shout; yell. 2. to complain loudly.
cry up, to shout praise of; praise highly.
in full cry, in eager pursuit: originally said of a pack of hunting dogs after a quarry.
SYN.—**cry** implies the expression of grief, sorrow, pain, or distress by making mournful, convulsive sounds and shedding tears; **weep** more specifically stresses the shedding of tears; to **sob** is to weep aloud with a catch in the voice and short, gasping breaths; **wail** implies the uttering of loud, prolonged, mournful cries in unsuppressed lamentation; **keen,** specifically an Irish term, signifies a wailing in lamentation for the dead; to **whimper** is to cry with low, whining, broken sounds, as a fretful or frightened child does; **moan** suggests the expression of sorrow or pain in a low, prolonged, mournful sound or sounds; **blubber,** a derisive term used chiefly of children, implies a contorting or swelling of the face with weeping, and broken, inarticulate speech.

cry·ba·by (krī′bā′bi), *n.* 1. a person, especially a child, who cries often or with little cause; hence, 2. a person who complains constantly or accepts defeat unwillingly.

cry·ing (krī′iŋ), *adj.* 1. that cries. 2. demanding immediate notice or remedy: as, a *crying* shame.

cry·o- (krī′ō, krī′ə), [< Gr. *kryos*, cold, frost; cf. CRUST], a combining form meaning *cold, freezing*, as in *cryogen.*

cry·o·gen (krī′ə-jən), *n.* [*cryo-* + *-gen*], a refrigerant.

cry·o·gen·ics (krī′ə-jen′iks), *n.pl.* [construed as sing.], [*cryogen* + *-ics*], the science that deals with the production of very low temperatures and their effect on the properties of matter.

cry·o·hy·drate (krī′ō-hī′drāt), *n.* [*cryo-* + *hydrate*], a crystalline solid formed by the combination of some substance, as salt, with ice at a temperature below the normal freezing point of water.

cry·o·lite (krī′ə-līt′), *n.* [*cryo-* + *-lite:* with reference to its icy appearance], a fluoride of sodium and aluminum, Na_3AlF_6, found in Greenland: it is used in the metallurgy of aluminum.

cry·om·e·ter (krī-om′ə-tẽr), *n.* [*cryo-* + *-meter*], a thermometer for measuring very low temperatures.

cry·os·co·py (krī-os′kə-pi), *n.* [*cryo-* + *-scopy*], the science dealing with the determination of the freezing points of liquids.

cry·o·stat (krī′ə-stat′), *n.* [*cryo-* + *-stat*], a regulator for maintaining a constant, low temperature.

cry·o·ther·a·py (krī′ō-ther′ə-pi), *n.* [*cryo-* + *therapy*], in *medicine*, treatment by the use of cold, as by the application of ice packs or by lowering the body temperature.

crypt (kript), *n.* [L. *crypta;* Gr. *kryptē* < *kryptos*, hidden < *kryptein*, to hide; IE. base **qra-u-*, **qru-*, to heap up, cover, hide; hence akin to OSlav. *kryti*, to hide, Lith. *kruvà*, heap], 1. an underground chamber or vault, especially one under the main floor of a church, serving as a burial place. 2. in *anatomy*, any of various recesses, glandular cavities, or follicles in the body.

cryp·tic (krip′tik), *adj.* [LL. *crypticus;* Gr. *kryptikos;* see CRYPT], 1. secret; occult; mysterious; hidden. 2. having a hidden or ambiguous meaning. 3. in *zoology*, serving to conceal, as the form or coloring of certain animals. —*SYN.* see **obscure.**

cryp·ti·cal (krip′ti-k'l), *adj.* cryptic.

cryp·to- (krip′tō, krip′tə), [< Gr. *kryptos;* see CRYPT], a combining form meaning *secret, hidden*, as in *cryptogram:* also, before a vowel, **crypt-**.

cryp·to·clas·tic (krip′tō-klas′tik), *adj.* [*crypto-* + *-clastic*], in *mineralogy*, consisting of fragmental grains too small to be seen with the unaided eye.

cryp·to·crys·tal·line (krip′tō-kris′t'l-in), *adj.* [*crypto-* + *crystalline*], in *mineralogy*, having a crystalline structure consisting, however, of crystals too small to be seen even with a microscope.

cryp·to·gam (krip′tə-gam′), *n.* [Fr. *cryptogame* < Gr. *kryptos* (see CRYPT) + *gamos*, marriage], a plant that bears no flowers or seeds but propagates by means of special cells called spores, as algae, mosses, ferns, etc.

cryp·to·gam·ic (krip′tə-gam′ik), *adj.* of or like cryptogams.

cryp·tog·am·ous (krip-tog′ə-məs), *adj.* cryptogamic.

cryp·to·gen·ic (krip′tə-jen′ik), *adj.* [*crypto-* + *-genic*], of unknown or obscure origin: said of a disease.

cryp·to·gram (krip′tə-gram′), *n.* [*crypto-* + *-gram*], something written in code or cipher.

cryp·to·gram·mic (krip′tə-gram′ik), *adj.* of or like a cryptogram.

cryp·to·graph (krip′tə-graf′, krip′tə-gräf′), *n.* a cryptogram.

cryp·tog·ra·pher (krip-tog′rə-fẽr), *n.* an expert in cryptography; person who writes in or deciphers secret writing.
cryp·to·graph·ic (krip′tə-graf′ik), *adj.* having to do with cryptography.
cryp·tog·ra·phist (krip-tog′rə-fist), *n.* a cryptographer.
cryp·tog·ra·phy (krip-tog′rə-fi), *n.* [*crypto-* + *-graphy*], 1. the art of writing in or deciphering secret writing or code. 2. a system of secret writing.
cryp·tol·o·gy (krip-tol′ə-ji), *n.* [*crypto-* + *-logy*], 1. cryptography. 2. secret language.
cryp·to·nym (krip′tə-nim′), *n.* [*crypt-* + *-onym*], a secret name.
cryp·ton·y·mous (krip-ton′i-məs), *adj.* [*cryptonym* + *-ous*], having a secret or concealed name; anonymous.
cryp·to·phyte (krip′tə-fīt′), *n.* a cryptogam.
Cryp·to·zo·ic (krip′tə-zō′ik), *adj.* [*crypto-* + *-zoic*], Proterozoic.
cryst., 1. crystalline. 2. crystallography.
Crys·tal (kris′t'l), *n.* a city in eastern Minnesota, near Minneapolis: pop., 24,000.
crys·tal (kris′t'l), *n.* [Latinized sp. of ME. & OFr. *cristal;* L. *crystallum,* crystal, ice < Gr. *krystallos* < *kryos;* see CRUST], 1. a clear, transparent quartz. 2. a piece of this cut in the form of an ornament. 3. a very clear, brilliant glass. 4. an article or articles made of such glass, as goblets, bowls, etc. 5. the transparent protective covering over the face of a watch. 6. anything clear and transparent like crystal. 7. a solidified form of a substance in which the atoms or molecules are arranged in a definite repeating pattern so that the external shape of a particle or mass of the substance is made up of plane faces in a symmetrical arrangement. 8. in *radio,* a crystal detector. *adj.* 1. of or composed of crystal. 2. like crystal; clear and transparent. 3. in *radio,* of or using a crystal.

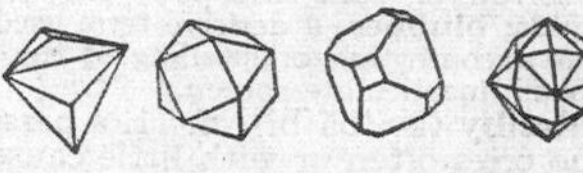
TYPES OF CRYSTAL

crystal ball, a large ball of rock crystal or, more commonly, of glass, used in crystal gazing.
crystal detector, in *radio,* a rectifier consisting of a semiconductor (e.g., silica) in contact with the sharp edge of a conductor (e.g., tungsten).
crystal gazing, the practice of gazing into a crystal ball and pretending to see certain images, especially of future events.
crys·tall- (kris′t'l), crystallo-.
crys·tal·lif·er·ous (kris′t'l-if′ẽr-əs), *adj.* [*crystall-* + *-iferous*], producing or containing crystals.
crys·tal·line (kris′t'l-in, kris′t'l-īn′), *adj.* [< Fr. & L.; Fr. *crystallin;* L. *crystallinus;* Gr. *krystallinos;* see CRYSTAL], 1. consisting or made of crystal. 2. like crystal; clear and transparent. 3. having the character or structure of a crystal. 4. consisting of crystals. Abbreviated **cryst.**
crystalline lens, the lens of the eye, a biconvex structure serving to focus light on the retina: see **eye,** illus.
crystalline system, any of the six groups (isometric, hexagonal, tetragonal, orthorhombic, monoclinic, and triclinic) into which crystalline species are classified on the basis of the relationships of their crystallographic axes (imaginary lines drawn from each face or edge through the center of the crystal).
crys·tal·lite (kris′t'l-īt′), *n.* [*crystall-* + *-ite*], a hairlike formation found in igneous and volcanic rocks that are beginning to crystallize.
crys·tal·lit·ic (kris′t'l-it′ik), *adj.* 1. of or containing crystallite. 2. of the nature of crystallite.
crys·tal·liz·a·ble (kris′t'l-īz′ə-b'l), *adj.* capable of crystallizing or being crystallized.
crys·tal·li·za·tion (kris′t'l-ə-zā′shən, kris′t'l-i-zā′shən), *n.* 1. a crystallizing or being crystallized. 2. a crystallized structure or substance.
crys·tal·lize (kris′t'l-īz′), *v.t.* [CRYSTALLIZED (-īzd′), CRYSTALLIZING], 1. to cause to form crystals or take on a crystalline structure. 2. to give a definite form to. 3. to coat with sugar. *v.i.* 1. to become crystalline in form. 2. to take on a definite form: as, our unfavorable impressions *crystallized* into a strong dislike.
crys·tal·lo- (kris′t'l-ō), [< Gr. *krystallos,* crystal], a combining form meaning *crystal,* as in *crystallography:* also, before a vowel, **crystall-.**
crys·tal·lo·graph·ic (kris′t'l-ə-graf′ik), *adj.* of or concerned with crystallography.
crys·tal·lo·graph·i·cal (kris′t'l-ə-graf′i-k'l), *adj.* crystallographic.
crys·tal·log·ra·phy (kris′t'l-og′rə-fi), *n.* [*crystallo-* + *-graphy*], the science of the form, structure, properties, and classification of crystals: abbreviated **cryst.**
crys·tal·loid (kris′t'l-oid′), *adj.* [*crystall-* + *-oid*], 1. like a crystal. 2. having the nature of a crystalloid. *n.* a substance, usually crystallizable, which, when in solution, readily passes through vegetable and animal membranes: opposed to *colloid.*
crys·tal·loi·dal (kris′t'l-oi′d'l), *adj.* of a crystalloid.
crys·tal·lose (kris′t'l-ōs′), *adj.* [*crystall-* + *-ose*], the sodium salt of saccharin, used for the same purposes as saccharin: also called *soluble saccharin.*
crystal pickup, a pickup with a quartz crystal, often used on electric phonographs: distinguished from *magnetic pickup.*
crystal set, a simple type of radio receiver with a crystal detector instead of an electron tube detector.
crystal violet, a rosaniline dye used in medicine as an antiseptic, an indicator, and a Gram stain for bacteria.
crystal vision, 1. the alleged faculty of divination by crystal gazing. 2. the images supposed to be seen in crystal gazing.
Cs, in *chemistry,* cesium.
cs., case; cases.
C.S., 1. Christian Science. 2. Confederate States.
C.S., c.s., 1. capital stock. 2. civil service.
C.S.A., Confederate States of America.
CSC, Civil Service Commission.
csc, cosecant.
csk., cask.
C.S.O., 1. Chief Signal Officer. 2. Chief Staff Officer.
C.S.T., Central Standard Time.
Ct., 1. Connecticut. 2. Count.
ct., 1. [*pl.* CTS.], cent. 2. *centum,* [L.], a hundred. 3. certificate. 4. county. 5. court.
CTC, Citizens' Training Corps.
cten·o- (ten′ō, tē′nə), [< Gr. *kteis, ktenos* < **pktenos;* akin to L. *pecten,* comb (see PECTINATE)], a combining form meaning *ctenoid scales, teeth,* etc., as in *ctenophore:* also, before a vowel, **cten-.**
cte·noid (tē′noid, ten′oid), *adj.* [*cten-* + *-oid*], having an edge with projections like the teeth of a comb, as the scales and teeth of certain fishes.
cte·noph·o·ran (ti-nof′ə-rən), *adj.* of a ctenophore. *n.* a ctenophore (sense 1).
cten·o·phore (ten′ə-fôr′, tē′nə-fōr′), *n.* [*cteno-* + *-phore*], 1. any of a large group of sea animals with a pair of long, streaming tentacles and an oval, transparent, jellylike body bearing eight rows of comblike plates that aid in swimming. 2. any of these plates.
Ctes·i·phon (tes′ə-fon′), *n.* an ancient city in Babylonia, on the Tigris River: its ruins are near Bagdad.
ctg., cartridge.
ctn, cotangent.
ctr., center.
cts., 1. centimes. 2. cents.
Cu, *cuprum,* [L.], in *chemistry,* copper.
Cu., cu., cumulus.
cu., cubic.
cub (kub), *n.* [Early Mod. Eng. *cubbe,* young fox; prob. < or via. Celt.; cf. Ir. *cuib,* whelp, OIr. *cū* (genit. *con*), dog; IE. base **kuon-,* dog, as also in L. *canis* (cf. CANINE) & Eng. *hound*], 1. a young fox, bear, lion, tiger, whale, etc.: term used only of certain mammals. 2. an inexperienced, awkward youth. 3. a novice or beginner, especially in newspaper reporting. 4. a member of a division of the Boy Scouts for boys between the ages of eight and eleven.
cub., cubic.
Cu·ba (kū′bə), *n.* a country on an island in the West Indies, south of Florida: area, 44,164 sq. mi.; pop., 6,743,000; capital, Havana.
cub·age (kū′bij), *n.* [*cube* + *-age*], cubic content.
Cuba lib·re (lē′brə), [Sp., lit., free Cuba], an alcoholic drink made by mixing a cola beverage with rum and fresh lime or lemon juice.
Cu·ban (kū′bən), *adj.* of Cuba, its people, or culture. *n.* a native or inhabitant of Cuba.
Cuban heel, a heel of medium height, used on some types of women's shoes.
cu·ba·ture (kū′bə-chẽr), *n.* [< L. *cubus* (see CUBE), after *quadrature*], 1. the determination of the cubic content of a solid. 2. cubic content; volume.
cub·by·hole (kub′i-hōl′), *n.* [children's word for snug place to play < Brit. dial. *cub,* little shed, enclosed place (for base see COVE); + *hole*], a small, enclosed space.
cube (kūb), *n.* [Fr.; L. *cubus;* Gr. *kybos,* a cube, die, vertebra; akin to AS. *hype,* hip, L. *cubare,* to lie down; all < IE. base **qeu-,* **qeub-,* to bend, turn], 1. in *geometry,* a solid with six equal, square sides. 2. in *mathematics,* the product obtained by multiplying a given number or quantity by its square; third power: as, the *cube* of 3 is 27 (3 × 3 × 3). *v.t.* [CUBED (kūbd), CUBING], 1. to raise to the third power; obtain the cube of (a number or quantity). 2. to form into the shape of a cube or cubes: as, *cube* the vegetables. 3. to measure the cubic content of.

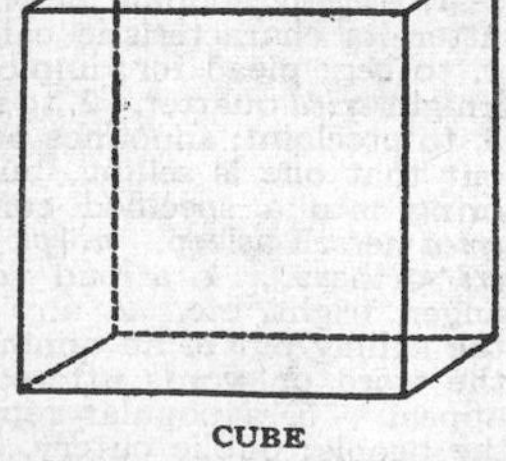
CUBE

cu·beb (kū′beb), *n.* [Fr. *cubèbe;* ML. *cubeba;* Ar. *kabābah*], 1. the small, spicy berry of an East Indian shrub of the pepper family, used in medicine. 2. a cigarette made from the crushed berries, sometimes used in treating catarrh.

cube root, the number or quantity of which a given number or quantity is the cube: as, the *cube root* of 8 is 2.

cu·bic (kū'bik), *adj.* [Fr. *cubique;* L. *cubicus;* Gr. *kybikos;* see CUBE], 1. having the shape of a cube. 2. having three dimensions: a cubic foot is the volume of a cube whose length, width, and breadth each measure one foot: abbreviated **cu., c., C., cub.** 3. in *mathematics,* of the third power or degree; relating to the cubes of numbers or quantities.

cu·bi·cal (kū'bi-k'l), *adj.* cube-shaped.

cu·bi·cal·ly (kū'bi-k'l-i, kū'bik-li), *adv.* according to cubic measure.

cu·bi·cle (kū'bi-k'l), *n.* [L. *cubiculum* < *cubare,* to lie down; see CUBE], 1. a small sleeping compartment, as in a dormitory. 2. any small compartment.

cubic measure, a system of measuring volume in cubic units; especially, the system in which
1,728 cubic inches = 1 cubic foot
27 cubic feet = 1 cubic yard
1,000 cubic millimeters = 1 cubic centimeter
1,000 cubic centimeters = 1 cubic decimeter
1,000 cubic decimeters = 1 cubic meter

cu·bic·u·lum (kyoo-bik'yoo-ləm), *n.* [*pl.* CUBICULA (-lə)], [L., lit., a sleeping chamber; cf. CUBICLE], a burial chamber, as in the Roman catacombs.

cu·bi·form (kū'bi-fôrm'), *adj.* having the form of a cube.

cub·ism (kūb'iz'm), *n* a school of modern art characterized by the use of cubes and other abstract geometric forms rather than by a realistic representation of nature.

cub·ist (kūb'ist), *n.* an adherent of cubism. *adj.* of cubism or cubists.

cu·bit (kū'bit), *n.* [L. *cubitum,* the elbow, cubit; akin to L. *cubare;* see CUBE], an ancient measure of length, about 18–22 inches; originally, the length of the arm from the end of the middle finger to the elbow.

cu·boid (kū'boid), *adj.* [Gr. *kyboeidēs;* see CUBE], 1. shaped like a cube. 2. designating a cubelike bone between the instep and the heel bone. *n.* 1. a six-sided figure each face of which is a rectangle. 2. the cuboid bone.

cu·boi·dal (kyoo-boi'd'l), *adj.* 1. cuboid. 2. of the cuboid bone.

cub reporter, an inexperienced newspaper reporter.

Cu·chul·ainn, Cu·chul·lin (kōō-kul'in, kōō'khool-in), *n.* [Ir.], in *Irish legend,* a hero and warrior who single-handedly defended his country against invaders.

cuck·ing stool (kuk'iŋ), [ME. *cokinge-stole,* lit., toilet seat < ME. *coken* < ON. *kūka,* to defecate: the instrument was orig. made to resemble a toilet seat to heighten the victim's indignity], a kind of chair in which disorderly women, scolds, dishonest tradespeople, etc. were fastened and exposed to public ridicule, or sometimes ducked.

cuck·old (kuk''ld), *n.* [ME. *cokewold, cukeweld;* OFr. *cucuault* < *cucu* (see CUCKOO): said to be in allusion to the bird's habit of laying its eggs in the nests of other birds], a man whose wife has committed adultery. *v.t.* to make a cuckold of.

cuck·old·ry (kuk''ld-ri), *n.* the act of making a cuckold of a husband; adultery.

cuck·oo (kook'ōō'; *also, esp. for adj.,* kōō'kōō'), *n.* [ME. < OFr. *coucou, cucu,* echoic of the bird's cry; akin to but not connected with L. *cuculus,* Gr. *kokkux,* etc., all echoic], 1. any of a family of birds with a long, slender body, grayish-brown on top and white below: the European species lays its eggs in the nests of other birds, but the American variety hatches and rears its own young. 2. the call of a cuckoo, which sounds somewhat like its name. 3. an imitation of this call. *v.i.* to utter or imitate this call. *v.t.* to repeat continually: from the cuckoo's habit of sounding its call again and again. *adj.* [Slang], crazy; foolish; silly.

cuckoo clock, a clock with a small toy figure of a cuckoo in it, which appears at regular intervals, usually on the hour, to the accompaniment of a sound imitating the bird's call.

cuck·oo·flow·er (kook'ōō-flou'ẽr, kōō'kōō-flou'ẽr), *n.* any of several plants; especially, *a)* a variety of cress bearing white or rose flowers. *b)* the ragged robin.

cuck·oo·pint (kook'ōō-pint', kōō'kōō-pint'), *n.* a European wild flower of the arum family, with large leaves and a flower shaped like that of the calla lily.

cuckoo spit (or **spittle**), 1. a frothy substance produced on plants by the nymphs of certain insects to envelop their larvae. 2. such an insect.

cu. cm., cubic centimeter; cubic centimeters.

cu·cu·li·form (kyoo-kū'li-fôrm'), *adj.* [< L. *cuculus,* cuckoo; + *-form*], of or like the cuckoos or the order of birds to which they belong.

cu·cul·late (kū'kə-lāt', kyoo-kul'āt), *adj.* hooded; shaped like a hood; cowled, as the leaves of violets.

cu·cum·ber (kū'kum-bẽr), *n.* [ME. *cocumber;* OFr. *cocombre;* Pr. *cogombre;* L. *cucumis, cucumere,* cucumber], 1. a long, green-skinned vegetable with firm, white flesh, used in salads and preserved as pickles. 2. the vine on which it grows.
cool as a cucumber, 1. comfortably cool. 2. calm and self-possessed.

cucumber tree, any of several kinds of American magnolia tree with large, green flowers and fruit resembling a small cucumber.

cu·cu·mi·form (kyoo-kū'mi-fôrm'), *adj.* [< L. *cucumis,* cucumber; + *-form*], shaped like a cucumber.

cu·cur·bit (kyoo-kũr'bit), *n.* [L. *cucurbita;* initial *cu-* prob. by analogy with *cucumis* (see CUCUMBER); akin to Sans. *carbhaṭa,* gourd], 1. any cucurbitaceous plant; gourd. 2. [Fr. *cucurbite* < L. *cucurbita:* so called in allusion to its shape], a large, gourd-shaped flask with a wide mouth, formerly used in distillation: also spelled **cucurbite.**

cu·cur·bi·ta·ceous (kyoo-kũr'bi-tā'shəs), *adj.* [< L. *cucurbita* (see prec.); + *-aceous*], of a large group of tendril-bearing, vinelike herbs of the gourd family, including the gourd, squash, melon, cucumber, etc.

cud (kud), *n.* [ME.; AS. *cwudu,* ball of cud, lit., what is rounded; akin to G. *koden,* double chin, paunch; IE. **geu-t,* etc. < base **geu-,* to curve, bend], a mouthful of previously swallowed food regurgitated from the first stomach of cattle and other ruminants back to the mouth, where it is chewed slowly a second time.
chew the cud, to recall and think over something; ruminate; ponder.

cud·bear (kud'bâr), *n.* [coined < *Cuthbert* by Dr. *Cuthbert* Gordon, who developed the dye], 1. a purple dye prepared from lichens. 2. any lichen that is the source of this dye.

cud·dle (kud''l), *v.t.* [CUDDLED (-'ld), CUDDLING], [Early Mod. Eng., to make comfortable; prob. < ME. (northern dial.) **cudelen* for **couthelen* (for *-d,* cf. FIDDLE) < *couth,* known, hence acquainted with, comfortable with (cf. UNCOUTH) + *-le,* freq. suffix], to hold lovingly and gently in one's arms; embrace and fondle. *v.i.* to lie close and snug; nestle; curl up. *n.* 1. a cuddling. 2. an embrace; hug. —*SYN.* see **caress.**

cud·dle·some (kud''l-səm), *adj.* [*cuddle* + *-some*], inviting cuddling; embraceable.

cud·dly (kud'li), *adj.* [CUDDLIER (-li-ẽr), CUDDLIEST (-li-ist)], fond of cuddling; cuddlesome.

cud·dy (kud'i), *n.* [*pl.* CUDDIES (-iz)], [17th-c.; date suggests borrowing < D. or Fris.; ? Gmc. base **kud-,* **kudd-* (< IE. **geu-,* to curve, bend); ult. akin to AS. *cofa, codda,* Eng. *cubby* in *cubbyhole*], 1. *a)* a small room or cabin on a ship. *b)* on a small ship, the cook's galley or a shelter cabin. 2. a small room, cupboard, or closet.

cud·dy (kud'i), *n.* [*pl.* CUDDIES (-iz)], [< *Cuddy,* dim. of *Cuthbert*], [Scot.], a donkey.

cud·dy (kud'i), *n.* [*pl.* CUDDIES (-iz)], [prob. < Scot. Gael. *cudaig*], [Scot.], a coalfish.

cudg·el (kuj'əl), *n.* [ME. (southwestern dial.) *kuggel;* AS. *cycgel,* lit., club with rounded or bulbous head; akin to G. *kugel,* ball, globe; IE. base **geu-,* to curve, bend], a short, thick stick or club. *v.t.* [CUDGELED or CUDGELLED (-əld), CUDGELING or CUDGELLING], to beat with a cudgel.
cudgel one's brains, to think hard.
take up the cudgels for, to come to the defense of.

cud·weed (kud'wēd'), *n.* [*cud* + *weed:* said to have been named from being given to cattle that had lost their cud], any of several plants with cottony or woolly leaves.

cue (kū), *n.* [< *q, Q,* used on plays in 16th & 17th c. to indicate actors' entrances; prob. abbrev. of some L. word (as *quando,* when, *qualis,* in what manner, etc.)], 1. a signal in dialogue, action, or music for an actor's entrance or speech, or for the working of curtains, lights, sound effects, etc. 2. the few notes or bars of music directly preceding an instrumentalist's or vocalist's part and serving as a signal for him to begin. 3. any signal or motion to begin or enter. 4. a hint; intimation; suggestion. 5. the part that an actor is assigned to play; hence, 6. a course of action. 7. frame of mind; mood; temperament. 8. in *psychology,* a secondary stimulus that guides behavior, often without entering consciousness. *v.t.* [CUED (kūd), CUING], [Colloq.], to give a cue to.

cue (kū), *n.* [< Fr. *queue,* pigtail; see QUEUE], 1. a queue (pigtail or waiting line). 2. a long, tapering, tipped rod used in billiards, pool, etc. to strike the cue ball. *v.t.* [CUED (kūd), CUING], to braid (hair, etc.).

cue ball, the ball that a player strikes with his cue in billiards or pool: it is usually white or yellowish.

Cuen·ca (kweŋ'kä), *n.* a city in southwestern Ecuador: pop., 54,000.

cues·ta (kwes'tə), *n.* [Sp.], a ridge or hill characterized by a steep escarpment on one side and a long gentle slope on the other.

cuff (kuf), *n.* [by sense extension < ME. *cuffe, coffe,* hand covering, hence mitten, glove; ? akin to ML. *cuffia, cuphia,* head covering, parallel with OFr. *coiffe;* see COIF], 1. a band at the wrist end of the sleeve of a garment, either fastened to the sleeve or separate. 2. the wrist end of a sleeve. 3. a turned-up fold at the bottom of a trouser leg. 4. a handcuff. *v.t.* to put a cuff or cuffs on.

off the cuff, [Slang], in an offhand manner; extemporaneously.

on the cuff, [Slang], with payment deferred.

cuff (kuf), *v.t.* [Early Mod. Eng.; ? < *cuff, n.* (in orig. sense "glove"); ? < ON.; cf. Sw. *kuffa,* to strike], to strike, especially with the open hand; slap. *n.* a slap.

cuff button, a button for the cuff of a shirt.

cuff link, a pair of linked buttons or similar small device for keeping a shirt cuff closed.

Cu·fic (kū'fik), *adj.* Kufic.

cu. ft., cubic foot; cubic feet.

‡**cui bo·no** (kwē' bō'nō, kī' bō'nō), [L., lit., to whom for a good], 1. for whose benefit? 2. to what purpose?

cu. in., cubic inch; cubic inches.

cui·rass (kwi-ras'), *n.* [Fr. *cuirasse;* It. *corazza;* LL. **coracea,* for L. (*vestis*) *coriacea,* leather (clothing) < *corium,* leather, hide; IE. base *(*s*)*qer-*(*t*)-, to cut, separate; akin to AS. *heortha,* deerskin, ON. *hörund,* skin], 1. a piece of close-fitting armor for protecting the breast and back: it was originally made of leather. 2. the breastplate of such armor. 3. in *zoology,* a protective structure of bony plates. *v.t.* to cover with or as with a cuirass.

cui·ras·sier (kwi'rə-sêr'), *n.* [Fr.], a cavalryman wearing a cuirass.

cuish (kwish), *n.* a cuisse.

cui·sine (kwi-zēn'), *n.* [Fr.; L. *coquina,* kitchen < *coquere,* to cook], 1. the kitchen. 2. the style of cooking; manner of preparing food. 3. the food prepared, as at a restaurant.

cuisse (kwis), *n.* [ME. *cuissues;* OFr. *cuisseaux,* pl. of *cuissel* < *cuisse,* thigh < L. *coxa,* hip; IE. base **qoksā:* cf. Sans. *kákṣā,* armpit, Fr. *cuisse,* thigh, G. *hächse* (OHG. *hahsa*), shin, OIr. *coss,* foot], *usually in pl.* a piece of armor for protection of the thigh; thigh piece: also **cuish**: see **armor,** illus.

culch (kulch), *n.* cultch.

cul-de-sac (kul'də-sak', kool'də-sak'; Fr. kü'd'-såk'), *n.* [*pl.* CUL-DE-SACS (-saks'); Fr. CULS-DE-SAC (kü'd'-såk')], [Fr., lit., bottom of a sack], 1. a passage or position with only one outlet; blind alley; hence, 2. a situation from which there is no escape.

-cule (kūl), [< Fr. or L.; Fr. *-cule;* L. *-culus, -cula, -culum*], a suffix added to nouns to indicate the diminutive, as in *animalcule:* see **-cle.**

Cu·le·bra Cut (kōō-lā'brə), Gaillard Cut: former name.

cu·let (kū'lit), *n.* [OFr., dim. of *cul,* posterior, bottom; L. *culus,* anus], the flat base of a diamond whose face is cut as a brilliant.

cu·lex (kū'leks), *n.* [L., a gnat; akin to OIr. *cuil,* gnat, Sans. *śula-,* spear, sharp stake], any of a large group of mosquitoes including the most common species found in North America and Europe.

cu·lic·id (kū-lis'id), *adj.* [< Mod. L. *Culicidae,* name of the family], of the mosquito family. *n.* a mosquito.

cu·li·nar·y (kū'lə-ner'i), *adj.* [L. *culinarius* < *culina,* kitchen], 1. of the kitchen. 2. of cookery. 3. suitable for or used in cooking.

Cu·lion (kōō-lyōn'), *n.* a small island in the western Philippines: site of a leper colony.

cull (kul), *v.t.* [ME. *cullen;* OFr. *cuillir;* L. *colligere;* see COLLECT], 1. to pick out; select. 2. to select and gather; pick (flowers, etc.). 3. to examine carefully in order to make a selection from; pick over. *n.* something picked out, especially something rejected as not up to standard.

Cul·len, Coun·tee (koun-tā' kul'ən), 1903–1946; American poet.

cul·len·der (kul'ən-dẽr), *n.* a colander.

cul·let (kul'it), *n.* [< Fr. *collet,* dim. of *col,* neck, with reference to glass debris at the neck of a bottle in blowing], scraps of waste glass that can be remelted.

cul·lion (kul'yən), *n.* [ME. *coillon;* Fr. *couillon,* coward, dullard; It. *coglione,* booby, wretch; LL. *coleone,* eunuch < **colea,* scrotum < L. *coleus,* testicles], [Obs.], a low, contemptible fellow.

cul·lis (kul'is), *n.* [Fr. *coulisse;* see COULISSE], in *architecture,* a gutter or groove.

cul·ly (kul'i), *n.* [*pl.* CULLIES (-iz)], [17th-c. thieves' slang; ? contr. (cf. MOB, CHUM) of *cullion*], 1. [Rare], a person easily deceived; dupe. 2. [British Slang], fellow; pal; buddy. *v.t.* [CULLIED (-id), CULLYING], [Obs.], to trick; deceive; cheat.

culm (kulm), *n.* [northern Brit. dial < ME. *colme,* lit., that which pours out < base (AS. **cwellan,* to pour forth) of AS. (*ge*)*collen,* swollen up; akin to G. *qualm,* smoke, steam (Dan. *kvalm,* D. *kwalm;* cf. OHG. *quellan,* to spring forth), G. *quelle,* a spring, fountain], 1. coal dust or slack; small pieces of anthracite. 2. in *geology,* a Lower Carboniferous formation of shale or sandstone containing beds of impure anthracite: also **culm measures.**

culm (kulm), *n.* [L. *culmus,* a stalk, stem; akin to G. *halm,* blade (of grass), Gr. *calamos,* reed, cane], the jointed stem of various grasses, usually hollow. *v.i.* to grow or develop into a culm.

cul·mif·er·ous (kul-mif'ẽr-əs), *adj.* [*culm* (coal dust) + *-iferous*], in *geology,* containing or producing culm.

cul·mi·nant (kul'mə-nənt), *adj.* [ML. *culminans,* ppr.], culminating; at the highest point or altitude.

cul·mi·nate (kul'mə-nāt'), *v.i.* [CULMINATED (-id), CULMINATING], [< ML. *culminatus,* pp. of *culminare* < L. *culmen, culminis,* peak, summit, contr. of *columen;* see COLUMN], 1. to reach its highest altitude: said of a celestial body. 2. to reach its highest point or climax; result (*in*).

cul·mi·na·tion (kul'mə-nā'shən), *n.* 1. a culminating; reaching of the highest altitude or point. 2. the highest point; that in which a thing culminates.

cu·lottes (koo-lots', kyoo-lots'), *n.pl.* [Fr.], knee-length trousers made full in the legs to resemble a skirt, worn by women and girls for sports, etc.

CULOTTES

‡**cul·pa** (kul'pə), *n.* [L.], 1. fault; guilt. 2. in *law,* negligence; carelessness.

cul·pa·bil·i·ty (kul'pə-bil'ə-ti), *n.* the fact of being culpable; liability to blame.

cul·pa·ble (kul'pə-b'l), *adj.* [ME. *coupable;* OFr. *coupable, culpable;* L. *culpabilis* < *culpa,* crime, fault, blame], deserving blame; blameworthy.

cul·pa·bly (kul'pə-bli), *adv.* in a culpable manner.

Cul·pep·er, Thomas (kul'pep'ẽr), second Baron Culpeper, 1635–1689; English governor of the colony of Virginia (1680–1683).

cul·prit (kul'prit), *n.* [< Anglo-Fr. *cul. prit,* contr. for phr. *culpable, prit* (*à averer nostre bille*), lit., guilty, ready (to prove our case): words used by prosecutor in opening case; *culpable* (see CULPABLE) + *prit,* for OFr. *prest* < LL. *praestus,* ready], 1. a person accused of a crime or offense, as in court; prisoner at the bar. 2. a person guilty of a crime or offense; offender.

cult (kult), *n.* [< Fr. & L.; Fr. *culte;* L. *cultus,* care, cultivation < *colere,* to till, cultivate; akin to ON. *hvel,* AS. *hweol;* cf. WHEEL], 1. a system of religious worship or ritual. 2. devoted attachment to, or extravagant admiration for, a person, principle, etc., especially when regarded as a fad: as, the *cult* of nudism. 3. a group of followers; sect.

cultch (kulch), *n.* [? < OFr. *culche, couche,* layer, deposit; see COUCH], 1. rubbish. 2. materials forming a spawning bed for oysters. Also spelled **culch.**

cul·ti·va·ble (kul'tə-və-b'l), *adj.* that can be cultivated.

cul·ti·vat·a·ble (kul'tə-vāt'ə-b'l), *adj.* cultivable.

cul·ti·vate (kul'tə-vāt'), *v.t.* [CULTIVATED (-id), CULTIVATING], [< ML. *cultivatus,* pp. of *cultivare* < *cultivus,* tilled < L. *cultus;* see CULT], 1. to prepare and use (soil, land, etc.) for growing crops; till. 2. to break up the surface soil around (plants) in order to destroy weeds, prevent crusting, and preserve moisture. 3. to grow (plants or crops) from seeds, bulbs, shoots, etc. 4. to improve or develop (plants) by various horticultural techniques. 5. to improve by care, training, or study; refine: as, *cultivate* your mind. 6. to promote the development or growth of; acquire and develop: as, he *cultivated* a social conscience. 7. to seek to develop a familiarity with; give one's attention to; pursue.

cul·ti·vat·ed (kul'tə-vāt'id), *adj.* [pp. of *cultivate*], 1. prepared and used for growing crops; tilled: as, *cultivated* land. 2. grown by cultivation: opposed to *wild.* 3. trained and developed; refined; cultured: as, a *cultivated* person.

cul·ti·va·tion (kul'tə-vā'shən), *n.* 1. the cultivating of land, plants, etc. 2. the giving of attention to the development or advancement of something. 3. training and development; refinement; culture.

cul·ti·va·tor (kul'tə-vā'tẽr), *n.* 1. a person who cultivates. 2. an implement or machine for loosening the earth and destroying weeds around growing plants.

cul·trate (kul'trāt), *adj.* [L. *cultratus,* knifelike < *culter,* a knife; cf. COLTER], sharp-edged and pointed, like some knives.

cul·tur·al (kul'chẽr-əl), *adj.* 1. of culture. 2. obtained by breeding.

cultural features, man-made landmarks, as cities, highways, dams, etc., especially as seen from the air.

cul·ture (kul'chẽr), *n.* [Fr.; L. *cultura* < *colere;* see CULT], 1. the cultivation of soil. 2. the raising, improvement, or development of some plant, animal, or product. 3. the growth of bacteria or other microorganisms in a specially prepared nourishing substance, as agar. 4. a colony of microorganisms thus grown. 5. improvement, refinement, or development by study, training, etc. 6. the training and refining of the mind, emotions, manners, taste, etc. 7. the result of this; refinement of thought, emotion, manners, taste, etc. 8. the concepts, habits, skills, arts, instruments, institutions, etc. of a given people in a given period; civilization. ***v.t.*** [CULTURED (-chẽrd), CULTURING], 1. to cultivate. 2. to grow (microorganisms) in a specially prepared medium.

cul·tured (kul′chẽrd), ***adj.*** 1. produced or obtained by cultivation. 2. having culture or refinement.

culture (or **cultural**) **diffusion,** in *sociology*, the spread of a culture trait or pattern from its point of origin to other areas.

culture (or **cultural**) **lag,** in *sociology*, the failure of one aspect of a cultural complex to keep pace with the changes in some other related aspect, as the failure of social institutions to keep pace with the rapid advances in science.

culture medium, a nutrient substance sterilized and suitably prepared for the controlled growth of microorganisms.

cul·tur·ist (kul′chẽr-ist), ***n.*** 1. a person engaged in the culture of plants or animals. 2. one who advocates, or is devoted to, general cultural advancement.

cul·tus (kul′təs), ***n.*** [L.], a religious cult.

cul·ver (kul′vẽr), ***n.*** [ME. *culfre;* AS. *culfer, culufre* (borrowing < L. *columba*, dove); IE. base ****qel-***, ****qāl-***, gray], a dove or pigeon, especially the wood pigeon.

cul·ver·in (kul′vẽr-in), ***n.*** [Fr. *coulevrine* < *couleuvre*, adder < LL. *culobra*, for L. *colubra*, a serpent, snake], 1. a kind of musket used in the Middle Ages. 2. a long, heavy cannon of the 16th and 17th centuries.

cul·vert (kul′vẽrt), ***n.*** [late 18th c.; prob. < name of unknown inventor], a drain or waterway of pipe or masonry crossing under a road or embankment.

CULVERT

cum (kum, koom) ***prep.*** [L.], with: used, usually in hyphenated compounds, with the general meaning *combined with, plus*, as, vaudeville-*cum*-burlesque.

Cu·mae (kū′mē), ***n.*** an ancient city in southwestern Italy, on the Bay of Naples: colonized by the Greeks.

Cu·mae·an (kyoo-mē′ən), ***adj.*** 1. of Cumae. 2. of a famous sibyl of Cumae: cf. **Sibylline Books.**

cum·ber (kum′bẽr), ***v.t.*** [ME. *cumbren, comberen* < OFr. *encombrer* (cf. ENCUMBER) < LL. *combrus*, barrier; prob. of Gmc. origin; akin to G. *kummer* (MHG. *kumber*), also < LL.; IE. base, prob. ****gem-***, to grip, get hold of], 1. to hinder by obstruction or interference; hamper. 2. to burden in a troublesome way. 3. [Obs.], to perplex or distress. ***n.*** anything that cumbers.

Cum·ber·land (kum′bẽr-lənd), ***n.*** 1. a county of northwestern England: pop., 285,000; county seat, Carlisle. 2. a river in Kentucky and Tennessee, flowing into the Ohio: length, 687 mi. 3. a city in northwestern Maryland: pop., 33,000.

Cumberland Gap, a pass through the Cumberland Mountains, at the joint boundary of Virginia, Kentucky, and Tennessee: height, 1,315 ft.

Cumberland Mountains, a mountain range of the Appalachians, in Kentucky, Virginia, and Tennessee.

Cumberland Plateau, the Cumberland Mountains.

cum·ber·some (kum′bẽr-səm), ***adj.*** [*cumber* + *-some*], burdensome; unwieldy; clumsy. —***SYN.*** see **heavy.**

cum·brance (kum′brəns), ***n.*** an encumbrance.

cum·brous (kum′brəs), ***adj.*** cumbersome.

‡cum gra·no sa·lis (kum grā′nō sā′lis), [L., lit., with a grain of salt], with due skepticism.

cum·in (kum′in), ***n.*** [ME.; AS. *cymen* < L. *cuminum;* ult. < Heb. *kammōn* or Ar. *kammūn* via Gr.; G. *kümmel* (cf. KÜMMEL) is of the same origin], 1. a small plant of the carrot family, bearing clusters of small, white or rose flowers. 2. its aromatic seeds, used for flavoring pickles, soups, etc. Also spelled **cummin.**

‡cum lau·de (kum lô′di, koom lou′de), [L.], with praise: phrase used to signify graduation with honors from a college: cf. **magna cum laude, summa cum laude.**

cum·mer (kum′ẽr), ***n.*** [Fr. *commère;* LL. *commater* < L. *com-*, with + *mater*, mother], [Scot.], 1. a godmother. 2. a woman companion. 3. a woman or girl.

cum·mer·bund (kum′ẽr-bund′), ***n.*** [Hind. & Per. *kamarband*, loin band < Ar.-Per. *kamar*, loins + Per. *band*, band], a sash for the waist, worn originally by men in India: also spelled **kummerbund.**

Cum·mings, E. E. (kum′iŋz), (*Edward Estlin Cummings*), 1894–1962; American poet and painter.

cum·quat (kum′kwot), ***n.*** a kumquat.

cum·shaw (kum′shô), ***n.*** [< dial. form of Chin. *kan hsieh*, grateful thanks; *kan*, to be thankful + *hsieh*, thanks], a tip; gratuity.

cu·mu·late (kūm′yə-lāt′; *for adj., usually* kūm′yə-lit), ***v.t. & v.i.*** [CUMULATED (-id), CUMULATING], [< L. *cumulatus*, pp. of *cumulare*, to heap up, amass < *cumulus;* see CUMULUS], to gather into a heap; accumulate. ***adj.*** gathered into a heap.

cu·mu·la·tion (kūm′yə-lā′shən), ***n.*** 1. a cumulating. 2. an accumulation; heap.

cu·mu·la·tive (kūm′yə-lā′tiv, kūm′yə-lə-tiv), ***adj.*** [see CUMULATE], 1. increasing in effect, size, quantity, etc. by successive additions; accumulated: as, *cumulative* interest is interest that is added to the principal and draws additional interest. 2. in *law*, designating additional evidence that gives support to earlier evidence.

cumulative voting, a system of voting for members of a legislature in which each voter is allowed as many votes as there are members to be elected: he may distribute his votes or give them all to one candidate.

cu·mu·li·form (kū′myoo-li-fôrm′), ***adj.*** [L. *cumuli*, pl. of *cumulus;* + *-form*], designating, or having the form of, a cumulus (cloud).

cu·mu·lo-cir·rus (kūm′yə-lō-sir′əs), ***n.*** a small cumulus that is white and filmy like a cirrus.

cu·mu·lo-nim·bus (kūm′yə-lō-nim′bəs), ***n.*** a thick, towering cloud formation, usually producing rain.

cu·mu·lo-stra·tus (kūm′yə-lō-strā′təs), ***n.*** a cumulus (cloud) with a horizontal base like a stratus.

cu·mu·lous (kūm′yə-ləs), ***adj.*** of, or having the form of, a cumulus (cloud), or consisting of cumuli.

cu·mu·lus (kūm′yə-ləs), ***n.*** [*pl.* CUMULI (-lī′)], [L., a heap < IE. ****ku-me-los***, a swelling, increase < base ****keu-***, to swell], 1. a heap; mass; pile. 2. a thick cloud formation with a horizontal base and rounded masses piled up on each other: abbreviated **cu., Cu.**

CUMULUS

Cuna, Credit Union National Association.

Cu·nax·a (kyoo-nak′sə), ***n.*** an ancient town near Babylon.

cunc·ta·tion (kuŋk-tā′shən), ***n.*** [L. *cunctatio* < *cunctari*, to hesitate, linger], [Rare], a delaying or delay.

cunc·ta·tive (kuŋk′tə-tiv), ***adj.*** [< base of L. *cunctatio*, delay (cf. CUNCTATION); + *-ive*], [Rare], characterized by delay; tardy; dilatory.

cunc·ta·tor (kuŋk-tā′tẽr), ***n.*** [L.; see CUNCTATION], [Rare], a person who delays.

cu·ne·al (kū′ni-əl), ***adj.*** [< L. *cuneus*, a wedge], wedge-shaped.

cu·ne·ate (kū′ni-it, kū′ni-āt′), ***adj.*** [L. *cuneatus* < *cuneus*, a wedge], in *botany*, wedge-shaped; tapering, as some leaves.

cu·ne·at·ed (kū′ni-āt′id), ***adj.*** cuneate.

cu·ne·at·ic (kū′ni-at′ik), ***adj.*** [see CUNEATE], cuneal.

cu·ne·i·form (kū-nē′ə-fôrm′, kū′ni-fôrm′), ***adj.*** [< L. *cuneus*, a wedge; + *-form*], wedge-shaped: said especially of the characters used in ancient Akkadian, Assyrian, Babylonian, and Persian inscriptions, or the inscriptions themselves. ***n.*** cuneiform characters or inscriptions.

THE SUN
GOD
MOUNTAIN
MAN
OX

CUNEIFORM CHARACTERS

cu·ni·form (kū′ni-fôrm′), ***adj. & n.*** cuneiform.

cun·ner (kun′ẽr), ***n.*** [Brit. var. *conner;* prob. < *con* (to direct) in sense "directing fishing boats to herring shoals"], either of two small, edible, salt-water fishes, related to the tautog or blackfish, found off the coasts of England and New England.

cun·ning (kun′iŋ), ***adj.*** [ME., having knowledge, knowing < ppr. of *cunnen*, to know (see CAN); for sense, cf. KNOWING], 1. skillful; clever; shrewd. 2. skillful in deception; sly; crafty. 3. attractive; pretty in a delicate way: as, a *cunning* child. 4. created with skill or ingenuity. ***n.*** 1. skill in deception; slyness; craftiness. 2. [Archaic], skill. —***SYN.*** see **clever, sly.**

cup (kup), ***n.*** [ME.; AS. *cuppe* < Gmc. ****kupp-***, of rounded shape; prob. influenced by LL. *cuppa* (< L. *cupa*, tub; see COOP); akin to AS. *copp*, summit, cup, G. *kopf*, head, lit., cup; IE. base ****geu-***, to curve, bend, arch; mutual interaction between L. *cupa*, tub & Gmc. base is undoubted but confused; cf. CUPEL, CUPOLA], 1. a small, open container for beverages, usually bowl-shaped and with a handle. 2. the bowl of a drinking container. 3. a cup and its contents. 4. as much as a cup will hold; cupful: usually half a pint. 5. anything shaped like a cup. 6. a cup-shaped ornament, usually of silver, given as a prize. 7. the chalice containing the wine at Communion; also, the wine. 8. one's portion, share, or allotment (*of* a given experience): as, his *cup* of happiness was full. 9. a drink made of wine sweetened, flavored, and iced: as, claret *cup*. 10. in *biology*, any cuplike organ or structure. 11. in *golf*, *a*) the metal container in a hole. *b*) a hole. 12. in *medicine*, a small glass bowl or similar object used in cupping. ***v.t.*** [CUPPED (kupt), CUPPING], 1. to treat with or subject to cupping. 2. to shape like a cup. 3. to take in or put into a cup.

in one's cups, drunk; intoxicated.

cup·bear·er (kup′bâr′ẽr), *n.* a person who fills and serves the wine cups, as in a king's palace.

cup·board (kub′ẽrd), *n.* [*cup* + *board* (plank)], 1. a closet or cabinet with shelves for holding cups, plates, food, etc. 2. [British], any small closet, cabinet, etc.

cupboard love, insincere professions of love, motivated by self-interest and a desire for gain.

cup·cake (kup′kāk′), *n.* a small cake, sometimes baked in a paper cup.

cu·pel (kū′pəl, kū-pel′), *n.* [Fr. *coupelle;* ML. *cupella,* dim. < L. *cupa;* see CUP], 1. a small cup, shallow and porous, used in assaying gold, silver, etc. 2. a receptacle or furnace bottom for refining silver. ***v.t.*** [CUPELED (-pəld) or CUPELLED (-peld′), CUPELING (-pəl-iŋ) or CUPELLING (-pel′iŋ)], to assay or refine in a cupel.

cu·pel·la·tion (kū′pə-lā′shən), *n.* the assaying or refining of precious metals in a cupel.

cup·ful (kup′fool′), *n.* [*pl.* CUPFULS (-foolz′)], 1. as much as a cup will hold. 2. in *cookery*, half a pint.

Cu·pid (kū′pid), *n.* [L. *Cupido* < *cupido*, desire, longing, passion < *cupidus*, eager, longing, passionate < *cupere*, to desire; IE. base **q(e)wep-*, to boil, smoke, be disturbed], 1. in *Roman mythology*, the god of love, son of Venus: usually represented as a winged boy with bow and arrow, and identified with the Greek god Eros. 2. [c-], a representation of Cupid as a naked, winged boy, as on a valentine.

cu·pid·i·ty (kū-pid′ə-ti), *n.* [Fr. *cupidité;* L. *cupiditas* < *cupidus;* see CUPID], strong desire, especially for wealth; avarice; greed.

cu·pid's-bow (kū′pidz-bō′), *adj.* in the shape of the bow that Cupid is usually pictured as carrying: as, a *cupid's-bow* mouth.

cup of tea, [British Colloq.], a favorite thing, activity, etc.: as, golf isn't his *cup of tea*.

cu·po·la (kū′pə-lə), *n.* [It.; L. *cupula*, dim. of *cupa;* see CUP], 1. a rounded roof or ceiling. 2. a small dome or similar structure on a roof. 3. a small furnace for melting metals. 4. a dome-shaped, armor-plated, revolving gun turret on a battleship. 5. in *anatomy*, a dome-shaped process or organ. ***v.t.*** [CUPOLAED (-ləd), CUPOLAING], 1. to provide with a cupola. 2. to make in the shape of a cupola.

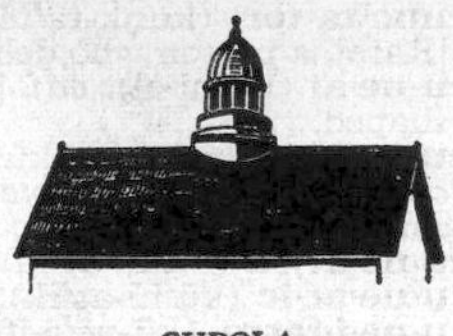

CUPOLA

cupped (kupt), *adj.* shaped like a cup.

cup·per (kup′ẽr), *n.* a person, as a physician, who practices cupping.

cup·ping (kup′iŋ), *n.* in *medicine*, the application of a glass cup to the surface of the skin for drawing blood to or through it by creating a partial vacuum.

cu·pre·ous (kū′pri-əs), *adj.* [L. *cupreus* < *cuprum;* see COPPER], 1. of, like, or containing copper. 2. copper-colored.

cu·pri- (kū′pri), [see CUPRO-], a combining form meaning *copper*, as in *cupriferous*.

cu·pric (kū′prik), *adj.* [< L. *cuprum* (see COPPER); + *-ic*], in *chemistry*, of or containing copper with a valence of two.

cu·prif·er·ous (kū-prif′ẽr-əs), *adj.* [*cupri-* + *-ferous*], containing copper.

cu·prite (kū′prīt), *n.* cuprous oxide, Cu_2O, a dark-red ore of copper.

cu·pro- (kū′prō), [< L. *cuprum;* see COPPER], a combining form meaning *copper and*, as in *cupromagnesite:* also, before a vowel, **cupr-**.

cu·pro·mag·ne·site (kū′prō-mag′ni-sīt′), *n.* a mineral containing copper and magnesium.

cu·prous (kū′prəs), *adj.* [< L. *cuprum* (see COPPER); + *-ous*], in *chemistry*, of or containing copper with a valence of one.

cu·prum (kū′prəm), *n.* [L.], copper: symbol, Cu (no period).

cu·pu·late (kū′pyoo-lāt′), *adj.* [< *cupule* + *-ate*], 1. shaped like a cupule. 2. having a cupule.

cu·pule (kū′pūl), *n.* [L. *cupula;* see CUPOLA], in *biology*, a cuplike structure, as the part of an acorn that holds the nut.

cur (kũr), *n.* [ME. *curre*, earlier *kurdogge;* prob. < ON. or MLG.; akin to Sw. dial. *kurre*, MLG. *korre*, dog; basic sense "snarling, growling" < ON. *kurra* or MLG. *korren*, to growl], 1. a dog of mixed breed; mongrel. 2. a person who is mean, contemptible, cowardly, etc.

cur., 1. currency. 2. current (of the present day, week, month, or year).

cur·a·bil·i·ty (kyoor′ə-bil′ə-ti), *n.* the state or quality of being curable.

cur·a·ble (kyoor′ə-b'l), *adj.* that can be cured.

Cu·ra·ça·o (kyoor′ə-sō′, kōō′rä-sou′), *n.* 1. the Netherlands Antilles: so called before 1949. 2. the largest island of the Netherlands Antilles: area 210 sq. mi.; pop. 111,000.

cu·ra·çao, cu·ra·çoa (kyoor′ə-sō′), *n.* [< *Curaçao*, where orig. made], a sweet liqueur made by flavoring distilled spirits with the dried peel of bitter oranges.

cu·ra·cy (kyoor′ə-si), *n.* [*pl.* CURACIES (-siz)], the position, office, or work of a curate.

cu·ra·re (kyoo-rä′ri), *n.* [Port. *curare, curari* or Sp. *curaré, urari* < native (Tupi) name], 1. a black, resinous substance prepared from the bark of certain South American plants and used by some Indians for poisoning arrows: it causes motor paralysis when introduced into the blood stream and is now used in medicine to reduce spasm in various conditions of muscular rigidity, as in tetanus and spastic paralysis. 2. any of certain plants from which this substance is prepared. Also **curari, curara, ourali, wourali, urari,** etc.

cu·ra·rize (kyoor′ə-rīz′, kyoo-rä′rīz), *v.t.* [CURARIZED (-rīzd′, -rīzd), CURARIZING], to treat or poison with curare.

cu·ras·sow (kyoor′ə-sō′, kyoo-ras′ō), *n.* [< *Curaçao*], a large, turkeylike bird of South and Central America.

cu·rate (kyoor′it), *n.* [ML. *curatus*, one responsible for the care of souls < L. *cura*, care; see CURE], 1. originally, a clergyman. 2. a clergyman who assists a vicar or rector.

cur·a·tive (kyoor′ə-tiv), *adj.* [Fr. *curatif* < L. *curare*, to take care of < *cura;* see CURE], 1. of or for the curing of disease. 2. curing, tending to cure, or having the power to cure. *n.* a thing that cures; remedy.

cu·ra·tor (kyoo-rā′tẽr), *n.* [< Fr. or L.; Fr. *curateur;* L. *curator* < *curare*, to take care of < *cura;* see CURE], 1. (*also* kyoor′ə-tẽr), in *law*, a guardian of a minor or of an incompetent. 2. a person who has charge, as of a museum, library, etc.

curb (kũrb), *n.* [Fr. *courbe*, curve, curb, orig., *adj.*, curved, bent < L. *curvus;* see CURVE], 1. a chain or strap passed around a horse's lower jaw and attached to the bit: the curb checks the horse when the reins are pulled. 2. anything that checks, restrains, or subdues. 3. an enclosing framework. 4. a raised margin around or along an edge, to strengthen or confine. 5. a stone or concrete edging of a sidewalk or pavement: British sp. **kerb.** 6. a market dealing in stocks and bonds not listed on the stock exchange: so called from the fact that early markets conducted their business on the street. ***v.t.*** 1. to restrain; check; control. 2. to provide with a curb. —***SYN.*** see **restrain.**

curb bit, a horse's bit with a curb.

curb·ing (kũrb′iŋ), *n.* 1. curbstones collectively. 2. material for curbstones. 3. a curb or part of a curb (sense 5). British sp. **kerbing.**

curb roof, a roof with a double slope on each side, the lower one being the steeper.

curb·stone (kũrb′stōn′), *n.* the stone or stones making up a curb; stone or concrete edging of a sidewalk or pavement: British sp. **kerbstone.**

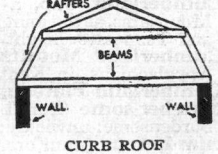

CURB ROOF

curch (kũrch), *n.* [a sing. formed < *curches* < OFr. *couvrechés*, pl. of *couvrechef;* cf. KERCHIEF], [Scot.], a woman's kerchief for the head.

cur·cu·li·o (kẽr-kū′li-ō′), *n.* [*pl.* CURCULIOS (-ōz′)], [L., corn worm, weevil; akin to *circulus* (see CIRCLE)], any of a group of beetles characterized by heads extending into long snouts: some are harmful to fruit.

cur·cu·ma (kũr′kyoo-mə), *n.* [Mod. L. < Ar. *kurkum;* see CROCUS], any of a group of tropical plants of the ginger family, with showy flowers and thick, tuberous rootstocks that yield starch: the turmeric of India, used as a condiment and dye, is a curcuma.

curd (kũrd), *n.* [15th-c. form, metathesized < ME. *crudde* < AS. *crudan*, to press (see CROWD); for sense development, cf. COAGULATE], the coagulated part of milk, from which cheese is made: it is formed when milk sours, and is distinguished from whey, the watery part. ***v.t. & v.i.*** to form into curd; curdle.

cur·dle (kũr′d'l), ***v.t. & v.i.*** [CURDLED (-d'ld), CURDLING], [< *curd* + *-le*, freq. suffix], to form into curd; coagulate; congeal.

curdle one's blood, to horrify or terrify one.

curd·y (kũrd′i), *adj.* 1. full of curd. 2. like curd.

cure (kyoor), *n.* [ME.; OFr.; L. *cura*, care, concern, trouble; OL. *coira-;* IE. base **kois-*, to sorrow], 1. a healing or being healed; getting well; restoration to health. 2. a thing that makes one well; remedy. 3. a system or method of medical treatment. 4. spiritual charge; care of souls. 5. the office or work of a curate. 6. the preserving of fish, meat, etc., as by salting or smoking. ***v.t.*** [CURED (kyoord), CURING], 1. to heal; make well; restore to health. 2. to get rid of or provide a remedy for (an ailment, evil, etc.). 3. to preserve (meat, etc.), as by salting or smoking. *v.i.* 1. to bring about a cure. 2. to be or become preserved.

SYN.—**cure** and **heal** both imply a restoring to health or soundness, **cure** specifically suggesting the elimination of disease, distress, evil, etc., and **heal**, the making or becoming whole of a wound, sore, lesion, etc. or, figuratively, the mending of a breach; **remedy** stresses the use of medication or a specific corrective treatment in relieving disease, injury, distress, etc.

cu·ré (kyoo-rā'), *n.* [Fr. < ML. *curatus;* see CURATE], in France, a parish priest.

cure-all (kyoor'ôl'), *n.* something supposed to cure all ailments or evils; panacea.

cu·ret·tage (kyoo-ret'ij, kyoor'ə-täzh'), *n.* [Fr.; see CURETTE], in *surgery*, the process of curetting.

cu·rette (kyoo-ret'), *n.* [Fr. < *curer*, to cleanse; see CURE, *v.*], a spoon-shaped instrument for the removal of tissue from the walls of body cavities. *v.t.* [CURETTED (-id), CURETTING], to clean or scrape with a curette.

cur·few (kũr'fū), *n.* [ME. *courfew;* Anglo-Fr. *coeverfu;* OFr. *covrefeu*, lit., cover fire < *covrir* (see COVER) + *feu*, fire < L. *focus*, fireplace (see FOCUS)], 1. in the Middle Ages, a regulation causing a bell to be rung every evening at a certain time as a signal for people to cover fires, put out lights, and retire. 2. the ringing of such a bell. 3. the time at which it was rung. 4. the bell. 5. a time, generally in the evening, set as a deadline beyond which children, inhabitants of cities occupied by the enemy in wartime, etc. may not appear on the streets or in public places. 6. the regulation establishing this time.

cu·ri·a (kyoor'i-ə), *n.* [*pl.* CURIAE (-ē')], [L. (in ML., court); prob. < **co-viria*, assembly of men < *co-*, together + **viro-*, man (see VIRILE)], 1. in ancient Rome, *a)* any of the ten political subdivisions into which the Latin, Sabine, and Etruscan tribes were each divided. *b)* its meeting place. *c)* the senate house at Rome. 2. a medieval judicial council or court held in the king's name. 3. [C-], the Curia Romana.

cu·ri·al (kyoor'i-əl), *adj.* of a curia.

Cu·ri·a Ro·ma·na (kyoor'i-ə rō-mā'nə), [L., lit., Roman Curia], the papal court, including all the officials and authorities that help the Pope in the government of the Roman Catholic Church.

cu·rie (kyoor'i, kyoo-rē'), *n.* [after Marie *Curie*], the unit used in measuring radioactivity: the quantity of any radioactive atom of a specific nuclear constitution in which the number of disintegrations per second is 3.700×10^{10}.

Cu·rie, Ma·rie Sklo·dow·ska (mȧ'rē' sklô-dôf'skä kü'rē'; Eng. kyoo-rē', kyoor'i), 1867–1934; wife of *Pierre;* Polish chemist and physicist in France; discovered radium and polonium, in collaboration with her husband; shared Nobel prize in physics, 1903; received Nobel prize in chemistry, 1911.

Curie, Pierre (pyâr), 1859–1906; French physicist and chemist: see **Curie, Marie Sklodowska.**

Curie's law, [after Pierre *Curie*], the law that the ratio of the magnetization of a paramagnetic substance to the magnetizing force is in inverse proportion to the absolute temperature.

cu·ri·o (kyoor'i-ō'), *n.* [*pl.* CURIOS (-ōz')], [contr. of *curiosity*], an art object valued as a curiosity or rarity.

cu·ri·o·sa (kyoor'i-ō'sə), *n.pl.* [L., lit., curious objects], curiosities; novelties; specifically, books, etc. dealing with unusual, especially pornographic, subjects.

cu·ri·os·i·ty (kyoor'i-os'ə-ti), *n.* [*pl.* CURIOSITIES (-tiz)], [ME. *curiosite;* OFr. *curioseté, curiosité;* L. *curiositas* < *curiosus;* see CURIOUS], 1. a desire to learn or know. 2. a desire to learn about things that do not necessarily concern one; inquisitiveness. 3. anything curious, strange, rare, or novel. 4. [Obs.], the quality of being careful, scrupulous, or fastidious.

cu·ri·ous (kyoor'i-əs), *adj.* [ME.; OFr. *curios, curius;* L. *curiosus*, careful, diligent, inquiring into, curious; akin to *cura*, care], 1. eager to learn or know. 2. unnecessarily inquisitive; prying. 3. careful; accurate; detailed. 4. arousing attention or interest; strange; unusual; odd. 5. [Obs.], very careful; scrupulous.

SYN.—**curious,** in this comparison, implies eagerness or anxiousness to find out things and may suggest a wholesome desire to be informed; **inquisitive** implies a habitual tendency to be curious, especially about matters that do not concern one, and an attempt to gain information by persistent questioning; **meddlesome** suggests unwelcome intrusion into the affairs of others; **prying** suggests an officious inquisitiveness and meddlesomeness that persist against resistance.

Cu·ri·ti·ba, Cu·ri·ty·ba (ko͞o'ri-tē'bə), *n.* a city in southeastern Brazil: pop., 361,000.

cu·ri·um (kyoor'i-əm), *n.* [after Pierre & Marie *Curie;* by analogy with *gadolinium*, which it resembles], one of the transuranic elements produced by atomic fission: symbol, Cm; at. wt., 242 (?); at. no., 96.

curl (kũrl), *v.t.* [ME. *curlen*, metathesized < *crulled, crolled*, curled < *crull, adj.*, curly (akin to D. *krul*, G. *krolle;* see CRULLER); Gmc. **kruzla* < IE. **greu-s* < base **ger-*, to turn, twist], 1. to wind or twist (hair, etc.) into ringlets or coils. 2. to cause to roll over or bend around. *v.i.* 1. to form curls; become curled. 2. to assume a spiral or curved shape. 3. to move in spirals; undulate. 4. to play the game of curling. *n.* 1. a ringlet of hair. 2. anything with a spiral or curled shape; coil. 3. a curling or being curled. 4. any of various diseases of plants in which the leaves curl up.
curl up, 1. to gather into spirals or curls; roll up. 2. to sit or lie with the legs drawn up. 3. [Colloq.], to collapse; break down.
in curl, curled.

curl·er (kũr'lẽr), *n.* 1. a person or thing that curls. 2. a person who plays the game of curling.

cur·lew (kũr'lo͞o, kũr'lū), *n.* [*pl.* CURLEWS (-lo͞oz, -lūz), CURLEW; see PLURAL, II, D, 1], [ME. *corleu, curlew;* OFr. *corlieu;* of echoic origin, but affected in form by association with *corlieu*, messenger, courier], any of several varieties of large, brownish wading birds with long legs and a long bill that curves downward.

curl·i·cue (kũr'li-kū'), *n.* [*curly* + *cue*], a fancy curve, flourish, etc., as in handwriting: also spelled **curlycue.**

curl·i·ness (kũr'li-nis), *n.* the quality or state of being curly.

curl·ing (kũr'liŋ), *n.* [so named from the curving path of the stone when slid], a game played by sliding a heavy, flat, polished stone along the ice at a mark (called the *tee*) 38 yards away.

curling iron (or **irons**), an instrument for curling or waving the hair, generally consisting of a kind of metal tongs: a lock of hair is lifted with the heated tongs and rolled into a ringlet.

curl·pa·per (kũrl'pā'pẽr), *n.* a piece of paper around which a lock of hair may be wrapped to make it curl.

curl·y (kũr'li), *adj.* [CURLIER (-li-ẽr), CURLIEST (-li-ist)], 1. curling or having a tendency to curl. 2. having curls. 3. having a curled or undulating grain, as certain woods.

curl·y·cue (kũr'li-kū'), *n.* a curlicue.

cur·mudg·eon (kẽr-muj'ən), *n.* [? < med. name *Curmegan* (for development, cf. RIBALD), ? equivalent to Fr. *coeur méchant*, evil heart (suggested by Johnson, 1755); sp. (1626) *curmegient*], a surly, ill-mannered, bad-tempered person; cantankerous fellow.

curn (kũrn), *n.* [var. of *corn*, grain; cf. KERNEL], [Scot.], 1. a grain; hence, 2. a small number or quantity; few.

curr (kũr), *v.i.* [echoic or < ON. *kurra;* see CUR], to make a murmuring, cooing sound.

cur·rach, cur·ragh (kur'əkh, kur'ə), *n.* [Ir. & Scot. Gael. *curach;* akin to W. *corwg*, skin boat; ? IE. base **qer-*, to cut], [Irish & Scot.], a coracle.

cur·ra·jong, cur·re·jong, cur·ri·jong (kũr'ə-joŋ'), *n.* a kurrajong.

cur·rant (kũr'ənt), *n.* [taken as sing. of *Corauntz* < Anglo-Fr. *(raisins de) Corauntz* < Fr. *(raisins de) Corinthe*, lit., raisins of Corinth: so named from being imported from Corinth], 1. the dried fruit of a small, seedless grape grown in the Mediterranean region, used in cooking. 2. [so named from resemblance to preceding], the small, sour, red, white, or black berry of a large group of hardy shrubs, used for jellies and jams. 3. the shrub bearing this fruit.

cur·ren·cy (kũr'ən-si), *n.* [*pl.* CURRENCIES (-siz)], [ML. **currentia*, a current < L. *currens;* see CURRENT], 1. a continual passing from hand to hand, as of a medium of exchange; circulation. 2. the money in circulation in any country: abbreviated **cur., cy.** 3. common acceptance; general use; prevalence: as, such superstitions now have little *currency*. 4. the time during which anything is current.

cur·rent (kũr'ənt), *adj.* [altered (after L.) < ME. *corant, courant;* OFr. *corant, curant*, ppr. of *curre, corre* < L. *currere*, to run], 1. [Rare], running or flowing. 2. now in progress; of this day, week, month, or year: as, the *current* issue of a magazine: abbreviated **cur., curr., curt.** 3. passing from hand to hand; circulating. 4. commonly accepted; generally used or known; prevalent. *n.* 1. a body of water or air flowing in a definite direction. 2. a running or flowing. 3. a general tendency or drift; course. 4. in *electricity*, the flow or rate of flow of electric force in a conductor, from a point of higher potential to one of lower potential. —*SYN.* see **prevailing, tendency.**

current density, the amount of electric current passing through a cross-sectional area of the conductor in a given unit of time: commonly expressed in amperes per square centimeter.

current expenses, the regular and continuing expenses of maintaining a going business.

cur·rent·ly (kũr'ənt-li), *adv.* 1. now. 2. generally; commonly; popularly.

cur·ri·cle (kũr'i-k'l), *n.* [L. *curriculum;* see CURRICULUM], a light, two-wheeled carriage drawn by two horses side by side.

cur·ric·u·lar (kə-rik'yoo-lẽr), *adj.* of a curriculum.

cur·ric·u·lum (kə-rik'yoo-ləm), *n.* [*pl.* CURRICULUMS (-ləmz), CURRICULA (-lə)], [L., a running, course, race.

career < *currere,* to run; fig. use], a specific course of study or, collectively, all the courses of study in a school, university, etc.

cur·ri·er (kũr'i-ẽr), *n.* [ME. *corier, coriour;* OFr. *corier;* L. *coriarius* < *corium,* hide, skin; affected in Eng. by association with *curry* (to rub)], 1. a person who curries tanned leather. 2. a person who curries horses, etc.

Cur·ri·er and Ives (kũr'i-ẽr ən īvz'), [after the founders, Nathaniel *Currier* (1813–1888) and James M. *Ives* (1824–1895)], 1. a 19th-century lithographing firm in the United States that published a series of prints showing the manners, people, and events of the times. 2. any of these prints.

cur·ri·er·y (kũr'i-ẽr-i), *n.* [*pl.* CURRIERIES (-iz)], the work or shop of a leather currier.

cur·rish (kũr'ish), *adj.* of or resembling a cur; snarling; bad-tempered; mean; ill-bred.

cur·ry (kũr'i), *v.t.* [CURRIED (-id), CURRYING], [ME. *curraien;* OFr. *correier, conreder,* to put in order; LL. **corredare* < L. *com-,* with + *-red-,* base appearing in **arredare;* see ARRAY], 1. to rub down and clean the coat of (a horse or other animal) with a currycomb or brush. 2. to prepare (tanned leather) by soaking, scraping, cleaning, beating, etc. 3. to beat; flog; drub.

curry favor, [altered < *curry favel;* OFr. *favel,* chestnut horse (taken as symbol of duplicity) < dial. form of OHG. *falo,* pale, pale-yellow; akin to AS. *fealu;* see FALLOW (pale)], to try to get favor by flattery, fawning, etc.

cur·ry (kũr'i), *n.* [*pl.* CURRIES (-iz)], [Tamil *kari,* sauce], 1. curry powder or a sauce made with this, used especially in the East Indies. 2. a kind of stew made with curry. *v.t.* [CURRIED (-id), CURRYING], to flavor with curry.

cur·ry·comb (kũr'i-kōm'), *n.* [*curry* (to rub) + *comb*], a comb with metal teeth, for rubbing down and cleaning a horse's coat. *v.t.* to rub down and clean with a currycomb; use a currycomb on.

curry powder, a powder prepared from turmeric and various spices and herbs, used as a seasoning in cooking.

curse (kũrs), *n.* [ME.; Late AS. *curs, n., cursian, v.;* ? base sense "wrath" (cf. *God's curse*) < Anglo-Fr. *curuz,* wrath (OFr. *coroz*) & Anglo-Fr. *curcier* (OFr. *corocier*), to call down wrath upon < LL. *corruptiare;* see CORRUPT], 1. a calling on God or the gods to send evil or injury down on some person or thing. 2. a blasphemous oath; imprecation. 3. a thing cursed. 4. evil or injury that seems to come in answer to a curse. 5. any cause of evil or injury. *v.t.* [CURSED or CURST (kũrst), CURSING], 1. to call evil or injury down on; damn. 2. to swear at; use blasphemous language against. 3. to bring evil or injury on; afflict. *v.i.* to utter a curse or curses; swear; blaspheme.

be cursed with, to be afflicted with; suffer from.

SYN.—**curse** is the general word for calling down evil or injury on someone or something; **damn** carries the same general meaning but, in strict usage, implies the use of the word "damn" in the curse (he *damned* his enemies = he said, "*Damn* my enemies!"); **execrate** suggests cursing prompted by great anger or abhorrence; **imprecate** suggests the calling down of relentless calamity on someone, especially from a desire for revenge; **anathematize** strictly refers to the formal utterance of a curse by ecclesiastical authority, but in general use it is equivalent to **imprecate.**—*ANT.* bless.

curs·ed (kũr'sid, kũrst), *adj.* 1. under a curse. 2. deserving to be cursed; evil; wicked; hateful; odious. 3. [Archaic], malevolent; quarrelsome: usually **curst.**

cur·sive (kũr'siv), *adj.* [ML. *cursivus* < L. *cursus;* see COURSE], flowing; designating writing in which the strokes of the letters are joined in each word. *n.* 1. a cursive character. 2. a manuscript in cursive writing. 3. in *printing,* a type face that looks like writing.

cur·so·ri·al (kẽr-sôr'i-əl, kẽr-sō'ri-əl), *adj.* [< *cursory* + *-al*], having legs or structural parts adapted for running.

cur·so·ri·ly (kũr'sẽr-i-li), *adv.* in a cursory manner.

cur·so·ri·ness (kũr'sẽr-i-nis), *n.* a cursory quality.

cur·so·ry (kũr'sẽr-i), *adj.* [L. *cursorius* < *cursor,* runner < *cursus;* see COURSE], hastily, hence often superficially, done, or passing rapidly over something without giving enough attention to details. —*SYN.* see **superficial.**

curst (kũrst), alternative past tense and past participle of **curse.** *adj.* cursed.

curt (kũrt), *adj.* [L. *curtus* < IE. *(*s*)*qr̥-tos,* cut off; akin to ON. *skarthr,* diminished, impaired & Eng. *short*], 1. short; shortened. 2. brief to the point of rudeness; terse and abrupt: as, a *curt* reply. —*SYN.* see **blunt.**

cur·tail (kẽr-tāl'), *v.t.* [altered (by association with *tail*) < *curtal;* see CURTAL], to cut short; reduce; abridge. —*SYN.* see **shorten.**

cur·tail·ment (kẽr-tāl'mənt), *n.* a curtailing.

cur·tain (kũr't'n, kũr'tin), *n.* [ME. & OFr. *cortine, curtine;* LL. *cortina,* little court, enclosure < L. *cors;* see COURT], 1. a piece of cloth, etc., sometimes arranged so that it can be drawn up or sideways, hung for decoration, as at a window, or to cover, conceal, or shut off something. 2. anything that conceals, covers, or shuts off as a curtain. 3. that part of a rampart and parapet between two bastions or gates. 4. in *architecture,* an enclosing wall that does not support a roof. 5. in the *theater,* *a*) the large drape or hanging screen at the front of the stage, which may be drawn up or aside to reveal the stage; hence, *b*) an effect, line, or situation in a play immediately before the fall of the curtain. 6. *pl.* [Slang], death; the end. *v.t.* 1. to provide or decorate with a curtain. 2. to conceal, cover, or shut off as with a curtain.

draw the curtain on, 1. to end. 2. to conceal.

lift the curtain on, 1. to begin. 2. to reveal.

curtain call, a call, usually by continued applause, for a performer to return to the stage at the end of a play, act, etc. and acknowledge the applause.

curtain lecture, a private scolding or reprimand given by a wife to her husband: so called from the curtained beds in which such reproofs were conventionally given.

curtain raiser, a short play or skit presented before a longer or more elaborate production.

curtain speech, a speech delivered from in front of the curtain at the end of a theatrical performance.

cur·tal (kũr't'l), *adj.* [OFr. *cortald, curtald;* prob. < *court,* short; L. *curtus;* see CURT], [Obs.], shortened; curtailed. *n.* [Obs.], 1. a horse with a docked tail. 2. anything cut short or shortened.

curtal ax, [altered < *cutlass*], [Archaic], a cutlass.

cur·tate (kũr'tāt), *adj.* [L. *curtatus,* pp. of *curtare,* to shorten < *curtus;* see CURT], shortened; abbreviated.

cur·te·sy (kũr'tə-si), *n.* [*pl.* CURTESIES (-siz)], [var. of *courtesy*], in *law,* the right that a husband has in the lands of his dead wife, when they have had children capable of inheriting.

cur·ti·lage (kũr't'l-ij), *n.* [OFr. *cortillage, curtillage* < *cortil, curtil, courtil,* dim. < ML. *cortis,* court; see COURT], in *law,* the fenced-in ground surrounding a house or dwelling.

Cur·tis (kũr'tis), [< Norm. Fr. *curteis* (OFr. *corteis*); see COURTEOUS] a masculine name.

Cur·tis, Charles (kũr'tis), 1860–1936; American statesman; vice-president of the United States (1929–1933).

Cur·tiss, Glenn Ham·mond (ham'ənd kũr'tis), 1878–1930; American inventor; developed the airplane.

cur·tle ax (kũr't'l), [see CURTAL AX], [Archaic], a cutlass.

curt·sy (kũrt'si), *n.* [*pl.* CURTSIES (-siz)], [var. of *courtesy*], a salutation made by bending the knees and dipping the body slightly, as a mark of respect or a step in dancing: now only of women and girls. *v.i.* [CURTSIED (-sid), CURTSYING], to make a curtsy. Also spelled **curtsey.**

cu·rule (kyoor'ool, kyoor'ōōl), *adj.* [L. *curulis* < *currus,* chariot; akin to *currere,* to run], 1. designating a chair shaped like a campstool, but with heavy curved legs and upholstered seat, in which only the highest civil officers of Rome were privileged to sit. 2. of the highest rank; privileged to sit in a curule chair.

cur·va·ceous (kũr-vā'shəs), *adj.* [< *curve* + *-aceous*], [Colloq.], having a full, shapely figure: said of a woman.

cur·va·ture (kũr'və-chẽr), *n.* [L. *curvatura* < *curvare;* see CURVE, *v.*], 1. a curving or being curved. 2. a curve; curved part of anything. 3. in *geometry,* the rate of deviation of a curve or curved surface from a straight line or plane surface tangent to it. 4. in *medicine,* an abnormal curving of a part: as, *curvature* of the spine.

curve (kũrv), *adj.* [L. *curvus,* bent; IE. base *(*s*)*qer-,* to turn, bend; hence akin to Gr. *korōnos* (see CORONA), Ir. *cor,* circle], curved. *n.* [L. *curvum* < the *adj.*], 1. a line having no straight part; bend having no angular part. 2. a thing or part having the shape of a curve. 3. a curving. 4. the amount of this. 5. in *baseball,* a pitched ball thrown with spin so that it curves to one side or the other before crossing the plate. 6. in *mathematics,* a line whose path is traced by an equation that can be applied to every point on it. *v.t. & v.i.* [CURVED (kũrvd), CURVING], 1. to form a curve by bending. 2. to move in a curved path.

SYN.—**curve** suggests a swerving or deflection in a line that follows or approximates the arc of a circle (he *curved* the next pitch); **bend** refers to the curving of something that is normally straight but that yields to pressure or tension (to *bend* a wire); **twist,** in this connection, implies greater resistance in the object to be bent and often connotes a wrenching out of the normal line (he *twisted* his arm); **turn,** in this comparison often interchangeable with **bend,** is used specifically where the object is curved back upon itself (to *turn* a bed sheet).

cur·vet (kũr'vit), *n.* [altered (after L. *curvus*) < earlier *corvetto;* It. *corvetta,* dim. < *corvo* < L. *curvus;* see CURVE], an upward leap made by a horse, in which the hind legs are raised from the ground just before the forelegs come down again. *v.i.* (kũr'vit, kẽr-vet'), [CURVETTED or CURVETED (-id), CURVETTING or CURVETING], 1. to make a curvet. 2. to leap; bound; frolic. *v.t.* to cause to curvet.

cur·vi- (kũr'və), [< L. *curvus,* curved], a combining form meaning *curved, bent,* as in *curvilinear.*

cur·vi·lin·e·al (kũr'və-lin'i-əl), *adj.* curvilinear.

cur·vi·lin·e·ar (kũr'və-lin'i-ẽr), *adj.* consisting of or enclosed by a curved line or lines.

Cur·zon, George Nathaniel (kũr'z'n), first Baron and first Marquis Curzon of Kedleston, 1859–1925; English statesman; viceroy of India (1899–1905).

Cus·co (kōōs'kō), *n.* a city in south central Peru:

former capital of the Inca empire: also spelled **Cuzco.**
cu·sec (kū′sek), *n.* [*cu*bic + *sec*ond], one cubic foot per second.
Cush (kush), *n.* [Heb. *kūsh*], in the *Bible,* 1. the oldest of Ham's sons. 2. the land inhabited by his descendants, thought to be Ethiopia. Also spelled **Kush.**
cush·at (kush′ət, koosh′ət), *n.* [northern Brit. dial. < ME. *cowschott;* AS. *cusceote, cuscote* as if < *cu-*, echoic of bird's cry (now *coo*) + base of *sceotan,* to shoot, dart (cf. SHOOT), in sense "cooing darter"], the European wood pigeon or ringdove.
cu·shaw (kə-shô′), *n.* [prob. < Chin. *k'u kua,* lit., bitter melon], a winter squash, usually oblong, with a large, smooth crookneck: also called *winter crookneck pumpkin, China squash.*
Cush·ing, Harvey (koosh′iŋ), 1869–1939; American surgeon and author.
cush·ion (koosh′ən), *n.* [ME. *cuisshin, quisschen;* Anglo-Fr. *quissine;* OFr. *coussin, coissin;* LL. *coxinum;* prob. (via **culcinum*) < L. *culcita,* cushion (see QUILT); prob. influenced by association with L. *coxa,* hip], 1. a pillow or soft pad for sitting or kneeling on, or reclining against. 2. a thing like a cushion in shape or use; specifically, *a*) a small pillow used in lacemaking. *b*) anything serving to absorb shock, as air or steam in some machines, or the elastic inner rim of a billiard table. *v.t.* 1. to provide with a cushion or cushions. 2. to seat or set on a cushion; prop up with cushions. 3. to hide, as if under a cushion. 4. to protect from shock by means of a cushion. 5. to absorb (shock).
Cush·it·ic (kush-it′ik), *adj.* [< *Cush;* cf. HAMITIC], designating or of a group of Hamitic languages spoken in Ethiopia and eastern Africa. *n.* this group of languages. Also spelled **Kushitic.**
cush·y (koosh′i), *adj.* [CUSHIER (-i-ēr), CUSHIEST (-i-ist)], [orig. Brit. army slang < Hind. *khush,* pleasant; Per. *khūsh*], [Slang], easy; comfortable: as, a *cushy* job.
cusk (kusk), *n.* [*pl.* CUSK, CUSKS (kusks); see PLURAL, II, D, 2], [Brit. local name; ? < ON. base of Norw. *kuse,* evil person, *kuseleg,* fearful, OSw. *kuskja,* to constrain, lit., to frighten (with reference to the burbot's evil appearance)], 1. a large, edible sea fish related to the cod. 2. the burbot, a fresh-water fish.
cusp (kusp), *n.* [L. *cuspis, cuspidis,* point, pointed end, spear], 1. a point or pointed end formed where two curves meet. 2. in *anatomy,* *a*) one of the elevations on the chewing surface of a tooth. *b*) one of the triangular parts of a heart valve. 3. in *architecture,* a projecting point where two arcs meet, as in the internal curve of an arch. 4. in *astronomy,* either horn of a crescent moon.
cus·pate (kus′pit, kus′pāt), *adj.* 1. having a cusp or cusps. 2. shaped like a cusp.
cus·pat·ed (kus′pā-tid), *adj.* cuspate.
cusped (kuspt), *adj.* cuspate.
cus·pid (kus′pid), *n.* [L. *cuspis;* see CUSP], a tooth with one cusp; canine tooth. *adj.* cuspidate.
cus·pi·dal (kus′pi-d'l), *adj.* 1. of or like a cusp. 2. having a cusp; pointed at the end.
cus·pi·date (kus′pi-dāt′), *adj.* [L. *cuspidatus,* pp. of *cuspidare,* to make pointed < *cuspis*], having a cusp or cusps; pointed at the end, as some leaves.
cus·pi·dat·ed (kus′pi-dā′tid), *adj.* cuspidate.
cus·pi·da·tion (kus′pi-dā′shən), *n.* the use of cusps for decoration, as in architecture.
cus·pi·dor (kus′pə-dôr′), *n.* [Port. *cuspideira* < *cuspir,* to spit < L. *conspuere* < *com-*, intens. + *spuere,* to spit out], a spittoon.
cuss (kus), *n.* [< *curse* (cf. BUST); in 2, ? < *customer*], [Colloq.], 1. a curse. 2. a person or animal, especially when regarded as queer or annoying: used humorously or contemptuously. *v.t. & v.i.* [Colloq.], to curse.
cuss·ed (kus′id), *adj.* [< *cuss* or *cursed*], [Colloq.], 1. cursed. 2. perverse; stubborn.
cus·tard (kus′tērd), *n.* [prob. altered < obs. *crustade,* spiced pie of meat, eggs, or the like < OFr. *croustade,* dish covered with a crust; see CRUST], a mixture of eggs, milk, sugar, flavoring, etc., either boiled or baked.
custard apple, [< *custard:* with reference to the flavor], 1. a species of small tree grown, especially in the West Indies, for its edible, heart-shaped fruit. 2. any of various related trees and shrubs, as the sweetsop, sugar apple, and soursop. 3. the fruit of any of these plants.
Cus·ter, George Arm·strong (ärm′strôŋ kus′tēr): 1836–1876; American army officer and Indian fighter, killed in a battle with Indians at Little Big Horn.
‡cus·to·des (kus-tō′dēz), *n.* plural of **custos.**
cus·to·di·al (kus-tō′di-əl), *adj.* of custody or custodians. *n.* a container for relics.
cus·to·di·an (kus-tō′di-ən), *n.* [< *custody*], 1. a person who has the care of something, as of the exhibits in a museum; caretaker; keeper. 2. a person responsible for the care and maintenance of a building; janitor.
cus·to·di·an·ship (kus-tō′di-ən-ship′), *n.* [*custodian* + *-ship*], the position or work of a custodian.
cus·to·dy (kus′tə-di), *n.* [*pl.* CUSTODIES (-diz)], [L. *custodia* < *custos,* a guard, keeper; IE. base *(*s*)*qeu-dh,* to hide; akin to AS. *hydan* (see HIDE, to conceal)], 1. a guarding or keeping safe; care; protection; guardianship. 2. detention; imprisonment.
in custody, in the keeping of the police; under arrest.
take into custody, to arrest.
cus·tom (kus′təm), *n.* [ME. *custom, custume, costume;* OFr. *custume, costume;* L. *consuetudo, consuetudinis* < *consuescere,* to accustom, habituate < *com-*, intens. + *suescere,* to become accustomed < *suere,* to be accustomed; IE. base **swe-*, refl.; akin to L. *suus,* one's own, Eng. *swain*], 1. a usual practice; habit; usage. 2. established usage; social conventions carried on by tradition and enforced by social disapproval of any violation. 3. a service, rent, etc. regularly paid to a feudal lord. 4. *pl.* *a*) duties or taxes imposed by a government on imported and, occasionally, exported goods. *b*) the government agency in charge of collecting these duties. 5. the regular support or patronage of a business establishment. 6. in *law,* such usage as by common consent and long-established, uniform practice has taken on the force of law. *adj.* 1. made to order: sometimes loosely said of a ready-made article regarded as resembling one made to order, extra fine, etc. 2. making things to order, or dealing in things made to order. —*SYN.* see **habit.**
cus·tom·a·ble (kus′təm-ə-b'l), *adj.* [Rare], subject to customs; taxable as imported.
cus·tom·ar·i·ly (kus′tə-mer′ə-li, kus′tə-mer′ə-li), *adv.* according to custom; usually.
cus·tom·ar·i·ness (kus′tə-mer′i-nis), *n.* the quality or state of being customary.
cus·tom·ar·y (kus′tə-mer′i), *adj.* [ML. *customarius;* see CUSTOM], 1. according to or established by custom, or usage; usual; habitual. 2. in *law,* *a*) subject to customs. *b*) holding or held by custom. *n.* [*pl.* CUSTOMARIES (-iz)], a collection of laws established by custom. —*SYN.* see **usual.**
cus·tom-built (kus′təm-bilt′), *adj.* built to order, according to the customer's specifications.
cus·tom·er (kus′təm-ēr), *n.* [Late Anglo-Fr. *custumer* (OFr. *coustumier*); see CUSTOM], 1. a person who buys, especially one who buys regularly: as, she is one of our *customers.* 2. [Colloq.], a person with whom one has to deal: as, he's a rough *customer.*
cus·tom·house (kus′təm-hous′), *n.* a building or office where duties are paid on imported and, sometimes, exported goods, and ships are cleared for entering or leaving: abbreviated **c.h.**
cus·tom-made (kus′təm-mād′), *adj.* made to order, according to the customer's specifications.
customs union, a union of two or more nations that agree to eliminate customs restrictions among them and to follow a common tariff policy toward all other nations.
‡cus·tos (kus′tos), *n.* [*pl.* CUSTODES (kus-tō′dēz)], [L.], a keeper; guardian; custodian.
cus·tu·mal (kus′tyoo-məl), *adj.* [ML. *custumalis*], of the customs of a manor, district, etc. *n.* a collection of the customs of a manor, district, etc.; a customary.
cut (kut), *v.t.* [CUT, CUTTING], [ME. *cutten, kitten, kytten, ketten;* Late AS. **cyttan* < Anglo-N.; cf. the only cognate forms, Sw. dial. *kuta, kota* (earlier *kotta*), Ice. *kuta,* to cut with a knife, Sw. dial. *kuta, kytti,* Ice. *kuti,* a knife; the word replaced AS. *ceorfan* (cf. CARVE), *snithan, scieran* (cf. SHEAR) as used in its basic senses], I. *denoting penetration or incision* 1. to make an opening in with a sharp-edged instrument; pierce; incise; gash. 2. to pierce or hit sharply so as to hurt. 3. to hurt the feelings of. 4. to get (a new tooth cutting its way through the gum). II. *denoting separation, removal, or division* 1. to remove or divide into parts with a sharp-edged instrument; sever. 2. to carve (meat). 3. to cause to fall by severing; fell; hew. 4. to mow or reap with a scythe, sickle, etc. 5. to pass through or across; intersect; divide: as, the path *cuts* the meadow diagonally. 6. to divide (a pack of cards) at random after shuffling and before dealing. 7. to castrate; geld. 8. [Colloq.], to pretend not to see or know (a person); snub. 9. [Colloq.], to stay away from (a school class, etc.) without being excused. 10. [Slang], to stop; discontinue: as, *cut* the noise. III. *denoting reduction* 1. to make less by or as by severing a part or parts; reduce; curtail: as, salaries were *cut.* 2. to make shorter by severing the ends of (hair, branches, fingernails, etc.); trim; shear; pare. 3. to dilute (alcohol, etc.). 4. to dissolve or break up the fat globules of: as, lye *cuts* grease. IV. *denoting performance by incision, etc.* to make, do, form, or decorate by or as by cutting; specifically, *a*) to make (an opening, clearing, channel, etc.) by incising, drilling, hacking, or excavating. *b*) to engrave; inscribe. *c*) to cut cloth so as to form the parts for (a garment). *d*) to perform: as, he *cut* a caper. *e*) in *motion pictures,* to edit (film) by deleting some scenes and assembling others into their proper sequence.

f) in *sports*, to hit, drive, or throw (a ball) so that it spins or is deflected. *v.i.* 1. to do the work of a sharp-edged instrument; pierce, sever, gash, etc. 2. to do cutting; work as a cutter. 3. to take cutting; be severed, etc.: as, wood *cuts* easily. 4. to use an instrument that cuts. 5. to hurt by or as by sharp, piercing strokes: as, the wind *cut* through his thin clothes. 6. in *motion pictures*, *a*) to stop the camera or cameras. *b*) to edit film. 7. in *sports*, *a*) to hit, drive, or throw a ball so that it spins or is deflected. *b*) to change direction suddenly while running. *adj.* 1. that has been cut. 2. made, formed, or decorated by cutting. 3. reduced; lessened. 4. castrated. 5. in *botany*, having an indented edge; incised, as some leaves or petals. *n.* 1. a cutting or being cut. 2. a stroke or blow with a sharp-edged instrument, whip, etc. 3. an opening, incision, wound, etc. made by a sharp-edged instrument. 4. the omission of a part. 5. a part omitted. 6. a piece cut; specifically, *a*) any of the divisions or segments of a meat animal. *b*) a slice from such a segment. 7. a reduction; lessening; decrease. 8. a route that is the shortest distance across: usually **short cut.** 9. a passage or channel cut out. 10. the style in which a thing is cut; fashion; form: as, her clothes have a stylish *cut.* 11. a cutting of a deck of cards. 12. an act, remark, etc. that hurts one's feelings. 13. a block or plate engraved for printing. 14. the impression from such a block or plate. 15. [Colloq.], a snub. 16. [Colloq.], an unauthorized absence from school, etc. 17. [Slang], a share, as of profits or loot. 18. in *sports*, a stroke that causes a ball to spin or be deflected from its course.

a cut above, [Colloq.], somewhat better than.

cut across, to take a shorter course by going straight across in a diagonal direction.

cut a figure, [Colloq.], 1. to attract attention. 2. to make a (specified kind of) showing or impression.

cut and dried, 1. prepared or arranged beforehand. 2. lifeless; dull; boring.

cut and run, 1. to cut the cable of a ship and set sail immediately; hence, 2. to get away quickly.

cut back, 1. to make shorter by cutting off the end. 2. to reduce or discontinue (a contract, etc.) before the completion of what was originally called for. 3. to go back, as in telling a story. 4. to change direction suddenly, as a football player running with the ball.

cut dead, [Colloq.], to snub completely.

cut down, 1. to cause to fall by cutting; fell. 2. to kill, as by striking with a sword. 3. to reduce; lessen.

cut in, 1. to move in suddenly. 2. to join in suddenly; interrupt. 3. to interrupt two people dancing together in order to dance with one of them.

cut it fine, [Colloq.], 1. to make exact calculations. 2. to make exact distinctions.

cut it out, [Colloq.], to stop doing what one is doing.

cut loose, 1. to cut a ship's moorings. 2. [Colloq.], to act or speak without restraint.

cut off, 1. to separate from other parts by cutting; sever. 2. to stop abruptly. 3. to shut off. 4. to interrupt. 5. to intercept. 6. to disinherit.

cut one's teeth on, to learn or use at an early age.

cut out, 1. to remove by cutting. 2. to remove; leave out; omit; eliminate. 3. to eliminate and take the place of (a rival). 4. to make or form by or as by cutting. 5. [Colloq.], to discontinue; stop.

cut out for, fitted for; suited for.

cut short, to stop abruptly before the end.

cut through, 1. to penetrate or go through by cutting. 2. to go straight through.

cut up, 1. to cut into pieces. 2. to inflict cuts or lacerations on. 3. [Colloq.], to cause to be dejected or distressed. 4. [Slang], to clown, play practical jokes, etc. to attract attention.

cut (kut), *n.* [? < W. *cwt*, lot (if not a loan < ME.) or OFr. *courte*, short; modified by ME. *cutten*], one of the bits of straw, stick, paper, etc. used in drawing lots to decide something.

cu·ta·ne·ous (kū-tā'ni-əs), *adj.* [ML. *cutaneus* < L. *cutis;* see CUTICLE], of or on the skin; affecting the skin.

cut·a·way (kut'ə-wā'), *n.* a coat with the front of the skirt cut so as to curve back to the tails, worn by men for formal daytime occasions: also **cutaway coat.**

CUTAWAY

cut·back (kut'bak'), *n.* 1. the act or result of shortening by cutting off the end. 2. reduction or discontinuance, as of a contract, before the completion of what was originally called for. 3. a sequence of earlier narrative events introduced at a later point in a novel, motion picture, etc. 4. in *football*, a play in which the player carrying the ball suddenly changes the direction of his run, as in avoiding opposing players.

Cutch (kuch), *n.* a state of western India: area, 8,461 sq. mi.; pop., 501,000 (est. 1950); capital, Abu.

Rann of Cutch (run), a large, marshy area near Cutch.

cutch (kuch), *n.* catechu.

cutch·er·ry (kə-cher'i), *n.* [*pl.* CUTCHERRIES (-iz)], [Hind. *kacahrī, kachĕrī*, audience hall], in India, a courthouse or administrative office.

cutch·er·y (kuch'ẽr-i), *n.* a cutcherry.

cute (kūt), *adj.* [< *acute*], [Colloq.], 1. clever; sharp; shrewd. 2. pretty or attractive, especially in a delicate or dainty way.

cut glass, glass, especially flint glass, shaped or ornamented by grinding and polishing.

cut-grass (kut'gras'), *n.* grass with many tiny hooks along the edges of the blades.

Cuth·bert (kuth'bẽrt), [AS. *Cuthbeorht*, lit., famously splendid < *cuth*, noted (pp. of *cunnan*, to know; see CAN, to be able) + *beorht* (see BRIGHT)], a masculine name.

Cuthbert, Saint, 635?–687 A.D.; English monk.

cut·i·cle (kū'ti-k'l), *n.* [L. *cuticula*, skin, dim. < *cutis*, skin; IE. base *(*s*)*qeu-t-*, to cover; hence akin to AS. *hyd* (see HIDE, skin)], 1. the outer layer of the skin; epidermis. 2. hardened skin, such as accumulates at the base and sides of a fingernail. 3. in *botany*, a delicate, skinlike layer over the outer surface of the epidermis of plants: it contains cutin and protects against water and gases.

cu·tic·u·la (kyoo-tik'yoo-lə), *n.* [*pl.* CUTICULAE (-lē')]; [L.; cf. CUTICLE], a cuticle; especially, the tough outer layer of skin of certain lower organisms.

cu·tic·u·lar (kyoo-tik'yə-lẽr), *adj.* of cuticle.

cu·tin (kū'tin), *n.* [< L. *cutis;* see CUTICLE], in *botany*, a waxy substance which, together with cellulose, forms the outer layer of the skin of many plants.

cut-in (kut'in'), *n.* in *motion pictures*, the close-up of a pertinent object, as a newspaper headline, a book, etc., inserted into the sequence of a scene: also called *insert.*

cu·tin·i·za·tion (kū'tin-ə-zā'shən), *n.* in *botany*, a process in which the outermost plant cells become thickened and covered with cutin, making them waterproof.

cu·tin·ize (kū'ti-nīz'), *v.i. & v.t.* [CUTINIZED (-nīzd'), CUTINIZING], to undergo or cause to undergo cutinization.

cu·tis (kū'tis), *n.* [L.; see CUTICLE], the layer of skin beneath the epidermis; derma; dermis; corium.

‡**cu·tis ve·ra** (kū'tis vêr'ə), [L., true skin], the cutis.

cut·lass, cut·las (kut'ləs), *n.* [Fr. *coutelas;* It. *coltellaccio* < *coltello*, knife; L. *cultellus*, dim. < *culter*, IE. **ql-tros* < base *(*s*)*qel-*, to cut, split; hence akin to L. *scalpere*, to cut (cf. SCALPEL), ON. *skalm*, short sword, knife], a short, thick, curving sword with a single cutting edge, formerly used especially by sailors.

cut·ler (kut'lẽr), *n.* [ME. *coteler;* Anglo-Fr. *cotillere;* OFr. *coutelier;* LL. *cultellarius*, one who makes knives < L. *cultellus;* see CUTLASS], a person who makes, sells, or repairs knives and other cutting tools.

cut·ler·y (kut'lẽr-i), *n.* [OFr. *cotelerie;* see CUTLER], 1. the work or business of a cutler. 2. cutting instruments; knives, scissors, etc. 3. implements used in eating; knives, forks, and spoons.

cut·let (kut'lit), *n.* [Fr. *côtelette*, dim. < *côte*, rib < L. *costa;* see COAST], 1. a small slice of meat from the ribs or leg, for frying or broiling, often served breaded. 2. a small, flat croquette of chopped meat or fish.

cut·off (kut'ôf'), *n.* 1. a road or passage that cuts across, shortening the distance. 2. a new and shorter channel cut by a river across a bend. 3. the water thus cut off. 4. the act of stopping steam, etc. from entering the cylinder of an engine. 5. a device for doing this, or the point at which this is done.

cut·out (kut'out'), *n.* 1. a switch or other device for breaking or closing an electric circuit. 2. a device for letting the exhaust gases of an internal-combustion engine pass directly into the air instead of through a muffler. 3. a design cut out of something, or to be cut out.

cut·o·ver (kut'ō'vẽr), *adj.* cleared of trees. *n.* land cleared of trees.

cut·purse (kut'pũrs'), *n.* 1. originally, a thief who stole purses by cutting them from the belts or girdles to which they were attached; hence, 2. a pickpocket.

cut-rate (kut'rāt'), *adj.* 1. on sale at a lower price. 2. having articles for sale at a lower price.

cut·tage (kut'ij), *n.* the method of propagating plants by means of cuttings.

cut·ter (kut'ẽr), *n.* 1. a device for cutting. 2. a person who cuts or whose work is cutting; specifically, a person whose work is cutting the patterned sections that are sewed together to form a garment. 3. any boat or small vessel that can cut swiftly through the water; specifically, *a*) a boat, motor-powered or rowed, carried aboard large ships as a communications tender: also **ship's cutter.** *b*) an armed, single-masted, gaff-rigged sailing vessel, formerly used by revenue authorities to pursue smugglers, etc.: also **revenue cutter.** *c*) an armed steamer or motor ship, now used by the coast guard for coastal or ocean patrol, etc.: also **coast-guard cutter.** *d*) a gaff-rigged racing yacht with a deep keel, single mast, large sail area, and narrow beam: also **British cutter.** *e*) a modern single-masted yacht or sailboat carrying two headsails under normal wind conditions: distinguished from *sloop*. 4. a small, lightweight sleigh, usually drawn by one horse.

cut·throat (kut′thrōt′), *n.* a person who cuts throats; murderer; assassin. *adj.* 1. murderous. 2. merciless; ruthless; relentless. 3. played by three people: said of some card games, as, *cutthroat* bridge.
cut·ting (kut′iŋ), *n.* 1. the act of a person or thing that cuts. 2. a thing or piece cut off. 3. the editing of a motion-picture film by deleting certain scenes and assembling others into their proper sequence. 4. [British], a clipping from a newspaper, etc. 5. a passage for trains, cars, etc., cut through a hill or high ground. 6. in *horticulture*, a slip or shoot cut away from a plant for rooting or grafting. *adj.* 1. that cuts; for cutting; edged; sharp. 2. chilling or piercing: as, a *cutting* wind. 3. wounding the feelings; sarcastic. —*SYN.* see **incisive.**
cut·tle (kut′'l), *n.* 1. a cuttlefish. 2. cuttlebone.
cut·tle·bone (kut′'l-bōn′), *n.* the internal shell of cuttlefish, used as a bird food and, when powdered, as a polishing agent.
cut·tle·fish (kut′'l-fish′), *n.* [*pl.* CUTTLEFISH, CUTTLEFISHES (-iz); see FISH], [ME. *codul, cotul;* AS. *cudele;* akin to Norw. dial. *kaule* (**kodle*), OLG. *cudele*, older D. *kuttlevisch*, etc.; sense "pouch fish" < same IE. base as *cod* (pod)], a squidlike sea mollusk that has ten sucker-bearing arms and a hard internal shell: when in danger, some cuttlefishes eject a black, inklike fluid: also **cuttle.**

CUTTLEFISH

cut·ty (kut′i), *adj.* [< *cut, v.*], [Scot. & Dial.], short. *n.* [*pl.* CUTTIES (-iz)], a short pipe or spoon.
cutty stool, [Scot.], 1. a low stool. 2. formerly, a seat in a church, in which offenders against chastity had to sit and be publicly rebuked by the minister.
cut·up (kut′up′), *n.* [Slang], a person who clowns, plays practical jokes, etc. to attract attention.
cut·wa·ter (kut′wô′tẽr, kut′wot′ẽr), *n.* 1. the fore part of a ship's prow. 2. the angular edge of the pier of a bridge.
cut·work (kut′wũrk′), *n.* openwork embroidery in which part of the cloth is cut away from the design.
cut·worm (kut′wũrm′), *n.* any of a number of caterpillars, especially the larvae of various night-flying moths, which live in the soil and attack young plants of cabbage, corn, etc., cutting them off at ground level.
Cu·vier, Georges (zhôrzh kü′vyā′, Eng. kōō′vi-ā′, kū′vi-ā′), Baron, 1769–1832; French naturalist.
Cu·ya·bá (kōō′yä-bä′), *n.* a city in western Brazil: pop., 50,000.
Cuyp, Aal·bert (äl′bẽrt koip), 1620?–1691; Dutch painter: also spelled **Kuyp.**
Cuz·co (kōōs′kō), *n.* Cusco.
cwt., hundredweight.
-cy (si), [ME. & OFr. *-cie;* L. *-cia, -tia;* Gr. *-kia, -keia, -tia, -teia*], a suffix meaning: 1. *quality, condition, state,* or *fact of being,* as in *hesitancy.* 2. *position, rank,* or *office of,* as in *captaincy, curacy.*
Cy., County.
cy., 1. capacity. 2. currency. 3. cycles.
cy·an- (sī′ən), cyano-.
cy·an·am·id (sī′ə-nam′id, sī-an′ə-mid), *n.* cyanamide.
cy·an·am·ide (sī′ə-nam′īd, sī-an′ə-mīd′, sī-an′ə-mid), *n.* [*cyan-* + *amide*], a white, crystalline compound, $CN \cdot NH_2$, prepared by the reaction of carbon dioxide and hot sodium amide, and by other reactions.
cy·a·nate (sī′ə-nāt′), *n.* a salt or ester of cyanic acid.
cy·an·ic (si-an′ik), *adj.* [*cyan-* + *-ic*], 1. of or containing cyanogen. 2. blue.
cyanic acid, a colorless, poisonous, unstable acid, HOCN, prepared by heating cyanuric acid.
cy·a·nid (sī′ə-nid), *n.* cyanide.
cy·a·nide (sī′ə-nīd′, sī′ə-nid), *n.* a substance composed of cyanogen in combination with some element or radical; especially, potassium cyanide, KCN, or sodium cyanide, NaCN, extremely poisonous, white, crystalline compounds with an odor of bitter almonds: used in extracting gold from low-grade ores, electroplating, case-hardening of steel, and as a fluxing material.
cyanide process, a process of extracting gold or silver from low-grade ores by treating them with a solution of sodium cyanide or potassium cyanide and then recovering the gold or silver by electrolysis.
cy·a·nine (sī′ə-nēn′, sī′ə-nin), *n.* [*cyan-* + *-ine*], a soluble, crystalline, blue dye, $C_{29}H_{35}N_2I$, derived from quiniline and used as a sensitizer in photography.
cy·a·nite (sī′ə-nīt′), *n.* [*cyan-* + *-ite*], a blue, crystalline silicate of aluminum, Al_2SiO_5: also **kyanite.**
cy·a·no- (sī′ə-nō, sī′ə-nə, sī-an′ə), [< Gr. *kyanos*, a dark-blue substance, the color blue], a combining form meaning: 1. *dark-blue,* as in *cyanosis.* 2. in *chemistry, of or containing cyanogen.* Also, before a vowel, **cyan-.**
cy·an·o·gen (sī-an′ə-jən), *n.* [*cyano-* + *-gen*], 1. a colorless, poisonous, inflammable gas, C_2N_2, with an odor like that of peach blossoms. 2. the univalent radical CN, occurring in cyanides.
cy·a·no·hy·drin (sī′ə-nō-hī′drin), *n.* [< *cyano-* + *hydro-* + *-in*], any of a class of organic chemical compounds containing both the CN and OH radicals.
cy·a·no·sis (sī′ə-nō′sis), *n.* [Mod. L.; Gr. *kyanōsis,* dark-blue color < *kyanos,* the color blue], a bluish coloration of the skin, caused by lack of oxygen in the blood.
cy·a·not·ic (sī′ə-not′ik), *adj.* of or characterized by cyanosis.
cy·an·o·type (sī-an′ə-tīp′), *n.* [*cyano-* + *-type*], a photographic print made on paper sensitized by a cyanide; blueprint.
cy·a·nu·ric (sī′ə-nyoor′ik), *adj.* [*cyan-* + *uric*], designating or of a white, crystalline acid, $C_3N_3(OH)_3$, made by heating urea, yielding cyanic acid when subjected to a heating process.
Cyb·e·le (sib′'l-ē′), *n.* [L.; Gr. *Kybelē*], in *ancient Phrygian mythology,* the goddess of nature: identified with the Greek goddess Rhea.
cy·ber·net·ics (sī′bẽr-net′iks), *n. pl.* [construed as sing.], [< Gr. *kybernetes,* helmsman; + *-ics*], a science dealing with the comparative study of complex electronic calculating machines and the human nervous system in an attempt to explain the nature of the brain.
cy·cad (sī′kad), *n.* [Mod. L. *Cycas, Cycadis;* Gr. *kykas,* scribal error for *koïkas,* acc. pl. of *koïx,* doum palm], any of various large, tropical plants resembling the palm and having fernlike leaves growing in a top cluster.
cyc·a·da·ceous (sik′ə-dā′shəs), *adj.* [*cycad* + *-aceous*], of or belonging to a group of primitive, tropical plants characterized by palmlike form and fernlike foliage.
Cyc·la·des (sik′lə-dēz′), *n. pl.* a group of Greek islands in the Aegean: area, 1,023 sq. mi.; pop., 130,000.
cyc·la·men (sik′lə-mən, sik′lə-men′), *n.* [*pl.* CYCLAMENS (-mənz, -menz′)], [Mod. L.; L. *cyclaminos;* Gr. *kyklaminos;* ? < *kyklos,* a circle (with reference to the form of the roots)], a plant of the primrose family, having heart-shaped leaves spotted with white along the veins, and white, pink, or red flowers with reflexed petals.
cy·cle (sī′k'l), *n.* [< Fr. & LL.; Fr. *cycle;* LL. *cyclus;* Gr. *kyklos,* a circle, cycle < IE. **qweqwlo-s,* redupl. of base **qwel-,* *(*s*)*qel-,* something curved; hence akin to AS. *hweol* (see WHEEL)], 1. a recurring period of a definite number of years, used as a measure of time. 2. a period of time within which a round of regularly recurring events or phenomena is completed: as, the business *cycle.* 3. a complete set of events or phenomena recurring in the same sequence. 4. a very long period of time; an age. 5. all of the traditional or legendary poems, songs, etc. connected with a hero or an event: as, the Charlemagne *cycle.* 6. a series of poems or songs on the same theme. 7. a bicycle, tricycle, or motorcycle. 8. in *astronomy,* the orbit of a heavenly body. 9. in *biology,* a recurring series of functional changes or events. 10. in *electricity,* one complete period of the reversal of an alternating current from positive to negative and back again. *v.i.* [CYCLED (-k'ld), CYCLING], 1. to occur or recur in cycles; pass through a cycle. 2. to ride a bicycle, tricycle, or motorcycle.
cy·clic (sī′klik, sik′lik), *adj.* 1. of, or having the nature of, a cycle; moving or occurring in cycles. 2. belonging to a cycle of legends, etc. 3. in *chemistry,* arranged in a ring or closed-chain structure: said of atoms.
cy·cli·cal (sī′kli-k'l, sik′li-k'l), *adj.* cyclic.
cy·clist (sī′klist), *n.* a person who rides a bicycle, etc.
cy·clo- (sī′klō, sī′klə, sik′lə), [< Gr. *kyklos,* a circle, wheel], a combining form meaning *of a circle, of a wheel, circular,* as in *cyclograph:* also, before a vowel, **cycl-.**
cy·clo·graph (sī′klə-graf′, sī′klə-gräf′), *n.* [*cyclo-* + *-graph*], 1. a camera that can take a panoramic view of half the surface of a spherical object. 2. an electronic tool for determining the hardness of metals.
cy·clo·hex·ane (sī′klō-hek′sān), *n.* [*cyclo-* + *hexane*], one of the saturated cyclic hydrocarbons, C_6H_{12}, present in petroleum.
cy·cloid (sī′kloid), *n.* [Gr. *kykloeidēs,* circular < *kyklos* (see CYCLE) + *eidos,* form], in *geometry,* a curve traced by any point on the circumference, or on a radius, of a circle making one complete revolution along a straight line in a single plane. *adj.* 1. circular. 2. designating or of a person who has cyclothymia.
cy·cloi·dal (sī-kloi′d'l), *adj.* of a cycloid.

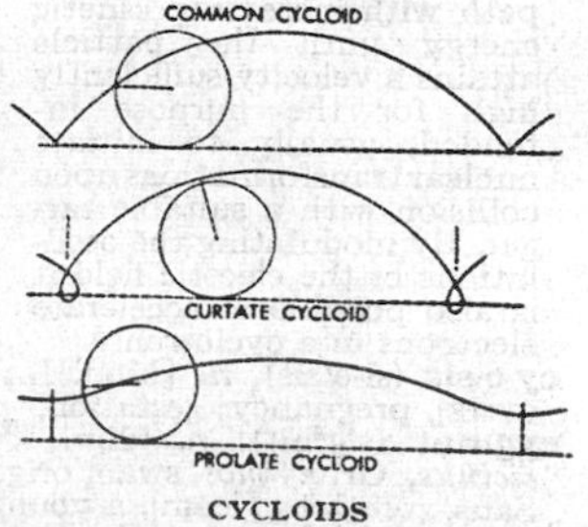

CYCLOIDS

cy·clom·e·ter (sī-klom′ə-tẽr), *n.* [*cyclo-* + *-meter*], 1. an instrument for measuring the arcs of circles. 2. an instrument for recording the revolutions of a wheel, hence measuring the distance traveled by a vehicle.

cy·clone (sī′klōn), *n.* [Gr. *kyklōn*, moving in a circle < *kykloein*, to circle around, whirl < *kyklos;* see CYCLE], 1. loosely, a windstorm with a violent, whirling movement; tornado or hurricane. 2. in *meteorology*, a storm with heavy rainfall and winds rotating about a moving center of low atmospheric pressure.

cyclone cellar, a deep cellar beneath a building, for shelter during heavy windstorms.

cy·clon·ic (sī-klon′ik), *adj.* of or like a cyclone.

cy·clon·i·cal (sī-klon′i-k'l), *adj.* cyclonic.

cy·clo·no·scope (sī-klō′nə-skōp′), *n.* [< *cyclone* + *-scope*], in *meteorology*, a device for locating the center of a cyclone.

Cy·clo·pe·an (sī′klə-pē′ən), *adj.* [L. *Cyclopeus;* Gr. *Kyklōpeios* < *Kyklōps*, Cyclops], 1. of the Cyclopes. 2. [c-], huge; gigantic; enormous; massive.

cy·clo·pe·di·a (sī′klə-pē′di-ə), *n.* [see ENCYCLOPEDIA], a book containing alphabetically arranged articles on aspects of many fields of knowledge, or dealing comprehensively with one subject; encyclopedia: abbreviated **cyc.**: also spelled **cyclopaedia.**

cy·clo·pe·dic (sī′klə-pē′dik), *adj.* 1. relating to a cyclopedia: abbreviated **cyc.** 2. of wide range; extensive and varied. Also spelled **cyclopaedic.**

cy·clo·pe·dist (sī′klə-pē′dist), *n.* a person who compiles or writes for a cyclopedia: also spelled **cyclopaedist.**

cy·clo·pen·tane (sī′klə-pen′tān), *n.* [*cyclo-* + *pentane*], a saturated, colorless liquid hydrocarbon, C_5H_{10}, derived from certain petroleums.

cy·clo·ple·gi·a (sī′klə-plē′ji-ə), *n.* [Mod. L.; see CYCLO- & -PLEGIA], paralysis of those muscles of the eye responsible for visual accommodation.

cy·clo·pro·pane (sī′klə-prō′pān), *n.* [*cyclo-* + *propane*], a colorless, inflammable gas, C_3H_6, used as a general anesthetic.

Cy·clops (sī′klops), *n.* [*pl.* CYCLOPES (sī-klō′pēz)], [L.; Gr. *Kyklōps*, lit., round-eyed < *kyklos* (see CYCLE) + *ōps*, eye], in *Greek mythology*, one of a race of giants supposedly living in Sicily, who had only one eye in the middle of the forehead.

cy·clo·ra·ma (sī′klə-ram′ə, sī′klə-rä′mə), *n.* [*cyclo-* + Gr. *horama*, sight], 1. a series of large pictures, as of a landscape, put on the wall of a circular room so as to appear in natural perspective to a spectator standing in the center. 2. a large, curved curtain or screen used as a background for stage settings.

cy·clo·ram·ic (sī′klə-ram′ik), *adj.* of or like a cyclorama.

cy·clos·to·mate (sī-klos′tə-māt′), *adj.* 1. having a round mouth. 2. of a cyclostome or the cyclostomes.

cy·clo·stom·a·tous (sī′klə-stom′ə-təs), *adj.* cyclostomate.

cy·clo·stome (sī′klə-stōm′, sik′lə-stōm′), *n.* [*cyclo-* + *-stome*], any of a group of primitive fishes, including the lamprey and hagfish, which are vertebrates with an eellike body and a circular, sucking mouth.

cy·clo·style (sī′klə-stīl′), *n.* [*cyclo-* + *style* (a pen)], an apparatus for producing a number of copies of a writing or drawing by means of a stencil in which very small holes are cut with a small, toothed wheel on a stylus.

cy·clo·thy·mi·a (sī′klə-thī′mi-ə), *n.* [Mod. L. < *cyclo-* + Gr. *thymos*, spirit], an abnormal condition characterized by alternate periods of elation and depression; manic-depressive psychosis.

cy·clo·thy·mic (sī′klə-thī′mik), *adj.* of, characteristic of, or having cyclothymia. *n.* a cyclothymic person.

cy·clo·tron (sī′klə-tron′), *n.* [*cyclo-* + elec*tron*], an apparatus for giving high energy to particles, usually protons and deuterons: through the combined action of a homogeneous magnetic field and an oscillating electrostatic field it causes a particle to move in a spiral path with increasing kinetic energy until the particle attains a velocity sufficiently high for the purpose intended, usually to initiate nuclear transformations upon collision with a suitable target. By modulating the oscillations of the electric field it is also possible to accelerate electrons in a cyclotron.

CYCLOTRON

cy·e·sis (sī-ē′sis), *n.* [Mod. L.; Gr. *kyēsis* < *kyein;* see CYME], pregnancy; gestation.

cyg·net (sig′nit), *n.* [dim. < Fr. *cygne*, swan; LL. *cicinus;* Gr. *kyknos*, swan, orig., the white one; akin to Sans. *çōcati*, to gleam], a young swan.

Cyg·nus (sig′nəs), *n.* [L. *Cygnus, Cycnus* (< *cygnus*, swan; Gr. *kyknos;* see CYGNET), mythical king of the Ligurians who was changed into a swan and placed among the stars], a northern constellation, the Swan, in the Milky Way: see **constellation,** chart.

cyl·in·der (sil′in-dẽr), *n.* [Fr. *cylindre;* L. *cylindrus;* Gr. *kylindros* < *kylindein*, to roll; akin to *kyklos;* see CYCLE], 1. in *geometry*, *a*) a solid figure described by the edge of a rectangle rotated around the parallel edge as axis: the ends of a cylinder are parallel and equal circles. 2. anything having the shape of a cylinder, whether hollow or solid; specifically, *a*) the turning part of a revolver, containing chambers for cartridges. *b*) a chamber in which force is exerted on the piston of a reciprocating engine. *c*) the barrel of a pump. *d*) on a printing press, a roller carrying the printing plates or the part receiving the impression. *e*) a roller-shaped stone with cuneiform inscriptions. Abbreviated **cyl.**

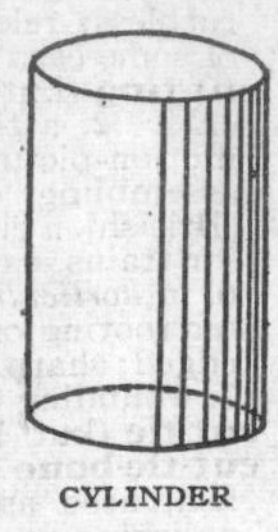

CYLINDER

cylinder head, the closed end, usually detachable, of a cylinder in an internal-combustion engine, often containing the seatings for the valves and the inlet and exhaust passages.

cy·lin·dric (si-lin′drik), *adj.* cylindrical.

cy·lin·dri·cal (si-lin′dri-k'l), *adj.* 1. having the shape of a cylinder. 2. of a cylinder. Abbreviated **cyl.**

cy·lin·dri·cal·i·ty (si-lin′dri-kal′ə-ti), *n.* the state or quality of being cylindrical.

cyl·in·droid (sil′in-droid′), *n.* [Gr. *kylindroeidēs;* see CYLINDER & -OID], a solid body resembling a cylinder, but with elliptical ends. *adj.* resembling a cylinder.

cy·lix (sī′liks, sil′iks), *n.* [*pl.* CYLICES (sil′i-sēz′)], [Gr. *kylix;* akin to *kyklos;* see CYCLE], a two-handled drinking cup with a stem and a wide, shallow bowl, used in ancient Greece: also **kylix.**

Cyl·le·ni·an (si-lē′ni-ən), *adj.* 1. of Mount Cyllene, in Greece; hence, 2. of Hermes, who was regarded as having been born there, or of the arts and practices of which he was the patron god.

Cym., Cymric.

cy·ma (sī′mə), *n.* [*pl.* CYMAE (-mē)], [Mod. L.; Gr. *kyma;* see CYME], in *architecture*, a molding of a cornice, whose profile is a line partly convex and partly concave.

cy·mar (si-mär′), *n.* [Fr. *simarre;* see SIMAR], a chemise or other loose, lightweight garment for women.

cy·ma·ti·um (si-mā′shi-əm), *n.* [*pl.* CYMATIA (-ə)], [L.; Gr. *kymation* < *kyma*, wave; see CYME], in *architecture*, 1. a cyma. 2. a molding topping an entablature.

cym·bal (sim′b'l), *n.* [ME. *symbal, cimbal;* partly < OFr. *cymble*, partly < AS. *cymbal;* both ult. < L. *cymbalum* < Gr. *kymbalon* < *kymbē*, hollow of a vessel (whence L. *cymba*, boat)], 1. either of a pair of circular, slightly concave plates made of brass, used as percussion instruments in orchestras or bands: when struck together they produce a sharp, ringing sound. 2. a single brass plate, struck with a drumstick.

CYMBALS

cym·bal·ist (sim′b'l-ist), *n.* a person who plays the cymbals.

Cym·bel·ine (sim′b'l-ēn′), *n.* a drama (1609) by Shakespeare, in which Iachimo unsuccessfully attempts to seduce Imogen after making a bet with her husband, Leonatus, that she would prove unfaithful.

cyme (sīm), *n.* [L. *cyma*, young sprout of cabbage; Gr. *kyma*, cyme, wave, orig., something swollen < *kyein*, to be pregnant; IE. base **keu-*, to swell, arch], a cluster of flowers in which each main and secondary stem bears a single flower, the bud on the main stem blooming first, as in phlox and sweet William.

cy·mene (sī′mēn), *n.* [Gr. *kyminon;* see CUMIN], a hydrocarbon, $C_{10}H_{14}$, occurring in three isomeric forms (*orthocymene, metacymene*, and *paracymene*), derived from benzene: the most common form, paracymene, is found in the oil of certain plants, as cumin and wild thyme.

cy·mo- (sī′mō, sī′mə), [Gr. *kymo-* < *kyma;* see CYME], a combining form meaning *wave*, as in *cymoscope.*

cy·mo·gene (sī′mə-jēn′), *n.* [< *cymene* + *-gene*], an inflammable distillate of petroleum which, when condensed, is used as a freezing mixture.

cy·mo·graph (sī′mə-graf′, sī′mə-gräf′), *n.* [*cymo-* + *-graph*], an instrument for making tracings, as of profiles, contours, etc.; kymograph.

cy·moid (sī′moid), *adj.* resembling a cyma or cyme.

cy·mom·e·ter (sī-mom′ə-tẽr), *n.* [*cymo-* + *-meter*], an instrument for measuring the frequency of electrical oscillations or radio waves.

cy·mo·phane (sī′mə-fān′), *n.* [*cymo-* + *-phane*], an opalescent variety of chrysoberyl.

cy·mo·scope (sī′mə-skōp′), *n.* [*cymo-* + *-scope*], an instrument for detecting the presence of electric waves.

cy·mose (sī′mōs, sī-mōs′), *adj.* [L. *cymosus* < *cyma*], 1. of or like a cyme. 2. bearing a cyme or cymes.

Cym·ric (kim′rik, sim′rik), *adj.* [< *Cymri*, western Britons, Welsh < W. *Cymry*, pl. of *Cymro* < *Cymru*, Wales; see CAMBRIA], 1. of the Celtic people of Wales.

2. of their language. *n.* the group of Brythonic Celtic languages that includes Welsh, Breton, and extinct Cornish. Abbreviated **Cym.** Also **Kymric.**

Cym·ry (kim′ri, sim′ri), *n.pl.* the Cymric Celts; the Welsh: also **Kymry.**

Cyn·e·wulf (kin′i-woolf′), *n.* Anglo-Saxon poet; fl. 750 A.D.

cyn·ic (sin′ik), *n.* [L. *Cynicus;* see CYNICAL], 1. [C-], a member of a sect of ancient Greek philosophers who held virtue to be the only good, and stressed independence from worldly needs and pleasures; they became critical of the rest of society and its material interests; hence, 2. a cynical person. 3. a person who believes that people are motivated in all their actions entirely by selfishness. *adj.* 1. [C-], of or like the Cynics or their doctrines. 2. cynical.

cyn·i·cal (sin′i-k'l), *adj.* [< L. *cynicus,* of the Cynics; Gr. *kynikos,* lit., canine, like a dog < *kyōn, kynos,* dog; IE. base **kuon-,* dog; hence akin to AS. *hund* (see HOUND, dog)], 1. inclined to question the sincerity and goodness of people's motives and actions, or the value of living. 2. morose, sarcastic, sneering, etc.
SYN.—**cynical** implies a contemptuous disbelief in human goodness and sincerity (he's *cynical* about recovering his lost watch); **misanthropic** suggests a deep-seated hatred or distrust of people in general (a *misanthropic* hermit); **pessimistic** implies an attitude, often habitual, of expecting the worst to happen (*pessimistic* about one's chances to win).—*ANT.* optimistic.

cyn·i·cism (sin′ə-siz'm), *n.* 1. [C-], the philosophy of the Cynics. 2. the attitude or beliefs of a cynic. 3. a cynical expression or view.

cy·no·sure (sī′nə-shoor′, sin′ə-shoor′), *n.* [< Gr. *kynosoura,* dog's tail, constellation of Ursa Minor; cf. CYNICAL], 1. [C-], the constellation Ursa Minor. 2. [C-], the North Star, which is in this constellation. 3. anything that guides or directs. 4. any person or thing that is a center of attention or interest.

Cyn·thi·a (sin′thi-ə), [L.; Gr. *Kynthia,* epithet of Artemis, orig. fem. of *Kynthios,* lit., of or from *Kynthos,* Cynthus, mountain in Delos, celebrated as the birthplace of Apollo and Artemis], a feminine name: diminutive, *Cindy. n.* 1. Artemis (or Diana), goddess of the moon; hence, 2. the moon personified.

cy·per·a·ceous (sī′pẽr-ā′shəs, sip′ẽr-ā′shəs), *adj.* [< Mod. L. *Cyperus,* sedge < Gr. *kypeiros;* + *-aceous*], of the sedge family of plants, which resemble the grasses but have solid stems and seeds in closed sheaths.

cy·pher (sī′fẽr), *n., v.t. & vi.* cipher.

cy pres (sē′ prā′), [Late Anglo-Fr.; OFr. *si pres,* so nearly], in *law,* as nearly as possible: applied to the interpretation of wills, as in cases of trust funds when the terms cannot be carried out literally and an effort is made to adhere to the general intent.

cy·press (sī′prəs), *n.* [ME. *cipres, cypres;* OFr. *cipres;* L. *cypressus, cupressus* < or akin to Gr. *kyparissos*], 1. any of a large group of evergreen, cone-bearing trees of the pine family, native to North America, Europe, and Asia: they have dark foliage and a distinctive symmetrical form. 2. the hard wood of one of these trees. 3. any of a number of related trees, including certain cedars and the bald cypresses. 4. the branches or sprigs of the cypress, used as a symbol of mourning.

cy·press (sī′prəs), *n.* [ME. *cipres;* OFr. *Cipre, Cypre, Cypres,* Cyprus], any of various textile fabrics, originally made in Cyprus; specifically, *a)* a cloth of gold. *b)* a heavy satin. *c)* a fine, gauzelike lawn or silk. Also spelled **cyprus.**

cypress vine, a tropical American climbing plant with showy, trumpet-shaped flowers of scarlet or white.

Cyp·ri·an (sip′ri-ən), *adj.* [L. *Cyprius;* Gr. *Kyprios* < *Kypros,* Cyprus], 1. of Cyprus, its people, or its language. 2. wanton; licentious: in reference to the worship of Aphrodite there in ancient times. *n.* 1. a native or inhabitant of Cyprus. 2. the Greek dialect of Cyprus. 3. [Obs.], a prostitute.

Cyprian, Saint, 1. ?–258 A.D.; Christian martyr; bishop of Carthage. 2. 476–546 A.D.; French prelate and writer; bishop of Toulon.

cy·pri·nid (si-prī′nid, sip′ri-nid), *adj. & n.* cyprinoid.

cy·prin·o·dont (si-prin′ə-dont′, si-prī′nə-dont′), *n.* [< Gr. *kyprinos,* carp; + *-odont*], any of a family of very small fishes with soft fins, including the killifishes.

cyp·ri·noid (sip′ri-noid′, si-prī′noid), *adj.* [< Gr. *kyprinos,* carp (akin to Eng. *carp*); + *-oid*], of or like the fishes of the carp family, including the carps, goldfishes, barbels, dace, etc. *n.* a cyprinoid fish.

Cyp·ri·ot (sip′ri-ət), *adj. & n.* Cyprian.

Cyp·ri·ote (sip′ri-ōt′), *adj. & n.* Cyprian.

cyp·ri·pe·di·um (sip′rə-pē′di-əm), *n.* [*pl.* CYPRIPEDIA (-ə)], [Mod. L., lady's-slipper < Gr. *Kypris,* Venus + *podion,* slipper, dim. < *pous, podis,* foot], any of a group of orchids with showy, drooping flowers, including lady's-slippers, moccasin flowers, etc.

Cy·prus (sī′prəs), *n.* a country on an island in the eastern Mediterranean, south of Turkey: a former British crown colony, it is now a member of the British Commonwealth of Nations: area, 3,572 sq. mi.; pop., 581,000; capital, Nicosia: abbreviated **Cyp.**

cy·prus (sī′prəs), *n.* cypress (cloth).

cyp·se·la (sip′sə-lə), *n.* [*pl.* CYPSELAE (-lē′)], [Mod. L.; Gr. *kypselē,* a hollow vessel], a kind of seed pod (*achene*) with two spore-bearing organs (*carpels*) and a calyx directly attached to it, as in the sunflower.

Cyrano de Bergerac, see **Bergerac, Cyrano de.**

Cy·re·na·ic (sir′ə-nā′ik, sī′rə-nā′ik), *adj.* 1. of Cyrenaica or Cyrene. 2. of the Greek school of philosophy founded by Aristippus of Cyrene, who considered pleasure the greatest good. *n.* 1. a native of Cyrenaica or Cyrene. 2. a philosopher of the Cyrenaic school.

Cyr·e·na·i·ca (sir′ə-nā′i-kə, sī′rə-nā′i-kə), *n.* 1. an ancient land in northern Africa, in the region of modern Cirenaica, Libya: also called *Barca.* 2. Cirenaica.

Cy·re·ne (sī-rē′ni), *n.* an ancient Greek city in northern Africa: capital of Cyrenaica.

Cyr·il (sir′əl), [LL. *Cyrillus;* Gr. *Kyrillos,* lit., lordly < *kyrios,* a lord], a masculine name.

Cyril, Saint, 1. 315?–386 A.D.; bishop of Jerusalem: his day is March 20. 2. 376–444 A.D.; archbishop of Alexandria: his day is February 9. 3. (born *Constantine*), 827–869 A.D.; apostle to the Slavs, born in Thessalonica: his day is July 5.

Cy·ril·lic (si-ril′ik), *adj.* designating or of the Slavic alphabet attributed to Saint Cyril, 9th-century apostle to the Slavs: in modified form, it is still used in Russia, Bulgaria, and other Slavic countries.

Cy·rus (sī′rəs), [L.; Gr. *Kyros;* OPer. *Kūrush*], a masculine name: diminutive, *Cy. n.* 1. Persian king; lived 600?–529 B.C.; founder of the Persian empire: called *the Great.* 2. brother of Artaxerxes II; 424?–401 B.C.; Persian prince; warred with his brother for the throne: called *the Younger.*

cyst (sist), *n.* [Mod. L. *cystis;* Gr. *kystis,* sac, bladder; akin to L. *cutis;* see CUTICLE], 1. any of certain saclike structures in plants or animals. 2. any saclike structure or pocket in the body, especially if filled with fluid or diseased matter.

cyst- (sist), cysto-.

-cyst (sist), [< Gr. *kystis;* see CYST], a suffix meaning *sac, pouch, bladder,* as in *encyst.*

cys·tec·to·my (sis-tek′tə-mi), *n.* [*pl.* CYSTECTOMIES (-miz)], [*cyst-* + *-ectomy*], 1. the surgical removal of a cyst. 2. the surgical removal of the gall bladder or of part of the urinary bladder.

cys·te·ine (sis′ti-ēn′, sis′ti-in), *n.* an amino acid, $C_3H_7O_2NS$, derived from cystine and produced by the acid hydrolysis of proteins in digestion.

cys·ti- (sis′ti), cysto-.

cyst·ic (sis′tik), *adj.* [Fr. *cystique;* Mod. L. *cysticus*], 1. of or like a cyst. 2. having or containing a cyst or cysts. 3. enclosed in a cyst. 4. in *anatomy,* of the gall bladder or the urinary bladder.

cys·ti·cer·coid (sis′tə-sũr′koid), *adj.* of or like a cysticercus. *n.* the larva of certain tapeworms, similar to a cysticercus but having a much smaller bladder.

cys·ti·cer·cus (sis′tə-sũr′kəs), *n.* [*pl.* CYSTICERCI (-sī)], [Mod. L. < *cysti-* + Gr. *kerkos,* tail], the larva of certain tapeworms, in which the head and neck are partly enclosed in a bladderlike cyst.

cystic fibrosis, a congenital disease of children, characterized by fibrosis and malfunctioning of the pancreas, and frequent respiratory infections.

cys·tin (sis′tin), *n.* cystine.

cys·tine (sis′tēn, sis′tin), *n.* [< Gr. *kystis* (see CYST); + *-ine:* so named from having been found first in urinary calculi], a crystalline amino acid, $C_4H_6(NH_2)_2S_2(COOH)_2$, produced in the digestion of proteins.

cys·ti·tis (sis-tī′tis), *n.* [*cyst-* + *-itis*], an inflammation of the urinary bladder.

cys·to- (sis′tō, sis′tə), [< Gr. *kystis,* bladder, sac; see CYST], a combining form meaning *of or like a bladder* or *sac,* as in *cystocele;* also **cyst-, cysti-.**

cys·to·carp (sis′tə-kärp′), *n.* [*cysto-* + *-carp*], a fruitlike structure (*sporocarp*) developed after fertilization in the red algae.

cys·to·cele (sis′tə-sēl′), *n.* [*cysto-* + *-cele*], a hernia of the urinary bladder.

cyst·oid (sis′toid), *adj.* like a cyst or bladder. *n.* a cystlike formation.

cys·to·lith (sis′tə-lith), *n.* [*cysto-* + *-lith*], 1. in *botany,* a crystalline deposit of calcium carbonate in a plant cell. 2. in *medicine,* a urinary calculus.

cys·to·scope (sis′tə-skōp′), *n.* [*cysto-* + *-scope*], an instrument for examining the interior of the urinary bladder. *v.t.* [CYSTOSCOPED (-skōpt′), CYSTOSCOPING], to examine with a cystoscope.

cys·tos·co·py (sis-tos′kə-pi), *n.* examination of the urinary bladder with the aid of a cystoscope.

cys·tot·o·my (sis-tot′ə-mi), *n.* [*cysto-* + *-tomy*], the surgical operation of making an incision into the urinary

bladder, as in order to remove calcium formations.
cyt- (sīt), cyto-.
cy·tas·ter (sī-tas′tẽr, sīt′as′tẽr), *n.* [*cyt-* + *-aster*], in *biology*, a star-shaped figure occurring in cells undergoing mitosis; aster.
-cyte (sīt), [< Gr. *kytos*, a hollow; akin to L. *cutis*; see CUTICLE], a terminal combining form meaning *a cell*, as in *lymphocyte*.
Cy·the·ra (si-thir′ə), *n.* Cerigo: the Latin name, used in English.
Cyth·er·e·a (sith′ə-rē′ə), *n.* [L.; Gr. *Kythereia* < *Kythera*, name of a Greek island near which the goddess is fabled to have arisen from the sea], Aphrodite; Venus.
cy·to- (sī′tō, sī′tə), [< Gr. *kytos*, a hollow; see -CYTE], a combining form meaning *of a cell* or *cells*, as in *cytology*, *cytoplasm*: also, before a vowel, **cyt-**.
cy·to·gen·e·sis (sī′tə-jen′ə-sis), *n.* [*cyto-* + *-genesis*], in *biology*, the formation and development of cells.
cy·to·ki·ne·sis (sī′tō-ki-nē′sis, sī′tō-kī-nē′sis), *n.* [Mod. L.; *cyto-* + *kinesis*], the changes that take place in the cytoplasm of a cell during the stages of its development.
cy·tol·o·gy (sī-tol′ə-ji), *n.* [*cyto-* + *-logy*], the branch of biology dealing with the structure, function, pathology, and life history of cells.
cy·tol·y·sis (sī-tol′ə-sis), *n.* [*cyto-* + *-lysis*], in *biology*, the degeneration of cells.
cy·to·plasm (sī′tə-plaz′m), *n.* [*cyto-* + *-plasm*], the protoplasm of a cell, exclusive of the nucleus.
cy·to·plas·mic (sī′tə-plaz′mik), *adj.* of or contained in cytoplasm.
cy·to·plast (sī′tə-plast′), *n.* cytoplasm.
Cyz·i·cus (siz′i-kəs), *n.* an ancient peninsular city on the southern shore of the Sea of Marmara: the Spartan fleet was defeated there (410 B.C.) by the Athenians.
C.Z., Canal Zone.
czar (zär), *n.* [Russ. *tsar′*, contr. of *tsesar*; OSlav. *cěsarĭ*; prob. via Goth. *kaisar* < L. *Caesar*; see CAESAR], 1. an emperor: title of any of the former emperors of Russia and, at various times, the sovereigns of other Slavic nations. 2. an autocrat; despot; absolute ruler. Also **tsar, tzar.**
czar·das (chär′däsh), *n.* [Hung. *csárdás*], 1. a Hungarian dance consisting of a fast movement and a slow movement. 2. the music for this dance.
czar·dom (zär′dəm), *n.* 1. the position or power of a czar. 2. the territory ruled over by a czar. Also **tsardom, tzardom.**
czar·e·vitch (zär′ə-vich′), *n.* [Russ. *tsarevich*, son of a czar], 1. the eldest son of a czar of Russia. 2. formerly, any son of a czar of Russia: in later times the title *grand duke* was borne by all sons but the eldest. Also **tsarevitch, tzarevich.**
cza·rev·na (zä-rev′nə), *n.* [Russ. *tsarevna*], 1. a Russian czar's daughter. 2. the wife of a czarevitch. Also **tsarevna, tzarevna.**
cza·ri·na (zä-rē′nə), *n.* [G. *zarin*, *czarin*, fem. of *zar*, *czar* (< Russ.), for Russ. *tsaritsa*], the wife of a czar; empress of Russia: also **tsarina, tzarina.**
czar·ism (zär′iz′m), *n.* czarist system of government; absolute rule; autocracy: also **tsarism, tzarism.**
czar·ist (zär′ist), *adj.* 1. of, characteristic of, or like the czars; autocratic. 2. of the time of the czars in Russia. 3. supporting a czar or czarism. *n.* a follower or supporter of a czar or czarism. Also **tsarist, tzarist.**
cza·rit·za (zä-rit′sə), *n.* [Russ.], czarina: also **tsaritza, tzaritza.**
Czech (chek), *n.* 1. a Bohemian, Moravian, or Silesian Slav. 2. the West Slavic language of the Czechs: also called *Bohemian*. *adj.* of Czechoslovakia, its people, or their language.
Czech·ic (chek′ik), *adj.* Czech.
Czech·ish (chek′ish), *adj.* Czech.
Czech·o·slo·vak, Czech·o-Slo·vak (chek′ə-slō′vak, chek′ə-slō′väk), *adj.* of Czechoslovakia, its people, or language. *n.* 1. a Czech or a Slovak living in Czechoslovakia. 2. the West Slavic language spoken there, including the Czech, Slovak, and Moravian dialects.
Czech·o·slo·va·ki·a, Czech·o-Slo·va·ki·a (chek′ə-slō-vä′ki-ə, chek′ə-slō-vak′yə), *n.* a country in central Europe, formed after World War I, consisting of Bohemia, Moravia and Silesia, and Slovakia: area, 54,244 sq. mi.; pop., 13,649,000; capital, Prague.
Czech·o·slo·vak·i·an, Czech·o-Slo·vak·i·an (chek′ə-slō-väk′i-ən, chek′ə-slō-vak′yən), *adj.* & *n.* Czechoslovak.
Czer·no·witz (cher′nə-vits′), *n.* Chernovtsy.
Czer·ny, Karl (kärl cher′ni), **1791–1857; Austrian** pianist and composer.
Czę·sto·cho·wa (chan′stô-Hô′vä), *n.* a city in western Poland: pop., 138,000.

D

D, d (dē), *n.* [*pl.* D's, d's, Ds, ds (dēz)], 1. the fourth letter of the English alphabet: from the Greek *delta*, a borrowing from the Phoenician: see **alphabet**, table. 2. the sound of D or d, normally a voiced tongue-apex stop. 3. a type or impression for D or d. 4. *a symbol for* the fourth in a sequence or group. *adj.* 1. of D or d. 2. fourth in a sequence or group.
D (dē), *n.* 1. an object shaped like D. 2. a Roman numeral for 500; with a superior bar ($\bar{D}$), 500,000, or, less often, 5,000. 3. in *chemistry, the symbol for*, *a*) deuterium. *b*) formerly, didymium. 4. in *education*, a grade fourth in quality, or merely passing: as, a *D* in history. 5. in *music*, *a*) the second tone or note in the scale of C major, or the fourth in the scale of A minor. *b*) a key, string, etc. producing this tone. *c*) the scale having D as the keynote. 6. in *physics, the symbol for* density. *adj.* shaped like D.
D., 1. December. 2. Democrat. 3. Democratic. 4. Department (of the United States Army). 5. *Deus*, [L.], God. 6. Doctor, as in *Ph. D.* 7. *Dominus*, [L.], Lord. 8. Don. 9. Duchess. 10. Duke. 11. Dutch.
d., 1. dam (in pedigrees). 2. date. 3. daughter. 4. day; days. 5. dead. 6. degree. 7. delete. 8. [L.], *denarius*, penny; *denarii*, pennies or pence: as, 6*d*. 9. density. 10. deputy. 11. deserter. 12. diameter. 13. died. 14. dime. 15. director. 16. dividend. 17. dollar. 18. dorsal. 19. dose. 20. dyne.
'd, 1. abbreviated spelling of *had* or *would* in contracted auxiliary forms, as *I'd, they'd*, etc. 2. -ed, as in *foster'd*.
da., 1. daughter. 2. day; days.
D.A., District Attorney.
dab (dab), *v.t.* & *v.i.* [DABBED (dabd), DABBING], [ME. *dabben*, to strike; akin to MD. *dabben* & Norw. *dabba*; IE. base **dhabh*, to strike], 1. to touch or strike lightly and quickly. 2. to peck. 3. to pat with something soft or moist. 4. to put on (paint, etc.) with light, quick strokes. *n.* 1. a light, quick blow; tap; pat. 2. a small, soft, or moist bit of something: as, a *dab* of rouge.
dab (dab), *n.* [< ME. *dabben*; see DAB, *v.*, 3 & *n.*, 2], 1. a small flounder. 2. any small, edible flatfish.
dab (dab), *n.* [contr. < Brit. *dab-hand*; see DAB, *v.*, 4 & DABSTER], [Colloq.], an expert.
dab·ber (dab′ẽr), *n.* 1. a person or thing that dabs. 2. a pad for applying ink, color, etc., used by printers and engravers.
dab·ble (dab′'l), *v.t.* [DABBLED (-'ld), DABBLING], [D. *dabbelen*, freq. of *dabben*, to strike, touch], 1. to dip lightly in and out of a liquid. 2. to wet by dipping, splashing, or sprinkling. *v.i.* 1. to play in water, as with the hands. 2. to do something superficially, not seriously (with *in* or *at*): as, he *dabbles* in art.
dab·bler (dab′lẽr), *n.* a person who dabbles; dilettante.
dab·chick (dab′chik′), *n.* [*dab*, *v.* + *chick*: from the manner of diving], 1. the European little grebe, a small diving bird. 2. the American pied-billed grebe.
dab·ster (dab′stẽr), *n.* 1. [British Dial.], an expert. 2. [Colloq.], a dabbler; clumsy, amateurish worker.
‡da ca·po (dä kä′pô), [It., from (the) head], in *music*, from the beginning: a direction to the performer to repeat a passage: abbreviated **D.C.**
Dac·ca (dak′ə), *n.* the capital of East Pakistan: pop., 600,000.
‡d'ac·cord (dȧ′kôr′), [Fr.], in accord; agreed.
dace (dās), *n.* [*pl.* DACE, DACES (-iz); see PLURAL, II, D, 2], [ME. *darse*, *darce*, orig., dial. form (with *-r* loss as in *bass*) < OFr. *dars*; ML. *darsus*; ? the same word as *dart*, from the fish's rapid motion; ? folk etym. for word of Gaul. origin], 1. a small fresh-water fish of the carp family, found in Europe. 2. any of a number of small North American fishes like or related to the carp, found in fresh-water streams or ponds.
Da·chau (dä′khou), *n.* a Nazi concentration camp

near Munich, Germany, especially for political prisoners.

dachs·hund (däks'hoond', daks'hund', dash'hund'; G. däkhs'hoont'), *n.* [G. *dachs,* badger + *hund,* dog], a small dog of German breed, with a long body, short legs, and drooping ears.

DACHSHUND (8–10 in. high)

Da·cia (dā'shə), *n.* an ancient Roman province between the Danube and the Carpathian Mountains: see **Roman Empire,** map.

Da·cian (dā'shən), *adj.* of Dacia or its people. *n.* a native or inhabitant of Dacia.

da·coit (də-koit'), *n.* [Hind. *ḍakait,* robber < *ḍākā,* attack by robbers], a member of a gang of robbers in India or Burma.

da·coit·y (də-koi'ti), *n.* [*pl.* DACOITIES (-tiz)], [Hind. *ḍakaitī;* see DACOIT], robbery by dacoits.

da·cron (dā'kron, dak'ron), *n.* a synthetic fiber, or a washable fabric made from this fiber that is resistant to wrinkling: a trade-mark (**Dacron**).

dac·tyl (dak'til, dak't'l), *n.* [L. *dactylus;* Gr. *daktylos,* a finger or (from the three joints) dactyl], 1. in *prosody,* a metrical foot of three syllables, the first accented and the others unaccented, as in English verse, or the first long and the others short, as in Greek and Latin verse. Example: "Nót ŏf thĕ | prínćĕs ănd | prélātes wĭth | pérĭwĭgged | chárĭŏ | téers." 2. in *zoology,* a finger or toe: also called *dactylus.*

-dac·tyl·i·a (dak-til'i-ə), -dactyly.

dac·tyl·ic (dak-til'ik), *adj.* of or made up of dactyls. *n.* a dactylic verse.

dac·ty·lo- (dak'ti-lō, dak-til'ə), [< Gr. *daktylos,* a finger], a combining form meaning *finger, toe, digit,* as in *dactylogram:* also, before a vowel, **dactyl-.**

dac·tyl·o·gram (dak-til'ə-gram'), *n.* [*dactylo-* + *-gram*], a fingerprint.

dac·ty·log·ra·phy (dak'ti-log'rə-fi), *n.* [*dactylo-* + *-graphy*], the study of fingerprints as a means of identification.

dac·ty·lol·o·gy (dak'ti-lol'ə-ji), *n.* [*dactylo-* + *-logy*], the study or use of the finger alphabet, as among deaf-mutes.

-dac·ty·ly (dak't'l-i), [< Gr. *daktylos,* a finger], a combining form meaning *a* (specified) *condition of the fingers, toes,* etc.: also **-dactylia.**

dad (dad), *n.* [< child's cry *dada*], [Colloq.], father.

Da·da (dä'dä, dä'də), *n.* [Fr.; prob. < child's cry; term chosen by Tristan Tsara, leader of cult, because of its meaninglessness], a cult (1916–1922) in painting, sculpture, and literature characterized by fantastic, symbolic, often formless expression of supposedly subconscious matter, and by nihilistic satire: also **Dadaism.**

Da·da·ism (dä'də-iz'm), *n.* Dada.

dad·dy (dad'i), *n.* [*pl.* DADDIES (-iz)], [see DAD], [Colloq.], father; dad.

dad·dy-long·legs (dad'i-lôŋ'legz', dad'i-loŋ'legz'), *n.* [*pl.* DADDY-LONGLEGS], 1. [British], the crane fly, an insect with two wings and very long legs. 2. the harvestman, an arachnid with four pairs of long legs.

da·do (dā'dō), *n.* [*pl.* DADOES (-dōz)], [It., a die, die-shaped part of pedestal, hence pedestal < L. *datum,* a die, lit., what is given; see DATE], 1. part of a pedestal between the cap and the base. 2. the lower part of the wall of a room if decorated differently from the upper part, as with panels or an ornamental border.

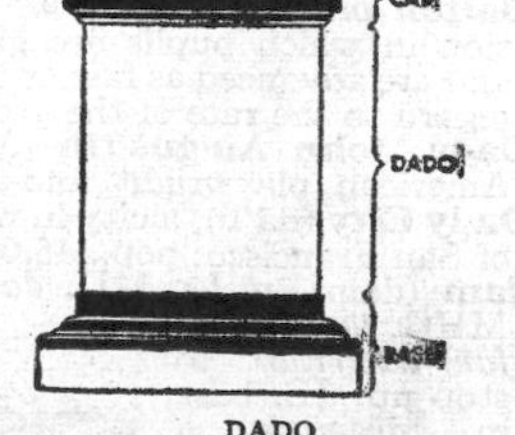

DADO

D.A.E., DAE, Dictionary of American English.

dae·dal (dē'd'l), *adj.* [L. *daedalus;* Gr. *daidalos* < *daidallein,* to work artfully; akin to L. *dolare,* to hew], 1. skillful in workmanship; ingenious. 2. highly wrought; intricate; varied. Also spelled **dedal.**

Dae·da·li·an, Dae·da·le·an (di-dā'li-ən, di-dāl'yən), *adj.* 1. of Daedalus. 2. [d-], daedal; ingenious or intricate. Also spelled **Dedalian, Dedalean.**

Daed·a·lus (ded'ə-ləs, dē'də-ləs), *n.* [L.; Gr. *Daidalos,* lit., the artful craftsman < *daidalos;* see DAEDAL], in *Greek legend,* the skillful artist and inventor who built the labyrinth in Crete for King Minos and was then imprisoned in it with his son Icarus: they escaped by means of wings that he had made.

dae·mon (dē'mən), *n.* [L.; Gr. *daimōn;* see DEMON], 1. in *Greek mythology,* any of the secondary divinities ranking between the gods and men; hence, 2. a guardian spirit; inspiring or inner spirit. 3. a demon; devil.

dae·mon·ic (di-mon'ik), *adj.* 1. of or possessed by a daemon. 2. demonic.

daff (daf), *v.i.* [ME. *daffe,* var. of *daft*], [Scot.], to act the part of a fool; talk or behave sportively.

daff (daf), *v.t.* [var. of *doff*], 1. [Obs.], to take off (an article of clothing); doff. 2. [Archaic], to turn or thrust aside.

daf·fa·down·dil·ly, daf·fy·down·dil·ly (daf'ə-doun-dil'i), *n.* [*pl.* DAFFADOWNDILLIES, DAFFYDOWNDILLIES (-iz)], [Poetic or Dial.], a daffodil.

daf·fo·dil (daf'ə-dil'), *n.* [ME. *affodille;* ML. *affodillus;* L. *asphodelus;* Gr. *asphodelos;* with playful *d-* as in *dandy;* cf. NED], 1. a narcissus that has long, narrow leaves and yellow flowers with a trumpetlike corona. 2. its flower. 3. yellow.

daf·fo·dil·ly (daf'ə-dil'i), *n.* [*pl.* DAFFODILLIES (-iz)], [Poetic or Dial.], a daffodil: also spelled **daffadilly.**

daf·fy (daf'i), *adj.* [DAFFIER (-i-ẽr), DAFFIEST (-i-ist)], [prob. < obs. *daff,* a fool, idiot; cf. DAFT], [Colloq.], crazy; idiotic; silly.

daft (daft, däft), *adj.* [ME. *dafte* < AS. (*ge*) *dæfte,* mild, gentle; for the sense development, see CRETIN, SILLY], 1. silly; foolish. 2. weak-minded. 3. insane.

Da·gan (dä'gän), *n.* [Assyr.-Babylonian *Dagān*], in *Babylonian mythology,* the god of the earth.

dag·ger (dag'ẽr), *n.* [ME. (12th c.), as if < *daggen,* to slit; akin to OFr. *dague,* It. & Sp. *daga,* G. *degen;* ? < L. **daca,* Dacian knife], 1. a short weapon with a sharp point, used for stabbing. 2. in *printing,* a reference mark (†) shaped like a dagger: the *double dagger* (‡) is also used. *v.t.* 1. to stab with a dagger. 2. to mark with a dagger.
look daggers at, to look at with anger or hatred.

dag·gle (dag''l), *v.t. & v.i.* [DAGGLED (-'ld), DAGGLING], [< dial. *dag,* to besprinkle, make muddy; prob. < ON. *dǫggva,* to bedew, besprinkle < *dǫgg,* genit. *dǫggvar,* dew; + *-le*], to make or become dirty by trailing through mud; draggle.

Da·ghe·stan Autonomous Soviet Socialist Republic (dä'ge-stän'), a division of the R.S.F.S.R. in the Caucasus, on the Caspian: area, 13,124 sq. mi.; pop., 1,063,000; capital, Makhachkala: also spelled **Dagestan.**

dag·lock (dag'lok'), *n.* [dial. *dag,* a loose, hanging end < ME. *daggen,* to slit; + *lock*], a lock of dirty or matted hair, fur, or wool.

Dag·mar (dag'mär), [Dan. < Gmc. *dag-,* day, brightness + *-mar;* akin to AS. *mære,* splendid, glorious], a feminine name.

Dag·ö (dä'gö), *n.* Hiiumaa, an island in the Baltic Sea.

da·go, Da·go (dā'gō), *n.* [*pl.* DAGOS, DAGOES (-gōz)], [Sp. *Diego,* a name equivalent to *James,* very common in Spanish], [Slang], a dark-skinned person of Italian, Spanish, Portuguese, or other Latin descent: vulgar term of prejudice and contempt.

Da·gon (dā'gon, dā'gən), *n.* [L.; Gr.; Heb. < *dāg,* a fish], the main god of the ancient Philistines and later of the Phoenicians, represented as half man and half fish.

da·guerre·o·type (də-ger'ə-tīp', də-ger'i-ə-tīp'), *n.* [after Louis J. M. *Daguerre* (1789–1851), Fr. painter, the inventor], 1. a photograph made by an early method on a plate of chemically treated metal or glass. 2. the method of making such photographs. *v.t.* to photograph by this method.

da·ha·be·ah, da·ha·bee·yah, da·ha·bi·ah (dä'hə-bē'ə), *n.* [Ar. *dhahabīya,* lit., golden one < *dhabab,* golden], a large passenger boat used on the Nile, originally equipped with lateen sails, now generally with steam or gasoline engines.

dahl·ia (dal'yə, däl'yə, dāl'yə), *n.* [after A. *Dahl,* 18th-c. Swed. botanist], 1. any of a group of perennial plants of the composite family, with tuberous roots and large, showy flowers in various bright colors. 2. the flower.

Da·ho·man (dä-hō'mən), *adj.* of Dahomey or its people. *n.* a native or inhabitant of Dahomey.

Da·ho·mey (dä-hō'mā; Fr. dà'ô'mā'), *n.* a country in west central Africa, on the Gulf of Guinea: a former French colony, it is now a member of the French Community: area, 44,696 sq. mi.; pop., 1,713,000; capital, Porto Novo.

Dail Eir·eann (dôl'âr'ən, doil', dīl'), [Ir. *dāil,* a gathering, assembly + *Éireann,* genit. of *Éire,* Ireland], the lower house of the legislature of Ireland.

dai·ly (dā'li), *adj.* [ME. *dayly;* AS. *dæglic* < *dæg,* day], relating to, done, happening, or published every day or every weekday. *n.* [*pl.* DAILIES (-liz)], a newspaper published every day or every weekday. *adv.* every day; day after day.

daily double, in *horse racing,* a bet the success of which depends on choosing both winners in two specified races during the day.

daily dozen, [Colloq.], gymnastic setting-up exercises (originally twelve) done daily.

dai·mio (dī'myō), *n.* [*pl.* DAIMIO, DAIMIOS (-myōz)],

[Japan. < Chin. *dai*, great + *mio*, name], a hereditary feudal nobleman of Japan under a former regime: also spelled **daimyo.**

dai·mon (dī′mōn), *n.* [see DAEMON], a daemon.

Dai Nip·pon (dī′ ni-pon′), [Japan., lit., great Nippon], Japan.

dain·ti·ly (dān′t'l-i), *adv.* in a dainty manner; delicately; gracefully; fastidiously.

dain·ti·ness (dān′ti-nis), *n.* the quality of being dainty.

dain·ty (dān′ti), *n.* [*pl.* DAINTIES (-tiz)], [ME. *deinte;* OFr. *deintė*, worth, value, delicacy < L. *dignitas*, worth, dignity], a delicacy. *adj.* [< the *n.*], 1. delicious and choice. 2. delicately pretty or lovely. 3. of delicate and refined taste. 4. fastidious; squeamish.
SYN.—**dainty**, in this comparison, suggests delicate taste and implies a tendency to reject that which does not fully accord with one's refined sensibilities (a *dainty* appetite); **nice** suggests fine or subtle discriminative powers, especially in intellectual matters (a *nice* distinction in definition); **particular** implies dissatisfaction with anything that fails to conform in detail with one's standards (*particular* in one's choice of friends); **fastidious** implies adherence to such high standards as to be disdainfully critical of even minor nonconformities (a *fastidious* taste in literature); **squeamish** suggests such extreme sensitiveness to what is unpleasant, or such prudishness, as to result in disgust or nausea (not too *squeamish* in his business dealings).

Dai·qui·ri (dī′kẽr-i, dak′ẽr-i), *n.* [after *Daiquirí*, Cuba, source of the rum first used in this drink], a cocktail made of rum, sugar, and lime or lemon juice.

Dai·ren (dī′ren′), *n.* a seaport in northeastern China, in Liaoning province, on the Yellow Sea: pop. (with nearby Port Arthur), 1,054,000. Chinese name, *Talien.*

dair·y (dâr′i), *n.* [*pl.* DAIRIES (-iz)], [ME. *deierie* < *deie*, dairymaid < AS. *dæge*, (female) breadmaker < *dag*, dough], 1. a place where milk and cream are kept and made into butter, cheese, etc. 2. a dairy farm. 3. a store where milk and milk products are sold. 4. dairying.

dairy cattle, cows raised mainly for their milk.

dairy farm, a farm in the business of dairying.

dair·y·ing (dâr′i-iŋ), *n.* the business of producing, making, or selling dairy products.

dair·y·maid (dâr′i-mād′), *n.* a girl or woman who works in a dairy.

dair·y·man (dâr′i-mən), *n.* [*pl.* DAIRYMEN (-mən)], 1. a man who works in or for a dairy. 2. a man who owns a dairy.

da·is (dā′is, dās), *n.* [*pl.* DAISES (dā′is-iz, dās′iz)], [ME. *deis, deys;* OFr. *deis, dois*, high table in a hall; LL. *discus*, table; L. *discus*, platter, quoit, discus], a platform raised above the floor at one end of a hall or room, as in a banquet room, classroom, etc.

Dai·sy (dā′zi), [< name of the flower], a feminine name.

dai·sy (dā′zi), *n.* [*pl.* DAISIES (-ziz)], [ME. *daies eige, daies ie;* AS. *dæges eage*, lit., day's eye; *dæges*, genit. of *dæg* + *eage*, an eye], 1. a common plant of the composite family, bearing flowers with white or pink rays around a yellow disk: often called *English daisy.* 2. its flower. 3. a related tall chrysanthemum with large flowers that have long, white rays around a yellow disk: also called *ox-eye.* 4. [Slang], something outstanding or notable.

daisy cutter, [Slang], in *baseball*, etc. a batted ball that travels close to the ground.

dak (däk, dôk), *n.* [Hind. *dāk*], in India, 1. a method of transporting passengers or news by relays of men and horses; hence, 2. the mail. Also spelled **dawk.**

Dak., Dakota.

Da·kar (dȧ′kär′), *n.* capital and seaport of Senegal, on the northwestern coast of Africa: pop., 234,500.

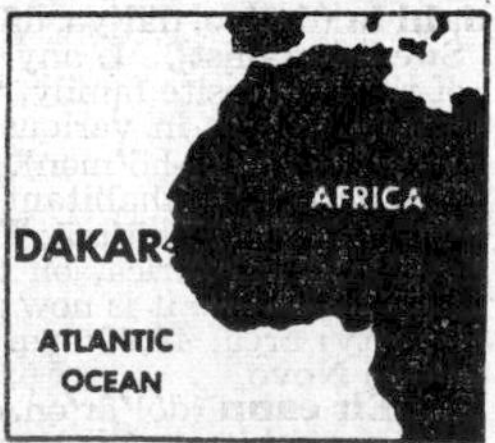

DAKAR

da·ker hen (dā′kẽr), a corn crake.

Da·kin's solution (dā′kinz), [after Henry D. *Dakin* (1880–1952), Eng. chemist in America], a mildly alkaline solution of sodium hypochlorite, used as an antiseptic in the treatment of wounds.

da·koit (də-koit′), *n.* a dacoit.

Da·ko·ta (də-kō′tə), *n.* 1. a member of a group of Siouan tribes that lived in North and South Dakota. 2. the Siouan language of the Dakotas. 3. a Sioux: Indian name. 4. a former Territory of the United States, which now forms North Dakota and South Dakota. *adj.* 1. of a Dakota. 2. of Dakota. 3. of North Dakota, South Dakota, or both.
the Dakotas, North Dakota and South Dakota.

Da·ko·tan (də-kō′tən), *adj.* Dakota. *n.* a native or inhabitant of North Dakota or South Dakota.

Da·la·dier, É·dou·ard (ā′dwâr′ dȧ′lȧ′dyā′), 1884– ; French statesman; premier (1933; 1934; 1938–1940).

Da·lai La·ma (dā-lī′ lä′mə), [Mong. *dalai*, ocean + *blama;* see LAMA], the highest priest of the Lamaist religion in Tibet and Mongolia; Grand Lama.

dale (dāl), *n.* [ME.; AS. *dæl, dalu*, influenced by ON. *dalr;* IE. base **dhel*, a hollowing], a small valley.

Dale, Sir **Thomas** (dāl), ?–1619; English colonial governor of Virginia.

dales·man (dālz′mən), *n.* [*pl.* DALESMEN (-mən)], a person living in a dale, specifically in northern Yorkshire, England.

da·leth, da·ledh (dä′led, dä′ləth), *n.* [Heb., door], the fourth letter of the Hebrew alphabet (ד), corresponding to English *D, d:* see **alphabet** table.

Dal·hou·sie, Earl of (dal-hōō′zi), (*George Ramsay*), 1770–1838; Scottish general; British colonial governor in Canada (1819–1828).

Dalhousie, Marquis of, (*James Andrew Ramsay*), 1812–1860; British governor general of India: son of *George Ramsay, Earl of Dalhousie.*

Da·li, Sal·va·dor (sal′və-dôr′ dä′li; Sp. säl′vä-thôr′ dä′lē), 1904– ; Spanish surrealist painter.

Dal·las (dal′əs), *n.* a city in northeastern Texas: pop., 680,000.

dalles (dalz), *n.pl.* [Fr., water trough, conduit; pl. of *dalle*, slab], rapids above a flat, slablike rock bottom in a narrow, troughlike part of a river: also **dells.**

dal·li·ance (dal′i-əns, dal′yəns), *n.* [ME. *daliance* < *dalien*], the act of dallying; flirting, toying, trifling, etc.

dal·li·er (dal′i-ẽr), *n.* a person who dallies.

dal·ly (dal′i), *v.i.* [DALLIED (-id), DALLYING], [ME. *dalien;* OFr. *dalier*, to converse, trifle], 1. to play, especially in making love; hence, 2. to flirt or toy: as, she *dallied* with the idea. 3. to loiter; waste time. *v.t.* to spend (time) in trifling (with *away*). —*SYN.* see **loiter, trifle.**

Dal·ma·tia (dal-mā′shə), *n.* a region of southwestern Yugoslavia; formerly a part of Austria.

Dal·ma·tian (dal-mā′shən), *adj.* of Dalmatia or its people. *n.* 1. a native or inhabitant of Dalmatia, especially a Slavic-speaking native. 2. a large, lean, short-haired dog with a black-and-white coat, of a breed supposed to have originated in Dalmatia: also called *coach dog.*

DALMATIAN (23 in. high)

dal·mat·ic (dal-mat′ik), *n.* [ME. *dalmatik;* OFr. *dalmatique;* LL. *dalmatica* < *Dalmatia*], 1. in the *Roman Catholic Church*, a loose outer garment with short, wide sleeves and open sides, worn by a deacon, or by a cardinal, bishop, or abbot under the chasuble at pontifical Mass. 2. a robe like this, worn by a king of England when being crowned.

Dal·ny (däl′ni), *n.* Dairen: the former name.

‡dal se·gno (däl se′nyô), [It.], in *music*, from the sign: a direction to return and repeat from the sign 𝄋: abbreviated **D.S., d.s.**

Dal·ton, John (dôl′t'n), 1766–1844; English chemist and physicist; originator of the atomic theory.

Dal·to·ni·an (dôl-tō′ni-ən), *adj.* 1. of John Dalton or his atomic theory. 2. of Daltonism.

Dal·ton·ism (dôl′t'n-iz'm), *n.* [after John *Dalton*, who had color blindness], color blindness, especially red-green blindness.

Dalton plan, [after *Dalton*, Mass.], a system of education in which pupils are given individual instruction and are advanced as fast as their ability allows, without regard to the rate of the group.

Da·ly, John Au·gus·tin (ô-gus′tin dā′li), 1838–1899; American playwright and theatrical manager.

Da·ly City (dā′li), a city in western California; a suburb of San Francisco: pop., 45,000.

dam (dam), *n.* [< MD. *damm;* akin to ON. *dammr*, MHG. *tam*, Goth. *faur-dammjan*, to stop up; IE. base in **dhəmnos*, a heap < **dhē*, to set, put in place], 1. a barrier built to hold back flowing water. 2. the water thus kept back. 3. a thing like a dam. *v.t.* [DAMMED (damd), DAMMING], 1. to put a dam in. 2. to keep back by means of a dam; hence, 3. to keep back or confine (usually with *in* or *up*).

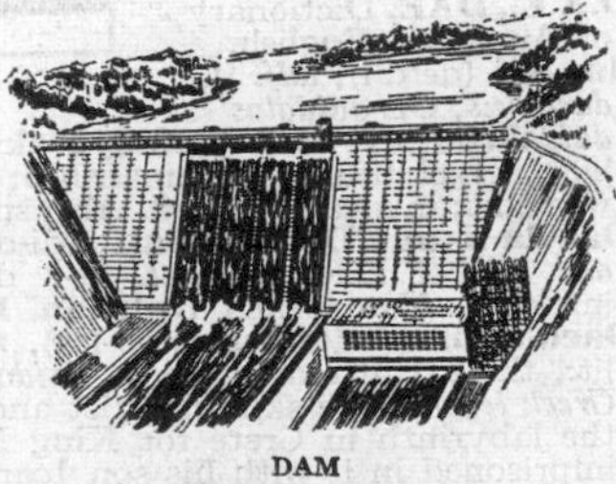
DAM

dam (dam), *n.* [var. of *dame*], 1. the female parent of any four-footed animal; hence, 2. [Archaic], a mother. Abbreviated **d.** (in pedigrees).

dam·age (dam′ij), *n.* [ME.; OFr. < *dam;* L. *damnum*, loss, injury], 1. injury; harm causing any loss. 2. the loss so caused. 3. *pl.* in *law*, money claimed by, or ordered paid to, a person to compensate for injury, loss, etc. that is the fault of someone else. 4. *usually pl.* [Colloq.], cost or expense. *v.t.* [DAMAGED (-ijd), DAMAGING], to do damage to. *v.i.* to incur damage. —*SYN.* see **injure.**

dam·age·a·ble (dam'ij-ə-b'l), *adj.* that can be damaged.

Da·man (dä'män'), *n.* Damão.

dam·an (dam'ən), *n.* [Ar., *damān Isrā'īl*, sheep of Israel], a mammal like the rodents but with modified hoofs, found in the Near East and parts of Africa: also called *hyrax*, and, in the Bible, *cony*.

Da·mão (dä-moun'), *n.* 1. a district of Portuguese India: area, 148 sq. mi.; pop., 57,000. 2. a seaport in this district. Also **Daman.**

Da·mas (dà'mä'), *n.* Damascus: the French name.

Dam·a·scene (dam'ə-sēn', dam'ə-sēn'), *adj.* [L. *Damascenus*, of Damascus, a city famous for armor and cloth], 1. of Damascus, its people, etc. 2. [d-], of damascening or damask. *n.* 1. a native or inhabitant of Damascus. 2. [d-], damascened work. 3. [d-], a small plum: see **damson.** *v.t.* [DAMASCENED (-sēnd', -sēnd'), DAMASCENING], [< the *adj.*], [d-], to decorate (metal) with wavy markings: also **damaskeen.**

Da·mas·cus (də-mas'kəs), *n.* the capital of Syria: it is one of the oldest cities in the world: pop., 286,000 (1943): French name, *Damas*.

Damascus steel, damask steel.

dam·ask (dam'əsk), *n.* [It. *damasco* < L. *Damascus*, the city], 1. a reversible fabric, usually of silk or linen, in figured weave. 2. a fine twilled table linen. 3. damascened steel. 4. the wavy markings of such steel. 5. deep pink or rose. *adj.* 1. of or from Damascus; named after Damascus. 2. made of damask (metal or cloth). 3. like damask. 4. deep-pink or rose. *v.t.* 1. to ornament with flowered designs or wavy lines, as in the cloth or metal. 2. to make deep-pink or rose.

dam·a·skeen (dam'ə-skēn'), *v.t.* to damascene.

damask rose, a variety of large rose, deep pink and fragrant, used in the Orient for making attar of roses.

damask steel, 1. steel decorated with wavy lines or inlaid gold and silver, originally made in Damascus and used for sword blades. 2. any steel like this.

dame (dām), *n.* [ME.; OFr.; L. *domina*, lady, fem. of *dominus*, a lord < base of *domus*, house + IE. affix *-no-*, denoting leadership], 1. a title formerly given to a woman in authority or head of a household: now only in *Dame Care, Dame Fortune*, etc. 2. a lady. 3. an elderly woman. 4. in Great Britain, *a)* the legal title of the wife or widow of a knight or baronet. *b)* a title awarded to a woman as the equivalent of a knight's title, *Sir:* used always with the given name, as, *Dame* Sybil Thorndike. 5. [Slang], a girl or woman.

Da·mien de Veus·ter, Jo·seph (zhô'zef' dà'myan' də vös'ter'; Eng. dā'mi-ən), 1840–1889; Belgian-born Roman Catholic priest and missionary to the leper colony at Molokai, Hawaiian Islands (1873–1889): called *Father Damien*.

Dam·i·et·ta (dam'i-et'ə), *n.* a city in Egypt, in the eastern Nile delta: pop., 40,000: Arabian name, *Dumyat*.

dam·mar, dam·mer (dam'ēr), *n.* [Malay *damar*], the resin from various pine trees of Australia, New Zealand, and the East Indies, used in making varnish.

damn (dam), *v.t.* [DAMNED (damd), DAMNING (-iŋ; *also, in adj. use*, -niŋ)], [ME. *damnen;* OFr. *damner;* L. *damnare*, to condemn, fine < *damnum*, loss, injury], 1. originally, to condemn as guilty; hence, 2. to condemn as bad, inferior, etc.: often used in the imperative as a curse. 3. to criticize adversely; hence, 4. to ruin the chances of for success; make fail. 5. to swear at by saying "damn": as, he *damned* the weather. 6. in *theology*, to condemn to eternal punishment, as in hell. *v.i.* to swear or curse; say "damn", etc. *n.* the saying of "damn" as a curse. *adj. & adv.* [Colloq.], damned: a clipped form, used as a curse or strong intensive. *interj.* an expression of anger, annoyance, disappointment, etc. Often euphemized as *darn, dog-gone*, etc. —*SYN.* see **curse.**

damn with faint praise, to condemn by praising without enthusiasm.

not care (or **give**) **a damn,** [Colloq.], not care at all.

dam·na·ble (dam'nə-b'l), *adj.* [ME.; OFr.; LL. *damnabilis* < *damnare;* see DAMN], 1. deserving damnation. 2. deserving to be sworn at; outrageous; execrable.

dam·na·bly (dam'nə-bli), *adv.* 1. in a damnable manner. 2. [Colloq.], very; extremely.

dam·na·tion (dam-nā'shən), *n.* [ME. *damnacioun;* Fr. *damnation;* L. *damnatio;* see DAMN], 1. a damning or being damned. 2. ruination by adverse criticism. 3. condemnation to endless punishment, as in hell. 4. endless punishment. *interj.* an expression of anger, annoyance, etc.

dam·na·to·ry (dam'nə-tôr'i, dam'nə-tō'ri), *adj.* [L. *damnatorius*], 1. threatening with damnation; damning. 2. condemning: as, *damnatory* evidence.

damned (damd; *also, in oratory or poetry*, dam'nid), *adj.* [pp. of *damn*], 1. condemned or deserving condemnation. 2. [Colloq.], cursed or deserving cursing; outrageous: as, a *damn(ed)* shame. 3. in *theology*, doomed to endless punishment, as in hell. *adv.* [Colloq.], very: as, you know *damn(ed)* well.

the damned, in *theology*, souls doomed to eternal punishment, as in hell.

dam·ni·fy (dam'nə-fī'), *v.t.* [DAMNIFIED (-fīd'), DAMNIFYING], [Early Mod. Eng.; OFr. *damnifier;* L. *damnificare*, to harm < *damnum;* cf. DAMN], in *law*, to cause injury, damage, or loss to.

damn·ing (dam'iŋ, dam'niŋ), *adj.* that damns or condemns; especially, that condemns as guilty; incriminating: as, *damning* evidence.

Dam·o·cles (dam'ə-klēz'), *n.* [L.; Gr. *Damoklēs*], in *Greek legend*, a courtier of ancient Syracuse who talked so much about the happiness of being a king that his own king, Dionysius, demonstrated the dangers of a ruler's life by seating him at a banquet just below a sword hanging by a hair.

sword of Damocles, any imminent danger.

dam·oi·selle, dam·o·sel, dam·o·zel (dam'ə-zel'), *n.* [Archaic], a damsel.

Da·mon and Pyth·i·as (dā'mən ən pith'i-əs), in *Roman legend*, friends so devoted to each other that when Pythias, condemned to death for plotting against King Dionysius of Syracuse, wanted time to arrange his affairs, Damon pledged his life that his friend would return: Pythias returned and was pardoned.

damp (damp), *n.* [MD., vapor, steam; akin to OHG., MHG., G. *dampf;* IE. base **dhem-*, to smoke, mist], 1. moisture; wetness. 2. a harmful gas sometimes found in mines; firedamp; chokedamp. 3. a dampened condition; dejected or depressed state. *adj.* 1. somewhat moist or wet; humid. 2. [Archaic], dejected. *v.t.* 1. to make damp; moisten. 2. to stifle; make choke. 3. to check or reduce (energy, action, etc.). 4. in *acoustics*, to check or deaden the vibration of (a string, etc.). 5. in *electricity*, to reduce the amplitude of (oscillations, waves, etc.). —*SYN.* see **wet.**

damp off, to wither and die because of mildew, as seedlings, plant shoots, etc.

damp-dry (damp'drī'), *v.t.* [DAMP-DRIED (-drīd'), DAMP-DRYING], to dry (laundry) so that some moisture is retained. *adj.* designating or of laundry so treated.

damp·en (dam'pən), *v.t.* 1. to make damp; moisten. 2. to depress; dishearten. 3. to deaden, reduce, or lessen. *v.i.* to become damp.

damp·er (dam'pēr), *n.* [see DAMP], 1. a person or thing that depresses or disheartens. 2. a movable plate or valve in the flue of a stove or furnace, for controlling the draft. 3. a device to check vibration in the strings of a stringed keyboard instrument. 4. a copper part in or near the poles of certain electric motors, generators, etc., to lessen variation from the proper rate of speed. 5. a device for lessening the oscillation of a magnetic needle, a moving coil, etc.

Dam·pier, William (dam'pêr, dam'pi-ēr, damp'yēr), 1652–1715; English explorer, pirate, and author.

damp·ing (dam'piŋ), *n.* in *physics*, a progressive reduction in amplitude of oscillations.

damp·ish (damp'ish), *adj.* somewhat damp.

damp·ness (damp'nis), *n.* damp quality or condition.

Dam·rosch, Walter Jo·han·nes (jō-han'əs dam'rosh), 1862–1950; American conductor and composer, born in Germany.

dam·sel (dam'z'l), *n.* [ME. *damesele;* OFr. *dameisele;* LL. **dominicella*, dim. of L. *domina;* see DAME], [Archaic], a girl; maiden: also **damosel, damozel, damoiselle, demoiselle.**

damsel fly, any of a species of slow-flying dragonfly with long wings that fold over its back when at rest.

dam·son (dam'z'n), *n.* [ME. *damasin;* OFr. *damascene*, plum of Damascus; L. *Damascenus*, of Damascus], 1. a kind of small, purple plum. 2. the tree it grows on.

Dan (dan), *n.* [Heb. *dān*, a judge], 1. in the *Bible*, the fifth son of Jacob. 2. the tribe of Israel descended from him, which settled in northern Palestine. 3. a town in northern Palestine: hence, *from Dan to Beersheba*, from end to end, as Beersheba was in southern Palestine.

Dan (dan), *n.* [ME.; OFr., *dan, danz* < L. *dominus*, a master, lord], [Archaic], master; sir: a title: as, *Dan* Cupid.

Dan., 1. Daniel. 2. Danish. 3. Danzig.

Da·na, Charles Anderson (dā' nə), 1819–1897; American newspaper editor.

Dana, James Dwight, 1813–1895; American geologist.

Dana, Richard Henry, 1815–1882; American lawyer and writer.

Dan·a·e, Dan·a·ë (dan'i-ē'), *n.* [Gr. *Danaē*], in *Greek mythology*, the mother of Perseus: she was visited by Zeus in the form of a shower of gold.

Da·na·i·des, Da·na·ï·des (də-nā'ə-dēz'), *n.pl.* [*sing.* DANAID, DANAÏD (dan'i-id)], [Gr.], in *Greek legend*, the fifty daughters of Danaus, who were married to their fifty cousins: forty-nine murdered their husbands at their father's command, and were condemned in Hades to pour water forever into a broken cistern or draw it with a sieve.

Dan·a·us, Dan·a·üs (dan'i-əs), *n.* in *Greek legend*, a king of Argos: see **Danaides.**

Dan·bur·y (dan'ber'i, dan'bēr-i), *n.* a city in southwestern Connecticut: pop., 23,000.

dance (dans, däns), *v.i.* [DANCED (danst, dänst), DANCING], [ME. *dansen, daunsen* < OFr. *danser* < OHG. *dansōn*, to draw out, extend; IE. base **ten-*, to pull, extend], 1. to move the body, especially the feet, in rhythm, ordinarily to music. 2. to move lightly and gaily about; caper. 3. to bob up and down. 4. to be stirred into rapid movement, as leaves in a wind. *v.t.* 1. to take part in (a dance); perform (a dance). 2. to cause to dance. 3. to bring into a specified condition by dancing: as, he *danced* her weary. 4. to dandle. *n.* 1. rhythmic movement of the feet or body, ordinarily to music. 2. a particular kind of dance, as the waltz, tango, etc. 3. the art of dancing. 4. one round of a dance. 5. a party to which people come to dance. 6. a piece of music for dancing. 7. rapid, lively movement.

dance attendance on, to be always near so as to wait on, lavish attentions on, etc.

dance to another tune, to alter one's actions or opinions as a result of changed conditions.

dance of death, a symbolic portrayal of a dance, often seen in medieval art, in which a skeleton, representing death, whirls people away one after another; danse macabre.

danc·er (dan'sēr, dän'sēr), *n.* a person who dances; specifically, a person whose profession is dancing.

dan·de·li·on (dan'di-lī'ən), *n.* [Fr. *dent de lion*, lit., tooth of the lion < L. *dens, dentis*, tooth + *de*, of + *leo*, lion: so called from the outline of the leaves], a common weed with yellow disk flowers, hollow stems, and jagged, edible leaves.

dan·der (dan'dēr), *n.* [? var. of Scot. *dunder*, resounding], [Colloq.], 1. anger. 2. temper.

get one's dander up, [Colloq.], to become angry; lose one's temper.

Dan·die Din·mont terrier (dan'di din'mənt), [after *Dandie* (Andrew) *Dinmont*, character in Scott's *Guy Mannering*], a small, active dog with drooping ears, short legs, and a rough coat, usually gray or tan, of a breed originated in Scotland.

dan·di·fy (dan'di-fī'), *v.t.* [DANDIFIED (-fīd'), DANDIFYING], to make look like a dandy; dress up.

dan·dle (dan'd'l), *v.t.* [DANDLED (-d'ld), DANDLING], [< or connected with It. (earlier) *dandolare*, (later) *dondolare*, to swing up and down, dally, trifle], 1. to dance (a child, etc.) up and down on the knee or in the arms. 2. to fondle; pet. —*SYN.* see **caress.**

dan·druff (dan'drəf), *n.* [folk etym. of earlier *dandro, dander;* prob. of Fr. origin; 2d element is Eng. dial. *hurf*, scab < ON. *hrufa*], little scales of dead skin formed on the scalp.

dan·dy (dan'di), *n.* [*pl.* DANDIES (-diz)], [playful Scot. form of *Andy* < *Andrew* (see MERRY-ANDREW); slang senses influenced by *dandy-*, convenient, small, as in *dandy-roll*, prob. dial. form of *handy* (with prefixed *d* as in *daffodil*], 1. a man who pays too much attention to his clothes and appearance; fop; coxcomb. 2. a kind of sloop or yawl. 3. in England, a kind of light cart with two wheels. 4. [Slang], something very good; first-class thing. *adj.* 1. dressed like a fop. 2. [Slang], very good; first-class.

dandy fever, dengue.

dan·dy·ish (dan'di-ish), *adj.* of or like a dandy.

dan·dy-roll (dan'di-rōl'), *n.* [see DANDY], in *papermaking*, a cylinder that puts on the watermark: also **dandy roll, dandy roller.**

Dane (dān), *n.* [< Anglo-N. form of AS. *Dene*, the Danes, orig., name of a continental Anglian people], a native or inhabitant of Denmark.

Dane·law, Dane·lagh (dān'lô'), *n.* [ME. *Danelagh* < Anglo-N.; AS. *Dena lagu*, Danes' law], 1. the code of Scandinavian laws established in eastern and northern England by Norse invaders and settlers in the 9th and 10th centuries A.D. 2. the eastern and northern section of England that was ruled under these laws.

dan·ger (dān'jēr), *n.* [ME. *daunger*, power, domination, arrogance; OFr. *danger*, absolute power of an overlord; LL. **dominarium* < L. *dominium*, lordship < *dominus*, a master; shift of sense ? influenced by LL. *damniarium* < *damnum*, injury, loss; see DAMN], 1. liability to injury, damage, loss or pain; peril. 2. a thing that may cause injury, pain, etc.

SYN.—**danger** is the general term for liability to injury or evil, of whatever degree or likelihood of occurrence (the *danger* of falling on icy walks); **peril** suggests great and imminent danger (the burning house put them in *peril* of death); **jeopardy** emphasizes exposure to extreme danger (liberty is in *jeopardy* under tyrants); **hazard** implies a foreseeable but uncontrollable possibility of danger, but stresses the element of chance (the *hazards* of hunting big game); **risk** implies the voluntary taking of a dangerous chance (he jumped at the *risk* of his life).—*ANT.* safety, security.

dan·ger·ous (dān'jēr-əs), *adj.* [ME. *dangerus;* OFr. *dangereus* < *danger;* see DANGER], full of danger; likely to cause injury, pain, etc.; unsafe; perilous.

dan·gle (daŋ'g'l), *v.i.* [DANGLED (-g'ld), DANGLING], [< ON.; akin to Dan. *dangle*, Ice. *dingla*, to dangle], 1. to hang swinging loosely. 2. to follow; be a hanger-on (usually with *after*). 3. in *grammar*, to lack clear connection with the proper substantive: in "Having broken his legs, the bystanders took the old man into the house," the participle ***having broken*** is *dangling*. *v.t.* to hold (something) so that it hangs and swings loosely; cause to dangle.

Dan·iel (dan'yəl), [Heb. *dānī'ēl*, lit., God is my judge], a masculine name: diminutive, *Dan.* *n.* in the *Bible*, 1. a Hebrew prophet whose faith saved him in the lions' den: Dan. 6:16–27. 2. the book of the Old Testament with his story and prophecies. Abbreviated **Dan., Danl.**

Dan·iel, Samuel (dan'yəl), 1562–1619; English poet.

Dan·iels, Josephus (dan'yəlz), 1862–1948; American statesman; secretary of the navy (1913–1921).

Dan·ish (dān'ish), *adj.* [ME.; AS. *Denise;* see DANE], of Denmark, the Danes, or their language. *n.* the North Germanic language of the Danes. Abbreviated **Dan., Da.**

Danish West Indies, the Virgin Islands now belonging to the United States: the former name.

Dan·ite (dan'īt), *adj.* of the Hebrew tribe of Dan. *n.* 1. a member of this tribe: Judg. 13:2. 2. a member of an alleged, secret Mormon organization, supposed to have been formed about 1837.

dank (daŋk), *adj.* [ME. *danke;* prob. < ON.; IE. base **dhem-;* see DAMP], disagreeably damp; moist and chilly. —*SYN.* see **wet.**

‡**dan·ke schön** (däŋ'kə shön'), [G.], thank you.

Danl., Daniel.

D'An·nun·zio, Ga·bri·e·le (gä'bri-e'le dä-nōōn'tsyô), 1863–1938; Italian poet, playwright, novelist, and political adventurer.

‡**danse ma·ca·bre** (däns' ma'kä'br'; Eng. däns' mə-kä'brə), [Fr.], dance of death.

dan·seuse (dän-sooz'; Fr. dän'söz'), *n.* [*pl.* DANSEUSES (-sooz'iz; Fr. -söz')], [Fr., fem. of *danseur*, dancer], a girl or woman dancer, especially a ballet dancer.

Dan·te A·li·ghie·ri (dän'te ä'lē-gyâr'ē; Eng. dan'ti), (born *Durante Alighieri*), 1265–1321; Italian poet; wrote *The Divine Comedy.*

Dan·te·an (dan'ti-ən, dan-tē'ən), *adj.* 1. of Dante or his writings. 2. Dantesque. *n.* a person who makes a special study of Dante and his writings.

Dan·tesque (dan-tesk'), *adj.* like Dante or his writings: see **Divine Comedy.**

Dan·ton, Georges Jacques (zhôrzh zhäk dän'tōn'; Eng. dan'tən), 1759–1794; French statesman; leader in the French Revolution.

Dan·ube (dan'ūb), *n.* a river in southern Europe, flowing from southwestern Germany eastward into the Black Sea: length, 1,725 mi.: German name, *Donau;* Hungarian name, *Duna;* Romanian name, *Dunărea.*

Da·nu·bi·an (dan-ū'bi-ən, də-nōō'bi-ən), *adj.* of the Danube or the regions and peoples near it.

Dan·ville (dan'vil), *n.* 1. a city in east central Illinois: pop., 42,000. 2. a city in south central Virginia: pop., 47,000.

Dan·zig (dan'tsig, dan'sig; G. dän'tsikh), *n.* a seaport in Poland on the Baltic Sea: formerly an autonomous region created by the Treaty of Versailles in 1920 (called *Free City of Danzig*), later a part of Germany (1939–1945): pop., 266,000: Polish name, *Gdańsk:* abbreviated **Dan.**

dap (dap), *v.i.* [DAPPED (dapt), DAPPING], [prob. var. of *dab*, influenced by *dip*], 1. to fish by dropping the bait gently on the water. 2. to dip lightly and suddenly into water, as a bird. 3. to bounce or skip, as a stone thrown along the surface of water. *n.* [Obs. or British Dial.], a bounce or hop, as of a ball or stone.

Daph·ne (daf'ni), [L.; Gr. < *daphnē*, the laurel or bay tree], a feminine name. *n.* 1. in *Greek mythology*, a nymph who escaped from Apollo by becoming a laurel tree. 2. [d-], the laurel tree. 3. [d-], a kind of shrub having fragrant flowers.

Daph·nis and Chlo·e (or **Chlo·ë**) (daf'nis ən klō'i), two lovers in an old Greek pastoral romance attributed to Longus (4th or 5th century A.D.).

dap·per (dap'ēr), *adj.* [ME. *daper*, agile, trim; ? < MD.; IE. base **dheb-*, heavy, strong, as in MD. *dapper*, heavy, powerful, agile, ON. *dapr*, heavy, OHG. *tapfar*, heavy, strong (G. *tapfer*, brave): the sense development is from "heavy, powerful" to "agile" to "trim, neat"], 1. small and active. 2. trim; neat; smart; spruce.

dap·ple (dap''l), *adj.* [ME. in comp. *dappel-grai*, dapple-gray; ON. *depill*, a spot, dot, splash of water < *dapi*, a pool], spotted; mottled; variegated. *n.* 1. a spotted condition. 2. an animal whose skin is spotted. *v.t.* [DAPPLED (-'ld), DAPPLING], to cover with spots.

dap·pled (dap''ld), *adj.* [pp. of *dapple*], spotted; mottled.

dap·ple-gray (dap''l-grā'), *adj.* gray spotted with darker gray. *n.* a dapple-gray horse.

Dap·sang (dəp-suŋ′), *n.* Godwin Austen, a mountain in India.
D.A.R., Daughters of the American Revolution.
Dar·by and Joan (där′bi ən jōn′), [< an old song (1753)], an old married couple who are devoted to each other and live in perfect harmony.
Dar·dan (där′dən), *adj. & n.* [L. *Dardanus;* Gr. *Dardanos* < *Dardanoi,* a people allied with the Trojans in Trojan War; later identified with them], Trojan.
Dar·da·nelles (där′də-nelz′), *n.* the strait joining the Aegean and the Sea of Marmara: length 40 mi.; width, 1–4 mi.: ancient name, *Hellespont.*

DARDANELLES

Dar·da·ni·an (där-dā′ni-ən), *adj. & n.* [L. *Dardanius;* Gr. *Dardanios;* see DARDAN], Trojan.
dare (dâr), *v.i.* [DARED (dârd) or *archaic* DURST (dŭrst), DARED, DARING; 3d pers. sing., pres. indic., DARE, DARES], [ME. *dar, der;* AS. *dear, dearr,* 1st pers. sing., pres. indic. of *durran,* to dare], to have enough courage or boldness for some act; be fearless; venture. *v.t.* 1. to have courage for; venture upon. 2. to face; oppose and defy. 3. to challenge (someone) to do something hard or dangerous as a test of courage. *n.* a challenge.
dare say, to think very likely; consider probable; as, I *dare say* you're right.
dare·dev·il (dâr′dev″'l), *adj.* reckless; bold; foolhardy. *n.* a bold, foolhardy fellow; reckless person.
Dar es Sa·laam (där′ es sə-läm′), seaport and capital of Tanganyika Territory, Africa: pop., 33,500: also spelled **Daressalam.**
Dar·fur (där-foor′), *n.* a province of Anglo-Egyptian Sudan: area, 144,100 sq. mi.; pop., 763,000.
dar·ic (dar′ik), *n.* [Gr. *dareikos* < Per. *dara,* king, or < *Darius,* name of king supposed to have coined it first], an ancient Persian gold coin.
Dar·i·en, Gulf of (dâr′i-en′; Sp. dä′rē-en′), a part of the Caribbean, between Panama and Colombia.
Darien, Isthmus of, the Isthmus of Panama: the former name.
dar·ing (dâr′iŋ), *adj.* [ppr. of *dare*], fearless; bold; intrepid. *n.* bold courage.
Da·ri·us I (də-rī′əs), 558?–486 B.C.; king of Persia (521–486 B.C.): called *the Great.*
dark (därk), *adj.* [ME. *derk;* AS. *deorc,* gloomy, cheerless, sinister; IE. base **dheregh-,* dirty, filthy, as in Lith. *dergia,* it is wretched weather, MLG. *dork,* place where dirt collects], 1. entirely or partly without light. 2. neither giving nor receiving light. 3. almost black. 4. not light in color or complexion; brunet. Abbreviated **dk.** 5. hidden. 6. not easily understood; hard to make clear. 7. gloomy. 8. evil; sinister. 9. ignorant; unenlightened. *n.* 1. the state of being dark. 2. night; nightfall. 3. obscurity. 4. secrecy. 5. lack of knowledge and culture. 6. a dark color or shade.
in the dark, uninformed; ignorant.
keep dark, to keep secret or hidden.
***SYN.*—dark,** the general word in this comparison, denotes an absence of light, entirely or partly (a *dark* night); **dim** implies so little light that objects can be seen only indistinctly; **dusky** suggests the grayish, shadowy light of twilight (a *dusky* winter evening); **murky** now usually suggests the thick, heavy darkness of fog or smoke-filled air (the *murky* ruins of a temple); **gloomy** suggests a cloudy, cheerless darkness (a *gloomy* forest). —*ANT.* light, bright.
Dark Ages, dark ages, 1. the period from the fall of the Western Roman Empire (476 A.D.) to the beginning of the modern era (c. 1450); Middle Ages. 2. the earlier part of the Middle Ages, to about the end of the 10th century. The term arose from the idea that the medieval period in Europe, especially the earlier part, was characterized by widespread ignorance, lack of progress, etc.
Dark Continent, Africa: so called because it was little known until the late 19th century.
dark·en (där′kən), *v.i.* to become dark or darker. *v.t.* to make dark or darker.
not darken one's door (or **doorway**), not come to one's home.
dark·ey, dark·ie (där′ki), *n.* see **darky.**
dark horse, [Colloq.], 1. an unexpected, almost unknown winner in a horse race, previously supposed to have little chance. 2. an almost unknown contestant regarded by only a few as having a chance to win. 3. in *politics,* a person who gets or may get the nomination unexpectedly, often as the result of a compromise.
dark·ish (där′kish), *adj.* somewhat dark.
dark lantern, a lantern with a shutter that can hide the light.
dar·kle (där′k'l), *v.i.* [DARKLED (-k'ld), DARKLING], [< *darkling*], 1. to appear dark or unclear. 2. to grow dark, gloomy, obscure, etc.
dark·ling (därk′liŋ), *adv.* [*dark* + *-ling*], [Poetic], in the dark. *adj.* [Poetic], 1. happening in darkness. 2. dark or growing dark; dusky; dim.
dark·ly (därk′li), *adv.* 1. in a dark manner. 2. in a gloomy or sinister manner. 3. mysteriously; obscurely.
dark·ness (därk′nis), *n.* 1. absence of light. 2. blackness. 3. blindness. 4. ignorance. 5. gloom. 6. obscurity; secrecy. 7. evil.
dark·room (därk′rōōm′, därk′room′), *n.* a room from which all actinic rays are excluded, so that photographs can be developed in it.
dark·some (därk′səm), *adj.* [Poetic], 1. dark; darkish. 2. dismal; gloomy. 3. obscure.
dark·y (där′ki), *n.* [*pl.* DARKIES (-kiz)], [Colloq.], a Negro: patronizing or contemptuous term: also spelled **darkey, darkie.**
Dar·lan, Jean Fran·çois (zhän fräN′swå′ dår′läN′); 1881–1942; French admiral; minister of defense (1941); chief of state in French Africa (1942); assassinated.
Dar·ling (där′liŋ), *n.* a river in southeastern Australia, flowing into the Murray River: length, 1,160 mi.
dar·ling (där′liŋ), *n.* [ME. *derling, deorling;* AS. *deorling,* dim. of *deor;* see DEAR], 1. a person much loved by another: often a term of affectionate address. 2. a favorite. *adj.* 1. very dear; beloved. 2. cherished; yearned for.
Darling Range, a mountain range along the southwestern coast of Australia.
Dar·ling·ton (där′liŋ-tən), *n.* a city in northern England: pop., 84,000 (est. 1946).
Darm·stadt (därm′shtät), *n.* the capital of Hesse, Germany: pop., 95,000 (est. 1946).
darn (därn), *v.t. & v.i.* [prob. < MFr. dial. *darner,* to piece together, mend < Bret. *darn,* a piece (torn out of something); IE. base **der-,* to pull off, split apart], to mend (cloth, etc.) or repair (a hole or tear in cloth) by sewing a network of stitches across the gap. *n.* 1. a darning. 2. a darned place in fabric. —*SYN.* see **mend.**
darn (därn), *v.t., n., adj., adv., interj.* [< *damn*], [Colloq.], damn: a euphemism for the curse.
dar·nel (där′n'l), *n.* [ME.; Fr. dial. *darnelle;* prob. < OFr. dial. *darnu,* stupefied < *Frank. *darn,* stupefied + OFr. *niella* < LL. *nigella,* black caraway < L. *niger,* black: so called from its supposed stupefying or intoxicating qualities], a poisonous weed resembling rye, often found in grain fields: also called *rye grass.*
darn·er (där′nẽr), *n.* 1. a person who darns. 2. a darning needle. 3. a wooden ball or similar device placed under a hole to be darned.
darn·ing (där′niŋ), *n.* 1. a mending with interlaced stitches. 2. things darned or to be darned.
darning needle, 1. a large needle for darning. 2. a dragonfly.
Darn·ley, Lord (därn′li), (*Henry Stewart*), 1545–1567; second husband of Mary, Queen of Scots; father of James VI (James I of Great Britain).
Dar·row, Clarence Sew·ard (sōō′ẽrd, sū′ẽrd dar′ō), 1857–1938; American lawyer.
dart (därt), *n.* [ME.; OFr. *dart* (Fr. *dard*) < Gmc. source; akin to AS. *daroth,* ON. *darrathr, darr,* a spear; IE. base **dhəro-,* pointed], 1. a small, pointed weapon for throwing or shooting. 2. anything resembling this. 3. a sudden, quick movement. 4. an insect's stinger. 5. a short, tapered seam to make a garment fit more closely. 6. *pl.* [construed as sing.], a game in which a number of small, pointed missiles are hurled at a target. *v.t. & v.i.* 1. to throw, shoot, etc. suddenly and fast. 2. to move suddenly and fast.
dart·er (där′tẽr), *n.* 1. a thing or animal that darts. 2. a snakebird: so called because it darts at its prey. 3. any of several small, perchlike, fresh-water fishes.
dar·tle (där′t'l), *v.t. & v.i.* [DARTLED (-t'ld), DARTLING], [*dart* + *-le,* freq.; see DART], to dart again and again; dart about.
Dart·moor (därt′moor′, därt′môr′), *n.* 1. a wild upland in Devonshire, England. 2. a celebrated prison there.
Dar·win (där′win), *n.* a seaport in Northern Territory, Australia: pop., 2,500 (1947).
Dar·win, Charles Robert (där′win), 1809–1882; English naturalist; originated theory of evolution by natural selection.
Darwin, Erasmus, 1731–1802; English physician, naturalist, and poet; grandfather of *Charles.*
Dar·win·i·an (där-win′i-ən), *adj.* of Darwin or his theory of evolution. *n.* a person who believes in the Darwinian theory; evolutionist.
Darwinian theory, Darwin's theory of evolution, which holds that all species of plants and animals

developed from earlier forms by hereditary transmission of slight variations in successive generations, those forms surviving which are best adapted to the environment (*natural selection* and *survival of the fittest*).

Dar·win·ism (där′win-iz'm), ***n.*** 1. the Darwinian theory. 2. adherence to the Darwinian theory.

Dar·win·ist (där′win-ist), ***n. & adj.*** Darwinian.

dash (dash), ***v.t.*** [ME. *daschen*, to rush or strike with violence; prob. < ON.], 1. to smash. 2. to strike violently against. 3. to throw, knock, or thrust (with *away, down*, etc.). 4. to splash. 5. to mix with a little of another substance. 6. to destroy. 7. to frustrate; discourage. 8. to abash. 9. to do, write, etc. hastily (with *off*). 10. [< the dash in *d—d*, a euphemistic form of *damned*], [Colloq.], to damn; usually in the imperative as a mild curse. ***v.i.*** 1. to strike violently against. 2. to rush. ***n.*** 1. a smash. 2. a splash. 3. a bit or pinch of something. 4. a rush. 5. a short, swift run or running race. 6. vigor; spirited quality; showy appearance or action. 7. a dashboard. 8. the mark (—), used in printing and writing to indicate a break in a sentence, a parenthetical element, or an omission. 9. in *telegraphy*, a long sound or signal, as in the Morse code: opposed to *dot*.

cut a dash, [Colloq.], to have a showy appearance.

dash·board (dash′bôrd′, dash′bōrd′), ***n.*** 1. a board or screen at the front or side of a carriage, boat, etc., for protection against splashing; splashboard. 2. a panel with instruments and gauges on it, as in an automobile.

da·sheen (da′shēn′), ***n*** [? < Fr. *de*, of + *Chine*, China,] the edible sprouts of the taro, a tropical plant.

dash·er (dash′ẽr), ***n.*** 1. a person or thing that dashes. 2. a rotating device for whipping cream in a churn or ice-cream freezer. 3. [Colloq.], a person full of dash or spirit.

dash·ing (dash′iŋ), ***adj.*** [ppr. of *dash*], 1. full of dash or spirit; bold and lively. 2. showy.

Dasht-i-Ka·vir (däsht′ē-kȧ-vêr′), ***n.*** the Kavir Desert, in Iran: the Persian name.

Dasht-i-Lut (däsht′ē-lōōt′), ***n.*** the Lut Desert, in Iran: the Persian name.

dash·y (dash′i), ***adj.*** [DASHIER (-i-ẽr), DASHIEST (-i-ist)], 1. having dash; showy. 2. full of dashes.

das·tard (das′tẽrd), ***n.*** [ME., a craven; akin to MD. *daasardt*, a fool, but prob. < ON. *dæstr*, exhausted < *dæsa*, to groan (see DAZE); + *-ard*], a mean, skulking coward. ***adj.*** dastardly.

das·tard·li·ness (das′tẽrd-li-nis), ***n.*** the state or quality of being dastardly.

das·tard·ly (das′tẽrd-li), ***adj.*** like or characteristic of a dastard; mean and skulking; cowardly and brutal. —***SYN.*** see **cowardly.**

das·y·ure (das′i-ūr′), ***n.*** [Gr. *dasys*, thick, hairy + *oura*, tail], any of a group of small Australian marsupials, such as the Tasmanian devil.

dat., dative.

da·ta (dā′tə, dat′ə, dä′tə), ***n.pl.*** [often construed as sing.], [see DATUM], things known or assumed; facts or figures from which conclusions can be inferred.

dat·a·ble (dāt′ə-b'l), ***adj.*** that can be dated.

da·ta·ry (dā′tə-ri), ***n.*** [*pl.* DATARIES (-riz)], [ML. *dataria* < L. *datarius*, for giving away < *datus*, pp. of *dare*, to give], in the *Roman Catholic Church*, a curial official in charge of examining candidates for papal benefices and handling the claims of those with rights to pensions.

date (dāt), ***n.*** [ME.; OFr.; L. *data*, neut. pl. of *datus*, pp. of *dare*, to give; the first word in Roman letters or documents, giving the place and time of writing, as *data Romae*, lit., given at Rome], 1. a statement on a writing, coin, etc. of when it was made: abbreviated **d.** 2. the time at which a thing happens. 3. the time that anything lasts or goes on. 4. [Rare], a season or period of time. 5. the day of the month. 6. [Colloq.], an appointment for a set time; specifically, a social appointment with a person of the opposite sex. 7. [Colloq.], a person of the opposite sex with whom one has such an appointment. ***v.t.*** [DATED (-id), DATING], 1. to mark (a letter, etc.) with a date. 2. to find out, determine, set, or give the date of. 3. to give a date to. 4. to reckon by dates. 5. [Colloq.], to have a social appointment with. ***v.i.*** 1. to be dated (usually with *from*). 2. to belong to, or have origin in, a definite period in the past (usually with *from*). 3. to be old-fashioned: see **dated.** 4. [Colloq.], to have social appointments with persons of the opposite sex.

out of date, old-fashioned; no longer in use.

to date, until now; as yet.

up to date, modern; now fashionable; in accord with present usage, the latest ideas, etc.

date (dāt), ***n.*** [ME.; OFr.; L. *dactylus*; Gr. *daktylos*, a date, lit., a finger: so named from its shape], 1. the sweet, fleshy fruit of the date palm, having a large, hard seed. 2. the date palm.

dat·ed (dāt′id), ***adj.*** [pp. of *date*], 1. marked with or showing a date. 2. out of date; old-fashioned.

date·less (dāt′lis), ***adj.*** 1. without a date. 2. without limit or end. 3. too old for its date to be fixed. 4. still good or interesting though old.

date line, 1. a line on which the date of writing or issue is given, as in a letter, a newspaper, etc. 2. an imaginary line drawn north and south through the Pacific Ocean, largely along the 180th meridian: it is the line at which, by international agreement, each calendar day begins at midnight, so that when it is Sunday just west of the line, it is Saturday just east of it.

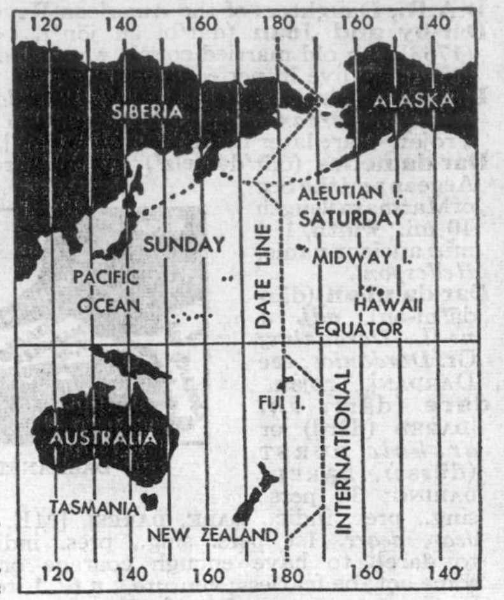

INTERNATIONAL DATE LINE

date palm, a palm tree that bears dates: some date palms have a tall, slender trunk with foliage at the top, others have a bushy appearance.

da·ti·val (dā-tī′v'l), ***adj.*** in the dative case.

da·tive (dā′tiv), ***adj.*** [L. *dativus*, relating to giving < *datus*, pp. of *dare*, to give; its grammatical use in LL. *casus dativus*, or simply *dativus*, dative case, translates Gr. *dotikē*, paraphrased by Varro as *casus dandi*, the case of giving; the term was made comprehensible by such L. examples as *pater filio librum dat*, lit., father *to son* (dat.) book *gave*], denoting or belonging to that case of a noun, pronoun, or adjective which expresses the indirect object of a verb and, in many languages, approach toward something. ***n.*** 1. the dative case: in English, the dative notion is expressed by *to, for*, or word order (e.g., I gave the book *to Jack*, I did the task *for Jack*, I gave *Jack* the book). 2. a word or phrase in the dative case. Abbreviated **dat.**

da·to (dä′tō; Sp. dä′tô), ***n.*** [*pl.* DATOS (-tōz; Sp. -tôs)], [< Malay *datóq*], 1. the chief of a Moslem Moro tribe in the Philippine Islands. 2. the chief of a barrio in Malay countries. Also spelled **datto.**

da·tum (dā′təm, dat′əm), ***n.*** [*pl.* DATA (-tə, -ə)], [L., what is given, hence gift, present; neut. of *datus*; see DATIVE], 1. *usually in pl.* something known or assumed; fact from which conclusions can be inferred. 2. a real or assumed thing, used as a basis for calculations; chiefly in combination, as *datum* point, line, etc.

datum plane, an assumed plane of reference from which elevations and depths are measured: sea level is often so used.

da·tu·ra (də-tyoor′ə), ***n.*** [Hind. *dhatūrā* < Sans. *dhattūra*], 1. any of a group of plants of the potato family, most of which are poisonous and have an unpleasant odor, as the jimson weed or thorn apple. 2. the flower of any of these plants.

dau., daughter.

daub (dôb), ***v.t. & v.i.*** [ME. *dauben, dawben*; OFr. *dauber*, to whiten, whitewash; L. *dealbare*, to whiten, whitewash < *de-*, intens. + *albus*, white], 1. to cover or smear with sticky, soft stuff, such as plaster, grease, etc. 2. to paint badly and coarsely. ***n.*** 1. anything daubed on, as plaster, grease, etc. 2. a daubing stroke or splash. 3. a poorly painted picture.

daub·er (dôb′ẽr), ***n.*** 1. a person who daubs; mediocre or inexpert painter. 2. a thing to daub with.

daub·er·y (dôb′ẽr-i), ***n.*** painting or work done in an inartistic or unskillful manner.

Dau·bi·gny, Charles Fran·çois (shȧrl frän′swȧ′ dō′bē′-nyē′), 1817–1878; French landscape painter.

daub·ing (dôb′iŋ), ***n.*** 1. the action of a person who daubs. 2. material used in daubing.

daub·ry (dôb′ri), ***n.*** daubery.

Dau·det, Al·phonse (ȧl′fōns′ dō′de′; Eng. dō-dā′), 1840–1897; French novelist.

Dau·ga·va (dou′gä-vä), ***n.*** Dvina River: Lettish name.

Dau·gav·pils (dou′gäf-pēls′), ***n.*** a city in southeastern Latvian S.S.R., on the Daugava (Dvina) River: pop., 45,000: Russian name, *Dvinsk*; German name, *Dünaberg*.

daugh·ter (dô′tẽr), ***n.*** [ME. *doughter*; AS. *dohtor*; akin to Goth. *dauhtar*, G. *tochter*, Sans. *duhitār*, etc.], 1. a girl or woman in her relationship to either or both parents: abbreviated **d., da., dau.** 2. a female descendant. 3. a female thought of as if in the relation of child to parent: as, a *daughter* of France. 4. anything thought of as like a daughter in relation to its source or origin: as, the colonies are the *daughters* of the mother country.

daugh·ter-in-law (dô'tẽr-'n-lô'), *n.* [*pl.* DAUGHTERS-IN-LAW], the wife of one's son.
daugh·ter·ly (dô'tẽr-li), *adj.* 1. of a daughter. 2. like, characteristic of, or proper to a daughter.
daughter of Eve, any woman or girl.
Dau·mier, Ho·no·ré (ō'nô'rā' dō'myā'), 1808–1879; French painter and caricaturist.
daunt (dônt, dänt), *v.t.* [ME. *daunten;* OFr. *danter, donter,* to daunt, subdue, tame < L. *domitare,* to tame, break in < *domare,* to tame, subdue], 1. to make afraid; intimidate. 2. to dishearten. —*SYN.* see **dismay.**
daunt·less (dônt'lis, dänt'lis), *adj.* that cannot be daunted or intimidated; brave.
dau·phin (dô'fin; Fr. dō'fan'), *n.* [Fr., lit., dolphin (see DOLPHIN); used as a proper name by the counts of Vienne, and hence as a title by the oldest son of the king after the province of Dauphiné (comprising Vienne and Auvergne) was ceded to the crown], the eldest son of the king of France: a title used from 1349 to 1830.
dau·phine (dô'fēn; Fr. dō'fēn'), *n.* [Fr., fem. of *dauphin*], a dauphiness.
Dau·phi·né (dō'fē'nā'), *n.* a former province of southeastern France, north of Provence.

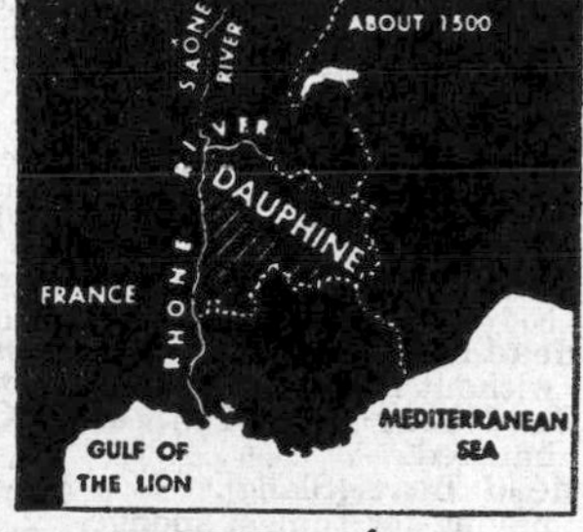

DAUPHINÉ

dau·phin·ess (dô'fin-is), *n.* the wife of a dauphin.
daut (dôt, dät), *v.t.* [Scot. Gael.; cf. *dalta,* foster son], [Scot.], to fondle; pet; caress: also spelled **dawt.**
D. A. V., Disabled American Veterans.
Da·vao (dä-vou'), *n.* a seaport in the Philippines, on Mindanao: pop., 111,000: see **Philippine Islands,** map.
D'Av·e·nant, Sir William (dav'ə-nənt), 1606–1668; English poet and dramatist: also **Davenant.**
Dav·en·port (dav'ən-pôrt', dav'ən-pōrt'), *n.* a city in eastern Iowa, on the Mississippi: pop., 89,000.
dav·en·port (dav'ən-pôrt', dav'ən-pōrt'), *n.* [< the name of orig. manufacturer (19th c.)], 1. a small desk with a hinged lid that opens out for writing. 2. a large couch or sofa, sometimes convertible into a bed.
Da·vid (dā'vid), [Heb. *dāvīd,* lit., beloved], a masculine name: diminutives, *Dave, Davy, Davey;* feminine, *Vida. n.* in the *Bible,* the second king of Israel and Judah, succeeding Saul and followed by his son Solomon: the reputed writer of the Psalms.
David I, 1084–1153; king of Scotland (1124–1153).
David, Saint, 6th century A.D.: patron saint of Wales: his day is March 1: also called *Saint Dewi.*
Da·vid, Jacques Lou·is (zhäk lwē dä'vēd'), 1748–1825; French painter.
Da·vid d'An·gers (dä'vēd' dän'zhā'), (born *Pierre Jean David*), 1788–1856; French sculptor.
Da·vid·son, Jo (jō dā'vid-s'n), 1883–1952; American sculptor.
da Vinci, da Gama, etc., see **Vinci, Gama,** etc.
Da·vis, Jefferson (dā'vis), 1808–1889; American statesman; president of the Confederacy (1861–1865).
Davis, Richard Harding, 1864–1916; American novelist, journalist, and editor.
Davis Strait, a part of the Atlantic, between Baffin Island, Canada, and Greenland: width, 200–500 mi.
dav·it (dav'it), *n.* [earlier *david, daviet;* OFr. *daviet, daviot,* dim. of *David:* with reference to the slaying of Goliath (see GOLIATH); cf. Fr. *davier,* a wrench, with the same connotation], 1. either of a pair of curved uprights projecting over the side of a ship for suspending or lowering a small boat. 2. a crane in a ship's bow, used to raise or lower the anchor.

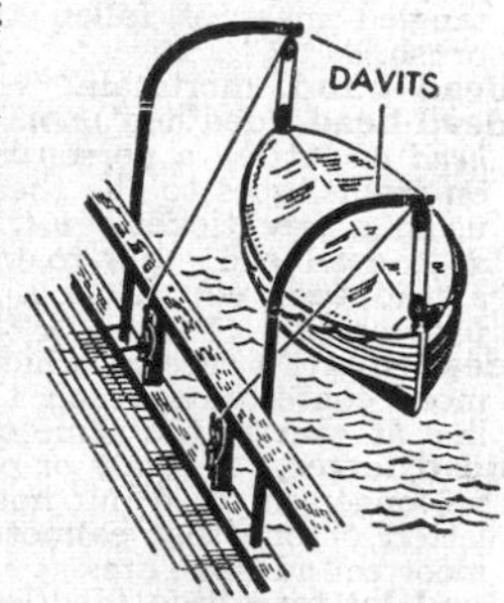

DAVITS

Da·vy, Sir **Hum·phry** (hum'fri dā'vi), 1778–1829; English chemist; evolved the electrolytic method of preparing potassium and sodium; invented the safety lamp.
Da·vy Jones (dā'vi jōnz'), the spirit of the sea: humorous name given by sailors.
Davy Jones's locker, the bottom of the sea; grave of those drowned at sea or buried there.
Davy lamp, [after Sir Humphry *Davy*], formerly, a miner's safety lamp in which the flame was enclosed by a screen of wire gauze as a protection against firedamp.
daw (dô), *n.* [ME. *dawe;* akin to OHG. *taha;* ? < IE. base **dhek-,* to hide away: with reference to its thieving habits; cf. GRACKLE], a kind of crow; jackdaw.
daw·dle (dô'd'l), *v.i.* & *v.t.* [DAWDLED (-d'ld), DAWDLING], [var. of dial. *daddle;* prob. akin to *dadder, dodder, didder,* Norw. dial. *dadra, darra, didra;* of echoic and redupl. origin], to waste (time) in trifling or in doing nothing; loiter (often with *away*). —**SYN.** see **loiter.**
Dawes, Charles Gates (dôz), 1865–1951; American financier and statesman; vice-president of the United States (1925–1929); received Nobel peace prize, 1925.
dawk (dôk), *n.* dak.
dawn (dôn), *v.i.* [ME. *dawnen;* AS. *dagian,* lit., to day (i.e., to dawn) < *dæg,* day, with added *-n* < ON.], 1. to begin to be day; grow light; hence, 2. to begin to appear, develop, etc. 3. to begin to be clear to the mind (usually with *on* or *upon*): as, the meaning suddenly *dawned* on me. *n.* 1. daybreak. 2. the beginning (*of* something): as, the *dawn* of the Atomic Age.
Daw·son (dô's'n), *n.* a city in Yukon Territory, Canada, on the Yukon River: pop., 850.
Daw·son, Sir **John William** (dô's'n), 1820–1899; Canadian geologist and educator.
Dawson Creek, a town in western Canada, at the southern end of the Alaska Highway.
dawt (dôt, dät), *v.t.* to daut.
day (dā), *n.* [ME. *dai, dei;* AS. *dæg,* pl. *dagas;* Gmc. **dag, *dog,* time the sun shines, as in ON. *dagr,* Goth. *dags,* OHG. *tag,* etc.; IE. base **dhegwh-,* to burn, shine], 1. the period of light between sunrise and sunset: abbreviated **da., d.** 2. daylight. 3. sunshine. 4. the time (24 hours) that it takes the earth to revolve once on its axis: the civil or legal day is from midnight to midnight, the astronomical day from noon to noon. 5. [often D-], a particular or special day: as, Decoration *Day, D-Day.* 6. a period of time; number of years: as, the best writer of his *day.* 7. a period of flourishing, power, glory, etc.: as, he has had his *day.* 8. the struggle or contest occurring on a certain day: as, we lost the *day.* 9. hours of work; shift: as, an eight-hour *day.* 10. an unspecified past or future: as, one of these *days.* 11. opportunity: as, my *day* has come. 12. *pl.* time; era: as, in *days* of old. 13. *pl.* life: as, he spent his *days* in study. 14. in *astronomy,* the time that it takes a celestial body to revolve once on its axis.
call it a day, [Colloq.], to stop working for the day.
day after day, every day.
day by day, each day.
day in, day out, every day.
from day to day, from one day to the next; without thought of or provision for the future.
day bed, a couch or sofa that can also be used as a bed.
day·book (dā'book'), *n.* 1. a diary. 2. in *bookkeeping,* a book used for keeping a record of the transactions of each day as they occur; journal: abbreviated **d.b.**
day·break (dā'brāk'), *n.* the time in the morning when light first appears; dawn.
day coach, a regular passenger car of a railroad train, as distinguished from a sleeping car, chair car, etc.
day·dream (dā'drēm'), *n.* 1. a pleasant, dreamy thought; reverie. 2. a pleasing but visionary notion or scheme. *v.i.* to have a daydream or daydreams.
day·flow·er (dā'flou'ẽr), *n.* 1. any of a number of related plants of the spiderwort family, with jointed stems, grasslike leaves, and short-lived, usually blue flowers. 2. the flower.
day·fly (dā'flī'), *n.* a May fly.
day in court, 1. a day on which one may present his case or claim in court; hence, 2. an opportunity to present one's arguments; hearing.
day laborer, an unskilled worker paid by the day.
day letter, a telegram with a minimum charge for fifty words or fewer, sent in the daytime: it is cheaper but slower than a regular telegram.
day·light (dā'līt'), *n.* 1. the light of day; sunlight. 2. dawn. 3. daytime. 4. understanding; solution (of a problem). 5. publicity: as, let *daylight* into the affair. 6. the approaching end of a task or an ordeal: as, we can now see *daylight* ahead. 7. *pl.* [Slang], the eyes; hence, consciousness: often used hyperbolically, as in *scare* (*beat, knock,* etc.) *the daylights out of.*
day·light-sav·ing time (dā'līt'sāv'iŋ), time that is one hour later than standard time, generally used in the summer to give an hour more of daylight at the end of the usual working day: also **Daylight Saving Time:** abbreviated **D.S.T.**
day lily, any of a number of lilies with long, narrow leaves and bright flowers that usually last only a day.
day·long (dā'lôŋ', dā'loŋ'), *adj.* & *adv.* through the entire day; all day.
day nursery, a nursery for taking care of small children during the daytime.

Day of Atonement, Yom Kippur, a Jewish holiday: see **Jewish holidays.**

Day of Judgment, in *theology*, the day of God's final judgment of all people; last day of the world.

day room, in *military usage*, a recreation room for a company, troop, or battery.

day school, 1. a school that has classes only in the daytime: opposed to *night school*. 2. a private school whose students live at home and attend classes daily: opposed to *boarding school*.

days·man (dāz'mən), *n.* [*pl.* DAYSMEN (-mən)], [Archaic; see Job 9:33], an arbiter or umpire.

days of grace, 1. extra time, usually three days, allowed by law in some States for payment of a note, bill, etc. after it is due; hence, 2. any extension of time.

day·spring (dā'spriŋ'), *n.* [ME. *dai-spring;* see DAY & SPRING], [Poetic], the dawn.

day·star (dā'stär'), *n.* [ME. *daisterre;* see DAY & STAR], 1. the morning star. 2. [Poetic], the sun.

day·time (dā'tīm'), *n.* the time of daylight, between dawn and sunset.

Day·ton (dā't'n), *n.* a city in southwestern Ohio, on the Miami River: pop., 262,000.

Day·to·na Beach (dā-tō'nə), a resort town on the northeastern coast of Florida: pop., 37,000.

day·work (dā'wûrk'), *n.* work done by the day or during the day.

daze (dāz), *v.t.* [DAZED (dāzd), DAZING], [ME. *dasen;* ON. *dasask*, to become weary < *dasi*, lazy, tired; IE. base **dhē-*, to wear away; cf. FATIGUE], 1. to stupefy, stun, or bewilder, as by a shock or blow. 2. to dazzle. *n.* a dazed condition; bewilderment.

daz·ed·ly (dāz'id-li), *adv.* in a dazed manner.

daz·zle (daz''l), *v.t.* [DAZZLED (-'ld), DAZZLING], [freq. of *daze*], 1. to overpower, or dim, the vision of with very bright light or moving lights. 2. to confuse, surprise, or overpower with brilliant qualities, display, etc. *v.i.* 1. to be overpowered by glare. 2. to arouse admiration by brilliant display. *n.* 1. a dazzling. 2. something that dazzles.

db, decibel.

D.B., Domesday Book.

d.b., daybook.

D.Bib., Douay Bible.

dbl., double.

D.C., 1. Dental Corps. 2. District of Columbia. 3. Doctor of Chiropractic. 4. in *music*, [It.], *da capo*.

D.C., d.c., direct current.

D.C.L., Doctor of Civil Law.

D.Cn.L., Doctor of Canon Law.

D.C.S., 1. Deputy Clerk of Sessions. 2. Doctor of Christian Science. 3. Doctor of Commercial Science.

D.D., 1. demand draft: also **D/D.** 2. *Divinitatis Doctor*, [L.], Doctor of Divinity.

dd., d/d, delivered.

D-Day (dē'dā'), *n.* [*D*, the first letter of *day* + *day:* the term was first used during World War I, in orders for the St. Mihiel offensive of the A.E.F.], 1. the unspecified day on which a military operation is to take place. 2. June 6, 1944, the day of the invasion of western Europe by Allied forces in World War II.

D.D.S., Doctor of Dental Surgery.

D.D.Sc., Doctor of Dental Science.

DDT, [*d*ichloro*d*iphenyl*t*richloroethane], a powerful insecticide effective upon contact.

de, De (də, dē), *prep.* [Fr.; OFr. *des;* L. *dis-;* see DIS-], 1. of. 2. from: in French family names, it indicates place of origin.

de- (di, də, de, dē), [L. a prefix signifying separation, cessation, intensification, or contraction; also < Fr. *dé-* < L. *de* or OFr. *des-* < L. *dis-;* see DIS-], a prefix meaning: 1. *away from, off*, as in *depilate, detrain*. 2. *down*, as in *depress, decline*. 3. *wholly, entirely*, as in *defunct*. 4. *undo, reverse the action of*, as in *defrost*.

D.E., Doctor of Engineering.

dea·con (dē'k'n), *n.* [ME. *deken, dekyn;* AS. *deacon;* LL. *diaconus*, deacon; Gr. *diakonos*, servant, messenger, deacon], 1. a clergyman ranking just below a priest in the Roman Catholic and Anglican churches. 2. in certain other Christian churches, a layman appointed to help the minister, especially in secular matters, etc. Abbreviated **Dea.** (as a title). *v.t.* 1. to read (a verse) aloud before it is sung by the congregation (usually with *off*). 2. to pack (fruit, etc.) with only the best showing; hence, 3. to do (something) dishonestly; adulterate.

dea·con·ess (dē'k'n-is), *n.* [after LL. *diaconissa*, fem. of *diaconus;* see DEACON & -ESS], a woman appointed as an assistant in a church, as, a woman who helps take care of the sick and poor of a parish.

dea·con·ry (dē'k'n-ri), *n.* [*pl.* DEACONRIES (-riz)], 1. the position or office of a deacon. 2. deacons collectively.

de·ac·ti·vate (dē-ak'tə-vāt'), *v.t.* [DEACTIVATED (-id), DEACTIVATING], in *military usage*, to place (a division, regiment, etc.) on a nonactive status; demobilize.

dead (ded), *adj.* [ME. *ded, deade;* AS. *dead;* akin to ON. *dauthr*, OHG. *tot*, Goth. *dauths;* orig. pp. of an old v. base appearing in ON. *deyja*, OS. *dojan*, OHG. *touwen*, all < IE. base **dheu-*, to become senseless], 1. no longer living; having died: abbreviated **d.** 2. without life. 3. deathlike: as, a face *dead* with fright. 4. lacking feeling, energy, sensitivity, warmth, etc. 5. motionless: as, *dead* waters. 6. inelastic: as, a *dead* tennis ball. 7. no longer used or significant; obsolete: as, *dead* languages, *dead* laws. 8. lacking interest, taste, zest, color, etc.; dull; flat: as, a *dead* picture. 9. barren; unproductive; unprofitable: as, *dead* soil. 10. certain as death; unerring; sure: as, a *dead* shot. 11. complete; absolute: as, a *dead* loss. 12. unvarying: as, a *dead* level. 13. unclaimed: as, *dead* letters. 14. [Colloq.], very tired; exhausted. 15. in *electricity*, with no current going through it; uncharged: as, a *dead* wire. 16. in *law*, deprived of civil rights. 17. in *printing*, *a)* set up but not to be used. *b)* already used: as, *dead* type. 18. in *radio*, not operating: as, a *dead* microphone. 19. in *sports*, not in actual play: as, a *dead* ball. *n.* the time of most cold, most darkness, etc.: as, the *dead* of night. *adv.* 1. completely; absolutely. 2. directly.
the dead, those who have died.
SYN.—**dead** is the general word for someone or something that was but is no longer alive; **deceased** and **departed** are both euphemistic, especially for one who has recently died, but the former is largely a legal, and the latter a religious, usage; **late** always precedes the name or title of one who has recently died or who preceded the incumbent in some office or function (the *late* Mr. Green, his *late* employer); **defunct,** applied to a person, is now somewhat jocularly rhetorical, but it is commonly used of something that because of failure no longer exists or functions (a *defunct* government); **extinct** is applied to a species, race, etc. that has no living member; **inanimate** refers to that which has never had life (*inanimate* rocks); **lifeless** is equivalent to either **dead** or **inanimate** (her *lifeless* body, *lifeless* blocks).—*ANT.* alive, living.

dead·beat (ded'bēt'), *adj.* in *mechanics*, making a beat without recoil. *n.* a beat without recoil.

dead-beat (ded'bēt'), *adj.* [Colloq.], tired out; exhausted.

dead beat [Slang], 1. a person who tries to evade paying for things; sponge. 2. a lazy, idle person.

dead center, in *mechanics*, 1. that position of a crank and a connecting rod in which both are in the same straight line, so that no force is exerted. 2. a nonrevolving center.

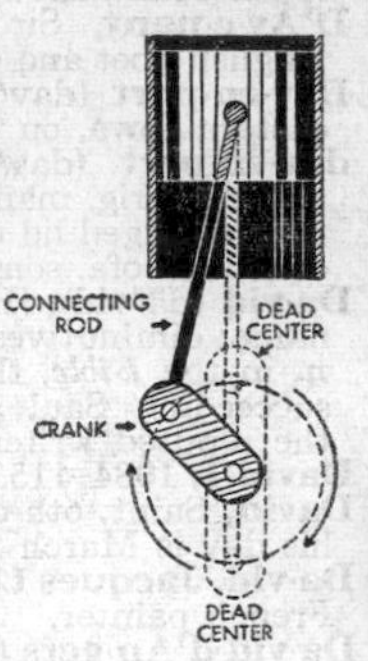

DEAD CENTER

dead·en (ded''n), *v.t.* [ME. *deden;* AS. *diedan, dydan* < *dead;* see DEAD], 1. to lessen the vigor or intensity of; dull; muffle. 2. to make numb; take away the sensitivity of. 3. to make soundproof. *v.i.* to become as if dead; lose vigor, intensity, etc.

dead-end (ded'end'), *adj.* 1. having one end closed: as, a *dead-end* street. 2. [Colloq.], [< *Dead End*, a play (1935) by Sidney Kingsley about New York slum life], of or characteristic of slums or slum life.

dead end, 1. a street, alley, etc. closed at one end; hence, 2. an impasse. 3. in *radio*, any part of a coil not connected with the circuit.

dead·en·ing (ded''n-iŋ), *n.* 1. material used to make rooms soundproof. 2. material used to take off gloss.

dead·eye (ded'ī'), *n.* a round, flat block of wood with three holes in it for the lanyard, used on a ship to fasten the shrouds.

dead·fall (ded'fôl'), *n.* 1. a trap for animals arranged so that a heavy weight is dropped on the prey, killing or maiming it. 2. a tangled mass of fallen trees and brush.

dead hand, mortmain.

dead·head (ded'hed'), *n.* [< *dead head* of cattle], a person who rides on trains, goes to the theater, etc. using a free ticket. *v.t.* to treat as a deadhead. *v.i.* to behave as a deadhead. *adv.* [Colloq.], without passengers.

dead heat, a race in which two or more contestants reach the finish line at exactly the same time; tie.

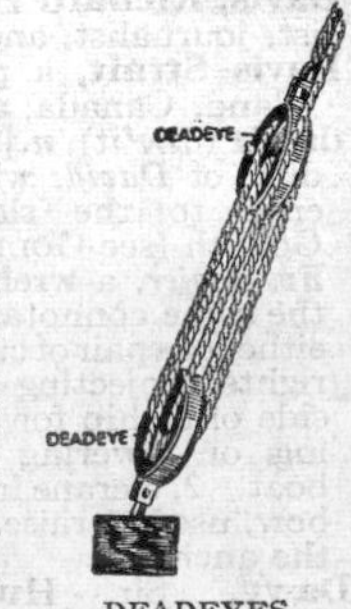

DEADEYES

dead letter, 1. a law or ordinance no longer enforced but not repealed. 2. an unclaimed letter, or one that cannot be delivered because of an incorrect address, etc.

dead-let·ter office (ded'let'ẽr), the postal department to which dead letters are sent to be opened and, if possible, returned to the writer, or destroyed.

dead lift, 1. a direct lifting without any mechanical assistance, as of a dead weight; hence, 2. a difficult task requiring all one's powers.

dead·light (ded'līt'), *n.* 1. a strong cover placed over a ship's porthole or cabin window in stormy weather. 2. a window of heavy glass in the deck or side of a ship. 3. a skylight made so as not to be opened.

dead·line (ded'līn'), ***n.*** 1. originally, a line around a prison beyond which a prisoner could go only at the risk of being shot by a guard. 2. a boundary which it is forbidden to cross. 3. a time limit, as for a payment, news story, etc.

dead·li·ness (ded'li-nis), ***n.*** the quality or state of being deadly.

dead load, in *engineering*, a uniform pressure or weight, as of a structure: opposed to *moving load*.

dead·lock (ded'lok'), ***n.*** a stoppage or standstill resulting from the action of equal and opposed forces. ***v.t.*** to bring to a deadlock. ***v.i.*** to come to a deadlock.

dead·ly (ded'li), ***adj.*** [DEADLIER (-li-ẽr), DEADLIEST (-li-ist)], [ME. *deadlich, deadlic;* AS. *deadlic;* see DEAD & -LY], 1. causing death; tending or liable to cause death; fatal. 2. until death: as, *deadly* combat. 3. as in death: as, *deadly* pallor. 4. excessive. 5. [Colloq.], unbearable: as, a *deadly* party. 6. in *theology*, causing spiritual death: as, the seven *deadly* sins. ***adv.*** [AS. *deadlice*], 1. like death. 2. as if dead. 3. extremely; excessively. —***SYN.*** see **fatal**.

deadly nightshade, the belladonna, a poisonous plant whose leaves and roots are used in medicine.

deadly sins, in *theology*, the seven capital sins (pride, covetousness, lust, anger, gluttony, envy, and sloth): so called because regarded as causing spiritual death.

dead march, solemn funeral music in slow march tempo; especially, a military funeral march.

dead-pan (ded'pan'), ***adj. & adv.*** [Slang], with an expressionless face.

dead pan, [Slang], 1. an expressionless face. 2. a person, as an actor, who has or assumes such a face.

dead point, dead center.

dead reckoning, [as if < *ded* (for *deduced*) *reckoning*], the finding of a ship's location by using compass readings and data recorded in the log (speed, course, and distance traveled) rather than astronomical observations: used in fog, etc.: abbreviated **d.r.**

Dead Sea, an inland body of salt water between Israel and Jordan: area, 370 sq. mi.; 1,290 ft. below sea level.

Dead Sea Scrolls, a number of scrolls dating from about 100 B.C. to about 70 A.D. and found variously since 1947 in caves near the Dead Sea: they contain Jewish Scriptural writings and religious writings of an Essene-like community.

dead set, 1. the unmoving position of a hunting dog in pointing game. 2. a resolute attack or effort. 3. [Colloq.], stubbornly determined: as, he was *dead set* on having his own way.

dead weight, 1. the weight of an inert person or thing. 2. a heavy burden: as, the *dead weight* of poverty. 3. the weight of a vehicle without a load. 4. freight for which charge is made by weight instead of bulk.

dead wind, a wind blowing in the direction opposite to a ship's course; head wind.

dead·wood (ded'wood'), ***n.*** 1. dead wood on trees; hence, 2. anything useless; burdensome person or thing. 3. the timbers or planks just above the keel of a ship, especially at the stern.

deaf (def), ***adj.*** [ME. *deaf, deef;* AS. *deaf;* akin to G. *taub*, Goth. *taubs;* IE. base **dheubh-*, misty, obscured < **dheu-*, to rise up as mist, smoke, dust, etc.], 1. totally or partially unable to hear. 2. unwilling to hear or listen; giving no heed: as, he was *deaf* to her pleas.

deaf-and-dumb (def'ən-dum'), ***adj.*** 1. deaf-mute. 2. of or for deaf-mutes. Now regarded as opprobrious.

deaf·en (def''n), ***v.t.*** 1. to make deaf. 2. to overwhelm with noise. 3. to drown out (a sound) with a louder sound. 4. to make soundproof.

deaf·en·ing (def''n-iŋ), ***adj.*** [ppr. of *deafen*], 1. making deaf. 2. very noisy. 3. making soundproof. ***n.*** material used in floors or walls to make them soundproof.

deaf-mute (def'mūt', def'mūt'), ***n.*** a person who is deaf, especially from birth, and therefore unable to speak: most deaf-mutes, having the necessary vocal organs, can be taught to speak. ***adj.*** unable to hear and speak, especially because deaf from birth.

deal (dēl), ***v.t.*** [DEALT (delt), DEALING], [ME. *delen;* AS. *dælan*, to divide, share; akin to G. *teilen;* see DEAL (an amount)], 1. to portion out. 2. to distribute. 3. to give; administer: as, he *dealt* his opponent a blow. 4. to distribute (playing cards) to the players. ***v.i.*** 1. to have to do (*with*): as, science *deals* with facts. 2. to act or conduct oneself (followed by *with*): as, *deal* fairly with others. 3. to take up or consider (followed by *with*): as, the committee will *deal* with these problems. 4. to do business; trade (*with* or *in*): as, we *deal* with the corner grocer, this firm *deals* in cutlery. 5. to distribute playing cards to the players. ***n.*** 1. a dealing. 2. *a*) the act of distributing playing cards. *b*) cards dealt. *c*) a player's turn to deal. *d*) the playing of one deal of cards. *e*) the privilege of dealing. 3. [Colloq.], a business transaction. 4. [Colloq.], a bargain or agreement, especially a secret one in politics. 5. [Colloq.], an arrangement, treatment, or plan, usually involving some sort of distribution: as, a fair *deal*.

deal (dēl), ***n.*** [ME. *dele, deel;* AS. *dæl*, a part, share; akin to G. *teil*, Goth. *dails;* IE. base **dhāi-*, var. of **dāi-*, to part, cut up, rend], an indefinite amount or quantity.

a good (or **great**) **deal,** 1. a large quantity or amount: as, you've wasted *a good deal* of time. 2. very much: as, I can't walk *a great deal* faster.

deal (dēl), ***n.*** [MD. *dele*, a board, plank; see DEAL (an amount)], 1. a fir or pine board of any of several sizes. 2. fir or pine wood. ***adj.*** made of deal.

deal·er (dēl'ẽr), ***n.*** a person who deals; specifically, *a*) the person who shuffles and distributes the cards in a card game. *b*) a buyer and seller; person engaged in trading: as, a *dealer* in furs. Abbreviated **dlr.**

deal·fish (dēl'fish'), ***n.*** [DEALFISH, DEALFISHES (-iz); see FISH], any of a number of related deep-sea fishes with a long, thin body; ribbonfish.

deal·ing (dēl'iŋ), ***n.*** 1. the act of a person who deals; distribution. 2. behavior; way of acting. 3. *usually pl.* transactions or relations, usually of business. 4. doing business. 5. way of doing business.

dealt (delt), past tense and past participle of **deal**.

dean (dēn), ***n.*** [ME. *deen, dene;* OFr. *deien*, dean; LL. *decanus*, a person who is head of ten (monks or soldiers) < L. *decem*, ten], 1. the presiding official of a cathedral or collegiate church. 2. a member of a college or university administration in charge of a school, faculty, or class, or of the men or women students. 3. the member of an association or group who has belonged to it longer than anyone else: as, the *dean* of English poets.

dean·er·y (dēn'ẽr-i), ***n.*** [*pl.* DEANERIES (-iz)], 1. the position, authority, or jurisdiction of a dean. 2. the official residence of a dean.

dean·ship (dēn'ship'), ***n.*** [see -SHIP], the position, rank, or term of office of a dean.

dear (dêr), ***adj.*** [ME. *deere, dere;* AS. *deore*, precious, costly, beloved; akin to D. *duur, dier*, G. *teuer* < Gmc. base prob. meaning "worthy of admiration"], 1. much loved; beloved. 2. much valued; highly thought of; esteemed: used as a polite form of address in speaking or letter writing: as, *Dear* Sir. 3. *a*) high-priced; costly. *b*) charging high prices. 4. earnest: as, our *dearest* hope. ***adv.*** 1. with deep affection. 2. at a high cost. ***n.*** a loved person; darling: often a term of affectionate address. ***interj.*** an expression of distress, surprise, pity, etc. —***SYN.*** see **costly**.

Dear·born (dêr'bẽrn, dêr'bôrn'), ***n.*** a city in Michigan, near Detroit: pop., 112,000.

dear·ly (dêr'li), ***adv.*** [ME. *deorliche, dereliche;* AS. *deorlic;* see DEAR & -LY], 1. with deep affection. 2. at a high cost. 3. earnestly: as, I *dearly* wish to go.

dearth (dũrth), ***n.*** [ME. *derth, derthe* < *deere, dere;* see DEAR & -TH], 1. originally, costliness; dearness; hence, 2. scarcity of food supply; famine. 3. scarcity; lack.

dear·y, dear·ie (dêr'i), ***n.*** [*pl.* DEARIES (-iz)], [Colloq.], dear; darling: now often ironic or humorous.

death (deth), ***n.*** [ME. *deth, deeth;* AS. *death;* akin to OS. *doth*, OHG. *tot*, ON. *dauthi;* see DEAD], 1. the act or fact of dying; permanent ending of all life in a person, animal, or plant. 2. [D-], the personification of death, usually pictured as a skeleton in a black robe, holding a scythe. 3. the state of being dead. 4. any ending resembling dying: as, the *death* of fascism. 5. any condition or experience thought of as like dying or being dead: as, it was *death* for her to have to see him again. 6. the cause of death: as, the atomic bomb was *death* to thousands. 7. murder or bloodshed. 8. [Obs.], pestilence: as, the Black *Death*.

at death's door, nearly dead.

do to death, to kill.

in at the death, 1. present at the death (of the quarry): hunter's term. 2. present at the end or culmination.

put to death, to kill; execute.

to death, to the extreme; very much: as, he worries me *to death*.

death·bed (deth'bed'), ***n.*** 1. the bed on which a person dies. 2. the last hours of a person's life. ***adj.*** done or made in the last hours of life: as, a *deathbed* will.

death bell, a bell tolled to announce a death.

death·blow (deth'blō'), ***n.*** 1. a blow that causes death; hence, 2. a thing destructive or fatal (*to* something).

death camass, a lilylike plant with a poisonous bulb and clusters of small greenish-white flowers.

death chamber, 1. a room in which someone has died. 2. a room in which condemned prisoners are executed.

death cup, a poisonous mushroom with a swollen, cuplike base.

death duty, [British], an inheritance tax.

death·ful (deth'fəl), ***adj.*** 1. deadly; murderous. 2. deathlike; deathly. 3. [Archaic], mortal.

death house, a place, as a cell block, where prisoners condemned to die are kept until the time of execution.

death·less (deth'lis), ***adj.*** that cannot die; forever alive; immortal: as, the *deathless* words of Lincoln.

death·like (deth′līk′), *adj.* like, or as in, death.
death·ly (deth′li), *adj.* 1. causing death; deadly; fatal. 2. like or characteristic of death. 3. [Poetic], of death. *adv.* 1. in a deathlike way; to a deadly degree. 2. extremely; deadly: as, *deathly* serious.
death mask, a cast of a person's face, taken soon after his death.
death rate, the number of deaths per year per thousand of population in a given community, area, or group: sometimes other units of time or population are used in giving the death rate.
death rattle, a sound that sometimes comes from the throat of a dying person, caused by breath passing through mucus.
death ray, a ray that can supposedly kill at a distance.
death's-head (deths′hed′), *n.* a human skull or a representation of it, symbolizing death.
death's-head moth, a large hawk moth with markings on its back that resemble a human skull.
deaths·man (deths′mən), *n.* [*pl.* DEATHSMEN (-mən)], [Archaic], an executioner.
death·trap (deth′trap′), *n.* 1. any unsafe building or other structure. 2. a very dangerous place, set of circumstances, etc.
Death Valley, a dry, hot region in eastern California: 276 ft. below sea level.
death warrant, 1. an official order to put a person to death; hence, 2. anything that ends hope, joy, etc.
death·watch (deth′woch′, deth′wôch′), *n.* 1. a vigil kept beside a dead or dying person. 2. a guard set over a person soon to be executed. 3. any of various insects, especially certain wood beetles, that make a ticking sound superstitiously regarded as an omen of death.
death·y (deth′i), *adj. & adv.* [Rare], deathly.
Deau·ville (dō′vil; Fr. dō′vēl′), *n.* a resort town in France, on the English Channel: pop., 4,700.
deave (dēv), *v.t.* [DEAVED (dēvd), DEAVING], [ME. *deven;* AS. *deafian* < *deaf*, deaf], [Scot. & British Dial.], to deafen, as with noise.
deb., debenture.
de·ba·cle (dā-bä′k'l, di-bak′'l), *n.* [Fr. *débâcle*, breakup, overthrow < *débâcler*, to break up], 1. a breaking up of ice in a river, etc. 2. a rush of debris-filled waters. 3. an overthrow; rout. 4. a sudden great disaster.
de·bar (di-bär′), *v.t.* [DEBARRED (-bärd′), DEBARRING], [Fr. *débarrer;* see DE- & BAR], 1. to bar out; exclude (*from* somewhere or something). 2. to prevent, hinder, or prohibit. —***SYN.*** see **exclude.**
de·bark (di-bärk′), *v.t.* [Fr. *débarquer;* see DE- & BARK (a ship)], to put ashore from a ship; unload. *v.i.* to go ashore from a ship; disembark.
de·bar·ka·tion (dē′bär-kā′shən), *n.* a putting ashore or going ashore from a ship; debarking.
de·bar·ment (di-bär′mənt), *n.* a debarring or being debarred.
de·base (di-bās′), *v.t.* [DEBASED (-bāst′), DEBASING], [*de-* + *base* (low)], to make lower in value, quality, character, dignity, etc.
SYN.*—debase** implies generally a lowering in quality, value, dignity, etc. (greed had *debased* his character); **deprave** suggests gross degeneration, especially with reference to morals (a mind *depraved* by crime); **corrupt** implies a deterioration or loss of soundness by some destructive or contaminating influence (a government *corrupted* by bribery); **debauch** implies a loss of moral purity or integrity as through dissipation or intemperate indulgence (*debauched* young profligates); **pervert** suggests a distorting of or departure from what is considered right, natural, or true (a *perverted* sense of humor). See also **degrade.**—ANT.*** elevate, improve.
de·base·ment (di-bās′mənt), *n.* 1. a debasing. 2. the fact or condition of being debased.
de·bat·a·ble (di-bāt′ə-b'l), *adj.* 1. that can be debated; open to question. 2. being disputed; undecided.
de·bate (di-bāt′), *v.i.* [DEBATED (-id), DEBATING], [ME.; OFr. *débatre*, to fight, contend, debate; see DE- & BATTER (to beat)], 1. to consider. 2. to discuss opposing reasons; argue. 3. to take part in a formal argument; be a debater. 4. [Obs.], to fight or quarrel. *v.t.* 1. to dispute about, especially in a meeting or legislature. 2. to argue (a question) formally. 3. to consider reasons for and against (*with* oneself, or *in* one's own mind). *n.* [ME. & OFr. *debat* < the *v.*], 1. discussion of opposing reasons; argument. 2. a formal contest of skill in reasoned argument, with two teams taking opposite sides of a specified question (the resolution). 3. the art or study of formal debate. —***SYN.*** see **discuss.**
de·bat·er (di-bāt′ẽr), *n.* a person who debates; person who takes part in a formal debate, usually as one of a team.
de·bauch (di-bôch′), *v.t.* [Fr. *débaucher;* OFr. *desbaucher*, to corrupt, seduce, draw away from work < *des-*, away from + *esbaucher*, to weed out < Gaul. **bodica*, fallow ground, plowed field; orig., a plowing metaphor], to lead astray morally; corrupt; deprave. *v.i.* to indulge in debauchery; dissipate. *n.* [Fr. *débauche* < the *v.*], 1. debauchery. 2. an orgy. —***SYN.*** see **debase.**
de·bauch·ed·ly (di-bôch′id-li), *adv.* in a debauched manner.
deb·au·chee (deb′ô-chē′, deb′ô-shē′), *n.* [Fr. *débauché*, pp. of *débaucher;* see DEBAUCH], a person who indulges in debauchery; dissipated or depraved person.
de·bauch·er·y (di-bôch′ẽr-i), *n.* [*pl.* DEBAUCHERIES (-iz)], [*debauch* + *-ery*], 1. extreme indulgence of one's appetites, especially for sensual pleasure; dissipation. 2. *pl.* orgies. 3. a leading astray morally.
de·bauch·ment (di-bôch′mənt), *n.* a debauching or being debauched.
de·ben·ture (di-ben′chẽr), *n.* [Fr. < L. *debentur*, 3d pers. pl., pres. indic., of *debere;* see DEBT: so called because receipts used to begin with the Latin words *debentur mihi*, there are owing to me], 1. a voucher or certificate acknowledging that a debt is owed by the signer. 2. a customhouse order for payment of a drawback, as to an importer. 3. a government voucher of indebtedness. 4. an interest-bearing bond issued, often without security, by a corporation. Abbreviated **deb., deben.**
de·bil·i·tate (di-bil′ə-tāt′), *v.t.* [DEBILITATED (-id), DEBILITATING], [< L. *debilitatus*, pp. of *debilitare*, to weaken < *debilis*, weak, not strong; *de-* (see DE-) + deriv. of IE. base **bel-*, strong], to make weak or feeble; enervate. —***SYN.*** see **weaken.**
de·bil·i·ta·tion (di-bil′ə-tā′shən), *n.* [L. *debilitatio*], a debilitating or being debilitated.
de·bil·i·ty (di-bil′ə-ti), *n.* [*pl.* DEBILITIES (-tiz)], [Fr. *débilité;* L. *debilitas*, weakness < *debilis;* see DEBILITATE], bodily weakness; feebleness.
deb·it (deb′it), *n.* [L. *debitum*, what is owing, debt; neut. pp. of *debere;* see DEBT], 1. an entry on the left-hand side of an account, as of money owed. 2. the total of such entries. 3. the left-hand side or column of an account, where such entries are made. Abbreviated **dr.** *adj.* relating to debt or debts. *v.t.* 1. to charge with a debt. 2. to enter as a debit or debits; enter on the left-hand side of an account.
deb·o·nair, deb·o·naire (deb′ə-nâr′), *adj.* [ME. *debonaire;* OFr. *de bon aire*, lit., of good breed or race; see AERIE], 1. affable; genial; courteous. 2. gay; jaunty.
‡**de bonne grace** (də bôn′ gräs′), [Fr.], with good grace; graciously.
Deb·o·rah (deb′ə-rə), [Heb. *debōrāh*, lit., a bee], a feminine name: diminutive, *Debby*. *n.* in the *Bible*, a prophetess and one of the judges of Israel, who helped the Israelites free themselves from the Canaanites: Judg. 4 & 5.
de·bouch (di-bo͞osh′), *v.i.* [Fr. *déboucher*, to emerge from < *dé-* (see DE-) + *bouche*, mouth, opening < L. *bucca*, cheek], 1. in *military usage*, to come forth from a narrow or shut-in place into open country; hence, 2. to come forth; emerge. *v.t.* to make come forth. *n.* a débouché.
‡**dé·bou·ché** (dā′bo͞o′shā′), *n.* [Fr., pp. of *déboucher;* see DEBOUCH], 1. an opening for troops to debouch through; hence, 2. an outlet, as for goods.
de·bouch·ment (di-bo͞osh′mənt), *n.* [Fr. *débouchement*], 1. a debouching. 2. a mouth (of a river); outlet.
De·bre·cen (de′bre-tsen′), *n.* a city in eastern Hungary: pop., 126,000.
‡**dé·bri·de·ment** (dā′brēd′män′), *n.* [Fr. < *débrider*, to unbridle], in *surgery*, the cutting away of dead or contaminated tissue from a wound to prevent infection.
de·bris, dé·bris (də-brē′, dā′brē; Brit. deb′rē), *n.* [Fr. *débris* < OFr. *desbrisier*, to break apart; see DE- & BRUISE], 1. broken, scattered remains; rubbish, especially that caused by destruction; ruins. 2. in *geology*, a heap or heaps of rock fragments, as from a glacier.
Debs, Eugene Victor (debz), 1855–1926; American labor leader; presidential candidate of the Socialist Party (1900; 1904; 1908; 1912; 1920).
debt (det), *n.* [Latinized sp. of ME. *det, dette;* OFr. *dette, debte* < L. *debitum*, neut. pp. of *debere*, to owe < *de-*, from + *habere*, to have], 1. something owed by one person to another or others. 2. an obligation or liability to pay or return something. 3. the condition of owing: as, to be in *debt*. 4. in *theology*, a sin.
debt of honor, a debt contracted in gambling or betting: not legally enforceable.
debt·or (det′ẽr), *n.* [Latinized sp. of ME. *dettur;* OFr. *detor;* L. *debitor* < *debitus*, pp. of *debere;* see DEBT], 1. a person, company, nation, etc. that owes something to another or others. 2. in *bookkeeping*, the left-hand (debit) side of an account: abbreviated **Dr., dr.**
de·bunk (di-buŋk′), *v.t.* [*de-* + *bunk* (nonsense)], [Colloq.], to expose the false or exaggerated claims, pretensions, glamour, etc. of.
De·bus·sy, A·chille Claude (á′shēl′ klōd də-bü′sē′; Eng. də-bū′si, deb′yoo-sē′), 1862–1918; French composer.
de·but, dé·but (di-bū′, dā′bū), *n.* [Fr. *début* < *débuter*, to lead off (at bowls, etc.) < (*jouer*) *de but*, (to play) for the mark; see DE- & BUTT (goal)], 1. a first appearance before the public, as of an actor. 2. the formal introduction of a girl to society. 3. the beginning of a career, course, etc.
deb·u·tant, dé·bu·tant (deb′yoo-tänt′, deb′yə-tant′), *n.* [Fr. *débutant*, ppr. of *débuter;* see DEBUT], a person making a debut.

deb·u·tante, dé·bu·tante (deb'yoo-tänt', deb'yə-tant'), *n.* [Fr., fem. of *débutant*], a girl or woman making a debut, especially into high society.
Dec., December.
dec., 1. deceased. 2. decimeter. 3. declaration. 4. declension. 5. declination. 6. decrease.
dec·a- (dek'ə), [< Gr. *deka*, ten], a combining form meaning *ten*, as in *decagon, decameter:* also, before a vowel, **dec-**, and in words referring to the metric system, **deka-**.
dec·ade (dek'ād, de-kād'), *n.* [Fr.; L. *decas;* Gr. *dekas* < *deka*, ten], 1. a group of ten. 2. a period of ten years.
de·ca·dence (di-kā'd'ns, dek'ə-dəns), *n.* [Fr. *décadence*, a falling away; ML. *decadentia* < L. *de-*, from + *cadens*, ppr. of *cadere*, to fall], a falling away; process, condition, or period of decline, as in morals, art, literature, etc.; deterioration; decay.
de·ca·den·cy (di-kā'd'n-si, dek'ə-dən-si), *n.* decadence.
de·ca·dent (di-kā'd'nt, dek'ə-dənt), *adj.* [Fr. *décadent:* term applied to themselves by young Fr. writers of late 19th c. who openly admired Roman decadence], in a state of decline; characterized by decadence. *n.* a decadent person, especially a decadent writer or artist.
dec·a·gon (dek'ə-gon'), *n.* [ML. *decagonum;* see DECA- & -GON], a plane figure with ten sides and ten angles.
de·cag·o·nal (de-kag'ə-n'l), *adj.* of, or having the form of, a decagon; ten-sided.
dec·a·gram, dec·a·gramme (dek'ə-gram'), *n.* [Fr. *décagramme;* see DECA- & GRAM], a measure of weight equal to 10 grams (0.3527 ounce): abbreviated **dkg.**
dec·a·he·dral (dek'ə-hē'drəl), *adj.* of, or having the form of, a decahedron.
dec·a·he·dron (dek'ə-hē'drən), *n.* [*pl.* DECAHEDRONS (-drənz), DECAHEDRA (-drə)], [Mod. L.; see DECA- & -HEDRON], a solid figure with ten plane surfaces.
de·cal (di-kal'), *n.* decalcomania.
de·cal·ci·fi·ca·tion (dē-kal'sə-fi-kā'shən), *n.* a decalcifying or being decalcified.
de·cal·ci·fi·er (dē-kal'sə-fi'ẽr), *n.* a thing that decalcifies.
de·cal·ci·fy (dē-kal'sə-fī'), *v.t.* [DECALCIFIED (-fīd'), DECALCIFYING], to remove calcium or lime from (bones, etc.).
de·cal·co·ma·ni·a (di-kal'kə-mā'ni-ə), *n.* [Fr. *décalcomanie* < *décalquer*, to counterdraw + Gr. *mania*, madness], 1. the process of transferring to glass, wood, etc. decorative pictures or designs printed on specially prepared paper. 2. a picture or design of this kind.
de·ca·les·cence (dē'kə-les''ns), *n.* [< L. *decalescens*, ppr. of *decalescere*, to become warm; *de-*, intens. + *calescere*, to grow hot < *calere*, to be warm, glow], a sudden decrease in the rate of temperature rise of heated metal after a certain degree of temperature has been reached (795°C. for iron), due to greater absorption of heat.
de·ca·les·cent (dē'kə-les''nt), *adj.* of or subject to decalescence.
dec·a·li·ter, dec·a·li·tre (dek'ə-lē'tẽr), *n.* [Fr. *décalitre;* see DECA- & LITER], a measure of capacity, equal to 10 liters (2.64 gallons liquid measure or 9.08 quarts dry measure): abbreviated **dkl.**
Dec·a·logue, Dec·a·log (dek'ə-lôg', dek'ə-log'), *n.* [ME. *decaloge;* Fr. *décalogue;* LL. *decalogus;* Gr. *dekalogos;* see DECA- & -LOGUE], [sometimes d-], the Ten Commandments: Exod. 20:2–17.
De·cam·er·on (di-kam'ẽr-ən), *n.* [It. *Decamerone* < Gr. *deka*, ten + *hēmera*, day], a collection of a hundred tales by Boccaccio (pub. 1353): so called because described as told by a group of Florentines to while away ten days during a plague.
dec·a·me·ter, dec·a·me·tre (dek'ə-mē'tẽr), *n.* [Fr. *décamètre;* see DECA- & METER], a measure of length, equal to 10 meters (32.808 feet): abbreviated **dkm.**
de·camp (di-kamp'), *v.i.* [Fr. *décamper*, to break camp; see DE- & CAMP], 1. to break or leave camp; hence, 2. to go away suddenly and secretly; run away.
de·camp·ment (di-kamp'mənt), *n.* a decamping.
dec·a·nal (dek'ə-n'l, di-kā'n'l), *adj.* [< LL. *decanus* (see DEAN); + *-al*], of a dean or deanery.
dec·ane (dek'ān), *n.* [< *deca-* + *-ane*], any of the isomeric hydrocarbons having the formula $C_{10}H_{22}$ and belonging to the methane series, present in petroleum or in certain petroleum products, such as kerosene.
de·cant (di-kant'), *v.t.* [Fr. *décanter;* ML. *decanthare* < L. *de-*, from + *canthus;* see CANT (edge)], 1. to pour off (a liquid) gently without stirring up the sediment. 2. to pour from one container into another.
de·cant·er (di-kan'tẽr), *n.* [*decant* + *-er*], a decorative glass bottle, generally with a stopper, used for serving wine, etc.
de·cap·i·tate (di-kap'ə-tāt'), *v.t.* [DECAPITATED (-id), DECAPITATING], [Fr. *décapiter* < ML. *decapitatus*, pp. of *decapitare* < L. *de-*, off + *caput*, the head], to cut off the head of; behead.
de·cap·i·ta·tion (di-kap'ə-tā'shən), *n.* [Fr.; ML. *decapitatio* < *decapitare;* see DECAPITATE], a beheading or being beheaded; execution by beheading.
de·cap·i·ta·tor (di-kap'ə-tā'tẽr), *n.* a person or thing that decapitates.
dec·a·pod (dek'ə-pod'), *adj.* [*deca-* + *-pod*], ten-legged. *n.* 1. any crustacean with ten legs, as a lobster, shrimp, etc. 2. any cephalopod with ten arms, as a squid.
De·cap·o·lis (di-kap'ə-lis), *n.* an ancient district of northeastern Palestine.
de·car·bon·ate (dē-kär'bə-nāt'), *v.t.* to remove carbon dioxide or carbonic acid from.
de·car·bon·ize (dē-kär'bə-nīz'), *v.t.* to remove carbon from.
de·car·box·y·la·tion (dē'kär-bok'sə-lā'shən), *n.* [*de-* + *carboxyl* + *-ation*], the removal of a molecule of carbon dioxide from amino acids and proteins by bacterial action, with the resultant formation of amines.
de·car·bu·rize (dē-kär'bə-rīz', dē-kär'byoo-rīz'), *v.t.* to decarbonize.
dec·are (dek'âr, dek-âr'), *n.* [Fr.; see DECA- & ARE, *n.*], a metric unit of surface measure equal to 10 ares (0.2471 acre).
dec·a·stere (dek'ə-stêr'), *n.* [Fr. *décastère;* see DECA- & STERE], a metric measure of volume, equal to 10 cubic meters (13.08 cubic yards).
dec·a·syl·lab·ic (dek'ə-si-lab'ik), *adj.* 1. having ten syllables. 2. of a decasyllable. *n.* a decasyllable.
dec·a·syl·la·ble (dek'ə-sil'ə-b'l), *n.* a line of verse having ten syllables.
de·cath·lon (di-kath'lon), *n.* [< *deca-* + Gr. *athlon*, a contest], an athletic contest in which each contestant takes part in ten events (100-meter dash, broad jump, 16-pound shot-put, high jump, 400-meter dash, 110-meter hurdles, discus throw, pole vault, javelin throw, and 1500-meter run): the winner is the contestant receiving the highest total of points.
De·ca·tur (di-kā'tẽr), *n.* 1. a city in central Illinois: pop., 78,000. 2. a city in northern Alabama: pop., 29,000.
De·ca·tur, Stephen (di-kā'tẽr), 1779–1820; American naval officer.
de·cay (di-kā'), *v.i.* [OFr. dial. *decair* < L. *decidere*, to fall down, fall away < *de-*, down + *cadere*, to fall], 1. to lose strength, health, beauty, prosperity, etc. gradually; waste away; deteriorate. 2. to rot. *v.t.* to cause to decay. *n.* 1. a gradual decline; deterioration. 2. a wasting away. 3. a rotting or chemical decomposition, as of vegetable matter. 4. rottenness. 5. the gradual disintegration of radioactive substances.
SYN.—**decay** implies gradual, often natural, deterioration from a normal or sound condition (his teeth have begun to *decay*); **rot** refers to the decay of organic, especially vegetable, matter, caused by bacteria, fungi, etc. (*rotting* apples); **putrefy** suggests the offensive, foul-smelling rotting of animal matter (bodies *putrefying* in the fields); **spoil** is the common informal word for the decay of foods (fish *spoils* quickly in summer); **molder** suggests a slow, progressive, crumbling decay (old buildings *molder* away); **disintegrate** implies the breaking up of something into parts or fragments so that the wholeness of the original is destroyed (the *disintegration* of rocks); **decompose** suggests the breaking up or separation of something into its component elements (to *decompose* a chemical compound): it is also a somewhat euphemistic substitute for **rot** and **putrefy.**
Dec·can (dek'ən), *n.* 1. that part of India south of the Narbada River. 2. sometimes, the region between the Narbada and Kistna Rivers.
de·cease (di-sēs'), *n.* [ME. *deces, deses;* OFr. *deces* < L. *decessus*, lit., departure, pp. of *decedere*, to depart, go away; *de-*, from + *cedere*, to go, move], death. *v.i.* [DECEASED (-sēst'), DECEASING], to die. —*SYN.* see **die.**
de·ceased (di-sēst'), *adj.* [pp. of *decease*], dead: abbreviated **dec.** —*SYN.* see **dead.**
the deceased, 1. the dead person. 2. dead persons; the dead.
de·ce·dent (di-sē'd'nt), *n.* [L. *decedens*, ppr. of *decedere;* see DECEASE], in *law*, the deceased; dead person.
de·ceit (di-sēt'), *n.* [ME. & OFr. *deceite;* see DECEIVE], 1. the act of representing as true what is known to be false; deceiving; lying. 2. a lie; dishonest action or trick. 3. the quality of being deceitful.
de·ceit·ful (di-sēt'fəl), *adj.* 1. tending to deceive; apt to lie or cheat. 2. intended to deceive; deceptive; false. —*SYN.* see **dishonest.**
de·ceiv·a·ble (di-sēv'ə-b'l), *adj.* [ME.; OFr. *decevable*], [Rare], that can be deceived.
de·ceive (di-sēv'), *v.t.* [DECEIVED (-sēvd'), DECEIVING], [ME.; OFr. *deceveir;* L. *decipere*, to ensnare, deceive < *de-*, from + *capere*, to take], 1. to make (a person) believe what is not true; delude; mislead. 2. [Archaic], to while away (time). *v.i.* to use deceit; lie, etc.
SYN.—**deceive** implies deliberate misrepresentation of facts by words, actions, etc., generally to further one's ends (*deceived* into buying fraudulent stocks); to **mislead** is to cause to follow the wrong course or to err in conduct or action, although not always by deliberate deception (*misled* by the sign into going to the wrong floor); **beguile** implies the use of wiles and enticing

prospects in deceiving or misleading (*beguiled* by promises of a fortune); to **delude** is to fool someone so completely that he accepts what is false as true; **betray** implies a breaking of faith while appearing to be loyal.

de·cel·er·ate (dē-sel′ẽr-āt′), *v.t. & v.i.* [DECELERATED (-id), DECELERATING], [*de-* + *accelerate*], to slow down: opposed to *accelerate*.

de·cel·er·a·tion (dē-sel′ẽr-ā′shən), *n.* a decelerating or being decelerated.

de·cel·er·a·tor (dē-sel′ẽr-ā′tẽr), *n.* a person or thing that decelerates.

De·cem·ber (di-sem′bẽr), *n.* [OFr. *decembre;* L. *December* < *decem*, ten: it was the tenth month to the early Romans, who reckoned from March], the twelfth and last month of the year, having 31 days: abbreviated **Dec., D.**

De·cem·brist (di-sem′brist), *n.* [*December* + *-ist*], in *Russian history*, one of the conspirators against Czar Nicholas I, in December, 1825.

de·cem·vir (di-sem′vẽr), *n.* [*pl.* DECEMVIRS (-vẽrz), DECEMVIRI (-ī′)], [L., sing. of *decemviri* < *decem*, ten + *vir*, a man], 1. a member of a council of ten magistrates in ancient Rome: in 450 B.C. this body drew up the first Roman code of laws. 2. a member of any authoritative group of ten men.

de·cem·vi·rate (di-sem′və-rit, di-sem′və-rāt′), *n.* [see DECEMVIR & -ATE], 1. the position or term of a decemvir. 2. any authoritative group of ten men.

de·cen·a·ry (di-sen′ə-ri), *adj.* [ML. *decenarius* < *decena*, a tithing < L. *decem*, ten], of a tithing. *n.* [*pl.* DECENARIES (-riz)], a tithing. Also spelled **decennary.**

de·cen·cy (dē′s′n-si), *n.* [*pl.* DECENCIES (-siz)], [L. *decentia* < *decens;* see DECENT], 1. the quality or condition of being decent; propriety of conduct and speech; proper observance of the requirements of modesty, good taste, etc. 2. *pl.* socially proper actions: as, observe the *decencies*. 3. *pl.* things needed for a proper or comfortable standard of living. —***SYN.*** see **decorum.**

de·cen·na·ry (di-sen′ə-ri), *n.* [*pl.* DECENNARIES (-riz)], [L. *decennis*, lasting ten years < *decem*, ten + *annus*, year; + *-ary*], a period of ten years. *adj.* ten-year; decennial.

de·cen·na·ry (di-sen′ə-ri), *adj. & n.* decenary.

de·cen·ni·al (di-sen′i-əl), *adj.* [LL. *decennium* < L. *decem*, ten + *annus*, year; + *-al*], 1. of or lasting ten years. 2. occurring every ten years. *n.* a tenth anniversary or its celebration.

de·cen·ni·um (di-sen′i-əm), *n.* [*pl.* DECENNIUMS (-əmz), DECENNIA (-ə)], [L. < *decennis;* see DECENNARY], a period of ten years; decade.

de·cent (dē′s′nt), *adj.* [Fr.; L. *decens*, ppr. of *decere*, to befit; see DÉCOR], 1. proper and fitting. 2. not immodest; not obscene; chaste. 3. conforming to approved social standards; respectable. 4. satisfactory; fairly good; adequate: as, *decent* wages. 5. fair; kind; generous: as, he is very *decent* to me. 6. [Colloq.], adequately clothed for propriety. —***SYN.*** see **chaste.**

de·cen·ter (dē-sen′tẽr), *v.t.* 1. to put out of center; make (a thing) eccentric. 2. to cut (a lens) so that the optical and geometrical centers are not the same. Also spelled **decentre.**

de·cen·tral·i·za·tion (dē-sen′trəl-i-zā′shən, dē′sen-trəl-i-zā′shən), *n.* a decentralizing or being decentralized.

de·cen·tral·ize (dē-sen′trəl-īz′), *v.t.* to break up the centralization of authority, as in a government or industry, and distribute among more places, local authorities, etc.

de·cep·tion (di-sep′shən), *n.* [Fr.; L. *deceptio* < pp. of *decipere;* see DECEIVE], 1. the act or practice of deceiving. 2. the fact or condition of being deceived. 3. something deceiving, as an illusion, or meant to deceive, as a fraud, imposture, etc.

SYN.—**deception** is applied to anything that deceives, whether by design or illusion; **fraud** suggests deliberate deception in dishonestly depriving a person of property, rights, etc.; **subterfuge** suggests an artifice or stratagem used to deceive others in evading something or gaining some end; **trickery** implies the use of tricks or ruses in fraudulently deceiving others; **chicanery** implies the use of petty trickery and subterfuge, especially in legal actions.

de·cep·tive (di-sep′tiv), *adj.* [Fr. *déceptif* < L. *deceptus*, pp. of *decipere;* see DECEIVE], deceiving or intended to deceive.

de·cern (di-sũrn′), *v.t.* [ME. *decernen;* OFr. *decerner;* L. *decernere*, to decide; cf. DISCERN], 1. to discern. 2. in *Scottish law*, to decree by judicial sentence.

dec·i- (des′ə), [Fr. *deci-* < L. *decimus*, tenth < *decem*, ten], a combining form, used especially in the metric system, meaning *one tenth of* (a specified unit), as in *decigram, decimeter*.

dec·i·are (des′i-âr′), *n.* [Fr.; see DECI- & ARE, *n.*], a metric measure of surface, equal to 1/10 are (10 square meters or 11.96 square yards).

dec·i·bel (des′ə-bel′), *n.* [*deci-* + *bel*], a unit for measuring the volume of a sound, equal to the logarithm of the ratio of the intensity of the sound to the intensity of an arbitrarily chosen standard sound: abbreviated **db** (no period).

de·cid·a·ble (di-sīd′ə-b′l), *adj.* that can be decided.

de·cide (di-sīd′), *v.t.* [DECIDED (-id), DECIDING], [Fr. *décider;* L. *decidere*, to cut off, decide < *de-*, off, from + *caedere*, to cut], 1. to end (a contest, etc.) or settle (an argument) by giving one side the victory or by passing judgment. 2. to cause to reach a decision. *v.i.* 1. to pass judgment. 2. to reach a decision; make up one's mind.

SYN.—**decide** implies the bringing to an end of vacillation, doubt, dispute, etc. by making up one's mind as to an action, course, or judgment; **determine** in addition suggests that the form, character, functions, scope, etc. of something are precisely fixed (the club *decided* on a lecture series and appointed a committee to *determine* the speakers, the dates, etc.); **settle** stresses finality in a decision, often one arrived at by arbitration, and implies the termination of all doubt or controversy; to **conclude** is to decide after careful investigation or reasoning; **resolve** implies firmness of intention to carry through a decision (he *resolved* to go to bed early every night).

de·cid·ed (di-sīd′id), *adj.* [pp. of *decide*], 1. definite; unmistakable; clear-cut. 2. unhesitating; determined.

de·cid·ed·ly (di-sīd′id-li), *adv.* 1. definitely; unmistakably; certainly. 2. without hesitation; determinedly.

de·cid·u·a (di-sij′ōō-ə, di-sij′ū-ə), *n.* [Mod. L., fem. of *deciduus;* see DECIDUOUS], a membrane formed in the uterus during pregnancy and cast off at childbirth.

de·cid·u·al (di-sij′ōō-əl, di-sij′ū-əl), *adj.* of the decidua.

de·cid·u·ous (di-sij′ōō-əs, di-sij′ū-əs), *adj.* [L. *deciduus* < *decidere*, to fall off < *de-*, off, down + *cadere*, to fall], 1. falling off at a certain season or stage of growth, as some leaves, antlers, the wings of certain insects, etc. 2. shedding leaves annually: opposed to *evergreen*. 3. short-lived; temporary.

dec·i·gram, dec·i·gramme (des′ə-gram′), *n.* [Fr.; see DECI- & GRAM], a metric weight, equal to 1/10 gram (1.5432 grains or .003527 ounce): abbreviated **dg.**

dec·ile (des′il), *n.* [< L. *decem*, ten + *-ile*], in *statistics*, any of the values in a series dividing the distribution of the individuals in the series into ten groups of equal frequency; also, any of these groups.

dec·i·li·ter, dec·i·li·tre (des′ə-lē′tẽr), *n.* [Fr. *décilitre;* see DECI- & LITER], a metric measure of volume, equal to 1/10 liter (3.38 fluid ounces or 6.1025 cubic inches): abbreviated **dl.**

de·cil·lion (di-sil′yən), *n.* [< L. *decem;* + *million*], 1. in the United States and France, 1 followed by 33 zeros. 2. in England and Germany, 1 followed by 60 zeros. *adj.* amounting to one decillion in number.

dec·i·mal (des′ə-m′l), *adj.* [OFr.; ML. *decimalis* < L. *decimus*, tenth < *decem*, ten], of or based upon the number ten; progressing by tens. *n.* a decimal fraction.

decimal fraction, a fraction with an unwritten denominator of ten or some power of ten, indicated by a point (*decimal point*) before the numerator: as, .5 = 5/10.

dec·i·mal·i·za·tion (des′ə-m′l-i-za′shən), *n.* a decimalizing or being decimalized.

dec·i·mal·ize (des′ə-m′l-īz′), *v.t.* [DECIMALIZED (-īzd′), DECIMALIZING], 1. to adopt a decimal system for (currency, etc.). 2. to change into a decimal or decimals.

dec·i·mal·ly (des′ə-mə-li), *adv.* 1. by tens. 2. by means of decimals.

decimal point, a period placed just to the left of a decimal fraction, as in 1.15, 0.9.

decimal system, a system of computation based on the number ten.

dec·i·mate (des′ə-māt′), *v.t.* [DECIMATED (-id), DECIMATING], [< L. *decimatus*, pp. of *decimare* < *decem*, ten], 1. to select by lot and kill every tenth one of; hence, 2. to destroy or kill a large part of: as, they *decimated* the enemy. 3. to take or destroy a tenth part of.

dec·i·ma·tion (des′ə-mā′shən), *n.* [L. *decimatio*], a decimating or being decimated.

dec·i·ma·tor (des′ə-mā′tẽr), *n.* a person or thing that decimates.

dec·i·me·ter, dec·i·me·tre (des′ə-mē′tẽr), *n.* [Fr.; see DECI- & METER], a metric measure of length, equal to 1/10 meter (3.937 inches): abbreviated **dec., decim., dm.**

de·ci·pher (di-sī′fẽr), *v.t.* [*de-* + *cipher*], 1. to translate from secret writing or code into comprehensible terms; decode. 2. to make out the meaning of (ancient inscriptions, blurred writing, etc.).

de·ci·sion (di-sizh′ən), *n.* [Fr. *décision;* L. *decisio*, a cutting short, decision < *decisus*, pp. of *decidere;* see DECIDE], 1. the act of deciding or settling a dispute or question by giving a judgment. 2. the act of making up one's mind. 3. a judgment or conclusion reached or given. 4. determination; firmness of mind: as, a man of *decision*. 5. in *boxing*, a victory on points instead of by a knockout.

de·ci·sive (di-sī′siv), *adj.* [ML. *decisivus* < L. *decisus;* see DECISION], 1. that settles or can settle a dispute, question, etc.; conclusive. 2. having the quality of decision; showing determination or firmness: as, a *decisive* tone of voice.

dec·i·stere (des′ə-stêr′), *n.* [Fr.; see DECI- & STERE], a metric measure of volume, equal to 1/10 cubic meter (3.53 cubic feet).

deck (dek), *n.* [MD. *decke*, *dek*, a covering, roof; akin to *thatch;* IE. base *(*s*)*teg-*, to cover, as in L. *tectum*, a roof; see PROTECT; sense 3 from the idea of one card covering

another], 1. a platform or roof over a section of a ship's hold, serving as a floor. 2. any platform or floor like a ship's deck. 3. a pack of playing cards. Abbreviated **dk.** *v.t.* [MD. *decken*, to hide, cover], 1. to cover or clothe with finery or ornaments; adorn; trim. 2. to furnish (a vessel) with a deck. 3. [Archaic], to cover.
clear the decks, 1. to remove unnecessary things from the decks of a ship, as for combat; hence, 2. to get ready for action.
hit the deck, [Slang], 1. to get out of bed; get up. 2. to get ready for action.
on deck, [Colloq.], 1. ready; on hand. 2. ready to take one's turn, as in some games.

deck chair, a lightweight folding chair, usually with arms and a leg rest, used on ship decks, etc.

-deck·er (dek'ēr), a combining form meaning *having* (a specified number of) *decks, layers*, etc., as in *two-decker, triple-decker*.

Decker, Thomas, Dekker, Thomas.

deck hand, a sailor, especially one who works on deck.

deck·house (dek'hous'), *n.* a small building or cabin erected on the upper deck of a ship.

deck·le, deck·el (dek''l), *n.* [G. *deckel*, dim. of *decke*, a cover; see DECK], in *papermaking*, 1. a wooden frame or curb to guide the pulp into a desired size or width. 2. a deckle edge.

deckle edge, the untrimmed edge of paper made in a deckle.

deck·le-edged (dek''l-ejd'), *adj.* having a deckle edge.

deck load, cargo carried above the upper deck of a ship.

deck tennis, a game somewhat like tennis, in which a small ring of rope, etc. is tossed back and forth over a net: so called because often played on passenger liners.

decl., 1. declension. 2. declensional.

de·claim (di-klām'), *v.i.* [ME. *declamen;* L. *declamare; de-*, intens. + *clamare*, to cry, shout], 1. to speak loudly and rhetorically. 2. to give a recitation, set speech, etc. 3. to attack in an emotional speech (with *against*). *v.t.* to recite or say loudly and rhetorically.

dec·la·ma·tion (dek'lə-mā'shən), *n.* [Fr.; L. *declamatio* < pp. of *declamare;* see DECLAIM], 1. a declaiming or being declaimed. 2. the art of declaiming; giving of formal speeches or recitations. 3. a formal speech, passage of poetry, etc. for declaiming. 4. a harangue; loud, emotional speech.

de·clam·a·to·ry (di-klam'ə-tôr'i, di-klam'ə-tō'ri), *adj.* [L. *declamatorius*], 1. of, characterized by, or fit for declaiming. 2. loud and rhetorical; oratorical.

dec·la·ra·tion (dek'lə-rā'shən), *n.* [ME. *declaracion;* L. *declaratio* < pp. of *declarare;* see DECLARE], 1. a declaring or being declared; announcement. 2. a thing declared. 3. a formal statement; proclamation. 4. a statement of taxable goods: as, a *declaration* at the customs office. 5. in *bezique*, an indication of the combination that a player holds, given by laying the cards face up on the table. 6. in *bridge*, a bid; especially, the winning bid. 7. in *law*, *a)* a statement of the plaintiff's cause for complaint in a court action. *b)* a witness's statement, subject to penalty in case of perjury: distinguished from *oath*. Abbreviated **dec.**

Declaration of Independence, the formal statement, written by Thomas Jefferson and adopted July 4, 1776, by the Second Continental Congress, declaring the thirteen American colonies free and independent of Great Britain: there were fifty-six signers.

de·clar·a·tive (di-klar'ə-tiv), *adj.* [LL. *declarativus;* see DECLARE], making a statement or assertion: as, a *declarative* sentence.

de·clar·a·to·ry (di-klar'ə-tôr'i, di-klar'ə-tō'ri), *adj.* [L. *declaratus*, pp. of *declarare;* + *-ory*], declarative.

de·clare (di-klâr'), *v.t.* [DECLARED (-klârd'), DECLARING], [ME. *declaren;* OFr. *declarer;* L. *declarare* < *de-*, intens. + *clarus*, clear], 1. to make clearly known; state or announce openly, formally, or in definite terms. 2. to show; reveal. 3. to say positively or emphatically. 4. to make a statement of (goods) for taxation. 5. in *bridge*, to bid to play the hand in (a specific suit or no trump). *v.i.* 1. to make a declaration. 2. to state openly a choice, opinion, etc. (with *for* or *against*).
declare oneself, 1. to state strongly one's opinion. 2. to reveal one's true character, identity, etc.
I declare! I am surprised, startled, etc.
SYN.—**declare** implies a making known openly by an explicit or clear statement, often one expressed formally (he *declared* his intention to run for office); to **announce** is to make something of interest known publicly or officially, especially something of the nature of news (to *announce* a sale); to **publish** is to make known through a medium that reaches the general public, now especially the medium of printing; **proclaim** implies official, formal announcement, made with the greatest possible publicity, of something of great moment or significance ("*Proclaim* liberty throughout all the land...."). See also **assert.**

de·clar·ed·ly (di-klâr'id-li), *adv.* in a declared manner; admittedly.

‡dé·clas·sé (dā'klá'sā'), *adj.* [Fr., pp. of *déclasser*, to cause to lose class; see DE- & CLASS], having lost class; lowered in social status.

de·classed (dē-klast', dē-kläst'), *adj.* déclassé.

de·clas·si·fy (dē-klas'ə-fī'), *v.t.* [DECLASSIFIED (-fīd'), DECLASSIFYING], to remove (governmental documents, reports, etc.) from secret or restricted classifications and make available to the public.

de·clen·sion (di-klen'shən), *n.* [prob. via ML. **declensio* < L. *declinatio*, a bending aside (< pp. of *declinare;* see DECLINE), modified in form by association with *descensio*, a going down, descending (see DESCEND)], 1. a bending or moving downward; sloping; descent. 2. a falling off or away; decline; deterioration. 3. a deviation, as from a faith or standard. 4. [Rare], a polite declining or refusal. 5. [see CASE], in *grammar*, *a)* a class of nouns, pronouns, or adjectives showing the same or a similar system of inflections. *b)* the inflection of such words: abbreviated **decl., dec.**

de·clen·sion·al (di-klen'shən-'l), *adj.* in *grammar*, of or connected with declension: abbreviated **decl.**

de·clin·a·ble (di-klīn'ə-b'l), *adj.* in *grammar*, that can be declined; having case inflections.

dec·li·na·tion (dek'lə-nā'shən), *n.* [ME. *declinacion;* L. *declinatio;* see DECLENSION, DECLINE], 1. a bending or sloping downward; deviation from the horizontal or vertical. 2. an oblique variation from some definite direction. 3. the angle that a freely turning magnetic needle makes with the imaginary line pointing to true north. 4. a polite declining or refusal. 5. [Archaic], decline; deterioration; decay. 6. in *astronomy*, the angular distance of a heavenly body north or south from the celestial equator. Abbreviated **dec.**

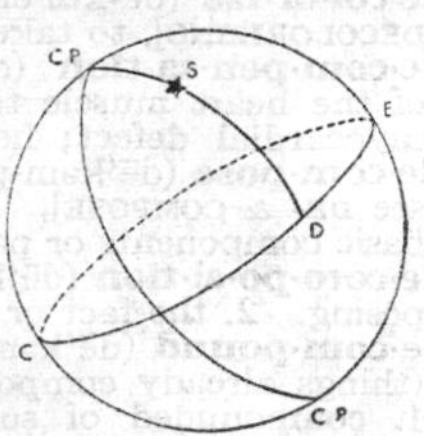

DECLINATION
CE, celestial equator; CP, celestial poles; DS, declination of star S

de·clin·a·to·ry (di-klīn'ə-tôr'i, di-klīn'ə-tō'ri), *adj.* of or expressing declination, or refusal.

de·cline (di-klīn'), *v.i.* [DECLINED (-klīnd'), DECLINING], [ME. *declinen;* OFr. *decliner*, to bend, turn aside; L. *declinare*, to bend from, inflect; *de-*, from + *clinare*, (in comb. only), to bend, incline], 1. to bend or slope downward or aside. 2. to sink, as the setting sun. 3. to lessen in force, health, value, etc.; deteriorate; decay. 4. to refuse something, especially in a polite manner. *v.t.* 1. to cause to bend or slope downward or aside. 2. to refuse, especially politely: as, I must *decline* your offer. 3. in *grammar*, to give the inflected forms of (a noun, pronoun, or adjective). *n.* 1. a declining, falling off or lower; sinking; deterioration; decay. 2. a failing (of health, etc.). 3. a period of decline; hence, 4. the last part: as, the *decline* of life. 5. a wasting disease, especially tuberculosis of the lungs. 6. a downward slope.
SYN.—**decline** implies courtesy in expressing one's nonacceptance of an invitation, proposal, etc. (he *declined* the nomination); **refuse** is a more direct, sometimes even blunt term, implying an emphatic denial of a request, demand, etc. (to *refuse* a person money); **reject** stresses a negative or antagonistic attitude and implies positive refusal to accept, use, believe, etc. (they *rejected* the damaged goods); **repudiate** implies the disowning, disavowal, or casting off with condemnation of a person or thing as having no authority, worth, validity, truth, etc. (to *repudiate* the claims of faith healers); to **spurn** is to refuse or reject with contempt or disdain (she *spurned* his attentions).—*ANT.* accept.

dec·li·nom·e·ter (dek'li-nom'ə-tēr), *n.* [see DECLINE & -METER,] an instrument for measuring declination.

de·cliv·i·tous (di-kliv'ə-təs), *adj.* [L. *declivitas* (see DECLIVITY); + *-ous*], fairly steep.

de·cliv·i·ty (di-kliv'ə-ti), *n.* [*pl.* DECLIVITIES (-tiz)], [L. *declivitas* < *declivis*, a sloping downward < *de-*, down, from + *clivus*, a slope, hill (akin to Goth. *hlaiw*, grave mound < IE. **kloi-wos*)], a downward slope or sloping, as of a hill: opposed to *acclivity*.

de·cli·vous (di-klī'vəs), *adj.* having a declivity.

de·coct (di-kokt'), *v.t.* [< L. *decoctus*, pp. of *decoquere*, to boil down; *de-*, down + *coquere*, to cook], to extract the essence, flavor, etc. of by boiling.

de·coc·tion (di-kok'shən), *n.* 1. a decocting or being decocted. 2. an extract produced by decocting.

de·code (dē-kōd'), *v.t.* [DECODED (-id), DECODING], to translate (something written in code) into comprehensible language.

de·cod·er (dē-kōd'ēr), *n.* 1. a person who deciphers messages written in code. 2. a device that automatically decodes scrambled messages sent by telephone.

de·co·here (dē'kō-hêr'), *v.t.* & *v.i.* [*de-* + *cohere*], in *electricity*, to change back to the normal condition of sensitivity: said of a coherer.

de·co·her·er (dē'kō-hêr'ēr), *n.* in *electricity*, a vibrating device for changing a coherer back to its normal condition of sensitivity after a current has gone through it.

de·co·he·sion (dē'kō-hē'zhən), *n.* a decohering or being decohered.

de·col·late (di-kol'āt), *v.t.* [DECOLLATED (-id), DECOLLATING], [< L. *decollatus*, pp. of *decollare*, to behead < *de-*, from + *collum*, the neck], to behead.

de·col·la·tion (dē'kə-lā'shən), *n.* [L. *decollatio;* see DECOLLATE], a beheading or being beheaded.

de·col·la·tor (dē'kə-lā'tēr), *n.* a person or thing that decollates.

‡**dé·col·le·tage** (dā'kôl'täzh'), *n.* [Fr. < *décolleter;* see DÉCOLLETÉ], 1. the neckline of a dress cut low so as to bare the neck and shoulders. 2. a décolleté dress, etc.

dé·col·le·té (dā'kol-tā', dā'ko-lə-tā'; Fr. dā'kôl'tā'), *adj.* [Fr., pp. of *décolleter*, to bare one's neck and shoulders < *dé-* (L. *de*), from + *collet*, dim. of *col*, collar, neck < L. *collum*, the neck], 1. cut low so as to bare the neck and shoulders, as some dresses. 2. wearing a décolleté dress, etc.

de·col·or (dē-kul'ēr), *v.t.* to decolorize.

de·col·or·ant (dē-kul'ēr-ənt), *adj.* decolorizing; bleaching. *n.* a substance that decolorizes; bleach.

de·col·or·ize (dē-kul'ēr-īz'), *v.t.* [DECOLORIZED (-īzd'), DECOLORIZING], to take the color out of; bleach.

de·com·pen·sa·tion (dē-kom'pən-sā'shən), *n.* failure of the heart muscle to compensate for a valvular or myocardial defect; heart failure.

de·com·pose (dē'kəm-pōz'), *v.t. & v.i.* [Fr. *décomposer;* see DE- & COMPOSE], 1. to break up or separate into basic components or parts. 2. to rot. —*SYN.* see **decay.**

de·com·po·si·tion (dē'kom-pə-zish'ən), *n.* 1. a decomposing. 2. the fact or state of being decomposed.

de·com·pound (dē'kəm-pound'), *v.t.* 1. to compound (things already compounded). 2. to decompose. *adj.* 1. compounded of substances already compounded. 2. in *botany*, having or made up of parts that are themselves compound, as some leaves.

de·com·press (dē'kəm-pres'), *v.t.* 1. to free from pressure. 2. to free (a worker in compressed air) from compression or air pressure by means of an air lock.

de·com·pres·sion (dē'kəm-presh'ən), *n.* 1. release from pressure. 2. the lowering of air pressure on deep-sea divers, tunnel workers, etc. 3. a surgical operation to relieve excessive pressure in the cranium: a flap of the skull is removed and replaced with a metal plate.

decompression sickness, a condition caused by the formation of air bubbles in the blood or body tissues as the result of a sudden lowering of pressure, as in deep-sea divers returning to the surface too quickly: it is characterized by tightness in the chest, pains in the joints, and convulsions and collapse in severe cases: commonly called *caisson disease, bends, diver's disease, tunnel disease.*

de·con·tam·i·nate (dē'kən-tam'ə-nāt'), *v.t.* to rid of a polluting or harmful substance, as poison gas.

de·con·trol (dē'kən-trōl'), *v.t.* [DECONTROLLED (-trōld'), DECONTROLLING], to free from controls. *n.* a decontrolling or being decontrolled.

dé·cor (dā-kôr'), *n.* [Fr.; L. *decor*, beauty, elegance, ornament < *decere*, to befit, be suitable], 1. decoration. 2. the decorative scheme of a room, stage set, etc.

dec·or·ate (dek'ə-rāt'), *v.t.* [DECORATED (-id), DECORATING], [< L. *decoratus*, pp. of *decorare*, to decorate, adorn < *decus*, an ornament], 1. to add something to so as to make more attractive; adorn; ornament. 2. to plan and furnish a color scheme, drapes, etc. for. 3. to paint or wallpaper: as, *decorate* a room. 4. to give a medal or similar sign of honor to: as, he was *decorated* for heroism. *v.i.* to put decorations on something; decorate a room, house, etc. —*SYN.* see **adorn.**

dec·o·ra·tion (dek'ə-rā'shən), *n.* [LL. *decoratio*], 1. a decorating. 2. the fact or state of being decorated. 3. anything used for decorating; ornament. 4. a medal, badge, or similar sign of honor.

Decoration Day, Memorial Day.

dec·o·ra·tive (dek'ə-rā'tiv, dek'ə-rə-tiv), *adj.* decorating; used for decorating; ornamental.

dec·o·ra·tor (dek'ə-rā'tēr), *n.* a person who decorates; specifically, an interior decorator.

dec·o·rous (dek'ə-rəs, di-kôr'əs, di-kō'rəs), *adj.* [L. *decorus*, becoming < *decor;* see DÉCOR], characterized by or showing decorum, propriety, good taste, etc.

de·cor·ti·cate (di-kôr'tə-kāt'), *v.t.* [< L. *decorticatus*, pp. of *decorticare* < *de-*, from + *cortex*, bark], to remove the bark, husk, or peel from.

de·cor·ti·ca·tor (di-kôr'tə-kā'tēr), *n.* a tool or machine for decorticating.

de·co·rum (di-kôr'əm, di-kō'rəm), *n.* [*pl.* DECORUMS (-əmz, -rəmz), DECORA (-ə, -rə)], [L., neut. of *decorus*, fit, proper < *decor;* see DÉCOR], 1. whatever is suitable or proper; propriety; congruity. 2. propriety and good taste in behavior, speech, dress, etc. 3. *often in pl.* an act or requirement of polite behavior.

SYN.—**decorum** implies stiffness or formality in rules of conduct or behavior established as suitable to the circumstances (levity not in keeping with *decorum*); **decency** implies observance of the requirements of modesty, good taste, etc. (have the *decency* to thank her); **propriety** suggests conformity with conventional standards of proper or correct behavior, manners, etc. (his offensive language oversteps the bounds of *propriety*); **dignity**, in this connection, implies conduct in keeping with one's position or one's self-respect; **etiquette** refers to the forms established by convention or prescribed by social arbiters for behavior in polite society.

de·coy (di-koi'; *also, for n.,* dē'koi), *n.* [earlier *coy* < D. *kooi*, a cage; W. Gmc. **kawia* < L. *cavea* < *cavus* (see CAVE); *de-* ? < D. article in *de kooi*, the cage], 1. a place into which wild ducks, etc. are lured for capture. 2. an artificial or trained bird or animal used to lure game to a place where it can be shot. 3. a thing or person used to lure or tempt into danger or a trap: as, a police *decoy*. *v.t. & v.i.* to lure or be lured into a trap, danger, etc. —*SYN.* see **lure.**

de·crease (di-krēs', dē'krēs'; *for n., usually* dē'krēs), *v.i. & v.t.* [DECREASED (-krēst'), DECREASING], [ME. *decresen;* OFr. *decreistre;* L. *decrescere; de-*, from, away + *crescere*, to grow, increase], to become or cause to become gradually less, smaller, etc.; diminish. *n.* 1. a decreasing; lessening; diminution. 2. amount of decreasing. Abbreviated **dec.**

on the decrease, decreasing.

SYN.—**decrease** and **dwindle** suggest a growing gradually smaller in bulk, size, volume, or number, but **dwindle** emphasizes a wasting away to the point of disappearance (his hopes *decreased* as his fortune *dwindled* away to nothing); **lessen** is equivalent to **decrease,** except that it does not imply any particular rate of decline (his influence *lessened* overnight); **diminish** emphasizes subtraction from the whole by some external agent (disease had *diminished* their ranks); **reduce** implies a lowering, or bringing down (to *reduce* prices).—*ANT.* increase.

de·cree (di-krē'), *n.* [ME. *decre;* OFr. *decret;* L. *decretum*, neut. of *decretus*, pp. of *decernere*, to decree; *de-*, from + *cernere*, to see, judge], 1. an official order, edict, or decision, as of a church, government, etc. 2. anything settled and unchangeable: as, a *decree* of fate. *v.t.* [DECREED (-krēd'), DECREEING], to order, decide, or appoint by decree or officially. *v.i.* to issue a decree.

dec·re·ment (dek'rə-mənt), *n.* [LL. *decrementum* < L. *decrescere;* see DECREASE], 1. a decreasing or decrease; loss; waste. 2. amount lost by decrease or waste: opposed to *increment*. 3. in *mathematics*, the quantity by which a variable decreases or is decreased.

de·crep·it (di-krep'it), *adj.* [Fr. *décrépit;* L. *decrepitus: de-*, intens. + *crepitus*, pp. of *crepere*, to creak, rattle; akin to Sans. *kṛpatē*, I wail, cry; ON. *hrafn*, raven; Cym. *cre, dychre*, cry, clamor], broken down or worn out by old age, illness, or long use. —*SYN.* see **weak.**

de·crep·i·tate (di-krep'ə-tāt'), *v.t.* [DECREPITATED (-id), DECREPITATING], [< *de-*, intens. + L. *crepitatus*, pp. of *crepitare*, to crackle, rattle, break with a noise < *crepere;* see DECREPIT], to roast or calcine (salts, minerals, etc.) until a crackling sound is caused or until this stops. *v.i.* to crackle when exposed to heat.

de·crep·i·ta·tion (di-krep'ə-tā'shən), *n.* 1. the process of decrepitating or being decrepitated. 2. a crackling noise caused by exposure of salts, etc. to heat.

de·crep·i·tude (di-krep'ə-to͞od', di-krep'ə-tūd'), *n.* [Fr. *décrépitude*], the condition of being decrepit; feebleness; infirmity, as from age.

de·cre·scen·do (dē'krə-shen'dō; It. de'kre-shen'dô), *adj. & adv.* [It.], in *music*, with a gradual decrease in loudness or intensity; diminuendo: abbreviated **decresc.** or indicated by the sign >. *n.* [*pl.* DESCRESCENDOS (-dōz)], in *music*, 1. a gradual decrease in loudness or intensity. 2. a passage played decrescendo.

de·cres·cent (di-kres''nt), *adj.* [L. *decrescens*, ppr. of *decrescere;* see DECREASE], decreasing; lessening; waning, as the moon in its final quarter.

de·cre·tal (di-krē't'l), *adj.* [Fr. *décrétal;* LL. *decretalis*], of or containing a decree. *n.* 1. a decree. 2. in the *Roman Catholic Church, a)* a decree by the Pope on a question of doctrine or ecclesiastical law. *b) usually pl.* a collection of such decrees forming a part of canon law.

de·cre·tist (di-krē'tist), *n.* [ML. *decretista* < L. *decretum;* see DECREE], an expert in canon law.

de·cre·tive (di-krē'tiv), *adj.* 1. of a decree. 2. having the power of a decree.

dec·re·to·ry (dek'rə-tôr'i, dek'rə-tō'ri), *adj.* [LL. *decretorius*], 1. having the nature of a decree. 2. of, involving, or settled by a decree.

de·cri·al (di-krī'əl), *n.* a decrying; noisy condemnation.

de·cry (di-krī'), *v.t.* [DECRIED (-krīd'), DECRYING], [Fr. *décrier;* OFr. *descrier;* see DE- & CRY], 1. to denounce or condemn openly; censure: as, we *decry* religious intolerance. 2. to depreciate (money, etc.) officially. —*SYN.* see **disparage.**

dec·u·man (dek'yoo-mən), *adj.* [L. *decumanus*, lit., of the tenth part, considerable, large < *decimus;* see DECIMAL], very large: as, a *decuman* wave: from the notion that every tenth wave was the largest.

de·cum·ben·cy (di-kum'bən-si), *n.* a decumbent condition or position.

de·cum·bent (di-kum'bənt), *adj.* [L. *decumbens*, ppr. of *decumbere*, to lie down < *de-*, down + *cumbere* (in comb. only), *cubare*, to recline, lie down], 1. lying down. 2. in *botany*, trailing on the ground and rising at the tip, as some stems.

dec·u·ple (dek'yoo-p'l), ***adj.*** [Fr. *décuple* < L. *decuplus*, tenfold < *decem*, ten + *plus*, more], 1. ten times as large; tenfold. 2. in tens. ***n.*** a number or quantity ten times as large as another one, or repeated ten times. ***v.t.*** [DECUPLED (-p'ld), DECUPLING], to make tenfold; multiply by ten.

de·cu·ri·on (di-kyoor'-ən), ***n.*** [L. *decurio* < *decuria*, company of ten men < *decem*, ten], in *Roman history*, 1. an officer having charge of ten men. 2. a member of a municipal or colonial senate.

de·cur·rent (di-kŭr'ənt), ***adj.*** [L. *decurrens*, ppr. of *decurrere* < *de-*, down + *currere*, to run], in *botany*, extending down along the stem, as the base of some leaves.

dec·u·ry (dek'yoo-ri), ***n.*** [*pl.* DECURIES (-riz)], [L. *decuria*, a group of ten], in *Roman history*, 1. the group commanded by a decurion. 2. any of various divisions or classes, as of the judges, the curiae, etc.

de·cus·sate (di-kus'āt; *also, for adj.*, di-kus'it), ***v.t. & v.i.*** [DECUSSATED (-id), DECUSSATING], [< L. *decussatus*, pp. of *decussare*, to cross in the form of an X < *decussis*, the figure ten (X) < *decem*, ten], to cross or cut so as to form an X; intersect. ***adj.*** 1. decussated. 2. in *botany*, arranged in pairs growing at right angles to those above and below: said of leaves or branches.

DECUSSATE LEAVES

de·cus·sa·tion (dē'kə-sā'shən), ***n.*** [L. *decussatio*], 1. a decussating or being decussated. 2. an intersection like an X.

de·dal (dē'd'l), ***adj.*** daedal.

De·da·li·an, De·da·le·an (di-dā'li-ən), ***adj.*** Daedalian.

De·de A·gach (de-de' ä-gäch'), Alexandroupolis, Greece: the former name: also written **Dedeagach.**

ded·i·cate (ded'ə-kāt'), ***v.t.*** [DEDICATED (-id), DEDICATING], [< L. *dedicatus*, pp. of *dedicare*, to consecrate, declare; *de-*, intens. + *dicare*, to proclaim, make known < *dicere*, to say, speak], 1. to set apart for a deity or religious purpose; devote to something sacred. 2. to set apart for a special purpose; devote to some work, duty, etc. 3. to address or inscribe (a book, artistic performance, etc.) to someone as a sign of honor, affection, etc. 4. to open formally (a public building, fair, etc.). 5. in *law*, to devote (land, etc.) to public use. ***adj.*** (ded'ə-kit), [Poetic & Archaic], dedicated. —***SYN.*** see **devote.**

ded·i·ca·tion (ded'ə-kā'shən), ***n.*** [L. *dedicatio*], 1. a dedicating or being dedicated. 2. an inscription in a book, etc., dedicating it to a person or cause.

ded·i·ca·tive (ded'ə-kā'tiv), ***adj.*** dedicatory.

ded·i·ca·tor (ded'ə-kā'tẽr), ***n.*** [L.], one who dedicates.

ded·i·ca·to·ry (ded'ə-kə-tôr'i, ded'ə-kə-tō'ri), ***adj.*** of or as a dedication.

de·duce (di-dōōs', di-dūs'), ***v.t.*** [DEDUCED (-dōōst', -dūst'), DEDUCING], [L. *deducere*, to lead or draw down, bring away; *de-*, down, away + *ducere*, to lead], 1. to trace the course or derivation of. 2. to infer from a general principle by deductive reasoning. 3. to conclude by reasoning. —***SYN.*** see **infer.**

de·duc·i·ble (di-dōōs'ə-b'l, di-dūs'ə-b'l), ***adj.*** that can be deduced.

de·duct (di-dukt'), ***v.t.*** [< L. *deductus*, pp. of *deducere*; see DEDUCE], to take away or subtract (a quantity).

de·duct·i·ble (di-duk'tə-b'l), ***adj.*** that can be deducted.

de·duc·tion (di-duk'shən), ***n.*** [L. *deductio*], 1. a deducting or being deducted; subtraction. 2. the sum or amount deducted. 3. in *logic*, *a)* the act or process of deducing; reasoning from a known principle to an unknown, from the general to the specific, or from a premise to a logical conclusion. *b)* a conclusion so deduced. Opposed to *induction* (in sense 2).

de·duc·tive (di-duk'tiv), ***adj.*** [L. *deductivus*], 1. of or based on deduction. 2. reasoning by deduction.

de·duc·tive·ly (di-duk'tiv-li), ***adv.*** by deductive reasoning.

Dee (dē), ***n.*** 1. a river in northeastern Scotland: length, 90 mi. 2. a river in northern Wales and England: length, 70 mi.

deed (dēd), ***n.*** [ME. *deed, dede;* akin to G. *tat* (OHG. *teta*), OD. *dede*, ON. *dāth*, Goth. *dēds;* all < base of *do*, *v.*], 1. a thing done; act. 2. a feat of courage, skill, etc. 3. action; doing. 4. in *law*, a document under seal that states a contract, transfer of property, etc. ***v.t.*** to transfer (property, etc.) by such a document.
in deed, in fact; really.

deem (dēm), ***v.t. & v.i.*** [ME. *demen;* AS. *deman*, to doom < *dom;* see DOOM], to think; believe; judge.

deem·ster (dēm'stẽr), ***n.*** [ME. *demester;* see DEEM & -STER], either of the two chief judges of the Isle of Man.

deep (dēp), ***adj.*** [ME. *deep, depe;* AS. *deop;* akin to G. *tief*, Goth. *diups;* IE. base **dheub-*, deep and hollow, as also in *dip, dump*], 1. extending far downward from the top or top edges, inward from the surface, backward from the front, or far to the sides or edge. 2. extending thus for a specified length or distance: as, eight feet *deep*. 3. placed far down or back. 4. coming from far down or back. 5. hard to understand; abstruse. 6. serious; extreme: as, *deep* disgrace. 7. strongly felt: as, *deep* love. 8. wise. 9. tricky and sly. 10. dark and rich: said of colors. 11. sunk in or absorbed by (with *in*): as, he was *deep* in thought. 12. great in degree; intense; profound: as, a *deep* sleep. 13. much involved: as, *deep* in debt. 14. of low pitch: said of sound. ***n.*** [ME. *deepe;* AS. *deop*, deep sea < the *adj.*], 1. a deep place, as in water or earth. 2. the extent of space, time, the unknown, etc. 3. the middle part; part that is darkest, most silent, etc.: as, in the *deep* of night. 4. in *nautical usage*, any unmarked point between two consecutive fathom marks on a sounding line. ***adv.*** [AS. *deope*], deeply; far down, far in, far back, far on, etc. —***SYN.*** see **broad.**
go off the deep end, 1. to dive or jump into deep water; hence, 2. [Colloq.], to plunge rashly into an enterprise. 3. [Colloq.], to become angry or excited.
the deep, [Poetic], the sea or ocean.

deep-chest·ed (dēp'ches'tid), ***adj.*** having or from a thick chest: as, a *deep-chested* roar.

deep-dish pie (dēp'dish'), a fruit pie baked in a deep dish and having only a top crust.

deep-dyed (dēp'dīd'), ***adj.*** 1. stained throughout. 2. thoroughgoing; unmitigated: as, a *deep-dyed* villain.

deep·en (dēp''n), ***v.t. & v.i.*** to make or become deep or deeper.

deep-freeze (dēp'frēz'), ***n.*** a refrigerator for keeping perishable foods at a very low temperature for long periods of time: a trade-mark (**Deepfreeze**). ***v.t.*** to put or keep (foods) in such a refrigerator.

deep-fry (dēp'frī'), ***v.t.*** [DEEP-FRIED (-frīd'), DEEP-FRYING], to fry in a deep pan of boiling fat.

deep-laid (dēp'lād'), ***adj.*** carefully worked out and kept secret: as, *deep-laid* plans.

deep-root·ed (dēp'rōōt'id, dēp'root'id), ***adj.*** 1. having deep roots; hence, 2. firmly established; hard to remove: as, *deep-rooted* prejudice.

deep-sea (dēp'sē'), ***adj.*** in or of the deeper parts of the sea: as, *deep-sea* fishing.

deep-seat·ed (dēp'sēt'id), ***adj.*** 1. placed or originating far beneath the surface; hence, 2. firmly established; hard to remove.

deep-set (dēp'set'), ***adj.*** 1. deeply set. 2. firmly established.

deep South, that region of the United States considered most typically Southern, including generally the southernmost parts of Georgia, Alabama, Mississippi, and Louisiana.

deer (dêr), ***n.*** [*pl.* DEER, *occas.* DEERS (dêrz)], [ME. *dere, deer;* AS. *deor*, wild animal; akin to G. *tier;* IE. base **dhewes-*, **dheus-*, etc. (as in L. *bestia* < IE. **dhwēs-dhiā*) in the sense "to breathe"; for the sense, cf. L. *anima*, breath, Eng. *animal*], 1. any of a family of hoofed, cud-chewing animals, as the moose, reindeer, caribou, etc., the males of which usually bear antlers that are shed annually: popularly used only of the smaller species of this family. 2. [Obs.], any animal; beast.

deer·fly (dêr'flī'), ***n.*** [*pl.* DEERFLIES (-flīz')], any of a group of blood-sucking flies related to the horsefly, but smaller and with mottled wings.

deer·hound (dêr'hound'), ***n.*** any of a Scottish breed of large, shaggy-haired dog, used in hunting deer.

deer lick, any damp, salty place where deer come to lick the salty earth.

deer mouse, 1. a small, white-footed mouse. 2. a light-brown jumping mouse. Both are American varieties.

deer·skin (dêr'skin'), ***n.*** 1. the hide of a deer. 2. leather made from this. ***adj.*** made of deerskin.

deer·stalk·er (dêr'stôk'ẽr), ***n.*** 1. a hunter who stalks deer. 2. a hunter's tight-fitting cap with a low crown.

deer·stalk·ing (dêr'stôk'iŋ), ***n.*** the hunting of deer by stalking.

def., 1. defendant. 2. defense. 3. deferred. 4. defined. 5. definite. 6. definition.

de·face (di-fās'), ***v.t.*** [DEFACED (-fāst'), DEFACING], [ME. *defacen;* OFr. *desfacier;* see DE- & FACE], 1. to spoil the appearance of; disfigure; mar. 2. to make illegible by injuring the surface of.

de·face·ment (di-fās'mənt), ***n.*** 1. a defacing or being defaced. 2. a thing that defaces.

‡**de fac·to** (dē fak'tō), [L.], in fact; actual (regardless of legal or moral considerations): as, *de facto* government: distinguished from *de jure*.

de·fal·cate (di-fal'kāt, di-fôl'kāt), ***v.i.*** [DEFALCATED (-id), DEFALCATING], [< ML. *defalcatus*, pp. of *defalcare*, to cut off < L. *de-*, from + *falx, falcis*, a sickle], to steal or misuse funds entrusted to one's care; embezzle.

de·fal·ca·tion (dē'fal-kā'shən, dē'fôl-kā'shən), ***n.*** [ML. *defalcatio;* see DEFALCATE], 1. the act of stealing or misusing funds entrusted to one's care; embezzlement. 2. the amount thus stolen or misused.

de·fal·ca·tor (di-fal'kā-tẽr, di-fôl'kā-tẽr), *n.* a person who defalcates; embezzler.

def·a·ma·tion (def'ə-mā'shən, dē'fə-mā'shən), *n.* a defaming or being defamed; calumny; slander or libel.

de·fam·a·to·ry (di-fam'ə-tôr'i, di-fam'ə-tō'ri), *adj.* [ML. *diffamatorius*], defaming or tending to defame.

de·fame (di-fām'), *v.t.* [DEFAMED (-fāmd'), DEFAMING], [ME. *defamen, diffamen;* OFr. *diffamer* or ML. *defamere, diffamere;* both < L. *diffamare,* to malign, defame < *dis-,* from + *fama;* see FAME], to attack the reputation of; calumniate; slander or libel.

de·fault (di-fôlt'), *n.* [ME. *defaulte;* OFr. *defaute* < L. *de-,* away + *fallere,* to fail, deceive], 1. failure to do something or be somewhere when required: as, he lost the tennis match by *default.* 2. failure to pay money due. 3. failure to appear in court to defend or prosecute a case. *v.i.* [ME. *defauten;* OFr. *defauter;* see the *n.*], 1. to fail to do something or be somewhere when required. 2. to fail to make payment when due. 3. to fail to appear in court. 4. to fail to take part in or finish a contest. 5. to lose by default. *v.t.* 1. to fail to do or pay (something) when required. 2. to fail to take part in or finish (a contest). 3. to lose (a contest, etc.) by default; forfeit.

in default of, in the absence of; through lack of.

de·fault·er (di-fôl'tẽr), *n.* 1. a person who defaults. 2. a defalcator; embezzler. 3. [British], a soldier guilty of a military offense.

de·fea·sance (di-fē'z'ns), *n.* [OFr. *defesance* < *defesant,* ppr. of *defaire, desfaire;* see DEFEAT], 1. the annulment of a contract or deed. 2. a clause stating a condition the fulfillment of which makes the deed, contract, etc. void in whole or in part.

de·fea·si·ble (di-fē'zə-b'l), *adj.* [see DEFEASANCE & -IBLE], that can be undone or made void.

de·feat (di-fēt'), *v.t.* [ME. *defeiten* < *defet,* dejected; OFr. *desfait,* pp. of *desfaire,* to undo; LL. *disfacere;* L. *dis-,* from + *facere,* to do], 1. to win victory over; overcome; beat. 2. to bring to nothing; frustrate. 3. to make null and void. 4. [Obs.], to undo; destroy. *n.* [< the *v.;* prob. after Fr. *défaite*], a defeating or being defeated; failure to win or succeed, frustration, etc. —***SYN.*** see **conquer.**

de·feat·ism (di-fēt'iz'm), *n.* the actions or state of mind of a defeatist.

de·feat·ist (di-fēt'ist), *n.* [Fr. *défaitiste*], a person who too readily accepts defeat for himself or his side, and acts accordingly. *adj.* of or characteristic of a defeatist.

de·fea·ture (di-fē'chẽr), *n.* [Early Mod. Eng.; OFr. *deffaiture* < *desfaire;* cf. DEFEAT], 1. [Archaic], disfigurement. 2. [Obs.], defeat or frustration.

def·e·cate (def'ə-kāt'), *v.t.* [DEFECATED (-id), DEFECATING], [< L. *defaecatus,* pp. of *defaecare,* to cleanse from dregs, strain < *de-,* from + *faex, faecis,* grounds, dregs], to remove impurities from; refine (sugar, wine, etc.) *v.i.* 1. to become free from impurities. 2. to excrete waste matter from the bowels.

def·e·ca·tion (def'ə-kā'shən), *n.* [L. *defaecatio*], the act or process of defecating.

def·e·ca·tor (def'ə-kā'tẽr), *n.* [see DEFECATE], a person or thing that defecates; specifically, an apparatus for removing impure matter, as in sugar refining.

de·fect (di-fekt', dē'fekt), *n.* [L. *defectus* < *deficere,* to undo, fail < *de-,* from + *facere,* to do], 1. lack of something necessary for completeness; shortcoming. 2. an imperfection; fault; flaw; blemish. *v.i.* (di-fekt'), to forsake a party, cause, etc.; desert.

SYN.—**defect** implies a lack of something essential to completeness or perfection (a *defect* in vision); an **imperfection** is any faulty detail that detracts from perfection (minor *imperfections* of style); a **blemish** is a superficial or surface imperfection that mars the appearance (skin *blemishes*); a **flaw** is an imperfection in structure or substance, such as a crack or gap, that mars the wholeness or continuity (a *flaw* in a metal bar).

de·fec·tion (di-fek'shən), *n.* [L. *defectio* < *defectus;* see DEFECT], 1. a failing; failure. 2. abandonment of loyalty, duty, principle, etc.; desertion.

de·fec·tive (di-fek'tiv), *adj.* [Fr. *défectif*], 1. having a defect or defects; incomplete; faulty. 2. in *grammar,* lacking some of the usual grammatical forms: as, *ought* is a *defective* verb. 3. subnormal in intelligence, memory, etc. *n.* 1. a person with some bodily or mental defect. 2. in *grammar,* a defective word.

de·fence (di-fens'), *n.* defense: British spelling.

de·fend (di-fend'), *v.t.* [ME. *defenden;* OFr. *defendre* (Fr. *défendre*); L. *defendere,* to ward off, repel; *de-,* away, from + *fendere,* to strike], 1. to guard from attack; keep from harm or danger; protect. 2. to support or maintain by speech or act. 3. to try to justify: as, he *defended* his conduct. 4. in *law, a*) to oppose (an action, etc.). *b*) to plead (one's cause) in defense. *c*) to act for (an accused). *v.i.* to make a defense.

SYN.—**defend** implies an active effort to repel an actual attack or invasion (to *defend* oneself in court); **guard** suggests a watching over to keep safe from any potential attack or harm (to *guard* a coast line); **protect** and **shield** imply a keeping safe from harm or injury by interposing a barrier (he built a fence to *protect* his garden), but **shield** also connotes a present or imminent attack or harmful agency (to *shield* one's eyes against a glare); **preserve** implies a keeping safe from encroaching deterioration or decay (to *preserve* civil liberties).—***ANT.*** attack.

de·fend·ant (di-fen'dənt), *adj.* [Fr. *défendant,* ppr. of *défendre*], defending. *n.* in *law,* the defending party; person sued or accused: opposed to *plaintiff:* abbreviated **def., deft.**

de·fend·er (di-fen'dẽr), *n.* one who defends; protector.

Defender of the Faith, a hereditary title of English sovereigns, first conferred upon Henry VIII by Pope Leo X (1521): abbreviated **D.F., F.D.**

de·fen·es·tra·tion (dē-fen'ə-strā'shən), *n.* [*de-* + *fenestration*], a throwing or being thrown out of a window.

de·fense (di-fens'), *n.* [ME.; OFr. < L. *defensus,* pp. of *defendere*], 1. a defending; guarding against attack; keeping from harm or danger. 2. the fact or state of being defended. 3. something that defends; means of defense. 4. justification or support by speech or writing. 5. an argument to justify or vindicate. 6. self-protection, as by boxing. 7. the side that is defending in any contest. 8. *a*) the arguments of the defendant or his lawyer in contesting a case. *b*) the defendant and his lawyer or lawyers, collectively. Abbreviated **def.**

de·fense·less (di-fens'lis), *adj.* lacking defense; unable to defend oneself; open to attack; helpless; unprotected.

defense mechanism (or **reaction**), 1. any self-protective physiological reaction of an organism. 2. in *psychology,* any behavior pattern in which there is an unconscious tendency to keep from oneself or others unpleasant or uncomfortable feelings, memories, etc.

de·fen·si·ble (di-fen'sə-b'l), *adj.* [ME. & OFr. *defensable;* L. *defensabilis* < *defensare* < *defendere;* see DEFEND], 1. that can be defended or protected. 2. that can be justified.

de·fen·sive (di-fen'siv), *adj.* [Fr. *défensif;* ML. *defensivus* < L. *defensus;* see DEFENSE], 1. defending. 2. of or for defense. *n.* 1. [Obs.], something that defends. 2. attitude, position, or operation of defense (often with *the*).

de·fer (di-fũr'), *v.t. & v.i.* [DEFERRED (-fũrd'), DEFERRING], [ME. *differren;* OFr. *differer;* see DIFFER], to put off to a future time; postpone; delay.

de·fer (di-fũr'), *v.i.* [DEFERRED (-fũrd'), DEFERRING], [Fr. *déférer,* to yield, impeach in court, pay deference to; L. *deferre,* to bring down; *de-,* down + *ferre,* to bear], to submit in opinion or judgment; yield with courtesy; be respectful: as, he *defers* to his father's decisions. —***SYN.*** see **yield.**

def·er·ence (def'ẽr-əns), *n.* [Fr. *déférence* < L. *deferens,* ppr. of *deferre;* see DEFER (to submit)], 1. a yielding in opinion, judgment, wishes, etc. 2. courteous regard or respect. —***SYN.*** see **honor.**

in deference to, because of regard or respect for (a person, his wishes, position, etc.).

def·er·ent (def'ẽr-ənt), *adj.* showing deference.

def·er·ent (def'ẽr-ənt), *adj.* [Fr. *déférent;* L. *deferens,* ppr. of *deferre;* see DEFER (to submit)], 1. carrying down or out. 2. in *anatomy,* carrying fluids, impulses, etc. away from an organ or part.

def·er·en·tial (def'ẽr-en'shəl), *adj.* showing deference; very respectful.

de·fer·ment (di-fũr'mənt), *n.* [see DEFER (to postpone)], postponement; putting off; delay.

de·ferred (di-fũrd'), *adj.* [pp. of *defer* (to postpone)], 1. postponed. 2. with rights, interest, etc. withheld until a certain date: as, a *deferred* annuity. 3. classified as not subject to immediate induction into the armed forces.

de·fer·rer (di-fũr'ẽr), *n.* a person who defers; postponer.

de·fi·ance (di-fī'əns), *n.* [ME. *defiaunce;* OFr. *defiance* < *defier;* see DEFY], 1. a defying; open, bold resistance to authority or opposition. 2. a challenge.

bid defiance to, to defy.

in defiance of, 1. defying. 2. in spite of.

set at defiance, to defy.

de·fi·ant (di-fī'ənt), *adj.* [Fr. *défiant,* ppr. of *défier*], full of defiance; challenging; openly and boldly resisting.

de·fi·cien·cy (di-fish'ən-si), *n.* [LL. *deficientia* < L. *deficiens,* ppr. of *deficere,* to lack, fail < *de-,* from + *facere,* to do], 1. the quality or state of being deficient; absence of something essential; incompleteness. 2. [*pl.* DEFICIENCIES (-siz)], *a*) a shortage. *b*) the amount of shortage; deficit.

deficiency disease, a disease, as rickets, scurvy, or pellagra, caused by a lack of vitamins, etc. in the diet.

deficiency judgment, in *law,* a judgment in favor of a mortgagee for the remainder of a debt not completely cleared by foreclosure of the mortgage.

de·fi·cient (di-fish'ənt), *adj.* [L. *deficiens;* see DEFICIENCY], 1. lacking in some essential; incomplete; defective. 2. inadequate in amount, quality, degree, etc.; not sufficient. *n.* a deficient person or thing.

def·i·cit (def'ə-sit), *n.* [L., there is lacking, 3d pers. sing., pres. indic., of *deficere,* to be wanting: from use as first word in inventory clauses], the amount by which a sum of money is less than what is expected, due, needed, etc.; shortage.

‡**de fi·de** (dē fī'di), [L.], of the faith: used in the Roman Catholic Church to designate a truth regarded as revealed.

de·fi·er (di-fī'ẽr), *n.* a person who defies.

def·i·lade (def'ə-lād'; *also, for n.,* def'ə-läd'), *v.t. & v.i.* [DEFILADED (-id), DEFILADING], [< Fr. *défilade*, a filing off, succession < *défiler;* see DEFILE (to march in file)], to arrange (troops and fortifications) so that the terrain will protect them, especially from enfilading fire. *n.* 1. the act of defilading. 2. the protection or concealment afforded by defilading.

de·file (di-fīl'), *v.t.* [DEFILED (-fīld'), DEFILING], [ME. *defoulen;* OFr. *defouler*, to tread underfoot, insult; influenced by ME. *filen*, to foul < AS. *fylan*, to make foul < *ful*, foul], 1. to make filthy; dirty; pollute. 2. to make ceremonially unclean. 3. to corrupt. 4. to profane; sully, as a person's name. 5. [Archaic], to violate the chastity of; deflower. —*SYN.* see **contaminate.**

de·file (di-fīl', dē'fīl), *v.i.* [DEFILED (-fīld', -fīld), DEFILING], [Fr. *défiler*, to file off, unravel < *dé-* (L. *de*), from + *file;* see FILE (a line)], 1. to march in a line, in single file. 2. to march by files. *n.* [Fr. *défilé* < the *v.*], 1. a narrow passage through which troops must defile; hence, 2. any narrow valley or mountain pass. 3. a march in single file or in files.

de·file·ment (di-fīl'mənt), *n.* 1. a defiling or being defiled. 2. a thing that defiles.

de·fil·er (di-fīl'ẽr), *n.* a person who defiles something.

de·fin·a·ble (di-fīn'ə-b'l), *adj.* that can be defined.

de·fine (di-fīn'), *v.t.* [DEFINED (-fīnd'), DEFINING], [ME. *definen;* OFr. *definer;* L. *definire*, to limit, define; *de-*, from + *finire*, to set a limit to, bound < *finis*, boundary], 1. to determine or set down the boundaries of; set down or show the precise outlines of. 2. to determine and state the limits and nature of; describe exactly. 3. to give the distinguishing characteristics of. 4. to state or explain the meaning or meanings of (a word, etc.). 5. to constitute the definition of: as, the characteristics that *define* man.

def·i·nite (def'ə-nit), *adj.* [L. *definitus*, pp. of *definire;* see DEFINE], 1. having exact limits. 2. precise and clear in meaning; explicit. 3. certain; positive: as, it's *definite* that he'll go. 4. in *grammar*, limiting or specifying: as, *the* is the *definite* article: abbreviated **def.** —*SYN.* see **explicit.**

def·i·ni·tion (def'ə-nish'ən), *n.* [OFr. *definicion;* L. *definitio* < pp. of *definire;* see DEFINE], 1. a defining or being defined. 2. a statement of what a thing is. 3. a statement or explanation of what a word or phrase means or has meant. 4. a putting or being in clear, sharp outline. 5. the power of a lens to show (an object) in clear, sharp outline. 6. the degree of distinctness of a photograph, etc. 7. in *radio & television*, the degree of accuracy with which sounds or images are reproduced. Abbreviated **def.**

de·fin·i·tive (di-fin'ə-tiv), *adj.* [OFr. *definitif;* L. *definitus*, pp. of *definire;* see DEFINE], 1. decisive; conclusive; final. 2. most nearly complete and accurate: as, a *definitive* edition of Shakespeare. 3. serving to define; limiting; distinguishing. 4. in *biology*, fully developed. *n.* in *grammar*, a word that defines or limits a noun, as *this, that, any, some*, etc.

de·fin·i·tude (di-fin'ə-tōōd', di-fin'ə-tūd'), *n.* [< L. *definitus* (see DEFINITE), after nouns ending in *-tude*, as *infinitude*], the quality of being definite; precision.

def·la·grate (def'lə-grāt'), *v.t. & v.i.* [DEFLAGRATED (-id), DEFLAGRATING], [< L. *deflagratus*, pp. of *deflagrare*, to burn, consume; *de-*, intens. + *flagrare*, to burn], to burn rapidly, with intense heat and dazzling light.

de·flate (di-flāt'), *v.t. & v.i.* [DEFLATED (-id), DEFLATING], [< L. *de-*, from + *flatus*, pp. of *flare*, to blow], 1. to collapse by letting out air or gas: as, *deflate* the tire; hence, 2. to lessen in amount, importance, etc., as currency. Opposed to *inflate.* —*SYN.* see **contract.**

de·fla·tion (di-flā'shən), *n.* 1. a deflating or being deflated. 2. a lessening of the amount of money in circulation, resulting in a relatively sharp and sudden rise in its value and fall in prices. See **inflation.**

de·fla·tion·ar·y (di-flā'shən-er'i), *adj.* of, causing, or characterized by deflation.

de·fla·tor (di-flā'tẽr), *n.* a person or thing that deflates.

de·flect (di-flekt'), *v.t. & v.i.* [L. *deflectere; de-*, from + *flectere*, to bend], to bend or turn to one side; swerve.

de·flec·tion (di-flek'shən), *n.* [LL. *deflexio* < L. *deflexus*, pp. of *deflectere;* see DEFLECT], 1. a deflecting or being deflected; bending; curving; deviation. 2. amount of this. 3. the deviation from the zero mark of the needle or pointer of a measuring instrument.

de·flec·tive (di-flek'tiv), *adj.* deflecting or tending to deflect.

de·flec·tor (di-flek'tẽr), *n.* a thing that deflects; especially, a device for deflecting a current of air, gas, sound, etc.

de·flex·ion (di-flek'shən), *n.* deflection: British spelling.

def·lo·ra·tion (def'lə-rā'shən), *n.* [Fr. *défloration;* L. *defloratio;* see DEFLOWER], the act of deflowering.

de·flow·er (di-flou'ẽr), *v.t.* [after Fr. *déflorer* & L. *deflorare;* see DE- & FLOWER], 1. to take away the virginity of (a woman). 2. to ravish; ravage; spoil. 3. to remove flowers from (a plant).

de·flux·ion (di-fluk'shən), *n.* [LL. *defluxio*, a flowing down < L. *defluens*, ppr. of *defluere; de-*, from + *fluere*, to flow], [Rare], in *medicine*, a flow or discharge, as from the nose.

De·foe, Daniel (di-fō'), 1659?–1731; English novelist and essayist: also spelled **De Foe.**

de·fo·li·ate (di-fō'li-āt'), *v.t.* [ML. *defoliatus*, pp. of *defoliare* < L. *de-*, from + *folium*, a leaf], to strip of leaves. *v.i.* to be stripped of leaves.

de·fo·li·a·tion (di-fō'li-ā'shən), *n.* a defoliating or being defoliated.

de·force (di-fôrs', di-fōrs'), *v.t.* in *law*, 1. to keep (property, etc.) from the true owner by force. 2. to keep (a person) from rightful possession by force.

de·for·ciant (di-fôr'shənt, di-fōr'shənt), *n.* in *law*, a person who deforces another or another's property.

de·for·est (dē-fôr'ist, dē-for'ist), *v.t.* to clear (land) of forests or trees.

De For·est, Lee (di fôr'ist, di for'ist), 1873–1961; American inventor of telegraphic, telephonic, and radio apparatus.

de·for·est·a·tion (dē-fôr'is-tā'shən, dē-for'is-tā'shən), *n.* a deforesting or being deforested.

de·form (di-fôrm'), *v.t.* [Fr. *déformer;* L. *deformare;* < *de-*, from + *forma*, form, shape], 1. to mar the form or shape of. 2. to make ugly; disfigure. 3. in *physics*, to change the shape of by pressure or stress. *v.i.* to become deformed.

SYN.—**deform** implies a marring of form, appearance, or character, as if by pressure or stress (a body *deformed* by disease); **distort** implies a twisting or wrenching out of the normal or proper shape or form (a mind *distorted* by fear); **contort** suggests an even more violent wrenching out of shape so as to produce a grotesque or unpleasant result (a face *contorted* by pain); **warp** implies a bending out of shape, as of wood in drying, and, hence, suggests a turning aside from the true or right course (judgment *warped* by prejudice).

de·form·a·ble (di-fôr'mə-b'l), *adj.* capable of being deformed, or changed in shape, as by pressure, etc.

de·for·ma·tion (dē'fôr-mā'shən, def'ẽr-mā'shən), *n.* [L. *deformatio*], 1. a deforming. 2. the fact or state of being deformed. 3. the result of deforming; disfigurement. 4. a change in form for the worse. 5. in *physics*, etc., *a)* change of form or shape. *b)* a changed form (of something).

de·formed (di-fôrmd'), *adj.* [pp. of *deform*], 1. changed, especially marred, in form; misshapen. 2. ugly, offensive, hateful, etc.

de·form·ed·ly (di-fôrm'id-li), *adv.* in a deformed way.

de·form·i·ty (di-fôr'mə-ti), *n.* [*pl.* DEFORMITIES (-tiz)], [OFr. *deformité;* L. *deformitas* < *deformis* < *de-*, from + *forma*, form, shape], 1. the condition of being deformed. 2. abnormal bodily formation. 3. a deformed part, as of the body. 4. ugliness; depravity. 5. a deformed person or thing.

de·fraud (di-frôd'), *v.t.* [ME. *defrauden;* OFr. *defrauder;* L. *defraudare; de-*, intens. + *fraudare*, to cheat < *fraus*, deceit, fraud], to take away or hold back property, rights, etc. from by fraud; cheat. —*SYN.* see **cheat.**

de·frau·da·tion (dē'frô-dā'shən), *n.* a defrauding or being defrauded.

de·fray (di-frā'), *v.t.* [Fr. *défrayer;* OFr. *defraier* < *de-* (L. *de*), from, off + *frai* (Fr. *frais, pl.*) expense, cost; prob. < ML. *fredum*, fine < OHG. *fridu*, peace; cf. OFr. *desfroi*, expense], to pay (the cost or expenses).

de·fray·al (di-frā'əl), *n.* a defraying; payment.

de·fray·ment (di-frā'mənt), *n.* defrayal.

de·frock (dē-frok'), *v.t.* to take priestly dress or church position from; unfrock.

de·frost (dē-frôst', dē-frost'), *v.t.* to remove frost or ice from. *v.i.* to become rid of frost or ice.

de·fros·ter (dē-frôs'tẽr, dē-fros'tẽr), *n.* any device for melting ice and frost or preventing their formation, as on an airplane wing, automobile windshield, etc.

deft (deft), *adj.* [ME. *defte, dafte;* see DAFT], skillful; dexterous. —*SYN.* see **dexterous.**

de·funct (di-fuŋkt'), *adj.* [L. *defunctus*, pp. of *defungi*, to do, finish, die; *de-*, from, off + *fungi*, to perform], no longer living or existing; extinct. —*SYN.* see **dead.**

de·fy (di-fī'; *also, for n.,* dē'fī), *v.t.* [DEFIED (-fīd'), DEFYING], [ME. *defien, diffyen;* OFr. *defier*, to distrust, repudiate, defy; LL. **disfidare* < L. *dis-*, from + *fidus*, faithful], 1. to resist or oppose boldly or openly. 2. to resist completely; foil: as, Stalingrad *defied* capture. 3. to dare (someone) to do or prove something. 4. [Archaic], to challenge (someone) to fight. *n.* [*pl.* DEFIES (-fīz', -fīz)], [Slang], a defiance; challenge.

deg., degree; degrees.

‡**dé·ga·gé** (dā′gȧ′zhā′), *adj.* [Fr.], unconstrained; easy and free in manner.

de·gas (dē-gas′), *v.t.* [DEGASSED (-gast′), DEGASSING], to remove gas from; specifically, *a*) to evacuate the gases from (a vacuum tube, etc.). *b*) to decontaminate (an area or person affected with a poison gas).

De·gas, Hi·laire Ger·main Ed·gar (ē′lâr′ zher′man′ ed′gär′ də-gä′), 1834–1917; French painter.

De Gaulle, Charles (shärl′ də-gōl′; Eng. də-gôl′), 1890– ; French general and statesman; premier (1958–1959); president (1959–).

de·gauss (di-gous′), *v.t.* [*de-* + *gauss*], to neutralize the magnetic field surrounding (a ship) as a protection against magnetic mines.

de·gen·er·a·cy (di-jen′ẽr-ə-si), *n.* 1. the condition or quality of being degenerate. 2. a degenerating.

de·gen·er·ate (di-jen′ẽr-it), *adj.* [L. *degeneratus*, pp. of *degenerare*, to become unlike one's race, fall off, degenerate < *degener*, not genuine, base < *de-*, from + *genus*, race, kind], having sunk below a former or normal condition, character, etc.; deteriorated. ***n.*** a degenerate person, especially one who is subnormal mentally or morally. ***v.i.*** (di-jen′ẽr-āt′), [DEGENERATED (-id), DEGENERATING], 1. to lose former, normal, or higher qualities. 2. in *biology*, to change gradually to a lower type; deteriorate: said of species, etc.

de·gen·er·a·tion (di-jen′ẽr-ā′shən, dē′jen-ẽr-ā′shən), *n.* [Fr. *dégénération*], 1. a degenerating. 2. a degenerate condition. 3. in *biology*, a gradual change to a lower form of development. 4. in *medicine*, biochemical change in tissues or organs, caused by injury or disease and leading to loss of vitality, of function, etc.

de·gen·er·a·tive (di-jen′ẽr-ā′tiv, di-jen′ẽr-ə-tiv), *adj.* 1. of, showing, or causing degeneration. 2. tending to degenerate.

de·glu·ti·nate (di-glōō′t'n-āt′), *v.t.* [DEGLUTINATED (-id), DEGLUTINATING], [< L. *deglutinatus*, pp. of *deglutinare*, to unglue; *de-*, from + *glutinare*, to glue < *gluten*, glue], to extract gluten from.

de·glu·ti·tion (dē′gloo-tish′ən), *n.* [Fr. *déglutition* < LL. *deglutire*, to swallow down; L. *de-*, from, down + *glutire*, to swallow], the act, process, or power of swallowing.

deg·ra·da·tion (deg′rə-dā′shən), *n.* [Fr. *dégradation*; ML. *degradatio* < LL. *degradare*; see DEGRADE], 1. a degrading or being degraded. 2. in *geology*, the lowering of surfaces by erosion.

de·grade (di-grād′), *v.t.* [DEGRADED (-id), DEGRADING], [ME. *degraden*; OFr. *degrader*; LL. *degradare*, to reduce in rank < L. *de-*, down + *gradus*; see GRADE], 1. to lower in rank or status; take a position of honor from: as, the sergeant was *degraded* to the rank of private. 2. to lower or corrupt in quality, moral character, etc. 3. to bring into dishonor or contempt. 4. to lower in value, price, quality, etc. 5. in *biology*, to place in a lower classification. 6. in *geology*, to lower (a surface) by erosion. ***v.i.*** to sink to a lower position or type; degenerate.

SYN.*—degrade** literally means to lower in grade or rank, but it commonly implies a lowering or corrupting of moral character, self-respect, etc.; **abase** suggests a loss, often merely temporary and self-imposed, of dignity, respect, etc. (he *abased* himself before his employer); **debase** implies a decline in value, quality, character, etc. (a *debased* mind); to **humble** is to lower the pride or increase the humility, especially of another, and, unqualified, suggests that such lowering is deserved (*humbled* by the frightening experience); to **humiliate** is to humble or shame (another) painfully and in public (*humiliated* by their laughter).—ANT.*** exalt, dignify.

de·grad·ed (di-grād′id), *adj.* [pp. of *degrade*], disgraced; debased; depraved.

de·grad·ing (di-grād′iŋ), *adj.* [ppr. of *degrade*], that degrades; debasing. —***SYN.*** see **base.**

‡**de gra·ti·a** (dē grā′shi-ə), [L.], in *law*, by grace or favor.

de·gree (di-grē′), *n.* [ME. *degre, degree*; OFr. *degre*, degree, step, rank; LL. **degradus* < *degradare*; see DEGRADE], 1. any of the successive steps or stages in a process or series: as, advance by *degrees*; hence, 2. a step in the direct line of descent: as, a cousin in the second *degree*. 3. social or official rank, position, or class: as, a man of low *degree*. 4. the relative condition, way, or respect: as, each contributing to victory in his *degree*. 5. intensity, extent, or amount: as, hungry to a slight *degree*, burns of the third *degree*. 6. in *algebra*, rank as determined by the sum of a term's exponents: as $a^3 c^2$ and x^5 are each of the fifth *degree*. 7. in *education*, a rank given by a college or university to a student who has completed a required course of study, or to a distinguished person as an honor: as, an M.A. *degree*, a Litt. D. *degree*. 8. in *grammar*, a grade of comparison of adjectives and adverbs: as, the positive *degree* of good is *good*, the comparative *degree* is *better*, and the superlative *degree* is *best*. 9. in *law*, the seriousness of a crime: as, murder in the first *degree*. 10. in *mathematics, astronomy, geography*, etc., a unit of measure for angles or arcs, one 360th part of the circumference of a circle: the measure of an angle is the number of degrees between its sides considered as radii of a circle: as, a right angle has 90 *degrees*. 11. in *music*, *a*) a line or space on the staff. *b*) the interval between any two notes on an adjacent line and space, as between E and F, E♭ and F♯, or G♯ and A♭. 12. in *physics*, *a*) a unit of measure for temperature: as, the boiling point of water is 212 *degrees* Fahrenheit (212°F.). *b*) a line marking a degree on a thermometer. Abbreviated **deg., d.**

by degrees, step by step; gradually.

to a degree, 1. to a great extent or amount. 2. somewhat.

de·gree-day (di-grē′dā′), *n.* a unit of heat measurement equal to one degree of variation from a standard temperature in the average temperature of one day.

de·gres·sion (di-gresh′ən), *n.* [LL. *degressio* < L. *degressus*, pp. of *degredi*, to go down; *de*, down + *gredi*, to go], a going down; descent or decrease; specifically, a decrease in the rate of taxation on sums below a specified amount.

de·gres·sive (di-gres′iv), *adj.* designating or of a system of taxation in which the rate of taxation becomes progressively lower on sums below a specified amount.

De Groot or **de Groot, Hugo** (də grōt′), see **Grotius.**

de·gust (di-gust′), *v.t.* & *v.i.* [Early Mod. Eng.; L. *degustare*], [Rare], to taste; especially, to taste attentively so as to perceive the flavor.

‡**de gus·ti·bus non dis·pu·tan·dum (est)** (dē gus′ti-bəs non dis′pū-tan′dəm est), [L.], there is no disputing about tastes.

de·hisce (di-his′), *v.i.* [DEHISCED (-hist′), DEHISCING], [L. *dehiscere*; *de-*, off, from + *hiscere*, to gape, yawn], to gape; burst or split open, as a seed pod.

de·his·cence (di-his′'ns), *n.* [see DEHISCENT], a bursting or splitting open, as of a pod, anther, etc. to discharge its contents.

de·his·cent (di-his′'nt), *adj.* [L. *dehiscens*, ppr. of *dehiscere*], dehiscing or tending to dehisce.

de·horn (dē-hôrn′), *v.t.* to remove the horns from.

de·hu·man·ize (dē-hū′mə-nīz′), *v.t.* to deprive of human qualities, as pity, kindness, etc.; make inhuman.

de·hu·mid·i·fy (dē′hū-mid′ə-fī′), *v.t.* [*de-* + *humidify*], to remove moisture from (the air, etc.).

de·hy·drate (dē-hī′drāt), *v.t.* [< *de-* + Gr. *hydōr*, water; + *-ate*], in *chemistry*, etc., to remove water from; dry: as, *dehydrate* fruits and vegetables to conserve them for future use. ***v.i.*** to lose water; become dry.

de·hy·dra·tion (dē′hī-drā′shən), *n.* a dehydrating or being dehydrated.

de·hy·dro·gen·ize (dē-hī′drə-jən-īz′), *v.t.* in *chemistry*, to remove hydrogen from.

de·hyp·no·tize (dē-hip′nə-tīz′), *v.t.* to arouse from a hypnotic trance.

De·ia·ni·ra, De·ia·nei·ra (dē′ə-nī′rə), *n.* [L. *Deianira*; Gr. *Dēianeira*], in *Greek mythology*, the second wife of Hercules, who unknowingly killed him by sending him a garment steeped in the poisoned blood of the centaur Nessus, thinking that it was a love charm.

de·ic·er (dē-ī′sẽr), *n.* a device for preventing or eliminating formations of ice, as on the wings of airplanes.

de·i·cide (dē′ə-sīd′), *n.* [< LL. *deicida* < *deus*, god + *caedere*, to kill], 1. the killer of a god. 2. [as if < ML. **deicidium*, after *homicide*], the killing of a god.

deic·tic (dīk′tik), *adj.* [Gr. *deiktikos* < *deiknynai*, to show, prove], 1. in *grammar*, pointing out; demonstrative: as, *that* is a *deictic* pronoun. 2. in *logic*, proving directly: opposed to *elenctic*. Also **dictic.**

de·if·ic (dē-if′ik), *adj.* [L. *deificus*], 1. deifying. 2. loosely, godlike.

de·i·fi·ca·tion (dē′ə-fi-kā′shən), *n.* [ME.; OFr.], 1. a deifying. 2. a deified person or embodiment.

de·i·form (dē′ə-fôrm′), *adj.* [ML. *deiformis* < L. *deus*, god + *forma*, form], 1. godlike in form. 2. divine.

de·i·fy (dē′ə-fī′), *v.t.* [DEIFIED (-fīd′), DEIFYING], [ME. *deifien*; OFr. *deifier*; LL. *deificare*, to make divine < L. *deus*, god + *facere*, to make], 1. to make a god of; rank among the gods. 2. to look upon as a god; worship. 3. to idealize; adore.

deign (dān), *v.i.* [ME. *deignen*; OFr. *deigner*; L. *dignare, dignari*, to deem worthy < *dignus*, worthy], to think befitting one's dignity (*to do* something); condescend; lower oneself. ***v.t.*** 1. to condescend to give; vouchsafe: as, will you *deign* no answer? 2. [Obs.], to condescend to accept. —***SYN.*** see **stoop.**

‡**De·i gra·ti·a** (dē′ī grā′shi-ə, dā′i grä′ti-ä), [L.], by the grace of God.

deil (dēl), *n.* [Scot.], 1. the devil. 2. a mischievous person.

de·i·on·ize (dē-ī′ə-nīz′), *v.t.* 1. to remove ions from. 2. to restore (gas that has become ionized) to its former condition.

De·iph·o·bus (dē-if′ə-bəs), *n.* [L.; Gr. *Dēiphobos*], in *Greek legend*, a Trojan hero, son of Priam and Hecuba: he married Helen after the death of Paris, and was eventually killed by Menelaus.

Deir·dre (dẽr′dri, der′dri), *n.* [OIr. *Derdriu*, lit., the raging one], in *Irish legend*, a princess of Ulster who eloped to Scotland with her lover: when he was treacherously killed by her guardian, she committed suicide.

de·ism (dē′iz'm), *n.* [Fr. *déisme* < L. *deus*, god], 1. the belief that God exists and created the world but thereafter assumed no control over it or the lives of people. 2. in *philosophy*, the belief that reason is sufficient to prove the existence of God, with the consequent rejection of revelation and authority.

de·ist (dē′ist), *n.* a believer in deism. —*SYN.* see **atheist.**

de·is·tic (dē-is′tik), *adj.* of deism or deists.

de·is·ti·cal (dē-is′ti-k'l), *adj.* deistic.

de·i·ty (dē′ə-ti), *n.* [*pl.* DEITIES (-tiz)], [ME. & OFr. *deite;* LL. *deitas*, divinity (formed by Augustine, c. 400 A.D., after L. *divinitas*) < L. *deus*, god], 1. the state of being a god; divine nature; godhood. 2. a god. 3. a goddess. **the Deity,** God.

‡dé·jà vu (dā′zhä′vü′), [Fr., lit., already seen], in *psychology*, the illusion that one has previously had a given experience.

de·ject (di-jekt′), *v.t.* [L. *dejectus*, pp. of *dejicere* < *de-*, down + *jacere*, to throw], to cast down in spirit; dishearten; depress. *adj.* [Archaic], dejected.

de·jec·ta (di-jek′tə), *n.pl.* [Mod. L., neut. pl. of *dejectus;* see DEJECT], excrements.

de·ject·ed (di-jek′tid), *adj.* [pp. of *deject*], depressed; discouraged; disheartened; downcast. —*SYN.* see **sad.**

de·jec·tion (di-jek′shən), *n.* [L. *dejectio;* see DEJECT], 1. lowness of spirits; depression; discouragement. 2. in *medicine*, *a*) an evacuation of the bowels. *b*) the matter evacuated; excrement.

‡dé·jeu·ner (dā′zhë′nā′), *n.* [Fr.; OFr. *desjeuner;* LL. **disjunare;* see DINE], 1. a breakfast, especially a late one; hence, 2. a luncheon.

‡de ju·re (dē joor′i), [L.], by right; in accordance with law: as, *de jure* government: distinguished from *de facto.*

dek·a- (dek′ə), deca-, as in *dekaliter*, *dekameter:* also, before a vowel, **dek-.**

De Kalb, Jo·hann (yô-hän′ də käl*p*′; Eng. də kalb), Baron De Kalb, 1721–1780; German military officer who served in the American Revolutionary Army.

Dek·ker, Thomas (dek′ẽr), 1572?–1632?; English dramatist: also spelled **Decker.**

De Ko·ven, Reginald (di-kō′vən), 1859–1920; American composer.

Del., Delaware.

del., 1. delete. 2. delegate. 3. *delineavit*, [L.], he (or she) drew it: used after an artist's signature on a painting.

De·la·croix, Fer·di·nand Vic·tor Eu·gène (fer′dē′nän′ vēk′tôr′ ë′zhen′ də-lȧ′krwä′), 1799–1863; French painter.

Del·a·go·a Bay (del′ə-gō′ə), an arm of the Indian Ocean, projecting into southern Mozambique, Africa: length, 55 mi.

de·laine (də-lān′), *n.* [for *muslin de laine;* Fr. *de laine*, of wool < L. *de-*, of, from + *lana*, wool], a lightweight cloth, formerly of wool, now usually of cotton and wool.

de la Mare, Walter John (də-lə-mâr′, del′ə-mâr′), 1873–1956; English poet and novelist.

de·lam·i·nate (dē-lam′ə-nāt′), *v.t. & v.i.* [*de-* + *laminate*], to separate into layers.

de·lam·i·na·tion (dē-lam′ə-nā′shən), *n.* a delaminating or being delaminated; specifically, in *embryology*, a splitting of the blastoderm into two layers of cells.

de·late (di-lāt′), *v.t.* [DELATED (-id), DELATING], [< L. *delatus*, pp. of *deferre;* see DEFER (to submit)], 1. [Chiefly Scot.], to accuse; inform against. 2. to relate; announce; make public.

de·la·tor (di-lā′tẽr), *n.* a person who delates; informer.

De·la·vigne, Jean Fran·çois Cas·i·mir (zhän′ frän′-swȧ′ kȧ′zē′mêr′ də-lȧ′vēn′y′), 1793–1843; French poet and playwright.

Del·a·ware (del′ə-wâr′), *n.* 1. an Eastern State of the United States: area, 2,057 sq. mi.; pop., 446,000; capital, Dover: abbreviated **Del.** 2. a river flowing between Pennsylvania and New Jersey into Delaware Bay: length, 296 mi. 3. a member of a tribe of Algonquian Indians who lived in the Delaware River valley. 4. a small, sweet, reddish American grape.

Del·a·war·e·an (del′ə-wâr′i-ən), *adj.* of Delaware. *n.* a native or inhabitant of Delaware.

Delaware Bay, the estuary of the Delaware River, separating Delaware from New Jersey.

De La Warr, Baron, (del′ə-wâr′), (*Thomas West;* known as *Lord Delaware*), 1577–1618; British soldier; colonial governor of Virginia (1610–1618).

de·lay (di-lā′), *v.t.* [ME. *delayen*, *delaien;* OFr. *delaier;* *de-*, from + *laier*, to leave, let], 1. to put off to a future time; postpone. 2. to make late; detain. *v.i.* to stop for a while; linger. *n.* a delaying or being delayed.

SYN.—**delay** implies the interference of something that causes a detainment or postponement (I was *delayed* by the storm); **retard** implies the action of something in causing a slowing down of movement or progress (the advancing army had been *retarded*); **slacken** suggests a slowing down by relaxation of activity or intensity (trade had *slackened* somewhat); **impede** implies interference with movement or progress by some obstruction (the muddy roads *impeded* our journey); **hinder** suggests a holding back or restraining of movement or action that has not yet begun (the search was *hindered* by his arrival).—*ANT.* hasten, expedite.

delaying action, maneuvers to cover a retreat, gain time, etc.

Del·cas·sé, Thé·o·phile (tā′ô′fēl′, del′kȧ′sā′), 1852–1923; French statesman; minister of foreign affairs (1898–1905; 1914–1915).

de·le (dē′li), *v.t.* [DELED (-lid), DELEING (-li-iŋ)], [L., imperative sing. of *delere;* see DELETE], in *printing*, to take out (a letter, etc.); delete: usually in the imperative as a direction to the printer. *n.* a mark (φ) showing that a letter, word, etc. is to be taken out.

de·lec·ta·bil·i·ty (di-lek′tə-bil′ə-ti), *n.* the quality of being delectable.

de·lec·ta·ble (di-lek′tə-b'l), *adj.* [L. *delectabilis* < *delectare;* see DELIGHT], enjoyable; delightful.

de·lec·ta·bly (di-lek′tə-bli), *adv.* in a delectable manner.

de·lec·ta·tion (dē′lek-tā′shən), *n.* [ME. *delectacioun;* OFr. *delectation;* L. *delectatio* < *delectare;* see DELIGHT], delight; enjoyment; entertainment.

De·led·da, Gra·zia (grä′tsyä de-led′dä), 1875–1936; Italian novelist; received Nobel prize in literature, 1926.

del·e·ga·cy (del′ə-gə-si), *n.* [*pl.* DELEGACIES (-siz)], 1. a delegating or being delegated. 2. authority to act as a delegate. 3. a delegation.

de·le·gal·ize (dē-lē′g'l-īz′), *v.t.* to make no longer legal.

del·e·gate (del′ə-gāt′; *also, for n.*, del′ə-git), *n.* [< L. *delegatus*, pp. of *delegare*, to send from one place to another, appoint, assign; *de-*, from + *legare*, to send, appoint], 1. a person authorized or sent to act for others; representative; deputy: abbreviated **del.** 2. a representative of a United States Territory in the House of Representatives, who has the right to speak but not to vote. 3. a member of a House of Delegates. *v.t.* [DELEGATED (-id), DELEGATING], 1. to authorize, send, or appoint as a delegate. 2. to entrust (authority, power, etc.) to a person acting as one's agent or representative. 3. in *law*, to assign (one's debtor) as debtor to one's creditor in place of oneself.

del·e·ga·tion (del′ə-gā′shən), *n.* [L. *delegatio*], 1. a delegating or being delegated. 2. the commission given to a delegate. 3. a delegate or group of delegates.

‡de·len·da est Car·tha·go (di-len′də est kär-thā′gō), [L.], Carthage must be destroyed: Roman view of the proper fate for a traditional enemy.

de·lete (di-lēt′), *v.t.* [DELETED (-id), DELETING], [< L. *deletus*, pp. of *delere*, to blot out, destroy < *de-*, from + base akin to *linere*, to daub, rub over], to take out (a printed or written letter, word, etc.); cross out; dele: abbreviated **del., d.** —*SYN.* see **erase.**

del·e·te·ri·ous (del′ə-têr′i-əs), *adj.* [ML. *deleterius;* Gr. *dēlētērios* < *dēlētēr*, a destroyer < *dēleisthai*, to injure, destroy], harmful to health, well-being, etc.; injurious. —*SYN.* see **pernicious.**

de·le·tion (di-lē′shən), *n.* [L. *deletio*], 1. a deleting or being deleted. 2. a deleted word, passage, etc.

delf (delf), *n.* delftware.

Delft (delft), *n.* a city in the western Netherlands: pop., 72,000.

delft (delft), *n.* delftware.

delft·ware (delft′wâr′), *n.* 1. glazed pottery, usually blue, which originated in Delft, Holland. 2. any similar ware. 3. brown earthenware covered with a white glaze and decorated.

Del·hi (del′i), *n.* 1. a small state of northern India: area, 574 sq. mi.; pop., 1,744,000. 2. its capital, on the Jumna River: pop., 915,000: also called *Old Delhi:* formerly the capital of India: see **New Delhi.**

Del·ia (dēl′yə), [L., fem. of *Delius*, of Delos], a feminine name. *n.* in *Greek mythology*, Artemis.

De·li·an (dē′li-ən), *adj.* of Delos or its people. *n.* a native or inhabitant of Delos.

de·lib·er·ate (di-lib′ẽr-it; *for v.*, di-lib′ẽr-āt′), *adj.* [L. *deliberatus*, pp. of *deliberare*, to consider, weigh well < *de-*, intens. + *librare*, to weigh < *libra*, a scales], 1. carefully thought out or formed; premeditated; done on purpose. 2. careful in considering; not rash or hasty: as, a *deliberate* judge. 3. slow; unhurried: as, take *deliberate* aim. *v.i.* [DELIBERATED (-id), DELIBERATING], 1. to consider carefully and fully. 2. to consider reasons for and against a thing in order to make up one's mind: as, a jury *deliberates*. *v.t.* to consider carefully. —*SYN.* see **think, voluntary.**

de·lib·er·a·tion (di-lib′ẽr-ā′shən), *n.* [ME. *deliberacioun;* OFr. *deliberation;* L. *deliberatio*], 1. a deliberating; considering carefully. 2. *often pl.* consideration and debate: as, the *deliberations* of statesmen. 3. the quality or condition of being deliberate; carefulness; slowness.

de·lib·er·a·tive (di-lib′ẽr-ā′tiv), *adj.* [L. *deliberativus*], 1. of or for deliberating; considering and debating: as, a *deliberative* assembly. 2. characterized by or resulting from deliberation.

de·lib·er·a·tor (di-lib'ẽr-ā'tẽr), *n.* [L.], a person who deliberates.

De·libes, Lé·o (lā'ō' də-lēb'), 1836–1891; French composer.

del·i·ca·cy (del'i-kə-si), *n.* [*pl.* DELICACIES (-siz)], [ME. *delicacie;* ML. *delicacia* < L. *delicatus;* see DELICATE], 1. the quality of being delicate. 2. fineness; frailty; graceful slightness, softness, etc.: as, the *delicacy* of a petal, of Venetian glass, of a child's face. 3. weakness of constitution or health: as, the invalid's *delicacy.* 4. the quality or condition of needing careful and deft handling: as, negotiations of great *delicacy.* 5. fineness of feeling, observing, or appreciating: as, *delicacy* of musical taste. 6. sensitiveness of response: as, the *delicacy* of a compass. 7. fineness of touch, skill, etc. 8. a fine regard for the feelings of others. 9. a sensitive distaste for what is considered improper or offensive. 10. a choice food: as, caviar and other *delicacies.*

del·i·cate (del'i-kit), *adj.* [ME. *delicat;* L. *delicatus,* giving pleasure, delightful; prob. < *deliciae,* delight, pleasure < *delicere,* to allure, entice < *de-,* intens. + *lacere;* see DELIGHT], 1. pleasingly and finely flavored. 2. deliciously mild, light, or soft: as, a *delicate* air, odor, color, etc. 3. beautifully fine in texture, quality, workmanship, etc.: as, *delicate* linen, a *delicate* ring, *delicate* skin. 4. slight and subtle: as, a *delicate* difference. 5. easily damaged, spoiled, disordered, etc.: as, a *delicate* vase, a *delicate* stomach. 6. frail in health: as, a *delicate* child. 7. needing careful handling: as, a *delicate* diplomatic question. 8. finely sensitive in feeling, understanding, or responding: as, a *delicate* ear for music, a *delicate* gauge. 9. finely skilled. 10. considerate and tactful. 11. having or showing a sensitive distaste for anything offensive or improper. *n.* [Archaic & Poetic], a delicacy; dainty.
SYN.—**delicate** and **dainty** are both used to describe things that are pleasing to highly refined tastes or sensibilities, **delicate** implying fragility, subtlety, or fineness, and **dainty,** smallness, fastidiousness, or delicate gracefulness; **exquisite** is applied to something so delicately wrought or subtly refined as to be appreciated by only the most keenly discriminating or fastidious.—***ANT.*** gross, crude, coarse.

del·i·ca·tes·sen (del'i-kə-tes''n), *n.pl.* [construed as sing. in sense 2 and often in sense 1], [G. *delikatessen,* as if < *delikat* (< Fr. *délicat*) + *essen,* food (<*essen,* to eat); actually < Fr. *délicatesse,* delicacy < *délicat;* L. *delicatus;* see DELICATE], 1. prepared cooked meats, smoked fish, cheeses, salads, relishes, etc. 2. a shop where such foods are sold.

de·li·cious (di-lish'əs), *adj.* [ME.; OFr. *delicieus;* L. *deliciosus* < *deliciae;* see DELICATE], 1. very agreeable or enjoyable; delightful. 2. very pleasing, especially to taste or smell. *n.* [D-], a variety of sweet, red winter apple.

de·lict (di-likt'), *n.* [L. *delictum,* a fault < *delinquere,* to leave undone; see DELINQUENCY], in *law,* an offense; misdemeanor.

de·light (di-līt'), *v.t.* [ME. *deliten;* OFr. *deliter;* L. *delectare,* to delight, freq. of *delicere* < *de-,* from + *lacere,* to entice, lit., to ensnare (cf. LACE): sp. influenced by *light,* etc.], to give great joy or pleasure to. *v.i.* 1. to give great joy or pleasure. 2. to be highly pleased; rejoice (often with *in* or an infinitive). *n.* [ME. & OFr. *delit* < the *v.*], 1. great joy or pleasure. 2. something giving great joy or pleasure. 3. [Poetic], the power of pleasing greatly. —***SYN.*** see **pleasure.**

de·light·ed (di-līt'id), *adj.* [pp. of *delight*], highly pleased; joyful; happy.

de·light·ful (di-līt'fəl), *adj.* giving delight; very pleasing; charming.

de·light·some (di-līt'səm), *adj.* [Archaic & Poetic], delightful.

De·li·lah (di-lī'lə), *n.* [Heb. *delīlāh,* lit., delicate], 1. in the *Bible,* the mistress of Samson, who betrayed him to the Philistines by having his hair cut off while he was asleep, thus depriving him of his strength: Judg. 16; hence, 2. a false woman; temptress; harlot.

de·lim·it (di-lim'it), *v.t.* [Fr. *délimiter;* L. *delimitare; de-,* from + *limitare*], to set the limits of; mark the boundaries of.

de·lim·i·tate (di-lim'ə-tāt') *v.t.* [DELIMITATED (-id), DELIMITATING], [< L. *delimitatus,* pp. of *delimitare*], to delimit.

de·lim·i·ta·tion (di-lim'ə-tā'shən, dē'lim-ə-tā'shən), *n.* 1. a delimiting or being delimited. 2. a thing that serves as a limit.

de·lin·e·ate (di-lin'i-āt'), *v.t.* [DELINEATED (-id), DELINEATING], [< L. *delineatus,* pp. of *delineare,* to mark out, sketch < *de-,* from + *linea,* a line], 1. to trace the outline of; sketch out. 2. to draw; depict; hence, 3. to depict in words; describe.

de·lin·e·a·tion (di-lin'i-ā'shən), *n.* [L. *delineatio*], 1. the act or art of delineating. 2. a drawing; sketch; portrait. 3. a word picture; description.

de·lin·e·a·tive (di-lin'i-ā'tiv), *adj.* of delineation or tending to delineate.

de·lin·e·a·tor (di-lin'i-ā'tẽr), *n.* 1. a person or thing that delineates. 2. a tailor's pattern that can be adjusted for cutting garments of various sizes.

‡**de·li·ne·a·vit** (di-lin'i-ā'vit), [L.], he (or she) drew (this): used with the artist's name on a painting, etc.: abbreviated **del., delt.**

de·lin·quen·cy (di-liŋ'kwən-si), *n.* [*pl.* DELINQUENCIES (-siz)], [LL. *delinquentia* < L. *delinquens,* ppr. of *delinquere,* to leave undone, commit a fault; *de-,* from + *linquere,* to leave], 1. failure or neglect to do what duty or law requires; guilt. 2. a fault; misdeed. 3. in *law,* the act or acts of a juvenile delinquent.

de·lin·quent (di-liŋ'kwənt), *adj.* [L. *delinquens;* see DELINQUENCY], 1. failing or neglecting to do what duty or law requires; guilty of a fault or misdeed. 2. overdue: as, *delinquent* taxes. *n.* a delinquent person; especially, a delinquent juvenile.

del·i·quesce (del'ə-kwes'), *v.i.* [DELIQUESCED (-kwest'), DELIQUESCING], [L. *deliquescere; de-,* from + *liquescere,* to melt < *liquere,* to be liquid], 1. to melt away. 2. in *biology, a*) to melt away in the course of growth or decay, as parts of certain fungi. *b*) to branch into many fine divisions, as leaf veins. 3. in *chemistry,* to become liquid by absorbing moisture from the air.

del·i·ques·cence (del'ə-kwes''ns), *n.* the act, process, result, or quality of deliquescing.

del·i·ques·cent (del'ə-kwes''nt), *adj.* [L. *deliquescens,* ppr. of *deliquescere;* see DELIQUESCE], that deliquesces; undergoing or characterized by deliquescence.

del·i·ra·tion (del'ə-rā'shən), *n.* [L. *deliratio;* see DELIRIUM], mental aberration; delirium; madness.

de·lir·i·ous (di-lir'i-əs), *adj.* [see DELIRIUM], 1. in a state of delirium; mentally wandering; incoherently raving. 2. of, characteristic of, or caused by delirium. 3. in a state of wild excitement: as, *delirious* with joy.

de·lir·i·um (di-lir'i-əm), *n.* [*pl.* DELIRIUMS (-əmz), DELIRIA (-ə)], [L., madness < *delirare,* to rave, be crazy, lit., to make the furrow awry in plowing, deviate from the straight line < *de-,* from + *lira,* a line, furrow], 1. a temporary state of extreme mental excitement, marked by restlessness, confused speech, and hallucinations: it sometimes occurs during fever, as in certain diseases, in some forms of insanity, etc. 2. an uncontrollably wild excitement or emotion: as, a *delirium* of joy. 3. wildly irrational, confused, or frenzied thought or speech. —***SYN.*** see **mania.**

delirium tre·mens (trē'mənz), [Mod. L. (1813), lit., trembling delirium], a violent delirium resulting from excessive drinking of alcoholic liquor, and characterized by sweating, trembling, anxiety, and hallucinations: abbreviated **D.t.'s, d.t.**

del·i·tes·cent (del'i-tes'n't), *adj.* [L. *delitescens,* ppr. of *delitescere,* to hide away, skulk behind < *de-,* from + *latescere,* to hide oneself < *latere,* to be hidden, lurk], lying hidden; not revealed; latent or inactive.

De·li·us, Frederick (dē'li-əs, dēl'yəs), **1863–1934;** English composer.

de·liv·er (di-liv'ẽr), *v.t.* [ME. *delivren;* OFr. *delivrer;* LL. *deliberare,* to set free, liberate; L. *de-,* from + *liberare,* to set free < *liber,* free], 1. to set free or save from evil, danger, etc.: as, *deliver* us from bondage. 2. to assist at the birth of (an offspring): as, the doctor *delivered* the child. 3. to give forth or express in words; utter: as, he *delivered* a speech. 4. to give up; give or hand over; transfer (with *to*). 5. to give out; distribute: as, *deliver* the mail. 6. to give forth: as, the well *delivers* much water. 7. to strike (a blow). 8. to throw or toss: as, the pitcher *delivered* a curve. 9. [Colloq.], to cause (votes, etc.) to be directed toward the support of a particular candidate or cause. *adj.* [Archaic], active or agile. —***SYN.*** see **rescue.**
be delivered of, to give birth to.
deliver oneself of, to express; utter.

de·liv·er·ance (di-liv'ẽr-əns), *n.* [ME.; OFr.; see DELIVER], 1. a setting free; rescue or release. 2. the fact or state of being freed. 3. an opinion, judgment, etc. formally or publicly expressed.

de·liv·er·y (di-liv'ẽr-i), *n.* [*pl.* DELIVERIES (-iz)], [Anglo-Fr. *delivrée,* orig. fem. of pp. of *délivrer;* see DELIVER], 1. a giving or handing over; transfer. 2. a giving out or distributing, as of goods or mail. 3. a giving birth; childbirth. 4. a giving forth in words; utterance. 5. any giving forth. 6. a striking (of a blow). 7. a throwing (of a ball). 8. the manner or style of speaking, singing, striking, throwing, etc.: as, an actor's poor *delivery.* 9. something delivered or to be delivered, as mail, parcels, a pitched ball, etc. 10. [Archaic], a setting free. 11. in *law, a*) the irrevocable transfer of a deed. *b*) the transfer of goods from a consignor to a consignee. Abbreviated **dlvy.**

dell (del), *n.* [ME. *delle;* AS. *dell;* akin to MHG. *telle,* D. *del,* ravine; IE. base **dhel-,* **dholo-,* cavity, hollow as in *dale*], a small, secluded valley, glen, or ravine, usually a wooded one.

Del·la (del'ə), a feminine name: see **Adela.**

della Robbia, Della Robbia, see **Robbia, della.**

dells (delz), *n.pl.* dalles.

de·lo·cal·ize (dē-lō'k'l-īz'), *v.t.* 1. to remove (a thing) from its locality. 2. to free (a thing) from limitations of locality; broaden, as in scope.

De·lorme, Phi·li·bert (fē'lē'bâr' də-lôrm'), 1515?–1570; French architect.

De·los (dē′los), *n.* one of the small islands of the Cyclades in the Aegean: legendary birthplace of Artemis and Apollo, and site of a famous ancient temple of Apollo.

de·louse (dē-lous′, dē-louz′), *v.t.* [DELOUSED (-loust′, -louzd′), DELOUSING], to rid of lice.

Del·phi (del′fi), *n.* a city in ancient Phocis, Greece: site of a celebrated oracle of Apollo: see **Greece,** map.

Del·phi·an (del′fi-ən), *adj.* Delphic.

Del·phic (del′fik), *adj.* 1. of Delphi or the oracle of Apollo there; hence, 2. oracular; obscure in meaning; ambiguous.

del·phi·nin (del′fə-nin), *n.* delphinine.

del·phi·nine (del′fə-nēn′, del′fə-nin), *n.* [*delphinium* + *-ine*], a poisonous, white crystalline substance prepared from the seeds of certain larkspurs and used in medicine to relieve neuralgia, rheumatism, etc.

del·phin·i·um (del-fin′i-əm), *n.* [Mod. L. < Gr. *delphinion*, larkspur < Gr. *delphis, delphin*, dolphin: so called from the resemblance of the nectary to a dolphin], any of a number of related plants bearing spikes of spurred, irregular flowers, usually blue, on tall stalks; larkspur.

Del·phi·nus (del-fi′nəs), *n.* [L., lit., dolphin; see DELPHINIUM], a small northern constellation between Pegasus and Aquila: see **constellation,** chart.

Del·sarte system (del-särt′), [after François *Delsarte* (1811–1871), Fr. teacher of music and dramatics], a system of calisthenics combined with singing, declamation, and dancing to develop bodily grace and poise.

del·ta (del′tə), *n.* [L.; Gr. *delta;* Heb. *daleth*, 4th letter of the alphabet; lit., door], 1. the fourth letter of the Greek alphabet (Δ, δ), corresponding to English *D, d:* see **alphabet,** table. 2. a deposit of sand and soil, usually triangular, formed at the mouth of some rivers, as of the Nile: so called from the resemblance to Δ.

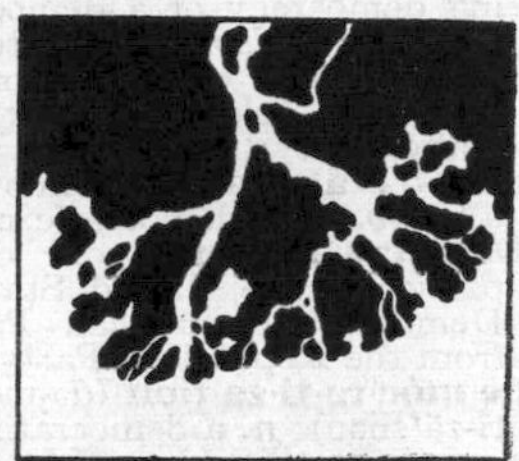

DELTA OF RIVER

del·ta·ic (del-tā′ik), *adj.* of, like, or forming a delta.

del·toid (del′toid), *adj.* [Gr. *deltoeidēs* < *delta* (Δ) + *eidos*, form], 1. shaped like a delta; triangular. 2. designating or of a large, triangular muscle of the shoulder, which raises the arm away from the side. *n.* this muscle.

de·lude (di-lōōd′, di-lūd′), *v.t.* [DELUDED (-id), DELUDING], [L. *deludere; de-*, from + *ludere*, to play, sport], 1. to mislead; beguile; deceive. 2. [Obs.], to elude; frustrate. —*SYN.* see **deceive.**

del·uge (del′ūj), *n.* [ME.; OFr.; L. *diluvium* < *diluere*, to wash away < *dis-*, off, from + *luere*, to wash], 1. a great flood. 2. a heavy rainfall. 3. an overwhelming, floodlike rush of anything: as, a *deluge* of visitors. *v.t.* [DELUGED (-ūjd), DELUGING], 1. to flood. 2. to overwhelm as with a flood.
the Deluge, in the *Bible*, the great flood in Noah's time: Gen. 7.

de·lu·sion (di-lōō′zhən, di-lū′zhən), *n.* [L. *delusio* < *delusus*, pp. of *deludere*], 1. a deluding. 2. the condition of being deluded. 3. a false belief or opinion. 4. in *psychiatry*, a false, persistent belief not substantiated by sensory evidence.
SYN.—**delusion** implies belief in something that is contrary to fact or reality, resulting from deception, a misconception, or a mental disorder (to have *delusions* of grandeur); **illusion** suggests the false perception or interpretation of something that has objective existence (perspective gives the *illusion* of depth in two dimensions); **hallucination** implies the apparent perception, in a nervous or mental disorder, of something external that is actually not present; **mirage** refers to an optical illusion caused by atmospheric conditions, and, in figurative use, implies an unrealizable hope or aspiration.

de·lu·sive (di-lōō′siv, di-lū′siv), *adj.* [L. *delusus* (see DELUSION); + *-ive*], tending to delude; misleading.

de·lu·so·ry (di-lōō′sə-ri, di-lū′sə-ri), *adj.* delusive.

de luxe (di looks′, di luks′; Fr. də lüks′), [Fr. lit., of luxury], of specially good quality; sumptuous; elegant.

delve (delv), *v.i.* [DELVED (delvd), DELVING], [ME. *delven;* AS. *delfan*, to dig; akin to OHG. (*bi*)*telban*, D. *delven;* IE. base **dhelbh-*, to dig out], 1. [Archaic or British Dial.], to dig; hence, 2. to make an investigation; search for facts: as, *delve* into books, into the past, etc. *v.t.* [Archaic or British Dial.], to dig or turn up (ground) with a spade.

Dem., 1. Democrat. 2. Democratic.

de·mag·net·i·za·tion (dē-mag′nə-ti-zā′shən, dē′mag-nə-tī-zā′shən), *n.* a demagnetizing or being demagnetized.

de·mag·net·ize (dē-mag′nə-tiz′), *v.t.* to deprive of magnetism or magnetic properties.

dem·a·gog (dem′ə-gôg′, dem′ə-gog′), *n.* a demagogue.

dem·a·gog·ic (dem′ə-goj′ik, dem′ə-gog′ik), *adj.* [Gr. *dēmagōgikos;* see DEMAGOGUE], of, like, or characteristic of a demagogue or demagogy.

dem·a·gog·i·cal (dem′ə-goj′i-k′l, dem′ə-gog′i-k′l), *adj.* demagogic.

dem·a·gog·i·cal·ly (dem′ə-goj′i-k′l-i, dem′ə-gog′ik-li), *adv.* 1. in the manner of a demagogue. 2. by means of demagogy.

dem·a·gog·ism (dem′ə-gôg′iz′m, dem′ə-gog′iz′m), *n.* the methods, actions, or principles of a demagogue: also spelled **demagoguism.**

dem·a·gogue (dem′ə-gôg′, dem′ə-gog′), *n.* [Gr. *dēmagōgos*, leader of the people < *dēmos*, the people + *agōgos*, leader < *agein*, to lead], 1. a person who tries to stir up the people by appeals to emotion, prejudice, etc. in order to become a leader and achieve selfish ends. 2. in *ancient history*, a leader of the common people.

dem·a·gog·uer·y (dem′ə-gôg′ẽr-i, dem′ə-gog′ẽr-i), *n.* demagogy.

dem·a·gog·y (dem′ə-gō′ji, dem′ə-gôg′i, dem′ə-gog′i), *n.* [Gr. *dēmagōgia*, control of the people], the methods, actions, or principles of a demagogue.

de·mand (di-mand′, di-mänd′), *v.t.* [OFr. *demander*, to demand; L. *demandare*, to give in charge; *de-*, away, from + *mandare*, to entrust, lit., to put in one's hands < *manus*, a hand + *dare*, to give], 1. to ask for boldly or urgently. 2. to ask for as a right or with authority. 3. to ask to know or be informed. 4. to require; need: as, the work *demands* patience. *v.i.* to make a demand. *n.* 1. a demanding. 2. a thing demanded. 3. a strong or authoritative request. 4. a requirement or claim. 5. an emphatic inquiry. 6. in *economics*, *a*) the desire for a commodity together with ability to pay for it. *b*) the amount people are ready and able to buy at a certain price. Opposed to *supply*. 7. in *law*, a legal claim.
in demand, demanded or sought.
on demand, when presented for payment.
SYN.—**demand** implies a calling for as owing or necessary, connoting a peremptory exercise of authority or an imperative need (to *demand* obedience); **claim** implies a demanding of something as allegedly belonging to one (to *claim* a throne); **require** suggests a pressing need, often one inherent in the nature of a thing, or the binding power of rules or laws (aliens are *required* to register); **exact** implies a demanding and the enforcing of the demand at the same time (an *exacting* foreman).

de·man·dant (di-man′dənt, di-män′dənt), *n.* in *law*, a plaintiff.

demand bill, a bill payable on demand.

demand deposit, in *banking*, a deposit that may be withdrawn on demand, without advance notice.

demand loan, a loan payable on demand; call loan: abbreviated **D/L.**

demand note, a promissory note payable on demand.

de·mar·cate (di-mär′kāt, dē′mär-kāt′), *v.t.* [DEMARCATED (-id), DEMARCATING], [< *demarcation*], 1. to set or mark the limits of; delimit; hence, 2. to distinguish; discriminate; separate.

de·mar·ca·tion (dē′mär-kā′shən), *n.* [Fr.; Sp. *demarcación* (in *linea de demarcación*, 1493) < *de-* (L. *de*), from + *marcar*, to mark boundaries < Gmc. *marka*, a boundary; cf. MARCH (limit)], 1. the act of setting and marking limits or boundaries. 2. a limit or boundary. 3. a separating. Also spelled **demarkation.**

‡dé·marche (dā′mȧrsh′), *n.* [Fr.; see DE- & MARCH (to walk)], 1. a line of action. 2. in *diplomacy*, a new line of action; change of policy.

de·ma·te·ri·al·ize (dē′mə-têr′i-ə-liz′), *v.t.* to cause to lose material form. *v.i.* to lose material form.

Dem·a·vend, Mount (dem′ə-vend′), the highest mountain of the Elburz Range, northern Iran: height, 18,603 ft.

deme (dēm), *n.* [Gr. *dēmos*, deme, common people, hence district], any of the hundred townships into which ancient Attica was divided.

de·mean (di-mēn′), *v.t.* [*de-* + *mean* (low): on analogy with *debase*], to lower in status or character; degrade; humble: as, he *demeaned* himself by taking the bribe.

de·mean (di-mēn′), *v.t.* [see DEMEANOR], to behave, conduct, or comport (oneself). —*SYN.* see **behave.**

de·mean·or (di-mēn′ẽr), *n.* [ME. *demeanure* < *demenen;* OFr. *demener*, to lead, drive; *de-* (L. *de*), from + *mener*, to lead < LL. *minare*, to drive, conduct < L. *minari*, to threaten], outward behavior; conduct; deportment; manner. —*SYN.* see **bearing.**

de·mean·our (di-mēn′ẽr), *n.* demeanor: British spelling.

de·ment (di-ment′), *v.t.* to cause dementia in; make insane.

de·ment·ed (di-men′tid), *adj.* [pp. of *dement* < L. *dementare* < *demens;* see DEMENTIA], mentally ill; affected with dementia.

‡dé·men·ti (dā′män′tē′), *n.* [Fr. < *dêmentir*, to give the lie to, contradict; *dé-* (L. *de*), from + *mentir* < L. *mentiri*, to lie], in *diplomacy*, an official denial, as of a rumor.

de·men·ti·a (di-men′shə, di-men′shi-ə), *n.* [L. < *demens*, *dementis*, out of one's mind; *de-*, out from, away +

mens, mentis, the mind], in *psychiatry,* loss or impairment of mental powers: distinguished from *amentia.* —*SYN.* see **insanity.**

dementia prae·cox (prē′koks), [L., lit., precocious dementia], a form of dementia, usually beginning in late adolescence, characterized by melancholia, withdrawal, hallucinations, delusions, etc.

de·mer·it (dē-mer′it), *n.* [Fr. *démérit;* LL. *demeritum,* transgression < *demerere,* to deserve ill, with prefix *de-* misunderstood as negative < L. *demerere,* to deserve well; *de-,* intens. + *merere,* to deserve], 1. a quality deserving blame; fault; defect. 2. a mark recorded against a student, etc. for unsatisfactory work or conduct. 3. [Obs.], merit.

dem·e·rol (dem′ə-rōl′, dem′ə-rol′), *n.* a synthetic drug used in medicine as a sedative and analgesic: a trademark (**Demerol**).

de·mesne (di-mān′, di-mēn′), *n.* [ME. *demaine;* OFr. *demaine* (Fr. *domaine*); see DOMAIN; intrusive *-s-* due prob. to association with OFr. *mesnee, mesnie,* household < L. *mansio;* see MANSION], 1. in *law,* possession (of real estate) as one's own. 2. formerly, the land or estate belonging to a lord and not rented or let but kept in his hands. 3. a lord's mansion and the land around it. 4. a region; domain. 5. a realm (of activity).

De·me·ter (di-mē′tẽr), *n.* [Gr. *Dēmētēr;* Doric Gr. *Damatēr*], in *Greek mythology,* the goddess of agriculture and fruitfulness, and protectress of marriage: identified by the Romans with Ceres.

de·mi (dē′mī), *n.* plural of **demos.**

dem·i- (dem′i), [Fr., half < L. *dimidius,* half < *dis-,* apart + *medius,* middle], a prefix meaning: 1. *half,* as in *demisemiquaver, demivolt;* hence, 2. *less than usual in size, power,* etc., as in *demigod, demitasse.*

dem·i·god (dem′i-god′), *n.* 1. in *mythology, a)* a lesser god; minor deity. *b)* the offspring of a human being and a god or goddess; hence, 2. a person regarded as partly divine. 3. a hero declared to be a god.

dem·i·john (dem′i-jon′), *n.* [Fr. *dame-jeanne,* demijohn, lit., Dame Jeanne; prob. orig. a fanciful name for the bottle], a large bottle of glass or earthenware, with a narrow neck and a wicker casing and handle.

de·mil·i·ta·ri·za·tion (dē-mil′ə-tə-ri-zā′shən, dē-mil′ə-tə-rī-zā′shən), *n.* a demilitarizing or being demilitarized.

de·mil·i·ta·rize (dē-mil′ə-tə-rīz′), *v.t.* 1. to free from organized military control. 2. to take away the military character or militarism of.

dem·i·lune (dem′i-lōōn′, dem′i-lūn′), *n.* [Fr.; *demi-* (see DEMI-) + *lune,* moon < L. *luna*], 1. a crescent. 2. a crescent-shaped outwork of a fortification.

dem·i·mon·daine (dem′i-mon-dān′), *n.* [Fr.], a woman of the demimonde.

dem·i·monde (dem′i-mond′, dem′i-mond′), *n.* [Fr.; *demi-* (see DEMI-) + *monde,* world, society < L. *mundus,* world], the class of women who have lost social standing because of sexual promiscuity.

dem·i·pique (dem′i-pēk′), *adj.* [< *demi-* + *peak;* sp. influenced by association with Fr. *pique,* a pike], having a low pommel: said formerly of certain military saddles. *n.* a demipique saddle.

dem·i·qua·ver (dem′i-kwā′vẽr), *n.* [*demi-* + *quaver*], in *music,* a sixteenth note; semiquaver.

dem·i·re·lief (dem′i-ri-lēf′), *n.* [*demi-* + *relief* (projection from a surface)], mezzo-relievo.

dem·i·rep (dem′i-rep′), *n.* [*demi-* + *rep*utation], a woman, or sometimes a man, of poor reputation, suspected of loose sexual behavior.

de·mis·a·ble (di-mīz′ə-b'l), *adj.* that can be demised.

de·mise (di-mīz′), *n.* [Fr. *démis, démise,* pp. of *démettre,* to dismiss, put away; L. *demittere;* see DEMIT], 1. the transfer of an estate by will or lease. 2. the transfer of sovereignty by death or abdication; hence, 3. death; decease. *v.t.* [DEMISED (-mīzd′), DEMISING], 1. to give, grant, or transfer (an estate) by will or lease. 2. to transfer (sovereignty) by death or abdication. *v.i.* to be passed on by bequest or inheritance.

dem·i·sem·i·qua·ver (dem′i-sem′i-kwā′vẽr), *n.* [*demi-* + *semi-* + *quaver*], in *music,* a thirty-second note (♬).

de·mis·sion (di-mish′ən), *n.* [Fr. *démission;* L. *demissio,* a letting down < *demissus,* pp. of *demittere*], a demitting; resignation or abdication (of an office).

de·mit (di-mit′), *v.t.* [DEMITTED (-id), DEMITTING], [L. *demittere,* to send down, let fall; *de-,* down + *mittere,* to send], 1. to resign (a position or office) voluntarily. 2. [Archaic], to dismiss. *v.i.* to resign.

dem·i·tasse (dem′i-tas′, dem′i-täs′), *n.* [Fr.; *demi-* (see DEMI-) + *tasse,* a cup], a small cup of or for after-dinner black coffee.

dem·i·urge (dem′i-ũrj′), *n.* [Gr. *dēmiourgos,* one who works for the people, skilled workman, creator < *dēmios,* belonging to the people (< *dēmos,* the people) + *-ergos,* worker (see ERG)], 1. [D-], in *Plato's philosophy,* a secondary deity, the creative spirit who made the world. 2. [D-], in *Gnostic philosophy,* a god subordinate to the supreme god, sometimes considered the originator of evil, or identified with the Jehovah of the Bible. 3. in *Greek history,* a magistrate in certain states.

dem·i·ur·gic (dem′i-ũr′jik), *adj.* 1. of the demiurge. 2. creative.

dem·i·volt (dem′i-vōlt′), *n.* [Fr. *demi-volte; demi-* (see DEMI-) + *volte,* a leap], in *horseback riding,* a half turn with the forelegs of the horse raised.

de·mobbed (dē-mobd′), *adj.* [British Slang], demobilized.

de·mo·bi·li·za·tion (dē′mō-b'l-i-zā′shən, di-mō′b'l-ī-zā′shən), *n.* a demobilizing or being demobilized.

de·mo·bi·lize (dē-mō′b'l-īz′), *v.t. & v.i.* 1. to disband or dismiss (troops that have been mobilized). 2. to change over from a war footing to a peace footing.

de·moc·ra·cy (də-mok′rə-si), *n.* [*pl.* DEMOCRACIES (-siz)], [Fr. *démocratie;* ML. *democratia;* Gr. *dēmokratia,* democracy, popular government < *dēmos,* the people + *kratein,* to rule], 1. government by the people, either directly or through elected representatives; rule by the ruled. 2. a country, state, community, etc. with such government. 3. majority rule. 4. the acceptance and practice of the principle of equality of rights, opportunity, and treatment; lack of snobbery: as, there is real *democracy* in this school. 5. the common people. 6. [D-], the Democratic Party of the United States, or the principles of this party. See also **republic.**

dem·o·crat (dem′ə-krat′), *n.* [Fr. *démocrate* < *démocratie;* see DEMOCRACY], 1. a person who believes in and upholds government by the people; advocate of rule by the majority. 2. a person who believes in and practices the principle of equality of rights, opportunity, and treatment. 3. [D-], a member or adherent of the Democratic Party: abbreviated **Dem., D.**

dem·o·crat·ic (dem′ə-krat′ik), *adj.* [Gr. *dēmokratikos,* suited to a democracy], 1. of, belonging to, or upholding democracy or a democracy. 2. of or for all the people: as, *democratic* entertainment. 3. considering and treating others as one's equals; not snobbish. 4. [D-], of, belonging to, or characteristic of the Democratic Party: abbreviated **Dem., D.**

dem·o·crat·i·cal·ly (dem′ə-krat′i-k'l-i, dem′ə-krat′ik-li), *adv.* in a democratic manner.

Democratic Party, one of the two major political parties in the United States: it descended from the Democratic-Republican Party (c. 1830), developed from the Republican Party led by Thomas Jefferson.

de·moc·ra·ti·za·tion (də-mok′rə-ti-zā′shən, də-mok′rə-tī-zā′shən), *n.* a democratizing or being democratized.

de·moc·ra·tize (də-mok′rə-tīz′), *v.t. & v.i.* [DEMOCRATIZED (-tīzd′), DEMOCRATIZING], [Fr. *démocratiser*], to make or become democratic.

De·moc·ri·te·an (di-mok′ri-tē′ən), *adj.* of or like Democritus or his philosophy.

De·moc·ri·tus (di-mok′ri-təs), *n.* Greek philosopher; exponent of atomism; 460?–362? B.C.

‡dé·mo·dé (dā′mô′dā′), *adj.* [Fr.], out-of-date; old-fashioned.

De·mo·gor·gon (dē′mə-gôr′gən, dem′ə-gôr′gən), *n.* [LL.; prob. of oriental origin, but influenced by L. *daemon* (see DEMON) + *Gorgo* (see GORGON)], a terrifying and mysterious god or demon of the underworld, to whom sinister powers were attributed: he is sometimes described in medieval writings as a primeval creator.

de·mo·graph·ic (dē′mə-graf′ik), *adj.* of demography.

de·mog·ra·phy (di-mog′rə-fi), *n.* [< Gr. *dēmos,* the people; + *-graphy*], the science of vital statistics, as of births, deaths, marriages, etc. of populations.

dem·oi·selle (dem′wä-zel′; Fr. də-mwȧ′zel′), *n.* [Fr. < OFr. *dameisele;* see DAMSEL], 1. a damsel. 2. a small crane of Africa, Asia, and Europe; Numidian crane. 3. any of various dragonflies with a small head, slender body, and wings held vertically when at rest.

de·mol·ish (di-mol′ish), *v.t.* [< root of Fr. *démolir;* L. *demoliri,* to pull down, destroy; *de-,* down + *moliri,* to build, construct, exert oneself < *moles,* a mass], 1. to pull or tear down (a building, etc.); hence, 2. to destroy; ruin. —*SYN.* see **destroy.**

de·mol·ish·ment (di-mol′ish-mənt), *n.* demolition.

dem·o·li·tion (dem′ə-lish′ən, dē′mə-lish′ən), *n.* [Fr.; L. *demolitio* < *demoliri;* see DEMOLISH], a demolishing or being demolished; destruction.

demolition bomb, a bomb designed primarily for demolishing buildings, fortifications, etc. by means of explosive force rather than the dispersal of fragments.

de·mon (dē′mən), *n.* [Fr. *démon;* L. *daemon;* see DAEMON], 1. a daemon. 2. a devil; evil spirit. 3. a person or thing regarded as evil, cruel, etc.: as, the *demon* of jealousy. 4. a person who has great energy or skill: as, a *demon* at golf.

demon., demonstrative.

de·mon·e·ti·za·tion (dē-mon′ə-ti-zā′shən, dē-mun′ə-tī-zā′shən), *n.* a demonetizing or being demonetized.

de·mon·e·tize (dē-mon′ə-tīz′, dē-mun′ə-tīz′), *v.t.* 1. to deprive (currency) of its standard value. 2. to stop using as money: as, silver was *demonetized.*

de·mo·ni·ac (di-mō′ni-ak′), *adj.* [L. *daemoniacus;* see DEMON, DAEMON], 1. possessed or influenced by a demon. 2. of a demon or demons. 3. like or characteristic of a demon or demons; devilish. 4. frenzied; frantic. *n.* a person supposedly possessed by a demon.

de·mo·ni·a·cal (dē′mə-nī′ə-k'l), *adj.* demoniac.

de·mon·ic (dē-mon′ik), *adj.* [LL. *daemonicus;* Gr. *daimonikos;* see DEMON, DAEMON], 1. of or like a demon or demons. 2. having a guiding spirit; daemonic; hence, 3. inspired.

de·mon·ism (dē′mən-iz′m), *n.* 1. belief in the existence and powers of demons. 2. demonolatry.

de·mon·ize (dē′mən-īz′), *v.t.* [DEMONIZED (-īzd′), DEMONIZING], 1. to make into, or like, a demon. 2. to bring under the influence of demons.

de·mon·o- (dē′mən-ō), [Gr. *daimono* < *daimōn;* see DAEMON], a combining form meaning *demon,* as in *demonology:* also, before a vowel, **demon-.**

de·mon·ol·a·ter (dē′mən-ol′ə-tẽr), *n.* a worshiper of demons.

de·mon·ol·a·try (dē′mən-ol′ə-tri), *n.* [*demono-* + *-latry*], the worship of demons.

de·mon·ol·o·gy (dē′mən-ol′ə-ji), *n.* [*demono-* + *-logy*], 1. the study of demons or of beliefs about them. 2. a treatise on demons.

de·mon·stra·bil·i·ty (di-mon′strə-bil′ə-ti, dem′ən-strə-bil′ə-ti), *n.* the quality or state of being demonstrable.

de·mon·stra·ble (di-mon′strə-b'l, dem′ən-strə-b'l), *adj.* [L. *demonstrabilis* < *demonstrare;* see DEMONSTRATE], that can be demonstrated, or proved.

de·mon·stra·bly (di-mon′strə-bli, dem′ən-strə-bli), *adv.* 1. in a demonstrable manner; plainly. 2. by means of demonstration.

de·mon·strant (di-mon′strənt), *n.* [< L. *demonstrans,* ppr. of *demonstrare;* see DEMONSTRATE], a person who takes part in a public demonstration.

dem·on·strate (dem′ən-strāt′), *v.t.* [DEMONSTRATED (-id), DEMONSTRATING], [< L. *demonstratus,* pp. of *demonstrare,* to point out, show; *de-,* out, from + *monstrare,* to show], 1. to show by reasoning; prove. 2. to explain or make clear by using examples, experiments, etc. 3. to show the operation or working of; hence, 4. to advertise by showing the working or use of (a commodity). 5. to show (feelings) plainly. *v.i.* 1. to show feelings or ideas by public meetings, parades, etc. 2. to show military power or preparedness.

dem·on·stra·tion (dem′ən-strā′shən), *n.* [ME. *demonstracion;* L. *demonstratio* < *demonstrare;* see DEMONSTRATE], 1. the act, process, or means of making evident or proving. 2. an explanation by example, experiment, etc.; practical showing of how something works or is used. 3. a display or outward show: as, a *demonstration* of grief. 4. a public show of feeling or opinion, as by a mass meeting or parade. 5. a show of military force or preparedness. 6. in *mathematics* & *logic,* the act or process of proving that certain results follow from certain premises.

de·mon·stra·tive (di-mon′strə-tiv), *adj.* [ME. *demonstratif;* Fr. *démonstratif;* L. *demonstrativus;* see DEMONSTRATE], 1. showing clearly; illustrative. 2. giving evidence or conclusive proof (usually with *of*). 3. having to do with demonstration: as, a *demonstrative* science. 4. showing feelings openly and frankly: as, she's a *demonstrative* child. 5. in *grammar,* pointing out: as, *that* is a *demonstrative* pronoun. *n.* in *grammar,* a demonstrative pronoun or adjective. Abbreviated **demon.**

dem·on·stra·tor (dem′ən-strā′tẽr), *n.* [L.], a person or thing that demonstrates, as a person who takes part in a public demonstration.

de·mor·al·i·za·tion (di-môr′ə-li-zā′shən, di-mor′ə-lī-zā′shən), *n.* a demoralizing or being demoralized.

de·mor·al·ize (di-môr′ə-līz′, di-mor′ə-līz′), *v.t.* [coined by Noah Webster < *de-* + *moralize*], 1. to corrupt the morals of; deprave. 2. to lower the morale of; weaken the spirit, courage, discipline, or staying power of. 3. to throw into confusion.

De Mor·gan, William Frend (frend də môr′gən), 1839–1917; English artist and novelist.

‡de mor·tu·is nil ni·si bo·num (dē môr′tū-is nil nī′sī bō′nəm), [L.], of the dead (say) nothing but good.

de·mos (dē′mos), *n.* [*pl.* DEMI (-mī)], [Gr. *dēmos,* the common people], 1. a deme. 2. the people or commonalty of an ancient Greek state; hence, 3. the common people; the people; the masses.

De·mos·the·nes (di-mos′thə-nēz′), *n.* Greek orator and statesman; lived 385?–322 B.C.

de·mote (di-mōt′), *v.t.* [DEMOTED (-id), DEMOTING], [*de-* + *-mote* as in *promote*], to reduce to a lower grade; lower in rank: opposed to *promote.*

de·mot·ic (di-mot′ik), *adj.* [Gr. *dēmotikos,* popular < *dēmos,* the people], 1. [Rare], of the people; popular. 2. in *ancient Egyptian history,* designating or of a simplified system of writing: distinguished from *hieratic.*

de·mot·ics (di-mot′iks), *n.pl.* [construed as sing.], sociology in its widest sense.

de·mo·tion (di-mō′shən), *n.* a demoting or being demoted.

de·mount (dē-mount′), *v.t.* to remove from a mounting or mounted position: as, *demount* the motor.

de·mount·a·ble (dē-moun′tə-b'l), *adj.* that can be demounted.

Demp·sey, Jack (demp′si), (born *William Harrison Dempsey*), 1895– ; American prize fighter; world heavyweight champion (1919–1926).

de·mul·cent (di-mul′s'nt), *adj.* [L. *demulcens,* ppr. of *demulcere,* to stroke down, soften; *de-,* down + *mulcere,* to stroke], soothing. *n.* a medicine or ointment that counteracts the irritation of inflamed surfaces.

de·mur (di-mũr′), *v.i.* [DEMURRED (-mũrd′), DEMURRING], [OFr. *demorer;* L. *demorari,* to delay; *de-,* from + *morari,* to delay < *mora,* a delay], 1. to hesitate; have scruples; object (with *at*). 2. in *law,* to enter a demurrer. *n.* 1. a demurring. 2. an objection raised or exception taken. —*SYN.* see **object.**

de·mure (di-myoor′), *adj.* [*de-* (prob. intens. < *demur*); + ME. *meur;* OFr. *meür;* prob. < L. *maturus,* mature, proper], 1. sober; serious; sedate. 2. affectedly modest or sedate; coy. —*SYN.* see **shy.**

de·mur·rage (di-mũr′ij), *n.* [OFr. *demorage,* a delay < *demorer, demurer;* see DEMUR], 1. the delaying of a ship, freight car, etc., as by the freighter's failure to load, unload, or sail within the time allowed. 2. the compensation paid for this.

de·mur·ral (di-mũr′əl), *n.* a demurring; demur; delay.

de·mur·rer (di-mũr′ẽr), *n.* [OFr. *demurer* (see DEMUR); inf. used as *n.*], 1. a plea for the dismissal of a lawsuit on the grounds that even if the statements of the opposition are true, they do not sustain the claim because they are insufficient or otherwise legally defective. 2. an objection; demur. 3. a person who demurs.

de·my (di-mī′), *n.* [*pl.* DEMIES (-mīz′)], [< *demi-*], 1. any of several sizes of writing and printing paper, averaging from 15 1/2 by 20 to 18 by 23 inches. 2. a foundation scholar at Magdalen College, Oxford.

den (den), *n.* [ME.; AS. *denn,* lair, pasture; akin to G. dial. *denn,* place where grass is trodden down, lair; IE. base **dhen-,* flattened place, flat of the hand], 1. the lair or hiding place of a wild animal. 2. a cage for a wild animal, as in a zoo. 3. a cave as a place to hide; hence, 4. a retreat or headquarters, as of thieves or vagrants; haunt. 5. a small, squalid room. 6. a small, cozy room where one can be alone to read, work, etc. *v.i.* [DENNED (dend), DENNING], to live or hide in or as in a den.

Den., Denmark.

de·nar·i·us (di-nâr′i-əs), *n.* [*pl.* DENARII (i-ī′)], [L., orig. adj., containing ten < *deni,* by tens < *decem,* ten], 1. an ancient Roman silver coin, the penny of the New Testament: the initial letter is now the symbol (d) for British pence. 2. an ancient Roman gold coin, worth 25 silver denarii.

den·a·ry (den′ə-ri, dē′nə-ri), *adj.* [see DENARIUS], having to do with the number ten; tenfold; decimal.

de·na·tion·al·ize (dē-nash′ə-n'l-īz′), *v.t.* [Fr. *dénationaliser;* see DE- & NATIONALIZE], to deprive of national rights, status, scope, etc.

de·nat·u·ral·ize (dē-nach′ẽr-əl-īz′), *v.t.* 1. to make unnatural. 2. to take citizenship away from.

de·na·tur·ant (dē-nā′chẽr-ənt), *n.* a denaturing agent.

de·na·tur·a·tion (dē-nā′chẽr-ā′shən), *n.* a denaturing or being denatured.

de·na·ture (dē-nā′chẽr), *v.t.* [DENATURED (-chẽrd), DENATURING], 1. to change the nature of; take natural qualities away from. 2. to make (alcohol, etc.) unfit as food or drink without spoiling for other uses.

denatured alcohol, ethyl alcohol mixed with a small amount of pyridine, methyl alcohol, or certain other compounds to make it unfit to drink: used as an antifreeze for automobile radiators, etc.

de·na·tur·ize (dē-nā′chẽr-īz′), *v.t.* [DENATURIZED (-īzd′), DENATURIZING], to denature.

de·na·zi·fy (dē-nät′sə-fī′), *v.t.* to rid of all Nazi elements, as by removal of Nazis from positions of importance, by education, etc.

Den·bigh (den′bi), *n.* 1. Denbighshire. 2. the county seat of Denbighshire: pop., 8,000.

Den·bigh·shire (den′bi-shir′), *n.* a county of northern Wales: pop., 158,000; county seat, Denbigh.

den·dri- (den′dri), dendro-.

den·dri·form (den′dri-fôrm′), *adj.* [*dendri-* + *-form*], shaped like a tree.

den·drite (den′drīt), *n.* [< Gr. *dendritēs,* of a tree < *dendron,* a tree], 1. a branching, treelike mark made by one mineral crystallizing in another. 2. a stone or mineral with such a mark. 3. the branched part of a nerve cell that carries impulses toward the cell body: also called *dendron, neurodendron.* 4. *pl.* the protoplasmic filaments of a nerve cell body.

den·drit·ic (den-drit′ik), *adj.* 1. of or like a dendrite or dendrites. 2. treelike; branching in form.

den·drit·i·cal (den-drit′i-k'l), *adj.* dendritic.

den·dro- (den′drō, den′drə), [< Gr. *dendron,* a tree], a combining form meaning *tree,* as in *dendrology:* also **dendri-,** or, before a vowel, **dendr-.**

den·droid (den′droid), *adj.* [Gr. *dendroeidēs* < *dendron,* a tree + *eidos,* form], treelike in form.

den·drol·o·gy (den-drol′ə-ji), *n.* [*dendro-* + *-logy*], the scientific study of trees.

-den·dron (den′drən), [< Gr. *dendron*, a tree], a combining form meaning *tree* or *treelike structure*, as in *rhododendron.*

dene (dēn), *n.* [var. of *dune*], [British Dial.], a low mound of loose sand near a seashore; dune.

Den·eb (den′eb), *n.* [Ar. *dhanab*, short for *dhanab al-dajājah*, tail of the hen], a first-magnitude star in the constellation Cygnus (Swan): see **constellation**, chart.

den·e·ga·tion (den′i-gā′shən), *n.* [Fr. *dénégation* < L. *denegatus*, pp. of *denegare;* see DENY], a denying; statement of denial.

den·gue (deŋ′gi, deŋ′gā), *n.* [W. Ind. Sp. < Swahili *dinga, dyenga,* cramplike attack; confused with Sp. *dengue,* affected contortion, prudery (with reference to the position of the neck and shoulders)], an infectious tropical disease transmitted by mosquitoes and characterized by severe pains in the joints and back, fever, and rash: also called *dandy fever, breakbone fever.*

de·ni·a·ble (di-nī′ə-b'l), *adj.* that can be denied.

de·ni·al (di-nī′əl), *n.* 1. a denying; saying "no" (to a request, etc.): opposed to *compliance.* 2. a contradiction: as, the *denial* of a statement: opposed to *affirmation.* 3. a disowning; repudiation: as, the *denial* of one's family. 4. a refusal to believe or accept (a doctrine, etc.). 5. a refusal to give. 6. abstinence from desired things: also **self-denial.**

de·nic·o·tin·ize (dē-nik′ə-tin-īz′), *v.t.* [DENICOTINIZED (-īzd′), DENICOTINIZING], [< *de-* + *nicotine* + *-ize*], to remove nicotine from (tobacco).

de·nier (də-nêr′; Fr. də-nyā′), *n.* [Fr.; L. *denarius;* see DENARIUS], 1. a small, obsolete French coin of little value, originally of silver, but after the 16th century, of copper. 2. (*usually* den′yẽr), a unit of weight for threads of silk, rayon, etc., equal to .05 gram per 450 meters.

de·ni·er (di-nī′ẽr), *n.* a person who denies.

den·i·grate (den′ə-grāt′), *v.t.* [DENIGRATED (-id), DENIGRATING], [< L. *denigratus*, pp. of *denigrare*, to blacken; *de-*, intens. + *nigrare*, to blacken < *niger*, black], 1. to blacken; hence, 2. to blacken the name of; defame.

den·i·gra·tion (den′ə-grā′shən), *n.* [L. *denigratio;* see DENIGRATE], 1. a blackening or becoming black. 2. a blackening of character; defamation.

den·i·gra·tor (den′ə-grā′tẽr), *n.* [< *denigrate* + *-or*], 1. a person or thing that blackens something. 2. a person who blackens another's character; defamer.

den·im (den′im), *n.* [contr. < Fr. *serge de Nîmes*, serge of Nîmes, town where first made], a coarse, twilled cotton cloth used for overalls, uniforms, etc.

Den·is (den′is), [Fr.; L. *Dionysius*], a masculine name: also spelled **Dennis.**

Denis, Saint, 3d century A.D.; patron saint of France and first bishop of Paris: also spelled **Denys.**

de·ni·trate (dē-nī′trāt), *v.t.* to remove nitric acid, the nitrate ion or radical, the nitro group, or the oxides of nitrogen from.

de·ni·tra·tion (dē′nī-trā′shən), *n.* the process of denitrating.

de·ni·tri·fy (dē-nī′trə-fī′), *v.t.* to remove nitrogen or its compounds from.

den·i·zen (den′i-z'n), *n.* [Anglo-Fr. *deinzein;* OFr. *denzein, deinzein,* native inhabitant < *deinz, denz,* within; LL. *de intus,* from within], 1. an inhabitant or occupant. 2. a foreigner granted specified rights of citizenship. 3. an animal, plant, foreign word, etc. that has become naturalized. *v.t.* 1. to naturalize. 2. [Rare], to furnish with denizens.

Den·mark (den′märk), *n.* a country in Europe, north of Germany, between the North and Baltic seas: area, 16,576 sq. mi.; pop., 4,448,000; capital, Copenhagen: abbreviated **Den.**

Denmark Strait, a strait between Greenland and Iceland: width, 130 mi.

Den·nis (den′is), a masculine name: see **Denis.**

de·nom·in·ate (di-nom′ə-nāt′; *for adj., usually* di-nom′ə-nit), *v.t.* [< L. *denominatus*, pp. of *denominare*, to name; *de-*, intens. + *nominare;* see NOMINATE], to name; call. *adj.* having a specified name: as, 3 lbs. and 15 ft. are *denominate* numbers.

de·nom·i·na·tion (di-nom′ə-nā′shən), *n.* [Fr.; L. *denominatio;* see DENOMINATE], 1. the act of naming. 2. a name. 3. the name of a class of things. 4. a class or kind (especially of units) having a specific name or value: as, coins of different *denominations.* 5. a religious sect: as, a Protestant *denomination.*

de·nom·i·na·tion·al (di-nom′ə-nā′shən-'l), *adj.* of, sponsored by, or under the control of, some religious sect or sects; sectarian.

de·nom·i·na·tion·al·ism (di-nom′ə-nā′shən-'l-iz'm), *n.* 1. denominational principles. 2. a denominational system. 3. acceptance or support of such principles or system. 4. division into denominations.

de·nom·i·na·tive (di-nom′ə-nā′tiv, di-nom′ə-nə-tiv), *adj.* [L. *denominativus*], 1. denominating; naming. 2. in *grammar*, formed from a noun or adjective stem: as, *to eye* is a *denominative* verb. *n.* a denominative word, especially a verb.

de·nom·i·na·tor (di-nom′ə-nā′tẽr), *n.* [ML.], 1. a person or thing that denominates. 2. in *arithmetic* & *algebra*, the term below or to the right of the line in a fraction, indicating the number of equal parts into which the whole is divided: as, 7 is the *denominator* of 6/7.

de·not·a·ble (di-nōt′ə-b'l), *adj.* that can be denoted.

de·no·ta·tion (dē′nō-tā′shən), *n.* [LL. *denotatio*], 1. a denoting. 2. a marking out or off. 3. the direct, explicit meaning or reference of a word or term: distinguished from *connotation.* 4. an indication or sign.

de·no·ta·tive (di-nō′tə-tiv, dē′nō-tā′tiv), *adj.* denoting; designative.

de·note (di-nōt′), *v.t.* [DENOTED (-id), DENOTING], [Fr. *dénoter;* L. *denotare*, to mark out, denote; *de-*, down + *notare*, to mark < *nota*, a mark], 1. to mark; indicate; designate; make known by a sign. 2. to mean; signify explicitly; refer to; be a name of: said of words, signs, or symbols, and distinguished from *connote.*

de·noue·ment, dé·noue·ment (dā-nōō′män; Fr. dā′-nōō′män′), *n.* [Fr. < *dénouer*, to untie; *dé-* (L. *dis-*), from, out + *nouer*, to tie < L. *nodare*, to knot < *nodus*, a knot], 1. the outcome, solution, unraveling, or clarification of a plot in a drama, story, etc. 2. the point in the plot where this occurs. 3. any final revelation or outcome.

de·nounce (di-nouns′), *v.t.* [DENOUNCED (-nounst′), DENOUNCING], [ME. *denouncen;* OFr. *denoncer;* L. *denuntiare;* see DENUNCIATION], 1. to accuse publicly; inform against: as, he *denounced* the traitor to the authorities. 2. to condemn strongly as evil. 3. to give formal notice of the ending of (a treaty, armistice, etc.). 4. [Obs.], to announce. —*SYN.* see **criticize.**

de·nounce·ment (di-nouns′mənt), *n.* denunciation.

‡**de no·vo** (dē nō′vō), [L.], anew; once more; again.

dense (dens), *adj.* [L. *densus*, compact], 1. having the parts crowded together; packed tightly together. 2. thick; impenetrable; hence, 3. thick-headed; stupid. 4. in *photography*, opaque, with good contrast in light and shade: said of a negative. —*SYN.* see **close, stupid.**

den·si·tom·e·ter (den′sə-tom′ə-tẽr), *n.* [< *density* + *-meter*], an optical device for measuring the density of a photographic negative.

den·si·ty (den′sə-ti), *n.* [*pl.* DENSITIES (-tiz)], [Fr. *densité;* L. *densitas*], 1. the quality or condition of being dense, thick, compact, or crowded. 2. quantity or number per unit, as of area: as, the *density* of population. 3. stupidity. 4. in *electricity, a*) the amount of a charge of electricity flowing through a unit of area in a unit of time. *b*) current density. 5. in *photography*, opaque quality; amount of light-stopping material on an exposed negative. 6. in *physics*, the ratio of the mass of an object to its volume: symbol, D (no period). Abbreviated **d.**

dent (dent), *n.* [ME., dial. var. of *dint*], a slight hollow made in a surface by a blow or pressure. *v.t.* to make a dent in. *v.i.* to become dented.

dent (dent), *n.* [Fr.; L. *dens, dentis*, a tooth], a toothlike projection as in a gearwheel, lock, etc.

dent., 1. dental. 2. dentist. 3. dentistry.

den·tal (den′t'l), *adj.* [Mod. L. *dentalis* < L. *dens, dentis*, a tooth; akin to Cym. *dant*, OHG. *zan, zand*, OS. *tand*, ON. *tönn*, Goth. *tunthus*, Pre-AS. **tanth*, AS. *toth*, Eng. *tooth;* see TOOTH], 1. of or for the teeth or dentistry. 2. in *phonetics*, formed by placing the tip of the tongue against or near the upper front teeth. *n.* in *phonetics*, a dental consonant, as *d, t, th.*

dental floss, thin, strong thread for removing food particles from between the teeth.

den·tate (den′tāt), *adj.* [L. *dentatus* < *dens, dentis*, a tooth], 1. having teeth or toothlike projections; toothed or notched. 2. in *botany*, having a toothed margin, as some leaves: see **leaf,** illus.

den·ta·tion (den-tā′shən), *n.* 1. the quality or condition of being dentate. 2. a toothlike projection, as on a leaf.

dent·ed (den′tid), *adj.* [see DENT (slight hollow)], 1. having a slight hollow or hollows in its surface. 2. indented.

dent·ed (den′tid), *adj.* [see DENT (toothlike projection)], toothed.

den·ti- (den′ti, den′tə), [< L. *dens, dentis*, a tooth], a combining form meaning: 1. *tooth* or *teeth*, as in *dentiform.* 2. in *phonetics, dental and*, as in *dentilabial.* Also, before a vowel, **dent-.**

den·ti·cle (den′ti-k'l), *n.* [L. *denticulus*, dim. of *dens, dentis*, a tooth], 1. a small tooth or toothlike projection. 2. a dentil.

den·tic·u·late (den-tik′yoo-lit, den-tik′yoo-lāt′), *adj.* [L. *denticulatus*], having denticles.

den·tic·u·lat·ed (den-tik′yoo-lā′tid), *adj.* denticulate.

den·tic·u·la·tion (den-tik′yoo-lā′shən), *n.* 1. the quality or condition of being denticulate. 2. a denticle.

den·ti·form (den′ti-fôrm′), *adj.* [*denti-* + *-form*], tooth-shaped.

den·ti·frice (den′tə-fris), *n.* [Fr.; L. *dentifricium*, tooth powder < *dens, dentis*, a tooth + *fricare*, to rub], any preparation for cleaning teeth, as a powder, paste, or liquid.

den·til (den'til), *n.* [MFr. *dentille;* It. *dentello,* dim. < L. *dens;* see DENTAL], in *architecture,* any of a series of small square blocks projecting like teeth, as from under a cornice.

den·ti·la·bi·al (den'ti-lā'bi-əl), *adj.* & *n.* [*denti-* + *labial*], labiodental.

den·ti·lin·gual (den'ti-liŋ'gwəl), *adj.* [*denti-* + *lingual*], in *phonetics,* pronounced with the tip of the tongue between the teeth, as the *th* in *thin:* now usually *interdental.*

den·tin (den'tin), *n.* dentine.

den·tine (den'tēn, den'tin), *n.* [< L. *dens, dentis,* a tooth; + *-ine*], the hard, dense, calcareous tissue forming the body of a tooth, under the enamel: see **tooth,** illus.

den·ti·phone (den'ti-fōn'), *n.* [*denti-* + *-phone*], an instrument held against the teeth to help the hearing by transmitting sound vibrations to the auditory nerve.

den·tist (den'tist), *n.* [Fr. *dentiste* < L. *dens, dentis,* a tooth], a person whose profession is the care of teeth, including the filling of cavities, the extraction of teeth beyond repair, and the replacement of missing teeth with artificial ones; doctor of dental surgery (**D.D.S.**): abbreviated **dent.**

den·tist·ry (den'tis-tri), *n.* the branch of medical science that deals with the teeth and their care; art or work of a dentist: abbreviated **dent.**

den·ti·tion (den-tish'ən), *n.* [L. *dentitio,* a teething < *dentire,* to cut teeth < *dens, dentis,* a tooth], 1. the teething process. 2. the number, sort, and arrangement of the teeth: as, the *dentition* of man differs from that of the dog.

den·to- (den'tō, den'tə), 1. denti-. 2. a combining form meaning *dental, dental and,* as in *dentosurgical.*

den·toid (den'toid), *adj.* [*dent-* + *-oid*], tooth-shaped.

den·to·sur·gi·cal (den'tō-sũr'ji-k'l), *adj.* relating to or used in both dentistry and surgery.

D'En·tre·cas·teaux Islands (dän'tr'-kȧs'tō'), a group of islands off southeastern New Guinea: a part of the Territory of Papua: area, 1,200 sq. mi.; pop., 33,000.

den·ture (den'chẽr), *n.* [Fr. < *dent;* L. *dens, dentis,* a tooth], a set of teeth; especially, a partial or complete set of artificial teeth.

den·u·date (den'yoo-dāt', di-nū'dāt), *v.t.* [DENUDATED (-id), DENUDATING], [< L. *denudatus,* pp. of *denudare,* to strip off < *de-,* off + *nudare,* to strip; cf. NUDE], to denude. *adj.* (di-nū'dit, den'yoo-dāt'), denuded.

den·u·da·tion (den'yoo-dā'shən, dē'nyoo-dā'shən), *n.* [Fr.; L. *denudatio;* see DENUDATE], 1. a denuding. 2. the fact or condition of being denuded.

de·nude (di-nōōd', di-nūd'), *v.t.* [DENUDED (-id), DENUDING], [L. *denudare;* see DENUDATE], 1. to make bare or naked; strip: as, the land was *denuded* of vegetation. 2. in *geology,* to lay bare by erosion. —*SYN.* see **strip.**

de·nun·ci·ate (di-nun'si-āt', di-nun'shi-āt'), *v.t.* & *v.i.* [DENUNCIATED (-id), DENUNCIATING], [< L. *denuntiatus;* see DENUNCIATION], to denounce.

de·nun·ci·a·tion (di-nun'si-ā'shən, di-nun'shi-ā'shən), *n.* [L. *denuntiatio,* announcement, forewarning < *denuntiatus,* pp. of *denuntiare,* to announce, denounce; *de-,* intens. + *nuntiare,* to announce], 1. a denouncing. 2. a threat or warning of evil, punishment, etc. 3. an informing against (someone) to the authorities; accusation. 4. a notice by a nation of its intention to end a treaty, armistice, etc. 5. [Obs.], an announcement.

de·nun·ci·a·tor (di-nun'si-ā'tẽr, di-nun'shi-ā'tẽr), *n.* [Fr. *dénonciateur;* L. *denuntiator,* police officer < *denuntiare;* see DENUNCIATION], a denouncer.

de·nun·ci·a·to·ry (di-nun'si-ə-tôr'i, di-nun'shi-ə-tō'ri), *adj.* of or characterized by denunciation.

Den·ver (den'vẽr), *n.* the capital of Colorado: pop., 494,000.

de·ny (di-nī'), *v.t.* [DENIED (-nīd'), DENYING], [ME. *denyen;* OFr. *denier;* L. *denegare; de-,* intens. + *negare,* to say "no," refuse, deny], 1. to declare (a statement) untrue; contradict. 2. to refuse to accept as true or right; reject as unfounded, unreal, etc. 3. to refuse to recognize; disown; repudiate. 4. to refuse access to. 5. to refuse to grant or give. 6. to refuse (a person who makes a request). 7. [Obs.], to forbid. *v.i.* to maintain a negative attitude; refuse compliance.

deny oneself, 1. to do without desired things. 2. to abstain from.

deny oneself to, to refuse access to (visitors).

SYN.—**deny** implies a refusal to accept as true, real, valid, existent, or tenable (he *denied* the charge); to **gainsay** is to dispute what a person says or to challenge the person saying it (facts that cannot be *gainsaid*); **contradict** not only implies emphatic denial, but, in addition, often suggests belief or evidence that the opposite or contrary is true; **impugn** implies a direct, forceful attack against that which one calls into question (she *impugned* his motives).

Den·ys, Saint (den'is; Fr. də-nē'), see **Denis,** Saint.

de·o·dand (dē'ə-dand'), *n.* [ML. *deodandum* < L. *Deo dandum,* lit., to be given to god; *Deo,* dat. of *Deus,* God + *dandum,* gerundive of *dare,* to give], in *early English law,* any property instrumental in a person's death, and consequently forfeited to the crown, to be used for some pious purpose.

de·o·dar (dē'ə-där'), *n.* [Hind. *deodār;* Sans. *devadāru; deva,* divine tree of the gods + *dāru,* wood], 1. a kind of cedar tree with durable, light-red wood, native to the Himalayas. 2. its wood.

de·o·dor·ant (dē-ō'dẽr-ənt), *adj.* [< *de-* + L. *odorans,* ppr. of *odorare,* to smell < *odor,* a smell], having the power of destroying or counteracting undesired odors. *n.* any deodorant substance or preparation.

de·o·dor·i·za·tion (dē-ō'dẽr-i-zā'shən, dē-ō'dẽr-ī-zā'shən), *n.* a deodorizing or being deodorized.

de·o·dor·ize (dē-ō'dẽr-īz'), *v.t.* [DEODORIZED (-īzd'), DEODORIZING], to remove or counteract the odor of.

‡De·o gra·ti·as (dē'ō grā'shi-as', dā'ō grä'ti-äs'), [L.], thanks to God.

de·on·to·log·i·cal (dē'on-tə-loj'i-k'l), *adj.* of, or with reference to, deontology.

de·on·tol·o·gy (dē'on-tol'ə-ji), *n.* [< Gr. *deon, deontos,* that which is binding, necessity < *dein,* to bind; + *-logy*], the theory of duty or moral obligation; ethics.

‡De·o vo·len·te (dē'ō vō-len'ti), [L.], (if) God is willing: abbreviated **D.V.**

de·ox·i·dize (dē-ok'sə-dīz'), *v.t.* to remove oxygen, especially chemically combined oxygen, from.

de·ox·y·gen·ate (dē-ok'sə-jə-nāt'), *v.t.* to remove oxygen, especially free oxygen, from (water, air, etc.).

dep., 1. department. 2. departs. 3. departure. 4. deponent. 5. deposed. 6. deposit. 7. depot. 8. deputy.

de·part (di-pärt'), *v.i.* [ME. *departen;* OFr. *despartir;* L. *dispartire,* to divide, separate; *dis-,* apart + *partire,* to divide < *pars, partis,* a part, share: orig. *v.t.,* to divide, as in earlier marriage service "till death us do depart"], 1. to go away (*from*); leave. 2. to start; set out. 3. to die. 4. to turn aside (*from* something): as, you *depart* from custom. *v.t.* [Archaic], to leave: now only in *depart this life.* *n.* [Obs.], a departure. —*SYN.* see **go.**

de·part·ed (di-pär'tid), *adj.* [pp. of *depart*], 1. gone away; past; bygone. 2. dead. —*SYN.* see **dead.**

the departed, 1. the dead person. 2. dead persons; the dead.

de·part·ment (di-pärt'mənt), *n.* [ME.; OFr. *departement* < *despartir;* see DEPART], 1. a separate part, division, or branch, as of a government or business: as, the police *department,* the accounting *department;* hence, 2. a field of knowledge or activity: as, rewriting is his *department.* 3. a government administrative district in France. 4. in *education,* a subdivision of a college or school, for the teaching and studying of a branch of knowledge: as, the *department* of sociology. Abbreviated **dept., dep., dpt.**

de·part·men·tal (di-pärt'men't'l, dē'pärt-men't'l), *adj.* 1. having to do with a department or departments. 2. arranged into or according to departments.

de·part·men·tal·ism (dē'pärt-men't'l-iz'm), *n.* 1. strict following of departmental rules, practices, etc. 2. bureaucracy.

department store, a large retail store for the sale of many kinds of goods arranged in departments.

de·par·ture (di-pär'chẽr), *n.* [OFr. *departeure* < *despartir;* see DEPART], 1. a departing; going away; leaving. 2. a starting out, as on a trip or new course of action: as, political action is a new *departure* for labor. 3. a deviation or turning aside (*from* something). 4. [Archaic], death. 5. in *nautical usage, a)* the distance of a ship due east or west from the meridian of its starting point. *b)* a ship's position in latitude and longitude at the start of a voyage, from which the dead reckoning is begun. Abbreviated **dep.**

de·pas·ture (di-pas'chẽr, di-päs'chẽr), *v.t.* 1. to consume the herbage of (a piece of land) by grazing: said of cattle, etc. 2. to pasture (cattle, etc.). *v.i.* to graze.

de·pend (di-pend'), *v.i.* [ME. *dependen;* OFr. *dependre;* L. *dependere,* to hang down from; *de-,* down + *pendere,* to hang], 1. to be influenced or determined by something else; be contingent (*on*). 2. to rely. 3. to rely for support or aid. 4. to be in suspense; be undecided. 5. [Archaic], to hang down. —*SYN.* see **rely.**

de·pend·a·bil·i·ty (di-pen'də-bil'ə-ti), *n.* the quality of being dependable.

de·pend·a·ble (di-pen'də-b'l), *adj.* that can be depended on; trustworthy; reliable. —*SYN.* see **reliable.**

de·pend·a·bly (di-pen'də-bli), *adv.* in a dependable manner.

de·pend·ence (di-pen'dəns), *n.* [Fr. *dépendance* < L. *dependens;* see DEPENDENT], 1. the condition or fact of being dependent. 2. the state of being contingent upon or influenced, controlled, or determined by something else. 3. subordination. 4. reliance (*on* someone else) for support or aid. 5. reliance; trust. 6. [Rare], a person or thing relied on. 7. [Archaic], anything suspended. Also spelled **dependance.**

de·pend·en·cy (di-pen′dən-si), *n.* [*pl.* DEPENDENCIES (-siz)], 1. dependence. 2. something dependent or subordinate. 3. a land or territory geographically distinct from the country governing it, but belonging to it and subject to its laws: as, Alaska was a *dependency* of the United States. Also spelled **dependancy.**

de·pen·dent (di-pen′dənt), *adj.* [Fr. *dépendant* < L. *dependens*, ppr. of *dependere;* see DEPEND], 1. hanging down. 2. influenced, controlled, or determined by something else; contingent. 3. relying (*on* someone or something) for support or aid. 4. subordinate. *n.* 1. a thing that depends. 2. a person who relies on someone else for existence, support, etc. Also spelled **dependant.**

dependent clause, in *grammar*, a subordinate clause.

de·peo·ple (dē-pē′p'l), *v.t.* to depopulate.

de·pict (di-pikt′), *v.t.* [< L. *depictus*, pp. of *depingere*, to paint, depict; *de-*, intens. + *pingere*, to paint], 1. to represent by drawing, painting, sculpturing, etc.; portray; picture. 2. to picture in words; describe.

de·pic·tion (di-pik′shən), *n.* [LL. *depictio*], 1. a depicting or being depicted. 2. a picture, sculpture, etc. depicting something. 3. description.

de·pic·ture (di-pik′chẽr), *v.t.* to represent in a picture or words; depict.

dep·i·late (dep′ə-lāt′), *v.t.* [DEPILATED (-id), DEPILATING], [< L. *depilatus*, pp. of *depilare*, to deprive of hair; *de-*, from + *pilare*, to pull out the hair < *pilus*, hair], to remove hair from (a part of the body).

dep·i·la·tor (dep′ə-lā′tẽr), *n.* [< *depilate* + *-or*], a person or instrument that removes hair.

de·pil·a·to·ry (di-pil′ə-tôr′i, di-pil′ə-tō′ri), *adj.* [< *depilate* + *-ory*], serving to remove hair, especially unwanted hair. *n.* [*pl.* DEPILATORIES (-iz, -riz)], a depilatory substance or device.

de·plete (di-plēt′), *v.t.* [DEPLETED (-id), DEPLETING], [< L. *depletus*, pp. of *deplere*, to empty; *de-*, from + *plere*, to fill], 1. to empty wholly or partly. 2. to exhaust, as of energy, funds, etc. 3. in *medicine*, to relieve of fluid, as congested blood, by draining.

de·ple·tion (di-plē′shən), *n.* 1. a depleting or being depleted. 2. a state of exhaustion resulting from excessive loss of blood.

de·plor·a·ble (di-plôr′ə-b'l, di-plō′rə-b'l), *adj.* to be deplored; lamentable; regrettable; unfortunate.

de·plor·a·bly (di-plôr′ə-bli, di-plō′rə-bli), *adv.* 1. in a deplorable manner. 2. to a deplorable extent.

de·plore (di-plôr′, di-plōr′), *v.t.* [DEPLORED (-plôrd′, -plōrd′), DEPLORING], [Fr. *déplorer;* L. *deplorare; de-*, intens. + *plorare*, to weep], to be regretful or sorry about; lament.

de·ploy (di-ploi′), *v.t. & v.i.* [Fr. *déployer*, to unfold, display; OFr. *desployer*, to unfold, unroll; LL. *displicare;* L. *dis-*, from + *plicare*, to fold], in *military science*, to spread out so as to form a wider front of narrow depth. *n.* [Rare], a deploying.

de·ploy·ment (di-ploi′mənt), *n.* a deploying or being deployed.

de·plu·ma·tion (dē′ploo-mā′shən), *n.* 1. a depluming or being deplumed. 2. the falling off of feathers, as in molting.

de·plume (di-ploom′), *v.t.* [Fr. *déplumer;* ML. *deplumare;* see DE- & PLUME], 1. to pull the feathers out of; pluck. 2. to strip of honor, riches, possessions, etc.

de·po·lar·i·za·tion (dē-pō′lẽr-i-zā′shən, dē′pō-lẽr-i-zā′shən), *n.* a depolarizing or being depolarized.

de·po·lar·ize (dē-pō′lẽr-īz′), *v.t.* to destroy or counteract the polarity or polarization of.

de·pone (di-pōn′), *v.t. & v.i.* [DEPONED (-pōnd′), DEPONING], [L. *deponere;* see DEPOSE], to declare in writing under oath; testify.

de·pon·ent (di-pō′nənt), *adj.* [L. *deponens*, ppr. of *deponere*, to lay down, set down; see DEPOSE], in *Latin & Greek grammar*, denoting a verb with a passive or middle voice form and an active meaning: so called because thought of as laying aside the original passive quality. *n.* 1. in *Latin & Greek grammar*, a deponent verb. 2. in *law*, *a*) a person who makes an affidavit. *b*) a person who gives written testimony under oath. Abbreviated **dep., dept., dpt.**

de·pop·u·late (dē-pop′yoo-lāt′), *v.t.* [< L. *depopulatus*, pp. of *depopulari*, to lay waste, devastate; *de-*, from + *populari*, to ravage, ruin < *populus*, the people], to rid of inhabitants; reduce the population of, especially by violence, pestilence, etc. *adj.* [Archaic], depopulated.

de·pop·u·la·tion (dē-pop′yoo-lā′shən, dē′pop-yoo-lā′shən), *n.* a depopulating or being depopulated.

de·pop·u·la·tor (dē-pop′yoo-lā′tẽr), *n.* a person or thing, as war or famine, that depopulates.

de·port (di-pôrt′, di-pōrt′), *v.t.* [OFr. *deporter; de-* (L. *de*), intens. + *porter* < L. *portare*, to carry, bear, endure], 1. to behave or conduct (oneself) in a specified way. 2. [Fr. *déporter;* L. *deportare*, to carry away, banish; *de-*, from + *portare*], to expel (someone) from a country; banish. *n.* [OFr. < *deporter*], [Obs.], deportment. —*SYN.* see **banish, behave.**

de·por·ta·tion (dē′pôr-tā′shən, dē′pōr-tā′shən), *n.* [Fr. *déportation;* L. *deportatio*, a carrying away, removal < *deportare;* see DEPORT], a deporting or being deported; expulsion, as of an undesirable alien, from a country.

de·por·tee (dē′pôr-tē′, dē′pōr-tē′), *n.* [Fr. *déporté*, pp. of *déporter;* see DEPORT & -EE], 1. a deported person. 2. a person sentenced to deportation.

de·port·ment (di-pôrt′mənt, di-pōrt′mənt), *n.* [OFr. *deportement;* see DEPORT], the manner of conducting or bearing oneself; behavior; demeanor. —*SYN.* see **bearing.**

de·pos·a·ble (di-pōz′ə-b'l), *adj.* that can be deposed.

de·pos·al (di-pōz′'l), *n.* a deposing from office; deposition.

de·pose (di-pōz′), *v.t.* [DEPOSED (-pōzd′), DEPOSING], [ME. *deposen*, to set aside, deprive of office, degrade; OFr. *deposer*, to set down, deposit; *de-* (L. *de*), from, away + *poser* (LL. *pausare;* see POSE, to lay down), to cease, lie down; confused in sense and form with L. *deponere* (pp. *depositus*) to lay down, lay aside; see DEPOSIT], 1. to remove from office or a position of power, especially from a throne; oust. 2. in *law*, to state under oath; testify. *v.i.* to bear witness.

de·pos·it (di-poz′it), *v.t.* [< L. *depositus*, pp. of *deponere;* see DEPOSE], 1. to place or entrust for safekeeping. 2. to put (money) in a bank, as for safekeeping or to earn interest. 3. to put down as a pledge or partial payment: as, they *deposited* $500 on a new house. 4. to put, lay, or set down. 5. to leave lying, as sediment. *n.* [L. *depositum* < *depositus;* see the *v.*], 1. the state of being placed or entrusted for safekeeping (with *on*). 2. something placed or entrusted for safekeeping. 3. money put in a bank. 4. a pledge or part payment. 5. a depositing. 6. a depository. 7. something deposited or left lying. 8. in *geology & mining*, sand, clay, mineral masses, etc. deposited by the action of wind, water, volcanic eruption, or ice. Abbreviated **dep.**

de·pos·i·tar·y (di-poz′ə-ter′i), *n.* [*pl.* DEPOSITARIES (-iz)], [LL. *depositarius* < L. *depositum;* see DEPOSIT], 1. a person, firm, etc. entrusted with something for safekeeping; trustee. 2. a depository; storehouse.

dep·o·si·tion (dep′ə-zish′ən, dē′pə-zish′ən), *n.* [OFr.; LL. *depositio*, a laying or putting down < L. *depositus;* see DEPOSIT], 1. a deposing or being deposed; removal from office or position of power. 2. a testifying. 3. testimony. 4. a depositing or being deposited. 5. something deposited; deposit. 6. in *law*, a written statement by a witness, made under oath, to be used as testimony in court.

de·pos·i·tor (di-poz′i-tẽr), *n.* [LL.], a person who deposits something, especially money in a bank.

de·pos·i·to·ry (di-poz′ə-tôr′i, di-poz′ə-tō′ri), *n.* [*pl.* DEPOSITORIES (-iz, -riz)], [ML. *depositorium;* see DEPOSIT], 1. a place where things are put for safekeeping; storehouse. 2. a trustee; depositary.

de·pot (dē′pō; *Brit. or military* dep′ō), *n.* [Fr. *dépôt*, a deposit, storehouse; OFr. *depost*, a deposit, pledge < L. *depositum;* see DEPOSIT], 1. a storehouse; warehouse. 2. a railroad station: used originally of a freight station. 3. in *military usage*, *a*) a storage place for supplies. *b*) a station for assembling either recruits for training or combat replacements for assignment to a unit. Abbreviated **dep.**

dep·ra·va·tion (dep′rə-vā′shən), *n.* [L. *depravatio* < pp. of *depravare*], 1. a depraving. 2. a depraved condition; depravity; corruption.

de·prave (di-prāv′), *v.t.* [DEPRAVED (-prāvd′), DEPRAVING], [ME. *depraven;* OFr. *depraver;* L. *depravare*, to make crooked < *de-*, intens. + *pravus*, crooked], to lead into bad habits; make morally bad; corrupt; pervert. —*SYN.* see **debase.**

de·praved (di-prāvd′), *adj.* [pp. of *deprave*], morally bad; corrupt; perverted.

de·prav·i·ty (di-prav′ə-ti), *n.* [obs. *pravity* (L. *pravitas*), after *deprave*], 1. a depraved condition; corruption. 2. [*pl.* DEPRAVITIES (-tiz)], a depraved act or practice.

dep·re·ca·ble (dep′rə-kə-b'l), *adj.* [LL. *deprecabilis*, that can be entreated], to be deprecated.

dep·re·cate (dep′rə-kāt′), *v.t.* [DEPRECATED (-id), DEPRECATING], [< L. *deprecatus*, pp. of *deprecari; de-*, off, from + *precari*, to pray], 1. to feel and express disapproval of; plead against. 2. [Archaic], to try to avert by prayer.

dep·re·ca·tion (dep′rə-kā′shən), *n.* [Fr. *déprécation;* L. *deprecatio*], a deprecating; disapproval or protest.

dep·re·ca·tive (dep′rə-kā′tiv), *adj.* deprecatory.

dep·re·ca·to·ry (dep′rə-kə-tôr′i, dep′rə-kə-tō′ri), *adj.* [L. *deprecatorius*], 1. deprecating. 2. apologetic.

de·pre·ci·a·ble (di-prē′shi-ə-b'l), *adj.* that can be depreciated; that may be lessened in value.

de·pre·ci·ate (di-prē′shi-āt′), *v.t. & v.i.* [DEPRECIATED (-id), DEPRECIATING], [L. *depretiatus*, pp. of *depretiare*, to lower the price of, make light of; *de-*, from + *pretiare*, to value < *pretium*, price], 1. to lessen in value or price. 2. to belittle; disparage. —*SYN.* see **disparage.**

de·pre·ci·a·tion (di-prē′shi-ā′shən), *n.* [see DEPRECIATE], 1. a decrease in value of property through wear, deterioration, or obsolescence. 2. the allowance made for this in bookkeeping, accounting, etc.: abbreviated **depr.** 3. a decrease in the purchasing power of money. 4. a belittling; disparagement.

de·pre·ci·a·tive (di-prē′shi-ā′tiv), *adj.* depreciatory.

de·pre·ci·a·tor (di-prē′shi-ā′tẽr), *n.* [L.], a person or thing that depreciates.

de·pre·ci·a·to·ry (di-prē′shi-ə-tôr′i, di-prē′shi-ə-tō′ri), *adj.* 1. tending to depreciate; lessening in value. 2. disparaging.

dep·re·date (dep′ri-dāt′), *v.t. & v.i.* [DEPREDATED (-id), DEPREDATING], [LL. *depraedatus*, pp. of *depraedare* < L. *de-*, intens. + *praedari*, to rob, plunder < *praeda*, booty, prey], [Archaic], to plunder.

dep·re·da·tion (dep′ri-dā′shən), *n.* [LL. *depraedatio;* see DEPREDATE], a plundering or laying waste; robbery.

dep·re·da·tor (dep′ri-dā′tēr), *n.* [LL.], a person or thing that depredates.

dep·re·da·to·ry (dep′rə-dā′tēr-i), *adj.* depredating.

de·press (di-pres′), *v.t.* [OFr. *depresser* < L. *depressus*, pp. of *deprimere*, to press down, plant deep, sink < *de-*, down + *premere*, to press], 1. to press down; push or pull down; lower. 2. to lower in spirits; make gloomy; discourage; sadden. 3. to decrease the force or activity of; weaken. 4. to lower in value, price, or amount. 5. in *music*, to lower the pitch of. 6. [Obs.], to suppress.

de·pres·sant (di-pres′ənt), *adj.* [*depress* + *-ant*], lowering the rate of muscular or nervous activity. *n.* a depressant medicine, drug, etc.; sedative.

de·pressed (di-prest′), *adj.* [pp. of *depress*], 1. pressed down. 2. lowered in position, intensity, amount, or degree. 3. flattened or hollowed, as if pressed down. 4. gloomy; dejected; sad. 5. in *botany*, flattened vertically, as if from downward pressure. 6. in *zoology*, having the horizontal diameter longer than the vertical; broader than high. —*SYN.* see **sad.**

de·pres·si·ble (di-pres′ə-b'l), *adj.* that can be depressed.

de·pres·sion (di-presh′ən), *n.* [ME. *depressioun;* OFr. *depression;* L. *depressio;* see DEPRESS], 1. a depressing or being depressed. 2. a depressed part or place; hollow or low place on a surface. 3. low spirits; gloominess; dejection; sadness. 4. a decrease in force, activity, amount, etc. 5. in *astronomy*, the angular distance of a heavenly body below the horizon. 6. in *economics*, a period marked by slackening of business activity, much unemployment, falling prices and wages, etc. 7. in *medicine*, a decrease in functional activity. 8. in *meteorology*, *a)* a lowering of the atmospheric pressure. *b)* the fall of mercury indicating this in a barometer. 9. in *psychology*, an emotional condition, either normal or pathological, characterized by discouragement, a feeling of inadequacy, etc.

de·pres·sive (di-pres′iv), *adj.* tending to depress; characterized by depression.

de·pres·so·mo·tor (di-pres′ō-mō′tēr), *adj.* slowing down or decreasing motor activity. *n.* any depressomotor drug or other agent.

de·pres·sor (di-pres′ēr), *n.* 1. a person or thing that depresses. 2. any of various muscles that draw down a part of the body. 3. a nerve the stimulation of which decreases the activity of a part of the body. 4. an instrument that presses a protruding part out of the way during a medical examination or operation: as, a tongue *depressor*.

de·priv·a·ble (di-prīv′ə-b'l), *adj.* that can be deprived.

de·priv·al (di-prīv′'l), *n.* deprivation.

dep·ri·va·tion (dep′rə-vā′shən), *n.* [LL. *deprivatio*], 1. a depriving or being deprived. 2. a loss. 3. dismissal from office.

de·prive (di-prīv′), *v.t.* [DEPRIVED (-prīvd′), DEPRIVING], [ME. *depriven;* OFr. *depriver* < L. *de-*, intens. + *privare*, to deprive, separate], 1. to take away from forcibly; dispossess: as, he was *deprived* of his property. 2. to keep from having, using, or enjoying: as, no citizen should be *deprived* of his rights. 3. to remove from office, especially ecclesiastical office.

‡de pro·fun·dis (dē′ prō-fun′dis), [L., out of the depths], 1. from the deepest distress. 2. [D- P-], Psalm 130: from the first words of the Latin version.

dep·sid (dep′sid), *n.* a depside.

dep·side (dep′sīd, dep′sid), *n.* [< Gr. *depsein*, to tan; + *-ide*], any of a class of anhydrides of phenol carboxylic acids, similar to esters.

dept., 1. department. 2. deponent. 3. deputy.

Dept·ford (det′fērd), *n.* a borough of London: pop., 95,000.

depth (depth), *n.* [ME. *depthe* < *dep*, deep (see DEEP); + *-th*], 1. the distance from the top straight downward, from the surface or edge inward, or from front to back. 2. the quality or condition of being deep; deepness. 3. intensity (of colors, silence, etc.). 4. deepness of thought; profundity. 5. strength (of emotion). 6. lowness (of tone). 7. the middle (of night or winter). 8. *usually pl.* the far inner or inmost part: as, the *depths* of a wood. 9. *usually pl.* the deep or deepest place or part (of the sea, earth, sky, etc.). 10. *usually pl.* emotional depression: as, in the *depths* of despair.
out of (or beyond) one's depth, 1. in water too deep for one. 2. past one's ability or understanding.

depth charge, a powerful explosive charge timed to explode at a certain depth, and used against submarines or other underwater targets: also called *depth bomb.*

dep·u·rate (dep′yoo-rāt′), *v.t.* [DEPURATED (-id), DEPURATING], [< ML. *depuratus*, pp. of *depurare*, to purify < L. *de-*, intens. + *purare*, to purify < *purus*, pure], to purify. *v.i.* to become purified.

dep·u·ra·tion (dep′yoo-rā′shən), *n.* a depurating; purifying.

dep·u·ra·tive (dep′yoo-rā′tiv, di-pyoor′ə-tiv), *adj.* depurating; purifying. *n.* a purifying substance.

dep·u·ta·tion (dep′yoo-tā′shən), *n.* [ME.; Fr. *députation*], 1. a deputing or being deputed. 2. a person or persons appointed to represent others; delegation.

de·pute (di-pūt′), *v.t.* [DEPUTED (-id), DEPUTING], [ME.; L. *deputare*, to cut off, prune down, detach, hence depute; *de-*, from + *putare*, lit., to cleanse, hence lop off, arrange, count, consider], 1. to give (authority, functions, etc.) to someone else as deputy. 2. to appoint as one's substitute, agent, or representative.

dep·u·tize (dep′yoo-tīz′), *v.t.* [DEPUTIZED (-tīzd′), DEPUTIZING], to appoint as deputy. *v.i.* to act as deputy.

dep·u·ty (dep′yoo-ti), *n.* [*pl.* DEPUTIES (-tiz)], [Fr. *député*, pp. of *députer;* see DEPUTE], 1. a person appointed to act for, or in the place of, another or others. 2. a member of a legislature such as the Chamber of Deputies of the Third French Republic. Abbreviated **dep., dept., d.** *adj.* acting as deputy. —*SYN.* see **agent.**

De Quin·cey, Thomas (di kwin′si), 1785–1859; English essayist.

der., 1. derivation. 2. derivative. 3. derived.

de·rac·i·nate (di-ras′ə-nāt′), *v.t.* [DERACINATED (-id), DERACINATING], [Fr. *déraciner* < *dé-* (L. *dis-*), from + *racine*, a root < LL. *radicina* < L. *radix, radicis*, a root], 1. to pull up by the roots; uproot. 2. to extirpate.

de·raign (di-rān′), *v.t.* [ME. *dereinen;* OFr. *derainier*, *deraisnier*, to plead, vindicate; *de-* (L. *de*), from + *raisnier* < LL. **rationare* < L. *ratio*, reason], [Rare], formerly, in *law*, to determine (an issue), especially by personal combat between the litigants.

de·rail (dē-rāl′), *v.t.* [Fr. *dérailler* < *dé-* (L. *de-*), from + *rail* < Eng. *rail*], to cause (a train, etc.) to run off the rails. *v.i.* to run off the rails.

de·rail·ment (dē-rāl′mənt), *n.* a derailing or being derailed.

De·rain, An·dré (än′drā′ də-ran′), 1880–1954; French postimpressionist painter.

de·range (di-rānj′), *v.t.* [DERANGED (-rānjd′), DERANGING], [Fr. *déranger;* OFr. *desrengier; des-* (L. *dis-*), apart + *rengier* (Fr. *ranger*); see RANGE], 1. to upset the arrangement or order of; disarrange; disorder. 2. to disturb the normal condition or working of; hence, 3. to make insane.

de·ranged (di-rānjd′), *adj.* [pp. of *derange*], 1. disordered. 2. disordered in mind; insane.

de·range·ment (di-rānj′mənt), *n.* [Fr. *dérangement;* see DERANGE], 1. an upsetting of order or arrangement; disorder. 2. mental disorder; insanity.

de·ray (di-rā′), *n.* [ME. *dereie, deraie;* OFr. *desrei;* cf. DIS- & ARRAY], [Obs.], disorder, disturbance, or confusion; especially, disorderly revelry, as in a dance.

Der·bent (der-bent′), *n.* a city in the Daghestan A.S.S.R., on the Caspian: pop., 27,000.

Der·by (dũr′bi; Brit. där′bi), *n.* [*pl.* DERBIES (-biz)], 1. the county seat of Derbyshire, England: pop., 139,000. 2. Derbyshire. 3. [after the twelfth Earl of *Derby*, who founded the race in 1780], a race for three-year-old horses, run annually at Epsom Downs in Surrey, near London. 4. any similar horse race, especially the Kentucky Derby. 5. [d-], a stiff felt hat with a round crown and curved brim: also called *bowler.*

DERBY

Der·by·shire (där′bi-shir′, dũr′bi-shir′), *n.* a county of central England: pop., 759,000 (est. 1945); county seat, Derby.

‡de rè·gle (də re′gl′), [Fr.], according to the rule or correct form.

der·e·lict (der′ə-likt′), *adj.* [L. *derelictus*, pp. of *derelinquere*, to forsake utterly, abandon; *de-*, intens. + *relinquere;* see RELINQUISH], 1. deserted by the owner; abandoned; forsaken. 2. neglectful of duty; remiss; negligent. *n.* 1. a property abandoned by the owner; especially, a ship deserted at sea. 2. a person or thing abandoned as worthless: as, the streets were full of shabby *derelicts*. 3. a person neglectful of duty or trust. 4. land exposed by the receding of the sea. —*SYN.* see **remiss.**

der·e·lic·tion (der′ə-lik′shən), *n.* [L. *derelictio;* see DERELICT], 1. an abandoning or forsaking. 2. the state of being abandoned or forsaken. 3. a neglect of, or failure in, duty; being remiss. 4. in *law*, *a)* the gaining of land from water by the gradual retreat of the sea below the usual watermark. *b*) the land so exposed.

de·ride (di-rīd′), *v.t.* [DERIDED (-id), DERIDING], [L. *deridere; de-* (giving bad sense to *v.*) + *ridere*, to laugh], to laugh at in contempt or scorn; make fun of; ridicule. —***SYN.*** see **ridicule**.

‡**de ri·gueur** (də rē′gër′), [Fr.], required by etiquette; according to good form.

de·ris·i·ble (di-riz′ə-b'l), *adj.* [< L. *derisus*, pp. of *deridere* (see DERIDE); + *-ible*], deserving to be derided.

de·ri·sion (di-rizh′ən), *n.* [LL. *derisio* < L. *derisus*, pp. of *deridere*], 1. a deriding or being derided; contempt or ridicule. 2. [Rare], a person or thing derided.

de·ri·sive (di-rī′siv), *adj.* [< L. *derisus*, pp. of *deridere* (see DERIDE); + *-ive*], showing derision; ridiculing.

de·ri·so·ry (di-rī′sə-ri), *adj.* [L. *derisorius*], derisive.

deriv., 1. derivation. 2. derivative. 3. derived.

de·riv·a·ble (di-riv′ə-b'l), *adj.* that can be derived.

der·i·va·tion (der′ə-vā′shən), *n.* [L. *derivatio* < pp. of *derivare*], 1. a deriving or being derived. 2. descent. 3. something derived; a derivative. 4. the source or origin of something. 5. the origin and development of a word; etymology. 6. the process of tracing this. 7. the process of forming words from bases by the addition of affixes, by internal phonetic change, etc. (e.g., *warmth* < *warm*, *deem* < *doom*). 8. in *mathematics*, the deriving of a solution expressed in terms of an equation; deducing of one function from another according to some definite principle. Abbreviated **deriv.**, **der.**

de·riv·a·tive (də-riv′ə-tiv), *adj.* [LL. *derivativus* < L. *derivatus*, pp. of *derivare;* see DERIVE], 1. derived; hence, 2. not original: as, *derivative* art. 3. of derivation. *n.* 1. something derived. 2. in *chemistry*, a substance derived from, or of such composition and properties that it may be considered as derived from, another substance by chemical change, especially by the substitution of one or more elements or radicals for one or more constituents of the original substance. Abbreviated **deriv.**, **der.** 3. in *linguistics*, a word derived from another or others. 4. in *mathematics*, a differential coefficient.

de·rive (də-rīv′), *v.t.* [DERIVED (-rīvd′), DERIVING], [ME. *deriven;* OFr. *deriver;* L. *derivare*, to turn a stream from its channel, derive < *de-*, from + *rivus*, a stream], 1. to get or receive (*from* a source). 2. to get by reasoning; deduce or infer. 3. to trace from or to a source; show the derivation of. 4. to originate (used reflexively). 5. in *chemistry*, to obtain or produce (a compound) from another compound by replacing one element with another. *v.i.* to proceed (*from* a source); be derived; originate. —***SYN.*** see **rise**.

derm- (dũrm), dermo-.

-derm (dũrm), [see DERMA], a suffix used in forming biological terms, meaning *skin* or *covering*, as in *blastoderm*, *endoderm*.

der·ma (dũr′mə), *n.* [Mod. L. < Gr. *derma*], dermis.

der·mal (dũr′məl), *adj.* of the skin or the dermis.

der·mat- (dũr′mət), dermato-.

der·ma·ti·tis (dũr′mə-tī′tis), *n.* [*dermat-* + *-itis*], inflammation of the dermis.

der·ma·to- (dũr′mə-tō, dũr-mat′ō), [Gr. *dermato-*, *dermat-* < *derma*, *dermatos*, skin, hide], a combining form meaning *skin* or *hide*, as in *dermatology*, *dermatogen:* also, before a vowel, **dermat-**.

der·mat·o·gen (dẽr-mat′ə-jen, dũr′mə-tə-jen′), *n.* [*dermato-* + *-gen*], in *botany*, a layer of dividing cells from which the epidermis is formed.

der·ma·toid (dũr′mə-toid′), *adj.* [*dermat-* + *-oid*], skinlike.

der·ma·tol·o·gist (dũr′mə-tol′ə-jist), *n.* an expert in dermatology; skin specialist.

der·ma·tol·o·gy (dũr′mə-tol′ə-ji), *n.* [*dermato-* + *-logy*], the branch of medicine dealing with the skin and its diseases.

der·ma·to·phyte (dũr′mə-tō-fīt′), *n.* [*dermato-* + *-phyte*], any plant parasitic on the skin, as the fungus that causes ringworm.

der·ma·to·plas·ty (dũr′mə-tō-plas′ti), *n.* [*dermato-* + *-plasty*], plastic surgery of the skin, as by skin grafts.

der·mic (dũr′mik), *adj.* of the skin; dermal.

der·mis (dũr′mis), *n.* [Mod. L. < Gr. *epidermis;* see EPIDERMIS], 1. the layer of skin just below the epidermis; derma. 2. the skin in general.

der·mo- (dũr′mō, dũr′mə), [< Gr. *derma*, the skin], dermato-: also, before a vowel, **derm-**.

der·moid (dũr′moid), *adj.* [*derm-* + *-oid*], dermatoid.

der·ni·er (dũr′ni-ẽr; Fr. der′nyā′), *adj.* [Fr.; OFr. *derrenier* < *derrein;* LL. **deretranus* < L. *de-*, from + *retro*, back], final; last.

‡**der·nier cri** (der′nyā′ krē′), [Fr., lit., the latest cry], the latest fashion; last word.

‡**der·nier res·sort** (der′nyā′ rə-sôr′), [Fr.], last resource.

der·o·gate (der′ə-gāt′), *v.t.* [DEROGATED (-id), DEROGATING], [< L. *derogatus*, pp. of *derogare*, to repeal part of (a law), take away, detract from; *de-*, from + *rogare*, to ask], 1. [Archaic], to take away (*from*) so as to lessen or impair; detract. 2. [Obs.], to disparage. *v.i.* 1. to detract. 2. to do something derogatory to oneself or one's position; degenerate.

der·o·ga·tion (der′ə-gā′shən), *n.* [Fr. *dérogation;* L. *derogatio;* see DEROGATE], 1. a lessening or weakening (*of* power, authority, position, etc.). 2. disparagement; detraction. 3. a decline; deterioration.

de·rog·a·tive (di-rog′ə-tiv), *adj.* derogatory.

de·rog·a·to·ri·ly (di-rog′ə-tôr′ə-li, di-rog′ə-tō′rə-li), *adv.* in a derogatory manner.

de·rog·a·to·ry (di-rog′ə-tôr′i, di-rog′ə-tō′ri), *adj.* [L. *derogatorius;* see DEROGATE], 1. tending to lessen or impair; detracting. 2. disparaging; belittling.

der·rick (der′ik), *n.* [after *Derrick*, London hangman of the early 17th c.: orig. applied to a gallows], 1. a large apparatus for lifting and moving heavy objects: it consists of a long, moving beam pivoted at the base of a vertical, stationary beam and guided by ropes running on pulleys. 2. a tall, tapering framework, as over an oil well, to support drilling machinery, etc.

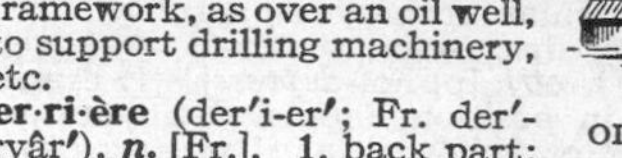
OIL WELL DERRICKS

der·ri·ère (der′i-er′; Fr. der′ryâr′), *n.* [Fr.], 1. back part; rear; hence, 2. the buttocks.

der·ring-do (der′iŋ-dōō′), *n.* [ME. *derrynge do*, *durring don*, lit., daring to do; misunderstood as abstract n. by Spenser and thence popularized as n. by Scott (*Ivanhoe*)], daring action; reckless courage.

der·rin·ger (der′in-jẽr), *n.* [< name of the inventor, Am. gunsmith, c. 1850], a small, short-barreled pistol of large caliber.

der·ris (der′is), *n.* [< Gr. *derris*, a covering], any of a group of woody, leguminous plants of the East Indies, from whose roots is extracted rotenone, used as an insecticide.

der·ry (der′i), *n.* [*pl.* DERRIES (-iz)], 1. a meaningless word in the refrains of old ballads; hence, 2. a ballad.

der·ry-down (der′i-doun′), *n.* a derry.

der·vish (dũr′vish), *n.* [Turk. *dervīsh;* Per. *darvīsh*, dervish, beggar], 1. a member of any of various Moslem orders, dedicated to a life of poverty and chastity: some dervishes practice whirling, howling, etc. as religious acts. 2. a follower of the Mahdi of Sudan.

Der·went (dũr′wənt), *n.* 1. a river in southeastern Tasmania: length, 125 mi. 2. any of three small rivers in England.

desc., descendant.

des·cant (des′kant), *n.* [OFr. *deschant;* ML. *discantus* < L. *dis-*, from, apart + *cantus*, song], 1. in *medieval music*, *a*) a counterpoint or melody sung above the main melody. *b*) the art of composing part music. *c*) a piece of part music. *d*) the highest voice in part singing. *e*) a variation on the chief melody. Also **discant**. 2. a varied song or melody. 3. [< the *v.*], a comment; criticism; discourse. *v.i.* (des-kant′, di-skant′), [OFr. *deschanter* < the *n.*], 1. to comment (*on* or *upon*). 2. to talk at length; discourse. 3. to sing or play a counterpoint to the main melody. 4. to sing.

Des·cartes, Re·né (rə-nā′ dā-kärt′; Fr. dā′kȧrt′), 1596–1650; French philosopher and mathematician.

de·scend (di-send′), *v.i.* [ME. *descenden;* OFr. *descendre;* L. *descendere*, to climb down, fall, descend < *de-*, down + *scandere*, to climb], 1. to move from a higher to a lower place; come down; go down. 2. to pass from an earlier to a later time, from greater to less, from general to particular, etc. 3. to slope or extend downward. 4. to come down (*from* a source): of ancestry, usually with auxiliary *be:* as, he *is descended* from pioneers. 5. to pass by inheritance or heredity: as, the estate *descended* to the nephew. 6. to lower oneself or stoop (*to* some act). 7. to make a sudden attack, raid, or visit (with *on* or *upon*). 8. in *astronomy*, to move toward the south or the horizon. 9. in *music*, to move down the scale. *v.t.* to move down, along, or through.

de·scend·a·ble (di-sen′də-b'l), *adj.* descendible.

de·scend·ant (di-sen′dənt), *adj.* [Fr. *descendant* < L. *descendens*, ppr. of *descendere;* see DESCEND], [Rare], descending. *n.* a person who is an offspring, however remote, of a certain ancestor, family, group, etc.: as, a *descendant* of the Vikings. Abbreviated **desc.**

de·scend·ent (di-sen′dənt), *adj.* [L. *descendens;* see DESCENDANT], descending.

de·scend·er (di-sen′dẽr), *n.* 1. a person or thing that descends. 2. in *typography*, *a*) a letter, such as *g* or *y*, that extends below the line. *b*) the part below the line.

de·scend·i·ble (di-sen′də-b'l), *adj.* 1. that may or does descend to an heir. 2. [Rare], that can be descended.

de·scent (di-sent′), *n.* [ME. *descent;* OFr. *descente* < *descendre;* see DESCEND], 1. a descending; coming down; going down; downward motion. 2. lineage; ancestry. 3. a generation (of a specified lineage). 4. a downward slope. 5. a way down or downward. 6. a sudden attack, raid, or invasion (with *on* or *upon*). 7. a decline; fall. 8. a stooping (*to* an act). 9. in *law*, transference (of property) to heirs or offspring by inheritance.

Des·chutes (dā-sho͞ot′), *n.* a river in central Oregon, flowing north into the Columbia River: length, 320 mi.
de·scrib·a·ble (di-skrīb′ə-b'l), *adj.* that can be described.
de·scribe (di-skrīb′), *v.t.* [DESCRIBED (-skrībd′), DESCRIBING], [ME. *descriven;* OFr. *descrivre;* L. *describere,* to write down or from, copy, transcribe, describe; *de-,* from + *scribere,* to write], 1. to tell or write about; give a detailed account of. 2. to picture in words. 3. to trace the outline of: as, his arm *described* an arc in the air. 4. to descry: so used through confusion.
de·scrip·tion (di-skrip′shən), *n.* [ME. *descripcioun;* OFr. *description;* L. *descriptio,* a marking out, delineation < pp. of *describere*], 1. the act, process, art, or technique of describing; picturing verbally; giving an account of in words. 2. a statement or passage that describes. 3. sort, kind, or variety: as, books of every *description.* 4. the act of tracing or outlining: as, the *description* of a circle.
de·scrip·tive (di-skrip′tiv), *adj.* describing; of or characterized by description: abbreviated **descr.**
descriptive geometry, a system of geometry that uses projections upon a plane to solve problems in space.
descriptive linguistics, the branch of linguistics which describes the structures of languages as they exist, without reference to their histories or to comparison with other languages.
de·scry (di-skrī′), *v.t.* [DESCRIED (-skrīd′), DESCRYING], [ME. *descryen, descrien;* OFr. *descrier,* to proclaim; *des-,* from + *crier;* see CRY], 1. to catch sight of; discern (distant or obscure objects). 2. to look for and discover; detect. —*SYN.* see **see.**
Des·de·mo·na (dez′də-mō′nə), *n.* in Shakespeare's *Othello,* the innocent wife of Othello, whom he smothers to death as a result of jealousy incited by Iago.
des·e·crate (des′i-krāt′), *v.t.* [DESECRATED (-id), DESECRATING], [formed by analogy with *consecrate* < OFr. *dessacrer* < L. *dis-,* apart + *sacrare,* to consecrate, make holy < *sacer,* sacred], to take away the sacredness of; treat as not sacred; profane.
des·e·crat·er (des′i-krāt′ẽr), *n.* a person who desecrates.
des·e·cra·tion (des′i-krā′shən), *n.* a desecrating or being desecrated. —*SYN.* see **sacrilege.**
des·e·cra·tor (des′i-krā′tẽr), *n.* a person who desecrates.
de·seg·re·gate (dē-seg′rə-gāt′), *v.t.* to abolish the segregation of races in (public schools, etc.).
de·sen·si·tize (dē-sen′sə-tīz′), *v.t.* 1. to take away the sensitivity of; make less sensitive. 2. in *photography,* to make (a plate or film) less sensitive to light, so that it may be developed in a brighter light than ordinarily. 3. in *physiology,* to make (a person, animal, or tissue) nonreactive or nonallergic to a substance by removing the antibodies from sensitized cells.
de·sert (di-zũrt′), *v.t.* [Fr. *déserter;* LL. *desertare* < *desertus,* pp. of L. *deserere,* to desert, abandon, lit., to disjoin; *de-,* from + *serere,* to join, unite], 1. to abandon; forsake; leave in the lurch. 2. to leave (one's post, military service, etc.) without permission. 3. to fail (one) when most needed. *v.i.* to leave one's post, military duty, etc. without permission: see **deserter.** —*SYN.* see **abandon.**
des·ert (dez′ẽrt), *n.* [ME.; OFr.; L. *desertum,* a desert, neut. of *desertus;* see DESERT, *v.*], 1. an uncultivated region without inhabitants; wilderness. 2. a dry, barren region, largely treeless and sandy. *adj.* [L. *desertus*], 1. of a desert or deserts. 2. wild and uninhabited: as, a *desert* island. —*SYN.* see **waste.**
de·sert (di-zũrt′), *n.* [ME. & OFr. *deserte* < *deservir;* see DESERVE], 1. the fact of deserving reward or punishment. 2. *often pl.* deserved reward or punishment: as, he got his just *deserts.* 3. the quality of deserving reward; merit.
de·sert·er (di-zũr′tẽr), *n.* 1. a person who deserts his duty, family, cause, etc. 2. a member of the armed forces who leaves his post without permission and with no intent to return or, in time of war, who leaves his post to avoid hazardous duty: abbreviated **d.**
de·ser·tion (di-zũr′shən), *n.* [Fr. *désertion* < LL. *desertio;* see DESERT, *v.*], 1. a deserting; action of a deserter. 2. the fact or state of being deserted.
de·serve (di-zũrv′), *v.t.* [DESERVED (-zũrvd′), DESERVING], [ME. *deserven;* OFr. *deservir,* to deserve < L. *deservire,* to serve diligently; *de-,* intens. + *servire,* to serve], to have a right to because of acts or qualities; be worthy of; merit. *v.i.* to be worthy.
de·served (di-zũrvd′), *adj.* [pp. of *deserve*], well earned; merited.
de·serv·ed·ly (di-zũr′vid-li), *adv.* in accordance with what is deserved; rightfully; justly.
de·serv·ing (di-zũr′viŋ), *adj.* that deserves; worthy (*of* help, reward, etc.). *n.* desert; merit or demerit.
des·ha·bille (dez′ə-bēl′), *n.* dishabille.
des·ic·cant (des′i-kənt), *adj.* [L. *desiccans,* ppr. of *desiccare;* see DESICCATE], drying. *n.* a substance, drug, etc. for drying something.
des·ic·cate (des′i-kāt′), *v.t.* [DESICCATED (-id), DESICCATING], [< L. *desiccatus,* pp. of *desiccare,* to dry up completely, drain; *de-,* intens. + *siccare,* to dry < *siccus,* dry], 1. to dry completely. 2. to preserve (food) by drying. *v.i.* to become dry.
des·ic·ca·tion (des′i-kā′shən), *n.* a desiccating or being desiccated.
des·ic·ca·tive (des′i-kā′tiv), *adj.* making dry; tending to make dry. *n.* a desiccant.
des·ic·ca·tor (des′i-kā′tẽr), *n.* 1. a person or thing that desiccates. 2. an apparatus for drying foods, etc.
de·sid·er·a·ta (di-sid′ẽr-ā′tə), *n.* plural of **desideratum.**
de·sid·er·ate (di-sid′ẽr-āt′), *v.t.* [DESIDERATED (-id), DESIDERATING], [< L. *desideratus,* pp. of *desiderare;* see DESIRE], to feel the lack of and desire for; want; miss.
de·sid·er·a·tive (di-sid′ẽr-ā′tiv), *adj.* [LL. *desiderativus;* see DESIDERATE], having to do with desire. *n.* in *Latin grammar,* a verb formed from another, showing desire to do the action of the original verb (e.g., *dicturio,* I wish to say < *dicto,* I say).
de·sid·er·a·tum (di-sid′ẽr-ā′təm), *n.* [*pl.* DESIDERATA (-tə)], [L., neut. of *desideratus,* pp. of *desiderare;* see DESIRE], something needed and wanted.
de·sign (di-zīn′), *v.t.* [OFr. *designer;* L. *designare,* to mark out, define; *de-,* out, from + *signare,* to mark < *signum,* a mark, sign], 1. to plan; make preliminary sketches of; sketch a pattern or outline for. 2. to form (plans, etc.) in the mind; contrive. 3. to plan to do; purpose; intend. 4. to intend or set apart for some purpose. *v.i.* 1. to make designs. 2. to make original plans, sketches, patterns, etc.: as, she *designs* for a coat manufacturer. *n.* [Fr. *dessein;* It. *disegno* < *disignare;* L. *designare*], 1. a plan; scheme; project. 2. purpose; intention; aim. 3. a thing planned for or outcome aimed at. 4. a working out by plan: as, do we find a *design* in history? 5. *pl.* a secret or sinister scheme (often with *on* or *upon*): as, he has *designs* on her property. 6. a plan or sketch to work from; pattern: as, a *design* for a house. 7. the art of making designs or patterns. 8. the arrangement of parts, details, form, color, etc., especially so as to produce a complete and artistic unit; artistic invention: as, the *design* of a rug. 9. a finished artistic work. —*SYN.* see **intend, plan.**
by design, with deliberate intent; purposely.
des·ig·nate (dez′ig-nit; *also, and for v. always,* dez′ig-nāt′), *adj.* [L. *designatus,* pp. of *designare;* see DESIGN], named for office, etc.; appointed: as, ambassador *designate.* *v.t.* [DESIGNATED (-id), DESIGNATING], 1. to point out; mark out; indicate; specify. 2. to name; entitle. 3. to name for an office or duty; appoint.
des·ig·na·tion (dez′ig-nā′shən), *n.* [L. *designatio;* see DESIGNATE], 1. a pointing out or marking out; specific indication. 2. a naming or being named for an office, post, etc. 3. a distinguishing name, title, etc.
des·ig·na·tive (dez′ig-nā′tiv), *adj.* designating.
des·ig·na·tor (dez′ig-nā′tẽr), *n.* [L.], a person or thing that designates.
de·signed (di-zīnd′), *adj.* [pp. of *design*], formed or done according to design; planned; purposed; intended.
de·sign·ed·ly (di-zīn′id-li), *adv.* by design; purposely.
des·ig·nee (dez′ig-nē′), *n.* a person designated.
de·sign·er (di-zīn′ẽr), *n.* 1. a person who designs. 2. a person who makes original sketches, patterns, etc.: as, a scene *designer.* 3. a schemer; plotter.
de·sign·ing (di-zīn′iŋ), *adj.* [ppr. of *design*], 1. that designs; of or for making designs, original patterns, etc. 2. planning. 3. scheming; crafty; artful. *n.* the art or work of making designs, original patterns, etc.
des·i·nence (des′i-nəns), *n.* [Fr. *désinence;* ML. *desinentia* < L. *desinens,* ppr. of *desinere,* to leave off], a termination, or ending; especially, in *grammar,* the formative ending of a word; suffix.
de·sir·a·bil·i·ty (di-zīr′ə-bil′ə-ti), *n.* the quality or state of being desirable.
de·sir·a·ble (di-zīr′ə-b'l), *adj.* [ME.; OFr. < *desirer,* after L. *desiderabilis;* see DESIRE], to be desired; worth wanting or having; pleasing, beautiful, excellent, etc.
de·sir·a·bly (di-zīr′ə-bli), *adv.* in accordance with what is desirable.
de·sire (di-zīr′), *v.t.* [DESIRED (-zīrd′), DESIRING], [ME. *desiren;* OFr. *desirer;* L. *desiderare,* to long for, desire, orig., prob., to await from the stars < *de-,* from + *sidus, sideris,* star; see CONSIDER], 1. to wish or long for; crave; covet. 2. to ask for; request. 3. to want sexually. *n.* 1. a wish or craving. 2. sexual appetite. 3. a request. 4. a thing or person desired.
SYN.—**desire,** generally interchangeable with the other words here in the sense of to long for, stresses intensity or ardor (to *desire* success); **wish** is not as strong a term as **desire** and has special application when an unrealizable longing is meant (he *wished* summer were here); **want,** specifically suggesting a longing for something lacking or needed, generally is a more informal equivalent of **wish** (she *wants,* or *wishes,* to go with us); **crave** suggests desire to gratify a physical appetite or an urgent need (to *crave* affection).
de·sir·ous (di-zīr′əs), *adj.* [ME.; OFr. *desireus;* LL.

desiderosus < *desiderare;* see DESIRE], desiring; having or characterized by desire: as, he is *desirous* of making a good impression.

de·sist (di-zist′), *v.i.* [OFr. *desister;* L. *desistere; de-*, from + *sistere*, to cause to stand < *stare*, to stand], to cease; stop; abstain: as, *desist* from the useless effort. —*SYN.* see **stop.**

desk (desk), *n.* [ME. *deske;* ML. *desca*, a table; It. *desco;* L. *discus;* Gr. *diskos;* see DISK], 1. a frame or table equipped with drawers, compartments, etc., and a flat or sloping top for writing, drawing, or reading. 2. a pulpit. 3. the post of a clerk, official, etc. in a department or office. 4. a musician's stand in an orchestra. 5. a (specified) position in an orchestra.

des·man (des′mən), *n.* [*pl.* DESMANS (-mənz)], [Sw., musk: the animal is so called from the scent], a molelike, insect-eating, aquatic mammal of Russia and the Pyrenees, with webbed feet and a long, flexible snout.

des·mid (des′mid), *n.* [Mod. L. *desmidium*, dim. < Gr. *desmos*, a chain], any of a number of related microscopic, one-celled, fresh-water algae, sometimes found joined in chainlike groups.

des·mid·i·an (des-mid′i-ən), *n.* a desmid.

des·moid (des′moid), *adj.* [< Gr. *desmos*, a band, ligament; + *-oid*], 1. like a ligament. 2. of fibrous texture, as certain tumors.

Des Moines (də-moin′, di-moinz′), 1. the capital of Iowa, on the Des Moines River: pop., 209,000. 2. a river in Iowa, flowing southeastward into the Mississippi: length, 327 mi.

Des·mou·lins, Ca·mille (kȧ′mē′y′ dā′mōō′lan′), 1760–1794; French revolutionist and writer; executed.

des·o·late (des′ə-lit; *for v.*, des′ə-lāt′), *adj.* [ME. *desolat;* L. *desolatus*, pp. of *desolare*, to leave alone, forsake, strip of inhabitants; *de-*, intens. + *solare*, to make lonely or desolate < *solus*, alone], 1. lonely; solitary. 2. uninhabited; deserted. 3. made uninhabitable; laid waste; in a ruinous state. 4. forlorn; wretched. *v.t.* [DESOLATED (-id), DESOLATING], [ME. *desolaten* < the *adj.*], 1. to make desolate; rid of inhabitants. 2. to make uninhabitable; lay waste; devastate. 3. to forsake; abandon. 4. to make forlorn, wretched, etc.

des·o·lat·er (des′ə-lāt′ẽr), *n.* a desolator.

des·o·la·tion (des′ə-lā′shən), *n.* 1. a making desolate; laying waste. 2. a desolate condition; ruin; waste. 3. lonely grief; misery. 4. loneliness. 5. a desolate place.

des·o·la·tor (des′ə-lā′tẽr), *n.* [LL.], a person or thing that desolates.

De So·to, Her·nan·do (hẽr-nan′dō di sō′tō; Sp. er-nän′dô de sô′tô), 1500?–1542; Spanish explorer; discovered Mississippi River (1541): also **de Soto.**

de·spair (di-spâr′), *v.i.* [ME. *despeiren;* OFr. *desperer;* L. *desperare*, to be without hope; *de-*, without + *sperare*, to hope < *spes*, hope], to lose or give up hope; be without hope (usually with *of*). *v.t.* [Archaic], to give up hope of. *n.* 1. a despairing; loss of hope. 2. a person or thing despaired of or causing despair.

de·spair·ing (di-spâr′iŋ), *adj.* [ppr. of *despair*], feeling or showing despair; hopeless. —*SYN.* see **hopeless.**

des·patch (di-spach′), *v.t.* & *n.* dispatch.

des·patch·er (di-spach′ẽr), *n.* a dispatcher.

des·per·a·do (des′pə-rā′dō, des′pə-rä′dō), *n.* [*pl.* DESPERADOES, DESPERADOS (-dōz)], [OSp. pp. of *desperar* < L. *desperare;* see DESPAIR], a dangerous, reckless criminal; bold outlaw.

des·per·ate (des′pẽr-it), *adj.* [L. *desperatus*, pp. of *desperare;* see DESPAIR], 1. driven to or resulting from desperation; rash or violent because of despair: as, a *desperate* criminal. 2. giving so little hope for improvement as to cause despair; extremely dangerous or serious: as, a *desperate* illness. 3. [Archaic], despairing; without hope. —*SYN.* see **hopeless.**

des·per·a·tion (des′pẽr-ā′shən), *n.* [ME. *desperacioun;* L. *desperatio*], 1. the state of being desperate. 2. recklessness resulting from despair.

des·pi·ca·ble (des′pik-ə-b′l, di-spik′ə-b′l), *adj.* [LL. *despicabilis;* see DESPISE], that is or should be despised; contemptible.

des·pi·ca·bly (des′pik-ə-bli, di-spik′ə-bli), *adv.* in a despicable manner.

de·spise (di-spīz′), *v.t.* [DESPISED (-spīzd′), DESPISING], [ME. *despisen;* OFr. *despirer, despis-* < L. *despicere*, to look down upon, despise < *de*, down, from + *specere*, to look at, behold], to look down on; be contemptuous or disdainful of; scorn.

SYN.—**despise** implies a strong emotional response toward that which one looks down upon with contempt (to *despise* a hypocrite); to **scorn** is to feel indignation toward or deep contempt for (to *scorn* the offer of a bribe); **disdain** implies a haughty or arrogant contempt for what one considers beneath his dignity (a *disdain* for flattery); **contemn**, chiefly a literary word, implies a vehement disapproval of a person or thing as base, vile, despicable, etc. See also **hate.**

de·spite (di-spīt′), *n.* [ME.; OFr. *despit;* L. *despectus*, a looking down upon, despising, contempt < *despicere;* see DESPISE], 1. a contemptuous act; insult; injury. 2. malice; spite. 3. [Archaic], contempt; scorn. *prep.* in spite of; notwithstanding. *v.t.* [Archaic], to scorn.

in despite of, 1. in defiance of. 2. in spite of.

de·spite·ful (di-spīt′fəl), *adj.* [see DESPITE], [Archaic], spiteful; malicious.

des·pit·e·ous (des-pit′i-əs), *adj.* [after *piteous* < obs. *despitous;* OFr. *despitos* < *despit;* see DESPITE], characterized by despite; despiteful.

de·spoil (di-spoil′), *v.t.* [ME. *despoilen;* OFr. *despoiller;* L. *despoliare; de-*, intens. + *spoliare*, to strip, rob, plunder], to deprive (*of* something) by force; rob; plunder. —*SYN.* see **ravage.**

de·spoil·ment (di-spoil′mənt), *n.* a despoiling or being despoiled; despoliation.

de·spo·li·a·tion (di-spō′li-ā′shən), *n.* [LL. *despoliatio;* see DESPOIL], robbery; pillage.

de·spond (di-spond′), *v.i.* [L. *despondere*, to lose (heart, etc.); *de-*, from + *spondere*, to promise], to lose courage, confidence, or hope; become disheartened; be depressed. *n.* despondency: now only in *slough of despond.*

de·spond·ence (di-spon′dəns), *n.* despondency.

de·spond·en·cy (di-spon′dən-si), *n.* [see DESPONDENT], loss of courage, confidence, or hope; dejection.

de·spond·ent (di-spon′dənt), *adj.* [L. *despondens*, ppr. of *despondere;* see DESPOND], showing or feeling despondency; disheartened; dejected. —*SYN.* see **hopeless.**

de·spond·ing (di-spon′diŋ), *adj.* despondent.

des·pot (des′pət, des′pot), *n.* [OFr.; Gr. *despotēs*, a master, lord], 1. originally, a title meaning "master," applied to certain classes of rulers, as Byzantine emperors, bishops of the Greek church, etc. 2. an absolute ruler; king with unlimited powers; autocrat. 3. a tyrant.

des·pot·ic (di-spot′ik), *adj.* [Fr. *despotique;* Gr. *despotikos*], of or like a despot; autocratic; tyrannical.

des·pot·i·cal (di-spot′i-k′l), *adj.* despotic.

des·pot·ism (des′pət-iz′m), *n.* [Fr. *despotisme*], 1. rule or government by a despot; autocracy. 2. the methods or acts of a despot; tyranny. 3. a government, political system, or state dominated by a despot.

de·spu·mate (di-spū′māt, des′pyoo-māt′), *v.t.* [DESPUMATED (-id), DESPUMATING], [< L. *despumatus*, pp. of *despumare*, to skim off; *de-*, off, from + *spumare*, to foam < *spuma*, foam], 1. to take the scum off; skim. 2. to throw off as froth. *v.i.* to become rid of scum.

des·pu·ma·tion (des′pyoo-mā′shən), *n.* [LL. *despumatio*], the process of despumating.

des·qua·mate (des′kwə-māt′), *v.i.* [DESQUAMATED (-id), DESQUAMATING], [< L. *desquamatus*, pp. of *desquamare*, to scale off < *de-*, off + *squama*, a scale], to fall off in scales; peel off.

des·qua·ma·tion (des′kwə-mā′shən), *n.* [see DESQUAMATE], the removal or peeling off of scales, as from skin.

Des·sau (des′ou), *n.* a city in east central Germany: pop., 88,000.

des·sert (di-zũrt′), *n.* [Fr. < *desservir*, to clear the table; *des-* (L. *de*), from + *servir* < L. *servire*, to serve], 1. a course of fruits, pudding, pie, ice cream, etc. served at the end of a meal. 2. [British], uncooked fruit and nuts served after the sweet course of cake, pudding, etc.

des·sert·spoon (di-zũrt′spōōn′), *n.* a spoon between a teaspoon and tablespoon in size, used for eating dessert.

des·sia·tine (des′yə-tēn′), *n.* [Russ. *dyesyatina*, lit., tithe < *dyesyat'*, ten], a Russian unit of land measure equal to about 2.7 acres.

de·ster·i·lize (dē-ster′ə-līz′), *v.t.* to bring back from a state of sterilization; especially, to return (sterilized gold) to a productive capacity as the basis for the further issuance of currency.

des·ti·na·tion (des′tə-nā′shən), *n.* [L. *destinatio*, settlement, appointment < *destinare;* see DESTINE], 1. [Rare], a destining or being destined. 2. the end for which something or someone is destined. 3. the place toward which someone or something is going or sent.

des·tine (des′tin), *v.t.* [DESTINED (-tind), DESTINING], [ME. *destenen;* OFr. *destiner;* L. *destinare*, to fasten down, secure, determine < *de-*, intens. + **stanare* < base of *stare*, to stand], 1. to predetermine, as by fate: usually in the passive. 2. to set apart for a certain purpose; intend.

destined for, 1. headed for; bound for: as, *destined for* Asia. 2. intended for: as, *destined for* leadership.

des·tin·y (des′tə-ni), *n.* [*pl.* DESTINIES (-niz)], [ME. & OFr. *destinee* < L. *destinare;* see DESTINE], 1. the inevitable or necessary succession of events. 2. what will necessarily happen to any person or thing; (one's) fortune. 3. that which determines events: said of either a supernatural agency or necessity. 4. [D-], in *Greek & Roman mythology*, *a*) the goddess of destiny. *b*) *pl.* the three Fates. —*SYN.* see **fate.**

des·ti·tute (des′tə-tōōt′, des′tə-tūt′), *adj.* [ME.; L. *destitutus*, pp. of *destituere*, to forsake, abandon < *de*, down, away + *statuere*, to set, put, place; see STATUTE], 1. lacking (with *of*): as, *destitute* of brains. 2. lacking the necessities of life; living in complete poverty. 3. [Obs.], abandoned. *v.t.* [DESTITUTED (-id), DESTITUTING], [Rare], 1. to deprive. 2. to leave destitute. —*SYN.* see **poor.**

des·ti·tu·tion (des′tə-tōō′shən, des′tə-tū′shən), *n.* [Fr.; L. *destitutio*, a forsaking], 1. the state of being destitute; lack. 2. complete poverty. —*SYN.* see **poverty.**

des·tri·er (des′tri-ẽr, des-trêr′), *n.* [Anglo-Fr. *destrer;*

OFr. *destrier* < LL. *dextrarius*, led by the right hand < *dextra*, right hand], Archaic], a war horse; charger.

de·stroy (di-stroi′), ***v.t.*** [ME. *destroyen;* OFr. *destruire;* L. *destruere; de-*, down + *struere*, to build], 1. to tear down; demolish. 2. to break up; spoil completely; ruin. 3. to put an end to; do away with. 4. to kill. 5. to neutralize the effect of. 6. to make useless.

***SYN.*—destroy** implies a tearing down or bringing to an end by wrecking, ruining, killing, eradicating, etc. and is the term of broadest application here (to *destroy* a city, one's influence, etc.); **demolish** implies such destructive force as to completely smash to pieces (the bombs *demolished* the factories); **raze** means to level to the ground, either destructively or by systematic wrecking with a salvaging of useful parts; to **annihilate** is to destroy so completely as to blot out of existence (rights that cannot be *annihilated*).

de·stroy·er (di-stroi′ẽr), ***n.*** 1. a person or thing that destroys. 2. [orig., *torpedo-boat destroyer*], a small, fast, powerful, heavily armed warship with high maneuverability.

de·struct·i·bil·i·ty (di-struk′tə-bil′ə-ti), ***n.*** the quality of being destructible.

de·struct·i·ble (di-struk′tə-b'l), ***adj.*** [LL. *destructibilis*], that can be destroyed; subject to destruction.

de·struc·tion (di-struk′shən), ***n.*** [ME.; OFr.; L. *destructio* < *destructus*, pp. of *destruere;* see DESTROY], 1. the act or process of destroying; demolition or slaughter. 2. the fact or state of being destroyed. 3. the cause or means of destroying. —***SYN.*** see **ruin.**

de·struc·tion·ist (di-struk′shən-ist), ***n.*** a person who believes in or favors destruction, as of the existing social order.

de·struc·tive (di-struk′tiv), ***adj.*** [OFr. *destructif;* LL. *destructivus* < *destructus*], 1. tending or likely to cause destruction. 2. destroying; causing or producing destruction. 3. tearing down: as, *destructive* criticism.

destructive distillation, the decomposition of a material, as coal, wood, etc., by heat in the absence of air, followed by the recovery of volatile products of the decomposition by condensation or other means.

de·struc·tiv·i·ty (dē′struk-tiv′ə-ti, di-struk′tiv′ə-ti), ***n.*** power or tendency to destroy; destructiveness.

de·struc·tor (di-struk′tẽr), ***n.*** [LL. < *destructus;* see DESTRUCTION], [British], an incinerator for rubbish.

des·ue·tude (des′wi-tōōd′, des′wi-tūd′), ***n.*** [Fr.; L. *desuetudo* < *desuetus*, pp. of *desuescere*, to disuse; *de-*, from + *suescere*, to be accustomed], disuse: as, laws fallen into *desuetude*.

de·sul·fur (dē-sul′fẽr), ***v.t.*** to desulfurize.

de·sul·fur·ize (dē-sul′fẽr-īz′), ***v.t.*** [DESULFURIZED (-īzd′), DESULFURIZING], to remove sulfur from.

des·ul·to·ri·ly (des′′l-tôr′i-li, des′′l-tō′ri-li), ***adv.*** in a desultory manner.

des·ul·to·ri·ness (des′′l-tôr′i-nis, des′′l-tō′ri-nis), ***n.*** the quality of being desultory.

des·ul·to·ry (des′′l-tôr′i, des′′l-tō′ri), ***adj.*** [L. *desultorius* < *desultor*, vaulter, jumper < *desultus*, pp. of *desilire*, to leap down < *de-*, down, from + *salire*, to leap], 1. jumping from one thing to another; disconnected; not methodical. 2. random: as, a *desultory* thought. —***SYN.*** see **random.**

det., detachment.

de·tach (di-tach′), ***v.t.*** [Fr. *détacher; dé-* (L. *dis-*), from + *-tacher* as in *attacher;* see ATTACH], 1. to unfasten and remove; separate; disconnect. 2. to send on special service or for a special task: said of troops, ships, etc.

de·tach·a·bil·i·ty (di-tach′ə-bil′ə-ti), ***n.*** the quality or state of being detachable.

de·tach·a·ble (di-tach′ə-b'l), ***adj.*** [see DETACH], that can be detached.

de·tached (di-tacht′), ***adj.*** [pp. of *detach*], 1. disconnected; separate. 2. not involved by emotion, interests, etc.; aloof; impartial. —***SYN.*** see **indifferent.**

de·tach·ment (di-tach′mənt), ***n.*** [Fr. *détachement*], 1. a detaching; separation. 2. the sending of troops or ships on special service. 3. a unit of troops or ships assigned to special service: abbreviated **det.** 4. the state of being on special service. 5. the state of being disinterested or impartial. 6. aloofness.

de·tail (di-tāl′; *also, for n.*, dē′tāl), ***n.*** [Fr. *détail* < the *v.*], 1. the act of dealing with things item by item. 2. a minute account; circumstantial story. 3. a small part or parts; item. 4. small secondary or accessory part or parts of a picture, statue, building, etc. 5. in *military usage, a*) one or more soldiers, sailors, etc. chosen for or sent on a special task. *b*) the special task. ***v.t.*** [Fr. *détailler;* to cut up, divide, tell in particulars; *dé-* (L. *de*), from + *tailler*, to cut; see TAILOR], 1. to give the particulars of; tell circumstantially or minutely. 2. in *military usage*, to choose for or send on a special task: as, *detail* a man for sentry duty. —***SYN.*** see **item.**

in detail, by items; with particulars.

detail drawing, a separate drawing of a small part or section, as of a machine.

de·tain (di-tān′), ***v.t.*** [OFr. *detenir;* L. *detinere*, to hold down or off, keep back, detain < *de-*, off, from + *tenere*, to hold], 1. to keep in custody; confine. 2. to keep; withhold. 3. to keep from going on; delay.

de·tain·er (di-tān′ẽr), ***n.*** 1. a person or thing that detains. 2. [Anglo-Fr. *detener*, inf. used as n. < OFr. *detenir;* see DETAIN], in *law, a*) the unlawful withholding of property from the rightful owner. *b*) the detention of a person without his consent. *c*) a writ for continuing to hold a person already in custody.

de·tain·ment (di-tān′mənt), ***n.*** [see DETAIN], detention.

de·tect (di-tekt′), ***v.t.*** [< L. *detectus*, pp. of *detegere*, to uncover; *de-*, from + *tegere*, to cover], 1. to discover; find out. 2. to discover the presence or existence of (anything hidden, not clear, etc.). 3. in *radio*, to rectify. 4. [Obs.], to uncover; reveal.

de·tect·a·ble, de·tect·i·ble (di-tek′tə-b'l), ***adj.*** that can be detected.

de·tec·tion (di-tek′shən), ***n.*** [LL. *detectio;* see DETECT], 1. a finding out or being found out: said especially of what tends to elude notice. 2. in *radio*, the process of separating a signal wave from its carrier wave in order to reproduce it as sound; rectification.

de·tec·tive (di-tek′tiv), ***adj.*** 1. of or for detection. 2. of detectives and their work. ***n.*** [< *detective policeman* or *officer*], a person, often a policeman, whose work is investigating and trying to solve crimes, watching suspected persons, getting information, etc.

de·tec·tor (di-tek′tẽr), ***n.*** [LL.], 1. a person or thing that detects. 2. an apparatus or device for indicating the presence of something, as electric waves. 3. in *radio*, a device, usually a vacuum tube, for separating a signal wave from its carrier wave in detection; rectifier.

de·tent (di-tent′), ***n.*** [Fr. *détente* < *détendre*, to relax, unbend; *dé-* (L. *dis-*), from + *tendre*, to stretch < L. *tendere*, to stretch out], in *mechanics*, a part that stops or releases a movement, as a catch for controlling the striking of a clock.

de·ten·tion (di-ten′shən), ***n.*** [L. *detentio* < *detentus*, pp. of *detinere;* see DETAIN], 1. a detaining or being detained. 2. a withholding; retention. 3. a keeping in custody; confinement. 4. an enforced delay.

de·ter (di-tũr′), ***v.t.*** [DETERRED (-tũrd′), DETERRING], [L. *deterrere; de-*, from + *terrere*, to frighten], to keep (a person) from doing something through fear, anxiety, doubt, etc.; discourage: as, the weather *deterred* them from going on a picnic.

de·terge (di-tũrj′), ***v.t.*** [DETERGED (-tũrjd′), DETERGING], [L. *detergere*, to wipe off, wipe away; *de-*, off, from + *tergere*, to wipe, cleanse], to cleanse, as a wound.

de·ter·gence (di-tũr′jəns), ***n.*** detergency.

de·ter·gen·cy (di-tũr′jən-si), ***n.*** a detergent quality or power.

de·ter·gent (di-tũr′jənt), ***adj.*** [L. *detergens*, ppr. of *detergere;* see DETERGE], cleansing. ***n.*** a cleansing substance, especially one that foams and cleans like soap but is made from the alkyl benzene sulfonates, the alkyl sulfates, etc. and not from fats and lye.

de·te·ri·o·rate (di-têr′i-ə-rāt′), ***v.t. & v.i.*** [DETERIORATED (-id), DETERIORATING], [< LL. *deterioratus*, pp. of *deteriorare*, to make worse < L. *deterior*, worse, inferior < obs. adj. **deter*, down < *de*, down], to make or become worse; lower in quality or value; depreciate.

de·te·ri·o·ra·tion (di-têr′i-ə-rā′shən), ***n.*** [Fr. *détérioration*], 1. a deteriorating. 2. a deteriorated condition.

de·te·ri·o·ra·tive (di-têr′i-ə-rā′tiv), ***adj.*** deteriorating or tending to deteriorate.

de·ter·ment (di-tũr′mənt), ***n.*** 1. a deterring. 2. a thing that deters.

de·ter·mi·na·ble (di-tũr′mi-nə-b'l), ***adj.*** [ME.; OFr.; LL. *determinabilis;* see DETERMINE], 1. that can be determined. 2. terminable.

de·ter·mi·nant (di-tũr′mə-nənt), ***adj.*** [L. *determinans*, ppr. of *determinare*], determining. ***n.*** 1. a thing or factor that determines. 2. in *mathematics*, the sum of the products formed, in accordance with certain laws, from a series of quantities arranged in an equal number of rows and columns. —***SYN.*** see **cause.**

de·ter·mi·nate (di-tũr′mə-nit), ***adj.*** [L. *determinatus*, pp. of *determinare;* see DETERMINE], 1. having exact limits; definite; distinct; fixed. 2. settled; decided; conclusive. 3. resolute. 4. in *botany*, having a flower at the end of the primary axis and of each secondary axis: said of the inflorescence of certain plants. 5. in *mathematics, a*) having a fixed value. *b*) of problems, having a fixed solution or solutions.

de·ter·mi·na·tion (di-tũr′mə-nā′shən), ***n.*** [L. *determinatio*], 1. a determining or being determined (in all senses of the verb). 2. a firm intention. 3. the quality of being resolute; firmness of purpose. 4. in *law*, the ending of an estate or of an interest in property.

de·ter·mi·na·tive (di-tũr′mə-nā′tiv, di-tũr′mə-nə-tiv), ***adj.*** [Fr. *déterminatif*], determining or serving to determine. ***n.*** a thing or factor that determines.

de·ter·mine (di-tũr′min), ***v.t.*** [DETERMINED (-mind),

DETERMINING], [ME. *determinen;* OFr. *determiner;* L. *determinare,* to bound, limit, prescribe; *de-,* from + *terminare,* to set bounds < *terminus,* an end], 1. to set limits to; bound; define. 2. to settle conclusively or beforehand; decide; resolve. 3. to reach a decision about after thought and investigation; decide upon. 4. to be the cause of; be the deciding or regulating factor in. 5. to find out exactly; ascertain; calculate; fix precisely. 6. to give a definite aim or direction to; direct. 7. to end; terminate. *v.i.* 1. to decide; resolve. 2. in *law,* to come to an end. —*SYN.* see **decide, learn.**

de·ter·mined (di-tũr′mind), *adj.* [pp. of *determine*], 1. having one's mind made up; decided; resolved. 2. resolute; unwavering.

de·ter·min·ism (di-tũr′min-iz'm), *n.* 1. the doctrine that everything is entirely determined by a sequence of causes. 2. the doctrine that one's choice of action is not free but is determined by a sequence of causes independent of his will.

de·ter·min·ist (di-tũr′min-ist), *n.* a person who believes in determinism. *adj.* of determinism or determinists.

de·ter·min·is·tic (di-tũr′mi-nis′tik), *adj.* determinist.

de·ter·rence (di-tũr′əns, di-ter′əns), *n.* 1. a deterring. 2. a deterrent.

de·ter·rent (di-tũr′ənt, di-ter′ənt), *adj.* [L. *deterrens,* ppr. of *deterrere*], deterring or tending to deter. *n.* a thing or factor that deters.

de·ter·sive (di-tũr′siv), *adj.* & *n.* [Fr. *détersif* < L. *detersus,* pp. of *detergere;* see DETERGE], (a) detergent.

de·test (di-test′), *v.t.* [Fr. *détester;* L. *detestari,* to curse by calling on the gods to witness, execrate, detest; *de-,* down + *testari,* to witness < *testis,* a witness], to dislike intensely; hate; abhor. —*SYN.* see **hate.**

de·test·a·bil·i·ty (di-tes′tə-bil′ə-ti), *n.* the quality of being detestable.

de·test·a·ble (di-tes′tə-b'l), *adj.* that is or should be detested; hateful; execrable; odious. —*SYN.* see **hateful.**

de·test·a·bly (di-tes′tə-bli), *adv.* in a detestable manner.

de·tes·ta·tion (dē′tes-tā′shən), *n.* [Fr. *détestation;* L. *detestatio;* see DETEST], 1. intense dislike; hatred; loathing. 2. a detested person or thing.

de·throne (dē-thrōn′), *v.t.* 1. to remove from a throne; depose; hence, 2. to oust from any high position.

de·throne·ment (dē-thrōn′mənt), *n.* a dethroning or being dethroned.

det·i·nue (det′i-nū′), *n.* [OFr. *detenue* < pp. of *detenir;* see DETAIN], in *law,* 1. the unlawful detention of personal property. 2. an action or writ for the recovery of property unlawfully detained, as in a pawnshop.

det·o·nate (det′ə-nāt′, dē′tō-nāt′), *v.i.* [DETONATED (-id), DETONATING], [< L. *detonatus,* pp. of *detonare,* to thunder, make a loud noise; *de-,* intens. + *tonare,* to make a sound], to explode violently and noisily. *v.t.* to cause to explode by setting off with a fuse, percussion cap, etc.: as, the bomb was *detonated* by remote control.

det·o·na·tion (det′ə-nā′shən, dē′tō-nā′shən), *n.* [Fr. *détonation*], 1. a detonating or being detonated. 2. a loud, violent explosion. 3. a loud noise.

det·o·na·tor (det′ə-nā′tẽr, dē′tō-nā′tẽr), *n.* [see DETONATE], 1. a fuse, percussion cap, etc. for setting off explosives. 2. an explosive.

de·tour (dē′toor, di-toor′), *n.* [Fr. *détour,* a turning, evasion, excuse < *détourner,* to turn aside, divert, evade; *dé-* (L. *de*), from + *tourner;* see TURN], 1. a roundabout way; deviation from the direct path. 2. a route used when the direct or regular route is closed to traffic. *v.i.* & *v.t.* to go or cause to go by way of a detour.

de·tract (di-trakt′), *v.t.* [Fr. *détracter;* L. *detractare,* to decline, depreciate < *detractus,* pp. of *detrahere,* to draw away; *de-,* from + *trahere,* to draw], 1. to take away. 2. [Rare], to belittle; disparage. *v.i.* to take something desirable away (*from*): as, anger *detracts* from her beauty.

de·trac·tion (di-trak′shən), *n.* 1. a detracting; taking away. 2. a belittling; disparagement.

de·trac·tive (di-trak′tiv), *adj.* 1. of the nature of detraction. 2. tending to take away. 3. disparaging.

de·trac·tor (di-trak′tẽr), *n.* a person who detracts or disparages.

de·trac·to·ry (di-trak′tə-ri), *adj.* detractive.

de·train (dē-trān′), *v.i.* to get off a railroad train. *v.t.* to cause to get off a railroad train.

de·train·ment (dē-trān′mənt), *n.* a detraining or being detrained.

det·ri·ment (det′rə-mənt), *n.* [Fr. *détriment;* L. *detrimentum,* a rubbing off, loss, damage < *detritus,* pp. of *deterere,* to rub off, wear away, weaken; *de-,* off, from + *terere,* to rub, wear], 1. damage; injury; harm. 2. anything that causes damage or injury.

det·ri·men·tal (det′rə-men′t'l), *adj.* [see DETRIMENT], causing damage; harmful. —*SYN.* see **pernicious.**

de·tri·tal (di-trī′t'l), *adj.* of detritus.

de·tri·tion (di-trish′ən), *n.* [< L. *detritus* (see DETRIMENT); + *-ion*], a wearing away or down by friction.

de·tri·tus (di-trī′təs), *n.* [L.; a rubbing away < pp. of *deterere;* see DETRIMENT], fragments of rock, etc. produced by disintegration or wearing away; debris.

De·troit (di-troit′), *n.* 1. a city in southeastern Michigan, on the Detroit River: pop., 1,670,000 (metropolitan area, 3,762,000). 2. a river connecting Lake St. Clair and Lake Erie: length, 25 mi.

‡**de trop** (də trō′), [Fr.], 1. literally, too much; too many; hence, 2. unwanted; superfluous.

de·trude (di-trōōd′), *v.t.* [DETRUDED (-id), DETRUDING], [L. *detrudere; de-,* down + *trudere,* to thrust], 1. to thrust down; force down. 2. to thrust away or out.

de·trun·cate (di-truŋ′kāt), *v.t.* [< L. *detruncatus,* pp. of *detruncare,* to cut or lop off; *de-,* from + *truncare;* see TRUNCATE], to shorten by cutting off a part.

Deu·ca·li·on (dōō-kā′li-ən, dū-kā′li-ən), *n.* [L.; Gr. *Deukaliōn*], in *Greek mythology,* a son of Prometheus: Deucalion and his wife, Pyrrha, were the only survivors of a great flood sent by Zeus to punish mankind for wickedness, and their son, Hellen, was the fabled ancestor of the Hellenic race.

deuce (dōōs, dūs), *n.* [Fr. *deux;* OFr. *deus;* L. *duos,* acc. of *duo,* two], 1. a playing card with two spots. 2. the side of a die bearing two spots, or a throw of the dice totaling two. 3. [< Fr. *à deux de jeu*], in *tennis,* a score of 40 each (or five games each) after which one player or side must get two successive points (or games) to win the game (or set).

deuce (dōōs, dūs), *n.* & *interj.* [orig. dicer's exclamation on making lowest score; associated with ME. *dewes!* God! < OFr. *Dieues* < *Dieu,* L. *deus,* god], bad luck, the devil, etc.: a mild curse or exclamation of annoyance, surprise, etc.

deu·ced (dōō′sid, dōōst, dū′sid, dūst), *adj.* [see DEUCE, *interj.*], devilish; confounded; extreme: used in mild cursing. *adv.* deucedly.

deu·ced·ly (dōō′sid-li, dū′sid-li), *adv.* [see DEUCE, *interj.*], devilishly; confoundedly; extremely.

‡**De·us** (dē′əs, dā′oos), *n.* [L.], God: abbreviated **D.**

‡**de·us ex ma·chi·na** (dē′əs eks mak′i-nə), [L., god from a machine], 1. in ancient Greek and Roman plays, a deity brought in by stage machinery to intervene in the action; hence, 2. any character or happening artificially, suddenly, or improbably introduced to resolve a situation, as in some fiction. 3. anyone who unexpectedly intervenes to change the course of events.

‡**De·us vo·bis·cum** (dē′əs vō-bis′kəm), [L.], (may) God (be) with you.

Deut., Deuteronomy.

deu·ter·ag·o·nist (dōō′tẽr-ag′ə-nist, dū′tẽr-ag′ə-nist), *n.* [< *deutero-* + Gr. *agōnizesthai* (see AGONIZE)], in *ancient Greek drama,* the character second in importance to the protagonist.

deu·te·ri·um (dōō-têr′i-əm, dū-têr′i-əm), *n.* [Mod. L.; see DEUTERO- & -IUM], the hydrogen isotope having an atomic weight of approximately 2; heavy hydrogen: symbol, D: with oxygen it forms deuterium oxide, D_2O (heavy water).

deu·ter·o- (dōō′tẽr-ō, dū′tẽr-ə), [< Gr. *deuteros,* second], a combining form meaning *second* or *secondary,* as in *deuteroplasm:* also **deuto-, deuter-, deut-.**

deu·ter·o·ca·non·i·cal (dōō′tẽr-ō-kə-non′i-k'l, dū′tẽr-ō-kə-non′i-k'l), *adj.* [*deutero-* + *canonical*], of or constituting a second or subsequent canon: as, the *deuterocanonical* (or, according to Protestants, apocryphal) books of the Bible.

deu·ter·og·a·my (dōō′tẽr-og′ə-mi, dū′tẽr-og′ə-mi), *n.* [Gr. *deuterogamia* < *deuteros,* second + *gamos,* marriage], a marriage after the death of the first spouse.

deu·ter·on (dōō′tẽr-on′, dū′tẽr-on′), *n.* [Mod. L.; see DEUTERIUM], the nucleus of an atom of deuterium: also **deutron, deuton.**

Deu·ter·on·o·my (dōō′tẽr-on′ə-mi, dū′tẽr-on′ə-mi), *n.* [LL. *Deuteronomium;* Gr. *Deuteronomion* < *deuteros,* second + *nomos,* law], the fifth book of the Pentateuch in the Old Testament, in which the law of Moses is set down in full for the second time: abbreviated **Deut.**

deu·ter·o·plasm (dōō′tẽr-ō-plaz'm, dū′tẽr-ə-plaz'm), *n.* deutoplasm.

deu·to- (dōō′tə, dū′tō), deutero-, as in *deutoplasm.*

deu·ton (dōō′ton, dū′ton), *n.* a deuteron.

deu·to·plasm (dōō′tə-plaz'm, dū′tə-plaz'm), *n.* [*deuto-* + *-plasm*], the substance in eggs or ova that provides food for the developing embryo.

deu·tron (dōō′tron, dū′tron), *n.* a deuteron.

Deut·sche·mark (doi′chə-märk′), *n.* [*pl.* DEUTSCHEMARK; Eng. DEUTSCHEMARKS (-märks′)], the monetary unit of West Germany, valued at $.24 in 1955: abbreviated **DM.**

‡**Deut·sches Reich** (doi′chəs riH′), [G., lit., German realm], Germany: the former official German name.

‡**Deutsch·land** (doich′länt′), *n.* [G.; *Deutsch,* German (same word as *Dutch*) + *land,* land; *Deutsch* < OHG. *diutisc,* of the people, popular < OHG. *thioda, diota* (Goth. *thiuda,* AS. *theod*), people, tribe + *-isc* (see -ISH); IE. base **teutā-,* crowd; folk, cf. TEUTONIC], Germany.

‡**Deutschland ü·ber al·les** (ü′bẽr äl′əs), [G.], Germany over everything: a nationalist slogan.

de·va (dā′və), *n.* [Sans. *deva,* god, deity], 1. in *Hindu mythology,* a god or good spirit. 2. in *Zoroastrian mythology,* a demon or evil spirit.

De Va·ler·a, Ea·mon (ā′mən dev′ə-lâr′ə, də-və-lêr′ə), 1882– ; Irish statesman born in the United States; prime minister of Ireland (1937–1948; 1951–1954; 1957–1959).

de·val·u·ate (dē-val′ū-āt′), *v.t.* [DEVALUATED (-id), DEVALUATING], to lessen the value of.

de·val·u·a·tion (dē-val′ū-ā′shən), *n.* 1. a devaluating or being devaluated. 2. the amount of this.

De·va·na·ga·ri (dā′və-nä′gə-rē′), *n.* [Sans. *devanāgarī*, city (writing) of the gods < *deva*, god + *nāgara*, city], the usual Sanskrit alphabet.

dev·as·tate (dev′əs-tāt′), *v.t.* [DEVASTATED (-id), DEVASTATING], [< L. *devastatus*, pp. of *devastare*, to lay waste; *de-*, intens. + *vastare*, to make empty < *vastus*, empty], to lay waste; make desolate; ravage; destroy. —*SYN.* see **ravage.**

dev·as·ta·tion (dev′əs-tā′shən), *n.* a devastating or being devastated; destruction; desolation.

dev·as·ta·tor (dev′əs-tā′tẽr), *n.* [L.], a person or thing that devastates.

dev·el (dev′'l), *n.* [prob. < *deaf* + *-le*, as if < ME. **devlen*], [Scot.], a heavy or stunning blow. *v.t.* to strike with such a blow.

de·vel·op (di-vel′əp), *v.t.* [Fr. *développer* < *dé-* (L. *dis-*), apart + OFr. *voluper*, to wrap; cf. Pr. *desvolopar*, Fr. *envelopper*, It. *inviluppare*, to wrap up; see ENVELOP], I. to cause to grow gradually in some way; cause to become gradually fuller, larger, better, etc.; especially, 1. to expand, as a business. 2. to strengthen, as muscles. 3. to bring into activity, as an idea. 4. to unfold gradually, as a bud. 5. to make more available or extensive, as electric power. 6. in *music*, to elaborate (a theme). 7. in *photography*, *a*) to put (an exposed film, plate, or printing paper) in various chemical solutions in order to make the picture visible. *b*) to make (a picture) visible by doing this. II. to show or work out by degrees; reveal; disclose; especially, 1. to make known gradually, as a plot. 2. to explain more clearly; enlarge upon. 3. in *mathematics*, to work out in detail or expand (a function or expression). *v.i.* 1. to come into being or activity. 2. to become larger, fuller, better, etc.; grow; evolve. 3. to become known or apparent; be disclosed. Also spelled **develope.**

de·vel·ope (di-vel′əp), *v.t. & v.i.* [DEVELOPED (-əpt), DEVELOPING], to develop.

de·vel·op·er (di-vel′əp-ẽr), *n.* 1. a person or thing that develops. 2. in *photography*, a chemical used to make the picture visible on an exposed film, plate, etc.

de·vel·op·ment (di-vel′əp-mənt), *n.* [Fr. *développement* < *développer*], 1. a developing or being developed (in all senses of the verb). 2. a step or stage in growth, advancement, etc.; hence, 3. an event or happening. 4. a thing that is developed; result of developing. 5. in *music*, *a*) the elaboration of a theme by rhythmic, harmonic, or melodic changes. *b*) the middle part of the sonata form. Also spelled **developement.**

de·vel·op·men·tal (di-vel′əp-men′təl), *adj.* of or connected with development.

Dev·e·reux, Robert (dev′ə-rōō′), see **Essex.**

de·vest (di-vest′), *v.t.* [OFr. *devester*; L. *devestire*, to undress < *dis-*, from + *vestire*, to dress < *vestis*, a dress, garment], 1. [Obs.], to undress; strip; hence, 2. in *law*, *a*) to take away (a right, etc.). *b*) [Archaic], to strip (*of* a title, etc.).

De·vi (dā′vē), *n.* [Sans., fem. of *deva*, god], a Hindu goddess, Sakti, the consort of Siva: also called **Maya.**

de·vi·ate (dē′vi-āt′; *for n.*, dē′vi-ət), *v.i.* [DEVIATED (-id), DEVIATING], [< LL. *deviatus*, pp. of *deviare*, to turn aside < L. *devius*; see DEVIOUS], to turn aside (*from* a course, direction, standard, doctrine, etc.); diverge; digress. *v.t.* to cause to deviate. *n.* a sexual pervert.

SYN.—**deviate** suggests a turning aside, often to only a slight degree, from the correct or prescribed course, standard, doctrine, etc. (to *deviate* from the truth); **swerve** implies a sudden or sharp turning from a path, course, etc. (the car *swerved* to avoid hitting us); **veer**, originally used of ships and wind, suggests a turning or series of turnings so as to change direction; **diverge** suggests the branching off of a single path or course into two courses constantly leading away from each other (the sides of an angle *diverge* from a single point); **digress** suggests a wandering, often deliberate and temporary, from the main topic in speaking or writing.

de·vi·a·tion (dē′vi-ā′shən), *n.* [ML. *deviatio*], 1. a deviating; turning aside from a course, standard, etc.; divergence. 2. the amount of this.

de·vi·a·tor (dē′vi-ā′tẽr), *n.* [LL.], a person or thing that deviates.

de·vice (di-vīs′), *n.* [ME. *devis*, intention, will; OFr. *devis*, fem. *devise*, division, will < *diviser*; see DEVISE], 1. a thing devised; plan; scheme. 2. an underhanded scheme; trick. 3. a mechanical contrivance for some purpose; invention. 4. an ornamental figure or design. 5. a design, often with a motto, on a coat of arms; heraldic emblem. 6. any motto or emblem. 7. [Archaic], the act or power of inventing or contriving.

leave to one's own devices, to allow to do as one wishes.

dev·il (dev′'l), *n.* [ME. *devel*; AS. *deofol*; LL. *diabolus*; Gr. *diabolos*, the devil, lit., slanderer < *diaballein*, to slander, lit., throw across; *dia-*, across + *ballein*, to throw], 1. [sometimes D-], in *theology*, *a*) the chief evil spirit, a supernatural being subordinate to, and the foe of, God and the tempter of man; Satan (with *the*): he is typically depicted as a man with horns, a tail, and cloven feet. *b*) any of such subordinate beings who reside in hell; demon. 2. something evil or bad: as, that *devil*, slavery. 3. a wicked or malevolent person. 4. a person who is sprightly, mischievous, energetic, etc. 5. an unlucky, unhappy person: as, that poor *devil* has had a hard time. 6. anything difficult; thing hard to operate or control, etc. 7. [orig. *printer's devil* (17th c.)], a printer's errand boy or apprentice. 8. any of various machines with teeth, as for tearing up rags. *v.t.* [DEVILED or DEVILLED (-'ld), DEVILING or DEVILLING], 1. [from the notion of heat], to prepare (food) with seasoning, condiments, etc. 2. to tear up (rags, etc.) with a special machine. 3. to annoy; torment; tease.

between the devil and the deep, between equally unpleasant alternatives.

give the devil his due, to acknowledge the ability or success of even a wicked or unpleasant person.

go to the devil, to fall into bad habits; degenerate morally: used also in the imperative as an expression of anger, annoyance, etc.

play the devil with, [Colloq.], to upset; cause to go awry.

raise the devil, 1. to conjure up the devil; hence, 2. [Colloq.], to make a commotion or have a boisterous good time.

the devil! [Colloq.], an exclamation of anger, surprise, negation, etc.: often in such phrases as *the devil you did!*, did you really?

the devil take the hindmost, leave the last, slowest, or least able to his fate without bothering about him.

the devil to pay, trouble as a consequence.

dev·iled (dev′'ld), *adj.* [pp. of *devil*: with reference to heat], prepared with strong seasoning: as, *deviled* ham: also spelled **devilled.**

dev·il·fish (dev′'l-fish′), *n.* [*pl.* DEVILFISH, DEVILFISHES (-iz); see FISH], 1. the largest kind of ray: so called because its pectoral fins are hornlike when rolled up. 2. any large cephalopod, especially the octopus.

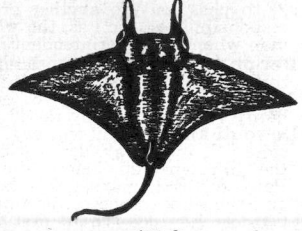

DEVILFISH (20 ft. across)

dev·il·ish (dev′'l-ish, dev′lish), *adj.* 1. of, like, or characteristic of a devil or devils; wicked; cruel; diabolical. 2. mischievous; energetic; reckless. 3. [Colloq.], extremely bad. 4. [Colloq.], extreme. *adv.* [Colloq.], extremely; excessively; very.

dev·il-may-care (dev′'l-mā-kâr′), *adj.* reckless; careless; happy-go-lucky.

dev·il·ment (dev′'l-mənt), *n.* 1. evil behavior or action. 2. mischief or mischievous action.

dev·il·ry (dev′'l-ri), *n.* [*pl.* DEVILRIES (-riz)], 1. evil or diabolical behavior; great wickedness or cruelty. 2. reckless mischief, fun, etc.; deviltry.

devil's advocate, [< L. *advocatus diaboli*], 1. in the *Roman Catholic Church*, the Promoter of the Faith, an official selected to examine critically the facts in the case of a dead person named for canonization; hence, 2. a person who upholds the wrong side, perversely or for argument's sake.

dev·il's-darn·ing-nee·dle (dev′'lz-där′niŋ-nē′d'l), *n.* a dragonfly.

dev·il's-food cake (dev′'lz-fōōd′), a rich cake made with chocolate or cocoa and baking soda.

Devil's Island, an island off the coast of French Guiana: site of a former French penal colony: French name, *Île du Diable.*

devil's tattoo, [cf. *tattoo* (a drumming); the reference may be to the feet of a hanged person], a rapid or nervous drumming with the fingers or feet.

dev·il·try (dev′'l-tri), *n.* [*pl.* DEVILTRIES (-triz)], [prob. < *devilry*], reckless mischief, fun, etc.; devilry.

dev·il·wood (dev′'l-wood′), *n.* a small evergreen tree of the olive family, with whitish bark, glossy leaves, greenish flowers, and hard wood: it grows in the southern United States.

de·vi·ous (dē′vi-əs), *adj.* [L. *devius* < *de-*, off, from + *via*, road], 1. roundabout; winding; rambling. 2. deviating from the proper course; going astray; crooked.

de·vis·a·ble (di-vīz′ə-b'l), *adj.* that can be devised.

de·vis·al (di-vīz′'l), *n.* a devising.

de·vise (di-vīz′), *v.t. & v.i.* [DEVISED (-vīzd′), DEVISING], [ME. *devisen*; OFr. *deviser*, to distribute, direct, regulate, talk; LL. *divisare* < L. *divisus*, pp. of *dividere*; see

DIVIDE], 1. to think out; contrive; plan; invent. 2. in *law*, to bequeath (real property) by will. 3. [Obs.], to divide. 4. [Obs.], to guess; divine. *n.* in *law*, 1. a gift of real property by will. 2. a will, or clause in a will, granting such a gift. 3. the property so granted.

dev·i·see (dev'i-zē', di-vīz'ē'), *n.* [*devise* + *-ee*], in *law*, the person to whom a devise has been bequeathed.

de·vis·er (di-vīz'ẽr), *n.* a person who devises; contriver.

de·vi·sor (di-vī'zẽr, di-vī'zôr), *n.* [OFr. *deviseor* < *devise*], in *law*, a person who devises property; testator.

de·vi·tal·i·za·tion (dē-vī't'l-i-zā'shən), *n.* 1. a devitalizing. 2. a devitalized condition.

de·vi·tal·ize (dē-vī't'l-īz'), *v.t.* 1. to kill; make lifeless. 2. to lower the vitality of; weaken.

de·vit·ri·fi·ca·tion (dē-vit'rə-fi-kā'shən), *n.* a devitrifying or being devitrified.

de·vit·ri·fy (dē-vit'rə-fī'), *v.t.* [DEVITRIFIED (-fīd'), DEVITRIFYING], 1. to take away or destroy the glassy qualities of. 2. to make (glass, etc.) opaque, hard, and crystalline, as by prolonged heating.

de·vo·cal·ize (dē-vō'k'l-īz'), *v.t.* in *phonetics*, to make (a voiced sound) voiceless.

de·void (di-void'), *adj.* [short form of ME. *devoided*, pp. of *devoiden*, to put away < OFr. *desvuidier; des-* (L. *dis-*), from + *vuidier;* see VOID], completely without; empty or destitute (*of*).

de·voir (də-vwär', dev'wär), *n.* [Fr., duty < *devoir*, to owe (OFr. *deveir, dever*) < L. *debere*, to owe, be indebted to], 1. duty. 2. an act of due respect or courtesy: now used in the plural, as, pay your *devoirs* to her.

dev·o·lu·tion (dev'ə-lōō'shən, dev''l-ū'shən), *n.* [ML. *devolutio*, a rolling back < L. *devolutus*, pp. of *devolvere;* see DEVOLVE], 1. originally, a rolling down or falling. 2. a passing down from stage to stage; hence, 3. the passing (of property, qualities, rights, authority, etc.) from one person to another. 4. a delegating (of duties) to a substitute or subordinate. 5. in *biology*, degeneration: opposed to *evolution*.

de·volve (di-volv'), *v.t. & v.i.* [DEVOLVED (-volvd'), DEVOLVING], [L. *devolvere*, to roll down; *de-*, down + *volvere*, to roll], 1. originally, to roll down or onward. 2. to pass (*on*) to another or others: said of duties, responsibilities, etc.: as, the work *devolves* on the foreman when the superintendent is ill.

Dev·on (dev'ən), *n.* 1. an island in the Northwest Territories, Canada, south of Ellesmere Island: area, 20,484 sq. mi. 2. Devonshire. 3. one of a breed of small, hardy cattle, originally raised in Devonshire.

De·vo·ni·an (də-vō'ni-ən), *adj.* 1. of Devon or Devonshire. 2. in *geology*, designating or of the period after the Silurian and before the Carboniferous in the Paleozoic Era, marked by the dominance of the fish and the appearance of the first amphibians: so called because its rocks were first studied in Devonshire. *n.* a native or inhabitant of Devon or Devonshire.

the Devonian, the Devonian Period: see **geology**, chart.

Dev·on·shire (dev'ən-shir'), *n.* a county of southwestern England: pop., 703,000 (est. 1945); county seat, Exeter.

de·vote (di-vōt'), *v.t.* [DEVOTED (-id), DEVOTING], [< L. *devotus*, pp. of *devovere*, to dedicate by vow; *de-*, from + *vovere*, to vow], 1. to dedicate; consecrate. 2. to give up or apply (oneself or one's time, energy, etc.) to some purpose, activity, or person. 3. [Rare], to consign to destruction; curse; doom.

***SYN.*—devote** suggests the giving up or applying of oneself or something with the seriousness or earnestness evoked by a formal vow (to *devote* one's life to a cause); to **dedicate** is to set apart or assign (something), as in a formal rite, to some serious, often sacred, purpose (to *dedicate* a temple); to **consecrate** is to set apart for some religious or holy use (to *consecrate* ground for a church); **hallow**, a stronger word, suggests an intrinsic holiness in the thing set apart (to *hallow* the Sabbath).

de·vot·ed (di-vōt'id), *adj.* [pp. of *devote*], 1. vowed; dedicated; consecrated. 2. very loyal; faithful. 3. [Rare], doomed.

dev·o·tee (dev'ə-tē'), *n.* 1. a person warmly devoted to something or someone: as, a *devotee* of the ballet. 2. a person deeply devoted to religion; zealot.

de·vo·tion (di-vō'shən), *n.* [ME. *devociun;* OFr. *devotion;* L. *devotio*, a devoting, consecrating], 1. the fact, quality, or state of being devoted. 2. piety; devoutness. 3. religious worship. 4. *pl.* prayers. 5. loyalty; faithfulness; deep affection. 6. the act of devoting.

de·vo·tion·al (di-vō'shən-'l), *adj.* of or characterized by devotion; having to do with worship.

de·vour (di-vour'), *v.t.* [ME. *devouren;* OFr. *devorer;* L. *devorare; de-*, intens. + *vorare*, to swallow whole], 1. to eat or eat up hungrily, greedily, or voraciously. 2. to consume; destroy. 3. to take in greedily with the eyes or ears: as, the child *devours* fairy tales. 4. to absorb completely; engross: as, he is *devoured* by curiosity. 5. to swallow up; engulf.

de·vout (di-vout'), *adj.* [ME.; OFr. *devot;* L. *devotus;* see DEVOTE], 1. very religious; pious. 2. showing reverence. 3. earnest; sincere; heartfelt.

SYN.*—devout** implies sincere, worshipful devotion to one's faith or religion; **pious** suggests scrupulous adherence to the forms of one's religion but may, in derogatory usage, connote hypocrisy (the *pious* burghers who defraud their tenants); **religious** stresses faith in a particular religion and constant adherence to its tenets (to lead a *religious* life); **sanctimonious** in current usage implies a hypocritical pretense of piety or devoutness and often connotes smugness or haughtiness (his *sanctimonious* disapproval of dancing).—ANT.*** impious.

De Vries, Hu·go (hü'gō də vrēs'), 1848–1935; Dutch botanist; formulated theory of mutation.

dew (dōō, dū), *n.* [ME.; AS. *deaw;* akin to G. *tau;* IE. base **dheu-*, to run, as in Sans. *dhāvati*, a spring, brook], 1. the atmospheric moisture that condenses after a warm day and appears during the night in little drops on cool surfaces. 2. anything regarded as refreshing, gently falling, pure, etc., like dew. 3. any moisture in small drops: as, the *dew* of his brow. *v.t.* to wet with or as with dew; make moist; bedew.

dew of youth, the early, fresh, or morninglike period of life: phrase from Psalm 110.

de·wan (di-wän', di-wôn'), *n.* [Ar. & Per. *dīwān, dīvān;* see DIVAN], in India, any of various governmental officials: also spelled **diwan.**

Dew·ar, Sir James (dū'ẽr), 1842–1923; Scottish chemist and physicist.

dew·ber·ry (dōō'ber'i, dū'ber'i), *n.* [*pl.* DEWBERRIES (-iz)], 1. any of various trailing blackberry plants. 2. the fruit of any of these plants.

dew·claw (dōō'klô', dū'klô'), *n.* 1. a functionless digit on the foot of some animals, as on the inner side of a dog's hind leg or above the true hoof in cattle, deer, etc. 2. the claw or hoof at the end of such a digit.

dew·drop (dōō'drop', dū'drop'), *n.* a drop of dew.

de Wet, Chris·ti·aan Ru·dolph (kris'ti-ån rü'dôlf də vet'), 1854–1922; Boer general and politician.

Dew·ey, George (dōō'i, dū'i), 1837–1917; American admiral in Spanish-American War.

Dewey, John, 1859–1952; American philosopher and educator; exponent of pragmatism.

Dewey, Mel·vil (mel'vil), 1851–1931; American librarian; originator of a decimal system for book classification in libraries.

dew·fall (dōō'fôl', dū'fôl'), *n.* 1. the formation of dew. 2. the time of the evening when this begins.

De·wi, Saint (dā'wi), see **David**, Saint.

dew·i·ly (dōō'ə-li, dū'ə-li), *adv.* in the manner of dew.

dew·i·ness (dōō'i-nis, dū'i-nis), *n.* the condition or quality of being dewy; moisture; freshness.

dew·lap (dōō'lap', dū'lap'), *n.* [ME. *dewlappe; dew*, prob. dew + *lappe*, a fold; AS. *lappa*], a loose fold of skin hanging from the throat of cattle and certain other animals.

dew·lapped (dōō'lapt', dū'lapt'), *adj.* having a dewlap.

dew point, the temperature at which dew starts to form or vapor to condense into liquid.

dew·y (dōō'i, dū'i), *adj.* [DEWIER (-i-ẽr), DEWIEST (-i-ist)], 1. wet or damp with dew. 2. of dew. 3. [Poetic], dewlike; refreshing, gentle, etc.: as, *dewy* slumber.

dex·e·drine (dek'sə-drin, dek'sə-drēn'), *n.* [*dextro-* + *ephedrine*], an isomer of amphetamine, similar to and used like benzedrine: a trade-mark (**Dexedrine**).

Dex·ter (dek'stẽr), [L.; see DEXTER, *adj.*], a masculine name.

dex·ter (dek'stẽr), *adj.* [L. *dexter*, right, to the right, skillful, fortunate], 1. of or on the right-hand side; hence, 2. [Obs.], favorable; auspicious. 3. in *heraldry*, on the right-hand side of a shield (the left of the viewer): opposed to *sinister*.

dex·ter·i·ty (dek-ster'ə-ti), *n.* [L. *dexteritas*, skillfulness, handiness < *dexter;* see DEXTER, *adj.*], 1. skill in using one's hands or body; adroitness. 2. skill in using one's mind; cleverness. 3. [Rare], right-handedness.

dex·ter·ous (dek'strəs, dek'stẽr-əs), *adj.* [L. *dexter* (see DEXTER, *adj.*); + *-ous*], 1. having or showing skill in the use of the hands or body. 2. having or showing mental skill. 3. [Rare], right-handed. Also **dextrous.**

SYN.*—dexterous** implies an expertness, natural or acquired, demonstrated in the ability to do things with skill and precision (a *dexterous* mechanic); **adroit** adds to this a connotation of cleverness and resourcefulness and is now generally used of mental facility (an *adroit* evasion); **deft** suggests a nimbleness and sureness of touch (a *deft* seamstress); **handy** suggests skill, usually without training, at a variety of small tasks (a *handy* man around the house).—ANT.*** clumsy, awkward, inept.

dextr-, dextro-.

dex·tral (dek'strəl), *adj.* [< L. *dextra*, right-hand side], 1. on the right-hand side; right. 2. right-handed. 3. having whorls that rise to the apex in counterclockwise spirals: said of the shells of certain mollusks. Opposed to *sinistral.*

dex·tral·i·ty (dek-stral'ə-ti), *n.* 1. the state of having the right side differing from the left. 2. right-handedness.

dex·tral·ly (dek'strə-li), *adv.* in a dextral way or direction.

dex·trin (dek'strin), *n.* [Fr. *dextrine* < L. *dexter*, right: so called from its property of rotating the plane of polarization to the right], a soluble, gummy substance obtained from starch and used as an adhesive, for sizing, etc.

dex·trine (dek'strin, dek'strēn), *n.* dextrin.

dex·tro (dek'strō), *adj.* in *chemistry*, dextrorotatory.

dex·tro- (dek′strə), [< L. *dexter*, right], a combining form meaning: 1. *toward* (or *on*) *the right-hand side*, as in *dextrorotatory*. 2. in *chemistry*, *dextrorotatory*. Also, before a vowel, **dextr-**.

dex·tro·gy·rate (deks′trə-jī′rāt), *adj.* [*dextro-* + *gyrate*], dextrorotatory.

dex·tro·ro·ta·ry (dek′strə-rō′tēr-i), *adj.* dextrorotatory.

dex·tro·ro·ta·tion (dek′strə-rō-tā′shən), *n.* dextrorotatory direction or movement.

dex·tro·ro·ta·to·ry (dek′strə-rō′tə-tôr′i, dek′strə-rō′tə-tō′ri), *adj.* [*dextro-* + *rotatory*], 1. turning or circling to the right, in a clockwise direction. 2. that turns the plane of polarized light clockwise: said of certain crystals, etc. Opposed to *levorotatory*.

dex·tror·sal (dek-strôr′s'l), *adj.* dextrorse.

dex·trorse (dek′strôrs, dek-strôrs′), *adj.* [L. *dextrorsum* or *dextrovorsum*, toward the right < *dexter*, right + *versus* or *vorsus*, pp. of *vertere* or *vortere*, to turn], in *botany*, twining upward to the right, as the stem of the hop: opposed to *sinistrorse*.

DEXTRORSE VINE (of morning-glory)

dex·trose (dek′strōs), *n.* [*dextr-* + *-ose*], a crystalline, dextrorotatory sugar, $C_6H_{12}O_6$, found in plants and animals and in the human body, and made commercially by the reaction of starch and sulfuric acid; glucose.

dex·trous (dek′strəs), *adj.* dexterous.

dey (dā), *n.* [Fr. *dey;* Turk. *dāi*, maternal uncle: orig., friendly title given to middle-aged or old people], 1. the former title of the governor of Algiers. 2. formerly, a pasha or ruler in Tunis or Tripoli.

Dezh·nev·a, Cape (dyezh-nyev′ä), the northeasternmost point of Asia, on the Bering Strait: also called *East Cape*.

D/F, in *radio*, direction-finding.

D.F., 1. Dean of the Faculty. 2. *Defensor Fidei*, [L.], Defender of the Faith. 3. *Districto Federal*, [Port.], Federal District. 4. *Distrito Federal*, [Sp.], Federal District (in Mexico).

D.F.C., Distinguished Flying Cross.

dg., decigram; decigrams.

d.h., *das heisst*, [G.], that is; namely; i.e.

‡dhar·ma (där′mə, dũr′mə), *n.* [Sans., law], in *Buddhism* & *Hinduism*, religious observances; conformity to the law; duty; **virtue**.

‡dhar·na (där′nə, dũr′nə), *n.* [Hind. *dharnā*], in India, a method of trying to get justice by sitting at the door of one's debtor or wrongdoer and fasting to death or until satisfaction is given: also **dhurna**.

Dhau·la·gi·ri (dou′lə-gē′ri), *n.* a mountain of the Himalayas, in central Nepal, India: height, 26,795 ft.

dhole (dōl), *n.* [*pl.* DHOLES (dōlz), DHOLE; see PLURAL, II, D, 1], [native name], a wild dog of India that hunts in packs, attacking even large game.

dho·ti, dhoo·ti (dō′ti), *n.* [Hind. *dhotī*], 1. the loincloth worn by Hindus. 2. the cloth used for it.

dhow (dou), *n.* [< Ar. *dāw*], a single-masted ship with a lateen sail, sharp prow, deep forefoot, and raised deck at the stern, used in the Red Sea and Indian Ocean.

dhur·na (dũr′nä), *n.* dharna.

di (dē), *n.* [arbitrary modification of *do*], in *music*, a syllable representing the tone intermediate between do and re of the diatonic scale: see **solfeggio**.

di- (dī), [Gr. *di-* < *dis*, twice; akin to L. *bis*, MHG. *zwis*, twice, and to base of Eng. *two*], a prefix meaning: 1. *twice, double, twofold*, as in *dichroism, dicotyledon*. 2. in *chemistry*, *having two* (atoms, molecules, radicals, etc.), as in *diacid*.

di- (di), dis- (*separation, deprivation*, etc.).

Di, in *chemistry*, didymium.

di., dia., diameter.

di·a- (dī′ə), [< Gr. *dia*, through, across], a prefix meaning: 1. *through, throughout, across*, as in *diaphragm, diagonal*. 2. *apart, between*, as in *diagnose, diacritical*. Also, before a vowel, **di-**.

di·a·base (dī′ə-bās′), *n.* [Fr. < Gr. *diabasis*, a crossing over < *dia-*, through + *bainein*, to go], 1. formerly, diorite. 2. a dark-colored igneous rock, made up largely of augite and feldspar.

di·a·be·tes (dī′ə-bē′tis, dī′ə-bē′tēz), *n.* [Mod. L.; L.; Gr. *diabētēs*, *diabetes*, a siphon < *diabainein*, to pass through; *dia-*, through + *bainein*, to go], a disease characterized by an excessive discharge of urine: there are various types of diabetes.

diabetes mel·li·tus (mə-lī′təs), [Mod. L.; lit., honey diabetes; L. *mellitus*, honeysweet, honey < *mel*, honey], a chronic form of diabetes characterized by excess of sugar in the blood and urine, hunger, thirst, and gradual loss of weight: also called *sugar diabetes*.

di·a·bet·ic (dī′ə-bet′ik, dī′ə-bē′tik), *adj.* of or having diabetes. *n.* a person who has diabetes.

di·a·ble·rie (di-ä′blə-ri), *n.* [Fr.; OFr. < *diable*, devil; LL. *diabolus;* see DEVIL], 1. devil's work; sorcery; witchcraft. 2. devil lore. 3. deviltry; mischief. Also spelled **diablery**.

di·a·bol·ic (dī′ə-bol′ik), *adj.* [Fr. *diabolique;* LL. *diabolicus* < *diabolus;* see DEVIL], 1. of the Devil or devils. 2. very wicked or cruel; fiendish; devilish; demoniacal.

di·a·bol·i·cal (dī′ə-bol′i-k'l), *adj.* diabolic.

di·ab·o·lism (dī-ab′ə-liz'm), *n.* [< LL. *diabolus* (see DEVIL); + *-ism*], 1. dealing or dealings with the Devil or devils; sorcery; witchcraft. 2. belief in or worship of the Devil or devils. 3. diabolical action or behavior. 4. the character or condition of the Devil or a devil.

di·ab·o·list (dī-ab′ə-list), *n.* 1. an authority on diabolism. 2. a devil worshiper.

di·ab·o·lo (di-ab′ə-lō′), *n.* [c. 1907; prob. < Gr. *dia-*, across + *bolē*, a throw < *ballein*, to throw, but associated with It. *diavolo*, a devil; LL. *diabolus;* see DEVIL], a game played with a wooden spool which is whirled and tossed on a string tied to two sticks held one in each hand.

di·a·caus·tic (dī′ə-kos′tik), *adj.* [*dia-* + *caustic* (sense 3)], designating or of a caustic curve or surface formed by refraction. *n.* a diacaustic curve or surface.

di·ach·y·lon (dī-ak′ə-lon′), *n.* [ML. < Gr. *diachylos*, very juicy; *dia-*, through + *chylos*, juice], in *medicine*, a plaster consisting essentially of lead oxide, olive oil, and water.

di·ach·y·lum (di-ak′ə-ləm), *n.* diachylon.

di·ac·id (dī-as′id), *adj.* 1. containing in each molecule two atoms of hydrogen replaceable by basic atoms or radicals: usually said of acids and acid salts. 2. capable of forming a salt or ester by reacting with one molecule of a diacid, or two of a monoacid: usually said of bases and alcohols. *n.* an acid having in each molecule two hydrogen atoms which can be replaced by a metal or react with basic substances.

di·ac·o·nal (dī-ak′ə-n'l), *adj.* [LL. *diaconalis* < *diaconus;* see DEACON], of a deacon or deacons.

di·ac·o·nate (dī-ak′ə-nit, dī-ak′ə-nāt′), *n.* [LL. *diaconatus* < *diaconus;* see DEACON], 1. the rank, office, or tenure of a deacon. 2. a group or board of deacons.

di·a·crit·ic (dī′ə-krit′ik), *adj.* [Gr. *diakritikos* < *diakrinein*, to distinguish, separate; *dia-*, across + *krinein*, to separate], 1. diacritical. 2. in *medicine*, diagnostic. *n.* a diacritical mark.

di·a·crit·i·cal (dī′ə-krit′i-k'l), *adj.* [see DIACRITIC], used to distinguish; distinguishing: as, a *diacritical* mark.

diacritical mark, a mark added to a letter to show pronunciation, etc. Examples: ä, ā, â, é.

di·ac·tin·ic (dī′ak-tin′ik), *adj.* capable of transmitting actinic rays of light.

di·a·del·phous (dī′ə-del′fəs), *adj.* [< *di-*, twice + Gr. *adelphos*, brother; + *-ous*], 1. arranged in two bundles or sets by the fusion of the filaments: said of stamens. 2. having the stamens so arranged.

DIADELPHOUS STAMENS (of pea)

di·a·dem (dī′ə-dem′), *n.* [ME. & OFr. *diademe;* L. *diadema;* Gr. *diadēma*, a band or fillet < *diadein*, to bind round, encircle; *dia-*, through + *dein*, to bind], 1. a crown. 2. an ornamental cloth headband worn as a crown by Eastern kings, especially in ancient Persia. 3. a thing like a crown. 4. kingly power, authority, or dignity. *v.t.* to put a diadem on; crown.

di·aer·e·sis (dī-er′ə-sis), *n.* [*pl.* DIAERESES (-sēz′)], dieresis.

di·ae·ret·ic (dī′ə-ret′ik), *adj.* dieretic.

diag., diagram.

Dia·ghi·lev, Ser·gei Pav·lo·vich (syer-gyā′i päv-lô′vich dyä′gi-lyef′), 1872–1929; Russian ballet producer and choreographer.

di·ag·nose (dī′əg-nōs′, dī′əg-nōz′), *v.t.* [DIAGNOSED (-nōst′, -nōzd′), DIAGNOSING], [< *diagnosis*], to make a diagnosis of; recognize and identify (a disease, etc.) by examination and observation. *v.i.* to make diagnoses.

di·ag·no·sis (dī′əg-nō′sis), *n.* [*pl.* DIAGNOSES (-sēz)], [L. < Gr. *diagnōsis*, a distinguishing, discrimination < *diagignōskein*, to distinguish; *dia-*, through, between + *gignōskein*, to know], 1. the act or process of deciding the nature of a diseased condition by examination. 2. a careful investigation of the facts to determine the nature of a thing. 3. the decision or opinion resulting from such examination or investigation.

di·ag·nos·tic (dī′əg-nos′tik), *adj.* [Gr. *diagnōstikos*], 1. of or constituting a diagnosis. 2. of value for a diagnosis; specifically characteristic. *n.* in *medicine*, 1. diagnosis. 2. a symptom.

di·ag·nos·ti·cal·ly (dī′əg-nos′ti-k'l-i, dī′əg-nos′tik-li), *adv.* 1. by diagnosis. 2. with regard to diagnosis.

di·ag·nos·ti·cate (dī′əg-nos′ti-kāt′), *v.t.* & *v.i.* [DIAGNOSTICATED (-id), DIAGNOSTICATING], to diagnose.

di·ag·nos·ti·cian (dī′əg-nos-tish′ən), *n.* a person who

makes diagnoses; specifically, a specialist in diagnostics.
di·ag·nos·tics (dī'əg-nos'tiks), ***n.pl.*** [construed as sing.], the branch of medical science that deals with diagnosis.
di·ag·o·nal (dī-ag'ə-n'l), ***adj.*** [L. *diagonalis;* Gr. *diagōnios* < *dia-*, through + *gōnia*, an angle, corner], 1. extending between the vertices of any two nonadjacent angles in a polygonal or polyhedral figure; extending slantingly between opposite corners. 2. having the general direction of a diagonal; slanting; oblique. 3. having slanting markings, lines, etc. ***n.*** 1. a diagonal line or plane. 2. any diagonal course, row, order, or part. 3. cloth woven with diagonal lines.

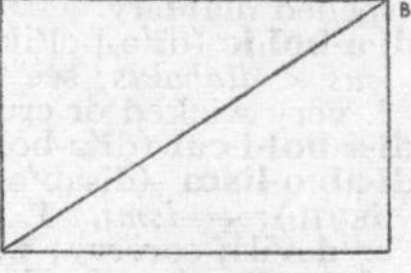

DIAGONAL (AB)

di·ag·o·nal·ly (dī-ag'ə-n'l-i), ***adv.*** in a diagonal manner or direction; obliquely.
di·a·gram (dī'ə-gram'), ***n.*** [Fr. *diagramme;* L. *diagramma;* Gr. *diagramma* < *diagraphein*, to mark out by lines, draw; *dia-*, through, across + *graphein*, to write], 1. a geometrical figure, often used to illustrate a theorem. 2. a sketch, drawing, or plan that explains a thing by outlining its parts, workings, etc. 3. a chart or graph explaining or illustrating ideas, statistics, etc. Abbreviated **diag., diagr.** ***v.t.*** [DIAGRAMED or DIAGRAMMED (-gramd'), DIAGRAMING or DIAGRAMMING], to show or represent by a diagram; make a diagram of.
di·a·gram·mat·ic (dī'ə-grə-mat'ik), ***adj.*** 1. of, or having the form of, a diagram or diagrams; hence, 2. merely outlined; sketchy.
di·a·gram·mat·i·cal (dī'ə-grə-mat'i-k'l), ***adj.*** diagrammatic.
di·a·gram·mat·i·cal·ly (dī'ə-grə-mat'i-k'l-i), ***adv.*** 1. in the form of a diagram. 2. by means of a diagram.
di·a·graph (dī'ə-graf', dī'ə-gräf'), ***n.*** [Fr. *diagraphe* < Gr. *diagraphein;* see DIAGRAM], an instrument for drawing figures or projections of objects; combination of a protractor and a scale, used in plotting.
di·a·ki·ne·sis (dī'ə-ki-nē'sis), ***n.*** [< *dia-* + Gr. *kinēsis*, motion; see KINEMATICS], in the meiosis of germ cells, a stage in which the maternal and paternal chromosomes have paired and lie near or on the nuclear membrane.
di·al (dī'əl, dīl), ***n.*** [ME.; ML. *dialis*, daily < L. *dies*, day], 1. a sundial. 2. the face of a watch or clock. 3. the clocklike face of an instrument for indicating, as by a moving pointer, the amount of something; face of a compass, gauge, or meter. 4. a vise to hold the stone in jewel cutting. 5. a graduated disk on a radio, especially one for tuning in stations. 6. a rotating disk on a telephone, used in making connections automatically. 7. a miner's compass. ***v.t. & v.i.*** [DIALED or DIALLED (-əld, dīld), DIALING or DIALLING], 1. to measure, survey, etc. with or as with a dial. 2. to show on a dial. 3. to tune in (a radio station, program, etc.). 4. to call by using a telephone dial.
dial., 1. dialect(al). 2. dialectic(al).
di·a·lect (dī'ə-lekt'), ***n.*** [Fr. *dialecte;* L. *dialectus;* Gr. *dialektos*, discourse, discussion, dialect < *dialegesthai*, to discourse, talk < *dia-*, between + *legein*, to choose, talk], 1. the sum total of local characteristics of speech. 2. the sum total of an individual's characteristics of speech. 3. any form of speech considered as deviating from a real or imaginary standard speech. 4. English speech as employed by a foreign-born or minority group: as, the Milwaukee Polish *dialect.* 5. loosely, any jargon, cant, or patois. 6. in ***linguistics***, the form or variety of a spoken language peculiar to a region, community, social group, or occupational group: in this sense, *dialects* are regarded as being, to some degree, mutually intelligible while ***languages*** are mutually unintelligible; hence, 7. any language as part of a larger group or family of languages: as, English is a West Germanic *dialect.* ***adj.*** of or in dialect: as, *dialect* ballads. Abbreviated **dial.**
SYN.**—dialect**, in this comparison, refers to a form of a language peculiar to a locality or group and differing from the standard language in matters of pronunciation, syntax, etc.; **vernacular** today commonly refers to the informal or colloquial variety of a language as distinguished from the formal or literary variety; **cant**, in this connection, refers to the distinctive stock words and phrases used by a particular sect, class, etc. (clergymen's *cant*); **jargon** is used of the special vocabulary and idioms of a particular class, occupational group, etc., especially by one who is unfamiliar with these; **argot** refers especially to the secret jargon of thieves and tramps; **lingo** is a humorous or mildly contemptuous term applied to any language, dialect, or jargon by one to whom it is unintelligible.
di·a·lec·tal (dī'ə-lek't'l), ***adj.*** of or characteristic of a dialect: abbreviated **dial.**
dialect atlas, a collection of maps illustrating the regional distribution of dialect characteristics.
di·a·lec·tic (dī'ə-lek'tik), ***n.*** [ME. *dialatik;* OFr. *dialetique;* L. *dialectica* (*ars*); Gr. *dialektikē* (*technē*), the dialectic (art) < *dialektikos;* see DIALECT], 1. the art or practice of examining opinions or ideas logically, often by the method of question and answer, so as to determine their validity: also **dialectics**. 2. logical argumentation. 3. the method of logic used by Hegel and adapted by Marx to his materialist philosophy: it is based on the concept of the contradiction of opposites (*thesis* and *antithesis*) and their continual resolution (*synthesis*). ***adj.***[L. *dialecticus;* Gr. *dialektikos*], 1. of or using dialectic. 2. dialectal. Abbreviated **dial.**
di·a·lec·ti·cal (dī'ə-lek'ti-k'l), ***adj.*** dialectic: abbreviated **dial.**
di·a·lec·ti·cal·ly (dī'-ə-lek'ti-k'l-i, dī'ə-lek'tik-li), ***adv.*** 1. in a dialectical manner. 2. by means of dialectic.
dialectical materialism, the philosophy originated by Karl Marx and Friedrich Engels, an application of Hegel's logical method (dialectic) to philosophical materialism: the official doctrine of Communism.
di·a·lec·ti·cian (dī'ə-lek-tish'ən), ***n.*** [Fr. *dialecticien*], an expert in dialectic; logician.
di·a·lec·ti·cism (dī'ə-lek'ti-siz'm), ***n.*** 1. the nature or effect of dialect. 2. a dialectical locution. 3. the use of dialectic.
di·a·lec·tics (dī'ə-lek'tiks), ***n.pl.*** [construed as sing.], dialectic (sense 1).
di·a·lec·tol·o·gy (dī'ə-lek-tol'ə-ji), ***n.*** the study of dialects.
di·al·ing, di·al·ling (dī'əl-iŋ), ***n.*** 1. the act of one who dials. 2. the art of making dials. 3. measurement of time by dials. 4. a method of surveying using a miner's compass.
di·al·lage (dī'ə-lij), ***n.*** [Fr.; Gr. *diallagē*, change, interchange < *dia-*, through + *allos*, other: so named from having unlike fracture planes], a green mineral that is a laminated variety of pyroxene.
di·a·log (dī'ə-lôg', dī'ə-log'), ***n.*** dialogue.
di·al·o·gism (dī-al'ə-jiz'm), ***n.*** [< *dialogue* + *-ism*], a discussion of some subject in the form of an imaginary dialogue.
di·al·o·gist (dī-al'ə-jist), ***n.*** 1. a writer of dialogue. 2. a person who takes part in a dialogue.
di·al·o·gize (dī-al'ə-jīz'), ***v.i.*** [DIALOGIZED (-jīzd'), DIALOGIZING], [Gr. *dialegesthai*], to carry on a dialogue.
di·a·logue (dī'ə-lôg', dī'ə-log'), ***n.*** [Fr.; L. *dialogus;* Gr. *dialogos* < *dialegesthai;* see DIALECT], 1. a talking together; conversation. 2. a written work in the form of a conversation. 3. the passages of talk in a play, story, radio act, etc. Abbreviated **dial.** ***v.i.*** [DIALOGUED (-lôgd', -logd'), DIALOGUING], to hold a conversation. ***v.t.*** to express in dialogue. Also spelled **dialog.**
dial tone, a low buzzing sound indicating to the user of a dial telephone that the line is open and a number may be dialed.
di·al·y·sis (dī-al'ə-sis), ***n.*** [*pl.* DIALYSES (-sēz')], [L.; Gr. *dialysis*, separation, dissolution < *dialyein*, to separate, dissolve; *dia-*, apart + *lyein*, to loose], 1. separation; dissolution. 2. in *chemistry*, the separation of crystalloids from colloids in solution by the faster diffusion of the former through a moist membrane.
di·a·lyt·ic (dī'ə-lit'ik), ***adj.*** [Gr. *dialytikos*], of or resembling dialysis.
di·a·lyt·i·cal·ly (dī'ə-lit'i-k'l-i, dī'ə-lit'ik-li), ***adv.*** by means of dialysis.
di·a·lyze (dī'ə-līz'), ***v.t.*** [DIALYZED (-līzd'), DIALYZING], to apply dialysis to; separate or get by dialysis.
diam., diameter.
di·a·mag·net·ic (dī'ə-mag-net'ik), ***adj.*** having or relating to diamagnetism. ***n.*** a diamagnetic substance, as bismuth or zinc.
di·a·mag·net·ism (dī'ə-mag'nə-tiz'm), ***n.*** 1. the property that certain substances have of being repelled by both poles of a magnet and hence taking a position at right angles to the magnet's line of influence. 2. diamagnetic force. 3. diamagnetic phenomena. 4. the science that deals with such phenomena and substances.
di·am·e·ter (dī-am'ə-tẽr), ***n.*** [ME. & OFr. *diametre;* L. *diametrus;* Gr. *diametros* < *dia-*, through + *metron*, a measure], 1. a straight line passing through the center of a circle, sphere, etc. from one side to the other. 2. the length of such a line; measurement across; width or thickness of a thing: as, the ***diameter*** of the tube is one inch. 3. in ***optics***, the unit of measure of the magnifying power of a lens. Abbreviated **diam., dia., d., di.**
di·a·met·ric (dī'ə-met'rik), ***adj.*** diametrical.
di·a·met·ri·cal (dī'ə-met'ri-k'l), ***adj.*** 1. of or along a diameter. 2. directly opposite; contrary. 3. direct; exact: said of opposites.
di·a·met·ri·cal·ly (dī'ə-met'ri-k'l-i, dī'ə-met'rik-li), ***adv.*** 1. in a diametrical way; as a diameter; straight through. 2. directly or exactly (with ***opposed, opposite***, etc.).
di·am·in (dī-am'in, dī'ə-min), ***n.*** diamine.
di·am·ine (dī-am'ēn, dī'ə-min), ***n.*** any of a group of chemical compounds containing two NH_2 radicals; double amine.
di·a·mond (dī'mənd, dī'ə-mənd), ***n.*** [ME. *diamaunde;* OFr. *diamant;* ML. *diamas, diamantis;* L. *adamas;* Gr. *adamas*, adamant, diamond], 1. nearly pure carbon in crystalline form: it is one of the hardest substances known, and has great brilliance. 2. a piece of this substance, used as a gem and in cutting tools, wire-drawing dies, etc. 3. a figure shaped like this ◇; lozenge. 4. a red, lozenge-shaped mark on some playing cards. 5. *pl.* the suit of cards with this mark. 6. a card of this suit. 7. in *baseball*, *a*) the infield. *b*) the

whole playing field. 8. in *printing*, a small size of type, 4½ point. This line is in diamond. *adj.* of, like, set with, or relating to a diamond or diamonds. *v.t.* to adorn with or as with diamonds.

diamond in the rough, 1. a diamond in its natural state; hence, 2. a person or thing having fine qualities but lacking in polish.

diamond anniversary, the sixtieth, or sometimes seventy-fifth, anniversary of an event.

di·a·mond·back (dī′mənd-bak′, dī′ə-mənd-bak′), *adj.* having diamond-shaped markings on the back: as, a *diamondback* rattlesnake. *n.* 1. a kind of moth. 2. a diamondback terrapin.

diamondback terrapin, an edible North American turtle with diamond-shaped ridges on its shell, found in salt marshes along the Atlantic and Gulf coasts.

diamond jubilee, a diamond anniversary.

diamond wedding, a sixtieth, or sometimes seventy-fifth, wedding anniversary.

Di·an (dī′ən), *n.* [Poetic], Diana.

Di·an·a (dī-an′ə), a feminine name: Fr. *Diane.* *n.* [L. < **Diviana* < *divus, dius,* divine, godly], 1. in *Roman mythology,* the goddess of the moon, of hunting, and of virginity: identified with the Greek Artemis; hence, 2. [Poetic], the moon.

DIANA

di·an·drous (dī-an′drəs), *adj.* [< *di-* + *andro-* + *-ous*], having two stamens.

di·a·no·et·ic (dī′ə-nō-et′ik), *adj.* [< Gr. *dianoētikos* < *dia-*, through + *noein,* to think over], relating to the thought process, particularly as proceeding from logical, rather than intuitive, reasoning.

di·an·thus (dī-an′thəs), *n.* [Mod. L. < Gr. *Dios* (genit. of *Zeus*) + *anthos,* a flower], any of a group of plants of the pink family, as the carnation, sweet William, etc.

di·a·pa·son (dī′ə-pā′z'n, dī′ə-pā′s'n), *n.* [L., contr. < Gr. *hē dia pasōn chordōn symphōnia,* concord through all of the notes; *dia,* through + *pasōn,* genit. pl. of *pas,* all; cf. CHORD & SYMPHONY], 1. the entire range of a musical instrument or voice. 2. either of two principal stops of an organ (*open diapason* and *stopped diapason*), covering the entire range: when either is used, any note played is sounded in two or more octaves. 3. a swelling burst of harmony. 4. a standard of musical pitch: as, *normal diapason.* 5. a tuning fork or pitch pipe. 6. [Obs.], the interval of an octave. 7. [Obs.], complete harmony.

di·a·per (dī′ə-pẽr), *n.* [ME. *diaper, diapery;* OFr. *diapre*-kind of ornamented cloth; ML. *diasprus,* kind of precious cloth; prob. < MGr. *diaspros,* ? white in spots or thoroughly white < Gr. *dia-*, through + *aspros,* white], 1. a white cotton or linen cloth woven in a pattern formed by a repeated, small, diamond-shaped figure. 2. such a pattern. 3. a towel or napkin of such cloth. 4. (*also* dī′pẽr), a small cloth usually of cotton, folded to form a baby's breechcloth. *adj.* 1. of diaper. 2. diapered. 3. for diapers. *v.t.* 1. to pattern with diamond-shaped figures. 2. to put a diaper on (a baby).

di·aph·a·nous (dī-af′ə-nəs), *adj.* [ML. *diaphanus;* Gr. *diaphanē,* transparent < *diaphainein,* to shine through; *dia-*, through + *phainein,* to show], transparent or translucent, as gauzy cloth.

di·a·phone (dī′ə-fōn′), *n.* [*dia-* + *-phone*], a group of sounds popularly recognized as being the same although pronounced with slight differences by various speakers: see **phoneme.**

di·a·pho·re·sis (dī′ə-fə-rē′sis), *n.* [LL.; Gr. *diaphorēsis,* a carrying away, perspiration < *diaphorein; dia-*, through + *phorein,* to bear], perspiration, especially when profuse and artificially induced.

di·a·pho·ret·ic (dī′ə-fə-ret′ik), *adj.* [LL. *diaphoreticus;* see DIAPHORESIS], producing or increasing perspiration. *n.* a diaphoretic medicine, treatment, etc.

di·a·phragm (dī′ə-fram′), *n.* [LL. *diaphragma, diaphragmatis;* Gr. *diaphragma; dia-*, through + *phragma,* a fence < *phrassein,* to enclose], 1. the partition of muscles and tendons between the chest cavity and the abdominal cavity; midriff. 2. any membrane or partition that separates one thing from another. 3. a device to regulate the amount of light entering the lens of a camera, microscope, etc. 4. a kind of contraceptive pessary. 5. a vibrating disk or cone that produces sound waves, as in an earphone, telephone receiver, or loud-speaker: see **telephone,** illus.

di·a·phrag·mat·ic (dī′ə-frag-mat′ik), *adj.* of or like a diaphragm.

di·a·phrag·mat·i·cal·ly (dī′ə-frag-mat′i-k'l-i), *adv.* by means of a diaphragm.

di·a·phys·i·al (dī′ə-fiz′i-əl), *adj.* of the diaphysis.

di·aph·y·sis (dī-af′ə-sis), *n.* [*pl.* DIAPHYSES (-sēz′)], [Mod. L.; Gr. *diaphysis,* line of separation, spinous process of the tibia < *diaphyein,* to grow through; *dia-*, through + *phyein,* to bring forth, produce], the shaft of a long bone, as distinguished from the growing ends.

di·ap·o·phys·i·al (dī′ap-ə-fiz′i-əl), *adj.* of a diapophysis.

di·a·poph·y·sis (dī′ə-pof′ə-sis), *n.* [*pl.* DIAPOPHYSES (-sēz′)], [see DIA- & APOPHYSIS], the transverse process of a vertebra.

Di·ar·bek·r (di-är′bek′ẽr), *n.* Diyarbekir.

di·arch·y (dī′är-ki), *n.* [*pl.* DIARCHIES (-kiz)], [*di-* + *-archy*], government shared by two rulers, powers, etc.: sometimes spelled **dyarchy.**

di·a·rist (dī′ə-rist), *n.* a person who keeps a diary.

di·ar·rhe·a, di·ar·rhoe·a (dī′ə-rē′ə), *n.* [LL. *diarrhoea;* Gr. *diarrhoia* < *dia-*, through + *rheein,* to flow], excessive frequency and looseness of bowel movements.

di·ar·rhe·al, di·ar·rhoe·al (dī′ə-rē′əl), *adj.* of or characterized by diarrhea.

di·ar·rhe·ic, di·ar·rhoe·ic (dī′ə-rē′ik), *adj.* diarrheal.

di·ar·thro·sis (dī′är-thrō′sis), *n.* [Mod. L.; Gr. *diarthrosis* < *diarthroun,* to divide by joints, articulate < *dia-*, through + *arthroun,* to connect by a joint < *arthron,* a joint], in *anatomy,* any articulation, as of the hip, permitting free movement in any direction.

di·a·ry (dī′ə-ri), *n.* [*pl.* DIARIES (-riz)], [L. *diarium,* daily allowance (of food or pay), hence record of this < *dies,* day], 1. a daily written record, especially of the writer's own experiences, thoughts, etc. 2. a book for keeping such a record. 3. a daily calendar or memorandum pad.

Di·as, Bar·tho·lo·me·u (bär′too-loo-me′oo dē′əsh; Eng. dē′əs), 1450?–1500; Portuguese navigator and explorer; discovered Cape of Good Hope (1488).

Di·as·po·ra (dī-as′pə-rə), *n.* [Gr. *diaspora,* a scattering < *dia-*, through + *speirein,* to sow], 1. the dispersion of the Jews after the Babylonian exile. 2. the Jews thus dispersed. 3. in the time of the apostles, Jewish Christians who lived outside of Palestine.

di·a·spore (dī′ə-spôr′, dī′ə-spōr′), *n.* [< Gr. *diaspora;* see DIASPORA], a native hydrate of aluminum, $HAlO_2$, which crackles and disperses when heated.

di·a·stase (dī′ə-stās′), *n.* [Fr.; Gr. *diastasis,* a standing apart, separation < *dia-*, apart + *histanai,* to stand], an enzyme that changes starches into maltose and later into dextrose; amylase.

di·a·stat·ic (dī′ə-stat′ik), *adj.* [Gr. *diastatikos*], of or having the properties of diastase; changing starch into sugar.

di·as·ter (dī-as′tẽr), *n.* [*di-* + *-aster*], the stage of mitosis in which there is a set of chromosomes near each pole of the spindle.

di·as·to·le (dī-as′tə-lē′), *n.* [LL.; Gr. *diastolē,* expansion, dilatation, distinction < *diastellein,* to separate, dilate; *dia-*, apart + *stellein,* to put, arrange], 1. the usual rhythmic dilatation of the heart, especially of the ventricles, following each contraction (*systole*), during which the heart muscle relaxes and the chambers fill with blood. 2. in *Greek & Latin prosody,* the lengthening of a short syllable. Opposed to *systole.*

di·as·tol·ic (dī′ə-stol′ik), *adj.* of the diastole.

di·as·tral (dī-as′trəl), *adj.* of or in the stage of diaster.

di·a·stroph·ic (dī′ə-strof′ik), *adj.* of diastrophism.

di·as·tro·phism (dī-as′trə-fiz′m), *n.* [< Gr. *diastrophē,* distortion < *diastrephein,* to turn aside, distort; *dia-*, aside + *strephein,* to turn; + *-ism*], 1. the process by which the earth's surface is reshaped through rock movements and displacements. 2. formations so made.

di·a·tes·sa·ron (dī′ə-tes′ə-ron′), *n.* [L. (Tatian, 2d c. A.D.) < Gr. *dia tessarōn,* through the four; *dia,* through + *tessarōn,* genit. of *tessares,* four], the four Gospels combined into a single account; Gospel harmony.

di·a·ther·man·cy (dī′ə-thũr′mən-si), *n.* [Fr. *diathermansie* < Gr. *dia-*, through + *thermansis,* a heating], the property of transmitting infrared or heat rays.

di·a·ther·ma·nous (dī′ə-thũr′mə-nəs), *adj.* diathermic.

di·a·ther·mi·a (dī′ə-thũr′mi-ə), *n.* [Mod. L.], diathermy.

di·a·ther·mic (dī′ə-thũr′mik), *adj.* [Fr. *diathermique*], 1. relating to diathermy. 2. letting heat rays pass through freely.

di·a·ther·mize (dī′ə-thũr′mīz), *v.t.* [DIATHERMIZED (-mīzd), DIATHERMIZING], to treat by diathermy.

di·a·ther·my (dī′ə-thũr′mi), *n.* [Mod. L. *diathermia* < Gr. *dia-*, through + *thermē,* heat], medical treatment in which heat is produced in the tissues beneath the skin by a high-frequency electric current.

di·ath·e·sis (dī-ath′ə-sis), *n.* [Mod. L.; Gr. *diathesis,* arrangement < *diatithenai,* to arrange; *dia-*, apart + *tithenai,* to place, put], congenital predisposition to certain diseases.

di·a·tom (dī′ə-təm, dī′ə-tom′), *n.* [Mod. L. *diatoma;* Gr. *diatomos,* cut in two < *diatemnein,* to cut through; *dia-*, through + *temnein,* to cut], any of a number of related microscopic algae, one-celled or in colonies, whose walls consist of two parts or valves and contain silica.

di·a·to·ma·ceous (dī'ə-tə-mā'shəs), *adj.* of, containing, or consisting of diatoms or their fossils.

di·a·tom·ic (dī'ə-tom'ik), *adj.* 1. having two atoms in the molecule. 2. having two replaceable atoms or radicals in the molecule; bivalent.

di·at·om·ite (dī-at'ə-mīt'), *n.* diatomaceous earth, forming, when dry, a fine powder used as an abrasive, as a pottery glaze, etc.

di·a·ton·ic (dī'ə-ton'ik), *adj.* [Fr. *diatonique;* LL. *diatonicus;* Gr. *diatonikos,* stretched through (the notes) < *dia-,* through + *teinein,* to stretch], in *music,* designating, of, or using any standard major or minor scale of eight tones without the chromatic intervals.

di·a·ton·i·cal·ly (dī'ə-ton'i-k'l-i, dī'ə-ton'ik-li), *adv.* in a diatonic manner; with reference to a diatonic scale.

di·a·tribe (dī'ə-trīb'), *n.* [Fr.; L. *diatriba,* learned discussion; Gr. *diatribē,* a wearing away, waste of time < *diatribein; dia-,* through + *tribein,* to rub], a bitter, abusive criticism or denunciation.

di·a·trop·ic (dī'ə-trop'ik), *adj.* of or showing diatropism.

di·at·ro·pism (dī-at'rə-piz'm), *n.* [*dia-* + *tropism*], in *botany,* the tendency of some plant parts to place themselves crosswise to the line of force of a stimulus.

di·az-, diazo-.

Diaz, Bartholomeu, see Dias, Bartholomeu.

Dí·az, Por·fi·rio (pôr-fē'ryô dē'äs; Eng. dē'as), 1830–1915; Mexican general and statesman; president of Mexico (1877–1880; 1884–1911).

Dí·az, Ro·dri·go (rô-*thrē*'gô dē'äth), see **Cid.**

di·a·zin (dī'ə-zin, dī-az'in), *n.* diazine.

di·a·zine (dī'ə-zēn', dī'ə-zin, dī-az'in), *n.* [*di-* + *az-* + *-ine*], any chemical compound with a molecular structure consisting of four atoms of carbon and two of nitrogen, arranged in a ring.

di·a·zo (dī-az'ō, dī-ā'zō), *adj.* [*di-* + *azo*], having a group of two nitrogen atoms combined directly with one hydrocarbon radical.

di·az·o- (dī-az'ō, dī-ā'zō), a combining form meaning *diazo:* also, **diaz-.**

di·az·o·am·i·no (dī-az'ō-ə-mē'nō, dī-ā'zō-ə-mē'nō), *adj.* denoting or of a diazo compound in which the N_2 group is attached to the nitrogen atom of an amino radical, replacing one of the atoms normally present in that radical.

di·a·zole (dī'ə-zōl', dī-az'ōl), *n.* [*diaz-* + *-ole*], 1. any chemical compound with a molecular structure consisting of three atoms of carbon and two of nitrogen, arranged in a ring. 2. a derivative of such a compound.

di·a·zo·ni·um (dī'ə-zō'ni-əm), *adj.* [*diaz-* + *ammonium*], designating or containing the bivalent organic radical $=N{:}N$ in which one nitrogen atom has a valence of three and the other a valence of five: it occurs in a series of aromatic compounds (*diazonium compounds*).

di·az·o·tize (dī-az'ə-tīz'), *v.t.* [DIAZOTIZED (-tīzd'), DIAZOTIZING], to convert chemically into a diazo compound.

dib (dib), *v.i.* [DIBBED (dibd), DIBBING], to dibble (*v.i.* 3).

di·bas·ic (dī-bās'ik), *adj.* 1. denoting or of an acid with two hydrogen atoms either or both of which may be replaced by basic radicals or atoms to form a salt. 2. having two atoms of a univalent metal.

dib·ber (dib'ẽr), *n.* a dibble.

dib·ble (dib''l), *n.* [Eng. dial. var. of *dabble*], a pointed tool used to make holes in the soil for seeds, bulbs, or young plants. *v.t.* [DIBBLED (-'ld), DIBBLING], 1. to make a hole in (the soil) with a dibble. 2. to plant with a dibble. *v.i.* 1. to use a dibble. 2. to dabble. 3. to dip bait gently into the water.

DIBBLE

di·bran·chi·ate (dī-braŋ'ki-it), *adj.* [< Mod. L. *dibranchiata* or *dibranchia,* name of the order < Gr. *di-,* two + *branchia,* gills of fish], of a group of cephalopods that have two gills, many armlike appendages, and a sac for ejecting an inky liquid. *n.* any such cephalopod, as a squid, octopus, etc.

di·cast (dī'kast, dik'ast), *n.* [Gr. *dikastēs* < *dikazein,* to judge, give a verdict < *dikē,* right, law, justice; akin to L. *dicere;* see DICTION], a judge of the high court of ancient Athens, chosen annually from 6,000 citizens.

dice (dīs), *n.pl.* [*sing.* DIE (dī), DICE], [see DIE, *n.*], 1. small cubes of bone, plastic, etc. marked on each side with a different number of spots (from one to six) and used in games of chance. 2. [construed as sing.], a gambling game played with dice. 3. any small cubes. *v.i.* [DICED (dīst), DICING], to play or gamble with dice, by throwing them to see what the spots on the upturned faces total. *v.t.* 1. to lose by gambling with dice. 2. to cut (vegetables, etc.) into small cubes. 3. to mark with a pattern of cubes or squares; checker.

di·cen·tra (dī-sen'trə), *n.* [Mod. L. < *di-,* two + Gr. *kentron,* a spur], any of a number of related plants with finely cut leaves and heart-shaped flowers of white, rose, etc., as the bleeding heart or Dutchman's-breeches.

di·ceph·a·lous (dī-sef'ə-ləs), *adj.* [Gr. *dikephalos* < *di-,* twice + *kephalē,* a head], having two heads, as certain fetal monsters.

di·cha·si·um (dī-kā'zhi-əm, dī-kā'zi-əm), *n.* [*pl.* DICHASIA (-ə)], [Mod. L. < Gr. *dichasis,* a division < *dichazein,* to divide into two < *dicha;* see DICHO-], in *botany,* a cyme whose stem forks into two branches.

di·chlo·rid (dī-klôr'id, dī-klō'rid), *n.* a dichloride.

di·chlo·ride (dī-klôr'īd, dī-klō'rid), *n.* any chemical compound in which two atoms of chlorine are combined with an element or radical.

di·chlo·ro·phe·nox·y·a·ce·tic acid (dī-klôr'ō-fi-nok'si-ə-sē'tik), a chlorine derivative of phenol and acetic acid, $C_7H_5Cl_2 \cdot O \cdot COOH$, used as a weed killer: also called *2,4-D.*

di·cho- (dī'kō, dī'kə), [Gr. *dicho-, dich-* < *dicha,* in two, asunder < *dis,* twice], an initial combining form meaning *in two* or *into two, asunder,* as in *dichotomy, dichogamy:* also, before a vowel, **dich-.**

di·chog·am·y (dī-kog'ə-mi), *n.* [*dicho-* + *-gamy*], in *botany,* the maturing of pistils and stamens at different times, preventing self-pollination: opposed to *homogamy.*

di·chot·o·mize (dī-kot'ə-mīz'), *v.t.* [DICHOTOMIZED (-mīzd'), DICHOTOMIZING], to divide into two parts; make a dichotomy of. *v.i.* in *botany,* to divide into two repeatedly, as a stem or root.

di·chot·o·mous (dī-kot'ə-məs), *adj.* 1. divided or dividing into two parts. 2. of or characterized by dichotomy.

di·chot·o·my (dī-kot'ə-mi), *n.* [*pl.* DICHOTOMIES (-miz)], [Gr. *dichotomia* < *dicha* (see DICHO-) + *temnein,* to cut], 1. division into two parts. 2. a division. 3. the phase of the moon or of a planet in which half of its apparently flat surface seems to be illuminated. 4. in *biology,* a dividing or forking into parts; bifurcation. 5. in *botany,* a system of branching by repeated divisions into two. 6. in *logic,* division of a class into two opposed subclasses, as *real* and *unreal.*

di·chro·ic (dī-krō'ik), *adj.* having or showing dichroism or dichromatism.

di·chro·ism (dī'krō-iz'm), *n.* [< Gr. *dichroos,* of two colors < *di-,* two + *chrōs,* skin, complexion, color; + *-ism*], 1. the property that some crystals have of reflecting two different colors when looked at from two different angles. 2. in *physics,* that property of a substance which results in its showing different colors of transmitted light, depending on the length of the light path in the substance: also called *dichromatism.*

di·chro·ite (dī'krō-īt'), *n.* [< Gr. *dichroos* (see DICHROISM); + *-ite:* so named because dichroic], iolite, a blue mineral.

di·chro·it·ic (dī'krō-it'ik), *adj.* dichroic.

di·chro·mate (dī-krō'māt, dī'krə-māt'), *n.* any salt of dichromic acid: also called *bichromate.*

di·chro·mat·ic (dī'krō-mat'ik), *adj.* [*di-,* two, twice + *chromatic*], 1. having two colors. 2. of or characterized by dichromatism. 3. in *biology,* having two varieties of coloration that are independent of sex or age, as certain species of insects, owls, parrots, etc.

di·chro·ma·tism (dī-krō'mə-tiz'm), *n.* 1. the quality or condition of being dichromatic. 2. color blindness characterized by inability to see more than two of the three primary colors, with their variants. 3. dichroism.

di·chro·mic (dī-krō'mik), *adj.* 1. able to distinguish only two of the three primary colors. 2. in *chemistry,* *a*) having two atoms of chromium per molecule; hence, *b*) designating an acid, $H_2Cr_2O_7$, which forms dichromates.

di·chro·o·scope (dī-krō'ə-skōp'), *n.* [< Gr. *dichroos;* + *-scope*], an instrument for studying dichroism.

di·chro·scope (dī'krə-skōp'), *n.* a dichrooscope.

dic·ing (dīs'iŋ), *n.* 1. the act or pastime of gambling with dice. 2. decoration of leather with stamped squares or diamonds. 3. leather so decorated. 4. a cutting into small cubes.

Dick (dik), a nickname for Richard. *n.* [d-], [Slang], a detective.

dick·cis·sel (dik-sis''l), *n.* [echoic of its cry], a migratory American bunting with a black throat and yellow breast.

dick·ens (dik''nz, dik'inz), *n. & interj.* [prob. < *Dickon,* nickname for *Richard*], [Colloq.], devil; deuce: a mild substitute for *devil,* as in *what the dickens!*

Dick·ens, Charles (dik''nz, dik'inz), (pseudonym *Boz*), 1812–1870; English novelist.

Dick·en·si·an (di-ken'zi-ən), *adj.* of or characteristic of Charles Dickens or his writings.

dick·er (dik'ẽr), *v.i. & v.t.* [< *dicker,* ten, ten hides < ME. *dycer;* akin to D. *daker,* G. *decher,* Dan. *deger,* ten hides < L. *decuria,* a division of ten < *decem,* ten, supposed unit of barter on Germanic frontier], to trade by bargaining, especially on a small scale; barter. *n.* [< the *v.*], the act of dickering.

dick·ey (dik'i), *n.* [*pl.* DICKEYS (-iz)], [< the nickname *Dick*], 1. a man's detachable shirt front. 2. a woman's detachable collar or blouse front. 3. a child's bib or pinafore. 4. a donkey. 5. a small bird. 6. the driver's seat in a carriage: also **dickey box.** 7. a back seat or rumble seat for servants in a carriage. Also spelled **dicky.**

DICKEY

Dick·in·son, Emily (dik'in-s'n), 1830–1886; American poet.

Dickinson, John, 1732–1808; American statesman and pamphleteer.

Dick test, [after G. F. *Dick* (1881–), Am. physician who devised it], a skin test for determining susceptibility or immunity to scarlet fever.

dick·y (dik'i), *n.* [*pl.* DICKIES (-iz)], a dickey.

di·cli·nism (dī'kli-niz'm), *n.* the quality or state of being diclinous.

di·cli·nous (dī'kli-nəs, dī-klī'nəs), *adj.* [< *di-* + Gr. *klinē*, bed; + *-ous*], 1. having the stamens and pistils in separate flowers. 2. having only stamens or only pistils, as some flowers.

di·cot·y·le·don (dī'kot-'l-ē'd'n, dī-kot''l-ē'd'n), *n.* a plant with two seed leaves (cotyledons); specifically, any plant belonging to that one of the two subclasses of seed plants which is characterized by embryos with two cotyledons, as most shrubs and deciduous trees.

di·cot·y·le·don·ous (dī'kot-'l-ē'd'n-əs, dī-kot''l-ed''n-əs), *adj.* having two cotyledons; belonging to the subclass of dicotyledons.

di·cou·mar·in (dī-kōō'mẽr-in), *n.* [*di-* + *coumarin*], a chemical compound extracted from spoiled sweet clover or prepared synthetically, used in medicine to retard the formation of blood clots.

di·crot·ic (dī-krot'ik), *adj.* [< Gr. *dikrotos*, double-beating (*di-*, two + *krotos*, rattling noise, clapping); + *-ic*], of or having a double pulse beat with each heart beat: as, a *dicrotic* artery.

di·cro·tism (dī'krə-tiz'm, dik'rə-tiz'm), *n.* the quality or state of being dicrotic.

dict., 1. dictated (by). 2. dictator. 3. dictionary.

dic·ta (dik'tə), *n.* alternative plural of **dictum.**

dic·ta·graph (dik'tə-graf', dik'tə-gräf'), *n.* a dictograph.

dic·ta·phone (dik'tə-fōn'), *n.* [< *dictate* + *-phone*], a machine for recording and reproducing words spoken into its mouthpiece, as for transcription by a stenographer: a trade-mark (**Dictaphone**).

dic·tate (dik'tāt; *also, for v.,* dik-tāt'), *v.t. & v.i.* [DICTATED (-id), DICTATING], [< L. *dictatus*, pp. of *dictare*, freq. of *dicere*, to speak], 1. to speak or read (something) aloud for someone else to write down. 2. to command expressly. 3. to impose or give (orders) with or as with authority; hence, 4. to give (orders or instructions) arbitrarily. *n.* an authoritative command.

dic·ta·tion (dik-tā'shən), *n.* [L. *dictatio;* see DICTATE], 1. the act of speaking or reading (something) aloud for someone else to write down. 2. the words so spoken, written down, or transcribed from shorthand. 3. the giving of authoritative orders or commands.

dic·ta·tor (dik'tā-tẽr, dik-tā'tẽr), *n.* [L.; see DICTATE], 1. in ancient Rome, a magistrate with supreme authority, appointed in times of emergency; hence, 2. a ruler with absolute power and authority. 3. a person whose word must be obeyed. 4. a person who speaks or reads aloud words for someone else to write down. Abbreviated **dict.**

dic·ta·to·ri·al (dik'tə-tôr'i-əl, dik'tə-tō'ri-əl), *adj.* of, like, or characteristic of a dictator; autocratic; imperious; domineering.

***SYN.*—dictatorial** implies the domineering, autocratic methods or manner of a dictator (the *dictatorial* enunciation of his opinions); **arbitrary** suggests the unreasoned, unpredictable use of one's power or authority in accord only with one's own will or desire (an *arbitrary* decision); **dogmatic** suggests the attitude of a religious teacher in asserting certain doctrines as absolute truths not open to dispute (the scientific method is not *dogmatic*); **doctrinaire** implies a rigid adherence to abstract doctrines or theories, without regard to their practical application.

dic·ta·tor·ship (dik-tā'tẽr-ship', dik'tā-tẽr-ship'), *n.* [*dictator* + *-ship*], 1. the position or office of a dictator. 2. a dictator's tenure of office; time that a dictator's rule lasts. 3. a dictatorial government; state ruled by a dictator. 4. absolute power or authority.

dictatorship of the proletariat, absolute control of economic and political power in a country by a government of the working class (proletariat): regarded in Communist theory as a means of effecting the transition from capitalism to socialism.

dic·tic (dik'tik), *adj.* deictic.

dic·tion (dik'shən), *n.* [< Fr. or L.; Fr. < L. *dictio*, a speaking < pp. of *dicere*, to say, orig. point out in words; IE. base **deik-*, to point out, show, as also in G. *zeigen*, to show, AS. *teon*, to accuse, etc.], 1. manner of expression in words; choice of words; wording. 2. manner of speaking or singing; enunciation.

dic·tion·ar·y (dik'shən-er'i; Brit. dik'shən-ẽr-i), *n.* [*pl.* DICTIONARIES (-iz)], [ML. *dictionarium* < L. *dictio;* see DICTION], 1. a book of alphabetically listed words in a language, with definitions, etymologies, pronunciations, and other information; lexicon: a dictionary is a record of generally accepted meanings, pronunciations, etc. which the words listed in it have acquired up to the time of its publication. 2. a book of alphabetically listed words in a language with their equivalents in another language: as, a Spanish-English *dictionary*. 3. any alphabetically arranged list of words or articles relating to a special subject: as, a medical *dictionary*. Abbreviated **dict.**

dic·to·graph (dik'tə-graf', dik'tə-gräf'), *n.* [< L. *dictus*, pp. of *dicere*, to speak; + *-graph*], a telephonic instrument with a small, very sensitive transmitter, used for secretly listening to or recording conversations carried on in another room: a trade-mark (**Dictograph**).

dic·tum (dik'təm), *n.* [*pl.* DICTUMS (-təmz), DICTA (-tə)], [L., something said, saying, word, witty remark; neut. of *dictus*, pp. of *dicere*, to speak], 1. a formal statement of opinion; authoritative pronouncement. 2. a saying. 3. in *law*, a judge's statement of opinion on some legal point other than the principal issue of the case.

Di·cu·ma·rol (dī-kōō'mə-rōl'), *n.* [< *dicoumarin*], an organic compound, a white crystalline powder, used in medicine to retard clotting of the blood: a trade-mark.

did (did), [ME. *dide;* AS. *dyde;* see DO], past tense of **do.**

Did·a·che (did'ə-kē'), *n.* [Gr. *didachē* (*tōn dōdeka apostolōn*), the teaching (of the twelve apostles)], an anonymous Christian treatise of the early 2d century.

di·dac·tic (dī-dak'tik), *adj.* [Gr. *didaktikos*, apt at teaching < *didaskein*, to teach], 1. used for teaching; intended for instruction. 2. morally instructive, or intended to be so. 3. too much inclined to teach others; pedantic: used generally in an unfavorable sense.

di·dac·ti·cal (dī-dak'ti-k'l), *adj.* didactic.

di·dac·ti·cism (dī-dak'tə-siz'm), *n.* 1. the quality of being didactic. 2. a didactic manner.

di·dac·tics (dī-dak'tiks), *n.pl.* [construed as sing.], [< *didactic*], the art or science of teaching; pedagogy.

di·dap·per (dī'dap'ẽr), *n.* [contr. < *dive dapper;* cf. AS. *dufedoppa* < *dufan*, to dive + *-doppa*, n. of agency < base of *dyppan;* see DIP], a small diving bird, the little grebe or dabchick.

did·dle (did''l), *v.i. & v.t.* [DIDDLED (-'ld), DIDDLING], [Eng. dial. *duddle, diddle*, to totter; akin to *dodder*], [Colloq.], to move back and forth jerkily; jiggle.

did·dle (did''l), *v.t. & v.i.* [DIDDLED (-'ld), DIDDLING], [? < Jeremy *Diddler*, character in the play *Raising the Wind* (1803), by James Kenney; name prob. < dial. *duddle*, to trick, ult. < AS. *dyderian*, to fool], [Colloq.], 1. to cheat; swindle; hence, 2. to ruin (a person). 3. to waste (time) in trifling.

Di·de·rot, De·nis (də-nē' dē'drō'; Eng. dē'də-rō'), 1713–1784; French philosopher and encyclopedist.

did·n't (did''nt), did not.

Di·do (dī'dō), *n.* [L.; Gr. *Didō*], in *Roman legend*, a Tyrian princess who founded Carthage and ruled there as queen: in Virgil's *Aeneid*, she greets Aeneas when he comes to Carthage after the fall of Troy, falls in love with him, and kills herself when he leaves.

di·do (dī'dō), *n.* [*pl.* DIDOS, DIDOES (-dōz)], [? < *Dido:* because of the story that Dido, on purchasing as much land as might be covered with the hide of a bull, ordered the hide cut into thin strips, with which she surrounded a large area], [Colloq.], a mischievous trick; prank.

didst (didst), archaic second person singular, past indicative, of **do**: used with *thou*.

di·dy (dī'di), *n.* [*pl.* DIDIES (-diz)], a diaper (sense 4).

di·dym (dī'dim), *n.* didymium.

di·dym·i·um (dī-dim'i-əm, di-dim'i-əm), *n.* [Mod. L. < Gr. *didymos*, twin (with lanthanum)], a rare metal, formerly considered an element but later found to be a mixture of two rare-earth elements, neodymium and praseodymium, usually found associated with cerium and lanthanum: symbol, D or Di (no period).

did·y·mous (did'ə-məs), *adj.* [< Gr. *didymos*, twin, double], in *botany & zoology*, growing in pairs; twin.

die (dī), *v.i.* [DIED (dīd), DYING (dī'iŋ)], [ME. *dien, deyen;* ON. *deyja;* akin to OS. *doian* & base of *death;* IE. base **dheu-*, to pass away, become senseless, as in W. *dyn*, (mortal) man], 1. to stop living; become dead; hence, 2. to suffer the agony of death, or an agony regarded as similar. 3. to stop functioning; end. 4. to lose force or activity; become weak, faint, etc. 5. to fade away; wither; become extinct. 6. to become indifferent (*to*), as if dead. 7. to pine away, as with desire. 8. [Colloq.], to wish very much, as if suffering or pining away: as, she's *dying* to learn the secret. 9. in *theology*, to suffer spiritual death.

die away, to become weaker and cease gradually.

die back, to wither to the roots or woody part.

die down, 1. to die away. 2. to wither to the ground.

die hard, to cling to life, a cause, etc.; resist to the last.

die off, to die one by one until all are gone.

die out, 1. to die away. 2. to go out of existence.

SYN.—**die** is the basic, simple, direct word meaning to stop living or to become dead; **decease, expire,** and **pass away** are all euphemisms, **decease** being also the legal term, **expire** meaning literally to breathe one's last breath, and **pass away** suggesting a coming to an end; **perish** implies death by a violent means or under difficult circumstances (six persons *perished* in the fire).

die (dī), *n.* [*pl.*, for 1 & 2, DICE (dīs); for 3 & 4, DIES (dīz)], [ME. *de, dee* (pl. *dees, dise*); OFr. *de* < LL. **datum* < L. *datus*, pp. of *dare*, to give, in the sense "to put out"], 1. either of a pair of dice; small, marked cube used in games of chance. 2. any small cube resembling this: as, vegetables cut into *dice*. 3. in *architecture*, a dado of a plinth or pedestal. 4. in *mechanics*, any of various tools or devices, originally cubical in form, for molding, stamping, cutting, or shaping; specifically, *a*) a piece of engraved metal used for stamping money, medals, etc. *b*) the stationary part of a machine for shaping or punching holes in sheet metal, etc.; matrix: distinguished from *punch*. *c*) the punch and matrix as a unit. *d*) a tool used for cutting threads, as of screws or bolts. *e*) a piece of metal with a hole through it, used in drawing wire, extruding rods, etc. *v.t.* [DIED (dīd), DIEING] to mold, stamp, cut, or shape with a die.

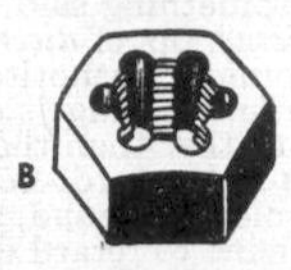

TYPES OF DIE
A, bolt die; B, rethreading die; C, adjustable dies

the die is cast, [after L. *jacta est alea*, ascribed to Caesar at the Rubicon], the decision has been made and is irrevocable.

die casting, 1. the process of making a casting by forcing molten metal into a metallic mold, or die, under great pressure. 2. a casting made in this way.

di·e·cious (dī-ē′shəs), *adj.* dioecious.

Die·fen·bak·er, John George (dē′f′n-bāk′ẽr), 1895– ; prime minister of Canada (1957–1963).

die-hard, die·hard (dī′härd′), *adj.* stubborn in resistance; unwilling to give in. *n.* a stubborn or resistant person; especially, an extreme conservative.

di·e·lec·tric (dī′ə-lek′trik), *n.* [< *dia-*, through, across + *electric:* so called because it permits the passage of the lines of force of an electrostatic field, but does not conduct the current], a material, as rubber or glass, that does not conduct electricity; insulator. *adj.* nonconducting; insulating.

di·en·ceph·a·lon (dī′en-sef′ə-lon′), *n.* [*di-* + *encephalon*], the posterior end of the prosencephalon, or forebrain.

Di·eppe (di-ep′; Fr. dyep), *n.* a port in northern France, on the English Channel: pop., 26,000.

di·er·e·sis (dī-er′ə-sis), *n.* [*pl.* DIERESES (-sēz′)], [LL. *diaeresis;* Gr. *diairesis*, division < *diairein*, to divide, separate < *dia-*, apart + *hairein*, to take], 1. the separation of two consecutive vowels, especially of a diphthong, into two syllables. 2. the mark (¨), placed over the second of two consecutive vowels to show that it is pronounced in a separate syllable: sometimes the dieresis is replaced by a hyphen (*coöperate, co-operate*). In this and some other dictionaries, the mark is also used to show a certain pronunciation of a vowel (ä, ë, ö, ü). 3. in *prosody*, a slight break or pause in a line of verse, resulting when the end of a metric foot coincides with the end of a word. Also spelled **diaeresis.**

di·e·ret·ic (dī′ə-ret′ik), *adj.* of dieresis.

Die·sel (dē′z'l, dē′s'l), *n.* [after Rudolf *Diesel* (1858–1913), G. inventor], a type of internal-combustion engine that burns fuel oil distilled from crude oil: the ignition is brought about by heat resulting from air compression, instead of by an electric spark as in a gasoline engine: also **diesel, Diesel engine** (or **motor**).

die·sink·er (dī′siŋ′kẽr), *n.* a maker of dies for stamping or shaping.

‡**Di·es I·rae** (dī′ēz ī′rē, dē′ās êr′ī), [L., Day of Wrath], 1. Judgment Day. 2. a medieval Latin hymn about Judgment Day, beginning *Dies Irae*, now often included in the Requiem Mass.

di·e·sis (dī′ə-sis), *n.* [*pl.* DIESES (-sēz′)], [L.; Gr. *diesis* < *diienai*, to send through < *dia-*, through + *hienai*, to send], a reference mark (‡) used in printing: also called *double dagger.*

‡**di·es non** (dī′ēz non′), [L. *dies non* (*juridicus*), not a (court) day], in *law*, a day on which the business of law courts cannot be transacted; legal holiday.

die·stock (dī′stok′), *n.* the frame to hold the dies for cutting threads, as on water pipes, screws, bolts, etc.

di·et (dī′ət), *n.* [ME. & OFr. *diete;* LL. *dieta;* L. *diaeta;* Gr. *diaita*, manner of, or place for, living], 1. what a person or animal usually eats and drinks; daily fare. 2. special, limited food and drink, chosen or prescribed for health or to gain or lose weight. 3. a regulated manner of living, with special reference to eating habits. *v.i.* & *v.t.* to eat or cause to eat a special selection of food and drink, especially for losing weight.

di·et (dī′ət), *n.* [OFr. *diete;* ML. *dieta*, assembly, day's journey < L. *dies*, day], 1. [Scot.], a day's session of an assembly. 2. a formal assembly. 3. in some countries, a national or, sometimes, local legislative assembly.

di·e·tar·y (dī′ə-ter′i), *n.* [*pl.* DIETARIES (-iz)], [LL. *dietarius*], 1. a system of diet. 2. daily food allowance, as in a hospital or jail. *adj.* 1. of diet. 2. of a dietary.

di·e·tet·ic (dī′ə-tet′ik), *adj.* [Gr. *diaitētikos*], of diet (food).

di·e·tet·i·cal (dī′ə-tet′i-k'l), *adj.* dietetic.

di·e·tet·i·cal·ly (dī′ə-tet′i-k'l-i), *adv.* with reference to dietetics.

di·e·tet·ics (dī′ə-tet′iks), *n.pl.* [construed as sing.], [< *dietetic*], the study of the kinds and quantities of food needed for health: abbreviated **diet.**

di·eth·yl·bar·bi·tu·ric acid (dī-eth″l-bär′bə-tyoor′ik), a compound, $C_8H_{12}O_3N_2$, derived from barbituric acid and used as a soporific: also called *veronal, barbital.*

di·e·ti·tian, di·e·ti·cian (dī′ə-tish′ən), *n.* an expert in dietetics; specialist in planning meals or diets.

diet kitchen, a kitchen, as in a hospital, where special diets for patients are planned by a dietitian.

‡**Dieu a·vec nous** (dyö′ ä′vek′ nōō′), [Fr.], God with us.

‡**Dieu et mon droit** (dyö′ ā mōn′ drwå′), [Fr.], God and my right: motto of British royalty.

dif- (dif), dis-: used before *f*, as in *differ.*

dif·fer (dif′ẽr), *v.i.* [ME. *differen;* OFr. *differer;* L. *differre*, to carry apart, differ < *dis-*, apart + *ferre*, to bring, carry], 1. to be unlike; be different (often with *from*): abbreviated **dif., diff.** 2. to be of opposite or different opinions; disagree. 3. to quarrel (*with*).

dif·fer·ence (dif′ẽr-əns, dif′rəns), *n.* [ME.; OFr.; L. *differentia* < *differens*, ppr. of *differre;* see DIFFER], 1. condition, quality, fact, or instance of being different. 2. the way or point in which people or things are different; distinguishing characteristic. 3. the state of holding an opinion unlike that of others; disagreement. 4. a dispute; quarrel. 5. a discrimination. 6. in *mathematics*, the amount by which one quantity is greater or less than another; remainder left when one quantity is subtracted from another. Abbreviated **dif., diff.** *v.t.* [DIFFERENCED (-ənst, -rənst), DIFFERENCING], to differentiate.

make a difference, 1. to have an effect; matter. 2. to change the outlook or situation. 3. to give different treatment; discriminate; differentiate.

split the difference, 1. to share equally what is left over. 2. to make a compromise.

what's the difference? [Colloq.], what does it matter?

dif·fer·ent (dif′ẽr-ənt, dif′rənt), *adj.* [Fr.; L. *differens;* see DIFFERENCE], 1. not alike; dissimilar (with *from*, or, more colloquially, *than*, and, in British usage, *to*). 2. not the same; distinct; separate. 3. various. 4. unlike most others; unusual. Abbreviated **dif., diff.**

SYN.—**different,** applied to things that are not alike, implies individuality (three *different* doctors) or contrast (the twins wore *different* hats); **diverse** more emphatically sets apart the things referred to, suggesting a conspicuous difference (*diverse* interests); **divergent** suggests a branching off in different directions with an ever-widening distance between, and stresses irreconciliability (*divergent* schools of thought); **distinct,** as applied to two or more things, stresses that each has a different identity and is unmistakably separate from the others, whether or not they are similar in kind, class, etc. (charged with two *distinct* offenses); **dissimilar** stresses absence of similarity in appearance, properties, or nature (*dissimilar* techniques); **disparate** implies essential or thoroughgoing difference, often stressing an absence of any relationship between things (*disparate* concepts); **various** emphasizes the number and diversity of kinds, types, etc. (*various* gifts).—*ANT.* alike, similar.

dif·fer·en·ti·a (dif′ẽr-en′shi-ə), *n.* [*pl.* DIFFERENTIAE (-shi-ē′)], [L.; see DIFFERENCE], in *logic*, a distinguishing characteristic, especially one that distinguishes one species from another of the same genus.

dif·fer·en·tial (dif′ẽr-en′shəl), *adj.* [ML. *differentialis* < L. *differentia;* see DIFFERENCE], 1. of, showing, or depending on a difference or differences: as, *differential* rates on a railroad. 2. constituting or making a specific difference; distinguishing. 3. having different effects or results; making use of differences: as, a *differential* gear. 4. in *mathematics* & *mechanics*, involving differentials. *n.* 1. a thing that is differential. 2. in *electricity*, one of two wire coils so arranged as to produce opposite polarities at some desired point of a circuit. 3. in *mathematics*, an infinitesimal difference between two consecutive values of a variable quantity. 4. in *me-*

chanics, a differential gear. 5. in *railroading,* a difference in rates, as between different routes.

differential calculus, the branch of higher mathematics that deals with the relations of differentials to the constant on which they depend.

differential coefficient, in *mathematics,* the measurement of the rate of change of a function in relation to its variable.

differential equation, in *mathematics,* an equation containing differentials or differential coefficients.

differential gear, a certain arrangement of gears (epicyclic train) connecting two axles in the same line and dividing the driving force between them, but allowing one axle to turn faster than the other: it is used in the rear axles of automobiles to permit a difference in axle speeds while turning curves.

dif·fer·en·tial·ly (dif'ẽr-en'shəl-i), ***adv.*** 1. in a differential manner. 2. distinctively.

differential quotient, a differential coefficient.

differential windlass, a windlass with two drums of different diameters to increase the lifting power.

dif·fer·en·ti·ate (dif'ẽr-en'shi-āt'), ***v.t.*** [DIFFERENTIATED (-id), DIFFERENTIATING], [ML. *differentiare* < L. *differentia;* see DIFFERENCE], 1. to constitute a difference in or between. 2. to make unlike; develop specialized differences in. 3. to perceive or express the difference in; distinguish between. 4. in *mathematics,* to work out the differential or differential coefficient of. ***v.i.*** 1. to become different or differentiated; develop new, distinguishing characteristics. 2. to perceive or express a difference. —*SYN.* see **distinguish.**

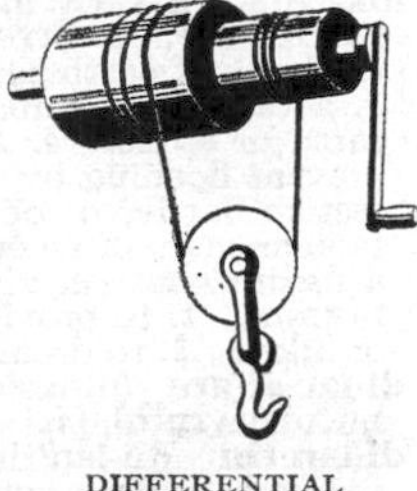

DIFFERENTIAL WINDLASS

dif·fer·en·ti·a·tion (dif'ẽr-en'shi-ā'shən), ***n.*** 1. a differentiating or being differentiated. 2. in *biology,* the modification of tissues, organs, etc. in structure or function during the course of development. 3. in *mathematics,* the working out of the differential or differential coefficient.

dif·fi·cile (dif'ə-sēl'; *earlier* di-fis''l), ***adj.*** [Fr. < L. *difficilis,* difficult; now used purely as a Fr. expression], hard, or difficult; especially, hard to deal with, please, or satisfy: said of persons.

dif·fi·cult (dif'i-kəlt, dif'i-kult'), ***adj.*** [< *difficulty*], 1. hard to do, make, understand, etc.; involving trouble, effort, or skill. 2. hard to satisfy, persuade, etc.: as, she is a *difficult* person. —*SYN.* see **hard.**

dif·fi·cul·ty (dif'i-kul'ti, dif'i-kəl-ti), ***n.*** [*pl.* DIFFICULTIES (-tiz)], [ME. & OFr. *difficulte;* L. *difficultas* < *dis-,* not + *facilis,* easy], 1. the condition or fact of being difficult. 2. something that is difficult; obstacle or objection. 3. trouble. 4. a disagreement or quarrel.

be in difficulties, to have financial troubles.

make a difficulty, 1. to cause a difficulty. 2. to offer objections; be reluctant; demur.

SYN.—**difficulty** is applied to anything hard to contend with, without restriction as to nature, intensity, etc. (a slight, or insurmountable, *difficulty*); **hardship,** stronger in connotation, suggests suffering, privation, or trouble that is extremely hard to bear (the *hardships* of the Pilgrims); **rigor** also suggests severe hardship, but in addition connotes that it is imposed by external, impersonal circumstances or by an inflexible discipline (the *rigors* of the Arctic winter); **vicissitude,** a bookish word, suggests a difficulty that is likely to occur in the course of something, often one inherent in a situation (the *vicissitudes* of political life).

dif·fi·dence (dif'i-dəns), ***n.*** [L. *diffidentia* < *diffidens,* ppr. of *diffidere,* to distrust < *dis-,* not + *fidere,* to trust], lack of confidence in oneself; hesitancy to assert oneself; shyness.

dif·fi·dent (dif'i-dənt), ***adj.*** [L. *diffidens;* see DIFFIDENCE], lacking confidence in oneself; hesitant to assert oneself; shy. —*SYN.* see **shy.**

dif·fract (di-frakt'), ***v.t.*** [< L. *diffractus,* pp. of *diffringere,* to break in pieces < *dis-,* apart + *frangere,* to break], 1. to break into parts. 2. to cause to undergo diffraction.

dif·frac·tion (di-frak'shən), ***n.*** [Mod. L. *diffractio* < L. *diffractus;* see DIFFRACT], 1. the breaking up of a ray of light into dark and light bands or into the colors of the spectrum, caused by the interference of one part of a beam with another when the ray is deflected at the edge of an opaque object or passes through a narrow slit. 2. a similar breaking up of other kinds of wave motion, as of sound or electricity.

diffraction grating, in *optics,* a plate of glass or polished metal ruled with a series of very close, equidistant, parallel lines, used to produce a spectrum by the diffraction of reflected or transmitted light.

dif·frac·tive (di-frak'tiv), ***adj.*** of or causing diffraction.

dif·fuse (di-fūs'; *for v.,* di-fūz'), ***adj.*** [L. *diffusus,* pp. of *diffundere,* to pour in different directions < *dis-,* apart + *fundere,* to pour], 1. spread out; not concentrated; hence, 2. using more words than are needed; long-winded; wordy. ***v.t. & v.i.*** [DIFFUSED (-fūzd'), DIFFUSING], 1. to pour in every direction; spread out; spread widely; scatter. 2. in *physics,* to mix by diffusion, as gases, liquids, etc. —*SYN.* see **wordy.**

dif·fus·er (di-fūz'ẽr), ***n.*** a person or thing that diffuses: also spelled **diffusor.**

dif·fus·i·ble (di-fūz'ə-b'l), ***adj.*** that can be diffused.

dif·fu·sion (di-fū'zhən), ***n.*** 1. a diffusing or being diffused; spreading; dissemination: as, the *diffusion* of cultural patterns. 2. wordiness. 3. the intermingling of the molecules of two or more substances. 4. a reflection, as of light, from an irregular surface.

dif·fu·sive (di-fū'siv), ***adj.*** 1. tending to diffuse. 2. characterized by diffusion. 3. diffuse.

dig (dig), ***v.t.*** [DUG (dug) or *archaic & poetic* DIGGED (digd), DIGGING], [ME. *diggen* < OFr. *diguer,* to excavate (cf. Fr. *digue,* dike); orig. base Gmc., as in MD. *diken,* AS. *dician,* to excavate, dig; see DITCH], 1. to break and turn up or remove (the ground, etc.) with a spade or other tool, or with hands, claws, snout, etc. 2. to make (a hole, cellar, one's way, etc.) by digging. 3. to get out by digging: as, *dig* potatoes; hence, 4. to find out, as by careful study or investigation; unearth (usually with *up* or *out*): as, we *dug* out the truth. 5. to thrust, nudge, or prod: as, he *dug* his elbow into my ribs. 6. [Slang], to understand; comprehend. ***v.i.*** 1. to dig the ground or any surface; excavate. 2. to make a way by digging (*through, into, under*). 3. [Colloq.], to work or study hard. ***n.*** 1. the act of digging. 2. [Colloq.], a thrust, poke, nudge, etc. 3. [Colloq.], a sarcastic comment; taunt; jeer.

dig in, 1. to dig trenches or foxholes for cover; hence, 2. to entrench oneself. 3. [Colloq.], to begin to work intensively.

dig into, 1. to penetrate by or as by digging. 2. [Colloq.], to work hard at.

dig., digest.

di·gam·ma (dī-gam'ə), ***n.*** [Gr.; *di-,* two + *gamma:* so called because it resembles two gammas (Γ) in form], the sixth letter (F, *F*) of the early Greek alphabet, derived from the Semitic *vav* and having the sound of English *w:* it was replaced in the Latin alphabet by *F.*

dig·a·mous (dig'ə-məs), ***adj.*** [L. *digamus;* Gr. *digamos*], 1. married a second time. 2. of digamy.

dig·a·my (dig'ə-mi), ***n.*** [L. & Gr. *digamia* < *di-,* two, twice + *gamos,* marriage], a second legal marriage; marriage to a second husband or wife after the death or divorce of the first.

di·gas·tric (dī-gas'trik), ***adj.*** [< *di-* + Gr. *gastēr,* belly], 1. having two fleshy parts with a connecting tendon between them: the *digastric muscle* depresses the lower jaw and indirectly moves the tongue. 2. of the digastric muscle.

di·gen·e·sis (dī-jen'ə-sis), ***n.*** [*di-* + *genesis*], in *biology,* successive reproduction by two processes, sexual in one generation and asexual in the next.

di·ge·net·ic (dī'jə-net'ik), ***adj.*** of or characterized by digenesis.

di·gest (dī'jest; *for v.,* di-jest', dī-jest'), ***n.*** [L. *digestum* (usually in pl. *digesta*) < *digestus,* pp. of *digerere,* to separate, explain; *di-,* apart + *gerere,* to bear, carry], 1. a body of condensed, comprehensive, systematic information; summary or synopsis, as of scientific material: abbreviated **dig.** 2. [D-], *often pl.* in *Roman law,* the Pandects of the Emperor Justinian. ***v.t.*** [< L. *digestus;* see the *n.*], 1. to arrange systematically, usually in condensed form; summarize. 2. [after L. *digerere cibum,* to cut up (dissolve) food], to change (food) in the mouth, stomach, and intestines by the action of gastric and intestinal juices, enzymes, and bacteria so that it can be absorbed by the body. 3. to aid the digestion of (food). 4. to think over and absorb. 5. to tolerate or accept. 6. in *chemistry,* to soften or make soluble with heat and moisture. ***v.i.*** 1. to be digested. 2. to digest food. —*SYN.* see **abridgment.**

di·gest·ant (di-jes'tənt, dī-jes'tənt), ***adj. & n.*** digestive.

di·gest·er (di-jes'tẽr, dī-jes'tẽr), ***n.*** 1. a person who makes a digest. 2. a heavy metal container in which substances are heated or cooked to soften them or extract soluble elements from them.

di·gest·i·bil·i·ty (di-jes'tə-bil'ə-ti, dī-jes'tə-bil'ə-ti), ***n.*** the quality of being digestible.

di·gest·i·ble (di-jes'tə-b'l, dī-jes'tə-b'l), ***adj.*** [ME., OFr.; LL. *digestibilis*], that can be digested.

di·gest·i·bly (di-jes'tə-bli, dī-jes'tə-bli), ***adv.*** in a digestible form.

di·ges·tion (di-jes'chən, dī-jes'chən), ***n.*** [ME. *digestioun;* OFr. *digestion;* L. *digestio*], 1. a digesting or being digested: said of food. 2. the ability to digest food. 3. the absorption of ideas; understanding.

di·ges·tive (di-jes′tiv, dī-jes′tiv), *adj.* [OFr. *digestif;* L. *digestivus* < *digestus;* see DIGEST], of, for, or aiding digestion. *n.* any substance, etc. that aids digestion.
digged (digd), original past tense and past participle of **dig,** now archaic or poetic.
dig·ger (dig′ẽr), *n.* 1. a person or thing that digs. 2. a tool or machine for digging. 3. the digging part of such a machine. 4. [D-], a member of any of several tribes of Indians in the western United States who dug up roots for food. 5. a digger wasp.
digger wasp, any of various wasps that dig a nest in the ground or in wood.
dig·gings (dig′iŋz), *n.pl.* 1. materials dug out. 2. [often construed as sing.], a place where digging or mining, especially gold mining, is carried on. 3. [Slang], originally, a gold miner's camp; hence, the place where one lives or stays; quarters.
dight (dīt), *v.t.* [DIGHT or DIGHTED (-id), DIGHTING], [ME. *dihten;* AS. *dihtan,* to arrange, dispose, appoint, direct, write, make, do < L. *dictare,* to say; see DICTATE], [Archaic & Poetic], 1. to adorn. 2. to equip.
dig·it (dij′it), *n.* [L. *digitus,* a finger, toe, inch], 1. a finger or toe. 2. the breadth of a finger, regarded as 3/4 inch. 3. any numeral from 0 to 9: so called because originally counted on the fingers. 4. in *astronomy,* one twelfth of the diameter of the sun or moon.
dig·it·al (dij′i-t′l), *adj.* [L. *digitalis*], 1. of or constituting a digit, especially a finger. 2. having digits. 3. like a digit. *n.* 1. a finger. 2. a key played with a finger, as on the piano.
digital computer, a computer using numbers, symbols, etc. consisting of coded digits to solve problems by means of arithmetic, especially in a binary system.
dig·i·ta·lin (dij′i-tal′in, dij′i-tā′lin), *n.* [< *digitalis* + *-in*], a poisonous crystalline glucoside, $C_{36}H_{56}O_{14}$, obtained from the seed of the digitalis.
dig·i·ta·lis (dij′i-tal′is, dij′i-tā′lis), *n.* [ML. *digitalis,* foxglove (see DIGIT): so named by Fuchs (1542) from its thimblelike flowers, after the G. name *fingerhut,* lit., finger hat, i.e., thimble], 1. any of a group of plants of the figwort family, with long spikes of thimblelike flowers; foxglove. 2. the dried leaves of the purple foxglove. 3. a medicine made from these leaves, used as a heart stimulant.
dig·i·tal·ism (dij′i-t′l-iz′m), *n.* a condition of the body caused by excessive use of digitalis.
dig·it·al·ly (dij′i-t′l-i), *adv.* [*digital* + *-ly*], with the finger or fingers.
dig·i·tate (dij′i-tāt′), *adj.* [L. *digitatus;* see DIGIT], 1. having separate fingers or toes. 2. like a digit; fingerlike. 3. in *botany,* having fingerlike divisions.
dig·i·tat·ed (dij′i-tā′tid), *adj.* digitate.
dig·i·ta·tion (dij′i-tā′shən), *n.* in *botany,* 1. a digitate condition. 2. a fingerlike part.
dig·i·ti- (dij′i-tə), [< L. *digitus;* see DIGIT], a combining form meaning *of the fingers* or *toes, fingerlike,* as in *digitigrade, digitiform.*
dig·i·ti·form (dij′i-tə-fôrm′), *adj.* [*digiti-* + *-form*], shaped like a finger; digitate.
dig·i·ti·grade (dij′i-tə-grād′), *adj.* [Fr.; see DIGITI- & -GRADE], walking on the toes with the heels not touching the ground, as cats, dogs, horses, etc. *n.* any animal that walks in this manner.
di·glot (dī′glot), *adj.* [Gr. *diglottos,* speaking two languages < *di-,* two + *glotta, glossa,* the tongue], in or using two languages; bilingual. *n.* a diglot edition.
dig·ni·fied (dig′nə-fīd′), *adj.* [pp. of *dignify*], having and showing dignity or stateliness.
dig·ni·fy (dig′nə-fī′), *v.t.* [DIGNIFIED (-fīd′), DIGNIFYING], [OFr. *dignifier;* ML. *dignificare* < L. *dignus,* worthy + *-ficare* < *facere,* to do, make], 1. to give dignity to; make worthy; honor; exalt. 2. to give a high-sounding name to: as, he *dignified* cowardice with the name of prudence.
dig·ni·tar·y (dig′nə-ter′i), *n.* [*pl.* DIGNITARIES (-iz)], [< L. *dignitas,* dignity; + *-ary*], a person holding a high, dignified position or office, as in a church.
dig·ni·ty (dig′nə-ti), *n.* [*pl.* DIGNITIES (-tiz)], [ME. & OFr. *dignite;* L. *dignitas,* worth, merit < *dignus,* worthy], 1. worthiness; nobility. 2. high repute; honor. 3. the degree of worth, repute, or honor. 4. a high position, rank, or title. 5. [Rare], a dignitary. 6. loftiness of appearance or manner; stateliness. 7. calm self-possession and self-respect. —*SYN.* see **decorum.**
di·graph (dī′graf, dī′gräf), *n.* [*di-* + *-graph*], a combination of two letters to represent one simple sound, as *read, show, graphic,* etc.
di·gress (də-gres′, dī-gres′), *v.i.* [< L. *digressus,* pp. of *digredi,* to go apart < *dis-,* apart + *gradi,* to go, step], to turn aside; depart temporarily from the main subject in talking or writing; ramble. —*SYN.* see **deviate.**
di·gres·sion (də-gresh′ən, dī-gresh′ən), *n.* [ME.; L. *digressio*], a digressing; temporary departure from the main subject in talking or writing.
di·gres·sion·al (də-gresh′ən-'l, dī-gresh′ən-'l), *adj.* digressive.
di·gres·sive (də-gres′iv, dī-gres′iv), *adj.* [L. *digressivus*], digressing; given to digression.

di·he·dral (dī-hē′drəl), *adj.* [< *di-* + Gr. *hedra,* a seat, base], 1. having two plane faces or sides: as, a *dihedral* angle. 2. having wings that form a dihedral angle with each other, as some airplanes. 3. in *solid geometry,* formed by two intersecting planes. *n.* 1. a dihedral angle. 2. the angle between either wing of an airplane and the horizontal plane of its transverse axis.

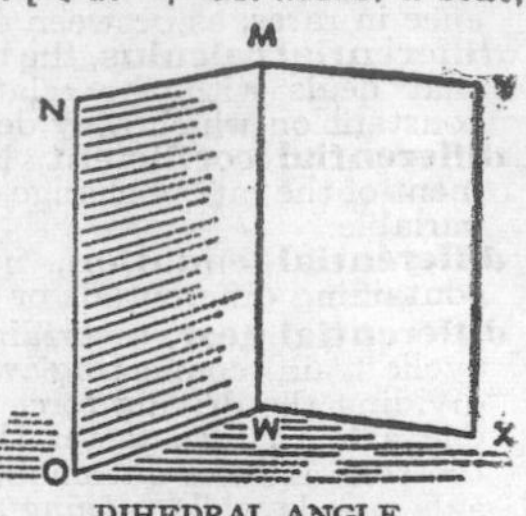

DIHEDRAL ANGLE
angle formed by planes MWON and MWXY

Di·jon (dē′zhōn′; Eng. dē′zhän), *n.* a city in east central France: pop., 113,000.
dik-dik (dik′dik′), *n.* [< the Ethiopian native name], a very small African antelope.
dike (dīk), *n.* [ME. *dike, dik;* AS. *dic,* influenced in form by ON. *dik;* see DITCH], 1. a ditch or watercourse. 2. the bank of earth thrown up in digging a ditch; hence, 3. a causeway, embankment, or low dividing wall of earth or stone. 4. an embankment or dam made to prevent flooding by the sea or by a stream. 5. a protective barrier or obstacle. 6. in *geology,* a hardened, tabular mass of igneous rock that has been forced into a fissure while in a melted state. *v.t.* [DIKED (dīkt), DIKING], 1. to provide, protect, or enclose with a dike or dikes. 2. to drain by a ditch. Also spelled **dyke.**
di·lac·er·ate (di-las′ə-rāt′), *v.t.* [DILACERATED (-id), DILACERATING], [*di-* + *lacerate*], to tear to pieces; rip.
di·lan·tin (di-lan′tin), *n.* [< *di*phenyl*hy*d*antoin* sodium], a drug used in the treatment of epileptic attacks: in full, **dilantin sodium:** a trade-mark (**Dilantin**).
di·lap·i·date (di-lap′ə-dāt′), *v.i. & v.t.* [DILAPIDATED (-id), DILAPIDATING], [< L. *dilapidatus,* pp. of *dilapidare,* to squander, consume, demolish, scatter like stones < *dis-,* apart + *lapidare,* to throw stones at < *lapis,* a stone], to become or cause to become partially ruined and in need of repairs.
di·lap·i·dat·ed (di-lap′ə-dāt′id), *adj.* [pp. of *dilapidate*], 1. falling to pieces or into disrepair; broken down; ruined; hence, 2. shabby and neglected.
di·lap·i·da·tion (di-lap′ə-dā′shən), *n.* 1. a dilapidating or becoming dilapidated. 2. a dilapidated condition. —*SYN.* see **ruin.**
di·lat·a·ble (dī-lāt′ə-b'l, di-lāt′ə-b'l), *adj.* that can be dilated.
di·lat·ant (dī-lāt′'nt, di-lāt′'nt), *adj.* [L. *dilatans,* ppr. of *dilatare*], 1. dilating or tending to dilate. 2. expanding in bulk when the shape changes: said of certain granular substances. *n.* 1. a thing that can dilate. 2. a surgical instrument for dilating; dilator.
dil·a·ta·tion (dil′ə-tā′shən, dī′lə-tā′shən), *n.* [ME. *dilatacioun;* OFr. *dilatation* < L.; see DILATE], 1. dilation. 2. in *medicine,* enlargement of an organ, cavity, duct, or opening of the body, beyond normal size.
di·late (dī-lāt′, di-lāt′), *v.t.* [DILATED (-id), DILATING], [L. *dilatare* < *dis-,* apart + *latus,* pp. of *ferre,* to bring], to make wider or larger; cause to expand or swell. *v.i.* 1. to become wider or larger; swell. 2. to speak or write in detail (*on* or *upon* a subject). —*SYN.* see **expand.**
di·lat·er (dī-lāt′ẽr, di-lāt′ẽr), *n.* a dilator.
di·la·tion (dī-lā′shən, di-lā′shən), *n.* 1. a dilating or being dilated. 2. a dilated part. Also **dilatation.**
di·la·tive (dī-lā′tiv, di-lā′tiv), *adj.* dilating or tending to dilate; producing dilation.
dil·a·tom·e·ter (dil′ə-tom′ə-tẽr), *n.* [see DILATE & -METER], an apparatus for measuring the dilatation, or expansion, of a substance.
di·la·tor (dī-lā′tẽr, di-lā′tẽr), *n.* 1. a person or thing that dilates. 2. any muscle that dilates a part of the body. 3. a surgical instrument for dilating an opening, wound, etc.
dil·a·to·ri·ly (dil′ə-tôr′ə-li, dil′ə-tō′rə-li), *adv.* in a dilatory manner.
dil·a·to·ri·ness (dil′ə-tôr′i-nis, dil′ə-tō′ri-nis), *n.* the quality of being dilatory; lateness or tardiness.
dil·a·to·ry (dil′ə-tôr′i, dil′ə-tō′ri), *adj.* [LL. *dilatorius* < L. *dilator,* dilatory person < *dilatus;* see DILATE], 1. causing or tending to cause delay; meant to gain time, defer action, etc. 2. inclined to delay; slow or late in doing things.
di·lem·ma (di-lem′ə), *n.* [LL.; Gr. *dilēmma; di-,* two + *lēmma,* proposition or assumption < *lambanein,* to take], 1. an argument necessitating a choice between equally unfavorable or disagreeable alternatives; hence, 2. any situation necessitating a choice between unpleasant alternatives; perplexing or awkward situation. —*SYN.* see **predicament.**
on the horns of a dilemma, faced with a choice between equally disagreeable alternatives.
dil·et·tan·te (dil′ə-tan′ti, dil′ə-tänt′), *n.* [*pl.* DILETTANTES (-tiz, -tänts′), DILETTANTI (-ti)], [It. < ppr. of *dilettare,* to delight < L. *delectare,* to charm, delight],

1. a person who loves the fine arts. 2. a person who follows an art or science only for amusement and in a superficial way; dabbler; trifler. *adj.* of or characteristic of a dilettante. —*SYN.* see **aesthete, amateur.**

dil·et·tan·te·ism (dil'ə-tan'ti-iz'm, dil'ə-tän'tiz'm), *n.* dilettantism.

dil·et·tan·ti (dil'ə-tan'ti), alternative plural of **dilettante.**

dil·et·tant·ish (dil'ə-tan'tish, dil'ə-tän'tish), *adj.* characterized by dilettantism.

dil·et·tant·ism (dil'ə-tan'tiz'm, dil'ə-tän'tiz'm), *n.* the quality, approach, etc. of a dilettante; superficial dabbling in art, literature, or science: also **dilettanteism.**

dil·i·gence (dil'ə-jəns), *n.* [ME.; OFr.; L. *diligentia* < *diligens*, ppr. of *diligere*, to esteem highly, select < *dis-*, apart + *legere*, to choose], 1. the quality of being diligent. 2. constant, careful effort; perseverance.

dil·i·gence (dil'ə-jəns; Fr. dē'lē'zhäns'), *n.* [Fr. < *carrosse de diligence*, lit., coach of diligence, i.e., fast coach < *faire diligence*, to hurry], a public stagecoach formerly much used in France and other European countries.

dil·i·gent (dil'ə-jənt), *adj.* [ME.; OFr.; L. *diligens*; see DILIGENCE], 1. persevering and careful in work; hardworking. 2. done with careful, steady effort; painstaking. —*SYN.* see **busy.**

dill (dil), *n.* [ME. *dille, dylle;* AS. *dile;* akin to OS. *dille*, OHG. *tilli;* prob. IE. base **dhewā-, dhū-*, to swell], 1. a plant of the carrot family, with aromatic seeds used to flavor pickles, etc.: the anise of the Bible. 2. the seeds.

dill pickle, a large cucumber pickle flavored with dill.

dil·ly·dal·ly (dil'i-dal'i), *v.i.* [DILLYDALLIED (-id), DILLYDALLYING], [redupl. form of *dally*], to waste time in hesitation or vacillation; loiter or trifle.

dil·u·ent (dil'ū-ənt), *adj.* [L. *diluens*, ppr. of *diluere;* see DILUTE], 1. diluting. 2. dissolving. *n.* a thing that dilutes or dissolves another thing.

di·lute (di-lo͞ot', dī-lūt'), *v.t.* [DILUTED (-id), DILUTING], [< L. *dilutus*, pp. of *diluere*, to wash away < *dis-*, off, from + *luere*, to wash], 1. to thin down or weaken by mixing with water or other liquid; hence, 2. to change or weaken (in brilliancy, force, etc.) by mixing with something else. *adj.* diluted. Abbreviated **dil.**

di·lu·tion (di-lo͞o'shən, dī-lū'shən), *n.* 1. a diluting or being diluted. 2. something diluted.

di·lu·vi·al (di-lo͞o'vi-əl, di-lū'vi-əl), *adj.* [LL. *diluvialis* < L. *diluvium;* see DILUVIUM], 1. of or caused by a flood, especially the Deluge. 2. of debris left by a flood or glacier.

di·lu·vi·an (di-lo͞o'vi-ən, di-lū'vi-ən), *adj.* diluvial.

di·lu·vi·um (di-lo͞o'vi-əm, di-lū'vi-əm), *n.* [*pl.* DILUVIUMS (-əmz), DILUVIA (-ə)], [L., a deluge < *diluere;* see DILUTE], in *geology*, a deposit of earth, rock, etc. left by a flood or glacier.

dim (dim), *adj.* [DIMMER (-ẽr), DIMMEST (-ist)], [ME. *dim;* AS. *dimm, dim;* akin to ON. *dimmr*, dark; IE. base **dhem-*, to be dusty, smoky, misty], 1. not bright; somewhat dark. 2. not clear; indistinct. 3. tarnished; without luster; dull. 4. not clearly seen, heard, perceived, or understood; vague. 5. not clearly seeing, hearing, understanding, etc. *v.t. & v.i.* [DIMMED (dimd), DIMMING], 1. to make or grow dim. 2. to make seem dim, as by comparison. —*SYN.* see **dark.**

take a dim view of, to view skeptically, pessimistically, without enthusiasm, etc.

dim., 1. dimension. 2. diminuendo. 3. diminutive.

dime (dīm), *n.* [ME. *dyme, disme;* OFr. *disme*, tithe, tenth; L. *decimus*, a tenth < *decem*, ten], a silver coin of the United States and Canada equal to ten cents; tenth of a dollar: abbreviated **d.**

a dime a dozen, [Colloq.], existing in great quantity and easily obtained; cheap.

dime novel, a cheap, melodramatic novel without literary worth, originally costing a dime.

di·men·sion (də-men'shən), *n.* [Fr.; L. *dimensio*, a measuring < *dimensus*, pp. of *dimetiri*, to measure off < *dis-*, off, from + *metiri*, to measure], 1. any measurable extent, as, length, breadth, thickness, etc. 2. *pl.* measurement in length, breadth, and, often, height. 3. extent; size; degree. 4. scope; importance. 5. in *algebra*, the sum of the exponents in a term: as, ab^2c^3 is of the sixth (1 + 2 + 3) *dimension*. Abbreviated **dim.**

di·men·sion·al (də-men'shən-'l), *adj.* 1. of dimension or dimensions. 2. having (a specified number of) dimensions: as, a three-*dimensional* figure.

dim·er·ous (dim'ẽr-əs), *adj.* [< *di-* + Gr. *meros*, a part; + *-ous*], 1. in *botany*, having two members in each whorl: said of flowers. 2. in *entomology*, having two-jointed tarsi.

dime store, a store where a wide variety of low-priced articles is sold, many for five or ten cents.

dim·e·ter (dim'ə-tẽr), *n.* [LL.; Gr. *dimetros* < *di-*, two + *metron*, a measure], in *prosody*, a line consisting of two measures (two or four feet).

di·met·ric (dī-met'rik), *adj.* [*di-* + *-metric*], in *crystallography*, tetragonal.

di·mid·i·ate (di-mid'i-āt', dī-mid'i-āt'), *adj.* [< L. *dimidiatus*, pp. of *dimidiare*, to divide into halves < *dimidium*, a half < *dis-*, apart, from + *medius*, middle], 1. halved. 2. in *biology*, having only one half developed. 3. in *botany*, split on one side, as some capsules. *v.t.* [DIMIDIATED (-id), DIMIDIATING], to reduce to half.

dimin., 1. diminuendo. 2. diminutive.

di·min·ish (də-min'ish), *v.t.* [combination of ME. *diminuen* (Fr. *diminuer;* L. *deminuere*, to make smaller, diminish; *de-*, from + *minuere*, to make smaller < *minus*, small) & Eng. *minish* < ME. *menusen;* OFr. *menusier;* LL. **minutiare* < *minutia*, smallness], 1. to make smaller; reduce in size, degree, importance, etc.; lessen. 2. in *music*, to reduce (a minor interval) by a semitone. *v.i.* to become smaller. —*SYN.* see **decrease.**

di·min·ished (də-min'isht), *adj.* [pp. of *diminish*], 1. made smaller; lessened; reduced. 2. in *music*, lessened by a semitone: said of intervals or of chords formed with such an interval.

di·min·ish·ing return (də-min'ish-iŋ), in *economics*, the proportionately smaller increase in productivity observed after a certain point in the increase of capital or labor.

di·min·u·en·do (də-min'ū-en'dō), *adj. & adv.* [It. < *diminuere;* see DIMINISH], in *music*, with gradually diminishing volume; decrescendo: symbol, >. *n.* [*pl.* DIMINUENDOS (-dōz)], 1. a gradual decrease in loudness. 2. a passage played diminuendo. Abbreviated **dim., dimin.**

dim·i·nu·tion (dim'ə-nū'shən, dim'ə-no͞o'shən), *n.* [ME.; OFr.; L. *diminutio, deminutio* < pp. of *deminuere;* see DIMINISH], 1. a diminishing or being diminished; lessening; decrease. 2. in *music*, the repetition of a theme in notes of one half or one quarter the length of those in the original.

di·min·u·tive (də-min'yoo-tiv), *adj.* [OFr. *diminutif;* LL. *diminutivus* < pp. of *deminuere;* see DIMINISH], 1. smaller than ordinary or average; very small; tiny. 2. in *grammar*, expressing smallness or diminution: as, a *diminutive* suffix. *n.* 1. a very small person or thing. 2. a word formed from another by the addition of a suffix expressing smallness in size and, sometimes, endearment, as *ringlet* (*ring* + *-let*), *sonny* (< *son* + *-y*), *lambkin* (*lamb* + *-kin*). Abbreviated **dim., dimin.** —*SYN.* see **small.**

dim·is·so·ry (dim'ə-sôr'i, dim'ə-sō'ri, də-mis'ẽr-i), *adj.* [LL. *dimissorius* < L. *dimissus*, pp. of *dimittere*, to send away < *dis-*, from + *mittere*, to send], giving leave to depart; dismissing: said chiefly of a bishop's letter permitting a clergyman to move to another diocese.

Di·mi·trov, Ge·or·gi (gye-ôr'gi di-mē'trôf), 1882–1949; Bulgarian statesman and Communist leader; prime minister (1946–1949).

dim·i·ty (dim'ə-ti), *n.* [*pl.* DIMITIES (-tiz)], [It. *dimiti*, pl. of *dimito;* ML. *dimitum* < Gr. *dimitos*, double-threaded < *dis-*, two + *mitos*, a thread; cf. TWILL], a thin, strong, corded cotton cloth, often figured, used for curtains, dresses, etc.

dim·ly (dim'li), *adv.* in a dim manner; obscurely, indistinctly, etc.

dim·mer (dim'ẽr), *n.* 1. a person that dims. 2. a device for dimming an electric light, as in automobile headlights or theater stage lights.

di·mor·phic (dī-môr'fik), *adj.* characterized by dimorphism.

di·mor·phism (dī-môr'fiz'm), *n.* [< Gr. *dimorphos*, having two forms < *di-*, two + *morphē*, form; + *-ism*], 1. in *botany*, the state of having two different kinds of leaves, flowers, stamens, etc. on the same plant or in the same species. 2. in *crystallography*, the property of crystallizing in two forms. 3. in *zoology*, the existence of two types, exclusive of sex, in the same species, distinct in coloring, size, etc.

di·mor·phous (dī-môr'fəs), *adj.* dimorphic.

dim-out (dim'out'), *n.* a dimming or reduction of the night lighting in a city, etc. to make it less easily visible, as to enemy aircraft; incomplete blackout.

dim·ple (dim'p'l), *n.* [Late ME. *dimpul* < base of Eng. dial. *dump*, deep pit filled with water + *-le*, dim. suffix; akin to MHG. *tumpfel*, G. *tümpel*, deep hole in water; IE. base **dheub-*, **dheup-*, hollow and deep, as in Eng. *deep, dip, dive*, etc.; ult. sense "little hole" parallels G. *grübchen*, lit., little pit, hence dimple], 1. a small, natural hollow on the body, as on the cheek or chin. 2. any little hollow, as on water. *v.t.* [DIMPLED (-p'ld), DIMPLING], to make dimples in. *v.i.* to show or form dimples; become dimpled.

dim·ply (dim'pli), *adj.* having dimples.

dim·wit (dim'wit'), *n.* [Slang], a stupid person; simpleton.

dim·wit·ted (dim'wit'id), *adj.* [Slang], like or characteristic of a dimwit.

din (din), *n.* [ME. *din, dyn;* AS. *dyne;* akin to ON. *dynr;* IE. base **dhwen-*, **dhun-*, to sound, boom, roar, as also in Sans. *dhrani*, sound, noise, thunder, word], a loud, continuous noise; confused clamor or uproar. *v.t.* [DINNED (dind), DINNING], 1. to strike with din. 2. to repeat insistently or noisily: as, *din* the idea into his ears. *v.i.* to make a din. —*SYN.* see **noise.**

Di·nah (dī'nə), [Heb. *dīnāh*, lit., judged], a feminine name.

di·nar (di-när'), *n.* [Ar. *dīnār;* Gr. *dēnarion;* L. *denarius;* see DENIER (coin)], 1. an ancient gold coin, used in some Moslem countries. 2. a monetary unit of Iraq valued at $2.80 in 1950. 3. a Persian coin of account. 4. a small coin of Yugoslavia valued at about $.02 in 1946.

Di·nar·ic Alps (di-nar'ik), a part of the Eastern Alps, along the Adriatic coast of Yugoslavia.

din·dle (din'd'l, din''l), *v.t.* & *v.i.* [DINDLED (-d'ld, -'ld), DINDLING], [prob. < *din* + *-le*, freq. suffix, with intrusive *-d-*], [Scot. & British Dial.], to tingle or vibrate, as with or from a loud sound, shock, etc. *n.* a tingling; thrill.

d'Indy, Vincent, see **Indy, Vincent d'.**

dine (dīn), *v.i.* [DINED (dīnd), DINING], [ME. *dinen, dynen;* OFr. *disner, disgner;* prob. < LL. **disjejunare;* L. *dis-* away, from + *jejunare*, to fast < *jejunus*, fasting, hungry], to eat dinner. *v.t.* to give a dinner to; entertain at dinner.

dine out, to eat dinner away from home.

din·er (dīn'ēr), *n.* 1. a person eating dinner. 2. a railroad car equipped to serve meals to passengers. 3. a small restaurant built to look like such a car.

di·ner·ic (dī-ner'ik), *adj.* [< *di-* + Gr. *nēron, nēros*, water; + *-ic*], in *physics*, constituting, or having to do with, the surface of contact between two liquids in the same container.

din·ette (dī-net'), *n.* [see DINE & -ETTE], an alcove or small, partitioned space used as a dining room.

ding (diŋ), *v.i.* [ME. *dingen*, to strike, beat < ON. *dengja*, to hammer (cf. *v.i.*, 2 & *v.t.*), merged with an echoic extension of *din*], 1. to make a sound like that of a bell; ring. 2. [Colloq.], to speak repetitiously and tiresomely. *v.t.* [Colloq.], to impress by vehement reiteration: as, he *dinged* the notion into us. *n.* the sound of a bell, or a similar sound.

ding·bat (diŋ'bat'), *n.* [Colloq.], 1. a stone, stick, or other object suitable for throwing. 2. a doohickey.

ding-dong (diŋ'dôŋ', diŋ'doŋ'), *n.* [echoic], 1. the sound of a bell struck repeatedly. 2. any similar sound. *adj.* [Colloq.], carried out, as a contest, fight, etc., with continual, successive changes in the lead or advantage; vigorously contested. *adv.* with a will; vigorously.

din·ghy (diŋ'gi), *n.* [*pl.* DINGHIES (-giz)], [Hind. *dīngī*, small boat], 1. originally, a rowboat used on the rivers of India. 2. a small boat carried on a warship. 3. a small boat, originally a rowboat, used as a tender to a yacht, motor cruiser, etc. 4. a small, undecked, single-masted racing boat, built on the lines of such a tender. Also spelled **dingey, dingy.**

din·gi·ly (din'ji-li), *adv.* in a dingy manner or condition.

din·gi·ness (din'ji-nis), *n.* the quality or condition of being dingy.

din·gle (diŋ'g'l), *n.* [ME. *dingel*, abyss < base of AS. *ding*, dungeon & ON. *dyngja*, cellar where women work; + *-le*, dim. suffix (cf. DIMPLE); IE. base **dhengh-*, to conceal; see DUNG], a small, deep, wooded valley; dell.

din·go (diŋ'gō), *n.* [*pl.* DINGOES (-gōz)], [native name], the Australian wild dog, with short, pointed ears and a bushy tail.

ding·us (diŋ'əs), *n.* [S.Afr.D. < *ding*, thing], [Slang], any device; contrivance; gadget: humorous substitute for a name not known or temporarily forgotten.

din·gy (din'ji), *adj.* [DINGIER (-ji-ēr), DINGIEST (-ji-ist)], [via. dial.; ? < *dung* + *-y*], 1. dirty-colored; not bright or clean; grimy; hence, 2. dismal; shabby.

din·gy (diŋ'gi), *n.* [*pl.* DINGIES (-giz)], a dinghy.

dining car, a railroad car equipped to serve meals to passengers.

dining room, a room in which people eat their meals, especially dinner.

di·ni·tro- (dī-nī'trō, dī-nī'trə), a combining form meaning *having two nitro groups per molecule*, as in *dinitrobenzene.*

di·ni·tro·ben·zene (dī-nī'trō-ben'zēn), *n.* a chemical compound, $C_6H_4(NO_2)_2$, formed by the reaction of nitric acid and benzene or nitrobenzene: it crystallizes as flexible needles.

dink (diŋk), *adj.* [Scot. dial.; ? < unrecorded Gael. word; cf. IE. base **dhengh-*, to cover, clothe, as in Lith. *apdanga*, clothing, OIr. *dingim*, to suppress; cf. DUNG], [Scot.], dressed in fine array; trim. *v.t.* [Scot.], to dress (oneself) in fine array; deck.

Din·ka (diŋ'kä), *n.* 1. a member of a group of Sudanic Negroid tribes living in the southern Anglo-Egyptian Sudan. 2. the East Sudanic language of the Dinkas.

din·key (diŋ'ki), *n.* [*pl.* DINKEYS (-kiz)], [see DINKY], [Colloq.], 1. a small locomotive for hauling cars, shunting, etc. in a railroad yard. 2. a small trolley car.

din·ky (diŋ'ki), *adj.* [DINKIER (-ki-ēr), DINKIEST (-ki-ist)], [Scot. & N. Eng. dial. *dink*, trim, neat; + *-y*], [Slang], small; of no consequence. *n.* a dinkey.

din·ner (din'ēr), *n.* [ME. *diner, dyner;* OFr. *disner* (Fr. *dîner*), inf. used as n.; see DINE], 1. the chief meal of the day, whether eaten in the evening or about noon. 2. a formal meal in honor of some person or event.

dinner dress, a woman's long, semiformal dress, usually with sleeves or worn with a jacket.

dinner jacket, a tuxedo jacket.

dinner ring, a ring with a large setting, worn on formal occasions.

din·ner·ware (din'ēr-wâr'), *n.* 1. plates, cups, saucers, etc., collectively. 2. a set of such dishes.

di·no- (dī'nə), [< Gr. *deinos*, terrible], a combining form meaning *terrible, dreadful*, as in *dinosaur.*

di·noc·er·as (dī-nos'ēr-əs), *n.* [Mod. L. < Gr. *deinos*, terrible + *keras*, a horn], a very large mammal of the Eocene Epoch, now extinct, with three pairs of horny projections on its head.

di·no·saur (dī'nə-sôr'), *n.* [< *dino-* + Gr. *sauros*, lizard] any of a group of extinct reptiles of the Mesozoic Era, with four limbs and a long, tapering tail: some dinosaurs were almost 100 feet long.

DINOSAUR (Tyrannosaurus; 18 ft. high)

di·no·sau·ri·an (dī'nə-sôr'i-ən), *adj.* of or like a dinosaur or dinosaurs. *n.* a dinosaur.

di·no·there (dī'nə-thêr'), *n.* [< *dino-* + Gr. *thēr* (akin to *fer-* in *feral*), wild beast], any of a number of related elephantlike animals of the Miocene Epoch, now extinct, with tusks curving downward from the lower jaw.

di·no·the·ri·um (dī'nə-thêr'i-əm), *n.* [*pl.* DINOTHERIA (-ə)], [Mod. L.], a dinothere.

dint (dint), *n.* [ME. *dint, dynt;* AS. *dynt*], 1. force; exertion: as, by *dint* of great effort he got what he wanted. 2. a dent. 3. [Archaic], a blow. *v.t.* to dent.

Din·wid·die, Robert (din-wid'i, din'wid-i), 1693–1770; British lieutenant governor of Virginia (1751–1758).

di·oc·e·san (dī-os'ə-s'n, dī'ə-sē's'n), *adj.* [ME. *dyocesan;* OFr. *diocesain*], of a diocese. *n.* the bishop of a diocese: abbreviated **dioc.**

di·o·cese (dī'ə-sēs', dī'ə-sis), *n.* [ME. & OFr. *diocise;* LL. *diocesis;* L. *dioecesis*, district, government; Gr. *dioikēsis*, administration < *dioikein*, to keep house < *dia-*, through + *oikos*, a house], the district under a bishop's jurisdiction; bishopric: abbreviated **dioc.**

Di·o·cle·tian (dī'ə-klē'shən), *n.* (*Gaius Aurelius Valerius Diocletianus*), Roman emperor (284–305 A. D.); lived 245–313 A.D.

di·ode (dī'ōd), *n.* [*di-* (separation) + *-ode* (path)], a vacuum tube with a cold anode and a heated cathode, used as a rectifier of alternating current.

di·oe·cious (dī-ē'shəs), *adj.* [< *di-* + Gr. *oikos*, a house; + *-ous*], in *biology*, having the male reproductive organs in one individual and the female organs in another; having separate sexes: also **diecious, dioicous.**

di·oes·trum (dī-es'trəm, dī-ēs'trəm), *n.* [Mod. L.; *di-* + *oestrum*], the interval between successive periods of sexual heat, especially in female animals.

Di·og·e·nes (dī-oj'ə-nēz'), *n.* Greek Cynic philosopher; 412?–323 B.C.: he supposedly lived in a tub to demonstrate his austerity, and searched with a lantern for an honest man.

di·oi·cous (dī-oi'kəs), *adj.* dioecious.

Di·o·med (dī'ə-med'), *n.* Diomedes.

Di·o·mede (dī'ə-mēd'), *n.* Diomedes.

Di·o·me·des (dī'ə-mē'dēz), *n.* [Gr. *Diomēdēs*, lit., Zeus-counseled < *Dios* (genit. of *Zeus*) + *mēdos*, counsel], 1. in *Greek legend*, a Greek warrior at the siege of Troy, who helped Odysseus steal the statue of Athena. 2. a Roman grammarian of the 4th century A.D.

di·o·nae·a (dī'ə-nē'ə), *n.* [Mod. L. < Gr. *Diōnē*, a name of Aphrodite (identified by the Romans with Venus)], a white-flowered swamp plant having leaves with two hinged blades that close upon insects: also called *Venus's-flytrap.*

Di·o·ny·si·a (dī'ə-nish'i-ə, dī'ə-nis'i-ə), *n.pl.* [L.; Gr. *Dionysia*, festival of Dionysus], any set of the various Greek festivals in honor of Dionysus, especially those at Athens from which the Greek drama originated.

Di·o·nys·i·ac (dī'ə-nis'i-ak), *adj.* [L. *Dionysiacus;* Gr. *Dionysiakos*], of Dionysus or the Dionysia.

Di·o·ny·sian (dī'ə-nish'ən, dī'ə-nis'i-ən), *adj.* 1. Dionysiac. 2. of any of several historical figures named Dionysius.

Di·o·ny·si·us Ex·ig·u·us (dī'ə-nish'i-əs eg-zig'ū-əs, dī'ə-nis'i-əs ek-sig'ū-əs), ?–540? A.D.; Roman monk and Christian theologian; believed to have devised the current system of reckoning dates with reference to the traditional year of the birth of Jesus.

Dionysius of Alexandria, Saint, 190?–265 A.D.; Christian bishop of Alexandria.

Dionysius of Hal·i·car·nas·sus (hal'i-kär-nas'əs), 54?–7? B.C.; Greek historian and rhetorician.

Dionysius the Elder, 430–367 B.C.; tyrant of Syracuse: he was victorious in his first two wars with Carthage but was defeated in the third.

Di·o·ny·sus, Di·o·ny·sos (dī'ə-nī'səs), *n.* [L.; Gr.

Dionysos], in *Greek mythology*, the god of vegetation and wine: identified with the Roman god Bacchus.

di·op·side (dī-op′sīd, dī-op′sid), *n.* [Fr. < *di-* (see DI-) + Gr. *opsis*, appearance, sight; associated in meaning with Gr. *diopsis*, transparency < *dia-*, through + *opsis*], in *mineralogy*, a kind of pyroxene, usually transparent.

di·op·tase (dī-op′tās), *n.* [Fr. < Gr. *dia-*, through + *optazein*, to see], a hydrous silicate of copper which occurs as green, glassy prisms; emerald copper ore.

di·op·ter (dī-op′tēr), *n.* [< L. *dioptra;* Gr. *dioptra*, instrument for leveling, taking altitudes, measuring angles < *dia-*, through + base of *opsis*, sight], a unit of measure of the refractive power of a lens, equal to the power of a lens with a focal distance of one meter.

di·op·tom·e·ter (dī′op-tom′ə-tēr), *n.* [*di-* + *optometer*], an instrument for testing the refraction of the eye.

di·op·tral (dī-op′trəl), *adj.* of a diopter.

di·op·tric (dī-op′trik), *adj.* [Gr. *dioptrikos*, relating to the use of the diopter; see DIOPTER], 1. of optical lenses or the method of numbering them according to their refractive powers; dioptral. 2. of dioptrics; refractive.

di·op·tri·cal (dī-op′tri-k'l), *adj.* dioptric.

di·op·trics (dī-op′triks), *n.pl.* [construed as sing.], [< *dioptric*], the branch of optics dealing with the refraction of light through lenses.

di·o·ra·ma (dī′ə-ram′ə, dī′ə-rä′mə), *n.* [< Gr. *dia-*, through + *horama*, a sight: by analogy with *panorama*], 1. a picture painted on a set of transparent cloth curtains and looked at through a small opening. 2. a miniature scene, wholly or partially three-dimensional, depicting figures in a naturalistic setting.

di·o·rite (dī′ə-rīt′), *n.* [Fr. < Gr. *diorizein*, to divide; *dia-*, through + *horizein*, to separate, bound < *horos*, boundary, limit], a dark-gray or greenish igneous rock, consisting chiefly of feldspar and hornblende.

Di·os·cu·ri (dī′ə-skyoor′ī), *n.pl.* [Gr. *Dioskouroi* < *Dios* (genit. of *Zeus*) + *kouroi*, pl. of *kouros*, boy, son], in *Greek mythology*, Castor and Pollux, twin sons of Zeus: after they died they became the constellation Gemini.

di·os·mose (dī-oz′mōs, dī-os′mōs), *n. & v.t.* osmose.

di·os·mo·sis (dī′oz-mō′sis, dī′os-mō′sis), *n.* osmosis.

di·ox·id (dī-ok′sid), *n.* a dioxide.

di·ox·ide (dī-ok′sīd), *n.* an oxide containing two atoms of oxygen per molecule.

dip (dip), *v.t.* [DIPPED (dipt) or, *occas.*, DIPT (dipt), DIPPING], [ME. *dippen;* AS. *dyppan, dippan*, to immerse < base of *deop*, deep; IE. base same as in *dimple, dive*], 1. to put into or under liquid for a moment and then immediately take out; immerse. 2. to dye in this way. 3. to baptize by immersion. 4. to clean (sheep) by bathing in disinfectant. 5. to make (a candle) by putting a wick in melted tallow or wax. 6. to plate or galvanize by immersion. 7. to get or take out by, or as if by, scooping up with a container, the hand, etc. 8. to lower and immediately raise again: as, *dip* the flag in salute. 9. to put (snuff) on the gums. *v.i.* 1. to plunge into water, etc. and quickly come out. 2. to sink or drop down suddenly. 3. to seem to sink: as, the sun *dips* into the ocean. 4. to slope down. 5. to lower a container, the hand, etc. into water, etc., especially in order to take something out. 6. to read here and there in a book, etc., or inquire into a subject superficially (with *into*). 7. in *aeronautics*, to drop suddenly before climbing. *n.* 1. a dipping or being dipped. 2. a plunge into water or other liquid. 3. a liquid into which something is dipped, as for dyeing. 4. whatever is removed by or used in dipping. 5. a candle made by dipping. 6. a downward slope or inclination. 7. the amount of this. 8. a slight hollow. 9. a short downward plunge, as of an airplane. 10. [Colloq.], liquid sauce. 11. [Slang], a pickpocket. 12. in *geology & mining*, the downward inclination of a stratum or vein, with reference to a horizontal plane. 13. in *gymnastics*, the act of lowering oneself by the arms between parallel bars until the chin reaches the bar level, and then raising oneself by straightening the arms. 14. in *physics*, the deviation of a dip needle from the horizontal; also, the amount of such deviation: also called *inclination*. 15. in *surveying*, the angular amount by which the horizon is below eye level.

di·pet·al·ous (dī-pet′'l-əs), *adj.* bipetalous.

di·phase (dī′fāz′), *adj.* [*di-* + *phase*], in *electricity*, generating, carrying, or run by two alternating currents whose phases differ by 90 degrees.

di·phas·ic (dī′fāz′ik), *adj.* diphase.

di·phen·yl (dī-fen′'l, dī-fē′n'l), *n.* a chemical compound, $(C_6H_5)_2$, the molecule of which consists of two chemically combined phenyl groups; biphenyl.

di·phen·yl·a·mine (dī-fen′'l-ə-mēn′, dī-fē′n'l-am′in), *n.* [*di-* + *phenyl* + *amine*], a colorless, crystalline chemical compound, $(C_6H_5)_2NH$, used as a stabilizer of explosives, as a test for nitric acid, and in making dyes.

di·phos·gene (dī-fos′jēn), *n.* a poisonous liquid compound, $ClCO_2CCl_3$, related to phosgene and used as a lung-irritant gas in chemical warfare.

diph·the·ri·a (dif-thêr′i-ə, dip-thêr′i-ə), *n.* [Fr. *diphthérie* (coined by Bretonneau, 1855) < Gr. *diphthera*, skin, leather < *dephein*, to tan hides], an acute infectious disease characterized by weakness, high fever, and the formation in the air passages of a membrane which interferes with breathing: it is caused by a bacillus.

diph·the·ri·al (dif-thêr′i-əl, dip-thêr′i-əl), *adj.* of or characteristic of diphtheria; diphtheritic.

diph·ther·ic (dif-ther′ik, dip-ther′ik), *adj.* diphtheritic.

diph·the·rit·ic (dif′thə-rit′ik, dip′thə-rit′ik), *adj.* [< Fr. *diphthérite*, Bretonneau's earlier name (1821) for the disease (see DIPHTHERIA); + *-ic*], 1. of, characteristic of, or like diphtheria. 2. having diphtheria.

diph·thong (dif′thôŋ, dip′thôŋ, dif′thoŋ), *n.* [Fr. *diphthongue;* LL. *diphthongus;* Gr. *diphthongos* < *di-*, two + *phthongos*, voice, sound < *phthengesthai*, to utter], in *phonetics*, a complex sound made by gliding continuously from the position for one vowel to that for another within the same syllable. Examples: *ou*, IPA [aʊ], in *house; oi*, IPA [ɔɪ], in *coil*. In many languages, diphthongs can be interpreted and phonetically written as a vowel followed by a semivowel (glide), as in the alternative IPA [haws], *house*, [kɔjl], *coil*.

diph·thon·gal (dif-thôŋ′g'l, dip-thôŋ′g'l, dif-thoŋ′g'l), *adj.* of, like, or constituting a diphthong.

diph·thong·i·za·tion (dif′thôŋ-i-zā′shən, dif′thoŋ-ī-zā′shən), *n.* a diphthongizing or being diphthongized.

diph·thong·ize (dif′thôŋ-īz′, dip′thôŋ-īz′, dif′thoŋ-īz′), *v.t.* [DIPHTHONGIZED (-īzd′), DIPHTHONGIZING], to make a diphthong of (a simple vowel); pronounce as a diphthong. *v.i.* to become a diphthong.

di·phyl·lous (dī-fil′əs), *adj.* [*di-* + *-phyllous*], in *botany*, having two leaves or sepals.

dip·lo- (dip′lō, dip′lə), [< Gr. *diploos*, double], a combining form meaning *two, double, twin*, as in *diplococcus:* also, before a vowel, **dipl-**.

dip·lo·coc·cus (dip′lə-kok′əs), *n.* [*pl.* DIPLOCOCCI (-kok′sī)], [*diplo-* + *coccus*], any of a group of parasitic bacteria occurring in pairs, as the pneumococcus that causes lobar pneumonia.

di·plod·o·cus (di-plod′ə-kəs), *n.* [Mod. L. < *diplo-* + Gr. *dokos*, a beam, shaft], a huge, herbivorous dinosaur of the Upper Jurassic of western North America.

dip·loid (dip′loid), *adj.* [*dipl-* + *-oid*], 1. twofold. 2. in *biology*, having twice the number of chromosomes normally occurring in a germ cell: most somatic cells are diploid. *n.* in *biology*, a diploid cell. Opposed to *haploid*.

di·plo·ma (di-plō′mə), *n.* [L.; Gr. *diplōma*, letter folded double < *diploos*, double], 1. an official state document or historical document; charter. 2. a certificate conferring honors, privileges, etc. 3. a certificate issued to a student by a school, college, or university, indicating the completion of a prescribed course of study, or conferring a degree.

di·plo·ma·cy (di-plō′mə-si), *n.* [*pl.* DIPLOMACIES (-siz)], [Fr. *diplomatie* < *diplomate;* see DIPLOMAT], 1. the conducting of relations between nations, as in making agreements. 2. skill in doing this; hence, 3. skill in dealing with people; tact. —*SYN.* see **tact**.

dip·lo·mat (dip′lə-mat′), *n.* [Fr. *diplomate* < *diplomatique* (after nouns ending in *-ate*, as *aristocrate*) < Mod. L. *diplomaticus, diplomatic* < L. *diploma;* see DIPLOMA, 1], 1. a representative of a government who conducts relations with another government in the interests of his own country; person whose career or profession is diplomacy: abbreviated **dipl.** 2. a person skilled in dealing with other people; tactful person.

dip·lo·mate (dip′lə-māt′), *n.* [< *diploma*], a doctor who is certified as a specialist by a board in a particular branch of medicine.

dip·lo·mat·ic (dip′lə-mat′ik), *adj.* [Fr. *diplomatique;* see DIPLOMAT], 1. of or connected with diplomacy: abbreviated **dipl.** 2. tactful and adroit in dealing with people. —*SYN.* see **suave**.

dip·lo·mat·i·cal·ly (dip′lə-mat′i-k'l-i, dip′lə-mat′ik-li), *adv.* in a diplomatic manner; with diplomacy.

diplomatic corps, all the foreign envoys in residence at the capital of a nation.

dip·lo·mat·ics (dip′lə-mat′iks), *n.pl.* [construed as sing.], 1. diplomacy. 2. the science of deciphering old official and historical documents, determining their authenticity and age, etc.

di·plo·ma·tist (di-plō′mə-tist), *n.* a diplomat.

di·plo·pi·a (di-plō′pi-ə), *n.* [Mod. L. < Gr. *diploos*, double + *ōps, ōpis*, the eye], an eye defect in which a single object appears double; double vision.

di·plop·ic (di-plop′ik), *adj.* of or having diplopia.

di·plo·sis (di-plō′sis), *n.* [Gr. *diplōsis*, a doubling], in *biology*, doubling of the number of chromosomes through the fusion of two haploid sets in the union of gametes.

dip needle, a magnetic needle vertically suspended and freely moving, used to indicate the direction of the earth's magnetism: it is horizontal at the magnetic equator (*aclinic line*) but vertical at the magnetic poles.

dip·no·an (dip′nō-ən), ***adj.*** [< Gr. *dipnoos*, double-breathed < *di-* + *pnoē*, breath; + *-an*], of a group of fishes with lungs as well as gills. ***n.*** a dipnoan fish.

di·pod·ic (dī-pod′ik), ***adj.*** of or in a dipody or dipodies.

dip·o·dy (dip′ə-di), ***n.*** [*pl.* DIPODIES (-diz)], [Gr. *dipodia* < *di-*, twice + *pous, podos*, the foot], a verse consisting of two feet; dimeter.

di·po·lar (dī-pō′lẽr), ***adj.*** of or like a dipole.

di·pole (dī′pōl′), ***n.*** in *physics & physical chemistry*, anything having two equal but opposite electric charges or magnetic poles, as a hydrogen atom with its positive nucleus and negative electron.

dip·per (dip′ẽr), ***n.*** 1. a person whose work is dipping something in liquid. 2. a thing for dipping, as a long-handled cup or similar container. 3. [D-], either of two groups of stars in the shape of a dipper, one (**Big Dipper**) in Ursa Major, the other (**Little Dipper**) in Ursa Minor: see **constellation**, chart. 4. in *zoology*, any of several dipping or diving birds, as the dabchick, grebe, and water ouzel.

dip·so·ma·ni·a (dip′sə-mā′ni-ə), ***n.*** [Mod. L. < Gr. *dipsa*, thirst + *mania*, madness], an abnormal and insatiable craving for alcoholic drink.

dip·so·ma·ni·ac (dip′sə-mā′ni-ak), ***n.*** a person who has dipsomania.

dip·so·ma·ni·a·cal (dip′sə-mə-nī′ə-k'l), ***adj.*** of, like, or having dipsomania.

dip·stick (dip′stik′), ***n.*** 1. a graduated metal rod for measuring the quantity or depth of a substance in its container, as of oil in an automobile crankcase. 2. a small stick used to put snuff on the gums.

dipt (dipt), occasional past tense and past participle of **dip.**

Dip·ter·a (dip′tẽr-ə), ***n.pl.*** [Mod. L. < Gr. *dipteros*; see DIPTEROUS], a large group of insects, including the housefly, mosquito, gnat, etc., having one pair of membranous wings.

dip·ter·al (dip′tẽr-əl), ***adj.*** 1. dipterous. 2. in *architecture*, surrounded by a double row of columns.

dip·ter·on (dip′tẽr-on′), ***n.*** [Gr. *dipteron*, neut. of *dipteros*; see DIPTEROUS], any dipterous insect.

dip·ter·ous (dip′tẽr-əs), ***adj.*** [Gr. *dipteros*, having two wings < *di-*, two + *pteron*, a wing], 1. having two wings, as some insects, or two winglike appendages, as some seeds. 2. of the Diptera.

dip·tych (dip′tik), ***n.*** [LL. *diptycha*, writing tablet of two leaves; Gr. *diptycha*, neut. pl. of *diptychos*, folded < *di-*, twice + *ptychē*, a fold < *ptyssein*, to fold, double], 1. anything folded so as to have two leaves. 2. an ancient writing tablet made up of a hinged pair of wooden or ivory pieces folding to protect the inner waxed writing surfaces. 3. a picture painted or carved on two hinged tablets.

dir·dum (dir′dəm, dũr′dəm), ***n.*** [Scot. & British Dial.], a loud outcry of blame or rebuke.

dire (dīr), ***adj.*** [DIRER (-ẽr), DIREST (-ist)], [L. *dirus*; fearful, dreadful; IE. base **dwei-*, to fear, as in Gr. *deinos*, fearful], dreadful; terrible; horrible; disastrous.

di·rect (də-rekt′, dī-rekt′), ***adj.*** [ME. & OFr. *directe*; L. *directus*, pp. of *dirigere*, to lay straight, put in a straight line, direct < *di-, dis-*, apart, from + *regere*, to keep straight, rule, control; cf. REGENT], 1. straight; not deviating; not roundabout; not turned aside; not interrupted. 2. straightforward; not vague; frank: as, a *direct* answer. 3. immediate. 4. with nothing or no one between: as, *direct* contact. 5. in an unbroken line of descent; lineal. 6. exact; complete: as, the *direct* opposite. 7. not needing a mordant: said of certain dyes. 8. by or of action of the people through popular vote instead of through representatives or delegates. 9. in *astronomy*, from west to east: opposed to *retrograde*. 10. in *mathematics*, designating or of a relation between variables in which one increases or decreases with the other: as, a *direct* proportion: opposed to *inverse*. ***v.t.*** 1. to manage the affairs of; guide; conduct; regulate; control. 2. to give authoritative instructions to (a person); ordain (*that* a thing be done); order; command. 3. to move, turn, or point (a person or thing) toward a place, object, or goal; aim; head. 4. to tell (a person) the way to a place. 5. to say (words, etc.) to a specific person or persons, or in a specific direction; address (remarks). 6. to write the address on (a letter, etc.). 7. to plan the action and effects of (a play, motion picture, etc.) and to supervise and instruct (the actors and technicians) in the carrying out of such a plan. ***v.i.*** 1. to give directions; make a practice of directing. 2. to be a director, as of a group of musicians. ***adv.*** in a direct manner; directly. —***SYN.*** see **command, conduct.**

direct action, action aimed directly at achieving an objective; especially, the use of strikes, demonstrations, etc. in disputes between labor and management.

direct current, an electric current flowing in one direction: abbreviated **D.C., d.c.**

direct discourse, quotation of a person's exact words.

di·rec·tion (də-rek′shən, dī-rek′shən), ***n.*** [L. *directio*, a making straight, act of directing; see DIRECT], 1. a directing; management; control. 2. the address on a letter or parcel. 3. *usually in pl.* instruction for doing, operating, using, preparing, etc. 4. an order; command. 5. the line in which or point toward which a moving person or thing goes. 6. the way a person or thing faces or points. 7. the line leading to a place: as, in the *direction* of Berlin. 8. an aspect, line of development, way, etc.: as, work in that *direction*. 9. in the *theater*, *a*) the director's plan for achieving certain effects, as of acting, lighting, etc. *b*) his instructions to the actors, etc. 10. in *music*, a word, phrase, or sign showing how a note, chord, passage, etc. is to be played.

di·rec·tion·al (də-rek′shən-'l, dī-rek′shən-'l), ***adj.*** 1. of direction in space. 2. in *radio*, *a*) for telling the direction from which signals are coming. *b*) for sending radio waves on one directed beam: as, a *directional* antenna.

direction finder, a device for finding out the direction from which radio waves or signals are coming, as a loop antenna that can be rotated freely on a vertical axis.

di·rec·tive (də-rek′tiv, dī-rek′tiv), ***adj.*** 1. directing; tending or intended to direct. 2. indicating direction. ***n.*** a general instruction or order issued by a central office, military unit, etc.

di·rect·ly (də-rekt′li, dī-rekt′li), ***adv.*** 1. in a direct way or line; straight. 2. without a person or thing coming between; immediately: as, *directly* responsible. 3. exactly; completely; as, *directly* opposite. 4. instantly; right away. ***conj.*** [Chiefly British], as soon as.

direct object, the word or words denoting the thing or person that receives the action of a transitive verb; goal of a verbal action, as ***ball*** in ***he hit the ball.***

Di·rec·toire (dē′rek′twär′), ***n.*** [Fr. < ML. *directorium*; see DIRECTORY], an executive body of five men in the First Republic in France, given office October 27, 1795 and ousted November 9, 1799. ***adj.*** of or characteristic of the Directoire period: said of furniture, dress, etc.

di·rec·tor (də-rek′tẽr, dī-rek′tẽr), ***n.*** [Anglo-Fr. *directour* < L. *directus*], 1. a person who directs or controls; supervisor; manager. 2. a member of a board chosen to direct the affairs of a corporation or institution. 3. a person who directs the production of a play or film, or the lighting, dancing, etc. 4. in *music*, a conductor.

di·rec·to·rate (də-rek′tə-rit, dī-rek′tə-rit), ***n.*** 1. the position of director. 2. a board of directors.

di·rec·to·ri·al (də-rek′tôr′i-əl, dī′rek-tō′ri-əl), ***adj.*** 1. of a director or directorate. 2. of directing or management.

di·rec·tor·ship (də-rek′tẽr-ship′, dī-rek′tẽr-ship′), ***n.*** [*director* + *-ship*], the position or term of a director.

di·rec·to·ry (də-rek′tə-ri, dī-rek′tə-ri), ***adj.*** [LL. *directorius* < L. *directus*], directing; guiding; advising. ***n.*** [*pl.* DIRECTORIES (-riz)], [ML. *directorium* < LL. *directorius*], 1. a thing that directs. 2. a book of directions. 3. a book listing the names and addresses (and, often, occupations) of a specific group of persons: as, a telephone *directory*. 4. a directorate. 5. in the *Anglican & Roman Catholic Churches*, directions for worship. 6. [D-], in *French history*, the Directoire.

direct primary election, a preliminary election at which candidates for public office are chosen by direct vote of the people instead of by delegates at a convention: also **primary (election)**: *closed primary elections* are those in which voters must declare party affiliation and are prohibited from voting for candidates of another party.

di·rec·tress (də-rek′tris, dī-rek′tris), ***n.*** a woman director.

di·rec·trix (də-rek′triks, dī-rek′triks), ***n.*** [*pl.* DIRECTRIXES (-trik-siz, trik-sēz′), DIRECTRICES (dī′rek-trī′sēz)], 1. a directress. 2. in *geometry*, a fixed line that serves as a guide in drawing a curve or surface.

direct tax, a tax levied directly on the person by whom it is to be paid, as an income tax or property tax.

dire·ful (dīr′fəl), ***adj.*** [*dire* + *-ful*], dreadful; terrible.

dirge (dũrj), ***n.*** [ME. *dirge, dorge* < L. *dirige*, imperative of *dirigere*, to direct: from the first word of the antiphon ***Dirige, Domine, Deus meus, in conspectu tuo viam meam*** (Direct, O Lord, my God, my way in thy sight), Psalm 5:8 in the Latin Office for the Burial of the Dead], 1. a funeral hymn or requiem mass. 2. a song, poem, or musical composition of grief or mourning; lament.

dir·i·gi·bil·i·ty (dir′i-jə-bil′ə-ti), ***n.*** the quality or state of being dirigible.

dir·i·gi·ble (dir′i-jə-b'l), ***adj.*** [< L. *dirigere* (see DIRECT); + *-ible*], that can be directed or steered. ***n.*** a balloon that can be steered, especially such a long, cigar-shaped, motor-driven balloon with a cabin underneath.

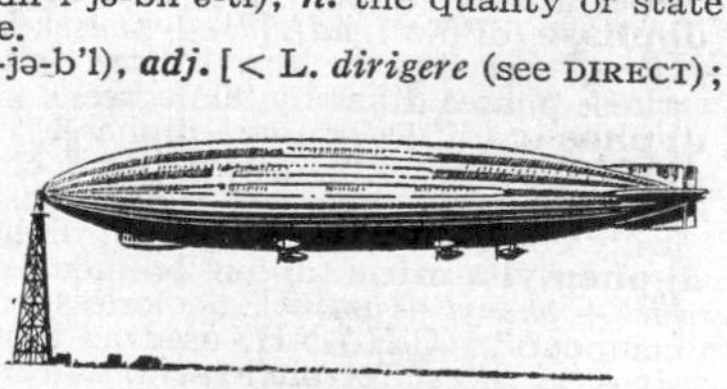

DIRIGIBLE

dir·i·ment (dir′ə-mənt), ***adj.*** [< L. *dirimens*, ppr. of *dirimere*, to interrupt; cf. Fr. *dirimant*], making absolutely void; nullifying; especially in ***diriment impediment***, in the *Roman Catholic Church*, any obstacle that automatically annuls a marriage.

dirk (dũrk), *n.* [so spelled by Dr. Johnson; earlier *dork, durk;* ? akin to G. *dolch,* Sw., LG. *dolk* (< IE. **dhelg,* to stab); ? influenced by name *Dirk;* cf. DERRICK], a short straight dagger. *v.t.* to stab with a dirk.

dirl (dirl, dũrl), *v.t. & v.i.* [var. of Scot. *thirl,* to pierce < ME. *thirlen, thrillen;* cf. THRILL], to vibrate or tingle.

dirn·dl (dũrn′d'l), *n.* [G., girl, dim. of *dirne,* girl, maid, hussy; OHG. *diorna,* servant girl (akin to OS. *thiorna,* ON. *therna*) < Gmc. **thiwairna,* servant's daughter, daughter of a vassal < **thiwa-,* servant; akin to AS. *theow,* servant, slave], 1. a kind of dress with a full skirt, gathered waist, and close-fitting bodice. 2. such a skirt without a bodice: also **dirndl skirt.**

dirt (dũrt), *n.* [ME. *dirt* < *drit;* ON. *dritr,* excrement, dirt; akin to LG., Fl. *dreet,* AS. *dritan,* to excrete; IE. base **dhreid,* to excrete], 1. any unclean or soiling matter, as mud, dust, trash, etc.; filth. 2. earth or garden soil. 3. anything common or filthy: as, he treats me like *dirt.* 4. dirtiness; uncleanness; meanness. 5. obscene writing or speaking; pornography. 6. malicious talk or gossip. 7. in *gold mining,* the gravel, soil, etc. from which gold is separated by washing or panning.

do one dirt, [Slang], to do harm to one, as by deception or malicious gossip.

dirt-cheap (dũrt′chēp′), *adj. & adv.* [Colloq.], as cheap as dirt; very cheap.

dirt farmer, [Colloq.], a farmer who does his own farming: distinguished from *gentleman-farmer.*

dirt·i·ly (dũr′t'l-i), *adv.* in a dirty manner.

dirt·i·ness (dũr′ti-nis), *n.* the quality or state of being dirty.

dirt·y (dũr′ti), *adj.* [DIRTIER (-ti-ẽr), DIRTIEST (-ti-ist)], 1. soiled or soiling with dirt; unclean. 2. obscene; pornographic: as, *dirty* jokes. 3. contemptible; mean. 4. grayish, muddy, or clouded: as, a *dirty* green. 5. producing much fallout: said of nuclear weapons. 6. in *nautical usage,* squally; rough: as, *dirty* weather. *v.t. & v.i.* [DIRTIED (-tid), DIRTYING], to make or become dirty; soil; tarnish; stain.

SYN.*—dirty** is applied to that which is covered or filled with any kind of dirt and is the broadest of these terms (a *dirty* face, a *dirty* room); **soiled** generally suggests the presence of superficial dirt in an amount sufficient to impair cleanness or freshness (a *soiled* shirt); **grimy** suggests soot or granular dirt deposited on or ingrained in a surface (a miner with a *grimy* face); **filthy** is applied to that which is disgustingly dirty (*filthy* as a pigpen); **foul** implies extreme filth that is grossly offensive or loathsome because of its stench, putridity, or corruption (*foul* air).—ANT.*** clean.

Dis (dis), *n.* [L.], in *Roman mythology,* 1. the god of the lower world: identified with the Greek god Pluto. 2. his realm; the lower world; Hades.

dis- (dis; *in some words,* diz), [< OFr. or (usually) L.; OFr. *des-* < L. *dis-* (*di-* before *b, d, g, v, m, n, l, r; dif-* before *f*) < IE. **dis-* (< **dwis-,* twice, in two; cf. BI-, TWO), whence also AS. *te-,* OS. & OFris. *te-, ti-,* OHG. *zi- ze-,* Goth. *dis-,* etc.; cf. DE-], a prefix denoting, in general, *separation, negation,* or *reversal:* 1. used to form verbs: *a*) from word bases not actually found as individual English words: meaning *away, apart,* as in *dismiss, disperse;* *b*) from nouns: meaning *deprive of, expel from,* as in *disfrock, disbar;* *c*) from adjectives: meaning *cause to be the opposite of,* as in *disable;* *d*) from other verbs: meaning *fail, cease, refuse to,* as in *dissatisfy, disappear, disallow; do the opposite of,* as in *disjoin, disintegrate;* intensifying the action, as in *disannul.* 2. used to form adjectives from other simple or verbal adjectives: meaning *not, un-, the opposite of,* as in *dishonest, dissatisfied, displeasing.* 3. used to form nouns from other simple or verbal nouns: meaning *opposite of, lack of,* as in *disease, disunion.*

dis- (dis), di- (twice, double).

dis., 1. distance. 2. distant. 3. distribute.

dis·a·bil·i·ty (dis′ə-bil′ə-ti), *n.* [*pl.* DISABILITIES (-tiz)], 1. a disabled condition. 2. that which disables, as illness. 3. a legal disqualification or incapacity.

disability clause, in *life insurance,* a clause entitling a policyholder who becomes totally and permanently disabled to cease premium payments and, often, to receive a specified monthly income, without losing any part of the life insurance given by the policy.

dis·a·ble (dis-ā′b'l), *v.t.* [DISABLED (-b'ld), DISABLING], [*dis-* + *able*], 1. to make unable or unfit; cripple; incapacitate. 2. to make legally incapable; disqualify legally. —***SYN.*** see **maim.**

dis·a·ble·ment (dis-ā′b'l-mənt), *n.* 1. a disabling or being disabled. 2. that which disables.

dis·a·buse (dis′ə-būz′), *v.t.* [*dis-* + *abuse*], to rid of false ideas; undeceive.

di·sac·cha·ride (dī-sak′ə-rīd′, dī-sak′ə-rid), *n.* [*di-* + *saccharide*], any of a group of sugars with a common formula, $C_{12}H_{22}O_{11}$, as sucrose, maltose, and lactose, which on hydrolysis yield two monosaccharides.

dis·ac·cord (dis′ə-kôrd′), *v.i.* [ME. *disacorden;* OFr. *desacorder;* see DIS- & ACCORD], to refuse to agree; disagree. *n.* lack of accord; discord; disagreement.

dis·ac·cred·it (dis′ə-kred′it), *v.t.* to cause to be no longer accredited, or authorized.

dis·ac·cus·tom (dis′ə-kus′təm), *v.t.* [OFr. *desacostumer;* see DIS- & ACCUSTOM], to rid of a habit; cause to be unaccustomed (*to* something).

dis·ad·van·tage (dis′əd-van′tij, dis′əd-vän′tij), *n.* [ME. *disadvauntage;* OFr. *desavantage;* see DIS- & ADVANTAGE], 1. an unfavorable situation or circumstance; drawback; handicap. 2. loss; injury; detriment. *v.t.* to act to the disadvantage of.

at a disadvantage, in an unfavorable situation (for doing something).

dis·ad·van·ta·geous (dis-ad′vən-tā′jəs, dis′ad-vən-tā′jəs), *adj.* causing or characterized by disadvantage; unfavorable; adverse.

dis·af·fect (dis′ə-fekt′), *v.t.* to cause to lose affection for; make unfriendly, discontented, or disloyal.

dis·af·fect·ed (dis′ə-fek′tid), *adj.* [pp. of *disaffect*], unfriendly, discontented, or disloyal, especially toward the government.

dis·af·fec·tion (dis′ə-fek′shən), *n.* the absence or withdrawal of affection or loyalty; discontent or disloyalty, especially toward the government.

dis·af·firm (dis′ə-fũrm′), *v.t.* [*dis-* + *affirm*], 1. to deny or contradict (a former statement). 2. in *law,* *a*) to refuse to abide by (a contract, agreement, etc.); repudiate. *b*) to reverse or set aside (a former decision).

dis·af·firm·ance (dis′ə-fũr′məns), *n.* a disaffirming; denial; repudiation.

dis·af·fir·ma·tion (dis′af-ẽr-mā′shən), *n.* disaffirmance.

dis·af·for·est (dis′ə-fôr′ist, dis′ə-for′ist), *v.t.* [ML. *disafforestare;* see DIS- & AFFOREST], 1. in *English law,* to reduce from the legal status of a forest to that of ordinary land. 2. to deforest.

dis·a·gree (dis′ə-grē′), *v.i.* [Fr. *désagréer;* see DIS- & AGREE], 1. to fail to agree; be different; differ. 2. to differ in opinion; hence, 3. to quarrel or dispute. 4. to be unsuitable or harmful (followed by *with*): as, midnight snacks *disagree* with me.

dis·a·gree·a·ble (dis′ə-grē′ə-b'l), *adj.* [Fr. *désagréable;* see DISAGREE], 1. not to one's taste; unpleasant; repugnant; offensive. 2. hard to get along with; quarrelsome.

dis·a·gree·a·bly (dis′ə-grē′ə-bli), *adv.* 1. in a disagreeable manner. 2. to a disagreeable extent.

dis·a·gree·ment (dis′ə-grē′mənt), *n.* 1. a disagreeing; refusal to agree. 2. difference; incongruity; discrepancy: as, there is *disagreement* between the accounts. 3. difference of opinion. 4. a quarrel or dispute.

dis·al·low (dis′ə-lou′), *v.t.* [ME. *disalouen;* OFr. *desalouer,* to blame, disapprove of; see DIS- & ALLOW], to refuse to allow; reject as untrue, invalid, or illegal.

dis·al·low·ance (dis′ə-lou′əns), *n.* a disallowing.

dis·an·nul (dis′ə-nul′), *v.t.* [*dis-,* intens. + *annul*], to cancel completely; annul.

dis·a·noint (dis′ə-noint′), *v.t.* [*dis-* + *anoint*], to annul the anointing or consecration of.

dis·ap·pear (dis′ə-pêr′), *v.i.* [*dis-* + *appear*], 1. to cease to be seen; go out of sight. 2. to cease being; go out of existence; become lost or extinct. —***SYN.*** see **vanish.**

dis·ap·pear·ance (dis′ə-pêr′əns), *n.* the act or fact of disappearing.

dis·ap·point (dis′ə-point′), *v.t.* [OFr. *desapointer;* see DIS- & APPOINT], 1. to fail to satisfy the hopes or expectations of. 2. to break one's promise to. 3. to prevent or undo the intended result of; balk; thwart: as, the weather *disappointed* their plans.

dis·ap·point·ed (dis′ə-poin′tid), *adj.* [pp. of *disappoint*], made unhappy by the failure of one's hopes or expectations.

disappointed of, prevented from fulfilling, achieving, or obtaining.

dis·ap·point·ment (dis′ə-point′mənt), *n.* 1. a disappointing. 2. the condition or feeling of being disappointed. 3. a person or thing that causes this.

dis·ap·pro·ba·tion (dis′ap-rə-bā′shən, dis-ap′rə-bā′shən), *n.* [*dis-* + *approbation*], disapproval; dislike.

dis·ap·prov·al (dis′ə-prōōv′'l), *n.* 1. a disapproving; failing to approve. 2. unfavorable opinion; dislike.

dis·ap·prove (dis′ə-prōōv′), *v.t.* [*dis-* + *approve*], 1. to have or express an unfavorable opinion of; consider (something) wrong; condemn. 2. to refuse to approve; reject. *v.i.* to have or express disapproval (*of*).

dis·ap·prov·ing·ly (dis′ə-prōōv′iŋ-li), *adv.* in a manner that shows disapproval.

dis·arm (dis-ärm′), *v.t.* [ME. *disarmen;* OFr. *desarmer;* see DIS- & ARM, *v.*], 1. to take away weapons from. 2. to deprive of the ability to hurt; make harmless. 3. to overcome the hostility of; make friendly. *v.i.* 1. to lay down arms. 2. to reduce or do away with armed forces and armaments.

dis·ar·ma·ment (dis-är′mə-mənt), *n.* 1. a disarming. 2. the reduction of armed forces and armaments, as to a limitation set by treaty. 3. a disarmed condition.

dis·arm·ing (dis-ärm′iŋ), *adj.* [ppr. of *disarm*], removing suspicions, fears, or hostility.
dis·ar·range (dis′ə-rānj′), *v.t.* [*dis-* + *arrange*], to put out of order or arrangement; unsettle; disorder.
dis·ar·range·ment (dis′ə-rānj′mənt), *n.* a disarranging or being disarranged.
dis·ar·ray (dis′ə-rā′), *v.t.* [OFr. *desareer;* see DIS- & ARRAY], 1. to throw into disorder or confusion; upset. 2. to take the clothes off; undress. *n.* [prob. < OFr. **desarei* (Fr. *désarroi*) < the *v.*], 1. disorder; confusion. 2. disorder or insufficiency of clothing. —*SYN.* see **confusion.**
dis·ar·tic·u·late (dis′är-tik′yoo-lāt′), *v.t.* [*dis-* + *articulate*], to separate or amputate at the joint or joints; disjoint.
dis·ar·tic·u·la·tion (dis′är-tik′yoo-lā′shən), *n.* a disarticulating or being disarticulated.
dis·as·sem·ble (dis′ə-sem′b'l), *v.t.* [*dis-* + *assemble*], to take apart.
dis·as·sem·bly (dis′ə-sem′bli), *n.* a disassembling or being disassembled.
dis·as·so·ci·ate (dis′ə-sō′shi-āt′), *v.t.* to dissociate.
dis·as·ter (di-zas′tẽr, di-zäs′tẽr), *n.* [OFr. *desastre;* It. *disastro* < L. *dis-* + *astrum* < Gr. *astron* (see ASTRAL), a star: from astrological notions; cf. ILL-STARRED], any happening that causes great harm or damage; serious or sudden misfortune; calamity.
SYN.—**disaster** implies great or sudden misfortune that results in loss of life, property, etc. or that is ruinous to an undertaking; **calamity** suggests a grave misfortune that brings deep distress or sorrow to an individual or to the people at large; **catastrophe** is specifically applied to a disastrous end or outcome; **cataclysm** suggests a great upheaval, especially a political or social one, that causes sudden and violent change with attending distress, suffering, etc.
dis·as·trous (di-zas′trəs, di-zäs′trəs), *adj.* [Fr. *désastreux*], of the nature of a disaster; causing great harm, damage, grief, etc.; calamitous.
dis·a·vow (dis′ə-vou′), *v.t.* [ME. *disavouen;* OFr. *desavouer;* see DIS- & AVOW], to deny any knowledge or approval of, or responsibility for; disclaim; disown; repudiate.
dis·a·vow·al (dis′ə-vou′əl), *n.* a disavowing; refusal to acknowledge, approve, etc.; repudiation.
dis·band (dis-band′), *v.t.* [MFr. *desbander;* see DIS- & BAND], 1. to break up (an association or organization). 2. to dismiss from military service. *v.i.* to cease to exist or function as an organization; scatter; disperse.
dis·band·ment (dis-band′mənt), *n.* a disbanding or being disbanded.
dis·bar (dis-bär′), *v.t.* [DISBARRED (-bärd′), DISBARRING], to expel (a lawyer) from the bar; deprive of the right to practice law. —*SYN.* see **exclude.**
dis·bar·ment (dis-bär′mənt), *n.* a disbarring or being disbarred.
dis·be·lief (dis′bi-lēf′), *n.* refusal to believe; absence of belief. —*SYN.* see **unbelief.**
dis·be·lieve (dis′bi-lēv′), *v.t.* to fail to believe; reject as untrue. *v.i.* to fail to believe (*in*).
dis·branch (dis-branch′, dis-bränch′), *v.t.* 1. to break or cut off (a branch). 2. to cut the branches from; prune.
dis·bur·den (dis-bûr′d'n), *v.t.* 1. to relieve of a burden or of anything burdensome. 2. to get rid of (a burden). *v.i.* to rid oneself of a burden.
dis·burs·a·ble (dis-bûr′sə-b'l), *adj.* that can be disbursed; to be disbursed.
dis·burse (dis-bûrs′), *v.t.* [DISBURSED (-bûrst′), DISBURSING], [OFr. *desbourser;* see DIS- & BOURSE], to pay out; expend.
dis·burse·ment (dis-bûrs′mənt), *n.* 1. a disbursing. 2. money disbursed; expenditure.
disc (disk), *n.* a disk.
disc., 1. discount. 2. discovered. 3. discoverer.
dis·calced (dis-kalst′), *adj.* [< L. *discalceatus,* unshod; *dis-,* not + *calceatus,* a sandal, shoe, etc. < pp. of *calceare,* to provide with shoes < *calceus,* a shoe < *calx,* a heel], barefooted: applied especially to members of certain religious orders.
dis·cant (dis′kant *for the n.,* dis-kant′ *for the v.*), *n. & v.i.* descant.
dis·card (dis-kärd′; *for n.,* dis′kärd), *v.t.* [OFr. *descarter;* prob. < *des-* + *carte;* see DIS- & CARD (stiff paper)], 1. in *card games, a*) to throw away (an undesired card or cards). *b*) to play (a card other than a trump and not in the suit led); hence, 2. to throw away, abandon, or get rid of as no longer valuable or useful. *v.i.* in *card games,* to make a discard. *n.* 1. a discarding. 2. the state of being discarded: as, that coat has been in *discard* for some time. 3. something discarded. 4. in *card games,* the card or cards discarded.
dis·cern (di-zũrn′, di-sũrn′), *v.t.* [ME. *discernen;* OFr. *discerner;* L. *discernere; dis-,* apart + *cernere,* to separate], 1. to separate (a thing) mentally from another or others; recognize as separate or different. 2. to perceive or recognize; make out clearly. *v.i.* to perceive or recognize the difference.
SYN.—**discern** implies a making out or recognizing of something visually or mentally (to *discern* one's motives); **perceive** implies recognition by means of any of the senses, and, with reference to mental apprehension, often implies keen understanding or insight (to *perceive* a change in attitude); **distinguish,** in this connection, implies a perceiving clearly or distinctly by sight, hearing, etc. (he *distinguished* the voices of men down the hall); **observe** and **notice** both connote some measure of attentiveness, and usually suggest use of the sense of sight (to *observe* an eclipse, to *notice* the brand of cigarettes a person smokes).
dis·cern·i·ble (di-zũrn′ə-b'l, di-sũrn′ə-b'l), *adj.* [LL. *discernibilis*], that can be discerned; perceptible.
dis·cern·i·bly (di-zũrn′ə-bli, di-sũrn′ə-bli), *adv.* so as to be discernible; noticeably; perceptibly.
dis·cern·ing (di-zũrn′iŋ, di-sũrn′iŋ), *adj.* [ppr. of *discern*], keenly perceptive; shrewd; astute.
dis·cern·ment (di-zũrn′mənt, di-sũrn′mənt), *n.* 1. a discerning. 2. the power of discerning; keen perception or judgment; insight; acumen.
dis·cerp·ti·ble (di-sũrp′tə-b'l), *adj.* [< L. *discerptus,* pp. of *discerpere,* to pluck to pieces (< *dis-,* apart + *carpere,* to pluck); + *-ible*], that can be torn apart or divided; separable; divisible.
dis·charge (dis-chärj′; *also, for n.,* dis′chärj′), *v.t.* [ME. *dischargen;* OFr. *descharger;* LL. **discarricare,* to unload < L. *dis-,* from + *carrus,* wagon, car], 1. to relieve of or release from something: as, *discharged* of suspicion, *discharged* from the army. 2. to relieve of or release from a burden; specifically, *a*) to remove the cargo of (a ship); unload. *b*) to release the charge of (a gun); fire. *c*) to relieve (a servant, jury, etc.) of office; dismiss from service. *d*) to release (a prisoner) from jail, (a defendant) from suspicion, (a patient) as cured, (a bankrupt) from obligations. 3. to release or remove (that with which a person or thing is burdened, etc.); specifically, *a*) to unload (a cargo). *b*) to shoot (a projectile). *c*) to remove (dye) from cloth. 4. to relieve oneself or itself of (a burden, load, etc.); specifically, *a*) to throw off; send forth; emit: as, the sore *discharges* pus. *b*) to get rid of; acquit oneself of; pay (a debt) or perform (a duty). 5. in *architecture,* to relieve (a wall, etc.) of excess pressure by distribution of weight; also, to distribute (weight) evenly over a supporting part. 6. in *electricity,* to remove stored energy from (a battery or condenser). 7. in *law,* to release (a person) from debt, duty, etc. *v.i.* 1. to get rid of a burden, load, etc. 2. to be released or thrown off. 3. to fire; go off: said of a gun, etc. 4. to emit waste matter: said of a wound, etc. *n.* [OFr. *descharge* < the *v.*], 1. a discharging or being discharged (in all senses). 2. that which discharges, as a legal order for release, a certificate of dismissal from military service, etc.; hence, 3. a seaman's record of service. 4. that which is discharged, as pus from a sore. 5. a flow of electricity across a gap, as in a spark. —*SYN.* see **free.**
dis·ci·ple (di-sī′p'l), *n.* [ME. < OFr. *disciple, deciple* or AS. *discipul;* both < L. *discipulus* < **discipere* (contrasted with *praecipere,* to teach; see PRECEPT), to learn, comprehend, treat, decide; orig., prob., to take apart completely < *dis-,* apart (see DIS-) + *-cipere* < *capere,* to hold, take, seize], 1. a pupil, follower, or adherent of any teacher or school of religion, learning, art, etc. 2. an early follower of Jesus, especially one of the twelve apostles. 3. [D-], a member of the Disciples of Christ. —*SYN.* see **follower.**
dis·ci·ple·ship (di-sī′p'l-ship′), *n.* [*disciple* + *-ship*], 1. the position of a disciple. 2. the duration of this.
Disciples of Christ, a Christian denomination which makes the Bible the only basis for faith and practice, holds Communion every Sunday, and baptizes by immersion: organized in 1809 by Alexander Campbell.
dis·ci·plin·a·ble (dis′ə-plin′ə-b'l), *adj.* [LL. *disciplinabilis*], that can or should be disciplined.
dis·ci·pli·nal (dis′ə-plī′n'l, dis′ə-plin-'l), *adj.* of, or having the nature of, discipline.
dis·ci·plin·ant (dis′ə-plin-ənt), *n.* a person who disciplines himself; specifically, [D-], any member of a former Christian sect in Spain who flagellated and otherwise tortured themselves publicly as a means of discipline.
dis·ci·pli·nar·i·an (dis′ə-pli-nâr′i-ən), *adj.* disciplinary. *n.* 1. a person who enforces discipline. 2. a believer in strict discipline.
dis·ci·pli·nar·y (dis′ə-pli-ner′i), *adj.* of or for discipline.
dis·ci·pline (dis′ə-plin), *n.* [ME.; OFr.; L. *disciplina* < *discipulus;* see DISCIPLE], 1. a branch of knowledge or learning. 2. training that develops self-control, character, or orderliness and efficiency. 3. the result of such training; self-control; orderly conduct. 4. acceptance of or submission to authority and control. 5. a system of rules or methods, as for the conduct of members of a monastic order. 6. treatment that corrects or punishes. *v.t.* [DISCIPLINED (-plind), DISCIPLINING], 1. to subject to discipline; train; control. 2. to punish. —*SYN.* see **punish.**
dis·claim (dis-klām′), *v.t.* [Anglo-Fr. & OFr. *desclamer;* see DIS- & CLAIM], 1. to give up or renounce any claim to or connection with; disown. 2. to refuse to acknowledge; deny; repudiate.
dis·claim·er (dis-klām′ẽr), *n.* [Anglo-Fr. *desclamer,* inf.

used as n.], a disclaiming; denial or renunciation, as of a claim, title, etc.
dis·cla·ma·tion (dis'klə-mā'shən), *n.* a disclaiming; renunciation; repudiation.
dis·close (dis-klōz'), *v.t.* [ME. *disclosen* < base of Fr. *desclore;* see DIS- & CLOSE, *v.*], 1. to uncover; bring into the open. 2. to reveal; make known. *n.* [Obs.], disclosure. —*SYN.* see **reveal.**
dis·clos·ure (dis-klō'zhẽr), *n.* 1. a disclosing or being disclosed; revealment. 2. a thing disclosed.
dis·cob·o·lus (dis-kob'ə-ləs), *n.* [L. < Gr. *diskobolos* < *diskos,* discus + *ballein,* to throw], 1. a discus thrower. 2. [D-], a famous Greek statue of a discus thrower, said to have been made by Myron (5th century B.C.).
dis·cog·ra·phy (dis-kog'rə-fi) *n.* [*pl.* DISCOGRAPHIES (-fiz)], [< *disk* (sense 4) + -(*o*)*graphy,* as in *bibliography*]. 1. the systematic study and cataloguing of phonograph records. 2. a list of the recordings of a particular performer, composition, classification, etc.
dis·coid (dis'koid), *adj.* [LL. *discoides;* Gr. *diskoeidēs,* disk-shaped < *diskos,* a disk + *eidos,* form], shaped like a disk. *n.* 1. anything shaped like a disk. 2. a dental instrument with a circular or disklike blade.
dis·coi·dal (dis-koi'd'l), *adj.* discoid.
dis·col·or (dis-kul'ẽr), *v.t. & v.i.* [ME. *descolouren;* OFr. *descolourer;* see DIS- & COLOR], to change in color; stain.
dis·col·or·a·tion (dis-kul'ẽr-ā'shən), *n.* 1. a discoloring or being discolored. 2. a discolored spot or mark.
dis·col·or·ment (dis-kul'ẽr-mənt), *n.* discoloration.
dis·col·our (dis-kul'ẽr), *v.t. & v.i.* to discolor: British spelling.
dis·com·fit (dis-kum'fit), *v.t.* [ME. *discomfiten* < OFr. *desconfit,* pp. of *desconfire;* LL. *disconficere;* L. *dis-* + *conficere;* see CONFECT], 1. originally, to defeat; overthrow; put to flight; hence, 2. to overthrow the plans or expectations of; thwart; frustrate. 3. to make uneasy; confuse; disconcert. —*SYN.* see **embarrass.**
dis·com·fi·ture (dis-kum'fi-chẽr), *n.* 1. a discomfiting or being discomfited. 2. confusion; embarrassment.
dis·com·fort (dis-kum'fẽrt), *n.* [ME.; OFr. *desconfort* < *desconforter,* to discourage; see DIS- & COMFORT], 1. absence of comfort; uneasiness; hardship; distress. 2. anything causing this. *v.t.* to cause discomfort to.
dis·com·fort·a·ble (dis-kum'fẽr-tə-b'l), *adj.* [Rare], causing discomfort; uncomfortable.
dis·com·mend (dis'kə-mend'), *v.t.* 1. *a*) to express disapproval of: opposed to *commend. b*) to speak of dissuasively: opposed to *recommend.* 2. [Obs.], to cause to be viewed or received with disfavor.
dis·com·mode (dis'kə-mōd'), *v.t.* [DISCOMMODED (-id), DISCOMMODING], [< *dis-* + L. *commodare,* to make suitable; see ACCOMMODATE], to inconvenience; disturb.
dis·com·mod·i·ty (dis'kə-mod'ə-ti), *n.* [*pl.* DISCOMMODITIES (-tiz)], 1. inconvenience; disadvantage. 2. in *economics,* anything that lacks utility.
dis·com·mon (dis-kom'ən), *v.t.* 1. at Oxford and Cambridge universities, to prohibit (a tradesman) from dealing with the undergraduates, as for some infraction of the rules. 2. in *law, a*) to deprive of the right of using a common, as for pasturage. *b*) to cause (a common) to become private property.
dis·com·pose (dis'kəm-pōz'), *v.t.* [*dis-* + *compose*], 1. to disturb the calm of; ruffle; agitate; disconcert. 2. to disorder; disarrange. —*SYN.* see **disturb.**
dis·com·po·sure (dis'kəm-pō'zhẽr), *n.* [< *discompose,* after *composure*], lack of composure; discomfiture.
dis·con·cert (dis'kən-sũrt'), *v.t.* [OFr. *desconcerter;* see DIS- & CONCERT], 1. to upset or frustrate (plans, etc.). 2. to upset the composure or self-possession of; embarrass; confuse. —*SYN.* see **embarrass.**
dis·con·form·i·ty (dis'kən-fôrm'ə-ti), *n.* lack of conformity.
dis·con·nect (dis'kə-nekt'), *v.t.* 1. to break or dissolve the connection between; separate; detach. 2. to turn off the current in (an electrical appliance) by breaking the connection with the main circuit.
dis·con·nect·ed (dis'kə-nek'tid), *adj.* [pp. of *disconnect*], 1. separated; detached; unrelated. 2. broken up into unrelated parts; incoherent.
dis·con·nec·tion (dis'kə-nek'shən), *n.* 1. a disconnecting. 2. the condition of being disconnected.
dis·con·so·late (dis-kon'sə-lit), *adj.* [ME. *disconsolat;* ML. *disconsolatus;* L. *dis-* + *consolatus,* pp. of *consolari;* see DIS- & CONSOLE, *v.*], 1. not to be comforted; inconsolable; hopeless; dejected; sad. 2. causing or suggesting discomfort or dejection; cheerless; gloomy.
dis·con·tent (dis'kən-tent'), *adj.* discontented. *n.* lack of contentment; dissatisfaction; restless desire for something more or different. *v.t.* to make discontented.
dis·con·tent·ed (dis'kən-ten'tid), *adj.* not contented.
dis·con·tent·ment (dis'kən-tent'mənt), *n.* discontent.
dis·con·tin·u·ance (dis'kən-tin'ū-əns), *n.* [Anglo-Fr.; see DISCONTINUE & -ANCE], 1. a stopping or being stopped; cessation or interruption. 2. in *law,* the interruption or ending of an action because of the plaintiff's failure to prosecute it properly, or because of a dismissal.
dis·con·tin·u·a·tion (dis'kən-tin'ū-ā'shən), *n.* [Fr.; ML. *discontinuatio*], discontinuance.
dis·con·tin·ue (dis'kən-tin'ū), *v.t.* [Fr. *discontinuer;* ML. *discontinuare;* see DIS- & CONTINUE], 1. to stop; cease; break off; give up. 2. in *law,* to effect a discontinuance of (a suit). *v.i.* to stop; end. —*SYN.* see **stop.**
dis·con·ti·nu·i·ty (dis'kon-tə-nōō'ə-ti, dis'kon-tə-nū'ə-ti), *n.* [< *discontinue,* after *continuity*], 1. lack of continuity; lack of logical sequence. 2. a gap or break.
dis·con·tin·u·ous (dis'kən-tin'ū-əs), *adj.* not continuous; broken up by interruptions or gaps; intermittent.
dis·cord (dis'kôrd), *n.* [ME. *discord, descord;* OFr. *descorde, discorde* < *descorder, discorder;* L. *discordare,* to be at variance, differ, be out of harmony < *discors,* unlike, discordant < *dis-,* apart + *cor, cordis,* heart], 1. lack of concord; disagreement; dissension; incompatibility; conflict. 2. a harsh or confused noise, as the sound of battle; clash; din. 3. in *music,* a lack of harmony in tones simultaneously sounded; inharmonious combination of tones; dissonance. *v.i.* (dis-kôrd'), to disagree; be inharmonious; clash.
SYN.—**discord** denotes disagreement or lack of concord and may imply quarreling between persons, clashing qualities in things, dissonance in sound, etc.; **strife** stresses the struggle to win out where there is a conflict or disagreement; **contention** suggests verbal strife as expressed in argument, controversy, dispute, etc.; **dissension** implies difference of opinion, usually suggesting contention between opposing groups in a body.—*ANT.* harmony, agreement.
dis·cord·ance (dis-kôr'd'ns), *n.* discord; disagreement.
dis·cord·an·cy (dis-kôr'd'n-si), *n.* [*pl.* DISCORDANCIES (-siz)], discordance.
dis·cord·ant (dis-kôr'd'nt), *adj.* [ME. *descordaunt;* OFr. *descordant,* ppr. of *descorder;* see DISCORD], 1. not in accord; disagreeing; dissenting; differing; incongruous. 2. not in harmony; dissonant; clashing; jarring.
dis·count (dis'kount), *n.* [Fr. *descompte* < *desconter,* to count off; OFr. *desconter* < LL. **discomputare;* see DIS- & COMPUTE], 1. a deduction from an original price or debt, allowed for paying promptly or in cash. 2. the interest deducted in advance by one who buys, or lends money on, a bill of exchange, promissory note, etc. 3. the rate of interest charged for discounting a bill, note, etc.: also called *discount rate.* 4. a discounting, as of a bill, note, etc. Abbreviated **disc., disct., dist.** *v.t.* (dis'kount, dis-kount'), [OFr. *desconter;* see the *n.*], 1. to deduct; subtract. 2. to pay or receive the present value of (a bill of exchange, promissory note, etc.), minus a deduction to cover interest for the purchaser. 3. to deduct from; reduce the quantity, cost, or value of; hence, 4. to take (a story, statement, opinion, etc.) at less than face value, allowing for exaggeration, bias, etc. 5. to disbelieve or disregard entirely; set aside as inaccurate or irrelevant. 6. to lessen the effect of by anticipating; reckon with in advance. *v.i.* to lend money with interest deducted in advance.
at a discount, 1. below the regular price; below face value. 2. worth little; unwanted and easily obtained.
dis·coun·te·nance (dis-koun'tə-nəns), *v.t.* [*dis-* + *countenance*], 1. to put to shame; disconcert; abash. 2. to refuse approval or support to; frown on; discourage.
discount house, a retail store that sells its goods at a marked discount below the advertised retail price.
dis·cour·age (dis-kũr'ij), *v.t.* [DISCOURAGED (-ijd), DISCOURAGING], [OFr. *descoragier;* see DIS- & COURAGE], 1. to deprive of courage; make less confident or hopeful; dishearten. 2. to advise or persuade (a person) to refrain. 3. to prevent or try to prevent by disapproving or raising objections or obstacles.
dis·cour·age·ment (dis-kũr'ij-mənt), *n.* [OFr. *descoragement*], 1. a discouraging. 2. the fact, state, or feeling of being discouraged. 3. anything that discourages.
dis·cour·ag·ing (dis-kũr'ij-iŋ), *adj.* that discourages; disheartening; depressing.
dis·course (dis'kôrs, dis'kōrs; *also, and for v. always,* dis-kôrs', dis-kōrs'), *n.* [OFr. *discours;* LL. *discursus,* discourse < L., pp. of *discurrere,* to run to and fro; *dis-,* from, in different directions + *currere,* to run], 1. communication by talking; conversation. 2. communication in general, especially as a subject of study. 3. a long and formal treatment of a subject, in speech or writing; lecture; sermon; treatise; dissertation. 4. [Archaic], ability to reason; rationality. *v.i.* [DISCOURSED (-kôrst', -kōrst'), DISCOURSING], 1. to carry on conversation; talk; confer. 2. to speak or write (*on* or *upon* a subject) formally and at some length. *v.t.* 1. to utter. 2. [Archaic], to tell. —*SYN.* see **speak.**
dis·cour·te·ous (dis-kũr'ti-əs), *adj.* not courteous; impolite; rude; ill-mannered. —*SYN.* see **rude.**
dis·cour·te·sy (dis-kũr'tə-si), *n.* 1. lack of courtesy; impoliteness; bad manners; rudeness. 2. [*pl.* DISCOURTESIES (-siz)], a rude or impolite act or remark.
dis·cov·er (dis-kuv'ẽr), *v.t.* [ME. *discoveren;* OFr. *descovrir;* LL. *discooperire,* to discover, reveal; see DIS- &

COVER], 1. to be the first to find out, see, or know about. 2. to find out; learn of the existence of; realize. 3. [Archaic], *a*) to reveal; disclose; expose. *b*) to uncover. —*SYN.* see **learn.**

dis·cov·ert (dis-kuv'ẽrt), ***adj.*** [ME.; OFr. *descovert*, lit., not covered, hence not protected; see DIS- & COVER], in *law*, having no husband: said of a spinster, widow, or divorcée.

dis·cov·er·y (dis-kuv'ẽr-i), ***n.*** [*pl.* DISCOVERIES (-iz)], [< *discover*, by analogy with *recovery*], 1. a discovering. 2. anything discovered.

Discovery Day, Columbus Day.

Discovery Inlet, an arm of the Ross Sea, Antarctica.

dis·cred·it (dis-kred'it), ***v.t.*** [*dis-* + *credit*], 1. to disbelieve. 2. to show reason for disbelieving or distrusting; cast doubt on. 3. to damage the credit or reputation of; disgrace. ***n.*** 1. absence or loss of belief or trust; disbelief; doubt. 2. damage to one's reputation; loss of respect or status; disgrace; dishonor. 3. something that causes disgrace or loss of status.

dis·cred·it·able (dis-kred'it-ə-b'l), ***adj.*** that discredits; damaging to one's reputation or status; disgraceful.

dis·cred·it·a·bly (dis-kred'it-ə-bli), ***adv.*** 1. in a discreditable manner. 2. to a discreditable extent.

dis·creet (dis-krēt'), ***adj.*** [ME. & OFr. *discret* < L. *descretus*, pp. of *discernere;* see DISCERN], careful about what one says or does; prudent. —*SYN.* see **careful.**

dis·crep·an·cy (dis-krep'ən-si), ***n.*** [OFr. *discrepance;* L. *discrepantia* < *discrepans*, ppr. of *discrepare*, to sound differently; *dis-*, from + *crepare*, to rattle, chatter], 1. disagreement; difference; inconsistency. 2. [*pl.* DISCREPANCIES (-siz)], an instance of this.

dis·crep·ant (dis-krep'ənt), ***adj.*** [OFr.], characterized by discrepancy; differing; inconsistent; at variance.

dis·crete (dis-krēt'), ***adj.*** [L. *discretus;* see DISCREET], 1. separate and distinct; unrelated. 2. made up of distinct parts.

dis·cre·tion (dis-kresh'ən), ***n.*** [ME. & OFr. *discrecion;* L. *discretio*, separation, distinction < *discretus;* see DISCREET], 1. the quality of being discrete; separation or distinction; discontinuity. 2. [Rare], the action or power of discerning; judgment. 3. the freedom or authority to make decisions and choices; power to judge or act. 4. the quality of being discreet; a being careful about what one does and says; prudence.

at one's discretion, in accordance with one's judgment.

dis·cre·tion·al (dis-kresh'ən-'l), ***adj.*** discretionary.

dis·cre·tion·ar·y (dis-kresh'ə-ner'i), ***adj.*** left to one's discretion; regulated by one's own judgment or choice.

dis·crim·i·nate (dis-krim'ə-nāt'), ***v.t.*** [DISCRIMINATED (-id), DISCRIMINATING], [< L. *discriminatus*, pp. of *discriminare*, to divide, distinguish < *discrimen*, division, distinction, interval; *dis-*, apart + *crimen*, verdict, judgment; see CRIME], 1. to constitute a difference between; differentiate. 2. to recognize as being different; tell the difference between; distinguish. ***v.i.*** 1. to see the difference (*between* things); distinguish. 2. to make distinctions in treatment; show partiality (*in favor of*) or prejudice (*against*). ***adj.*** (dis-krim'ə-nit), 1. distinct; distinguished. 2. involving discrimination; distinguishing carefully. —*SYN.* see **distinguish.**

dis·crim·i·nat·ing (dis-krim'ə-nāt'iŋ), ***adj.*** [ppr. of *discriminate*], 1. that discriminates; differentiating. 2. able to make or see fine distinctions; discerning. 3. treating differently; differential, as a tariff.

dis·crim·i·na·tion (dis-krim'ə-nā'shən), ***n.*** [L. *discriminatio*], 1. a discriminating; making or perceiving differences and distinctions. 2. the ability to make or perceive distinctions; perception; discernment. 3. a showing of difference or favoritism in treatment.

dis·crim·i·na·tive (dis-krim'ə-nā'tiv), ***adj.*** discriminating; distinguishing, discerning, or differential.

dis·crim·i·na·tor (dis-krim'ə-nā'tẽr), ***n.*** [LL.], a person who discriminates.

dis·crim·i·na·to·ry (dis-krim'ə-nə-tôr'i, dis-krim'ə-nə-tō'ri), ***adj.*** characterized by discrimination.

dis·crown (dis-kroun'), ***v.t.*** to take the crown away from; dethrone; depose.

dis·cur·sive (dis-kũr'siv), ***adj.*** [ML. *discursivus* < L. *discursus;* see DISCOURSE], 1. wandering from one topic to another; skimming over many apparently unconnected subjects; rambling; desultory; digressive. 2. in *philosophy*, going from premises to conclusions in a series of logical steps: distinguished from *intuitive*.

dis·cus (dis'kəs), ***n.*** [*pl.* DISCUSES (-iz), DISCI (dis'ī)], [L.; Gr. *diskos*, see DISK], 1. a disk of metal or stone, thrown for distance as a test of strength and skill. 2. the throwing of the discus as a contest of strength and skill: often **discus throw.**

DISCUS THROWER

dis·cuss (dis-kus'), ***v.t.*** [ME. *discussen*, to examine, scatter < L. *discussus*, pp. of *discutire*, to strike asunder, shake apart, scatter < *dis-*, apart + *quatere*, to shake, beat], 1. to talk or write about; take up in conversation or in a discourse; consider and argue the pros and cons of. 2. [Colloq.], to eat or drink (something) with enjoyment.

SYN.—**discuss** implies a talking about something in a deliberative fashion, with varying opinions offered constructively and, usually, amicably, so as to settle an issue, decide on a course of action, etc.; **argue** implies the citing of reasons or evidence to support or refute an assertion, belief, proposition, etc.; **debate** implies a formal argument, usually on public questions, in contests between opposing groups; **dispute** implies argument in which there is a clash of opposing opinions, often presented in an angry or heated manner.

dis·cuss·i·ble (dis-kus'ə-b'l), ***adj.*** that can be discussed.

dis·cus·sion (dis-kush'ən), ***n.*** [LL. *discussio*], a discussing; talk or writing in which the pros and cons of a subject are considered.

under discussion, being discussed.

dis·dain (dis-dān'), ***v.t.*** [ME. *disdainen;* OFr. *desdaignier;* LL. **disdignari;* L. *dis-*, not + *dignari*, to deign, deem worthy < *dignus*, worthy; see DIGNITY], to regard as unworthy or beneath one's dignity or status; treat, refuse, or reject with aloof contempt or scorn. ***n.*** the feeling, attitude, or expression of disdaining; aloof contempt or scorn. —*SYN.* see **despise.**

dis·dain·ful (dis-dān'fəl), ***adj.*** feeling or expressing disdain; scornful and aloof. —*SYN.* see **proud.**

dis·ease (di-zēz'), ***n.*** [ME. *disese;* OFr. *desaise;* orig., a euphemism; see DIS- & EASE], 1. any departure from health; illness in general. 2. a particular destructive process in an organism, with a specific cause and characteristic symptoms; specific illness; ailment. 3. an evil or destructive tendency or state of affairs: as, bigotry is a *disease* of society. ***v.t.*** [DISEASED (-zēzd'), DISEASING], [ME. *disesen;* OFr. *desaaisier* < the *n.*], to cause disease in; make ill; infect; derange; corrupt.

SYN.—**disease** may apply generally to any deviation of the body from its normal or healthy state or it may refer to a particular disorder with a specific cause and characteristic symptoms; **affection** refers to a disorder of a specific organ or part (an *affection* of the spleen); **malady** usually refers to a deep-seated chronic disease, frequently one that is ultimately fatal; **ailment** refers to a chronic, annoying disorder of whatever degree of seriousness (the minor *ailments* of the aged).

dis·eased (di-zēzd'), ***adj.*** [pp. of *disease*], 1. showing the symptoms of a disease; having an illness. 2. abnormal; unhealthy; disordered; deranged.

dis·em·bark (dis'im-bärk'), ***v.t.*** [Fr. *désembarquer;* see DIS- & EMBARK], to put (passengers or goods) ashore from a ship; unload. ***v.i.*** to go ashore from a ship; land.

dis·em·bar·ka·tion (dis'em-bär-kā'shən, dis-em'bär-kā'shən), ***n.*** a disembarking or being disembarked.

dis·em·bar·rass (dis'im-bar'əs), ***v.t.*** [*dis-* + *embarrass*], to rid or relieve of something embarrassing, annoying, entangling, perplexing, or burdensome.

dis·em·bod·ied (dis'im-bod'id), ***adj.*** [pp. of *disembody*], freed from the body; incorporeal.

dis·em·bod·i·ment (dis'im-bod'i-mənt), ***n.*** a disembodying or being disembodied.

dis·em·bod·y (dis'im-bod'i), ***v.t.*** [DISEMBODIED (-id), DISEMBODYING], [*dis-* + *embody*], to free (a spirit, etc.) from bodily existence; make incorporeal.

dis·em·bogue (dis'im-bōg'), ***v.t. & v.i.*** [DISEMBOGUED (-bōgd'), DISEMBOGUING], [Sp. *desembocar*, to come out of the mouth of a river or haven; *des-* (L. *dis-*), apart + *embocar*, to enter by the mouth < L. *in*, in + *bucca*, cheek], 1. to pour out (its waters) at the mouth; empty (itself): said of a stream, etc. 2. [Archaic], to sail out of an estuary or harbor.

dis·em·bos·om (dis'im-booz''m, dis'im-bōōz''m), ***v.t. & v.i.*** [*dis-* + *embosom*], to reveal (a secret, etc.); unbosom (oneself).

dis·em·bow·el (dis'im-bou'əl, dis'im-boul'), ***v.t.*** [DISEMBOWELED or DISEMBOWELLED (-əld, -bould'), DISEMBOWELING or DISEMBOWELLING], [*dis-* + *em-* + *bowel*], to take out the bowels of; remove the entrails of; eviscerate.

dis·em·bow·el·ment (dis'im-bou'əl-mənt, dis'im-boul'mənt), ***n.*** a disemboweling or being disemboweled.

dis·en·a·ble (dis'en-ā'b'l), ***v.t.*** [DISENABLED (-b'ld), DISENABLING], to cause to become unable or incapable; prevent or disable.

dis·en·chant (dis'in-chant', dis'in-chänt'), ***v.t.*** [Fr. *désenchanter;* see DIS- & ENCHANT], to set free from an enchantment or illusion.

dis·en·chant·ment (dis'in-chant'mənt, dis'in-chänt'mənt), ***n.*** 1. a disenchanting. 2. the fact or state of being disenchanted.

dis·en·cum·ber (dis'in-kum'bẽr), ***v.t.*** [*dis-* + *encumber*], to relieve of a burden; free from a hindrance or annoyance.

dis·en·fran·chise (dis'in-fran'chīz), ***v.t.*** to disfranchise.

dis·en·gage (dis'in-gāj'), ***v.t.*** [*dis-* + *engage*], to release or loosen from something that binds, holds, complicates, or entangles; unfasten; detach; extricate; disentangle. ***v.i.*** to release oneself; get loose.

dis·en·gaged (dis'in-gājd'), ***adj.*** [pp. of *disengage*], 1. having no engagements; at leisure; at liberty. 2. detached; set loose.

dis·en·gage·ment (dis'in-gāj'mənt), ***n.*** 1. a disengag-

ing or being disengaged. 2. freedom from obligation, occupation, etc.; ease; leisure.
dis·en·gag·ing action (dis'in-gāj'iŋ), a voluntary tactical withdrawal of troops in a critical situation: sometimes a euphemism for *retreat.*
dis·en·tan·gle (dis'in-taŋ'g'l), *v.t.* 1. to free from something that entangles, confuses, etc.; extricate; disengage. 2. to straighten out (anything tangled, confused, etc.); unravel; untangle. *v.i.* to get free from a tangle.
dis·en·tan·gle·ment (dis'in-taŋ'g'l-mənt), *n.* a disentangling or being disentangled.
dis·en·thrall, dis·en·thral (dis'in-thrôl'), *v.t.* [*dis-* + *enthrall*], to free from bondage or slavery; liberate.
dis·en·throne (dis'in-thrōn'), *v.t.* to dethrone; depose.
dis·en·ti·tle (dis'in-tī't'l), *v.t.* to deprive of a right, title, or claim.
dis·en·tomb (dis'in-to͞om'), *v.t.* to take out of a tomb; disinter.
dis·en·twine (dis'in-twīn'), *v.t. & v.i.* to disentangle; untwine; unwind.
di·sep·al·ous (dī-sep''l-əs), *adj.* in *botany,* having two sepals.
dis·es·tab·lish (dis'ə-stab'lish), *v.t.* 1. to deprive of the status of being established. 2. to deprive (a state church) of official connection with the government.
dis·es·tab·lish·ment (dis'ə-stab'lish-mənt), *n.* a disestablishing or being disestablished.
dis·es·teem (dis'ə-stēm'), *v.t.* to hold in low esteem; dislike; despise; slight. *n.* lack of esteem; disfavor.
‡**di·seuse** (dē'zëz'), *n.* [Fr.; lit., feminine speaker < base *dis-* of *dire* (L. *dicere*), to say, speak], a woman entertainer who performs monologues, dramatic impersonations, etc.
dis·fa·vor (dis-fā'vẽr), *n.* 1. an unfavorable opinion; dislike; disapproval. 2. the state of being disliked or disapproved of; disesteem: as, he fell into *disfavor* with his patron. *v.t.* to regard or treat unfavorably; slight.
dis·fea·ture (dis-fē'chẽr), *v.t.* [DISFEATURED (-chẽrd), DISFEATURING], to impair the features of; disfigure.
dis·fig·u·ra·tion (dis'fig-yẽr-ā'shən, dis-fig'yẽr-ā'shən), *n.* disfigurement.
dis·fig·ure (dis-fig'yẽr), *v.t.* [ME. *disfiguren;* OFr. *desfigurer* < L. *dis-* (in sense of "spoiling"; see DIS-) + *figurare,* to fashion, form < *figura,* a figure], to hurt the appearance or attractiveness of; deform; deface; mar.
dis·fig·ure·ment (dis-fig'yẽr-mənt), *n.* 1. a disfiguring. 2. the fact or state of being disfigured. 3. anything that disfigures; blemish; defect; deformity.
dis·for·est (dis-fôr'ist, dis-for'ist), *v.t.* 1. to disafforest. 2. to deforest.
dis·fran·chise (dis-fran'chīz), *v.t.* [*dis-* + *franchise*], 1. to deprive of the rights of citizenship, as of the right to vote or hold office. 2. to deprive of a privilege, right, or power.
dis·fran·chise·ment (dis-fran'chiz-mənt), *n.* a disfranchising or being disfranchised.
dis·frock (dis-frok'), *v.t.* to unfrock.
dis·gorge (dis-gôrj'), *v.t. & v.i.* [OFr. *desgorger;* see DIS- & GORGE], 1. to force (something swallowed) out through the throat; vomit; hence, 2. to give up (something wrongfully obtained). 3. to pour forth (its contents); empty (itself).
dis·grace (dis-grās'), *n.* [Fr. *disgrâce;* It. *disgrazia; dis-* (L. *dis-*), not + *grazia,* favor < L. *gratia;* see GRACE], 1. the state of being in disfavor because of bad conduct, etc.: as, he is in *disgrace.* 2. loss of favor or respect; public dishonor; ignominy; disrepute; shame. 3. a person or thing that brings shame, dishonor, or reproach (*to* one, etc.). *v.t.* [DISGRACED (-grāst'), DISGRACING], [Fr. *disgracier;* It. *disgraziare* < the *n.*] 1. to bring shame or dishonor upon; be a discredit to; be unworthy of: as, his theft *disgraced* his family. 2. to dismiss from a position of favor; punish by degrading; humiliate.
SYN.—**disgrace** refers to a loss of favor or respect and a sense of humiliation brought on by one's own or another's actions (I felt *disgrace* at his expulsion); **dishonor** implies a loss of honor or self-respect brought on by one's own actions; **shame** emphasizes the humiliation felt at a loss of esteem (his guilt brought him no *shame*); **infamy** stresses the notoriety occasioned by a great disgrace; **ignominy** stresses the contemptible nature of that which causes disgrace; **odium** refers to the disgrace or infamy brought on by hateful action; **scandal,** in this connection, stresses the severe criticism, gossip, etc. brought on by a shameful or infamous act.—*ANT.* honor, respect, esteem.
dis·grace·ful (dis-grās'fəl), *adj.* causing or characterized by disgrace; not honorable; shameful.
dis·grun·tle (dis-grun't'l), *v.t.* [DISGRUNTLED (-t'ld), DISGRUNTLING], [*dis-* + obs. *gruntle,* freq. of *grunt*], to make peevishly discontented or disappointed; displease and make sulky.
dis·guise (dis-gīz'), *v.t.* [DISGUISED (-gīzd'), DISGUISING], [ME. *disguisen;* OFr. *desguiser,* to change costume; see DIS- & GUISE], 1. to make appear, sound, etc. different from usual so as to be unrecognizable: as, *disguise* your voice. 2. to hide or obscure the real nature of: as, she *disguised* her hatred. *n.* 1. any clothes, equipment, manner, etc. used for disguising. 2. the state of being disguised. 3. the act or practice of disguising.
dis·guis·ed·ly (dis-gīz'id-li), *adv.* 1. in a manner that disguises. 2. in disguise; incognito.
dis·gust (dis-gust'), *n.* [MFr. *desgoust,* distaste < *des-* (see DIS-) + L. *gustus,* a taste, relish; see GUSTO], a sickening distaste or dislike; deep aversion; repugnance. *v.t.* [MFr. *desgouster* < *des-* (see DIS-) + L. *gustare,* to taste, enjoy < *gustus*], to cause to feel disgust; be sickening, repulsive, or very disagreeable to.
dis·gust·ful (dis-gust'fəl), *adj.* disgusting.
dis·gust·ing (dis-gus'tiŋ), *adj.* [ppr. of *disgust*], sickening; repulsive; very disagreeable.
dish (dish), *n.* [ME. *dissh, disch;* AS. *disc,* a dish, plate < L. *discus;* see DISK], 1. any container, generally shallow and concave, for serving or holding food: dishes are usually made of porcelain, earthenware, glass, metal, or plastic, and comprise plates, bowls, saucers, cups, etc. 2. the food in a dish; particular kind of food: as, my favorite *dish* is baked beans. 3. a dishful. 4. a dish-shaped object. 5. a dishlike concavity. 6. the amount of such concavity. *v.t.* 1. to serve (food) in a dish (usually with *up* or *out*). 2. to shape (an object, surface, or hole) like a dish; make concave (usually with *out*). 3. [Slang, chiefly British], to baffle; cheat; frustrate. *v.i.* to be or become dish-shaped; cave in.
dish it out, [Slang], to administer punishment, reprimands, etc.
dis·ha·bille (dis'ə-bēl'), *n.* [Fr. *déshabillé;* pp. of *déshabiller,* to undress; *dés-* (see DIS-) + *habiller,* to clothe, dress; OFr., to clothe, orig., to make ready, fit < *abille, habile,* fit, suitable < L. *habilis* (see ABLE); meaning influenced by Fr. *habit,* dress], 1. the state of being dressed only partially or in night clothes. 2. clothing or garment worn in this state. Also **deshabille.**
dis·har·mo·ni·ous (dis'här-mō'ni-əs), *adj.* not harmonious; discordant.
dis·har·mo·nize (dis-här'mə-nīz'), *v.t. & v.i.* to put or be out of harmony; make or be discordant.
dis·har·mo·ny (dis-här'mə-ni), *n.* absence of harmony; discord.
dish·cloth (dish'klôth', dish'kloth'), *n.* a cloth for washing dishes; dishrag.
dis·heart·en (dis-här't'n), *v.t.* [*dis-* + *hearten*], to deprive of courage or enthusiasm; discourage; depress.
dis·heart·en·ment (dis-här't'n-mənt), *n.* a disheartening or being disheartened.
dished (disht), *adj.* [pp. of *dish*], 1. dish-shaped; concave. 2. farther apart at the top than at the bottom: said of parallel wheels.
dis·helm (dis-helm'), *v.t. & v.i.* [*dis-* + *helm* (helmet), after OFr. *desheaulmer*], to take the helmet off.
dis·her·i·son (dis-her'ə-z'n), *n.* [OFr. *desheriteisun* < L. *dis-,* not + *hereditas;* see HEREDITY], [Archaic], a disinheriting or being disinherited.
dis·her·it (dis-her'it), *v.t.* [OFr. *desheriter*], to disinherit.
di·shev·el (di-shev''l), *v.t.* [DISHEVELED or DISHEVELLED (-əld), DISHEVELING or DISHEVELLING], [ME. *dischevelen;* OFr. *descheveler; des-* (L. *dis-*), apart + *cheveler,* to tousle, tear out (hair) < *chevel,* hair < L. *capillus,* hair], 1. to cause (hair, clothing, etc.) to become disarranged and untidy, as by pulling or loosening, etc.; tousle; rumple. 2. to cause the hair or clothes of (a person) to become thus disarranged.
di·shev·eled, di·shev·elled (di-shev''ld), *adj.* [pp. of *dishevel*], 1. disarranged and untidy; tousled; rumpled: said of hair or clothing. 2. having disheveled hair or clothing.
di·shev·el·ment (di-shev''l-mənt), *n.* a disheveled condition.
dish·ful (dish'fool'), *n.* as much as a dish holds.
dis·hon·est (dis-on'ist), *adj.* [ME. *dishoneste;* OFr. *deshoneste;* LL. *dishonestus (see DIS-), for L. *dehonestus;* see DE- & HONEST], not honest; lying, cheating, etc.
SYN.—**dishonest** implies the act or practice of telling a lie, or of cheating, deceiving, stealing, etc. (a *dishonest* official); **deceitful** implies an intent to make someone believe what is not true, as by giving a false appearance, using fraud, etc. (a *deceitful* advertisement); **lying** suggests only the act of telling a falsehood (curb your *lying* tongue); **untruthful** is used as a somewhat softened substitute for **lying,** especially with reference to statements, reports, etc. (an *untruthful* account). —*ANT.* honest.
dis·hon·es·ty (dis-on'is-ti), *n.* [ME. *dishonestee* < OFr.], 1. the quality of being dishonest; dishonest behavior; deceiving, stealing, etc. 2. [*pl.* DISHONESTIES (-tiz)], a dishonest act or statement; fraud, lie, etc.
dis·hon·or (dis-on'ẽr), *n.* [ME. *deshonour;* OFr. *deshonor;* see DIS- & HONOR], 1. loss of honor; loss of status, respect, or reputation; shame; disgrace; ignominy. 2. a person, thing, or action that brings dishonor; discredit; insult. 3. the act of refusing or failing to pay a check, draft, bill of exchange, etc. *v.t.* 1. to treat disrespect-

fully; insult. 2. to bring shame or discredit upon; disgrace. 3. to violate the virginity or chastity of. 4. to refuse or fail to pay (a check, draft, bill of exchange, etc.). —*SYN.* see **disgrace.**

dis·hon·or·a·ble (dis-on′ẽr-ə-b'l), *adj.* causing or deserving dishonor; not honorable; shameful; disgraceful.

dis·hon·or·a·bly (dis-on′ẽr-ə-bli), *adv.* 1. in a dishonorable manner. 2. with dishonor: as, *dishonorably* discharged.

dish·pan (dish′pan′), *n.* a pan in which dishes and cooking utensils are washed.

dish·rag (dish′rag′), *n.* a dishcloth.

dish·wash·er (dish′wôsh′ẽr, dish′wosh′ẽr), *n.* a person or machine that washes dishes and cooking utensils.

dish·wa·ter (dish′wô′tẽr, dish′wot′ẽr), *n.* water in which dishes and cooking utensils are, or have been, washed.

dis·il·lu·sion (dis′i-lōō′zhən, dis′i-lū′zhən), *v.t.* to free from illusion; disenchant. *n.* disillusionment.

dis·il·lu·sion·ment (dis′i-lōō′zhən-mənt, dis′i-lū′zhən-mənt), *n.* 1. a disillusioning. 2. the fact or state of being disillusioned.

dis·im·pris·on (dis′im-priz″n), *v.t.* to free from imprisonment.

dis·in·cli·na·tion (dis′in-klə-nā′shən, dis-in′klə-nā′shən), *n.* [*dis-* + *inclination*], a dislike or lack of desire (*for*); aversion (*to*); reluctance.

dis·in·cline (dis′in-klīn′), *v.t.* [see DIS- & INCLINE], to make unwilling. *v.i.* to be unwilling.

dis·in·clined (dis′in-klīnd′), *adj.* [pp. of *disincline*], unwilling; reluctant. —*SYN.* see **reluctant.**

dis·in·fect (dis′in-fekt′, dis″n-fekt′), *v.t.* [Fr. *désinfecter;* see DIS- & INFECT], to destroy or make inactive the harmful bacteria, viruses, etc. in; sterilize.

dis·in·fect·ant (dis′in-fek′tənt, dis″n-fek′tənt), *adj.* [Fr. *désinfectant*], disinfecting. *n.* anything that disinfects; means for destroying harmful bacteria, viruses, etc., or for making them inactive.

dis·in·fec·tion (dis′in-fek′shən, dis″n-fek′shən), *n.* a disinfecting or being disinfected.

dis·in·fec·tor (dis′in-fek′tẽr, dis″n-fek′tẽr), *n.* a person or thing that disinfects.

dis·in·gen·u·ous (dis′in-jen′ū-əs, dis″n-jen′ū-əs), *adj.* [*dis-* + *ingenuous*], not straightforward; not candid; insincere.

dis·in·her·it (dis′in-her′it, dis″n-her′it), *v.t.* [*dis-* + *inherit* (in obs. sense "to make heir")], to deprive of an inheritance or the right to inherit.

dis·in·her·i·tance (dis′in-her′ə-təns, dis″n-her′ə-təns), *n.* 1. a disinheriting. 2. the state of being disinherited.

dis·in·te·grate (dis-in′tə-grāt′), *v.t. & v.i.* [see DIS- & INTEGRATE], to separate into parts or fragments; lose or cause to lose wholeness; disunite. —*SYN.* see **decay.**

dis·in·te·gra·tion (dis-in′tə-grā′shən), *n.* 1. a disintegrating or being disintegrated. 2. the breaking up of rocks subjected to the action of water, wind, frost, etc.

dis·in·te·gra·tor (dis-in′tə-grā′tẽr), *n.* a person or thing that causes something to disintegrate.

dis·in·ter (dis′in-tũr′), *v.t.* [DISINTERRED (-tũrd′), DISINTERRING], [Fr. *désenterrer;* see DIS- & INTER], 1. to remove from a grave, tomb, etc.; dig up (what is buried); exhume. 2. to bring (something hidden) to light.

dis·in·ter·est·ed (dis-in′tẽr-is-tid, dis-in′tris-tid), *adj.* 1. not influenced by personal interest or selfish motives; impartial; unbiased. 2. [Colloq.], uninterested; indifferent. —*SYN.* see **indifferent.**

dis·in·ter·ment (dis′in-tũr′mənt), *n.* 1. a disinterring or being disinterred. 2. anything disinterred.

dis·ject (dis-jekt′), *v.t.* [< L. *disjectum,* pp. of *disjicere,* to throw apart < *dis-,* apart + *jacere,* to throw], to throw or break apart; disperse.

‡dis·jec·ta mem·bra (dis-jek′tə mem′brə), [L.], scattered parts or fragments.

dis·join (dis-join′), *v.t.* [OFr. *desjoindre;* L. *disjungere;* see DIS- & JOIN], to prevent the joining of; separate; detach. *v.i.* to become separated.

dis·joint (dis-joint′), *adj.* [ME.; OFr. *desjoint,* pp. of *desjoindre;* see DISJOIN], [Obs.], disjointed. *v.t.* [< the *adj.*], 1. to put out of joint; dislocate. 2. to take apart joint by joint; dismember. 3. to destroy the unity, connections, or orderliness of. *v.i.* to come apart at the joints; go out of joint.

dis·joint·ed (dis-join′tid), *adj.* [pp. of *disjoint*], 1. out of joint. 2. dismembered. 3. disconnected; without unity or coherence.

dis·junct (dis-juŋkt′), *adj.* [L. *disjunctus,* pp. of *disjungere;* see DISJOIN], disjoined; separated.

dis·junc·tion (dis-juŋk′shən), *n.* [< OFr. or L.; OFr. *disjunction;* L. *disjunctio* < pp. of *disjungere;* see DISJOIN], 1. a disjoining or being disjoined; separation. 2. in *logic,* the relation between two or more alternatives of a disjunctive proposition.

dis·junc·tive (dis-juŋk′tiv), *adj.* [LL. *disjunctivus* < L. *disjunctus;* see DISJUNCT], 1. disjoining; separating or causing to separate. 2. having to do with disjunction. 3. in *grammar,* indicating a contrast or an alternative between ideas, clauses, etc.: as, *either . . . or, but,* and *although* are *disjunctive* conjunctions. 4. in *logic,* presenting alternatives: as, a *disjunctive* proposition. *n.* 1. in *grammar,* a disjunctive conjunction. 2. in *logic,* a disjunctive proposition. Example: Either all men are free, or no man is free.

dis·junc·ture (dis-juŋk′chẽr), *n.* [ML. *disjunctura*], disjunction.

disk (disk), *n.* [L. *discus;* Gr. *diskos,* quoit, discus, dish, disk], 1. a thin, flat, circular thing of any material. 2. anything resembling this in shape: as, the moon's *disk.* 3. the disk-shaped center of certain composite flowers: as, the *disk* of the sunflower. 4. a phonograph record. 5. in *zoology,* a disk-shaped part or structure. 6. [Obs.], a discus. Also spelled **disc,** especially in sense 5.

disk flower, any of the little flowers that make up the central disk of a composite flower; floret.

disk harrow, a harrow with sharp disks that can revolve, used to break up the soil for sowing.

disk jockey, a person who conducts a radio program of recorded music, interspersed with chatter, jokes, commercials, etc.

disk wheel, a wheel made solid from rim to hub instead of with spokes.

dis·like (dis-līk′), *v.t.* to have a feeling of not liking; feel aversion to; have objections to. *n.* a feeling of not liking; distaste; aversion; antipathy.

dis·limn (dis-lim′), *v.t.* [Obs. or Poetic], to obliterate or efface the outlines of (a picture, etc.); blot out.

dis·lo·cate (dis′lō-kāt′, dis-lō′kāt), *v.t.* [< ML. *dislocatus,* pp. of *dislocare;* see DIS- & LOCATE], 1. to put out of joint; disjoint. 2. to upset the order of; disarrange.

dis·lo·ca·tion (dis′lō-kā′shən), *n.* [OFr.], 1. a dislocating. 2. the condition of being dislocated.

dis·lodge (dis-loj′), *v.t.* [DISLODGED (-lojd′), DISLODGING], [OFr. *desloger;* see DIS- & LODGE], to remove from a position or place of lodgment; force out; drive out. *v.i.* to go from such a place or position.

dis·lodg·ment (dis-loj′mənt), *n.* a dislodging or being dislodged.

dis·loy·al (dis-loi′əl), *adj.* [OFr. *disloial*], not loyal or faithful, as to one's country, duty, etc.; perfidious. —*SYN.* see **faithless.**

dis·loy·al·ty (dis-loi′əl-ti), *n.* 1. the quality of being disloyal. 2. [*pl.* DISLOYALTIES (-tiz)], a disloyal act.

dis·mal (diz′m'l), *adj.* [< ME. *dysmal,* pl. *dismale,* evil days (of the medieval calendar) < OFr. *dis mal* < L. *dies mali,* evil days], 1. causing gloom or misery; depressing. 2. dark and gloomy; bleak; dreary. 3. depressed; miserable.

Dismal Swamp, a marshy region north of Albemarle Sound, North Carolina: length, c. 30 mi.

dis·man·tle (dis-man′t'l), *v.t.* [DISMANTLED (-t'ld), DISMANTLING], [OFr. *desmanteller,* to take off one's cloak; see DIS- & MANTLE], 1. to strip of covering. 2. to strip (a house, ship, etc.) of furniture, equipment, means of defense, etc. 3. to take apart; raze; make unusable for its original purpose. —*SYN.* see **strip.**

dis·mast (dis-mast′, dis-mäst′), *v.t.* to remove or destroy the mast or masts of.

dis·may (dis-mā′), *v.t.* [ME. *dismayen;* Anglo-Fr. **desmaier;* prob. < *des-* + OFr. **smaier,* to deprive of power; ? < L. *ex-,* from + Gmc. base *mag,* power; see MAIN], to make afraid or discouraged at the prospect of trouble or danger; fill with apprehension or alarm; daunt. *n.* a loss of courage or confidence at the prospect of trouble or danger; consternation.

SYN.—**dismay** suggests fear or, especially in modern usage, discouragement at the prospect of some difficulty or problem which one does not quite know how to resolve (I was *dismayed* at his lack of understanding); **appall** suggests terror or (now more commonly) dismay at a shocking but apparently unalterable situation (an *appalling* death rate); **horrify** suggests horror or loathing (or, in a weakened sense, irritation) at that which shocks or offends one (*horrified* at the suggestion); **daunt** implies a becoming disheartened in the performance of an act that requires some courage (never *daunted* by adversity). See also **fear.**

dis·mem·ber (dis-mem′bẽr), *v.t.* [ME. *dismembren;* OFr. *desmembrer;* see DIS- & MEMBER], 1. to remove the limbs of by cutting or tearing; tear limb from limb. 2. to cut or pull to pieces; separate into parts.

dis·mem·ber·ment (dis-mem′bẽr-mənt), *n.* a dismembering or being dismembered.

dis·miss (dis-mis′), *v.t.* [< LL. *dismissus,* for L. *dimissus,* pp. of *dimittere,* to send away; *di-,* from + *mittere,* to send], 1. to send away; request or allow to go away. 2. to remove or discharge from a duty, office, position, or employment. 3. to put out of one's mind: as, he *dismissed* his fears. 4. in *law,* to discontinue or reject (a claim or action). —*SYN.* see **eject.**

dis·miss·al (dis-mis′'l), *n.* 1. a dismissing or being dismissed. 2. an order for the dismissing of someone.

dis·miss·i·ble (dis-mis′ə-b'l), *adj.* that can be dismissed.

dis·mis·sion (dis-mish′ən), *n.* [Rare], dismissal.

dis·mount (dis-mount′), *v.i.* [*dis-* + *mount*], to get off or down, as from a horse, bicycle, etc.; alight. *v.t.* 1. to remove (a thing) from its mounting or setting. 2. to cause to get off or down. 3. to take (a machine) apart.

dis·na·ture (dis-nā′chẽr), *v.t.* [DISNATURED (-chẽrd), DISNATURING], to cause to lose its natural quality, appearance, etc.; make unnatural.

Dis·ney, Walt (wôlt diz′ni), (*Walter E. Disney*), 1901– ;

American motion-picture producer, especially of animated cartoons.

dis·o·be·di·ence (dis'ə-bē'di-əns), *n.* [ME.; OFr.; see DIS- & OBEDIENCE], refusal to obey; failure to follow commands; insubordination.

dis·o·be·di·ent (dis'ə-bē'di-ənt), *adj.* not obedient; refusing or failing to obey; insubordinate; refractory.

dis·o·bey (dis'ə-bā'), *v.t. & v.i.* [ME. *disobeien;* OFr. *desobeir;* LL. **disobedire* (for L. *inoboedire*)], to refuse to obey; fail to obey.

dis·o·blige (dis'ə-blīj'), *v.t.* [Fr. *désobliger*], 1. to refuse to oblige; not do for (another) what he wants done. 2. to slight; offend. 3. to inconvenience.

dis·or·der (dis-ôr'dẽr), *n.* [prob. after Fr. *désordre*], 1. a lack of order; confusion; jumble. 2. a breach of public peace; riot. 3. a disregard of system; irregularity. 4. an upset of normal function; disease. *v.t.* 1. to throw into disorder; disarrange; muddle. 2. to upset the normal functions or health of. —*SYN.* see **confusion.**

dis·or·dered (dis-ôr'dẽrd), *adj.* [pp. of *disorder*], 1. put out of order; jumbled. 2. ill; deranged: as, a *disordered* stomach, a *disordered* mind.

dis·or·der·ly (dis-ôr'dẽr-li), *adj.* 1. not orderly; untidy; messy; unsystematic. 2. causing a disturbance; unruly; riotous. 3. in *law,* violating public peace, safety, or order. *adv.* in a disorderly manner.

disorderly conduct, in *law,* any petty offense against public peace, safety, or order.

disorderly house, in *law,* any establishment where offenses against public peace, safety, or order habitually occur, as a house of prostitution or a gambling house.

dis·or·gan·i·za·tion (dis-ôr'gə-ni-zā'shən, dis'ôr-gə-nī-zā'shən), *n.* 1. a disorganizing. 2. the condition of being disorganized.

dis·or·gan·ize (dis-ôr'gə-nīz'), *v.t.* [Fr. *désorganiser;* see DIS- & ORGANIZE], to break up the order, arrangement, or system of; throw into confusion or disorder.

dis·o·ri·ent (dis-ôr'i-ent', dis-ō'ri-ent'), *v.t.* [Fr. *désorienter;* see DIS- & ORIENT, *v.*], 1. to turn away from the east; hence, 2. to cause to lose one's bearings; confuse.

dis·o·ri·en·tate (dis-ôr'i-en-tāt', dis-ō'ri-en-tāt'), *v.t.* to disorient.

dis·o·ri·en·ta·tion (dis-ôr'i-en-tā'shən, dis-ō'ri-en-tā'shən), *n.* a loss of orientation; specifically, in *psychiatry,* a condition of mental confusion with respect to time, place, and the identity of persons and objects.

dis·own (dis-ōn'), *v.t.* to refuse to acknowledge as one's own; repudiate; cast off.

dis·par·age (dis-par'ij), *v.t.* [DISPARAGED (-ijd), DISPARAGING], [ME. *disparagen;* OFr. *desparagier,* to marry one of inferior rank < *des-* (see DIS-) + *parage,* rank < *per;* see PEER, *n.*], 1. to lower in esteem; discredit. 2. to speak slightingly of; show disrespect for; belittle.

SYN.—to **disparage** is to attempt to lower in esteem, as by insinuation, invidious comparison, faint praise, etc.; to **depreciate** is to lessen (something) in value as by implying that it has less worth than is usually attributed to it (he *depreciated* her generosity); **decry** implies vigorous public denunciation, often from the best of motives (to *decry* corruption in government); **belittle** is equivalent to **depreciate,** but stresses a contemptuous attitude in the subject; **minimize** suggests an ascription of the least possible value or importance (don't *minimize* your own efforts).—*ANT.* extol, praise, magnify.

dis·par·age·ment (dis-par'ij-mənt), *n.* 1. a disparaging; detraction. 2. anything that detracts or discredits.

dis·par·ag·ing (dis-par'ij-iŋ), *adj.* that disparages; slighting; belittling.

dis·pa·rate (dis'pə-rit), *adj.* [L. *disparatus,* pp. of *disparare,* to separate; *dis-* apart, not + *parare,* to make equal < *par,* equal], essentially not alike; distinct or different in kind; unequal. —*SYN.* see **different.**

dis·par·i·ty (dis-par'ə-ti), *n.* [*pl.* DISPARITIES (-tiz)], [Fr. *disparité;* LL. *disparitas;* see DIS- & PARITY], 1. inequality or difference, as in rank, amount, degree, excellence, etc. 2. unlikeness; incongruity.

dis·part (dis-pärt'), *v.t. & v.i.* [prob. < OFr. *despartir;* L. *dispartire,* to divide, distribute; *dis-,* apart, from + *partire,* to part, divide < *pars, partis,* a part], to divide into parts; separate. *n.* 1. the difference in radius of the bore between the muzzle end and the breech end of a firearm. 2. a sight on the muzzle of a firearm to compensate for this.

dis·pas·sion (dis-pash'ən), *n.* freedom from passion, from emotion, or from bias.

dis·pas·sion·ate (dis-pash'ən-it), *adj.* free from passion, emotion, or bias; calm; impartial. —*SYN.* see **fair.**

dis·patch (dis-pach'), *v.t.* [Sp. *despachar* & It. *dispacciare,* to send off, hasten; lit., prob., to remove hindrances or impediments, hence facilitate; formed with *dis-* (see DIS-) as counterpart to Sp. *empachar* & It. *impacciare,* to trouble, pain, impede < LL. **impedicare,* to halt, hinder < *in-,* intens. + **pedicare,* to snare < L. *pedica,* a snare, trap, fetter < *pes, pedis,* a foot], 1. to send off or out, usually on a specific errand or official business. 2. to put an end to; kill. 3. to finish quickly or promptly. 4. [Colloq.], to eat up. *n.* 1. a dispatching; sending out or off. 2. a putting to death; killing. 3. speed; haste; promptness. 4. a message, especially an official message. 5. a news story sent to a paper, as by a syndicate or special reporter. 6. a dispatching agency. —*SYN.* see **haste, kill.**

dis·patch·er (dis-pach'ẽr), *n.* 1. a person who dispatches. 2. a transportation worker who sends out trains, busses, trucks, etc. according to a schedule.

dis·pel (dis-pel'), *v.t.* [DISPELLED (-peld'), DISPELLING], [L. *dispellere; dis-,* apart, away + *pellere,* to drive], to scatter and drive away; cause to vanish; disperse. —*SYN.* see **scatter.**

dis·pend (dis-pend'), *v.t.* [ME. *despenden;* OFr. *despendre* (Fr. *dependre*); LL. *dispendere,* to weigh out; see DISPENSE], [Obs.], to spend; especially, to spend lavishly; squander.

dis·pen·sa·bil·i·ty (dis-pen'sə-bil'ə-ti), *n.* the quality of being dispensable.

dis·pen·sa·ble (dis-pen'sə-b'l), *adj.* [ML. *dispensabilis*], 1. that can be dispensed; that can be dealt out or administered. 2. that can be dispensed with; not important. 3. admitting of dispensation, as a sin, etc.; condonable. 4. that can be considered not binding.

dis·pen·sa·ry (dis-pen'sə-ri), *n.* [*pl.* DISPENSARIES (-riz)], [*dispense* + *-ary*], 1. a room in a hospital, physician's office, school, factory, etc. where medicines are made up and given out. 2. a place where medicines and medical treatment are given free or for a small fee.

dis·pen·sa·tion (dis'pən-sā'shən, dis'pen-sā'shən), *n.* [ME. *dispensacioun;* OFr. *despensation;* L. *dispensatio,* management, charge < pp. of *dispensare*], 1. a dispensing; giving out; distribution. 2. anything dispensed or distributed. 3. the system by which anything is administered; management. 4. any release from an obligation; special exemption or remission. 5. in *law,* the suspension of a statute in a specific case for extenuating reasons. 6. in the *Roman Catholic Church,* an official exemption or release from the provisions of a specific church law: as, a papal *dispensation* for divorce. 7. in *theology, a*) the ordering of events under divine authority. *b*) any religious system: as, the Moslem *dispensation* differs from the Christian.

dis·pen·sa·tor (dis'pen-sā'tẽr), *n.* [Anglo-Fr. *dispensatour;* OFr. *dispensateur;* L. *dispensator,* manager, steward < pp. of *dispensare*], [Rare], a person who dispenses; distributor or administrator.

dis·pen·sa·to·ry (dis-pen'sə-tôr'i, dis-pen'sə-tō'ri), *n.* [*pl.* DISPENSATORIES (-iz, -riz)], [ML. *dispensatorium* < LL. *dispensatorius,* of management or control < L. *dispensare;* see DISPENSE], 1. a handbook on the preparation and use of medicines; pharmacopoeia: abbreviated **disp.** 2. [Archaic], a dispensary. *adj.* [L. *dispensatorius*], granting privilege by dispensation.

dis·pense (dis-pens'), *v.t.* [DISPENSED (-penst'), DISPENSING], [ME. *dispensen;* OFr. *despenser;* L. *dispensare,* to weigh out, pay out < pp. of *dispendere,* to weigh out; *dis-,* out + *pendere,* to weigh], 1. to give out; deal out; distribute. 2. to prepare and give out (medicines, prescriptions, etc.). 3. to administer: as, he *dispensed* the law justly. 4. to exempt; excuse. —*SYN.* see **distribute.**

dispense with, 1. to get rid of; do away with. 2. to do without; manage without.

dis·peo·ple (dis-pē'p'l), *v.t.* to strip of all or many inhabitants; depopulate.

di·sper·mous (dī-spũr'məs), *adj.* [*di-* + *spermous*], in *botany,* having two seeds.

dis·per·sal (dis-pũr's'l), *n.* a dispersing or being dispersed; distribution.

dis·perse (dis-pũrs'), *v.t.* [DISPERSED (-pũrst'), DISPERSING], [Fr. *disperser* < L. *dispersus,* pp. of *dispergere,* to scatter abroad < *dis-,* out + *spargere,* to scatter, strew], 1. to break up and scatter in all directions; spread about or out; distribute widely. 2. to dispel (mist, etc.). 3. to break up (light) into its component colored rays. *v.i.* to move in different directions; scatter. —*SYN.* see **scatter.**

dis·pers·i·ble (dis-pũr'sə-b'l), *adj.* that can be dispersed.

dis·per·sion (dis-pũr'shən, dis-pũr'zhən), *n.* [Fr.; L. *dispersio*], 1. a dispersing or being dispersed. 2. the breaking up of light into its component colored rays, as by means of a prism. 3. the similar breaking up of electric waves, etc.

the Dispersion, the Diaspora.

dis·per·sive (dis-pũr'siv), *adj.* dispersing or tending to disperse.

dis·pir·it (di-spir'it), *v.t.* to lower the spirits of; depress; dishearten; deject.

dis·pit·e·ous (dis-pit'i-əs), *adj.* [var. of *despiteous*], without pity or mercy; ruthless.

dis·place (dis-plās'), *v.t.* [OFr. *desplacer*], 1. to move or shift (something) from its customary place. 2. to remove from office; discharge. 3. to take the place of; replace: as, a ship *displaces* a certain amount of water. —*SYN.* see **replace.**

dis·placed person (dis-plāst′), a person left homeless in a foreign country as a result of war: abbreviated **D. P.**
dis·place·ment (dis-plās′mənt), *n.* 1. a displacing or being displaced. 2. the weight or volume of air, water, or other fluid displaced by a floating object, as a balloon or a ship. 3. the difference between a later position of a thing and its original position; hence, 4. in *geology*, a fault. 5. in *psychiatry*, the transference of an emotion to a logically inappropriate object.
dis·plant (dis-plant′, dis-plänt′), *v.t.* [Obs.], to move from the normal or settled place; specifically, *a*) to transplant. *b*) to dislodge or displace.
dis·play (dis-plā′), *v.t.* [ME. *displeien;* OFr. *despleier;* L. *displicare*, to scatter, unfold; *dis-*, apart + *plicare*, to fold], 1. to unfold; spread out; unfurl. 2. to unfold to the eye; show off; exhibit to advantage. 3. to unfold to the mind; disclose; reveal. 4. to print conspicuously, as in large or fancy type. *n.* 1. a displaying; exhibition. 2. anything displayed; exhibit. 3. ostentation; show. 4. a manifestation: as, a *display* of courage. 5. in *printing*, the variation of type faces to attract attention. —*SYN.* see **show.**
dis·please (dis-plēz′), *v.t. & v.i.* [ME. *displesen;* OFr. *desplaisir;* LL. **displacere* < L. *displicere* < *dis-*, not + *placere;* see PLEASE], to fail to please; annoy; offend.
dis·pleas·ure (dis-plezh′ẽr), *n.* [OFr. *desplaisir*, inf. used as n.; see DISPLEASE], 1. the fact or feeling of being displeased; dissatisfaction; disapproval; annoyance. 2. [Archaic], discomfort; trouble. 3. [Archaic], an injury; offense. —*SYN.* see **offense.**
dis·plode (dis-plōd′), *v.t. & v.i.* [DISPLODED (-id), DISPLODING], [L. *displodere* < *dis-*, apart + *plaudere*, to strike, beat; cf. EXPLODE], [Obs.], to explode.
dis·plume (dis-plōōm′), *v.t.* [Rare], to deplume.
dis·port (dis-pôrt′, dis-pōrt′), *v.i.* [ME. *disporten*, to bear, support, manage; OFr. *desporter; des-* (see DIS-) + *porter* < L. *portare*, to carry], to indulge in amusement; play; frolic. *v.t.* to amuse or divert (oneself). *n.* [Archaic], a disporting; amusement; play.
dis·pos·a·ble (dis-pō′zə-b'l), *adj.* 1. that can be disposed of; easy to get rid of. 2. that can be disposed; not put to any particular use; subject to disposal.
dis·pos·al (dis-pō′z'l), *n.* 1. a disposing; arrangement in a particular order: as, the *disposal* of the furniture in this room suits me. 2. a dealing with matters; settling affairs. 3. a giving away; transfer; bestowal. 4. a disposing of; getting rid of. 5. the power to dispose of. 6. management; control.
at one's disposal, available to be used as one wishes.
dis·pose (dis-pōz′), *v.t.* [DISPOSED (-pōzd′), DISPOSING], [ME. *disposen;* OFr. *disposer*, to put apart, hence arrange; see DIS- & POSE], 1. to place in a certain order or arrangement. 2. to arrange (matters); settle or regulate (affairs). 3. to make some use of; employ. 4. to make willing; incline: as, I am *disposed* to agree with you. 5. to make susceptible or liable: as, the climate *disposes* the people to laziness. *v.i.* to have the power or privilege of disposing.
dispose of, 1. to deal with; arrange; settle. 2. to give away; bestow. 3. to sell. 4. to get rid of; throw away. 5. to do away with by eating or drinking.
dis·posed (dis-pōzd′), *adj.* [see DISPOSE], inclined; having a certain tendency (usually preceded by an adverb): as, he feels well-*disposed* toward you.
dis·po·si·tion (dis′pə-zish′ən), *n.* [ME.; OFr.; L. *dispositio* < *dispositus*, pp. of *disponere*, to arrange, dispose; *dis-*, apart + *ponere*, to place, put], 1. a putting in order or being put in order; proper or orderly arrangement: as, the *disposition* of crowds in a mob scene. 2. arrangement or management of affairs. 3. the giving away or giving up (*of* something). 4. the power or authority to arrange, settle, or manage; control. 5. an inclination or tendency: as, a *disposition* to quarrel. 6. [from astrological use as applied to planets], one's customary frame of mind; one's nature or temperament.
SYN.—**disposition** refers to the normal or prevailing aspect of one's nature (a genial *disposition*); **temperament** refers to the balance of traits that are manifested in one's behavior or thinking (an artistic *temperament*); **temper** refers to one's basic emotional nature, especially as regards relative quickness to anger (a hot *temper*, an even *temper*); **character** is applied to the sum of moral qualities associated with a distinctive individual (a weak *character*) and, unqualified, suggests moral strength, self-discipline, etc. (a man of *character*); **personality** is applied to the sum of physical, mental, and emotional qualities that distinguish one as a person (a negative *personality*) and, unqualified, suggests attractiveness or charm (a girl with *personality*).
dis·pos·sess (dis′pə-zes′), *v.t.* to deprive of the possession of something, especially land, a house, etc.; oust.
dis·pos·ses·sion (dis′pə-zesh′ən), *n.* a dispossessing or being dispossessed.
dis·pos·ses·sor (dis′pə-zes′ẽr), *n.* a person who dispossesses.
dis·po·sure (dis-pō′zhẽr), *n.* [Rare], disposition or disposal (in various senses).
dis·praise (dis-prāz′), *v.t.* [ME. *dispreisen;* OFr. *despreisier*, to blame; see DIS- & PRAISE], to speak of with disapproval or disparagement; blame; censure. *n.* a dispraising; blame; reproach.
dis·prize (dis-prīz′), *v.t.* [OFr. *despriser*, var. of *despreisier;* see DISPRAISE], [Archaic], to regard as of low value; not prize.
dis·proof (dis-prōōf′), *n.* 1. a disproving; refutation. 2. evidence that disproves.
dis·pro·por·tion (dis′prə-pôr′shən, dis′prə-pōr′shən), *n.* a lack of proportion; lack of symmetry; disparity. *v.t.* to cause to be disproportionate.
dis·pro·por·tion·al (dis′prə-pôr′shən-'l, dis′prə-pōr′shən-'l), *adj.* disproportionate.
dis·pro·por·tion·al·ly (dis′prə-pôr′shən-'l-i, dis′prə-pōr′shən-'l-i), *adv.* not proportionally; not equally.
dis·pro·por·tion·ate (dis′prə-pôr′shən-it, dis′prə-pōr′shən-it), *adj.* not proportionate; not in proportion.
dis·pro·por·tion·ate·ly (dis′prə-pôr′shən-it-li, dis′prə-pōr′shən-it-li), *adv.* 1. in a manner characterized by disproportion. 2. to a disproportionate extent.
dis·prov·al (dis-prōōv′'l), *n.* a disproving or disproof.
dis·prove (dis-prōōv′), *v.t.* [ME. *disproven;* OFr. *desprover*], to prove (something or someone) to be false or in error; refute.
SYN.—**disprove** implies the presenting of evidence or reasoned arguments that demonstrate an assertion, etc. to be false or erroneous; **refute** implies a more thorough assembly of evidence and a more careful development of argument and hence suggests conclusiveness of proof against; **confute** suggests the overwhelming or silencing of a person by argument or proof; **controvert** implies a disputing or denying of statements, arguments, etc. in an endeavor to refute them; **rebut** stresses formality in argument such as is observed in debate, court procedure, etc.
dis·pu·ta·ble (dis-pū′tə-b'l, dis′pyoo-tə-b'l), *adj.* [L. *disputabilis*], that can be disputed; debatable.
dis·pu·ta·bly (dis-pū′tə-bli, dis′pyoo-tə-bli), *adv.* in a disputable manner.
dis·pu·tant (dis′pyoo-tənt, dis-pū′t'nt), *adj.* [L. *disputans*, ppr. of *disputare*], disputing. *n.* a person who disputes, or debates.
dis·pu·ta·tion (dis′pyoo-tā′shən), *n.* [L. *disputatio*], 1. a disputing; dispute. 2. controversial discussion; debate. 3. [Obs.], discussion or conversation.
dis·pu·ta·tious (dis′pyoo-tā′shəs), *adj.* inclined to dispute; fond of arguing; contentious.
dis·put·a·tive (dis-pū′tə-tiv), *adj.* [LL. *disputativus*], 1. disputatious. 2. having to do with disputation.
dis·pute (dis-pūt′), *v.i.* [DISPUTED (-id), DISPUTING], [ME. *disputen;* OFr. *desputer* < L. *disputare*, lit., to compute, hence estimate, discuss, hence argue about; *dis-*, apart + *putare*, to think], 1. to argue; debate. 2. to quarrel. *v.t.* 1. to argue or debate (a question); discuss pro and con. 2. to question the truth of; doubt. 3. to oppose in any way; resist. 4. to try to win (a game, prize, etc.). *n.* 1. a disputing; argument; debate; controversy. 2. a quarrel. 3. [Obs.], a fight. —*SYN.* see **argument, discuss.**
beyond dispute, 1. not open to dispute or question; settled. 2. indisputably.
in dispute, still being argued about; not settled.
dis·qual·i·fi·ca·tion (dis-kwôl′ə-fi-kā′shən, dis′kwäl-ə-fi-kā′shən), *n.* 1. a disqualifying or being disqualified. 2. anything that disqualifies.
dis·qual·i·fy (dis-kwôl′ə-fī′, dis-kwäl′ə-fī′), *v.t.* 1. to make unfit or unqualified; disable; incapacitate. 2. to make or declare ineligible; take a right or privilege away from, as of further participation in a sport, for breaking rules.
dis·qui·et (dis-kwī′ət), *v.t.* [*dis-* + *quiet*], to make anxious, uneasy, or restless; disturb; fret. *n.* anxiety; restlessness; uneasiness. *adj.* [Rare], restless; uneasy.
dis·qui·e·tude (dis-kwī′ə-tōōd′, dis-kwī′ə-tūd′), *n.* [see DISQUIET], restlessness; uneasiness; anxiety.
dis·qui·si·tion (dis′kwə-zish′ən), *n.* [L. *disquisitio* < *disquisitus*, pp. of *disquirere*, to investigate, inquire < *dis-*, apart + *quaerere*, to seek], a formal discussion of some subject, often in writing; a discourse or treatise.
Dis·rae·li, Benjamin (diz-rā′li), first Earl of Beaconsfield, 1804–1881; English statesman and writer; prime minister of England (1868; 1874–1880).
dis·rate (dis-rāt′), *v.t.* to lower in rating, or rank, as a naval petty officer; degrade.
dis·re·gard (dis′ri-gärd′), *v.t.* [*dis-* + *regard*], 1. to pay little or no attention to. 2. to treat without due respect; slight. *n.* 1. lack of attention. 2. lack of due regard or respect; disdain. —*SYN.* see **neglect.**
dis·re·gard·ful (dis′ri-gärd′fəl), *adj.* showing disregard; neglectful.
dis·rel·ish (dis-rel′ish), *n. & v.t.* [*dis-* + *relish*], dislike.
dis·re·mem·ber (dis′ri-mem′bẽr), *v.t.* [Dial. & Colloq.], to forget; be unable to remember.
dis·re·pair (dis′ri-pâr′), *n.* the condition of needing repairs; state of neglect; dilapidation.
dis·rep·u·ta·ble (dis-rep′yoo-tə-b'l), *adj.* 1. not reputable; discreditable. 2. not respectable.
dis·rep·u·ta·bly (dis-rep′yoo-tə-bli), *adv.* in a disreputable manner.
dis·re·pute (dis′ri-pūt′), *n.* lack or loss of repute; bad reputation; disgrace; disfavor.
dis·re·spect (dis′ri-spekt′), *n.* lack of respect or esteem; discourtesy. *v.t.* to have or show lack of respect for.

dis·re·spect·a·ble (dis'ri-spek'tə-b'l), ***adj.*** not respectable; unworthy of respect.
dis·re·spect·ful (dis'ri-spekt'fəl), ***adj.*** having or showing lack of respect; discourteous; impolite; rude.
dis·robe (dis-rōb'), ***v.t. & v.i.*** [*dis-* + *robe*], to undress.
dis·root (dis-rōōt', dis-root'), ***v.t.*** to tear out by the roots; uproot.
dis·rupt (dis-rupt'), ***v.t. & v.i.*** [< L. *disruptus*, pp. of *disrumpere*, to break or burst apart; *dis-*, apart + *rumpere*, to break], to break apart; split up; rend asunder. ***adj.*** disrupted.
dis·rup·tion (dis-rup'shən), ***n.*** [L. *disruptio, diruptio*], 1. a disrupting; breaking up; splitting. 2. the fact or state of being disrupted.
dis·rup·tive (dis-rup'tiv), ***adj.*** 1. causing disruption. 2. produced by disruption.
dis·rup·tor (dis-rup'tẽr), ***n.*** a person who disrupts something: also spelled **disrupter.**
dis·sat·is·fac·tion (dis'sat-is-fak'shən), ***n.*** 1. the condition of being dissatisfied or displeased; discontent. 2. anything that dissatisfies.
dis·sat·is·fac·to·ry (dis'sat-is-fak'tə-ri), ***adj.*** not satisfying; unsatisfactory.
dis·sat·is·fied (dis-sat'is-fīd'), ***adj.*** [pp. of *dissatisfy*], 1. not satisfied; displeased; discontented. 2. showing displeasure or dissatisfaction.
dis·sat·is·fy (dis-sat'is-fī'), ***v.t.*** [DISSATISFIED (-fīd'), DISSATISFYING], to fail to satisfy; discontent; displease.
dis·seat (dis-sēt'), ***v.t.*** to unseat.
dis·sect (di-sekt'), ***v.t.*** [< L. *dissectus*, pp. of *dissecare*, to cut apart, cut up; *dis-*, apart + *secare*, to cut], 1. to cut apart piece by piece; separate into parts, as a body for purposes of study; anatomize. 2. to examine or analyze closely.
dis·sect·ed (di-sek'tid), ***adj.*** [pp. of *dissect*], 1. cut up into parts. 2. in *botany*, consisting of many lobes or segments, as some leaves. 3. in *physical geography*, cut up by valleys and ravines.
dis·sec·tion (di-sek'shən), ***n.*** [L. *dissectio*], 1. a dissecting or being dissected. 2. anything dissected, as a plant or animal for study. 3. analysis part by part; detailed examination.
dis·sec·tor (di-sek'tẽr), ***n.*** 1. a person who dissects. 2. an instrument used in dissecting.
dis·seize, dis·seise (dis-sēz'), ***v.t.*** [ME. *disseisen;* OFr. *dessaisir;* see DIS- & SEIZE], in *law*, to deprive wrongfully of real property; dispossess unlawfully.
dis·sei·zee, dis·sei·see (dis'sē-zē', dis-sēz'ē'), ***n.*** in *law*, a disseized person.
dis·sei·zin, dis·sei·sin (dis-sē'zin), ***n.*** [ME. *disseisine;* OFr. *dessaisine* < *dessaisir*], in *law*, a disseizing or being disseized; unlawful dispossession.
dis·sei·zor, dis·sei·sor (dis-sē'zẽr, dis-sē'zôr), ***n.*** in *law*, a person who disseizes.
dis·sem·blance (di-sem'bləns), ***n.*** [< *dissemble* + *-ance*], 1. a dissembling; dissimulating. 2. [OFr. *dessemblance;* see DIS- & SEMBLANCE], [Archaic], lack of resemblance.
dis·sem·ble (di-sem'b'l), ***v.t.*** [DISSEMBLED (-b'ld), DISSEMBLING], [earlier *dissimule* < OFr. *dissimuler;* L. *dissimulare* (see DISSIMULATE); re-formed after *resemble*], 1. to conceal under a false appearance: as, he *dissembled* his hatred by pretending to be friendly. 2. to resemble falsely; simulate; feign: as, vice sometimes *dissembles* virtue. 3. to pretend not to observe; feign ignorance of. ***v.i.*** to conceal one's true feelings, motives, etc. by pretense; behave hypocritically.
dis·sem·i·nate (di-sem'ə-nāt'), ***v.t.*** [DISSEMINATED (-id), DISSEMINATING], [< L. *disseminatus*, pp. of *disseminare*, lit., to scatter seed, hence disseminate; *dis-*, apart + *seminare*, to sow < *semen*, seed], to scatter far and wide; spread abroad, as if sowing; promulgate widely.
dis·sem·i·na·tion (di-sem'ə-nā'shən), ***n.*** [L. *disseminatio*], a disseminating or being disseminated.
dis·sem·i·na·tor (di-sem'ə-nā'tẽr), ***n.*** [L.], a person or thing that disseminates.
dis·sen·sion (di-sen'shən), ***n.*** [ME. *dissencion;* OFr. *dissension;* L. *dissensio* < *dissensus*, pp. of *dissentire;* see DISSENT], 1. a difference of opinion; disagreement. 2. strife; quarreling; wrangling. —***SYN.*** see **discord.**
dis·sent (di-sent'), ***v.i.*** [ME. *dissenten;* L. *dissentire; dis-*, apart + *sentire*, to feel, think], 1. to disagree; think differently (often with *from*): as, one judge *dissented* from the others. 2. to refuse to accept the doctrines and forms of an established church. ***n.*** 1. a dissenting; difference of opinion. 2. the rendering of a minority opinion in the decision of a law case.
dis·sent·er (di-sen'tẽr), ***n.*** 1. a person who dissents. 2. [D-], in England and Scotland, a Protestant who refuses to accept the doctrines and forms of the established state church.
dis·sen·tient (di-sen'shənt), ***adj.*** [L. *dissentiens*, ppr. of *dissentire*], dissenting, especially from the majority opinion. ***n.*** a person who dissents; dissenter.
dis·sen·tious (di-sen'shəs), ***adj.*** [Rare], of or inclined to dissension; quarrelsome; contentious.
dis·sep·i·ment (di-sep'i-mənt), ***n.*** [L. *dissaepimentus* < *dis-*, from + *saepire*, to fence in, enclose], in *botany* & *zoology*, a partition in some organ or part; septum.
dis·sert (di-sũrt'), ***v.i.*** [< pp. of *disserer*, to argue, discuss; *dis-*, apart + *serere*, to join, connect], [Rare], to dissertate.
dis·ser·tate (dis'ẽr-tāt'), ***v.i.*** [DISSERTATED (-id), DISSERTATING], [< L. *dissertatus*, pp. of *dissertare*, to discuss, argue, freq. of *disserere;* see DISSERT], [Rare], to discuss formally; discourse.
dis·ser·ta·tion (dis'ẽr-tā'shən), ***n.*** [LL. *dissertatio;* see DISSERTATE], a formal and lengthy discussion in speech or writing; a discourse or treatise, especially one required by colleges and universities as partial fulfillment of requirements for a degree; thesis.
dis·ser·ta·tor (dis'ẽr-tā'tẽr), ***n.*** [LL.], a person who dissertates.
dis·serve (dis-sũrv'), ***v.t.*** [*dis-* + *serve*], [Rare], to harm; do a disservice to.
dis·serv·ice (dis-sũr'vis), ***n.*** [*dis-* + *service*], harmful action; injury.
dis·sev·er (di-sev'ẽr), ***v.t.*** [ME. *disseveren;* OFr. *dessevrer;* LL. *disseparare* < L. *dis-* apart (intens.) + *separare*, to sever], 1. to sever; separate; cut apart. 2. to divide into parts. ***v.i.*** to separate or part; disunite.
dis·si·dence (dis'ə-dəns), ***n.*** [L. *dissidentia* < *dissidens*, ppr. of *dissidere*, to disagree; *dis-*, apart + *sidere*, to sit], disagreement; dissent.
dis·si·dent (dis'ə-dənt), ***adj.*** [L. *dissidens*, ppr. of *dissidere;* see DISSIDENCE], not agreeing; dissenting. ***n.*** a dissident person; dissenter.
dis·sil·i·ent (di-sil'i-ənt), ***adj.*** [L. *dissiliens*, ppr. of *dissilire*, to leap or burst apart < *dis-*, apart + *salire*, to leap], 1. springing apart; bursting apart. 2. in *botany*, bursting open with force, as some plant capsules or pods.
dis·sim·i·lar (di-sim'ə-lẽr, dis-sim'ə-lẽr), ***adj.*** not similar; not alike; different. —***SYN.*** see **different.**
dis·sim·i·lar·i·ty (di-sim'ə-lar'ə-ti, dis-sim'ə-lar'ə-ti), ***n.*** 1. absence of similarity; unlikeness; difference. 2. [*pl.* DISSIMILARITIES (-tiz)], an instance or point of difference, or unlikeness.
dis·sim·i·late (di-sim'ə-lāt', dis-sim'ə-lāt'), ***v.t.*** [DISSIMILATED (-id), DISSIMILATING], 1. to make dissimilar. 2. to cause to undergo dissimilation.
dis·sim·i·la·tion (di-sim'ə-lā'shən, dis'sim-ə-lā'shən), ***n.*** 1. a making or becoming dissimilar. 2. in *linguistics*, *a)* the mutual repulsion of sounds (phonemes) which are identical, similar, or formed with neighboring tongue positions; especially, *b)* the replacement or disappearance of a sound (usually *l*, *r*, or *n*) when it recurs within the same word or form. Examples: It. pel*l*egrino < L. pe*r*egrinus; Eng. mar*b*le < OFr. mar*b*re.
dis·si·mil·i·tude (dis'si-mil'ə-tōōd', dis'si-mil'ə-tūd'), ***n.*** [*dis-* + *similitude*], dissimilarity; difference.
dis·sim·u·late (di-sim'yoo-lāt'), ***v.t. & v.i.*** [DISSIMULATED (-id), DISSIMULATING], [< L. *dissimulatus;* see DISSIMULATION], to hide (one's feelings, motives, etc.) by pretense; dissemble.
dis·sim·u·la·tion (dis-sim'yoo-lā'shən), ***n.*** [ME.; OFr.; L. *dissimulatio* < *dissimulare*, to dissemble < *dis-*, not + *similis*, like], pretense; hypocrisy; deception.
dis·sim·u·la·tor (di-sim'yoo-lā'tẽr), ***n.*** a person who dissimulates.
dis·si·pate (dis'ə-pāt'), ***v.t.*** [DISSIPATED (-id), DISSIPATING], [< L. *dissipatus*, pp. of *dissipare*, to scatter, disperse; *dis-*, apart + *sipare*, *supare*, to throw], 1. to scatter; dispel; disperse. 2. to drive completely away; make disappear. 3. to waste; squander. ***v.i.*** 1. to be dissolved or dispelled; vanish. 2. to waste one's time and energy on frivolities; indulge in pleasure, especially drinking, gambling, etc., to the point of harming oneself; be dissolute. —***SYN.*** see **scatter.**
dis·si·pat·ed (dis'ə-pāt'id), ***adj.*** [pp. of *dissipate*], 1. scattered. 2. squandered; wasted. 3. wasting time and energy on frivolities; indulging in pleasure to excess; dissolute. 4. showing the harmful effects of dissipation.
dis·si·pa·tion (dis'ə-pā'shən), ***n.*** [L. *dissipatio;* see DISSIPATE], 1. a scattering or being scattered; dispersion. 2. a wasting or squandering. 3. any wasteful use of time or energy; frivolous diversion. 4. wasteful or excessive indulgence in pleasure; intemperance; dissoluteness.
dis·si·pa·tor (dis'ə-pā'tẽr), ***n.*** a person who dissipates: also spelled **dissipater.**
dis·so·ci·a·ble (di-sō'shi-ə-b'l, di-sō'shə-b'l), ***adj.*** [Fr.; L. *dissociabilis* < *dissociare;* see DISSOCIATE], 1. that can be dissociated; separable; distinguishable. 2. ill-matched; incongruous. 3. (di-sō'shə-b'l), [*dis-*, not + *sociable*], unsociable.
dis·so·cial (di-sō'shəl), ***adj.*** not social, or friendly; unsociable.
dis·so·ci·ate (di-sō'shi-āt'), ***v.t.*** [DISSOCIATED (-id), DISSOCIATING], [< L. *dissociatus*, pp. of *dissociare; dis-*, apart + *sociare*, to join < *socius*, companion], 1. to break the ties or connection between; sever association with; separate; disunite. 2. to think of as separate or

distinct. 3. in *chemistry*, to cause to undergo dissociation. *v.i.* 1. to part company; stop associating. 2. in *chemistry*, to undergo dissociation.

dissociate oneself from, to deny or repudiate any connection with.

dis·so·ci·a·tion (di-sō′si-ā′shən, di-sō′shi-ā′shən), *n.* [L. *dissociatio*], 1. a dissociating or being dissociated; separation. 2. in *chemistry*, the breaking up of a compound into simpler components. 3. in *psychology*, the process in which a group of mental activities breaks away from the main stream of consciousness and functions as a separate unit: an intensified dissociation can lead to multiple personality.

dis·so·ci·a·tive (di-sō′shi-ā′tiv), *adj.* 1. relating to dissociation. 2. causing or tending to cause dissociation.

dis·sol·u·bil·i·ty (di-sol′yoo-bil′ə-ti), *n.* the quality or state of being dissoluble; solubility.

dis·sol·u·ble (di-sol′yoo-b'l), *adj.* [L. *dissolubilis* < *dissolvere;* see DISSOLVE], that can be dissolved.

dis·so·lute (dis′ə-lōōt′, dis′ə-lūt′), *adj.* [L. *dissolutus*, loosened, lax, unrestrained; pp. of *disolvere;* see DISSOLVE], dissipated and immoral; profligate; debauched.

dis·so·lu·tion (dis′ə-lōō′shən, dis′ə-lū′shən), *n.* [L. *dissolutio* < *dissolutus;* see DISSOLVE], 1. a dissolving or being dissolved. 2. a breaking up or into parts; disintegration. 3. an ending; termination. 4. the ending of life; death. 5. the adjournment of a formal meeting. 6. in *finance*, the surrender of a charter; liquidation. 7. in *law*, the annulment of a contract.

dis·solv·a·ble (di-zol′və-b'l), *adj.* that can be dissolved.

dis·solve (di-zolv′), *v.t. & v.i.* [DISSOLVED (-zolvd′), DISSOLVING], [ME. *dissolven* < L. *dissolvere*, to loosen; *dis-*, apart + *solvere*, to loosen; see SOLVE], 1. to make or become liquid; liquefy; melt. 2. to merge with a liquid; pass or make pass into solution. 3. to break up; disunite; decompose; disintegrate. 4. to end by or as by breaking up; terminate. 5. to disappear or make disappear. 6. in *motion pictures*, to fade or make fade into or out of view. *n.* in *motion pictures*, 1. a fade-in. 2. a fade-out. —*SYN.* see **adjourn, melt.**

dissolved in tears, weeping.

dis·sol·vent (di-zol′vənt), *adj.* [L. *dissolvens*, ppr. of *dissolvere*], that can dissolve other substances. *n.* a dissolvent substance; solvent.

dis·so·nance (dis′ə-nəns), *n.* [Fr.; LL. *dissonantia* < L. *dissonans*, ppr. of *dissonare*, to be discordant, disagree in sound < *dis-*, apart + *sonus*, a sound], 1. an inharmonious sound or combination of sounds; discord. 2. any lack of harmony or agreement; incongruity. 3. in *music*, a chord that sounds harsh and incomplete until resolved to a harmonious chord.

dis·so·nant (dis′ə-nənt), *adj.* 1. characterized by or constituting a dissonance; discordant. 2. opposing in opinion, temperament, etc.; incompatible; incongruous.

dis·suade (di-swād′), *v.t.* [DISSUADED (-id), DISSUADING], [L. *dissuadere; dis-*, away, from + *suadere*, to persuade], to turn (a person) aside (*from* a course, etc.) by persuasion or advice.

dis·sua·sion (di-swā′zhən), *n.* [L. *dissuasio* < pp. of *dissuadere*], a dissuading.

dis·sua·sive (di-swā′siv), *adj.* trying to dissuade; meant to dissuade.

dis·syl·lab·ic (dis′si-lab′ik, dis′i-lab′ik), *adj.* having or consisting of two syllables: also **disyllabic.**

dis·syl·la·ble (di-sil′ə-b'l, dis′sil′ə-b'l), *n.* [Fr. *dissyllabe* < L. *disyllabus;* Gr. *disyllabos*, of two syllables < *di-*, two + *syllabē*, syllable], a word of two syllables, as *receive*: also **disyllable.**

dis·sym·met·ric (dis′si-met′rik), *adj.* dissymmetrical.

dis·sym·met·ri·cal (dis′si-met′ri-kəl), *adj.* 1. not symmetrical. 2. symmetrical in opposite directions, as are a person's hands.

dis·sym·me·try (dis-sim′ə-tri), *n.* [*pl.* DISSYMMETRIES (-triz)], 1. a lack or deficiency of symmetry. 2. symmetry in opposite directions, as of a person's hands.

dist., 1. discount. 2. distance. 3. distant. 4. distinguish. 5. distinguished. 6. district.

dis·taff (dis′taf, dis′täf), *n.* [ME. *distaf, dystaf;* AS. *distæf; dis-*, flax + *stæf*, a staff], 1. a staff on which flax, wool, etc. is wound for use in spinning; hence, 2. woman's work or concerns; hence, 3. woman or women in general.

DISTAFF AND SPINDLE

distaff side, the maternal side or female line of a family.

dis·tain (dis-tān′), *v.t.* [OFr. *desteindre* < L. *dis-* + *tingere*, to wet, tinge, dye], [Archaic], 1. to discolor; dye; stain. 2. to stain the honor of; disgrace.

dis·tal (dis′t'l), *adj.* [*distant* + *-al;* formed in contrast to *proximal*], in *anatomy*, farthest from the center or the point of attachment or origin; terminal: opposed to *proximal*.

dis·tance (dis′təns), *n.* [ME.; OFr.; L. *distantia* < *distans*, ppr. of *distare*, to stand apart, be separate < *dis-*, apart + *stare*, to stand], 1. the fact or condition of being separated or removed in space or time; remoteness. 2. a gap or space between two points. 3. an interval between two points in time. 4. the measure of a space or interval: as, the *distance* was one mile. 5. a remoteness in relationship: as, the *distance* between health and illness. 6. a remoteness in behavior; coolness of manner; reserve. 7. a far-away place: as, the bird flew away into the *distance*. 8. a far-away point of time: as, at this *distance* we cannot know Neanderthal man. 9. in *music*, an interval between two tones. 10. in *painting*, the depicting of distance, as in a landscape. 11. in *racing*, a space that is a certain distance back from the finish line: in order to be qualified for future heats, a horse must have reached this space by the time the winner has completed the course. Abbreviated **dis., dist.** *v.t.* [DISTANCED (-tənst), DISTANCING], 1. to place or hold at some distance. 2. to make appear to be far away: as, he *distances* his landscapes well. 3. to do better or more than; leave behind; outdo; best.

keep at a distance, to treat aloofly; be reserved or cool toward (someone).

keep one's distance, to be or remain aloof or reserved.

dis·tant (dis′tənt), *adj.* [OFr.; L. *distans;* see DISTANCE], 1. having a gap or space between; separated. 2. widely separated; far apart or far away in space or time. 3. away: as, New York is 100 miles *distant*. 4. far apart in relationship; remote: as, a *distant* cousin. 5. cool in manner; aloof; reserved; standoffish. 6. from or at a distance: as, a *distant* sound. Abbreviated **dis., dist.** —*SYN.* see **far.**

dis·taste (dis-tāst′), *n.* [*dis-* + *taste*], dislike; aversion (with *for*). *v.t.* [Obs.], 1. to have a distaste for; dislike. 2. to displease; offend.

dis·taste·ful (dis-tāst′fəl), *adj.* causing distaste; unpleasant; disagreeable.

Dist. Atty., District Attorney.

dis·tem·per (dis-tem′pẽr), *v.t.* [ME. *distemperen;* OFr. *destemprer;* ML. *distemperare*, to derange, disorder (esp. the "tempers," or four humors); L. *dis-*, apart + *temperare*, to mix in due proportion, be moderate], 1. to disturb; ruffle. 2. to upset or unbalance the functions of; derange; disorder. *n.* 1. a mental or physical derangement or disorder; disease. 2. an infectious virus disease of young dogs. 3. strangles, a disease of horses. 4. formerly, any of several other infectious diseases of animals, characterized by catarrh, fever, etc. 5. civil disorder or turmoil.

dis·tem·per (dis-tem′pẽr), *v.t.* [OFr. *destemprer, destremper;* ML. *distemperare*, to mix, dilute; L. *dis-*, intens. + *temperare*, to compound thoroughly, mix in due proportion], 1. to mix (colors or pigments) with water and egg yolks or some other binding medium. 2. to paint with such a mixture. *n.* 1. a method of painting using distempered pigment, as in murals. 2. a painting done in this way. 3. distempered paint.

dis·tem·per·a·ture (dis-tem′prə-chẽr, dis-tem′pẽr-ə-chẽr), *n.* [< *distemper*, after *temperature*], [Archaic], a disordered condition, especially of the body or the mind.

dis·tend (di-stend′), *v.t. & v.i.* [L. *distendere; dis-*, apart + *tendere*, to stretch], 1. to stretch out. 2. to expand, as by pressure from within; make or become swollen. —*SYN.* see **expand.**

dis·ten·si·ble (di-sten′sə-b'l), *adj.* [< LL. *distensus* (L. *distentus*, pp. of *distendere*)], that can be distended.

dis·ten·tion, dis·ten·sion (di-sten′shən), *n.* [L. *distentio* < pp. of *distendere*], a distending or being distended; inflation; expansion.

dis·tich (dis′tik), *n.* [L. *distichon;* Gr. *distichon* < *distichos*, having two rows; *di-*, two + *stichos*, a row, rank], two lines of verse regarded as a unit; couplet.

dis·tich·ous (dis′ti-kəs), *adj.* [Gr. *distichos;* see DISTICH], in *botany*, arranged in two vertical rows, as leaves on opposite sides of a stem.

dis·till, dis·til (di-stil′), *v.i.* [DISTILLED (-stild′), DISTILLING], [ME. *distillen;* OFr. *distiller;* L. *distillare, destillare*, to drop, trickle down; *de-*, down + *stillare*, to drop < *stilla*, a drop], 1. to fall in drops; trickle; drip. 2. to undergo distillation. *v.t.* 1. to cause or allow to fall in drops. 2. to subject to distillation; change or extract by distillation. 3. to purify, rectify, or refine by or as by distillation.

dis·til·late (dis′t'l-it, dis′t'l-āt′), *n.* [< L. *distillatus*, pp. of *distillare*], a product of distillation; liquid obtained by distilling.

dis·til·la·tion (dis′t'l-ā′shən), *n.* [ME.; OFr.; L. *distillatio* < pp. of *distillare*], 1. a distilling. 2. the process of first heating a mixture to separate the more volatile from the less volatile parts, and then cooling and condensing the resulting vapor so as to produce a more nearly pure or refined substance: nonvolatile impurities remain in the residue. 3. anything distilled; distillate. 4. the essence of anything.

dis·tilled (di-stild′), *adj.* produced by distilling.

dis·till·er (di-stil'ẽr), *n.* 1. a person or apparatus that distills. 2. a person, company, etc. in the business of making alcoholic liquors produced by distillation.
dis·till·er·y (di-stil'ẽr-i), *n.* [*pl.* DISTILLERIES (-iz)], 1. a place where distilling is carried on. 2. an establishment or industrial plant where distilled alcoholic liquors are made.
dis·till·ment, dis·til·ment (di-stil'mənt), *n.* distillation.
dis·tinct (di-stiŋkt'), *adj.* [ME. & OFr. < L. *distinctus*, pp. of *distinguere;* see DISTINGUISH], 1. not alike; different. 2. not the same; separate; individual. 3. clearly marked off; clear; plain. 4. well-defined; unmistakable; definite. 5. [Poetic], marked; decorated; variegated. —*SYN.* see **different.**
dis·tinc·tion (di-stiŋk'shən), *n.* [ME. *distinctiun;* OFr. *distinction;* L. *distinctio* < pp. of *distinguere;* see DISTINGUISH], 1. the act of making or keeping distinct; differentiating between or among things. 2. that which makes or keeps distinct; particular quality, mark, or feature that differentiates: as, the *distinction* of this building is its height. 3. the state of getting special recognition or honor; fame; eminence: as, a singer of *distinction.* 4. the quality that makes one seem superior or worthy of special recognition or honor: as, he fought with *distinction.* 5. a mark or sign of special recognition or honor: as, the professor was loaded with *distinctions.*
dis·tinc·tive (di-stiŋk'tiv), *adj.* making distinct; distinguishing from others; characteristic. —*SYN.* see **characteristic.**
dis·tinct·ly (di-stiŋkt'li), *adv.* in a distinct manner; clearly; definitely.
dis·tin·gué (dis'taŋ-gā', di-staŋ'gā; Fr. dēs'tan'gā'), *adj.* [*fem.* DISTINGUÉE (-gā', -gā; Fr. -gā')], distinguished; having an air of distinction.
dis·tin·guish (di-stiŋ'gwish), *v.t.* [< L. *distinguere* + Eng. *-ish;* L. *distinguere,* to separate, discriminate, punctuate < *dis-*, apart + *-stinguere,* to prick, pierce; IE. base **steig-*, to prick, pierce, as in Eng. *stick,* G. *sticken,* to pierce, embroider, Gr. *stigma,* etc.], 1. to separate or mark off by differences; perceive or show the difference in; differentiate. 2. to be an essential characteristic of; characterize. 3. to perceive clearly; recognize plainly by any of the senses. 4. to separate and classify: as, *distinguish* colors into primary and secondary. 5. to make famous or eminent; give distinction to: as, he *distinguished* himself in battle. *v.i.* to make a distinction (often with *between* or *among*). Abbreviated **dist., disting.**
SYN.—**distinguish** implies a recognizing or marking apart from others by special features or characteristic qualities (to *distinguish* good from evil); **discriminate,** in this connection, suggests a distinguishing of minute or subtle differences between similar things (to *discriminate* scents); **differentiate** suggests the noting or ascertaining of specific differences between things by comparing in detail their distinguishing qualities or features. See also **discern.**
dis·tin·guish·a·ble (di-stiŋ'gwish-ə-b'l), *adj.* that can be distinguished; separable or perceptible.
dis·tin·guished (di-stiŋ'gwisht), *adj.* [pp. of *distinguish*], 1. celebrated; eminent: abbreviated **dist.** 2. having an air of distinction. —*SYN.* see **famous.**
Distinguished Flying Cross, 1. a decoration given by the United States for heroism or extraordinary achievement in aerial flight against the enemy: instituted in 1917. 2. a similar decoration given by the British government to members of the Royal Air Forces. Abbreviated **D.F.C.**
Distinguished Service Cross, 1. a cross of bronze awarded in the United States Army for extraordinary heroism in battle. 2. a British Royal Navy cross of silver awarded officers below the rank of lieutenant commander for distinguished service against the enemy. Abbreviated **D.S.C.**
Distinguished Service Medal, 1. a bronze medal awarded in the armed forces of the United States for meritorious service in a duty of great responsibility. 2. a bronze medal awarded to enlisted men in the British Royal Navy or Marines for distinguished service in time of war. Abbreviated **D.S.M.**
dis·tort (di-stôrt'), *v.t.* [< L. *distortus,* pp. of *distorquere,* to twist out of shape, distort; *dis-*, intens. + *torquere,* to twist], 1. to twist out of shape; change the usual shape or appearance of; hence, 2. to misrepresent; misstate; pervert: as, you *distort* the facts. —*SYN.* see **deform.**
dis·tor·tion (di-stôr'shən), *n.* [L. *distortio*], 1. a distorting; twisting. 2. the fact or condition of being distorted. 3. anything distorted.
distr., 1. distributed. 2. distribution. 3. distributor.
dis·tract (di-strakt'), *v.t.* [ME. *distracten* < L. *distractus,* pp. of *distrahere,* to draw apart; *dis-*, apart + *trahere,* to draw, pull], 1. to draw (the mind, etc.) away in another direction; divert. 2. to draw (the thoughts) in conflicting directions; harass; confuse. 3. to derange the mind of; craze.
dis·tract·i·ble (di-strak'tə-b'l), *adj.* that can be distracted.
dis·trac·tion (di-strak'shən), *n.* [ME. *distractioun;* L. *distractio*], 1. a distracting or being distracted; confusion. 2. anything that distracts; cause of confusion. 3. anything that gives mental relaxation or freedom from worry, grief, etc.; amusement; diversion. 4. great mental agitation or derangement; madness.
dis·trac·tive (di-strak'tiv), *adj.* distracting; confusing.
dis·train (di-strān'), *v.t. & v.i.* [ME. *distreinen;* OFr. *destreindre;* LL. *distringere,* to force by seizure of goods < L. *distringere,* to pull asunder, detain, etc.; *dis-*, apart + *stringere,* to draw tight, stretch], in *law,* to seize and hold (property) as security or indemnity for a debt.
dis·train·ee (dis'trā-nē'), *n.* [*distrain* + *-ee*], a person whose goods have been seized as security or indemnity for a debt.
dis·train·er (di-strān'ẽr), *n.* a distrainor.
dis·train·or (di-strān'ẽr, dis'trā-nôr'), *n.* a creditor who distrains the property of another.
dis·traint (di-strānt'), *n.* [OFr. *destreinte,* distress < pp. of *destreindre*], in *law,* a distraining; distress.
dis·trait (di-strā'; Fr. dēs'tre'), *adj.* [Fr., pp. of *distraire,* to distract; L. *distrahere;* see DISTRACT], absent-minded; inattentive. —*SYN.* see **absent-minded.**
dis·traught (di-strôt'), *adj.* [prob. var. sp. of *distrait* or of *distract,* used as adj.], 1. distracted; harassed; mentally confused. 2. driven mad; crazed. —*SYN.* see **absent-minded.**
dis·tress (di-stres'), *v.t.* [ME. *distressen;* OFr. *destresser, destrecier,* orig., to constrain (to do something); LL. **districtiare* < L. *districtus,* pp. of *distringere;* see DISTRAIN], 1. to cause sorrow, misery, or suffering to; make unhappy, anxious, etc.; pain; afflict; trouble. 2. in *law,* to distrain. *n.* 1. the state of being distressed; pain; grief; anxiety; suffering. 2. anything that distresses; affliction. 3. a state of danger or trouble; bad straits. 4. in *law, a)* distraint. *b)* the property distrained.
SYN.—**distress** implies mental or physical strain imposed by pain, trouble, worry, or the like and usually suggests a state or situation that can be relieved (*distress* caused by famine); **suffering** stresses the actual enduring of pain, distress, or tribulation (the *suffering* of the wounded); **agony** suggests mental or physical torment so excruciating that the body or mind is convulsed with the force of it (in mortal *agony*); **anguish** has equal force but is more often applied to acute mental suffering (the *anguish* of despair).
dis·tress·ful (di-stres'fəl), *adj.* 1. causing distress; painful; grievous. 2. feeling or expressing distress.
dis·trib·ut·a·ble (di-strib'yoo-tə-b'l), *adj.* that can be distributed.
dis·trib·u·tar·y (di-strib'yoo-ter'i), *n.* [*pl.* DISTRIBUTARIES (-iz)], [< *distribute;* formed in contrast to *tributary*], any branch of a river that flows away from the main stream and does not rejoin it: opposed to *tributary.*
dis·trib·ute (di-strib'yoot), *v.t.* [DISTRIBUTED (-id), DISTRIBUTING], [< L. *distributus,* pp. of *distribuere,* to distribute; *dis-*, apart + *tribuere,* to allot, give < *tribus,* division of the people, tribe], 1. to divide and give out in shares; allot. 2. to scatter or spread out, as over a surface. 3. to divide and arrange according to a classification; classify. 4. to put (things) in various distinct places. 5. [Archaic], to administer, as justice. 6. in *law,* to apportion (an intestate's property) to those entitled to it. 7. in *logic,* to use (a term) in its full or extended meaning, so as to refer to every individual denoted. 8. in *printing,* to break up (type) and put the letters back in the proper boxes. Abbreviated **dis., distr.**
SYN.—**distribute** implies a dealing out of portions or a spreading about of units among a number of recipients (to *distribute* leaflets); **dispense** suggests the careful measuring out of that which is distributed (to *dispense* drugs); **divide** suggests separation of a whole into parts to be shared (an inheritance *divided* among five children); **dole** implies a distributing of money, food, etc. in charity or in a sparing or niggardly manner.
dis·tri·bu·tion (dis'trə-bū'shən), *n.* [L. *distributio*], 1. a distributing or being distributed. 2. the manner of being distributed: as, an equal *distribution* of property. 3. anything distributed; portion; share. 4. the system or process of distributing commodities to consumers. Abbreviated **distr.**
dis·trib·u·tive (di-strib'yoo-tiv), *adj.* [Fr. *distributif;* LL. *distributivus*], 1. distributing or tending to distribute. 2. relating to distribution. 3. referring to each member of a group regarded individually. 4. in *logic,* distributed in a given proposition: said of a term. *n.* a distributive word or expression, as *any* or *each.*
dis·trib·u·tive·ly (di-strib'yoo-tiv-li), *adv.* in a distributive manner or sense; singly; individually.
dis·trib·u·tor (di-strib'yoo-tẽr), *n.* [L.], 1. a person or thing that distributes. 2. an agent or business firm that distributes goods to consumers. 3. a device for distributing electric current to the spark plugs of a gasoline engine so that they fire in proper order. Abbreviated **distr.**

dis·trict (dis′trikt), *n.* [Fr.; ML. *districtus*, orig., power of constraint, control; hence, in feudal law, a territory within which a lord had the right to administer jurisdiction, district < L. *districtus*, pp. of *distringere;* see DISTRAIN], 1. a geographical or political division made for a specific purpose: as, a school *district.* 2. any region; part of a country, city, etc.: as, the business *district.* Abbreviated **dist.** *v.t.* to divide into districts.

district attorney, a lawyer elected or appointed in a specified district to serve as a prosecutor for the state in criminal cases: abbreviated **D.A., Dist. Atty.**

district court, 1. the federal trial court sitting in each district of the United States. 2. in some States, the court of general jurisdiction.

District of Columbia, a federal district of the United States, on the north bank of the Potomac River: area, 69 sq. mi.; pop., 764,000: occupied by the city of Washington: abbreviated **D.C.**

dis·trust (dis-trust′), *n.* a lack of trust, of faith, or of confidence; doubt; suspicion. *v.t.* to have no trust, faith, or confidence in; doubt; suspect.

dis·trust·ful (dis-trust′fəl), *adj.* distrusting; doubting. **distrustful of,** suspicious of; having no confidence in.

dis·turb (di-stũrb′), *v.t.* [ME. *distorben;* OFr. *destorber, distourber;* L. *disturbare,* to drive asunder, tear in pieces; *dis-,* apart (intens.) + *turbare,* to disorder, throw into confusion < *turba,* a mob], 1. to break up the quiet or serenity of; agitate (what is quiet or still). 2. to agitate the mind of; make uneasy or anxious. 3. to break up the settled order or orderly working of: as, don't *disturb* my things. 4. to break in on; interrupt; interfere with. 5. to inconvenience: as, don't *disturb* yourself.

***SYN.*—disturb** implies the unsettling of normal mental calm or powers of concentration by worry, interruption, etc. (to *disturb* one's train of thought); **discompose** implies the upsetting of one's self-possession (her sudden outburst *discomposed* him); to **perturb** is to cause to have a troubled or alarmed feeling (the bad news *perturbed* him); **agitate** suggests an arousing of intense mental or emotional excitement (he was so *agitated,* he could not answer).

dis·turb·ance (di-stũr′bəns), *n.* [ME.; OFr. *destourbance*], 1. a disturbing or being disturbed. 2. anything that disturbs. 3. the state of being worried, troubled, or anxious. 4. commotion; disorder.

di·sul·fate (dī-sul′fāt), *n.* 1. a salt of disulfuric acid. 2. a chemical compound containing two sulfate groups per molecule. 3. a bisulfate.

di·sul·fide (dī-sul′fīd, di-sul′fid), *n.* [*di-* + *sulfide*], a chemical compound in which two sulfur atoms are united with a single radical or with a single atom of an element: as, carbon *disulfide,* CS_2.

di·sul·fu·ric acid (dī′sul-fyoor′ik), an acid, $H_2S_2O_7$, whose molecule is composed of two molecules of sulfuric acid minus one molecule of water: also called *pyrosulfuric acid.*

dis·un·ion (dis-ūn′yən), *n.* [*dis-* + *union*], 1. a breaking of a tie or bond; separation. 2. absence of unity; dissension; disagreement; discord.

dis·un·ion·ist (dis-ūn′yən-ist), *n.* 1. a person who advocates or tries to cause disunion. 2. a person who advocated secession of some State or States from the United States (during the Civil War period).

dis·u·nite (dis′yoo-nīt′), *v.t.* to destroy or take away the unity of; make disagree; separate. *v.i.* to become separate; come apart.

dis·un·i·ty (dis-ūn′ə-ti), *n.* a lack of unity; disunion.

dis·use (dis-ūz′; *for n.,* dis-ūs′), *v.t.* to stop using. *n.* the fact or state of being or becoming unused; lack of use.

dis·u·til·i·ty (dis′yoo-til′ə-ti), *n.* a lack of utility; quality of being harmful; inconvenience.

dis·val·ue (dis-val′ū), *v.t.* [Rare], to regard as of no value; depreciate; disparage.

di·syl·lab·ic (dis′i-lab′ik), *adj.* dissyllabic.

di·syl·la·ble (di-sil′ə-b′l), *n.* a dissyllable.

dis·yoke (dis-yōk′), *v.t.* to free from, or as from, a yoke; unyoke.

ditch (dich), *n.* [ME. *dich, dic;* AS. *dic,* a ditch, drain; akin to OFris., ON. *dik,* G. *deich, teich,* lit., cut-out place; IE. base **dhēig-,* to pierce, stab, as in L. *figere,* to pin together, pierce, thrust in], a long, narrow cut in the earth, usually for carrying water; channel for drainage or irrigation of the soil. *v.t.* 1. to border with a ditch. 2. to make a ditch in. 3. to throw into a ditch; derail (a train). 4. to set (a disabled aircraft) down on water and abandon it. 5. [Slang], to desert or get rid of. *v.i.* to dig a ditch or ditches.

di·the·ism (dī′thi-iz′m), *n.* [*di-* + *theism*], 1. the belief in two supreme gods; dualism. 2. the belief in two universal forces, as of good and of evil.

dith·er (dith′ẽr), *n.* [var. of *didder;* see DIDDLE], a trembling or excited condition. *v.i.* to be in a dither.

di·thi·on·ic acid (dī′thī-on′ik, dith′i-on′ik), [*di-* + *thionic*], an acid, $H_2S_2O_6$, having two sulfur atoms in each molecule and existing only in salts or solutions.

dith·y·ramb (dith′ə-ram′, dith′ə-ramb′), *n.* [L. *dithyrambus;* Gr. *dithyrambos*], 1. in ancient Greece, a wild and emotional choric hymn in honor of Dionysus; hence, 2. any wildly emotional, song, speech, or writing.

dith·y·ram·bic (dith′ə-ram′bik), *adj.* 1. of or like a dithyramb. 2. wildly emotional or enthusiastic. *n.* a dithyrambic verse; dithyramb.

dit·ta·ny (dit′ə-ni), *n.* [*pl.* DITTANIES (-niz)], [ME. *ditane, detany;* OFr. *ditan, ditain;* L. *dictamnum;* Gr. *diktamnon* < *Dikte,* Mount Dicte, in Crete, where the plant grew], 1. a pink-flowered mint. 2. a shrubby plant with flowers that give off an inflammable vapor; fraxinella. 3. a plant of the mint family, with oval leaves and clusters of purplish flowers.

dit·to (dit′ō), *n.* [*pl.* DITTOS (-ōz)], [It. < L. *dictum,* a saying < *dicere,* to say], 1. the same (as something said or appearing above or before). 2. a duplicate; another of the same. 3. a ditto mark. *adv.* as said above; as before; likewise. Abbreviated **do.** *v.t.* [DITTOED (-ōd), DITTOING], to repeat; duplicate; copy.

dit·tog·ra·phy (di-tog′rə-fi), *n.* [< Gr. *dittos,* form of *dissos,* double; + *-graphy*], the accidental repetition of a letter or letters in writing or copying.

ditto machine, a machine for duplicating writings or drawings: a trade-mark (**Ditto machine**).

ditto mark, a mark (") used in itemized lists or tables to show that a word, figure, or passage above is to be repeated. Example: 4 hrs. overtime Sat.
2 " " Mon.

dit·ty (dit′i), *n.* [*pl.* DITTIES (-iz)], [ME. *dite;* OFr. *dité* < L. *dictatum,* thing dictated; neut. pp. of *dictare;* see DICTATE], a short, simple song.

ditty bag (or **box**), [< obs. *dutty,* coarse calico, orig. E. Ind.; cf. Hind. *dhōtī,* loincloth], a small bag (or box) used by sailors or soldiers for carrying sewing equipment, toilet articles, etc.

Di·u (dē′oo), *n.* 1. a district of Portuguese India, consisting of a small island and a section of the adjacent mainland in northwestern India: area, 14 sq. mi.; pop., 20,000. 2. the island of this district.

di·u·re·sis (dī′yoo-rē′sis), *n.* [Mod. L. < Gr. *diourein* < *dia-,* through + *ourein,* to urinate < *ouron,* urine], an increased or excessive secretion or flow of urine.

di·u·ret·ic (dī′yoo-ret′ik), *adj.* [LL. *diureticus;* Gr. *diourētikos* < *diourein;* see DIURESIS], increasing the secretion and flow of urine. *n.* a diuretic drug.

di·ur·nal (dī-ũr′n′l), *adj.* [ME.; L. *diurnalis* < *diurnus,* daily < *dies,* day], 1. daily; happening each day. 2. of the daytime: opposed to *nocturnal.* 3. in *entomology,* living for one day. 4. in *zoology,* active in the daytime. *n.* [Archaic], 1. a diary. 2. a daily newspaper. 3. in *ecclesiastical usage,* a service book containing the prayers for the canonical hours of the daytime.

di·ur·nal·ly (dī-ũr′n′l-i), *adv.* [*diurnal* + *-ly*], 1. daily. 2. by day; in or during the daytime.

Div., Divinity.

div., 1. diversion. 2. divide. 3. dividend. 4. divine. 5. division. 6. divisor. 7. divorced.

di·va (dē′və), *n.* [*pl.* DIVAS (-vəz); It. DIVE (-ve)], [It.; L., goddess, fem. of *divus,* god], a prima donna; leading woman singer, especially in grand opera.

di·va·gate (dī′və-gāt′), *v.i.* [DIVAGATED (-id), DIVAGATING], [< pp. of L. *divagari,* to wander about < *dis-,* from + *vagari,* to wander], 1. to wander about; hence, 2. to stray from the subject; digress.

di·va·ga·tion (dī′və-gā′shən), *n.* a divagating; wandering; digression.

di·va·lent (dī-vā′lənt, div′ə-lənt), *adj.* 1. having a valence of two. 2. having two valences. Also, esp. for 2, **bivalent.**

di·van (di-van′ *for 1;* dī′van *or* di-van′ *for 2 & 3*), *n.* [Turk. *dīwān;* Per. *dīvān, dīwān,* orig., bundle of written sheets, hence accounts, office of accounts, customhouse, council room, appropriate furniture, council, etc.], 1. in Oriental countries, a royal council or council room. 2. a large, low couch or sofa, usually without arm rests or back. 3. a coffee room, café, or smoking room.

di·var·i·cate (də-var′ə-kāt′, dī-var′ə-kāt′), *v.i.* [DIVARICATED (-id), DIVARICATING], [< L. *divaricatus,* pp. of *divaricare,* to spread apart < *dis-,* apart + *varicare,* to straddle < *varicus,* straddling; cf. PREVARICATE], to split into two parts; fork; branch. *v.t.* to spread or branch widely apart. *adj.* widely diverging; spreading or branching far apart.

di·var·i·ca·tion (də-var′ə-kā′shən, dī-var′ə-kā′shən), *n.* 1. a divaricating; forking. 2. a difference of opinion.

di·var·i·ca·tor (də-var′ə-kā′tẽr, dī-var′ə-kā′tẽr), *n.* [see DIVARICATE], the muscle that stretches apart the shells of a bivalve.

dive (dīv), *v.i.* [DIVED (dīvd) or DOVE (dōv), DIVED, DIVING], [ME. *diven, dyven;* AS. *dyfan,* to immerse, caus. of *dufan,* to dive; akin to ON. *dȳfa, deyfa,* to plunge, *dūfa,* a wave; IE. base **dheup-,* deep and hollow; cf. DIP], 1. to plunge head first into water. 2. to go suddenly under water: as, a submarine *dives.* 3. to plunge the hand or body suddenly into a substance or opening: as, he *dived* into his foxhole. 4. to vanish from sight suddenly. 5. in *aviation,* to make a steep, sudden descent. *v.t.* 1. to plunge (a hand, head, etc.) into something. 2. to explore or penetrate by or as by diving. 3. to send (one's airplane) into a dive. *n.* 1. a diving; sudden plunge into water head first. 2. any sudden plunge or submersion. 3. in *aviation,* a sharp descent. 4. [Colloq.], a cheap, disreputable saloon, gambling place, etc.

dive bomber, a kind of airplane that releases its bombs while diving at the target.

di·er (dīv′ẽr), *n.* 1. a person or thing that dives. 2. a person whose occupation is diving or working under water. 3. any of several kinds of diving water birds, as the grebe or loon.

di·verge (də-vũrj′, dī-vũrj′), *v.i.* [DIVERGED (-vũrjd′), DIVERGING], [Mod. L. *divergere* < L. *dis-*, apart + *vergere*, to turn, incline], 1. to go or be in different directions from a common point or from each other; branch off. 2. to vary from a norm; differ. —*SYN.* see **deviate.**

di·ver·gence (də-vũr′jəns, dī-vũr′jəns), *n.* [Mod. L. *divergentia* < ppr. of *divergere*], 1. a diverging; branching off. 2. variation from a norm; difference; deviation.

di·ver·gen·cy (də-vũr′jən-si, dī-vũr′jən-si), *n.* [*pl.* DIVERGENCIES (-siz)], divergence.

di·ver·gent (də-vũr′jənt, dī-vũr′jənt), *adj.* [Mod. L. *divergens*, ppr. of *divergere*], 1. diverging. 2. varying from a norm; deviating; different. —*SYN.* see **different.**

di·vers (dī′vẽrz), *adj.* [ME.; OFr. < L. *diversus*, pp. of *divertere*, to turn in different directions < *dis-*, apart + *vertere*, to turn], 1. various or sundry; several. 2. [Archaic], diverse.

di·verse (də-vũrs′, dī-vũrs′, dī′vũrs), *adj.* [see DIVERS], 1. different; dissimilar. 2. varied; diversified. —*SYN.* see **different.**

di·verse·ly (də-vũrs′li, dī-vũrs′li), *adv.* in diverse directions or ways; differently; variously.

di·ver·si·fi·ca·tion (də-vũr′sə-fi-kā′shən, dī-vũr′sə-fi-kā′shən), *n.* a diversifying or being diversified; variety; variation.

di·ver·si·fied (də-vũr′sə-fīd′, dī-vũr′sə-fīd′), *adj.* [pp. of *diversify*] made diverse; varied.

di·ver·si·form (də-vũr′sə-fôrm′, dī-vũr′sə-fôrm), *adj.* [see DIVERS & -FORM], of various forms, or shapes.

di·ver·si·fy (də-vũr′sə-fī′, dī-vũr′sə-fī′), *v.t.* [DIVERSIFIED (-fīd′), DIVERSIFYING], [Fr. *diversifier;* ML. *diversificare*, to make different < L. *diversus*, different + *facere*, to make], to make diverse; give variety to; vary.

di·ver·sion (də-vũr′zhən, dī-vũr′shən), *n.* [ML. *diversio* < L. *diversus;* see DIVERS], 1. a diverting; turning aside (*from*): as, *diversion* of funds from the treasury: abbreviated **div.** 2. distraction of attention: as, *diversion* of the enemy. 3. anything that diverts or distracts the attention; hence, 4. a pastime; amusement.

di·ver·sion·ar·y (də-vũr′zhən-er′i, dī-vũr′shən-er′i), *adj.* having the nature of a diversion; especially, in *military usage*, serving to distract the enemy from the main point of attack: as, *diversionary* tactics.

di·ver·si·ty (də-vũr′sə-ti, dī-vũr′sə-ti), *n.* [*pl.* DIVERSITIES (-tiz)], 1. quality, state, fact, or instance of being diverse; difference. 2. variety; multiformity.

di·vert (də-vũrt′, dī-vũrt′), *v.t.* [ME. *diverten;* OFr. *divertir;* L. *divertere;* see DIVERS], 1. to turn (a person or thing) aside (*from* a course); deflect. 2. to distract the attention of; hence, 3. to amuse; entertain. —*SYN.* see **amuse.**

di·ver·tic·u·lum (dī′vẽr-tik′yoo-ləm), *n.* [*pl.* DIVERTICULA (-lə)], [L. *diverticulum, deverticulum*, a bypath, side way < *divertere, devertere*, to turn aside; *de-*, from + *vertere*, to turn], in *anatomy*, a pouch or sac opening out from a tubular organ or main cavity.

di·ver·ti·men·to (di-ver′ti-men′tō), *n.* [*pl.* DIVERTIMENTI (-ti)], [It.; see DIVERT], any of various light, melodic instrumental compositions in several movements.

di·vert·ing (də-vũr′tiŋ, dī-vũr′tiŋ), *adj.* that diverts; especially, amusing or entertaining.

‡di·ver·tisse·ment (dē′ver′tēs′män′), *n.* [Fr.; see DIVERT], 1. a diversion; amusement. 2. a short ballet, etc. performed between the acts of a play or opera; entr'acte. 3. a divertimento.

Di·ves (dī′vēz), *n.* [L., wealthy], 1. in the *Bible*, the rich man in the parable: Luke 16:19–31. 2. any rich man.

di·vest (də-vest′, dī-vest′), *v.t.* [< earlier *devest* (< OFr. *desvestir; des-*, from + *vestir* < L. *vestire*, to dress < *vestis*, a garment) after ML. *divestire*, contr. < *disvestire;* L. *dis-*, from + *vestire*], 1. to strip (*of* clothing, arms, etc.). 2. to deprive or dispossess (*of* rank, rights, etc.). —*SYN.* see **strip.**

di·vest·i·ture (də-ves′tə-chẽr, dī-ves′tə-chẽr), *n.* a divesting or being divested: also **divesture.**

di·vest·ment (də-vest′mənt, dī-vest′mənt), *n.* divestiture.

di·ves·ture (də-ves′chẽr, dī-ves′chẽr), *n.* divestiture.

di·vid·a·ble (də-vīd′ə-b'l), *adj.* that can be divided; divisible.

di·vide (də-vīd′), *v.t.* [DIVIDED (-id), DIVIDING], [ME. *deviden, dividen;* L. *dividere*, to separate, divide, distribute < *di-* (< *dis-*, apart) + base seen in *vidua*, a widow < IE. base **weidh-, *widh-*, to separate], 1. to separate into parts; split up; sever. 2. to separate into groups; classify. 3. to make or keep separate by or as by a boundary or partition. 4. to give out in shares; apportion. 5. to cause disagreement between or among; alienate. 6. in *mathematics*, *a*) to separate into equal parts by a divisor. *b*) to be a divisor of. 7. in *mechanics*, to mark off the divisions of; graduate; gradate. *v.i.* 1. to be or become separate; part. 2. to disagree; differ in opinion. 3. to separate into groups in voting on a question. 4. to share. *n.* a ridge that divides two drainage areas; watershed. Abbreviated **div.** —*SYN.* see **distribute, separate.**

di·vid·ed (də-vīd′id), *adj.* [pp. of *divide*], 1. separated into parts; parted. 2. in *botany*, segmented.

divided payments, payments in installments.

‡di·vi·de et im·pe·ra (div′ə-dē′ et im′pə-rə), [L.], divide and rule.

div·i·dend (div′ə-dend′), *n.* [Fr. *dividende;* L. *dividendum*, that which is to be divided < *dividendus*, gerundive of *dividere*], 1. the number or quantity to be divided. 2. a sum or quantity, usually of money, to be divided among stockholders, creditors, members of a co-operative, etc. 3. an individual's share of such a sum or quantity. 4. in *insurance*, the refund made to the insured from the year's surplus profit. Abbreviated **div., d.** —*SYN.* see **bonus.**

di·vid·ers (də-vīd′ẽrs), *n.pl.* an instrument for dividing lines, measuring or marking off distances, etc.; compasses.

div·i-div·i (div′i-div′i), *n.* [Sp. < Caribbean word], 1. a small tropical American tree of the pea family. 2. its curled, astringent pods, which yield tannic and gallic acids and are used in medicine, dyeing, and tanning.

di·vid·u·al (də-vij′o͞o-əl), *adj.* [< L. *dividuus*], 1. divided; separate. 2. divisible; separable. 3. distributed; shared.

div·i·na·tion (div′ə-nā′shən), *n.* [ME.; OFr.; L. *divinatio* < *divinatus*, pp. of *divinare;* see DIVINE, *v.*], 1. the act or practice of trying to foretell the future or the unknown by occult means. 2. a prophecy; augury. 3. a successful guess; clever conjecture.

di·vin·a·to·ry (də-vin′ə-tôr′i, də-vin′ə-tō′ri), *adj.* of or by divination.

di·vine (də-vīn′), *adj.* [ME.; OFr. *divin, devin;* L. *divinus* < *divus*, god, deity; IE. **deiwos*, god < base **dej-, *deja-, *dja-*, to glow, shine], 1. of or like God or a god. 2. given or inspired by God; holy; sacred. 3. devoted to God; religious; sacrosanct. 4. having to do with theology. 5. supremely great, good, etc. 6. [Colloq.], very pleasing, attractive, etc.: a feminine intensive. *n.* 1. a clergyman. 2. a theologian. Abbreviated **div.** *v.t.* [DIVINED (-vīnd′), DIVINING], [ME. *devinen;* OFr. *deviner;* L. *divinare* < *divinus*], 1. to prophesy. 2. to guess; conjecture. 3. to find out by intuition. *v.i.* to engage in divination. —*SYN.* see **holy.**

Divine Comedy, an elaborate narrative poem in Italian, written (1302–1321) by Dante Alighieri: it deals with the author's imaginary journey through Hell, Purgatory, and Paradise.

di·vine·ly (də-vīn′li), *adv.* 1. in a divine manner. 2. by a divine agency; by God's power. 3. supremely.

di·vin·er (də-vīn′ẽr), *n.* [ME. *devinour;* OFr. *devineor* < *deviner;* see DIVINE, *v.*], 1. a person who engages in divination. 2. a divining rod.

divine right of kings, the supposedly God-given right to rule formerly attributed to monarchs.

diving bell, a large, hollow, bell-shaped apparatus in which divers can work under water: air is pumped into it through a hose.

diving board, a board projecting horizontally over a swimming pool, lake, etc. in such a way that by jumping on the end of it a diver can propel himself farther into the air before plunging into the water.

diving suit, a heavy, waterproof garment covering the body, worn by divers working under water: it has a detachable helmet into which air is pumped through a hose.

DIVING SUIT

divining rod, a forked branch or stick allegedly useful in discovering water, minerals, etc. hidden underground.

di·vin·i·ty (də-vin′ə-ti), *n.* [*pl.* DIVINITIES (-tiz)], [ME. & OFr. *divinite;* L. *divinitas* < *divinus*, divine], 1. the quality or condition of being divine. 2. a divine being; a god; deity. 3. a divine power or quality; supreme virtue or excellence. 4. the study of religion; theology. 5. a soft, creamy kind of candy. **the Divinity,** God; the Lord.

div·i·nize (div′ə-nīz′), *v.t.* [DIVINIZED (-nīzd′), DIVINIZING], to make or regard as divine; deify.

di·vis·i·bil·i·ty (də-viz′ə-bil′ə-ti), *n.* the quality of being divisible.

di·vis·i·ble (də-viz′ə-b'l), *adj.* [L. *divisibilis*], 1. that can be divided; dividable. 2. in *mathematics*, that can be divided without leaving a remainder.

di·vi·sion (də-vizh′ən), *n.* [ME.; OFr.; L. *divisio* < *divisus*, pp. of *dividere*], 1. a dividing or being divided; separation. 2. a sharing or apportioning; distribution. 3. a difference of opinion; disagreement. 4. a separation into groups in voting. 5. anything that divides; partition; boundary. 6. anything partitioned off or separated; department; compartment; section; segment. 7. in *biology*, a group of organisms constituting part of a larger group. 8. in *mathematics*, the process of finding how many times a number (the *divisor*) is contained in another number (the *dividend*): the number of times constitutes the *quotient*. 9. in *military science*, a section of an army corps, consisting generally of three regiments and auxiliary troops, under the command of a major general. 10. in *naval science*, a group of several ships, usually four, under a single commander. Abbreviated **div.** —*SYN.* see **part.**

di·vi·sion·al (də-vizh′ən'l), *adj.* of or constituting a division.

division sign (or **mark**), the symbol (÷), indicating that the preceding number is to be divided by the following number. Example: 8 ÷ 4 = 2.

di·vi·sive (də-vī′siv), *adj.* [< L. *divisus*; + *-ive*], 1. causing or showing division. 2. causing disagreement or dissension.

di·vi·sor (də-vī′zẽr), *n.* [L.], in *mathematics*, 1. the number or quantity by which the dividend is divided to produce the quotient. 2. a number or quantity by which another can be divided without leaving a remainder; factor. Abbreviated **div.**

di·vorce (də-vôrs′, də-vōrs′), *n.* [ME. *divors*; OFr. *divorce*; L. *divortium* < *diversus*, pp. of *divertere*, earlier *divortere*, to turn or go different ways; see DIVERS], 1. legal and formal dissolution of a marriage. 2. complete separation; disunion: as, a *divorce* of municipal and state functions. *v.t.* [DIVORCED (-vôrst′, -vōrst′), DIVORCING], 1. to dissolve legally a marriage between; separate (one of a married couple) from the other by divorce. 2. to rid oneself of (one's husband or wife) by divorce. 3. to separate; disunite. *v.i.* to get a divorce.

di·vor·cé (də-vôr′sā′, də-vōr′sā′), *n.* [Fr.], a divorced man.

di·vor·cée (də-vôr′sā′, də-vōr′sā′), *n.* [Fr.], a divorced woman.

di·vor·cee (də-vôr′sē′, də-vōr′sē′), *n.* a divorced person.

di·vorce·ment (də-vôrs′mənt, də-vōrs′mənt), *n.* divorce; a divorcing or being divorced.

div·ot (div′ət), *n.* [Scot. dial.; ? re-formed < MLG. *dövicke*, a plug, or < ON.; prob. IE. base **dheubh-*, **dhub-*, a plug, lump; see DOWEL], 1. [Scot.], a thin slice of turf used for roofing, burning, etc. 2. in *golf*, a lump of turf dislodged by a player's club in making a stroke.

di·vul·gate (də-vul′gāt), *v.t.* [DIVULGATED (-id), DIVULGATING], [< L. *divulgatus*, pp. of *divulgare*], to divulge.

di·vulge (də-vulj′), *v.t.* [DIVULGED (-vuljd′), DIVULGING], [L. *divulgare*; *di-*, *dis-*, apart + *vulgare*, to make public < *vulgus*, the common people], to make known; make public; disclose; reveal. —*SYN.* see **reveal.**

di·vulge·ment (də-vulj′mənt), *n.* [Rare], a divulging or being divulged.

di·vul·gence (də-vul′jəns), *n.* a divulging; revealing; disclosure.

di·vul·sion (də-vul′shən), *n.* [via. Fr. < L. *divulsionem*], a tearing or being torn apart; violent rending or separation.

div·vy (div′i), *v.t.* & *v.i.* [DIVVIED (-id), DIVVYING], [clipped form of *divide*], [Slang], to share (often with *up*). *n.* [*pl.* DIVVIES (-iz)], [Slang], a share; portion.

di·wan (di-wän′, di-wôn′), *n.* a dewan.

Dix·ie (dik′si), *n.* [? < *dixie*, popular name for a ten-dollar bank note issued in Louisiana prior to the Civil War: so called from the large *dix* (ten) printed on one side], 1. the Southern States of the United States, collectively. 2. a song celebrating the South, composed in 1859 by D. D. Emmett: it became popular in the Confederacy during the Civil War.

Dix·ie·land (dik′si-land′), *adj.* in, of, or like the style of jazz associated with New Orleans, characterized by a fast, ragtime tempo.

Dixie Land, Dixie.

dix·it (dik′sit), *n.* [L., 3d pers. sing., perf. indic., of *dicere*; see DICTATE], a statement made without confirmation; dogmatic assertion: also **ipse dixit.**

Di·yar·be·kir (dē-yär′be-kir′), *n.* a city in southeastern Turkey: pop., 81,000: also **Diarbekr.**

diz·en (diz′'n, dī′z'n), *v.t.* [MD. *disen*, to put flax on a distaff < LG. *dise*, bunch of flax; akin to *dis-*, flax, in AS. *distæf*; see DISTAFF], 1. originally, to put flax on a distaff. 2. to dress up in finery; deck out; bedizen.

diz·zi·ly (diz′'l-i), *adv.* in a dizzy or dizzying manner.

diz·zi·ness (diz′i-nis), *n.* the state or sensation of being dizzy; vertigo.

diz·zy (diz′i), *adj.* [DIZZIER (-i-ẽr), DIZZIEST (-i-ist)], [ME. *disie*, *desie*; AS. *dysig*, foolish; akin to MLG. *dūsich*, insensitive, giddy, Eng. *doze*; IE. base **dhwes-* (< **dhewes-*) in the sense "to eddy, whirl, vacillate"; cf. DUSK], 1. feeling giddy or unsteady. 2. causing or likely to cause dizziness: as, *dizzy* heights. 3. confused; bewildered. 4. [Colloq.], silly; foolish. *v.t.* [DIZZIED (-id), DIZZYING], to make dizzy.

Dja·kar·ta (jä-kär′tä), *n.* Jakarta, the capital of Indonesia, in Java.

djeb·el (jeb′əl), *n.* [Fr.; Ar. *jebel*], a hill: often used in Arabic place names.

Djeb·el Druze (jeb′əl drōōz′), a territory of southern Syria: area, 2,400 sq. mi.; pop., 90,000.

Dji·bou·ti (ji-bōō′ti; Fr. jē′bōō′tē′), *n.* the capital of French Somaliland, on the Gulf of Aden: pop., 41,000: also spelled **Jibuti.**

DJIBOUTI

Djok·ja·kar·ta (jôk′yä-kär′tä), *n.* Jokjakarta, a city in Java.

dk., 1. deck. 2. dock.

dkg., decagram; decagrams.

dkl., decaliter.

dkm., decameter.

D/L, demand loan.

dl., deciliter; deciliters.

D. Lit., *Doctor Literarum*, [L.], Doctor of Literature.

D. Litt., *Doctor Litterarum*, [L.], Doctor of Letters.

dlr., dealer.

D.L.S., Doctor of Library Science.

dlvy., delivery.

Dm., Deutschemark.

dm., decimeter; decimeters.

D. Mus., Doctor of Music.

DNA, [< *d*eoxyribo*n*ucleic *a*cid], a nucleic acid within the chromatin of a living cell, which contains the genetic code and transmits the hereditary pattern.

D.N.B., Dictionary of National Biography (British).

Dne·pr (nē′pẽr; Russ. dnye′p'r), *n.* a river in western U.S.S.R., flowing into the Black Sea: length, 1,400 mi.

Dne·pro·pe·trovsk (dnye′prô-pye-trôfsk′), *n.* an industrial city in the Ukrainian S.S.R., on the Dnepr: pop., 658,000: formerly called *Ekaterinoslav*.

Dnes·tr (nēs′tẽr; Russ. dnye′st'r), *n.* a river in the southwestern U.S.S.R., flowing into the Black Sea: length, 800 mi.: Romanian name, *Nistru*.

Dnie·per (nē′pẽr), *n.* the Dnepr.

Dnies·ter (nēs′tẽr), *n.* the Dnestr.

do (dōō), *v.t.* [DID (did), DONE (dun), DOING], [ME. *doon*, *don*; AS. *don*; akin to G. *tun* (OHG. *tuon*), OLG. *don*; IE. base **dhē-*, to put, set, place, as also in Sans. *dadhāmi*, Gr. *tithēmi*, I place, put, L. *-dere* in *condere*, to set down, ground, establish], 1. to perform (an action, etc.); carry out; fulfill: as, *do* a deed, *do* one's duty. 2. to finish; bring to completion: used in the perfect tenses, as, dinner has been *done* for an hour. 3. to cause; bring about: as, it *does* no harm, who *did* this to you? 4. to exert (efforts, etc.): as, *do* your best. 5. to deal with as is required; attend to: as, *do* the ironing, *do* one's nails. 6. to work at; have as one's work or occupation. 7. to work out; solve: as, he *did* the problem. 8. to produce (a play, etc.): as, we *did Hamlet*. 9. to play the role of: as, I *did* Polonius. 10. to cover (distance): as, he *does* a mile in record time. 11. to visit as a sightseer; tour: as, they *did* England in two months. 12. to translate: as, he *did* Horace into English. 13. to give; render: as, he *did* honor to the great dead. 14. to suit; be convenient to: as, this will *do* me very well. 15. [Colloq.], to cheat; swindle: as, you've been *done*. 16. [Colloq.], to serve (a jail term). *v.i.* 1. to behave: as, he *does* well when treated well. 2. to be active; work: as, *do*, don't talk. 3. to finish: used in the perfect tenses, as, have *done* with dreaming. 4. to get along; fare: as, mother and child are *doing* well. 5. to be adequate or suitable; serve the purpose: as, the black dress will *do*. Auxiliary uses of *do:* 1. to give emphasis: as, please *do* stay. 2. to ask a question: as, *did* you write? 3. to emphasize negation or prohibition: as, *don't* go. 4. to serve as a substitute verb: as, love me as I *do* (love) you. 5. to form inverted constructions after some adverbs: as, little *did* he realize. *n.* [British Colloq.], 1. a hoax; swindle. 2. a party.

do away with, 1. to get rid of. 2. to destroy; kill.

do by, to act toward or for; behave in respect to or in behalf of.

do for, [Colloq.], to ruin; destroy.

do in, [Slang], to kill.

do oneself well, [after G. *sich gütlich tun*], to achieve success for oneself.

do over, [Colloq.], to redecorate.

do to death, [Archaic], to kill.

do up, [Colloq.], 1. to clean and prepare (laundry, etc.). 2. to wrap up; tie up. 3. to arrange or wear (the hair) so that it is off the neck and shoulders. 4. to tire out; exhaust.

do with, to make use of; find helpful.

do without, to get along without; dispense with.

have to do with, to have relation with or to.

make do, to manage with what is available.

do (dō), *n.* [It. (? < *dominus*, first word of a Latin hymn); used instead of earlier *ut;* see GAMUT], in *music*, a syllable representing the first or last tone of the diatonic scale: see **solfeggio.**

do., ditto.

D/O, d.o., delivery order.

D.O., 1. District Office. 2. Doctor of Optometry. 3. Doctor of Osteopathy.

do·a·ble (do͞o'ə-b'l), *adj.* that can be done.

do-all (do͞o'ôl'), *n.* a person who does all kinds of things or who manages all aspects of some business or affair.

doat (dōt), *v.i.* to dote.

doat·y (dō'ti), *adj.* doty.

dob·ber (dob'ẽr), *n.* [? < D. *dobber*], the float on a fisherman's line.

dob·bin (dob'in), *n.* [rhyme alteration < *Robin*], a horse, especially a plodding, patient horse.

dob·by weave (dob'i), [< *Dobbie*, dim. of *Dob*, rhymed nickname for *Robin, Robert*], a weave with small, simple patterns.

Do·ber·man pin·scher (dō'bẽr-mən pin'shẽr), [G.; *Dobermann*, name of the first breeder + *pinscher*, terrier < *Pinzgau*, area in northern Austria known for breeding of dogs and horses; cf. G. *Pinzgauer*, variety of horse orig. bred in Pinzgau], a breed of terrier with short, smooth, dark hair and tan markings.

do·bla (dō'blä), *n.* [Sp. < *doble*, double < L. *duplus;* see DOUBLE], an obsolete gold coin of Spain.

do·bra (dō'brə), *n.* [Port. < *dobre*, double < L. *duplus;* (see DOUBLE): so named because double the value of another coin, e.g., the *peça*], any of several obsolete gold coins of Portugal.

Do·bru·ja, Do·bru·dja (dō'broo-jə), *n.* a district of southeastern Romania, along the Black Sea.

Dob·son, Austin (dob's'n), (*Henry Austin Dobson*), 1840–1921; English poet, critic, and biographer.

dob·son fly (dob's'n), [fisherman's term < the name *Dobson*], a large insect with grayish-white wings: the larva (called *hellgrammite*) is used as fishing bait.

do·by (dō'bi), *n.* [*pl.* DOBIES (-biz)] & *adj.* [Colloq.], adobe.

doc (dok), *n.* [Slang], doctor: often used as a general term of address like *Mac, Bud, Jack*, etc.

doc., document.

do·cent (dō's'nt; G. dō-tsent'), *n.* [G., teacher, academic lecturer < L. *docens*, ppr. of *docere*, to teach], in some American universities, a teacher or lecturer not on the regular faculty.

doc·ile (dos''l, dos'il), *adj.* [Fr.; L. *docilis*, easily taught < *docere*, to teach], 1. easy to teach; teachable. 2. easy to discipline; tractable. —*SYN.* see **obedient.**

do·cil·i·ty (dō-sil'ə-ti, do-sil'ə-ti), *n.* [Fr. *docilité;* L. *docilitas*], the quality of being docile.

dock (dok), *n.* [orig., mud channel made by a vessel's bottom at low tide; hence, fenced-in channel for docking; MD. *docke*, runnel, channel; It. *doccia* or ML. *ductia*, channel < L. *ductio*, a leading away; see DUCT, DOUCHE], 1. a large excavated basin equipped with floodgates, used for receiving ships between voyages. 2. a landing pier; wharf. 3. the area of water between two docks. 4. a platform at which trucks or freight cars are loaded and unloaded. Abbreviated **dk.** *v.t.* to bring or pilot (a ship) to a dock. *v.i.* to come into a dock.

dock (dok), *n.* [< Fl. *docke, dok*, hutch, pen, cage], the place where the accused stands or sits in court.

dock (dok), *n.* [ME. *docke, dokke;* AS. *docce;* akin to MHG. *tocke*, bundle, tuft, cluster; IE. **dhŭk, dheuk*, prob. in the sense "to roll together, make thick"], any of several coarse weeds of the buckwheat family, with small, green flowers and large leaves.

dock (dok), *n.* [ME. *doc, dok;* ON. *dockr*, a short, stumpy tail < same base as *dock* (the weed)], 1. the solid part of an animal's tail, excluding the hair. 2. an animal's bobbed tail. *v.t.* [ME. *docken* < the *n.*], 1. to cut off the end of (a tail, etc.); clip or bob. 2. to shorten the tail of by cutting. 3. to deduct a part from (wages, etc.). 4. to deduct a part from the wages of.

dock·age (dok'ij), *n.* [*dock* (wharf) + *-age*], 1. the fee charged for the use of a dock. 2. docking accommodations. 3. the docking of ships.

dock·age (dok'ij), *n.* [*dock* (to cut off) + *-age*], a cutting off or down; curtailment; deduction.

dock·er (dok'ẽr), *n.* a dock worker; longshoreman.

dock·er (dok'ẽr), *n.* [*dock* (to cut off) + *-er*], a person or thing that docks.

dock·et (dok'it), *n.* [merging of *cocket*, a seal, anything sealed or approved & obs. *doggette*, abstract of approved papers, register, custom warrant < It. *doghetta*, small heraldic bend, dim. of *doga*, barrel stave], 1. a summary, abridged statement, or list of legal decisions. 2. a list of cases to be tried by a law court. 3. any list or summary of things to be done; agenda. 4. a label listing the contents of a package, directions, etc. *v.t.* 1. to enter in a docket. 2. to put a docket on; label; ticket.

dock·mack·ie (dok'mak-i), *n.* [? via D. < Am. Ind. (Lenape) *dogekumak*], a shrub of the honeysuckle family, with maplelike leaves, small clusters of yellow-white flowers, and purple or black berries.

dock·yard (dok'yärd'), *n.* a place with docks, machinery, and supplies for repairing or building ships.

doc·tor (dok'tẽr), *n.* [ME. *doctour, doctur*, doctor (of medicine, law, or divinity); OFr. *doctour;* L. *doctor*, teacher < pp. of *docere*, to teach], 1. a person on whom a university or college has conferred the doctorate: a Doctor of Medicine, Dentistry, Philosophy, Divinity, etc. is properly addressed as *Doctor:* abbreviated **Dr.** (as a title), **D.** (as in *Ph.D., D.Litt.*, etc.). 2. a physician or surgeon (M.D.). 3. a person licensed to practice any of the healing arts, as an osteopath, chiropractor, etc. 4. a witch doctor or medicine man. 5. a makeshift device or apparatus for making emergency repairs. 6. a bright-colored artificial fly used in angling. 7. [Rare], a teacher. 8. [Archaic], a learned man, especially one of the Schoolmen of the Middle Ages. *v.t.* [Colloq.], 1. to try to heal; apply medicine to. 2. to repair; mend. 3. to tamper with: as, he *doctored* the evidence. *v.i.* [Colloq.], 1. to practice medicine. 2. to be under a doctor's care; take treatments, medicine, etc.

doc·tor·al (dok'tẽr-əl), *adj.* 1. of a doctor or doctorate: as, a *doctoral* dissertation. 2. having a doctorate.

doc·tor·ate (dok'tẽr-it), *n.* [ML. *doctoratus*], the degree or status of doctor conferred by a university.

doc·tri·naire (dok'tri-nâr'), *n.* [Fr. < *doctrine;* see DOCTRINE: coined (c. 1815) by extremists to apply to opponents holding the "doctrine" of compromise; now applied to extremists themselves], a person who tries to apply theories regardless of practical problems which affect them; visionary. *adj.* impractical; visionary. —*SYN.* see **dictatorial.**

doc·tri·nal (dok'tri-nəl), *adj.* [LL. *doctrinalis*], of, based on, or containing doctrine.

doc·trine (dok'trin), *n.* [ME.; L. *doctrina* < *doctor;* see DOCTOR], 1. something taught; teachings. 2. something taught as the principles or creed of a religion, political party, etc.; tenet or tenets; belief; dogma.

SYN.—**doctrine** refers to a theory based on carefully worked out principles and taught or advocated by its adherents (scientific or social *doctrines*); **dogma** refers to a belief or opinion that is handed down by authority as true and indisputable, and usually connotes arbitrariness, arrogance, etc. (religious *dogma*); **tenet** emphasizes the maintenance or defense, rather than the teaching, of a theory or principle (the *tenets* of a political party); **precept** refers to an injunction or dogma intended as a rule of action or conduct (to teach by example rather than by *precept*).

doc·u·ment (dok'yoo-mənt; *for v.*, dok'yoo-ment'), *n.* [Fr.; L. *documentum*, lesson, example, proof < *docere*, to teach], 1. anything printed, written, etc., relied upon to record or prove something: abbreviated **doc.** 2. anything serving as proof. *v.t.* 1. to provide with a document or documents. 2. to provide (a book, pamphlet, etc.) with references as proof or support of things said. 3. to prove or support, as by reference to documents.

doc·u·men·tal (dok'yoo-men't'l), *adj.* of a document or documents.

doc·u·men·ta·ry (dok'yoo-men'tə-ri), *adj.* 1. consisting of, supported by, contained in, or serving as a document or documents. 2. designating or of a motion picture that records news events or shows social conditions without fictionalization. *n.* [*pl.* DOCUMENTARIES (-riz)], a documentary motion picture.

doc·u·men·ta·tion (dok'yoo-men-tā'shən), *n.* 1. the supplying of documents or supporting references; use of documentary evidence. 2. the documents or references thus supplied.

dod·der (dod'ẽr), *v.i.* [var. of dial. *dudder, dither;* akin to or < AS. *dyderian*, to confuse, delude; akin to Norw. *dudra*, to tremble, quake, MLG. *dotten, dutten*, to be bewildered, be crazy; IE. base **dheudh-*, to whirl around confusedly, shake, be senseless; cf. DIDDLE], 1. to shake or tremble as from old age. 2. to totter.

dod·der (dod'ẽr), *n.* [ME. *doder;* Late AS. *dodder* < same base as *dodder, v.;* cf. dial. *dodder*, quaking-grass & G. *dotter* (AS. *dydrin*), egg yolk], any of several parasitic plants lacking leaves, roots, and chlorophyll: the threadlike stem is equipped with special suckers for drawing nourishment from the host.

dod·dered (dod'ẽrd), *adj.* [Dryden's form (influenced by *dodder*) of older *doddard, dotard*, an old, decaying oak; see DOTARD], having lost its branches or top because of age, decay, etc.: said of a tree.

dod·der·ing (dod'ẽr-iŋ), *adj.* [ppr. of *dodder*], trembling, shaky, or tottering, as from old age.

do·dec·a- (dō'dek-ə), [< Gr. *dōdeka*, twelve; *dō-*, two < **dwo-* < IE. **dwō-* (see TWO) + Gr. *deka*, ten (see DECA-)], a prefix meaning *twelve*, as in *dodecagon:* also, before a vowel, **dodec-**.

do·de·ca·gon (dō-dek'ə-gon', dō-dek'ə-gən), *n.* [Gr.

dōdekagōnon; see DODECA- & -GON], a plane figure with twelve angles and twelve sides.

do·dec·a·he·dral (dō'dek-ə-hē'drəl), *adj.* of, or having the form of, a dodecahedron.

do·dec·a·he·dron (dō'dek-ə-hē'drən), *n.* [*pl.* DODECAHEDRONS (-drənz), DODECAHEDRA (-drə)], [Gr. *dōdekaedron;* see DODECA- & -HEDRON], a solid figure with twelve plane faces.

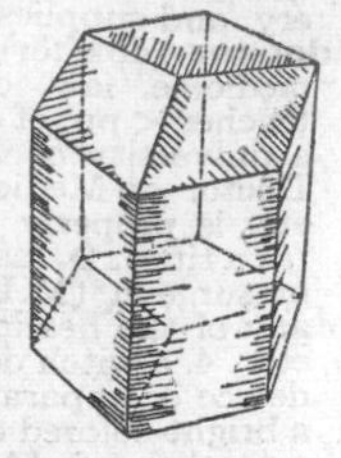
DODECAHEDRON

Do·dec·a·nese (dō-dek'ə-nēs', dō'-dek-ə-nēs'), *n.* a group of Greek islands in the Aegean, off southwestern Turkey: area, 974 sq. mi.; pop., 121,000.

dodge (doj), *v.i.* [DODGED (dojd), DODGING], [late 16th c.; phonetic form (cf. SLEDGE beside SLED) suggests Scot. *dod,* to jog; for the base, see DODDER]. 1. to move or twist quickly aside; shift suddenly, as to avoid a blow. 2. to use tricks, deceits, or evasions; be shifty. *v.t.* 1. to avoid (a blow, etc.) by moving or shifting quickly aside. 2. to evade by cunning, trickery, cleverness, etc. *n.* 1. a dodging. 2. a trick used in cheating or evading. 3. a clever device, plan, etc.

dodg·er (doj'ẽr), *n.* 1. a person who dodges. 2. a tricky, dishonest person; shifty rascal. 3. a bread or cake made of corn meal. 4. a small handbill.

Dodg·son, Charles Lut·widge (lut'wij doj's'n), see **Carroll, Lewis.**

do·do (dō'dō), *n.* [*pl.* DODOS, DODOES (-dōz)], [Port. *doudo,* lit., foolish, stupid], a large bird, now extinct, that had a hooked bill, short neck and legs, and rudimentary wings useless for flying: formerly found on Mauritius.

DODO (2 ft. high)

Do·do·nae·an, Do·do·ne·an (dō'də-nē'ən), *adj.* [< Gr. *Dōdōnē,* Dodona], 1. of the ancient Greek town of Dodona in Epirus. 2. of the famous oracle of Zeus there, in a grove of oaks.

Doe (dō), [same word as *doe;* John Doe and Richard Roe were orig. fictitious plaintiff and defendant in a form of ejection action], a name (*John Doe, Jane Doe*) used in law courts, legal papers, etc. to refer to any person whose name is unknown.

doe (dō), *n.* [*pl.* DOES (dōz), DOE; see PLURAL, II, D, 1], [ME. *doo, do;* AS. *da* < Corn. *da* (or Cymric); ult. < IE. **domā, *demā, *dəmə,* to make domestic, tame (< **dem-,* to build, house), as in LL. *dama,* fallow deer, buck, L. *domare,* to tame (see TAME); base apparently first used of domesticated horned animals], the female of the deer, or of the antelope, rabbit, or almost any other animal the male of which is called a buck.

do·er (do͞o'ẽr), *n.* 1. a person who does something or acts in a specified manner: as, a *doer* of good. 2. a person who gets things done; active or energetic person.

does (duz), the third person singular, present indicative, of **do.**

doe·skin (dō'skin'), *n.* 1. the skin of a female deer. 2. leather made from this. 3. a fine, soft, smooth woolen cloth used for suits, upholstery, etc.

does·n't (duz''nt), does not.

do·est (do͞o'ist), archaic second person singular, present indicative, of **do:** used with *thou,* and in auxiliary uses shortened to **dost.**

do·eth (do͞o'ith), archaic third person singular, present indicative of **do:** in auxiliary uses shortened to **doth.**

doff (dof, dôf), *v.t.* [< *do + off*], 1. to take off (clothes, etc.). 2. to remove or lift (one's hat), as in greeting. 3 to put aside; get rid of; give up.

dog (dôg), *n.* [*pl.* DOGS (dôgz), DOG; see PLURAL, II, D, 1], [ME. *dog, dogge;* generalized in sense < late, rare AS. *docga, dogga* (usual AS. *hund;* see HOUND), dog of native breed (whence Fr. *dogue,* G. *dogge,* Eng. *dog,* mastiff); akin to or borrowed in ON. *dugga,* headstrong, intractable person; the form *dog* instead of *dodge* (< AS. *docga*) suggests ON. transmission; IE. base **dheugh-,* to be strong, be of use, avail; cf. DOUGHTY], 1. any of a large and varied group of domesticated animals related to the fox, wolf, and jackal. 2. the male of any of these animals. 3. a low, contemptible fellow. 4. a prairie dog, dogfish, or other animal thought of as resembling a dog. 5. [< orig. shape; cf. Fr. *chenet*], an andiron; firedog. 6. [Colloq.], a boy or man: as, lucky *dog,* gay *dog.* 7. *pl.* [Slang], feet. 8. [D-], in *astronomy,* either of two constellations near Orion, separated from each other by the Milky Way; the Great Dog (*Canis Major*) or the Little Dog (*Canis Minor*). 9. in *mechanics,* any of several devices for holding or grappling. 10. in *meteorology,* a parhelion; sundog, seadog, or fog-dog. *v.t.* [DOGGED (dôgd), DOGGING], 1. to follow, hunt, or track down like a dog. 2. to hold down with a mechanical dog. *adv.* very; completely: used in combination, as, *dog*-tired.

a dog's age, [Colloq.], a long time.
a dog's life, a wretched existence.
dog eat dog, ruthless and savage competition.
dog in the manger, a person who keeps others from using something which he has but cannot or will not use: from the fable of the dog that kept the ox from eating the hay.
every dog has his day, something good or lucky happens to everyone at one time or another.
go to the dogs, [Colloq.], to deteriorate; degenerate.
let sleeping dogs lie, to let well enough alone; not disturb things as they are for fear of something worse.
put on the dog, [Slang], to make a show of being very elegant, wealthy, etc.
teach an old dog new tricks, to induce a person of settled habits to adopt new methods or ideas.

dog ape, a baboon.

dog·bane (dôg'bān'), *n.* [so named because said to be poisonous to dogs], a perennial plant with clusters of small, pink or white flowers and a milky juice used in medicine.

dog·ber·ry (dôg'ber'i, dôg'bẽr-i), *n.* [*pl.* DOGBERRIES (-iz)], 1. the berry or fruit of the European dogwood, the chokeberry, the yellow clintonia, or the mountain ash. 2. in Great Britain, the fruit of certain cranberries. 3. any of these plants. 4. [D-], a stupid, egotistical constable in Shakespeare's *Much Ado About Nothing* (1600).

dog biscuit, 1. a hard biscuit containing ground bones, meat, etc., for feeding dogs. 2. [Slang], an army field-ration biscuit.

dog·cart (dôg'kärt'), *n.* 1. a small, light cart drawn by dogs. 2. a small, light, open carriage, usually with two wheels, having two seats arranged back to back: so called because originally it had a box under the seat for a sportsman's dogs.

dog days, the hot, uncomfortable days in July and August: so called because during that period the Dog Star rises and sets with the sun.

doge (dōj), *n.* [It. < L. *dux,* leader < *ducere,* to lead], the chief magistrate of either of the former republics of Venice and Genoa.

dog-ear (dôg'êr'), *n.* a turned-down corner of the leaf of a book. *v.t.* to turn down the corner or corners of (a leaf or leaves in a book).

dog·face (dôg'fās'), *n.* [Slang], an enlisted man in the army, especially an infantryman.

dog fennel, the mayweed.

dog·fight (dôg'fīt'), *n.* a rough, violent fight between, or as between, dogs; specifically, in *military usage,* combat between fighter planes or tanks at close quarters.

dog·fish (dôg'fish'), *n.* [*pl.* DOGFISH, DOGFISHES (-iz); see FISH], 1. any of various small, voracious sharks. 2. any of several other fishes, as the bowfin, or mudfish.

dog fox, a male fox.

dog·ged (dôg'id), *adj.* [see DOG], not giving in readily; persistent; stubborn. —*SYN.* see **stubborn.**

dog·ger (dôg'ẽr), *n.* [ME. *doggere* (whence ODan. *dogge,* D. *doggerboat,* etc.) < *dog;* cf. CAT, CATBOAT], a two-masted boat with a broad beam, used by fishermen in the North Sea.

Dog·ger Bank (dôg'ẽr, dog'ẽr), a shallow part of the North Sea, off the northern English coast: depth, 36–120 ft.: a fishing area.

dog·ger·el (dôg'ẽr-əl, dog'ẽr-əl), *n.* [ME. *dogerel* (Chaucer); prob. < It. *doga,* barrel stave, but influenced by *dog* as in *dog Latin;* cf. G. *knüttelvers,* lit., cudgel verse, Pr. *bastonnet,* little stick, type of verse], trivial, inartistic, weakly constructed verse, usually of a burlesque or comic sort; jingle. *adj.* designating or of such verse. Also **doggrel.**

dog·ger·y (dôg'ẽr-i), *n.* [*pl.* DOGGERIES (-iz)], 1. mean or surly behavior like that of a snappish dog. 2. dogs collectively; hence, 3. the rabble; riffraff.

dog·gish (dôg'ish), *adj.* 1. of or like a dog. 2. snarling; snapping. 3. [Colloq.], stylish and showy.

dog-gone (dôg'gôn'), *interj.* [? < *dog* (pox) *on it!,* an imprecation (cf. Scot. *dagone, dagont*), or ? euphemistic remodeling of *God damn*], damn! darn!: an exclamation used variously to express anger, irritation, surprise, pleasure, etc. *v.t.* [DOG-GONED (-gônd'), DOG-GONING], [Colloq.], to damn: usually in the past participle, as, I'll be *dog-goned* if I'll go.

dog·grel (dôg'rəl, dog'rəl), *n. & adj.* doggerel.

dog·gy (dôg'i), *n.* [*pl.* DOGGIES (-iz)], a little dog: often used as a pet name for any dog: also spelled **doggie.** *adj.* [DOGGIER (-i-ẽr), DOGGIEST (-i-ist)], 1. of or like a dog. 2. [Colloq.], stylish and showy.

dog·house (dôg'hous'), *n.* a dog's shelter; kennel.
in the doghouse, [Slang], in disfavor.

do·gie (dō'gi), *n.* [Texas dial.; also earlier *doughgy;* ? < Southwest dial. *dough,* cereal grain still soft and milky before maturity], in the western United States, a stray or motherless calf: also spelled **dogy.**

dog Latin, 1. incorrect or ungrammatical Latin. 2. a jargon made up in imitation of Latin.

dog-leg·ged (dôg′leg′id, dôg′legd′), *adj.* bent like the hind leg of a dog.
dog·ma (dôg′mə, dog′mə), *n.* [*pl.* DOGMAS (-məz), DOGMATA (-mə-tə)], [L.; Gr. *dogma*, that which one thinks true, opinion, decree < *dokein*, to think, believe], 1. a doctrine; tenet; belief. 2. doctrines, tenets, or beliefs, collectively. 3. a positive, arrogant assertion of opinion. 4. in *theology*, a doctrine or body of doctrines formally and authoritatively affirmed. —*SYN.* see **doctrine.**
dog·mat·ic (dôg-mat′ik, dog-mat′ik), *adj.* [L. *dogmaticus;* Gr. *dogmatikos*], 1. of or like dogma. 2. asserted a priori or without proof. 3. stating opinion in a positive or arrogant manner. —*SYN.* see **dictatorial.**
dog·mat·i·cal (dôg-mat′i-k′l, dog-mat′i-k′l), *adj.* dogmatic.
dog·mat·ics (dôg-mat′iks, dog-mat′iks), *n.pl.* [construed as sing.], the study of religious dogmas, especially those of Christianity.
dog·ma·tism (dôg′mə-tiz′m, dog′mə-tiz′m), *n.* [Fr. *dogmatisme;* ML. *dogmatismus* < Gr. *dogmatizein*, to lay down a decree; see DOGMA], dogmatic assertion of opinion, usually without reference to evidence.
dog·ma·tist (dôg′mə-tist, dog′mə-tist), *n.* a person who utters dogmas or is dogmatic.
dog·ma·tize (dôg′mə-tīz′, dog′mə-tīz′), *v.i.* [DOGMATIZED (-tīzd′), DOGMATIZING], [Fr. *dogmatiser;* ML. *dogmatizare;* Gr. *dogmatizein;* see DOGMA], to speak or write dogmatically. *v.t.* to formulate or express as dogma.
dog rose, [transl. of L. *rosa canina*], a European wild rose with single, pink flowers and hooked thorns.
dog salmon, a large salmon of the Pacific coast.
dog's-ear (dôgz′êr′), *n.* & *v.t.* dog-ear.
dog sled (or **sledge**), a sled (or sledge) drawn by dogs.
dog's letter, [transl. of L. *litera canina*], the letter R, especially when trilled: so called because of its supposed resemblance to a dog's growl.
dog's-tail (dôgz′tāl′), *n.* a coarse kind of grass; yard grass; wire grass: also **dog's-tail grass.**
Dog Star, 1. Sirius, the brightest star in the constellation Canis Major. 2. Procyon, a bright star in the constellation Canis Minor.
dog's-tongue (dôgz′tuŋ′), *n.* hound's-tongue.
dog's-tooth violet (dôgz′to͞oth′), dogtooth violet.
dog tag, 1. an identification tag or license tag for a dog. 2. [Slang], a military identification tag worn about the neck.
dog-tired (dôg′tīrd′), *adj.* [Colloq.], very tired.
dog·tooth (dôg′to͞oth′), *n.* [*pl.* DOGTEETH (-tēth′)], 1. a canine tooth; eyetooth: also **dog tooth.** 2. an ornamental molding in some medieval buildings, consisting of a series of toothlike projections.
dogtooth violet, 1. an American plant of the lily family, with two mottled leaves and either a yellow or a white flower: it is not related to the violet family: also called *adder's-tongue.* 2. a related similar European plant with a purple flower. Also **dog's-tooth violet.**
dog·trot (dôg′trot′), *n.* a slow, easy trot, like a dog's.
dog·vane (dôg′vān′), *n.* a small vane of bunting, etc. placed on the weather gunwale of a ship to indicate the direction of the wind.
dog·watch (dôg′wôch′, dôg′wäch′), *n.* in *nautical usage*, either of two duty periods (from 4 to 6 P.M. and from 6 to 8 P.M.) half the length of the normal period.
dog·wood (dôg′wood′), *n.* [shortened < *dogberry wood, dogberry tree*, etc.], 1. a tree with pink or white flowers early in the spring and clusters of small red berries in the fall. 2. any tree or shrub of the same family. 3. the hard, close-grained wood of any of these trees.
do·gy (dō′gi), *n.* [*pl.* DOGIES (-giz)], a dogie.
doiled (doild), *adj.* [var. of *dold*, orig. pp. of ME. *dollen*, to make dull; cf. AS. *dol*, stupid], [Scot. & British Dial.], demented, stupid, foolish, etc.
doi·ly (doi′li), *n.* [*pl.* DOILIES (-liz)], [after a 17th-c. London draper named *Doily* or *Doyley*], a small napkin or mat of linen, paper, etc., used as decoration or protection for a tray, table, or other furniture.
do·ings (do͞o′iŋz), *n.pl.* 1. things done; deeds; actions; activities. 2. behavior.
doit (doit), *n.* [D. *duit*], 1. a small, obsolete Dutch coin that was worth about 1/4 cent. 2. anything of trifling value: as, not worth a *doit.*
doit·ed (doi′tid), *adj.* [var. of *doted;* cf. DOTE], [Scot.], foolish, as from old age; senile.
do-it-your·self (do͞o′it-yoor-self′), *n.* the practice of constructing, repairing, redecorating, etc. by oneself instead of hiring another to do it. *adj.* of, used for, or engaged in do-it-yourself.
dol., 1. [*pl.* DOLS.], dollar. 2. in *music*, dolce.
do·lab·ri·form (dō-lab′rə-fôrm′), *adj.* [< L. *dolabra*, pickax (< *dolare*, to chip); + *-form*], shaped like the head of an ax, as certain leaves.
‡**dol·ce** (dôl′che), *adj.* [It., sweet], 1. sweet and soft; hence, 2. in *music*, smooth in performance: abbreviated **dol.** *n.* [*pl.* DOLCI (-chē)], a soft-toned organ stop.
‡**dol·ce far nien·te** (dôl′che fär nyen′te), [It., (it is) sweet doing nothing], pleasant idleness or inactivity.
dol·drums (dol′drəmz), *n.pl.* [? < *dull*, by analogy with *tantrum*], 1. low spirits; dull, gloomy, listless feeling. 2. *a*) equatorial ocean regions noted for dead calms and light fluctuating winds. *b*) the dead calms and light, fluctuating winds characteristic of these regions.
dole (dōl), *n.* [ME. *dole, dale;* AS. *dal*, parallel to *dæl;* see DEAL], 1. a giving out of money or food in charity. 2. that which is thus given out; alms. 3. anything given out sparingly. 4. a form of payment by a government to the unemployed, as in England. 5. [Archaic], a person's destiny or lot. *v.t.* [DOLED (dōld), DOLING], to give sparingly or as a dole (usually with *out*). —*SYN.* see **distribute.**
on the dole, receiving government relief funds.
dole (dōl), *n.* [see DOLEFUL], [Archaic], sorrow; dolor.
dole·ful (dōl′fəl), *adj.* [ME. *deolful; deol, doel*, sorrow, grief < OFr. *doel* < LL. *dolus*, grief, pain < L. *dolere*, to suffer; + *-ful*], sad; sorrowful; mournful; melancholy; dismal. —*SYN.* see **sad.**
dol·er·ite (dol′ẽr-īt′), *n.* [Fr. < Gr. *doleros*, deceptive < *dolos*, deceit: so called from its close resemblance to diorite], 1. a coarse-grained variety of basalt. 2. loosely, diabase or any of various other igneous rocks whose composition cannot be analyzed without microscopic examination.
dole·some (dōl′səm), *adj.* [see -SOME], [Rare], doleful.
dol·i·cho·ce·phal·ic (dol′i-kō′sə-fal′ik), *adj.* [< Gr. *dolichos*, long; + *-cephalic*], having a relatively long skull; having a skull whose width is less than 80 per cent of its length: opposed to *brachycephalic:* see also **cephalic index.**
dol·i·cho·ceph·a·lous (dol′i-kō-sef′ə-ləs), *adj.* dolichocephalic.
dol·i·cho·ceph·a·ly (dol′i-kō-sef′ə-li), *n.* the condition of being dolichocephalic.
doll (dol), *n.* [orig., nickname for *Dorothy*], 1. a children's toy made to resemble a baby, child, or grown person. 2. a pretty but rather stupid or silly girl or woman. 3. a pretty child. 4. [Slang], any girl or young woman. *v.t.* & *v.i.* [Slang], to dress carefully and stylishly or showily (with *up*).
dol·lar (dol′ẽr), *n.* [LG. & Early Mod. D. *daler;* G. *thaler* (now *taler*), contr. < *Joachimsthaler*, coin made (orig. in 1519) at *Joachimstal*, Bohemia < *St. Joachim* (name of the village) + *thal, tal*, valley (see DALE)], 1. the monetary unit of the United States, equal to 100 cents: symbol, $, as, $1.00. 2. the standard monetary unit of Canada and Liberia and of British Guiana and some other British colonies, valued at about 88 cents in 1950. 3. a standard monetary unit of China: in full, *People's Dollar.* 4. the Mexican peso. 5. any of several monetary units used only in trade, as the British Hong Kong dollar, the Straits Settlements dollar, the Levant dollar of Austria, etc. 6. a coin or piece of paper money of the value of a dollar. 7. [Obs.], a Spanish coin (piece of eight) used in American Revolutionary times. Abbreviated **dol., d.**
dollar diplomacy, the policy of using the economic power or influence of a government to promote in other countries the business interests of its private citizens, corporations, etc.
dol·lar·fish (dol′ẽr-fish′), *n.* [*pl.* DOLLARFISH, DOLLARFISHES (-iz); see FISH], any of several salt-water food fishes with short, compressed bodies and smooth scales.
Doll·fuss, Eng·el·bert (eŋ′g′l-bert′ dôl′fo͞os; Eng. dol′fəs), 1892–1934; Austrian statesman; chancellor (1932–1934); assassinated.
doll·y (dol′i), *n.* [*pl.* DOLLIES (-iz)], [< *doll*], 1. a doll: child's term. 2. a stick or board for stirring, used in laundering clothes or washing ore; dasher. 3. a tool used to hold a rivet at one end while a head is hammered out of the other end. 4. any of several kinds of low, flat, wheeled frames for transporting heavy objects, as in a factory. 5. a narrow-gauge locomotive for railroad yard work. 6. in *motion pictures & television*, a low, wheeled platform on which the camera is mounted for moving it about the set. *v.i.* to move a dolly forward (*in*), backward (*out*), etc. in photographing or televising the action.
Dolly Var·den (vär′d′n), [after the character in Dickens' *Barnaby Rudge*], 1. a dress of sheer figured muslin worn over a bright-colored petticoat. 2. a woman's flower-trimmed hat with a large brim, bent down on one side. 3. a kind of red-spotted trout found in streams west of the Rocky Mountains: so named from its coloring.
dol·man (dol′mən), *n.* [*pl.* DOLMANS (-mənz)], [Fr., hussar's jacket; Pol. *doloman* < Turk. *dōlāmān*, long robe], 1. a long Turkish robe. 2. a hussar's showy, gold-braided jacket worn like a cape with the sleeves hanging free. 3. a woman's coat or wrap with dolman sleeves, or with capelike arm pieces instead of sleeves.
dolman sleeve, a kind of sleeve for a woman's coat or dress, tapering from a wide opening at the armhole to a narrow one at the wrist.

dol·men (dol′men), *n.* [Fr.; prob. < Corn. *tolmen*, hole of stone], a prehistoric tomb or monument consisting of a large, flat stone laid across upright stones; cromlech.

DOLMEN

dol·o·mite (dol′ə-mīt′), *n.* [after the Fr. geologist *Dolomieu* (1750–1801)], rock consisting mainly of magnesium carbonate and calcium carbonate; limestone or marble with much magnesium carbonate in it.

Dol·o·mites (dol′ə-mīts′), *n.pl.* that part of the Alps in northeastern Italy (formerly Tyrol): highest peak, Mt. Marmolada, 10,964 ft.: also **Dolomite Alps.**

do·lor (dō′lẽr), *n.* [ME. & OFr. *dolour;* L. *dolor* < *dolere*, to suffer], [Poetic], sorrow; distress; grief.

Do·lor·es (də-lôr′is, də-lō′ris, də-lō′rez), [Sp. < *Maria de los Dolores*, lit., Mary of the sorrows], a feminine name.

‡do·lo·ro·so (dô′lô-rô′sô), *adj. & adv.* [It.], in *music*, with sorrow or plaintive quality.

dol·or·ous (dol′ẽr-əs, dō′lẽr-əs), *adj.* [OFr. *dolerous;* LL. *dolorosus;* see DOLOR], 1. sad; mournful. 2. painful.

do·lour (dō′lẽr), *n.* dolor: British spelling.

dol·phin (dol′fin), *n.* [ME. *dolphyn;* OFr. *daulphin, dalphin;* L. *delphinus;* Gr. *delphinos*, genit. of *delphis;* see DAUPHIN], 1. any of several mammals of the whale family, with a beaklike snout and teeth in the upper jaw. 2. either of two swift marine fishes with colors that brighten and change when the fish is taken out of water. 3. [D-], in *astronomy*, a northern constellation west of Pegasus: also called *Delphinus.* 4. in *nautical usage*, a buoy or spar used in mooring a boat.

DOLPHIN (about 8 ft.)

dolphin striker, a small spar under the bowsprit of a vessel, helping to form a truss which supports the jib boom: also called *martingale.*

dols., dollars.

dolt (dōlt), *n.* [16th c.; ? < *dull*], a stupid, slow-witted person; blockhead.

dolt·ish (dōl′tish), *adj.* [see DOLT], stupid; slow-witted.

Dom (dom), *n.* [Port. < L. *dominus*, a lord, master], 1. a title given to certain Roman Catholic monks, priests, or other church dignitaries. 2. a title of respect formerly given by royal decree to gentlemen of Brazil and Portugal: used with the given name.

-dom (dəm), [ME. & AS. < *dom*, state, condition, power; see DOOM], a noun-forming suffix meaning: 1. *the rank of, position of, domain of, dominion of*, as in *kingdom, earldom.* 2. *the fact of being, state of being*, as in *wisdom, martyrdom.* 3. *a total of all who are*, as in *officialdom.*

Dom., 1. Dominica. 2. Dominican.

dom., 1. domestic. 2. dominion.

do·main (dō-mān′), *n.* [Fr. *domaine;* L. *dominium*, right of ownership, dominion < *dominus*, a lord, master; see DEMESNE], 1. territory under one government or ruler; dominion. 2. land belonging to one person; estate. 3. field or sphere of activity or influence: as, the *domain* of science.

dome (dōm), *n.* [sense 1 < L. *domus*, house; others < early Fr. *dôme* < It. *duomo* or LL. *doma*, building, cathedral building, cathedral roof < L. *domus;* IE. base *dem-, *demā-, to put together, build; seen also in Gr. *demein*, Goth. *timrjan* (AS. *timbrian*), to build; (cf. TIMBER)], 1. [Poetic], a mansion or stately building. 2. a roof formed by a series of rounded arches or vaults on a round or many-sided base; cupola. 3. any dome-shaped structure or object. 4. [Slang], the head. *v.t.* [DOMED (dōmd), DOMING], 1. to cover with or as with a dome. 2. to form into a dome. *v.i.* to have, or take on, the form of a dome; swell out like a dome.

Do·mei (dō-mā′), *n.* [Japan., lit., united < *dō*, same + *mei*, together, joint], a Japanese agency for gathering and distributing news.

Do·me·ni·co (dô-me′nē-kô′), see **El Greco.**

domes·day (dōōmz′dā′, dōmz′dā′), *n.* doomsday.

Domesday Book, [said to be so named because it spared none and judged all men without bias, like the Last Judgment], the record of a survey of England made under William the Conqueror in 1086, listing all landowners and showing the value and extent of their holdings: abbreviated **D.B.:** also **Doomsday Book.**

do·mes·tic (də-mes′tik), *adj.* [OFr. *domestique;* L. *domesticus* < *domus;* see DOME], 1. having to do with the home; of the house or family: as, *domestic* happiness. 2. of one's homeland: as, *domestic* and foreign issues arose; hence, 3. made or produced in the home country; native. 4. domesticated; tame: said of animals. 5. home-loving; enjoying household affairs. Abbreviated **dom.** (in senses 2 & 3). *n.* 1. a domestic worker; maid, cook, butler, etc. 2. *pl.* native products.

do·mes·ti·cal·ly (də-mes′ti-k'l-i, də-mes′tik-li), *adv.* 1. in a domestic manner. 2. with regard to domestic matters.

do·mes·ti·cate (də-mes′tə-kāt′), *v.t.* [DOMESTICATED (-id), DOMESTICATING], [< ML. *domesticatus*, pp. of *domesticare*, to tame, live in a family < L. *domesticus* < *domus;* see DOME], 1. originally, to cause to be at home. 2. to accustom to home life; make domestic. 3. to cause (animals or plants) to be no longer wild; tame. 4. to civilize. *v.i.* to become domestic.

do·mes·ti·ca·tion (də-mes′tə-kā′shən), *n.* 1. a domesticating. 2. the fact or state of being domesticated.

do·mes·tic·i·ty (dō′mes-tis′ə-ti), *n.* [*pl.* DOMESTICITIES (-tiz)], [*domestic* + *-ity*], 1. home life; family life. 2. devotion to home and family life. 3. *pl.* household affairs or duties.

domestic relations court, a municipal court with jurisdiction over cases involving relations within the family or household, as between husband and wife or parent and child.

domestic science, the study of cooking, sewing, and other household affairs; home economics.

domestic worker, a person employed to do household work in another's home, as a maid, cook, butler, etc.

dom·ic (dōm′ik, dom′ik), *adj.* domical.

dom·i·cal (dōm′i-k'l, dom′i-k'l), *adj.* 1. of or like a dome. 2. having a dome, domes, or domelike structure.

dom·i·cile (dom′ə-sil, dom′ə-sīl′), *n.* [Fr.; L. *domicilium*, a dwelling, home < *domus;* see DOME], 1. a customary or permanent dwelling place; home; residence. 2. in *law*, one's official or legal residence. *v.t.* [DOMICILED (-sild, -sīld′), DOMICILING], to establish (oneself or another) in a domicile. *v.i.* [Rare], to dwell; reside.

dom·i·cil·i·ar·y (dom′ə-sil′i-er′i), *adj.* [ML. *domiciliarius* < L. *domicilium*], of or connected with a domicile.

dom·i·cil·i·ate (dom′ə-sil′i-āt′), *v.t. & v.i.* [DOMICILIATED (-id), DOMICILIATING], to domicile.

dom·i·nance (dom′ə-nəns), *n.* [< *dominant*], a dominating; being dominant; control; authority.

dom·i·nan·cy (dom′ə-nən-si), *n.* dominance.

dom·i·nant (dom′ə-nənt), *adj.* [Fr.; L. *dominans*, ppr. of *dominari;* see DOMINATE], 1. dominating; ruling; prevailing; exercising authority or influence. 2. in *genetics*, designating or relating to that one of any pair of opposite Mendelian characters which, when factors for both are present in the germ plasm, dominates over the other and appears in the organism: opposed to *recessive*: see **Mendel's laws.** 3. in *music*, of or based upon the fifth tone of a diatonic scale. *n.* 1. in *genetics*, *a)* a dominant character or factor. *b)* an organism having such characters. 2. in *music*, the fifth note of a diatonic scale.

***SYN.*—dominant** refers to that which dominates or controls, or has the greatest effect (*dominant* characteristics in genetics); **predominant** refers to that which is at the moment uppermost in importance or influence (the *predominant* reason for his refusal); **paramount** is applied to that which ranks first in importance, authority, etc. (of *paramount* interest to me); **pre-eminent** implies prominence because of surpassing excellence (the *pre-eminent* writer of his time); **preponderant** implies superiority in amount, weight, power, importance, etc. (the *preponderant* religion of a country).

dom·i·nate (dom′ə-nāt′), *v.t. & v.i.* [< L. *dominatus*, pp. of *dominari*, to rule < *dominus*, a master], 1. to rule or control by superior power: as, she *dominates* her husband. 2. to tower over (other things); rise high above (the surroundings, etc.): as, this building *dominates* the city.

dom·i·na·tion (dom′ə-nā′shən), *n.* 1. a dominating or being dominated; rule; control; ascendancy. 2. *pl.* in *theology*, the fourth order of angels.

dom·i·na·tive (dom′ə-nā′tiv), *adj.* [ML. *dominativus*], inclined to dominate; ruling.

dom·i·na·tor (dom′ə-nā′tẽr), *n.* [Fr. *dominateur;* L. *dominator*], a person who dominates; ruler.

dom·i·neer (dom′ə-nêr′), *v.i.* [D. *domineren;* Fr. *dominer;* L. *dominari;* see DOMINATE], to rule (*over*) in a harsh or arrogant way; bully; tyrannize; impose one's own opinion and wishes.

dom·i·neer·ing (dom′ə-nêr′iŋ), *adj.* [ppr. of *domineer*], arrogant; overbearing; tyrannical.—***SYN.*** see **masterful.**

Dom·in·ic (dom′ə-nik), [L. *Dominicus*, lit., belonging to a lord < *dominus*, a master, lord], a masculine name: variant, *Dominick.*

Dominic, Saint, (*Domingo de Guzmán*), 1170–1221; Spanish founder of the Dominican order.

Dom·i·ni·ca (də-min′i-kə, dom′ə-nē′kə), *n.* a British island of the Windward group in the West Indies: area, 305 sq. mi.; pop., 48,000 (1946): abbreviated **Dom.**

do·min·i·cal (də-min′i-k'l), *adj.* [ML. *dominicalis* < L. *dominicus*, of a lord < *dominus*, a lord, master], 1. having to do with Jesus as the Lord. 2. having to do with the Lord's day (Sunday).

dominical letter, any of the first seven letters in the alphabet as used in church calendars to indicate Sundays: the letters are assigned to the first seven days of January, and the letter falling to Sunday is the arbitrary symbol for Sunday the rest of the year: as, the *dominical letter* of 1945 was G.

Do·min·i·can (də-min'i-kən), *adj.* 1. of Saint Dominic. 2. designating or of the orders of friars and nuns founded by him. 3. of the Dominican Republic. *n.* 1. in the *Roman Catholic Church,* a member of one of the orders of mendicant friars and nuns founded in 1215 by Saint Dominic. 2. a native or inhabitant of the Dominican Republic. Abbreviated **Dom.**

Dominican Republic, a country in the eastern part of Hispaniola, in the West Indies: area, 18,700 sq. mi.; pop., 3,205,000; capital, Santo Domingo: formerly called *Santo Domingo:* abbreviated **Dom. Rep.**

Dom·i·nick (dom'ə-nik), a masculine name: see **Dominic.** *n.* a Dominique.

dom·i·nie (dom'ə-ni), *n.* [< vocative case (*domine*) of L. *dominus,* a master], 1. in Scotland, a schoolmaster. 2. (*usually* dō'mə-ni), in the United States, a pastor of the Dutch Reformed Church; hence, 3. [Colloq.], any pastor or clergyman.

do·min·ion (də-min'yən), *n.* [Fr. (obs.); ML. *dominio* < L. *dominus,* a master, lord], 1. rule or power to rule; sovereign authority; sovereignty. 2. a governed territory or country: abbreviated **dom.** 3. [D-], a self-governing commonwealth of the British Empire: as, the *Dominion* of New Zealand. —*SYN.* see **power.**

Dominion Day, in Canada, July 1, a legal holiday commemorating the anniversary of the proclamation in 1867 of the establishment of the Dominion of Canada.

Dom·i·nique (dom'ə-nēk'), *n.* [Fr., Dominica], one of an American breed of domestic chickens with yellow legs and gray, barred plumage: also spelled **Dominick.**

do·min·i·um (dō-min'i-əm), *n.* [L.; see DOMAIN], in *law,* ownership or control of a property or right.

dom·i·no (dom'ə-nō'), *n.* [*pl.* DOMINOES, DOMINOS (-nōz')], [Fr. & It., hooded cloak (worn by cathedral canons) < L. *dominus,* a lord, master: in reference to the costume of one addressed as "sir"], 1. a loose cloak or robe with wide sleeves, hood, and mask, worn at masquerades. 2. a small mask for the eyes; half mask: it is generally black. 3. a person dressed in such a cloak or mask. 4. [Fr. < Sp.: in reference to the blackness of the piece], a small, oblong piece of wood, bone, or plastic marked into halves, each half being blank or having from one to six dots marked on it. 5. *pl.* [construed as sing.], a game played with twenty-eight such pieces, which the players must match according to the number of dots on each half.

‡**Do·mi·nus** (dom'ə-nəs), *n.* [L.], the Lord.

‡**Do·mi·nus vo·bis·cum** (dom'ə-nəs vō-bis'kəm), [L.], the Lord be with you.

Do·mi·tian (də-mish'ən), *n.* (*Titus Flavius Domitianus Augustus*), Roman emperor (81–96 A.D.); lived 51–96 A.D.

Dom·re·my (dōn'rə-mē'), *n.* a village in northeastern France: birthplace of Joan of Arc.

Dom·re·my-la-Pu·celle (dōn'rə-mē'là'pü'sel'), *n.* Domremy.

Dom. Rep., Dominican Republic.

Don (don; *also, for 1,* Russ. dôn), *n.* 1. a river in the European U.S.S.R., flowing into the Sea of Azov: length, 1,100 mi.: also called *Duna.* 2. a river in Aberdeen, Scotland: length, 80 mi. 3. a river in Yorkshire, England: length, 65 mi.

don (don), *n.* [Sp. < L. *dominus,* a lord, master], 1. [D-], Sir; Mr.: a Spanish title of respect, used with the given name, as, *Don* Pedro: abbreviated **D.** 2. a Spanish nobleman or gentleman. 3. a distinguished man. 4. [Colloq.], a head, tutor, or fellow of any college of Oxford or Cambridge.

don (don), *v.t.* [DONNED (dond), DONNING], [contr. of *do on*], to put on (a garment, etc.); dress in (a certain color or material).

‡**Do·ña** (dô'nyä), *n.* [Sp. < L. *domina,* mistress, lady], 1. Lady; Madam: a Spanish title of respect, used with the given name. 2. [d-], a Spanish lady.

‡**Do·na** (dô'nə), *n.* [Port.; see DOÑA], 1. Lady; Madam; a Portuguese title of respect, used with the given name. 2. [d-], a Portuguese lady.

Don·ald (don''ld), [Ir. *Donghal,* lit., brown stranger; or Gael. *Domhnall,* lit., world ruler], a masculine name: diminutive, *Don.*

Do·nar (dō'när), *n.* [OHG.; see THUNDER], in *Germanic mythology,* the god of thunder, corresponding to the Norse god Thor.

do·nate (dō'nāt), *v.t.* [DONATED (-id), DONATING], [< L. *donatus,* pp. of *donare* < *donus,* gift < *dare,* to give], to give, especially to some philanthropic or religious cause; present; contribute. —*SYN.* see **give.**

Do·na·tel·lo (dô'nä-tel'lô; Eng. don'ə-tel'ō), *n.* (*Donato di Niccolò di Betto Bardi*), Italian sculptor; 1386?–1466.

do·na·tion (dō-nā'shən), *n.* [Fr.; L. *donatio* < *donatus*], 1. a donating; giving; presenting. 2. a gift or contribution, as to a charitable organization. —*SYN.* see **present.**

Don·a·tist (don'ə-tist), *n.* [ML. *Donatista* < *Donatus,* Bishop of Casae Nigrae, founder of the sect], a member of a Christian religious sect formed in North Africa in the 4th century A.D. *adj.* of this sect or its doctrines.

don·a·tive (don'ə-tiv, dō'nə-tiv), *n.* [L. *donativum* < *donativus* < *donare;* see DONATE], a donation; gift.

do·na·tor (dō'nā-tẽr), *n.* [L.], a person who donates.

don·a·to·ry (don'ə-tôr'i, dō'nə-tō'ri), *n.* [*pl.* DONATORIES (-iz, -riz)], [ML. *donatorius* < L. *donatus;* see DONATE], in *law,* the person who receives a gift or donation; donee.

Do·nau (dō'nou), *n.* the Danube: the German name.

Don·cas·ter (doŋ'kas-tẽr; Brit. doŋ'kəs-tẽr), *n.* a city in Yorkshire, England, on the River Don: pop., 85,000.

Don Cossack, a member of the eastern branch of the Cossacks, living along the Don.

done (dun), past participle of **do.** *adj.* 1. completed; ended. 2. sufficiently cooked.

done in, [Colloq.], completely exhausted; worn out.

do·nee (dō-nē'), *n.* [< base of *donor* + *-ee*], a person who receives a gift or donation.

Don·e·gal (don'i-gôl', don'i-gôl'), *n.* a county on the northern coast of Ireland, in Ulster province: pop., 114,000; county seat, Lifford.

Do·nets (do-nets'; Russ. dô-nyets'), *n.* a river in the European U.S.S.R., flowing into the Don: length, 675 mi.

dong (dôŋ, doŋ), *n.* [echoic], a sound imitating or representing that of a large bell.

Don·go·la leather (doŋ'gə-lə), [< *Dongola,* province of former Anglo-Egyptian Sudan], a goatskin or calfskin tanned to resemble kid.

Do·ni·zet·ti, Ga·e·ta·no (gä'e-tä'nô dô'nē-dzet'tē; Eng. don'ə-zet'i), 1797–1848; Italian operatic composer.

don·jon (dun'jən, don'jən), *n.* [old sp. of *dungeon*], the heavily fortified inner tower or keep of a castle.

Don Ju·an (don jōō'ən; Sp. dôn Hwän'), 1. in *Spanish legend,* a dissolute nobleman and seducer of women, the hero of many poems, plays, and operas; hence, 2. any man who seduces women or has one love affair after another; libertine; philanderer; rake.

don·key (doŋ'ki, duŋ'ki), *n.* [*pl.* DONKEYS (-kiz)], [also earlier *donky;* late slang, rhyming with and patterned after *monkey;* either < *Duncan* (cf. *dicky,* etc.) or < *dun, adj.* + *-key,* dim. ending], 1. a small domestic animal resembling the horse but with longer ears and a shorter mane; ass. 2. a person regarded as stupid, foolish, or obstinate. 3. a donkey engine.

donkey engine, a small, portable steam engine, especially one used on a ship to lift cargo, etc.

Don·na (don'ə), [It. < L. *domina,* fem. of *dominus,* a lord, master], a feminine name. *n.* (It. dôn'nä), 1. Lady; Madam: an Italian title of respect, used with the given name. 2. [d-], an Italian lady.

Donne, John (dun), 1573–1631; English poet and clergyman.

don·nered, don·nard (don'ẽrd), *adj.* [< Scot. dial. *donner,* to stun, freq. of ME. *donen, donien,* to sound], [Scot.], stunned; stupefied.

don·nish (don'ish), *adj.* of, characteristic of, or like a university don.

don·ny·brook (don'i-brook'), *n.* [Slang], [< *Donnybrook* Fair], a rough, rowdy fight or free-for-all.

Don·ny·brook Fair (don'i-brook'), 1. the yearly fair formerly held at Donnybrook, Ireland, during which there was much fighting, drinking, and love-making; hence, 2. any fair or celebration like this.

do·nor (dō'nẽr), *n.* [OFr. *doneor;* L. *donator*], a person who donates; giver: as, a blood *donor.*

Don Quix·ote (don kwik'sət, don ki-hō'ti; Sp. dôn kē-Hô'te), 1. a satirical romance by Miguel de Cervantes, published in two parts (1605, 1615). 2. the hero of this romance, who tries in a chivalrous but unrealistic way to rescue the oppressed and fight evil.

don't (dōnt), 1. do not. 2. does not: in this sense now generally considered a substandard usage.

do·nut (dō'nut'), *n.* a doughnut.

don·zel (don'z'l), *n.* [Early Mod. Eng. < It. *donzello* < LL. *domnicellus,* lit., little master < L. *dominus;* cf. DON], [Obs.], a young gentleman who attended upon a knight; squire.

doo·dad (dōō'dad'), *n.* [see DOO-HICKEY], [Colloq.], 1. any small object whose name does not readily occur to one; gadget. 2. a bauble; gimcrack.

doo·dle (dōō'd'l), *v.t.* [DOODLED (-d'ld), DOODLING], [G. *dudeln,* to play (the bagpipe), hence to trifle, dawdle (< Pol. *dudlić* < *dudy,* a bagpipe < Turk. *düdük,* a flute); reinforced by echoic *tootle* & *dawdle*], 1. [Archaic], originally, to play (the bagpipe). 2. [Dial.], to make a fool of; fool. *v.i.* 1. to move aimlessly or foolishly; dawdle. 2. to scribble aimlessly, especially when the attention is elsewhere; make doodles. *n.* 1. a foolish person; simpleton. 2. a mark, design, figure, etc. made in aimless scribbling.

doo·dle·bug (dōō'd'l-bug'), *n.* [*doodle* + *bug:* from the notion that it emerges from the ground when one calls "doodle"], the larva of the ant lion.

doo·dle·sack (dōō'd'l-sak'), *n.* [G. *dudelsack,* bagpipe

< *dudeln*, to play on the bagpipe, tootle + *sack*, sac, bag], a bagpipe.

doo·hick·ey (do͞o′hik′i), ***n.*** [fanciful extension of *do*, as also in *doodad*, etc.], [Colloq.], any device; contrivance; gadget: humorous substitute for a name not known or temporarily forgotten.

doom (do͞om), ***n.*** [ME. & AS. *dom*, lit., what is laid down, judgment, decree; akin to Goth. *doms*, judgment; IE. base **dhē-*, to place, set, lay down, as in *-dere* in L. *credere*, to believe, lit., to set to heart; see DEEM], 1. in *history*, a statute; decree. 2. a judgment; sentence; condemnation. 3. destiny; fate. 4. tragic fate; ruin or death. 5. Judgment Day. ***v.t.*** 1. to pronounce judgment on; condemn; sentence. 2. to destine to a tragic fate. 3. to ordain as a penalty. —***SYN.*** see **fate.**

doom (do͞om), ***n.*** [Fr. *doum;* Ar. *dawm*], an African palm tree bearing an edible fruit about as large as an apple: also spelled **doum.**

dooms·day (do͞omz′dā′), ***n.*** [ME. *domesdai;* AS. *domes dæg; domes*, genit. of *dom*, doom + *dæg*, day], 1. Judgment Day; Last Judgment. 2. any day of judgment.

Doomsday Book, Domesday Book.

Doon (do͞on), ***n.*** a small river in southern Scotland, flowing into the Firth of Clyde.

door (dôr, dōr), ***n.*** [ME. *dore, door, dur;* AS. *duru* fem. (orig., pair of doors), *dor* neut.; akin to G. *tür*, door, *tor*, gate; IE. base **dhwer-, *dhwōr-*, etc., pair of doors], 1. a movable structure for opening or closing the entrance to a building or room, or giving access to a closet, cupboard, etc.: most doors turn on hinges, slide in grooves, or revolve on an axis. 2. the room or building to which a door belongs: as, two *doors* down the hall. 3. anything resembling a door, as the shutter of a cupboard. 4. any opening with a door in it; doorway. 5. any way to go in or out; passage; access.
lay at the door of, to blame (a person) for.
lie at one's door, to be imputable or chargeable to one.
out of doors, outside a house, building, etc.; outdoors.
show a person the door, to ask or command a person to leave one's house, room, etc.

door·bell (dôr′bel′, dōr′bel′), ***n.*** a bell that rings inside a building or room when an outside push button, lever, etc. is worked by someone wishing to enter.

door·jamb (dôr′jam′, dōr′jam′), ***n.*** a vertical piece of wood, etc. constituting the side of a doorway.

door·keep·er (dôr′kēp′ẽr, dōr′kēp′ẽr), ***n.*** 1. a person guarding the entrance of a house, hotel, etc.; gatekeeper; porter. 2. a doorman.

door·knob (dôr′nob′, dōr′nob′), ***n.*** a small knob or lever on a door, usually for releasing the latch.

door·man (dôr′man′, dôr′mən, dōr′man′), ***n.*** [*pl.* DOORMEN (-men′, -mən)], 1. a man whose work is opening the street door of a public building for those who enter or leave, hailing taxicabs, etc. 2. a doorkeeper.

door mat, a mat for people to wipe their shoes on before entering a house, room, etc.

door·nail (dôr′nāl′, dōr′nāl′), ***n.*** a large-headed nail used as studding on some doors.
dead as a doornail, dead beyond a doubt.

door·plate (dôr′plāt′, dōr′plāt′), ***n.*** a metal plate on an entrance door, bearing the number, occupant's name, etc.

door·post (dôr′pōst′, dōr′pōst′), ***n.*** a doorjamb.

door·sill (dôr′sil′, dōr′sil′), ***n.*** [*door* + *sill*], a board, piece of metal, etc. along the bottom of a doorway; threshold.

door·step (dôr′step′, dōr′step′), ***n.*** a step that leads from an outer door to a path, lawn, etc.

door·stop (dôr′stop′, dōr′stop′), ***n.*** 1. a weight, spring, or other device used to hold a door open at a desired position or prevent it from closing too forcibly. 2. a thin wooden strip affixed to the frame of a doorway, against which the door closes.

door·way (dôr′wā′, dōr′wā′), ***n.*** 1. an opening in a wall that can be closed by a door; portal. 2. a means of access: as, the *doorway* to China.

door·yard (dôr′yärd′, dōr′yärd′), ***n.*** a yard onto which a door of a house opens.

dope (dōp), ***n.*** [D. *doop*, sauce, dip, baptism < *doopen*, to dip, baptize], 1. any thick liquid or pasty substance used to lubricate or absorb something. 2. a dressing, varnish, or filler used as protection on a surface, as on the cloth covering of airplane wings. 3. a drug used to stimulate race horses. 4. [Slang], any drug or narcotic. 5. [Slang], advance information on a race horse's condition; hence, 6. [Slang], any information; especially, advance information for prediction. 7. [Slang], a user of narcotics; hence, 8. [Slang], a slow-witted, stupid, or lethargic person. 9. in *photography*, a developer. ***v.t.*** [DOPED (dōpt), DOPING], 1. to give dope to; treat with dope; hence, 2. to drug or stupefy. 3. [Slang], to make out or figure out; also, to predict after analyzing the available information (usually with *out*).

dope fiend, [Slang], a drug addict.

dope·y (dō′pi), ***adj.*** [DOPIER (-pi-ẽr), DOPIEST (-pi-ist)], [*dope* + *-y*], [Slang], 1. under the influence of a narcotic; in a stupor; hence, 2. mentally slow or confused; lethargic; stupid.

‡Dop·pel·gäng·er (dô′p′l-geŋ′ẽr), ***n.*** [G.], a double-ganger.

Dop·pler effect (dop′lẽr), [after Christian *Doppler* (1803–1853), Austrian mathematician and physicist], the apparent change of frequency of sound waves or light waves, varying with the relative velocity of the source and the observer: if the source and observer are drawing closer together, the frequency is increased.

dor (dôr), ***n.*** a dorbeetle: also spelled **dorr.**

Dor., 1. Doric. 2. Dorian.

Dor·a (dôr′ə, dō′rə), a feminine name: see **Dorothea, Theodora.**

Do·ra·do (də-rä′dō), ***n.*** [Sp., a dolphin, lit., gilded], a small southern constellation: see **constellation,** chart.

dor·bee·tle (dôr′bē′t′l), ***n.*** [< ME. *dore;* AS. *dora*, a beetle, cockchafer; + *beetle*], 1. the European dung beetle or cockchafer. 2. any beetle that flies with a buzzing sound. Also **dorrbeetle, dor,** etc.

dor·bug (dôr′bug′), ***n.*** a dorbeetle.

Dor·cas (dôr′kəs), [L.; Gr. *dorkas*, gazelle], a feminine name. ***n.*** in the *Bible*, a woman who spent her life making clothes for the poor: Acts 9:36–41.

Dorcas Society, any of various women's sewing societies which make clothes for the poor.

Dor·ches·ter (dôr′ches′tẽr, dôr′chis-tẽr), ***n.*** the county seat of Dorsetshire, England: pop., 10,000.

Dor·dogne (dôr′dōn′y′), ***n.*** a river in southwestern France, flowing into the Garonne River: length, 300 mi.

Dor·drecht (dôr′dreHt), ***n.*** a city in the southern Netherlands: pop., 68,000 (1947): also called *Dort.*

Do·ré, Paul Gus·tave (pôl güs′täv′ dô′rā′; Eng. dô-rā′), 1833–1883; French illustrator and painter.

Do·ri·an (dôr′i-ən, dō′ri-ən), ***adj.*** [< L. *Dorius;* Gr. *Dōrios* < *Doris*], Doric. ***n.*** a native of Doris; member of a race that formed one of the four main divisions of the ancient Greeks. Abbreviated **Dor.**

Dor·ic (dôr′ik, dor′ik), ***adj.*** [L. *Doricus*, Gr. *Dōrikos*], 1. of Doris, its people, their language, or culture. 2. designating or relating to the architectural style of Doris, characterized by simplicity of form: see TYPES OF ARCHITECTURE, p. 77. ***n.*** 1. the Greek dialect of Doris; hence, 2. the Scottish dialect as contrasted with Standard English. Abbreviated **Dor.**

Doric order, the oldest and plainest of the three orders (Doric, Ionic, Corinthian) of classical Greek architecture: it is characterized by fluted, heavy columns with simple capitals.

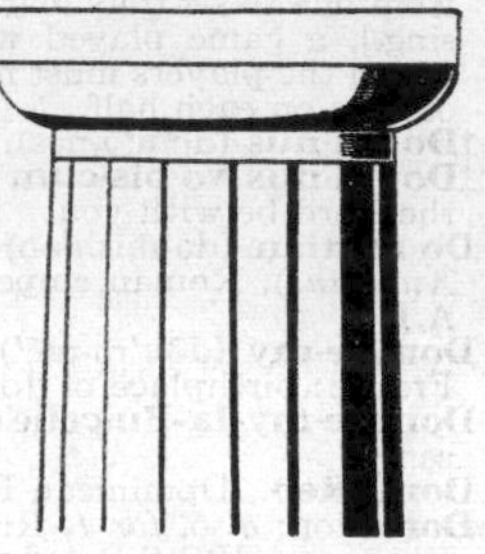
DORIC CAPITAL

Dor·is (dôr′is, dor′is), [L.; Gr. *Dōris*], a feminine name. ***n.*** an ancient region of Greece: see **Greece,** map.

Dor·king (dôr′kiŋ), ***n.*** [< *Dorking*, England], one of the oldest breeds of domestic fowl, having a large, heavy body, short legs, five-toed feet, and plumage of varying colors.

dorm (dôrm), ***n.*** [Colloq.], a dormitory.

dor·man·cy (dôr′mən-si), ***n.*** [< *dormant*], the state of being dormant.

dor·mant (dôr′mənt), ***adj.*** [ME.; OFr., ppr. of *dormir;* L. *dormire*, to sleep], 1. sleeping. 2. as if asleep; quiet; still. 3. inoperative; inactive. 4. in *biology*, torpid in winter: as, *dormant* snakes. 5. in *botany*, not vegetating: as, *dormant* plants. 6. in *heraldry*, in a sleeping position: as, a lion *dormant.* —***SYN.*** see **latent.**

dor·mer (dôr′mẽr), ***n.*** [OFr. *dormeour*, orig., dormitory; L. *dormitorium;* see DORMITORY], 1. a window set upright in a sloping roof. 2. the roofed projection in which this window is set. Also **dormer window.**

DORMER

dor·mi·to·ry (dôr′mə-tôr′i, dôr′mə-tō′ri), ***n.*** [*pl.* DORMITORIES (-iz, -riz)], [L. *dormitorium*, place for sleeping < *dormitorius*, of or for sleeping < *dormire*, to sleep], 1. a room, building, or part of a building with sleeping accommodations for a number of people. 2. a building with many rooms that provide sleeping and living accommodations for a number of people, as in most colleges.

dor·mouse (dôr′mous′), ***n.*** [*pl.* DORMICE (-mīs′)], [ME. *dormous;* prob. < Eng. dial. *dorm*, to doze < Fr. *dormir* < L. *dormire*, to sleep; + *mouse*], any of several small, hibernating European rodents that resemble squirrels.

dor·my, dor·mie (dôr′mi), ***adj.*** [prob. < Scot. dial. *dorm*, to doze (see DORMOUSE): when a player is dormy, he has no further need of effort], in *golf*, ahead of an opponent by as many holes as are yet to be played.

dor·nick (dôr′nik), ***n.*** [< *Doornik*, Fl. name of Tournai, Belgium, where it was originally made], a heavy damask used for hangings, vestments, etc.

dor·nick (dôr′nik), ***n.*** [Ir. Gael. *dornóg*, Scot. Gael.

doirneag < *dorn*, hand], a stone of a size suitable for throwing.

dor·nock (dor′nək), *n.* dornick (damask).

Dor·o·the·a (dôr′ə-thē′ə, dor′ə-thē′ə), [L.; Gr. *Dōrothea*, lit., gift of God < *dōron*, gift + *theos*, God], a feminine name: variant, *Dorothy;* diminutives, *Dolly, Dora, Dot, Dotty*.

Dor·o·thy (dôr′ə-thi, dor′ə-thi, dôr′thi), a feminine name: see **Dorothea.**

dorp (dôrp), *n.* [D.; akin to G. *dorf*, Eng. *thorpe*], a village; hamlet.

Dor·pat (dôr′pät), *n.* Tartu, a city in Estonian S.S.R.: the German name.

dorr (dôr), *n.* a dor; dorbeetle.

dorr·bee·tle (dôr′bē′t'l), *n.* a dorbeetle.

dor·sal (dôr′s'l), *adj.* [Fr.; ML. *dorsalis;* L. *dorsualis* < *dorsum*, the back], 1. of, on, or near the back. 2. in *botany*, on or of the underside of a surface: abbreviated **d.**

dor·sal, dor·sel (dôr′s'l), *n.* a dossal.

dor·sal·ly (dôr′s'l-i), *adv.* in a dorsal location or direction.

dor·ser (dôr′sẽr), *n.* a dosser.

Dor·set (dôr′sit), *n.* Dorsetshire.

Dorset Horn, any of a breed of large-horned sheep having wool of medium length: originally from Dorsetshire, England.

Dor·set·shire (dôr′sit-shir′), *n.* a county on the southern coast of England: pop., 243,000 (est. 1945); county seat, Dorchester.

dor·si- (dôr′si), [see DORSO-], a combining form meaning *of, on,* or *along the back:* often identical with *dorso-*.

dor·si·ven·tral (dôr′si-ven′trəl), *adj.* 1. in *botany*, having both dorsal and ventral surfaces. 2. in *zoology*, dorsoventral.

dor·so- (dôr′sō), [< L. *dorsum*, back], a combining form meaning: 1. *relating to the back.* 2. *the back and.*

dor·so·ven·tral (dôr′sō-ven′trəl), *adj.* 1. in *botany*, dorsiventral. 2. in *zoology*, from the back to the front; from the dorsum to the ventral side.

dor·sum (dôr′səm), *n.* [*pl.* DORSA (-sə)], [L.], 1. the back (of an animal). 2. any part like the back: as, the *dorsum* of the hand.

Dort (dôrt), *n.* Dordrecht.

Dort·mund (dôrt′moont; Eng. dôrt′mənd), *n.* a city in Westphalia, Germany: pop., 453,000 (1946).

dort·y (dôr′ti), *adj.* [< Scot. dial. *dort*, to sulk + *-y; dort* is prob. < Scot. Gael. & akin to Ir. *dord*, W. *dordd*, noise, clamor], [Scot.], bad-tempered; sullen.

do·ry (dôr′i, dō′ri), *n.* [*pl.* DORIES (-iz, -riz)], [Am. Ind. (Central America) *dori, duri*, a dugout], a small, flat-bottomed fishing boat with high, outward curving sides.

do·ry (dôr′i, dō′ri), *n.* [*pl.* DORIES (-iz, -riz)], [Fr. *dorée*, lit., gilt; fem. of *doré*, pp. of *dorer;* LL. *deaurare*, to gild; L. *de-*, intens. + *aurare*, to gild < *aurum*, gold], 1. the John Dory, a small, edible salt-water fish of a golden color. 2. any of several fishes related to this, as the wall-eyed pike.

dos-à-dos (dō′zä-dō′), *adv.* [Fr.], back to back. *n.* 1. [*pl.* DOS-A-DOS (-dōz′)], any seat, sofa, carriage, etc. built so that the occupants sit back to back. 2. (*usually* dō′sē-dō′), a movement in various folk dances, in which two dancers approach each other, pass back to back, and return to their original positions.

dos·age (dōs′ij), *n.* 1. the giving of medicine in prescribed doses. 2. the amount of medicine in a single dose. 3. the adding of an ingredient to wine, etc. to flavor or strengthen it.

dose (dōs), *n.* [Fr.; ML. *dosis;* Gr. *dosis*, gift < *didonai*, to give], 1. exact amount of a medicine to be given or taken at one time or at stated intervals: abbreviated **d.** 2. amount of a remedy, punishment, etc. given or taken at one time; something administered. 3. any ingredient added to wine, etc. to flavor or strengthen it. 4. [Slang], a venereal infection, especially gonorrhea. *v.t.* [DOSED (dōst), DOSING], [< the *n.*], 1. to give a dose or doses of medicine, etc. to. 2. to give (medicine, etc.) in doses. 3. to add something to (wine, etc.) to flavor or strengthen it. *v.i.* to take a dose or doses of medicine.

do·sim·e·ter (dō-sim′ə-tẽr), *n.* [see DOSE & -METER], 1. a device for measuring very small quantities of liquid, as of doses of medicine. 2. a small device carried by a person, usually in the pocket, for measuring the number of roentgens he has absorbed.

do·sim·e·try (dō-sim′ə-tri), *n.* the measurement of liquids as with a dosimeter.

Dos Pas·sos, John (dos pas′ōs), 1896– ; American novelist.

doss (dos), *n.* [< Fr. *dos*, a back; LL. **dossum;* L. *dorsum*, the back], [British Slang], 1. a bed or bunk, especially in a cheap lodging house. *v.i.* [British Slang], to sleep.

dos·sal, dos·sel (dos′'l), *n.* [ML. *dossale*, var. of *dorsale* < *dorsalis;* see DORSAL, *adj.*], 1. an ornamental upholstery at the back of a chair, throne, etc. 2. an ornamental cloth hung behind an altar, at the back of a chancel, etc.

dos·ser (dos′ẽr), *n.* [ME.; OFr. *dossier* < *dos*, the back; LL. **dossum;* L. *dorsum*, the back], 1. a large basket that can be carried on the back; especially, one of a pair of baskets slung over the back of a pack animal; pannier. 2. a dossal.

doss house, [see DOSS], [British Slang], a place where a night's lodging can be had for a few cents.

dos·si·er (dos′i-ā′, dos′i-ẽr), *n.* [Fr., bundle of papers], a collection of documents recording information about some person or matter.

dos·sil (dos′'l), *n.* [ME. *dosil*, faucet < OFr.], 1. a plug of cotton or cloth for a wound; folded bandage used as a compress; pledget. 2. in *printing*, a wad of cloth for cleaning the ink from a plate.

dost (dust), [cf. DOEST], archaic second person singular, present indicative, of **do:** used with *thou.*

Dos·to·ev·ski, Fe·o·dor Mi·khai·lo·vich (fyô′dôr mi-khī′lô-vich dôs′tô-yef′ski), 1821–1881; Russian novelist.

dot (dot), *n.* [AS. *dott*, head of boil; prob. reinforced (16th c.) by D. *dot;* akin to G. *dütte*, nipple, D. *dodde*, a plug, *dot*, wisp of cloth, little child, Norw., LG. *dott*, little heap or swelling, wisp of straw, etc.; all these prob. metaphors < base of *dodder*], 1. a tiny spot, speck, or mark; any mark made with or as with a pointed object. 2. a small, round spot. 3. anything resembling a dot. 4. the short sound used in the Morse code of telegraphy, written as a dot: distinguished from *dash.* 5. in *mathematics*, *a*) a decimal point. *b*) a symbol of multiplication. 6. in *music*, *a*) a mark after a note or rest, increasing its time value by one half: two dots increase the time value by three quarters. *b*) a staccato mark. 7. in *printing & writing*, *a*) the mark used above an *i* or *j:* originally a stroke distinguishing *i* from *n, m, u,* etc. *b*) the similar mark indicating a full stop; period. *v.t.* [DOTTED (-id), DOTTING], 1. to mark with or as with a dot. 2. to make or form with dots: as, a *dotted* line. 3. to cover with or as with dots; be dotlike parts in: as, gas stations *dotted* the landscape. *v.i.* to make a dot or dots.

dot one's *i's* and cross one's *t's*, to be minutely correct or detailed in doing or saying something.

on the dot, [Colloq.], at the exact time.

dot (dot), *n.* [Fr. < L. *dos, dotis* < *dare*, to give (*do*, I give)], a woman's dowry at marriage.

dot·age (dōt′ij), *n.* [ME. < *dotien, doten*, to dote], 1. feeble and childish state due to old age; senility. 2. a doting; foolish or excessive affection.

do·tal (dō′t'l), *adj.* [Fr.; see DOT (dowry)], of or constituting a dowry.

do·tard (dō′tẽrd), *n.* [ME. < *dotien, doten*, to dote; cf. DODDERED], a person in his dotage; foolish and doddering old person.

do·ta·tion (dō-tā′shən), *n.* [ME. (via OFr.) < L. *dotatio* < *dotare;* cf. DOS, DOT (dowry)], an endowing or endowment.

dote (dōt), *v.i.* [DOTED (-id), DOTING], [ME. *dotien, doten* < Anglo-Fr. **doter* (Fr. *radoter*); ult. < Gmc. (cf. D. *doten*, to dote) < base of *dodder*], 1. to be foolish or weak-minded, especially because of old age. 2. to be excessively or foolishly fond (with *on* or *upon*).

doth (duth), [cf. DOETH], archaic third person singular, present indicative, of **do,** in auxiliary uses.

dot·ing (dōt′iŋ), *adj.* [ppr. of *dote*], 1. foolishly or excessively fond. 2. in *botany*, doty; decaying from age.

dot·ter·el (dot′ẽr-əl), *n.* [*pl.*, for 1 & 2, DOTTERELS (-əlz), DOTTEREL; see PLURAL, II, D, 1], [< *dote;* so called because regarded as stupid and easy to catch], 1. the European plover, a short-billed shore bird. 2. any of several related shore birds with a short bill. 3. [Dial.], an easy dupe. Also **dottrel.**

dot·tle, dot·tel (dot′'l), *n.* [? dim. of *dot* (spot)], tobacco left in the bowl of a pipe after it has been smoked.

dot·trel (dot′rəl), *n.* a dotterel.

dot·ty (dot′i), *adj.* [DOTTIER (-i-ẽr), DOTTIEST (-i-ist)], [< *dot*, a spot], 1. covered with dots; dotted. 2. [Colloq.], feeble; unsteady; shaky; hence, 3. [Colloq.], feeble-minded; mentally weak or queer; crazy.

dot·y (dō′ti), *adj.* [DOTIER (-ti-ẽr), DOTIEST (-ti-ist)], [< *dote*], in *botany*, discolored and decayed from age.

Dou, Ge·rard (gä′rärt dou), 1613–1675; Dutch painter; pupil of Rembrandt: also spelled **Dow.**

Dou·ai, Dou·ay (dōō′ā′), *n.* a city in northern France: pop., 37,000 (1946).

Douay Bible, an English version of the Bible translated from the Latin Vulgate edition for the use of Roman Catholics: the New Testament was published at Reims (1582), the Old Testament at Douai (1609–1610): abbreviated **D. Bib.:** also **Douay Version.**

dou·ble (dub′'l), *adj.* [ME.; OFr.; L. *duplus*, lit., twofold < *duo*, two (see TWO) + *-plus* < IE. **pel-*, to fold; hence akin to L. *plicare*, to fold, ON. *fel*, a furrow, fold], 1. two combined; twofold; duplex. 2. having two layers; folded in two. 3. having two of one kind; paired; repeated: as, a *double* consonant. 4. being of two kinds; dual: as, a *double* standard. 5. having two meanings; ambiguous. 6. twice as much, as many, as large, etc.: as, pay *double* fare. 7. of extra size, value, strength, or quantity. 8. designed or made for two: as, a *double* bed. 9. having duplicity; two-faced; deceiving. 10. having a tone an octave lower: said of musical instruments. 11. in *botany*, having more than one set of petals. ***adv.*** 1. twofold. 2. twice. 3. two together; in or by pairs. ***n.*** 1. anything twice as much, as many, or as large as normal. 2. an exact repetition or duplication of something; counterpart: as, I have a *double* in my son. 3. a substitute actor or singer; hence, 4. a stand-in or substitute, as in motion pictures. 5. a fold; second ply. 6. a sharp turn or shift of direction. 7. a trick; shift. 8. in *baseball*, a hit on which the batter reaches second base. 9. in *bridge*, *a*) the doubling of an opponent's bid. *b*) a hand that makes this possible. 10. *pl.* a game of tennis, handball, etc. with two players on each side, usually played on a larger area than singles. Abbreviated **dbl.** ***v.t.*** [DOUBLED (-'ld), DOUBLING], 1. to make double; make twice as much or many; multiply by two: as, *double* the recipe. 2. to fold; add another ply to: as, *double* the bandage. 3. to repeat or duplicate. 4. to be the double of. 5. in *bridge*, to increase the point value or penalty of (an opponent's bid). 6. in *music*, to supply the upper or lower octave to (another part or voice): as, *double* the tenor in brass. 7. in *nautical usage*, to sail around: as, they *doubled* Cape Horn. ***v.i.*** 1. to become double; increase twofold. 2. to bend or turn sharply backward: as, the animal *doubled* on its tracks. 3. to serve as a double, serve two purposes, etc. 4. in *baseball*, to hit a double.

double back, 1. to fold back. 2. to turn and go back in the direction from which one came.

double in brass, [Slang], 1. in *jazz music*, originally, to be capable of playing another (especially, brass-wind) instrument in addition to one's usual instrument. 2. to do or be capable of doing something additional to one's specialty.

double up, 1. to fold completely; clench (one's fist). 2. to bend over, as in laughter or pain. 3. to share a room, etc. with someone.

on the double, [Colloq.], 1. in double time. 2. quickly.

double bar, in *music*, two parallel vertical lines drawn through the staff to indicate the end of a movement.

dou·ble-bar·reled (dub''l-bar''ld), ***adj.*** 1. having two barrels, as a kind of shotgun. 2. having two purposes. 3. that can be taken in two ways; ambiguous.

dou·ble-bass (dub''l-bās'), ***adj.*** contrabass.

double bass, the largest and deepest-toned musical instrument of the violin family, with a range of approximately three octaves; contrabass; bass viol: see **contrabass,** illus.

double bassoon, a large bassoon pitched an octave lower than the bassoon proper; contrabassoon.

double bed, a bed large enough for two people: the standard width is 54 inches.

double (Black·wall) hitch (blak'wôl'), a kind of knot: see **knot,** illus.

double boiler, a cooking utensil consisting of two pans, one of which fits into the other: the heat from water boiling in the lower one cooks the food in the upper without scorching.

dou·ble-breast·ed (dub''l-bres'tid), ***adj.*** overlapping so as to provide a double thickness of material across the breast, and having a double row of buttons, as a coat.

double chin, a fold of flesh beneath the chin.

dou·ble-cross (dub''l-krôs'), ***v.t.*** [Slang], to betray (a person) by doing the opposite of, or intentionally failing to do, what one has promised; cheat.

double cross, [Slang], double-crossing; treachery.

double dagger, a mark (‡) used in printing and writing to indicate a note or cross reference; diesis.

double date, [Colloq.], a social engagement in which two couples go somewhere or do something together.

dou·ble-deal·er (dub''l-dēl'ẽr), ***n.*** a person who behaves with duplicity.

dou·ble-deal·ing (dub''l-dēl'iŋ), ***n.*** the act of doing the opposite of what one pretends to do; duplicity.

dou·ble-deck·er (dub''l-dek'ẽr), ***n.*** 1. any structure or vehicle with an upper deck or floor. 2. [Colloq.], a sandwich with two layers of filling and three slices of bread.

double eagle, a United States gold coin with a face value of $20: it is no longer in circulation.

dou·ble-edged (dub''l-ejd'), ***adj.*** 1. having two cutting edges. 2. applicable against as well as for: said of an argument, etc.

‡**dou·ble-en·ten·dre** (dōō'bl'-än'tän'dr'), ***n.*** [Fr.; prob. altered < *double entente*], 1. a word or phrase with two meanings, especially when one of these has a risqué or indecorous connotation. 2. the use of such a term or terms; ambiguity.

‡**dou·ble en·tente** (dōō'bl' än'tänt'), [Fr.], a double meaning; ambiguity.

double entry, a system of bookkeeping in which every transaction is entered as both a debit and a credit.

double exposure, in *photography*, 1. the making of two exposures on the same film or plate, either by mistake or for a composite photograph. 2. such a photograph.

dou·ble-faced (dub''l-fāst'), ***adj.*** 1. having two faces or aspects. 2. having a finished nap on both sides: said of cloth. 3. hypocritical; insincere.

double feature, two full-length motion pictures on the same program.

double first, in *British universities*, 1. a degree with first-class honors in two subjects. 2. a student winning such a degree.

dou·ble·gang·er (dub''l-gaŋ'ẽr), ***n.*** [G. *doppelgänger* < *doppel*, double + *gänger*, goer, walker], the supposed ghost or wraith of a living person.

double harness, 1. a harness for a pair of horses; hence, 2. close association or companionship, as in marriage.

dou·ble-head·er (dub''l-hed'ẽr), ***n.*** 1. a train pulled by two locomotives. 2. in *baseball*, two games played in succession by the same two teams on the same day.

double indemnity, a clause in life insurance policies providing for the payment of twice the face value of the contract in the case of accidental death.

dou·ble-joint·ed (dub''l-join'tid), ***adj.*** having joints that permit limbs, fingers, etc. to bend at other than the usual angles.

dou·ble-lock (dub''l-lok'), ***v.t.*** 1. to lock by two turns of the key. 2. to lock doubly or with special care.

dou·ble-mind·ed (dub''l-mīnd'id), ***adj.*** undecided in mind; vacillating.

dou·ble-park (dub''l-pärk'), ***v.t. & v.i.*** to park (an automobile), usually unlawfully, alongside another that is properly parked next to a curb.

double play, in *baseball*, a play by which two players are put out.

double pneumonia, pneumonia of both lungs.

dou·ble-quick (dub''l-kwik'), ***adj.*** very quick. ***n.*** a double-quick marching pace; double time. ***v.i. & v.t.*** to go or cause to go at this pace. ***adv.*** in this pace.

dou·ble-reed (dub''l-rēd'), ***adj.*** designating or of any of a group of wood-wind instruments, as the oboe or bassoon, having two reeds separated by a narrow opening, that are vibrated against each other by the breath. ***n.*** a double-reed instrument.

dou·ble-rip·per (dub''l-rip'ẽr), ***n.*** a long sled for coasting, made up of two sleds fastened together, one behind the other, by a plank: also called *double-runner*.

double salt, in *chemistry*, 1. a salt, as sodium potassium tartrate, which in solution produces two different cations or anions. 2. any compound that may be regarded as a combination of two different salts.

double sharp, a symbol (× or ※) indicating that a note must be raised two half tones above the natural pitch.

double standard, the moral code imposing a different and more restrictive standard of behavior on women than on men, especially in matters of sex.

double star, two stars so close to each other that only by means of a telescope can they be seen to be separate.

dou·ble-stop (dub''l-stop'), ***v.i.*** to produce two tones at once by drawing the bow over two strings of the violin, etc. at the same time: the strings may or may not be stopped with the fingers, depending upon what tones are desired. ***n.*** 1. the two tones thus produced. 2. the notes showing these.

dou·blet (dub'lit), ***n.*** [ME. *dublet;* OFr. *doublet*, dim. of *double*, orig., something folded, doubled; see DOUBLE], 1. a man's close-fitting jacket with or without sleeves, worn chiefly from the 14th century to the 16th. 2. either of a pair of similar things. 3. a pair; couple. 4. *pl.* a pair of dice thrown so that identical sides are uppermost. 5. a simulated gem produced by cementing two crystals together with a layer of colored glass between them. 6. in *linguistics*, either of two words which derive ultimately from the same source but have changed in form (e.g., *card, chart; regal, royal*).

DOUBLET

double tackle, a tackle having two grooved wheels in the same pulley block.

double take, a delayed reaction to some unusual or unexpected situation, statement, etc., in which there is first unthinking acceptance and then a startled and obvious understanding of the true meaning: used especially as a piece of comic business in acting.

double talk, 1. ambiguous and deceptive talk. 2. meaningless syllables made to sound like talk; gibberish.

double time, 1. a rate of payment twice as high as usual, as for overtime on Sundays. 2. a marching cadence of 180 three-foot steps a minute, used in the United States Army: normal cadence is 120 steps a minute. 3. double-quick. 4. in *music*, duple time.

dou·ble-tongue (dub''l-tuŋ'), ***v.i.*** to vibrate the tongue in playing the flute, cornet, etc. so as to produce staccato tones.

dou·ble-tongued (dub''l-tuŋd'), ***adj.*** deceitful.

dou·ble·tree (dub″'l-trē'), *n.* [< *double*, after *singletree*], a crossbar on a wagon, carriage, plow, etc., to each end of which the singletrees are attached when two horses are harnessed abreast.
dou·bloon (du-blōōn'), *n.* [Fr. *doublon;* Sp. *doblón* < *doble* (< L. *duplus*), double], an obsolete Spanish gold coin which varied in value from about $16 to about $5.
‡dou·blure (dōō'blür'), *n.* [Fr., lining < *double;* see DOUBLE], an ornamental lining, as of leather, on the inner side of a book cover.
dou·bly (dub'li), *adv.* 1. twice; to twice the degree or quantity. 2. two at a time. 3. [Archaic], in a deceitful manner; with duplicity.
Doubs (dōō), *n.* a river in eastern France, flowing into the Saône River: length, 270 mi.
doubt (dout), *v.i.* [ME. *douten;* OFr. *douter;* L. *dubitare*, to waver in opinion (see DUBIOUS); *-b-* erroneously inserted, after L., by Renaissance pedants; cf. DEBT, ISLE], 1. to be unsettled in opinion or belief; be uncertain or undecided. 2. to be inclined to disbelief. 3. [Archaic], to hesitate. *v.t.* 1. to be uncertain about; question; feel distrust of. 2. to be inclined to disbelieve. 3. [Archaic], to be fearful, apprehensive, or suspicious of. *n.* 1. a wavering of opinion or belief; lack of conviction; feeling of uncertainty. 2. a condition of uncertainty: as, the outcome was in *doubt* until the end. 3. an unsettled point or matter; difficulty. 4. [Obs.], apprehension; fear. —*SYN.* see **uncertainty.**
beyond doubt, certainly.
in doubt, not certain; not sure.
no doubt, 1. certainly. 2. very likely; probably.
without doubt, certainly.
doubt·ful (dout'fəl), *adj.* 1. in doubt; not clear or definite; ambiguous. 2. uncertain; unsure. 3. giving rise to doubt or suspicion; of questionable reputation. 4. feeling doubt; unsettled in opinion or belief.
SYN.—**doubtful** implies strong uncertainty as to the probability, value, honesty, validity, etc. of something (a *doubtful* remedy); **dubious** is less strong, suggesting merely vague suspicion or hesitancy (*dubious* about the future); **questionable** strictly suggests only that there is some reason for doubt, but it is often used as a euphemism to imply strong suspicion, almost amounting to certainty, of immorality, dishonesty, etc. (a *questionable* reputation); **problematical** implies only uncertainty with no suggestion of a moral question (a *problematical* success).—*ANT.* certain, sure.
doubt·ing Thomas (dout'iŋ), [after the apostle *Thomas*, who doubted Jesus' resurrection: John 20:24–29], a person who habitually doubts; chronic skeptic.
doubt·less (dout'lis), *adj.* [Rare], feeling no doubt; sure. *adv.* 1. without doubt; certainly. 2. probably.
douce (dōōs), *adj.* [< Fr. *doux* < L. *dulcis;* cf. DOUR], [Scot.], pleasant; sweet-natured; hospitable.
‡dou·ceur (dōō'sẽr'), *n.* [Fr., lit., sweetness], a gratuity; tip; bribe.
douche (dōōsh), *n.* [Fr.; It. *doccia*, water jet, runnel (cf. DOCK, wharf); LL. **ductia*, a pipe < L. *ductio*, a leading away < *ductus*, pp. of *ducere*, to lead, bring], 1. a jet of liquid applied externally or internally to some part of the body, especially as a bath or treatment. 2. a bath or treatment of this kind. 3. a device for douching. *v.t. & v.i.* [DOUCHED (dōōsht), DOUCHING], to apply a douche to (some part of the body, especially the vagina).
dough (dō), *n.* [ME. *dough, dogh;* AS. *dag;* akin to Goth. *daigs*, G. *teig;* IE. base **dheigh-*, to knead (clay, etc.); hence, to form (plastic) masses, objects, etc.; seen also as L. *-fig-* (cf. EFFIGY, FIGURE)], 1. a mixture of flour, liquid, and other ingredients, worked into a soft, thick mass for baking into bread, pastry, etc. 2. any pasty mass like this. 3. [Slang], money.
dough·boy (dō'boi'), *n.* 1. a boiled dumpling. 2. [Colloq.], a United States infantryman.
dough·nut (dō'nut'), *n.* a small, usually ring-shaped cake of sweetened, leavened dough, fried in deep fat.
dough·ti·ly (dou't'l-i), *adv.* in a doughty manner.
dough·ti·ness (dou'ti-nis), *n.* a doughty quality.
dough·ty (dou'ti), *adj.* [DOUGHTIER (-ti-ẽr), DOUGHTIEST (-ti-ist)], [ME.; AS. *dohtig;* altered < *dyhtig* after *dohte*, past tense of *dugan*, to avail; akin to G. *tüchtig*, fit, good, excellent; IE. base **dheugh-*, to be strong, avail; cf. DOG], valiant; brave; bold; strong: now used humorously with a somewhat archaic flavor.
dough·y (dō'i), *adj.* [DOUGHIER (-i-ẽr), DOUGHIEST (-i-ist)], of or like dough; soft, pasty, flabby, etc.
Doug·las (dug'ləs), [< Celt.; lit., dark, gray], a masculine name: diminutive, *Doug.* *n.* the capital of the Isle of Man: pop., 20,000.
Doug·las, Stephen Arnold, (dug'ləs), 1813–1861; American statesman; debated with Lincoln (1858).
Douglas, William Orville, 1898– ; American jurist; associate justice, United States Supreme Court (1939–).
Douglas fir (or **spruce, pine, hemlock**), [after David *Douglas* (1798–1834), Scot. botanist in America], a tall evergreen tree of the pine family, found in the western part of North America and valued for its hard wood.
Doug·lass, Frederick (dug'ləs), 1817?–1895; American Negro leader, journalist, and statesman.
Dou·kho·bors (dōō'kə-bôrz'), *n.pl.* Dukhobors.
doum (dōōm), *n.* the doom (palm tree).
Dou·ma (dōō'mä), *n.* Duma.
dour (door, door, dour), *adj.* [ME. *dowre;* L. *durus*, hard], 1. [Scot.], hard; unbending; stern; severe. 2. [Scot.], obstinate. 3. sullen; gloomy; forbidding.
dou·ra, dou·rah (door'ə), *n.* durra.
dou·rine (doo-rēn'), *n.* [Fr.], a disease of horses and mules, caused by a protozoan and transmitted in copulation.
Dou·ro (dō'roo), *n.* the Duero: the Portuguese name.
douse (dous), *v.t.* [DOUSED (doust), DOUSING], [16th-c. slang, prob. < LG.; cf. MD. *dossen* (later *doezen*), to beat noisily], 1. originally, to hit forcefully. 2. to pull down (sails), especially in a hurried and sudden manner; hence, 3. [Colloq.], to pull off (shoes, clothes, etc.). 4. [Colloq.], to put out (a light or fire) quickly; extinguish. Also spelled **dowse.**
douse (dous), *v.t.* [DOUSED (doust), DOUSING], [same as prec. *douse*, influenced by *souse*], 1. to plunge or thrust suddenly into liquid. 2. to drench; pour liquid over. *v.i.* to be immersed or drenched. Also spelled **dowse.**
douze·pers (dōōz'pârz'), *n. pl.* [OFr. *douze pers*, lit., twelve peers], 1. in *French history*, the twelve great peers of the realm. 2. in *medieval romance*, the twelve great paladins or knights of Charlemagne.
dove (duv), *n.* [ME.; ON. *dūfa;* akin to Goth. *dūbō*, G. *taube;* IE. base **dheubh-*, smoky, misty, dark (of color); cf. DEAF], 1. a bird of the pigeon family, especially the smaller species, with a full-breasted body, short legs, and a typical cooing cry: the dove is used as a symbol of the Holy Spirit and of peace. 2. a person regarded as gentle, innocent, or beloved.
dove (dōv), alternative past tense of **dive.**
dove·cot (duv'kot'), *n.* a dovecote.
dove·cote (duv'kōt', duv'kot'), *n.* [*dove* + *cote* (< AS. *cote*, fem. form of *cot*), cottage; see COT (cottage)], a small house or box with compartments for nesting pigeons, usually on a pole, etc. above the ground.
dove·kie, dove·key (duv'ki) *n.* [*dove* + *-kie, -key*, dim. suffix], 1. the black guillemot. 2. the rotche.
Do·ver (dō'vẽr), *n.* 1. the capital of Delaware: pop., 7,000. 2. a city in England, on the Strait of Dover, opposite Calais: pop., 35,000.
Dover, Strait (or **Straits**) **of,** the strait between France and England, joining the English Channel and the North Sea: narrowest point, 20 mi.: French name, *Pas de Calais.*
Do·ver's powder, [after Thomas *Dover* (1660–1742), Brit. physician], a preparation of opium, ipecac, etc., used to relieve pain and induce perspiration.
dove·tail (duv'tāl'), *n.* 1. a part or thing shaped like a dove's tail; specifically, a projecting, wedge-shaped part (called *tenon*) that fits into a corresponding indentation (called *mortise*) to form a joint. 2. a joint thus formed. *v.t.* 1. to join or fasten together by means of dovetails. 2. to piece together (facts, etc.) so as to make a logically connected whole. *v.i.* to fit together closely or logically.

DOVETAIL JOINT

Dow, Gerard, see **Dou, Gerard.**
dow·a·ger (dou'ə-jẽr), *n.* [OFr. *douagiere* < *douage*, dowry; see DOWER], 1. a widow with a title or property derived from her dead husband: often used in combination with the title, as, queen *dowager*, *dowager* duchess. 2. [Colloq.], an elderly woman of wealth and dignity.
Dow·den, Edward (dou'd'n), 1843–1913; Irish literary critic and Shakespearean scholar.
dow·di·ly (dou'd'l-i), *adv.* in a dowdy manner.
dow·di·ness (dou'di-nis), *n.* the quality of being dowdy.
dow·dy (dou'di), *adj.* [DOWDIER (-di-ẽr), DOWDIEST (-di-ist)], [< ME. *doude*, a slut], not neat, fashionable, or smart in dress or appearance; shabby; slovenly. *n.* [*pl.* DOWDIES (-diz)], a dowdy woman.
dow·el (dou'əl), *n.* [ME. *duvel, dowle;* prob. < MLG. *dövel* via Fr.; akin to G. *döbel*, a plug; IE. base **dheubh-*, **dhubh-*, a peg, wooden pin, plug], a peg or pin of wood, metal, etc., usually fitted into corresponding holes in two pieces to fasten them together. *v.t.* [DOWELED or DOWELLED (-əld), DOWELING or DOWELLING], to fasten with dowels; furnish with dowels.
dow·er (dou'ẽr), *n.* [ME. *dowere;* OFr. *douaire;* ML. *dotarium* < L. *dos, dotis;* see DOT (dower)],

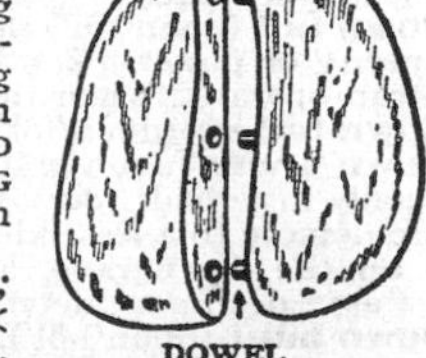

DOWEL

1. that part of a husband's property which his widow inherits for life. 2. a dowry. 3. a natural talent, gift, or endowment. *v.t.* 1. to give a dower to. 2. to bestow a talent or power upon; endow (*with*).
dow·er·y (dou'ẽr-i), *n.* [*pl.* DOWERIES (-iz)], a dowry.
dow·itch·er (dou'ich-ẽr), *n.* [*pl.* DOWITCHERS (-ẽrz), DOWITCHER; see PLURAL, II, D, 1], [prob. of Am. Ind. origin], a shore bird related to the American snipe.
dow·las (dou'ləs), *n.* [< *Daoulas*, near Brest in Brittany], 1. originally, a coarse linen. 2. a heavy calico.
Down (doun), *n.* a county of Ulster Province, Northern Ireland: pop., 241,000.
down (doun), *adv.* [ME. *down, doun* < *adune*, adown; AS. *adun, adune, ofdune*, from the hill; *a-, of-*, off, from + *dune*, dat. of *dun*, hill], 1. from a higher to a lower place; toward the ground. 2. in or on a lower position or level; on the ground. 3. in a direction or place thought of as lower or below: as, *down*town. 4. below the horizon. 5. from an earlier to a later period or person: as, *down* from the Middle Ages. 6. into a low or dejected mental or emotional condition. 7. into a low or prostrate physical condition: as, he came *down* with pneumonia. 8. in an inferior position; in check: as, they held him *down*. 9. to a lower amount or bulk: as, things have come *down* in price. 10. to a heavier consistency: as, boil *down*. 11. to a less excited or active condition; into a tranquil state: as, the waves settled *down*. 12. in a serious or earnest manner: as, get *down* to work. 13. completely; to the full extent: as, loaded *down*. 14 in cash or when bought: as, five dollars *down* and the remainder in installments. 15. in writing; on record: as, take *down* his name. *adj.* 1. descending; directed toward a lower position. 2. in a lower place; on the ground. 3. gone, brought, pulled, paid, etc. down. 4. dejected; discouraged. 5. prostrate; ill. 6. in *sports*, *a*) not in play: said of a football. *b*) trailing an opponent with reference to the number of points, goals, or strokes. *c*) in *baseball*, put out. *prep.* down toward, along, through, into, or upon. *v.t.* to put, bring, get, throw, or knock down. *v.i.* to go, come, or get down. *n.* 1. a descent. 2. a reverse; misfortune: as, the ups and *downs* of a career. 3. in *football*, *a*) one of four consecutive plays in which the team in possession of the ball must either score or advance the ball a total of at least ten yards in order to keep possession. *b*) the declaring of the ball as down, or the play just before this.
down and out, 1. in *boxing*, knocked out. 2. in the state of being penniless, friendless, ill, etc.
down on, [Colloq.], hostile to because of a grievance against; angry or annoyed with.
down with, 1. put down. 2. overthrow; do away with: an expression of disfavor.
down (doun), *n.* [ME. *doun, dun;* ON. *dūnn;* akin to Goth. *dauns*, fume, smoke; IE. base **dheu-*, to fly like dust, steam, mist, etc., as in L. *fumus* (cf. FUME)], 1. soft, fine feathers, as on young birds: see **feather**, illus. 2. soft, fine hair or hairy growth.
down (doun), *n.* [ME. *doun;* AS. *dun*, a hill; akin to OD. *duna*, D. *duin*, LG. *düne*, sandhill (see DUNE)], *usually in pl.* 1. an expanse of open, high, grassy land. 2. [confused with *dune*], a sandy mound formed by the wind.
the Downs, 1. the treeless, hilly uplands of Kent and Sussex in southeastern England. 2. a roadstead off the coast of Kent, England.
down-beat (doun'bēt'), *n.* in *music*, the downward stroke of the conductor's hand or baton to indicate the first accent in each measure.
down-bow (doun'bō'), *n.* a stroke on a violin, etc. in which the bow is drawn across the strings from the handle to the tip: symbol, ⊓.
down·cast (doun'kast', doun'käst'), *adj.* 1. directed downward. 2. sad; very discouraged; dejected. *n.* 1. a casting down. 2. in *mining*, a ventilating shaft.
down·come (doun'kum'), *n.* 1. a comedown; downfall; humiliation. 2. a downcomer.
down·com·er (doun'kum'ẽr), *n.* a pipe through which the gases from blast furnaces come down into hot-blast stoves and boilers.
down-east (doun'ēst'), *adj.* [Colloq.], of New England, especially Maine.
down-east·er (doun'ēs'tẽr), *n.* [Colloq.], a native of New England, especially of Maine.
Dow·ney (doun'i), *n.* a city in southwestern California, near Los Angeles: pop., 83,000.
down·fall (doun'fôl'), *n.* 1. a sudden fall, as from prosperity or power. 2. a heavy fall of rain or snow. 3. a trap operated when the prey causes a weight to drop.
down·fall·en (doun'fôl''n), *adj.* fallen; ruined.
down·grade (doun'grād'), *n.* a downward slope, especially in a road. *adv. & adj.* downhill; downward. *v.t.* to demote to a less skilled job at lower pay.
on the downgrade, losing success, influence, health, etc.; declining; deteriorating.
down·haul (doun'hôl'), *n.* a rope or series of ropes for hauling down a sail.
down·heart·ed (doun'här'tid), *adj.* discouraged; dejected; despondent.
down·hill (doun'hil', doun'hil'), *adv.* toward the bottom of a hill; downward. *adj.* sloping or going downward.
go downhill, to lose success, health, etc.; decline.
down·i·ness (doun'i-nis), *n.* the quality of being downy.
Down·ing Street (doun'iŋ), [after Sir George *Downing* (1623–1684)], 1. a street in the West End of London, location of some of the principal government offices, including the official residence of the Prime Minister (No. 10); hence, 2. the British government or cabinet.
down·pour (doun'pôr', doun'pōr'), *n.* a heavy rain.
down·right (doun'rīt', doun'rīt'), *adv.* [ME. *dun rihte;* see DOWN, *adv.* & RIGHT], 1. thoroughly; utterly. 2. [Rare], straight down. 3. [Archaic], plainly. *adj.* 1. absolute; thoroughgoing; utter: as, a *downright* insult. 2. straightforward; plain; frank: as, a *downright* fellow. 3. [Rare], going straight downward.
down·stage (doun'stāj'), *adv.* toward the front of the stage. *adj.* having to do with the front of the stage.
down·stair (doun'stâr'), *adv. & adj.* [Rare], downstairs.
down·stairs (doun'stârz', doun'stârz'), *adv.* 1. down the stairs. 2. on or to a lower floor. *adj.* situated on a lower floor. *n.* a lower floor or floors.
down·stream (doun'strēm', doun'strēm'), *adv. & adj.* in the direction of the current of a stream.
down·throw (doun'thrō'), *n.* a throwing down or being thrown down; overthrow.
down·town (doun'toun', doun'toun'), *adj.* 1. of or in the geographically lower part of a city or town: opposed to *uptown*. 2. of, in, or like the main business section of a city or town. *adv.* to, toward, or in the geographically lower part or main business section of a city or town. *n.* the main business section of a city or town.
down·trod (doun'trod'), *adj.* [Archaic], downtrodden.
down·trod·den (doun'trod''n), *adj.* 1. trampled on or down. 2. oppressed; subjugated; tyrannized over.
down under, [Colloq.], Australia or New Zealand.
down·ward (doun'wẽrd), *adv. & adj.* [ME. *dounward, duneward;* AS. *aduneweard; adune*, adown, down + *-weard*, -ward], 1. toward a lower place, position, state, etc. 2. from an earlier to a later time.
down·wards (doun'wẽrdz), *adv.* downward.
down-wash (doun'wäsh', doun'wôsh'), *n.* the air that an airplane wing pushes downward while moving through the air.
down·y (doun'i), *adj.* [DOWNIER (-i-ẽr), DOWNIEST (-i-ist)], 1. of or covered with soft, fine feathers or hair. 2. soft and fluffy, like down.
dow·ry (dou'ri), *n.* [*pl.* DOWRIES (-riz)], [Anglo-Fr. *douarie* < OFr. *doaire;* see DOWER], 1. the property that a woman brings to her husband at marriage. 2. a natural talent, gift, or endowment: as, poetry was his *dowry*. 3. [Archaic], a widow's dower. 4. [Archaic], a gift by a man to his bride.
dowse (dous), *v.t.* [DOWSED (doust), DOWSING], to douse.
dowse (douz), *v.i.* [DOWSED (douzd), DOWSING], [? Corn.], to search for a source of water or minerals with a divining rod.
dows·ing rod (dou'ziŋ), [prob. < Corn. merging of G. dial. *deuten*, to declare, with *douse* (to plunge); earlier form *deusing rod*], a divining rod.
Dow·son, Ernest (dou's'n), 1867–1900; English poet.
dox·ol·o·gy (doks-ol'ə-ji), *n.* [*pl.* DOXOLOGIES (-jiz)], [ML. *doxologia;* Gr. *doxologia*, a praising; *doxologos*, giving or uttering praise < *doxa*, praise, opinion < *dokein*, to think + *logos*, a word < *legein*, to speak], any of several hymns of praise to God; specifically, *a*) the **greater doxology**, which begins *Gloria in Excelsis* (glory to God in the highest). *b*) the **lesser doxology**, which begins *Gloria Patri* (glory to the Father). *c*) a hymn beginning "Praise God from whom all blessings flow."
dox·y (dok'si), *n.* [< words ending in *-doxy*, as *orthodoxy, heterodoxy*], a doctrine, creed, or ism, especially in religion.
dox·y (dok'si), *n.* [*pl.* DOXIES (-siz)], [orig., slang for "beggar's mistress"; ? < obs. *docke*, rump, or archaic D. *docke*, doll, of same origin], [Slang], a hussy; wench.
‡**doy·en** (dwȧ'yan'; Eng. doi'ən), *n.* [Fr.; see DEAN], the senior member, or dean, of a group.
‡**doy·enne** (dwȧ'yen'; Eng. doi'en'), *n.* [Fr.], feminine of **doyen.**
Doyle, Sir **Arthur Co·nan** (kō'nən doil), 1859–1930; English physician and novelist; known for his *Sherlock Holmes* stories.
doy·ley (doi'li), *n.* [*pl.* DOYLEYS (-liz)], a doily.
doy·ly (doi'li), *n.* [*pl.* DOYLIES (-liz)], a doily.
D'Oyly Carte, Richard, see **Carte, Richard D'Oyly.**
doz., dozen; dozens.
doze (dōz), *v.i.* [DOZED (dōzd), DOZING], [orig., to stupefy < LG.; cf. LG. *dös*, tiredness, sleepiness, *dösig*, dizzy, tired, whence Dan. *döse*, to make tired, etc.; for the ult. base, see DIZZY], to sleep lightly or fitfully; nap; be half asleep. *v.t.* to spend (time) in dozing (often with *away* or *out*). *n.* a light sleep; nap.
doze off, to fall into a light sleep.
doz·en (duz''n), *n.* [*pl.* DOZENS (-'nz); *before a noun, and usually when preceded by a specific number*, DOZEN], [ME. *dozeine;* OFr. *dozaine* < *douze*, twelve; L. *duodecim*, twelve < *duo*, two + *decem*, ten], a set of twelve: abbreviated **doz., dz.**: see also **baker's dozen.**
doz·enth (duz''nth), *adj.* twelfth.

doz·y (dōz′i), *adj.* [DOZIER (-i-ẽr), DOZIEST (-i-ist)], [see DOZE], sleepy; drowsy.

D.P., displaced person.

dpt., 1. department. 2. deponent.

D.P.W., Department of Public Works.

Dr., Doctor.

dr., 1. debit. 2. debtor. 3. dram; drams. 4. drawer.

drab (drab), *n.* [< Fr. *drap*, cloth; LL. *drappus;* prob. < IE. **dh(e)rābh-*, dark-colored, dirty, etc., via Gmc. or Celt.; cf. DRAPE], 1. a kind of cloth, especially a yellowish-brown woolen. 2. a dull yellowish brown. *adj.* [DRABBER (-ẽr), DRABBEST (-ist)], 1. of a dull yellowish-brown color. 2. dull; lacking brightness; monotonous.

drab (drab), *n.* [< Celt.; akin to Ir. *drabog*, Gael. *drabag*, slattern; cf. prec. DRAB], 1. a slovenly woman; slattern; slut. 2. a prostitute. *v.i.* [DRABBED (drabd), DRABBING], [< the *n.*], to be a prostitute.

drab·bet (drab′it), *n.* [< *drab* (cloth)], [British], a coarse, unbleached linen.

drab·ble (drab′'l), *v.t.* [DRABBLED (-'ld), DRABBLING], [ME. *drabelen, drablen;* ? < LG. *drabbeln*, to walk in mud or water], to make wet and dirty by dragging in mud and water; draggle. *v.i.* to become drabbled.

dra·cae·na (drə-sē′nə), *n.* [Mod. L. < Gr. *drakaina*, she-dragon; see DRAGON], any of a number of related tropical shrubs and trees of the lily family found in the Eastern Hemisphere: also **dracaena palm.**

drachm (dram), *n.* [ME. *dragmē, drame;* OFr. *dragme;* L. *drachma* < Gr.], 1. a drachma. 2. a dram.

drach·ma (drak′mə), *n.* [*pl.* DRACHMAS (-məz), DRACHMAE (-mē)], [L.; Gr. *drachmē* < *drachma*, handful < *drassesthai*, to grasp, take by handfuls; IE. base **dhergh-*, to be firm, hold firmly; cf. TARGET], 1. an ancient Greek silver coin. 2. an ancient Greek unit of weight approximately equal to the weight of this coin. 3. any of several modern weights or measures: see **dram.** 4. a modern Greek monetary unit: in 1949, about 1,700 drachmas equaled one dollar.

Dra·co (drā′kō), *n.* 1. Athenian statesman and lawgiver of the 7th century B.C. 2. [L.; see DRAGON], the Dragon, a northern constellation lying partially between the Big Dipper and the Little Dipper: see **constellation,** chart.

Dra·co·ni·an (drā-kō′ni-ən), *adj.* 1. of Draco (sense 1). 2. of the very harsh code of laws which he drew up in 621 B.C.; hence, 2. [sometimes d-], inhumanly severe or cruel. 3. [d-], draconic.

dra·con·ic (drā-kon′ik), *adj.* [< L. *draco;* see DRAGON], 1. of or like a dragon. 2. [D-], Draconian.

draff (draf), *n.* [ME. *draf;* ON. *draf;* akin to *treb-* in G. *treber;* IE. base **dh(e)rābh-*, dark, dirty, smelly, dirt, refuse, etc.; cf. DRAB], dregs; lees; sediment; refuse.

draff·y (draf′i), *adj.* full of, or as if full of, draff, or dregs; worthless.

draft (draft, dräft), *n.* [ME. *draught, draht*, a drawing, pulling, pull, stroke < AS. *dragan*, to draw, drag, pull; see DRAW], 1. a drawing or pulling, as of a vehicle or load. 2. the thing, quantity, or load pulled. 3. a drawing in of a fish net. 4. the amount of fish caught in one drawing in of the net. 5. a drawing of liquid into the mouth; drinking. 6. the amount taken at one drink. 7. a drink. 8. a drawing into the lungs, as of air or smoke. 9. the air, smoke, etc. drawn in. 10. a drawing, as of beer, from a cask when ordered. 11. a rough or preliminary sketch of a writing. 12. a plan or drawing of a work to be done. 13. a current of air, as in a room, heating system, etc. 14. a device for regulating the current of air in a heating system. 15. a written order issued by one person, bank, firm, etc., directing the payment of money to another; check. 16. a drawing of money or stock. 17. a drain; heavy demand. 18. the choosing or taking of individuals from a group for some special purpose. 19. the taking of qualified persons for compulsory military service. 20. those thus chosen or taken. 21. [Slang], influence. 22. in *commerce*, a deduction allowed for waste or loss in weight. 23. in *hydraulics*, the size of an opening for the flow of water. 24. in *masonry*, a narrow border along the edge or across the face of a stone. 25. in *mechanics*, the taper given to a pattern or die so that the work can be removed easily. 26. in *nautical usage*, the depth of water that a ship draws, or displaces. *v.t.* 1. to choose or take for some special purpose, as compulsory military service, by drawing from a group. 2. to draw off or away. 3. to make a preliminary sketch of or working plans for. *adj.* 1. used for pulling loads: as, *draft* animals. 2. drawn from a cask on order: as, *draft* beer. Also spelled **draught** in all senses, especially *n.* 3–10, inclusive, and *adj.* 2.

on draft, ready to be drawn directly from the cask.

draft animal, an animal used for pulling heavy loads.

draft board, an official board of civilians designated to select qualified persons for compulsory service in the United States armed forces.

draft′dodger, a person who avoids or tries to avoid being drafted into the armed forces.

draf·tee (draf-tē′, dräf-tē′), *n.* a person drafted, especially one drafted for service in the armed forces.

draft·i·ly (draf′t'l-i, dräf′t'l-i), *adv.* in a drafty manner: also spelled **draughtily.**

draft·i·ness (draf′ti-nis, dräf′ti-nis), *n.* the condition of being drafty: also spelled **draughtiness.**

drafts (drafts, dräfts), *n.pl.* checkers: see **draughts.**

drafts·man (drafts′mən, dräfts′mən), [*pl.* DRAFTSMEN (-mən)], 1. a person who draws plans of structures or machinery. 2. a person who draws up legal documents, speeches, etc. Also spelled **draughtsman.**

drafts·man·ship (drafts′mən-ship′, dräfts′mən-ship′), *n.* [*draftsman* + *-ship*], the work or skill of a draftsman: also spelled **draughtsmanship.**

draft·y (draf′ti, dräf′ti), *adj.* [DRAFTIER (-ti-ẽr), DRAFTIEST (-ti-ist)], 1. in, or exposed to, a draft (current of air). 2. letting in, causing, or having a draft or drafts: as, a *drafty* house. Also spelled **draughty.**

drag (drag), *v.t.* [DRAGGED (dragd), DRAGGING], [ME. *draggen, dragen;* AS. *dragan* or ON. *draga;* see DRAW], 1. to pull or draw with force or effort, especially along the ground or other surface; haul. 2. to pull a grapnel, net, or other device over the bottom of (a river, lake, etc.) in searching for or catching something; dredge. 3. to draw a harrow over (land). 4. to draw (something) out over a period of time; continue tediously or painfully. 5. to bring (a subject) into conversation or into a piece of writing, etc. unnecessarily or as if by force. *v.i.* 1. to be dragged; be pulled along the ground or other surface; trail. 2. to lag behind. 3. to be prolonged tediously; move or pass too slowly. 4. to search a river, lake, etc. with a grapnel, net, or other device. 5. to cause the sensation of dragging or tugging: as, a *dragging* fear. *n.* 1. something dragged or pulled along the ground; specifically, *a)* a harrow used for breaking ground. *b)* a heavy sledge (vehicle). *c)* a large, heavy coach with seats inside and on top. 2. a device used to catch and haul up something under water; grapnel, dragnet, etc. 3. a thing that checks motion, as a brake on the wheel of a vehicle; hence, 4. anything that hinders or obstructs. 5. the amount by which anything drags. 6. a dragging; slow, cumbersome movement. 7. something for dragging heavy objects. 8. [Slang], influence. 9. [Slang], a puff of a cigarette, pipe, etc. 10. [Slang], a dance. 11. [Slang], a race between hot rods to test their rates of acceleration, generally held on a short stretch of road or other straight course (*drag strip*) set aside for this purpose. 12. in *aeronautics*, the resistance to movement brought to bear on an airplane by the air through which it passes. 13. in *billiards*, a backspin given to the cue ball to cause it to stop upon hitting another ball. 14. in *hunting*, *a)* a trail of scent left by an animal. *b)* something dragged over the ground to leave a trail of scent. *c)* a hunt over such a trail. —*SYN.* see **pull.**

drag on (or **out**), to prolong or be prolonged tediously.

‡dra·gée (drȧ′zhā′), *n.* [Fr.], a sugar-coated candy or pill.

drag·gle (drag′'l), *v.t.* [DRAGGLED (-'ld), DRAGGLING], [freq. of *drag*], to make wet and dirty by dragging in mud or water. *v.i.* 1. to be or become draggled; trail on the ground. 2. to lag behind; straggle.

drag·gle·tail (drag′'l-tāl′), *n.* a slovenly woman with draggled skirts; slattern; slut.

drag·hound (drag′hound′), *n.* in *hunting*, a hound trained to follow a drag, or trail of scent.

drag·line (drag′līn′), *n.* a dragrope or guide rope.

drag link, a link connecting the cranks of two engine shafts.

drag·net (drag′net′), *n.* 1. a net dragged along the bottom of a river, lake, etc. for catching fish. 2. a net for catching small game. 3. an organized system or network for gathering in or catching people wanted by the authorities, as criminals, etc.

drag·o·man (drag′ə-mən), *n.* [*pl.* DRAGOMANS (-mənz), DRAGOMEN (-mən)], [Fr.; Late Gr. *dragoumanos;* OAr. *targumān* < *targama*, to interpret], in the Near East, an interpreter or professional guide for travelers.

drag·on (drag′ən), *n.* [ME. *dragoun;* OFr. *dragon;* L. *draco;* Gr. *drakōn*, dragon, serpent, lit., the seeing one < *derkesthai*, to see; IE. base **derk-*, to see], 1. a mythical monster, usually represented as a large reptile with wings and claws, breathing out fire and smoke. 2. a fierce person; especially, a fiercely watchful female guardian; strict chaperon. 3. formerly, a short musket fastened to a soldier's belt. 4. a soldier armed with such a musket: see **dragoon.** 5. [Archaic], a large serpent or snake. 6. [D-], in *astronomy*, the constellation Draco. 7. in the *Authorized Version of the Bible*, a word used to translate several Hebrew words now understood to mean *serpent, jackal, Old Serpent* (Satan), etc. 8. in *botany*, any of several plants of the arum family. 9. in *zoology*, a small Asiatic tree lizard with winglike mem-

branes that enable it to glide from tree to tree.
drag·on·et (drag′ən-it), *n.* [ME.; OFr., dim. of *dragon*], 1. literally, a small dragon. 2. any of a large group of small, bright-colored sea fishes related to the goby.
drag·on·fly (drag′ən-flī′), *n.* [*pl.* DRAGONFLIES (-flīz′)], a large, harmless insect with a long, slender body and four filmy wings: it flies swiftly and feeds on flies, gnats, etc.

DRAGONFLY

drag·on·head (drag′ən-hed′), *n.* a kind of mint with blue, purple, or white flowers.
drag·on·nade (drag′ə-nād′), *n.* [Fr. < *dragon*, dragoon; see DRAGON], 1. the persecution of the French Protestants by the troops of Louis XIV, especially by the dragoons. 2. any persecution or raid in which troops are used.
dragon's blood, any of several red, resinous substances obtained from various tropical plants and trees, used for coloring varnishes and in photoengraving.
drag·on's-head (drag′ənz-hed′), *n.* 1. dragonhead. 2. in *astronomy*, dragon's head.
dragon's head, 1. the ascending node of a planet or of the moon: symbol, ☊. 2. dragonhead.
dragon's tail, the descending node of a planet or of the moon: symbol, ☋.
dragon tree, a tall tree of the lily family, from which a red, resinous substance (called *dragon's blood*) is obtained: it grows in the Canary Islands.
dra·goon (drə-gōōn′), *n.* [Fr. *dragon;* see DRAGON], 1. formerly, a soldier armed with a short musket, capable of fighting on horseback or on foot; mounted infantryman. 2. a heavily armed cavalryman. 3. [Obs.], a short musket: also called *dragon. v.t.* 1. to harass or persecute by dragoons. 2. to force by persecution (*into* doing something).
drag·rope (drag′rōp′), *n.* 1. a rope for dragging something, as a cannon. 2. a rope hung from a balloon or dirigible for use as a variable ballast or mooring line.
drag sail (or **sheet**), a sea anchor made from a sail.
drag strip, see **drag,** *n.* 11.
drag strut, any of the internal reinforcing ribs of an airplane wing.
drain (drān), *v.t.* [AS. *dreahnian*, to strain off, lit., to dry out < base of *dryge;* see DRY], 1. to draw off (liquid, etc.) gradually. 2. to draw water or any liquid from gradually; dry or empty in this way: as, the doctor *drained* the abscess. 3. to drink all the liquid from (a cup, glass, etc.). 4. to exhaust gradually; use up slowly: said of strength, resources, etc. 5. to filter. *v.i.* 1. to flow off or trickle through gradually. 2. to become dry by the drawing or flowing off of liquid. 3. to discharge its waters: said of a region, as, Central Europe *drains* into the Danube. *n.* 1. a channel or pipe for carrying off water, sewage, etc. 2. a draining or exhausting; that which gradually exhausts strength, resources, etc. 3. in *surgery*, a tube or other device for drawing off discharge, as from an abscess.
drain·age (drān′ij), *n.* 1. the act, process, or method of draining. 2. a system of drains; arrangement of pipes, etc. for carrying off waste matter. 3. that which is drained off. 4. a region or area drained, as by a river.
drainage basin, the land drained by a river system.
drainage tube, a small tube used for draining pus from an incision or a wound.
drain·er (drān′ẽr), *n.* 1. a person who lays pipes for draining, makes field drains, etc. 2. a container for drawing off liquid.
drain·pipe (drān′pīp′), *n.* a large pipe used to carry off water, sewage, etc.
drake (drāk), *n.* [ME. < West Gmc. **drako*, male duck (? L. *draco*, dragon); prob. via LG.; cf. LG. *drake*, G. dial. *draak, endedrach*, lit., duck-drake], a male duck.
drake (drāk), *n.* [ME.; AS. *draca* < L. *draco;* see DRAGON], 1. a small cannon of the 17th and 18th centuries. 2. a May fly, used as a fishing bait: also **drake fly.** 3. [Archaic], a dragon.
Drake, Sir **Francis** (drāk), 1545?–1596; English admiral; first Englishman to sail around the world.
Dra·kens·berg Mountains (drä′kənz-bũrg′), a mountain range in the eastern part of the Union of South Africa: length, 600 mi.: also called *Quathlamba.*
Drake Passage, the body of water between the southern tip of South America and the Antarctic Archipelago.
dram (dram), *n.* [ME. & OFr. *dragme;* L. *drachma;* see DRACHMA], 1. in *apothecaries' weight*, a unit equal to 60 grains (1/8 ounce): symbol, ʒ. 2. in *avoirdupois weight*, a unit equal to 27 1/3 grains (1/16 ounce). 3. a fluid dram; 1/128 pint. 4. a small drink of alcoholic liquor. 5. a small amount of anything. Abbreviated **dr.**
dra·ma (drä′mə, dram′ə), *n.* [LL.; Gr., a deed, action (see ACT), drama, tragedy < *dran*, to do], 1. a literary composition that tells a story, usually of human conflict, by means of dialogue and action, to be performed on the stage by actors; stage play: see also **closet drama.** 2. the art or profession of writing, acting, or producing plays; institution of the theater (often with *the*). 3. plays collectively: as, Elizabethan *drama.* 4. a series of events so interesting, vivid, etc. as to resemble those of a play. 5. the quality of being dramatic.
Dram·a·mine (dram′ə-mēn′), *n.* a drug used to prevent and relieve seasickness, airsickness, etc.: a trade-mark.
dra·mat·ic (drə-mat′ik), *adj.* [LL. *dramaticus;* Gr. *dramatikos*], 1. of or connected with drama. 2. having the characteristics of a drama, especially conflict; like a play; hence, 3. full of action; highly emotional; vivid, exciting, etc. Abbreviated **dram.**
dra·mat·i·cal (drə-mat′i-k'l), *adj.* dramatic.
dra·mat·i·cal·ly (drə-mat′i-k'l-i, drə-mat′ik-li), *adv.* 1. in a dramatic manner. 2. from the viewpoint of drama.
dra·mat·ics (drə-mat′iks), *n.pl.* [construed as sing.], 1. the art of performing or producing plays. 2. plays performed and produced by amateurs.
dramatic tenor, 1. a tenor voice of a lower range and a heavier, more powerful quality than a lyric tenor: it is especially suited to dramatic or heroic roles, as in the operas of Wagner. 2. a singer with such a voice. Also called *heroic tenor.*
dram·a·tis per·so·nae (dram′ə-tis pẽr-sō′nē), [L. < LL. *dramatis*, genit. of *drama*, drama + L. *personae*, pl. of *persona*, character], 1. the characters in a play. 2. a list of these. Abbreviated **dram. pers.**
dram·a·tist (dram′ə-tist), *n.* [see DRAMA], a playwright.
dram·a·ti·za·tion (dram′ə-ti-zā′shən, dram′ə-tī-zā′shən), *n.* 1. a dramatizing. 2. that which is dramatized; dramatized version, as of a novel.
dram·a·tize (dram′ə-tīz′), *v.t.* [DRAMATIZED (-tīzd′), DRAMATIZING], [< LL. *drama, dramatis*, drama; + *-ize*], 1. to make into a drama; arrange (a story, events, etc.) as a play; adapt for performance on the stage, screen, etc. 2. to look at, interpret, or present (things, actions, oneself, etc.) as though in a play; give dramatic quality to. *v.i.* to be capable of being dramatized.
dram·a·turge (dram′ə-tũrj′), *n.* a dramatist.
dram·a·tur·gic (dram′ə-tũr′jik), *adj.* of dramaturgy.
dram·a·tur·gi·cal·ly (dram′ə-tũr′ji-k'l-i), *adv.* 1. in a dramaturgic manner. 2. from the viewpoint of dramaturgy.
dram·a·tur·gist (dram′ə-tũr′jist), *n.* a dramatist.
dram·a·tur·gy (dram′ə-tũr′ji), *n.* [Fr. *dramaturgie;* Gr. *dramatourgia* < *drama* (see DRAMA) + *ergon*, work], the art of writing plays or producing them.
dram. pers., dramatis personae.
dram·shop (dram′shop′), *n.* [Now Rare], a bar; saloon.
‡Drang nach Os·ten (drāŋk näkh ôs′t'n), [G.], the thrust toward the East: in reference to the aims of German imperialists who advocated such expansion.
drank (draŋk), past tense and archaic past participle of **drink.**
drape (drāp), *v.t.* [DRAPED (drāpt), DRAPING], [OFr. *draper*, to make into cloth < *drap*, cloth; LL. *drappus*, cloth; see DRAB], 1. to cover, hang, or decorate with or as with cloth or clothes in loose folds. 2. to arrange (a garment, cloth, etc.) artistically in folds or hangings. *v.i.* to hang or fall in folds, as a garment, cloth, etc. *n.* [Fr. *drap*, cloth], 1. *usually in pl.* cloth hanging in loose folds; drapery; curtain. 2. the manner in which cloth hangs: as, his suit had an English *drape.*
drap·er (drāp′ẽr), *n.* [ME. < OFr. *drapier;* see DRAPE], 1. originally, a maker of cloth. 2. [British], a dealer in cloth and dry goods.
Dra·per, Henry (drā′pẽr), 1837–1882; American astronomer.
Draper, John William, 1811–1882; American scientist and historian; father of *Henry.*
dra·per·ied (drā′pẽr-id), *adj.* hung with drapery.
dra·per·y (drā′pẽr-i), *n.* [*pl.* DRAPERIES (-iz)], [ME. & OFr. *draperie;* see DRAPE], 1. cloth; fabric; textile. 2. [British], the business of a draper. 3. hangings or clothing arranged in loose folds. 4. an artistic arrangement of such hangings or clothing, especially in sculpture, painting, etc. 5. *pl.* curtains.
dras·tic (dras′tik), *adj.* [Gr. *drastikos*, active < *dran*, to do, act], acting with force; having a violent or strong effect; severe; harsh; extreme.
dras·ti·cal·ly (dras′ti-k'l-i, dras′tik-li), *adv.* in a drastic manner.
drat (drat), *interj.* [< *'od rot* < *God rot*], a mild expletive expressing annoyance, like *confound, darn*, etc.
D ration, a United States Army emergency field ration consisting of a specially prepared chocolate bar having a highly concentrated food value: three bars constitute one day's ration.
drat·ted (drat′id), *adj.* [cf. DRAT], [Colloq.], darned.
Drau (drou), *n.* the Drava: the German name.
draught (draft, dräft), *n., v.t., adj.* draft.
draught·i·ly (draf′t'l-i, dräf′t'l-i), *adv.* draftily.
draught·i·ness (draf′ti-nis, dräf′ti-nis), *n.* draftiness.
draughts (drafts, dräfts), *n.pl.* [British], the game of checkers: also spelled **drafts.**
draughts·man (drafts′mən, dräfts′mən), *n.* [*pl.* DRAUGHTSMEN (-mən)], 1. a draftsman. 2. [British], any of the pieces used in playing draughts.
draughts·man·ship (drafts′mən-ship′, dräfts′mən-ship′), *n.* draftsmanship.

draught·y (draf′ti, dräf′ti), ***adj.*** [DRAUGHTIER (-ti-ẽr), DRAUGHTIEST (-ti-ist)], drafty.
Dra·va (drä′vä), ***n.*** a river in Austria, Hungary, and Yugoslavia, flowing into the Danube: length, 450 mi.: German name, *Drau.*
Dra·ve (drä′və), ***n.*** the Drava.
drave (drāv), archaic past tense of **drive.**
Dra·vid·i·an (drə-vid′i-ən), ***n.*** [coined by Bishop R. Caldwell < Sans. *Drāvida,* name of district in southern India], 1. any member of a group of intermixed races in southern India and southern Ceylon. 2. the family of non-Indo-European languages spoken by these races, including Tamil, Malayalam, Kanarese, Kurukh, Telugu, etc.; it is characterized by a caste classification of nouns, inclusive and exclusive plurals of the pronoun of the first person, and extensive use of verbal auxiliaries. ***adj.*** of the Dravidians or their languages.
Dra·vid·ic (drə-vid′ik), ***adj.*** Dravidian.
draw (drô), ***v.t.*** [DREW (drōō), DRAWN (drôn), DRAWING], [ME. *drawen;* AS. *dragan;* akin to ON. *draga* (see DRAG), G. *tragen,* to bear, carry; IE. base **dheragh-,* to pull, draw along, prob. also in L. *trahere,* to pull, draw (cf. TRACTION)], I. *indicating traction* 1. to make move toward one; cause to follow along after by exerting physical force; pull; haul; drag: as, a horse *draws* the cart. 2. *a*) to pull up, as a sail. *b*) to pull down, as a window shade. *c*) to pull in, as a dragnet. *d*) to pull aside or together, as a curtain. 3. to pull back the drawstring of (a bow). 4. to displace (a specified depth of water) in floating; need (a specified depth of water) to float in: said of a ship. 5. in *billiards,* to give backspin to (the cue ball). 6. in *cricket,* to deflect (the ball) to the side of the field on which the batsman stands, by a slight turn of the bat. II. *indicating attraction* 1. to attract; charm; entice. 2. to take into the lungs; breathe in; inhale. 3. to bring forth; elicit: as, his challenge *drew* no reply. 4. to bring about as a result; cause to happen; bring on: as, the airplane *drew* the enemy's fire. 5. in *medicine,* to cause a flow of (blood, pus, etc.) to some part. III. *indicating extraction* 1. to pull out; take out; remove; extract, as a tooth, cork, sword, etc. 2. to take out (a liquid, etc.) by sucking, draining, distilling, seeping, etc. 3. to bring up, as water from a well; cause (liquid) to flow out of an opening, tap, etc.: as, he *drew* a bath, the knife *draws* blood. 4. to take out the viscera of; disembowel. 5. to get or receive from some source: as, he *draws* a good salary. 6. to take out or withdraw (money) held in an account; hence, 7. to write (a check or draft). 8. to extract (a conclusion or inference); deduce. 9. to get or win in a lottery. 10. in *card games, a*) to take or get (cards). *b*) to cause (a card or cards) to be played out: as, *draw* your opponent's trump. IV. *indicating tension* 1. to pull out so as to make longer or larger; stretch; make tense; extend: as, they *drew* the rope tight. 2. to pull out of shape; distort. 3. to stretch, flatten, or shape (metal) by die stamping, hammering, etc. 4. to make metal into (wire) by pulling it through holes. V. *indicating delineation* (to "pull" across paper, etc.). 1. to make (lines, figures, pictures, etc.), as with a pencil, pen, brush, or stylus; delineate; sketch; diagram; hence, 2. to describe. 3. to make (comparisons, etc.); formulate. ***v.i.*** 1. to draw something (in various senses of the *v.t.*). 2. to be drawn. 3. to come; move; approach: as, we *drew* near to town. 4. to shrink; contract. 5. to produce a draft; allow a draft of air, smoke, etc. to move through: as, the chimney *draws* well. 6. in *hunting, a*) to track game by following its scent. *b*) to move slowly toward the game after pointing: said of hounds. ***n.*** 1. a drawing or being drawn (in various senses). 2. the result of drawing. 3. a thing drawn. 4. [from the former withdrawal of stakes in such a case], a tie; stalemate: as, the game ended in a *draw.* 5. a thing that attracts. 6. the movable part of a drawbridge. 7. a land basin that water drains into or through. —***SYN.*** see **pull.**
beat to the draw, 1. to draw one's weapon sooner than one's opponent does; hence, 2. to do something sooner than someone else.
draw and quarter, in *medieval history,* 1. to execute by tying each arm and leg to a different horse, and then driving the horses in four different directions. 2. to eviscerate after hanging: so used in the phrase *hanged, drawn, and quartered.*
draw on, to approach.
draw oneself up, 1. to assume a straighter posture; stand or sit straight. 2. to bridle.
draw out, 1. to extend; lengthen; prolong. 2. to get (a person) to answer or talk.
draw up, 1. to arrange in order; marshal. 2. to compose (a document) in due form; draft. 3. to stop.
draw·back (drô′bak′), ***n.*** 1. money paid back from a charge previously made; refund or rebate, especially of import duties when the taxed commodities are later exported. 2. anything that prevents or lessens full satisfaction; shortcoming; detriment; disadvantage.
draw·bar (drô′bär′), ***n.*** the bar bearing the couplings by which railroad cars are joined.
draw·bore (drô′bôr′, drô′bōr′), ***n.*** in *carpentry,* a hole so bored in a tenon that the pin driven into it will tighten the joint.
draw·bridge (drô′brij′), ***n.*** a bridge that can be raised, lowered, or drawn aside.
draw·ee (drô′ē′), ***n.*** the person on whom an order, bill of exchange, or draft is drawn.
draw·er (drô′ẽr), ***n.*** 1. a person or thing that draws. 2. a person who draws liquor, as at a bar. 3. a person who draws an order for the payment of money. 4. a draftsman. 5. (drôr), a sliding box in a table, bureau, chest, etc., which can be drawn out and then pushed back into place. Abbreviated **dr.** (in senses 3 & 4).
draw·ers (drôrz), ***n.pl.*** [< *draw,* because drawn on], an undergarment for the lower part of the body, sometimes covering the legs; underpants.

DRAWBRIDGE

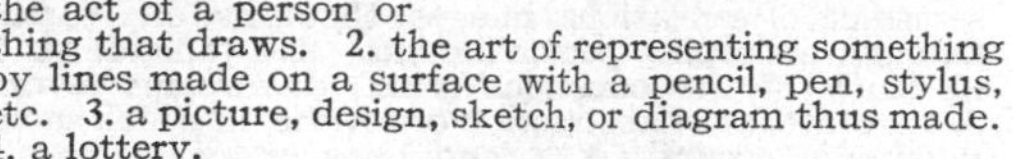

DRAWBRIDGES

draw·ing (drô′iŋ), ***n.*** 1. the act of a person or thing that draws. 2. the art of representing something by lines made on a surface with a pencil, pen, stylus, etc. 3. a picture, design, sketch, or diagram thus made. 4. a lottery.
drawing account, 1. an account showing money paid for expenses or as advances on salary, commissions, etc., as to a salesman. 2. the privilege of such an account.
drawing board, a flat, smooth board on which paper, canvas, etc. is fastened for making drawings.
drawing card, an entertainer, speaker, show, etc. that normally can be expected to draw a large audience.
drawing room, [< *withdrawing room:* orig. so called because it was the room into which guests withdrew after dinner], 1. a room where guests are received or entertained; living room or parlor. 2. those assembled in such a room. 3. a formal reception. 4. a private compartment on a railroad sleeping car, with accommodations for several people.
draw·knife (drô′nīf′), ***n.*** [*pl.* DRAWKNIVES (-nīvz′)], a knife with a handle at each end, usually at right angles to the blade: the user draws it toward him in shaving a surface: also **drawing knife.**
drawl (drôl), ***v.t. & v.i.*** [prob. freq. of *draw*], 1. to speak slowly, prolonging the syllables. 2. to speak in such a manner that vowels are broken at the points where word pitch changes: as, many Southerners *drawl.* ***n.*** a manner of speech characterized by slowness and prolongation of syllables.

DRAWKNIFE

drawn (drôn), past participle of **draw.** ***adj.*** 1. pulled out of the sheath. 2. [prob. < *withdrawn,* orig. applied to bets], with neither side winning or losing; even; tied. 3. disemboweled; eviscerated. 4. tense; haggard.
drawn butter, melted butter, sometimes thickened, used as a sauce.
drawn work, ornamental work done on textiles by pulling out threads and embroidering or hemstitching the edges.
draw·plate (drô′plāt′), ***n.*** a metal plate with holes in it through which wire is drawn to get the desired thickness.
draw poker, a form of poker in which each player is dealt five cards, and unwanted cards (usually not more than three) may be discarded and replacements drawn from the deck before betting begins.
draw·shave (drô′shāv′), ***n.*** a drawknife.
draw·string (drô′striŋ′), ***n.*** a string drawn through a hem, as in the waist of a garment or mouth of a bag, to fasten or close it by taking up the fullness.
draw·tube (drô′tōōb′, drô′tūb′), ***n.*** a tube sliding within another tube, as in a microscope: see **microscope,** illus.
dray (drā), ***n.*** [ME. *dreie,* orig., a drag, sled; AS. *dræge,* lit., something drawn < *dragan;* see DRAG, DRAW], a low,

sturdily built cart with detachable sides, for carrying heavy loads. *v.t.* to carry or haul on a dray. *v.i.* to drive a dray.
dray·age (drā'ij), *n.* 1. the hauling of a load by dray. 2. the charge made for this.
dray·man (drā'mən), *n.* [*pl.* DRAYMEN (-mən)], a man who drives a dray.
Dray·ton, Michael (drā't'n), 1563–1631; English poet.
dread (dred), *v.t. & v.i.* [ME. *dreden;* AS. *on-drædan, a-drædan;* akin to OS. *andrādan,* OHG. *intrāten;* not formed by faulty separation of **ond-hrædan* but < IE. base **dhrēdh-*, to be uneasy, fear], 1. to anticipate with fear, misgiving, or distaste; fear intensely. 2. [Archaic], to regard with awe. *n.* 1. intense fear; apprehensive terror. 2. fear mixed with awe or reverence. *adj.* 1. dreaded or dreadful. 2. inspiring awe or reverence; awesome; solemn. —*SYN.* see **awe, fear.**
dread·ful (dred'fəl), *adj.* 1. inspiring dread; terrible or awesome. 2. [Colloq.], very bad, offensive, disagreeable, etc.
dread·ful·ly (dred'fəl-i), *adv.* 1. in a dreadful manner. 2. [Colloq.], very; extremely: as, I am *dreadfully* tired.
dread·nought, dread·naught (dred'nôt'), *n.* 1. a coat made of a thick woolen cloth. 2. the cloth. 3. [D-], a heavy, armored British battleship built in 1906, the first to have a large battery of 12-inch guns capable of being fired simultaneously in the same direction. 4. any large, powerful, heavily armored battleship of this sort.
dream (drēm), *n.* [ME. *dream, dreem;* in form < AS. *dream,* joy, music (OS. *drōm);* in sense < ON. *draum* (OFris. *drām,* MD. *droom,* G. *traum*), a dream; Gmc. **draugma,* phantom < IE. base **dhreugh-*, to deceive, as in G. *trügen,* to deceive & ON. *draugr,* ghost], 1. a sequence of sensations, images, thoughts, etc. passing through a sleeping person's mind. 2. a fanciful vision or fancy of the conscious mind; daydream; reverie. 3. the state, as of abstraction or reverie, in which such a daydream occurs. 4. a fond hope or aspiration. 5. anything so lovely, charming, transitory, etc. as to seem dreamlike. *v.i.* [DREAMED (drēmd) or DREAMT (dremt), DREAMING], 1. to have dreams. 2. to have daydreams. 3. to have vague notions or any conception (*of*). *v.t.* 1. to dream of. 2. to spend in dreaming (with *away* or *out*). 3. to imagine as possible; fancy; suppose.
dream up, [Colloq.], to conceive of, imagine, or devise, as by giving free rein to the imagination.
dream·er (drēm'ẽr), *n.* 1. a person who dreams. 2. an impractical person; visionary.
dream·i·ly (drēm''l-i), *adv.* in a dreamy manner.
dream·i·ness (drēm'i-nis), *n.* the quality or state of being dreamy.
dream·land (drēm'land'), *n.* 1. a place that seems to appear to one in dreams. 2. any lovely but imaginary place. 3. sleep.
dreamt (dremt), alternative past tense and past participle of **dream.**
dream world, a fanciful, pleasant world such as may be seen in a dream or imagined.
dream·y (drēm'i), *adj.* [DREAMIER (-i-ẽr), DREAMIEST (-i-ist)], 1. filled with dreams. 2. fond of daydreaming; given to reverie; visionary; impractical: as, a *dreamy* idealist. 3. like something in a dream; shadowy; vague; misty: as, a *dreamy* scene. 4. lulling; soft and soothing: as, a *dreamy* melody.
drear (drêr), *adj.* [Poetic], dreary; melancholy.
drear·i·ly (drêr''l-i), *adv.* in a dreary manner.
drear·i·ness (drêr'i-nis), *n.* the quality or state of being dreary.
drear·y (drêr'i), *adj.* [DREARIER (-i-ẽr), DREARIEST (-i-ist)], [ME. *drery, dreri;* AS. *dreorig,* sad, mournful, orig., bloody, gory < *dreor,* blood < base of *dreosan,* to drip], 1. gloomy; cheerless; depressing; dismal; dull. 2. [Archaic], sad.
dredge (drej), *n.* [< obs. D. *dregghe, dregge* or AS. **dreig* (< *dragan);* for base, see DRAG, DRAW], 1. a device consisting of a net attached to a frame, dragged along the bottom of a river, bay, etc. to gather shellfish or other things. 2. a dredging machine. *v.t.* [DREDGED (drejd), DREDGING], 1. to search for or gather with a dredge. 2. to enlarge or clean out (a river channel, harbor, etc.) with a dredge. *v.i.* to use a dredge.

DREDGE

dredge (drej), *v.t.* [DREDGED (drejd), DREDGING], [< ME. *dragge, dragie,* sweetmeat; OFr. *dragee;* prob. < L. *tragemata* < Gr. *tragēmata,* sweetmeats, confectionery], 1. to sprinkle with flour or other powdery substance. 2. to sprinkle or sift (flour, etc.).
dredg·er (drej'ẽr), *n.* 1. a person who operates or uses a dredge. 2. a boat with a dredge for gathering shellfish. 3. a dredging machine.
dredg·er (drej'ẽr), *n.* [< *dredge* (to sprinkle) + *-er*], a perforated container for sprinkling powdered substances.
dredging machine, [see DREDGE, *n.* & *v.*], an apparatus for scooping up mud, sand, etc., as in deepening or clearing channels, harbors, or river beds.
dree (drē), *v.t.* [DREED (drēd), DREEING], [AS. *dreogan*], [Scot. & Archaic], to endure; suffer. *adj.* [Scot. & Archaic], dreary; tedious.
dreg·gy (dreg'i), *adj.* [DREGGIER (-i-ẽr), DREGGIEST (-i-ist)], full of, or having the nature of, dregs; foul.
dregs (dregz), *n.pl.* [ME. *dregges;* ON. *dregg,* barm, lees; IE. **dherēgh,* residue (< base **dher-*, dark, dirty, smelly, etc.); see DARK, DRAB], 1. the particles of solid matter that go to the bottom in a liquid; lees; hence, 2. the most worthless part of anything: as, the *dregs* of society. 3. *sing.* a small amount remaining; residue.
‡**Drei·bund** (drī'boont'), *n.* [G.; *drei,* three + *bund,* a league], 1. a triple alliance. 2. the alliance of Austria-Hungary, Germany, and Italy (1882–1915).
Drei·ser, Theodore (drī'sẽr, drī'zẽr), 1871–1945; American novelist.
drench (drench), *v.t.* [ME. *drenchen;* AS. *drencan,* to make drink, drown, caus. of *drincan,* to drink; akin to OHG. *trenkan* (Goth. *dragkjan*) < Gmc. **drankjan; *drank-*, preterit stem of **drinkan* (see DRINK) + *-jan,* caus. suffix], 1. to make (a horse, cow, etc.) drink something, especially medicine. 2. to wet all over; soak or saturate in liquid. *n.* 1. a large dose or draught, especially for a sick animal. 2. a drenching. 3. a thing that drenches; solution for soaking. —*SYN.* see **soak.**
Dres·den (drez'dən; G. drās'dən), *n.* 1. the capital of the state of Saxony, Germany: pop., 625,000. 2. a fine porcelain or chinaware made near Dresden. *adj.* designating such porcelain or chinaware.
dress (dres), *v.t.* [DRESSED or DREST (drest), DRESSING], [ME. *dressen,* to make straight, direct; OFr. *dresser,* to set up, arrange; LL. **directiare* < L. *directus;* see DIRECT], 1. to put clothes on; clothe. 2. to provide with clothing. 3. to decorate; trim; adorn. 4. to arrange a display in: as, he *dresses* store windows. 5. to arrange or do up (the hair). 6. to arrange (troops, etc.) in a straight line or lines. 7. to apply medicines and bandages to (a wound, sore, etc.). 8. to prepare; make ready for use; especially, *a*) to clean and draw (a fowl). *b*) to till, cultivate, or prune (fields or plants). *c*) to curry (a horse, leather, etc.). *d*) to smooth and polish (stone, wood, etc.). *v.i.* 1. to put on clothes; wear clothes. 2. to dress in formal clothes. 3. to get into a straight line; take up proper alignment. *n.* 1. clothes; clothing; apparel. 2. the usual outer garment worn by women, generally of one piece with a skirt. 3. formal clothes. 4. external covering or appearance. *adj.* 1. of or for dresses: as, *dress* material. 2. worn on formal occasions: as, a *dress* suit.
dress down, [Colloq.], 1. to reprimand; scold. 2. to give a beating to; thrash.
dress ship, to raise the ensign and put up all code flags and bunting on a ship.
dress up, 1. to dress in formal clothes, or in clothes less informal or more elegant, showy, etc. than one is wearing or usually wears. 2. to arrange in a straight line, as troops.
dress circle, a section of seats in a theater or concert hall, usually behind and above the orchestra: so called because formal dress was formerly customary there.
dress coat, a black or very dark blue coat with tails, part of a man's formal dress.
dress·er (dres'ẽr), *n.* 1. a person who dresses another person; valet, etc. 2. a person who dresses something, as store windows, leather, wounds, etc. 3. a tool used for dressing wood, stone, etc. 4. a person who dresses elegantly or in a certain way: as, a fancy *dresser.*
dress·er (dres'ẽr), *n.* [Fr. *dressoir* < OFr. *dresser;* see DRESS], 1. a kitchen table on which food is prepared for serving. 2. a cupboard for dishes and kitchen utensils. 3. a chest of drawers for clothes, with a mirror: also called *bureau.*
dress goods, cloth for dresses.
dress·i·ly (dres''l-i), *adv.* in a dressy manner.
dress·i·ness (dres'i-nis), *n.* the quality of being dressy.
dress·ing (dres'iŋ), *n.* 1. the act of a person or thing that dresses. 2. that which is used to dress a person (as clothes) or a thing (as manure applied to soil, medicines and bandages applied to wounds, etc.). 3. a substance used to stiffen fabric during manufacture. 4. a sauce added to salads and other dishes: as, French *dressing.* 5. a stuffing, as of bread, seasoning, etc., for roast fowl. 6. [Colloq.], a dressing-down.
dressing case, a case fitted with brushes, combs, etc.
dress·ing-down (dres'iŋ-doun'), *n.* [Colloq.], 1. a reprimand; scolding. 2. a thrashing; beating.
dressing gown, a loose robe for wear when one is undressed or lounging.
dressing room, a room for getting dressed in; especially, in the *theater,* a room backstage where actors dress and make up for their roles.
dressing table, a low stand or table with a mirror, for use while putting on cosmetics, etc.
dress·mak·er (dres'māk'ẽr), *n.* a person who makes women's dresses and the like. *adj.* designating or of a woman's suit, coat, etc. not cut on severe, mannish lines: distinguished from *tailored.*

dress·mak·ing (dres′māk′iŋ), *n.* the art, process, work, or business of making dresses.
dress parade, a parade in dress uniform, as of troops on review.
dress rehearsal, a final rehearsal, as of a play, ceremony, or military engagement, performed in exactly the manner in which it is to take place.
dress suit, a man's formal suit for evening wear.
dress·y (dres′i), *adj.* [DRESSIER (-i-ẽr), DRESSIEST (-i-ist)], [Colloq.], 1. wearing showy, elaborate clothes. 2. stylish; elegant; smart: said of clothes, parties, etc.
drest (drest), alternative past tense and past participle of **dress.**
drew (drōō), past tense of **draw.**
Drew, John (drōō), 1853–1927; American actor.
Drey·fus, Alfred (drā′fəs, drī′fəs; Fr. dre′füs′), 1859–1935; French army officer convicted of treason and imprisoned but later released and restored to his rank when investigation showed him to be the victim of anti-Semitism and conspiracy.
drib (drib), *v.i. & v.t.* [DRIBBED (dribd), DRIBBING], [< *drip*], [Obs.], to fall, or let fall, in or as in driblets.
 dribs and drabs, [< N. Brit. dial. *drib*, driblet, drop-let + *drab* for *drap*, dial. form of *drop*, *n.*], [Colloq.], small amounts.
drib·ble (drib′'l), *v.i. & v.t.* [DRIBBLED (-'ld), DRIBBLING], [freq. of *drib & drip*], 1. to flow, or let flow, in drops or driblets; trickle. 2. to slaver; drool. 3. in *basketball*, to bounce (the ball) or move (the ball) forward by repeated bounces. 4. in *soccer*, etc., to move (the ball) forward by a rapid succession of short kicks. *n.* 1. a small drop; driblet; dribbling flow. 2. the act of dribbling a ball. 3. [Colloq.], a drizzling rain.
drib·let, drib·blet (drib′lit), *n.* [*drib* (see DRIBBLE) + *-let*], a small amount; bit: as, he pays his debt in *driblets*.
dried (drīd), past tense and past participle of **dry.**
driegh (drēkh), *adj.* [Scot.], dree.
dri·er (drī′ẽr), *n.* 1. a person or thing that dries. 2. an apparatus for drying by heating, blowing, etc. 3. a substance added to paint, varnish, etc. to make it dry fast. Also spelled **dryer.** *adj.* comparative of **dry.**
dri·est (drī′ist), *adj.* superlative of **dry.**
drift (drift), *n.* [ME. *drift*, *dryft* (akin to D. *drift*, OHG. *trift*, herd, drifting) < AS. *drifan*; see DRIVE], 1. a driving. 2. a drifting; being driven or carried along, as by a current of air or water. 3. the course on which something is directed. 4. the deviation of a ship or airplane from its path, caused by side currents or winds. 5. a tendency; inclination; trend. 6. meaning; intent; tenor. 7. something driven, as rain, snow, dust, or smoke driven before the wind, or floating matter driven by water currents. 8. a heap of snow, sand, etc., piled up by the wind. 9. in *geology*, rocks, gravel, sand, etc., carried away from one place and deposited in another by a river or glacier. 10. in *mechanics*, *a)* a tool used for ramming or driving down a heavy object. *b)* a tool for enlarging or shaping holes. 11. in *mining*, a horizontal passageway driven into or along the path of a vein or rock layer. 12. in *physical geography*, a slow ocean current. *v.i.* 1. to be carried along by or as by a current; hence, 2. to be carried along by circumstances; go along aimlessly. 3. to accumulate in heaps by force of wind or water. *v.t.* to cause to drift. —*SYN.* see **tendency, wash.**
drift·age (drif′tij), *n.* 1. a drifting. 2. the deviation caused by drifting. 3. that which has drifted; anything that drifts about or is washed ashore.
drift anchor, a drag anchor.
drift·er (drif′tẽr), *n.* 1. a person or thing that drifts. 2. a boat carrying nets that are allowed to drift with the tide: distinguished from *trawler*.
drift·wood (drift′wood′), *n.* wood drifting in the water or washed ashore: often used figuratively.
drift·y (drif′ti), *adj.* [DRIFTIER (-ti-ẽr), DRIFTIEST (-ti-ist)], having drifts or a tendency to form drifts.
drill (dril), *n.* [D. *dril* < the *v.*], 1. a tool or apparatus for boring holes in wood, metal, stone, etc. 2. a snail that bores into the shells of oysters and kills them. 3. military or physical exercise and training, especially of a group, as in marching and the manual of arms; hence, 4. the process of training or teaching by making those trained repeat an exercise again and again. 5. the method or style of drilling. *v.t.* [D. *drillen* < MD. *drille*, a hole; akin to Eng. *-tril*, as in *nostril*; cf. THRILL], 1. to bore a hole in with or as with a drill. 2. to train in military or physical exercises. 3. to teach or train by having do repeated exercises. *v.i.* 1. to bore a hole or holes. 2. to engage in, or be put through, military, physical, or mental exercises. —*SYN.* see **practice.**

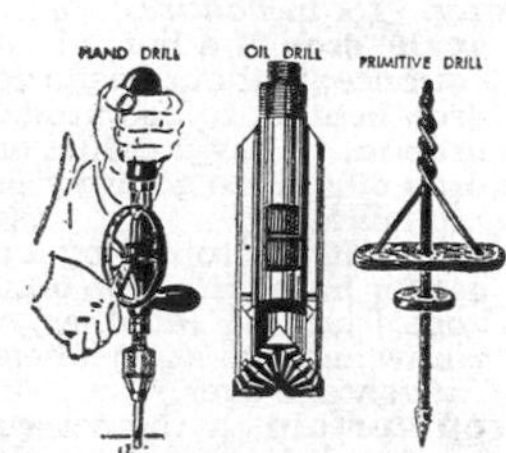

TYPES OF DRILL

drill (dril), *n.* [? ult. same word as *drill* (a tool)], 1. a furrow in which seeds are planted. 2. a row of planted seeds. 3. a machine for making holes or furrows and dropping seeds into them. *v.t.* 1. to sow (seeds) in rows. 2. to plant (a field) in drills.
drill (dril), *n.* [earlier *drilling* < MHG. *dril(i)ch* (G. *drillich*), cloth woven with three threads < L. *trilix*, three-threaded], a coarse linen or cotton cloth with a diagonal weave, used for work clothes, etc.
drill (dril), *n.* [? < Fr. *drill*, a soldier], a baboon native to western Africa, like the mandrill but smaller.
drill·er (dril′ẽr), *n.* a person or thing that drills.
dril·ling (dril′iŋ), *n.* drill (kind of cloth).
drill·mas·ter (dril′mas′tẽr, dril′mäs′tẽr), *n.* 1. an instructor in military drill. 2. a person who teaches by drilling.
drill press, a machine tool for drilling holes in metal, etc.
drill·stock (dril′stok′), *n.* that part of a drilling machine or tool which holds the shank of a drill or bit.
dri·ly (drī′li), *adv.* dryly.
drink (driŋk), *v.t.* [DRANK (draŋk) or *archaic* DRUNK (druŋk), DRUNK or *archaic* DRUNKEN or DRANK, DRINKING], [ME. *drinken*; AS. *drincan*; akin to D. *drinken*, OFris. *drinka*, OHG. *trinkan*, Goth. *drigkan*], 1. to take (liquid) into the mouth and swallow it. 2. to absorb (liquid or moisture). 3. to swallow the contents of. 4. to drink in honor of; drink a toast to. *v.i.* 1. to take liquid into the mouth and swallow it. 2. to absorb anything as if in drinking. 3. to drink alcoholic liquor. 4. to drink alcoholic liquor habitually or excessively. *n.* 1. any liquid for drinking; beverage. 2. alcoholic liquor. 3. habitual or excessive use of alcoholic liquor. 4. a portion of liquid drunk or for drinking. 5. [Slang], any body of water; especially, the ocean.
 drink in, to take in with the senses or the mind, especially in an eager manner.
 drink to, to drink in honor of; drink a toast to.
drink·a·ble (driŋk′ə b'l), *adj.* suitable for drinking. *n.* *usually in pl.* a thing to drink; beverage.
drink·er (driŋk′ẽr), *n.* 1. a person who drinks. 2. a person who drinks alcoholic liquor habitually.
Drink·er respirator (driŋk′ẽr), [after the Am. inventor, Philip *Drinker* (1893–)], an apparatus for maintaining artificial respiration: also called *iron lung*.
drinking song, a song celebrating the pleasures of drinking alcoholic liquors; song for a drinking party.
Drink·wa·ter, John (driŋk′wô′tẽr, driŋk′wä′tẽr), 1882–1937; English poet, critic, and dramatist.
drip (drip), *v.i. & v.t.* [DRIPPED or DRIPT (dript), DRIPPING], [ME. *dryppen*; AS. *dryppan*, intens. form (< Gmc. **drupjan*); akin to AS. *dreopan* (G. *triefen*), to drop, drip; IE. base **dhreub-*, to break away, crumble; cf. DROP], to fall, or let fall, in drops. *n.* 1. a falling in drops; trickling. 2. moisture or liquid falling in drops. 3. the sound made by liquid falling in drops. 4. a projecting part of a sill, cornice, etc. that sheds rain water. 5. [Slang], a person regarded as unpleasant or insipid.
drip-dry (drip′drī′), *adj.* designating or of fabrics that dry quickly when hung soaking wet and require little or no ironing.
drip grind, a fine grind of coffee, for use in a dripolator.
drip·o·la·tor (drip′ə-lā′tẽr), *n.* [*drip* + *-olator* as in *percolator*], a kind of coffeepot in three sections: boiling water in the top section seeps slowly through small holes into finely ground coffee in the perforated middle section, and then drips into the one below.
drip·ping (drip′iŋ), *adj.* [ppr. of *drip*], thoroughly wet. *n.* 1. a falling of liquid drop by drop. 2. *usually pl.* anything that drips; especially, the fat and juices that drip from roasting meat.
dripping pan, a pan to catch the drippings from meat being cooked: also **drip pan.**
drip·stone (drip′stōn′), *n.* 1. a projecting part of a sill, cornice, etc. that sheds rain water. 2. calcium carbonate, $CaCO_3$, deposited by dripping water in the form of stalactites or stalagmites. 3. a porous stone used as a filter.
dript (dript), alternative past tense and past participle of **drip.**
drive (drīv), *v.t.* [DROVE (drōv), DRIVEN (driv′'n), DRIVING], [ME. *driven*; AS. *drifan*; akin to Goth. *dreiban*, G. *treiben*, ON. *drīfa*; ? < IE. base **dhreibh-*, to push, force on], 1. to force to go; urge onward; push forward. 2. to force into or from a state or act: as, ambition *drove* him to crime. 3. to force to work, usually to excess. 4. to force by a blow, thrust, or stroke; throw, hit, or cast hard and swiftly: as, the batter *drove* the ball into the bleachers. 5. to cause to go through; make penetrate. 6. to make or produce by doing this: as, he *drove* an oil well. 7. to control the movement or direct

the course of (an automobile, wagon, locomotive, etc.); hence, 8. to transport in an automobile or other vehicle. 9. to impel or propel as motive power; set or keep going; cause to function: as, a gasoline engine *drives* a motorboat. 10. to carry on with vigor; push (a bargain, etc.) through. 11. in *hunting*, *a*) to chase (game) from thickets into the clear or into nets, traps, etc. *b*) to cover (an area) in this way. *v.i.* 1. to advance violently; dash. 2. to drive a blow, ball, missile, etc. 3. to be driven; operate: said of an automobile. 4. to go or be conveyed in a vehicle. 5. to operate a motor vehicle. *n.* 1. a driving. 2. a trip in a vehicle. 3. a road for automobiles, etc. 4. a rounding up of animals for branding, killing, etc. 5. a hard, swift blow, thrust, etc., as of a ball in a game. 6. the manner in which a ball, etc. is driven. 7. an organized movement to achieve some purpose; campaign. 8. energy; push: as, a person with initiative and *drive*. 9. that which is urgent or pressing; pressure. 10. a collection of logs floating down a river. 11. the apparatus controlling the propulsion of a motor vehicle: as, a gear *drive*. 12. a device that communicates motion to a machine or machine part. 13. [Colloq.], a driveway. 14. in *psychology*, any of the basic impulses or urges.

drive at, 1. to aim at. 2. to mean; intend.

let drive, to hit or aim.

drive-in (drīv′in′), *adj.* 1. designating a place where people can drive up in automobiles and be served food, make bank deposits, etc. without having to get out. 2. designating a kind of outdoor theater where people can see a motion picture while sitting in parked automobiles. *n.* such a restaurant, theater, etc.

driv·el (driv′'l), *v.i.* [DRIVELED or DRIVELLED (-'ld), DRIVELING or DRIVELLING], [ME. *drivelen*, *drevelen* < AS. *dreflian*, to slobber], 1. to let saliva flow from one's mouth; drool; slobber. 2. to flow from the mouth like saliva. 3. to speak in a silly or stupid manner; talk childish nonsense. *v.t.* 1. to let run from the mouth. 2. to say in a silly, stupid, or nonsensical manner. *n.* 1. saliva running from the mouth. 2. silly, stupid talk; childish nonsense; twaddle.

driv·el·er, driv·el·ler (driv′'l-ẽr), *n.* one who drivels.

driv·en (driv′'n), past participle of **drive**. *adj.* 1. moved along and piled up by the wind: as, *driven* snow. 2. forced into a (specified) condition: as, *driven* mad.

driv·er (drīv′ẽr), *n.* 1. a person who drives; specifically, *a*) one who drives an automobile, horse, locomotive, etc. *b*) one who herds cattle. *c*) one who makes his subordinates work hard. 2. a thing that drives; specifically, *a*) a mallet, hammer, tamper, etc. *b*) a wooden-headed golf club with little loft, used in hitting the ball from the tee: see **golf club**, illus. *c*) any machine part that communicates motion to another part.

driver ant, any of several African stinging ants that travel together in large numbers.

drive·way (drīv′wā′), *n.* 1. a path leading from a garage or house to the street, used especially by automobiles. 2. a road for automobiles, etc.; drive.

driv·ing (drīv′iŋ), *adj.* [ppr. of *drive*], 1. transmitting force or motion: as, a *driving* belt. 2. moving with force and violence: as, a *driving* rain.

driving iron, a golf club with an iron head and a nearly straight face.

driving wheel, a wheel that transmits motion from one part of a mechanism to another, as one of the large wheels of a locomotive which receive power from the engine by means of the connecting rod.

driz·zle (driz′'l), *v.i.* [DRIZZLED (-'ld), DRIZZLING], [< ME. *dresen* (< AS. *dreosan*), to fall in drops; + *-le*, freq. suffix], to rain in fine, mistlike drops. *n.* a rain of this kind.

driz·zly (driz′li), *adj.* drizzling; characterized by a drizzle.

Dro·ghe·da (dro′hē-də, drô′i-də), *n.* a town at the mouth of the Boyne River, eastern Ireland: pop., 14,500: its people were massacred by Cromwell when he captured the town (1649).

dro·gher (drō′gẽr), *n.* [16th-c. Fr. *drogueur* < D. *drogher*, *drooger*, lit., drier (< MD. *droghe*, dry), ship in which fish were dried or smoked after catching; cf. D. *droogen haring*, smoked herring], a slow, awkward coasting sailboat, originally of the West Indies.

droit (droit; Fr. drwå), *n.* [Fr. < OFr. *dreit;* LL. *directum*, right, justice < L. *directus;* see DIRECT], 1. a legal right. 2. that to which one has legal claim.

droll (drōl), *adj.* [Fr. *drôle;* used earlier as n., buffoon, jester < D. *drol*, short, stout fellow, lit., bowling pin], amusing in a quaint way; humorously odd. *n.* a droll person; jester; buffoon. *v.i.* to joke; play the jester. —*SYN.* see **funny**.

droll·er·y (drōl′ẽr-i), *n.* [*pl.* DROLLERIES (-iz)], 1. anything quaintly amusing; droll act, remark, etc. 2. the act of joking. 3. a droll quality; quaint humor.

drol·ly (drōl′li), *adv.* in a droll manner.

-drome (drōm), [< Gr. *dromas;* see DROMEDARY], a suffix meaning *running*, *racecourse*, as in *hippodrome*.

drom·e·dar·y (drom′ə-der′i), *n.* [*pl.* DROMEDARIES (-iz)], [ME. *dromedarie;* OFr. *dromadaire;* LL. *dromedarius* (*camelus*), dromedary (camel) < L. *dromas*, dromedary; Gr. *dromas*, *dromad-*, a runner, running < *dramein*, to run], a camel trained for fast riding; especially, the one-humped Arabian camel.

drom·on (drom′'n), *n.* a dromond.

drom·ond (drom′ənd, drum′ənd), *n.* [ME.; OFr. *dromon*(*t*), swift ship < Byzantine Gr. *dromon;* see DROMEDARY], a large, swift-sailing ship of the Middle Ages.

-dro·mous (drō′məs, drə-məs), [see -DROME], a suffix meaning *running*, *moving*, as in *catadromous*.

drone (drōn), *n.* [ME.; AS. *dran;* OS. *dran;* akin to MLG. *drone* (whence G. *drohne*)*;* IE. base **dhren-*, etc., to hum, murmur, as in Goth. *drunjus*, sound, noise], 1. a male bee, especially a male honeybee, which serves only in a reproductive capacity, has no sting, and does no work: see **bee**, illus. 2. a person who does no work but lives by the work of others; idler; loafer. 3. a pilotless airplane whose flight is radio-controlled by an operator in an accompanying craft or on the ground. *v.i.* [DRONED (drōnd), DRONING], to live in idleness; loaf.

drone (drōn), *v.i.* [DRONED (drōnd), DRONING], [ME. *dronen*, to sound; prob. < *drone* (bee)], 1. to make a continuous and monotonous humming or buzzing sound. 2. to talk in a monotonous voice. *v.t.* to utter in a dull, monotonous tone. *n.* 1. a continuous and monotonous humming or buzzing sound. 2. a bagpipe. 3. its bass pipe. 4. a bass voice or part, sustaining a single low tone. 5. such a tone.

drool (drōōl), *v.i.* [< *drivel*], 1. to let saliva flow from one's mouth; drivel. 2. to flow from the mouth, as saliva. 3. [Slang], to speak in a silly or stupid manner; talk childish nonsense. *v.t.* 1. to let run from the mouth: as, he *drooled* tobacco juice over his chin. 2. [Slang], to say in a silly, stupid, or nonsensical manner. *n.* 1. saliva running from the mouth. 2. [Slang], silly, stupid talk; childish nonsense; twaddle; drivel.

droop (drōōp), *v.i.* [ME. *droupen;* ON. *drūpa* < base of *drop*, drip; see DROP], 1. to sink down; hang or bend down. 2. to lose vitality or strength; become weakened; languish. 3. to become dejected or dispirited. *v.t.* to let sink or hang down. *n.* a drooping.

droop·i·ness (drōōp′i-nis), *n.* the quality or state of being droopy.

droop·y (drōōp′i), *adj.* [DROOPIER (-i-ẽr), DROOPIEST (-i-ist)], drooping or tending to droop.

drop (drop), *n.* [ME. *drope;* AS. *dropa;* akin to G. *tropf-* in *tropfen;* for the base, see DRIP], 1. a small quantity of liquid that is somewhat spherical or pear-shaped, as when falling. 2. a very small quantity of liquid. 3. *pl.* liquid medicine taken in drops. 4. a very small quantity of anything. 5. a thing like a drop in shape, size, etc., as a pendent earring or a small piece of candy. 6. a dropping; sudden fall, descent, slump, or decrease: as, a *drop* in prices. 7. anything that drops or is used for dropping or covering something, as a drop curtain, a drop hammer, a trap door, or a slot for depositing letters. 8. the distance between a higher and lower level; depth to which or distance through which anything falls or sinks. 9. in *football*, a drop kick. *v.i.* [DROPPED or, *occas.*, DROPT (dropt), DROPPING], 1. to fall in drops. 2. to fall; come down. 3. to sink to the ground exhausted, wounded, or dead. 4. to fall into a specified state; pass into a less active or less desirable condition: as, she *dropped* off to sleep. 5. to come to an end or to nothing: as, let the matter *drop*. 6. to slump; become lower or less, as temperatures, prices, etc. 7. to move down with a current of water or air. 8. to be born: said of animals. *v.t.* 1. to let fall in drops. 2. to sprinkle with drops. 3. to let fall; release hold of. 4. to give birth to: said of animals. 5. to utter (a suggestion, hint, etc.) casually. 6. to send (a letter). 7. to cause to fall, as by wounding or killing. 8. to dismiss; have done with. 9. to lower. 10. to omit (a letter or letters) in a word. 11. to poach (an egg). 12. [Colloq.], to leave (a person or thing) at a specified place. 13. [Slang], to lose (money). 14. in *football*, *a*) to drop-kick (a ball). *b*) to make (a goal) in this way. 15. in *nautical usage*, to outdistance.

at the drop of a hat, 1. at a signal. 2. immediately; at once; without hesitation or reluctance.

drop behind, to be outdistanced; fall behind.

drop in, to pay a casual or unexpected visit.

drop off, 1. to go away or out of sight. 2. [Colloq.], to fall asleep.

drop out, to stop being a member or participant.

get (or **have**) **the drop on**, [Slang], 1. to draw and aim one's gun at (another) more quickly than he can draw and aim at one; hence, 2. to get (or have) any advantage over.

drop curtain, a theater curtain that can be lowered and raised.

drop-forge (drop′fôrj′, drop′fōrj′), *v.t.* to pound (heated metal) between dies with a drop hammer.

drop hammer, 1. a machine for pounding metal into shape, with a heavy weight that is raised and then dropped on the metal. 2. this weight.

drop-kick (drop′kik′), *v.t.* & *v.i.* to give a drop kick to (a football).

drop kick, in *football*, a kick in which the player drops

the ball in front of him and kicks it just as it rebounds from the ground.
drop-leaf (drop'lēf'), *adj.* having a drop leaf.
drop leaf, a hinged board attached to the side or end of a table as an extension of the surface: it hangs down when not in use.
drop·let (drop'lit), *n.* a very small drop.
drop letter, a letter posted at and delivered from the same office.
drop·light (drop'līt'), *n.* a light so suspended from a fixture that it can be raised or lowered as desired.
drop·out (drop'out'), *n.* a student who withdraws from school, especially high school, before graduating.
drop·per (drop'ẽr), *n.* 1. a person or thing that drops. 2. a small glass tube with openings at both ends, one reduced, the other usually capped by a hollow rubber piece that is squeezed to draw liquid into the other end or to release it in drops.
drop·ping (drop'iŋ), *n.* 1. the act of a person or thing that drops. 2. that which drops or falls in drops. 3. *pl.* dung of animals.
drop press, a drop hammer.
drop shot, 1. shot made by letting molten metal fall in drops to solidify in a container of water below. 2. in *tennis*, a stroke by which the ball is made to drop just over the net and with very little bounce.
drop·si·cal (drop'si-k'l), *adj.* 1. of or like dropsy. 2. having dropsy.
drop·sied (drop'sid), *adj.* having dropsy.
drop·sy (drop'si), *n.* [ME. *dropsie, dropesie* < *ydropesie;* OFr. *idropisie;* L. *hydropisis* < Gr. *hydrōps*, dropsy < *hydōr*, water], an abnormal accumulation of serous fluid in cavities or tissues of the body.
dropt (dropt), occasional past tense and past participle of **drop.**
drop·wort (drop'wũrt'), *n.* a tall plant of the rose family, with fernlike leaves and white or reddish flowers: it resembles the meadowsweet.
drosh·ky (drosh'ki, drôsh'ki), *n.* [*pl.* DROSHKIES (-kiz)], [Russ. *drozhki*, dim. of *drogi*, a wagon < *droga*, a bar between front and back axles, lit., a plank], 1. a low, open, four-wheeled Russian carriage with a long, narrow bench which the passengers straddle. 2. any of various other carriages.

DROSHKY

dros·ky (dros'ki), *n.* [*pl.* DROSKIES (-kiz)], a droshky.
dro·soph·i·la (drō-sof'ə-lə, drə-sof'ə-lə), *n.* [*pl.* DROSOPHILAE (-lē')], [Mod. L. < Gr. *drosos*, dew, liquid + *philos*, loving], a small fly used in laboratory experiments in heredity because of its short life cycle and great reproductivity: also called *fruit fly.*
dross (drôs, dros), *n.* [ME. *drosse;* AS. *dros*, dregs < *dreosan*, to fall; see DREARY, DRIZZLE], 1. a scum formed on the surface of molten metal. 2. waste matter; worthless stuff; refuse; rubbish.
dross·i·ness (drôs'i-nis, dros'i-nis), *n.* the quality or state of being drossy.
dross·y (drôs'i, dros'i), *adj.* [DROSSIER (-i-ẽr), DROSSIEST (-i-ist)], of, like, or containing dross.
drought (drout), *n.* [ME. *drougth, drugthe;* AS. *drugoth*, dryness, dry ground < base of *dryge;* see DRY], 1. dryness; absence of moisture, especially of rain. 2. prolonged dry weather. 3. [Archaic], thirst. Also **drouth.**
drought·y (drout'i), *adj.* 1. characterized by or suffering from drought. 2. without moisture; dry; arid. 3. [Archaic or Dial.], thirsty.
drouth (drouth), *n.* drought.
drouth·y (drouth'i), *adj.* droughty.
drove (drōv), *n.* [ME. *drof;* AS. *draf* < *drifan;* see DRIVE], 1. a number of cattle, hogs, sheep, etc. driven or moving along as a group; flock; herd. 2. a moving crowd of people. 3. in *stonecutting*, *a)* a drove chisel. *b)* drove work. *v.t.* & *v.i.* [DROVED (drōvd), DROVING], to finish (stone) with a drove chisel. —***SYN.*** see **group.**
drove (drōv), past tense of **drive.**
drove chisel, a broad-faced chisel for smoothing stone.
dro·ver (drō'vẽr), *n.* 1. a person who takes a drove of animals to market. 2. a cattle dealer.
drove work, in *stonecutting*, the grooved surface of finished stone.
drown (droun), *v.i.* [ME. *drounen* < Anglo-N. **drun(k)na*, form of ON. *drukkna* without assimilated *n;* cf. obs. Dan. *drone;* akin to AS. *druncnian*, to become drunk, be drowned < *druncen*, pp. of *drincan;* see DRINK, DRUNK], to die by suffocation in water or other liquid. *v.t.* 1. to kill by suffocation in water or other liquid. 2. to cover with water; flood; inundate; soak. 3. to deaden or muffle (sound, etc.): as, the few boos were *drowned* out by applause. 4. to cause to disappear; get rid of: as, he *drowned* his worries in drink.
drowse (drouz), *v.i.* [DROWSED (drouzd), DROWSING], [< archaic D. *droosen;* akin to AS. *drusian*, to sink, become sluggish < base of *dreosan*, to fall; see DREARY, DRIZZLE], to be sleepy or almost asleep; doze. *v.t.* 1. to make sleepy; make sluggish or dull, as with sleep. 2. to spend (time) in drowsing. *n.* the quality or state of being sleepy or almost asleep; doze.
drow·si·head (drou'zi-hed'), *n.* [< *drowsy* + *-head*, -hood], [Archaic], drowsiness.
drow·si·hood (drou'zi-hood'), *n.* [< *drowsy* + *-hood*], [Archaic], drowsiness.
drow·si·ly (drou'z'l-i), *adv.* in a drowsy manner; sleepily.
drow·si·ness (drou'zi-nis), *n.* the quality or state of being drowsy; sleepiness.
drow·sy (drou'zi), *adj.* [DROWSIER (-zi-ẽr), DROWSIEST (-zi-ist)], [see DROWSE], 1. being or making sleepy or half asleep; lethargic or soporific. 2. brought on by sleepiness. —***SYN.*** see **sleepy.**
drub (drub), *v.t.* [DRUBBED (drubd), DRUBBING], [Turk. *durb* < Ar. *darb*, a beating < *daraba*, to cudgel, bastinado], 1. to beat with a stick or club; cudgel; thrash. 2. to defeat soundly in a fight, contest, etc. *n.* a blow with a club; thump.
drub·bing (drub'iŋ), *n.* [see DRUB], a sound beating, thrashing, or defeat.
drudge (druj), *n.* [? < base in AS. *dreogan;* see DREE], a person who does hard, menial, or unpleasant work. *v.i.* [DRUDGED (drujd), DRUDGING], to do such work.
drudg·er·y (druj'ẽr-i), *n.* [*pl.* DRUDGERIES (-iz)], [see DRUDGE], work that is hard, menial, or unpleasant.
drug (drug), *n.* [ME. *drogge;* OFr. *drogue;* prob. < LG. *drooge (fat)*, dry (cask), the adj. being taken wrongly as the name of the contents], 1. any substance used as a medicine or as an ingredient in a medicine: some drugs are poisonous. 2. formerly, any substance used in chemistry, dyeing, etc. 3. a narcotic, especially one that is habit-forming. *v.t.* [DRUGGED (drugd), DRUGGING], 1. to put a harmful drug in (a beverage, etc.). 2. to stupefy or poison with or as with a drug. 3. to administer something nauseating to.
drug on the market, a commodity for which there is little or no demand because the supply is so plentiful.
drug addict, a habitual user of narcotics.
drug·get (drug'it), *n.* [Fr. *droguet*, dim. of *drogue*, stuff, trash; prob. of same origin as *drug*], 1. formerly, a woolen or part-woolen material used for clothing. 2. a coarse fabric used as a floor covering, carpet lining, etc. 3. a coarse rug from India made of jute or cotton and hair: also **India drugget.**
drug·gist (drug'ist), *n.* [Fr. *droguiste* < *drogue;* see DRUG], 1. a dealer in drugs, medical equipment, etc. 2. a person authorized to fill prescriptions; pharmacist.
drug·store (drug'stôr', drug'stōr'), *n.* a store where medical prescriptions are filled and drugs and medical supplies are sold: most drugstores now also sell cosmetics, tobacco, ice cream, books, etc.
dru·id, Dru·id (drōō'id), *n.* [Fr. *druide* < L. *druides, pl.* < Celt.; IE. **dru-wid*, lit., oak-wise (< base **derew-*, oak), hence prob. "very wise" in OIr. *drūi*, the druids, etc.], a member of a Celtic religious order of priests, soothsayers, judges, poets, etc. in ancient Britain, Ireland, and France, influential especially before the Celts were Christianized.
dru·id·ic (drōō-id'ik), *adj.* of druids or druidism.
dru·id·i·cal (drōō-id'i-k'l), *adj.* druidic.
dru·id·ism (drōō'id-iz'm), *n.* the religious and philosophic system of the druids.
drum (drum), *n.* [Englishing of D. *trom* or MLG. *trumme;* akin to ON., OS., OHG. *trumba*, trumpet, trumpet call, MHG. *trumpe*, trumpet, drum (see TRUMP) < Gmc. echoic base; ? influenced by L. *triumphare* (see TRIUMPH)], 1. a percussion instrument consisting of a hollow cylinder or hemisphere with a membrane stretched tightly over the end or ends, played by beating with the hands, sticks, etc. 2. the sound produced by beating a drum, or any sound like this. 3. any of various drumlike cylindrical objects. 4. a metal spool or cylinder around which cable, etc. is wound in a machine. 5. a barrellike metal container for oil, etc. 6. in *anatomy*, *a)* the middle ear. *b)* the eardrum. 7. in *architecture*, *a)* one of the cylindrical blocks making up the shaft of a stone column. *b)* the circular or polygonal wall supporting a dome. *v.i.* [DRUMMED (drumd), DRUMMING], 1. to beat a drum. 2. to beat or tap continually or rhythmically, as with the fingers. 3. to make a loud, reverberating sound by quivering the wings: said of the ruffed grouse, etc. *v.t.* 1. to play (a piece) on a drum. 2. to assemble by beating a drum.
drum into, to make known to by continued repetition.
drum out of, 1. originally, to expel from (the army) with drums beating. 2. to expel from in disgrace.
drum up, 1. to summon by or as by beating a drum. 2. to get (business, etc.) by canvassing or soliciting.
drum (drum), *n.* a drumlin.
drum·beat (drum'bēt'), *n.* a sound made by beating a drum.

drum·ble (drum'b'l, droom''l), *v.i.* [DRUMBLED (-b'ld, -'ld), DRUMBLING], [echoic var. < dial. *dummel* < *dumb*], [Obs. or British Dial.], to act or move sluggishly.
drum·fire (drum'fīr'), *n.* heavy and continuous gunfire, thought of as resembling drumbeats.
drum·fish (drum'fish'), *n.* [*pl.* DRUMFISH, DRUMFISHES (-iz); see FISH], any of various salt-water and fresh-water fishes that make a drumming noise.
drum·head (drum'hed'), *n.* 1. the membrane stretched over the open end or ends of a drum. 2. the eardrum. 3. the top of a capstan, into which bars are inserted for leverage in turning it.
drumhead court-martial, a court-martial held in the field for trial of offenses committed during military operations or troop movements: so called because the head of a drum was formerly used as the judges' table.
drum·lin (drum'lin), *n.* [< Ir. *druim*, narrow ridge; + *-lin*, dim. suffix < *-ling*], a long ridge or oval-shaped hill formed by glacial drift.
drum major, a person who leads a marching band, or one who precedes it, often twirling a baton and prancing.
drum ma·jor·ette (mā'jēr-et'), *n.* a girl drum major.
drum·mer (drum'ēr), *n.* 1. a drum player. 2. [see DRUM, phr. *drum up*], [Colloq.], a traveling salesman.
Drum·mond light (drum'ənd), [after Scot. inventor, T. *Drummond* (1797–1840)], limelight (calcium light).
drum·stick (drum'stik'), *n.* 1. a stick for beating a drum. 2. the lower half of the leg of a cooked fowl.
drunk (druŋk), [ME. *dronke* < *drunken;* see DRUNKEN], past participle and archaic past tense of **drink.** *adj.* (used in the predicate) 1. overcome by alcoholic liquor to the point of losing control over one's faculties; intoxicated. 2. overcome by any powerful emotion: as, *drunk* with joy, happiness, etc. *n.* [Slang], 1. a drunken person. 2. a drinking spree.
SYN.—**drunk** is the simple, direct word, always used in the predicate, for one who is overcome by alcoholic liquor (he is *drunk*); **drunken,** usually used attributively, is equivalent to **drunk** but sometimes implies habitual intemperate addiction to drink (a *drunken* bum); **intoxicated** and **inebriated** are euphemisms, the former often expressing slight drunkenness and the latter, a state of drunken exhilaration; there are many euphemistic and slang terms in English expressing varying degrees of drunkenness: e.g., **tipsy** (slight), **tight** (moderate, but without loss of muscular co-ordination), **blind** (great), **blotto** (to the point of unconsciousness), etc.—*ANT.* sober.
drunk·ard (drun'kērd), *n.* [*drunk* + *-ard;* ? after D. *dronkaard*], a person who often gets drunk; inebriate.
drunk·en (druŋ'kən), [ME.; AS., pp. of *drincan*, to drink], archaic past participle of **drink.** *adj.* (used before the noun) 1. intoxicated or habitually intoxicated; drunk. 2. caused by or occurring in a drunken condition. —*SYN.* see **drunk.**
drunk·en·ness (druŋ'kən-nis), *n.* the state or habit of being drunk; intoxication.
dru·pa·ceous (droo-pā'shəs), *adj.* 1. of or like a drupe. 2. producing drupes.
drupe (droop), *n.* [L. *drupa;* Gr. *dryppa*, overripe olive], any fruit with a soft, fleshy part (called *epicarp*) around an inner stone (called *endocarp*) that contains the seed, as an apricot, cherry, plum, etc.
drupe·let (droop'lit), *n.* a small drupe: a loganberry or blackberry consists of many drupelets.
Dru·ry Lane (droor'i), a street in London, famous in the 17th and 18th centuries for its theaters.
Druse (drooz), *n.* [Ar. *Duruz, pl.* < Ismail al-*Darazi* (lit., tailor), the founder (11th c.)], a member of a religious sect in Syria whose creed is basically Moslem with a mixture of Christian elements.
Dru·si·an, Dru·se·an (droo'zi-ən), *adj.* of the Druses or their religion.
Dru·sil·la (droo-sil'ə), [L., dim. of *Drusus*, familiar Roman name in the Livian family], a feminine name.
Dru·sus (droo'səs), *n.* (*Nero Claudius Drusus Germanicus*), Roman general; lived 38–9 B.C.
dry (drī), *adj.* [DRIER (drī'ēr), DRIEST (drī'ist)], [ME. *drye;* AS. *dryge;* akin to G. *trock-* in *trocken*, dry, D. *droog* (see DROGHER, DRUG); IE. **dhereugh*, fast, firm, solid (< base **dher-*, to hold out, hold fast, hold up), as in Fris. *dreegh*, firm, stable], 1. not watery; not under water: as, *dry* land. 2. having no moisture; not wet; not damp or moist. 3. not shedding tears. 4. lacking rain or water: as, a *dry* summer. 5. having lost moisture; arid; withered. 6. needing water or drink; thirsty. 7. not yielding milk or other liquid. 8. without butter, jam, etc. on it: as, *dry* toast. 9. solid: opposed to *liquid.* 10. [in reference to the effect on the palate], not sweet; unsweetened; sec: as, *dry* wine. 11. having no mucous or watery discharge: as, a *dry* cough. 12. without bleeding: as, a *dry* death. 13. prohibiting or opposed to the use or sale of alcoholic liquors: as, Kansas was a *dry* State. 14. unemotional; plain; matter-of-fact: as, *dry* facts. 15. unfruitful: as, a *dry* interview. 16. insipid; boring; dull: as, a *dry* lecture. *n.* [*pl.* DRYS (drīz)], [Colloq.], a person opposed to the use or sale of alcoholic liquors; prohibitionist. *v.t. & v.i.* [DRIED (drīd), DRYING], to make or become dry.
dry up, 1. to make or become thoroughly dry; parch; wither. 2. [Slang], to stop talking.
not dry behind the ears, [Colloq.], immature; inexperienced; naive.
SYN.—**dry** suggests a lack or insufficiency of moisture, in either a favorable or unfavorable sense (a *dry* climate, a *dry* river bed); **arid** implies an abnormal, intense dryness, especially with reference to a region or climate, and connotes barrenness or lifelessness (an *arid* waste).—*ANT.* wet, moist.
dry·ad, Dry·ad (drī'ad, drī'ad), *n.* [*pl.* DRYADS (-ədz, -adz), DRYADES (-ə-dēz')], [L. *dryas, dryadis;* Gr. *dryas* < *drys*, an oak, tree; cf. DRUID], in *Greek mythology*, any nymph living in a tree; wood nymph.
dry·ad·ic (drī-ad'ik), *adj.* of or like a dryad.
dry battery, 1. an electric battery made up of several connected dry cells. 2. a dry cell.
dry cell, a voltaic cell either sealed or treated with an absorbent so that its contents cannot spill.

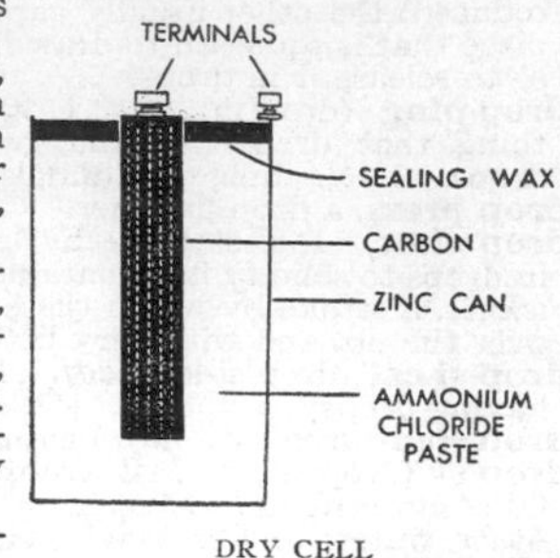

DRY CELL

dry-clean (drī'klēn', drī'klēn'), *v.t.* to clean (garments, etc.) with some solvent other than water, as naphtha, or gasoline.
dry cleaner, 1. a solvent such as naphtha, benzine, gasoline, carbon tetrachloride, etc., used in dry cleaning. 2. a person whose business or work is dry cleaning.
dry cleaning, the cleaning of garments, etc. with solvents such as naphtha or gasoline instead of with soap and water.
dry-cleanse (drī'klenz'), *v.t.* [DRY-CLEANSED (-klenzd'), DRY-CLEANSING], to dry-clean.
Dry·den, John (drī'd'n), 1631–1700; English poet, critic, and dramatist; poet laureate (1670–1688).
dry-dock (drī'dok'), *v.t. & v.i.* to place in or go into a dry dock.
dry dock, a dock from which the water can be emptied, used for building and repairing ships.
dry·er (drī'ēr), *n.* a drier.
dry-eyed (drī'īd'), *adj.* not weeping; shedding no tears.
dry-farm (drī'färm'), *v.i. & v.t.* to do dry farming on (land).
dry farmer, a farmer who does dry farming.
dry farming, farming in an almost rainless region without the help of irrigation: it is done by conserving the natural moisture of the soil and by planting crops that can resist drought.

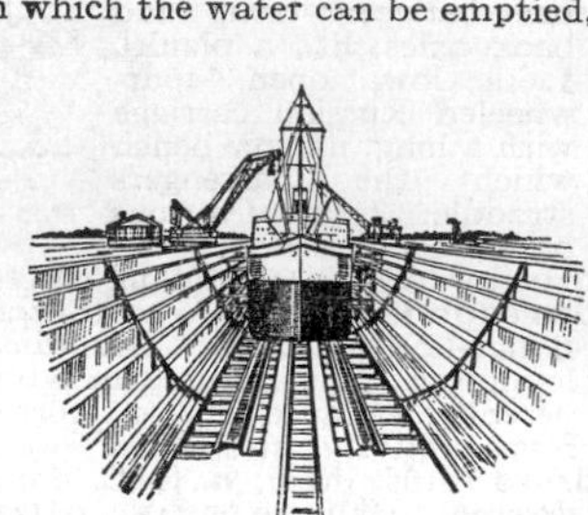
DRY DOCK

dry goods, [< use of *dry measure*], cloth, cloth products, thread, etc.
dry ice, carbon dioxide highly compressed and in a solid state, used as a refrigerant because it changes back to gas without becoming liquid.
dry kiln, an enclosed place in which lumber is dried and seasoned by artificial heat.
dry law, a law prohibiting the manufacture and sale of alcoholic liquors.
dry·ly (drī'li), *adv.* in a dry manner; without emotion; matter-of-factly.
dry measure, a system of measuring the volume of dry things, such as grain, vegetables, etc.; especially, the system in which 2 pints = 1 quart, 8 quarts = 1 peck, and 4 pecks = 1 bushel.
dry·ness (drī'nis), *n.* the quality or state of being dry.
dry-nurse (drī'nũrs'), *v.t.* to be a dry nurse to.
dry nurse, a nurse who takes care of a baby without breast-feeding it: opposed to *wet nurse.*
dry point, 1. a fine, hard needle for engraving lines on a copper plate without using acid. 2. a picture printed from such a plate. 3. this way of engraving.
dry rot, 1. a fungous decay causing seasoned timber to become brittle and crumble to powder. 2. a similar fungous disease of plants, fruits, and vegetables. 3. any of various fungi causing such decay. 4. any internal moral or social decay, generally resulting from lack of new or progressive influences.
dry run, [Military Slang], 1. practice in firing small arms or guns without using live ammunition; hence, 2. a rehearsal for any event.
dry-salt (drī'sôlt'), *v.t.* to salt and dry (meat, etc.) in order to preserve it.
dry·salt·er (drī'sôl'tēr), *n.* [British], a dealer in dried and salted goods, paints, drugs, etc., or in canned goods, pickles, etc.
dry·salt·er·y (drī'sôl'tēr-i), *n.* [*pl.* DRYSALTERIES (-iz)],

[British], the stock, shop, or trade of a drysalter.
dry-shod (drī'shod'), *adj.* with dry shoes on; without getting one's feet wet.
Dry Tor·tu·gas (tôr-tōō'gəz), a group of small islands in the Gulf of Mexico, west of the Florida Keys: they belong to Florida.
dry wash, laundry washed and dried but not ironed.
Ds, in *chemistry*, dysprosium.
d.s., 1. daylight saving. 2. in *commerce*, days after sight.
D.S., d.s., *dal segno*, [It.], (repeat) from this sign.
D.S., D.Sc., Doctor of Science.
D.S.C., Distinguished Service Cross.
D.S.M., Distinguished Service Medal.
D.S.T., Daylight Saving Time.
D. Surg., Dental Surgeon.
d.t., 1. delirium tremens. 2. double time.
D.Th., D.Theol., Doctor of Theology.
D.T.'s (dē'tēz'), [Slang], delirium tremens.
Du., 1. Duke. 2. Dutch.
du·ad (dōō'ad, dū'ad), *n.* [see DYAD], two together; pair; couple.
du·al (dōō'əl, dū'əl), *adj.* [L. *dualis* < *duo*, two], 1. of two. 2. having or composed of two parts; double; twofold: as, he has a *dual* nature. *n.* in *linguistics*, 1. dual number. 2. a word having dual number.
du·al·ism (dōō'əl-iz'm, dū'əl-iz'm), *n.* 1. the state of being dual; duality. 2. in *philosophy*, the theory that the world is ultimately composed of, or explicable in terms of, two basic entities, as mind and matter. 3. in *theology*, *a*) the doctrine that there are two mutually antagonistic principles in the universe, good and evil. *b*) the doctrine that man has two natures, physical and spiritual.
du·al·ist (dōō'əl-ist, dū'əl-ist), *n.* a believer in dualism.
du·al·is·tic (dōō'əl-is'tik, dū'əl-is'tik), *adj.* 1. of or based on dualism. 2. dual.
du·al·is·tic·al·ly (dōō'əl-is'ti-k'l-i, dū'əl-is'tik-li), *adv.* 1. in a dualistic manner. 2. from the viewpoint of dualism.
du·al·i·ty (dōō-al'ə-ti, dū-al'ə-ti), *n.* [LL. *dualitas*], the state or quality of being dual.
dual number, in some languages, a grammatical number indicating *two, a pair:* distinguished by inflection from *singular* (indicating *one*) and *plural* (indicating *more than two*), as in Sanskrit *vṛkas*, wolf (*singular*), *vṛkau*, two wolves (*dual*), *vṛkās*, more than two wolves (*plural*); the dual occurs regularly in Sanskrit, Old Iranian, Old Irish, Old Slavonic, etc., with traces in Greek, Gothic, and Anglo-Saxon.
dual personality, in *psychology*, the abnormal condition of having two different personalities, shown alternately or simultaneously.
du·al-pur·pose (dōō'əl-pũr'pəs, dū'əl-pũr'pəs), *adj.* having, or meant to have, two uses.
dub (dub), *v.t.* [DUBBED (dubd), DUBBING], [ME. *dubben;* AS. *dubbian*, to strike (akin to East Fris. *dubben*, to beat, push, D. *dof*, a blow, etc.); ? influenced in senses 4 & 5 by LG. or Fr. *adouber* (< same Gmc. base); IE. base **dheubh-*, **dhub-*, a club, wooden pin, etc.; cf. DOWEL], 1. to hit; strike; thrust; poke. 2. to beat (a drum). 3. to make (a man) a knight by tapping on the shoulder with a sword; hence, 4. to confer a title or rank upon; name or nickname. 5. to make (wood, etc.) smooth, as by hammering or scraping. 6. to dress (leather) by rubbing. 7. [Slang], to be obliged to repeat (a stroke, etc.); bungle (a golf stroke, etc.). *n.* 1. a drumbeat. 2. [Slang], a clumsy, unskillful player; hence, 3. [Slang], any clumsy, unskillful person.
dub (dub), *v.t.* [DUBBED (dubd), DUBBING], [< *double*], to make a new recording of (a piece of music) by playing the old record: distinguished from *re-press*. *n.* dialogue, music, etc. inserted in the sound track of a motion picture.
dub in, in *motion pictures*, 1. to insert (dialogue, music, etc.) in the sound track. 2. to insert (synchronized dialogue in another language) in place of the original dialogue.
Du Bar·ry, Ma·rie Jeanne Bé·cu (má'rē' zhän' bā'kü' dü' bá'rē'; Eng. dōō' bar'i, dū' bar'i), Comtesse, 1746?–1793; mistress of Louis XV of France.
dub·bin (dub'in), *n.* [< *dubbing;* see DUB (to hit), *v.*, sense 6], a greasy preparation for softening and waterproofing leather: also **dubbing**.
du·bi·e·ty (dōō-bī'ə-ti, dū-bī'ə-ti), *n.* [L. *dubietas*], 1. the quality of being dubious; doubtfulness. 2. [*pl.* DUBIETIES (-tiz)], a doubtful thing. —*SYN.* see **uncertainty.**
du·bi·os·i·ty (dōō'bi-os'ə-ti, dū'bi-os'ə-ti), *n.* [*pl.* DUBIOSITIES (-tiz)], dubiety. —*SYN.* see **uncertainty.**
du·bi·ous (dōō'bi-əs, dū'bi-əs), *adj.* [L. *dubiosus*, doubtful < *dubius*, doubting, uncertain < *du-*, felt as stem of *duo*, two + IE. base **bhu-*, to be], 1. causing doubt; ambiguous; vague: as, a *dubious* remark. 2. feeling doubt; hesitating; skeptical. 3. with the outcome undecided or hanging in the balance: as, *dubious* battle. 4. rousing suspicion; questionable; shady: as, a *dubious* character. —*SYN.* see **doubtful.**
du·bi·ta·ble (dōō'bi-tə-b'l, dū'bi-tə-b'l), *adj.* [L. *dubitabilis*], to be doubted; uncertain.
du·bi·ta·tion (dōō'bə-tā'shən, dū'bə-tā'shən), *n.* [Fr.; L. *dubitatio*], doubt.
du·bi·ta·tive (dōō'bə-tā'tiv, dū'bə-tā'tiv), *adj.* [LL. *dubitativus*], 1. doubting; hesitating. 2. expressing doubt or hesitancy.
Dub·lin (dub'lin), *n.* the capital of Ireland: seaport on the Irish Sea: pop., 539,000.
DuBois, William Edward Burg·hardt (bũrg'härt dōō-bois'), 1868–1963; American historian, educator, and Negro leader.
du·bon·net (dōō'bə-nā'; Fr. dü'bô'ne'), *n.* [name of Fr. manufacturer], 1. a fortified French red wine, often served as an apéritif: a trade-mark (**Dubonnet**). 2. a light maroon color, as of this wine. *adj.* of this color.
Du·brov·nik (dōō'brôv-nik), *n.* a seaport in southern Yugoslavia: pop., 23,000: Italian name, *Ragusa.*
Du·buque (də-būk'), *n.* a city in eastern Iowa, on the Mississippi: pop., 57,000.
du·cal (dōō'k'l, dū'k'l), *adj.* [LL. *ducalis*, of a leader < L. *dux, ducis*, leader], 1. of a duke. 2. of a dukedom.
duc·at (duk'ət), *n.* [OFr.; It. *ducato*, ducat, duchy < LL. *ducatus;* see DUCHY], 1. any of several gold or silver coins formerly used in some European countries: their values varied from about 83¢ to about $2.32. 2. [Slang], a ticket, especially an admission ticket.
‡**du·ce** (dōō'che), *n.* [It.; L. *dux, ducis*], chief; leader: title (*Il Duce*) assumed by Benito Mussolini, Fascist head of Italy (1922–1943).
duch·ess (duch'is), *n.* [ME. & OFr. *duchesse* < LL. *ducissa* < L. *dux, ducis*, leader], 1. the wife or widow of a duke. 2. a woman who holds in her own right the sovereignty of a duchy. Abbreviated **D.** (as a title).
duch·y (duch'i), *n.* [*pl.* DUCHIES (-iz)], [ME. *duchee;* OFr. *duché, duchée;* LL. *ducatus*, military command, territory of a duke < L. *dux, ducis*, leader], the territory ruled by a duke or duchess; dukedom.
duck (duk), *n.* [ME. *duk, duke;* AS. *duce*, lit., diver, ducker < base of *duck, v.;* replaces AS. *ened* (G. *ente*, etc.), common Gmc. word for the bird], 1. [*pl.* DUCKS (duks), DUCK; see PLURAL, II, D, 1], any of several swimming birds with a flat bill, short neck and legs, and webbed feet. 2. a female duck: opposed to *drake*. 3. the flesh of a duck as food. 4. [Colloq.], a darling; dear. 5. [Slang], a person: as, he's a queer *duck.* 6. [Military Slang], an amphibious motor vehicle.
like water off a duck's back, with no effect.
duck (duk), *v.t. & v.i.* [ME. *duken, douken* < AS. **ducan*, to plunge, dive; akin to OHG. *tūhan* (G. *tauchen*), MLG. *dūken* (D. *duiken*), to dive; altered after *duck* (the bird)], 1. to plunge or dip under water for a moment. 2. to lower, turn, or bend (the head, body, etc.) suddenly, as in avoiding a blow or hiding. 3. [Colloq.], to avoid (a task, person, etc.). 4. [Slang], to move (*in* or *out*) quickly. *n.* a ducking.
duck (duk), *n.* [D. *doek;* akin to G. *tuch*, cloth], 1. a cotton or linen cloth somewhat like canvas but finer and lighter in weight. 2. *pl.* [Colloq.], white trousers made of this cloth.
duck·bill (duk'bil'), *n.* a small, egg-laying water mammal with webbed feet, a tail like a beaver's, and a bill like a duck's: also called *platypus.*

DUCKBILL (1 1/2 ft. long)

duck·board (duk'bôrd', duk'bōrd'), *n.* a board or boards forming a slightly raised surface or flooring on a muddy road, wet place, etc.
duck·er (duk'ẽr), *n.* 1. a person who raises ducks. 2. a duck hunter.
duck·er (duk'ẽr), *n.* [see DUCK (to dip)], 1. a person who ducks. 2. a diving bird; dabchick or little grebe.
duck-foot·ed (duk'foot'id), *adj.* having the hind toe pointing forward, as on a duck's foot: said of fowls.
duck hawk, 1. the North American peregrine falcon. 2. in England, the marsh harrier, a kind of buzzard.
ducking stool, a chair in which a culprit was tied and then ducked into water; cucking stool: a form of punishment formerly used, as in New England, especially for quarrelsome women.

DUCKING STOOL

duck·ling (duk'liŋ), *n.* a young duck.
duck·pins (duk'pinz'), *n.pl.* [so named when a spec-

tator at the first game said that the pins, on being struck, "flew like ducks"], 1. [construed as sing.], a game like bowling or tenpins, played with smaller pins and balls. 2. the pins used in this game.

ducks and drakes, the game of throwing a small, flat stone or shell across the surface of water so that it will skip along several times before sinking.
make ducks and drakes of, 1. to deal with recklessly. 2. to squander. Also **play ducks and drakes with.**

duck·weed (duk′wēd′), *n.* any of a family of very small flowering plants which float on fresh water like a green scum: so called because eaten by ducks.

duck·y (duk′i), *adj.* [DUCKIER (-i-ẽr), DUCKIEST (-i-ist)], [early 19th-c. term of endearment; *duck* + *-y*], [Slang], excellent, pleasing, delightful, etc.

duct (dukt), *n.* [L. *ductus*, a leading, conducting, pp. of *ducere*, to lead; see DOCK, DOUCHE], 1. a tube, channel, or canal through which a gas, liquid, etc. moves. 2. a tube in the body for the passage of excretions or secretions, as from a gland. 3. a pipe or conduit with wires or cables running through it.

duc·tile (duk′t'l, duk′til), *adj.* [L. *ductilis* < *ductus*; see DUCT], 1. that can be stretched, drawn, or hammered thin without breaking; not brittle: said of metals. 2. easily molded; plastic; pliant. 3. easily led; tractable. —*SYN.* see **pliable.**

duc·til·i·ty (duk-til′ə-ti), *n.* the quality or condition of being ductile.

duct·less gland (dukt′lis), any of certain glands, as the thyroid and pituitary, which have no excretory ducts and send their secretions directly into the lymph or blood stream.

dud (dud), *n.* [ult. < D. *dood*, dead], [Slang], 1. a bomb or shell that fails to explode; hence, 2. a person or thing that fails or is ineffectual.

dud·dy, dud·die (dud′i), *adj.* [< dial. *dud*, coarse cloak (cf. DUDS) + *-y*], [Scot.], ragged; tattered.

dude (dōōd, dūd), *n.* [invented term, 1883], 1. a man too much concerned with his manners and appearance; dandy; fop. 2. [Western Slang], a city fellow or tourist, especially an Easterner.

du·deen (dōō-dēn′), *n.* [< Ir. *dūidīn*, a little pipe < *dūd*, a pipe], [Irish], a short-stemmed clay tobacco pipe.

dude ranch, a ranch or farm operated as a resort for tourists, with horseback riding and similar sports.

Du·de·vant (düd′vän′), Baronne, see **Sand, George.**

dudg·eon (duj′ən), *n.* [16th-c. (*take*) *in dudgeon*; also *endugine*; prob. Anglo-Fr. *en digeon*, with reference to the hand on the dagger hilt; see DUDGEON (dagger hilt)], an angry or offended feeling; resentment.
in high dudgeon, very angry, offended, or resentful.

dudg·eon (duj′ən), *n.* [ME. *dogeon*, Anglo-Fr. *digeon*], [Obs.], 1. a wood, perhaps boxwood, used for dagger hilts. 2. such a hilt. 3. a dagger with such a hilt.

dud·ish (dōōd′ish, dūd′ish), *adj.* like a dude; foppish.

Dud·ley (dud′li), [< Celt.; lit., fair field], a masculine name. *n.* a city in central England: pop., 62,000.

Dud·ley, Robert (dud′li), see **Leicester,** Earl of.

duds (dudz), *n.pl.* [ME. *dudde*, cloth, cloak; prob. < ON. *duthi*, swaddling clothes < *dutha*, to swathe], [Slang], 1. clothes; clothing. 2. trappings; belongings.

due (dōō, dū), *adj.* [ME.; OFr. *deu*, pp. of *devoir*, to owe; L. *debere*, to owe], 1. owed or owing as a debt; payable: as, the first payment is *due*. 2. suitable; fitting; proper: as, give him *due* respect. 3. as much as is required; enough; adequate: as, *due* care, in *due* time. 4. expected or scheduled to arrive or be ready; timed for a certain hour or date: as, the plane is *due* at 6:30 P.M. *adv.* exactly; directly: as, *due* west. *n.* anything due.
become (or **fall**) **due,** to become payable as previously arranged.
due to, 1. caused by; owing to. 2. [Colloq.], because of: widely so used despite purists' objections.
give (**a person**) **his due,** to concede deserved credit to (a person).

due bill, a written acknowledgment of a debt to a person named, but neither payable to his order nor transferable by indorsement: distinguished from *promissory note.*

du·el (dōō′əl, dū′əl), *n.* [Fr.; It. *duello* < ML. & OL. *duellum* (L. *bellum*), war, fight < *duo*, two], 1. a formal fight between two persons armed with deadly weapons: it is prearranged and witnessed by two others, called *seconds*, one for each combatant. 2. any contest or encounter suggesting such a fight, usually between two persons: as, a verbal *duel*. *v.i. & v.t.* [DUELED or DUELLED (-əld), DUELING or DUELLING], to fight a duel with (a person or persons).

du·el·ist, du·el·list (dōō′əl-ist, dū′əl-ist), *n.* 1. a person who fights a duel. 2. an expert at dueling.

du·el·lo (dōō-el′ō, dū-el′ō), *n.* [*pl.* DUELLOS (-ōz)], [It.], 1. the art, rules, or code of dueling. 2. [Obs.], a duel.

du·en·na (dōō-en′ə, dū-en′ə), *n.* [Sp. *dueña* < L. *domina*, mistress, lady], 1. an elderly woman who has charge of the girls and young unmarried women of a Spanish or Portuguese family. 2. a chaperon or governess.

Due·ro (dwe′rô), *n.* a river in northern Spain and Portugal, flowing into the Atlantic: length, 475 mi.: Portuguese name, *Douro.*

dues (dōōz, dūz), *n.pl.* [see DUE], 1. a fee or tax. 2. the sum of money paid, or to be paid, by a member to an organization, usually for the rights of membership.

du·et (dōō-et′, dū-et′), *n.* [It. *duetto*, dim. of *duo*, duet < L. *duo*, two], in *music*, 1. a composition for two voices or two instruments. 2. the two performers of such a composition; duo.

duff (duf), *n.* [dial. var. of *dough*, with *ff* for ME. *-gh* (cf. *laugh, enough*), orig. pronounced (kh) as in G. *nacht*], 1. a thick flour pudding boiled in a cloth bag. 2. [? < other source], decaying vegetable matter on the ground in a forest. 3. coal dust or slack.

duf·fel, duf·fle (duf′'l), *n.* [D. < *Duffel*, Belgium], 1. a coarse woolen cloth with a thick nap. 2. essential clothing and equipment carried by a woodsman, hunter, or yachtsman. 3. a camper's kit or equipment.

duffel bag, a large cloth bag for carrying clothing and personal belongings.

duf·fer (duf′ẽr), *n.* [< thieves' slang *duff*, to counterfeit, fake], 1. [Obs.], a peddler of cheap jewelry, etc. 2. [Slang], an incompetent, awkward, or stupid person.

dug (dug), past tense and past participle of **dig.**

dug (dug), *n.* [< same base as Dan. *dægge* (Sw. *dägga*), to suckle, caus. of Dan. *die*, to suck], a female animal's nipple or teat.

du·gong (dōō′goŋ), *n.* [Malay *dūyung*], a large, whale-like mammal that lives in tropical seas and feeds on plants: also called *sea cow.*

dug·out (dug′out′), *n.* 1. a boat or canoe hollowed out of a log. 2. a large hole dug in the ground or the side of a hill and often covered or reinforced with logs, beams, etc., used as a dwelling or bomb shelter. 3. in *baseball*, a covered shelter near the diamond for the players to sit in when not at bat or in the field.

dui·ker (dī′kẽr), *n.* [*pl.* DUIKERS (-kẽrz), DUIKER; see PLURAL, II, D, 1], [D. *duiker*, a diver: the animal dives into the bush], a small, horned antelope of South Africa.

dui·ker·bok (dī′kẽr-bok′), *n.* [*pl.* DUIKERBOK, DUIKERBOKS (-boks′); see PLURAL, II, D, 2.], [D. *duiker* + *bok*, a buck], a duiker.

dui·ker·buck (dī′kẽr-buk′), *n.* [*pl.* DUIKERBUCK, DUIKERBUCKS (-buks′); see PLURAL II, D, 2], a duiker.

Duis·burg-Ham·born (düs′boorkh-häm′bôrn), *n.* a city in the Rhine Province, Germany, on the Rhine: pop., 431,000.

duke (dōōk, dūk), *n.* [ME. *duke, duk, duc*; OFr. *duc, dux*; L. *dux*, leader, general], 1. a prince who is the ruler of an independent duchy. 2. a nobleman of the highest hereditary rank below that of prince. Abbreviated **D., Du.** (as a title).

duke·dom (dōōk′dəm, dūk′dəm), *n.* 1. the territory ruled by a duke; duchy. 2. the title or rank of a duke.

dukes (dōōks, dūks), *n.pl.* [< *duke*, short for *Duke of York*, used in 19th-c. Eng. rhyming slang for *fork*, hence fingers, hence fist], [Slang], the fists or hands.

Du·kho·bors (dōō′kə-bôrz′), *n.pl.* [Russ. *dukhobortsy*, lit., spirit wrestlers; *dukh*, spirit + *bortsy*, wrestlers: so called from their struggle against the doctrine of the Holy Spirit], a Russian religious sect separated from the Orthodox Church in 1785: many Dukhobors emigrated to Canada in the 1890's to escape military conscription, which they considered sinful.

Du·kho·bor·tsy (dōō-kho-bôr′tsi), *n.pl.* Dukhobors.

dul·cet (dul′sit), *adj.* [ME. & OFr. *doucet*, dim. of *douz*, sweet; L. *dulcis*, sweet; Eng. sp. fashioned after L.], 1. soothing or pleasant to hear; melodious. 2. [Archaic], sweet to taste or smell. *n.* an organ stop of sweet, mellow tone, one octave higher in pitch than the dulciana.

dul·ci·an·a (dul′si-an′ə), *n.* [ML. < L. *dulcis*, sweet], an organ stop with a sweet, mellow tone like that of a stringed instrument.

dul·ci·fy (dul′sə-fī′), *v.t.* [DULCIFIED (-fīd′), DULCIFYING], [< L. *dulcis*, sweet; + *-fy*], 1. [Rare], to sweeten. 2. to make pleasant or agreeable; mollify.

dul·ci·mer (dul′sə-mẽr), *n.* [OFr. *doulcimer* < L. *dulce melos*; *dulce*, neut. of *dulcis*, sweet + *melos* < Gr. *melos*, a song, strain], 1. a musical instrument with metal strings, which are struck with two small hammers by the player. 2. in the *Bible*, the psaltery, a kind of harp: see Dan. 3:10.

DULCIMER

Dul·cin·e·a (dul-sin′i-ə, dul′sə-nē′ə), *n.* [Sp. < *dulce*, sweet; L. *dulcis*], 1. the plain peasant girl whom Don Quixote imagines to be a beautiful lady and falls in love with; hence, 2. any idealized sweetheart.

du·li·a (dōō-lī′ə, dū-lī′ə), *n.* [ML. < Gr. *douleia*, service < *doulos*, a slave], in the *Roman Catholic Church*, the homage paid to angels and saints.

dull (dul), *adj.* [ME.; AS. *dol*, foolish, stupid; akin to G. *toll;* IE. base **dh(e)wel-*, turbid, dark, obscure, as in OIr., W. *dall*, blind], 1. mentally slow; stupid. 2. lacking sensitivity; unfeeling: as, *dull* to grief. 3. physically slow; slow-moving; sluggish. 4. lacking spirit; not lively; depressed. 5. causing boredom; tedious: as, a *dull* party. 6. not keen; not pointed; blunt: as, a *dull* blade. 7. not felt keenly; not acute: as, a *dull* headache. 8. not vivid; not brilliant; dim: as, a *dull* color. 9. not distinct; muffled: as, a *dull* thud. 10. gloomy; cloudy: as, *dull* weather. 11. slack: as, business is *dull*. *v.t. & v.i.* to make or become dull.
SYN.—**dull** is specifically applied to a point or edge that has lost its previous sharpness (a *dull* knife) and generally connotes a lack of keenness, zest, spirit, intensity, etc. (a *dull* book, pain, etc.); **blunt** is often equivalent to **dull**, but specifically refers to a point or edge that is intentionally not sharp (a *blunt* fencing saber); **obtuse** literally applies to a pointed end whose sides form an angle greater than 90°, and figuratively connotes great dullness of understanding or lack of sensitivity (too *obtuse* to comprehend). See also **stupid.**—*ANT.* sharp, keen.

dull·ard (dul′ẽrd), *n.* [*dull* + *-ard*], a stupid person.

Dul·les, John Fos·ter (fôs′tẽr dul′əs), 1888–1959; United States secretary of state (1953–1959).

dull·ish (dul′ish), *adj.* somewhat dull.

dull·ness, dul·ness (dul′nis), *n.* a dull state or quality.

dul·ly (dul′li, dul′i), *adv.* in a dull manner.

dulse (duls), *n.* [Ir. & Gael. *duileasg*], any of several edible seaweeds with large, red, wedge-shaped fronds.

Du·luth (də-lōōth′), *n.* a city in eastern Minnesota, on Lake Superior: pop., 107,000.

du·ly (dōō′li, dū′li), *adv.* 1. in a due manner; as due; rightfully; properly; fittingly. 2. when due; at the right time; on time. 3. as required; sufficiently.

Du·ma (dōō′mä), *n.* the former Russian parliament, set up as a consultative body in 1905 by Czar Nicholas II: ended by the revolution of 1917: also spelled **Douma.**

Du·mas, A·lex·an·dre (å′lek′sän′dr′ dü′må′; Eng. dōō-mä′, dōō′mä), 1. 1802–1870; French novelist and dramatist: called *Dumas père.* 2. 1824–1895; son of the above; French dramatist and novelist: called *Dumas fils.*

du Mau·ri·er, George Louis Pal·mel·la Bus·son (pal-mel′ə bōō-sôn′ dōō′ môr′i-ā′, dū′ môr′i-ā′), 1834–1896; English novelist and illustrator.

dumb (dum), *adj.* [ME.; AS.; akin to G. *dumm* (Goth. *dumbs*), dumb, stupid (cf. sense 6); all < nasalized var. of IE. **dheubh*, misty, dark, obscured; cf. DEAF], 1. lacking the power of speech; mute. 2. unwilling to talk; silent; reticent. 3. not accompanied by speech. 4. temporarily speechless, as from fear, grief, etc. 5. producing no sound. 6. [< G. *dumm*], [Colloq.], stupid; moronic. —*SYN.* see **voiceless.**

dumb ague, a form of malarial fever in which the chill and other symptoms are slight or entirely obscured.

Dum·bar·ton (dum-bär′t'n), *n.* 1. a county of western Scotland, on the Clyde River: pop., 177,000. 2. its county seat: pop., 24,000.

dumb·bell (dum′bel′), *n.* [*dumb* + *bell:* from orig. shape], 1. a device consisting of two heavy weights, usually metal balls, joined by a short bar of metal or wood: it is lifted or swung about with the hand to help develop the muscles of the arm, shoulder, and back. 2. [cf. DUMB, sense 6], [Slang], a stupid person.

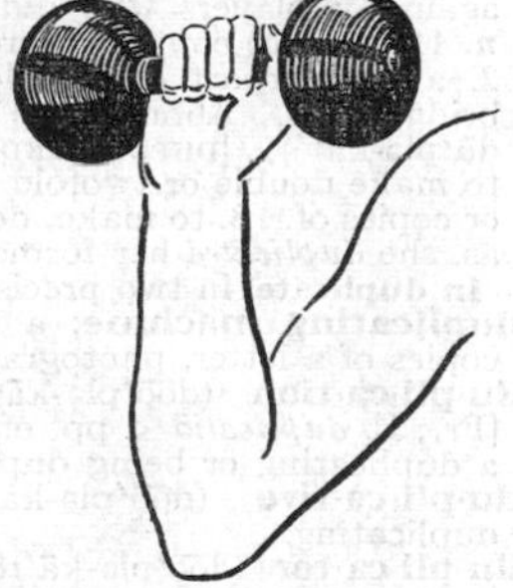

DUMBBELL

dumb·found (dum′-found′), *v.t.* to dumfound.

dumb show, 1. formerly, a part of a play done in pantomime. 2. gestures without speech.

dumb-wait·er (dum′wāt′-ẽr), *n.* 1. a small, portable serving stand placed near a dining table. 2. a small, hand-operated elevator used for sending food, trash, etc. from one floor to another.

dum·dum (bullet) (dum′dum), *n.* [< *Dumdum*, arsenal near Calcutta, India], a soft-nosed bullet that expands when it hits, inflicting a large, jagged wound.

dum·found (dum′found′), *v.t.* [< *dumb* + *confound*], to make speechless by surprising; amaze; astonish: also spelled **dumbfound.** —*SYN.* see **puzzle.**

Dum·fries (dum-frēs′), *n.* 1. a county of southern Scotland, on Solway Firth: pop., 89,000. 2. its county seat: pop., 26,000.

dum·my (dum′i), *n.* [*pl.* DUMMIES (-iz)], [< *dumb*], 1. a person unable to talk; mute: now vulgar in this sense.

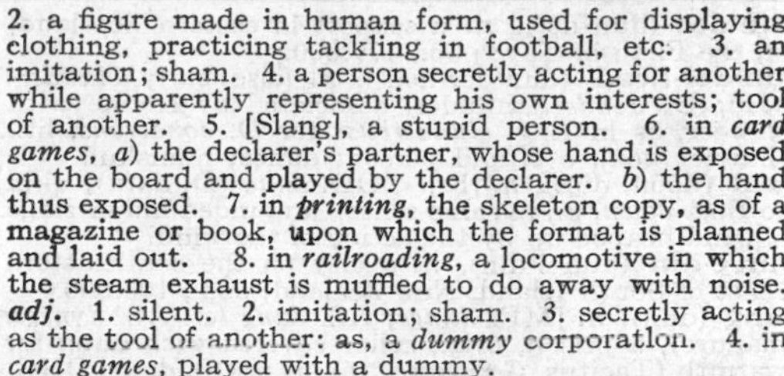

2. a figure made in human form, used for displaying clothing, practicing tackling in football, etc. 3. an imitation; sham. 4. a person secretly acting for another while apparently representing his own interests; tool of another. 5. [Slang], a stupid person. 6. in *card games*, *a)* the declarer's partner, whose hand is exposed on the board and played by the declarer. *b)* the hand thus exposed. 7. in *printing*, the skeleton copy, as of a magazine or book, upon which the format is planned and laid out. 8. in *railroading*, a locomotive in which the steam exhaust is muffled to do away with noise. *adj.* 1. silent. 2. imitation; sham. 3. secretly acting as the tool of another: as, a *dummy* corporation. 4. in *card games*, played with a dummy.

dump (dump), *v.t.* [ME. *dumpen*, to fall down, throw down; prob. < ON.; cf. Dan. *dumpe*, Sw. *dompa*], 1. to throw down (the contents of, etc.); empty out or unload in a heap or mass. 2. to throw away as rubbish; get rid of. 3. to throw (a large quantity of goods) on the market, especially abroad, at low prices. *v.i.* 1. to fall in a heap or mass. 2. to unload rubbish. 3. to dump commodities. *n.* 1. a rubbish pile. 2. a place for dumping. 3. in *military usage*, a temporary supply center in the field, as of ammunition, food, or clothing. 4. [Slang], a place that is unpleasant, ugly, uncomfortable, etc. 5. [Slang], loosely, any place.

dump (dump), *n.* [prob. < D. *domp*, haze, dullness], [Archaic], 1. a sad tune or song. 2. any tune or song. **in the dumps,** in low spirits; in a depressed condition.

dump (dump), *n.* [? < *dumpy* (stumpy)], [British], a small, shapeless lump or chunk, as of lead.

dump·i·ly (dump′'l-i), *adv.* in a dumpy manner.

dump·i·ness (dump′i-nis), *n.* the quality or state of being dumpy.

dump·ish (dump′ish), *adj.* [see DUMP (sad tune)], [Rare], gloomy; depressed; melancholy.

dump·ling (dump′liŋ), *n.* [*dump* (shapeless lump) + *-ling*], 1. a small piece of dough, steamed or boiled and served with meat or soup. 2. a crust of dough filled with fruit and steamed or baked. 3. [Colloq.], a short, fat person or animal.

dump truck, a truck whose contents are unloaded by tilting the truck bed backward with the tail gate open.

dump·y (dump′i), *adj.* [DUMPIER (-i-ẽr), DUMPIEST (-i-ist)], [< *dump, v.;* reinforced by echoism], short and thick; squat; stumpy.

dump·y (dump′i), *adj.* [DUMPIER (-i-ẽr), DUMPIEST (-i-ist)], [see DUMP (sad tune)], melancholy; depressed.

Dum·yat (doom-yät′), *n.* Damietta: the Arabian name.

dun (dun), *adj.* [ME.; AS. *dunn;* akin to OS. *dun*, chestnut-brown; IE. **dhus-no* < **dhus*, dust-colored, mist-gray, as also in *dusk, dust*], dull grayish-brown. *n.* 1. a dull grayish brown. 2. an artificial fly of this color: also **dun fly.** 3. a May fly. *v.t.* [DUNNED (dund), DUNNING], to give a dun color to.

dun (dun), *v.t. & v.i.* [DUNNED (dund), DUNNING], [prob. Eng. western dial. var. of *din;* ? influenced or reinforced by name *Dunn*, whether Joe *Dun*, bailiff of Lincoln, or John *Dun*, fictitious legal figure like John Doe], to ask (a debtor) insistently or repeatedly for payment. *n.* 1. a person who duns. 2. an insistent demand for payment of a debt.

Du·na (dōō′nå), *n.* 1. the Danube: the Hungarian name. 2. the Don: the Russian name.

Dü·na (dü′nä), *n.* the Dvina (1): the German name.

Dü·na·burg (dü′nä-boorkh′), *n.* Daugavpils, a city in the Latvian S.S.R.: the German name.

Dun and Brad·street (dun′ 'nd brad′strēt′), an agency that furnishes subscribers with information as to the financial standing and credit rating of businesses.

Du·nă·re·a (doo′nə-ryä), *n.* Danube: Romanian name.

Dun·bar, Paul Laurence (dun′bär), 1872–1906; American poet and novelist.

Dun·bar, William (dun-bär′), 1460?–1520?; Scottish poet.

Dun·can (duŋ′kən), [Gael. *Donnchadh*, lit., brown warrior], a masculine name. *n.* in Shakespeare's *Macbeth*, the aged king of Scotland, murdered by Macbeth.

Dun·can, Isadora (duŋ′kən), 1878–1927; American dancer.

Duncan Phyfe, designating or of furniture in a modified Empire and Directoire style designed by Duncan Phyfe (1768–1854), American cabinetmaker.

dunce (duns), *n.* [< John *Duns* Scotus, called the "Subtle Doctor" (died c. 1308), whose followers, called *Dunsmen, Duncemen* and ult. *Dunses, Dunces*, were regarded as foes of Renaissance humanism; the word came to be applied to any opponent of education, and then to any stupid person], 1. a dull, ignorant person. 2. a person who learns more slowly than others.

dunce cap, a cone-shaped hat, sometimes marked D, which children slow at learning were formerly forced to wear in school.

Dun·dalk (dun′dôk), *n.* a town in central Maryland; a suburb of Baltimore: pop., 82,000.

Dun·dee (dun-dē′), *n.* a seaport in eastern Scotland, on the Firth of Tay: pop., 179,000.

dun·der·head (dun′dẽr-hed′), *n.* [also early *blunderhead;* D. *donder,* thunder, associated by rhyme with *blunder,* as in Eng. *blunderbuss* for D. *donderbus,* lit., thunder box], a stupid person; dunce; numskull.

dune (dōōn, dūn), *n.* [Fr. < OD. *duna* (D. *duin*); akin to Eng. *down, n.,* in same sense], a rounded hill or ridge of sand heaped up by the action of the wind.

Dun·e·din (dun-ē′din), *n.* a city on the southeastern coast of South Island, New Zealand: pop., 103,000.

dung (duŋ), *n.* [ME. *dunge;* AS. *dung* (cf. AS. *dyncge,* manure), a prison, orig., cellar covered with dung for warmth (Tacitus, *Germania,* 16), as in OS. *dung,* OHG. *tung* (ON. *dyngia*), cellar where women weave; IE. base **dheng-,* to cover, covering layer], 1. animal excrement; manure; hence, 2. filth. *v.t.* to spread or cover with dung, as in fertilizing.

dun·ga·ree (duŋ′gə-rē′), *n.* [Hind. *dungrī*], 1. a coarse cotton cloth used for tents, sails, work clothing, etc. 2. *pl.* work trousers or overalls made of this cloth.

dung beetle, any of various beetles, chafers, and scarabs that breed in dung and feed on it.

dun·geon (dun′jən), *n.* [ME. *dungeon, dongon;* OFr. *donjon;* prob. < Frank. *dungjo,* earth-covered cellar for storing fruits; see DUNG], 1. the main keep or fortified tower of a medieval castle; donjon. 2. a dark underground cell, vault, or prison. *v.t.* [Rare], to confine in a dungeon.

dung·hill (duŋ′hil′), *n.* 1. a heap of dung. 2. anything vile or filthy.

dung·y (duŋ′i), *adj.* [DUNGIER (-i-ẽr), DUNGIEST (-i-ist)], soiled with dung; filthy like dung.

dunk (duŋk), *v.t. & v.i.* [G. *tunken,* to steep, dip, soak < OHG. *dunchôn;* akin to L. *tinguere,* to moisten, immerse], to dip (bread, cake, etc.) into soup, coffee, etc. before eating it.

Dunk·ards (duŋ′kẽrdz), *n.pl.* Dunkers.

Dun·kerque (dōn′kerk′), *n.* Dunkirk: French name.

Dunk·ers (duŋ′kẽrz), *n.pl.* [G. *tunker,* dipper < *tunken;* see DUNK], a sect of German-American Baptists opposed to military service and the taking of oaths; Dunkards: properly called *German Baptist Brethren, Church of the Brethren.*

Dun·kirk (dun′kẽrk), *n.* a town in northern France, on the Strait of Dover: pop., 11,000: scene of evacuation of Allied troops under enemy fire (1940).

dun·lin (dun′lin), *n.* [*pl.* DUNLINS (-linz), DUNLIN; see PLURAL, II, D, 1], [< *dunling; dun,* dark brown + *-ling*], a sandpiper which has a black stripe on its abdomen during the breeding season.

Dun·more (dun′môr′, dun′mōr′), *n.* a town in northeastern Pennsylvania: pop., 19,000.

dun·nage (dun′ij), *n.* [also early *dinnage, denage;* ? lit., *thin* + *-age* < MD. *dun,* MLG. *dünne,* thin, via OFr. or ML.; cf. ML. *dennagio,* dunnage (1336)], 1. a loose packing of any bulky material put around cargo for protection. 2. personal baggage or belongings.

Dunne, Finley Peter (dun), 1867–1936; American journalist and humorist.

dun·nite (dun′īt), *n.* [after B. W. *Dunn,* Am. chemist who invented it], an explosive derived from picric acid, used as the bursting charge for armor-piercing projectiles.

Dun·sa·ny, Edward John More·ton Drax Plun·kett (mōr′tən draks pluŋ′kit dun-sā′ni), eighteenth Baron, 1878–1957; Irish poet and playwright: called *Lord Dunsany.*

Dun·si·nane (dun′sə-nān′, dun′sə-nān′), *n.* a hill in central Scotland: ruined fort at its summit thought to be site of Macbeth's defeat in the play by Shakespeare.

Duns Sco·tus, John (dunz skō′təs), 1265?–1308?; Scottish scholar and theologian.

Dun·stan, Saint (dun′stən), 925?–988 A.D.; English churchman; archbishop of Canterbury (961–988 A.D.).

dunt (dunt, doont), *n.* [ME. *dunte,* var. of *dint,* a blow; cf. DINT], [Scot. & British Dial.], 1. a heavy, dull-sounding blow or stroke. 2. a wound caused by such a blow. *v.t. & v.i.* [Scot. & British Dial.], to strike with such a blow.

du·o (dōō′ō, dū′ō), *n.* [*pl.* DUOS (-ōz), DUI (-ē)], [It.], a duet (especially in sense 2).

du·o- (dōō′ə, dū′ə), [< L. *duo,* two], a combining form meaning *two, double,* as in *duologue.*

du·o·dec·i·mal (dōō′ə-des′ə-m'l, dū′ə-des′ə-m'l), *adj.* [< L. *duodecim,* twelve (< *duo,* two + *decem,* ten); + *-al*], 1. relating to twelve or twelfths. 2. consisting of or counting by twelves or powers of twelve. *n.* 1. one twelfth. 2. *pl.* in *mathematics,* a system of numeration with twelve as its base: distinguished from the *decimal* system, which has ten as its base.

du·o·dec·i·mo (dōō′ə-des′ə-mō′, dū′ə-des′ə-mō′), *n.* [*pl.* DUODECIMOS (-mōz′)], [short for L. *in duodecimo,* (in) twelve; see DUODECIMAL], 1. the page size of a book made up of printer's sheets folded into twelve leaves, each leaf being approximately 5 by 7 1/2 inches. 2. a book consisting of pages of this size: also called *twelvemo,* and written *12mo* or *12°.* *adj.* consisting of pages of this size.

du·o·de·nal (dōō′ə-dē′n'l, dū′ə-dē′n'l, dōō-od′i-n'l), *adj.* in or of the duodenum.

du·o·den·a·ry (dōō′ə-den′ə-ri, dū′ə-dē′nə-ri), *adj.* [L. *duodenarius,* containing twelve < *duodeni,* twelve each], 1. having to do with twelve; in or increasing by twelves. 2. having to do with duodecimal numeration.

du·o·de·ni·tis (dōō′ə-di-nī′tis, dū′ə-di-nī′tis), *n.* [< *duodenum* + *-itis*], inflammation of the duodenum.

du·o·de·num (dōō′ə-dē′nəm, dū′ə-dē′nəm, dōō-od′i-nəm), *n.* [*pl.* DUODENA (-nə)], [ML. < L. *duodeni,* twelve each: so called because its length is about twelve fingers' breadth], the first section of the small intestine, between the stomach and the jejunum.

du·o·logue (dōō′ə-lôg′, dū′ə-log′), *n.* [*duo-* + *monologue*], a conversation between two people, especially in a dramatic performance.

‡**duo·mo** (dwô′mô), *n.* [*pl.* DUOMI (-mē)], [It.; see DOME], a cathedral.

du·o·tone (dōō′ə-tōn′, dū′ə-tōn′), *adj.* showing a two-tone color effect. *n.* a picture having such an effect.

du·o·type (dōō′ə-tīp′, dū′ə-tīp′), *n.* in *photoengraving,* an illustration printed from a pair of half-tone plates etched separately from a single negative.

dup., duplicate.

dup·a·ble (dōōp′ə-b'l, dūp′ə-b'l), *adj.* that can be duped.

dupe (dōōp, dūp), *n.* [Fr.; OFr. *dupe, duppe* < L. *upupa,* hoopoe, stupid bird], a person easily tricked or fooled. *v.t.* [DUPED (dōōpt, dūpt), DUPING], [Fr. *duper* < the *n.*], to deceive by trickery; cheat. —***SYN.*** see **cheat.**

dup·er·y (dōōp′ẽr-i, dūp′ẽr-i), *n.* [*pl.* DUPERIES (-iz)], a duping or being duped; deception.

du·ple (dōō′p'l, dū′p'l), *adj.* [L. *duplus;* see DOUBLE], 1. double; twofold. 2. in *music,* containing an even number of beats (i.e., two or a multiple of two) to the measure: as, *duple* time.

Du·ples·sis-Mor·nay (dü′ple′sē′ môr′nā′), see **Mornay.**

du·plex (dōō′pleks, dū′pleks), *adj.* [L. < *duo,* two + base akin to *plaga,* region, area (Gr. *plax,* surface, area) < IE. **plaq-, *plag-,* broad, flat], 1. double; twofold. 2. relating to duplex telegraphy. 3. in *machinery,* having two units operating in the same way or simultaneously. *n.* 1. a duplex apartment or house. 2. either of two small, private compartments forming one unit in a railroad car.

duplex apartment, an apartment with rooms on two floors and a private inner stairway.

duplex house, a house consisting of two separate family units.

du·plex·i·ty (dōō-plek′sə-ti, dū-plek′sə-ti), *n.* the quality or state of being duplex.

duplex process, a method of making steel, in which refining of the raw materials is begun in one sort of furnace and finished in another.

duplex telegraphy, a system of telegraphy in which two messages may be sent simultaneously over one wire, one in either direction.

du·pli·ca·ble (dōō′pli-kə-b'l, dū′pli-kə-b'l), *adj.* that can be duplicated.

du·pli·cate (dōō′plə-kit, dū′plə-kit), *adj.* [L. *duplicatus,* pp. of *duplicare,* to double; see DUPLEX], 1. double. 2. having two similar parts. 3. corresponding exactly. 4. designating a way of playing bridge, etc. in which, for comparative scoring, the same hands are played off again by players who did not hold them originally. *n.* 1. an exact copy or reproduction; replica; facsimile. 2. a counterpart or double. 3. a duplicate game of bridge, etc. Abbreviated **dup.** *v.t.* (dōō′plə-kāt′, dū′plə-kāt′), [DUPLICATED (-id), DUPLICATING], 1. to make double or twofold. 2. to make an exact copy or copies of. 3. to make, do, or cause to happen again: as, she *duplicated* her former success. —***SYN.*** see **copy.**
in duplicate, in two precisely similar forms.

duplicating machine, a machine for making exact copies of a letter, photograph, drawing, etc.

du·pli·ca·tion (dōō′plə-kā′shən, dū′plə-kā′shən), *n.* [Fr.; L. *duplicatio* < pp. of *duplicare;* see DUPLEX], 1. a duplicating or being duplicated. 2. a copy; replica.

du·pli·ca·tive (dōō′plə-kā′tiv, dū′plə-kā′tiv), *adj.* duplicating.

du·pli·ca·tor (dōō′plə-kā′tẽr, dū′plə-kā′tẽr), *n.* [LL., doubler < *duplicare;* see DUPLEX], a machine for making exact copies of written or typewritten matter.

du·plic·i·ty (dōō-plis′ə-ti, dū-plis′ə-ti), *n.* [*pl.* DUPLICITIES (-tiz)], [Fr. *duplicité;* LL. *duplicitas;* see DUPLEX], hypocritical cunning or deception; double-dealing.

Du Pont, É·leu·thère I·ré·née (ā′lë′târ′ ē′rā′nā′ dü′pōn′; Eng. dōō′pont, dū′pont), 1771–1834; French industrialist in America.

Du·quesne (dōō-kān′, dū-kān′), *n.* a city in Pennsylvania, near Pittsburgh: pop., 15,000.

Dur., Durango.

du·ra (dyoor′ə), *n.* the dura mater.

du·ra·bil·i·ty (door′ə-bil′ə-ti, dyoor′ə-bil′ə-ti), *n.* [Fr. *durabilité;* LL. *durabilitas*], the quality of being durable; ability to last in spite of frequent use or hard wear.

du·ra·ble (door′ə-b'l, dyoor′ə-b'l), *adj.* [Fr.; L. *durabilis* < *durare,* to last, harden < *durus,* hard], 1. lasting in spite of hard wear or frequent use. 2. continuing to exist; stable. 3. [Archaic], able to endure.

du·ra·bly (door′ə-bli, dyoor′ə-bli), *adv.* in a durable manner; so as to last.
du·ral (dyoor′əl), *adj.* of the dura mater.
du·ral·u·min (doo-ral′yoo-min′, dyoo-ral′yoo-min′), *n.* [*durable* + *aluminum*], a strong, lightweight alloy of aluminum with copper, manganese, magnesium, and silicon: a trade-mark (**Duralumin**).
du·ra ma·ter (dyoor′ə mā′tẽr), [ML., lit., hard mother, transl. of an Ar. term], the outermost, toughest, and most fibrous of the three membranes covering the brain and spinal cord: also **dura.**
du·ra·men (dyoo-rā′min), *n.* [L., hardness < *durare;* see DURABLE], the hard wood at the center of the trunk of any tree that grows by annual rings; heartwood.
dur·ance (door′əns, dyoor′əns), *n.* [OFr.; L. *durans*, ppr. of *durare*, to last; see DURABLE], 1. imprisonment, especially when long continued. 2. [Archaic], duration.
Du·ran·go (doo-räŋ′gô), *n.* 1. a state of northern Mexico: area, 42,272 sq. mi.; pop., 756,000. 2. its capital: pop., 59,000. Abbreviated **Dur.**
du·ra·tion (doo-rā′shən, dyoo-rā′shən), *n.* [ME. *duracioun;* LL. *duratio* < pp. of L. *durare;* see DURABLE], 1. continuance in time. 2. the time that a thing continues or lasts.
Dur·ban (dũr′bən), *n.* a city on the coast of Natal, Union of South Africa: pop., 480,000.
dur·bar (dũr′bär), *n.* [Hind. & Per. *darbār*, a ruler's court; *dar*, portal + *bār*, court], 1. in India, an official reception or audience held by a native prince, or by a British ruler or governor. 2. the place or hall where this is held.
dure (dyoor, door), *adj.* [L. *durus*, hard], [Obs.], hard; stern. *v.i. & v.t.* [DURED (dyoord, doord), DURING], [Obs. & Dial.], to last; continue; endure.
Dü·rer, Al·brecht (äl′breHt dü′rẽr), 1471–1528; German painter and wood engraver.
du·ress (doo-res′, dyoo-res′, door′is, dyoor′is), *n.* [ME. & OFr. *duresse;* L. *duritia*, hardness, harshness < *durus*, hard], 1. imprisonment. 2. coercion or compulsion: as, a confession signed under *duress.*
Dur·ham (dũr′əm), *n.* 1. a county of northern England: pop., 1,464,000. 2. its county seat: pop., 19,000. 3. one of a breed of short-horned beef cattle, originally bred in Durham county. 4. a city in north central North Carolina: pop., 78,000.
du·ri·an, du·ri·on (door′i-ən), *n.* [Malay < *duri*, thorn, prickle], 1. the oval, edible fruit of a tree that grows in the East Indies. 2. the tree.
dur·ing (door′iŋ, dyoor′iŋ), *prep.* [ME. *duringe, prep.*, orig. ppr. of *duren*, to last; OFr. *durer* < L. *durare;* see DURABLE], 1. throughout the entire time of; all through: as, he was happy *during* his lifetime. 2. at some point in the entire time of; in the course of: as, he left *during* the lecture.
dur·mast (dũr′mast, dũr′mäst), *n.* [apparently (T. Nichols, 1791) for *dun mast oak*, dark acorned oak], a variety of European oak valued for its dark, heavy, tough wood.
du·ro (doo′rō; Sp. doo′rô), *n.* [*pl.* DUROS (-rōz; Sp. -rôs)], [Sp., for *duro peso*, lit., hard peso], the silver peso, or dollar, of Spain and Spanish America.
Du·roc-Jer·sey (door′ok-jũr′zi, dyoor′ok-jũr′zi), *n.* any of a breed of large, red hog: also **Duroc.**
dur·ra (door′ə), *n.* [Ar. *dhurah*], a variety of grain-producing sorghum; Indian millet: also spelled **doura, dourah.**
durst (dũrst), archaic past tense of **dare.**
du·rum (door′əm, dyoor′əm), *n.* [L., neut. of *durus*, hard], a variety of hard wheat: flour made from it is used in macaroni, spaghetti, etc.
Du·se, E·le·o·no·ra (e′le-ô-nô′rä doo′ze), 1859–1924; Italian actress.
dusk (dusk), *adj.* [ME. *dusk, dosk;* AS. *dosc, dox*, dark-colored; see DUN, *adj.*], [Poetic], dark in color; dusky; shadowy. *n.* 1. the beginning of darkness in the evening; dark part of twilight. 2. gloom; dusky quality. *v.t. & v.i.* to make or become dusky or shadowy.
dusk·i·ly (dus′k'l-i), *adv.* in a dusky manner; dimly.
dusk·i·ness (dus′ki-nis), *n.* a dusky quality or state.
dusk·y (dus′ki), *adj.* [DUSKIER (-ki-ẽr), DUSKIEST (-ki-ist)], [*dusk* + *-y*], 1. somewhat dark in color; shadowy; swarthy. 2. lacking light; dim. 3. gloomy; melancholy.
***SYN.*—dusky** suggests a darkness of color or an absence of light, verging on blackness (*dusky* twilight); **swarthy** and **tawny** both refer only to color, **swarthy** suggesting a dark-brown verging on black (a *swarthy* complexion) and **tawny**, a yellowish-brown, or tan (*tawny* hair). See also **dark.**
Düs·sel·dorf (düs′əl-dôrf′), *n.* a city in west central Germany, on the Rhine: pop., 685,000.
dust (dust), *n.* [ME.; AS.; akin to ON. *dust;* IE. base **dhus-* (< **dhewes;* see DEER), to fly like dust, dust-colored, etc.; cf. DUN, DUSK], 1. powdery earth or any powdered matter fine enough to be easily suspended in air. 2. a cloud of such matter; hence, 3. confusion; turmoil. 4. earth. 5. mortal remains disintegrated or thought of as disintegrating to earth or dust. 6. a humble or lowly condition. 7. anything worthless. 8. [British], ashes, rubbish, etc. 9. [Rare], a particle. 10. pollen. 11. tiny gold particles obtained by washing gold deposits; hence, 12. [Slang], money. *v.t.* 1. to sprinkle with or as with dust; powder. 2. to sprinkle (powder, etc.) on. 3. to make dusty. 4. to rid of dust, as by brushing, shaking, or wiping (often with *off*). *v.i.* 1. to remove dust, especially from furniture, floors, etc. 2. to bathe in dust: said of a bird. 3. to become dusty.
bite the dust, to fall in battle; be defeated.
lick the dust, 1. to fall in battle; be defeated. 2. to be servile; grovel.
make the dust fly, 1. to act energetically. 2. to move swiftly.
shake the dust off one's feet, to leave in anger or contempt: Matt. 10:14.
throw dust in (someone's) eyes, to mislead or practice deception on (someone).
dust·bin (dust′bin′), *n.* [British], a container for dust, rubbish, etc.; ash can.
dust bowl, those parts of the Great Plains of the United States where the eroded topsoil of fallow land was blown away by winds so that a vast desert area resulted, largely reclaimed during the administration of Franklin D. Roosevelt: also **Dust Bowl.**
dust·er (dus′tẽr), *n.* 1. a person or thing that dusts. 2. a brush or cloth for removing dust from furniture, etc. 3. a device for dusting a powder on. 4. a device for sprinkling sugar, ground cinnamon, etc. 5. a lightweight coat worn to protect the clothes from dust, as formerly in open automobiles.
dust·i·ly (dus′t'l-i), *adv.* 1. in a dusty manner. 2. with dust.
dust·i·ness (dus′ti-nis), *n.* a dusty quality or state.
dust jacket, a removable paper covering folded around the binding of a book for protection and ornament.
dust·less (dust′lis), *adj.* having or causing no dust: as, a *dustless* room, *dustless* chalk.
dust·man (dust′mən), *n.* [*pl.* DUSTMEN (-mən)], 1. [British], a man whose work is removing rubbish, ashes, garbage, etc. 2. a character in folklore supposed to make children sleepy by sprinkling dust in their eyes.
dust·pan (dust′pan′), *n.* a shovellike receptacle into which floor dust is swept.
dust·proof (dust′proof′), *adj.* keeping out dust; protecting from dust.
dust storm, a wind storm that sweeps up clouds of dust when passing over an arid region.
dust·y (dus′ti), *adj.* [DUSTIER (-ti-ẽr), DUSTIEST (-ti-ist)], [ME. *dusti;* AS. *dystig* < *dust*], 1. covered with dust; full of dust. 2. like dust; powdery. 3. of the color of dust.
Dutch (duch), *adj.* [orig. applied to Germans; *Netherlands* sense from 17th-c. onward; see DEUTSCHLAND], 1. of the Netherlands, its people, language, or culture. 2. [Slang], German. *n.* 1. the language of the Netherlands. 2. [Slang], German. 3. [construed as pl.], the people of the Netherlands. 4. [construed as pl.], [Slang], the German people. Abbreviated **D., Du.**
beat the Dutch, [Slang], to be very unusual or extraordinary; surpass what has hitherto been considered remarkable.
go Dutch, [Colloq.], to have every participant pay his own expenses.
in Dutch, [Slang], in difficulties or disfavor.
Dutch Belted, any of a breed of dairy cattle that are black with a broad white stripe around the body.
Dutch Borneo, formerly, the part of Borneo that belonged to the Netherlands.
Dutch cheese, 1. a hard, round cheese made of skim milk, and usually colored red outside, as Edam cheese. 2. cottage cheese.
Dutch courage, [Colloq.], 1. courage stimulated by drinking alcoholic liquor; hence, 2. alcoholic liquor.
Dutch door, a door with upper and lower halves that can be opened separately.
Dutch East Indies, the Netherlands Indies.
Dutch Guiana, Surinam, a part of the kingdom of the Netherlands, in South America.
Dutch Harbor, a town in Unalaska, in the Aleutian Islands: site of a United States naval station.
Dutch·man (duch′mən), *n.* [*pl.* DUTCHMEN (-mən)], 1. a native or inhabitant of the Netherlands; Hollander. 2. a Dutch ship. 3. [Slang], a German. 4. [Nautical Slang], a German ship.
Dutch·man's-breech·es (duch′mənz-brich′iz), *n. sing. & pl.* a wild flower that grows in the spring, with a formation on its yellow-tipped white flowers that is shaped somewhat like wide breeches.
Dutch·man's-pipe (duch′mənz-pīp′), *n.* [from the resemblance of the curved flowers to a pipe bowl], a hardy, woody vine with U-shaped flowers.
Dutch metal, tombac, an alloy of copper and zinc.

Dutch New Guinea, Netherlands New Guinea.
Dutch oven, 1. an iron kettle for baking, with a tight-fitting convex lid, on which live coals can be placed. 2. a metal container for roasting meats, etc., with an open side placed so that it is toward the fire. 3. a brick oven whose walls are preheated for cooking.
Dutch treat, [Colloq.], any entertainment, party, etc. in which each participant pays his own expenses.
Dutch uncle, [Colloq.], a person who bluntly and sternly lectures or scolds someone else.
Dutch West Indies, the Netherlands Antilles.
du·te·ous (dōō′ti-əs, dū′ti-əs), ***adj.*** dutiful; obedient.
du·ti·a·ble (dōō′ti-ə-b'l, dū′ti-ə-b'l), ***adj.*** necessitating payment of a duty or tax, as imported goods.
du·ti·ful (dōō′ti-fəl, dū′ti-fəl), ***adj.*** 1. showing, or resulting from, a sense of duty. 2. performing one's duty or duties; obedient; respectful.
du·ty (dōō′ti, dū′ti), ***n.*** [*pl.* DUTIES (-tiz)], [ME. *dute, deute;* OFr. *duete,* what is due (owing); see DUE & -TY], 1. conduct owed to one's parents, older people, etc.; behavior showing a proper regard or sense of obligation; obedience; respect. 2. any action necessary in or appropriate to one's occupation or position. 3. conduct resulting from a sense of justice, morality, etc. 4. a sense or feeling of obligation: as, *duty* calls. 5. a payment due to the government, especially a tax imposed on imports, exports, or manufactured goods. 6. [British], the performance of a machine as measured by the output of work per unit of fuel. 7. the amount of work that a machine is meant to do: as, a heavy-*duty* tractor. 8. in *agriculture,* the amount of water needed for irrigation per acre per crop: also **duty of water.**
do duty for, to be a substitute for; serve as.
off duty, temporarily relieved from one's work.
on duty, at one's assigned work.
SYN.—**duty** refers to the general conduct required by one's sense of justice, morality, etc. or by the dictates of one's conscience (*duty* to one's fellow men); **obligation** refers to what one is bound to do to fulfill a particular contract, promise, social requirement, etc. (you are under *obligation* to care for her); **responsibility** refers to a particular task, trust, etc. for which one is accountable or answerable (the garden is her *responsibility*). See also **function.**
du·ty-free (dōō′ti-frē′, dū′ti-frē′), ***adj. & adv.*** with no payment of a duty or tax required.
du·um·vir (dōō-um′vẽr, dū-um′vẽr), ***n.*** [*pl.* DUUMVIRS (-vẽrz), DUUMVIRI (-vi-rī′)], [L. < *duo,* two + *vir,* a man], either of two magistrates in ancient Rome who held office jointly.
du·um·vi·rate (dōō-um′və-rit, dū-um′və-rit), ***n.*** [L. *duumviratus,* office of a *duumvir*], 1. governmental position or authority held jointly by two men. 2. two men jointly holding such position or authority.
du·ve·tyn, du·ve·tyne, du·ve·tine (dōō′və-tēn′, dōō′-və-tēn′), ***n.*** [< Fr. *duvet,* eider down], a soft textile with a short, velvety nap, made of wool mixed with some other fiber, as mercerized cotton or spun silk.
D.V., 1. *Deo volente,* [L.], God willing. 2. Douay Version (of the Bible).
Dvi·na (dvi-nä′), ***n.*** 1. a river in Russia and Latvia, flowing northwestward into the Gulf of Riga: length, 640 mi.: German name, *Düna;* Lettish name, *Daugava.* 2. a river in Russia: see **Northern Dvina.**
Dvina Bay, the estuary of the Northern Dvina in the White Sea: also called *Gulf of Archangel, Gulf of Dvinsk.*
Dvinsk (dvēnsk), ***n.*** Daugavpils: the Russian name.
D.V.M., Doctor of Veterinary Medicine.
Dvo·řák, An·ton (än′tôn dvôr′zhäk, dvôr′zhak), 1841–1904; Czech composer.
D.V.S., Doctor of Veterinary Surgery.
D/W, dock warrant.
dwarf (dwôrf), ***n.*** [ME. *dwerf* (see DUFF), *dwergh;* AS. *dweorh;* akin to G. *zwerg;* IE. base **dhwergh-* (< **dhwer-,* to delude), deceptive (i.e., magic-making) being, little devil], 1. any human being, animal, or plant that is much smaller than the usual one of its species. 2. in *folklore,* an ugly little being to whom magic powers are attributed. ***v.t.*** 1. to keep from growing to full natural size; stunt the growth of. 2. to make smaller. 3. to make seem small in comparison; tower over; outshine. ***v.i.*** to become stunted or dwarfed. ***adj.*** undersized; dwarfish; stunted.
SYN.—**dwarf** refers to any individual that is considerably smaller than the average for the species and sometimes implies malformation or disproportion of parts; **midget** refers to a normally formed and proportioned, but diminutive, human being; **Pygmy** strictly refers to a member of any of several small-sized African or Asiatic peoples, but it is sometimes used (written **pygmy**) as a synonym for **dwarf** or **midget.**
dwarf alder, a small buckthorn tree with leaves like those of an alder.
dwarf chestnut, 1. the chinquapin, a small chestnut tree. 2. its edible nut.
dwarf·ish (dwôrf′ish), ***adj.*** 1. like a dwarf. 2. abnormally small; diminutive.
dwell (dwel), ***v.i.*** [DWELT (dwelt) or DWELLED (dweld), DWELLING], [ME. *dwellen;* AS. *dwellan* & ON. *dvelja,* to deceive, hence hold up, hinder, stop; repatterned in sense after ON. *dveljask* (reflexive of *dvelja*), lit., to hold up or stop oneself, hence to stay, remain; IE. base **dh(e)wel-,* to obscure, make dull; also, dark, dirty; cf. DULL], to reside; make one's home.
dwell on (or **upon**), to linger over in thought or speech; think or express oneself about at length.
dwell·er (dwel′ẽr), ***n.*** a person who dwells (in a specified place); inhabitant or permanent resident.
dwell·ing (dwel′iŋ), ***n.*** [ME.; see DWELL], a place to live in; residence; house; abode: also **dwelling place.**
dwelling house, the house, room, apartment, etc. that is one's residence.
dwelt (dwelt), alternative past tense and past participle of **dwell.**
Dwight (dwīt), [Gmc., wise person], a masculine name.
dwin·dle (dwin′d'l), ***v.i. & v.t.*** [DWINDLED (-d'ld), DWINDLING], [dim. of ME. *dwinen;* AS. *dwinan* (akin to D. *dwijnen*), to waste away], to make or become smaller or less; diminish; shrink. —***SYN.*** see **decrease.**
dwine (dwīn), ***v.i.*** [DWINED (dwīnd), DWINING], [ME. *dwinen;* AS. *dwinan;* akin to ON. *dvīna;* IE. base **dheu-,* to vanish, die; cf. DEATH, DWINDLE], [Archaic or British Dial.], to pine away; languish; fade; wither.
dwt., [*denarius weight*], pennyweight; pennyweights.
DX, D.X., in *radio,* 1. distance. 2. distant.
Dy, in *chemistry,* dysprosium.
dy·ad (dī′ad), ***n.*** [LL. *dyas, dyadis;* Gr. *dyas, dyados,* two], 1. two units regarded as one; pair. 2. in *biology,* a double chromosome resulting from the division of a tetrad; half of a tetrad. 3. in *chemistry,* an atom, element, or radical with a valence of two. ***adj.*** consisting of two.
dy·ad·ic (dī-ad′ik), ***adj.*** of or consisting of a dyad, or group of two.
Dy·ak (dī′ak), ***n.*** [Malay *dayak,* savage], a member of various related tribes of native inhabitants of Borneo.
dy·arch·y (dī′är-ki), ***n.*** [*pl.* DYARCHIES (-kiz)], [< Gr. *dyo,* two; + *-archy*], a dual governmental system, especially that instituted in the nine major provinces of India under the reformed Indian constitution of 1919, which divided governmental functions between the British governor and the provincial governor.
dye (dī), ***n.*** [differentiated sp. of earlier *die;* ME. *dehe;* AS. *deah;* IE. **dh(e)wĕk,* etc., dark color, secret mystery, as also in OS. *dōgal-,* OHG. *tougal,* dark, secret], 1. color produced in a substance by saturating it with a coloring agent; tint; hue. 2. any substance used to give color to fabric, hair, etc.; coloring matter or a solution containing it. ***v.t.*** [DYED (dīd), DYEING], [ME. *deien, deagen;* AS. *deagian, degian* < *deag*], 1. to color with or as with a dye. 2. to make (something) a specified color by or as by the use of dye. ***v.i.*** to take on color in dyeing.
of deepest dye, of the worst or most villainous sort.
dyed-in-the-wool (dīd′'n-thə-wool′), ***adj.*** 1. having the yarn dyed before being woven; hence, 2. thoroughgoing; unchangeable.
dye·ing (dī′iŋ), ***n.*** the process or work of coloring fabrics with dyes.
dy·er (dī′ẽr), ***n.*** a person whose work or business is dyeing fabrics.
dy·er's-weed (dī′ẽrz-wēd′), ***n.*** any of a number of plants that yield a dyestuff, as the indigo plant.
dye·stuff (dī′stuf′), ***n.*** any substance constituting or yielding a dye.
dye·weed (dī′wēd′), ***n.*** the woodwaxen, a small, shrubby plant with yellow flowers yielding a yellow dye.
dye·wood (dī′wood′), ***n.*** any wood yielding a dye.
dy·ing (dī′iŋ), present participle of **die.** ***adj.*** 1. at the point of death; about to die. 2. drawing to a close; about to end: as, a *dying* social order. 3. of or connected with death or dying. ***n.*** the act or process of ceasing to live or exist.
dyke (dīk), ***n. & v.t.*** dike.
dyn., dynamics.
dy·na- (dī′nə), a combining form meaning *power,* as in *dynameter:* also, before a vowel, **dyn-.**
dy·nam- (dī′nəm), dynamo-.
dy·nam·e·ter (dī-nam′ə-ter), ***n.*** [*dyna-* + *-meter*], an instrument for finding the magnifying power of a telescope.
dy·nam·ic (dī-nam′ik), ***adj.*** [Fr. *dynamique;* Gr. *dynamikos* < *dynamis,* power, strength], 1. relating to energy or physical force in motion: opposed to *static.* 2. relating to dynamics. 3. energetic; vigorous; forceful. 4. relating to or tending toward change. 5. in *medicine,* functional: opposed to *organic.*
dy·nam·i·cal (dī-nam′i-k'l), ***adj.*** dynamic.
dy·nam·ics (dī-nam′iks), ***n.pl.*** [construed as sing. in senses 1, 3 & 4], [< *dynamic*], 1. the branch of physics that treats of the action of force on bodies in motion or at rest; kinetics, kinematics, and statics, collectively. 2. the various forces, physical or moral, operating in any field. 3. the study of forces operating in any field. 4. that aspect of musical expression which deals with the various degrees of loudness and softness in performance: distinguished from *tempo, rhythm,* etc. Abbreviated **dyn.**
dy·na·mism (dī′nə-miz'm), ***n.*** [*dynam-* + *-ism*], 1. the theory that force or energy, rather than mass or motion, is the basic principle of all phenomena. 2. the quality

of being energetic, vigorous, etc.; dynamic quality.
dy·na·mite (dī'nə-mīt'), *n.* [< Gr. *dynamis*, power; + *-ite*], a powerful explosive made by soaking nitroglycerin into some absorbent, such as sodium nitrate and wood pulp. *v.t.* [DYNAMITED (-id), DYNAMITING], to blow up or destroy with dynamite.
dy·na·mo (dī'nə-mō') *n.* [*pl.* DYNAMOS (-mōz')], [< *dynamo electric machine*], a device for converting mechanical energy into electrical energy, usually by expending the mechanical energy in producing a relative periodic motion of a conductor and a surrounding magnetic field.

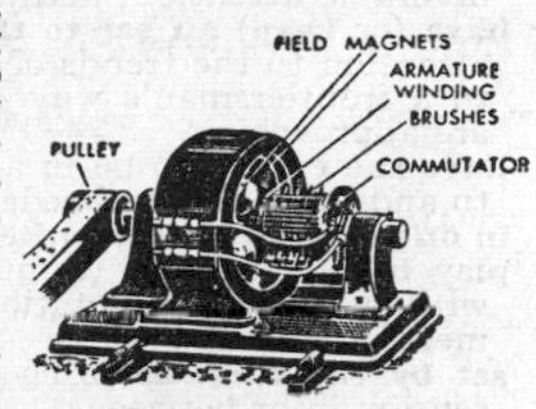

DYNAMO

dy·na·mo- (dī'nə-mō), [< Gr. *dynamis*, power], a combining form meaning *power*, as in *dynamoelectric:* also, before a vowel, **dynam-**.
dy·na·mo·e·lec·tric (dī'nə-mō-i-lek'trik), *adj.* [*dynamo-* + *electric*], having to do with the production of electrical energy from mechanical energy, or of mechanical energy from electrical energy.
dy·na·mo·e·lec·tri·cal (dī'nə-mō-i-lek'tri-k'l), *adj.* dynamoelectric.
dy·na·mom·e·ter (dī'nə-mom'ə-tẽr), *n.* [Fr. *dynamomètre;* see DYNAMO- & -METER], an apparatus for measuring force or energy.
dy·na·mo·met·ric (dī'nə-mō-met'rik), *adj.* of dynamometry, or the measurement of force.
dy·na·mom·e·try (dī'nə-mom'ə-tri), *n.* [*dynamo-* + *-metry*], the process of measuring forces at work.
dy·na·mo·tor (dī'nə-mō'tẽr), *n.* an electrical generator combining dynamo and motor, for transforming current of one voltage to that of another voltage.
dy·nast (dī'nast, dī'nəst), *n.* [L. *dynastes;* Gr. *dynastēs* < *dynasthai*, to be able or strong], a ruler, especially a hereditary ruler.
dy·nas·tic (dī-nas'tik), *adj.* [Gr. *dynastikos*], of or connected with a dynasty.
dy·nas·ti·cal (dī-nas'ti-k'l), *adj.* dynastic.
dy·nas·ty (dī'nəs-ti), *n.* [*pl.* DYNASTIES (-tiz)], [Fr. *dynastie;* LL. *dynastia;* Gr. *dynasteia*, lordship, rule < *dynastēs;* see DYNAST], 1. a succession of rulers who are members of the same family. 2. the period during which a certain family reigns.
dy·na·tron (dī'nə-tron'), *n.* [Mod. L.; *dyna-* + *electron*], 1. a three-electrode vacuum tube in which the plate and grid potentials are such that the secondary discharge of electrons from the plate causes a decrease in the plate current simultaneously with an increase in the plate potential: it is often used as an oscillator. 2. a mesotron.
dyne (dīn), *n.* [Fr. < Gr. *dynamis*, power], the amount of force that causes a mass of one gram to alter its speed by one centimeter per second for each second during which the force acts: the unit of force in the C.G.S. (metric) system: abbreviated **d.**
dys- (dis), [Gr. *dys-;* akin to Goth. *tuz-*, OHG. *zur-* (G. *zer-*)], a prefix meaning *bad, ill, difficult*, etc., as in *dysgenic.*
dys·en·ter·ic (dis''n-ter'ik), *adj.* 1. of or like dysentery. 2. having dysentery.
dys·en·ter·y (dis''n-ter'i), *n.* [OFr. *dysenterie;* L. *dysenteria;* Gr. *dysenteria* < *dys-*, bad + *enteron*, pl. *entera*, bowels], any of various intestinal diseases characterized by inflammation, abdominal pain, toxemia, and diarrhea with bloody, mucous feces.
dys·func·tion (dis-fuŋk'shən), *n.* [*dys-* + *function*], in *medicine*, abnormal, impaired, or incomplete functioning of an organ or part.
dys·gen·ic (dis-jen'ik), *adj.* [*dys-* + *-genic*], causing deterioration of hereditary qualities: opposed to *eugenic.*
dys·gen·ics (dis-jen'iks), *n.pl.* [construed as sing.], 1. the study of dysgenic trends in a population: opposed to *eugenics.* 2. intermarriage of hereditarily defective individuals.
dys·lo·gis·tic (dis'lə-jis'tik), *adj.* [*dys-* + *eulogistic*], not favorable; antagonistic: opposed to *eulogistic.*
dys·men·or·rhe·a (dis'men-ə-rē'ə), *n.* [< *dys-* + Gr. *mēn*, month + *rhoia*, a flowing], painful or difficult menstruation.
dys·pep·sia (dis-pep'shə, dis-pep'si-ə), *n.* [L.; Gr. < *dyspeptos; dys-*, bad + *peptos* < *peptein*, to soften, cook, digest], impaired digestion; indigestion.
dys·pep·sy (dis-pep'si), *n.* [Now Dial. or Colloq.], dyspepsia.
dys·pep·tic (dis-pep'tik), *adj.* [< Gr. *dyspeptos* (see DYSPEPSIA); + *-ic*], 1. of, causing, or having dyspepsia; hence, 2. gloomy; grouchy. *n.* a person who suffers from dyspepsia.
dys·pep·ti·cal·ly (dis-pep'ti-k'l-i), *adv.* 1. in the manner of a dyspeptic. 2. with dyspepsia.
dys·pha·gi·a (dis-fā'ji-ə), *n.* [Mod. L.; *dys-* + *-phagia*], in *medicine*, difficulty in swallowing.
dys·pha·si·a (dis-fā'zhə, dis-fā'zhi-ə), *n.* [Mod. L. *dys-* + *-phasia*], impairment of the ability to speak or, sometimes, to understand language, as the result of brain injury.
dys·pho·ni·a (dis-fō'ni-ə), *n.* [Gr. *dysphōnia* < *dys-*, bad + *phōnē*, voice], any impairment of the voice; difficulty in producing speech sounds.
dys·pho·ri·a (dis-fôr'i-ə, dis-fō'ri-ə), *n.* [Mod. L.; Gr. *dysphoria* < *dys-*, hard + *pherein*, to bear], in *psychology*, a generalized feeling of ill-being; especially, an abnormal feeling of anxiety, discontent, physical discomfort, etc.
dysp·ne·a, dysp·noe·a (disp-nē'ə), *n.* [L. *dispnoea;* Gr. *dyspnoia* < *dys-*, hard + *pnoē*, breathing < *pnein*, to breathe], difficult or painful breathing.
dysp·ne·al, dysp·noe·al (disp-nē'əl), *adj.* of dyspnea.
dysp·ne·ic, dysp·noe·ic (disp-nē'ik), *adj.* having or caused by dyspnea.
dysp·no·ic (disp-nō'ik), *adj.* dyspneic.
dys·pro·si·um (dis-prō'si-əm, dis-prō'shi-əm), *n.* [Mod. L. < Gr. *dysprositos*, difficult of access; *dys-*, hard + *prositos*, approachable], a chemical element of the rare-earth group: symbol, Dy; at. wt., 162.46; at. no., 66: it is the most magnetic of all known substances: abbreviated **Ds** (no period).
dys·tro·phy (dis'trə-fi), *n.* [Mod. L. *dystrophia; dys-* + *-trophy*], faulty nutrition: cf. **muscular dystrophy.**
dys·u·ri·a (dis-yoor'i-ə), *n.* [LL.; Gr. *dysouria* < *dys-*, hard + *ouron*, urine], difficult or painful urination.
Dyu·sham·be (dyoo-shäm'be), *n.* Stalinabad, capital of the Tadzhik S.S.R.: the former name.
dz., dozen; dozens.
Dzher·zinsk (jer-zinsk'), *n.* a city in the Soviet Union, near Moscow: pop., 103,000.
Dzhu·gash·vi·li (joo͞'gä-shvē'lē), *n.* see **Stalin, Joseph.**
Dzun·ga·ri·a (zoon-gar'i-ə), *n.* a district of northern Sinkiang, China.

E

E, e (ē), *n.* [*pl.* E's, e's, Es, es (ēz)], 1. the fifth letter of the English alphabet: from the Greek *epsilon*, a borrowing from the Phoenician: see **alphabet**, table. 2. a sound of E or e: in English, usually the mid front unrounded vowel, IPA [ɛ], of *bed*, or the high front unrounded vowel, IPA [i], of *equal;* also used in written diphthongs (*ea, ei, ie*, etc.) and as a silent final letter (originally, a vocalized inflectional ending in Middle English) to indicate a long quality in the preceding vowel, as in *note, site, fate*, etc. 3. a type or impression for E or e. 4. *a symbol for* the fifth in a sequence or group. *adj.* 1. of E or e. 2. fifth in a sequence or group.
E (ē), *n.* 1. an object shaped like E. 2. a Roman numeral for 250; with a superior bar (Ē), 250,000. 3. in *chemistry, the symbol for* einsteinium. 4. in *education, a)* a grade fifth in quality, often equivalent to *condition. b)* sometimes, a grade first in quality, meaning *excellent.* 5. in *music, a)* the third tone or note in the scale of C major, or the fifth in the scale of A minor. *b)* a key, string, etc. producing this tone. *c)* the scale having E as the keynote. 6. in *physics, the symbol for, a)* the

modulus of elasticity. *b*) electromotive force. *adj.* shaped like E.

e- (ē; *unstressed*, i, ə), a prefix meaning *out, out of, from, without*, as in *eject, egress:* see **ex-**.

E., 1. Earl. 2. Easter. 3. English. 4. in *physics*, modulus of elasticity.

E, E., e, e., east.

E., e., 1. earth. 2. eastern. 3. engineer(ing). 4. in *baseball*, errors. 5. in *physics*, electromotive force.

ea., each.

E. A., in *psychology*, educational age.

each (ēch), *adj. & pron.* [ME. *ech, elc*, each, every; AS. *ælc* < *a*, ever + *gelic*, alike; for retained *-l-*, cf. Scot. form *ilk*], every one of two or more considered separately. *adv.* apiece: as, give them two apples *each.*

each other, each the other: in formal usage restricted to two and distinguished from *one another*.

Eads, James Buchanan (ēdz), 1820–1887; American engineer and inventor of the diving bell.

ea·ger (ē'gẽr), *adj.* [ME. *eger, egre;* OFr. *egre, aigre;* L. *acer, acris*, sharp, keen, hence acute, ardent, eager], 1. keenly desiring; wanting very much; impatient or anxious; ardent. 2. [Archaic], sharp; keen; cutting.

SYN.—**eager** implies great enthusiasm, zeal, or sometimes impatience, in the desire for or pursuit of something (he was *eager* to begin work); **avid** suggests an intense, sometimes greedy, desire to enjoy or possess something (*avid* for power); **keen** implies deep interest and a spirited readiness to achieve something (the team was *keen* on winning); **anxious,** in this connection, suggests an eagerness that is accompanied with some uneasiness over the outcome (*anxious* to do his best).

ea·gle (ē'g'l), *n.* [ME. *egle;* OFr. *egle, aigle;* L. *aquila*, eagle; form of *aquilus*, dark-colored, brown], 1. any of a number of large, strong, flesh-eating birds of prey belonging to the falcon family, noted for their sharp vision and powerful wings: see **American eagle,** illus. 2. a representation of the eagle, used as a symbol or emblem of a nation, etc.; especially, *a*) the military standard of the Roman Empire. *b*) the national emblem of the United States, or the seal bearing this emblem. *c*) the military insigne of a colonel in the United States armed forces (captain in the United States Navy). 3. a former gold coin of the United States, worth $10. 4. [E-], the constellation Aquila. 5. in *golf*, a score of two below par on any hole with a par of over three.

ea·gle-eyed (ē'g'l-īd'), *adj.* having keen vision.

ea·gle·stone (ē'g'l-stōn'), *n.* [so called because fabled to be found in eagles' nests], in *mineralogy*, a hollow, rounded mass of clay ironstone, formed by concretion.

ea·glet (ē'glit), *n.* [Fr. *aiglette*, dim. of *aigle*], a young eagle.

ea·gre (ē'gẽr, ā'gẽr), *n.* [Brit. eastern dial. form, prob. with loss of *h-* and orig. ME. lowered and lengthened vowel, for western form represented by Early Mod. Eng. *hyger, higre, higer;* ML. *higra* suggests AS. **higere*, lit., roarer < base of AS. *higian*, to strive, hasten, lit., breathe hard], a tidal wave in an estuary: also called *bore.*

Ea·kins, Thomas (ā'kinz), 1844–1916; American painter and sculptor.

eal·dor·man, eal·der·man (ôl'dẽr-mən), *n.* [Obs.], an alderman (especially sense 3).

EAM, [< Mod. Gr. *E*thniko *A*peleftherotiko *M*etopo, National Liberation Front], the National Liberation Front, a Greek underground movement in World War II formed by a coalition of leftist political parties and other groups to offer resistance to the Nazi occupation: cf. **ELAS.**

-e·an (ē'ən), [< L. *-ae-, -e-, -i-* & Gr. *-ai-, -ei-* (stem endings of nouns and adjectives); + *-an*], a suffix meaning *of, belonging to, like*, used to form adjectives and nouns, as *European, Aegean:* also **-aean, -ian.**

E. & O.E., errors and omissions excepted.

E. and P., Extraordinary and Plenipotentiary.

ean·ling (ēn'liŋ), *n.* [Obs.], a young lamb or kid: usually **yeanling.**

ear (êr), *n.* [ME. *ere;* AS. *eare;* akin to Goth. *auso*, G. *ohr;* IE. base **au-*, to perceive, hear, as also in L. *auris* (cf. AURICULAR) & *aus-cultare*, to listen (cf. AUSCULTATE)], 1. the part of the body specialized for the perception of sound; organ of hearing: the human ear consists of *a*) the external ear (pinna and external auditory canal); *b*) the inner ear (labyrinth), containing the cochlea and semicircular canals; and *c*) the middle ear (tympanum), a cavity connected to the external ear by the tympanic membrane, to the pharynx by the Eustachian tube, and to the inner ear by a series of three small bones called the *hammer, anvil,* and *stirrup.* 2. the visible, external part of the ear. 3. the sense of hearing. 4. the ability to recognize slight differences in sound, especially in the pitch, rhythm, etc. of musical tones. 5. anything shaped or placed like an ear. 6. in *journalism*, a small box in either upper corner of the front page of a newspaper, containing weather reports, advertising, etc.

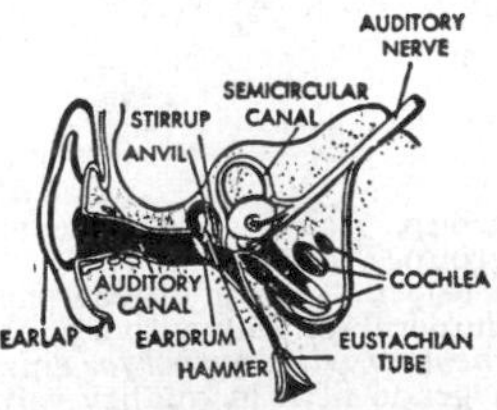

HUMAN EAR

be all ears, to be listening attentively or eagerly.

fall on deaf ears, to be ignored or unheeded.

give (or **lend**) **ear,** to listen; give attention, especially favorable attention; heed.

have (or **keep**) **an ear to the ground,** to give careful attention to the trends of public opinion: in allusion to a frontiersman's way of learning that horsemen are approaching.

have the ear of, to be in a favorable position to talk to and influence; be heeded by.

in one ear and out the other, heard but without effect.

play by ear, to play (a musical instrument or piece) without the use of notation, improvising an arrangement.

set by the ears, to bring about controversy or dissension in or between.

turn a deaf ear, to be unwilling to listen or heed.

up to the ears, very deeply: said of involvement in debt, trouble, etc.

ear (êr), *n.* [ME.; AS. *ear;* akin to G. *ähre*, Goth. *ahs;* IE. base **âk-*, sharp, as also in L. *acus*, chaff], the grain-bearing spike of a cereal plant: as, an *ear* of corn. *v.i.* to sprout ears; form ears.

ear (êr), *v.t.* [ME. *erien;* AS. *erian;* akin to Goth. *arjan;* IE. base **arā-*, to plow], [Archaic], to plow.

ear·ache (êr'āk'), *n.* an ache or pain in the (middle or inner) ear; otalgia.

ear·drop (êr'drop'), *n.* a hanging ornament for the ear; earring.

ear drops, any of various liquid medicines to be inserted in the ear in drops.

ear·drum (êr'drum'), *n.* 1. the middle ear; tympanum. 2. the tympanic membrane; thin membrane that separates the middle ear from the external ear and vibrates when struck by sound waves. See **ear,** illus.

eared (êrd), *adj.* having ears (in various senses): often used in combination, as, long-*eared.*

ear·flaps (êr'flaps'), *n.pl.* two pieces of cloth or fur attached to a cap and turned down to cover the ears in cold weather.

ear·ful (êr'fool'), *n.* [Colloq.], 1. enough or too much of what is heard: as, I got an *earful* of that. 2. important or startling news or gossip. 3. a scolding.

Ear·hart, Amelia (âr'härt'), (*Mrs. George Palmer Putnam*), 1898–1937; American flyer; first woman to fly across the Atlantic; lost on flight over the Pacific.

ear·ing (êr'iŋ), *n.* [< *ear* (organ of hearing), sense 6], a small rope for attaching the upper corner of a sail to the yard or gaff.

Earl, Earle (ũrl), [see next entry], a masculine name.

earl (ũrl), *n.* [ME. *erl*, nobleman, count; AS. *eorl*, warrior, brave man (influenced in Late AS. by ON. *jarl*, leader, ruler, noble); base sense may be "eagle," hence "renowned fighter" < IE. base **er-*, great bird, eagle], a British nobleman ranking above a viscount and below a marquis: the wife or widow of an earl is called a *countess*: abbreviated **E.** (as a title).

ear·lap (êr'lap'), *n.* [*ear* + *lap* (overlapping part)], 1. an earflap. 2. the ear lobe. 3. the external ear: see **ear,** illus.

earl·dom (ũrl'dəm), *n.* [ME. & AS. *eorldom;* see EARL (nobleman) & -DOM], 1. the territory ruled by an earl. 2. the rank or title of an earl.

ear·li·ness (ũr'li-nis), *n.* the quality or state of being early.

earl·ship (ũrl'ship'), *n.* [*earl* + *-ship*], the rank or title of an earl.

ear·ly (ũr'li), *adv. & adj.* [EARLIER (-li-ẽr), EARLIEST (-li-ist)], [ME. *erli;* rare AS. *ærlice, adv.* (whence *ærlic, adj.*) < *ær*, before (see ERE) + *-lice*, adv. suffix (see -LY, LIKE); akin to ON. *arliga*], 1. near the beginning of a given period of time or series of actions, events, or things. 2. before the expected or customary time. 3. in the far distant past; in ancient or remote times. 4. in the near future; before much time has passed.

Ear·ly, Ju·bal Anderson (jōō'b'l ũr'li), 1816–1894; Confederate general in the Civil War.

early bird, [Colloq.], a person who arrives early or gets up early in the morning.

Early Modern English, the English language as spoken and written from about 1450 to about 1750: as compared to Middle English, it is characterized by a sweeping change in the vowel system, whereby the long high vowels were diphthongized, the long mid and low vowels raised, and the short vowels lowered, and by a great increase in vocabulary, based on borrowings from Latin, Greek, and the Romance languages.

ear·mark (êr'märk'), *n.* 1. an identification mark or brand put on the ear of a domestic animal to show ownership; hence, 2. an identifying mark or feature; characteristic; sign. *v.t.* 1. to mark the ears of (livestock) for identification; hence, 2. to set a distinctive or informative mark upon; identify. 3. to set aside or reserve for a special purpose: as, *earmark* these supplies for the army.

ear·muffs (êr′mufs′), *n.pl.* a pair of cloth or fur coverings for the ears, worn in cold weather.

earn (ũrn), *v.t.* [ME. *ernien, ernen;* AS. *earnian,* to gain, labor for, lit., to harvest; akin to G. *ernte,* harvest, OHG. *arnōn,* to bring to harvest; IE. base **es-en,* summer, harvest time, as also in L. *annona,* a year's proceeds], 1. to receive (salary, wages, etc.) for one's labor or service. 2. to get as a result of merit: as, his remarks *earned* him the praise of everyone. 3. to do enough to deserve; get as a consequence: as, she *earned* that spanking. 4. to gain (interest, etc.) as profit.

Ear·nest (ũr′nist), a masculine name: see **Ernest.**

ear·nest (ũr′nist), *adj.* [ME. *erneste, ernest;* AS. *eornoste* < *eornost,* earnestness, zeal; akin to G. *ernst,* seriousness, gravity (OHG. *ernust*); IE. base **er-,* to set oneself in motion, excite, arouse (cf. RUN)], 1. serious and intense; not joking or playful; zealous and sincere; deeply convinced. 2. important; not petty or trivial: as, *earnest* matters. —*SYN.* see **serious.**

in earnest, 1. serious; not joking; zealous. 2. in a serious or zealous manner; with determination.

ear·nest (ũr′nist), *n.* [ME. *ernest, ernes;* OFr. *erres;* L. *arrae,* pl. of *arra, arrha, arrhabo,* earnest money; Gr. *arrabōn;* Heb. *'ērābōn;* influenced in ME. by *erneste,* seriousness], 1. money given as a part payment and pledge in binding a bargain: in full, **earnest money.** 2. something given or done as an indication or assurance of what is to come; token; pledge. —*SYN.* see **pledge.**

earn·ings (ũr′niŋz), *n.pl.* 1. money, etc. earned by labor or service; wages or other recompense. 2. money made by an investment or an enterprise; profits.

ear·phone (êr′fōn′), *n.* a receiver for radio, telephone, etc., usually part of a headset; headphone.

ear·reach (êr′rēch′), *n.* earshot.

ear·ring (êr′riŋ′), *n.* a ring or other small ornament for the lobe of the ear, either passed through a hole pierced in the lobe or fastened with a screw or clip.

ear shell, 1. an abalone, a kind of mollusk. 2. its shell, shaped somewhat like the human ear.

ear·shot (êr′shot′), *n.* [by analogy with *bowshot,* etc.], the distance within which a sound, especially that of the unaided human voice, can be heard.

ear·split·ting (êr′split′iŋ), *adj.* so loud as to hurt the ears; very loud; deafening.

ear stone, a small, calcareous mass formed in the inner ear of a vertebrate; otolith.

earth (ũrth), *n.* [ME. *erthe;* AS. *eorthe;* akin to G. *erde;* IE. base **er-t,* as also in MIr. *ert,* ground], 1. the planet that we live on; terrestrial globe: it is the fifth largest planet of the solar system and the third in distance from the sun: diameter, 7,918 mi.; symbol, ⊕: abbreviated **E., e.** 2. this world, as distinguished from heaven and hell. 3. all the people on the earth. 4. land, as distinguished from sea or sky; the ground. 5. [Poetic], a land or country. 6. the soft, granular or crumbly part of land; soil; ground. 7. [Poetic], *a)* the substance of the human body. *b)* the human body. *c)* human concerns; worldly matters. 8. the hole of a burrowing animal; lair. 9. in *chemistry,* any of the metallic oxides, formerly classed as elements, which are reduced with difficulty, as alumina, zirconia, strontia, etc. *v.t.* 1. to embed in or cover (*up*) with soil for protection, as seeds, plants, or roots. 2. to chase (an animal) into a hole or burrow in the ground. *v.i.* to hide in a burrow: said of a fox, etc.

come back (or **down**) **to earth,** to stop being impractical; return to reality.

down to earth, practical; realistic.

move heaven and earth, to make every effort.

run to earth, [< use in fox hunting], 1. to hunt down. 2. to find by search.

SYN.—**earth** is applied to the globe or planet we live on, but in religious use is opposed to heaven or hell; **universe** refers to the whole system of planets, stars, space, etc. and to everything that exists in it; **world** is equivalent to **earth,** especially in its relation to man and his activities, but it is sometimes a generalized synonym for **universe.**

earth·born (ũrth′bôrn′), *adj.* 1. born on or springing from the earth; hence, 2. human; mortal.

earth-bound, earth·bound (ũrth′bound′), *adj.* 1. confined to or by the earth and earthly things. 2. headed for the earth.

earth·en (ũr′thən), *adj.* 1. made of earth. 2. made of baked clay. 3. earthly.

earth·en·ware (ũr′thən-wâr′), *n.* 1. the coarser sort of containers, tableware, etc. made of baked clay. 2. baked clay. *adj.* made of earthenware.

earth·i·ness (ũr′thi-nis), *n.* an earthy quality or state.

earth·light (ũrth′līt′), *n.* earthshine.

earth·li·ness (ũrth′li-nis), *n.* the quality or state of being earthly.

earth·ling (ũrth′liŋ), *n.* 1. a person who lives on the earth; human being. 2. a worldly person; worldling.

earth·ly (ũrth′li), *adj.* [AS. *eorthlic*], 1. of the earth; specifically, *a)* terrestrial. *b)* worldly. *c)* temporal or secular: opposed to *heavenly, spiritual.* 2. conceivable; possible: as, a thing of no *earthly* good.

SYN.—**earthly** is applied to that which belongs to the earth or to the present life and is chiefly contrasted with *heavenly* (*earthly* pleasures); **terrestrial,** having as its opposite *celestial* (both Latin-derived parallels of the preceding terms), has special application in formal and scientific usage (*terrestrial* magnetism); **worldly** implies reference to the material concerns or pursuits of mankind and is chiefly contrasted with *spiritual* (*worldly* wisdom); **mundane,** although often used as a close synonym of **worldly,** now especially stresses the commonplace or practical aspects of life (to return to *mundane* matters after a flight of fancy).

earth·nut (ũrth′nut′), *n.* 1. the root, tuber, or underground pod of various plants, as the peanut. 2. an edible underground fungus; truffle.

earth·pea (ũrth′pē′), *n.* a vine of the pea family, whose pods ripen underground.

earth·quake (ũrth′kwāk′), *n.* a shaking or trembling of the crust of the earth, caused by underground volcanic forces or by breaking and shifting of rock beneath the surface: also used figuratively.

earth·shine (ũrth′shīn′), *n.* the faint illumination of the dark part of the moon by sunlight reflected from the earth, seen about the time of the new moon.

earth·star (ũrth′stär′), *n.* a fungus whose outer covering splits into a starlike form.

earth·ward (ũrth′wẽrd), *adv. & adj.* [*earth* + *-ward*], toward the earth.

earth·wards (ũrth′wẽrdz), *adv.* earthward.

earth·work (ũrth′wũrk′), *n.* 1. a fortification made by piling up earth; defensive embankment. 2. in *engineering,* the work of excavating and building embankments.

earth·worm (ũrth′wũrm′), *n.* a round, segmented worm that burrows in the soil.

earth·y (ũr′thi), *adj.* [EARTHIER (-thi-ẽr), EARTHIEST (-thi-ist)], 1. of or like earth or soil. 2. of this world; hence, 3. *a)* coarse; gross. *b)* simple and natural; hearty and unashamed: as, *earthy* humor.

ear trumpet, a trumpet-shaped tube formerly used as a hearing aid by the partially deaf: it funneled the sound into the small end, which was held to the ear.

ear·wax (êr′waks′), *n.* the yellowish, waxlike secretion found in the canal of the outer ear; cerumen.

ear·wig (êr′wig′), *n.* [AS. *earwicga* < *eare,* ear + *wicga,* beetle, worm: so called from the baseless notion that it creeps into a person's ear], 1. any of a group of insects with thick, short forewings, many-jointed feelers, and a pincerlike part at the tail end. 2. any of a number of related small centipedes.

ease (ēz), *n.* [ME. *eaise, eise, ese;* OFr. *aise, aaise;* LL. **adjaces* < L. *adjacens,* lying nearby, hence easy to reach; see ADJACENT], 1. freedom from pain, worry, or trouble; comfort. 2. freedom from constraint, formality, or awkwardness; poise; natural, easy manner. 3. freedom from difficulty; facility; readiness; adroitness: as, he writes with *ease.* 4. freedom from poverty; state of being financially comfortable; affluence. 5. rest; leisure; relaxation. *v.t.* [EASED (ēzd), EASING], 1. to free from pain, worry, or trouble; comfort. 2. to lessen or alleviate (pain, anxiety, etc.). 3. to make easier; facilitate. 4. to reduce the strain, tension, or pressure of; loosen; slacken (a rope, sail, etc.): often with *away, down, up,* or *off.* 5. to fit or move by careful shifting, relaxing, etc.: as, they *eased* the piano into place. *v.i.* 1. to move or be moved by careful shifting, relaxing, etc. 2. to lessen in tension, speed, pain, etc.

at ease, 1. having no anxiety, pain, or discomfort. 2. in *military usage, a)* in a relaxed position but maintaining attention and silence. *b)* a command to take such a position.

ease the helm (or **rudder**), to bring the helm back a little when it is hard over, in order to reduce the strain on the rudder.

take one's ease, to relax and be comfortable.

ease·ful (ēz′fəl), *adj.* characterized by or full of ease.

ea·sel (ē′z'l), *n.* [17th & 18th c. < D. *ezel* (G. *esel*), ass; for sense, cf. Fr. *chevalet,* easel, lit., little horse & see SAWHORSE, CHEVAL GLASS], an upright frame or tripod to hold a canvas on which an artist is painting, or to hold a picture on display, etc.

EASEL

ease·ment (ēz′mənt), *n.* [ME. *esement, aisiement;* OFr. *aisement*], 1. an easing or being eased. 2. something that gives ease; a comfort, relief, or convenience. 3. in *law,* a right or privilege that a person may have in another's land, as the right of way.

eas·i·ly (ē′z'l-i, ēz′i-li), *adv.* 1. with ease; without much difficulty or effort. 2. without pain or discomfort. 3. in a smooth, free manner: as, the machine ran *easily*. 4. without a doubt; by far: as, she is *easily* the best dancer. 5. very likely: as, the train may *easily* be late.

eas·i·ness (ēz′i-nis), *n.* 1. the quality or state of being easy to do or get. 2. careless indifference; nonchalance. 3. ease of manner; freedom from constraint; poise.

east (ēst), *n.* [ME. *est*, also *esten, adv.*; AS. *east, eastan, adv., east, adj., easte, n.*; akin to G. *osten*, ON. *austr*; Gmc. base **aust-*, dawn < IE. **aues-*, to shine, dawn, as also in L. *aurora*, dawn (cf. AURORA) & *aurum*, gold (cf. AUREATE); cf. EASTER], 1. the direction to the right of a person facing north; direction in which sunrise occurs: it is properly the point on the horizon at which the center of the sun rises at the equinox. 2. the point on a compass at 90°, directly opposite west. 3. a region or district in or toward this direction. 4. [E-], the eastern part of the earth, especially Asia and the nearby islands; Orient. *adj.* 1. in, of, to, toward, or facing the east. 2. from the east: as, an *east* wind. 3. [E-], designating the eastern part of a continent, country, etc.: as, *East* Africa, *East* Ohio. 4. designating or in the part of a church containing the altar, conventionally the eastern end. *adv.* in or toward the east; in an easterly direction. Abbreviated **E, E., e, e.**

down East, [Colloq.], 1. New England, especially Maine. 2. in, to, or toward this region.

the East, the eastern part of the United States; specifically, *a*) the part east of the Allegheny Mountains, from Maine through Maryland. *b*) the part east of the Mississippi and north of the Ohio.

East Anglia, 1. a former Anglo-Saxon kingdom of eastern England. 2. the district of eastern England comprising Norfolk and Suffolk.

East Bengal, the eastern territories of Bengal: since 1948 part of East Pakistan (see **Pakistan**).

east·bound (ēst′bound′), *adj.* bound east; going eastward.

East·bourne (ēst′bôrn′, ēst′bōrn′, ēst′bẽrn), *n.* a city in eastern England, on the English Channel: pop., 58,000.

east by north, the direction, or the point on a mariner's compass, halfway between due east and east-northeast; 11° 15′ north of due east: abbreviated **E b N, E by N** (no period).

east by south, the direction, or the point on a mariner's compass, halfway between due east and east-southeast; 11° 15′ south of due east: abbreviated **E b S, E by S** (no period).

East Chicago, a city in northwestern Indiana, near Chicago: pop., 58,000.

East China Sea, a sea off eastern China, separated from the South China Sea by Formosa: area, 482,000 sq. mi.; average depth, 618 ft.: also called *Eastern Sea*.

East Cleveland, a city in northeastern Ohio: suburb of Cleveland: pop., 38,000.

East Detroit, a city in southeastern Michigan: suburb of Detroit: pop., 46,000.

East·er (ēs′tẽr), *n.* [ME. *ester, esterne*; AS. *eastre*, in pl. *eastron* (akin to G. *Ostern*), spring, Easter; orig., name of pagan vernal festival almost coincident in date with paschal festival of the church < *Eastre*, dawn goddess (see EAST)], 1. an annual Christian festival celebrating the resurrection of Jesus, held on the first Sunday after the date of the first full moon that occurs on or after March 21: abbreviated **E.** 2. the Sunday of this festival: often **Easter Sunday.**

Easter egg, a colored egg or an egg-shaped piece of candy, etc., used as an Easter gift or ornament.

Easter Island, a Chilean island in the South Pacific: native name, *Rapa Nui*.

east·er·ly (ēs′tẽr-li), *adj.* 1. in, of, or toward the east. 2. from the east: as, an *easterly* wind. *adv.* 1. toward the east. 2. from the east: as, the wind blew *easterly*.

east·ern (ēs′tẽrn), *adj.* [ME. *esterne*; AS. *easterne*], 1. in, of, toward, or facing the east. 2. from the east: as, an *eastern* wind. 3. [E-], of or characteristic of the East. *n.* an easterner. Abbreviated **East., east.**

Eastern Church, 1. originally, the Christian Church in the Eastern Roman Empire, consisting of the four patriarchates in eastern Europe, western Asia, and Egypt, headed by the Bishops of Constantinople, Alexandria, Antioch, and Jerusalem: distinguished from the *Western Church*, the patriarchate in western Europe and North Africa, headed by the Bishop of Rome. 2. the Orthodox Eastern Church. 3. all Catholics who practice the Eastern rite but acknowledge the supreme authority of the Pope; Uniats.

Eastern Empire, the Byzantine Empire.

east·ern·er (ēs′tẽr-nẽr), *n.* 1. a native or inhabitant of the east. 2. [E-], a native or inhabitant of the eastern part of the United States.

Eastern Hemisphere, that half of the earth which includes Europe, Africa, Asia, and Australia.

east·ern·most (ēs′tẽrn-mōst′), *adj.* farthest east.

Eastern Roman Empire, the empire formed by the division of the Roman Empire at the death of Theodosius I in 395 A.D.: it was ended by the Turkish conquest of Constantinople, its capital, in 1453.

Eastern Shore, the eastern shore of Chesapeake Bay, especially the part in Maryland.

Eastern Standard Time, one of the four standard times in the United States, corresponding to the mean local time of the 75th meridian west of Greenwich, England: it is five hours behind Greenwich time: abbreviated **E.S.T.**

East·er·tide (ēs′tẽr-tīd′), *n.* [*Easter* + *tide* (time)], the period after Easter, extending in various churches to Ascension Day, Whitsunday, or Trinity Sunday.

East Flanders, a province of western Belgium: area, 1,147 sq. mi.; pop., 1,261,000; capital, Ghent.

East Ham, a city in Essex, England: suburb of London: pop., 110,000.

East Hartford, a town in central Connecticut, near Hartford: pop., 44,000.

East India, the East Indies: abbreviated **E.I.**

East India Company, any of several European companies for exploiting trade with the East Indies, having special trading rights and government support; especially, such an English company, first chartered in 1600 and dissolved in 1874.

East Indian, 1. of the East Indies, its people, etc. 2. a native of the East Indies. Abbreviated **E. Ind., E.I.**

East Indies, 1. the islands southeast of Asia; Malay Archipelago. 2. the Malay Archipelago, the Malay Peninsula, the Indochinese peninsula, and India. Abbreviated **E. I.** Also called *East India*.

east·ing (ēs′tiŋ), *n.* in *nautical usage*, 1. the distance covered sailing in an easterly direction. 2. a turning, or veering, to the east. 3. an easterly direction.

East Lansing, a city in central Michigan: suburb of Lansing: pop., 30,000.

East Liverpool, a city in eastern Ohio: pop., 22,000.

East London, a city on the southeastern coast of the Union of South Africa: pop., 91,000.

East Los Angeles, a town in southwestern California: suburb of Los Angeles: pop., 104,000.

East Lo·thi·an (lō′*thi*-ən), a county of southeastern Scotland, on the Firth of Forth: pop., 52,000; county seat, Haddington.

East·man, George (ēst′mən), 1854–1932; American industrialist and inventor of photographic equipment.

east-north·east (ēst′nôrth′ēst′; *in nautical usage*, ēst′nôr-ēst′), *n.* the direction, or the point on a mariner's compass, halfway between due east and northeast; 22° 30′ north of due east. *adj. & adv.* 1. in or toward this direction. 2. from this direction: as, an *east-northeast* wind. Abbreviated **ENE, E.N.E., e.n.e.**

Eas·ton (ēs′tən), *n.* a city in east central Pennsylvania, on the Delaware River: pop., 32,000.

East Orange, a city in northeastern New Jersey, near Newark: pop., 77,000.

East Point, a city in north central Georgia: suburb of Atlanta: pop., 36,000.

East Providence, a city in eastern Rhode Island, near Providence: pop., 42,000.

East Prussia, a former province of Prussia, Germany, on the Baltic Sea, separated from Germany proper by the Polish Corridor: now divided between the R.S.F.S.R. and Poland: German name, *Ostpreussen*.

East Rid·ing (rīd′iŋ), a division of Yorkshire, England: pop., 511,000.

East River, a narrow strait connecting Long Island Sound and New York Bay and separating Manhattan Island from Long Island: length, 15 mi.

east-south·east (ēst′south′ēst′), *n.* the direction, or the point on a mariner's compass, halfway between due east and southeast; 22° 30′ south of due east. *adj. & adv.* 1. in or toward this direction. 2. from this direction: as, an *east-southeast* wind. Abbreviated **ESE, E.S.E., e.s.e.**

East St. Louis, a city in western Illinois, on the Mississippi, opposite St. Louis: pop., 82,000.

east·ward (ēst′wẽrd), *adv. & adj.* [see -WARD], toward the east. *n.* an eastward direction, point, or region.

east·ward·ly (ēst′wẽrd-li), *adv. & adj.* 1. toward the east. 2. from the east: as, an *eastwardly* wind.

east·wards (ēst′wẽrdz), *adv.* eastward.

eas·y (ēz′i), *adj.* [EASIER (-i-ẽr), EASIEST (-i-ist)], [ME. *aisie*; OFr. *aaisie* < *aise*; see EASE], 1. that can be done, got, mastered, etc. with ease; not difficult; not exacting. 2. free from trouble, anxiety, pain, etc. 3. conducive to comfort, rest, or relaxation; comfortable; pleasant. 4. fond of comfort, ease, or idleness. 5. free from constraint; not stiff, awkward, or embarrassed. 6. not strict, harsh, or severe; lenient; tolerant. 7. readily influenced; compliant; tractable. 8. unhurried; not fast; moderate. 9. in *business*, *a*) in little demand: said of a commodity. *b*) lacking firmness in prices: said of a market. *c*) with funds plentiful and interest rates low: said of a money market. Opposed to *tight*. 10. in *card games*, evenly divided between opponents: as, *easy* aces. *adv.* [Colloq.], easily.

easy come—easy go, got and spent or lost with equal ease: implying a carefree attitude toward money.

on easy street, well-to-do; in easy circumstances.

take it easy, [Colloq.], 1. to refrain from anger, violence, haste, etc. 2. to refrain from hard work; relax; rest. Sometimes used as a farewell.

SYN.—**easy** is the broadest term here in its application to that which demands little effort or presents little difficulty (*easy* work); **facile** means occurring, moving, working, etc. easily and quickly, sometimes unfavorably suggesting a lack of thoroughness or depth (a *facile* style); **effortless**, in contrast, favorably suggests expert skill or knowledge as responsible for performance that seems to require no effort (the *effortless* grace of the skater); **smooth** suggests freedom from or riddance of irregularities, obstacles, or difficulties as bringing ease of movement (a *smooth* path to success); **simple**, in this connection, suggests freedom from complication, elaboration, or involvement as making something easy to understand (a *simple* explanation). —***ANT.*** hard, difficult.

easy chair, a stuffed or padded armchair.

eas·y·go·ing, eas·y-go·ing (ē'zi-gō'iŋ), *adj.* 1. having an even, comfortable gait: said of a horse. 2. dealing with things in an unworried, unhurried manner; not strenuous or agitated.

easy mark, [Colloq.], a person easily duped or taken advantage of.

eat (ēt), *v.t.* [ATE (āt; Brit. et) or *archaic & dial.* EAT (et, ēt), EATEN (ēt''n) or *archaic* EAT (et, ēt), EATING], [ME. *eten;* AS. *etan;* akin to G. *essen;* IE. base **ed-*, to eat, as also in L. *edere* (cf. EDIBLE)], 1. to put in the mouth, chew, and swallow (food). 2. to use up, devour, destroy, or waste as by eating; consume or ravage (usually with *away* or *up*). 3. to penetrate and destroy, as acid does; corrode. 4. to make by or as by eating: as, termites *eat* their way through wood, acid *ate* holes in my suit. *v.i.* to eat food; have a meal or meals.
  eat into, 1. to penetrate and destroy, as acid does. 2. to use up or consume part of.
  eat one's heart out, [Colloq.], to brood or feel keenly unhappy for some time over some frustration, etc.
  eat one's words, to retract something said earlier.
  eat up, 1. to consume, devour, or use up thoroughly. 2. to engross deeply: as, *eaten up* with curiosity.

eat·a·ble (ēt'ə-b'l), *adj.* fit to be eaten; edible. *n. usually in pl.* a thing fit to be eaten; food.

eat·en (ēt''n), past participle of **eat.**

eat·ing (ēt'iŋ), *n.* 1. the action of a person or thing that eats. 2. something edible, with reference to its quality as food: as, the army meals were poor *eating.*

eats (ēts), *n.pl.* [Colloq.], food; meals.

‡**eau** (ō), *n.* [*pl.* EAUX (ō)], [Fr.; L. *aqua*, water], water.

Eau Claire (ō'klâr'), a city in western Wisconsin: pop., 38,000.

eau de Co·logne (ō' də kə-lōn'), [Fr., lit., water of Cologne: it was orig. made at Cologne, Germany], a perfumed toilet water made up of alcohol and aromatic oils; cologne.

‡**eau de Ja·velle** (ō' də zhȧ'vel'), [Fr.], Javel water.

‡**eau de vie** (ō'd'vē', ōd'vē'), [Fr., lit., water of life], brandy.

eaves (ēvz), *n.pl.* [*mod. sing.* EAVE (ēv)], [orig. sing. now regarded as pl.; ME. *euese* (also *euesen, pl.*); AS. *efes*, edge, border, eaves; akin to ON. *ups*, church porch, OHG. *obiza*, porch; IE. base **upo-*, up from behind, as also in L. *summus* (< **supmos;* cf. SUMMIT) & Eng. *up*], the edge or edges of a roof, usually projecting beyond the sides of a building.

EAVES

eaves·drop (ēvz'drop'), *n.* [earlier *eavesdrip*], 1. water that drips from the eaves. 2. the ground on which it drips. *v.i.* [EAVESDROPPED (-dropt'), EAVESDROPPING], [from the orig. sense of standing under eaves to overhear through a window], to listen secretly to the private conversation of others.

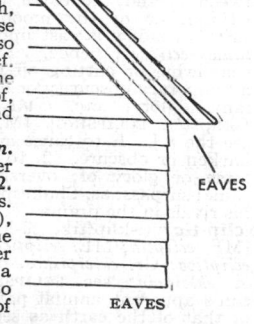

eaves·drop·per (ēvz'drop'ẽr), *n.* one who eavesdrops.

Eb, in *chemistry,* erbium.

ebb (eb), *n.* [ME. *ebbe;* AS. *ebba, æbba;* common LG. as in MLG. *ebbe* (whence G. *ebbe*), OFris. *ebba*, etc.; Gmc. **abjan*, a going back; prob. IE. base **apo-*, from, away from, as also in AS. *æf, of,* (cf. OFF)], 1. the flowing of the tide back toward the sea; receding of the tide. 2. a passing away; weakening or lessening; decline: as, the *ebb* of one's hopes. *v.i.* [ME. *ebben;* AS. *ebbian;* see the *n.*], 1. to flow back or out; recede, as the tide. 2. to weaken or lessen; decline. —***SYN.*** see **wane.**

ebb tide, the outgoing tide; falling tide: opposed to *flood tide.*

Eb·en·e·zer (eb'ə-nē'zẽr), [Heb. *eben-ha-'ēzer*, lit., stone of help: see I Sam. 7:12], a masculine name.

E·bert, Fried·rich (frē'driH ā'bẽrt), 1871–1925; German Social Democratic statesman; first president of the German Republic (1919–1925).

Eb·lis (eb'lis), *n.* [Ar. *Iblīs* < Gr. *diabolos;* see DEVIL], Satan: the Moslem name.

E b N, east by north.

eb·on (eb'ən), *adj. & n.* [ME. *eban;* L. *ebenus, hebenus;* Gr. *ebenos;* Egypt. *hebni*], [Poetic], ebony.

eb·on·ite (eb'ən-īt'), *n.* [< *ebony* + *-ite*], a black, hard rubber, vulcanized with sulfur: used for electric insulation, combs, fountain pens, etc.; vulcanite.

eb·on·ize (eb'ən-īz'), *v.t.* [EBONIZED (-īzd'), EBONIZING], to make (wood, etc.) black; make look like ebony.

eb·on·y (eb'ən-i), *n.* [*pl.* EBONIES (-iz)], [prob. < L. *ebeninus, hebeninus* < *ebenus;* see EBON], 1. the hard, heavy, dark, durable wood of any of various trees, especially of a group of persimmons native to tropical Africa, Asia, and Ceylon: it is used for furniture and decorative woodwork. 2. any tree that yields this wood. *adj.* 1. made of ebony. 2. like ebony, especially in color; dark; black.

Eb·o·ra·cum (eb'ə-rā'kəm), *n.* York, a city in England: the ancient name.

E·bro (ē'brō; Sp. e'brô), *n.* a river in northeastern Spain, flowing into the Mediterranean: length, 465 mi.

E b S, east by south.

e·bul·li·ence (i-bul'yəns, i-bul'i-əns), *n.* [see EBULLIENT], 1. a bubbling or boiling up. 2. an overflow of enthusiasm, high spirits, etc.; exuberance.

e·bul·li·en·cy (i-bul'yən-si, i-bul'i-ən-si), *n.* ebullience.

e·bul·li·ent (i-bul'yənt, i-bul'i-ənt), *adj.* [L. *ebulliens*, ppr. of *ebullire*, to boil up; *e-*, out + *bullire*, to boil], 1. bubbling; boiling; effervescent. 2. overflowing with enthusiasm, high spirits, etc.; exuberant.

e·bul·li·tion (eb'ə-lish'ən), *n.* [L. *ebullitio* < pp. of *ebullire;* see EBULLIENT], 1. a boiling or bubbling up; effervescence. 2. a sudden outburst, as of some emotion.

e·bur·na·tion (ē'bẽr-nā'shən, eb'ẽr-nā'shən), *n.* [< L. *eburnus*, of ivory < *ebur*, ivory], an abnormal condition of bone or cartilage in which it becomes hard like ivory.

ec- (ek), [Gr. *ek-;* see EX-], a prefix meaning *out of*, as in *eccentric, ecstasy:* used before consonants: see **ex-.**

E.C., 1. Engineering Corps. 2. Established Church.

e.c., *exempli causa*, [L.], for the sake of example.

é·car·té (ā'kär-tā'; Brit. ā-kär'tā; Fr. ā'kȧr'tā'), *n.* [Fr., pp. of *écarter*, to discard, set aside: so called because any or all of the cards dealt may be discarded and replaced from the pack], a card game for two persons played with thirty-two cards (sevens up through aces).

Ec·bat·a·na (ek-bat'ə-nə), *n.* the capital of ancient Media, on the site of modern Hamadan.

ec·bol·ic (ek-bol'ik), *adj.* [Gr. *ekbolē*, a throwing out < *ek-*, out + *ballein*, to throw; + *-ic*], helping to bring forth the fetus in birth, or causing abortion, by contracting the uterus: said of certain drugs. *n.* an ecbolic drug.

‡**ec·ce** (ek'si, ek'e), *interj.* [L.], behold! lo! see!

‡**ec·ce ho·mo** (ek'si hō'mō, ek'e hō'mō), [L.], 1. literally, behold the man: the Vulgate version of Pilate's words when he presented Jesus to the populace before the crucifixion: John 19:5; hence, 2. a picture or statue of Jesus wearing the crown of thorns.

ec·cen·tric (ik-sen'trik, ek-sen'trik), *adj.* [ML. *eccentricus* < LL. *eccentros*, out of the center, eccentric; Gr. *ekkentros* < *ek-*, out of (see EX-) + *kentron*, center], 1. not having the same center; having different centers, as two circles: opposed to *concentric.* 2. not having the axis exactly in the center; off center: as, an *eccentric* wheel. 3. not exactly circular in shape or motion. 4. irregular; out of the ordinary; capricious; hence, 5. deviating from the norm, as in conduct; odd; whimsical; peculiar; unconventional. *n.* 1. a circle or sphere not having the same center as another partly within or around it. 2. a disk set off center on a shaft and revolving inside a strap attached to one end of a rod, thereby converting the circular motion of the shaft into back-and-forth motion of the rod. 3. an odd or unconventional person.

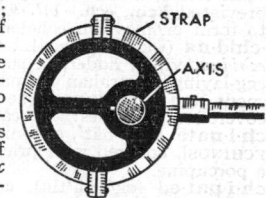

ECCENTRIC (sense 2)

ec·cen·tri·cal·ly (ik-sen'tri-k'l-i, ek-sen'trik-li), *adv.* in an eccentric manner.

ec·cen·tric·i·ty (ek'sən-tris'ə-ti, ek'sen-tris'ə-ti), *n.* [*pl.* ECCENTRICITIES (-tiz)], [see ECCENTRIC], 1. the state, quality, or amount of being off center or not concentric. 2. deviation from circular shape. 3. deviation from what is ordinary or customary, as in conduct or manner; oddity; peculiarity; whimsicality; unconventionality. 4. in *mathematics*, the ratio of the distances from any point on a curve of a conic section to the focus and to the directrix. 5. in *mechanics*, the distance between the center (as of an eccentric wheel) and the axis; throw. —***SYN.*** see **idiosyncrasy.**

ec·chy·mo·sis (ek'i-mō'sis), *n.* [Mod. L.; Gr. *ekchymōsis* < *ekchymousthai*, to pour out, extravasate < *ek-*, out of (see EX-) + *cheein*, to pour], in *medicine*, 1. an oozing of blood from a blood vessel into the tissues, as the result of a bruise. 2. a black-and-blue or yellowish mark caused by this.

eccl., eccles., ecclesiastical.

Eccles., Eccl., Ecclesiastes.

ec·cle·si·a (i-klē'zhi-ə, i-klē'zi-ə), *n.* [*pl.* ECCLESIAE (-ē')], [L.; Gr. *ekklēsia*, assembly of the people < *ekklētos*, summoned < *ekkalein*, to summon, call out; *ek-*, out + *kalein*, to call], 1. in ancient Greek states, a general assembly of citizens for political purposes. 2. the members of a church. 3. a church building.

Ec·cle·si·as·tes (i-klē'zi-as'tēz), *n.* [L.; Gr., lit., preacher (< *ekklēsia;* see ECCLESIA); name first used in the Septuagint as transl. of Heb. *qōheleth*, of uncertain meaning, but understood by the translators as "one who addresses an assembly or ecclesia"], a book of the Old Testament, ascribed to Solomon.

ec·cle·si·as·tic (i-klē'zi-as'tik), *adj.* [L. *ecclesiasticus;* Gr. *ekklēsiastikos;* see ECCLESIA], ecclesiastical. *n.* a clergyman or priest.

ec·cle·si·as·ti·cal (i-klē'zi-as'ti-k'l), *adj.* of the church, the organization of the church, or the clergy.

ec·cle·si·as·ti·cism (i-klē'zi-as'tə-siz'm), *n.* 1. ecclesiastical principles, rituals, customs, etc. 2. strong attachment to these things.

Ec·cle·si·as·ti·cus (i-klē'zi-as'ti-kəs), *n.* [L. *Ecclesiasticus*, short for *ecclesiasticus liber*, lit., the church book (see ECCLESIASTIC): so named by the Latin church fathers from its frequent use for catechetical teaching in the churches], a book of proverbs in the Apocrypha, included as canonical in the Douay Bible: abbreviated **Ecclus.**

ec·cle·si·ol·o·gy (i-klē'zi-ol'ə-ji), *n.* [< *ecclesia* + *-logy*], 1. the study or science of the building and decorating of churches. 2. a treatise about churches.

ec·cri·nol·o·gy (ek'ri-nol'ə-ji), *n.* [< Gr. *ekkrinein*, to secrete (*ek-*, out of + *krinein*, to separate); + *-logy*], the branch of physiology that deals with secretions and excretions.

ec·dy·sis (ek'di-sis), *n.* [Mod. L.; Gr. *ekdysis*, a getting out, stripping < *ekdyein*, to strip off; *ek-*, out of + *dyein*, to enter], in *zoology*, the shedding of an outer layer of skin or integument, as by snakes, insects, crustaceans, etc.

E·che·ga·ray, Jo·se (hô-se' e'che-gä-rä'ē), 1832–1916; Spanish dramatist, statesman, and mathematician; received Nobel prize in literature, 1904.

ech·e·lon (esh'ə-lon'), *n.* [Fr. *échelon*, ladder rung < *échelle;* OFr. *eschelle;* L. *scala*, ladder], 1. a steplike formation of units of troops, in which each unit is progressively to the left or right of the one preceding it. 2. any subdivision of a combat force (as an assault *echelon*), or of a headquarters (as a rear *echelon*). 3. any of various formations of ships, aircraft, etc. Abbreviated **Ech., ech.** *v.t. & v.i.* to form or move in echelon.

AIRPLANES FLYING IN ECHELON

e·chid·na (i-kid'nə), *n.* [L.; Gr. *echidna*, viper, adder], a small, egg-laying Australian mammal with a long, tapering snout and a sticky tongue: it feeds on ants and is covered with spines: also called *spiny anteater*.

ech·i·nate (ek'i-nāt', ek'i-nit), *adj.* [L. *echinatus;* see ECHINUS], covered with prickles; prickly; bristling, as a porcupine.

ech·i·nat·ed (ek'i-nā'tid), *adj.* echinate.

e·chi·no- (i-kī'nə, ek'i-nō), [< Gr. *echinos*, sea urchin], a combining form meaning *prickly, spiny*, as in *echinoderm*: also, before a vowel, **echin-.**

e·chi·no·derm (i-kī'nə-dũrm', ek'i-nə-dũrm'), *n.* [*echino-* + *-derm*], any of various small sea animals with a hard, spiny shell and radial body, including the starfishes and sea urchins.

e·chi·no·der·ma·tous (i-kī'nə-dũr'mə-təs, ek'i-nə-dũr'mə-təs), *adj.* 1. of the echinoderms. 2. like an echinoderm.

e·chi·noid (i-kī'noid, ek'i-noid'), *adj.* [*echin-* + *-oid*], of or like a sea urchin. *n.* a sea urchin; echinus.

e·chi·nus (i-kī'nəs), *n.* [*pl.* ECHINI (-nī)], [L.; Gr. *echinos*, hedgehog, sea urchin], 1. a sea urchin. 2. in *architecture*, *a)* molding under the abacus of the capital of a Doric column. *b)* any of several similar moldings.

ech·o (ek'ō), *n.* [*pl.* ECHOES (-ōz)], [L.; Gr. *ēchō*, reverberated sound, echo < *ēchē*, *ēchos*, a sound, noise], 1. the repeating of a sound, produced by reflection of sound waves from a surface. 2. a sound so produced. 3. any repeating or imitating of the words, style, ideas, etc. of another. 4. a person who repeats or imitates the words, style, ideas, etc. of another. 5. sympathetic response. 6. in *bridge & whist*, the playing of an informative card in answer to a card led by one's partner. 7. in *music*, *a)* a soft repetition of a phrase. *b)* an organ stop for producing the effect of echo. 8. [E-], in *Greek mythology*, a nymph who, because of her unreturned love for Narcissus, pined away until only her voice remained. 9. in *poetry*, the repetition of the terminal syllables of one line at or near the beginning of the next line. *v.i.* [ECHOED (-ōd), ECHOING], 1. to resound with an echo; reverberate: as, the empty room *echoed*. 2. to be repeated or given back from a surface: as, his voice *echoed* in the hall. *v.t.* 1. *a)* to repeat (another's words, ideas, etc.). *b)* to repeat the words, etc. of (another person). 2. to repeat or reflect (sound) from a surface.

e·cho·ic (e-kō'ik), *adj.* 1. having the nature of an echo; hence, 2. imitative in sound; onomatopoeic: a term in linguistics used, as in the etymologies of this dictionary, to indicate that a word is formed in approximate imitation of some sound, as *blare, tinkle*, etc.

ech·o·ism (ek'ō-iz'm), *n.* [*echo* + *-ism*], formation of words approximately imitating sounds; onomatopoeia.

Eck·hart, Jo·han·nes (yō-hä'nəs ek'härt), 1260?–1327?; German philosopher, theologian, and mystic: called *Meister Eckhart.*

é·clair (ā-klâr', i-klâr'), *n.* [Fr., lit., a flash, lightning], a small, oblong pastry shell filled with flavored custard or whipped cream and covered with frosting.

‡é·clair·cisse·ment (ā'klâr'sēs'män'), *n.* [Fr. < *éclaircir*, to clear up; OFr. *esclarcir* < L. *clarus*, clear], 1. a clearing up, as of a disputed or difficult point; clarification; explanation. 2. [E-], the Enlightenment.

ec·lamp·si·a (ek-lamp'si-ə), *n.* [Mod. L. < Late Gr. *eklampsis*, a shining forth < *ek-*, out + *lampein*, to shine], an attack of convulsions, caused by any of various toxic conditions of the body and occurring especially in the latter stages of pregnancy and in childbirth.

é·clat (ā-klä', i-klä'), *n.* [Fr., noise, clap, splendor < *éclater*, to burst (out), shine; Pr. *esclatar;* ? < LL. **exclapitare* < *ex-*, intens. + Gmc. **klap-*, clap], 1. brilliant or conspicuous success. 2. acclaim. 3. *a)* brilliance of reputation; fame; renown. *b)* notoriety.

ec·lec·tic (ik-lek'tik, ek-lek'tik), *adj.* [Gr. *eklektikos* < *eklegein*, to select, pick out; *ek-*, out + *legein*, to choose, pick], 1. choosing; selecting from various systems, doctrines, or sources; adhering to the principles of eclecticism. 2. composed of material gathered from various sources, systems, etc. *n.* a person who uses eclectic methods in philosophy, science, or art.

ec·lec·ti·cal·ly (ik-lek'ti-k'l-i, ek-lek'tik-li), *adv.* in an eclectic manner.

ec·lec·ti·cism (ik-lek'tə-siz'm, ek-lek'tə-siz'm), *n.* 1. an eclectic method or system of thought. 2. the using or upholding of such a method or system.

e·clipse (i-klips'), *n.* [ME.; OFr.; L. *eclipsis;* Gr. *ekleipsis*, an abandoning, eclipse, failing < *ekleipein*, to leave out, pass over, fail; *ek-*, out + *leipein*, to leave], 1. the partial or total apparent darkening of the sun when the moon comes between it and the earth (called *solar eclipse*), or of the moon when the earth's shadow is cast upon it (called *lunar eclipse*); hence, 2. any overshadowing or cutting off of light. 3. a temporary obscurity or dulling, as of fame, glory, etc. *v.t.* [ECLIPSED (-klipst'), ECLIPSING], [ME. *eclipsen;* see the *n.*], 1. to cause an eclipse of; darken or obscure. 2. to obscure the fame or glory of; overshadow; outshine; surpass: as, Shakespeare *eclipsed* his rivals in the drama.

ECLIPSE STAGES

e·clip·tic (i-klip'tik, ē-klip'tik), *n.* [ME. *ecliptik;* ML. *ecliptica;* L. (*linea*) *ecliptica;* Gr. *ekleiptikos*, of an eclipse < *ekleipein;* see ECLIPSE], 1. the sun's apparent annual path, or orbit, or that of the earth as seen from the sun; great circle of the celestial sphere. 2. the plane of the earth's orbit, cutting this circle and inclined at an angle of about 23 1/2 degrees to the celestial equator. 3. a great circle drawn on a terrestrial globe, at the same angle to the terrestrial equator, corresponding to the sun's ecliptic. *adj.* of eclipses or the ecliptic.

e·clip·ti·cal (i-klip'ti-k'l, ē-klip'ti-k'l), *adj.* ecliptic.

ec·lo·gite (ek'lə-jit'), *n.* [Gr. *eklogē*, choice, selection; see ECLOGUE], a metamorphic rock consisting mainly of a green pyroxene, red garnet, and other minerals.

ec·logue (ek'lôg, ek'log), *n.* [Fr. *éclogue;* L. *ecloga;* Gr. *eklogē*, selection, especially of poems < *eklegein;* see ECLECTIC], a short pastoral poem, usually in the form of a dialogue between two shepherds.

ecol., 1. ecological. 2. ecology.

‡é·cole (ā'kôl'), *n.* [Fr.], school.

ec·o·log·ic (ek'ə-loj'ik, ē'kə-loj'ik), *adj.* ecological.

ec·o·log·i·cal (ek'ə-loj'i-k'l, ē'kə-loj'i-k'l), *adj.* of or by ecology: abbreviated **ecol.**

e·col·o·gist (ē-kol'ə-jist), *n.* a student of or expert in ecology.

e·col·o·gy (ē-kol'ə-ji), *n.* [< Gr. *oikos*, house; + *-logy*],

1. the branch of biology that deals with the relations between living organisms and their environment. 2. in *sociology*, the relationship between the distribution of human groups with reference to material resources, and the consequent social and cultural patterns. Abbreviated **ecol.**

econ., 1. economic. 2. economics. 3. economy.

e·co·nom·ic (ē'kə-nom'ik, ek'ə-nom'ik), *adj.* [L. *oeconomicus*; Gr. *oikonomikos* < *oikonomia;* see ECONOMY], 1. of the management of the income, expenditures, etc. of a household, private business, community, or government. 2. of the production, distribution, and consumption of wealth. 3. of economics. 4. of the satisfaction of the material needs of people: as, *economic* biology. Abbreviated **econ.**

e·co·nom·i·cal (ē'kə-nom'i-k'l, ek'ə-nom'i-k'l), *adj.* 1. not wasting money, time, fuel, etc.; thrifty: as, an *economical* person, an *economical* stove. 2. of economics; economic. —*SYN.* see **thrifty.**

e·co·nom·i·cal·ly (ē'kə-nom'i-k'l-i, ek'ə-nom'ik-li), *adv.* 1. in an economical manner. 2. from the viewpoint of economics.

economic geography, the branch of geography that deals with the relation of economic conditions to physical geography and natural resources.

e·co·nom·ics (ē'kə-nom'iks, ek'ə-nom'iks), *n.pl.* [construed as sing.], the science that deals with the production, distribution, and consumption of wealth, and with the various related problems of labor, finance, taxation, etc.; political economy: abbreviated **econ.**

e·con·o·mist (i-kon'ə-mist, ē-kon'ə-mist), *n.* 1. an economical person. 2. a specialist in economics.

e·con·o·mize (i-kon'ə-mīz', ē-kon'ə-mīz'), *v.i.* [ECONOMIZED (-mīzd'), ECONOMIZING], to avoid waste or needless expenditure; be thrifty; reduce expenses. *v.t.* to manage or use with thrift.

e·con·o·miz·er (i-kon'ə-mīz'ēr, ē-kon'ə-mīz'ēr), *n.* 1. a person who economizes. 2. any mechanical apparatus that helps save fuel, heat, etc.

e·con·o·my (i-kon'ə-mi, ē-kon'ə-mi), *n.* [*pl.* ECONOMIES (-miz)], [L. *oeconomia;* Gr. *oikonomia,* management of a household or state, public revenue < *oikonomos,* manager, administrator < *oikos,* house (< IE. **woiko-s;* hence akin to L. *vicus,* group of houses, village, whence AS. *wic,* house, village) + *nomos,* managing < *nemein,* to distribute, manage (akin to AS. *niman,* to take)], 1. the management of the income, expenditures, etc. of a household, private business, community, or government. 2. careful management of wealth, resources, etc.; avoidance of waste by careful planning and use; thrift or thrifty use. 3. an instance of this. 4. a tendency to economize. 5. an orderly management or arrangement of parts; organization or system: as, the *economy* of the human body. 6. a system of producing, distributing, and consuming wealth. Abbreviated **econ.**

‡é·cra·seur (ā'krā'zẽr'), *n.* [Fr. < *écraser,* to crush], a surgical instrument consisting of a looped wire or cord, which is gradually tightened about a part so as to cut it off.

ec·ru (ek'rōō, ā'krōō, ā-krōō'), *adj. & n.* [Fr. *écru,* unbleached, raw; OFr. *escru* < L. *ex,* out + *crudus,* raw: in reference to the color of unbleached linen], light tan; beige.

ec·sta·sy (ek'stə-si), *n.* [*pl.* ECSTASIES (-siz)], [ME. & OFr. *extasie;* LL. *ecstasis;* Gr. *ekstasis,* a being put out of its place, distraction, astonishment, trance < *ek-,* out + *histanai,* to place], 1. a state of being overpowered with emotion, especially joy; being beside oneself with feeling: as, an *ecstasy* of delight. 2. a feeling of overpowering joy; great delight; rapture: as, he listened to the music with *ecstasy.* 3. a trance, especially one resulting from great religious fervor.

SYN.—**ecstasy** implies extreme emotional exaltation, now usually intense delight, that overpowers the senses and lifts one into a trancelike state; **bliss** implies a state of great happiness and contentment, often literally or figuratively suggesting heavenly joy; **rapture** now generally suggests the mental exaltation experienced when one's entire attention is captured by something that evokes great joy or pleasure; **transport** implies a being carried away by any powerful emotion.

ec·stat·ic (ik-stat'ik, ek-stat'ik), *adj.* [Gr. *ekstatikos*], 1. of, having the nature of, or characterized by ecstasy. 2. causing, or caused by, ecstasy. 3. subject to ecstasy. *n.* a person subject to fits of ecstasy.

ec·stat·i·cal·ly (ik-stat'i-k'l-i, ek-stat'ik-li), *adv.* in an ecstatic manner.

ec·to- (ek'tō, ek'tə), [< Gr. *ektos,* outside], a combining form meaning *outside, external,* used mainly in forming biological terms, as *ectoderm, ectoplasm*: also, before a vowel, **ect-.**

ec·to·blast (ek'tə-blast'), *n.* [*ecto-* + *blast*], the outer layer of an embryo in the earliest (gastrula) stage; epiblast.

ec·to·blas·tic (ek'tə-blas'tik), *adj.* of the ectoblast.

ec·to·derm (ek'tə-dũrm'), *n.* [*ecto-* + *-derm*], 1. the outer layer of cells of an animal embryo in its early stage, from which the nervous system, skin, teeth, etc. are developed. 2. the outer layer of cells of certain organisms, as the coelenterates.

ec·to·der·mal (ek'tə-dũr'm'l), *adj.* of the ectoderm.

ec·to·der·mic (ek'tə-dũr'mik), *adj.* ectodermal.

ec·to·en·zyme (ek'tō-en'zīm, ek'tō-en'zim), *n.* an enzyme secreted by a cell and acting outside it; exoenzyme.

ec·to·gen·ic (ek'tə-jen'ik), *adj.* [*ecto-* + *-genic*], that can develop outside the host: said of certain parasitic bacteria.

ec·tog·e·nous (ik-toj'ə-nəs, ek-toj'ə-nəs), *adj.* ectogenic.

ec·to·mere (ek'tə-mêr'), *n.* [*ecto-* + *-mere*], any of the early cells that form the ectoderm of an embryo.

ec·to·mer·ic (ek'tə-mer'ik), *adj.* of an ectomere.

ec·to·mor·phic (ek'tə-môr'fik), *adj.* [*ecto-* + *-morphic*], designating or of the slender physical type, characterized by predominance of the structures developed from the ectodermal layer of the embryo (i.e., skin, nerves, brain, and sense organs); asthenic: distinguished from *endomorphic.*

-ec·to·my (ek'tə-mi), [< Gr. *ektomē,* a cutting out < *ek-,* out + *temnein,* to cut], a combining form meaning *a surgical excision of,* as in *appendectomy, tonsillectomy.*

ec·to·par·a·site (ek'tō-par'ə-sīt'), *n.* any parasite that lives on the outer surface of an animal: opposed to *endoparasite.*

ec·to·plasm (ek'tə-plaz'm), *n.* [*ecto-* + *-plasm*], 1. in *biology,* the outer layer of the cytoplasm of a cell: distinguished from *endoplasm.* 2. in *spiritualism,* the vaporous, luminous substance supposed to emanate from the medium's body during a trance.

ec·to·plas·mic (ek'tə-plaz'mik), *adj.* of ectoplasm.

ec·to·sarc (ek'tə-särk'), *n.* [< *ecto-* + Gr. *sarx, sarkos,* flesh], the outer layer of certain one-celled animals.

ec·tos·to·sis (ek'tos-tō'sis), *n.* [Mod. L.; *ect-* + *ostosis*], formation of bone under the membranous covering of cartilage, or replacing it.

ec·ty·pal (ek'ti-p'l), *adj.* of, or having the nature of, an ectype.

ec·type (ek'tīp'), *n.* [L. *ectypus*; Gr. *ektypos,* engraved in relief, formed in outline; *ek-,* out + *typos,* a figure, outline], a copy; reproduction of an original: opposed to *archetype, prototype.*

‡é·cu (ā'kü'), *n.* [*pl.* ÉCUS (-kü')], [Fr.; OFr. *escu;* L. *scutum,* a shield], any of various French silver or gold coins, especially a silver crown of the 17th and 18th centuries.

Ec·ua·dor (ek'wə-dôr'), *n.* a country on the northwestern coast of South America: area, 275,000 sq. mi.; pop., 4,298,000; capital, Quito.

Ec·ua·do·ran (ek'wə-dôr'ən, ek'wə-dō'rən), *adj. & n.* Ecuadorian.

Ec·ua·do·ri·an, Ec·ua·do·re·an (ek'wə-dôr'i-ən, ek'wə-dō'ri-ən), *adj.* of Ecuador, its people, or their culture. *n.* a native or inhabitant of Ecuador.

ec·u·men·ic (ek'yoo-men'ik), *adj.* ecumenical.

ec·u·men·i·cal (ek'yoo-men'i-k'l), *adj.* [LL. *oecumenicus;* Gr. *oikoumenikos,* of or from the whole world < *oikoumenē* (*gē*) the inhabited (world) < *oikein,* to dwell, inhabit < *oikos,* a house], general; universal; especially, of the Christian Church as a whole: also spelled **oecumenical.**

ec·ze·ma (ek'sə-mə, eg'zi-mə; *now sometimes* eg-zē'mə), *n.* [Mod. L.; Gr. *ekzema* < *ek-,* out of + *zeein,* to boil (see YEAST)], a disease of the skin characterized by inflammation, itching, and the formation of scales.

ec·zem·a·tous (eg-zem'ə-təs), *adj.* 1. having the nature of eczema. 2. having or resulting from eczema.

-ed (*as a separate syllable,* id, əd; *after a voiced consonant in the same syllable,* d; *after a voiceless consonant in the same syllable,* t), 1. [as ending of past tense < AS. *-ede, -ode, -ade, -de;* as ending of past participles and analogous forms < AS. *-ed, -od, -ad*], a suffix used: *a*) to form the past tense and past participle of weak verbs, as in *walked, wanted:* also, formerly and now poetically, **-t,** as in *dreamt.* *b*) to form adjectives from nouns or verbs, as in *cultured, versed,* or from other adjectives ending in *-ate,* as in *echinated.* 2. [< AS. *-ede*], a suffix added to nouns, meaning: *having, provided with, characterized by,* as in *bearded, sugared, small-mouthed.*

ed., [*pl.,* for 2 & 3, EDS.], 1. edited. 2. edition. 3. editor.

E.D., 1. Eastern Department. 2. ex dividend.

e·da·cious (i-dā'shəs), *adj.* [< L. *edax, edacis* < *edere,* to eat; + *-ious*], voracious; consuming; devouring.

e·dac·i·ty (i-das'ə-ti), *n.* [L. *edacitas*], the state of being edacious; huge capacity for eating: now humorous.

E·dam (ē'dəm, ē'dam), *n.* 1. (*also D.* ā-däm'), a town in the western Netherlands: pop., 3,700. 2. Edam cheese.

Edam cheese, [< *Edam,* Holland, where orig. made], a mild yellow cheese, made in a round mold and generally colored red on the outside.

Ed.B., Bachelor of Education.

Ed.D., Doctor of Education.

Ed·da (ed′ə), *n.* [ON. *Edda;* prob. akin to ON. *óthr,* poetry, AS. *wod* (G. *wut*), rage, madness; IE. base **wat-,* to be mentally excited, as also in L. *vates,* soothsayer, poet & ON. *Odinn,* AS. *Woden* (cf. ODIN, WEDNESDAY)], either of two early Icelandic literary works: *a*) the *Prose,* or *Younger, Edda* (c. 1230), a summary of Norse mythology with two treatises on the writing of poetry, attributed to Snorri Sturluson. *b*) the *Poetic,* or *Elder, Edda* (c. 1200), a collection of old Norse poetry.

Ed·da·ic (i-dā′ik, e-dā′ik), *adj.* Eddic.

Ed·dic (ed′ik), *adj.* of or like the Eddas.

Ed·ding·ton, Sir **Arthur Stanley** (ed′iŋ-tən), 1882–1944; English astronomer and physicist.

ed·do (ed′ō), *n.* [*pl.* EDDOES (-ōz)], [prob. < native name in W. Africa], 1. the edible root of the taro. 2. the root of any of several other related tropical plants.

ed·dy (ed′i), *n.* [*pl.* EDDIES (-iz)], [ME. *ydy;* prob. < ON. *itha,* an eddy, whirlpool], a current of air, water, etc. moving against the main current and with a circular motion; little whirlpool or whirlwind. *v.i.* [EDDIED (-id), EDDYING], to move with a circular motion against the main current; whirl; move in an eddy.

Ed·dy, Mary Baker (ed′i), 1821–1910; American religious leader; founder of Christian Science.

Ed·dy·stone Light (ed′i-stən), a lighthouse on the Eddystone Rocks off the coast of Cornwall, England.

e·del·weiss (ā′d'l-vīs′), *n.* [G.; *edel,* noble, precious + *weiss,* white], a small plant native to the Swiss Alps, having white, woolly leaves arranged in star-shaped clusters with small, yellow flower heads at their center.

e·de·ma (i-dē′mə), *n.* [*pl.* EDEMATA (-mə-tə)], [Gr. *oidēma,* a swelling, tumor < *oidein,* to swell], an abnormal accumulation of fluid in cells, tissues, or cavities of the body, resulting in swelling; dropsy: also spelled **oedema.**

e·dem·a·tose (i-dē′mə-tōs′), *adj.* edematous.

e·dem·a·tous (i-dē′mə-təs), *adj.* of, or having the nature of, an edema.

E·den (ē′d'n), *n.* [LL.; Heb. *'edēn,* Eden, lit., delight], 1. in the *Bible,* the garden where Adam and Eve first lived; Paradise; hence, 2. any delightful place or state; a paradise.

E·den, Sir **Anthony** (ē′d'n), (*Robert Anthony Eden*), 1897– ; British prime minister (1955–1957).

e·den·tate (ē-den′tāt, i-den′tāt), *adj.* [L. *edentatus,* pp. of *edentare,* to render toothless < *e-,* out + *dens, dentis,* tooth], in *biology,* 1. without teeth. 2. of the edentates. *n.* any of a group of mammals having only molars, or no teeth at all, as the sloths, armadillos and anteaters.

EDES, [< Mod. Gr. *E*thnikos *D*imokratikos *E*llenikos *S*yndesmos, National Democratic Hellenic Union], the National Democratic Hellenic Union, a Greek resistance movement in World War II formed by a coalition of conservative parties and other groups.

E·des·sa (i-des′ə), *n.* an ancient city in Mesopotamia, on the site of modern Urfa, Turkey.

Ed·gar (ed′gẽr), [AS. *Eadgar* < *ead,* riches, prosperity, happiness (< Gmc. **autha-;* hence akin to Goth. *audags,* fortunate, OHG. *ot,* wealth) + *gar,* a spear (see GORE)], a masculine name: diminutives, *Ed, Ned.*

edge (ej), *n.* [ME. *egge, ege;* AS. *ecg;* akin to G. *ecke,* corner; IE. base **ak-,* sharp, pointed, as also in L. *acer,* sharp (cf. ACRID)], 1. the thin, sharp, cutting part of a blade. 2. the quality of being sharp or keen. 3. the projecting ledge or brink, as of a cliff. 4. the part farthest from the middle; line where something begins or ends; border, or part nearest the border; margin. 5. [Colloq.], advantage: as, you have the *edge* on me. *v.t.* [EDGED (ejd), EDGING], 1. to form or put an edge on; provide an edge for. 2. to make (one's way) sideways, as through a crowd. 3. to move gradually or cautiously. *v.i.* 1. to move sideways. 2. to move gradually or cautiously: as, she *edged* away from the fierce-looking dog. —*SYN.* see **border.**

on edge, 1. so tense or nervous as to be easily upset; irritable. 2. eager; impatient.

set one's teeth on edge, 1. to give one a sensation of tingling discomfort, as the sound of a fingernail scraped on a slate; hence, 2. to irritate; provoke.

take the edge off, to dull the intensity, force, or pleasure of.

edge·bone (ej′bōn′), *n.* an aitchbone.

edge tool, a chisel or similar tool that has a cutting edge.

edge·ways (ej′wāz′), *adv.* with the edge foremost; on, by, with, or toward the edge.

get a word in edgeways, to manage to say something oneself in a conversation being monopolized by another or others.

edge·wise (ej′wīz′), *adv.* edgeways.

Edge·worth, Maria (ej′wẽrth), 1767–1849; Irish novelist.

edg·ing (ej′iŋ), *n.* something forming an edge or placed along the edge; fringe, trimming, etc. for a border.

edg·y (ej′i), *adj.* 1. having an edge or edges; sharp. 2. irritable; on edge. 3. having outlines that are too sharp: said of drawings, paintings, etc.

edh (eth), *n.* a letter of the Anglo-Saxon alphabet (ð, Ð), replaced in the 13th century by *th:* it was generally pronounced as a voiced fricative (*th*) whose unvoiced equivalent was the thorn (þ): also called *eth.*

ed·i·bil·i·ty (ed′ə-bil′ə-ti), *n.* the quality of being edible.

ed·i·ble (ed′ə-b'l), *adj.* [LL. *edibilis* < *edere,* to eat], fit to be eaten; eatable. *n. usually pl.* anything fit to be eaten; food.

e·dict (ē′dikt), *n.* [L. *edictum;* neut. pp. of *edicere,* to proclaim; *e-,* out + *dicere,* to speak], an official public proclamation or order issued by authority; decree.

e·dic·tal (i-dik′t'l), *adj.* of, or in the form of, an edict.

ed·i·fi·ca·tion (ed′ə-fi-kā′shən), *n.* [ME.; L. *aedificatio*], an edifying or being edified; instruction; especially, moral or spiritual instruction or improvement.

ed·i·fi·ca·to·ry (ed′ə-fi-kā′tẽr-i, i-dif′ə-kə-tôr′i, i-dif′ə-kə-tō′ri), *adj.* edifying or intended to edify.

ed·i·fice (ed′ə-fis), *n.* [Fr. *édifice;* L. *aedificium,* a building < *aedificare,* to build < *aedes, aedis,* a building, temple + *-ficare* < *facere,* to make], a building, especially a large one of imposing appearance: often used figuratively. —*SYN.* see **building.**

ed·i·fi·er (ed′ə-fī′ẽr), *n.* a person who edifies.

ed·i·fy (ed′ə-fī′), *v.t.* [EDIFIED (-fīd′), EDIFYING], [ME. *edifien;* OFr. *edifier;* L. *aedificare,* to build, construct, edify < *aedes,* a dwelling, house, temple, orig., hearth, fireplace (akin to Gr. *aithein,* to burn, AS. *ad,* pyre < IE. base **ai-dh-,* to burn) + *-ficare,* to make; see -FY], 1. to instruct; especially, to instruct or improve morally or spiritually. 2. [Archaic], to build; establish.

e·dile (ē′dīl), *n.* [see AEDILE], in ancient Rome, an official in charge of buildings, roads, sanitation, public games, etc.: also spelled **aedile.**

Ed·in·burgh (ed′'n-bũr′ō, ed′'n-bũr′ə), *n.* 1. the capital of Scotland, near the Firth of Forth: pop., 471,000 (est. 1946): abbreviated **Edin.** 2. Midlothian, a county of Scotland: the former name.

E·dir·ne (e-dẽr′ne), *n.* Adrianople: the Turkish name.

Ed·i·son, Thomas Alva (ed′i-s'n), 1847–1931; American inventor of the incandescent lamp, phonograph, etc.: called the *Wizard of Menlo Park.*

ed·it (ed′it), *v.t.* [< L. *editus,* pp. of *edere,* to give out, put forth, publish < *e-,* out + *dare,* to give], 1. to prepare (an author's works, journals, letters, etc.) for publication, by selection, arrangement, and annotation. 2. to revise and make ready (a manuscript) for publication. 3. to govern the policy of (a newspaper or periodical); decide what is to be printed, etc.

edit., 1. edited. 2. edition. 3. editor.

E·dith (ē′dith), [AS. *Eadgyth* < *ead* (see EDGAR) + **gyth* < *guth,* combat, battle, war], a feminine name.

e·di·tion (i-dish′ən), *n.* [Fr. *édition;* L. *editio,* a bringing forth, publishing < *edere;* see EDIT], 1. the size, style, or form in which a book is published: as, a pocket *edition.* 2. *a*) the total number of copies of a book, newspaper, etc. printed from the same plates, type, etc. and published at about the same time. *b*) a single copy of such a printing. 3. the issue of a well-known work distinguished by its editor or publisher: as, the Skeat *edition* of Chaucer. Abbreviated **ed., edit.**

‡**e·di·ti·o prin·ceps** (i-dish′i-ō prin′seps), [L.], first edition.

ed·i·tor (ed′i-tẽr), *n.* [L.], 1. a person who edits. 2. a writer of editorials. 3. a device for examining, cutting, and splicing motion-picture film. Abbreviated **ed., edit.**

ed·i·to·ri·al (ed′ə-tôr′i-əl, ed′ə-tō′ri-əl), *adj.* 1. of an editor or editing; written by an editor. 2. characteristic of an editor or editorial; expressing opinion in the manner of an editor: as, *editorial* comment has no place in news stories. *n.* an article in a newspaper, etc. explicitly stating opinions of the editor or publisher.

ed·i·to·ri·al·ize (ed′ə-tôr′i-əl-īz′, ed′ə-tō′ri-əl-īz′), *v.t.* & *v.i.* [EDITORIALIZED (-īzd′), EDITORIALIZING], 1. to express editorial opinions about (something). 2. to put editorial opinions into (a newspaper article, etc.).

ed·i·to·ri·al·ly (ed′ə-tôr′i-əl-i, ed′ə-tō′ri-əl-i), *adv.* 1. in an editorial manner; as an editor. 2. in or by an editorial or editorials.

editor in chief, [*pl.* EDITORS IN CHIEF], the editor who heads or supervises the editorial staff of a publication.

ed·i·tor·ship (ed′i-tẽr-ship′), *n.* [*editor* + *-ship*], the position, functions, guidance, or authority of an editor.

Ed.M., Master of Education.

Ed·mond, Ed·mund (ed′mənd), [AS. *Eadmund* < *ead* (see EDGAR) + *mund,* hand, protection; akin to L. *manus* (see MANUAL); hence, wealthy protector], a masculine name: diminutives, *Ed, Ned.*

Ed·mon·ton (ed′mən-tən), *n.* 1. the capital of Alberta, Canada: pop., 160,000. 2. a city in Middlesex, England, north of London: pop., 103,000.

Ed·na (ed′nə), [Gr. *Edna* < Heb. *'ēdnāh,* rejuvenation], a feminine name.

Ed·o (ed′ō), *n.* Tokyo: a former name.

E·dom (ē′dəm), *n.* 1. in the *Bible,* Esau, Jacob's brother. 2. an ancient kingdom south of the Dead Sea: Greek name, *Idumea.*

E·dom·ite (ē′dəm-īt′), *n.* in the *Bible,* a descendant of Edom, or Esau; inhabitant of Edom: Gen. 36.

E·dom·it·ish (ē′dəm-ī′tish), *adj.* 1. of Edom. 2. characteristic of the Edomites.

educ., 1. education. 2. educational. 3. educator.

ed·u·ca·ble (ej′oo-kə-b'l), ***adj.*** that can be educated.

ed·u·cate (ej′oo-kāt′), ***v.t.*** [EDUCATED (-id), EDUCATING], [<L. *educatus*, pp. of *educare*, to bring up, rear, or train < *educere; e-*, out + *ducere*, to lead, draw, bring], 1. to give knowledge or training to; train or develop the knowledge, skill, mind, or character of, especially by formal schooling or study; teach; instruct. 2. to form and develop (one's taste, etc.). 3. to pay for the schooling of (a person). —***SYN.*** see **teach.**

ed·u·ca·tion (ej′oo-kā′shən), ***n.*** [L. *educatio;* see EDUCATE], 1. the process of training and developing the knowledge, skill, mind, character, etc., especially by formal schooling; teaching; training. 2. knowledge, ability, etc. thus developed. 3. *a)* formal schooling. *b)* a kind or stage of this: as, a medical *education*, a high-school *education*. 4. systematic study of the problems, methods, and theories of teaching and learning. Abbreviated **educ.**

ed·u·ca·tion·al (ej′oo-kā′shən-'l), ***adj.*** 1. relating to education. 2. educating; giving instruction or information: as, an *educational* film. Abbreviated **educ.**

ed·u·ca·tion·al·ly (ej′oo-kā′shən-'l-i), ***adv.*** 1. by means of education. 2. from the viewpoint of education.

ed·u·ca·tion·ist (ej′oo-kā′shən-ist), ***n.*** an educator; especially, an authority on educational theory: often a disparaging term with varying connotations of inflexibility, antitraditionalism, intellectual limitations, etc.

ed·u·ca·tive (ej′oo-kā′tiv), ***adj.*** educating or tending to educate; instructive.

ed·u·ca·tor (ej′oo-kā′tẽr), ***n.*** [L.], 1. a person whose work is to educate others; teacher. 2. a specialist in the science of education; authority on educational problems, theories, and methods. Abbreviated **educ.**

e·duce (i-dōōs′, ē-dūs′), ***v.t.*** [EDUCED (-dōōst′, -dūst′), EDUCING], [L. *educere; e-*, out + *ducere*, to lead, draw], 1. to draw out; elicit; evolve. 2. to deduce; infer from data. —***SYN.*** see **extract.**

e·duc·i·ble (i-dōō′sə-b'l, ē-dū′sə-b'l), ***adj.*** that can be educed.

e·duct (ē′dukt), ***n.*** [L. *eductum*, neut. pp. of *educere*], 1. something educed. 2. a substance separated unchanged from another substance: distinguished from *product*.

e·duc·tion (i-duk′shən, ē-duk′shən), ***n.*** [L. *eductio* < pp. of *educere*], 1. an educing. 2. something educed.

e·duc·tive (i-duk′tiv, ē-duk′tiv), ***adj.*** educing or tending to educe.

e·dul·co·rate (i-dul′kə-rāt′), ***v.t.*** [EDULCORATED (-id), EDULCORATING], [<LL. *edulcoratus*, pp. of *edulcorare*, to sweeten; L. *e-*, out + *dulcorare*, to sweeten < *dulcor*, sweetness < *dulcis*, sweet], 1. to purify or soften. 2. in *chemistry*, to free from acids or other soluble impurities by washing.

Ed·ward (ed′wẽrd), [AS. *Eadward, Eadweard* < *ead* (see EDGAR) + *weard*, guardian, protector (see WARD, *n.*); hence, wealthy (or fortunate) guardian], a masculine name: diminutives, *Ed, Ned*: equivalents, Fr. *Édouard*, G. *Eduard*, It. & Sp. *Eduardo*, Scand. *Edvard*. ***n.*** Prince of Wales; 1330–1376; son of Edward III: called the *Black Prince*.

Edward I, 1239–1307; king of England (1272–1307).

Edward II, 1284–1327; son of Edward I; king of England (1307–1327); defeated at battle of Bannockburn by Robert Bruce.

Edward III, 1312–1377; son of Edward II; king of England (1327–1377).

Edward IV, 1442–1483; king of England (1461–1470; 1471–1483).

Edward V, 1470–1483; son of Edward IV; king of England (1483); murdered by order of his uncle, Richard III.

Edward VI, 1537–1553; son of Henry VIII and Jane Seymour; king of England (1547–1553).

Edward VII, (*Albert Edward*), 1841–1910; son of Queen Victoria; king of England (1901–1910).

Edward VIII, see **Windsor,** Duke of.

Edward, Lake, a lake on the boundary of Congo (sense 2) and Uganda: area, 840 sq. mi.

Ed·ward·i·an (ed-wôr′di-ən), ***adj.*** designating or of the reigns of any of the English kings named Edward; specifically, *a)* designating, or in the style of, the architecture of the period of the first three Edwards. *b)* of or characteristic of the time of Edward VII, with reference to the literature and art produced then.

Ed·wards, Jonathan (ed′wẽrdz), 1703–1758; American theologian and preacher.

Edward the Confessor, 1002?–1066; king of England (1042–1066).

Ed·win (ed′win), [AS. *Eadwine* < *ead* (see EDGAR) + *wine*, friend < Gmc. *weniz < IE. base meaning "to become accustomed to, like, desire" (hence akin to Eng. *wish, winsome*); lit., wealthy (or fortunate) friend], a masculine name: diminutive, *Ed;* feminine, *Edwina*.

Ed·win·a (ed-wē′nə, ed-win′ə, ed′win-ə), [fem. of *Edwin*], a feminine name.

-ee (ē), [< Anglo-Fr. *-é*, masc. ending of pp. of verbs in *-er* < L. *-atus;* see -ATE], a noun-forming suffix, designating: 1. *the recipient of a specified action, grant, or benefit*, as in *appointee, selectee, mortgagee*. 2. *a person in a specified condition*, as in *absentee, refugee, employee*. 3. *a person or thing associated in some way with another*, as in *bargee, goatee*.

-ee (ē), a suffix forming substandard singulars from nouns ending in *-ese*, as in *Chinee, Portugee*.

E.E., 1. Early English. 2. Electrical Engineering.

E.E.C., European Economic Community: see **Common Market.**

eel (ēl), ***n.*** [*pl.* EELS (ēlz), EEL; see PLURAL, II, D, 1], [ME. *ele;* AS. *æl;* akin to G. *aal;* prob. < IE. base **ēlo-*, snakelike fish; ? connected with IE. **angwi-*, snake (cf. L. *anguis*, snake) through the development seen in L. *anguilla*, eel], 1. any of a group of fishes with long, slippery, snakelike bodies and no pelvic fins. 2. any of various similar snakelike fishes, including the electric eel and lamprey.

EEL (2 ft. long)

eel·grass (ēl′gras′, ēl′gräs′), ***n.*** a plant with long, narrow leaves, that grows under water in shallow inlets of the sea, especially of the North Atlantic.

eel·pout (ēl′pout′), ***n.*** [*pl.* EELPOUT, EELPOUTS (-pouts′); see PLURAL, II, D, 2], [AS. *ælepute;* see EEL & POUT (fish)], 1. any of a group of salt-water fishes resembling the blenny. 2. the burbot, a fresh-water fish of the cod family.

eel·y (ēl′i), ***adj.*** like an eel; slippery.

e'en (ēn), ***adv.*** [Poetic], even. ***n.*** [Poetic or Dial.], even (evening).

e'er (âr), ***adv.*** [Poetic], ever.

-eer (êr), [Fr. *-ier;* L. *-arius*], a suffix used to form: 1. nouns meaning *a) a person or thing that has to do with*, as *auctioneer, engineer, muffineer*. *b) a person who writes, makes*, etc., as *pamphleteer, sonneteer, profiteer*: sometimes derogatory. 2. verbs meaning *to have to do with*, as *electioneer*.

ee·rie (êr′i, ē′ri), ***adj.*** [EERIER (-i-ẽr, -ri-ẽr), EERIEST (-i-ist, -ri-ist)], [northern Eng. dial. & Scot.; ME. *eri*, timid; var. of *erg*, cowardly, timid (AS. *earg*, akin to G. *arg*, bad, wicked) or < *erg* + *-y*], 1. originally, timid or frightened; uneasy because of superstitious fear. 2. inspiring fear; weird; uncanny. Also spelled **eery.** —***SYN.*** see **weird.**

ee·ri·ly (êr′ə-li, ē′rə-li), ***adv.*** in an eerie manner.

ee·ri·ness (êr′i-nis, ē′ri-nis), ***n.*** an eerie quality.

ee·ry (êr′i, ē′ri), ***adj.*** [EERIER (-i-ẽr, -ri-ẽr), EERIEST (-i-ist, -ri-ist)], eerie.

ef- (ef, if, əf), ex-: used before *f*, as in *efferent*.

ef·face (i-fās′, e-fās′), ***v.t.*** [EFFACED (-fāst′), EFFACING], [Fr. *effacer* < L. *ex*, out + *facies*, form, appearance, look], 1. to rub out, as from a surface; erase; blot out; wipe out; obliterate; blur: as, it seemed that the very memory of her was *effaced* from his mind. 2. to cause (oneself) to remain inconspicuous; withdraw (oneself) from notice. —***SYN.*** see **erase.**

ef·face·ment (i-fās′mənt, e-fās′mənt), ***n.*** an effacing or being effaced.

ef·fect (ə-fekt′, i-fekt′), ***n.*** [ME.; L. *effectus*, pp. of *efficere*, to bring to pass, accomplish < *ex-*, out + *facere*, to do], 1. anything brought about by a cause or agent; result. 2. the power or ability to bring about results; efficacy. 3. influence or action on something: as, the drug had a cathartic *effect*. 4. purport; meaning; tenor: as, he spoke to this *effect*. 5. the combination of color or form in a picture, landscape, etc.: as, cubist *effects* differ from those of the impressionists. 6. the impression produced on the mind of the observer or hearer, as by artistic design or manner of speaking, acting, etc.: as, she did that just for *effect*. 7. the condition or fact of being operative or in force; fulfillment (with *in, into*, or *to*). 8. *pl.* belongings; property: as, household *effects*. ***v.t.*** 1. to bring about; cause to happen; accomplish; produce as a result. 2. to make; produce; construct.

give effect to, to put into practice; make operative.

in effect, 1. in result; actually; in fact. 2. in essence; virtually. 3. in practice; in operation; in force.

of no effect, producing no results; in vain.

take effect, to begin to act or produce results.

to the effect, with the purport or meaning.

SYN.**—effect** is applied to that which is directly produced by an action, process, or agent and is the exact correlative of *cause;* **consequence** suggests that which follows something else on which it is dependent in some way, but does not connote as direct a connection with *cause;* **result** stresses that which is finally brought about by the effects or consequences of an action, process, etc.; **issue**, in this connection, suggests a result in which there is emergence from difficulties or conflict; **outcome** refers to the result of something that was in doubt. See also **perform**.—*ANT.* cause.

ef·fec·tive (ə-fek′tiv, i-fek′tiv), *adj.* [Fr. *effectif;* L. *effectivus*], 1. having an effect; producing a result. 2. producing a definite or desired result; efficient. 3. operative; active; in effect. 4. making a striking impression; impressive. 5. equipped and ready for combat, as a sailor or ship. *n. usually in pl.* a member or unit of the armed forces equipped and ready for combat.

SYN.—**effective** is applied to that which produces a definite effect or result (an *effective* speaker); **efficacious** refers to that which is capable of producing the desired effect or result (an *efficacious* remedy); **effectual** specifically implies the production of the desired effect or result in a decisive manner (an *effectual* reply to his charge); **efficient** implies skill and economy of energy in producing the desired result and is often applied to persons (an *efficient* worker).—*ANT.* futile.

ef·fec·tor (ə-fek′tẽr, i-fek′tẽr), *n.* [L., a producer < *effectus;* see EFFECT], 1. a muscle, gland, etc. capable of responding to a stimulus, especially to a nerve impulse. 2. that part of a nerve which transmits an impulse to an organ of response.

ef·fec·tu·al (ə-fek′choo-əl, i-fek′choo-əl), *adj.* [ME.; OFr. *effectuel;* LL. *effectualis*], 1. producing, or capable of producing, the desired effect: as, penicillin is *effectual* in treating some types of pneumonia. 2. having legal force; valid. —*SYN.* see **effective**.

ef·fec·tu·al·ly (ə-fek′choo-əl-i, i-fek′chool-i), *adv.* with the desired effect; completely; effectively.

ef·fec·tu·ate (ə-fek′choo-āt′, i-fek′choo-āt′), *v.t.* [EFFECTUATED (-id), EFFECTUATING], [< Fr. *effectuer* (< L. *effectus;* see EFFECT), with ending after verbs in *-ate* (e.g., actu*ate*)], to bring about; cause to happen; effect; accomplish.

ef·fec·tu·a·tion (ə-fek′choo-ā′shən, i-fek′choo-ā′shən), *n.* an effectuating; accomplishment.

ef·fem·i·na·cy (ə-fem′ə-nə-si, i-fem′ə-nə-si), *n.* [*pl.* EFFEMINACIES (-siz)], 1. the quality or state of being effeminate. 2. an instance of this.

ef·fem·i·nate (ə-fem′ə-nit, i-fem′ə-nit), *adj.* [L. *effeminatus*, pp. of *effeminare*, to make womanish < *ex-*, out + *femina*, a woman], 1. having the qualities generally attributed to women, as weakness, gentleness, delicacy, etc.; unmanly. 2. characterized by such qualities; weak; soft, decadent, etc.: as, *effeminate* art. *v.t. & v.i.* (ə-fem′ə-nāt′, i-fem′ə-nāt′), [EFFEMINATED (-id), EFFEMINATING], to make or become effeminate. —*SYN.* see **female**.

ef·fen·di (i-fen′di), *n.* [*pl.* EFFENDIS (-diz)], [Turk. *efendi* < Mod. Gr. *aphentēs;* Gr. *authentēs*, a master, ruler], Sir; Master: a Turkish title of respect.

ef·fer·ent (ef′ẽr-ənt), *adj.* [L. *efferens, efferentis*, ppr. of *efferre*, to carry out < *ex-*, out + *ferre*, to bear], carrying or carried away: said especially of a duct or blood vessel that carries a secretion or blood away from a part, or a nerve that carries impulses away from a nerve center: opposed to *afferent*. *n.* 1. a stream that carries off water from a pond. 2. an efferent nerve, duct, etc.

ef·fer·vesce (ef′ẽr-ves′), *v.i.* [EFFERVESCED (-vest′), EFFERVESCING], [L. *effervescere*, to boil up, foam up < *ex-*, out + *fervescere*, to begin to boil < *fervere*, to be hot, boil], 1. to give off gas bubbles, as carbonated beverages; bubble; foam. 2. to come out in bubbles; rise in bubbles in a liquid. 3. to be lively and high-spirited; be vivacious.

ef·fer·ves·cence (ef′ẽr-ves′′ns), *n.* [< L. *effervescens*, ppr.; see EFFERVESCE], 1. a bubbling up; foaming. 2. liveliness; high spirits; vivacity; exuberance.

ef·fer·ves·cen·cy (ef′ẽr-ves′′n-si), *n.* effervescence.

ef·fer·ves·cent (ef′ẽr-ves′′nt), *adj.* [L. *effervescens*, ppr.; see EFFERVESCE], 1. giving off gas bubbles; bubbling up; foaming. 2. lively and high-spirited; vivacious.

ef·fete (e-fēt′, i-fēt′), *adj.* [L. *effetus*, that has brought forth offspring, exhausted < *ex-*, out + *fetus*, that has brought forth], no longer capable of producing; worn out; exhausted; spent and sterile.

ef·fi·ca·cious (ef′ə-kā′shəs), *adj.* [L. *efficax, efficacis* < *efficere*, to bring to pass, accomplish (see EFFECT); + *-ous*], producing or capable of producing the desired effect; having the intended result; effective: as, an *efficacious* drug. —*SYN.* see **effective**.

ef·fi·ca·cy (ef′i-kə-si), *n.* [*pl.* EFFICACIES (-siz)], [L. *efficacia* < *efficax;* see EFFICACIOUS], power to produce effects or intended results; effectiveness.

ef·fi·cien·cy (ə-fish′ən-si, i-fish′ən-si), *n.* [*pl.* EFFICIENCIES (-siz)], [L. *efficientia*], 1. ability to produce the desired effect with a minimum of effort, expense, or waste; quality or fact of being efficient. 2. the ratio of effective work to the energy expended in producing it, as of a machine; output divided by input.

efficiency expert, a person whose work is to increase the efficiency and productivity of a business or industrial plant by finding better methods of performing various operations, cutting down waste, etc.

ef·fi·cient (ə-fish′ənt, i-fish′ənt), *adj.* [L. *efficiens*, ppr. of *efficere;* see EFFECT], 1. directly producing an effect or result; causative; effective: as, the *efficient* cause. 2. producing the desired effect or result with a minimum of effort, expense, or waste; working well; competent; able; capable. —*SYN.* see **effective**.

ef·fi·gy (ef′ə-ji), *n.* [*pl.* EFFIGIES (-jiz)], [Fr. *effigie;* L. *effigies*, a copy, image, likeness < *effingere* < *ex-*, out + *fingere*, to form], a portrait, statue, or other image, usually of a person; likeness; often, a crude representation of a person who is hated or held in contempt.

burn (or **hang**) **in effigy**, to burn (or hang) an image of a person who is hated or held in contempt.

ef·flo·resce (ef′lô-res′, ef′lō-res′), *v.i.* [EFFLORESCED (-rest′), EFFLORESCING], [L. *efflorescere*, to blossom, flourish < *ex-*, out + *florescere*, to begin to blossom < *florere*, to blossom < *flos, floris*, a flower], 1. to blossom out; flower. 2. in *chemistry*, *a*) to change from a crystalline to a powdery state through loss of the water of crystallization when exposed to air. *b*) to develop a powdery crust as a result of evaporation or chemical change.

ef·flo·res·cence (ef′lô-res′′ns, ef′lō-res′′ns), *n.* [Fr. < L. *efflorescens*, ppr. of *efflorescere;* see EFFLORESCE], 1. a flowering; blooming. 2. the time of flowering; hence, 3. the peak or fulfillment, as of an art or career. 4. in *chemistry*, *a*) the changing of certain crystalline compounds to a whitish powder or powdery crust through loss of their water of crystallization. *b*) the powder or crust thus formed. 5. in *medicine*, an eruption on the skin; rash or other skin lesion.

ef·flo·res·cent (ef′lô-res′′nt, ef′lō-res′′nt), *adj.* [L. *efflorescens*, ppr.; see EFFLORESCE], 1. blossoming; flowering. 2. in *chemistry*, *a*) changing from a crystalline to a powdery state through loss of the water of crystallization when exposed to air. *b*) covered with a powdery crust as a result of evaporation or chemical change.

ef·flu·ence (ef′loo-əns), *n.* [L. *effluens*, ppr. of *effluere*, to flow out < *ex-*, out + *fluere*, to flow], 1. a flowing out or forth; emanating. 2. a thing that flows out or forth; emanation.

ef·flu·ent (ef′loo-ənt), *adj.* [L. *effluens;* see EFFLUENCE], flowing out or forth. *n.* a thing that flows out or forth; specifically, *a*) a stream flowing out of a body of water. *b*) the outflow of a sewer, sewage tank, etc.

ef·flu·vi·a (e-floo′vi-ə, i-floo′vi-ə), *n.* alternative plural of **effluvium**.

ef·flu·vi·al (e-floo′vi-əl, i-floo′vi-əl), *adj.* of or like effluvia; noxious.

ef·flu·vi·um (e-floo′vi-əm, i-floo′vi-əm), *n.* [*pl.* EFFLUVIA (-ə), EFFLUVIUMS (-əmz)], [LL., a flowing out, outlet; see EFFLUENCE, FLOW], 1. a real or supposed outflow in the form of a vapor or stream of invisible particles; aura. 2. a disagreeable or noxious vapor or odor.

ef·flux (ef′luks), *n.* [< L. *effluxus*, pp. of *effluere;* see EFFLUENCE, FLUX], 1. a flowing out; emanating. 2. a thing that flows out; outflow; emanation.

ef·fort (ef′ẽrt), *n.* [Fr.; OFr. *esforz* < *esforcier*, to make an effort < LL. **exfortiare* < L. *ex-*, intens. + *fortis*, strong], 1. the using of energy to get something done; exertion of strength or mental power. 2. a try, especially a hard try; attempt; endeavor. 3. a product or result of working or trying; achievement.

SYN.—**effort** implies a conscious attempt to achieve a particular end (make some *effort* to be friendly); **exertion** implies an energetic, even violent, use of power, strength, etc., often without reference to any particular end (she feels faint after any *exertion*); **endeavor** suggests an earnest, sustained attempt to accomplish a particular, usually meritorious, end (a life spent in the *endeavor* to do good); **pains** suggests a laborious, diligent attempt (to take *pains* with one's work).—*ANT.* ease.

ef·fort·less (ef′ẽrt-lis), *adj.* making, requiring, or showing virtually no effort. —*SYN.* see **easy**.

ef·fron·ter·y (e-frun′tẽr-i, i-frun′tẽr-i), *n.* [*pl.* EFFRONTERIES (-iz)], [Fr. *effronterie* < *effronté*, shameless, bold; LL. **effrontatus* < L. *effrons, effrontis*, barefaced, shameless < *ex-*, from + *frons*, forehead], impudence; unashamed boldness; presumption. —*SYN.* see **temerity**.

ef·fulge (e-fulj′, i-fulj′), *v.t. & v.i.* [EFFULGED (-fuljd′), EFFULGING], [L. *effulgere;* see EFFULGENCE], to shine or flash out.

ef·ful·gence (e-ful′jəns, i-ful′jəns), *n.* [L. *effulgens*, ppr. of *effulgere* < *ex-*, forth + *fulgere*, to shine, gleam], great brightness; radiance; luster; splendor.

ef·ful·gent (e-ful′jənt, i-ful′jənt), *adj.* [L. *effulgens;* see EFFULGENCE], brightly shining; radiant; resplendent.

ef·fuse (e-fūz′, i-fūz′; *for adj.*, e-fūs′, i-fūs′), *v.t. & v.i.* [EFFUSED (-fūzd′), EFFUSING], [< L. *effusus*, pp. of *effundere*, to pour forth < *ex-*, out + *fundere*, to pour], 1. to pour out or forth. 2. to spread; diffuse. *adj.* 1. in *botany*, spread out loosely, without form: said of a flower. 2. in *zoology*, with the lips divided by a gap: said of a shell.

ef·fu·sion (e-fū′zhən, i-fū′zhən), *n.* [L. *effusio;* see EFFUSE], 1. a pouring forth. 2. unrestrained or emotional expression in speaking or writing. 3. in *medicine*, *a*) an escape of fluid from glands, blood vessels, etc. into body cavities or tissues. *b*) the fluid thus escaping.

ef·fu·sive (e-fū′siv, i-fū′siv), *adj.* [see EFFUSE], 1. pouring out or forth; overflowing. 2. expressing excessive emotion in an unrestrained manner; too demonstrative.

eft (eft), ***n.*** [ME. *euete;* AS. *efeta;* older, dial., & literary form of *newt*], a newt or small lizard.

eft (eft), ***adv.*** [ME. & AS. *eft*, orig. compar. (Gmc. **aftis*) of *aft;* cf. AFT], [Archaic], 1. again. 2. afterwards.

eft·soon (eft-sōōn'), ***adv.*** [ME. *eftsone(s);* AS. *eftsona;* *eft* (see EFT, *adv.*) + *sona* (see SOON)], [Archaic], 1. immediately afterward; forthwith. 2. at frequent intervals; often. 3. again.

eft·soons (eft-sōōnz'), ***adv.*** Archaic], eftsoon.

Eg., 1. Egypt. 2. Egyptian. 3. Egyptology.

e.g., *exempli gratia*, [L.], for the sake of example; for example.

e·gad (i-gad', ē-gad'), ***interj.*** [prob. < *ah God*], a softened or euphemistic oath.

e·gal·i·tar·i·an (i-gal'ə-târ'i-ən, ē-gal'ə-târ'i-ən), ***adj. & n.*** [< Fr. *égalitaire* < *égalité;* OFr. *equalité;* see EQUALITY], equalitarian.

‡é·ga·li·té (ā'gà'lē'tā'), ***n.*** [Fr.], equality.

Eg·bert (eg'bērt), [AS. *Ecgbeorht* < *ecg* (see EDGE) + *beorht* (see BRIGHT); hence, bright sword], a masculine name. ***n.*** king of the West Saxons (802–839 A.D.); first overlord of England (828–839 A.D.); lived 775?–839 A.D.

E·ger (ā'gēr), ***n.*** the Ohře River: the German name.

E·ge·ri·a (i-jêr'i-ə), ***n.*** [L.; Gr. *Ēgeria*], 1. in *Roman mythology*, a nymph who advised, and dictated laws to, Numa, second king of Rome. 2. any woman adviser.

e·gest (ē-jest'), ***v.t.*** [< L. *egestus*, pp. of *egerere*, to bear out, discharge; *e-*, out + *gerere*, to bear], to pass off (perspiration, excrement, etc.); excrete.

e·ges·ta (ē-jes'tə), ***n.pl.*** [Mod. L. < L. *egestus;* see EGEST], egested matter; feces, perspiration, etc.

e·ges·tion (ē-jes'chən), ***n.*** [L. *egestio*], 1. an egesting. 2. egested matter.

e·ges·tive (ē-jes'tiv), ***adj.*** relating to egestion.

egg (eg), ***n.*** [ME. *egg, egge* < ON. *egg*, replacing native form *ey* < AS. *æg;* akin to G. *ei* (pl. *eier*); prob. IE. base **owjom-*, **ojom-*, laid by a bird (as also in L. *ovum;* see OVUM) < **awei-*, bird (as in L. *avis;* see AVIARY)], 1. the oval or round body laid by a female bird, fish, reptile, insect, etc., containing the germ of a new individual along with food for its development, and having an enclosing shell or membrane. 2. a reproductive cell produced by the female; ovum. 3. a hen's egg, raw or cooked in any way. 4. a thing resembling a hen's egg. 5. [Slang], a person: as, he's a good *egg*. 6. [Slang], an aerial bomb, hand grenade, or torpedo. ***v.t.*** 1. to mix or cover with the yolk or white of eggs, as in cooking. 2. [Colloq.], to throw eggs at.

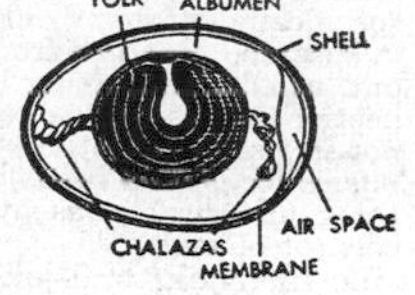

HEN'S EGG

lay an egg, [Slang], to fail completely: said of a joke, theatrical performance, etc.

put (or have) all one's eggs in one basket, to risk all that one has on a single venture, method, etc.

egg (eg), ***v.t.*** [ME. *eggen* < ON. *eggja*, lit., to give edge to; replacing Early Mod. Eng. *to edge*, in the same sense; cf. EDGE], to urge or incite (with *on*).

egg and dart, a decorative molding used in architecture and cabinetwork, consisting of an egg-shaped form alternating with a form shaped like an arrow, anchor, or tongue: also **egg and anchor, egg and tongue.**

egg cell, a reproductive cell produced by the female.

egg coal, any of various sizes of coal between 1 1/2 and 4 inches in diameter.

egg·er (eg'ēr), ***n.*** [apparently *egg, n.* + *-er*: from the egg-shaped cocoon of the moth], any of various moths whose larvae feed on the leaves of trees.

egg·head (eg'hed'), ***n.*** [Slang], an intellectual: usually a term of contempt or derision as used by anti-intellectuals.

Eg·gle·ston, Edward (eg''l-stən), 1837–1902; American novelist, historian, and preacher.

egg·nog (eg'nog'), ***n.*** [*egg, n.* + *nog*, strong beer or ale], a thick drink made of beaten eggs, milk, sugar, and nutmeg, usually containing whisky, rum, wine, etc.

egg·plant (eg'plant', eg'plänt'), ***n.*** 1. a plant with a large, pear-shaped, usually purple-skinned fruit, which is eaten as a vegetable. 2. the fruit.

egg·shell (eg'shel'), ***n.*** the hard, brittle covering of a bird's egg. ***adj.*** 1. fragile and thin, like an eggshell. 2. yellowish-ivory.

e·gis (ē'jis), ***n.*** [see AEGIS], 1. in *Greek mythology*, a shield or breastplate used by Zeus and, later, by his daughter Athena; hence, 2. a protection. 3. sponsorship; auspices. Also spelled **aegis.**

eg·lan·tine (eg'lən-tīn', eg'lən-tēn'), ***n.*** [Fr. *églantine* < OFr. *aiglent*, sweetbrier; LL. *aculentus* < L. *aculeus*, a sting, prickle, dim. of *acus*, a point, sting], a sweet-smelling wild rose with pink flowers and a prickly stem; sweetbrier: used in Milton's *L'Allegro* to refer to another flower, probably the honeysuckle.

e·go (ē'gō, eg'ō), ***n.*** [*pl.* EGOS (ē'gōz, eg'ōz)], [L., I], 1. the self; the individual as aware of himself. 2. [Colloq.], egotism; conceit. 3. in *philosophy*, the self, variously conceived as an absolute spiritual substance on which experience is superimposed, the series of acts and mental states introspectively recognized, etc. 4. in *psychoanalysis*, that part of the psyche which, developing from the id, experiences the external world through the senses, and consciously controls the impulses of the id: distinguished from *superego, id.*

e·go·cen·tric (ē'gō-sen'trik, eg'ō-sen'trik), ***adj.*** 1. viewing everything in relation to oneself; self-centered. 2. in *philosophy*, existing only as conceived in the individual mind: said of the world. ***n.*** an egocentric person.

e·go·cen·tric·i·ty (ē'gō-sen-tris'ə-ti, eg'ō-sen-tris'ə-ti), ***n.*** the quality or state of being egocentric.

e·go·ism (ē'gō-iz'm, eg'ō-iz'm), ***n.*** [Fr. *égoïsme* < L. *ego*, I], 1. the tendency to be self-centered, or to consider only oneself and one's own interests; selfishness. 2. egotism; conceit. 3. in *ethics*, the doctrine that self-interest is the proper goal of all human actions: opposed to *altruism*.

e·go·ist (ē'gō-ist, eg'ō-ist), ***n.*** [Fr. *égoïste* < L. *ego*, I], 1. a person who is self-centered or selfish. 2. a conceited person; egotist. 3. in *philosophy*, a person who accepts the doctrine of egoism.

e·go·is·tic (ē'gō-is'tik, eg'ō-is'tik), ***adj.*** 1. self-centered or selfish. 2. egotistic; conceited. 3. of an egoist or egoism.

e·go·is·ti·cal (ē'gō-is'ti-k'l, eg'ō-is'ti-k'l), ***adj.*** egoistic.

e·go·ma·ni·a (ē'gō-mā'ni-ə, eg'ō-mā'ni-ə), ***n.*** [*ego* + *-mania*], abnormally excessive egotism.

e·go·ma·ni·ac (ē'gō-mā'ni-ak', eg'ō-mā'ni-ak'), ***n.*** a person characterized by egomania.

e·go·tism (ē'gə-tiz'm, eg'ə-tiz'm), ***n.*** [L. *ego*, I + *-tism* for *-ism* after *nepotism*, etc.], 1. constant, excessive reference to oneself in speaking or writing. 2. self-conceit. 3. selfishness: see also **egoism;** the terms are sometimes used interchangeably, but *egotism* is generally considered the more opprobrious term.

e·go·tist (ē'gə-tist, eg'ə-tist), ***n.*** a person characterized by egotism.

e·go·tis·tic (ē'gə-tis'tik, eg'ə-tis'tik), ***adj.*** characterized by egotism.

e·go·tis·ti·cal (ē'gə-tis'ti-k'l, eg'ə-tis'ti-k'l), ***adj.*** egotistic.

e·gre·gious (i-grē'jəs, i-grē'ji-əs), ***adj.*** [L. *egregius*, chosen or separated from the herd, hence select, choice, eminent < *e-*, out + *grex, gregis*, a herd], 1. outstanding for undesirable qualities; remarkably bad; flagrant. 2. [Archaic], outstanding; remarkable.

e·gress (ē'gres), ***n.*** [L. *egressus;* pp. of *egredi*, to go out < *e-*, out + *gradi*, to step, go], 1. a going out; emergence. 2. the right to go out. 3. a way out; exit.

e·gres·sion (i-gresh'ən), ***n.*** a going out; egress.

e·gret (ē'grit, eg'ret), ***n.*** [ME. *egrete;* Fr. *aigrette*, kind of heron, tuft of feathers; Pr. *aigreta* < *aigron;* OHG. *haigiro*, heron], 1. [*pl.* EGRETS (-grits, -rets), EGRET; see **PLURAL, II, D,** 1], any of various herons with long, white plumes. 2. such a plume: usually **aigrette.**

E·gypt (ē'jipt), ***n.*** a country in northeastern Africa, on the Mediterranean and Red Seas: since 1958 a part of the United Arab Republic: area, 386,000 sq. mi.; pop., 23,400,000: (est.) abbreviated **Eg.**

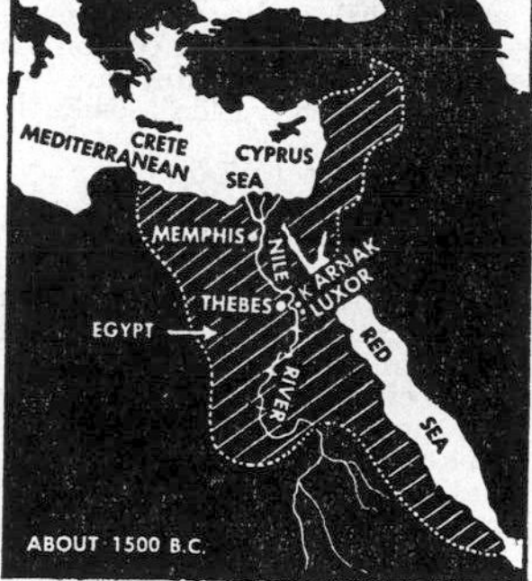

ANCIENT EGYPT

E·gyp·tian (i-jip'shən, ē-jip'shən), ***adj.*** 1. of Egypt, its people, or their culture. 2. of the Egyptian language. 3. [Obs.], gypsy. ***n.*** 1. a native or inhabitant of Egypt. 2. the Hamitic language of the ancient Egyptians. 3. [Obs.], a gypsy. Abbreviated **Egypt., Eg.**

Egyptian pound, the gold monetary unit of Egypt, valued at slightly more than a British pound: symbol, £E.

E·gyp·tol·o·gist (ē'jip-tol'ə-jist), ***n.*** a student of or specialist in Egyptology.

E·gyp·tol·o·gy (ē'jip-tol'ə-ji), ***n.*** the science or study of ancient Egyptian architecture, inscriptions, language, customs, etc.: abbreviated **Egyptol., Eg.**

eh (ā, e), ***interj.*** a sound expressing: 1. surprise. 2. doubt or inquiry: equivalent to *a)* "What did you say?" *b)* "Don't you think so?"

Ehr·lich, Paul (poul âr′liH; Eng. âr′lik), 1854–1915; German bacteriologist and physician; received Nobel prize in medicine, 1908.

E.I., 1. East India. 2. East Indian. 3. East Indies.

ei·der (ī′dẽr), *n.* [ON. *æthar*, genit. of *æthr*, eider duck via earlier Swed. *eider*], 1. [*pl.* EIDERS (-dẽrz), EIDER; see PLURAL, II, D, 1], any of a number of large sea ducks that live in northern regions: often **eider duck.** 2. the down of this duck.

eider down, [< ON. *æthar-dūn* via Sw.], 1. the soft, fine breast feathers, or down, of the eider duck, used as a stuffing for quilts, pillows, etc. 2. a bed quilt stuffed with such feathers.

ei·do·lon (ī-dō′lən), *n.* [*pl.* EIDOLA (-lə)], [Gr. *eidōlon*, an image; see IDOL], a phantom; apparition; image.

Eif·fel Tower (ī′f′l), an iron tower in Paris, 984 feet high, designed by A. Eiffel for the Exposition of 1889.

eight (āt), *adj.* [ME. *eihte, eyght;* AS. *eahta;* akin to G. *acht;* IE. base **oktō(u)*-, as also in L. *octo*], totaling one more than seven. *n.* 1. the cardinal number between seven and nine; 8; VIII. 2. any group of eight people or things, as a crew of eight oarsmen. 3. anything shaped like an eight: as, a figure *eight* in skating. 4. a playing card marked with the number 8 and eight spots of its suit.

eight ball, a black ball with the number eight on it, used in playing pool: in one form of the game, if a player pockets this ball before all the other balls are pocketed, he immediately loses the game.

behind the eight ball, [Slang], in a very unfavorable position: from having the cue ball directly behind the eight ball in the game of pool, so that the shooter runs the risk of pocketing the eight ball.

eight·een (ā′tēn′), *adj.* [ME. *eyghtene;* see EIGHT & -TEEN], eight more than ten. *n.* the cardinal number between seventeen and nineteen; 18; XVIII.

eight·een·mo (ā′tēn′mō′), *n. & adj.* octodecimo; 18mo: a size of book.

eight·eenth (ā′tēnth′), *adj.* [ME. *eihtetenthe;* see EIGHTEEN & -TH], 1. preceded by seventeen others in a series; 18th. 2. designating any of the eighteen equal parts of something. *n.* 1. the one following the seventeenth. 2. any of the eighteen equal parts of something; 1/18.

eight·fold (āt′fōld′), *adj.* [see -FOLD], 1. having eight parts. 2. having eight times as much or as many. *adv.* eight times as much or as many.

eighth (ātth, āth), *adj.* [ME. *eihtithe*, etc.; AS. *eahtotha* < *eahta;* see EIGHT & -TH], 1. preceded by seven others in a series; 8th. 2. designating any of the eight equal parts of something. *n.* 1. the one following the seventh. 2. any of the eight equal parts of something; 1/8. 3. in *music*, the interval of an octave.

eighth·ly (ātth′li, āth′li), *adv.* in the eighth place.

eighth note, in *music*, a note (♪) having one eighth the duration of a whole note: also called *quaver.*

eight·i·eth (ā′ti-ith), *adj.* [ME. *eigtithe;* see EIGHTY & -TH], 1. preceded by seventy-nine others in a series; 80th. 2. designating any of the eighty equal parts of something. *n.* 1. the one following the seventy-ninth. 2. any of the eighty equal parts of something; 1/80.

eight·y (ā′ti), *adj.* [ME. *eigteti, eygty;* AS. (*hund*)*eahtatig;* see EIGHT & -TY (tens)], eight times ten. *n.* [*pl.* EIGHTIES (-tiz)], the cardinal number between seventy-nine and eighty-one; 80; LXXX.

the eighties, the years from eighty through eighty-nine (of a century or a person's age).

ei·kon (ī′kon), *n.* an icon.

Ei·leen (ī-lēn′, ī′lēn′, ā-lēn′), a feminine name: see **Helen.**

E. Ind., East Indian.

Eind·ho·ven (īnt′hō′vən), *n.* a city in the southern Netherlands: pop., 163,000.

Ein·stein, Albert (īn′stīn′; G. īn′shtīn′), 1879–1955; Geman-born physicist; became American citizen in 1940; introduced theory of relativity; received Nobel prize in physics, 1921.

Ein·stein·i·an (īn-stīn′i-ən), *adj.* of Albert Einstein or his theories.

ein·stein·i·um (īn-stīn′i-əm), *n.* [after A. *Einstein*], a radioactive chemical element produced by bombarding uranium with nuclear particles: symbol, E; at. wt., 247 (?); at. no., 99.

Eir·e (âr′ə), *n.* the Republic of Ireland: a former name: see **Ireland.**

Ei·sen·ach (ī′z′n-äkh′), *n.* a city in east central Germany: pop., 52,000.

Ei·sen·how·er, Dwight David (ī′z′n-hou′ẽr), 1890– ; American general; supreme Allied commander in Europe (1943–1945; 1950–1952); thirty-fourth president of the United States (1953–1961): nicknamed *Ike.*

Eisk (āsk), *n.* a seaport in southwestern R.S.F.S.R., on the Sea of Azov: pop., 55,000: also spelled **Eysk.**

eis·tedd·fod (ā-steth′vod, es-teth′vod), *n.* [*pl.* EISTEDDFODS (-vodz); Welsh EISTEDDFODAU (es′teth-vôd′ī)], [W., a sitting, session, assembly < *eistedd*, to sit], a yearly congress in Wales of poets, musicians, etc., at which prizes are given for compositions and performances: 19th century revival of an old Welsh custom.

ei·ther (ē′thẽr, ī′thẽr), *adj.* [ME.; AS. *æghwæther* < *a* (*æ*), always (see AY) + *gehwæther*, each of two (cf. WHETHER); akin to, and of same formation as, OHG. *eogihwedar* (MHG. *iegeweder*)], 1. one or the other (of two): as, use *either* hand. 2. each (of two); the one and the other: as, he had a tool in *either* hand. *pron.* one or the other (of two). *conj.* the first element of the pair of disjunctive correlatives *either . . . or*, implying a choice of alternatives: as, *either* go or stay. *adv.* 1. any more than the other; also (following negative expressions): as, if she doesn't go, he won't *either.* 2. [Colloq.], an intensifier in a negative statement, usually in answer to an affirmative: as, "You took it." "I didn't *either!*"

e·jac·u·late (i-jak′yoo-lāt′, ē-jak′yoo-lāt′), *v.t.* [EJACULATED (-id), EJACULATING], [< L. *ejaculatus*, pp. of *ejaculari*, to cast out, throw out; *e-*, out + *jaculari*, to throw < *jaculum*, a dart, missile < *jacere*, to throw], 1. to eject or discharge (fluids) suddenly. 2. to utter suddenly and vehemently; exclaim.

e·jac·u·la·tion (i-jak′yoo-lā′shən, ē-jak′yoo-lā′shən), *n.* [see EJACULATE], 1. a sudden ejection of fluid, especially of seminal fluid, from the body. 2. a sudden, vehement utterance; exclamation.

e·jac·u·la·tive (i-jak′yoo-lā′tiv, ē-jak′yoo-lə-tiv), *adj.* of, or having the nature of, an ejaculation.

e·jac·u·la·tor (i-jak′yoo-lā′tẽr, ē-jak′yoo-lā′tẽr), *n.* a person or thing that ejaculates.

e·jac·u·la·to·ry (i-jak′yoo-lə-tôr′i, ē-jak′yoo-lə-tō′ri), *adj.* 1. ejaculating; of or for ejaculation: as, the *ejaculatory* ducts of the male. 2. having the nature of an ejaculation; exclamatory: as, *ejaculatory* words.

e·ject (i-jekt′, ē-jekt′), *v.t.* [< L. *ejectus*, pp. of *ejicere*, to throw out < *e-*, out + *jacere*, to throw], 1. to throw out; cast out; expel; emit; discharge: as, the chimney *ejects* smoke. 2. to drive out; evict: as, the heckler was *ejected* from the meeting.

***SYN.*—eject,** the term of broadest application here, implies generally a throwing or casting out from within (to *eject* saliva from the mouth); **expel** suggests a driving out, as by force, specifically, a forcing out of a country, organization, etc., often in disgrace (*expelled* from school); **evict** refers to the forcing out, as of a tenant, by legal procedure; **dismiss,** in this connection, refers to the removal of an employee, etc. but does not in itself suggest the reason for the separation (he was *dismissed* for lack of funds); **oust** implies the getting rid of something undesirable, as by force or the action of law (to *oust* corrupt officials).

e·jec·ta (i-jek′tə, ē-jek′tə), *n.pl.* [L., neut. pl. of *ejectus*], ejected matter; waste matter; refuse.

e·jec·tion (i-jek′shən, ē-jek′shən), *n.* [L. *ejectio*], 1. an ejecting or being ejected. 2. anything ejected.

e·jec·tive (i-jek′tiv, ē-jek′tiv), *adj.* of or causing ejection.

e·ject·ment (i-jekt′mənt, ē-jekt′mənt), *n.* 1. an ejecting; ousting; eviction. 2. in *law*, an action to secure or regain possession of hereditary property.

e·jec·tor (i-jek′tẽr, ē-jek′tẽr), *n.* a person or thing that ejects.

E·ka·te·rin·burg (ye-kä′tye-rin-boorH′), *n.* Sverdlovsk, a city in western Siberia: the former name.

E·ka·te·ri·no·dar (ye-kä′tye-rē′nô-där′), *n.* Krasnodar, a city in the Caucasus: the former name.

E·ka·te·ri·no·slav (ye-kä′tye-rē′nô-släf′), *n.* Dnepropetrovsk, a city in the Ukraine: the former name.

eke (ēk), *v.t.* [EKED (ēkt), EKING], [ME. *eken*, to increase; chiefly < *eke*, addition (cf. NICKNAME), partly < AS. *eacan*, to increase], [Archaic or Dial.], to make larger or longer; increase.

eke out, 1. to add something missing to; supplement: as, he *eked out* his income by writing stories. 2. to manage to make (a living) with difficulty.

eke (ēk), *adv. & conj.* [ME.; AS. *eac;* akin to G. *auch;* IE. base **au-*, again, on the other hand, as also in L. *aut*, or *autem*, on the other hand], [Archaic], also.

el (el), *n.* 1. [so called because shaped like an L], an extension or wing at right angles to the main structure; ell. 2. [< *elevated*], [Colloq.], an elevated railway.

e·lab·o·rate (i-lab′ẽr-it; *for v.*, i-lab′ə-rāt′), *adj.* [L. *elaboratus*, pp. of *elaborare*, to work out, labor greatly; *e-*, out + *laborare* < *labor*, labor, work], worked out carefully; developed in great detail; highly wrought; complicated; painstaking. *v.t.* [ELABORATED (-id), ELABORATING], 1. to produce by effort; develop by labor. 2. to work out carefully; develop in great detail. *v.i.* to state something in detail; give additional information; be more specific (usually with *on* or *upon*).

e·lab·o·ra·tion (i-lab′ə-rā′shən), *n.* 1. an elaborating or being elaborated. 2. a thing elaborated.

e·lab·o·ra·tive (i-lab′ə-rā′tiv, i-lab′ẽr-ə-tiv), *adj.* elaborating or tending to elaborate.

e·lab·o·ra·tor (i-lab′ə-rā′tẽr), *n.* a person who elaborates.

el·ae·op·ten (el′i-op′ten), *n.* elaeoptene.

el·ae·op·tene (el′i-op′tēn), *n.* [< Gr. *elaion*, olive oil, oil + *ptēnos*, winged], that part of an essential oil which does not become solid: distinguished from *stearoptene.*

El·a·gab·a·lus (el′ə-gab′ə-ləs), *n.* Heliogabalus.

E·laine (i-lān′), a feminine name: see **Helen.** *n.* in *Arthurian legend*, any of several women; specifically, *a*)

Elaine of Astolat, who loved Sir Lancelot. *b*) the mother of Sir Galahad.

E·lam (ē′ləm), *n.* an ancient kingdom in the region of modern Khuzistan, Iran.

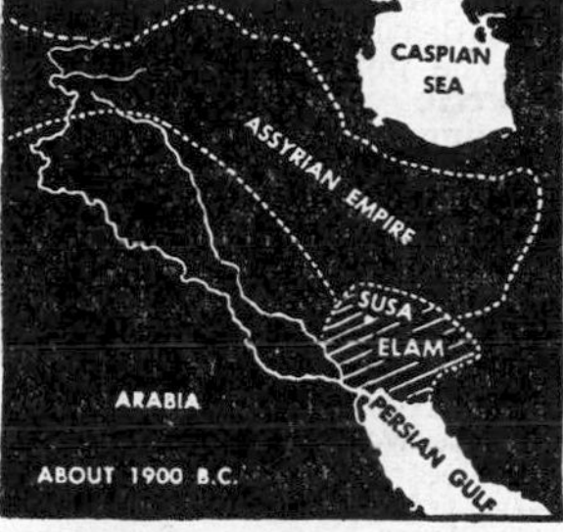

ELAM

E·lam·ite (ē′ləm-īt′); *n.* a native or inhabitant of Elam. *adj.* of Elam or the Elamites.

E·lam·it·ic (ē′lə-mit′-ik), *n.* the group of languages spoken by the Elamites. *adj.* 1. designating or of these languages. 2. Elamite.

‡é·lan (ā′län′), *n.* [Fr., a start, outburst, impetuosity < *élancer,* to dart, throw; *é-,* out + *lancer,* to throw a lance, hence throw < LL. *lanceare* < *lancea;* see LANCE], ardor; enthusiasm; vigor; impetuosity.

e·land (ē′lənd), *n.* [*pl.* ELAND, ELANDS (-ləndz); see PLURAL, II, D, 2], [D. *eland,* elk], a large, heavy African antelope with long, twisted horns.

‡é·lan vi·tal (ā′län′ vē′tål′), [Fr., lit., vital force], in *Bergsonian philosophy,* the original life force, the creative linking principle in the evolution of all organisms.

e·lapse (i-laps′), *v.i.* [ELAPSED (-lapst′), ELAPSING], [< L. *elapsus,* pp. of *elabi,* to glide away; *e-,* out + *labi,* to glide, fall], to slip by; pass: said of time.

ELAS, [< Mod. Gr. *E*thnikos *L*aikos *A*peleftherotikos *S*tratos, National Popular Liberation Army], the Hellenic Popular Liberation Army, the military branch of the EAM in World War II.

e·las·mo·branch (i-las′mə-braŋk′, i-laz′mə-braŋk′), *adj.* [< Mod. L. *elasmobranchii* < Gr. *elasmos,* beaten metal + L. *branchia,* gills], designating or of a group of fishes characterized by cartilaginous skeletons, platelike scales, and lack of air bladders. *n.* any fish of this group, as the shark, skate, ray, etc.

e·las·tic (i-las′tik), *adj.* [Late Gr. *elastikos* < Gr. *elaunein,* to drive, set in motion; akin to L. *alacer,* lively, animated < IE. base **ela-,* to stimulate], 1. having the property of immediately returning to its original size, shape, or position after being stretched, squeezed, flexed, expanded, etc.; flexible; springy; hence, 2. having the ability to recover easily from dejection, fatigue, etc.; buoyant: as, an *elastic* temperament kept her optimistic. 3. readily changed to suit circumstances; adaptable: as, *elastic* regulations. *n.* 1. a loosely woven fabric made flexible by strands of rubber running through it. 2. a band, garter, etc. of this material. 3. a rubber band.

SYN.—**elastic** implies ability to return without permanent injury to the original size or shape after being stretched, expanded, etc. (an *elastic* garter); **resilient** implies ability to spring back quickly into shape after being deformed, especially by compression (a healthy, *resilient* skin); **flexible** refers to anything that can be bent without breaking, whether or not it returns to its original form (a *flexible* wire); **supple** is applied to that which is easily bent, twisted, or folded without breaking, cracking, etc. (kidskin is *supple*).—***ANT.*** rigid, stiff.

e·las·ti·cal·ly (i-las′ti-k′l-i, i-las′tik-li), *adv.* in an elastic manner.

e·las·tic·i·ty (i-las′tis′ə-ti, ē′las-tis′ə-ti); *n.* [*pl.* ELASTICITIES (-tiz)], the quality or condition of being elastic; specifically, *a*) springiness; flexibility; resilience. *b*) buoyancy of spirit. *c*) adaptability.

e·las·ti·cize (i-las′tə-sīz′), *v.t.* [ELASTICIZED (-sīzd′), ELASTICIZING], [*elastic* + *-ize*], to make (fabric) elastic, as by interweaving with rubber strands.

elastic tissue, a connective tissue consisting largely of yellow, elastic fibers, occurring especially in the walls of arteries and veins.

e·las·tin (i-las′tin), *n.* [< *elastic* + *-in*], an albuminoid that is the basic constituent of elastic tissue, characterized by its elasticity when moist.

e·late (i-lāt′, ē-lāt′), *v.t.* [ELATED (-id), ELATING], [< L. *elatus,* pp. of *efferre,* to bring out, lift up < *ex-,* out + *ferre,* to bear, bring], to raise the spirits of; make proud, happy, or joyful. *adj.* [Poetic], elated.

e·lat·ed (i-lāt′id, ē-lāt′id), *adj.* [pp. of *elate*], in high spirits; proud or happy; joyful.

el·a·ter (el′ə-tẽr), *n.* [Mod. L. < Gr. *elatēr,* driver < *elaunein;* see ELASTIC], 1. [Obs.], elasticity. 2. in *botany,* an elastic filament that scatters the ripe reproductive cells, found in certain plants, as in the capsule of a liverwort. 3. in *entomology,* a beetle that can snap itself over onto its feet when turned on its back, as the click beetle.

e·lat·er·id (i-lat′ẽr-id), *n.* in *biology,* an elater (the beetle). *adj.* in *biology,* of an elater or the elaters.

e·lat·er·in (i-lat′ẽr-in), *n.* [*elaterium* + *-in*], a white, crystalline substance, $C_{20}H_{28}O_5$, the active principle of elaterium.

e·lat·er·ite (i-lat′ẽr-īt′), *n.* [*elater* (sense 2) + *-ite*], a dark-brown, rubberlike, elastic mineral hydrocarbon.

el·a·te·ri·um (el′ə-têr′i-əm), *n.* [L.; Gr. *elatērion,* neut. of *elatērios,* driving < *elaunein,* to drive], a cathartic and diuretic obtained from the dried juice of the wild cucumber, used in the treatment of dropsy.

e·la·tion (i-lā′shən, ē-lā′shən), *n.* [L. *elatio*], a feeling of exultant joy, pride, or happiness; high spirits.

El·ba (el′bə), *n.* an Italian island between Corsica and Italy: area, 86 sq. mi.; pop., 30,000: site of Napoleon's first exile (1814–1815).

El·be (el′bə), *n.* a river in Bohemia and Germany, flowing into the North Sea: length, 725 mi.: Czech name, *Labe.*

El·ber·feld (el′bẽr-felt′), *n.* a former city in western Germany: now a part of Wuppertal.

El·bert (el′bẽrt), a masculine name: see **Albert.**

Elbert, Mount, the highest peak of the Sawatch Range, central Colorado: height, 14,431 ft.

El·bing (el′biŋ), *n.* a city in northern Poland, formerly in East Prussia: pop., 72,000: Polish name, *Elbląg.*

El·bląg (el′blôŋg), *n.* Elbing: the Polish name.

el·bow (el′bō), *n.* [ME. *elbowe;* AS. *elboga, elnboga* < *eln,* forearm, hence ell + *boga,* a bow; akin to G. *ellenbogen*], 1. the joint between the upper and lower arm; especially, the outer part of the curve of a bent arm. 2. anything bent like an elbow. *v.t.* to shove or jostle with or as with the elbows. *v.i.* to make one's way by shoving or jostling.

at one's elbow, very close to one; easy to reach.

out at (the) elbows, shabby; poverty-stricken.

rub elbows with, to associate or mingle with (famous or prominent people, etc.).

up to the elbows, deeply engaged (*in* work, etc.).

elbow grease, [Colloq.], vigorous physical effort.

el·bow·room (el′bō-ro͞om′, el′bō-room′), *n.* room enough to move or work in; ample space or scope.

El·brus (or **El·bruz**), **Mount** (el′broos, äl′bro͞os), a volcanic mountain in the Caucasus: height, 18,468 ft.

El·burz Mountains (el-bo͞orz′), a mountain range in northern Iran, along the Caspian.

El Cap·i·tan (el kap′i-tan′; Sp. el kä′pē-tän′), a mountain in Yosemite National Park: height, 7,564 ft.

eld (eld), *n.* [ME. *elde;* AS. *eldo, ildu,* etc. < base of *ald, eald* (see OLD); akin to Goth. *alths*], [Archaic], 1. old age. 2. ancient times; antiquity; days of yore.

eld·er (el′dẽr), *adj.* [ME.; AS. (Mercian) *eldra, ældra;* compar. < base of *ald, eald* (see OLD); akin to OHG. *altiro, eltiro* (G. *älter*), Goth. *althiza*], 1. older; born or brought forth earlier than another or others; exceeding another in age; senior. 2. superior in rank, position, validity, etc. 3. earlier; former; ancient. Now only attributive. *n.* 1. an older person. 2. an aged person. 3. a forefather; ancestor; predecessor. 4. an older person with some authority or dignity in a tribe or community. 5. any of certain leaders in a church organization, as in the Presbyterian Church. 6. in the *Mormon Church,* a person appointed to the higher order of priesthood.

el·der (el′dẽr), *n.* [ME. *ellerne* & (with intrusive *-d-* as in *alder*) *eldore;* AS. *ellern, ellen;* akin to MLG. *ellern, eldern;* IE. base **el-* (cf. ELM, ALDER), as also in L. *alnus,* elder], 1. any of a large group of plants of the honeysuckle family, with white or pink flowers and red or blackish berries. 2. any of various similar, unrelated plants.

el·der·ber·ry (el′dẽr-ber′i, el′dẽr-bẽr-i), *n.* [*pl.* ELDERBERRIES (-iz)], 1. the elder (tree). 2. the berry, or drupe, of the elder, used for making wines, jelly, etc.

eld·er·ly (el′dẽr-li), *adj.* somewhat old; past middle age; approaching old age.

eld·er·ship (el′dẽr-ship′), *n.* [*elder* (church leader) + *-ship*], 1. the position or duties of an elder in a church. 2. a group of elders; presbytery.

elder statesman, 1. formerly, in Japan, any of a number of retired statesmen who served informally as a group of advisors to the emperor. 2. any elderly retired statesman who continues to be consulted on governmental matters.

eld·est (el′dist), *adj.* [ME.; AS. *eldest(a), ieldest(a),* etc., superl. of *ald, eald* (see OLD); akin to OHG. *altist-* (G. *ältest-*) & Goth. *althist(a)*], oldest; especially, first-born or oldest surviving: now only attributive.

El Do·ra·do (el′ də-rä′dō), [*pl.* EL DORADOS (-dōz)], [Sp., the gilded; *dorado,* pp. of *dorar,* to gild; LL. *deaurare,* to gild < L. *de-,* intens. + *aurum,* gold], 1. an imaginary country in South America, fabled to be rich in gold and precious stones: it was the object of much search by early Spanish explorers; hence, 2. any fabulously rich place. Also spelled **Eldorado.**

El·dred (el′drid), [AS. *Ealdred* < *eald* (see OLD) + *ræd,* counsel (see READ)], a masculine name.

el·dritch (el′drich), *adj.* [Early Mod. Eng. *elrich* with intrusive *-d-* as in *alder;* Scot. form *elphrish* suggests orig. connection with *elf*], [Scot.], weird; eerie; ghastly.
El·ea·nor (el′ə-nẽr, el′i-nôr′), [OFr. *Elienor, Alienor;* see HELEN], a feminine name: diminutives, *Ella, Nell, Nora;* variant, *Leonora:* also spelled **Elinor.**
El·e·at·ic (el′i-at′ik), *adj.* [L. *Eleaticus* < *Elea* (Velia), ancient Greek colony in Italy], designating or of an ancient Greek school of philosophy, centering in Elea during the 5th and 6th centuries B.C., which held that the singular and unchangeable "Being" was the only reality and that plurality, change, and motion were only illusory: Parmenides and Zeno were its outstanding adherents. *n.* an Eleatic philosopher.
El·e·a·zar, El·e·a·zer (el′i-ā′zẽr), *n.* [LL. *Eleazar;* Gr. *Eleazar;* Heb. *el'āzār*, lit., God has helped], in the *Bible,* Aaron's son and successor as high priest of Israel: Numb. 20:28.
elec., elect., 1. electric. 2. electrical. 3. electricity.
el·e·cam·pane (el′i-kam-pān′), *n.* [ML. *enula campana;* L. *inula;* Gr. *helenion,* elecampane; *campana* < L. *campus,* field], 1. a hardy, perennial plant of the composite family, with large clusters of yellow flowers. 2. a candy flavored with the root of this plant.
e·lect (i-lekt′, ə-lekt′), *adj.* [ME.; L. *electus,* pp. of *eligere,* to pick out, choose < *e-,* out + *legere,* to pick, choose, select], 1. chosen; given preference. 2. elected but not yet installed in office: as, mayor-*elect.* 3. in *theology,* chosen by God for salvation and eternal life. *n.* a person who is elect. *v.t.* 1. to select (a person) for some office by voting. 2. to choose; select. 3. in *theology,* to choose for eternal salvation: used only in the passive, with *God* as the implied subject. *v.i.* to make a choice by vote. —*SYN.* see **choose.**
the elect, 1. persons belonging to a specially privileged group. 2. in *theology,* those chosen by God for salvation and eternal life.
e·lec·tion (i-lek′shən, ə-lek′shən), *n.* [ME. *eleccioun;* OFr. *election;* L. *electio* < *electus*; see ELECT], 1. a choosing or choice. 2. a choosing for office by vote. 3. in *theology,* the selection by God of certain people for salvation and eternal life; predestination.
e·lec·tion·eer (i-lek′shən-êr′, ə-lek′shən-êr′), *v.i.* to canvass votes for, or otherwise work for the success of, a candidate, political party, etc. in an election.
e·lec·tive (i-lek′tiv, ə-lek′tiv), *adj.* [Fr. *électif*], 1. filled by election: as, an *elective* office. 2. chosen by election. 3. having the power or authority to choose; electoral. 4. that may be chosen but is not required; optional. *n.* an optional course or subject in a school or college curriculum.
elective affinity, a tendency to combine chemically with a certain substance or substances rather than with another or others.
e·lec·tor (i-lek′tẽr, ə-lek′tẽr), *n.* [L.], 1. a person who elects; specifically, a qualified voter. 2. a member of the electoral college. 3. [usually E-], [transl. of G. *kurfürst,* lit., choosing prince], any of the princes of the Holy Roman Empire who took part in the election of the emperor.
e·lec·tor·al (i-lek′tẽr-əl, ə-lek′tẽr-əl), *adj.* 1. of an election or electors. 2. made up of electors: as, an *electoral* college.
electoral college, an assembly elected by the voters to perform the formal duty of electing the president and the vice-president of the United States: the electors of each State, equal in number to its members in Congress, are expected to cast their votes for the candidates selected by the popular vote in their State.
e·lec·tor·ate (i-lek′tẽr-it, ə-lek′tẽr-it), *n.* 1. all those qualified to vote in an election. 2. a division or district of voters; electoral district. 3. the rank of an elector in the Holy Roman Empire. 4. the territory ruled by such an elector.
E·lec·tra (i-lek′trə), *n.* [L.; Gr. *Ēlektra,* lit., shining one; see ELECTRIC], in *Greek legend,* 1. the daughter of Agamemnon and Clytemnestra: she persuaded her brother, Orestes, to kill their mother and their mother's lover, who together had murdered Agamemnon. 2. one of the Pleiades.
Electra complex, in *psychoanalysis,* the unconscious tendency of a daughter to be attached to her father and hostile toward her mother: see **Oedipus complex.**
e·lec·tric (i-lek′trik, ə-lek′trik), *adj.* [Mod. L. *electricus* < L. *electrum;* Gr. *ēlektron,* amber (akin to *ēlektōr,* shining, the sun): so called from effect of friction upon amber], 1. of, charged with, or conveying electricity: as, an *electric* wire. 2. producing, or produced by, electricity: as, an *electric* generator. 3. operated by electricity: as, an *electric* iron. 4. electrifying; magnetic; exciting; tense. *n.* 1. a substance, as glass, amber, etc., which does not conduct electricity but can be used to store or excite an electrical charge. 2. a train, etc. operated by electricity. Abbreviated **elec., elect.**
e·lec·tri·cal (i-lek′tri-k'l, ə-lek′tri-k'l), *adj.* 1. electric. 2. connected with the science or use of electricity: as, an *electrical* engineer. Abbreviated **elec., elect.**
e·lec·tri·cal·ly (i-lek′tri-k'l-i, ə-lek′trik-li), *adv.* by or with electricity.
electrical transcription, in *radio broadcasting,* 1. a large, long-playing phonograph record for recording programs. 2. the use of such records for broadcasting.
electric chair, 1. an apparatus in the form of a chair, used in electrocuting criminals; hence, 2. [Colloq.], the death sentence or punishment by electrocution: as, he got the *electric chair.*
electric eel, an eel-shaped fish of South America, having special organs that can give electric shocks.
electric eye, a photoelectric cell: used for controlling various sorts of apparatus, as for opening doors, etc.
electric furnace, an electrically heated furnace used in the reduction of ore, manufacture of carbides, etc.
electric guitar, a kind of guitar whose tones are transmitted to an amplifier and loudspeaker through an electrical pickup attached to the bridge.
e·lec·tri·cian (i-lek′trish′ən, ē′lek-trish′ən), *n.* a person whose work is the construction, repair, or installation of electric apparatus.
e·lec·tric·i·ty (i-lek′tris′ə-ti, ē′lek-tris′ə-ti), *n.* [see ELECTRIC], 1. a form of energy generated by friction, induction, or chemical change, and having magnetic, chemical, and radiant effects: it is a property of the basic particles of all matter, consisting of protons (positive charges) and electrons (negative charges), which attract each other. 2. *a*) an electric current; stream of moving electrons: it sets up a magnetic field of force through which it produces kinetic energy. *b*) static electricity; charge of stationary particles: it sets up a field of force having potential energy. 3. the branch of physics dealing with electricity. 4. electric current supplied as a public utility for lighting, heating, etc. Abbreviated **elec., elect.** 5. a state of strong emotional tension, anticipation, etc.: as, her entrance created *electricity* in the room.
electric needle, a high-frequency electrode in the form of a needle, used in surgery to cut through tissue, searing it at the same time to prevent bleeding.

ELECTRIC NEEDLE

electric organ, a musical instrument resembling an organ, but producing tones by means of vacuum tubes instead of pipes.
electric ray, any of a group of rays (fish) with special organs that can give electric shocks.
electric steel, steel processed in an electric furnace.
e·lec·tri·fi·ca·tion (i-lek′trə-fi-kā′shən, ə-lek′trə-fi-kā′shən), *n.* 1. an electrifying or being electrified. 2. all the installation and equipment required for electrifying.
e·lec·tri·fi·er (i-lek′trə-fi′ẽr, ə-lek′trə-fi′ẽr), *n.* a person or thing that electrifies.
e·lec·tri·fy (i-lek′trə-fī′, ə-lek′trə-fī′), *v.t.* [ELECTRIFIED (-fīd′), ELECTRIFYING], 1. to charge with electricity. 2. to give an electric shock to. 3. to excite; thrill; shock. 4. to equip for the use of electricity.
e·lec·trize (i-lek′trīz, ə-lek′trīz), *v.t.* [ELECTRIZED (-trīzd), ELECTRIZING], to electrify.
e·lec·tro (i-lek′trō, ə-lek′trō), *n.* [*pl.* ELECTROS (-trōz)], 1. an electrotype. 2. an electroplate.
e·lec·tro- (i-lek′trō, ə-lek′trə), [< Gr. *ēlektron,* amber; see ELECTRIC], a combining form meaning: 1. *electric,* as in *electromagnet.* 2. *electrically,* as in *electrocute.* 3. *electricity,* as in *electrostatics.* 4. *electrolysis,* as in *electrodeposit.*
e·lec·tro·a·nal·y·sis (i-lek′trō-ə-nal′ə-sis, ə-lek′trō-ə-nal′ə-sis), *n.* analysis by means of electrolysis.
e·lec·tro·car·di·o·gram (i-lek′trō-kär′di-ə-gram′, ə-lek′trō-kär′di-ə-gram′), *n.* a tracing showing the changes in electric potential produced by the contractions of the heart.
e·lec·tro·car·di·o·graph (i-lek′trō-kär′di-ə-graf′, ə-lek′trō-kär′di-ə-gräf′), *n.* an instrument for making an electrocardiogram.
e·lec·tro·chem·i·cal (i-lek′trō-kem′i-k'l, ə-lek′trō-kem′i-k'l), *adj.* relating to electrochemistry.
e·lec·tro·chem·is·try (i-lek′trō-kem′is-tri, ə-lek′trō-kem′is-tri), *n.* the science that deals with the chemical effects of electrical action: abbreviated **electrochem.**
e·lec·tro·cul·ture (i-lek′trō-kul′chẽr, ə-lek′trō-kul′chẽr), *n.* the stimulation of plant growth by treating the soil, seeds, etc. with electricity.
e·lec·tro·cute (i-lek′trə-kūt′, ə-lek′trə-kūt′), *v.t.* [ELECTROCUTED (-id), ELECTROCUTING], [*electro-* + *execute*], 1. to execute (a criminal) by electricity. 2. to kill accidentally by electricity.
e·lec·tro·cu·tion (i-lek′trə-kū′shən, ə-lek′trə-kū′shən), *n.* an electrocuting or being electrocuted.
e·lec·trode (i-lek′trōd, ə-lek′trōd), *n.* [*electro-* + *-ode*], either of the two terminals of an electric source, such as a battery; anode or cathode.
e·lec·tro·de·pos·it (i-lek′trō-di-poz′it, ə-lek′trō-di-poz′it), *v.t.* to deposit (a metal) electrolytically. *n.* a deposit made by an electric current, as in electroplating.

e·lec·tro·dy·nam·ic (i-lek′trō-dī-nam′ik, ə-lek′trō-dī-nam′ik), ***adj.*** 1. of electricity in motion. 2. of electrodynamics.

e·lec·tro·dy·nam·ics (i-lek′trō-dī-nam′iks, ə-lek′trō-dī-nam′iks), ***n.pl.*** [construed as sing.], the branch of physics dealing with the phenomena of electric currents and associated magnetic forces.

e·lec·tro·dy·na·mom·e·ter (i-lek′trō-dī′nə-mom′ə-tẽr, ə-lek′trō-dī′nə-mom′ə-tẽr), ***n.*** [*electro-* + *dynamometer*], an instrument for measuring the strength of an electric current by means of the interaction between the different parts of a single circuit carrying the current.

e·lec·tro·en·ceph·a·lo·gram (i-lek′trō-en-sef′ə-lə-gram′, ə-lek′trō-en-sef′ə-lə-gram′), ***n.*** a tracing showing the changes in electric potential produced by the brain.

e·lec·tro·en·ceph·a·lo·graph (i-lek′trō-en-sef′ə-lə-graf′, i-lek′trō-en-sef′ə-lə-gräf′), ***n.*** an instrument for making electroencephalograms.

e·lec·tro·graph (i-lek′trə-graf′, ə-lek′trə-gräf′), ***n.*** [*electro-* + *-graph*], 1. the graphic record made by an electrometer or other device for recording the action of electricity. 2. an electrical device for etching or engraving plates. 3. a machine for preparing rollers that print fabrics and wallpaper. 4. an X-ray picture. 5. a telegraphic instrument for transmitting photographs, drawings, etc. 6. the transmitted picture; wirephoto.

e·lec·tro·jet (i-lek′trə-jet′, ə-lek′trə-jet′), ***n.*** an atmospheric stream of electric energy that girdles the earth above the magnetic equator.

e·lec·tro·ki·net·ics (i-lek′trō-ki-net′iks, ə-lek′trō-kī-net′iks), ***n.pl.*** [construed as sing.], the branch of electrodynamics dealing with electricity in motion, or electric currents: opposed to *electrostatics*.

e·lec·trol·y·sis (i-lek′trol′ə-sis, ə-lek′trol′ə-sis), ***n.*** [*electro-* + *-lysis*], 1. the decomposition into ions of a chemical compound in solution by the action of an electric current passing through the solution. 2. the removal of unwanted hair from the body by destroying the hair roots with an electrified needle.

e·lec·tro·lyte (i-lek′trə-līt′, ə-lek′trə-līt′), ***n.*** [*electro-* + *-lyte*], any substance which in solution is dissociated into ions and is thus made capable of conducting an electric current: when an electric current is passed through an electrolyte, a gas is generated or a solid deposited at the electrodes.

e·lec·tro·lyt·ic (i-lek′trə-lit′ik, ə-lek′trə-lit′ik), ***adj.*** 1. of or produced by electrolysis. 2. of an electrolyte.

e·lec·tro·lyt·i·cal·ly (i-lek′trə-lit′i-k′l-i, ə-lek′trə-lit′ik-li), ***adv.*** by electrolysis.

e·lec·tro·lyze (i-lek′trə-līz′, ə-lek′trə-līz′), ***v.t.*** [ELECTROLYZED (-līzd′), ELECTROLYZING], to subject to, or decompose by, electrolysis.

e·lec·tro·mag·net (i-lek′trō-mag′nit, ə-lek′trō-mag′nit), ***n.*** a soft iron core that temporarily becomes a magnet when an electric current flows through a coil of wire surrounding it.

e·lec·tro·mag·net·ic (i-lek′trō-mag-net′ik, ə-lek′trō-mag-net′ik), ***adj.*** 1. of or produced by an electromagnet. 2. having to do with electromagnetism.

e·lec·tro·mag·net·i·cal·ly (i-lek′trō-mag-net′i-k′l-i, ə-lek′trō-mag-net′ik-li), ***adv.*** by means of an electromagnet or electromagnetism.

electromagnetic wave, in *radio, television,* etc. a wave of electric energy radiated from an antenna.

ELECTROMAGNET

e·lec·tro·mag·net·ism (i-lek′trō-mag′nə-tiz′m, ə-lek′trō-mag′nə-tiz′m), ***n.*** 1. magnetism produced by an electric current. 2. the branch of physics that deals with the relations between electricity and magnetism.

e·lec·tro·met·al·lur·gy (i-lek′trō-met′′l-ũr′ji, ə-lek′trō-met′′l-ũr′ji), ***n.*** the branch of metallurgy having to do with the use of electricity for producing heat in smelting, refining, etc., or for separating metals from their ores by electrolysis: abbreviated **electrometal.**

e·lec·trom·e·ter (i-lek′trom′ə-tẽr, ə-lek′trom′ə-tẽr, ē′lek-trom′ə-tẽr), ***n.*** [*electro-* + *-meter*], a device for detecting or measuring differences of potential by means of electrostatic forces.

e·lec·tro·met·ric (i-lek′trō-met′rik, ə-lek′trō-met′rik), ***adj.*** of an electrometer or electrometry.

e·lec·trom·e·try (i-lek′trom′ə-tri, ə-lek′trom′ə-tri, ē′lek-trom′ə-tri), ***n.*** the science of making electrical measurements; measurement by an electrometer.

e·lec·tro·mo·tion (i-lek′trə-mō′shən, ə-lek′trə-mō′shən), ***n.*** 1. the motion of an electric current. 2. motion produced by electricity.

e·lec·tro·mo·tive (i-lek′trə-mō′tiv, ə-lek′trə-mō′tiv), ***adj.*** 1. producing an electric current through differences in potential. 2. relating to electromotive force or electromotion. Abbreviated **E.M.**

electromotive force, the force that can alter the motion of electricity, measured in terms of the energy per unit charge imparted to electricity passing through the source of this force: abbreviated **E.M.F., e.m.f., EMF, emf, E, E., e.**

e·lec·tro·mo·tor (i-lek′trə-mō′tẽr, ə-lek′trə-mō′tẽr), ***n.*** 1. any apparatus that produces or excites an electric current, as a dynamo. 2. an electric motor.

e·lec·tron (i-lek′tron, ə-lek′tron), ***n.*** [Mod. L.; Gr. *ēlektron;* see ELECTRIC], any of the nonnuclear, negatively charged particles that form a part of all atoms, each carrying one negative charge 1.6 × 10^{-19} coulombs in size: the mass of an electron is about 1/1800 of that of a proton, and the number of electrons circulating around a nucleus is equal to the number of positive charges on the nucleus.

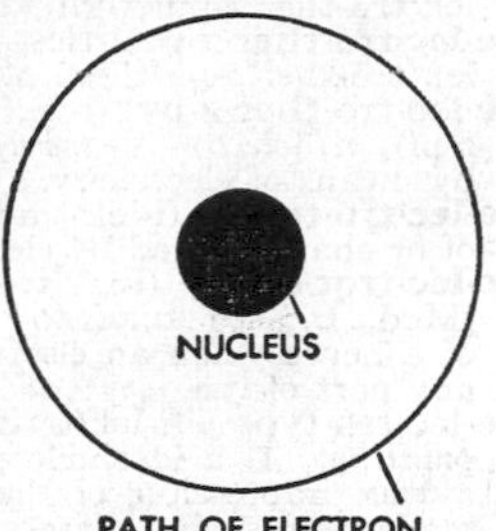

ELECTRON
(diagram of hydrogen atom)

e·lec·tro·neg·a·tive (i-lek′trō-neg′ə-tiv, ə-lek′trō-neg′ə-tiv), ***adj.*** 1. having a negative electrical charge; tending to move to the positive electrode, or anode, in electrolysis; hence, 2. acid; not metallic. ***n.*** an electronegative substance.

electron gun, the part of a cathode-ray tube that collects, focuses, and emits the electrons.

e·lec·tron·ic (i-lek′tron′ik, ə-lek′tron′ik), ***adj.*** 1. of an electron or electrons. 2. operated, operating, produced, or done by the action of electrons.

electronic brain, an electronic calculator, computer, etc.

e·lec·tron·ics (i-lek′tron′iks, ə-lek′tron′iks), ***n.pl.*** [construed as sing.], the science that deals with electronic action in vacuums and gases, and with the use of vacuum tubes, transistors, photoelectric cells, etc.

electron microscope, an instrument for focusing rays of electrons, rather than light rays, to form an enlarged image of the object: it is much more powerful than any optical microscope.

electron optics, the branch of electronics having to do with the control of electron rays by means of electric and magnetic fields, which act upon the rays in the same way that lenses act on light rays.

electron tube, a type of vacuum tube whose functioning is largely dependent on the motion of electrons, as an X-ray tube: see also **vacuum tube.**

e·lec·tron-volt (i-lek′tron-vōlt′, ə-lek′tron-vōlt′), ***n.*** in *physics,* a unit of energy equal to that attained by an electron falling unimpeded through a potential difference of one volt; 1.602 × 10^{-12} erg: abbreviated **ev** (no period).

e·lec·trop·a·thy (i-lek′trop′ə-thi, ə-lek′trop′ə-thi), ***n.*** [*electro-* + *-pathy*], electrotherapeutics.

e·lec·tro·pho·re·sis (i-lek′trō-fə-rē′sis, ə-lek′trō-fə-rē′sis), ***n.*** cataphoresis.

e·lec·troph·o·rus (i-lek′trof′ə-rəs, ə-lek′trof′ə-rəs, el′ek-trof′ə-rəs), ***n.*** [*pl.* ELECTROPHORI (-rī′)], [< *electro-* + Gr. *-phoros,* bearing < *pherein,* to bear], an apparatus consisting of an insulated disk of resin, shellac, etc. and a metal plate, used in generating static electricity by induction.

e·lec·tro·plate (i-lek′trə-plāt′, ə-lek′trə-plāt′), ***v.t.*** to deposit a coating of metal on by electrolysis. ***n.*** anything so plated; especially, silver-plated tableware.

e·lec·tro·pos·i·tive (i-lek′trə-poz′ə-tiv, ə-lek′trə-poz′ə-tiv), ***adj.*** 1. having a positive electrical charge; tending to move toward the negative electrode, or cathode, in electrolysis; hence, 2. basic; not acid. ***n.*** any electropositive substance.

e·lec·tro·scope (i-lek′trə-skōp′, ə-lek′trə-skōp′), ***n.*** [*electro-* + *-scope*], an instrument for detecting very small charges of electricity, and indicating whether they are positive or negative, as by the divergence of strips of gold leaf.

ELECTROSCOPE

e·lec·tro·scop·ic (i-lek′trə-skop′ik, ə-lek′trə-skop′ik), ***adj.*** of, measured by, or capable of being detected by, an electroscope.

e·lec·tro·stat·ic (i-lek′trə-stat′ik, ə-lek′trə-stat′ik), ***adj.*** [*electro-* + *static*], relating to electricity at rest or to stationary electric particles; of static electricity.

e·lec·tro·stat·ics (i-lek′trə-stat′iks, ə-lek′trə-stat′iks), ***n.pl.*** [construed as sing.], the branch of electrodynamics dealing with electricity at rest, or static electricity: opposed to *electrokinetics.*

e·lec·tro·sur·ger·y (i-lek'trō-sũr'jẽr-i, ə-lek'trō-sũr'jẽr-i), *n.* in *surgery*, the use of electrically operated instruments to cut through tissues or destroy them.

e·lec·tro·syn·the·sis (i-lek'trō-sin'thə-sis, ə-lek'trō-sin'-thə-sis), *n.* in *chemistry*, synthesis produced by means of an electric current.

e·lec·tro·ther·a·peu·tic (i-lek'trō-ther'ə-pū'tik, ə-lek'-trō-ther'ə-pū'tik), *adj.* relating to electrotherapeutics.

e·lec·tro·ther·a·peu·ti·cal (i-lek'trō-ther'ə-pū'ti-k'l, ə-lek'trō-ther'ə-pū'ti-k'l), *adj.* electrotherapeutic.

e·lec·tro·ther·a·peu·tics (i-lek'trō-ther'ə-pū'tiks, ə-lek'trō-ther'ə-pū'tiks), *n.* electrotherapy.

e·lec·tro·ther·a·py (i-lek'trō-ther'ə-pi, ə-lek'trō-ther'-ə-pi), *n.* [*electro-* + *therapy*], the treatment of disease by means of electricity.

e·lec·tro·ton·ic (i-lek'trə-ton'ik, ə-lek'trə-ton'ik), *adj.* of or characterized by electrotonus.

e·lec·trot·o·nus (i-lek'trot'ə-nəs, ə-lek'trot'ə-nəs), *n.* [Mod. L.; see ELECTRO- & TONE], the changed state of a nerve when an electric current is passed through any part of it.

e·lec·tro·type (i-lek'trə-tīp', ə-lek'trə-tīp'), *n.* in *printing*, 1. a facsimile plate made by electroplating a wax impression of the original plate. 2. a print made from such a plate. *v.t.* to make such a facsimile plate or plates of. *v.i.* to make such plates.

e·lec·tro·typ·ic (i-lek'trə-tip'ik, ə-lek'trə-tip'ik), *adj.* 1. of electrotypy. 2. using, produced by, or having the nature of, an electrotype or electrotypes.

e·lec·tro·typ·y (i-lek'trə-tīp'i, ə-lek'trə-tīp'i), *n.* the making of electrotypes.

e·lec·trum (i-lek'trəm, ə-lek'trəm), *n.* [L. < Gr. *ēlektron*; see ELECTRIC], 1. a light-yellow alloy of gold and silver, used in ancient times. 2. an alloy of copper, nickel, and zinc, used for keys, tableware, etc.: also called *German silver, nickel silver.*

e·lec·tu·ar·y (i-lek'choo-er'i, ə-lek'choo-er'i), *n.* [*pl.* ELECTUARIES (-iz)], [ME. *lectuarie, electuarie*; LL. *electuarium* < Gr. *ekleikton* < *ekleichein*, to lick out; *ek-*, out + *leichein*, to lick], a medicine made by mixing drugs with honey or sirup to form a paste.

el·ee·mos·y·nar·y (el'ə-mos''n-er'i, el'i-ə-mos''n-er'i), *adj.* [ML. *eleemosynarius* < *eleemosyna*; Gr. *eleēmosynē*, alms], 1. of or for charity or alms; charitable. 2. supported by or dependent on charity. 3. given by charity; gratuitous; free.

el·e·gance (el'ə-gəns), *n.* [Fr. *élégance*; L. *elegantia*], 1. the quality of being elegant; dignified richness and grace, as of manner, dress, design, style, etc.; restrained opulence; tasteful luxury. 2. anything elegant.

el·e·gan·cy (el'ə-gən-si), *n.* elegance.

el·e·gant (el'ə-gənt), *adj.* [Fr. *élégant*; L. *elegans*, ppr. of **elegare*; *e-*, out + *legare*, to choose, select], 1. characterized by dignified richness and grace, as of manner, dress, design, style, etc.; luxurious or opulent in a restrained, tasteful manner. 2. characterized by a sense of propriety or refinement; fastidious in manners and tastes. 3. [Colloq.], excellent; fine; first-rate.

el·e·gi·ac (el'ə-jī'ək, i-lē'ji-ak'), *adj.* [L. *elegiacus*; Gr. *elegeiakos*], 1. of or composed in dactylic hexameter couplets, the second line (sometimes called a pentameter) having only an accented syllable in the third and sixth feet: the form was used for Greek and Latin elegies and various other lyric poems. Scansion:

[scansion marks]

2. of, like, or fit for an elegy. 3. sad; mournful; plaintive. *n.* 1. an elegiac couplet. 2. *pl.* a series of such couplets; poem or poems written in such couplets.

el·e·gi·a·cal (el'ə-jī'ə-k'l), *adj.* elegiac.

el·e·gist (el'ə-jist), *n.* a writer of an elegy or elegies.

e·le·git (i-lē'jit), *n.* [L., 3d pers. sing., perf. indic., of *eligere*, to choose; see ELECT], in *law*, a writ of execution by which a plaintiff is given possession of the defendant's goods until his claim is satisfied.

el·e·gize (el'ə-jīz'), *v.i.* [ELEGIZED (-jīzd'), ELEGIZING], to write elegies. *v.t.* to commemorate or lament in or as in an elegy.

el·e·gy (el'ə-ji), *n.* [*pl.* ELEGIES (-jiz)], [Fr. *élégie*; L. *elegia*; Gr. *elegeia* < *elegos*, a lament], 1. a poem of lament and praise for the dead, as Shelley's "Adonais." 2. any poem in elegiac verse. 3. a poem written in a mournfully contemplative tone: as, Gray's "*Elegy* in a Country Churchyard."

elem., 1. element. 2. elementary. 3. elements.

el·e·ment (el'ə-mənt), *n.* [ME.; OFr.; L. *elementum*, first principle, element], 1. any of the four substances—earth, air, fire, water—formerly believed to constitute all physical matter. 2. any of these four substances thought of as the natural environment of a class of living beings; hence, 3. the natural or fitting environment for a person or thing. 4. a component, feature, or principle of something; basic part. 5. in *chemistry*, any substance that cannot be separated into different substances except by nuclear disintegration: all matter is composed of such substances: see table, p. 469. 6. *pl.* in *ecclesiastical usage*, the bread and wine of the Eucharist. 7. in *electricity*, *a*) either of a pair of metallic substances that act together in an electrolyte to produce electricity. *b*) a positive or negative electrode. *c*) the working part of an electrical appliance: as, the heating *element* of an iron. 8. in *mathematics*, *a*) an infinitesimal part of any magnitude; differential. *b*) the point, line, etc. that generates a line, suface, etc. 9. in *military aviation*, the basic unit of an air force, consisting of one or more aircraft: it is a subdivision of a flight. Abbreviated **elem.** (in senses 5, 7, 8).

in one's element, in a situation, surroundings, etc. suited to one.

the elements, 1. the first or basic principles; rudiments. 2. wind, rain, etc.; forces of the atmosphere.

SYN.—**element**, in its general use, is the broadest term for any of the basic, irreducible parts or principles of anything, concrete or abstract (the *elements* of a science); **component** and **constituent** both refer to any of the simple or compound parts of some complex thing or concept, but **constituent** also implies that the part is essential to the complex (hemoglobin is a *constituent* of blood); **ingredient** refers to any of the substances (sometimes non-essential) that are mixed together in preparing a food, medicine, etc. (the *ingredients* of a cocktail); **factor** applies to any of the component parts that are instrumental in determining the nature of the complex (luck was a *factor* in his success).

el·e·men·tal (el'ə-men't'l), *adj.* 1. of any or all of the four elements (earth, air, fire, and water) believed in by ancient philosophers. 2. of or like natural forces; characteristic of the physical universe; hence, 3. basic and powerful; primal: as, hunger and sex are *elemental* drives. 4. of first principles; elementary; basic; rudimentary; simple. 5. being an essential part or parts. 6. in *chemistry*, of an element; not a compound.

el·e·men·ta·ri·ly (el'ə-men'tẽr-ə-li), *adv.* in an elementary manner.

el·e·men·ta·ri·ness (el'ə-men'tẽr-i-nis), *n.* the quality of being elementary.

el·e·men·ta·ry (el'ə-men'tẽr-i, el'ə-men'tri), *adj.* [L. *elementarius*], 1. elemental. 2. of first principles; of the rudiments or fundamentals of something; introductory. 3. consisting of one chemical element; not a compound. 4. of a chemical element or elements. Abbreviated **elem.**

elementary school, 1. in educational systems having no junior high school, a school of eight grades, where basic subjects are taught. 2. in educational systems having a junior high school, a similar school of six grades. Also called *grade school, grammar school.*

el·e·mi (el'ə-mi), *n.* [Fr. *élémi*; prob. < Ar. *al-lāmī*], a resin obtained from various tropical trees, used in medicinal ointments and in varnishes: also **gum elemi.**

El·e·na (el'ə-nə), a feminine name: see **Helena.**

e·len·chus (i-leŋ'kəs), *n.* [*pl.* ELENCHI (-kī)], [L.; Gr. *elenchos*, cross-examination, disproof, refutation], in *logic*, a syllogism that refutes a proposition by proving the direct contrary of its conclusion.

e·lenc·tic (i-leŋk'tik), *adj.* [Gr. *elenktikos*, fond of cross-examining, critical], in *logic*, 1. of elenchus; refuting. 2. of cross-examination.

el·e·phant (el'ə-fənt), *n.* [*pl.* ELEPHANTS (-fənts), ELEPHANT; see PLURAL, II, D, 2], [ME. *elifaunt, olifaunt*; OFr. *olifant* (Fr. *éléphant*); L. *elephantus*; Gr. *elephas, elephantos*, elephant, ivory], a huge, thick-skinned, almost hairless mammal, the largest of extant four-footed animals, with a long, flexible snout (called a *trunk*) and two ivory tusks growing out of the upper jaw: the two existing species are the Indian elephant and the African elephant, which is larger and has a flatter head and larger ears.

Elephant Butte, a dam and reservoir in New Mexico, on the Rio Grande: height, 306 ft.

el·e·phan·ti·a·sis (el'ə-fən-tī'ə-sis), *n.* [L.; Gr. *elephantiasis* < *elephas*, elephant: so called from resemblance of the skin to the elephant's hide], a chronic disease of the skin characterized by the enlargement of certain parts of the body, especially the legs and genitals, and by the hardening and ulceration of the surrounding skin: it is caused by small, threadlike worms (*filariae*) which obstruct the lymphatic glands.

el·e·phan·tine (el'ə-fan'tēn, el'ə-fan'tin, el'ə-fan'tīn), *adj.* [L. *elephantinus*; Gr. *elephantinos*], 1. of an elephant or elephants. 2. like an elephant in size or gait; huge, heavy, slow, clumsy, ungainly, etc.

el·e·phant's-ear (el'ə-fənts-êr'), *n.* any of several plants with large, ornamental leaves shaped like the ears of an elephant, as the taro or begonia.

el·e·phant's-foot (el'ə-fənts-foot'), *n.* a vine of the yam family, with a large root somewhat resembling an elephant's foot.

El·eu·sin·i·an (el'yoo-sin'i-ən), *adj.* of Eleusis.

Eleusinian mysteries, secret religious rites of ancient Greece, celebrated every spring at Eleusis in honor of Demeter and Persephone: they symbolized the annual death and resurrection of vegetation.

E·leu·sis (e-loo'sis, el-ū'sis), *n.* a city in ancient Greece, northwest of Athens.

el·e·vate (el'ə-vāt'), *v.t.* [ELEVATED (-id), ELEVATING], [< L. *elevatus*, pp. of *elevare*, to raise, lift up; *e-*, out +

CHEMICAL ELEMENTS

With International Atomic Weights. Oxygen at 16 is the standard.

	Symbol	Atomic Number	Atomic Weight
Actinium	Ac	89	227(?)
Aluminum	Al	13	26.97
Americium	Am	95	241(?)
Antimony	Sb	51	121.76
Argon	A	18	39.944
Arsenic	As	33	74.91
Astatine	At	85	211(?)
Barium	Ba	56	137.36
Berkelium	Bk	97	243(?)
Beryllium	Be	4	9.02
Bismuth	Bi	83	209.00
Boron	B	5	10.82
Bromine	Br	35	79.916
Cadmium	Cd	48	112.41
Calcium	Ca	20	40.08
Californium	Cf	98	244(?)
Carbon	C	6	12.01
Cerium	Ce	58	140.13
Cesium	Cs	55	132.91
Chlorine	Cl	17	35.457
Chromium	Cr	24	52.01
Cobalt	Co	27	58.94
Copper	Cu	29	63.54
Curium	Cm	96	242(?)
Dysprosium	Dy	66	162.46
Einsteinium	E	99	247(?)
Erbium	Er	68	167.2
Europium	Eu	63	152.0
Fermium	Fm	100	254(?)
Fluorine	F	9	19.00
Francium	Fr	87	223(?)
Gadolinium	Gd	64	156.9
Gallium	Ga	31	69.72
Germanium	Ge	32	72.60
Gold	Au	79	197.2
Hafnium	Hf	72	178.6
Helium	He	2	4.003
Holmium	Ho	67	164.94
Hydrogen	H	1	1.0080
Indium	In	49	114.76
Iodine	I	53	126.92
Iridium	Ir	77	193.1
Iron	Fe	26	55.85
Krypton	Kr	36	83.7
Lanthanum	La	57	138.92
Lawrencium	Lw	103	257(?)
Lead	Pb	82	207.21
Lithium	Li	3	6.940
Lutetium	Lu	71	174.99
Magnesium	Mg	12	24.32
Manganese	Mn	25	54.93
Mendelevium	Mv	101	256(?)
Mercury	Hg	80	200.61
Molybdenum	Mo	42	95.95
Neodymium	Nd	60	144.27
Neon	Ne	10	20.183
Neptunium	Np	93	239
Nickel	Ni	28	58.69
Niobium	Nb	41	92.91
Nitrogen	N	7	14.008
Nobelium	No	102	255(?)
Osmium	Os	76	190.2
Oxygen	O	8	16.0000
Palladium	Pd	46	106.7
Phosphorus	P	15	30.98
Platinum	Pt	78	195.23
Plutonium	Pu	94	239
Polonium	Po	84	210.0
Potassium	K	19	39.096
Praseodymium	Pr	59	140.92
Promethium	Pm	61	147(?)
Protactinium	Pa	91	231
Radium	Ra	88	226.05
Radon	Rn	86	222
Rhenium	Re	75	186.31
Rhodium	Rh	45	102.91
Rubidium	Rb	37	85.48
Ruthenium	Ru	44	101.7
Samarium	Sm	62	150.43
Scandium	Sc	21	45.10
Selenium	Se	34	78.96
Silicon	Si	14	28.06
Silver	Ag	47	107.880
Sodium	Na	11	22.997
Strontium	Sr	38	87.63
Sulfur	S	16	32.06
Tantalum	Ta	73	180.88
Technetium	Tc	43	99(?)
Tellurium	Te	52	127.61
Terbium	Tb	65	159.2
Thallium	Tl	81	204.39
Thorium	Th	90	232.12
Thulium	Tm	69	169.4
Tin	Sn	50	118.70
Titanium	Ti	22	47.90
Tungsten	W	74	183.92
Uranium	U	92	238.07
Vanadium	V	23	50.95
Wolfram	*alt. name for* TUNGSTEN		
Xenon	Xe	54	131.3
Ytterbium	Yb	70	173.04
Yttrium	Y	39	88.92
Zinc	Zn	30	65.38
Zirconium	Zr	40	91.22

levare, to make light, lift < *levis*, light], 1. to raise, lift up. 2. to raise the pitch or volume of (the voice, etc.). 3. to raise (a person) in rank or position. 4. to raise to a higher intellectual or moral level. 5. to raise the spirits of; elate; exhilarate. —*SYN.* see **lift.**

el·e·vat·ed (el′ə-vāt′id), *adj.* [pp. of *elevate*], 1. raised; lifted up; high. 2. exalted; dignified; lofty. 3. high-spirited; joyful. *n.* [Colloq.], an elevated railway.

elevated railway, a railway elevated above a street on a framework so that the street is left free for traffic.

el·e·va·tion (el′ə-vā′shən), *n.* [ME. *elevacioun;* OFr. *elevacion;* L. *elevatio*], 1. an elevating or being elevated. 2. a high place or position. 3. height above the surface of the earth. 4. dignity; eminence; loftiness. 5. a flat scale drawing of the front, rear, or side of a building, etc. 6. in *astronomy*, the angular altitude of any heavenly body above the horizon. 7. in *geography*, height above sea level; altitude. Abbreviated **elev.** —*SYN.* see **height.**

el·e·va·tor (el′ə-vā′tẽr), *n.* [LL.; see ELEVATE], 1. a person or thing that raises or lifts up. 2. a machine for hoisting or lowering goods or people by means of a suspended cage or car; also, the cage or car itself: in British usage, a *lift*. 3. a machine, usually consisting of buckets or scoops fastened to an endless belt, for hoisting grain, etc., as in a warehouse. 4. a warehouse, often cylindrical, for storing, hoisting, and discharging grain; granary. 5. a movable airfoil like a horizontal rudder, usually hinged to the tail section of an aircraft, for making the craft go up or down: see **airplane,** illus.

e·lev·en (i-lev′′n, ə-lev′′n), *adj.* [ME. *elevyn, enleve(ne);* AS. *endleofan*, lit., one left over (after ten); akin to OFris. *andlofa, elleva,* OHG. *einlif* (G. *elf*); Gmc. **ainlif* < **ain-* (AS. *an;* cf. Eng. *articles* A, AN), one + *-lif*, left over, left behind < IE. base **leiqw-*, to leave, leave behind (as in L. *linquere*, to leave; cf. RELINQUISH); cf. TWELVE], totaling one more than ten. *n.* 1. the cardinal number between ten and twelve; 11; XI. 2. in *football* & *cricket*, a team.

e·lev·en·fold (i-lev′′n-fōld′, ə-lev′′n-fōld′), *adj.* [see -FOLD], 1. having eleven parts. 2. having eleven times as much or as many. *adv.* eleven times as much or as many.

e·lev·enth (i-lev′′nth, ə-lev′′nth), *adj.* [ME. *eleventh*, earlier *enlefte;* AS. *endlyfta;* see ELEVEN & -TH], 1. preceded by ten others in a series; 11th. 2. designating any of the eleven equal parts of something. *n.* 1. the one following the tenth. 2. any of the eleven equal parts of something; 1/11.

at the eleventh hour, [< Matt. 20], at the last possible time; just before it is too late.

elf (elf), *n.* [*pl.* ELVES (elvz)], [ME. *elfe;* AS. *ælf;* akin to OHG. *alþ* (G. *alp*, nightmare); prob. IE. base **albho-*, white, as also in L. *albus*, white (cf. ALBUM, ALBUMEN); prob. basic sense "whitish figure" (in the mist)], 1. in *folklore*, a small sprite or fairy, supposedly exercising magic powers and haunting woods and hills; pixie. 2. a mischievous child or small person.

El Faiyum, see **Faiyum, El.**

elf·in (el′fin), *adj.* [prob. < ME. *elvene*, genit. pl. of *elfe;* see ELF], of, appropriate to, or like an elf or elves; fairylike. *n.* an elf.

elf·ish (el′fish), *adj.* like or characteristic of an elf or elves; elfin; impish; mischievous.

elf·lock (elf′lok′), *n.* a lock of hair tangled as if by elves.

El·gar, Sir **Edward** (el′gẽr, el′gär), 1857–1934; English composer.

El·gin (el′jin), *n.* a city in northeastern Illinois: pop., 49,000.

El·gon (el′gon), *n.* a volcanic mountain between Uganda and Kenya, Africa: height, 14,136 ft.

El Grec·o (el grek′ō), (born *Kyriakos Theotokopoulos*), 1548?–1614?; painter and sculptor in Italy and Spain, born in Crete: also called *Domenico*.

E·li (ē′lī), [Heb. *'ēlī*, lit., high], a masculine name. *n.* in the *Bible*, a high priest of Israel and teacher of Samuel: I Sam. 3.

E·li·a (ē′li-ə, ēl′yə), see **Lamb, Charles.**

E·li·as (i-lī′əs), [L.; Gr. *Ēlias* < Heb.; see ELIJAH], a masculine name. *n.* in the *Bible*, Elijah: Greek form of the name.

e·lic·it (i-lis′it), *v.t.* [< L. *elicitus*, pp. of *elicere*, to draw out < *e-*, out + *lacere*, to entice], to draw forth; evoke: as, his irony *elicited* an angry reply. —*SYN.* see **extract.**

e·lic·i·ta·tion (i-lis′ə-tā′shən), *n.* an eliciting or being elicited.

e·lide (i-līd′), *v.t.* [ELIDED (-id), ELIDING], [L. *elidere*, to strike out < *e-*, out + *laedere*, to hurt; cf. LESION], 1. to leave out; suppress. 2. to leave out or slur over (a vowel, syllable, etc.) in pronunciation.

e·lid·i·ble (i-līd′ə-b′l), *adj.* that can be elided.

el·i·gi·bil·i·ty (el′i-jə-bil′ə-ti), *n.* 1. the quality or state of being eligible. 2. [*pl.* ELIGIBILITIES (-tiz)], *usually in pl.* a quality that makes eligible.

el·i·gi·ble (el′i-jə-b′l), *adj.* [Fr. *éligible* < L. *eligere;* see ELECT], fit to be chosen; legally or morally qualified; suitable; desirable. *n.* an eligible person.

el·i·gi·bly (el′i-jə-bli), *adv.* in an eligible manner.

E·li·hu (el′ə-hū′), [Heb. *elīhū*, lit., my God is he], a masculine name. *n.* (i-lī′hū), in the *Bible*, the youngest of the four men who visited Job in his affliction: Job: 32–37.

E·li·jah (i-lī′jə, ə-lī′jə), [Heb. *'ēlīyāhū*, lit., Jehovah is God], a masculine name: variant, *Elias;* diminutive, *Lige*. *n.* in the *Bible*, a prophet of Israel in the 9th century B.C.: I Kings 17–19, II Kings 2:1–11.

e·lim·i·nate (i-lim′ə-nāt′, ə-lim′ə-nāt′), *v.t.* [ELIMINATED (-id), ELIMINATING], [< L. *eliminatus*, pp. of *eliminare*, to turn out of doors, banish < *e-*, out + *limen*, threshold, door], 1. to take out; remove; get rid of. 2. to leave out of consideration; reject; omit. 3. in *algebra*, to get rid of (an unknown quantity) by combining equations. 4. in *physiology*, to expel (waste products) from the body; excrete. —*SYN.* see **exclude.**

e·lim·i·na·tion (i-lim′ə-nā′shən, ə-lim′ə-nā′shən), *n.* an eliminating or being eliminated.

e·lim·i·na·tive (i-lim′ə-nā′tiv, ə-lim′ə-nā′tiv), *adj.* having to do with elimination; tending to eliminate.

e·lim·i·na·tor (i-lim′ə-nā′tẽr, ə-lim′ə-nā′tẽr), *n.* a person or thing that eliminates.

e·lim·i·na·to·ry (i-lim′ə-nə-tôr′i, ə-lim′ə-nə-tō′ri), *adj.* eliminating.

El·i·nor (el′ə-nẽr, el′i-nôr′), a feminine name: see **Eleanor.**

El·i·ot (el′i-ət), [< *Ellis*], a masculine name: also spelled **Elliot, Elliott.**

El·i·ot, Charles William (el′i-ət), 1834–1926; American educator; president of Harvard University (1869–1909).

Eliot, George, (pseudonym of *Mary Ann Evans*), 1819–1880; English novelist.

Eliot, John, 1604–1690; American theologian; known for missionary work among American Indians: called *Apostle of the Indians*.

Eliot, T.S., (*Thomas Stearns Eliot*), 1888– ; American poet, critic, and essayist in England; received Nobel prize in literature, 1948.

E·lis (ē′lis), *n.* 1. a division of ancient Greece, in the western Peloponnesus. 2. its capital. See **Greece,** map.

E·lis·a·beth (i-liz′ə-bəth, ə-liz′ə-bəth), a feminine name: see **Elizabeth.** *n.* in the *Bible*, the mother of John the Baptist and a kinswoman of Mary: Luke 1.

E·li·sa·vet·grad (ye-lē′sä-vet-grät′), *n.* Kirovograd, a city in the Ukraine: the former name.

E·li·sa·vet·pol (ye-lē′sä-vet-pôl′y′), *n.* Kirovabad, a city in Transcaucasia: the former name.

E·li·sha (i-lī′shə, ə-lī′shə), [Heb. *elīshā'*, lit., God is salvation], a masculine name: variant, *Ellis;* diminutive, *Lish*. *n.* in the *Bible*, a prophet of Israel, ordained by Elijah as his successor: I Kings 19:16,19, II Kings 2.

e·li·sion (i-lizh′ən), *n.* [L. *elisio* < pp. of *elidere*], an eliding or being elided; specifically, the omission or slurring over of a vowel, syllable, etc. in pronunciation: often used in poetry, especially when a word ends with a vowel before another word beginning with a vowel or silent *h* (e.g., "th' inevitable hour").

e·lite, é·lite (i-lēt′, ā-lēt′), *n.* [Fr. < *élite*, choice, select; pp. of *élire;* L. *eligere;* see ELECT], 1. [also construed as pl.], the choice or most carefully selected part of a group, as of a society or profession. 2. a size of type for typewriters, equivalent to 10-point.

Elite Guard, the Schutzstaffel.

e·lix·ir (i-lik′sẽr), *n.* [ME.; ML.; Ar. *al-iksīr*, philosopher's stone; *al*, the + *iksīr*, philosopher's stone; prob. < Gr. *xērion*, powder for drying wounds < *xēros*, dry], 1. a hypothetical substance sought for by medieval alchemists to change base metals into gold or to prolong life indefinitely: also called *philosopher's stone, elixir of life;* hence, 2. [Rare], the quintessence; underlying principle. 3. a remedy for all ailments; panacea. 4. in *pharmacy*, a medicine made of drugs in alcoholic solution, usually sweetened; tincture.

Eliz., Elizabethan.

E·li·za (i-lī′zə), a feminine name: diminutive, **Liza:** see **Elizabeth.**

E·liz·a·beth (i-liz′ə-bəth, ə-liz′ə-bəth), [L. *Elisabeth;* Heb. *elīsheba'*, lit., God is (my) oath], a feminine name: diminutives, *Bess, Bessie, Beth, Betsy, Betty, Elsie, Libby, Lizzie;* variant, *Eliza:* also spelled **Elisabeth.** *n.* 1. (*Elizaveta Petrovna*), daughter of Peter the Great; 1709–1762; empress of Russia (1741–1762). 2. a city in northeastern New Jersey: pop., 108,000.

Elizabeth I, 1533–1603; daughter of Henry VIII and Anne Boleyn; queen of England (1558–1603).

Elizabeth II, 1926– ; daughter of George VI; queen of England (1952–).

Elizabeth, Saint, 1207–1231; Hungarian princess and religious mystic: her day is November 19.

E·liz·a·be·than (i-liz′ə-bē′thən, ə-liz′ə-beth′ən), *adj.* of or characteristic of the time when Elizabeth I was queen of England: as, *Elizabethan* poetry. *n.* an English person, especially a writer, statesman, etc., of the time of Queen Elizabeth I. Abbreviated **Eliz.**

Elizabethan sonnet, a sonnet form: see **Shakespearean sonnet.**

elk (elk), *n.* [*pl.* ELK, ELKS (elks); see PLURAL, II, D,

2], [Late ME. *elke*, a special development (with *-k*) < AS. *elh, eolh;* akin to G. *elch;* Gmc. base **alxis;* IE. base **el-*, stag, hart, as also in W. *elain*, hind], 1. a large, mooselike deer of northern Europe and Asia, with broad antlers. 2. the wapiti, a North American deer. 3. a light, flexible leather of horsehide, calf, etc.

Elk·hart (elk′härt′), *n.* a city in north central Indiana: pop., 40,000.

ell (el), *n.* 1. the letter L. 2. something shaped like an L; specifically, *a)* an extension or wing at right angles to the main structure. *b)* an L-shaped joint of piping or tubing.

ell (el), *n.* [ME. *elle, ellen, elne;* AS. *eln;* akin to G. *elle;* Gmc. **ălinā*, lit., arm, hence arm's length; IE. base **elei-*, to bend, as also in L. *ulna*, arm, elbow (< **olenā*) & Gr. *ōlenē*, elbow; cf. ELBOW], a former measure of length, used mainly in measuring cloth: it varied from 27 inches in Holland, etc. to 45 inches in England.

El·la (el′ə), a feminine name: see **Eleanor.**

El·len (el′ən), a feminine name: see **Helen.**

Elles·mere Island (elz′mêr), an island in the Northwest Territories, Canada, west of northwestern Greenland: area, 76,600 sq. mi.

El·lice Islands (el′is), a group of British islands in the South Pacific, between the Gilbert and Fiji Islands: area, 9 1/2 sq. mi.; pop., 5,000: old name *Lagoon Islands.*

El·li·ot, El·li·ott (el′i-ət), a masculine name: see **Eliot.**

el·lipse (i-lips′, ə-lips′), *n.* [*pl.* ELLIPSES (-lip′siz)], [L. *ellipsis;* Gr. *elleipsis*, a want, defect, ellipsis < *elleipein*, to fall short, leave undone < *en-*, in + *leipein*, to leave], in *geometry*, the path of a point that moves so that the sum of its distances from two fixed points (called *foci*) is constant; closed curve produced when a cone is cut by a plane inclined obliquely to the axis and not touching the base.

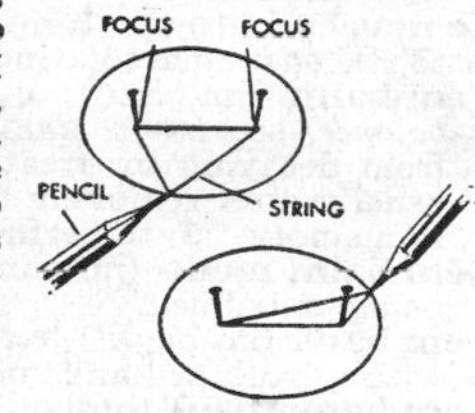

ELLIPSE

el·lip·sis (i-lip′sis, ə-lip′sis), *n.* [*pl.* ELLIPSES (-sēz)], [L. *ellipsis;* see ELLIPSE], 1. in *grammar*, the omission of a word or words necessary for complete construction but understood in the context. Example: "If (it is) possible, (you) come early." 2. in *writing & printing*, a mark (. . . or * * *) indicating an omission of words or letters.

el·lips·oid (i-lip′soid, ə-lip′soid), *n.* [< *ellipse* + *-oid*], in *geometry*, 1. a solid whose plane sections are all ellipses or circles. 2. the surface of such a solid. *adj.* of or shaped like an ellipsoid.

el·lip·soi·dal (i-lip′soi′d'l, el′ip-soi′d'l), *adj.* ellipsoid.

el·lip·tic (i-lip′tik, ə-lip′tik), *adj.* elliptical.

el·lip·ti·cal (i-lip′ti-k'l, ə-lip′ti-k'l), *adj.* [< Gr. *elleiptikos* (see ELLIPSE); + *-al*], 1. of, or having the form of, an ellipse, as some leaves: see **leaf,** illus. 2. of or characterized by ellipsis; with a word or words omitted.

el·lip·ti·cal·ly (i-lip′ti-k'l-i, ə-lip′tik-li), *adv.* 1. so as to form an ellipse. 2. with the use of ellipsis.

el·lip·tic·i·ty (i-lip′tis′ə-ti, el′ip-tis′ə-ti), *n.* 1. the condition of being elliptical; elliptical form. 2. the degree of deviation of an ellipse, elliptical orbit, etc. from circular form, or of a spheroid from spherical form.

El·lis (el′is), a masculine name: see **Elisha.**

El·lis, Have·lock (hav′lok, hav′lək el′is), (*Henry Havelock Ellis*), 1859–1939; English psychologist, scientist, and author.

El·lis Island (el′is), a small island in New York harbor: immigrants were formerly examined there before being allowed into the United States.

Ells·worth, Lincoln (elz′wẽrth), 1880–1951; American polar explorer.

Ellsworth, Oliver, 1745–1807; American jurist; chief justice, United States Supreme Court (1796–1799).

elm (elm), *n.* [ME. *elme;* AS. *elm;* akin to OHG. *elm;* IE. base **el-* (cf. ALDER, ELDER, tree), as also in L. *ulmus*, elm], 1. any of a group of tall, hardy shade trees, growing largely in the North Temperate Zone. 2. the hard, heavy wood of this tree.

El·man, Mi·scha (mish′ə, mē′shə el′mən), 1891– ; American violinist, born in Russia.

elm beetle, any of various beetles that feed on the leaves or bark of elm trees.

El·mer (el′mẽr), [? < AS. *Æthelmær* (< *æthel*, noble + *mære*, famous); or ? < *Egilmær* (< *egil-* < *ege*, awe, dread + *mære*)], a masculine name.

El·mi·ra (el-mī′rə), *n.* a city in south central New York: pop., 47,000.

el·o·cu·tion (el′ə-kū′shən), *n.* [L. *elocutio* < pp. of *eloqui;* see ELOQUENT], 1. style or manner of speaking or reading in public. 2. the art of public speaking or declaiming: often associated with a studied or artificial style of speaking.

el·o·cu·tion·ar·y (el′ə-kū′shən-er′i), *adj.* 1. of or in elocution. 2. artificial and declamatory.

el·o·cu·tion·ist (el′ə-kū′shən-ist), *n.* 1. a person who teaches elocution. 2. a person skilled in elocution.

E·lo·him (e-lō′him; Heb. e-lō-hēm′), *n.* [Heb. *elōhīm*, pl. of *elōah*, God], God: Hebrew name used in parts of the Old Testament: see also **Jehovah.**

E·lo·hist (e-lō′hist), *n.* the unknown author of those parts of the Old Testament in which the term *Elohim*, instead of *Yahweh* (Jehovah), is used as the name for God.

El·o·his·tic (el′ō-his′tik), *adj.* 1. of or written by the Elohist. 2. designating those parts of the Old Testament in which the term *Elohim*, instead of *Yahweh* (Jehovah), is used as the name for God.

e·loign, e·loin (i-loin′), *v.t.* [Fr. *éloigner;* OFr. *esloignier;* LL. **exlongare* for *elongare;* see ELONGATE], 1. to carry away (property). 2. in *law*, to remove (private property) beyond the jurisdiction of a sheriff, etc.

El·o·ise (el′ō-ēz′, el′ə-wēz′, el′ə-wēz′), a feminine name: equivalent, Fr. *Héloïse:* see **Louise.**

e·lon·gate (i-lôŋ′gāt), *v.t. & v.i.* [ELONGATED (-id), ELONGATING], [< LL. *elongatus*, pp. of *elongare*, to prolong < L. *e-*, out + *longus*, long], to lengthen; stretch; extend. *adj.* 1. lengthened; stretched. 2. in *botany*, long and narrow, as certain leaves. —*SYN.* see **extend.**

e·lon·ga·tion (i-lôn′gā′shən, ē′lôŋ-gā′shən), *n.* [ME. *elongacioun;* LL. *elongatio*], 1. an elongating or being elongated; lengthening; extension. 2. something elongated; lengthened part; continuation. 3. the distance of a planet from the sun, measured in degrees.

e·lope (i-lōp′, ə-lōp′), *v.i.* [ELOPED (-lōpt′), ELOPING], [Anglo-Fr. *aloper;* prob. < ME. *aleapen, alopen*, to leap up, run away; AS. *ahleapan* influenced by cognate ON. *hlaupa*, to run (cf. LOPE); *a-*, away + *hleapan*, to run, leap], 1. to run away secretly, especially in order to get married: said of lovers. 2. to run away; escape; abscond.

e·lope·ment (i-lōp′mənt, ə-lōp′mənt), *n.* an eloping.

el·o·quence (el′ə-kwəns), *n.* [Fr. *éloquence* < L. *eloquentia;* see ELOQUENT], 1. speech or writing that is vivid, forceful, fluent, graceful, and persuasive. 2. *a)* the art or manner of such speech or writing. *b)* the power to persuade with speech or writing.

el·o·quent (el′ə-kwənt), *adj.* [Fr. *éloquent;* L. *eloquens*, ppr. of *eloqui*, to speak out, utter; *e-*, out + *loqui*, to speak], 1. having, or characterized by, eloquence; fluent, forceful, and persuasive. 2. vividly expressive: as, an *eloquent* sigh.

El Pas·o (el pas′ō), a city in northwestern Texas, on the Rio Grande: pop., 277,000.

El·sa (el′sə), [G.; apparently orig. name of a certain water sprite], a feminine name.

El Sal·va·dor (el sal′və-dôr′; Sp. el säl′vä-thôr′), a country in western Central America, on the Pacific: area, 8,259 sq. mi.; pop., 2,613,000; capital, San Salvador: see **Central America,** map.

else (els), *adj.* [ME. & AS. *elles*, adv. genit. of n. base *el-*, other, seen in AS. *el-land*, foreign land, *el-theod*, foreign people (cf. G. *elend*, lit., banishment); akin to Goth. *aljis*, OHG. *elles*, of same formation; IE. base **al-*, that, yonder one, as also in L. *alius*, another, *alienus*, belonging to another (cf. ALIEN)], 1. different; other: as, somebody *else.* 2. in addition; more: as, is there anything *else? Else* follows the word modified. *adv.* 1. in a different time, place, or manner; differently; otherwise: as, where *else* can I go? 2. if not: as, study, (or) *else* you will fail.

else·where (els′hwâr′), *adv.* [ME. *elleswhere;* AS. *elleshwær*], in, at, or to some other place; somewhere else.

El·sie (el′si), a feminine name: see **Alice, Elizabeth, Elsa.**

El·si·nore (el′sə-nôr′, el′sə-nōr′), *n.* Helsingör, Denmark, scene of Shakespeare's *Hamlet:* the English name.

El·speth (el′spəth), [Scot. form of *Elizabeth*], a feminine name.

e·lu·ci·date (i-lōō′sə-dāt′, i-lū′sə-dāt′), *v.t.* [ELUCIDATED (-id), ELUCIDATING], [< LL. *elucidatus*, pp. of *elucidare*, to make light or clear < L. *e-*, out + *lucidus*, light, clear < *lux*, light], to make clear; explain. —*SYN.* see **explain.**

e·lu·ci·da·tion (i-lōō′sə-dā′shən, i-lū′sə-dā′shən), *n.* an elucidating; explanation.

e·lu·ci·da·tor (i-lōō′sə-dā′tẽr, i-lū′sə-dā′tẽr), *n.* a person who elucidates.

e·lude (i-lōōd′, i-lūd′), *v.t.* [ELUDED (-id), ELUDING], [L. *eludere*, to finish play, parry a blow, frustrate, deceive; *e-*, out + *ludere*, to play], 1. to avoid or escape from by quickness, cunning, etc. 2. to escape detection by; evade; baffle: as, the point that you're trying to make *eludes* me. —*SYN.* see **escape.**

E·lul (e-lōōl′; Heb. el′ool), *n.* [Heb. *elūl*], the twelfth month of the Jewish year: see **Jewish calendar.**

e·lu·sion (i-lōō′zhən, i-lū′zhən), *n.* [ML. *elusio* < L. *elusus*, pp. of *eludere*], an eluding; escape or avoidance by quickness or cunning; evasion.

e·lu·sive (i-lo͞o′siv, i-lū′siv), *adj.* [< L. *elusus* (see ELUSION); + *-ive*], 1. tending to elude. 2. hard to grasp or retain mentally; baffling.

e·lu·so·ry (i-lo͞o′sẽr-i, i-lū′sẽr-i), *adj.* [ML. *elusorius*], elusive: said especially of mental impressions.

e·lu·tri·ate (i-lo͞o′tri-āt′, i-lū′tri-āt′), *v.t.* [ELUTRIATED (-id), ELUTRIATING], [< L. *elutriatus*, pp. of *elutriare*, to wash out, rack off < *eluere; e-*, out + *luere*, to wash], 1. to purify by washing and straining; decant. 2. to separate the lighter particles from the heavier particles of by washing.

el·ver (el′vẽr), *n.* [for *eelfare*, the passage of young eels up a stream], a young eel, especially a young conger eel.

elves (elvz), *n.* plural of **elf.**

El·vi·ra (el-vī′rə, el-vêr′ə), [Sp.; prob. < Goth. *alwera* < Gmc. *ala*, complete, whole + *wer-* < IE. base **wer-*, to close up, cover, protect by covering], a feminine name.

elv·ish (el′vish), *adj.* like an elf; elfish.

E·ly (ē′li), *n.* a town in the county of Isle of Ely: pop., 10,000: site of a famous ancient cathedral.

Ely, Isle of, an administrative county in Cambridgeshire, England: area, 373 sq. mi.; pop., 89,000.

El·yot, Sir **Thomas** (el′i-ət, el′yət), 1490?–1546; English author, diplomat, and lexicographer.

E·lyr·i·a (i-lêr′i-ə, ə-lêr′yə), *n.* a city in northern Ohio: pop., 44,000.

E·ly·sian (i-lizh′ən, i-lizh′i-ən), *adj.* 1. in or like Elysium; hence, 2. happy; blissful; delightful.

E·ly·si·um (i-lizh′i-əm, i-liz′i-əm), *n.* [L.; Gr. *Ēlysion* (*pedion*), Elysian (plain), plain of the departed], 1. in *Greek mythology*, the place where virtuous people went after death. 2. any place or condition of ideal bliss or complete happiness; paradise. Also **Elysian fields.**

el·y·tra (el′i-trə), *n.* 1. plural of **elytron.** 2. plural of **elytrum.**

el·y·troid (el′i-troid′), *adj.* like an elytron.

el·y·tron (el′i-tron′), *n.* [*pl.* ELYTRA (-trə)], [Mod.L.; Gr. *elytron*, a covering, sheath < *elyein*, to roll round, wrap up], either of the front pair of modified wings in certain insects, which act as protective covering for the rear wings; wing cover.

el·y·trum (el′i-trəm), *n.* [*pl.* ELYTRA (-trə)], an elytron.

El·ze·vir (el′zə-vẽr, el′zə-vêr′), *adj.* [< Latinized form, *Elzevirius*, of the Dutch *Elzevier*], 1. designating or of books printed and published by the Elzevirs, a family of 17th-century printers in the Netherlands. 2. designating a type face introduced by the Elzevirs.
This line is in Elzevir type.

El·ze·vir, Bon·a·ven·ture (bon′ə-ven′chẽr el′zə-vêr′, el′zə-vẽr), 1583–1652; son of *Louis;* Dutch printer.

Elzevir, Louis, 1540?–1617; Dutch printer.

em (em), *n.* 1. the letter M, m. 2. in *printing*, formerly the letter M of any given font, now a square of any size of type, used as a unit of measure, as of column width; especially, an em pica, equal to about 1/6 of an inch.

'em (əm, 'm), *pron.* [ME. *hem*, dat. pl. of 3d pers. pron. used as acc.; it was replaced by *them* (< ON.) in stressed positions], [Colloq.], them.

em- (im, em: *although in many of the following words beginning with unstressed em- only* im *is given,* em *is also heard*), en-: used before bilabial consonants (*p, b, m*), as in *empower, embrace, emmarble.*

EM, in the *United States Army*, enlisted man (or men).

Em., in *chemistry*, emanation.

E.M., 1. Earl Marshal. 2. electromotive. 3. Engineer of Mines.

e·ma·ci·ate (i-mā′shi-āt′), *v.t.* [EMACIATED (-id), EMACIATING], [< L. *emaciatus*, pp. of *emaciare*, to make lean, cause to waste away; *e-*, out + *maciare*, to be lean < *macies*, leanness], to cause to become abnormally lean; cause to lose much flesh or weight.

e·ma·ci·at·ed (i-mā′shi-āt′id), *adj.* [pp. of *emaciate*], abnormally lean; wasted away, as from starvation or disease.

e·ma·ci·a·tion (i-mā′shi-ā′shən, i-mā′si-ā′shən), *n.* 1. an emaciating; wasting away. 2. abnormal leanness, caused by starvation, disease, etc.

em·a·nate (em′ə-nāt′), *v.i.* [EMANATED (-id), EMANATING], [< L. *emanatus*, pp. of *emanare*, to flow out, arise; *e-*, out + *manare*, to flow], to come forth; issue, as from a source. *v.t.* [Rare], to send forth; emit. —*SYN.* see **rise.**

em·a·na·tion (em′ə-nā′shən), *n.* 1. an emanating; coming forth. something that comes forth from a source; thing emitted. 3. in *chemistry*, a gas given off by some radioactive substance: abbreviated **Em.**

em·a·na·tive (em′ə-nā′tiv), *adj.* emanating or tending to emanate having to do with emanation.

e·man·ci·pate (i-man′sə-pāt′), *v.t.* [EMANCIPATED (-id), EMANCIPATING], [< L. *emancipatus*, pp. of *emancipare; e-*, out + *mancipare*, to deliver up or make over as property, by means of a formal act called *mancipium* < *manceps*, purchaser, contractor < *manus*, the hand + *capere*, to take], 1. to set free (a slave, etc.); release from bondage. 2. to free from restraint or influence, as of convention. 3. in *law*, to release (a child) from a father's control: used especially in Roman law. —*SYN.* see **free.**

e·man·ci·pa·tion (i-man′sə-pā′shən), *n.* [L. *emancipatio;* see EMANCIPATE], a setting free or being set free from servitude, bondage, or restraint.

Emancipation Proclamation, a proclamation issued by President Lincoln in September, 1862, effective January 1, 1863, freeing the slaves in all territory still at war with the Union.

e·man·ci·pa·tor (i-man′sə-pā′tẽr), *n.* [LL.], a person who emancipates.

e·man·ci·pa·to·ry (i-man′sə-pə-tôr′i, i-man′sə-pə-tō′ri), *adj.* emancipating or serving to emancipate.

E·man·u·el (i-man′ū-əl, i-man′ū-el′), a masculine name: see **Emmanuel.**

e·mar·gi·nate (i-mär′jə-nit, i-mär′jə-nāt′), *adj.* [L. *emarginatus;* see E- & MARGINATE], having a notched margin or tip, as some leaves or wings: see **leaf,** illus.

e·mar·gi·nat·ed (i-mär′jə-nā′tid), *adj.* emarginate.

e·mas·cu·late (i-mas′kyoo-lāt′), *v.t.* [EMASCULATED (-id), EMASCULATING], [< L. *emasculatus*, pp. of *emasculare* < *e-*, out + *masculus*, male], 1. to remove the testicles of, so as to deprive of the power to reproduce; castrate; hence, 2. to weaken; destroy the strength or vigor of: as, the novel was *emasculated* by censorship. *adj.* (i-mas′kyoo-lit), deprived of virility, strength, or vigor; effeminate.

e·mas·cu·la·tion (i-mas′kyoo-lā′shən), *n.* an emasculating or being emasculated.

e·mas·cu·la·tive (i-mas′kyoo-lā′tiv), *adj.* that tends to emasculate; emasculatory.

e·mas·cu·la·tor (i-mas′kyoo-lā′tẽr), *n.* a person or thing that emasculates.

e·mas·cu·la·to·ry (i-mas′kyoo-lə-tôr′i, i-mas′kyoo-lə-tō′ri), *adj.* emasculating; depriving of vigor.

em·balm (im-bäm′), *v.t.* [ME. *enbaumen;* OFr. *embaumer;* see EN- & BALM], 1. to keep (a dead body) from decaying by treating it with various chemicals, usually after removing the viscera, etc. 2. to preserve in memory. 3. to perfume; make fragrant.

em·balm·ment (im-bäm′mənt), *n.* an embalming or being embalmed.

em·bank (im-baŋk′), *v.t.* to protect, support, or enclose with a bank or banks of earth, rubble, etc.

em·bank·ment (im-baŋk′mənt), *n.* 1. the act or process of embanking. 2. a bank (of earth, rubble, etc.) used to keep back water, hold up a roadway, etc.

em·bar (em-bär′), *v.t.* [Fr. *embarrer* < *en-* (see EN-) + *barre* (see BAR)], 1. to bar in; confine; imprison. 2. to stop; arrest.

em·bar·go (im-bär′gō), *n.* [*pl.* EMBARGOES (-gōz)], [Sp. < *embargar;* LL. **imbarricare* < L. *in*, in, on + *barra*, a bar], 1. a government order prohibiting the entry or departure of commercial ships at its ports, especially as a war measure. 2. any restriction imposed on commerce by law; especially, a prohibition of trade in a particular commodity. 3. restriction; restraint; prohibition. *v.t.* to put an embargo upon.

em·bark (im-bärk′), *v.t.* [Fr. *embarquer* < L. *in*, in + LL. *barca*, small boat, bark], 1. to put aboard ship. 2. to take aboard: said of a ship. 3. to engage (a person) or invest (money, etc.) in an enterprise. *v.i.* 1. to go aboard a ship; hence, 2. to begin a journey. 3. to engage in an enterprise.

em·bar·ka·tion, em·bar·ca·tion (em′bär-kā′shən), *n.* [Fr. *embarcation*], an embarking.

em·bark·ment (im-bärk′mənt), *n.* an embarking.

‡em·bar·ras des ri·chesses (än′bå′rä′ dā′ rē′shes′), [Fr.], literally, an embarrassment of wealth (of good things); hence, too much to choose from.

em·bar·rass (im-bar′əs), *v.t.* [Fr. *embarrasser*, lit., to encumber, obstruct; It. *imbarazzare*, to embarrass < *im-* (L. *in*), in + LL. *barra*, a bar], 1. to cause to feel self-conscious, confused, and ill at ease; disconcert; fluster. 2. to hinder; impede; cause difficulties to. 3. to cause to be in debt; cause financial difficulties to. 4. to complicate; make more difficult.

SYN.—to **embarrass** is to cause to feel ill at ease so as to result in a loss of composure (*embarrassed* by their compliments); **abash** implies a sudden loss of self-confidence and a growing feeling of shame or inadequacy (I stood *abashed* at his rebukes); **discomfit** implies a frustration of plans or expectations and often connotes a resultant feeling of discomposure or humiliation; to **disconcert** is to cause to lose quickly one's self-possession so as to result in confusion or mental disorganization (his interruptions were *disconcerting*); **rattle** and **faze** are colloquial equivalents for **disconcert,** but the former emphasizes emotional agitation, and the latter is most commonly used in negative constructions (danger does not *faze* him).—*ANT.* compose, assure.

em·bar·rass·ing (im-bar′əs-iŋ), *adj.* [ppr. of *embarrass*], that embarrasses.

em·bar·rass·ment (im-bar′əs-mənt), *n.* 1. an embarrassing or being embarrassed. 2. a thing that embarrasses.

em·bas·sa·dor (im-bas′ə-dẽr), *n.* ambassador.

em·bas·sage (em′bə-sij), *n.* [Archaic], embassy.

em·bas·sy (em′bə-si), *n.* [*pl.* EMBASSIES (-siz)], [earlier *ambassy;* OFr. *ambassée;* It. *ambasciata;* Pr. *ambaisada* < **ambaisa* or ML. *ambactia*, mission < L. *ambactus*, vassal; Goth. *andbahts*, servant; see AMBASSADOR], 1. the position, functions, or business of an ambassador. 2. the sending of ambassadors. 3. the official residence or offices of an ambassador in a foreign country: also called *legation.* 4. an ambassador and his staff. 5. a person or group sent on an official mission to a foreign government. 6. any important or official mission, errand, or message.

em·bat·tle (em-bat'ʼl), ***v.t.*** [EMBATTLED (-'ld), EMBATTLING], [ME. *enbatailen;* see EN- & BATTLEMENT], to provide with battlements; build battlements on.

em·bat·tle (em-bat'ʼl), ***v.t.*** [EMBATTLED (-'ld), EMBATTLING], [ME. *embatailen;* OFr. *embataillier* < *en-* (L. *in*), in + *bataille;* see BATTLE], 1. [Rare, except in pp.], to prepare, array, or set in line for battle. 2. to fortify.

em·bay (em-bā'), ***v.t.*** 1. to put or force (a boat, etc.) into a bay for protection or shelter. 2. to shut in; enclose or surround, as in a bay. 3. to form (a shore) into bays.

em·bay·ment (em-bā'mənt), ***n.*** 1. a forming into a bay. 2. a bay or a formation resembling a bay.

em·bed (im-bed'), ***v.t.*** [EMBEDDED (-id), EMBEDDING], 1. to set (flowers, etc.) in earth. 2. to set or fix firmly in a surrounding mass: as, the knife was *embedded* in the wood. 3. to fix in the mind, memory, etc.

em·bel·lish (im-bel'ish), ***v.t.*** [ME. *enbelisen* < base of OFr. *embellir* < *em-* (L. *in*) + *bel* < L. *bellus,* beautiful], 1. to improve the appearance of; decorate; ornament; adorn. 2. to improve (a story, etc.) by adding details, often of a fictitious kind; touch up. —***SYN.*** see **adorn.**

em·bel·lish·ment (im-bel'ish-mənt), ***n.*** 1. an embellishing or being embellished; ornamentation. 2. something that embellishes; specifically, *a*) an ornament; decoration. *b*) a detail or touch, often fictitious, added to improve a story, etc.

em·ber (em'bẽr), ***n.*** [ME. *emer, eimer* & (with intrusive *-b-*) *eymbre* < AS. *æmerge* influenced by cognate ON. *eimyrja;* akin to Dan. *emmer,* G. dial. *ammer,* glowing ashes; AS. *æmerge* < *æm-* (akin to ON. *eimr,* steam, white smoke) + *-yrge* (akin to ON. *ysja,* fire) < IE. base **eus-,* to burn, as also in L. *urere,* to burn], 1. a glowing piece of coal, wood, peat, etc. from a fire; especially, such a piece smoldering among ashes. 2. *pl.* the smoldering remains of a fire; ashes with glowing pieces of coal, etc. still among them.

em·ber (em'bẽr), ***adj.*** [ME. (southeastern dial.) *embyr-,* in *embyr-dayes,* etc.; AS. *ymbren,* lit., a coming around < *ymbrene, ymbryne,* circuit, revolution < *ymb,* round (akin to *ambi-*) + *ryne,* a running (< base of *run*)], designating or of three days (called *Ember days*) set aside for prayer and fasting in a specified week of each of the four seasons of the year: observed in the Roman Catholic, Anglican, and certain other churches.

em·bez·zle (im-bez'ʼl), ***v.t.*** [EMBEZZLED (-'ld), EMBEZZLING], [Anglo-Fr. *enbesiler;* OFr. *embesillier* < *en-* (see EN-) + *besillier,* to destroy], to steal (money, etc. entrusted to one's care); take by fraud for one's own use.

em·bez·zle·ment (im-bez'ʼl-mənt), ***n.*** an embezzling; theft or fraudulent appropriation of money, etc. entrusted to one's care.

em·bit·ter (im-bit'ẽr), ***v.t.*** 1. to make bitter; make resentful or morose. 2. to make more bitter; exacerbate; aggravate.

em·bit·ter·ment (im-bit'ẽr-mənt), ***n.*** an embittering or being embittered.

em·blaze (em-blāz'), ***v.t.*** [EMBLAZED (-blāzd'), EMBLAZING], [*em-* + *blaze* (a flame)], 1. to light up; illuminate. 2. to set on fire; kindle.

em·blaze (em-blāz'), ***v.t.*** [EMBLAZED (-blāzd'), EMBLAZING], [*em-* + *blaze* (to proclaim)], to emblazon.

em·bla·zon (em-blā'z'n), ***v.t.*** [see BLAZON], 1. to decorate (*with* coats of arms, etc.); adorn. 2. to display brilliantly; decorate with bright colors; make resplendent. 3. to spread the fame of; praise; celebrate; extol.

em·bla·zon·ment (em-blā'z'n-mənt), ***n.*** 1. an emblazoning or being emblazoned. 2. a thing emblazoned.

em·bla·zon·ry (em-blā'z'n-ri), ***n.*** [*pl.* EMBLAZONRIES (-riz)], 1. heraldic decoration; emblazoning. 2. any brilliant decoration or display.

em·blem (em'bləm), ***n.*** [orig., inlaid work; OFr. *embleme;* L. *emblema,* inlaid work; Gr. *emblēma,* insertion < *emballein* < *en-,* in + *ballein,* to throw, put], 1. formerly, a picture with a motto or verses, allegorically suggesting some moral truth, etc. 2. a visible symbol of a thing, idea, class of people, etc.; object or representation that stands for or suggests something else: as, the cross is an *emblem* of Christianity. 3. a sign, badge, or device. ***v.t.*** [Rare], to emblematize.

em·blem·at·ic (em'blə-mat'ik), ***adj.*** of, containing, or serving as an emblem; symbolic.

em·blem·at·i·cal (em'blə-mat'i-k'l), ***adj.*** emblematic.

em·blem·at·i·cal·ly (em'blə-mat'i-k'l-i, em'blə-mat'ikli), ***adv.*** by means of an emblem.

em·blem·a·tist (em-blem'ə-tist), ***n.*** a person who makes or designs emblems.

em·blem·a·tize (em-blem'ə-tīz'), ***v.t.*** [EMBLEMATIZED (-tīzd'), EMBLEMATIZING], 1. to be an emblem of; symbolize. 2. to represent by or as by an emblem.

em·ble·ments (em'blə-mənts), ***n.pl.*** [OFr. *emblaement, sing.* < *emblaer* (Fr. *emblaver*); LL. *imbladare,* to sow with grain < L. *in,* in + *bladum,* grain], in *law,* 1. growing crops. 2. the profits from such crops.

em·bod·i·ment (im-bod'i-mənt), ***n.*** 1. an embodying or being embodied. 2. that in which some idea, quality, etc. is embodied; concrete expression or incarnation of some idea, quality, etc.: as, she is the *embodiment* of virtue. 3. anything embodied.

em·bod·y (im-bod'i), ***v.t.*** [EMBODIED (-id), EMBODYING], 1. to give bodily form to; make corporeal; incarnate. 2. to give definite, tangible, or visible form to; make concrete: as, his speech *embodied* democratic ideals. 3. to collect and include (material) in a book, system, statute, etc. 4. to make (something) part of an organized whole; incorporate: as, our ideas are *embodied* in the committee's report.

em·bold·en (im-bōl'd'n), ***v.t.*** [*em-* + *bold* + *-en*], to give courage to; cause to be bold or bolder.

em·bo·lec·to·my (em'bə-lek'tə-mi), ***n.*** the removal of an embolus by surgery.

em·bol·ic (em-bol'ik), ***adj.*** 1. of or caused by embolism or an embolus. 2. in *embryology,* pushing or growing inward, as an invagination.

em·bo·lism (em'bə-liz'm), ***n.*** [LL. *embolismus;* Gr. *embolismos,* intercalary < *embolos;* see EMBOLUS], 1. the insertion of a day or other period of time into a calendar, as in leap year; intercalation. 2. the time intercalated. 3. in *medicine, a*) the obstruction of a blood vessel by an embolus too large to pass through it. *b*) loosely, an embolus.

em·bo·lus (em'bə-ləs), ***n.*** [*pl.* EMBOLI (-lī')], [L.; Gr. *embolos,* anything put in, wedge < *emballein* < *en-,* in + *ballein,* to throw, cast], any foreign matter, as a blood clot or air bubble, carried in the blood stream.

‡**em·bon·point** (än'bōn'pwan'), ***n.*** [Fr.; OFr. *en bon point,* lit., in good condition], stoutness; corpulence.

em·bos·om (em-booz'əm, em-boo'zəm), ***v.t.*** 1. to take to one's bosom; embrace; cherish. 2. to enclose protectively; surround; shelter.

em·boss (im-bôs', im-bos'), ***v.t.*** [OFr. *embosser;* see EN- & BOSS (raised ornament)], 1. to decorate or cover with designs, patterns, etc. raised above the surface. 2. to carve, raise, or print (a design, etc.) so that it is raised above the surface; raise in relief. 3. to embellish; ornament.

em·boss·ment (im-bôs'mənt, im-bos'mənt), ***n.*** 1. an embossing or being embossed. 2. something embossed; figure or design carved or molded in relief. 3. a bulge.

em·bou·chure (om'boo-shoor'; Fr. än'boo'shür'), ***n.*** [Fr. < *emboucher,* to put into the mouth; ML. **imbuccare* < L. *in,* in + *bucca,* the cheek], 1. the mouth of a river. 2. the opening out of a river valley into flat ground. 3. in *music, a*) the mouthpiece of a wind instrument. *b*) the way of applying the lips and tongue to the mouthpiece of a wind instrument.

em·bow (em-bō'), ***v.t.*** [Late ME. **enbowe,* inferred < *enbowed, adj.*], [Archaic except in pp.], to bend into the form of an arch or bow: as, a dolphin *embowed* on the shield.

em·bow·el (em-bou'əl, em-boul'), ***v.t.*** [EMBOWELED or EMBOWELLED (-əld, -bould'), EMBOWELING or EMBOWELLING], [OFr. *enboweler,* altered < *esboueler* < *es-* (L. *ex*), out of + *bouel,* bowel], 1. [Rare], to disembowel. 2. [*em-* + *bowel*], [Obs.], to put deep; embed.

em·bow·er (em-bou'ẽr), ***v.t.*** to enclose or shelter in or as in a bower.

em·brace (im-brās'), ***v.t.*** [EMBRACED (-brāst'), EMBRACING], [ME. *embracen;* OFr. *embracier* < LL. **imbrachiare* < L. *im-,* in + *brachium,* an arm], 1. to clasp in the arms, usually as an expression of affection or desire; hug. 2. to accept readily; avail oneself of: as, he *embraced* the opportunity. 3. to take up; enter upon; adopt: as, he *embraced* a new profession. 4. to encircle; surround; enclose. 5. to include; comprise; contain. 6. to take in mentally; perceive: as, his glance *embraced* the scene. ***v.i.*** to clasp or hug one another in the arms. ***n.*** an embracing; hug. —***SYN.*** see **include.**

em·brace (em-brās'), ***v.t.*** [EMBRACED (-brāst'), EMBRACING], [OFr. *embraser,* to set on fire, incite, instigate < *en-,* in + *braise,* live coals], in *law,* to try illegally to influence or instruct (a jury).

em·brace·or, em·bra·cer (em-brās'ẽr), ***n.*** [Anglo-Fr. *embraceor;* OFr. *embraseor;* see EMBRACE (to influence)], in *law,* a person guilty of embracery.

em·brac·er·y (em-brās'ẽr-i), ***n.*** [< *embrace* (to influence)], in *law,* an illegal attempt to influence or instruct a jury.

em·branch·ment (em-branch'mənt, em-bränch'mənt), ***n.*** a branching out or off, as of a river, etc.; ramification.

em·bran·gle (em-braŋ'g'l), ***v.t.*** [EMBRANGLED (-g'ld), EMBRANGLING], [*em-* + dial. *brangle,* to wrangle, prob. var. of *wrangle* influenced by Fr. *branler,* to shake, confuse], to entangle; mix up; confuse; perplex.

em·bran·gle·ment (em-braŋ'g'l-mənt), ***n.*** an embrangling or being embrangled.

em·bra·sure (em-brā'zhẽr), *n.* [Fr. < *embraser* (now *ébraser*), to widen an opening < *em-* (L. *in*), in + *braser*, to groove, bevel], 1. an opening (for a door, window, etc.) with the sides slanted so that it is wider on the inside than on the outside. 2. an opening (in a wall or parapet) with the sides slanting outward to increase the angle of fire of a gun.

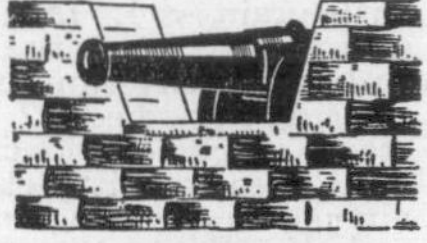
EMBRASURE

em·bro·cate (em'brō-kāt'), *v.t.* [EMBROCATED (-id), EMBROCATING], [< ML. *embrocatus*, pp. of *embrocare*, to foment < L. *embrocha*, wet poultice; Gr. *embrochē* < *embrechein* < *en-*, in + *brechein*, to wet], to moisten and rub (a part of the body) with an oil, liniment, etc.

em·bro·ca·tion (em'brō-kā'shən), *n.* 1. an embrocating. 2. a liquid used in embrocating; liniment or lotion.

em·broi·der (im-broi'dẽr), *v.t.* [OFr. *embroder;* see EN- & BROIDER], 1. to ornament (fabric) with a design in needlework. 2. to make (a design, etc.) on fabric with needlework. 3. to embellish (a story, etc.); add fanciful details to; exaggerate. *v.i.* to do embroidery.

em·broi·der·y (im-broi'dẽr-i), *n.* [*pl.* EMBROIDERIES (-iz)], [ME. *embrouderie* < OFr. *embroder;* see EMBROIDER & -ERY], 1. the art or work of ornamenting fabric with needlework; embroidering. 2. embroidered work or fabric; ornamental needlework. 3. embellishment, as of a story.

em·broil (em-broil'), *v.t.* [Fr. *embrouiller;* see EN- & BROIL (to dispute)], 1. to confuse (affairs, etc.); mix up; muddle; entangle. 2. to cause (a person, government, etc.) to take part in a quarrel or fight; involve.

em·broil·ment (em-broil'mənt), *n.* an embroiling or being embroiled.

em·brown (em-broun'), *v.t.* to make darker in color; make brown or tan.

em·brue (em-brōō'), *v.t.* [EMBRUED (-brōōd'), EMBRUING], to imbrue; wet.

em·bry- (em'bri), embryo-.

em·bry·ec·to·my (em'bri-ek'tə-mi), *n.* the surgical removal of an embryo, especially in cases of pregnancy outside of the uterus.

em·bry·o (em'bri-ō'), *n.* [*pl.* EMBRYOS (-ōz')], [ML. < Gr. *embryon*, embryo, fetus, thing newly born; neut. of *embryos*, growing in < *en-*, in + *bryein*, to swell, be full], 1. an animal in the earliest stages of its development in the uterus: the human organism in the first three months after conception is called an *embryo*, thereafter a *fetus*. 2. *a*) an early or undeveloped stage of something. *b*) anything in such a stage. 3. the rudimentary plant contained in a seed. *adj.* embryonic.

em·bry·o- (em'bri-ō, em'bri-ə), a combining form meaning *embryo, embryonic*, as in *embryology*.

em·bry·o·gen·e·sis (em'bri-ō-jen'ə-sis), *n.* embryogeny.

em·bry·o·ge·net·ic (em'bri-ō-jə-net'ik), *adj.* of embryogeny.

em·bry·og·e·ny (em'bri-oj'ə-ni), *n.* [*embryo-* + *-geny*], 1. the formation and development of the embryo. 2. the study of this.

em·bry·o·log·ic (em'bri-ə-loj'ik), *adj.* embryological.

em·bry·o·log·i·cal (em'bri-ə-loj'i-k'l), *adj.* of embryology.

em·bry·ol·o·gist (em'bri-ol'ə-jist), *n.* a specialist in embryology.

em·bry·ol·o·gy (em'bri-ol'ə-ji), *n.* [*embryo-* + *-logy*], the branch of biology dealing with the formation and development of embryos: abbreviated **embryol.**

em·bry·on (em'bri-on'), *n.* [Mod.L.; see EMBRYO], [Rare], an embryo: used technically.

em·bry·on·ic (em'bri-on'ik), *adj.* 1. of or like an embryo; hence, 2. in an early stage; undeveloped; rudimentary.

embryo sac, in *botany*, a thin-walled cell in the central part of a seed, where the egg undergoes development after fertilization.

em·cee (em'sē'), *v.t.* [EMCEED (-sēd'), EMCEEING], [< *M.C.*, Master of Ceremonies], [Slang], to act as master of ceremonies for (a radio program, etc.). *n.* [Slang], a master of ceremonies.

Em·den (em'dən), *n.* a seaport in northwestern Hanover, Germany: pop., 34,000.

e·meer (ə-mêr'), *n.* an emir.

e·meer·ate (ə-mêr'it), *n.* an emirate.

Em·e·line (em'ə-līn', em'ə-lēn'), a feminine name: also spelled **Emmeline:** see **Emily.**

e·mend (i-mend'), *v.t.* [L. *emendare*, to correct < *e-*, out + *menda*, a fault, blemish], to correct or improve; specifically, to make scholarly corrections in (a literary text, etc.); suggest a different reading for (a passage, etc.).

e·men·date (ē'mən-dāt'), *v.t.* [EMENDATED (-id), EMENDATING], [< L. *emendatus*, pp. of *emendare*], to emend (a text).

e·men·da·tion (ē'men-dā'shən, em'ən-dā'shən), *n.* [L. *emendatio* < pp. of *emendare*], 1. an emending. 2. correction or alteration made in a literary text, etc., as in an attempt to restore the original reading.

e·men·da·tor (ē'mən-dā'tẽr, em'ən-dā'tẽr), *n.* [L.], a person who emendates.

e·mend·a·to·ry (i-men'də-tôr'i, i-men'də-tō'ri), *adj.* having to do with emendation; emending.

em·er·ald (em'ẽr-əld, em'rəld), *n.* [ME. *emeraude;* OFr. *esmeraude, esmeralde;* LL. *smaraldus;* L. *smaragdus;* Gr. *smaragdos, maragdos;* prob. via Prakrit *maragada;* ult. < Heb. *bāreqeth*], 1. a bright-green, transparent precious stone; green variety of beryl. 2. a similar variety of corundum. 3. bright green. 4. in *printing*, a size of type between minion and nonpareil, about 6 1/2 point. This line is in emerald. *adj.* 1. bright-green. 2. made of or with an emerald or emeralds.

Emerald Isle, Ireland: probably so called, with reference to the green of the landscape, from Drennan's song "Erin" (1795).

e·merge (i-mũrj'), *v.i.* [EMERGED (-mũrjd'), EMERGING], [L. *emergere; e-*, out + *mergere*, to dip, immerse], 1. to rise from or as from a fluid. 2. to come forth into view; become visible, apparent, or known.

e·mer·gence (i-mũr'jəns), *n.* [LL. *emergentia* < ppr. of *emergere*], 1. an emerging. 2. an outgrowth from beneath the outer layer of a plant, as a rose thorn.

e·mer·gen·cy (i-mũr'jən-si), *n.* [*pl.* EMERGENCIES (-siz)], [orig. sense, emergence; see EMERGENCE], a sudden, generally unexpected occurrence or set of circumstances demanding immediate action. *adj.* for use in case of sudden necessity: as, an *emergency* brake.

***SYN.*—emergency** refers to any sudden or unforeseen situation that requires immediate action (the flood had created an *emergency*); **exigency** may refer either to such a situation or to the need or urgency arising from it (the *exigencies* of the moment require drastic action); **contingency** is used of an emergency regarded as remotely possible in the future (prepare for any *contingency*); **crisis** refers to an event regarded as a turning point which will decisively determine an outcome (an economic *crisis*); **strait** (or **straits**) refers to a trying situation from which it is difficult to extricate oneself (the loss left them in dire *straits*).

e·mer·gent (i-mũr'jənt), *adj.* 1. emerging. 2. arising unexpectedly or as a new development.

e·mer·i·tus (i-mer'ə-təs), *adj.* [L., having served one's time as a soldier; pp. of *emereri*, to serve out one's time; *e-*, out + *mereri*, to serve, earn, merit], retired from active service, usually for age, but retaining one's rank or title: as, professor *emeritus*.

e·mersed (i-mũrst'), *adj.* [L. *emersus;* see EMERGE], having emerged above the surface; specifically, standing out above the water, as the leaves of certain aquatic plants.

e·mer·sion (ē-mũr'shən, ē-mũr'zhən), *n.* [< L. *emersus*, pp. of *emergere*], an emerging; emergence.

Em·er·son, Ralph Wal·do (wôl'dō em'ẽr-s'n), 1803–1882; American essayist, philosopher, and poet.

Em·er·y (em'ẽr-i), [prob. by way of OFr. *Aimeri* < OHG. *Almarich, Amalrich*, lit., work ruler < **amal-*, work (in battle) + **rich*, ruler, leader (akin to L. *rex*, king)], a masculine name: equivalents, L. *Almericus*, G. *Emmerich*, It. *Amerigo*: also spelled **Emmery, Emory.**

em·er·y (em'ẽr-i, em'ri), *n.* [*pl.* EMERIES (-iz, -riz)], [Fr. *émeri;* OFr. *emeril;* LL. *smericulum;* It. *smeriglio* < Gr. *smēris, smyris*, emery; IE. base **smer-*, to smear (cf. SMEAR)], a dark, very hard, coarse variety of corundum used for grinding, polishing, etc.

emery board, a small, flat stick coated with powdered emery, used as a manicuring instrument.

emery cloth, cloth coated with a mixture of powdered emery and glue, used for polishing and cleaning metal.

em·e·sis (em'ə-sis), *n.* [Mod.L.; Gr. *emesis;* see EMETIC], vomiting.

e·met·ic (i-met'ik), *adj.* [L. *emeticus;* Gr. *emetikos* < *emeein*, to vomit; IE. base **wemē-*, to vomit], causing vomiting. *n.* a medicine or other substance that causes vomiting.

em·e·tin (em'ə-tin), *n.* emetine.

em·e·tine (em'ə-tēn', em'ə-tin), *n.* [*emetic* + *-ine*], an alkaloid, $C_{29}H_{40}N_2O_4$, obtained from ipecac root, used as an expectorant and an emetic.

e·meu (ē'mū), *n.* an emu.

‡é·meute (ā'möt'; Eng. i-mūt'), *n.* [Fr. < pp. of *émouvoir*, to agitate, stir up; L. *emovere*, to agitate; *e-*, out + *movere*, to move], a popular uprising; riot.

E.M.F., e.m.f., EMF, emf, electromotive force.

-e·mi·a (ē'mi-ə), [Mod.L. < Gr. *-aimia* < *haima*, blood], a suffix meaning *a* (specified) *condition* or *disease of the blood*, as in *leukemia:* also spelled **-aemia.**

em·i·grant (em'ə-grənt, em'ə-grant'), *adj.* [L. *emigrans*, ppr. of *emigrare*], 1. emigrating. 2. of emigrants or emigration. *n.* a person who emigrates.

em·i·grate (em'ə-grāt'), *v.i.* [EMIGRATED (-id), EMIGRATING], [< L. *emigratus*, pp. of *emigrare*, to move away, depart from a place; *e-*, out + *migrare*, to move, depart], to leave one country or region to settle in another: opposed to *immigrate*. —***SYN.*** see **migrate.**

em·i·gra·tion (em'ə-grā'shən), *n.* 1. an emigrating. 2. emigrants collectively; body of emigrants.

‡é·mi·gré (ā'mē'grā'; Eng. em'ə-grā'), *n.* [*pl.* ÉMIGRÉS (-grā'; Eng. -grāz')], [Fr.; pp. of *émigrer;* L. *emigrare;* see EMIGRATE], 1. an emigrant. 2. a Royalist who fled from France during the French Revolution. 3. an opponent of the Soviet regime who fled from the Soviet

Union after the revolution of 1918. —*SYN.* see **alien.**

E·mil (ā'm'l, ē'm'l, em''l), [G. < Fr. *Émile* < L. *Aemilius*, name of a Roman gens < L. *aemulus;* see EMULATE], a masculine name: feminine, *Emily.*

E·mil·i·a (i-mil'i-ə, i-mil'yə), a feminine name: see **Emily.** *n.* (e-mēl'yä), a department of northern Italy.

Em·i·ly (em''l-i), [Fr. *Émilie;* L. *Aemilia*, fem. of *Aemilius;* see EMIL], a feminine name: variants, *Emilia, Emeline, Emmeline.*

em·i·nence (em'ə-nəns), *n.* [L. *eminentia* < *eminens*, excellent, prominent, ppr. of *eminere*, to stand out, project; *e-*, out + **minere*, to project < IE. base **men-*, to project; hence akin to L. *mons* (see MOUNT)], 1. a high or lofty place, thing, etc., as a hill. 2. superiority in rank, position, character, achievement, etc.; greatness; celebrity. 3. [E-], in the *Roman Catholic Church*, a title of honor given to a cardinal. 4. in *anatomy*, a raised area, usually on the surface of a bone.

em·i·nen·cy (em'ə-nən-si), *n.* [*pl.* EMINENCIES (-siz)], 1. [Obs.], eminence. 2. prominence; importance.

em·i·nent (em'ə-nənt), *adj.* [L. *eminens;* see EMINENCE], 1. rising above other things or places; high; lofty. 2. projecting; prominent; protruding. 3. standing high by comparison with others; renowned; exalted; distinguished. 4. outstanding; remarkable; noteworthy: as, a man of *eminent* good sense. —*SYN.* see **famous.**

eminent domain, in *law*, the right of a government to take, or to authorize the taking of, private property for public use, just compensation being given to the owner.

em·i·nent·ly (em'ə-nənt-li), *adv.* in an eminent manner or degree; notably; conspicuously.

e·mir (ə-mêr'), *n.* [Ar. *amīr, emīr*, commander, ruler, prince], 1. an Arabian ruler, prince, or military commander. 2. a title given Mohammed's descendants through his daughter Fatima. 3. a Turkish honorary title. Also spelled **emeer.**

e·mir·ate (ə-mêr'it), *n.* the rule or jurisdiction of an emir.

em·is·sar·y (em'ə-ser'i), *n.* [*pl.* EMISSARIES (-iz)], [L. *emissarius* < pp. of *emittere;* see EMIT], a person or agent, especially a secret agent, sent on a specific mission. *adj.* of, or serving as, an emissary or emissaries.

e·mis·sion (i-mish'ən), *n.* [L. *emissio* < pp. of *emittere*], 1. an emitting; issuance. 2. something emitted; discharge. 3. in *medicine*, a discharge of fluid from the body; especially, an involuntary discharge of semen.

e·mis·sive (i-mis'iv), *adj.* [< L. *emissus*, pp. of *emittere;* + *-ive*], emitting or having the power to emit.

em·is·siv·i·ty (em'ə-siv'ə-ti), *n.* 1. the capacity or tendency to emit. 2. the rate of emission.

e·mit (i-mit'), *v.t.* [EMITTED (-id), EMITTING], [L. *emittere; e-*, out + *mittere*, to send], 1. to send out; give forth; discharge: as, geysers *emit* water. 2. to utter (sounds, etc.). 3. to issue (paper money, etc.); put into circulation.

Em·ma (em'ə), [G. < *Erma* < names beginning with *Erm-* (e.g., *Ermenhilde*); see IRMA], a feminine name.

Em·man·u·el (i-man'ū-əl), [Gr. *Emmanouēl;* Heb. *'immānūēl*, lit., God with us], a masculine name: variants, *Immanuel, Manuel:* also spelled **Emanuel.** *n.* the Messiah: see **Immanuel.**

Em·me·line (em'ə-lin', em'ə-lēn'), a feminine name: also spelled **Emeline:** see **Emily.**

em·men·a·gogue (i-men'ə-gôg', i-mē'nə-gog'), *n.* [< Gr. *emmēna, n.pl.*, menses (< *en-*, in + *mēn*, month); + *-agogue*], in *medicine*, anything used to stimulate the menstrual flow.

Em·mer·y (em'ēr-i), a masculine name: see **Emery.**

em·met (em'it), *n.* [see ANT], [Archaic], an ant.

Em·met, Robert (em'it), 1778–1803; Irish nationalist; hanged after leading an unsuccessful rising against the British.

em·me·tro·pi·a (em'i-trō'pi-ə), *n.* [Mod.L. < Gr. *emmetros*, in measure, fit < *en-*, in + *metron*, measure; + *-opia*], the condition of normal refraction of light in the eye, in which vision is perfect.

em·me·trop·ic (em'ə-trop'ik), *adj.* of or characterized by emmetropia.

Em·my (em'i), *n.* [Slang], any of the statuettes awarded annually in the United States for special achievement in the television industry.

EmnE., EMnE., Early Modern English.

e·mol·li·ent (i-mol'yənt, i-mol'i-ənt), *adj.* [L. *emolliens*, ppr. of *emollire*, to soften; *e-*, out + *mollire*, to soften < *mollis*, soft], softening; soothing. *n.* a preparation or medicine that has a softening or soothing effect on surface tissues.

e·mol·u·ment (i-mol'yoo-mənt), *n.* [L. *emolumentum*, the result of exertion, gain, profit, advantage < *emolere*, to grind out; *e-*, out + *molere*, to grind], gain from employment or position; payment received for work; salary; wages; fees. —*SYN.* see **wage.**

Em·or·y (em'ēr-i), a masculine name: see **Emery.**

e·mote (i-mōt'), *v.i.* [EMOTED (-id), EMOTING], [< *emotion*, by analogy with *devote*, etc.], [Colloq.], to conduct oneself in an emotional or theatrical manner; behave as though acting an emotional role: often used humorously.

e·mo·tion (i-mō'shən), *n.* [Fr.; prob. after *motion* < pp. of L. *emovere*, to move out, stir up, agitate; *e-*, out + *movere*, to move], 1. strong, generalized feeling; psychical excitement. 2. any specific feeling; any of various complex reactions with both psychical and physical manifestations, as love, hate, fear, anger, etc. —*SYN.* see **feeling.**

e·mo·tion·al (i-mō'shən-'l), *adj.* 1. of emotion or the emotions. 2. showing emotion. 3. easily aroused to emotion; quick to weep, be angry, etc. 4. appealing to the emotions; moving people to tears, anger, etc.

e·mo·tion·al·ism (i-mō'shən-'l-iz'm), *n.* 1. emotional character. 2. the tendency to be emotional or to show emotion quickly and easily. 3. display of emotion. 4. an appeal to emotion, especially to sway an audience to some belief.

e·mo·tion·al·ist (i-mō'shən-'l-ist), *n.* 1. a very emotional person. 2. a person who uses or relies on emotion or emotional effects, as in oratory, art, etc.

e·mo·tion·al·i·ty (i-mō'shən-al'ə-ti), *n.* the quality or state of being emotional.

e·mo·tion·al·ize (i-mō'shən-'l-īz'), *v.t.* [EMOTIONALIZED (-īzd'), EMOTIONALIZING], to treat, present, or interpret in an emotional way; make emotional.

e·mo·tion·al·ly (i-mō'shən-'l-i), *adv.* 1. in an emotional manner. 2. with reference to the emotions.

e·mo·tive (i-mō'tiv), *adj.* 1. characterized by, expressing, or producing emotion. 2. relating to the emotions.

Emp., 1. Emperor. 2. Empire. 3. Empress.

em·pale (im-pāl'), *v.t.* [EMPALED (-pāld'), EMPALING], to impale.

em·pan·el (im-pan''l), *v.t.* [EMPANELED or EMPANELLED (-'ld), EMPANELING or EMPANELLING], 1. to enter the name or names of on a jury list. 2. to choose (a jury) from such a list. Also spelled **impanel.**

em·path·ic (em-path'ik), *adj.* of or characterized by empathy.

em·pa·thy (em'pə-thi), *n.* [< Gr. *empatheia*, affection, passion < *en-*, in + *pathos*, feeling; used as translation of G. *einfühlung* (< *ein-*, in + *fühlung*, feeling)], 1. the projection of one's own personality into the personality of another in order to understand him better; intellectual identification of oneself with another. 2. the projection of one's own personality into an object, with the attribution to the object of one's own emotions, responses, etc.: also called *pathetic fallacy.*

Em·ped·o·cles (em-ped'ə-klēz'), *n.* Greek philosopher; 5th century B.C.

‡**em·pen·nage** (än'pe'nȧzh'; Eng. em'pi-nij), *n.* [Fr. < *empenner*, to feather an arrow < *em-*, in + *penne*, a feather; see PEN (quill)], the stabilizing tail assembly of an airplane, consisting of vertical and horizontal airfoils, and including the fin, rudder, stabilizer, and elevator.

em·per·or (em'pẽr-ẽr), *n.* [ME. *emperour* < OFr. *empereor, emperere*, lit., ruler of the Holy Roman Empire; L. *imperator*, commander in chief, orig. a title voted to a successful general by the Roman army, then conferred by the senate on Caesar & Augustus, then revived by the Pope at the crowning of Charlemagne (800 A.D.) < pp. of *imperare*, to command < *in-*, in + *parare*, to set in order, prepare], 1. a man who rules an empire: abbreviated **Emp.** (as a title). 2. any of various large butterflies.

em·per·or·ship (em'pẽr-ẽr-ship'), *n.* [*emperor* + *-ship*], the position, rank, or reign of an emperor.

em·per·y (em'pẽr-i), *n.* [*pl.* EMPERIES (-iz)], [ME. *emperie;* OFr. *emperie* < *emperer*, to rule; L. *imperare;* see EMPEROR], [Poetic], 1. the sovereignty of an emperor; empire; hence, 2. broad dominion or authority.

em·pha·sis (em'fə-sis), *n.* [*pl.* EMPHASES (-sēz')], [L. < Gr. *emphasis*, an appearing in, outward appearance < *en-*, in + *phasis*, appearance, information; akin to *phainein*, to show, appear], 1. force of expression, thought, feeling, action, etc.: as, sincerity gives *emphasis* to his contention. 2. special stress given to a syllable, word, phrase, etc. in speaking: abbreviated **emph.** 3. special attention given to something so as to make it stand out; importance; stress; weight: as, too much *emphasis* was placed on athletics.

em·pha·size (em'fə-sīz'), *v.t.* [EMPHASIZED (-sīzd'), EMPHASIZING], to give emphasis to; give special force or prominence to; stress.

em·phat·ic (im-fat'ik), *adj.* [Gr. *emphatikos*], 1. expressed, felt, or done with emphasis. 2. using emphasis in speaking, etc.: abbreviated **emph.** 3. forcible; striking; definite: as, an *emphatic* defeat.

em·phat·i·cal·ly (im-fat'i-k'l-i, im-fat'ik-li), *adv.* in an emphatic manner; with emphasis; forcefully; decidedly.

em·phy·se·ma (em'fi-sē'mə), *n.* [Mod.L.; Gr. *emphysēma*, inflation < *emphysaein*, to inflate, blow in < *en-*, in + *physaein*, to blow], 1. an abnormal swelling of body tissues caused by the accumulation of air; especially, such a swelling of the alveoli or of the tissue connecting the alveoli in the lungs. 2. heaves, a disease of horses.

em·phy·sem·a·tous (em′fi-sem′ə-təs, em′fi-sē′mə-təs), *adj.* 1. of or like emphysema. 2. having emphysema.

em·pire (em′pīr), *n.* [ME. *enpir;* OFr. *empire;* L. *imperium* < *imperare;* see EMPEROR], 1. supreme rule; absolute power or authority; dominion. 2. government by an emperor or empress. 3. the period during which such government prevails. 4. a group of states or territories under one sovereign power; dominion of an emperor or empress. 5. a state uniting many territories and peoples under one ruler. Abbreviated **Emp.** *adj.* (*also* äm-pêr′), [E-], of or characteristic of the first French Empire (1804–1815), under Napoleon; specifically, *a*) designating a style of furniture of this period, characterized by rectangular massiveness, swelling curves, and the use of heavy textiles and bronze ornamentation. *b*) designating a gown fashioned in the style of the period, with a short waist, décolleté bodice, flowing skirt, and short, puffed sleeves.

the Empire, a specified or understood empire; especially, *a*) the British Empire. *b*) the Holy Roman Empire. *c*) the first French Empire, under Napoleon.

Empire Day, May 24, Queen Victoria's birthday, celebrated as a holiday throughout the British Empire.

Empire State, New York State.

em·pir·ic (em-pir′ik), *n.* [L. *empiricus;* Gr. *empeirikos*, experienced < *empeiria*, experience < *en-*, in + *peira*, a trial, experiment], 1. a person who is ignorant of scientific principles and relies solely on practical experience. 2. a person who lacks regular training and proper qualifications; charlatan; quack. *adj.* empirical.

em·pir·i·cal (em-pir′i-k'l), *adj.* [see EMPIRIC], 1. relying or based solely on experiment and observation: as, the *empirical* method. 2. relying or based on practical experience without reference to scientific principles: as, an *empirical* remedy.

em·pir·i·cism (em-pir′ə-siz'm), *n.* 1. experimental method; search for knowledge by observation and experiment. 2. *a*) a disregarding of scientific methods and relying solely on experience; hence, *b*) quackery. 3. in *philosophy*, the theory that sensory experience is the only source of knowledge.

em·pir·i·cist (em-pir′ə-sist), *n.* 1. a person who uses methods of experiment and observation. 2. *a*) a person who disregards or is ignorant of scientific principles and relies solely on practical experience; hence, *b*) a quack. 3. a believer in the philosophical theory of empiricism.

em·place·ment (im-plās′mənt), *n.* [Fr. < *emplacer*, to put in position; see EN- & PLACE], 1. a placing in position; assigning to a location. 2. in *military science*, the prepared position from which a heavy gun is fired.

em·ploy (im-ploi′), *v.t.* [Fr. *employer;* L. *implicare*, to enfold, engage, hence bend attention on < *in-*, in + *plicare*, to fold; cf. IMPLY], 1. to make use of; use. 2. to keep busy or occupied; take up the attention, time, etc. of; devote: as, he *employed* himself in study during his vacation. 3. to provide work and pay for: as, public works *employ* thousands of men. 4. to engage the services or labor of; hire. *n.* the state of being employed; paid service; employment. —***SYN.*** see **use**.

em·ploy·a·ble (im-ploi′ə-b'l), *adj.* that can be employed; specifically, *a*) physically or mentally fit to be hired for work. *b*) meeting the minimum requirements for a specified kind of work or position of employment.

em·ploy·ee, em·ploy·e (im-ploi′ē, em′ploi-ē′), *n.* [Fr. *employé* (fem. *employée*); pp. of *employer*; see EMPLOY], a person hired by another, or by a business firm, etc., to work for wages or salary: also spelled **employé.**

em·ploy·er (im-ploi′ẽr), *n.* [see EMPLOY], 1. a person, business firm, etc. that hires one or more persons to work for wages or salary. 2. a user.

em·ploy·ment (im-ploi′mənt), *n.* 1. an employing or being employed. 2. the thing at which one is employed; work; occupation; profession; job.

em·poi·son (em-poi′z'n), *v.t.* [Fr. *empoisonner;* see EN- & POISON], 1. to make poisonous; taint or corrupt; hence, 2. to embitter; envenom.

Em·po·ri·a (em-pôr′i-ə, em-pō′ri-ə), *n.* a city in eastern Kansas: pop., 18,000.

em·po·ri·um (em-pôr′i-əm, em-pō′ri-əm), *n.* [*pl.* EMPORIUMS (-əmz), EMPORIA (-ə)], [L. < Gr. *emporion*, trading place, mart < *emporios*, pertaining to trade, commerce < *emporos*, traveler < *en-*, in + *poros*, way], 1. a place of commerce; trading center; market place. 2. a large store with a wide variety of things for sale.

em·pow·er (im-pou′ẽr), *v.t.* 1. to give power or authority to; authorize: as, the president is *empowered* to veto legislation. 2. to give ability to; enable; permit: as, science *empowers* men to control natural forces more effectively. Also spelled **impower.**

em·press (em′pris), *n.* [ME. *emperice, emperesse;* OFr. *empereis, emperesse*, fem. of *emperere;* see EMPEROR], 1. the wife of an emperor. 2. a woman ruler of an empire; hence, 3. a woman with great power or influence: as, the *empress* of his heart. Abbreviated **Emp.** (as a title).

‡**em·presse·ment** (äṉ′pres′mäṉ′), *n.* [Fr., eagerness < *s'empresser*, to be eager, hasten; see IMPRESS], effusive regard or cordiality.

em·prise, em·prize (em-prīz′), *n.* [ME. *emprise;* OFr. *emprise, emprinse* < pp. of *emprendre*, to undertake < LL. **imprehendere;* L. *im-*, in + *prehendere*, to take], [Archaic], 1. an enterprise or adventure. 2. prowess or daring: as, knights of great *emprise*.

emp·ti·ly (emp′tə-li), *adv.* in an empty manner; as though empty.

emp·ti·ness (emp′ti-nis), *n.* the quality or condition of being empty.

emp·ty (emp′ti), *adj.* [EMPTIER (-ti-ẽr), EMPTIEST (-ti-ist)], [ME. *emtie* & (with intrusive *-p-*; cf. EMBER) *empti;* AS. *æmettig*, unoccupied, lit., at leisure < *æmetta*, leisure, rest + *-ig* (see -Y); AS. *æmetta* < *æ-*, without, not + base of *mot*, a meeting (cf. MOOT)], 1. containing nothing; having nothing in it. 2. having no one in it; unoccupied; vacant: as, an *empty* house. 3. carrying or bearing nothing; bare. 4. worthless; not substantial; unsatisfying: as, *empty* pleasures. 5. meaningless; insincere; vain: as, *empty* promises. 6. [Colloq.], hungry. *v.t.* [EMPTIED (-tid), EMPTYING], 1. to make empty. 2. *a*) to pour out or remove (the contents) of something. *b*) to transfer (the contents) *into* something else. *v.i.* 1. to become empty. 2. to pour out; discharge: as, the St. Lawrence *empties* into the Atlantic. *n.* [*pl.* EMPTIES (-tiz)], an empty freight car, truck, bottle, etc.

empty of, lacking; without; devoid of.

SYN.—**empty** means having nothing in it (an *empty* box, street, stomach, etc.); **vacant** means lacking that which appropriately or customarily occupies or fills it (a *vacant* apartment, position, etc.); **void**, as discriminated here, specifically stresses complete or vast emptiness (*void* of judgment); **vacuous**, now rare in its physical sense, suggests the emptiness of a vacuum. See also **vain.**—***ANT.*** full.

emp·ty-hand·ed (emp′ti-han′did), *adj.* bringing or carrying away nothing.

emp·ty-head·ed (emp′ti-hed′id), *adj.* frivolous and stupid; silly and ignorant.

em·pur·ple (em-pũr′p'l), *v.t.* to make purple.

em·py·e·ma (em′pi-ē′mə, em′pī-ē′mə), *n.* [*pl.* EMPYEMATA (-ē′mə-tə, -em′ə-tə)], [Mod. L.; Gr. *empyēma* < *empyein*, to suppurate < *en-*, in + *pyon*, pus], the accumulation of pus in a body cavity, especially in the cavity containing the lungs.

em·pyr·e·al (em-pir′i-əl, em′pə-rē′əl, em′pī-rē′əl), *adj.* [LL. *empyrius, empyreus;* Gr. *empyrios*, in fire < *en-*, in + *pyr*, a fire], of the empyrean; heavenly; sublime.

em·py·re·an (em′pə-rē′ən, em′pī-rē′ən), *n.* [< LL. *empyreus;* see EMPYREAL], 1. the highest heaven; specifically, *a*) among the ancients, the sphere of pure light or fire. *b*) among Christian poets, the abode of God. 2. the sky; the celestial vault; firmament. *adj.* empyreal.

e·mu (ē′mū), *n.* [prob. < Port. *ema*, a crane], a large, nonflying Australian bird, like the ostrich but smaller: also spelled **emeu.**

EMU (6 ft. high)

E.M.U., e.m.u., emu, electromagnetic units.

em·u·late (em′yoo-lāt′), *v.t.* [EMULATED (-id), EMULATING], [< L. *aemulatus*, pp. of *aemulari* < *aemulus*, trying to equal or excel], 1. to try to equal or surpass. 2. to rival successfully. *adj.* [Obs.], (em′yoo-lit), ambitious.

em·u·la·tion (em′yoo-lā′shən), *n.* [L. *aemulatio*], 1. an emulating. 2. desire or ambition to equal or surpass. 3. [Obs.], *a*) ambitious rivalry. *b*) envious dislike. —***SYN.*** see **competition.**

em·u·la·tive (em′yoo-lā′tiv), *adj.* of, characterized by, or resulting from emulation.

em·u·la·tor (em′yoo-lā′tẽr), *n.* a person who emulates.

em·u·lous (em′yoo-ləs), *adj.* [L. *aemulus;* see EMULATE], 1. desirous of equaling or surpassing. 2. [Obs.], jealous; envious. 3. emulative. —***SYN.*** see **ambitious.**

e·mul·si·fi·ca·tion (i-mul′sə-fi-kā′shən), *n.* an emulsifying or being emulsified.

e·mul·si·fi·er (i-mul′sə-fī′ẽr), *n.* a substance, as gelatin, gum arabic, etc., for emulsifying a fixed oil.

e·mul·si·fy (i-mul′sə-fī′), *v.t.* & *v.i.* [EMULSIFIED (-fīd′), EMULSIFYING], to form into an emulsion.

e·mul·sion (i-mul′shən), *n.* [Mod. L. *emulsio* < L. *emulsus*, pp. of *emulgere*, to milk or drain out; *e-*, out + *mulgere*, to milk], a fluid, as milk, formed by the suspension of a very finely divided oily or resinous liquid in another liquid; specifically, *a*) in *pharmacy*, a preparation of an oily substance held in suspension in a watery liquid by means of a gummy substance: as, an *emulsion* of cod-liver oil. *b*) in *photography*, a suspension of a salt of silver in gelatin or collodion, used to coat plates and film.

e·mul·sive (i-mul′siv), *adj.* 1. having the nature of an emulsion. 2. capable of emulsifying.
e·munc·to·ry (i-muŋk′tẽr-i), *n.* [*pl.* EMUNCTORIES (-iz)], [LL. *emunctorium*, pair of snuffers < pp. of L. *emungere*, to blow the nose, cleanse; *e-*, out + *mungere*, to blow the nose], any organ or part of the body that gives off waste products, as the kidneys, lungs, and skin. *adj.* giving off waste products; excretory.
en (en), *n.* 1. the letter N, n. 2. in *printing*, a space half the width of an em.
en- (in, en), [ME. *en-*; OFr. *en-*; L. *in-* < prep. *in*, in, into], a prefix, used to form verbs from nouns, adjectives, and other verbs, meaning: 1. *to put into* or *on*, as in *enthrone; to cover* or *wrap with*, as in *enrobe:* prefixed to nouns. 2. *to make, make into* or *like, cause to be*, as in *endanger, enfeeble:* prefixed to nouns or adjectives. 3. *in* or *into*, as in *enclose, enliven:* prefixed to verbs. *En-* often has the force of an intensifier as in *enliven, encourage*. Many words beginning *en-* are also spelled *in-* (e.g., *enquire, inquire*). See also **em-**.
en- (in, en), [Gr. *en-* < prep. *en*, in], a prefix meaning *in*, used chiefly in Greek derivatives, as *endemic*.
-en (ən, ′n), the common form taken by several suffixes, variously used: 1. [ME. *-en, -ien;* AS. *-nian*], to form verbs, usually transitive, meaning: *a) to become* or *cause to be:* added to adjectives, as in *darken, weaken*. *b) to come to have, cause to have:* added to nouns, as in *heighten, hearten, strengthen*. 2. [ME.; AS.], to form adjectives from concrete nouns, meaning *made of*, as in *wooden, woolen*. 3. [ME.; AS.], to form the past participle of strong verbs, as in *risen, written*. 4. [AS. *-an*], to form plurals, as in *children, brethren*. 5. [AS.], to form feminines of nouns, as in *vixen* (AS. *fyxen*). 6. [AS.], to form diminutives, as in *chicken*.
en·a·ble (in-ā′b′l), *v.t.* [ENABLED (-b′ld), ENABLING], 1. to make able; provide with means, opportunity, power, or authority (*to* do something). 2. [Obs.], to make possible or effective.
en·act (in-akt′), *v.t.* 1. to make (a bill, etc.) into a law; pass (a law); decree; ordain. 2. to do; accomplish: usually in the passive, as, the place where the shooting was *enacted*. 3. to represent in or as in a play; act out.
en·ac·tive (in-ak′tiv), *adj.* enacting or having the power to enact.
en·act·ment (in-akt′mənt), *n.* 1. an enacting or being enacted. 2. something enacted, as a law or decree.
en·am·el (i-nam′′l), *n.* [ME. *enamyl;* see the *v.*], 1. a glassy, colored, opaque substance fused to surfaces of metals, glass, and pottery as an ornamental or protective coating. 2. any smooth, hard, glossy coating or surface like enamel. 3. the hard, white, glossy coating of the crowns of teeth: see **tooth**, illus. 4. anything enameled; enameled ware. 5. paint or varnish that produces a smooth, hard, glossy surface when it dries. 6. liquid nail polish that produces such a surface. *v.t.* [ENAMELED or ENAMELLED (-′ld), ENAMELING or ENAMELLING], [ME. *enamelen;* Anglo-Fr. *enamayller* < *en-* (see EN-) + *amayl* < OFr. *esmail*, enamel < Gmc. **smalts*, a glaze, melted substance; see SMELT, *v.*], 1. to inlay or cover with enamel. 2. to decorate in various colors, as if with enamel. 3. to form an enamellike coating or surface on.
en·am·el·er, en·am·el·ler (i-nam′′l-ẽr), *n.* a person or thing that enamels.
en·am·el·ware (i-nam′′l-wâr′), *n.* kitchen utensils, etc. made of enameled metal.
en·am·or, en·am·our (in-am′ẽr), *v.t.* [ME. *enamuren;* OFr. *enamourer, enamorer* < *en-*, in + *amour* < L. *amor*, love; cf. INAMORATA], to fill with love and desire; charm; captivate.
en·am·ored, en·am·oured (in-am′ẽrd), *adj.* [pp. of *enamor*], greatly in love; charmed; captivated.
enamored of, in love with; captivated by.
‡en ar·rière (än′ nȧ′ryâr′), [Fr.], 1. in the rear; behind. 2. in arrears.
en·ar·thro·sis (en′är-thrō′sis), *n.* [Mod. L.; Gr. *enarthrōsis* < *enarthros*, jointed < *en-*, in + *arthron*, a joint], a joint in which the head of one bone fits into the socket of another, as the hip joint.
‡en a·vant (än′ nȧ′vän′), [Fr.], forward; onward: used chiefly as a command.
en bloc (en blok′; Fr. än′ blôk′), [Fr., lit., in a block], in one lump; as a whole; all together.
‡en bro·chette (än′ brô′shet′), [Fr.], broiled on small spits or skewers.
enc., 1. enclosed. 2. enclosure. 3. encyclopedia.
en·cae·ni·a (en-sē′ni-ə, en-sēn′yə), *n.* [ME. *encennia;* L.; Gr. *enkainia* < *en-*, in + *kainos*, new], 1. a festival commemorating the founding of a city, church, etc. 2. [E-], in England, the annual ceremony commemorating the founding of Oxford University.
en·cage (in-kāj′), *v.t.* to shut up in a cage; confine: also spelled **incage**.
en·camp (in-kamp′), *v.i.* to make, and stay in, a camp. *v.t.* 1. to put in a camp. 2. to make into a camp.
en·camp·ment (in-kamp′mənt), *n.* 1. an encamping or being encamped. 2. a camp or camp site.
en·car·nal·ize (in-kär′n′l-īz′), *v.t.* [ENCARNALIZED (-īzd′), ENCARNALIZING], 1. to incarnate. 2. to make carnal; make sensual.
en·case (in-kās′), *v.t.* 1. to cover completely; enclose. 2. to put into a case or cases. Also spelled **incase**.
en cas·se·role (en kas′ə-rōl′; Fr. än′ kȧs′rôl′), [Fr.], (baked and served) in a casserole.
en·caus·tic (en-kôs′tik), *adj.* [L. *encausticus;* Gr. *enkaustikos* < *enkaustos*, burnt in < *enkaiein*, to burn in; *en-*, in + *kaiein*, to burn], burnt in; done by a process of burning in; prepared by heat: as, *encaustic* tile. *n.* a method of painting or decorating in which colors in wax are fused with hot irons.
-ence (əns), [< Fr. & L.; Fr. *-ence;* L. *-entia* < *-ent-* (see -ENT) + *-ia*, n. ending], a suffix used to form abstract nouns corresponding to adjectives ending in *-ent*. It means *act, fact, quality, state, result*, or *degree*, as in *conference, excellence:* see also **-ance, -ency**.
‡en·ceinte (än′sant′; Eng. en-sānt′), *n.* [Fr. < pp. of *enceindre* < L. *incingere*, to gird about; *in-*, in + *cingere*, to surround], in *military science*, 1. the line of works enclosing a fortified place. 2. the space so enclosed.
‡en·ceinte (än′sant′; Eng. en-sānt′), *adj.* [Fr.; LL. *incincta*, orig. fem. of *incinctus*, ungirt; L. *in-*, not + *cinctus*, pp. of *cingere*, to gird, surround], pregnant; carrying an unborn child.
En·cel·a·dus (en-sel′ə-dəs), *n.* [L.; Gr. *Enkelados*], in *Greek mythology*, a giant with a hundred arms, who fought against the gods: he was killed by Zeus and buried beneath Mt. Etna.
en·ce·phal·ic (en′sə-fal′ik), *adj.* [see ENCEPHALON], of or near the brain.
en·ceph·a·lit·ic (en′sef-ə-lit′ik, en-sef′ə-lit′ik), *adj.* 1. of encephalitis. 2. having encephalitis.
en·ceph·a·li·tis (en′sef-ə-lī′tis, en-sef′ə-lī′tis), *n.* [*encephal-* + *-itis*], inflammation of the brain.
encephalitis le·thar·gi·ca (li-thär′ji-kə), sleeping sickness.
en·ceph·a·lo- (en-sef′ə-lō), [< Gr. *enkephalos*, the brain], a combining form meaning *of the brain*: also, before a vowel, **encephal-**, as in *encephalitis*.
en·ceph·a·lo·gram (en-sef′ə-lə-gram′), *n.* an electroencephalogram.
en·ceph·a·lo·graph (en-sef′ə-lə-graf′, en-sef′ə-lə-gräf′), *n.* an electroencephalograph.
en·ceph·a·lo·ma (en′sef-ə-lō′mə, en-sef′ə-lō′mə), *n.* [*pl.* ENCEPHALOMATA (-mə-tə), ENCEPHALOMAS (-məz)], [Mod. L.; see ENCEPHALO- & -OMA], 1. a tumor of the brain. 2. a hernia of the brain.
en·ceph·a·lon (en-sef′ə-lon′), *n.* [*pl.* ENCEPHALA (-lə)], [Mod. L. < Gr. *enkephalos*, (what is) in the head < *en-*, in + *kephalē*, the head], in *anatomy*, the brain.
en·chain (en-chān′), *v.t.* [OFr. *enchainer;* see EN- & CHAIN], 1. to put in chains; bind or hold with chains; fetter; hence, 2. to hold fast; captivate.
en·chain·ment (en-chān′mənt), *n.* an enchaining or being enchained.
en·chant (in-chant′, in-chänt′), *v.t.* [ME. *enchanten;* OFr. *enchanter;* L. *incantare*, to bewitch, enchant, mutter in a magic formula; *in-*, in + *cantare*, to sing], 1. to cast a spell over, as by magic; bewitch; hence, 2. to charm greatly; delight. —*SYN.* see **attract**.
en·chant·ing (in-chan′tiŋ, in-chän′tiŋ), *adj.* 1. charming; delightful. 2. bewitching; fascinating.
en·chant·ment (in-chant′mənt, in-chänt′mənt), *n.* [ME. & OFr. *enchantement;* see ENCHANT & -MENT], 1. the act of casting a spell over; use of magic to charm. 2. the state of being under the influence of a magic spell or charm. 3. a magic spell or charm. 4. something that charms or delights greatly. 5. great delight or pleasure.
en·chant·ress (in-chan′tris, in-chän′tris), *n.* [ME. *enchaunteresse;* OFr. *enchanteresse;* see ENCHANT], 1. a sorceress; witch. 2. a fascinating or charming woman.
en·chase (en-chās′), *v.t.* [Fr. *enchâsser* < *en-*, in + *châsse;* see CHASE (groove)], 1. to put in a setting; serve as a setting for; incase. 2. to ornament by engraving, embossing, cutting, or inlaying with gems, etc. 3. to engrave or carve (designs, etc.).
en·chi·la·da (en′chi-lä′də), *n.* [Sp. < *en-* (see EN-) + *chile* (see CHILI) + *-ada* (see -ADE)], a Mexican dish flavored with chili.
en·chi·rid·i·on (en′kī-rid′i-ən, en′kə-rid′i-ən), *n.* [LL.; Gr. *encheiridion* < *en-*, in + *cheir*, hand], a handbook.
en·chon·dro·ma (en′kon-drō′mə), *n.* [*pl.* ENCHONDROMATA (-mə-tə), ENCHONDROMAS (-məz)], [Mod. L.; Gr. *en*, in + *chondr-* + *-oma*], a cartilaginous tumor.
en·chon·drom·a·tous (en′kon-drom′ə-təs, en′kon-drō′mə-təs), *adj.* 1. of or like an enchondroma. 2. having an enchondroma.
en·cho·ri·al (en-kôr′i-əl, en-kō′ri-əl), *adj.* [< Gr. *enchōrios*, native < *en-*, in + *chōra*, country, place], of or used in a particular country; native; popular;

domestic: used especially to designate the popular, or demotic, writing of ancient Egypt.
en·chor·ic (en-kôr′ik, en-kō′rik), *adj.* enchorial.
en·ci·na (en-sē′nə), *n.* [Sp. < LL. *ilicina*, holm oak < L. *ilex*, kind of oak], the live oak, especially the California live oak.
en·cir·cle (in-sũr′k'l), *v.t.* 1. to make a circle around; enclose within a circle; surround. 2. to move in a circle around.
en·cir·cle·ment (in-sũr′k'l-mənt), *n.* an encircling or being encircled.
en·clasp (en-klasp′, en-kläsp′), *v.t.* to hold in a clasp; embrace.
en·clave (en′klāv), *n.* [< ME. *enclaven;* OFr. *enclaver*, to enclose, lock in; LL. *inclaver* < L. *in*, in + *clavis*, a key or *clavus*, a nail], foreign territory surrounded by a specified country: as, East Prussia was an *enclave* of Poland: distinguished from *exclave*.
en·clit·ic (en-klit′ik), *adj.* [LL. *encliticus;* Gr. *enklitikos* < *enklinein*, to lean toward, incline; *en-*, in + *klinein*, to lean], in *grammar*, dependent for its stress on the preceding word: said of a word that has lost its stress in combination (e.g., *man* in *layman*). *n.* any such word or particle.
en·close (in-klōz′), *v.t.* [ME. *enclosen; en-* + *closen* (after OFr. *enclos*, pp. of *enclore*, to enclose); see EN- & CLOSE, *v.*], 1. to shut in all around; surround; hem in; fence in. 2. to put into a receptacle. 3. to insert in an envelope, wrapper, etc. together with a letter. 4. to contain. Also spelled **inclose.**
en·clo·sure (in-klō′zhẽr), *n.* [OFr. < *enclos;* see EN-CLOSE & -URE], 1. an enclosing or being enclosed. 2. something that encloses, as a fence, wall, etc. 3. something enclosed; specifically, *a*) an enclosed place or area. *b*) a document, money, etc. enclosed with a letter: abbreviated **enc., encl.** Also spelled **inclosure.**
en·co·mi·ast (en-kō′mi-ast′), *n.* [Gr. *enkōmiastēs* < *enkōmiazein*, to praise < *enkōmion*], a person who speaks or writes encomiums; eulogist.
en·co·mi·as·tic (en-kō′mi-as′tik), *adj.* 1. of an encomiast. 2. of or like an encomium; eulogistic.
en·co·mi·as·ti·cal (en-kō′mi-as′ti-k'l), *adj.* encomiastic.
en·co·mi·um (en-kō′mi-əm), *n.* [*pl.* ENCOMIUMS (-əmz), ENCOMIA (-ə)], [L.; Gr. *enkōmion*, hymn to a victor, song of praise; neut. of *enkōmios* < *en-*, in + *kōmos*, a revel], a formal expression of high praise; elaborate commendation; eulogy; panegyric. —*SYN.* see **tribute.**
en·com·pass (in-kum′pəs), *v.t.* 1. to shut in all around; surround; encircle. 2. to contain; include.
en·com·pass·ment (in-kum′pəs-mənt), *n.* an encompassing or being encompassed.
en·core (äŋ′kôr, än-kōr′), *interj.* [Fr.; It. *ancora*, yet, still, again; prob. < L. *in hanc horam*, to this hour], again; once more. *n.* (äŋ′kôr, än′kōr), 1. a demand by the audience, shown by continued applause, for the repetition of a piece of music, etc., or for further performance or another appearance of the performer or performers. 2. the repetition, further performance, etc. in answer to such a demand. 3. the piece of music, etc. performed in answer to such a demand. 4. the performance of something added to the regular program. *v.t.* (äŋ-kôr′, än′kōr), [ENCORED (-kôrd′, -kōrd), ENCORING], to demand a repetition of (a piece of music, etc.) or from (a performer) by applauding.
en·coun·ter (in-koun′tẽr), *v.t.* [ME. *encontren;* OFr. *encontrer* < L. *in*, in + *contra*, against], 1. to meet unexpectedly; come upon. 2. to meet in conflict; engage in battle. 3. to meet with; face (difficulties, trouble, etc.). *v.i.* to meet accidentally or in opposition. *n.* 1. a meeting in conflict; battle; fight. 2. an unexpected meeting. —*SYN.* see **battle.**
en·cour·age (in-kũr′ij), *v.t.* [ENCOURAGED (-ijd), ENCOURAGING], [OFr. *encoragier, encourager;* see EN- & COURAGE], 1. to give courage, hope, or confidence to; embolden; hearten. 2. to help; give support to; be favorable to; foster.
en·cour·age·ment (in-kũr′ij-mənt), *n.* [OFr. *encoragement*], 1. an encouraging or being encouraged. 2. something that encourages.
en·cour·ag·ing (in-kũr′ij-iŋ), *adj.* [ppr. of *encourage*], giving courage, hope, or confidence.
en·crim·son (en-krim′z'n), *v.t.* to make crimson.
en·cri·nite (en′kri-nīt′), *n.* [< Mod. L. *Encrinus* (< Gr. *en*, in + *krinon*, lily), name of the genus; + *-ite*], in *paleontology*, 1. a fossil crinoid, a spiny sea invertebrate. 2. occasionally, any crinoid.
en·croach (in-krōch′), *v.i.* [ME. *encrochen;* OFr. *encrochier, encrocier*, to seize upon, take; *en-*, in + *croc, croche*, a hook; cf. CROCHET], 1. to trespass or intrude (*on* or *upon* the rights, property, etc. of another). 2. to advance beyond the proper, original, or customary limits; make inroads (*on* or *upon*). —*SYN.* see **trespass.**
en·croach·ment (in-krōch′mənt), *n.* 1. an encroaching. 2. something gained by encroaching.
en·crust (in-krust′), *v.t.* 1. to cover or line with a crust. 2. to decorate richly and heavily, as with jewels. *v.i.* to form, or form into, a crust.
en·cum·ber (in-kum′bẽr), *v.t.* [ME. *encombren;* OFr. *encombrer;* see EN- & CUMBER], 1. to hold back the motion or action of, as with a burden; hinder; hamper. 2. to load or fill in such a way as to obstruct; block up; obstruct. 3. to burden; load or weigh down, as with claims, debts, etc. Also spelled **incumber.**
en·cum·brance (in-kum′brəns), *n.* [OFr. *encombrance*], 1. something that encumbers; hindrance; obstruction; burden. 2. [Rare], a dependent, especially a child. 3. in *law*, a claim or lien attached to property, as a mortgage. Also spelled **incumbrance.**
-en·cy (ən-si), [L. *-entia*], a suffix equivalent to *-ence*, used to form abstract nouns corresponding to adjectives ending in *-ent*. It means *act, fact, quality, state, result*, or *degree*, as in *dependency, emergency, efficiency*: see also **-ancy.**
en·cy·clic (en-sik′lik, en-sī′klik), *adj.* & *n.* encyclical.
en·cy·cli·cal (en-sik′li-k'l, en-sī′kli-k'l), *adj.* [LL. *encyclicus* < Gr. *enkyklios*, in a circle, general, common < *en-*, in + *kyklos*, a circle], for general circulation. *n.* in the *Roman Catholic Church*, a letter sent by the Pope to the clergy, having to do with church matters.
en·cy·clo·pe·di·a, en·cy·clo·pae·di·a (in-sī′klə-pē′di-ə), *n.* [Mod. L. *encyclopaedia* < Gr. *enkyklopaideia*, false reading for *enkyklios paideia*, instruction in the circle of the arts and sciences; *enkyklios* (*en-*, in + *kyklos*, a circle) in a circle, general + *paideia*, education < *paideuein*, to educate, bring up a child < *pais, paidos*, child], 1. a book or set of books giving information on all branches of knowledge, generally in articles alphabetically arranged. 2. a similar work giving information on one field of knowledge. Abbreviated **enc., ency., encyc., encycl.**
en·cy·clo·pe·dic, en·cy·clo·pae·dic (in-sī′klə-pē′dik), *adj.* 1. of or like an encyclopedia. 2. giving information about many subjects; comprehensive in scope.
en·cy·clo·pe·di·cal, en·cy·clo·pae·di·cal (in-sī′klə-pē′di-k'l), *adj.* encyclopedic.
en·cy·clo·pe·dism, en·cy·clo·pae·dism (in-sī′klə-pē′diz'm), *n.* 1. encyclopedic knowledge or learning. 2. [E-], the doctrines or work of the Encyclopedists.
en·cy·clo·pe·dist, en·cy·clo·pae·dist (in-sī′klə-pē′dist), *n.* 1. a person who compiles or helps compile an encyclopedia. 2. [E-], *pl.* the writers of the French Encyclopedia (1751–1765) edited by Diderot and d'Alembert, which contained the advanced ideas of the period.
en·cyst (en-sist′), *v.t.* & *v.i.* to enclose or become enclosed in a cyst, capsule, or sac.
en·cyst·ment (en-sist′mənt), *n.* an encysting.
end (end), *n.* [ME. & AS. *ende;* akin to G. *ende*, Goth. *andeis;* basic sense "the opposite boundary or extremity"; IE. base **anti-*, **anta-*, opposite, in front of, as also in L. *ante*, lit., in front of, opposite one in space], 1. a limit or limiting part; boundary; point of beginning or stopping. 2. the last part of anything; final point; finish; completion; conclusion. 3. a ceasing to exist; death or destruction; also, the cause or manner of this. 4. the part at, toward, or near either of the extremities of anything; tip. 5. an aim; object; purpose; intention. 6. an outcome; result; upshot; consequence. 7. a piece left over; fragment; remnant. 8. the reason for being; final cause. 9. in *football*, *a*) a player at either end of the line of scrimmage. *b*) his position. *v.t.* 1. to bring to an end; finish; stop; conclude. 2. to be or form the end of. 3. [Obs.], to kill. *v.i.* 1. to come to an end; terminate. 2. to die. *adj.* at the end; final: as, *end* man, *end* product. —*SYN.* see **close, intention.**
at loose ends, [orig. nautical, with reference to rope], 1. in an unsettled or indefinite condition. 2. in a disorganized or confused condition.
end for end, with the ends, or the position, reversed.
end on, with the end foremost; not sideways.
end to end, in a line so that the ends touch or meet.
end up, 1. in an upright position. 2. to come to an end; finish.
make an end of, 1. to finish; stop. 2. to do away with.
make both ends meet, [cf. Fr. *joindre les deux bouts*], 1. to keep one's expenses within one's income. 2. to manage merely to exist on one's income.
no end, [Colloq.], a great deal; very much or many.
on end, 1. in an upright position. 2. one after the other.
put an end to, 1. to stop; finish. 2. to do away with.
end., endorsed.
end-all (end′ôl′), *n.* 1. the end of everything. 2. that which ends everything.
en·da·moe·ba, en·da·me·ba (en′də-mē′bə), *n.* [see ENDO- & AMOEBA], any of a large group of amoebas, some species of which are found as parasites in the internal organs of man and certain other animals, causing amoebic dysentery and some other diseases.
en·dan·ger (in-dān′jẽr), *v.t.* to expose to danger, harm, or loss; imperil.
en·dear (in-dêr′), *v.t.* to make dear or beloved: as, she *endeared* herself to the children by her generosity.
en·dear·ment (in-dêr′mənt), *n.* 1. an endearing or being endeared; affection. 2. an expression of affection; caress. 3. something that endears.
en·deav·or (in-dev′ẽr), *v.i.* [ME. *endever* < *en-* (see EN-) + *dever, devor* < OFr. *deveir* (Fr. *devoir*), duty: from the use of these words in such expressions as *se mettre en*

deveir, to try to do, set about; *deveir* < L. *debere*, to owe, be under obligation], to try hard; exert effort; make an earnest attempt; strive. ***v.t.*** [Archaic], to try to achieve; attempt. ***n.*** an earnest attempt; effort to accomplish something. British spelling **endeavour.** —***SYN.*** see **effort, try.**

En·de·cott, John (en′di-kot′, en′di-kət), 1589?–1665; first English governor of Massachusetts Bay colony: also spelled **Endicott.**

en·dem·ic (en-dem′ik), ***adj.*** [< Gr. *endēmos, endēmios; en-*, in + *dēmos*, the people; + *-ic*], prevalent in or restricted to a particular nation, region, locality, or group; indigenous: as, an *endemic* plant, an *endemic* disease. ***n.*** an endemic disease. —***SYN.*** see **native.**

en·dem·i·cal (en-dem′i-k′l), ***adj.*** endemic.

En·der·by Land (en′dẽr-bi), a region in Antarctica, south of Africa.

en·der·mic (en-dũr′mik), ***adj.*** [< Gr. *en*, in + *derma*, the skin; + *-ic*], in *medicine*, applied to the skin and acting by absorption through it.

‡en dés·ha·bil·lé (än′ dā′zȧ′bē′yā′), [Fr., in undress], 1. partly undressed. 2. dressed in a robe, negligee, etc.

Endicott, John, see **Endecott, John.**

end·ing (en′diŋ), ***n.*** [AS. *endung*; see END, *v.*], 1. an end; specifically, *a*) the last part; finish; conclusion. *b*) death. 2. in *grammar*, the final letter or letters added to a word or word base to make a derivative or inflectional form: as, *-ed* is the *ending* in *wanted.*

en·dive (en′dīv, än′dēv), ***n.*** [Fr.; ML. *endivia*; MGr. *indivi* < L. *intibus, intubus, intybus*, (LL. *intiba*); Gr. *entybon, entybion;* prob. < Egypt. *tybi*, January (during which month it is said to grow in Egypt)], 1. a kind of chicory with ragged, curly leaves which are used in salads, etc.: also called *escarole.* 2. another kind of chicory whose long leaves are blanched for use in salads.

end leaf, an end paper.

end·less (end′lis), ***adj.*** [AS. *endeleas* (see END & -LESS)], 1. having no end; going on forever; eternal; infinite. 2. lasting too long; interminable: as, an *endless* speech. 3. with the ends joined to form a closed ring that can move continuously over wheels, etc.: as, an *endless* chain.

end·long (end′lôŋ′), ***adv.*** 1. lengthwise. 2. on end.

end man, 1. a man at the end of a row. 2. in a minstrel show, the performer at each end of the first row, who tells jokes with the help of the interlocutor.

end·most (end′mōst′), ***adj.*** at or nearest to the end; farthest; most remote; last.

en·do- (en′dō, en′də), [< Gr. *endon*, within], a combining form meaning *within, inner*, as in *endocrine, endoderm:* also, before a vowel, **end-.**

en·do·blast (en′də-blast′), ***n.*** [*endo-* + *-blast*], the endoderm; hypoblast.

en·do·car·di·al (en′də-kär′di-əl), ***adj.*** 1. within the heart. 2. of the endocardium.

en·do·car·di·tis (en′dō-kär-dī′tis), ***n.*** [Mod. L.; see -ITIS], inflammation of the endocardium.

en·do·car·di·um (en′də-kär′di-əm), ***n.*** [Mod. L. < *endo-* + Gr. *kardia*, the heart], the thin endothelial membrane lining the cavities of the heart.

en·do·carp (en′də-kärp′), ***n.*** [*endo-* + *-carp*], the inner layer of a ripened ovary or fruit, as the pit of a plum.

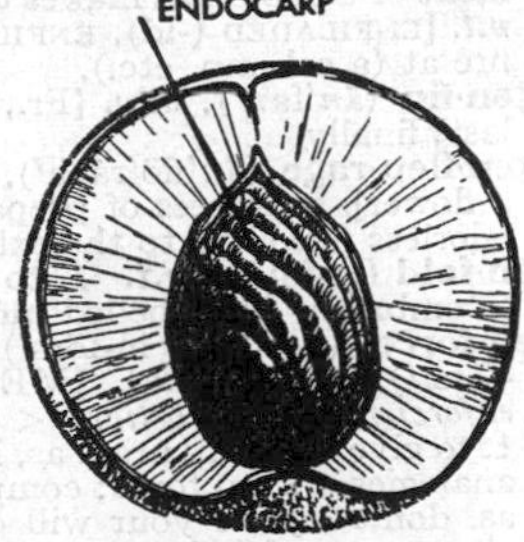

ENDOCARP OF PEACH

en·do·crin (en′də-krin′), ***n.*** endocrine.

en·do·cri·nal (en′də-krī′-n′l), ***adj.*** endocrinous.

en·do·crine (en′də-krīn′, en′də-krin), ***adj.*** [< *endo-* + Gr. *krinein*, to separate], 1. designating or of any gland producing one or more internal secretions that are carried by the blood or lymph to some part whose functions they regulate or control. 2. designating or of such a secretion. ***n.*** any such gland or its secretion: the thyroid, adrenal, and pituitary glands are endocrines.

en·do·crin·ic (en′də-krin′ik), ***adj.*** endocrinous.

en·do·cri·nol·o·gy (en′dō-krī-nol′ə-ji, en′dō-kri-nol′ə-ji), ***n.*** the study of the endocrine glands and the internal secretions of the body.

en·doc·ri·nous (en-dok′ri-nəs), ***adj.*** of an endocrine gland or its secretion.

en·do·derm (en′də-dũrm′), ***n.*** [*endo-* + *-derm*], the inner layer of cells of the embryo, from which is formed the lining of the digestive tract and of other internal organs; endoblast; hypoblast.

en·do·en·zyme (en′dō-en′zīm, en′dō-en′zim), ***n.*** an enzyme that functions within the cell.

en·do·gam·ic (en′də-gam′ik), ***adj.*** endogamous.

en·dog·a·mous (en-dog′ə-məs), ***adj.*** 1. of endogamy. 2. practicing endogamy.

en·dog·a·my (en-dog′ə-mi), ***n.*** [*endo-* + *-gamy*], the custom of marrying only within one's own tribe or social group; inbreeding: opposed to *exogamy.*

en·do·gen (en′də-jen′), ***n.*** [*endo-* + *-gen*: so called because the stems were formerly believed to grow from within], any plant that grows by adding tissue irregularly throughout the stem; monocotyledon: distinguished from *exogen.*

en·dog·e·nous (en-doj′ə-nəs), ***adj.*** 1. developing from within; originating internally. 2. in *biology*, growing or developing from or on the inside. 3. in *physiology & biochemistry*, of the anabolism of cells.

en·dog·e·ny (en-doj′ə-ni), ***n.*** [*endo-* + *-geny*], in *biology*, growth from within; endogenous formation of cells.

en·do·lymph (en′də-limf′), ***n.*** [*endo-* + *lymph*], in *anatomy*, the fluid in the membranous labyrinth of the ear.

en·do·morph (en′də-môrf′), ***n.*** [*endo-* + *-morph*], a mineral, especially a crystal, enclosed within another.

en·do·mor·phic (en′də-môr′fik), ***adj.*** 1. of an endomorph. 2. of or caused by endomorphism. 3. designating or of the abdominal physical type, characterized by predominance of the structures developed from the endodermal layer of the embryo (i.e., the internal organs): distinguished from *ectomorphic.*

en·do·mor·phism (en′də-môr′fiz′m), ***n.*** 1. the state or fact of being endomorphic. 2. structural change caused in an intrusive rock by the action of the surrounding rock.

en·do·par·a·site (en′də-par′ə-sīt′), ***n.*** a parasite that inhabits the internal organs of an animal; hookworm, tapeworm, endamoeba, etc.

en·do·phyte (en′də-fīt′), ***n.*** [*endo-* + *-phyte*], in *botany*, any plant that grows within another plant.

en·do·plasm (en′də-plaz′m), ***n.*** [*endo-* + *-plasm*], the inner part of the cytoplasm of a cell: distinguished from *ectoplasm.*

en·do·plas·mic (en′də-plaz′mik), ***adj.*** of endoplasm.

end organ, any specialized structure at the peripheral end of nerve fibers having either sensory or motor functions: see **nerve,** illus.

en·dors·a·ble (in-dôr′sə-b′l), ***adj.*** that can be endorsed: also spelled **indorsable.**

en·dorse (in-dôrs′), ***v.t.*** [ENDORSED (-dôrst′), ENDORSING], [with altered sp. after L. < ME. *endossen;* OFr. *endosser* < ML. *indorsare* < L. *in*, on, upon + *dorsum*, the back], 1. to write on the back of (a document); specifically, *a*) to sign one's name as payee on the back of (a check, money order, etc.). *b*) to make (a check, etc.) payable to another person by thus signing one's name and adding "payable to the order of ——" on the back. 2. to give support or approval to; sanction: as, civic leaders have *endorsed* the housing project. Also spelled **indorse.** —***SYN.*** see **approve.**

en·dor·see (in-dôr′sē′, en′dôr′sē′), ***n.*** the person to whom a check, note, etc. is made over by endorsement: also spelled **indorsee.**

en·dorse·ment (in-dôrs′mənt), ***n.*** 1. the act of writing on the back of a check, note, etc. 2. something written on the back of a check, note, etc., as the signature of a payee, by which money or property is made over to someone. 3. a change, as of coverage or beneficiary, written on or added to an insurance policy, and signed by an agent of the insurer. 4. approval; sanction. Also spelled **indorsement.**

en·do·sarc (en′də-särk′), ***n.*** [*endo-* + Gr. *sarx, sarkos*, flesh], the endoplasm of certain protozoa.

en·do·scope (en′də-skōp′), ***n.*** [*endo-* + *-scope*], an instrument for examining the inside of a hollow organ of the body, as the bladder or rectum.

en·dos·co·py (en-dos′kə-pi), ***n.*** the examination of hollow organs of the body by means of an endoscope.

en·do·skel·e·ton (en′də-skel′ə-t′n), ***n.*** the internal bony supporting structure, or true skeleton, in vertebrates: distinguished from *exoskeleton.*

en·dos·mo·sis (en′dos-mō′sis, en′doz-mō′sis), ***n.*** [Mod. L.; *end-* + *osmosis*], in osmosis, the more rapid diffusion of the less dense fluid through the semipermeable membrane to mingle with the more dense: opposed to *exosmosis.*

en·dos·mot·ic (en′dos-mot′ik, en′doz-mot′ik), ***adj.*** of endosmosis.

en·do·sperm (en′də-spũrm′), ***n.*** [*endo-* + *sperm*], the nourishment for the embryo, which surrounds the embryo in the seed of a plant.

en·do·spore (en′də-spôr′, en′də-spōr′), ***n.*** 1. in *bacteriology*, an asexual spore formed within a special spore case. 2. in *botany*, the endosporium.

en·do·spo·ri·um (en′də-spôr′iəm, en′də-spō′ri-əm), ***n.*** [*pl.* ENDOSPORIA (-ə)], [Mod. L.; see ENDO- & SPORE], the inner layer of the covering of a spore.

en·dos·te·um (en-dos′ti-əm), ***n.*** [*pl.* ENDOSTEA (-ə)],

[Mod. L. < *end-* + Gr. *osteon*, a bone], the vascular connective tissue lining the marrow cavities of bones.
en·dos·to·sis (en'dos-tō'sis), ***n.*** [Mod. L.; *end-* + *ostosis*], the formation of bone within cartilage.
en·do·the·li·al (en'də-thē'li-əl), ***adj.*** of the endothelium.
en·do·the·li·oid (en'də-thē'li-oid'), ***adj.*** of or like the endothelium.
en·do·the·li·um (en'də-thē'li-əm), ***n.*** [*pl.* ENDOTHELIA (-ə)], [Mod. L. < *endo-* + Gr. *thēlē*, nipple], the layer of squamous cells lining the inside of blood and lymph vessels, of the heart, and of some other closed cavities.
en·doth·e·loid (en-doth'ə-loid'), ***adj.*** endothelioid.
en·do·ther·mal (en'də-thũr'm'l), ***adj.*** endothermic.
en·do·ther·mic (en'də-thũr'mik), ***adj.*** [*endo-* + *thermic*], designating or of a chemical change in which there is an absorption of heat: opposed to *exothermic*.
en·do·tox·in (en'də-tok'sin), ***n.*** [*endo-* + *toxin*], any of a group of toxic substances found in certain disease-producing bacteria and liberated by the disintegration of the bacterial cell: they harm certain tissue cells.
en·dow (in-dou'), ***v.t.*** [ME. *endowen;* OFr. *endouer; en-*, in + *douer* < L. *dotare*, to give], 1. to provide with some talent, quality, etc.: as, he was *endowed* with courage. 2. to give money or property so as to provide an income for the support of (a college, hospital, etc.); bequeath. 3. [Obs.], to provide with a dower.
en·dow·ment (in-dou'mənt), ***n.*** 1. an endowing. 2. that with which something is endowed; bequest; gift. 3. a gift of nature; talent; ability.
endowment policy, an insurance policy by which a stated amount is paid to the insured after the period of time specified in the contract, or to the beneficiaries in case the insured dies within the time specified.
end paper, a folded sheet of paper one half of which is pasted to the inside of either cover of a book, the other half forming the first (or last) page of the book: also called *end leaf*.
end product, the final result of any series of changes, processes, or chemical reactions.
end table, a small table to be placed at either end of a sofa, beside a chair, etc.
en·due (in-dōō', in-dū'), ***v.t.*** [ENDUED (-dōōd', -dūd'), ENDUING], [ME. *endewen;* OFr. *enduire;* L. *inducere*, to lead in; *in-*, in + *ducere*, to lead; form and sense affected by L. *induere*, to put on (see INDUE); confused in Eng. with *endow*], 1. [Rare], to put on; clothe; cover. 2. to provide (*with* something); specifically, to endow (*with* qualities, talents, etc.). Also spelled **indue.**
en·dur·a·ble (in-door'ə-b'l, in-dyoor'ə-b'l), ***adj.*** that can be endured; bearable.
en·dur·ance (in-door'əns, in-dyoor'əns), ***n.*** 1. an enduring. 2. the power of enduring; specifically, *a*) ability to last, continue, or remain. *b*) ability to stand pain, distress, fatigue, etc.; fortitude. 3. [Rare], that which is endured; hardship. 4. duration. —***SYN.*** see **patience.**
en·dure (in-door', in-dyoor'), ***v.t.*** [ENDURED (-doord', -dyoord'), ENDURING], [ME. *enduren;* OFr. *endurer* < L. *indurare; in-*, in + *durare*, to harden, hold out, last < *durus*, hard], 1. to stand (pain, fatigue, etc.); bear; undergo. 2. to put up with; tolerate. ***v.i.*** 1. to last; continue; remain. 2. to bear pain, etc. without flinching; hold out. Also spelled **indure.** —***SYN.*** see **bear, continue.**
en·dur·ing (in-door'iŋ, in-dyoor'iŋ), ***adj.*** [ppr. of *endure*], 1. lasting; permanent. 2. long-suffering.
end·ways (end'wāz'), ***adv.*** 1. on end; upright. 2. with the end foremost. 3. lengthwise. 4. end to end.
end·wise (end'wīz'), ***adv.*** endways.
En·dym·i·on (en-dim'i-ən), ***n.*** [L.; Gr. *Endymiōn*], in *Greek legend*, a beautiful young shepherd loved by Selene and caressed by her as he slept.
-ene (ēn), [after L. *-enus*, adj. suffix], a suffix used: 1. to form names for certain hydrocarbons, especially of the olefin or ethylene series, as in *benzene, acetylene*. 2. to form commercial names for some products.
ENE, E.N.E., e.n.e., east-northeast.
‡en ef·fet (äṅ'ne'fe'), [Fr., lit., in effect], in reality; in fact; indeed.
en·e·ma (en'ə-mə), ***n.*** [LL.; Gr. *enema*, injection < *enienai*, to send in; *en-*, in + *hienai*, to send], 1. a liquid injected into the rectum either as a purgative or a medicine; clyster. 2. the injection of such a liquid. 3. the apparatus used for this.
en·e·my (en'ə-mi), ***n.*** [*pl.* ENEMIES (-miz)], [ME. & OFr. *enemi;* L. *inimicus*, unfriendly, hostile, hence enemy < *in-*, not + *amicus*, friend], 1. a person who hates another, and wishes or tries to injure him; person hostile to an idea, cause, etc.; adversary; foe. 2. *a*) a nation or force hostile to another. *b*) troops, fleet, ship, member, etc. of a hostile nation. 3. anything hostile or injurious. ***adj.*** 1. of an enemy; of a hostile nation. 2. [Obs.], hostile. —***SYN.*** see **opponent.**
enemy alien, an alien residing or interned in a country with which his own country is at war.
en·er·ge·sis (en'ēr-jē'sis), ***n.*** [Mod. L. < Gr. *energein*, to be in action; see ENERGY], in *botany*, the process by which energy is liberated through catabolic action in the cell.
en·er·get·ic (en'ēr-jet'ik), ***adj.*** [Gr. *energētikos*], having or showing energy; vigorous; forceful. —***SYN.*** see **active.**
en·er·get·i·cal·ly (en'ēr-jet'i-k'l-i, en'ēr-jet'ik-li), ***adv.*** in an energetic manner; with energy.
en·er·get·ics (en'ēr-jet'iks), ***n.pl.*** [construed as sing.], the science that deals with the laws of energy.
en·er·gize (en'ēr-jīz'), ***v.t.*** [ENERGIZED (-jīzd'), ENERGIZING], to give energy to; activate. ***v.i.*** to show energy; be active.
en·er·gu·men (en'ēr-gū'men), ***n.*** [LL. *energumenos;* Gr. *energoumenos*, ppr. pass. of *energein*, to work on; see ENERGY], 1. a person supposedly possessed by an evil spirit; demoniac; hence, 2. a fanatic; enthusiast.
en·er·gy (en'ēr-ji), ***n.*** [*pl.* ENERGIES (-jiz)], [LL. *energia;* Gr. *energeia* < *energēs*, active, at work < *en-*, in + *ergon*, work], 1. force of expression or utterance. 2. potential forces; inherent power; capacity for vigorous action. 3. *pl.* such powers, especially in action: as, apply all your *energies* to the cause. 4. strength or power efficiently exerted. 5. in *physics*, the capacity for doing work and overcoming resistance: see **matter,** 2. —***SYN.*** see **strength.**
en·er·vate (en'ēr-vāt'), ***v.t.*** [ENERVATED (-id), ENERVATING], [< L. *enervatus*, pp. of *enervare* < *enervis*, nerveless, weak < *e-*, out + *nervus*, a nerve, sinew], to deprive of nerve, force, vigor, etc.; weaken physically, mentally, or morally; devitalize; debilitate. ***adj.*** (i-nũr'vit), enervated; weakened. —***SYN.*** see **unnerve, weaken.**
en·er·va·tion (en'ēr-vā'shən), ***n.*** [LL. *enervatio*], an enervating or being enervated.
en·er·va·tor (en'ēr-vā'tēr), ***n.*** a thing that enervates.
E·ne·sco, Georges (zhôrzh e-ne'skō), 1881–1955; Romanian violinist, composer, and conductor.
en·face (en-fās'), ***v.t.*** to write or print on the face of (a document, check, etc.).
en·face·ment (en-fās'mənt), ***n.*** something written or printed on the face of a document.
‡en famille (äṅ' fà'mē'y'), [Fr., lit., in (one's) family], 1. with one's family; at home. 2. in an informal way.
‡en·fants per·dus (äṅ'fäṅ' pâr'dü'), [Fr., lit., lost children], a forlorn hope: military term, applied to troops in a hopelessly dangerous position.
‡en·fant ter·ri·ble (äṅ'fäṅ' te'rē'bl'), [Fr., lit., terrible child], 1. an unmanageable, mischievous child. 2. a person who causes trouble by making frank, bold remarks at the wrong times.
en·fee·ble (in-fē'b'l), ***v.t.*** [ENFEEBLED (-b'ld), ENFEEBLING], [ME. *enfeblen;* OFr. *enfeblir*], to make feeble.
en·fee·ble·ment (in-fē'b'l-mənt), ***n.*** an enfeebling or being enfeebled.
en·feoff (en-fef', en-fēf'), ***v.t.*** [ME. *enfeffen* (Anglo-Fr. *enfeoffer*); OFr. *enfeofer, enfeffer;* see EN- & FIEF], in *law*, to invest with an estate held in fee.
en·feoff·ment (en-fef'mənt, en-fēf'mənt), ***n.*** 1. an enfeoffing or being enfeoffed. 2. a deed or instrument that enfeoffs. 3. a fief. 4. the possession of a fief.
en·fet·ter (in-fet'ēr), ***v.t.*** to bind in or as in fetters.
En·field (en'fēld), ***n.*** a city in Middlesex, England, near London: pop., 92,000.
en·fi·lade (en'fə-lād'), ***n.*** [Fr. *enfiler*, to thread, string, rake with fire < *en-* (L. *in*), in + *fil* (L. *filum*), a thread], 1. gunfire directed from either flank along the length of a column or line of troops. 2. a disposition or placement of troops that makes them vulnerable to such fire. ***v.t.*** [ENFILADED (-id), ENFILADING], to direct such gunfire at (a column, etc.).
‡en·fin (äṅ'faṅ'), ***adv.*** [Fr., lit., in the end], lastly; at last; finally.
‡en·fleu·rage (äṅ'flö'ràzh'), ***n.*** [Fr. < *en-*, in + *fleur*, a flower], a process of preparing perfumes by exposing odorless fixed oils to the exhalations of certain flowers.
en·fold (in-fōld'), ***v.t.*** 1. to wrap in folds; wrap up. 2. to embrace. Also spelled **infold.**
en·force (in-fôrs', in-fōrs'), ***v.t.*** [ENFORCED (-fôrst', -fōrst'), ENFORCING], [ME. *enforcen;* OFr. *enforcer, enforcier;* LL. *infortiare* < L. *in*, in + *fortis*, strong], 1. to give force to; urge: as, he *enforced* his argument by analogies. 2. to force; compel. 3. to impose by force: as, don't *enforce* your will on the child. 4. to compel observance of (a law, etc.).
en·force·ment (in-fôrs'mənt, in-fōrs'mənt), ***n.*** an enforcing or being enforced.
en·fran·chise (en-fran'chīz), ***v.t.*** [ENFRANCHISED (-chīzd), ENFRANCHISING], [OFr. *enfranchiss-*, stem of *enfranchir*, to set free, enfranchise; *en-*, in + *franchir*, to set free < *franc;* see FRANK, *adj.*], 1. to free from slavery, bondage, legal obligation, etc. 2. to give a franchise to; admit to citizenship, especially to the right to vote.
en·fran·chise·ment (en-fran'chiz-mənt), ***n.*** an enfranchising or being enfranchised.
Eng., 1. England. 2. English.
eng., 1. engine. 2. engineer. 3. engineering. 4. engraved. 5. engraver. 6. engraving.
en·gage (in-gāj'), ***v.t.*** [ENGAGED (-gājd'), ENGAGING], [Fr. & OFr. *engager;* see EN- & GAGE], 1. originally, to give or assign as security for a debt, etc. 2. to bind (oneself) by a promise; pledge: as, she *engaged* herself to do the job. 3. to bind by a promise of marriage; be-

troth: as, he became *engaged* to a childhood sweetheart. 4. to arrange for the services of; hire; employ: as, he *engaged* Smith as his lawyer. 5. to arrange for the use of; reserve: as, he *engaged* a hotel room. 6. to entangle. 7. to draw into; involve: as, *engage* him in conversation. 8. to attract and hold (the attention, etc.). 9. to employ the efforts, thoughts, etc. of; keep busy; occupy: as, reading *engages* all my spare time. 10. to enter into conflict with (the enemy). 11. to interlock with; mesh together: as, *engage* the gears. ***v.i.*** 1. to pledge oneself; promise; undertake; agree: as, don't *engage* to do it unless you have time. 2. to occupy or involve oneself; take part; be active: as, she *engaged* in dramatics. 3. to enter into conflict. 4. to interlock; mesh.

en·gaged (in-gājd′), ***adj.*** [pp. of *engage*], 1. pledged. 2. pledged in marriage; betrothed. 3. occupied; employed; busy. 4. involved in combat, as troops. 5. attached to or partly set into (a wall, etc.): as, *engaged* columns. 6. interlocked; meshed; in gear.

en·gage·ment (in-gāj′mənt), ***n.*** 1. an engaging or being engaged; specifically, *a)* a promise; pledge. *b)* a promise of marriage; betrothal. *c)* an arrangement to go somewhere, do something, meet someone, etc.; appointment; obligation. *d)* employment or period of employment. *e)* a conflict; battle. *f)* *usually pl.* in *business*, financial obligations; commitments. *g)* an interlocking; being in gear. 2. something that engages. ***—SYN.*** see **battle.**

en·gag·ing (in-gāj′iŋ), ***adj.*** [ppr. of *engage*], attractive; pleasant; winning; charming.

‡en garde (än′gärd′), [Fr.], in *fencing*, on guard: the opening position in which the fencer is prepared either to attack or defend.

en·gar·land (en-gär′lənd), ***v.t.*** to put a garland or garlands on or around.

Eng. D., Doctor of Engineering.

Eng·els, Frie·drich (frē′driH eŋ′əls), 1820–1895; German socialist, manufacturer, and author; close associate of Karl Marx.

en·gen·der (in-jen′dẽr), ***v.t.*** [ME. *engendren;* OFr. *engendrer;* L. *ingenerare*, to beget; *in-*, in + *generare;* see GENERATE], 1. [Rare], to beget. 2. to bring into being; cause; produce; bring about: as, pity *engendered* love.

en·gine (en′jən), ***n.*** [orig., genius, ingenuity, or a result of ingenuity; ME. *engin*, native talent, hence something produced by this; OFr. *engin;* L. *ingenium*, natural ability, genius (cf. INGENIOUS) < *in-*, in + base of *gignere*, to produce], 1. any machine that uses energy to develop mechanical power; especially, a machine for starting motion in some other machine. 2. a railroad locomotive. Abbreviated **eng.** 3. any instrument or machine; apparatus: as, *engines* of warfare, *engines* of torture. 4. [Archaic], any means, agent, or device.

en·gi·neer (en′jə-nêr′), ***n.*** [< *engine* + *-eer*, for earlier *enginer;* ME. *enginour;* OFr. *engigneur*], 1. [Rare], a person who makes engines. 2. a person skilled or occupied in some branch of engineering: as, a mechanical *engineer*, an electrical *engineer*. 3. the operator of an engine; especially, the driver of a railroad locomotive. 4. in *military science*, a member of that branch of the army which is concerned with the construction and demolition of bridges, roads, and fortifications, the laying and sapping of mines, etc. Abbreviated **E., e., eng., engin., engr.** ***v.t.*** 1. to plan, construct, or manage as an engineer; hence, 2. to contrive; manage skillfully; superintend; guide (a measure, action, etc. *through*).

en·gi·neer·ing (en′jə-nêr′iŋ), ***n.*** 1. the planning, designing, construction, or management of machinery, roads, bridges, buildings, fortifications, waterways, etc.; science, profession, or work of an engineer: abbreviated **E., e., eng., engin.** 2. a maneuvering or managing.

engine house, a building in which fire engines are housed.

en·gine·man (en′jən-mən), ***n.*** [*pl.* ENGINEMEN (-mən)], the operator of an engine, especially a stationary engine.

en·gine·ry (en′jən-ri), ***n.*** 1. [Rare], engines collectively; machinery. 2. [Obs.], *a)* instruments of war. *b)* the art of making such instruments or military works.

engine shaft, a mine shaft in which the pumping machinery is housed.

engine turning, ornamentation on metal, as on some watch cases, consisting of finely engraved lines radiating from a center.

en·gird (en-gũrd′) ***v.t.*** to encircle; encompass; gird.

Eng·land (iŋ′glənd), ***n.*** [ME. *Englonde, Yngelonde* (with vowel change as in Eng. *wing*, ME. *weng*); AS. *Engla land*, lit., land of the Angles (as opposed to the Saxons), hence England; cf. ANGLES], a division of Great Britain, bounded by Wales and Scotland: area, 50,874 sq. mi.; pop., 41,159,000; capital, London: abbreviated **Eng.**: see **Great Britain, United Kingdom.**

Eng·land·er (iŋ′glən-dẽr), ***n.*** a native of England.

Eng·lish (iŋ′glish), ***adj.*** [ME. *Englysch;* AS. *englisc*, *ænglisc*, lit., of the Angles; see ANGLES & -ISH], 1. of England, its people, their culture, etc. 2. of their language. ***n.*** 1. the people of England. 2. the language of the English, spoken also in the United States and most parts of the British Empire. 3. the English language of a specific period or place: see **American English, British English, Old English, Middle English, Modern English.** 4. a characteristic way of using this language: as, the professor's *English* was pedantic. 5. the equivalent in the English language; English translation. 6. a school course or class in the English language or its literature. 7. [sometimes e-], in *billiards, bowling*, etc., a spinning motion given to a ball, as by striking it on one side. 8. in *printing*, a size of type, 14 point. Abbreviated **E., Eng.** ***v.t.*** 1. to translate into English. 2. to apply the principles of English pronunciation, spelling, etc. to; Anglicize, as a foreign word. 3. [sometimes e-], in *billiards, bowling*, etc., to give a spinning motion to (a ball), as by striking it on one side.

English Channel, an arm of the Atlantic, between England and France: width, 20-100 mi.

English daisy, see **daisy.**

English horn, a double-reed instrument of the woodwind family, similar to the oboe but larger and a fifth lower in pitch.

Eng·lish·ism (iŋ′glish-iz′m), ***n.*** 1. a characteristic or the characteristics of the English people. 2. an idiom of British English; Briticism. 3. an attachment to English ways and things.

Eng·lish·man (iŋ′glish-mən), ***n.*** [*pl.* ENGLISHMEN (-mən)], 1. a native or inhabitant of England, especially a man. 2. a person of English ancestry, especially a man, as in Canada, Australia, etc. 3. an English ship.

Englishman's tie, a kind of knot: see **knot,** illus.

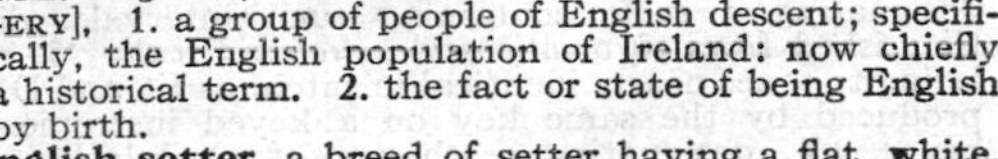

ENGLISH HORN

Eng·lish·ry (iŋ′glish-ri), ***n.*** [Anglo-Fr. *englescherie* < *englesche* < ME. *englisch;* see ENGLISH & -ERY], 1. a group of people of English descent; specifically, the English population of Ireland: now chiefly a historical term. 2. the fact or state of being English by birth.

English setter, a breed of setter having a flat, white, long-haired coat with black, yellow, or orange spots, and feathery hair on the legs and tail.

English sonnet, see **Shakespearean sonnet.**

English sparrow, the common street sparrow, a small brownish-gray European finch now found extensively in North America.

English walnut, 1. an Asiatic walnut tree now grown in Europe and North America. 2. its nut.

Eng·lish·wom·an (iŋ′glish-woom′ən), ***n.*** [*pl.* ENGLISHWOMEN (-wim′ən)], 1. a woman who is a native or inhabitant of England. 2. a woman of English ancestry, as in Canada, Australia, etc.

en·glut (en-glut′), ***v.t.*** [OFr. *englotir;* LL. *inglutire;* see EN- & GLUT (to swallow)], [Obs.], 1. to swallow; gulp down. 2. to glut.

en·gorge (en-gôrj′), ***v.t.*** [Fr. *engorger* < *en-*, in + *gorge*], 1. to gorge; glut. 2. to devour greedily. 3. in *medicine*, to congest (a blood vessel, tissue, etc.) with blood or other fluid. ***v.i.*** to eat greedily; feed ravenously.

en·gorge·ment (en-gôrj′mənt), ***n.*** an engorging or being engorged.

engr., 1. engineer. 2. engraved. 3. engraver. 4. engraving.

en·graft (en-graft′, en-gräft′), ***v.t.*** 1. to insert (a shoot or graft from one tree or plant) into another for propagation; graft. 2. to implant; establish firmly: as, patriotism was *engrafted* in his soul. Also **ingraft.**

en·grail (en-grāl′), ***v.t.*** [Fr. *engrêler* < *en-*, in + *grêle* < OFr. *gresle*, hail], 1. to indent (an edge or line) with concave, curved notches. 2. to decorate with such an indented edge or outline.

en·grail·ment (en-grāl′mənt), ***n.*** 1. an engrailing or being engrailed. 2. the engrailed inner edge of a coin or medal.

en·grain (in-grān′), ***v.t.*** [ME. *engreinen;* OFr. *engrainer*, to dye scarlet < *en-* (see EN-) + *graine*, seed, cochineal dye; associated in both Fr. & Eng. with *grain* (fiber)], 1. to ingrain. 2. to grain or color in imitation of wood.

en·gram (en′gram), ***n.*** [*en-* + *-gram*], 1. in *biology*, a permanent change produced by a stimulus in the protoplasm of a tissue. 2. in *psychology*, a permanent effect produced in the psyche as a result of stimulation: it serves as the basis for memory.

en·grave (in-grāv′), ***v.t.*** [ENGRAVED (-grāvd′), ENGRAVING], [*en-* + *grave* (to carve), after Fr. *engraver*], 1. to carve into (a surface); cut or etch letters, designs, etc. in or on. 2. to impress deeply or permanently on the mind or memory, as though by engraving. 3. to cut or etch (a picture, letters, etc.) into a metal plate, wooden block, etc. for printing. 4. to print by means of such a plate, block, etc.

en·grav·er (in-grāv'ẽr), *n.* a person who engraves designs, letters, etc. on metal plates, wooden blocks, etc. for printing: abbreviated **eng., engr.**

en·grav·ing (in-grāv'iŋ), *n.* 1. the act, process, or art of cutting or etching designs or letters on metal plates, wooden blocks, etc. for printing. 2. an engraved plate, design, etc. 3. any printed impression made from an engraved surface. Abbreviated **eng., engr.**

en·gross (in-grōs'), *v.t.* [< Anglo-Fr. *engrosser* < *en-* (see EN-) + *gros*, large (< L. *grossus;* see GROSS); also < OFr. *engroissier*, to become thick < LL. **ingrossiare* < L. *in*, in + *grossus*], 1. to write in large, distinct letters, as for a legal document; hence, 2. to express formally or in legal form. 3. to take the entire attention of; occupy wholly; absorb: as, this work *engrosses* me. 4. [Archaic], to monopolize.

en·gross·ing (in-grōs'iŋ), *adj.* [ppr. of *engross*], taking one's entire attention; very interesting; absorbing.

en·gross·ment (in-grōs'mənt), *n.* 1. an engrossing or being engrossed. 2. something engrossed, as a document.

en·gulf (in-gulf'), *v.t.* [*en-*, in + *gulf*, after OFr. *engolfer*], 1. to swallow up; overwhelm. 2. to plunge, as into a gulf. Also spelled **ingulf.**

en·hance (in-hans', in-häns'), *v.t.* [ENHANCED (-hanst', -hänst'), ENHANCING], [ME. *enhansen;* Anglo-Fr. *enhauncer;* prob. < OFr. *enhaucer; enhaucier;* LL. **inaltiare; in-*, in + **altiare*, to raise < L. *altus*, high], to make greater, as in cost, value, attractiveness, etc.; heighten; intensify; augment. *v.i.* [Archaic], to rise; increase. —*SYN.* see **intensify.**

en·hanced (in-hanst', in-hänst'), *adj.* [pp. of *enhance*], 1. made greater; heightened; intensified. 2. in *heraldry*, placed higher than usual on the shield.

en·hance·ment (in-hans'mənt, in-häns'mənt), *n.* an enhancing or being enhanced.

en·har·mon·ic (en'här-mon'ik), *adj.* [L. *enharmonicus;* Gr. *enarmonikos;* see EN- & HARMONY], in *music*, 1. *a)* designating or of an interval less than a half step. *b)* designating a quarter step in early Greek music. 2. designating a scale containing such intervals: distinguished from *chromatic scale, diatonic scale.* 3. relating to tones nearly identical in pitch, as E♭ and D♯, produced by the same key on a keyed instrument; hence, 4. designating a change of modulation in notation without change in sound of the given tone.

E·nid (ē'nid), [Celt., lit., spotless purity], a feminine name. *n.* 1. in *Arthurian legend*, the wife of Geraint: she was a model of constancy, loyalty, and patience. 2. a city in north central Oklahoma: pop., 39,000.

e·nig·ma (i-nig'mə), *n.* [*pl.* ENIGMAS (-məz)], [L. *aenigma;* Gr. *ainigma* < *ainissesthai*, to speak in riddles < *ainos*, tale, story], 1. a perplexing statement; riddle; hence, 2. a perplexing, baffling, or seemingly inexplicable matter, person, etc. —*SYN.* see **mystery.**

e·nig·mat·ic (en'ig-mat'ik, ē'nig-mat'ik), *adj.* of or like an enigma; perplexing; baffling. —*SYN.* see **obscure.**

e·nig·mat·i·cal (en'ig-mat'i-k'l, ē'nig-mat'i-k'l), *adj.* enigmatic.

en·isle (en-īl'), *v.t.* [ENISLED (-īld'), ENISLING], 1. to make (something) into or like an island. 2. to place on or as on an island; isolate.

E·ni·we·tok (en'ə-wē'tok, ə-nē'wə-tôk'), *n.* a large atoll in the Marshall Islands: site of United States atomic and hydrogen bomb tests.

en·jamb·ment, en·jambe·ment (in-jam'mənt; Fr. än'zhänb'män'), *n.* [Fr. *enjambement* < *enjamber*, to encroach < *en-* (see EN-) + *jambe*, leg], in *prosody*, the running on of a sentence from one couplet or line into the next without pause at the line end.

en·join (in-join'), *v.t.* [ME. *enjoignen;* OFr. *enjoindre;* L. *injungere*, to join or fasten into, charge, put upon; *in-*, in + *jungere*, to join], 1. to command; order; urge or impose with authority: as, the teacher *enjoined* silence on the class. 2. to prohibit, especially by legal injunction; forbid: as, the company was *enjoined* from using false advertising. —*SYN.* see **command, forbid.**

en·joy (in-joi'), *v.t.* [ME. *enjoyen;* OFr. *enjoier*, to give joy to], 1. to have or experience with joy; get pleasure from; relish. 2. to have the use or benefit of; have as one's lot or advantage.

enjoy oneself, to have a good time; have pleasure.

en·joy·a·ble (in-joi'ə-b'l), *adj.* capable of being enjoyed or giving enjoyment; agreeable. —*SYN.* see **pleasant.**

en·joy·a·bly (in-joi'ə-bli), *adv.* in an enjoyable manner.

en·joy·ment (in-joi'mənt), *n.* 1. an enjoying; specifically, *a)* a having the use or benefit of something; having as one's lot or advantage. *b)* a having or experiencing with joy; getting pleasure from. 2. something enjoyed. 3. pleasure; gratification; joy. —*SYN.* see **pleasure.**

en·kin·dle (en-kin'd'l), *v.t.* [*en-* + *kindle*], 1. to make blaze up; arouse (passions, etc.). 2. to light up.

enl., 1. enlarge. 2. enlarged. 3. enlisted.

en·lace (in-lās'), *v.t.* [ME. *enlacen;* OFr. *enlacer;* LL. **inclaciare* < *in-*, in + **lacius* < L. *laqueus*, a noose; see LACE], 1. to wind about as with a lace or laces; encircle; enfold. 2. to entangle; interlace. 3. to cover with or as with lace.

en·large (in-lärj'), *v.t. & v.i.* [ENLARGED (-lärjd'), ENLARGING], [ME. *enlargen;* OFr. *enlargier*], 1. to make or become larger; increase in size, volume, extent, etc.; broaden; expand. 2. in *photography*, to reproduce or be capable of being reproduced on a larger scale. —*SYN.* see **increase.**

enlarge on (or **upon**), to speak or write at greater length or in greater detail about; expatiate on.

en·large·ment (in-lärj'mənt), *n.* 1. an enlarging or being enlarged. 2. something that enlarges by being added: as, the index is an *enlargement* to the book. 3. a reproduction, as of a photograph, on a larger scale.

en·light·en (in-līt''n), *v.t.* 1. to give the light of fact and knowledge to; reveal truths to; endow with discernment; free from ignorance, prejudice, or superstition. 2. to inform; give clarification to (a person) as to meanings, intentions, etc. 3. [Archaic], to light up.

en·light·en·ment (in-līt''n-mənt), *n.* an enlightening or being enlightened.

the Enlightenment, an 18th-century European philosophical movement characterized by rationalism, an impetus toward learning, and a spirit of skepticism and empiricism in social and political thought.

en·list (in-list'), *v.t.* 1. to enroll for service in some branch of the armed forces. 2. to win the support of; get the help or services of: as, we'll *enlist* him in our movement. 3. to get (the help, support, etc. of someone): as, we'll *enlist* his aid in our cause. *v.i.* 1. to join some branch of the armed forces (often with *in*). 2. to join or support a cause or movement (with *in*).

enlisted man, any man in the armed forces who is not a commissioned or warrant officer: abbreviated **EM** (no period).

en·list·ment (in-list'mənt), *n.* 1. an enlisting or being enlisted. 2. the period of time for which one enlists.

en·liv·en (en-līv'ən), *v.t.* [*en-* + *life* (or *live, adj.*) + *-en*], to make active, vivacious, interesting, or cheerful; invigorate or brighten.

en masse (en mas'; Fr. än'màs'), [Fr., lit., in mass], in a group; as a whole; altogether.

en·mesh (en-mesh'), *v.t.* to entangle; catch in or as in the meshes of a net: also **inmesh.**

en·mi·ty (en'mə-ti), *n.* [*pl.* ENMITIES (-tiz)], [ME. *enemite;* OFr. *enemistie* < LL. **inimicitas* < L. *inimicus;* see ENEMY], the attitude or feelings of an enemy or enemies; hostility; antagonism.

SYN.—**enmity** denotes a strong, settled feeling of hatred, whether concealed, displayed, or latent; **hostility** usually suggests enmity expressed in active opposition, attacks, etc.; **animosity** suggests bitterness of feeling that tends to break out in open hostility; **antagonism** stresses the mutual hostility or enmity of persons, forces, etc.

en·ne·ad (en'i-ad'), *n.* [Gr. *enneas, enneados* < *ennea*, nine], a group or set of nine (books, gods, etc.).

en·ne·a·gon (en'i-ə-gon'), *n.* [< Gr. *ennea*, nine + *gōnia*, an angle], a plane figure having nine angles and nine sides; nonagon.

en·ne·a·he·dral (en'i-ə-hē'drəl), *adj.* of, or having the form of, an enneahedron.

en·ne·a·he·dron (en'i-ə-hē'drən), *n.* [*pl.* ENNEAHEDRONS (-drənz), ENNEAHEDRA (-drə)], [Mod. L. < Gr. *ennea*, nine; + *-hedron*], a solid figure with nine plane surfaces.

en·no·ble (i-nō'b'l, en-nō'b'l), *v.t.* [ENNOBLED (-b'ld), ENNOBLING], [Fr. *ennoblir;* see EN- & NOBLE], 1. to raise to the rank of nobleman; make (a person) a member of the nobility. 2. to give nobility to; dignify.

en·no·ble·ment (i-nō'b'l-mənt, en-nō'b'l-mənt), *n.* an ennobling or being ennobled.

en·nui (än'wē; Fr. än'nwē'), *n.* [*pl.* ENNUIS (-wēz; Fr. -nwē')], [Fr.; see ANNOY], weariness and dissatisfaction resulting from inactivity or lack of interest; boredom.

E·noch (ē'nək), [Gr. *Enōch;* Heb. *ḥānōkh*, lit., dedicated], a masculine name. *n.* in the *Bible*, 1. the eldest son of Cain: Gen. 4:17. 2. the father of Methuselah: Gen. 5:21.

e·nor·mi·ty (i-nôr'mə-ti), *n.* [*pl.* ENORMITIES (-tiz)], [Fr. *enormité;* L. *enormitas* < *enormis*, irregular, immoderate, immense < *e-*, out, + *norma*, rule], 1. great wickedness: as, the *enormity* of the crime. 2. a monstrous or outrageous act; very wicked crime.

e·nor·mous (i-nôr'məs), *adj.* [< L. *enormis* (see ENORMITY); + *-ous*], 1. very much exceeding the usual size, number, or degree; of great size; huge; vast; immense. 2. [Archaic], outrageous; very wicked; monstrous.

SYN.—**enormous** implies an exceeding by far what is normal in size, amount, or degree (an *enormous* nose, *enormous* expenses); **immense**, basically implying immeasurableness, suggests size beyond the regular run of measurements but does not connote abnormality in that which is very large (redwoods are *immense* trees); **huge** usually suggests an immense mass or bulk (a *huge* building, *huge* profits); **gigantic, colossal,** and **mammoth** basically imply a likeness to specific objects of great size (respectively, a giant, the Colossus of Rhodes, and the huge, extinct elephant) and therefore emphasize the idea of great magnitude, force, importance, etc., now often hyperbolically; **tremendous**, literally suggesting that which inspires awe or amazement because of its great size, is also used loosely as an intensive term.

e·nor·mous·ly (i-nôr′məs-li), *adv.* to an enormous extent; greatly; extremely; immeasurably.
E·nos (ē′nəs), [Gr. *Enōs;* Heb. *enōsh*, lit., man], a masculine name.
e·nough (i-nuf′), *adj.* [ME. *inouh;* AS. *genoh* (akin to G. *genug*) < *ge-*, intens. + **noh*, sufficient (akin to **negh* in *geneah*), it suffices (Goth. *ganah*); IE. base **enek-*, **nek-*, to reach, attain, as also in L. *nactus*, obtained, gained; cf. ENOW], as much or as many as necessary or desirable; sufficient; adequate. *n.* the amount or number needed or desired; sufficiency. *adv.* 1. as much or as often as necessary; to the required degree or amount; sufficiently. 2. fully; quite: as, he was thankful *enough* to escape. 3. just adequately; tolerably; fairly: as, he played well *enough*. *interj.* no more! that's enough! —*SYN.* see **sufficient.**
e·nounce (ē-nouns′, i-nouns′), *v.t.* [ENOUNCED (-nounst′), ENOUNCING], [Fr. *énoncer* < L. *enuntiare; e-*, out + *nuntiare*, to speak, declare < *nuntius*, messenger], 1. to state publicly or formally; proclaim. 2. to speak; utter; enunciate; pronounce.
e·now (i-nou′), *adj.*, *n.*, *adv.* [ME. *ynoghe, inou* (the former with traces of pl.; *enow* was considered pl. of *enough* by Johnson, as still in Scot. dial.); AS. *genog*, orig. form of *genoh;* see ENOUGH], [Archaic], enough.
‡**en pas·sant** (än′ pȧ′sän′), [Fr.], in passing; incidentally; by the way: used, in chess, of the capture of an opponent's pawn, which has taken its first move of two squares, by one's own pawn that dominates the first of those squares.
en·phy·tot·ic (en′fi-tot′ik), *adj.* [< *en-* + Gr. *phyton*, a plant], affecting certain plants of an area at regular intervals: said of various plant diseases.
en·plane (en-plān′), *v.i.* [ENPLANED (-plānd′), ENPLANING], [*en-* + *plane*, after *entrain*], to board an airplane.
en·quire (in-kwīr′), *v.t. & v.i.* [ENQUIRED (-kwīrd′), ENQUIRING], to inquire.
en·quir·y (in-kwīr′i), *n.* [*pl.* ENQUIRIES (-iz)], an inquiry.
en·rage (in-rāj′), *v.t.* [ENRAGED (-rājd′), ENRAGING], [OFr. *enrager*], to put into a rage; make very angry; infuriate.
‡**en rap·port** (än′ rȧ′pôr′), [Fr.], in harmony; in sympathy; in accord.
en·rapt (in-rapt′), *adj.* enraptured; rapt.
en·rap·ture (in-rap′chẽr), *v.t.* [ENRAPTURED (-chẽrd), ENRAPTURING], [*en-* + *rapture*], to fill with pleasure or delight; entrance; enchant.
en·rav·ish (en-rav′ish), *v.t.* [*en-* + *ravish*], to enrapture.
en·reg·is·ter (en-rej′is-tẽr), *v.t.* [Fr. *enregistrer*], to enter in a register; enroll; record.
‡**en rè·gle** (än′ reg′l′), [Fr.], according to rule; in order.
‡**en re·traite** (än′ rə-tret′), [Fr.], in retreat; in retirement.
en·rich (in-rich′), *v.t.* [ME. *enrichen;* OFr. *enrichir*], to make rich or richer; as, *a*) to give more wealth to. *b*) to give greater value or importance to: as, music has *enriched* my life. *c*) to fertilize (soil). *d*) to decorate; adorn. *e*) to add vitamins, minerals, etc. to (bread, etc.) so as to increase the food value.
en·rich·ment (in-rich′mənt), *n.* 1. an enriching or being enriched. 2. something that enriches.
en·robe (en-rōb′), *v.t.* to dress in or as in a robe.
en·roll, en·rol (in-rōl′), *v.t.* [ENROLLED (-rōld′), ENROLLING], [ME. *enrollen;* OFr. *enroller* (Fr. *enrôler*); see EN- & ROLL], 1. to record in a list. 2. to enlist. 3. to accept as a member; make (a person) a member. 4. [Rare], to roll up; wrap up. 5. [Obs.], to inscribe (a document); engross. *v.i.* 1. to have one's name recorded on a list. 2. to enlist. 3. to become a member.
en·roll·ment, en·rol·ment (en-rōl′mənt), *n.* 1. an enrolling or being enrolled. 2. a list of those enrolled. 3. the number of those enrolled.
en·root (en-rōōt′, en-root′), *v.t.* [*en-* + *root*], to implant firmly or deeply.
en route (än rōōt′; Fr. än′rōōt′), [Fr.], on the way; along the way.
‡**ens** (enz), *n.* [*pl.* ENTIA (en′shi-ə)], [LL. *ens, entis*, a being or thing; ppr. of *esse*, to be], in *philosophy*, 1. abstract being; existence, in the most general sense. 2. that which has being, either concrete or abstract.
Ens., Ensign.
en·sam·ple (en-sam′p'l, en-säm′p'l), *n.* [ME.; OFr.; altered < *essample;* see EXAMPLE], [Archaic], an example.
en·san·guine (en-saŋ′gwin), *v.t.* [ENSANGUINED (-gwind), ENSANGUINING], [*en-* + L. *sanguis, sanguinem*, blood; prob. after It. *insanguinare*], to stain or cover with blood; make bloody.
en·sconce (en-skons′), *v.t.* [ENSCONCED (-skonst′), ENSCONCING], [*en-* + *sconce* (small fortification)], 1. to hide; conceal; shelter. 2. to place comfortably, snugly, or securely: as, he *ensconced* himself on the sofa.
en·sem·ble (än-säm′b'l; Fr. än′sän′bl′), *n.* [Fr.; OFr.; LL. *insimul*, at the same time; *in-*, in + *simul*, at the same time], 1. all the parts considered as a whole; total effect. 2. a whole costume; costume of matching parts. 3. in *music*, *a*) the performance together of all the instruments of an orchestra or of all the voices in a chorus. *b*) a small group of musicians playing or singing together. *c*) the instruments or voices constituting such a group. 4. in the *theater*, *a*) the entire company. *b*) their appearance together on the stage.
en·sep·ul·cher, en·sep·ul·chre (en-sep′′l-kẽr), *v.t.* to put into a sepulcher; entomb.
en·shrine (in-shrīn′), *v.t.* [ENSHRINED (-shrīnd′), ENSHRINING], 1. to enclose in or as in a shrine. 2. to hold as sacred; cherish.
en·shrine·ment (in-shrīn′mənt), *n.* 1. an enshrining or being enshrined. 2. something that enshrines.
en·shroud (en-shroud′), *v.t.* to cover as if with a shroud; hide; veil; obscure.
en·si·form (en′si-fôrm′), *adj.* [< L. *ensis*, sword; + *-form*], sword-shaped, as an iris leaf; xiphoid.
en·sign (en′sīn), *n.* [OFr. *ensigne, enseigne;* L. *insigna*, standard, badge < *insigne*, neut. of *insignis*, distinguished by a mark, remarkable; *in-* + *signum*, a sign, mark], 1. a badge, symbol, or token of office or authority. 2. a flag or banner, especially a military or naval banner. 3. in the *British Army*, formerly, a commissioned officer who served as standard-bearer. 4. (en′s'n), [after Fr. *enseigne de vaisseau*, ship's ensign, midshipman], in the *United States Navy*, a commissioned officer of the lowest rank, corresponding to a second lieutenant in the Army: abbreviated **Ens.** (as a title). 5. [Obs.], a signal or sign.
en·sign·cy (en′s'n-si), *n.* ensignship.
en·sign·ship (en′s'n-ship′), *n.* [*ensign* + *-ship*], the rank or position of an ensign in the armed forces.
en·si·lage (en′s'l-ij), *n.* [Fr. < *ensiler*, to preserve in an underground granary; Sp. *ensilar* < *en-*, in + *silo;* see SILO], 1. the preserving of green fodder by storage in a silo. 2. green fodder so preserved; silage. *v.t.* [ENSILAGED (-ijd), ENSILAGING], to ensile.
en·sile (en-sīl′, en′sīl), *v.t.* [ENSILED (-sīld′, -sīld), ENSILING], [Fr. *ensiler;* see ENSILAGE], to store (fodder) in a silo for preservation.
en·slave (in-slāv′), *v.t.* [ENSLAVED (-slāvd′), ENSLAVING], 1. to put into slavery; make a slave of; hence, 2. to dominate; subjugate.
en·slave·ment (in-slāv′mənt), *n.* an enslaving or being enslaved; bondage.
en·snare (en-snâr′), *v.t.* to catch in or as in a snare; trap: also **insnare.**
en·sor·cell, en·sor·cel (en-sôr′s'l), *v.t.* [OFr. *ensorceler*, for **ensorcerer;* see EN- & SORCERY], to bewitch.
en·soul (en-sōl′), *v.t.* 1. to take or put into the soul. 2. to endow with a soul. Also **insoul.**
en·sphere (en-sfêr′), *v.t.* [ENSPHERED (-sfērd′), ENSPHERING], 1. to enclose in or as in a sphere. 2. to form into a sphere. Also **insphere.**
en·sue (en-sōō′, en-sū′), *v.i.* [ENSUED (-sōōd′, -sūd′), ENSUING], [ME. *ensuen;* OFr. *enseu*, pp. of *ensuivre* < LL. *insequere* < L. *insequi; in-* + *sequi*, to follow], 1. to come afterward; follow immediately. 2. to happen as a consequence; result. *v.t.* [Obs.], to follow; pursue; strive for. —*SYN.* see **follow.**
‡**en suite** (än′ swēt′; Eng. än swēt′), [Fr.], in a series; in a set; following one another in order.
en·sure (in-shoor′), *v.t. & v.i.* [ENSURED (-shoord′), ENSURING], [Late ME. *ensuren;* Anglo-Fr. *enseurer* (OFr. *asseurer;* see ASSURE) < *en-* (see EN-) + *seur*, sure], to insure.
en·swathe (en-swāth′), *v.t.* to wrap or bind in or as in a bandage; swathe: also **inswathe.**
-ent (ənt), [< Fr. & L.; Fr. *-ent;* L. *-ent-*, stem ending of present participles of certain verbs], a suffix used to form: 1. adjectives from verbs, corresponding to the present participles, as *insistent*. 2. nouns of agency from verbs, as *superintendent, solvent*. See also **-ant.**
en·tab·la·ture (en-tab′lə-chẽr), *n.* [MFr.; It. *intavolatura* < *intavolare* < *in-*, in + *tavola*, table, base < L. *tabula*, a board, tablet], in *architecture*, a horizontal superstructure supported by columns and composed of architrave, frieze, and cornice.

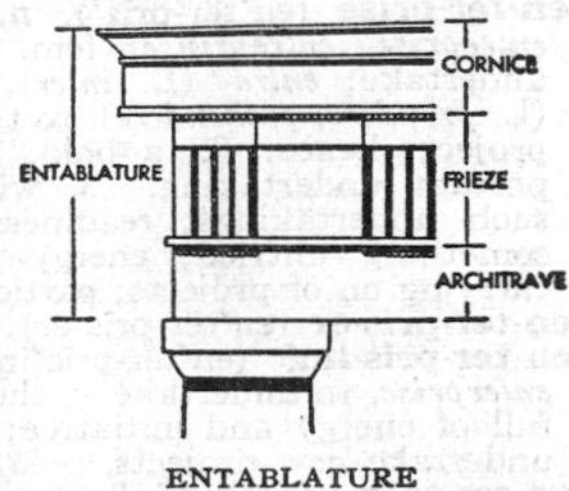

ENTABLATURE

en·ta·ble·ment (en-tā′b'l-mənt), *n.* [Fr.; OFr. < *entabler;* see EN-, TABLE, & -MENT], 1. an entablature. 2. the platform or series of platforms directly beneath a statue and on top of the dado and the base.
en·tail (in-tāl′), *v.t.* [ME. *entailen* < *en-*, in + *taile, talie*, an agreement; OFr. *taillé, taillié*, pp. of *taillier*, to cut; see TAILOR], 1. in *law*, to limit the inheritance of (property) to a specific line of heirs in such a way

that it can never be legally transferred. 2. to cause or require as a necessary consequence; involve; necessitate: as, the plan *entails* work. *n.* 1. an entailing or being entailed. 2. that which is entailed, as an inheritance. 3. necessary sequence, as the order of descent for an entailed inheritance.

en·tail·ment (in-tāl'mənt), *n.* an entailing or being entailed.

en·ta·moe·ba (en'tə-mē'bə), *n.* [*pl.* ENTAMOEBAE (-bē), ENTAMOEBAS (-bəz)], an endamoeba: also spelled **entameba.**

en·tan·gle (in-taŋ'g'l), *v.t.* 1. to involve in or as in a tangle; catch, as in a net, vine, etc., so that escape is difficult; ensnare; hence, 2. to involve in difficulty; confuse; perplex. 3. to cause to be tangled; complicate.

en·tan·gle·ment (in-taŋ'g'l-mənt), *n.* 1. an entangling or being entangled. 2. something that entangles.

en·ta·sis (en'tə-sis), *n.* [Mod. L.; Gr. *entasis,* lit., a stretching < *enteinein,* to entend in], in *architecture,* a slight, convex swelling in the shaft of a column.

En·teb·be (en-teb'e), *n.* the capital of Uganda, Africa, on Lake Victoria: pop., 7,200.

en·tel·e·chy (en-tel'ə-ki), *n.* [*pl.* ENTELECHIES (-kiz)], [L. *entelechia;* Gr. *entelecheia,* actuality < *en telei echein; en,* in + *telei,* dat. of *telos,* end, completion + *echein,* to hold], in *Aristotelian philosophy,* complete actuality: distinguished from *potentiality.*

en·tel·lus (en-tel'əs), *n.* [after *Entellus,* an ancient Sicilian hero, famous as an athlete], a small, long-tailed monkey of the East Indies.

en·tente (än-tänt'; Fr. än'tänt'), *n.* [Fr.; pp. of *entendre,* to understand], 1. an understanding or agreement, as between governments. 2. the parties to this.

‡**en·tente cor·diale** (än'tänt' kôr'dyȧl'), [Fr., lit., cordial understanding], a friendly understanding or agreement, especially between nations.

en·ter (en'tẽr), *v.t.* [ME. *entren;* OFr. *entrer;* L. *intrare* < *intra,* within, inside; see INTRA-], 1. to come or go into or upon. 2. to force a way into; penetrate; pierce: as, the bullet *entered* his body. 3. to put into; insert. 4. to write down in a record, list, diary, etc.; make an entry of. 5. to list by name in a competition, race, etc. 6. to join; become a part or member of; gain admission to (a political party, school, club, etc.). 7. to get (a person, etc.) admitted: as, he *entered* his son at a private school. 8. to begin; start upon: as John is *entering* business. 9. to register (a ship or cargo) at a customhouse. 10. in *law,* to place (a record, evidence, etc.) before a court. *v.i.* 1. to come or go into some place; make an entrance. 2. to pierce; penetrate.

enter into, 1. to engage in; take part in: as, he *entered into* the conversation. 2. to form a part or component of; be or become a factor in. 3. to deal with; discuss. 4. to sympathize with; appreciate and share: as, she *entered into* the spirit of the occasion.

enter on (or **upon**), 1. to begin; set out on; start. 2. to begin to possess or enjoy; take possession of.

en·ter·ic (en-ter'ik), *adj.* intestinal; of the enteron.

enteric fever, typhoid fever.

en·ter·i·tis (en'tə-rī'tis), *n.* [*enter-* + *-itis*], inflammation of the intestine, especially the small intestine.

en·ter·o- (en'tə-rō), [< Gr. *enteron,* intestine], a combining form meaning *intestine,* as in *enterocolitis*: also, before a vowel, **enter-.**

en·ter·o·co·li·tis (en'tə-rō'kə-lī'tis), *n.* [*entero-* + *colitis*], inflammation of the colon and the small intestine.

en·ter·on (en'tə-ron'), *n.* [Gr. *enteron,* intestine], the alimentary canal.

en·ter·os·to·my (en'tə-ros'tə-mi), *n.* [*pl.* ENTEROSTOMIES (-miz)], [*entero-* + *-stomy*], the surgical operation of making an artificial opening into the intestine through the abdominal wall, as for drainage.

en·ter·prise (en'tẽr-prīz'), *n.* [ME. *entrepryse;* OFr. *entreprise, entreprinse;* fem. pp. of *entreprendre,* to undertake; *entre-* (L. *inter*), in, between + *prendre* (L. *prendere, prehendere*), to take], 1. an undertaking; project; hence, 2. a bold, hard, dangerous, or important undertaking. 3. willingness to venture on such undertakings; readiness to take risks or try something untried; energy and initiative. 4. the carrying on of projects; participation in undertakings.

en·ter·pris·er (en'tẽr-prīz'ẽr), *n.* an entrepreneur.

en·ter·pris·ing (en'tẽr-prīz'iŋ), *adj.* [< archaic v. *enterprise,* to undertake < the *n.*], showing enterprise; full of energy and initiative; willing to take risks or undertake new projects. —*SYN.* see **ambitious.**

en·ter·tain (en'tẽr-tān'), *v.t.* [Fr. *entretenir* < OFr. *entre* (L. *inter*), between + *tenir* (L. *tenere*), to hold], 1. to hold the attention of; interest; divert; amuse. 2. to give hospitality to; have as a guest. 3. to consider: as, he refused to *entertain* the idea. 4. to keep in the mind; maintain: as, he *entertains* thoughts of revenge. 5. [Archaic], to keep up; continue. *v.i.* to have guests: as, they often *entertain* at dinner. —*SYN.* see **amuse.**

en·ter·tain·er (en'tẽr-tān'ẽr), *n.* a person who entertains; especially, one whose work is singing, dancing, etc., as at nightclubs.

en·ter·tain·ing (en'tẽr-tān'iŋ), *adj.* [ppr. of *entertain*], interesting; diverting; amusing.

en·ter·tain·ment (en'tẽr-tān'mənt), *n.* 1. an entertaining or being entertained; specifically, *a*) amusement. *b*) hospitality given or received. *c*) the consideration of an idea, etc. *d*) a keeping in mind. 2. something that entertains; interesting, diverting, or amusing thing, as a show or performance.

en·thet·ic (en-thet'ik), *adj.* [Gr. *enthetikos,* fit to put in < *enthetos,* verbal adj. of *entithenai; en-,* in + *tithenai,* to put], in *medicine,* coming from outside; exogenous: as, syphilis is an *enthetic* disease.

en·thrall, en·thral (in-thrôl'), *v.t.* [ENTHRALLED (-thrôld'), ENTHRALLING], [*en-* + *thrall*], 1. to make a slave of; enslave; hence, 2. to put or hold under strong influence; captivate; enchant; fascinate. Also spelled **inthrall, inthral.**

en·thrall·ment, en·thral·ment (in-thrôl'mənt), *n.* an enthralling or being enthralled.

en·throne (in-thrōn'), *v.t.* [ENTHRONED (-thrōnd'), ENTHRONING], 1. to place on a throne, as a king or bishop; make a king or bishop of; hence, 2. to accord the highest place to; revere; exalt. Also spelled **inthrone.**

en·throne·ment (in-thrōn'mənt), *n.* an enthroning or being enthroned.

en·thuse (in-thōōz', in-thūz'), *v.t.* & *v.i.* [ENTHUSED (-thōōzd', -thūzd'), ENTHUSING], [back-formation < *enthusiasm*], [Colloq.], 1. to make or become enthusiastic. 2. to show or cause to show enthusiasm.

en·thu·si·asm (in-thōō'zi-az'm, in-thū'zi-az'm), *n.* [Gr. *enthousiasmos* < *enthousiazein,* to be inspired, be possessed by a god, inspire < *enthous, entheos,* possessed by a god; *en-,* in + *theos,* god], 1. originally, supernatural inspiration or possession; inspired prophetic or poetic ecstasy. 2. intense or eager interest; zeal; fervor. 3. something arousing such interest or zeal. 4. [Archaic], religious frenzy. —*SYN.* see **passion.**

en·thu·si·ast (in-thōō'zi-ast, in-thū'zi-ast), *n.* [Gr. *enthousiastēs*], 1. a person full of enthusiasm. 2. a religious zealot, fanatic, or visionary. —*SYN.* see **zealot.**

en·thu·si·as·tic (in-thōō'zi-as'tik, in-thū'zi-as'tik), *adj.* 1. having or showing enthusiasm; ardent. 2. of, or having the nature of, enthusiasm.

en·thu·si·as·ti·cal·ly (in-thōō'zi-as'ti-k'l-i, in-thū'zi-as'tik-li), *adv.* in an enthusiastic manner; with enthusiasm.

en·thy·meme (en'thə-mēm'), *n.* [L. *enthymema;* Gr. *enthymēma* < *enthymeisthai,* to consider, reflect upon < *en-,* in + *thymos,* mind], 1. originally, in Aristotle, an argument from probabilities. 2. in *logic,* an argument in which one of the premises or, sometimes, the conclusion is not expressed but implied.

en·tice (in-tīs'), *v.t.* [ENTICED (-tīst'), ENTICING], [ME. *entisen;* OFr. *enticier, enticher,* to set afire, hence excite, entice; LL. **intitiare* < L. *in,* in + *titio,* a burning brand], to attract by offering hope of reward or pleasure; tempt; allure. —*SYN.* see **lure.**

en·tice·ment (in-tīs'mənt), *n.* 1. an enticing or being enticed. 2. something that entices; an allurement.

en·tire (in-tīr'), *adj.* [ME. *enter;* OFr. *entier;* L. *integer,* whole, untouched, undiminished; see INTEGER], 1. not lacking any of the parts; whole; complete; total. 2. unbroken; intact. 3. being wholly of one piece; undivided; continuous. 4. not castrated. 5. [Obs.], not mixed or alloyed; pure. 6. in *botany,* having an unbroken margin, without notches or indentations, as some leaves: see **leaf,** illus. *n.* 1. the whole; entirety. 2. a stallion. —*SYN.* see **complete.**

en·tire·ly (in-tīr'li), *adv.* 1. wholly; completely; totally; fully. 2. solely; only.

en·tire·ty (in-tīr'ti), *n.* [*pl.* ENTIRETIES (-tiz)], [OFr. *entierté*], 1. the state or fact of being entire; wholeness; completeness. 2. an entire thing; whole; total. 3. in *law,* undivided or sole possession.

in its entirety, as a whole; completely.

en·ti·tle (in-tī't'l), *v.t.* [ENTITLED (-t'ld), ENTITLING], [ME. *entitlen;* OFr. *entituler;* LL. *intitulare* < L. *in,* in + *titulus,* a title], 1. to give a title or name to; hence, 2. to honor or dignify by a title. 3. to give a right, claim, or legal title to; qualify (a person *to* do something). Also spelled **intitle.**

en·ti·ty (en'tə-ti), *n.* [*pl.* ENTITIES (-tiz)], [Fr. *entité;* ML. *entitas* < L. *ens, entis,* ppr. of *esse,* to be], 1. being; existence. 2. a thing that has real and individual existence, in reality or in the mind; anything real in itself.

en·to- (en'tə), [< Gr. *entos,* within], a combining form meaning *within* or *inner,* as in *entophyte, entozoon*: also, before a vowel, **ent-.**

en·to·blast (en'tə-blast'), *n.* [*ento-* + *-blast*], endoderm.

en·to·derm (en'tə-dũrm'), *n.* endoderm.

en·tomb (in-tōōm'), *v.t.* [OFr. *entoumber* (Fr. *entomber*)], 1. to place in a tomb or grave; bury. 2. to be a tomb for. Also spelled **intomb.**

en·tomb·ment (in-tōōm'mənt), *n.* an entombing or being entombed.

en·to·mo- (en'tə-mə), [< Gr. *entoma* (*zōa*), notched animals, insects < *entomos,* cut, notched (< *en-,* in + *temnein,* to cut): so named from their structure (see INSECT)], a combining form meaning *insect, insects,* as in *entomology.*

en·to·mo·log·ic (en'tə-mə-loj'ik), *adj.* entomological.

en·to·mo·log·i·cal (en'tə-mə-loj'i-k'l), *adj.* having to do with entomology: abbreviated **entom.**

en·to·mol·o·gist (en'tə-mol'ə-jist), *n.* a student of or specialist in entomology.

en·to·mol·o·gy (en'tə-mol'ə-ji), *n.* [Fr. *entomologie;* see ENTOMO- & -LOGY], the branch of zoology that deals with insects: abbreviated **entom.**

en·to·phyte (en'tə-fit'), *n.* [*ento-* + *-phyte*], a plant that lives inside the body of another plant or of an animal.

en·to·phyt·ic (en'tə-fit'ik), *adj.* of, or having the nature of, an entophyte.

en·tou·rage (än'too-räzh'; Fr. än'tōō'räzh'), *n.* [Fr. < *entourer*, to surround < *en tour*, around; *en*, in + *tour*, round], 1. surroundings; environment. 2. a group of associates or attendants; retinue.

en·to·zo·a (en'tə-zō'ə), *n.* plural of **entozoon.**

en·to·zo·an (en'tə-zō'ən), *n.* an entozoon. *adj.* of the entozoa.

en·to·zo·ic (en'tə-zō'ik), *adj.* [see ENTOZOON], 1. in *botany*, living inside animals, usually as a parasite: said of certain fungi, etc. 2. in *zoology*, living inside another animal: said especially of certain intestinal worms.

en·to·zo·on (en'tə-zō'on), *n.* [*pl.* ENTOZOA (-ə)], [*ento-* + Gr. *zōon*, animal], an animal parasite, especially an intestinal worm, living inside another animal.

en·tr'acte (än-trakt'; Fr. än'träkt'), *n.* [Fr. < *entre-*, between + *acte*, an act], 1. the interval between two acts of a play, opera, etc.; intermission. 2. a musical selection, dance, etc. performed during this interval.

en·trails (en'trālz, en'trəlz), *n.pl.* [ME. & OFr. *entrailles;* LL. *intralia* < L. *interanea*, pl. of *interaneum*, intestine < *interaneus*, internal < *inter*, between, among], 1. the inner organs of men or animals; specifically, the intestines; viscera; guts. 2. [Rare], the inner parts of a thing.

en·train (in-trān'), *v.t.* [coined after *embark*], to put (troops, etc.) aboard a train. *v.i.* to go aboard a train.

en·trance (en'trəns), *n.* [OFr. < *entrant*, ppr. of *entrer;* see ENTER], 1. the act or point of entering: as, at the famous singer's *entrance*, the audience rose and cheered. 2. a place for entering; door, gate, etc. 3. the permission, right, or power to enter; admission.

en·trance (in-trans', in-träns'), *v.t.* [ENTRANCED (-transt', -tränst'), ENTRANCING], 1. to put into a trance; hence, 2. to delight; charm; enrapture; enchant.

en·trance·ment (in-trans'mənt, in-träns'mənt), *n.* 1. an entrancing or being entranced. 2. something that entrances.

en·trant (en'trənt), *n.* [Fr.; OFr.; see ENTRANCE, *n.*], 1. a person who enters. 2. a person entering a profession, an organization, etc. 3. a participant in a contest or competition.

en·trap (in-trap'), *v.t.* [OFr. *entraper, entrapper*], 1. to catch in or as in a trap. 2. to deceive or trick into difficulty; ensnare.

en·treat (in-trēt'), *v.t.* & *v.i.* [ME. *entreten*, to treat or deal with, beseech; OFr. *entraiter*, to treat of, entertain; *en-*, in + *traiter;* see TREAT], 1. to ask earnestly; beg; beseech; implore. 2. [Archaic], to treat. 3. [Obs.], *a*) to persuade by imploring. *b*) to induce. Also spelled **intreat.** —*SYN.* see **beg.**

en·treat·y (in-trēt'i), *n.* [*pl.* ENTREATIES (-iz)], [< *entreat*], an earnest request; supplication; prayer.

‡en·tre·chat (än'trə-shä'), *n.* [Fr. < It. (*capriola*) *intrecciata*, intricate (leap) < *intrecciare* < *in-*, in + *treccia*, a pleat], in *ballet*, a leap straight upward in which the dancer crosses his legs or strikes his heels together, usually several times, while coming down.

en·tree, en·trée (än'trā; Fr. än'trā'), *n.* [Fr. *entrée;* fem. pp. of *entrer;* see ENTER], 1. the right, permission, or freedom to enter; access. 2. the main course of a meal. 3. formerly, and still in some countries, a dish served before the roast or between the main courses, as between the fish and the meat.

en·tre·mets (än'trə-mā'; Fr. än'trə-me'), *n.* [*pl.* ENTREMETS (-māz'; Fr. -me')], [Fr.; *entre-*, between + *mets*, a dish; see MESS, *n.*], a dish served between the main courses or as a side dish.

en·trench (in-trench'), *v.t.* [*en-* + *trench*, after Fr. *retrancher*], 1. to surround or fortify with a trench or trenches; hence, 2. to establish securely: used in the passive voice or with a reflexive pronoun, as, the right to trial by jury is *entrenched* in our legal system. *v.i.* to encroach; infringe; trespass. Also spelled **intrench.**

en·trench·ment (in-trench'mənt), *n.* 1. an entrenching or being entrenched. 2. a trench or system of trenches, usually fortified with mounds of earth, rubble, etc.; hence, 3. any fortification or defense.

‡en·tre nous (än'tr' nōō'), [Fr., lit., between us], between ourselves; confidentially.

en·tre·pôt (än'trə-pō'; Fr. än'trə-pō'), *n.* [Fr. < *entreposer;* see INTER- & POSE, *v.*], 1. a place for the storage of goods; warehouse. 2. a distributing center for goods.

en·tre·pre·neur (än'trə-prə-nũr'; Fr. än'trə-prə-nër'), *n.* [Fr. < *entreprendre;* see ENTERPRISE], a person who organizes and manages a business undertaking, assuming the risk for the sake of the profit.

en·tre·sol (en'tẽr-sol'; Fr. än'trə-sôl'), *n.* [Fr.; *entre-*, between + *sol*, ground], a low story or floor just above the street floor, as in some hotels and department stores: also called *mezzanine.*

en·tro·py (en'trə-pi), *n.* [(after *energy*) < Gr. *tropē*, a turning < *trepein*, to turn], in *physics*, the theoretical measure of energy, as of steam, which cannot be transformed into mechanical work in a thermodynamic system: symbol, Φ.

en·trust (in-trust'), *v.t.* 1. to trust; charge or invest with a trust or duty: as, he *entrusted* his friend with the property. 2. to assign the care of; turn over for safekeeping: as, *entrust* your books to me while you are away. Also spelled **intrust.** —*SYN.* see **commit.**

en·try (en'tri), *n.* [*pl.* ENTRIES (-triz)], [ME. & OFr. *entree;* LL. *intrata* < pp. of L. *intrare;* see ENTER], 1. an entering; entrance. 2. a way or passage by which to enter; door, hall, etc.; entryway. 3. the writing down of an item, note, etc. in a list, journal, etc. 4. a thing thus written down. 5. the registration of a ship or cargo at a customhouse. 6. one entered in a race, competition, etc.; entrant. 7. in *law*, *a*) the taking possession of buildings, land, etc. by entering or setting foot upon them. *b*) the entering upon premises with the intention of committing burglary or some other crime.

en·try·way (en'tri-wā'), *n.* a way or passage by which to enter.

en·twine (in-twīn'), *v.t.* & *v.i.* to twine, weave, or twist together or around: also spelled **intwine.**

en·twist (en-twist'), *v.t.* 1. to twist together or in (*with*). 2. to make into a twist. Also **intwist.**

e·nu·cle·ate (i-nōō'kli-āt', i-nū'kli-āt'), *v.t.* [< L. *enucleatus*, pp. of *enucleare* < *e-*, out + *nucleus*, a kernel], 1. to extract (a kernel, etc.) from a shell or husk; hence, 2. to make clear; explain. 3. in *biology*, to remove the nucleus of. 4. in *surgery*, to remove (a tumor, etc.) as a whole from its enclosing sac. *adj.* (i-nōō'kli-it, i-nū'kli-it), enucleated.

e·nu·cle·a·tion (i-nōō'kli-ā'shən, i-nū'kli-ā'shən), *n.* an enucleating or being enucleated.

e·nu·cle·a·tor (i-nōō'kli-ā'tẽr, i-nū'kli-ā'tẽr), *n.* a person or thing that enucleates.

e·nu·mer·ate (i-nōō'mə-rāt', i-nū'mə-rāt'), *v.t.* [< L. *enumeratus*, pp. of *enumerare; e-*, out + *numerare*, to count < *numerus*, number], 1. to count; count one by one. 2. to name one by one; specify, as in a list.

e·nu·mer·a·tion (i-nōō'mə-rā'shən, i-nū'mə-rā'shən), *n.* [L. *enumeratio*], 1. an enumerating or being enumerated. 2. a detailed list.

e·nu·mer·a·tive (i-nōō'mə-rā'tiv, i-nū'mẽr-ə-tiv), *adj.* 1. enumerating. 2. of enumeration.

e·nu·mer·a·tor (i-nōō'mə-rā'tẽr, i-nū'mə-rā'tẽr), *n.* a person who enumerates.

e·nun·ci·a·ble (i-nun'si-ə-b'l, i-nun'shi-ə-b'l), *adj.* that can be enunciated.

e·nun·ci·ate (i-nun'si-āt', i-nun'shi-āt'), *v.t.* [ENUNCIATED (-id), ENUNCIATING], [< L. *enuntiatus*, pp. of *enuntiare; e-*, out + *nuntiare*, to announce < *nuntius*, a messenger], 1. to state definitely. 2. to announce; proclaim. 3. to pronounce (words); especially, to pronounce clearly and distinctly. *v.i.* to pronounce words; articulate. —*SYN.* see **utter.**

e·nun·ci·a·tion (i-nun'si-ā'shən, i-nun'shi-ā'shən), *n.* [L. *enunciatio*], 1. an enunciating or being enunciated. 2. an announcement; declaration. 3. the manner of enunciating words.

e·nun·ci·a·tive (i-nun'si-ā'tiv, i-nun'shi-ə-tiv), *adj.* [L. *enunciativus*], 1. enunciating; declaratory. 2. having to do with enunciation.

e·nun·ci·a·tor (i-nun'si-ā'tẽr, i-nun'shi-ā'tẽr), *n.* [LL. *enuntiator*], a person who enunciates.

en·ure (in-yoor'), *v.t.* & *v.i.* to inure.

en·u·re·sis (en'yoo-rē'sis), *n.* [Mod. L. < Gr. *enourein;* see EN- & URINE], involuntary emission of urine.

en·vel·op (in-vel'əp), *v.t.* [ME. *envelupen;* OFr. *envoluper, enveloper* (Fr. *envelopper*); see EN- & DEVELOP], 1. to wrap up; cover completely. 2. to surround. 3. to conceal; hide; obscure. *n.* an envelope.

en·ve·lope (en'və-lōp', än'və-lōp'), *n.* [Fr. *enveloppe* < *envelopper* (OFr. *enveloper*); see ENVELOP], 1. a thing that envelops; wrapper; covering. 2. a folded paper container for letters, etc., usually with a gummed flap for sealing. 3. the outer covering of a dirigible or balloon. 4. the bag that contains the gas in a dirigible or balloon. 5. in *astronomy*, a cloudy mass surrounding the head of a comet on the side toward the sun. 6. in *biology*, any enclosing membrane, skin, or shell. 7. in *botany*, any surrounding structure, as the calyx. 8. in *geometry*, the locus of the ultimate intersections of a series of curves or surfaces. Abbreviated **env.**

en·vel·op·ment (in-vel'əp-mənt), *n.* 1. an enveloping

or being enveloped. 2. something that envelops; wrapper; covering.

en·ven·om (en-ven′əm), *v.t.* [ME. *envenimen;* OFr. *envenimer*], 1. to put venom or poison on or into; make poisonous; hence, 2. to fill with hate; embitter.

en·vi·a·ble (en′vi-ə-b'l), *adj.* to be envied or desired.

en·vi·er (en′vi-ẽr), *n.* a person who envies.

en·vi·ous (en′vi-əs), *adj.* [ME.; OFr. *envieus;* L. *invidiosus* < *invidia,* envy], 1. characterized by envy; feeling, showing, or resulting from envy. 2. [Obs.], *a)* emulous. *b)* spiteful.

en·vi·ron (in-vī′rən), *v.t.* [ME. *envirounen;* OFr. *environner* < *environ,* about; see ENVIRONS], to surround; encircle; enclose.

en·vi·ron·ment (in-vī′rən-mənt; *sometimes* in-vī′ẽrn-mənt), *n.* [*environ* + *-ment*], 1. a surrounding or being surrounded. 2. something that surrounds; surroundings. 3. all the conditions, circumstances, and influences surrounding, and affecting the development of, an organism or group of organisms: often contrasted with *heredity.*

en·vi·ron·men·tal (in-vī′rən-men′t'l), *adj.* of environment.

en·vi·rons (in-vī′rənz, en′və-rənz), *n. pl.* [ME. *environ* (sing.); OFr. *environ* < *en-,* in + *viron,* a circuit < *virer,* to turn; see VEER], the districts surrounding a town or city; suburbs; vicinity.

en·vis·age (en-viz′ij), *v.t.* [ENVISAGED (-ijd), ENVISAGING], [Fr. *envisager;* see EN- & VISAGE], 1. to face; confront: as, you must *envisage* realities. 2. to form an image of in the mind; visualize.

en·vi·sion (en-vizh′ən), *v.t.* [*en-* + *vision*], to imagine (something not yet in existence); picture in the mind.

en·voy (en′voi), *n.* [Fr. *envoyé,* pp. of *envoyer,* to send; OFr. *envoier* < *en-* (L. *in*), in + *voie* (L. *via*), way], 1. a messenger; agent. 2. an agent sent by a government or ruler to transact diplomatic business: an envoy ranks just below an ambassador.

en·voy (en′voi), *n.* [ME. *envoye;* OFr. *envoy,* lit., a sending < *envoier,* to send; see ENVOY (messenger)], 1. originally, a dedication or postscript to a poem, essay, or book, directing it to a specific person's attention. 2. a concluding stanza added to a ballade and some other verse forms. Often **l'envoi. l'envoy.**

en·vy (en′vi), *n.* [*pl.* ENVIES (-viz)], [ME. & OFr. *envie;* L. *invidia* < *invidus,* having hatred or ill will < *invidere,* to look askance at; *in-,* in, upon + *videre,* to look, see], 1. a feeling of discontent and ill will because of another's advantages, possessions, etc.; resentful dislike of another who has something desirable. 2. desire for some advantage or possession belonging to another. 3. an object of envious feeling: as, he was the *envy* of other boys because he had a bicycle. 4. [Obs.], *a)* ill will; spite. *b)* odium. *v.t.* [ENVIED (-vid), ENVYING], to feel envy toward, at, or because of; regard with envy. *v.i.* [Obs.], to feel or show envy.

SYN.—to **envy** another is to feel ill will, jealousy, or discontent at his possession of something that one keenly desires to have or achieve oneself; **begrudge** implies an unwillingness that someone should possess or enjoy something that he needs or deserves; to **covet** is to long ardently and wrongfully for something that belongs to another.

en·womb (en-wōōm′), *v.t.* to enclose in or as in a womb.

en·wrap (en-rap′), *v.t.* to wrap; envelop: also **inwrap.**

en·wreathe (en-rēth′), *v.t.* to encircle or surround with or as with a wreath: also **inwreathe.**

en·zo·ot·ic (en′zō-to′ik), *adj.* [< Gr. *en-,* in + *zōion,* animal; + *-otic* (as in *chaotic,* etc.)], affecting animals in a certain area, climate, or season: said of diseases: cf. **endemic.** *n.* an enzootic disease.

en·zym (en′zim), *n.* an enzyme.

en·zy·mat·ic (en′zī-mat′ik, en′zi-mat′ik), *adj.* of, like, or derived from an enzyme or enzymes.

en·zyme (en′zīm, en′zim), *n.* [G. *enzym;* LGr. *enzymos,* leavened < Gr. *en-,* in + *zymē,* leaven], any of various organic substances that are produced in plant and animal cells and cause changes in other substances by catalytic action: as, pepsin is a digestive *enzyme.*

e·o- (ē′ə, ē′ō), [< Gr. *ēōs,* dawn], a prefix used in forming terms in geology, paleontology, etc., meaning *early, early part of a period,* as in *Eocene, eolithic.*

e.o., ex officio.

E·o·an·thro·pus (ē′ō-an-thrō′pəs), *n.* [Mod. L. < *eo-* + Gr. *anthrōpos,* man], Piltdown man, a species of prehistoric man.

E·o·cene (ē′ə-sēn′), *adj.* [*eo-* + Gr. *kainos,* new], designating or of the earliest epoch of the Tertiary Period in the Cenozoic Era, during which mammals became the dominant animals.

the Eocene, the Eocene Epoch or its rocks: see **geology,** chart.

e·o·hip·pus (ē′ō-hip′əs), *n.* [Mod. L. < *eo-* + Gr. *hippos,* horse], the extinct, prehistoric ancestor of the modern horse: it was about the size of a fox and had toes instead of hoofs.

E·o·li·an (ē-ō′li-ən), *adj. & n.* Aeolian.

E·ol·ic (ē-ol′ik), *adj. & n.* Aeolic.

‡é·o·lienne (ā′ô′lyen′), *n.* [Fr., orig., fem. of *éolien,* aeolian: so named from its lightness], a cloth of silk and wool or silk and cotton, like poplin but lighter.

e·o·lith (ē′ə-lith′), *n.* [*eo-* + *-lith*], any of the crude stone tools used in the early part of the Stone Age.

e·o·lith·ic (ē′ə-lith′ik), *adj.* [*eo-* + *lithic*], designating or of that early stage of human culture in which crude stone tools were first used.

e.o.m., end of the month.

e·on (ē′ən, ē′on), *n.* [see AEON], an extremely long, indefinite period of time; thousands and thousands of years: also spelled **aeon.** —***SYN.*** see **period.**

e·o·ni·an (ē-ō′ni-ən), *adj.* lasting forever; eternal: also spelled **aeonian.**

‡e·o no·mi·ne (ē′ō nom′i-nē′), [L.], by that name.

E·os (ē′os), *n.* [L.; Gr. *Ēōs;* see EO-], in *Greek mythology,* the goddess of dawn: identified with the Roman goddess Aurora.

e·o·sin (ē′ə-sin), *n.* [< Gr. *ēōs,* dawn; + *-in*], 1. a rose-colored dye and acid-base indicator, extracted from coal tar. 2. any of various other red dyes obtained from coal tar.

e·o·sine (ē′ə-sin, ē′ə-sēn′), *n.* eosin.

e·o·sin·ic (ē′ə-sin′ik), *adj.* of or containing eosin.

-e·ous (i-əs), [L. *-eus;* + *-ous*], an adjectival suffix meaning *having the nature of, like,* as in *beauteous.*

E·o·zo·ic (ē′ə-zō′ik), *adj.* [*eo-* + Gr. *zōon,* animal; + *-ic*], pre-Paleozoic: see also **Proterozoic, Algonkian.**

ep- (ep), epi-.

Ep., Epistle.

e·pact (ē′pakt), *n.* [Fr. *épacte;* LL. *epacta;* Gr. *epaktē* < *epaktos,* intercalary, brought in < *epagein,* to bring in, intercalate < *epi-,* on, in + *agein,* to bring, lead], 1. the period of about eleven days by which the solar year exceeds the lunar year of twelve months. 2. the age, in days, of the calendar moon on the first of the year.

E·pam·i·non·das (i-pam′ə-non′dəs), *n.* a Theban (Greek) general and statesman; 418?–362 B.C.

ep·arch (ep′ärk), *n.* [Gr. *eparchos* < *epi-,* over + *archein,* to rule], 1. the governor of a province in ancient Greece. 2. the governor of an eparchy in modern Greece. 3. in the *Orthodox Eastern Church,* a metropolitan, or bishop.

ep·ar·chi·al (ep-är′ki-əl), *adj.* of an eparch or eparchy.

ep·arch·y (ep′är-ki), *n.* [*pl.* EPARCHIES (-kiz)], [Gr. *eparchia* < *eparchos;* see EPARCH], 1. in modern Greece, a political subdivision of a province. 2. in the *Orthodox Eastern Church,* a diocese.

ep·au·let, ep·au·lette (ep′ə-let′), *n.* [Fr. *épaulette,* dim. of *épaule,* the shoulder < OFr. *espale* < L. *spatula;* see SPATULA], 1. a shoulder ornament for certain uniforms, especially military uniforms. 2. any similar ornament, as on a woman's dress.

ep·ax·i·al (ep-ak′si-əl), *adj.* [*ep-* + *axial*], in *anatomy,* upon or above an axis.

e·pee (e-pā′), *n.* [Fr.; OFr. *espee;* L. *spatha,* broad, flat instrument, broad two-edged sword without a point; Gr. *spathē,* any broad blade, broad blade of a sword; see SPADE], a sword, especially a thin, pointed sword without a cutting edge, like a foil but heavier and more rigid, used in fencing: also spelled **épée.**

e·pee·ist (e-pā′ist), *n.* a person who fences with an epee: also spelled **épéeist.**

e·pei·ro·gen·e·sis (e-pī′rə-jen′ə-sis), *n.* epeirogeny.

e·pei·ro·ge·net·ic (e-pī′rə-jə-net′ik), *adj.* epeirogenic.

e·pei·ro·gen·ic (e-pī′rə-jen′ik), *adj.* of epeirogeny: also spelled **epirogenic.**

ep·ei·rog·e·ny (ep′ī-roj′ə-ni), *n.* [< Gr. *ēpeiros,* mainland; + *-geny*], the changes in the earth's surface that produce continents, ocean basins, etc.: also spelled **epirogeny.**

ep·en·ceph·a·lon (ep′en-sef′ə-lon′), *n.* [Mod. L. < Gr. *epi,* on, near + *enkephalos,* the brain; *en-,* in + *kephalos,* the head], 1. the front part of the most posterior primary vesicle of an embryo's brain: it develops into the pons and part of the cerebellum. 2. [Rare], the cerebellum.

ep·en·dy·ma (ep-en′di-mə), *n.* [Gr. *ependyma,* a wrap], the membrane lining the central cavities of the brain and spinal cord.

ep·en·the·sis (ep-en′thə-sis), *n.* [*pl.* EPENTHESES (-sēz′)], [LL.; Gr. *epenthesis* < *epi-,* upon + *en-,* in + *tithenai,* to put, place], 1. the insertion or development of an unhistorical sound or syllable in a word to make its pronunciation easier, as the *b* in *mumble* (< ME. *momelen*). 2. any such letter or syllable so occurring.

ep·en·thet·ic (ep′ən-thet′ik), *adj.* of, or having the nature of, epenthesis.

e·pergne (i-pũrn′, ā-pern′), *n.* [Fr.; prob. < *épargner,* to save], an ornamental dish with several compartments for fruit, cookies, candy, etc., used as a centerpiece for a dining table.

ep·ex·e·ge·sis (ep-ek′sə-jē′sis), *n.* [Mod. L.; Gr. *epexēgēsis,* detailed account, explanation < *epexēgeisthai,* to recount in detail < *epi-,* on, in + *exēgeisthai,* to point out; see EXEGESIS], additional explanation; further clarification, as by the addition of a word or words.

ep·ex·e·get·ic (ep-ek′sə-jet′ik), *adj.* epexegetical.

ep·ex·e·get·i·cal (ep-ek′sə-jet′i-k'l), *adj.* of, or having the nature of, epexegesis.

eph- (ef), epi-.

Eph., Ephesians.

e·phah, e·pha (ē'fə), *n.* [Heb. *'ēphāh*], an ancient Hebrew dry measure, equal to about 37 quarts.

e·phe·bic (e-fē'bik), *adj.* [L. *ephebicus;* Gr. *ephebikos*], of, or having the nature of, an ephebus.

e·phe·bos (e-fē'bəs, e-fē'bos), *n.* [*pl.* EPHEBOI (-boi)], an ephebus.

e·phe·bus (e-fē'bəs), *n.* [*pl.* EPHEBI (-bī)], [L.; Gr. *ephēbos* < *epi-*, at, upon + *hēbē*, early manhood], in ancient Greece, a youth who had just become a citizen.

e·phed·rin (e-fed'rin), *n.* ephedrine.

e·phed·rine (e-fed'rin, ef'ə-drēn'), *n.* [< *Ephedra*, name of a genus of desert shrubs containing the alkaloid < L. *ephedra*, horsetail; Gr. *ephedra* < *ephedros*, sitting by or upon < *epi-*, on, near + *hedra*, a seat], an alkaloid, $C_{10}H_{15}NO$, derived from certain plants, used to relieve nasal congestion, as in asthma, hay fever, etc.: it causes constriction of the swollen or inflamed blood vessels.

e·phem·er·a (ə-fem'ēr-ə), *n.* [*pl.* EPHEMERAS (-əz), EPHEMERAE (-ē')], [Mod. L. < Gr. *ephēmeros*, for the day, short-lived < *epi-*, upon + *hēmera*, a day], 1. an ephemerid; May fly. 2. an ephemeral thing.

e·phem·er·al (ə-fem'ēr-əl), *adj.* [< Gr. *ephemeros* (see EPHEMERA); + *-al*], 1. lasting only one day. 2. short-lived; transitory: as, *ephemeral* glory. *n.* an ephemeral thing. —*SYN.* see **transient.**

e·phem·er·id (ə-fem'ēr-id), *n.* [< *ephemera* + *-id*], any of a group of delicate insects with gauzy wings, which live for only a few hours or a few days, although the larvae live for several years; May fly: also called *ephemera, ephemeron.*

e·phem·er·is (ə-fem'ēr-is), *n.* [*pl.* EPHEMERIDES (ef'ə-mer'ə-dēz')], [L.; Gr. *ephēmeris*, diary, calendar < *ephēmeros;* see EPHEMERA], 1. a table giving the computed positions of a heavenly body for every day of a given period. 2. an astronomical almanac containing such tables. 3. [Obs.], *a*) an almanac; calendar. *b*) a diary; journal.

e·phem·er·on (ə-fem'ə-ron'), *n.* [*pl.* EPHEMERA (-rə), EPHEMERONS (-ronz')], [Gr. *ephēmeron*, short-lived insect < *ephēmeros;* see EPHEMERA], a May fly; ephemerid.

E·phe·sian (i-fē'zhən), *adj.* of Ephesus or its people. *n.* a native or inhabitant of Ephesus.

E·phe·sians (i-fē'zhənz), *n.pl.* [construed as sing.], the Epistle to the Ephesians, a book of the New Testament which was a message from the Apostle Paul to the Christians of Ephesus: abbreviated **Eph., Ephes.**

Eph·e·sus (ef'ə-səs), *n.* an ancient city in Asia Minor.

eph·od (ef'əd, ē'fod), *n.* [Heb. *ēphōd* < *āphad*, to put on], a richly embroidered outer vestment worn by Jewish priests in ancient times.

EPHESUS

eph·or (ef'ôr, ef'ēr), *n.* [*pl.* EPHORS (-ôrz, -ērz), EPHORI (-ə-rī')], [L. *ephorus;* Gr. *ephoros*, overseer < *ephoran* < *epi-*, over + *horan*, to see], 1. in ancient Greece, a magistrate; especially, any of the five chief magistrates annually elected by the people of Sparta. 2. in modern Greece, any of various governmental officials.

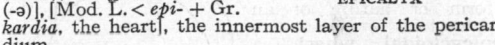

E·phra·im (ē'fri-əm), [LL.; Gr. *Ephraim;* Heb. *ephrayim*, lit., very fruitful], a masculine name. *n.* in the *Bible*, 1. the younger son of Joseph. 2. the tribe of Israel descended from him; hence, 3. the kingdom of Israel.

E·phra·im·ite (ē'fri-əm-īt'), *n.* a descendant of Ephraim; member of the tribe of Ephraim.

ep·i- (ep'ə, ep'i), [< Gr. *epi*, at, on, upon, over, besides, etc.], a prefix meaning *on, upon, over, on the outside, anterior, beside, besides, among*, as in *epiglottis, epidemic, epidermis:* it becomes **ep-** before a vowel, as in *eparch*, and **eph-** in an aspirated word, as in *ephemeral.*

ep·i·blast (ep'ə-blast'), *n.* [*epi-* + *-blast*], the outer layer of cells of an embryo.

ep·i·bol·ic (ep'ə-bol'ik), *adj.* having to do with epiboly.

e·pib·o·ly (i-pib'ə-li), *n.* [Gr. *epibolē*, a throwing upon < *epiballein*, to throw upon; *epi-*, on, upon + *ballein*, to throw], in *embryology*, the growth of a group of cells around another group, resulting from the more rapid division of the former.

ep·ic (ep'ik), *n.* [L. *epicus;* Gr. *epikos, adj.*, epic < *epos*, a word, speech, tale, song, epic], 1. a long narrative poem about the deeds of a traditional or historical hero or heroes of high station; typically, *a*) a poem like the *Iliad* and *Odyssey*, with a background of warfare and the supernatural, a dignified style, and certain formal characteristics of structure (beginning *in medias res*, catalogue passages, invocations of the muse, etc.); *classical epic. b*) a poem like Milton's *Paradise Lost* or Tasso's *Jerusalem Delivered*, in which such structure and conventions are applied to later or different materials; *art epic; literary epic. c*) a poem like *Beowulf*, the *Nibelungenlied*, and the *Chanson de Roland*, considered as expressing the early ideals, character, and traditions of a people or nation as the *Iliad* and *Odyssey* expressed those of the Greeks; *folk epic; national epic.* 2. any long narrative poem regarded as having the style, structure, and importance of an epic: as, Dante's *Divine Comedy* is the *epic* of the Ages of Faith. 3. a prose narrative, play, motion picture, etc. regarded as having the qualities of an epic. 4. a series of events regarded as a proper subject for an epic. *adj.* 1. of an epic. 2. having the nature of an epic; specifically, *a*) heroic; grand; majestic; imposing. *b*) dealing with or characterized by events of historical or legendary importance.

ep·i·cal (ep'i-k'l), *adj.* epic.

ep·i·ca·lyx (ep'ə-kā'liks, ep'ə-kal'iks), *n.* [*pl.* EPICALYXES (-lik-siz, -ik-siz), EPICALYCES (-li-sēz', -i-sēz')], [Mod. L.; see EPI- & CALYX], a ring of leaflets (called *bracts*) at the base of certain flowers, resembling an extra outer calyx.

EPICALYX

ep·i·can·thus (ep'ə-kan'thəs), *n.* [Mod. L. < *epi-* + Gr. *kanthos*, the corner of the eye], a small fold of skin sometimes covering the inner corner of the eye.

ep·i·car·di·al (ep'ə-kär'di-əl), *adj.* of the epicardium.

ep·i·car·di·um (ep'ə-kär'di-əm), *n.* [*pl.* EPICARDIA (-ə)], [Mod. L. < *epi-* + Gr. *kardia*, the heart], the innermost layer of the pericardium.

ep·i·carp (ep'ə-kärp'), *n.* [*epi-* + *-carp*], the outer layer of a ripened ovary or fruit, as the rind of an apple; exocarp.

EPICANTHUS

ep·i·ce·di·um (ep'ə-sē'di-əm, ep'ə-si-dī'əm), *n.* [*pl.* EPICEDIA (-ə)], [L.; Gr. *epikēdeion* < *epikēdeios*, funereal < *epi-*, in, on + *kēdos*, grief, funeral rites], a funeral ode or hymn; dirge.

ep·i·cene (ep'ə-sēn'), *adj.* [L. *epicoenus;* Gr. *epikoinos*, common; *epi-*, upon, to + *koinos*, common], 1. in *grammar*, designating a word having only one form for both the masculine and the feminine, or of the same gender regardless of the sex of the being referred to, as some Greek and Latin nouns. 2. belonging to, having characteristics of, or common to both sexes. *n.* an epicene person.

ep·i·cen·ter (ep'i-sen'tēr), *n.* [*epi-* + *center*], 1. the area of the earth's surface directly above the place of origin, or focus, of an earthquake. 2. a focal point. Also spelled **epicentre.**

ep·i·cen·tral (ep'i-sen'trəl), *adj.* of an epicenter.

ep·i·cen·trum (ep'i-sen'trəm), *n.* [*pl.* EPICENTRA (-trə)], [Mod. L.], an epicenter.

ep·i·cot·yl (ep'ə-kot''l), *n.* [< *epi-* + *cotyledon*], in *botany*, that part of the stem of a seedling or embryo just above the cotyledons.

e·pic·ri·sis (i-pik'rə-sis), *n.* [Gr. *epikrisis*, judgment < *epikrinein*, to judge; *epi-*, upon + *krinein*, to judge], a detailed critique of some literary work.

ep·i·crit·ic (ep'ə-krit'ik), *adj* [Gr. *epikritikos*, determinative < *epikrisis*, determination < *epikrinein*, to judge; *epi-*, upon + *krinein*, to judge], designating or of the nerve fibers in the skin that transmit the sensations of touch and temperature.

Ep·ic·te·tus (ep'ik-tē'təs), *n.* Greek Stoic philosopher who lived in Rome; 1st century A.D.

ep·i·cure (ep'i-kyoor'), *n.* [< L. *Epicurus;* Gr. *Epikouros;* see EPICURUS], 1. a person who enjoys and has a discriminating taste for foods and liquors. 2. a person who is especially fond of luxury and sensuous pleasure.

SYN.—an **epicure** is a person who has a highly refined taste for fine foods and liquors and takes great pleasure in indulging it; a **gourmet** is a connoisseur in eating and drinking who discriminatingly appreciates differences in flavor or quality; **gourmand,** occasionally equivalent to **gourmet,** is more often applied to a person who has a hearty liking for good food or one who is inclined to eat to excess; a **gastronome** is an expert in all phases of the art or science of good eating; a **glutton** is a greedy, voracious eater and drinker.

Ep·i·cu·re·an (ep'i-kyoo-rē'ən), *adj.* [L. *Epicureus;* Gr. *Epikoureios* < *Epikouros*], 1. of Epicurus or his philosophy. 2. [e-], fond of luxury and sensuous pleasure, especially that of eating and drinking. 3. [e-], suited to or characteristic of an epicure. *n.* 1. a follower of

Epicurus or his philosophy. 2. [e-], an epicure. —*SYN.* see **sensuous.**

Ep·i·cu·re·an·ism (ep'i-kyoo-rē'ən-iz'm), ***n.*** 1. the philosophy of Epicurus or his school. 2. adherence to or practice of this philosophy. 3. [e-], epicurism.

ep·i·cur·ism (ep'i-kyoo-riz'm), ***n.*** 1. the tastes, habits, or outlook of an epicure. 2. [E-], Epicureanism.

Ep·i·cu·rus (ep'i-kyoor'əs), ***n.*** Greek philosopher; 342?–270 B.C.; founder of the Epicurean school, which held that the goal of man should be a life of pleasure regulated by morality, temperance, serenity, and cultural development.

ep·i·cy·cle (ep'ə-sī'k'l), ***n.*** [ME. *epicicle;* Fr. *epicycle;* LL. *epicyclus;* Gr. *epikyklos; epi-*, upon + *kyklos*, a circle], 1. a circle whose center moves along the circumference of another, larger circle: said chiefly of the orbit described by a planet. 2. in *geometry,* a circle that rolls around either the interior or exterior of the circumference of another circle.

ep·i·cy·clic (ep'ə-sī'klik, ep'ə-sik'lik), ***adj.*** of, or having the nature of, an epicycle or epicycles.

ep·i·cy·cli·cal (ep'ə-sī'kli-k'l, ep'ə-sik'li-k'l), ***adj.*** epicyclic.

epicyclic train, a system of cogwheels, belt pulleys, etc., in which at least one wheel axis moves around the circumference of another fixed or moving axis, permitting an unusual velocity ratio with relative simplicity of parts.

ep·i·cy·cloid (ep'ə-sī'kloid), ***n.*** [< *epicycle* + *-oid*], in *geometry,* the curve traced by a point on the circumference of a circle that rolls around the outside of another circle.

ROTATING CIRCLE
EPICYCLOID
P
FIXED CIRCLE

EPICYCLOID
P, point of rotating circle

ep·i·cy·cloi·dal (ep'ə-sī-kloi'd'l), ***adj.*** having the form or nature of an epicycloid.

epicycloidal wheel, a wheel of an epicyclic train.

ep·i·dem·ic (ep'ə-dem'ik), ***adj.*** [Fr. *épidémique* < *épidémie;* LL. *epidemia;* Gr. *epidēmia* < *epidēmios, epidēmos,* among the people, general; *epi-*, among + *dēmos,* people], prevalent and spreading rapidly among many people in a community at the same time; widespread: said especially of a contagious disease. ***n.*** 1. an epidemic disease. 2. the rapid spreading of such a disease. 3. the rapid, widespread occurrence of a fad, fashion, etc.

ep·i·dem·i·cal (ep'ə-dem'i-k'l), ***adj.*** epidemic.

ep·i·dem·i·cal·ly (ep'ə-dem'i-k'l-i, ep'ə-dem'ik-li), ***adv.*** in the manner of an epidemic.

epidemic encephalitis, sleeping sickness.

ep·i·de·mi·ol·o·gy (ep'ə-dem'i-ol'ə-ji, ep'ə-dē'mi-ol'ə-ji), ***n.*** [Gr. *epidēmios* (see EPIDEMIC); + *-logy*], the branch of medicine that investigates the causes and control of epidemics.

ep·i·der·mal (ep'ə-dũr'm'l), ***adj.*** of or from the epidermis.

ep·i·der·mic (ep'ə-dũr'mik), ***adj.*** epidermal.

ep·i·der·mis (ep'ə-dũr'mis), ***n.*** [LL. *epidermis;* Gr. *epidermis* < *epi-*, upon + *derma,* the skin], 1. the outermost layer of the skin in vertebrates, having no blood vessels and consisting of several layers of cells, covering the dermis: see **skin,** illus. 2. the outermost layer of cells covering seed plants and ferns. 3. the outer layer of the shells of many mollusks. 4. any of various other integuments.

ep·i·der·moid (ep'ə-dũr'moid), ***adj.*** like, or having the nature of, epidermis.

ep·i·did·y·mal (ep'ə-did'ə-m'l), ***adj.*** of the epididymis.

ep·i·did·y·mis (ep'ə-did'i-mis), ***n.*** [*pl.* EPIDIDYMIDES (ep'ə-di-dim'ə-dēz')], [Mod. L.; Gr. *epididymis* < *epi-*, upon + *didymos,* testicle], a long, oval-shaped structure attached to the rear upper surface of each testicle, consisting mainly of the excretory ducts of the testicles.

ep·i·dote (ep'ə-dōt'), ***n.*** [Fr. *épidote* < Gr. *epididonai,* to give besides, increase < *epi-*, over + *didonai,* to give: so named because some of the secondary crystal forms show enlargement of the base of the primary], any one of several hydrous silicates of calcium, aluminum, and iron, yellowish-green to black in color, found in the form of monoclinic crystals, grains, or fibers, and including allanite, piedmontite, and zoisite.

ep·i·dot·ic (ep'ə-dot'ik), ***adj.*** of, or having the nature of, epidote.

ep·i·fo·cal (ep'ə-fō'k'l), ***adj.*** over the focus, or center of disturbance, of an earthquake.

ep·i·gas·tric (ep'ə-gas'trik), ***adj.*** of or located within the epigastrium.

ep·i·gas·tri·um (ep'ə-gas'tri-əm), ***n.*** [Mod. L.; Gr. *epigastrion,* neut. of *epigastrios,* over the stomach < *epi-*, upon + *gastēr, gastros,* the stomach], in *anatomy,* the upper middle portion of the abdomen, including the area over and in front of the stomach; epigastric region.

ep·i·ge·al (ep'ə-jē'əl), ***adj.*** 1. in *botany,* epigeous. 2. in *zoology,* living close to the ground: said of certain insects.

ep·i·ge·an (ep'ə-jē'ən), ***adj.*** epigeal.

ep·i·gene (ep'ə-jēn'), ***adj.*** [Fr. *épigène* < Gr. *epigenēs,* born late < *epi-*, after, upon + *gignesthai,* to produce], in *geology,* produced or formed on the earth's surface: as, *epigene* boulders: opposed to *hypogene.*

ep·i·gen·e·sis (ep'ə-jen'ə-sis), ***n.*** [Gr. *epi,* after, upon + *genesis,* birth, descent], 1. in *biology,* the theory that the germ cell is structureless and that the embryo develops as a new creation through the action of the environment on the protoplasm: opposed to *preformation.* 2. in *geology,* metamorphism. 3. in *medicine, a*) the appearing of secondary symptoms. *b*) a secondary symptom.

ep·i·ge·net·ic (ep'i-jə-net'ik), ***adj.*** of, or having the nature of, epigenesis.

e·pig·e·nous (e-pij'ə-nəs), ***adj.*** [*epi-* + *-genous*], in *botany,* growing on the surface, especially the upper surface, of an organ or part, as fungi on a leaf: cf. **hypogenous.**

ep·i·ge·ous (ep'ə-jē'əs), ***adj.*** [Gr. *epigeios,* on the earth < *epi-*, upon + *gē,* the earth; + *-ous*], in *botany,* growing on or above the ground; specifically, directed above ground after germination: opposed to *hypogeous.*

ep·i·glot·tis (ep'ə-glot'is), ***n.*** [Gr. *epiglōttis* < *epi-*, upon + *glōtta, glōssa,* the tongue], the thin, triangular lid of cartilage that folds back to cover the opening of the windpipe during swallowing, thus preventing food, etc. from entering the lungs.

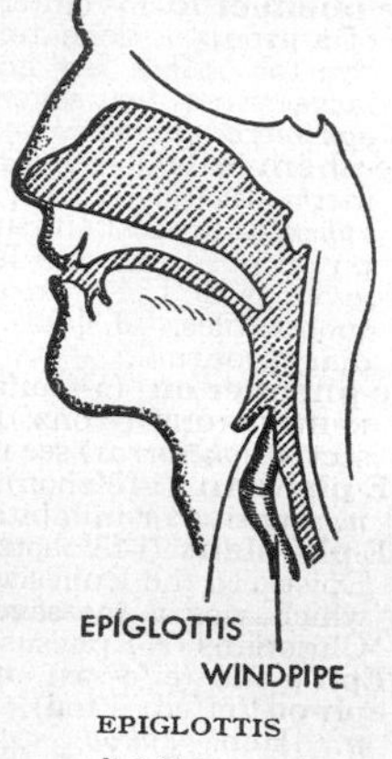

EPIGLOTTIS

ep·i·gram (ep'ə-gram'), ***n.*** [L. *epigramma;* Gr. *epigramma,* inscription, epigram < *epigraphein; epi-*, upon + *graphein,* to write], 1. a short poem with a witty or satirical point; hence, 2. any terse, witty, pointed statement, often antithetical. Example: "Crying is the refuge of plain women, but the ruin of pretty ones." 3. the use of epigrams. —*SYN.* see **saying.**

ep·i·gram·mat·ic (ep'i-grə-mat'ik), ***adj.*** [L. *epigrammaticus;* Gr. *epigrammatikos*], 1. of or full of epigram or epigrams. 2. having the nature of an epigram; terse, witty, etc.

ep·i·gram·mat·i·cal·ly (ep'i-grə-mat'i-k'l-i, ep'i-grə-mat'ik-li), ***adv.*** in an epigrammatic manner; in the form of an epigram.

ep·i·gram·ma·tist (ep'ə-gram'ə-tist), ***n.*** a person who makes epigrams.

ep·i·gram·ma·tize (ep'ə-gram'ə-tiz'), ***v.t.*** [EPIGRAMMATIZED (-tīzd'), EPIGRAMMATIZING,] to express (something) epigrammatically; deal with in an epigram. ***v.i.*** to make epigrams; write or speak epigrammatically.

ep·i·graph (ep'ə-graf', ep'ə-gräf'), ***n.*** [Gr. *epigraphē,* inscription < *epigraphein;* see EPIGRAM], 1. an inscription on a building, monument, etc. 2. a motto or quotation at the beginning of a book, chapter, etc.

e·pig·ra·pher (e-pig'rə-fẽr), ***n.*** an epigraphist.

ep·i·graph·ic (ep'ə-graf'ik), ***adj.*** having to do with an epigraph or epigraphy.

ep·i·graph·i·cal (ep'ə-graf'i-k'l), ***adj.*** epigraphic.

e·pig·ra·phist (e-pig'rə-fist), ***n.*** a specialist in epigraphy.

e·pig·ra·phy (e-pig'rə-fi), ***n.*** [see EPIGRAPH], 1. inscriptions collectively. 2. the study that deals with deciphering, interpreting, and classifying inscriptions, especially ancient inscriptions.

e·pig·y·nous (e-pij'ə-nəs), ***adj.*** [*epi-* + *-gynous*], designating petals, sepals, and stamens that are attached to the top of the ovary as though inserted: opposed to *hypogynous.*

EPIGYNOUS BLOSSOM
(of pear)

e·pig·y·ny (e-pij'ə-ni), ***n.*** the fact or quality of being epigynous.

ep·i·lep·sy (ep'ə-lep'si), ***n.*** [Fr. *épilepsie;* L. *epilepsia;* Gr. *epilēpsia, epilēpsis,* lit., a seizure, hence epilepsy < *epilambanein,* to seize upon; *epi-*, upon + *lambanein,* to seize], a chronic disease of the nervous system, characterized by convulsions and, often, unconsciousness: also called *falling sickness:* see **grand mal, petit mal.**

ep·i·lep·tic (ep'ə-lep'tik), ***adj.*** [Fr. *épileptique;* L. *epilepticus;* Gr. *epileptikos*], 1. of, like, or having the nature of, epilepsy. 2. having epilepsy. ***n.*** a person who has epilepsy.

ep·i·lep·ti·cal·ly (ep'ə-lep'ti-k'l-i, ep'ə-lep'tik-li), ***adv.*** in the manner of an epileptic.

ep·i·lep·toid (ep'ə-lep'toid), ***adj.*** like epilepsy.

ep·i·logue, ep·i·log (ep'ə-lôg', ep'ə-log'), ***n.*** [Fr. *épilogue;* L. *epilogus;* Gr. *epilogos,* conclusion, epilogue, peroration < *epilegein,* to say in addition, add; *epi-*, upon + *legein*, to say, speak], 1. a closing section added to a novel, play, etc., providing further comment, interpretation, or information. 2. a short speech or poem spoken to the audience by one of the actors at the end of a play. 3. the actor or actors who speak this.

Ep·i·me·theus (ep'ə-mē'thi-əs, ep'ə-mē'thūs), *n.* [L.; Gr. *Epimētheus*, lit., "Afterthinker"], in *Greek mythology*, a Titan, the brother of Prometheus and husband of Pandora: he was given the task, by the gods, of making man and the animals, and distributing the various faculties to them.

ep·i·nas·ty (ep'ə-nas'ti), *n.* [< *epi-* + Gr. *nastos*, pressed close; + *-y*], in *botany*, the condition in which an organ, as a leaf, turns downward because of the more rapid growth of the upper layers of cells: opposed to *hyponasty*.

ep·i·neph·rin (ep'ə-nef'rin), *n.* epinephrine.

ep·i·neph·rine (ep'ə-nef'rin, ep'ə-nef'rēn), *n.* [< *epi-* + Gr. *nephros*, kidney; + *-ine*], 1. the hormone produced by the adrenal glands. 2. a drug made from the adrenal glands of animals, or synthetically: see **adrenalin.**

ep·i·neu·ri·um (ep'ə-nyoor'i-əm), *n.* [Mod. L. < *epi-* + Gr. *neuron*, a nerve], the layer of connective tissue surrounding a peripheral nerve.

E·piph·a·ny (i-pif'ə-ni), *n.* [*pl.* EPIPHANIES (-niz)], [ME. *epiphani;* OFr. *epiphanie;* LL. *epiphania;* Gr. *epiphaneia*, appearance < *epiphainein*, to show forth, manifest; *epi-*, upon + *phainein*, to show], 1. [e-], an appearance or manifestation of a god or other supernatural being. 2. in most Christian churches, a yearly festival, held January 6, commemorating the revealing of Jesus as the Christ to the Gentiles in the persons of the Magi at Bethlehem: also called *Twelfth Night.*

ep·i·phe·nom·e·non (ep'i-fə-nom'ə-non'), *n.* [*pl.* EPIPHENOMENA (-nə)], [Mod. L.], 1. a phenomenon that occurs with and seems to result from another. 2. in *medicine*, a secondary or additional occurrence in the course of a disease.

ep·i·phys·e·al, ep·i·phys·i·al (ep'ə-fiz'i-əl), *adj.* of, or having the nature of, an epiphysis.

e·piph·y·sis (i-pif'ə-sis), *n.* [*pl.* EPIPHYSES (-sēz')], [Mod. L.; Gr. *epiphysis*, a growth upon, excrescence < *epiphyein*, to grow upon; *epi-*, upon + *phyein*, to grow], 1. that part of a bone which is at first separated from the main part by cartilage, but later fuses with it by ossification. 2. the pineal body.

ep·i·phyte (ep'ə-fīt'), *n.* [*epi-* + *-phyte*], 1. a nonparasitic plant that grows on another plant but gets its nourishment from the air, as certain orchids, mosses, and lichens; air plant. 2. a fungus that is a parasite on an animal.

ep·i·phyt·ic (ep'ə-fit'ik), *adj.* having the nature of an epiphyte.

ep·i·phyt·i·cal (ep'ə-fit'i-k'l), *adj.* epiphytic.

ep·i·phy·tot·ic (ep'i-fī-tot'ik), *adj.* [< *epi-* + Gr. *phyton*, a plant; + *-otic*], epidemic among plants.

e·pi·ro·gen·ic (e-pī'rə-jen'ik), *adj.* epeirogenic.

ep·i·rog·e·ny (ep'ī-roj'ə-ni), *n.* epeirogeny.

E·pi·rus (e-pī'rəs), *n.* a former country in the northwestern part of ancient Greece: see **Greece**, map.

Epis., Epistle.

Epis., Episc., 1. Episcopal. 2. Episcopalian.

e·pis·co·pa·cy (i-pis'kə-pə-si), *n.* [*pl.* EPISCOPACIES (-siz)], [< LL. *episcopatus*, office of a bishop < *episcopus*, bishop; Gr. *episkopos*, overseer, watcher < *episkopein*, to look upon, examine; *epi-*, upon + *skopein*, to look], 1. the system of church government by bishops. 2. the position, rank, or term of office of a bishop; episcopate. 3. bishops collectively.

e·pis·co·pal (i-pis'kə-p'l), *adj.* [Fr. *épiscopal;* LL. *episcopalis;* see EPISCOPACY], 1. of or governed by bishops. 2. [E-], designating or of any of various churches governed by bishops, as the Protestant Episcopal or the Anglican Church.

E·pis·co·pa·li·an (i-pis'kə-pā'li-ən, i-pis'kə-pāl'yən), *adj.* 1. [e-], of church government by bishops. 2. Episcopal. *n.* 1. [e-], a member of an episcopal church or a person believing in episcopal government. 2. a member of the Protestant Episcopal Church.

E·pis·co·pa·li·an·ism (i-pis'kə-pā'li-ən-iz'm, i-pis'kə-pāl'yən-iz'm), *n.* the beliefs and ritual of Episcopalians.

e·pis·co·pal·ism (i-pis'kə-p'l-iz'm), *n.* the theory or doctrine that the authority to govern a church rests in a body of bishops and not in any individual: it was rejected by the Vatican Council of the Roman Catholic Church in 1870.

e·pis·co·pate (i-pis'kə-pit, i-pis'kə-pāt'), *n.* [see EPISCOPACY], 1. the position, rank, or term of office of a bishop. 2. a bishop's see. 3. bishops collectively.

e·pis·co·pa·ture (i-pis'kə-pə-choor'), *n.* an episcopate (in senses 2 & 3).

ep·i·sode (ep'ə-sōd'), *n.* [Gr. *epeisodion*, addition, episode; neut. of *epeisodios*, following upon the entrance, coming in besides < *epi-*, besides + *eisodos*, an entrance < *eis-*, into + *hodos*, way, road], 1. the part of an ancient Greek tragedy between two choral songs: it corresponds to an act. 2. in a novel, poem, etc., any part of the story, or a digression, that is complete in itself; incident. 3. any event or series of events complete in itself but forming part of a larger one: as, an *episode* in the war. 4. any installment of a serialized story or drama. 5. in *music*, any incidental passage between repetitions of the main theme, especially in a fugue or rondo. —*SYN.* see **occurrence.**

ep·i·sod·ic (ep'ə-sod'ik), *adj.* 1. having the nature of an episode; incidental. 2. divided into episodes.

ep·i·sod·i·cal (ep'ə-sod'i-k'l), *adj.* episodic.

ep·i·sod·i·cal·ly (ep'ə-sod'i-k'l-i, ep'ə-sod'ik-li), *adv.* in an episodic manner; in episodes.

ep·i·spas·tic (ep'ə-spas'tik), *adj.* [Gr. *epispastikos*, drawing to oneself, adapted < *epispastos*, drawn upon oneself < *epispan*, to draw upon; *epi-*, upon + *span*, to draw, suck], in *medicine*, causing blistering or a serous discharge. *n.* a blistering agent; vesicant.

ep·i·stax·is (ep'ə-stak'sis), *n.* [Mod. L. < Gr. *epistazein*, to bleed at the nose; *epi-*, upon + *stazein*, to fall in drops], in *medicine*, nosebleed; nasal hemorrhage.

e·pis·te·mo·log·i·cal (i-pis'tə-mə-loj'i-k'l), *adj.* having to do with epistemology.

e·pis·te·mol·o·gy (i-pis'tə-mol'ə-ji), *n.* [*pl.* EPISTEMOLOGIES (-jiz)], [< Gr. *epistēmē*, knowledge; + *-logy*], the study or theory of the origin, nature, methods, and limits of knowledge.

ep·i·ster·nal (ep'ə-stūr'n'l), *adj.* of, on, or near the episternum.

ep·i·ster·num (ep'ə-stūr'nəm), *n.* [*pl.* EPISTERNA (-nə)], [Mod. L.; see EPI- & STERNUM], 1. the uppermost part of the sternum in mammals; manubrium. 2. the bone between the clavicles and in front of the sternum in certain vertebrates; interclavicle.

e·pis·tle (i-pis''l), *n.* [ME.; OFr.; L. *epistola, epistula;* Gr. *epistolē*, a letter, message < *epistellein*, to send to; *epi-*, upon, to + *stellein*, to send, summon], 1. a letter, especially a long, formal, instructive letter: now used humorously. 2. [E-], *a*) in the *New Testament*, any of the letters written by an Apostle: abbreviated **Ep., Epis.** *b*) a selection, usually from these Epistles, read as part of Mass, Communion, etc. in various churches.

e·pis·to·lar·y (i-pis'tə-ler'i), *adj.* [Fr. *épistolaire;* L. *epistolaris* < *epistola;* see EPISTLE], 1. of or suitable to letters or letter writing. 2. contained in, conducted by, or made up of letters.

ep·i·style (ep'i-stīl'), *n.* [L. *epistylium;* Gr. *epistylion* < *epi-*, upon + *stylos*, column], an architrave.

ep·i·taph (ep'ə-taf', ep'ə-täf'), *n.* [ME. *epitaf;* OFr. *epitaphe;* L. *epitaphium*, eulogy; Gr. *epitaphios*, at the tomb < *epi-*, upon, at + *taphos*, tomb < *thaptein*, to bury], 1. an inscription on a tomb, in memory of a dead person; hence, 2. a short composition in prose or verse, written as a tribute to a dead person.

ep·i·tha·la·mi·on (ep'i-thə-lā'mi-ən), *n.* [*pl.* EPITHALAMIA (-ə)], [< Mod. L. & Gr.; Gr. *epithalamion*], an epithalamium.

ep·i·tha·la·mi·um (ep'i-thə-lā'mi-əm), *n.* [*pl.* EPITHALAMIUMS (-əmz), EPITHALAMIA (-ə)], [L.; Gr. *epithalamion* < *epithalamios*, nuptial < *epi-*, at + *thalamos*, bride chamber], a song or poem in honor of a bride or bridegroom, or of both; nuptial song.

ep·i·the·li·al (ep'ə-thē'li-əl), *adj.* of, or having the nature of, epithelium.

ep·i·the·li·o·ma (ep'ə-thē'li-ō'mə), *n.* [*pl.* EPITHELIOMATA (-tə), EPITHELIOMAS (-məz)], [Mod. L. < *epithelium* + *-oma*], a malignant tumor of epithelial cells, particularly of the skin, mouth, larynx, or urinary bladder.

ep·i·the·li·um (ep'ə-thē'li-əm), *n.* [*pl.* EPITHELIUMS (-əmz), EPITHELIA (-ə)], [Mod. L. < Gr. *epi-*, upon + *thēlē*, nipple], cellular tissue that covers surfaces, forms glands, and lines most cavities of the body: it consists of one or several layers of cells with only little intercellular material.

ep·i·thet (ep'ə-thet'), *n.* [L. *epitheton;* Gr. *epitheton* < *epitithenai*, to put on; *epi-*, on + *tithenai*, to put], 1. an adjective, noun, or phrase expressing some quality considered characteristic of a person or thing: as, that *black-hearted* villain. 2. a descriptive name or title applied to a person: as, Ivan *the Terrible.*

ep·i·thet·ic (ep'ə-thet'ik), *adj.* epithetical.

ep·i·thet·i·cal (ep'ə-thet'i-k'l), *adj.* 1. of or used as an epithet. 2. full of epithets.

e·pit·o·me (i-pit'ə-mi), *n.* [*pl.* EPITOMES (-miz)], [L.; Gr. *epitomē*, abridgment < *epitemnein*, to cut short, cut upon; *epi-*, upon + *temnein*, to cut], 1. a short statement of the main points of a book, report, incident, etc.; abstract; summary. 2. a part or thing that is representative or typical of the characteristics or general quality of the whole. —*SYN.* see **abridgment.**

e·pit·o·mize (i-pit′ə-mīz′), ***v.t.*** [EPITOMIZED (-mīzd′), EPITOMIZING], to make or be an epitome of.

ep·i·zo·on (ep′ə-zō′on), ***n.*** [*pl.* EPIZOA (-ə)], [Mod. L.; *epi-* + Gr. *zōion*, animal], a parasite on the outside of an animal's body.

ep·i·zo·ot·ic (ep′i-zō-ot′ik), ***adj.*** [Fr. *épizootique* < *épizootie*, epizooty, formed by analogy with *épidémie* (see EPIDEMIC) < Gr. *epi*, upon + *zōion*, animal], designating a disease temporarily prevalent among many animals. ***n.*** a disease of this kind.

ep·i·zo·o·ty (ep′ə-zō′ə-ti), ***n.*** an epizootic disease.

‡**e plu·ri·bus u·num** (ē ploor′ə-bəs ū′nəm), [L.], out of many, one: a motto of the United States.

ep·och (ep′ək; *chiefly* Brit., ē′pok), ***n.*** [LL. *epocha;* Gr. *epochē*, a check, cessation, pause < *epechein*, to hold in, check < *epi-*, upon + *echein*, to hold], 1. the beginning of a new and important period in the history of anything: as, the invention of radio marked an *epoch* in communication. 2. a period of time considered in terms of noteworthy and characteristic events, developments, persons, etc.: as, an *epoch* of social revolution. 3. in *astronomy*, *a*) an arbitrary date for which are given the relative data determining the position of a heavenly body. *b*) the position of the heavenly body at that time. 4. in *geology*, a subdivision of a geological period: as, the Eocene *Epoch*: see also **era, period, age.** —***SYN.*** see **period.**

ep·och·al (ep′ə-k′l), ***adj.*** of, characteristic of, or marking an epoch.

ep·ode (ep′ōd), ***n.*** [Fr. *épode;* L. *epodos;* Gr. *epōidos*, aftersong, lit., singing, or sung, to music < *epaeidein*, to sing to accompaniment < *epi-*, upon + *aeidein*, to sing; see ODE], 1. a form of lyric poem in which a short line follows a longer one: it was used by Horace. 2. that part of a lyric ode which follows the strophe and antistrophe.

ep·o·nym (ep′ə-nim′), ***n.*** [< Gr. *epōnymos;* see EPONYMOUS], 1. a real or mythical person from whose name the name of a nation, institution, etc. is derived or is supposed to have been derived: as, William *Penn* is the *eponym* of *Penn*sylvania. 2. *a*) a person whose name has become closely associated with some period, movement, theory, etc. *b*) the name applied to the period, etc., as *Elizabethan* or *Einsteinian.*

ep·on·y·mous (e-pon′ə-məs), ***adj.*** [Gr. *epōnymos* < *epi-*, upon + *onyma*, a name], 1. giving one's name to a people, nation, etc.: as, an *eponymous* founder. 2. of an eponym.

ep·o·pee (ep′ə-pē′, ep′ə-pē′), ***n.*** [Fr. *épopée;* Gr. *epopoiia*, the making of epics < *epos*, song + *poiein*, to make], 1. an epic poem. 2. epic poetry.

ep·o·poe·ia (ep′ə-pē′ə), ***n.*** [Mod. L.], epopee.

ep·os (ep′os), ***n.*** [L.; Gr. *epos;* see EPIC], 1. epic poetry. 2. a primitive epic poem, handed down by word of mouth. 3. a series of epic events.

ep·ox·y (ep-ok′si), ***adj.*** [*ep-* + *oxy*gen], designating a compound in which an oxygen atom is joined to each of two other connected atoms; specifically, designating a resin that polymerizes spontaneously when its components are mixed, forming a strong, hard, resistant adhesive used in glues, enamel coatings, etc.

ep·si·lon (ep′sə-lon′, ep′sə-lən), ***n.*** [Gr.; *e*, e + *psilon*, plain, simple], the fifth letter of the Greek alphabet (Ε, ε), corresponding to English *E, e*, sounded as in *let*: see **alphabet**, table.

Ep·som (ep′səm), ***n.*** a town in England, south of London: pop., 27,000: site of Epsom Downs, where the Derby is run.

Epsom salts (or **salt**), [< *Epsom*, England, famous for its mineral waters], a white, crystalline salt, magnesium sulfate, $MgSO_4 \cdot 7H_2O$, used chiefly as a cathartic.

Ep·stein, Sir **Jacob** (ep′stīn), 1880–1959; British sculptor, born in the United States.

Ep·worth League (ep′wẽrth), [after *Epworth*, England, birthplace of John Wesley], an American organization of young people of the Methodist Episcopal Church.

eq., 1. equal. 2. equalizer. 3. equation. 4. equator. 5. equivalent.

eq·ua·bil·i·ty (ek′wə-bil′ə-ti, ē′kwə-bil′ə-ti), ***n.*** [L. *aequabilitas*], the quality or state of being equable.

eq·ua·ble (ek′wə-b′l, ē′kwə-b′l), ***adj.*** [L. *aequabilis* < *aequare*, to make equal < *aequus*, equal], 1. not varying or fluctuating much; steady; uniform: as, an *equable* temperature. 2. even; tranquil; serene: as, an *equable* temperament. —***SYN.*** see **steady.**

eq·ua·bly (ek′wə-bli, ē′kwə-bli), ***adv.*** in an equable manner.

e·qual (ē′kwəl), ***adj.*** [ME.; L. *aequalis*, equal < *aequus*, plain, even, flat], 1. of the same quantity, size, number, value, degree, intensity, etc.: abbreviated **eq.** 2. having the same rights, privileges, ability, rank, etc. (with *to* or *with*): as, I am *equal* with him in skill. 3. evenly proportioned; balanced or uniform in effect or operation. 4. [Archaic], fair; just; impartial. 5. [Archaic], level; smooth and flat. 6. [Obs.], equable. ***n.*** any thing or person that is equal: as, this book is the *equal* of the other. ***v.t.*** [EQUALED or EQUALLED (-kwəld), EQUALING or EQUALLING], 1. [Archaic], to make equal; equalize. 2. to be equal to; match. 3. to do or make something equal to: as, you can *equal* his record. 4. to recompense in full. —***SYN.*** see **same.**

equal to, having the necessary ability, strength, power, capacity, or courage for.

e·qual·i·tar·i·an (i-kwäl′ə-târ′i-ən, i-kwôl′ə-târ′i-ən), ***adj.*** of, or holding, the belief that all men should have equal political and social rights. ***n.*** a person who holds this belief.

e·qual·i·ty (i-kwäl′ə-ti, i-kwôl′ə-ti), ***n.*** [*pl.* EQUALITIES (-tiz)], [OFr. *équalité;* L. *aequalitas*], state or instance of being equal; especially, the state of being equal in political, economic, and social rights.

e·qual·i·za·tion (ē′kwə-lə-zā′shən), ***n.*** an equalizing or being equalized.

e·qual·ize (ē′kwəl-īz′), ***v.t.*** [EQUALIZED (-īzd′), EQUALIZING], 1. to make equal. 2. to make uniform.

e·qual·iz·er (ē′kwəl-īz′ẽr), ***n.*** 1. a person who equalizes. 2. a thing that equalizes; especially, an electrical conductor of low resistance, used to equalize voltages: abbreviated **eq.**

e·qual·ly (ē′kwəl-i), ***adv.*** in an equal manner; in or to an equal extent or degree; uniformly; impartially.

equal mark (or **sign**), the arithmetical sign (=), indicating that the terms on either side of the sign are equal: as, $2 + 2 = 4$.

e·qua·nim·i·ty (ē′kwə-nim′ə-ti, ek′wə-nim′ə-ti), ***n.*** [L. *aequanimitas* < *aequanimis* < *aequus*, even, plain + *animus*, the mind], the quality of remaining calm and undisturbed; evenness of mind or temper; composure.

SYN.—**equanimity** implies an inherent evenness of temper or disposition that is not easily disturbed; **composure** implies the disciplining of one's emotions in a trying situation or habitual self-possession in the face of excitement; **serenity** implies a lofty, clear peace of mind that is not easily clouded by ordinary stresses or excitements; **nonchalance** implies a casual indifference to or a cool detachment from situations that might be expected to disturb one emotionally; **sang-froid** implies great coolness and presence of mind in dangerous or trying circumstances.

e·quate (i-kwāt′), ***v.t.*** [EQUATED (-id), EQUATING], [< L. *aequatus*, pp. of *aequare*, to make equal < *aequus;* see EQUAL], 1. in *mathematics*, to state or express the equality of; put in the form of an equation. 2. to make equal or equivalent; treat, regard, or express as equal or equivalent.

e·qua·tion (i-kwā′zhən, i-kwā′shən), ***n.*** [ME. *equacion;* L. *aequatio*], 1. an equating or being equated. 2. *a*) variation in computation due to personal errors in observation, judgment, etc., or the correction to compensate for this: in full, **personal equation.** *b*) the amount of such error or correction, as in astronomical computations. 3. in *chemistry*, an expression in which symbols and formulas are used to represent a chemical reaction: as, $H_2SO_4 + 2NaCl = 2HCl + Na_2SO_4$. 4. in *mathematics*, an expression of equality between two quantities, as shown by the equal mark (=): as, a quadratic *equation*. Abbreviated **eq.**

e·qua·tor (i-kwā′tẽr), ***n.*** [ME. & LL. *aequator* < L. *aequare;* see EQUABLE], 1. an imaginary circle around the earth, equally distant at all points from both the North Pole and the South Pole: it divides the earth's surface into the Northern Hemisphere and the Southern Hemisphere. 2. any circle that divides a sphere or other body into two equal and symmetrical parts. 3. in *astronomy*, the imaginary circle formed by the intersection of the plane of the earth's equator with the observed celestial sphere: in full, **celestial equator.** Abbreviated **eq.**

e·qua·to·ri·al (ē′kwə-tôr′i-əl, ek′wə-tō′ri-əl), ***adj.*** 1. of or near the earth's equator. 2. of an equator. 3. like or characteristic of conditions near the earth's equator: as, *equatorial* heat. ***n.*** a telescope mounted in such a way as to have two axes of motion, one (called *polar axis*) parallel to the earth's axis, the other (called *declination axis*) perpendicular to it: by rotation on the polar axis it can follow the apparent motion of a heavenly body.

eq·uer·ry (ek′wẽr-i; *occas.* i-kwer′i), ***n.*** [*pl.* EQUERRIES (-iz)], [Fr. *écurie;* OFr. *escurie;* prob. < ML. *scuria, scura*, a stable < OHG. *sciura*, a shed; associated in Eng. with L. *equus*, horse], 1. formerly, an officer in charge of the horses of a royal or noble household. 2. a personal attendant on some member of the king's family, as in England.

e·ques·tri·an (i-kwes′tri-ən), ***adj.*** [< L. *equester* < *eques*, horseman < *equus*, a horse; + *-ian*], 1. of horses, horsemen, horseback riding, or horsemanship. 2. on horseback, or so represented: as, an *equestrian* statue. ***n.*** a rider or circus performer on horseback.

e·ques·tri·enne (i-kwes′tri-en′), ***n.*** [< *equestrian* + Fr. fem. suffix *-enne*], a girl or woman who rides or performs on horseback.

e·qui- (ē′kwə-, ē′kwi), [< L. *aequus*, equal], a combining form meaning *equal, equally*, as in *equivalent, equidistant.*

e·qui·an·gu·lar (ē′kwi-aŋ′gyoo-lẽr), ***adj.*** having all angles equal.

e·qui·dis·tance (ē′kwə-dis′təns), ***n.*** equal distance.

e·qui·dis·tant (ē′kwə-dis′tənt), ***adj.*** equally distant.

e·qui·lat·er·al (ē'kwə-lat'ẽr-əl), ***adj.*** [LL. *aequilateralis* < L. *aequus*, equal + *latus*, *lateris*, side], having all sides equal: as, an *equilateral* triangle. ***n.*** 1. a figure having equal sides. 2. a side exactly equal to another or others.

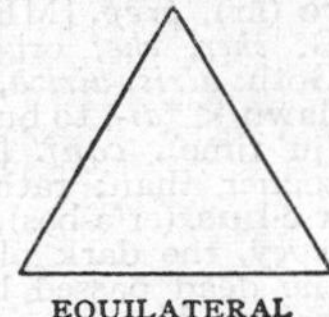
EQUILATERAL TRIANGLE

e·quil·i·brant (ē-kwil'ə-brənt), ***n.*** [Fr. *équilibrant*, ppr. of *équilibrer*, to equilibrate < *équilibre*, equilibrium < L. *aequilibrium*; see EQUILIBRIUM], in *physics*, a force or combination of forces that can balance another force or forces.

e·qui·li·brate (ē'kwə-lī'brāt, i-kwil'ə-brāt'), ***v.t. & v.i.*** [EQUILIBRATED (-id), EQUILIBRATING], [< LL. *aequilibratus*, in equilibrium, level (taken as pp. of **aequilibrare*) < L. *aequus*, equal + *libra*, balance], to bring into or be in equilibrium; balance or counterbalance.

e·qui·li·bra·tion (ē'kwə-lī-brā'shən, i-kwil'ə-brā'shən), ***n.*** an equilibrating or being equilibrated.

e·qui·li·bra·tor (ē'kwə-li'brā-tẽr, i-kwil'ə-brā'tẽr), ***n.*** a thing that equilibrates; device that helps maintain equilibrium.

e·quil·i·brist (i-kwil'ə-brist), ***n.*** [Fr. *équilibriste* < *équilibre*; see EQUILIBRANT], a performer who does tricks of balancing, as a tightrope walker.

e·qui·lib·ri·um (ē'kwə-lib'ri-əm), ***n.*** [*pl.* EQUILIBRIUMS (-əmz), EQUILIBRIA (-ə)], [L. *aequilibrium* < *aequilibris*, evenly balanced < *aequus*, even, equal + *libra*, a balance], 1. a state of balance or equality between opposing forces. 2. a state of balance or adjustment of conflicting desires, interests, etc. 3. in *chemistry*, the stage in a reversible chemical change at which the products of the forward or direct reaction are consumed by the reverse reaction at the same rate as they are formed. 4. in *radioactivity*, the stage of a radioactive material at which the rate of disintegration and the rate of formation are equal.

eq·ui·mo·lec·u·lar (ē'kwi-mə-lek'yoo-lẽr), ***adj.*** having an equal number of molecules.

e·quine (ē'kwīn), ***adj.*** [L. *equinus* < *equus*, horse], of, like, or characteristic of a horse. ***n.*** a horse.

e·qui·noc·tial (ē'kwə-nok'shəl), ***adj.*** [ME. *equinoxial*; L. *aequinoctialis*], 1. relating to either of the equinoxes. 2. occurring at or about the time of the equinox, when night and day are equal in length. 3. equatorial. ***n.*** 1. the celestial equator. 2. a storm occurring at or about the time of either of the equinoxes.

equinoctial circle (or **line**), the celestial equator: when the sun crosses it, the days and nights are equally long in all parts of the earth.

e·qui·nox (ē'kwə-noks'), ***n.*** [Fr. *équinoxe*; LL. *aequinoxium*; L. *aequinoctium* < *aequus*, equal + *nox*, night], 1. the time when the sun crosses the equator, making night and day of equal length in all parts of the earth: the vernal equinox occurs about March 21, the autumnal equinox about September 22-23. 2. either of the two points on the celestial equator where the sun crosses it on these dates: also called *equinoctial point.*

e·quip (i-kwip'), ***v.t.*** [EQUIPPED (-kwipt'), EQUIPPING], [Fr. *équiper*; OFr. *equiper*, *esquiper*, to embark, put out to sea; prob. < AS. *scipian*, to embark < *scip* (see SHIP); or ? < ON. *skipa*, to arrange, make ready], 1. to furnish with the necessities for an undertaking; fit out: as, the soldiers were *equipped* for battle; hence, 2. to prepare intellectually; train. 3. to dress (oneself) for a certain purpose. —***SYN.*** see **furnish.**

eq·ui·page (ek'wə-pij), ***n.*** [OFr. < *equiper*; see EQUIP], 1. the furnishings, accessories, or outfit of a ship, army, expedition, etc.; equipment. 2. a carriage, especially one with horses and liveried servants. 3. [Archaic], *a*) toilet articles. *b*) a case for these. 4. [Archaic], retinue; train; following, as of a person of rank.

e·quip·ment (i-kwip'mənt), ***n.*** 1. an equipping or being equipped. 2. whatever a person, group, or thing is equipped with; furnishings; outfit. 3. in *transportation*, cars, trucks, etc.; rolling stock, as distinguished from stationary property.

e·qui·poise (ek'wə-poiz', ē'kwə-poiz'), ***n.*** [*equi-* + *poise*], 1. equal distribution of weight; state of balance, or equilibrium. 2. counterpoise; counterbalance.

e·qui·pol·lence (ē'kwə-pol'əns), ***n.*** [Fr. *équipollence*; see EQUIPOLLENT], equality of force, value, meaning, etc.

e·qui·pol·len·cy (ē'kwə-pol'ən-si), ***n.*** equipollence.

e·qui·pol·lent (ē'kwə-pol'ənt), ***adj.*** [Fr. *équipolent*; L. *aequipollens* < *aequus*, equal + *pollens*, ppr. of *pollere*, to be strong], 1. equal in force, weight, validity, etc. 2. equivalent in meaning or result. ***n.*** something equipollent.

e·qui·pon·der·ance (ē'kwə-pon'dẽr-əns), ***n.*** [< *equiponderant*], equality of weight; equilibrium; balance.

e·qui·pon·der·an·cy (ē'kwə-pon'dẽr-ən-si), ***n.*** equiponderance.

e·qui·pon·der·ant (ē'kwə-pon'dẽr-ənt), ***adj.*** [ML. *aequiponderans*, ppr. of *aequiponderare* < L. *aequus*, equal + *ponderare*, to weigh], of the same weight; evenly balanced (often with *to* or *with*).

e·qui·pon·der·ate (ē'kwə-pon'dẽr-āt'), ***v.t.*** [EQUIPONDERATED (-id), EQUIPONDERATING], [< pp. of ML. *aequiponderare*; see EQUIPONDERANT], 1. to counterbalance. 2. to make evenly balanced.

e·qui·po·ten·tial (ē'kwi-pō-ten'shəl), ***adj.*** 1. having equal potentiality or power. 2. in *physics*, of the same potential.

eq·ui·se·tum (ek'wə-sē'təm), ***n.*** [*pl.* EQUISETUMS (-təmz), EQUISETA (-tə)], [L. *equisaetum*, *equisetum*, horsetail < *equus*, horse + *saeta*, *seta*, bristle], any of a genus of flowerless plants with hard, jointed stems, useful in preventing erosion; the horsetail; scouring rush.

eq·ui·ta·ble (ek'wi-tə-b'l), ***adj.*** [Fr. *équitable* < *équité*], 1. characterized by equity; fair; just: said of actions, results of actions, etc. 2. in *law*, *a*) having to do with equity, as distinguished from common or statute law. *b*) valid in equity.

eq·ui·ta·bly (ek'wi-tə-bli), ***adv.*** in an equitable manner; according to the principles of equity.

eq·ui·tant (ek'wi-tənt), ***adj.*** [L. *equitans*, ppr. of *equitare*; see EQUITATION], in *botany*, overlapping: said of leaves whose bases overlap the leaves within or above them, as in the iris.

eq·ui·ta·tion (ek'wi-tā'shən), ***n.*** [L. *equitatio* < *equitatus*, pp. of *equitare*, to ride < *eques*, horseman < *equus*, horse], the art of riding on horseback; horsemanship.

eq·ui·tes (ek'wə-tēz'), ***n.pl.*** [L., pl. of *eques*; see EQUESTRIAN], members of a specially privileged class of citizens in ancient Rome, from which the cavalry was formed; equestrian order of knights.

eq·ui·ty (ek'wə-ti), ***n.*** [*pl.* EQUITIES (-tiz)], [ME. *equitee*; OFr. *equité*; L. *aequitas*, equality < *aequus*, equal], 1. fairness; impartiality; justice. 2. anything that is fair or equitable. 3. the value of property beyond the total amount owed on it. 4. in *law*, *a*) resort to general principles of fairness and justice whenever existing law is inadequate. *b*) a system of rules and doctrines, as in the United States, supplementing common and statute law and superseding such law when it proves inadequate for just settlement. *c*) an equitable right or claim. *d*) an equity of redemption.

equity of redemption, the right of a mortgagor to redeem his forfeited estate by payment of capital and interest within a reasonable time: it is granted by a court of equity.

e·quiv·a·lence (i-kwiv'ə-ləns), ***n.*** [Fr. *équivalence*; ML. *aequivalentia* < LL. *aequivalens*], 1. the condition of being equivalent; equality of quantity, value, force, meaning, etc. 2. in *chemistry*, equality of combining capacity; the principle that different weights of different substances are equivalent in chemical reactions.

e·quiv·a·len·cy (i-kwiv'ə-lən-si), ***n.*** equivalence.

e·quiv·a·lent (i-kwiv'ə-lənt), ***adj.*** [Fr.; LL. *aequivalens*, ppr. of *aequivalere*, to have equal power < L. *aequus*, equal + *valere*, to be strong], 1. equal in quantity, value, force, meaning, etc. 2. in *chemistry*, having the same valence. 3. in *geometry*, equal in area, volume, etc., but not of the same shape. ***n.*** 1. an equivalent thing. 2. in *chemistry*, the quantity by weight (of a substance) that combines with one gram of hydrogen or eight grams of oxygen. Abbreviated **eq., equiv.** —***SYN.*** see **same.**

e·quiv·o·cal (i-kwiv'ə-k'l), ***adj.*** [< LL. *aequivocus* (see EQUIVOCATE); + *-al*], 1. that can have more than one interpretation; having two or more meanings; purposely vague, misleading, or ambiguous: as, an *equivocal* reply. 2. uncertain; undecided; doubtful: as, an *equivocal* outcome. 3. suspicious; questionable: as, *equivocal* conduct. —***SYN.*** see **obscure.**

e·quiv·o·cate (i-kwiv'ə-kāt'), ***v.i.*** [EQUIVOCATED (-id), EQUIVOCATING], [LL. *aequivocatus*, pp. of *aequivocari*, to have the same sound, be called by the same name < *aequivocus*, of like sound < L. *aequus*, equal + *vox*, *vocis*, voice, sound], to use equivocal terms in order to deceive or mislead; be purposely ambiguous; hedge. —***SYN.*** see **lie.**

e·quiv·o·ca·tion (i-kwiv'ə-kā'shən), ***n.*** 1. an equivocating. 2. an equivocal, or ambiguous, expression.

e·quiv·o·ca·tor (i-kwiv'ə-kā'tẽr), ***n.*** a person who equivocates.

eq·ui·voque, eq·ui·voke (ek'wi-vōk'), ***n.*** [< Fr. or LL.; Fr. *équivoque*; LL. *aequivocus*; see EQUIVOCATE], 1. an ambiguous expression or term. 2. *a*) a pun. *b*) punning. 3. verbal ambiguity; double meaning.

E·qu·le·us (i-kwōō'li-əs), ***n.*** [L., dim. of *equus*, a horse], a very small constellation on the equator: see **constellation,** chart.

er (*approx.* ə, u; ẽr, ũr *is a sp. pronun.*), ***interj.*** a conventionalized expression of the sound often made by a speaker when hesitating briefly; vocalized pause.

-er (ẽr), a suffix of various origins, functions, and meanings: 1. [ME. *-er(e)*; AS. *-ere*; WGmc. **-arj*,

*-ārj; reinforced by L. *-arius, -arium*, agentive suffixes, (Anglo-Fr. *-er, -ier*), L. *-arem* (OFr. *-er*), L. *-aturam* (OFr. *-ëure*), L. *-atorium* (OFr. *-ëor*, Fr. *-oir*), L. *-atorem* (OFr. *-ëor*)], *a*) added to nouns, meaning ***a person having to do with***, as in *hatter, cottager*: also **-ier** or **-yer** after *-w* and in a few words with Anglo-French *-ier*, as in *lawyer, hosier*. *b*) added to place names, meaning ***a person living in***, as in *New Yorker*. *c*) in colloquial usage, added to nouns, noun compounds, and noun phrases, meaning ***a thing or action connected with***, as in *diner, double-header*. *d*) added to verbs, meaning ***a person or thing that***, as in *sprayer, roller*; see also **-ar, -or**. 2. [ME. *-re, -er*; AS. *-ra*], added to many adjectives and adverbs to form the comparative degree, as in *later, greater*. 3. [ME.; Anglo-Fr. inf. suffix], added to verb bases in legal language, meaning ***the action of —ing***, as in *demurrer, waiver*. 4. [ME. *-ren, -rien*; AS. *-rian*, freq. suffix], added to verbs and verb bases, meaning ***repeatedly***, as in *flicker, patter*.

Er, in *chemistry*, erbium.

e·ra (êr′ə), ***n.*** [LL. *aera*, era; earlier senses, "counters," "items of account" < pl. of L. *aes, aeris*, brass], 1. a system of reckoning time by numbering the years from some important occurrence or given point of time: as, the Christian *Era* is dated from approximately four years after Jesus' birth. 2. an event or date that marks the beginning of a new or important period in the history of something. 3. a period of time measured from some important occurrence or date. 4. a period of time considered in terms of noteworthy and characteristic events, developments, men, etc.: as, an *era* of progress. 5. any of the five main divisions of geological time: as, the Paleozoic *Era*: see also **epoch, period, age.** —***SYN.*** see **period.**

e·ra·di·ate (ē-rā′di-āt′), ***v.i. & v.t.*** to shoot out, as light rays; radiate.

e·rad·i·ca·ble (i-rad′i-kə-b'l), ***adj.*** that can be eradicated.

e·rad·i·cate (i-rad′i-kāt′), ***v.t.*** [ERADICATED (-id), ERADICATING], [L. *eradicatus*, pp. of *eradicare*, to root out < *e-*, out + *radix, radicis*, a root], 1. to tear out by the roots; uproot; hence, 2. to get rid of; wipe out; destroy; annihilate. —***SYN.*** see **exterminate.**

e·rad·i·ca·tion (i-rad′i-kā′shən), ***n.*** an eradicating or being eradicated; total destruction; annihilation.

e·rad·i·ca·tive (i-rad′i-kā′tiv, i-rad′i-kə-tiv), ***adj.*** eradicating or tending to eradicate.

e·rad·i·ca·tor (i-rad′i-kā′tẽr), ***n.*** a person or thing that eradicates: chemical ink removers are called *eradicators*.

e·ras·a·ble (i-rās′ə-b'l), ***adj.*** that can be erased.

e·rase (i-rās′), ***v.t.*** [ERASED (-rāst′), ERASING], [< L. *erasus*, pp. of *eradere*, to scratch out; *e-*, out + *radere*, to scrape, scratch], 1. to rub, scrape, or wipe out, as written or engraved letters; efface; expunge. 2. to remove all marks of; obliterate, as from the mind. 3. [Slang], to kill.

SYN.—**erase** implies a scraping or rubbing out of something written or drawn, or figuratively, the removal of an impression; to **expunge** is to remove or wipe out completely; **efface** implies a rubbing out from a surface, and, in extended use, suggests a destroying of the distinguishing marks, or even of the very existence, of something; **obliterate** implies a thorough blotting out of something so that all visible traces of it are removed; **delete** implies the marking of written or printed matter for removal, or the removal of the matter itself.

e·ras·er (i-rās′ẽr), ***n.*** a thing that erases; specifically, a device made of rubber, for erasing marks made with ink or pencil, or a pad of felt or cloth, for removing chalk marks from a blackboard.

e·ra·sion (i-rā′zhən), ***n.*** 1. an erasing. 2. in *surgery*, the removal of diseased tissue by scraping with a curette.

E·ras·mi·an (i-raz′mi-ən), ***adj.*** of Desiderius Erasmus or his ideas. ***n.*** a follower of Erasmus.

E·ras·mus (i-raz′məs), [LL. < Gr. *erasmios*, lovely < *eran*, to love], a masculine name.

E·ras·mus, Des·i·der·i·us (des′i-dêr′i-əs i-raz′məs), (born *Gerhard Gerhards*), 1466?–1536; Dutch humanist, theologian, and writer.

E·ras·tian (i-ras′chən, i-ras′ti-ən), ***adj.*** of or supporting Thomas Erastus or his doctrines, especially that advocating the supreme authority of the state in church matters. ***n.*** a follower of Erastus or his doctrines.

E·ras·tus (i-ras′təs), [L.; Gr. *Erastos*, lit., beloved, lovely < *eran*, to love], a masculine name.

E·ras·tus, Thomas (i-ras′təs), 1524–1583; German-Swiss theologian and physician.

e·ra·sure (i-rā′shẽr, i-rā′zhẽr), ***n.*** 1. an erasing. 2. an erased word, mark, etc. 3. the place on a surface where some word, mark, etc. has been erased.

Er·a·to (er′ə-tō′), ***n.*** [L.; Gr. *Eratō*], in *Greek mythology*, the Muse of lyric poetry and love poetry.

Er·a·tos·the·nes (er′ə-tos′thə-nēz′), ***n.*** Greek mathematician and astronomer; 3d century B.C.

Er·bil (ẽr-bēl′), ***n.*** Arbela, Iraq: the modern name.

er·bi·um (ũr′bi-əm), ***n.*** [Mod. L. < *Ytterby*, Sweden, where gadolinite, the mineral containing this substance, is found], a metallic chemical element of the rare-earth group: symbol, Er, E; at. wt. 167.2; at. no., 68.

ere (âr), ***prep.*** [ME.; AS. *ær, adv., prep., conj.*; akin to G. *eher, ehe*; orig. compar. as seen in the cognate Goth. *airis, airiza*, earlier < *air*, early; IE. base **aier-*, dawn < **ai-*, to burn, shine], [Archaic or Poetic], before (in time). ***conj.*** [Archaic or Poetic], 1. before. 2. sooner than; rather than.

Er·e·bus (er′ə-bəs), ***n.*** [L.; Gr. *Erebos*], in *Greek mythology*, the dark place under the earth through which the dead passed before entering Hades.

Erebus, Mount, a volcanic mountain in Victoria Land, Antarctica: height, 13,202 ft.

Er·ech·thei·on (er′ik-thī′on), ***n.*** the Erechtheum.

Er·ech·the·um (er′ik-thē′əm), ***n.*** [Gr. *Erechtheion* < *Erechtheus*, lit., the render, a mythical king of Athens < *erechthein*, to rend, break], a temple on the Acropolis in Athens: it was completed about 409 B.C. and contains outstanding examples of Ionic architecture.

e·rect (i-rekt′), ***adj.*** [L. *erectus*, pp. of *erigere*, to set up; *e-*, out, up + *regere*, to make straight], 1. upright; vertical; pointing upward. 2. bristling; stiff: said of hair, etc. 3. [Archaic], *a*) not depressed; uplifted. *b*) alert. ***v.t.*** 1. to raise or construct (a building, etc.). 2. to set up; cause to arise: as, they *erected* arbitrary social barriers. 3. to set in an upright position; raise. 4. to set up; assemble. 5. [Archaic], to establish; found. 6. in *geometry*, to construct or draw (a perpendicular, figure, etc.) upon a base line. 7. in *physiology*, to cause to become swollen and hard by being filled with blood. ***v.i.*** in *physiology*, to become swollen and hard by being filled with blood.

e·rec·tile (i-rek′t'l, i-rek′til), ***adj.*** [Fr. < L. *erectus*], that can become erect: used especially to designate tissue, as in the penis, that becomes swollen and hard when filled with blood.

e·rec·til·i·ty (i-rek′til′ə-ti, ē′rek-til′ə-ti), ***n.*** the condition of being erectile.

e·rec·tion (i-rek′shən), ***n.*** 1. an erecting or being erected. 2. something erected; structure, building, etc. 3. in *physiology*, a becoming or being hard and swollen by filling with blood: said of erectile tissue.

e·rec·tor (i-rek′tẽr), ***n.*** a person or thing that erects.

ere·long (âr′lôŋ′), ***adv.*** [Archaic or Poetic], ere long; before long; soon.

er·e·mite (er′ə-mīt′), ***n.*** [ME. < OFr. or LL.; OFr. *ermite, hermite*; see HERMIT], a hermit; religious recluse.

er·e·mit·ic (er′ə-mit′ik), ***adj.*** of or characteristic of an eremite.

er·e·mit·i·cal (er′ə-mit′i-k'l), ***adj.*** eremitic.

ere·now (âr′nou′), ***adv.*** [Archaic or Poetic], ere now; before now; heretofore.

er·e·thism (er′ə-thiz'm), ***n.*** [Gr. *erethismos*, irritation < *erethizein*, to irritate], [Rare], in *physiology*, extreme irritability or sensitivity (of an organ, tissue, etc.).

ere·while (âr′hwīl′), ***adv.*** [ME. *erwhile*], [Archaic], a short while before; a short time ago.

ere·whiles (âr′hwīlz′), ***adv.*** [Archaic], erewhile.

Er·furt (er′foort), ***n.*** a city in Saxony, Germany: pop., 145,000.

erg (ũrg), ***n.*** [< Gr. *ergon*, work], in *physics*, the unit of work or energy in the C.G.S. (metric) system, being the amount of work done by one dyne acting through a distance of one centimeter; ergon: abbreviated **e.**

‡er·go (ũr′gō), ***conj. & adv.*** [L.], therefore; consequently; hence.

er·go·graph (ũr′gō-graf′, ũr′gō-gräf′), ***n.*** [< Gr. *ergon*, work; + *-graph*], an instrument for measuring and recording the amount of work done in muscular exertion: used especially for measuring the rate of fatigue.

er·gom·e·ter (ẽr-gom′ə-tẽr), ***n.*** [< Gr. *ergon*, work; + *-meter*], an instrument for measuring the amount of energy used or work done.

er·gon (ũr′gon), ***n.*** [Mod. L.; Gr. *ergon*, work; see WORK], in *physics*, 1. work, in terms of its equivalent in heat. 2. an erg.

er·gos·ter·ol (ẽr-gos′tə-rōl′), ***n.*** [< *ergot* + *sterol*], an alcohol, $C_{28}H_{44}O$, of high molecular weight, formerly prepared from ergot but now chiefly from yeast: when exposed to ultraviolet rays it produces a vitamin (D_1) used to prevent or cure rickets.

er·got (ũr′gət), ***n.*** [Fr.; OFr. *argot*, a rooster's spur, hence (from the shape) the disease growth in the plant], 1. a fungous growth on the grains of rye, other cereal plants, and some grasses. 2. the disease in which this occurs. 3. the fungus causing this disease. 4. the dried fungus, used as a drug to stop bleeding and to contract muscles, as of the uterus during labor.

er·got·ism (ũr′gə-tiz'm), ***n.*** a diseased condition resulting from the excessive or improper use of ergot or the eating of grain infested with ergot fungus.

Er·ic (er′ik), [Scand.; ON. *Eirikr* < Gmc. **aizo*, honor (akin to G. *ehre*, honor) + base akin to L. *rex* (see RICH); hence, lit., honorable ruler], a masculine name.

er·i·ca·ceous (er′ə-kā′shəs), ***adj.*** [Mod. L. *Erica*, name of the genus (< L. *erice*, heath, broom; Gr. *ereikē*; akin to Russ. *veresŭ*, OIr. *froech*); + *-aceous*], of the heath family of plants and shrubs, including the rhododendrons, laurels, azaleas, etc.

Er·ic·son, Leif (lēf, lāv er'ik-s'n), fl. 1000 A.D.; son of Eric the Red; Norwegian discoverer of America.

Er·ics·son, John (er'ik-s'n), 1803–1889; American naval engineer, born in Sweden; builder of the *Monitor.*

Eric the Red, fl. 10th century A.D.; Norwegian navigator; discovered and colonized Greenland.

E·rid·a·nus (i-rid'ə-nəs), *n.* [L., poetic name of the Po River], a long constellation extending from the equator to the southern horizon: see **constellation,** chart.

Er·ie (êr'i), *n.* [short for Am. Ind. (Huron) *Erieehronous,* the Erie, apparently < *eri'e,* at the place of the cat], 1. [*pl.* ERIE, ERIES (-iz)], a member of a tribe of Iroquoian Indians who lived in an area east and southeast of Lake Erie. 2. one of the Great Lakes, between Lake Huron and Lake Ontario: area, 9,940 sq. mi.; length, 240 mi: usually **Lake Erie.** 3. a port on Lake Erie, in northwestern Pennsylvania: pop., 138,000.

Erie Canal, a former barge canal from Buffalo on Lake Erie to Albany on the Hudson, opened in 1825: see **New York State Barge Canal.**

e·rig·er·on (i-rij'ə-ron'), *n.* [L., groundsel; Gr. *ērigerōn* < *ēri,* early + *gerōn,* old man: so named from the hoary down appearing on certain varieties], any of a group of plants with asterlike rayed flower heads of white, rose, or violet.

Er·in (âr'in, êr'in), *n.* [OIr. *Ērinn,* dat. of *Ēriu,* Eire], [Poetic], Ireland.

er·i·na·ceous (er'i-nā'shəs), *adj.* [< L. *erinaceus,* a hedgehog], of, or having the nature of, a hedgehog.

e·rin·go (i-riŋ'gō), *n.* eryngo.

E·rin·y·es (i-rin'i-ēz'), *n.pl.* [*sing.* ERINYS (i-rin'is, i-rī'-nis)], [L. < Gr. *Erinys*], in *Greek mythology,* the Furies.

E·ris (êr'is, er'is), *n.* [L.; Gr. *Eris* (see ERISTIC)], in *Greek mythology,* the goddess of strife and discord.

er·is·tic (er-is'tik), *adj.* [Gr. *eristikos* < *erizein,* to strive, dispute < *eris,* strife], 1. of argument or controversy. 2. argumentative; controversial. *n.* 1. a disputant; controversialist. 2. the art of disputation.

Er·i·tre·a (er'i-trē'ə), *n.* an autonomous unit of Ethiopia, in eastern Africa, on the Red Sea: it is a former Italian colony: area, 48,000 sq. mi.; pop., 1,100,000; capital, Asmara.

Er·i·tre·an (er'i-trē'ən), *adj.* of Eritrea or its people. *n.* a native or inhabitant of Eritrea.

Er·i·van (er'i-vän'y'), *n.* the capital of the Armenian S.S.R.: pop., 509,000.

erl·king (ûrl'kiŋ'), *n.* [after G. *erlkönig* < misunderstanding by Herder (1779) of Dan. *ellerkonge,* var. of *elverkonge,* king of the elves], in *Germanic folklore,* a spirit who does mischief and evil, especially to children.

er·mine (ûr'min), *n.* [*pl.* ERMINES (-minz), ERMINE; see PLURAL, II, D, 1], [ME.; OFr. *ermine, hermine;* prob. < MHG. *hermin,* erminelike < *harme,* ermine; OHG. *harmo,* weasel (AS. *hearma*); or < or confused with L. (*mus*) *Armenius,* Armenian (mouse)], 1. any of several weasels of northern regions, whose fur is brown in summer but white with a black-tipped tail in winter: also called *stoat.* 2. the soft, white fur of this animal, used for women's coats, trimming, etc. 3. the position, rank, or functions of a judge, whose state robe, in European countries, is trimmed with ermine as an emblem of honor and purity: as, he has worn the *ermine* for ten years. 4. in *heraldry,* the representation of fur, consisting of a white field with black spots.

ERMINE (15 in. long)

er·mined (ûr'mind), *adj.* 1. trimmed with ermine. 2. wearing ermine.

er·mi·nois (ûr'mi-noiz', ûr'mi-nois'), *n.* [OFr. *erminois, herminois* < *ermine, hermine;* see ERMINE], in *heraldry,* a fur represented by a golden field with black spots.

erne, ern (ûrn), *n.* [ME. *ern, arn;* AS. *earn;* akin to MLG. *arn* (D. *arend*); IE. base **er-,* **or-,* great bird, eagle, seen also in G. *aar,* eagle & Gr. *ornis,* bird], a kind of eagle that lives near the sea; sea eagle.

Er·nest (ûr'nist), [G. *Ernst;* OHG. *Ernust, Ernost,* lit., resolute fighter < *ernust;* see EARNEST], a masculine name: diminutive, *Ernie;* feminine, *Ernestine;* equivalents, It. & Sp. *Ernesto,* G. *Ernst:* also spelled **Earnest.**

Er·nes·tine (ûr'nəs-tēn'), [G., fem. < *Ernst;* see ERNEST], a feminine name.

e·rode (i-rōd'), *v.t.* [ERODED (-id), ERODING], [Fr. *éroder;* L. *erodere; e-,* out, off + *rodere,* to gnaw], 1. to eat into; wear away; disintegrate: as, acid *erodes* metal. 2. to form by wearing away gradually: as, the running water *eroded* a gully. *v.i.* to become eroded.

e·rod·ent (i-rō'd'nt), *adj.* causing erosion; erosive.

e·rog·e·nous (i-roj'ə-nəs), *adj.* [< Gr. *erōs,* love; + *-genous*], designating or of those zones, or parts, of the body the stimulation of which tends to arouse sexual desire.

-er·oo (ə-rōō'), [prob. < *buckaroo;* use apparently encouraged by double talk], a humorous slang suffix.

E·ros (êr'os, er'os), *n.* [L.; Gr. *Erōs,* Cupid, god of love < *erōs,* love], in *Greek mythology,* the god of love, son of Aphrodite: identified by the Romans with Cupid.

e·rose (i-rōs'), *adj.* [L. *erosus,* pp. of *erodere;* see ERODE], 1. irregular, as if gnawed away. 2. in *botany,* having an irregularly notched edge, as some leaves.

e·ro·sion (i-rō'zhən), *n.* [L. *erosio* < *erosus,* pp. of *erodere*], an eroding or being eroded: as, soil *erosion* can often be prevented by planting trees, terracing, etc.

e·ro·sive (i-rō'siv), *adj.* causing erosion; eroding.

e·rot·ic (i-rot'ik), *adj.* [Gr. *erōtikos* < *erōs, erōtos,* love], of or causing sexual feelings or desires; having to do with sexual love; amatory. *n.* 1. a person abnormally sensitive to sexual stimulation. 2. an erotic poem.

e·rot·i·ca (i-rot'i-kə), *n.pl.* erotic books, pictures, etc.

e·rot·i·cal·ly (i-rot'i-k'l-i, i-rot'ik-li), *adv.* in an erotic manner.

e·rot·i·cism (i-rot'ə-siz'm), *n.* 1. erotic quality or character. 2. sexual instincts and behavior. 3. preoccupation with sex.

er·o·tism (er'ə-tiz'm), *n.* eroticism (especially in sense 2).

ERP, E.R.P., European Recovery Program.

err (ûr), *v.i.* [ME. *erren;* OFr. *errer;* L. *errare,* to wander, go astray, err], 1. to be wrong or mistaken; fall into error. 2. to deviate from the established moral code; do wrong. 3. [Obs.], to go astray; wander.

er·ran·cy (er'ən-si), *n.* [L. *errentia* < *errans;* see ERRANT], 1. the state of erring. 2. a tendency to err.

er·rand (er'ənd), *n.* [ME. *erande, erende;* AS. *ærende,* message, mission, news, lit., that delivered by messenger < base of AS. *ar,* messenger; akin to OS. *ārundi,* OHG. *ārunti*], 1. a trip to carry a message or do a definite thing; especially, a short trip to do a thing for someone else. 2. the thing to be done on such a trip; purpose or object for which one is sent.

er·rant (er'ənt), *adj.* [ME. *erraunt;* OFr. *errant,* ppr. of *errer* < LL. **iterare,* to travel < L. *iter,* a journey; cf. ERR], 1. roving in search of adventure; wandering; itinerant: as, a knight-*errant.* 2. [OFr., ppr. of *errer* (see ERR); confused with *errer,* to rove, travel], erring; straying from what is right; wrong. 3. [Obs.], arrant.

er·rant·ry (er'ənt-ri), *n.* the condition or behavior of a knight-errant; spirit or deeds of chivalry.

er·ra·ta (i-rā'tə, e-rä'tə), *n.* plural of **erratum:** used chiefly of errors in printing.

er·rat·ic (ə-rat'ik), *adj.* [ME. *erratik;* OFr. *erratique;* L. *erraticus,* wandering; pp. of *errare,* to wander], 1. having no fixed course or purpose; irregular; wandering. 2. deviating from the conventional or customary course, eccentric; queer. 3. in *geology,* designating a boulder or rock formation transported some distance from its original source, as by a glacier. *n.* an erratic person.

er·rat·i·cal·ly (ə-rat'i-k'l-i, ə-rat'ik-li), *adv.* in an erratic manner.

er·ra·tum (i-rā'təm, e-rä'təm), *n.* [*pl.* ERRATA (-tə)], [L., neut. of *erratus* < pp. of *errare,* to wander], an error in printing or writing: see **errata.**

er·rhine (er'īn, er'in), *adj.* [Gr. *errhinon* < *en-,* in + *rhis, rhinos,* nose], increasing nasal discharge and, hence, causing sneezing. *n.* an errhine medicine.

err·ing (ûr'iŋ; *occas.* er'iŋ), *adj.* that errs or has erred.

er·ro·ne·ous (ə-rō'ni-əs, e-rō'ni-əs), *adj.* [L. *erroneus,* wandering about < *errare,* to wander], containing or based on error; mistaken; wrong: abbreviated **erron.**

er·ror (er'ẽr), *n.* [ME. *errour;* OFr. & L. *error* < L. *errare,* to wander], 1. the state of believing what is untrue, incorrect, or wrong. 2. a wrong belief; incorrect opinion. 3. something incorrectly done through ignorance or carelessness; mistake. 4. a departure from the accepted moral code; transgression; wrongdoing. 5. the difference between a computed or estimated result and the actual value, as in mathematics. 6. in *baseball,* any misplay (by a member of the team in the field) of a chance that should have resulted in an out for the team at bat, or that permits a runner to advance: a passed ball and a wild pitch are not classed as errors.

SYN.—**error** implies deviation from truth, accuracy, correctness, right, etc. and is the broadest term in this comparison (an *error* in judgment, in computation, etc.); **mistake** suggests an error resulting from carelessness, inattention, misunderstanding, etc. and does not in itself carry a strong implication of criticism (a *mistake* in reading a blueprint); **blunder** implies stupidity, clumsiness, inefficiency, etc. and carries a suggestion of more severe criticism (the tactical *blunder* cost them the war); a **slip** is a mistake, usually slight, made inadvertently in speaking or writing; a **faux pas** is a social blunder or error in etiquette that causes embarrassment; **boner,** a slang term, is applied to a silly or ridiculous blunder.

er·satz (er-zäts'), *n.* & *adj.* [G., lit., replacement < *ersetzen,* to replace < *setzen,* to set, place], substitute:

the word usually suggests inferior quality. —*SYN.* see **artificial.**

Erse (ũrs), *adj.* & *n.* [Scot. var. of *Irish*], 1. formerly, Scottish Gaelic. 2. in *linguistics*, Irish Gaelic.

Er·skine, John (ũr′skin), 1. 1695–1768; Scottish jurist and writer. 2. 1879–1951; American educator, critic, and novelist.

erst (ũrst), *adv.* [ME. *erest, erste;* AS. *ærest*, superl. of *ær;* see ERE], 1. [Obs.], at first; originally. 2. [Archaic], formerly; long ago. *adj.* [Obs.], first.

erst·while (ũrst′hwīl′), *adv.* [Archaic], formerly; some time ago. *adj.* former; of an earlier time: as, my *erstwhile* friend.

er·u·bes·cent (er′oo-bes′′nt), *adj.* [L. *erubescens*, ppr. of *erubescere*, to redden; *e-*, out + *rubescere*, to grow red; see RUBESCENT], reddish; reddening; blushing.

e·ruct (i-rukt′), *v.t.* & *v.i.* [L. *eructare; e-*, out + *ructare*, to belch], to belch.

e·ruc·tate (i-ruk′tāt), *v.t.* & *v.i.* [ERUCTATED (-id), ERUCTATING], [< L. *eructatus*, pp. of *eructare;* see ERUCT], to belch.

e·ruc·ta·tion (i-ruk′tā′shən, ē′ruk-tā′shən, er′ək-tā′shən), *n.* [L. *eructatio*], 1. an eructating; belching. 2. that which is belched up.

er·u·dite (er′yoo-dīt′, er′oo-dīt′), *adj.* [L. *eruditus*, pp. of *erudire*, to instruct < *e-*, out + *rudis*, rude, untrained], having a wide knowledge gained from reading; learned; scholarly.

er·u·di·tion (er′yoo-dish′ən, er′oo-dish′ən), *n.* [L. *eruditio;* see ERUDITE], learning acquired by reading and study; scholarship. —*SYN.* see **information.**

e·rupt (i-rupt′), *v.i.* [< L. *eruptus*, pp. of *erumpere*, to break out, burst forth; *e-*, out + *rumpere*, to break], 1. to burst forth or out, as lava from a volcano. 2. to throw forth lava, water, steam, etc.: as, geysers and volcanoes *erupt.* 3. to break out in a rash. 4. to break through the gums and become visible: said of new teeth. *v.t.* to cause to burst forth; throw forth; eject.

e·rup·tion (i-rup′shən), *n.* [L. *eruptio;* see ERUPT], 1. a bursting forth or out, as of lava from a volcano. 2. a throwing forth of lava, water, steam, etc. 3. a sudden outburst, as of emotion or social discontent. 4. in *medicine*, *a*) a breaking out in a rash. *b*) a rash.

e·rup·tive (i-rup′tiv), *adj.* 1. erupting or tending to erupt. 2. of, produced by, or formed by eruption: as, *eruptive* rock. 3. in *medicine*, causing or characterized by a skin eruption. *n.* in *geology*, a rock thrown out by volcanic eruption.

E.R.V., English Revised Version (of the Bible).

Er·vine, St. John Greer (sin′jən grêr ũr′vin), 1883– ; Irish writer.

Er·win (ũr′win), [G. *Erwin*, earlier *Herwin* < OHG. *hari, heri*, host, crowd, army (akin to AS. *here;* see HARRY, *v.*) + *wini, wine* (see EDWIN); hence, lit., friend of hosts], a masculine name: also spelled **Irwin.**

-er·y (ẽr-i), [ME. *-erie;* OFr. *-erie* < LL. *-aria*, or by addition of *-ie* (L. *-ia*) to OFr. nouns of agency in *-ier*], a suffix used to form nouns from verbs or other nouns, meaning: 1. *a place to*, as in *tannery, brewery.* 2. *a place for*, as in *nunnery, vinery.* 3. *the practice, act*, or *occupation of*, as in *surgery, robbery.* 4. *the product* or *goods of*, as in *pottery, millinery.* 5. *a collection of*, as in *jewelry, crockery.* 6. *the state* or *condition of*, as in *drudgery, slavery.* Also **-ry.**

Er·y·man·thi·an (er′i-man′thi-ən), *adj.* [L. *Erymanthius*], in *Greek mythology*, 1. of Mount Erymanthus. 2. designating a savage boar captured by Hercules.

Er·y·man·thus, Mount (er′i-man′thəs), a mountain between Arcadia and Achaia.

e·ryn·go (i-riŋ′gō), *n.* [< (? via L. *eryngion* < Gr. *ēryngion*, dim.) Gr. *ēryngos*], 1. a plant of the carrot family, with broad, spiny, grayish-blue leaves and pale-blue flowers: also called *sea holly.* 2. [Obs.], the candied root of this plant, formerly used as an aphrodisiac. Also spelled **eringo.**

er·y·sip·e·las (er′ə-sip′′l-əs, êr′ə-sip′ə-ləs), *n.* [L.; Gr. *erysipelas* < *erythros*, red + *pella*, skin], an acute infectious disease of the skin or mucous membranes caused by any of several kinds of streptococcus: it is characterized by local inflammation and fever.

er·y·si·pel·a·tous (er′ə-si-pel′ə-təs, êr′ə-si-pel′ə-təs), *adj.* of or having erysipelas.

er·y·the·ma (er′ə-thē′mə), *n.* [Mod. L.; Gr. *erythēma* < *erythainein, erythrainein*, to redden, blush < *erythros*, red], an abnormal redness of the skin resulting from the congestion of small capillaries.

er·y·the·mat·ic (er′ə-thi-mat′ik), *adj.* erythematous.

er·y·them·a·tous (er′ə-them′ə-təs, er′ə-thē′mə-təs), *adj.* of or characterized by erythema.

er·y·the·mic (er′ə-thē′mik), *adj.* erythematous.

e·ryth·rism (i-rith′riz′m, e-rith′riz′m), *n.* [< *erythro-* + *-ism*], excessive redness, especially of the hair of mammals or the feathers of birds.

e·ryth·rite (i-rith′rīt), *n.* [< *erythro-* + *-ite*], 1. erythritol. 2. a hydrous cobalt arsenate, $CO_3(AsO_4)_2 \cdot 8H_2O$, usually rose-colored.

e·ryth·ri·tol (i-rith′ri-tōl′, i-rith′ri-tol′), *n.* [< *erythro-* + *-ite* + *-ol:* so named because found in an alkaloid obtained from plants of the genus *Erythrina*], a sweet, colorless crystalline compound, $CH_2OH(CHOH)_2CH_2OH$, obtained from some lichens and algae.

e·ryth·ro- (i-rith′rō, e-rith′rō), [< Gr. *erythros*, red], a combining form meaning: 1. *red*, as in *erythrocyte, erythrophyll.* 2. *erythrocyte*, as in *erythroblast.* Also, before a vowel, **erythr-.**

e·ryth·ro·blast (i-rith′rō-blast′, e-rith′rō-blast′), *n.* [*erythro-* + *-blast*], any of the small nucleated cells, found normally in the marrow of bones, from which the erythrocytes develop.

e·ryth·ro·blas·to·sis (i-rith′rō-blas-tō′sis, e-rith′rō-blas-tō′sis), *n.* an increase in the number of erythroblasts in the fetus, believed to result from the incompatability of Rh positive and negative factors.

e·ryth·ro·cyte (i-rith′rō-sīt′, e-rith′rō-sīt′), *n.* [*erythro-* + *-cyte*], a red blood corpuscle: it is a very small, circular disk with both faces concave, and contains hemoglobin, which carries oxygen to the body tissues.

e·ryth·ro·cy·tom·e·ter (i-rith′rō-sī-tom′ə-tẽr, er′ith-rō′sī-tom′ə-tẽr), *n.* [< *erythrocyte* + *-meter*], a device for counting red blood corpuscles.

e·ryth·ro·phyll (i-rith′rō-fil′, e-rith′rō-fil′), *n.* [*erythro-* + *-phyll*], in *botany*, a red coloring matter in certain leaves, which gives them the red color seen in the fall.

Er·zu·rum, Er·ze·rum (er′zə-rōōm′), *n.* a city in northeastern Turkey: pop., 91,000.

-es (iz, əz), a suffix used: 1. [ME.; AS. *-as*, pl. inflection of masc. nouns], to form the plural of some nouns, as in *fishes:* also **-s, -'s.** 2. [ME.; Northumbrian AS. *-s*, 3d pers. sing., pres. tense inflection of verbs], to form the third person singular, present indicative, of verbs, as in (he) *kisses:* also **-s.** 3. [ME.; AS. *-es*, genit. inflection of masc. & neut. nouns], formerly, to form the possessive case of nouns, as in *Godes, Wednesday* (*Woden's day*): now written **'s.** In all these uses, the full (i.e., dissimilated) form of this suffix is pronounced when the preceding consonant is sibilant (s, sh, ch), as in *rushes, matches, Walsh's;* when the preceding consonant is other than sibilant, the suffix is assimilated to it, becoming (s) after voiceless consonants, as in *lips, Philip's*, he *limps*, and (z) after voiced consonants, as in *reeds, Red's*, he *reads.*

E·sau (ē′sô), *n.* [L.; Gr. *Ēsau;* Heb. *'ēsāw*, lit., hairy], in the *Bible*, the son of Isaac and Rebekah, who sold his birthright to his younger twin brother, Jacob: Gen. 25: 21–34, 27.

es·ca·drille (es′kə-dril′; Fr. es′kä′drē′y′), *n.* [Fr., dim. of *escadre*, fleet; It. *squadra;* LL. **exquadra;* see SQUAD], 1. a squadron of airplanes, usually six, with their men and equipment, as in the French armed forces of World War I. 2. a squadron of warships, usually eight.

es·ca·lade (es′kə-lād′), *n.* [Fr.; Sp. *escalada* < *escalar*, to climb < L. *scala*, ladder], the act of scaling or climbing the walls of a fortified place by ladders. *v.t.* [ESCALADED (-id), ESCALADING], to climb (a wall, etc.) or enter (a fortified place) by ladders.

es·ca·late (es′kə-lāt′), *v.i.* [ESCALATED (-id), ESCALATING], [back formation < *escalator*], 1. to rise on or as on an escalator. 2. to expand, as from a local conflict into a general nuclear war. *v.t.* to cause to escalate.

es·ca·la·tion (e′skə-lā′shən), *n.* an escalating or being escalated.

es·ca·la·tor (es′kə-lā′tẽr), *n.* [Mod. L. < Fr. *escalader*, to scale; see ESCALADE], a moving stairway consisting of treads linked in an endless belt, used in department stores, subway stations, etc.: a former trademark (**Escalator**).

ESCALATOR

escalator clause, a clause in a contract between an employer and a labor union providing for increases or decreases in pay, as in accordance with fluctuations in the cost of living.

es·cal·op, es·cal·lop (e-skol′əp, e-skal′əp), *n.* [OFr. *escalope*, a shell; see SCALLOP], 1. the scallop, a mollusk that has a ribbed shell with a wavy edge. 2. a decorative curve resembling that of a scallop shell. *v.t.* 1. to trim in curves. 2. to bake with crumbs or in a cream sauce.

es·ca·pade (es′kə-pād′, es′kə-pād′), *n.* [Fr. < Sp. *escapada* < *escapar*, to escape, flee; LL. **excappare;* see ESCAPE], 1. an escaping from restraint or confining rules. 2. a reckless adventure or prank.

es·cape (ə-skāp′, e-skāp′), *v.i.* [ESCAPED (-skāpt′), ESCAPING], [ME. *escapen;* OFr. *escaper*, var. of *eschaper;* LL. **excappare* < L. *ex-*, out of + *cappa*, cloak (i.e., leave one's cloak behind)], 1. to get free; get away; break loose, as from a prison. 2. to avoid an illness, accident, pain, etc.: as, two were killed, but he *escaped.* 3. to flow, drain, or leak away: as, water *escapes* rapidly from the drainpipe. 4. to slip away; disappear: as, the image *escaped* from her memory. *v.t.* 1. to get away from; flee. 2. to avoid; manage to keep away from: as, he *escaped* punishment. 3. to come from involuntarily or unintentionally: as, a scream *escaped* his lips. 4. to

slip away from; be missed, unperceived, or forgotten by: as, the exact date *escapes* me. ***n.*** [Fr. *échappe*], 1. an escaping. 2. the state of having escaped. 3. a means or way of escape. 4. an outward flow or leakage. 5. a temporary mental release from reality: as, movies are an *escape*. 6. in *botany*, a garden plant growing wild. ***adj.*** 1. giving temporary mental release from reality. 2. giving a basis for evading a claim, responsibility, etc.
SYN.—**escape**, as compared here, implies a getting out of, a keeping away from, or simply a remaining unaffected by an impending or present danger, evil, confinement, etc. (to *escape* death, criticism, etc.); **avoid** suggests the display of conscious effort in keeping clear of something undesirable or harmful (to *avoid* crowds during a flu epidemic); to **evade** is to escape or avoid by artifice, cunning, adroitness, etc. (to *evade* pursuit, one's duty, etc.); to **elude** is to escape the grasp of someone or something by artful or slippery dodges or because of a baffling quality (the criminal *eluded* the police, the meaning *eluded* him).
es·cape·ment (ə-skāp′mənt, e-skāp′mənt), ***n.*** [*escape* + *-ment*, after Fr. *échappement*], 1. [Rare], an escaping or means of escape. 2. the part in a clock or watch that controls the speed and regularity of the balance wheel or pendulum, and thereby of the entire mechanism, by the movement of a notched wheel, one tooth of which is permitted to escape from the detaining catch at a time. 3. the mechanism in typewriters that regulates the horizontal movement of the carriage.
escape wheel, the notched wheel in the escapement of a watch or clock.

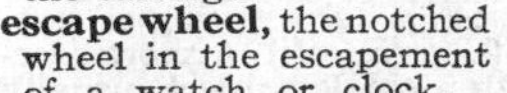

ESCAPEMENT (of clock)

es·cap·ism (ə-skāp′iz'm, e-skāp′iz'm), ***n.*** 1. a tendency to escape from reality, the responsibilities and routine of real life, etc., especially by unrealistic imaginative activity. 2. behavior characterized by this tendency. 3. literature, art, etc. expressing, catering to, or providing an outlet for this tendency.
es·cap·ist (ə-skāp′ist, e-skāp′ist), ***adj.*** characterized by escapism. ***n.*** a person whose behavior, writing, etc. is escapist.
‡es·car·got (es′kår′gō′), ***n.*** [Fr.], a snail, especially an edible variety.
es·ca·role (es′kə-rōl′), ***n.*** [Fr.; ML. *escariola* < L. *escarius*, pertaining to food, fit for eating < *esca*, food (see ESCULENT)], a kind of endive, a plant whose leaves are used in salads.
es·carp (e-skärp′), ***n.*** [Fr. *escarpe* < It. *scarpa*], a scarp; escarpment. ***v.t.*** [Fr. *escarper* < the *n.*], to make into, or provide with, an escarp or escarps.
es·carp·ment (e-skärp′mənt), ***n.*** [Fr. < *escarper;* see ESCARP, SCARP], 1. a steep slope or cliff. 2. ground formed into a steep slope as part of a fortification.
Es·caut (es′kō′), ***n.*** the Scheldt, a river in France, Belgium, and the Netherlands: the French name.
-esce (es), [L. *-escere*], a suffix used to form verbs that designate an action just begun or still incomplete, as *coalesce:* such verbs are called *inceptive* or *inchoative*.
-es·cence (es′'ns), [L. *-escentia* < *-escens;* see -ESCENT], a noun suffix corresponding to the adjective suffix *-escent*, as in *opalescence, obsolescence.*
-es·cent (es′'nt), [L. *-escens, -escentis*, ppr. ending of inceptive or inchoative verbs in *-escere*], an adjective suffix meaning *in process of* ——*ing, starting to be, being*, or *becoming* (as indicated), as in *convalescent, obsolescent.*
esch·a·lot (esh′ə-lot′, esh′ə-lot′), ***n.*** [Fr. *eschallotte;* OFr. *eschalotte*, var. < *eschalogne;* see SHALLOT, SCALLION], a small onion.
es·char (es′kär), ***n.*** [< Fr. & L.; Fr. *eschare;* L. *eschara;* Gr. *eschara*, a hearth, burn; see SCAB], a dry scab that forms as the result of a burn or of action by some corrosive substance.
es·cha·rot·ic (es′kə-rot′ik), ***adj.*** [LL. *escharoticus;* Gr. *escharōtikos*], producing or tending to produce an eschar; corrosive; caustic. ***n.*** a corrosive or caustic substance.
es·cha·tol·o·gy (es′kə-tol′ə-ji), ***n.*** [< Gr. *eschatos*, furthest; + *-logy*], 1. the branch of theology dealing with the last things, such as death, resurrection, judgment, immortality, etc. 2. the doctrines concerning these.
es·cheat (es-chēt′), ***n.*** [ME. *eschete;* OFr. *escheoite*, lit., that which falls to one < pp. of *escheoir*, to fall to one's share < LL. **excadere*, to fall upon; L. *ex-*, out + *cadere*, to fall], in *law*, 1. the reverting of property to the lord of the manor (in feudal law), to the crown (in England), or to the government (in the United States) when there are no legal heirs. 2. property so reverting. 3. escheatage. ***v.t.*** to cause to escheat; confiscate. ***v.i.*** to revert or go by escheat.
es·cheat·age (es-chēt′ij), ***n.*** [*escheat* + *-age*], the right to take by escheat.
es·chew (es-chōō′, es-chū′), ***v.t.*** [ME. *eschewen;* Anglo-Fr. *eschuer;* OFr. *eschiver;* OHG. *sciuhan*, to fear (see SHY)], to keep away from (something harmful or bad); shun; avoid; abstain from.
es·chew·al (es-chōō′əl, es-chū′əl), ***n.*** an eschewing.
Es·cor·i·al (e-skôr′i-əl; Sp. es′kō-rē-äl′), ***n.*** [Sp. *escorial*, lit., place where a mine has been exhausted < *escoria;* L. *scoria*, dross], a huge granite structure near Madrid, built in the 16th century by Philip II of Spain: it encloses a monastery, palace, tomb, etc.: also **Escurial.**
es·cort (es′kôrt), ***n.*** [Fr. *escorte;* It. *scorta* < *scortare* < *scorgere*, to perceive, lead; LL. **excorrigere;* L. *ex-*, out + *corrigere*, to set right, correct], 1. one or more persons (or ships, airplanes, etc.) accompanying another or others to give protection or show honor. 2. a man or boy accompanying a woman or girl in public. 3. accompaniment as an escort. ***v.t.*** (i-skôrt′), [Fr. *escorter;* It. *scortare*], to go with as an escort; accompany to protect or show honor or courtesy to. —***SYN.*** see **accompany.**
es·cri·toire (es′kri-twär′, es′kri-twôr′), ***n.*** [OFr. *escriptoire* (Fr. *écritoire*); LL. *scriptorium*, place or apparatus for writing < pp. of L. *scribere*, to write], a writing desk or table: sometimes called *secretary.*
es·crow (es′krō, e-skrō′), ***n.*** [OFr. *escroe, escroue*, roll of writings, bond; see SCROLL], in *law*, a written agreement, as a bond or deed, put in the care of a third party and not in effect until certain conditions are fulfilled.
in escrow, in *law*, put in the care of a third party until certain conditions are fulfilled, as a bond, deed, or contract.
es·cu·do (es-kōō′dō; Sp. es-kōō′thô), ***n.*** [*pl.* ESCUDOS (-dōz; Sp. -thôs)], [Sp., a shield, gold coin < L. *scutum*, a shield], 1. any of several obsolete coins of Spain, Portugal, and their former colonies. 2. (Port. es-kōō′thoo), *a)* the gold monetary unit of Portugal, equal to 100 centavos, and valued at about 3 1/2 cents in 1950. *b)* a Portuguese coin of this value.
Es·cu·la·pi·an (es′kyoo-lā′pi-ən), ***adj.*** & ***n.*** Aesculapian.
es·cu·lent (es′kyoo-lənt), ***adj.*** [L. *esculentus* < *esca*, food < IE. **ēds-qa*, food < base **ēdes-* < **ed-*, to eat; hence akin to L. *edere*, to eat], fit for food; eatable; edible. ***n.*** something fit for food, especially a vegetable.
Es·cu·ri·al (e-skyoor′i-əl), ***n.*** the Escorial.
es·cutch·eon (i-skuch′ən), ***n.*** [ONorm. Fr. *escuchon;* LL. **scutio* < L. *scutus*, shield], 1. a shield or shield-shaped surface on which a coat of arms is displayed. 2. something shaped like an escutcheon; specifically, *a)* an ornamental shield or plate, as that around a keyhole. *b)* the space on a ship's stern bearing the name.
a blot on one's escutcheon, a stain on one's honor; disgrace to one's reputation.

ESCUTCHEON

Es·dra·e·lon (es′dri-ē′lən, ez′dri-ē′lən), ***n.*** a plain in northern Israel: site of several ancient battles: also called *Plain of Jezreel.*
Es·dras (ez′drəs), ***n.*** [Gr. *Esdras*, Ezra], 1. either of two books about Ezra in the Protestant Apocrypha. 2. either of two books of the Old Testament, Ezra and Nehemiah: in the *Douay Bible* they are called *1* and *2 Esdras.* Abbreviated **Esd.**
-ese (ēz; *formerly & still occas.* ēs), [OFr. *-eis;* L. *-ensis*], a suffix used: 1. to form adjectives meaning: *a) of* (a country or place), as in *Portuguese, Javanese.* *b) in the language* or *dialect of*, as in *Chinese, Cantonese.* *c) in the style of*, as in *Carlylese, journalese.* 2. to form nouns corresponding to these adjectives, meaning: *a) a native* or *inhabitant of.* *b) the language* or *dialect of.* *c) the style of.*
-ese (ēz), [< *-ase*], in *biochemistry*, a suffix added to the name of a substance, meaning *acted upon by a synthetic enzyme*, as in *Celanese.*
ESE, E.S.E., e.s.e., east-southeast.
Esk., Eskimo.
es·ker, es·kar (es′kẽr), ***n.*** [Ir. *eiscir*, a ridge], a winding, narrow ridge of sand or gravel, probably deposited by a stream flowing in or under glacial ice.
Es·ki·mau·an (es′kə-mō′ən), ***adj.*** Eskimoan.
Es·ki·mo (es′kə-mō′), ***n.*** [said to be < Am. Ind. (Labrador-Algonquian) *eskimantik*, eater of raw flesh], 1. [*pl.* ESKIMOS (-mōz′), ESKIMO (-mō′)], a member of a race living in Greenland, the Arctic and Hudson Bay coasts of North America, the Labrador coast, Alaska, and the northeastern tip of Asia. 2. the language of the Eskimos, comprising a number of closely related dialects now classified as members of the Eskimo-Aleut language group. ***adj.*** of the Eskimos or their language. Abbreviated **Esk.** Also spelled **Esquimau.**

Es·ki·mo·an (es′kə-mō′ən), *adj.* of the Eskimos, their language, or culture.

Eskimo dog, a strong breed of dog native to Greenland and Labrador, with a bushy tail and grayish, shaggy fur: it is used by the Eskimos to pull sleds.

ESKIMO DOG (20 in. high)

Es·ki·şe·hir, Es·ki·she·hir (es-kē′she-hêr′), *n.* a city in western Turkey: pop., 80,000 (1945).

e·so·phag·e·al (ē′sə-faj′i-əl), *adj.* of the esophagus: also spelled **oesophageal.**

e·soph·a·gus (i-sof′ə-gəs), *n.* [*pl.* ESOPHAGI (-jī′)], [L. *oesophagus* < Gr. *oisophagos,* lit., passage for food < *oisein,* fut. inf. of *pherein,* to carry + *phagein,* to eat], the passage for food from the pharynx to the stomach; gullet: also spelled **oesophagus:** see **alimentary canal,** illus.

es·o·ter·ic (es′ə-ter′ik), *adj.* [Gr. *esōterikos* < *esōteros,* inner, compar. of *esō,* within], 1. intended for or understood by only a chosen few; of or for only an inner group of disciples or initiates: said of ideas, doctrines, literature, etc. 2. confidential; private; withheld: as, an *esoteric* plan. Opposed to *exoteric.*

es·o·ter·i·cal·ly (es′ə-ter′i-k'l-i, es′ə-ter′ik-li), *adv.* in an esoteric manner.

ESP, E.S.P., extrasensory perception.

esp., especially.

es·pal·ier (e-spal′yẽr), *n.* [Fr.; It. *spalliera,* support for the shoulders < *spalla,* the shoulder < L. *spatula;* see SPATULA], 1. a lattice or trellis on which trees and shrubs are trained to grow flat. 2. a plant, tree, etc. so trained. *v.t.* 1. to train as or on an espalier. 2. to provide with an espalier.

ESPALIER

Es·pa·ña (es-pä′nyä), *n.* Spain: the Spanish name.

es·par·to (es-pär′tō), *n.* [Sp.; L. *spartum;* Gr. *sparton, spartos*], either of two kinds of long, coarse grass growing in Spain and Algeria, used to make cordage, baskets, shoes, and paper: also **esparto grass.**

es·pe·cial (ə-spesh′əl), *adj.* [ME. & OFr.; L. *specialis;* see SPECIAL], special; particular; outstanding; exceptional. —*SYN.* see **special.**

es·pe·cial·ly (ə-spesh′ə-li), *adv.* particularly; mainly; to a marked degree; unusually: abbreviated **esp., espec.**

Es·pe·ran·to (es′pə-rän′tō, es′pə-ran′tō), *n.* [after pseudonym of Dr. L. L. Zamenhof, who invented the language (1887), lit. (in Esperanto), one who hopes, substantive form of *esperant,* ppr. of *esperi,* to hope < Romance forms (Fr. *esperer,* Sp. *esperar,* Port. *esperar*) < L. *sperare,* to hope], an artificial language for international (chiefly European) use, based on word bases common to the main European languages: it has self-evident parts of speech (all nouns end in *-o,* all adjectives in *-a,* etc.), a single and regular conjugation of verbs, a few simplified inflections, etc.

es·pi·al (ə-spī′əl), *n.* [ME. & OFr. *espiaille* < *espier;* see ESPY], 1. an espying or being espied; observation. 2. discovery. 3. [Obs.], a spy.

es·pi·o·nage (es′pi-ə-nij; Fr. es′pyô′näzh′), *n.* [Fr. *espionnage* < *espionner,* to spy < *espion;* It. *spione* < *spia,* a spy; of Gmc. origin (see ESPY)], 1. spying. 2. the use of spies, especially for military purposes.

es·pla·nade (es′plə-nād′, es′plə-näd′), *n.* [Fr.; Sp. *esplanada;* It. *spianata* < *spianare,* to level < L. *explanare,* to level; see EXPLAIN], 1. a level, open space of ground; especially, a public walk or roadway, often along a shore; promenade. 2. a level or sloping, open space separating the citadel of a fortification from the town, so as to leave attacking troops exposed to fire.

es·pous·al (i-spou′z'l), *n.* [ME. *espousaile, esponsailles* (*pl*); OFr. *espousailles* (*pl.*); L. *sponsalia* < *sponsus* (fem. *sponsa*), one betrothed, pp. of *spondere;* see ESPOUSE], 1. *usually pl. a*) a betrothal or betrothal ceremony. *b*) a marriage or wedding. 2. an espousing (of some cause, idea, etc.); adoption or advocacy.

es·pouse (i-spouz′), *v.t.* [ESPOUSED (-spouzd′), ESPOUSING], [OFr. *espouser;* LL. *sponsare* < L. *sponsus;* see SPOUSE], 1. to take as a spouse; marry: generally said of a man. 2. to give in marriage. 3. to take up; support, advocate, or adopt (some cause, idea, etc.).

‡es·prit (es′prē′), *n.* [Fr.], 1. spirit. 2. lively intelligence or wit.

‡es·prit de corps (es′prē′ də kôr′), [Fr., lit., spirit of a body (of persons)], group spirit; sense of pride, honor, etc. in common interests and activities, as of those in the same profession.

es·py (ə-spī′), *v.t.* [ESPIED (-spīd′), ESPYING], [ME. *espien;* OFr. *espier;* prob. < OHG. *spehōn,* to spy], to catch sight of; make out; spy; descry. —*SYN.* see **see.**

Esq., Esqr., Esquire.

-esque (esk), [Fr. *-esque;* It. *-esco;* OHG. *-isc*], a suffix used to form adjectives, meaning: 1. *in the manner* or *style of,* as in *Romanesque, Dantesque:* some adjectives so formed are also used as nouns, as *arabesque, burlesque.* 2. *having the quality of, like,* as in *picturesque, statuesque.*

Es·qui·line (es′kwə-līn′), *n.* [L. (*Mons*) *esquilinus* < *Esquiliae,* name of the hill < base akin to *colere,* to till (see CULTIVATE)], one of the Seven Hills of Rome.

Es·qui·mau (es′kə-mō′), *n.* [*pl.* ESQUIMAUX (-mō′, -mōz′)] & *adj.* Eskimo.

es·quire (ə-skwīr′; *now occas. for n.* es′kwīr), *n.* [Late ME. *esquyer;* ME. *squyer;* OFr. *esquier;* LL. *scutarius,* a squire, shield-bearer < L. *scutum,* a shield], 1. formerly, a candidate for knighthood, acting as attendant and shield-bearer for a knight. 2. in England, a member of the gentry ranking just below a knight. 3. [E-], a title of courtesy, usually abbreviated **Esq., Esqr.,** placed after a man's surname and corresponding, more ceremoniously, to *Mr.* 4. a landed country gentleman. 5. a man escorting a woman in public; escort. *v.t.* [ESQUIRED (-skwīrd′), ESQUIRING], 1. to attend (a knight) as esquire. 2. to raise to the rank of esquire. 3. to address as Esquire. 4. to escort (a woman or girl).

ess (es), *n.* [*pl.* ESSES (es′iz)], 1. the letter S, s. 2. something shaped like an S.

-ess (is, əs; *occas.* es), [ME. *-esse, -isse;* OFr. *-esse;* LL. *-issa;* Gr. *-issa*], a suffix used to form feminine nouns, as in *lioness:* in nouns of agent ending *-tor* or *-ter,* the vowel is usually dropped before the addition of *-ess* (e.g., *actress*).

es·say (ə-sā′, e-sā′), *v.t.* [OFr. *essayer;* LL. **exagiare* < L. *exagium,* a weight, weighing < *ex-,* out of + *agere,* to do, drive], 1. to test the quality of; try out. 2. to try; attempt. *n.* 1. (e-sā′, es′ā), *a*) a trying or testing. *b*) an attempt; trial. 2. (es′ā, es′i), a short literary composition dealing with a single subject, usually from a personal point of view and without attempting completeness. —*SYN.* see **try.**

es·say·ist (es′ā-ist, es′i-ist), *n.* one who writes essays.

‡es·se (es′i), *n.* [L., to be], being; existence; essence.

Es·sen (es′'n), *n.* a city in the Rhine Province, Germany: pop., 521,000 (est. 1946).

es·sence (es′'ns), *n.* [Fr.; L. *essentia* < ppr. of *esse,* to be], 1. something that is, or exists; entity. 2. that which makes something what it is; intrinsic, fundamental nature (of something); essential being. 3. a substance that keeps, in concentrated form, the flavor, fragrance, or other properties of the plant, drug, food, etc. from which it is extracted; essential oil. 4. a solution of such a substance or oil in alcohol. 5. a perfume. 6. in *philosophy,* the inward nature of anything, underlying its manifestations; true substance.

Es·sene (es′ēn, e-sēn′), *n.* [LL. *Esseni;* Gr. *Essēnoi,* the Essenes; prob. < Heb. *tsenū'im,* lit., the pious ones], a member of an ancient Jewish sect of ascetics and mystics, which existed from the 2d century B.C. to the 2d century A.D.

es·sen·tial (ə-sen′shəl), *adj.* [LL. *essentialis;* see ESSENCE], 1. of or constituting the intrinsic, fundamental nature of something; basic; inherent: as, there is an *essential* difference between fascism and communism. 2. absolute; complete; perfect; pure: as, *essential* happiness. 3. necessary to make a thing what it is; indispensable; requisite: as, water is *essential* to life. 4. containing, or having the properties of, a concentrated extract of a plant, drug, food, etc.: as, an *essential* oil. *n.* something necessary or fundamental; indispensable, inherent or basic feature or principle.

SYN.—**essential,** in strict usage, is applicable to that which constitutes the absolute essence or the fundamental nature of a thing and therefore must be present for the thing to exist, function, etc. (food is *essential* to life); an **indispensable** person or thing cannot be done without if the specified or implied purpose is to be achieved; **requisite** is applied to that which is required by the circumstances or for the purpose and generally suggests a requirement that is imposed externally rather than an inherent need (the *requisite* experience for a position); **necessary** implies a pressing need but does not always connote absolute indispensability.

es·sen·ti·al·i·ty (ə-sen′shi-al′ə-ti), *n.* [*pl.* ESSENTIALITIES (-tiz)], essential quality, fact, or thing.

es·sen·tial·ly (ə-sen′shəl-i), *adv.* in essentials or essence; in a characteristic manner.

essential oil, any volatile oil that gives distinctive odor, flavor, etc. to a plant, flower, or fruit.

Es·se·qui·bo (es′ə-kē′bō), *n.* a river in British Guiana, flowing northward to the Atlantic: length, 600 mi.

Es·sex (es′iks), *n.* 1. a former Anglo-Saxon kingdom of eastern England. 2. a county on the eastern coast of England: pop., 1,625,000 (est. 1945); county seat, Chelmsford.

Essex, second Earl of, (*Robert Devereux*), 1566–1601; English soldier and statesman; favorite of Queen Elizabeth; executed for treason.

es·so·nite (es′ə-nīt′), *n.* [< Gr. *hēssōn,* inferior to (i.e., less hard than real hyacinth); + *-ite*], a dark-brown kind of garnet: also called *hessonite, cinnamon stone.*

-est (ist, əst; *occas.* est), a suffix used to form: 1. [ME.; AS. *-est, -ost, -ast*, superl. suffix of adjectives & adverbs], the superlative degree of most adjectives and adverbs of one or two syllables, as in *greatest, soonest.* 2. [ME.; AS. *-est*, 2d pers. sing., pres. tense inflection], the archaic second person singular, present indicative, of verbs, as in *goest*: also **-st.**

E.S.T., Eastern Standard Time.

es·tab·lish (ə-stab′lish), ***v.t.*** [ME. *establissen;* OFr. *establir;* L. *stabilire* < *stabilis*, stable], 1. to make stable; make firm; settle. 2. to order, ordain, or appoint (officials, laws, etc.) permanently. 3. to set up (a government, nation, business, etc.); found; institute. 4. to settle in an office or position; set up in business or a profession: as, he *established* himself as a grocer. 5. to make a state institution of (a church). 6. to set up (a precedent, theory, reputation, etc.) permanently; cause to be accepted or recognized. 7. to prove; demonstrate; vindicate: as, the plaintiff *established* his case. 8. in *card games*, to win control of (a suit) so that one is sure of taking all the remaining tricks.

es·tab·lished church (ə-stab′lisht), a church officially recognized by the government and supported as a national institution; specifically, [E- C-], the Church of England: abbreviated **E.C.**

es·tab·lish·ment (ə-stab′lish-mənt), ***n.*** [*establish* + *-ment*, after OFr. *establissement*], 1. an establishing or being established. 2. a thing established, as a business, military organization, household, etc.
the Establishment, 1. the Church of England. 2. the Presbyterian Church of Scotland. 3. in England, a complex consisting of the church, the royal family, and the plutocracy, regarded as holding the chief measure of power and influence. 4. the ruling inner circle of any nation, institution, etc.

‡es·ta·mi·net (es′tȧ′mē′nā′), ***n.*** [Fr.], a café.

‡es·tan·cia (es-tän′syä), ***n.*** [Sp., orig., a stop, stopping place], a large estate, especially a cattle ranch, in Spanish America.

es·tate (ə-stāt′), ***n.*** [ME. & OFr. *estat* (Fr. *état*); L. *status*, a state, condition, pp. of *stare*, to stand], 1. a condition or stage of life: as, he came to man's *estate* at the age of 21. 2. formerly, especially in feudal times, any of the three social classes having specific political powers: the first estate was the Lords Spiritual (clergy), the second estate the Lords Temporal (nobility), and the third estate the Commons (bourgeoisie). 3. property; possessions; capital; fortune. 4. the assets and liabilities of a dead or bankrupt person. 5. landed property; individually owned piece of land containing a residence: it is usually large and maintained by great wealth. 6. [Archaic], *a*) the degree of a person's wealth, influence, etc. *b*) display of wealth; pomp. 7. in *law*, the degree, nature, extent, and quality of interest or ownership that one has in land, etc.: abbreviated **est.**
the fourth estate, [cf. sense 2], journalism or journalists.

Es·tates-Gen·er·al (ə-stāts′jen′ẽr-əl), ***n.*** the legislature of France before 1789, to which each of the three estates (clergy, nobility, and bourgeoisie) sent delegates.

es·teem (ə-stēm′), ***v.t.*** [Fr. *estimer;* L. *aestimare*, to value, appraise, estimate; prob. < **aes-tema*, one who cuts copper, mints money < *aes*, brass, copper + base akin to Gr. *temnein*, to cut], 1. to value highly; have great regard for or a favorable opinion of; prize; respect: as, ability is always *esteemed.* 2. to consider; regard; hold to be: as, we *esteem* this theory useless. ***n.*** 1. favorable opinion; high regard; respect: as, he is held in high *esteem.* 2. [Archaic], an opinion; estimation. —***SYN.*** see **appreciate, regard.**

Es·tel·la (e-stel′ə), [Sp. < L. *Stella*, lit., star; see STELLAR], a feminine name: variants, *Estelle, Stella.*

Es·telle (es-tel′), [Fr.], a feminine name: see **Estella.**

es·ter (es′tẽr), ***n.*** [G.; synthesis of *äther*, ether + *säure*, acid], an organic compound, comparable to an inorganic salt, formed by the reaction of an acid and an alcohol: the organic radical of the alcohol replaces the acid hydrogen of the acid.

es·ter·ase (es′tẽr-ās′), ***n.*** any of a group of enzymes by whose action the hydrolysis of esters is accelerated.

es·ter·i·fy (es-ter′ə-fī′), ***v.t. & v.i.*** [ESTERIFIED (-fīd′), ESTERIFYING], to change into an ester: said of an acid.

Es·tes Park (es′tiz), a mountain resort in northern Colorado.

Es·ther (es′tẽr), [L.; Heb. *estēr;* prob. < Bab. *Ishtar*, Ishtar], a feminine name: variants, *Hester, Hesther.* ***n.*** in the *Bible*, 1. the Jewish wife of the Persian king Ahasuerus (Xerxes): she saved her people from slaughter by Haman. 2. the book of the Old Testament that tells her story. Abbreviated **Esth.**

es·the·si·a (es-thē′zhə, es-thē′zhi-ə), ***n.*** [see AESTHESIA], the ability to feel sensations: also spelled **aesthesia.**

es·thete (es′thēt), ***n.*** [see AESTHETE], 1. a person highly sensitive to art and beauty. 2. a person who exaggerates the value of artistic sensitivity or makes a cult of art and beauty; believer in art for art's sake. Also spelled **aesthete.**

es·thet·ic (es-thet′ik), ***adj.*** [see AESTHETIC], 1. of esthetics. 2. of beauty. 3. sensitive to art and beauty; showing good taste; artistic. Also spelled **aesthetic.**

es·thet·i·cal (es-thet′i-k′l), ***adj.*** esthetic.

es·thet·i·cal·ly (es-thet′i-k′l-i, es-thet′ik-li), ***adv.*** 1. in an esthetic manner. 2. from the point of view of esthetics. Also spelled **aesthetically.**

es·the·ti·cian (es′thə-tish′ən), ***n.*** an expert or specialist in esthetics: also spelled **aesthetician.**

es·thet·i·cism (es-thet′ə-siz′m), ***n.*** 1. esthetic doctrine; cult of beauty, art, and good taste. 2. sensitivity to art and beauty. Also spelled **aestheticism.**

es·thet·ics (es-thet′iks), ***n.pl.*** [construed as sing.], the study or philosophy of beauty; theory of the fine arts and of people's responses to them: also spelled **aesthetics.**

Es·tho·ni·a (es-thō′ni-ə, es-tō′ni-ə), ***n.*** Estonia.

Es·tho·ni·an (es-thō′ni-ən, es-tō′ni-ən), ***adj. & n.*** Estonian.

Es·tienne, Hen·ri (äN′rē′ es′tyen′), 1528?–1598; son of *Robert;* French printer, editor, and writer.

Estienne, Ro·bert (rô′bâr′), 1503–1559; French printer and scholar.

es·ti·ma·ble (es′tə-mə-b′l), ***adj.*** [Fr.; L. *aestimabilis* < *aestimare;* see ESTEEM], 1. that can be estimated or evaluated; calculable. 2. worthy of esteem; deserving to be respected or valued highly.

es·ti·ma·bly (es′tə-mə-bli), ***adv.*** in an estimable manner.

es·ti·mate (es′tə-māt′; *for n., usually* es′tə-mit), ***v.t.*** [ESTIMATED (-id), ESTIMATING], [< L. *aestimatus*, pp. of *aestimare;* see ESTEEM], 1. to form an opinion or judgment about; gauge. 2. to judge or determine roughly (the size, value, cost, requirements, etc.); calculate approximately. ***v.i.*** to make an estimate or estimates. ***n.*** 1. a rough calculation of size, value, etc.; especially, an approximate computation of the probable cost of a piece of work, made by a person undertaking to do the work. 2. a written statement of this: abbreviated **est.** 3. an opinion or judgment.
***SYN.*—estimate,** in this comparison, refers broadly to the forming of a personal opinion or judgment; **appraise** implies the aim of giving an accurate or expert judgment, as of value or worth (to *appraise* a new house); **evaluate** also connotes an attempt at an exact judgment, but rarely with reference to value in terms of money (let us *evaluate* the evidence); **rate** implies assignment of comparative value, quality, etc. (he is *rated* the best in his field). See also **calculate.**

es·ti·ma·tion (es′tə-mā′shən), ***n.*** [ME. *estimacioun;* OFr. *estimation;* L. *aestimatio*], 1. an estimating. 2. an opinion or judgment. 3. esteem; regard; respect.

es·ti·ma·tive (es′tə-mā′tiv), ***adj.*** 1. serving as an estimate. 2. estimating or capable of estimating.

es·ti·ma·tor (es′tə-mā′tẽr), ***n.*** a person who estimates.

e·stip·u·late (ē-stip′yoo-lit), ***adj.*** exstipulate.

es·ti·val (es′tə-v′l, es-tī′v′l), ***adj.*** [see AESTIVAL], of summer: also spelled **aestival.**

es·ti·vate (es′tə-vāt′), ***v.i.*** [ESTIVATED (-id), ESTIVATING], [see AESTIVATE], 1. to spend the summer. 2. to spend the summer in a dormant condition: opposed to *hibernate.* Also spelled **aestivate.**

es·ti·va·tion (es′tə-vā′shən), ***n.*** 1. in *zoology*, the habit or state of estivating. 2. in *botany*, the arrangement of petals in a flower bud before it opens: see **vernation.** Also **aestivation.**

‡est mo·dus in re·bus (est mō′dəs in rē′bəs), [L.], there is a measure in things; temperance is a virtue: a quotation from Horace.

Es·to·ni·a (es-tō′ni-ə), ***n.*** a country in northeastern Europe annexed as the Estonian Soviet Socialistic Republic in August, 1940: also **Esthonia.**

Es·to·ni·an (es-tō′ni-ən), ***adj.*** of Estonia, its people, their language, or culture. ***n.*** 1. a native or inhabitant of Estonia. 2. the Finno-Ugric language of the Estonians. Also **Esthonian.**

Estonian Soviet Socialist Republic, a republic of the U.S.S.R., on the Baltic Sea: area, 18,050 sq. mi.; pop., 1,221,000; capital, Tallinn.

es·top (e-stop′), ***v.t.*** [ESTOPPED (-stopt′), ESTOPPING], [< Anglo-Fr. *estopper* & OFr. *estoper;* LL. **stuppare*, to stop with tow, cram < L. *stuppa*, oakum, tow; see STOP], 1. originally, to stop up. 2. to stop; obstruct; prevent; bar. 3. in *law*, to bar or prevent by estoppel.

es·top·page (e-stop′ij), ***n.*** [< *estop* + *-age*], an estopping or being estopped; stoppage.

es·top·pel (e-stop′′l), ***n.*** [prob. < OFr. *estoupail*, stopper, bung < *estoper;* see ESTOP], in *law*, the prevention of a person from making an affirmation or denial because it is contrary to a previous affirmation or denial that he has made.

es·to·vers (e-stō′vẽrz), ***n.pl.*** [OFr. *estover, estovoir*, to be necessary; inf. used as n.], certain necessaries allowed by law, as wood given to a tenant for fuel or repairs, alimony for a divorced wife, etc.

es·trange (ə-strānj′), *v.t.* [ESTRANGED (-strānjd′), ESTRANGING], [OFr. *estranger*, to remove < LL. *extraneare*, to treat as a stranger < L. *extraneus*, foreign < *extra*, beyond, without; cf. STRANGE], 1. to remove, as from usual surroundings or associates; keep apart or away. 2. to turn away; divert; alienate. 3. to turn (a person) from an affectionate or friendly attitude to an indifferent, unfriendly, or hostile one; alienate the affections of; separate.

es·trange·ment (ə-strānj′mənt), *n.* an estranging or being estranged; alienation.

es·tray (e-strā′), *n.* [Anglo-Fr. < *estraier;* see STRAY], 1. any person or thing out of its usual place. 2. in *law*, a stray and unclaimed domestic animal. *v.i.* [Archaic], to stray.

es·treat (e-strēt′), *n.* [Anglo-Fr. *estrete;* OFr. *estraite* < LL. *extracta* < pp. of L. *extrahere;* see EXTRACT], a true copy or extract of an original record entered in a law court, as of fines. *v.t.* 1. to take from the records of a law court for purposes of prosecution. 2. to take as a levy, fine, etc.

Es·tre·ma·du·ra (es′tre-mä-*thōō*′rä; *for 2,* esh′trə-mə-dōō′rə), *n.* 1. a former province of southwestern Spain. 2. a province of western Portugal.

ESTREMADURA

es·trin (es′trin, ēs′trin), *n.* [Rare], estrone: also spelled **oestrin.**

es·tri·ol (es′trī-ōl′), *n.* a female sex hormone, $C_{18}H_{24}O_3$, used to treat conditions of estrogen deficiency, especially in menopause; theelol.

es·tro·gen (es′trə-jən), *n.* any of several estrus-producing compounds, as estriol and estrone.

es·tro·gen·ic (es′trə-jen′ik), *adj.* 1. of estrogen. 2. of or producing estrus.

es·trone (es′trōn), *n.* [< *estrus* + *-one*], a female sex hormone, $C_{18}H_{22}O_2$, injected into the muscles to treat conditions of estrogen deficiency; theelin: it is more active than estriol.

es·trous (es′trəs, ēs′trəs), *adj.* of, or having the characteristics of, estrus: also spelled **oestrous.**

es·trum (es′trəm, ēs′trəm), *n.* estrus.

es·trus (es′trəs, ēs′trəs), *n.* [L. *oestrus*, gadfly, horsefly, frenzy; Gr. *oistros*, gadfly, sting, frenzy; akin to ON. *eisa*, to rush on, L. *ira*, ire, Lith. *aistra*, violent passion], 1. a strong impulse; overwhelming desire; frenzy. 2. the sexual excitement, or heat, of female mammals, corresponding to *rut* in males. 3. the period of this, characterized by sexual desire and changes in the sex organs. Also spelled **oestrus.**

es·tu·ar·i·al (es′chōō-er′i-əl), *adj.* of an estuary.

es·tu·ar·ine (es′chōō-ẽr-in, es′chōō-ə-rīn′, *adj.* formed or deposited in an estuary.

es·tu·ar·y (es′chōō-er′i), *n.* [*pl.* ESTUARIES (-iz)], [L. *aestuarium* < *aestus*, the tide], an inlet or arm of the sea; especially, the wide mouth of a river, where the tide meets the current: abbreviated **est.**

e·su·ri·ence (i-soor′i-əns, i-syoor′i-əns), *n.* [see ESURIENT], hunger; greed; voracity.

e·su·ri·en·cy (i-soor′i-ən-si, i-syoor′i-ən-si), *n.* esurience.

e·su·ri·ent (i-soor′i-ənt, i-syoor′i-ənt), *adj.* [L. *esuriens*, ppr. of *esurire*, to be hungry < pp. of *edere*, to eat], hungry; voracious; greedy.

‡et (et; Fr. ā), [L., or Fr. < L.], and.

-et (it, ət), [ME. *-et;* OFr. *-et*, masc., *-ete* (Fr. *-ette*), fem.], a suffix added to nouns, meaning *little*, as in *rivulet, islet*: it has lost its diminutive sense in most words, as in *bullet, hatchet, pocket, pullet, sonnet*, etc.

Et, et, in *chemistry*, ethyl.

e·ta (ā′tə, ē′tə), *n.* the seventh letter of the Greek alphabet (Η, η), corresponding in sound to English *a*, as in *fate:* in English transliteration, as in the etymologies of this dictionary, it is shown as *ē*: see **alphabet,** table.

E.T.A., Estimated Time of Arrival.

et al., [L.], 1. *et alibi.* 2. *et alii.*

‡et a·li·bi (et al′ə-bī′), [L.], and elsewhere: abbreviated **et al.**

‡et a·li·i (et ā′li-ī′), [L.], and others: abbreviated **et al.**

et·a·mine (et′ə-mēn′), *n.* [Fr. *étamine*], a loosely woven cotton or worsted cloth, similar to bunting or voile.

etaoin shrdlu, two sequences of letters on a linotype machine: if the machine jams, the entire slug may drop, so that these sequences may accidentally appear in print.

‡é·tape (ā′tȧp′), *n.* [Fr.; OFr. *estaple;* MD. *stapel*, storage place, depot; see STAPLE (storehouse)], 1. a halting place; specifically, a place where troops encamp after a day's march. 2. the length of a day's march.

etc., et cetera.

et cet·er·a, et caet·er·a (et set′ẽr-ə, et set′rə), [L.], and others; and the like; and the rest; and so forth: abbreviated etc., &c.

et·cet·er·as (et-set′ẽr-əz, et-set′rəz), *n.pl.* additional things; odds and ends; customary extras.

etch (ech), *v.t.* [D. *etsen;* G. *ätzen*, to feed, corrode < MHG. *etzen*, to cause to eat, caus. of *ezzen* (G. *essen*), to eat], 1. to make (a drawing, design, etc.) on metal, glass, etc. by the action of an acid: usually done by coating the surface with wax and letting acid eat into the lines or areas laid bare with a special needle. 2. to engrave (a metal plate, glass, etc.) in this way, for use in printing such drawings or designs. 3. to produce (designs, etc.) by this process. *v.i.* to make etchings.

etch·ing (ech′iŋ), *n.* 1. the art, process, or act of producing drawings or designs on plates of metal, glass, etc. by the action of acid. 2. an etched plate, drawing, or design. 3. a print made from an etched plate.

E·te·o·cles (i-tē′ə-klēz′), *n.* [L.; Gr. *Eteoklēs*], in *Greek legend*, a son of Oedipus and Jocasta: see **Seven against Thebes.**

e·ter·nal (i-tũr′n′l), *adj.* [OFr. (Fr. *éternel*); LL. *aeternalis;* L. *aeturnus* < *aevum*, an age; IE. base **aiw-, *āju-*, a life, lifetime; akin to AS. *a*, always], 1. without beginning or end; existing through all time; everlasting. 2. timeless. 3. forever the same; always true or valid; unchangeable: as, *eternal* principles. 4. always going on or coming back; never stopping; perpetual. 5. seeming never to stop; happening very often. —*SYN.* see **continual.**

the Eternal, God.

Eternal City, Rome.

e·ter·nal·ize (i-tũr′n′l-īz′), *v.t.* [ETERNALIZED (-īzd′), ETERNALIZING], to make eternal; eternize.

e·ter·nal·ly (i-tũr′n′l-i), *adv.* 1. continuing through eternity; for all time; without beginning or end. 2. always. 3. continuously; without stopping; constantly.

e·terne (i-tũrn′), *adj.* [Archaic or Poetic], eternal.

e·ter·ni·ty (i-tũr′nə-ti), *n.* [*pl.* ETERNITIES (-tiz)], [ME. *eternite;* OFr. *eternité;* L. *aeternitas*], 1. the quality, state, or fact of being eternal; eternal existence or duration; continuance without end. 2. infinite time; time without beginning or end. 3. a long period of time that seems endless: as, an *eternity* of waiting. 4. *a*) the endless time after death; hence, *b*) future life; immortality.

e·ter·ni·za·tion (i-tũr′nə-zā′shən, i-tũr′nī-zā′shən), *n.* an eternizing or being eternized.

e·ter·nize (i-tũr′nīz), *v.t.* [ETERNIZED (-nīzd), ETERNIZING], [Fr. *éterniser;* ML. *aeternizare* < L. *aeternus;* see ETERNAL], 1. to make eternal; cause to last forever. 2. to make famous forever; immortalize.

e·te·sian (i-tē′zhən), *adj.* [L. *etesius*, annual, pertaining to the etesian winds (L. *etesiae;* Gr. *etēsiai*); Gr. *etēsios* < *etos*, year], annual: said of certain Mediterranean winds that blow from the northwest for several weeks every summer.

eth (*eth*), *n.* an edh.

-eth (əth, ith), [expanded form < ME. *-the*], a suffix used in forming ordinal numerals from bases ending in a vowel, as in *fortieth;* see also **-th.**

-eth (əth, ith), [ME. *-(e)th;* AS. *-(a)th;* orig., 3d pers. sing., pres. indic. ending of verbs in the South East Midland, Southeastern, Southern, South West Midland, and Central West Midland dialects of Middle English; displaced in 14th- & 15th-c. South East Midland by *-(e)s* < Northern & North East Midland dialects; in 16th- & 17th-c. Eng., written *-(e)th* was actually pronounced (*-s, -z, -iz*), the present pronun. being due to spelling], archaic ending of the third person singular, present indicative, of verbs, as in *asketh, bringeth*: see also **-th.**

Eth., 1. Ethiopia. 2. Ethiopian. 3. Ethiopic.

E·than (ē′thən), [L.; Heb. *ēthān*, strength, firmness], a masculine name.

eth·ane (eth′ān), *n.* [< *ether* + *-ane*], an odorless, colorless, gaseous hydrocarbon, CH_3CH_3, of the methane series: it is found in natural gas and illuminating gas, and is used as a refrigerant.

Eth·a·nim (eth′ə-nim), *n.* [Heb.], Tishri: the early Hebrew name: see **Jewish calendar.**

eth·a·nol (eth′ə-nōl′, eth′ə-nol′), *n.* [< *ethane* + *-ol*], ethyl alcohol: see **alcohol.**

Eth·el (eth′əl), [AS. *Æthelu* < *æthel*, noble; akin to G. *adel;* see ADELAIDE], a feminine name.

Eth·el·bert (eth′əl-bẽrt), [AS. *Æthelbryht*, lit., noble bright < *æthele*, noble + *beorht*, bright; hence akin to *Adelbert;* see ALBERT], a masculine name. *n.* king of Kent; lived 552?–616 A.D.

Eth·el·red II (eth′əl-red′), 968?–1016 A.D.; king of England (978–1016 A.D.): called *the Unready.*

eth·ene (eth′ēn), *n.* ethylene.

e·ther (ē′thẽr), *n.* [L. *aether;* Gr. *aithēr* < *aithein*, to kindle, burn], 1. an imaginary substance regarded by the ancients as filling all space beyond the sphere of the moon, and making up the stars and planets. 2. the upper regions of space; clear sky. 3. [Rare], the air. 4. in *chemistry*, any of a class of organic compounds that are oxides of hydrocarbon radicals; specifically, a volatile, colorless, highly inflammable liquid, $(C_2H_5)_2O$, with an aromatic odor, prepared by the reaction of sulfuric acid and ethyl alcohol: it is used as an anesthetic and a solvent for resins and fats: also called *diethyl ether.* 5. in *physics*, a hypothetical invisible substance postulated (in older theory) as pervading space and serving as the medium for the transmission of light waves and other forms of radiant energy. Also spelled **aether** (in senses 1, 2, 3).

e·the·re·al (i-thêr′i-əl), *adj.* [< L. *aetherius;* Gr. *aitherios;* + *al*], 1. of or like the ether, or upper regions of space; hence, 2. very light; airy; delicate: as, the *ethereal* grace of her dancing. 3. heavenly; celestial; not earthly. 4. in *chemistry*, of, like, or containing ether. Also spelled **aethereal** (in senses 1, 2, 3).

e·the·re·al·i·ty (i-thêr′i-al′ə-ti), *n.* ethereal quality.

e·the·re·al·ize (i-thêr′i-ə-līz′), *v.t.* [ETHEREALIZED (-līzd′), ETHEREALIZING], to make, or treat as being, ethereal.

Eth·er·ege, Sir George (eth′ẽr-ij), 1635?–1691; English playwright of the Restoration.

e·ther·i·fy (i-ther′ə-fī′, ē′thẽr-ə-fī′), *v.t.* [ETHERIFIED (-fīd′), ETHERIFYING], to change (an alcohol) into ether.

e·ther·i·za·tion (ē′thẽr-ə-zā′shən, ē′thẽr-ī-zā′shən), *n.* 1. an etherizing; especially, giving ether as an anesthetic. 2. the fact or process of being or becoming etherized.

e·ther·ize (ē′thə-rīz′), *v.t.* [ETHERIZED (-rīzd′), ETHERIZING], 1. to change into ether; etherify. 2. to cause to inhale ether fumes so as to make unconscious; anesthetize with ether.

eth·ic (eth′ik), *n.* [Fr. *éthique;* L. *ethica;* Gr. *ēthikē* (*technē*), ethical (art); see ETHICAL], ethics or a system of ethics. *adj.* ethical.

eth·i·cal (eth′i-k′l), *adj.* [< L. *ethicus;* Gr. *ēthikos*, ethical, moral < *ēthos*, character, custom, man's normal state; IE. base **swedh-*, **swēdh-*, essential quality, own character; akin to Goth. *swēs*, one's own], 1. having to do with ethics or morality; of or conforming to moral standards. 2. conforming to the standards of conduct of a given profession: as, it is not *ethical* for a judge to hear a case involving his own interests. —*SYN.* see **moral.**

eth·i·cal·ly (eth′i-k′l-i, eth′ik-li), *adv.* 1. in an ethical manner. 2. according to ethics.

eth·i·cize (eth′ə-sīz′), *v.t.* [ETHICIZED (-sīzd′), ETHICIZING], to make, or regard as, ethical.

eth·ics (eth′iks), *n.pl.* [construed as sing. in 1 & 2], 1. the study of standards of conduct and moral judgment; moral philosophy. 2. a treatise on this study; book about morals. 3. the system or code of morals of a particular philosopher, religion, group, profession, etc.

E·thi·op (ē′thi-op′), *n. & adj.* Ethiopian.

E·thi·o·pi·a (ē′thi-ō′pi-ə), *n.* 1. an ancient region in northeastern Africa, south of Egypt. 2. a country in eastern Africa: area, 395,000 sq. mi.; pop., c. 20,000,000; capital, Addis Ababa: Eritrea became federated with Ethiopia in 1952 (cf. **Eritrea**): also called *Abyssinia.* Abbreviated **Eth.**

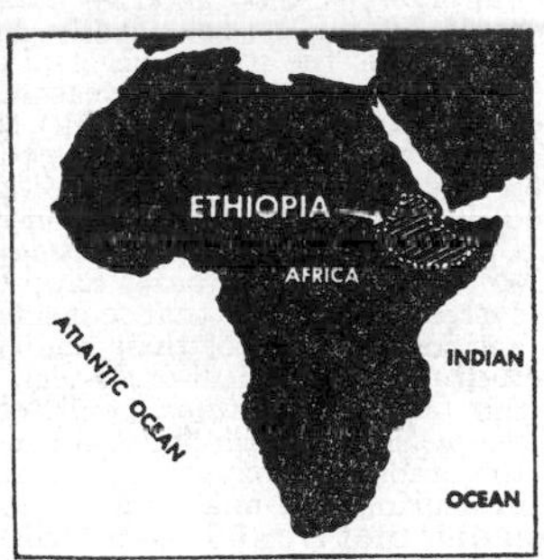

ETHIOPIA

E·thi·o·pi·an (ē′thi-ō′pi-ən), *adj.* of Ethiopia, its people, culture, or Semitic language. *n.* 1. a native or inhabitant of Ethiopia. 2. loosely, a Negro. 3. Ethiopic. Abbreviated **Eth.**

E·thi·op·ic (ē′thi-op′ik, ē′thi-ō′pik), *adj.* 1. Ethiopian. 2. of the Semitic language of the Ethiopians. *n.* this language. Abbreviated **Eth.**

eth·moid (eth′moid), *adj.* [Gr. *ēthmoeidēs* < *ēthmos*, strainer, sieve (< *ētheein*, to strain) + *eidos*, form], 1. like a sieve. 2. designating or of the perforated bone or bones at the front part of the base of the skull, forming part of the septum and walls of the nasal cavity: the olfactory nerves pass through the perforations. *n.* an ethmoid bone.

eth·narch (eth′närk), *n.* [Gr. *ethnarchēs* < *ethnos*, nation, people + *archein*, to rule], the governor of a people or province.

eth·narch·y (eth′när-ki), *n.* [*pl.* ETHNARCHIES (-kiz)], [Gr. *ethnarchia*], 1. the position or rank of an ethnarch. 2. a province ruled by an ethnarch.

eth·nic (eth′nik), *adj.* [Fr. *ethnique;* L. *ethnicus;* Gr. *ethnikos* < *ethnos*, nation, people, *ta ethnē*, the (gentile) nations, heathens], 1. of nations or groups neither Christian nor Jewish; heathen. 2. designating or of any of the basic divisions or groups of mankind, as distinguished by customs, characteristics, language, etc.; ethnological.

eth·ni·cal (eth′ni-k′l), *adj.* ethnic.

eth·ni·cal·ly (eth′ni-k′l-i, eth′nik-li), *adv.* according to ethnic groups or characteristics.

eth·no- (eth′nə), [< Gr. *ethnos*, nation], a combining form meaning *race, peoples,* as in *ethnocentrism, ethnology*: also, before a vowel, **ethn-.**

eth·no·cen·trism (eth′nə-sen′triz′m), *n.* [< *ethno-* + *center* + *-ism*], the emotional attitude that one's own race, nation, or culture is superior to all others.

ethnog., 1. ethnographic. 2. ethnography.

eth·nog·e·ny (eth-noj′ə-ni), *n.* [*ethno-* + *-geny*], 1. the branch of ethnology that deals with the origins of races and peoples. 2. racial origin.

eth·nog·ra·pher (eth-nog′rə-fẽr), *n.* a student of or specialist in ethnography.

eth·no·graph·ic (eth′nə-graf′ik), *adj.* of ethnography: abbreviated **ethnog.**

eth·no·graph·i·cal (eth′nə-graf′i-k′l), *adj.* ethnographic.

eth·no·graph·i·cal·ly (eth′nə-graf′i-k′l-i, eth′nə-graf′ik-li), *adv.* 1. by ethnography. 2. from the viewpoint of ethnography.

eth·nog·ra·phy (eth-nog′rə-fi), *n.* [*ethno-* + *-graphy*], the branch of anthropology that deals descriptively with specific cultures, especially those of primitive peoples or groups: abbreviated **ethnog.**

eth·no·log·ic (eth′nə-loj′ik), *adj.* ethnological.

eth·no·log·i·cal (eth′nə-loj′i-k′l), *adj.* of ethnology: abbreviated **ethnol.**

eth·no·log·i·cal·ly (eth′nə-loj′i-k′l-i, eth′nə-loj′ik-li), *adv.* 1. by ethnology. 2. from the viewpoint of ethnology.

eth·nol·o·gist (eth-nol′ə-jist), *n.* a student of or specialist in ethnology.

eth·nol·o·gy (eth-nol′ə-ji), *n.* [*ethno-* + *-logy*], the branch of anthropology that deals with the comparative cultures of various peoples, including their distribution, characteristics, folkways, etc.: abbreviated **ethnol.**

e·thos (ē′thos), *n.* [Gr. *ēthos*, disposition, character], 1. the characteristic and distinguishing attitudes, habits, etc. of a racial, political, occupational, or other group. 2. the universal or objective elements in a work of art, as distinguished from the emotional or subjective elements: opposed to *pathos.*

eth·yl (eth′əl), *n.* [< *ether* + *-yl*], 1. the monovalent hydrocarbon radical CH_3CH_2, which forms the base of common alcohol, ether, and many other compounds: symbol, Et, et (no period). 2. *a*) tetraethyl lead, $Pb(C_2H_5)_4$, a poisonous, colorless lead compound: a trade-mark (**Ethyl**). *b*) any of various gasolines or motor fuels that contain tetraethyl lead to increase power and prevent knocking. *adj.* containing ethyl (sense 1) or tetraethyl lead.

ethyl alcohol, common alcohol: see **alcohol.**

eth·yl·ate (eth′ə-lāt′), *v.t.* [ETHYLATED (-id), ETHYLATING], to compound with one or more ethyl groups. *n.* (eth′ə-lit, eth′ə-lāt′), a compound formed by the replacement of the hydrogen atom in the hydroxyl group of ethyl alcohol by an active metal.

eth·yl·ene (eth′ə-lēn′), *n.* [*ethyl* + *-ene*], a colorless, inflammable, gaseous hydrocarbon of the olefin series, $CH_2{\cdot}CH_2$, with a disagreeable odor: it is obtained from natural or coal gas, by the action of sulfuric acid on alcohol, etc., and is used as a fuel and anesthetic, and in hastening the ripening of fruits: also called *ethene.*

ethylene glycol, the simplest polyhydric alcohol, $OH{\cdot}CH_2{\cdot}CH_2{\cdot}OH$: see **glycol.**

ethyl hydride, ethane.

e·thyl·ic (i-thil′ik), *adj.* of, obtained from, or containing ethyl.

ethyl oxide, diethyl ether.

e·ti·o·late (ē′ti-ə-lāt′), *v.t. & v.i.* [ETIOLATED (-id), ETIOLATING], [Fr. *étioler* < OFr. *estioler, estieuler*, to become slender or puny < *tieulê*, tile-colored < *tieule*, tile < L. *tegula;* see TILE], in *botany*, to blanch or bleach by deprivation of sunlight.

e·ti·o·log·i·cal (ē′ti-ə-loj′i-k′l), *adj.* of (an) etiology.

e·ti·ol·o·gy (ē′ti-ol′ə-ji), *n.* [*pl.* ETIOLOGIES (-jiz)], [LL. *aetiologia;* Gr. *aitologia* < *aitia*, cause + *logia*, description], 1. the assignment of a cause: as, the *etiology* of a folkway. 2. the science of causes or origins. 3. science or theory of the causes or origins of diseases. Also spelled **aetiology.**

et·i·quette (et′i-ket′, et′i-kət), *n.* [Fr. *étiquette*, a ticket, label; OFr. *estiquette* < *estiquer*, to stick; prob. < MHG. *stecken*, to stick], 1. the forms, manners, and ceremonies established by convention as acceptable or required in society, in a profession, or in official life. 2. the rules for such forms, manners, and ceremonies. —*SYN.* see **decorum.**

Et·na (et′nə), *n.* 1. a volcanic mountain in eastern Sicily: height, 10,741 ft.: also spelled **Aetna.** 2. [e-], a lamp for heating or vaporizing liquids: it consists of a cup set in a saucer in which alcohol is burned.

E·ton (ē′t'n), ***n.*** 1. a town on the Thames, near London: pop., 3,200. 2. a private preparatory school (called *public school* in England) for boys, at this town: in full, **Eton College.**

ETON COLLAR AND JACKET

Eton coat, an Eton jacket.
Eton collar, 1. a broad, white linen collar worn with an Eton jacket. 2. a collar resembling this.
E·to·ni·an (ē-tō′ni-ən), ***adj.*** of Eton. ***n.*** a student or former student at Eton.
Eton jacket, 1. a boys' short, waist-length jacket with broad lapels, left open in front: worn by students at Eton. 2. a similar jacket, as worn by girls and women.
E·tru·ri·a (i-troor′i-ə), ***n.*** an ancient country in the central part of western Italy, now forming Tuscany and part of Umbria.
E·trur·i·an (i-troor′i-ən), ***adj. & n.*** Etruscan.
E·trus·can (i-trus′kən), ***adj.*** of Etruria, its people, their language, or culture. ***n.*** 1. a native or inhabitant of Etruria. 2. the language of the Etruscans.

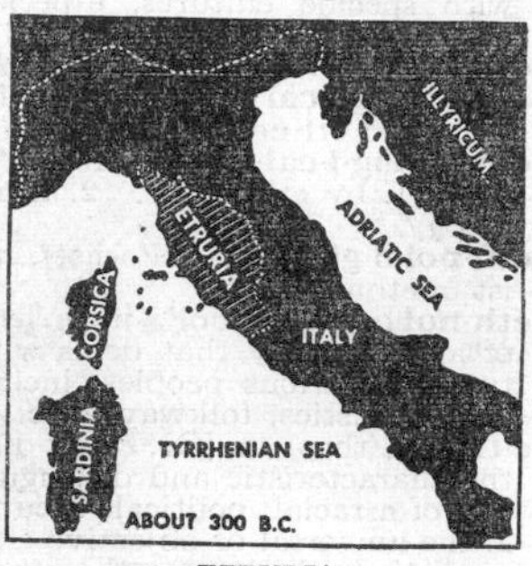

ETRURIA

‡et se·quens (et sē′kwənz), [L.], and the following: abbreviated **et seq.**
‡et se·quen·tes (et si-kwen′tēz), [L.], and those that follow: abbreviated **et seq., et seqq.**
‡et se·quen·ti·a (et si-kwen′shi-ə), [L.], and those that follow: abbreviated **et seq., et seqq.**
Et·ta (et′ə), a feminine name: see **Henrietta.**
-ette (et), [Fr., fem. of *-et*], a suffix used to form nouns, meaning: 1. *little,* as in *dinette, statuette.* 2. *female,* as in *suffragette.* 3. *a substitute for,* as in *leatherette.*
‡et tu, Bru·te! (et tōō brōō′te, tū brōō′ti), [L.], and you (too), Brutus!: said to be Julius Caesar's words on seeing his friend Brutus among his assassins: used as a reproachful exclamation implying betrayal.
é·tude (ā′tōōd, ā′tūd; Fr. ā-tüd′), ***n.*** [Fr.; see STUDY], 1. a study. 2. a musical composition for a solo instrument, designed to give practice in some special point of technique, but often performed for its artistic worth.
e·tui (ā-twē′, e-twē′, et′wē), ***n.*** [Fr. *étui;* OFr. *estui;* prob. < *estuier,* to place in a cover, enclose, hence hide, save < LL. **studiare,* to treat with care < L. *studium;* see STUDY], a case for small articles, as needles.
e·twee (e-twē′, et′wē), ***n.*** an etui.
ety., etym., etymol., 1. etymological. 2. etymology.
et·y·mo·log·i·cal (et′ə-mə-loj′i-k'l), ***adj.*** [LL. *etymologicus;* Gr. *etymologikos*], of or according to the etymology or the principles of etymology.
et·y·mo·log·i·cal·ly (et′ə-mə-loj′i-k'l-i, et′ə-mə-loj′ik-li), ***adv.*** by or according to etymology or its principles.
et·y·mol·o·gist (et′ə-mol′ə-jist), ***n.*** an expert in etymology.
et·y·mol·o·gize (et′ə-mol′ə-jīz′), ***v.t. & v.i.*** [ETYMOLOGIZED (-jīzd′), ETYMOLOGIZING], to trace the etymology of, or give or suggest an etymology for (a word or words).
et·y·mol·o·gy (et′ə-mol′ə-ji), ***n.*** [*pl.* ETYMOLOGIES (-jiz)], [Fr. *étymologie;* L. *etymologia;* Gr. *etymologia;* see ETYMON & -LOGY], 1. the origin and development of a word; tracing a word back as far as possible, generally by the methods of comparative linguistics. 2. an account of this: in this dictionary etymologies are given in brackets following the part-of-speech label. 3. the branch of linguistics that deals with the origin and development of words. Abbreviated **etym., etymol., ety.**
et·y·mon (et′ə-mon′), ***n.*** [*pl.* ETYMONS (-monz′), ETYMA (-mə)], [L.; Gr. *etymon,* literal sense of a word, etymology; neut. of *etymos,* true; IE. base **s-eto-* < **es-,* to be (whence L. *sum, est,* Eng. *is*)], the original form of a word, from which its derivatives have developed.
Et·zel (et′s'l), ***n.*** [< Goth. *Attila;* see ATTILA], in *German legend,* the king who married Kriemhild, after Siegfried's death.
eu- (ū, yoo), [Gr. *eu-,* good, well], a prefix meaning *good, well,* as in *eulogy, eugenic*: opposed to *dys-, caco-.*
Eu, in *chemistry,* europium.
Eu·boe·a (yoo-bē′ə), ***n.*** Evvoia: the ancient name.
eu·caine (ū-kān′, ū′kə-in′), ***n.*** [< *eu-* + *cocaine*], either of two synthetic alkaloids, α-eucaine, $C_{19}H_{27}NO_4$, and β-eucaine, $C_{15}H_{21}NO_2$, made from piperidine: their hydrochlorides have been used as local anesthetics.
eu·ca·lypt (ū′kə-lipt′), ***n.*** a eucalyptus tree.
eu·ca·lyp·te·ol (ū′kə-lip′ti-ōl, ū′kə-lip′ti-ol′), ***n.*** [< *eucalyptus* + *-ol*], a crystalline compound made from eucalyptus oil: it is used as an intestinal antiseptic.
eu·ca·lyp·tole, eu·ca·lyp·tol (ū′kə-lip′tōl, ū′kə-lip′tol), ***n.*** [*eucalyptus* + *-ole, -ol*], cineole, a liquid found in certain essential oils.
eu·ca·lyp·tus (ū′kə-lip′təs), ***n.*** [*pl.* EUCALYPTUSES (-iz), EUCALYPTI (-tī)], [Mod. L. < Gr. *eu-,* well + ***kalyptos,*** covered (from the covering of the buds) < ***kalyptein,*** to cover, conceal], any of a group of subtropical evergreen trees of the myrtle family, native to Australia, valued for their timber, gums, and oil.
eucalyptus oil, an essential oil derived from eucalyptus leaves, used as an antiseptic and disinfectant.
eu·cha·ris (ū′kə-ris), ***n.*** [Mod. L.; LL.; Gr. *eucharis,* charming, gracious; see EUCHARIST], any of a group of South American plants of the amaryllis family, with white, bell-shaped flowers.
Eu·cha·rist (ū′kə-rist), ***n.*** [ME. & OFr. *eucariste;* LL. *eucharistia;* Gr. *eucharistia,* thankfulness, gratitude < *eucharistos,* grateful, thankful < *eu-,* well + *charizesthai,* to show favor to < *charis,* favor], in *Christian churches,* 1. Holy Communion; Lord's Supper. 2. the consecrated bread and wine used in this.
Eu·cha·ris·tic (ū′kə-ris′tik), ***adj.*** of or connected with the Eucharist.
Eu·cha·ris·ti·cal (ū′kə-ris′ti-k'l), ***adj.*** Eucharistic.
eu·chre (ū′kẽr), ***n.*** [earlier also *yuker, uker;* use of *bower* for nontrump knave in game (see BOWER) suggests G. dial. origin (cf. G. *juchs,* joke, game) with Creole Fr. or Sp. sp.; ? influenced by Creole Sp. *ser yuca,* to best, outdo; prob. not < Fr. *écarté*], 1. a card game for two, three, or four players, played with thirty-two cards, all the cards below seven except the ace being removed. 2. a euchring or being euchred. ***v.t.*** [EUCHRED (-kẽrd), EUCHRING], 1. to gain an advantage of two points over (an opponent at euchre) by his failure to take three tricks; hence, 2. [Colloq.], to outwit or defeat, as in scheming (often with *out*).
Euck·en, Ru·dolf Chris·toph (rōō′dôlf kris′tôf oi′k'n), 1846–1926; German writer and philosopher; received Nobel prize in literature, 1908.
eu·clase (ū′klās), ***n.*** [< *eu-* + Gr. *klasis,* a breaking < *klan,* to break: so named from breaking easily], a crystalline silicate of aluminum and beryllium, $HBeAlSiO_5$, colored pale green or blue: used as a gem.
Eu·clid (ū′klid), ***n.*** [L. *Euclides;* Gr. *Eukleidēs*], 1. Greek mathematician; fl. c. 300 B.C. 2. his *Elements,* a basic work in geometry. 3. Euclidean geometry. 4. a city in northeastern Ohio: a suburb of Cleveland: pop., 63,000.
Eu·clid·e·an, Eu·clid·i·an (ū-klid′i-ən), ***adj.*** [L. *Euclideus*], of Euclid or his geometric principles.
eu·dae·mo·ni·a (ū′di-mō′ni-ə), ***n.*** [Gr. *eudaimonia,* happiness < *eu-,* good + *daimōn,* one's demon, fate, soul], happiness; specifically, in Aristotle's philosophy, happiness, the main universal goal, derived from a life of activity governed by reason.
eu·dae·mon·ic (ū′di-mon′ik), ***adj.*** [Gr. *eudaimonikos;* see EUDAEMONIA], conducive to happiness.
eu·dae·mon·i·cal (ū′di-mon′i-k'l), ***adj.*** eudaemonic.
eu·dae·mon·ism (yoo-dē′mən-iz'm), ***n.*** [Gr. *eudaimonismos,* a calling happy < *eudaimonizein,* to call happy < *eudaimōn,* fortunate, happy; see EUDAEMONIA], the system of ethics that considers the moral value of actions in terms of their ability to produce happiness.
eu·di·om·e·ter (ū′di-om′ə-tẽr), ***n.*** [< Gr. *eudios,* clear, fair (*eu-,* good + *dios,* genit. of *Zeus,* god of the sky); + *-meter*], 1. originally, an instrument for measuring the amount of oxygen in the air. 2. an instrument for measuring and analyzing gases.
eu·di·o·met·ric (ū′di-ə-met′rik), ***adj.*** of eudiometry.
eu·di·o·met·ri·cal (ū′di-ə-met′ri-k'l), ***adj.*** eudiometric.
eu·di·om·e·try (ū′di-om′ə-tri), ***n.*** the analysis of gases by means of a eudiometer.
Eu·gene (yoo-jēn′, ū′jēn), [Fr. *Eugène;* L. *Eugenius;* Gr. *Eugenios* < *eugenēs,* well-born; see EUGENIC], a masculine name: diminutive, *Gene;* feminine, *Eugenia.* ***n.*** a city in western Oregon: pop., 51,000.
Eu·gene, Prince (Fr. ë′zhen′), (*François Eugène de Savoie-Carignon*), 1663–1736; Prince of Savoy; Franco-Austrian general.
Eu·ge·ni·a (yoo-jē′ni-ə), [L.; Gr. *Eugenia;* see EUGENE], a feminine name: diminutive, *Genie.*
eu·gen·ic (yoo-jen′ik), ***adj.*** [Gr. *eugenēs,* well-born; see EU- & GENESIS], improving, or relating to the improvement of, the race; relating to the bearing of healthy offspring.
eu·gen·i·cal·ly (yoo-jen′i-k'l-i, yoo-jen′ik-li), ***adv.*** 1. in a eugenic manner. 2. by or according to eugenics.
eu·gen·i·cist (yoo-jen′ə-sist), ***n.*** a specialist in or advocate of eugenics.
eu·gen·ics (yoo-jen′iks), ***n.pl.*** [construed as sing.], [< Gr. *eugenēs* (see EUGENIC); + *-ics*], the science that deals with the improvement of races and breeds, especially the human race, through the control of hereditary factors: distinguished from *euthenics.*
Eu·gé·nie (ë′zhā′nē′; Eng. yoo-jē′ni), ***n.*** (*Marie Eugénie de Montijo de Guzmán*), wife of Louis Napoleon; 1826–1920; empress of the French (1853–1871).

eu·ge·nist (ū'jə-nist), *n.* a specialist in eugenics.

eu·ge·nol (ū'jə-nōl', ū'jə-nol'), *n.* [< Mod. L. *Eugenia*, a genus of tropical trees; + *-ol*], a colorless, aromatic liquid compound, $C_{10}H_{12}O_2$, found in oil of cloves and used in perfumes, as an antiseptic in dentistry, etc.

eu·gle·na (yoo-glē'nə), *n.* [Mod. L.; *eu-* + Gr. *glēnē*, pupil of the eye], a green protozoan with a single flagellum and a characteristic red pigment spot.

eu·he·mer·ism (yoo-hē'mẽr-iz'm, yoo-hem'ẽr-iz'm), *n.* [< L. *Euhemerus* (< Gr. *Euhēmeros*); + *-ism*], the doctrine of the Sicilian philosopher Euhemerus (4th century B.C.) that the gods of mythology were deified human beings; theory that myths are based on traditional accounts of real people and events.

eu·he·mer·ist (yoo-hē'mẽr-ist, yoo-hem'ẽr-ist), *n.* a believer in euhemerism. *adj.* euhemeristic.

eu·he·mer·is·tic (yoo-hē'mẽr-is'tik, yoo-hem'ẽr-is'tik), *adj.* of or based on euhemerism.

eu·he·mer·ize (yoo-hē'mẽr-īz', yoo-hem'ẽr-īz'), *v.t.* [EUHEMERIZED (-īzd'), EUHEMERIZING], to interpret (myths, etc.) by euhemerism.

Eu·la·li·a (yoo-lā'li-ə, yoo-lā'lyə), [L.; Gr. *Eulalia*, lit., fair (in) speech < *eu-*, well + *lalein*, to talk], a feminine name.

Eulalia, Saint, ?-304 A.D.; Spanish martyr; patroness of sailors and of Barcelona: her day is February 12.

Eu·ler, Le·on·hard (lā'ôn-härt' oi'lẽr), 1707–1783; Swiss mathematician; originated the calculus of variation.

eu·lo·gi·a (yoo-lō'ji-ə), *n.* [LL.; New Testament Gr. *eulogia*, the Eucharist, act of blessing; see EULOGY], 1. originally, the Eucharist. 2. bread (formerly bread of the Eucharist) blessed but not consecrated, and given in small pieces to the noncommunicants at Mass, especially in the Orthodox Eastern Church.

eu·lo·gist (ū'lə-jist), *n.* a person who eulogizes.

eu·lo·gis·tic (ū'lə-jis'tik), *adj.* of or expressing eulogy; praising highly; laudatory.

eu·lo·gis·ti·cal·ly (ū'lə-jis'ti-k'l-i, ū'lə-jis'tik-li), *adv.* in a eulogistic manner.

eu·lo·gi·um (yoo-lō'ji-əm), *n.* [*pl.* EULOGIUMS (-əmz), EULOGIA (-ə)], [ML.], eulogy.

eu·lo·gize (ū'lə-jīz'), *v.t.* [EULOGIZED (-jīzd'), EULOGIZING], to praise highly; compose a eulogy about; extol. —*SYN.* see **praise**.

eu·lo·gy (ū'lə-ji), *n.* [*pl.* EULOGIES (-jiz)], [ML. *eulogia*; Gr. *eulogia* < *eulegein*, to speak well of, praise (in New Testament, to bless); see EU- & -LOGY], 1. speech or writing in praise of a person, event, or thing; especially, a formal speech or statement praising a dead person. 2. high praise; commendation. —*SYN.* see **tribute**.

Eu·men·i·des (ū-men'ə-dēz'), *n.pl.* [L.; Gr. *Eumenides*, lit., the gracious ones < *eumenēs*, well-disposed, gracious < *eu-*, well + *menos*, the mind, temper: a propitiatory euphemism], in *Greek mythology*, the Furies; Erinyes.

Eu·nice (ū'nis), [L.; Gr. *Eunikē*, lit., good victory < *eu-*, well + *nikē*, victory], a feminine name.

eu·nuch (ū'nək), *n.* [L. *eunuchus*; Gr. *eunouchos*, guardian of the bed, chamberlain, eunuch < *eunē*, bed + *echein*, to have, hold], 1. a castrated man in charge of an Oriental harem or employed as a chamberlain or officer by an Oriental potentate. 2. any castrated man.

eu·on·y·mus (ū-on'ə-məs), *n.* [L. *euonymos*; Gr. *euōnymos* < *eu-*, good + *onyma*, dial. form of *onoma*, name], any of a group of evergreen shrubs with highly colored fruit: also **evonymus**.

eu·pa·to·ri·um (ū'pə-tôr'i-əm, ū'pə-tō'ri-əm), *n.* [Mod. L.; Gr. *eupatorion*, hemp agrimony < *Eupator*, king of Pontus, by whom said to have been first used], any of a group of plants of the composite family, including the mistflower, joe-pye weed, snakeroot, boneset, etc.

eu·pat·rid (yoo-pat'rid, ū'pə-trid'), *n.* [*pl.* EUPATRIDAE (yoo-pat'ri-dē'), EUPATRIDS (-ridz, -tridz')], [Gr. *eupatridēs* < *eu-*, well, good + *patēr*, father], [also E-], any of the hereditary aristocrats of ancient Athens and other Greek states, who were the lawmakers and administrators. *adj.* (ū'pə-trid'), of these aristocrats.

eu·pep·si·a (yoo-pep'shə, yoo-pep'si-ə), *n.* [Mod. L.; Gr. *eupepsia* < *eu-*, well + *peptein*, to digest], good digestion.

eu·pep·tic (yoo-pep'tik), *adj.* [< Gr. *eupeptos* (see EUPEPSIA); + *-ic*], 1. of or having good digestion. 2. aiding digestion.

Eu·phe·mi·a (yoo-fē'mi-ə), [L.; Gr. *Euphēmia*, lit., (of) fair report < *eu-*, well + *phēmē*, speech, report], a feminine name: diminutives, *Effie*, *Phemie*.

eu·phe·mism (ū'fə-miz'm), *n.* [Gr. *euphēmismos* < *euphēmizein*, to use a good or auspicious word for an evil or inauspicious < *euphēmos*, of good sound or omen < *eu-*, good + *phēmē*, voice < *phanai*, to speak], 1. the use of a word or phrase that is less expressive or direct but considered less distasteful, less offensive, etc. than another. 2. a word or phrase so substituted (e.g., *remains* for *corpse*).

eu·phe·mist (ū'fə-mist), *n.* a user of euphemisms.

eu·phe·mis·tic (ū'fə-mis'tik), *adj.* of, containing, having the nature of, or intended as euphemism.

eu·phe·mis·ti·cal (ū'fə-mis'ti-k'l), *adj.* euphemistic.

eu·phe·mis·ti·cal·ly (ū'fə-mis'ti-k'l-i, ū'fə-mis'tik-li), *adv.* in a euphemistic manner; by euphemism.

eu·phe·mize (ū'fə-mīz'), *v.t. & v.i.* [EUPHEMIZED (-mīzd'), EUPHEMIZING], to speak or write (of) euphemistically.

eu·phon·ic (yoo-fon'ik), *adj.* 1. of euphony. 2. euphonious.

eu·phon·i·cal (yoo-fon'i-k'l), *adj.* euphonic.

eu·pho·ni·ous (yoo-fō'ni-əs), *adj.* characterized by euphony; having a pleasant sound; harmonious.

eu·pho·ni·um (yoo-fō'ni-əm), *n.* [Mod. L. < Gr. *euphōnos*; see EUPHONY], a brass-wind instrument, now rarely used, resembling the tuba but having a slightly higher range and more mellow tone.

EUPHONIUM

eu·phon·ize (ū'fə-nīz'), *v.t.* [EUPHONIZED (-nīzd'), EUPHONIZING], to make euphonious.

eu·pho·ny (ū'fə-ni), *n.* [*pl.* EUPHONIES (-niz)], [LL. *euphonia*; Gr. *euphōnia* < *euphōnos*, sweet-voiced, musical < *eu-*, well + *phōnē*, voice], 1. the quality of having a pleasing sound; pleasant effect of a combination of agreeable sounds, as in speech or music. 2. in *phonetics*, the tendency to make pronunciation easier, as by assimilation, dissimilation, etc., resulting from normal causes of sound change and not from an attempt at pleasanter sound, as formerly believed.

eu·phor·bi·a (yoo-fôr'bi-ə), *n.* [Mod. L.; L. *euphorbea*; Gr. *euphorbion* < *Euphorbos*, Gr. physician], any of a large group of cactuslike plants with a thick, milky juice, including the poinsettia, etc.; spurge.

eu·phor·bi·a·ceous (yoo-fôr'bi-ā'shəs), *adj.* of the family of plants typified by the euphorbias, found in many parts of the world.

eu·pho·ri·a (yoo-fôr'i-ə, yoo-fō'ri-ə), *n.* [Mod. L. < Gr. *euphoria*, power of bearing easily < *euphoros*, bearing well < *eu-*, well + *pherein*, to bear], a feeling of well-being; especially, in *psychology*, an abnormal feeling of buoyant vigor and health.

eu·phor·ic (yoo-fôr'ik, yoo-for'ik), *adj.* of or characterized by euphoria.

eu·phra·sy (ū'frə-si), *n.* [ML. *euphrasia*; Gr. *euphrasia* < *euphrasein*, to cheer < *eu-*, well + *phrēn*, mind], eyebright, an herb.

Eu·phra·tes (ū-frā'tēz), *n.* a river flowing through eastern Turkey, Syria, and Iraq, into the Persian Gulf: length, 1,700 mi.

eu·phroe (ū'frō, ū'vrō), *n.* [< D. *juffrouw*, lit., young woman < *jong*, young + *vrouw*, woman], a long, perforated, cylindrical block to fasten and tighten the ropes supporting an awning on shipboard, a tent, etc.: also spelled **uphroe**.

Eu·phros·y·ne (ū-fros'ə-nē', ū-froz'ə-nē'), *n.* [L.; Gr. *Euphrosynē* < *euphrōn*, cheerful], in *Greek mythology*, Joy, one of the three Graces.

eu·phu·ism (ū'fū-iz'm), *n.* [< *Euphues*, fictitious character in two prose romances by John Lyly < Gr. *euphyēs*, shapely, graceful < *eu-*, well + *phyē*, growth < *phyein*, to grow], 1. the artificial, affected, high-flown style of speaking or writing used by John Lyly and his imitators, characterized by alliteration, balanced sentences, antithesis, farfetched figures of speech, etc. 2. any artificial, high-flown style of speech or writing. 3. an instance of this.

eu·phu·ist (ū'fū-ist), *n.* a person who uses euphuism.

eu·phu·is·tic (ū'fū-is'tik), *adj.* 1. having the nature of euphuism; high-flown, affected, etc. 2. characterized by euphuism. —*SYN.* see **bombastic**.

eu·phu·is·ti·cal (ū'fū-is'ti-k'l), *adj.* euphuistic.

eu·plas·tic (yoo-plas'tik), *adj.* [*eu-* + *-plastic*], in *physiology*, easily formed into or adapted to the formation of tissue. *n.* a euplastic material.

eup·ne·a, eup·noe·a (yoop-nē'ə), *n.* [Mod. L.; Gr. *eupnoia* < *eu-*, well + *pnoē*, breathing < *pnein*, to breathe], normal breathing: opposed to *dyspnea*.

Eur., 1. Europe. 2. European.

Eur·a·sia (yoo-rā'zhə, yoo-rā'shə), *n.* Europe and Asia, considered as a unit.

Eur·a·sian (yoo-rā'zhən, yoo-rā'shən), *adj.* 1. of Eurasia. 2. of mixed European and Asiatic descent. *n.* 1. a person of mixed European and Asiatic descent. 2. a member of a people of both Europe and Asia.

eu·re·ka (yoo-rē'kə), *interj.* [Gr. *heurēka*, 1st pers., perf. indic. act., of *heuriskein*, to find, discover], 1. I have found (it) : exclamation supposedly uttered by Archimedes when he discovered a way to determine the purity of gold by applying the principle of specific gravity; hence, 2. any exclamation of triumphant achievement, equivalent to "I've got it!"

eu·rhyth·mic (yoo-rith'mik), *adj.* eurythmic.

eu·rhyth·mi·cal (yoo-rith'mi-k'l), *adj.* eurythmical.

eu·rhyth·mics (yoo-rith'miks), *n.pl.* [construed as sing.], eurythmics.

eu·rhyth·my (yoo-rith'mi), *n.* eurythmy.

Eu·rip·i·des (yoo-rip'ə-dēz'), *n.* Greek tragic dramatist; 5th century B.C.

eu·ri·pus (yoo-rī'pəs), *n.* [*pl.* EURIPI (-pī)], [L.; Gr. *euripos* (orig., in sense 2) < *eu-*, well + *rhipē*, rush, impetus], 1. [E-], a channel between the island of Euboea and Boeotia in Greece, noted for the violent and unpredictable flow of water in both directions. 2. any strait or channel with such a current or tide.

Eu·roc·ly·don (yoo-rok'li-don'), *n.* [Mod. L.; New Testament Gr. *euroklydōn* < *euros*, southeast wind + *klydōn*, wave; prob. false reading for *euraklyōn* < LL. *Euraquilo*, northeast wind < L. *Eurus*, east wind (see EURUS) + *Aquilo*, north wind < *aquilus*, dark, stormy, orig., watery < *aqua*, water], 1. in the *Bible*, a stormy northeast wind of the Mediterranean, mentioned in the account of Paul's voyage to Rome: Acts 27:14; hence, 2. any stormy wind.

Eu·ro·pa (yoo-rō'pə), *n.* [L.; Gr. *Eurōpē*], in *Greek mythology*, a Phoenician princess loved by Zeus: taking on the form of a white bull, he carried her off across the sea to Crete.

Eu·rope (yoor'əp), *n.* [L. *Europa*; Gr. *Eurōpē*: named after *Europa*], the continent west of Asia: area, 3,872,000 sq. mi.; pop., c. 560,000,000: abbreviated **Eur.**

Eu·ro·pe·an (yoor'ə-pē'ən), *adj.* of Europe, its people, their culture, etc. *n.* a native or inhabitant of Europe. Abbreviated **Eur.**

Eu·ro·pe·an·ize (yoor'ə-pē'ən-īz'), *v.t.* [EUROPEANIZED (-īzd'), EUROPEANIZING], to make European in habits, dress, culture, scope, etc.

European plan, a system of hotel operation in which guests are charged for rooms and service, and pay for meals separately if they wish them: distinguished from *American plan.*

eu·ro·pi·um (yoo-rō'pi-əm), *n.* [Mod. L. < *Europe* + *-ium*], a chemical element of the rare-earth group: symbol, Eu; at. wt., 152.0; at. no., 63.

Eu·rus (yoor'əs), *n.* [L.; Gr. *euros*], in *Greek mythology*, the east wind or the god of the east wind.

eu·ry- (yoor'i), [Gr. *eury-* < *eurys*, wide, broad; IE. base **ewer-*, broad; hence akin to Sans. *uru*, Goth. *iusiza*, better], a combining form meaning *wide, broad.*

Eu·ryd·i·ce (yoo-rid'ə-sē'), *n.* [L.; Gr. *Eurydikē*], in *Greek legend*, the wife of Orpheus: after she died, he got permission to bring her back from Hades, but she had to return there when Orpheus broke his agreement with Pluto by turning to see whether she was following him: also spelled **Euridice.**

eu·ryp·ter·id (yoo-rip'tə-rid'), *n.* [< Mod. L. *Eurypterida* (pl.), name of the order < Gr. *eurys*, broad + *pteron*, feather, wing: so named from a pair of broad swimming appendages], any of a group of large fossil crustaceans related to the king crabs: they abounded in the Silurian and Devonian Periods of the Paleozoic Era.

eu·ryth·mic (yoo-rith'mik), *adj.* 1. characterized by perfect proportion and harmony, or by movement in rhythm. 2. of eurythmics. Also spelled **eurhythmic.**

eu·ryth·mi·cal (yoo-rith'mi-k'l), *adj.* eurythmic.

eu·ryth·mics (yoo-rith'miks), *n.pl.* [construed as sing.], [< *eurythmy*], the art of performing various bodily movements in rhythm, usually to musical accompaniment: also spelled **eurhythmics.**

eu·ryth·my (yoo-rith'mi), *n.* [L. *eurythmia*; Gr. *eurythmia* < *eurythmos*, rhythmical < *eu-*, well + *rhythmos*, rhythm], proportion or motion characterized by harmony: also spelled **eurhythmy.**

Eu·se·bi·us Pam·phi·li (ū-sē'bi-əs pam'fə-lī'), 260?–340? A.D.; ecclesiastical historian.

eu·sol (ū'sōl, ū'sol), *n.* [*E*dinburgh *U*niversity *sol*ution], an antiseptic solution made of chlorinated lime and boric acid, and containing hypochlorous acid.

Eus·tace (ūs'tis), [OFr.; L. *Eustachius*; Gr. *Eustachios* < *eustachys*, rich in corn, blooming, fruitful < *eu-*, well + *stachys*, ear of grain], a masculine name.

Eu·sta·chi·an tube (yoo-stā'ki-ən, yoo-stā'shi-ən, yoo-stā'shən), [after Bartolommeo *Eustachio* (1520–1574), It. anatomist], a slender tube between the middle ear and the pharynx, which serves to equalize air pressure on both sides of the eardrum: see **ear,** illus.

eu·tax·y (ū'tak-si), *n.* [Fr. *eutaxie* < Gr. *eutaxia*; see EU- & -TAXY], good or proper arrangement or order.

eu·tec·tic (yoo-tek'tik), *adj.* [Gr. *eutēkos*, easily fused < *eu-*, well + *tēkein*, to melt; + *-ic*], fusing at the lowest possible temperature. *n.* an alloy with a melting point lower than that of any other combination of the same components.

eu·tec·toid (yoo-tek'toid), *adj.* like a eutectic. *n.* an alloy like a eutectic, as pearlite.

Eu·ter·pe (ū-tũr'pi), *n.* [L.; Gr. *Euterpē* < *euterpēs*, charming < *eu-*, well + *terpein*, to delight, charm], in *Greek mythology*, the Muse of music and lyric poetry.

eu·tha·na·si·a (ū'thə-nā'zhə, ū'thə-nā'zhi-ə), *n.* [Mod. L.; Gr. *euthanasia*, painless, happy death < *eu-*, well + *thanatos*, death], 1. an easy and painless death. 2. act or method of causing death painlessly, so as to end suffering: advocated by some as a way to deal with victims of incurable diseases.

eu·then·ics (yoo-then'iks), *n.pl.* [construed as sing.], [< Gr. *euthēnein*, to flourish; + *-ics*], the science that deals with the improvement of races and breeds, especially the human race, through the control of environmental factors: distinguished from *eugenics.*

eux·e·nite (ūk'sə-nīt'), *n.* [< Gr. *euxenos*, hospitable (*eu-*, well + *xenos*, stranger, guest); + *-ite*: so named from containing several rare elements], a lustrous, brown-black mineral containing columbium, titanium, yttrium, erbium, cerium, and uranium.

Eux·ine Sea (ūk'sin, ūk'sīn), the Black Sea: the ancient name.

E.V., English Version (of the Bible).

E·va (ē'və, ev'ə), a feminine name: see **Eve.**

e·vac·u·ant (i-vak'ū-ənt), *adj.* [L. *evacuans*, ppr. of *evacuare*; see EVACUATE], causing evacuation, especially of the bowels or stomach; cathartic or emetic. *n.* an evacuant medicine; cathartic or emetic.

e·vac·u·ate (i-vak'ū-āt'), *v.t.* [EVACUATED (-id), EVACUATING], [< L. *evacuatus*, pp. of *evacuare*; *e-*, out + *vacuare*, to make empty < *vacuus*, empty], 1. to make empty; remove the contents of. 2. to discharge (excrement, etc.); void; emit. 3. to move or remove; send away. 4. to give up military occupation of; withdraw from. *v.i.* to withdraw, as from a besieged town.

e·vac·u·a·tion (i-vak'ū-ā'shən), *n.* [L. *evacuatio* < pp. of *evacuare*], 1. an evacuating or being evacuated. 2. in *medicine*, *a*) an emptying or discharging of waste matter, as from the bowels, urinary bladder, etc. *b*) matter so discharged. 3. a withdrawal of troops from a fortified place, or of civilians from an inhabited area.

e·vac·u·a·tor (i-vak'ū-ā'tẽr), *n.* a person or thing that evacuates.

e·vac·u·ee (i-vak'ū-ē', i-vak'ū-ē'), *n.* a person evacuated from an area of danger.

e·vad·a·ble, e·vad·i·ble (i-vād'ə-b'l), *adj.* that can be evaded.

e·vade (i-vād'), *v.i.* [EVADED (-id), EVADING], [Fr. *évader*; L. *evadere*; *e-*, out, from + *vadere*, to go], 1. [Rare], to escape; get away. 2. to use evasion; be deceitful or clever in avoiding or escaping. *v.t.* 1. to avoid or escape from by deceit or cleverness; keep out of the way of; elude. 2. to avoid doing or answering directly; get around; get out of. —*SYN.* see **escape.**

e·vag·i·nate (i-vaj'ə-nāt'), *v.t. & v.i.* [EVAGINATED (-id), EVAGINATING], [< L. *evaginatus*, pp. of *evaginare*, to unsheath < *e-*, from + *vagina*, a sheath], 1. to turn inside out; evert. 2. to protrude by eversion.

e·vag·i·na·tion (i-vaj'ə-nā'shən), *n.* 1. an evaginating or being evaginated. 2. an evaginated part.

e·val·u·ate (i-val'ū-āt'), *v.t.* [EVALUATED (-id), EVALUATING], [Fr. *évaluer* < *é-* (L. *ex-*), out + *value*; see VALUE], 1. to find the value or amount of; determine the worth of; appraise. 2. in *mathematics*, to find the numerical value of; express in numbers. —*SYN.* see **estimate.**

e·val·u·a·tion (i-val'ū-ā'shən), *n.* 1. an evaluating or being evaluated. 2. valuation.

Ev·an (ev'ən), [< Celt. *Eoghan*, young man, youth], a masculine name.

ev·a·nesce (ev'ə-nes'), *v.i.* [EVANESCED (-nest'), EVANESCING], [L. *evanescere*; *e-*, out + *vanescere*, to vanish < *vanus*, vain, empty], to fade from sight, like mist or smoke; disappear; vanish.

ev·a·nes·cence (ev'ə-nes''ns), *n.* [Fr. *évanescence* < ppr. of L. *evanescere*; see EVANESCE], 1. a fading from sight; vanishing. 2. a tendency to fade from sight; evanescent quality; transitoriness.

ev·a·nes·cent (ev'ə-nes''nt), *adj.* [Fr. *évanescent*; L. *evanescens*, ppr.; see EVANESCE], tending to fade from sight; vanishing; ephemeral. —*SYN.* see **transient.**

evang., evangelical.

e·van·gel (i-van'jəl), *n.* [ME. & OFr. *evangile*; LL. *evangelium*, gospel; New Testament Gr. *euangelion*, good news, gospel < Gr. *euangelos*, bringing good news; *eu-*, well + *angelos*, messenger], 1. the gospel. 2. [E-], any of the four Gospels. 3. good news. 4. [Gr. *euangelos*], an evangelist.

e·van·gel·ic (ē'van-jel'ik, ev'ən-jel'ik), *adj.* evangelical.

e·van·gel·i·cal (ē'van-jel'i-k'l, ev'ən-jel'i-k'l), *adj.* [< LL. *evangelicus* (see EVANGEL); + *-al*], 1. in, of, or according to the Gospels or the teachings of the New Testament. 2. of those Protestant churches, as the Methodist and Baptist, that emphasize salvation by faith in the atonement of Jesus, and reject the efficacy of the sacraments and good works alone: also called *orthodox.* 3. of the Low Church party in the Church of England. 4. evangelistic. *n.* a member of an evangelical church. Abbreviated **evang.**

e·van·gel·i·cal·ism (ē'van-jel'i-k'l-iz'm, ev'ən-jel'i-k'l-iz'm), *n.* 1. evangelical church doctrines. 2. acceptance of such doctrines.

e·van·gel·i·cal·ly (ē'van-jel'i-k'l-i, ev'ən-jel'ik-li), *adv.* in an evangelical manner; by or according to the Gospels or evangelical doctrines.

E·van·ge·line (i-van'jə-lin, i-van'jə-līn', i-van'jə-lēn'),

[Fr. *Évangeline* < LL. *evangelium;* see EVANGEL], a feminine name.

e·van·gel·ism (i-van′jə-liz'm), *n.* 1. a preaching of, or zealous effort to spread, the gospel, as in revival meetings. 2. the work of an evangelist. 3. evangelicalism.

e·van·gel·ist (i-van′jə-list), *n.* [ME. & OFr. *evangeliste;* LL. *evangelista;* Gr. *euangelistēs;* see EVANGEL], 1. [E-], any of the four writers of the Gospels; Matthew, Mark, Luke, or John. 2. anyone who preaches the gospel; especially, a traveling preacher; revivalist; home missionary. 3. in the *Mormon Church,* a patriarch.

e·van·gel·is·tic (i-van′jə-lis′tik), *adj.* 1. of any of the Evangelists or an evangelist. 2. evangelical.

e·van·gel·is·ti·cal·ly (i-van′jə-lis′ti-k'l-i, i-van′jə-lis′tikli), *adv.* in an evangelistic manner; by or according to evangelism.

e·van·gel·i·za·tion (i-van′jə-li-zā′shən), *n.* an evangelizing or being evangelized.

e·van·gel·ize (i-van′jə-līz′), *v.t.* [EVANGELIZED (-lizd′), EVANGELIZING], [ME. *evangelizen;* OFr. *evangelizer;* LL. *evangelizare;* New Testament Gr. *euangelizesthai;* see EVANGEL & -IZE], 1. to preach the gospel to. 2. to convert to Christianity.

e·van·ish (i-van′ish), *v.i.* [< OFr. *evaniss-,* base of *esvanir*], [Poetic], to fade from sight; vanish.

Ev·ans, Sir Arthur John (ev′ənz), 1851–1941; English archaeologist.

Evans, Mary Ann, see **Eliot, George.**

Evans, Maurice, 1901– ; English actor.

Ev·ans·ton (ev′ən-stən, ev′ənz-tən), *n.* a city in Illinois, near Chicago: pop., 79,000.

Ev·ans·ville (ev′ənz-vil′), *n.* a city in southwestern Indiana, on the Ohio River: pop., 142,000.

e·vap·o·ra·bil·i·ty (i-vap′ẽr-ə-bil′ə-ti), *n.* the quality of being evaporable.

e·vap·o·ra·ble (i-vap′ẽr-ə-b'l), *adj.* that can be evaporated.

e·vap·o·rate (i-vap′ə-rāt′), *v.t.* [EVAPORATED (-id), EVAPORATING], [< L. *evaporatus,* pp. of *evaporare; e-,* out, from + *vaporare,* to emit vapor < *vapor,* steam, vapor], 1. to change (a liquid or solid) into vapor; drive out or draw off in the form of vapor. 2. to remove moisture from (milk, vegetables, fruits, etc.) by heating or drying so as to get a concentrated product. *v.i.* 1. to become vapor; pass off in the form of vapor. 2. to give off vapor. 3. to disappear like vapor; vanish.

evaporated milk, canned, unsweetened milk thickened by evaporation: distinguished from *condensed milk.*

e·vap·o·ra·tion (i-vap′ə-rā′shən), *n.* [Fr.; L. *evaporatio;* see EVAPORATE], 1. a changing or being changed into vapor. 2. the removal of moisture, as from milk, fruit, or vegetables. 3. the result or product of evaporating.

e·vap·o·ra·tor (i-vap′ə-rā′tẽr), *n.* anything that causes evaporation; specifically, an apparatus for evaporating the moisture from a food.

Ev·arts, William Maxwell (ev′ẽrts), 1818–1901; American lawyer and statesman.

e·va·sion (i-vā′zhən), *n.* [L. *evasio* < *evasus,* pp. of *evadere;* see EVADE], 1. an avoiding of a duty, question, fact, etc. by deceit or cleverness. 2. a means of doing this; subterfuge; equivocation; excuse.

e·va·sive (i-vā′siv), *adj.* [Fr. *évasif* < L. *evasus;* see EVASION], 1. tending or seeking to evade; not straightforward; tricky; equivocal: as, *evasive* talk. 2. elusive.

Eve (ēv), [ME.; AS. *Efe;* LL. *Eva, Heva;* Heb. *hawwāh,* lit., ? life], a feminine name: variant, *Eva.* *n.* in the *Bible,* Adam's wife, the first woman: Gen. 3:20.

eve (ēv), *n.* [ME.; shortened < *even* (evening)], 1. [Poetic], evening. 2. the evening or day before a holiday: as, Christmas *Eve;* hence, 3. the period immediately before some event: as, on the *eve* of victory.

e·vec·tion (i-vek′shən), *n.* [L. *evectio,* a going up, carrying away or out < *evectus,* pp. of *evehere; e-,* out, from + *vehere,* to carry], a periodical variation in the motion of the moon in its orbit, caused by the attraction of the sun.

Ev·e·li·na (ev′ə-lī′nə), a feminine name: see **Eveline.**

Ev·e·line (ev′ə-lin′, ev′ə-lin), [< Celt., lit., pleasant], a feminine name: variants, *Evelina, Evelyn.*

Ev·e·lyn (ev′ə-lin, ēv′lin), a feminine and masculine name: see **Eveline.**

Eve·lyn, John (ēv′lin), 1620–1706; English diarist.

e·ven (ē′vən, ē′v'n), *adj.* [ME. *evene, even;* AS. *efne,* flat, level; akin to G. *eben;* IE. base **im-nos-,* what is the same < adv. base **im-,* just like], 1. flat; level; smooth: as, *even* country. 2. not irregular; not varying; uniform; constant: as, an *even* tempo. 3. calm; tranquil; serene; placid: as, an *even* disposition. 4. in the same plane or line; in line: as, the water was *even* with the rim. 5. equally balanced. 6. owing and being owed nothing; hence, 7. revenged for a wrong, insult, etc. 8. just; equitable; fair: as, an *even* exchange. 9. equal or identical in number, quantity, degree, etc. 10. exactly divisible by two: said of numbers, and opposed to *odd.* 11. exact: as, an *even* mile. *adv.* 1. [Obs.], in an even manner. 2. *used as an intensive or emphatic particle a) emphasizing the limit of what is possible or probable:* though it may seem improbable; moreover; indeed; fully: as, *even* unto death, *even* a fool could understand. *b) emphasizing precise correspondence:* exactly; precisely; just; in no other way but: as, it happened *even* as I expected. *c) emphasizing coincidence, concurrence, or simultaneity:* just as; while: as, *even* as he spoke, I left. *d) emphasizing a comparison:* still; yet: as, his error was *even* worse. *e)* [Archaic], *emphasizing identity:* namely; particularly: as, one there was, *even* John. *v.t. & v.i.* to make, become, or be even; level off; equalize or be equalized. —*SYN.* see **level, steady.**

break even, [Slang], to finish as neither a winner nor loser.

even if, though; despite the fact that.

e·ven (ē′vən), *n.* [Poetic or Dial.], evening.

e·ven·fall (ē′vən-fôl′), *n.* [Poetic], the fall of evening; twilight; dusk.

e·ven·hand·ed (ē′vən-han′did), *adj.* impartial; fair; just; unbiased.

eve·ning (ēv′niŋ), *n.* [ME.; AS. *æfnung,* verbal n. < *æfnian,* to grow toward evening < *æfen;* akin to G. *abend;* IE. base **epi-,* **opi-,* after, later; basic sense "later part of the day"], 1. the last part of the day; close of the day and early part of night; period between sunset or the last meal of the day and bedtime. 2. in some parts of the South, in rural areas, and in parts of England, the period from noon through sunset and twilight. 3. the last period, as of life, a career, etc. 4. a part of the night spent in a specified way: as, a musical *evening.* *adj.* in, for, or of the evening.

evening dress (or **clothes**), formal clothes worn on formal occasions in the evening and at night.

evening gown, a woman's evening dress, usually long and décolleté.

evening prayer, evensong.

evening primrose, any of a group of plants with spikes of yellowish fragrant flowers, which open at night.

evening star, a bright planet, usually Venus, that can be seen in the western sky soon after sunset: also called *Vesper, Hesperus.*

e·ven-mind·ed (ē′vən-mīn′did), *adj.* having evenness of mind or temper; characterized by equanimity; equable; placid.

e·ven·ness (ē′vən-nis), *n.* an even quality or state.

e·ven·song (ē′vən-sôŋ′), *n.* [ME.; AS. *æfensang;* see EVEN, *n.* & SONG], 1. in the *Roman Catholic Church,* vespers. 2. in the *Church of England,* the service of evening prayer. 3. a song sung at evening. 4. [Archaic], evening.

e·vent (i-vent′), *n.* [OFr.; L. *eventus,* event, occurrence, pp. of *evenire,* to happen; *e-,* out + *venire,* to come], 1. a happening; occurrence, especially an important occurrence. 2. a result; consequence; outcome. 3. a particular contest or item in a program: as, the pole vault, high jump, and other *events.* —*SYN.* see **occurrence.**

at all events, no matter what happens; anyhow: also **in any event.**

in the event of, if there should happen to be; in case of.

e·ven-tem·pered (ē′vən-tem′pẽrd), *adj.* not quickly angered or excited; placid; calm.

e·vent·ful (i-vent′fəl), *adj.* 1. full of outstanding events: as, an *eventful* year. 2. having an important outcome; momentous: as, an *eventful* conversation.

e·ven·tide (ē′vən-tīd′), *n.* [ME.; AS. *æfentid;* see EVEN, *n.* & TIDE, *n.*], [Archaic or Poetic], evening.

e·ven·tu·al (i-ven′chōō-əl), *adj.* [Fr. *éventuel* < L. *eventus*], 1. depending on future events or conditions; contingent or possible. 2. happening at the end of, or as a result of, a series of events; ultimate; final: as, blunders leading to *eventual* disaster.

e·ven·tu·al·i·ty (i-ven′chōō-al′ə-ti), *n.* [*pl.* EVENTUALITIES (-tiz)], a possible event, outcome, or condition; contingency: as, we must be ready for any *eventualities.*

e·ven·tu·al·ly (i-ven′chōō-ə-li, i-ven′choo-li), *adv.* [*eventual* + *-ly*], finally; ultimately; in the end.

e·ven·tu·ate (i-ven′chōō-āt′), *v.i.* [EVENTUATED (-id), EVENTUATING], [< L. *eventus* (see EVENT); + *-ate*], to happen in the end; result (often with *in*).

ev·er (ev′ẽr), *adv.* [ME.; AS. *æfre;* prob. < WGmc. bases of AS. *a,* always, ever (see AY) + *byre,* time, occurrence], 1. always; at all times: as, he is *ever* the same. 2. repeatedly. 3. at any time: as, have you *ever* seen an eclipse? 4. at all; by any chance; in any case: as, if it *ever* starts, we can go. *Ever* is also used colloquially as an intensifier: as, was she *ever* tired!

ever and anon, [Archaic], from time to time; now and then; once in a while.

ever so, [Colloq.], very; extremely.

for ever and a day, always.

Ev·er·ard (ev′ẽr-ärd′), [OFr. *Everart;* OHG. *Eberhard* < *eber,* wild boar + *hard,* strong (see HARD); hence, lit., strong (as a) wild boar], a masculine name: equivalents, Fr. *Evraud,* G. *Eberhard, Ebert,* It. *Everardo, Eberardo.*

Ev·er·est, Mount (ev′ẽr-ist, ev′rist), a peak of the Himalayas, between Tibet and Nepal: height, 29,002 ft.: the highest known mountain in the world.
Ev·er·ett (ev′ẽr-it, ev′rit), [D. *Evert, Everhart;* see EVERARD], a masculine name. *n.* 1. a city in eastern Massachusetts, near Boston: pop., 44,000. 2. a city in northwestern Washington, on Puget Sound: pop., 40,000.
Ev·er·ett, Edward (ev′ẽr-it, ev′rit), 1794–1865; American statesman, orator, and writer.
ev·er·glade (ev′ẽr-glād′), *n.* [as if < *ever* + *glade;* prob. folk etym. < lost native name], a tract of marshy land covered in places with tall grass; swampland.
the Everglades, a large tract of swampland in southern Florida: length, 140 mi.; width, 50 mi.
Everglades National Park, a national park in the southern part of the Everglades, created in 1947: area, 423 sq. mi.

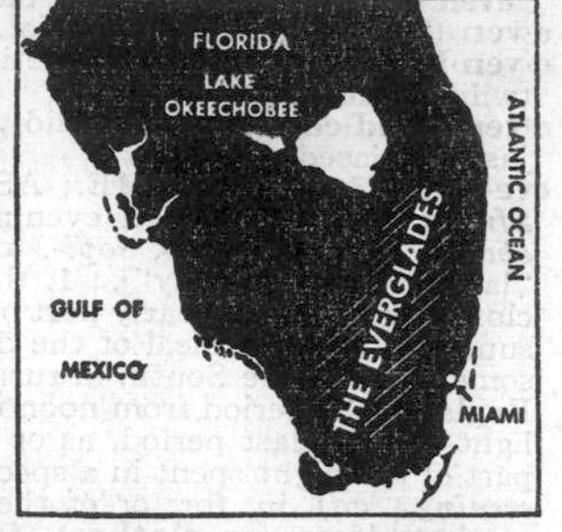

THE EVERGLADES

ev·er·green (ev′ẽr-grēn′), *adj.* having green leaves throughout the year: opposed to *deciduous.* *n.* 1. an evergreen plant or tree, including most conifers. 2. *pl.* the branches and twigs of evergreens, used for decoration.
ev·er·last·ing (ev′ẽr-las′tiŋ, ev′ẽr-läs′tiŋ), *adj.* 1. never coming to an end; lasting forever; eternal. 2. going on for a long time; lasting indefinitely; durable. 3. going on too long; seeming never to stop; happening very often. *n.* 1. eternity. 2. any of various plants whose blossoms keep their color and shape when dried; immortelle. 3. a durable ribbed woolen cloth; lasting.
the Everlasting, God.
ev·er·more (ev′ẽr-môr′, ev′ẽr-mōr′), *adv.* forever; always: used also as a substantive, as, for *evermore.*
e·ver·si·ble (ē-vũr′sə-b'l), *adj.* [< pp. of L. *evertere*], that can be everted.
e·ver·sion (ē-vũr′shən, ē-vũr′zhən), *n.* [L. *eversio* < *eversus,* pp. of *evertere*], an everting or being everted.
e·vert (ē-vũrt′), *v.t.* [L. *evertere; e-,* out, from + *vertere,* to turn], to turn outward or inside out, as an eyelid.
e·ver·tor (ē-vũr′tẽr), *n.* a muscle that everts a part, especially the foot.
ev·er·y (ev′ri, ev′ẽr-i), *adj.* [ME. *everiche, everilc;* AS. *æfre ælc,* lit., ever each], 1. all, taken individually and separately; each of all, without exception: as, *every* man among you. 2. all possible: as, he was given *every* chance to do the job. 3. each interval of (a specified number or time): as, he arrives *every* three days.
every now and then, from time to time; now and then.
every other, each alternate, as the first, third, fifth, etc., or the second, fourth, sixth, etc.
every so often, [Colloq.], every now and then.
every which way, [Colloq.], in every direction; in complete disorder.
ev·er·y·bod·y (ev′ri-bod′i, ev′ri-bud′i), *pron.* every person; everyone.
ev·er·y·day (ev′ri-dā′), *adj.* 1. daily: as, one's *everyday* routine. 2. suitable for every ordinary day: as, *everyday* shoes. 3. usual; common: as, an *everyday* occurrence.
ev·er·y·one (ev′ri-wun′, ev′ri-wən), *pron.* every person; everybody.
every one, 1. everyone. 2. every person or thing.
ev·er·y·thing (ev′ri-thiŋ′), *pron.* 1. every thing; all things; all. 2. all things pertinent. 3. the most important thing: as, money is *everything* to some people.
ev·er·y·where (ev′ri-hwâr′), *adv.* in every place; in all places.
e·vict (i-vikt′), *v.t.* [< L. *evictus,* pp. of *evincere; e-,* from + *vincere,* to conquer], in *law,* 1. formerly, to recover (property) through court judgment or superior claim. 2. to put (a tenant) out by legal procedure, as for failure to pay rent. —*SYN.* see **eject.**
e·vic·tion (i-vik′shən), *n.* an evicting or being evicted.
ev·i·dence (ev′ə-dəns), *n.* [ME.; OFr.; L. *evidentia* < *evidens,* clear, evident; *e-,* from + *videns,* ppr. of *videre,* to see], 1. the condition of being evident. 2. something that makes another thing evident; indication; sign. 3. something that tends to prove; ground for belief. 4. in *law,* *a*) something legally presented before a court, as a statement of a witness, an object, etc., which bears on or establishes the point in question: distinguished from *testimony* and *proof.* *b*) a person who presents testimony; witness: as, state's *evidence.* *v.t.* [EVIDENCED (-dənst), EVIDENCING], 1. to make evident; indicate; show. 2. to bear witness to; attest. —*SYN.* see **proof.**
in evidence, plainly visible or perceptible.
turn state's evidence, to give testimony against an accomplice.
ev·i·dent (ev′ə-dənt), *adj.* [ME.; OFr.; L. *evidens, evidentis;* see EVIDENCE], easy to see or perceive; clear; obvious; plain; patent; apparent.
SYN.—**evident** and **apparent** apply to that which can be readily perceived or easily inferred, but **evident** implies the existence of external signs (his *evident* disappointment) and **apparent** suggests the use of deductive reasoning (it's *apparent* he'll win); **manifest** applies to that which is immediately, often intuitively, clear to the understanding; **obvious** refers to that which is so noticeable or obtrusive that no one can fail to perceive it; **palpable** applies especially to that which can be perceived through some sense other than that of sight (*palpable* signs of fever); **clear** implies that there is no confusion or obscurity to hinder understanding (*clear* proof); **plain** implies such simplicity or lack of complexity as to be easily perceptible (the *plain* facts are these).
ev·i·den·tial (ev′ə-den′shəl), *adj.* 1. of, serving as, or based on evidence. 2. providing, or having the nature of, evidence.
ev·i·dent·ly (ev′ə-dənt-li, ev′ə-dent′li), *adv.* in an evident manner; clearly; obviously; plainly; apparently.
e·vil (ē′v'l), *adj.* [ME. *eville, ivel, uvel;* AS. *yfel;* akin to G. *übel;* IE. base **upo-,* up from under, as also in Eng. *up,* L. *summus*], 1. morally bad or wrong; wicked; depraved. 2. causing pain or trouble; harmful; injurious. 3. threatening or bringing misfortune; unlucky; disastrous; unfortunate: as, an *evil* hour. 4. resulting from or based on conduct regarded as immoral: as, an *evil* reputation. *n.* 1. anything morally bad or wrong; wickedness; depravity; sin. 2. anything that causes harm, pain, misery, disaster, etc. 3. [Obs.], king's evil, a skin disease. —*SYN.* see **bad.**
the Evil One, the Devil; Satan.
e·vil·do·er (ē′v'l-dōō′ẽr), *n.* a person who does evil.
e·vil-do·ing, e·vil·do·ing (ē′v'l-dōō′iŋ), *n.* a doing of evil.
evil eye, the supposed power of harming others by merely looking at them, superstitiously attributed to some people.
e·vil·ly (ē′v'l-i), *adv.* in an evil manner.
e·vil-mind·ed (ē′v'l-mīn′did), *adj.* having an evil mind or disposition; specifically, *a*) malicious; wicked. *b*) putting an evil interpretation on innocent things; salacious; prurient.
e·vince (i-vins′), *v.t.* [EVINCED (-vinst′), EVINCING], [L. *evincere,* to conquer, overcome; *e-,* out, from + *vincere,* to conquer], 1. to show plainly; indicate; make manifest; especially, to show that one has (a quality, feeling, etc.): as, he *evinced* his desire to go home. 2. [Obs.], to overcome.
e·vin·ci·ble (i-vin′sə-b'l), *adj.* that can be evinced.
e·vin·cive (i-vin′siv), *adj.* [see EVINCE], proving or tending to prove.
e·vis·cer·ate (i-vis′ə-rāt′), *v.t.* [EVISCERATED (-id), EVISCERATING], [< L. *evisceratus,* pp. of *eviscerare* < *e-,* out + *viscera;* see VISCERA], 1. to remove the entrails from; disembowel; hence, 2. to deprive of an essential part; take away the force, significance, etc. of.
e·vis·cer·a·tion (i-vis′ə-rā′shən), *n.* an eviscerating or being eviscerated.
ev·i·ta·ble (ev′ə-tə-b'l), *adj.* [L. *evitabilis*], avoidable.
ev·o·ca·ble (ev′ə-kə-b'l), *adj.* [Fr. *évocable;* see EVOKE], that can be called forth.
ev·o·ca·tion (ev′ō-kā′shən), *n.* [L. *evocatio* < pp. of *evocare*], an evoking; calling forth; summons.
e·voc·a·tive (i-vok′ə-tiv, i-vō′kə-tiv), *adj.* evoking or tending to evoke.
ev·o·ca·tor (ev′ə-kā′tẽr), *n.* a person who evokes.
e·voke (i-vōk′), *v.t.* [EVOKED (-vōkt′), EVOKING], [Fr. *évoquer;* L. *evocare; e-,* out, from + *vocare,* to call < *vox, vocis,* the voice], to call forth; summon; elicit, as a response, a mental image, etc. —*SYN.* see **extract.**
ev·o·lute (ev′ə-lōōt′, ev′ə-lūt′), *n.* [< L. *evolutus,* pp. of *evolvere;* see EVOLVE], in *geometry,* a curve that is either the locus of the center of curvature of another curve (called the *involute*), or the envelope of the perpendiculars, or normals, of the involute.

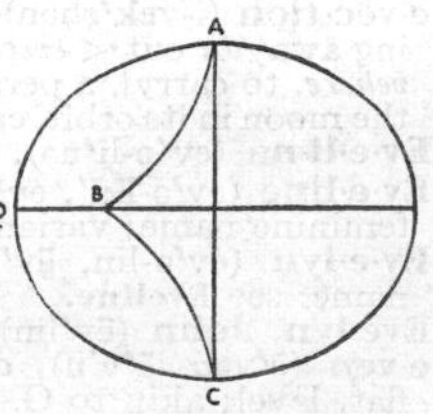

EVOLUTE
ABC, evolute of ADC

ev·o·lu·tion (ev′ə-lōō′shən, ev′'l-ū′shən), *n.* [L. *evolutio,* an unrolling or opening < *evolutus,* pp. of *evolvere;* see EVOLVE], 1. an unfolding, opening out, or working out; process of development, formation, or growth. 2. a result or product of this; thing evolved. 3. *a*) a movement that is part of a series or pattern. *b*) a pattern produced, or seemingly produced, by such a series of movements: as, the *evolutions* of a fancy skater. 4. a setting free; giving off; emission or disengaging. 5. in *biology,* *a*) the development of a species, organism, or organ from its original or rudimentary state to its present or completed state; phylogeny or ontogeny. *b*) the obsolete theory that the germ cell contains the fully developed individual in miniature form; theory of preformation. *c*) the theory, now generally accepted, that all species of plants and animals developed from earlier forms by hereditary transmission of slight variations in successive generations: see also **Darwinian theory, Lamarckism, mutation, natural selection.** 6. in *mathematics, a)* the extracting of a root from a given power: opposed to *involution. b)* the development of a curve from which an involute can be formed. 7. in *military & naval usage,* any of various movements or maneuvers by which troops, ships, etc. change formation.

ev·o·lu·tion·al (ev'ə-lōō'shən-'l, ev''l-ū'shən-'l), *adj.* evolutionary.

ev·o·lu·tion·ar·y (ev'ə-lōō'shən-er'i, ev''l-ū'shən-er'i), *adj.* 1. of evolution; developmental. 2. in accordance with the theory of evolution. 3. of or by evolutions.

ev·o·lu·tion·ist (ev'ə-lōō'shən-ist, ev''l-ū'shən-ist), *n.* 1. a person who believes in the theory of evolution. 2. a person who believes in the possibility of political and social progress by gradual, peaceful steps. *adj.* 1. of the theory of evolution. 2. of evolutionists.

e·volve (i-volv'), *v.t.* [EVOLVED (-volvd'), EVOLVING], [L. *evolvere,* to roll out or forth; *e-,* out + *volvere,* to roll], 1. to unfold; open out; work out; develop gradually. 2. to set free or give off (gas, heat, etc.); emit or disengage. 3. to produce or change by evolution. *v.i.* 1. to develop gradually; reach a highly developed state by a process of growth and change. 2. to unfold; become disclosed.

e·volve·ment (i-volv'mənt), *n.* an evolving or being evolved.

ev·on·y·mus (e-von'ə-məs), *n.* euonymus.

e·vul·sion (i-vul'shən), *n.* [L. *evulsio* < *evulsus,* pp. of *evellere,* to pull or pluck out], a pulling out by force; plucking or rooting out.

Ev·voi·a (ev'ē-ə), *n.* a large Greek island in the Aegean: area, 1,585 sq. mi.; pop., 154,000: ancient name, *Euboea;* Italian name, *Negroponte.*

ewe (ū; *dial.* yō), *n.* [ME. *ewe,* also *yowe;* AS. *eowu,* fem. of *eow,* sheep; akin to G. *au-* in *aulamm,* ewe lamb; IE. base **owi-s,* sheep, as also in L. *ovis*], a female sheep.

Ew·ell, Richard Stod·dert (stod'ẽrt ū'əl), 1817–1872; American Confederate general.

ewe-necked (ū'nekt'), *adj.* having a thin, badly arched neck: said of a horse.

ew·er (ū'ẽr), *n.* [ME.; Anglo-Fr. *ewer, ewiere;* OFr. *ewere, aiguier,* water carrier, water pitcher < LL. *aquaria,* water pitcher < L. *aquarius,* for water < *aqua,* water], a large water pitcher with a wide mouth, used with a basin on washstands.

ex (eks), *prep.* [L.], in *business & finance,* 1. without; exclusive of: as, *ex* dividend, *ex* interest. 2. out of; free of: *ex warehouse* means "free of charges until removed from the warehouse."

ex (eks), *n.* [*pl.* EXES (ek'siz)], 1. the letter X, x. 2. something shaped like an X.

ex- (eks), [< L. *ex;* Gr. *ex,* out, from], 1. (*also* iks, igz, egz: *in the following words compounded with* ex-, *although only* iks *and* igz *are given,* eks *and* egz *are often also heard*), a prefix meaning: *a) forth, from, out,* as in *expel, exert, exempt, excoriate. b) beyond,* as in *excess. c) away from, out of,* as in *expropriate, expatriate. d) thoroughly,* as in *exterminate. e) upward,* as in *exalt. f) without, not having,* as in *exanimate.* It appears as *ef-* before *f,* as in *efface; e-* before *b, d, g, h, l, m, n, r,* and *v,* as in *educe, egress, elect, emit,* etc.; often *ec-,* before *c* or *s,* as in *eccentric, ecstasy;* and, in many words of French origin, *es-,* as in *escape.* 2. [orig. < L. phrases like *ex consule, ex magistro*], a prefix meaning *former, previous, previously,* used to form hyphenated compounds with nouns denoting position, rank, occupation, status, etc., as in *ex-president, ex-convict,* etc.

ex- (eks), exo-.

Ex., Exodus.

ex., 1. examined. 2. example. 3. except. 4. excepted. 5. exception. 6. exchange. 7. excursion. 8. executed. 9. executive. 10. export. 11. extra. 12. extract.

ex·ac·er·bate (ig-zas'ẽr-bāt', ik-sas'ẽr-bāt'), *v.t.* [EXACERBATED (-id), EXACERBATING], [< L. *exacerbatus,* pp. of *exacerbare,* to exasperate, make angry < *ex-,* intens. + *acerbus,* bitter, harsh, sour], 1. to make more intense or sharp; aggravate (disease, pain, annoyance, etc.). 2. to exasperate; annoy; irritate; embitter.

ex·ac·er·ba·tion (ig-zas'ẽr-bā'shən, ik-sas'ẽr-bā'shən), *n.* [L. *exacerbatio;* see EXACERBATE], 1. intensification or aggravation, as of a disease, pain, etc. 2. irritation; annoyance; embitterment.

ex·act (ig-zakt'), *adj.* [L. *exactus* < pp. of *exigere,* to drive out, measure, determine < *ex-,* out + *agere,* to drive], 1. characterized by, requiring, or capable of accuracy of detail; methodical; very accurate; correct: as, an *exact* science. 2. leaving no room for error, deviation, or doubt; precise: as, put it on the *exact* spot. 3. strict; severe; rigorous: as, an *exact* disciplinarian. *v.t.* 1. to force payment of; extort (with *from* or *of*). 2. to demand and get by authority or force; insist on (with *from* or *of*). 3. to require; call for; make necessary. —*SYN.* see **correct, demand, explicit.**

ex·act·ing (ig-zak'tiŋ), *adj.* [ppr. of *exact*], 1. making severe or excessive demands; tyrannical; not easily satisfied: as, an *exacting* teacher. 2. demanding great care, patience, effort, etc.; arduous: as, an *exacting* job. —*SYN.* see **onerous.**

ex·ac·tion (ig-zak'shən), *n.* [ME. *exaccioun;* Fr.; L. *exactio*], 1. an exacting, as of strength, money, time, etc. 2. an excessive demand; extortion. 3. something exacted; enforced fee, tax, etc.

ex·act·i·tude (ig-zak'tə-tōōd', ig-zak'tə-tūd'), *n.* [Fr.], the quality of being exact; precision; accuracy.

ex·act·ly (ig-zakt'li), *adv.* in an exact manner; accurately; correctly; precisely: also used as an affirmative reply, equivalent to "I agree," "quite true."

ex·ag·ger·ate (ig-zaj'ə-rāt'), *v.t.* [EXAGGERATED (-id), EXAGGERATING], [< L. *exaggeratus,* pp. of *exaggerare,* to heap up, increase, exaggerate; *ex-,* out, up + *aggerare,* to heap up < *agger,* a heap, mound], 1. to think, speak, or write of (something) as greater than it is; magnify beyond the fact; overstate. 2. to increase or enlarge to an abnormal degree; overemphasize; intensify. *v.i.* to give an exaggerated description or account of something; use exaggeration.

ex·ag·ger·a·tion (ig-zaj'ə-rā'shən), *n.* 1. an exaggerating or being exaggerated. 2. a thing that is exaggerated; especially, an overstatement or hyperbole.

ex·ag·ger·a·tive (ig-zaj'ə-rā'tiv), *adj.* tending to exaggerate or characterized by exaggeration.

ex·ag·ger·a·tor (ig-zaj'ə-rā'tẽr), *n.* a person or thing that exaggerates.

ex·alt (ig-zôlt'), *v.t.* [OFr. *exalter;* L. *exaltare* < *ex-,* out, up + *altus,* high], 1. to raise on high; elevate; lift up: no longer used in the physical sense. 2. to raise in status, dignity, power, honor, wealth, etc. 3. to praise; glorify; extol. 4. to fill with joy, pride, etc.; elate. 5. to heighten or intensify the effect of (colors, etc.).

ex·al·ta·tion (eg'zôl-tā'shən), *n.* [ME. *exaltacioun;* LL. *exaltatio* < pp. of L. *exaltare*], 1. an exalting or being exalted. 2. a feeling of great or excessive joy, pride, power, etc.; elation; rapture.

ex·am (ig-zam'), *n.* [Colloq.], examination.

exam., examination.

ex·a·men (ig-zā'men), *n.* [L.; see EXAMINE], in *ecclesiastical usage,* examination.

ex·am·in·a·ble (ig-zam'ə-nə-b'l), *adj.* that can be examined.

ex·am·i·nant (ig-zam'ə-nənt), *n.* [< L. *examinans,* ppr. of *examinare*], a person who examines; examiner.

ex·am·i·na·tion (ig-zam'ə-nā'shən), *n.* [Fr.; L. *examinatio,* examination, (earlier) equilibrium], 1. an examining or being examined; investigation; inspection; scrutiny; inquiry; testing. 2. means or method of examining. 3. a set of questions asked or answers given in testing; test: abbreviated **exam.**

ex·am·ine (ig-zam'in), *v.t.* [EXAMINED (-ind), EXAMINING], [ME. *examinen;* OFr. *examiner;* L. *examinare,* to weigh, ponder, examine < *examen,* tongue of a balance, examination < **ex-agsmen* < *ex-,* out + base of *agere,* to lead, move, conduct], 1. to look at or into critically or methodically in order to find out the facts, physical condition, etc. of; investigate; inspect; scrutinize; inquire into. 2. to test by questioning carefully in order to find out the knowledge, skill, qualifications, etc. of (a student, witness, etc.). —*SYN.* see **scrutinize.**

ex·am·i·nee (ig-zam'ə-nē'), *n.* a person being examined; candidate for examination.

ex·am·ple (ig-zam'p'l, ig-zäm'p'l), *n.* [ME. *ensample, ansaumple;* OFr. *exemple, essample;* L. *exemplum,* selection from a larger quantity, sample, example < **ex-em-lom* < *eximere,* to take out < *ex-,* out + *emere,* to buy; cf. SAMPLE], 1. something selected to show the nature or character of the rest; single part or unit used as a sample; typical instance. 2. a case that serves as a warning or caution: as, the teacher made an *example* of the impudent pupil by sending him home. 3. a person or thing to be imitated; model; pattern; precedent. 4. a problem in mathematics, etc. designed to illustrate a principle or method: abbreviated **ex.** *v.t.* [EXAMPLED (-p'ld), EXAMPLING], [Obs. except in the passive], to exemplify. —*SYN.* see **instance, model.**

set an example, to behave so as to be a pattern or model for others to imitate.

without example, having no precedent.

ex·an·i·mate (ig-zan'ə-mit, ig-zan'ə-māt'), *adj.* [L. *exanimatus,* pp. of *exanimare,* to deprive of air, kill, die < *ex-,* out of + *anima,* air, spirit], 1. dead; inanimate. 2. without animation; spiritless; inert.

ex·an·them (ek-san'thəm), *n.* exanthema.

ex·an·the·ma (ek'san-thē'mə), *n.* [*pl.* EXANTHEMATA (-them'ə-tə, -thē'mə-tə), EXANTHEMAS (-thē'məz)], [LL.; Gr. *exanthēma,* efflorescence, eruption < *exanthein,* to bloom, blossom; *ex-,* out + *anthein,* to flower < *anthos,* a flower], 1. a skin eruption or rash occurring in certain infectious diseases, as scarlet fever. 2. an infectious disease characterized by such eruptions.

ex·arch (ek′särk), *n.* [LL. *exarchus;* Gr. *exarchos,* governor, superintendent; *ex-*, out, away + *archos,* a guide; see -ARCH], 1. a governor of an outlying province in the ancient Byzantine empire. 2. the supreme head of the independent Orthodox Church of Bulgaria. 3. in the *Orthodox Eastern Church,* originally, an archbishop, or patriarch; later, a bishop or other clergyman serving as a patriarch's deputy or legate.

ex·arch·ate (ek′sär-kāt′, ik-sär′kāt), *n.* [ML. *exarchatus*], the position, rank, or province of an exarch.

ex·as·per·ate (ig-zas′pə-rāt′), *v.t.* [EXASPERATED (-id), EXASPERATING], [< L. *exasperatus,* pp. of *exasperare; ex-*, out, from + *asperare,* to roughen < *asper,* rough], 1. to irritate or annoy very much; make angry; vex; incense; infuriate. 2. to intensify (a feeling, disease, etc.); aggravate. —*SYN.* see **irritate.**

ex·as·per·a·tion (ig-zas′pə-rā′shən), *n.* an exasperating or being exasperated; great irritation or annoyance.

Exc., Excellency.

exc., 1. excellent. 2. except. 3. excepted. 4. exception. 5. exchange.

Ex·cal·i·bur (eks-kal′ə-bẽr), *n.* [OFr. *Escalibor;* ML. *Caliburnus* < Celt.], in *Arthurian legend,* King Arthur's sword: in one version of the legend, he drew it out of a stone; in another, it was given to him by Vivian, the Lady of the Lake.

ex ca·the·dra (eks kə-thē′drə, eks kath′i-drə), [L., lit., from the chair], with authority, as of a rank or office; from the seat of authority: as, the Pope spoke *ex cathedra.*

ex·cau·date (eks-kô′dāt), *adj.* [*ex-* + *caudate*], in *zoology,* lacking a tail; tailless.

ex·ca·vate (eks′kə-vāt′), *v.t.* [EXCAVATED (-id), EXCAVATING], [< L. *excavatus,* pp. of *excavare; ex-*, out + *cavare,* to make hollow < *cavus,* hollow], 1. to make a hole or cavity in, as by digging; hollow out. 2. to form by hollowing out; dig: as, *excavate* a tunnel. 3. to uncover or expose by digging; unearth. 4. to dig out; remove (earth, soil, etc.).

ex·ca·va·tion (eks′kə-vā′shən), *n.* [L. *excavatio*], 1. an excavating or being excavated. 2. a hole or hollow made by excavating. 3. something unearthed by excavating. —*SYN.* see **hole.**

ex·ca·va·tor (eks′kə-vā′tẽr), *n.* a person or thing that excavates: dredges and steam shovels are *excavators.*

ex·ceed (ik-sēd′), *v.t.* [ME. *exceden;* OFr. *exceder;* L. *excedere; ex-*, out, beyond + *cedere,* to go], 1. to go or be beyond (a limit, limiting regulation, measure, etc.): as, he *exceeded* the speed limit. 2. to be more than; be greater than; surpass; outdo: as, the concert *exceeded* our expectations. *v.i.* to surpass others, as in a quality or quantity; be outstanding.

ex·ceed·ing (ik-sēd′iŋ), *adj.* [ppr. of *exceed*], surpassing; extraordinary; extreme. *adv.* [Archaic], exceedingly.

ex·ceed·ing·ly (ik-sēd′iŋ-li), *adv.* extremely; to a great degree; extraordinarily.

ex·cel (ik-sel′), *v.i. & v.t.* [EXCELLED (-seld′), EXCELLING], [OFr. *exceller;* L. *excellere,* to raise, raise oneself, surpass, excel; *ex-*, out of, from + *-cellere,* to rise, project; IE. base **qel-*, to project; hence akin to L. *culmen* (cf. CULMINATE) & Eng. *hill*], to be better or greater than, or superior to (another or others): as, he *excels* in wit.
SYN.—**excel** implies superiority in some quality, skill, achievement, etc. over all or over the one (or ones) specified (to *excel* at chess); **surpass** implies a going beyond (someone or something specified) in degree, amount, or quality (no one *surpasses* him in selfishness); **transcend** suggests a surpassing to an extreme degree (it *transcends* all understanding); **outdo** implies a going beyond someone else or a previous record in performance (he will not be *outdone* in bravery).

ex·cel·lence (ek′s'l-əns), *n.* [ME.; OFr.; L. *excellentia* < ppr. of *excellere,* to surpass, excel], 1. the fact or condition of excelling; superiority; surpassing goodness, merit, etc. 2. something in which a person or thing excels; particular virtue. 3. [E-], Excellency.

ex·cel·len·cy (ek′s'l-ən-si), *n.* [*pl.* EXCELLENCIES (-siz)], [< L. *excellentia*], 1. [E-], a title of honor applied to various persons of high position, as an ambassador, bishop, governor, etc. (with *His, Her,* or *Your*): abbreviated **Exc.** 2. [Archaic], excellence (in senses 1 & 2).

ex·cel·lent (ek′s'l-ənt), *adj.* [ME.; OFr.; L. *excellens;* see EXCELLENCE], 1. unusually good of its kind; of exceptional merit, virtue, etc.: abbreviated **exc.** 2. [Obs.], excelling; surpassing.

ex·cel·si·or (ek-sel′si-ôr′; *for n.,* ik-sel′si-ẽr), *adj. & interj.* [L., compar. of *excelsus,* lofty, high, pp. of *excellere;* see EXCEL: *n.* senses < orig. use as trademark], higher; always upward: used as a motto (as on the New York State seal) and trade-mark. *n.* 1. long, thin wood shavings used for packing or as stuffing in some upholstered furniture. 2. in *printing,* a size of type, 3 point. This line is in excelsior.

ex·cept (ik-sept′), *v.t.* [ME. *excepten;* Fr. *excepter;* L. *exceptare,* to take out, except < *exceptus,* pp. of *excipere* < *ex-*, out + *capere,* to take], to leave out or take out; exclude; omit; make an exception of. *v.i.* to object; take exception (with *against*): as, I *except* against his statement. *prep.* [ME. < L. *exceptus*], leaving out; other than; but: as, everyone present *except* me liked the play. *conj.* [Archaic], unless. Abbreviated **exc., ex.**

ex·cept·ing (ik-sep′tiŋ), *prep.* [ppr. of *except*], except; leaving out; but. *conj.* [Archaic], unless.

ex·cep·tion (ik-sep′shən), *n.* [L. *exceptio*], 1. an excepting or being excepted; omission; exclusion. 2. a person or thing omitted or excluded; case to which a rule, general principle, etc. does not apply. 3. a person or thing different from others of the same class; anything deviating from the usual pattern or course. 4. in *law,* a formal objection or reservation to court action or opinion in the course of a trial: abbreviated **ex., exc.**
take exception, 1. to object; demur. 2. to resent; feel offended.
the exception proves the rule, the exception tests the rule: often used to mean "the exception establishes the rule."

ex·cep·tion·a·ble (ik-sep′shən-ə-b'l), *adj.* liable to exception; open to objection.

ex·cep·tion·a·bly (ik-sep′shən-ə-bli), *adv.* in an exceptionable manner.

ex·cep·tion·al (ik-sep′shən-'l), *adj.* constituting, or having the nature of, an exception; unusual; extraordinary.

ex·cep·tion·al·ism (ik-sep′shən-'l-iz'm), *n.* the fact or state of being an exception to some rule or general principle.

ex·cep·tive (ik-sep′tiv), *adj.* [LL. *exceptivus*], 1. of, containing, or forming an exception. 2. inclined to take exception; captious.

ex·cerpt (ik-sũrpt′; *for n.,* ek′sẽrpt), *v.t.* [< L. *excerptus,* pp. of *excerpere,* to pick out, choose < *ex-*, out + *carpere,* to pick, pluck], to select, take out, or quote (passages from a book, etc.); make extracts from (a book, etc.); extract. *n.* a passage selected or quoted from a book, article, etc.; extract.

ex·cerp·tion (ik-sũrp′shən), *n.* [L. *excerptio*], 1. an excerpting or being excerpted. 2. something excerpted.

ex·cess (ik-ses′; *for adj., usually* ek′ses′), *n.* [ME. & OFr. *exces;* L. *excessus,* pp. of *excedere;* see EXCEED], 1. action or conduct that goes beyond the usual, reasonable, or lawful limit; hence, 2. intemperance; immoderation; overindulgence. 3. an amount or quantity greater than is necessary, desirable, usable, etc.; too much; superfluity. 4. the amount or degree by which one thing is greater or more than another; remainder; surplus. *adj.* more than usual; extra; surplus: as, *excess* profits.
in excess of, more than.
to excess, to too great an extent or degree; too much.

ex·ces·sive (ik-ses′iv), *adj.* [OFr. *excessif;* LL. *excessivus*], characterized by excess; immoderate; inordinate.
SYN.—**excessive** applies to that which goes beyond what is proper, right, or usual (*excessive* demands); **exorbitant** is applied to that which is unreasonably excessive and often connotes a greedy desire for more than is just or due (*exorbitant* prices); **extravagant** and **immoderate** both imply excessiveness resulting from a lack of restraint or of prudence (*extravagant* praise, *immoderate* laughter); **inordinate** implies a going beyond the orderly limits of convention or the bounds of good taste (his *inordinate* pride).

ex·ces·sive·ly (ik-ses′iv-li), *adv.* to an excessive extent; too much.

ex·cess-prof·its tax (ek′ses-prof′its), a tax on business profits that are greater than the statistical average of profits over a certain period of years.

exch., 1. exchange. 2. exchequer.

ex·change (iks-chānj′), *v.t.* [EXCHANGED (-chānjd′), EXCHANGING], [ME. *eschaungen;* OFr. *eschangier;* LL. *excambiare;* see EX- & CHANGE], 1. *a*) to give, hand over, or transfer (*for* another thing in return). *b*) to receive or give another thing for (something returned). 2. to give and receive (equivalent or similar things); interchange: as, John *exchanges* gifts with Mary at Christmas. 3. to give up for a substitute or alternative: as, she *exchanged* honor for wealth. *v.i.* 1. to make an exchange; barter; trade. 2. in *finance,* to pass in exchange: as, the currency of this country *exchanges* at par. *n.* 1. a giving or taking of one thing for another; trade; barter. 2. a reciprocal giving; giving and receiving: as, an *exchange* of greetings. 3. the substituting of one thing for another: as, an *exchange* of tears for smiles. 4. a thing given or received in exchange. 5. a place for exchanging; place where business is carried on by brokers, merchants, etc.: as, a stock *exchange:* abbreviated **exch., ex., exc.** 6. a central office, or a system operated by it, providing telephone communication in a community or in part of a city: usually identified by some assigned call name. 7. in *commerce & finance,* *a*) the payment of debts by negotiable drafts or bills of exchange, without actual transfer of money. *b*) a bill of exchange. *c*) a fee paid for settling accounts or collecting a draft, bill of exchange, etc. *d*) an exchanging of a sum of money of one country or of a depreciated issue for the equivalent in the money of another country or of a current issue. *e*) the rate of exchange; value of one currency in terms of the other; difference in value between currencies. *f*) *pl.* the checks, drafts, etc. presented for exchange and settlement between banks in a clearinghouse. 8. in *law,* a contract by which parties agree to exchange one thing for another. *adj.* 1. exchanged: as, an *exchange* student. 2. having to do with an exchange: as, an *exchange* broker.

ex·change·a·bil·i·ty (iks-chān'jə-bil'ə-ti), *n.* the quality or state of being exchangeable.

ex·change·a·ble (iks-chān'jə-b'l), *adj.* that can be exchanged.

exchange broker, a broker who deals in foreign bills of exchange and currencies.

ex·cheq·uer (iks-chek'ẽr, eks'chek-ẽr), *n.* [ME. *escheker,* lit., chessboard, court of revenue, treasury; OFr. *eschequier;* LL. *scaccarium,* chessboard], 1. [E-], *a*) under the Norman kings of England, an administrative and judicial state department in charge of revenue: so called from a table marked into squares, on which accounts of revenue were kept with counters. *b*) later, the British Court of Exchequer, which had jurisdiction over all cases relating to government revenue, now merged in the Queen's Bench Division of the High Court of Justice. *c*) [sometimes e-], the British state department in charge of the national revenue; hence, 2. the funds in the British treasury. 3. a treasury, as of a country or organization: abbreviated **exch., excheq.** 4. money in one's possession; funds; finances.

ex·cide (ik-sīd'), *v.t.* [EXCIDED (-id), EXCIDING], [L. *excidere* < *ex-*, out + *caedere,* to cut], to cut out.

ex·cip·i·ent (ik-sip'i-ənt), *n.* [L. *excipiens,* ppr. of *excipere;* see EXCEPT], in *pharmacy,* any of various inert substances added to a prescription to give the desired consistency or form.

ex·cis·a·ble (ik-sīz'ə-b'l), *adj.* subject to excise.

ex·cise (ik-sīz'; *for n., also* ek'sīz), *n.* [earlier *accise;* prob. < MD. *accijs;* OFr. *aceis* < LL. **accensus* < *accensare,* to tax < L. *ad-*, to + *census,* a tax], 1. a tax; a tax or duty on the manufacture, sale, or consumption of various commodities within a country, as liquor, tobacco, etc.: also **excise tax.** 2. a fee paid for a license to carry on certain occupations, sports, etc. *v.t.* [EXCISED (-sīzd'), EXCISING], to force payment of an excise from.

ex·cise (ik-sīz'), *v.t.* [EXCISED (-sīzd'), EXCISING], [< L. *excisus,* pp. of *excidere;* see EXCIDE], to cut out or away; remove, as a tumor.

ex·cise·man (ik-sīz'mən), *n.* [*pl.* EXCISEMEN (-mən)], in Great Britain, a government official who collects excises and enforces the laws concerning them.

ex·ci·sion (ik-sizh'ən), *n.* [L. *excisio* < pp. of *excidere;* see EXCIDE], 1. a cutting out or being cut out; removal by or as by cutting. 2. excommunication.

ex·cit·a·bil·i·ty (ik-sī'tə-bil'ə-ti), *n.* 1. the quality of being easily excited. 2. in *physiology,* the capacity or degree of response to the proper stimulus.

ex·cit·a·ble (ik-sī'tə-b'l), *adj.* 1. that can be excited; easily excited. 2. in *physiology,* capable of responding to the proper stimulus.

ex·cit·ant (ik-sī'tənt, ek'sə-tənt), *adj.* [L. *excitans,* ppr. of *excitare;* see EXCITE], stimulating. *n.* a stimulant.

ex·ci·ta·tion (ek'sī-tā'shən, ek'si-tā'shən), *n.* 1. an exciting or being excited; excitement. 2. in *physics, a*) the production of electricity, magnetism, or a magnetic field. *b*) the raising of an atom or molecule to an energy state higher than its normal, or ground, state.

ex·cit·a·tive (ik-sīt'ə-tiv), *adj.* exciting or tending to excite.

ex·cit·a·to·ry (ik-sīt'ə-tôr'i, ik-sīt'ə-tō'ri), *adj.* excitative.

ex·cite (ik-sīt'), *v.t.* [EXCITED (-id), EXCITING], [ME. *exciten;* OFr. *exciter;* L. *excitare,* to call out or forth, stimulate, excite < *ex-*, out + pp. of *ciere,* to call, summon], 1. to put into motion or activity; stir up: as, the injections of adrenalin *excited* the rats. 2. to arouse; call forth; provoke: as, she *excited* his jealousy. 3. to arouse the feelings or passions of: as, the news *excited* us. 4. in *electricity, a*) to produce an electric or magnetic field in. *b*) to set (an electric current) in motion. 5. in *physiology,* to produce or increase the response of (an organism, organ, tissue, etc.) to a proper stimulus. —*SYN.* see **provoke.**

ex·cit·ed (ik-sīt'id), *adj.* [pp. of *excite*], 1. emotionally aroused; agitated. 2. in *physics,* in a state of excitation.

ex·cite·ment (ik-sīt'mənt), *n.* 1. an exciting or being excited; agitation. 2. something that excites.

ex·cit·er (ik-sīt'ẽr), *n.* 1. a person or thing that excites. 2. in *electricity,* a small generator that provides field current for a large dynamo or motor.

ex·cit·ing (ik-sīt'iŋ), *adj.* [ppr. of *excite*], causing excitement; arousing keen interest, agitation, etc.; stirring; thrilling.

ex·ci·tor (ik-sī'tẽr), *n.* 1. an exciter. 2. in *physiology,* a nerve which, when stimulated, causes increased activity of the part that it supplies.

excl., 1. exclamation. 2. excluding. 3. exclusive.

ex·claim (iks-klām'), *v.i. & v.t.* [Fr. *exclamer;* L. *exclamare; ex-*, out + *clamare,* to cry, shout], to cry out; speak or say suddenly and vehemently, as in surprise, emotion, etc.

ex·cla·ma·tion (eks'klə-mā'shən), *n.* [OFr.; L. *exclamatio* < pp. of *exclamare*], 1. an exclaiming; sudden, vehement utterance; outcry. 2. something exclaimed; exclamatory word or phrase; interjection: abbreviated **excl., exclam.**

exclamation mark (or **point**), a mark (!) used after a word or sentence in writing or printing to show surprise, strong emotion, etc.: it symbolizes the unusually high pitch and stress heard in actual speech.

ex·clam·a·to·ry (iks-klam'ə-tôr'i, iks-klam'ə-tō'ri), *adj.* [< L. *exclamatus,* pp. of *exclamare* (see EXCLAIM); + *-ory*], of, containing, expressing, or using exclamation.

ex·clave (eks'klāv), *n.* [*ex-* (out) + *-clave,* as in *enclave*], a territory (of a specified country) surrounded by foreign territory: as, East Prussia was an *exclave* of Germany: distinguished from *enclave.*

ex·clo·sure (eks-klō'zhẽr), *n.* [< *ex-*, after *enclosure*], an area protected by various devices against the entrance of animal and insect pests.

ex·clud·a·ble (iks-klōōd'ə-b'l), *adj.* that can be excluded.

ex·clude (iks-klōōd'), *v.t.* [EXCLUDED (-id), EXCLUDING], [ME. *excluden;* L. *excludere* < *ex-*, out + *claudere,* to shut], 1. to refuse to admit, consider, include, etc.; shut out; keep from entering, happening, or being; reject; bar. 2. to put out; force out; expel; banish.

SYN.—**exclude** implies a keeping out or prohibiting of that which is not yet in (to *exclude* someone from membership); **debar** connotes the existence of some barrier, as legal authority or force, which excludes someone from a privilege, right, etc. (to *debar* certain groups from voting); **disbar** refers only to the expulsion of a lawyer from the group of those who are permitted to practice law; **eliminate** implies the removal of that which is already in, usually connoting its undesirability or irrelevancy (to *eliminate* waste products); **suspend** refers to the removal, usually temporary, of someone from some organization, institution, etc., as for the infraction of some rule (to *suspend* a student from school). —*ANT.* admit, include.

ex·clu·sion (iks-klōō'zhən), *n.* [L. *exclusio* < pp. of *excludere*], 1. an excluding or being excluded. 2. a thing excluded.

to the exclusion of, so as to keep out, bar, etc.

ex·clu·sion·ist (iks-klōō'zhən-ist), *n.* a person in favor of excluding another or others from something.

ex·clu·sive (iks-klōō'siv), *adj.* [ML. *exclusivus* < L. *exclusus,* pp. of *excludere*], 1. excluding all others; shutting out other considerations, happenings, existences, occupations, etc.: as, *vegetable* and *mineral* are *exclusive* terms. 2. having the tendency or power to exclude all others. 3. excluding all but what is specified: as, only is an *exclusive* particle. 4. not shared or divided; sole; single: as, an *exclusive* right to sell something. 5. excluding certain people or groups for social or economic reasons; hence, 6. snobbish; undemocratic. 7. [Colloq.], charging high prices: as, an *exclusive* shop.

exclusive of, excluding; not including or allowing for.

ex·clu·sive·ly (iks-klōō'siv-li), *adv.* with all others excluded; only.

ex·cog·i·tate (eks-koj'ə-tāt'), *v.t.* [< L. *excogitatus,* pp. of *excogitare;* see EX- & COGITATE], to think out; contrive; devise; invent.

ex·cog·i·ta·tion (eks-koj'ə-tā'shən), *n.* 1. an excogitating or being excogitated. 2. a thing excogitated.

ex·com·mu·ni·ca·ble (eks'kə-mū'ni-kə-b'l), *adj.* deserving, liable to, or punishable by excommunication.

ex·com·mu·ni·cate (eks'kə-mū'nə-kāt'; *for adj. & n., also* eks'kə-mū'ni-kit), *v.t.* [EXCOMMUNICATED (-id), EXCOMMUNICATING], [< LL. *excommunicatus,* pp. of *excommunicare;* see EX- & COMMUNICATE], to cut off from communion with a church; exclude from membership in or the privileges of a church by ecclesiastical authority. *adj.* excommunicated. *n.* an excommunicated person.

ex·com·mu·ni·ca·tion (eks'kə-mū'nə-kā'shən), *n.* 1. an excommunicating or being excommunicated. 2. a formal sentence that excommunicates.

ex·com·mu·ni·ca·tive (eks'kə-mū'nə-kā'tiv, eks'kə-mū'ni-kə-tiv), *adj.* excommunicating; of or decreeing excommunication.

ex·com·mu·ni·ca·tor (eks'kə-mū'nə-kā'tẽr), *n.* a person who excommunicates.

ex·com·mu·ni·ca·to·ry (eks'kə-mū'ni-kə-tôr'i, eks'kə-mū'ni-kə-tō'ri), *adj.* of, causing, or decreeing excommunication.

ex·co·ri·ate (ik-skôr'i-āt', ik-skō'ri-āt'), *v.t.* [EXCORIATED (-id), EXCORIATING], [< L. *excoriatus,* pp. of *excoriare* < *ex-*, out, off + *corium,* the skin], 1. to strip, scratch, or peel off the skin of; abrade; chafe; hence, 2. to denounce strongly.

ex·co·ri·a·tion (ik-skôr'i-ā'shən, eks'kō-ri-ā'shən), *n.* 1. an excoriating or being excoriated. 2. an excoriated spot; abrasion; sore.

ex·cre·ment (eks'krə-mənt), *n.* [Fr. *excrément;* L. *excrementum,* that which is sifted out, refuse < *excretus;* see EXCRETE], waste matter from the bowels; feces.

ex·cre·men·tal (eks'krə-men't'l), *adj.* of, or having the nature of, excrement.

ex·cre·men·ti·tious (eks'krə-men-tish'əs), *adj.* of, or having the nature of, excrement; excremental.
ex·cres·cence (iks-kres''ns), *n.* [L. *excrescentia*, excrescences < *excrescere*, to grow out; *ex-*, out + *crescere*, to grow], 1. a normal outgrowth; natural appendage, as fingernails, hair, etc. 2. an abnormal or disfiguring outgrowth or addition, as a bunion.
ex·cres·cen·cy (iks-kres''n-si), *n.* 1. the condition of being excrescent. 2. [*pl.* EXCRESCENCIES (-siz)], an excrescence.
ex·cres·cent (iks-kres''nt), *adj.* [L. *excrescens*, ppr. of *excrescere*], 1. forming an excrescence; growing abnormally; superfluous. 2. designating or of a sound that has entered a word as a result of the natural position of the vocal organs in pronouncing the contiguous or neighboring sounds, as the *b* in *chamber:* the term *unhistoric* is preferred by linguists.
ex·cre·ta (eks-krē'tə), *n.pl.* [L., neut. pl. of *excretus*], waste matter excreted from the body, as sweat or urine: the term is sometimes applied to feces.
ex·crete (iks-krēt'), *v.t.* & *v.i.* [EXCRETED (-id), EXCRETING], [< L. *excretus*, pp. of *excernere*, to sift out; *ex-*, out of + *cernere*, to sift (see CERTAIN)], 1. to separate (waste matter) from the blood or tissue and eliminate from the body, as through the kidneys or sweat glands. 2. in *botany*, to eliminate (waste matter) from the cells.
ex·cre·tion (iks-krē'shən), *n.* 1. the act or process of excreting. 2. waste matter excreted; sweat, urine, etc.
ex·cre·tive (iks-krē'tiv), *adj.* excreting or promoting excretion.
ex·cre·to·ry (eks'kri-tôr'i, eks'kri-tō'ri), *adj.* [LL. *excretorius*], of or for excretion. *n.* an excretory organ.
ex·cru·ci·ate (iks-kroo'shi-āt'), *v.t.* [EXCRUCIATED (-id), EXCRUCIATING], [< L. *excruciatus*, pp. of *excruciare; ex-*, intens. + *cruciare*, to torture, crucify < *crux, crucis*, a cross], 1. to torture; cause intense bodily pain to. 2. to subject to mental anguish; torment.
ex·cru·ci·at·ing (iks-kroo'shi-āt'iŋ), *adj.* [ppr. of *excruciate*], causing intense physical or mental pain; torturing; unbearably intense; agonizing; tormenting.
ex·cru·ci·a·tion (iks-kroo'shi-ā'shən, iks-kroo'si-ā'shən), *n.* 1. an excruciating or being excruciated. 2. torture; agony; anguish.
ex·cul·pa·ble (ik-skul'pə-b'l), *adj.* that can be exculpated.
ex·cul·pate (eks'kəl-pāt', ik-skul'pāt), *v.t.* [EXCULPATED (-id), EXCULPATING], [< L. *ex*, out + *culpatus*, pp. of *culpare*, to blame < *culpa*, fault], to free from blame; declare or prove guiltless.
ex·cul·pa·tion (eks'kəl-pā'shən), *n.* [ML. *exculpatio*], 1. an exculpating or being exculpated. 2. a thing that exculpates; vindication; evidence of being guiltless.
ex·cul·pa·to·ry (ik-skul'pə-tôr'i, ik-skul'pə-tō'ri), *adj.* exculpating or tending to exculpate; vindicatory.
ex·cur·rent (eks-kũr'ənt), *adj.* [L. *excurrens*, ppr. of *excurrere*, to run out, project; *ex-*, out + *currere*, to run], 1. running out or forth. 2. in *botany*, *a*) projecting beyond the tip, as the midrib of certain leaves. *b*) having an undivided main stem, as fir trees. 3. in *zoology*, of ducts, tubes, or passages whose contents flow outward.
ex·cur·sion (ik-skũr'zhən, ik-skũr'shən), *n.* [L. *excursio*, a running out or forth < *excursus*, pp. of *excurrere;* see EXCURRENT], 1. a short trip taken with the intention of returning to the point of departure; short journey for health or pleasure. 2. a round trip (on a train, bus, ship, etc.) at reduced rates, usually with limits set on the time of departure and return. 3. a group taking such a trip or journey. 4. a deviation or digression. 5. [Obs.], a military sortie; raid. 6. in *physics*, *a*) a single movement outward from the mean position in an oscillating or alternating motion. *b*) the distance involved in such a movement. *adj.* for an excursion or excursions: as, *excursion* rates. Abbreviated **ex.**
ex·cur·sion·ist (ik-skũr'zhən-ist, ik-skũr'shən-ist), *n.* a person who goes on an excursion.
ex·cur·sive (ik-skũr'siv), *adj.* 1. having the character of an excursion: as, *excursive* trips. 2. rambling; desultory: as, *excursive* reading. 3. digressive; wandering.
ex·cur·sus (eks-kũr'səs), *n.* [*pl.* EXCURSUSES (-iz), or, rarely, EXCURSUS], [L. *excursus*, a running forth, digression, pp. of *excurrere;* see EXCURRENT], 1. a detailed discussion of some point in a work, added as an appendix. 2. a digression, as in a literary work.
ex·cus·a·ble (ik-skūz'ə-b'l), *adj.* [ME.; OFr.; L. *excusabilis*], that can be excused; pardonable; justifiable.
ex·cus·a·bly (ik-skūz'ə-bli), *adv.* so as to be excusable.
ex·cus·a·to·ry (ik-skūz'ə-tôr'i, ik-skūz'ə-tō'ri), *adj.* of or containing an excuse or excuses; apologetic.
ex·cuse (ik-skūz'; *for n.*, ik-skūs'), *v.t.* [EXCUSED (-skūzd'), EXCUSING], [ME. *excusen;* OFr. *excuser;* L. *excusare*, to free from a charge < *ex-*, from + *causa*, a charge, cause], 1. to try to free (a person) of blame; seek to exonerate. 2. to try to minimize or pardon (a fault); apologize or give reasons for. 3. to consider (an offense or fault) as unimportant; overlook: as, *excuse* my rudeness. 4. to release from an obligation, duty, promise, etc. 5. to permit to leave. 6. to serve as an explanation or justification for; justify; exculpate; absolve: as, his honesty *excuses* his mistake. *n.* 1. a plea or explanation given in defense of one's conduct; apology. 2. a release from obligation, duty, etc. 3. something that excuses; extenuating or justifying factor. 4. a pretended reason for conduct; pretext.
excuse oneself, 1. to ask that one's fault be overlooked; apologize. 2. to ask for permission to leave.
exec., 1. executive. 2. executor.
ex·e·cra·ble (ek'si-krə-b'l), *adj.* [L. *execrabilis*], 1. deserving to be execrated; abominable; detestable. 2. very inferior; of very poor quality.
ex·e·cra·bly (ek'si-krə-bli), *adv.* in an execrable manner.
ex·e·crate (ek'si-krāt'), *v.t.* [EXECRATED (-id), EXECRATING], [< L. *execratus*, pp. of *execrare*, to curse < *ex-*, out + *sacrare*, to consecrate < *sacer*, sacred], 1. to call down evil upon; curse; hence, 2. to loathe; detest; abhor; abominate. *v.i.* to curse. —***SYN.*** see **curse.**
ex·e·cra·tion (ek'si-krā'shən), *n.* [L. *execratio;* see EXECRATE], 1. a cursing. 2. a detesting; loathing; abhorrence. 3. a curse; imprecation. 4. a person or thing cursed or detested.
ex·e·cra·tor (ek'si-krā'tẽr), *n.* a person who execrates.
ex·e·cra·to·ry (ek'si-krə-tôr'i, ek'si-krā'tẽr-i), *adj.* of or characterized by execration.
ex·e·cut·a·ble (ek'si-kū'tə-b'l, ig-zek'yoo-tə-b'l), *adj.* that can be executed; that can be done or effected.
ex·ec·u·tant (ig-zek'yoo-tənt), *n.* [Fr. *exécutant*, ppr. of *exécuter;* see EXECUTE], a person who does something; performer, especially on a musical instrument.
ex·e·cute (ek'si-kūt'), *v.t.* [EXECUTED (-id), EXECUTING], [ME. *executen;* OFr. *executer* < L. *executus, exsecutus*, pp. of *exequi, exsequi*, to follow out, pursue; *ex-*, out + *sequi*, to follow], 1. to follow out or carry out; do; perform; fulfill: as, he *executed* the captain's orders. 2. to carry into effect; administer (laws, etc.). 3. to put to death in accordance with a legally imposed sentence. 4. to create or produce in accordance with an idea, plan, blueprints, etc.: as, he *executed* a statue in marble. 5. to perform (a piece of music, a part in a play, etc.). 6. in *law*, to complete or make valid (a deed, contract, etc.), as by signing, sealing, and delivering. —***SYN.*** see **kill, perform.**
ex·e·cu·tion (ek'si-kū'shən), *n.* [ME. *execucion;* OFr. *execution;* L. *executio, exsecutio*], 1. an executing; specifically, *a*) a carrying out; doing; performing; fulfilling. *b*) a carrying into effect; administration. *c*) a putting to death in accordance with a legally imposed sentence. *d*) a producing according to a plan, idea, etc. 2. *a*) the manner of doing or producing something. *b*) the manner of performing a piece of music, part in a play, etc. 3. effective action, especially of a destructive nature: as, the bombs did heavy *execution*. 4. in *law*, *a*) a writ, issued by a court, giving authority to put a judgment into effect. *b*) the act of carrying out the provisions of such a writ. *c*) the making valid of a legal instrument, as by signing, sealing, and delivering.
ex·e·cu·tion·er (ek'si-kū'shən-ẽr), *n.* a person who carries out the death penalty imposed by a court; hangman, headsman, etc.
ex·ec·u·tive (ig-zek'yoo-tiv), *adj.* [< L. *executus* (see EXECUTE); + *-ive*], 1. of, capable of, or fit for, carrying out duties, functions, etc.: as, *executive* ability. 2. empowered and required to administer (laws, government affairs, etc.); administrative: distinguished from *legislative, judicial*. *n.* 1. a person, group of people, or branch of government empowered and required to administer the laws and affairs of a nation. 2. any person whose function is to administer or manage affairs, as of a corporation, school, etc. Abbreviated **exec., ex.**
Executive Mansion, 1. the White House (in Washington, D.C.), official home of the President of the United States. 2. the official home of the governor of a State.
ex·ec·u·tor (ek'si-kū'tẽr; *for 2*, ig-zek'yoo-tẽr), *n.* [ME. & OFr. *executour;* L. *executor, exsecutor* < pp. of *exequi, exsequi;* see EXECUTE], 1. a person who does something; performer of actions. 2. a person appointed to carry out the provisions of another's will: abbreviated **exr., exec.**
ex·ec·u·to·ry (ig-zek'yoo-tôr'i, ig-zek'yoo-tō'ri), *adj.* [LL. *executorius, exsecutorius* < L. *exsecutus;* see EXECUTE], 1. executive; administrative. 2. in force; effective, as a law, decree, etc. 3. in *law*, designed to be, or capable of being, put into effect at the appropriate time; contingent.
ex·ec·u·trix (ig-zek'yoo-triks), *n.* [*pl.* EXECUTRIXES (-iz), EXECUTRICES (ig-zek'yoo-trī'sēz)], [ML.], a woman executor: abbreviated **exrx.**
ex·e·dra (ek'si-drə, ik-sē'drə), *n.* [*pl.* EXEDRAE (-drē')], [L.; Gr. *exedra* < *ex-*, out + *hedra*, a seat], 1. in ancient Greece, a room, building, or outdoor area with seats, where conversations and discussions were held. 2. a large, semicircular, outdoor bench of wood or stone, usually with a high, solid back.
ex·e·ge·sis (ek'sə-jē'sis), *n.* [*pl.* EXEGESES (-sēz)], [L. < Gr. *exēgēsis*, explanation < *exēgeisthai*, to show the way, lead, explain < *ex-*, out + *hēgeisthai*, to lead, guide; IE. base **seg-, *sag-*, to trace, suspect; akin to L. *sagire*,

to perceive quickly, Eng. *seek* (see SEEK)], explanation, critical analysis, or interpretation of a word, literary passage, etc., especially of the Bible.

ex·e·gete (ek′sə-jēt′), *n.* an expert in exegesis.

ex·e·get·ic (ek′sə-jet′ik), *adj.* [Gr. *exēgētikos*], of, or having the nature of, exegesis; explanatory; expository.

ex·e·get·i·cal (ek′sə-jet′i-k′l), *adj.* exegetic.

ex·e·get·ics (ek′sə-jet′iks), *n.pl.* [construed as sing.], the study, art, or practice of exegesis.

ex·em·plar (ig-zem′plẽr, ig-zem′plär), *n.* [ME. & OFr. *exemplaire;* LL. *exemplarium* < L. *exemplum*, a pattern, copy; respelled after L. *exemplar*, of same origin], 1. a person or thing regarded as worthy of imitation; model; pattern; archetype. 2. a sample; specimen; example.

ex·em·pla·ry (ig-zem′plə-ri), *adj.* [LL. *exemplaris;* see EXEMPLAR], 1. serving as a model or example; worth imitating: as, *exemplary* behavior. 2. serving as a warning or deterrent: as, *exemplary* punishment. 3. serving as a sample, instance, type, etc.; typical.

exemplary damages, in *law*, damages beyond the actual loss, imposed as a punishment.

ex·em·pli·fi·ca·tion (ig-zem′plə-fi-kā′shən), *n.* [ML. *exemplificatio* < *exemplificare;* see EXEMPLIFY], 1. a showing by example. 2. something that exemplifies; example. 3. in *law*, a legally attested or certified copy.

ex·em·pli·fy (ig-zem′plə-fī′), *v.t.* [EXEMPLIFIED (-fīd′), EXEMPLIFYING], [ML. *exemplificare* < L. *exemplum*, an example + *facere*, to make], 1. to show by example; serve as an example of. 2. to make a legally attested or certified copy of (a document, etc.) under seal.

‡ex·em·pli gra·ti·a (eg-zem′plī grā′shi-ə), [L., lit., for the sake of example], for example; for instance: abbreviated e.g.

ex·em·plum (ig-zem′pləm), *n.* [*pl.* EXEMPLA (-plə)], [L.; see EXAMPLE], 1. an example; illustration. 2. a moralized tale or anecdote, especially as used to illustrate the text of a medieval sermon.

ex·empt (ig-zempt′), *v.t.* [ME. *exempten;* OFr. *exempter* < L. *exemptus*, pp. of *eximere*, to take out, deliver, set free < *ex-*, out + *emere*, to take, buy], to free from a rule or obligation which others must observe; excuse; release. *adj.* [L. *exemptus*], exempted; freed from a rule, obligation, etc. which binds others; excused; released. *n.* an exempted person.

ex·empt·i·ble (ig-zemp′tə-b′l), *adj.* deserving or qualified to be exempted.

ex·emp·tion (ig-zemp′shən), *n.* 1. an exempting. 2. the state of being exempted; freedom or release from a liability, obligation, etc.; immunity. 3. *a)* the exempting from an individual's taxable income of a specified sum for himself and each of his dependents. *b)* the sum specified. *c)* any such dependent.

SYN.—**exemption** implies a release from some obligation or legal requirement, especially where others are not so released (an *exemption* from the military draft); **immunity** implies freedom from or protection against something disagreeable or menacing to which all or many are liable (*immunity* from penalty, disease, taxes); **impunity** specifically implies freedom from punishment (to commit a crime with *impunity*).—*ANT.* liability.

ex·en·ter·ate (eks-en′tə-rāt′), *v.t.* [EXENTERATED (-id), EXENTERATING], [< L. *exenteratus*, pp. of *exenterare* < *ex-*, out of + Gr. *enteron*, intestine (formed in L. after Gr. *exenterizein*)], 1. [Rare], to disembowel: now only figurative. 2. in *surgery*, to take out (an organ).

ex·e·qua·tur (ek′si-kwā′tẽr), *n.* [L., 3d pers. sing., pres. subj., of *exequi, exsequi*, to follow out, perform; see EXECUTE], an official document given to a consul or commercial agent by the government of the country in which he is stationed, authorizing him to perform his duties there.

ex·e·quy (ek′si-kwi), *n.* [*pl.* EXEQUIES (-kwiz)], [OFr. *exequies* (pl.) < L. *exequiae* < *exequi;* see EXECUTE], 1. *pl.* funeral rites; obsequies. 2. a funeral procession.

ex·er·cis·a·ble (ek′sẽr-sīz′ə-b′l), *adj.* that can be exercised.

ex·er·cise (ek′sẽr-sīz′), *n.* [ME. & OFr. *exercice;* L. *exercitium* < pp. of *exercere*, to drive out (farm animals to work), hence drill, exercise < *ex-*, out + *arcere*, to enclose, shut up]. 1. active use or operation; employment: as, writing requires the *exercise* of imagination. 2. activity for the purpose of training or developing the body or mind; systematic practice; especially, bodily exertion for the sake of health. 3. *usually in pl.* a regular series of movements designed to strengthen or develop some part of the body or some faculty: as, finger *exercises* for the piano. 4. a problem or group of written examples, passages, etc. to be studied and worked out for developing technical skill, as in mathematics, grammar, etc. 5. *pl.* a series of ceremonial acts; program of speeches, etc., as at graduation. *v.t.* [EXERCISED (-sīzd′), EXERCISING], 1. to put into action; use; employ: as, he *exercised* self-control. 2. to use habitually; practice; train: used reflexively or in the passive, as, she was *exercised* in virtue. 3. to put into action for the purpose of training or developing, as the body, a muscle, the mind, a mental faculty, etc. 4. to drill (troops). 5. to take up the attention of; especially, to worry; perplex; harass; trouble: used especially in the passive, as, he was greatly *exercised* about the decision. 6. to carry out (duties, etc.); perform; fulfill. 7. to exert, wield, or have (influence, control, authority, etc.). *v.i.* to take exercise; do exercises. —*SYN.* see **practice.**

ex·er·cis·er (ek′sẽr-sīz′ẽr), *n.* 1. a person who exercises. 2. a mechanical apparatus for exercising the muscles.

ex·er·ci·ta·tion (ig-zẽr′si-tā′shən), *n.* [ME. *exercitacioun;* OFr. *exercitation;* L. *exercitatio* < *exercitare*, intens. of *exercere;* see EXERCISE], 1. exercise. 2. an essay, oration, etc. that serves as an exercise.

ex·ergue (ig-zũrg′, ek′sũrg), *n.* [Fr. *exergue*, lit., that which is out of the work, accessory, exergue of a coin; ML. *exergum* < Gr. *ex*, out, outside of + *ergon*, work], 1. the space on a coin or medal between the rim and the bottom of the picture or design: it is often used for the date, place, etc. 2. the inscription in this space.

ex·ert (ig-zũrt′), *v.t.* [L. *exertare, exsertare* < *exerere, exserere*, to stretch out, put forth; *ex-*, out + *serere*, to join, fasten together], 1. to put forth energetically; exercise; put into action: as, *exert* your will power. 2. [Obs.], to put forth; disclose; reveal.

exert oneself, to put forth effort; try or work hard.

ex·er·tion (ig-zũr′shən), *n.* 1. the act, fact, or process of exerting; active use of strength, power, etc.; exercise. 2. energetic activity; effort. —*SYN.* see **effort.**

ex·er·tive (ig-zũr′tiv), *adj.* exerting or tending to exert.

Ex·e·ter (ek′si-tẽr), *n.* a city in Devonshire, England: pop., 74,000 (est. 1946).

ex·e·unt (ek′si-ənt, ek′si-oont′), [L., 3d pers. pl., pres. indic., of *exire;* see EXIT], they go off (the stage): a stage direction applying to two or more (specified) characters.

exeunt om·nes (om′nēz), [L.], all (of the characters who are on stage) go off: a stage direction.

‡ex fa·ci·e (eks fā′shi-ē′), [L.], on the face (of a legal document, etc.).

ex·fo·li·ate (eks-fō′li-āt′), *v.t. & v.i.* [EXFOLIATED (-id), EXFOLIATING], [< LL. *exfoliatus*, pp. of *exfoliare*, to strip of leaves < *ex-*, out + *folium*, a leaf], to cast or come off in flakes, scales, or layers, as skin, bark, etc.

ex·fo·li·a·tion (eks-fō′li-ā′shən), *n.* 1. an exfoliating or being exfoliated. 2. something exfoliated, as scales, layers of bark, etc.

ex·fo·li·a·tive (eks-fō′li-ā′tiv), *adj.* causing or characterized by exfoliation.

ex·hal·ant (eks-hāl′ənt, ig-zāl′ənt), *adj.* [L. *exhalans*, ppr. of *exhalare*], 1. exhaling. 2. for exhaling. *n.* an organ or duct for exhaling.

ex·ha·la·tion (eks′hə-lā′shən, eg′zə-lā′shən), *n.* [L. *exhalatio* < pp. of *exhalare*], 1. an exhaling or being exhaled; expiration or evaporation. 2. something exhaled, as air, steam, or an odor; emanation; effluvium.

ex·hale (eks-hāl′, ig-zāl′), *v.i.* [EXHALED (-hāld′, -zāld′), EXHALING], [Fr. *exhaler;* L. *exhalare; ex-*, out + *halare*, to breathe], 1. to breathe forth air; expire. 2. to be given off or rise into the air as vapor; evaporate. *v.t.* 1. to breathe forth (air or smoke). 2. to give off (vapor, fumes, etc.).

ex·haust (ig-zôst′), *v.t.* [< L. *exhaustus*, pp. of *exhaurire*, to draw out, exhaust; *ex-*, out + *haurire*, to draw, drain], 1. to draw off or let out (air, gas, etc.), as from a container. 2. to use up; expend completely: as, he *exhausted* his resources. 3. to empty completely; draw off the contents of; drain: as, they *exhausted* the well. 4. to drain of power, resources, etc.: as, war *exhausts* nations. 5. to tire out; make very weary; weaken. 6. to deal with, study, or develop completely and thoroughly: as, she has *exhausted* the subject. *v.i.* to be discharged or let out, as gas or steam from an engine. *n.* 1. a creating of an outflowing current of air by means of a partial vacuum. 2. an apparatus for doing this, as in getting rid of fumes, dust, stale air, etc. 3. the discharge or release of used steam, gas, etc. from the cylinders of an engine at the end of every working stroke of the pistons. 4. the pipe through which such steam, gas, etc. is released. 5. something given off or let out, as fumes from a gasoline engine.

ex·haust·i·bil·i·ty (ig-zôs′tə-bil′ə-ti), *n.* the quality of being exhaustible; capacity for being exhausted.

ex·haust·i·ble (ig-zôs′tə-b′l), *adj.* that can be exhausted.

ex·haus·tion (ig-zôs′chən), *n.* 1. an exhausting. 2. the state of being exhausted; especially, *a)* great fatigue or weariness. *b)* the condition of being used up; complete consumption.

ex·haus·tive (ig-zôs′tiv), *adj.* exhausting or tending to exhaust; specifically, leaving nothing out; complete; thorough: as, *exhaustive* research.

ex·haust·less (ig-zôst′lis), *adj.* that cannot be exhausted; inexhaustible.

ex·hib·it (ig-zib′it), *v.t.* [< L. *exhibitus*, pp. of *exhibere*, to hold forth, present < *ex-*, out + *habere*, to hold, have], 1. to present or expose to view; show; display. 2. to present to public view for entertainment, instruction, advertising, judgment in a competition, etc. 3. to give evidence of; reveal: as, he *exhibited* impatience. 4. in *law*, to present (a piece of evidence, etc.) officially to a court. 5. in *medicine*, to administer (a drug, etc.) as a remedy. *v.i.* to put pictures, wares, etc. on public display. *n.* 1. a show; display; presentation. 2. a thing exhibited; especially, an object or objects displayed publicly. 3. in *law*, a document or object produced as evidence in a court. —*SYN.* see **proof, show.**

ex·hib·it·er (ig-zib'ə-tẽr), *n.* an exhibitor.

ex·hi·bi·tion (ek'sə-bish'ən), *n.* [OFr. *exhibicion;* LL. *exhibitio* < pp. of L. *exhibere;* see EXHIBIT], 1. the act or fact of showing publicly; presentation. 2. the thing or things shown. 3. a public show or display, as of pictures, merchandise, athletic feats, etc. 4. [British], a financial endowment for a university scholarship.

ex·hi·bi·tion·er (ek'sə-bish'ən-ẽr), *n.* [see EXHIBITION, 4], [British], a university student who holds a scholarship allowance.

ex·hi·bit·ion·ism (ek'sə-bish'ən-iz'm), *n.* 1. a tendency to call attention to oneself or show off one's talents, skill, etc. 2. in *psychology*, *a*) a tendency to expose parts of the body that are conventionally concealed. *b*) an instance of such exposure.

ex·hi·bi·tion·ist (ek'sə-bish'ən-ist), *n.* a person who indulges in exhibitionism.

ex·hib·i·tive (ig-zib'ə-tiv), *adj.* serving or tending to exhibit (usually with *of*).

ex·hib·i·tor (ig-zib'ə-tẽr), *n.* [LL.], one that exhibits; especially, *a*) a person, company, etc. that enters an exhibit in a fair, show, competition, etc. *b*) the owner or manager of a motion-picture theater.

ex·hib·i·to·ry (ig-zib'ə-tôr'i, ig-zib'ə-tō'ri), *adj.* [LL. *exhibitorius*], 1. exhibiting. 2. of or for exhibition.

ex·hil·a·rant (ig-zil'ə-rənt), *adj.* [Fr.; L. *exhilarans*, ppr. of *exhilarare*], exhilarating. *n.* a thing that exhilarates.

ex·hil·a·rate (ig-zil'ə-rāt'), *v.t.* [EXHILARATED (-id), EXHILARATING], [< L. *exhilaratus*, pp. of *exhilarare*, to gladden; *ex-*, intens. + *hilarare*, to gladden < *hilaris*, glad], to make cheerful, merry, or lively; enliven; stimulate; invigorate. —*SYN.* see **animate.**

ex·hil·a·ra·tion (ig-zil'ə-rā'shən), *n.* [LL. *exhiliratio*], 1. an exhilarating. 2. an exhilarated condition or feeling; liveliness; animation; high spirits; stimulation.

ex·hil·a·ra·tive (ig-zil'ə-rā'tiv), *adj.* exhilarating or tending to exhilarate.

ex·hort (ig-zôrt'), *v.t. & v.i.* [ME. *exhorten;* L. *exhortari*, to exhort; *ex-*, out + *hortari*, to urge, incite], to urge earnestly by advice, warning, etc. (*to* do what is proper or required); admonish strongly. —*SYN.* see **urge.**

ex·hor·ta·tion (eg'zôr-tā'shən, ek'sẽr-tā'shən), *n.* [ME. *exhortacion;* OFr.; L. *exhortatio* < pp. of *exhortari*], 1. an exhorting. 2. a plea, sermon, etc. that exhorts.

ex·hor·ta·tive (ig-zôr'tə-tiv), *adj.* exhortatory.

ex·hor·ta·to·ry (ig-zôr'tə-tôr'i, ig-zôr'tə-tō'ri), *adj.* [LL. *exhortatorius*], of, or having the nature of, exhortation; meant to exhort; admonitory.

ex·hu·ma·tion (eks'hyoo-mā'shən), *n.* an exhuming; disinterment.

ex·hume (iks-hūm', ig-zūm'), *v.t.* [EXHUMED (-hūmd', -zūmd'), EXHUMING], [Fr. *exhumer;* ML. *exhumare* < L. *ex*, out + *humus*, the ground], 1. to dig out of the earth; disinter; hence, 2. to unearth; disclose; reveal.

ex·i·gence (ek'sə-jəns), *n.* exigency.

ex·i·gen·cy (ek'sə-jən-si), *n.* [*pl.* EXIGENCIES (-siz)], [ML. *exigentia*], 1. the condition or quality of being exigent; urgency. 2. a situation calling for immediate action or attention. 3. *pl.* pressing needs; demands; requirements. —*SYN.* see **emergency, need.**

ex·i·gent (ek'sə-jənt), *adj.* [L. *exigens*, ppr. of *exigere*, to drive out, drive forth < *ex-*, out + *agere*, to drive], 1. calling for immediate action or attention; urgent; pressing; critical. 2. requiring more than is reasonable; demanding; exacting.

ex·i·gi·ble (ek'sə-jə-b'l), *adj.* [< L. *exigere* (see EXIGENT); + *-ible*], that can be demanded or exacted.

ex·i·gu·i·ty (ek'sə-gū'ə-ti), *n.* [L. *exiguitas* < *exiguus;* see EXIGUOUS], scantiness; littleness; smallness.

ex·ig·u·ous (ig-zig'ū-əs, ik-sig'ū-əs), *adj.* [L. *exiguus*, small < *exigere*, to weigh], scanty; little; small; meager.

ex·ile (eg'zīl, ek'sīl), *n.* [ME. *exil, exile;* OFr. *exil, essil;* L. *exilium, exsilium* < *exul, exsul*, an exile, one banished < *ex-*, out + IE. base **al-*, to wander aimlessly; hence akin to Gr. *alaomai*, I wander, roam, am banished], 1. a prolonged living away from one's country, community, etc., usually enforced; banishment, sometimes self-imposed. 2. a person in exile. *v.t.* (*also* ig-zīl'), [EXILED (-zīld, -sīld, -zīld'), EXILING], to force (a person) to leave his own country, community, etc.; banish. —*SYN.* see **banish.**

the Exile, the period in the 6th century B.C. during which the Jews were held in captivity in Babylon.

ex·il·ic (ig-zil'ik, ik-sil'ik), *adj.* of exile, especially the exile of the Jews in Babylon.

ex·ist (ig-zist'), *v.i.* [Fr. *exister;* L. *existere, exsistere*, to step or come forth, stand forth; *ex-*, out + *sistere*, to cause to stand, set, place, caus. of *stare*, to stand], 1. to be; have reality or actual being. 2. to occur; be present; be (*in* a given condition or place): as, water *exists* in milk. 3. to continue being; live.

ex·ist·ence (ig-zis'təns), *n.* [ME.; OFr.; LL. *existentia* < ppr. of L. *existere*], 1. an existing; state or fact of being. 2. life; living; continuance of being. 3. occurrence; specific manifestation. 4. a manner of existing, being, or living: as, sharecroppers have a poor *existence*. 5. a being; entity; thing that exists.

ex·ist·ent (ig-zis'tənt), *adj.* 1. existing; having existence or being. 2. existing now; present; immediate.

ex·is·ten·tial (eg'zis-ten'shəl, ek'sis-ten'shəl), *adj.* [LL. *existentialis*], of or based on existence.

ex·is·ten·tial·ism (eg'zis-ten'shəl-iz'm), *n.* a literary-philosophic cult of nihilism and pessimism, popularized in France after World War II, chiefly by Jean-Paul Sartre: it holds that each man exists as an individual in a purposeless universe, and that he must oppose his hostile environment through the exercise of his free will.

ex·it (eg'zit, ek'sit), *n.* [L. *exitium* < *exitus*, pp. of *exire*, to go out; *ex-*, out + *ire*, to go], 1. an actor's departure from the stage. 2. a going out; departure. 3. a way out; doorway or passage leading out. 4. [L., 3d pers. sing., pres. indic., of *exire*], he (or she) goes off (the stage): a stage direction for a (specified) character.

‡ex li·bris (eks lī'bris, eks lē'bris), [L., lit., from the books (of)], 1. belonging to the library of: an inscription followed by the owner's name, often used on book plates. 2. a bookplate. Abbreviated **ex lib.**

Ex·moor (eks'moor), *n.* a moorland region in Somersetshire and Devonshire, England.

‡ex ni·hi·lo ni·hil fit (eks nī'hil-ō nī'hil fit), [L.], out of nothing comes nothing; nothing is made from nothing.

ex·o- (ek'sō, ek'sə), [< Gr. *exō*, without; cf. ECTO-], a prefix meaning *outside, outer, outer part*, as in *exogamy, exogenous*: also, before a vowel, **ex-.**

ex·o·carp (ek'sō-kärp'), *n.* [*exo-* + *-carp*], the outer layer of a ripened ovary or fruit; epicarp.

Exod., Exodus.

ex·o·don·ti·a (ek'sə-don'shə, ek'sə-don'shi-ə), *n.* [Mod. L. < L. *ex*, out + Gr. *odōn, odontos*, tooth; + *-ia*], the branch of dentistry having to do with the extraction of teeth.

ex·o·dus (ek'sə-dəs), *n.* [L. < Gr. *exodos*, a going out < *ex-*, out + *hodos*, way], 1. a going out or forth; departure. 2. [E-], the departure of the Israelites from Egypt (with *the*). 3. [E-], the second book of the Old Testament, which describes this: abbreviated **Ex., Exod.**

ex·o·en·zyme (ek'sō-en'zīm, ek'sō-en'zim), *n.* an ectoenzyme.

ex of·fi·ci·o (eks ə-fish'i-ō'), [L., lit., from office], by virtue of one's office, or position: abbreviated **e.o.**

ex·o·gam·ic (ek'sə-gam'ik), *adj.* of exogamy.

ex·og·a·mous (eks-og'ə-məs), *adj.* of, having the nature of, or characterized by, exogamy.

ex·og·a·my (eks-og'ə-mi), *n.* [*exo-* + *-gamy*], the custom, often inviolable, of marrying only outside the tribe, clan, etc.; outbreeding: opposed to *endogamy*.

ex·o·gen (ek'sə-jen'), *n.* [*exo-* + *-gen*], a seed plant that grows by adding layers on its outside; dicotyledon.

ex·og·e·nous (eks-oj'ə-nəs), *adj.* [*exo-* + *-genous*], 1. developing from without; originating externally. 2. in *biology*, growing or developing from or on the outside.

ex·on·er·ate (ig-zon'ə-rāt'), *v.t.* [EXONERATED (-id), EXONERATING], [< L. *exoneratus*, pp. of *exonerare*, to disburden; *ex-*, out + *onerare*, to load < *onus, oneris*, a load, burden], 1. originally, to relieve of (a burden, obligation, etc.); unload; hence, 2. to free (a person) from a charge or the imputation of guilt; declare or prove blameless; exculpate. —*SYN.* see **absolve.**

ex·on·er·a·tion (ig-zon'ə-rā'shən), *n.* [L. *exoneratio*], an exonerating or being exonerated.

ex·on·er·a·tor (ig-zon'ə-rā'tẽr), *n.* one who exonerates.

ex·o·path·ic (ek'sə-path'ik), *adj.* [*exo-* + *-pathic*], designating or of a disease having its cause or source outside the body.

ex·oph·thal·mi·a (ek'sof-thal'mi-ə), *n.* [Mod.L. < Gr. *exophthalmos*, with prominent eyes; *ex-*, out + *ophthalmos*, an eye], abnormal protrusion of the eyeball, caused by disease: also **exophthalmos, exophthalmus.**

ex·oph·thal·mic (ek'sof-thal'mik), *adj.* of, or having the nature of, exophthalmia.

ex·oph·thal·mos (ek'sof-thal'mos), *n.* exophthalmia.

ex·oph·thal·mus (ek'sof-thal'məs), *n.* exophthalmia.

ex·o·ra·ble (ek'sẽr-ə-b'l), *adj.* [L. *exorabilis* < *exorare*, to move by entreaty; *ex-*, out + *orare*, to pray], that can be persuaded or moved by pleas.

ex·or·bi·tance (ig-zôr'bə-təns), *n.* [L. *exorbitans*], 1. a going beyond what is right or reasonable, as in demands, prices, etc.; extravagance. 2. [Archaic], lawlessness.

ex·or·bi·tan·cy (ig-zôr'bə-tən-si), *n.* [*pl.* EXORBITANCIES (-siz)], exorbitance.

ex·or·bi·tant (ig-zôr'bə-tənt), *adj.* [L. *exorbitans*, ppr. of *exorbitare*, to go out of the track < *ex-*, out + *orbita*, a track, orbit], going beyond what is reasonable, just, proper, usual, etc.; excessive; extravagant; immoderate: said of charges, prices, etc. —*SYN.* see **excessive.**

ex·or·bi·tant·ly (ig-zôr'bə-tənt-li), *adv.* to an exorbitant degree; extravagantly.
ex·or·cise (ek'sôr-sīz'), *v.t.* [EXORCISED (-sīzd'), EXORCISING], [OFr. *exorciser;* LL. *exorcizare;* New Testament Gr. *exorkiein,* to drive away an evil spirit by adjuration, (earlier) to swear a person, administer an oath < Gr. *ex-,* out + *horkizein,* to make one swear < *horkos,* an oath; cf. CONJURE], 1. to drive (a supposed evil spirit or spirits) out or away by ritual charms or incantation. 2. to summon or command (such a spirit or spirits). 3. to free from such a spirit or spirits. Also spelled **exorcize.**
ex·or·cism (ek'sôr-siz'm), *n.* [LL. *exorcismus;* Gr. *exorkismos*], 1. an exorcising. 2. a verbal formula or ritual used in exorcising.
ex·or·cist (ek'sôr-sist), *n.* a person who exorcises.
ex·or·cize (ek'sôr-sīz'), *v.t.* [EXORCIZED (-sīzd'), EXORCIZING], to exorcise.
ex·or·di·al (ig-zôr'di-əl, ik-sôr'di-əl), *adj.* containing, or having the nature of, an exordium; introductory.
ex·or·di·um (ig-zôr'di-əm, ik-sôr'di-əm), *n.* [*pl.* EXORDIUMS (-əmz), EXORDIA (-ə)],[L. < *exordiri,* to begin a web, hence begin (a speech, etc.); *ex-,* from + *ordiri,* to begin], 1. a beginning. 2. the opening part of a speech, treatise, etc.
ex·o·skel·e·ton (ek'sō-skel'ə-t'n), *n.* in *zoology,* any hard external supporting structure, as the shell of an oyster, lobster, etc.: distinguished from *endoskeleton.*
ex·os·mo·sis (ek'sos-mō'sis, ek'soz-mō'sis), *n.* [Mod.L.; *ex-* + *osmosis*], in osmosis, the slower diffusion of the more dense fluid through the semipermeable membrane to mingle with the less dense: opposed to *endosmosis.*
ex·o·spore (ek'sə-spôr', ek'sə-spōr'), *n.* [*exo-* + *spore*], in *botany,* the outer layer of the covering of a spore.
ex·os·to·sis (ek'sos-tō'sis), *n.* [*pl.* EXOSTOSES (-sēz)], [Mod.L.; Gr. *exostōsis* < *ex-,* outside + *osteon,* a bone], an abnormal bony growth on the surface of a bone or tooth.
ex·o·ter·ic (ek'sə-ter'ik), *adj.* [LL. *exotericus;* Gr. *exōterikos,* external < compar. of *exō,* outside], 1. of the outside world; external. 2. not intended for only a chosen few or an inner group of disciples; suitable for outsiders or the uninitiated. 3. that can be understood by the public; popular. Opposed to *esoteric.*
ex·o·ter·i·cal·ly (ek'sə-ter'i-k'l-i, ek'sə-ter'ik-li), *adv.* in an exoteric manner.
ex·o·ther·mic (ek'sō-thūr'mik), *adj.* [*exo-* + *thermic*], designating or of a chemical change in which there is a liberation of heat, as in combustion: opposed to *endothermic.*
ex·ot·ic (ig-zot'ik), *adj.* [L. *exoticus;* Gr. *exōtikos* < *exō,* outside], 1. foreign; imported; hence, 2. having the charm or fascination of the unfamiliar; strangely beautiful, enticing, etc. *n.* 1. a foreign or imported thing 2. a plant that is not native.
ex·ot·i·cal·ly (ig-zot'i-k'l-i, ig-zot'ik-li), *adv.* in an exotic manner.
ex·o·tox·in (ek'sō-tok'sin), *n.* any of a group of toxic substances excreted by certain disease-producing bacteria: also called *true toxin.*
exp., 1. expenses. 2. export. 3. exported. 4. express.
ex·pand (ik-spand'), *v.t.* [L. *expandere; ex-,* out + *pandere,* to spread, extend], 1. to spread out; open out; stretch out; unfold: as, the eagle *expanded* his wings. 2. to cause to fill more space; increase in size, bulk, area, etc.; enlarge; dilate; extend. 3. to enlarge upon (a topic, idea, etc.); develop in detail. 4. in *algebra,* to develop (an equation, etc.) to its completed or enlarged form through a series of steps. *v.i.* to become expanded; spread out, unfold, enlarge, etc.
SYN.—**expand** implies an increasing in size, bulk, or volume and is the broadest term here, being applicable when the enlarging force operates from either the inside or the outside or when the increase comes about by unfolding, puffing out, spreading, or opening; **swell** implies expansion beyond the normal limits or size; **distend** implies a swelling as a result of pressure from within that forces a bulging outward; **inflate** suggests the use of air or gas, or of something insubstantial, to distend or swell a thing; **dilate** suggests a widening or stretching of something circular. —*ANT.* contract.
ex·pand·ed (ik-span'did), *adj.* [pp. of *expand*], in *printing,* extended.
ex·panse (ik-spans'), *n.* [ME. *expans* < L. *expansum* < *expansus,* pp. of *expandere;* see EXPAND], 1. a large, open area or unbroken surface; wide extent; great breadth. 2. expansion. 3. the amount of expansion.
ex·pan·si·bil·i·ty (ik-span'sə-bil'ə-ti), *n.* capacity for expansion.
ex·pan·si·ble (ik-span'sə-b'l), *adj.* that can be expanded.
ex·pan·sile (ik-span's'l), *adj.* 1. expansible. 2. tending to expand. 3. of or characteristic of expansion.
ex·pan·sion (ik-span'shən), *n.* [LL. *expansio* < L. *expansus;* see EXPANSE], 1. an expanding or being expanded; enlargement; dilatation. 2. an expanded thing or part. 3. the amount, degree, or extent of expansion. 4. a development or full treatment, as of a topic. 5. in *algebra,* the process or result of developing an equation, etc. to a fuller form through a series of steps. 6. in *mechanics,* the expanding in volume of steam in the cylinder of a steam engine after cutoff, or of gas in the cylinder of an internal-combustion engine after explosion.
expansion bolt, a bolt with an attachment that expands and acts as a wedge as it is screwed inward, used in holes drilled in stone, concrete, etc.
ex·pan·sion·ism (ik-span'shən-iz'm), *n.* the policy of expanding a nation's territory or its sphere of influence, often at the expense of other nations.
ex·pan·sion·ist (ik-span'shən-ist), *n.* a person who believes in or advocates expansionism.
ex·pan·sive (ik-span'siv), *adj.* [< L. *expansus* (see EXPANSE); + *-ive*], 1. tending to expand; that can expand. 2. of, or working by means of, expansion. 3. widely extended; broad; extensive; comprehensive. 4. characterized by a free and generous nature; sympathetic; demonstrative; open: as, an *expansive* person. 5. in *psychiatry,* characterized by expansiveness.
ex·pan·sive·ness (ik-span'siv-nis), *n.* 1. the quality or state of being expansive. 2. in *psychiatry,* a state characterized by overestimation of the ego, delusions of grandeur, etc.; megalomania.
ex par·te (eks pär'ti), [L., lit., from the side or party; see EX- & PART], on, or in the interest of, one side only; one-sided.
ex·pa·ti·ate (ik-spā'shi-āt'), *v.i.* [EXPATIATED (-id), EXPATIATING], [< L. *expatiatus,* pp. of *expatiari, exspatiari,* to go out of one's course, wander; *ex-,* out + *spatiari,* to walk, roam < *spatium,* space], 1. originally, to roam or wander freely; hence, 2. to speak or write at length; elaborate or enlarge (*on* or *upon*).
ex·pa·ti·a·tion (ik-spā'shi-ā'shən), *n.* 1. an expatiating. 2. a lengthy account of something.
ex·pa·tri·ate (eks-pā'tri-āt'; *for adj. & n., also* eks-pā'tri-it), *v.t. & v.i.* [EXPATRIATED (-id), EXPATRIATING], [< L. *ex,* out of + *patria,* native country, fatherland < *pater,* father], 1. to drive (a person) from his native land; exile. 2. to withdraw (oneself) from one's native land. *adj.* expatriated. *n.* an expatriated person. —*SYN.* see **banish.**
ex·pa·tri·a·tion (eks-pā'tri-ā'shən, eks'pā-tri-ā'shən), *n.* an expatriating or being expatriated.
ex·pect (ik-spekt'), *v.t.* [L. *expectare, exspectare; ex-,* out + *spectare,* to look < pp. of *specere,* to see], 1. originally, to await; wait for. 2. to look forward to; look for as likely to occur or appear; anticipate: as, I *expected* you yesterday. 3. to look for as due, proper, or necessary: as, some parents *expect* too much from their children. 4. [Colloq.], to suppose; presume; guess.
be expecting, [Colloq.], to be pregnant.
SYN.—**expect** implies a considerable degree of confidence that an event will happen (to *expect* guests to dinner); **anticipate** implies a looking forward to something with a foretaste of the pleasure or distress it promises, or a realizing of something in advance, and a taking steps to meet it (to *anticipate* trouble); **hope** implies a desire for something, accompanied by some confidence in the belief that it can be realized (to *hope* for the best); **await** implies a waiting for, or a being ready for a person or thing (a hearty welcome *awaits* you).
ex·pect·ance (ik-spek'təns), *n.* expectancy.
ex·pect·an·cy (ik-spek'tən-si), *n.* [*pl.* EXPECTANCIES (-siz)], [ML. *expectantia* < L. *expectans;* see EXPECTANT], 1. an expecting or being expected; expectation. 2. that which is expected, especially on a statistical basis: as, life *expectancy.*
ex·pect·ant (ik-spek'tənt), *adj.* [ME.; OFr.; L. *expectans,* ppr. of *expectare*], expecting; specifically, *a)* having or showing expectation. *b)* waiting, as for a position, etc. *n.* a person who expects something.
expectant mother, a pregnant woman.
ex·pec·ta·tion (ek'spek-tā'shən), *n.* [L. *expectatio* < pp. of *expectare;* see EXPECT], 1. a looking forward to; anticipation. 2. a looking for as due, proper, or necessary. 3. a thing looked forward to. 4. *also pl.* a reason or warrant for looking forward to something; prospect for the future, as of advancement or prosperity. 5. the degree of probability of the occurrence, duration, etc. of something.
in expectation, in the state of being looked for.
expectation of life, the number of years that a person can expect to live after any given age, as indicated by statistics of mortality.
ex·pect·a·tive (ik-spek'tə-tiv), *adj.* [ML. *expectativus*], of or characterized by expectation.
ex·pec·to·rant (ik-spek'tə-rənt), *adj.* [L. *expectorans,* ppr. of *expectorare*], causing or stimulating expectoration. *n.* any expectorant medicine.
ex·pec·to·rate (ik-spek'tə-rāt'), *v.t. & v.i.* [EXPECTORATED (-id), EXPECTORATING], [< L. *expectoratus,* pp. of *expectorare,* to banish from the mind, expel from the breast < *ex-,* out + *pectus, pectoris,* breast], 1. to

cough up and spit (phlegm, mucus, etc.). 2. to spit.
ex·pec·to·ra·tion (ik-spek'tə-rā'shən), *n.* 1. an expectorating. 2. what is expectorated, as phlegm, etc.
ex·pe·di·ence (ik-spē'di-əns), *n.* expediency.
ex·pe·di·en·cy (ik-spē'di-ən-si), *n.* [*pl.* EXPEDIENCIES (-siz)], 1. the quality or state of being expedient; suitability for a given purpose; appropriateness to the conditions. 2. the doing or consideration of what is of selfish use or advantage rather than what is right or just; self-interest.
ex·pe·di·ent (ik-spē'di-ənt), *adj.* [ME.; OFr.; L. *expediens*, ppr. of *expedire;* see EXPEDITE], 1. useful for effecting a desired result; suited to the circumstances or the occasion; advantageous; convenient. 2. based on or offering what is of use or advantage rather than what is right or just; guided by self-interest; advisable; politic. *n.* 1. an expedient thing; means to an end. 2. a device used in an emergency; makeshift; resource. —*SYN.* see **resource.**
ex·pe·di·en·tial (ik-spē'di-en'shəl), *adj.* based on or guided by expediency.
ex·pe·dite (ek'spi-dīt'), *v.t.* [EXPEDITED (-id), EXPEDITING], [< L. *expeditus*, pp. of *expedire*, lit., to free one caught by the feet, hence hasten, dispatch < *ex-*, out + *pes*, *pedis*, foot], 1. to speed up or make easy the progress or action of; hasten; facilitate. 2. to do quickly. 3. [Rare], to send off; dispatch; issue officially. *adj.* 1. without impediment; free. 2. prompt, ready, or alert. 3. convenient.
ex·pe·dit·er (ek'spi-dīt'ẽr), *n.* a person who expedites, especially one employed by an industry, government agency, etc. to expedite urgent or involved projects.
ex·pe·di·tion (ek'spi-dish'ən), *n.* [Fr.; L. *expeditio* < pp. of *expedire;* see EXPEDITE], 1. a sending forth or embarking upon a voyage, march, etc. for some definite purpose, as exploration or battle. 2. a journey for such a purpose. 3. the people, ships, equipment, etc. on such a journey. 4. efficient speed; dispatch. —*SYN.* see **haste, trip.**
ex·pe·di·tion·ar·y (ek'spi-dish'ən-er'i), *adj.* of or constituting an expedition.
ex·pe·di·tious (ek'spi-dish'əs), *adj.* done with or characterized by expedition; efficient and speedy; prompt.
ex·pel (ik-spel'), *v.t.* [EXPELLED (-speld'), EXPELLING], [ME. *expellen;* L. *expellere; ex-*, out + *pellere*, to thrust, drive], 1. to drive out by force; make leave; eject. 2. to dismiss or send away by authority; deprive of rights, membership, etc.: as, he was *expelled* from school because of misconduct. —*SYN.* see **eject.**
ex·pel·la·ble (ik-spel'ə-b'l), *adj.* that can be or deserves to be expelled.
ex·pel·lant, ex·pel·lent (ik-spel'ənt), *adj.* expelling or tending to expel. *n.* an expellant medicine.
ex·pend (ik-spend'), *v.t.* [L. *expendere*, to weigh out, pay out; *ex-*, out + *pendere*, to weigh], to spend; consume by using; use up.
ex·pend·a·ble (ik-spen'də-b'l), *adj.* 1. that can be expended. 2. in *military usage*, *a)* designating supplies or equipment expected to be used up or destroyed in service and therefore not entered on a certificate of expenditure; hence, *b)* designating equipment or men considered replaceable and therefore worth sacrificing to gain an objective.
ex·pend·i·ture (ik-spen'di-chẽr), *n.* [< ML. *expenditus*, irreg. pp. for L. *expendere;* + *-ure*], 1. an expending; spending or using up of money, time, etc. 2. the amount of money, time, etc. expended.
ex·pense (ik-spens'), *n.* [ME.; Anglo-Fr. *expense;* LL. *expensa* (*pecunia*), paid out (money); L. *expensum;* neut. of *expensus*, pp. of *expendere*], 1. an expending; paying out of money. 2. *also in pl.* cost; fee; charge. 3. *pl.* *a)* charges met with in carrying out a task, one's work, etc. *b)* money to pay for these charges: abbreviated **exp.** 4. a cause of spending; drain on one's finances: as, a car can be a considerable *expense.* 5. loss; sacrifice.
at the expense of, 1. with the payment borne by. 2. with the loss of.
ex·pen·sive (ik-spen'siv), *adj.* necessitating or involving much expense; high-priced; dear. —*SYN.* see **costly.**
ex·pe·ri·ence (ik-spêr'i-əns), *n.* [ME.; OFr.; L. *experientia*, trial, proof, experiment < *experiens*, ppr. of *experiri*, to try, put to test; *ex-*, out + base appearing in *peritus*, experienced < IE. base **per-*, to attempt, venture; akin to Gr. *peira*, experience, attempt, and prob. to AS. *frasian*, to inquire, try], 1. an actual living through an event or events; personally undergoing or observing something or things in general as they occur. 2. anything observed or lived through: as, our trip was a pleasant *experience.* 3. all that has happened to one; everything that one has seen or done: as, it hasn't happened in my *experience.* 4. effect on one of anything or everything that has happened to him; individual reaction to events, feelings, etc.: as, what was your *experience* with the work? 5. *a)* activity that includes training, observation of practice, and personal participation. *b)* the period of such activity: as, teaching *experience.* 6. knowledge, skill, or practice resulting from this. *v.t.* [EXPERIENCED (-ənst), EXPERIENCING], to have experience of; undergo; feel; meet with.
ex·pe·ri·enced (ik-spêr'i-ənst), *adj.* 1. having had much experience, as in a particular occupation or activity. 2. having learned from experience; made wise, competent, etc. by experience.
experience table, a table showing life expectancy at given ages, based upon the experience of actuaries.
ex·pe·ri·en·tial (ik-spêr'i-en'shəl), *adj.* [< L. *experientia;* + *-al*], of or based on experience; empirical.
ex·per·i·ment (ik-sper'ə-mənt), *n.* [ME.; OFr.; L. *experimentum*, a trial, test < *experiri;* see EXPERIENCE], 1. a test or trial of something; specifically, *a)* any action or process undertaken to discover something not yet known or to demonstrate something known. *b)* something tried to find out whether it will be effective: as, giving students complete freedom to choose their courses is an educational *experiment.* 2. the conducting of such tests or trials; experimentation. *v.i.* to make an experiment or experiments. —*SYN.* see **trial.**
ex·per·i·men·tal (ik-sper'ə-men't'l, ek'sper-ə-men't'l), *adj.* 1. of or based on experience rather than theory or authority. 2. based on, tested by, or having the nature of, experiment. 3. for the sake of experiment; testing; hence, 4. tentative. 5. of or used for experiments.
ex·per·i·men·tal·ism (ik-sper'ə-men't'l-iz'm, ek'sper-ə-men't'l-iz'm), *n.* 1. the theory or practice of depending on experimentation; empiricism. 2. fondness for making experiments.
ex·per·i·men·tal·ly (ik-sper'ə-men't'l-i), *adv.* 1. by experiments. 2. as an experiment.
ex·per·i·men·ta·tion (ik-sper'ə-men-tā'shən), *n.* an experimenting; using experiments.
ex·pert (ek'spẽrt; *also, for adj.*, ik-spũrt'), *adj.* [ME.; OFr.; L. *expertus*, pp. of *experiri;* see EXPERIENCE], 1. very skillful; having much training and knowledge in some special field. 2. of or from an expert: as, an *expert* opinion. *n.* [Fr.], 1. a person who is very skillful or highly trained and informed in some special field. 2. in the *United States Army*, *a)* the highest of the three ratings of proficiency of a rifleman: see also **sharpshooter, marksman.** *b)* a soldier with this rating.
ex·pert·ise (ek'spẽr-tēz'), *n.* [Fr.], the skill or knowledge of an expert.
ex·pi·a·ble (ek'spi-ə-b'l), *adj.* [Fr.], that can be expiated.
ex·pi·ate (ek'spi-āt'), *v.t.* [EXPIATED (-id), EXPIATING], [< L. *expiatus*, pp. of *expiare*, to make satisfaction or atonement; *ex-*, out + *piare*, to appease, propitiate < *pius*, devout, pious], to make amends or reparation for (wrongdoing or guilt); atone for; pay the penalty of.
ex·pi·a·tion (ek'spi-ā'shən), *n.* [L. *expiatio;* see EXPIATE], 1. atonement; making amends for wrongdoing or guilt. 2. the means of atonement; amends.
ex·pi·a·tor (ek'spi-ā'tẽr), *n.* a person who expiates.
ex·pi·a·to·ry (ek'spi-ə-tôr'i, ek'spi-ə-tō'ri), *adj.* [LL. *expiatorius*], expiating; intended or serving to expiate.
ex·pi·ra·tion (ek'spə-rā'shən), *n.* [L. *expiratio*, *exspiratio* < pp. of *expirare;* see EXPIRE], 1. a breathing out, as of air from the lungs. 2. *a)* something breathed out. *b)* a sound, etc. made by breathing out. 3. a breathing one's last; dying; hence, 4. a coming to an end; close.
ex·pir·a·to·ry (ik-spīr'ə-tôr'i, ik-spīr'ə-tō'ri), *adj.* of expiration; relating to breathing out air from the lungs.
ex·pire (ik-spīr'), *v.t.* [EXPIRED (-spīrd'), EXPIRING], [Fr. *expirer;* L. *expirare, exspirare; ex-*, out + *spirare*, to breathe], 1. to breathe out: as, air is *expired* from the lungs. 2. [Obs.], to give off (an odor, etc.). *v.i.* 1. to breathe out air from the lungs. 2. to breathe one's last breath; die. 3. to come to an end; terminate; stop; cease: as, the lease *expires* soon. —*SYN.* see **die.**
ex·pi·ry (ik-spī'ri, ek'spə-ri), *n.* [*pl.* EXPIRIES (-riz)], [< *expire* + *-y*], 1. a coming to an end; termination. 2. [Archaic], death.
ex·plain (iks-plān'), *v.t.* [L. *explanare*, to flatten, spread out; *ex-*, out + *planare*, to make level < *planus*, level, plain; sp. influenced by *plain*], 1. to make clear, plain, or understandable. 2. to give the meaning or interpretation of; expound. 3. to account for; state reasons for. *v.i.* to give an explanation.
explain away, to state reasons for so as to justify or make understandable.
explain oneself, 1. to make clear what one means. 2. to give reasons justifying one's conduct.
SYN.—**explain** implies a making clear or intelligible of something that is not known or understood (to *explain* how a machine operates); **expound** implies a systematic and thorough explanation, often one made by a person having expert knowledge (to *expound* a theory); **explicate** implies a scholarly analysis or exposition that is developed in detail (the *explication* of a Biblical passage); **elucidate** implies a shedding light upon by clear and specific explanation, illustration, etc. (to *elucidate* the country's foreign policy); to **interpret** is to bring out meanings not immediately apparent, as by translation, searching insight, or special knowledge (how do you *interpret* his silence?); **construe** suggests a particular interpretation of something whose meaning is ambiguous (his statement is not to be lightly *construed*).
ex·pla·na·tion (eks'plə-nā'shən), *n.* [L. *explanatio* < pp. of *explanare*], 1. an explaining. 2. something that explains. 3. the interpretation, meaning, or sense given

in explaining. 4. a mutual defining of terms, declaration of motives, etc. to clear up a misunderstanding or settle a dispute.

ex·plan·a·to·ri·ly (iks-plan'ə-tôr'ə-li, iks-plan'ə-tō'rə-li), ***adv.*** in an explanatory manner; as an explanation.

ex·plan·a·to·ry (iks-plan'ə-tôr'i, iks-plan'ə-tō'ri), ***adj.*** [LL. *explanatorius*], tending or intended to explain.

ex·ple·tive (eks'pli-tiv), ***n.*** [LL. *expletivus*, serving to fill < L. *expletus*, pp. of *explere*, to fill; *ex-*, out, up + *plere*, to fill], 1. an oath or exclamation. 2. a word, phrase, etc. not needed for the sense but used merely to fill out a sentence or metrical line, for rhythm, balance, etc. ***adj.*** used to fill out a sentence, line, etc.

ex·ple·to·ry (eks'plə-tôr'i, eks'plə-tō'ri), ***adj.*** expletive.

ex·pli·ca·ble (eks'pli-kə-b'l; *sometimes* iks-plik'ə-b'l), ***adj.*** [L. *explicabilis* < *explicare;* see EXPLICATE], that can be explained.

ex·pli·cate (eks'pli-kāt'), ***v.t.*** [EXPLICATED (-id), EXPLICATING], [< L. *explicatus*, pp. of *explicare*, to unfold, spread out; *ex-*, out + *plicare*, to fold], to make clear or explicit (something obscure or implied); explain. —***SYN.*** see **explain.**

ex·pli·ca·tion (eks'pli-kā'shən), ***n.*** [Fr.; L. *explicatio;* see EXPLICATE], 1. an exposition and interpretation; explanation. 2. a detailed account, as of the implications of a statement.

ex·pli·ca·tive (eks'pli-kā'tiv, iks-plik'ə-tiv), ***adj.*** explicating or tending to explicate; explanatory.

ex·pli·ca·to·ry (eks'pli-kə-tôr'i, eks'pli-kə-tō'ri), ***adj.*** explicative; explanatory.

ex·plic·it (iks-plis'it), ***adj.*** [L. *explicitus*, pp. of *explicare;* see EXPLICATE], 1. clearly stated; distinctly expressed; leaving nothing implied; definite: distinguished from *implicit*. 2. saying what is meant, without reservation or disguise; outspoken.

SYN.—**explicit** is applied to that which is so clearly stated or distinctly set forth that there should be no doubt as to the meaning; **express** adds to **explicit** the ideas of directness and positiveness; **exact** and **precise**, in this connection, both suggest that which is strictly defined, accurately stated, or made fastidiously clear; **definite** implies precise limitations as to the nature, character, meaning, etc. of something; **specific** implies the pointing up of details or the particularizing of references. —***ANT.*** vague, ambiguous.

ex·plode (iks-plōd'), ***v.t.*** [EXPLODED (-id), EXPLODING], [orig., to drive off the stage by clapping and hooting; L. *explodere* < *ex-*, off + *plaudere*, to applaud], 1. to discredit; cause to be rejected; expose as false: as, that theory is *exploded*. 2. to make burst with a loud noise; blow up; detonate. 3. to cause to change suddenly and violently from a solid or liquid to a quickly expanding gas. ***v.i.*** 1. to be exploded; burst noisily and violently. 2. to break forth noisily: as, he *exploded* with anger.

exploded view, a photograph or drawing showing in proper sequence and relationship the various parts of an assembly, as of a machine.

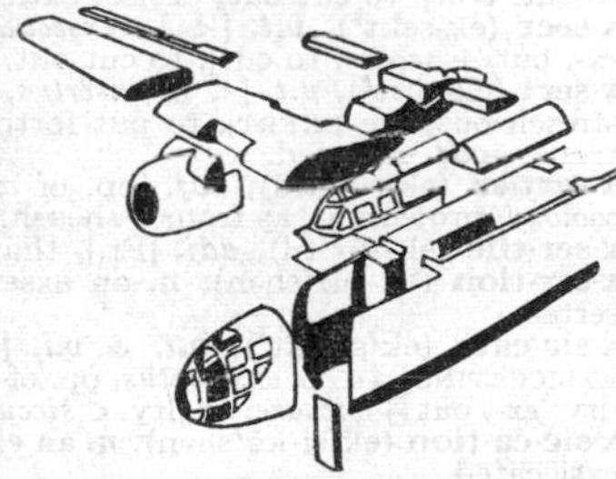

EXPLODED VIEW
(fuselage and wing of airplane)

ex·ploit (eks'ploit, iks-ploit'), ***n.*** [ME. *esploit, espleit;* OFr. *esploit*, an exploit, action, deed; L. *explicitus*, pp. of *explicare;* see EXPLICIT], an act remarkable for brilliance or daring; bold deed. ***v.t.*** (iks-ploit'), 1. to make use of; utilize; turn to account. 2. to make unethical use of for one's own advantage or profit; turn selfishly or unfairly to one's own account. 3. in *advertising*, to stir up interest in; promote: as, to *exploit* a product. 4. in *Marxism*, to make profit from the labor of (others).

ex·ploi·ta·tion (eks'ploi-tā'shən), ***n.*** an exploiting or being exploited; especially, unethical utilization for selfish purposes.

ex·ploit·a·tive (iks-ploi'tə-tiv), ***adj.*** 1. exploiting. 2. of exploitation.

ex·ploi·ter (iks-ploit'ẽr), ***n.*** a person who exploits. ***v.t.*** [Fr.], [Rare], to exploit.

ex·plo·ra·tion (eks'plə-rā'shən, eks'plô-rā'shən), ***n.*** [L. *exploratio* < pp. of *explorare;* see EXPLORE], 1. the act of looking into closely; careful scrutiny; examination. 2. the act of traveling for purposes of discovery in regions previously little known. 3. in *medicine*, the examination or probing of an organ, wound, etc.

ex·plor·a·tive (iks-plôr'ə-tiv, iks-plō'rə-tiv), ***adj.*** 1. exploratory. 2. tending to explore.

ex·plor·a·to·ry (iks-plôr'ə-tôr'i, iks-plō'rə-tō'ri), ***adj.*** [L. *exploratorius*], of, in, or for exploration.

ex·plore (iks-plôr', iks-plōr'), ***v.t.*** [EXPLORED (-plôrd', -plōrd'), EXPLORING], [L. *explorare*, to search out, investigate; *ex-*, out + *plorare*, to cry out, wail], 1. to look into closely; examine carefully; investigate. 2. to travel in (a region previously unknown or little known) in order to learn about its natural features, inhabitants, etc. 3. in *medicine*, to examine or probe (an organ, etc.). ***v.i.*** to make explorations.

ex·plor·er (iks-plôr'ẽr, iks-plō'rẽr), ***n.*** 1. a person who explores; especially, one who explores an unknown or little-known region. 2. an instrument used in exploring, or examining, as a medical or dental probe.

ex·plo·sion (iks-plō'zhən), ***n.*** [L. *explosio*, a driving off the stage by applause < pp. of *explodere;* see EXPLODE], 1. an exploding; especially, a blowing up; bursting with a loud noise; detonation. 2. the noise made by exploding. 3. a noisy outburst; loud breaking forth: as, an *explosion* of wrath. 4. in *phonetics*, the sudden release of breath in the articulation of a plosive.

ex·plo·sive (iks-plō'siv), ***adj.*** 1. of, causing, or having the nature of, an explosion. 2. tending to explode; especially, tending to burst forth noisily. 3. in *phonetics*, pronounced with a sudden release of breath, as the consonants *b, d, g, k, p,* and *t* when used as initial sounds. ***n.*** 1. a substance that can explode, as gunpowder. 2. an explosive consonant: see **stop.**

ex·po·nent (ik-spō'nənt), ***adj.*** [L. *exponens*, ppr. of *exponere;* see EXPOUND], setting forth; explaining; expounding; interpreting. ***n.*** 1. a person who sets forth, expounds, or interprets (principles, methods, etc.). 2. a person or thing that is an example or symbol (*of* something). 3. in *algebra*, a small figure or symbol placed above and at the right of another figure or symbol to show how many times the latter is to be multiplied by itself (e.g., $b^3 = b \times b \times b$).

ex·po·nen·tial (ek'spō-nen'shəl), ***adj.*** in *algebra*, relating to exponents; especially, involving the variable or unknown quantity as an exponent.

ex·po·ni·ble (ik-spō'nə-b'l), ***adj.*** [< L. *exponere;* see EXPOUND], 1. needing to be explained. 2. in *logic*, designating a proposition that needs to be restated for inclusion in a syllogism. ***n.*** an exponible proposition.

ex·port (ik-spôrt', ik-spōrt'; *also, and for n. & adj. always*, ek'spôrt), ***v.t.*** [L. *exportare; ex-*, out + *portare*, to carry], to carry or send (goods, etc.) from one country to another, especially for purposes of sale. ***n.*** 1. something exported. 2. the act or process of exporting; exportation. ***adj.*** of exporting or exports; for exportation. Abbreviated **exp., ex.**

ex·por·ta·tion (ek'spôr-tā'shən, ek'spōr-tā'shən), ***n.*** 1. the act or process of exporting. 2. an export.

ex·port·er (ik-spôr'tẽr, ik-spōr'tẽr), ***n.*** a person or company in the export trade.

ex·pos·al (ik-spō'z'l), ***n.*** exposure.

ex·pose (ik-spōz'), ***v.t.*** [EXPOSED (-spōzd'), EXPOSING], [OFr. *exposer;* prob. < L. *expositus*, pp. of *exponere* (see EXPOUND), but associated in OFr. with *poser* < L. *pausare;* see POSE], 1. *a*) to lay open (*to* danger, attack, ridicule, etc.); leave unprotected. *b*) to make accessible or subject (*to* an influence or action). 2. to put or leave out in an unprotected place; abandon: as, some ancient peoples *exposed* unwanted infants. 3. to allow to be seen; disclose; reveal; exhibit; display. 4. *a*) to make (a crime, fraud, etc.) known; unmask. *b*) to make known the crimes, etc. of (a person). 5. in *photography*, to subject (a sensitized film or plate) to the action of actinic rays. —***SYN.*** see **show.**

ex·po·sé (ek'spō-zā'), ***n.*** [Fr., pp. of *exposer;* see EXPOSE], a public disclosure of a scandal, crime, etc.

ex·po·si·tion (ek'spə-zish'ən), ***n.*** [ME. *exposicioun;* OFr. *exposition;* L. *expositio* < *expositus*, pp. of *exponere;* see EXPOUND], 1. a setting forth of facts, ideas, etc.; detailed explanation. 2. writing or speaking that sets forth or explains: distinguished from *description, narration, argumentation*. 3. [< Fr.], a large public exhibition or show, often international in scope. 4. that part of a play, etc. which reveals what has happened before, who the characters are, etc. 5. the first section of certain musical forms, as the sonata, fugue, etc., which introduces the main theme or themes. 6. [Obs.], an exposing or being exposed.

ex·pos·i·tive (ik-spoz'ə-tiv), ***adj.*** expository; explanatory; descriptive.

ex·pos·i·tor (ik-spoz'ə-tẽr), ***n.*** [OFr. *expositeur;* L. *expositor* < *expositus*, pp. of *exponere;* see EXPOUND], a person, piece of writing, etc. that sets forth or explains.

ex·pos·i·to·ry (ik-spoz'ə-tôr'i, ik-spoz'ə-tō'ri), ***adj.*** [ML. *expositorius;* see EXPOSITOR], of, containing, or having the nature of, exposition; explanatory.

ex post fac·to (eks pōst fak'tō), [L., from the (thing) done afterward], done or made after something, but having retroactive effect: as, an *ex post facto* law.

ex·pos·tu·late (ik-spos'chə-lāt'), ***v.i.*** [EXPOSTULATED (-id), EXPOSTULATING], [< L. *expostulatus*, pp. of *expostulare*, to demand vehemently, require; *ex-*, intens.

+ *postulare*, to demand], to reason with a person earnestly, objecting to his actions or intentions; remonstrate (*with*). —*SYN.* see **object.**

ex·pos·tu·la·tion (ik-spos'chə-lā'shən), *n.* [L. *expostulatio*], an expostulating; earnest protest or remonstrance.

ex·pos·tu·la·tor (ik-spos'chə-lā'tẽr), *n.* a person who expostulates.

ex·pos·tu·la·to·ry (ik-spos'chə-lə-tôr'i, ik-spos'chə-lə-tō'ri), *adj.* of or expressing expostulation.

ex·po·sure (ik-spō'zhẽr), *n.* [< *expose*, after *enclosure*, etc.], 1. an exposing or being exposed (in various senses). 2. a location, as of a house, in relation to the sun, winds, etc.: as, an eastern *exposure*. 3. in *photography*, *a*) the subjection of a sensitized film or plate to the action of actinic rays. *b*) a sensitized surface or section of a film for making one picture. *c*) the time during which such a surface or film is exposed.

exposure meter, in *photography*, an instrument for measuring the intensity of light on the subject and thus determining the correct exposure.

ex·pound (ik-spound'), *v.t.* [ME. *expounden*, *expounen*; OFr. *expondre*; L. *exponere*, to put forth, expose, expound; *ex-*, out + *ponere*, to put], 1. to set forth point by point; state in detail. 2. to explain; make plain; interpret; clarify. —*SYN.* see **explain.**

ex·press (iks-pres'), *v.t.* [ME. *expressen*; OFr. *expresser*, *espresser* < L. *ex*, out + *pressare*; see PRESS], 1. to press out or squeeze out (juice, etc.). 2. to get by pressure; elicit by force; extort. 3. to put into words; represent by language; state. 4. to make known; reveal; show: as, his face *expressed* sorrow. 5. to picture, represent, or symbolize in music, art, etc. 6. to show by a sign; symbolize; signify: as, the sign + *expresses* addition. 7. to send by express. *adj.* [ME. *expresse*; OFr. *expres*; L. *expressus*, pp. of *exprimere* < *ex-*, out + *premere*; see PRESS], 1. expressed and not implied; explicit; hence, 2. exact: as, the *express* image of a person. 3. for a definite or special purpose: as, his *express* reason for going; hence, 4. [orig., for the *express* purpose of running to one station], fast, direct, and making few stops: as, an *express* train: distinguished from *local*; hence, 5. characterized by speed or velocity; specifically, *a*) for fast driving: as, an *express* highway. *b*) high-speed: as, an *express* bullet. *c*) for high-speed projectiles: as, an *express* rifle. *d*) having to do with railway express, pony express, etc.: see the *n.* *adv.* by express. *n.* 1. a special messenger; courier. 2. a message delivered by such a messenger; dispatch sent swiftly. 3. *a*) an express train, bus, truck, etc. *b*) an express rifle. 4. the pony express. 5. a method or service for transporting goods or sending money rapidly: express is usually more expensive and faster than freight. 6. the goods transported or money sent by express. 7. any method or means of swift transmission. 8. a business concern operating such a system. Abbreviated **exp.** —*SYN.* see **explicit, utter.**

express oneself, 1. to state one's thoughts. 2. to give expression to one's feelings, imagination, etc., especially in creative or artistic activity.

ex·press·age (iks-pres'ij), *n.* [see -AGE], 1. the carrying of packages, etc. by express. 2. the charge for this.

ex·press·i·ble (iks-pres'ə-b'l), *adj.* that can be expressed.

ex·pres·sion (iks-presh'ən), *n.* [L. *expressio* < *expressus*; see EXPRESS, *adj.*], 1. a pressing out or squeezing out, as of juice. 2. a putting into words; representing in language; stating. 3. a picturing, representing, or symbolizing in art, music, etc. 4. a manner of expressing; especially, a meaningful and eloquent manner of speaking, singing, etc.: as, she reads with *expression*. 5. a particular word, phrase, or sentence: as, "catch cold" is an idiomatic *expression*. 6. a showing of feeling, character, etc.: as, laughter is often the *expression* of joy. 7. a look, intonation, sign, etc. that conveys meaning or feeling: as, there was a quizzical *expression* on his face. 8. a symbol or set of symbols expressing some algebraic fact, as a quantity or operation. 9. a showing by a symbol, sign, figures, etc.

ex·pres·sion·ism (iks-presh'ən-iz'm), *n.* an early 20th-century movement in the arts, especially in drama, characterized by the nonobjective use of symbols, stereotyped characters, stylization, etc. to give objective expression to inner experience.

ex·pres·sion·ist (iks-presh'ən-ist), *adj.* of or characterized by expressionism. *n.* an expressionist artist, writer, etc.

ex·pres·sion·is·tic (iks-presh'ən-is'tik), *adj.* expressionist.

ex·pres·sion·is·ti·cal·ly (iks-presh'ən-is'ti-k'l-i, iks-presh'ən-is'tik-li), *adv.* in an expressionistic manner.

ex·pres·sive (iks-pres'iv), *adj.* 1. of or characterized by expression. 2. expressing; indicating; serving as a sign: as, a song *expressive* of joy. 3. full of expression; forcible; significant: as, an *expressive* nod.

ex·press·ly (iks-pres'li), *adv.* 1. plainly; definitely; explicitly. 2. especially; particularly; on purpose.

ex·press·man (iks-pres'mən), *n.* [*pl.* EXPRESSMEN (-mən)], a person employed by an express company; especially, a driver of an express truck, who collects and delivers packages.

express rifle, a hunting rifle using a large charge and a light bullet of large caliber, discharged with a high initial velocity: used to kill large game at short range.

express train, a fast railroad train that makes few stops.

ex·press·way (iks-pres'wā'), *n.* a highway for high-speed traffic, usually divided and of limited access.

ex·pro·pri·ate (eks-prō'pri-āt'), *v.t.* [EXPROPRIATED (-id), EXPROPRIATING], [< ML. *expropriatus*, pp. of *expropriare*, to deprive of one's own < L. *ex*, out + *proprius*, one's own], 1. to take (land, property, etc.) from its owner; especially, to take for public use or in the public interest, as by right of eminent domain. 2. to transfer (property) from one person, nation, etc. to another. 3. to deprive of ownership; dispossess.

ex·pro·pri·a·tion (eks-prō'pri-ā'shən, eks'prō-pri-ā'shən), *n.* an expropriating or being expropriated.

ex·pro·pri·a·tor (eks-prō'pri-ā'tẽr), *n.* a person, nation, etc. that expropriates.

ex·pul·sion (ik-spul'shən), *n.* [L. *expulsio* < *expulsus*, pp. of *expellere*], 1. an expelling; forcing out. 2. the fact or state of being expelled.

ex·pul·sive (ik-spul'siv), *adj.* [< L. *expulsus* (see EXPULSION); + *-ive*], expelling or capable of expelling.

ex·punc·tion (ik-spuŋk'shən), *n.* [LL. *expunctio* < L. *expunctus*, pp.], an expunging or being expunged.

ex·punge (ik-spunj'), *v.t.* [EXPUNGED (-spunjd'), EXPUNGING], [L. *expungere*; *ex-*, out + *pungere*, to prick, strike], to blot, wipe, or strike out; erase; delete; cancel; efface. —*SYN.* see **erase.**

ex·pur·gate (ek'spẽr-gāt'), *v.t.* [EXPURGATED (-id), EXPURGATING], [< L. *expurgatus*, pp. of *expurgare*, to purge, cleanse; *ex-*, out + *purgare*, to cleanse], 1. to remove passages considered obscene or otherwise objectionable from (a book, etc.). 2. [Obs.], to clear; purge.

ex·pur·ga·tion (ek'spẽr-gā'shən), *n.* [L. *expurgatio*], an expurgating or being expurgated.

ex·pur·ga·tor (ek'spẽr-gā'tẽr), *n.* one who expurgates.

ex·pur·ga·to·ry (ik-spũr'gə-tôr'i, ik-spũr'gə-tō'ri), *adj.* 1. of expurgation. 2. tending to expurgate or purify.

ex·qui·site (eks'kwi-zit, ik-skwiz'it), *adj.* [orig., carefully sought out, choice; L. *exquisitus*, pp. of *exquirere*, to search out < *ex-*, out + *quaerere*, to ask], 1. carefully done or elaborately made: as, *exquisite* designing. 2. very beautiful or lovely, especially in a delicate or carefully wrought way: as, *exquisite* lace. 3. of highest quality; admirable. 4. highly sensitive; keenly discriminating; fastidious: as, an *exquisite* ear for music. 5. intense; keen: as, *exquisite* pain. *n.* a person who makes a great show of being very sensitive, refined, and fastidious in his tastes, etc. —*SYN.* see **delicate.**

ex·san·guine (eks-saŋ'gwin), *adj.* bloodless; anemic.

ex·scind (ek-sind'), *v.t.* [L. *exscindere*; *ex-*, out + *scindere*, to cut, tear], to cut out; excise; extirpate.

ex·sect (ek-sekt'), *v.t.* [< L. *exsectus*, pp. of *exsecare*; *ex-*, out + *secare*, to cut], to cut out.

ex·sert (ek-sũrt'), *v.t.* [< L. *exsertus*, pp. of *exserere*, to stretch out; see EXERT], to put forth; thrust out; protrude. *adj.* exserted.

ex·sert·ed (ek-sũr'tid), *adj.* [pp. of *exsert*], in *botany* & *zoology*, projecting, as from a sheath, pod, etc.

ex·ser·tile (ek-sũr'til), *adj.* [Fr.], that can be exserted.

ex·ser·tion (ek-sũr'shən), *n.* an exserting or being exserted.

ex·sic·cate (ek'si-kāt'), *v.t.* & *v.i.* [EXSICCATED (-id), EXSICCATING], [< L. *exsiccatus*, pp. of *exsiccare*, to make dry; *ex-*, out + *siccare*, to dry < *siccus*, dry], to dry up.

ex·sic·ca·tion (ek'si-kā'shən), *n.* an exsiccating or being exsiccated.

ex·sic·ca·tor (ek'si-kā'tẽr), *n.* in *chemistry*, a container in which substances are exsiccated, or dried.

ex·stip·u·late (eks-stip'yoo-lit, eks-stip'yoo-lāt'), *adj.* in *botany*, having no stipules.

ex·suf·fli·cate (eks-suf'li-kit, eks-suf'li-kāt'), *adj.* [arbitrary extension of obs. *exsufflate* < L. *ex*, out + *sufflare*, to blow], [Obs.], inflated; puffed up: *Othello*, III, iii.

ext., 1. extension. 2. external. 3. extinct. 4. extra.

ex·tant (ek'stənt, ik-stant'), *adj.* [L. *extans*, *exstans*, ppr. of *extare*, *exstare*, to stand out or forth; *ex-*, out + *stare*, to stand], 1. still existing; not extinct; not lost or destroyed. 2. [Archaic], standing out; conspicuous.

ex·tem·po·ral (ik-stem'pẽr-əl), *adj.* [L. *extemporalis*], [Archaic], extemporaneous.

ex·tem·po·ra·ne·ous (ik-stem'pə-rā'ni-əs), *adj.* [LL. *extemporaneus* < L. *ex*, out + *tempus*, *temporis*, time], 1. made, done, or spoken without any preparation; unpremeditated; offhand: as, an *extemporaneous* speech. 2. in *speech classes*, etc., spoken with preparation but not written out or memorized: distinguished from *impromptu*. 3. speaking or adept at speaking without preparation. 4. made for the occasion; improvised: as, an *extemporaneous* fireplace. —*SYN.* see **impromptu.**

ex·tem·po·rar·i·ly (ik-stem'pə-rer'ə-li, ik-stem'pə-rer'ə-li), *adv.* in an extemporary manner.

ex·tem·po·rar·i·ness (ik-stem'pə-rer'i-nis, ik-stem'pə-rer'i-nis), *n.* the quality of being extemporary.

ex·tem·po·rar·y (ik-stem'pə-rer'i), *adj.* extemporaneous. —*SYN.* see **impromptu.**

ex·tem·po·re (ik-stem′pə-ri, ik-stem′pə-rē′), *adv. & adj.* [L., lit., out of the time; *ex*, from, out of + *tempore*, abl. of *tempus, temporis*, time], without preparation; offhand: as, a speech given *extempore*. —*SYN.* see **impromptu.**

ex·tem·po·ri·za·tion (ik-stem′pẽr-i-zā′shən, ik-stem′pẽr-i-zā′shən), *n.* 1. an extemporizing. 2. something extemporized.

ex·tem·po·rize (ik-stem′pə-rīz′), *v.i. & v.t.* [EXTEMPORIZED (-rīzd′), EXTEMPORIZING], to speak, perform, or compose extempore; improvise.

ex·tend (ik-stend′), *v.t.* [ME. *extenden;* L. *extendere; ex-*, out + *tendere*, to stretch], 1. to stretch out or draw out to a certain point, or for a certain distance or time. 2. to prolong; continue. 3. to enlarge in area, scope, influence, meaning, etc.; widen; broaden; expand; spread. 4. to stretch forth; hold out; proffer; hence, 5. to offer; accord; grant. 6. to stretch or straighten out (a limb of the body): opposed to *flex.* 7. in *commerce*, to allow a period of time for the payment of (a debt) beyond that originally set. 8. in *cooking*, to make larger portions of (a scarce or expensive food) by combining with other cheaper foods. 9. in *law*, *a)* in Great Britain, to assess; value. *b)* to seize or levy upon, as by a writ of extent. *v.i.* to be extended.

SYN.—**extend** and **lengthen** both imply a making longer in space or time, but **extend**, in addition, may signify an enlarging in area, scope, influence, meaning, etc.; **elongate** is a synonym for **lengthen** in the spatial sense and is more commonly used in technical applications; **prolong** and **protract** both primarily imply an extending in time, **prolong** suggesting continuation beyond the usual or expected time, and **protract** a being drawn out needlessly or wearyingly.

ex·tend·ed (ik-sten′did), *adj.* [pp. of *extend*], 1. stretched out; spread out. 2. prolonged; continued. 3. enlarged in influence, meaning, scope, effect, etc.; extensive; widespread. 4. in *printing*, designating type with a wider face than is standard for the height.

ex·tend·i·ble (ik-sten′də-b'l), *adj.* extensible.

ex·ten·si·bil·i·ty (ik-sten′sə-bil′ə-ti), *n.* the quality of being extensible.

ex·ten·si·ble (ik-sten′sə-b'l), *adj.* [Fr. < L. *extensus*, pp. of *extendere*], that can be extended.

ex·ten·sile (ik-sten′s'l, ik-sten′sil), *adj.* [< L. *extensus* (see EXTENSIBLE); + *-ile*], 1. that can be thrust forth, as a claw or tentacle. 2. extensible.

ex·ten·sim·e·ter (eks′ten-sim′ə-tẽr), *n.* an extensometer.

ex·ten·sion (ik-sten′shən), *n.* [L. *extensio* < pp. of *extendere*], 1. an extending or being extended. 2. the amount or degree to which something is or can be extended; range; extent. 3. an extended part; continuation; addition: as, an *extension* to a factory. 4. a branch of a university for students who cannot attend the university proper. 5. an extra telephone connected to the same line as the main telephone. 6. in *biology*, the straightening of a limb or other part. 7. in *commerce*, an extra period of time allowed a debtor for making payment. 8. in *logic*, the total number of objects to which a single term applies; denotation: opposed to *intension.* 9. in *physics*, that property of a body by which it occupies space. Abbreviated **ext.**

ex·ten·si·ty (ik-sten′sə-ti), *n.* 1. the quality of extension. 2. in *psychology*, that quality of sensation which permits the perception of space or size.

ex·ten·sive (ik-sten′siv), *adj.* [L. *extensivus* < *extensus;* see EXTENSIBLE], 1. having great extent; covering a large area; vast. 2. having a wide scope, effect, influence, etc.; far-reaching; comprehensive. 3. of or characterized by extension. 4. in *agriculture*, using large areas of land with comparatively little cultivation: as, *extensive* farming: opposed to *intensive.*

ex·ten·som·e·ter (eks′ten-som′ə-tẽr), *n.* [< L. *extensus* (see EXTENSIBLE); + *-meter*], an instrument for measuring extremely small degrees of expansion, contraction, or deformation of something: also **extensimeter.**

ex·ten·sor (ik-sten′sẽr), *n.* [LL. *extensor*, stretcher, one who stretches a victim on the rack, torturer < L. *extensus;* see EXTENSIBLE], any of various muscles that extend or straighten some part of the body, especially an arm or leg: opposed to *flexor.*

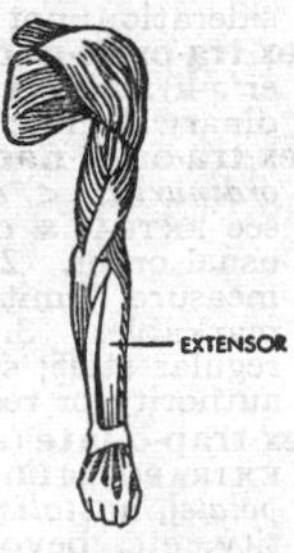

EXTENSOR

ex·tent (ik-stent′), *n.* [ME. *extente;* Anglo-Fr. *extente, estente;* OFr. *estente* < *estendre* < L. *extendere*], 1. the space, amount, or degree to which a thing extends; size; length; breadth. 2. scope; limits; comprehensiveness; coverage. 3. an extended space; vast area: as, an *extent* of woodland. 4. in *British history*, an assessment or valuation, as of land. 5. in *law*, *a)* in Great Britain, a writ (*writ of extent*) by which the person, goods, and property of a debtor could formerly be seized to force payment. *b)* seizure by such a writ. *c)* in the United States, a writ giving to a creditor temporary ownership of his debtor's property.

ex·ten·u·ate (ik-sten′ū-āt′), *v.t.* [EXTENUATED (-id), EXTENUATING], [< L. *extenuatus*, pp. of *extenuare; ex-*, out + *tenuare*, to make thin < *tenuis*, thin], 1. originally, to make thin; hence, 2. to diminish; weaken. 3. to underrate; underestimate. 4. to lessen or seem to lessen the seriousness of (an offense, guilt, etc.) by giving excuses or serving as an excuse.

extenuating circumstances, in *law*, circumstances that tend to lessen the severity of a crime and its punishment.

ex·ten·u·a·tion (ik-sten′ū-ā′shən), *n.* 1. an extenuating or being extenuated; especially, mitigation, as of the seriousness of a crime, offense, etc. 2. a thing that extenuates; partial excuse.

ex·ten·u·a·tive (ik-sten′ū-ā′tiv), *adj.* extenuatory.

ex·ten·u·a·tor (ik-sten′ū-ā′tẽr), *n.* a person or thing that extenuates.

ex·ten·u·a·to·ry (ik-sten′ū-ə-tôr′i, ik-sten′ū-ə-tō′ri), *adj.* extenuating or tending to extenuate.

ex·te·ri·or (ik-stêr′i-ẽr), *adj.* [L., compar. of *exter, exterus*, on the outside; see EXTRA], 1. outer; outermost; on the outside: as, an *exterior* wall. 2. originating outside; acting or coming from without: as, *exterior* forces. 3. foreign; of foreign affairs. *n.* 1. an outside or outside surface; hence, 2. an outward appearance: as, a misleading *exterior.*

exterior angle, 1. any of the four angles formed on the outside of two straight lines by a straight line cutting across them. 2. an angle formed by any side of a polygon and the extension of the adjacent side.

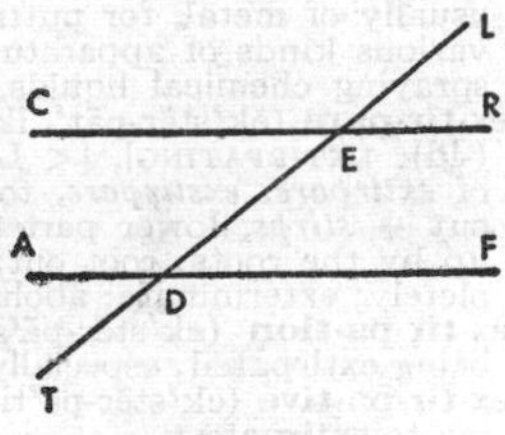

EXTERIOR ANGLES (CEL, LER, ADT, TDF)

ex·ter·mi·nate (ik-stũr′mə-nāt′), *v.t.* [EXTERMINATED (-id), EXTERMINATING], [< L. *exterminatus*, pp. of *exterminare*, lit., to drive beyond the boundaries, hence drive out, destroy < *ex-*, out + *terminus*, boundary], to destroy entirely; wipe out; annihilate.

SYN.—**exterminate** implies the complete, wholesale destruction of living beings or things whose existence is considered undesirable; **extirpate** and **eradicate** both suggest the extinction or abolition of something, **extirpate** implying a deliberate and violent destruction at the very source so that the thing cannot be regenerated, and **eradicate** connoting less violence and, often, the working of natural processes or a methodical plan.

ex·ter·mi·na·tion (ik-stũr′mə-nā′shən), *n.* an exterminating or being exterminated; annihilation.

ex·ter·mi·na·tive (ik-stũr′mə-nā′tiv), *adj.* exterminatory.

ex·ter·mi·na·tor (ik-stũr′mə-nā′tẽr), *n.* [LL.], a person or thing that exterminates; specifically, *a)* a person whose work or business is exterminating rats, cockroaches, and other vermin. *b)* any of various powders, liquids, etc. for exterminating vermin.

ex·ter·mi·na·to·ry (ik-stũr′mə-nə-tôr′i, ik-stũr′mə-nə-tō′ri), *adj.* of extermination; tending to exterminate.

ex·tern (ek′stẽrn, ik-stũrn′), *n.* [Fr. *externe* < L. *externus;* see EXTERNAL], a person connected with, but not living in, an institution, as a nonresident doctor in a hospital: opposed to *intern.*

ex·ter·nal (ik-stũr′n'l), *adj.* [< L. *externus*, outward, external < *exter, exterus*, on the outside, compar. form < *ex*, out of; + *-al*], 1. on the outside; outer; exterior. 2. on, or for use on, the outside of the body: as, a medicine for *external* use only. 3. outwardly visible; material; existing apart from the mind. 4. originating outside; acting or coming from without: as, an *external* force. 5. for outward appearance or show; superficial: as, *external* politeness. 6. having to do with foreign countries and international affairs. Abbreviated **ext.** *n.* 1. an outside or outward surface or part. 2. *pl.* outward appearance or behavior; form; superficialities: as, he judges by mere *externals.*

ex·ter·nal·i·ty (ek′stẽr-nal′ə-ti), *n.* 1. the quality or state of being external. 2. [*pl.* EXTERNALITIES (-tiz)], an external thing.

ex·ter·nal·i·za·tion (ik-stũr′n'l-i-zā′shən, ik-stũr′n'l-ī-zā′shən), *n.* 1. an externalizing. 2. an externalized thing; embodiment.

ex·ter·nal·ize (ik-stũr′n'l-īz′), *v.t.* [EXTERNALIZED (-īzd′), EXTERNALIZING], 1. to make external. 2. to regard as having external existence.

ex·ter·nal·ly (ik-stũr′n'l-i), *adv.* on or from the outside.

ex·ter·o·cep·tive (ek′stẽr-ō-sep′tiv), *adj.* [L. *exter*, on the outside; + *-o* + *receptive*], designating, of, or affected by stimuli from outside the body, as in touching, seeing, smelling, tasting, etc.

ex·ter·o·cep·tor (ek'stẽr-ō-sep'tẽr), ***n.*** [Mod. L.], a sense organ or sensory receptor that responds to exteroceptive stimuli.

ex·ter·ri·to·ri·al (eks'ter-ə-tôr'i-əl, eks'ter-ə-tō'ri-əl), ***adj.*** outside the territorial limits or jurisdiction of the country, state, etc.; extraterritorial.

ex·tinct (ik-stiŋkt'), ***adj.*** [L. *extinctus, exstinctus*, pp. of *exstinguere;* see EXTINGUISH], 1. having died down or gone out; extinguished: as, an *extinct* fire. 2. no longer in existence; having come to an end; having no living descendant: abbreviated **ext.** —***SYN.*** see **dead.**

ex·tinc·tion (ik-stiŋk'shən), ***n.*** [L. *exstinctio* < *exstinctus;* see EXTINCT, EXTINGUISH], 1. a putting out or being put out; quenching. 2. the fact or state of being or becoming extinct; dying out, as of a race, species of animal, etc. 3. a destroying or being destroyed; wiping out; annihilation; abolition.

ex·tinc·tive (ik-stiŋk'tiv), ***adj.*** [*extinct* + *-ive*], serving or tending to extinguish.

ex·tin·guish (ik-stiŋ'gwish), ***v.t.*** [L. *extinguere, exstinguere*, to quench, destroy; prob. < *ex-*, intens. + *tinguere*, older form of *tingere*, to wet, bathe, soak (see TINGE); *-ish* after *abolish, banish*], 1. to put out (a fire, etc.); quench; smother. 2. to put an end to; cause to die out; wipe out; destroy. 3. to put in the shade; eclipse; obscure: as, her beauty *extinguished* all others. 4. in *law*, to nullify.

ex·tin·guish·er (ik-stiŋ'gwish-ẽr), ***n.*** a person or thing that extinguishes; specifically, *a*) a hollow cone, usually of metal, for putting out a candle. *b*) any of various kinds of apparatus for extinguishing a fire by spraying chemical liquids, powders, etc.

ex·tir·pate (ek'stẽr-pāt', ik-stũr'pāt), ***v.t.*** [EXTIRPATED (-id), EXTIRPATING], [< L. *extirpatus, exstirpatus*, pp. of *extirpare, exstirpare*, to root out, eradicate < *ex-*, out + *stirps*, lower part of a tree, root], 1. to pull up by the roots; root out; hence, 2. to destroy completely; exterminate; abolish. —***SYN.*** see **exterminate.**

ex·tir·pa·tion (ek'stẽr-pā'shən), ***n.*** an extirpating or being extirpated; especially, extermination.

ex·tir·pa·tive (ek'stẽr-pā'tiv), ***adj.*** extirpating or tending to extirpate.

ex·tir·pa·tor (ek'stẽr-pā'tẽr), ***n.*** [L.], a person or thing that extirpates.

ex·tol, ex·toll (ik-stōl', ik-stol'), ***v.t.*** [EXTOLLED (-stōld', -stold'), EXTOLLING], [L. *extollere*, to raise up, lift up; *ex-*, out, up + *tollere*, to raise], to praise highly; laud. —***SYN.*** see **praise.**

ex·tol·ler (ik-stōl'ẽr, ik-stol'ẽr), ***n.*** a person who extols.

ex·tol·ment, ex·toll·ment (ik-stōl'mənt, ik-stol'mənt), ***n.*** an extolling.

ex·tort (ik-stôrt'), ***v.t.*** [< L. *extortus*, pp. of *extorquere*, to twist or turn out; *ex-*, out + *torquere*, to twist], to get (money, etc.) by violence, threats, misuse of authority, etc.; exact or wrest (*from*). —***SYN.*** see **extract.**

ex·tor·tion (ik-stôr'shən), ***n.*** [ME. *extorcioun;* OFr. *extorcion, extorsion;* LL. *extorsio* < L. *extortus*], 1. an extorting; getting money, etc. by violence, threats, misuse of authority, etc.: sometimes applied to the exaction of too high a price. 2. something extorted.

ex·tor·tion·ar·y (ik-stôr'shən-er'i), ***adj.*** extortionate.

ex·tor·tion·ate (ik-stôr'shən-it), ***adj.*** 1. characterized by, or having the nature of, extortion. 2. excessive; exorbitant: as, an *extortionate* price.

ex·tor·tion·er (ik-stôr'shən-ẽr), ***n.*** a person guilty of extortion.

ex·tor·tion·ist (ik-stôr'shən-ist), ***n.*** an extortioner.

ex·tra (eks'trə), ***adj.*** [contr. < *extraordinary;* also < L. *extra*, additional, extra < *extra, adv.*, more than, outside; see EXTRA-], more, larger, or better than what is normal, expected, usual, necessary, etc.; additional. ***n.*** an extra person or thing; specifically, *a*) *often in pl.* an additional charge. *b*) a special edition of a newspaper, put out between regular editions to cover news of unusual interest or importance. *c*) something of unusually good quality. *d*) an extra worker. *e*) in *cricket*, a run not made from a hit, as a bye. *f*) in *motion pictures*, an actor hired by the day to play a minor part, as a member of a mob scene, etc. ***adv.*** more than usually; especially; exceptionally: as, *extra* good quality. Abbreviated **ex., ext.**

ex·tra- (eks'trə), [L. < *exter, exterus;* see EXTERNAL], a prefix meaning *outside, outside the scope* or *region of, beyond, besides*, used to form adjectives such as *extracurricular, extramural*. The following list shows others:

extracellular	**extraparental**
extracerebral	**extraparliamentary**
extracorporeal	**extraparochial**
extragovernmental	**extraprofessional**
extrahistoric	**extrasocial**
extramarital	**extravaginal**
extraofficial	**extravisceral**

ex·tra·bold (eks'trə-bōld'), ***n.*** in *printing*, a style of type heavier than boldface.

ex·tra·ca·non·i·cal (eks'trə-kə-non'i-k'l), ***adj.*** not included in the canon; not among the authorized books.

ex·tra-con·densed (eks'trə-kən-denst'), ***adj.*** in *printing*, designating a style of type narrower than condensed.

ex·tract (iks-trakt'; *for n.*, eks'trakt), ***v.t.*** [< L. *extractus*, pp. of *extrahere*, to draw out; *ex-*, out + *trahere*, to draw], 1. to draw out by effort; pull out: as, a dentist *extracts* teeth, we *extracted* a promise from him. 2. to obtain by pressing, distilling, etc.: as, *extract* juice from fruit. 3. to obtain as if by drawing out; deduce; derive; manage to get. 4. to copy out (a passage from a book, etc.); make a selection or quotation of. 5. in *mathematics*, to find out (the root of a quantity). ***n.*** something extracted; specifically, *a*) a concentrated form, whether solid, viscid, or liquid, of a food, flavoring, etc.: as, vanilla *extract*. *b*) a passage from a book, etc.; excerpt; quotation. *c*) in *pharmacy*, the substance obtained by treating a drug with some solvent, as ether or alcohol, and then evaporating the preparation. Abbreviated **ex., ext.**

SYN.—**extract** implies a drawing out of something, as if by pulling, sucking, etc. (to *extract* a promise); **educe** suggests a drawing out or evolving of something that is latent or undeveloped (laws were *educed* from tribal customs); **elicit** connotes difficulty or skill in drawing out something hidden or buried (his jokes *elicited* no smiles); **evoke** implies a calling forth or summoning, as of a mental image, by stimulating the emotions (the odor *evoked* a memory of childhood); **extort** suggests a forcing or wresting of something, as by violence or threats (to *extort* a ransom).

ex·tract·a·ble, ex·tract·i·ble (iks-trak'tə-b'l), ***adj.*** that can be extracted.

ex·trac·tion (iks-trak'shən), ***n.*** 1. an extracting or being extracted. 2. origin; lineage; descent: as, he is of French *extraction*. 3. a thing extracted; extract.

ex·trac·tive (iks-trak'tiv), ***adj.*** 1. extracting or tending to extract. 2. extractable. 3. having the nature of an extract. ***n.*** 1. an extractive substance. 2. an extract.

ex·trac·tor (iks-trak'tẽr), ***n.*** a person or thing that extracts; specifically, the part of a breech-loading gun that withdraws the cartridge case from the chamber.

ex·tra·cur·ric·u·lar (eks'trə-kə-rik'yoo-lẽr), ***adj.*** not part of the curriculum; outside the regular course of study: as, debating is an *extracurricular* activity.

ex·tra·dit·a·ble (eks'trə-dīt'ə-b'l), ***adj.*** 1. that can be extradited. 2. making liable to extradition.

ex·tra·dite (eks'trə-dīt'), ***v.t.*** [EXTRADITED (-id), EXTRADITING], [< *extradition*], 1. to turn over (an alleged criminal, fugitive, etc.) to the jurisdiction of another country, state, etc. 2. to obtain the extradition of.

ex·tra·di·tion (eks'trə-dish'ən), ***n.*** [Fr. < L. *ex*, out + *traditio*, a surrender < *traditus*, pp. of *tradere*, to give up], the turning over of an alleged criminal, fugitive, or prisoner by one country, state, etc. to another.

ex·tra·dos (eks-trā'dos), ***n.*** [Fr. < L. *extra*, beyond + Fr. *dos* < L. *dorsum*, back], in *architecture*, the outside curved surface of an arch.

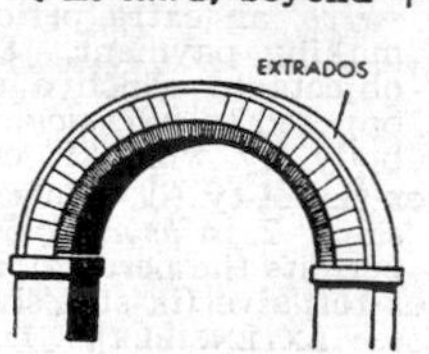

EXTRADOS

ex·tra·ju·di·cial (eks'trə-jōō-dish'əl), ***adj.*** 1. outside or beyond the jurisdiction of a court. 2. outside the usual course of justice.

ex·tra·le·gal (eks'trə-lē'g'l), ***adj.*** outside of legal control or authority.

ex·tra·mun·dane (eks'trə-mun'dān), ***adj.*** [see EXTRA- & MUNDANE], outside the physical world; not of this world.

ex·tra·mu·ral (eks'trə-myoor'əl), ***adj.*** [see EXTRA- & MURAL], outside the walls or limits of a city, university, etc.: as, *extramural* classes.

ex·tra·ne·ous (iks-trā'ni-əs), ***adj.*** [L. *extraneus*, external, strange, foreign < *extra;* see EXTRA- & STRANGE], 1. coming from outside; foreign: as, an *extraneous* substance. 2. not belonging to the matter under consideration; not pertinent. —***SYN.*** see **extrinsic.**

ex·tra·or·di·nar·i·ly (iks-trôr'd'n-er'ə-li, iks-trôr'd'n-er'ə-li), ***adv.*** in an extraordinary manner; to an extraordinary degree; exceptionally.

ex·tra·or·di·nar·y (iks-trôr'd'n-er'i), ***adj.*** [L. *extraordinarius* < *extra ordinem*, out of the usual order; see EXTRA- & ORDINARY], 1. not ordinary; out of the usual order. 2. going far beyond the ordinary degree, measure, limit, etc.; very unusual; exceptional; remarkable. 3. (eks'trə-ôr'd'n-er'i), outside of the regular staff; sent on a special errand; having special authority or responsibility: as, an envoy *extraordinary*.

ex·trap·o·late (eks-trap'ə-lāt', eks'trə-pə-lāt'), ***v.t. & v.i.*** EXTRAPOLATED (-id), EXTRAPOLATING], [*extra* + *interpolate*], in *statistics*, to estimate or infer (a value, quantity, etc. beyond the known range) on the basis of certain variables within the known range, from which the estimated value is assumed to follow: as, sales figures for next year may be *extrapolated* from the known sales figures for preceding years.

ex·trap·o·la·tion (eks-trap'ə-lā'shən, eks'trə-pə-lā'shən), ***n.*** an extrapolating or being extrapolated.

ex·tra·sen·so·ry (eks'trə-sen'sə-ri), *adj.* outside the realm of the senses; apart from sense perception.

ex·tra·ter·ri·to·ri·al (eks'trə-ter'ə-tôr'i-əl, eks'trə-ter'ə-tō'ri-əl), *adj.* 1. outside the territorial limits or jurisdiction of the country, state, etc. 2. of extraterritoriality: as, *extraterritorial* rights.

ex·tra·ter·ri·to·ri·al·i·ty (eks'trə-ter'ə-tôr'i-al'ə-ti, eks'trə-ter'ə-tō'ri-al'ə-ti), *n.* 1. freedom from the jurisdiction of the country in which one lives, as in the case of an ambassador or foreign agent. 2. jurisdiction of a country over its citizens in foreign lands.

ex·tra·u·ter·ine (eks'trə-ū'tẽr-in), *adj.* outside the uterus.

ex·trav·a·gance (iks-trav'ə-gəns), *n.* [Fr.; see EXTRAVAGANT], 1. a going beyond reasonable or moderate limits in conduct or speech; unreasonable excess. 2. a spending of more than is reasonable or necessary; excessive expenditure; wastefulness. 3. an instance of excess in spending, behavior, or speech.

ex·trav·a·gan·cy (iks-trav'ə-gən-si), *n.* [*pl.* EXTRAVAGANCIES (-siz)], extravagance.

ex·trav·a·gant (iks-trav'ə-gənt), *adj.* [Fr.; ML. *extravagans*, ppr. of *extravagari*, to stray < L. *extra*, beyond + *vagari*, to wander], 1. going beyond reasonable limits; excessive: as, *extravagant* prices. 2. spending too much; wasteful. —*SYN.* see **excessive, profuse.**

ex·trav·a·gan·za (iks-trav'ə-gan'zə), *n.* [respelled after L. < It. *estravaganza*, extravagance], a literary or dramatic composition characterized by a loose structure, farce, and fantastic plot; now, a spectacular, elaborate theatrical production, as some musical shows.

ex·trav·a·gate (iks-trav'ə-gāt'), *v.i.* [EXTRAVAGATED (-id), EXTRAVAGATING], [< ML. *extravagatus*, pp.; see EXTRAVAGANT], [Rare], 1. to stray; wander. 2. to go beyond reasonable limits; be extravagant.

ex·trav·a·sate (iks-trav'ə-sāt'), *v.t.* [EXTRAVASATED (-id), EXTRAVASATING], [*extra-* + L. *vas*, a vessel; + *-ate*], to let flow or force (blood, etc.) from its normal containers into the surrounding body tissues. *v.i.* to flow out or escape into surrounding tissues, as blood, lymph, etc.

ex·trav·a·sa·tion (iks-trav'ə-sā'shən), *n.* 1. an extravasating. 2. extravasated matter; especially, blood that has flowed into the tissues, as from a bruise.

ex·tra·vas·cu·lar (eks'trə-vas'kyoo-lẽr), *adj.* 1. not contained in blood and lymph vessels; outside the vascular system. 2. not vascular.

ex·tra·ver·sion (eks'trə-vũr'zhən, eks'trə-vũr'shən), *n.* extroversion (sense 2).

ex·tra·vert (eks'trə-vũrt'), *n.* an extrovert.

ex·treme (iks-trēm'), *adj.* [OFr.; L. *extremus*, last, outermost, superl. of *exterus*, outer, outward], 1. at the end or outermost point; farthest away; most remote; utmost. 2. last; final. 3. going to great lengths; in or to the greatest degree; very great or greatest; excessive; immoderate: as, *extreme* poverty. 4. advanced; radical: as, *extreme* views. 5. very severe; drastic. *n.* 1. either of two things that are as different or far as possible from each other. 2. an extreme degree. 3. an extreme act, expedient, etc. 4. an extreme state or condition: as, an *extreme* of distress. 5. [Obs.], an extreme point; extremity. 6. in *mathematics*, the first or last term of a ratio, proportion, or series: opposed to *mean.*

go to extremes, to be excessive or immoderate in speech or action.

in the extreme, to the utmost degree.

ex·treme·ly (iks-trēm'li), *adv.* to an extreme degree; very much; very.

extreme unction, in the *Roman Catholic Church*, the sacrament administered by a priest or bishop to a person who is dying or in danger of death through sickness.

ex·trem·ism (iks-trēm'iz'm), *n.* the quality or state of going to extremes.

ex·trem·ist (iks-trēm'ist), *n.* 1. a person who goes to extremes. 2. a person who holds extreme, or advanced, views, or advocates extreme measures. *adj.* of extremism or extremists.

ex·trem·i·ty (iks-trem'ə-ti), *n.* [*pl.* EXTREMITIES (-tiz)], [L. *extremitas* < *extremus;* see EXTREME], 1. the outermost or utmost point or part; end. 2. the greatest degree. 3. a state of extreme necessity, danger, etc. 4. the end of life; dying. 5. *usually in pl.* an extreme measure; severe or strong action: as, we must resort to *extremities* when all else fails. 6. *pl.* the hands and feet.

ex·tri·ca·ble (eks'tri-kə-b'l), *adj.* that can be extricated.

ex·tri·cate (eks'tri-kāt'), *v.t.* [EXTRICATED (-id), EXTRICATING], [< L. *extricatus*, pp. of *extricare*, to disentangle < *ex-*, out + *tricae*, trifles, toys], 1. to set free; release; disentangle (*from* a net, difficulty, embarrassment, etc.). 2. to cause (a gas, heat, etc.) to be emitted.

ex·tri·ca·tion (eks'tri-kā'shən), *n.* an extricating or being extricated; disentanglement, liberation, etc.

ex·trin·sic (eks-trin'sik), *adj.* [Fr. *extrinsèque;* L. *extrinsecus*, from without, outer < *exter*, without + *secus*, otherwise, besides], 1. not belonging to the real nature of a thing; not inherent. 2. being, coming, or acting from the outside; extraneous. Opposed to *intrinsic.*

SYN.—**extrinsic** refers to that which coming from outside a thing is not inherent in its real nature (the *extrinsic* advantages of wealth); **extraneous**, often synonymous with **extrinsic**, may connote the possibility of integration of the external object into the thing to which it is added (*extraneous* grace notes); **foreign** implies that the external object is organically so different that it cannot become assimilated (a *foreign* substance in the blood); **alien** emphasizes the incompatibility of the external object with the subject in question (nothing human is *alien* to me). —*ANT.* intrinsic.

ex·trin·si·cal·ly (eks-trin'si-k'l-i, eks-trin'sik-li), *adv.* in an extrinsic manner; externally; from outside.

ex·tro- (eks'trə), extra- (when opposed to *intro-*).

ex·trorse (eks-trôrs'), *adj.* [Fr.; LL. *extrorsus* < L. *extra*, outside + *versus*, pp. of *vertere*, to turn], in *botany*, turned outward or away from the axis of growth: opposed to *introrse.*

ex·tro·ver·sion (eks'trō-vũr'zhən, eks'trō-vũr'shən), *n.* [< *extra* + L. *versus*, pp. of *vertere*, to turn], 1. in *medicine*, the turning inside out of an organ; especially, such a congenital condition of the urinary bladder. 2. in *psychology*, an attitude in which a person directs his interest to phenomena outside himself rather than to his own experiences and feelings: opposed to *introversion:* also **extraversion.**

ex·tro·vert (eks'trō-vũrt'), *n.* [see EXTROVERSION], in *psychology*, a person whose interest is more in his environment and in other people than in himself; person who is active and expressive, or other than introspective: opposed to *introvert:* also **extravert.**

ex·trude (iks-trōōd'), *v.t.* [EXTRUDED (-id), EXTRUDING], [L. *extrudere*, to thrust out or forth; *ex-*, out + *trudere*, to thrust], to push or force out; expel: as, plastic material is *extruded* through very small holes to form fibers. *v.i.* to stick out; protrude; project.

ex·tru·sion (iks-trōō'zhən), *n.* an extruding or being extruded.

ex·tru·sive (iks-trōō'siv), *adj.* 1. extruding or tending to extrude. 2. in *geology*, forced out in a molten state through the earth's crust; volcanic: as, *extrusive* rock.

ex·u·ber·ance (ig-zōō'bẽr-əns, ig-zū'bẽr-əns), *n.* [Fr. *exubérance;* LL. *exuberantia* < L. *exuberans*, ppr. of *exuberare*, to come forth in abundance; *ex-*, intens. + *uberare*, to bear abundantly < *uber*, udder], 1. the state or quality of being exuberant; great abundance; luxuriance. 2. an instance of this; especially, action or speech showing high spirits.

ex·u·ber·an·cy (ig-zōō'bẽr-ən-si, ig-zū'bẽr-ən-si), *n.* [*pl.* EXUBERANCIES (-siz)], exuberance.

ex·u·ber·ant (ig-zōō'bẽr-ənt, ig-zū'bẽr-ənt), *adj.* [L. *exuberans;* see EXUBERANCE], 1. growing profusely; luxuriant; prolific: as, *exuberant* vegetation. 2. overflowing; lavish; effusive: as, *exuberant* spirits. 3. overflowing with good health and spirits: said of a person.

ex·u·ber·ate (ig-zōō'bə-rāt', ig-zū'bə-rāt'), *v.i.* [EXUBERATED (-id), EXUBERATING], [< L. *exuberatus*], [Rare], to be exuberant; abound.

ex·u·date (eks'yoo-dāt'), *n.* [L. *exudatus, exsudatus*, pp. of *exsudare;* see EXUDE], matter exuded.

ex·u·da·tion (eks'yoo-dā'shən), *n.* [< obs. *exudate*, to exude], 1. an exuding. 2. something exuded, as sweat.

ex·ude (ig-zōōd', ik-sūd'), *v.i.* & *v.t.* [EXUDED (-id), EXUDING], [L. *exudare, exsudare; ex-*, out + *sudare*, to sweat < *sudor*, sweat], to pass out in drops, as through pores, an incision, etc.; ooze; discharge.

ex·ult (ig-zult'), *v.i.* [Fr. *exulter;* L. *exultare, exsultare*, to leap up, leap for joy < *ex-*, intens. + *saltare*, freq. of *salire*, to leap], 1. to rejoice greatly; be jubilant; glory. 2. [Obs.], to leap up; leap with joy.

ex·ult·an·cy (ig-zul't'n-si), *n.* exultation.

ex·ult·ant (ig-zul't'nt), *adj.* [L. *exsultans*, ppr. of *exsultare*], exulting; triumphant; jubilant.

ex·ul·ta·tion (eg'zul-tā'shən, ek'sul-tā'shən), *n.* [L. *exultatio, exsultatio* < pp. of *exsultare*], an exulting; rejoicing; jubilation; triumph.

ex·ur·ban·ite (eks-ũr'bən-īt'), *n.* [coined, (1955), after *suburbanite*, by A. C. Spectorsky], a person of the upper middle class who lives in the semirural areas beyond the suburbs but who works in the metropolis, especially in advertising, publishing, the theater, etc.: exurbanites are regarded as conforming to social and cultural patterns as standardized as those of suburban life.

ex·u·vi·ae (ig-zōō'vi-ē', ik-sū'vi-ē'), *n.pl.* [*sing.* EXUVIA (-ə)], [L., that which is stripped off, spoils < *exuere*, to strip off; cf. INDUE], in *zoology*, cast-off coverings of animals, as the skins of snakes, crab shells, etc.

ex·u·vi·al (ig-zōō'vi-əl, ik-sū'vi-əl), *adj.* of exuviae.

ex·u·vi·ate (ig-zōō'vi-āt', ik-sū'vi-āt'), *v.t.* & *v.i.* [EXUVIATED (-id), EXUVIATING], [< *exuviae* + *-ate*], to cast off (a skin, shell, etc.); molt.

ex·u·vi·a·tion (ig-zōō'vi-ā'shən, ik-sū'vi-ā'shən), *n.* 1. an exuviating. 2. an exuviated covering.

-ey (ē, i), -y (adjective-forming suffix): used especially after words ending in *y*.

ey·as (ī′əs), *n.* [faulty division (influenced by ME. *ey*, an egg) of *a nyas, a niais;* Fr. *niais*, nestling < LL. **nidax* < L. *nidus*, a nest], 1. a young hawk taken from its nest for training in falconry. 2. an unfledged bird; nestling.

Eyck, Huy·brecht van (hoi′breHt vän īk′; Eng. van īk′), 1366?–1426; brother of *Jan;* Flemish painter: also **Hubert van Eyck.**

Eyck, Jan van (yän), 1370?–1440?; Flemish painter.

eye (ī), *n.* [ME. *ey, eie*, etc.; AS. *eage;* akin to G. *auge;* IE. base **oqw-*, to see, as also in L. *oculus* (cf. OCULIST)], 1. organ of sight in man and animals. 2. the eyeball. 3. the iris: as, she has brown *eyes.* 4. the area around the eye, including the eyelids: as, he was fighting and got a black *eye.* 5. sight; vision. 6. a look; glance; gaze: as, cast your *eye* on this. 7. attention; regard; observation. 8. the power of judging, estimating, discriminating, etc. by eyesight: as, a good *eye* for distances. 9. *often in pl.* judgment; opinion; estimation: as, in the *eyes* of the law. 10. a thing like an eye in appearance or function; specifically, *a*) a bud of a potato. *b*) the spot on a peacock's tail feather. *c*) the center of a target; bull's-eye. *d*) a hole in a tool, as for a handle. *e*) the threading hole in a needle. *f*) a loop of metal or thread. *g*) an organ sensitive to light, as in certain lower forms of life. *h*) a photoelectric cell. 11. in *meteorology*, the calm, low-pressure center (of a hurricane), around which winds of high velocity move. *v.t.* [EYED (īd), EYING or EYEING], 1. to look at; observe; watch carefully; scrutinize. 2. to provide with eyes, or holes. *v.i.* [Obs.], to appear (to the eyes).

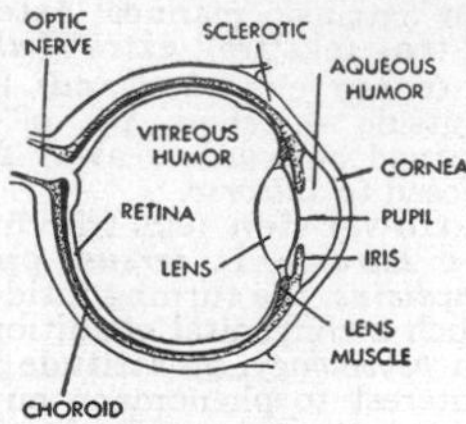

HUMAN EYE

an eye for an eye, punishment or retaliation similar or equivalent to the injury suffered.
catch one's eye, to attract one's attention.
eyes right (or **left**), in *military usage*, a command to turn the head to the right (or left) while marching, as a salute when passing in review.
feast one's eyes on, to look at with pleasure or admiration.
give (a person) the eye, [Slang], to look at (a person), especially with admiration or invitation.
have an eye for, to have the ability to notice with discernment and appreciation.
have an eye to, to watch out for; attend to.
in a pig's eye, [Slang], never; under no circumstances.
in the eye of the wind, in *nautical usage*, in a direction opposite to that of the wind; close to the wind.
in the public eye, 1. much seen in public. 2. often brought to public attention; well-known.
keep an eye on, to look after; watch carefully.
keep one's eyes open, to be on the lookout; be watchful.
lay (or **set** or **clap**) **eyes on,** to see; look at.
make eyes at, to look at lovingly or flirtatiously.
my eye! [Slang], an exclamation of contradiction, astonishment, etc.
open one's eyes, to make one aware of the facts, real reasons, etc.
run one's eye over, to glance over; look at hurriedly.
see eye to eye, to hold precisely the same view.
see with half an eye, to see or understand (something) easily because it is so evident.
shut one's eyes to, to be unwilling to see or think about.
with an eye to, paying attention to; considering.

eye·ball (ī′bôl′), *n.* the ball-shaped part of the eye, enclosed by the socket and eyelids.

eye·beam (ī′bēm′), *n.* a beam, or glance, of the eye; quick look.

eye·bright (ī′brīt′), *n.* a small European plant with white, yellow, or purple flowers, used in treating diseases of the eye: also called *euphrasy.*

eye·brow (ī′brou′), *n.* 1. the bony arch over each eye. 2. the arch of hair growing on this.

eye·cup (ī′kup′), *n.* a small cup whose rim is shaped to fit over the eye, used in applying medicine to the eyes or washing them.

eyed (īd), *adj.* 1. having eyes: often used in compounds, as in *blue-eyed.* 2. having markings that look like eyes; spotted.

eye·ful (ī′fool′), *n.* 1. a quantity of something in the eye: as, an *eyeful* of water. 2. as much as can be seen in one glance. 3. [Slang], a person or thing that looks striking or unusual.
get an eyeful, [Colloq.], 1. to get a good look. 2. to see something very interesting.

eye·glass (ī′glas′, ī′gläs′), *n.* 1. a lens to help or correct faulty vision; monocle. 2. *pl.* a pair of such lenses, usually in a frame: also called *glasses*, or, less commonly, *spectacles.* 3. an eyepiece. 4. an eyecup.

eye·hole (ī′hōl′), *n.* 1. the socket for the eyeball. 2. a peephole. 3. an opening for receiving a rope, cord, pin, etc.; eyelet.

eye·lash (ī′lash′), *n.* 1. any of the hairs on the edge of the eyelid. 2. a fringe of these hairs.

eye·less (ī′lis), *adj.* without eyes; blind.

eye·let (ī′lit), *n.* [ME. *oylet;* OFr. *oeillet*, dim. of *oeil*, eye < L. *oculus*, eye], 1. a small hole for receiving a rope, cord, hook, etc. 2. a metal ring or short tube for lining such a hole. 3. a small hole edged by stitching in embroidered work. 4. a peephole or loophole. 5. a small eye; ocellus. *v.t.* to make eyelets in; provide with eyelets.

eye·let·eer (ī′lə-têr′), *n.* a pointed instrument for making eyelet holes; bodkin.

eye·lid (ī′lid′), *n.* [ME. *eielid, eien lidd;* see EYE & LID], either of the two movable folds of flesh that cover and uncover the front of the eyeball.

ey·en (ī′ən), *n.* archaic and dialectal plural of **eye.**

eye opener, 1. something that causes the eyes to open in astonishment or realization, as a piece of news, discovery, etc. 2. [Slang], an alcoholic drink, especially one taken early in the day.

eye·piece (ī′pēs′), *n.* in a telescope, microscope, or other optical instrument, the lens or lenses nearest the viewer's eye: see **microscope,** illus.

eye·pit (ī′pit′), *n.* the eye socket.

eye·serv·ant (ī′sũr′vənt), *n.* [Archaic], a servant who does his work only when watched.

eye·serv·ice (ī′sũr′vis), *n.* 1. work done only under the observation of a supervisor. 2. admiring glances.

eye shadow, a cosmetic paste of various colors, usually green or blue, applied to the eyelids.

eye·shot (ī′shot′), *n.* the distance that a person can see; range of vision.

eye·sight (ī′sīt′), *n.* 1. the power of seeing; sight; vision. 2. the range of vision.

eye·sore (ī′sôr′, ī′sōr′), *n.* a thing that is disagreeable to look at.

eye splice, a splice made by turning the end of a rope back and interlacing it with the rope, forming an end loop, or eye: see **splice,** illus.

eye·spot (ī′spot′), *n.* 1. a spot of color that looks like an eye. 2. in *zoology*, a simple form of eye, found in many invertebrates.

eye·stalk (ī′stôk′), *n.* in certain crustaceans, as the lobster or shrimp, a movable stalk with an eye at the tip.

eye·stone (ī′stōn′), *n.* a small calcareous object with one side flat and the other convex, passed under the eyelid to remove cinders, dust, etc. from the eye.

eye·strain (ī′strān′), *n.* a tired or strained condition of the eye muscles, caused by too much or incorrect use of the eyes, faulty vision, etc.

eye·tooth (ī′tōōth′), *n.* [*pl.* EYETEETH (-tēth′)], either of the two pointed teeth in the upper jaw between the bicuspids and the incisors; upper canine tooth.
cut one's eyeteeth, to become experienced or sophisticated.

eye·wash (ī′wôsh′, ī′wäsh′), *n.* 1. a lotion for the eyes. 2. [Slang], *a*) nonsense. *b*) flattery. *c*) something done only to impress an observer.

eye·wa·ter (ī′wô′tẽr, ī′wä′tẽr), *n.* 1. the natural moisture of the eye. 2. a lotion for the eyes.

eye·wink (ī′wiŋk′), *n.* 1. a wink, look, or glance; hence, 2. an instant.

eye·wink·er (ī′wiŋk′ẽr), *n.* 1. an eyelash. 2. any foreign particle in the eye that causes blinking.

eye·wit·ness (ī′wit′nis), *n.* 1. a person who sees or has seen something happen, as an accident, crime, etc. 2. a person who testifies to what he has seen.

eyre (âr), *n.* [ME. *eire;* OFr. *eire, erre* < *errer*, to travel; see ERRANT], 1. a tour or circuit: as, justices in *eyre.* 2. in *English history*, a circuit court held by justices in eyre.

Eyre, Lake (âr), a salt lake in northeastern South Australia: area, 4,000 sq. mi.

Eyre's Peninsula (ârz), a peninsula in South Australia.

ey·rie, ey·ry (âr′i, êr′i), *n.* [*pl.* EYRIES (-iz)], [see AERIE], 1. the nest of an eagle or other bird of prey that builds in a high place; hence, 2. a house or stronghold on a high place. 3. the young (of an eagle, hawk, etc.) in the nest. Also spelled **aerie.**

Eysk (āsk), *n.* Eisk.

Ez., Ezra.

E·zek·i·el (i-zē′ki-əl, i-zē′kyəl), [LL. *Ezechiel;* Gr. *Iezekiēl;* Heb. *yeḥezq'ēl*, lit., God strengthens], a masculine name: diminutive, *Zeke.* *n.* 1. a Hebrew prophet who lived in the 6th century B.C. 2. a book of the Old Testament containing his prophetic writings. Abbreviated **Ezek.**

Ez·ra (ez′rə), [LL.; Heb. *ezrā*, lit., help], a masculine name. *n.* 1. a Hebrew scribe, prophet, and religious reformer of the 5th century B.C. 2. a book of the Old Testament telling of his life and teachings. Abbreviated **Ez., Ezr.**

F

F, f (ef), *n.* [*pl.* **F's, f's, Fs, fs** (efs)], 1. the sixth letter of the English alphabet: a modification of the Old Greek digamma (Ϝ), ultimately from the Phoenician: see **alphabet**, table. 2. the sound of F or f, normally an unvoiced labiodental fricative. 3. a type or impression for F or f. 4. *a symbol for* the sixth in a sequence or group. 5. in *genetics, the symbol for* filial generation. 6. in *photography, the symbol for* F number. *adj.* 1. of F or f. 2. sixth in a sequence or group.

F (ef), *n.* 1. an object shaped like F. 2. a medieval Roman numeral for 40: with a superior bar ($\bar{F}$), 40,000. 3. in *chemistry, the symbol for* fluorine. 4. in *education, a)* a grade meaning *failure. b)* sometimes, a grade third in quality, meaning *fair.* 5. in *mathematics, the symbol for* function. 6. in *music, a)* the fourth tone or note in the scale of C major, or the sixth in the scale of A minor. *b)* a key, string, etc. producing this tone. *c)* the scale having F as the keynote. *d) a symbol for* the bass clef. 7. in *physics, a symbol for* farad. 8. in *printing, a symbol for* folio. *adj.* shaped like F.

F/, f/, f:, *f.*, F number.

F., 1. Fahrenheit. 2. February. 3. Fellow. 4. France. 5. French. 6. Friday.

F., f., 1. farad. 2. farthing. 3. father. 4. fathom. 5. feet. 6. feminine. 7. filly. 8. fine. 9. fluid. 10. folio; folios. 11. following. 12. foot. 13. form. 14. franc; francs. 15. from. 16. in *baseball,* finished by a substitute pitcher. 17. in *music,* forte. 18. [L.], in *pharmacy, a) fac,* make. *b) fiat,* let there be made.

fa (fä), *n.* [It. < *fa*muli; see GAMUT], in *music,* a syllable representing the fourth tone of the diatonic scale: see **solfeggio.**

FA, F.A., 1. Field Artillery. 2. Fine Arts.

f.a., 1. fire alarm. 2. freight agent.

F.A.A.A.S., Fellow of the American Association for the Advancement of Science.

fa·ba·ceous (fə-bā'shəs), *adj.* [L. *fabaceus* < *faba,* a bean], of the pea family of plants.

Fa·bi·an (fā'bi-ən), *adj.* [L. *Fabianus,* of Fabius; see FABIUS], 1. using a cautious strategy of delay and avoidance of battle. 2. of the Fabian Society. *n.* a member of the Fabian Society; Fabian socialist.

Fa·bi·an·ism (fā'bi-ən-iz'm), *n.* the principles and methods of the Fabian Society.

Fabian Society, an organization of English socialists, established in 1884, aiming to bring about socialism by gradual reforms rather than drastic means.

Fa·bi·us (fā'bi-əs), (*Quintus Fabius Maximus*), *n.* Roman general and statesman; 3d century B.C.; defeated Hannibal in the Second Punic War by a cautious strategy of delay and avoidance of battle: called *Cunctator (the Delayer).*

fa·ble (fā'b'l), *n.* [ME.; OFr. < L. *fabula,* a story < *fari,* to speak; see FAME], 1. a fictitious story meant to teach a moral lesson: the characters are usually animals. 2. a myth or legend. 3. a story that is not true; falsehood. 4. [Archaic], the plot of a literary work. *v.i. & v.t.* [FABLED (-b'ld), FABLING], to write or tell (fables, fiction, falsehoods).

fa·bled (fā'b'ld), *adj.* [pp. of *fable*], 1. told in fables; mythical; legendary. 2. unreal; fictitious; invented.

fab·li·au (fab'li-ō'; Fr. fá'bli'ō'), *n.* [*pl.* FABLIAUX (-ōz'; Fr. -ō')], [OFr. < ML. **fabulellus,* dim. < L. *fabula;* see FABLE], in medieval literature, especially French and English literature, a short metrical story, often in eight-syllable lines, telling comic incidents of ordinary life, usually with blunt realism and earthy humor: the genre arose in France in the 12th and 13th centuries.

Fa·bre, Jean Hen·ri (zhän än'rē' fá'br'), 1823–1915; French entomologist.

fab·ric (fab'rik), *n.* [Fr. *fabrique;* L. *fabrica,* a workshop, trade, product of a trade, fabric < *faber,* a workman, artisan; cf. FORGE], 1. anything made of parts put together; structure; building; framework. 2. the style or plan of construction; texture. 3. any woven, knitted, or felted cloth.

fab·ri·cant (fab'ri-kənt), *n.* [Fr. < L. *fabricans,* ppr.; see FABRICATE], a person who makes or builds; manufacturer.

fab·ri·cate (fab'ri-kāt'), *v.t.* [FABRICATED (-id), FABRICATING], [< L. *fabricatus,* pp. of *fabricari,* to construct, frame, build < *fabrica;* see FABRIC], 1. to make; build; construct; manufacture. 2. to make or build by assembling parts: as, we *fabricate* engines. 3. to make up (a story, reason, lie, etc.); invent. —*SYN.* see **lie, make.**

fab·ri·ca·tion (fab'ri-kā'shən), *n.* 1. a fabricating or being fabricated; construction; manufacture. 2. a fabricated thing; especially, a falsehood, false excuse, etc.

fab·ri·ca·tor (fab'ri-kā'tẽr), *n.* [L.], a person who fabricates; specifically, *a)* a maker; manufacturer. *b)* a liar.

fab·ri·koid (fab'ri-koid'), *n.* [see FABRIC & -OID], a fabric made to resemble leather, used for upholstery, etc.: a trade-mark (**Fabrikoid**).

fab·u·list (fab'yoo-list), *n.* [Fr. *fabuliste* < L. *fabula;* see FABLE], 1. a person who writes, tells, or invents fables. 2. a liar.

fab·u·lous (fab'yoo-ləs), *adj.* [L. *fabulosus,* fabled < *fabula;* see FABLE], 1. of or like a fable; imaginary; fictitious; mythical; legendary. 2. incredible; hard to believe; astounding. —*SYN.* see **fictitious.**

fac., facsimile.

fa·çade (fə-säd'), *n.* [Fr.; It. *facciata* < *faccia;* LL. *facia;* see FACE], 1. the front of a building; part of a building facing a street, courtyard, etc.; hence, 2. the front part of anything: often used figuratively, with implications of an imposing appearance concealing something inferior.

FAÇADE (of temple)

face (fās), *n.* [ME.; OFr.; LL. *facia* < L. *facies,* the face, appearance], 1. the front of the head from the top of the forehead to the bottom of the chin, and from ear to ear; visage; countenance. 2. the expression of the countenance. 3. the surface of a thing; especially, *a)* the main surface or side. *b)* the front, upper, or outer surface or part. 4. the side or surface that is marked, as of a clock, playing card, domino, etc., or finished, as of fabric, leather, etc. 5. the appearance; outward aspect. 6. [< Chin. idiom], dignity; self-respect; prestige: as, Japan lost *face* by her defeat. 7. the value printed or written on a note: usually **face value.** 8. the topography (of an area). 9. the functional side (of a tool, etc.). 10. [Colloq.], an expressive distortion of the face; grimace. 11. [Colloq.], effrontery; audacity. 12. in *law,* what is shown by the language of a document, without explanation or addition. 13. in *military science,* any of the sides of a formation, especially of a square formation. 14. in *mineralogy,* any surface of a stone or crystal. 15. in *mining,* the end of a working excavation. 16. in *typography, a)* the type surface on which a letter is cut; printing part of a letter or plate. *b)* the design of type. *v.t.* [FACED (fāst), FACING], [ME. *facen* < the *n.*], 1. to turn, or have the face turned, toward; be in a position opposite to: as, the building *faces* the square. 2. to meet squarely or face to face. 3. to confront with boldness, courage, etc. 4. to realize and be ready to meet (a condition, fact, etc.). 5. to cover with a new surface. 6. to give a false appearance to: as, alcohol is *faced* with caramel to make it look like whisky. 7. to put a smooth surface on (a stone, tool, etc.). 8. to turn (a card, etc.) with the face up. 9. in *military science,* to cause (a formation of soldiers) to pivot by giving the appropriate command. 10. in *sewing,* to add a piece of cloth to (another material) for lining, trimming, etc. *v.i.* 1. to turn, or have the face turned, toward a specified thing or person, or in a specified direction. 2. in *hockey, lacrosse,* etc., to start play by tossing the ball or puck between the two

opposing centers (with *off*). 3. in *military science*, to pivot in a specified direction: usually in the form of a command, as, right *face!*
face down, 1. to disconcert or overcome by a confident, bold manner. 2. with the face down; prone, or wrong side up.
face to face, 1. confronting one another; hence, 2. very near; in the presence: followed by *with*.
face up to, 1. to face with courage; confront and resist. 2. to realize and be ready to meet (a fact, condition, etc.).
fly in the face of, to be rashly defiant of.
in the face of, 1. in the presence of. 2. in spite of.
on the face of it, to all appearances; apparently.
pull (or **wear**) **a long face,** to look sad, glum, disappointed, disapproving, etc.
put a bold face on, to seem bold or confident about.
set one's face against, to be determinedly against; disapprove of; resist; oppose.
show one's face, to come and be seen; appear.
to one's face, confronting one; in one's presence; openly and without fear.
SYN.—**face** is the basic, direct word for the front of the head; **countenance** refers to the face as it reflects the emotions or feelings and is, hence, often applied to the facial expression (his happy *countenance*); **visage** refers to the form, proportions, and expression of the face, especially as indicative of general temperament (a man of stern *visage*); **physiognomy** refers to the general cast of features, especially as characteristic of an ethnic group or as supposedly indicative of character (the *physiognomy* of an honest man).

face card, any king, queen, or jack in a deck of cards.

face lifting, plastic surgery for removing wrinkles, sagging flesh, etc. from the face.

face powder, a cosmetic powder, as of flesh-colored talc, applied to the face to dull the shine, conceal skin blemishes, etc.

fac·er (fās'ẽr), *n.* 1. a person or thing that faces. 2. [Colloq.], a sudden blow in the face; hence, 3. [Colloq.], any sudden, unexpected difficulty.

fac·et (fas'it), *n.* [Fr. *facette*, dim. of *face;* see FACE], 1. any of the small, polished plane surfaces of a cut gem; hence, 2. any of a number of sides or aspects, as of a personality. 3. in *anatomy*, any small, smooth surface on a bone or other hard part. 4. in *architecture*, the raised plane between the flutes of a column. 5. in *zoology*, any of the many small surfaces of a compound eye, as in some insects. *v.t.* to cut or make facets on. —***SYN.*** see **phase.**

fa·ce·ti·ae (fə-sē'shi-ē'), *n.pl.* [L., pl. of *facetia*, a jest, bit of humor < *facetus*, elegant, witty], 1. witty sayings. 2. ribald or coarsely witty books.

fa·ce·tious (fə-sē'shəs), *adj.* [Fr. *facétieux* < L. *facetia;* see FACETIAE & -OUS], lightly joking; jocular; jocose, especially at an inappropriate time. —***SYN.*** see **witty.**

face value, 1. the value printed or written on a bill, bond, etc.; hence, 2. the seeming value: as, I took his promise at *face value*.

fa·cial (fā'shəl), *adj.* [Fr.; ML. *facialis* < LL. *facia;* see FACE], of or for the face. *n.* [Colloq.], a treatment for the skin of the face, consisting of the application of astringents and creams, massage, etc.

facial angle, the angle made by the intersection of two lines drawn from the base of the nostrils, one to the base of the skull and the other to the most prominent part of the forehead.

A B

FACIAL ANGLE
A, New Guinea native;
B, European woman

facial index, the ratio of the length to the width of the face $\left(\frac{\text{length} \times 100}{\text{width}}\right)$: abbreviated **F.I.**

fa·ci·end (fā'shi-end'), *n.* [< neut. of L. *faciendus*, gerundive of *facere*, to make, do], in *mathematics*, the number or factor to be multiplied by another; multiplicand.

-fa·cient (fā'shənt), [*L. faciens, facientis*, ppr. of *facere*, to make, do], a suffix used to form adjectives, meaning *making* or *causing to become*, as in *liquefacient*.

fac·ile (fas''l, fas'il), *adj.* [Fr. < L. *facilis* < *facere*, to make, do], 1. not hard to do; easy. 2. moving or working easily and quickly; fluent: as, a *facile* mind. 3. easy to influence or persuade; affable. —***SYN.*** see **easy.**

‡**fa·ci·le prin·ceps** (fas'ə-li prin'seps), [L.], easily first or foremost; pre-eminent.

‡**fa·ci·lis de·scen·sus A·ver·no** (fas'ə-lis di-sen'səs ə-vũr'nō), [L.], the descent to Avernus (hell) is easy: a quotation from Virgil.

fa·cil·i·tate (fə-sil'ə-tāt'), *v.t.* [FACILITATED (-id), FACILITATING], [Fr. *faciliter*, after It. *facilitare* < L. *facilis;* see FACILE], 1. to make easy or easier. 2. to lighten the work of; assist; help.

fa·cil·i·ta·tion (fə-sil'ə-tā'shən), *n.* 1. a facilitating. 2. in *psychology*, increased ease of performance of any action, resulting from the lessening of nerve resistance by the continued successive application of the necessary stimulus: opposed to *inhibition*.

fa·cil·i·ty (fə-sil'ə-ti), *n.* [*pl.* FACILITIES (-tiz)], [Fr. *facilité;* L. *facilitas*, easiness < *facilis*, easy], 1. ease of doing or making; absence of difficulty. 2. a ready ability; skill; dexterity; fluency. 3. a tendency to be easygoing, yielding, etc. 4. *pl.* the means by which something can be more easily done; conveniences: as, good transportation *facilities*.

fac·ing (fās'iŋ), *n.* 1. a lining or trimming, often decorative, sewn on the inside or outside edge or part of a dress, coat, etc. 2. any material used for this. 3. a covering of contrasting material to decorate or protect a building. 4. *pl.* the trimmings, collar, and cuffs of certain military coats. 5. *pl.* the turning movements executed by soldiers in drilling.

fac·sim·i·le (fak-sim'ə-li), *n.* [L. *fac*, imperative of *facere*, to make + *simile*, neut. of *similis*, like], 1. an exact reproduction or copy: abbreviated **fac., facsim.** 2. the transmission and reproduction of printed matter by a process involving the use of radio broadcast: the transmitted signals, formed by a photoelectric cell that picks up the differences in light and dark in the subject matter as it is scanned by a beam of light, are converted into a facsimile of the original matter by a mechanism attached to the radio receiver. *adj.* of, or having the nature of, a facsimile. *v.t.* [FACSIMILED (-lid), FACSIMILEING], to make a facsimile of. —***SYN.*** see **copy.**
in facsimile, as an exact likeness; in exact reproduction.

fact (fakt), *n.* [L. *factum*, that which is done, deed, fact; neut. pp. of *facere*, to do, act < IE. base **dhē-*, to put, place, seen also in AS. *don*, to do & Gr. *tithēmi*, I place], 1. originally, a deed; act. 2. a thing that has actually happened or is true; thing that has been or is. 3. the state of things as they are; reality; actuality; truth. 4. something said to have occurred or supposed to be true. 5. in *law*, an actual or alleged incident or condition, as distinguished from its legal consequence.
as a matter of fact, to tell the truth; really: also **in fact, in point of fact.**

fac·tion (fak'shən), *n.* [< Fr. & L.; Fr. *faction;* L. *factio*, a making, doing, company, faction < pp. of *facere;* see FACT], 1. a group of people in an organization who have common interests, usually in opposition to the principles or aims of the main body or leadership; clique. 2. dissension; partisan conflict within an organization or a country.

fac·tion·al (fak'shən-əl), *adj.* 1. of a faction or factions; partisan. 2. causing or characterized by faction.

fac·tion·al·ism (fak'shən-əl-iz'm), *n.* factional quarreling; spirit of faction.

fac·tious (fak'shəs), *adj.* [L. *factiosus* < *factio*], 1. producing or tending to produce faction; causing dissension. 2. produced or characterized by faction.

fac·ti·tious (fak-tish'əs), *adj.* [L. *facticius* < pp. of *facere;* see FACT], not natural, genuine, or spontaneous; forced or artificial: as, the *factitious* needs of our era.

fac·ti·tive (fak'tə-tiv), *adj.* [Mod. L. < L. *factus;* see FACT], designating or of a verb that expresses the idea of making, calling, or thinking something to be of a certain character, using a noun, pronoun, or adjective as a complement to its direct object; taking a complementary object. Examples: *make* the dress *short, elect* him *president*.

fac·tor (fak'tẽr), *n.* [Fr. *facteur;* OFr. *factour;* L. *factor*, doer, maker, performer < pp. of *facere*, to do, make], 1. *a*) a person who carries on business transactions for another; commission merchant; agent for the sale of goods. *b*) a person legally appointed to take care of forfeited or sequestered property. *c*) [Scot.], a person who manages an estate for another; steward; bailiff. 2. [< fig. use of 4], any of the circumstances, conditions, etc. that bring about a result; element or constituent that makes a thing what it is. 3. in *biology*, a gene. 4. in *mathematics*, any of two or more quantities which form a product when multiplied together. *v.t.* in *mathematics*, to resolve into factors; factorize. —***SYN.*** see **agent, element.**

fac·tor·age (fak'tẽr-ij), *n.* 1. the business of a factor; buying and selling on commission. 2. a factor's commission.

fac·to·ri·al (fak-tôr'i-əl, fak-tō'ri-əl), *adj.* 1. of a factor. 2. [Rare], of a factory. 3. in *mathematics*, of factors or factorials. *n.* the product of a given series of consecutive whole numbers beginning with 1: as, the *factorial* of 5 is $1\times2\times3\times4\times5$, or 120.

fac·tor·ize (fak'tə-rīz'), *v.t.* [FACTORIZED (-rīzd'), FACTORIZING], in *mathematics*, to separate (a product) into factors.

factor of safety, the ratio of the maximum strength of a piece of material or a part to the probable maximum load to be applied to it.

fac·to·ry (fak'tə-ri, fak'tri), *n.* [*pl.* FACTORIES (-riz, -triz)], [Fr. *factorie* < *facteur;* see FACTOR], 1. a building or buildings in which things are manufactured; manufacturing plant. 2. [after Port. *feitoria*], a trading settlement maintained by factors.

fac·to·tum (fak-tō'təm), *n.* [ML.; L. *fac*, imperative of *facere*, to do + *totum*, neut. of *totus*, all, the whole], a person hired to do all sorts of work; handy man.

fac·tu·al (fak'choo-əl), *adj.* [< L. *factum* (see FACT); + *-al*], 1. of or containing facts. 2. having the nature of fact; real; actual.

fac·ture (fak'chẽr), *n.* [Fr., L. *factura* < *facere*, to make], 1. the act or method of making something. 2. the thing made.

fac·u·la (fak'yoo-lə), *n.* [*pl.* FACULAE (-lē')], [L., dim. of *fax, facis*, torch], a bright streak or spot on the sun's surface.

fac·ul·ta·tive (fak''l-tā'tiv), *adj.* [Fr. *facultatif* < L. *facultas;* see FACULTY], 1. *a*) granting a faculty, or permission; permissive; hence, *b*) optional. 2. that may or may not happen; contingent. 3. having to do with a faculty or faculties. 4. in *biology*, capable of living under conditions other than the usual: said of parasites, etc.

fac·ul·ty (fak''l-ti), *n.* [*pl.* FACULTIES (-tiz)], [ME. *faculte;* OFr. *faculté;* L. *facultas* < *facilis;* see FACILE], 1. formerly, the power to do; ability to perform any action. 2. any natural or specialized power of a living organism: as, the *faculty* of hearing, speech, etc. 3. power or ability to do some particular thing; skill developed by practice; knack; special aptitude: as, she has a *faculty* for making friends. 4. [< L. *facultas*, transl. of Aristotle's *dynamis*, branch of learning], any of the departments of learning in a university: as, the *faculty* of law, the science *faculty*. 5. all the teachers of a school, college, or university. 6. all the members of any of the learned professions. 7. a power conferred by authority; authorization. 8. [Archaic], what a person is trained to do; trade. 9. in *psychology*, any of the powers formerly thought of as composing the mind, such as will, reason, etc. 10. in the *Roman Catholic Church*, authorization to do something normally forbidden; dispensation. —*SYN.* see **talent.**

fad (fad), *n.* [19th c. < Brit. Midland dial.], a custom, style, etc. that many people are interested in for a short time; passing fashion, craze, or hobby. —*SYN.* see **fashion.**

fad·dish (fad'ish), *adj.* 1. having the nature of a fad. 2. fond of fads; following fads.

fad·dist (fad'ist), *n.* a person who has a fad or follows fads.

fad·dy (fad'i), *adj.* faddish.

fade (fād), *v.i.* [FADED (-id), FADING], [ME. *faden;* OFr. *fader* < *fade*, pale; prob. < L. *vapidus*, stale; influenced by L. *fatuus*, foolish, silly], 1. to become less distinct; lose color or brilliance; dim. 2. to lose freshness or strength; wither; languish; droop; wane. 3. to disappear slowly; die out. *v.t.* 1. to cause to fade. 2. [Slang], to meet the bet of; cover: dice player's term. —*SYN.* see **vanish.**

fade back, in *football*, to move back from the line of scrimmage, as in order to throw a forward pass.

fade in, in *motion pictures, radio & television*, to appear gradually; become more distinct.

fade out, in *motion pictures, radio & television*, to disappear gradually; become less distinct.

fade-in (fād'in'), *n.* in *motion pictures, radio & television*, a fading in; gradual appearance or becoming distinct of a scene or sound.

fade·less (fād'lis), *adj.* that will not fade; unfading.

fade-out (fād'out'), *n.* in *motion pictures, radio & television*, a fading out; gradual disappearance or becoming indistinct of a scene or sound.

fae·cal (fē'k'l), *adj.* fecal.

fae·ces (fē'sēz), *n.pl.* feces.

Fa·en·za (fä-en'tsä), *n.* a city in northern Italy: pop., 47,000.

fa·er·ie, fa·er·y (fâr'i), *n.* [var. of *fairy*, first used by Spenser], [Archaic], 1. (fā'ẽr-i), fairyland. 2. a fairy. *adj.* [Archaic], fairy. Also spelled **faërie, faëry.**

Faer·oe Islands (fâr'ō), a group of Danish islands between Great Britain and Iceland: area, 540 sq. mi.; pop., 30,000 (est. 1947): also spelled **Faroe.**

Faer·oes (fâr'ōz), *n.pl.* the Faeroe Islands.

Faf·nir (fäv'nir, fäf'nẽr), *n.* [ON. *Fáfnir*], in *Norse legend*, a giant who, in the form of a dragon, guarded the Nibelung treasure: he was killed by Sigurd.

fag (fag), *v.i.* [FAGGED (fagd), FAGGING], [earlier form of *flag, v.;* basic sense "to droop, decline, hang loosely"], 1. to work hard and become very tired. 2. to serve as a fag. *v.t.* 1. to make tired by hard work. 2. to employ (a boy) as a fag. *n.* [British Colloq.], 1. *a*) hard, tiring work; drudgery. *b*) fatigue; weariness. 2. a boy in an English public school who acts as a servant for another boy in a higher form, or class.

fag (fag), *n.* [< *fag end*], [Slang], a cigarette.

fag·a·ceous (fə-gā'shəs), *adj.* [< Mod. L. *Fagaceae*, name of the family < L. *fagus;* see BEECH], of the beech family of plants, including the beech, oak, and chestnut.

fag end, [*fag* in earlier *n.* sense of "thing hanging loosely"], 1. *a*) the last part or coarse end of a piece of cloth. *b*) the frayed, untwisted end of a rope; hence, 2. the last and worst part of anything; remnant.

fag·got (fag'ət), *n.* & *v.t.* fagot.

fag·got·ing (fag'ət-iŋ), *n.* fagoting.

Fa·gin (fā'gin), *n.* in Dickens' *Oliver Twist*, an old villain who trains children to be thieves.

fag·ot (fag'ət), *n.* [ME.; OFr., with change of suffix < LL. **facellum* < Gr. *phakelos*, a bundle], 1. a bundle of sticks, twigs, or branches, especially for use as fuel. 2. in *metallurgy*, a bundle or heap of iron or steel pieces to be worked into bars by hammering or rolling at welding temperature. *v.t.* 1. to make into a fagot; form fagots of. 2. in *sewing*, to decorate with fagoting. Also spelled **faggot.**

fag·ot·ing (fag'ət-iŋ), *n.* 1. a decorative stitch made by pulling horizontal threads out of the fabric and tying the cross threads together in bunches. 2. openwork decoration in which the thread is drawn in crisscross stitches across the open seam. Also spelled **faggoting.**

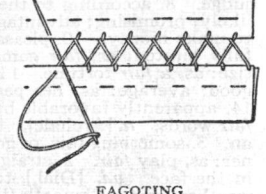

FAGOTING

Fah., Fahrenheit.

‡Fahl·band (fäl'bänt'; Eng. fäl'band'), *n.* [G. < *fahl*, pale (akin to Eng. *fallow*) + *band*, a strip: from the faded appearance upon decomposition], a layer of rock containing metallic sulfides.

Fahr·en·heit (far'ən-hīt', fär'ən-hīt'), *adj.* [< Gabriel Daniel *Fahrenheit* (1686–1736), G. physicist who devised the scale], designating or of a thermometer on which the boiling point of pure water is 212° and the freezing point 32°, under standard atmospheric pressure. *n.* this thermometer or its scale. Abbreviated **F., Fah., Fahr.**

fa·ience (fī-äns', fā-äns'; Fr. fà'yäns'), *n.* [Fr.; It. *faenza* < *Faenza*, Italy, original place of its manufacture], a fine grade of painted and glazed pottery or porcelain.

fail (fāl), *v.i.* [ME. *failen;* OFr. *faillir*, to fail, miss; L. *fallere*, to deceive, disappoint], 1. to be lacking or insufficient; fall short. 2. to lose power or strength; weaken; die away. 3. to be deficient or negligent in an obligation, duty, or expectation; default. 4. to be unsuccessful in obtaining a desired end; be unable to do or become; miss. 5. to become bankrupt. 6. in *education*, to get a grade of failure; not pass. *v.t.* 1. to be useless or not helpful to; be inadequate for; disappoint. 2. to leave; abandon: as, his courage *failed* him. 3. to neglect or omit: used with an infinitive, as, he *failed* to go. 4. in *education*, *a*) to give a grade of failure to (a pupil). *b*) to get a grade of failure in (a subject). *n.* [ME. *faile;* OFr. *faile* < the *v.*], failure: now only in *without fail*, without failing (to occur, do something, etc.).

fail of, to fail to achieve; be without.

fail·ing (fāl'iŋ), *n.* 1. a failure. 2. a weakness; slight fault or defect: as, tardiness was one of his *failings*. *prep.* without; in the lack of: as, *failing* the shipment, the store lost sales. —*SYN.* see **fault.**

faille (fāl, fīl; Fr. fà'y'), *n.* [Fr.], a ribbed, soft, plainly woven fabric of silk or rayon, for dresses, etc.

fail·ure (fāl'yẽr), *n.* [< earlier *failer;* Anglo-Fr. *failer;* OFr. *faillir*, orig. inf. in legal use (cf. DISCLAIMER); see FAIL], 1. the state or fact of being lacking or insufficient; falling short. 2. a losing of power or strength; weakening; dying away. 3. a not doing; neglect or omission: as, *failure* to obey rules. 4. a not succeeding in doing or becoming. 5. a person or thing that does not succeed. 6. a becoming bankrupt. 7. in *education*, *a*) a failing to pass. *b*) a grade or mark (usually *F*) indicating a failing to pass.

fain (fān), *adj.* [ME. *fain, faegen*, joyful, joyfully; AS. *fægen, fægn*, glad; akin to ON. *feginn;* IE. base **pek-*, to be satisfied], [Archaic & Poetic], 1. glad; ready. 2. compelled by circumstances; reluctantly willing. 3. eager. *adv.* with eagerness; gladly: used with *would*, as, he *would fain* stay.

fai·naigue (fə-nāg'), *v.i.* [FAINAIGUED (-nāgd'), FAINAIGUING], [clipped form < *finagle*], 1. to fail to follow suit in playing cards; renege. 2. to cheat; finagle.

fai·né·ant (fā'ni-ənt; Fr. fe'nā'än'), *adj.* [Fr. < OFr. *faignant*, an idler, orig. ppr. of *faindre* (see FEIGN); altered by association with Fr. *faire*, to do + *néant*, nothing], lazy; idle. *n.* a lazy, idle person.

faint (fānt), *adj.* [ME. *faint, feint*, weak; OFr. *feint*, lit., sluggish, pp. of *feindre;* see FEIGN], 1. without strength; weak; feeble. 2. without courage or vigor; timid. 3. done without strength, vigor, or enthusiasm. 4. feeling weak and dizzy, as if about to swoon. 5. dim; indistinct; unclear. *n.* a condition of temporary loss of consciousness as a result of an inadequate flow of blood to the brain; swoon. *v.i.* 1. to fall into a faint; swoon (often with *away*). 2. [Archaic or Poetic], to weaken; languish.

faint·heart (fānt'härt'), *n.* a fainthearted person.

faint·heart·ed (fānt′här′tid), *adj.* cowardly; timid.

faints (fānts), *n.pl.* [see FAINT], the crude, impure spirits given off in the first and last stages of the distillation of liquors.

fair (fâr), *adj.* [ME.; AS. *fæger*, beautiful; akin to Goth. *fagrs*, apt, fit; IE. base **pāk-*, to fasten, as also in L. *pax, pacis*, peace (cf. PEACE, PACIFY); orig. opposed to *foul*, as still in phrases], 1. attractive; beautiful; lovely: as, *fair* women. 2. unblemished; clean: as, a *fair* reputation. 3. [< idea that dark coloring was *foul*], light in color; blond: as, *fair* hair. 4. clear and sunny; unclouded; free from storm or the threat of storm: as, *fair* weather. 5. without obstacles; clear and open: as, a *fair* road. 6. smooth and even: said of a ship's lines. 7. just and honest; impartial; unprejudiced: as, a *fair* judge. 8. according to the rules: as, a *fair* defeat. 9. likely; promising; advantageous: as, he is in a *fair* way to make money. 10. pleasant and courteous. 11. lawfully hunted: as, *fair* game. 12. of moderately good size: as, a *fair* fortune. 13. neither very bad nor very good; average: as, her performance was merely *fair*. 14. apparently favorable but really false; specious: as, *fair* words. *n.* [Archaic], 1. beauty. 2. a pretty woman. 3. something fair, or good. *adv.* 1. in a fair manner: as, play *fair*. 2. straight; squarely: as, struck *fair* in the face. *v.i.* [Dial.], to become clear: said of the weather. *v.t.* to smooth (timbers, etc.).

bid fair, to appear likely; have a reasonable chance.

fair and square, [Colloq.], with justice and honesty.

fair to middling, [Colloq.], moderately good; passable.

SYN.*—fair,** the general word, implies the treating of both or all sides alike, without reference to one's own feelings or interests (a *fair* exchange); **just** implies adherence to a standard of rightness or lawfulness without reference to one's own inclinations (a *just* decision); **impartial** and **unbiased** both imply freedom from prejudice for or against any side (an *impartial* chairman, an *unbiased* account); **dispassionate** implies the absence of passion or strong emotion, hence, connotes cool, disinterested judgment (a *dispassionate* critic); **objective** implies a viewing of persons or things without reference to oneself, one's feelings, interests, etc. (an *objective* newspaper). See also **beautiful.** —ANT.*** prejudiced, biased.

fair (fâr), *n.* [ME. & OFr. *feire* (Fr. *foire*); LL. *feria;* L. *feriae, pl.*, feast days, holidays; OL. *fesiae;* like L. *festus* (see FESTIVE) < Oscan *fíísnú*, temple, akin to L. *fanum*, holy place < IE. base **dhēs-*, used in religious terms], 1. originally, a gathering of people held at regular intervals for barter and sale of goods. 2. a festival or carnival where there is entertainment and things are sold, often for charity; bazaar. 3. an exhibition, often competitive, of farm, household, and manufactured products, usually with various amusement facilities and educational displays; kind of exposition.

fair ball, in *baseball*, a batted ball that stops in the infield, or first strikes the ground there, and does not pass the foul line before first or third base, or that first strikes the ground inside the foul line after passing first or third base: opposed to *foul ball*.

Fair·banks (fâr′baŋks), *n.* a city in central Alaska: pop., 13,000.

fair catch, in *football*, a catch of a kicked ball made after giving the proper signal that no attempt will be made to run with the ball: the opposing players are penalized if they interfere with the catcher.

fair copy, an exact copy of a document after final corrections have been made on it.

fair employment practices, the employment of persons without prejudicial regard to matters that are irrelevant to the work, such as race, religion, sex, etc.

Fair·field (fâr′fēld′), *n.* a town in southwestern Connecticut: pop., 46,000.

fair green, in *golf*, a fairway.

fair·ground (fâr′ground′), *n.* an open space where fairs are held.

fair-haired (fâr′hârd′), *adj.* 1. having blond hair. 2. [Colloq.], favorite: as, the *fair-haired* boy of the family.

fair·i·ly (fâr′i-li), *adv.* in a fairylike manner; gracefully.

fair·ing (fâr′iŋ), *n.* [*fair, v.* + *-ing*], in *engineering*, an additional part or structure added to an aircraft, etc. to smooth the outline and thus reduce drag.

fair·ing (fâr′iŋ), *n.* [Archaic], a gift got at a fair.

fair·ish (fâr′ish), *adj.* moderately good, well, large, etc.

Fair Lawn, a town in northeastern New Jersey: pop., 36,000.

fair-lead (fâr′lēd′), *n.* [< earlier *fair-leader*], in *nautical usage*, a ring, block, or piece of wood with holes in it that acts as a guide for the running rigging or a rope, to prevent its being cut or chafed.

fair·ly (fâr′li), *adv.* [ME. *fairliche;* see FAIR, *adj.*], 1. justly; equitably. 2. moderately; somewhat: as, he plays *fairly* well. 3. clearly; distinctly. 4. completely or really: as, his voice *fairly* rang. 5. [Obs.], *a)* softly. *b)* courteously.

fair-mind·ed (fâr′mīn′did), *adj.* just; impartial; unbiased; unprejudiced.

Fair·mont (fâr′mont), *n.* a city in northern West Virginia: pop., 27,000.

fair play, the act or fact of abiding by the rules in sports, games, or any other activity; fairness and honor in dealing with competitors, customers, etc.

fair sex, women.

fair-spo·ken (fâr′spō′kən), *adj.* speaking or spoken civilly and pleasantly; polite; courteous; bland; plausible.

fair-trade (fâr′trād′), *adj.* designating or of an agreement whereby a distributor undertakes to charge no less than the minimum price set by a manufacturer on a specified trade-marked commodity. *v.t.* to sell (a commodity) under a fair-trade agreement.

fair·way (fâr′wā′), *n.* 1. a navigable channel in a river, harbor, etc. 2. that part of a golf course between the tees and the putting greens where the grass is cut short.

fair-weath·er (fâr′weth′ẽr), *adj.* 1. suitable only for fair weather; hence, 2. helpful, dependable, etc. only in agreeable, easy circumstances; failing in times of distress or need: as, *fair-weather* friends.

Fair·weath·er, Mount (fâr′weth′ẽr), a mountain between Alaska and British Columbia: height, 15,399 ft.

fair·y (fâr′i), *n.* [*pl.* FAIRIES (-iz)], [ME. *faierie*, fairyland, enchantment, fairy; OFr. *faerie* (Fr. *féerie*); see FAY], 1. a tiny, graceful, delicate imaginary being in human form, supposed to have magic powers. 2. [Slang], a male homosexual: contemptuous term. *adj.* 1. of fairies. 2. fairylike; graceful; delicate. Formerly also spelled **faerie, faery, faërie, faëry** (except in *n.* 2).

fair·y·land (fâr′i-land′), *n.* 1. the imaginary land where the fairies live. 2. a lovely, enchanting place.

fairy ring, a circle of contrasting color often seen on grass-covered ground, caused by underground fungi: so called because formerly thought to have been made by the dancing of fairies.

fairy tale, 1. a story about fairies, giants, magic deeds, etc.; hence, 2. an unbelievable or untrue story; lie.

Fai·sal I (fī′səl), 1885–1933; Arabian military officer and statesman; king of Syria (1920); king of Iraq (1921–1933): also spelled **Feisal, Feisul.**

‡**fait ac·com·pli** (fe′tà′kōn′plē′), [Fr., lit., an accomplished fact], a thing already done, so that opposition or argument is useless.

Faith (fāth), [see next entry], a feminine name.

faith (fāth), *n.* [ME. *feith;* OFr. *feid, fei* (Fr. *foi*); L. *fides* < *fidere*, to trust, confide in], 1. unquestioning belief. 2. unquestioning belief in God, religion, etc. 3. a religion or a system of religious beliefs: as, the Catholic *faith*. 4. anything believed. 5. complete trust, confidence, or reliance: as, children usually have *faith* in their parents. 6. loyalty; allegiance to some person or thing. ***interj.*** indeed; in faith. —***SYN.*** see **belief.**

bad faith, insincerity; dishonesty; duplicity.

break faith, 1. to be disloyal to one's beliefs, principles, etc. 2. to break a promise.

good faith, sincerity; honesty.

in faith, indeed; really.

keep faith, 1. to be loyal to one's beliefs, principles, etc. 2. to keep a promise.

faith cure, 1. a method of trying to cure illness by having faith, praying, etc. 2. a cure allegedly caused by such methods.

faith·ful (fāth′fəl), *adj.* 1. keeping faith; worthy of trust; honest; loyal. 2. reliable; dependable. 3. accurate; exact; true: as, a *faithful* copy. 4. [Rare], full of faith, especially religious faith.

the faithful, 1. the true believers (in any specified religion). 2. the loyal adherents.

SYN.*—faithful** implies continued, steadfast adherence to a person or thing to whom one is bound by an oath, duty, obligation, etc. (a *faithful* wife); **loyal** implies undeviating allegiance to a person, cause, institution, etc. which one feels morally bound to support or defend (a *loyal* friend); **constant** suggests freedom from fickleness in affections or loyalties (a *constant* lover); **stanch** (or **staunch**) implies such strong allegiance to one's principles or purpose as not to be turned aside by any cause (a *stanch* defender of the truth); **resolute** stresses unwavering determination, often in adhering to one's personal ends or aims (she was *resolute* in her decision to stay). —ANT.*** faithless.

faith healer, a person who attempts faith cures.

faith·less (fāth′lis), *adj.* 1. not keeping faith; dishonest; disloyal. 2. unreliable; undependable. 3. [Rare], without faith, especially religious faith.

SYN.*—faithless** implies failure to adhere to an oath, duty, obligation, etc. (a *faithless* wife); **false,** in this connection more or less synonymous with **faithless,** stresses failure in devotion to someone or something that has a moral claim to one's support (a *false* friend); **disloyal** implies a breach of allegiance to a person, cause, institution, etc. (*disloyal* to one's family); **traitorous** strictly implies the commission of an act of treason; **treacherous** suggests an inclination to commit treason or a tendency to betray a trust (his *treacherous* colleagues); **perfidious** adds to the meaning of **treacherous** a connotation of sordidness or depravity (a *perfidious* informer). —ANT.*** faithful.

fai·tour (fā′tẽr), *n.* [OFr. *faitor*, doer, maker < L. *factor*], [Obs.], an impostor; rogue.

Fai·yum (fī-yōōm′), *n.* 1. a division of northern Egypt: area, 670 sq. mi.; pop., 764,000. 2. a city in this region: pop., 101,000. Also spelled **Fayum, Fayyum.**

fake (fāk), *v.t.* & *v.i.* [FAKED (fākt), FAKING], [earlier *feague, feake;* ? < G. *fegen*, to clean, sweep in 17th-c. thieves' slang], [Colloq.], 1. to make (something) seem real, satisfactory, etc. by any sort of deception; practice deception by simulating or tampering with (something); counterfeit. 2. in *jazz*, to improvise (a chorus, solo passage, etc.). *n.* [Colloq.], anything or anyone not genuine; fraud; counterfeit. *adj.* [Colloq.], fraudulent; not genuine; sham; false. —*SYN.* see **false.**

fake (fāk), *n.* [prob. < base of AS. *fæc*, interval, division, interval of time, either directly (cf. Scot. *faik*, a fold) or with influence < LG. cognates (cf. MLG. *vak*); IE. base **paĝ-*, to fasten], in *nautical usage*, a loop of coiled rope, cable, etc. *v.t.* [FAKED (fākt), FAKING], to coil (a rope, cable, etc.).

fa·keer (fə-kêr′), *n.* a fakir.

fak·er (fāk′ẽr), *n.* [Colloq.], 1. a person who fakes; fraud; especially, a swindler. 2. a peddler of trinkets.

fa·kir (fə-kêr′, fā′kẽr), *n.* [Ar. *faqīr*, lit., poor, a poor man], 1. a member of a Moslem holy sect who lives by begging. 2. any Moslem itinerant beggar, often one claiming to perform miracles. 3. any Hindu ascetic.

fa la, fal la (fä′lä, fə-lä′), 1. syllables used as a refrain in some old songs. 2. a type of part song with this refrain.

Fa·lange (fā′lanj; Sp. fä-läŋ′hä), *n.* [Sp., lit., phalanx; L. *phalanx;* see PHALANX], a fascist organization established in Spain in 1934: it helped to overthrow the republic in the Spanish civil war (1936–1939) and became the only official political party under Franco's regime.

Fa·lang·ist (fə-lan′jist), *n.* a member of the Falange.

Fa·la·sha (fä-lä′shə), *n.* a member of a Hamitic tribe living in Ethiopia and practicing the Jewish religion.

fal·ba·la (fal′bə-lə), *n.* [Fr.], a furbelow; flounce; frill.

fal·be·lo (fal′bə-lō′), *n.* a falbala.

fal·cate (fal′kāt), *adj.* [L. *falcatus* < *falx, falcis*, a sickle], sickle-shaped; curved; hooked: as, a *falcate* leaf.

fal·chion (fôl′chən, fôl′shən), *n.* [ME. & OFr. *fauchon;* LL. **falcio* < L. *falx*, a sickle; see FALCATE], 1. a medieval sword with a short, broad, slightly curved blade; hence, 2. [Poetic], any sword.

fal·ci·form (fal′si-fôrm′), *adj.* [< L. *falx, falcis*, a sickle; + *-form*], falcate; curved: as, *falciform* cartilages.

fal·con (fôl′k'n, fô′k'n), *n.* [ME. *faucun, faukon;* OFr. *faucon, falcun;* LL. *falco;* prob. < L. *falx, falcis*, a sickle: ? so named from its curved beak, talons, or wings], 1. any hawk trained to hunt and kill small game, as in the Middle Ages: cf. **tercel.** 2. any of several related birds of prey, with long, pointed wings and a short, curved, notched beak. 3. a small cannon used from the 15th to the 17th centuries.

FALCON (17 in. long)

fal·con·er (fôl′k'n-ẽr, fô′k'n-ẽr), *n.* [ME. *fauconer;* OFr. *faulconier*], 1. a person who breeds and trains falcons. 2. a person who hunts with falcons.

fal·con·et (fôl′k'n-et′, fô′k'n-et′), *n.* [dim. of *falcon*], 1. a small falcon, especially any of various Asiatic kinds. 2. [It. *falconetto* < OIt. *falcone* (It. *falco*); cf. FALCON], an obsolete type of light cannon.

fal·con-gen·tle (fôl′k'n-jen′t'l, fô′k'n-jen′t'l), *n.* [Fr. *faucon gentil;* see FALCON & GENTLE], the female of the European goshawk.

fal·con·ry (fôl′k'n-ri, fô′k'n-ri), *n.* [OFr. *fauconnerie*], 1. the art of training falcons to hunt game. 2. the sport of hunting with falcons.

fal·de·ral (fal′də-ral′), *n.* [nonsense syllables], 1. a trifle; gewgaw. 2. mere nonsense. 3. a refrain in some old songs. Also **falderol, folderol.**

fal·de·rol (fal′də-rol′), *n.* a falderal.

fald·stool (fôld′stōōl′), *n.* [OFr. *faldestoel;* LL. *faldistolium;* OHG. *faltstuol*, lit., folding stool < *faldan*, to fold + *stuol*, a chair, stool], 1. a portable stool or desk used in praying. 2. in the *Roman Catholic Church*, a backless chair used by a bishop when officiating in a church other than his own, or when not on his throne. 3. in the *Anglican Church*, a desk at which the litany is read.

Fal·ken·hayn, E·rich von (ā′riH fôn fäl′kən-hīn′), 1861–1922; German general; chief of staff (1914–1916).

Fal·kirk (fôl′kẽrk, fô′kẽrk), *n.* a city in Stirlingshire, Scotland: pop., 37,000 (est. 1946): site of a battle (1298) in which Scotland under Wallace was defeated by England.

Falk·land Islands (fôk′lənd), a group of British islands, east of southern tip of South America: area, 4,618 sq. mi.; pop., 2,400; capital, Port Stanley: abbreviated **F.I.**

Falk·ner, William (fôk′nẽr), see **Faulkner, William.**

fall (fôl), *v.i.* [FELL (fel), FALLEN (fôl′'n), FALLING], [ME. *fallen;* AS. *feallan*, to fall; akin to G. *fallen;* IE. base **phol-*, to fall], I. to come down by the force of gravity; drop; descend. 1. to come down because detached, pushed, dropped, etc.; move down and land forcibly: as, apples *fall* from the tree. 2. to come down suddenly from a standing or sitting position; tumble; topple; become prostrate: as, the child stumbled and *fell.* 3. to be wounded or killed in battle. 4. to come down in ruins; collapse: as, the building *fell.* 5. to hang down: as, the coat *falls* well from the shoulders. 6. to strike; hit: as, the arrow *fell* wide of its mark. II. to pass from a position, condition, etc. regarded as higher to one regarded as lower. 1. to take a downward direction: as, her glance *fell*, the river *falls* to the sea. 2. to become lower in amount, number, degree, intensity, value, etc.; lessen: as, prices are *falling*, his temperature *fell.* 3. to lose power; be overthrown: as, the government has *fallen.* 4. to lose status, reputation, dignity, etc. 5. to yield to temptation; do wrong; sin; especially (of women), to lose chastity. 6. to be captured or conquered: as, Berlin *fell* to the Allies. 7. to pass into a particular mental or physical state: as, the child *fell* ill. 8. to take on a look of disappointment or dejection: as, her face *fell.* 9. to become lower in pitch or volume: as, her voice *fell.* III. to happen as if by dropping. 1. to take place; occur: as, the meeting *fell* on a Friday. 2. to come by chance, lot, or distribution: as, the prize *fell* to the lucky girl. 3. to come as a right or inheritance: as, the estate *falls* to the widow. 4. to come at a specified place: as, the accent *falls* on the third syllable. 5. to be directed: as, his eye *fell* on a misspelled word. 6. to be spoken: as, the news *fell* from his lips. 7. to be born: said of animals. 8. to be divided (*into*): as, these poems *fall* into two classes. *n.* [< the *v.*], 1. a dropping; descending; coming down. 2. a coming down suddenly from a standing or sitting position. 3. a hanging down. 4. a downward direction or slope. 5. a becoming lower or less; reduction in value, price, etc. 6. a capture; overthrow; ruin. 7. a loss of status, reputation, etc. 8. a yielding to temptation; wrongdoing; moral lapse. 9. *a)* a birth: said of animals. *b)* the number of animals born at one birth; litter. 10. something that has fallen: as, a *fall* of leaves. 11. the season when leaves fall; autumn. 12. the amount of what has fallen: as, a six-inch *fall* of snow. 13. the distance that something falls: as, the stream had a *fall* of three feet. 14. *usually pl.* water falling over a cliff, etc.; cascade. 15. a broad, turned-down ruff or collar. 16. a piece of cloth hanging from a woman's hat, usually in back; kind of veil. 17. in *mechanics*, the loose end of a cable or chain of a tackle. 18. in *nautical usage*, *a)* a break in the level of a deck line. *b) pl.* a hoisting apparatus. 19. *a)* in *wrestling*, the act of throwing an opponent on his back so that both shoulders touch the floor. *b)* a bout or division of a wrestling match. *adj.* of, for, or in the autumn.

fall among, to come among by chance.

fall away, 1. to take away friendship, support, etc.; desert. 2. to become less in size, strength, etc.; specifically, to grow thin and weak.

fall back, to withdraw; give way; retreat; recede.

fall back on (or **upon**), 1. to turn, or return, to for security or help. 2. to retreat to.

fall behind, 1. to drop back; lag behind. 2. to fail to pay on time; be in arrears.

fall down on, [Slang], to be unsuccessful in; fail in.

fall flat, to fail to have the desired effect; be completely unsuccessful.

fall for, [Slang], 1. to fall in love with; become infatuated with. 2. to be tricked or duped by.

fall foul (or **afoul**) **of,** 1. to become entangled with. 2. to have trouble with; get into a quarrel with. 3. [orig. sense], in *nautical usage*, to collide with.

fall from grace, to sin; lapse in the observance of moral or religious prescriptions.

fall in, 1. to bend inward; cave in. 2. to agree. 3. to line up in proper formation.

fall in with, 1. to meet by chance. 2. to meet and join. 3. to agree with; comply with.

fall off, 1. to drop. 2. to become smaller, less, etc. 3. to become worse; decline. 4. in *nautical usage*, to swing to leeward or off the wind.

fall on (or **upon**), 1. to attack. 2. to be the duty of.

fall out, 1. to have a disagreement; quarrel. 2. to happen; result. 3. to leave one's place in line.

fall short, 1. to be lacking. 2. to fail to meet a standard or goal (with *of*).

fall through, to fail; come to nothing.

fall to, 1. to begin; start. 2. to start attacking; hence, 3. to start eating. 4. to close or move into position by itself.

fall under, 1. to come under (an influence, etc.). 2. to be listed or classified as.

ride for a fall, to behave in a manner likely to cause one trouble or injury.

the Fall (of Man), in *Christian theology*, Adam's sin of yielding to temptation in eating the forbidden fruit, and his subsequent loss of grace: see **original sin**.

Fal·la, Ma·nu·el de (mä-nwel′ *the* fä′lyä), 1876–1946; Spanish composer.

fal·la·cious (fə-lā′shəs), *adj.* [L. *fallaciosus*], 1. based on a fallacy; faulty in logic; erroneous: as, *fallacious* reasoning. 2. misleading and disappointing; deceptive: as, *fallacious* expectations.

fal·la·cy (fal′ə-si), *n.* [*pl.* FALLACIES (-siz)], [ME. & OFr. *fallace;* L. *fallacia*, deception, artifice < *fallax, fallacis*, deceptive, deceitful < *fallere*, to deceive], 1. originally, deception. 2. aptness to mislead; being deceptive; delusive quality: as, the *fallacy* of the senses. 3. a false or mistaken idea, opinion, etc.; error. 4. false reasoning; illogical or misleading argument.

fal-lal (fal′lal′), *n.* [arbitrary formation], a useless piece of finery or frippery.

fall·en (fôl′n), *adj.* [ME.; pp. of *fall*], 1. having come down; dropped. 2. prostrate; on the ground. 3. having lost status or moral reputation; degraded. 4. captured; overthrown. 5. ruined; destroyed. 6. dead.

fall guy, [Slang], a person made the victim, or left to face the consequences, of a scheme that has miscarried.

fal·li·bil·i·ty (fal′ə-bil′ə-ti), *n.* the quality of being fallible.

fal·li·ble (fal′ə-b'l), *adj.* [ME.; ML. *fallibilis* < L. *fallere*, to deceive], 1. liable to be mistaken or deceived. 2. liable to be erroneous or inaccurate.

falling sickness, [Rare], epilepsy.

falling star, a meteor.

fall line, 1. the geographical line indicating the beginning of a plateau, usually marked by many waterfalls and rapids. 2. [F- L-], the line east of the Appalachian Mountains, marking the end of the coastal plains and the beginning of the Piedmont Plateau.

Fal·lo·pi·an tube (fə-lō′pi-ən), [after Gabriel *Fallopio* (or *Fallopius*), Italian anatomist (1523–1562), who discovered them], either of two slender tubes that carry ova from the ovaries to the uterus: also called *oviduct*.

fall·out (fôl′out′), *n.* 1. the descent to earth of radioactive particles after a nuclear explosion. 2. these particles.

fal·low (fal′ō), *n.* [ME. *falow;* AS. *fealh;* akin to AS. *fealh*, harrow, felloe (of wheel); IE. **pel-k* < base **qwel-*, to turn], 1. land plowed but not seeded for one or more growing seasons, to kill weeds, make the soil richer, etc. 2. the plowing of land to be left idle for one or more growing seasons. *adj.* 1. left uncultivated or unplanted. 2. untrained; inactive: said of the mind. *v.t.* [ME. *falwen, falgen;* AS. *fealgian* < *fealh*, fallow land; associated with *fealwian*, to fade < *fealu;* see FALLOW (yellow)], to leave (land) unplanted after plowing.

fal·low (fal′ō), *adj.* [ME. *falow, falwe;* AS. *fealo;* akin to G. *fahl*, fallow; Gmc. **falwa* < IE. base **pel-*, gray, pale; cf. PALE], pale-yellow; brownish-yellow.

fallow deer, a small European deer having a yellowish coat spotted with white in summer.

Fall River, a seaport in southeastern Massachusetts: pop., 100,000.

false (fôls), *adj.* [ME. & OFr. *fals;* L. *falsus*, pp. of *fallere*, to deceive], 1. not accurate; not true; in error; incorrect; wrong; mistaken: as, a *false* argument. 2. untruthful; lying; dishonest: as, a *false* witness. 3. disloyal; unfaithful: as, a *false* friend. 4. deceiving or meant to deceive; misleading: as, a *false* scent. 5. not real; sham; artificial; counterfeit. 6. not properly so named; deceptively resembling: as, the *false* sunflower. 7. in *mechanics*, temporary, inessential, or added on for protection, disguise, etc.: as, a *false* drawer. 8. in *music*, pitched incorrectly. *adv.* in a false manner.

play (a person) false, to deceive, cheat, hoodwink, or betray (a person).

put (a person) in a false position, to cause misunderstanding of (a person's) intentions, opinions, etc.

SYN.—**false**, in this comparison, refers to anything that is not in essence that which it purports to be and may or may not connote deliberate deception (*false* hair); **sham** refers to an imitation or simulation of something and usually connotes intent to deceive (*sham* piety); **counterfeit** and the colloquial **bogus** apply to a very careful imitation and always imply intent to deceive or defraud (*counterfeit*, or *bogus*, money); **fake** is a colloquial term for any person or thing that is not genuine (a *fake* doctor, chimney, etc.). See also **faithless**. —*ANT.* genuine, real.

false bottom, 1. a bottom (of a box, drawer, etc.) between which and the real bottom there is a secret compartment. 2. the bottom of a whisky glass, etc. raised or narrowed in such a way as to give a deceptive appearance to the true capacity of the glass.

false face, a mask; usually, a comical or grotesque mask.

false foxglove, a tall plant with large, yellow, thimble-like flowers, resembling the foxglove.

false·heart·ed (fôls′här′tid), *adj.* disloyal; deceitful.

false·hood (fôls′hood), *n.* 1. lack of accuracy or truth; falsity; deception. 2. the telling of lies; lying. 3. a false statement; lie. 4. a false belief, theory, idea, etc.

false imprisonment, unlawful imprisonment.

false keel, a narrow keel below the main keel, for protection and increased steadiness.

false pretenses, in *law*, deliberate misrepresentation of fact in speech or action in order to defraud someone of the title to a certain property or money.

false ribs, the five lower ribs on each side of the body: so called because they are not directly attached to the breastbone.

false step, 1. a misstep; stumble; hence, 2. a blunder.

false teeth, an artificial denture, especially, a complete denture.

fal·set·to (fôl-set′ō), *n.* [*pl.* FALSETTOS (-ōz)], [It. *falsetto*, dim. of *falso*, false < L. *falsus;* see FALSE], 1. an artificial way of singing, used especially by tenors, in which the voice is placed in a register much higher than that of the natural voice. 2. the voice used in such singing, usually characterized by a soft, nasal quality. 3. a person singing in falsetto. *adj.* of or singing in falsetto. *adv.* in falsetto.

fals·ies (fôl′siz), *n.pl.* [Colloq.], pads worn with a brassiere to make the breasts look fuller.

fal·si·fi·ca·tion (fôl′sə-fi-kā′shən), *n.* [OFr.; LL. *falsificatio*], a falsifying or being falsified.

fal·si·fi·er (fôl′sə-fī′ẽr), *n.* a person who falsifies.

fal·si·fy (fôl′sə-fī′), *v.t.* [FALSIFIED (-fīd′), FALSIFYING], [Fr. *falsifier;* ML. *falsificare* < L. *falsificus*, that acts falsely < *falsus* (see FALSE) + *facere*, to make], 1. to make false; specifically, *a*) to misrepresent; give an untrue or misleading account of. *b*) to alter (a record, etc.) fraudulently. *c*) to alter from the accepted rule or form: as, a poet sometimes *falsifies* accent. 2. to prove to be untrue or unfounded. *v.i.* to tell falsehoods; lie.

fal·si·ty (fôl′sə-ti), *n.* [*pl.* FALSITIES (-tiz)], 1. the condition or quality of being false; specifically, *a*) incorrectness. *b*) dishonesty. *c*) deceitfulness. *d*) disloyalty. 2. something false; especially, a lie.

Fal·staff, Sir John (fôl′staf, fôl′stäf), in Shakespeare's *Henry IV* (Parts I and II) and *The Merry Wives of Windsor*, a fat, jovial, witty knight, bold and brazen in talk but cowardly on the battlefield.

Fal·staff·i·an (fôl-staf′i-ən), *adj.* of or like Falstaff or his ragged followers; boastful, witty, brazen, etc.

Fal·ster (fäl′stẽr), *n.* one of the islands of Denmark: area, 199 sq. mi.; pop., 46,000.

falt·boat (fält′bōt′), *n.* [G. *faltboot* < *falten*, to fold (akin to Eng. *fold*) + *boot*, a boat (akin to Eng. *boat*)], a light, collapsible boat made like a kayak: also **foldboat**.

fal·ter (fôl′tẽr), *v.i.* [ME. *faltren*, prob. < ON.; cf. ON. *faltra*(*sk*), to be encumbered], 1. to move uncertainly or unsteadily; totter; stumble. 2. to stumble in speech; speak haltingly; stammer. 3. to act hesitantly; show uncertainty; waver; flinch: as, the front ranks *faltered* before the enemy fire. *v.t.* to say haltingly, hesitantly, or timidly. *n.* 1. a faltering. 2. a faltering sound. —*SYN.* see **hesitate**.

fam., 1. familiar. 2. family.

F.A.M., Free and Accepted Masons.

fame (fām), *n.* [ME.; OFr.; L. *fama*, fame, reputation; like *fari*, to speak < IE. base **bhā-*, to speak, seen also in Gr. *phēmē*, utterance, report & AS. *ben*, a request], 1. [Rare or Archaic], public report; rumor. 2. reputation, especially for good. 3. the state of being well known or much talked about; renown; celebrity. *v.t.* [FAMED (fāmd), FAMING], [Archaic], 1. to tell about widely. 2. to make famous.

famed (fāmd), *adj.* [pp. of *fame*], 1. reported; reputed; popularly believed. 2. widely known; celebrated; renowned (*for* something).

Fa·meuse (fə-mūz′; Fr. fà′möz′), *n.* [Fr., fem. of *fameux*, famous], a late fall variety of apple.

fa·mil·ial (fə-mil′yəl), *adj.* [< L. *familia*, a family], of, involving, or common to a family.

fa·mil·iar (fə-mil′yẽr), *adj.* [ME. & OFr. *familier;* L. *familiaris*, of a household, domestic < *familia;* see FAMILY], 1. originally, having to do with a family. 2. friendly; intimate; close: as, *familiar* conversation. 3. too friendly; presumptuous; unduly intimate or bold. 4. closely acquainted (*with*). 5. well-known; common; ordinary: as, accidents are a *familiar* sight. 6. domesticated: said of animals. Abbreviated **fam.** *n.* 1. a close friend. 2. formerly, a spirit believed to act as an intimate servant. 3. [Obs.], a member of the family. 4. in the *Roman Catholic Church*, a lay servant in a monastery or bishop's household.

SYN.—**familiar** is applied to that which is known through constant association, and, with reference to persons, suggests informality, or even presumption, such as might prevail among members of a family; **close** is applied to persons or things very near to one in affection, attraction, interests, etc.; **intimate** implies very close association, acquaintance, relationship, etc. or suggests something of a very personal or private nature; **confidential** implies a relationship in which there is mutual trust and a sharing of private thoughts, problems, etc. See also **common**.

fa·mil·i·ar·i·ty (fə-mil′i-ar′ə-ti, fə-mil′yar′ə-ti), *n.* [*pl.* FAMILIARITIES (-tiz)], [ME. & OFr. *familiarite;* L. *familiaritas* < *familiaris;* see FAMILIAR], 1. intimacy. 2. free and intimate behavior; absence of formality and ceremony. 3. undue intimacy. 4. *usually pl.* an act, remark, etc. permitted only by intimacy or close relationship. 5. close acquaintance (*with* something).

fa·mil·iar·i·za·tion (fə-mil'yẽr-ə-zā'shən), *n.* a familiarizing or being familiarized.

fa·mil·iar·ize (fə-mil'yə-rīz'), *v.t.* [FAMILIARIZED (-rīzd'), FAMILIARIZING], [*familiar* + *-ize*], 1. to make commonly known: as, the war *familiarized* terms like *radar* and *jeep*. 2. to make (another or oneself) accustomed or fully acquainted: as, *familiarize* yourself with the job.

fam·i·ly (fam'ə-li, fam'li), *n.* [*pl.* FAMILIES (-liz)], [L. *familia*, servants in a household, household < *famulus*, servant; ? < IE. **dhe-mo-*, house (< **dhē-*; see FACT), seen also in Sans. *dhāman*, household; cf. DOOM], 1. all the people living in the same house. 2. *a*) a group consisting of the two parents and their children. *b*) the children of the same parents. *c*) one's husband (or wife) and children. 3. a group of people related by blood or marriage; relatives. 4. all those descended from a common ancestor; tribe, clan, or race. 5. *a*) descent; lineage. *b*) good or noble lineage. 6. a group of things having a common source or similar features: as, a *family* of languages. 7. in *biology*, a subdivision in the classification of plants or animals, ranking above a genus and below an order: family names of plants have the suffix *-aceae*, those of animals, *-idae*. Abbreviated **fam.**

in a family way, [Colloq.], pregnant; with child.

family circle, 1. a group consisting of the members of a family and intimate friends. 2. in some theaters, a section in the upper balcony.

family man, 1. a man with a family. 2. a man devoted to his family and home.

family name, a surname.

family tree, 1. a chart showing the relationship of all the ancestors and descendants in a given family. 2. all the ancestors and descendants in a given family.

fam·ine (fam'in), *n.* [ME.; OFr.; LL. **famina* < L. *fames*, hunger], 1. *a*) an acute and general shortage of food. *b*) the time of this. 2. starvation; great hunger. 3. an acute and general lack of anything.

fam·ish (fam'ish), *v.t. & v.i.* [< ME. *famen*; OFr. *afamer* < L. *ad*, to + *fames*, hunger], 1. to be or make very hungry; weaken with hunger. 2. to kill or die with hunger; starve.

fa·mous (fā'məs), *adj.* [ME.; OFr. *fameus*; L. *famosus* < *fama*; see FAME], 1. much talked about; having fame, or celebrity; renowned. 2. [Colloq.], excellent; very good; first-rate. 3. [Archaic], notorious.

SYN.—**famous** is applied to persons or things that have received wide public attention and are generally known and talked about; **renowned** suggests a being named publicly again and again for some outstanding quality, achievement, etc.; **celebrated** is applied to persons or things that have received much public honor or praise; **noted** implies a being brought to the wide notice of the public for some particular quality; **notorious,** in current usage, suggests a being widely but unfavorably known or talked about; **distinguished** implies a being noted as superior in its class or of its kind; **eminent** more strongly stresses the conspicuous superiority of persons or things; **illustrious** suggests a reputation based on brilliance of achievement or splendidness of character. —*ANT.* obscure, unknown.

fam·u·lus (fam'yoo-ləs), *n.* [*pl.* FAMULI (-lī')], [L., a servant; see FAMILY], an attendant or assistant, especially of a medieval sorcerer or scholar.

fan (fan), *n.* [ME. *fan*, *fann*; AS. *fann* < L. *vannus*, basket for winnowing grain < IE. base **wē-*, to blow, flutter, seen also in Eng. *wind* (air), *winnow*], 1. originally, a device for separating grain from chaff by throwing the grain into the air so as to cause the chaff to be blown away; hence, 2. any device or machine used to set up a current of air for ventilating or cooling; specifically, *a*) any flat surface moved by hand. *b*) a folding device made of paper, cloth, etc. which when opened has the shape of a sector of a circle. *c*) a device consisting of one or more revolving blades or vanes attached to a rotary hub and operated by a motor. 3. anything in the shape of a fan (2, b), as the tail of a bird. 4. in a windmill, a small vane that keeps the large vanes, or sails, at right angles to the wind. *v.t.* [FANNED (fand), FANNING], [ME. *fannien* < the *n.*], 1. to move or agitate (air) with or as with a fan; set up a current of (air) with a fan. 2. to direct a current of air toward or on with or as with a fan; blow on. 3. to stir up; excite. 4. to blow away (flies, etc.) with a fan. 5. to spread out into the shape of a fan (*n.* 2, b). 6. to separate (grain) from chaff. 7. [< *v.i.*, 2], [Slang], in *baseball*, to strike (a batter) out. *v.i.* 1. to scatter or spread (*out*) like a fan (*n.* 2, b). 2. [< idea of *fanning* the air], [Slang], in *baseball*, to strike out.

fan the air, to strike at but fail to hit something.

fan (fan), *n.* [prob. < *fanatic*, influenced by *fancier* & *the fancy*], [Colloq.], a person enthusiastic about a specified sport, pastime, or performer; devotee: as, a baseball *fan*, movie *fan*.

fa·nat·ic (fə-nat'ik), *adj.* fanatical. *n.* a fanatical person. —*SYN.* see **zealot.**

fa·nat·i·cal (fə-nat'i-k'l), *adj.* [< L. *fanaticus*, of a temple, hence enthusiastic, inspired < *fanum*, a temple (cf. FANE); + *-al*], unreasonably enthusiastic; overly zealous: as, *fanatical* devotion to a cause.

fa·nat·i·cism (fə-nat'ə-siz'm), *n.* [see FANATICAL & -ISM], excessive and unreasonable enthusiasm or zeal: as, religious *fanaticism*.

fan·cied (fan'sid), *adj.* [pp. of *fancy*], imaginary; imagined.

fan·ci·er (fan'si-ẽr), *n.* [see FANCY, *v.t.*], 1. a person given to fancies. 2. a person with a special interest in and knowledge of something, particularly of the breeding of plants or animals: as, a dog *fancier*.

fan·ci·ful (fan'si-fəl), *adj.* 1. full of fancy; indulging in fancies; imaginative; whimsical. 2. created in the fancy; imaginary; not real: as, a *fanciful* tale. 3. showing fancy in construction or design; quaint; odd: as, *fanciful* costumes. —*SYN.* see **imaginary.**

fan·ci·less (fan'si-lis), *adj.* without fancy, or imagination.

fan·cy (fan'si), *n.* [*pl.* FANCIES (-siz)], [contr. < ME. *fantasy*; see FANTASY], 1. *a*) originally, imagination in general. *b*) decorative, light, whimsical, playful, or capricious imagination: the current literary sense. See **imagination.** 2. illusion or delusion. 3. a mental image. 4. an arbitrary idea; notion; caprice; whim. 5. an inclination, liking, or fondness, often temporary. 6. critical taste or judgment in art, dress, etc. *adj.* [FANCIER (-si-ẽr), FANCIEST (-si-ist)], 1. based on fancy; capricious; whimsical; fanciful. 2. higher than real value; extravagant: as, a *fancy* price. 3. made or added to please the fancy; ornamental; decorated; not plain; elaborate: as, a *fancy* necktie. 4. of superior skill; intricate and difficult: as, *fancy* diving. 5. of superior quality, and therefore costing more: as, canned goods graded *fancy*. 6. for expensive tastes: as, a *fancy* shop, *fancy* groceries. 7. bred for some special feature or excellence of type: said of animals. *v.t.* [FANCIED (-sid), FANCYING], 1. to imagine. 2. to have a liking for; be fond of. 3. to believe without conviction; suppose. 4. to breed (animals) for some special feature or excellence of type.

fancy (that)! can you imagine (that)!

the fancy, formerly, the enthusiasts of some sport or hobby, especially boxing.

fancy dress, a masquerade costume.

fan·cy-free (fan'si-frē'), *adj.* 1. free to fall in love; not married, engaged, etc. 2. carefree.

fancy man, 1. a man supported by a woman, especially by a prostitute. 2. a man who gambles, especially on horse racing.

fancy woman, 1. a mistress. 2. a prostitute.

fan·cy·work (fan'si-wũrk'), *n.* embroidery, crocheting, and other ornamental needlework.

fan·dan·go (fan-daŋ'gō), *n.* [*pl.* FANDANGOS (-gōz)], [Sp.], 1. a lively Spanish dance in rhythm varying from slow to quick 3/4 time. 2. music for this.

fane (fān), *n.* [L. *fanum*, sanctuary, temple < base of *fari*; see FAME], [Archaic & Poetic], a temple or church.

Fan·euil Hall (fan''l, fan'yəl), an old market building and public hall in Boston, Massachusetts: called the *Cradle of Liberty* because of its use by Revolutionary patriots as a meeting place.

fan·fare (fan'fâr'), *n.* [Fr. < *fanfarer*, to blow trumpets < *fanfaron*, braggart, blusterer; see FANFARONADE], 1. a loud blast or flourish of trumpets. 2. noisy or showy display.

fan·fa·ron·ade (fan'fẽr-ə-nād'), *n.* [Fr.; Sp. *fanfarronada* < Sp. *fanfarron*, *fafarron*, boaster < Ar. *farfār*, boastful], 1. boasting talk or action. 2. fanfare.

fang (faŋ), *n.* [ME., lit., that which catches; AS. *fang*, a catching, seizing < base of *fon* (Gmc. **faŋxan-*), to seize, akin to G. *fangen*; IE. base **pak-*, to fasten, fix, as also in L. *pangere*, to fasten], 1. *a*) one of the long, pointed teeth with which meat-eating animals seize and tear their prey; canine tooth. *b*) one of the long, hollow or grooved teeth through which poisonous snakes inject their venom. 2. the pointed part of something; tusk; talon. 3. formerly, the root of a tooth. —*SYN.* see **tooth.**

FANGS
FANGS (of bushmaster)

fanged (faŋd), *adj.* having fangs.

fan·light (fan'līt'), *n.* a semicircular window, often with sash bars in a fanlike arrangement, over a door or larger window.

fan mail, letters received by a prominent or well-known person, as an author or actor, especially, letters of praise or adulation from strangers.

fan·ner (fan′ẽr), *n.* a person or thing that fans; especially, a machine for separating grain from chaff.

Fan·nie, Fan·ny (fan′i), a feminine name: see **Frances.**

fan·ny (fan′i), *n.* [contraction of *Aunt Fanny*, fanciful euphemism], [Slang], the buttocks.

fan·o (fan′ō), *n.* a fanon.

fan·on (fan′ən), *n.* [OFr.; OHG. *fano*, piece of cloth], 1. a narrow band worn hanging over the left arm by priests celebrating Mass; maniple. 2. a capelike vestment worn by the Pope at Mass. Also **fano, fanum, phano.**

fan palm, any palm tree with broad, fan-shaped leaves.

fan·tail (fan′tāl′), *n.* 1. a part, tail, or end spread out like an opened fan. 2. a variety of domestic pigeon, Australian flycatcher, or goldfish with such a tail.

fan-tan (fan′tan′), *n.* [< Chin. *fan*, number of times + *t'an*, apportion], 1. a Chinese gambling game in which the players must guess the number of beans, counters, etc. that will be left from a pile after it has been counted off in fours. 2. a card game in which the players discard their cards in proper sequence, the winner being the one who first gets rid of all his cards.

fan·ta·si·a (fan-tā′zi-ə, fan-tā′zhə, fan-tä′zi-ə, fan′tə-zē′ə), *n.* [It. < LL. *phantasia;* see FANTASY], 1. a musical composition of no fixed form, with a structure determined by the composer's fancy. 2. a medley of familiar tunes.

fan·tasm (fan′taz'm), *n.* a phantasm.

fan·tast (fan′tast), *n.* an impractical dreamer; visionary.

fan·tas·tic (fan-tas′tik), *adj.* [OFr. *fantastique;* ML. *fantasticus;* LL. *phantasticus;* Gr. *phantastikos*, able to present or represent to the mind < *phantazein*, to make visible < *phainein*, to show], 1. existing in the imagination; imaginary; unreal: as, the *fantastic* notions of the insane. 2. having a strange or weird appearance; grotesque; odd; quaint: as, a *fantastic* hat. 3. thought of by unrestrained fancy; extravagant; capricious; eccentric: as, her whims are *fantastic*. *n.* a person who is fantastic in behavior, dress, etc.; eccentric.

SYN.—**fantastic** implies a lack of restraint in imagination, suggesting that which is extravagantly fanciful or unreal in design, conception, construction, etc. (*fantastic* notions); **bizarre** suggests that which is extraordinarily eccentric or strange because of startling incongruities, extreme contrasts, etc. (music with a *bizarre* atonality); **grotesque** suggests a ludicrously unnatural distortion of the normal or real, or a fantastic combination of elements (the *grotesque* grimaces of the comedian). See also **imaginary.**

fan·tas·ti·cal (fan-tas′ti-k'l), *adj.* fantastic.

fan·ta·sy (fan′tə-si, fan′tə-zi), *n.* [*pl.* FANTASIES (-siz, -ziz)], [ME. & OFr. *fantasie;* LL. *phantasia*, idea, notion; Gr. *phantasia*, look or appearance of a thing, lit., a making visible < *phainein*, to show], 1. imagination or fancy; especially, wild, visionary fancy. 2. an unreal mental image; illusion; phantasm. 3. a whim; queer notion; caprice. 4. an imaginative poem, play, etc. 5. in *music*, a fantasia. 6. in *psychology*, a mental image, as in a daydream, usually pleasant and with some vague continuity. Also spelled **phantasy.**

fan·tom (fan′təm), *n.* & *adj.* phantom.

fan tracery, the decoration on fan vaulting.

fan·um (fan′əm), *n.* a fanon.

fan vaulting, in *architecture*, vaulting in which the ribs are spread out like those of a fan.

fan·wise (fan′wīz′), *adv.* opened out like a folding fan.

fan·wort (fan′wũrt′), *n.* a water plant with submerged, finely divided leaves: it is used in aquariums.

far (fär), *adj.* [FARTHER (-thẽr), FARTHEST (-*th*ist); see also FURTHER, FURTHEST], [ME. *farre* & *ferre* (whence dial. form *fur*); AS. *feor, feorr;* akin to OHG. *fer;* IE. ***per-**, thither, thither from, seen also in *per-* & L. *semper*, always], 1. distant in space or time; not near; remote: as, a *far* land, in the *far* future. 2. extending a long way: as, a *far* journey. 3. more distant: as, the *far* side of the stage. 4. very different in quality or nature. 5. advanced; well along, as in years. *adv.* 1. very distant in space, time, or degree. 2. to or from a distance in time or position. 3. very much; considerably: as, this book is *far* better than that. *n.* a distant place: used in certain phrases, as *from far*.

as far as, to the distance, extent, or degree that.
by far, considerably; to a great degree.
far and away, very much; beyond doubt.
far and near, everywhere.
far and wide, widely; everywhere.
far be it from me, I would not presume or wish.
go far, 1. to cover much extent; last long. 2. to have a strong tendency. 3. to accomplish much; achieve much success.
in so far as, to the extent or degree that.
so far, 1. to that extent. 2. up to that point; up to now.
so far as, to the extent or point that.
so far, so good, up to this point everything is all right.

SYN.—**far** generally suggests that which is an indefinitely long way off in space, time, relation, etc. (a *far* cry); **distant**, although also suggesting a considerable interval of separation (a *distant* sound), is the term used when the measure of any interval is specified (desks four feet *distant* from one another); **remote** is applied to that which is far off in space, time, connection, etc. from a place, thing, or person understood as a point of reference (a *remote* village); **removed**, used predicatively, stresses separateness, distinctness, or lack of connection more strongly than **remote.** —***ANT.*** near, close.

far·ad (far′əd, far′ad), *n.* [after M. *Faraday*], an electromagnetic unit of capacitance, equal to the amount that permits the storing of one coulomb of charge for each volt of applied potential difference: symbol, F: abbreviated **F., f.**

far·a·day (far′ə-dā′), *n.* [after M. *Faraday*], a unit of quantity of electricity, used especially in electrolysis, equal to the amount necessary to free one gram atomic weight of a univalent element: its value is approximately 96,494 coulombs.

Far·a·day, Michael (far′ə-dā′), 1791–1867; English chemist and physicist; discovered electromagnetic induction; formulated the laws of electrolysis.

fa·rad·ic (fə-rad′ik), *adj.* [see FARAD], in *electricity*, inductive; induced.

far·a·dize (far′ə-dīz′), *v.t.* [FARADIZED (-dīzd′), FARADIZING], [Fr. *faradiser*, after Michael *Faraday;* see -IZE], in *medicine*, to treat or stimulate with induced electricity.

fa·ran·do·la (fə-ran′dō-lə), *n.* a farandole.

far·an·dole (far′ən-dōl′), *n.* [Fr.; Pr. *farandoulo;* prob. < *fa*, to make + *roundelō*, round dance (cf. ROUNDEL)], 1. a lively French dance in 6/8 time. 2. the music for such a dance.

far·a·way (fär′ə-wā′), *adj.* 1. distant in time, place, degree, etc. 2. dreamy; abstracted: as, a *faraway* look.

farce (färs), *n.* [Fr., stuffing, hence farce < *farcer*, to stuff; L. *farcire*, to stuff, fill in: so called because early farces were used to fill in the interludes between parts of a play], 1. an exaggerated comedy based on broadly humorous situations; play intended only to be funny. 2. broad humor of the kind found in such plays. 3. something absurd or ridiculous: as, his work was just a *farce*. 4. the stuffing for a fowl. *v.t.* [FARCED (färst), FARCING], to fill out with or as with stuffing or seasoning: as, he *farced* his play with old jokes.

‡far·ceur (får′sẽr′), *n.* [Fr.], 1. an actor in farces. 2. a writer of farces. 3. a joker; humorist; wag.

far·cial (fär′shəl), *adj.* farcical.

far·ci·cal (fär′si-k'l), *adj.* of, or having the nature of, a farce; absurd; ridiculous; ludicrous. —***SYN.*** see **funny.**

far·ci·cal·i·ty (fär′si-kal′ə-ti), *n.* 1. the quality of being farcical. 2. [*pl.* FARCICALITIES (-tiz)], a farcical action or remark.

far cry, a great distance or extent; long way.

far·cy (fär′si), *n.* [Fr. *farcin* < LL. *farciminum* < L. *farcire*, to stuff, cram], a disease of horses affecting the lymphatic glands: a form of glanders.

far·del (fär′d'l), *n.* [ME.; OFr., dim. < *farde*, a bundle, pack; Ar. *fardah*, a bundle, camel's load], [Archaic], 1. a pack; bundle. 2. a burden; misfortune.

fare (fâr), *v.i.* [FARED (fârd), FARING], [ME. *faren;* AS. *faran*, to go, wander; akin to G. *fahren;* IE. base ***per-**, (to go) thither, (come) hither, etc. (cf. FAR), seen also in L. *portare*, to carry, lit., to bring hither or thither], 1. [Poetic], to travel; go. 2. to happen; result: as, how did it *fare* with him? 3. to be in a specified condition or position; get on; go through an experience: as, he *fared* well in his business. 4. to eat or be given food. *n.* 1. the amount of money paid for transportation. 2. a passenger in a train, bus, taxi, etc. 3. food; diet. 4. [Archaic], the condition of things. —***SYN.*** see **food.**

Far East, eastern Asia, including China, Japan, etc.

Far Eastern Region, Khabarovsk Territory, U.S.S.R.

fare·well (fâr′wel′), *interj.* [*fare* (imperative) + *well*], good-by. *n.* (fâr′wel′), 1. parting words; expression at parting, usually of good wishes. 2. a leave-taking. *adj.* (fâr′wel′), parting; last: as, a *farewell* gesture.

Fare·well, Cape (fâr′wel′), the southernmost tip of Greenland.

far-famed (fär′fāmd′), *adj.* widely famous.

far-fetched (fär′fecht′), *adj.* 1. not naturally resulting or introduced; strained; forced. 2. [Archaic], brought from a distance.

far-flung (fär′fluŋ′), *adj.* extending for a great distance.

Far·go (fär′gō), *n.* a city in southeastern North Dakota, on the Red River: pop., 47,000.

fa·ri·na (fə-rē′nə), *n.* [L., ground corn, meal < *far*, sort of grain, spelt], 1. flour or meal made from cereal grains, potatoes, nuts, beans, etc., eaten as a cooked cereal. 2. potato starch or other starch.

far·i·na·ceous (far′ə-nā′shəs), *adj.* [LL. *farinaceus* < L. *farina;* see FARINA], 1. containing, consisting of, or made from flour or meal. 2. like meal. 3. starchy.

far·i·nose (far′ə-nōs′), *adj.* [LL. *farinosus*], 1. producing farina. 2. full of meal; mealy. 3. in *botany* & *zoology*, covered with a powderlike substance.

far·kle·ber·ry (fär′k'l-ber′i), *n.* [*pl.* FARKLEBERRIES (-iz)], [?], a shrub or small tree of the heath family, with large, white flowers and round, black, inedible berries, found in the southern United States.

farm (färm), *n.* [ME. & Fr. *ferme;* ML. *firma*, fixed payment < *firmare*, to fix < *firmus*, steadfast, stable], 1. *a*) originally, a fixed sum payable at regular intervals, as rent, taxes, etc., or an amount collected in place of taxes, etc.; hence, *b*) the letting out, for a fixed amount, of the collection of taxes, with the privilege of keeping all that is collected; hence, *c*) the condition of being let out, or farmed out, at a fixed rent. 2. a district of a country leased out by a government for the collection of taxes. 3. a piece of land (with house, barns, etc.) on which crops or animals are raised: originally, such land let out to tenants. 4. something similar to this: as, a tract of water for raising fish is a fish *farm.* 5. in *baseball*, a minor-league team owned and operated by a major-league team to train young or inexperienced players. *v.t.* 1. to cultivate (land). 2. to collect the taxes and other fees of (a business) on a commission basis or for a fixed amount. 3. to rent (a business, land, etc.) in return for a fixed payment (usually with *out*). 4. to send (work) from the main shop, office, etc. to workers on the outside (with *out*). 5. to let out the labor of (a convict, etc.) for a fixed amount. 6. to arrange for the care of (children, paupers, etc.). 7. in *baseball*, to assign to a farm (usually with *out*). *v.i.* to work on or operate a farm; be a farmer.

farm·er (fär′mẽr), *n.* [ME. *fermour*, farmer, bailiff; Anglo-Fr. *fermer;* OFr. *fermier* < *ferme;* see FARM], 1. a person who earns his living by farming; especially, one who manages or operates a farm. 2. a person who contracts to collect taxes or revenues by paying a fixed sum to the government for the right to do so.

farm·er·ette (fär′mẽr-et′), *n.* [Colloq.], a girl or woman farm worker.

farm·er-gen·er·al (fär′mẽr-jen′ẽr-əl), *n.* [*pl.* FARMERS-GENERAL], [Fr. *fermier général*], any of the men who farmed certain taxes in France before the Revolution.

Farm·er-La·bor Party (fär′mẽr-lā′bẽr), 1. a political party in Minnesota, founded in 1919, which favored taxation reforms, social-security legislation, etc.: it merged with the Democratic Party in 1944. 2. a United States political party (1920–1924), which favored nationalization of basic industries and banks.

farm·house (färm′hous′), *n.* a house on a farm; especially, the main dwelling house on a farm.

farm·ing (fär′miŋ), *adj.* of or for agriculture. *n.* 1. the business of operating a farm; agriculture. 2. the letting out to farm of land, revenue, etc.

farm·stead (färm′sted′), *n.* the land and buildings of a farm.

farm·yard (färm′yärd′), *n.* the yard surrounding or enclosed by the farm buildings.

far·o (fâr′ō), *n.* [Fr. *pharaon*: ? so called from the representation of an ancient king of Egypt (*pharaoh*) on the back of one of the cards], a gambling game in which the players bet on the cards to be turned up from the top of the dealer's pack.

Far·oe Islands (fâr′ō), the Faeroe Islands.

Far·o·ese (fâr′ō-ēz′), *n.* 1. [*pl.* FAROESE], a native or inhabitant of the Faeroe Islands. 2. the Norse dialect of the Faeroe Islands, akin to Icelandic.

far-off (fär′ôf′), *adj.* distant; remote.

Fa·rouk I (fä-rōōk′), see **Faruk I.**

Far·quhar, George (fär′kwẽr, fär′kẽr), 1678–1707; Anglo-Irish dramatist.

far·ra·go (fə-rā′gō, fə-rä′gō), *n.* [*pl.* FARRAGOES (-gōz)], [L., mixed fodder for cattle, mixture, medley < *far, farris*, kind of grain, meal; see FARINA], a confused mixture; jumble; medley; hodgepodge.

Far·ra·gut, David Glasgow (far′ə-gət), 1801–1870; American admiral; Union naval commander in the Civil War.

Far·rar, Geraldine (fə-rär′), 1882– ; American dramatic soprano.

far-reach·ing (fär′rēch′iŋ), *adj.* having a wide range, extent, influence, or effect.

Far·rell, James Thomas (far′′l), 1904– ; American novelist.

far·ri·er (far′i-ẽr), *n.* [OFr. *ferrier* < L. *ferrarius*, of iron, hence worker with iron, blacksmith < *ferrum*, iron], 1. a man who shoes horses; blacksmith. 2. [Obs.], a veterinary, especially one who treats horses.

far·ri·er·y (far′i-ẽr-i), *n.* [*pl.* FARRIERIES (-iz)], 1. the shoeing of horses. 2. a place where horses are shod.

far·row (far′ō), *n.* [dial. also *farry;* form influenced by *farrow, adj.;* ME. *farh, farr;* AS. *fearh*, young pig; akin to D. *vark-* in dim. *varken;* IE **porkos;* cf. PORK, AARDVARK], 1. a litter of pigs. 2. [Obs.], a young pig. *v.t. & v.i.* to give birth to (a litter of pigs).

far·row (far′ō), *adj.* [earlier *ferow, furrow*; prob. < LG.; cf. Early Mod. D. *verrekoe*, barren cow, Fris. *fear*, barren], not bearing a calf in a given season: said of a cow.

Fars (färs), *n.* a province of southern Iran: pop., 750,000; capital, Shiraz.

far·see·ing (fär′sē′iŋ), *adj.* 1. capable of seeing far. 2. planning ahead; provident.

far·sight·ed (fär′sīt′id), *adj.* 1. farseeing. 2. having better vision for distant objects than for near ones; hypermetropic.

fart (färt), *v.i. & v.t.* [ME.; akin to *faren*, to go; orig., a euphemism], to pass, or emit as, gas from the intestines through the anus. *n.* [< the *v.*], a passing of gas in this way; breaking wind. Now a vulgar term.

far·ther (fär′thẽr), *adj.* [comparative of *far*], [ME. *ferther*, var. of *further*, substituted for regular *ferrer*, compar.; AS. *fyrre*, more remote, farther, compar. of *feorr, fiorr*, far; see FURTHER], 1. more distant or remote. 2. additional; more: now usually *further.* *adv.* [comparative of *far*], 1. at or to a greater distance or more remote point in space or time. 2. to a greater degree or extent. 3. in addition; moreover: now usually *further.*

Farther India, Indo-China.

far·ther·most (fär′thẽr-mōst′, fär′thẽr-məst), *adj.* most distant; most remote; farthest.

far·thest (fär′thist), *adj.* [superlative of *far*], [ME. *ferthest;* see FARTHER], 1. most distant; most remote. 2. most extended; longest. *adv.* [superlative of *far*]; 1. at or to the greatest distance or most remote point in space or time. 2. to the greatest degree or extent.

far·thing (fär′thiŋ), *n.* [ME. *ferthing;* AS. *feorthing*, lit., a fourthling, fourth part of a thing; dim. of *feortha*, fourth], 1. a small British coin, equal to half of a British halfpenny, worth about half a cent in United States money: abbreviated **F., f.** 2. [Obs.], anything small in amount or value; trifle.

far·thin·gale (fär′thiŋ-gāl′), *n.* [OFr. *verdugalle, vertugalle*, farthingale; Sp. *verdugado*, provided with hoops, farthingale < *verdugo*, young shoot of a tree, rod, hoop < *verde;* L. *viridis*, green], a hoop formed of a framework of whalebone, etc., or a skirt or petticoat covering such a hoop, worn by women in the 16th and 17th centuries.

FARTHINGALE

Fa·ruk I (fä-rōōk′), 1920– ; son of *Fuad I;* king of Egypt (1936–52); abdicated: also spelled **Farouk.**

f.a.s., free alongside ship.

fas·ces (fas′ēz), *n.pl.* [L., pl. of *fascis*, a bundle, fagot, packet; cf. FASCISM], a bundle of rods bound about an ax with projecting blade, carried before ancient Roman magistrates as a symbol of authority: later the symbol of Italian fascism.

fas·ci·a (fash′i-ə), *n.* [*pl.* FASCIAE (-ē′)], [L., a band, sash, fillet], 1. a band; flat strip; fillet. 2. in *anatomy*, a thin layer of connective tissue covering, supporting, or connecting the muscles or inner organs of the body. 3. in *architecture*, a wooden or stone band between moldings. 4. in *surgery*, a bandage. 5. in *zoology*, a broad, distinct band of color.

fas·ci·al (fash′i-əl), *adj.* of a fascia.

fas·ci·ate (fash′i-āt′), *adj.* [L. *fasciatus*, pp. of *fasciare*, to swathe, wrap with bands < *fascia*, a band, fillet], 1. bound with a band or fillet. 2. in *botany*, *a*) abnormally enlarged and flattened, as some plant stems. *b*) growing in a fascicle. 3. in *zoology*, marked by broad colored bands.

fas·ci·at·ed (fash′i-ā′tid), *adj.* fasciate.

FASCES

fas·ci·a·tion (fash′i-ā′shən), *n.* [Fr.], 1. the condition of being fasciate. 2. a binding up. 3. the way in which something is bound up. 4. in *botany*, an abnormal enlargement and flattening of plant stems.

fas·ci·cle (fas′i-k′l), *n.* [L. *fasciculus*, dim. of *fascis;* see FASCES], 1. a small bundle. 2. an installment of a book published in parts. 3. in *botany*, a small tuft or cluster of fibers, leaves, or flowers.

fas·ci·cled (fas′i-k′ld), *adj.* growing in a fascicle.

fas·cic·u·lar (fə-sik′yoo-lẽr), *adj.* fasciculate.

fas·cic·u·late (fə-sik′yoo-lit, fə-sik′yoo-lāt′), *adj.* [< L. *fasciculus*, dim. of *fascis* (see FASCES); + *-ate*], formed of, or growing in, bundles or clusters.

fas·cic·u·lat·ed (fə-sik′yoo-lā′tid), *adj.* fasciculate.

fas·ci·cule (fas′i-kūl′), *n.* [Fr.], a fasciculus.

fas·cic·u·lus (fə-sik′yoo-ləs), *n.* [*pl.* FASCICULI (-lī′)], [L., dim. of *fascis*, a bundle], a small bundle of fibers; specifically, a bundle of nerve fibers in the central nervous system: also **fascicle.**

fas·ci·nate (fas′′n-āt′), *v.t.* [FASCINATED (-id), FASCINATING], [L. *fascinatus*, pp. of *fascinare*, to bewitch, charm < *fascinum*, an enchanting, witchcraft], 1. originally, to bewitch; put under a spell. 2. to attract or hold motionless, as by a fixed look or by inspiring terror. 3. to attract by delightful qualities; charm. —*SYN.* see **attract.**

fas·cin·a·tion (fas″n-ā′shən), *n.* 1. a fascinating or being fascinated. 2. strong attraction; charm; allure.

fas·ci·na·tor (fas′′n-ā′tẽr), *n.* 1. a person who fascinates. 2. a woman's scarf made of lace, net, yarn, etc., worn around the head and neck.

fas·cine (fa-sēn′), *n.* [Fr.; OFr.; L. *fascina*, a bundle of sticks, a fagot < *fascis;* see FASCES], a bundle of sticks bound together, used to fill ditches, strengthen the sides of trenches, etc.

fas·cism (fash′iz'm), *n.* [It. *fascismo* < *fascio*, political group, organization, club < L. *fascis;* see FASCES], 1. [F-], the doctrines, methods, or movement of the Fascisti. 2. [sometimes F-], a system of government characterized by rigid one-party dictatorship, forcible suppression of the opposition (unions, other, especially leftist, parties, minority groups, etc.), the retention of private ownership of the means of production under centralized governmental control, belligerent nationalism and racism, glorification of war, etc.: first instituted in Italy in 1922. 3. *a)* the political philosophy and movement based on such doctrines and policies. *b)* fascist behavior. See also **Nazism.**

fas·cist (fash′ist), *n.* [It. *fascista*], 1. [F-], *a)* a member of the Fascisti. *b)* a member of some similar party; Nazi, Falangist, etc. 2. a person who believes in or practices fascism. *adj.* 1. [F-], of Fascists or Fascism. 2. of, believing in, or practicing fascism.

Fa·scis·ti (fə-shis′ti; It. fä-shē′stē), *n.pl.* [*sing.* FASCISTA (-tə; -stä)], [It. < *fasci* < L. *fasces;* see FASCES], an Italian political organization, founded in 1919, which seized power in Italy and set up an antidemocratic dictatorship (1922–1943) under the leadership of Benito Mussolini; Fascists.

fa·scis·tic (fə-shis′tik), *adj.* fascist.

fa·scis·ti·cal·ly (fə-shis′ti-k'l-i, fə-shis′tik-li), *adv.* in a fascist manner.

fash (fash), *v.t. & v.i.* [< OFr. *faschier* (Fr. *fâcher*), to annoy, vex; LL. **fastidicare* < L. *fastidium;* cf. FASTIDIOUS], [Scot.], to annoy; trouble; vex.

fash·ion (fash′ən), *n.* [ME. *fasoun;* OFr. *façon;* L. *factio*, a making < pp. of *facere*, to make], 1. the make, form, or shape of a thing. 2. kind; sort. 3. the way in which something is made or done; manner. 4. the current style or mode of dress, speech, conduct, etc. 5. something fashionable. 6. those people who conform to the fashions of society. *v.t.* 1. to make; form; shape; mold. 2. to contrive. 3. to fit; accommodate (with *to*).

after (or **in**) **a fashion**, in some manner; to some extent; not too well.

SYN.—**fashion** is the prevailing custom in dress, manners, speech, etc. of a particular place or time, especially as established by the dominant section of society or the leaders in the fields of art, literature, etc.; **style**, often a close synonym for **fashion**, in discriminating use suggests a distinctive fashion, especially the elegant way of dressing, living, etc. that distinguishes persons with money and taste; **mode**, the French word expressing this idea, suggests the height of fashion in dress, behavior, etc. at any particular time; **vogue** stresses the general acceptance or great popularity of a certain fashion; **fad** stresses the impulsive enthusiasm with which a fashion is taken up for a short time; **rage** and **craze** both stress an intense, sometimes irrational enthusiasm for a passing fashion. See also **make, method.**

fash·ion·a·ble (fash′ən-ə-b'l), *adj.* 1. following the current style; in fashion; stylish. 2. of, characteristic of, or used by people who follow the current style of dress, speech, conduct, etc. *n.* a fashionable person.

fash·ion·a·bly (fash′ən-ə-bli), *adv.* in a fashionable manner.

fashion plate, 1. a picture showing a current style in dress. 2. a fashionably dressed person.

Fa·sho·da (fä-shō′dä), *n.* Kodok: the former name.

fast (fast, fäst), *adj.* [ME.; AS. *fæst;* akin to G. *fest*, firm, stable; IE. base **pasto-*, fixed, secure], 1. not easily moved; firm. 2. firmly fastened. 3. loyal; devoted: as, *fast* friends. 4. complete; sound. 5. unfading: said of colors. 6. rapid in movement; swift; quick; speedy. 7. permitting or promoting swift movement: as, a *fast* highway. 8. taking or lasting a short time. 9. ahead of time; showing a time in advance of standard: as, a *fast* clock. 10. *a)* living in a reckless, wild, dissipated way. *b)* having loose morals; promiscuous. 11. in *bacteriology*, resistant to staining or destruction, as certain bacteria. 12. in *photography*, having a high shutter speed. *adv.* [ME. *faste;* AS. *fæste* < *adj.*], 1. firmly; fixedly. 2. thoroughly; soundly: as, the child was *fast* asleep. 3. rapidly; swiftly; quickly; speedily. 4. in a reckless, dissipated way; wildly. 5. [Obs. or Poetic], close; near: as, *fast* by the river.

play fast and loose, to behave with reckless duplicity, insincerity, and inconstancy.

SYN.—**fast** and **rapid** are generally interchangeable in expressing the idea of a relatively high rate of movement or action, but **fast** more often refers to the person or thing that moves or acts, and **rapid** to the action (a *fast* typist, *rapid* transcription); **swift** implies great rapidity, but in addition often connotes smooth, easy movement; **fleet** suggests a nimbleness or lightness in that which moves swiftly; **quick** implies promptness of action, or occurrence in a brief space of time, rather than velocity (a *quick* reply); **speedy** intensifies the idea of quickness, but may also connote high velocity (a *speedy* recovery, a *speedy* flight); **hasty** suggests hurried action and may connote carelessness, rashness, or impatience. —*ANT.* slow.

fast (fast, fäst), *v.i.* [ME. *festen, fasten;* AS. *fæstan;* akin to G. *fasten*, Goth. *fastan;* all ult. < base of *fast, adj.*], 1. to keep from eating all or certain foods, as in observing a holy day. 2. to eat very little or nothing. *n.* 1. a fasting. 2. a day or period of fasting.

break one's fast, to eat food for the first time after fasting, or for the first time in the day.

fast day, a religious holy day, etc. observed by fasting.

fas·ten (fas′′n, fäs′′n), *v.t.* [ME. *fastnen, festnen;* AS. *fæstnian* < base of *fæst* (see FAST, *adj.*); akin to G. *festnen*, make firm, secure], 1. to attach; join; connect. 2. to make fast or secure, as by locking, shutting, buttoning, etc.; fix firmly in place. 3. to hold, fix, or direct (the attention, gaze, etc.) steadily (*on*). 4. to cause to be connected or attributed; impute: as, he *fastened* the crime on me. *v.i.* 1. to become attached or joined. 2. to take hold; cling. —*SYN.* see **tie.**

fasten on (or **upon**), 1. to clutch; seize; cling to. 2. to concentrate on.

fas·ten·er (fas′′n-ẽr, fäs′′n-ẽr), *n.* 1. a person who fastens. 2. a device for fastening things together.

fas·ten·ing (fas′′n-iŋ, fäs′′n-iŋ), *n.* 1. the act or way of making something fast, or secure. 2. anything used to fasten; bolt, clasp, hook, lock, button, etc.

fas·tid·i·ous (fas-tid′i-əs), *adj.* [L. *fastidiosus* < *fastidium*, a loathing, disgust < *fastus*, disdain, contempt], 1. not easy to please; very critical. 2. daintily refined; oversensitive; easily disgusted. —*SYN.* see **dainty.**

fas·ti·gi·ate (fas-tij′i-it, fas-tij′i-āt′), *adj.* [L. *fastigatus* < *fastigium*, a slope, roof], sloping toward a point; conelike, as the blossom of a plant.

fast·ness (fast′nis, fäst′nis), *n.* [ME. *fastnesse;* AS. *fæstnes;* see FAST, *adj.* & -NESS], 1. the quality or condition of being fast. 2. a secure place; stronghold.

fast time, [Colloq.], daylight saving time, war time, etc., as distinguished from standard time.

fat (fat), *adj.* [FATTER (-ẽr), FATTEST (-ist)], [ME. *fatt, fat;* AS. *fætt*, contracted pp. of v. represented by AS. *fættian*, to fatten; akin to G. *feist*, orig. pp. < OHG. *feizzen*, to make fat; IE. base **poi-*, **pī-*, damp, soft, yielding, as also in L. *o-pi-mus*, well-nourished], 1. *a)* containing or full of fat; oily; greasy. *b)* having much fat in relation to lean: said of meat. 2. *a)* fleshy; plump. *b)* too plump; corpulent; obese. 3. thick; broad. 4. containing something valuable in great quantity; fertile; productive: as, *fat* land. 5. profitable; lucrative: as, a *fat* job. 6. prosperous. 7. supplied plentifully; ample. 8. stupid; dull. *n.* 1. *a)* an oily, yellow or white substance formed in the bodies of animals. *b)* a similar substance occurring in vegetable matter, especially in the seeds of certain plants. 2. either of these substances used in cookery. 3. fleshiness; plumpness; corpulence. 4. the richest part of anything. 5. in *chemistry*, a class of glyceryl esters of fatty acids, insoluble in water. *v.t. & v.i.* [FATTED (-id), FATTING], [ME. *fatten;* AS. *fættian*], to make or become fat.

a fat chance, [Slang], very little or no chance.

a fat lot, [Slang], very little or nothing.

chew the fat, [Slang], to talk together; chat.

the fat is in the fire, the thing has happened and cannot be prevented.

the fat of the land, [after Vulg. L. *medulla terrae*, Gen. 45:18], the best things obtainable; great luxury.

fa·tal (fā′t'l), *adj.* [ME.; OFr.; L. *fatalis* < *fatum*, fate], 1. originally, fated; destined; inevitable. 2. fateful; decisive: as, the *fatal* day arrived. 3. resulting in death. 4. destructive; ruinous; disastrous. 5. concerned with or determining fate: as, the *fatal* sisters are the Fates.

SYN.—**fatal** implies the inevitability or actual occurrence of death or disaster (a *fatal* disease, a *fatal* mistake); **deadly** is applied to a thing that can and probably (but not inevitably) will cause death (a *deadly* poison); **mortal** implies that death has occurred and is applied to the immediate cause of the death (he has received a *mortal* blow); **lethal** is applied to that which in its nature or purpose is a cause of death (a *lethal* weapon).

fa·tal·ism (fā′t'l-iz'm), *n.* 1. the belief that all events are determined by fate and are therefore inevitable. 2. the acceptance of every event as inevitable.

fa·tal·ist (fā′t'l-ist), *n.* a person who believes in fatalism.

fa·tal·is·tic (fā′t'l-is′tik), *adj.* of, based on, or characterized by fatalism.

fa·tal·is·ti·cal·ly (fā′t'l-is′ti-k'l-i, fā′t'l-is′tik-li), *adv.* in a fatalistic manner.

fa·tal·i·ty (fə-tal′ə-ti, fā-tal′ə-ti), *n.* [*pl.* FATALITIES (-tiz)], [Fr. *fatalité;* LL. *fatalitas* < L. *fatalis;* see FATAL], 1. the agency of fate or necessity; subjection to fate. 2. an inevitable liability to disaster. 3. a fatal quality; deadliness; deadly effect: as, the *fatality* of any specified disease. 4. an event resulting in death; death: as, accidents in the home cause many *fatalities.*

fa·tal·ly (fā′t'l-i), *adv.* 1. as determined by fate; inevitably. 2. so as to cause death or disaster; mortally.

Fa·ta Mor·ga·na (fä′tə môr-gä′nə), [It., lit., fairy Morgan, after Anglo-Fr. *Morgan-le-Fey*, sorceress sister of King Arthur], 1. Morgan le Fay, a fairy in some medieval legends and romances. 2. [f- m-], a mirage, especially one sometimes seen off the coast of Sicily near the Strait of Messina: so called because formerly supposed to be the work of Morgan le Fay.

fate (fāt), *n.* [ME.; L. *fatum*, prophetic declaration, oracle; neut. pp. of *fari*, to speak; see FAME], 1. the power supposed to determine the outcome of events before they occur; destiny. 2. something inevitable, supposedly determined by this power; hence, 3. what happens or has happened to a person; lot; fortune: as, it was his *fate* to be a bachelor. 4. final outcome. 5. death; destruction; doom. *v.t.* [FATED (-id), FATING], [Obs. except in passive], to destine.

the Fates, in *Greek & Roman mythology*, the three goddesses who control human destiny and life: the first (Clotho) spins the thread of life, the second (Lachesis) determines its length, and the third (Atropos) cuts it off.

***SYN.*—fate** refers to the inevitability of a course of events as supposedly predetermined by a god or other agency beyond human control; **destiny** also refers to an inevitable succession of events as determined supernaturally or by necessity, but often implies a favorable outcome (it was her *destiny* to become famous); **portion** and **lot** refer to what is supposedly distributed in the determining of fate, but **portion** implies an equitable apportionment and **lot** implies a random assignment; **doom** always connotes an unfavorable or disastrous fate.

fat·ed (fāt′id), *adj.* [pp. of *fate*], 1. ordained by fate; destined. 2. destined to destruction; doomed.

fate·ful (fāt′fəl), *adj.* 1. revealing what is to come; prophetic. 2. having important consequences; significant; decisive. 3. controlled by or as if by fate. 4. bringing about death or destruction. —*SYN.* see **ominous.**

fat·head (fat′hed′), *n.* a stupid person; blockhead.

fat·head·ed (fat′hed′id), *adj.* stupid; dull; obtuse.

fa·ther (fä′*th*ẽr), *n.* [ME. *fader, father;* AS. *fæder;* common Gmc.; akin to G. *vater;* IE. **pətér*, whence also L. *pater*, Gr. *patēr*, Sans. *pitár*, etc.; ult. origin echoic, as in *papa*], 1. a male parent. 2. a person regarded as a male parent; protector. 3. [F-], God. 4. *usually in pl.* a forefather; ancestor; forebear. 5. an originator; founder; creator; inventor. 6. anyone deserving respect or reverence because of age, position, etc. 7. a senator of ancient Rome. 8. *pl.* the leaders of a city, assembly, etc. 9. [often F-], any of the early Christian religious writers considered reliable authorities on the doctrines and teachings of the Church. 10. in the *Roman Catholic Church*, *a*) any priest. *b*) his title. Abreviated **F., f., Fr.** *v.t.* 1. to be the father of; beget. 2. to act as a father to; protect as a father. 3. to originate; found; create; invent; make. 4. to take the responsibility for.

father confessor, 1. a priest who listens to confessions, as in the Roman Catholic Church. 2. a person to whom people habitually tell private matters.

fa·ther·hood (fä′*th*ẽr-hood′), *n.* [ME. *fadirhode;* see -HOOD], the state of being a father; paternity.

fa·ther-in-law (fä′*th*ẽr-′n-lô′), *n.* [*pl.* FATHERS-IN-LAW], 1. the father of one's wife or husband. 2. [Rare], a stepfather.

fa·ther·land (fä′*th*ẽr-land′), *n.* [often after D. *vaderland*, G. *vaterland*], a person's native land or, sometimes, the land of his ancestors.

fa·ther·less (fä′*th*ẽr-lis), *adj.* [ME. *faderles;* AS. *fæderleas*], 1. not having a father living, or lacking a father's protection. 2. not knowing who one's father is.

fa·ther·li·ness (fä′*th*ẽr-li-nis), *n.* a fatherly quality.

fa·ther·ly (fä′*th*ẽr-li), *adj.* [AS. *fæderlic*], 1. belonging to a father: as, *fatherly* duties. 2. like or characteristic of a father; kindly; protective. *adv.* [Archaic], in a fatherly manner.

Father of His Country, George Washington.

Father of Medicine, Hippocrates.

Father of Waters, the Mississippi River: translation of the Indian name.

Father's Day, the third Sunday in June, a day set aside to honor fathers.

Father Time, time personified as a very old man carrying a scythe and an hourglass.

fath·om (fa*th*′əm), *n.* [ME. *fadym, fathem;* AS. *fæthm* (parallel with OFris. *fethm*, OS. pl. *fathmōs*), the two arms outstretched (to embrace, measure, etc.); akin to G. *faden*, thread, lit., as much as will extend between outstretched arms; IE. base **pet-*, to stretch out, as also in L. *patere*, to stretch out], a unit of measure equal to 6 feet, used mainly in measuring the depth of water or the length of a rope or cable: abbreviated **f., F., fth., fthm., fm.** *v.t.* [in form < ME. *fadmen, fathmen* < AS. *fæthmian*, to embrace with extended arms; present sense Early Mod. Eng.], 1. to measure the depth of; sound; hence, 2. to get to the bottom of; understand thoroughly.

fath·om·less (fa*th*′əm-lis), *adj.* [*fathom* + *-less*], 1. too deep to be measured. 2. incomprehensible.

fa·tid·ic (fə-tid′ik), *adj.* [L. *fatidicus*, prophesying < *fatum*, fate + *dicere*, to say, speak], of divination or prophecy; prophetic.

fat·i·ga·ble (fat′i-gə-b′l), *adj.* that can be fatigued; easily tired.

fa·tigue (fə-tēg′), *n.* [Fr. < *fatiguer;* L. *fatigare*, to weary, fatigue], 1. physical or mental exhaustion; weariness. 2. the cause of this; hard work; toil. 3. fatigue duty. 4. *pl.* fatigue clothes. 5. a weakening in metal, wood, etc. caused by strain or long use. 6. in *physiology*, the decreased ability of an organism or one of its parts to function because of prolonged exertion, which causes a toxic decomposition in the muscle and nerve cells. *v.t.* [FATIGUED (-tēgd′), FATIGUING], 1. to tire out; weary; exhaust. 2. to weaken by continued use.

fatigue clothes, clothing of denim or twill worn in doing fatigue duty.

fatigue duty, any labor, other than drill or instruction, assigned to soldiers in training.

Fat·i·ma (fat′i-mə, fä′ti-mə; *now often* fə-tē′mə), *n.* 1. the daughter of Mohammed; lived 606–632 A.D. 2. Bluebeard's last wife.

Fat·i·mid (fat′i-mid), *adj.* 1. descended from Mohammed's daughter, Fatima. 2. of or characteristic of the Fatimid dynasty or the period during which it was in power. *n.* a Moslem ruler descended from Fatima and the Caliph Ali: the Fatimids formed a dynasty that ruled over Egyptian Islam and parts of northern Africa (909–1171).

Fat·i·mite (fat′i-mīt′), *adj. & n.* Fatimid.

fat·ling (fat′liŋ), *n.* [*fat* + *-ling*, n. suffix], a calf, lamb, kid, or young pig fattened before being slaughtered.

Fat·shan (fät′shän′), *n.* a city in Kwangtung, China, near Canton: pop., c. 500,000.

fat·so (fat′sō), *n.* [Slang], a fat person.

fat-sol·u·ble (fat′sol′yoo-b′l), *adj.* soluble in fats.

fat·ten (fat′'n), *v.t.* 1. to make fat, or plump, as by feeding. 2. to make (land) fertile. 3. to make richer, larger, etc.: as, he *fattened* his purse by robbing the poor. *v.i.* to become fat.

fat·ti·ness (fat′i-nis), *n.* the quality of being fatty.

fat·tish (fat′ish), *adj.* somewhat fat.

fat·ty (fat′i), *adj.* [FATTIER (-i-ẽr), FATTIEST (-i-ist)], 1. containing, covered with, or made of fat. 2. resembling fat; greasy; oily. *n.* [Colloq.], a fat person.

fatty acid, any of a series of saturated organic acids having the general formula $C_nH_{2n}O_2$: some occur as glyceryl esters in natural fats.

fatty degeneration, in *pathology*, the abnormal occurrence of fat particles in tissue cells.

fa·tu·i·tous (fə-tū′ə-təs, fə-tōō′ə-təs), *adj.* characterized by fatuity.

fa·tu·i·ty (fə-tū′ə-ti, fə-tōō′ə-ti), *n.* [*pl.* FATUITIES (-tiz)], [Fr. *fatuité;* L. *fatuitas* < *fatuus*, foolish], 1. stupidity, especially complacent stupidity; foolishness; folly. 2. something fatuous. 3. [Rare], idiocy or imbecility.

fat·u·ous (fach′ōō-əs), *adj.* [L. *fatuus*, foolish], 1. complacently stupid or inane; silly; foolish. 2. [Rare], unreal; illusory: cf. **ignis fatuus.** —*SYN.* see **silly.**

‡fau·bourg (fō′bōōr′; Eng. fō′boorg), *n.* [Fr. for earlier *faux bourg*, lit., false town, folk etym. form of OFr. *forsbourg, forbourg*, lit., outside town, hence suburb < OFr. *fors* (Fr. *hors*), outside + *bourg*, town], a suburb or district within a city.

fau·cal (fô′kəl), *adj.* [< L. *fauces*, throat; + *-al*], of or produced in the fauces: said of certain vocal sounds.

fau·ces (fô′sēz), *n.pl.* [L., throat, gullet], the passage leading from the back of the mouth into the pharynx.

fau·cet (fô′sit), *n.* [ME. *fauset;* Fr. *fausset;* prob. < OFr. *faulser*, to make a breach in, falsify < L. *falsus;* see FALSE], a device with a hand-operated valve for regulating the flow of a liquid from a pipe, barrel, etc.: also called *cock, tap.*

fau·cial (fô′shəl), *adj.* faucal.

faugh (fô: *conventionalized pronun.; actually, an expulsion of air between the upper teeth and lower lip*), *interj.* [echoic], an exclamation of disgust, scorn, etc.: also spelled **foh.**

Faulk·ner, William (fôk′nẽr), 1897–1962; American novelist; received Nobel prize in literature, 1949: also **William Falkner.**

fault (fôlt), *n.* [Latinized sp. < ME. *faut, faute;* OFr. *faute, faulte*, a lack, fault < pp. of L. *fallere*, to deceive; in some phrases, contr. < *default*], 1. originally, failure to have or do what is required; lack; default; neglect. 2. something that mars the appearance, character, structure, etc.; flaw; failing; imperfection; defect. 3.

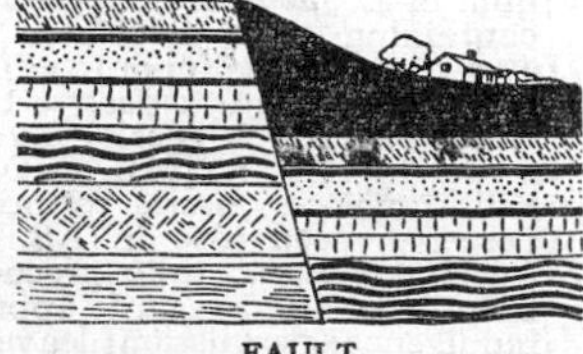
FAULT

something done wrongly; specifically, *a*) a misdeed; offense. *b*) an error; mistake. 4. responsibility for something wrong; blame: as, it was her *fault* that they were delayed. 5. in *electricity*, a defect or point of defect in a circuit, which prevents the current from following the intended course. 6. in *geology*, a break in rock strata or veins that causes a section to become dislocated along the line of fracture. 7. in *hunting*, a dog's loss of the scent. 8. in *tennis, squash*, etc., *a*) failure to serve the ball into the proper court. *b*) a served ball that does not land in the proper court. *v.t.* 1. [Rare], to blame. 2. in *geology*, to cause a fault in. *v.i.* 1. [Archaic], to make a mistake; blunder. 2. in *geology*, to develop a fault.

at fault, 1. unable to find the scent, as hunting dogs; hence, 2. not knowing what to do; perplexed. 3. guilty of error; in the wrong; deserving blame.

find fault, to seek and point out faults; complain.

find fault with, to be dissatisfied with; object to.

in fault, guilty of error; in the wrong; deserving blame.

to a fault, too much; excessively.

SYN.—**fault,** in this comparison, refers to a definite, although not strongly condemnatory, imperfection in character (her only *fault* is stubbornness); **failing** implies an even less serious shortcoming, usually one of those common to mankind (tardiness was one of his *failings*); **weakness** applies to a minor shortcoming that results from a lack of perfect self-control (fattening foods are her *weakness*); **foible** refers to a slight weakness that is regarded more as an amusing idiosyncracy than an actual defect in character (nervous giggling is one of her *foibles*); **vice,** although stronger in its implication of moral failure than any of the preceding terms, does not in this connection suggest actual depravity or wickedness (gambling is his only *vice*). —*ANT.* virtue.

fault·find·er (fôlt'fīn'dẽr), *n.* a person given to finding fault; chronic, captious complainer.

fault·find·ing (fôlt'fīn'diŋ), *n. & adj.* finding fault; calling attention to defects. —*SYN.* see **critical.**

fault·i·ly (fôl'tə-li), *adv.* in a faulty manner.

fault·i·ness (fôl'ti-nis), *n.* the quality or condition of being faulty.

fault·less (fôlt'lis), *adj.* without any fault; perfect.

fault·y (fôl'ti), *adj.* [FAULTIER (-ti-ẽr), FAULTIEST (-ti-ist)], [ME. *fauti*], 1. having a fault or faults; containing defects, blemishes, imperfections, or errors; imperfect. 2. [Obs.], guilty of error; deserving blame.

faun (fôn), *n.* [ME.; L. *Faunus;* see FAUNUS], any of a class of minor Roman rural deities, usually represented as having the body of a man, but the horns, pointed ears, tail, and hind legs of a goat: see also **satyr.**

FAUN

fau·na (fô'nə), *n.* [Mod. L. < LL. *Fauna*, Roman goddess, sister or wife of Faunus; adopted by Linnaeus (1746) as term parallel to *flora*], 1. [*pl.* FAUNAS (-nəz), FAUNAE (-nē)], the animals of a specified region or time: as, the *fauna* and flora of North America. 2. a treatise on such animals.

fau·nal (fô'nəl), *adj.* of fauna.

Fau·nus (fô'nəs), *n.* [L.; prob. < IE. *dhaunos, wolf, strangler < base *dhau-, to strangle; akin to Gr. *Daunos;* associated even in classical folk etym. with L. *favere*, to favor], in *Roman mythology*, a god of nature, the patron of farming and animals, and a giver of oracles: identified with the Greek Pan.

Faust (foust), *n.* [G. (Dr. Johann Faust) < L. *faustus*, fortunate < base of *favere;* see FAVOR], the hero of several medieval legends, an old philosopher who sells his soul to the devil in exchange for knowledge and power: the theme of several literary and operatic works, notably a play by Marlowe, a two-part dramatic poem written by Goethe between 1773 and 1831, and an opera by Gounod based on Goethe's poem.

Faus·tus (fôs'təs), *n.* Faust: Latin form of the name, used by Marlowe in his poetic drama *The Tragical History of Doctor Faustus* (1593).

‡**fau·teuil** (fô'tẽ'y'), *n.* [Fr.], an armchair.

faux pas (fō'pä'), [*pl.* FAUX PAS (fō'päz'; Fr. fō'pä')], [Fr., lit., false step], a social blunder; error in etiquette; tactless act or remark. —*SYN.* see **error.**

fa·ve·o·late (fə-vē'ə-lāt'), *adj.* [< Mod. L. *faveolus*, dim. of L. *favus*, a honeycomb; + *-ate*], honeycombed; containing cells; alveolate.

fa·vo·ni·an (fə-vō'ni-ən), *adj.* [L. *Favonianus* < *Favonius*, west wind < *favere*, to favor], 1. of the west wind; hence, 2. gentle; favoring.

fa·vor (fā'vẽr), *n.* [ME. & OFr. *favour;* L. *favor*, good will, favor < *favere*, to favor; IE. base *ghou-, to perceive, seen also in AS. (*ofer*)*gumian*, to neglect, Czech *hověti*, to take precautions (with), spare], 1. friendly or kind regard; approval; liking. 2. *a*) kind indulgence; permission; leave. *b*) too kind indulgence; unfair partiality. 3. help; assistance: as, he escaped under *favor* of night. 4. a kind, obliging, friendly, or generous act: as, he asked a *favor* of me. 5. *pl.* consent (of a woman) to sexual intimacy. 6. a small gift, souvenir, or token (originally, a love token): as, the ladies received compacts as *favors* at the banquet. 7. a letter; note; communication: as, your *favor* of the 15th June has been received. 8. [Obs.], attractiveness; charm. *v.t.* 1. to regard with favor; consider kindly; approve; like. 2. to be indulgent or too indulgent toward; be partial to; prefer unfairly. 3. to support; advocate; be for; endorse. 4. to make easier; help; assist: as, the sudden commotion *favored* his escape. 5. to do a kindness for. 6. to look like; resemble in facial features: as, the baby *favors* its mother. 7. to use gently; spare: as, the boxer *favored* his injured hand.

find favor, to be regarded with favor; be pleasing to.

in favor, favored; liked.

in favor of, 1. approving; supporting; endorsing. 2. to the advantage of. 3. payable to, as a check, etc.

in one's favor, to one's advantage or credit.

out of favor, not favored; not liked.

fa·vor·a·ble (fā'vẽr-ə-b'l), *adj.* [ME.; OFr.; L. *favorabilis*], favoring; specifically, *a*) approving. *b*) helpful.

SYN.—**favorable** applies to that which is distinctly helpful or advantageous in gaining an end (a *favorable* climate for citrus fruits); **auspicious** refers to something regarded as a good omen of some undertaking (he made an *auspicious* debut); **propitious** is now usually applied to a circumstance or a time that appears favorable for doing or beginning something (a *propitious* moment). —*ANT.* adverse, unfavorable.

fa·vored (fā'vẽrd), *adj.* 1. regarded or treated with favor; specifically, *a*) provided with advantages; talented. *b*) specially privileged. 2. having (specified) features: often in hyphenated compounds, as, *ill-favored.*

fa·vor·ite (fā'vẽr-it, fāv'rit), *n.* [MFr. *favorit;* It. *favorito*, pp. of *favorire*, to favor < *favore* (L. *favor*); see FAVOR], 1. a person or thing regarded with special liking, or more highly than others. 2. a person liked very much and granted special privileges by a king, high official, etc. 3. a contestant regarded as most likely to win. *adj.* held in special regard; preferred.

favorite son, 1. a famous man honored and praised in his native city, district, etc. because of his achievements. 2. a candidate favored by the political leaders of his own State, city, etc., as for presidential nomination.

fa·vor·it·ism (fā'vẽr-it-iz'm, fāv'rit-iz'm), *n.* 1. the showing of more kindness and indulgence to some person or persons than to others; being unfairly partial. 2. the condition of being a favorite.

fa·vour (fā'vẽr), *n. & v.t.* favor: British spelling.

fa·vus (fā'vəs), *n.* [L., a honeycomb], an infectious skin disease caused by a fungus and characterized by itching and the formation of yellow crusts about the hair follicles, especially on the scalp.

Fawkes, Guy (fôks, foks), 1570–1606; English conspirator; executed for participating in the Gunpowder Plot, a plot to blow up the Parliament building.

fawn (fôn), *v.i.* [ME. *fauhnen, fahnen;* AS. *fagnian*, var. of *fægnian*, to rejoice < *fagen*, var. of *fægen;* see FAIN], 1. to show affection by leaping about, licking the hand, wagging the tail, etc.: said of a dog. 2. to act servilely; cringe and flatter: as, the courtiers *fawned* on the king.

fawn (fôn), *n.* [ME.; OFr. *faon, feon;* LL. **feton* < L. *fetus;* see FETUS], 1. a young deer less than one year old. 2. a pale, yellowish brown. *adj.* of this color.

Fay (fā), [< ME. & OFr. *fei;* see FAITH], a feminine name: variant spelling, *Faye.*

fay (fā), *n.* [ME. *fai;* OFr. *fae, faie;* LL. *fata*, one of the fates < *fatum;* see FATE], a fairy.

fay (fā), *n.* [ME. & OFr. *fei;* see FAITH], [Archaic], faith: used in oaths, as, by my *fay.*

fay (fā), *v.t. & v.i.* [ME. *feien, fegen;* AS. *fegan*, to join, fit < same base as *fæger;* see FAIR, *v.*], in *shipbuilding*, to fit closely or exactly; join.

Fa·yal (fä-yäl'), *n.* one of the islands forming the Azores: area, 64 sq. mi.; pop., 24,000.

Fay·ette·ville (fā'ət-vil), *n.* a city in south central North Carolina: pop., 47,000.

Fa·yum, Fay·yum (fī-yōōm'), *n.* Faiyum.

faze (fāz), *v.t.* [FAZED (fāzd), FAZING], [form of *feeze;* ? influenced by Scand.; cf. Norw. *föise*, Sw. *fösa*, corresponding to ON. **feysa*], [Colloq.], to disturb; agitate; disconcert: also **feaze, feeze.** —*SYN.* see **embarrass.**

fb., in *football*, fullback.

FBI, F.B.I., Federal Bureau of Investigation.

f.c., in *printing*, follow copy.

fcap., fcp., foolscap.

FCC, F.C.C., Federal Communications Commission.

F clef, the bass clef: see **clef,** illus.

F.D., 1. *Fidei Defensor*, [L.], Defender of the Faith: one of the titles of the king of England. 2. Fire Department.

FDA, F.D.A., Food and Drug Administration.

FDR, F.D.R., Franklin Delano Roosevelt.

Fe, *ferrum*, [L.], in *chemistry*, iron.

fe·al·ty (fē'əl-ti), *n.* [*pl.* FEALTIES (-tiz)], [ME. *fealte;* OFr. *feaulte, fealte, feelte;* L. *fidelitas;* see FIDELITY], 1. the duty and loyalty owed by a vassal or tenant to his feudal lord. 2. [Archaic or Poetic], loyalty; fidelity. —*SYN.* see **allegiance.**

fear (fêr), *n.* [ME. *fere;* AS. *fær*, lit., sudden attack; akin to OHG. *fāra*, ambush, snare & *-fahr* in G. *gefahr*, danger, peril; basic sense, "trap"; prob. IE. base **per-*, to test, entice, etc., seen also in the L. element *per-* in *experimentum, periculum;* cf. EXPERIMENT, PERIL], 1. a feeling of anxiety and agitation caused by the presence or nearness of danger, evil, pain, etc.; timidity; dread; terror; fright; apprehension. 2. respectful dread; awe; reverence. 3. a feeling of uneasiness; disquiet; anxiety; concern: as, I have a *fear* that you will be late. 4. a cause for fear; possibility; chance: as, there was no *fear* of difficulty. ***v.t.*** 1. to be afraid of; dread. 2. to feel reverence or awe for. 3. to expect with misgiving; suspect: as, I *fear* the guests are late. ***v.i.*** 1. to feel fear; be afraid. 2. to be uneasy, anxious, or doubtful.

for fear of, in order to avoid or prevent; lest.

SYN.—**fear** is the general term for the anxiety and agitation felt at the presence of danger; **dread** refers to the fear or depression felt in anticipating something dangerous or disagreeable (to live in *dread* of poverty); **fright** applies to a sudden, shocking, usually momentary fear (the mouse gave her a *fright*); **alarm** implies the fright felt at the sudden realization of danger (he felt *alarm* at the sight of the pistol); **dismay** implies a loss of courage or a feeling of consternation at the prospect of trouble or danger; **terror** applies to an overwhelming, often paralyzing fear (the *terror* of soldiers in combat); **panic** refers to a frantic, unreasoning fear, often one that spreads quickly and leads to irrational, aimless action (the cry of "fire!" created a *panic*).

Fear, Cape, a cape on Smith Island, off North Carolina.

fear·ful (fêr′fəl), ***adj.*** 1. causing fear; terrifying; dreadful. 2. feeling fear; afraid. 3. showing or resulting from fear: as, a *fearful* look. 4. [Colloq.], very bad, offensive, great, etc.: as, a *fearful* liar. —***SYN.*** see **afraid.**

fear·ful·ly (fêr′fəl-i), ***adv.*** 1. in a fearful manner. 2. to a fearful extent. 3. [Colloq.], very much; very: as, he's *fearfully* busy.

fear·less (fêr′lis), ***adj.*** without fear; not afraid; brave.

fear·nought, fear·naught (fêr′nôt′), ***n.*** 1. a heavy woolen cloth used for coats. 2. a coat made of this.

fear·some (fêr′səm), ***adj.*** 1. causing fear; dreadful; frightful. 2. frightened; timid; timorous.

fea·sance (fē′z'ns), ***n.*** [Anglo-Fr. *fesance* (Fr. *faisance*) < *faire,* to do; L. *facere;* see FACT], in *law,* the carrying into effect of a condition, obligation, etc.

fea·si·bil·i·ty (fē′zə-bil′ə-ti), ***n.*** [*pl.* FEASIBILITIES (-tiz)], the quality of being feasible, or possible; practicability.

fea·si·ble (fē′zə-b'l), ***adj.*** [OFr. *faisible, faisable* < *faire,* to make, do; L. *facere*], 1. capable of being done or carried out; practicable; possible: as, a *feasible* scheme. 2. likely; reasonable; probable: as, a *feasible* story. 3. capable of being used or dealt with successfully; suitable: as, land *feasible* for cultivation. —***SYN.*** see **possible.**

feast (fēst), ***n.*** [ME. & OFr. *feste* (Fr. *fête*) < L. *festa,* pl. of *festum,* holiday, festival, feast < *festus,* festal, joyful], 1. a celebration or festival, especially a religious festival. 2. a rich and elaborate meal; banquet; hence, 3. anything that gives pleasure because of its abundance or richness; special treat. ***v.i.*** [ME. *festen;* OFr. *fester* < the *n.*], to have a feast; eat a rich, elaborate meal. ***v.t.*** 1. to give a feast to; entertain at a banquet. 2. to give pleasure to; delight: as, he *feasted* his eyes on her.

Feast of Lots, Purim: see **Jewish holidays.**

feat (fēt), ***n.*** [ME. & OFr. *feet, fait* < L. *factum,* a deed; neut. pp. of *facere,* to make, do; see FACT], an act or accomplishment showing unusual daring, skill, endurance, etc.; remarkable deed; exploit.

feat (fēt), ***adj.*** [ME. *fete, fet;* OFr. *fait, feit,* made, pp. of *faire,* to do, make (L. *facere*); see FACT], [Archaic], 1. fitting; suitable. 2. neat. 3. skillful; adroit.

feath·er (feth′ẽr), ***n.*** [ME. *fether, feder;* AS. *fether;* akin to G. *feder;* IE. base **pet-,* to stretch out, seen also in L. *penna,* a feather, Gr. *pterōn,* a wing, Eng. *fathom*], 1. any of the growths covering the body of a bird and making up a large part of the wing surface: it consists typically of a horny central shaft, partly hollow, from which light, soft, narrow barbs extend to form a thin, flat surface. 2. a feather or featherlike part fastened to the shaft of an arrow to help control its flight. 3. anything like or suggesting a feather or feathers in appearance, lightness, etc.; specifically, *a*) a trifle. *b*) a fin or rib projecting from a casting for stiffening it. *c*) a thin, wedge-shaped projection for fitting into a groove. *d*) an irregular flaw in a gem. *e*) the wake left by a submarine's periscope. *f*) the fringe of hair along the tail and back of the legs of some dogs. 4. *pl.* *a*) plumage; hence, *b*) attire; dress. 5. class; kind: as, birds of a *feather.* 6. frame of mind; mood; humor; temper; vein. 7. the act of feathering an oar or propeller. ***v.t.*** 1. to provide (an arrow, etc.) with a feather. 2. to cover, fit, adorn, or fringe with or as with feathers. 3. to join by inserting a wedge-shaped part into a groove. 4. to turn (the blade of an oar) to a horizontal or nearly horizontal position between strokes so as to offer the least resistance to the water. 5. to turn (the blade of a propeller) on its shaft so that its leading and trailing edges are nearly parallel with the airplane's line of flight, thus offering minimum resistance or drag when idle. ***v.i.*** 1. to grow feathers; become covered with feathers. 2. to move, grow, or extend like feathers. 3. to look like feathers. 4. to feather an oar or propeller.

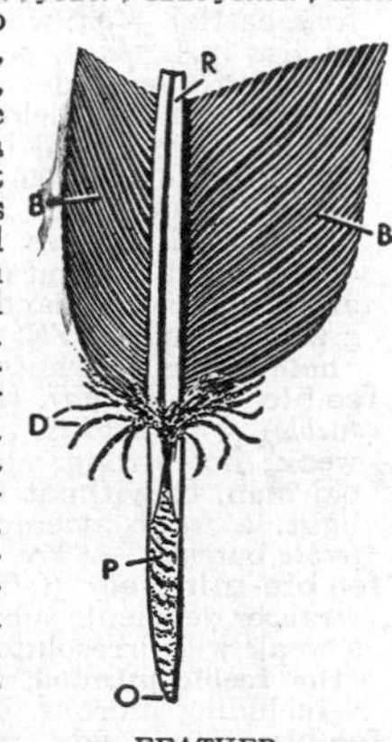

FEATHER

B, barbs (with barbules); D, down; R, shaft; O, opening at end of shaft; P, pith

feather in one's cap, a distinctive accomplishment; achievement worthy of pride.

feather one's nest, to grow rich by taking advantage of circumstances.

in feather, feathered.

in fine (or **high** or **good**) **feather,** in very good humor, health, or form.

show the white feather, [from the notion that a white feather in a rooster's tail is a sign of cowardice], to show cowardice.

feath·er·bed (feth′ẽr-bed′), ***adj.*** designating rules or regulations designed to accomplish featherbedding. ***v.i.*** to take advantage of such rules.

feather bed, a large, heavy quilt thickly filled with feathers or down, used as a mattress.

feath·er·bed·ding (feth′ẽr-bed′iŋ), ***n.*** the practice of limiting work or output in order to provide more jobs and prevent unemployment.

feath·er·bone (feth′ẽr-bōn′), ***n.*** a substitute for whalebone prepared from the quills of domestic fowls.

feath·er·brain (feth′ẽr-brān′), ***n.*** a featherbrained person.

feath·er·brained (feth′ẽr-brānd′), ***adj.*** silly; foolish; frivolous.

feath·er·cut (feth′ẽr-kut′), ***n.*** a style of hairdressing in which the hair is cut short and unevenly so as to form small, upswept curls with feathery tips.

feath·ered (feth′ẽrd), ***adj.*** 1. having feathers; covered or decorated with or as with feathers. 2. winged; swift.

feath·er·edge (feth′ẽr-ej′), ***n.*** a very thin edge, as on a board or tool, that can be easily broken or curled.

feath·er·edged (feth′ẽr-ejd′), ***adj.*** having a featheredge.

feath·er·head (feth′ẽr-hed′), ***n.*** a featherbrain.

feath·er·i·ness (feth′ẽr-i-nis), ***n.*** the condition or quality of being feathery.

feath·er·ing (feth′ẽr-iŋ), ***n.*** an especially delicate and light method of bowing rapid passages on the violin.

feather merchant, [Slang], a slacker in time of war.

feather palm, any palm with featherlike, or pinnate, leaves.

feath·er·stitch (feth′ẽr-stich′), ***n.*** [so called from resemblance to the arrangement of barbs on a feather], an embroidery stitch forming a zigzag line. ***v.t.*** & ***v.i.*** to embroider with such stitches.

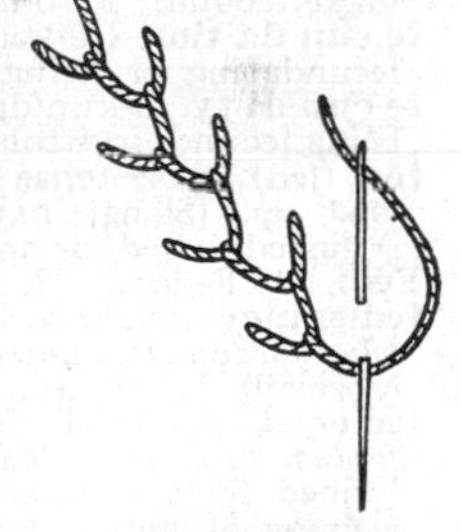

FEATHERSTITCH

feath·er·weight (feth′ẽr-wāt′), ***n.*** 1. any person or thing of comparatively light weight or small size; hence, 2. an unimportant person or thing. 3. a boxer or wrestler who weighs between 119 and 126 pounds. 4. the minimum weight that a race horse may carry in a handicap. ***adj.*** 1. of featherweights. 2. light or trivial.

feath·er·wood (feth′ẽr-wood′), ***n.*** a hardwood tree of Australia with wood like hickory.

feath·er·y (feth′ẽr-i), ***adj.*** 1. covered with or as with feathers. 2. resembling feathers; soft, light, etc.

feat·ly (fēt′li), ***adv.*** [ME. *fetli* < *fet;* see FEAT, *adj.*], [Archaic], 1. suitably; aptly. 2. neatly. 3. skillfully; adroitly. ***adj.*** [Archaic], neat; graceful.

fea·ture (fē′chẽr), ***n.*** [ME. *feture, fetour;* OFr. *faiture, feture* < L. *factura,* a making, formation < pp. of *facere,* to make; see FACT], 1. originally, *a*) the make, shape, form, or appearance of a person or thing; hence, *b*) attractive appearance; physical beauty. 2. *a*) *pl.* the form or cast of the face; facial appearance. *b*) any of the parts of the face, as the eyes, nose, mouth, etc. 3. a distinct or outstanding part, quality, or characteristic of something: as, the island's chief *feature* was its beauty. 4. a prominently displayed attraction or item, as of an entertainment, store, etc. 5. a special story, article, etc. in a newspaper or magazine, often prominently displayed. 6. a full-length motion picture. ***v.t.*** [FEATURED (-chẽrd), FEATURING], 1. to portray; represent. 2. to make outstanding or prominent; make a specialty of. 3. to sketch or show the features of. 4. to be a feature of. 5. [Slang], to imagine; conceive of.

fea·tured (fē′chērd), *adj.* 1. having (a specified kind of) facial features: as, *broad-featured.* 2. formed; shaped. 3. given special prominence.
fea·ture-length (fē′chēr-leŋth′), *adj.* full-length: said of a motion picture, magazine article, etc.
fea·ture·less (fē′chēr-lis), *adj.* without features; without anything striking, outstanding, or distinctive.
feaze (fēz, fāz), *v.t.* [FEAZED (fēzd, fāzd), FEAZING], to faze or feeze.
feaze (fēz), *v.t. & v.i.* [FEAZED (fēzd), FEAZING], [prob. < LG. or D.; cf. MD. *vese, veze,* frayed edge; akin to AS. *fæs,* a fringe, ME. *faselen*], [Dial.], to unravel.
Feb., February.
feb·ri- (feb′ri), [< L. *febris*], a combining form meaning *fever,* as in *febrific, febrifuge.*
fe·bric·i·ty (fi-bris′ə-ti), *n.* [see FEBRILE], the condition of being feverish.
feb·ri·fuge (feb′ri-fūj′), *n.* [Fr. *fébrifuge;* see FEBRI- & -FUGE], any substance for reducing or removing fever. *adj.* reducing or removing fever.
fe·brile (fē′brəl, feb′rəl), *adj.* [Fr. *fébrile* < L. *febris,* fever], 1. of or characterized by fever; feverish. 2. caused by fever.
Feb·ru·ar·y (feb′roo-er′i; *now often, by dissimilation,* feb′yoo-er′i), *n.* [L. *Februarius* (*mensis*), orig. month of expiation < *februa,* Roman festival of purification held Feb. 15, pl. of *februum,* means of purification], the second month of the year, having 28 days in regular years and 29 days in leap years: abbreviated **Feb., F.**
fe·cal (fē′kəl), *adj.* of feces: also spelled **faecal.**
fe·ces (fē′sēz), *n.pl.* [L. *faeces,* pl. of *faex,* dregs, lees], 1. waste matter expelled from the bowels; excrement. 2. dregs; sediment. Also spelled **faeces.**
Fech·ner, Gus·tav The·o·dor (goos′täf tā′ô-dōr feH′nēr), 1801–1887; German physicist, philosopher, and psychologist.
‡**fe·cit** (fē′sit), [L.], he (or she) made (it): formerly used with an artist's signature on a painting, etc.: abbreviated **fec.**
feck·less (fek′lis), *adj.* [Scot. < *effectless; effect* + *-less*], 1. weak; ineffective; spiritless. 2. thoughtless; careless; irresponsible.
fec·u·lence (fek′yoo-ləns), *n.* [Fr. *féculence;* L. *faeculentia* < *faecula,* dim. of *faex;* see FECES], 1. the state or quality of being feculent. 2. *a*) dregs; sediment. *b*) filth.
fec·u·lent (fek′yoo-lənt), *adj.* [Fr. *féculent* < L. *faeculentus* < *faec-,* stem of *faex;* see FECES], containing, or having the nature of, feces; filthy; foul.
fe·cund (fē′kənd, fek′ənd), *adj.* [Fr. *fécond;* L. *fecundus,* fertile], fruitful; productive; prolific. —*SYN.* see **fertile.**
fe·cun·date (fē′kən-dāt′, fek′ən-dāt′), *v.t.* [FECUNDATED (-id), FECUNDATING], [< L. *fecundatus,* pp. of *fecundare,* to make fruitful < *fecundus,* fertile], 1. to make fecund. 2. to impregnate; pollinate.
fe·cun·da·tion (fē′kən-dā′shən, fek′ən-dā′shən), *n.* a fecundating or being fecundated; fertilization.
fe·cun·di·ty (fi-kun′də-ti), *n.* the quality or power of being fecund; fruitfulness; fertility; productiveness.
fed (fed), past tense and past participle of **feed.**
fed up, [Slang], having had enough to become disgusted, bored, or annoyed; surfeited.
Fed., 1. Federal. 2. Federation.
fed·er·a·cy (fed′ēr-ə-si), *n.* [*pl.* FEDERACIES (-siz)], [< LL. *foederatus,* federate], 1. [Rare], an alliance, especially by treaty. 2. a confederacy.
fed·er·al (fed′ēr-əl, fed′rəl), *adj.* [Fr. *fédéral* < L. *foedus, foederis,* a league, compact, treaty], 1. of or formed by a compact; specifically, designating or of a union of states, groups, etc. in which each member agrees to subordinate its power to that of the central authority in common affairs. 2. designating, of, or having to do with a central government of this sort. 3. [usually F-], designating, of, or having to do with the central government of the United States. 4. [F-], of or supporting the Federalist Party or its principle of centralized government. 5. [F-], of or supporting the central government of the United States in the Civil War (1861–1865); Union; pro-Union. *n.* 1. [F-], a Federalist. 2. [F-], a supporter or soldier of the Federal government in the Civil War. Abbreviated **Fed.**
Federal Bureau of Investigation, a branch of the United States Department of Justice whose duty is to investigate and bring to trial all violators of Federal criminal laws, except violators of currency, tax, and postal laws: abbreviated **FBI, F.B.I.**
Federal Capital Territory, Australian Capital Territory: the former name.
fed·er·al·ism (fed′ēr-əl-iz′m, fed′rəl-iz′m), *n.* 1. the federal principle of government or organization. 2. [F-], the principles of the Federalist Party.
fed·er·al·ist (fed′ēr-əl-ist, fed′rəl-ist), *n.* 1. a person who believes in or supports federalism. 2. [F-], a member or supporter of the Federalist Party. *adj.* 1. of or supporting federalism. 2. [F-], of or supporting the Federalist Party or its principles.
The Federalist, a set of eighty-five articles by Alexander Hamilton, James Madison, and John Jay, published in 1787 and 1788, analyzing the Constitution of the United States and urging its adoption.
fed·er·al·is·tic (fed′ēr-əl-is′tik, fed′rəl-is′tik), *adj.* federalist.
Federalist (or **Federal**) **Party,** a political party in the United States (1789–1816), led by Alexander Hamilton and John Adams, which advocated the adoption of the Constitution and the establishment of a strong, centralized government.
fed·er·al·i·za·tion (fed′ēr-əl-i-zā′shən, fed′rəl-ī-zā′shən), *n.* a federalizing or being federalized.
fed·er·al·ize (fed′ēr-əl-īz′, fed′rəl-īz′), *v.t.* [FEDERALIZED (-īzd′), FEDERALIZING], 1. to unite (states, etc.) in a federal union. 2. to put under the authority of a federal government.
Federal Reserve Bank, any of the twelve district banks of the Federal Reserve System: abbreviated **FRB, F.R.B.**
Federal Reserve Board, a board composed of seven (originally eight) members which directs the Federal Reserve System: in 1935, the name was changed to *Board of Governors of the Federal Reserve System*: abbreviated **FRB, F.R.B.**
Federal Reserve System, a centralized banking system in the United States, consisting of twelve Federal Reserve banks, each acting as the central bank for its district, and over 10,000 affiliated banks: it was established by the Federal Reserve Act of 1913 to develop a currency which would fluctuate with business demands, and to regulate the member banks of each district.
Federal Security Agency, a Federal agency created in 1939 to supervise matters of social and economic security, educational opportunity, and health in the United States: it administers the Social Security Board, the Public Health Service, the Food and Drug Administration, etc.: abbreviated **FSA, F.S.A.**
Federal Trade Commission, a Federal agency created in 1915 to investigate unfair methods of competition in business, fraudulent advertising, etc., and to prosecute those guilty of such practices: abbreviated **FTC, F.T.C.**
fed·er·ate (fed′ēr-it; *for v.,* fed′ēr-āt′), *adj.* [L. *foederatus,* pp. of *foederare,* to league together < *foedus;* see FEDERAL], united by common agreement under a central government or authority. *v.t. & v.i.* [FEDERATED (-id), FEDERATING], to unite in a federation.
Federated Malay States, a former division of the Malay Peninsula, including the native states of Pahang, Perak, Negri Sembilan, and Selangor: area, 27,540 sq. mi.: now a part of the Federation of Malaya.
Federated Press, a privately owned agency for gathering news and distributing it among member newspapers.
fed·er·a·tion (fed′ə-rā′shən), *n.* [Fr. *fédération;* ML. *federatio* < L. *foederatus;* see FEDERATE], 1. a uniting by compact; union of states, groups, etc. by agreement of each member to subordinate its power to that of the central authority in common affairs. 2. a federated organization; league; federal union of states, nations, etc. Abbreviated **Fed.** (in a title or name).
fed·er·a·tive (fed′ēr-ā′tiv, fed′ēr-ə-tiv), *adj.* of, forming, or having the nature of, a federation.
fe·do·ra (fi-dôr′ə), *n.* [Fr. < *Fédora* (1882), play by Sardou], a soft felt hat with the crown creased lengthwise and a somewhat curved brim.
fee (fē), *n.* [ME. *fee, feo,* fief, payment; Anglo-Fr. *fee, fie* (OFr. *feu, fiu, fief*); associated with ME. *feo, feoh* (< AS. *feoh*), cattle, hence property, chattels; sense influences < ML. *feodum, feudum,* prob. lit., cattle-wealth < Gmc. **fexu-,* (whence OHG. *fihu,* G. *vieh,* AS. *feoh,* cattle) + *od,* wealth; IE. base **pek-,* sheep, cattle, as also in L. *pecu, pecus,* cattle; cf. PECUNIARY, PECULIAR, &, for sense development, CHATTEL], 1. originally, *a*) heritable land held from a feudal lord in return for service; fief; feudal benefice: also called *feud.* *b*) the right to hold such land. *c*) payment, service, or homage due to a superior. 2. a payment asked or given for professional services, admissions, licenses, tuition, etc.; charge. 3. a present of money; tip; gratuity. 4. in *law,* an inheritance in land: see **fee simple, fee tail.** *v.t.* to give a fee to. —*SYN.* see **wage.**
hold in fee, to own; possess.
fee·ble (fē′b'l), *adj.* [ME. *feble;* OFr. *feble, foible* (Fr. *faible*) < L. *flebilis,* to be wept over < *flere,* to weep], weak; not strong; specifically, *a*) infirm: as, a *feeble* old man. *b*) without force or effectiveness: as, a *feeble* light, a *feeble* attempt. *c*) easily broken; frail: as, a *feeble* barrier. —*SYN.* see **weak.**
fee·ble-mind·ed (fē′b'l-min′did), *adj.* 1. mentally weak or deficient; subnormal in intelligence. 2. having a weak will; irresolute.
the feeble-minded, those who are mentally deficient, including morons, imbeciles, and, sometimes, idiots.
fee·bly (fē′bli), *adv.* in a feeble manner.
feed (fēd), *v.t.* [FED (fed), FEEDING], [ME. *feden;* AS. *fedan* < **fodjan* < base of AS. *fod,* food (see FOOD); akin to OFris. *fēda,* OHG. *fuotan,* etc.], 1. to give food to; provide food for. 2. to serve or provide as food: as, the farmer *fed* oats to the horses. 3. to provide something necessary for the growth, development, or existence of; nourish; sustain: as, the blood *feeds* the body tissue, the news *fed* his anger. 4. to provide (material to be used up): as, *feed* coal to the stove.

5. to provide with material: as, *feed* the stove. 6. to provide satisfaction for; gratify: as, the incident *fed* his vanity. 7. in *sports*, to pass the ball, puck, etc. to (a player intending to make a shot, try for a goal, etc.). 8. in the *theater*, to give (an actor) the necessary cue lines. ***v.i.*** to eat: said chiefly of animals. ***n.*** 1. food given to animals; fodder. 2. the amount of fodder given at one time. 3. the material supplied to a machine. 4. the part of the machine supplying this material. 5. the supplying of this material. 6. [Colloq.], a meal.

feed on (or **upon**), 1. to take as food; be nourished by. 2. to get satisfaction, support, etc. from.

off one's feed, [Slang], without appetite for food; somewhat sick: originally said of horses, etc.

feed·back (fēd′bak′), ***n.*** in *electronics*, the feeding back of part of the output to the input at the proper phase: used in radio to amplify or decrease the strength of a signal, or to make a circuit oscillatory.

feed-back (fēd′bak′), ***adj.*** in *electricity*, regenerative.

feed bag, a bag filled with grain, fastened over a horse's muzzle for feeding: also called *nose bag*.

put on the feed bag, [Slang], to eat a meal.

feed·er (fēd′ẽr), ***n.*** 1. a person or thing that feeds; especially, one that supplies material to a machine. 2. anything that supplies or leads into something else, as a stream of water, a railroad, an air route, etc.; subsidiary; tributary. 3. in *electricity*, a conductor supplying energy to a center from which the energy is distributed into various channels.

feel (fēl), ***v.t.*** [FELT (felt), FEELING], [ME. *felen;* AS. *felan;* akin to G. *fühlen;* IE. base **pāl-*, to finger, touch, seen also in L. *palpare*, to touch softly (cf. PALPABLE, PALPITATE); prob. not connected with *palm*, etc.], 1. to touch; touch or handle in order to become aware of; examine by touching or handling. 2. to perceive or be aware of through physical sensation: as, he *felt* tears run down his cheeks. 3. to be influenced or moved by; be sensitive to or emotionally disturbed by. 4. to be aware of through intellectual perception: as, I *feel* the weight of his argument. 5. to think; believe; consider. ***v.i.*** 1. to have physical sensation; be sentient. 2. to appear to be to the senses, especially to the sense of touch: as, the water *feels* warm. 3. to try to find by touching; grope. 4. to be aware of the condition of being: as, I *feel* sad. 5. to be moved to sympathy, pity, etc. ***n.*** 1. the act of feeling; perception by the senses. 2. the sense of touch. 3. the nature of a thing perceived through touch: as, the *feel* of wet sawdust. 4. an emotional sensation.

feel (a person) out, to find out the opinions or attitude of (a person) by a cautious and indirect approach.

feel like, [Colloq.], to have an inclination or desire for.

feel (like) oneself, to feel normally healthy, fit, etc.

feel up to, [Colloq.], to feel capable of.

feel·er (fēl′ẽr), ***n.*** 1. a person or thing that feels. 2. a specialized organ of touch in an animal or insect, as a tentacle or antenna. 3. an action, remark, question, etc. made to feel out another or others.

feel·ing (fēl′iŋ), ***adj.*** [ME. *feling;* see FEEL & -ING], full of emotion or sensitivity; sympathetic. ***n.*** 1. that one of the senses by which sensations of contact, pressure, temperature, and pain are transmitted through the skin; sense of touch. 2. the power or faculty of experiencing physical sensation. 3. an awareness; consciousness; sensation: as, a *feeling* of pain. 4. an emotion. 5. *pl.* sensitivities; susceptibilities: as, her *feelings* are easily hurt. 6. a kindly, generous attitude; sympathy; pity. 7. *a*) an opinion or sentiment: as, it is my *feeling* that events are moving slowly. *b*) a premonition: as, I have a *feeling* that something unpleasant will happen. 8. what is attributed to something as a result of one's own impression or emotion; air; atmosphere: as, a great city has a *feeling* of strain and hurry. 9. discriminating and sensitive taste: as, he has a *feeling* for music. 10. the emotional quality in a work of art.

***SYN.*—feeling,** when unqualified in the context, refers to any of the subjective reactions, pleasurable or unpleasurable, that one may have to a situation and usually connotes an absence of reasoning (I can't trust my own *feelings*); **emotion** implies an intense feeling with physical as well as mental manifestations (her breast heaved with *emotion*); **passion** refers to a strong or overpowering emotion, connoting especially sexual love or intense anger; **sentiment** applies to a feeling, often a tender one, accompanied by some thought or reasoning (what are your *sentiments* in this matter?).

feel·ing·ly (fēl′iŋ-li), ***adv.*** in a manner resulting from or expressing strong emotion.

fee simple, [Anglo-Fr.; see FEE & SIMPLE], ownership (of land) with unrestricted rights of disposition.

feet (fēt), ***n.*** plural of **foot**: abbreviated **ft., f., F.**

carry (or **sweep**) **off one's feet,** 1. to fill with enthusiasm. 2. to make a deep impression on.

on one's feet, 1. in a standing position. 2. firmly established.

sit at the feet of, to be an admiring disciple or pupil of.

stand on one's own feet, to be independent.

fee tail, [Anglo-Fr. *fee tailé; fee* (see FEE) + *tailé*, pp. of *taillir*, to cut, limit (OFr. *taillier*); see TAILOR], ownership (of land) restricted to a specified class of heirs.

feeze (fēz, fāz), ***v.t.*** [FEEZED (fēzd, fāzd), FEEZING], [ME. *fesen, fesien*, to drive, put to flight; AS. *fesan, fesian*, to drive; cf. FAZE], 1. [Obs. or Dial.], *a*) to drive; drive off. *b*) to frighten. *c*) to beat; chastise. 2. [var. of *faze*], [Colloq.], to disturb; agitate; disconcert. Also **feaze.** ***n.*** [< the *v.*], 1. [Brit. Dial.], a rush, hard impact, or rub. 2. [Colloq.], perturbation; agitation.

feh (fā), ***n.*** [Heb.], a variant of peh, the seventeenth letter of the Hebrew alphabet (פ, פ), corresponding to English *F, f:* see **alphabet**, table.

feign (fān), ***v.t.*** [ME. *feinen;* OFr. *feindre* (ppr. *feignant*) < L. *fingere*, to touch, handle, shape; cf. FICTION, FIGURE], 1. originally, to form; shape. 2. to make up (a story, excuse, etc.); invent; fabricate. 3. to imagine. 4. to make a false show of; pretend; imitate; simulate. ***v.i.*** to pretend; dissemble. —***SYN.*** see **assume.**

feigned (fānd), ***adj.*** 1. fictitious; imagined. 2. pretended; simulated; sham.

feint (fānt), ***n.*** [Fr. *feinte* < pp. of *feindre;* see FEIGN], 1. a false show; pretense; sham: as, he made a *feint* of working. 2. a pretended blow or attack intended to take the opponent off his guard, as in boxing, fencing, warfare, etc. ***v.i.*** to deliver such a blow or attack.

Fei·sal I (fī′səl), see **Faisal I:** also spelled **Feisul.**

feld·spar (feld′spär′, fel′spär′), ***n.*** [G. *feldspat(h); feld*, field + *spat(h)*, spar], any of several crystalline minerals made up mainly of aluminum silicates, usually glassy and moderately hard, found in igneous rocks: also **felspar.**

feld·spath·ic (feld-spath′ik, fel-spath′ik), ***adj.*** containing or resembling feldspar.

feld·spath·ose (feld-spath′ōs, fel-spath′ōs), ***adj.*** feldspathic.

Fe·li·ci·a (fə-lish′i-ə, fə-lish′ə), a feminine name: see **Felix.**

fe·li·cif·ic (fē′lə-sif′ik), ***adj.*** [< L. *felix, felicis*, happy; + *-fic*], producing or tending to produce happiness.

fe·lic·i·tate (fə-lis′ə-tāt′), ***v.t.*** [FELICITATED (-id), FELICITATING], [< L. *felicitatus*, pp. of *felicitare*, to make happy < *felix, felicis*, happy], 1. to congratulate; wish happiness to. 2. [Rare], to make happy. ***adj.*** [Obs.], made happy.

fe·lic·i·ta·tion (fə-lis′ə-tā′shən), ***n.*** congratulation.

fe·lic·i·tous (fə-lis′ə-təs), ***adj.*** [< *felicity* + *-ous*], 1. used or expressed in a way suitable to the occasion; appropriate; aptly chosen. 2. having the knack of appropriate and pleasing expression, style, etc.

fe·lic·i·ty (fə-lis′ə-ti), ***n.*** [*pl.* FELICITIES (-tiz)], [ME. *felicite;* OFr. *felicité;* L. *felicitas*, happiness < *felix, felicis*, happy], 1. happiness; bliss. 2. anything producing happiness; good fortune. 3. a quality or faculty of appropriate and pleasing expression in writing, speaking, painting, etc. 4. an apt expression or thought.

fe·lid (fē′lid), ***n.*** [< Mod. L. *Felidae*, the cat family < L. *felis;* see FELINE], any animal of the cat family.

fe·line (fē′lin), ***adj.*** [L. *felinus* < *feles, felis*, a cat], 1. of a cat or the cat family. 2. catlike; crafty; sly; stealthy. ***n.*** any animal of the cat family, including the cat, leopard, lion, lynx, panther, puma, tiger, etc.

fe·lin·i·ty (fi-lin′ə-ti), ***n.*** the quality of being feline.

Fe·lix (fē′liks), [L., lit., happy], a masculine name: feminine, *Felicia.*

fell (fel), past tense of **fall.**

fell (fel), ***v.t.*** [ME. *fellen;* AS. *fellan, fiellan* (< Gmc. **falljan*), caus. of *feallan* (< Gmc. **fallan*), to fall (see FALL, *v.*); akin to G. *fällen*], 1. to cause to fall; knock down: as, the boxer *felled* his opponent with a blow. 2. to cut down (a tree or trees). 3. in *sewing*, to turn over (the rough edge of a seam) and sew down flat. ***n.*** 1. the trees cut down in one season. 2. in *sewing*, a felled seam.

fell (fel), ***adj.*** [ME., AS. & OFr. *fel*, cruel, furious (orig. nom. of *felon*); LL. **fello;* see FELON], 1. fierce; terrible; cruel. 2. [Archaic or Poetic], causing death; deadly: as, a *fell* plague.

fell (fel), ***n.*** [ME. *felle, fel;* AS. *fel;* akin to G. *fell;* IE. base **pel-*, skin, hide, seen also in L. *pellis*, skin (cf. PELLICLE) & AS. *filmen*, membrane (cf. **FILM**)], an animal's hide or skin.

fell (fel), ***n.*** [ME. *fell* < Anglo-N.; cf. ON. *fjall*, mountain; akin to G. *fels* (OHG. *felis*)], [British], 1. a rocky or barren hill. 2. a moor; down.

fel·lah (fel′ə), ***n.*** [*pl.* FELLAHS (fel′əz); Ar. FELLAHEEN, FELLAHIN (fel′ə-hēn′)], [Ar. *fellāḥ* (pl. *fellaḥīn*) < *falāḥa*, to plow], a peasant or laborer in Egypt or some other countries where Arabic is spoken.

fell·er (fel′ẽr), ***n.*** [Slang or Dial.], a fellow; man or boy.

fell·er (fel′ẽr), ***n.*** 1. a person or thing that fells. 2. a sewing-machine attachment for felling seams.

fell·mon·ger (fel′muŋ′gẽr), ***n.*** [*fell* (a hide) + *monger*],

a dealer in sheepskins or other animal skins.
fel·loe (fel'ō), *n.* a felly.
fel·low (fel'ō, fel'ə), *n.* [ME. *felaghe, felauh, felawe,* etc.; late AS. *feolaga,* formed < *feoh,* cattle, property, money (cf. FEE) + *laga,* a laying down (cf. LAW, LAY), after ON. *félagi,* partner, comrade, of the same ult. derivation; basic sense, "one laying down money or property for a joint undertaking"; senses 5, 6, 7 after L. *socius* (cf. ASSOCIATE)], 1. originally, a person who shares; partner or accomplice. 2. a companion; associate. 3. a person of the same class or rank; equal; peer. 4. either of a pair of similar things; mate. 5. a graduate student who holds a fellowship in a university or college. 6. a member of a learned society. 7. [British], a member of a governing body of a college, as at Oxford University. 8. [Obs.], *a*) a person of a lower social class. *b*) a coarse, rough man. 9. [Colloq.], *a*) a man or boy: often in familiar address. *b*) a person; one: as, a *fellow* must eat. 10. [Colloq.], a suitor; beau. Abbreviated **F.** (in senses 5, 6, 7). *adj.* having the same ideas, position, work, etc.; in the same condition; associated: as, *fellow* workers, *fellow* students.
fellow feeling, sympathy; mutual understanding.
fel·low·ship (fel'ō-ship'), *n.* [ME. *felawschip;* see FELLOW & -SHIP], 1. companionship; friendly association. 2. a mutual sharing, as of experience, activity, interest, etc. 3. a group of people with the same interests; company; brotherhood. 4. an endowment, or a sum of money paid from such an endowment, for the support of a graduate student in a university or college. 5. the rank or position of a fellow in a university or college.
fellow traveler, [transl. of Russ. *popuchiki*], a nonmember who supports or approves the cause of a party, especially the Communist Party.
fel·ly (fel'i), *n.* [*pl.* FELLIES (-iz)], [ME. *felowe, felge;* AS. *felg;* akin to G. *felge;* IE. **pel-k* < base **pel-,* **qwel-,* to turn; cf. FALLOW (field)], 1. the rim of a spoked wheel. 2. a segment of such a rim. Also **felloe.**
fel·ly (fel'li), *adv.* in a fell manner; with cruelty.
‡**fe·lo-de-se** (fē'lō-di-sē', fel'ō-di-sē'), *n.* [*pl.* FELOS-DE-SE (fē'lōz-, fel'ōz-), FELONES-DE-SE (fel'ō-nēz'-)], [Anglo-L., lit., felon of (one)self], in *law,* (a) suicide.
fel·on (fel'ən), *n.* [ME. *felon, feloun, n.* & *adj.,* criminal; OFr. *felon, felun* < LL. **fello;* ? < L. *fel, fellis,* gall], 1. [Rare], a villain. 2. in *law,* a person guilty of a major crime; criminal. *adj.* wicked; base; criminal.
fel·on (fel'ən), *n.* [ME.; prob. < same base as prec.], a painful, pus-producing infection at the end of a finger or toe, near the nail; whitlow.
fe·lo·ni·ous (fə-lō'ni-əs), *adj.* 1. wicked; base; criminal. 2. in *law,* of, like, or constituting a felony.
fel·on·ry (fel'ən-ri), *n.* felons collectively.
fel·o·ny (fel'ə-ni), *n.* [*pl.* FELONIES (-niz)], [ME. & OFr. *felonie;* LL. *felonia,* treason, treachery < **fello;* see FELON], a major crime, as murder, arson, rape, etc., for which statute provides a greater punishment than for a misdemeanor: the penalty is usually death or imprisonment in a penitentiary.
fel·site (fel'sīt), *n.* [*felspar* + *-ite*], an igneous rock consisting mainly of feldspar and quartz.
fel·spar (fel'spär'), *n.* [mistakenly altered (1794) by Kirwan < *feldspar,* after G. *fels,* rock], feldspar.
felt (felt), *n.* [ME. & AS.; akin to G. *filz,* D. *filt;* basic sense, "cloth made by pounding or beating" < IE. base **pel-,* to beat, strike, seen also in L. *pellere,* to beat, drive (cf. IMPEL, EXPEL), Eng. *anvil*], 1. a fabric of wool, often mixed with fur or hair, worked together by pressure, heat, chemical action, etc. without weaving or knitting. 2. anything made of felt. *adj.* made of felt. *v.t.* 1. to make into felt. 2. to cover with felt.
felt (felt), past tense and past participle of **feel.**
felt·ing (fel'tiŋ), *n.* 1. the making of felt. 2. the material of which felt is made. 3. felted cloth.
fe·luc·ca (fə-luk'ə, fe-luk'ə), *n.* [It. *feluca;* Sp. *faluca;* ? < Ar. *fulk,* a ship], a small, narrow ship with two or three masts, propelled by oars or lateen sails or both, used especially along the Mediterranean coasts.
fem., feminine.
fe·male (fē'māl), *adj.* [ME. & OFr. *femelle;* L. *femella,* dim. of *femina,* a woman < IE. base **dhē-,* **dhə-,* to suck, suckle, seen also in L. *felare,* to suck, *filius,* son, orig., a suckling, Gr. *thēlazein,* to suckle], 1. designating or of the sex that produces ova and bears offspring: opposed to *male:* biological symbol, ♀. 2. of, characteristic of, or suitable to members of this sex; feminine. 3. consisting of women or girls. 4. in *botany, a*) having a pistil and no stamens. *b*) designating or of a reproductive structure or part containing large gametes that can be fertilized by smaller, motile gametes. *c*) designating or of any structure or part that produces fruit after it is fertilized. 5. in *mechanics,* designating or having a hollow part shaped to receive a corresponding inserted part (called *male*): said of a gauge, electric plug, etc. *n.* a female person, animal, or plant.
SYN.—**female** is the basic term applied to members of the sex that is biologically distinguished from the male sex and is used of animals or plants as well as of human beings; **feminine** is now the preferred term for references, other than those basically biological, to qualities characteristic of women or things appropriate to them; **womanly** suggests the noble qualities one associates with a woman, especially one who has maturity of character; **womanish,** in contrast, suggests the weaknesses and faults that are regarded as characteristic of women; **effeminate,** used chiefly in reference to a man, implies delicacy, softness, or lack of virility; **ladylike** refers to manners, conduct, etc. such as are expected from a refined or well-bred woman. See also **woman.** —*ANT.* male, masculine, manly, mannish.
feme (fem), *n.* [OFr. *feme* (Fr. *femme*) < L. *femina,* woman], 1. in *law,* a wife. 2. [Obs.], a woman.
feme covert, [OFr., lit., woman covered], in *law,* a married woman.
feme sole, [OFr., lit., woman alone], in *law,* an unmarried woman; spinster, divorcee, or widow.
fem·i·na·cy (fem'ə-nə-si), *n.* [*pl.* FEMINACIES (-siz)], feminine nature.
fem·i·nal·i·ty (fem'ə-nal'ə-ti), *n.* [*pl.* FEMINALITIES (-tiz)], [< OFr. *feminal, adj.,* female < L. *femina*], the state or quality of being female; femininity.
fem·i·ne·i·ty (fem'ə-nē'ə-ti), *n.* [*pl.* FEMINEITIES (-tiz)], [< L. *femineus,* feminine < *femina*], 1. femininity. 2. effeminacy.
fem·i·nine (fem'ə-nin), *adj.* [< L. *feminus* < *femina,* woman], 1. female; of women or girls. 2. having qualities regarded as characteristic of women and girls, as gentleness, weakness, delicacy, modesty, etc.; womanly. 3. suitable to or characteristic of a woman. 4. effeminate; womanish: said of men. 5. in *grammar,* designating or of the gender of words denoting or referring to females or things originally regarded as female. *n.* in *grammar,* 1. the feminine gender. 2. a word or form in this gender. Abbreviated **fem., f., F.** —*SYN.* see **female.**
feminine rhyme, a rhyme of two or, sometimes, three syllables of which only the first is stressed (e.g., fashion, passion; haziness, laziness).
fem·i·nin·i·ty (fem'ə-nin'ə-ti), *n.* [*pl.* FEMININITIES (-tiz)], 1. the quality or state of being feminine; womanliness. 2. women in general; womankind.
fem·i·nism (fem'ə-niz'm), *n.* [< L. *femina,* woman; + *-ism*], 1. *a*) the theory that women should have political, economic, and social rights equal to those of men. *b*) the movement to win such rights for women. 2. [Rare], feminine qualities.
fem·i·nist (fem'ə-nist), *n.* an advocate or supporter of feminism. *adj.* of feminism or feminists.
fem·i·nis·tic (fem'ə-nis'tik), *adj.* feminist.
fem·i·ni·za·tion (fem'ə-ni-zā'shən, fem'ə-nī-zā'shən), *n.* a feminizing.
fem·i·nize (fem'ə-nīz'), *v.t.* & *v.i* [FEMINIZED (-nīzd'), FEMINIZING], [< L. *femina,* woman; + *-ize*], to make or become feminine or effeminate.
‡**femme** (fåm), *n.* [Fr.], a woman or wife.
‡**femme cou·verte** (fåm'ko͞o'vert'), [Fr., lit., covered woman], a married woman.
‡**femme de cham·bre** (fåm' də shän'br'), [Fr.], a chambermaid; lady's maid.
fem·o·ra (fem'ẽr-ə), *n.* alternative plural of **femur.**
fem·o·ral (fem'ẽr-əl), *adj.* [ML. *femoralis*], of the femur.
fe·mur (fē'mẽr), *n.* [*pl.* FEMURS (-mẽrz), FEMORA (fem'ẽr-ə)], [L., thigh], the thighbone: see **skeleton,** illus.
fen (fen), *n.* [ME.; AS. *fen, fenn;* akin to G. *fenne,* marsh, Goth. *fani,* mud; IE. base **pan-,* wet, slime, mire], low, flat, marshy land; swamp; bog.
fe·na·gle (fi-nā'g'l), *v.i.* & *v.t.* [FENAGLED (-g'ld), FENAGLING], to finagle.
fence (fens), *n.* [ME., abbrev. of *defence;* see DEFENSE], 1. originally, a protection; defense. 2. a barrier of wooden posts, wire, iron, etc., used as a boundary or means of protection or confinement. 3. the art of self-defense with foil, saber, etc.; fencing. 4. expertness in conversation or debate. 5. a person who buys and sells stolen goods. 6. a place where stolen goods are bought and sold. *v.t.* [FENCED (fenst), FENCING], 1. to enclose with or as with a fence (often with *in*). 2. [Archaic], to ward off; protect; defend. *v.i.* 1. to practice the art of fencing. 2. to avoid giving a direct reply; parry; evade. 3. to buy or sell stolen goods.
fence with, to be evasive with; avoid answering directly.
on the fence, not having chosen to join one side or the other in a controversy.
fenc·er (fen'sẽr), *n.* 1. a person who fences with a foil, saber, etc. 2. one who makes or repairs fences.
fen·ci·ble (fen'sə-b'l), *adj.* [abbrev. of *defensible*], [Scot.], that can defend or be defended. *n. usually in pl.* [Archaic], a soldier who enlists only for home service.
fenc·ing (fen'siŋ), *n.* [< *fence, v.*], 1. the art or sport of fighting with a foil or other sword. 2. debating. 3. material for making fences. 4. a system of fences.
fend (fend), *v.t.* [ME. *fenden,* abbrev. of *defenden;* see DEFEND], [Archaic or Poetic], to defend. *v.i.* to resist; parry.
fend for oneself, to manage by oneself; get along without help.
fend off, to ward off; turn aside; repel.

fend·er (fen′dẽr), *n.* anything that fends off or protects something else; specifically, *a*) any of the metal frames over the wheels of an automobile or other vehicle to protect against splashing mud, etc.; mudguard. *b*) a device on the front of a streetcar or locomotive to catch or push aside anything on the track; cowcatcher. *c*) a screen or guard placed in front of a fireplace to keep the hot coals in. *d*) a pad or cushion of rope, wood, etc. hung over a ship's side to protect it in docking.

Fé·ne·lon, Fran·çois de Sa·li·gnac de la Mothe (frän′-swȧ′ də sȧ′lē′nyȧk′ də lȧ mōt′ fān′lōn′; Eng. fen′'l-on′), 1651–1715; French churchman and writer.

fen·es·tel·la (fen′is-tel′ə), *n.* [L., dim. of *fenestra*, window], a small window or opening, especially one for displaying relics in an altar.

fe·nes·tra (fi-nes′trə), *n.* [*pl.* FENESTRAE (-trē)], [L., window], 1. a small windowlike opening, as in the inner wall of the middle ear. 2. a small, transparent spot, as in the wings of some insects.

fe·nes·tral (fi-nes′trəl), *adj.* 1. of a window. 2. of or having a fenestra or fenestrae. *n.* a frame fitted with cloth or paper instead of glass, serving as a window.

fe·nes·trate (fi-nes′trit, fi-nes′trāt), *adj.* [L. *fenestratus*, pp. of *fenestrare*, to furnish with windows or openings < *fenestra*, window], 1. containing small openings or perforations. 2. in *zoology*, having fenestrae.

fe·nes·trat·ed (fi-nes′trā′tid), *adj.* 1. having windows. 2. in *zoology*, having fenestrae.

fen·es·tra·tion (fen′is-trā′shən), *n.* [< *fenestrate* + *-tion*], 1. the arrangement of the windows in a building. 2. the surgical operation of making a fenestra, or perforation, as in the middle ear.

Feng·kieh (fuŋ′kyu′), *n.* a city in eastern Szechwan province, China: pop., 25,000.

Feng·tien (fuŋ′tyen′), *n.* Liaoning: the former name.

Fe·ni·an (fē′ni-ən, fēn′yən), *n.* [< *Fiann* or *Fianna*, the old militia of Ireland, so called from *Finn*, *Fionn*, hero of Irish tradition; associated with OIr. *fēne*, inhabitant of Ireland], 1. any of a group of legendary military heroes of ancient Ireland. 2. a member of a secret Irish revolutionary brotherhood established in New York about 1858 for the purpose of freeing Ireland from English rule. *adj.* of the Fenians.

Fe·ni·an·ism (fē′ni-ən-iz′m, fēn′yən-iz′m), *n.* the principles, aims, and methods of the Fenians.

fen·nec (fen′ek), *n.* [Ar. *fanak*], a small, fawn-colored African fox with large ears.

fen·nel (fen′'l), *n.* [ME. *fenil;* AS. *finul, finugl* < L. *feniculum, faeniculum*, dim. of *fenum, faenum*, hay], a tall herb of the carrot family, with yellow flowers: its aromatic seeds are used as a seasoning and in medicine.

fen·nel·flow·er (fen′'l-flou′ẽr), *n.* [so named from being confused with the *fennel*], 1. a hardy herb of the buttercup family, with blue, yellow, or white flowers: its seeds are often used for seasoning. 2. its flower.

fen·ny (fen′i), *adj.* [ME. *fenni;* AS. *fennig*], 1. full of fens; marshy; boggy. 2. of or found in fens.

Fen·rir (fen′rẽr), *n.* [ON.], in *Norse mythology*, a great wolf, bound by the gods with a magic rope.

Fen·ris-wolf (fen′ris-woolf′), *n.* Fenrir.

fen·u·greek (fen′yoo-grēk′), *n.* [Fr. *fenugrec;* L. *fenumgraecum, faenum Graecum*, lit., Greek hay], an herb of the pea family, whose seeds are used to flavor curry.

feod (fūd), *n.* [var. of *feud*], an estate held under a feudal lord; fee; fief.

feo·dal (fū′d'l), *adj.* of feods or feudalism; feudal.

feoff (fef, fēf), *v.t.* [Early ME. *feoffen;* Anglo-Fr. *feoffer;* OFr. *fieuffer, fieffer* < *fieu, fief*], to give or sell a fief to; enfeoff. *n.* a fief.

feoff·ee (fef-ē′, fēf-ē′), *n.* [Anglo-Fr. *feoffé*, pp. of *feoffer*], a person to whom land is given as a fief.

feoff·ment (fef′mənt, fēf′mənt), *n.* [Anglo-Fr. *feoffement*], the granting of land as a fief; enfeoffing.

feof·for, feoff·er (fef′ẽr, fēf′ẽr), *n.* [Anglo-Fr. *feoffour*], a person granting a feoffment.

FEPC, Fair Employment Practices Committee.

-fer (fẽr), [see -FEROUS], a suffix meaning *one that bears* or *produces*, as in *conifer*: used to form nouns corresponding to adjectives in *-ferous*.

fe·ra·cious (fə-rā′shəs), *adj.* [< L. *ferax, feracis* < *ferre*, to bear; + *-ous*], producing abundantly; fruitful.

fe·rac·i·ty (fə-ras′ə-ti), *n.* the state of being feracious.

‡fe·rae na·tu·rae (fē′rē nə-tū′rē), [L.], 1. of a wild nature. 2. in *law*, nondomesticated animals and fowls that are not the private property of anyone.

fe·ral (fêr′əl), *adj.* [< L. *fera*, wild animal < *ferus* (see FIERCE); + *-al*], 1. untamed; wild. 2. savage; brutal.

fe·ral (fêr′əl), *adj.* [L. *feralis*, of the dead, of funeral rites], 1. deadly; fatal. 2. gloomy; funereal.

Fer·ber, Edna (fũr′bẽr), 1887– ; American writer.

fer·de·lance (fâr′də-läns′), *n.* [Fr., iron tip of a lance], a large, poisonous snake related to the rattlesnake, found in tropical American countries.

Fer·di·nand (fũr′d'n-and′), [Fr.; prob. < Gmc. **frithu-*, peace (see FREDERICK) + **nanths*, courage; cf. Goth. (*ana*)*nanthjan*, to be bold, take courage, AS. *nethan*, to venture on, dare; hence, lit., bold (in) peace], a masculine name: feminine, *Fernanda;* equivalents, It. *Ferdinando, Ferrando*, Sp. *Fernando, Hernando.*

Ferdinand I, 1. ?–1065; king of Castile (1033–1065); emperor of Spain (1056–1065): called *the Great.* 2. (*Maximilian Karl Leopold Maria*), 1861–1948; father of *Boris III;* king of Bulgaria (1908–1918); abdicated.

Ferdinand V, 1452–1516; king of Castile (1474–1516); as Ferdinand II, king of Aragon (1479–1516); as Ferdinand III, king of Naples (1504–1516): called *the Catholic.*

fere (fêr), *n.* [ME. *fere;* AS. (Anglian) *fera*, aphetic form of *gefera; ge-*, together + *-fera* < base of *faran*, to go (cf. FARE, *v.*)], [Archaic], 1. a companion; mate. 2. a husband or wife.

fer·e·to·ry (fer′ə-tôr′i, fer′ə-tō′ri), *n.* [*pl.* FERETORIES (-iz, -riz)], [altered < ME. *fertre;* OFr. *fiertre;* L. *feretrum*, a litter, bier; Gr. *pheretron* < *pherein*, to bear; akin to Eng. *bier, bear*], 1. a shrine for the relics of saints. 2. a bier. 3. the place in a church where shrines were kept.

Fer·gus (fũr′gəs), [MIr. & MGael. < base meaning "manly strength"], a masculine name. *n.* in *Irish legend*, a hero of the army that attacked Cuchulain at Ulster.

fe·ri·a (fêr′i-ə), *n.* [*pl.* FERIAE (-ē′)], [LL.; see FAIR (festival)], 1. *pl.* holidays; festivals. 2. any weekday, especially one not designated by the church as a holiday.

fe·ri·al (fêr′i-əl), *adj.* [ME. *ferialle;* OFr. *ferial;* ML. *ferialis* < L. *feriae;* see FAIR (festival)], 1. having to do with a weekday, especially one not a church holiday. 2. having to do with a holiday.

fe·rine (fêr′īn), *adj.* [L. *ferinus* < *ferus*, wild], feral.

Fe·rin·gi, Fe·rin·ghee (fə-riŋ′gi), *n.* [Per. *Farangi;* Ar. *Faranji*, adapted < OFr. *Franc*, a Frank], in India, a European or a Eurasian, especially one of Portuguese-Indian descent.

fer·i·ty (fer′ə-ti), *n.* [L. *feritas* < *ferus*, wild], the state or quality of being wild, savage, or untamed.

‡fer·ma·ta (fer-mä′tä), *n.* [It.], in *music*, 1. the holding of a tone or rest beyond its written value, at the discretion of the performer. 2. the sign (⌒) indicating this. Also called *pause, hold.*

fer·ment (fũr′mənt; *for v.*, fẽr-ment′), *n.* [Fr. < L. *fermentum*, leaven, yeast < *fervere*, to boil, be agitated; cf. BARM], 1. a substance causing fermentation in other substances, as yeast, bacteria, enzymes, etc. 2. fermentation. 3. a state of excitement; agitation; commotion; unrest. *v.t.* 1. to cause fermentation in. 2. to excite; agitate. *v.i.* 1. to be in the process of fermentation. 2. to be excited or agitated; seethe.

fer·men·ta·tion (fũr′mən-tā′shən, fũr′men-tā′shən), *n.* [L. *fermentatio*, see FERMENT, *v.*], 1. the breakdown of complex molecules in organic compounds, caused by the influence of a ferment: as, bacteria cause milk to curdle by *fermentation.* 2. excitement; unrest; agitation.

fer·ment·a·tive (fẽr-men′tə-tiv), *adj.* causing or resulting from fermentation.

Fer·mi, En·ri·co (en-re′kô fâr′mē), 1901–1954; Italian physicist in America; instrumental in development of atomic bomb; awarded Nobel Prize in physics in 1938.

fer·mi·um (fâr′mi-əm), *n.* [after E. *Fermi*], a radioactive chemical element produced by nuclear bombardment in a cyclotron: symbol, Fm; at. wt., 254 (?); at. no., 100.

fern (fũrn), *n.* [ME.; AS. *fearn;* akin to G. *farn;* IE. base **per-* (< **petr-*), wing, feather, as in Sans. *parṇá-m*, feather], any of a large group of shrubby, nonflowering plants having roots, stems, and fronds, and reproducing by spores instead of by seeds.

Fer·nan·da (fẽr-nan′də), a feminine name: see **Ferdinand.**

Fer·nán·dez, Juan (hwän fer-nän′deth; Eng. fẽr-nan′-diz), 1536?–1602; Spanish navigator and discoverer of islands in the Pacific.

Fer·nan·do de No·ro·nha (fer-nän′thoo thə nô-rô′nyə), an island in the South Atlantic, northeast of Natal, Brazil: a Brazilian penal colony: area, 10 sq. mi.

Fer·nan·do Po (fẽr-nan′dō pō′), an island in the Gulf of Guinea, part of the colony of Spanish Guinea: area, 786 sq. mi.; pop., 47,000; capital, Santa Isabel.

Fer·nan·do Pó·o (fer-nän′dô pô′ô), Fernando Po: the Spanish name.

Fern·dale (fũrn′dāl′), *n.* a city in southeastern Michigan: pop., 31,000.

fern·er·y (fũr′nẽr-i), *n.* [*pl.* FERNERIES (-iz)], a place where ferns are grown; collection of growing ferns.

fern seed, the dustlike spores of ferns: formerly believed to make invisible the person who carried them.

fern·y (fũr′ni), *adj.* 1. full of ferns. 2. of or like ferns.

fe·ro·cious (fi-rō′shəs), *adj.* [< L. *ferox, ferocis* < *ferus*, wild, fierce; + *-ous*], 1. fierce; savage; violently cruel. 2. [Colloq.], very great: as, a *ferocious* appetite.

fe·roc·i·ty (fi-ros′ə-ti), *n.* [*pl.* FEROCITIES (-tiz)], [Fr. *férocité;* L. *ferocitas*], the quality or condition of being ferocious; fierceness; savagery.

-fer·ous (fẽr-əs), [L. *-fer* < *ferre*, to bear; + *-ous*] a suffix meaning *bearing, producing, yielding,* as in *coniferous, odoriferous.*

Fer·ra·ra (fə-rä′rə; It. fer-rä′rä), *n.* a city in northern Italy: pop., 133,000 (1947).

fer·rate (fer′āt), *n.* [< L. *ferrum*, iron; + *-ate*], a salt of ferric acid.

fer·re·ous (fer′i-əs), *adj.* [L. *ferreus* < *ferrum*, iron], 1. of or containing iron. 2. like iron in hardness, etc.

fer·ret (fer′it), *n.* [It. *fioretto*, dim. of *fiore*, a flower; L. *flos, floris*, a flower], a narrow ribbon of cotton, wool, silk, etc.: also **ferreting.**

fer·ret (fer′it), *n.* [ME. *feret, foret;* OFr. *furet*, dim. of *furon;* LL. *furo*, a ferret < L. *fur*, thief], a kind of weasel, easily tamed and used for hunting or killing rabbits, rats, etc. *v.t.* 1. to force out of hiding with a ferret; hence, 2. to look for carefully; search out; investigate thoroughly. *v.i.* 1. to hunt with ferrets. 2. to search.

FERRET (about 1 1/2 ft. long)

fer·ret·y (fer′it-i), *adj.* like a ferret (animal).

fer·ri- (fer′i, fer′ī), [< L. *ferrum*, iron], a combining form meaning *containing ferric iron:* see **ferro-.**

fer·ri·age (fer′i-ij), *n.* [< *ferry* + *-age*], 1. transportation by ferry. 2. the charge for this.

fer·ric (fer′ik), *adj.* [< L. *ferrum*, iron; + *-ic*], 1. of, containing, or derived from iron. 2. in *chemistry*, designating or of iron with a valence higher than two, or compounds containing such iron: distinguished from *ferrous.*

fer·ri·cy·an·ic (fer′i-sī-an′ik, fer′ī-sī-an′ik), *adj.* [*ferri-* + *cyanic*], designating or of a brown, crystalline, unstable acid, $H_3Fe(CN)_6$.

fer·ri·cy·a·nide (fer′i-sī′ə-nīd′, fer′ī-sī′ə-nid), *n.* a salt of ferricyanic acid.

fer·rif·er·ous (fe-rif′ẽr-əs), *adj.* [< L. *ferrum*, iron; + *-ferous*], bearing or containing iron.

Fer·ris wheel (fer′is), [after George W. G. *Ferris* (1859–1896), Am. engineer who constructed the first one for the World's Fair in Chicago in 1893], a large, upright wheel revolving on a fixed axle and having seats hanging from the frame: used in amusement parks, etc.

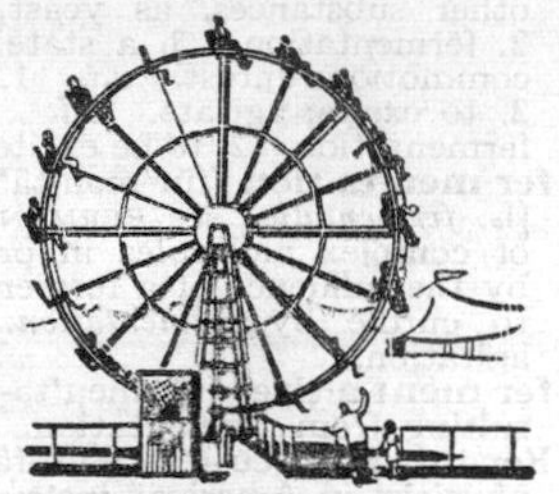
FERRIS WHEEL

fer·rite (fer′īt), *n.* [< L. *ferrum*, iron; + *-ite*], 1. any yellowish or reddish-brown substance occurring in rocks and containing iron compounds. 2. one of the forms of pure metallic iron, having high magnetic permeability and occurring as a constituent of ordinary iron and steel. 3. any of various compounds in which ferric oxide may be regarded as combined with a more basic metallic oxide, as calcium ferrite, $Ca(FeO_2)_2$.

fer·ro- (fer′ō), [< L. *ferrum*, iron], a combining form meaning: 1. *iron, connection with iron,* as in *ferromagnetic.* 2. *iron and,* as in *ferromanganese.* 3. in *chemistry, containing ferrous iron,* as in *ferrocyanide.*

fer·ro·al·loy (fer′ō-ə-loi′), *n.* any of various alloys of iron used in the manufacture of steel: named from the added metal, as ferrochromium, ferromanganese, etc.

fer·ro·cal·cite (fer′ō-kal′sīt), *n.* in *mineralogy*, a calcite containing ferrous carbonate, $FeCO_3$.

fer·ro·chro·mi·um (fer′ō-krō′mi-əm), *n.* an alloy of iron and chromium.

fer·ro·con·crete (fer′ō-kon′krēt, fer′ō-kon-krēt′), *n.* concrete having an iron or steel framework embedded in it: also called *reinforced concrete, armored concrete.*

fer·ro·cy·an·ic (fer′ō-sī-an′ik), *adj.* [*ferro-* + *cyanic*], designating or of a colorless crystalline acid, $H_4Fe(CN)_6$.

fer·ro·cy·a·nide (fer′ō-sī′ə-nīd′, fer′ō-sī′ə-nid), *n.* a salt of ferrocyanic acid.

fer·ro·mag·ne·sian (fer′ō-mag-nē′shən), *adj.* in *mineralogy*, having iron and magnesium as constituents.

fer·ro·mag·net·ic (fer′ō-mag-net′ik), *adj.* highly magnetic, as iron, nickel, etc.: distinguished from *paramagnetic.*

fer·ro·mag·net·ism (fer′ō-mag′nə-tiz′m), *n.* the quality of being ferromagnetic.

fer·ro·man·ga·nese (fer′ō-maŋ′gə-nēs′, fer′ō-maŋ′gə-nēz′), *n.* an alloy of iron and manganese, used for making hard steel.

fer·ro·sil·i·con (fer′ō-sil′i-kən), *n.* a compound of iron and silicon, used in making steel.

fer·ro·type (fer′ō-tīp′), *n.* [*ferro-* + *-type*], 1. a positive photograph taken directly on a thin plate of iron coated with a sensitized film: also called *tintype.* 2. the process of making such photographs.

fer·rous (fer′əs), *adj.* [< L. *ferrum*, iron; + *-ous*], 1. of, containing, or derived from iron. 2. in *chemistry*, designating or of bivalent iron or compounds containing it: distinguished from *ferric.*

fer·ru·gi·nous (fə-rōō′ji-nəs), *adj.* [L. *ferruginus* < *ferrugo*, iron rust, color of iron rust < *ferrum*, iron], 1. of, containing, or having the nature of, iron. 2. having the color of iron rust; reddish-brown.

fer·rule (fer′əl, fer′ool), *n.* [formerly *verrel;* OFr. *virole*, iron ring to put around the end of a staff < LL. *virola*, a ring, bracelet; L. *viriola*, dim. of *viriae*, bracelets, armlets; prob. via Celt. < IE. base **weir-*, wire, twisted work (seen also in Eng. *wire*) < **wei-*, to bend, twist, seen in L. *viere*, to twist, bind around; sp. altered after L. *ferrum*, iron], 1. a metal ring or cap put around the end of a stick, tool, cane, etc. to prevent splitting or to give added strength. 2. in *mechanics*, a short tube or bushing for tightening a joint. *v.t.* [FERRULED (-əld, -oold), FERRULING], to furnish with a ferrule.

fer·ry (fer′i), *v.t.* [FERRIED (-id), FERRYING], [ME. *ferien;* AS. *ferian*, to carry, convey, especially by water, caus. of *faran*, to go (see FARE, *v.*); akin to Goth. *farjan*, ON. *ferja*], 1. to take across a river or narrow body of water in a boat. 2. to cross (a river, etc.), as on a ferry. 3. to deliver (airplanes) by flying to the destination. *v.i.* to cross a narrow body of water in a ferryboat. *n.* [*pl.* FERRIES (-iz)], 1. a transportation system for carrying people, goods, etc. across a narrow body of water. 2. a boat for this purpose. 3. the place where a ferryboat crosses. 4. the legal right to transport in this way for a fee. 5. the delivery of airplanes from one point to another by flying them.

fer·ry·boat (fer′i-bōt′), *n.* a boat for transporting people, goods, etc. across a narrow body of water.

fer·ry·man (fer′i-mən), *n.* [*pl.* FERRYMEN (-mən)], a man who owns, manages, or works on a ferry.

fer·tile (fũr′t′l), *adj.* [OFr. *fertil;* L. *fertilis* < stem **fert-* < *ferre*, to bear], 1. producing abundantly; rich in resources or invention; fruitful; prolific. 2. causing or helping fertility: as, the sun's *fertile* warmth. 3. able to produce young, seeds, fruit, etc. 4. capable of development into a new individual; fertilized: as, *fertile* eggs.

SYN.—**fertile** implies a producing, or power of producing, fruit or offspring, and may be used figuratively of the mind; **fecund** implies the abundant production of offspring or fruit, or, figuratively, of creations of the mind; **fruitful** specifically suggests the bearing of much fruit, but it is also used to imply fertility (of soil), favorable results, profitableness, etc.; **prolific,** a close synonym for **fecund,** more often carries derogatory connotations of overly rapid production or reproduction. —*ANT.* sterile, barren.

fer·til·i·ty (fẽr-til′ə-ti), *n.* [*pl.* FERTILITIES (-tiz)], the quality or state of being fertile; fecundity; productivity.

fer·ti·liz·a·ble (fũr′t′l-iz′ə-b′l), *adj.* that can be fertilized.

fer·ti·li·za·tion (fũr′t′l-i-zā′shən, fũr′t′l-ī-zā′shən), *n.* a fertilizing or being fertilized (in all senses).

fer·ti·lize (fũr′t′l-iz′), *v.t.* [FERTILIZED (-īzd′), FERTILIZING], 1. to make fertile; make fruitful or productive; enrich: as, nitrates *fertilize* soil. 2. to spread fertilizer on 3. in *biology*, to make (the female reproductive cell or female individual) fruitful by introducing the male germ cell; impregnate or pollinate.

fer·ti·liz·er (fũr′t′l-īz′ẽr), *n.* a person or thing that fertilizes; specifically, *a)* any material put on or in the soil to improve the quality or quantity of plant growth, as manure, chemicals, etc. *b)* in *botany*, something that helps bring about fertilization: as, bees are *fertilizers* of flowers.

fer·u·la (fer′yoo-lə, fer′oo-lə), *n.* [L., giant fennel, hence (because used to punish slaves or schoolboys), whip, rod; prob. akin to *festuca*, blade of grass, wild hay (< IE. base **dhwes-*, to scatter, fly about)], 1. any of a group of herbs related to parsley, valuable as sources of gums and medicinal agents. 2. a ferule. 3. a scepter, especially that of the emperor in the Byzantine Empire.

fer·u·la·ceous (fer′yoo-lā′shəs, fer′oo-lā′shəs), *adj.* [L. *ferulaceus;* see FERULA], like a reed or cane.

fer·ule (fer′əl, fer′ōōl), *n.* [L. *ferula;* see FERULA], a flat stick or ruler used for punishing children. *v.t.* [FERULED (-əld, -ōōld), FERULING], to strike or punish with a ferule.

fer·ven·cy (fũr′vən-si), *n.* [OFr. *fervence* < L. *fervens;* see FERVENT], great warmth of feeling; intense devotion or earnestness; ardor; zeal.

fer·vent (fũr′vənt), *adj.* [L. *fervens, ferventis*, ppr. of *fervere*, to glow, boil, rage], 1. hot; burning; glowing. 2. having or showing great warmth of feeling; intensely earnest; ardent. —*SYN.* see **passionate.**

fer·vid (fũr′vid), *adj.* [L. *fervidus* < *fervere*, to boil, glow], 1. hot; burning; glowing. 2. impassioned; fervent. —*SYN.* see **passionate.**

‡**Fer·vi·dor** (fâr′vē′dôr′; Eng. fũr′vi-dôr′), *n.* [Fr. < L. *fervidus;* see FERVID], Thermidor, the eleventh month of the French Revolutionary Calendar.

fer·vor (fũr′vẽr), *n.* [ME. & OFr. *fervor;* L. *fervor* < *fervere;* see FERVENT], 1. intense heat. 2. great warmth of emotion; ardor; zeal. —*SYN.* see **passion.**

fer·vour (fũr′vẽr), *n.* fervor: British spelling.

Fes·cen·nine (fes′ə-nīn′, fes′ə-nin), *adj.* [L. *Fescenninus* < *Fescennia,* city in Etruria noted for scurrilous verse], vulgar; obscene; scurrilous.

fes·cue (fes′kū), *n.* [ME. & OFr. *festu* < L. *festuca,* a stock, straw], 1. any of a group of tough meadow grasses, used for pasture. 2. [Rare], a long stick, straw, etc., used as a teacher's pointer.

fess, fesse (fes), *n.* [OFr. *fesse, faisse* < L. *fascia,* a band], in *heraldry,* a horizontal band forming the middle third of an escutcheon.

fess point, in *heraldry,* the center point in an escutcheon.

-fest (fest), [< G. *fest,* a feast, celebration], a combining form used in forming colloquial and slang words, meaning *an occasion of much,* as in *songfest, funfest, slugfest.*

fes·tal (fes′t'l), *adj.* [OFr. < L. *festum,* feast], of, or having the character of, a feast or festival; gay; joyous.

fes·ter (fes′tẽr), *n.* [ME.; OFr. *festre;* L. *fistula;* see FISTULA], a small sore producing pus; pustule. *v.i.* [ME. *festren* < the *n.*], 1. to form pus; ulcerate. 2. to grow embittered; rankle. 3. to decay. *v.t.* 1. to cause the formation of pus in. 2. to make rankle; embitter.

‡fes·ti·na len·te (fes-tī′nə len′tē), [L.], make haste slowly.

fes·ti·nate (fes′tə-nāt′), *v.t. & v.i.* [FESTINATED (-id), FESTINATING], [< L. *festinatus,* pp. of *festinare,* to hurry], [Obs.], to hurry; speed. *adj.* (fes′tə-nit), [Obs.], hurried.

fes·ti·na·tion (fes′tə-nā′shən), *n.* [L. *festinatio,* haste], an involuntary inclination to hurry in walking, especially as a symptom of certain nervous diseases.

fes·ti·val (fes′tə-v'l), *n.* [ME., *n.* & *adj.* < OFr.; LL. *festivalis* < L. *festivus;* see FESTIVE], 1. a time or day of feasting or celebration, especially a periodic religious celebration. 2. a celebration, entertainment, or series of performances of a certain kind, often held periodically: as, the Bach *festival.* 3. merrymaking; festivity. *adj.* of, for, or fit for a festival.

fes·tive (fes′tiv), *adj.* [L. *festivus* < *festus,* festive, joyful < *festum* (see FEAST)], of, for, or suitable for a feast or festival; merry; gay; joyous; jovial.

fes·tiv·i·ty (fes-tiv′ə-ti), *n.* [*pl.* FESTIVITIES (-tiz)], [L. *festivitas* < *festivus;* see FESTIVE], 1. merrymaking; gaiety; mirth. 2. *a)* a festival. *b) pl.* festive proceedings; things done in celebration.

fes·toon (fes-to͞on′), *n.* [Fr. *feston;* It. *festone* < *festa,* feast; see FEAST], 1. a wreath or garland of flowers, leaves, paper, etc. hanging in a loop or curve. 2. any carved or molded decoration resembling this, as on furniture. *v.t.* 1. to adorn or hang with festoons. 2. to form into a festoon or festoons. 3. to join by festoons.

fes·toon·er·y (fes-to͞on′ẽr-i), *n.* an arrangement of festoons in decoration.

‡Fes·tung Eu·ro·pa (fes′tooŋ oi-rō′pä), [G., lit., fortress Europe], Europe, exclusive of the Soviet Union, considered as an impregnable stronghold: term of Nazi geopolitics before and during World War II.

fe·tal (fē′t'l), *adj.* 1. of, or having the nature of, a fetus. 2. characteristic of a fetus. Also spelled **foetal.**

fe·ta·tion (fē-tā′shən), *n.* the development or formation of a fetus; pregnancy: also spelled **foetation.**

fetch (fech), *v.t.* [ME. *fecchen;* AS. *feccan,* earlier *fetian;* prob. < base of AS. *fæt* (see VAT) and akin to OHG. *fazzōn,* G. *fassen,* to grasp], 1. to go after and come back with; bring; get. 2. to cause to come; produce; elicit. 3. to draw (a breath); heave (a sigh, groan, etc.). 4. to derive; infer. 5. [Dial.], to come to; reach. 6. to bring as a price; sell for. 7. [Colloq.], to attract; charm; captivate. 8. [Colloq.], to deliver or deal (a blow, stroke, etc.). *v.i.* 1. to go after things and bring them back; hence, 2. to retrieve game: said of hounds. 3. in *nautical usage, a)* to take or hold a course. *b)* to veer. *n.* 1. a fetching. 2. a trick; dodge. —*SYN.* see **bring.**
fetch and carry, to do minor tasks or chores.
fetch up, to reach; stop.

fetch (fech), *n.* [prob. Anglo-Ir. form of *fetch-life*], the apparition of a living person; wraith.

fetch·ing (fech′iŋ), *adj.* [ppr. of *fetch*], [Colloq.], attractive; charming; captivating.

fete, fête (fāt), *n.* [Fr. *fête* < OFr. *feste;* see FEAST], a festival; entertainment; especially, a gala entertainment held outdoors. *v.t.* [FETED, FÊTED (-id), FETING, FÊTING], to celebrate or honor with a fete; entertain.

‡fête cham·pê·tre (fet′ shän′pe′tr′), [Fr., rural festival], an outdoor feast or entertainment.

fet·e·ri·ta (fet′ə-rē′tə), *n.* [prob. < Ar. *faṭīrah,* kind of unleavened bread], a grain-yielding sorghum of the southwestern United States.

fe·tial (fē′shəl), *n.* [*pl.* FETIALES (fē′shi-ā′lēz)], [L. *fetialis* < *fetiales, pl.,* college of priests < OL. **fetis* < IE. **dhē-ti-s,* statute, compact < base **dhē-* (see FACT)], in ancient Rome, any of a group of twenty priests who conducted diplomatic negotiations, declared war when necessary, and presided at ceremonies at the end of a war. *adj.* of these priests or their functions.

fe·ti·a·lis (fē′shi-ā′lis), *n.* [*pl.* FETIALES (-lēz)], a fetial.

fe·tich (fē′tish, fet′ish), *n.* a fetish.

fe·tich·ism (fē′tish-iz'm, fet′ish-iz'm), *n.* fetishism.

fe·tich·ist (fē′tish-ist, fet′ish-ist), *n.* a fetishist.

fe·tich·is·tic (fē′ti-shis′tik, fet′i-shis′tik), *adj.* fetishistic.

fe·ti·cide (fē′tə-sīd′), *n.* [< *fetus* + *-cide*], the killing of a fetus; illegal abortion: also spelled **foeticide.**

fet·id (fet′id, fē′tid), *adj.* [L. *fetidus, foetidus* < *fetere, foetere,* to stink], having a bad smell; stinking. —*SYN.* see **stinking.**

fe·tip·a·rous (fi-tip′ẽr-əs), *adj.* [< *fetus* + *-parous*], designating or of animals whose young are born incompletely developed, as marsupials: also spelled **foetiparous.**

fe·tish (fē′tish, fet′ish), *n.* [Fr. *fétiche;* Port. *feitiço,* a charm, sorcery; orig. *adj.* < L. *facticius, factitius,* artificial < pp. of *facere,* to make], 1. any object believed by primitive peoples to have magic power; hence, 2. anything held in unreasoning devotion: as, she makes a *fetish* of dress. 3. in *psychiatry,* any nonsexual object, such as a foot or a glove, that excites erotic feelings. Also spelled **fetich.**

fe·tish·ism (fē′tish-iz'm, fet′ish-iz'm), *n.* 1. worship of or belief in fetishes. 2. in *psychiatry,* an abnormal condition in which erotic feelings are excited by a nonsexual object, as a foot, glove, etc. Also spelled **fetichism.**

fe·tish·ist (fē′tish-ist, fet′ish-ist), *n.* a worshiper of fetishes: also spelled **fetichist.**

fe·ti·shis·tic (fē′ti-shis′tik, fet′i-shis′tik), *adj.* having to do with a fetish: also spelled **fetichistic.**

fet·lock (fet′lok′), *n.* [ME. *fetlak, fitlok;* akin to MHG. *fiszlach,* G. *fiszloch;* prob. < MLG. or MD.; cf. D. *vitlok, vitslok,* LG. *fitlock;* understood as compound of *foot, feet* + *lock* (of hair)], 1. a tuft of hair on the back of a horse's leg just above the hoof. 2. the joint or projection bearing this tuft. Also **fetterlock.**

fe·tor (fē′tẽr, fē′tôr), *n.* [L. *fetor, foetor* < *fetere,* to stink], a strong, disagreeable smell; stench: also spelled **foetor.**

fet·ter (fet′ẽr), *n.* [ME. *feter, fetter;* AS. *feter* < base of *fot* (see FOOT); akin to MHG. *fesser* (G. *fessel*), D. *veter,* lace, orig., a chain], 1. *usually pl.* a shackle or chain for the feet; hence, 2. anything that holds in check; restraint. *v.t.* [ME. *feterien* < AS. *gefeterian*], 1. to bind with fetters; shackle; chain. 2. to hold in check; restrain; confine. —*SYN.* see **hamper.**

fet·ter·bush (fet′ẽr-boosh′), *n.* an ornamental evergreen shrub with white or pink flowers, growing in the southern United States.

fet·ter·lock (fet′ẽr-lok′), *n.* a fetlock.

fet·tle (fet′'l), *v.t.* [FETTLED (-'ld), FETTLING], [ME. *fetlen,* to make ready; prob. < AS. *fetel,* belt; sense of "to prepare" prob. < idea of "to gird up"], 1. [Dial.], to put in order or readiness; arrange. 2. to beat (a person). 3. in *metallurgy,* to line or cover (the hearth of a puddling furnace) with ore, silica, or other loose material. *n.* 1. condition; state; trim: as, the speaker was in fine *fettle.* 2. in *metallurgy,* the lining for the hearth of a puddling furnace.

fet·tling (fet′liŋ), *n.* [see FETTLE], in *metallurgy,* a loose material, as ore, silica, etc., used to line and protect the hearth of a puddling furnace.

fe·tus (fē′təs), *n.* [*pl.* FETUSES (-iz)], [L. *fetus, foetus,* a bringing forth, bearing, progeny; as *adj.,* pregnant, fruitful], 1. the unborn young of an animal while still in the uterus or egg, especially in its later stages. 2. in man, the offspring in the womb from the end of the third month of pregnancy until birth: distinguished from *embryo.* Also spelled **foetus.**

feu (fū), *n.* [Scot. for *fee;* see FEE], in *Scottish history & law,* 1. a fee; feudal estate. 2. a renting of land paid for by the holder in grain or money rather than in military service. 3. the land so held. *v.t.* in *Scottish history & law,* to grant (land) on feu.

feu·ar (fū′ẽr), *n.* a person who held a feu.

Feucht·wang·er, Li·on (lē′ôn foiHt′väŋ-gẽr), 1884–1959; German novelist.

feud (fūd), *n.* [ME. *fede, feide;* OFr. *faide;* prob. < MHG. *vede, vehede* < OHG. *fehida,* enmity, revenge; base as in *foe*], a bitter, deadly quarrel; especially, such a quarrel between clans or families, lasting through several generations. *v.i.* to carry on a feud; quarrel.

feud (fūd), *n.* [ML. *feudum, feodum;* see FEE], in the feudal system, land held from a lord in return for service given him: also **fee, fief, feoff, feod.**

feu·dal (fū′d'l), *adj.* [ML. *feudalis*], 1. of or having to do with land held in feud. 2. of or having to do with feudalism: abbreviated **feud.**

feu·dal (fū′d'l), *adj.* having to do with a feud, or quarrel.

feu·dal·ism (fū′d'l-iz'm), *n.* the feudal system; economic, political, and social organization of medieval

Europe, in which land, worked by serfs attached to it, was held by vassals in exchange for military and other services given to overlords: abbreviated **feud.**

feu·dal·is·tic (fū′d'l-is′tik), *adj.* 1. of, or having the nature of, feudalism. 2. inclined toward feudalism.

feu·dal·i·ty (fū-dal′ə-ti), *n.* [*pl.* FEUDALITIES (-tiz)], [Fr. *feodalité*], 1. the quality or state of being feudal; feudalism. 2. a feudal holding or estate; fief.

feu·dal·i·za·tion (fū′d'l-i-zā′shən, fū′d'l-ī-zā′shən), *n.* a feudalizing or being feudalized.

feu·dal·ize (fū′d'l-īz′), *v.t.* [FEUDALIZED (-īzd′), FEUDALIZING], to make feudal; establish feudalism in.

feu·dal·ly (fū′d'l-i), *adv.* 1. according to feudalism. 2. under feudal tenure.

feudal system, feudalism.

feu·da·to·ry (fū′də-tôr′i, fū′də-tō′ri), *n.* [*pl.* FEUDATORIES (-iz, -riz)], [ML. *feudatorius* < pp. of *feudare,* to enfeoff < *feodum, feudum;* see FEE], 1. a person who holds land by feudal tenure; vassal. 2. a feudal estate; fief. *adj.* 1. of the feudal relationship between vassal and lord. 2. owing feudal allegiance (*to*).

feud·ist (fū′dist), *n.* a participant in a feud, or quarrel.

feud·ist (fū′dist), *n.* in *law,* a specialist in feudal law.

‡**feuil·le·ton** (fö′yə-tōn′), *n.* [Fr. < *feuillet,* a leaf, sheet], 1. that part of a French newspaper which contains fiction, critical notices, etc. 2. an article or story in this section.

fe·ver (fē′vẽr), *n.* [ME. *fevere, fevre;* AS. *fefer, fefor;* L. *febris,* fever], 1. a state of abnormally increased body temperature; pyrexia. 2. any disease characterized by a rise in body temperature and usually accompanied by a quickened pulse, delirium, etc. 3. a restless, emotional excitement. *v.t.* to cause fever in.

fever blister, fever sore; cold sore.

fe·vered (fē′vẽrd), *adj.* [pp. of *fever*], 1. having fever; feverish. 2. excited; agitated.

fe·ver·few (fē′vẽr-fū′), *n.* [ME. *fevyrfue;* AS. *feverfuge* & Anglo-Fr. *fewerfue,* both < LL. *febrifugia* < L. *febris,* fever + *fugia, fuga* < *fugare,* to drive away], a plant of the aster family, with small, white, daisylike flowers.

fe·ver·ish (fē′vẽr-ish), *adj.* 1. having fever, especially slight fever. 2. of, like, or having the nature of, fever. 3. causing fever. 4. infested by fever: said of countries. 5. excited; agitated.

fe·ver·ous (fē′vẽr-əs), *adj.* feverish.

fe·ver·root (fē′vẽr-ro͞ot′, fē′vẽr-root′), *n.* [so called because the roots are sometimes used medicinally], a coarse herb of the honeysuckle family, with small, purplish flowers: also called *horse gentian.*

fever sore, an acute infectious disease caused by a virus and characterized by small blisters of the skin and mucous membranes, especially about the mouth; fever blister; cold sore: see **herpes.**

fever therapy, the treatment of a disease by artificially inducing a rise in bodily temperature to kill or make ineffective the organisms causing the disease.

few (fū), *adj.* [ME. *fewe, few;* AS. *feawe, feawa, pl.;* akin to OFris. *fē,* Goth. *fawai, pl.;* IE. base **pōu-,* etc., small, little, as also in L. *paucus,* little (cf. PAUCITY)], not many; of small number. *pron. & n.* not many; a small number.

quite a few, [Colloq.], a rather large number; a good many.

the few, the minority: contrasted with *the many.*

fey (fā), *adj.* [ME. *feie, fey;* AS. *fæge,* fated: akin to G. *feige,* cowardly (OHG. *feigi,* doomed); IE. base **peig-,* **peik-,* evil-minded, of evil intention, as also in L. *piger,* averse, Eng. *foe*], [Archaic & Scot.], 1. fated; doomed to death. 2. in an unusually excited or gay state, formerly believed to portend sudden death.

Fez (fez), *n.* one of the traditional capitals of the sultanate of Morocco: pop., 144,000.

fez (fez), *n.* [*pl.* FEZZES (-iz)], [Fr. < Turk. *fes* < *Fez,* city in Morocco], a tapering felt cap, usually red, with a black tassel hanging from the crown: formerly worn by Turkish men.

FEZ

Fez·zan (fez-zan′), *n.* an area of oases in the Sahara Desert, central Libya.

ff., 1. folios. 2. following (pages). 3. in *music,* fortissimo.

f.f., in *photography,* fixed focus.

F.F.A., f.f.a., in *nautical usage,* free from alongside.

F.F.I., French Forces of the Interior: see **maquis.**

F.G.S.A., Fellow of the Geological Society of America.

FHA, F. H. A., Federal Housing Administration.

fi (fē), *n.* [arbitrary modification of *fa*], in *music,* a syllable representing the tone intermediate between fa and sol of the diatonic scale: see **solfeggio.**

F.I., 1. facial index. 2. Falkland Islands.

fi·a·cre (fi-ä′kẽr), *n.* [Fr., after the Hotel St. *Fiacre* in Paris], in France, a small carriage for hire.

fi·an·cé (fē′än-sā′, fē-än′sā), *n.* [Fr., pp. of *fiancer* < *fiance,* a promise], the man to whom a woman is engaged to be married.

fi·an·cée (fē′än-sā′, fē-än′sā), *n.* [Fr., fem. pp. of *fiancer;* see FIANCÉ], the woman to whom a man is engaged to be married.

Fi·an·na (fē′ə-nə), *n.* the Fenians.

fi·as·co (fi-as′kō), *n.* [*pl.* FIASCOES, FIASCOS (-kōz)], [It., lit., a bottle; cf. FLASK], a complete failure; action that comes to a ridiculous end.

fi·at (fī′ət, fī′at), *n.* [L. *fiat,* 3d pers. sing., pres. subj., of *fieri,* to become, come into existence], 1. an order issued by legal authority, usually beginning with *fiat* (let it be done); decree. 2. a sanction; authorization.

‡**fi·at lux** (fī′ət luks), [L.], let there be light.

fiat money, paper currency made legal tender by law or fiat, although not backed by gold or silver and not necessarily redeemable in coin.

fib (fib), *n.* [16th- & 17th-c. slang; said to be clipped form of obs. *fible-fable,* redupl. form of *fable*], a lie about something unimportant. *v.i.* [FIBBED (fibd), FIBBING], to tell such a lie or lies. —***SYN.*** see **lie.**

fib·ber (fib′ẽr), *n.* a person who tells fibs.

fi·ber, fi·bre (fī′bẽr), *n.* [Fr. *fibre* < L. *fibra*], 1. a slender, threadlike structure that combines with others to form animal or vegetable tissue. 2. any substance that can be separated into threads or threadlike structures for weaving, etc. 3. a threadlike root. 4. the texture of something: as, a fabric of coarse *fiber;* hence, 5. character; nature; quality: as, a man of strong moral *fiber.*

fi·ber·board, fi·bre·board (fī′bẽr-bôrd′, fī′bẽr-bōrd′), *n.* 1. a boardlike material made from pressed fibers, used in building. 2. a piece of this material.

fi·ber·glas (fī′bẽr-glas′, fī′bẽr-gläs′), *n.* finespun filaments of glass made into yarn that is woven into textiles or used in woolly masses as insulation material: a trademark (**Fiberglas).**

fibr-, fibro-.

fi·bri·form (fī′bri-fôrm′), *adj.* fiberlike.

fi·bril (fī′brəl), *n.* [< Mod. L. *fibrilla,* dim. of L. *fibra,* a fiber, filament], 1. a small fiber. 2. a hairlike subdivision of a root; root hair.

fi·bril·lar (fī′bri-lẽr), *adj.* of fibrils.

fi·bril·lar·y (fī′bri-ler′i), *adj.* fibrillar.

fi·bril·lose (fī′bri-lōs′), *adj.* of or like fibrils.

fi·bril·lous (fī′bri-ləs), *adj.* fibrillose.

fi·brin (fī′brin), *n.* 1. an elastic, threadlike, insoluble protein formed from fibrinogen by the action of thrombin in the clotting of blood, and forming the network of the clot. 2. a substance resembling this in plant tissues; gluten: often called *plant fibrin, vegetable fibrin.*

fi·bri·no- (fī′bri-nō), a combining form meaning *fibrin,* as in *fibrinosis:* also, before a vowel, **fibrin-.**

fi·brin·o·gen (fi-brin′ə-jən, fī′brin-ə-jen′), *n.* [*fibrino-* + *-gen*], a blood protein that is converted to fibrin by the action of the enzyme thrombin in the clotting of blood.

fi·brin·o·gen·ic (fī′bri-nō-jen′ik), *adj.* fibrinogenous.

fi·bri·nog·e·nous (fī′brin-oj′ə-nəs), *adj.* 1. of or like fibrinogen. 2. able to form fibrin.

fi·brin·ous (fī′bri-nəs), *adj.* of, like, or having the texture of, fibrin.

fi·bro- (fī′brō), [< L. *fibra,* fiber], a combining form used in anatomy, geology, etc., meaning *of fibrous matter* or *structure,* as in *fibrosis:* also, before a vowel, **fibr-.**

fi·broid (fī′broid), *adj.* [*fibr-* + *-oid*], like, composed of, or forming fibrous tissue. *n.* a fibrous tumor.

fi·bro·in (fī′brō-in), *n.* [*fibro-* + *-in*], a white albuminoid of which cobwebs and raw silk are mainly composed.

fi·bro·ma (fi-brō′mə), *n.* [*pl.* FIBROMAS (-məz), FIBROMATA (-mə-tə)], [Mod. L. < *fibr-* + *-oma*], a nonmalignant tumor composed largely of fibrous tissue.

fi·brom·a·tous (fi-brom′ə-təs, fi-brō′mə-təs), *adj.* of, like, or containing a fibroma.

fi·bro·sis (fi-brō′sis), *n.* [Mod. L. < *fibr-* + *-osis*], an abnormal increase in the amount of fibrous connective tissue in an organ, part, or tissue.

fi·brous (fī′brəs), *adj.* [Mod. L. *fibrosus*], 1. containing or composed of fibers. 2. like fiber.

fib·ster (fib′stẽr), *n.* [Colloq.], a person who tells fibs.

fib·u·la (fib′yoo-lə), *n.* [*pl.* FIBULAE (-lē′), FIBULAS (-ləz)], [L., a clasp, buckle, pin: so called because the bone, as it appears in man, is like a clasp], 1. the long, thin outer bone of the human leg below the knee: see **skeleton,** illus. 2. a similar bone in the hind leg of animals. 3. in ancient Greece or Rome, a buckle or clasp for fastening garments.

fib·u·lar (fib′yoo-lẽr), *adj.* of or near the fibula.

-fic (fik), [< Fr. & L.; Fr. *-fique;* L. *-ficus* < unstressed form of *facere,* to make], an adjectival suffix meaning *making, creating,* as in *terrific, scientific.*

-fi·ca·tion (fi-kā′shən), [< Fr. & L.; Fr. *-fication;* L. *-ficatio* < *-ficare,* unstressed combining form of *facere,* to make, do], a suffix meaning *a making, creating, causing,* as in *calcification, glorification.*

Fich·te, Jo·hann Gott·lieb (yō′hän gôt′lēp fiH′tə), 1762–1814; German Kantian philosopher.

Fich·te·an (fiH′ti-ən), *adj.* of Fichte or his philosophy. *n.* a student or follower of Fichte or his philosophy.

fich·u (fish′o͞o; Fr. fē′shü′), *n.* [Fr.], a three-cornered lace or muslin cape worn over the shoulders by women.

fick·le (fik′'l), *adj.* [ME. *fikel;* AS. *ficol,* tricky < base of *befician,* to deceive; akin to AS. *gefic,* betrayal, deceit; IE. base as in *fey*], changeable or unstable in affection, interest, etc.; capricious. —***SYN.*** see **inconstant.**

fi·co (fē′kō), *n.* [*pl.* FICOES (-kōz)], [It., a fig; L. *ficus*], 1. a worthless trifle. 2. [Obs.], a gesture of derisive contempt made by thrusting the thumb between the first two fingers or under the upper teeth.

fic·tile (fik′t'l, fik′til), *adj.* [L. *fictilis* < pp. of *fingere;* see FICTION], 1. that can be molded; plastic. 2. formed of molded clay. 3. of pottery or ceramics.

fic·tion (fik′shən), *n.* [Fr.; L. *fictio,* a making, counterfeiting < pp. of *fingere,* to form, mold, devise], 1. a making up of imaginary happenings; feigning. 2. anything made up or imagined, as a statement, story, etc. 3. *a*) any literary work portraying imaginary characters and events, as a novel, play, etc. *b*) such works collectively; especially, novels and stories: abbreviated **fict.** 4. in *law,* something accepted as fact for the sake of convenience, although not necessarily true.

fic·tion·al (fik′shən-'l), *adj.* of, or having the nature of, fiction.

fic·tion·ist (fik′shən-ist), *n.* a writer of fiction.

fic·ti·tious (fik-tish′əs), *adj.* [L. *fictitius, ficticius* < pp. of *fingere*], 1. of or like fiction; imaginary; not real. 2. false; assumed for deception: as, a *fictitious* name. ***SYN.*—fictitious** refers to that which is invented by the imagination and therefore not real, true, or actually existent (Tom Jones is a *fictitious* character); **fabulous** suggests that which is incredible or astounding, but does not necessarily connote nonexistence (the man's wealth is *fabulous*); **legendary** refers to something that may have a historical basis in fact but, in popular tradition, has undergone great elaboration and exaggeration (the *legendary* amours of Don Juan); **mythical** basically applies to the highly imaginary explanation of natural or historical phenomena by a people and, therefore, connotes that what it qualifies is a product of the imagination; **apocryphal** suggests that which is of doubtful authenticity or authorship. —***ANT.*** real, true, factual.

fic·tive (fik′tiv), *adj.* [Fr. *fictif*], 1. able to produce fiction. 2. of fiction. 3. imaginary; feigned; sham.

fid (fid), *n.* [Early Mod. Eng. naut. term; ? < L. *findere,* to split, via Fr. or It.], 1. a hard, tapering pin for separating the strands of a rope in splicing. 2. a wood or metal bar or pin for supporting something. 3. in *nautical usage,* a square bar for supporting a topmast.

-fid (fid), [L. *-fidus,* split < base of *findere,* to cleave, divide], a combining form meaning *separated into* (a specified number of) *parts, split,* as in *palmatifid.*

fid., fiduciary.

fid·dle (fid′'l), *n.* [ME. *fithele;* AS. *fithele;* ML. *vidula;* L. *vitula*], 1. *a*) a violin. *b*) any instrument of the viol class. Now usually humorous or deprecatory. 2. in *nautical usage,* a frame or railing on a ship's table to keep dishes, etc. from falling off in rough weather. *v.t.* [FIDDLED (-'ld), FIDDLING], 1. [Colloq.], to play (a tune) on the violin. 2. to waste (time). *v.i.* 1. [Colloq.], to play on a violin. 2. to fidget.
 fit as a fiddle, in excellent health; physically fit.
 play second fiddle, to act in a subordinate position.

fid·dle·dee·dee (fid′'l-dē′dē′), *n.* & *interj.* [prob. < *fiddle,* with addition of nonsense syllables], nonsense; also **fiddle-de-dee,** etc.

fid·dle-fad·dle (fid′'l-fad′'l), *n.* & *interj.* [prob. < *fiddle* + obs. *faddle,* to trifle], [Colloq.], nonsense. *v.i.* [FIDDLE-FADDLED (-'ld), FIDDLE-FADDLING], [Colloq.], to be concerned with trifles; fuss.

fid·dle·head (fid′'l-hed′), *n.* a carved decoration on a ship's bow, curved like the scroll of a violin head.

fid·dler (fid′lẽr), *n.* 1. a person who fiddles; violinist. 2. a fiddler crab.

fiddler crab, a small, burrowing crab of the Atlantic coast, which has one claw much larger than the other.

fiddler's green, the heaven to which souls of sailors are regarded as going.

fid·dle·stick (fid′'l-stik′), *n.* 1. a violin bow. 2. a trifle; mere nothing.

fid·dle·sticks (fid′'l-stiks′), *interj.* nonsense!

FIDDLER CRAB
(1 in. across)

fid·dle·wood (fid′'l-wood′), *n.* 1. any of several tropical American timber trees valuable for their hard wood. 2. the wood.

fid·dling (fid′liŋ, fid′'l-iŋ), *adj.* [ppr. of *fiddle*], 1. that plays the fiddle. 2. trifling; useless; petty.

‡Fi·de·i De·fen·sor (fī′dē-ī di-fen′sẽr), [L.], Defender of the Faith: one of the titles of the kings of England: abbreviated, as on coins, **Fid. Def.**

fi·del·i·ty (fi-del′ə-ti, fə-del′ə-ti), *n.* [*pl.* FIDELITIES (-tiz)], [L. *fidelitas* < *fidelis,* faithful, trusty < *fides,* faith, trust], 1. a faithful devotion to duty or to one's obligations or vows; loyalty; faithfulness. 2. accuracy of reproduction: as, the manuscript was copied with complete *fidelity.* —***SYN.*** see **allegiance.**

fidg·et (fij′it), *n.* [< obs. *fidge,* to fidget < ME. *fiken* < ON. *fīkja,* to fidget, hurry about], 1. the state of being restless, nervous, or uneasy. 2. a restless, nervous, uneasy person. *v.i.* to be restless, nervous, or uneasy; make nervous, spasmodic movements: as, she *fidgeted* with her necklace. *v.t.* to cause to fidget.
 the fidgets, a restless, uneasy condition, shown by slight nervous movements.

fidg·et·i·ness (fij′it-i-nis), *n.* the quality or condition of being fidgety.

fidg·et·y (fij′it-i), *adj.* restless; nervous; uneasy.

fi·du·cial (fi-dōō′shəl, fi-dū′shəl), *adj.* [L. *fiducialis* < *fiducia,* trust < *fidere,* to trust], 1. based on firm belief or faith. 2. of or like a trust; fiduciary. 3. in *astronomy, physics,* etc., used as a standard of reference for measurement or calculation: as, a *fiducial* point.

fi·du·ci·ar·y (fi-dōō′shi-er′i, fi-dū′shi-er′i), *adj.* [L. *fiduciarius* < *fiducia,* trust, thing held in trust < *fidere,* to trust], 1. designating or of a person who holds something in trust for another; of a trustee or trusteeship: as, a *fiduciary* guardian for a minor child. 2. held in trust: as, *fiduciary* property. 3. valuable only because of public confidence and support: said of certain paper money. *n.* [*pl.* FIDUCIARIES (-iz)], a trustee. Abbreviated **fid.**

‡fi·dus A·cha·tes (fī′dəs ə-kā′tēz), [L.], 1. faithful Achates, the companion of Aeneas. 2. a true friend.

fie (fī), *interj.* [ME. & OFr. *fi, fy;* L. *fi,* expression of disgust], shame!: now often used humorously to indicate a pretense of shock or a mild reproach.

fief (fēf), *n.* [Fr.; see FEE], in the feudal system, *a*) heritable land held from a lord in return for service; feudal benefice. *b*) the right to hold such land. Also **fee, feud, feoff, feod.**

field (fēld), *n.* [ME. & AS. *feld;* akin to G. *feld,* D. *veld;* IE. base **pelā-*, broad and even, seen also in L. *planus* (IE. *plā-no-s*), even, level (cf. PLANE)], 1. *often pl.* a wide stretch of open land; plain. 2. a piece of cleared land, set off or enclosed, for raising crops or pasturing livestock. 3. a piece of land used for some particular purpose: as, a football *field.* 4. an area of land producing some natural resource: as, a gold *field.* 5. any wide, unbroken space: as, a *field* of ice. 6. *a*) a battlefield. *b*) a battle. 7. *a*) an area of military operations. *b*) a military area away from the post or headquarters. 8. a realm of knowledge or of special work or opportunity: as, the *field* of television. 9. an area of observation, as in a microscope. 10. the background, as on a flag or coin. 11. in *athletics* & *sports,* *a*) an area where games or athletic events are held. *b*) the part of such an area, usually inside a closed racing track, where contests in the high jump, broad jump, shot-put, pole vault, etc. are held. *c*) in baseball, the outfield. *d*) all the entrants in a contest. *e*) all the active players on the field, as in baseball or football. *f*) all the entrants in a contest except the one or ones specified. *g*) the team not at bat, as in baseball, cricket, etc. 12. in *heraldry,* the surface or part of the surface of a shield. 13. in *physics,* a space within which magnetic or electrical lines of force are active. *adj.* 1. of, in, or for the field or fields. 2. growing in fields; having a field or fields as its habitat. 3. in *athletics,* of or held on the field: distinguished from *track.* *v.t.* in *baseball, cricket,* etc. 1. to stop or catch and return (a ball) in play. 2. to put (a player) into a field position. *v.i.* in *baseball, cricket,* etc., to play in a field position.
 keep the field, to continue activity, as in games, military operations, etc.
 play the field, to take a broad area of operations; not confine one's activities to one object.
 take the field, to begin activity in a game, military operation, etc.

Field, Cyrus West (fēld), 1819–1892; American capitalist; projector of the first Atlantic cable.

Field, Eugene, 1850–1895; American poet and journalist.

field army, the largest unit of an army, consisting of two or more corps and usually headed by a lieutenant general: often called *army.*

field artillery, 1. movable artillery capable of accompanying an army into battle. 2. [F- A-], the branch of the army that uses such artillery: distinguished from *Coast Artillery*: abbreviated **FA, F.A.**

field battery, a number of field artillery pieces, usually four, employed as a unit.

field day, 1. a day devoted to military exercises and display. 2. a day of athletic events and contests. 3. a day spent in outdoor scientific study. 4. a day of pleasantly exciting events or successful activity.

field·er (fēl′dẽr), *n.* in *baseball* & *cricket,* a player in the field.

field·er's choice (fēl′dẽrz), in *baseball,* an attempt by a fielder to retire a runner already on base rather than the batter: the batter is not credited with a base hit if he reaches first base safely.

field·fare (fēld′fâr′), *n.* [ME. *feldefare;* AS. *feldeware*, usually taken as miswriting of *feldefare*, lit., field-goer < *feld* (see FIELD) + *fare* (see FARE, *v.*), but *feldeware* may be genuine form meaning "field-dweller"; ? folk etym.], a European thrush with a grayish head, brown wings, and a black tail.

field glass, field glasses, a small, portable, binocular telescope with considerable magnifying power.

field goal, 1. in *basketball*, a basket toss made from play, counting two points. 2. in *football*, a goal kicked from the field, counting three points.

field gun, a mobile artillery piece for use in the field: also called *fieldpiece*.

field hand, 1. originally, a plantation slave who worked in the fields. 2. now, any hired farm laborer.

field hockey, a hockey game played on a field: there are ordinarily eleven players on each side.

field hospital, a temporary military hospital near the combat zone, for emergency treatment.

Fiel·ding, Henry (fēl′diŋ), 1707–1754; English novelist.

field magnet, the magnet used to create and maintain the magnetic field in a motor or generator.

field marshal, in some European armies, an officer ranking just below the commander in chief: abbreviated **F.M.** (as a title).

field mouse, any of several kinds of mice that live in fields.

field music, 1. military musicians, as buglers, drummers, etc. 2. their music.

field officer, a colonel, lieutenant colonel, or major in the army: abbreviated **F.O., f.o.**

field of force, in *physics*, the region under the influence of some force, as gravitational, electrical, etc.

field of honor, 1. originally, a dueling place. 2. a battleground.

field·piece (fēld′pēs′), *n.* a field gun.

fields·man (fēldz′mən), *n.* [*pl.* FIELDSMEN (-mən)], in *cricket*, a fielder.

field sports, athletic events, as pole vaulting, shot-putting, etc., as distinguished from races held on a track.

field trip, a trip away from the classroom to permit the gathering of data at first hand.

field winding, the winding of a field magnet.

field·work (fēld′wũrk′), *n.* any temporary breastwork, dugout, or other defensive fortification made by troops in the field.

field work, the work of collecting scientific data in the field, as by a geologist, botanist, etc.

field·work·er (fēld′wũr′kẽr), *n.* a scientist, technician, or student who does field work.

fiend (fēnd), *n.* [ME. *fend, feend;* AS. *feond*, lit., the one hating, orig. ppr. < base of *feogan*, to hate; akin to Goth. *fijands* < *fijan*, to hate; IE. base as in *fey, foe*], 1. an evil spirit; devil. 2. an inhumanly wicked person. 3. [Colloq.], *a*) a person addicted to some activity, habit, etc.: as, a cigarette *fiend*, a bridge *fiend*. *b*) a person who is excellent at some activity: as, he's a *fiend* at tennis.
the Fiend, the Devil; Satan.

fiend·ish (fēn′dish), *adj.* like or characteristic of a fiend; inhumanly wicked or cruel; devilish.

fiend·like (fēnd′līk′), *adj.* like a fiend; fiendish.

fierce (fêrs), *adj.* [FIERCER (-ẽr), FIERCEST (-ist)], [ME. *fers;* OFr. *fers, fier, fer* < L. *ferus*, wild, savage < IE. base *ĝhwer-*, wild animal, seen also in Gr. *thēr*, animal], 1. of a violently cruel nature; savage; wild: as, a *fierce* dog. 2. violent; uncontrolled: as, a *fierce* storm. 3. intensely eager; intense; ardent: as, *fierce* labor, *fierce* envy. 4. [Slang], very distasteful, disagreeable, bad, etc.

‡fi·er·i fa·ci·as (fī′ə-rī′ fā′shi-as′), [L., lit., cause it to be done], in *law*, a writ authorizing the proper legal officer to collect a judgment of debt from the property of a person against whom the judgment has been made.

fi·er·i·ly (fīr′i-li, fī′ẽr-i-li), *adv.* in a fiery manner.

fi·er·i·ness (fīr′i-nis, fī′ẽr-i-nis), *n.* the quality or state of being fiery.

fi·er·y (fīr′i, fī′ẽr-i), *adj.* [FIERIER (-ri-ẽr, -i-ẽr), FIERIEST (-ri-ist, -i-ist)], 1. containing or consisting of fire. 2. like fire; glaring, hot, etc. 3. characterized by strong emotion; ardent; spirited: as, *fiery* words. 4. easily stirred up; excitable: as, a *fiery* nature. 5. easily set on fire; inflammable, as coal damp in a mine. 6. inflamed: said of a sore.

fiery cross, 1. a wooden cross with charred or bloody ends, used by ancient Scottish clans as a signal calling men to battle. 2. a burning cross, used by the Ku Klux Klan as an emblem or to inspire terror.

Fie·so·le, Gio·van·ni da (jô-vän′nē dä fye′zô-le), see **Angelico, Fra.**

fi·es·ta (fi-es′tə; Sp. fyes′tä), *n.* [Sp.; ML. *festa;* see FEAST], 1. a religious festival; saint's day. 2. any gala celebration; holiday.

Fife (fif), *n.* a county of eastern Scotland, on the Firth of Forth: pop., 290,000 (est. 1946); county seat, Cupar.

fife (fif), *n.* [prob. < G. *pfeife*, a pipe, tube, fife; MHG. *pfife* (or ? via Fr. *fifre* < MHG. *pfife*); OHG. *pfifa* < ML. **pipa*, a pipe, reed; see PIPE], a small, shrill-toned musical instrument resembling a flute, used mainly with drums to make music for marching. *v.t.* & *v.i.* [FIFED (fift), FIFING], to play on a fife.

fife rail, a rail around a ship's mast to hold belaying pins for the rigging.

Fife·shire (fif′shir), *n.* Fife.

fif·teen (fif′tēn′), *adj.* [ME. *fiftene;* AS. *fiftene, fiftyne;* see FIVE & TEEN], five more than ten. *n.* 1. the cardinal number between fourteen and sixteen; 15; XV. 2. a group of fifteen persons or things.

fif·teenth (fif′tēnth′), *adj.* [ME. *fifteneth, fiftethe;* AS. *fifteotha* < *fiftene;* see FIFTEEN & -TH], 1. preceded by fourteen others in a series; 15th. 2. designating any of the fifteen equal parts of something. *n.* 1. the one following the fourteenth. 2. any of the fifteen equal parts of something; 1/15.

fifth (fifth), *adj.* [ME. *fifthe, fifte;* AS. *fifta* < *fif*, five], 1. preceded by four others in a series; 5th. 2. designating any of the five equal parts of something. *n.* 1. the one following the fourth. 2. any of the five equal parts of something; 1/5. 3. a fifth of a gallon. 4. in *music*, *a*) an interval of five degrees in a diatonic scale. *b*) a tone five degrees above or below a given tone. *c*) the combination of two notes separated by this interval. *d*) the fifth note of a diatonic scale; dominant.

fifth column, [said to have been used first in a radio address by the Spanish Nationalist General Mola, then (1939) besieging Madrid with four columns from the outside and the "fifth" from within], 1. those people in Madrid who gave aid and support to the forces led by Francisco Franco in his uprising against the Spanish republic (1936–1939); hence, 2. any similar group of people who give aid and support to the enemy.

fifth columnist, a member of a fifth column.

fifth·ly (fifth′li), *adv.* in the fifth place.

Fifth Republic, the republic set up in France in 1958.

fifth wheel, 1. a horizontal wheellike structure placed over the front axle of a carriage to support it on turns. 2. any unnecessary or superfluous person or thing.

fif·ti·eth (fif′ti-ith), *adj.* [ME. *fiftithe, fiftugethe;* AS. *fiftigotha* < *fiftig;* see FIFTY & -TH], 1. preceded by forty-nine others in a series; 50th. 2. designating any of the fifty equal parts of something. *n.* 1. the one following the forty-ninth. 2. any of fifty equal parts of something; 1/50.

fif·ty (fif′ti), *adj.* [ME. *fifti;* AS. *fiftig;* see FIVE & -TY (tens)], five times ten. *n.* [*pl.* FIFTIES (-tiz)], the cardinal number between forty-nine and fifty-one; 50; L.
the fifties, the years from fifty through fifty-nine (of a century or a person's age).

fif·ty-fif·ty (fif′ti-fif′ti), *adj.* [Colloq.], having equal shares; equal; even. *adv.* [Colloq.], equally.

fig (fig), *n.* [ME.; OFr. *figue, fige;* LL. **fica;* L. *ficus*, fig tree, fig], 1. a small, pear-shaped fruit with sweet, pulpy, seed-filled flesh: it is usually dried or preserved for eating. 2. the tree bearing this fruit. 3. a trifling amount; little bit: as, their opinion wasn't worth a *fig*. 4. a gesture of contempt or disdain made as by placing the thumb between the first and second fingers; fico.

A B

FIG
A, cross section;
B, leaves and fruit

fig (fig), *v.t.* [FIGGED (figd), FIGGING], [altered < obs. *feague*, to whip, polish; confused with the contr. for *figure*, prob. from the use of this contracted form in reference to plates in books of fashions], to dress showily (with *out* or *up*). *n.* [Colloq.], 1. dress; appearance. 2. shape; condition: as, he was in poor *fig*.
in full fig, [Colloq.], completely dressed or outfitted, especially in a showy manner.

fig., 1. figurative. 2. figuratively. 3. figure; figures.

fig·eat·er (fig′ēt′ẽr), *n.* a large beetle that eats ripe fruit; the June bug of the southern United States.

fight (fīt), *v.i.* [FOUGHT (fôt), FIGHTING], [ME. *fihten, fehten;* AS. *feohtan;* akin to G. *fechten;* IE. base **pek-*, to pluck or tousle hair or wool, as also in L. *pecten*, a comb], 1. to take part in a physical struggle or battle; struggle. 2. to struggle against opposition; try to overcome someone or something; contend. *v.t.* 1. to oppose physically or in battle, as with fists, weapons, etc. 2. to try to overcome; struggle against; contend with as by argument, legislation, etc. 3. to engage in or carry on (a war, conflict, case, etc.). 4. to gain by struggle: as, he *fought* his way to the top. 5. to cause to fight; manage (a boxer, gamecock, etc.). *n.* [ME.; AS. *feoht* < the *v.*], 1. a physical struggle; battle; combat. 2. any struggle, contest, or quarrel. 3. power or readiness to fight; pugnacious spirit: as, he still had some *fight* in him. —***SYN.*** see **conflict.**
fight it out, to fight until one side is defeated.
fight off, to fight to keep away; struggle to avoid.

fight·er (fīt′ẽr), *n.* 1. one that fights or is inclined to fight. 2. a prizefighter; pugilist. 3. a small, light, highly maneuverable airplane for aerial combat: often **fighter plane:** see TYPES OF AIRPLANE, p. 32.

fighting chance, a chance to win or succeed, but only after a hard struggle.

fig marigold, any of several plants with showy flowers of pink or white, found in hot, dry climates.

fig·ment (fig′mənt), *n.* [L. *figmentum* < *fingere*, to make, devise, invent], something imagined or made up in the mind; fictitious story.

fig·u·line (fig′yoo-lin, fig′yoo-lin′), *adj.* [L. *figulinus* < *figulus*, a potter < *fingere;* see FIGMENT], made of clay or pottery. *n.* 1. a piece of pottery or porcelain; small statue. 2. clay for pottery.

fig·u·rant (fig′yoo-rant′; Fr. fē′gü′rän′), *n.* [Fr., masc. ppr. of *figurer*, to figure], 1. a ballet dancer. 2. a supernumerary on the stage.

fig·u·rante (fig′yoo-rant′; Fr. fē′gü′ränt′), *n.* feminine of **figurant.**

fig·u·ra·tion (fig′yoo-rā′shən), *n.* [Fr.; L. *figuratio* < *figuratus;* see FIGURATIVE], 1. a forming; shaping. 2. form; appearance. 3. an ornamenting with or representing by figures or symbols.

fig·ur·a·tive (fig′yoor-ə-tiv), *adj.* [LL. *figurativus* < L. *figuratus*, pp. of *figurare*, to form, fashion < *figura;* see FIGURE], 1. representing by means of a figure, symbol, or likeness. 2. having to do with figure drawing, painting, etc. 3. not in its original, usual, literal, or exact sense or reference; representing one concept in terms of another that may be thought of as analogous with it; metaphorical: to call a fierce fighting man a tiger is a figurative use of *tiger*: abbreviated **fig.** 4. containing or using figures of speech.

fig·ure (fig′yoor), *n.* [ME.; OFr.; L. *figura* < *fingere*, to form, shape], 1. the outline or shape of something; form. 2. the shape of the human body; human form. 3. a person, especially one seen or thought of in a specified way: as, Roosevelt was one of the greatest *figures* of his time. 4. a likeness or representation of a person or thing. 5. an illustration; diagram; picture; drawing: abbreviated **fig.** 6. an artistic design in fabrics, etc.; pattern. 7. the symbol for a number: as, the *figure* 5. 8. *pl.* calculation with such symbols; arithmetic: as, she has a poor head for *figures*. 9. a sum of money. 10. in *dancing*, a series of steps and movements. 11. in *geometry*, a surface or space bounded on all sides by lines or planes. 12. in *logic*, the form of a syllogism with reference to the position of the middle term. 13. in *music*, a series of consecutive tones or chords forming a distinct group which with other similar groups completes a phrase or theme. 14. in *rhetoric*, a figure of speech. *v.t.* [FIGURED (-yoord), FIGURING], [ME. *figuren* < the *n.*], 1. to represent in definite form; give a shape to. 2. to represent mentally; imagine. 3. to ornament with a design. 4. to compute with figures. 5. [Colloq.], to believe; consider; predict. 6. in *music*, to indicate chords for (the bass) by writing the appropriate figures next to the notes. 7. in *rhetoric*, to represent by a figure of speech. *v.i.* 1. to appear prominently; be conspicuous. 2. to do arithmetic. 3. [Colloq.], to consider; calculate. —***SYN.*** see **form.**

figure on, 1. to count on; rely on. 2. to consider as part of a scheme or project; plan on.

figure out, 1. to solve; compute. 2. to understand; reason out.

figure up, to add; total.

fig·ured (fig′yoord), *adj.* [ME., pp.; see FIGURE, *v.*], 1. shaped; formed. 2. represented or shown by a picture, diagram, etc. 3. having a design or pattern. 4. in *music*, marked with figures representing the appropriate accompanying chords: said of the bass.

fig·ure·head (fig′yoor-hed′), *n.* 1. a carved figure on the bow of a ship. 2. a person put in a position of leadership because of his name, rank, importance, etc., but having no real power, authority, or responsibility.

fig·ure-of-eight knot (fig′yoor-əv-āt′), a kind of knot: see **knot,** illus.

figure of speech, an expression using words in an unusual or nonliteral sense to give beauty or vividness of style; metaphor, personification, simile, litotes, hyperbole, metonymy, synecdoche, etc.; trope.

figure skating, ice skating in which the performer traces various elaborate figures on the ice.

fig·u·rine (fig′yoo-rēn′), *n.* [Fr.; It. *figurina*, dim. of *figura* < L.; see FIGURE], a small sculptured or molded figure; statuette.

fig·wort (fig′wûrt′), *n.* any of a group of tall, coarse, strong-smelling plants with small flowers, including the snapdragon, mullein, etc.

Fi·ji (fē′jē), *n.* 1. the Fiji Islands. 2. a native of the Fiji Islands. 3. a British colony including the Fiji Islands: area, 7,083 sq. mi.; pop., 227,000.

Fi·ji·an (fē′jē-ən), *adj.* of the Fiji Islands, their people, language, or culture. *n.* 1. a Fiji. 2. the Melanesian language of the Fijis.

Fiji Islands, a group of British islands in the South Pacific, east of the New Hebrides: area, 7,069 sq. mi.; pop., 221,000; capital, Suva.

fil·a·ment (fil′ə-mənt), *n.* [Fr.; LL. *filamentum* < *filare*, to spin < L. *filum;* see FILE (container)], 1. a very slender thread or fiber. 2. a threadlike part; specifically, the fine metal wire in a light bulb or vacuum tube, which becomes incandescent when heated by an electric current. 3. in *botany*, the stalk of a stamen bearing the anther.

fil·a·men·ta·ry (fil′ə-men′tēr-i), *adj.* made of, like, or having a filament or filaments.

fil·a·men·tous (fil′ə-men′təs), *adj.* 1. threadlike. 2. having filaments.

fi·lar (fī′lẽr), *adj.* [< L. *filum*, a thread], 1. of a thread. 2. having fine threads or hairs stretched across the field of view: said of a micrometer, microscope, etc.

fi·la·ri·a (fi-lâr′i-ə), *n.* [*pl.* FILARIAE (-ē′)], [Mod.L. < L. *filum;* see FILE (container)], any of several kinds of threadlike parasitic worms that live in the blood and tissues of vertebrate animals: they are often carried and transmitted by mosquitoes and other invertebrates.

fi·lar·i·al (fi-lâr′i-əl), *adj.* of, having the nature of, carrying, or caused by filariae.

fi·lar·i·an (fi-lâr′i-ən), *adj.* filarial.

fil·a·ri·a·sis (fil′ə-rī′ə-sis), *n.* [Mod.L.; see FILARIA], a diseased condition caused by filarial worms, which are transmitted by mosquitoes and invade lymphatic vessels and lymphoid tissue.

fil·a·ture (fil′ə-chẽr), *n.* [Fr. < pp. of L. *filare*, to spin < *filum*, a thread; see FILE (container)], 1. a spinning into threads. 2. a reeling of raw silk from cocoons. 3. *a*) a reel for this. *b*) a place where this is done.

fil·bert (fil′bẽrt), *n.* [ME. *filberde, philliberd;* prob. via Norm. Fr. (*noix de*) *filbert*, (nut of) Philibert < St. *Philibert*, whose feast came in the nutting season], 1. the hazelnut, especially the cultivated variety. 2. the tree bearing this nut.

filch (filch), *v.t.* [16th-c. thieves' argot < *filch, n.*, staff with a hook on the end; hence, orig., "to steal with a filch"; cf. obs. *file*, to pick pockets, Fr. *filou*, pickpocket], to steal (usually something small or petty); pilfer. —***SYN.*** see **steal.**

file (fīl), *n.* [Fr.; OFr. *fil*, a file, rank, row; LL. *fila*, a string, series < L. *filum*, a thread; IE. **gwhis-lom*], 1. a container, as a folder, cabinet, etc., for keeping papers in order. 2. an orderly arrangement of papers, cards, etc., as for reference. 3. a line of persons or things situated one behind another: distinguished from *rank*. 4. in *chess*, any of the rows of squares running vertically along the length of the board. *v.t.* [FILED (fīld), FILING], 1. to arrange (papers, etc.) in order for future reference. 2. to put (a paper, etc.) in its proper place or order. 3. to put (a legal document) on public record. *v.i.* to move in a line: as, the children *filed* out of the building.

in file, in line, one behind another.

on file, kept in order for reference; in a file.

file (fīl), *n.* [ME.; AS. *feol* (Mercian *fīl*); akin to G. *feile* (OHG. *fihila*), D. *vijl;* IE. **peik-*, to cut], a steel tool with a rough, ridged surface for smoothing, grinding down, or cutting through something. *v.t.* [FILED (fīld), FILING], to smooth, grind down, or cut through with or as with a file.

FLAT
HALF ROUND
TRIANGULAR
ROUND
TYPES OF FILE

file (fīl), *v.t.* [FILED (fīld), FILING], [ME. *filen, fulen;* AS. *-fylan* < *ful*, dirty, filthy; see FOUL], [Archaic], to make foul; defile.

file clerk, a person employed to keep office files in order.

file·fish (fīl′fish′), *n.* [*pl.* FILEFISH, FILEFISHES (-iz); see FISH], any of various fishes, as the triggerfish, with hard, rough spines instead of scales.

fi·let (fi-lā′, fil′ā, fil′it; Fr. fē′le′), *n.* [Fr.; see FILLET], 1. a net or lace with a simple pattern on a square mesh background. 2. a fillet (of fish or meat).

fi·let mi·gnon (fi-lā′ min-yōn′, fi-lā′ min-yon′, fil′ā min′-yon; Fr. fē′le′mē′nyōn′), [Fr.], a round cut of lean beefsteak broiled, usually with mushrooms and bacon.

fil·i·al (fil′i-əl, fil′yəl), *adj.* [LL. *filialis*, of a son or daughter < L. *filius*, son, *filia*, daughter], 1. of, suitable to, or due from a son or daughter: as, *filial* devotion. 2. in *genetics*, designating or of any generation following the parental: symbol, F (e.g., F_1 means "first filial," F_2, "second filial," etc.).

fil·i·a·tion (fil′i-ā′shən), *n.* [Fr.; ML. *filiatio* < L. *filius*, a son, *filia*, a daughter], 1. the state or fact of being a son or daughter; relation of a child to its parent. 2. descent from or as from a parent; derivation. 3. *a*) the forming of a new branch or affiliation of a society, etc. *b*) such an affiliated branch. 4. in *law*, the determination by a court of the paternity of an illegitimate child.

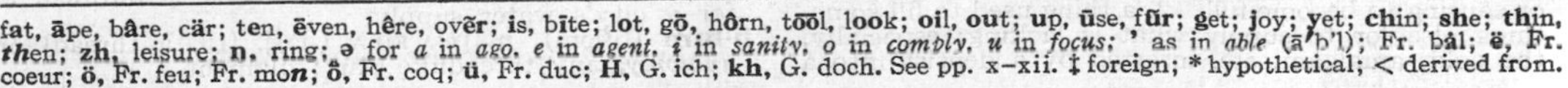

fil·i·beg (fil′ə-beg′), *n.* [Gael. *feileadh beag; feileadh,* a fold + *beag,* little], a kilt.
fil·i·bus·ter (fil′ə-bus′tẽr), *n.* [Sp. *filibustero* < Fr. *flibustier, fribustier* < D. *vrijbuiter,* freebooter < *vrij,* free + *buit,* booty], 1. an adventurer who engages in unauthorized warfare against a country with which his own country is at peace; freebooter. 2. a member of a minority group of a legislative body, especially the Senate, who obstructs the passage of a bill by making long speeches, introducing irrelevant issues, etc. 3. the deliberate obstruction of the passage of a bill by such methods. *v.i.* 1. to engage in unauthorized warfare as a freebooter. 2. to obstruct the passage of a bill by making long speeches, etc. *v.t.* to obstruct the passage of (a bill) by such methods.
fil·i·cid·al (fil′ə-sīd′'l), *adj.* having to do with filicide.
fil·i·cide (fil′ə-sīd′), *n.* [< L. *filius,* son, *filia,* daughter; + *-cide*], 1. the act of murdering one's child. 2. a parent who murders his child.
fil·i·form (fil′ə-fôrm′, fī′lə-fôrm′), *adj.* [< L. *filum,* a thread; + *-form*], having the form of a thread or filament.
fil·i·gree (fil′ə-grē′), *n.* [altered from earlier *filigrain;* Fr. *filigrane;* It. *filigrana* < L. *filum,* a thread + *granum,* grain], 1. delicate, lacelike ornamental work of intertwined wire of gold, silver, etc. 2. any delicate work or figure like this. *adj.* like, made of, or made into filigree. *v.t.* [FILIGREED (-grēd′), FILIGREEING], to ornament with, or work in, filigree.
fil·ing (fil′iŋ), *n.* *usually in pl.* a small piece of metal, etc. scraped off with a file.
Fil·i·pine (fil′ə-pēn′), *adj.* Philippine.
Fil·i·pi·no (fil′ə-pē′nō), *n.* [*pl.* FILIPINOS (-nōz)], [Sp.], a native or citizen of the Philippines. *adj.* Philippine.
fill (fil), *v.t.* [ME. *fillen, fullen;* AS. *fyllan* < base of *full, adj.*], 1. to put as much as possible into (a container or space); make full. 2. to take up the whole of; occupy: as, the crowd *filled* the room. 3. to occupy (an office, position, etc.). 4. to put a person into (an office, position, etc.). 5. to supply the things needed or called for in (an order, requisition, prescription, etc.). 6. to close or plug (holes, cracks, etc.). 7. *a*) to feed. *b*) to satisfy the hunger of. 8. to be plentiful in. 9. to put into a container so as to fill it, or as if to fill it. 10. to add earth, etc. to (low land) until a required level is reached. 11. in *nautical usage, a*) to swell (a sail). *b*) to trim (a yard) so as to catch the wind on the after side of the sail. *v.i.* to become full. *n.* 1. all that is needed to make full. 2. all that is needed to satisfy. 3. anything that fills or is used to fill a space. 4. a piece of land artificially raised to a required level, as a railroad embankment.
  fill in, 1. to fill with some substance. 2. to make complete by inserting or supplying something. 3. to insert or supply for completion. 4. to be a substitute.
  fill one in on, [Colloq.], to provide one with additional facts, details, etc. of.
  fill out, 1. to make or become larger, rounder, shapelier, etc. 2. to make (a document, etc.) complete by inserting or supplying information.
  fill up, to make or become completely full.
fill·a·gree (fil′ə-grē′), *n.* filigree.
‡fille (fē′y′), *n.* [Fr.], 1. a daughter. 2. a girl; maid. 3. a spinster. 4. a prostitute. See also **jeune fille.**
‡fille de cham·bre (fē′y′ də shän′br′), [Fr.], a chambermaid; lady's maid.
‡fille de joie (fē′y′ də zhwä′), [Fr., lit., daughter of joy], a prostitute.
filled gold, brass or other base metal covered with a layer of gold, used as a substitute for solid gold.
filled milk, skimmed milk with vegetable oils added to increase the fat content.
fill·er (fil′ẽr), *n.* a person or thing that fills; specifically, *a*) matter added to some other to increase bulk, as sand in fertilizer. *b*) a preparation used to fill in the cracks, grain, etc. of wood before painting or varnishing. *c*) the tobacco rolled in the leaf of a cigar. *d*) a short, space-filling item in a newspaper. *e*) a pad of loose-leaf paper for a notebook.
fil·lér (fēl′lâr), *n.* [Hung.], a Hungarian bronze coin equal to 1/100 of a forint (or, formerly, of a pengö).
fil·let (fil′it), *n.* [OFr. *filet,* dim. of *fil;* see **FILE** (a line, row)], 1. a narrow band worn around the head for ornament or to hold the hair in place. 2. a thin strip or band. 3. in *architecture,* a flat, square molding separating other moldings; narrow band between two flutings in a column. 4. in *bookbinding,* a line impressed on a book cover. 5. (fil′ā, fil′it), in *cookery,* a boneless, lean piece of fish or meat: also spelled **filet.** 6. in *heraldry,* a horizontal band on a shield, just below the chief and one-fourth its width. *v.t.* 1. to bind or decorate with a band, molding, etc. 2. (fil′ā, fi-lā′, fil′it), in *cookery,* to bone and slice (meat or fish).
fill-in (fil′in′), *n.* 1. a person or thing that fills a vacancy or gap, often temporarily. 2. [Colloq.], a brief summary of the pertinent facts. *adj.* of or by a fill-in.
fill·ing (fil′iŋ), *n.* 1. the act of one that fills; a becoming or causing to become full. 2. a thing used to fill something else, or to supply what is lacking; especially, the gold, amalgam, etc. inserted by a dentist into a prepared cavity in a tooth. 3. the horizontal threads crossing the warp in a woven fabric; woof.
filling station, a place where gasoline, oil, services, etc. for automobiles and other motor vehicles are sold at retail.
fil·lip (fil′əp), *n.* [echoic extension of *flip;* cf. CHIRRUP, CHIRP], 1. the snap made by a finger which is held down toward the palm by the thumb and then suddenly released. 2. a light blow or tap given in this way. 3. anything that stirs up or arouses; tonic; stimulus. *v.t.* 1. to jerk or toss with a fillip. 2. to stir up; arouse; stimulate. *v.i.* to make a fillip.
fil·li·peen (fil′ə-pēn′), *n.* a game of forfeits or the forfeit made: see **philopena.**
fil·lis·ter (fil′is-tẽr), *n.* [corresponds in form with G. *filister* (Dan. *filister*), lit., Philistine, first recorded in sense "pikeman, member of the town watch"; ? modified < some such word as *fenester* (cf. FENESTRATE)], 1. a plane for cutting grooves. 2. a groove, as for receiving the glass in a window frame.
Fill·more, Mill·ard (mil′ẽrd fil′môr, fil′mōr), 1800–1874; thirteenth president of the United States (1850–1853).
fil·ly (fil′i), *n.* [*pl.* FILLIES (-iz)], [ME. *fillie* < ON. *fylja,* fem. of *foli,* a foal; see FOAL], 1. a young mare. 2. [Colloq.], a vivacious young woman or girl.
film (film), *n.* [ME. *fylme;* AS. *filmen,* membrane, foreskin, ult. derived < base of *fel,* skin, hide (see FELL, skin); akin to OFris. *filmene;* IE. base **pel-,* as also in L. *pellis,* skin], 1. a fine, thin skin or coating. 2. a sheet or roll of a flexible cellulose material covered with a substance sensitive to light and used in taking photographs. 3. a thin veil, haze, or blur, as over the eyes. 4. a motion picture. 5. a fine thread. *v.t.* 1. to cover with or as with a film. 2. to take a photograph of. 3. to make a motion picture of: as, they *filmed* the story. *v.i.* 1. to be or become covered with a film. 2. to be filmed or suitable for filming: as, this story won't *film* well.
film·i·ly (fil′mə-li), *adv.* in a filmy manner; with or through a film.
film·i·ness (fil′mi-nis), *n.* the quality of being filmy.
film pack, several sheets of photographic film in a frame that fits in the back of a camera.
film·y (fil′mi), *adj.* [FILMIER (-mi-ẽr), FILMIEST (-mi-ist)], 1. of or like a film; hazy, gauzy, etc. 2. covered with or as with a film; blurred.
fi·lose (fī′lōs), *adj.* [< L. *filum;* + *-ose*], 1. threadlike. 2. having a threadlike projection.
‡fils (fēs), *n.* [Fr.], a son or a youth: often used like English *Jr.,* as Dumas *fils.*
fil·ter (fil′tẽr), *n.* [Fr. *filtre;* LL. *filtrum, feltrum,* felt fulled wool (used for straining liquors); see FELT, *n.*], 1. a device for separating solid particles, impurities, etc. from a fluid by passing it through a porous substance. 2. any porous substance used for this purpose, as sand, charcoal, felt, etc. 3. in *physics, a*) a device or substance that passes electric currents of certain frequencies or frequency ranges while preventing the passage of others. *b*) a device or substance that partially or completely absorbs certain light rays: as, a color *filter* for a camera lens. *v.t.* [Fr. *filtrer* < the *n.*], 1. to pass (fluids) through a filter. 2. to remove or separate (solid particles, impurities, etc.) from a fluid by means of a filter. 3. to act as a filter for (electric currents of certain frequencies, etc.). *v.i.* 1. to be filtered; hence, 2. to move or pass slowly: as, the news *filtered* through town.
fil·ter·a·bil·i·ty (fil′tẽr-ə-bil′ə-ti), *n.* the quality or state of being filterable.
fil·ter·a·ble (fil′tẽr-ə-b'l), *adj.* 1. that can be filtered. 2. that goes through a filter. Also **filtrable.**
filter bed, a tank with a sand or gravel bottom, used to filter water, sewage, etc.
filter paper, a porous paper for straining liquids.
filth (filth), *n.* [ME. *filthe, fulthe, felthe;* AS. *fylthe* < base of *ful* (see FOUL) + *-th,* nominal suffix], 1. foul dirt; disgusting matter. 2. moral corruption or something causing it; indecency; obscenity.
filth·i·ly (fil′thə-li), *adv.* in a filthy manner.
filth·i·ness (fil′thi-nis), *n.* 1. the quality or state of being filthy. 2. a filthy thing.
filth·y (fil′thi), *adj.* [FILTHIER (-thi-ẽr), FILTHIEST (-thi-ist)], 1. full of, or having the nature of, filth; foul. 2. morally corrupt; obscene; lewd. —*SYN.* see **dirty.**
fil·tra·bil·i·ty (fil′trə-bil′ə-ti), *n.* filterability.
fil·tra·ble (fil′trə-b'l), *adj.* filterable.
filtrable virus, any virus of ultramicroscopic size, capable of passing through filters that bacteria cannot pass through: some such viruses cause measles, influenza, poliomyelitis, etc.
fil·trate (fil′trāt; *also, for n.,* fil′trit), *v.t.* [FILTRATED (-id), FILTRATING], [< Mod. L. *filtratus,* pp. of *filtrare,* to filter], to strain; filter. *n.* a filtered liquid.
fil·tra·tion (fil-trā′shən), *n.* [Fr. < *filtrer*], a filtering or being filtered.
filtration plant, a place where water is purified, as for a city's water supply.
fi·lum (fī′ləm), *n.* [*pl.* FILA (-lə)], [L., a thread], in *anatomy,* any threadlike part; filament.

fim·bri·a (fim′bri-ə), *n.* [*pl.* FIMBRIAE (-ē′)], [L.], in *botany & zoology*, a fringe or border of hairs, fibers, etc.
fim·bri·ate (fim′bri-āt′), *adj.* [L. *fimbriatus*, fringed < *fimbria*, a fringe, border], having a fringe of hairs, fibers, etc., as certain plants. *v.t.* [FIMBRIATED (-id), FIMBRIATING], to fringe; put a border on.
fim·bri·at·ed (fim′bri-āt′id), *adj.* fimbriate.
fim·bri·a·tion (fim′bri-ā′shən), *n.* [< *fimbriate* + *-tion*], 1. the condition of being fringed. 2. a fringe.
fin (fin), *n.* [ME. & AS. *finn;* akin to D. *vin*, G. *finne;* IE. base **pet-*, feather, wing, whence also L. *penna*, (< **pet-nā*), a wing, feather (cf. PEN)], 1. any of several winglike, membranous organs on the body of a fish, dolphin, etc., used in swimming, turning, and balancing. 2. anything like a fin in shape or use; specifically, *a*) a fine edge formed on a casting by metal forced through the halves of the mold. *b*) [Slang], the hand. *c*) in *aeronautics*, any fixed or movable airfoil whose chief function is to give stability in flight. *d*) in *nautical usage*, a projection on boats or submarines; also, a fin keel. 3. [Slang], a five-dollar bill. *v.t.* [FINNED (find), FINNING], to cut the fins from. *v.i.* to move the fins, especially in a violent way.
Fin., 1. Finland. 2. Finnish.
fin., 1. finance. 2. financial.
fin·a·ble (fin′ə-b'l), *adj.* liable to a fine: also spelled **fineable.**
fin·a·ble (fin′ə-b'l), *adj.* [< *fine*, to refine + *-able*], that can be refined or purified: also spelled **fineable.**
fi·na·gle (fi-nā′g'l), *v.i.* [FINAGLED (-g'ld), FINAGLING], [prob. respelling of *Feinagel*, G. mesmerist and whist expert of the Regency; cf. FAINAIGUE], 1. in *card games*, to renege; revoke; hence, 2. to use trickery; be sly or crafty; cheat. *v.t.* 1. to cheat. 2. to get or manage by trickery, slyness, or craftiness. Also **fenagle.**
fi·na·gler (fi-nā′glẽr), *n.* a person who finagles.
fi·nal (fī′n'l), *adj.* [ME.; OFr.; L. *finalis* < *finis*, end], 1. of or coming at the end; last; concluding. 2. leaving no further chance for action, discussion, or change; deciding; conclusive: as, a *final* decree. 3. of purpose or result: as, a *final* cause. *n.* 1. anything final. 2. *pl.* the last of a series of athletic contests, tests, etc. 3. *often in pl.* [Colloq.], a final examination. —*SYN.* see **last.**
fi·na·le (fi-nä′li; It. fē-nä′le), *n.* [It. < L. *finalis;* see FINAL], 1. the concluding movement or passage of a musical composition. 2. the last scene or feature of an entertainment. 3. the conclusion or last part; end.
fi·nal·ist (fī′n'l-ist), *n.* a contestant who participates in the final and deciding contest or contests of a series.
fi·nal·i·ty (fi-nal′ə-ti), *n.* 1. the quality or condition of being final, settled, or complete; conclusiveness. 2. [*pl.* FINALITIES (-tiz)], anything final or conclusive.
fi·nal·ize (fī′n'l-īz′), *v.t.* [FINALIZED (-īzd′), FINALIZING], [U.S. neologism], to make final; bring to completion.
fi·nal·ly (fī′n'l-i), *adv.* [see FINAL & -LY], 1. at the end; in conclusion. 2. decisively; conclusively; irrevocably.
fi·nance (fə-nans′, fī′nans), *n.* [ME. *finaunce*, a fine, forfeit; OFr. *finance*, wealth, revenue < *finer*, to end, settle accounts, pay ransom < *fin;* see FINE (end)], 1. *pl.* the money resources, income, etc. of a nation, organization, or person. 2. the science of managing money matters: abbreviated **fin.** *v.t.* [FINANCED (-nanst′, -nanst), FINANCING], 1. to supply money for. 2. to manage the money of.
fi·nan·cial (fə-nan′shəl, fī-nan′shəl), *adj.* of finance, finances, or financiers: abbreviated **fin.**
SYN.—**financial** implies reference to money matters, especially where large sums are involved (a *financial* success); **fiscal** is used with reference to government revenues and expenditures or the administering of the financial affairs of an organization or corporation (a *fiscal* year); **monetary** refers directly to money itself and is used in connection with coinage, circulation, standards, relative values, etc. (the *monetary* unit of a country); **pecuniary** is applied to money matters of a practical or personal nature (*pecuniary* motives).
fi·nan·cial·ly (fə-nan′shəl-i, fi-nan′shəl-i), *adv.* in regard to finance or finances.
fin·an·cier (fin′ən-sêr′, fī′nən-sêr′), *n.* [Fr.], 1. a person trained or skilled in finance. 2. a person who engages in financial operations on a large scale. *v.t.* to finance.
fin·back (fin′bak′), *n.* a large whalebone whale with a dorsal fin; rorqual: also **finback whale.**
finch (finch), *n.* [ME.; AS. *finc;* akin to G. *fink;* IE. echoic base *(*s*)*pingo-*, chirping bird, as also in W. *pink*, Fr. *pinson*, finch], any of a large group of small, short-beaked, seed-eating songbirds, including the bunting, canary, cardinal, goldfinch, and sparrow.
find (find), *v.t.* [FOUND (found), FINDING], [ME. *finden;* AS. *findan;* akin to G. *finden*, Goth. *finthan;* IE. base **pent-*, to walk, go, as also in L. *pons, pontis*, a plank causeway, bridge; for sense development, cf. INVENT], 1. to happen on; come upon; meet with; discover by chance. 2. to get by searching. 3. to get sight or knowledge of; perceive; learn. 4. *a*) to recover (something lost). *b*) to recover the use of. 5. to consider; think. 6. to reach; attain: as, the blow *found* his chin. 7. to decide: as, the jury *found* him innocent. 8. to supply; furnish. *v.i.* to reach and announce a decision: as, the jury *found* for the accused. *n.* 1. a finding. 2. something found, especially something interesting or valuable.
find oneself, to learn what one's real talents and inclinations are, and begin to apply them.
find out, 1. to discover; learn. 2. to learn the true character or identity of (someone or something).
find·er (fin′dẽr), *n.* 1. a person or thing that finds. 2. a camera device, as a special lens, that helps in adjusting the position of the camera by showing what will appear in the photograph. 3. a small, low-powered telescope attached to a larger one, used to locate objects for closer view with the more powerful telescope.
‡**fin de siè·cle** (fan′də-sye′kl′), [Fr., lit., end of the century], of or characteristic of the last years of the 19th century: formerly used to refer to progressive ideas and customs, but now generally used to indicate decadence.
find·ing (fin′diŋ), *n.* [see FIND], 1. discovery. 2. something found or discovered. 3. *pl.* *a*) the tools, materials, etc. ordinarily provided by a worker. *b*) miscellaneous small supplies used by a worker: as, thread, bindings, etc. are *findings* in dressmaking. 4. the conclusion reached after an examination or consideration of facts by a judge, coroner, scholar, etc.
Find·lay (find′li), *n.* a city in northwestern Ohio: pop., 30,000.
fine (fin), *adj.* [FINER (-ẽr), FINEST (-ist)], [ME. *fin, fine;* OFr. *fin;* LL. *finus* < L. *finitus*, lit., finished, pp. of *finire*, to bound, limit < *finis*, an end, limit, bound; see FINISH], 1. originally, finished; perfected; hence, 2. superior in quality; above the average; excellent; very good: as, a *fine* sample. 3. of exceptional character or ability: as, a *fine* teacher. 4. with no impurities; refined. 5. containing a specified proportion of pure metal: said of gold or silver: abbreviated **F., f.** 6. clear and bright: said of the weather. 7. not heavy, gross, or coarse: as, *fine* sand. 8. very thin or slender: as, *fine* thread. 9. sharp; keen: as, a knife with a *fine* edge. 10. discriminating; subtle: as, *fine* distinctions. 11. of delicate composition: as, *fine* lace. 12. good-looking; handsome: as, a *fine* baby. 13. trained and developed physically to maximum ability: said of athletes, horses, etc. 14. too elegant; showy: as, *fine* writing. *adv.* [Colloq.], 1. very well. 2. in *billiards & pool*, so that the cue ball touches the object ball lightly on the side in passing and is deflected very little. *v.t. & v.i.* [FINED (find), FINING], to make or become fine or finer.
fine (fin), *n.* [ME. *fin, fine;* OFr. *fin;* L. *finis;* see FINISH], 1. originally, a finish; end; conclusion. 2. a sum of money paid to settle a matter; especially, a sum required to be paid as punishment for an offense. *v.t.* [FINED (find), FINING], to require the payment of a fine from.
in fine, 1. in conclusion. 2. in brief.
‡**fi·ne** (fē′ne), *n.* [It. < L. *finis;* see FINISH], in *music*, the end: a direction marking the close of a repeated passage.
fine·a·ble (fin′ə-b'l), *adj.* finable.
fine arts, [so called because orig. considered purely aesthetic, as distinguished from the "useful" arts], the graphic arts, generally including drawing, painting, sculpture, ceramics, and, occasionally, architecture: literature, music, dramatic art, and dancing are sometimes included: abbreviated **FA, F.A.**
fine-cut (fin′kut′), *adj.* cut into small, narrow shreds of equal width: said of tobacco, and distinguished from *rough-cut.*
fine-draw (fin′drô′), *v.t.* [*fine, adj.* & *adv.* + *draw, v.*], 1. to sew together (two pieces of cloth, as the edges of a tear) so carefully that the seam cannot be seen. 2. to draw (wire, etc.) out to extreme fineness; hence, 3. to extend (reasoning, etc.) to a high degree of subtleness.
fine-drawn (fin′drôn′), *adj.* [pp. of *fine-draw*], 1. drawn out until very fine, as wire. 2. extremely subtle: said of reasoning, arguments, etc.
fine-grained (fin′grānd′), *adj.* having a fine, smooth grain, as some kinds of wood, leather, etc.
fine·ly (fin′li), *adv.* [ME. *finliche*], in a fine manner.
fine·ness (fin′nis), *n.* 1. the quality or state of being fine. 2. the proportion of pure gold or silver in an alloy.
fin·er·y (fin′ẽr-i), *n.* [*pl.* FINERIES (-iz)], showy, gay, elaborate decoration, especially clothes, jewelry, etc.
fin·er·y (fin′ẽr-i), *n.* [*pl.* FINERIES (-iz)], [Fr. *finerie* < *finer*, to refine; OIt. **finare*, lit., to finish < L. *finis;* see FINISH], a refinery where malleable iron or steel is made.
fine-spun (fin′spun′), *adj.* 1. spun or drawn out to extreme fineness; delicate; fragile. 2. extremely subtle. 3. too subtle; not practical.
fi·nesse (fi-nes′), *n.* [Fr. < *fin, fine;* see FINE, *adj.*], 1. skill; adroitness and delicacy of performance. 2. the ability to handle delicate and difficult situations skill-

fully and diplomatically; hence, 3. cunning; artfulness; craft. 4. in *bridge, whist*, etc., an attempt to take a trick with a lower card while holding a higher card not in sequence with this, in the hope that an intervening card will not be played. *v.t.* [FINESSED (-nest′), FINESSING], 1. to change by finesse; bring by finesse (into a certain condition). 2. in *bridge, whist*, etc., to make a finesse with (a card). *v.i.* to use or make a finesse.

fine-toothed comb (fīn′tōōtht′), a comb with fine, closely set teeth.

go over with a fine-toothed comb, to examine very carefully and thoroughly.

Fin·gal's Cave (fiŋ′g'lz), a large cavern on Staffa Island, in the Hebrides.

fin·ger (fiŋ′gẽr), *n.* [ME.; AS.; akin to G. *finger*, Goth. *figgrs*, etc.; IE. base **peŋqwe-*, five, seen also in L. *quinque*, Goth. *fimf*, five, etc.], 1. any of the five parts at the end of the hand; especially, any of these other than the thumb. 2. the part of a glove covering one of these parts. 3. anything resembling a finger in shape or use. 4. a unit of measurement based on the breadth of a finger (3/4 inch to 1 inch) or the length of the middle finger (about 4 1/2 inches). 5. in *mechanics*, a projecting part coming into contact with another part and controlling its motion. *v.t.* 1. to touch with the fingers; put or use the fingers on; handle. 2. to take; steal. 3. in *music*, *a)* to play (an instrument) by using the fingers on strings, keys, etc. to produce the tones. *b)* to mark (a score) with directions for the way to use the fingers. *v.i.* 1. to use the fingers in a certain way on a musical instrument to produce the tune. 2. to be fingered: said of musical instruments.

burn one's fingers, to cause oneself trouble by being too inquisitive, meddlesome, etc.

have a finger in the pie, 1. to help do something; participate. 2. to be meddlesome.

put one's finger on, to indicate or ascertain exactly.

put the finger on, [Slang], 1. to identify as for the police; inform on. 2. to indicate as the place to be robbed, victim to be shot, etc.

twist (or **turn**) **around one's little finger**, to be able to handle or manage with ease.

finger board, 1. a strip of hard wood in the neck of a stringed instrument, as a violin, mandolin, etc., against which the strings are pressed with the fingers to produce the desired tones: see **violin**, illus. 2. the keyboard of a piano, organ, etc.

finger bowl, a small bowl to hold water for rinsing the fingers at table after a meal.

fin·ger·breadth (fiŋ′gẽr-bredth′), *n.* the breadth of a finger; almost an inch.

fin·gered (fiŋ′gẽrd), *adj.* 1. having fingers (of a specified kind or number): in hyphenated compounds, as, *light-fingered*. 2. soiled or marred by touching. 3. in *botany*, *a)* digitate. *b)* fingerlike in form. 4. in *music*, marked to show the fingering: said of a score.

fin·ger·ing (fiŋ′gẽr-iŋ), *n.* 1. a touching or handling with the fingers. 2. in *music*, *a)* act or technique of applying the fingers to the strings, keys, etc. of an instrument to produce the tones. *b)* directions on a musical score for using the fingers in a certain way.

Finger Lakes, a series of long, narrow glacial lakes in central New York.

fin·ger·ling (fiŋ′gẽr-liŋ), *n.* [ME. *fingirling*; see FINGER & -LING], 1. any small object. 2. a small fish about the length of a finger: see **parr**.

finger mark, a mark or smudge left by a finger.

fin·ger-marked (fiŋ′gẽr-märkt′), *adj.* having finger marks on it.

fin·ger·nail (fiŋ′gẽr-nāl′), *n.* the horny substance growing on the upper part of the end joint of a finger: it consists of epithelial cells that develop from the skin.

fin·ger-paint (fiŋ′gẽr-pānt′), *v.i. & v.t.* to paint with finger paints.

finger painting, 1. the art or process of painting by using the fingers, hand, or arm to spread finger paints on moistened paper. 2. a painting made in this manner.

finger paints, paints composed of starch, water, glycerin, and pigments, used in finger painting.

finger post, a post with a sign, often shaped like a pointing finger or hand, indicating a direction.

fin·ger·print (fiŋ′gẽr-print′), *n.* an impression of the lines and whorls on the inner surface of the last joint of the finger, used in the identification of a person. *v.t.* to take the fingerprints of.

fin·ger·print·ing (fiŋ′gẽr-print′iŋ), *n.* the act or science of taking and comparing fingerprints for identification.

finger reading, the use of the fingers to read Braille.

fin·ger·stall (fiŋ′gẽr-stôl′), *n.* a protective covering of rubber, leather, etc. for an injured finger.

finger tip, 1. the tip of a finger. 2. a shield to protect the end of a finger, as from the bowstring in archery.

FINGERPRINT

have at one's finger tips, 1. to have available for instant use. 2. to be completely familiar with.

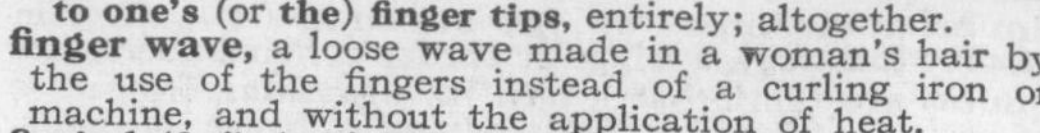

to one's (or **the**) **finger tips**, entirely; altogether.

finger wave, a loose wave made in a woman's hair by the use of the fingers instead of a curling iron or machine, and without the application of heat.

fin·i·al (fin′i-əl, fī′ni-əl), *n.* [ME.; *finis* + *-ial*], 1. an ornament at the top of a spire, gable, etc., or at the end of certain structures. 2. the highest point; apex.

fin·i·cal (fin′i-k'l), *adj.* [< *fine, adj.*], too particular; too dainty or exacting; fussy; fastidious.

fin·i·cal·i·ty (fin′i-kal′ə-ti), *n.* a finical quality.

fin·ick·ing (fin′i-kiŋ), *adj.* [< *finical*], finical; finicky.

fin·ick·y (fin′i-ki), *adj.* finical.

fin·i·kin (fin′i-kin), *adj.* finicking; finical.

fin·ing (fin′iŋ), *n.* [< *fine*, to refine], 1. the refining or clarifying of liquids, metals, etc. 2. *pl.* any substance used for clarifying liquors.

fi·nis (fī′nis; *now often* fin′is), *n.* [*pl.* FINISES (-iz)], [L.], the end; finish; conclusion: often used at the end of a book or motion picture.

fin·ish (fin′ish), *v.t.* [ME. *finissen* < stem of OFr. *fenir* (Fr. *finir*); L. *finire*, to end < *finis*, an end, limit < OL. *-fig-snis*, fixed object, boundary stake < IE. base **dheig-*, to prick, thrust in, seen also in L. *figere*, to prick, fasten], 1. to come to the end of; end. 2. to complete; accomplish. 3. to use up; consume entirely. 4. to remove all blemishes from; perfect; polish. 5. to give (cloth, leather, etc.) a desired surface effect. 6. [Colloq.], to overthrow completely; kill. 7. [Colloq.], to reduce to worthlessness; cause to be of no value. *v.i.* to come to an end; stop; terminate. *n.* 1. the last part; end. 2. anything used to finish something else, as polish, wax, etc. 3. completeness; perfection. 4. the manner or method of completion. 5. the way in which the surface, as of furniture, is smoothed, polished, etc. 6. refinement in manners, speech, etc.; polish in social or cultural matters. 7. in *carpentry*, *a)* joiner work, as doors, stairs, panels, etc., which completes the interior of a building. *b)* high-quality lumber used for this. —***SYN.*** see **close**.

finish off, 1. to end or complete. 2. to kill or destroy.

finish up, 1. to end or complete. 2. to consume all of.

finish with, 1. to end or complete. 2. to end relations with; become indifferent to.

in at the finish, in attendance or activity at the conclusion, as of a contest.

fin·ished (fin′isht), *adj.* [pp. of *finish*], 1. ended; concluded. 2. completed. 3. made perfect; accomplished; excellent. 4. smoothed and polished: said of furniture. 5. reduced to worthlessness; no longer of value.

fin·ish·er (fin′ish-ẽr), *n.* 1. a person or thing that finishes, especially one that adds final touches. 2. [Colloq.], a decisive blow or happening.

fin·ish·ing (fin′ish-iŋ), *adj.* [ppr. of *finish*], last. *n.* 1. an ending. 2. a completing or perfecting. 3. *pl.* the fixtures for lighting, plumbing, etc. in a building.

finishing school, a private school that trains girls for life in society, as by teaching music, languages, etc.

Fin·is·terre, Cape (fin′is-ter′), a promontory at the westernmost point of Spain.

fi·nite (fī′nīt), *adj.* [L. *finitus*, pp. of *finire*; see FINISH], 1. having measurable or definable limits; not infinite. 2. in *grammar*, having limits of person, number, and tense: said of a verb that can be used in a predicate. 3. in *mathematics*, *a)* capable of being reached or surpassed by counting: said of numbers. *b)* neither infinite nor infinitesimal: said of a magnitude. *n.* anything that has measurable limits; finite thing.

fin·i·tude (fin′ə-tōōd′, fī′nə-tūd′), *n.* the state or quality of being finite.

fink (fiŋk), *n.* [? < name of notorious Am. strikebreaker], [Slang], an informer or strikebreaker; especially, a professional strikebreaker.

fin keel, a deep, narrow metal keel, shaped somewhat like a dorsal fin, used on some sailboats to give stability and prevent lateral drift.

Fin·land (fin′lənd), *n.* a country in northern Europe, northeast of the Baltic Sea: area, 119,113 sq. mi.; pop., 4,464,000; capital, Helsinki: abbreviated **Fin.**: Finnish name, *Suomi*.

Finland, Gulf of, an arm of the Baltic Sea, south of Finland: length, 260 mi.

Fin·lay, Fin·ley (fin′li), [of Celt. origin; first element < base meaning "white"], a masculine name.

Finn (fin), *n.* 1. a native or inhabitant of Finland. 2. any person speaking a Finnic language.

Finn., Finnish.

fin·nan had·die (fin′ən had′i), [prob. < *Findhorn haddock*, after fishing port and river of *Findhorn*, Scotland; often associated with *Findon*, Scotland], smoked haddock: also **finnan haddock**.

finned (find), *adj.* having a fin or fins.

Finn·ic (fin′ik), *adj.* 1. Finnish. 2. designating or of the group of languages to which Finnish belongs: see **Finno-Ugric**.

fin·nick·ing (fin′ik-iŋ), *adj.* finicking.

fin·nick·y (fin′i-ki), *adj.* finicky.

Finn·ish (fin′ish), *adj.* 1. of Finland. 2. of the Finns, their language, or culture. *n.* the language of the Finns; Suomi. Abbreviated **Finn., Fin.**

Fin·no- (fin'ō), a combining form meaning *Finn* or *Finnish*, as in *Finno-Ugric.*
Fin·no-U·gri·an (fin'ō-ōō'gri-ən, fin'ō-ū'gri-ən), *adj.* & *n.* Finno-Ugric.
Fin·no-U·gric (fin'ō-ōō'grik, fin'ō-ū'grik), *adj.* designating or of a subfamily of the Uralic group of languages spoken in northeastern Europe, western Siberia, and Hungary: it includes Finnish, Estonian, Hungarian (Ugric, Magyar), Lapp, etc. *n.* this subfamily of languages.
fin·ny (fin'i), *adj.* 1. having fins. 2. like a fin. 3. of fish. 4. [Poetic], full of fish.
Fin·ster·aar·horn (fin'stēr-är'hôrn), *n.* the highest mountain of the Bernese Alps, southern Switzerland: height, 14,026 ft.
fiord (fyôrd, fyōrd), *n.* [Norw. < ON. *fjörthr;* akin to AS. *ford*], a narrow inlet or arm of the sea bordered by steep cliffs, especially in Norway: also spelled **fjord.**

FIORD

fip·pen·ny bit (fip'ən-i, fip'ni), [altered < *five-penny bit*], a Spanish or Mexican silver coin worth about six cents, circulated in the United States before 1857.
fip·ple (fip''l), *n.* [? akin to ON. *flipi*, horse's lip], a plug near the mouthpiece of certain wind instruments, as the recorder, to divert the breath in producing the tones.
fir (fūr), *n.* [ME. *firre;* AS. *fyrh, furh;* akin to G. *föhre;* IE. base **perqwo-*, name of trees, seen also in L. *quercus*, oak; prob. applied orig. to a species of oak], 1. any of a group of cone-bearing evergreen trees somewhat like a pine. 2. the wood of any of these.
Fir·dau·si (fir-dou'sē), *n.* (born *Abul Qasim Mansur*), Persian epic poet; 940?–1020? A.D.
Fir·dou·si, Fir·du·si (fir-dōō'sē), Firdausi.
fire (fīr), *n.* [ME. *fyre;* AS. *fyr;* akin to G. *feuer;* IE. base **pewōr-*, seen also in Gr. *pūr*, fire (cf. PYRE); not connected with *pure*], 1. the active principle of burning, characterized by the heat and light of combustion. 2. something burning, as fuel in a furnace. 3. a destructive burning: as, a forest *fire.* 4. any preparation that will burn and make a brilliant display: as, red *fire.* 5. anything like a fire in heat, brilliance, etc.: as, the *fire* of lightning. 6. torture or trial by fire. 7. great trouble; tribulation. 8. a feverish condition of the body or part of the body. 9. strong feeling; excitement; ardor: as, the *fire* of patriotism. 10. vivid imagination. 11. a discharge of firearms or artillery; shooting; hence, 12. anything like this in speed and continuity of action: as, a *fire* of criticism. *v.t.* [FIRED (fīrd), FIRING], [ME. *firen;* AS. *fyrian*], 1. to apply fire to; make burn; ignite. 2. to supply with fuel; tend the fire of: as, he *fired* the furnace. 3. to cauterize. 4. to bake in a kiln, as bricks, pottery, etc. 5. to dry by heat. 6. to make bright; illuminate, as if by fire. 7. to excite; stimulate; inflame. 8. to shoot; discharge (a gun, bullet, etc.). 9. [Colloq.], to direct with force and suddenness; hurl: as, *fire* a rock, *fire* questions. 10. [pun on *discharge*], [Colloq.], to dismiss from a position; discharge: as, the right to hire and *fire.* *v.i.* 1. to start burning; flame. 2. to tend a fire. 3. to become excited or aroused. 4. to react in a specified way to firing in a kiln: as, this glaze will *fire* a bright blue. 5. to shoot a firearm. 6. to discharge a projectile: as, the gun *fired.*
between two fires, between two attacks; shot at, criticized, etc. from both sides.
catch fire, to begin burning; ignite.
fire away, [Colloq.], to begin; start; especially, to start to talk or ask questions.
fire up, 1. to start a fire in a furnace, stove, etc. 2. to become suddenly angry.
go through fire and water, to undergo great difficulties or dangers.
hang fire, 1. to fail to fire, or delay in firing: said of a gun. 2. to be slow in acting or happening.
lay a fire, to place fuel ready for starting a fire, as in a fireplace.
miss fire, 1. to fail to fire, as a gun. 2. to fail in an attempt.
on fire, 1. burning. 2. greatly excited; full of ardor.
open fire, 1. to begin to shoot. 2. to begin; start.
play with fire, to do something risky.
rapid fire, the firing of the rounds in a firearm in rapid succession.
running fire, 1. rapid fire. 2. a rapid series of criticisms, questions, etc.
set fire to, to make burn; ignite.
set on fire, 1. to make burn. 2. to excite greatly; arouse the feelings or passions of.
set the world on fire, to become very successful, famous, etc.
strike fire, to make a spark, as with tinder.
take fire, 1. to begin to burn. 2. to become excited.
under fire, 1. under attack by the enemy. 2. under attack; criticized; censured.
fire alarm, 1. a signal to announce the outbreak of a fire. 2. a bell, siren, whistle, etc. to give this signal. Abbreviated **f. a.**
fire·arm (fīr'ärm'), *n.* any weapon from which a shot is fired by the force of an explosion; especially, such a weapon small enough to be carried, as a rifle, pistol, etc.
fire·ball (fīr'bôl'), *n.* 1. something resembling a ball of fire, as a kind of lightning. 2. a large, bright meteor. 3. a ball containing material to cause an explosion or a fire: formerly used as a weapon thrown in battle.
fire·bird (fīr'būrd'), *n.* any of various birds with brilliant coloring, as the scarlet tanager and the Baltimore oriole.
fire boat, a boat equipped with fire-fighting equipment, used along water fronts.
fire·box (fīr'boks'), *n.* 1. the place for the fire in a locomotive engine, stove, etc. 2. [Obs.], a tinderbox.
fire·brand (fīr'brand'), *n.* 1. a piece of burning wood. 2. a person who stirs up others to revolt or strife.
fire·break (fīr'brāk'), *n.* a strip of land cleared to stop the spread of fire, as in a forest or prairie.
fire·brick (fīr'brik'), *n.* a brick made to withstand great heat, used to line fireplaces, furnaces, etc.
fire brigade, a body of men organized to fight fires.
fire·bug (fīr'bug'), *n.* [Colloq.], a person who deliberately sets fire to buildings, etc.; pyromaniac; incendiary.
fire clay, a kind of clay capable of resisting intense heat, used for making firebricks, furnace linings, etc.
fire company, 1. a body of men organized to fight fires. 2. [British], a business firm selling fire insurance.
fire·crack·er (fīr'krak'ēr), *n.* a roll of paper that contains an explosive and an attached fuse, and makes a sharp noise when exploded: used at celebrations, etc.
fire-cure (fīr'kyoor'), *v.t.* to cure and season (tobacco) over wood fires.
fire·damp (fīr'damp'), *n.* a gas, largely methane, formed in coal mines, which is explosive when mixed with a certain proportion of air.
fire department, a municipal department whose work is fighting fires and preventing their occurrence.
fire·dog (fīr'dôg', fīr'dog'), *n.* [for sense, cf. Fr. *chenet*, andiron, dim. of *chien*, dog], a metal support for wood or logs in a fireplace; andiron.
fire·drake (fīr'drāk'), *n.* [see FIRE & DRAKE], in *Germanic mythology*, a fire-breathing dragon.
fire drill, a drill in which buildings are vacated, fire stations manned, etc. in a quick, orderly way to teach proper procedure in case of fire.
fire-eat·er (fīr'ēt'ēr), *n.* 1. a performer at circuses, etc. who pretends to eat fire. 2. a hot-tempered person always ready to quarrel or fight.
fire engine, 1. a machine for spraying water, chemicals, etc. to extinguish fires: it is often part of a specially designed motor truck; hence, 2. loosely, any motor truck for carrying firemen and equipment to a fire.
fire escape, any device, as a ladder, chute, outside stairway, etc., for escape from a burning building.
fire extinguisher, a portable device containing chemicals that can be sprayed on a fire to extinguish it.
fire·fly (fīr'flī'), *n.* [*pl.* FIREFLIES (-flīz')], any of several winged beetles whose abdomen glows with a phosphorescent light: the larvae and wingless females are called *glowworms.*

FIREFLY (1/2 in. long)

fire·guard (fīr'gärd'), *n.* a metal screen set in front of a fireplace.
fire·house (fīr'hous'), *n.* a fire station.
fire insurance, insurance against loss or damage resulting from fire.
fire irons, the poker, shovel, and tongs used for tending a fireplace.
fire·less (fīr'lis), *adj.* without a fire.
fireless cooker, an insulated container which when heated stays hot and finishes cooking food placed in it, or keeps the food warm.
fire·light (fīr'līt'), *n.* the light from a fire, especially an open fire.
fire·lock (fīr'lok'), *n.* 1. an early type of gunlock in which the priming was ignited by sparks; wheel lock or flintlock; hence, 2. an early type of musket with such a lock.
fire·man (fīr'mən), *n.* [*pl.* FIREMEN (-mən)], 1. a man whose work is fighting fires; member of a fire department. 2. a man who tends a fire in a furnace, locomotive engine, etc.

fire-new (fīr′nōō′, fīr′nū′), *adj.* [Archaic], direct from the fire or forge; brand-new.
Fi·ren·ze (fē-ren′dze), *n.* Florence, Italy: the Italian name.
fire·place (fīr′plās′), *n.* a place for a fire, especially an open place built in a wall, at the base of a chimney.
fire·plug (fīr′plug′), *n* a street hydrant to which a hose can be attached for fighting fires.
fire pot, 1. formerly, a pot filled with a burning substance, thrown against an enemy. 2. the fire holder in a stove, furnace, etc. 3. a crucible.
fire·pow·er (fīr′pou′ēr), *n.* in *military usage,* 1. the effectiveness of a weapon in terms of the accuracy and volume of its fire. 2. the capacity of a given unit to deliver fire.
fire·proof (fīr′prōōf′), *adj.* virtually impossible to set fire to or destroy by fire; very hard to burn. *v.t.* (fīr′prōōf′), to make fireproof.
fire sale, a sale at lowered prices of goods damaged in a fire.
fire screen, a screen to be set in front of a fire to protect against heat or to stop sparks.
fire ship, a ship filled with materials that will explode and burn when set afire: it is floated among an enemy's ships to destroy them.
fire·side (fīr′sīd′), *n.* 1. the space around a fireplace; hearth; hence, 2. home. 3. home life; family life. *adj.* of or at the hearth or home.
fire station, place where fire engines are kept; engine house.
fire·stone (fīr′stōn′), *n.* 1. formerly, flint or iron pyrites used for striking fire. 2. a stone that can withstand intense heat: used especially of a variety of sandstone in England.
fire tower, a tower, usually in a forest, where a lookout is posted to watch for fires and give the alarm.
fire·trap (fīr′trap′), *n.* a building unsafe in case of fire because it will burn easily or because it lacks adequate exits or fire escapes.
fire wall, a fireproof wall to prevent the spread of fire from one room or compartment to the next.
fire·ward (fīr′wôrd), *n.* a firewarden.
fire·ward·en (fīr′wôr′d'n), *n.* an official assigned to prevent or fight fires, as in forests, public buildings, etc.
fire·wa·ter (fīr′wô′tēr, fīr′wä′tēr), *n.* [Am. Ind. term for whisky, rum, etc.], alcoholic liquor: now humorous.
fire·weed (fīr′wēd′), *n.* any of a number of weeds that grow readily on cleared or burned-over land, as the Jimson weed.
fire·wood (fīr′wood′), *n.* wood used as fuel.
fire·works (fīr′wũrks′), *n.pl.* 1. *sometimes used in sing.* firecrackers, rockets, etc., exploded or burned, as in celebrations, to produce noises or brilliant lighting effects. 2. a display of or as of fireworks.
fir·ing (fīr′iŋ), *n.* 1. the application of heat to harden or glaze pottery. 2. the tending of a fire or furnace. 3. the shooting of firearms, etc. 4. fuel for a fire.
firing line, 1. the line from which gunfire is, or is intended to be, directed against the enemy. 2. the troops stationed along this line. 3. the front position in any kind of activity.
firing order, the order in which explosions occur in the cylinders of an internal-combustion engine.
firing pin, that part in the bolt or breech of a firearm which strikes the primer and explodes the charge.
firing squad (or **party**), a group of soldiers detailed to shoot to death someone so sentenced by a military court, or to fire a volley of shots over the grave at a military funeral.
fir·kin (fũr′kin), *n.* [< *ferdekyn* < D. *vierdekin; vierde,* a fourth + *-kin,* -kin], 1. a small wooden tub for butter, lard, etc. 2. a measure of capacity equal to 1/4 barrel.
firm (fũrm), *adj.* [ME. & OFr. *ferme* < L. *firmus*], 1. not yielding easily under pressure; solid; hard. 2. not moved or shaken easily; fixed; stable. 3. continued steadily; remaining the same: as, a *firm* pressure. 4. unchanging; resolute; constant: as, a *firm* faith. 5. showing determination; positive: as, a *firm* command. 6. legally or formally concluded; definite; final: as, a *firm* contract, a *firm* order. 7. in *commerce,* not rising or falling considerably; steady: said of prices, etc. *v.t. & v.i.* 1. to make or become firm. 2. [Archaic], to establish; confirm.
stand firm, to be steadfast in conviction; remain unchanged by attack, persuasion, etc.
SYN.—**firm,** in referring to material consistency, suggests a compactness that does not yield easily to, or is very resilient under, pressure (*firm flesh*); **hard** is applied to that which is so firm that it is difficult to penetrate, cut, or crush it (*hard* as rock); **solid** suggests a dense consistency throughout a mass or substance that is firm or hard and often connotes heaviness or substantialness (*solid* brick); **stiff** implies resistance to bending or stretching (a *stiff* collar).
firm (fũrm), *n.* [It. *firma,* signature, hence title of a business < L. *firmare,* to strengthen < *firmus;* see FIRM, *adj.*], a business company or partnership of two or more persons: distinguished from *corporation*: in the United States and England, a firm is not legally recognized as a person apart from the members forming it.
fir·ma·ment (fũr′mə-mənt), *n.* [L. *firmamentum,* a strengthening, support (LL. the firmament) < *firmare,* to strengthen < *firmus;* see FIRM, *adj.*], the sky, viewed poetically as a solid arch or vault.
fir·man (fũr′mən, fẽr-män′), *n.* [*pl.* FIRMANS (-mənz, -mänz′)], [Per. *fermān*], a decree or sanction given by an Oriental ruler.
firm·er (fũr′mẽr), *adj.* [Fr. *fermoir,* altered < *formoir* < *former,* to form (see FORM, *v.*)], designating a chisel with a thin blade fixed in a handle. *n.* a firmer chisel.
firn (firn), *n.* [G. < *firn,* of last year, old; akin to AS. *fyrn,* former], the granular snow, not in a completely compacted mass, at the top of a glacier; névé.
fir·ry (fũr′i), *adj.* 1. full of firs. 2. made of fir.
first (fũrst), *adj.* [ME. *firste;* AS. *fyrst,* lit., foremost, superl. of *fore,* before (see FORE); akin to OHG. *furist,* G. *fürst,* prince, lit., foremost man], 1. preceding all others in a series; before any others; 1st: used as the ordinal of *one.* 2. happening or acting before all others; earliest. 3. ranking before all others; foremost in rank, quality, importance, etc.; principal. 4. in *music,* of highest pitch; playing or singing the upper part or the part highest in pitch. *adv.* 1. before any other person or thing; at the beginning. 2. for the first time. 3. sooner; preferably. *n.* 1. the one before the second. 2. any person, thing, class, place, etc. that is first. 3. the first day of a month. 4. the first year of a reign, era, etc. 5. the beginning; start. 6. *pl.* the best quality of merchandise: as, these stockings are *firsts.* 7. the winning place, as in racing. 8. the first or lowest forward gear ratio of a motor vehicle; low gear. 9. [usually F-], in British universities, *a*) the highest rank in examinations for honors. *b*) a holder of this rank. 10. in *music,* the highest or leading voice or instrument in an ensemble.
first thing, as the first thing; before anything else.
in the first place, firstly; to begin with.
first-aid (fũrst′ād′), *adj.* of or used for first aid.
first aid, emergency treatment for injury or sudden illness, given before regular medical care is available.
first base, in *baseball,* the first position on the diamond, to the right of home plate, which a batter who has hit fairly must reach ahead of the ball.
get to first base, [Slang], to accomplish the first step of an undertaking.
first-born (fũrst′bôrn′), *adj.* born first in a family; oldest. *n.* the first-born child.
first cause, 1. a primary or original cause of anything; source. 2. in *theology,* God as the prime mover.
first-class (fũrst′klas′, fũrst′kläs′), *adj.* 1. of the highest class, rank, excellence, etc.; of the best quality. 2. designating or of the best accommodations: as, a *first-class* cabin on a ship. 3. designating or of a class of mail consisting of sealed matter in writing, as letters, and all other matter sealed against ready inspection: such mail carries the highest regular postage rates. *adv.* 1. with the best accommodations: as, we traveled to Europe *first-class.* 2. as or by first-class mail.
first cousin, the son or daughter of one's uncle or aunt: cf. **cousin.**
first day, Sunday; term used by the Society of Friends.
first estate, see **estate** (sense 2).
first finger, the finger next to the thumb; index finger.
first floor, 1. the ground floor of a building. 2. in Europe and Great Britain, the floor above the ground floor: also sometimes so designated in hotels, etc. in the United States.
first fruits, 1. the earliest produce of the season. 2. the first products, results, or profits of any activity.
first·hand (fũrst′hand′), *adj. & adv.* from the original producer or source; direct.
First International, a workingmen's association founded in London in 1864 by Karl Marx and Friedrich Engels to spread their philosophy of socialism.
first lady, the wife of the president of the United States.
first lieutenant, an officer ranking above a second lieutenant and below a captain, as in the United States Army or Marine Corps.
first·ling (fũrst′liŋ), *n.* 1. the first of a kind. 2. the first fruit, produce, etc. 3. the first-born of an animal.
first·ly (fũrst′li), *adv.* in the first place; first: used chiefly in enumerating topics.
first mate, a ship's officer next in rank below the captain.
first mortgage, a mortgage having priority over all others as a lien on property.
first night, the opening night of a play, opera, etc.
first-night·er (fũrst′nīt′ẽr), *n.* a person who regularly attends the opening performances of plays, operas, etc.
first offender, a person who has committed a legal offense for the first time.
first officer, in *nautical usage,* a first mate.
first papers, the documents by which an alien makes preliminary application for United States citizenship.
first person, that form of a pronoun or verb which refers to the speaker or speakers: in *I* (or *we*) *do, I* (or *we*) and *do* are in the first person.
first quarter, 1. the time of month between new moon and first half-moon. 2. the moon's shape at this time.
first-rate (fũrst′rāt′), *adj.* [orig. applied to the highest

of the rates, or classes, of warships], 1. of the highest class, rank, etc.; of the best quality. 2. [Colloq.], very good; excellent. *adv.* [Colloq.], very well.

First Republic, the republic established in France in 1792 after the Revolution, and lasting until the establishment of an Empire by Napoleon in 1804.

first sergeant, in *military usage,* the highest ranking noncommissioned officer of a company, battery, etc., serving as administrative assistant to the unit commander: eliminated (1948) in the United States Army as a title of rank, but retained as an occupational designation: see **master sergeant.**

first water, the best quality and purest luster: said of diamonds, pearls, etc., but also used figuratively.

firth (fũrth), *n.* [< ON. *fjörthr*], a narrow inlet or arm of the sea; estuary.

fisc (fisk), *n.* [Fr.; L. *fiscus;* see FISCAL], [Rare], a royal or state treasury; exchequer.

fis·cal (fis'k'l), *adj.* [Fr.; LL. *fiscalis* < L. *fiscus,* basket of rushes, money bag, public chest], 1. having to do with the public treasury or revenues. 2. financial. *n.* in some European countries, a legal official corresponding to public prosecutor. —*SYN.* see **financial.**

fiscal year, the twelve-month period between settlements of financial accounts: in the United States the government fiscal year legally ends June 30.

fish (fish), *n.* [Fr. *fiche,* a stake, pin, peg < *ficher,* to fix; OFr. *fichier;* LL. **figicare,* intens. for L. *figere;* see FIX], a piece of wood, etc. fastened to another or to a joint to strengthen it. *v.t.* to strengthen or join by using such a piece of wood, etc.

fish (fish), *n.* [*pl.* FISH; in referring to different species, FISHES (-iz); see PLURAL, II, D, 2], [ME. *fissh;* AS. *fisc;* akin to G. *fisch;* IE. base **p(e)isq-,* as also in L. *piscis* (cf. PISCATORIAL)], 1. any of a large group of cold-blooded animals living in water and having backbones, permanent gills for breathing, fins, and, usually, scales. 2. loosely, any animal living in water only, as a crab, oyster, etc. 3. the flesh of a fish used as food. 4. [Colloq.], a person thought of as like a fish in being easily lured by bait, lacking intelligence or emotion, etc.: as, the poor *fish* was taken in easily, he's a cold *fish.* 5. [F-], in *astronomy,* either of the two groups of stars supposedly outlining a fish and forming the constellation Pisces. 6. in *nautical usage,* a device for raising the anchor. *v.i.* [AS. *fiscian*], 1. to catch or try to catch fish. 2. to try to get something indirectly or by cunning. *v.t.* 1. to catch or try to catch fish in: as, we *fished* the stream. 2. to get by fishing. 3. to grope for, find, and bring to view: often with *out* or *up,* as, he *fished* a coin out of his pocket. 4. to raise (the anchor) with a fish (*n.* 6). *adj.* 1. of fish or fishing. 2. selling fish.

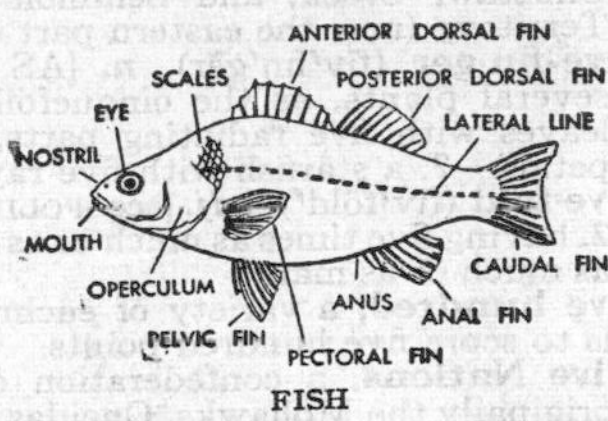

FISH

drink like a fish, to drink heavily.
fish for, to search for or try to get, especially by cunning or indirect means.
fish in troubled waters, to try to gain something by taking advantage of a confused or troubled situation.
fish out, to deplete the stock of fish in (a lake, etc.).
like a fish out of water, out of one's element; in unfamiliar surroundings; not adapted.
neither fish, flesh, nor fowl (or **nor good red herring**), not anything definite or recognizable.
other fish to fry, other, more important things to attend to.

Fish, Hamilton (fish), 1808–1893; American statesman; secretary of state (1869–1877).

fish and chips (chips), [Chiefly British], small fillets of fish and strips of potato French fried and eaten hot.

fish ball (or **cake**), a fried patty of minced fish, often mixed with mashed potato.

fish·bolt (fish'bōlt'), *n.* a bolt used to fasten fishplates to rails.

fish·bowl (fish'bōl'), *n.* a glass bowl in which goldfish, snails, etc. are kept; small aquarium: also **fish bowl.**

fish crow, a small, fish-eating crow found along the eastern coast of the United States.

fish·er (fish'ẽr), *n.* 1. a person who fishes; fisherman. 2. a boat used in fishing. 3. [*pl.* FISHERS (-ẽrz), FISHER; see PLURAL, II, D, 1], an animal that catches and eats fish; especially, a fish-eating animal of the marten family that is like a weasel but larger.

Fish·er, Dorothy Can·field (kan'fēld fish'ẽr), 1879–1958; American novelist.

fish·er·man (fish'ẽr-mən), *n.* [*pl.* FISHERMEN (-mən)], 1. a person who fishes for sport or for a living. 2. a ship used in fishing.

fish·er·man's bend (fish'ẽr-mənz), a kind of knot: see **knot,** illus.

fish·er·y (fish'ẽr-i), *n.* [*pl.* FISHERIES (-iz)], 1. the business of catching, packing, or selling fish or other products of lakes, rivers, or the sea. 2. a place where fish, etc. are caught; fishing ground. 3. a legal right to catch fish in certain waters or at certain times. 4. a place where fish are bred.

fish·gig (fish'gig'), *n.* [altered, after *fish* < *fizgig, fisgig* < Sp. *fisga,* harpoon with three hooks < *fisgar,* to fish with a harpoon < LL. **fixicare,* to attach (to), fasten < pp. of L. *figere;* see FIX], a pronged spear for catching fish: also **fizgig.**

fish hawk, the osprey, a large, fish-eating hawk.

fish·hook (fish'hook'), *n.* a hook, usually barbed, for catching fish.

fish·i·ly (fish'ə-li), *adv.* in a fishy manner.

fish·i·ness (fish'i-nis), *n.* the quality of being fishy.

fish·ing (fish'iŋ), *n.* 1. the catching of fish for sport or for a living. 2. a place to fish.

fishing banks (or **grounds**), a place where fish are abundant, as off Newfoundland.

fishing rod, a slender pole with an attached line, hook, and, sometimes, a reel, used in fishing.

fishing tackle, the equipment, as hooks, lines, rods, reels, etc., used in fishing.

fish joint, a joint, as of two railroad rails, held together by fishplates along the sides.

fish ladder, a series of steps in the rocks which help fish, especially salmon, to go up a waterfall.

fish line, a line, usually with a hook at one end, used in fishing.

fish meal, dried fish, ground and used as fertilizer or fodder.

fish·mon·ger (fish'muŋ'gẽr), *n.* a dealer in fish.

fish·plate (fish'plāt'), *n.* [prob. < Fr. *fiche,* means of fixing, confused with *fish*], either of a pair of iron or steel plates bolting two rails together lengthwise, as on a railroad.

FISHPLATE

fish pole, a fishing rod.

fish pond (fish'pond'), *n.* a pond where fish are kept or bred.

fish·pound (fish'pound'), *n.* [Dial.], a submerged net for catching fish; weir.

fish·skin disease (fish'skin'), ichthyosis.

fish story, [from the conventional exaggeration by fishermen of the size of fish that escaped being caught], [Colloq.], an unbelievable story; exaggeration.

fish tackle, hook and tackle for raising the flukes of an anchor up to the gunwale of a ship.

fish·tail (fish'tāl'), *v.i.* [Colloq.], to retard the speed of an airplane by swinging the tail from side to side in approaching the ground for a landing.

fish warden, an officer in charge of fisheries and the enforcement of the fishing laws in his district.

fish·wife (fish'wif'), *n.* [*pl.* FISHWIVES (-wīvz')], 1. a woman who sells fish. 2. a coarse, scolding woman.

fish·worm (fish'wũrm'), *n.* worm used for bait in fishing.

fish·y (fish'i), *adj.* [FISHIER (-i-ẽr), FISHIEST (-i-ist)], 1. of or full of fish. 2. like a fish in odor, taste, etc. 3. like that of a fish; dull; without expression; lusterless: as, a *fishy* stare. 4. [Colloq.], questionable; suspicious.

Fiske, John (fisk), 1842–1901; American historian and writer.

Fiske, Minnie Mad·dern (mad'ẽrn), 1865–1932; American actress.

fis·sile (fis''l, fis'il), *adj.* [L. *fissilis* < *fissus,* pp. of *findere,* to cleave, split], that can be split; easily cleft.

fis·sil·i·ty (fi-sil'ə-ti), *n.* the quality of being fissile.

fis·sion (fish'ən), *n.* [L. *fissio* < *fissus,* pp. of *findere,* to cleave, split], 1. a splitting apart; division into parts; cleavage. 2. in *biology,* a form of asexual reproduction, found in various simple plants and animals, in which the parent organism divides into two or more parts, each becoming an independent individual. 3. in *physics,* nuclear fission.

fis·sion·a·ble (fish'ən-ə-b'l), *adj.* that can undergo fission; specifically, designating a substance, as uranium, whose nuclei can undergo fission.

fis·sip·a·rous (fi-sip'ẽr-əs), *adj.* [<L. *fissus* (see FISSION); + *-parous*], reproducing by fission.

fis·si·ros·tral (fis'i-ros'trəl), *adj.* [< L. *fissi,* cloven + *rostrum,* beak; + *-al*], 1. broad and deeply cleft: said of the beaks of certain birds. 2. having such a beak: said of certain birds, as the swifts and swallows.

fis·sure (fish'ẽr), *n.* [Fr.; L. *fissura* < *fissus,* pp. of *findere,* to cleave, split], 1. a cleft or crack. 2. a dividing or breaking into parts. 3. in *anatomy,* a groove between lobes or parts of an organ, as in the brain. *v.t.* & *v.i.* [FISSURED (-ẽrd), FISSURING], to break into parts; crack or split apart.

fist (fist), *n.* [ME.; AS. *fyst;* akin to G. *faust* (OHG.

fūst); IE. base **pn̥sti-*, fist or ? < IE. **pn̥qsti* < **peŋqwe-*, five (cf. FINGER), in the sense "clenched five fingers"], 1. a hand with the fingers closed tightly into the palm; clenched hand. 2. [Colloq.], *a*) a hand. *b*) the grasp. *c*) handwriting. 3. in *printing*, the sign (☛), used to point out something. ***v.t.*** 1. to hit with the fist. 2. in *nautical usage*, to grasp or handle.

fist·ful (fist′fool), ***n.*** a handful.

fist·ic (fis′tik), ***adj.*** [Colloq.], having to do with boxing; fought with the fists; pugilistic.

fis·ti·cuffs (fis′ti-kufs′), ***n.pl.*** [< *fist* + *cuff* (a blow)], 1. a fight with the fists; boxing match. 2. blows with the fists; punches. 3. the science of boxing.

fis·tu·la (fis′choo-lə), ***n.*** [*pl.* FISTULAS (-ləz), FISTULAE (-lē′)], [L., a pipe, cane, ulcer], 1. a pipe or tube. 2. an abnormal hollow passage from an abscess, cavity, or hollow organ to the skin or to another abscess, cavity, or organ.

fis·tu·lar (fis′choo-lẽr), ***adj.*** fistulous.

fis·tu·lous (fis′choo-ləs), ***adj.*** [L. *fistulosus* < *fistula*], 1. shaped like a pipe or tube; tubular. 2. consisting of tubular parts. 3. of a fistula.

fit (fit), ***v.t.*** [FITTED (-id) or FIT, FITTED, FITTING], [< the *adj.*], 1. to be suitable or adapted to: as, his actions *fit* his words. 2. to be the proper size, shape, etc. for: as, the coat *fits* him. 3. to make or alter so as to fit. 4. to make suitable or qualified. 5. to insert exactly: as, he *fitted* the key in the lock. 6. to equip; outfit. ***v.i.*** 1. to be suitable or proper. 2. to be adjusted as specified in size, shape, etc.: as, his coat *fits* well. ***adj.*** [FITTER (-ẽr), FITTEST (-ist)], [Late ME. *fyt*, prob. var. of *fete*, fitting, adapted < OFr. *fait*, lit., made < L. *factus* (see FACT); senses influenced by *v.t.* and prob. by other words], 1. adapted, adjusted, qualified, or suited to some purpose, aim, function, etc. 2. proper; right; appropriate. 3. prepared; ready; trained. 4. in good physical condition; healthy. ***n.*** [prob. < the *v.*], 1. the condition of fitting or being fitted. 2. the manner of fitting: as, a tight *fit*. 3. anything that fits.

fit out (or **up**), to equip; outfit, as a ship.

SYN.—**fit**, the broadest term here, means having the qualities or qualifications to meet some condition, circumstance, purpose, or demand (*fit* for a king); **suitable** is applied to that which accords with the requirements or needs of the occasion or circumstances (shoes *suitable* for hiking); **proper** implies reference to that which naturally or rightfully belongs to something or suggests a fitness or suitability dictated by good judgment (*proper* respect for one's elders); that is **appropriate** which is especially or distinctively fit or suitable; **fitting** is applied to that which accords harmoniously with the character, spirit, or tone of something; **apt**, in this connection, is used of that which is nicely adapted to the purpose (an *apt* phrase).

fit (fit), ***n.*** [ME.; AS. (rare) *fitt*, conflict; sense development: conflict—moment of danger—mortal crisis—paroxysm], 1. any sudden, uncontrollable attack; paroxysm: as, a *fit* of coughing. 2. *a*) a sharp, brief display of feeling: as, a *fit* of anger. *b*) a transient mood: as, a *fit* of the blues. 3. a temporary burst of activity: as, he works by *fits*. 4. in *medicine*, a convulsion in which the victim loses consciousness.

by fits and starts, in an irregular way; in bursts of activity followed by periods of inactivity.

have (or **throw**) **a fit**, [Colloq.], to become very angry or upset.

fit (fit), ***n.*** [ME. *fitte*; AS. *fitt*; akin to OS. (Latinized) pl. *vitteas*, sections of a poem (the *Heliand*); for IE. base see FOOT], [Archaic], a short section of a poem, ballad, or song; canto.

fitch (fich), ***n.*** fitchew.

Fitch, Clyde (fich), (*William Clyde Fitch*), 1865–1909; American playwright.

Fitch, John, 1743–1798; American inventor of a steamboat.

Fitch·burg (fich′bẽrg), ***n.*** a city in northern Massachusetts: pop., 43,000.

fitch·et (fich′it), ***n.*** fitchew.

fitch·ew (fich′o͞o), ***n.*** [ME. < *ficheux*, dial. form of OFr. *fissau*, *fissel*, dim. <MD. *fisse*, *vitsche*; OHG. *wiessa* < Gmc. **wis(j)o*, musky animal (seen also in Eng. *weasel*) < IE. base **weis-*, to melt, flow: used of animal sperm and of the moisture or odor of decaying vegetation; seen also in L. *vissio*, stench, *virus*, slime, poison & prob. in Gmc. **wisunt*, bison (from the musky odor)], 1. the European polecat. 2. its fur. Also **fitch, fitchet.**

FITCHEW (24 in. long)

fit·ful (fit′fəl), ***adj.*** [*fit* (paroxysm) + *-ful*], characterized by irregular bursts of activity followed by periods of inactivity; intermittent; spasmodic; irregular.

fit·ly (fit′li), ***adv.*** 1. in a fit manner; suitably. 2. at the right time.

fit·ter (fit′ẽr), ***n.*** a person who fits; specifically, *a*) a person who alters or adjusts garments to fit. *b*) a person who supplies, installs, or adjusts machinery, pipes, etc.

fit·ting (fit′iŋ), ***adj.*** [ppr. of *fit*], suitable; proper; appropriate. ***n.*** 1. an adjustment or trying on of clothes, etc. for fit. 2. something used in an adjustment: as, a pipe *fitting*. 3. *pl.* the fixtures, furnishings, or decorations of a house, office, automobile, etc. —***SYN.*** see **fit.**

fitz- (fits), a prefix meaning *son of*, as in *Fitzgibbon*: formerly used in surnames, especially to denote an illegitimate son of a prince.

Fitz·Ger·ald, Edward (fits-jer′əld), 1809–1883; English poet and translator: also written **Fitzgerald.**

Fitzgerald, F. Scott, (*Francis Scott Key Fitzgerald*), 1896–1940; American novelist.

Fiu·me (fū′me), ***n.*** a seaport in Yugoslavia, on the Adriatic; in Italy 1924–1947: pop., 54,000: cf. **Rieka.**

five (fīv), ***adj.*** [ME.; AS. *fif*, *fife*, with assimilated nasal (cf. OFris. *fif*); akin to G. *fünf* (OHG., Goth. *fimf*); Gmc. **fimfi-*; for IE. base see FINGER], totaling one more than four. ***n.*** 1. the cardinal number between four and six; 5; V. 2. anything having five units or members; specifically, *a*) a basketball team. *b*) a playing card or domino with five spots. *c*) [Colloq.], a five-dollar bill.

five-and-dime (fīv′′n-dīm′), ***n.*** [Colloq.], a five-and-ten-cent store.

five-and-ten-cent store (fīv′′n-ten′sent′), a store that sells a wide variety of merchandise, originally with many articles priced at five or ten cents: also **five-and-ten**: also called *dime store.*

Five Civilized Nations, the Cherokee, Chickasaw, Choctaw, Creek, and Seminole tribes of the Indian Territory (now the eastern part of Oklahoma).

five-fin·ger (fīv′fiŋ′gẽr), ***n.*** [AS. *fiffingre*], 1. any of several plants, as the cinquefoil or the oxlip, having leaves with five radiating parts, or flowers with five petals. 2. a starfish with five rays.

five·fold (fīv′fōld′), ***adj.*** [see -FOLD], 1. having five parts. 2. having five times as much or as many. ***adv.*** five times as much or as many.

five hundred, a variety of euchre in which the object is to score five hundred points.

Five Nations, a confederation of Iroquoian Indians, originally the Mohawks, Oneidas, Onondagas, Cayugas, and Senecas, and later including the Tuscaroras.

fiv·er (fīv′ẽr), ***n.*** [Slang], 1. a five-dollar bill. 2. something that scores five in a game. 3. [British], a five-pound note.

fives (fīvz), ***n.*** [? < *five* fingers of the hand], a kind of handball played in England.

Five-Year Plan (fīv′yêr′), any of several five-year programs for the development of the socialized industry, agriculture, etc. of the Soviet Union: the first Five-Year Plan was begun in 1928.

fix (fiks), ***v.t.*** [FIXED or FIXT (fikst), FIXING], [ME. *fixen* < *fix*, fixed or < ML. *fixare*, to fix; both < *fixus*, pp. of *figere*, to fasten, attach; for IE. base see FINISH], 1. to make firm, stable, or secure; fasten or attach firmly. 2. to set firmly in the mind. 3. to direct steadily: as, the child *fixed* his eyes on the clown. 4. to direct one's eyes steadily at. 5. to make rigid. 6. to make permanent or lasting: as, color is *fixed* in dyeing. 7. to arrange definitely; establish; set: as, he *fixed* the rent at forty dollars. 8. to reach a decision about; find out with certainty: as, the city of Homer's birth has never been *fixed*. 9. to arrange properly; set in order; adjust. 10. to repair; mend. 11. to bank, refuel, and tend (a fire). 12. to prepare and cook (food or meals). 13. [Colloq.], to influence the result or action of (a horse race, jury, election, etc.) to one's advantage by bribery, trickery, etc. 14. [Colloq.], to punish; revenge oneself on; get even with. 15. in *chemistry*, *a*) to make solid or nonvolatile. *b*) to cause (atmospheric nitrogen) to combine with other elements or compounds to form nitrates, ammonia, etc. 16. in *photography*, to make (a film, slide, etc.) permanent and prevent from fading by washing in a chemical solution. ***v.i.*** 1. to become fixed. 2. [Colloq. or Dial.], to prepare or intend: as, I'm *fixing* to go hunting. ***n.*** 1. [Colloq.], a difficult or awkward situation; predicament. 2. in *aviation*, *navigation*, etc., a position determined from the bearings of two or more known points. 3. [Slang], a person or situation that can be fixed (sense 13). —***SYN.*** see **predicament.**

fix on (or **upon**), to choose; settle on.

fix up, [Colloq.], 1. to repair; mend. 2. to arrange properly; set in order. 3. to make arrangements for.

fix·ate (fik′sāt), ***v.t.*** & ***v.i.*** [FIXATED (-id), FIXATING], [< ML. *fixatus*, pp. of *fixare*; see FIX], to make or become fixed; specifically, 1. in *psychology*, *a*) to direct and focus (the eyes). *b*) to direct and focus the eye on (a point). 2. in *psychoanalysis*, to attach or arrest (one of the component impulses of the libido) at an early stage of psychosexual development.

fix·a·tion (fik-sā′shən), ***n.*** [ME.; ML. *fixatio*, < *fixatus*; see FIX], 1. *a*) a fixing or being fixed. *b*) a fixating or being fixated. 2. in *chemistry*, *a*) reduction into a solid or nonvolatile form. *b*) the fixing of atmospheric nitrogen: see **nitrogen fixation.** 3. in *photography*, the treatment of a film, print, etc. to make it permanent. 4. in *psychology*, *a)* the directing and focusing of the eyes on a point. *b)* popularly, a morbid preoccupation; obsession. 5. in *psychoanalysis*, an attaching or arresting of one of the component impulses of the libido at an early stage of psychosexual development.

fix·a·tive (fik'sə-tiv), ***adj.*** [*fix* + *-ative*], that can or tends to make permanent, prevent fading, etc. ***n.*** a substance that makes something permanent, prevents fading, etc., as a mordant.

fixed (fikst), ***adj.*** [ME.; see FIX], 1. firm; not movable. 2. established; settled; set: as, a *fixed* price. 3. steady; unmoving; resolute: as, a *fixed* purpose. 4. persisting in the mind, sometimes to the point of delusion, and tending to control the thoughts and action; obsessive: as, a *fixed* idea. 5. in *chemistry*, *a)* nonvolatile: as, *fixed* oils. *b)* incorporated into a stable compound from its free state, as atmospheric nitrogen.

fixed charge, any of certain charges, as taxes, rent, interest, etc., which must be paid, usually at regular intervals, without being changed or shifted, and without reference to the amount of business done.

fix·ed·ly (fik'sid-li), ***adv.*** in a fixed manner; steadily; intently.

fix·ed·ness (fik'sid-nis), ***n.*** the state of being fixed.

fixed oil, a nonvolatile oil, especially one found in fatty animal tissue and the seeds of some plants.

fixed star, a star whose great distance from the earth makes it appear to keep the same position in relation to other stars.

fix·er (fik'sẽr), ***n.*** 1. a person or thing that fixes. 2. [Colloq.], a person who pays bribes or uses his influence to keep himself or others from being punished for illegal acts.

fix·ings (fik'siŋz), ***n.pl.*** [Colloq.], furnishings; accessories; trimmings.

fix·i·ty (fik'sə-ti), ***n.*** 1. the quality or state of being fixed; steadiness; stability; permanence. 2. [*pl.* FIXITIES (-tiz)], anything fixed.

fixt (fikst), poetic past tense and past participle of **fix.**

fix·ture (fiks'chẽr), ***n.*** [< obs. *fixure* (L. *fixura*), after *mixture*], 1. anything firmly in place. 2. *usually in pl.* any of the fittings or furniture of a house, store, etc., attached to the building and considered legally as a part of it: as, bathroom *fixtures*. 3. [Colloq.], a person who remains in one job or place for a long time.

fiz·gig (fiz'gig'), ***n.*** [*fizz*, *v.* + *gig* (light carriage)], 1. a giddy, flirtatious girl. 2. a kind of firework that makes hissing noises when it explodes.

fiz·gig (fiz'gig'), ***n.*** a fishgig.

fizz, fiz (fiz), ***n.*** [echoic], 1. a hissing, sputtering sound. 2. a drink, as champagne, soda water, etc., that hisses and bubbles; effervescent drink. ***v.i.*** [FIZZED (fizd), FIZZING], to make a hissing or bubbling sound.

fiz·zle (fiz''l), ***v.i.*** [FIZZLED (-'ld), FIZZLING], [echoic], 1. to make a hissing or sputtering sound. 2. [Colloq.], to fail, especially after a successful beginning (often with *out*). ***n.*** 1. a hissing or sputtering sound. 2. [Colloq.], an attempt that ends in failure; fiasco.

fiz·zy (fiz'i), ***adj.*** [FIZZIER (-i-ẽr), FIZZIEST (-i-ist)], fizzing; bubbling; effervescent.

fjeld (fyeld), ***n.*** [Norw.; ON. *fiall*, *fjall*, a fell; cf. FELL (rocky hill)], a barren Scandinavian plateau.

fjord (fyôrd, fyōrd), ***n.*** a fiord.

Fl, in *chemistry*, fluorine.

Fl., 1. Flanders. 2. Flemish.

fl., 1. floor. 2. florin; florins. 3. *floruit*, [L.], (he or she) flourished. 4. flower. 5. fluid. 6. flute.

Fla., Florida.

flab·ber·gast (flab'ẽr-gast'), ***v.t.*** [18th-c. slang; prob. < *flabby* + *aghast*], [Colloq.], to make speechless with amazement; astonish. —***SYN.*** see **surprise.**

flab·bi·ly (flab'ə-li), ***adv.*** in a flabby manner.

flab·bi·ness (flab'i-nis), ***n.*** a flabby quality or state.

flab·by (flab'i), ***adj.*** [FLABBIER (-i-ẽr), FLABBIEST (-i-ist)], [var. of *flappy* < *flap*], 1. lacking firmness; limp and soft; flaccid: as, *flabby* muscles. 2. lacking force; weak.

fla·bel·late (flə-bel'āt), ***adj.*** [< *flabellum* + *-ate*], fan-shaped.

fla·bel·li·form (flə-bel'ə-fôrm'), ***adj.*** [< *flabellum* + *-form*], fan-shaped.

fla·bel·lum (flə-bel'əm), ***n.*** [*pl.* FLABELLA (-ə)], [L., a fan, dim. of *flabrum*, a breeze < *flare*, to blow], 1. a large fan carried by the Pope's attendants on ceremonial occasions. 2. in *botany & zoology*, a fan-shaped part or structure.

flac·cid (flak'sid), ***adj.*** [Fr. *flaccide*; L. *flaccidus* < *flaccus*, flabby], 1. hanging in loose folds or wrinkles; soft and limp; flabby: as, *flaccid* muscles. 2. lacking force; weak; feeble.

flac·cid·i·ty (flak-sid'ə-ti), ***n.*** the quality or state of being flaccid.

‡**fla·con** (flȧ'kōn'), ***n.*** [Fr.; see FLAGON], a small flask or bottle with a stopper, for holding perfume, etc.

flag (flag), ***n.*** [Late ME. *flagge*; prob. < *flag*, *v.i.* in sense "to flutter"; akin to Dan. *flag*, Sw. *flagg*, etc.], 1. a piece of cloth or bunting, often attached to a staff, with definite colors, patterns, or symbolic devices, used as a national or state symbol, or to indicate membership in an organization, to signal, etc.; banner; standard; ensign. 2. *pl.* *a)* the quills on the second joint of a bird's wing. *b)* the long feathers on the leg of a hawk, owl, etc. 3. the tail of a deer. 4. the bushy tail of certain dogs, as setters and some hounds. ***v.t.*** [FLAGGED (flagd), FLAGGING], 1. to decorate or mark with flags. 2. to signal with or as with a flag: as, he *flagged* the train. 3. to send (a message) by signaling.

dip the flag, to salute by lowering a flag briefly.

flag down, to flag (a train, etc.) as a signal to stop.

strike the (or **one's**) **flag,** 1. to lower the flag; hence, 2. to give up; surrender.

flag (flag), ***n.*** [ON. *flaga*, slab of stone, lit., flake; cf. FLAKE], 1. any hard stone split into flat pieces and used for paving; flagstone. 2. a piece of this stone. ***v.t.*** [FLAGGED (flagd), FLAGGING], to pave with flagstones.

flag (flag), ***n.*** [ME. *flagge*, *flegge*; prob. < or akin to *flag*, *v.i.* in sense "to flutter"; akin to D. *flag*, Dan. *flæg*], 1. any of several plants, especially an iris or a sweet flag, with sword-shaped leaves and purple, blue, yellow, or white flowers. 2. the flower or leaf of any of these plants.

flag (flag), ***v.i.*** [FLAGGED (flagd), FLAGGING], [16th c.; prob. var. of ME. *flacken*, to flutter, influenced by OFr. *flaquir*, to be flaccid & by echoism; for IE. base see FLAW], 1. to become limp; droop. 2. to lose strength; grow weak or tired: as, his enthusiasm *flagged*.

Flag Day, 1. June 14, anniversary of the day in 1777 when the United States flag was adopted. 2. [f- d-], in England, a day when people contribute to some special fund for charity and get small flags in receipt.

fla·gel·la (flə-jel'ə), ***n.*** alternative plural of **flagellum.**

flag·el·lant (flaj'ə-lənt, flə-jel'ənt), ***n.*** [L. *flagellans*, ppr. of *flagellare*; see FLAGELLATE], a person who whips; especially, one who whips himself or has himself whipped as a religious discipline or in abnormal eroticism. ***adj.*** engaging in flagellation.

flag·el·late (flaj'ə-lāt'), ***v.t.*** [FLAGELLATED (-id), FLAGELLATING], [< L. *flagellatus*, pp. of *flagellare*, to whip, scourge < *flagellum*, a whip, scourge], to whip; flog. ***adj.*** 1. having flagella. 2. shaped like a flagellum.

flag·el·lat·ed (flaj'ə-lāt'id), ***adj.*** flagellate.

flag·el·la·tion (flaj'ə-lā'shən), ***n.*** [ME.; L. *flagellatio*; see FLAGELLATE], a whipping or flogging, especially as religious discipline or in abnormal eroticism.

flag·el·la·tor (flaj'ə-lā'tẽr), ***n.*** a flagellant.

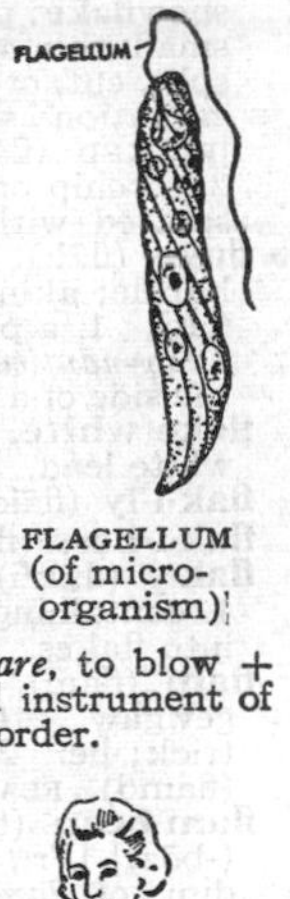

flag·el·la·to·ry (flaj'ə-lə-tôr'i, flaj'ə-lə-tō'ri), ***adj.*** having to do with flagellation.

fla·gel·li·form (flə-jel'i-fôrm'), ***adj.*** [< *flagellum* + *-form*], shaped like a whiplash or flagellum; long, slender, round, and tapering.

fla·gel·lum (flə-jel'əm), ***n.*** [*pl.* FLAGELLA (-ə), FLAGELLUMS (-əmz)], [L., a whip, dim. of *flagrum*, a scourge], 1. a whip. 2. in *biology*, a whiplike or taillike part serving as an organ of locomotion in bacteria, protozoa, and certain cells. 3. in *botany*, a threadlike shoot or runner.

FLAGELLUM (of micro-organism)

flag·eo·let (flaj'ə-let'), ***n.*** [Fr., dim. of OFr. *flageol*, *flajeol* (Pr. *flaujol*), a pipe, flute < LL. **flabeolum*, a flute < L. *flare*, to blow + ending of *flabellum*, a fan], a small wind instrument of the fipple flute family, similar to a recorder.

flag·ging (flag'iŋ), ***adj.*** [ppr. of *flag*, *v.i.*], weakening; drooping.

flag·ging (flag'iŋ), ***n.*** [< *flag* (flagstone)], 1. a pavement made of flagstones. 2. flagstones.

flag·gy (flag'i), ***adj.*** full of flags (the plants).

flag·gy (flag'i), ***adj.*** of or like flagstone.

fla·gi·tious (flə-jish'əs), ***adj.*** [L. *flagitiosus* < *flagitium*, shameful or disgraceful act < *flagitare*, to demand, demand fiercely], shamefully wicked; vile and scandalous; heinous.

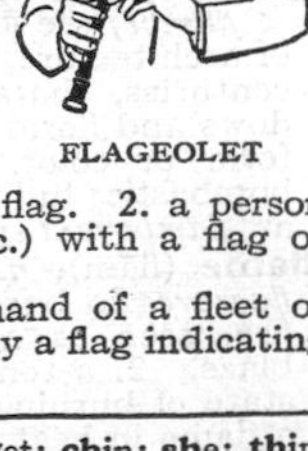

FLAGEOLET

flag·man (flag'mən), ***n.*** [*pl.* FLAGMEN (-mən)], 1. a person who carries a flag. 2. a person whose work is signaling (trains, etc.) with a flag or lantern, as at a railroad crossing.

flag officer, a naval officer in command of a fleet or squadron and hence entitled to display a flag indicating his rank or command.

flag of truce, a white flag shown to an enemy to indicate a desire for surrender or conference.
flag·on (flag′ən), *n.* [ME. *flakon;* OFr. *flacon, flascon;* It. *fiascone* < *fiasca;* see FLASK], 1. a container for liquids, usually having a handle, a narrow neck, a spout, and, sometimes, a lid. 2. the contents of such a container.
flag·pole (flag′pōl′), *n.* a pole on which a flag is raised and flown.
fla·grance (flā′grəns), *n.* flagrancy; notoriety; outrage.
fla·gran·cy (flā′grən-si), *n.* the quality or state of being flagrant.
fla·grant (flā′grənt), *adj.* [L. *flagrans,* ppr. of *flagrare,* to flame, blaze], glaringly bad; notorious; scandalous; outrageous.
SYN.—**flagrant** applies to anything that is so obviously bad or wrong as to be notorious (a *flagrant* violation of the law); **glaring** is used of something bad that is even more conspicuous so that it is immediately perceived (a *glaring* error in arithmetic); **gross** implies an even greater degree of badness or wrongness, so as to deserve censure (*gross* negligence); **rank,** in this connection, is used contemptuously to imply that no exaggeration is intended in the description (it was *rank* folly to send the letter). See also **outrageous.**
‡**fla·gran·te de·lic·to** (flə-gran′tē di-lik′tō), [L., lit., during the blazing of the crime], in the very act of committing the crime; red-handed.
flag·ship (flag′ship′), *n.* the ship that carries the commander of a fleet or squadron and displays his flag.
Flag·staff (flag′staf′, flag′stäf′), *n.* a city in central Arizona, site of the Lowell Observatory: pop., 18,000.
flag·staff (flag′staf′, flag′stäf′), *n.* a flagpole.
flag station, a railroad station at which trains stop only when signaled.
flag·stone (flag′stōn′), *n.* a large, flat paving stone.
flail (flāl), *n.* [ME. *fleil, flegl;* OFr. *flaiel* < L. *flagellum,* a whip, scourge], an implement consisting of a free-swinging stick tied to the end of another stick, used to thresh grain by hand. *v.t.* 1. to thresh with a flail. 2. to whip; beat; thrash.

FLAIL

flair (flâr), *n.* [ME.; OFr., odor < *flairer,* to emit an odor < LL. *flagrare* < L. *fragrare,* to emit an odor: orig. in sense of "keen sense of smell"], 1. keen natural discernment. 2. a natural talent or ability; aptitude; knack.
flak (flak), *n.* [< G. *Fl*iegerabwehr*k*anone, antiaircraft gun], antiaircraft fire.
flake (flāk), *n.* [ME. < ON. *flaki;* cf. Dan. *sneflage,* snowflake; prob. IE. base **plāg-,* **plăg-,* to beat], 1. a small, thin mass: as, a *flake* of snow. 2. a thin piece split, cut, or peeled from anything; chip. 3. a kind of carnation with single-colored stripes. *v.t.* & *v.i.* [FLAKED (flākt), FLAKING], 1. to form into flakes. 2. to chip or peel off in flakes. 3. to make or become spotted with flakes.
flake (flāk), *n.* [ME. *flake, fleke* < ON. *flaki, fleki,* hurdle; akin to MD. *vlāke;* IE. base **plāg-,* wide and flat], 1. a platform or rack for storing or drying food. 2. in *nautical usage,* an adjustable scaffold hung over the side of a ship for supporting men doing repair work.
flake white, a white coloring matter made of flakes of white lead.
flak·i·ly (flāk′ə-li), *adv.* in a flaky manner.
flak·i·ness (flāk′i-nis), *n.* a flaky quality or state.
flak·y (flāk′i), *adj.* [FLAKIER (-i-ẽr), FLAKIEST (-i-ist)], 1. containing or made up of flakes. 2. breaking easily into flakes.
flam (flam), *n.* [prob. contr. of obs. *flamfew,* a trifle, gewgaw < OFr. *fanfelue,* a bubble], 1. a deceptive trick; lie. 2. blarney; humbug. *v.t.* & *v.i.* [FLAMMED (flamd), FLAMMING], to deceive by lying or flattery.
flam·beau (flam′bō), *n.* [*pl.* FLAMBEAUX, FLAMBEAUS (-bōz)], [Fr., dim. of *flambe;* OFr. *flamble* < L. *flammula,* dim. of *flamma,* a flame], 1. a lighted torch. 2. a large, ornamental candlestick.
flam·boy·ance (flam-boi′əns), *n.* the quality or state of being flamboyant.
flam·boy·an·cy (flam-boi′ən-si), *n.* flamboyance.
flam·boy·ant (flam-boi′ənt), *adj.* [Fr., ppr. of *flamboyer* < *flambe;* see FLAMBEAU], 1. designating or of a kind of architecture, as French Gothic of the 15th and 16th centuries, characterized by flamelike tracery of windows and florid decoration. 2. flamelike or brilliant in form or color. 3. ornate; too showy. 4. flowery; bombastic; full of exaggerations and figures of speech: as, *flamboyant* speech.
flame (flām), *n.* [ME. & OFr. *flamme;* L. *flamma* < *flagrare,* to burn], 1. the burning gas or vapor of a fire, seen as a shimmering light of various colors; blaze. 2. a tongue of light rising from a fire. 3. the state of burning with a blaze of light. 4. a thing like a flame in heat, brilliance, etc. 5. an intense emotion; strong passion. 6. [Slang], a sweetheart. *v.i.* [FLAMED (flāmd), FLAMING], [ME. *flammen;* OFr. *flamer* < the *n.*], 1. to burn with a blaze of light; burst into flame. 2. to act or be like a flame. 3. to light up with color as if blazing; grow red or hot: as, her face *flamed* with anger 4. to show intense emotion; become very excited. *v.t.* 1. to burn or heat with flame. 2. [Poetic], to arouse (emotions); inflame. —*SYN.* see **blaze.**
flame up (or **out**), to burst out in or as in flames.
fla·men (flā′men), *n.* [*pl.* FLAMENS (-menz), FLAMINES (flam′ə-nēz′)], [L.], in ancient Rome, a priest in the service of one particular god.
fla·men·co (flä-meŋ′kō), *n.* [Sp., Flemish], 1. the Spanish gypsy style of dance (characterized by stamping, clapping, etc.) or music (typically very emotional and mournful). 2. a song or dance in this style.
flame thrower, [transl. of G. *flammenwerfer*], a weapon for shooting a stream of flaming liquid, as oil, at enemy troops and positions.
flam·ing (flām′iŋ), *adj.* 1. burning with flames; blazing. 2. like a flame in brilliance or heat. 3. intensely emotional; ardent; passionate. 4. startling; flagrant.
fla·min·go (flə-miŋ′gō), *n.* [*pl.* FLAMINGOS, FLAMINGOES (-gōz)], [Port. *flamingo, flamengo;* Sp. *flamenco,* a flamingo, lit., Fleming; associated with *flama,* flame, because of the color], any of a group of tropical wading birds with long legs, webbed feet, long necks, downward-curving beaks, and bright pink or red feathers.
flam·ma·ble (flam′ə-b′l), *adj.* [L. *flammare,* to set on fire, burn; + *-able*], easily set on fire; that will burn readily or quickly; inflammable.
flam·y (flām′i), *adj.* of or like flame; flaming.
flan (flan; Fr. flän), *n.* [Fr.; OFr. *flaon* (whence ME. *flawn,* flan); ML. *flado, fladonis;* OHG. *flado,* flat cake; akin to ME. *flathe;* for IE. base see FLAT], 1. a tart filled with cheese, custard, fruit, etc. 2. a piece of shaped metal ready to be made into a coin by the stamp of a die; blank.
Flan·ders (flan′dẽrz), *n.* a former country in Europe, on the coast of the North Sea: now the Belgian provinces of East Flanders and West Flanders, and part of northern France: abbreviated **Fl.**

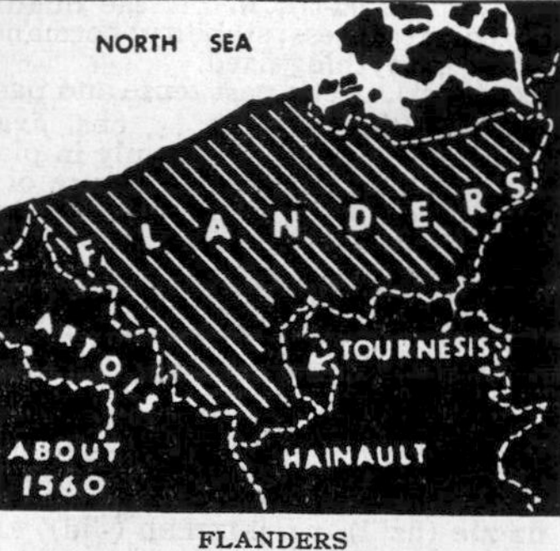

FLANDERS

‡**flâ·ne·rie** (flä′n′-rē′), *n.* [Fr. < *flâner,* to stroll, waste time, lounge in bed < Early Mod. Fr. *flaine,* bed linen, pillowcase; LL. **fluxina* < L. *fluxus,* a flowing (in LL., folds, drapery); see FLUX], idle walking; loafing.
‡**flâ·neur** (flä′nẽr′), *n.* [Fr.; see FLÂNERIE], a person who wanders about idly; loafer; trifler.
flange (flanj), *n.* [prob. < OFr. *flangir,* to turn], 1. a projecting rim or collar on a wheel, pipe, rail, etc., to hold it in place, give it strength, guide it, or attach it to something else. 2. a tool for making flanges. *v.t.* [FLANGED (flanjd), FLANGING], to put a flange on.

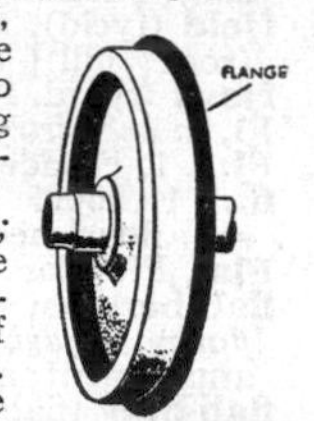

FLANGE

flank (flaŋk), *n.* [ME. *flanke;* OFr. *flanc;* OHG. *hlanka,* a hip, flank], 1. the fleshy side of a person or animal between the ribs and the hip. 2. a cut of beef from this part: see **beef,** illus. 3. loosely, the side of the upper part of the human thigh. 4. the side of anything. 5. in *military science,* *a)* the right or left side of a formation or force. *b)* the territory surrounding either side. *c)* either of the sides of the projecting part of a bastion. *adj.* of or having to do with the flank. *v.t.* 1. to be at the side of. 2. in *military science,* *a)* to protect the side of (a friendly unit). *b)* to attack the side of (an enemy unit). *c)* to pass around the side of (an enemy unit). *v.i.* to be in a flanking position (with *on* or *upon*).
flank·er (flaŋ′kẽr), *n.* in *military science,* 1. a fortified position at either flank for protection or attack. 2. any of several men sent out to protect the flanks of a marching column.
flan·nel (flan′'l), *n.* [earlier *flannen;* prob. < W. *gwlanen* < *gwlan,* wool], 1. a lightweight, loosely woven woolen cloth. 2. *pl.* clothes, especially trousers, made of this cloth. 3. flannelette. 4. [Colloq.], *pl.* heavy woolen underwear. *v.t.* [FLANNELED or FLANNELLED (-'ld), FLANNELING or FLANNELLING], 1. to wrap or clothe in flannel. 2. to rub with flannel.
flan·nel·ette, flan·nel·et (flan′'l-et′), *n.* a soft cotton cloth resembling flannel.
flan·nel·mouth (flan′'l-mouth′), *n.* [prob. from its soft mouth], the catfish found in the Great Lakes.

flap (flap), *n.* [ME. *flap, flappe,* a stroke, blow, loose and flexible part of a garment; < the *v.;* cf. D. *flap,* a stroke, blow], 1. anything flat and broad that hangs loose and is attached at one end: as, the *flap* of a pocket. 2. the movement of such a part: as, the *flap* of an awning. 3. the sound made by such a movement. 4. a slap. 5. in *aeronautics,* a movable hinged rear section of an airfoil; especially, a section hinged to the trailing edge of a wing between the aileron and the fuselage, usually used to lessen landing speed. 6. in *surgery,* a section of flesh partly detached from the surrounding flesh, as for grafting. *v.t.* [FLAPPED (flapt), FLAPPING], [ME. *flappen;* cf. D. *flappen;* prob. echoic], 1. to strike with something flat and broad; slap. 2. to move back and forth or up and down as in beating the air, usually with some noise: as, the bird *flapped* its wings. *v.i.* 1. to be flapping; flutter. 2. to fly by flapping the wings. 3. to hang down as a flap.

flap·doo·dle (flap'dōō'd'l), *n.* [arbitrary formation], [Colloq.], nonsense; foolish talk.

flap·drag·on (flap'drag'ən), *n.* [prob. after dial. *snapdragon*], an old game played by snatching raisins or other sweets from burning brandy and eating them.

flap·jack (flap'jak'), *n.* [see FLAP, *v.* & JACK-], a large pancake or griddlecake.

flap·per (flap'ẽr), *n.* 1. a person or thing that flaps; especially, *a)* a flap. *b)* a broad fin or flipper. *c)* something broad and flat for striking. 2. a young wild duck, partridge, etc. just learning to fly; hence, 3. [Colloq.], in the 1920's, a young girl considered bold and unconventional in actions and dress.

flare (flâr), *v.i.* [FLARED (flârd), FLARING], [earlier also *flear;* orig. sense "to flutter"; prob. thieves' slang borrowing of D. *vlederen* (G. *flattern*), to flutter, or the like], 1. to blaze up brightly and unsteadily. 2. to signal by flares. 3. to curve or spread outward, as the sides of a ship; bulge. *v.t.* 1. to make flare. 2. to signal with flares. *n.* 1. a bright, unsteady blaze of light lasting only a little while; outburst of flame. 2. a dazzling light lasting only a little while, used as a signal, to illuminate a landing field, etc. 3. a sudden, brief outburst, as of emotion or sound. 4. a curving outward, as of a skirt. 5. a part that curves or spreads outward. 6. in *photography,* a foggy spot on film, caused by a reflection of light from the lens. —*SYN.* see **blaze.**

flare up (or **out**), 1. to burst into flame. 2. to become suddenly angry, excited, violent, etc.

flare·back (flâr'bak'), *n.* a flame shooting out backward or otherwise abnormally from a furnace, a cannon, etc.

flare-up (flâr'up'), *n.* 1. a sudden outburst of flame. 2. a sudden, brief outburst of emotion, violence, etc.

flar·ing (flâr'iŋ), *adj.* [ppr. of *flare*], 1. blazing brightly and unsteadily for a little while. 2. gaudy; lurid. 3. curving or spreading outward.

flash (flash), *v.i.* [orig., to rush along with a splashing sound; splash; dash; ME. *flasken, flaschen,* to splash; prob. echoic], 1. to send out a sudden, brief blaze or light. 2. to be brilliant; sparkle; gleam: as, her eyes *flashed* with anger. 3. to come, move, or pass swiftly and suddenly; be seen or realized for an instant like a flash of light: as, the automobile *flashed* by, an idea *flashed* through his mind. *v.t.* 1. to send out (light, etc.) in sudden, brief spurts; cause to flash. 2. to send (news, messages, etc.) swiftly or suddenly. 3. to cover (a roof, etc.) with material for weatherproofing. 4. [Colloq.], to show briefly or ostentatiously: as, he *flashed* a roll of money. 5. in *glassmaking, a)* to make (glass) into sheets. *b)* to put (a colored film of glass) on other glass. *c)* to coat with a colored film of glass. *n.* 1. a sudden, brief light. 2. a brief time; moment. 3. a sudden, brief display of thought, understanding, feeling, etc.: as, a *flash* of wit. 4. a brief message or item of news sent by telegraph or radio. 5. a gaudy display; showiness. 6. the language of thieves, sharpers, etc. 7. *a)* a sudden raising of the water in a channel to help boats over a dam, etc. *b)* the mechanism for this. 8. a preparation containing burnt sugar, used for coloring liquors. 9. anything that flashes or produces a flash. *adj.* 1. flashy. 2. of thieves, sharpers, etc.

flash in the pan, 1. an ineffectual flash of the priming in the pan of a flintlock musket, which fails to explode the charge. 2. a sudden, apparently brilliant effort that fails. 3. a person who fails after such an effort.

SYN.—**flash** implies a sudden, brief, brilliant light; **glance** refers to a darting light, especially one that is reflected from a surface at an angle; **gleam** suggests a steady, narrow ray of light shining through a background of relative darkness; **sparkle** implies a number of brief, bright, intermittent flashes; **glitter** implies the reflection of such bright, intermittent flashes; **glisten** suggests the reflection of a lustrous light, as from a wet surface; **shimmer** refers to a soft, tremulous reflection of light, as from a slightly disturbed body of water.

flash-back (flash'bak'), *n.* 1. an interruption in the continuity of a story, play, etc. by the narration or portrayal of some earlier episode. 2. such an episode.

flash·board (flash'bôrd', flash'bōrd'), *n.* an extra board or boards placed alongside a dam to increase the depth or force of the stream.

flash bulb, an electric light bulb giving a brief, dazzling light, for taking photographs indoors or at night.

flash burn, injury or destruction of body tissue caused by exposure to a flash or sudden release of intense radiant heat, especially the heat of a nuclear explosion.

flash·er (flash'ẽr), *n.* a person or thing that flashes; specifically, *a)* a device for causing lights to go on and off intermittently by closing and opening an electric circuit. *b)* a beacon, buoy, etc. whose light goes on and off intermittently.

flash flood, a sudden, violent flood, as after a heavy rain.

flash gun, in *photography,* a synchronized device that simultaneously sets off a flash bulb and works the camera shutter.

flash·i·ly (flash'ə-li), *adv.* in a flashy manner.

flash·i·ness (flash'i-nis), *n.* the quality of being flashy.

flash·ing (flash'iŋ), *n.* 1. the action of a person or thing that flashes. 2. the sudden raising of water in a channel. 3. sheets of metal or other material used to weatherproof joints, edges, etc., especially of a roof.

flash·light (flash'līt'), *n.* 1. a light that shines in flashes, used for signaling, as in lighthouses, airplane beacons, etc. 2. a portable electric light, usually operated by a small storage battery. 3. a brief, dazzling light for taking photographs at night or indoors.

flash point, the lowest temperature at which the vapor of a volatile oil will ignite with a flash.

flash·y (flash'i), *adj.* [FLASHIER (-i-ẽr), FLASHIEST (-i-ist)], 1. flashing; dazzling or bright for a little while. 2. gaudy; showy; tawdry. —*SYN.* see **gaudy.**

flask (flask, fläsk), *n.* [Fr. *flasque;* OFr. *flasque, flasche;* ML. *flasca, flasco* (whence AS. *flasce,* It. *fiasca*), wine bottle, orig., straw jacket for bottle; prob. of Gmc. origin], 1. any small, bottle-shaped container with a narrow neck, used in laboratories, etc. 2. a small, flattened container for liquor, etc., to be carried in the pocket. 3. the frame for a mold of sand in a foundry.

flask·et (flas'kit, fläs'kit), *n.* [OFr. *flasquet,* dim. of *flasque;* see FLASK], 1. a small flask. 2. [Archaic], a long, shallow basket.

flat (flat), *adj.* [FLATTER (-ẽr), FLATTEST (-ist)], [ME. < ON. *flatr;* akin to OHG. *flaz;* IE. base **plet-,* **plēt-,* etc., wide and level, as also in AS. *flet,* floor; cf. next entry], 1. having a smooth, level surface; having little or no depression or elevation. 2. lying extended or spread out; at full length. 3. having little depth or thickness; broad, even, and thin. 4. absolute; positive: as, a *flat* denial. 5. without variation; not fluctuating: as, a *flat* rate. 6. without much business activity: as, a *flat* market. 7. having little or no sparkle or taste; insipid: as, a *flat* drink. 8. having little or no interest; monotonous; dull. 9. not clear or full; blurred: as, a *flat* sound. 10. emptied of air: as, a *flat* tire. 11. [Colloq.], completely without money; penniless. 12. in *art, a)* designating figures lacking relief or perspective. *b)* uniform in tint. *c)* without gloss. 13. in *grammar, a)* not having the sign *to:* said of an infinitive (e.g., *come* in *make him come home*). *b)* not having an inflectional ending: said of a noun used as an adjective (e.g., *orange* in *orange juice*), or of an adverb not having an adverbial ending (e.g., *fast* in *drive fast*). 14. in *music, a)* below the true pitch. *b)* lower in pitch by a half note: as, *D-flat.* 15. in *phonetics, a)* designating or of a vowel sounded with the tongue in a relatively level position (e.g., *a* in *can*). *b)* designating or of a voiced consonant. *adv.* 1. flatly (in various senses). 2. in a prone or supine position: as, he fell *flat.* 3. exactly; precisely: as, he ran the 100-yard dash in ten seconds *flat.* 4. in *finance,* with no interest. 5. in *music,* below the true pitch. *n.* 1. a flat surface or part: as, the *flat* of the hand, of a sword, etc. 2. an expanse of level land. 3. a low-lying marsh. 4. a shallow; shoal. 5. any of various flat things; specifically, *a)* a shallow box or container. *b)* a flat-bottomed boat. *c)* a flatcar. *d)* a piece of theatrical scenery on a flat frame. *e)* a deflated tire. *f) pl.* flat-heeled shoes. 6. in *music, a)* a note or tone one half step below another. *b)* the symbol (♭) indicating such a note: opposed to *sharp.* *v.t.* & *v.i.* [FLATTED (-id), FLATTING], to make or become flat. —*SYN.* see **insipid, level.**

fall flat, to fail in desired effect; arouse no response.

flat (flat), *n.* [altered < Scot. dial. *flet* (ME. & AS. *flet*), a floor (of a dwelling); see prec. entry], an apartment or suite of rooms on one floor of a building.

flat·boat (flat'bōt'), *n.* a flat-bottomed boat for carrying freight in shallow waters or on rivers.

flat-bot·tomed (flat'bot'əmd), *adj.* having a flat bottom: said especially of boats.

flat·car (flat'kär'), *n.* a railroad car without sides or a roof, for carrying some kinds of freight.

flat·fish (flat'fish'), *n.* [*pl.* FLATFISH, FLATFISHES (-iz); see FISH], a fish with a flat body and both eyes on the uppermost side, as the flounder, halibut, sole, etc.

flat·foot (flat′foot′), *n.* 1. a condition in which the instep arch of the foot has been flattened. 2. [Slang], a policeman: so called from the notion that a policeman's feet are flattened by walking his beat.

flat foot, a foot having a flattened instep arch.

flat-foot·ed (flat′foot′id), *adj.* 1. having feet with flattened instep arches; having flatfoot. 2. designating a manner of walking, with the toes pointed outward, seen in people with flatfoot. 3. [Colloq.], downright and firm; plain and uncompromising.
  catch flat-footed, [Colloq.], 1. to catch unprepared to escape; take by surprise. 2. to catch in the act of committing some offense.

Flat·head (flat′hed′), *n.* 1. [erroneously so named by confusion with other tribes (such as the Chinooks) which practiced head-flattening], a member of a tribe of American Indians who lived in northwestern Montana. 2. a Chinook Indian. 3. a lake in northwestern Montana: length, 30 mi.; width, 15 mi.

flat·i·ron (flat′ī′ẽrn), *n.* a device which, when heated, is used for pressing clothes or cloth: it consists of a handle and a heavy, shaped piece of iron or steel that is flat and smooth on the undersurface.

flat knot, a reef knot: see **knot,** illus.

flat·ling (flat′liŋ), *adv.* [ME.; see FLAT & -LING], [Archaic], 1. flatly; at full length. 2. with the flat side, as of a sword. *adj.* [Archaic], struck with the flat side: as, a *flatling* blow.

flat·lings (flat′liŋz), *adv.* [Obs.], flatling.

flat·long (flat′lôŋ), *adv.* [Obs.], flatling.

flat silver, silver knives, forks, spoons, etc., as distinguished from silver trays, teapots, etc.

flat·ten (flat′'n), *v.t.* 1. to make flat or flatter. 2. to knock down; make prostrate. *v.i.* 1. to become flat or flatter. 2. to become prostrate.
  flatten out, 1. to make or become flat or flatter by spreading out. 2. in *aeronautics, a*) to return (an airplane) to a horizontal position after diving or climbing. *b*) to become horizontal; level off.

flat·ter (flat′ẽr), *v.t.* [ME. *flateren;* prob. < OFr. *flater,* to smooth, touch gently], 1. to praise too much, untruly, or insincerely. 2. to try to ingratiate oneself, please, or get the favor of, by praise and attention. 3. to make seem more attractive than is so: as, this photographer *flatters* his subjects. 4. to make feel pleased or honored; gratify the vanity of. 5. to please (the eye, ear, etc.). *v.i.* to use flattery.
  flatter oneself, to be pleased with the idea or belief (*that*); delude oneself into thinking (*that*): as, don't *flatter* yourself that he will forgive you.

flat·ter (flat′ẽr), *n.* 1. a person who flattens something. 2. a die plate for drawing flat strips. 3. a smith's forging tool with a broad, flat face.

flat·ter·y (flat′ẽr-i), *n.* [*pl.* FLATTERIES (-iz)], [ME. & OFr. *flaterie* (Fr. *flatterie*) < *flater*], 1. the act of flattering. 2. excessive, untrue, or insincere praise; exaggerated compliment or attention; blandishment.

flat·ting (flat′iŋ), *n.* the act or process of making flat; specifically, *a*) the rolling out of sheet metal. *b*) the application of paint so as to dry without gloss.

flat tire, 1. a tire from which all or most of the air has escaped. 2. [Slang], a boring, uninteresting person.

flat·tish (flat′ish), *adj.* somewhat flat.

flat·top, flat-top (flat′top′), *n.* [Slang], an aircraft carrier.

flat·u·lence (flach′ə-ləns, flach′yoo-ləns), *n.* [Fr. < Mod. L. *flatulentus;* see FLATULENT], 1. gas in the stomach or intestines. 2. windiness or emptiness of speech; vanity; pomposity.

flat·u·len·cy (flach′ə-lən-si, flach′yoo-lən-si), *n.* flatulence.

flat·u·lent (flach′ə-lənt, flach′yoo-lənt), *adj.* [Fr.; Mod. L. *flatulentus* < L. *flatus;* see FLATUS], 1. of or having gas in the stomach or intestines. 2. producing gas in the stomach or intestines, as certain foods. 3. windy or empty in speech; vain; pompous; pretentious.

fla·tus (flā′təs), *n.* [*pl.* FLATUSES (-iz)], [L. < *flare,* to blow; for IE. base see BLADDER], 1. gas in the stomach or intestines. 2. a breath or puff of wind.

flat·ware (flat′wâr′), *n.* flat table utensils, as knives, forks, and spoons, or plates, platters, etc.

flat·ways (flat′wāz′), *adv.* with the flat side foremost, uppermost, or in contact: opposed to *edgeways.*

flat·wise (flat′wīz′), *adv.* flatways.

flat·work (flat′wũrk′), *n.* laundered articles, as sheets, napkins, and other flat pieces, that can be pressed quickly in a mangle.

flat·worm (flat′wũrm′), *n.* any of a large group of worms with a flattened, unsegmented body, as the liver fluke and the tapeworm; any platyhelminth or planarian: many flatworms are parasitic.

Flau·bert, Gus·tave (güs′tàv′ flō′bâr′), 1821–1880; French novelist.

flaunt (flônt), *v.i.* [15th c. & 16th c.; prob. < dial.; cf. Eng. dial. *flant,* to strut coquettishly, akin to Norw. *flanta* (Dan. *flane*), to coquet; ult. source prob. ON., either directly or via Anglo-Fr.], 1. to make a gaudy, ostentatious, conspicuous, impudent, or defiant display: as, brazen women *flaunt* through the town. 2. to flutter or wave freely. *v.t.* to show off proudly, defiantly, or impudently: as, he *flaunts* his guilt. *n.* a flaunting. —*SYN.* see **show.**

flaunt·y (flônt′i), *adj.* [Rare], flaunting; showy.

flau·tist (flô′tist), *n.* [It. *flautista;* see FLUTE], a person who plays the flute: also **flutist.**

fla·ves·cent (flə-ves′'nt), *adj.* [L. *flavescens,* ppr. of *flavescere,* to become yellow < *flavus,* yellow], turning a pale yellow; yellowish.

fla·vin (flā′vin, flav′in), *n.* [< L. *flavus,* yellow], 1. a complex heterocyclic ketone, $C_{10}H_6N_4O_2$. 2. any of a group of yellow pigments occurring in certain plant and animal products or prepared by synthesis; specifically, riboflavin; lactoflavin. 3. quercetin.

fla·vine (flā′vēn, flav′in), *n.* flavin.

fla·vone (flā′vōn, flə-vōn′, flav′ōn), *n.* [< L. *flavus,* yellow; + *-one*], 1. a colorless crystalline compound, $C_{15}H_{10}O_2$, obtained from certain plants or prepared synthetically: it forms a base for some yellow dyes. 2. any derivative of this compound.

fla·vo·pro·te·in (flā′vō-prō′tē-in, flā′vō-prō′tēn), *n.* any of a group of proteins linked chemically with flavins, especially one that yields riboflavin upon hydrolysis.

fla·vo·pur·pu·rin (flā′vō-pũr′pẽr-in), *n.* [< L. *flavus,* yellow; + *purpurin*], a yellowish, crystalline chemical compound, $C_{14}H_8O_5$, used in making dyes.

fla·vor (flā′vẽr), *n.* [ME.; OFr. *flaor, fleur;* prob. < L. *flatus* (see FLATUS) + *foetor,* foul smell; Eng. *-v-* by analogy with *savor*], 1. an odor; smell; aroma. 2. that quality of a substance which gives it a characteristic taste. 3. any substance added to a food to give it a particular taste; flavoring. 4. the characteristic quality of something; distinctive nature: as, the *flavor* of adventure. *v.t.* to give flavor to.

fla·vor·ing (flā′vẽr-iŋ), *n.* an essence, extract, etc. added to a food or drink to give it a certain taste.

fla·vor·ous (flā′vẽr-əs), *adj.* full of flavor; having a pleasant flavor.

fla·vor·y (flā′vẽr-i), *adj.* flavorous.

fla·vour (flā′vẽr), *n. & v.t.* flavor: British spelling.

flaw (flô), *n.* [ME. *flaw(e), flay;* prob. < ON. *flaga,* slab, *fla,* break in a cliff; IE. base **plāg-,* broad and wide; cf. FLAKE (hurdle)], 1. a crack; broken or faulty place; blemish: as, a *flaw* in a diamond. 2. a defect; fault; error: as, a *flaw* in a legal document, in a person's reasoning, etc. *v.t. & v.i.* to make or become faulty. —*SYN.* see **defect.**

flaw (flô), *n.* [prob. < ON. *flaga,* sudden onset, or cognate D. *vlage;* cf. Dan. *flage;* Sw. *flaga,* sudden gust; IE. base **plāq-,* **plāg-,* etc., to strike, beat, as also in L. *plangere,* to beat (the breast); cf. PLANGENT], a sudden, brief gust of wind, often with rain or snow; squall.

flaw·less (flô′lis), *adj.* having no flaw; perfect.

flax (flaks), *n.* [ME. *flax, flex;* AS. *fleax;* akin to G. *flachs;* IE. base **plek-,* to plait, interweave, seen also in L. *plectere* (cf. PLAIT)], 1. any of several slender, erect plants with delicate blue flowers and narrow leaves: the seeds are used to make linseed oil, and the fibers of the stem are spun into linen thread. 2. the threadlike fibers of these plants, ready for spinning. 3. any of a number of flaxlike plants.

flax·en (flak′s'n), *adj.* 1. of or made of flax. 2. like flax in color; pale-yellow; straw-colored.

flax·seed (flaks′sēd′, flak′sēd′), *n.* the seed of the flax; linseed: it is used in medicine and for making linseed oil.

flax·y (flak′si), *adj.* of or like flax.

flay (flā), *v.t.* [ME. *flan, flean, flagen;* AS. *flean;* akin to MD. *vlaen;* IE. base **plek-,* etc., to tear off; cf. FLESH], 1. to strip off the skin or hide of, as by whipping. 2. to criticize or scold mercilessly. 3. to rob; pillage; fleece.

F.L.B., Federal Land Bank.

flea (flē), *n.* [ME. *fle, flee;* AS. *fleah;* akin to G. *floh;* same Gmc. base as *flee*], any of several small, wingless, jumping insects that are parasitic and bloodsucking.
  flea in one's ear, a sharp, stinging rebuke, rebuff, or hint.

FLEA (1/8 in. long)

flea·bane (flē′bān′), *n.* any of several plants of the composite family that are supposed to drive away fleas.

flea·bite (flē′bīt′), *n.* 1. the bite of a flea. 2. the red spot on the skin caused by the bite of a flea. 3. a minor pain or trifling inconvenience.

flea-bit·ten (flē′bit′'n), *adj.* 1. bitten by a flea or fleas. 2. infested with fleas. 3. wretched; decrepit. 4. light-colored with reddish-brown spots: said of horses.

fleam (flēm), *n.* [OFr. *flieme* < LL. **fleutomum* for *flebotomus, phlebotomus;* see PHLEBOTOMY], a lancet, or surgical knife, especially one used for opening veins: also called *phlebotome.*

flea·wort (flē′wũrt′), *n.* 1. a European aromatic herb with rough leaves and yellow flowers. 2. a plantain whose seeds, which more or less resemble fleas, are used as a laxative.

flèche (flāsh; Fr. flesh), *n.* [Fr., lit., an arrow; prob. < MD. *vleke*, an arrow; akin to AS. *flacor*, flying (of arrows); for IE. base, cf. FLAW (gust)], 1. a projecting, arrow-shaped outwork in a fortification. 2. a slender spire, especially one over the intersection of the nave and the transept in some Gothic churches.

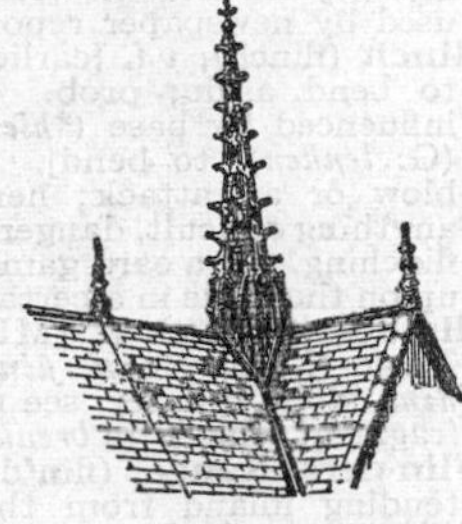
FLÈCHE

fleck (flek), *n.* [ON. *flekkr;* akin to G. *fleck;* prob. IE. base **plek-*, to tear off], 1. a spot or small patch of color, etc.; speck: as, *flecks* of sunlight. 2. a small piece; particle; flake. *v.t.* [ME. *flecken, flekken* < the *n.* or < ON. *flekka* < *flekkr*], to cover or sprinkle with flecks; spot; speckle.

flec·tion (flek′shən), *n.* [L. *flexio* < pp. of *flectere*, to bend], 1. a bending; flexing. 2. a bent part or bend. 3. in *grammar*, inflection. Also spelled **flexion.**

flec·tion·al (flek′shən-'l), *adj.* of or like flection: also spelled **flexional.**

fled (fled), past tense and past participle of **flee.**

fledge (flej), *v.i.* [FLEDGED (flejd), FLEDGING], [Early Mod. Eng. < ME. *flegge, adj.*, fit to fly, SE. Midland form < AS. (*un*)*flycge*, (un)fledged; AS. *-flycge* is akin to G. *flügge* (< LG.); Gmc. base as in FLY], to grow the feathers necessary for flying. *v.t.* 1. to rear (a young bird) until it is able to fly. 2. to supply or cover (an arrow, etc.) with feathers.

fledg·ling, fledge·ling (flej′liŋ), *n.* [see FLEDGE & -LING], 1. a young bird just fledged. 2. a young, inexperienced person.

flee (flē), *v.i.* [FLED (fled), FLEEING], [ME. *fleen;* AS. *fleon;* akin to G. *fliehen;* cf. FLEA], 1. to run away or escape from danger, pursuit, unpleasantness, etc. 2. to pass away quickly and suddenly; disappear; vanish: as, night had *fled.* 3. to move rapidly; go swiftly. *v.t.* to run away or try to escape from; avoid; shun.

fleece (flēs), *n.* [ME. *flees;* AS. *fleos, flies;* akin to G. *flies(s);* IE. base **pleus-*, to pluck out, etc., seen also in L. *pluma*, a feather, down (< **plus-mā*); cf. PLUME], 1. the wool covering a sheep or similar animal. 2. the amount of wool cut from a sheep in one shearing. 3. a covering like a sheep's: as, a *fleece* of hair. 4. a soft, warm, napped fabric, used for linings, etc. *v.t.* [FLEECED (flēst), FLEECING], 1. to shear the fleece from (sheep, etc.). 2. to steal from by fraud; cheat; swindle.

fleec·i·ness (flēs′i-nis), *n.* the quality of being fleecy.

fleec·y (flēs′i), *adj.* [FLEECIER (-i-ẽr), FLEECIEST (-i-ist)], 1. made of or covered with fleece. 2. like a fleece; soft and light: as, *fleecy* snow.

fleer (flêr), *v.i.* [ME. *flerien;* prob. < ON.; cf. Dan. dial., Norw. *flire*, to snicker, laugh; prob. IE. base *(*s*)*plei-*, to split, in sense "to make a gap with the lips"], to jeer; laugh derisively; sneer. *v.t.* to laugh derisively at. *n.* a mocking or derisive grimace, laugh, or remark; gibe.

fle·er (flē′ẽr), *n.* [Rare], a person who flees.

fleet (flēt), *n.* [ME. *flete;* AS. *fleot* < *fleotan*, to float; see FLEET, *v.*], 1. *a*) a number of warships acting together and under one command, usually in a definite area of operation. *b*) the entire naval force of a country; navy. 2. any group of ships, trucks, busses, airplanes, etc. acting together or under one control. 3. a set of fishing nets, pots, etc. worked together.

fleet (flēt), *v.i.* [ME. *fleten;* AS. *fleotan;* akin to G. *fliessen;* IE. **pleu-d* < base **pleu-*, to flow, run, as also in L. *pluere*, to rain], 1. originally, to float; swim. 2. to move swiftly; flit; fly. 3. [Archaic], to pass away swiftly; disappear. 4. in *nautical usage*, to change position. *v.t.* 1. [Rare], to pass away (time). 2. in *nautical usage*, to cause to change position. *adj.* 1. swift; rapid. 2. [Poetic], evanescent. —*SYN.* see **fast.**

fleet (flēt), *n.* [ME. *flete;* AS. *fleot;* akin to D. *vliet;* base as in FLEET, *v.*], [Obs. or Dial.], a small inlet; creek.
the Fleet, 1. a former small creek in London, now a covered sewer. 2. Fleet Prison, a debtor's prison which stood near this creek.

fleet·ing (flēt′iŋ), *adj.* [AS. *fleotende*, floating; see FLEET, *v.*], passing swiftly; not lasting. —*SYN.* see **transient.**

Fleet Street (flēt), 1. an old street in London, where many newspaper and printing offices are now located; hence, 2. the London press.

Flem·ing (flem′iŋ), *n.* 1. a native of Flanders. 2. a Belgian who speaks Flemish.

Fleming, Sir **Alexander,** 1881–1955; British bacteriologist; one of the discoverers of penicillin; received Nobel prize in medicine, 1945.

Flem·ish (flem′ish), *adj.* of Flanders, the Flemings, or their language. *n.* the Low German language of the Flemings. Abbreviated **Fl., Flem.**
the Flemish, the people of Flanders.

Flemish knot, a figure-of-eight knot: see **knot,** illus.

flench (flench), *v.t.* to flense.

flense (flens), *v.t.* [FLENSED (flenst), FLENSING], [< D. *vlenzen* or Dan. *flense*], to cut blubber or skin from (a whale, seal, etc.).

flesh (flesh), *n.* [ME. *flesch;* AS. *flæsc;* akin to G. *fleisch;* IE. base **plek-*, etc., to tear off; cf. FLAY], 1. the soft substance of the body (of a person or animal) between the skin and the bones; especially, the muscular tissue. 2. the pulpy or edible part of fruits and vegetables. 3. the flesh of any animal as food; meat; especially, meat other than fish or fowl. 4. the human body, as distinguished from the soul: as, more than *flesh* can stand. 5. the nature of the human body; especially, the sensual nature. 6. all human beings; mankind. 7. all living beings: as, the way of all *flesh.* 8. the surface of the human body: as, Renoir's technique in painting *flesh.* 9. the usual color of a white person's skin; yellowish pink. *v.t.* 1. to feed (animals) with flesh so as to incite them to hunt or kill. 2. to prepare for or incite to bloodshed, etc. by a foretaste. 3. to harden; inure. 4. to plunge (a weapon) into flesh. 5. to clothe with flesh. 6. to put flesh on; fatten. 7. to remove flesh from (a hide). *v.i.* [Colloq.], to grow fat.
flesh and blood, the human body, especially as subject to its natural limitations.
in the flesh, 1. alive. 2. actually present; in person.
one's (own) flesh and blood, a person or persons closely related to one by birth.

flesh-col·ored (flesh′kul′ẽrd), *adj.* having the color of the surface of a white person's body; yellowish-pink.

flesh-eat·ing (flesh′ēt′iŋ), *adj.* habitually eating flesh; carnivorous.

flesh fly, [ME. *fleschflie*], any of a number of flies that lay their eggs on flesh: also called *blowfly.*

flesh·i·ness (flesh′i-nis), *n.* a fleshy quality or state.

flesh·ings (flesh′iŋz), *n.pl.* 1. flesh-colored tights, worn by acrobats, etc. 2. pieces of flesh scraped from hides.

flesh·li·ness (flesh′li-nis), *n.* the quality of being fleshly.

flesh·ly (flesh′li), *adj.* [FLESHLIER (-li-ẽr), FLESHLIEST (-li-ist)], [ME. *fleschlich;* AS. *flæsclic;* see FLESH & -LY], 1. of the body and its nature; corporeal. 2. fond of bodily pleasures; sensual. 3. fleshy. *adv.* [Archaic], in a fleshly manner. —*SYN.* see **carnal.**

flesh·pot (flesh′pot′), *n.* 1. a pot for cooking meat. 2. [after Ex. 16:3], *pl.* bodily comfort and pleasures; luxury, especially when regarded with envy or longing.

flesh wound, a wound that does not reach the bones or vital organs.

flesh·y (flesh′i), *adj.* [FLESHIER (-i-ẽr), FLESHIEST (-i-ist)], 1. having much flesh; fat; plump. 2. of or like flesh. 3. having a firm pulp; pulpy: said of some fruits.

fletch (flech), *v.t.* [? altered < *fledge*, by analogy with *fletcher*], to put a feather on (an arrow).

fletch·er (flech′ẽr), *n.* [ME.; OFr. *flechier* < *fleche*, an arrow], [Archaic], a person who makes or feathers arrows.

Fletch·er, John (flech′ẽr), 1579–1625; English dramatist; collaborated with Francis Beaumont.

Fletcher, John Gould, 1886– ; American poet.

Fletch·er·ism, fletch·er·ism (flech′ẽr-iz′m), *n.* [after Horace *Fletcher* (1849–1919), Am. dietician], the practice of chewing food slowly and thoroughly, advocated as an aid to digestion.

fleur-de-lis (flũr′də-lē′, flũr′də-lēs′), *n.* [*pl.* FLEURS-DE-LIS (flũr′də-lēz′)], [Fr., flower of the lily], 1. the iris (plant or flower). 2. the coat of arms of the former French royal family. 3. in *heraldry*, an emblem resembling a lily or iris: also **fleur-de-lys, flower-de-luce.**

FLEUR-DE-LIS

flew (flōō), past tense of **fly.**

flew (flōō), *n.* a flue (fishing net).

flews (flōōz), *n.pl.* [earlier technical use in falconry, etc. suggests OFr. origin and connection with OFr. *fluir*, to flow], the loose, hanging parts of the upper lip of a hound or other dog.

flex (fleks), *v.t.* & *v.i.* [< L. *flexus*, pp. of *flectere*, to bend, curve], 1. to bend, as an arm. 2. to contract, as a muscle.

flex·i·bil·i·ty (flek′sə-bil′ə-ti), *n.* [Fr. *flexibilité;* LL. *flexibilitas*], the quality of being flexible.

flex·i·ble (flek′sə-b'l), *adj.* [L. *flexibilis* < *flexus;* see FLEX], 1. able to bend without breaking; not stiff or rigid; pliant; easily bent. 2. easily persuaded or influenced; tractable. 3. adjustable to change; capable of modification: as, a *flexible* voice. —*SYN.* see **elastic.**

flex·i·bly (flek′sə-bli), *adv.* in a flexible manner.

flex·ile (flek′sil), *adj.* [L. *flexilis*], flexible; pliant; mobile.

flex·ion (flek′shən), *n.* flection.

flex·ion·al (flek′shən-əl), *adj.* flectional.

Flex·ner, Abraham (fleks′nẽr), 1866–1959; American educator; brother of *Simon.*

Flexner, Simon, 1863–1946; American pathologist.
flex·or (flek′sẽr, flek′sôr), *n.* [Mod. L. < L. *flexus;* see FLEX], any muscle that bends a limb or other part of the body.
flex·u·os·i·ty (flek′shōō-os′ə-ti), *n.* 1. the quality or state of being flexuous. 2. [*pl.* FLEXUOSITIES (-tiz)], a curve or winding.
flex·u·ous (flek′shōō-əs), *adj.* [L. *flexuosus* < *flexus;* see FLEX], 1. full of bends; winding. 2. wavering.
flex·ure (flek′shẽr), *n.* [L. *flexura*], 1. a bending, curving, or flexing, as of a heavy object under its own weight, or a stratum under pressure. 2. a bend; curve; fold.
flib·ber·ti·gib·bet (flib′ẽr-ti-jib′it), *n.* [extended < earlier *flibbergib* (? after *gibbet*); ? echoic imitation of nonsense chatter; ? < Fr. **foubert-ageter, v.* < *foubert*, a dupe (< *Fulbert*, proper name, with semantic influence < *fou*, crazy) + *-age* (< L. *-aticus*) + *-eter*, dim. v. suffix; said to be orig. name of a devil in the morris dance], 1. a person, especially a woman, who chatters constantly; hence, 2. an irresponsible, flighty person.
flick (flik), *n.* [prob. partly echoic (like Fr. *flic, flicflac*) & partly back-formation < *flicker* as *flick-* + freq. suffix *-er*], 1. a light, quick, stroke or blow, as with a whip; sudden, jerky movement; snap. 2. a light, snapping sound, as of the flick of a whip. 3. a fleck; splotch; streak; dash. *v.t.* 1. to strike, throw, remove, etc. with a light, quick, snapping stroke. 2. to make a light, quick, snapping stroke with (a whip, etc.). *v.i.* to move quickly and jerkily; flutter.
flick·er (flik′ẽr), *v.i.* [ME. *flikeren, flekeren;* AS. *flicorian;* akin to D. *flikkeren*, to sparkle, AS. *flacor*, flying (of arrows); IE. base **plāg-*, **plāq-*, etc., to beat; see FLAW (gust)], 1. to flap the wings rapidly, as in hovering; flutter: said of a bird. 2. to move with a quick, light, wavering motion. 3. to burn or shine unsteadily, as a candle in the wind. *v.t.* to cause to flicker or waver. *n.* 1. a flickering. 2. a dart of flame or light, as in a flickering fire. 3. a brief, passing feeling: as, a *flicker* of fear. 4. *pl.* [Earlier Slang], the motion pictures. —*SYN.* see **blaze.**
flick·er (flik′ẽr), *n.* [echoic of its cry], a North American woodpecker with a red, crescent-shaped mark on the back of the head, and wings colored golden on the underside.
flied (flid), past tense and past participle of **fly** (only in reference to baseball; see **fly,** *v.i.*).
fli·er (flī′ẽr), *n.* 1. a thing that flies. 2. an aviator. 3. a bus, train, etc. that has a fast schedule. 4. any step in a straight stairway. 5. a small handbill widely distributed. 6. [Slang], a reckless gamble or speculation, as in the stock market. Also spelled **flyer.**
flight (flīt), *n.* [ME. *fliht;* AS. *flyht* (akin to OS. *fluht*, D. *vlucht*) < base of *fleogan*, to fly + nominal suffix *-t;* see FLY], 1. the act, manner, or power of flying. 2. the distance flown or that can be flown at one time by an airplane, bird, projectile, etc. 3. a group of things flying through the air together: as, a *flight* of birds, arrows, etc. 4. *a*) a formation of military airplanes in flight. *b*) a basic organizational unit of an air force, consisting of a small number of planes of the same type. 5. an airplane scheduled to fly a certain route at a certain time. 6. a trip by airplane. 7. an outburst or soaring above the ordinary: as, a *flight* of fancy. 8. a set of stairs, especially between landings. 9. in *angling*, tackle that spins the bait around rapidly. 10. in *archery*, *a*) a contest in distance shooting. *b*) a special arrow for such shooting: also **flight arrow.** *v.i.* to fly in numbers; migrate: said of birds. —*SYN.* see **group.**
flight (flīt), *n.* [ME. *fliht, fluht;* AS. **flyht* < base of *fleon*, to flee + nominal suffix *-t;* see FLEE], a fleeing; running away from or as from danger.
put to flight, to force to run away; make flee.
take to flight, to run away; flee.
flight formation, the orderly arrangement of two or more airplanes flying together as a unit in close proximity, as for their mutual protection in warfare.
flight·i·ly (flīt′′l-i), *adv.* in a flighty manner.
flight·i·ness (flīt′i-nis), *n.* a flighty quality or state.
flight·less (flīt′lis), *adj.* not able to fly.
flight officer, an officer in the United States Air Force ranking just below a second lieutenant.
flight·y (flīt′i), *adj.* [FLIGHTIER (-i-ẽr), FLIGHTIEST (-i-ist)], [*flight* (a flying) + *-y*], 1. given to sudden whims or fancies; unsettled; fickle; frivolous. 2. mentally unbalanced; slightly demented.
flim·flam (flim′flam′), *n.* [reduplicated echoic term; cf. FLAM], 1. nonsense; rubbish; humbug. 2. a sly trick or deception. *adj.* 1. nonsensical. 2. tricky; deceptive. *v.t.* [FLIMFLAMMED (-flamd′), FLIMFLAMMING], [Colloq.], to cheat; trick; swindle; deceive.
flim·si·ly (flim′z′l-i), *adv.* in a flimsy manner.
flim·si·ness (flim′zi-nis), *n.* the quality or state of being flimsy.
flim·sy (flim′zi), *adj.* [FLIMSIER (-zi-ẽr), FLIMSIEST (-zi-ist)], [said to be < *film* + *-y*, with inserted *s* as in *clumsy, tipsy*, etc.; prob. < W. *llymsi*, flimsy (with *fl-* for W. *ll-*, as in *flummery*), hence var. of U.S. dial. *limpsy*, weak, fragile (of same origin)], 1. thin and easily broken or damaged; fragile; frail. 2. without adequate substance or sense; trivial; ineffectual: as, a *flimsy* excuse. *n.* 1. thin paper, as transfer paper, used by newspaper reporters. 2. copy written on this.
flinch (flinch), *v.i.* [earlier also *flench* < OFr. *flenchir*, to bend aside; prob. < OFr. *fleschier* (Fr. *flêchir*) influenced by base (**hlenc-*, **hlank-*) of MHG. *lenken* (G. *lenken*), to bend], 1. to draw back, as from a blow or an attack; hence, 2. to draw back from anything difficult, dangerous, or painful; wince. *n.* 1. a flinching. 2. a card game played by building the cards up on the table in a certain order. —*SYN.* see **recoil.**
flin·der (flin′dẽr), *n.* [ME. (northern) *flender;* prob. < Anglo-N.; cf. Norw. *flindra*, a splinter & Early Dan. *flint*, stone splinter; see FLINT], a little piece; splinter; fragment: chiefly in *break* (or *fly*) *into flinders.*
Flin·ders Range (flin′dẽrz), a mountain range extending inland from the coast of South Australia.
fling (fliŋ), *v.t.* [FLUNG (fluŋ), FLINGING], [ME. *flingen*, to rush; prob. < ON. **flinga, v.i.;* cf. ON. *flengja*, to whip (Norw. dial., to throw), OSw. *flängia*, to beat (Sw. *flänga*, to rush forward); nasalized < IE. base **plāq-*, etc.; see FLAW (gust)], 1. to throw, especially with force or violence; hurl; cast. 2. to put abruptly or violently: as, the crowd was *flung* into confusion. 3. to throw down; overthrow. 4. to move (one's arms, legs, head, etc.) suddenly or impulsively: as, he *flung* his arms about her. 5. to move or enter into hastily and with spirit: used reflexively, as, he *flung* himself into the task. 6. to throw aside; disregard: as, she *flung* caution to the winds. 7. to give out; emit; diffuse (a fragrance, etc.). *v.i.* 1. to move suddenly and violently; rush; dash: as, she *flung* out of the room. 2. to talk wildly or abusively. *n.* 1. a flinging. 2. a taunting remark; sneer. 3. a brief time of wild actions and unrestrained pleasures: as, youth must have its *fling.* 4. a spirited dance: as, the Highland *fling.* 5. [Colloq.], a trial effort: as, he had a *fling* at working. —*SYN.* see **throw.**
Flint (flint), *n.* 1. a city in eastern Michigan: pop., 197,000. 2. Flintshire.
flint (flint), *n.* [ME.; AS. *flint;* akin to Norw. *flint*, stone splinter; IE. base *(*s*)*plei-*, to split (off), as also in *split, splint, splinter, flinder*, etc.], 1. a very hard stone, a kind of quartz, which produces sparks when struck against steel: it is usually brown, black, or gray. 2. a piece of this stone, used to start a fire, as material for primitive tools and weapons, etc. 3. anything extremely hard or firm like flint.
flint corn, a variety of Indian corn with very hard kernels.
flint glass, a hard, bright glass containing lead, used for lenses, crystal, etc.
flint·i·ness (flint′i-nis), *n.* a flinty quality or state.
flint·lock (flint′lok′), *n.* 1. a gunlock in which the powder is exploded by a spark produced by the striking of a flint in the hammer against a metal plate. 2. an old-fashioned gun with such a lock.

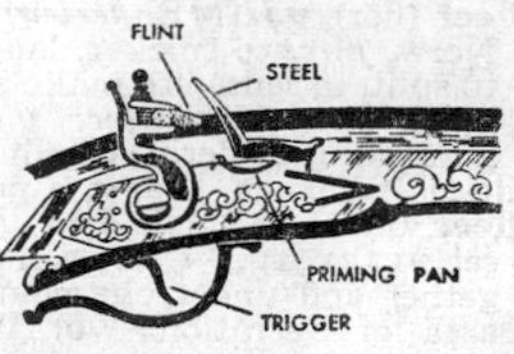

FLINTLOCK

Flint·shire (flint′shir), *n.* a county of northeastern Wales: pop., 145,000; county seat, Mold.
flint·y (flin′ti), *adj.* [FLINTIER (-ti-ẽr), FLINTIEST (-ti-ist)], 1. made of or containing flint. 2. like flint; extremely hard and firm: as, a *flinty* heart.
flip (flip), *v.t.* [FLIPPED (flipt), FLIPPING], [echoic], 1. to toss or move with a quick jerk; flick; fillip: as, *flip* the drawer shut. 2. to toss (a coin, etc.) by snapping with the thumb against the finger. *v.i.* 1. to make a quick, light stroke, as with the finger or a whip; snap. 2. to move jerkily. *n.* a flipping; snap, tap, or jerk.
flip up, to toss a coin in the air and see which side will land uppermost, as in determining a choice.
flip (flip), *n.* [prob. < *flip*, to toss], a hot, sweetened drink of beer, cider, etc. with spices and, sometimes, milk and eggs.
flip (flip), *adj.* [FLIPPER (-ẽr), FLIPPEST (-ist)], [Colloq.], flippant; saucy; pert; impertinent.
flip·pan·cy (flip′ən-si), *n.* 1. the quality or state of being flippant. 2. [*pl.* FLIPPANCIES (-siz)], a flippant act or remark.
flip·pant (flip′ənt), *adj.* [Early Mod. Eng. *flippant, flippent*, nimble; prob. < *flip, v.*, with *-ant, -ent* < dial. ppr. suffix *-ind, -end, -and*], 1. [Rare], glib; talkative. 2. frivolous and disrespectful; saucy; impertinent.
flip·per (flip′ẽr), *n.* [< *flip, v.*], 1. a broad, flat part or limb adapted for swimming, as in seals, turtles, whales, etc. 2. [Slang], the hand.
flirt (flũrt), *v.t.* [16th & 17th c.; also earlier *flert, flurt;* ? echoic (cf. E. Fris. *flirtje*, giddy girl), but strongly influenced by OFr. *fleureter*, to touch lightly, lit., move from flower to flower], 1. to throw quickly and jerkily. 2. to move jerkily; wave back and forth quickly: as, the bird *flirted* its tail. *v.i.* 1. to move jerkily or unevenly. 2. to make love without serious intentions; play at love;

coquet. 3. to trifle; play; toy: as, he *flirted* with the idea of quitting his job. *n.* 1. a quick, jerky movement; flutter. 2. a quick, jerky throw or toss. 3. a person who plays at love. —*SYN.* see **trifle.**

flir·ta·tion (flũr-tā'shən), *n.* 1. a playing at love without serious intentions; flirting. 2. a superficial, rather playful love affair.

flir·ta·tious (flũr-tā'shəs), *adj.* 1. inclined to flirt, or play at love. 2. of or characteristic of flirtation.

flirt·y (flũrt'i), *adj.* flirtatious.

flit (flit), *v.i.* [FLITTED (-id), FLITTING], [ME. *flitten;* ON. *flytja;* for base see FLEET, *v.*], 1. to pass lightly and rapidly: as, memories *flitted* through his mind. 2. to fly lightly and rapidly; flutter: as, birds *flit* about in the trees. 3. [Dial.], to go away. 4. [Scot. & Brit. Dial.], to move to other quarters, especially by stealth. 5. [Obs.], to be changing or evanescent. *v.t.* [Archaic], to move (furnishings, etc.) to other quarters. *n.* a flitting; light, rapid movement. —*SYN.* see **fly.**

flitch (flich), *n.* [ME. *flicche;* AS. *flicce;* akin to ON. *flikki;* IE. base **pleik-*, **plik-*, to tear (off)], 1. the cured and salted side of a hog; side of bacon. 2. a lengthwise strip from the outer part of a tree trunk. *v.t.* [< the *n.*], to cut so as to form flitches.

flite (flīt), *v.i.* & *v.t.* [ME. *fliten;* AS. *flitan;* akin to OHG. *flīzan*, to strive (cf. G. *fleiss*, diligence, assiduity); ? < IE. base *(*s*)*plei-*, to split; cf. FLINT], [Archaic or Dial.], 1. to quarrel with (a person). 2. to scold. *n.* [AS. *flit*], [Archaic or Dial.], a quarrel; dispute. Also spelled **flyte.**

flit·ter (flit'ẽr), *v.i.* & *v.t.* [freq. of *flit*], [Chiefly Dial.], to move rapidly and lightly; flutter.

flit·ter (flit'ẽr), *n.* a person or thing that flits.

flit·ter·mouse (flit'ẽr-mous'), *n.* [*pl.* FLITTERMICE (-mīs')], [*flitter, v.i.* + *mouse*], [Obs.], a bat (animal).

fliv·ver (fliv'ẽr), *n.* [arbitrary coinage], [Slang], a small, cheap automobile, airplane, etc. *v.i.* [Slang], to fail.

float (flōt), *n.* [ME. *flote;* AS. *flota*, that which floats, ship < base of *fleotan* (see FLEET, *v.*); influenced in some senses by OFr. *flote, flot* (Fr. *flotte*) and by the *v.*], 1. anything that stays, or causes something else to stay, on the surface of a liquid; specifically, *a*) an air-filled bladder in a fish. *b*) a cork on a fishing line. *c*) a floating ball that regulates water level, as in a boiler or tank. *d*) a raft. *e*) a life preserver. *f*) the landing gear on an amphibious airplane. 2. a low, flat, decorated vehicle for carrying exhibits, tableaux, etc. in a parade. 3. a flat tool for smoothing cement, plaster, etc. 4. *often pl.* a row of footlights on a stage. 5. [Rare], a floating. *v.i.* [ME. *flotien;* AS. *flotian*], 1. to stay on the surface of a liquid. 2. to drift gently; move without effort on water, in air, etc.: as, the leaves *floated* down from the trees. 3. to move or drift about vaguely and without purpose: as, idle thoughts *floated* through his mind. *v.t.* 1. *a*) to cause to stay on the surface of a liquid. *b*) to bring to the surface and cause to stay there. 2. to hold up; bear: as, enough water to *float* a fleet. 3. to flood. 4. to put into circulation; place on the market; start: as, they *floated* a bond issue. 5. to smooth (cement, plaster, etc.). 6. to refine or make (pigments) smooth by grinding them and floating them in a stream of water.

float·age (flōt'ij), *n.* flotage.

float·a·tion (flō-tā'shən), *n.* flotation.

float·er (flōt'ẽr), *n.* 1. a person or thing that floats. 2. a person who illegally casts a vote at each of several polling places. 3. [Colloq.], a person who changes his place of residence or work at frequent intervals; especially, a transient laborer.

float-feed (flōt'fēd'), *adj.* having the flow of fuel regulated by a float, as some carburetors.

float·ing (flōt'iŋ), *adj.* [ppr. of *float*], 1. that floats. 2. not fixed; not remaining in one place; moving about: as, the *floating* population in wartime industry. 3. in *finance*, *a*) designating an unfunded, short-time debt resulting from current operations and having no specified date for repayment. *b*) not permanently invested; used for current expenses: as, *floating* capital. 4. in *medicine*, displaced, especially downward, from the normal position: as, a *floating* kidney.

floating dock, a dock that can be lowered in the water for the entrance of a ship, and then raised for use as a dry dock.

floating island, 1. a floating mass of earth resembling an island. 2. a boiled custard dessert topped with meringue or whipped cream.

floating ribs, the eleventh and twelfth pairs of ribs, which are not attached to the breastbone or to other ribs.

floating supply, the supply of stocks, securities, etc. that can be readily bought on the open market.

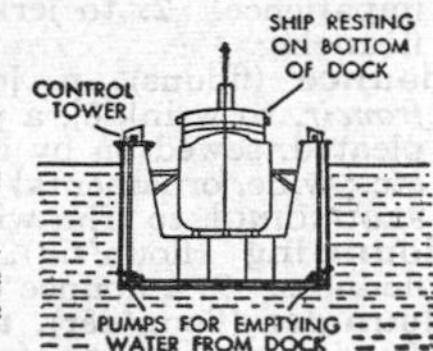

FLOATING DOCK

float valve, a valve regulated by a float.

floc (flok), *n.* [< *floccule*], a very fine, fluffy mass formed by the aggregation of fine suspended particles, as in smoke: also spelled **flock.**

floc·cil·la·tion (flok'sə-lā'shən), *n.* [< L. *floccus*, flock of wool + *-ill(us)*, dim. ending; + *-ation*], a plucking at bedclothes by a delirious patient.

floc·cose (flok'ōs, flo-kōs'), *adj.* [LL. *floccosus* < L. *floccus*, a flock of wool], 1. covered with soft wool or hair; flocculent. 2. in *botany*, covered with woollike tufts.

floc·cu·late (flok'yoo-lāt'), *v.t.* & *v.i.* [FLOCCULATED (-id), FLOCCULATING], to collect, as soils, clouds, etc., into small, flocculent lumps or masses.

floc·cule (flok'ūl), *n.* [see FLOCCULUS], a small, detached mass of matter resembling a soft tuft of wool; floc.

floc·cu·lence (flok'yoo-ləns), *n.* the quality or state of being flocculent.

floc·cu·lent (flok'yoo-lənt), *adj.* [< L. *floccus*, flock of wool], 1. woolly; fluffy. 2. containing or consisting of small woolly masses. 3. covered with a waxy, woollike substance, as some insects.

floc·cu·lus (flok'yoo-ləs), *n.* [*pl.* FLOCCULI (-lī')], [Mod. L. dim. < L. *floccus*, flock of wool], 1. a small, woolly or hairy tuft. 2. in *anatomy*, a small lobe on the underside of each half of the cerebellum. 3. in *astronomy*, a woolly, cloudlike mass of vapor in the sun's atmosphere.

floc·cus (flok'əs), *n.* [*pl.* FLOCCI (-sī)], [L.], a tuft of wool or hair, especially the tuft at the end of the tail in some animals; floccule.

flock (flok), *n.* [ME. *floc;* AS. *flocc*, a troop, band; akin to ON. *flokkr;* ? var. of AS. *folc*, folk], 1. a group of certain animals, as goats, sheep, or birds, living, feeding, etc. together. 2. a large number of people or things. 3. the members of a church. 4. the children in one family. *v.i.* to assemble or travel in a flock or flocks; gather or go in a crowd. —*SYN.* see **group.**

flock (flok), *n.* [ME. *flocke;* OFr. *floc;* L. *floccus*], 1. a small tuft or lock of wool. 2. wool or cotton waste used to stuff upholstered furniture, mattresses, etc. 3. the inferior wool fibers added to low-grade fabrics to give weight. 4. a floc. *v.t.* to stuff or cover with flock.

flock·y (flok'i), *adj.* flocculent; floccose.

Flod·den (flod''n), *n.* a hill in County Northumberland, England: site of the defeat (1513) of James IV of Scotland by the English.

floe (flō), *n.* [ON. *flo*, a layer, expanse], 1. a large, flat field or sheet of floating ice formed at the surface of a sea, etc. 2. a piece of such a field or sheet broken off and floating free.

flog (flog, flôg), *v.t.* [FLOGGED (flogd, flôgd), FLOGGING], [? cant abbrev. of L. *flagellare*, to whip], to beat with a strap, stick, whip, etc.; punish by whipping severely. —*SYN.* see **beat.**

flog·ger (flog'ẽr, flôg'ẽr), *n.* a person or thing that flogs.

flood (flud), *n.* [ME. *flode;* AS. *flod*, akin to G. *flut;* for IE. base see FLOW], 1. an overflowing of water on land usually dry; inundation; deluge. 2. *a*) the flowing of the tide toward the shore; rising of the tide: opposed to *ebb*. *b*) the rising tide: also **flood tide.** 3. a great flow or outpouring: as, a *flood* of words. 4. [Colloq.], a floodlight. 5. [Archaic or Poetic], *a*) water, as opposed to land. *b*) a large body of water; ocean, sea, lake, or river. *v.t.* 1. to cover or fill with a flood; overflow; inundate. 2. to cover, fill, or overwhelm like a flood: as, music *flooded* the room, he was *flooded* with invitations. 3. to put much or too much water on or in: as, the sprinkler *flooded* the lawn. *v.i.* 1. to rise in a flood. 2. to come out like a flood; gush out.
the Flood, in the *Bible*, the great flood in Noah's time: Gen. 7.

flood control, the protection of land from floods by the construction of river embankments, soil conservation, reforestation, etc.

flood·gate (flud'gāt'), *n.* 1. a gate in a stream or canal, to control the height and flow of the water; sluice. 2. anything like this in controlling a flow or an outburst: as, the *floodgates* of anger.

flood·light (flud'līt'), *n.* 1. an artificial light of high intensity, usually with a reflector that causes it to shine in a broad beam. 2. such a beam of light. *v.t.* [FLOODLIGHTED (-id) or FLOODLIT (-lit), FLOODLIGHTING], to throw a broad beam of light on; illuminate by a floodlight.

flood plain, a plain along a river, formed from soil deposited by floods.

flood tide, the incoming tide; rising tide: opposed to *ebb tide*.

floor (flôr, flōr), *n.* [ME. & AS. *flor;* akin to G. *flur*, a plain, field; IE. base **p(e)lā-*, broad and flat, seen also in L. *planus* (cf. PLANE)], 1. the inside bottom surface of a room, porch, etc.; part that one stands on in a room, etc. 2. the corresponding surface of anything: as, the ocean *floor*. 3. a level or story in a building; as, their apartment is on the sixth *floor*: abbreviated **fl.** 4. the platform of a bridge, pier, etc. 5. the part of a legislative chamber, stock exchange, etc. occupied by the members and not including the gallery or platform; hence, 6. the right to speak in an assembly: as, the chairman gave him the *floor*. 7. a minimum price level for any commodity. 8. in *nautical usage*, the flat part of a ship's bottom. *v.t.* 1. to cover or furnish with a floor. 2. to knock down; hence, 3. [Colloq.], *a*) to defeat; put to silence. *b*) to puzzle; perplex; confuse: as, the problem *floored* us.

floor·age (flôr'ij, flōr'ij), *n.* [see -AGE], the area of a floor; floor space.

floor·cloth (flôr'klôth', flōr'kloth'), *n.* 1. linoleum, oilcloth, etc. for covering floors. 2. a cloth for washing or mopping floors.

floor·ing (flôr'iŋ, flōr'iŋ), *n.* 1. a floor. 2. floors collectively. 3. material for making a floor.

floor leader, a member of a legislature who is chosen by fellow members of his political party to direct their actions on the floor.

floor plan, an architectural scale drawing showing the size and arrangement of rooms, halls, etc. on one floor of a house or other building.

floor show, an entertainment, as singing, dancing, etc., presented in a cleared space on the floor of a restaurant or night club.

floor·walk·er (flôr'wôk'ẽr, flōr'wôk'ẽr), *n.* a person employed by a department store to direct customers, supervise sales, etc.: now often **floor manager.**

floo·zy, floo·zie, (flōō'zi), *n.* [*pl.* FLOOZIES (-ziz)], [cf. FLOSSY], [Slang], 1. a loose, disreputable woman or girl. 2. any woman or girl. Also spelled **floosy.**

flop (flop), *v.t.* [FLOPPED (flopt), FLOPPING], [var. of *flap*], to flap, strike, throw, or cause to drop noisily and clumsily. *v.i.* 1. to move or flap around loosely or clumsily, usually with a thud or thuds. 2. to fall or drop in this way: as, he *flopped* wearily into a chair. 3. to make a sudden change. 4. [Colloq.], to fail. 5. [Slang], to sleep. *n.* 1. a flopping. 2. the sound of flopping. 3. [Colloq.], a failure. 4. [Slang], a place to sleep. *adv.* with a flop.

flop·house (flop'hous'), *n.* a kind of hotel where a night's lodging can be had very cheaply.

flop·py (flop'i), *adj.* [FLOPPIER (-i-ẽr), FLOPPIEST (-i-ist)], [Colloq.], flopping or inclined to flop.

flor., *floruit*, [L.], he (or she) flourished.

Flo·ra (flôr'ə, flō'rə), [L. < *flos, floris*, a flower; in sense 2, used and popularized by Linnaeus (1745)], a feminine name. *n.* 1. in *Roman mythology*, the goddess of flowers. 2. [f-], [*pl.* FLORAS (-əz, -rəz), FLORAE (-ē, -rē)], the plants of a specified region or time: as, the *flora* and fauna of Africa. 3. [f-], a treatise on such plants.

flo·ral (flôr'əl, flō'rəl), *adj.* [L. *floralis*, of Flora; see FLORA], of, made of, or like flowers.

floral emblem, any flower or plant that is the symbol of a city, country, state, etc.

floral envelope, the perianth, or external covering, of a flower.

‡Flo·ré·al (flō'rā'ál'; Eng. flôr'i-əl), *n.* [Fr. < L. *flos, floris*, blossom; + *-al*], the eighth month (April 20-May 19) of the French Revolutionary Calendar, adopted by the First Republic in 1793.

Flor·ence (flôr'əns, flor'əns), [Fr.; L. *Florentia*, lit., a flowering, blooming < *florens*, ppr. of *florere*, to bloom, blossom < *flos, floris;* see FLORA], a feminine name: diminutives, *Flo, Flossie;* equivalents, G. *Florenz*, It. *Fiorenza*, Sp. *Florencia*. *n.* a city in Tuscany, Italy: pop., 391,000: Italian name, *Firenze*.

Flor·en·tine (flôr'ən-tēn', flor'ən-tēn'), *adj.* of Florence, Italy, or its people, culture, or art. *n.* a native or inhabitant of Florence.

Flo·res (flô'res), *n.* 1. one of the Sunda Islands of Indonesia, west of Timor: area, 5,509 sq. mi.; pop., c. 500,000. 2. a western island in the Azores: area, 57 sq. mi.; pop., 8,000.

flo·res·cence (flô-res''ns, flō-res''ns), *n.* [L. *florescens*, ppr. of *florescere*, to begin to bloom, incept. of *florere*, to bloom < *flos, floris*, a flower], 1. a blooming; blossoming. 2. the condition or period of blooming; hence, 3. a period of success or achievement.

flo·res·cent (flô-res''nt, flō-res''nt), *adj.* [see FLORESCENCE], breaking into flower; blossoming.

Flores Sea, a part of the Pacific, between Celebes and Flores.

flo·ret (flôr'it, flō'rit), *n.* [ME. *flourette;* OFr. *florete*, dim. of *flor* (Fr. *fleur*); L. *flos, floris*, a flower], 1. a small flower. 2. any of the small flowers making up the head of a composite flower, as the daisy or aster.

Flo·ri·a·nop·o·lis (flôr'i-ə-nop'ə-lis, flō'ri-ə-nop'ə-lis), *n.* a city on Santa Catarina Island, off southern Brazil: pop., 49,000.

flo·ri·at·ed (flôr'i-ā'tid, flō'ri-ā'tid), *adj.* having floral decorations.

flo·ri·cul·ture (flôr'i-kul'chẽr, flō'ri-kul'chẽr), *n.* [< L. *flos, floris*, a flower + *cultura*, cultivation], the cultivation of flowers, especially of decorative flowering plants.

flo·ri·cul·tur·ist (flôr'i-kul'chẽr-ist, flō'ri-kul'chẽr-ist), *n.* an expert in floriculture.

flor·id (flôr'id, flor'id), *adj.* [L. *floridus*, flowery < *flos, floris*, a flower], 1. rosy; ruddy; highly colored: said of the complexion. 2. highly decorated; gaudy; showy; ornate: as, a *florid* passage in music, etc. 3. [Rare], decorated with flowers; flowery. —*SYN.* see **rosy.**

Flor·i·da (flôr'i-də, flor'i-də), *n.* a State on a peninsula in the southeastern United States: area, 58,560 sq. mi.; pop., 4,952,000; capital, Tallahassee: abbreviated **Fla., Flor.**: nicknamed *Everglade State*.

Florida Keys, a chain of islands off southern Florida.

Flor·i·dan (flôr'i-dən, flor'i-dən), *adj. & n.* Floridian.

Florida Strait, the strait connecting the Gulf of Mexico and the Atlantic, between Florida and the Bahama Islands and Cuba.

Flo·rid·i·an (flô-rid'i-ən, flō-rid'i-ən, flo-rid'i-ən), *adj.* of Florida. *n.* a native or inhabitant of Florida.

flo·rid·i·ty (flô-rid'ə-ti, flō-rid'ə-ti), *n.* the state or quality of being florid.

flo·rif·er·ous (flô-rif'ẽr-əs, flō-rif'ẽr-əs), *adj.* [L. *florifer* < *flos, floris*, a flower + *ferre*, to bear; + *-ous*], bearing flowers; blooming abundantly.

flor·in (flôr'in, flor'in), *n.* [ME.; OFr.; It. *fiorino* < *fiore*, a flower < L. *flos, floris*, so named from the figure of a lily stamped on the original coins], 1. originally, a gold coin of medieval Florence, issued in 1252. 2. an English silver coin equal to two shillings. 3. any of various European silver or gold coins. Abbreviated **fl.**

Flo·ri·o, John (flôr'i-ō', flō'ri-ō'), 1553?–1625; English writer; translator of Montaigne's *Essays*.

flo·rist (flôr'ist, flō'rist, flor'ist), *n.* [< L. *flos, floris*, a flower; + *-ist*], a person who cultivates or sells flowers.

-flo·rous (flə-rəs), [L. *-florus* < *flos, floris*, a flower], a suffix meaning *having many* or *a* (specified) *number of flowers*, as in *multiflorous, triflorous*.

‡flo·ru·it (flō'rōō-it, flor'yōō-it), [L.], he (or she) flourished: used when dates of birth and death are unknown: abbreviated **fl., flor.**

flos fer·ri (flos' fer'ī), [L., flower of iron], a coralloid variety of aragonite, usually found in iron ore.

floss (flôs, flos), *n.* [prob. < Fr. *floche*, downy, woolly (in *soie floche*, floss silk) < L. *floccus;* see FLOCK (a lock)], 1. the rough silk covering a silkworm's cocoon. 2. the short, downy waste fibers of silk. 3. floss silk. 4. a soft, silky substance resembling floss, as in corn tassels or milkweed pods.

floss silk, soft, untwisted silk fibers, used in embroidery and cheap silk fabrics.

floss·y (flôs'i, flos'i), *adj.* [FLOSSIER (-i-ẽr), FLOSSIEST (-i-ist)], 1. of or like floss; downy; light; fluffy. 2. [Slang], showy and frilly; elegant; fancy. *n.* [Slang], 1. a woman or girl of showy dress and light morals. 2. any woman or girl. Also spelled **flossie** (for the *n.*).

flo·tage (flō'tij), *n.* [*float, v.* + *-age;* but cf. OFr. *flotage*], 1. the act, condition, or power of floating. 2. anything that floats; especially, floating debris; flotsam. Also spelled **floatage.**

flo·ta·tion (flō-tā'shən), *n.* [earlier *floatation*, respelled as if < Fr. *flottaison*], 1. the act or condition of floating or launching. 2. the act of beginning or financing a business by selling an entire issue of bonds, securities, etc.; hence, 3. the act of beginning; becoming established. 4. in *mining*, a method of ore separation in which finely powdered ore is introduced into a bubbling solution to which oils are added: certain minerals float on the surface, and others sink. Also spelled **floatation.**

flo·til·la (flō-til'ə), *n.* [Sp., dim. of *flota*, a fleet], 1. a small fleet. 2. a fleet of boats or small ships.

Flo·tow, Frie·drich von (frē'driH fôn flō'tō), Baron, 1812–1883; German composer.

flot·sam (flot'səm), *n.* [Anglo-Fr. *floteson;* OFr. *flotaison*, a floating < *floter*, to float < AS. *flotian*, to float], the wreckage of a ship or its cargo found floating on the sea: distinguished from *jetsam*.

flotsam and jetsam, 1. the wreckage of a ship or its cargo found floating on the sea or washed ashore. 2. miscellaneous trifles or worthless things. 3. transient, unemployed people; drifters; vagrants.

flounce (flouns), *v.i.* [FLOUNCED (flounst), FLOUNCING], [Early Mod. Eng., orig., to dive; hence prob. Scand. & akin to Sw. dial. *flunsa*, to dive, dip; ? merged with native echoic word after *bounce*], 1. to move with quick, flinging motions of the body, as in anger or impatience. 2. to jerk; twist or turn abruptly. *n.* a flouncing.

flounce (flouns), *n.* [earlier *frounce;* OFr. *fronce* < *froncir*, to wrinkle], a piece of cloth, often gathered or pleated, sewed on by its upper edge to a skirt, sleeve, etc.; wide, ornamental ruffle. *v.t.* [FLOUNCED (flounst), FLOUNCING], to trim with a flounce or flounces.

flounc·ing (floun'siŋ), *n.* 1. material for making flounces. 2. a flounce or flounces.

floun·der (floun'dẽr), *v.i.* [16th & 17th c.; also earlier *flunder;* prob. var. of *founder*, with symbolistic *fl-* < dial. *flodder*, of same senses], 1. to struggle awkwardly to move, as in deep mud or snow; plunge about in a stumbling manner; hence, 2. to speak or act in an awkward, confused manner, with hesitation and frequent mistakes. *n.* a floundering.

floun·der (floun'dẽr), *n.* [*pl.* FLOUNDERS (-dẽrz), FLOUNDER; see PLURAL, II, D, 1], [ME.; Anglo-Fr. *floundre;* OFr. *flondre;* prob. < Scand.; cf. Sw. *flundra*], any of a large group of flatfishes caught for food, including the halibut and the plaice.

flour (flour), *n.* [var. sp. of *flower* (ME. *flour*); a fig. use as "best, prime" in "flour of wheat," after Fr. *fleur de farine*, lit., flower of meal], 1. a fine, powdery substance produced by grinding and sifting grain, especially wheat. 2. any finely powdered substance. *v.t.* 1. to put flour in or on. 2. to grind and sift (grain); make into flour.

flour·ish (flũr′ish), *v.i.* [ME. *florischen, florissen;* OFr. *florir*, to bloom, blossom; LL. **florire* < L. *florere*, to blossom, flower < *flos, floris*, a flower], 1. originally, to blossom. 2. to grow vigorously; succeed; thrive; prosper. 3. to be at the peak of development, activity, influence, production, etc.; be in one's prime. 4. to make showy, wavy motions, as of the arms. 5. to write in an ornamental style. 6. in *music, a*) to play a showy passage. *b*) to perform a fanfare, as of trumpets. *v.t.* 1. to ornament with something flowery or fanciful. 2. [after Wyclif's transl. of the Bible], to wave (a sword, arm, etc.) in the air; brandish. *n.* 1. [Rare], a thriving state; success; prosperity. 2. anything done in a showy or flaunting way. 3. a waving in the air; brandishing. 4. a decorative or curved line or lines in writing. 5. an ornate musical passage; fanfare. 6. [Obs.], a blooming. —***SYN.*** see **succeed.**

flour mill, 1. a place where grain is ground into flour. 2. a machine for grinding grain into flour.

flour·y (flour′i), *adj.* 1. of flour. 2. like flour in color or texture; powdery or white. 3. covered with flour.

flout (flout), *v.t.* [? special use of ME. *flouten*, to play on the flute], to mock or scoff at; show scorn or contempt for. *v.i.* to be scornful; show contempt; jeer; scoff. *n.* a scornful or contemptuous action or speech; mockery; scoffing; insult. —***SYN.*** see **scoff.**

flow (flō), *v.i.* [ME. *flowen;* AS. *flowan;* akin to ON. *floa*, to flood, OHG. *flouwen*, to wash; IE. base **pleu-*, to run, flow, as also in L. *pluere*, to rain; cf. FLOOD], 1. to move as a liquid does; move in a stream, like water. 2. to move in a way suggestive of a liquid; stream: as, the crowds *flowed* past. 3. *a*) to move gently, smoothly, and easily; glide. *b*) to have smooth and pleasing continuity: as, the lines in this painting *flow.* 4. to stream forth; pour out. 5. to be derived; spring; proceed. 6. to fall in waves; hang loose: as, her hair *flowed* down her back. 7. to come in; rise, as the tide: opposed to *ebb.* 8. to be overflowing or plentiful. *v.t.* 1. to overflow; flood. 2. [Archaic], to cause to flow. *n.* 1. the act or manner of flowing. 2. the rate of flow. 3. anything that flows; stream or current. 4. the rising of the tide. —***SYN.*** see **rise.**

flow·age (flō′ij), *n.* [see -AGE], 1. a flowing, overflowing, or flooding. 2. a flooded condition. 3. what flows or overflows.

flow·er (flou′ẽr, flour), *n.* [ME. *flowre, flour, flur;* OFr. *flor, flur, flour* (Fr. *fleur*); L. *flos, floris*, a flower; for IE. base see BLOOM (flower)], 1. the part of a plant containing or consisting of the reproductive organs; especially, this part in seed-producing plants, usually including a surrounding structure of brightly colored leaves or petals; blossom; bloom. 2. a plant cultivated for its blossoms; flowering plant. 3. the best or finest part or example: as, the *flower* of the country's youth. 4. the best period of a person or thing; time of flourishing. 5. something decorative; especially, a figure of speech. 6. *pl.* in *chemistry*, a substance in powder form, made from condensed vapors: as, *flowers* of sulfur. Abbreviated **fl.** *v.i.* 1. to produce blossoms; bloom. 2. to reach the best or most vigorous stage: as, his genius *flowered* early. *v.t.* to decorate with flowers or floral patterns.

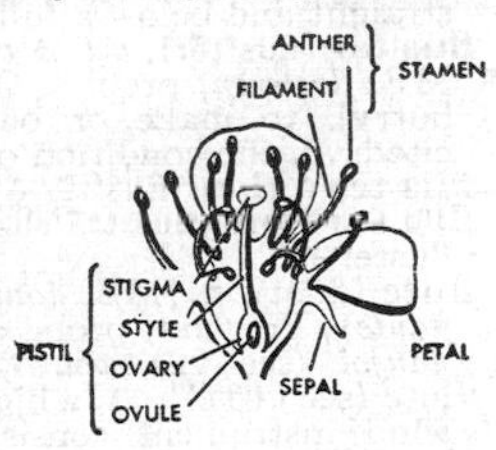

DIAGRAM OF FLOWER

in flower, in a state of flowering.

flow·er·age (flou′ẽr-ij, flou′rij), *n.* [see -AGE], 1. flowers collectively. 2. a flowering.

flow·er-de-luce (flou′ẽr-di-lōōs′, flour′di-lōōs′), *n.* 1. the fleur-de-lis. 2. the iris.

flow·ered (flou′ẽrd), *adj.* 1. bearing or containing flowers. 2. decorated with flowers or a floral design.

flow·er·et (flou′ẽr-it, flou′rit), *n.* [ME. *flourette*, dim. of *flour;* see FLOWER], 1. a small flower. 2. a floret.

flower girl, 1. a girl or woman who sells flowers in the streets. 2. a little girl who carries flowers and attends the bride at a wedding.

flower head, in *botany*, a capitulum.

flow·er·i·ly (flou′ẽr-ə-li, flou′rə-li), *adv.* in a flowery manner.

flow·er·i·ness (flou′ẽr-i-nis, flou′ri-nis), *n.* the quality or state of being flowery.

flow·er·ing (flou′ẽr-iŋ, flou′riŋ), *adj.* 1. having flowers; in bloom. 2. having conspicuous flowers.

flow·er·pot (flou′ẽr-pot′, flour′pot′), *n.* a container, usually made of porous clay, in which to grow plants.

flow·er·y (flou′ẽr-i, flou′ri), *adj.* [FLOWERIER (-i-ẽr, -ri-ẽr), FLOWERIEST (-i-ist, -ri-ist)], 1. covered or decorated with flowers. 2. like flowers. 3. full of figurative and ornate expressions and fine words: said of language, style, etc. —***SYN.*** see **bombastic.**

flown (flōn), past participle of **fly:** sometimes used in hyphenated compounds, as *far-flown, high-flown.*

flown (flōn), *adj.* [obs. pp. of *flow*], 1. flushed; excited; exalted. 2. having colors combined or flowing into each other: as, *flown* porcelain.

flow·sheet (flō′shēt′), *n.* a diagram showing the materials, operations, etc. involved in a manufacturing process, used in calculating costs: also **flow sheet.**

Floyd (floid), [var. of *Lloyd;* for *Fl-*, cf. FLIMSY], a masculine name.

fl. oz., fluid ounce; fluid ounces.

flu (flōō), *n.* [Colloq.], influenza.

fluc·tu·ant (fluk′chōō-ənt), *adj.* [L. *fluctuans*, ppr. of *fluctuare*], fluctuating; varying; undulating.

fluc·tu·ate (fluk′chōō-āt′), *v.i.* [FLUCTUATED (-id), FLUCTUATING], [< L. *fluctuatus*, pp. of *fluctuare* < *fluctus*, a flowing, wave < pp. stem of *fluere*, to flow], 1. to move back and forth or up and down; rise and fall, as waves. 2. to be continually changing or varying in an irregular way: as, the cost of sugar *fluctuates.* *v.t.* to cause to fluctuate. —***SYN.*** see **swing.**

fluc·tu·a·tion (fluk′chōō-ā′shən), *n.* [L. *fluctuatio*], 1. a moving back and forth or up and down; rising and falling, as of waves. 2. continual or irregular variation.

flue (flōō), *n.* [orig., a chimney; variously derived < dial. *flew*, flaring (Tudor chimneys were flared), OFr. *flue*, a flowing, Eng. *flow*, D. *vloei-* in *vloei-pijp*, air-shaft, lit., flowpipe; ? a blend of some of these], 1. a tube, pipe, or shaft for the passage of smoke, hot air, gas, etc., as in a chimney. 2. a flue pipe in an organ. 3. the opening or passage for air in such a flue pipe.

flue (flōō), *n.* [altered < *fluke*], a barbed point; fluke.

flue (flōō), *n.* [ME. *fluwe, flowe;* Fl. *vluwe* < Fr. *velu*, woolly; LL. **villutus*, shaggy < L. *villus*, shaggy hair], a loose, downy mass; fluff.

flue (flōō), *n.* [ME. *flew;* MD. *vluwe*], any of various kinds of fishing net: also spelled **flew.**

flue-cured (flōō′kyoord′), *adj.* cured or dried by hot air passed through flues: said of tobacco.

flu·en·cy (flōō′ən-si), *n.* [L. *fluentia* < *fluens;* see FLUENT], 1. the quality of flowing smoothly and easily. 2. the ability to write or speak easily, smoothly, and expressively; readiness or smoothness of speech.

flu·ent (flōō′ənt), *adj.* [L. *fluens, fluentis*, ppr. of *fluere*, to flow], 1. flowing or going smoothly and easily: as, *fluent* verse. 2. able to write or speak easily, smoothly, and expressively.

flue pipe, an organ pipe in which the tone is produced by a current of air striking the lip of the mouth, or opening, in the pipe.

fluff (fluf), *n.* [? a merging of *flue* (soft mass) & *puff*], 1. soft, light down. 2. a loose, soft mass of fur, dust, hair, etc. 3. in the *theater, radio*, etc. an error in reading lines. *v.t.* 1. to shake or pat until loose, feathery, and fluffy. 2. in the *theater, radio*, etc. to make an error in reading (a word, one's lines, etc.). *v.i.* to become fluffy.

fluf·fi·ness (fluf′i-nis), *n.* the quality of being fluffy.

fluf·fy (fluf′i), *adj.* [FLUFFIER (-i-ẽr), FLUFFIEST (-i-ist)], 1. like fluff; feathery; downy. 2. covered with fluff.

‡Flü·gel·horn (flü′g'l-hôrn′; Eng. flōō′g'l-hôrn′), *n.* [G.; *flügel*, wing + *horn*, horn: because of shape], a brass-wind instrument like the cornet in design but with a tone like that of the French horn.

flu·id (flōō′id), *adj.* [Fr. *fluide;* L. *fluidus* < *fluere*, to flow], 1. that can flow; not solid; able to move and change shape without separating when under pressure. 2. of a fluid or fluids. 3. like a fluid; that can change rapidly or easily; not settled; mobile or plastic: as, *fluid* beliefs. *n.* any substance that can flow; liquid or gas. Abbreviated **fl., f.** —***SYN.*** see **liquid.**

fluid dram (or **drachm**), a liquid measure equal to 1/8 fluid ounce.

flu·id·ex·tract (flōō′id-eks′trakt), *n.* in *pharmacy*, a concentrated fluid preparation of a vegetable drug, containing alcohol either as a preservative or a solvent, and of such strength that one cubic centimeter of the solution is equal in activity to one gram of the dry, powdered drug.

flu·id·ic (flōō-id′ik), *adj.* of, or having the nature of, a fluid.

flu·id·i·ty (flōō-id′ə-ti), *n.* a fluid state or quality.

flu·id·ounce (flōō′id-ouns′), *n.* a fluid ounce.

fluid ounce, a liquid measure equal to 8 fluid drams, 1/16 pint, or 29.6 cc. (in Great Britain, 1/20 imperial pint, or 28.4 cc.): abbreviated **fl. oz.**

fluid pressure, pressure of, or like that of, a fluid: it is constant and uniform in every direction.

fluke (flo͞ok), *n.* [ME. *floke;* AS. *floc;* akin to ON. *floki;* IE. base **p(e)lāg-*, wide and flat, as also in G. *flach,* flat, level], 1. a flatfish; especially, a flounder. 2. any of a number of flat, parasitic worms, living especially in sheep's livers.

fluke (flo͞ok), *n.* [prob. < prec. *fluke,* with reference to shape], 1. either of the two triangular, pointed blades on the arms of an anchor, which catch in the ground: see **anchor**, illus. 2. a barb or barbed head of an arrow, lance, harpoon, etc. 3. either of the two lobes of a whale's tail.

fluke (flo͞ok), *n.* [19th-c. billiard slang; ? orig. "dupe stroke" < slang *fluke,* person easily duped < *fluke,* flatfish (which is easily caught)], [Slang], 1. an accidentally good or lucky stroke in billiards, pool, etc.; hence, 2. a lucky chance; stroke of luck: as, we won the football game by a *fluke.* ***v.i.*** [FLUKED (flo͞okt), FLUKING], [Slang], to make a fluke. ***v.t.*** [Slang], to hit or get by a fluke.

fluk·y, fluk·ey (flo͞ok'i), *adj.* [FLUKIER (-i-ẽr), FLUKIEST (-i-ist)], [< *fluke* (lucky stroke)], [Slang], 1. resulting from chance; lucky. 2. constantly changing; uncertain; fitful: as, a *fluky* breeze.

flume (flo͞om), *n.* [ME. *flum, flun,* river, stream; OFr. *flum;* L. *flumen* < *fluere,* to flow], 1. an artificial channel, usually an inclined chute or trough, for carrying water to furnish power, transport logs down a mountainside, etc. 2. a narrow gorge or ravine with a stream running through it. ***v.t.*** [FLUMED (flo͞omd), FLUMING], to send (logs, etc.) down a flume.

flum·mer·y (flum'ẽr-i), *n.* [*pl.* FLUMMERIES (-iz)], [W. *llymru,* soured oatmeal < *llymus,* of a sharp quality; cf. FLIMSY], 1. any soft, easily eaten food; especially, *a*) thick, boiled oatmeal or flour. *b*) a soft custard or blancmange. 2. meaningless flattery or silly talk.

flum·mox (flum'əks), *v.t.* [< dial. *flummocks* or thieves' slang; prob. echoic], [Slang], to confuse; perplex.

flump (flump), *v.t. & v.i.* [prob. echoic], to drop or move heavily and noisily. *n.* the act or sound of flumping.

flung (fluŋ), past tense and past participle of **fling**.

flunk (fluŋk), *v.t.* [19th-c. college slang; ? < *funk* (orig., Oxford Univ. slang) or echoic], [Colloq.], 1. to fail in (schoolwork): as, he *flunked* the English examination. 2. to give a mark of *failure* to; grade as having failed. 3. to cause to fail: as, continued absence will *flunk* a student. ***v.i.*** [Colloq.], 1. to fail, especially in schoolwork. 2. to give up; retreat. *n.* [Colloq.], 1. a failure. 2. a mark or grade of *failure.*

flunk out, [Colloq.], to go or send away from school or college because of unsatisfactory work.

flunk·ey (fluŋ'ki), *n.* [*pl.* FLUNKEYS (-kiz)], a flunky.

flunk·y (fluŋ'ki), *n.* [*pl.* FLUNKIES (-kiz)], [orig. Scot.; ? < Fr. *flanquer,* to flank, run along by the side of, be at one's elbow to render assistance < *flanc;* see FLANK], 1. a liveried manservant, as a footman: term of contempt. 2. a flattering, servile person; toady.

flunk·y·ism, flunk·ey·ism (fluŋ'ki-iz'm), *n.* the behavior or spirit of a flunky.

flu·o (flo͞o'ō), *adj.* of or containing fluorine.

flu·o- (flo͞o'ə), [< *fluor*], a combining form meaning: 1. *fluorine.* 2. *fluorescent.*

flu·o·bo·ric (flo͞o'ə-bôr'ik, flo͞o'ə-bō'rik), *adj.* of, or in combination with, fluorine and boron.

flu·or (flo͞o'ẽr, flo͞o'ôr), *n.* [L., flux < *fluere,* to flow; used as transl. of G. *fluss* and orig. applied to certain minerals used as smelting fluxes, but later limited to those containing fluorine], fluorite.

flu·o·resce (flo͞o'ə-res'), *v.i.* [FLUORESCED (-rest'), FLUORESCING], to produce, show, or undergo fluorescence; be or become fluorescent.

flu·o·res·ce·in (flo͞o'ə-res'i-in), *n.* [*fluoresce* + *-in:* from its bright fluorescence in solution], a yellowish-red, crystalline compound, $C_{20}H_{12}O_5$, made synthetically from resorcin and phthalic anhydride: an alkaline solution appears green by reflected light and red by transmitted light.

flu·o·res·ce·ine (flo͞o'ə-res'i-ēn', flo͞o'ə-res'i-in), *n.* fluorescein.

flu·o·res·cence (flo͞o'ə-res''ns), *n.* [< *fluor* spar (which exhibits the property) + ending of *phosphorescence*], 1. the property of a substance, such as fluorite, of producing light while it is being acted upon by radiant energy, such as ultraviolet rays or X rays. 2. the production of such light. 3. light so produced.

flu·o·res·cent (flo͞o'ə-res''nt, floor-es''nt), *adj.* having or resulting from fluorescence.

fluorescent lamp, a glass tube coated on the inside with a fluorescent substance that gives off light (*fluorescent light*) when acted upon by a stream of electrons from the cathode.

flu·or·ic (flo͞o-ôr'ik, flo͞o-or'ik), *adj.* of or obtained from fluorine or fluorite.

flu·o·rid (flo͞o'ə-rid), *n.* fluoride.

flu·o·ri·date (flo͞o'ə-ri-dāt'), *v.t.* [FLUORIDATED (-id), FLUORIDATING], to add fluorides to (a water supply) in order, as is claimed, to reduce the incidence of caries in the teeth.

flu·o·ride (flo͞o'ə-rīd', flo͞o'ə-rid), *n.* a compound of fluorine and one or more elements or radicals.

flu·o·rin (flo͞o'ə-rin), *n.* fluorine.

flu·o·rine (flo͞o'ə-rēn', flo͞o'ə-rin), *n.* [so named from occurring in *fluor*ite, with ending after related chlor*ine*], a very active chemical element of the halogen family, a corrosive, greenish-yellow gas: symbol, F, Fl; at. wt., 19.00; at. no., 9.

flu·o·rite (flo͞o'ə-rīt'), *n.* [*fluor* + *-ite*], calcium fluoride, CaF_2, a transparent, crystalline mineral having many colors and perfect cleavage: it is used as a flux, in glassmaking, etc.: also called *fluor, fluor spar.*

flu·o·ro- (flo͞o'ə-rō), a combining form meaning: 1. *fluorine.* 2. *fluorescence.* Also, before a vowel, **fluor-**.

flu·o·ro·scope (floor'ə-skōp', flo͞o'ə-rə-skōp'), *n.* [*fluoro-* + *-scope*], a machine for examining internal structures by viewing the shadows cast on a fluorescent screen by objects or parts through which X rays are directed: the shadows vary in intensity according to the density of the object or part.

flu·or·os·co·py (floor-os'kə-pi, flo͞o'ə-ros'kə-pi), *n.* examination by means of the fluoroscope.

fluor spar, fluorite.

flur·ry (flũr'i), *n.* [*pl.* FLURRIES (-iz)], [extension of obs. dial. *flur,* to whir, prob. echoic], 1. a sudden, brief rush of wind; gust. 2. a gust of rain or snow. 3. a sudden confusion, commotion, or agitation. ***v.t.*** [FLURRIED (-id), FLURRYING], to confuse; agitate.

flush (flush), *v.i.* [complex of several words, with senses < *flash, v.* & ME. *flusschen,* to fly up suddenly, blended with echoic elements; "flow" senses prob. < or akin to OFr. *fluir* (*fluiss-*), to flow (cf. FLUENT)], 1. to flow and spread suddenly and rapidly: as, the blood *flushed* in his face. 2. to become red in the face, as with embarrassment or anger; blush. 3. to glow. 4. to become cleaned, washed, or emptied out with a sudden flow of water, etc. 5. to start up from cover: said of birds. ***v.t.*** 1. to clean, wash, or empty out with a sudden flow of water, etc. 2. to make blush or glow. 3. to excite; animate; exhilarate. 4. to drive (birds) from cover. 5. to make level or even: as, the mason *flushed* the joint with mortar. *n.* 1. a sudden and rapid flow, as of water in washing out something. 2. a sudden, vigorous growth: as, the first *flush* of youth. 3. a sudden feeling of excitement or exhilaration. 4. a blush; glow. 5. a sudden feeling of great heat, as in a fever. ***adj.*** 1. well supplied, especially with money. 2. abundant; plentiful. 3. lavish; profuse. 4. full of vigor; hence, 5. having a ruddy color; glowing. 6. making an even or unbroken line or surface; adjusted to a margin, edge, etc.: as, the door is *flush* with the walls. 7. direct; full: as, a blow *flush* in the face. ***adv.*** 1. in an even manner; so as to be level or in alignment. 2. directly; squarely.

flush (flush), *n.* [Fr. *flux;* see FLUX], a hand of cards all in the same suit: in poker, a flush is just above a straight and below a full house.

flus·ter (flus'tẽr), *v.t. & v.i.* [orig., to excite with liquor; ME. *flosteren;* prob. < ON.; cf. Ice. *flaustra,* to bustle, hurry], to make or be confused, nervous, and excited. *n.* the condition of being flustered.

flus·ter·a·tion (flus'tẽr-ā'shən), *n.* flustration.

flus·tra·tion (flus-trā'shən), *n.* the condition of being flustered.

flute (flo͞ot), *n.* [ME. *floute, fluite;* OFr. *fleüte, flaute* (It. *flauto*); Pr. *fläut;* prob. < *flauja* < *flaujol* (see FLAGEOLET) + *laüt,* lute (see LUTE)], 1. a high-pitched wind instrument consisting of a long, slender tube, played by blowing across a hole near the upper end: by fingering the holes and keys along its length, the player can produce various tones. 2. a thing shaped like such an instrument, as a roll of bread, a wineglass, etc. 3. an ornamental groove in cloth, etc. 4. in *architecture,* a long, rounded groove in the shaft of a column. 5. in *music,* a flue organ stop with a flutelike tone. Abbreviated fl. ***v.t.*** [FLUTED (-id), FLUTING], 1. to sing, speak, whistle, etc. in a flutelike tone. 2. to play on the flute. 3. to make long, rounded grooves in (a column, etc.). ***v.i.*** 1. to play on the flute. 2. to sing, speak, whistle, etc. in a flutelike tone.

FLUTE

flut·ed (flo͞ot'id), *adj.* [pp. of *flute*], 1. having a flutelike tone; fluty. 2. having long, rounded grooves.

flut·er (flo͞ot'ẽr), *n.* [ME. *floutour;* OFr. *flauteur*], 1. [Rare], a flutist. 2. a person or tool that makes flutings.

flut·i·ly (flo͞ot''l-i), *adv.* in a fluty manner.

flut·i·ness (flo͞ot'i-nis), *n.* the quality of being fluty.

flut·ing (flo͞ot'iŋ), *n.* [< *flute, v.* + *-ing*], 1. a decoration consisting of long, rounded grooves, as in a column. 2. a groove or grooves, as in a column or ruffle. 3. the act of making such grooves. 4. the act of playing the flute. 5. a singing, etc. in a flute-like tone.

fluting iron, an iron with a corrugated surface, for pressing ruffles.

fluting machine, a machine for corrugating sheet metal.

flut·ist (flōōt′ist), *n.* a person who plays the flute: also **flautist.**

flut·ter (flut′ẽr), *v.i.* [ME. *flotteren;* AS. *flotorian,* freq. formation < base of *fleotan;* see FLEET, *v.*], 1. to flap the wings rapidly, as in short flight, or without flying at all. 2. to wave or vibrate rapidly and irregularly: as, the flag *fluttered* in the wind. 3. to move with quick vibrations, flaps, etc. 4. to be in a state of tremulous excitement; tremble; quiver. 5. to move restlessly; bustle. *v.t.* 1. to cause to move in quick, irregular motions. 2. to throw into a state of excitement or confusion. *n.* 1. a fluttering movement; vibration. 2. a state of excitement or confusion. 3. a condition of the heart beat in which the contractions are very rapid but regular: in *impure flutter* they are irregular. —*SYN.* see **fly.**

flutter kick, a swimming kick in which the legs are moved continually up and down in short, rapid strokes.

flutter wheel, a water wheel at the bottom of a chute, turned by the falling water.

flut·ter·y (flut′ẽr-i), *adj.* fluttering or apt to flutter.

flut·y (flōōt′i), *adj.* [FLUTIER (-i-ẽr), FLUTIEST (-i-ist)], flutelike in tone; soft, clear, and high-pitched.

flu·vi·al (flōō′vi-əl), *adj.* [ME.; OFr.; L. *fluvialis* < *fluvius,* a river < *fluere,* to flow], of, found in, or produced by a river or rivers.

flu·vi·a·tile (flōō′vi-ə-til), *adj.* [Fr.; L. *fluviatilis* < *fluvius*], fluvial.

flu·vi·o·ma·rine (flōō′vi-ō′mə-rēn′), *adj.* [< L. *fluvius* (see FLUVIAL); + *marine*], in *geology,* of or made by the combined action of the ocean and a river flowing into it.

flux (fluks), *n.* [ME.; OFr.; L. *fluxus,* a flowing, flow, pp. of *fluere,* to flow], 1. a flowing or flow. 2. a coming in of the tide. 3. a continuous movement; continual change: as, fashion is always in a state of *flux.* 4. any excessive or unnatural discharge of fluid matter from the body. 5. a substance, as borax or rosin, used to help metals to fuse together, as in soldering. 6. in *physics,* the rate of flow of energy, fluids, etc. over a surface. *v.t.* 1. to fuse (metals) by melting. 2. in *medicine,* to purge. *v.i.* [Archaic], to flow or stream out.

flux density, in *physics,* the quantity of a fluid or energy emitted per unit of time through a unit of surface area.

flux·ion (fluk′shən), *n.* [Fr.; L. **fluxio* for *fluctio,* a flowing < pp. of *fluere,* to flow], 1. a flowing. 2. continuous change. 3. something that flows; discharge. 4. [adopted by Newton], in *mathematics,* the rate of continuous change in variable quantities; a differential.

flux·ion·al (fluk′shən-'l), *adj.* of a fluxion or fluxions.

flux·ion·ar·y (fluk′shən-er′i), *adj.* fluxional.

fly (flī), *v.i.* [FLEW (flōō), FLOWN (flōn), FLYING], [ME. *flien, flyhen, fleien,* etc.; AS. *fleogan, fliogan;* akin to G. *fliegen;* IE. **pleu-q-* < **pleu-,* to move forward (by swimming, flying, running, etc.), extension < **pel-,* to flow, pour; hence, akin to *flow, fleet*], 1. to move through the air; specifically, *a*) to move through the air by using wings, as a bird. *b*) to travel through the air in an aircraft. *c*) to be propelled through the air, as a bullet. 2. to operate an aircraft. 3. to wave or float in the air, as a flag or kite. 4. to move swiftly or suddenly: as, the door *flew* open. 5. to appear to pass swiftly: as, time *flies.* 6. to be used up swiftly: said of money, etc. 7. to run away from danger or evil; flee. 8. [FLIED (flīd), FLYING], in *baseball,* to hit a fly. 9. in *hawking,* to hunt with a hawk. *v.t.* 1. to cause to move or float in the air: as, *fly* a kite. 2. to operate (an aircraft). 3. to go over in an aircraft: as, he *flew* the Pacific. 4. to carry or transport in an aircraft. 5. to run away from; flee from; avoid. 6. in *hawking,* to hunt with a hawk. *n.* [*pl.* FLIES (flīz)], [< the *v.*], 1. a flap of cloth that conceals buttons or other fasteners in a garment; especially, such a flap in the front of a pair of trousers. 2. *a*) a flap serving as the door of a tent. *b*) a piece of fabric serving as an outer or second top on a tent. 3. *a*) the width of an extended flag. *b*) the part of a flag farthest from the staff. 4. a flywheel. 5. a flyleaf. 6. [British], a hackney carriage. 7. in *baseball,* a ball batted high in the air within the foul lines. 8. *pl.* in the *theater,* the space behind and above the proscenium arch, containing overhead lights, machinery for raising and lowering sets, etc.

fly at, to attack suddenly by or as by flying or springing toward.

fly in the face of, to be openly opposed to or defiant of.

fly into, to have a violent outburst of.

fly off, to go away quickly or suddenly; hurry off.

fly out, in *baseball,* to be put out by hitting a fly that is caught by a fielder before it touches the ground.

let fly (at), 1. to shoot or throw (at). 2. to direct a verbal attack (at).

on the fly, 1. while in flight. 2. [Slang], while in a hurry.

SYN.—**fly** is the general word implying movement through the air on wings (birds, insects, airplanes *fly*); **flit** suggests a series of quick, brief flights from place to place (sparrows *flitted* about in the trees); to **hover** is to remain suspended at a point in the air by special movements of the wings (a butterfly *hovered* over the flower); **soar** implies a flying high into the air in a straight, almost vertical line (the lark *soared* into the sky), or it may also describe a gliding on air currents high in the air (eagles *soaring* near the craggy peaks); **flutter** suggests a rapid but unsteady flapping of the wings, as in the short flight of a young or injured bird.

fly (flī), *n.* [*pl.* FLIES (flīz)], [ME. *flie, flege;* AS. *fleoge, flyge* (akin to G. *fliege*) < base of *fleogan;* see FLY, *v.*], 1. *a*) a housefly. *b*) any of a large group of insects with two transparent wings, including the housefly, gnat, mosquito, and Mayfly. 2. a device made of feathers, colored silk, etc. to resemble an insect, used as bait in fishing. 3. in *printing,* *a*) formerly, the person whose work was removing sheets from the press as they were printed. *b*) a fingered device on the press for removing the printed sheets.

fly in the ointment, anything, especially a little thing, that reduces or destroys the value or usefulness of something else.

fly (flī), *adj.* [FLIER (flī′ẽr), FLIEST (flī′ist)], [orig., thieves' slang; prob. renders D. *vlug* in same sense], [Slang], 1. quick; agile; nimble. 2. alert and knowing; sharp.

fly agaric, a common, very poisonous mushroom with an orange-colored cap full of white warts: also called *fly amanita.*

fly·a·way (flī′ə-wā′), *adj.* 1. flying in the wind; streaming: as, *flyaway* hair. 2. flighty. *n.* 1. a runaway. 2. a flighty person.

fly·blow (flī′blō′), *n.* a blowfly's egg or larva. *v.t. & v.i.* [FLYBLEW (-blōō′), FLYBLOWN (-blōn′), FLYBLOWING], 1. to deposit eggs in (meat, etc.): said of a fly; hence, 2. to contaminate; spoil; taint.

fly·blown (flī′blōn′), *adj.* 1. full of flies' eggs or larvae; hence, 2. contaminated; spoiled; tainted.

fly·boat (flī′bōt′), *n.* [D. *vlieboot,* after the *Vlie,* channel connecting the North Sea and the Zuyder Zee], 1. a fast, flat-bottomed Dutch boat. 2. any of several fast sailing vessels.

fly book, a booklike case to hold artificial fishing flies.

fly-by-night (flī′bī-nīt′), *adj.* not trustworthy; financially unsound. *n.* a debtor who runs away from his debts.

fly·catch·er (flī′kach′ẽr), *n.* 1. any of a group of small birds, including the kingbird, pewee, phoebe, and crested flycatcher, that catch insects in flight. 2. any of a number of plants that catch and ingest insects.

fly·er (flī′ẽr), *n.* a flier.

fly-fish (flī′fish′), *v.i.* to fish with flies, especially artificial flies, as bait.

fly·ing (flī′iŋ), *adj.* [ppr. of *fly;* cf. AS. *fleogende,* glossing, L. *volucer*], 1. that flies or can fly. 2. moving as if flying; moving swiftly; fast. 3. like flight through the air. 4. waving or streaming in the air: as, with flags *flying.* 5. hasty and brief: as, a *flying* trip. 6. of or for aircraft or aviators: as, a *flying* field, *flying* suit. *n.* the action of a person or thing that flies.

send flying, to set in rapid motion.

flying boat, an airplane with a hull that permits it to land on and take off from water: see TYPES OF AIRPLANE, p. 32.

flying buttress, a buttress connected with a wall at some distance from it by an arch or part of an arch: it serves to resist outward pressure.

FLYING BUTTRESS

flying colors, 1. flags flying in the air; hence, 2. victory or success.

flying column, a detachment of soldiers lightly equipped for rapid movement and operations independent of the main force.

Flying Dutchman, 1. a fabled Dutch sailor condemned for his sins to sail the seas until Judgment Day. 2. his ghostlike ship, considered a bad omen by sailors who think they see it. The subject of an opera (1843) by Richard Wagner.

flying field, a field prepared for the landing, taking off, and minor servicing of aircraft: distinguished from *airport.*

flying fish, any of a number of warm-water sea fishes with winglike pectoral fins that enable them to leap through the air.

FLYING FISH

flying fox, any of several fruit-eating bats with foxlike heads.

flying frog, a frog found in Borneo and the East Indies that has webbed

feet which permit it to make long, gliding leaps.
flying gurnard, any of various fishes with winglike fins, capable of flying short distances.
flying jib, a small, triangular sail in front of the jib, usually on an extension of the jib boom or bowsprit: see sail, illus.
flying lemur, an East Indian tree-dwelling mammal capable of making long, gliding leaps from tree to tree by means of a membrane extending like a wing from its neck to its tail.
flying machine, any aircraft, especially an airplane.
flying mare, in *wrestling*, a throw made by seizing the opponent's wrist, turning, and throwing him over one's back.
flying phalanger, any of several small Australian marsupials capable of leaping like flying squirrels.
flying saucer, any of various unidentified objects frequently reported since 1947 to have been seen flying at great heights and high speeds, and variously regarded as light phenomena, hallucinations, secret military missiles, etc.
flying squirrel, any of a number of squirrels with winglike folds of skin attached to the legs and body which enable them to make long, gliding leaps.
flying start, 1. the start of a race in which the contestants are already moving when the starting signal is given. 2. any rapid beginning.
flying wing, an airplane consisting of a single wing of thick section tapered toward the tips and having no fuselage or tail group.
fly·leaf (flī'lēf'), *n.* [*pl.* FLYLEAVES (-lēvz')], a blank leaf at the beginning or end of a book, etc.
fly net, a net to protect animals or people from flies and other insects.
fly·pa·per (flī'pā'pēr), *n.* a sticky or poisonous paper set out to catch or kill flies: also **fly paper.**
Fly River, a river in New Guinea, flowing southeastward through Papua Territory: length, c. 800 mi.
fly sheet, [< earlier *flying sheet*], a pamphlet.
fly·speck (flī'spek'), *n.* 1. a speck of excrement left by a fly. 2. any tiny spot. ***v.t.*** to make flyspecks on.
flyte (flīt), *v.i., v.t. & n.* flite.
fly·trap (flī'trap'), *n.* 1. any device for catching flies. 2. a plant that catches insects; pitcher plant or Venus's-flytrap.
fly·weight (flī'wāt'), *n.* a boxer who weighs 112 pounds or less. *adj.* of flyweights.
fly·wheel (flī'hwēl'), *n.* a heavy wheel for regulating the speed and uniformity of motion of the machine to which it is attached.
FM, frequency modulation.
Fm, in *chemistry*, fermium.
fm., 1. fathom. 2. from.
F.M., 1. Field Marshal. 2. Foreign Missions.
F number, in *photography*, the measurement of the ratio of a lens diameter to its focal distance: symbol, f/, F/, f, F, f:, *f.*: the lower the F number, the shorter the exposure required.
fo., folio.
F.O., 1. Foreign Office. 2. field officer: also **f.o.**
foal (fōl), *n.* [ME. *fole;* AS. *fola;* akin to OHG. *folo* (G. *fohlen*); IE. base **pōu-*, etc., little, small, seen also in *pauper & pullet;* cf. FILLY], a young horse, mule, donkey, etc.; colt or filly. ***v.t. & v.i.*** to give birth to (a foal).
foam (fōm), *n.* [ME. *fome, foom;* AS. *fam;* akin to G. *feim*, scum; IE. base **(s)poimno-*, foam, seen also in *spume*], 1. the whitish mass of bubbles formed on liquids by violent shaking, fermentation, etc. 2. something like foam, as the heavy sweat of horses, or frothy saliva. 3. [Poetic], the sea. ***v.i.*** to form, produce, or gather foam; froth. ***v.t.*** to cause to foam.
foam at the mouth, to be very angry; rage.
foam·flow·er (fōm'flou'ēr), *n.* a small American herb of the saxifrage family, with white flowers that bloom in the spring.
foam·i·ly (fōm'ə-li), *adv.* in a foamy manner.
foam·i·ness (fōm'i-nis), *n.* a foamy quality or state.
foam rubber, rubber prepared in a firm spongy mass, used in upholstered seats, mattresses, etc.
foam·y (fōm'i), *adj.* [FOAMIER (-i-ēr), FOAMIEST (-i-ist)], [ME. *fomi;* AS. *famig*], 1. foaming or covered with foam. 2. consisting of foam. 3. like foam.
fob (fob), *n.* [prob. < dial. G. *fuppe*, a pocket], 1. a small pocket in the front of a man's trousers, for carrying a watch, etc.; watch pocket. 2. a short ribbon or chain attached to a watch and hanging out of such a pocket. 3. any ornament worn at the end of such a ribbon or chain.
fob (fob), *v.t.* [FOBBED (fobd), FOBBING], [< ME. *fobbe, fobbere*, cheater, prob. var. of *foppe* (see FOP)], [Obs.], to cheat; trick; deceive: also **fub.**
fob off, 1. to trick or put off (a person) with something second-rate or undesired. 2. to get rid of (something worthless) by deceit or trickery; palm off.
F.O.B., f.o.b., free on board: used in quoting prices of goods at the place of manufacture, not including transportation charges.
fo·cal (fō'k'l), *adj.* of or placed at a focus.
focal distance, the distance from the optical center of a lens to the point where the light rays converge; length of the focus: also **focal length.**
focal infection, a localized infection, as in the gall bladder, teeth, or tonsils, from which bacterial toxins may be liberated into the blood stream so as to cause infection in another part of the body.
fo·cal·i·za·tion (fō'k'l-i-zā'shən, fō'k'l-ī-zā'shən), *n.* a focalizing or being focalized.
fo·cal·ize (fō'k'l-īz'), *v.t. & v.i.* [FOCALIZED (-īzd'), FOCALIZING], 1. to adjust or become adjusted to a focus. 2. in *medicine*, to limit or be limited to a small area: said of an infection.
Foch, Fer·di·nand (fer'dē'nän' fôsh), 1851–1929; French commander in chief of Allied armies (1918).
fo·ci (fō'sī), *n.* alternative plural of **focus.**
fo'c's'le (fōk's'l), *n.* forecastle: a phonetic spelling.
fo·cus (fō'kəs), *n.* [*pl.* FOCUSES (-iz), FOCI (fō'sī)], [L., fireplace, hearth; adopted by Kepler (1604) in math. senses], 1. the point where rays of light, heat, etc. or waves of sound come together, or from which they spread or seem to spread; specifically, the point where rays of light reflected by a mirror or refracted by a lens meet (called *real focus*), or the point where they would meet if prolonged backward through the lens or mirror (called *virtual focus*). 2. the focal distance. 3. an adjustment of this distance to make a clear image: as, he brought the camera into *focus*. 4. any center of activity, attention, etc.; hence, 5. a part of the body where an infection is localized or most active. 6. in *mathematics*, *a*) either of the two fixed points used in determining an ellipse. *b*) any analagous point for a parabola or hyperbola. 7. in *seismology*, the starting point of an earthquake. ***v.t.*** [FOCUSED OR FOCUSSED (-kəst), FOCUSING OR FOCUSSING], 1. to bring into focus. 2. to adjust the focal distance of (the eye, a lens, etc.) in order to produce a clear image. 3. to fix on one object; concentrate: as, *focus* your attention on study. ***v.i.*** to meet at a focus.

LIGHT RAYS LENS FOCUS

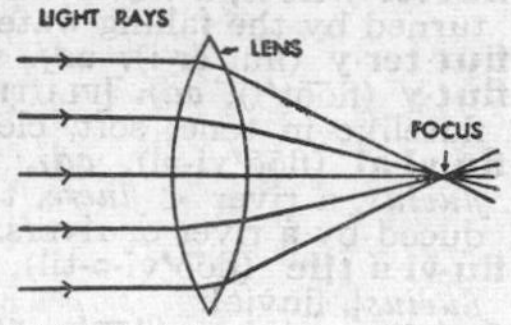

LIGHT RAYS BROUGHT INTO FOCUS BY LENS

in focus, clear; distinct; sharply defined.
out of focus, indistinct; blurred; not sharply defined.
fod·der (fod'ēr), *n.* [ME. *foder, foddre;* AS. *fodor* (akin to G. *futter*) < base of *foda;* see FOOD], coarse food for cattle, horses, sheep, etc., as cornstalks, hay, and straw. ***v.t.*** to feed with fodder.
foe (fō), *n.* [ME. *fo, ifo;* AS. *fah*, hostile, *(ge)fah*, enemy; akin to OHG. *gefēh*, at feud, hostile; for IE. base see FEUD], an enemy; opponent. —*SYN.* see **opponent.**
foehn (fān; G. fön), *n.* [G. dial. *föhn;* MHG. *phönne;* OHG. *fonno;* LL. **faunjo* < L. *Favonius*, west wind], a warm, dry wind blowing down into the valleys of a mountain, especially in the Alps.
foe·man (fō'mən), *n.* [*pl.* FOEMEN (-mən)], [AS. *fahmann*, lit., hostile person], [Archaic or Poetic], a foe; enemy.
foe·tal (fē't'l), *adj.* fetal.
foe·tus (fē'təs), *n.* a fetus.
fog (fôg, fog), *n.* [said to be back-formation < *foggy* (in basic early senses "covered with rank grass, hence damp, moist") < *fog* (coarse grass); ? a merging of this with an ON. word; cf. Dan. *snefog*, driving snowstorm, Norw. dial. *fuka*, sea mist], 1. a large mass of water vapor condensed to fine particles, at or just above the earth's surface. 2. a similar mass of smoke, dust, etc. obscuring the atmosphere. 3. a state of mental dimness and confusion; blurred, bewildered condition. 4. a blur on a photograph or film. ***v.i.*** [FOGGED (fôgd, fogd), FOGGING], 1. to become surrounded or covered by fog. 2. to be or become blurred, dimmed, or obscured. ***v.t.*** 1. to surround or cover with fog. 2. to blur; dim; obscure. 3. to confuse; bewilder. 4. in *photography*, to make blurred. —*SYN.* see **mist.**
fog (fôg, fog), *n.* [ME. *fogge;* ME. dial. distribution suggests ON. origin; cf. Norw. dial. *fogg*, long grass in moist place; ? akin to AS. *fuht*, G. *feucht*, moist], 1. a new growth of grass after cutting or grazing. 2. long, rank grass left uncut or ungrazed. 3. [Dial.], moss.
fog bank, a dense mass of fog.
fog·bound (fôg'bound', fog'bound'), *adj.* prevented from sailing because of fog.
fog·dog (fôg'dôg', fog'dôg'), *n.* a bright spot sometimes seen at the horizon in a fog.
fo·gey (fō'gi), *n.* [*pl.* FOGEYS (-giz)], a fogy.
Fog·gia (fôd'jä), *n.* a city in southeastern Italy: pop., 67,000 (1947).
fog·gi·ly (fôg'ə-li, fog'ə-li), *adv.* in a foggy manner.
fog·gi·ness (fôg'i-nis, fog'i-nis), *n.* the quality or state of being foggy.
fog·gy (fôg'i, fog'i), *adj.* [FOGGIER (-i-ēr), FOGGIEST (-i-ist)], [Early Mod. Eng., orig., covered with or like *fog* (coarse grass)], 1. full of fog; misty; murky. 2. dim; blurred; clouded. 3. confused; perplexed.
fog·horn (fôg'hôrn', fog'hôrn'), *n.* 1. a horn blown to give warning to ships in a fog. 2. a loud, strident voice.

fo·gy (fō′gi), *n.* [*pl.* FOGIES (-giz)], [earlier also *foggy;* said to be < *foggy, adj.* in obs. sense of "flabby, fat"], a person who is old-fashioned or overly conservative in ideas and actions: also spelled **fogey.**
fo·gy·ish (fō′gi-ish), *adj.* of or like a fogy; old-fashioned.
foh (fô), *interj.* faugh.
foi·ble (foi′b'l), *n.* [obs. form of Fr. *faible;* see FEEBLE], 1. a small weakness; slight frailty in character. 2. the weaker part of a sword blade, from the middle to the point. —*SYN.* see **fault.**
foil (foil), *v.t.* [ME. *foilen;* OFr. *fuler, fouler,* to trample on, subdue; LL. *fullare,* to full (cloth) by trampling or beating < L. *fullo,* a fuller], 1. to keep from being successful; baffle; balk; thwart; frustrate: as, he was *foiled* in his attempt. 2. in *hunting,* to make (a scent, trail, etc.) confused, as by trampling, in order to balk the pursuers. *n.* 1. the scent or trail of an animal. 2. a long, thin fencing sword with a button on the point to prevent injury. 3. the art or sport of fencing with foils. 4. [Archaic], a thwarting. —*SYN.* see **frustrate.**
foil (foil), *n.* [ME. *foile;* OFr. *foil, fuil* (Fr. *feuille*), a leaf, sheet of paper or metal < L. *folia,* pl. of *folium,* a leaf; IE. **bholjom* < base **bhel-, *bhlō-,* to swell; cf. BLADE], 1. a leaflike, rounded space or design between cusps or in windows, etc., as in Gothic architecture. 2. a very thin sheet or leaf of metal: as, gold *foil,* tin *foil.* 3. a thin leaf of polished metal placed under a gem to give it brilliance, or under other substances to make them seem precious, as in some jewelry. 4. a person or thing that sets off or enhances another by contrast: as, Laertes is a *foil* to Hamlet. *v.t.* 1. to cover or back with foil. 2. [Rare], to serve as a contrast to. 3. to decorate (windows, etc.) with foils.
foils·man (foilz′mən), *n.* [*pl.* FOILSMEN (-mən)], a fencer who uses a foil.
foin (foin), *v.i. & n.* [ME. *foinen* < OFr. *foine, foisne,* fish spear < L. *fuscina,* a trident], [Archaic], lunge; thrust.
Fo·ïsm (fō′iz'm), *n.* [< Chin. *Fo,* Buddha], the Buddhism of China.
foi·son (foi′z'n), *n.* [ME. *foison, foisoun;* OFr. *foison, fuison;* L. *fusio,* a pouring; see FUSION], 1. [Archaic], a plentiful crop; good harvest; plenty. 2. [Obs. or Dial.], *a*) vitality; strength; ability. *b*) *pl.* resources.
foist (foist), *v.t.* [prob. < dial. D. *vuisten,* to hold in the hand, hence, in dicing, to conceal in the hand, palm off < *vuist,* a fist], 1. to put in slyly or stealthily; insert surreptitiously, as a clause into a contract. 2. to pass off (something false) as genuine (with *on* or *upon*); impose by fraud; palm off.
Fo·kine, Mi·chel (mi-shel′ fô-kēn′), 1880–1942; American choreographer, born in Russia.
Fok·ker, Anthony Herman Gerard (fok′ẽr), 1890–1939; Dutch airplane designer and constructor in Germany and, later, the United States.
fol., 1. folio. 2. following.
fold (fōld), *v.t.* [ME. *folden;* AS. *faldan* (W.S. *fealdan*); akin to G. *falten;* IE. **pel-to* < base **pel-,* to fall, seen also in *sim-pl-e, du-pl-e, tri-pl-e,* etc.], 1. to bend or press (something) so that one part is over another; double up on itself. 2. to draw together and intertwine: as, *fold* your arms. 3. to draw close to the body: as, a bird *folds* its wings. 4. to clasp in the arms; embrace. 5. to wrap up; envelop. *v.i.* 1. to be or become folded. 2. [Slang], to fail; be forced to close: said of a play, etc. *n.* 1. a folding. 2. a folded part or layer. 3. a mark made by folding. 4. a hollow or crease produced by folded parts or layers. 5. in *geology,* a rock layer folded by pressure.
  fold up, 1. to make or become more compact by folding. 2. [Slang], to fail; be forced to close: said of a play, etc.
fold (fōld), *n.* [ME. *fold;* AS. *falod, falud;* akin to D. *vaalt,* enclosed place, Dan. *fold,* sheep pen; IE. base **pel-,* to fall (cf. prec.); basic sense "enclosed (? with wickerwork)"], 1. a pen in which to keep sheep. 2. sheep kept together; flock of sheep; hence, 3. *a*) the members of a church. *b*) a church. *c*) any group or organization with common interests, aims, etc. *v.t.* to keep or confine (sheep) in a pen.
-fold (fōld), [ME. *-fold, -fald;* AS. *-feald;* see FOLD (to double up)], a suffix meaning: 1. *having* (a specified number of) *parts.* 2. (a specified number of) *times as many, as much, as large,* as in *tenfold, hundredfold.*
fold·boat (fōld′bōt′), *n.* a faltboat.
fold·er (fōl′dẽr), *n.* 1. a person or thing that folds. 2. a sheet of cardboard or heavy paper folded as a holder for papers. 3. a pamphlet or booklet folded but not stitched.
fol·de·rol (fol′də-rol′), *n.* falderal.
folding doors, a pair of doors with hinged leaves that unfold from either side of a wide doorway and meet in the middle to close it.
fo·li·a (fō′li-ə), *n.* alternative plural of **folium.**
fo·li·a·ceous (fō′li-ā′shəs), *adj.* [L. *foliaceus* < *folium,* a leaf], 1. of or like the leaf of a plant. 2. having leaves. 3. consisting of thin layers, as certain rocks.
fo·li·age (fō′li-ij), *n.* [earlier *foillage;* OFr. *foillage, feuillage* < *foille, feuille,* a leaf < L. *folia,* pl. of *folium,* a leaf], 1. leaves, as of a plant or tree; mass of leaves; leafage. 2. a decoration consisting of a representation of leaves, branches, flowers, etc.
fo·li·aged (fō′li-ijd), *adj.* having foliage: usually in hyphenated compounds, as, *dark-foliaged.*
fo·li·ar (fō′li-ẽr), *adj.* [Mod. L. *foliaris* < L. *folium,* a leaf], of or like a leaf or leaves.
fo·li·ate (fō′li-āt′), *v.t.* [FOLIATED (-id), FOLIATING], [< L. *foliatus,* pp. of *foliare,* to put forth leaves < *folium,* a leaf], 1. *a*) to divide into thin layers. *b*) to beat into foil. 2. to decorate with leaflike layers or ornamentation. 3. to number (the leaves of a book). *v.i.* 1. to separate into layers. 2. to send out leaves. *adj.* (fō′li-it, fō′li-āt′), 1. having or covered with leaves. 2. like a leaf or leaves.
fo·li·a·tion (fō′li-ā′shən), *n.* [< *foliate* + *-tion*], 1. a growing of or developing into a leaf or leaves; leaf formation. 2. the state of being in leaf. 3. the act or process of beating metal into layers. 4. *a*) a splitting into leaflike layers: said of certain minerals and rocks. *b*) the property of splitting into such layers. *c*) such layers. 5. the process of covering glass with metal foil or some other reflecting substance to make a mirror. 6. the consecutive numbering of leaves, rather than pages, of a book. 7. a leaflike decoration consisting of small arcs or foils. 8. in *botany,* the way leaves are arranged in the bud; vernation.
fo·li·a·ture (fō′li-ə-chẽr), *n.* [L. *foliatura;* see FOLIATE], foliage.
fo·lic acid (fō′lik), [< L. *folium,* a leaf; + *-ic*],a nitrogenous acid found in green leaves and in certain other plant and animal tissues, believed to be one of the vitamin B complex.
fo·li·o (fō′li-ō′, fōl′yō), *n.* [*pl.* FOLIOS (-li-ōz′, -yōz)], [L., in phr. *in folio,* in a sheet; *folio,* abl. of *folium,* a leaf], 1. a large sheet of paper folded once, so that it forms two leaves, or four pages, of a book, manuscript, etc. 2. a book, usually more than 30 centimeters or 11 inches in height, made of sheets folded in this way: it is the largest regular size of book. 3. a leaf of a manuscript, book, etc. numbered on only one side. 4. the number of a page in a book, etc. 5. a set number of words (100 in the United States, 72 or 90 in England) considered as a unit in measuring the length of a legal or official document. 6. in *bookkeeping,* a page of a ledger, or facing pages with the same number. Symbol, F (in senses 1 & 2). Abbreviated **F., f.** (*pl.* **ff.**), **fo., fol.** (in senses 3, 4, 6). *adj.* having sheets folded once; of the size of a folio. *v.t.* [FOLIOED (-ōd′, -yōd′), FOLIOING], to number the pages of (a book, etc.) consecutively; page.
  in folio, in the form or size of a folio.
fo·li·ose (fō′li-ōs′), *adj.* [L. *foliosus,* leafy < *folium,* a leaf], covered with leaves; leafy.
-fo·li·ous (fō′li-əs), [< L. *folium,* a leaf], a terminal combining form meaning *leaf,* used to form adjectives.
‡fo·li·o ver·so (fō′li-ō′ vũr′sō), [L.], on the back of the page: abbreviated **f.v.**
fo·li·um (fō′li-əm), *n.* [*pl.* FOLIUMS (-əmz), FOLIA (-ə)], [L.; see FOIL], 1. in *geology,* a thin layer or stratum, as in metamorphic rock. 2. in *geometry,* the part of a curve enclosed by the intersection of the two ends at its node; loop.
folk (fōk), *n.* [*pl.* FOLK, FOLKS (fōks)], [ME.; AS. *folc;* akin to G. *volk;* IE. base **pel-,* to fill (prob. specialized < **pel-,* to pour, flow), seen also in Eng. *full,* L. *plere,* to fill up, *plenus,* full (cf. PLENUM), *plebs,* the common people (cf. PLEBEIAN), *populus,* people, nation (cf. PEOPLE, POPULAR), redupl. < **po-pel-os;* basic sense prob. "crowd"], 1. a people; race; tribe; nation; ethnic group. 2. *pl.* people; persons: as, *folks* don't agree, town *folk* are not like farmers. *adj.* of or existing among the common people: often distinguished from *art,* as, *folk* ballads differ from art ballads.
  just folks, [Dial. or Colloq.], simple and unassuming; not snobbish; not putting on airs.
  (one's) folks, [Colloq.], (one's) family or relatives.
folk dance, 1. a traditional dance of the common people of a country or region. 2. music for this.
Folke·stone (fōk′stən), *n.* a seaport in southeastern England on the Strait of Dover: pop., 39,000 (est. 1946).
‡Fol·ke·ting, Fol·ke·thing (fōl′kə-tiŋ′), *n.* [Dan. < *folke,* people (see FOLK) + *ting, thing,* assembly (see THING)], 1. formerly, the lower branch of the Danish legislature. 2. now, the unicameral legislature of Denmark.
folk etymology, 1. the change that occurs in the form of a word over a period of prolonged usage so as to give it an apparent connection with some other well-known word: as, *cole slaw* becomes *cold slaw* through

folk etymology: see also **bridegroom, crawfish, sparrowgrass**, etc. 2. unscientific etymology; popular but incorrect notion of the origin and derivation of a word. Also called *popular etymology*.

folk·lore (fōk′lôr′, fōk′lōr′), *n.* [*folk* + *lore;* suggested (1846) by W. J. Thoms to replace earlier *popular antiquities*], 1. the traditional beliefs, legends, sayings, customs, etc. of a people. 2. the study of these.

folk·lor·ist (fōk′lôr′ist, fōk′lōr′ist), *n.* a specialist or expert in folklore.

folk·moot (fōk′mōōt′), *n.* [AS. *folcmot, folcgemot;* see FOLK & MOOT], [Obs. or Hist.], a general meeting of the people of a town, county, etc.

folk·mote, folk·mot (fōk′mōt′), *n.* a folkmoot.

folk music, music made and handed down among the common people.

folk song, [after G. *volkslied*], 1. a song made and handed down among the common people: folk songs are usually of anonymous authorship and often have many versions. 2. a song composed in imitation of such a song.

folk·sy (fōk′si), *adj.* [Colloq.], 1. of or like the common people. 2. sociable.

folk tale, a story, often with legendary or mythical elements, made and handed down among the common people: also **folk story.**

folk·way (fōk′wā′), *n.* [term first used in 1907 by William Graham Sumner, Am. sociologist (1840–1910)], any way of thinking, feeling, behaving, etc. common to members of the same social group.

foll., following.

fol·li·cle (fol′i-k′l), *n.* [L. *folliculus*, a small bag, husk, pod; dim. of *follis*, bellows, windbag, moneybag], 1. in *anatomy*, any small sac, cavity, or gland for excretion or secretion: as, a hair *follicle*: see **skin**, illus. 2. in *botany*, a dry, one-celled seed capsule or pod, which opens along only one side to release its seeds, as a milkweed pod. 3. in *zoology*, a cocoon.

fol·lic·u·lar (fə-lik′yoo-lẽr), *adj.* 1. of or like a follicle. 2. growing out of a follicle or follicles.

fol·lic·u·late (fə-lik′yoo-lāt′), *adj.* 1. having or consisting of a follicle or follicles. 2. enclosed in a cocoon.

fol·lic·u·lat·ed (fə-lik′yoo-lā′tid), *adj.* folliculate.

fol·lies (fol′iz), *n.pl.* [construed as sing.], [pl. of *folly*], a revue: used as part of the title.

fol·low (fol′ō), *v.t.* [ME. *folwen;* AS. *folgian;* akin to G. *folgen;* found only in Gmc.; said to be orig. a compound formed from a phrase containing *full* + *go* with basic sense "to accompany" (cf. AS. *ful-gan, fulgangan*, actually of this origin and sense)], 1. to come or go after. 2. to accompany; attend. 3. to go after in order to catch; chase; pursue. 4. to go along: as, *follow* the right road. 5. to come or occur after in time, in a series, etc. 6. to take the place of in rank, position, etc.: as, he *followed* his father as manager. 7. to take up; engage in: as, he *follows* the plumber's trade. 8. to result from: as, disease often *follows* malnutrition. 9. to take as a model; act in accordance with; imitate. 10. to accept the authority of; obey: as, we *followed* the rules of the game. 11. to support or advocate the ideas, opinions, etc. of. 12. to watch or listen to closely; observe: as, she *followed* their conversation intently. 13. to be interested in or attentive to current developments in: as, he *follows* local politics. 14. to understand the continuity or logic of: as, do you *follow* me? *v.i.* 1. to come, go, or happen after or next after some thing or person in place, sequence, or time. 2. to attend. 3. to occur as a consequence; result. *n.* 1. the act of following. 2. in *billiards*, a shot that causes the cue ball to continue rolling after striking the ball at which it was aimed: also **follow shot.**

as follows, as will next be told or explained.

follow out, to carry out fully.

follow through, 1. to continue and complete a stroke after hitting the ball, as in golf or tennis; hence, 2. to continue and complete an action.

follow up, 1. to follow closely and persistently. 2. to carry out fully. 3. to add to the effectiveness of by doing something more.

SYN.—**follow** is the general word meaning to come or occur after, but it does not necessarily imply a causal relationship with what goes before (sunshine *followed* by rain); **ensue** implies that what follows comes as a logical consequence of what preceded (clouds appeared and rain *ensued*); **succeed** implies that what follows takes the place of what preceded (who *succeeded* Polk to the Presidency?); **result** stresses a definite relationship of cause and effect between what follows and what preceded (superstition *results* from ignorance). —***ANT.*** precede.

fol·low·er (fol′ō-ẽr, fol′ə-wẽr), *n.* [ME. *folwere;* AS. *folgere*], 1. a person or thing that follows; specifically, *a*) a person who follows another's beliefs or teachings; disciple. *b*) a servant or attendant. 2. a part (of a machine) that is given motion by another part.

SYN.—**follower** is the general term for one who follows or believes in the teachings or theories of someone (a *follower* of Freud); **supporter** applies to one who upholds or defends opinions or theories that are disputed or under attack (a *supporter* of technocracy); **adherent** refers to a close, active follower of some theory, cause, etc. (the *adherents* of a political party); **disciple** implies a personal, devoted relationship to the teacher of some doctrine or leader of some movement (Aristotle was a *disciple* of Plato); **partisan,** in this connection, refers to an unswerving, often blindly devoted, adherent of some person or cause.

fol·low·ing (fol′ō-iŋ, fol′ə-wiŋ), *adj.* [ppr. of *follow*], 1. that follows; next after: abbreviated, usually with reference to pages, **f.** (*pl.* **ff.**), **fol., foll., F.** 2. to be mentioned immediately; to be dealt with next: as, the *following* people were chosen. 3. moving in the same direction that a ship is moving: said of the tide or wind. *n.* a group of followers or attendants.

the following, 1. the one or ones to be mentioned immediately. 2. what follows; what comes next.

fol·low-through (fol′ō-thrōō′), *n.* 1. the act or manner of continuing the swing of a club, racket, etc. to its natural end after striking the ball, as in tennis, golf, baseball, etc. 2. the final part of the stroke after the ball has been hit.

fol·low-up (fol′ō-up′, fol′ə-wup′), *adj.* designating or of anything that follows something else as a repetition or addition: as, *follow-up* visits, a *follow-up* letter. *n.* 1. a follow-up thing or event. 2. the use of follow-up letters, visits, etc. 3. a following up.

fol·ly (fol′i), *n.* [*pl.* FOLLIES (-iz)], [ME. *folye, folie;* OFr. *folie* < *fol;* see FOOL], 1. a lack of understanding, sense, or rational conduct; a being foolish. 2. any foolish action or belief. 3. any foolish and fruitless but expensive undertaking. 4. [Archaic], a crime. See also **follies.**

Fol·som man (fol′səm), [< *Folsom*, New Mexico, where remains have been found], a member of a race of people believed to have lived in North America at the time of the last glacial age.

Fo·mal·haut (fō′m'l-hôt′), *n.* a star in the constellation Piscis Australis: see **constellation**, chart.

fo·ment (fō-ment′), *v.t.* [Fr. *fomenter;* L. *fomentare* < *fomentum*, warm application, poultice < *fovere*, to keep warm], 1. to treat with warm water, medicated lotions, etc. 2. to stir up; arouse; instigate; incite: as, the unjust tax *fomented* rebellion. —***SYN.*** see **incite.**

fo·men·ta·tion (fō′mən-tā′shən), *n.* [LL. *fomentatio* < L. *fomentum;* see FOMENT], 1. treatment of bodily pain or injury by the application of warm, moist substances. 2. any liquid lotion, compress, etc. so applied. 3. a stirring up; arousing; instigation; incitement.

fond (fond), *adj.* [ME., contr. of *fonned*, foolish, pp. of *fonnen*, to be foolish; cf. FONDLE, FUN], 1. [Now Rare], foolishly naive, credulous, or hopeful. 2. [Dial.], insane; crazed. 3. foolishly tender and affectionate; too loving; doting. 4. affectionate; loving; tender: as, *fond* caresses. 5. cherished with great or unreasoning affection; doted on: as, my *fondest* wish.

fond of, having a liking or affection for.

‡**fond** (fōn; Eng. fond), *n.* [Fr.; see FUND], 1. foundation; basis; essential nature. 2. supply; fund.

fon·dant (fon′dənt), *n.* [Fr., ppr. of *fondre*, to melt], a soft, creamy candy made of sugar, used especially as a filling for other candies.

Fond du Lac (fon′joo-lak′, fon′də-lak′, fon′də-lak′), a city in Wisconsin, on Lake Winnebago: pop., 33,000.

fon·dle (fon′d'l), *v.t.* [FONDLED (-d'ld), FONDLING], [freq. of obs. *fond, v.* < *fond, adj.*], 1. to caress; stroke or handle tenderly; pet. 2. [Obs.], to pamper; coddle. —***SYN.*** see **caress.**

fond·ly (fond′li), *adv.* [ME.; see FOND, *adj.* & -LY], 1. naively; with simple trust: as, he *fondly* believed that all men were his friends. 2. lovingly; affectionately. 3. [Archaic], foolishly.

fon·due (fon′dōō, fon-dōō′; Fr. fōn′dü′), *n.* [Fr., fem. pp. of *fondre*, to melt], a dish made of cheese, eggs, etc.

‡**fons et o·ri·go** (fonz′ et ō-rī′gō), [L.], source and origin.

font (font), *n.* [ME.; AS. < L. *fons, fontis*, fountain, spring], 1. a bowl, usually of stone, to hold the water used in baptismal services. 2. a basin for the holy water used in symbolic washing on entering certain churches. 3. [Poetic], a fountain or spring; hence, 4. a source; origin; beginning.

font (font), *n.* [Fr. *fonte* < *fondre*, to cast, found; see FOUND (to cast)], in *printing*, a complete assortment of type in one size and style: also **fount.**

Fon·taine·bleau (fōn′ten′blō′; Eng. fon′tin-blō′, fon′tin-blō′), *n.* a town near Paris: pop., 15,000: site of a palace of former kings of France.

font·al (font′'l), *adj.* [ML. *fontalis;* see FONT (bowl) & -AL], 1. of a spring or source; original. 2. baptismal.

fon·ta·nel, fon·ta·nelle (fon′tə-nel′), *n.* [Fr. *fontanelle*, dim. of *fontain*, fountain], 1. originally, *a*) an outlet. *b*) [Obs.], an opening in the body for the discharge of secretions. 2. any of the soft, boneless areas in the skull of a baby or young animal, which are later closed up by the formation of bone.

Foo·chow (fōō′chou′; Chin. fōō′jō′), *n.* the capital of Fukien province, China: pop., 331,000: also **Minhow.**

food (fōōd), *n.* [ME. *fode;* AS. *foda;* IE. **pā-t*, to eat < base **pā-*, to pasture cattle, hence to fodder, seen also in *pasture, pastor, pabulum*], 1. any substance taken into and assimilated by a plant or animal to keep it alive and enable it to grow; nourishment; nutriment.

2. solid substances of this sort: distinguished from *drink.* 3. a specified kind of food. 4. anything that nourishes or stimulates; whatever helps something to keep active, grow, etc.: as, *food* for thought.

SYN.—**food** is the general term for all matter that is taken into the body for nourishment; **fare** refers to the range of foods eaten by a particular organism or available at a particular time and place (the *fare* of horses, a bill of *fare*); **victuals** is a dialectal or colloquial word for human fare or diet; **provisions,** in this connection, refers to a stock of food assembled in advance (*provisions* for the hike); **ration** refers to a fixed allowance or allotment of food (the weekly *ration*) and in the plural (**rations**) to food in general (how are the *rations* in this outfit?).

food·stuff (fōōd′stuf′), *n.* any material made into or used as food.

fool (fōōl), *n.* [ME. & OFr. *fol* (Fr. *fou*), a fool, idiot; LL. *follus, follis,* a fool, foolish < L. *follis,* a pair of bellows, windbag], 1. a person with little or no judgment, common sense, wisdom, etc.; silly person; simpleton. 2. a man formerly kept in the household of a nobleman or king to entertain by acting as a clown; professional jester. 3. a victim of a joke or trick; dupe. *v.i.* 1. to act like a fool; be silly. 2. to joke; be playful. *v.t.* to make a fool of; trick; deceive; dupe.

be no (or **nobody's**) **fool,** to be shrewd and capable.

fool around, [Colloq.], to do foolish, useless things; trifle.

fool away, [Colloq.], to waste like a fool; squander.

fool with, [Colloq.], to trifle or meddle with.

play the fool, to act like a fool; do silly things; clown.

fool (fōōl), *n.* [Early Mod. Eng., kind of trifle (confection); hence, prob. < *fool* (silly person) by analogy with *trifle*], stewed fruit with cream, especially whipped cream.

fool·er·y (fōōl′ẽr-i), *n.* [*pl.* FOOLERIES (-iz)], foolish behavior or action.

fool·har·di·ly (fōōl′här′d'l-i), *adv.* in a foolhardy manner.

fool·har·di·ness (fōōl′här′di-nis), *n.* the quality of being foolhardy.

fool·har·dy (fōōl′här′di), *adj.* [FOOLHARDIER (-di-ẽr), FOOLHARDIEST (-di-ist)], [ME. *folherdi;* OFr. *fol hardi; fol,* foolish, a fool + *hardi,* pp. of *hardir,* to make bold], foolishly daring; thoughtlessly bold; rash.

fool·ing (fōōl′iŋ), *n.* [< *fool, v.*], a joking or clowning.

fool·ish (fōōl′ish), *adj.* [ME.; see FOOL & -ISH], 1. without good sense or wisdom; silly; imprudent; unwise. 2. ridiculous; absurd. 3. [Archaic], humble; worthless. —*SYN.* see **absurd.**

fool·ish·ness (fōōl′ish-nis), *n.* 1. the quality or state of being foolish; nonsense. 2. a foolish action or thing.

fool·proof (fōōl′prōōf′), *adj.* so harmless, simple, or indestructible as not to be mishandled, injured, misunderstood, etc. even by a fool.

fools·cap (fōōlz′kap′), *n.* 1. (*also* fōōl′skap′), [so called from the fool's head and cap formerly used as a watermark], any of various sizes of writing paper measuring from 12 by 15 inches to 13 1/2 by 17 inches: abbreviated **fcap., fcp., fp.** 2. a fool's cap.

fool's cap, a cap, usually with bells, formerly worn by a court fool or jester.

fool's errand, a foolish, fruitless task or undertaking.

fool's gold, iron pyrites or copper pyrites, like gold in color.

fool's paradise, a state of deceptive happiness, based on illusions.

fool's-pars·ley (fōōlz′pärs′li), *n.* a nauseating, poisonous European weed resembling parsley.

foot (foot), *n.* [*pl.* FEET (fēt)], [ME. & AS. *fot;* akin to G. *fuss;* IE. base **pĕd-,* **pōd-,* foot, to go, seen also in L. *pes, pedis* (cf. PEDAL)], 1. the end part of the leg, on which a person or animal stands or moves. 2. a thing like a foot in some way; specifically, *a*) the part that a thing stands on; base. *b*) the lowest part; bottom: as, the *foot* of a page. *c*) the last of a series: as, go to the *foot* of the line. *d*) the part of a sewing machine that holds the cloth steady. 3. the end of a bed, grave, etc. toward which the feet are directed. 4. the part of a stocking, etc. that covers the foot. 5. [alternative *pl.* FOOT, generally regarded as substandard], a measure of length, equal to 12 inches, from the approximate length of the human foot: symbol, ′ (e.g., 10′): abbreviated **ft.** (*sing. & pl.*), **F., f.** 6. foot soldiers; infantry. 7. [*pl.* FOOTS (foots)], the sediment in a liquid. 8. a group of syllables serving as a unit of meter in verse; especially, such a unit having a specified placement of the stressed or long syllable or syllables, as a trochee, dactyl, spondee, etc. *v.i.* 1. to dance. 2. to go on foot; walk. 3. to proceed; move along, as a ship. *v.t.* 1. to walk, dance, or run on, over, or through; tread. 2. to make or put on the foot of (a stocking, etc.). 3. to add (a column of figures) and set down a total. 4. [Colloq.], to pay (costs, expenses, etc.): as, he *footed* the bill.

foot it, [Colloq.], to dance, walk, or run.

foot up, to add up, as items in a bill.

have one foot in the grave, [Colloq.], to be near death; be very old or ill.

on foot, 1. standing. 2. walking or running. 3. going on; in process.

put one's best foot forward, [Colloq.], 1. to walk or run at top speed. 2. *a*) to do the best that one can. *b*) to try to appear at one's best.

put one's foot down, [Colloq.], to be firm; act decisively.

put one's foot in it (or **one's mouth**), [Colloq.], to make an embarrassing or troublesome blunder.

under foot, 1. on the surface of the ground; on the floor, etc. 2. in the way. 3. under one's control.

-foot (foot), a combining form meaning (a specified number of) *feet long, high, tall,* or *deep,* used to form hyphenated adjectives, as *six-foot.*

foot·age (foot′ij), *n.* [*foot* + *-age*], the length expressed in feet: said especially of motion-picture film.

foot-and-mouth disease (foot′'n-mouth′), an acute, contagious disease of cattle and deer, caused by a virus and characterized by fever and blisters in the mouth and around the hoofs: it can be transmitted to other domestic animals and man.

foot·ball (foot′bôl′), *n.* [ME. (Scots) *fut ball* (1424)], 1. any of several games played with an inflated leather ball by two teams on a field with goals at each end, the object being to get the ball across the opponents' goal: in *association football,* or *soccer,* the form most closely related to the original, the players are not allowed to use their hands or arms in advancing the ball, which is propelled chiefly by kicking; in *Rugby,* a form popular in England, the players may kick, throw, or run with the ball, but are not permitted to be in front of it while it is being carried or kicked by a teammate; in U.S. & Canadian *football,* the elaborated form developed from Rugby, the players may run ahead of the ball variously for interference, forward passes, etc. 2. *a*) the elliptical, inflated ball used in playing U.S., Canadian, or Rugby football. *b*) the spherical, inflated ball used in playing soccer. 3. any issue, problem, etc. that is passed about or shunted from one group to another: as, a political *football.*

foot·board (foot′bôrd′, foot′bōrd′), *n.* 1. a board or small platform for supporting the feet. 2. a vertical piece across the foot of a bed.

foot·boy (foot′boi′), *n.* [cf. FOOTMAN], a young manservant or page.

foot brake, a brake worked by pressure of the foot, as in an automobile.

foot·bridge (foot′brij′), *n.* a narrow bridge for use by pedestrians only.

foot-can·dle (foot′kan′d'l), *n.* a unit for measuring illumination: it is equal to the amount of direct light thrown by one international candle on a square foot of surface every part of which is one foot away.

foot·cloth (foot′klôth′), *n.* [*pl.* FOOTCLOTHS (-klôthz′, -klôths′)], 1. originally, an ornamental cloth put over a horse's back. 2. a carpet or rug.

foot·ed (foot′id), *adj.* having a foot or feet; especially, having (a specified number or kind of) feet: generally used in hyphenated compounds, as *four-footed.*

-foot·er (foot′ẽr), a combining form meaning *a person* or *thing* (a specified number of) *feet tall* or *high:* used in hyphenated compounds, as *six-footer.*

foot·fall (foot′fôl′), *n.* 1. a footstep. 2. the sound of a footstep or footsteps.

foot fault, in *tennis,* failure to keep both feet behind the base line when serving, counted as a point against the server.

foot·gear (foot′gêr′), *n.* covering for the feet; shoes, boots, etc.

foot·hill (foot′hil′), *n.* a low hill at or near the foot of a mountain or mountain range.

foot·hold (foot′hōld′), *n.* 1. a place to put the feet in standing or climbing. 2. a secure position: as, the rumor had gained a *foothold.*

foot·ing (foot′iŋ), *n.* [ME. *fotinge;* see FOOT, *v.* & -ING], 1. a moving on the feet; walking, dancing, etc. 2. a secure placing of the feet: as, if you lose your *footing,* you'll fall. 3. a secure place to put the feet; something to stand on: as, the icy hill provided no *footing.* 4. a secure position or basis: as, this business must be put on a sound *footing.* 5. a basis for relationship; position in relation to others: as, he was on a friendly *footing* with them. 6. *a*) the making of a foot for a stocking, etc. *b*) the material used for this. 7. *a*) the adding of a column of figures. (*b* the sum obtained. 8. in *architecture,* the projecting base of a column, pedestal, wall, etc.

foot·less (foot′lis), *adj.* [ME. *fotelesse*], 1. without a foot or feet; hence, 2. not supported; without basis or substance. 3. [Colloq.], clumsy; not skillful or efficient.

foot·lights (foot′līts′), *n.pl.* 1. a row of lights along the front of a stage, about on a level with the actors' feet. 2. the theater; the stage; acting as a profession.

foot·ling (foot′liŋ), *adj.* [ppr. of *footle,* to trifle, talk foolishly; altered (prob. after *futile*) < dial. *footer*, to trifle < Fr. *foutre*, orig., to copulate with; L. *futuere*], [Colloq.], trivial; trifling; silly and unimportant.

foot·lock·er (foot'lok'ẽr), *n.* a small trunk containing the clothing and personal belongings of a soldier, usually kept at the foot of his bed.

foot-loose (foot'lōōs'), *adj.* free to go wherever one likes or do as one likes.

foot·man (foot'mən), *n.* [*pl.* FOOTMEN (-mən)], [orig., man who ran on foot beside his master's horse or carriage], 1. a male servant who waits on table, opens the door, accompanies his employer in an automobile or carriage, etc. 2. [Archaic], a foot soldier; infantryman.

foot·mark (foot'märk'), *n.* a footprint.

foot·note (foot'nōt'), *n.* a note of comment or reference at the bottom of a page. *v.t.* 1. to add such a note or notes to. 2. to add confirmatory evidence to (a statement, etc.).

foot·pace (foot'pās'), *n.* a walking pace; normal speed of walking.

foot·pad (foot'pad'), *n.* [see PAD (path)], a highway robber or holdup man who travels on foot.

foot·path (foot'path', foot'päth'), *n.* a narrow path for use by pedestrians only.

foot-pound (foot'pound'), *n.* a unit of energy, equal to the amount of energy required to raise a weight of one pound a distance of one foot: abbreviated **ft-lb, fp., F.P., f.p.**

foot-pound·al (foot'pound''l), *n.* a unit of work, equal to the work done when a mass of one pound, accelerating at the rate of one foot per second per second, has moved a distance of one foot.

foot·print (foot'print'), *n.* an impression or mark made by a foot.

foot·rest (foot'rest'), *n.* a support to rest the feet on.

foot·rope (foot'rōp') *n.* 1. the part of a boltrope sewn into the lower edge of the sail. 2. a piece of wire rope supported beneath a yard, upon which sailors stand when furling or reefing sail.

foot rule, a ruler, or measuring stick, one foot long.

foot soldier, a soldier who moves and fights largely on foot; infantryman.

foot·sore (foot'sôr', foot'sōr'), *adj.* having sore or tender feet, as from much walking.

foot·stalk (foot'stôk'), *n.* 1. the stalk of a flower or stem of a leaf. 2. a stalklike part of an animal, as the muscle by which a barnacle attaches itself.

foot·step (foot'step'), *n.* 1. a person's step. 2. the distance covered in a step. 3. the sound of a step; footfall. 4. a footprint. 5. a step by which to go up or down.

follow in (someone's) footsteps, to repeat or imitate (someone's) actions.

foot·stone (foot'stōn'), *n.* a stone put at the foot of a grave.

foot·stool (foot'stōōl'), *n.* a low stool for supporting the feet of a seated person.

foot-ton (foot'tun'), *n.* a unit of energy, equal to the amount of energy required to raise a weight of one ton a distance of one foot.

foot·way (foot'wā'), *n.* 1. a footpath. 2. [British], a sidewalk.

foot·wear (foot'wâr'), *n.* anything to wear on the feet; shoes, boots, slippers, etc.

foot·work (foot'wũrk'), *n.* the manner of using the feet, as in boxing, dancing, tennis, football, etc.

foot·worn (foot'wôrn', foot'wōrn'), *adj.* 1. having tired feet, as from much walking. 2. worn down by feet: as, *footworn* stairs.

foo·zle (fōō'z'l), *v.t. & v.i.* [FOOZLED (-z'ld), FOOZLING], [? < G. *fuseln*, to bungle], to make or do (something) awkwardly; bungle (a stroke in golf, etc.). *n.* 1. an awkward, unskillful act or stroke. 2. [Colloq.], an awkward, dull person.

fop (fop), *n.* [ME. *foppe*, a fool; prob. < MD. or MLG.; cf. D. *foppen*, to befool (Early Mod. Eng. *foppe*, to hoax); see FOB, *v.*], 1. originally, a foolish person; hence, 2. a vain, affected man who pays too much attention to his clothes, appearance, etc.; dandy.

fop·per·y (fop'ẽr-i), *n.* [*pl.* FOPPERIES (-iz)], 1. the actions, dress, etc. of a fop. 2. something foppish.

fop·pish (fop'ish), *adj.* of, characteristic of, or fit for a fop; vain and affected.

for (fôr; *unstressed* fẽr), *prep.* [ME.; AS. *for*, weakened form of *fore*, before (see FORE); akin to G. *für;* IE. base **per-*, as also in L. *per-*, *pro-*, *prae-*, etc.], 1. in place of; instead of: as, we used blankets *for* coats. 2. as representative of; in the interest of: as, his agent acted *for* him in the negotiations. 3. in defense of; in favor of; on the side of: as, he fought *for* liberty. 4. in honor of: as, the baby was named *for* his grandfather, the banquet was given *for* him. 5. with the aim or purpose of; with a view to: as, he carried a gun *for* protection. 6. with the purpose of going to: as, she has just left *for* home. 7. in order to be, become, get, have, keep, etc.: as, the air corps trains men *for* flyers, we walk *for* exercise, he fought *for* his life. 8. in search of: as, the child looked *for* his dog. 9. meant to be received by or belong to a specified person or thing, or to be used in a specified way: as, flowers *for* a girl, money *for* paying bills. 10. suitable to; appropriate to; adapted to: as, a room *for* sleeping. 11. with a yearning or other feeling toward: as, the child cried *for* his mother, he has an ear *for* music. 12. as affecting (a person or thing) in a specified way: as, that will be bad *for* you. 13. as being: as, we left him *for* dead, I know *for* a fact. 14. considering the nature of; as concerns: as, it is cool *for* July, she is clever *for* a child. 15. because of; as a result of: as, he cried *for* pain. 16. in spite of; notwithstanding: as, she is stupid *for* all her learning. 17. in proportion to; corresponding to: as, a good day *for* every ten bad ones. 18. to the amount of; equal to: as, a bill *for* $50: when preceded and followed by the same noun, *for* indicates an equality between things compared or contrasted (e.g., dollar *for* dollar). 19. at the price or payment of: as, he sold the house *for* $10,000. 20. to the length, duration, or extent of; throughout; through: as, the movie lasts *for* an hour, the road runs *for* five miles. 21. at (a specified time): as, an appointment *for* two o'clock. 22. [Obs.], before. *conj.* because; seeing that: more formal than *because* and used to introduce evidence or explanation for an immediately preceding statement.

for (a person or thing) **to,** that (a person or thing) will, should, ought, must, etc.: as, she wrote an order *for* the grocer *to* fill.

O! for, I wish that I had.

for- (fôr, fẽr), [ME.; AS. *for-*, replacing *fer-, fær-;* akin to G. *ver-;* IE. base **per-*, as in *fore, for;* basic Eng. sense "too thoroughly"], an Anglo-Saxon and Middle English prefix used chiefly with verbs, meaning: 1. *away, apart, off*, as in *forbid, forget, forgo*: the original senses are now largely obscured. 2. *very much, intensely*, as in *forweep, forfrighted.*

for., 1. foreign. 2. forestry.

for·age (fôr'ij, for'ij), *n.* [ME.; OFr. *fourage* < *forrer*, to forage < *forre, fuerre*, fodder < Frank. *fodr*, food], 1. food for domestic animals; fodder. 2. a search for food or provisions. *v.i.* [FORAGED (-ijd), FORAGING], [Fr. *fourrager* < the *n.*], 1. to search for food or provisions. 2. to search for what one needs or wants (with *for* or *about*). *v.t.* 1. *a)* to get or take food or provisions from. *b)* to ravage; plunder. 2. to provide with forage; feed. 3. to get by foraging.

For·a·ker, Mount (fôr'ə-kẽr, for'ə-kẽr), a mountain of the Alaska Range, central Alaska: height, 17,000 ft.

for·a·men (fō-rā'mən), *n.* [*pl.* FORAMINA (-ram'i-nə), FORAMENS (-rā'mənz)], [L., a hole < *forare*, to bore], a small opening, especially a natural one in a bone.

‡fo·ra·men mag·num (fō-rā'mən mag'nəm), [L., large opening], the large opening at the base of the skull through which the lower part of the medulla oblongata passes.

for·a·min·i·fer (for'ə-min'ə-fẽr), *n.* [*pl.* FORAMINIFERA (fə-ram'ə-nif'ẽr-ə)], [< L. *foramen, foraminis* (see FORAMEN); + *-fer*], any of several very small, one-celled sea animals with hard shells full of tiny holes through which slender filaments project.

fo·ram·i·nous (fō-ram'i-nəs), *adj.* containing foramina.

for·as·much (fôr'əz-much'), *conj.* inasmuch (followed by *as*).

for·ay (fôr'ā, for'ā), *v.t. & v.i.* [ME. *forraien;* prob. back-formation < *forreier* < OFr. *forrier*, forager < *forrer;* see FORAGE], to raid for spoils; plunder; pillage. *n.* [ME. *forrai, ferrai*], a raid, as for spoils.

for·bade, for·bad (fẽr-bad', fôr-bad'), past tense of **forbid.**

for·bear (fôr-bâr', fẽr-bâr'), *v.t.* [FORBORE (-bôr', -bōr') or *archaic* FORBARE (-bâr'), FORBORNE (-bôrn', -bōrn'), FORBEARING], [ME. *forberen;* AS. *forberan;* see FOR- & BEAR (to carry)], 1. to refrain from; avoid (doing, saying, etc.). 2. [Archaic or Dial.], to endure; tolerate. *v.i.* 1. to refrain or abstain. 2. to keep oneself in check; control oneself. —*SYN.* see **refrain.**

for·bear (fôr'bâr'), *n.* a forebear; ancestor.

for·bear·ance (fôr-bâr'əns, fẽr-bâr'əns), *n.* 1. the act of forbearing. 2. the quality of being forbearing; self-control; patient restraint. 3. in *law*, an extension of time for the payment of a debt. —*SYN.* see **patience.**

Forbes-Rob·ert·son, Sir **Johnston** (fôrbz'rob'ẽrt-s'n), 1853–1937; English actor.

for·bid (fẽr-bid', fôr-bid'), *v.t.* [FORBADE or FORBAD (-bad'), FORBIDDEN (-bid''n) or *archaic* FORBID, FORBIDDING], [ME. *forbeden;* AS. *forbeodan;* see FOR- & BID, *v.*], 1. to rule against; prohibit; not permit. 2. to command to stay away from; exclude or bar from. 3. to make impossible; prevent.

SYN.—**forbid** is the basic, direct word meaning to command a person to refrain from some action; **prohibit** implies a forbidding by law or official decree; **interdict** implies legal or ecclesiastical prohibition, usually for a limited time, as an exemplary punishment or to forestall unfavorable developments; **enjoin** implies a legal order from a court prohibiting (or ordering) a given action, under penalty; **ban** implies legal or ecclesiastical prohibition with an added connotation of strong condemnation or censure. —*ANT.* permit, allow.

for·bid·dance (fẽr-bid''ns, fôr-bid''ns), *n.* [Rare], the act of forbidding; prohibition.

for·bid·den (fẽr-bid′'n, fôr-bid′'n), *adj.* [pp. of *forbid*], not permitted; prohibited.

Forbidden City, [so called from having been closed to the public], a walled section of Peking, China, containing the royal palaces of the former Chinese Empire.

forbidden fruit, 1. in the *Bible*, the fruit of the tree of knowledge, forbidden to Adam and Eve: Gen. 2:17; 3:3. 2. something desired but prohibited.

for·bid·ding (fẽr-bid′iŋ, fôr-bid′iŋ), *adj.* [ppr. of *forbid*], looking dangerous, threatening, or disagreeable; frightening; repellent.

for·bore (fôr-bôr′, fôr-bōr′), past tense of **forbear.**

for·borne (fôr-bôrn′, fôr-bōrn′), past participle of **forbear.**

for·by, for·bye (fôr-bī′), *prep.* [ME. *forbi* (see FOR & BY); akin to G. *vorbei*], [Scot. or Archaic], 1. close by; near; next to. 2. besides. *adv.* [Scot. or Archaic], 1. to one side; aside. 2. past. 3. besides.

force (fôrs, fōrs), *n.* [ME. *force, fors;* OFr. *force;* LL. **forcia*, **fortia* < L. *fortis*, strong; see FORT], 1. strength; energy; vigor; power. 2. the intensity of power; impetus: as, the *force* of the blow knocked him down. 3. *a*) physical power or strength exerted against a person or thing: as, he used *force* in opening the door. *b*) the use of physical power to overcome or restrain a person; physical coercion; violence: as, the police resorted to *force* to disperse them. 4. the power of a person to act effectively and vigorously; moral strength: as, *force* of character. 5. the power to control, persuade, influence, etc.; effectiveness. 6. military, naval, or air power. 7. any organized group of soldiers, sailors, etc. 8. any group of people organized for some activity: as, a sales *force.* 9. in *law*, binding power; validity. 10. in *physics*, the cause of motion, or of change or stoppage of motion, of a body. *v.t.* [FORCED (fôrst, fōrst), FORCING], 1. to make (a person or animal) do something by force; compel. 2. to rape (a woman). 3. *a*) to break open, into, or through by force. *b*) to make (a way, etc.) by force. *c*) to overpower or capture by breaking into, through, etc.: as, we *forced* the enemy's stronghold. 4. to get or take by force; wrest; extort: as, I *forced* the gun from his hand. 5. to drive by or as by force; cause to move against resistance; impel: as, you may strip the thread if you *force* the bolt, hunger *forced* him to steal. 6. to impose by or as by force (with *on* or *upon*): as, he *forced* his attentions on her. 7. to effect or produce by or as by force; produce by unusual or unnatural effort: as, she *forced* a smile. 8. to exert beyond the natural limits or capacity; strain: as, she *forced* her voice. 9. to cause (plants, fruit, etc.) to develop or grow faster by artificial means. 10. [Obs.], *a*) to give or add force to. *b*) to put in force. 11. in *baseball*, *a*) to cause (a base runner) to be put out at an advanced base by occupying the base behind him. *b*) to send (a runner) home to score by walking the batter with the bases full. *c*) to cause (a run) to be scored in this way. 12. in *card games*, *a*) to play so as to cause (an opponent) to play a particular card. *b*) to cause (a particular card) to be played in this way.

in force, 1. in full strength; in full number. 2. in effect; operative; valid.

SYN.—**force** implies the exertion of power in causing a person or thing to act, move, or comply against his or its resistance and may refer to physical strength or to any impelling motive (circumstances *forced* him to lie); **compel** implies a driving irresistibly to some action, condition, etc.; to **coerce** is to compel submission or obedience by the use of superior power, intimidation, threats, etc.; **constrain** implies the operation of a restricting force and therefore suggests a strained, repressed, or unnatural quality in that which results (a *constrained* laugh). See also **strength.**

forced (fôrst, fōrst), *adj.* [pp. of *force*], 1. done or brought about by force; not voluntary; compulsory: as, *forced* labor. 2. produced or kept up by unusual effort; not natural; not spontaneous; strained; constrained: as, a *forced* smile.

forc·ed·ly (fôr′sid-li), *adv.* in a forced manner; by compulsion.

forced march, in *military usage*, a long march at a pace faster than usual.

forced sale, a property sale under the authority of a court for payment of a debt; foreclosure sale.

force feed, a method of pressure lubrication used in internal-combustion engines.

force·ful (fôrs′fəl, fōrs′fəl), *adj.* full of force; powerful; strong; vigorous; effective; cogent.

‡force ma·jeure (fôrs′mȧ′zhẽr′), [Fr.], 1. overpowering force. 2. in *Roman law*, an act of God.

force·meat (fôrs′mēt′, fōrs′mēt′), *n.* [altered < *farce meat;* obs. *farce* < Fr. *farcir*, to stuff], meat chopped up and seasoned, usually for stuffing.

force-out (fôrs′out′, fōrs′out′), *n.* in *baseball*, an out scored against a base runner when he is forced from a base by a teammate's hit and fails to reach the advance base before the ball does.

for·ceps (fôr′səps, fôr′seps), *n.* [*pl.* FORCEPS, rarely FORCEPSES (-iz)], [L., orig., smith's tongs < *formus*, hot + *capere*, to take], small tongs or pincers for grasping, compressing, and pulling, used especially by surgeons and dentists.

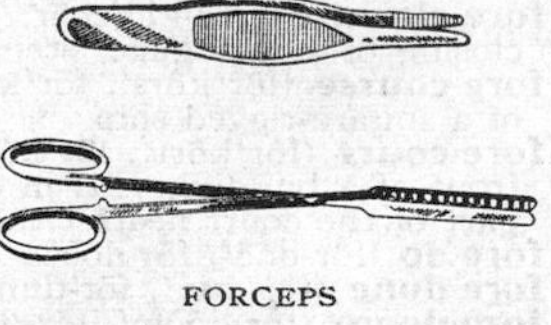

FORCEPS

force pump, a pump with a valveless plunger for forcing a liquid through a pipe, especially for sending water under pressure to a considerable height.

for·ci·ble (fôr′sə-b'l, fōr′sə-b'l), *adj.* [ME.; OFr.], 1. done or effected by force; involving the use of force. 2. having force; forceful.

for·ci·bly (fôr′sə-bli, fōr′sə-bli), *adv.* in a forcible manner.

ford (fôrd, fōrd), *n.* [ME.; AS.; akin to G. *furt;* IE. **pr̥-tu*, passage, seen also in L. *portus*, door, harbor (cf. PORTAL, PORT)], a shallow place in a stream, river, etc. that can be crossed by walking or by riding on horseback, in an automobile, etc. *v.t.* to cross (a stream, etc.) in this way.

Ford, Henry (fôrd, fōrd), 1863–1947; American capitalist, inventor, and automobile manufacturer.

Ford, John 1586?–1639?; English dramatist.

for·do (fôr-do͞o′), *v.t.* [for prin. pts. see DO], [ME. & AS. *fordon; for-* + *don*, to do], [Archaic], 1. to destroy, kill, ruin, etc. 2. to cause to become exhausted: only in the past participle. Also **foredo.**

for·done (fôr-dun′), *adj.* [ME. *fordon*, pp. of *fordon*, to ruin, destroy; AS. *fordon;* see FOR- & DO, *v.*], [Archaic], completely exhausted: also spelled **foredone.**

fore (fôr, fōr), *adv.* [ME.; AS. *fore;* akin to G. *vor;* IE. base **per-*, through, throughout, before, etc., as also in L. *per-;* cf. FOR, FOR-], at, in, or toward the front: now only with reference to the front part, or bow, of a ship, and opposed to *aft. adj.* situated in front or in front of some other thing or part. *n.* the thing or part in front. *prep.* [Obs.], before: used chiefly in oaths. *interj.* in *golf*, a shout warning those ahead that one is about to drive the ball.

to the fore, 1. to the front; into view; into prominence. 2. at hand; available. 3. alive; still active.

'fore (fôr), *prep.* [Poetic], before.

fore- (fôr, fōr), [ME.; AS.; see FORE, *adv.*], a prefix meaning: 1. *before in time, place, order,* or *rank*, as in *forecast, forenoon.* 2. *the front part of*, as in *forearm, forehead.*

fore-and-aft (fôr′'n-aft′, fōr′'n-äft′), *adj.* in *nautical usage*, from the bow to the stern; lengthwise; set lengthwise: as, *fore-and-aft* rig differs from square rig.

fore and aft, in *nautical usage*, 1. from the bow to the stern; lengthwise; set lengthwise. 2. at, in, or toward both the bow and the stern.

fore-and-aft·er (fôr′'n-af′tẽr, fōr′'n-äf′tẽr), *n.* [Colloq.], a schooner, ketch, or other ship with fore-and-aft rig.

fore·arm (fôr′ärm′, fōr′ärm′), *n.* the part of the arm between the elbow and the wrist.

fore·arm (fôr-ärm′, fōr-ärm′), *v.t.* to arm in advance; prepare beforehand for a fight or any difficulty.

fore·bear (fôr′bâr′, fōr′bâr′), *n.* [< *fore* + *be* + *-er*], an ancestor: also spelled **forbear.**

fore·bode (fôr-bōd′, fōr-bōd′), *v.t. & v.i.* [AS. *forebodian;* see FORE- & BODE], 1. to foretell; predict; indicate beforehand; portend: usually of something bad or harmful. 2. to have a presentiment of (something bad or harmful). —*SYN.* see **foretell.**

fore·bod·ing (fôr-bōd′iŋ, fōr-bōd′iŋ), *n.* [see FOREBODE], a prediction, portent, or presentiment, especially of something bad or harmful. —*SYN.* see **ominous.**

fore·brain (fôr′brān′, fōr′brān′), *n.* 1. the front part of the brain of an embryo. 2. the part of the fully developed brain evolved from this.

fore·cast (fôr-kast′, fôr′kast′, fōr-käst′, fōr′käst′), *v.t.* [FORECAST or FORECASTED (-id), FORECASTING], [*fore-* + *cast, v.*], 1. to plan in advance; foresee. 2. to estimate or calculate in advance; predict; prophesy. 3. to serve as a prediction or prophecy of. *n.* (fôr′kast′, fōr′käst′), 1. [Rare], foresight; forethought. 2. a prediction or prophecy, as of the weather. —*SYN.* see **foretell.**

fore·cas·tle (fōk′s'l; fôr′kas′'l & fōr′käs′'l *are sp. pronuns.*), *n.* [*fore* + *castle*: so called from the foremost of the two castlelike structures set on the hull of a medieval vessel to command an enemy's decks], 1. the upper deck of a ship in front of the foremast. 2. the front part of a merchant ship, where the sailors' quarters are located. Also **fo'c's'le.**

fore·close (fôr-klōz′, fōr-klōz′), *v.t.* [FORECLOSED (-klōzd′), FORECLOSING], [ME. *forclosen* < OFr. *forclos*, pp. of *forclore*, to exclude < *fors* (< L. *foris*), outside + *clore* (< L. *claudere*), to close], 1. to shut out; exclude; bar. 2. to deprive of the right to redeem a mortgage when regular payments have not been kept up. 3. to take away the right to redeem (a mortgage, etc.). *v.i.* to foreclose a mortgage, etc.

fore·clo·sure (fôr-klō'zhẽr, fōr-klō'zhẽr), *n.* the foreclosing of a mortgage, etc.

fore·course (fôr'kôrs', fōr'kōrs'), *n.* the fore mainsail of a square-rigged ship.

fore·court (fôr'kôrt', fōr'kōrt'), *n.* 1. a court at the front of a building. 2. in *tennis, badminton*, etc., the part of the court nearest the net.

fore·do (fôr-do͞o', fōr-do͞o'), *v.t.* [Archaic], to fordo.

fore·done (fôr-dun', fōr-dun'), *adj.* [Archaic], fordone.

fore·doom (fôr-do͞om', fōr-do͞om'), *v.t.* to doom in advance; condemn beforehand. *n.* (fôr'do͞om', fōr'do͞om'), a sentence or judgment in advance; destiny.

fore·fa·ther (fôr'fä'thẽr, fōr'fä'thẽr), *n.* [ME. *forefader*, after ON. *forfathir;* see FORE- & FATHER], an ancestor.

Fore·fa·thers' Day (fôr'fä'thẽrz, fōr'fä'thẽrz), December 22, anniversary of the day in 1620 when the Pilgrims landed at Plymouth, Massachusetts.

fore·feel (fôr-fēl', fōr-fēl'), *v.t.* [FOREFELT (-felt'), FOREFEELING], to feel beforehand; have a premonition of. *n.* [Rare], a forefeeling; premonition.

fore·fend (fôr-fend', fōr-fend'), *v.t.* [Archaic], to forfend.

fore·fin·ger (fôr'fiŋ'gẽr, fōr'fiŋ'gẽr), *n.* [ME.], the finger nearest the thumb; index finger; first finger.

fore·foot (fôr'foot', fōr'foot'), *n.* [ME. *forefot*], 1. either of the front feet of an animal with four or more feet. 2. the meeting point of the keel and the stem of a ship.

fore·front (fôr'frunt', fōr'frunt'), *n.* 1. the extreme front. 2. the position of most activity, importance, etc.

fore·gath·er (fôr-gath'ẽr, fōr-gath'ẽr), *v.i.* to forgather.

fore·go (fôr-gō', fōr-gō'), *v.t. & v.i.* [FOREWENT (-went'), FOREGONE (-gôn', -gon'), FOREGOING], 1. [ME. *forgon;* AS. *foregan*], to go before in place, time, or degree; precede. 2. [see FORGO], to forgo; do without.

fore·go·ing (fôr'gō'iŋ, fōr'gō'iŋ), *adj.* [ppr. of *forego*], preceding; previously said, written, etc. —*SYN.* see **previous.**

the foregoing, 1. the one or ones previously mentioned. 2. what has already been said or written.

fore·gone (fôr-gôn', fōr'gon), *adj.* [pp. of *forego*], 1. that has gone before; previous; former. 2. *a*) previously determined; known beforehand; confidently anticipated. *b*) inevitable; unavoidable: said of a conclusion.

fore·ground (fôr'ground', fōr'ground'), *n.* 1. *a*) the part of a scene, landscape, etc. nearest to the viewer. *b*) the part of a picture represented in perspective as nearest to the viewer. 2. the most noticeable or conspicuous place.

fore-gut (fôr'gut', fōr'gut'), *n.* the front part of the alimentary canal in vertebrate embryos: the duodenum, stomach, esophagus, and pharynx develop from it.

fore·hand (fôr'hand', fōr'hand'), *adj.* 1. foremost; front. 2. designating or of a stroke, as in tennis, made with the palm of the hand turned forward. *n.* 1. the position in front or above; advantage. 2. the part of a horse in front of the rider. 3. *a*) a method of making a forehand stroke, as in tennis. *b*) such a stroke.

fore·hand·ed (fôr'han'did, fōr'han'did), *adj.* 1. looking ahead to, or making provision for, the future; thrifty; prudent. 2. done beforehand; early; timely. 3. in *tennis*, forehand.

fore·head (fôr'id, for'əd; *also, sp. pronun.*, fôr'hed'), *n.* [ME. *forheued, forheed;* AS. *forheafod;* see FORE- & HEAD], 1. the part of the face between the eyebrows and the line where the hair normally begins. 2. the front part of anything.

for·eign (fôr'in, for'ən), *adj.* [ME. *forein, foreyn;* OFr. *forain* < LL. **foranus*, outside, exterior < L. *foras*, out of doors, orig. acc. pl. of OL. *fora*, door], 1. situated outside one's own country, province, locality, etc. 2. of, from, characteristic of, or dealing with another country or countries: as, a *foreign* language, *foreign* population, *foreign* trade: often opposed to *domestic*: abbreviated **for.** 3. coming from or having to do with another person or thing; not originating in the person or thing specified; not belonging; not characteristic: as, unkindness is *foreign* to his nature. 4. not organically connected: said of substances found in parts of the body or in organisms where they do not naturally occur. —*SYN.* see **extrinsic.**

foreign affairs, matters concerning the policy of a country in its relations with other countries.

foreign bill, an authorization for the payment of a specified sum of money to someone in another state or country: also **foreign bill of exchange, foreign draft.**

for·eign-born (fôr'in-bôrn', for'ən-bôrn'), *adj.* born in some other country; not native.

for·eign·er (fôr'in-ẽr, for'ən-ẽr), *n.* 1. a person born in another country; alien. 2. loosely or humorously, a person regarded as an outsider or stranger. 3. something, especially a ship, from another country. —*SYN.* see **alien.**

foreign exchange, 1. the transfer of credits to a foreign country to settle debts or accounts between residents of the home country and those of the foreign country. 2. foreign bills, collectively.

for·eign·ism (fôr'in-iz'm, for'ən-iz'm), *n.* a foreign idiom, mannerism, custom, etc.

foreign legion, a military force composed mainly of volunteers from foreign countries; especially, [F- L-], such a French force, based in North Africa.

foreign mission, 1. a religious mission established by foreigners, especially in a non-Christian country. 2. a group of governmental representatives sent on diplomatic or other business to a foreign nation.

foreign office, in some countries, the office of government in charge of foreign affairs: abbreviated **F.O.**

fore·judge (fôr-juj', fōr-juj'), *v.t.* 1. to consider or decide before knowing the facts; judge beforehand. 2. [see FORJUDGE], to forjudge.

fore·know (fôr-nō', fōr-nō'), *v.t.* [FOREKNEW (-no͞o', -nū'), FOREKNOWING], to know beforehand.

fore·knowl·edge (fôr'nol'ij, fōr-nol'ij), *n.* knowledge of something before it happens or exists; prescience.

fore·la·dy (fôr'lā'di, fōr'lā'di), *n.* a forewoman.

fore·land (fôr'lənd, fōr'lənd), *n.* 1. a headland; cape; promontory. 2. a strip of land fronting an embankment or wall of a fortification. 3. land in relation to the territory lying behind it: opposed to *hinterland.*

fore·leg (fôr'leg'), *n.* either of the front legs of an animal with four or more legs.

fore·lock (fôr'lok', fōr'lok'), *n.* a lock of hair growing just above the forehead.

take time by the forelock, to anticipate and be ready for any chance; act without delay.

fore·lock (fôr'lok', fōr'lok'), *n.* a cotter pin or linchpin. *v.t.* to fasten with such a pin or pins.

fore·man (fôr'mən, fōr'mən), *n.* [*pl.* FOREMEN (-mən)], [orig., foremost man, leader], 1. a man who is chairman and spokesman of a jury. 2. a man in charge of a department or group of workers in a factory, mill, etc.

fore·man·ship (fôr'mən-ship', fōr'mən-ship'), *n.* [see -SHIP], the position or duties of a foreman.

fore·mast (fôr'mast', fōr'mäst'), *n.* the mast nearest the bow of a ship.

fore·most (fôr'mōst', fōr'məst), *adj.* [ME. *foremeste;* AS. *formest* (akin to OFris. *formest*, Goth. *frumists*, etc.), superl. (cf. -EST) of AS. *forma*, itself a superl. of *fore* (see FORE); later understood and spelled as *fore* + *most*], 1. first in place or time. 2. first in rank or importance; leading. *adv.* first. —*SYN.* see **chief.**

fore·name (fôr'nām', fōr'nām'), *n.* a first name; name before the surname.

fore·named (fôr'nāmd', fōr'nāmd'), *adj.* named before; previously mentioned.

fore·noon (fôr'no͞on', fōr-no͞on'), *n.* the time from sunrise to noon; morning. *adj.* of, in, or for the forenoon.

fo·ren·sic (fə-ren'sik), *adj.* [< L. *forensis*, public < *forum*, market place + adj. suffix *-ensis;* + *-ic*], of, characteristic of, or suitable for a law court or public debate.

fo·ren·si·cal·ly (fə-ren'si-k'l-i, fə-ren'sik-li), *adv.* in a forensic manner; by or with debate.

fore·or·dain (fôr'ôr-dān', fōr'ôr-dān'), *v.t.* to ordain beforehand; predestine.

fore·or·di·na·tion (fôr'ôr-d'n-ā'shən, fōr'ôr-d'n-ā'shən), *n.* a foreordaining; predestination.

fore·part (fôr'pärt', fōr'pärt'), *n.* fore part.

fore part, the part in front; first or early part.

fore·passed, fore·past (fôr-past', fōr-päst'), *adj.* [Rare], past; bygone.

fore·paw (fôr'pô', fōr'pô'), *n.* an animal's front paw.

fore·peak (fôr'pēk', fōr'pēk'), *n.* the part of a ship's hold in the angle of the bow.

fore·quar·ter (fôr'kwôr'tẽr, fōr'kwôr'tẽr), *n.* the front half of a side of beef, pork, mutton, etc.

fore·reach (fôr-rēch', fōr-rēch'), *v.t.* 1. to overtake; pass, especially in a sailboat. 2. to get an advantage over; get the better of. *v.i.* 1. to move closer; gain. 2. to move forward swiftly and suddenly, as a ship.

fore·run (fôr-run', fōr-run'), *v.t.* [Rare or Archaic], 1. to run before; go before; precede. 2. to be the precursor of; be a prediction or sign of (a thing to follow); foreshadow. 3. to forestall.

fore·run·ner (fôr-run'ẽr, fōr'run'ẽr), *n.* [ME., after L. *praecursor*], 1. a person sent before or going before to announce or prepare the way for another or for something to follow; herald. 2. a sign that tells or warns of something to follow; prognostic. 3. *a*) a predecessor. *b*) an ancestor.

SYN.—**forerunner** and **precursor** both refer to a person or thing that comes before (and presages the appearance of) another, **precursor** more specifically suggesting preparation for the work or achievements of the one that follows; **herald,** originally applied to one who made public proclamations or carried messages of state, now refers to any person or thing that announces something or bears news; **harbinger,** originally applied to one sent in advance to secure lodgings as for a royal party, now applies to one that announces the coming of something for which preparations must be made.

fore·said (fôr'sed', fōr'sed'), *adj.* aforesaid.

fore·sail (fôr'sāl', fôr's'l, fō's'l), *n.* 1. the main, square sail on the foremast of a square-rigged ship. 2. the main triangular sail on the mast of a fore-and-aft-rigged ship. 3. *pl.* any sails on the foremast or before the mast. See **sail,** illus.

fore·see (fôr-sē', fōr-sē'), *v.t.* [FORESAW (-sô'), FORE-

SEEN (-sēn′), FORESEEING], [AS. *foreseon*], to see beforehand; know beforehand.
fore·se·er (fôr-sē′ẽr, fōr-sē′ẽr), *n.* a person who foresees.
fore·shad·ow (fôr-shad′ō, fōr-shad′ō), *v.t.* to indicate or suggest beforehand; prefigure; presage.
fore·shank (fôr′shaŋk′, fōr′shaŋk′), *n.* 1. the upper part of the front legs of cattle. 2. meat from this part. See **beef**, illus.
fore·sheet (fôr′shēt′, fōr′shēt′), *n.* 1. one of the ropes used to trim a foresail. 2. *pl.* the space in the bows of an open boat.
fore·shore (fôr′shôr′, fōr′shōr′), *n.* the part of a shore between high-water mark and low-water mark.
fore·short·en (fôr-shôr′t'n, fōr-shôr′t'n), *v.t.* in *drawing, painting,* etc., to represent the lines of (an object) as shorter than they actually are in order to give the illusion of proper relative size, in accordance with the principles of perspective.

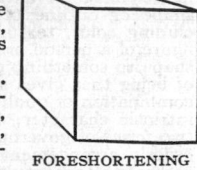

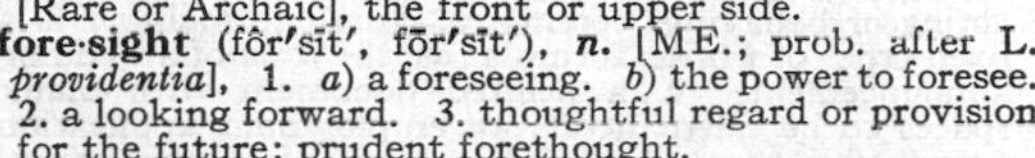
FORESHORTENING OF PLANES OF A BLOCK

fore·show (fôr-shō′, fōr-shō′), *v.t.* [FORESHOWED (-shōd′), FORESHOWN (-shōn′) or FORESHOWED, FORESHOWING], [AS. *foresceawian*], to show beforehand; indicate beforehand; foretell; prefigure.
fore·side (fôr′sīd′, fōr′sīd′), *n.* [ME. *foresyde*; akin to G. *vorseite*], [Rare or Archaic], the front or upper side.
fore·sight (fôr′sīt′, fōr′sīt′), *n.* [ME.; prob. after L. *providentia*], 1. *a*) a foreseeing. *b*) the power to foresee. 2. a looking forward. 3. thoughtful regard or provision for the future; prudent forethought.
fore·sight·ed (fôr′sīt′id, fōr′sīt′id), *adj.* having or indicating foresight.
fore·skin (fôr′skin′, fōr′skin′), *n.* the fold of skin that covers the end (*glans*) of the penis and is removed in circumcision; prepuce.
fore·speak (fôr-spēk′, fōr-spēk′), *v.t.* [ME.; see FORE- & SPEAK], [Rare], 1. to foretell; prophesy; predict. 2. to apply for or demand in advance; bespeak.
fore·spent (fôr-spent′, fōr-spent′), *adj.* [Archaic or Poetic], forspent.
for·est (fôr′ist, for′ist), *n.* [ME.; OFr. (Fr. *forêt*) < ML. (*silva*) *forestis*, (wood) unenclosed < L. *foris*, out of doors], 1. a large tract of land covered with trees and underbrush; woodland: often used figuratively. 2. the trees on such a tract. 3. in Great Britain, a tract of woodland or wasteland, usually the property of the king, preserved for game. *adj.* of or in a forest; sylvan. *v.t.* to plant with trees; change into a forest; afforest.
fore·stall (fôr-stôl′, fōr-stôl′), *v.t.* [ME. *forestallen* < AS. *foresteall*, ambush; *fore-* + *steall*, a standing], 1. to prevent or hinder by doing something beforehand. 2. to act in advance of; get ahead of; anticipate. 3. to interfere with the trading in (a market) by buying up goods in advance, getting sellers to raise prices, etc. 4. [Obs.], *a*) to intercept. *b*) to obstruct by force. —*SYN.* see **prevent.**
for·est·a·tion (fôr′is-tā′shən, for′is-tā′shən), *n.* the planting or care of forests; afforestation.
fore·stay (fôr′stā′, fōr′stā′), *n.* [ME. *forstie;* see FORE- & STAY], a rope or cable reaching from the head of a ship's foremast to the bowsprit, for helping to support the foremast.
fore·stay·sail (fôr′stā′sāl′, fōr′stā′s'l), *n.* a triangular sail set from the forestay.
for·est·er (fôr′is-tẽr, for′is-tẽr), *n.* [ME.; OFr. *forestier*], 1. a person trained in forestry. 2. a person in charge of a forest or trees. 3. a person or animal that lives in a forest. 4. any of several related moths.
fore·stick (fôr′stik′, fōr′stik′), *n.* a log placed at the front of a hearth fire, parallel to the back log.
for·est·ry (fôr′is-tri, for′is-tri), *n.* [OFr. *foresterie*], 1. [Rare], wooded land; forest land. 2. the science of planting and taking care of forests. 3. systematic forest management for the production of timber, conservation, etc. Abbreviated **for.** (in senses 2 & 3).
fore·taste (fôr′tāst′, fōr′tāst′), *n.* [ME. *fortaste*], a preliminary or first taste; slight experience of something to be enjoyed, endured, etc. in the future; anticipation. *v.t.* (fôr-tāst′, fōr-tāst′), [Rare], to taste beforehand; have a foretaste of.
fore·tell (fôr-tel′, fōr-tel′), *v.t.* [FORETOLD (-tōld′), FORETELLING], [ME.], to tell, announce, or indicate beforehand; prophesy; predict.
SYN.—**foretell** is the general term for a telling or indicating beforehand and does not in itself suggest the means used (to *foretell* the future); **predict**, often interchangeable with **foretell**, more often suggests deduction from facts already known or the use of scientific calculation (the Chaldeans could *predict* eclipses); **forecast** comes close to **predict**, now commonly implying estimation of the probable course or future condition of things (to *forecast* the weather); **prophesy**, in discriminating use, implies prediction by divine inspiration or occult knowledge (Jeremiah *prophesied* the Captivity); to **prognosticate** is to foretell by the study of signs or symptoms (to *prognosticate* a depression); **presage** and **forebode** are more often used of things than of persons, **presage** referring to either favorable or unfavorable prognostications, and **forebode** to those of an unfavorable nature, based on premonition, presentiment, etc.
fore·thought (fôr′thôt′, fōr′thôt′), *n.* [ME. *forethouht;* see FORE- & THOUGHT], 1. a thinking or planning beforehand; previous consideration. 2. prudent thought for the future; foresight.
fore·time (fôr′tīm′, fōr′tīm′), *n.* the past; former time.
fore·to·ken (fôr′tō′kən, fōr′tō′kən), *n.* [ME. *foretokne;* AS. *foretacn;* see FORE- & TOKEN], a prophetic sign; omen; prognostic. *v.t.* (fôr-tō′kən, fōr-tō′kən), to be a prophetic sign or omen of; foreshadow.
fore·told (fôr-tōld′), past tense and past participle of **foretell.**
fore·tooth (fôr′tōōth′, fōr′tōōth′), *n.* [*pl.* FORETEETH (-tēth′)], [ME. & AS. *foretoth*], a front tooth; incisor.
fore·top (fôr′top′, fōr′top′; *also, for 1,* fôr′təp, fōr′təp), *n.* [ME.; see FORE- & TOP], 1. the platform at the top of a ship's foremast. 2. a horse's (or, formerly, a person's) forelock.
fore-top·gal·lant (fôr′top-gal′ənt, fōr′tə-gal′ənt), *adj.* designating or of the mast, sail, etc. just above the fore-topmast: see **sail, illus.**
fore-top·mast (fôr-top′mast′, fōr-top′mäst′, fôr-top′məst), *n.* the section of mast extending above the foremast.
fore-top·sail (fôr-top′sāl′, fōr-top′s'l), *n.* a sail set on the fore-topmast, above the foresail: see **sail, illus.**
for·ev·er (fẽr-ev′ẽr, fôr-ev′ẽr), *adv.* 1. for eternity; for always; endlessly. 2. always; at all times.
for·ev·er·more (fẽr-ev′ẽr-môr′, fôr-ev′ẽr-mōr′), *adv.* for always: emphatic for *forever.*
fore·warn (fôr-wôrn′, fōr-wôrn′), *v.t.* to warn beforehand.
fore·went (fôr-went′, fōr-went′), past tense of **forego.**
fore·wom·an (fôr′woom′ən, fōr′woom′ən), *n.* [*pl.* FOREWOMEN (-wim′in)], a woman serving as a foreman.
fore·word (fôr′wũrd′, fōr′wũrd′), *n.* [transl. of G. *vorwort; vor,* fore + *wort,* word], an introductory remark, preface, or prefatory note. —*SYN.* see **introduction.**
fore·worn (fôr-wôrn′, fōr-wôrn′), *adj.* [Archaic], forworn.
fore·yard (fôr′yärd′, fōr′yärd′), *n.* the lowest yard on a ship's foremast.
For·far (fôr′fẽr, fôr′fär′), *n.* 1. Angus, a county of Scotland: the former name. 2. its county seat: pop., 9,800.
for·feit (fôr′fit), *n.* [ME. *forfet;* OFr. *forfait,* pp. of *forfaire,* to transgress; ML. *forisfacere,* to do wrong, lit., to do beyond < L. *foris, foras,* out of doors, outside, beyond (see FOREIGN) + *facere* (see FACT)], 1. something that a person loses or has to give up because of some crime, fault, or neglect of duty; hence, 2. a fine; penalty. 3. a thing taken away as a penalty for making some mistake in a game, and redeemable by a specified action. 4. *pl.* any game in which such forfeits are taken from players. 5. the act or process of paying a penalty for a crime, fault, etc.; forfeiture. *adj.* lost, given up, or taken away as a forfeit. *v.t.* to lose, give up, or be deprived of as a forfeit for some crime, fault, etc.
for·fei·ture (fôr′fi-chẽr), *n.* 1. a forfeiting; payment of a penalty or fine. 2. anything forfeited; penalty or fine.
for·fend (fôr-fend′), *v.t.* [ME. *forfenden;* see FOR- & FEND], [Archaic], 1. to forbid. 2. to ward off; avert; prevent. Also **forefend.**
for·fi·cate (fôr′fə-kit), *adj.* [< L. *forfex, forficis,* pair of shears; + *-ate*], deeply forked, as some birds' tails.
for·gat (fôr-gat′), archaic past tense of **forget.**
for·gath·er (fôr-gath′ẽr), *v.i.* [*for-* + *gather;* ? after D. *vergaderen*], 1. to meet; come together; assemble. 2. to meet by chance; encounter. 3. to associate or have friendly social relations (*with*). Also **foregather.**
for·gave (fẽr-gāv′, fôr-gāv′), past tense of **forgive.**
forge (fôrj, fōrj), *n.* [ME.; OFr. < L. *fabrica,* workshop, fabric < *faber,* workman, artisan], 1. a furnace for heating metal to be wrought. 2. a place where metal is heated and hammered or wrought into shape; smithy. 3. a place where wrought iron is made from pig iron or iron ore. *v.t.* [FORGED (fôrjd, fōrjd), FORGING], [ME. *forgen;* OFr. *forgier, forger* < L. *fabricari, fabricare,* to make, construct < *fabrica*], 1. to form or shape (metal) by heating and hammering; beat into shape. 2. to make (something) by or

FORGE

fat, āpe, bâre, cär; ten, ēven, hêre, ovẽr; is, bīte; lot, gō, hôrn, tōōl, look; oil, out; up, ūse, fũr; get; joy; yet; chin; she; thin, *th*en; zh, leisure; ŋ, ring; ə for *a* in *ago, e* in *agent, i* in *sanity, o* in *comply, u* in *focus;* ′ as in *able* (ā′b'l); Fr. bál; ë, Fr. coeur; ö, Fr. feu; Fr. mon; ô, Fr. coq; ü, Fr. duc; H, G. ich; kh, G. doch. See pp. x–xii. ‡ foreign; * hypothetical; < derived from.

as by this method; form; shape; produce. 3. to make (something false) to be passed off as genuine; imitate for purposes of deception or fraud; counterfeit (a check, etc.). *v.i.* 1. to shape metal, as a blacksmith does; work at a forge. 2. to make an imitation of something for purposes of deception or fraud; commit forgery.

forge (fôrj, fōrj), *v.t.* & *v.i.* [FORGED (fôrjd, fōrjd), FORGING], [prob. altered < *force*], to move forward consistently but slowly, as if against difficulties (often with *ahead*).

forg·er (fôr'jẽr, fōr'jẽr), *n.* a person who forges; specifically, *a*) one who tells false stories. *b*) one who forges metal. *c*) one who commits forgery.

for·ger·y (fôr'jẽr-i, fōr'jẽr-i), *n.* [*pl.* FORGERIES (-iz)], 1. the act or legal offense of imitating or counterfeiting documents, signatures, etc. to deceive. 2. anything forged. 3. [Poetic], literary invention.

for·get (fẽr-get', fôr-get'), *v.t.* [FORGOT (-got') or *archaic* FORGAT (-gat'), FORGOTTEN (-got''n) or FORGOT, FORGETTING], [ME. *forgeten, forgiten;* AS. *forgietan, forgetan;* akin to G. *vergessen;* see FOR- & GET], 1. to lose (facts, knowledge, etc.) from the mind; fail to recall; be unable to remember. 2. to fail to do (what one intended) because of carelessness or thoughtlessness; overlook, omit, or neglect unintentionally: as, she *forgot* to write. 3. to overlook, omit, or neglect intentionally: as, the successful candidate *forgot* the wishes of the voters. *v.i.* to forget things; be forgetful. —*SYN.* see **neglect.**

forget oneself, 1. to think only of others; be altruistic or unselfish. 2. to behave in an improper or unseemly manner.

for·get·ful (fẽr-get'fəl, fôr-get'fəl), *adj.* 1. apt to forget; having a poor memory. 2. heedless; negligent. 3. [Poetic], causing to forget: as, *forgetful* sleep.

for·get-me-not (fẽr-get'mi-not'), *n.* 1. a plant of the borage family, with hairy leaves and clusters of small, blue flowers generally considered an emblem of faithfulness and friendship. 2. any of a number of other plants related or similar to this.

for·get·ter (fẽr-get'ẽr, fôr-get'ẽr), *n.* a person who easily forgets.

forg·ing (fôr'jiŋ, fōr'jiŋ), *n.* something forged; especially, a forged piece of metal.

for·giv·a·ble (fẽr-giv'ə-b'l, fôr-giv'ə-b'l), *adj.* that can be forgiven; pardonable.

for·give (fẽr-giv', fôr-giv'), *v.t.* [FORGAVE (-gāv'), FORGIVEN (-giv'ən), FORGIVING], [ME. *forgeven, forgiven;* AS. *forgiefan, forgifan;* akin to G. *vergeben;* see FOR- & GIVE], 1. to give up resentment against or the desire to punish; stop being angry with; pardon. 2. to give up all claim to punish or exact penalty for (an offense); overlook. 3. to cancel or remit (a debt). *v.i.* to show forgiveness; be inclined to forgive. —*SYN.* see **absolve.**

for·give·ness (fẽr-giv'nis, fôr-giv'nis), *n.* 1. a forgiving or being forgiven; pardon. 2. inclination to forgive; willingness to pardon.

for·giv·ing (fẽr-giv'iŋ, fôr-giv'iŋ), *adj.* [ppr. of *forgive*], that forgives; inclined to forgive.

for·go (fôr-gō'), *v.t.* [FORWENT (-went'), FORGONE (-gôn', -gon'), FORGOING], [ME. *forgon;* AS. *forgan;* see FOR- & GO], 1. to do without; abstain from; give up. 2. [Archaic], *a*) to go past. *b*) to overlook; neglect. *c*) to leave. Also **forego.** —*SYN.* see **relinquish.**

for·gone (fẽr-gôn', fôr-gon'), past participle of **forgo.**

for·got (fẽr-got', fôr-got'), past tense and alternative past participle of **forget.**

for·got·ten (fẽr-got''n, fôr-got''n), past participle of **forget.**

for·int (fôr'int; Hung. fô-rent'), *n.* [Hung.], the monetary unit of Hungary, equal to about 9 cents in 1947.

for·judge (fôr-juj'), *v.t.* [ME. *forjugen;* OFr. *forjugier* < *fors,* outside (< L. *foris;* see FORFEIT) + *jugier;* see JUDGE], in *law,* to expel or dispossess by court judgment: also **forejudge.**

fork (fôrk), *n.* [ME. *forke;* AS. *forca, force* < L. *furca,* hayfork, etc.; reinforced by Anglo-Fr. *forque* (Fr. *fourche*), of the same origin (cf. G. *furke,* pitchfork, < L.)], 1. an instrument consisting of a handle and two or more pointed prongs at one end: forks are variously used for picking up, spearing, holding, or pitching objects. 2. something resembling a fork in shape: as, a tuning *fork.* 3. a division into branches; bifurcation. 4. the point where a river, road, etc. is divided into two or more branches, or where such branches join to form a river, road, etc. 5. one of these branches. *v.i.* to divide into branches; be bifurcated: as, the river *forks* here. *v.t.* 1. to make into the shape of a fork. 2. to pick up, spear, or pitch with a fork. 3. in *chess,* to attack (two chessmen) simultaneously with a knight, etc.

fork over (or **out, up**), [Colloq.], to pay out; hand over; give up.

forked (fôrkt; *poetic,* fôr'kid), *adj.* [pp. of *fork*], 1. having a fork or forks; divided into branches; cleft. 2. having prongs: often in hyphenated compounds, as *five-forked.* 3. zigzag: as, *forked* lightning.

For·lì (fôr-lē'), *n.* a city in northeastern Italy: pop., 73,000 (1947).

for·lorn (fẽr-lôrn', fôr-lôrn'), *adj.* [ME. & AS. *forloren,* pp. of ME. *forlesen* & AS. *forleosan,* to lose utterly (see FOR- & LOSE); the *r,* as compared with the infinitive *s,* results from the Gmc. stress assimilation known as Verner's phenomenon], 1. left behind; abandoned; deserted. 2. in pitiful condition; wretched; miserable. 3. without hope; desperate. 4. bereft or deprived (*of*).

forlorn hope, [altered < D. *verloren hoop,* lit., lost group; *verloren,* pp. of *verliezen,* to lose + *hoop,* a band, group (akin to Eng. *heap*)], 1. a group of soldiers detached from the main group for a very dangerous mission; hence, 2. a desperate undertaking; enterprise with very little chance of success. 3. [through confusion with *hope*], a faint hope.

form (fôrm), *n.* [ME. & OFr. *forme;* L. *forma,* a shape, figure, image; ? akin to *ferire,* to cut, beat], 1. the shape or outline of anything; figure; structure, excluding color, texture, and density. 2. the body or figure of a person or animal. 3. anything used to give shape to something else; mold. 4. the particular way of being that gives something its nature or character; combination of qualities making something what it is; intrinsic character: as, democracy and autocracy are two *forms* of government. 5. arrangement; especially, orderly arrangement; way that something is put together; pattern; style: distinguished from *content.* 6. a way of doing something: as, his *form* in serving at tennis is good. 7. an established or customary way of acting or behaving; ceremony; ritual; formality. 8. a fixed order of words; formula: as, the *form* of a wedding announcement. 9. a printed document with blank spaces to be filled in: as, an employment application *form.* 10. a particular kind, or type, of a larger group; species or variety: as, man is a *form* of animal life. 11. a condition of mind or body in regard to mental or physical performances of skill, speed, etc.: as, the boxer was in good *form* for the fight. 12. the lair or hiding place of a hare, etc. 13. (*occas.* fōrm), a long, wooden bench without a back, as formerly in a schoolroom. 14. a grade or class in school. 15. [Archaic], beauty. 16. in *grammar,* any of the different appearances of a word in changes of inflection, spelling, or pronunciation: as, *am* is a *form* of the verb *be.* 17. in *printing,* the type, plates, etc. locked in a frame or chase for printing. Abbreviated **F., f.** *v.t.* 1. to give shape or form to; fashion; make, as in some particular way: as, a school *formed* after the model of Oxford. 2. to mold or shape by training and discipline; train; instruct. 3. to develop (habits). 4. to think of; frame in the mind; conceive. 5. to come together into; take the formation of; organize into: as, the boys *formed* lines. 6. to make up; act as; constitute; create out of separate elements: as, thirteen States *formed* the original Union. 7. in *grammar,* to build (words) from bases, prefixes, etc.; construct or make up (a sentence, phrase, etc.). *v.i.* 1. to be formed; assume shape. 2. to come into being; take form. 3. to take a definite or specific form or shape.

bad form, conduct not in accord with social custom.

good form, conduct in accord with social custom.

SYN.—**form** denotes the arrangement of the parts of a thing that gives it its distinctive appearance and is the broadest term here, applying also to abstract concepts; **figure** is applied to physical form as determined by the bounding lines or surfaces; **outline** is used of the lines bounding the limits of an object and, in an extended sense, suggests an undetailed general plan; **shape,** although also stressing outline, is usually applied to something that has mass or bulk and may refer to nonphysical concepts; **configuration** stresses the relative disposition of the inequalities of a surface. See also **make.**

-form (fôrm), [L. *-formis* < *forma;* see FORM], a suffix meaning: 1. *having the form of, shaped like,* as in *cuneiform, oviform.* 2. *having* (a specified number of) *forms,* as in *uniform.*

for·mal (fôr'm'l), *adj.* [L. *formalis* < *forma;* see FORM], 1. of external form or structure, rather than nature or content; apparent. 2. of the internal form; relating to the character or nature; essential. 3. of or according to prescribed or fixed customs, rules, ceremonies, etc.: as, a *formal* wedding; hence, 4. *a*) made or done for outward appearance only. *b*) stiff; prim; ceremonious. 5. *a*) designed for use or wear at ceremonies, elaborate parties, etc.: as, *formal* dress. *b*) requiring clothes of this kind: as, the dance will be *formal.* 6. done or made in orderly, regular fashion; methodical. 7. very regular or orderly in arrangement, pattern, etc.; rigidly symmetrical: as, a *formal* garden. 8. done or made according to the forms that make explicit, definite, valid, etc.: as, a *formal* contract. 9. designating education in schools, colleges, etc. 10. designating or of that level of language usage characterized by expanded vocabulary, complete syntactical constructions, complex sentences, etc.: distinguished from *colloquial* or *informal.* *n.* [Colloq.], 1. a dance requiring evening dress of the persons attending. 2. a woman's evening dress.

go formal, [Colloq.], to go dressed in evening clothes.

form·al·de·hyde (fôr-mal'də-hīd'), *n.* [< *formic* + *aldehyde*], a colorless, pungent gas, HCHO, used in solution as a strong disinfectant and preservative.

for·ma·lin (fôr'mə-lin), *n.* [< *formaldehyde* + *-in*], a 40 per cent solution of formaldehyde in water, used as an antiseptic.

for·mal·ism (fôr'm'l-iz'm), *n.* strict or excessive attention to or insistence on outward forms and customs, as in art or religion.

for·mal·ist (fôr'm'l-ist), *n.* a person who likes and practices formalism.

for·mal·is·tic (fôr'm'l-is'tik), *adj.* of or characterized by formalism.

for·mal·i·ty (fôr-mal'ə-ti), *n.* [*pl.* FORMALITIES (-tiz)], [Fr. *formalité;* LL. *formalitas* < L. *formalis;* see FORMAL], 1. the quality or state of being formal; specifically, *a)* a following or observing of prescribed customs, rules, ceremonies, etc.; propriety. *b)* careful or too careful attention to order, regularity, precision, or conventionality; stiffness. 2. a formal or conventional act or requirement; ceremony or form, often without practical meaning: as, saying "How do you do?" to acknowledge an introduction is a *formality.* —***SYN.*** see **ceremony.**

for·mal·i·za·tion (fôr'm'l-ə-zā'shən, fôr'm'l-ī-zā'shən), *n.* a formalizing or being formalized.

for·mal·ize (fôr'm'l-īz'), *v.t.* [FORMALIZED (-īzd'), FORMALIZING], 1. to give definite form to; shape. 2. to make formal. *v.i.* to behave with formality; be formal.

for·mal·ly (fôr'm'l-i), *adv.* 1. in a formal manner. 2. with regard to form, arrangement, or outline.

for·mat (fôr'mat; Fr. fôr'mä'), *n.* [Fr. < L. (*liber*) *formatus,* (a book) formed, pp. of *formare;* see FORM], 1. the shape, size, binding, type, paper, and general make-up or arrangement of a book, magazine, etc. 2. general arrangement, as of a television program.

for·mate (fôr'māt), *n.* a salt or ester of formic acid.

for·ma·tion (fôr-mā'shən), *n.* [L. *formatio* < pp. of *formare;* see FORM], 1. a forming or being formed. 2. a thing formed. 3. the way in which something is formed or arranged; arrangement; structure; order. 4. in *geology,* a series or group of strata of the same sort of rock or mineral, or having common characteristics. 5. in *military usage,* the arrangement or disposition of troops, ships, etc.

form·a·tive (fôr'mə-tiv), *adj.* [OFr. *formatif* < L. *formatus,* pp. of *formare;* see FORM & -IVE], 1. giving or able to give form; helping to shape, develop, or mold: as, a teacher is a *formative* influence on a child. 2. of formation or development: as, a child's *formative* years. 3. in *grammar,* serving to form words. *n.* in *grammar,* 1. an element, as a prefix or suffix, used with other elements to form words. 2. a word thus formed.

form class, in *linguistics,* a class made up of words having certain formal features in common, as the form class *noun,* made up of all words to which both the plural and possessive suffixes may be added.

for·mer (fôr'mẽr), *adj.* [ME. *formere,* compar., back-formation < *formest;* see FOREMOST], 1. preceding in time; earlier; past: as, in *former* times. 2. first mentioned of two: opposed to *latter;* often used absolutely (with *the*), as, Jack and Bill are twins, but the *former* is taller than the latter. —***SYN.*** see **previous.**

form·er (fôr'mẽr), *n.* a person or thing that forms.

for·mer·ly (fôr'mẽr-li), *adv.* at or in a former time; in the past; some time ago: abbreviated **form.**

for·mic (fôr'mik), *adj.* [< L. *formica,* an ant], 1. of ants. 2. designating or of a colorless acid, HCOOH, that is irritating to the skin: it is found in ants, spiders, etc. as well as in nettles and some other plants, and is prepared commercially from oxalic acid and glycerine.

For·mi·ca (fôr-mī'kə), *n.* a laminated thermosetting plastic used, as for table and sink tops, because of its resistance to heat, chemicals, etc.: a trade-mark.

for·mi·car·y (fôr'mi-ker'i), *n.* [*pl.* FORMICARIES (-iz)], [ML. *formicarium* < **formicarius,* of ants < L. *formica,* ant], an ant hill; ants' nest.

for·mi·cate (fôr'mi-kāt'), *v.i.* [FORMICATED (-id), FORMICATING], [< L. *formicatus,* pp. of *formicare,* to crawl < *formica,* ant], to crawl or swarm like or with ants.

for·mi·da·bil·i·ty (fôr'mi-də-bil'ə-ti), *n.* the quality of being formidable.

for·mi·da·ble (fôr'mi-də-b'l), *adj.* [Fr.; L. *formidabilis* < *formidare,* to fear, dread < *formido,* fear], 1. causing dread, fear, or awe. 2. hard to handle or overcome.

for·mi·da·bly (fôr'mi-də-bli), *adv.* in a formidable manner; so as to be formidable.

form·less (fôrm'lis), *adj.* having no definite or regular form or plan; shapeless; amorphous.

form letter, a letter of standardized form, usually one of a number printed or run off on a duplicating machine, with the date, address, etc. filled in separately.

For·mo·sa (fôr-mō'sə), *n.* Taiwan, an island province off southeastern China: see **Taiwan.**

Formosa Strait, the strait between Formosa and China.

for·mu·la (fôr'myoo-lə), *n.* [*pl.* FORMULAS (-ləz), FORMULAE (-lē')], [L., dim. of *forma;* see FORM], 1. a fixed form of words, especially one that has lost its original meaning or force and is now used only as a conventional or ceremonial expression: as, "Very truly yours" is a *formula* used in letters. 2. any conventional rule or method for doing something, especially when used, applied, or repeated without thought. 3. an exact statement of religious faith or doctrine. 4. a prescribed method or prescription for preparing a medicine, a baby's food, etc. 5. a set of algebraic symbols expressing a mathematical fact, principle, rule, etc.: as, $A = \pi r^2$ is the *formula* for determining the area of a circle. 6. in *chemistry,* an expression of the composition of a compound (or a radical, etc.) by a combination of symbols and figures to show the constituents in their exact proportions: an *empirical formula* shows the kinds of atoms and the number of each kind in any molecule of the substance (e.g., C_6H_6, benzene); a *structural formula* shows, in addition, how the atoms are arranged

```
            H
            C
      HC        CH
in the molecule (e.g.,        , benzene; C6H5-
      HC        CH
            C
            H
```

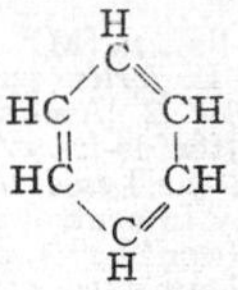

COOH, benzoic acid).

for·mu·lar·ize (fôr'myoo-lə-rīz'), *v.t.* [FORMULARIZED (-rīzd'), FORMULARIZING], to formulate.

for·mu·lar·y (fôr'myoo-ler'i), *n.* [*pl.* FORMULARIES (-iz)], [Fr. *formulaire* < L. *formula;* see FORMULA], 1. a collection of formulas; book of prescribed forms, as prayers, rituals, etc. 2. a formula. 3. in *pharmacy,* a list of medicines with their formulas and directions for compounding them. *adj.* of, or having the nature of, a formula or formulas.

for·mu·late (fôr'myoo-lāt'), *v.t.* [FORMULATED (-id), FORMULATING], 1. to express in or reduce to a formula. 2. to express, as a theory, in a systematic way.

for·mu·la·tion (fôr'myoo-lā'shən), *n.* 1. a formulating or being formulated. 2. a formulated expression.

for·mu·la·tor (fôr'myoo-lā'tẽr), *n.* one who formulates.

for·mu·lism (fôr'myoo-liz'm), *n.* 1. reliance on or belief in formulas. 2. a system of formulas.

for·mu·lis·tic (fôr'myoo-lis'tik), *adj.* of or characterized by formulism.

for·mu·li·za·tion (fôr'myoo-lə-zā'shən, fôr'myoo-lī-zā'shən), *n.* a formulizing.

for·mu·lize (fôr'myoo-līz'), *v.t.* [FORMULIZED (-līzd'), FORMULIZING], to formulate.

for·myl (fôr'mil), *n.* [< *formic* + *-yl*], the radical, HCO, of formic acid.

For·nax (fôr'naks), *n.* [L., a furnace], a southern constellation: see **constellation,** chart.

for·nent (fẽr-nent'), *prep.* [*fore, adv.* + *anent*], 1. [British Dial.], directly opposite to; facing. 2. [Obs.], in connection with; with regard to.

for·ni·cate (fôr'ni-kāt'), *v.i.* [FORNICATED (-id), FORNICATING], [< LL. *fornicatus,* pp. of *fornicari,* to fornicate < L. *fornix, fornicis,* a vault, brothel], to commit fornication.

for·ni·ca·tion (fôr'ni-kā'shən), *n.* [ME. *fornicatioun;* OFr. *fornication;* L. *fornicatio* < *fornicatus;* see FORNICATE], 1. voluntary sexual intercourse between an unmarried woman and a man, especially an unmarried man: it is generally forbidden by law. 2. in the *Bible,* *a)* any unlawful sexual intercourse, including adultery. *b)* worship of idols.

for·ni·ca·tor (fôr'ni-kā'tẽr), *n.* a person who fornicates.

for·nix (fôr'niks), *n.* [*pl.* FORNICES (-ni-sēz')], [L., an arch], a structure in the brain composed of arched nerve fibers: it is part of the olfactory pathways in the brain.

for·sake (fẽr-sāk', fôr-sāk'), *v.t.* [FORSOOK (-sook'), FORSAKEN (-sāk'ən), FORSAKING], [ME. *forsaken;* AS. *forsacan,* to oppose, refuse, forsake; *for-* + *sacan,* to contend, strive], 1. to give up; renounce (a habit, idea, etc.). 2. to leave; desert. —***SYN.*** see **abandon.**

for·sak·en (fẽr-sāk'ən, fôr-sāk'ən), *adj.* [pp. of *forsake*], abandoned; desolate; forlorn.

for·sook (fẽr-sook', fôr-sook'), past tense of **forsake.**

for·sooth (fẽr-sōōth', fôr-sōōth'), *adv.* [AS. *forsoth* < *for, prep.* + *soth,* truth], [Archaic], in truth; no doubt; indeed: now only in ironic use.

for·spent (fôr-spent'), *adj.* [pp. of obs. *forspend* < AS. *forspendan,* to use up; see FOR- & SPEND], [Archaic or Poetic], exhausted with toil; fatigued: also **forespent.**

For·ster, E. M. (fôr'stẽr), (*Edward Morgan Forster*), 1879– ; English novelist.

for·swear (fôr-swâr'), *v.t.* [FORSWORE (-swôr', -swōr'), FORSWORN (-swôrn', -swōrn'), FORSWEARING], [ME. *forswerien;* AS. *forswerian;* see FOR- & SWEAR], 1. to renounce on oath; promise earnestly to give up. 2. to deny earnestly or on oath. *v.i.* to swear falsely; fail to keep an oath or promise; commit perjury.

forswear oneself, to swear falsely; perjure oneself.

for·sworn (fôr-swôrn′, fôr-swōrn′), past participle of **forswear.** *adj.* having sworn falsely; perjured.

for·syth·i·a (fẽr-sith′i-ə, fôr-sī′thi-ə), *n.* [Mod.L., after William *Forsyth* (1737–1804), Eng. botanist who introduced it to England], a shrub with yellow bell-shaped flowers, which appear in early spring before the leaves.

fort (fôrt, fōrt), *n.* [Fr., orig. *adj.*, strong; L. *fortis*, strong, powerful; OL. **forctis;* IE. base **bherĝh-*, to raise, high, seen also in Sans. *brinhati*, strengthens, elevates, OHG. *berg*, hill], 1. an enclosed place or fortified building for military defense, usually equipped with earthworks, guns, etc. 2. a permanent army post, as distinguished from a temporary training camp. Abbreviated **ft.**

hold the fort, to make a defensive stand.

For·ta·le·za (fôr-tä-le′zə; Eng. fôr′tə-lā′zə), *n.* a city on the coast of northern Brazil: pop., 205,000: also called *Ceará*.

for·ta·lice (fôr′tə-lis), *n.* [ME. *forteletes;* OFr. *fortelesse;* ML. *fortalitia* < L. *fortis*, strong], 1. a small fort or defensive outwork. 2. [Archaic], a fortress.

Fort-de-France (fôr′də-fräns′), *n.* seaport and capital of Martinique, in the Lesser Antilles: pop., 61,000.

Fort Dodge, a city in central Iowa: pop., 28,000.

Fort Don·el·son (don″l-s′n), a fort on the Cumberland River, northern Tennessee, captured by Grant in 1862.

Fort Du·quesne (dōō-kān′, dū-kān′), a French fort that stood on the site of Pittsburgh, captured (1758) by the English in the French and Indian War.

forte (fôrt), *n.* [Fr. *fort;* fem. ending *-e* added through association with *morale, locale*, etc.; see FORT], 1. the thing that a person does particularly well; one's special accomplishment or strong point. 2. the strongest part of the blade of a sword, between the middle and the hilt: opposed to *foible*.

for·te (fôr′ti, fôr′tā), *adj. & adv.* [It. < L. *fortis*, strong], in *music*, loud: a direction to the performer, opposed to *piano*: abbreviated **f., F.** *n.* a forte note or passage.

‡**for·te·pi·a·no** (fôr′te-pyä′nô), *adj. & adv.* [It.; see FORTE & PIANO], in *music*, loud and then soft: a direction to the performer: abbreviated **fp., F.P., f.p.**

Forth (fôrth, fōrth), *n.* a river in eastern Scotland, flowing into the North Sea: length, 50 mi.

forth (fôrth, fōrth), *adv.* [ME.; AS.; akin to *fore*], 1. forward in place, time, or degree; onward. 2. out; into view, as from hiding or obscurity. 3. [Archaic], abroad. *prep.* [Archaic], out from; out of. See also idiomatic phrases under **hold, show,** etc.

and so forth, and so on; and other such things: equivalent to *etc.*

Forth, Firth of (fôrth, fōrth), the long estuary of the Forth River, eastern Scotland: length, 48 mi.

FIRTH OF FORTH

forth·com·ing (fôrth′kum′iŋ, fōrth′kum′iŋ), *adj.* 1. approaching; about to appear: as, the author's *forthcoming* book. 2. available or ready when needed: as, the promised money was not *forthcoming*. *n.* a coming forth; appearing or approaching.

Fort Henry, a fort in northern Tennessee, captured by Grant in 1862.

forth·right (fôrth′rīt′, fōrth′rīt′), *adj.* [AS. *forth riht;* see FORTH & RIGHT], 1. originally, going straight forward. 2. straightforward; direct; frank. *adv.* 1. straight forward; directly onward. 2. immediately; at once. *n.* [Archaic], a straight path or course.

forth·with (fôrth′with′, fōrth′with′), *adv.* [ME. *forth with*, for AS. *forth mid;* see FORTH & WITH], immediately; without delay; at once.

for·ti·eth (fôr′ti-ith), *adj.* [ME. *feowertigthe;* AS. *feowertigotha;* see FORTY & -TH], 1. preceded by thirty-nine others in a series; 40th. 2. designating any of the forty equal parts of something. *n.* 1. the one following the thirty-ninth. 2. any of the forty equal parts of something; 1/40.

for·ti·fi·a·ble (fôr′tə-fī′ə-b′l), *adj.* that can be fortified.

for·ti·fi·ca·tion (fôr′tə-fi-kā′shən), *n.* [Fr.; LL. *fortificatio* < pp. of *fortificare*], 1. the act or science of fortifying. 2. something used in fortifying; especially, a fort or defensive earthwork, wall, etc. 3. a fortified place or position. Abbreviated **fort., ft.**

for·ti·fi·er (fôr′tə-fī′ẽr), *n.* a person or thing that fortifies.

for·ti·fy (fôr′tə-fī′), *v.t.* [FORTIFIED (-fīd′), FORTIFYING], [Fr. *fortifier;* LL. *fortificare* < L. *fortis*, strong + *facere*, to make], 1. to make strong or stronger; strengthen physically or structurally. 2. to strengthen against attack, as by building or furnishing with forts, walls, etc. 3. to support; corroborate: as, he *fortified* his argument with statistics. 4. to strengthen (liquor, etc.) by adding alcohol. 5. to add vitamins, minerals, etc. to (bread, etc.) so as to increase the food value. *v.i.* to build military defenses.

for·tis (fôr′tis), *adj.* [L., strong], in *phonetics*, strongly articulated: as, a *fortis* stop. *n.* a strongly articulated speech sound, especially a stop. Opposed to *lenis*.

for·tis·si·mo (fôr-tis′ə-mō′; It. fôr-tēs′sē-mô′), *adj. & adv.* [It., superl. of *forte;* see FORTE, *adj. & adv.*], in *music*, very loud: a direction to the performer, opposed to *pianissimo*: abbreviated **ff.** *n.* [*pl.* FORTISSIMOS (-mōz′), FORTISSIMI (-mē′)], a passage to be performed fortissimo.

for·ti·tude (fôr′tə-tōōd′, fôr′tə-tūd′), *n.* [Fr.; L. *fortitudo* < *fortis*, strong], firm courage; patient endurance of misfortune, pain, etc.

SYN.—**fortitude** refers to the courage that permits one to endure patiently misfortune, pain, etc. (to face a calamity with *fortitude*); **grit** applies to an obstinate sort of courage that refuses to succumb under any circumstances; **backbone** refers to the strength of character and resoluteness that permits one to face opposition unflinchingly; **pluck** and **guts** both refer originally to visceral organs, hence **pluck** implies a strong heart in the face of danger or difficulty and **guts**, a slang word, suggests the sort of stamina that permits one to "stomach" a disagreeable or frightening experience. See also **patience.** —*ANT.* cowardice.

for·ti·tu·di·nous (fôr′tə-tōō′də-nəs, fôr′tə-tū′də-nəs), *adj.* having fortitude; courageous.

Fort Lau·der·dale (lô′dẽr-dāl′), a city on the southeastern coast of Florida: pop., 84,000.

Fort Mc·Hen·ry (mək-hen′ri), a fort in Baltimore harbor, Maryland, where the British were repulsed in 1814.

fort·night (fôrt′nīt, fôrt′nit), *n.* [ME. *fourte(n) niht;* AS. *feowertyne niht*, lit., fourteen nights; cf. SENNIGHT], [Chiefly British], two weeks.

fort·night·ly (fôrt′nīt-li), *adv.* once in every fortnight; at two-week intervals. *adj.* happening or appearing at two-week intervals. *n.* [*pl.* FORTNIGHTLIES (-liz)], a periodical issued at two-week intervals.

for·tress (fôr′tris), *n.* [ME.; OFr. *fortresse, fortelesce;* see FORTALICE], a fortified place; fort: often used figuratively. *v.t.* to protect by or supply with a fortress.

Fort Smith, a city in western Arkansas, on the Arkansas River: pop., 53,000.

Fort Sum·ter (sum′tẽr), a fort in Charleston harbor, South Carolina, where Confederate troops fired the first shots of the Civil War, on April 12, 1861.

for·tu·i·tism (fôr-tōō′ə-tiz′m, fôr-tū′ə-tiz′m), *n.* [*fortuitous* + *-ism*], in *philosophy*, the doctrine that natural phenomena occur by chance rather than by the design of some higher intelligence.

for·tu·i·tous (fôr-tōō′ə-təs, fôr-tū′ə-təs), *adj.* [L. *fortuitus* < *fors, fortis*, chance, luck], happening by chance; accidental. —*SYN.* see **accidental.**

for·tu·i·ty (fôr-tōō′ə-ti, fôr-tū′ə-ti), *n.* [*pl.* FORTUITIES (-tiz)], [Fr. *fortuité* < *fortuit*, accidental < L. *fortuitus;* see FORTUITOUS], chance; accident.

For·tu·na (fôr-tū′nə, fôr-tōō′nə), *n.* [L. < *fortuna*], in *Roman mythology*, the goddess of fortune.

for·tu·nate (fôr′chə-nit), *adj.* [ME.; L. *fortunatus*, pp. of *fortunare*, to make fortunate < *fortuna;* see FORTUNE], 1. having good luck; lucky. 2. bringing, or coming by, good luck; favorable; auspicious. —*SYN.* see **lucky.**

for·tune (fôr′chən), *n.* [ME.; OFr.; L. *fortuna*, chance, hap, fate, fortune < *fors, fortis*, chance, luck], 1. the supposed power considered to bring good or bad to people; luck; chance; fate: often personified. 2. what happens or is going to happen to one; one's lot, good or bad; especially, one's future lot. 3. good luck; success; prosperity. 4. wealth; riches; large estate; extensive possessions: as, she inherited a *fortune*. *v.t.* [FORTUNED (-chənd), FORTUNING], [Rare], to provide with wealth. *v.i.* [Archaic], to happen; chance.

tell one's fortune, to profess to tell what is going to happen in one's life, as by palmistry, cards, etc.

fortune hunter, a person who tries to become rich, especially by marrying a rich person.

for·tune·tell·er (fôr′chən-tel′ẽr), *n.* a person who professes to foretell events in other people's lives.

Fort Wayne, a city in northeastern Indiana: pop., 162,000.

Fort William, a city in southern Ontario, Canada, on Lake Superior: pop., 35,000.

Fort Worth, a city in northern Texas: pop., 356,000.

for·ty (fôr′ti), *adj.* [ME. *fourti;* AS. *feowertig;* akin to G. *vierzig*, Goth. *fidwor tigjus;* see FOUR & -TY (tens)], four times ten. *n.* [*pl.* FORTIES (-tiz)], the cardinal number between thirty-nine and forty-one; 40; XL.

the forties, the years from forty through forty-nine (of a century or a person's age).

for·ty-nin·er, For·ty-Nin·er (fôr′ti-nīn′ẽr), *n.* [Colloq.], a person who went to California in the gold rush of 1849.

forty winks, [Colloq.], a short sleep; nap.

fo·rum (fôr′əm, fō′rəm), *n.* [*pl.* FORUMS (-əmz, -rəmz), FORA (-ə, -rə)], [L., orig., prob., place boarded off or fenced in; IE. base **bhor-*, wood cut into planks, seen also in L. *forus*, gangplank, gaming board, MHG. *bar*, a beam], 1. the public square or market place of an ancient Roman city or town, where legal and political business was conducted. 2. a law court; tribunal. 3. an assembly for the discussion of public matters or current questions.

the Forum, the forum of ancient Rome.

for·ward (fôr′wẽrd), ***adj.*** [ME. *foreward, forwarde;* AS. *foreweard, adj. & adv.;* see FORE & -WARD], 1. at, toward, or of the front, or fore part. 2. advanced; specifically, *a*) ahead of time; early. *b*) mentally advanced; precocious. *c*) advanced socially, politically, etc.; progressive. 3. moving toward a point in front; onward; advancing. 4. prompt; ready; eager: as, he was *forward* in helping. 5. bold; pushing; presumptuous; pert. 6. of or for the future: as, *forward* buying. ***adv.*** 1. toward the front or a point in front; ahead; onward. 2. toward the future: as, look *forward.* 3. into view or prominence: as, he brought *forward* an opinion. ***n.*** in *basketball, hockey, football,* etc., any of the players in the front line or in a front position. ***v.t.*** 1. to help advance; promote. 2. to send; dispatch; transmit. 3. to send on to one's new address: as, *forward* her mail to New York. 4. to make (a book) ready for the finisher by adding the cover, etc. —***SYN.*** see **advance.**

for·ward·er (fôr′wẽr-dẽr), ***n.*** a person or thing that forwards; specifically, a transmitting agent; person who receives goods and delivers them to the regular transportation agent for transmission to the proper destination.

for·ward·ly (fôr′wẽrd-li), ***adv.*** 1. at or toward the front, or fore part. 2. readily; eagerly. 3. boldly; presumptuously; pertly.

for·ward·ness (fôr′wẽrd-nis), ***n.*** the quality or state of being forward; specifically, *a*) an advanced state of development or progress. *b*) readiness; eagerness. *c*) boldness; presumption; pertness.

forward pass, in *football,* a pass made from behind the line of scrimmage to a teammate in a position toward the opponent's goal.

for·wards (fôr′wẽrdz), ***adv.*** [ME. *forewardes; foreward* + adv. genit. *-es;* akin to G. *vorwärts*], forward.

for·went (fôr-went′), past tense of **forgo.**

for·why (fôr-hwī′), ***adv.*** [ME. *forwhi;* AS. *for hwy,* wherefore; *for* (see FOR, *prep.*) + *hwy,* instrumental case of *hwæt* (see WHAT)], [Archaic], why; wherefore. *conj.* [Archaic], because.

for·worn (fôr-wôrn′), ***adj.*** [Early Mod. Eng. *forworen,* pp. of obs. v. *forwear,* to wear out; see FOR- & WEAR], [Archaic], worn out: also **foreworn.**

for·zan·do (fôr-tsän′dō), ***adj.*** [It. < *forzare,* to force; LL. ***fortiare;* see FORCE, *v.*], in *music,* with force; with stress; sforzando: a direction to the performer: symbol, ∧, <; abbreviated **fz.**

fos·sa (fos′ə), ***n.*** [*pl.* FOSSAE (-ē)], [L., a ditch, trench], in *anatomy,* a cavity, pit, or small hollow.

fosse (fôs, fos), ***n.*** [ME.; OFr.; L. *fossa* < *fossa* (*terra*), dug (earth) < *fossus;* see FOSSIL], a ditch or moat, especially one used in fortifications: also spelled **foss.**

fos·sette (fô-set′, fo-set′), ***n.*** [Fr., dim. of *fosse;* see FOSSE], 1. a small hollow. 2. a dimple.

fos·sil (fos′'l; *now often* fô's'l), ***n.*** [< Fr. *fossile* < L. *fossilis,* dug out, dug up < *fossus,* pp. of *fodere,* to dig up], 1. originally, any rock or mineral dug out of the earth; hence, 2. any hardened remains or traces of plant or animal life of some previous geological period, preserved in rock formations in the earth's crust. 3. [Colloq.], a person who is old-fashioned or has outmoded, fixed ideas. ***adj.*** 1. of, having the nature of, or forming a fossil or fossils. 2. belonging to the past; unchanged by progress; antiquated.

fos·sil·if·er·ous (fos′'l-if′ẽr-əs), ***adj.*** [< L. *fossilis* (see FOSSIL); + *-ferous*], containing fossils.

fos·sil·i·za·tion (fos′'l-ə-zā′shən, fos′'l-i-zā′shən), ***n.*** 1. a fossilizing or being fossilized. 2. a fossilized thing.

fos·sil·ize (fos′'l-iz′), ***v.t.*** [FOSSILIZED (-īzd′), FOSSILIZING], 1. to change into a fossil or fossils; petrify. 2. to make out of date, rigid, or incapable of change. ***v.i.*** 1. to become fossilized. 2. [Rare], to collect or search for fossils.

fos·so·ri·al (fo-sôr′i-əl, fo-sō′ri-əl), ***adj.*** [< LL. *fossorius* < L. *fossor,* digger < *fossus* (see FOSSIL); + *-al*], digging or adapted for digging; burrowing: as, *fossorial* claws.

fos·ter (fôs′tẽr, fos′tẽr), ***v.t.*** [ME. *fostren;* AS. *fostrian,* to nourish, bring up < *fostor,* food, nourishment < base of *foda,* food; see FOOD], 1. to bring up; rear. 2. to help to develop; stimulate; promote: as, hunger *fosters* disease. 3. to cherish; harbor fondly in one's mind: as, she *fostered* hopes of becoming an actress. ***adj.*** giving, receiving, or sharing affection, care, etc., as if related by blood; having the standing of a specified member of a family but not by birth: as, a *foster* brother. ***n.*** [Obs.], a foster parent.

Fos·ter, Stephen Collins (fôs′tẽr, fos′tẽr), 1826–1864; American composer of songs.

Foster, William Zeb·u·lon (zeb′yoo-lən), 1881–1961; American labor organizer and Communist Party leader.

fos·ter·age (fôs′tẽr-ij, fos′tẽr-ij), ***n.*** [*foster* + *-age*], 1. the rearing of a foster child. 2. the state of being a foster child. 3. the act of giving a child over to foster parents. 4. a promoting, stimulating, or encouraging.

foster brother, [AS. *fostorbrothor*], a boy in his relationship to the child or children of his foster parents.

foster child, [AS. *fostorcild*], a child reared by anyone other than his mother or father.

foster father, [AS. *fostorfæder*], a man who acts as a father to a child not his own.

fos·ter·ling (fôs′tẽr-liŋ, fos′tẽr-liŋ), ***n.*** [AS. *fostorling;* see -LING], a foster child.

foster mother, [AS. *fostormodor*], a woman who acts as a mother to a child not her own.

foster parent, a foster father or foster mother.

foster sister, [AS. *fostorsweostor*], a girl in her relationship to the child or children of her foster parents.

Foth·er·in·ghay (foth′ẽr-iŋ-gā′, foth′riŋ-gā′), ***n.*** a village in Northamptonshire, England: site of the castle where Mary Queen of Scots was imprisoned and beheaded (1587).

Fou·cault, Jean Ber·nard Lé·on (zhän ber′når′ lā′ōn′ fōō′kō′), 1819–1868; French physicist.

fou·droy·ant (fōō-droi′ənt; Fr. fōō′drwå′yän′), ***adj.*** [Fr., ppr. of *foudroyer,* to strike by lightning < *foudre,* lightning < LL. *fulgere* for L. *fulgur*], attacking suddenly and severely; fulminant: said of a disease.

fought (fôt), [ME. *fauht, faht;* AS. *feaht,* 3d pers. sing., past indic., of *feohtan*], past tense and past participle of **fight.**

fought·en (fôt′'n), archaic past participle of **fight.**

foul (foul), ***adj.*** [ME.; AS. *ful;* akin to G. *faul,* rotten, putrid, lazy; IE. base ***pū-,** ***pu-,** etc., to stink (? < exclamation of disgust), seen also in *pus, putrid*], 1. so offensive to the senses as to cause disgust; stinking; loathsome: as, a *foul* odor. 2. extremely dirty; disgustingly filthy. 3. full of or covered with dirt or foreign objects: as, a *foul* pipe. 4. putrid; rotten: said of food. 5. indecent; obscene; profane: as, *foul* language. 6. wicked; abominable: as, a *foul* murder. 7. not clear; stormy; unfavorable: as, *foul* weather, winds, etc. 8. tangled; caught; jammed: as, a *foul* rope: opposed to *clear.* 9. not according to the rules of a game; unfair, either by accident or intention. 10. treacherous; dishonest. 11. [Archaic], ugly. 12. [Colloq.], unpleasant, disagreeable, etc. 13. in *baseball,* relating to or having to do with foul balls or foul lines. 14. in *printing,* full of errors or changes: as, *foul* copy. ***n.*** anything foul; specifically, *a*) a collision of boats, contestants, etc. *b*) an infraction of the rules, as of a game or sport. *c*) in *baseball,* a foul ball. ***v.t.*** 1. to make foul; dirty; soil; defile. 2. to dishonor; disgrace. 3. to impede; obstruct; specifically, *a*) ‡to fill up; encrust; choke: as, grease often *fouls* sink drains. *b*) to cover (the bottom of a ship) with impeding growths. *c*) to entangle; catch: as, the rope was *fouled* in the shrouds: opposed to *clear. d*) to collide with. 4. to make a foul against in a contest or game. 5. in *baseball,* to bat (the ball) so that it falls outside the foul lines. ***v.i.*** 1. to become dirty. 2. to be clogged or choked. 3. to become tangled. 4. to collide. 5. to break the rules of a game. 6. in *baseball, a*) to bat the ball so that it falls outside the foul lines. *b*) to be retired by a catch of such a ball (with *out*). —***SYN.*** see **dirty.**

foul up, [Colloq.], to make a mess of; make disordered or confused; entangle or bungle.

go (or **fall** or **run**) **foul of,** 1. to collide with and become tangled in. 2. to get into conflict or trouble with.

fou·lard (fōō-lärd′), ***n.*** [Fr. < Swiss Fr. *foulat,* lit., fulled (cloth) < *fouler,* to full; cf. FULL, *v.,* FELT, *n.*], 1. a lightweight material of silk, rayon, or silk and cotton, usually printed with a small design. 2. a necktie, scarf, or handkerchief made of this material.

foul ball, in *baseball,* a batted ball that falls outside the foul lines: opposed to *fair ball.*

foul line, 1. in *baseball,* either of the lines extending from home plate through the outside corners of first base or third base and onward to the end of the outfield. 2. in *basketball,* the line from which a player makes the free throw or throws granted to him when he is fouled. 3. in *tennis, bowling,* etc., any of various lines bounding the playing area, outside of which the ball must not be hit, the player must not go, etc.

foul·mouthed (foul′mouthd′, foul′moutht′), ***adj.*** using obscene, profane, or scurrilous language.

foul·ness (foul′nis), ***n.*** 1. the quality or condition of being foul. 2. something foul.

foul play, 1. unfair play; action that breaks the rules of the game. 2. treacherous action or violence.

foul shot, in *basketball,* any of one or more free throws at the basket allowed to a player as a penalty imposed on the opponents for some infraction of the rules:

each throw if successful counts for one point.

foul tip, in *baseball*, a batted ball barely tipped by the bat: it is counted as a strike, but if it is the third strike, it must be caught by the catcher for the batter to be out.

fou·mart (fōō′märt), *n.* [ME. *fulmard, fulmart* < AS. *ful*, foul + *mearth*, marten], the European polecat.

found (found), [ME. *funden;* AS. *fundon*, pp. of *findan*], past tense and past participle of **find.** *adj.* provided with all the necessaries, especially room and board.

found (found), *v.t.* [ME. *founden;* OFr. *funder, fonder;* L. *fundare* < *fundus*, bottom], 1. to lay the base of; set for support; base: as, this statement is *founded* on facts. 2. to begin the construction of; establish: as, the city was *founded* in 1815. *v.i.* [Rare], to be based.

found (found), *v.t.* [Fr. *fondre* < L. *fundere*, to pour, melt (metal)], 1. to melt and pour (metal or materials for glass) into a mold. 2. to make by pouring molten metal into a mold; cast.

foun·da·tion (foun-dā′shən), *n.* [ME. *foundacioun;* OFr. *fondation;* L. *fundatio* < pp. of *fundare;* see FOUND (to base)], 1. a founding or being founded; establishment. 2. the establishment of an institution with provision for its upkeep. 3. a fund or endowment to maintain a hospital, school, charity, etc. 4. an institution maintained by an endowment. 5. the supporting part of a wall, house, etc.; base. 6. the fundamental principle on which something is founded; basis. 7. a supporting material or part beneath an outer part, as in a dress. 8. a foundation garment. —*SYN.* see **base.**

foundation garment, a woman's corset or girdle, often with an attached brassiere.

foundation stone, 1. a stone that is part of the foundation of a building. 2. a cornerstone.

foun·der (foun′dẽr), *v.i.* [ME. *foundren;* OFr. *fondrer*, to fall in, sink < *fond*, bottom; L. *fundus*, bottom], 1. *a*) to stumble, fall, or go lame. *b*) to have founder: said of a horse. 2. to fill with water and sink: said of a ship. 3. to break down; collapse; fail. *v.t.* to cause to founder. *n.* [< the *v.i.*, 1], an inflammation of a horse's foot; laminitis.

found·er (foun′dẽr), *n.* [ME. *foundeor;* OFr. *fondeor;* L. *fundator*], a person who founds, or establishes.

found·er (foun′dẽr), *n.* a person who founds, or casts, metals, etc.

foun·der·ous (foun′dẽr-əs), *adj.* causing or likely to cause foundering: as, a *founderous* road.

found·ers' shares (foun′dẽrz), shares of corporation stock, sometimes carrying special privileges, issued to the founders or organizers of a company: now seldom issued except in England.

found·ling (found′liŋ), *n.* [ME. *foundeling* < *founde(n)*, pp. of *finden* (cf. FIND) + *-ling;* cf. D. *vondeling*, akin in formation], a child found after it has been abandoned by its unknown parents.

found·ry (foun′dri), *n.* [*pl.* FOUNDRIES (-driz)], [Fr. *fonderie* < *fondre;* see FOUND (to cast)], 1. the act, process, or work of melting and molding metals; casting. 2. metal castings. 3. a place where metal is cast.

foundry proof, in *printing*, proof submitted for a final reading before plates are cast.

fount (fount), *n.* [Fr. *font;* L. *fons, fontis*, a fountain], 1. a fountain; spring. 2. a source.

fount (fount), *n.* in *printing*, a font: British form.

foun·tain (foun′t'n), *n.* [Late ME. *fontayne;* OFr. *funtaine, fontaine;* LL. *fontana*, fem. of L. *fontanus* < *fons, fontis*, fountain], 1. a natural spring of water. 2. the source or beginning of a stream. 3. the origin of anything; source. 4. *a*) an artificial spring, jet, or flow of water. *b*) the basin, pipes, etc. where this flows. *c*) a drinking fountain; bubbler or similar device. *d*) a soda fountain. 5. a storage place for liquid; container or reservoir, as for ink, oil, etc.

foun·tain·head (foun′t'n-hed′, foun′tin-hed′), *n.* 1. a spring that is the source of a stream. 2. the original or main source of anything.

Fountain of Youth, a legendary spring supposed to restore the health and youth of anyone who drank from it: it was sought by Ponce de León and other Spanish explorers in America and the West Indies.

fountain pen, a pen in which a nib or ball at the end is fed writing fluid from a supply in the reservoir or from a replaceable cartridge in the holder.

four (fôr, fōr), *adj.* [ME. *foure;* AS. *feower;* akin to G. *vier*, Goth. *fidwōr*, etc.; IE. **qwetwor*, four, seen also in L. *quattuor* (whence Fr. *quatre*, etc.)], totaling one more than three. *n.* 1. the cardinal number between three and five; 4; IV. 2. something that has four of anything as its outstanding characteristic, as a playing card or domino marked with four spots.

on all fours, 1. on all four feet. 2. on hands and knees (or feet).

four-bag·ger (fôr′bag′ẽr, fōr′bag′ẽr), *n.* [Slang], in *baseball*, a home run.

four·chette (foor-shet′), *n.* [Fr., dim. of *fourche;* see FORK], in *anatomy*, 1. the wishbone of a bird. 2. the frog of a hoof. 3. a small fold of skin connecting the inner lips (*labia minora*) of the vulva at the lower end.

four-col·or (fôr′kul′ẽr, fōr′kul′ẽr), *adj.* designating or of a process in which printing is done with separate plates in yellow, red, blue, and black, so that any desired color or colors can be produced.

four-cy·cle (fôr′sī′k'l, fōr′sī′k'l), *n.* a cycle of four strokes, as in some internal-combustion engines.

four-di·men·sion·al (fôr′di-men′shən-'l, fōr′di-men′shən-'l), *adj.* of or in four dimensions.

Four·drin·i·er (foor-drin′i-ẽr), *adj.* [after Sealy and Henry *Fourdrinier*, who developed the machine in England early in the 19th century], designating or of a paper-making machine that produces paper in a continuous strip or roll. *n.* such a machine.

four-flush (fôr′flush′, fōr′flush′), *v.i.* 1. in *poker*, to pretend that one's hand has five cards of the same suit when it has only four (*four flush*); hence, 2. [Slang], to bluff.

four·flush·er (fôr′flush′ẽr, fōr′flush′ẽr), *n.* 1. a poker player who four-flushes; hence, 2. [Slang], a person who bluffs.

four·fold (fôr′fōld′, fōr′fōld′), *adj.* [see -FOLD], 1. having four parts. 2. having four times as much or as many. *adv.* four times as much or as many.

four-foot·ed (fôr′foot′id, fōr′foot′id), *adj.* [ME. *fourfoted*], having four feet; quadruped.

Four Freedoms, freedom of speech, freedom of religion, freedom from want, and freedom from fear: the establishment of these freedoms everywhere in the world was declared an objective of United States foreign policy by President Roosevelt in his message to Congress, January 6, 1941.

‡**four·gon** (fōōr′gōn′), *n.* [Fr.], a wagon or car for baggage.

four-hand·ed (fôr′han′did, fōr′han′did), *adj.* 1. having four hands. 2. for four players, as some games. 3. in *music*, for two performers, as a piano duet.

Four-H club, 4-H club (fôr′āch′, fōr′āch′), [< the aim to improve the *h*ead, *h*ands, *h*eart, and *h*ealth], a rural youth organization sponsored by the Department of Agriculture, offering instruction in scientific agriculture and home economics.

four hundred, [popularized by C. J. Allen, New York *Sun* society reporter, from a remark by Ward McAllister: "There are only 400 people in New York that one really knows"; ? from limited capacity of Mrs. J. J. Astor's ballroom], the social set regarded as wealthiest and most exclusive (with *the*).

Fou·rier, Fran·çois Ma·rie Charles (frän′swå′ må′rē′ shårl fōō′ryā′; Eng. foor′i-ẽr), 1772–1837; French socialist and reformer.

Fourier, Jean Bap·tiste Jo·seph (zhän bå′tēst′ zhō′zef′), Baron, 1768–1830; French mathematician and physicist.

Fou·ri·er·ism (foor′i-ẽr-iz'm), *n.* the doctrines of F. M. C. Fourier; especially, his proposed system for reorganizing society into small, co-operative communities.

four-in-hand (fôr′in-hand′, fōr′in-hand′), *n.* 1. a team of four horses. 2. a coach drawn by such a team. 3. a necktie tied in a slipknot with the ends left hanging. *adj.* designating or of a four-in-hand.

four-leaf clover (fôr′lēf′, fōr′lēf′), a clover with four leaves, popularly supposed to bring good luck to the finder.

four-letter word (fôr′let′ẽr, fōr′let′ẽr), any of several short words having to do with sex or excrement and generally regarded as objectionable and unprintable.

four-o'clock (fôr′ə-klok′, fōr′ə-klok′), *n.* any of several plants with bright foliage and long-tubed yellow, red, and white blossoms that open late in the afternoon and close again late in the morning; marvel-of-Peru.

four·pence (fôr′pəns, fōr′pəns), *n.* 1. the sum of four pence; four British pennies. 2. a former British silver coin of this value, or about eight cents.

four·pen·ny (fôr′pen′i, fōr′pən-i), *adj.* 1. costing or valued at fourpence. 2. designating a size of nail: see **-penny.** *n.* fourpence.

four-post·er (fôr′pōs′tẽr, fōr′pōs′tẽr), *n.* a large bedstead with tall corner posts that sometimes support a canopy or curtains.

‡**four·ra·gère** (fōō′rå′zhâr′), *n.* [Fr. < *fourrager;* see FORAGE, *v.*], a military decoration awarded to an entire unit of troops, consisting of a colored and braided cord to be worn on the left shoulder by every member of the unit.

four·score (fôr′skôr′, fōr′skōr′), *adj.* & *n.* [ME.], [Archaic or Poetic], four times twenty; eighty.

four·some (fôr′səm, fōr′səm), *adj.* [*four* + *-some*], [Scot.], of or for four people, as some games. *n.* 1. a group of four people. 2. in *golf*, *a*) a game involving four players, usually two to a team. *b*) the players in such a game.

four·square (fôr′skwâr′, fōr′skwâr′), *adj.* 1. square. 2. unyielding; unhesitating; firm. 3. frank; forthright. *adv.* in a square form; squarely. *n.* a square.

four·teen (fôr′tēn′, fōr′tēn′), *adj.* [ME. *fowertene;* AS. *feowertyne;* see FOUR & -TEEN], four more than ten. *n.* the cardinal number between thirteen and fifteen; 14; XIV.

four·teenth (fôr′tēnth′, fōr′tēnth′), *adj.* [ME. *fourteothe;* AS. *feowerteotha* < *feowertyne;* form repatterned after *fourteen* + *-th*], 1. preceded by thirteen others in a series; 14th. 2. designating any of the fourteen equal parts of something. *n.* 1. the one following the thirteenth. 2. any of the fourteen equal parts of something; 1/14.

fourth (fôrth, fōrth), *adj.* [ME. *feorthe, ferthe;* AS. *feortha;* see FOUR & -TH], 1. preceded by three others in a series; 4th. 2. designating any of the four equal parts of something. *n.* 1. the one following the third. 2. any of the four equal parts of something; 1/4. 3. in *music,* *a*) the tone four degrees above a given tone in a diatonic scale. *b*) the interval between these tones. *c*) a combination of these tones.

fourth-class (fôrth′klas′, fōrth′kläs′), *adj.* of the class, rank, excellence, etc. next below the third; specifically, designating or of a class of mail consisting of merchandise or printed matter not first-class or second-class: also called *parcel post.* *adv.* as or by fourth-class mail.

fourth dimension, a dimension in addition to those of length, width, and depth: in the theory of relativity, time is regarded as the fourth dimension: see **space-time continuum.**

fourth·ly (fôrth′li, fōrth′li), *adv.* in the fourth place: used in enumerating topics.

Fourth of July, the holiday celebrating the adoption of the Declaration of Independence on July 4, 1776: also called *Independence Day.*

Fourth Republic, the republic established in France in 1945, after the liberation in World War II, lasting until 1958.

four-way (fôr′wā′, fōr′wā′), *adj.* giving passage in four directions: as, a *four-way* valve.

four-wheel (fôr′hwēl′, fōr′hwēl′), *adj.* 1. four-wheeled. 2. affecting four wheels: as, a *four-wheel* drive.

four-wheeled (fôr′hwēld′, fōr′hwēld′), *adj.* having or running on four wheels.

fou·ter, fou·tre (fōō′tẽr), *n.* [< OFr. *foutre,* to copulate with < L. *futuere*], [Obs.], a fig: euphemism for a strong term of contempt.

fo·ve·a (fō′vi-ə), *n.* [*pl.* FOVEAE (-ē′)], [L.], a small pit, hollow, or depression.

fovea cen·tra·lis (sen-trā′lis), a depression at the back of the retina, the point where the vision is most acute.

fo·ve·ate (fō′vi-it, fō′vi-āt′), *adj.* having a fovea or foveae; pitted.

fo·ve·o·la (fə-vē′ə-lə), *n.* [*pl.* FOVEOLAE (-lē′)], [Mod.L., dim. of L. *fovea*], a small fovea.

fo·ve·o·late (fō′vi-ə-lāt′), *adj.* in *biology,* foveate; pitted.

fo·ve·ole (fō′vi-ōl′), *n.* a foveola.

fowl (foul), *n.* [*pl.* FOWLS (foulz), FOWL; see PLURAL, II, D, 1], [ME. *foule, fowel, foghel;* AS. *fugol, fugel;* akin to G. *vogel,* bird; IE. base **pōu-,* etc., small, little, seen also in *puerile, pauper, foal, pullet,* etc.], 1. originally, any bird: used now in combination, as, wild *fowl.* 2. any of the larger domestic birds used as food; specifically, *a*) the chicken. *b*) the duck, goose, etc. *c*) a full-grown chicken, as distinguished from a springer, etc. 3. the flesh of any of these birds used for food. *v.i.* to catch, trap, hunt, or shoot wild birds for food or sport.

fowl·er (foul′ẽr), *n.* [ME. *foulere;* AS. *fugelere;* see FOWL & -ER], a person who hunts, traps, or shoots wild birds.

fowl·ing (foul′iŋ), *n.* the hunting of wild fowl.

fowling piece, a type of shotgun for fowling.

Fox (foks), *n.* 1. a member of a tribe of Algonquian Indians who lived in Illinois and southwestern Wisconsin. 2. this tribe: merged with the Sac tribe (1760).

fox (foks), *n.* [*pl.* FOXES (-iz), FOX; see PLURAL, II, D, 1], [ME.; AS.; akin to G. *fuchs;* Gmc. base **fuh-;* prob. < IE. base **puq-,* **peuq-,* thick-haired, bushy, seen also in Sans. *púccha,* tail; animal prob. so named from its bushy tail], 1. any of a group of small, wild, flesh-eating animals of the dog family, with bushy tails and, commonly, reddish-brown fur: the fox is conventionally thought of as sly and crafty: see also **red fox, silver fox, blue fox, cross fox.** 2. its fur. 3. a sly, crafty, deceitful person. 4. in *nautical usage,* a strand of ropes twisted together. 5. [Obs.], a kind of sword. *v.t.* 1. to make (beer, etc.) sour by fermenting. 2. [from the color of a fox], to stain (book leaves, prints, etc.) with reddish-brown or yellowish discolorations. 3. to trick or deceive by slyness or craftiness. 4. to repair (boots, shoes, etc.) with new upper leather. *v.i.* 1. to become sour: said of beer, etc. 2. to become stained: said of book leaves, etc.

FOX (3 1/2 ft. long including tail)

Fox, Charles James (foks), 1749–1806; British orator and statesman.

Fox, George, 1624–1691; English theologian; founded the Society of Friends, c. 1650.

fox brush, the tail of a fox, especially when regarded as the trophy of a fox hunt.

foxed (fokst), *adj.* [pp. of *fox*], 1. soured, as beer. 2. stained or discolored, as an old book. 3. tricked. 4. repaired, as shoes.

fox·glove (foks′gluv′), *n.* [ME. *foxes glove;* AS. *foxes glofa,* fox's glove], any of a number of plants of the figwort family, with long spikes full of thimblelike flowers: one species is a source of digitalis.

fox·hole (foks′hōl′), *n.* a hole dug in the ground as a temporary protection for one or two soldiers against enemy gunfire or tanks.

fox·hound (foks′hound′), *n.* any of a breed of hounds having great strength and speed and a keen scent: they are bred and trained to hunt foxes and other game.

FOXHOUND (24 in. high)

fox-hunt (foks′-hunt′), *v.i.* to take part in a fox hunt or fox hunts.

fox hunt, a sport in which hunters on horses ride after dogs in pursuit of a fox.

fox·i·ly (fok′s′l-i), *adv.* in a foxy manner; slyly.

fox·i·ness (fok′si-nis), *n.* the quality of being foxy; slyness.

fox·ing (fok′siŋ), *n.* [see FOX, *v.*], a piece of leather for repairing or decorating the upper of a shoe.

fox squirrel, the North American tree squirrel.

fox·tail (foks′tāl′), *n.* 1. the tail, or brush, of a fox. 2. any of several tall grasses with long spikes of brushlike flowers.

fox terrier, any of a breed of small, active terriers with a smooth or wire-haired coat, usually white with dark patches: they were formerly trained to drive foxes out of hiding.

WIRE-HAIRED FOX TERRIER (15 in. high at shoulder)

fox-trot (foks′trot′), *v.i.* 1. to go at a fox trot, or mixed pacing and trotting gait: said of a horse. 2. to dance the fox trot.

fox trot, 1. a slow, mixed gait of a horse in which it trots with the forelegs and paces with the hind legs; hence, 2. a dance in 4/4 time with a variety of steps, both fast and slow. 3. the music for such a dance.

fox·y (fok′si), *adj.* [FOXIER (-si-ẽr), FOXIEST (-si-ist)], 1. foxlike; crafty; wily; sly. 2. having the reddish-brown color of a fox. 3. covered with brownish or yellowish stains, as an old book. 4. sour: said of beer, wine, etc. not properly fermented. —*SYN.* see **sly.**

foy (foi), *n.* [MD. *foy, fooy, voye;* prob. < OFr. *voie* < L. *via,* way, journey; see VIA], [Dial.], 1. a feast, present, etc. given by or to a person departing on a journey. 2. a feast at the end of a harvest or fishing season.

foy·er (foi′ẽr, foi′ā; Fr. fwȧ′yā′), *n.* [orig., greenroom of a theater; Fr., hearth, lobby < LL. **focarium* < L. *focus,* hearth, fireplace], an entrance hall or lobby, especially in a theater, hotel, or apartment house.

fp., 1. foolscap. 2. in *music, fortepiano.*

fp., F.P., f.p., foot-pound; foot-pounds.

F.P., f.p., 1. fireplug. 2. fully paid. 3. in *insurance,* *a*) fire policy. *b*) floating policy. 4. in *music, fortepiano.*

f.p., fp, fp., freezing point.

FPC, F.P.C., Federal Power Commission.

Fr, in *chemistry,* francium.

Fr., 1. Father. 2. France. 3. *Frau.* 4. French. 5. Friar. 6. Friday.

fr., 1. fragment. 2. franc; francs. 3. frequent. 4. from.

Fra (frä), *n.* [It., abbrev. of *frate* < L. *frater,* brother], brother: title given to a friar or monk, as, *Fra* Lippo Lippi.

fra·cas (frā′kəs), *n.* [Fr.; It. *fracasso* < *fracassare,* to smash < *fra-,* intens. (< L. *infra,* below) + *cassare,* to quash, break < L. *quassare;* see QUASH], a noisy dispute or fight; loud quarrel or disturbance; brawl.

frac·tion (frak′shən), *n.* [Fr.; L. *fractio,* a breaking < pp. of *frangere,* to break], 1. a breaking; dividing: now only of the Eucharistic bread. 2. a small part broken off; small part, amount, degree, etc.; fragment; scrap. 3. in *chemistry,* a part separated by fractional crystallization, distillation, etc. 4. in *mathematics,* *a*) a quantity less than a whole number expressed as a decimal (.4) or with a numerator and denominator (1/2, 2/3). *b*) any quantity expressed in terms of a numerator and denominator, as 13/4. See also **common**

fraction, compound fraction, complex fraction, etc. —*SYN.* see **part.**

frac·tion·al (frak'shən-'l), *adj.* 1. of or forming a fraction or fractions. 2. very small; unimportant; insignificant. 3. in *chemistry*, designating or of any of various processes for separating the constituents of a mixture by taking advantage of differences in their solubility, boiling points, etc.: as, *fractional* distillation. 4. in *commerce*, being less than the unit of transaction, usually 100 shares, in stock exchanges.

fractional currency, small coins or paper money in circulation, worth less than the monetary unit: as, the dime is *fractional currency*, worth less than the dollar.

frac·tion·ar·y (frak'shən-er'i), *adj.* 1. fractional. 2. fragmentary.

frac·tion·ate (frak'shən-āt'), *v.t.* [FRACTIONATED (-id), FRACTIONATING], in *chemistry*, to separate into fractions by crystallization, distillation, etc.

frac·tion·a·tion (frak'shən-ā'shən), *n.* the act or process of fractionating.

frac·tion·ize (frak'shən-īz'), *v.t. & v.i.* [FRACTIONIZED (-īzd'), FRACTIONIZING], to divide into fractions.

frac·tious (frak'shəs), *adj.* [prob. altered < *factious*, after *fraction* (in obs. sense of "brawling") or *refractory* (cf. CAPTIOUS)], 1. unruly; rebellious; refractory. 2. peevish; irritable; fretful; cross.

frac·to- (frak'tō, frak'tə), [< L. *fractus*, pp. of *frangere*, to break], a combining form used in hyphenated compounds, meaning ***a ragged mass of*** (a specified kind of) *cloud*, as in *fracto-stratus*.

frac·to-cu·mu·lus (frak'tō-kū'myoo-ləs), *n.* a mass of small, ragged clouds torn from a cumulus.

frac·to-nim·bus (frak'tō-nim'bəs), *n.* a mass of ragged, shapeless clouds torn from a nimbus.

frac·to-stra·tus (frak'tō-strā'təs), *n.* a ragged cloud in long, threadlike layers, torn from a stratus.

frac·tur·al (frak'chẽr-əl), *adj.* of, having the nature of, or caused by a fracture.

frac·ture (frak'chẽr), *n.* [Fr.; L. *fractura*, a breaking, breach, cleft < pp. of *frangere*, to break], 1. a breaking or being broken. 2. a break; crack; split. 3. a break in a bone or, occasionally, a tear in a cartilage: see also **compound fracture, simple fracture.** 4. the texture of the surface of a mineral broken across the normal line of cleavage. *v.t. & v.i.* [FRACTURED (-chẽrd), FRACTURING], to break; crack; split. —*SYN.* see **break.**

frae (frā), *prep.* [Scot.], from. *adv.* [Scot.], fro.

frae·num (frē'nəm), *n.* a frenum.

frag·ile (fraj'əl), *adj.* [L. *fragilis* < *frangere*, to break], easily broken, shattered, damaged, or destroyed; brittle; frail; delicate.

SYN.—**fragile** implies such delicacy of structure as to be easily broken (a *fragile* china teacup); **frangible** adds to this the connotation of liability to being broken because of the use to which the thing is put (the handle on this axe seems *frangible*); **brittle** implies such inelasticity as to be easily broken or shattered by pressure or a blow (the bones of the body become *brittle* with age); **crisp** suggests a desirable sort of brittleness, as of fresh celery or soda crackers; **friable** is applied to something that is easily crumbled or crushed into powder (*friable* rock). —*ANT.* tough, sturdy.

fra·gil·i·ty (frə-jil'ə-ti, fra-jil'ə-ti), *n.* [ME. & OFr. *fragilite;* L. *fragilitas*], the quality of being fragile.

frag·ment (frag'mənt), *n.* [Fr.; L. *fragmentum* < *frangere*, to break], 1. a part broken away from a whole; broken piece: abbreviated **fr.** 2. a detached, isolated, or incomplete part: as, *fragments* of the melody remained in her mind. 3. the part that exists of a literary or other work left incomplete or unfinished: as, this poem is only a *fragment*. —*SYN.* see **part.**

frag·men·tal (frag-men't'l), *adj.* 1. fragmentary. 2. in *geology*, designating or of rocks formed of the fragments of rocks that had existed previously; clastic.

frag·men·tar·i·ly (frag'mən-ter'ə-li), *adv.* in a fragmentary manner.

frag·men·tar·i·ness (frag'mən-ter'i-nis), *n.* the quality or condition of being fragmentary.

frag·men·tar·y (frag'mən-ter'i), *adj.* consisting of fragments; not complete; disconnected.

frag·men·ta·tion (frag'mən-tā'shən), *n.* a breaking into fragments.

fragmentation bomb, an antipersonnel bomb that scatters the broken, jagged pieces of the bomb case over a wide area when it explodes.

frag·ment·ed (frag'mən-tid), *adj.* broken into fragments.

frag·ment·ize (frag'mən-tīz'), *v.t.* [FRAGMENTIZED (-tīzd'), FRAGMENTIZING], to break into fragments.

Fra·go·nard, Jean Ho·no·ré (zhän ô'nô'rā' frà'gô'nàr'), 1732–1806; French painter.

fra·grance (frā'grəns), *n.* [OFr.; L. *fragrantia*], 1. the quality of being fragrant. 2. a sweet smell; pleasant odor. —*SYN.* see **odor.**

fra·gran·cy (frā'grən-si), *n.* [*pl.* FRAGRANCIES (-siz)], [Rare], fragrance.

fra·grant (frā'grənt), *adj.* [< Fr. or L.; Fr. *fragrant;* L. *fragrans, fragrantis*, ppr. of *fragrare*, to emit a (sweet) smell], having a pleasant odor; sweet-smelling.

frail (frāl), *adj.* [ME. *frele;* OFr. *frele, fraile* < L. *fragilis;* see FRAGILE], 1. easily broken, shattered, damaged, or destroyed; fragile; delicate. 2. slender and delicate; not robust; weak. 3. easily tempted; morally weak; liable to sin or misbehave. *n.* [Slang], a woman or girl. —*SYN.* see **weak.**

frail (frāl), *n.* [ME. *fraiel;* OFr. *frael, fraiel, flael*, rush basket; ML. *fraellum;* L. *flagellum*, young branch, shoot, whip], 1. a basket made of rushes, for packing figs, raisins, etc. 2. the varying quantity of raisins, etc. packed in such a basket, usually 50 or 75 pounds.

frail·ty (frāl'ti), *n.* [ME. *frelete;* OFr. *frailete*], 1. the quality or condition of being frail; weakness; especially, moral weakness. 2. [*pl.* FRAILTIES (-tiz)], any fault or failing arising from such weakness.

fraise (frāz), *n.* [Fr., orig., a ruff < *fraiser*, to ruffle; Pr. *frezar* < *fres*, a border, curl < Frank. **frisi*, a curl, edging; akin to AS. *fris*, crisped, curled], 1. a ruff or high collar. 2. in *military usage*, a palisading or barrier consisting of an inclined or horizontal fence of barbed wire, or, formerly, of wooden stakes.

fram·be·si·a, fram·boe·si·a (fram-bē'zhi-ə, fram-bē'zi-ə), *n.* [Mod. L. < Fr. *framboise*, raspberry; LL. **frambosia* < L. *fraga ambrosia*, ambrosial berry], the yaws, a contagious tropical disease.

frame (frām), *v.t.* [FRAMED (frāmd), FRAMING], [ME. *framen, framien;* partly < AS. *framian*, to be helpful (< *fram, adj.*, forward; see FROM), partly < ON. *frama, fremja*, to further, execute (of same ult. origin); mod. senses largely < ME. sense "to prepare (timber) for use"], 1. to shape, fashion, or form, usually according to a pattern; design: as, they *framed* a constitution. 2. to put together the parts of; construct. 3. to compose; put into words; devise; contrive; conceive: as, he *framed* a theory of progress. 4. to utter: as, his lips *framed* the words. 5. to adapt for a particular use; adjust; fit: as, the law was *framed* to equalize the tax burden. 6. to enclose in a border; provide a border for, as a mirror or picture. 7. [Slang], to falsify evidence, testimony, etc. beforehand in order to make (a person) appear guilty. *n.* [chiefly < the *v.* but orig. with sense of "advantage" < ON. *frami*, furtherance], 1. *a*) anything made of parts fitted together according to a design; basic or skeletal structure; framework, as of a house, ship, etc. *b*) any of various machines built on or in a framework. 2. the human skeleton; body structure in general; build. 3. the case or border into which a window, door, etc. is set and which serves as a structural support. 4. an ornamental border surrounding and sometimes supporting a picture. 5. the way that anything is constructed or put together; organization; form. 6. mood; humor; temper. 7. an established order or system, especially of government. 8. [Slang], a framing (sense 7). 9. [Colloq.], in *baseball*, an inning. 10. in *bowling*, etc., any of the ten divisions of a game, in each of which the pins are set up anew. 11. in *motion pictures*, each of the small exposures composing a strip of film. 12. in *pool*, *a*) the triangular form in which the balls are set up at the beginning of a game. *b*) the balls so set up before the break. *c*) the period of play required to pocket all the balls. 13. in *shipbuilding*, any of the transverse structures that form the ribs of a ship's hull and extend from the gunwale to the bilge or to the keel: called *square frame* when set at a right angle to the vertical plane of the keel, and *cant frame* when set at an oblique angle. 14. in *television*, a single scanning of the field of vision by the televisor.

frame house, a house with a wooden framework, usually covered with boards.

frame of mind, mental or emotional state; mood.

frame-up (frām'up'), *n.* [Colloq.], 1. a falsifying of evidence, testimony, etc. to make an innocent person seem guilty. 2. a surreptitious, underhand arrangement or scheme made beforehand.

frame·work (frām'wũrk'), *n.* 1. a structure, usually rigid, serving to hold the parts of something together or to support something constructed or stretched over or around it; skeletal structure: as, the *framework* of a house. 2. the basic structure, arrangement, or system.

fram·ing (frām'iŋ), *n.* 1. the act of a person or thing that frames. 2. the way in which something is framed. 3. *a*) a frame or framework. *b*) a system of frames.

Fram·ing·ham (frā'miŋ-ham'), *n.* a town in eastern Massachusetts: pop., 45,000.

franc (fraŋk), *n.* [Fr. < L. *Francorum rex*, king of the French, device on the coin in 1360], 1. *a*) the monetary unit and a coin of France, valued at about 1/5 cent in 1959: it was replaced in 1960 by a new franc (abbrev. **NF**) equal to 100 old francs, or about $.20. *b*) an obsolete French coin of gold or silver. 2. *a*) the monetary unit of Belgium, equal to about $.02 in 1961. *b*) the monetary unit of Switzerland, equal to about $.23 in 1961. Abbreviated **fr., F., f.**

France (frans, fräns), *n.* a country in western Europe: area, 212,737 sq. mi.; pop., 45,355,000; capital, Paris: abbreviated **Fr., F.**

France, A·na·tole (à'nà'tôl' fräns; Eng. an'ə-tōl' frans, fräns), (pseudonym of *Jacques Anatole François Thibault*), 1844–1924; French novelist and literary critic; received Nobel prize in literature, 1921.

Fran·ces (fran′sis, frän′sis), [< OFr. fem. form of *Franceis;* see FRANCIS], a feminine name: diminutives, *Fran, Fannie, Fanny.*

Fran·ces·ca, Pie·ro del·la (pye′rô del′lä frän-ches′kä), 1420?–1492; Umbrian painter.

Franche-Com·té (fränsh′kōn′tā′), *n.* a former province of eastern France.

FRANCHE-COMTÉ

fran·chise (fran′chīz), *n.* [ME.; OFr. < *franc,* free; see FRANK, *adj.*], 1. originally, freedom from some restriction, servitude, etc.; hence, 2. *a)* any special right or privilege granted by the government, as to be a corporation, operate a public utility, etc. *b)* the jurisdiction over which this extends. 3. the right to vote; suffrage. 4. the right to market a product, often exclusive for a specified area, as granted by the manufacturer.

fran·chised (fran′chīzd), *adj.* holding a franchise: as, *a franchised* dealer.

Fran·cis (fran′sis, frän′sis), [OFr. *Franceis;* LL. *Franciscus* < Gmc. **Franco;* see FRANK, *adj.*], a masculine name: diminutive, *Frank;* feminine, *Frances;* equivalents, Fr. *François,* G. *Franz,* It. *Francesco, Franco,* Sp. *Francisco.*

Francis I, 1. 1494–1547; king of France (1515–1547). 2. title of Francis II as emperor of Austria.

Francis II, 1768–1835; last emperor of the Holy Roman Empire (1792–1806); as Francis I, first emperor of Austria (1804–1835).

Fran·cis·can (fran-sis′kən), *adj.* [< ML. *Franciscus,* Francis], 1. of Saint Francis of Assisi. 2. designating or of the monastic order founded by him in 1209: it is now divided into three independent branches. *n.* any member of this order.

Francis Ferdinand, 1863–1914; nephew of Francis Joseph I; archduke of Austria: his assassination led to the outbreak of World War I.

Francis Joseph I, (*Franz Josef*), 1830–1916; emperor of Austria (1848–1916); king of Hungary (1867–1916).

Francis of Assisi, Saint, 1182–1226; Italian founder of the Franciscan order: his day is October 4.

Francis of Sales, Saint (sālz; Fr. sål), 1567–1622; French ecclesiastic: his day is January 29.

fran·ci·um (fran′si-əm), *n.* [< *France* + *-ium*], a metallic chemical element of the alkali group: symbol, Fr; at. wt., 223 (?); at. no., 87.

Franck, Cé·sar Au·guste (sā′zär′ ō′güst′ fränk; Eng. fräŋk), 1822–1890; French composer, born in Belgium.

Fran·co, Fran·cis·co (frän-thēs′kô fräŋ′kô; Eng. fraŋ′kō), 1892– ; Spanish general; leader of the successful fascist revolt against the Spanish republic (1936–1939); dictator of Spain (1939–): called *El Caudillo.*

Fran·co- (fraŋ′kō, fraŋ′kə), [ML. < *Francus,* a Frank], a combining form meaning: 1. *Frankish.* 2. *of France, of the French,* as in *Francophobe.* 3. *France and, the French and,* as in *Franco-German.*

fran·co·lin (fraŋ′kə-lin), *n.* [Fr.; It. *francolino* < *franco,* free; cf. FRANK, *adj.*], any of several African and Asiatic partridges.

Fran·co·ni·a (fraŋ-kō′ni-ə), *n.* a former duchy of southwestern Germany.

FRANCONIA

Fran·co·phil (fraŋ′kə-fil), *n.* & *adj.* Francophile.

Fran·co·phile (fraŋ′kə-fīl′), *n.* [*Franco* + *-phile*], a person who admires or is extremely fond of France, its people, customs, influence, etc. *adj.* of Francophiles.

Fran·co·phobe (fraŋ′kə-fōb′), *n.* [*Franco-* + *-phobe*], a person who hates or fears France, its people, customs, etc. *adj.* of Francophobes.

Fran·co-Prus·sian War (fraŋ′kō-prush′ən), a war (1870–1871) in which Prussia defeated France.

‡franc-ti·reur (frän′tē′rër′), *n.* [*pl.* FRANCS-TIREURS (frän′tē′rër′)], [Fr.; *franc,* free + *tireur,* a gunner < *tirer,* to shoot], any of a group of French irregular soldiers serving variously as light infantry, scouts, etc.

fran·gi·bil·i·ty (fran′jə-bil′ə-ti), *n.* the quality or state of being frangible.

fran·gi·ble (fran′jə-b'l), *adj.* [OFr. *frangible* < L. *frangere,* to break], breakable; fragile. —*SYN.* see **fragile.**

fran·gi·pane (fran′jə-pān′), *n.* frangipani.

fran·gi·pan·i (fran′ji-pan′i, fran′ji-pä′ni), *n.* [said to be after a Marquis *Frangipani,* major general under Louis XIV], 1. any of several tropical American shrubs with large, fragrant flowers; especially, the red jasmine. 2. a perfume obtained from this flower or imitating its scent. Also **frangipane.**

Frank (fraŋk), a masculine name: see **Francis.** *n.* [ME.; AS. *Franca;* see FRANK, *adj.*], 1. a member of the Germanic tribes that established the Frankish Empire, which, at its height (beginning of the 9th century A.D.), extended over what is now France, Germany, and Italy. 2. any native or inhabitant of Europe, especially western Europe: term used by Moslems and Greeks.

frank (fraŋk), *adj.* [ME.; OFr. *franc,* free, frank; ML. *francus* < *Francus,* a Frank, hence free man (i.e., member of the ruling race in Gaul); OHG. *Franco,* a Frank; prob. < **francho,* a spear, javelin; akin to AS. *franca,* ON. *frakka;* cf. SAXON], 1. [Rare], free in giving; generous; liberal. 2. free in expressing what one thinks or feels; outspoken; candid. 3. free from reserve, disguise, or guile; clearly evident; plain: as, *frank* rebellion. *v.t.* 1. to send (mail) free of postage. 2. to mark (mail) so that it can be sent free. 3. to make easy the coming or going of (a person); allow to pass free of charge. 4. to free; release from; exempt. *n.* 1. the right to send mail free. 2. a mark or signature authorizing mail to be sent free. 3. any letter, etc. sent free.

SYN.—**frank** applies to a person, remark, etc. that is free or blunt in expressing the truth or an opinion, unhampered by conventional reticence (a *frank* criticism); **candid** implies a basic honesty that makes deceit or evasion impossible, sometimes to the embarrassment of the listener (a *candid* opinion); **open** implies a lack of concealment and often connotes an ingenuous quality (her *open* admiration for him); **outspoken** suggests a lack of restraint or reserve in speech, especially when reticence might be preferable.

frank (fraŋk), *n.* [Slang], a frankfurter.

Frank., 1. Frankish. 2. Franconian.

Frank·en·stein (fraŋk′ən-stīn′), *n.* 1. the title character in a novel (1818) by Mary Wollstonecraft Shelley: he is a young medical student who creates a monster that destroys him. 2. any person destroyed by his own creation. 3. *a)* popularly, Frankenstein's monster. *b)* anything that becomes dangerous to its creator.

Frank·fort (fraŋk′fẽrt), *n.* 1. the capital of Kentucky, on the Kentucky River: pop., 18,000. 2. Frankfurt am Main. 3. Frankfurt an der Oder.

Frank·furt am Main (fräŋk′foort äm mīn′), a city in western Germany, on the Main River: pop., 648,000.

Frankfurt an der O·der (än dẽr ō′dẽr), a city in eastern Germany, on the Oder River: pop., 52,000.

frank·furt·er, frank·fort·er (fraŋk′fẽr-tẽr), *n.* [G. < *Frankfurt,* Germany], a smoked sausage of beef or beef and pork, usually enclosed in a membranous casing and made in cylindrical links a few inches long; wiener: also **frankfurt (or frankfort) sausage, frank.**

Frank·furt·er, Felix (fraŋk′fẽr-tẽr), 1882– ; American jurist, born in Austria; associate justice, United States Supreme Court (1939–).

frank·in·cense (fraŋk′in-sens′), *n.* [ME. *frankincens, frankensence;* OFr. *franc encens;* see FRANK, *adj.* & INCENSE], a gum resin from various Asiatic and East African trees of the balsam family, burned as incense.

Frank·ish (fraŋk′ish), *adj.* of the Franks, their language, or culture. *n.* the West Germanic language of the Franks: abbreviated **Frank.**

Frank·lin (fraŋk′lin), [see FRANKLIN (freeman)], a masculine name. *n.* a district in the northern part of Northwest Territories, Canada: area, 554,030 sq. mi.

frank·lin (fraŋk′lin), *n.* [ME. *frankelein, franklen;* Anglo-Fr. *fraunkelain;* ML. *francelanus, francelengus* < *francus* (see FRANK, *adj.*) + Gmc. **-ling* (see -LING)], a freeholder; specifically, in England in the 14th and 15th centuries, a landowner of free but not noble birth, ranking just below the gentry.

Frank·lin, Benjamin (fraŋk′lin), 1706–1790; American statesman, scientist, inventor, and writer.

Franklin, Sir **John,** 1786–1847; English explorer.

frank·lin·ite (fraŋk′lin-īt′), *n.* [after *Franklin,* New Jersey, where it is found], a brilliant black mineral, an oxide of iron, manganese, and zinc.

Franklin stove, a type of open, iron stove resembling a fireplace, invented by Benjamin Franklin.

frank·pledge (fraŋk′plej′), *n.* [Anglo-Fr. *frank-plege* (see FRANK, *adj.* & PLEDGE); prob. a mistransl. of AS. *frith-borh,* lit., peace pledge], in *English history,* 1. the system which made each man in a tithing responsible

for the actions of other members. 2. a member under this system. 3. the tithing.
fran·tic (fran′tik), ***adj.*** [ME. *frenetik, frantik;* OFr. *frenetique;* L. *phreneticus;* Gr. *phrenitikos*, suffering from inflammation of the brain < *phrenitis*, inflammation of the brain < *phrēn*, mind], 1. greatly excited by anger, grief, pain, etc.; frenzied. 2. [Archaic], insane.
fran·ti·cal·ly (fran′ti-k'l-i, fran′tik-li), ***adv.*** in a frantic manner.
fran·tic·ly (fran′tik-li), ***adv.*** [Rare], frantically.
Franz Jo·sef (fränts yō′zef; Eng. fränts jō′zəf), see **Francis Joseph I.**
Franz Josef Land, Fridtjof Nansen Land.
frap (frap), ***v.t.*** [FRAPPED (frapt), FRAPPING], [prob. < OFr. *fraper*, to strike; Fr. *frapper* is used in same sense], in *nautical usage*, 1. to strengthen or bind together by cables, ropes, etc. 2. to tighten (slack ropes).
frap·pé (fra-pā′; Fr. frȧ′pā′), ***adj.*** [Fr., pp. of *frapper*, to strike], partly frozen; iced; cooled. ***n.*** 1. a dessert made of partly frozen beverages, fruit juices, etc. 2. a drink made of some beverage poured over shaved ice.
Fra·ser (frā′zẽr), ***n.*** a river in British Columbia, Canada, flowing southward into Georgia Strait: length, 695 mi.
frat (frat), ***n.*** [Slang], a fraternity, as at a college.
fra·ter (frā′tẽr), ***n.*** [ME. *fraitour;* OFr. *freitor*, contr. < *refreitor, refeitor;* ML. *refectorium*], [Obs.], the eating room, or refectory, in a monastery.
fra·ter (frā′tẽr), ***n.*** [L., lit., brother; see BROTHER], [Obs.], 1. a comrade; brother. 2. a friar.
fra·ter·nal (frə-tũr′n'l), ***adj.*** [ML. *fraternalis* < L. *fraternus*, brotherly < *frater*, a brother; see BROTHER], 1. of or characteristic of a brother or brothers; brotherly. 2. of or like a fraternal order. 3. designating twins (boys, girls, or boy and girl) developed from separately fertilized ova and thus having hereditary characteristics as different as if they were not twins: distinguished from *identical*.
fra·ter·nal·ism (frə-tũr′n'l-iz'm), ***n.*** 1. a fraternal relationship or spirit; brotherliness. 2. the organization and customs of fraternal orders.
fraternal order (or **society, association**), a society, often secret, of members banded together for mutual benefit or for work toward a common goal.
fra·ter·ni·ty (frə-tũr′nə-ti), ***n.*** [*pl.* FRATERNITIES (-tiz)], [ME. *fraternite;* OFr. *fraternité;* L. *fraternitas* < *fraternus;* see FRATERNAL], 1. the state or quality of being a brother or brothers; fraternal relationship or spirit; brotherliness. 2. a group of men (or, rarely, women) joined together by common interests, for fellowship, etc.: as, certain religious orders and Greek-letter organizations are called *fraternities*. 3. a group of people with the same beliefs, interests, work, etc.: as, the writing *fraternity*, the medical *fraternity*.
frat·er·ni·za·tion (frat′ẽr-nə-zā′shən, frat′ẽr-nī-zā′shən), ***n.*** a fraternizing.
frat·er·nize (frat′ẽr-nīz′), ***v.i.*** [FRATERNIZED (-nīzd′), FRATERNIZING], [Fr. *fraterniser* < L. *fraternus;* see FRATERNAL], 1. to associate in a brotherly manner; be on friendly terms. 2. [Colloq.], to have sexual relations with one of the enemy: said of soldiers in and after World War II. ***v.t.*** [Rare], to bring into fraternal association.
frat·ri·cid·al (frat′rə-sīd″'l, frā′trə-sīd″'l), ***adj.*** 1. relating to fratricide. 2. relating to the killing of relatives or fellow-countrymen, as in a civil war.
frat·ri·cide (frat′rə-sīd′, frā′trə-sīd′), ***n.*** [Fr.; LL. *fratricidium* < L. *fratricida*, one who kills a brother < *frater*, brother + *caedere*, to kill], 1. the act of killing one's own brother or sister. 2. [Fr.; L. *fratricida*], a person who kills his own brother or sister.
‡**Frau** (frou), ***n.*** [*pl.* FRAUEN (frou′ən)], [G.; cf. FROW (wife)], a married woman; wife: used in Germany as a title corresponding to *Mrs.*: abbreviated **Fr.**
fraud (frôd), ***n.*** [ME. & OFr. *fraude;* L. *fraus, fraudis*], 1. *a)* deceit; trickery; cheating. *b)* in *law*, intentional deception to cause a person to give up property or some lawful right. 2. something said or done to deceive; trick; artifice. 3. [Colloq.], a person who deceives or is not what he pretends to be; impostor; cheat. —***SYN.*** see **deception.**
fraud·u·lence (frô′jə-ləns), ***n.*** [OFr.; LL. *fraudulentia*], the quality or state of being fraudulent.
fraud·u·len·cy (frô′jə-lən-si), ***n.*** fraudulence.
fraud·u·lent (frô′jə-lənt), ***adj.*** [ME.; OFr.; L. *fraudulentus* < *fraus;* see FRAUD], 1. acting with fraud; deceitful. 2. based on or characterized by fraud. 3. done or obtained by fraud.
fraught (frôt), ***adj.*** [ME. *fraught*, pp. of *frahten*, to freight; MD. *vrachten* < *vracht*, a load, cargo, freight], filled, charged, or loaded (*with*): as, the situation is *fraught* with danger.
‡**Fräu·lein** (froi′lin), ***n.*** [*pl.* FRÄULEIN], [G.; *frau* (see FRAU) + dim. suffix *-lein*], an unmarried woman: used in Germany as a title corresponding to *Miss.*
Fraun·ho·fer lines (froun′hō′fẽr), [after Joseph von *Fraunhofer* (1787-1826), Bavarian optician, who first observed and mapped them accurately], the dark lines visible in the solar spectrum.
frax·i·nel·la (frak′si-nel′ə), ***n.*** [Mod.L., dim. of L. *fraxinus*, ash tree: the leaves resemble those of the ash], a perennial plant of the rue family, with thick foliage and white flowers: also called *burning bush*, in reference to the fact that its vapor is inflammable on hot nights.
fray (frā), ***n.*** [< *affray*], 1. a noisy quarrel; brawl. 2. a fight; conflict. ***v.t.*** [Archaic], to frighten. ***v.i.*** [Archaic], to quarrel or fight; brawl.
fray (frā), ***v.t. & v.i.*** [Fr. *frayer;* OFr. *freier;* L. *fricare*, to rub], to make or become worn or ragged by rubbing.
Fra·zer, Sir **James George** (frā′zẽr), 1854–1941; Scottish anthropologist; author of *The Golden Bough.*
fraz·zle (fraz″'l), ***v.t. & v.i.*** [FRAZZLED (-'ld), FRAZZLING], [Brit. (E. Anglian) dial. & U.S.; prob. < LG.; cf. MLG. *vrāsen*, to consume, wear out (akin to G. *fressen*, to devour; see FRET); the *-le* is prob. freq.], [Colloq.], 1. to wear or become worn to rags or tatters; fray. 2. to make or become tired or exhausted. ***n.*** [Colloq.], 1. the state of being frazzled. 2. a worn end; shred.
FRB, F.R.B., 1. Federal Reserve Bank. 2. Federal Reserve Board.
F.R.C.P., Fellow of the Royal College of Physicians.
F.R.C.S., Fellow of the Royal College of Surgeons.
freak (frēk), ***n.*** [Early Mod. Eng.; ? via dial. < AS. *frician*, to dance; sense 3 < *freak of nature*, after L. *lusus naturae*], 1. a sudden fancy; odd notion; whim. 2. a whimsical nature; capriciousness. 3. any abnormal animal, person, or plant; monstrosity. ***adj.*** oddly different from what is usual or normal; queer; abnormal.
freak (frēk), ***v.t.*** [? < Eng. dial. *freck*, to streak, after *freak* (sudden fancy); cf. FRECKLE], [Poetic], to fleck; streak; checker; dapple. ***n.*** [Poetic], a fleck or streak.
freak·ish (frēk′ish), ***adj.*** 1. full of or characterized by freaks; whimsical; capricious. 2. having the nature of a freak; odd; queer.
freak·y (frēk′i), ***adj.*** [FREAKIER (-i-ẽr), FREAKIEST (-i-ist)], freakish.
freck·le (frek″'l), ***n.*** [ME. *fracel*, var. of *frekne, frakyn* < ON.; cf. Norw. dial. *frokle*, freckle & Norw. *frekna*, Dan. *fregne*, Sw. *fräkne*, ON. *freknōttr*, freckled; IE. base **(s)p(h)ereg-*, to strew, sprinkle, etc., as also in L. *spargere*, to strew, Eng. *sprinkle*, etc.], a small, yellowish-brown spot on the skin, especially on parts of the body exposed to the sun, as arms, face, and neck. ***v.t.*** [FRECKLED (-'ld), FRECKLING], to cause freckles to appear on. ***v.i.*** to become spotted with freckles.
freck·ly (frek′li), ***adj.*** covered with freckles.
Fre·da (frē′də), a feminine name: see **Frieda.**
Fred·er·i·ca (fred′ə-rē′kə), [see FREDERICK], a feminine name.
Fred·er·ick, Fred·er·ic (fred′ẽr-ik, fred′rik), [Fr. *Frédéric;* G. *Friedrich;* OHG. *Fridurih* < Gmc. **frithu-*, peace (< *fri-*, to love, protect + *-thu-*, substantive particle; akin to Eng. *free*) + **rik-*, king, ruler (akin to L. *rex*, G. *reich*)], a masculine name: diminutive, *Fred;* feminine, *Frederica;* equivalents, Fr. *Frédéric*, G. *Friedrich, Fritz*, It. & Sp. *Federico:* also **Fredric, Fredrick.**
Frederick I, 1. 1123?–1190; emperor of the Holy Roman Empire (1152–1190): called *Frederick Barbarossa.* 2. 1657–1713; son of Frederick William; first king of Prussia (1701–1713); as Frederick III, elector of Brandenburg (1688–1701).
Frederick II, 1. 1194–1250; emperor of the Holy Roman Empire (1215–1250); as Frederick I, king of Sicily (1198–1212). 2. Frederick the Great.
Frederick III, 1463–1525; elector of Saxony (1486–1525); protected Luther in opposition to the diet at Worms.
Frederick IX, 1899– ; king of Denmark (1947–).
Fred·er·icks·burg (fred′riks-bũrg′, fred′ẽr-iks-bũrg′), ***n.*** a city in northeastern Virginia: pop., 14,000: scene of a battle (1862) of the Civil War, in which the Confederate forces under Lee defeated the Union troops led by Burnside.
Frederick the Great, (*Frederick II*), 1712–1786; son of Frederick William I; king of Prussia (1740–1786).
Frederick William, 1620–1688; elector of Brandenburg (1640–1688): called *the Great Elector.*
Frederick William I, 1688–1740; father of Frederick the Great; king of Prussia (1713–1740).
Frederick William II, 1744–1797; grandson of Frederick William I; king of Prussia (1786–1797).
Frederick William III, 1770–1840; son of Frederick William II; king of Prussia (1797–1840); one of the original co-signatories of the Holy Alliance.
Fred·er·ic·ton (fred′ẽr-ik-tən, fred′rik-tən), ***n.*** the capital of New Brunswick, Canada, on the St. John River: pop., 18,000.
Fred·er·iks·berg (fred′ẽr-iks-bũrg′, fred′riks-bũrg′; Dan. freth′ə-rēks-berkh′), ***n.*** a city in Denmark: pop., 114,000: suburb of Copenhagen.
Fred·ric, Fred·rick (fred′rik), a masculine name: see **Frederick.**
free (frē), ***adj.*** [FREER (frē′ẽr), FREEST (frē′ist)], [ME. *fre, free;* AS. *freo*, not in bondage, noble, glad, illustrious; akin to G. *frei*, etc.; IE. base **prei-*, to be fond of, hold dear, as also in Sans. *priyá-*, dear, desired, Eng. *friend;* basic sense of *free* prob. "dear to (i.e., akin to) the chief," hence "not enslaved"], 1. *a)* not under the control of some other person or some arbi-

trary power; able to act or think without compulsion or arbitrary restriction; having liberty; independent. *b*) characterized by or resulting from liberty. 2. *a*) having, or existing under, a government that does not impose arbitrary restrictions on the right to speak, assemble, petition, vote, etc.; having political liberty: as, a *free* people. *b*) not under control of a foreign government. 3. able to move in any direction; not held, as in chains, etc.; not kept from motion; loose. 4. not held or confined by a court, the police, etc.; acquitted. 5. not held or burdened by obligations, debts, discomforts, etc.; unhindered; unhampered: as, *free* from pain. 6. not confined to the usual rules or patterns; not limited by convention or tradition. 7. not literal; not exact; as, a *free* translation. 8. not held or confined by prejudice or bias. 9. able to choose for itself; not restricted by anything except its own limitations or nature: as, *free* will. 10. not busy; available for other work, use, etc.: as, what time will you be *free*? 11. ready; readily done or made; spontaneous: as, a *free* offer. 12. not constrained or stilted; smooth, easy, and graceful: as, a *free* gait. 13. *a*) generous; liberal; lavish: as, a *free* spender. *b*) profuse; abundant; copious. 14. frank; straightforward. 15. too frank or familiar in speech, action, etc.; forward; indecorous. 16. without cost or payment; gratis: as, a *free* ticket. 17. not liable to (trade restrictions, etc.); exempt from certain impositions, as taxes or duties. 18. clear of obstructions; open and unimpeded: as, a *free* road ahead. 19. open to all: as, a *free* market, *free* port. 20. not in contact or connection; not fastened: as, the *free* end of a rope. 21. not united; not combined: as, *free* oxygen. 22. in *nautical usage*, not opposed; favoring: as, a *free* wind is a wind blowing from a direction more than six points from straight ahead. 23. in *phonetics*, designating a stress whose position varies in inflected forms of the same word. ***adv.*** 1. without cost or payment. 2. in a free manner; without obstruction, hindrance, burden, obligation, etc. 3. in *nautical usage*, with a favorable wind. ***v.t.*** to make free; specifically, *a*) to release from bondage or arbitrary power, authority, obligation, etc. *b*) to clear of obstruction, entanglement, etc.; disengage.

free and easy, not constrained by formality or conventionality; informal; unceremonious.

free from (or **of**), 1. lacking; without. 2. released or removed from. 3. beyond; outside of.

give (or **have**) **a free hand,** to give (or have) liberty to act according to one's judgment.

make free with, 1. to use freely; use or treat as if one owned. 2. to be too familiar with.

set free, to cause to be free; liberate; release; disengage.

with a free hand, with generosity; lavishly.

SYN.—**free** is the general term meaning to set loose from any sort of restraint, entanglement, burden, etc. (to *free* a convict, one's conscience, etc.); **release,** more or less interchangeable with **free,** stresses a setting loose from confinement, literally or figuratively (*release* me from my promise); **liberate** emphasizes the state of liberty into which the freed person or thing is brought (to *liberate* prisoners of war); **emancipate** refers to a freeing from the bondage of slavery or of social institutions or conventions regarded as equivalent to slavery (*emancipated* from medieval superstition); **discharge,** in this connection, implies a being permitted to leave that which confines or restrains (*discharged* at last from the army). —***ANT.*** restrain, bind, confine.

free alongside ship (or **vessel**), delivered to the dock with freight charges paid by the shipper: said of goods to be hauled by ship: abbreviated **f.a.s.**

free association, in *psychoanalysis*, the technique of having the patient talk as freely as possible about something, bringing in whatever ideas, memories, etc. are associated with it in his mind: used to discover and clarify repressions.

free·board (frē′bôrd′, frē′bōrd′), ***n.*** the part of a ship's side between the deck or gunwale and the water line.

free·boot (frē′bōōt′), ***v.i.*** [< *freebooter*], [Rare], to act as a freebooter.

free·boot·er (frē′bōōt′ẽr), ***n.*** [D. *vrijbuiter* < *vrijbuiten*, to plunder < *vrij*, free + *buit*, plunder], a plunderer; pirate; buccaneer.

free·born (frē′bôrn′), ***adj.*** 1. born free, not in slavery or serfdom. 2. of or fit for such a person or people.

free city, a city that is an autonomous and independent state: Hamburg, Lübeck and Bremen were called *free cities* in the Middle Ages because they had no feudal obligations except to the emperor.

free coinage, the system by which a government is legally required to coin for a person, either free or at cost, any gold, silver, or other specified metal that he brings to the mint.

free company, in the Middle Ages, any of the groups of mercenary soldiers (called *free companions*) who fought for whoever hired them.

freed·man (frēd′mən), ***n.*** [*pl.* FREEDMEN (-mən)], a man legally freed from slavery or bondage.

free·dom (frē′dəm), ***n.*** [ME. *fredom;* AS. *freodom;* see -DOM], 1. the state or quality of being free; especially, *a*) exemption or liberation from the control of some other person or some arbitrary power; liberty; independence. *b*) exemption from arbitrary restrictions on a specified civil right; political liberty: as, *freedom* of speech. *c*) exemption or immunity from a specified obligation, discomfort, etc.: as, *freedom* from want. *d*) exemption or release from imprisonment. *e*) a being able to act, move, use, etc. without hindrance or restraint. *f*) a being able of itself to choose or determine action freely: as, *freedom* of the will. *g*) ease of movement or performance; facility. *h*) a being free from the usual rules, patterns, etc. *i*) frankness; straightforwardness. *j*) an excessive frankness or familiarity. 2. a privilege held by a city, corporation, etc.; franchise.

SYN.—**freedom,** the broadest in scope of these words, implies the absence of hindrance, restraint, confinement, repression, etc. (*freedom* of speech); **liberty,** often interchangeable with **freedom,** strictly connotes past or potential restriction, repression, etc. (civil *liberties*); **license** implies freedom that consists in violating the usual rules, laws, or practices, either by consent (poetic *license*) or as an abuse of liberty (slander is *license* of the tongue). —***ANT.*** repression, constraint.

freedom of the city, 1. originally, citizenship in a city, granted as an honor to nonresidents. 2. now, honorary citizenship in a city, given ceremoniously to distinguished visitors.

freedom of the press, freedom to publish any opinions in newspapers, magazines, books, etc. without government interference or censorship: usually modified to exclude libel, sedition, and obscenity.

freedom of the seas, the principle that merchant ships of any country may freely travel any part of the open seas at any time, without restriction.

freed·wom·an (frēd′woom′ən), ***n.*** [*pl.* FREEDWOMEN (-wim′in)], a woman freed from slavery or bondage.

free enterprise, the economic doctrine or practice of permitting private industry to operate with a minimum of control by the government.

free-for-all (frē′fẽr-ôl′), ***n.*** 1. a contest, race, etc. that anyone may enter. 2. a disorganized fight in which many take part; brawl. ***adj.*** open to anyone.

Free French, in World War II, those Frenchmen who continued resistance against Germany and the French collaborationists after the surrender of France in 1940.

free gold, 1. formerly, gold in the United States Treasury above the amount needed to redeem gold certificates. 2. in *mining*, pure gold.

free·hand (frē′hand′), ***adj.*** drawn, sketched, etc. by hand without the use of instruments, measurements, or similar aids.

free·hand·ed (frē′han′did), ***adj.*** generous; openhanded.

free·heart·ed (frē′här′tid), ***adj.*** [ME. *frehertid*], frank, open, generous, impulsive, etc.

free·hold (frē′hōld′), ***n.*** 1. the holding of a piece of land, an office, etc. for life or with the right to pass it on through inheritance. 2. an estate, office, etc. held in this way. ***adj.*** of or held by freehold.

free·hold·er (frē′hōl′dẽr), ***n.*** a possessor of a freehold.

free-lance (frē′lans′, frē′läns′), ***adj.*** of or acting as a free lance. ***v.i.*** to work as a free lance (sense 3).

free lance, 1. a medieval soldier who sold his services to any state or military leader; mercenary. 2. a person who acts according to his principles and is not influenced by any group; independent. 3. a writer, actor, etc. who is not under contract for regular work but sells his writings or services to any buyer.

free list, 1. a list of goods not subject to import or export tariff duties. 2. a list of people, as newspaper reporters, admitted free to entertainments, etc.

free liver, a person who freely indulges in eating, drinking, and similar pleasures.

free-liv·ing (frē′liv′iŋ), ***adj.*** 1. indulging freely in eating, drinking, and similar pleasures. 2. in *biology*, living independently of any other organism; not parasitic or symbiotic.

free love, the principle or practice of sexual relations unrestricted by conventions of marriage, religion, etc.

free·man (frē′mən), ***n.*** [*pl.* FREEMEN (-mən)], 1. a person not in slavery or bondage. 2. a citizen; person who has all civil and political rights in a city or state.

Free·man, Mary Eleanor Wilkins (frē′mən), 1862–1930; American novelist.

free·mar·tin (frē′mär′tin), ***n.*** [understood as *free martin;* 2d element ? < Celt.; cf. Scot. Gael. *mart*, heifer], an imperfectly developed female calf, usually sterile, born as the twin of a male.

Free·ma·son (frē′mā′s'n, frē′mā′s'n), ***n.*** [< obs. *freemason*, member of a class of skilled itinerant masons: so named prob. from being free to move from town to town, without restraint by local guilds], a member of an international secret society having as its principles brotherliness, charity, and mutual aid: also called *Free and Accepted Mason, Mason.*

Free·ma·son·ry (frē′mā′s'n-ri, frē′mā′s'n-ri), ***n.*** 1. the

principles, rituals, etc. of Freemasons; Masonry. 2. the Freemasons. 3. [f-], a natural sympathy and understanding among persons with similar experiences.
free on board, delivered (by the seller) aboard the train, ship, etc. at the point of shipment, without further charge to the buyer: abbreviated **f.o.b., F.O.B.**
Free·port (frē′pôrt′, frē′pōrt′), *n.* 1. a city in northern Illinois: pop., 27,000. 2. a village in southeastern New York: pop., 34,000.
free port, a port or guarded district in a port, open equally to ships of all countries, where imported and exported goods are not subject to duties or taxes.
free·si·a (frē′zhi-ə, frē′zhə, frē′si-ə), *n.* [Mod.L., after E. M. *Fries* (1794–1878), Swed. botanist], any of several South African plants of the iris family, with fragrant white or yellow flowers.
free silver, the free coinage of silver, especially at a fixed ratio to the gold coined in the same period.
free-soil (frē′soil′), *adj.* opposed to the extension of slavery.
free soil, territory in which there is no slavery; especially, any territory in the United States where slavery was prohibited before the Civil War.
Free-Soil Party (frē′soil′), a former United States political party (1848–1854) that opposed the spread of slavery into the Territories.
free-spo·ken (frē′spō′kən), *adj.* frank; outspoken.
Free State, 1. any State in which slavery was forbidden before the Civil War. 2. the Irish Free State.
free·stone (frē′stōn′), *n.* [transl. of OFr. *franche pere,* lit., excellent stone], 1. a stone, especially sandstone or limestone, that can be cut easily without splitting. 2. a peach, plum, etc. in which the pit does not cling to the pulp of the ripened fruit. *adj.* having such a pit.
free-swim·ming (frē′swim′iŋ), *adj.* capable of swimming about freely, as certain protozoa.
free·think·er (frē′thiŋk′ẽr), *n.* a person who forms his opinions about religion independently of tradition, authority, or established belief. —*SYN.* see **atheist.**
free·think·ing (frē′thiŋk′iŋ), *n.* free thought. *adj.* 1. of freethinkers or free thought. 2. believing in free thought.
free thought, opinions about religion formed independently of tradition, authority, or established belief.
Free·town (frē′toun′), *n.* seaport and capital of Sierra Leone, Africa: pop., 100,000.
free trade, 1. trade carried on without governmental regulations; especially, international trade conducted without protective tariffs, customs duties, etc. 2. [Archaic], smuggling.
free·trad·er (frē′trād′ẽr), *n.* a person who believes in, advocates, or engages in free trade: also **free trader.**
free verse, verse characterized by much rhythmic variation, irregular or unusual stanzaic forms, and either no rhyme or a loose rhyme pattern: also **vers libre.**
free·way (frē′wā′), *n.* a multiple-lane highway designed to move traffic along smoothly and quickly, as by the use of interchanges.
free·wheel (frē′hwēl′) *n.* 1. in a bicycle, a device in the rear hub that permits the rear wheel to go on turning when the pedals are stopped. 2. in some automobiles, a device that permits the drive shaft to go on turning when its speed exceeds that of the engine shaft, thus allowing free coasting with the gears engaged.
free·wheel·ing (frē′hwēl′iŋ), *n.* 1. a freewheel. 2. the use of a freewheel. *adj.* 1. of, having, or using a freewheel. 2. [Slang], unrestrained, exuberant, etc.
free·will (frē′wil′), *adj.* 1. voluntary; freely given or done. 2. of or holding the doctrine of free will.
free will, 1. the human will regarded as free from restraints, compulsions, or any antecedent conditions; freedom of decision or choice. 2. the doctrine that people have this: opposed to *determinism.*
freeze (frēz), *v.i.* [FROZE (frōz), FROZEN (frō′z′n), FREEZING], [ME. *fresen, freesen;* AS. *freosan;* akin to OHG. *friosan* (G. *frieren*); IE. base **preus-,* to freeze, burn like cold, seen also in L. *pruina* (< **pruswina*), hoarfrost, *pruna,* glowing coals, etc.], 1. to be formed into ice; be hardened or solidified by cold. 2. to become covered or clogged with ice. 3. to be or become very cold. 4. to become fixed or attached by freezing: as, the automobile tires *froze* to the ground. 5. to die or be damaged by exposure to cold. 6. to become motionless or stiff. 7. to be chilled or made momentarily rigid by a strong, sudden emotion: as, his face *froze* with terror. 8. to become formal, haughty, or unfriendly. 9. in *mechanics,* to stick or become tight as a result of expansion of parts caused by overheating. *v.t.* 1. to cause to form into ice; harden or solidify by cold. 2. to cover or clog with ice. 3. to make very cold; chill. 4. to preserve (food) by rapid refrigeration. 5. to make fixed or attached by freezing. 6. to kill or damage by exposure to cold. 7. to make or keep motionless or stiff. 8. to frighten or discourage by cool behavior, unfriendliness, etc. 9. to make formal, haughty, or unfriendly. 10. [Colloq.], to fix (prices, employment, an employee, etc.) at a given level or place by authoritative regulation. *n.* 1. a freezing or being frozen. 2. a period of cold, freezing weather; a frost.
freeze (on) to, [Colloq.], to cling to; hold fast to.
freeze out, [Colloq.], to keep out or force out by a cold manner, competition, etc.
freeze over, to cover or become covered with ice.
freez·er (frēz′ẽr), *n.* 1. a person or device that freezes; especially, a machine for making ice cream and sherbet. 2. a refrigerator tmaintaining emperatures at or below 0° F., for freezing and storing perishable foods.
freez·ing (frēz′iŋ), *adj.* [ppr. of *freeze*], very cold.
freezing point, the temperature at which a liquid freezes or becomes solid: the freezing point of water under laboratory conditions is 32° F. or 0° C.: abbreviated **f.p., fp, fp.**
Frei·burg (frī′boorkh; Eng. frī′bẽrg), *n.* 1. a city in southwestern Germany: pop., 136,000. 2. Fribourg.
freight (frāt), *n.* [ME. *freyght, freit, freyte* < MD. *vraht* (cf. FRAUGHT); sp. prob. influenced by Fr. *fret,* of same origin], 1. a method or service for transporting goods, usually bulky goods, by water, land, or air: freight is usually cheaper and slower than express. 2. the cost for such transportation. 3. the goods transported; lading; cargo. 4. a freight train. 5. any load or burden. Abbreviated **frt.** *v.t.* 1. to load with freight. 2. to load; burden. 3. to transport as or send by freight.
freight·age (frāt′ij), *n.* 1. the charge for transporting goods. 2. freight; cargo. 3. the transportation of goods.
freight car, a railroad car for transporting freight.
freight·er (frāt′ẽr), *n.* 1. a person who loads a ship. 2. a person who sends goods by freight. 3. a person who receives freighted goods and forwards them to their destination. 4. a ship for carrying freight; cargo vessel.
freight house, a depot where freight is received and stored until claimed.
freight train, a railroad train made up of freight cars.
Fre·man·tle (frē′man′t'l), *n.* a seaport in Western Australia, near Perth: pop., 22,000.
fremd (fremd), *adj.* [ME.; AS. *fremde;* cf. G. *fremd*], [Obs. or Dial.], strange, foreign, alien, etc.
frem·i·tus (frem′i-təs), *n.* [*pl.* FREMITUS], [L., a roaring < *fremere,* to roar, growl], in *medicine,* a vibration, especially one felt in palpation of the chest.
Fré·mont, John Charles (frē′mont, fri-mont′), 1813–1890; American politician, general, and explorer.
French (french), *adj.* [ME. *Frenkisch, Frensche;* AS. *Frencisc* < *Franca,* a Frank; see FRANK, *adj.*], of France, its people, their language, or culture. *n.* the Romance language spoken by the French. Abbreviated **Fr., F.**
the French, the people of France.
French, Daniel Chester (french), 1850–1931; American sculptor.
French and Indian War, the American phase (1754–1763) of the Seven Years' War (between England and France).
French chalk, a very soft soapstone chalk used for marking lines on cloth or removing grease spots.
French Community, a political union comprising France and its overseas departments and territories, and eleven other fully independent member states: Mauritania, Senegal, Upper Volta, Niger, Ivory Coast, Dahomey, Gabon, Congo, Central African Republic, Chad, and Malagasy Republic.
French cuff, a double cuff on the sleeve of a shirt; cuff turned back on itself and fastened with a link.
French doors, two adjoining doors that have glass panes from top to bottom and are hinged at opposite sides of a doorway so that they open in the middle.
French dressing, a salad dressing made of vinegar, oil, and various seasonings.
French Equatorial Africa, a former federation of French colonies in west central Africa.
French fried, fried in very hot, deep fat until crisp: French fried potatoes (colloquially called *French fries*) are first cut lengthwise into strips.
French Guiana, a French overseas department in northern South America, on the Atlantic: area, 34,740 sq. mi.; pop., 32,000; capital, Cayenne.
French Guinea, a former French colony in western Africa: now, the independent country of Guinea.
French heel, a curved high heel on a woman's shoe.
French horn, a brass-wind instrument with three rotary valves and a long, coiled tube ending in a wide, flaring bell: it has a range of 3 1/2 octaves and a mellow tone.
French ice cream, very rich ice cream made with cream and eggs.
French·i·fy (fren′chə-fī′), *v.t. & v.i.* [FRENCHIFIED (-fīd′), FRENCHIFYING], to make or become French or like the French in customs, ideas, manners, etc.
French India, formerly five small dependencies of France along the coast of India: incorporated into India since 1954.
French Indochina, former French federation in south-

FRENCH HORN

eastern Asia, including North Vietnam, South Vietnam, Cambodia, and Laos: see **Indochina, Vietnam.**

French leave, [< 18th-c. custom, prevalent in France, of leaving receptions without taking leave of the host or hostess], an unauthorized, unnoticed, or unceremonious departure; act of leaving secretly or in haste.

French·man (french′mən), *n.* [*pl.* FRENCHMEN (-mən)], 1. a native or inhabitant of France, especially a man. 2. a French ship.

French Morocco, formerly, the French zone of the sultanate of Morocco: in 1956 it became, with Spanish Morocco and Tangier, the independent state of Morocco.

French Oceania, French Polynesia: the former name.

French pastry, rich pastry, usually filled with preserved fruit, whipped cream, etc.

French Polynesia, a French overseas territory in the South Pacific, consisting of five scattered island groups: area, 1,544 sq. mi.; pop., 77,000; capital, Papeete. Former name, *French Oceania.*

French Revolution, the revolution of the people against the monarchy in France: it began in 1789, resulted in the establishment of a republic, and ended in 1799 with the Consulate under Napoleon.

French Revolutionary Calendar, the official calendar of the first French republic, adopted in 1793 and abolished in 1805: it consisted of twelve months, each containing thirty days and divided into three periods called *decades,* with five extra days in the regular year.

French seam, a narrow seam sewed on both sides to hide the raw edges of the cloth.

French Somaliland, a French overseas territory in eastern Africa, on the Gulf of Aden: area, 8,996 sq. mi.; pop., 69,000; capital, Djibouti.

French Sudan, a former French colony in western Africa: since 1960, the independent republic of Mali.

French telephone, a telephone mouthpiece and receiver mounted together on a handle; handset.

French toast, sliced bread dipped in a batter of egg and milk and then fried.

French Union, a political union consisting of France, its colonies, territories, etc. established in 1946: succeeded by the French Community in 1958.

French West Africa, a former group of French colonies in western Africa, consisting of Senegal, Ivory Coast, Dahomey, French Sudan, Mauritania, Upper Volta, and Niger: all are now member states in the French Community except French Sudan, now Mali.

French West Indies, French overseas departments in the West Indies, including Guadeloupe and Martinique.

French windows, a pair of casement windows, usually extending to the floor, that have glass panes from top to bottom and are hinged at opposite sides of a window frame so that they open in the middle.

French·wom·an (french′woom′ən), *n.* [*pl.* FRENCHWOMEN (-wim′in)], a woman who is a native or inhabitant of France.

French·y (fren′chi), *adj.* [FRENCHIER (-chi-ẽr), FRENCHIEST (-chi-ist)], of, characteristic of, or like the French. *n.* [*pl.* FRENCHIES (-chiz)], [Colloq.], a Frenchman.

Fre·neau, Philip Mo·rin (mô-ran′ fri-nō′), 1752–1832; American poet and journalist.

fre·net·ic (frə-net′ik), *adj.* [see PHRENETIC], frantic; frenzied. *n.* a frantic person.

fre·net·i·cal (frə-net′i-k'l), *adj.* frenetic.

fre·num (frē′nəm), *n.* [*pl.* FRENUMS (-nəmz), FRENA (-nə)], [L., a bridle], a fold of skin or mucous membrane that is attached to a part of the body and checks or controls its motion, as the fold under the tongue: also spelled **fraenum.**

fren·zied (fren′zid), *adj.* wildly excited; frantic.

fren·zy (fren′zi), *n.* [*pl.* FRENZIES (-ziz)], [ME. & OFr. *frenesie;* LL. *phrenesia;* L. *phrenesis;* Late Gr. *phrenēsis* < Gr. *phrenitis,* madness, inflammation of the brain < *phrēn,* mind], wild or frantic outburst; brief delirium that is almost insanity. *v.t.* [FRENZIED (-zid), FRENZYING], to make frantic; drive mad. —*SYN.* see **mania.**

fre·on (frē′on), *n.* [*fluorine* + *refrigerant* + *-on* as in *neon,* etc.], a colorless gas, CCl_2F_2, used especially as a refrigerant: a trade-mark (**Freon**).

freq., 1. frequent. 2. frequentative. 3. frequently.

fre·quence (frē′kwəns), *n.* [Fr. *fréquence;* L. *frequentia;* see FREQUENT], frequency.

fre·quen·cy (frē′kwən-si), *n.* [*pl.* FREQUENCIES (-siz)], [L. *frequentia;* see FREQUENT], 1. originally, *a*) the condition of being crowded. *b*) a crowd. 2. the fact of occurring often or repeatedly; frequent occurrence. 3. the number of times any action or occurrence is repeated in a given period. 4. in *mathematics & statistics, a*) the ratio of the number of actual occurrences to the number of possible occurrences in a given period. *b*) the ratio of the number of individuals occurring in a specific class to the total number of individuals under survey. 5. in *physics, a*) the number of vibrations or cycles per unit of time. *b*) the number of cycles per second of an alternating electric current.

frequency modulation, 1. the changing of the frequency of the transmitting radio wave in accordance with the sound being broadcast. 2. broadcasting that uses this, characterized by freedom from static and more faithful reproduction of sound. Abbreviated **FM, F.M.** Distinguished from *amplitude modulation.*

fre·quent (frē′kwənt; *for v.,* fri-kwent′), *adj.* [Fr. *fréquent* < L. *frequens, frequentis,* ppr. of **frequere,* to cram, stuff; akin to *farcire,* to stuff; see FARCE], 1. originally, crowded; filled. 2. occurring often; happening repeatedly at brief intervals: abbreviated **freq., fr.** 3. constant; habitual. *v.t.* to go to constantly; be at or in habitually: as, she *frequents* the theater.

fre·quen·ta·tion (frē′kwən-tā′shən), *n.* [Fr. *fréquentation;* L. *frequentatio* < pp. of *frequentare*], the act or practice of frequenting.

fre·quen·ta·tive (fri-kwen′tə-tiv), *adj.* [LL. *frequentativus* < L. *frequentare;* see FREQUENT, *v.*], in *grammar,* expressing frequent and repeated action. *n.* in *grammar,* a frequentative verb: *prickle* is a frequentative of *prick.* Abbreviated **freq.**

fre·quent·er (fri-kwen′tẽr), *n.* a person who frequents; constant visitor.

fre·quent·ly (frē′kwənt-li), *adv.* at frequent or brief intervals; often: abbreviated **freq., fr.**

‡**frère** (frâr), *n.* [Fr.], 1. a brother. 2. a friar.

fres·co (fres′kō), *n.* [*pl.* FRESCOES, FRESCOS (-kōz)], [It., fresh, cool, hence coolness, freshness < OHG. *frisc;* see FRESH (recently produced)], 1. the art or technique of painting with water colors on wet plaster. 2. a painting or design so made. *v.t.* to paint in fresco.
in fresco, with water colors on wet plaster.

fresh (fresh), *adj.* [ME. *fresshe;* AS. *fersc,* not salt; influenced by OFr. *freis, fresche* < same Gmc. base; akin to G. *frisch;* IE. **proisko-s,* **prisko-s,* not sour, not fermented], 1. recently produced, obtained, or grown; newly made: as, make some *fresh* coffee. 2. having original strength, vigor, quality, taste, etc.; especially, *a*) not salted, preserved, pickled, etc.: as, *fresh* meat. *b*) not spoiled, rotten, or stale. *c*) not tired; vigorous; lively: as, he felt *fresh* even after six sets of tennis. *d*) not worn, soiled, faded, etc.; vivid; bright; clean. *e*) youthful or healthy in appearance: as, a *fresh* complexion. 3. new; recent; not known before: as, *fresh* information on an old subject. 4. additional; further: as, he made a *fresh* start. 5. inexperienced; unaccustomed; untutored. 6. original, spontaneous, and stimulating: as, the conversation was *fresh* and delightful. 7. cool and refreshing; invigorating: as, a *fresh* spring day. 8. brisk; strong: said of the wind. 9. not salt: said of water. 10. designating or of a cow that has newly come into the state of a milker, as after having borne a calf. —*SYN.* see **new.**
fresh out of, [Slang], having just sold or used up.

fresh (fresh), *adj.* [< G. *frech,* bold, impudent; confused with *fresh* (recently produced)], [Slang], 1. bold; saucy; impertinent; impudent. 2. drunk; tipsy.

fresh·en (fresh′ən), *v.t.* to make fresh, or vigorous, clean, etc. *v.i.* 1. to become fresh. 2. to have a calf: said of a cow; hence, 3. to come into milk.

fresh·et (fresh′it), *n.* [*fresh, n.* + *-et*], 1. a stream or rush of fresh water flowing into the sea. 2. a sudden overflowing of a stream because of melting snow or heavy rain.

fresh·ly (fresh′li), *adv.* [ME. *freschli*], 1. in a fresh manner. 2. recently; just now: followed by a past participle, as, bread *freshly* baked.

fresh·man (fresh′mən), *n.* [*pl.* FRESHMEN (-mən)], [*fresh* (recently produced) + *man*], 1. a beginner; novice. 2. a first-year student in a high school or college. 3. a person in his first year at any enterprise: as, Senator Smith is a *freshman* in Congress. *adj.* of or for first-year students: as, the *freshman* curriculum.

fresh-wa·ter (fresh′wô′tẽr, fresh′wät′ẽr), *adj.* 1. of or living in water that is not salty. 2. accustomed to sailing only on rivers or lakes, not on the sea; hence, 3. inexperienced; unskilled. 4. in or of the hinterland; inland; hence, 5. somewhat provincial, obscure, etc.: as, a *fresh-water* college.

Fres·no (frez′nō), *n.* a city in central California: pop., 134,000.

fret (fret), *v.t.* [FRETTED (-id), FRETTING], [ME. *freten;* AS. *fretan,* to devour, eat up; akin to G. *fressen,* Goth. *fra-itan;* Gmc. prefix **fra-* (AS. *for-;* see FOR-, 2) + **itan,* to eat (AS. *etan;* see EAT)], 1. to eat away; gnaw. 2. to wear away by gnawing, rubbing, chafing, corroding, rusting, etc. 3. to make or form by wearing away. 4. to make rough; disturb: as, the wind *frets* the water. 5. to irritate; vex; annoy; worry. *v.i.* 1. to gnaw (*into, on,* or *upon*). 2. to become eaten, corroded, worn, frayed, etc. 3. to become rough or disturbed. 4. to be irritated, annoyed, or querulous; worry. *n.* 1. a wearing away. 2. a worn place. 3. irritation; annoyance; worry.

fret (fret), *n.* [ME. *frette;* prob. merging of OFr. *frete* (Fr. *frette*), interlaced work, with AS. *frætwa,* trappings, ornament, which may itself have influenced, or be the source of, the OFr. word], 1. an ornamental net or network, especially one formerly worn by women as a headdress. 2. an ornamental pattern of small, straight bars intersecting or joining one another at right angles to form a regular design, as for a border. 3. in *architecture*, an ornamental pattern of this kind in relief; fretwork. 4. in *heraldry*, a transverse cross interlaced with a hollow, diamond-shaped figure. *v.t.* [FRETTED (-id), FRETTING], to ornament with a fret or fretwork.

fret (fret), *n.* [Fr., a band, ring < OFr. *freter*, to make fast: frets were orig. rings of gut], any of several narrow, lateral ridges fastened across the finger board of a banjo, guitar, mandolin, etc. to regulate the fingering. *v.t.* [FRETTED (-id), FRETTING], to furnish with frets.

fret·ful (fret′fəl), *adj.* tending to fret; irritable and discontented; peevish.

fret saw, a saw with a long, narrow, fine-toothed blade, for cutting thin wooden boards or metal plates into patterns.

FRET SAW

fret·ted (fret′id), past tense and past participle of **fret** (to ornament). *adj.* decorated with frets.

fret·ted (fret′id), past tense and past participle of **fret** (to vex). *adj.* 1. worn away; chafed. 2. worried; anxious; discontented.

fret·work (fret′wũrk′), *n.* work ornamented with frets; decorative carving or openwork, usually of interlacing lines.

Freud, Sigmund (froid; G. froit), 1856–1939; Austrian physician and psychiatrist; founder of psychoanalysis.

Freud·i·an (froi′di-ən), *adj.* of or according to Freud or his theories and practice. *n.* a person who believes in Freud's theories or uses Freud's methods in psychoanalysis. See **psychoanalysis.**

Freud·i·an·ism (froi′di-ən-iz'm), *n.* the theories and practice of Freud.

Frey (frā), *n.* [ON. *Freyr*], in *Norse mythology*, the god of the crops, fruitfulness, love, peace, and prosperity.

Frey·a, Frey·ja (frā′ə), *n.* [ON. *Freyja*], in *Norse mythology*, the goddess of love and beauty, sister of Frey.

Freyr (frâr), *n.* Frey.

F.R.G.S., Fellow of the Royal Geographical Society.

Fri., Friday.

fri·a·bil·i·ty (frī′ə-bil′ə-ti), *n.* the state or quality of being friable.

fri·a·ble (frī′ə-b'l), *adj.* [Fr.; L. *friabilis* < *friare*, to rub, crumble; IE. base **bhrēi-, *bhrī-*, to cut, scrape, seen also in Russ. *briti*, to shave, L. *frivolus* (cf. FRIVOLOUS)], easily crumbled or crushed into powder. —*SYN.* see **fragile.**

fri·ar (frī′ẽr), *n.* [< ME. & OFr. *frere* (with dial. vowel development as in *briar, choir*); L. *frater*, brother; see BROTHER], in the *Roman Catholic Church*, a member of any of several religious orders, especially those living as mendicant traveling ministers: an Augustinian, Carmelite, Dominican, or Franciscan: abbreviated **Fr.**

fri·ar·bird (frī′ẽr-bũrd′), *n.* any of several Australian birds that eat the honey or nectar from flowers and have a naked, featherless head.

fri·ar's lantern (frī′ẽrz), a will-o'-the-wisp; ignis fatuus.

fri·ar·y (frī′ẽr-i), *n.* [*pl.* FRIARIES (-iz)], 1. a place where friars live; monastery. 2. a brotherhood of friars.

frib·ble (frib′'l), *adj.* [altered < Fr. *frivole* (cf. FRIVOLOUS), ? under echoic influence], of little value or importance; trifling. *n.* 1. a person who wastes time. 2. any trifling act or thought. *v.i.* [FRIBBLED (-'ld), FRIBBLING], to waste time; behave in a foolish, trifling, frivolous way.

Fri·bourg (frē′bo͝or′), *n.* 1. a canton of western Switzerland: pop., 152,000. 2. its capital: pop., 26,000. German spelling, *Freiburg.*

fric·an·deau (frik′ən-dō′), *n.* [*pl.* FRICANDEAUX (-dōz′)], [Fr.], roasted or stewed meat, usually veal, served in sauce: also spelled **fricando.**

fric·as·see (frik′ə-sē′), *n.* [Fr. *fricassée*, fem. pp. of *fricasser*, to cut up and fry], meat cut into pieces, stewed or fried, and served in a sauce of its own gravy. *v.t.* [FRICASSEED (-sēd′), FRICASSEEING], to prepare (meat) by this method.

fric·a·tive (frik′ə-tiv), *adj.* [< L. *fricatus*, pp. of *fricare*, to rub; + *-ive*], formed and pronounced by forcing the breath through a narrow opening between the teeth, lips, etc.: said of certain consonants, as *f, s, v,* and *z*, characterized by local frictional noises. *n.* a fricative consonant; friction consonant.

Frick, Henry Clay (frik), 1849–1919; American coal and steel magnate.

fric·tion (frik′shən), *n.* [Fr.; L. *frictio* < pp. of *fricare*, to rub], 1. a rubbing, especially of one object against another. 2. disagreement or conflict because of differences of opinion, temperament, etc. 3. in *mechanics*, the resistance to motion of two moving objects or surfaces that touch.

fric·tion·al (frik′shən-'l), *adj.* of or caused by friction.

fric·tion·al·ly (frik′shən-'l-i), *adv.* by or with friction.

friction match, a match that lights by friction.

friction tape, an adhesive tape for insulating exposed electrical wires, etc.

Fri·day (frī′di), *n.* [ME. *fridai;* AS. *frigedæg*, lit., day of the goddess *Frig* (ON. *Frigg;* see FRIGG), wife of *Wodan* (ON. *Odinn;* cf. WEDNESDAY), transl. L. *Veneris dies*, (Fr. *vendredi*), Venus' day; akin to G. *freitag; Frig* is prob. confused with *Freya*, Gmc. goddess of love; for the Gmc. & IE. base see FREE], 1. the sixth day of the week: abbreviated **Fri., F., Fr.** 2. the devoted servant of Robinson Crusoe; hence, 3. a faithful follower or helper: usually **man Friday.**

Fridt·jof Nan·sen Land (frēt′yôf nän′sən), islands of the U.S.S.R., north of Novaya Zemlya, in the Arctic Ocean: also called *Franz Josef Land.*

fried (frīd), [ME. *ifrid*, pp. of *frien;* see FRY], past tense and past participle of **fry.** *adj.* 1. cooked by frying. 2. [Slang], drunk; intoxicated.

Frie·da (frē′də), [G. < OHG. *fridu*, peace; see FREDERICK], a feminine name: also spelled **Freda.**

fried·cake (frīd′kāk′), *n.* a small cake fried in deep fat; doughnut or cruller.

friend (frend), *n.* [ME. *frend;* AS. *freond*, friend, lover; akin to G. *freund;* formed < ppr. of the Gmc. *v.* "to love," represented in AS. by *freon, freogan;* for the IE. base see FREE], 1. a person whom one knows well and is fond of; intimate associate; close acquaintance: applied loosely to any associate or acquaintance, or, as a term of address, even to a stranger. 2. a person on the same side in a struggle; ally: opposed to *foe.* 3. a supporter or sympathizer: as, a *friend* of labor. 4. [F-], a member of the Society of Friends; Quaker. *v.t.* [Rare], to act as a friend to; befriend.

be (or **make**) **friends with,** to be (or become) a friend of.

friend at court, a person in an influential position who is friendly toward one and able to help him.

friend·less (frend′lis), *adj.* without friends.

friend·li·ness (frend′li-nis), *n.* the quality or condition of being friendly.

friend·ly (frend′li), *adj.* [FRIENDLIER (-li-ẽr), FRIENDLIEST (-li-ist)], 1. like, characteristic of, or suitable for a friend, friends, or friendship; kindly. 2. not hostile; amicable. 3. supporting; helping; favorable. 4. desiring friendship. 5. [F-], of the Friends, or Quakers. *adv.* in a friendly manner; as a friend; amicably.

Friendly Islands, Tonga Islands.

friend·ship (frend′ship), *n.* [AS. *freondscipe;* see -SHIP], 1. the state of being friends. 2. attachment between friends. 3. friendly feeling or attitude.

fri·er (frī′ẽr), *n.* a fryer.

Frie·sian (frē′zhən), *adj.* & *n.* Frisian.

Fries·ic (frē′zik), *adj.* & *n.* Frisian.

Fries·land (frēz′lənd, frēz′land′), *n.* a province of the northern Netherlands: capital, Leeuwarden.

frieze (frēz), *n.* [Fr. *frise;* ML. *frisium* (seen also in It. *freggio*) < Frank. **frisi*, a curl, border; cf. FRAISE], 1. a decoration or series of decorations forming an ornamental band around a room, mantel, etc. 2. in *architecture*, a horizontal band, usually decorated with sculpture, between the architrave and cornice of a building: see **entablature,** illus.

frieze (frēz), *n.* [Fr. & MD. *frise;* akin to Frank. **frisi;* see prec. entry], a heavy wool cloth with a shaggy, uncut nap on one side.

frig·ate (frig′it), *n.* [OFr. *frégate;* It. *fregata*], a fast, medium-sized sailing warship of the 18th and early 19th centuries, which carried from 28 to 60 guns.

frigate bird, a strong-winged tropical sea bird that robs other birds of their prey: also called *man-of-war bird.*

Frigg (frig), *n.* [ON.], in *Norse mythology*, the wife of Odin and goddess of heaven, presiding over marriage and the home.

Frig·ga (frig′ä, frig′ə), *n.* Frigg.

fright (frīt), *n.* [ME. *fryhte, fyrhte;* AS. (Mercian) *fyrhto;* by metathesis < *fryhto*, fear; akin to G. *furcht*, fear; IE. base **perg-*, fear, to be afraid, seen also in Arm. *erkiul*, fear], 1. sudden fear or terror; alarm. 2. [Colloq.], an ugly, ridiculous, startling, or unusual person or thing. *v.t.* [ME. *frigten;* AS. *fyrhtan* < base of the *n.*], [Rare & Poetic], to frighten; terrify. —*SYN.* see **fear.**

fright·en (frīt′'n), *v.t.* 1. to cause to feel fright; make suddenly afraid; scare; terrify. 2. to make go (*away* or *into* a specified condition) or to force (*out* or *off*) by frightening: as, we *frightened* him into confessing. *v.i.* to become suddenly afraid.

SYN.—**frighten** is the broadest of these terms and implies, usually, a sudden, temporary feeling of fear (*frightened* by a mouse) but sometimes, a state of continued dread (she's *frightened* when she's alone); **scare,** often equivalent to **frighten,** in stricter use implies a fear that causes one to flee or to stop doing something (I *scared* him from the room); **alarm** suggests a sudden fear or apprehension at the realization of an approaching danger (*alarmed* by his warning); to **terrify** is to cause to feel an overwhelming, often paralyzing fear (*terrified* at the thought of war); **terrorize** implies deliberate intention to terrify by threat or intimidation (the gangsters *terrorized* the city).

fright·ened (frīt′'nd), *adj.* [pp. of *frighten*], filled with fright; terrified; afraid. —*SYN.* see **afraid.**

fright·ful (frīt′fəl), *adj.* 1. causing fright; terrifying; alarming. 2. shocking; disgusting. 3. [Colloq.], *a*) unpleasant; annoying. *b*) great: as, a *frightful* bore.
fright·ful·ly (frīt′fəl-i), *adv.* 1. in a frightful manner. 2. [Colloq.], very.
frig·id (frij′id), *adj.* [L. *frigidus* < *frigere*, to be cold < *frigus*, coldness, frost; IE. base **srīg-*, coldness, seen also in Gr. *hrigos*, frost], 1. extremely cold; without heat or warmth. 2. without warmth of feeling or manner; stiff and forbidding; formal. 3. sexually cold; habitually failing to become sexually aroused: said of women.
frig·id·aire (frij′i-dâr′), *n.* [arbitrary coinage < *frigid* + *air*], an electric refrigerator: trade-mark (**Frigidaire**).
fri·gid·i·ty (fri-jid′ə-ti), *n.* the quality or state of being frigid.
Frigid Zone, 1. the Arctic Zone. 2. the Antarctic Zone. See **zone**, illus.
frig·o·rif·ic (frig′ə-rif′ik), *adj.* [Fr. *frigorifique;* L. *frigorificus* < *frigus* (see FRIGID) + *facere*, to make], making cold; freezing or cooling.
fri·jol, fri·jole (frē′hōl), *n.* [*pl.* FRIJOLES (-hōlz; Sp. frē-hô′les)], [Sp. *frijol, fréjol;* prob. < L. *phaselus;* Gr. *phasēlos*, kind of bean, kidney bean], any bean cultivated for food, especially a variety much used in Mexico and the southwestern United States.
frill (fril), *n.* [Early Mod. Eng., prob. with orig. sense "mesentery of a cow" (cf. Fr. *fraise*, mesentery, ruff, G. *gekröse*, giblets, plaited ruff); ? < OFr. *fresel*, dim. of *fraise*, influenced in sense by OFr. *friller*, to shiver], 1. a fold or fringe of hair or feathers around the neck of a bird or animal. 2. [Colloq.], any unnecessary ornament; superfluous thing added for show. 3. an edging or trimming of lace, etc., gathered or pleated and attached at one end but free at the other; ruffle. 4. in *photography*, the wrinkling of the edge of a film. *v.t.* 1. to make a ruffle of; crimp. 2. to decorate with a ruffle. *v.i.* in *photography*, to become wrinkled, as a film.
frill·ing (fril′iŋ), *n.* 1. frills. 2. material for frills.
frill·y (fril′i), *adj.* [FRILLIER (-i-ẽr), FRILLIEST (-i-ist)], 1. full of or covered with frills. 2. like a frill or frills.
‡**Fri·maire** (frē′mâr′), *n.* [Fr. < *frimas*, frost < Frank. **hrim;* akin to AS. *hrim*, rime], the third month (November 21—December 20) of the French Revolutionary Calendar.
fringe (frinj), *n.* [ME. *frenge;* OFr. *frenge, fringe* < LL. **frimbia*, metathesis of L. *fimbria*, a fringe, border], 1. a border or trimming of cords or threads, hanging loose or tied in bunches at the top. 2. a thing like this; outer edge; border; margin: as, the *fringes* of civilization. 3. in *optics*, any of the light or dark bands resulting from the interference or diffraction of light. *v.t.* [FRINGED (frinjd), FRINGING], 1. to decorate with or as with fringe. 2. to be a fringe for; line: as, trees *fringed* the lawn. *adj.* at the outer edge or border: as, a *fringe* area of television reception.
fringe benefit, 1. a payment other than wages or salary made to an employee, as in the form of a pension, vacation, insurance, etc. 2. an additional benefit.
fringed gentian, a gentian of eastern North America, with blue, fringed flowers.
fringe tree, either of two small trees of the olive family, with fluffy clusters of white flowers, found in the southeastern United States.
fring·y (frin′ji), *adj.* 1. like a fringe. 2. having a fringe or fringes.
frip·per·y (frip′ẽr-i), *n.* [*pl.* FRIPPERIES (-iz)], [orig., old clothes, castoff clothes; Fr. *friperie;* OFr. *freperie* < *frepe*, a rag], 1. cheap, gaudy clothes; tawdry finery; hence, 2. showy display in dress, manners, speech, etc.; affectation of elegance.
Fris., Frisian.
Frisch·es Haff (frish′əs häf′), a bay of the Baltic Sea, off East Prussia.
Fris·co (fris′kō), *n.* [Colloq.], San Francisco.
fri·sé (fri-zā′), *n.* [Fr. < *friser*, to curl; cf. FRIZZ], a type of upholstery fabric having a thick pile consisting of uncut loops or, sometimes, with some loops cut to form a design.
fri·sette (fri-zet′), *n.* [Fr. < *friser*, to curl], a fringe of curls or fluffy bangs worn on the forehead by women: also spelled **frizette.**
‡**fri·seur** (frē′zẽr′), *n.* [Fr. < *friser*, to curl], a hairdresser.
Fri·sian (frizh′ən, frizh′i-ən), *adj.* of Friesland, the Frisian Islands, their people, or their language. *n.* 1. a native or inhabitant of Friesland or the Frisian Islands. 2. a member of an ancient Teutonic tribe of northern Holland. 3. the Low German, West Germanic language of the Frisians: it is the most closely related to English of all the Continental European languages. Abbreviated **Fris., Frs.**
Frisian Islands, a chain of islands in the North Sea off the coast of the Netherlands and Germany.
frisk (frisk), *adj.* [OFr. *frisque;* prob. < OHG. *frisc*, new, cheerful, lively; see FRESH (recently produced)], [Obs.], lively; frisky. *n.* a lively, playful movement; frolic; gambol. *v.t.* 1. to move in a playful, lively manner: as, the puppy *frisked* its tail. 2. [Slang], to search (a person) for concealed weapons, stolen articles, etc. by passing the hands quickly over his clothing. 3. [Slang], to steal something from (a person) thus. *v.i.* to dance or move about in a playful, lively manner; frolic; gambol.
frisk·i·ly (fris′kə-li), *adv.* in a frisky manner.
frisk·i·ness (fris′ki-nis), *n.* a frisky quality or state.
frisk·y (fris′ki), *adj.* [FRISKIER (-ki-ẽr), FRISKIEST (-ki-ist)], inclined to frisk about; lively; playful; frolicsome.
frit (frit), *n.* [Fr. *fritte;* It. *fritta*, fried, pp. of *friggere* < L. *frigere*, to fry], 1. the partly fused mixture of sand and fluxes of which glass is made. 2. a partly fused substance used as a basis for certain glazes. 3. a partly fused substance of which soft porcelain is made. *v.t. & v.i.* [FRITTED (-id), FRITTING], to prepare (materials for glass) by heating; make into frit. Also spelled **fritt.**
frit fly, [prob. < prec., with ref. to the glazed, shining appearance of the fly's body], a small, two-winged European fly that destroys grain.
frith (frith), *n.* [var. of *firth*], a narrow inlet or arm of the sea; estuary; firth.
frit·il·lar·y (frit′ə-ler′i), *n.* [*pl.* FRITILLARIES (-iz)], [< Mod.L. *Fritillaria*, name of the genus of plants < L. *fritillus*, dice box: from markings on the petals or wings], 1. any of a group of plants of the lily family, with spotted, bell-shaped, drooping flowers. 2. any of a large group of butterflies having wings spotted with many colors.
fritt (frit), *n., v.t. & v.i.* frit.
frit·ter (frit′ẽr), *n.* [OFr. *fraiture;* L. *fractura;* see FRACTURE], [Rare], a small piece; fragment; shred. *v.t.* [< the *n.*], 1. [Rare], to break, cut, or tear into small pieces. 2. to waste (energy, money, time, etc.) bit by bit on trifling or petty things (usually with *away*).
frit·ter (frit′ẽr), *n.* [Fr. *friture;* LL. **frictura* < pp. of *frigere*, to fry], a small cake of fried batter, usually containing corn, fruit, or other filling.
Fri·u·li-Ve·ne·zia Giulia (frē-ōō′lē-ve-ne′tsyä), see **Venezia Giulia.**
friv·ol (friv″l), *v.i. & v.t.* [FRIVOLED or FRIVOLLED (-′ld), FRIVOLING or FRIVOLLING], [< *frivolous*], [Colloq.], to waste (time) on frivolous or trifling things.
fri·vol·i·ty (fri-vol′ə-ti), *n.* [Fr. *frivolité*], 1. the quality of being frivolous. 2. [*pl.* FRIVOLITIES (-tiz)], a frivolous act or thing.
friv·o·lous (friv′ə-ləs), *adj.* [L. *frivolus*, brittle, crumbling (cf. FRIABLE), hence silly], 1. of little value or importance; trifling; trivial; paltry. 2. not properly serious or sensible; silly and light-minded; giddy.
friz (friz), *v.t. & v.i.* [FRIZZED (frizd), FRIZZING], [Fr. *friser*, to curl], 1. to form into small, tight curls: said of hair. 2. to form into small, hard knots or tufts: said of the nap of cloth. *n.* something frizzed; especially, hair formed into small, tight curls. Also spelled **frizz.**
fri·zette (fri-zet′), *n.* a frisette.
frizz (friz), *v.t. & v.i.* to friz.
frizz (friz), *v.t. & v.i.* [< *fry*, with echoic *-zz*], to fry with a sputtering, hissing noise; sizzle.
friz·zle (friz″l), *v.t. & v.i.* [FRIZZLED (-′ld), FRIZZLING], [prob. echoic extension of *fry*, influenced by *sizzle, frazzle, fizzle*, etc.], 1. to make or cause to make a sputtering, hissing noise, as in frying; sizzle. 2. to make or become crisp by broiling or frying thoroughly.
friz·zle (friz″l), *v.t. & v.i.* [FRIZZLED (-′ld), FRIZZLING], [prob. < *friz* (*frieze, freeze*) in earlier sense "raise a nap on cloth" + *-le*, freq. suffix (cf. FRIEZE); prob. akin to Fris. *frislen*, to plait (the hair)], to form into small, tight curls; friz; crimp. *n.* a small, tight curl.
friz·zly (friz′li), *adj.* [< *frizzle*, *n.* + *-y*], full of or covered with small, tight curls.
friz·zy (friz′i), *adj.* frizzly.
fro (frō), *adv.* [ME. *fra, fro* < ON. *frā;* akin to AS. *fram* (see FROM)], away; backward; back: now only in *to and fro.* *prep.* [Scot. or Dial.], from.
to and fro, forward and backward; back and forth.
Fro·bish·er, Sir **Martin** (frō′bish-ẽr), 1535?–1594; English navigator and explorer.
frock (frok), *n.* [ME. *frok, froc;* OFr. *froc*, monk's cowl or habit; ML. *froccus* < OHG. *hroc*, a cloak], 1. *a*) a robe worn by friars, monks, etc.; hence, *b*) the office of a priest, etc. 2. any of various other garments; specifically, *a*) a tunic, mantle, or long coat formerly worn by men. *b*) a shirtlike overall; smock. *c*) a woolen jersey worn by sailors. *d*) a dress; gown. *e*) a frock coat. *v.t.* to clothe in a frock.
frock coat, a man's double-breasted dress coat with a full skirt reaching to the knees both in front and in back, worn chiefly in the 19th century.
froe (frō), *n.* [also *frow* (*frower*), *frau;* dial. synonymous *fromward, frommard* suggests shortening of *froward*, in sense "handle turned away," but ? associated with D.

vrouw, G. *frau*, wife], a wedge-shaped cleaving tool with a handle set into the blade at right angles to the back: also spelled **frow**.

Froe·bel, Frie·drich (frē′driH frö′bəl; Eng. frā′b'l), 1782–1852; German educational reformer; originated the kindergarten system: also spelled **Fröbel**.

frog (frôg, frog), *n.* [ME. *frogge;* AS. *frogga;* basically akin to G. *frosch;* for prob. IE. base see FROTH], 1. *a)* any of a group of small, four-legged, leaping animals with long, powerful hind legs, short forelegs, webbed feet, and no tail: it develops from a tadpole and, when grown, is able to live either in water or on land. *b)* an animal resembling this, as a tree frog. 2. [prob. from the shape], a horny pad in the middle of the sole of a horse's foot. 3. a corded or braided loop used as a fastener or decoration on clothing. 4. a device on railroad tracks for keeping cars on the proper rails at intersections or switches: so called from its resemblance to the structure of a frog's hind leg. 5. [Slang], a Frenchman: term of contempt or derision, from the fondness of the French for eating frogs' legs.

STAGES IN DEVELOPMENT OF FROG

FROGS ON JACKET

frog in the throat, a hoarseness due to throat irritation.

frog·fish (frôg′fish′, frog′fish′), *n.* [*pl.* FROGFISH, FROGFISHES (-iz); see FISH], any of a number of angler fishes with compressed bodies, large mouths, and flipperlike fins.

frog·gy (frôg′i, frog′i), *adj.* [FROGGIER (-i-ẽr), FROGGIEST (-i-ist)], 1. of or like a frog. 2. full of frogs.

frog·hop·per (frôg′hop′ẽr, frog′hop′-ẽr), *n.* any of a group of leaping insects whose larvae produce frothy masses in plants.

Froh·man, Charles (frō′mən), 1860–1915; American theatrical manager and producer.

Frois·sart, Jean (zhän frwȧ′sȧr′; Eng. froi′särt), 1333?–1400?; French historian and poet.

frol·ic (frol′ik), *adj.* [D. *vroolijk* < MD. *vrō*, merry; akin to G. *froh*], full of fun and pranks; gay; merry. *n.* 1. a gay trick. 2. a gay party or game. 3. merriment; gaiety; fun. *v.i.* [FROLICKED (-ikt), FROLICKING], to make merry; have fun; gambol. —***SYN.*** see **play**.

frol·ick·er (frol′ik-ẽr), *n.* a person who frolics.

frol·ick·y (frol′ik-i), *adj.* frolicsome.

frol·ic·some (frol′ik-səm), *adj.* [*frolic* + *-some*], full of gaiety or high spirits; playful; merry; sportive.

from (frum, from; *unstressed* frəm), *prep.* [ME.; AS. *from, fram;* akin to Goth. *fram*, forward, away, further, ON. *frā* (see FRO); IE. base **pro-* (var. of **per-;* cf. FORE, FOR-), seen also in AS. *forma*, the first (cf. FORMER, FOREMOST)], a particle used generally in the four basic senses below, which come out of the primary sense of *forward*, hence *away, apart, out of*: it is used with verbs or other words to indicate I. *a point of departure for motion, duration, distance, action, etc.; source or beginning of ideas, action, etc.* 1. beginning at: as, he walked *from* the door. 2. starting with (the first of two named limits): as, I stayed *from* three to six. 3. out of; derived or coming out of: as, he took a comb *from* his pocket. 4. with (a person or thing) as the maker, sender, speaker, teacher, etc.: as, a letter *from* Mary, facts learned *from* reading. II. *distance, absence, removal, obstruction, exclusion, prevention, freedom, etc.* 1. at a place not near to; out of contact with: as, keep away *from* me, he is far *from* home. 2. out of the whole of; out of unity or alliance with: as, take two *from* four. 3. out of the possibility or use of: as, he kept me *from* going. 4. out of the possession or control of: as, they released him *from* jail. III. *difference, distinction, etc.* as not being like: as, he didn't know me *from* Adam. IV. *reason, cause, motive, etc.* by reason of; caused by; because of: as, he trembled *from* fear. Abbreviated **fr., fm.**

fro·men·ty (frō′mən-ti), *n.* frumenty, a kind of pudding.

frond (frond), *n.* [L. *frons, frondis*, leafy branch, foliage], 1. the leaflike organ of a fern, differing from a true leaf in that it bears the reproductive cells on its surface. 2. the leaflike part, or shoot, of a lichen, seaweed, etc. 3. [Poetic], a leaf; especially, the compound palm leaf.

‡**Fronde** (frōnd), *n.* [Fr., lit., a sling], 1. in French history, a political party organized during the minority of Louis XIV to oppose the court and Cardinal Mazarin; hence, 2. violent political opposition.

frond·ed (fron′did), *adj.* having fronds.

fron·des·cence (fron-des′'ns), *n.* [see FRONDESCENT], 1. the process, state, or period of putting forth leaves. 2. leaves; foliage.

fron·des·cent (fron-des′ənt), *adj.* [L. *frondescens*, ppr. of *frondescere*, to become leafy < *frondere*, to put forth leaves], putting forth new leaves or fronds.

front (frunt), *n.* [ME.; OFr.; L. *frons, frontis*, forehead, front], 1. the forehead; hence, 2. the face; countenance. 3. attitude or appearance, as of the face, indicating state of mind; external behavior when facing a problem, etc.: as, he puts on a bold *front* in spite of his fears. 4. impudence; effrontery. 5. the part of something that faces forward or is regarded as facing forward; most important side; fore part. 6. first part; beginning. 7. the place or position before a person or thing: as, it's right in *front* of you. 8. the first or most available bellhop or page, as in a hotel: generally used as a call. 9. the land bordering a lake, ocean, street, etc. 10. a promenade along a body of water. 11. the advanced line, or the whole area, of contact between opposing sides in warfare; combat zone. 12. a broad movement in which different groups are united for the achievement of certain common political or social aims. 13. a person who serves as a public representative of a business, group, etc., usually because of his prestige; hence, 14. a person or group whose work or reputation serves to obscure the real activity or objectives of a business, society, etc. 15. a stiff shirt bosom, worn with formal clothes. 16. [Colloq.], an appearance, usually pretended or assumed, of social standing, wealth, etc. 17. in *architecture*, a face of a building; especially, the face with the principal entrance. 18. in *meteorology*, the boundary between two masses of air that are different, as in density. *adj.* 1. at, to, in, on, or of the front. 2. in *phonetics*, articulated with the front of the tongue: as, *i* (in *bid*) and *e* (in *met*) are *front* vowels. *v.t.* 1. to face; be opposite to. 2. to be before in place. 3. to meet: confront. 4. to defy; oppose. 5. to supply with a front. *v.i.* to face in a certain direction: as, the castle *fronted* on the sea.

in front of, before; in a position ahead of.

front., frontispiece.

front·age (frun′tij), *n.* [see -AGE], 1. the front part of a building. 2. the direction toward which this faces; exposure. 3. the land between the front edge of a building and the street. 4. *a)* the front boundary line of a lot facing a street. *b)* the length of this line. 5. land bordering a street, river, lake, etc.

fron·tal (frun′t'l), *adj.* [Mod. L. *frontalis*], 1. of the front; in, on, at, or against the front. 2. of or for the forehead. *n.* the bone of the forehead: see **skull**, illus.

fron·tal (frun′t'l), *n.* [ME. *frountel;* OFr. *frontel;* ML. *frontale;* L. *frontalia*, *pl.* < *frons;* see FRONT & -AL], 1. an ornamental band or piece of armor worn on the forehead or over the face. 2. an ornamental cover or drapery for the front of an altar. 3. *a)* a façade. *b)* a small pediment over a door, window, etc.

frontal attack, 1. an attack made against the whole of an enemy's front in a given sector: distinguished from *flanking attack*. 2. any direct attack.

Fron·te·nac, Lou·is de Bu·ade de (lwē′ də bü-ȧd′ də frōnt′nȧk′; Eng. fron′tə-nak′), Comte, 1620–1698; French governor of Canada (1672–1682; 1689–1698).

fron·tier (frun-têr′, fron′têr), *n.* [ME. *frontere;* OFr. *frontier* < *front;* see FRONT], 1. that part of a country which faces or borders on another country. 2. that part of a settled, civilized country which lies next to an unexplored or undeveloped region. 3. any new or incompletely investigated field of learning, thought, etc.: often in the plural, as, the *frontiers* of medicine are still being extended. *adj.* of, on, or near the frontier.

fron·tiers·man (frun-têrz′mən), *n.* [*pl.* FRONTIERSMEN (-mən)], a man who lives on the frontier.

fron·tis·piece (frun′tis-pēs′, fron′tis-pēs′), *n.* [OFr. *frontispiece*, frontispiece, front of a house; ML. *frontispicium*, front of a church, front view < L. *frons, frontis*, front + *specere*, to look, view], 1. formerly, *a)* the first page or title page of a book. *b)* a preface; foreword; hence, 2. an illustration facing the first page or title page of a book or division of a book: abbreviated **front.** 3. in *architecture*, *a)* the main façade. *b)* a small pediment over a door, window, etc.

front·let (frunt′lit), *n.* [OFr. *frontelet*, dim. of *frontel;* see FRONTAL (band for forehead)], 1. a band or fillet worn on the forehead; frontal; phylactery. 2. the forehead of an animal. 3. the forehead of a bird, when distinguishable by the color or texture of the plumage. 4. an ornamental border for an altar cover.

fron·to- (frun′tō, fron′tō), [< L. *frons, frontis;* see FRONT], a combining form meaning: 1. *of* or *connected with the frontal bone* or *region and*, as in *fronto-parietal*. 2. *of* or *connected with a meteorological front*, as in *frontogenesis*.

fron·to·gen·e·sis (frun′tō-jen′ə-sis), *n.* [Mod.L.; see FRONTO- & GENESIS], the coming into contact of two atmospherically different masses or currents of air, thereby forming a meteorological front and usually causing clouds, rain, snow, etc.

fron·tol·y·sis (frun-tol′ə-sis), *n.* [Mod.L.; see FRONTO- & -LYSIS], the process that tends to destroy a meteorological front, as by mixture or divergence of the frontal air.

front-page (frunt′pāj′), *adj.* printed or fit to be printed on the front page of a newspaper; important or sensational.

Front Range, a mountain range in north central Colorado.

front room, a room in the front of a house, especially a living room.

frore (frôr, frōr), *adj.* [ME. *frore(n)*, frozen, pp. of *fresen* (see FREEZE); for the *r* beside infinitive *s*, cf. FORLORN], [Archaic or Poetic], very cold; frosty; frozen.

frosh (frosh) *n.* [*pl.* FROSH], [< G. *frosch*, lit., a frog, slang term for a first-year student at certain German universities c. 1900; cf. FROG], [Slang], a freshman.

frosh (frosh), *n.* [ME. *frosch;* AS. *frox, forsc;* akin to G. *frosch* (cf. FROG)], [Dial.], a frog.

frost (frôst, frost), *n.* [ME.; AS. *forst, frost* (akin to G. *frost*, etc.) < pp. base of *freosan* (see FREEZE) + *-t* (Gmc. **-ta*), nominal suffix], 1. a freezing or state of being frozen. 2. temperature causing freezing; temperature below the freezing point of water. 3. frozen dew or vapor; moisture frozen as a white, crystalline coating on a surface; hoarfrost. 4. coolness of action, feeling, manner, etc. 5. [Slang], a failure, especially of something meant to entertain or interest. *v.t.* 1. to cover with frost. 2. to damage, wither, or kill by freezing. 3. to cover with frosting, or icing. 4. to make frostlike in appearance, as some nontransparent glass.

Frost, Robert Lee (frôst, frost), 1874–1963; American poet.

frost·bite (frôst′bīt′, frost′bīt′), *v.t.* [FROSTBIT (-bit′), FROSTBITTEN (-bit′′n), FROSTBITING], to injure the tissues of (a part of the body) by exposure to intense cold; nip with frost. *n.* injury caused by such exposure.

frost·bit·ten (frôst′bit′′n, frost′bit′′n), *adj.* [pp. of *frostbite*], injured by exposure to intense cold.

frost·ed (frôs′tid, fros′tid), *adj.* 1. covered or whitened with frost. 2. frostbitten. 3. covered with frosting, or icing. 4. having a surface made to resemble frost, as some nontransparent glass.

frost·fish (frôst′fish′, frost′fish′), *n.* [*pl.* FROSTFISH, FROSTFISHES (-iz); see FISH], 1. the tomcod, common along the New England coast in early winter. 2. the common American smelt.

frost·flow·er (frôst′flou′ẽr, frost′flou′ẽr), *n.* 1. a small plant of the lily family. 2. its white, star-shaped flower. 3. any of various asters.

frost·i·ly (frôs′t'l-i, fros′t'l-i), *adv.* in a frosty manner.

frost·i·ness (frôs′ti-nis, fros′ti-nis), *n.* the quality or state of being frosty.

frost·ing (frôs′tiŋ, fros′tiŋ), *n.* 1. a mixture of sugar, water or other liquid, flavoring, and, sometimes, whites of eggs, etc., for covering a cake; icing. 2. a dull, frostlike finish on glass, metal, etc. 3. a mixture of ground glass, varnish, etc., used in ornamental work.

frost line, the limit of penetration of frost.

frost·work (frôst′wũrk′, frost′wũrk′), *n.* 1. the tracery formed by frost on glass, etc. 2. ornamentation like this, as on silver.

frost·y (frôs′ti, fros′ti), *adj.* [FROSTIER (-ti-ẽr), FROSTIEST (-ti-ist)], 1. cold enough to produce frost; characterized by frost; freezing. 2. covered with or as with frost; glistening. 3. cold in manner or feeling; austere; unfriendly. 4. having white or gray hair; hoary; hence, 5. *a)* old. *b)* of or like old age.

froth (frôth, froth), *n.* [ME. *frothe;* ON. *frotha, frauth;* basically akin to AS. *(a)-freothan*, to froth up; IE. **preu-th*, a snorting, slavering (< base **per-*, to sprinkle, scatter), seen also in *frog*], 1. foam. 2. foaming saliva caused by disease or great excitement. 3. anything of a light, trifling, or worthless nature, as conversation, ideas, etc. *v.t.* [< the *n.*], 1. to cause to foam. 2. to cover with foam. 3. to spill forth in the form of foam. *v.i.* to produce froth; foam.

froth·i·ly (frôth′ə-li, froth′ə-li), *adv.* in a frothy manner.

froth·i·ness (frôth′i-nis, froth′i-nis), *n.* the quality or state of being frothy.

froth·y (frôth′i, froth′i), *adj.* [FROTHIER (-i-ẽr), FROTHIEST (-i-ist)], 1. of, like, or covered with froth; foamy. 2. light; trifling; worthless.

Froude, James Anthony (frōōd), 1818–1894; English historian.

frou·frou (frōō′frōō′), *n.* [Fr.; echoic], 1. a rustling or swishing as of a silk skirt when the wearer moves. 2. [Colloq.], excessive or affected elegance, fanciness, etc.

frounce (frouns), *v.t.* & *v.i.* [FROUNCED (frounst), FROUNCING], [ME. *frouncen;* OFr. *froncier, froncir*, to wrinkle < Frank. **hrunkja*, a wrinkle, akin to ON. *hrukka*], [Archaic], 1. to make or become curled. 2. to crease; wrinkle. *n.* [ME.; OFr. *fronce* < the *v.*], [Archaic], 1. a curl or crease; hence, 2. showy display.

frou·zy, frou·sy (frou′zi), *adj.* frowzy.

frow (frou), *n.* [ME. *frowe;* MD. *vrouwe;* akin to G. *frau;* for Gmc. & IE. base see FURNISH], 1. a Dutch or German woman or wife; hence, 2. [Archaic or Rare], any woman or wife.

frow (frō), *n.* a froe.

fro·ward (frō′ẽrd, frō′wẽrd), *adj.* [Early ME. *fraward;* see FRO & -WARD], 1. not easily controlled; stubbornly willful; contrary; refractory. 2. [Obs.], adverse; unfavorable.

frown (froun), *v.i.* [ME. *frounen;* OFr. *frognier;* prob. of Gmc. origin], 1. to contract the brows, as in sternness, displeasure, or concentrated thought. 2. to look with displeasure or disapproval (*on* or *upon*). *v.t.* 1. to silence, subdue, etc. with a disapproving look (with *down*). 2. to express (disapproval, disgust, etc.) by contracting the brows. *n.* 1. a contracting of the brows in sternness, thought, etc. 2. any expression of displeasure or disapproval.

SYN.—**frown, scowl,** and **glower** all denote the making of a wry or gloomy face, **frown** implying a contracting of the brows in disapproval, annoyance, or deep thought, **scowl** a puckering and lowering of the brows in irritation or sullenness, and **glower**, a staring fiercely in great anger or contempt. —*ANT.* smile.

frow·zi·ly, frow·si·ly (frou′z'l-i), *adv.* in a frowzy manner.

frow·zi·ness, frow·si·ness (frou′zi-nis), *n.* the quality or state of being frowzy.

frow·zy (frou′zi), *adj.* [FROWZIER (-zi-ẽr), FROWZIEST (-zi-ist)], [prob. akin to or < Brit. dial. *frowsty*, musty; ? < OFr. *frouste*, decayed, ruined], 1. [Rare], bad-smelling; musty. 2. dirty and untidy; slovenly; unkempt. Also spelled **frowsy, frouzy, frousy.**

froze (frōz), past tense of **freeze.**

fro·zen (frō′z'n), [ME.], past participle of **freeze.** *adj.* 1. turned into or covered with ice; congealed by cold. 2. injured, damaged, or killed by freezing. 3. having heavy frosts and extreme cold: as, the *frozen* polar wastes. 4. preserved by freezing, as food. 5. affected as if turned into ice: as, *frozen* with terror. 6. without warmth or affection in behavior, manners, etc. 7. prohibited in sale or exchange; not marketable because of legal restrictions or unfavorable economic conditions. 8. prohibited from changing to another job.

frozen custard, a food resembling ice cream, but with less butterfat content and of a looser consistency.

Frs., Frisian.

frs., francs.

F.R.S., Fellow of the Royal Society.

F.R.S.L., Fellow of the Royal Society of Literature.

F.R.S.S., Fellow of the Royal Statistical Society.

frt., freight.

‡**Fruc·ti·dor** (frük′tē′dôr′; Eng. fruk′ti-dôr′), *n.* [Fr. < L. *fructus*, fruit + Gr. *dōron*, gift: so named from being the month of harvest], the twelfth month (August 18—September 16) of the French Revolutionary Calendar, adopted by the First Republic in 1793.

fruc·tif·er·ous (fruk-tif′ẽr-əs), *adj.* [< L. *fructifer* (< *fructus*, fruit + *ferre*, to bear); + *-ous*], producing fruit; fruit-bearing.

fruc·ti·fi·ca·tion (fruk′tə-fi-kā′shən), *n.* [LL. *fructificatio* < pp. of L. *fructificare*], 1. the act or process of fructifying. 2. the fruit of a plant.

fruc·ti·fy (fruk′tə-fī′), *v.i.* [FRUCTIFIED (-fīd′), FRUCTIFYING], [ME. *fructifien;* OFr. *fructifier;* L. *fructificare;* see FRUIT & -FY], to bear fruit; become fruitful. *v.t.* to cause to bear fruit; fertilize; make fruitful.

fruc·tose (fruk′tōs, frook′tōs), *n.* [< L. *fructus*, fruit; + *-ose*], a crystalline sugar, $C_6H_{12}O_6$, found in sweet fruits and in honey: also called *fruit sugar, levulose.*

fruc·tu·ous (fruk′chōō-əs), *adj.* [ME.; OFr.; L. *fructuosus* < *fructus*, fruit], fruitful; productive.

fru·gal (frōō′g'l), *adj.* [L. *frugalis* < *frugi*, fit for food, hence proper, worthy, frugal, orig. dative of *frux, frugis*, fruits, produce; for IE. base see FRUIT], 1. not wasteful; not spending freely or unnecessarily; saving; economical. 2. *a)* not costly or luxurious; inexpensive. *b)* sparingly provided: as, a *frugal* meal. —*SYN.* see **thrifty.**

fru·gal·i·ty (frōō-gal′ə-ti), *n.* [*pl.* FRUGALITIES (-tiz)], [Fr. *frugalité;* L. *frugalitas*], quality or instance of being frugal; careful economy; thrift.

fru·giv·o·rous (frōō-jiv′ə-rəs), *adj.* [< L. *frux, frugis* (see FRUGAL); + *-vorous*], in *zoology*, fruit-eating.

fruit (frōōt), *n.* [see PLURAL, II, D, 3], [ME.; OFr. *fruit, fruict;* L. *fructus*, enjoyment, means of enjoyment, fruit, produce, profit < pp. of *frui*, to partake of, enjoy; IE. base **bhrūg-*, fruit, to enjoy, seen also in Eng. *brook* (to put up with)], 1. *usually in pl.* any plant product, as grain, flax, vegetables, etc. 2. the edible part of a plant or tree, consisting of the seeds and pulpy surrounding tissues: usually distinguished from *vegetable* only when the latter also consists of leaves, root, etc. 3. the result, product, or consequence of any action: as, prosperity is the *fruit* of planning. 4. [Archaic], the young of animals or man. 5. in *botany*, the mature ovary of a plant or tree, including the seed, its envelope, and any closely connected parts, as the pit and flesh of a peach, or a pea and its pod. *v.i.* to produce or bear fruit. *v.t.* to cause to bear fruit.

fruit·age (frōōt′ij), *n.* [OFr.; see -AGE], 1. the bearing

of fruit; fruiting. 2. a crop of fruit; fruits collectively. 3. a result; product; consequence.
fruit·cake (frōōt′kāk′), *n.* a rich cake containing nuts, preserved fruit, citron, spices, etc.
fruit cup, mixed fruits cut into small pieces and served in a sherbet glass, etc. as an appetizer or dessert.
fruit·er (frōōt′ẽr), *n.* 1. a person who grows fruit. 2. a tree that bears fruit. 3. a ship for transporting fruit.
fruit·er·er (frōōt′ẽr-ẽr), *n.* [ME. *ffruterer* (with redundant *-er*)], [Chiefly British], 1. a person who deals in fruit. 2. a ship for transporting fruit.
fruit fly, 1. any of several small flies whose larvae feed on fruits and vegetables, as the Mediterranean fruit fly. 2. the drosophila.
fruit·ful (frōōt′fəl), *adj.* 1. bearing much fruit. 2. producing much; productive; prolific. 3. producing results; profitable: as, a *fruitful* plan. —*SYN.* see **fertile.**
fruit·i·ness (frōō′ti-nis), *n.* the quality or condition of being fruity.
fru·i·tion (frōō-ish′ən), *n.* [OFr.; L. *fruitio*, enjoyment < pp. of *fruire*, to use, enjoy], 1. a pleasure obtained from using or possessing something; enjoyment. 2. [by association with *fruit*], the bearing of fruit; hence, 3. a coming to fulfillment; realization: as, success was the *fruition* of his years of work.
fruit jar, a jar, usually of glass, for containing canned fruit, preserves, etc., sealed airtight with a cap.
fruit·less (frōōt′lis), *adj.* [ME. *fruitles*], 1. without results; unprofitable; unsuccessful; vain. 2. bearing no fruit; sterile; barren. —*SYN.* see **futile.**
fruit sugar, fructose: also called *levulose.*
fruit tree, a tree that bears edible fruit.
fruit·y (frōōt′i), *adj.* [FRUITIER (-i-ẽr), FRUITIEST (-i-ist)], 1. like fruit in taste or smell; rich in flavor: as, a *fruity* wine. 2. rich in tone; mellow; sonorous: as, a *fruity* voice. 3. [Colloq.], rich in interest; spicy; juicy: as, a *fruity* story.
fru·men·ta·ceous (frōō′men-tā′shəs), *adj.* [LL. *frumentaceus* < L. *frumentum*, corn], of, having the nature of, or like wheat or other grain.
fru·men·ty (frōō′mən-ti), *n.* [ME. *frumentee, furmente;* OFr. *frumentée* < L. *frumentum*, corn], hulled wheat boiled in milk, sweetened, and flavored with cinnamon, etc.: also **fromenty, furmenty, furmety.**
frump (frump), *n.* [prob. shortened n. form < ME. *fromplen*, to wrinkle < earlier D. *frompelen, verrompelen* < *rompelen* (see RUMPLE); early sense of *frump*, "sneer, derisive wrinkling, jeer," suggests basic modern sense, "one whose appearance causes a grimace"], 1. a dowdy, and sometimes ill-tempered, woman or, rarely, man. 2. *pl.* [British Dial.], sulks; sulky mood.
frump·ish (frump′ish), *adj.* dowdy, and sometimes ill-tempered.
frump·y (frump′i), *adj.* [FRUMPIER (-i-ẽr), FRUMPIEST (-i-ist)], frumpish.
Frun·ze (frōōn′ze), *n.* the capital of Kirghiz S.S.R.: pop., 93,000.
frus·trate (frus′trāt), *v.t.* [FRUSTRATED (-id), FRUSTRATING], [< L. *frustratus*, pp. of *frustrare, frustrari*, to disappoint, deceive, trick < *frustra*, in vain], 1. to cause to have no effect; bring to nothing; counteract; nullify: as, he *frustrated* our plans. 2. to prevent from achieving an objective; foil; baffle; defeat: as, he *frustrated* his opponents. 3. in *psychology*, to prevent from gratifying certain impulses and desires, either conscious or unconscious. *adj.* [Archaic], baffled; defeated.
SYN.—**frustrate** implies a depriving of effect or a rendering worthless of efforts directed to some end; **thwart** implies a frustrating by blocking or acting in opposition to a person or thing moving toward some objective; **foil** implies a throwing something off its course (literally, by confusing the scent or trail) so as to discourage further effort or make it of no avail; to **baffle** is to defeat the efforts of by bewildering or confusing (the crime *baffled* the police); to **balk** is to frustrate by setting up obstacles or obstructions.
frus·tra·tion (frus-trā′shən), *n.* 1. a frustrating or being frustrated. 2. something that frustrates.
frus·tule (frus′chōōl′), *n.* [Fr.; L. *frustulum*, dim. of *frustum*, a piece, bit, part], the hard shell of a diatom.
frus·tum (frus′təm), *n.* [*pl.* FRUSTUMS (-təmz), FRUSTA (-tə)], [L., a piece, bit, part], 1. the solid figure formed when the top of a cone or pyramid is cut off by a plane parallel to the base. 2. the part of a solid figure contained between two planes, especially two parallel planes.

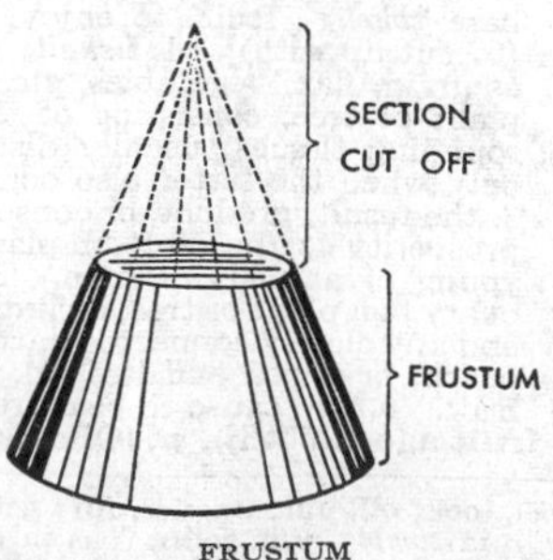

FRUSTUM

fru·tes·cence (frōō-tes′ns), *n.* shrubbiness; frutescent state.
fru·tes·cent (frōō-tes′-′nt), *adj.* [< L. *frutex*, a shrub; + *-escent*], shrubby or becoming shrubby.
fru·ti·cose (frōō′ti-kōs′), *adj.* [L. *fruticosus* < *frutex fruticis*, a shrub], of or like a shrub; shrubby.
fry (frī), *v.t.* [FRIED (frīd), FRYING], [ME. *frien;* OFr. *frire;* L. *frigere*, to fry], 1. to cook in hot fat or oil over direct heat. 2. [Obs.], to torment; agitate. *v.i.* 1. to be cooked in hot fat or oil. 2. [Obs.], to seethe; be agitated. *n.* [*pl.* FRIES (frīz)], 1. a dish of fried food, especially meat. 2. a social gathering, usually outdoors, at which food is fried and eaten: as, a fish *fry.*
fry (frī), *n.* [*pl.* FRY], [ME. *frie, fry;* a merging of ON. *frio*, seed, offspring (akin to Goth. *fraiw*) with Anglo-Fr. *frei* (OFr. *froi*, Fr. *frai*), spawn < the same Gmc. base or < L. *fricare*, to rub], 1. young fish. 2. small adult fish, especially when in large groups. 3. young; offspring; children.
small fry, 1. children. 2. unimportant people or things.
fry·er (frī′ẽr), *n.* 1. a person or thing that fries. 2. food to be cooked by frying; especially, a chicken young and tender enough to fry. Also spelled **frier.**
frying pan, a shallow metal pan with a long handle, for frying food.
out of the frying pan into the fire, from a bad situation into a worse one.
F.S., 1. Field Service. 2. Fleet Surgeon.
FSA, F.S.A., 1. Farm Security Administration. 2. Federal Security Agency.
ft., 1. foot; feet. 2. fort. 3. fortification. 4. fortified.
FTC, F.T.C., Federal Trade Commission.
fth., fthm., fathom.
ft-lb, foot-pound.
Fu·ad I (fōō-äd′), (*Ahmed Fuad Pasha*), 1868–1936; king of Egypt (1922–1936).
fub (fub), *v.t.* [FUBBED (fubd), FUBBING], to fob (trick).
fub·sy (fub′zi), *adj.* [FUBSIER (-zi-ẽr), FUBSIEST (-zi-ist)], [< dial. *fub*, plump child], fat and squat; plump.
fuch·si·a (fū′shə, fū′shi-ə), *n.* [Mod.L., after Leonard *Fuchs* (1501–1566), G. botanist], 1. any of several shrubby plants of the evening primrose family, with pink, red, or purple flowers hanging from the ends of the branches. 2. purplish red. *adj.* purplish-red.
fuch·sin (fook′sin), *n.* [< *fuchsia* + *-in*: from the color], a purplish-red aniline dye: also called *aniline red, magenta.*
fuch·sine (fook′sin, fook′sēn), *n.* fuchsin.
fu·coid (fū′koid), *adj.* [< *fucus* + *-oid*], of or like seaweed, especially rockweed. *n.* a seaweed; especially, rockweed.
fu·cus (fū′kəs), *n.* [*pl.* FUCI (-sī), FUCUSES (-iz)], [L., rock lichen; also, red or purple paint obtained from it; Gr. *phykos*, rock lichen, orchil, rouge < Sem.; cf. Heb. *puk*, cosmetic for the eyes], 1. originally, *a)* a kind of paint for the face. *b)* any paint or dye. 2. an olive-green or brown seaweed with flat, leathery fronds.
fud·dle (fud′′l), *v.t.* [FUDDLED (-′ld), FUDDLING], [Early Mod. Eng.; date & freq. form suggest D., LG. origin via thieves' slang; cf. D. *vod*, slack, loose, G. dial. *fuddeln*, to swindle], to muddle, confuse, or stupefy with or as with alcoholic liquor; befuddle. *v.i.* [Rare], to drink heavily; tipple. *n.* a fuddled condition.
fud·dy-dud·dy (fud′i-dud′i), *n.* [*pl.* FUDDYDUDDIES (-iz)], [prob. reduplicating echoism, suggested by *fuddle* or dial. *fud*, buttocks], [Slang], 1. a fussy, critical person. 2. an old-fashioned person.
fudge (fuj), *n.* [? developments of an echoic interj.; ? after G. *futsch!* no good!], 1. a false story; empty talk; nonsense. 2. a soft candy made of butter, milk, sugar, flavoring, etc. 3. in *printing*, a short piece of last-minute news or other matter, often printed in color, inserted in a newspaper page. *interj.* nonsense! *v.t.* [FUDGED (fujd), FUDGING], to make or put together dishonestly or carelessly; fake.
Fu·e·gi·an (fū-ē′ji-ən, fwā′ji-ən), *adj.* of Tierra del Fuego, its Indians, or their culture. *n.* 1. a member of a tribe of South American Indians who live in Tierra del Fuego. 2. a native or inhabitant of Tierra del Fuego.
‡**Fueh·rer** (fü′rẽr; Eng. fyoor′ẽr), *n.* [G.], Führer.
fu·el (fū′′l), *n.* [ME. *fouaile;* OFr. *fouaille;* LL. **focalia*, pl. of **focalis*, of fire < L. *focus*, fireplace; see FOCUS], 1. any material, as coal, oil, gas, wood, etc., burned to supply heat or power. 2. anything that maintains or intensifies strong feeling, etc. *v.t.* [FUELED OR FUELLED (-′ld), FUELING OR FUELLING], to supply with fuel. *v.i.* to get fuel.
fu·el·er, fu·el·ler (fū′′l-ẽr), *n.* a person or thing that fuels.
fu·ga·cious (fū-gā′shəs), *adj.* [< L. *fugax, fugacis* (< *fugere*, to flee); + *-ious*], 1. fleeing or apt to flee; passing quickly away; fleeting; evanescent; ephemeral. 2. in *botany*, falling soon after blooming, as some flowers.
fu·gac·i·ty (fū-gas′ə-ti), *n.* the quality of being fugacious.
fu·gal (fū′g′l), *adj.* of, or having the nature of, a fugue.
-fuge (fūj), [Fr. < L. *fugere*, to flee], a noun suffix meaning *something that drives away or out*, as in *febrifuge, vermifuge.*
fu·gi·tive (fū′jə-tiv), *adj.* [ME. & OFr. *fugitif;* L. *fugitivus* < pp. of *fugere*, to flee; IE. base **bheug-*, to flee,

akin to *bheugh-, to bend; cf. BOW (to bend)], 1. fleeing, apt to flee, or having fled, as from danger, justice, etc. 2. passing quickly away; not lasting long; fleeting; evanescent; ephemeral. 3. having to do with matters of temporary interest: as, *fugitive* essays. 4. roaming; shifting. *n.* 1. a person who flees or has fled from danger, justice, etc. 2. a fleeting or elusive thing.

fu·gle (fū'g'l), *v.i.* [FUGLED (-g'ld), FUGLING], [< *fugleman*], 1. to act as a fugleman; be the guide or director. 2. to motion in or as in signaling.

fu·gle·man (fū'g'l-mən), *n.* [*pl.* FUGLEMEN (-mən)], [altered by dissimilation < G. *flügelmann*, file-leader, lit., wing-man < *flügel*, wing + *mann*, man], 1. originally, a soldier expert in drilling, detailed to stand at the head of his unit and serve as a model and guide for others; hence, 2. a leader or exemplar.

fugue (fūg), *n.* [Fr.; It. *fuga;* L. *fuga*, a flight < *fugere;* see FUGITIVE], 1. a musical form or composition in which a theme is taken up and developed by the various instruments or voices in succession according to the strict laws of counterpoint. 2. in *psychiatry*, a state of psychological amnesia during which a patient seems to behave in a conscious and rational way, although upon return to normal consciousness he cannot remember the period of time nor what he did during it; temporary flight from reality.

‡**Füh·rer** (fü'rēr; Eng. fyoor'ĕr), *n.* [G. < *führen*, to lead], leader: title assumed by Adolf Hitler as head of Nazi Germany (1933–1945): also spelled **Fuehrer.**

Fu·ji (fōō'jē), *n.* Fujiyama.

Fu·ji·san (fōō'jē-sän'), *n.* Fujiyama.

Fu·ji·ya·ma (fōō'jē-yä'mä), *n.* a volcanic mountain near Tokyo, Japan: height, 12,395 ft.

Fu·kien (fōō'kyen'), *n.* a province of southeastern China: area, 46,514 sq. mi.; pop., 13,143,000; capital, Foochow.

Fu·ku·o·ka (fōō'kōō-ô'kä), *n.* a city on the northern coast of Kyushu, Japan: pop., 544,000.

-ful (fəl, f'l), [< *full, adj.*], a suffix meaning: 1. *full of, characterized by, having*, as in *joyful, painful.* 2. *having the qualities of*, as in *masterful.* 3. *having the ability or tendency to, apt to*, as in *helpful, forgetful.* 4. *the quantity that fills or would fill*, as in *teaspoonful, handful.*

Fu·lah, Fu·la (fōō'lä), *n.* [*pl.* FULAH, FULA], [< native name], 1. a Moslem people of the Egyptian Sudan, basically Hamitic but with an admixture of Negro stock. 2. their language.

ful·crum (ful'krəm), *n.* [*pl.* FULCRUMS (-krəmz), FULCRA (-krə)], [L., bedpost < *fulcire*, to prop, support], 1. the support or point of support on which a lever turns in raising or moving something; hence, 2. a means of exerting influence, pressure, etc.

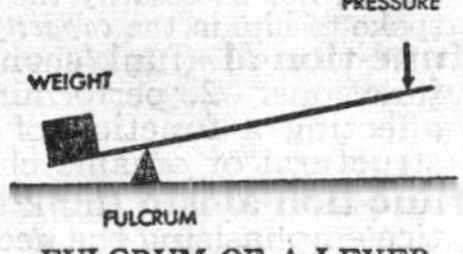

FULCRUM OF A LEVER

ful·fill, ful·fil (fool-fil'), *v.t.* [FULFILLED (-fild'), FULFILLING], [ME. *fulfillen;* AS. *fullfyllan*: a pleonasm (see FULL, *adj.* & FILL, *v.*)], 1. to carry out (something promised, desired, expected, predicted, etc.); cause to be or happen. 2. to do (something required); obey. 3. to fill the requirements of; satisfy (a condition); answer (a purpose). 4. to bring to an end; complete. —*SYN.* see **perform.**

fulfill oneself, to realize completely one's ambitions, potentialities, etc.

ful·fill·er (fool-fil'ĕr), *n.* a person who fulfills.

ful·fill·ment, ful·fil·ment (fool-fil'mənt), *n.* 1. a fulfilling or being fulfilled. 2. a thing that fulfills.

ful·gent (ful'jənt), *adj.* [ME.; L. *fulgens, fulgentis*, ppr. of *fulgere*, to flash, shine], [Poetic], very bright; radiant.

ful·gu·rate (ful'gyoo-rāt'), *v.i.* [FULGURATED (-id), FULGURATING], [< L. *fulguratus*, pp. of *fulgurare*, to flash < *fulgur*, lightning], to give off flashes of or like lightning.

ful·gu·rat·ing (ful'gyoo-rāt'iŋ), *adj.* [ppr. of *fulgurate*], in *medicine*, like lightning: used to describe sharp, sudden pains.

ful·gu·rite (ful'gyoo-rīt'), *n.* [L. *fulgur*, lightning; + *-ite*], a glassy substance, usually tube-shaped, formed by fusion when sand, rock, etc. are struck by lightning.

ful·gu·rous (ful'gyoo-rəs), *adj.* [L. *fulgur*, lightning; + *-ous*], like or full of lightning; flashing.

ful·ig·i·nous (fyoo-lij'ə-nəs), *adj.* [L. *fuliginosus* < *fuligo*, soot], 1. full of smoke or soot. 2. dark; dusky.

full (fool), *adj.* [ME.; AS.; akin to G. *voll*, Goth. *fulls;* IE. **pl-no* < base **pel-*, to fill, as also in *plenty, plenary*, etc.], 1. having in it all there is space for; holding or containing as much as possible; filled: as, the pail is *full.* 2. having eaten all that one wants. 3. using or occupying all of a given space: as, a *full* load. 4. having a great deal or number of; crowded with: as, a room *full* of people. 5. well supplied, stocked, or provided with; rich or abounding in: as, woods *full* of game. 6. filling the required number, capacity, measure, etc.; complete: as, a *full* dozen. 7. having reached the greatest development, size, extent, intensity, etc.: as, a *full* moon, *full* speed. 8. entirely visible: as, a *full* view. 9. having clearness, volume, and depth: as, a *full* tone. 10. plump; round; filled out; chubby: as, a *full* face. 11. with loose, wide folds; with plenty of material; ample; flowing: as, a *full* skirt. 12. *a*) greatly affected by emotion, etc. *b*) occupied or engrossed with ideas, thoughts, etc. *n.* the greatest amount, extent, number, size, etc. *adv.* 1. completely; to the greatest degree: as, a *full*-grown boy. 2. directly; exactly: as, the blow landed *full* in his face. *v.t.* to make with loose folds; gather, as a skirt. —*SYN.* see **complete.**

at the full, at the state or time of fullness.

full many, [Archaic & Poetic], very many.

full of, 1. filled by or with. 2. having had all that one wants of. 3. occupied or engrossed with.

full well, very well.

in full, 1. to, for, or with the full amount, value, etc. 2. with all the words or letters; not abbreviated.

to the full, fully; completely; thoroughly.

full (fool), *v.t. & v.i.* [ME. *fullen;* OFr. *fuler* < LL. **fullare*, to full < L. *fullo*, cloth fuller], to clean, shrink, and thicken (cloth) with moisture, heat, andressure.

full admiral, in the *United States Navy*, a four-star admiral, ranking below an Admiral of the Fleet and above a vice-admiral: corresponds to *full general.*

full·back (fool'bak'), *n.* in *football*, 1. a player whose position is behind the scrimmage line together with, and usually behind, the halfbacks and the quarterback. 2. the position played by a fullback.

full blood, [from obs. notion that blood is the medium of heredity], 1. the relationship between brothers and sisters of the same parents. 2. unmixed breed or race.

full-blood·ed (fool'blud'id), *adj.* 1. vigorous; lusty. 2. of unmixed breed or race; thoroughbred.

full-blown (fool'blōn'), *adj.* 1. in full bloom; open: said of flowers. 2. fully grown or developed; matured.

full-bod·ied (fool'bod'id), *adj.* having a rich flavor and much strength: as, a *full-bodied* wine.

full-dress (fool'dres'), *adj.* 1. of full dress: as, a *full-dress* suit. 2. formal: as, a *full-dress* dinner.

full dress, formal clothes worn on important or ceremonial occasions; especially, formal evening clothes.

full·er (fool'ĕr), *n.* [ME.; AS. *fullere;* L. *fullo*], a person whose work is to full cloth.

full·er (fool'ĕr), *n.* [? < obs. *full*, to make full, complete < *full, adj.*], 1. a tool used by blacksmiths to hammer grooves into iron. 2. a groove so made.

Ful·ler, George (fool'ĕr), 1822–1884; American painter.

Fuller, Margaret, (*Sarah Margaret Fuller*), 1810–1850; American writer, editor, and social reformer.

Fuller, Melville Wes·ton (wes't'n), 1833–1910; American jurist; chief justice, United States Supreme Court (1888–1910).

full·er's earth (fool'ĕrz), a highly absorbent, claylike substance used to remove grease from woolen cloth in fulling, to purify oil, etc.

Ful·ler·ton (fool'ĕr-tən), *n.* a city in southwestern California, near Los Angeles: pop., 56,000.

full·face (fool'fās'), *n.* in *printing*, boldface. *adv.* with the face turned directly toward the speaker or spectator.

full-faced (fool'fāst'), *adj.* 1. having a round face. 2. with the face turned directly toward the spectator or in a specified direction.

full-fash·ioned (fool'fash''nd), *adj.* knitted to conform to the shape of the foot and leg: said of stockings.

full-fledged (fool'flejd'), *adj.* 1. having a complete set of feathers: said of birds. 2. completely developed or trained; of full rank or status.

full general, in the *United States Army*, a four-star general, ranking below a General of the Army and above a lieutenant general: corresponds to *full admiral.*

full-grown (fool'grōn'), *adj.* fully grown; full-sized.

full house, in *poker*, a hand containing three cards of one denomination and a pair of another, as three jacks and two fives: it is higher than a flush but lower than four of a kind: sometimes called *full hand.*

full-length (fool'leŋkth', fool'leŋth'), *adj.* 1. showing the whole length of an object. 2. showing all of a person's figure: said of a portrait or mirror. 3. of the original, unabridged, or standard length; not shortened: as, a *full-length* novel, *full-length* sofa.

full moon, 1. the moon seen as a circle when its whole disk reflects the sun's light. 2. the time of month when such a moon is seen.

full-mouthed (fool'mouthd'), *adj.* 1. having a full set of teeth: said of cattle, etc. 2. uttered loudly.

full nelson, [see NELSON, *n.*], in *wrestling*, a hold in which both arms are placed under the opponent's armpits from behind with the hands pressed against the back of his neck.

full·ness (fool'nis), *n.* [ME. *fulnesse*], the quality or state of being full (in various senses): also spelled **fulness.**

fullness of time, the appointed or allotted time.

full professor, see **professor.**

full-rigged (fool′rigd′), *adj.* 1. having the maximum number of masts and sails: said of a ship; hence, 2. fully equipped.
full sail, 1. the complete number of sails. 2. with every sail set; hence, 3. with the greatest possible speed and energy.
full stop, a period (punctuation mark).
full swing, full activity; operation at full capacity.
full tilt, full force; full speed.
full·y (fool′i), *adv.* [ME. *fulli;* AS. *fullice* < *full;* see FULL, *adj.*]. 1. to the full; completely; entirely; thoroughly. 2. exactly. 3. abundantly; amply. 4. at least: as, there were *fully* 200 people in the room.
ful·mar (fool′mẽr), *n.* [prob. < ON. *fūll*, foul, unpleasant + *mār, mōr,* seagull], a sea bird of the petrel family, common in Arctic regions.
ful·mi·nant (ful′mə-nənt), *adj.* [< Fr. or L.; Fr. *fulminant;* L. *fulminans,* ppr.], 1. fulminating. 2. in *medicine,* developing suddenly and severely, as a disease.
ful·mi·nate (ful′mə-nāt′), *v.i.* [FULMINATED (-id), FULMINATING], [< L. *fulminatus,* pp. of *fulminare,* to lighten, strike with lightning < *fulmen,* lightning, thunderbolt], 1. [Rare], to thunder and lighten. 2. to explode with sudden violence; detonate. 3. to shout or thunder forth denunciations, decrees, etc. *v.t.* 1. to cause to explode. 2. to shout or thunder forth (denunciations, decrees, etc.). *n.* any highly explosive compound.
fulminating powder, any highly explosive powder, especially one containing mercuric fulminate.
ful·mi·na·tion (ful′mə-nā′shən), *n.* 1. a fulminating. 2. a loud explosion. 3. a violent denunciation.
ful·mi·na·tor (ful′mə-nā′tẽr), *n.* a person who fulminates.
ful·mi·na·to·ry (ful′mə-nə-tôr′i, ful′mə-nə-tō′ri), *adj.* [Fr. *fulminatoire*], fulminating; thundering; denouncing.
ful·mine (ful′min), *v.i. & v.t.* [FULMINED (-mind), FULMINING], [Fr. *fulminer*], [Rare], to fulminate.
ful·min·ic (ful-min′ik), *adj.* [< L. *fulmen,* lightning; + *-ic*], 1. explosive. 2. designating or of an unstable acid, C:N·O·H, that forms highly explosive salts of certain metals, especially of mercury.
ful·mi·nous (ful′mə-nəs), *adj.* [L. *fulmineus* < *fulmen,* lightning], of or like thunder and lightning.
ful·ness (fool′nis), *n.* fullness.
ful·some (fool′səm, ful′səm), *adj.* [ME. *fulsum, fulsom,* full, fat (see FULL, *adj.* & -SOME); but influenced by *ful, foul,* foul], disgusting or offensive, especially because of excess or insincerity: as, *fulsome* flattery.
Ful·ton, Robert (fool′t'n), 1765–1815; American inventor and engineer; designer of the first commercially successful American steamboat, the *Clermont* (c. 1807).
ful·vous (ful′vəs), *adj.* [L. *fulvus*], dull reddish-yellow or brownish-yellow; tawny.
fu·mar·ic (fyoo-mar′ik), *adj.* [< L. *fumus* (see FUME); + *-ar* + *-ic*], designating or of a white, crystalline, unsaturated organic acid, $C_2H_2(COOH)_2$, occurring in Iceland moss, various fungi, and other plants, or produced synthetically from malic acid.
fu·ma·role (fū′mə-rōl′), *n.* [Fr. *fumarolle;* It. *fumaruolo* < LL. *fumariolum,* smoke hole, dim. of *fumarium,* chimney < *fumus,* smoke], an opening in a volcanic area, from which smoke and gases arise.
fu·ma·to·ri·um (fū′mə-tôr′i-əm, fū′mə-tō′ri-əm,) *n.* [*pl.* FUMATORIA (-ə), FUMATORIUMS (-əmz)], [Mod.L.], a fumatory.
fu·ma·to·ry (fū′mə-tôr′i, fū′mə-tō′ri), *n.* [*pl.* FUMATORIES (-iz, -riz)], [< Mod.L. *fumatorium* < pp. of L. *fumare,* to smoke, fume], a place used for smoking or fumigating. *adj.* of smoke or smoking.
fum·ble (fum′b'l), *v.i. & v.t.* [FUMBLED (-b'ld), FUMBLING], [var. of ME. *famelen;* prob. < ON. *famla* (Sw. *fumla,* Dan. *fumle*), to grope; for *-b-* cf. THIMBLE; Gmc. base occurs in AS. *folm,* hand (akin to L. *palma;* cf. PALM); Mod. Eng. form akin to D. *fommelen*], 1. to search (*for* a thing) by feeling about awkwardly with the hands; grope clumsily. 2. to handle (a thing) clumsily or unskillfully; bungle. 3. in *football,* etc., to fail to catch, hold, or handle (the ball) properly. *n.* 1. a clumsy groping or handling. 2. a failing to catch, hold, or handle the ball properly.
fum·bler (fum′blẽr), *n.* a person who fumbles; bungler.
fume (fūm), *n.* [ME.; OFr. *fum;* L. *fumus*], 1. a gas, smoke, or vapor, especially if offensive or suffocating. 2. anything imaginary or without substance. 3. [Rare], an outburst of anger, annoyance, etc. *v.i.* [FUMED (fūmd), FUMING], [Fr. *fumer;* L. *fumare* < *fumus*], 1. to give off gas, smoke, or vapor. 2. to rise up or pass off in fumes. 3. to show, or give way to, anger, annoyance, etc. *v.t.* to expose to fumes; treat or fill with fumes.
fumed oak, oak wood given a darker color and more distinct markings by exposure to ammonia fumes.
fu·mi·gate (fū′mə-gāt′), *v.t.* [FUMIGATED (-id), FUMIGATING], [< L. *fumigatus,* pp. of *fumigare,* to smoke < *fumus,* smoke + *agere,* to do, make], 1. to expose to the action of fumes, especially in order to disinfect or kill the vermin in. 2. [Rare or Archaic], to perfume.
fu·mi·ga·tion (fū′mə-gā′shən), *n.* [ME. *fumigacioun,* generation of fumes in sorcery; OFr.; ML. *fumigatio* < L. *fumigatus*], a fumigating or being fumigated.
fu·mi·ga·tor (fū′mə-gā′tẽr), *n.* 1. a person who fumigates. 2. a device for fumigating.
fu·mi·to·ry (fū′mə-tôr′i, fū′mə-tō′ri), *n.* [*pl.* FUMITORIES (-iz, -riz)], [ME. *fumeter;* OFr. *fumeterre* < LL. *fumus terrae,* lit., smoke of the earth: so called from its smell], any of a group of erect or climbing plants, especially one with clusters of pink or purple flowers, formerly used as a medicine.
fum·y (fūm′i), *adj.* [FUMIER (-i-ẽr), FUMIEST (-i-ist)], full of fumes; producing fumes; vaporous.
fun (fun), *n.* [< obs. *v. fon* (< ME. *fonnen*), to act foolishly; see FOND], 1. lively, gay play or playfulness; merriment; amusement; sport; recreation; joking. 2. a source or cause of amusement or merriment, as an amusing person or thing: as, he's good *fun. Fun* is never preceded by *a.* *v.i.* [FUNNED (fund), FUNNING], [< the *n.*], [Colloq.], to make fun; play or joke.
for (or **in**) **fun,** not seriously; playfully or jokingly.
like fun, [Slang], by no means; not at all: used to express emphatic negation or doubt.
make fun of, to ridicule; mock laughingly.
fu·nam·bu·list (fyoo-nam′byoo-list), *n.* [< L. *funambulus* < *funis,* a rope + *ambulare,* to walk; + *-ist*], a tightrope walker.
Fun·chal (foon-shäl′), *n.* seaport and capital of the Madeira Islands: pop., 48,000.
func·tion (fuŋk′shən), *n.* [OFr. (Fr. *fonction*); L. *functio* < pp. of *fungi,* to perform; akin to Sans. *bhuṅktē,* (he) enjoys], 1. the normal or characteristic action of anything; especially, any of the natural, specialized actions of an organ or part of an animal or plant: as, the procreative *function.* 2. a special duty or performance required of a person or thing in the course of work or activity: as, the *function* of a policeman is to protect and assist the public. 3. occupation; employment. 4. a formal ceremony or elaborate social occasion. 5. a thing that depends on and varies with something else. 6. in *mathematics,* a variable quantity whose value depends on and varies with that of another quantity or quantities: symbol, F (no period). *v.i.* to act in a required or expected manner; work; be used.
SYN.—**function** is the broad, general term for the natural, required, or expected activity of a person or thing (the *function* of the liver, of education, etc.); **office,** in this connection, refers to the function of a person, as determined by his position, profession, or employment (the *office* of a host); **duty** is applied to a task necessary in or appropriate to one's occupation, rank, status, etc. and carries a strong connotation of obligation (the *duties* of a vicar); **capacity** refers to a specific function or status, not necessarily the usual or customary one (the judge spoke to him in the *capacity* of a friend).
func·tion·al (fuŋk′shən-'l), *adj.* 1. of a function or functions. 2. performing a function. 3. in *medicine,* affecting a function of some organ without apparent structural or organic changes: as, a *functional* disease.
func·tion·al·ism (fuŋk′shən-'l-iz'm), *n.* theory or practice emphasizing the necessity of adapting the structure or design of anything to its function.
func·tion·al·ly (fuŋk′shən-'l-i), *adv.* 1. in a functional manner. 2. from the standpoint of function.
func·tion·ar·y (fuŋk′shən-er′i), *n.* [*pl.* FUNCTIONARIES (-iz)], [*function* + *-ary,* after Fr. *fonctionnaire*], a person who performs a certain function; official.
fund (fund), *n.* [L. *fundus,* bottom, land, estate; meaning affected by Fr. *fond,* stock, provision < same source], 1. a supply that can be drawn upon; stock; store: as, a *fund* of good humor. 2. *a*) a sum of money set aside for some particular purpose. *b*) *pl.* money available for use; ready money. 3. *pl.* [British], a permanent government debt on which interest is paid; public securities (with *the*). *v.t.* 1. to provide money for the payment of interest on (a debt). 2. to put or convert into a long-term debt that bears interest. 3. to put in a fund; collect.
fun·da·ment (fun′də-mənt), *n.* [ME. & OFr. *fondement;* L. *fundamentum* < *fundare,* to lay the bottom < *fundus,* the bottom], 1. the buttocks. 2. the anus.
fun·da·men·tal (fun′də-men′t'l), *adj.* [Late ME.; ML. *fundamentalis* < L. *fundamentum;* see FUNDAMENT], 1. of or forming a foundation or basis; basic; essential. 2. in *music,* designating or of the lowest, or root, tone of a chord. 3. in *physics,* designating or of a fundamental. *n.* 1. a principle, theory, law, etc. serving as a basis; essential part. 2. in *music,* the lowest, or root, tone of a chord. 3. in *physics,* the component having the lowest frequency in a complex vibration; tone produced by the whole of a vibrating body, as distinguished from any of the tones (called *harmonics*) produced by the vibration of any part.
fundamental bass, in *music,* the harmonic part consisting of the root tones of the chords.
fun·da·men·tal·ism (fun′də-men′t'l-iz'm), *n.* [sometimes F-], 1. orthodox religious beliefs based on a literal interpretation of the Bible (e.g., complete acceptance of the story of creation as given in Genesis and rejection of the theory of evolution) and regarded as fundamental to the Christian faith. 2. among some American Protestants, the movement based on this belief: opposed to *modernism.*

fun·da·men·tal·ist (fun'də-men't'l-ist), *n.* a person who adheres to fundamentalism. *adj.* of fundamentalism or fundamentalists.

fun·da·men·tal·ly (fun'də-men't'l-i), *adv.* [*fundamental* + *-ly*], at, from, or to the foundation; basically; essentially.

fund·ed (fun'did), *adj.* [pp. of *fund*], made into a long-term debt bearing regular interest.

funded debt, the part of a public debt represented by long-term, interest-bearing bonds.

fun·dus (fun'dəs), *n.* [L., bottom], in *anatomy*, the base of a hollow organ, or the part farthest from the opening.

Fun·dy, Bay of (fun'di), an arm of the Atlantic, between New Brunswick and Nova Scotia, noted for its high tides.

Fü·nen (fü'nən), *n.* Fyn: the German name.

fu·ner·al (fū'nẽr-əl), *adj.* [ME.; OFr.; ML. *funeralis* < L. *funus, funeris*, a funeral], of, like, or suitable for burial or cremation ceremonies. *n.* [OFr. *funeraille* < ML. *funeralia*, neut. pl. of *funeralis;* see the *adj.*], 1. the ceremonies connected with burial or cremation of the dead; obsequies. 2. the procession accompanying the body to the place of burial or cremation.

fu·ner·ar·y (fū'nẽr-er'i), *adj.* [LL. *funerarius*], having to do with a funeral or burial.

fu·ne·re·al (fū-nêr'i-əl), *adj.* [L. *funereus*], suitable for a funeral; sad and solemn; gloomy; dismal; lugubrious.

Fünf·kir·chen (fünf'kir'Hən), *n.* Pécs, a city in Hungary: the German name.

fun·gal (fuŋ'gəl), *adj. & n.* fungus.

fun·gi (fun'jī), *n.* alternative plural of **fungus.**

fun·gi·ble (fun'jə-b'l), *adj.* [ML. *fungibilis* < L. *fungi*, to perform], in *law*, designating goods, as grain, any unit or part of which can replace another unit, as in discharging a debt; capable of being used in place of another. *n.* [ML. (*res*) *fungibilis*], a fungible thing.

fun·gi·cid·al (fun'jə-sīd''l), *adj.* serving as a fungicide.

fun·gi·cide (fun'jə-sīd'), *n.* [*fungi-* + *-cide*], any substance that kills fungi or checks the growth of spores.

fun·go (fuŋ'gō), *adj.* [< ?], in *baseball*, designating or of a manner of batting, as for fielding practice, in which the batter himself tosses the ball lightly into the air and hits it as it falls.

fun·goid (fuŋ'goid), *adj.* like or characteristic of a fungus. *n.* a fungus.

fun·gous (fuŋ'gəs), *adj.* [L. *fungosus*, spongy < *fungus*], 1. of, like, or caused by a fungus or fungi. 2. growing or arising suddenly, but not lasting or substantial.

fun·gus (fuŋ'gəs), *n.* [*pl.* FUNGI (fun'jī), FUNGUSES (-iz)], [L., a mushroom, fungus; altered (after *fungi*, to perform) < Gr. *spongos, sphongos;* see SPONGE], 1. any of a group of plants, including mildews, molds, mushrooms, rusts, and toadstools, that have no leaves, flowers, or green color and reproduce by means of spores. 2. something that grows suddenly and rapidly like a fungus. 3. in *medicine*, a spongy, granular growth on the body, sometimes malignant. *adj.* fungous.

fu·ni·cle (fū'ni-k'l), *n.* [L. *funiculus*, dim. of *funis*, a cord, rope], a little cord or fiber; funiculus.

fu·nic·u·lar (fū-nik'yoo-lẽr), *adj.* [< L. *funiculus* (see FUNICLE); + *-ar*], 1. of or like a funiculus or funiculi. 2. of, worked by, or hanging from a rope or cable: as, a *funicular* railway is a mountain railway on which the cars are pulled up and lowered by cables. *n.* a funicular railway.

fu·nic·u·late (fū-nik'yoo-lit, fū-nik'yoo-lāt'), *adj.* having or constituting a funiculus or funiculi.

fu·nic·u·lus (fū-nik'yoo-ləs), *n.* [*pl.* FUNICULI (-lī')], [L., small cord, dim. of *funis*, a cord, rope], 1. in *anatomy*, a cord; specifically, *a*) the spermatic cord. *b*) the umbilical cord. 2. in *botany*, the slender stalk of an ovule or seed.

funk (fuŋk), *n.* [? < Fl. *fonck*, dismay; via thieves' slang & university slang], [Colloq.], 1. a cowering or flinching through fear; panic. 2. a person who cowers or flinches through fear. *v.i.* [Colloq.], to be in a funk; try to back out. *v.t.* [Colloq.], 1. to be afraid of. 2. to avoid because of fear; shrink from; shirk. 3. to frighten.

fun·nel (fun''l), *n.* [ME. *fonel* < (prob. via an OFr. form) Pr. *fonilh, enfonilh* < L. *fundibulum, infundibulum*, a funnel, hopper of a mill < *infundere*, to pour in; *in-*, in + *fundere*, to pour], 1. an instrument consisting of an inverted cone with a hole at the small end, or a tapering or cylindrical tube with a wide, cone-shaped mouth, for pouring liquids and powders into containers that have small openings. 2. a thing shaped like a funnel. 3. a cylindrical chimney or smokestack, as of a locomotive or steamship. 4. a flue. *v.i. & v.t.* [FUNNELED or FUNNELLED (-'ld), FUNNELING or FUNNELLING], to move or pour through, or as if through, a funnel.

fun·neled, fun·nelled (fun''ld), *adj.* 1. having a funnel. 2. shaped like a funnel.

fun·ni·ly (fun'ə-li), *adv.* in a funny manner.

fun·ni·ness (fun'i-nis), *n.* the state or quality of being funny.

fun·ny (fun'i), *adj.* [FUNNIER (-i-ẽr), FUNNIEST (-i-ist)], [see FUN & -Y], 1. causing laughter; laughable; amusing; humorous. 2. [Colloq.], out of the ordinary; strange; queer. *n.* [*pl.* FUNNIES (-iz)], *usually in pl.* [Colloq.], a comic strip.

SYN.—**funny** is the simple, general term for anything that excites laughter or mirth; **laughable** applies to that which is fit to be laughed at and may connote contempt or scorn; that is **amusing** which provokes smiles, laughter, or pleasure by its pleasant, entertaining quality; that is **droll** which amuses one because of its quaintness or strangeness, or its wry or waggish humor; **comic** is applied to that which contains the elements of comedy (in a dramatic or literary sense) and amuses one in a thoughtful way; **comical** suggests that which evokes laughter of a more spontaneous, unrestrained kind; **farcical** suggests a broad comical quality based on nonsense, extravagantly boisterous humor, etc. See also **absurd.**

funny bone, [from its reaction to impact, but prob. suggested also by its relation to the *humerus* (hence, "humorous")], a place on the elbow where the ulnar nerve passes close to the surface: a sharp impact at this place causes a sudden, painful, tingling sensation in the arm: also called *crazy bone.*

funny paper, the comic-strip section of a newspaper.

fur (fũr), *n.* [ME. *forre, furre*, orig., a case, covering, lining; OFr. *forre, fuerre*, a case, sheath; Gmc. *fodr*, a sheath, lining], 1. the soft, thick hair covering the bodies of certain animals. 2. *a*) a skin bearing such hair, when stripped and processed for use as material; dressed pelt. *b*) *pl.* skins of this kind; peltry. 3. any garment, neckpiece, trimming, etc. made of such skins. 4. any furlike or fuzzy coating, as diseased matter on the tongue in illness. *adj.* [OFr. *forrer* < the *n*], of fur. *v.t.* [FURRED (fũrd), FURRING], 1. to line, cover, make, or trim with fur. 2. to coat with a deposit. 3. to make level, as a floor, wall, etc., by using furring. *v.i.* to become coated with a deposit.

make the fur fly, to cause dissension or fighting.

fu·ran (fyoor'an, fyoo-ran'), *n.* [< L. *furfur*, bran; + *-an*], a colorless liquid, C_4H_4O, prepared from wood tar, used as a solvent or tanning agent.

fu·rane (fyoor'ān), *n.* furan.

fur·be·low (fũr'bə-lō'), *n.* [altered (after *fur*) < New Pr. *farbello*, a fringe, flounce, var. of Fr. *falbala*, a 17th-c. coinage], 1. a flounce or ruffle. 2. *usually pl.* showy, useless trimming or ornamentation. *v.t.* to decorate with or as with furbelows.

fur·bish (fũr'bish), *v.t.* [ME. *forbischen* < OFr. *forbir, fourbir;* OHG. *furban*, to clean, polish], 1. to brighten by rubbing or scouring; polish; burnish. 2. to put into usable condition again; renovate (usually with *up*).

fur·cate (fũr'kāt; *also, for adj.*, fũr'kit), *adj.* [ML. *furcatus*, cloven < L. *furca*, a fork], forked. *v.i.* [FURCATED (-id), FURCATING], to branch; fork.

fur·ca·tion (fẽr-kā'shən), *n.* 1. a furcating; forking. 2. a forklike part; branch.

fur·cu·lum (fũr'kyoo-ləm), *n.* [*pl.* FURCULA (-lə)], [Mod. L., dim. of *furca*, a fork], in *anatomy* & *zoology*, any forked part or organ; especially, the wishbone.

fur·fur (fũr'fẽr), *n.* [*pl.* FURFURES (-ēz')], [L., bran], 1. dandruff; scurf. 2. *pl.* bits of skin; dandruff scales.

fur·fu·ra·ceous (fũr'fyoo-rā'shəs), *adj.* [L. *furfuraceus;* see FURFUR], 1. of or like bran. 2. covered with dandruff; scurfy.

fur·fur·al (fũr'fẽr-al'), *n.* [L. *furfur*, bran; + *-al*], a colorless, sweet-smelling oily liquid, $C_5H_4O_2$, produced from corncobs, oat hulls, and other cereal wastes, used to make dyes, lacquers, synthetic resins, etc.

fur·fur·an (fũr'fẽr-an'), *n.* furan.

fur·fur·ane (fũr'fẽr-ān'), *n.* furan.

Fu·ries (fyoor'iz), *n.pl.* [L. *Furiae*, pl. of *furia;* see FURY], in *Greek & Roman mythology*, the three terrible female spirits with snaky hair (Alecto, Tisiphone, and Megaera) who punished the doers of unavenged crimes: also called *Erinyes, Eumenides.*

fu·ri·ous (fyoor'i-əs), *adj.* [ME.; OFr. *furieus;* L. *furiosus* < *furia;* see FURY], 1. full of fury or intense feeling; frantic; violent. 2. moving violently; violently overpowering: as, a *furious* attack.

furl (fũrl), *v.t.* [prob. < Fr. *ferler;* OFr. *fermlier;* L. *firmum ligare; firmum*, firm + *ligare*, to lay], to roll up tightly and make secure to a staff or mast, as a flag, sail, etc. *v.i.* to become curled or rolled up. *n.* 1. a roll or coil of something furled. 2. a furling or being furled.

fur·long (fũr'lôŋ), *n.* [ME.; AS. *furlang*, a measure, lit., length of a furrow < *furh*, a furrow + *lang*, long], a measure of distance equal to 1/8 of a mile, or 220 yards.

fur·lough (fũr'lō), *n.* [earlier *furloff* < D. *verlof;* after G. *verlaub*, leave], a leave of absence; especially, in *military usage*, a leave granted to enlisted personnel for a specified period of more than three days. *v.t.* to grant a furlough to.

fur·men·ty (fũr'mən-ti), *n.* frumenty.

fur·met·y (fũr'mə-ti), *n.* frumenty.

fur·nace (fũr′nis), ***n.*** [ME. *forneis, fornais;* OFr. *fornais;* L. *fornax, fornacis,* furnace, kiln < *fornus, furnus,* oven], 1. an enclosed chamber or structure in which heat is produced for heating a building, reducing ores and metals, baking pottery, etc. 2. any extremely hot place. 3. a grueling test; severe trial.

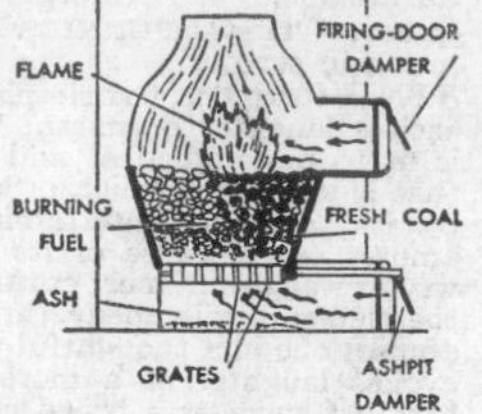

COAL FURNACE

Fur·ness, Horace Howard (fũr′nis), 1833–1912; American Shakespearean scholar.

fur·nish (fũr′nish), ***v.t.*** [< OFr. *furniss-,* inflectional base of *furnir, fornir* < Frank. **fronjan,* to do feudal or compulsory service < *fron-,* lord; Gmc. **frawan,* **fraujan,* lord (seen also in AS. *frea,* Goth. *frauja,* lord); IE. **prowon* < base **pr̥w(ĵ)o-,* former, first], 1. to supply, provide, or equip with whatever is necessary or useful; especially, to put furniture into (a room, apartment, etc.). 2. to supply; provide; give.

SYN.—**furnish,** as compared here, implies the provision of all the things requisite for a particular service, action, etc. (to *furnish* a house); to **equip** is to furnish with what is requisite for efficient action (a car *equipped* with overdrive); to **outfit** is to equip completely with the articles needed for a specific undertaking, occupation, etc. (to *outfit* a hunting expedition); **appoint,** a formal word now generally used in the past participle, implies the provision of all the requisites and accessories for proper service (a well-*appointed* studio); **arm** literally implies equipment with weapons, etc. for war but, in extended use, connotes provision with what is necessary to meet any circumstance.

fur·nish·ings (fũr′nish-iŋz), ***n.pl.*** 1. the furniture and fixtures for a room, apartment, etc. 2. articles of dress; things to wear.

fur·ni·ture (fũr′ni-chẽr), ***n.*** [Fr. *fourniture* < *fournir;* see FURNISH], 1. originally, a furnishing. 2. the movable things in a room, apartment, etc., which equip it for living, as chairs, sofas, tables, beds, etc. 3. the necessary equipment of a machine, ship, trade, etc. 4. [Archaic], all articles necessary to equip a man and horse, as armor, harness, etc. Abbreviated **furn.**

fu·ror (fyoor′ôr), ***n.*** [< Fr. or L.; Fr. *fureur;* L. *furor,* rage, madness; see FURY], 1. fury; rage; frenzy. 2. a poetic or religious frenzy. 3. a great, widespread outburst of admiration or enthusiasm; craze; rage.

fu·rore (fyoor′ôr, fyoo-rō′ri), ***n.*** [It. < L. *furor*], a furor (sense 3).

furred (fũrd), ***adj.*** [pp. of *fur;* also *fur, n.* + *-ed*], 1. made, trimmed, or lined with fur. 2. having fur: said of an animal. 3. wearing fur. 4. coated with diseased or waste matter.

fur·ri·er (fũr′i-ẽr, fũr′yẽr), ***n.*** 1. a dealer in furs. 2. a person who processes furs or makes and repairs garments, etc. of fur.

fur·ri·er·y (fũr′i-ẽr-i), ***n.*** [*pl.* FURRIERIES (-iz)], 1. furs collectively. 2. the business or work of a furrier.

fur·ri·ness (fũr′i-nis), ***n.*** a furry quality or state.

fur·ring (fũr′iŋ), ***n.*** 1. fur used for trimming or lining. 2. the act of trimming, lining, etc. with fur. 3. a coating of diseased or waste matter, as on the tongue. 4. the formation of such a coating. 5. in *architecture, a*) the leveling of a floor, wall, etc. or the creating of air spaces with thin strips of wood or metal before adding boards or plaster. *b*) the strips so used.

fur·row (fũr′ō), ***n.*** [ME. *forowe, forge,* etc.; AS. *furh;* akin to G. *furche* (OHG. *furuh*); IE. base **perk-,* **pr̥k-,* seen also in L. *porca,* furrow, ridge (cf. synonymous Norw. dial. *fere*)], 1. a narrow groove made in the ground by a plow. 2. anything resembling this, as a deep, narrow rut or track made by a wheel, a deep wrinkle on the face, etc. 3. [Poetic], a plowed field. ***v.t.*** [< the *n.*], 1. to make a furrow or furrows in. 2. to cleave through (the sea). ***v.i.*** 1. to make furrows. 2. to become wrinkled.

fur·ry (fũr′i), ***adj.*** [FURRIER (-i-ẽr), FURRIEST (-i-ist)], 1. of or made of fur. 2. covered with or wearing fur. 3. lined or trimmed with fur. 4. like fur, as in texture.

fur seal, any of several seals with soft, thick underfur.

Fürth (fürt), ***n.*** a city in Bavaria, Germany: pop., 77,000.

fur·ther (fũr′thẽr), ***adj.*** [ME. *further, forther;* AS. *furthra* (akin to G. *vorder*), usually regarded as containing the base of AS. *fore* (see FORE) + the compar. suffix in *af-ter, o-ther,* etc.], 1. more distant or remote; farther. 2. additional; more. ***adv.*** [ME. *furthere, forthere;* AS. *furthor,* orig. a neut. acc. of the *adj.*], 1. at or to a greater distance or more remote point in space or time. 2. to a greater degree or extent. 3. in addition; moreover. *Further* is now generally interchangeable with *farther* in senses 1 & 2 of the *adv.* and 1 of the *adj.*, though preference is often given to *farther* in reference to space and to *further* in reference to time, degree, or addition. Abbreviated **fur.** ***v.t.*** [ME. *furthren, ferthren, firthren;* AS. *fyrthran, fyrthrian* < *furthra, furthor, adj.* & *adv.*], to promote; give aid to. —***SYN.*** see **advance.**

fur·ther·ance (fũr′thẽr-əns), ***n.*** [ME.], 1. a furthering, or helping forward; advancement; promotion. 2. something that helps; aid.

fur·ther·more (fũr′thẽr-môr′, fũr′thẽr-mōr′), ***adv.*** [ME. *further more*], besides; moreover; in addition.

fur·ther·most (fũr′thẽr-mōst′), ***adj.*** [ME. (northern) *forthirmast*], most distant; furthest.

fur·thest (fũr′thist), ***adj.*** [ME., formed as superl. on analogy of *further*], most distant; farthest. ***adv.*** 1. at or to the greatest distance or most remote point in space or time. 2. to the greatest degree or extent.

fur·tive (fũr′tiv), ***adj.*** [Fr. *furtif;* L. *furtivus,* stolen, concealed, hidden < *furtum,* theft < *fur,* a thief], done or acting in a stealthy manner; surreptitious; stealthy; sly; shifty. —***SYN.*** see **secret.**

fu·run·cle (fyoor′uŋ-k′l), ***n.*** [L. *furunculus,* thief, pilferer, boil, dim. of *fur,* thief], a small skin abscess; boil.

fu·ry (fyoor′i), ***n.*** [*pl.* FURIES (-iz)], [ME. & OFr. *furie;* L. *furia* < *furere,* to rage; prob. < IE. base **dhus-,* to rage, storm, seen also in Gr. *thyein,* to storm; akin to base of AS. *dysig* (Eng. *dizzy*)], 1. *a*) violent anger; wild rage. *b*) a fit of this. 2. violence; vehemence; fierceness. 3. a violent, uncontrollable person, especially a woman. 4. [F-], one of the Furies. 5. [Archaic], frenzy of inspiration. —***SYN.*** see **anger.**

like fury, [Colloq.], 1. with violence. 2. swiftly.

furze (fũrz), ***n.*** [ME. *firs;* AS. *fyrs;* IE. base **pūro-,* cereal, cereal grain, seen also in Russ. *pyrej,* couch grass], any of several prickly evergreen shrubs with dark-green spines and yellow flowers, common in Europe, especially on wastelands: also called *gorse, whin.*

furz·y (fũr′zi), ***adj.*** 1. full of or covered with furze. 2. of or like furze.

fu·sain (fū-zān′; Fr. fü′zan′), ***n.*** [Fr., orig., spindle tree < L. *fusus,* a spindle], 1. a type of fine charcoal pencil prepared from the wood of the spindle tree. 2. a drawing made with this.

Fu·san (fōō′sän′), ***n.*** a seaport in southeastern Korea: pop., 214,000.

fus·cous (fus′kəs), ***adj.*** [L. *fuscus*], dark in color; dusky.

fuse (fūz), ***v.t. & v.i.*** [FUSED (fūzd), FUSING], [< L. *fusus,* pp. of *fundere,* to pour out, shed; IE. **ĝhund* < base **ĝhud-,* to pour, seen also in AS. *geotan,* to pour, flow], 1. to make or become liquid by great heat; melt. 2. to unite as if by melting together; blend. Also spelled **fuze.** —***SYN.*** see **mix.**

fuse (fūz), ***n.*** [It. *fuso,* a cord, tube, casing, covering < L. *fusus,* hollow spindle or casing], 1. a narrow tube filled with combustible material or a wick saturated with such material for setting off an explosive charge. 2. any of various other devices for setting off bombs and explosive charges: as, a chemical *fuse,* electrical *fuse,* or percussion *fuse.* 3. in *electricity,* a wire or strip of easily melted metal placed in a circuit as a safeguard: when the current becomes too strong, the metal melts, thus breaking the circuit. Also spelled **fuze.**

fu·see (fū-zē′), ***n.*** [Fr. *fusée,* spindleful, rocket, hence fusee; ML. *fusata* < L. *fusus;* see FUSE, *n.*], 1. a friction match with a large head, intended to burn in a wind. 2. a colored flare used as a railroad signal. 3. in an old-fashioned clock or watch, a grooved cone upon which the cord from the spring container was unwound to equalize the force of the spring. 4. a bony growth on a horse's leg. Also spelled **fuzee.**

fu·se·lage (fū′z′l-ij, fū′s′l-ij, fū′zə-läzh′), ***n.*** [Fr.; prob. < OFr. *fusel,* dim. of L. *fusus,* a spindle + *-age* (see -AGE)], the body of an airplane, exclusive of the wings and tail assembly: see **airplane,** illus.

fu·sel oil (fū′z′l, fū′s′l), [G. *fusel,* inferior liquor], an oily, acrid, poisonous liquid occurring in alcoholic products that have not been distilled sufficiently to separate the ethyl alcohol from other substances with a low boiling point: it consists generally of a mixture of amyl, butyl, propyl, and isoamyl alcohols: also **fusel.**

fu·si·bil·i·ty (fū′zə-bil′ə-ti), ***n.*** 1. the quality of being fusible. 2. the degree to which this quality is present.

fu·si·ble (fū′zə-b′l), ***adj.*** [ME.; OFr.], that can be fused or easily fused: as, lead is a *fusible* metal.

fu·si·form (fū′zə-fôrm′), ***adj.*** [< L. *fusus,* a spindle; + *-form*], shaped like a spindle; rounded, broadest in the middle, and tapering toward each end.

fu·sil (fū′z′l, fū′s′l), ***adj.*** [L. *fusilis* < *fusus;* see FUSE (to melt)], 1. [Rare], fusible or fusing. 2. fused; melted. 3. made by melting and molding, or casting; founded. Also **fusile.**

fu·sil (fū′z′l), ***n.*** [Fr., orig., steel for striking sparks < LL. **focile* < L. *focus,* hearth (in LL., fire)], an old-fashioned light flintlock musket.

fu·sile (fū′z′l, fū′s′l, fū′sīl), ***adj.*** fusil.

fu·sil·ier, fu·sil·eer (fū′z′l-êr′), ***n.*** [Fr. *fusilier* < *fusil;* see FUSIL, *n.*], [Obs.], a soldier armed with a fusil: the term *Fusiliers* is still applied to certain British regiments formerly so armed.

fu·sil·lade (fū′z′l-ād′), ***n.*** [Fr. < *fusiller,* to shoot < *fusil;* see FUSIL, *n.*], 1. a simultaneous or rapid and continuous discharge of many firearms. 2. something like this: as, a *fusillade* of questions. ***v.t.*** [FUSILLADED (-id), FUSILLADING], to shoot down or attack with a fusillade.

fu·sion (fū′zhən), *n.* [L. *fusio*], 1. a fusing; melting or melting together. 2. *a*) the union of different things by or as if by melting; blending; coalition: as, a *fusion* of political parties. *b*) the state or fact of being so united. 3. anything made by fusing.
fusion bomb, a hydrogen bomb.
fu·sion·ism (fū′zhən-iz′m), *n.* the theory or practice of bringing about a fusion, or coalition, of political parties, factions, races, etc.
fu·sion·ist (fū′zhən-ist), *n.* an adherent of fusionism or a participant in a political fusion. *adj.* of fusionism or fusionists.
fuss (fus), *n.* [17th-c. slang, prob. echoic, used esp. in phr. *keep a fuss with* (now, *make a fuss about*)], 1. a nervous, excited activity or state; unnecessary bother or worry; bustle. 2. a fussy person. *v.i.* to bustle about or worry, especially over trifles. *v.t.* [Colloq.], to bother or worry unnecessarily; make nervous.
fuss-budg·et (fus′buj′it), *n.* [*fuss* + *budget*, prob. in sense of "bag, sack"], [Colloq.], a fussy person.
fuss·i·ly (fus′'l-i), *adv.* in a fussy manner.
fuss·i·ness (fus′i-nis), *n.* a fussy quality or state.
fuss·y (fus′i), *adj.* [FUSSIER (-i-ẽr), FUSSIEST (-i-ist)], 1. habitually fussing; bustling about or worrying over trifles. 2. showing or needing careful attention. 3. full of details, especially if unnecessary or showy.
fus·tian (fus′chən), *n.* [ME. *fustane, fustyane;* OFr. *fustaine, fustaigne;* ML. *fustaneum;* prob. < *fustis*, wooden stick, transl. of Gr. *xylinon*, wooden], 1. originally, a coarse cloth of cotton and linen. 2. now, a thick cotton cloth with a short nap, as corduroy, velveteen, etc. 3. pompous, pretentious talk or writing; bombast; rant; high-sounding nonsense. *adj.* 1. made of fustian. 2. pompous and pretentious but empty.
fus·tic (fus′tik), *n.* [Fr. & Sp. *fustoc;* Ar. *fustuq;* prob. < Gr. *pistakē*, pistachio], 1. a tropical American tree of the mulberry family, from whose wood a yellow dye is extracted. 2. the dye. 3. any of several other woods from which dyes are extracted.
fus·ti·gate (fus′tə-gāt′), *v.t.* [FUSTIGATED (-id), FUSTIGATING], [< L. *fustigatus*, pp. of *fustigare*, to beat with a stick < *fustis*, a stick], to beat with a stick; cudgel.
fust·i·ness (fus′ti-nis), *n.* a fusty quality or state.
fust·y (fus′ti), *adj.* [FUSTIER (-ti-ẽr), FUSTIEST (-ti-ist)], [< *fust*, moldiness; OFr. *fust*, cask, orig. tree trunk < L. *fustis*, wooden stick], 1. musty; moldy; smelling stale or stuffy. 2. not up-to-date; old-fashioned.
fut., future.
fu·thark (fōō′thärk), *n.* [< the first six letters: *f, u, þ* (*th*), *ǫ* (or *a*), *r, c*], the runic alphabet: formerly also **futharc, futhorc, futhork.**
fu·tile (fū′t'l), *adj.* [< Fr. or L.; Fr. *futile;* L. *futilis*, lit., that easily pours out, hence untrustworthy, worthless, futile < base of *fundere;* see FUSE (to melt)], 1. useless; ineffectual; vain. 2. trifling; unimportant.
SYN.—**futile** is applied to that which fails completely of the desired end or is incapable of producing any result; **vain** also implies failure but does not have as strong a connotation of intrinsic inefficacy as **futile; fruitless** stresses the idea of great and prolonged effort that is profitless or fails to yield results; that is **abortive** which fails to succeed or miscarries at an early stage of its development; that is **useless** which has proved to be ineffectual in practice or is theoretically considered to be of no avail. —*ANT.* effective, fruitful, effectual.
fu·til·i·tar·i·an (fyoo-til′ə-târ′i-ən), *adj.* [< *futility*, after *utilitarian*], based on or having the belief that everything in life is futile. *n.* a person who has this belief.
fu·til·i·ty (fū-til′ə-ti), *n.* [*pl.* FUTILITIES (-tiz)], [Fr. *futilité;* L. *futilitas* < *futilis;* see FUTILE], 1. the quality of being useless or ineffectual. 2. the quality of being frivolous or unimportant. 3. something futile.
fut·tock (fut′ək), *n.* [? pronun. sp. of *foot* + *hook*], any of the upright curved timbers forming the ribs of a wooden ship.
futtock plate, an iron plate put horizontally around the top of a ship's lower mast to hold the futtock shrouds.
futtock shroud, one of the iron rods extended from a futtock plate to a band around the lower mast to brace the mast.
fu·tur·al (fū′chẽr-əl), *adj.* of the future or futures.
fu·ture (fū′chẽr), *adj.* [ME.; OFr. *futur;* L. *futurus*, about to be, used as fut. part. of *esse*, to be], 1. that is to be or come; of days, months, or years ahead. 2. indicating time to come: as, the *future* tense of a verb. *n.* 1. the time that is to come; days, months, or years ahead. 2. what will happen; what is going to be: as, no one can foretell the *future*. 3. the prospective or potential condition of a person or thing; chance to achieve, succeed, etc.: as, he has a great *future* in politics. 4. *pl.* commodities bought or sold by speculators, theoretically to be delivered in time to come. 5. in *grammar*, *a*) the future tense. *b*) a verb form in this tense: abbreviated **fut.**
fu·ture·less (fū′chẽr-lis), *adj.* having no hopes, plans, or prospects for the future.
future life, in *religion*, the state of the soul after death.
future perfect tense, 1. a tense indicating an action or state as completed in relation to a specified time in the future. 2. a verb form in this tense (e.g., will have gone, shall have said).
fu·tur·ism (fū′chẽr-iz′m), *n.* a movement in art, literature, music, etc., shortly before and during World War I, which opposed traditionalism and tried to depict dynamic movement by the elimination of conventional form, balance, and rhythm and by stressing the violence and speed of the machine age.
fu·tur·ist (fū′chẽr-ist), *n.* an adherent of futurism. *adj.* of or relating to futurism or futurists.
fu·tu·ri·ty (fū-toor′ə-ti, fū-tyoor′ə-ti), *n.* [*pl.* FUTURITIES (-tiz)], 1. the future. 2. a future condition or event. 3. the quality of being future. 4. a futurity race.
futurity race, a race, usually a horse race, in which the contestants are selected long beforehand.
futurity stakes, 1. stakes competed for in a futurity race. 2. a futurity race.
fuze (fūz), *n.* a fuse.
fuze (fūz), *v.t. & v.i.* [FUZED (fūzd), FUZING], to fuse.
fu·zee (fū-zē′), *n.* a fusee.
fuzz (fuz), *n.* [said to be echoic, but cf. earlier D. *voos*, spongy, loose-textured (akin to Norw. *fos*) & the common dial. application to fungus in *fuzzball*], very loose, light particles of down, wool, etc.; fine hairs or fibers: as, the *fuzz* on a peach. *v.i. & v.t.* to cover or become covered with fuzz.
fuzz·ball (fuz′bôl′), *n.* a giant puffball.
fuzz·i·ly (fuz′'l-i), *adv.* in a fuzzy manner.
fuzz·i·ness (fuz′i-nis), *n.* the quality or condition of being fuzzy.
fuzz·y (fuz′i), *adj.* [FUZZIER (-i-ẽr), FUZZIEST (-i-ist)], 1. of, like, or covered with fuzz. 2. not clear; blurred.
f.v., *folio verso*, [L.], on the back of the page.
-fy (fī), [ME. *-fyen, -fien;* OFr. *-fier;* L. *-ficare* < *facere*, to make, do], a suffix used to form verbs, meaning: 1. *to make, cause to be or become*, as in *liquefy*. 2. *to cause to have, imbue with*, as in *glorify*. 3. *to become*, as in *emulsify*.
fyke (fīk), *n.* [D. *fuik*, a bow net], a fish net in the form of a long bag.
fyl·fot (fil′fot), *n.* [< *fill* + *foot*: so called because used to fill the foot of a colored window], a swastika.
Fyn (fün), *n.* a Danish island, between Jutland and Zealand island: area, 1,150 sq. mi.; pop., 328,000: German name, *Fünen*.
fytte (fit), *n.* [Obs.], a fit (division of a long poem).
Fyz·a·bad (fī′zä-bäd′), *n.* a city in Uttar Pradesh, India: pop., 66,000.
F.Z.S., Fellow of the Zoological Society.

G

G, g (jē), *n.* [*pl.* G's, g's, Gs, gs (jēz)], 1. the seventh letter of the English alphabet: from the Latin: see **alphabet**, table. 2. a sound of G or g: in English, it represents the voiced back-tongue stop, (g), of *get* or the voiced affricate, (j), IPA [dʒ], of *siege*. 3. a type or impression for G or g. 4. *a symbol for* the seventh in a sequence or group. *adj.* 1. of G or g. 2. seventh in a sequence or group.

G (jē), *n.* 1. a Roman numeral for 400: with a superior bar (Ḡ), 400,000. 2. [< *grand*, slang term for $1,000], [Slang], one thousand dollars. 3. in *education*, a grade of *good*. 4. in *music*, *a)* the fifth tone or note in the scale of C major, or the seventh in the scale of A minor. *b)* a key string, etc. producing this tone. *c)* the scale having G as the keynote. *adj.* shaped like G.
G., 1. German. 2. Germany. 3. specific gravity.
G., g., 1. gauge. 2. gold. 3. grain. 4. gram; grams. 5. grand. 6. guide. 7. guinea; guineas. 8. gulf. 9. in *electricity*, conductance.
g, 1. in *physics*, *a)* gravity. *b)* acceleration of gravity. 2. in *psychology*, general intelligence.
g., 1. gender. 2. general. 3. genitive.
Ga, in *chemistry*, gallium.
Ga., 1. Gaelic. 2. Gallic. 3. Georgia.
G.A., 1. General Agent. 2. General Assembly.
G.A., G/A, g.a., in *insurance*, general average.
gab (gab), *v.i.* [GABBED (gabd), GABBING], [ME. *gabben; prob.* < ON. *gabba*, to mock, reinforced by OFr. *gaber*, to boast, deride; the base occurs in AS. *gaffetung*, a scoffing, mocking & *gaf-spræc*, foolish speech; IE. base **ĝhabh-* < **ĝhei*, etc., to yawn, have the mouth open], [Colloq.], to talk much or idly; chatter; gabble. *n.* [Colloq.], chatter, talkativeness.
gift of (the) gab, [Colloq.], the ability to speak fluently; eloquence; glibness.
gab·ar·dine (gab′ẽr-dēn′, gab′ẽr-dēn′), *n.* [var. of *gaberdine*], 1. a woolen, cotton, or rayon cloth twilled on one side and having a fine, diagonal weave, used for suits, coats, dresses, etc. 2. a gaberdine.
gab·ber (gab′ẽr), *n.* [Colloq.], a person who gabs.
gab·ble (gab′'l), *v.i.* [GABBLED (-'ld), GABBLING], [< *gab* + *-le*, freq. suffix; ? suggested by MD. *gabbeln*, to chatter], 1. to talk rapidly and incoherently; jabber; chatter. 2. to utter rapid, meaningless sounds, as a goose. *v.t.* to utter rapidly and incoherently. *n.* rapid, incoherent talk or meaningless utterance.
gab·bler (gab′lẽr), *n.* a person who gabbles.
gab·bro (gab′rō), *n.* [It. < L. *glaber*, bare, smooth], any of a group of dark, heavy igneous rocks, composed chiefly of pyroxene and feldspar.
gab·by (gab′i), *adj.* [see GAB], [Colloq.], talkative; inclined to chatter.
ga·belle (gə-bel′), *n.* [Fr.; It. *gabella;* Ar. *gabālah*], a tax levied in certain countries; especially, a tax on salt, levied in France before the Revolution of 1789.
gab·er·dine (gab′ẽr-dēn′, gab′ẽr-dēn′), *n.* [earlier *gawbardyne;* OFr. *gauvardine, galvardine* < MHG. *walvart*, pilgrimage < *wallen*, to wander about + *vart* a trip < *varen*, to travel], 1. a loose coat or cloak made of coarse cloth, worn in the Middle Ages, especially by Jews. 2. gabardine.
gab·er·lun·zie (gab′ẽr-lun′zi; Scot. gȧb′ẽr-lün′yi), *n.* [Scot.; printing form of *gaberlunyie* (with printed *z* for *y* as in pers. name *Menzies*); earlier also *gaberloonie;* prob. < Scot. Gaelic], a wandering beggar.
ga·bi·on (gā′bi-ən), *n.* [Fr.; It. *gabbione*, large cage < *gabbia*, cage, coop < L. *cavea*, cave, cage], 1. a cylinder of wicker filled with earth or stones, formerly used in building fortifications. 2. a similar cylinder of metal, used in building dams, foundations, etc.
ga·bi·on·ade (gā′bi-ən-ād′), *n.* [Fr. *gabionnade*], a defensive embankment or structure made of gabions.
ga·ble (gā′b'l), *n.* [ME.; OFr.; prob. < ON. *gafl*, gable; basic sense, "forked twig" seen in G. *gabel*, a fork], 1. *a)* the triangular wall enclosed by the sloping ends of a ridged roof. *b)* popularly, the whole section, including wall, roof, and space enclosed. 2. the end wall of a building, the upper part of which is a gable. 3. a triangular decorative feature in architecture, such as that over a door or window. *v.t.* [GABLED (-b'ld), GABLING], to put a gable or gables on. *v.i.* to be in the form of, or end in, a gable.

GABLE (sense 3)

gable roof, a ridged roof forming a gable at one end or both ends
gable window, 1. a window in a gable (sense 2). 2. a window with a gable (sense 3) over it.
Ga·bon (gȧ′bôn′), *n.* a country in west central Africa, on the Gulf of Guinea: a former French colony, it is now a member of the French Community: area, 102,300 sq. mi.; pop., 420,000; capital, Libreville: also **Gabun**.
Ga·bo·riau, É·mile (ā′mēl′ gȧ′bô′ryō′), 1835–1873; French writer of detective stories.
Ga·bri·el (gā′bri-əl), [Heb. *gabhrī'ēl*, lit., God is (my) strength], a masculine name: diminutive, *Gabe;* feminine, *Gabriella, Gabrielle*. *n.* in the *Bible*, one of the seven archangels, the angel of the Annunciation and the herald of good news: Luke 1:26, Dan. 8, 9.
Ga·bri·el·la (gā′bri-el′ə, gab′ri-el′ə), [It. & Sp.], a feminine name: see **Gabriel**.
Ga·bri·elle (gā′bri-el′, gab′ri-el′), [Fr.], a feminine name: see **Gabriel**.
Ga·bri·lo·witsch, Os·sip (ô′süp gȧ-vri-lô′vich; Eng. gä′bri-luv′ich, gə-bril′ə-wich′), 1878–1936; American pianist and conductor, born in Russia.
Ga·bun (gə-bōōn′), *n.* Gabon.
ga·by (gā′bi), *n.* [*pl.* GABIES (-biz)], [< Brit. Midland dial.; also *gawby;* ? echoic formation < *gape, gaup*, after *baby;* cf. ON. *gapi*, reckless person], [Colloq.], a foolish person; simpleton.
Gad (gad), *n.* [Heb. *gādh*, lit., fortune], 1. in the *Bible*, a son of Jacob; hence, 2. a tribe of Israel descended from him. 3. the land where this tribe lived.
Gad, gad (gad), *interj.* [cf. EGAD, etc.], a mild oath or expression of surprise, disgust, etc.: a euphemism for *God*.
gad (gad), *v.i.* [GADDED (-id), GADDING], [? a back-formation < ME. *gadeling*, vagabond; AS. *gædeling*], to roam about in an aimless or restless manner; go about seeking excitement. *n.* [Colloq.], a gadding.
gad (gad), *n.* [ME. *gadd;* ON. *gaddr;* influenced in sense by AS. *gad* (cf. GOAD); akin to Goth. *gazds*, thorn; IE. base **ghasto-*, rod, pole, as also in L. *hasta*, rod, shaft, spear, missile], 1. a goad. 2. a spike; any of several chisellike or pointed bars used in mining. *v.t.* [GADDED (-id), GADDING], 1. to goad. 2. in *mining*, to break up or loosen (ore) with a gad.
gad·a·bout (gad′ə-bout′), *n.* [Colloq.], a person who gads about; one who goes about looking for fun, excitement, etc. *adj.* fond of gadding.
gad·der (gad′ẽr), *n.* a person who gads; gadabout.
gad·fly (gad′flī′), *n.* [*pl.* GADFLIES (-flīz′)], [*gad* (goad) + *fly*], 1. a large fly that stings cattle, etc.; horsefly. 2. a person who annoys or irritates others.
gadg·et (gaj′it), *n.* [< engineering jargon; ? suggested by Scot. *gadge*, form of *gauge*, measuring device + *-et*, dim. suffix], 1. any small mechanical contrivance or device. 2. any small object, especially something relatively useless or superfluous.
Ga·dhel·ic (gə-del′ik, gə-dē′lik, gad′ə-lik), *adj. & n.* Goidelic.
ga·did (gā′did), *n.* [< Mod. L. *Gadidae*, name of the family < *gadus*, cod < Gr. *gados*, kind of fish], any fish of the cod family, as the cod, haddock, pollack, etc.
ga·doid (gā′doid), *adj.* [< Mod. L. *gadus* (see GADID); + *-oid*], of the cod family of fishes, a large family of soft-finned, large-mouthed food fishes with a somewhat lengthened body and wide gill openings, including the codfish, haddock, hake, etc. *n.* any fish of this family.
gad·o·lin·ite (gad′ə-lin-īt′), *n.* [see GADOLINIUM], a brown or black silicate mineral, containing some metals of the rare-earth group in combination with iron.
gad·o·lin·i·um (gad′ə-lin′i-əm), *n.* [after J. *Gadolin*, 18th-c. Finn. chemist], a chemical element of the rare-earth group: symbol, Gd; at. wt., 156.9; at. no., 64.
ga·droon (gə-drōōn′), *n.* [Fr. *godron* < *goder*, to crease, pucker], any of various oval-shaped beadings, flutings, or reedings used to decorate molding, silverware, etc.: also spelled **godroon**.
Gads·den (gadz′dən), *n.* a city in northeastern Alabama: pop., 58,000.
Gadsden, James, 1788–1858; American army officer and diplomat; negotiated purchase of land from Mexico (1853).
gad·wall (gad′wôl), *n.* [*pl.* GADWALLS (-wôlz), GADWALL; see PLURAL, II, D, 1], a grayish-brown wild duck living in the northern fresh-water regions of America.
Gad·zooks (gad′zōōks′, gad′zooks′), *interj.* [< *God's hooks*, nails of the Cross], [Archaic], a mild oath or expletive.
gae (gā), *v.i.* [GAED (gād), GAEN (gān), GAEING], [Scot.], to go.
gae (gā), [Scot.], past tense of **give**.
Gae·a (jē′ə), *n.* [Gr. *Gaia* < *gē*, earth], in *Greek mythology*, the earth personified as a goddess, mother of Uranus, the Titans, etc.; Mother Earth: identified by the Romans with Tellus: also **Gaia, Ge**.
Gaek·wad (gīk′wäd, jēk′wäd), *n.* Gaekwar.
Gaek·war (gīk′wär, jēk′wär), *n.* [Prakrit *Gāekvāḍ*, name of the family (lit., cowherd)], the title of the native prince ruling Baroda, India: also **Gaikwar**.
Gael (gāl), *n.* [contr. < Gael. *Gaidheal;* akin to Ir. *Gaedheal*, OIr. *Góidel*, W. *gwyddel* (Irishman)], a Celt of Scotland, Ireland, or the Isle of Man; especially, a Celt of the Scottish Highlands.
Gael·ic (gāl′ik), *adj.* [< Gael. *Gaidhealach*], 1. of the Gaels. 2. of the Goidelic subfamily of languages or its components; especially, of Scottish Gaelic. *n.* 1. the Goidelic subfamily of languages. 2. one of these languages, especially that of the Scottish Highlands (*Scottish Gaelic*). Abbreviated **Gael.**
gaff (gaf), *n.* [ME. & MFr. *gaffe*, prob. of Celt. origin; cf. Ir. *gaf, gafa*, a hook; for the IE. base, cf. GABLE], 1. a large, strong hook on a pole, or a barbed spear, used in landing large fish. 2. a sharp metal spur fastened to the leg of a gamecock. 3. [British Slang], [earlier in sense of "fair": prob. < fact that visitors

were *gaffed* there], a cheap theater, dance hall, etc. 4. a spar or pole extending diagonally upward from the after side of a mast and supporting a fore-and-aft sail. *v.t.* 1. to strike or land (a fish) with a gaff; hence, 2. [Slang, chiefly British], to cheat; hoax; trick.
stand the gaff, [Slang], to bear up well under difficulties, punishment, ridicule, etc.; be game.

‡gaffe (gaf), *n.* [Fr.], a blunder; faux pas.

gaf·fer (gaf′ẽr), *n.* [altered < *godfather*], 1. an old man, especially one from the country: often used contemptuously or humorously: see also **gammer.** 2. [British], a foreman of a group of workers.

gaff sail, a fore-and-aft sail fastened to a gaff.

gaff-top·sail (gaf′top′s'l, gaf′top′sāl′), *n.* a topsail set above a gaff.

gag (gag), *v.t.* [GAGGED (gagd), GAGGING], [ME. *gaggen;* of echoic origin], 1. to cause to retch or choke. 2. to put something over or into the mouth of, so as to keep from talking, crying out, etc.; hence, 3. to keep (a person) from speaking or expressing himself freely, by intimidation, etc. 4. to prevent or limit speech in (a legislative body). 5. in *mechanics,* to choke or stop up (a valve, etc.). *v.i.* 1. to retch or choke. 2. [Slang], to make a gag or gags; joke. *n.* 1. something put into or over the mouth to prevent talking, crying out, etc. 2. any restraint of free speech. 3. a device for holding the mouth open, as in dentistry. 4. a strong bit for breaking in a horse. 5. *a)* a joke, especially one with an unexpected turn. *b)* a practical joke; hoax or bit of comic business, as on the stage.

gage (gāj), *n.* [ME.; OFr. *gage, guage,* a pledge, pawn < Gmc.; ? < Goth. *wadi,* a surety, pledge, bail, via LL. **wadium;* see WED], 1. something deposited or pledged to insure that an obligation will be fulfilled; security. 2. a pledge to appear and fight, as a glove thrown down by a knight challenging another; hence, 3. a challenge. *v.t.* [GAGED (gājd), GAGING], [Archaic], 1. to offer as a pledge; wager. 2. to bind by a pledge.

gage (gāj), *n.* & *v.t.* gauge.

gage (gāj), *n.* [< *greengage*], any of several varieties of plums: see **greengage.**

Gage, Thomas (gāj), 1721–1787; British general in the American Revolution.

gag·er (gāj′ẽr), *n.* a gauger.

gag·ger (gag′ẽr), *n.* a person or thing that gags; specifically, a piece of iron to keep a core in place in a mold.

gag man, a man who devises jokes, bits of comic business, etc., as for professional comedians.

gag rule (or **law**), a rule or law limiting or preventing discussion: as, in 1836 Congress adopted a *gag rule* to prevent discussion of anything relating to slavery.

gahn·ite (gän′īt), *n.* [after J. G. *Gahn* (1745–1818), Swed. chemist], a zinc aluminate, $ZnAl_2O_4$, found as almost opaque crystals of green, brown, or black.

Gai·a (gā′ə, gī′ə), *n.* Gaea; Ge.

gai·e·ty (gā′ə-ti), *n.* [*pl.* GAIETIES (-tiz)], [Fr. *gaieté*], 1. the state or quality of being gay; cheerfulness. 2. merrymaking; festivity. 3. finery; showy display: as, *gaiety* of plumage. Also spelled **gayety.**

Gaik·war (gīk′wär), *n.* Gaekwar.

Gail (gāl), [contr. or dim. of *Gaylord,* masculine name], a masculine name.

Gail (gāl), a feminine name: see **Abigail.**

Gail·lard Cut (gā′lärd), [after Col. D. DuB. *Gaillard* (1859–1913), Am. army engineer], a section of the Panama Canal, cut through a hill about 10 miles from the city of Panama: length, 7–8 mi.: formerly called *Culebra Cut.*

gail·lar·di·a (gā-lär′di-ə), *n.* [Mod. L., after the Fr. botanist *Gaillard* de Marentonneau], any of a group of American composite plants having large, showy flower heads with yellow or reddish rays and purple disks.

gai·ly (gā′li), *adv.* [ME.], in a gay manner; specifically, *a)* happily; merrily; joyously. *b)* brightly; in bright colors; with bright display. Also spelled **gayly.**

gain (gān), *n.* [ME. *gain, gein;* OFr. *gain, gaaigne* < *gaaignier;* see the *v.*], 1. an increase; addition; specifically, *a) often in pl.* an increase in wealth, earnings, etc.; profit; winnings. *b)* an increase in advantage; advantage; improvement. Opposed to *loss.* 2. in radio, sound reproduction, etc., an increase in signal power from one stage to another in an amplifying system, usually expressed in decibels. 3. the act of getting something; acquisition; accumulation. *v.t.* [ME. *gainen, geinen,* to profit, be of use < OFr. *gaaignier* < OHG. ** weidanjan,* to work, gain < *weidenon,* to pasture < *weide,* pasture], 1. to get by labor; earn. 2. to get by effort or merit, as in competition; win. 3. to get as an increase, addition, profit, or advantage. 4. to get to; arrive at; reach. *v.i.* to make progress; improve or advance, as in health, business, etc. —*SYN.* see **get, reach.**
gain on, 1. to draw nearer to (an opponent in a race, etc.). 2. to make more progress than (a competitor).
gain over, to win over to one's side.

gain (gān), *n.* [prob. < *gain* (increase) with special technical application of sense of "addition"], in *carpentry,* a joining notch, groove, or mortise. *v.t.* to fasten or join by, or fit into, such a notch or groove.

gain·er (gān′ẽr), *n.* 1. a person or thing that gains. 2. a fancy dive in which the diver faces forward and does a backward somersault in the air.

Gaines·ville (gānz′vil), *n.* a city in northern Florida: pop., 30,000.

gain·ful (gān′fəl), *adj.* producing gain; profitable.

gain·ly (gān′li), *adj.* [ME. *geinliche* < *gein,* convenient, ready < ON. *gegn,* straight, favorable; cf. UNGAINLY], shapely and graceful; comely.

gain·say (gān′sā′), *v.t.* [GAINSAID (-sed′, -sād′), GAINSAYING], [ME. *geinseggen; gein-* < AS. *gegn,* against + *seggen* (see SAY)], 1. to deny. 2. to contradict. 3. to speak or act against; oppose; forbid. *n.* (gān′sā′), a gainsaying. —*SYN.* see **deny.**

Gains·bor·ough, Thomas (gānz′bũr′ō, gānz′bẽr-ə), 1727–1788; English painter.

'gainst, gainst (genst, gānst), *prep.* [Poetic], against.

gait (gāt), *n.* [ME. *gate; gaite* (N. & Scot.); special application of ON. *gata,* path between hedges, street, akin to G. *gasse,* lane], 1. manner of moving on foot; way of walking or running. 2. any of the various foot movements of a horse, as a trot, pace, canter, or gallop. *v.t.* to train (a horse) to certain gaits.

gait·ed (gāt′id), *adj.* having a (specified) gait: used in hyphenated compounds, as *heavy-gaited.*

gai·ter (gā′tẽr), *n.* [Fr. *guêtre,* earlier *guietre*], 1. a cloth or leather covering for the instep and ankle, and, sometimes, the calf of the leg; spat or legging. 2. a shoe with elastic in the sides and no lacing. 3. formerly, a variety of high-topped shoe.

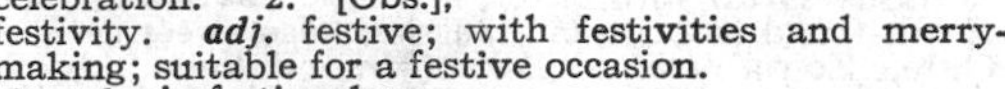
GAITERS

gal (gal), *n.* [Slang], a girl.

Gal., Galatians.

gal., gallon; gallons.

ga·la (gā′lə, gal′ə, gä′lə), *n.* [< Fr. & It.; Fr. *gala;* It. *gala* < OFr. *gale,* enjoyment, pleasure, prob. <MD.*wale,*riches,wealth; akin to Eng. *weal*], 1. a festive occasion; festival; celebration. 2. [Obs.], festivity. *adj.* festive; with festivities and merrymaking; suitable for a festive occasion.
in gala, in festive dress.

ga·lac·ta·gogue (gə-lak′tə-gôg′, gə-lak′tə-gog′), *adj.* [< Gr. *gala, galaktos,* milk + *agōgos,* bringing], that stimulates the secretion of milk. *n.* a galactagogue medicine.

ga·lac·tic (gə-lak′tik), *adj.* [Gr. *galaktikos,* milky < *gala, galaktos,* milk], 1. of or obtained from milk; lactic. 2. in *astronomy,* of the Milky Way, or Galaxy. 3. in *medicine,* of or increasing the flow of milk.

ga·lac·to- (gə-lak′tō, gə-lak′tə), [Gr. *gala, galaktos,* milk], a combining form meaning *milk, milky,* as in *galactometer:* also, before a vowel, **galact-.**

gal·ac·tom·e·ter (gal′ak-tom′ə-tẽr), *n.* [*galacto-* + *-meter*], a hydrometer for testing milk by measuring its specific gravity.

ga·lac·tose (gə-lak′tōs), *n.* [*galact-* + *-ose*], a white, crystalline sugar, $C_6H_{12}O_6$, prepared by the hydrolysis of lactose.

Gal·a·had (gal′ə-had′), *n.* 1. in late Arthurian legend, a knight who was successful in the quest for the Holy Grail because of his purity and nobility of spirit: he was the son of Lancelot and Elaine. 2. any man regarded as very pure and noble.

gal·a·lith (gal′ə-lith′), *n.* [Gr. *gala,* milk (see GALAXY); + *-lith*], an insulating material made from casein.

ga·lan·gal (gə-laŋ′gəl), *n.* galingale.

gal·an·gale (gal′ən-gāl′), *n.* galingale.

gal·an·tine (gal′ən-tēn′), *n.* [ME. & OFr. *galentine;* ML. *galatina,* jelly < L. *gelata,* fem. pp. of *gelare,* to congeal], a mold of boned, seasoned, boiled white meat, as chicken or veal, chilled and served in its own jelly.

ga·lan·ty show (gə-lan′ti), [earlier also *galanté;* prob. < It. *galante,* gallant: from the stories portrayed], a pantomime made by throwing the shadows of puppet figures on a screen or wall.

Ga·lá·pa·gos Islands (gə-lä′pə-gōs′; Sp. gä-lä′pä-gôs′), a group of islands in the Pacific, on the equator: a possession of Ecuador: area, 2,868 sq. mi.; pop., 1,700: also called *Colón Archipelago.*

Ga·la·ta (gä′lä-tä), *n.* a suburb of Istanbul, Turkey.

Gal·a·te·a (gal′ə-tē′ə), *n.* [L.; Gr. *Galateia*], in *Greek legend,* a statue of a maiden carved in ivory by Pygmalion, king of Cyprus: he fell in love with it and it was given life by Aphrodite.

gal·a·te·a (gal′ə-tē′ə), *n.* [after *Galatea*, name of an English warship: the fabric was used to make sailor suits for little boys], a strong cotton cloth, usually striped, used chiefly for children's clothing.

Ga·la·ţi (gȧ-läts′), *n.* a city in eastern Romania, on the Danube: pop., 100,000.

Ga·la·tia (gə-lā′shə), *n.* an ancient kingdom, and later a Roman province, in central Asia Minor: see **Roman Empire**, map.

Ga·la·tian (gə-lā′shən), *adj.* of Galatia or its people. *n.* a native or inhabitant of Galatia.

Ga·la·tians (gə-lā′shənz), *n.* the Epistle to the Galatians, a book of the New Testament which was a message from the Apostle Paul to the Christians of Galatia: abbreviated **Gal.**

Ga·latz (gä′läts), *n.* Galati.

gal·a·vant (gal′ə-vant′), *v.i.* to gallivant.

ga·lax (gā′laks), *n.* [Mod. L. < Gr. *gala*, milk: from its white flower], an evergreen herb with shiny leaves (often used in wreaths) and small, white flowers, found in mountain regions of the southeastern United States.

gal·ax·y (gal′ək-si), *n.* [Fr. *galaxie;* L. *galaxias;* Gr. *galaxias*, Milky Way < *gala, galaktos*, milk], 1. [often G-], the Milky Way, a grouping of millions of stars apparently merging into a luminous band that extends across the sky. 2. [*pl.* GALAXIES (-siz)], any similar but smaller grouping of stars. 3. *a)* an assembly of brilliant or famous people. *b)* a brilliant array of things.

Gal·ba (gal′bə, gôl′bə), *n.* (*Servius Sulpicius Galba*), Roman emperor (68–69 A.D.); lived 5? B.C.–69 A.D.

gal·ba·num (gal′bə-nəm), *n.* [L.; Gr. *chalbanē;* Heb. *ḥelbenāh*], a bitter, bad-smelling Asiatic gum resin, used in medicine and the arts.

Gal·cha (gal′chä), *n.* [< the native name], 1. [*pl.* GALCHA], a member of a people living in the Pamirs, west central Asia: also called *Pamiri.* 2. their Iranian language: also called *Pamir.*

gale (gāl), *n.* [prob. < Anglo-N. *gaul (ON. *gol*), wind, blast of wind, with softened meaning as in Norw. *gul*, steady wind, *gaul*, moderate gale; akin to ON. *gola*, Eng. *yowl*, to howl (IE. base **ghēu-*, to bark, yawn)], 1. a strong wind; specifically, in *meteorology*, one ranging in speed from 32 to 63 miles per hour: designated as moderate (32–38 mph), fresh (39–46 mph), strong (47–54 mph), and whole (55–63 mph). 2. [Poetic], a breeze. 3. an outburst: as, a *gale* of laughter. 4. [Colloq.], a state of excitement or hilarity. —*SYN.* see **wind.**

gale (gāl), *n.* [ME. *gawel;* AS. *gagel;* akin to G. *gagel*], a hardy shrub with bitter, aromatic leaves and yellow fruit, found in bogs and marshes: also **sweet gale.**

Gale, Zo·na (zō′nə gāl), (*Mrs. William Llywelyn Breese*), 1874–1938; American novelist and playwright.

ga·le·a (gā′li-ə), *n.* [*pl.* GALEAE (-ē′)], [L., a helmet; prob. < Gr. *galeē*, a weasel, marten (hence, leather, hide, then article made of leather)], in *botany & zoology*, a helmet-shaped part, as of a flower.

ga·le·ate (gā′li-āt′), *adj.* [L. *galeatus*, pp. of *galeare*, to cover with a helmet < *galea*, a helmet], 1. wearing a helmet. 2. helmet-shaped. 3. having a galea.

ga·le·at·ed (gā′li-ā′tid), *adj.* galeate.

Ga·len (gā′lən), *n.* (*Claudius Galen*), Greek physician and writer of the 2nd century A.D.

ga·le·na (gə-lē′nə), *n.* [L., lead ore, dross of melted lead; ? < Gr. *galēnē*, lit., stillness of the sea, calm, anything that produces tranquillity, hence antidote to poison], native lead sulfide, PbS, a lead-gray mineral with metallic luster: it is the principal ore of lead, often also containing silver: also called *galenite.*

Ga·len·ic, ga·len·ic (gə-len′ik), *adj.* of Galen or his medical teachings or methods.

Ga·len·i·cal, ga·len·i·cal (gə-len′i-kəl), *adj.* Galenic.

ga·len·ite (gə-lē′nīt), *n.* galena.

Gales·burg (gālz′bẽrg), *n.* a city in northwestern Illinois: pop., 37,000.

Ga·li·bi (gä-lē′bē), *n.* any member of a subdivision of Carib Indians living in the Guianas.

Ga·li·cia (gə-lish′ə), *n.* 1. (*also*, Sp. gä-lē′thyä), a former province of northwestern Spain. 2. a former province of southern Poland: now divided between Poland and the Ukrainian S.S.R.

Ga·li·cian (gə-lish′ən), *adj.* 1. of Spanish Galicia, its people, or language. 2. of Polish Galicia or its people. *n.* 1. a native or inhabitant of Spanish Galicia. 2. the Portuguese dialect of the Spanish Galicians. 3. a native or inhabitant of Polish Galicia.

Gal·i·le·an (gal′ə-lē′ən), *adj.* of Galilee or its people. *n.* 1. a native or inhabitant of Galilee. 2. a Christian. **the Galilean**, Jesus.

Gal·i·le·an (gal′ə-lē′ən), *adj.* of Galileo.

Gal·i·lee (gal′ə-lē′), *n.* an ancient division of northern Palestine: see **Samaria**, map.

gal·i·lee (gal′ə-lē′), *n.* [OFr. *galilee, galileye;* ML. *galilaea* < L. *Galilaea*, Galilee: so named apparently because, being at the less sacred western end, it was compared with the scriptural "Galilee of the Gentiles," considered inferior by the Jews], a porch or chapel at the western entrance of certain medieval churches.

Galilee, Sea of, a small lake in northeastern Palestine: also called *Sea of Tiberias.*

Gal·i·le·o (gal′ə-lē′ō), *n.* (*Galileo Galilei*), Italian astronomer and physicist; 1564–1642; demonstrated the truth of the Copernican theory with the telescope; condemned for heresy by the Inquisition.

gal·i·ma·ti·as (gal′ə-mā′shi-əs, gal′ə-mat′i-əs), *n.* [Fr.; < ?; cf. GALLIMAUFRY], meaningless talk; gibberish.

gal·in·gale (gal′in-gāl′), *n.* [ME.; OFr. *galingal;* ML. *galanga;* Ar. *khalanjān;* ? via Per. < Chin.], 1. the pungent, aromatic root stem of various East Indian plants of the ginger family. 2. a sedge with a pungent root, growing in the south of England; sweet sedge. Also **galangal, galangale.**

gal·i·ot (gal′i-ət), *n.* [ME. *galiote;* OFr., dim. of *galie* < ML. *galea;* see GALLEY], 1. a small, swift galley with sails and oars, formerly used on the Mediterranean. 2. a light, Dutch merchant ship of shallow draught, with a single mast and leeboards, somewhat resembling a sailing barge. Also spelled **galliot.**

gal·i·pot (gal′i-pot′), *n.* [Fr.; earlier *garipot*, apparently altered < MD. *harpois*, boiled resin], crude turpentine from certain pine trees of southern Europe: also spelled **gallipot.**

gall (gôl), *n.* [ME. *galle, gawle;* AS. (Anglian) *galla* (W.S. *gealla*); akin to G. *galle;* IE. base **ĝhel-*, etc., "to shine, yellow," seen also in L. *fel*, gall, Gr. *cholē*, bile (cf. CHOLER, CHOLERA)], 1. a bitter, greenish fluid secreted by the liver of an animal and stored in the gall bladder; bile. 2. the gall bladder. 3. something that is bitter or distasteful. 4. bitter feeling; rancor. 5. [Colloq.], impudence; audacity; effrontery. —*SYN.* see **temerity.**

gall (gôl), *n.* [ME. *galle;* AS. *gealla;* ? < L. *galla*, a gallnut, but prob. connected with OFr. *galle*, an itching, sore (of same origin)], 1. a sore on the skin caused by rubbing or chafing; especially, such a sore on a horse. 2. *a)* irritation; annoyance; vexation. *b)* a cause of this. 3. a spot worn bare; flaw or weak spot. *v.t.* [ME. *gallen;* prob. back-formation < AS. *geallede*, galled < the *n.*], 1. to make (the skin) sore by rubbing or chafing; chafe. 2. to irritate; annoy; vex. *v.i.* to become sore from rubbing or chafing.

gall (gôl), *n.* [ME. & OFr. *galle;* L. *galla*, gallnut, orig., prob., spherical growth < IE. base **gel-*, to form into a ball], a tumor on plant tissue caused by irritation due to fungi, insects, or bacteria: galls formed on oak trees have a high tannic acid content and are used commercially.

Gal·la (gal′ə), *n.* [ult. < Ar. *ghaliz*, wild], 1. a member of one of the Hamitic tribes living in British Somaliland and southern Ethiopia. 2. the language of the Gallas.

gal·la·lith (gal′ə-lith′), *n.* galalith.

gal·lant (gal′ənt), *adj.* [OFr. *galant*, gay, brave, ppr. of *galer*, to rejoice, make merry < *gale;* see GALA], 1. fine; showy; gay: as, *gallant* attire. 2. stately; imposing; grand: as, a *gallant* ship. 3. brave and noble; high-spirited and daring: as, a *gallant* warrior. 4. (gə-lant′, gal′ənt), *a)* polite and attentive to women in a courtly way. *b)* having to do with love; amorous. *n.* (gal′ənt, gə-lant′), 1. a high-spirited, brave, noble man. 2. a man attentive and polite to women. 3. *a)* a lover. *b)* a paramour. *v.t.* (gə-lant′), 1. to court (a woman). 2. to escort or accompany (a woman). *v.i.* to behave like a gallant. —*SYN.* see **civil.**

gal·lant·ry (gal′ən-tri), *n.* [*pl.* GALLANTRIES (-triz)], [Fr. *gallanterie* < *galant;* see GALLANT], 1. nobility of behavior or spirit; heroic courage. 2. the behavior of a gallant; courtly manner. 3. *usually in pl.* an act or speech characteristic of a gallant. 4. amorous intrigue. 5. [Archaic], gay or showy appearance or display.

Gal·la·tin, Albert (gal′ə-tin), 1761–1849; American statesman, born in Switzerland; secretary of the treasury (1801–1814).

gall bladder, a membranous sac attached to the liver, in which excess gall or bile is stored and concentrated.

Galle (gäl), *n.* a seaport in southwestern Ceylon: pop., 56,000.

gal·le·ass (gal′i-as′, gal′i-əs), *n.* [Fr. *galéasse;* OFr. *galeace;* It. *galeazza* < *galea;* ML. *galea;* see GALLEY], a large, three-masted vessel having sails and oars and carrying heavy guns: used on the Mediterranean in the 16th and 17th centuries.

gal·le·on (gal′i-ən), *n.* [Fr. *galion* (< OFr. *galie*, a galley) or Sp. *galeon;* both < ML. *galea;* see GALLEY], a large, heavy Spanish ship of the 15th and 16th centuries, with three or four decks at the stern and one or more at the bow: it was used as both a warship and a trader.

GALLEON

gal·ler·ied (gal′ẽr-id), *adj.* [pp. of *gallery*], having a gallery or galleries.

gal·ler·y (gal′ẽr-i), *n.* [*pl.* GALLERIES (-iz)], [Fr. *galerie, gallerie,* long portico, gallery; ML. *galeria;* ? < *galilaea;* see GALILEE (a porch)], 1. a covered walk or porch open at one side or having the roof supported by pillars; colonnade; portico. 2. a long, narrow platform on the outside of a building, above the ground; balcony. 3. a platform or balcony at the quarters or around the stern of an early sailing ship. 4. a platform or projecting upper floor attached to the back wall or sides of a church, theater, etc.; especially, the highest of a series of such platforms in a theater, with the cheapest seats; hence, 5. the cheapest seats in a theater. 6. the people occupying these seats, sometimes regarded as exemplifying popular tastes; hence, 7. popular, or uncultivated, tastes. 8. any group of spectators at a sporting event, legislative meeting, etc. 9. a long, narrow corridor or room. 10. a place or establishment for art exhibitions. 11. a collection of paintings, statues, etc. 12. a place or establishment, originally resembling a gallery (sense 9), for taking photographs, shooting at targets, etc.: as, a shooting *gallery.* 13. an underground passage, as one made by an animal, or one used in mining or military engineering. *v.t.* [GALLERIED (-id), GALLERYING], to furnish with a gallery, or balcony. *v.i.* to make a gallery, or underground passage.

play to the gallery, 1. in the *theater,* to act in a manner that will please those in the gallery; hence, 2. to try to win the applause or approval of the public, especially by obvious or easy means.

gal·let (gal′it), *n.* [Fr. *galet,* pebble, dim. < dial. *gal,* stone, round stone < ON. *valr,* round, oval], a chip of stone. *v.t.* in *masonry,* to fill (joints) with gallets.

gal·ley (gal′i), *n.* [*pl.* GALLEYS (-iz)], [ME. *galeie;* OFr. *galie, galee;* ML. *galea;* MGr. *galaia,* kind of ship], 1. a long, low, usually single-decked ship propelled by oars and sails, used especially in ancient and medieval times: the oars were usually manned by chained slaves or convicts. 2. a large rowboat on British warships, for the captain's use. 3. a ship's kitchen. 4. in *printing, a)* a shallow oblong tray for holding composed type. *b)* a galley proof.

GALLEY

galley proof, printer's proof taken from type in a galley to permit correction of errors before the type is made up in pages.

galley slave, 1. a slave or convict sentenced or compelled to pull an oar on a galley; hence, 2. anyone who must do hard, monotonous work; drudge.

gal·ley-west (gal′i-west′), *adv.* [Colloq.], completely; into smithereens: only in the phrase *knock galley-west.*

gall·fly (gôl′flī′), *n.* [*pl.* GALLFLIES (-flīz′)], an insect whose eggs cause galls when deposited on plant stems.

Gal·li·a (gal′i-ə), *n.* Gaul: the Latin name.

gal·liard (gal′yərd), *adj.* [ME. & OFr. *gaillard,* thorough, sturdy, gay (prob. by association with *gai,* gay); prob. of Celt. origin (cf. Cymric *gallu,* ability)], [Obs.], 1. valiant; sturdy. 2. lively. *n.* 1. a lively French dance in triple time, for two dancers, popular in the 16th and 17th centuries. 2. music for this.

gal·li·ass (gal′i-as′), *n.* a galleass.

Gal·lic (gal′ik), *adj.* [L. *Gallicus* < *Galli,* the Gauls], 1. of ancient Gaul or its people. 2. French.

gal·lic (gal′ik), *adj.* [Fr. *gallique* < *galle;* L. *galla,* gallnut], designating or of an acid, $(OH)_3C_6H_2 \cdot COOH$, prepared from nutgalls, tannin, etc. and used in the manufacture of inks, dyes, etc.

Gal·li·can (gal′i-kən), *adj.* [L. *Gallicanus,* of the Roman province of Gallia < *Gallicus*], 1. Gallic. 2. of the Roman Catholic Church in France, especially before 1870. 3. of Gallicanism. *n.* 1. a French Roman Catholic. 2. a supporter of Gallicanism.

Gal·li·can·ism (gal′i-kən-iz′m), *n.* [< L. *Gallicanus* (see GALLICAN); + *-ism*], the principles enunciated by the French Roman Catholic Church in 1682, claiming limited autonomy.

Gal·li·cism, gal·li·cism (gal′ə-siz′m), *n.* [Fr. *Gallicisme* < L. *Gallicus;* see GALLIC], 1. French idiom or expression, used in another language (e.g., "it gives one furiously to think"). 2. French custom, way of thought, etc.

Gal·li·cize (gal′ə-sīz′), *v.t.* & *v.i.* [GALLICIZED (-sīzd′), GALLICIZING], [see GALLIC], to make or become French or like the French in thought, language, etc.

Gal·li-Cur·ci, A·me·li·ta (ä′me-lē′tä gäl′lē-kōōr′chē; Eng. gal′i-kûr′chi), 1889– ; American coloratura soprano, born in Italy.

gal·li·gas·kins (gal′i-gas′kinz), *n.pl.* [altered < Fr. *garguesque* < OFr. *garguesque, greguesque;* It. *grechesca* < *Grechesca,* Grecian (hence, orig., "Grecian breeches"); form altered by association with *Gascony* & *galley*], 1. loosely fitting breeches worn in the 16th and 17th centuries: later applied humorously to any loose breeches. 2. [British Dial.], leggings or gaiters.

gal·li·mau·fry (gal′ə-mô′fri), *n.* [*pl.* GALLIMAUFRIES (-friz)], [Fr. *galimafrée*], 1. a hash made of meat scraps; hence, 2. a hodgepodge; jumbled assortment.

gal·li·na·cean (gal′ə-nā′shən), *adj.* gallinaceous. *n.* any gallinaceous bird.

gal·li·na·ceous (gal′ə-nā′shəs), *adj.* [L. *gallinaceus* < *gallina,* hen < *gallus,* a cock], of, or having the nature of, a large group of birds that nest on the ground, including common poultry, pheasants, grouse, etc.

gall·ing (gôl′iŋ), *adj.* [ppr. of *gall* (to wear away)], chafing; irritating; vexing.

gal·li·nip·per (gal′ə-nip′ẽr), *n.* [< *galley* + *nipper;* humorous formation; cf. GALLEY-WEST], [Colloq.], a large mosquito or other insect that can bite or sting painfully.

gal·li·nule (gal′ə-nūl′, gal′ə-nōōl′), *n.* [L. *gallinula,* dim. of *gallina;* see GALLINACEOUS], any of several wading birds of the rail family.

gal·li·ot (gal′i-ət), *n.* a galiot.

Gal·lip·o·li (gə-lip′ə-li), *n.* 1. a peninsula in European Turkey, along the north shore of the Dardanelles. 2. a city on this peninsula, at the entrance to the Sea of Marmara: pop., 25,000.

gal·li·pot (gal′ə-pot′), *n.* [prob. < *galley* + *pot;* such pots were orig. shipped from Italy], a small pot or jar of glazed earthenware, especially one used by druggists as a container for medicine.

gal·li·pot (gal′i-pot′), *n.* galipot.

gal·li·um (gal′i-əm), *n.* [Mod. L. < L. *Gallia,* Gaul; also a pun on L. *gallus,* a cock, transl. of *Lecoq,* first name of the discoverer, Lecoq de Boisbaudran], a soft, bluish-white, metallic chemical element with an unusually low melting point (29.75° C. or 85.5° F.), used as a substitute for mercury in thermometers, dental amalgam, etc.: symbol, Ga; at. wt., 69.72; at. no., 31.

gal·li·vant (gal′ə-vant′, gal′ə-vant′), *v.i.* [arbitrary elaboration of *gallant*], 1. to play the gallant or beau; go about with members of the opposite sex. 2. to go about in search of amusement or excitement; gad.

gal·li·wasp (gal′i-wäsp′, gal′i-wôsp′), *n.* [< *galley* + *wasp:* apparently first used of a West Indian wasp that infested ships], a large, harmless lizard found in marshes in the West Indies and Central America.

gall midge, any of several very small flies that produce galls on trees, etc.

gall·nut (gôl′nut′), *n.* a nutlike gall, especially on oaks.

Gal·lo- (gal′ō), [L. < *Gallus,* a Gaul], a combining form meaning: 1. *French,* as in *Gallophile.* 2. *French and.*

gal·lo·glass (gal′ō-glas′), *n.* [Ir. ‡*gallōglach,* servant, heavily armed soldier; *gall,* foreigner + *ōglach,* a youth, servant, soldier], an armed follower of any of the old Irish chieftains: also spelled **gallowglass.**

gal·lon (gal′ən), *n.* [ME. *galoun;* ONorm.Fr. *galon;* OFr. *jalon* < base of LL. *galleta,* a jug, liquid measure], 1. a liquid measure, equal to 4 quarts (231 cubic inches): the British imperial gallon equals 277.42 cubic inches. 2. a dry measure, equal to 1/8 bushel. 3. any container with a capacity of one gallon. Abbreviated **gal., gall.**

gal·loon (gə-lōōn′), *n.* [Fr. *galon* < *galonner,* to braid, adorn with lace], 1. a cotton, silk, or worsted braid or ribbon used for trimming or binding. 2. such braid woven of gold or silver thread.

gal·loot (gə-lōōt′), *n.* [Slang], a galoot.

gal·lop (gal′əp), *n.* [OFr. *galop* < *galoper,* to gallop, for *waloper* < Frank. **walahlaupan,* to run well; *wala,* well + *hlaupan,* to run], 1. the fastest gait of a horse or other animal, consisting of a succession of leaping strides with all the feet off the ground at one time. 2. a ride on a galloping animal. 3. [Colloq.], any fast pace, speedy action, or rapid progression. *v.i.* 1. to go at a gallop. 2. to move, progress, or act very fast; hurry. *v.t.* to cause to gallop.

gal·lo·pade (gal′ə-pād′), *n.* [Fr. *galopade* < *galoper;* see GALLOP & -ADE], 1. a lively dance of Hungarian origin. 2. music for this.

gal·lop·er (gal′əp-ẽr), *n.* 1. a person or animal that gallops. 2. formerly, *a)* a light, two-wheeled gun carriage used as a mount for a light cannon. *b)* the gun mounted on this.

gal·lous (gal′əs), *adj.* [*gallium* + *-ous*], in *chemistry,* containing gallium with a valence of two.

Gal·lo·way (gal′ə-wā′), *n.* 1. a district of southwestern Scotland, consisting of Wigtown, Kircudbright, and Dumfries counties. 2. a horse of a small, hardy breed originated in Galloway. 3. a breed of beef cattle.

gal·low·glass (gal′ō-glas′), *n.* a galloglass.

gal·lows (gal′ōz), *n.* [*pl.* GALLOWSES (-iz), GALLOWS], [ME. *galowes, galwes,* pl. of *galwe, galge;* AS. *galga;* akin to G. *galgen;* IE. base **ghalgh-,* pliant branch of a tree, pole (the earliest gallows was a pulled-down branch that carried the victim with it when allowed to spring back into normal position; cf. GALLOWS TREE)], 1. an upright frame with a crossbeam, for hanging condemned persons. 2. any structure like this, used for suspending or supporting. 3. the punishment of hanging. 4. a gallows bird.

gallows bird, [Colloq.], a person who deserves to be hanged.

gallows tree, [for AS. *galgtreow*], a gallows.

gall·stone (gôl′stōn′), *n.* a small, solid mass sometimes formed in the gall bladder or bile duct; biliary calculus: it is formed of cholesterol or, occasionally, of calcium salts, and can obstruct the flow of bile, causing a painful diseased condition.

gal·lus·es (gal′əs-iz), *n.pl.* [< *gallus*, dial. var. of *gallows*], [Colloq.], suspenders; braces.

ga·loot (gə-lo͞ot′), *n.* [orig., naval slang; ? < D. *gelubt*, eunuch (so according to Weekley); cf. LUBBER], [Slang], a person, especially an awkward, ungainly person: also spelled **galloot.**

gal·op (gal′əp), *n.* [Fr.; see GALLOP], 1. a lively dance in 2/4 time. 2. music for this. *v.i.* to dance a galop.

ga·lore (gə-lôr′), *adv.* [Ir. *go leōr*, enough; *go*, to + *leōr*, enough], in abundance; plentifully: as, she has dresses *galore*. *n.* [Rare], abundance.

ga·losh, ga·loshe (gə-losh′), *n.* [ME. & OFr. *galoche*; prob. ult. < Gr. *kalopous*, wooden shoe, shoemaker's last < *kalon*, wood + *pous*, the foot], 1. originally, *a)* a heavy shoe; clod. *b)* any boot or shoe. 2. *usually in pl.* any protective overshoe; especially, a high, warmly lined overshoe of rubber and waterproof fabric: also spelled **golosh, goloshe.**

gals., gallons.

Gals·wor·thy, John (gôlz′wũr′*th*i, galz′wũr′*th*i), 1867–1933; English novelist and dramatist; received Nobel prize in literature, 1932.

Gal·ton, Sir **Francis** (gôl′t′n), 1822–1911; English anthropologist, meteorologist, and writer; pioneer in eugenics.

ga·lumph (gə-lumf′), *v.i.* [coined by Lewis Carroll < *gallop* + *triumph*], to march or prance along in a self-satisfied, triumphant manner.

Gal·va·ni, Lu·i·gi (lo͞o-ē′jē gäl-vä′nē; Eng. gal-vä′ni), 1737–1798; Italian physiologist and physicist: see **galvanism.**

gal·van·ic (gal-van′ik), *adj.* [< *galvanism* + *-ic*], 1. of, caused by, or producing an electric current, especially from a battery: abbreviated **galv.** 2. stimulating or stimulated as if by electric shock; startling.

gal·van·i·cal (gal-van′i-k′l), *adj.* galvanic.

gal·va·nism (gal′və-niz′m), *n.* [Fr. *galvanisme*; It. *galvanismo*: so called after the first investigator in the field, L. *Galvani*], 1. electricity produced by chemical action. 2. the branch of physics that deals with this. 3. the use of electricity in the treatment of disease.

gal·va·ni·za·tion (gal′və-ni-zā′shən, gal′və-nī-zā′shən), *n.* a galvanizing or being galvanized.

gal·va·nize (gal′və-nīz′), *v.t.* [GALVANIZED (-nīzd′), GALVANIZING], [Fr. *galvanizer* < *galvanisme*; see GALVANISM], 1. to apply an electric current to. 2. to stimulate as if by electric shock; startle; excite. 3. to plate (metal) with zinc, originally by galvanic action.

galvanized iron, iron coated with zinc as a protection against rust.

gal·va·no- (gal′və-nō, gal-van′ō), a combining form meaning *galvanic, galvanism*, as in *galvanometer*.

gal·va·nom·e·ter (gal′və-nom′ə-tẽr), *n.* [*galvano-* + *-meter*], an instrument for detecting, and determining the intensity and direction of, an electric current.

gal·va·no·met·ric (gal′və-nō-met′rik), *adj.* 1. having to do with a galvanometer or galvanometry. 2. measured by a galvanometer.

gal·va·nom·e·try (gal′və-nom′ə-tri), *n.* the determining of the intensity and direction of electric currents by means of a galvanometer.

gal·va·no·plas·tics (gal′və-nō-plas′tiks, gal-van′ō-plas′tiks), *n.pl.* [construed as sing.], [*galvano-* + *plastics*], the process of coating things with metal by means of electrolysis; especially, electrotypy.

gal·va·no·scope (gal-van′ə-skōp′, gal′və-nō-skōp′), *n.* [*galvano-* + *-scope*], an instrument for detecting very weak electric currents and indicating their direction.

gal·va·nos·co·py (gal′və-nos′kə-pi), *n.* the use of a galvanoscope, especially in medical diagnosis.

gal·va·no·ther·my (gal′və-nō-thũr′mi, gal-van′ō-thũr′mi), *n.* [< *galvano-* + Gr. *thermē*, heat], the production of heat by galvanism, as for medical treatment.

Gal·ves·ton (gal′vis-t′n), *n.* a seaport in southeastern Texas: pop., 67,000.

Galveston Bay, an arm of the Gulf of Mexico, southeast of Texas.

Gal·way (gôl′wā), *n.* 1. a county of Connaught province, Ireland: pop., 156,000. 2. its capital.

Gal·we·gian (gal-wē′jən), *adj.* of Galloway or its people. *n.* a native or inhabitant of Galloway.

gal·yak, gal·yac (gal′yak), *n.* [< word used in Bokhara for a premature lamb < Russ. *golyak*, bare, naked < IE. base **gal-*, seen also in Eng. *callow*], a flat, glossy fur made from the pelts of lambs or kids.

gam (gam), *n.* [prob. < Scand.; cf. Norw., Sw. dial. *gams*, loose conversation, light behaviour < synonymous ON. *gems*; akin to Eng. *game, gammon* (cf. GAME)], 1. a social visit. 2. an exchange of visits between the crews of whaling ships at sea. 3. a school of whales. *v.i.* [GAMMED (gamd), GAMMING], 1. to visit socially, especially at sea. 2. to come together; congregate: said of whales. *v.t.* to have a social visit with, especially at sea.

gam (gam), *n.* [var. of *gamb*], [Slang], a leg; especially, a woman's leg.

Gam·a, Vas·co da (vas′kō də gam′ə; Port. dä gä′mä), 1469?–1524; Portuguese navigator; discovered the sea route around Africa to India.

Ga·ma·li·el (gə-mā′li-əl, gə-māl′yəl), [L.; Gr. *Gamaliēl*; Heb. *gamlī'ēl*, lit., reward of God], a masculine name. *n.* in the *Bible*, 1. a teacher of Saul of Tarsus: Acts 22:3. 2. a ruler of Manasseh: Numb. 10:23.

gamb, gambe (gamb), *n.* [dial. Fr. *gambe* (Fr. *jambe*); ML. *gamba*, a leg (in LL., a hoof) < Gr. *kampē*, a turn, bend (of a limb), joint], an animal's leg or shank, especially as shown on a coat of arms.

gam·bade (gam-bād′), *n.* a gambado.

gam·ba·do (gam-bā′dō), *n.* [*pl.* GAMBADOS, GAMBADOES (-dōz)], 1. [Sp. *gambada*; It. *gambata*, a kick < *gamba*, a leg; see GAMB], a curvetting leap, by or as by a horse; hence, 2. a prank or antic. 3. [< It. *gamba*, a leg], a long legging or gaiter attached to a saddle to serve as a stirrup; hence, 4. any long gaiter.

gam·be·son (gam′bi-s′n), *n.* [ME.; OFr. *gambeson*, *gambaison* < *gambais, wambais*; ML. *wambasium* < LGr. *bambax*, cotton; see BOMBAST], a medieval coat, made of leather or quilted cloth, worn as armor.

Gam·bet·ta, Lé·on (lā′ōn′ gän′be′tȧ′; Eng. gam-bet′ə), 1838–1882; French statesman; premier (1881–1882).

Gam·bi·a (gam′bi-ə), *n.* 1. *a)* a British protectorate on the western coast of Africa. *b)* a colony in this protectorate. Bathurst is the capital of both colony and protectorate: area (of both), 3,977 sq. mi.; pop. (of both), 289,000. 2. a river flowing from Guinea, through Gambia, to the Atlantic: length, 500 mi.

gam·bier (gam′bêr′), *n.* [Malay *gambir*], an astringent substance extracted from the leaves of a Malayan plant, used in medicine, tanning, and dyeing.

Gam·bier Islands (gam′bêr′), a group of French islands in the Tuamotu Archipelago, South Pacific: area, 12 sq. mi.; pop., 7,000; chief island, Mangareva.

gam·bit (gam′bit), *n.* [Fr.; OFr. *gambet*; Sp. *gambeta*, *gambito*, a tripping < *gamba*, a leg; LL. *gamba*; see GAMB], in *chess*, an opening in which a pawn or other piece is sacrificed to get an advantage in position.

gam·ble (gam′b′l), *v.i.* [GAMBLED (-b′ld), GAMBLING], [prob. dial. var. of ME. *gamen, gamenen*; AS. *gamenian*, to play, game; akin to G. dial. *gammeln, gameln*, to sport, make merry; form may be influenced by *gambol* (but cf. THIMBLE)], 1. to play games of chance for money or some other stake. 2. to take a risk in order to gain some advantage. *v.t.* 1. to squander or lose in gambling (with *away*). 2. to bet; wager. *n.* an act or undertaking involving risk of a loss.

gam·bler (gam′blẽr), *n.* a person who gambles or is fond of gambling; especially, one who makes a living by gambling.

gam·boge (gam-bōj′, gam-bo͞ozh′), *n.* [Mod. L. *gambogium* < *Cambodia*], 1. a gum resin extracted from certain Asiatic trees, used as a yellow pigment and as a cathartic. 2. bright yellow.

gam·bol (gam′bəl), *n.* [earlier *gambolde* < Fr. *gambade*, a gambol; It. *gambata*, a kick < *gamba*, a leg; see GAMBIT], a jumping and skipping about in play; frolic. *v.i.* [GAMBOLED or GAMBOLLED (-bəld), GAMBOLING or GAMBOLLING], to jump and skip about in play; frolic. —*SYN.* see **play.**

gam·brel (gam′brəl), *n.* [OFr. *gamberel*; prob. < *gambe*, leg; It. *gamba*, a leg; see GAMBIT], 1. the hock of a horse or similar animal. 2. a frame shaped like a horse's hind leg, used by butchers for hanging carcasses. 3. a gambrel roof.

gambrel roof, a roof with two slopes on each side, the lower steeper than the upper, which form the ridge: also **gambrel.**

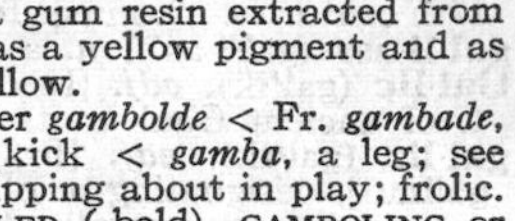

GAMBREL ROOF

game (gām), *n.* [ME. *game(n), gamme(n)*; AS. *gamen*; akin to OFris. *game*, OHG. *gaman*, etc.; IE. base **ghem-*, to leap joyfully, spring, seen also in MHG. *gampen*, to leap; cf. GAM, GAMMON], 1. any form of play or way of playing; amusement; recreation; sport; frolic; play. 2. *a)* any specific amusement or sport involving competition under specific rules: as, football and chess are *games*. *b)* a single contest in such a competition: as, he went to a basketball *game*. 3. *a)* the number of points required for winning: as, the *game* is 25. *b)* the score at any given point in a competition: as, at the half the *game* was 7 to 6. *c)* that which is gained by winning; victory; win. 4. a set of equipment for a competitive amusement: as, toys and *games* are sold here. 5. a way or quality of playing in competition: as, that halfback plays a good *game*. 6. any test of skill, courage, or endurance: as, the *game* of life. 7. a project; scheme; plan: as, he saw through my *game*. 8. wild birds, fish, or animals hunted for sport or for use as food. 9. the flesh of such creatures used as food. 10. [Colloq.], any object of pursuit. 11. [Slang], a business or vocation, especially one with an element of risk: as, the stock-market *game*. ***v.i.*** [GAMED (gāmd), GAMING], to play cards, etc. for stakes; gamble. ***v.t.*** to squander or lose in gambling (with *away*). ***adj.*** 1. designating or of wild birds, fish, etc. hunted for sport or for use as food. 2. [Colloq.], *a*) plucky; courageous. *b*) having enough spirit or enthusiasm; ready: as, he's *game* for anything.

big game, 1. large wild animals, as gorillas, elephants, lions, etc., hunted for sport; hence, 2. [Slang], any important objective difficult or dangerous to pursue.

die game, to die bravely and still fighting.

make game of, to make fun of; make the butt of jokes, teasing, etc.; ridicule.

play the game, [Colloq.], 1. to act according to the rules of a game; hence, 2. to behave as fairness or custom requires.

the game is up, all chances for a successful completion are gone: said of enterprises involving risk or danger.

game (gām), ***adj.*** [also dial. *gammy*; ? < Fr. dial. *gambi*, limping], [Colloq.], lame or injured: said especially of a leg.

game bag, a bag to hold game killed by a hunter.

game·cock (gām′kok′), ***n.*** a specially bred rooster trained for cockfighting.

game fowl, any of a breed of fowl trained for cockfighting.

game·keep·er (gām′kēp′ẽr), ***n.*** a person employed to take care of game birds and animals on public lands or private estates, to prevent poaching, etc.

game laws, laws regulating hunting and fishing in order to preserve game.

game·ly (gām′li), ***adv.*** in a game, or plucky, manner.

game·ness (gām′nis), ***n.*** a game, or plucky, quality.

game·some (gām′səm), ***adj.*** [ME. *gamsum*; see GAME (play) & -SOME], playful; sportive; frolicsome; merry.

game·ster (gām′stẽr), ***n.*** [*game*, *n.* + *-ster*], a gambler.

gam·e·tan·gi·um (gam′i-tan′ji-əm), ***n.*** [*pl.* GAMETANGIA (-ə)], [Mod. L.; see **GAMETO-** & **ANGIO-**], in *botany*, that part of a plant in which the gametes are produced.

gam·ete (gam′ēt, gə-mēt′), ***n.*** [Mod. L. *gameta* < Gr. *gametē*, a wife < *gamein*, to marry < *gamos*, marriage], a reproductive cell that can unite with another similar one to form the cell that develops into a new individual: see also **zygote.**

ga·met·ic (gə-met′ik), ***adj.*** of, or having the nature of, a gamete or gametes.

ga·me·to- (gə-mē′tō, gə-mē′tə), a combining form meaning *gamete*, as in *gametophore, gametophyte.*

ga·me·to·phore (gə-mē′tə-fôr′, gə-mē′tə-fōr′), ***n.*** [*gameto-* + *-phore*], that part of a plant bearing the organs that produce gametes.

ga·me·to·phyte (gə-mē′tə-fit′), ***n.*** [*gameto-* + *-phyte*], the gamete-bearing phase of a plant in the alternation of generations: distinguished from *sporophyte*.

game warden, an official in charge of enforcing the game laws in a certain area.

gam·ic (gam′ik), ***adj.*** [< Gr. *gamos*, marriage; + *-ic*], in *biology*, 1. sexual. 2. that can develop only after fertilization.

gam·i·ly (gām′ə-li), ***adv.*** in a gamy manner; pluckily.

gam·in (gam′in), ***n.*** [Fr.], a homeless or neglected child left to roam the streets; street urchin; street Arab.

gam·i·ness (gām′i-nis), ***n.*** the quality of being gamy.

gam·ing (gām′iŋ), ***n.*** the playing of games of chance for stakes; gambling.

gam·ma (gam′ə), ***n.*** [ME.; L.; Gr. < Sem.; cf. Heb. *gīmel*, akin to *gāmāl*, camel], 1. the third letter of the Greek alphabet (Γ, γ), corresponding to English *G*, *g*: see **alphabet**, table. 2. the symbol for the third in any series. 3. a microgram.

gam·ma·di·on (gə-mā′di-ən), ***n.*** [*pl.* GAMMADIA (-ə)], [MGr., dim. < Gr. *gamma*], a figure made by four capital gammas radiating from a center; especially, such a figure in the form of a swastika.

gamma globulin, that fraction of blood serum which contains most antibodies: it has been used since 1951 in experimental inoculation against poliomyelitis.

gamma rays, one of the three kinds of rays emitted by radioactive substances: they are similar to X rays, but shorter in wave length: see **alpha rays, beta rays.**

gam·mer (gam′ẽr), ***n.*** [altered < *godmother*], an old woman, especially one from the country: often used contemptuously or humorously: see also **gaffer.**

gam·mon (gam′ən), ***n.*** [ONorm. Fr. *gambon* (Fr. *jambon*) < *gambe*; see GAMB], 1. the bottom end of a side of bacon. 2. the ham of a hog or a side of bacon, smoked or cured.

gam·mon (gam′ən), ***n.*** [ME. *gammen*, form of *game(n)*; see GAME (play)], in *backgammon*, a victory in which the winner gets rid of all his men before his opponent gets rid of any. ***v.t.*** to defeat by scoring a gammon.

gam·mon (gam′ən), ***v.t.*** [? *gammon* (bacon) with ref. to tying up], to lash (the bowsprit) to the stem of a vessel.

gam·mon (gam′ən), ***n.*** & ***interj.*** [prob. < *gammon* (bacon) with jocular allusion, but influenced by *gammon* (game)], [Colloq.], nonsense intended to deceive, humbug. ***v.t.*** & ***v.i.*** [Colloq.], to talk humbug (to)

gam·o- (gam′ō, gam′ə), [< Gr. *gamos*, marriage], a combining form meaning: 1. ***sexually united***, as in *gamogenesis*. 2. *joined*, as in *gamosepalous*.

gam·o·gen·e·sis (gam′ə-jen′ə-sis), ***n.*** [*gamo-* + *-genesis*], reproduction by the uniting of gametes; sexual reproduction.

gam·o·pet·al·ous (gam′ə-pet′'l-əs), ***adj.*** [*gamo-* + *petalous*], having the petals united so as to form a tubelike corolla.

GAMOPETALOUS FLOWER (morning glory)

gam·o·sep·al·ous (gam′ə-sep′'l-əs), ***adj.*** [*gamo-* + *-sepalous*], having the sepals united.

-ga·mous (gə-məs), [< Gr. *gamos*, marriage], a combining form meaning ***marrying, uniting sexually***, as in *heterogamous, polygamous.*

gamp (gamp), ***n.*** [in allusion to the umbrella of Mrs. Sairey *Gamp* in Dickens' *Martin Chuzzlewit*], a large umbrella, especially one that is bulky or awkwardly wrapped.

gam·ut (gam′ət), ***n.*** [ML. *gamma ut*; *gamma*, the gamut, name used by Guido d'Arezzo for the lowest note of his scale < Gr. *gamma*, third letter of the Gr. alphabet + *ut* < L. *ut*, that, used as a musical note, taken from a medieval song whose phrases began on successive ascending major tones: *Ut* queant laxis *Re*sonare fibris, *Mi*ra gestorum *Fa*muli tuorum, *Sol*ve polluti *La*bii reatum, *S*ancte *I*ohannes], 1. in *music*, *a*) the lowest note of the medieval scale, corresponding to modern G below middle C. *b*) the complete medieval scale. *c*) the entire series of recognized notes in modern music. *d*) any complete musical scale, especially the major scale. 2. the entire range or extent of anything: as, she ran the *gamut* of emotions. —***SYN.*** see **range.**

gam·y (gām′i), ***adj.*** [GAMIER (-i-ẽr), GAMIEST (-i-ist)], 1. having a strong, tangy flavor like that of cooked game; hence, 2. strong in smell or taste; slightly tainted. 3. plucky; high-spirited.

-ga·my (gə-mi), [Gr. *-gamia* < *gamos*, marriage], a combining form meaning ***marriage, sexual union***, as in *polygamy*.

gan (gan), past tense of **gin** (to begin).

Gand (gän), ***n.*** Ghent: the French name.

gan·der (gan′dẽr), ***n.*** [ME.; AS. *gan(d)ra*; akin to G. dial., D., LG. *gander*, all with inserted *-d*; for the base **gans-*, cf. G. *gans*, GOOSE], 1. a male goose. 2. a stupid or silly fellow. 3. [Slang], a look: chiefly in the phrase *take a gander*.

Gan·dhi, Mo·han·das Ka·ram·chand (mō′hən-däs′ kə-rəm-chund′ gän′dē; Eng. gan′di), 1869–1948; Indian nationalist leader and social reformer; assassinated; called *Mahatma Gandhi*.

Gan·dhi·ism (gän′di-iz'm, gan′di-iz'm), ***n.*** the political theories of Gandhi, especially his theories of passive resistance and civil disobedience to achieve reform.

gan·dy dancer (gan′di), [? < *gander*: from the worker's gait in using a tamping bar along a railroad track], [Slang], a worker in a railroad section gang.

Gand·zha (gän′jä), ***n.*** Kirovabad: a former name.

ga·nef (gä′nəf), ***n.*** [see GANOV], a thief.

gang (gaŋ), ***n.*** [ME.; AS. *gang*, a going, journey < base of *gangan* (see GANG *v.*) & *gan* (see GO); mod. senses may be influenced by the related AS. *genge*, a troop, band; orig. sense survives in *gangway*], 1. a group of people associated together in some way; specifically, *a*) a group of workers directed by a foreman. *b*) an organized group of criminals. *c*) a squad of convicts at work. *d*) a group of children or youths from the same neighborhood banded together for social reasons. 2. a set of like tools or machines designed or arranged to work together: often used attributively, as, a *gang* plow. ***v.i.*** to form a gang; be associated in a gang (often with *up*). ***v.t.*** [Colloq.], to attack as a gang.

gang up on, [Slang], to attack or oppose as a group.

gang (gaŋ), ***v.i.*** [AS. *gangan* < IE. base ****ghengh-***, to step, seen also in ON. *ganga*, Goth. *gaggan*, to go (see GO)], [Scot.], to go; walk.

gang (gaŋ), ***n.*** gangue.

gang·er (gaŋ′ẽr), ***n.*** a foreman of a gang of workers.

Gan·ges (gan′jēz), ***n.*** a river in northern India, flowing from the Himalaya Mountains into the Bay of Bengal: length, 1,550 mi.

gan·gli- (gaŋ'gli), ganglio-.

gan·gli·a (gaŋ'gli-ə), *n.* plural of **ganglion.**

gan·gli·ate (gaŋ'gli-it), *adj.* gangliated.

gan·gli·at·ed (gaŋ'gli-ā'tid), *adj.* having ganglia.

gan·gling (gaŋ'gliŋ), *adj.* [form suggests ppr. < **gangle,* to keep going < *gang, v.* + *-le,* freq. suffix], thin, tall, and awkward; of loose, lanky build; spindling.

gan·gli·o- (gaŋ'gli-ō, gaŋ'gli-ə), a combining form meaning *ganglion,* as in *ganglioplexus.*

gan·gli·on (gaŋ'gli-ən), *n.* [*pl.* GANGLIA (-ə), GANGLIONS (-ənz)], [LL. < Gr. *ganglion,* tumor], 1. a mass of nerve cells serving as a center from which nerve impulses are transmitted. 2. a center of force, energy, activity, etc. 3. a small tumor growing on a tendon.

gan·gli·on·ic (gaŋ'gli-on'ik), *adj.* of, or having the nature of, a ganglion.

gan·gli·o·plex·us (gaŋ'gli-ə-plek'səs), *n.* a network of nerve fibers in a ganglion.

gan·gly (gaŋ'gli), *adj.* gangling.

gang·plank (gaŋ'plaŋk'), *n.* [*gang* (in obs. sense of "act of going"; see GANG, a group) + *plank*], a narrow, movable platform forming a bridge by which to board or leave a ship.

gang plow, a plow with a number of shares fastened side by side for making several furrows at a time.

gan·grel (gaŋ'grəl, gaŋ'rəl), *n.* [*gang, v.* + ending seen also in *wastrel*], [Dial. or Archaic], a roving beggar.

gan·grene (gaŋ'grēn), *n.* [OFr.; L. *gangraena;* Gr. *gaggraina* < *grainein,* to gnaw, eat], decay of tissue in a part of the body when the blood supply is obstructed by injury, disease, etc. *v.t.* [GANGRENED (-grēnd), GANGRENING], to cause gangrene in. *v.i.* to develop gangrene; decay.

gan·gre·nous (gaŋ'gri-nəs), *adj.* of or having gangrene.

gang·ster (gaŋ'stẽr), *n.* 1. a member of a gang, especially of a gang of criminals; hence, 2. any criminal or tough.

gangue (gaŋ), *n.* [Fr.; G. *gang,* metallic vein, passage], the commercially worthless minerals associated with economically valuable metallic minerals in a deposit; matrix: also spelled **gang.**

gang·way (gaŋ'wā'), *n.* [AS. *gangweg,* thoroughfare (see GANG, in obs. sense "a going" & WAY)], a passageway or space through which to enter, leave, or go past; specifically, *a)* an opening in a ship's side for loading and unloading freight or for passengers. *b)* a gangplank. *c)* an accommodation ladder. *d)* a passageway between rows of seats. *e)* the aisle across the British House of Commons. *f)* a main level in a mine. *g)* an incline for logs, leading from the water to a saw mill. *interj.* make room! clear the way!

gan·is·ter (gan'is-tẽr), *n.* [G. dial. *ganster;* MHG. *ganster, ganeister,* a spark], a hard, siliceous rock sometimes found underlying coal beds or produced synthetically, used for lining metallurgical furnaces.

gan·net (gan'it), *n.* [*pl.* GANNETS (-its), GANNET; see PLURAL, II, D, 1], [ME. *ganat, gante;* AS. *ganot,* solan goose, lit., a gander; akin to D. *gent,* OHG. *ganazzo,* gander; for IE. base see GOOSE; cf. GANDER], any of several varieties of large, white, web-footed water birds, related to the herons and somewhat resembling pelicans: they nest on the rocks in northern seas.

gan·oid (gan'oid), *adj.* [Fr. *ganoide* < Gr. *ganos,* brightness; + *-oid*], of a group of fishes that are covered by rows of hard, glossy, enameled scales or plates: the group includes the sturgeons, gars, bowfins, and paddlefishes. *n.* a ganoid fish.

ga·nov (gä'nəf), *n.* [Yid. < Heb.], a thief: also spelled **ganef, ganof, gonof, gonoph,** etc.

gant·let (gônt'lit, gant'lit), *n.* [earlier *gantlope;* Sw. *gatlopp,* a running down a lane < *gata,* street or lane + *lopp,* a course or run], 1. a former military punishment in which the offender had to run between two rows of men who struck him with clubs, etc. as he passed. 2. a series of troubles or difficulties. 3. a section of railroad track over a narrow passage where two lines of track overlap, one rail of each line being within the rails of the other. *v.t.* to overlap (railroad tracks) so as to make a gantlet. Also spelled **gauntlet.**

run the gantlet, 1. to be punished by means of the gantlet; hence, 2. to proceed or act while under attack from both sides, as by criticism, gossip, etc.

gant·let (gônt'lit, gant'lit), *n.* a glove: see **gauntlet.**

gan·try (gan'tri), *n.* [*pl.* GANTRIES (-triz)], [altered < OFr. *gantier, chantier;* L. *canterius, cantherius,* beast of burden, trellis, rafter; Gr. *kanthēlios,* a pack ass < *kanthōn,* of same meaning], 1. a frame on which barrels can be set horizontally. 2. a framework supported at each end so that it spans a distance, used for carrying a traveling crane or displaying railroad signals. Also **gauntry.**

Gan·y·mede (gan'ə-mēd'), *n.* [L. *Ganymedes;* Gr. *Ganymēdēs*], 1. in *Greek mythology,* a beautiful youth carried off by Zeus to be the cupbearer to the gods. 2. one of the satellites of the planet Jupiter.

gaol (jāl), *n.* a jail: British spelling.

gaol·er (jāl'ẽr), *n.* a jailer: British spelling.

gap (gap), *n.* [ME. *gappe;* ON. *gap* < *gapa,* to yawn, gape], 1. a hole or opening, as in a wall or fence, made by breaking or parting; breach. 2. a mountain pass, cleft, or ravine. 3. an interruption of continuity; blank space; hiatus; lacuna. 4. a distance or difference between ideas, natures, etc.: as, there is a *gap* between his thinking and mine. *v.t.* [GAPPED (gapt), GAPPING], to make an opening in; breach.

gape (gāp), *v.i.* [GAPED (gāpt), GAPING], [ME. *gapen* < ON. *gapa,* to yawn, gape], 1. to open the mouth wide, as in yawning or hunger. 2. to stare with the mouth open, as in wonder or surprise. 3. to open or be opened wide, as a chasm. *n.* 1. the act of gaping; specifically, *a)* an open-mouthed stare. *b)* a yawn. 2. a wide gap or opening. 3. in *zoology,* the measure of the widest possible opening of a mouth or beak. —*SYN.* see **look.**

the gapes, 1. a disease of poultry and birds, characterized by gaping: see **gapeworm.** 2. a fit of yawning.

gape·worm (gāp'wũrm'), *n.* a parasitic roundworm infesting the larger respiratory passages of young poultry and causing the gapes.

gap·y (gāp'i), *adj.* having the gapes.

gar (gär), *n.* [*pl.* GAR, GARS (gärz); see PLURAL, II, D, 2], [ME.; AS. *gar,* a spear: so called from the pointed snout], any of a group of marine and fresh-water ganoid fishes characterized by elongated bodies covered with very hard scales, long beaklike snouts, and many sharp teeth: also called *garfish, needlefish.*

G.A.R., Grand Army of the Republic.

ga·rage (gə-räzh', gə-räj'; Brit. gar'ij), *n.* [Fr. < *garer,* to protect, preserve; Pr. *garar;* prob. < Frank. *waron,* to watch, protect], 1. a shelter or storage place for an automobile or automobiles. 2. a business establishment where automobiles are stored, repaired, washed, greased, etc. *v.t.* [GARAGED (-räzhd', -räjd'; Brit. -ijd), GARAGING], to put or keep in a garage.

Gar·a·mond (gar'ə-mond'), *n.* a style of type based on that designed by Claude Garamond, 16th-century French type founder.

Gar·and rifle (gar'ənd, gə-rand'), [after John C. *Garand* (1888–), Am. who invented it], a semiautomatic, rapid-firing, .30-caliber rifle: the standard infantry weapon of the United States Army in World War II.

garb (gärb), *n.* [OFr. *garbe,* gracefulness; It. *garbo,* elegance < OHG. *garawi, garwi,* preparation, dress < *garawen,* to prepare, dress < Gmc. **garwjan* < **garwo,* ready, seen also in AS. *gearu* (cf. YARE), ON. *gqrr,* ready], 1. clothing; manner or style of dress, especially as characteristic of an occupation, profession, or rank. 2. external form, covering, or appearance. 3. [Obs.], style; manner. *v.t.* to clothe; dress; attire.

gar·bage (gär'bij), *n.* [ME., entrails of fowls], 1. waste parts of food, as from a market or kitchen; animal or vegetable matter that is thrown away. 2. any worthless or offensive matter: as, literary *garbage.*

gar·ble (gär'b'l), *v.t.* [GARBLED (-b'ld), GARBLING], [OFr. *garbeler, grabeler;* It. *garbellare* < Ar. *gharbala* < LL. *cribellare,* to sift < *cribellum,* small sieve, dim. of *cribrum,* a sieve], 1. [Rare], to cleanse or sort by sifting. 2. [Rare], to select the best parts of. 3. to select, suppress, improperly emphasize, or otherwise distort parts of (a story, etc.) in telling, in order to mislead or misrepresent. 4. to confuse or mix up (a quotation, story, etc.) innocently.

gar·board (gär'bôrd', gär'bōrd'), *n.* [D. *gaarbord* < *garen* (contr. of *gaderen,* to gather) + *boord,* a board; cf. Fr. *gabord* < D.], in *shipbuilding,* the planks or plates adjoining the keel: also **garboard strake.**

‡gar·çon (gȧr'sōn'), *n.* [*pl.* GARÇONS (gȧr'sōn')], [Fr.], 1. a boy, youth, or young man. 2. a waiter or servant.

Gard, Ro·ger Mar·tin du (rô'zhā' mȧr'tan' dü' gȧr'), 1881–1958; French novelist; received Nobel prize in literature, 1937.

Gar·da, Lake (gär'dä), a lake in northern Italy: area, 145 sq. mi.

gar·dant (gär'dənt), *adj.* [Fr., ppr. of *garder;* see GUARD, WARD], in *heraldry,* guardant.

gar·den (gär'd'n), *n.* [ME. & ONorm. Fr. *gardin* < Frank. *gardo;* akin to G. *garten,* AS. *geard;* see YARD, GARTH], 1. a piece of ground for the growing of fruits, flowers, or vegetables: it is usually close to a house. 2. a well-cultivated region; area of fertile, developed land. 3. *often pl.* a place for public enjoyment, planted with trees, flowers, etc., and often having special displays of animal or plant life. *v.i.* to make, work in, or take care of a garden, lawn, etc. *v.t.* to make a garden of. *adj.* 1. of, for, used in, or grown in a garden; hence, 2. *a)* ordinary; commonplace. *b)* hardy.

Gar·den, Mary (gär'd'n), 1877– ; American operatic soprano, born in Scotland.

gar·den·er (gärd'nẽr, gär'd'n-ẽr), *n.* 1. a person who makes, or works in, a garden. 2. a person whose occupation is gardening.

Garden Grove, a city in southwestern California, near Los Angeles: pop., 84,000.

gar·de·ni·a (gär-dēn'yə, gär-dē'ni-ə), *n.* [Mod. L.; after Alexander *Garden* (1730–1791), Am. botanist], 1. a white or yellowish flower with fragrant, waxy petals. 2. the tropical tree or shrub on which it grows.

Gar·di·ner, Samuel Raw·son (rô′s'n gärd′nẽr, gär′d'n-ẽr), 1829–1902; English historian.

gar·dy·loo (gär′di-lo͞o′), *n.* [< Fr. *gare l'eau,* beware (of) the water < *garer,* to beware < MHG. *waren*; cf. BEWARE], formerly, in Edinburgh, a cry warning people below that slops were being thrown from the windows into the street.

Gar·eth (gar′ith), *n.* [ME. < AS. *Garrath;* see GARRET], in *Arthurian legend,* one of the knights of the Round Table, a nephew of King Arthur.

Gar·field (gär′fēld), *n.* a city in New Jersey, on the Passaic River: pop., 29,000.

Garfield, James Abram, 1831–1881; twentieth president of the United States (1881); assassinated.

Garfield Heights, a city in northeastern Ohio: a suburb of Cleveland: pop., 38,000.

gar·fish (gär′fish′), *n.* [*pl.* GARFISH, GARFISHES (-iz); see FISH], a gar.

gar·ga·ney (gär′gə-ni), *n.* [prob. < It. dial. *garganello;* origin prob. echoic of the cry], a European water bird of the duck family, living near fresh water and resembling the American blue-winged teal.

Gar·gan·tu·a (gär-gan′cho͞o-ə), *n.* a giant king, the main character of *Gargantua and Pantagruel,* a social and political satire by Rabelais (completed in 1552).

Gar·gan·tu·an (gär-gan′cho͞o-ən), *adj.* like Gargantua; gigantic; huge; prodigious.

gar·get (gär′git), *n.* [ME.; OFr. *gargate,* throat; prob. < L. *gurges,* abyss, whirlpool], 1. a disease of cattle or swine characterized by swelling of the throat, etc. 2. an inflammation of the udders of cows, ewes, etc.

gar·gle (gär′g'l), *v.t.* [GARGLED (-g'ld), GARGLING], [Fr. *gargouiller* < *gargouille,* throat, waterspout, gargoyle; L. *gurgulio,* throat, windpipe], 1. to rinse or wash (the throat) with a liquid kept in motion in the throat by the slow expulsion of air from the lungs. 2. to utter with the sound of gargling. *v.i.* to gargle the throat. *n.* a liquid used for gargling.

gar·goyle (gär′goil), *n.* [ME. *gargulie;* OFr. *gargouille;* see GARGLE], 1. a waterspout, usually in the form of an elaborately carved animal or fantastic creature, projecting from the gutter of a building. 2. a projecting ornament (on a building) like a gargoyle in appearance.

GARGOYLE

gar·i·bal·di (gar′ə-bôl′di), *n.* a woman's loose, high-necked blouse with full sleeves, patterned after the shirt worn by the followers of Garibaldi.

Gar·i·bal·di, Giu·sep·pe (jo͞o-zep′pe gä′rē-bäl′dē; Eng. gar′ə-bôl′di), 1807–1882; Italian patriot; helped unify Italy.

gar·ish (gâr′ish), *adj.* [earlier *gaurish;* prob. < ME. *gauren,* to stare], too bright or gaudy; showy; glaring. —*SYN.* see **gaudy.**

gar·land (gär′lənd), *n.* [ME.; OFr. *garlande* (Fr. *guirlande* < It.)], 1. a wreath of flowers, leaves, etc., worn on the head or used as decoration. 2. an anthology of poems, songs, etc. 3. in *heraldry,* a wreath of laurel or oak leaves. 4. in *nautical usage, a*) a band or ring of rope used to hoist spars. *b*) a kind of net used as a food bag. *v.t.* to form into or decorate with a garland or garlands.

Gar·land (gär′lənd), *n.* a city in northeastern Texas: a suburb of Dallas: pop., 39,000.

Gar·land, Ham·lin (ham′lin gär′lənd), 1860–1940; American novelist.

gar·lic (gär′lik), *n.* [ME. *garlek;* AS. *garleac; gar,* a spear + *leac,* a leek: from the spearlike leaves], 1. a bulbous plant of the lily family. 2. the strong-smelling bulb of this plant, made up of small sections called cloves, used as seasoning in meats, salads, etc.

gar·lick·y (gär′lik-i), *adj.* having the smell or taste of garlic.

gar·ment (gär′mənt), *n.* [ME.; OFr. *garnement* < *garnir;* see GARNISH], 1. *a*) any article of clothing. *b*) *pl.* clothes; costume. 2. a covering. *v.t.* to cover with a garment; clothe.

gar·ner (gär′nẽr), *n.* [ME. *gerner;* OFr. *gernier, grenier;* L. *granarium,* granary < *granum,* grain], 1. a place for storing grain; granary. 2. a store of something. *v.t.* to gather up and store in or as in a granary.

Gar·ner, John Nance (nans gär′nẽr), 1868– ; vice-president of the United States (1933–1941).

gar·net (gär′nit), *n.* [ME. *gernet;* OFr. *grenat;* ML. *granatus,* a garnet < *granatus,* having seeds < L. *granum,* a grain, seed: from the resemblance to pomegranate seeds], 1. a hard, glasslike silicate mineral of various colors: the most precious variety, used as a gem, is of a deep, transparent red. 2. deep red.

gar·net (gär′nit), *n.* [prob. < D. *granaat, kranaat,* apparently folk-etymologized forms of Fr. *garant,* fall tackle < Bret. *garan,* a crane], in *nautical usage,* a hoisting tackle for loading and unloading cargo.

gar·ni·er·ite (gär′ni-ẽr-īt′), *n.* [after Jules *Garnier,* Fr. geologist], in *mineralogy,* an apple-green hydrated silicate of magnesium and nickel.

gar·nish (gär′nish), *v.t.* [ME. *garnischen* < base of OFr. *garnir, guarnir, warnir,* to protect; prob. < MHG. *warnen,* to equip oneself, prepare, protect], 1. to decorate; adorn; embellish; trim. 2. to decorate (food) with something that adds color or flavor: as, a steak is often *garnished* with parsley. 3. in *law,* to bring garnishment proceedings against; garnishee. *n.* 1. a decoration; ornament. 2. something put on or around food to add color or flavor, as parsley or nuts. 3. [Obs.], a fee; specifically, a fee formerly extorted from new prisoners by inmates of English jails or by the jailer.

gar·nish·ee (gär′ni-shē′), *n.* [*garnish, v.* + *-ee*], in *law,* a person who has money or other property of a defendant in his possession, and is ordered not to dispose of it pending settlement of the lawsuit. *v.t.* [GARNISHEED (-shēd′), GARNISHEEING], in *law, a*) to attach (a debtor's property, wages, etc.) by the authority of a court, so that it can be used to pay the debt. *b*) to order (a person) not to dispose of the defendant's money or property in his possession pending settlement of the lawsuit.

gar·nish·ment (gär′nish-mənt), *n.* [*garnish, v.* + *-ment*], 1. a decoration; embellishment. 2. in *law, a*) a summons to a person other than the litigants to appear in a lawsuit. *b*) a notice ordering a person not to dispose of a defendant's property or money in his possession pending settlement of the lawsuit.

gar·ni·ture (gär′ni-chẽr), *n.* [Fr. < *garnir;* see GARNISH], an ornament; decoration; embellishment; trimming.

Ga·ronne (gȧ′rôn′), *n.* a river in southwestern France, flowing from the Pyrenees to the Gironde: length, 355 mi.

ga·rotte (gə-rot′), *n.* & *v.t.* garrote.

gar pike, a North American fresh-water fish of the gar family.

gar·ret (gar′it), *n.* [ME. & OFr. *garite,* watchtower < *garir,* to watch < Gmc. **warjan,* to protect], the room or rooms just below the roof of a house, especially when unplastered and under a sloping roof; attic.

Gar·ret, Gar·rett (gar′it), [< AS. *Garrath,* lit., swift spear < *gar,* spear + *rathe, hrathe,* quick, ready (see RATHER); also < LG. *Gerrit, Gerd,* contr. < *Gerhard;* see GERARD], a masculine name.

Gar·rick, David (gar′ik), 1717–1779; English actor and theater manager.

gar·ri·son (gar′i-s'n), *n.* [ME. & OFr. *garison* < *garir* (see GARRET, attic); meaning affected by association with ME. & OFr. *garnison,* a garrison, provisions < *garnir,* to furnish (see GARNISH)], 1. troops stationed in a fort or fortified place. 2. a fortified place with troops, guns, etc.; military post or station. *v.t.* 1. to station troops in (a fortified place) for its defense. 2. to place (troops) on duty in a garrison.

Gar·ri·son, William Lloyd (gar′i-s'n), 1805–1879; American editor, lecturer, and abolitionist leader.

garrison cap, a military cap with a round, flat crown and leather visor: distinguished from *overseas cap.*

gar·rote (gə-rot′, gə-rōt′), *n.* [Sp., orig., a stick used to wind a cord < Celt.], 1. a Spanish method of execution by strangling with an iron collar tightened by a screw. 2. the iron collar so used. 3. a cord, thong, or length of wire for strangling an enemy outpost or sentry in a surprise attack. 4. *a*) a disabling by strangling, as in an attack for robbery; strangulation. *b*) strangulation and robbery. *v.t.* [GARROTED or GARROTTED (-id), GARROTING or GARROTTING], 1. to execute or attack with a garrote or by strangling. 2. *a*) to disable by strangling, as in an attack for robbery. *b*) to strangle and rob. Also **garote, garrotte.**

gar·rotte (gə-rot′), *n.* & *v.t.* garrote.

gar·ru·li·ty (gə-ro͞o′lə-ti), *n.* [L. *garrulitas*], the quality of being garrulous; talkativeness.

gar·ru·lous (gar′oo-ləs, gar′yoo-ləs), *adj.* [L. *garrulus* < *garrire,* to chatter, prattle], talking much, often about unimportant things; loquacious. —*SYN.* see **talkative.**

gar·ter (gär′tẽr), *n.* [ME.; ONorm. Fr. *gartier* < OFr. *garet, jaret,* small of the leg behind the knee < Celt.; cf. Bret. *gar, garr,* shank of the leg], 1. an elastic band, or a strap suspended from an undergarment, for holding a stocking in position. 2. [G-], *a*) the badge of the Order of the Garter, the highest order of British knighthood, instituted about 1344 by Edward III. *b*) the order itself. *c*) membership in it. *v.t.* to bind, support, or fasten with or as with a garter.

garter belt, a belt, usually of elastic fabric, with garters suspended from it, worn by women.

garter snake, any of various small, harmless, striped snakes, common in North America.

garth (gärth), *n.* [ME.; ON. *garthr;* akin to AS. *geard* (see YARD)], [Archaic], an enclosed yard or garden.

Gar·y (gâr'i), [contr. < *Garret;* or < AS. **Garwig*, lit., spear (of) battle < *gar*, a spear + *wig* < Gmc. **wiga-*, battle; IE. base **wīk-*, to be bold, seen in L. *vincere*, to conquer], a masculine name. *n.* a city in northwestern Indiana, on Lake Michigan: pop., 178,000.

gas (gas), *n.* [word invented by the Belgian chemist, Van Helmont (1577–1644), on basis of Gr. *chaos*, chaos], 1. the fluid form of a substance in which it can expand indefinitely and completely fill its container; form that is neither liquid nor solid; vapor. 2. any mixture of inflammable gases used for lighting or heating. 3. any gas used as an anesthetic, as nitrous oxide. 4. any substance, as phosgene, intentionally dispersed through the atmosphere, as in war, to act as a poison or irritant. 5. [Colloq.], *a)* gasoline. *b)* the accelerator or throttle in an automobile, etc. 6. [Slang], empty, idle, or boastful talk. 7. in *mining*, a mixture of firedamp with air that explodes if ignited. *v.t.* [GASSED (gasd), GASSING], 1. to supply with gas. 2. to subject to the action of gas. 3. to attack with gas; injure or kill by gas, as in war. *v.i.* 1. to give off gas. 2. [Slang], to talk in an empty, idle, or boastful way. *adj.* of, using, or operated by gas: as, a *gas* range.

step on the gas, [Slang], 1. to press on the accelerator of an automobile, etc.; hence, 2. to hurry; move or act faster.

gas bacillus, a rod-shaped microorganism that infects wounds and causes gas to form in them.

gas·bag (gas'bag'), *n.* 1. a bag to hold gas, as in a balloon or dirigible. 2. [Slang], a person who talks too much.

gas black, a dense carbon deposited in gas retorts.

gas burner, 1. a gas jet. 2. a stove or furnace in which gas is used as fuel.

gas coal, soft coal from which illuminating gas is distilled.

Gas·cogne (gås'kôn'y'), *n.* Gascony: the French name.

Gas·con (gas'kən), *adj.* [Fr.], 1. of Gascony or its people, who were famous for their boastfulness; hence, 2. [g-], boastful; swaggering. *n.* 1. a native of Gascony. 2. [g-], a boaster; swaggerer.

gas·con·ade (gas'kə-nād'), *n.* [Fr. *gasconnade;* see GASCON & -ADE], boastful or blustering talk; brag. *v.i.* [GASCONADED (-id), GASCONADING], to boast or bluster.

Gas·co·ny (gas'kə-ni), *n.* a former province of southwestern France.

gas·e·lier (gas'ə-lêr'), *n.* [*gas* + chan*delier*], an early kind of chandelier with branches ending in gas jets.

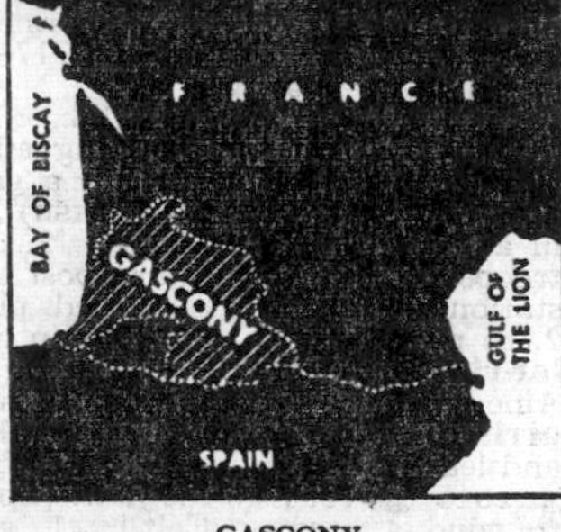

GASCONY

gas engine, an engine in which the explosion of gas in a cylinder drives the piston; internal-combustion engine.

gas·e·ous (gas'i-əs, gas'yəs), *adj.* of, having the nature of, or in the form of, gas.

gas fitter, a person whose work is installing and repairing gas pipes and fixtures.

gas fixture, a device that carries gas from the pipe to a jet or burner.

gas furnace, 1. a furnace that distills gas from coal, etc. 2. a furnace that burns gas as fuel.

gas gangrene, gangrene in which gas bacilli cause the diseased tissues of dirty wounds to become filled with gas and a liquid discharge.

gash (gash), *v.t.* [earlier *garse;* ME. *garsen;* OFr. *garser*], to make a long, deep cut in; slash. *n.* [ME. *garse* < the *v.*], a long, deep cut.

gas·house (gas'hous'), *n.* a place where gas for heating and lighting is prepared; gasworks: used figuratively to suggest slum areas, roughness, etc.

gas·i·fi·ca·tion (gas'ə-fi-kā'shən), *n.* a gasifying or being gasified.

gas·i·form (gas'ə-fôrm'), *adj.* in the form of gas; gaseous.

gas·i·fy (gas'ə-fī'), *v.t. & v.i.* [GASIFIED (-fīd'), GASIFYING], to change into gas.

gas jet, 1. a flame of illuminating gas. 2. a nozzle or burner at the end of a gas fixture.

Gas·kell, Elizabeth Cleg·horn (kleg'hôrn' gas'k'l), 1810–1865; English novelist.

gas·ket (gas'kit), *n.* [prob. < It. *gaschetta*, a rope end], 1. a piece or ring of rubber, metal, paper, etc. placed around a piston or joint to make it leakproof. 2. in *nautical usage*, a rope or cord by which a furled sail is tied to the yard.

gas·kin (gas'kin), *n.* [contr. < *galligaskins*], 1. *pl.* [Obs.], galligaskins. 2. the upper part of the hind leg of a horse or similar animal.

gas·light (gas'līt'), *n.* 1. the light produced by the burning of illuminating gas. 2. a gas jet or burner. *adj.* of or characteristic of the period of gaslight illumination: as, *gaslight* melodrama.

gas log, an imitation log in the form of a hollow, perforated cylinder, used as a gas heater in a fireplace.

gas main, a large underground pipe that conducts gas into smaller pipes leading into houses, factories, etc.

gas·man (gas'man'), *n.* [*pl.* GASMEN (-men')], 1. an employee of a gasworks who regularly reads consumers' gas meters to determine the amount of gas used. 2. a gas fitter. 3. in *mining*, a person whose work is checking the ventilation and guarding against firedamp.

gas mantle, a tube of fabric treated with certain incandescent metals and fastened over a gas burner to give off light when heated by the flame.

gas mask, a device worn over the face to prevent the breathing in of poisonous gases by filtering them out of the air.

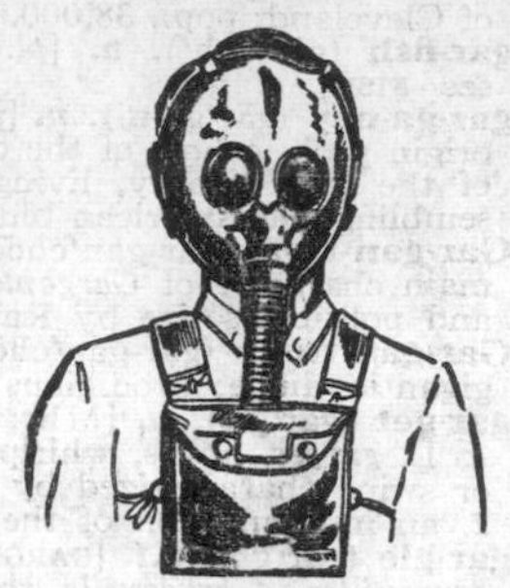
GAS MASK

gas meter, an instrument for measuring the quantity of a gas, especially of illuminating gas consumed as fuel.

gas·o·line, gas·o·lene (gas'-'l-ēn', gas''l-ēn'), *n.* [< *gas* + L. *oleum*, oil; + *-ine, -ene*], a volatile, highly inflammable, colorless liquid produced by the fractional distillation, or cracking, of petroleum and used chiefly as a fuel in internal-combustion engines: also called *petrol* (in England, etc.).

gas·om·e·ter (gas-om'ə-tẽr), *n.* [Fr. *gazometre;* see GAS & -METER], 1. a container for holding and measuring gas. 2. a gas reservoir.

gas·om·e·try (gas-om'ə-tri), *n.* the science of measuring gases; especially, the determination of the amount of a gas in a mixture.

gasp (gasp), *v.i.* [ME. *gaspen, gayspen;* ON. *geispa*, to yawn, by metathesis < **geip-sa* (cf. LG. *gapsen*); akin to *gape*], to catch the breath suddenly or with effort, as in surprise or in choking. *v.t.* to say or tell with gasps: as, he *gasped* out his story. *n.* a gasping; catching of the breath with difficulty.

at the last gasp, 1. just before death; hence, 2. just before the end; at the last moment.

Gas·pé Peninsula (gås'pā'), a peninsula in Quebec, Canada, between the St. Lawrence River and the Gulf of St. Lawrence.

gas shell, an explosive shell filled with poisonous or irritant gas, used in war.

gas station, a place for the sale of gasoline, oil, services, etc. for motor vehicles.

gas·sy (gas'i), *adj.* [GASSIER (-i-ẽr), GASSIEST (-i-ist)], 1. full of or containing gas. 2. like gas. 3. [Colloq.], full of talk, especially pretentious or boastful talk.

gas·ter·o·pod (gas'tẽr-ə-pod'), *n.* a gastropod.

Gas·to·ni·a (gas-tō'ni-ə), *n.* a city in southern North Carolina: pop., 37,000.

gastr-, gastro-.

gas·tral·gi·a (gas-tral'ji-ə), *n.* [Mod. L.; *gastr-* + *-algia*], a pain in the stomach or epigastrium.

gas·trec·to·my (gas-trek'tə-mi), *n.* [*pl.* GASTRECTOMIES (-miz)], [*gastr-* + *-ectomy*], the surgical removal of part of the stomach.

gas·tric (gas'trik), *adj.* [*gastr-* + *-ic*], of, in, or near the stomach.

gastric juice, the thin, acid digestive fluid produced by glands in the mucous membrane lining the stomach: it contains enzymes and hydrochloric acid.

gastric ulcer, an ulcer of the lining of the stomach.

gas·trin (gas'trin), *n.* [*gastr-* + *-in*], a hormone that is formed in the stomach and stimulates the production of the gastric juice: it is now regarded as identical with histamine.

gas·tri·tis (gas-trī'tis), *n.* [Mod. L.; *gastr-* + *-itis*], inflammation of the stomach, especially of the stomach lining.

gas·tro- (gas'trō, gas'trə), [< Gr. *gastēr*, the stomach], a combining form meaning: 1. *the stomach*, as in *gastroenteritis*. 2. *the stomach and*, as in *gastrocolic*. Also, before a vowel, **gastr-**.

gas·tro·col·ic (gas'trō-kol'ik), *adj.* of or attached to the stomach and the transverse colon.

gas·tro·en·ter·i·tis (gas'trō-en'tẽr-ī'tis), *n.* [Mod. L.; *gastro-* + *enter-* + *-itis*], an inflammation of the lining of the stomach and the intestines.

gas·tro·in·tes·ti·nal (gas'trō-in-tes'ti-n'l), *adj.* of the stomach and the intestines: abbreviated **g.i., G.I.**

gas·tro·lith (gas'trə-lith), *n.* [*gastro-* + *-lith*], in *medicine*, a stony concretion formed in the stomach.

gas·tro·nome (gas'trə-nōm'), *n.* [Fr. < *gastronomie;* see GASTRONOMY], a person who enjoys and has a discriminating taste for foods. —*SYN.* see **epicure.**

gas·tron·o·mer (gas-tron'ə-mẽr), *n.* a gastronome.

gas·tro·nom·ic (gas'trə-nom'ik), *adj.* of gastronomy.

gas·tro·nom·i·cal (gas'trə-nom'-i-k'l), *adj.* gastronomic.

gas·tron·o·mist (gas-tron'ə-mist), *n.* a gastronome.

gas·tron·o·my (gas-tron'ə-mi), *n.* [Fr. *gastronomie;* Gr. *gastronomia* < *gastēr*, the stomach + *nemein*, to regulate < *nomos*, a rule, law], the art or science of good eating; epicurism.

gas·tro·pho·tog·ra·phy (gas'trō-fə-tog'rə-fi), *n.* a method of photographing the inside of the stomach by introducing a small camera into it.

gas·tro·pod (gas'trə-pod'), *n.* [*gastro-* + *-pod*], any of a large group of mollusks having one-piece spiral shells, as the snail, limpet, etc., or no shells at all, as certain slugs: gastropods move by means of a broad, muscular, ventral disk. *adj.* gastropodous. Also **gasteropod.**

gas·trop·o·dous (gas-trop'ə-dəs), *adj.* of or like a gastropod.

gas·tro·scope (gas'trə-skōp'), *n.* [*gastro-* + *-scope*], an instrument for inspecting the inside of the stomach.

gas·tro·scop·ic (gas'trə-skop'ik), *adj.* of a gastroscope or gastroscopy.

gas·tros·co·py (gas-tros'kə-pi), *n.* inspection of the inside of the stomach with a gastroscope.

gas·trot·o·my (gas-trot'ə-mi), *n.* [*pl.* GASTROTOMIES (-miz)], [*gastro-* + *-tomy*], surgical incision into the stomach, as for removing gastroliths.

gas·tro·vas·cu·lar (gas'trō-vas'kyoo-lẽr), *adj.* 1. having both a digestive and a circulatory function. 2. of organs with such a dual function.

gas·tru·la (gas'troo-lə), *n.* [*pl.* GASTRULAE (-lē'), GASTRULAS (-ləz)], [Mod. L., dim. < Gr. *gastēr*, the stomach], an embryo in the early stage of development, consisting of a sac with two layers, the ectoderm and endoderm, enclosing a central cavity that opens to the outside through the blastopore.

CELLS

GASTRULA

gas·tru·la·tion (gas'troo-lā'shən), *n.* the formation of a gastrula.

gas·works (gas'wũrks'), *n.* a place where gas for heating and lighting is prepared; gashouse: see **gashouse.**

gat (gat), archaic past tense of **get.**

gat (gat), *n.* [< Scand.; cf. ON. *gat*, an opening passage; cf. also KATTEGAT], a narrow ship channel between cliffs or sandbanks.

gat (gat), *n.* [< *Gat*ling gun], [Slang], a pistol.

gate (gāt), *n.* [ME. < AS. pl. type *gatu* of *geat*, a gate; akin to OFris. *jet*, D. & ON. *gat*, opening (cf. GAT); IE. base **ĝhed-*, to void], 1. a movable framework or solid structure, especially one that swings on hinges, controlling entrance or exit through an opening in a fence or wall. 2. an opening providing passageway through a fence or wall, with or without such a structure; gateway. 3. any means of entrance or exit: as, the *gate* to one's heart. 4. a mountain gap. 5. a movable barrier, as at a railroad crossing. 6. a structure controlling the flow of water, as in a pipe, canal, etc. 7. a saw frame. 8. *a*) the total amount of money received in admission prices to a performance or exhibition. *b*) the total number of spectators who pay to see such an event. *v.t.* [British], to confine (a student) to the college grounds.

give the gate, [Slang], to send away; get rid of; dismiss.

gate (gāt), *n.* [< AS. *gēotan*, to pour], 1. a channel through which molten metal is poured into a mold. 2. the waste part of a casting formed at this channel.

gate·house (gāt'hous'), *n.* a house beside or over a gateway, used as a porter's lodge, etc.

gate-leg table (gāt'leg'), a table with drop leaves supported by gatelike legs that are swung back against the frame to permit the leaves to drop: also **gate-legged table.**

gate·post (gāt'pōst'), *n.* an upright post at the side of a gate, either the one on which the gate is hung or the one to which it is fastened when closed.

Gates, Horatio (gāts), 1728?–1806; American general in the Revolutionary War.

Gates·head (gāts'hed'), *n.* a city in northeastern England: pop., 114,000 (est. 1946).

gate·way (gāt'wā'), *n.* 1. an entrance in a wall, fence, etc. fitted with a gate. 2. a means of going in or out; means of getting at something.

Gath (gath), *n.* [Heb., lit., wine press], in the *Bible*, one of the five great Philistine cities: II Sam. 1:20.

gath·er (gath'ẽr), *v.t.* [ME. *gaderen, gethuren*, etc.; AS. *gad(e)rian;* akin to OFris. *gaduria*, D. *gaderen;* IE. base **ghadh-*, to unite, join, seen also in (*to*)*gether* & G. *gatte*, spouse, mate], 1. to cause to come together in one place or group. 2. to get or collect gradually from various places, sources, etc.; amass; accumulate. 3. to pick, pluck, or collect by picking; cull: as, *gather* a harvest, flowers, etc. 4. to get (an idea, impression, etc.); infer; conclude: as, I *gather* that you disagree. 5. to prepare or collect (oneself, one's energies) to meet a situation. 6. to gain or acquire gradually: as, the car *gathered* speed. 7. to draw (cloth) into fixed folds or pleats. 8. to wrinkle (one's brow). *v.i.* 1. to come together; assemble. 2. to fester; form pus; come to a head, as a boil. 3. to increase. 4. to become wrinkled: said of the brow. *n.* a pleat.

be gathered to one's fathers, to die.

gather up, 1. to pick up and assemble. 2. to draw together; make more compact.

SYN.—**gather** is the general term for a bringing or coming together (to *gather* scattered objects, people *gathered* at the corners); **collect** usually implies careful choice in gathering from various sources, a bringing into an orderly arrangement, etc. (he *collects* coins); **assemble** applies especially to the gathering together of persons for some special purpose (*assemble* the students in the auditorium); **muster** applies to a formal assembling, especially of troops for inspection, roll call, etc. See also **infer.**

gath·er·ing (gath'ẽr-iŋ), *n.* 1. the act of one that gathers. 2. what is gathered; specifically, *a*) a meeting; assemblage; crowd. *b*) a collection for charity. *c*) a series of small pleats in cloth. 3. a boil; abscess.

Gat·ling gun (gat'liŋ), [after R. J. *Gatling* (1818–1903), Am. inventor], an obsolete kind of machine gun consisting of a cluster of barrels arranged parallel with and around an axis, designed to be successively discharged when rotated by a crank.

Ga·tun (gä-tōōn'), *n.* a town in the Panama Canal Zone. 2. a dam near by: length, 1 1/2 mi. 3. a lake formed by Gatun Dam: area, 164 sq. mi.

gauche (gōsh), *adj.* [Fr. < MFr. *gauchir*, to become crooked, warped, ult. < Frank. *walkan*, to pull, beat; akin to Eng. *walk*], awkward; tactless; lacking grace, especially social grace.

gau·che·rie (gō'shə-rē', gō'shə-rē'), *n.* [Fr.; see GAUCHE], 1. awkwardness; tactlessness. 2. an awkward or tactless act or expression.

Gau·cho (gou'chō; Sp. gou'chô), *n.* [*pl.* GAUCHOS (-chōz; Sp. -chôs)], [Sp., of S. Am. (Araucan) origin], a cowboy of mixed Indian and Spanish ancestry, living on the South American pampas.

gaud (gôd), *n.* [ME. *gaude, gawde;* a jewel, ornament; prob. < OFr. *gaudir*, to make merry < L. *gaudere*, to rejoice], 1. a cheap, tasteless, showy ornament or bit of finery; trinket. 2. *pl.* showy gaieties.

‡**gau·de·a·mus** (gô'di-ā'məs), *n.* [L., lit., let us be joyful: the beginning of a famous medieval student song], a merrymaking, especially of college students.

gaud·er·y (gôd'ẽr-i), *n.* gaudy, or ostentatious, appearance, clothes, etc.; finery.

gaud·i·ly (gôd''l-i), *adv.* in a gaudy manner.

gaud·i·ness (gôd'i-nis), *n.* the quality of being gaudy.

gaud·y (gôd'i), *adj.* [GAUDIER (-i-ẽr), GAUDIEST (-i-ist)], [*gaud* + *-y*], bright and showy, but lacking in good taste; cheaply brilliant and ornate.

SYN.—**gaudy** applies to that which is brightly colored and gay, but inappropriately so or in bad taste (*gaudy* furniture); **tawdry** is used of something cheap and flimsy that is also gaudy (*tawdry* embroidery); **garish** implies a glaring brightness of color and excessive ornamentation (*garish* wallpaper); **flashy** and **showy** imply a conspicuous brightness and display, but **flashy** connotes that it is offensive to subdued tastes (a *flashy* sport coat), while **showy** does not necessarily connote this (*showy* blossoms). —*ANT.* subdued, quiet.

gauf·fer (gôf'ẽr), *v.t. & n.* goffer.

gauge (gāj), *n.* [ONorm.Fr. < the *v.*], 1. a measure; standard measure or scale of measurement. 2. dimensions; capacity; extent. 3. any device for measuring something, as rainfall, the thickness of wire or metal, the dimensions of a part being machined, the amount of liquid in a container, steam pressure, etc. 4. any means of estimating or judging. 5. the distance between the two rails of a railway: *standard gauge* in most countries is 56 1/2 inches: any larger gauge is called *broad* (or *wide*) *gauge*, and any smaller gauge is called *narrow gauge*. 6. the distance between the parallel wheels on opposite sides of a vehicle. 7. the size of the bore of a firearm, especially of a shotgun, as determined by the number per pound of spherical projectiles fitting the bore. 8. in *building*, *a*) a row of shingles, slates, etc. *b*) the part of a slate or shingle remaining exposed when laid. 9. in *carpentry*, a tool for scoring a line parallel with the edge of a board. 10. in *nautical usage*, *a*) the position of a ship in relation to another ship and the wind. *b*) the depth to which a ship with a full cargo is submerged in water. 11. in *plastering*, the amount of plaster of Paris used with common plaster to quicken its setting. Abbreviated **G., g.** (in senses 5, 6, 7, 10). *v.t.* [GAUGED (gājd), GAUGING], [ME. *gaugin;* ONorm.Fr. *gauger;* LL. **galicare*, to gauge, ult. < **gal-*, measuring rod < Celt.], 1. to measure accurately by means of a gauge. 2. to measure the size, amount, extent, or capacity of. 3. to estimate; judge; appraise. 4. to bring to correct gauge; make conform with a standard. 5. in *plastering,* to mix (plaster) in the right proportions, depending on the required drying time. Also spelled **gage.** —*SYN.* see **standard.**

gaug·er (gāj'ẽr), *n.* [Anglo-Fr. *gaugeour* < *gauger*], 1. a person or thing that gauges; especially, an official who measures the contents of casks of liquor, etc. to be taxed; hence, 2. a collector of excise taxes. Also spelled **gager.**

Gau·guin, Paul (pôl gō'gan'), (*Eugène Henri Paul Gauguin*), 1848–1903; French painter; in Tahiti after 1890.

Gaul (gôl), *n.* 1. an ancient division of the Roman Empire, consisting of France and Belgium, northern Italy, and parts of the Netherlands, Germany, and Switzerland: Latin name, *Gallia*: see **Roman Empire,** map. 2. any of the Celtic-speaking people of ancient Gaul. 3. a Frenchman.

‡**Gau·lei·ter** (gou'lī'tẽr), *n.* [G.], the administrator of a province or district under the Nazi regime.

Gaul·ish (gôl'ish), *adj.* of Gaul or the Gauls. *n.* the continental branch of the Celtic languages, spoken in ancient Gaul.

gaul·the·ri·a (gôl-thêr'i-ə), *n.* [Mod. L., after M. *Gaulthier*, Canad. botanist], any of a widely distributed group of evergreen shrubs, including the American wintergreen.

gaunt (gônt, gänt), *adj.* [ME. *gawnte* beside later *gant;* this sp. & the basic ME. sense "nicely slender" suggest OFr. origin < *gentr*, elegant, as prob. in the early surname, *le Gant;* ? sense change < merging with ON. *gandr*, thin pole, via E. Anglian ME. dialects], 1. thin and bony; emaciated; hollow-eyed and haggard, as from great hunger or age. 2. looking grim, forbidding, or desolate. —*SYN.* see **lean.**

gaunt·let (gônt'lit, gänt'lit), *n.* [ME. & OFr. *gantelet*, dim. of *gant*, a glove < Frank. *want*, a mitten], 1. a medieval glove, usually of leather covered with metal plates, worn to protect the hand from injury in combat: see **armor,** illus. 2. a long glove with a flaring cuff covering the lower part of the arm. 3. the part of such a glove covering the lower part of the arm. Also **gantlet.**

take up the gauntlet, 1. to accept a challenge. 2. to undertake the defense of a person, etc.

throw down the gauntlet, to challenge, as to combat.

gaunt·let (gônt'lit, gänt'lit), *n.* a gantlet (form of punishment).

gaunt·let·ed (gônt'lit-id, gänt'lit-id), *adj.* having or wearing a gauntlet, or glove.

gaun·try (gôn'tri), *n.* [*pl.* GAUNTRIES (-triz)], a gantry.

gauss (gous), *n.* [after Karl F. *Gauss* (1777–1855), G. mathematician & physicist], in *electricity*, a unit used in measuring magnetic induction or magnetic intensity, equal to one line of magnetic force per square centimeter.

Gau·ta·ma (gou'tə-mə, gô'tə-mə), *n.* see **Buddha.**

Gau·tier, Thé·o·phile (tā'ô'fēl' gō'tyā'), 1811–1872; French poet, critic, and novelist.

gauze (gôz), *n.* [Fr. *gaze;* said to be < *Gaza* in Palestine, where made], 1. any very thin, light, transparent, loosely woven material, as of cotton, silk, or wire. 2. a thin mist or haze. *adj.* made of or like gauze.

gauz·i·ness (gôz'i-nis), *n.* the quality of being gauzy.

gauz·y (gôz'i), *adj.* [GAUZIER (-i-ẽr), GAUZIEST (-i-ist)], thin, light, and transparent, like gauze; diaphanous.

gave (gāv), past tense of **give.**

gav·el (gav''l), *n.* [use only in U.S. suggests D. or dial. G. origin; ? akin to MD. *gaffele*, dial. Eng. *gaffle*, a fork, spur, lever; sense 2 < 1 via Freemasonry], 1. a mason's hammer for breaking off the rough edges of stones. 2. a small mallet rapped on the table by a presiding officer in calling for attention or silence.

gav·el·kind (gav''l-kīnd'), *n.* [ME. *gavelkynde, gavelkende* (orig. Kentish) < *gavel*, tribute, tax, rent (< AS. *gafol* < base of *giefan;* see GIVE) + *kynde, kinde* (see KIND, *n.*)], 1. formerly, a system of land tenure by which: (a) the property of a man dying intestate was divided equally among his sons; (b) the tenant could dispose of his land by feoffment at the age of fifteen; (c) the land did not escheat upon the conviction of the tenant as a felon. 2. a similar system of land tenure still practiced in Kent and Wales.

ga·vi·al (gā'vi-əl), *n.* [Fr. < Hind. *ghaṛiyāl*], a large crocodile of India, with a long, slender muzzle.

ga·vot (gə-vot', gav'ət), *n.* a gavotte.

ga·votte (gə-vot'), *n.* [Fr.; Pr. *gavoto*, dance of the *Gavots*, Pr. name of people of Hautes-Alpes, France, where the dance originated], 1. a 17th-century dance like the minuet, but faster and livelier. 2. the music for this, in 4/4 time.

G.A.W., guaranteed annual wage.

Ga·wain (gä'win), *n.* [prob. < W. *Gwalchmai;* ? lit., courteous], in *Arthurian legend*, a knight of the Round Table, nephew of King Arthur.

gawk (gôk), *n.* [prob. dial. var. of *gowk*, cuckoo, stupid person (< ON. *gaukr*, cuckoo); akin to synonymous G. *gauch;* the etym. crux created by forms *gawk-hand, gallock-hand*, left hand, is prob. illusory: cf. forms *golke, goilk* of *gowk*], a clumsy, stupid fellow; simpleton. *v.i.* [Colloq.], to stare like a gawk, in a stupid way.

gawk·i·ly (gôk'ə-li), *adv.* in a gawky manner.

gawk·i·ness (gôk'i-nis), *n.* the quality of being gawky.

gawk·y (gôk'i), *adj.* [GAWKIER (-i-ẽr), GAWKIEST (-i-ist)], awkward; clumsy; ungainly. *n.* a gawk.

gay (gā), *adj.* [ME. & OFr. *gai*], 1. joyous and lively; merry; happy; light-hearted. 2. bright; brilliant: as, *gay* colors. 3. given to social life and pleasures: as, a *gay* life; hence, 4. wanton; licentious: as, a *gay* dog. —*SYN.* see **lively.**

Gay, John (gā), 1685–1732; English poet and playwright; wrote *The Beggar's Opera.*

Ga·ya (gä'yə), *n.* a city in Bihar, India: pop., 105,000.

gay·e·ty (gā'ə-ti), *n.* [*pl.* GAYETIES (-tiz)], gaiety.

Gay-Lus·sac, Jo·seph Lou·is (zhô'zef' l'wē' gā'lü'sàk'), 1778–1850; French chemist and physicist.

gay·ly (gā'li), *adv.* gaily.

Gay-Pay-Oo (gā'pā'ōō'), *n.* [< first letters of Russ. *Gosudarstvennoye Politicheskoye Upravlyeniye*, governmental political department], formerly, the state security police, or secret service, of the Soviet Union, succeeding the Cheka in 1922 and succeeded by the NKVD in 1934: also called *G.P.U., Ogpu:* see **MVD.**

gay·wings (gā'wiŋz'), *n.* a trailing pink wildflower of the eastern United States and Canada.

Ga·za (gā'zə), *n.* 1. an ancient city in Asia Minor, one of the five royal cities of the Philistines: Samson died there: Judg. 16:1. 2. (*usually* gä'zə), a city in southwestern Palestine on the same site; pop., 20,000.

gaze (gāz), *v.i.* [GAZED (gāzd), GAZING], [ME. *gazen, gasen;* prob. < ON.; cf. Norw. & Sw. dial. *gasa*, to stare], to look intently and steadily; stare, as in wonder or expectancy. *n.* a steady look. —*SYN.* see **look.**

ga·ze·bo (gə-zē'bō), *n.* [*pl.* GAZEBOS, GAZEBOES (-bōz)], [said to be jocular formation (after L. *videbo*, I shall see), replacing earlier *gazing room* but ? altered < an Oriental word], a turret or windowed balcony from which one can gaze at the surrounding scenery.

gaze·hound (gāz'hound'), *n.* a dog that hunts by sight instead of scent.

ga·zelle (gə-zel'), *n.* [*pl.* GAZELLES (-zelz'), GAZELLE; see PLURAL, II, D, 1], [Fr.; Ar. *ghazāl*], any of various small, swift, graceful antelopes of Africa, the Near East, and Asia, with spirally twisted, backward-pointing horns and large, lustrous eyes.

ga·zette (gə-zet'), *n.* [Fr.; It. *gazzetta* < dial. (Venetian) *gazeta*, a small coin, price paid for the paper; orig., prob. dim. of *gaza*, magpie], 1. a newspaper: now used mainly in some newspaper titles. 2. in England, any of various official publications, as of the government or a university, containing announcements and bulletins: abbreviated **gaz.** *v.t.* [GAZETTED (-id), GAZETTING], to publish, announce, or list in a gazette.

gaz·et·teer (gaz'ə-têr'), *n.* [Fr. *gazettier, gazetier*], 1. *a*) a person who writes for a gazette. *b*) an official appointed to publish a gazette. 2. [prob. after Eachard's use for his geographical dict. (1693)], a dictionary or index of geographical names: abbreviated **gaz.**

Ga·zi·an·tep (gä'zi-än-tep'), *n.* a city in southern Turkey: pop., 63,000 (1945): also called *Aintab.*

G.B., Great Britain.

g-cal., gram calorie; gram calories.

G.C.D., g.c.d., greatest common divisor.

G.C.F., g.c.f., greatest common factor.

G clef, the treble clef: see **clef,** illus.

G.C.M., g.c.m., greatest common measure.

Gd, in *chemistry*, gadolinium.

gd., guard.

G.D., 1. Grand Duchess. 2. Grand Duke.

Gdańsk (g'dänsk), *n.* Danzig: the Polish name.

gds., goods.

Gdy·nia (g'dēn'yä), *n.* a seaport in Poland, on the Bay of Danzig: pop., 120,000.

Ge (jē, gē), *n.* Gaea; Gaia.

Ge, in *chemistry*, germanium.

ge·an·ti·cli·nal (jē'an-ti-klī'n'l), *n.* a geanticline. *adj.* of, or having the nature of, a geanticline.

ge·an·ti·cline (jē'an'ti-klīn'), *n.* [Gr. *gē*, earth; + *anticline*], in *geology*, a great upward folding of the earth's crust, often several hundred miles in breadth.

gear (gêr), *n.* [ME. *geare, gere;* ON. *gervi*, preparation, ornament; akin to AS. *gearwe* (see YARE)], 1. *a*) clothing; apparel. *b*) originally, the clothing and equipment of a soldier, knight, etc.; hence, 2. apparatus or equipment for some particular task, as a workman's tools, the rigging of a ship, a harness, etc. 3. in *mechanics*, *a*) a system of two or more toothed wheels meshed together so that the motion of one is passed on to the others. *b*) a gear wheel. *c*) adjustment or proper working order: as, out of *gear*. *d*) a specific adjustment: as, high *gear* is for greater speed. *e*) a part of a mechanism performing a specific function: as, a steering *gear*. *f*) the diameter of a hypothetical wheel whose circumference is equal to the distance trav-

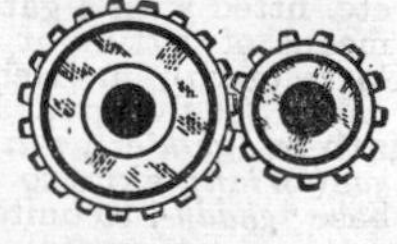
GEARS

eled by a bicycle with one revolution of the pedal. *v.t.* 1. to furnish with gear; harness. 2. to adapt (one thing) so as to conform with another: as, they *geared* production to the new demand. 3. in *mechanics, a*) to connect by gears. *b*) to furnish with gears. *c*) to put into gear. *v.i.* in *mechanics,* to be in, or come into, proper adjustment or working order.

high gear, 1. in a multiple gear system, the arrangement of gears providing the greatest speed but little power. 2. [Colloq.], high speed.
in gear, 1. connected to the motor; in adjustment for use; hence, 2. in order.
low gear, 1. in a multiple gear system, the arrangement of gears providing little speed but great power. 2. [Colloq.], low speed.
out of gear, 1. not connected to the motor; not in adjustment for use; hence, 2. out of order.
reverse gear, in a multiple gear system, the arrangement of gears providing reverse, or backward, motion.
shift gears, in a multiple gear system, to change from one gear arrangement to another.

gear·box (gêr'boks'), *n.* 1. the unit consisting of the transmission gears in a power-transmission system. 2. a case enclosing gears to protect them from dirt.

gear·ing (gêr'iŋ), *n.* 1. *a*) the fitting of a machine with gears. *b*) the manner in which the gears are fitted. 2. in *mechanics,* a system of gears or other parts for transmitting motion.

gear·shift (gêr'shift'), *n.* a device for connecting any of a number of sets of transmission gears to a motor, etc., or for disconnecting them.

gear·wheel (gêr'hwēl'), *n.* a toothed wheel designed to mesh with another or others in a system of gears; cogwheel: also **gear wheel.**

geb., *geboren,* [G.], born.

geck·o (gek'ō), *n.* [*pl.* GECKOS, GECKOES (-ōz)], [Malay *gekoq,* echoic of its cry], any of a group of soft-skinned, insect-eating lizards with short, stout bodies, large heads, weak limbs, and suction pads on their feet.

Ged·des, Norman Bel (bel ged'iz), 1893–1958; American stage and industrial designer.

gee (jē), *interj. & n.* [Early Mod. Eng.; cf. *haw*], a word of command to a horse, ox, etc. being driven without reins, meaning "turn to the right!" or (usually *gee up*) "go ahead!" *v.t. & v.i.* [GEED (jēd), GEEING], 1. to turn to the right. 2. to evade. Also spelled **jee.** Opposed to *haw.*

gee (jē), *interj.* [euphemistic contraction of *Jesus*], [Slang], an exclamation of surprise, etc.

Gee·long (jē-lôŋ'), *n.* a seaport in Victoria, Australia: pop., 39,000.

Geel·vink Bay (khāl'viŋk), a large inlet on the northern coast of Netherlands New Guinea.

geese (gēs), *n.* plural of **goose.**

geest (gēst), *n.* [LG. *geest,* sandy soil < *güst,* barren; ? akin to AS. *gæsne,* barren, destitute], in *geology,* a loose gravel deposit not of recent origin; alluvium.

gee·zer (gē'zẽr), *n.* [< dial. *guiser,* a mummer < *guise*], [Slang], an eccentric old man, or, rarely, woman.

ge·fil·te fish (ge-fil'tə), [Yid.; altered < G. *gefüllter fisch* < *gefüllt,* pp. of *füllen,* to fill + *fisch,* a fish], chopped fish, usually a mixture, as of whitefish, pike, and carp, mixed with chopped onion, egg, seasoning, etc., put into a casing of the skin, and boiled, often with vegetables.

Ge·hen·na (gi-hen'ə), *n.* [LL.; Gr. *Geenna;* Heb. *gēhinnōm*], 1. in the *Bible,* the valley of Hinnom, near Jerusalem, where refuse was dumped and fires were kept continually burning to prevent pestilence; hence, 2. *a*) a place of torment and burning. *b*) in the *New Testament,* hell.

Gei·ger counter (gī'gẽr), [after Hans *Geiger* (1882–1945), G. physicist], an instrument for detecting and counting ionizing particles that pass through it: it consists of a needlelike electrode inside a hollow metallic cylinder filled with gas which, when ionized by the radiation, sets up a current in an electric field.

Gei·ger-Mül·ler counter (gī'gẽr-mü'lẽr), an instrument similar to the Geiger counter but with an amplifying system, for detecting and measuring radioactivity.

Gei·gers (gī'gẽrz), *n.pl.* radioactive particles, etc., as measured by a Geiger counter.

gei·sha (gā'shə), *n.* [*pl.* GEISHA, GEISHAS (-shəz)], [Japan.], a Japanese professional singing and dancing girl.

Geiss·ler tube (gis'lẽr), [< Heinrich *Geissler* (1814–1879), G. physicist who invented it], a glass tube having two electrodes and containing a gas which, when electrified, takes on a luminous glow of a color characteristic of the gas: used in spectroscopy, etc.

gei·to·nog·a·my (gī'tə-nog'ə-mi), *n.* [< Gr. *geitōn,* a neighbor; + *-gamy*], the fertilization of a flower by pollen from another of the same plant: distinguished from *xenogamy.*

gel (jel), *n.* [< *gelatin*], a jellylike substance formed by a colloidal solution in its solid phase: opposed to *sol.* *v.i.* [GELLED (jeld), GELLING], to form a gel; jellify: often used figuratively.

gel·a·tin, gel·a·tine (jel'ə-t'n), *n.* [Fr. *gélatine;* It. *gelatina* < *gelata,* a jelly < pp. of L. *gelare,* to freeze], 1. *a*) the tasteless, odorless, brittle substance extracted by boiling bones, hoofs, and animal tissues. *b*) a similar vegetable substance: gelatin dissolves in hot water, forming a jellylike substance when cool, and is used in the preparation of various foods, medicine capsules, photographic film, etc. 2. a jelly made with gelatin.

ge·la·ti·nate (ji-lat''n-āt'), *v.t. & v.i.* [GELATINATED (-id), GELATINATING], to change into gelatin or gelatinous matter.

ge·lat·i·nize (ji-lat''n-īz'), *v.t.* [GELATINIZED (-īzd'), GELATINIZING], 1. to change into gelatin or gelatinous matter. 2. in *photography,* to coat with gelatin. *v.i.* to be changed into gelatin or gelatinous matter.

ge·lat·in·oid (ji-lat''n-oid', jel'ə-t'n-oid'), *adj.* like gelatin. *n.* a gelatinoid substance.

ge·lat·i·nous (ji-lat''n-əs), *adj.* [Fr. *gélatineux*], 1. of or containing gelatin. 2. like gelatin or jelly; having the consistency of gelatin or jelly; viscous.

ge·la·tion (jel-ā'shən, jə-lā'shən), *n.* [L. *gelatio* < pp. of *gelare,* to freeze], solidification by cooling or freezing.

geld (geld), *v.t.* [GELDED (-id) or GELT (gelt), GELDING], [ME. *gelden;* ON. *gelda,* to castrate < *geldr,* barren], 1. to remove the testicles of (a horse, etc.); castrate; hence, 2. to deprive of anything essential; weaken.

geld (geld), *n.* [ML. (Domesday Bk.) *geldum* < AS. *gield, geld, gyld,* payment, tribute (akin to G. *geld,* money); for IE. base see YIELD], a tax paid to the crown by English landholders in the times of the Anglo-Saxon and Norman kings.

Gel·der·land (gel'dẽr-lənd; D. khel'dẽr-länt'), *n.* a province of the eastern Netherlands: area, 1,940 sq. mi.; pop., 1,034,000 (1947); capital, Arnhem.

geld·ing (gel'diŋ), *n.* [ME.; ON. *geldingr*], 1. a gelded animal, especially a horse. 2. [Archaic], a eunuch.

gel·id (jel'id), *adj.* [L. *gelidus* < *gelu,* frost, cold; see GLACIER], frozen; frosty; extremely cold.

ge·lid·i·ty (jə-lid'ə-ti), *n.* the state of being gelid.

gel·se·mi·um (jel-sē'mi-əm), *n.* [Mod. L. < It. *gelsomino,* jessamine < Per. *yāsamīn;* see JASMINE], 1. any of a group of twining shrubs. 2. the root of one variety (*yellow jasmine*), used as a sedative.

Gel·sen·kir·chen (gel'zən-kir'Hən), *n.* a city in Westphalia, Germany: pop., 313,000.

gelt (gelt), alternative past tense and past participle of **geld.**

gem (jem), *n.* [ME. & OFr. *gemme* (AS. *gim*); L. *gemma,* a swelling, bud, precious stone], 1. a precious or, occasionally, semiprecious stone, cut and polished for use as a jewel. 2. anything prized for its beauty and value, especially if small and perfect of its kind. 3. a kind of muffin. *v.t.* [GEMMED (jemd), GEMMING], to adorn or set with or as with gems.

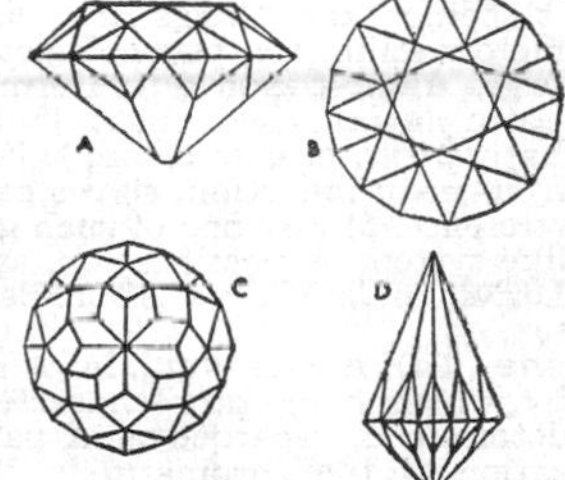

CUTS OF GEMS

A, American (side view); B, American (top view); C, 20th century (top view); D, briolette

Ge·ma·ra (gə-môr'ə, gə-mä'rä), *n.* [Aram. *gemārā,* completion], the second and supplementary part of the Talmud, providing a commentary on the first part (the Mishna).

gem·el (jem'əl), *n.* [ME.; OFr. < L. *gemellus,* dim. of *geminus,* a twin], 1. in *heraldry,* either of two bars placed together across a shield. 2. in *mechanics,* either of two units, as a hook and loop, together forming a hinge: often used attributively, as, *gemel* hinge.

gem·i·nate (jem'ə-nāt'), *adj.* [< L. *geminatus,* pp. of *geminare,* to double < *geminus,* twin], growing or combined in pairs; coupled. *v.t.* [GEMINATED (-id), GEMINATING], to double; arrange in pairs. *v.i.* to become doubled or paired.

gem·i·na·tion (jem'ə-nā'shən), *n.* [L. *geminatio* < pp. of *geminare;* see GEMINATE], a doubling; duplication; especially, the doubling of a consonant or consonant sound.

Gem·i·ni (jem'ə-nī'), *n.pl.* [L., twins], 1. a northern constellation between Cancer and Taurus, containing the stars Castor and Pollux, represented as twins sitting together. 2. the third sign of the zodiac (Ⅱ or □ or ♊), entered by the sun about May 21: see **zodiac,** illus.

gem·ma (jem'ə), *n.* [*pl.* GEMMAE (-ē)], [L.; cf. GEM], in *biology,* 1. a bud. 2. a budlike outgrowth which be-

comes detached and develops into a new organism.
gem·mate (jem′āt), *adj.* [L. *gemmatus*, pp. of *gemmare*, to put forth buds < *gemma*, a bud], having or reproducing by gemmae. *v.i.* [GEMMATED (-id), GEMMATING], to have, or reproduce by, gemmae; bud.
gem·ma·tion (jem-ā′shən), *n.* [Fr. < L. *gemmatus*, pp. of *gemmare;* see GEMMATE], formation of or reproduction by gemmae.
gem·mip·a·rous (jem-ip′ēr-əs), *adj.* [< L. *gemma*, a bud; + *-parous*], in *biology*, of or reproducing by gemmation; budding.
gem·mu·la·tion (jem′yoo-lā′shən), *n.* formation of or reproduction by gemmules.
gem·mule (jem′ūl), *n.* [Fr.; L. *gemmula*, dim. of *gemma*, a bud], in *biology*, a small gemma.
gem·my (jem′i), *adj.* [ME.], 1. set with gems. 2. like a gem; glittering.
gems·bok (gemz′bok′), *n.* [*pl.* GEMSBOK, GEMSBOKS (-boks′); see PLURAL, II, D, 2], [D.; G. *gemsbock; gemse*, chamois + *bock*, a buck], a large, South African antelope with long, straight horns.
‡**ge·müt·lich** (gə-müt′liH), *adj.* [G.], agreeable, cheerful, cozy, etc.: indicating a general sense of well-being.
-gen (jen, jən), [Fr. *-gène;* Gr. *-genēs*, born < base of *gignesthai*, to be born, become; see GENUS], a suffix used to form nouns meaning: 1. *something that produces*, as in *oxygen, hydrogen*. 2. *something produced* (in a specified way), as in *endogen*.
Gen., 1. General. 2. Genesis. 3. Geneva.
gen., 1. gender. 2. genera. 3. general. 4. generally. 5. generator. 6. generic. 7. genitive. 8. genus.
gen·darme (zhän′därm; Fr. zhän′dȧrm′), *n.* [*pl.* GENDARMES (-därmz; Fr. -dȧrm′)], [Fr. < *gens d'armes*, men-at-arms < L. *gens*, a people, nation + *de*, of, from + *arma*, arms], 1. formerly, a French cavalryman commanding a squad. 2. in France, Belgium, etc., an armed policeman; hence, 3. any policeman: humorous or literary usage.
gen·dar·me·rie (zhän′där-mēr-i; Fr. zhän′dȧr′m′rē′), *n.* [Fr.], gendarmes collectively; the police.
gen·darm·er·y (zhän′där-mēr-i), *n.* gendarmerie.
gen·der (jen′dēr), *n.* [ME.; OFr. *gendre*, with unhistoric *-d-* < L. *genus, generis*, descent, origin, translating Gr. (Aristotle) *gēnos;* see GENUS], 1. in *grammar, a)* the classification by which nouns and pronouns (and often accompanying modifiers) are grouped and inflected, or changed in form, in relation to sex or their lack of it: gender is *natural* when, as in English, Persian, and Armenian, animate beings and inanimate things are classified as masculine, feminine, and neuter (e.g., *man*, masc.; *woman*, fem.; *tree*, neut.); gender is *grammatical* when, as in the majority of languages possessing it, beings and things are classified according to remotely animistic, psychological, or formal associations (e.g., Anglo-Saxon *wif*, German *weib*, woman, neut.; Latin *fluvius*, river, masc. [but *flumen*, stream, neut.]; Latin *pirus*, pear tree, fem.): English, now virtually free from noun inflection, shows gender chiefly by pronoun reference. *b)* any one of such groupings. *c)* any gender-like system of classification, as the caste-system of the Dravidian languages. Abbreviated **gen., g.** 2. [Colloq.], sex.
gene (jēn), *n.* [see -GEN], in *genetics*, any of the elements by which hereditary characters are transmitted and determined, regarded as a particular state of organization of the chromatin in the chromosome; factor: theoretically each mature reproductive cell carries a gene for every inheritable characteristic, and thus an individual resulting from the union of two such cells receives a set of genes from each of its parents: see **dominant character, recessive character.**
gen·e·a·log·i·cal (jē′ni-ə-loj′i-k'l, jen′i-ə-loj′i-k'l), *adj.* 1. of genealogy. 2. tracing a line of descent.
gen·e·a·log·i·cal·ly (jē′ni-ə-loj′i-k'l-i, jen′i-ə-loj′ik-li), *adv.* 1. in a genealogical manner. 2. according to genealogy.
gen·e·al·o·gist (jē′ni-al′ə-jist, jen′i-äl′ə-jist), *n.* a person who studies genealogies or traces them.
gen·e·al·o·gy (jē′ni-al′ə-ji, jen′i-äl′ə-ji), *n.* [*pl.* GENEALOGIES (-jiz)], [ME. *genelogi;* OFr. *genealogie;* LL. *genealogia;* Gr. *genealogia* < *genea*, race, stock (cf. GENUS) + *logos*, a discourse < *legein*, to speak], 1. a recorded history of the descent of a person or family from an ancestor or ancestors. 2. the science or study of family descent. 3. descent from an ancestor; pedigree; lineage. Abbreviated **geneal.**
gen·er·a (jen′ēr-ə), *n.* plural of **genus**: abbreviated **gen.**
gen·er·a·ble (jen′ēr-ə-b'l), *adj.* [L. *generabilis*], that can be generated.
gen·er·al (jen′ēr-əl, jen′rəl), *adj.* [ME.; OFr.; L. *generalis* < *genus, generis*, kind, class; see GENUS], 1. of, for, or from the whole or all; not particular; not local: as, a *general* anesthetic, the *general* welfare. 2. of, for, or applying to a whole genus, kind, class, order, or race: as, animal, vegetable, and mineral are the three *general* classifications of matter. 3. existing or occurring extensively; common; widespread: as, there is a *general* unrest in the country; hence, 4. most common; usual: as, what is the *general* pronunciation of that word? 5. concerned with the main or over-all features; lacking in details; not specific: as, these are the *general* characteristics; hence, 6. vague; not precise: as, he spoke in *general* terms. 7. senior or highest in rank: as, the attorney *general*. 8. not connected with or limited to one branch or department of learning, business, etc.; not specialized: as, a *general* store. Abbreviated **gen., genl., g.** (in senses 1, 2, 4, 8). *n.* 1. the main or over-all fact, condition, idea, etc.: opposed to *particular*. 2. the head of a religious order. 3. [Archaic], the public; populace. 4. in *military usage, a)* a full general: see **full general, lieutenant general, major general, brigadier general, General of the Army.** *b)* any general officer: a shortened title. *c)* in some foreign armies, an officer ranking immediately below a marshal. Abbreviated **Gen.** (as a title in all military senses). —*SYN.* see **common, universal.**
in general, 1. in the main; usually. 2. without specific details. 3. with reference to all spoken of.
General American, the English language as conversationally spoken by most people in the greater part of the United States, exclusive of much of New England and most of the South.
General Assembly, 1. in some States of the United States, the legislative assembly: abbreviated **G.A.** 2. the legislative assembly of the United Nations.
General Court, 1. originally, a Colonial legislative assembly with judicial powers. 2. now, the legislature of New Hampshire or Massachusetts: the official title.
general court-martial, the most formal military court, for judging the gravest offenses: it consists of five or more officers or (since 1948) enlisted men, and can impose the death sentence.
gen·er·al·cy (jen′ēr-əl-si, jen′rəl-si), *n.* [*pl.* GENERALCIES (-siz)], the rank, commission, tenure of office, or authority of a general.
general delivery, 1. delivery of mail at the post office to addressees who call for it. 2. the department of the post office responsible for such delivery.
general election, a final election to choose between the candidates nominated in the primary elections.
general headquarters, in *military usage*, the headquarters of a commanding general in the field: abbreviated **G.H.Q.**
gen·er·al·is·si·mo (jen′ēr-əl-is′ə-mō′, jen′rəl-is′ə-mō′), *n.* [*pl.* GENERALISSIMOS (-mōz′)], [It. superl. of *generale*, general; see GENERAL], 1. in certain countries, the commander in chief of all the armed forces. 2. the commanding officer of several armies in the field.
gen·er·al·i·ty (jen′ə-ral′ə-ti), *n.* [*pl.* GENERALITIES (-tiz)], [Fr. *généralité;* LL. *generalitas* < L. *generalis*], 1. the condition or quality of being general, or applicable to all. 2. a general, or nonspecific, statement, expression, idea, principle, etc.: as, he spoke in *generalities*. 3. the bulk; main body; majority; mass.
gen·er·al·i·za·tion (jen′ēr-əl-i-zā′shən, jen′rəl-ī-zā′-shən), *n.* 1. the act or process of generalizing. 2. a general idea, statement, etc. resulting from this; inference applied generally.
gen·er·al·ize (jen′ēr-əl-īz′, jen′rəl-īz′), *v.t.* [GENERALIZED (-īzd′), GENERALIZING], to make general; especially, *a)* to state in terms of a general law or precept. *b)* to infer (a general law or precept) from particular instances. *c)* to draw, infer, or induce general principles, etc. from. *d)* to emphasize the general character rather than specific details of; make vague. *e)* to cause to be widely known or used; popularize. *v.i.* 1. to formulate general principles or inferences from particulars. 2. to talk in generalities; make vague or indefinite statements.
gen·er·al·ly (jen′ēr-əl-i, jen′rəl-i), *adv.* 1. widely; popularly; extensively; to or by most people: as, it is *generally* believed that he is innocent. 2. in most instances; usually; as a rule. 3. in a general way or sense; without reference to details or individual cases; not specifically. Abbreviated **gen.**
general officer, in *military usage*, any officer above a colonel in rank.
General of the Armies, in the *United States Army*, the honorary rank given General John J. Pershing on his retirement from active service.
General of the Army, the highest rank in the United States Army, having the insigne of five stars.
general paralysis (or **paresis**), see **paresis.**
general post office, the main post office of a city or area having branch offices: abbreviated **G.P.O.**
general practitioner, a practicing physician who does not specialize in any particular field of medicine: abbreviated **G.P., g.p.**
gen·er·al·ship (jen′ēr-əl-ship′, jen′rəl-ship′), *n.* [see -SHIP], 1. *a)* the rank, commission, tenure of office, or authority of a general. *b)* the military skill of a general; hence, 2. skillfulness of directing or managing; leadership.
general staff, in *military usage*, a group of specially trained officers who assist the commander of a division or higher unit in planning and supervising military operations: abbreviated **G.S., g.s.**
general store, a store where many sorts of merchandise are sold.

general strike, a strike by the workers in an entire industry or in all or many of the industries in a community or country.

gen·er·ate (jen′ə-rāt′), *v.t.* [GENERATED (-id), GENERATING], [< L. *generatus*, pp. of *generare*, to beget, produce < *genus*, *generis*, race, kind; see GENUS], 1. to produce (offspring); beget; procreate. 2. to bring into being; cause to be; produce; originate. 3. in *mathematics*, to trace out or form (a line, plane, figure, or solid) by the motion of a point, line, or plane.

gen·er·a·tion (jen′ə-rā′shən), *n.* [L. *generatio* < *generatus;* see GENERATE], 1. the act or process of producing offspring; procreation. 2. the act or process of bringing into being; origination; production. 3. a single stage or degree in the succession of natural descent: as, father, son, and grandson are three *generations*. 4. the period of time (about thirty years) between the birth of one generation and that of another. 5. all the people born at about the same time or living in the same period of time. 6. in *mathematics*, the formation of a line, figure, plane, or solid by the motion of a point, line, or plane.

gen·er·a·tive (jen′ə-rā′tiv, jen′ẽr-ə-tiv), *adj.* [ME. *generatif*], 1. of the production of offspring; procreative. 2. having the power of producing or originating.

gen·er·a·tor (jen′ə-rā′tẽr), *n.* [L.], a person or thing that generates; especially, *a)* a machine for producing gas or steam. *b)* a machine for changing mechanical energy into electrical energy; dynamo. Abbreviated **gen.**

gen·er·a·trix (jen′ə-rā′triks), *n.* [*pl.* GENERATRICES (-ẽr-ə-trī′sēz)], [L., fem. of *generator*], in *mathematics*, a point, line, or plane whose motion generates a line, plane, figure, or solid.

ge·ner·ic (jə-ner′ik), *adj.* [< L. *genus*, *generis*, race, kind (see GENUS); + *-ic*], 1. of, applied to, or referring to a kind, class, or group; inclusive or general: opposed to *specific*, *special*. 2. in *biology*, of or characteristic of a genus. Abbreviated **gen.** —*SYN.* see **universal.**

ge·ner·i·cal·ly (jə-ner′i-k′l-i, jə-ner′ik-li), *adv.* in a generic manner.

gen·er·os·i·ty (jen′ə-ros′ə-ti), *n.* [ME. & OFr. *generosite;* L. *generositas* < *generosus*], 1. the quality of being generous; specifically, *a)* nobility of mind; magnanimity. *b)* willingness to give or share; being unselfish. 2. [*pl.* GENEROSITIES (-tiz)], a generous act.

gen·er·ous (jen′ẽr-əs), *adj.* [ME. *generus;* OFr. *generous;* L. *generosus*, of noble birth, excellent, generous < *genus*, *generis*, race, kind; see GENUS], 1. originally, of noble birth; hence, 2. having qualities attributed to people of noble birth; noble-minded; gracious; not mean; magnanimous. 3. willing to give or share; unselfish; bountiful; liberal. 4. large; ample: as, *generous* portions. 5. rich in yield; fertile: said of land, soil, etc. 6. rich, full-flavored, and strong: said of wine.

Gen·e·see (jen′ə-sē′), *n.* a river in western New York, flowing northward into Lake Ontario: length, 120 mi.

gen·e·sis (jen′ə-sis), *n.* [*pl.* GENESES (-sēz′)], [AS.; L.; Gr. *genesis*, birth, origin < base of *gignesthai*, to be born, become; see GENUS], 1. [G-], the first book of the Old Testament, giving an account of the creation of the universe: abbreviated **Gen.** 2. a beginning; origin; creation; way in which something is formed.

-gen·e·sis (jen′ə-sis), [see GENESIS], a noun-forming combining form, meaning *origination*, *creation*, *formation*, *evolution* (of something specified), as in *parthenogenesis*.

gen·et (jen′it, jə-net′), *n.* [ME.; OFr. *genette;* Sp. *gineta;* Ar. *jarnayt*], 1. any of a group of small, spotted African animals related to the civet. 2. *a)* the fur of this animal. *b)* fur made in imitation of this. Also spelled **genette.**

gen·et (jen′it), *n.* jennet.

ge·net·ic (jə-net′ik), *adj.* [< *genesis*, by analogy with *antithesis*, *antithetic*], 1. of the genesis, or origin, of something. 2. of genetics. 3. genic.

ge·net·i·cal·ly (jə-net′i-k′l-i, jə-net′ik-li), *adv.* **1.** with reference to origin, beginning, or genesis. 2. according to the principles of genetics.

ge·net·i·cist (jə-net′ə-sist), *n.* a specialist in genetics.

ge·net·ics (jə-net′iks), *n.pl.* [construed as sing.], [< *genetic*], 1. the branch of biology that deals with heredity and variation in similar or related animals and plants. 2. the genetic features or constitution of an individual, group, or kind.

ge·nette (jə-net′), *n.* a genet (catlike animal).

Ge·ne·va (jə-nē′və), *n.* 1. a city in Switzerland, on Lake Geneva: pop., 124,000: French name, *Genève*. 2. a lake between southwestern Switzerland and France: area, 225 sq. mi.: also called *Lake Léman*.

ge·ne·va (jə-nē′və), *n.* [D. *genever;* OFr. *genevre*, juniper berry < L. *juniperus*, juniper], gin (liquor); Holland gin.

Geneva bands, two linen strips hanging from the front of the neck, worn with clerical or academic dress.

Geneva Convention, an international agreement signed at Geneva in 1864, establishing a code for the care and treatment in wartime of the sick, wounded, and prisoners of war, including protection of hospitals, ambulances, etc. having the emblem of the Red Cross.

Geneva cross, a red Greek cross on a white background: see **red cross.**

Geneva gown, a long, loose, wide-sleeved black gown, first worn by the Calvinistic clergy of Geneva.

Ge·ne·van (jə-nē′vən), *adj.* 1. of Geneva or its people. 2. having to do with the doctrines or followers of John Calvin, who established a theocratic state in Geneva; Calvinistic. *n.* 1. a native or inhabitant of Geneva. 2. a follower of Calvin.

Ge·nève (zhə-nev′), *n.* Geneva: the French name.

Gen·e·vese (jen′ə-vēz′), *adj. & n. sing. & pl.* Genevan.

Gen·e·vieve (jen′ə-vēv′, jen′ə-vēv′), [Fr. *Geneviève;* LL. *Genovefa;* ? < Celt.], a feminine name.

Genevieve, Saint, 422?–512 A.D.; patron saint of Paris.

Gen·ghis Khan (jen′giz kän′, jeŋ′gis kän′), 1167–1227; Mongol conqueror of central Asia: also spelled **Jenghiz Khan.**

gen·ial (jēn′yəl; *for 1,* jē′ni-əl), *adj.* [L. *genialis*, of generation or birth, nuptial < *genius*, guardian deity; see GENIUS], 1. [Rare], of marriage or generation. 2. good for life and growth; pleasantly warm and mild: as, a *genial* climate. 3. cheerful, friendly, and sympathetic; cordial and kindly; amiable. 4. [Rare], of or characterized by genius. —*SYN.* see **amiable.**

ge·ni·al (ji-nī′əl), *adj.* [< Gr. *geneion*, a chin (< *genys*, a jaw; cf. CHIN); + *-al*], having to do with the chin.

ge·ni·al·i·ty (jē′ni-al′ə-ti, jēn-yal′ə-ti), *n.* the quality of being genial; especially, cheerful friendliness; sympathetic cordiality.

gen·ic (jen′ik), *adj.* of, having the nature of, or caused by a gene or genes; genetic.

-gen·ic (jen′ik), a combining form used to form adjectives corresponding to nouns ending in *-gen* or *-geny*, as in *endogenic*, *phylogenic*.

ge·nic·u·late (jə-nik′yoo-lit), *adj.* [L. *geniculatus* < *geniculum*, dim. of *genu*, knee], having a kneelike joint or joints; bent like a knee.

ge·nie (jē′ni), *n.* [Fr. *génie;* L. *genius;* see GENIUS, JINNI], a jinni; spirit; demon.

ge·ni·i (jē′ni-ī′), *n.* occasional plural of **genius.**

gen·i·pap (jen′i-pap′), *n.* [Port. *genipapo* < the W. Ind. (Tupi) name], 1. the brown, edible fruit, about the size of an orange, of a certain tropical American tree. 2. the tree.

genit., genitive.

gen·i·tal (jen′ə-t′l), *adj.* [ME.; OFr.; L. *genitalis* <*genitus*, pp. of *genere*, *gignere*, to beget; see GENUS], of reproduction or the sexual organs.

gen·i·ta·li·a (jen′ə-tāl′yə, jen′ə-tā′li-ə), *n.pl.* [L., short for *genitalia* (*membra*)], genitals.

gen·i·tals (jen′ə-t′lz), *n.pl.* [< *genital*], the reproductive organs; especially, the external sex organs.

gen·i·ti·val (jen′ə-tī′v′l), *adj.* of or in the genitive case.

gen·i·tive (jen′ə-tiv), *adj.* [OFr. *genitif;* L. *genitivus*, of birth, genitive case < *genitus*, pp. of *genere*, *gignere*, to beget, produce; see GENUS, GENITIVE CASE], of or in the genitive case. *n.* 1. the genitive case. 2. a word or construction in the genitive case. Abbreviated **gen., genit., g.**

genitive case, [after L. *casus genitivus*, lit., case relating to birth, for "case of origin"; mistransl. < Gr. *genikē*, generic (case), (case) of genus < Gr. *gēnos*, genus], 1. in *Latin grammar*, a relational case shown by inflection of nouns, pronouns, and adjectives, chiefly expressing possession (L. *liber Petri*, lit., book of Peter, hence Peter's book), material or substance (L. *virga lauri*, twig of laurel), and partition (L. *pars mundi*, part of the world): originally a generic case and almost adjectival in force. 2. in *linguistics*, loosely, any generic case with functions resembling or thought to resemble those of the Latin genitive; specifically, in English grammar, the possessive case, considered as adjectival by many linguists.

gen·i·to- (jen′ə-tō), a combining form meaning *genital and*, as in *genitourinary*.

gen·i·to·u·ri·nar·y, gen·i·to-u·ri·nar·y (jen′i-tō-yoor′ə-ner′i), *adj.* designating or of the genital and urinary organs together: abbreviated **g.u.**

gen·ius (jēn′yəs, jē′ni-əs), *n.* [*pl.* for 3, 4, 5, 6 GENIUSES (-iz), for 1 & 2 GENII (jē′ni-ī′)], [L., guardian deity or spirit of a person, spirit, natural ability, genius < base of *genere*, *gignere*, to produce; see GENUS], 1. *a)* [often G-], according to ancient Roman belief, a guardian spirit assigned to a person at birth; tutelary deity; hence, *b)* [often G-], the guardian spirit of any person, place, etc. *c)* either of two spirits, one good and one evil, supposed to influence one's destiny. *d)* a person considered as having strong influence over another. 2. a jinni; spirit; demon. 3. particular character or essential spirit or nature of a nation, place, age, etc. 4. natural ability; strong disposition or inclination; innate ability (with *to* or *for*). 5. great mental capacity and inventive ability; especially, great and original creative ability in some art, science, etc. 6. a person having such capacity or ability. —*SYN.* see **talent.**

‡**ge·ni·us lo·ci** (jē′ni-əs lō′sī), [L., lit., the (guardian) spirit of a place], the general atmosphere of a place.

genl., general.

Gen·o·a (jen′ō-ə, ji-nō′ə), *n.* 1. a seaport in northwestern Italy: pop., 649,000 (1947). 2. a former republic of Italy. Italian name, *Genova*.

gen·o·cide (jen′ə-sīd′), *n.* [< Gr. *genos*, race, kind; + *-cide*: first applied to the attempted extermination of the Jews by Nazi Germany], the systematic killing or extermination of a whole people or nation.

Gen·o·ese (jen′ō-ēz′), *adj.* of Genoa, its people, etc. *n.* [*pl.* GENOESE], a native or inhabitant of Genoa.

gen·o·type (jen′ə-tīp′), *n.* [< Gr. *genos*, race, kind (see GENUS); + *-type*], 1. the fundamental constitution of an organism in terms of its hereditary factors. 2. a group of organisms each having the same combination of hereditary characteristics.

-gen·ous (jə-nəs), [*-gen* + *-ous*], a suffix used to form adjectives derived from nouns ending in *-gen*, *-geny*, meaning: 1. *producing, generating*, as in *nitrogenous*. 2. *produced by, generated in*, as in *autogenous*.

Ge·no·va (je′nô-vä′), *n.* Genoa: the Italian name.

gen·re (zhän′rə; Fr. zhän′r′), *n.* [Fr.; L. *genus, generis;* see GENUS, GENDER], 1. a kind; sort; type: said of works of literature, art, etc. 2. genre painting.

genre painting, painting in which subjects from everyday life are treated realistically.

gen·ro (gen′rō′), *n.* [Japan., lit., first (of the) elders], in Japan, formerly, a group of retired statesmen assembled to advise the emperor: see **elder statesman.**

gens (jenz), *n.* [*pl.* GENTES (jen′tēz)], [L., orig., that belonging together by birth or descent < base of *gignere*, to beget, produce; see GENUS], 1. in ancient Rome, a clan united by descent through the male line from a common ancestor and having both a name and religious observances in common. 2. any tribe or clan; especially, an exogamous group reckoning descent only through the male line.

Gen·san (gen′sän′), *n.* a seaport in eastern Korea: pop., 67,000: Japanese name, *Wonsan*.

Gent (gent), *n.* Ghent: the Flemish name.

gent (jent), *n.* [Slang], a gentleman; man: humorous or vulgar term.

gent (jent), *adj.* [ME.; OFr.; L. *genitus*, born, pp. of *gignere*, to beget, produce; see GENUS], [Obs.], 1. of good birth and social standing. 2. pretty; graceful.

Gent., gent., gentleman; gentlemen.

gen·teel (jen-tēl′), *adj.* [< Fr. *gentil* (of same origin as *gentle* & *jaunty*, but reborrowed in 16th c.)], 1. formerly, gentlemanly or ladylike; well-bred; refined; polite; elegant; fashionable. 2. excessively, affectedly, or pretentiously well-bred, refined, polite, etc.

gen·tian (jen′shən), *n.* [ME. *genciane;* OFr. *gentiane;* L. *gentiana* < *Gentius*, Illyrian king who discovered its properties], 1. any of a large group of plants with blue, white, red, or yellow flowers. 2. the bitter root of the yellow gentian, used as a gastrointestinal tonic.

gen·ti·a·na·ceous (jen′shi-ə-nā′shəs), *adj.* [< Mod.L. *Gentianaceae*, name of the family], of the gentian family.

gentian violet, a violet dye used as an antiseptic and as a stain in microscopy.

gen·tile (jen′tīl; *for adj. 4 & 5, usually* jen′til), *n.* [< Fr. & L.; Fr. *gentil;* L. *gentilis*, of the same gens, clan, or race; also, foreigner (in opposition to Roman), pagan, heathen (in opposition to Jew and Christian); see GENTLE], 1. any person not a Jew. 2. formerly, among Christians, a heathen; pagan. 3. among Mormons, any person not a Mormon. *adj.* 1. not Jewish. 2. heathen; pagan. 3. not Mormon. 4. of a clan, tribe, people, or nation. 5. in *grammar*, designating a nationality or country: as, French is a *gentile* word. Also [G-] for *n.* & *adj.* 1 & 3. —*SYN.* see **pagan.**

gen·ti·lesse (jen′t'l-es′), *n.* [ME.; OFr. *gentillise* < *gentil;* see GENTLE], [Archaic], the quality of being gentle, or polite; courtesy; good breeding.

gen·til·i·ty (jen-til′ə-ti), *n.* [*pl.* GENTILITIES (-tiz)], [ME. & OFr. *gentilite;* L. *gentilitas* < *gentilis;* see GENTLE, GENTEEL], 1. originally, gentle birth; position of a person of the upper classes. 2. politeness; refinement; respectability: now sometimes ironic.

gen·tle (jen′t'l), *adj.* [GENTLER (-tlẽr), GENTLEST (-tlist)], [ME. & OFr. *gentil*, noble, of noble birth; L. *gentilis*, of the same gens, clan, or race (in LL., of a good family) < *gens;* see GENS], 1. belonging to a family of social standing; of the upper classes; of good birth. 2. having qualities considered appropriate to those of good birth; refined; polite. 3. [Archaic], noble; chivalrous: as, a *gentle* knight; hence, 4. generous; kind: in the phrase *gentle reader*. 5. easily handled; tame: as, a *gentle* dog. 6. kindly; serene; patient: as, a *gentle* disposition. 7. mild; moderate; not violent, harsh, or rough: as, a *gentle* tap, a *gentle* rebuke. 8. designating a mild breeze, usually one with a velocity of no more than 12 miles per hour. 9. gradual: as, a *gentle* slope. *n.* 1. [so called because soft], the larva of the bluebottle fly. 2. *usually in pl.* [Archaic], a person born into a family of social standing. *v.t.* [GENTLED (-t'ld), GENTLING], [Rare], 1. to make gentle. 2. to tame or train (a horse). 3. [Obs.], to raise to the social status of a gentleman; make a noble of. —*SYN.* see **soft.**

the gentle craft (or **art**), 1. fishing. 2. [Obs.], shoemaking.

the gentle sex, women; womankind.

gen·tle·folk (jen′t'l-fōk′), *n.pl.* people of good birth and social standing: also **gentlefolks.**

gen·tle·man (jen′t'l-mən), *n.* [*pl.* GENTLEMEN (-mən)], [ME. *gentilman* (after OFr. *gentilz hom*); see GENTLE & MAN], 1. a man of good birth and social standing. 2. a well-bred, courteous, gracious, considerate man. 3. a man in attendance on a person of rank. 4. *often in pl.* any man: polite term, as of address. Abbreviated **Gent., gent.** (*sing.* & *pl.*).

the gentleman from ——, in the United States House of Representatives, the member from (a specified State).

gen·tle·man-at-arms (jen′t'l-mən-ət-ärmz′), *n.* [*pl.* GENTLEMEN-AT-ARMS], in Great Britain, any of a group of forty gentlemen who accompany the sovereign as a guard on important occasions.

gen·tle·man-farm·er (jen′t'l-mən-fär′mẽr), *n.* [*pl.* GENTLEMEN-FARMERS], a wealthy man who owns and manages a farm, but usually does not work on it.

gentleman in waiting, a man of social standing serving as an attendant for a king or prince.

gen·tle·man·like (jen′t'l-mən-līk′), *adj.* gentlemanly.

gen·tle·man·ly (jen′t'l-mən-li), *adj.* [ME.], of, characteristic of, or fit for a gentleman; well-mannered.

gentleman of fortune, an adventurer; specifically, *a*) a pirate. *b*) a cheating gambler.

gentleman's (or **gentlemen's**) **agreement,** an informal, unwritten agreement secured only by the parties' pledge of honor and not legally binding.

gentleman's gentleman, [*pl.* GENTLEMEN'S GENTLEMEN], a valet.

gen·tle·wom·an (jen′t'l-woom′ən), *n.* [*pl.* GENTLEWOMEN (-wim′in)], 1. a woman of good birth and social standing; lady. 2. a well-bred, courteous, gracious, considerate woman. 3. formerly, a woman in attendance on a lady of rank.

gen·tly (jen′tli), *adv.* in a gentle manner; specifically, *a*) so as to be a gentleman or gentlewoman: as, *gently* born. *b*) in the manner of gentlefolk: as, *gently* bred. *c*) softly, mildly, lightly, tenderly, etc.: as, treat the child *gently*. *d*) gradually: as, the hill sloped *gently*.

Gen·too (jen-tōō′), *n.* [*pl.* GENTOOS (-tōōz′)], [Port. *gentio*, heathen, gentile < L. *gentilis;* see GENTILE], 1. a Hindu, as distinguished from a Moslem of India. 2. the language of the Gentoos. *adj.* of the Gentoos.

gen·try (jen′tri), *n.* [ME. *genterie*, noble or high birth; apparently taken as sing. of *genterise*, gentility of birth; OFr. *genterise, gentilise* < *gentil;* see GENTEEL], 1. [Obs.], rank resulting from birth; especially, high rank. 2. people of good birth and social standing; especially, in Great Britain, the class of people ranking just below the nobility. 3. people of a particular class or group: usually humorous or disparaging, as, the newspaper *gentry*.

ge·nu (jē′nū), *n.* [*pl.* GENUA (jen′ū-ə)], [L., knee; for IE. base see KNEE], 1. the knee. 2. a kneelike part.

gen·u·flect (jen′yoo-flekt′), *v.i.* [ML. *genuflectere;* see GENUFLECTION], to bend the knee, as in reverence or worship.

gen·u·flec·tion, gen·u·flex·ion (jen′yoo-flek′shən), *n.* [ML. *genuflexio* < L. *genu*, the knee + *flectere*, to bend; see FLEX], a genuflecting, as in reverence or worship.

gen·u·ine (jen′ū-in), *adj.* [L. *genuinus*, orig., inborn, native, hence authentic, genuine < base of *gignere*, to be born; see GENUS], 1. of the original stock; purebred. 2. really being what it is said to be; actually coming from the alleged source or origin; real; true; authentic; not counterfeit or artificial. 3. sincere and frank; honest and forthright. —*SYN.* see **authentic.**

ge·nus (jē′nəs), *n.* [*pl.* GENERA (jen′ẽr-ə), sometimes GENUSES (jē′nəs-iz)], [L., birth, origin, race, species, kind, class < IE. base *ĝen-, *ĝenē-, *ĝenō-, to beget, produce, seen also in L. *gignere*, to beget; Gr. *genos*, race, *gignesthai*, to be born; G. *kind*, child; AS. (*ge*)*cynd*, kind, *cennan*, to beget; also, with loss of initial *g-* in L. *nascor*, to be born, *natura*, nature], 1. a class; kind; sort. 2. in *logic*, any class of things made up of subordinate classes, or species. 3. in *biology*, a classification of plants or animals with common distinguishing characteristics: a genus is the main subdivision of a family and includes one or more species; the genus name is capitalized and precedes the species name, which is not capitalized (e.g., *Homo sapiens*, the scientific name for man): abbreviated **gen.**

-gen·y (jə-ni), [Gr. *-geneia;* see -GEN], a suffix meaning *manner of origin, production*, or *development*, as in *phylogeny*.

ge·o- (jē′ō, jē′ə), [Gr. *geō-* < *gaia, gē*, the earth], a combining form meaning *earth, of the earth*, as in *geocentric, geophyte*.

ge·o·cen·tric (jē′ō-sen′trik), *adj.* [*geo-* + *centric*], 1. measured or viewed as from the center of the earth. 2. having or regarding the earth as a center.

ge·o·cen·tri·cal (jē′ō-sen′tri-k'l), *adj.* geocentric.

ge·o·chem·is·try (jē′ō-kem′is-tri), *n.* the science dealing with the chemical composition of the earth's crust.

ge·ode (jē′ōd), *n.* [Fr. *géode;* L. *geodes;* Gr. *gaiōdēs, geōdēs,* earthlike < *gē,* earth + *eidos,* form], 1. a stone having a cavity lined with crystals. 2. *a*) such a cavity. *b*) any formation like this.

ge·o·des·ic (jē′ə-des′ik, jē′ə-dē′sik), *adj.* of or determined by geodesy; geodetic.

ge·od·e·sy (jē-od′ə-si), *n.* [Fr. *géodésie;* Mod. L. *geodaesia;* Gr. *geōdaisia* < *gē,* the earth + *daiein,* to divide], the branch of applied mathematics concerned with measuring, or determining the shape of, the earth or a large part of its surface, or with locating exactly points on its surface: abbreviated **geod.**

ge·o·det·ic (jē′ə-det′ik), *adj.* of or determined by geodesy; geodesic: abbreviated **geod.**

ge·o·det·i·cal·ly (jē′ə-det′i-k′l-i), *adv.* by or according to geodesy.

ge·o·det·ics (jē′ə-det′iks), *n.pl.* [construed as sing.], [< *geodetic*], geodesy.

ge·od·ic (jē-od′ik), *adj.* of or like a geode.

Geof·frey (jef′ri), [< Fr. or OFr.; Fr. *Geoffroi;* OFr. *Jofrei;* ML. *Gaufridus, Galfridus,* var. of *Godefridus;* OHG. *Godafrid;* see GODFREY], a masculine name: diminutives, *Geof, Jeff;* variant, *Jeffrey.*

Geoffrey of Monmouth, 1100?–1154; Welsh chronicler; transmitter of the Arthurian legend.

geog., 1. geographer. 2. geographical. 3. geography.

ge·og·no·sy (jē-og′nə-si), *n.* [Fr. *géognosie* < Gr. *gē,* earth + *gnōsis,* knowledge < *gignōskein,* to know], the branch of geology dealing with the composition of the earth and the distribution of its various strata and mineral deposits.

ge·og·ra·pher (jē-og′rə-fẽr, jē-ôg′rə-fẽr), *n.* [< ML. *geographus* (Gr. *geōgraphos*); + *-er*], a student of or specialist in geography: abbreviated **geog.**

ge·o·graph·ic (jē′ə-graf′ik), *adj.* geographical.

ge·o·graph·i·cal (jē′ə-graf′i-k′l), *adj.* of or according to geography: abbreviated **geog.**

geographical linguistics, the branch of linguistics which describes the differentiations of languages and dialects within a speech area.

ge·o·graph·i·cal·ly (jē′ə-graf′i-k′l-i, jē′ə-graf′ik-li), *adv.* by or according to geography.

geographical mile, a measure of length, equal to one minute of longitude at the equator; about 6,076 feet.

ge·og·ra·phy (jē-og′rə-fi, jē-ôg′rə-fi), *n.* [*pl.* GEOGRAPHIES (-fiz)], [L. *geographia;* Gr. *geōgraphia,* geography; *geō-* (see GEO-) + *graphein,* to write], 1. the descriptive science dealing with the surface of the earth, its division into continents and countries, and the climate, plants, animals, natural resources, inhabitants, and industries of the various divisions. 2. the physical features, especially the surface features, of a region, area, or place. 3. a book about geography. Abbreviated **geog.**

ge·oid (jē′oid), *n.* [*geo-* + *-oid,* after Gr. *geoeidēs,* earthlike; cf. GEODE], a hypothetical figure of the earth with the entire surface represented as at mean sea level.

ge·o·log·ic (jē′ə-loj′ik), *adj.* geological: abbreviated **geol.**

ge·o·log·i·cal (jē′ə-loj′i-k′l), *adj.* of or according to geology: abbreviated **geol.**

ge·o·log·i·cal·ly (jē′ə-loj′i-k′l-i, jē′ə-loj′ik-li), *adv.* by or according to geology.

ge·ol·o·gist (jē-ol′ə-jist), *n.* a student of or specialist in geology: abbreviated **geol.**

ge·ol·o·gize (jē-ol′ə-jīz′), *v.i.* [GEOLOGIZED (-jīzd′), GEOLOGIZING], to study geology or make a geological study of an area, etc. *v.t.* [Rare], to study geologically.

ge·ol·o·gy (jē-ol′ə-ji), *n.* [*pl.* GEOLOGIES (-jiz)], [*geo-* + *-logy*], 1. the science dealing with the structure of the earth's crust and the formation and development of its various layers: it includes the study of individual rock types and early forms of life found as fossils in rocks. 2. the structure of the earth's crust in a given region, area, or place; rocks, rock formations, etc. 3. a book about geology. Abbreviated **geol.** See chart, p. 606.

geom., 1. geometer. 2. geometric. 3. geometrical. 4. geometrician. 5. geometry.

ge·o·man·cer (jē′ə-man′sẽr), *n.* a person who practices geomancy.

ge·o·man·cy (jē′ə-man′si), *n.* [ME. & OFr. *geomancie;* ML. *geomantia;* Late Gr. *geōmanteia* < Gr. *geō-* (see GEO-) + *manteia,* divination], divination by random figures formed when a handful of earth is cast on the ground, or by dots or lines drawn at random.

ge·o·man·tic (jē′ə-man′tik), *adj.* having to do with geomancy.

ge·om·e·ter (jē-om′ə-tẽr), *n.* [L. *geometres;* Gr. *geōmetrēs* < *geō-* (see GEO-) + *metron,* measure], a geometrician: abbreviated **geom.**

ge·o·met·ric (jē′ə-met′rik), *adj.* [L. *geometricus;* Gr. *geōmetrikos*], 1. of or according to geometry: abbreviated **geom.** 2. characterized by straight lines, triangles, circles, or similar regular forms: as, a *geometric* pattern.

ge·o·met·ri·cal (jē′ə-met′ri-k′l), *adj.* geometric: abbreviated **geom.**

ge·o·met·ri·cal·ly (jē′ə-met′ri-k′l-i, jē′ə-met′rik-li), *adv.* by or according to geometry.

ge·om·e·tri·cian (jē′ə-mə-trish′ən, jē-om′ə-trish′ən), *n.* a specialist in geometry; geometer: abbreviated **geom.**

geometric progression, a sequence of terms in which the ratio of each term to the preceding one is the same throughout the sequence: 1, 2, 4, 8, 16, 32, etc. are in *geometric progression.*

ge·om·e·trid (jē-om′ə-trid), *n.* [< Mod.L. *Geometridae,* name of the family < L. *geometres;* see GEOMETER], any of a group of small moths whose larvae move by looping their bodies: the larvae are called ***looping caterpillars*** or *measuring worms.*

ge·om·e·trize (jē-om′ə-trīz′), *v.i.* [GEOMETRIZED (-trīzd′), GEOMETRIZING], 1. to study geometry. 2. to work by geometric principles. *v.t.* [Rare], to work out geometrically.

ge·om·e·try (jē-om′ə-tri), *n.* [*pl.* GEOMETRIES (-triz)], [ME. & OFr. *geometrie;* L. *geometria;* Gr. *geōmetria* measurement of land, geometry < *gē,* earth, land + *metria,* measurement < *metrein,* to measure], 1. the branch of mathematics that deals with points, lines, planes, and solids, and examines their properties, measurement, and mutual relations in space: see also **plane geometry, solid geometry.** 2. a book about geometry. Abbreviated **geom.**

ge·oph·a·gy (jē-of′ə-ji), *n.* [*geo-* + *-phagy*], the eating of earth, either as a psychotic symptom or to make up for lack of food, as in famine areas.

ge·o·phys·i·cal (jē′ō-fiz′i-k′l), *adj.* having to do with geophysics.

ge·o·phys·ics (jē′ō-fiz′iks), *n.pl.* [construed as sing.], the physics of the earth; science that deals with weather, winds, tides, etc. and their effect on the earth.

ge·o·phyte (jē′ō-fīt′), *n.* [*geo-* + *-phyte*], a plant that grows in earth, especially one with underground buds.

ge·o·pol·i·tics (jē′ō-pol′ə-tiks), *n.pl.* [construed as sing.], [< G. *geopolitik;* see GEO- & POLITICS], the study of the relation of politics to geography; specifically, the Nazi doctrine of aggressive geographical and political expansion to acquire more living space and promote German domination of the world.

ge·o·pon·ic (jē′ə-pon′ik), *adj.* [Gr. *geōponikos; geō-* (see GEO-) + *ponikos,* toilsome < *ponos,* work, toil], [Rare], 1. having to do with agriculture or farming; hence, 2. rural; bucolic: humorous usage.

George (jôrj), [< Fr. & L.; Fr. *George, Georges;* LL. *Georgius;* Gr. *Geōrigios* < *geōrgos,* husbandman, lit., earthworker < *gaia, gē,* earth, ground + base of *ergon,* work (see WORK)], a masculine name: diminutive, *Georgie;* feminine, *Georgia, Georgiana, Georgina;* equivalents, Fr. *George, Georges,* G. & Scand. *Georg,* It. *Giorgio,* Sp. *Jorge.* *n.* a jeweled figure of St. George slaying the dragon, one of the insignia of the Order of the Garter.

George I, 1. 1660–1727; great-grandson of James I; king of England (1714–1727). 2. 1845–1913; king of Greece (1863–1913); assassinated.

George II, 1. 1683–1760; son of George I; king of England (1727–1760). 2. 1890–1947; son of Constantine I; king of Greece (1922–1923; 1935–1947).

George III, 1738–1820; grandson of George II; king of England (1760–1820).

George IV, 1762–1830; son of George III; king of England (1820–1830).

George V, 1865–1936; son of Edward VII; king of England (1910–1936).

George VI, 1895–1952; son of George V; king of England (1936–1952).

George, Saint, ?–303? A.D.; Cappadocian martyr; patron saint of England: his day is April 23.

George, David Lloyd, see **Lloyd George.**

George, Henry (jôrj), 1839–1897; American political economist; advocate of single tax.

George, Lake, a lake in eastern New York: length, 36 mi.

George·town (jôrj′toun′), *n.* 1. the capital of British Guiana: pop., 120,000. 2. a seaport in the state of Penang, Malaya: pop., 235,000: also called *Penang:* also written **George Town.**

geor·gette (jôr-jet′), *n.* [after *Georgette* de la Plante, Parisian modiste], a thin, transparent, slightly crinkled cloth of silk, etc., used for women's dresses, blouses, etc.: also **georgette crepe.**

Geor·gia (jôr′jə), a feminine name: see **George.** *n.* 1. a Southern State of the United States: area, 58,876 sq. mi.; pop., 3,943,000; capital, Atlanta: one of the thirteen original States: abbreviated **Ga.** 2. Georgian S.S.R.

Geor·gi·an (jôr′jən, jôr′ji-ən), *adj.* 1. *a*) of the reigns of George I, II, III, and IV of England (1714–1830); especially, *b*) designating or of the artistic style of this period. 2. of the Georgian S.S.R., its people, language, or culture. 3. of the State of Georgia. *n.* 1. a native or inhabitant of the Georgian S.S.R. 2. a native or inhab-

Geological Time Chart

ERAS	PERIODS (OF TIME) or SYSTEMS (OF ROCK)	EPOCHS (OF TIME) or SERIES (OF ROCK)	APPROXIMATE TIME IN YEARS SINCE BEGINNING OF EACH	PHYSICAL & BIOLOGICAL FEATURES
CENOZOIC	QUATERNARY	RECENT	50,000	Development of modern man.
		PLEISTOCENE	1,000,000	Ice sheets over Europe and North America; appearance of early man.
	TERTIARY	PLIOCENE	12,000,000	Development of modern plants and animals; formation of mountains in western America.
		MIOCENE	30,000,000	Highest development of larger mammals; formation of mountains, including the Alps, Andes, and Himalayas.
		OLIGOCENE	40,000,000	Development of higher mammals.
		EOCENE (& PALEOCENE)	60,000,000	Rise to dominance of mammals; appearance of ancestral horse and primates.
MESOZOIC	CRETACEOUS		120,000,000	Extinction of dinosaurs; development of early mammals and flowering plants; deposit of chalk beds.
	JURASSIC		155,000,000	Appearance of flying reptiles and birds; dominance of dinosaurs; appearance of primitive mammals; abundance of coniferous trees.
	TRIASSIC		190,000,000	Appearance of dinosaurs; dominance of reptiles; appearance of cycadaceous trees.
PALEOZOIC	PERMIAN		215,000,000	Development of reptiles; decline of huge plants of the Carboniferous.
	CARBONIFEROUS PENNSYLVANIAN MISSISSIPPIAN		300,000,000	Age of coal; formation of coal beds from luxuriant plant life in warm, swampy forests; great, fernlike trees; appearance of primitive conifers; abundance of insect life; first appearance of reptiles; development of amphibians.
	DEVONIAN		350,000,000	Age of the fish; appearance of primitive amphibians; development of primitive plant life on dry continents.
	SILURIAN		390,000,000	Appearance of scorpions, the first animals to live on land; extensive coral reefs.
	ORDOVICIAN		480,000,000	Floods and recessions of shallow seas; deposits of limestone, lead, and zinc ores; abundance of marine invertebrate life; appearance of a few primitive, fishlike vertebrates.
	CAMBRIAN		550,000,000	Shallow seas over much of the land; formation of sedimentary rocks; development of marine invertebrate life, including brachiopods, snails, sponges, and trilobites.
PRE-CAMBRIAN: PROTEROZOIC			1,200,000,000	Formation of mountains; deposits of iron ore; abundance of lime-secreting algae; appearance of sponges.
PRE-CAMBRIAN: ARCHEOZOIC			2,000,000,000	Great volcanic activity; formation of igneous rocks; some microscopic algae; probably some protozoa.

itant of the State of Georgia. 3. the language of the Transcaucasian Georgians: see **Caucasian.**

Geor·gi·an·a (jôr-jan′ə, jôr′ji-an′ə), a feminine name: see **George.**

Georgian Bay, the northeast part of Lake Huron, in Ontario, Canada.

Georgian Soviet Socialist Republic, a republic of the U.S.S.R., in the Transcaucasus, on the Black Sea: area, 26,875 sq. mi.; pop., 3,722,000; capital, Tiflis: also called *Georgia.*

Georgia pine, 1. a kind of pine growing in the southern United States, valued for its wood and as a source of turpentine. 2. its wood. Also called *longleaf, long-leaf.*

Georgia Strait, an arm of the Pacific, between Vancouver Island and British Columbia.

geor·gic (jôr′jik), *adj.* [L. *georgicus;* Gr. *geōrgikos*, agricultural < *geōrgos*, husbandman, farmer; see GEORGE], having to do with agriculture or husbandry. *n.* [L. (Virgil) *georgicum (carmen)*, georgic (song)], a poem dealing with farming or rural life.

the Georgics, a long poem about farming, by Virgil: it consists of four parts.

ge·o·stat·ic (jē′ō-stat′ik), *adj.* [*geo-* + *static*], 1. having to do with pressure of earth or a similar substance. 2. capable of supporting such pressure, as a kind of arch.

ge·o·stat·ics (jē′ō-stat′iks), *n.pl.* [construed as sing.], [< *geostatic*], the branch of physics dealing with the mechanics of the equilibrium of forces in rigid bodies; statics of rigid bodies.

ge·o·syn·cline (jē′ō-sin′klīn), *n.* [*geo-* + *syncline*], a very large, troughlike depression in the earth's surface: opposed to *geanticline.*

ge·o·tac·tic (jē′ō-tak′tik), *adj.* of or influenced by geotaxis.

ge·o·tax·is (jē′ō-tak′sis), *n.* [Mod.L.; see GEO- & -TAXIS], any movement of a freely moving organism, determined by the force of gravity: cf. **geotropism.**

ge·o·tec·ton·ic (jē′ō-tek-ton′ik), *adj.* [*geo-* + *tectonic*], having to do with the structure, distribution, shape, etc. of rocks at the earth's surface.

ge·o·ther·mic (jē′ō-thūr′mik), *adj.* [*geo-* + *thermic*], having to do with the heat of the earth's interior.

ge·o·trop·ic (jē′ō-trop′ik), *adj.* of, characterized by, influenced by, or having the nature of, geotropism.

ge·ot·ro·pism (jē-ot′rə-piz′m), *n.* [*geo-* + *-tropism*], any movement or growth of a living organism in response to the force of gravity: movement toward the center of the earth, as of the roots of plants growing downward, is *positive geotropism*: movement away from the center of the earth, as of shoots extending upward, is *negative geotropism*: cf. **geotaxis.**

Ger., 1. German. 2. Germany.

ger., gerund.

ge·rah (gē′rə), *n.* [Heb. *gērāh*, lit., a bean], an ancient Hebrew coin or weight, equal to 1/20 of a shekel.

Ge·raint (jə-rānt′), *n.* [< Celt.], in *Arthurian legend*, a knight of the Round Table, husband of Enid.

Ger·ald (jer′əld), [< OFr. or OHG.; OFr. *Giraut, Giralt;* OHG. *Gerald, Gerwald* < *ger*, spear (akin to AS. *gar*) + base of *waldan*, to rule], a masculine name: feminine, *Geraldine.*

Ger·al·dine (jer′əl-dēn′, jer′əl din), [Fr.], a feminine name: see **Gerald.**

ge·ra·ni·a·ceous (ji-rā′ni-ā′shəs), *adj.* [< Mod. L. *Geraniaceae*, name of the family < L. *geranium*], of the geranium family of plants, having flowers with five petals and leaves with many lobes.

ge·ra·ni·um (ji-rā′ni-əm), *n.* [L. < Gr. *geranion* < *geranos*, a crane], 1. any of a large group of plants having strong-smelling flowers of pink or purple and leaves with many lobes; cranesbill. 2. any of a group of plants related to these; pelargonium.

Ger·ard (ji-rärd′), [OFr. *Girart, Gerart;* OHG. *Gerhart* < *ger*, spear (see GERALD) + *hart*, hard (see HARD); hence, lit., hard spear], a masculine name.

ger·bil, ger·bille (jūr′bil), *n.* [Fr. *gerbille;* Mod. L. *gerbillus* < *gerbo*, jerboa; see JERBOA], any of a group of burrowing rodents related to the mouse, native to Africa and Asia.

ger·ent (jêr′ənt), *n.* [< L. *gerens, gerentis*, ppr. of *gerere*, to bear, conduct], [Rare], a person who manages, directs, governs, or rules.

ger·fal·con (jūr′fôl′k'n, jūr′fô′k'n), *n.* [see GYRFALCON], a large falcon of northern regions: also spelled **gyrfalcon.**

ger·i·at·rics (jer′i-at′riks), *n.pl.* [construed as sing.], [< Gr. *gēras*, old age; + *-iatrics*], the branch of medicine that deals with the diseases and hygiene of old age.

germ (jūrm), *n.* [Fr. *germe* < L. *germen*, sprig, offshoot, sprout, bud, germ, embryo < IE. **gen-men* (cf. Sans. *janiman-*, birth, origin) < base **gen-;* see GENUS], 1. the rudimentary form from which a new organism is developed; seed, bud, etc. 2. any microscopic organism, especially one of the bacteria, that can cause disease. 3. that from which something can develop or grow; origin: as, the *germ* of an idea.

Ger·man (jūr′mən), *adj.* [L. *Germanus;* prob. < Celt.], of or like Germany, its people, language, or culture. *n.* 1. a native or inhabitant of Germany. 2. the Germanic language of the Germans, technically called *New High German*: see also **Old High German, Middle High German, High German, Low German.** Abbreviated **G., Ger.**

ger·man (jūr′mən), *adj.* [ME. *germain, german;* OFr. *germain;* L. *germanus*, akin to *germen*, a sprout, bud; see GERM], closely related; specifically, *a)* having the same parents: as, a brother-*german*, sister-*german*. *b)* having the same grandparents on either the father's side or the mother's: a cousin-german is a first cousin.

ger·man (jūr′mən), *n.* [short for *German cotillion*], 1. a complicated dance for many couples in which partners are changed often; cotillion. 2. a party at which the german is danced.

German Africa, the former German colonies in Africa, consisting of German East Africa (now Tanganyika Territory), German Southwest Africa (now South West Africa), Kamerun (now the British and French Cameroons), and Togo (now British and French Togo).

German Baptist Brethren, a sect of German-American Baptists: see **Dunkers.**

ger·man·der (jẽr-man′dẽr), *n.* [ME. *germaunder;* OFr. *germandree;* ML. *germandra;* Late Gr. *chamandrya;* Gr. *chamaidrys; chamai*, on the ground + *drys*, tree], 1. any of a group of shrubby plants of the mint family, with showy flowers and mintlike leaves. 2. a kind of speedwell, a plant of the figwort family, with long spikes of blue flowers.

ger·mane (jẽr-mān′), *adj.* [var. of *german* (closely related)], 1. closely related; appropriate; pertinent; to the point. 2. akin; german. —*SYN.* see **relevant.**

German East Africa, a former German colony in eastern Africa: now mostly in Tanganyika Territory.

Ger·man·ic (jẽr-man′ik), *adj.* [L. *Germanicus*, of the Germans: the term, never used by the Germanic peoples themselves, orig. applied to a particular tribe, perhaps Germanic but prob. Celtic], 1. of Germany or the Germans; German. 2. designating or of the original language of the German peoples, or its speakers; Teutonic. 3. designating or of the languages descended from this language or their speakers. *n.* 1. the original language of the German peoples: usually **Primitive Germanic**: also called *Primitive Teutonic.* 2. a principal branch of the Indo-European family of languages, comprising this language and the languages descended from it: these include the extant languages Norwegian, Icelandic, Swedish, Danish (all *North Germanic*), New High German, Yiddish, Plattdeutsch, Dutch, Afrikaans, Flemish, Frisian, Modern English, and Modern Scottish (all *West Germanic*); and the extinct languages Gothic (*East Germanic*), Old Icelandic, Old Norwegian, Old Danish, Old Swedish (all *North Germanic*), Old High German, Middle High German, Old Saxon, Middle Low German, Middle Dutch, Old Frisian, Old English, Middle English, and Middle Scottish (all *West Germanic*). Abbreviated **Gmc.**

Ger·man·ism (jūr′mən-iz′m), *n.* 1. a German idiom or expression, used in another language. 2. a German custom, way of thought, etc. 3. fondness for or imitation of German ways.

Ger·man·ist (jūr′mən-ist), *n.* a student of or specialist in German life or Germanic linguistics and literature.

ger·ma·ni·um (jẽr-mā′ni-əm), *n.* [Mod. L. < L. *Germania*, Germany], a rare, grayish-white, metallic chemical element of the carbon family: symbol, Ge; at. wt., 72.60; at. no., 32.

Ger·man·ize (jūr′mə-nīz′), *v.t.* [GERMANIZED (-nīzd′), GERMANIZING], 1. to make German or like the Germans in thought, language, etc. 2. to translate into German. *v.i.* to adopt German habits, methods, etc.

German knot, a figure-of-eight knot: see **knot,** illus.

German measles, an acute, contagious disease characterized by slight fever, sore throat, pain in the limbs, and small skin eruptions: it resembles measles but is less severe: also called *rubella.*

Ger·ma·no- (jūr′mə-nō, jẽr-man′ō), a combining form meaning *German, of Germany, of the Germans,* as in *Germanophobe.*

German Ocean, the North Sea.

Ger·man·o·phile (jẽr-man′ə-fīl′, jẽr-man′ə-fil), *n.* [*Germano-* + *-phile*], a person who admires or is extremely fond of Germany, its people, customs, influence, etc.

Ger·man·o·phobe (jẽr-man′ə-fōb′), *n.* [*Germano-* + *-phobe*], a person who hates or fears Germany, its people, customs, influence, etc.

German sausage, a large sausage made of spiced, partly cooked meat.

German shepherd dog, a breed of dog somewhat like a wolf in form and size, notable for its intelligence: it was first developed by the Germans and is used in sheepherding, police work, etc.: also called *(German) police dog.*

German silver, a white alloy of zinc, nickel, and copper: abbreviated **GS**: also called *nickel silver*.
German Southwest Africa, a former German colony, now South West Africa.
German text, the modern German black-letter type, somewhat like Old English. This line is in German text.
Ger·man·town (jũr'mən-toun'), *n.* the northwest part of Philadelphia: formerly a town where a battle of the Revolutionary War was fought in 1777.
Ger·ma·ny (jũr'mə-ni), *n.* a country in north central Europe, on the North and Baltic Seas: area, 137,555 sq. mi.; pop., 80,528,000: in 1945, Germany was divided into four zones of occupation, administered respectively by France, Great Britain, the Soviet Union, and the United States; in 1949, it was divided into *a*) the Federal Republic of Germany (*West Germany*), comprising the United States, British, and French zones: area, 95,734 sq. mi.; pop., 55,016,000; capital, Bonn, and *b*) the German Democratic Republic (*East Germany*), comprising the Soviet zone: area 41,635 sq. mi.; pop., 17,079,000; capital, East Berlin. German name, *Deutschland*: abbreviated **Ger., G.**
germ cell, a cell from which a new organism can develop; egg or sperm cell: opposed to *somatic cell*.
ger·men (jũr'min), *n.* [*pl.* GERMENS (-minz), GERMINA (-mi-nə)], [L.], a germ: now used only figuratively.
ger·mi·cid·al (jũr'mə-sī'd'l), *adj.* destroying germs.
ger·mi·cide (jũr'mə-sīd'), *n.* [< *germ* + *-cide*], anything used to destroy germs, especially those causing diseases.
‡Ger·mi·nal (zhâr'mē'nál'; Eng. jũr'mə-n'l), *n.* [Fr. < Mod. L. *germinalis* (see GERMINAL): so named from being the seed month], the seventh month (March 21-April 19) of the French Revolutionary Calendar, adopted by the First Republic in 1793.
ger·mi·nal (jũr'mə-n'l), *adj.* [ML. *germinalis* < L. *germen, germinis* (see GERM)], 1. of, like, or characteristic of germs or germ cells. 2. in an embryonic stage; in the first stage of growth or development.
germinal disk, 1. a disklike spot in a fertilized ovum in which the first traces of the embryo are visible. 2. the disklike spot on the yolk of an egg where segmentation begins after fertilization.
germinal vesicle, 1. in *botany*, an oösphere. 2. in *embryology*, the nucleus of an egg before segmentation begins.
ger·mi·nant (jũr'mə-nənt), *adj.* germinating.
ger·mi·nate (jũr'mə-nāt'), *v.i.* & *v.t.* [GERMINATED (-id), GERMINATING], [< L. *germinatus*, pp. of *germinare*, to sprout, bud < *germen*, a sprout, bud], to start developing or growing; sprout or cause to sprout, as from a spore, seed, or bud.
ger·mi·na·tion (jũr'mə-nā'shən), *n.* [L. *germinatio*], a germinating; sprouting; beginning of growth.
ger·mi·na·tive (jũr'mə-nā'tiv, jũr'mə-nə-tiv), *adj.* of or capable of germination or growth.
Ger·mis·ton (jũr'mis-tən), *n.* a city in the Transvaal, South Africa: pop., 205,000.
germ layer, in *embryology*, any of the three primary layers of cells (ectoderm, endoderm, and mesoderm) from which the various organs and parts of the organism develop by further differentiation.
germ plasm (or **plasma**), the substance in germ cells by which hereditary characteristics are believed to be transmitted.
germ theory, 1. the generally accepted theory that all living organisms develop only from germ cells. 2. the generally accepted theory that infectious diseases are transmitted by specific germs, or microorganisms.
Ge·ron·i·mo (jə-ron'ə-mō'), 1829–1909; American Indian chief of the Apache tribe.
ger·on·toc·ra·cy (jer'ən-tok'rə-si), *n.* [Gr. *geronto-* < *gerōn*, old man; + *-cracy*], 1. government by old men. 2. [*pl.* GERONTOCRACIES (-siz)], a governing group composed of old men.
ger·on·tol·o·gy (jer'ən-tol'ə-ji), *n.* [Gr. *geronto-* < *gerōn*, old man; + *-logy*], the scientific study of the process of aging and of the problems of aged people.
-ger·ous (jẽr-əs), [L. *-ger* < *gerere*, to bear; + *-ous*], a suffix meaning *producing* or *bearing*, as in *dentigerous*.
Ger·ry, El·bridge (el'brij ger'i), 1744–1814; vice-president of the United States (1813–1814).
ger·ry·man·der (ger'i-man'dẽr, jer'i-man'dẽr), *v.t.* [< Elbridge *Gerry*, governor of Massachusetts when the method was employed (1812) + *salamander*, from the shape of the redistricted Essex County], 1. to divide (a voting area) in such a way as to give an unfair advantage to one political party. 2. to manipulate unfairly; falsify to gain advantage. *v.i.* to engage in gerrymandering. *n.* a redistricting of voting districts to the advantage of one party.
Gersh·win, George (gũrsh'win), 1898–1937; American composer.
Ger·trude (gũr'trood), [< Fr. & G.; Fr. *Gertrude*; G. *Gertrud* < OHG. *ger*, spear (see GERALD) + *trut*, dear, beloved], a feminine name: diminutives, *Gertie, Trudy*. *n.* [g-], a baby's underdress, or slip.
ger·und (jer'ənd), *n.* [L. *gerundium* < *gerere*, to do or carry out], 1. in *Latin grammar*, a verbal noun used in all cases but the nominative (e.g., *probandi* in *onus probandi*, the burden of proving). 2. in *English grammar*, a verbal noun ending in *-ing*: it has all the uses of the noun but retains certain characteristics of the verb, such as the ability to take an object or an adverbial modifier (e.g., *playing* in "Playing the piano was one of his hobbies"). Abbreviated **ger.**
ge·run·di·al (jə-run'di-əl), *adj.* 1. of or like a gerund. 2. used as a gerund.
ge·run·dive (jə-run'div), *adj.* [L. *gerundivus* < *gerundium*; see GERUND], gerundial. *n.* 1. a Latin verbal adjective with a typical gerund stem form, used as a future passive participle expressing duty, necessity, fitness, etc. (e.g., *delenda est Carthago*, Carthage must be destroyed). 2. a similar form in any language.
Ge·ry·on (jêr'i-ən, ger'i-ən), *n.* [L.; Gr. *Gēryōn* or *Gēryonēs*], in *Greek mythology*, a winged, three-bodied monster: after killing him, Hercules captured his oxen.
ges·so (jes'ō), *n.* [It., gypsum, chalk < L. *gypsum*; see GYPSUM], plaster of Paris prepared for use in sculpture or bas-reliefs, or as a surface for painting.
gest, geste (jest), *n.* [ME. & OFr. *geste*; L. *gesta*, deeds, pl. of pp. of *gerere*, to do, act], 1. an adventure; deed; exploit. 2. a romantic story of daring adventures, especially one in verse.
gest (jest), *n.* [Fr. *geste*; L. *gestus*, posture, gesture < pp. of *gerere*, to bear, behave], [Archaic], 1. bearing; deportment; carriage. 2. a gesture.
gest., *gestorben*, [G.], died.
‡Ge·stalt (gə-shtält'), *n.* [*pl.* GESTALTEN (-ən)], [G.; lit., shape, form, configuration < MHG. *gestalt*, pp. of *stellen*, to arrange, fix, form], in *Gestalt psychology*, any of the integrated structures or patterns that make up all experience and have specific properties which can neither be derived from the elements of the whole nor considered simply as the sum of these elements.
Gestalt psychology, [see prec. entry], a school of psychology, developed in Germany, which affirms that all experience consists of Gestalten, and that the response of an organism to a situation is a complete and unanalyzable whole rather than a sum of the responses to specific elements in the situation.
Ge·sta·po (gə-stä'pō, gə-stap'ō; G. gə-shtä'pō), *n.* [< G. *Geheime Staatspolizei*, secret state police], the German state police, organized in 1933 under the Nazi regime to operate against political opposition, and abolished as a result of Germany's defeat in World War II.
Ges·ta Ro·ma·no·rum (jes'tə rō'mə-nôr'əm, rō'mə-nō'rəm), [L., doings of the Romans], a 14th-century, European collection of tales in Latin, used as a source of plots by Chaucer, Shakespeare, etc.
ges·tate (jes'tāt), *v.t.* [GESTATED (-id), GESTATING], [< L. *gestatus*, pp. of *gestare*, to bear < *gerere*, to bear, carry], to carry in the uterus during pregnancy.
ges·ta·tion (jes-tā'shən), *n.* [L. *gestatio* < pp. of *gestare*; see GESTATE], 1. the act or period of carrying young in the uterus from conception to birth; pregnancy. 2. the development of a plan in the mind.
ges·tic (jes'tik), *adj.* [*gest* (bearing) + *-ic*], having to do with bodily movement, as dancing.
ges·ti·cal (jes'ti-k'l), *adj.* gestic.
ges·tic·u·late (jes-tik'yoo-lāt'), *v.i.* [GESTICULATED (-id), GESTICULATING], [< L. *gesticulatus*, pp. of *gesticulari*, to make mimic gestures < *gesticulus*, dim. of *gestus*, a gesture, pp. of *gerere*, to bear, carry, do], 1. to make or use gestures to help express one's meaning, as in speaking. 2. to make or use many energetic gestures. *v.t.* to express by gesticulating.
ges·tic·u·la·tion (jes-tik'yoo-lā'shən, jes'tik-yoo-lā'shən), *n.* [L. *gesticulatio*], 1. a gesticulating. 2. a gesture; especially, an energetic gesture.
ges·tic·u·la·tive (jes-tik'yoo-lā'tiv, jes-tik'yoo-lə-tiv), *adj.* making, or done with, gestures.
ges·tic·u·la·tor (jes-tik'yoo-lā'tẽr), *n.* a person who gesticulates.
ges·tic·u·la·to·ry (jes-tik'yoo-lə-tôr'i, jes-tik'yoo-lə-tō'ri), *adj.* of, like, or expressing by gesticulation.
ges·ture (jes'chẽr), *n.* [ML. *gestura*, mode of action < L. *gestus*, pp. of *gerere*, to bear, carry], 1. movement of the body, or of part of the body, to express or emphasize ideas, emotions, etc. 2. any action, statement, or characteristic of utterance intended to convey a state of mind, intention, etc.; demonstration of power, principles, etc., often one made only for effect: as, his speech was a *gesture* of friendship. *v.i.* [GESTURED (-chẽrd), GESTURING], to make or use a gesture or gestures.
‡Ge·sund·heit (gə-zoont'hīt'), *n.* [G.], (your) health: spoken as a toast or as an expression of good wishes to someone who has just sneezed.
get (get), *v.t.* [GOT (got), or *archaic* & *dial.* GAT (gat), GOT or GOTTEN (-'n), GETTING], [ME. *geten*; ON. *geta*, to obtain, get, beget; akin to AS. *-gietan* (see BEGET, FORGET, etc.), G. *-gessen* in *vergessen*, forget, etc.; IE. base **ghend-*, to seize, get hold of, seen also in L. *praehendere*, to grasp, seize, understand (see APPREHEND, PREHENSILE)], 1. to come into the state of having (anything); become the owner or receiver of; receive; win; gain; obtain; acquire. 2. to reach; arrive at: as, we *got* home early; hence, 3. to set up communication with, as on a radio, telephone, etc.: as, did you *get*

Paris? 4. *a*) to go and bring. *b*) to bring: as, go *get* your books. 5. to catch; capture; gain hold of. 6. to learn; commit to memory. 7. to find out or discover to be as the result of experiment or calculation: as, when you add two and two you *get* four. 8. to influence or persuade (a person) to do something: as, please *get* him to leave. 9. to cause (something) to act in a certain way: as, can you *get* the door to shut? 10. *a*) to cause to be: as, he *got* his hands dirty. *b*) to cause to arrive at: as, *get* this copy to the printer. 11. to take (oneself) away: often used absolutely. 12. to be sentenced to: as, he *got* ten years. 13. to prepare: as, will you *get* breakfast for us? 14. to give birth to; procreate; beget: usually said of animals. 15. [Colloq.], to be obliged to; feel a necessity to (with *have* or *has*): as, he has *got* to pass. 16. [Colloq.], to own; possess (with *have* or *has*): as, he has *got* red hair. 17. [Colloq.], to be or become the master of; especially, *a*) to overpower; have complete control of: as, narcotics will *get* him. *b*) to puzzle; baffle: as, this problem *gets* me. *c*) to take into custody, wound, or kill. *d*) in *baseball*, etc., to put (an opponent) out, as by catching a batted ball. 18. [Colloq.], to strike; hit: as, the blow *got* him in the eye. 19. [Colloq.], to catch the meaning or import of; understand. 20. [Slang], to cause an emotional response in; irritate, please, thrill, etc.: as, a ride on the roller coaster *gets* me. 21. [Slang], to notice or observe: as, did you *get* the look on his face? ***v.i.*** 1. to come, go, or arrive (with *from, to, into*, etc.): as, when do we *get* to New York? 2. to be; become; come to be (doing something); come to be (in a situation, condition, etc.): as, he *got* caught in the rain, *get* in touch with me. *Get* is used as a linking verb in idiomatic phrases, and as an informal auxiliary for emphasis in passive constructions: as, we *got* beaten yesterday. ***n.*** 1. the young of an animal; offspring; breed. 2. a begetting. 3. in *tennis*, etc., a retrieving of a shot seemingly out of reach.

get about, 1. to move from place to place. 2. to go to many social events, places, etc. 3. to circulate, as news; come to the notice of many.

get across, [Colloq.], 1. to clarify or explain convincingly. 2. to be clear; be understood. 3. to succeed, as in making oneself understood or conveying one's personality to an audience.

get ahead, to succeed; prosper.

get ahead of, to outdo; excel; surpass.

get along, 1. to proceed; make progress. 2. to leave; go away. 3. to succeed or be fairly successful, as in making a living. 4. to agree; be compatible.

get around, 1. to move from place to place. 2. to go to many social events, places, etc. 3. to circulate, as news; come to the notice of many. 4. to circumvent or overcome. 5. to influence, outwit, or gain favor with by cajoling, flattering, etc.

get at, 1. to approach or reach. 2. to apply oneself to (work, etc.). 3. to find out; ascertain. 4. [Colloq.], to influence by bribery or intimidation.

get away, 1. to go away; leave. 2. to escape. 3. to start, as in a race.

get away with, [Slang], to succeed in doing or taking without being discovered or punished.

get back, 1. to return. 2. to recover. 3. [Slang], to retaliate; get revenge (usually with *at*).

get by, 1. to pass. 2. [Colloq.], to succeed without being discovered or punished. 3. [Colloq.], to survive; manage.

get down, to descend; dismount.

get down to, to begin to consider or act on.

get in, 1. to enter; join in. 2. to arrive. 3. to put in. 4. to become familiar or closely associated (*with*).

get it, [Colloq.], 1. to understand. 2. to be punished.

get nowhere, to make no progress; accomplish nothing.

get off, 1. to come off, down, or out of. 2. to leave; go away. 3. to take off. 4. to escape. 5. *a*) to help to escape sentence or punishment. *b*) to lessen the sentence or punishment of. 6. to start, as in a race. 7. to utter (a joke, retort, etc.).

get on, 1. to go on or into. 2. to put on. 3. to proceed; make progress. 4. to grow older. 5. to succeed, as in making a living. 6. to agree; be compatible.

get out, 1. to go out. 2. to go away. 3. to take out. 4. to become no longer a secret. 5. to publish.

get out of, 1. to go out from. 2. *a*) to escape from or avoid. *b*) to help to escape from or avoid. 3. to go beyond (sight, etc.). 4. to find out from.

get over, 1. to recover from. 2. to forget or overlook. 3. [Colloq.], to get across (in all senses).

get there, [Colloq.], to succeed.

get through, 1. to finish. 2. manage to survive.

get to, [Colloq.], 1. to succeed in (followed by an infinitive). 2. to succeed in reaching or communicating with. 3. to influence, as by bribery or intimidation.

get together, 1. to bring together; accumulate. 2. to come together. 3. [Colloq.], to reach an agreement.

get up, 1. to rise (from a chair, from sleep, etc.). 2. to contrive; organize. 3. to dress elaborately. 4. to advance; make progress. 5. to climb or mount.

SYN.—**get** is the word of broadest application meaning to come into possession of, with or without effort or volition (to *get* a job, an idea, a headache, etc.); **obtain** implies that there is effort or desire in the getting (he has *obtained* aid); **procure** suggests active effort or contrivance in getting or bringing to pass (to *procure* a settlement of the dispute); **secure**, in strict discrimination, implies difficulty in obtaining something and in retaining it (to *secure* a lasting peace); **acquire** implies a lengthy process in the getting and connotes collection or accretion (he *acquired* a fine education); **gain** always implies effort in the getting of something advantageous or profitable (to *gain* fame).—***ANT.*** lose, forgo.

get·at·a·ble (get′at′ə-b'l), ***adj.*** easy to reach or ascertain; accessible.

get·a·way (get′ə-wā′), ***n.*** 1. the act of starting, as in a race. 2. the act of escaping.

Geth·sem·a·ne (geth-sem′ə-ni), ***n.*** [Gr. *Gethsēmanē;* Aram. *gath shemānī(m)*, lit., oil press: prob. so named because such a press was located there], 1. in the *Bible*, a garden outside of Jerusalem, scene of the agony, betrayal, and arrest of Jesus: Matt. 26:36; hence, 2. [often g-], any scene or occasion of agony.

get·ta·ble (get′ə-b'l), ***adj.*** that can be got; obtainable.

get-to·geth·er (get′tə-geth′ẽr), ***n.*** an informal social gathering or meeting.

Get·tys·burg (get′iz-bũrg′), ***n.*** a town in southern Pennsylvania: pop., 8,000: site of a crucial battle (July 1–3, 1863) of the Civil War: now the site of Gettysburg National Military Park.

Gettysburg Address, the speech made by Abraham Lincoln in 1863 at the dedication of the National Cemetery on the battlefield of Gettysburg.

get-up (get′up′), ***n.*** [Colloq.], 1. general arrangement or composition of a thing. 2. costume; outfit; dress. 3. driving ambition; vigor; energy.

gew·gaw (gū′gô), ***n.*** [ME. *giuegoue, gugaw*, etc., redupl. formation like Fr. *joujou*, toy & D. *giegagen*, to heehaw; ? < ME. *gawen, gowen*, to gape, stare < ON. *gā*, to heed], something showy but worthless or useless; bauble; trinket. ***adj.*** showy but worthless or useless.

gey·ser (gī′zẽr, gī′sẽr; *for* 2, Brit. gē′zẽr), ***n.*** [Ice. *Geysir*, name of a certain hot spring in Iceland; lit., gusher < ON. *göysa*, to gush], 1. a spring from which columns of boiling water and steam gush into the air at intervals. 2. [British], a small, gas, hot-water heater of the coil type.

gey·ser·ite (gī′zẽr-īt′, gī′sẽr-īt′), ***n.*** an opaline mineral deposited on the edges of geysers and hot springs.

Ge·zi·ra (jə-zē′rə), ***n.*** a region in the Sudan, between the Blue Nile and the White Nile.

G.F.T.U., General Federation of Trade Unions.

g.gr., great gross.

Gha·na (gä′nə), ***n.*** a country in western Africa, on the Gulf of Guinea: formed (1957) by a merger of the Gold Coast and British Togoland, it is a member of the British Commonwealth of Nations: area, 91,843 sq. mi.; pop., 6,691,000; capital, Accra.

ghast·li·ness (gast′li-nis, gäst′li-nis), ***n.*** the quality or state of being ghastly.

ghast·ly (gast′li, gäst′li), ***adj.*** [GHASTLIER (-li-ẽr), GHASTLIEST (-li-ist)], [ME. *gastlie, gasteliche;* AS. *gastlic, gæstlic*, lit., ghostly, hence spectral, dreary: var. of *ghostly* with specialized meaning], 1. horrible; frightful. 2. ghostlike; pale; haggard. 3. [Colloq.], very bad; very unpleasant. ***adv.*** in a ghastly manner.

SYN.—**ghastly** suggests the horror aroused by the sight or suggestion of death (a *ghastly* smile on the dead man's face); **grim** implies hideously repellent aspects (a *grim* joke); **grisly** suggests an appearance that causes one to shudder with horror (the *grisly* sights of Buchenwald); **gruesome** suggests the fear and loathing aroused by something horrible and sinister (the *gruesome* details of a murder); **macabre** implies concern with the gruesome aspects of death (a *macabre* tale).

ghat, ghaut (gôt), ***n.*** [Hind. *ghāṭ*], 1. in India, a mountain pass. 2. a chain of mountains; especially, either of the Ghats ranges. 3. in India, a flight of steps leading down to a river landing for ritual bathers.

Ghats (gôts, gäts), ***n.pl.*** two mountain ranges along the coasts of southern India: the Western Ghats are higher than the Eastern Ghats.

gha·zi (gä′zē), ***n.*** [Ar. *ghāzī*, ppr. of *ghazā*, to fight], 1. a Moslem hero, especially one who wages war against infidels. 2. [G-], in Turkey, a title of honor meaning "victorious warrior."

Ghe·ber, Ghe·bre (gā′bẽr, gē′bẽr), ***n.*** [Fr. *guèbre;* Per. *gabr;* prob. < Ar. *kāfir*, infidel; see KAFFIR, GIAOUR], any of the Zoroastrian fire worshipers who remained in Persia after the Moslem conquest in 637 A.D.

ghee (gē), ***n.*** [Hind. *ghī*], in India, the liquid butter remaining when butter from buffalo milk is melted, boiled, and strained.

Ghent (gent), ***n.*** the capital of East Flanders, Belgium: pop., 161,000: Flemish name, *Gent;* French name, *Gand.*

gher·kin (gũr′kin), *n.* [< D. dim. of *agurk*, cucumber; Czech *okurka;* Late Gr. *angourion*], 1. a variety of cucumber bearing small, prickly fruit. 2. the fruit of this plant, used for pickles. 3. the immature fruit of the common cucumber when pickled.
ghet·to (get′ō), *n.* [*pl.* GHETTOS (-ōz)], [It.], 1. in certain European cities, a section to which Jews are, or were, restricted: the word is also applied, often in an unfriendly sense, to any section (of a city) in which many Jews live; hence, 2. any section of a city in which many members of some national or racial group live, or to which they are restricted.
Ghib·el·line (gib″'l-in, gib″'l-ēn′), *n.* [It. *Ghibellino*, for G. *Waiblingen*, Hohenstaufen estate in Franconia], any member of a political party in medieval Italy that supported the authority of the German emperors in Italy in opposition to the papal party of the Guelphs. *adj.* of this party.
Ghi·ber·ti, Lo·ren·zo (lô-ren′tsô gē-ber′tē), 1378–1455; Florentine sculptor and painter.
Ghir·lan·da·jo (gêr′län-dä′yô), *n.* (pseudonym of *Domenico di Tommaso Bigordi*), Florentine painter; 1449–1494.
ghost (gōst), *n.* [early printers' sp. (prob. after Fl. *gheest*) of ME. *goste, goost;* AS. *gast* (also *gæst*), soul, spirit, demon, etc.; akin to G. *geist;* IE. base **gheiz*(*d*)-, startled, angered, seen also in Sans. *hed-*, to be angry], 1. originally, the spirit or soul: now only in *give up the ghost*, to die; hence, 2. the supposed disembodied spirit of a dead person, conceived of as appearing to the living as a pale, shadowy apparition. 3. a haunting memory. 4. a faint, shadowy semblance; inkling; slight trace: as, not a *ghost* of a chance. 5. [Colloq.], a ghost writer. 6. in *optics & television*, an unwanted secondary image or bright spot. 7. [often G-], in *theology*, the Divine Spirit: now only in *Holy Ghost*. *v.i.* [Colloq.], to work as a ghost writer. *v.t.* 1. to haunt. 2. [Colloq.], to be the ghost writer of.
ghost dance, a North American Indian religious dance, dedicated to the dead.
ghost·li·ness (gōst′li-nis), *n.* the quality of being ghostly.
ghost·ly (gōst′li), *adj.* [GHOSTLIER (-li-ẽr), GHOSTLIEST (-li-ist)], [ME. *gostlich;* AS. *gastlic;* see GHASTLY], 1. of, like, or characteristic of a ghost or other apparition; spectral. 2. having to do with the soul or religion; spiritual.
ghost word, [term invented by W. W. Skeat], a word created through misreading of manuscripts, misunderstanding of grammatical elements, etc. and hence possessing a ghost-existence in a language. Examples: *derring-do*, desperate courage (misunderstanding of ME. *derring do*, lit., daring to do).
ghost writer, a person who writes speeches, articles, etc. for another who professes to be the author.
ghoul (gōōl), *n.* [Ar. *ghūl*, demon of the mountains < *ghāla*, to seize], 1. in *Oriental folklore*, an evil spirit that robs graves and feeds on the flesh of the dead; hence, 2. a robber of graves. 3. a person who performs horrible acts or enjoys loathsome things.
ghoul·ish (gōōl′ish), *adj.* like or characteristic of a ghoul; horrible; fiendish; loathsome.
GHQ, G.H.Q., General Headquarters.
ghyll (gil), *n.* a gill (ravine, stream).
gi., gill; gills.
GI, G.I. (jē′ī′), *adj.* 1. in *military usage*, *a*) originally, galvanized iron: as, a *GI* can. *b*) now, government issue: designating clothing, equipment, etc. issued to military personnel; hence, 2. [Colloq.], *a*) of or characteristic of the United States armed forces or their personnel: as, a *GI* haircut. *b*) inclined to a strict observance of military regulations and customs: as, our captain is very *GI*. *c*) of or for veterans of World War II. *n.* [Colloq.], any member of the United States armed forces; especially, an enlisted soldier.
g.i., G.I., gastrointestinal.
gi·ant (jī′ənt), *n.* [ME. *geant;* ONorm. Fr. *gaiant* (OFr. *jaiant*); LL. **gagante* < L. *gigas, gigantes;* Gr. *gigas, gigantos*], 1. in *Greek mythology*, any of a race of huge beings of human form who warred with the gods. 2. any imaginary being of human form but of superhuman size and strength. 3. a person or thing of great size, strength, intellect, etc. *adj.* like a giant; of great size, strength, etc.
gi·ant·ess (jī′ən-tis), *n.* a female giant.
gi·ant·ism (jī′ən-tiz'm), *n.* gigantism.
giant panda, a panda (sense 2).
giant powder, an explosive that is like dynamite.
Giants' Causeway, an unusual formation of columnar basalt on the northern coast of Ireland, extending about 500 feet into the sea.
giaour (jour), *n.* [Turk. *giaur;* Per. *gaur, gabr;* see GHEBER], a non-Moslem: term applied by Moslems to unbelievers, especially Christians.
gib (gib), *n.* [? < OFr. *gibe*, staff; cf. GIBBET], 1. the hook of gristle that appears on the lower jaw of a male salmon after spawning. 2. an adjustable piece of metal or wood for keeping the moving parts of a machine in place: as, a *gib* and cotter. *v.t.* [GIBBED (gibd), GIBBING], to fasten or keep in place with a gib.
gib (gib), *n.* [short for *Gilbert*, used as a proper name for a cat], 1. a cat; especially, a tomcat. 2. [Dial.], a castrated cat.
Gib., Gibraltar.
gibbed (gibd), *adj.* [< *gibbed cat*, var. of *gib cat* (see GIB, a cat), but treated as if < an assumed *gib*, to castrate], castrated: said of a cat.
gib·ber (jib′ẽr, gib′ẽr), *v.i. & v.t.* [echoic], to speak or utter rapidly and incoherently; chatter unintelligibly. *n.* unintelligible chatter; gibberish.
gib·ber·ish (jib′ẽr-ish, gib′ẽr-ish), *n.* [prob. < *gibber*], rapid and incoherent talk; unintelligible chatter; jargon.
gib·bet (jib′it), *n.* [ME. & OFr. *gibet*, gallows, forked stick; dim. < Frank. *gibb*, forked stick], 1. a gallows. 2. a structure like a gallows, from which bodies of criminals already executed were hung and exposed to public scorn. *v.t.* 1. to execute by hanging. 2. to hang on a gibbet. 3. to expose to public scorn.
gib·bon (gib′ən), *n.* [Fr.], a small, slender, long-armed ape of India, southern China, and the East Indies.

GIBBON (3 ft. high)

Gib·bon, Edward (gib′ən), 1737–1794; English historian.
Gib·bons, Orlando (gib′ənz), 1583–1625; English composer and organist.
gib·bose (gib′ōs, gi-bōs′), *adj.* gibbous.
gib·bos·i·ty (gi-bos′ə-ti), *n.* [< L. *gibbosus;* + *-ity*], 1. the state or quality of being gibbous. 2. [*pl.* GIBBOSITIES (-tiz)], a rounded swelling or protuberance.
gib·bous (gib′əs), *adj.* [< L. *gibbus* or *gibba*, a hump; + *-ous*], 1. protuberant; rounded and bulging. 2. designating the moon when it is in a phase between half-moon and full moon and the curves forming its outline are convex. 3. humpbacked.
gibe (jīb), *v.i. & v.t.* [GIBED (jībd), GIBING], [? < OFr. *giber*, to handle roughly], to jeer; taunt; sneer or scoff (at). *n.* a jeer; taunt; sneer; scoff. Also spelled **jibe.** —*SYN.* see **scoff.**
gib·er (jīb′ẽr), *n.* a person who gibes: also spelled **jiber.**
gib·let (jib′lit), *n.* [ME. & OFr. *gibelet*, stew made of game], *usually in pl.* any of the edible internal parts of a fowl, as the gizzard.
Gi·bral·tar (ji-brôl′tẽr), *n.* 1. a British colony and fortress on the Rock of Gibraltar: area, 1 7/8 sq. mi.; pop., 21,000: abbreviated **Gib.** 2. any strong fortification; unassailable fortress.
Gibraltar, Rock of, a large rock forming a peninsula in southern Spain, at the entrance to the Mediterranean.
Gibraltar, Strait of, the strait between Spain and Africa, joining the Atlantic and the Mediterranean: width, 8 1/2 – 23 mi.
Gib·son, Charles Dana (gib′sən), 1867–1944; American painter and illustrator.
Gibson Desert, a large desert in west central Australia.
Gibson girl, the American girl of the 1890's as depicted by Charles Dana Gibson.
gi·bus (jī′bəs; Fr. zhē′büs′), *n.* [Fr.: after the name of the 19th-c. inventor], an opera hat; collapsible top hat: also **gibus hat.**
gid (gid), *n.* [< *giddy*], a brain disease of sheep; staggers.
gid·di·ly (gid″'l-i), *adv.* in a giddy manner.
gid·di·ness (gid′i-nis), *n.* a giddy quality or state.
gid·dy (gid′i), *adj.* [GIDDIER (-i-ẽr), GIDDIEST (-i-ist)], [ME. *gidie, gedie, guydi;* AS. *gydig*, insane, prob. < base **gud-* of AS. *god*, a god (see GOD) + *-ig* (see -Y); hence, basic meaning "possessed by a god"], 1. having a whirling, dazed sensation; dizzy; lightheaded. 2. causing or likely to cause such a sensation: as, a *giddy* height. 3. turning or circling around very rapidly; whirling. 4. *a*) inconstant; fickle. *b*) frivolous; flighty; heedless. *v.t. & v.i.* [GIDDIED (-id), GIDDYING], to make or become giddy.
Gide, An·dré (än′drā′ zhēd), 1869–1951; French novelist and critic: received Nobel prize in literature, 1947.
Gid·e·on (gid′i-ən), [Heb. *gid'ōn*, lit., hewer], a masculine name. *n.* in the *Bible*, a hero of Israel who led his people in the defeat of the Midianites and became a judge of Israel for forty years: Judg. 6: 11 ff.
Gideon Society, an organization for placing Bibles in hotel rooms, etc., founded in 1899 by a group of commercial travelers.
gie (gē, gi), *v.t. & v.i.* [GIED (gēd), GAE (gā), GIEN (gē′ən), GIEING], [Scot. & British Dial.], to give.
Gif·ford (gif′ẽrd), [< Eng. place name *Gifford*, Early ME. *Giddingford*, the ford of Gydda's people; cf. Eng. surname *Gidding, Gedding*], a masculine name.
gift (gift), *n.* [ME.; AS. < *giefan* (see GIVE) + *-t;* influ-

enced by the cognate ON. *gipt, gift*, what is given; akin to G. *gift*, poison], 1. something given or bestowed; present. 2. the act, power, or right of giving. 3. a natural ability; talent: as, Mozart had a great *gift*. —*SYN*. see **present, talent.**

look a gift horse in the mouth, to be critical of something given to one: from the practice of judging a horse's age by its teeth.

gift·ed (gif'tid), *adj.* [see GIFT], having a natural ability or aptitude; talented.

gift-wrap (gift'rap'), *v.t.* to wrap (a gift) attractively, with decorative wrapping, ribbon, etc.

gig (gig), *n.* [ME. *gigge*, whirligig, spinning top; prob. < ON.; cf. Dan. *gig*, whirling object, top, Norw. dial. *giga*, to shake, totter, with same base (IE. **ghei-gh-*) as Eng. *giggle;* senses prob. influenced by *jig*], 1. a light, two-wheeled, open carriage drawn by one horse. 2. a long, light ship's boat with oars and sail, usually reserved for the commanding officer. 3. a rowboat used in racing. 4. [for *gig mill*], a machine for raising nap on cloth. *v.i.* [GIGGED (gigd), GIGGING], to travel in a gig.

gig (gig), *n.* [< *fishgig* or *fizgig*], a fish spear. *v.t. & v.i.* [GIGGED (gigd), GIGGING,]to fish or spear with a gig.

gig (gig), *n.* [prob. < ME. *gigge* (see GIG, carriage, etc.) in sense "something light or trivial"], [Slang], 1. an official record or report of a minor delinquency, as in the army, school, etc.; demerit. 2. punishment for such a delinquency. *v.t.* [GIGGED (gigd), GIGGING], [Slang], 1. to give a gig to. 2. to punish with a gig.

gi·gan·te·an (jī'gan-tē'ən), *adj.* [< L. *giganteus* < *gigas* (see GIANT); + *-an*], gigantic; huge.

gi·gan·tesque (jī'gan-tesk'), *adj.* [Fr.; It. *gagantesco* < *gigante;* see GIANT], like or fit for a giant.

gi·gan·tic (jī-gan'tik), *adj.* [< L. *gigas, gigantis* (see GIANT); + *-ic*], 1. of, like, characteristic of, or fit for a giant; hence, 2. very big; huge; colossal; enormous; immense. —*SYN*. see **enormous.**

gi·gan·ti·cal·ly (jī-gan'ti-k'l-i, jī-gan'tik-li), *adv.* to a gigantic degree; on a gigantic scale.

gi·gan·tism (jī'gan-tiz'm, ji-gan'tiz'm), *n.* [< L. *gigas, gigantis* (see GIANT); + *-ism*], abnormal growth of the body, believed to be caused by a disease of the anterior lobe of the pituitary gland: also **giantism.**

gi·gan·tom·a·chy (jī'gan-tom'ə-ki), *n.* [LL. *gigantomachia;* Gr. *gigantomachia* < *gigas, gigantos*, giant + *machē*, battle], 1. [G-], in *Greek mythology*, the struggle between the giants and the gods. 2. any war between giants or giant powers.

gig·gle (gig''l), *v.i.* [GIGGLED (-'ld), GIGGLING], [16th c.; ? < MD. or LG.; cf. D. *giggelen*, from the base of ME. *gigge*, whirligig (see GIG, carriage, etc.) + *-le*, freq. suffix; IE. base **ĝhei-gh-* < **ĝhēi-*, to yawn, yelp, etc.], to laugh with a series of uncontrollable, rapid, high-pitched sounds, suggestive of foolishness, nervousness, etc.; titter. *n.* such a laugh. —*SYN*. **see laugh.**

gig·gler (gig'lẽr), *n.* a person who giggles.

gig·gly (gig'li), *adj.* inclined to giggle.

gig·o·lo (jig'ə-lō'; Fr. zhē'gô'lō'), *n.* [*pl.* GIGOLOS (-lōz'; Fr. -lō')], [Fr. < *gigolette*, a prostitute, concubine, dim. of *gigole*, tall, thin woman < *gigue*, long-legged, thin girl, thigh, leg < *giguer*, to dance, jig < *gigue*, a fiddle; see GIGOT], 1. a man who is paid to be a dancing partner or escort for women. 2. a man supported by a prostitute.

gig·ot (jig'ət), *n.* [Fr.; OFr., leg of mutton, dim. of *gigue*, a fiddle; OHG. *giga*, a fiddle], 1. a leg of mutton, lamb, veal, etc. 2. a leg-of-mutton sleeve; sleeve close-fitting from the wrist to the elbow and then flaring out to fullness at the shoulder: also **gigot sleeve.**

‡gigue (zhēg), *n.* [Fr.], a jig.

GI Joe, [Slang], any man in the United States armed forces; especially, an enlisted soldier of World War II.

Gi·la (hē'lə), *n.* 1. a river in southern Arizona, flowing into the Colorado: length, 630 mi. 2. a Gila monster.

Gi·la monster (hē'lə), [< the *Gila* River], a stout, sluggish, poisonous lizard with a short, stumpy tail and a body covered with beadlike scales arranged in alternating rings of black and orange: it is found in desert regions of the southwestern United States.

Gil·bert (gil'bẽrt), [OFr. *Guillebert;* OHG. *Williberht* < *willo, willeo*, will, wish (see WILL) + *beraht*, bright (see BRIGHT)], a masculine name: diminutive, *Gil*.

gil·bert (gil'bẽrt), *n.* [after William *Gilbert* (1544–1603), English physician & physicist], the C.G.S. unit for magnetomotive force, equal to 0.7958 ampere turn.

Gilbert, Cass (kas), 1859–1934; American architect.

Gilbert, Sir **Humphrey,** 1539?–1583; English navigator and colonizer.

Gilbert, Sir **William Schwen(c)k** (shweŋk), 1836–1911; English humorous poet and librettist; collaborated with Sir Arthur Sullivan in writing comic operas.

Gilbert and Ellice Islands, a British colony comprising the Gilbert and the Ellice islands and several other small islands: capital, Tarawa.

Gil·ber·ti·an (gil-bûr'ti-ən), *adj.* 1. of Sir William S. Gilbert. 2. of or like his style or humor.

Gilbert Islands, a group of British islands on the equator, in the Pacific between the Marshall and Ellice Islands: area, 116 sq. mi.; pop., 31,000.

gild (gild), *v.t.* [GILDED (-id) or GILT (gilt), GILDING], [ME. *gilden;* AS. *gyldan* < base (**guld-*) of AS. *gold* (see GOLD)], 1. *a)* to overlay with a thin layer of gold. *b)* to coat with a gold color. 2. to make appear bright and attractive. 3. to make (something) seem more attractive or more valuable than it is.

gild (gild), *n.* a guild.

gil·der (gil'dẽr), *n.* a person whose work is gilding.

gil·der (gil'dẽr), *n.* a guilder.

gild·ing (gil'diŋ), *n.* 1. the art or process of applying gold or a substance like gold to surfaces of metal, stone, wood, etc. 2. the substance so applied. 3. an outward appearance covering unpleasant facts, reality, etc.

Gil·e·ad (gil'i-əd), *n.* 1. a region in ancient Palestine, east of the Jordan: Gen. 37:25. 2. a city in this region.

Gilead, Mount, a mountain in Jordan, northeast of the Dead Sea: height, 3,580 ft.

Giles (jīlz), [OFr. *Gilles;* L. *Aegidius* < *aegis;* see AEGIS], a masculine name.

Giles, Saint, 7th century A.D.; Greek hermit in France; patron saint of cripples, beggars, and lepers.

Gil·ga·mesh (gil'gə-mesh'), *n.* [< Bab.], a legendary Babylonian king, hero of an epic (*Gilgamesh Epic*) completed about 2000 B.C. and containing an account of the Biblical Flood.

Gil·ga·mish (gil'gə-mish), *n.* Gilgamesh.

gill (gil), *n.* [ME. *gile, gille;* prob. < Anglo-N.; cf. ON. *gjolnar*, jaws, gills, older Dan. (*fiske*) *gæln*, Sw. *gäl;* IE. base **ghelunā-*, jaw, seen also in Gr. *chelynē*, lip, jaw], 1. the organ for breathing of most animals that live in water, as fish, lobsters, etc. 2. *often pl. a)* a red flap of flesh hanging below the beak of a fowl; wattle. *b)* the flesh under and about the chin and lower jaw of a person. 3. *pl.* the thin, leaflike, radiating plates on the undersurface of a mushroom.

gill (jil), *n.* [ME. *gille, gylle;* OFr. *gille*, measure for wine; L. *gillo*, cooling vessel], a liquid measure, equal to 1/4 pint: abbreviated **gi.** (*sing. & pl.*).

gill (jil), *n.* [contr. of *Gillian*, proper name < L. *Juliana*, fem. of *Julianus*, given name], a girl or woman; sweetheart: also spelled **jill.**

gill (gil), *n.* [ME. *gille, gylle;* ON. *gil*], 1. a wooded ravine or glen with a stream flowing through it. 2. a narrow stream; brook. Also spelled **ghyll.**

Gil·lette, William (ji-let'), 1855–1937; American actor.

gill fungus (gil), an agaric.

gil·lie (gil'i), *n.* [*pl.* GILLIES (-iz)], [Scot. < Gael. *gille*, lad, page], 1. in the Scottish Highlands, a sportsman's attendant or servant. 2. a servant. Also spelled **gilly.**

gil·li·flow·er (jil'i-flou'ẽr), *n.* a gillyflower.

gill net (gil), a net set upright in the water so that fish are caught in it when their gills become entangled in its meshes.

gil·ly (gil'i), *n.* [*pl.* GILLIES (-iz)], a gillie.

gil·ly·flow·er (jil'i-flou'ẽr), *n.* [altered < ME. *gilofre, gelofer;* OFr. *gilofre, girofle*, gillyflower; LL. *caryophyllum;* Gr. *karyophyllon*, clove tree, lit., nut leaf < *karyon*, nut + *phyllon*, leaf], 1. any of several plants with clove-scented flowers, including the clove pink, the European wallflower, and the common stock. 2. a variety of apple.

Gi·lo·lo (ji-lō'lō), *n.* Halmahera, an island in the Moluccas, Netherlands Indies.

gil·son·ite (gil'sən-it'), *n.* [after S. H. *Gilson*, of Salt Lake City, Utah], uintaite, a pure asphalt found mainly in Utah.

gilt (gilt), alternative past tense and past participle of **gild.** *adj.* gilded. *n.* a thin layer of gold, or a substance like gold, covering a surface; gilding. Abbreviated **glt., gt.**

gilt (gilt), *n.* [ME. *gilte;* ON. *gyltr;* akin to ON. *göltr*, a boar], [Dial.], a young female pig; immature sow.

gilt-edge (gilt'ej'), *adj.* gilt-edged.

gilt-edged (gilt'ejd'), *adj.* 1. having the edge or edges gilded, as the pages of a book. 2. of the highest quality, grade, or value: said of bonds, securities, etc.

gilt·head (gilt'hed'), *n.* any of a number of sea fishes with gold markings on the head, as the sparoid fish of the Mediterranean or the English cunner.

gim·bals (jim'b'lz, gim'b'lz), *n.pl.* [altered < ME. *gemel;* OFr. *gemelle*, twin < L. *gemellus*, dim. of *geminus*, twin, double], a device consisting of a pair of rings pivoted on axes at right angles to each other so that one is free to swing within the other: a ship's compass, lantern, etc. will keep a horizontal position when suspended in gimbals.

gim·crack (jim'krak'), *adj.* [? < ME. *gibecrake*, inlaid wood], showy but cheap and useless. *n.* a cheap, showy, useless thing; knickknack.

gim·el (gim'əl), *n.* [Heb. *gīmel*, lit., camel; cf. GAMMA], the third letter of the Hebrew alphabet (ג), corresponding to English *G, g:* see **alphabet,** table.

gim·let (gim′lit), *n.* [ME. *gymelot;* OFr. *guinbelet, guimbelet* (Fr. *gibelet*), dim. form < MD. *wimpel;* see WIMBLE], a small boring tool with a handle at right angles to a shaft having at the other end a spiral, pointed cutting edge. *v.t.* to make a hole in with or as with a gimlet.

GIMLET

gim·let-eyed (gim′lit-īd′), *adj.* having a piercing glance; sharp-eyed.

gim·mal (gim″l, jim′'l), *n.* [var. of *gemel*], a ring formed of two or more interlocked circlets.

gim·mick (gim′ik), *n.* [? < G. *gemach,* lit., a convenience, via. G. dial. with stress shift], [Slang], 1. a secret means of controlling a prize wheel, etc. 2. a trick device used by a magician. 3. anything that tricks or mystifies; deceptive or secret device. 4. any gadget or contrivance whose name is unknown or not recalled.

gimp (gimp), *n.* [Fr. *guimpe,* wimple; OFr. *guimple,* wimple; OHG. *wimpal* (see WIMPLE); meaning affected in Fr. prob. by *guipure* (see GUIPURE)], a ribbonlike silk, worsted, or cotton braided fabric, sometimes stiffened with wire, used to trim garments, furniture, etc.

gin (jin), *n.* [< *geneva*], 1. a strong, aromatic alcoholic liquor distilled from rye and other grains and flavored with juniper berries. 2. a similar liquor differently flavored. 3. alcoholic liquor generally.

gin (jin), *n.* [ME. *gin, ginne,* ingenuity, contrivance, machine, engine, abbrev. of *engin, engyn;* see ENGINE], 1. a snare, net, or trap, as for game or fish. 2. a machine for hoisting heavy objects. 3. a machine for separating cotton fibers from the seeds: usually **cotton gin.** *v.t.* [GINNED (jind), GINNING], 1. to catch in a trap. 2. to remove seeds from (cotton) with a gin.

gin (gin), *v.t. & v.i.* [GAN (gan), GINNING], [ME. *ginnen,* aphetic form of *beginnen* (see BEGIN) & *onginnen* (AS. *onginnan,* to attempt)], [Archaic & Poetic], to begin.

gin (gin), *conj.* [? contr. < *given;* ? influenced by Scot. prep. *gin,* by (a certain time)], [Scot.], if; whether.

gin (jin), *n.* gin rummy. *v.i.* [GINNED (jind), GINNING], to win in gin rummy by knocking, or exposing one's cards, with no unmatched cards left in one's hand, thus gaining additional points.

gin·gal, gin·gall (jin′gôl), *n.* a jingal.

gin·ge·li, gin·gel·ly (jin′ji-li), *n.* gingili.

gin·ger (jin′jẽr), *n.* [ME. *gingere, gingivere,* partly < AS. *gingiber, gingifer* < LL. *zingiber* & partly < OFr. *gimgibre, gingimbre* (Fr. *gingembre*) of the same origin; Gr. *ziggiber-;* Sans. *śṛṅgavēra,* lit., horn body; ? < Dravidian], 1. any of a group of tropical herbs grown commercially in the East Indies, Africa, and China for their aromatic rootstalks, used for flavoring foods and in medicine. 2. the rootstalk of the ginger plant. 3. the spice made from this. 4. a sandy or reddish color. 5. [Colloq.], vigor; spirit. *v.t.* 1. to flavor with ginger. 2. to invigorate; enliven.

ginger ale, an effervescent, nonalcoholic drink flavored with ginger.

ginger beer, a ginger-flavored drink similar to ginger ale, popular in England.

gin·ger·bread (jin′jẽr-bred′), *n.* 1. a cake flavored with ginger and molasses. 2. cheap, showy ornamentation, as cheap, fancy carvings on furniture, front porches, etc. *adj.* cheap and showy; tawdry; gaudy.

gin·ger·ly (jin′jẽr-li), *adv.* [*ginger* (? < OFr. *genzor,* compar. of *gent,* delicate) + *-ly*], cautiously; carefully; timidly. *adj.* cautious; careful; timid.

gin·ger·snap (jin′jẽr-snap′), *n.* a crisp, spicy cooky flavored with ginger and molasses.

gin·ger·y (jin′jẽr-i), *adj.* 1. like or flavored with ginger; spicy; pungent. 2. sandy or reddish in color.

ging·ham (giŋ′əm), *n.* [D. *gingang* (Fr. *guingan*); prob. < Malay *giṅgaṅ,* striped (cloth): transmission to Europe prob. via D.], a yarn-dyed cotton cloth, usually woven in stripes, checks, or plaids: it is used for aprons, house dresses, etc. *adj.* made of gingham.

gin·gi·li (jin′ji-li), *n.* [Hind. *jinjali*], 1. sesame seed. 2. the oil of this seed. Also spelled **gingeli, gingelly.**

gin·gi·val (jin-jī′v'l, jin′jə-v'l), *adj.* [< L. *gingiva,* the gum; + *-al*], of the gums; alveolar. *n.* an alveolar consonant.

gin·gi·vi·tis (jin′jə-vī′tis), *n.* [Mod. L. < L. *gingiva,* the gum; + *-itis*], inflammation of the gums.

ging·ko (giŋ′kō), *n.* [*pl.* GINGKOES (-kōz)], a ginkgo.

gink (giŋk), *n.* [? < dial. *gink,* a trick (whence Scot. *ginkie,* term of reproach applied to a woman)], [Slang], a person, especially one regarded as odd, queer, etc.

gink·go (giŋ′kō, jiŋ′kō), *n.* [*pl.* GINKGOES (-kōz)], [Japan. *ginko, gingko* < Chin. *yin-hing,* silver apricot], a large tree with fan-shaped leaves and edible yellow fruit, native to northern China and Japan: also **gingko.**

gin mill (jin), [Slang], a saloon.

gin·ner (jin′ẽr), *n.* a person who gins cotton.

gin rummy, [? a play on *gin* (liquor), suggested by *rum* (liquor)], a variety of the card game rummy, for two or more players: when his unmatched cards total not more than ten points, a player may knock, or expose his hand, either winning the number of points by which his opponent's unmatched cards exceed his or losing that by which his exceed his opponent's, plus an added penalty: see also **gin** (gin rummy).

gin·seng (jin′seŋ), *n.* [Chin. *jen shen*], 1. an herb with a thick, forked, aromatic root: some species are found in China and North America. 2. the root of this plant, used medicinally by the Chinese.

Gio·con·da, La (lä′ jō-kon′də; It. jô-kôn′dä), *n.* [It., lit., the cheerful one], 1. a portrait by Leonardo da Vinci, more commonly called *Mona Lisa.* 2. an Italian opera (1876) by Ponchielli.

‡**gio·co·so** (jô-kô′sô), *adj. & adv.* [It.; see JOCOSE], in *music,* with a gay, playful quality: a direction to the performer.

Gior·gio·ne Il (ēl jôr-jô′ne), (*Giorgio Barbarelli*), 1478?–1511; Venetian painter: also **Giorgione da Castelfranco** (dä käs′tel-fräŋ′kô).

Giot·to di Bon·do·ne (jôt′tô dē bôn-dô′ne; Eng. jot′ō), 1276?–1337?; Florentine painter and architect: often **Giotto.**

gip (jip), *n., v.t. & v.i.* gyp.

gi·pon (ji-pon′, jip′on), *n.* [ME.; OFr. *gipon, jupon;* see JUPON], a jacket or tunic formerly worn over or under armor: also **jupon.**

gip·sy (jip′si), *n.* [*pl.* GIPSIES (-siz)], *adj., v.i.* [GIPSIED (-sid), GIPSYING], gypsy.

gipsy moth, a gypsy moth.

gi·raffe (jə-raf′, jə-räf′), *n.* [*pl.* GIRAFFES (-rafs′, -räfs′), GIRAFFE; see PLURAL, II, D, 1], [Fr.; via Sp. & Port. *girafa* or It. *giraffa* < Ar. *zarāfah*], 1. a large cud-chewing animal of Africa, with a very long neck and legs: it often grows to a height of 18 feet and is the tallest of existing animals: also called *camelopard.* 2. [G-], the constellation Camelopard.

gi·ran·do·la (ji-ran′də-lə), *n.* a girandole.

gir·an·dole (jir′ən-dōl′), *n.* [Fr.; It. *girandola,* chandelier, fire wheel < L. *gyrare,* to turn < *gyrus,* a circle], 1. a revolving cluster of fireworks. 2. a revolving water jet. 3. a branched candleholder. 4. a pendant or earring with small stones grouped around a larger one.

Gi·rard, Stephen (ji-rärd′), 1750–1831; American financier and philanthropist.

gir·a·sol (jir′ə-sol′, jir′ə-sōl′), *n.* [Fr.; It. *girasole,* fire opal, sunflower < *girare* (< L. *gyrare*), to turn + *sole* (< L. *sol, solis*), the sun], 1. [Rare], a tall sunflower with edible, potatolike roots: usually called *Jerusalem artichoke.* 2. a variety of opal that has a reddish gleam in a bright light; fire opal. Also spelled **girosol.**

gir·a·sole (jir′ə-sōl′), *n.* a girasol.

gird (gũrd), *v.t.* [GIRT (gũrt) or GIRDED (-id), GIRDING], [ME. *girden, gerden, gurden;* AS. *gyrdan;* akin to G. *gürten;* IE. base ***ghердh-**, to enclose, surround, seen also in *garth, girth*], 1. to encircle with a belt or band. 2. to fasten with a belt or band. 3. to encircle; enclose. 4. to equip; furnish; clothe; endue; invest. 5. to prepare (oneself) for action.

gird (gũrd), *n., v.i. & v.t.* [ME. *girden, gerden, gurden,* to strike, hence strike with scorn; the forms suggest a Late AS. (W.S.) **gyrdan* for **gierdan,* lit., to rod < AS. *gierd, gerd,* a rod (see YARD, a measure); influenced by prec. *gird*], gibe; taunt; scoff; jeer.

gird·er (gũr′dẽr), *n.* [*gird* (to encircle) + *-er*], a large beam, usually horizontal, of timber or steel, for supporting the joists of a floor, the framework of a building, the superstructure of a bridge, etc.

gir·dle (gũr′d'l), *n.* [ME. *girdil, gerdelle, gurdil;* AS. *gyrdel* < base of *gyrdan* (see GIRD), to encircle + *-el,* prob. dim. suffix; akin to G. *gürtel*], 1. a belt or sash for the waist. 2. anything that surrounds or encircles. 3. a light, flexible, corsetlike garment, for supporting or molding the waist and hips. 4. the rim of a cut gem. 5. a ring around the trunk of a tree, made by removing bark. 6. in *anatomy,* a bony arch or zone supporting the limbs: as, the pelvic *girdle.* *v.t.* [GIRDLED (-d'ld), GIRDLING], 1. to surround or bind, as with a girdle. 2. to encircle. 3. to cut a ring of bark from (a tree).

gir·dler (gũr′dlẽr, gũr′d'l-ẽr), *n.* [ME. *gyrdlere;* see GIRDLE], 1. a person who makes girdles. 2. a person or thing that girdles, or encircles. 3. a beetle that cuts girdles in tree branches or trunks.

girl (gũrl), *n.* [ME. in forms *girle, gurle, gerle,* youngster of either sex; these indicate an AS. **gyrele, *gyrela* (recorded as *gyrl-*), strongly substantiated by Brit. southern dial. *girls,* primrose blooms, *girlopp,* a lout; for possible jocular allusion as sense basis, cf. LAD; ? connected with (late) LG. *goere,* young person (of either sex) & (rare) AS. *gyr,* fir tree], 1. a female child. 2. a young, unmarried woman. 3. a female servant. 4. [Colloq.], a woman of any age, married or single. 5. [Colloq.], a sweetheart.

girl guide, a member of a British organization (*Girl Guides*) that is like the Girl Scouts.

girl·hood (gũrl′hood), *n.* [*girl* + *-hood*], 1. the state or time of being a girl. 2. girls collectively.

girl·ish (gũr′lish), *adj.* 1. of or like a girl or girls. 2.

characteristic of or suitable for a girl or girlhood.

girl scout, a member of the Girl Scouts.

Girl Scouts, an organization founded by Juliette Low in Savannah, Georgia in 1912 (as *Girl Guides*) to provide healthful, character-building activities for girls.

girn (gũrn), ***n., v.i. & v.t.*** [var. of *grin*, to snarl], [British Dial.], snarl.

Gi·ronde (jə-rond′; Fr. zhē′rōnd′), ***n.*** 1. an estuary formed by the Garonne and Dordogne Rivers, on the southwestern coast of France: length, 45 mi. 2. a department of France, on the southwestern coast. 3. [so named because led by deputies from this department], a French political party (1791–1793) that advocated moderate republican principles: it was suppressed by the Jacobins.

Gi·ron·dist (jə-ron′dist), ***n.*** a member of the Gironde. ***adj.*** of this party.

gir·o·sol (jir′ə-sol′, jir′ə-sōl′), ***n.*** a girasol.

girt (gũrt), past tense and past participle of **gird** (to encircle).

girt (gũrt), ***v.t.*** [< *gird;* also < *girt, n.*], 1. to gird; girdle. 2. to fasten with a girdle, belt, etc. 3. to measure the girth of. ***v.i.*** to measure in girth.

girt (gũrt), ***n.*** [var. of *girth*], girth.

girth (gũrth), ***n.*** [ME. *gerthe, girthe;* Anglo-N. **gerthu* (ON. *gjörth*) < base of ON. *gyrtha*, to encircle, akin to AS. *gyrdan* (see GIRD, to encircle)], 1. a band put around the belly of a horse or other animal for holding a saddle, pack, etc. 2. the circumference, as of a tree trunk or person's waist. 3. a girdle. ***v.t.*** 1. to girdle; encircle; surround. 2. to fasten or bind with a girth. ***v.i.*** to measure in girth.

gi·sarme (gi-zärm′), ***n.*** [ME.; OFr. < OHG. *getisarn*, lit., weeding iron < *getan*, to weed + *isarn*, iron (cf. IRON)], a battle-ax or halberd with a long shaft, formerly carried by foot soldiers.

Gis·sing, George Robert (gis′iŋ), 1857–1903; English novelist.

gist (jist), ***n.*** [OFr. *giste*, abode, lodgings, point at issue < 3d pers. sing., pres. indic. act., of *gesir*, to lie < L. *jacere*, to lie; special sense influenced by Anglo-Fr. legal phrase *l'action gist*, lit., the action lies], 1. the grounds for action in a lawsuit; hence, 2. the essence or main point, as of an article or argument.

git·tern (git′ẽrn), ***n.*** [ME. *giterne;* OFr. *guiterne* < L. *cithara;* Gr. *kithara*, guitar, cithara; cf. CITHER], an obsolete, wire-strung musical instrument somewhat resembling a guitar.

Giu·ba (jōō′bä), ***n.*** the Juba, a river in eastern Africa.

give (giv), ***v.t.*** [GAVE (gāv), GIVEN (-′n), GIVING], [ME. *give(n), geve(n)* (with *g-* < ON. *gefa*, to give), *yive(n), yeve(n);* AS. *giefan, gefan;* akin to G. *geben;* IE. base **ghabh-*, **ghap-* (< *qap*, to seize), seen also in L. *habere*, to have, *habilis* (cf. ABLE, ABILITY), etc.; the special Gmc. sense of this base results from its use as a substitute for IE. **dō-* (as in L. *dare*, to give)], 1. to turn over the possession or control of to someone without cost or exchange; hand over as a gift. 2. to hand or pass over; cause to be in the trust or keeping of someone; deliver: as, he *gave* the porter his bag to carry, her father *gave* Dorothy in marriage. 3. to hand or pass over in exchange for something else, as money, services, etc.; sell for a price; pay: as, I'll *give* you five dollars for the book. 4. to cause to have; produce in a person or thing; impart: as, Marlowe *gave* form to Elizabethan drama. 5. to cause to have as an honor or favor; confer (a title, position, etc.). 6. to let have in answer to a petition; grant; allow: as, God *give* me strength. 7. to be the source, origin, or cause of; produce; supply: as, cows *give* milk. 8. to part with for some cause; devote to some occupation, pursuit, etc.: as, he *gave* his life for his men. 9. to surrender; yield; concede: as, I'll *give you* that point. 10. to put forward to be taken or not; offer; proffer: as, may I *give* a suggestion? 11. to make (gestures, etc.): as, she *gave* him a cold glance. 12. to utter, emit, or produce (words, etc.); put in words; communicate; state: as, *give* a reply. 13. to perform: as, they *gave* a concert. 14. to inflict or impose (punishment, sentence, etc.): as, they *gave* him a whipping. ***v.i.*** 1. to make gifts; be in the habit of giving. 2. to bend, sink, move, etc. from force or pressure; yield: as, the floor *gave* under the weight of the piano. 3. to be springy; be resilient. ***n.*** 1. a bending, moving, sinking, etc. under pressure. 2. a tendency to be springy; resiliency.

give and take, to exchange on an even basis.

give away, 1. to make a gift of; donate; bestow. 2. in the marriage ceremony, to give (the bride) to the bridegroom. 3. [Colloq.], to reveal; expose; betray.

give back, to return; restore.

give forth, to send forth; emit; issue.

give in, 1. to hand in. 2. to abandon a claim, fight, or argument; yield.

give it to, [Colloq.], to punish; beat or scold.

give off, to send forth or out; emit.

give out, 1. to send forth or out; emit. 2. to cause to be known; make public. 3. to distribute. 4. to become worn out, spent, or consumed; fail to last.

give over, 1. to hand over. 2. to stop; cease.

give to understand (or **know**, etc.), to cause to understand (or know, etc.).

give up, 1. to hand over; turn over; relinquish; surrender. 2. to stop; cease. 3. to admit failure and stop trying. 4. to lose hope for; despair of. 5. to sacrifice; devote wholly.

SYN.—**give** is the general word meaning to transfer from one's own possession to that of another; **grant** implies that there has been a request or an expressed desire for the thing given (to *grant* a favor); **present** implies a certain formality in the giving and often connotes considerable value in the gift (he *presented* the school with a library); **donate** is used especially of a giving to some philanthropic or religious cause; **bestow** stresses that the thing is given gratuitously and often implies condescension in the giver (to *bestow* charity upon the poor); **confer** implies that the giver is a superior and the thing given, an honor or privilege (to *confer* a title, a college degree, etc.).

give-and-take (giv′ən-tāk′), ***n.*** 1. an exchange on equal terms. 2. an exchange of talk, repartee, etc. on equal terms; banter.

give·a·way (giv′ə-wā′), ***n.*** [Colloq.], 1. an unintentional revelation or betrayal. 2. something given free or at low cost to attract buyers. ***adj.*** [Colloq.], in *radio* & *television*, designating a type of program in which prizes are given to contestants, as for answering questions correctly.

giv·en (giv′′n), past participle of **give.** ***adj.*** 1. bestowed; presented. 2. accustomed, as from habit or inclination; prone: as, he is *given* to drink. 3. stated; specified. 4. in *logic* & *mathematics*, taken as a premise; assumed; granted. 5. in *law*, issued; executed.

given name, the first name of a person; name given at birth or baptism, as distinguished from the surname.

giv·er (giv′ẽr), ***n.*** a person who gives: often in compounds, as *lawgiver, almsgiver.*

Gî·za, El (el gē′zə), a city in Egypt, near Cairo: pop., 38,000: site of the pyramids and the Sphinx: also spelled **El Gîzeh.**

giz·zard (giz′ẽrd), ***n.*** [< ME. & OFr. *giser* (with unhistoric *-d*) < L. *gigeria*, neut. pl., cooked entrails of poultry], 1. the second stomach of a bird: it has thick muscular walls and a tough lining for grinding food that has been partially digested in the first stomach. 2. [Colloq.], the stomach: humorous usage.

Gjel·le·rup, Karl (yel′ə-roop), 1857–1919; Danish poet and novelist; received Nobel prize in literature, 1917.

Gk., Greek.

Gl, in *chemistry*, glucinum.

gl., 1. glass. 2. gloss.

gla·bel·la (glə-bel′ə), ***n.*** [*pl.* GLABELLAE (-ē)], [Mod. L. < L. *glabellus*, without hair < *glaber;* see GLABROUS], the smooth prominence on the forehead between the eyebrows and just above the nose.

gla·brate (glā′brāt), ***adj.*** [< L. *glabratus*, pp. of *glabrare*, lit., to make smooth, deprive of hair < *glaber;* see GLABROUS], in *botany* & *zoology*, glabrous.

gla·brous (glā′brəs), ***adj.*** [< L. *glaber*, smooth, bald (< IE. **ghladh-ros* < base **ĝhel-*, **ghlō-*, **ghle-*, to gleam; cf. GLAD, GLOW, GOLD); + *-ous*], without hair, down, or fuzz; smooth; bald.

‡gla·cé (glȧ′sā′; Eng. gla-sā′), ***adj.*** [Fr., pp. of *glacer*, to turn into ice, freeze < *glace* < L. *glacies*, ice], 1. having a smooth, glossy surface. 2. covered with icing or sugar, as fruits; candied. 3. frozen; iced. ***v.t.*** to cover with icing; glaze.

gla·cial (glā′shəl, glā′shi-əl), ***adj.*** [L. *glacialis*, icy, frozen < *glacies*, ice], 1. of ice or glaciers. 2. of or produced by a glacial epoch or period. 3. like ice; cold and hard; icy. 4. in *chemistry*, having an icelike, crystalline appearance: as, *glacial* acetic acid.

glacial epoch, 1. any period of geological time when a large part of the earth was covered with glaciers. 2. the latest of these periods, during the Pleistocene, when a large part of the Northern Hemisphere was covered with glaciers.

gla·cial·ist (glā′shəl-ist, glā′shi-əl-ist), ***n.*** 1. a student of glaciers and their action. 2. a person who accepts the established theory that certain surface changes of the earth were caused by glaciers.

glacial period, the period including the glacial epochs; ice age.

gla·ci·ate (glā′shi-āt′), ***v.t.*** [GLACIATED (-id), GLACIATING], [< L. *glaciatus*, pp. of *glaciare*, to turn into ice, freeze; see GLACIAL & -ATE], 1. *a*) to cover over with ice or a glacier. *b*) to form into ice; freeze. 2. to expose to or change by glacial action. 3. to give a frosted or icelike appearance to.

gla·ci·a·tion (glā′shi-ā′shən, glā′si-ā′shən), ***n.*** a glaciating.

gla·cier (glā′shẽr), ***n.*** [Fr. (orig., Savoy dial., whence also G. *gletscher*); LL. **glaciarium* < *glacia* (whence Fr. *glace*), for L. *glacies*, ice (akin to *gelu*, frost, cold)

< IE. base *gel, seen also in *cool, chill*, etc.], a large mass of ice and snow that forms in areas where the rate of snowfall constantly exceeds the rate at which the snow melts: it moves slowly down a mountain slope or valley until it melts or breaks away.
Glacier National Park, a national park in northwestern Montana, containing 250 lakes and 60 small glaciers: area, 1,538 sq. mi.
gla·cis (glā′sis, glas′is), *n.* [Fr. < OFr. *glacier*, to slip < *glace*, ice; see GLACIER], 1. a gradual slope. 2. an embankment sloping gradually up to a fortification so that attackers will be exposed to defending gunfire.
glad (glad), *adj.* [GLADDER (-ẽr), GLADDEST (-ist)], [ME. *gladd(e); AS. glæd*; akin to G. *glatt*, smooth, representing the orig. Gmc. sense; IE. **ghlădh-*, shining, smooth (< **ĝhel-, *ghel-*, to shine); cf. GLABROUS, GLOW, GOLD], 1. feeling or characterized by pleasure or joy; happy; pleased. 2. causing pleasure or joy; making happy. 3. pleased; willing: as, I'm *glad* to do it. 4. bright; beautiful. *v.t. & v.i.* [GLADDED (-id), GLADDING], [Archaic], to gladden. —***SYN.*** see **happy.**
glad (glad), *n.* [Slang], a gladiolus.
Glad·bach-Rheydt (glät′bäkh-rīt′), *n.* city in the Rhine Province, Germany: pop., 194,000.
glad·den (glad′′n), *v.t. & v.i.* [ME. *gladen, gladien*; AS. *gladian*], to make or become glad.
glade (glād), *n.* [prob. akin to *glad*; orig. sense prob. "bright, smooth place"; cf. G. *lichtung*, glade < *licht*, light, Fr. *clairière* < *clair*, clear], 1. an open space in a wood or forest. 2. an everglade.
glad eye, [Slang], an inviting or flirtatious glance: usually in *give* (or *get*) *the glad eye.*
glad hand, [Slang], cordial welcome.
glad·i·ate (glad′i-āt′, glā′di-āt′), *adj.* [< L. *gladius*, sword; + *-ate*], in *botany*, sword-shaped.
glad·i·a·tor (glad′i-ā′tẽr), *n.* [L. < *gladius*, sword], 1. in ancient Rome, a man who fought other men or animals with a sword or other weapon in an arena, for the entertainment of spectators: gladiators were slaves, captives, or paid performers. 2. any person involved in a controversy or fight.
glad·i·a·to·ri·al (glad′i-ə-tôr′i-əl, glad′i-ə-tō′ri-əl), *adj.* of gladiators or their fights.
glad·i·o·la (glad′i-ō′lə, glə-dī′ə-lə), *n.* [Mod. L.], a gladiolus.
glad·i·o·lus (glad′i-ō′ləs, glə-dī′ə-ləs), *n.* [*pl.* GLADIOLUSES (-iz), GLADIOLI (-lī, -lī′)], [L., sword lily, small sword, dim. of *gladius*, sword], a plant of the iris family, with swordlike leaves and tall spikes of funnel-shaped flowers in various colors.
glad·ly (glad′li), *adv.* in a glad manner; willingly.
glad rags, [Slang], fine or dressy clothes.
glad·some (glad′səm), *adj.* [see GLAD, *adj.* & -SOME], 1. giving joy; cheering; delightful. 2. joyful; cheerful.
Glad·stone (glad′stōn′, glad′stən), *n.* [after William Ewart *Gladstone*], 1. a four-wheeled carriage with two inside seats for passengers, and places for driver and footman. 2. a Gladstone bag.
Glad·stone, William Ew·art (ū′ẽrt glad′stōn′, glad′stən), 1809–1898; British statesman; prime minister of England (1868–1874; 1880–1885; 1886; 1892–1894).
Gladstone bag, a traveling bag hinged so that it can open flat into two compartments of equal size.
Glad·ys (glad′is), [W. *Gwladys*; prob. < L. *Claudia*; see CLAUDIA], a feminine name.
glair (glâr), *n.* [ME. *gleyre*; OFr. *glaire* < LL. **claria* < L. *clarus*, clear], 1. raw white of egg, used in sizing or glossing. 2. a size or glaze made from this. 3. any sticky matter resembling white of egg. *v.t.* to cover with glair.
glair·e·ous (glâr′i-əs), *adj.* glairy.
glair·y (glâr′i), *adj.* like glair; covered with glair.
glaive (glāv), *n.* [ME.; OFr., a lance < L. *gladius*, sword], [Archaic], 1. a kind of halberd with a sword-like blade. 2. a sword; especially, a broadsword. Also spelled **glave.**
glam·or (glam′ẽr), *n.* glamour.
Gla·mor·gan (glə-môr′gən), *n.* Glamorganshire.
Gla·mor·gan·shire (glə-môr′gən-shir′), *n.* a county of southeastern Wales, on the Bristol Channel: pop., 1,155,000; capital, Cardiff: also **Glamorgan.**
glam·or·ize (glam′ẽr-īz′), *v.t.* [GLAMORIZED (-īzd′), GLAMORIZING], to make glamorous.
glam·or·ous (glam′ẽr-əs), *adj.* full of glamour; fascinating; alluring.
glam·our (glam′ẽr), *n.* [Scot. var. of *grammar* in sense of *gramarye*, popularized by Sir Walter Scott; orig. esp. in *cast the glamour*, to cast an enchantment], 1. originally, magic; enchantment; magic spell or charm; hence, 2. seemingly mysterious and elusive fascination or allure, as of some person, object, scene, etc.; bewitching charm; delusive enticement: the current sense.
glamour girl, [Slang], a young woman whose natural allure is emphasized by cosmetics, dress, etc.
glam·our·ous (glam′ẽr-əs), *adj.* glamorous.
glance (glans, gläns), *v.i.* [GLANCED (glanst, glänst), GLANCING], [< OFr. *glacier*, to slide, slip; ? influenced in sp. by D. *glanzen*, to shine, glint < MHG.], 1. to strike obliquely and go off at an angle. 2. to make an indirect or passing reference. 3. to flash; gleam. 4. to look suddenly and briefly. *v.t.* to cause to strike (a surface) at an angle and be deflected. *n.* 1. a glancing off; deflected impact. 2. a flash or gleam. 3. a quick glimpse. —***SYN.*** see **flash.**
glance (glans, gläns), *n.* [G. *glanz*, lit., luster; akin to Eng. *glint*], any of various ores with a metallic luster: now applied to only a few metallic ores, such as silver glance (argentite) and lead glance (galena).
gland (gland), *n.* [Fr. *glande*; OFr. *glandre*; L. *glandula*, dim. of *glans, glandis*, acorn: so called prob. from the shape], any organ that separates certain elements from the blood and secretes them in the form of a substance for the body to use, as adrenalin, or throw off, as urine: there are two kinds of glands, those which have ducts and empty into an organ, as the liver and kidneys, and those without ducts (*ductless glands*), which pass their secretions directly into the blood stream, as the thyroid and adrenals.
gland (gland), *n.* [Fr. < L. *glans*; see GLAND (organ)], in *mechanics*, a movable part that compresses the packing on a stuffing box.
glan·dered (glan′dẽrd), *adj.* having glanders.
glan·der·ous (glan′dẽr-əs), *adj.* of, having, or like glanders.
glan·ders (glan′dẽrz), *n.pl.* [construed as sing.], [OFr. *glandres*, lit., glands; see GLAND (organ)], a contagious disease of horses, mules, etc. characterized by fever, swelling of glands beneath the lower jaw, inflammation of the nasal mucous membranes, etc.: it can be transmitted to certain other animals and man.
glan·du·lar (glan′joo-lẽr), *adj.* [Fr. *glandulaire*; see GLANDULE], of, like, consisting of, or having a gland or glands.
glandular fever, an infectious disease characterized by fever and a generalized swelling of the lymph nodes: also called *infectious mononucleosis.*
glan·dule (glan′jōōl), *n.* [Fr.; L. *glandula*, dim. of *glans*; see GLAND (organ)], a small gland.
glan·du·lous (glan′joo-ləs), *adj.* glandular.
glans (glanz), *n.* [*pl.* GLANDES (glan′dēz)], [L., acorn; see GLAND (organ)], 1. the glans penis. 2. the glans clitoridis.
glans cli·tor·i·dis (klī-tor′ə-dis), the end of the clitoris, corresponding to the glans penis.
glans penis, the head, or end, of the penis.
glare (glâr), *v.i.* [GLARED (glârd), GLARING], [ME. *glaren*; prob. < OD. or OLG.; cf. MD., MLG. *glaren*, to gleam, glare, akin to AS. *glær*, amber; for the IE. base see GLASS], 1. to shine with a strong, steady, dazzling light. 2. to be too bright and showy. 3. to stare fiercely or angrily. *v.t.* to send forth or express with a glare. *n.* 1. a strong, steady, dazzling light or brilliant reflection, as from sunlight on ice. 2. a fierce or angry stare. 3. a too bright or showy display. —***SYN.*** see **blaze, look.**
glare (glâr), *n.* [prob. < *glare*, brightness, as from sunlight on ice], a smooth, bright, glassy surface, as of ice. *adj.* smooth, bright, and glassy.
glar·ing (glâr′iŋ), *adj.* [ppr. of *glare*], 1. dazzlingly and steadily bright. 2. too bright and showy. 3. staring in a fierce, angry manner. 4. too obvious to be overlooked; flagrant: as, a *glaring* mistake. —***SYN.*** see **flagrant.**
glar·y (glâr′i), *adj.* [GLARIER (-i-ẽr), GLARIEST (-i-ist)], glaring.
Glas·gow (glas′gō, gläs′kō), *n.* a city in Scotland, on the River Clyde: pop., 1,076,000 (est. 1946).
Glas·gow, Ellen (glas′gō), 1874–1945; American novelist.
Glas·pell, Susan (glas′pel), 1882–1948; American novelist and dramatist.
glass (glas, gläs), *n.* [ME. *glas*; AS. *glæs*; akin to G. *glas*; IE. base **ĝhel-, *ghel-*, to shine, seen also in *glad, glare, glow*, etc.], 1. a hard, brittle substance, usually transparent or translucent, made by fusing silicates with soda or potash, lime, and, sometimes, various metallic oxides. 2. any substance like glass in composition or properties. 3. glassware. 4. *a*) an article made partly or wholly of glass, as a drinking container, mirror, windowpane, telescope, barometer, etc. *b*) *pl.* eyeglasses. *c*) *pl.* binoculars. 5. the quantity contained in a drinking glass: as, he drank a *glass* of milk: abbreviated **gl.** *v.t.* 1. to enclose in glass. 2. to put into glass jars for preserving. 3. to mirror; reflect. 4. to equip with glass; glaze. *adj.* of or made of glass.
Glass, Carter (glas, gläs), 1858–1946; American statesman; senator from Virginia (1902–1918; 1920–1946); secretary of the treasury (1918–1920).
glass blower, a person or machine that does glass blowing.
glass blowing, the art or process of shaping molten glass into any desired form by blowing air into a mass of it at the end of a tube.
glass cutter, 1. a person whose work is cutting sheets of glass to desired sizes or shapes. 2. a person whose work is inscribing designs on glass. 3. a tool for cutting, or inscribing designs on, glass.
glass·ful (glas′fool′, gläs′fool′), *n.* [*pl.* GLASSFULS (-foolz′)], the amount that will fill a glass.

glass·house (glas′hous′, gläs′hous′), *n.* a greenhouse or hothouse.
glass·i·ly (glas′ə-li, gläs′ə-li), *adv.* in a glassy manner.
glass·ine (gla-sēn′), *n.* [*glass* + *-ine*], a thin but tough, glazed, nearly transparent paper, used for the windows of envelopes, etc.
glass·i·ness (glas′i-nis, gläs′i-nis), *n.* the quality or state of being glassy.
glass·mak·er (glas′māk′ẽr, gläs′māk′ẽr), *n.* a person who makes glass.
glass·man (glas′mən, gläs′mən), *n.* [*pl.* GLASSMEN (-mən)], 1. a person who sells glassware. 2. a glassmaker. 3. a glazier.
glass snake, a legless lizard found in the southern United States: so called because its long tail breaks off easily.
glass·ware (glas′wâr′, gläs′wâr′), *n.* articles made of glass.
glass·work (glas′wũrk′, gläs′wũrk′), *n.* 1. *pl.* [construed as sing. or pl.], a factory for making glass. 2. the making or ornamentation of glass and glassware. 3. glassware.
glass·work·er (glas′wũrk′ẽr, gläs′wũrk′ẽr), *n.* a person who works with glass.
glass·wort (glas′wũrt′, gläs′wũrt′), *n.* [*glass* + *wort*], any of several European plants of the goosefoot family, with fleshy, leafless stems, growing in salt-water marshes: its ash is rich in soda and was formerly used in glassmaking.
glass·y (glas′i, gläs′i), *adj.* [GLASSIER (-i-ẽr), GLASSIEST (-i-ist)], [ME. *glasi*], 1. like or suggesting glass in appearance or quality; smooth; transparent. 2. expressionless or lifeless: as, a *glassy* stare.
Glas·we·gi·an (glas-wē′jən, gläs-wē′ji-ən), *adj.* of Glasgow. *n.* a native or inhabitant of Glasgow.
Glau·ber's salt (or **salts**) (glou′bẽrz), [after Johann R. *Glauber* (1604–1668), G. chemist], sodium sulfate, $Na_2SO_4 \cdot 10H_2O$, a crystalline salt used as a cathartic, etc.: also **Glauber salt** (or **salts**).
glau·co- (glô′kō, glô′kə), [< Gr. *glaukos*, orig., gleaming], a combining form meaning *bluish-green, silvery,* or *gray,* as in *glauconite.*
glau·co·ma (glô-kō′mə), *n.* [L.; Gr. *glaukōma* < *glaukos;* see GLAUCO-], a disease of the eye, characterized by increased tension within, and hardening of, the eyeball: it leads to a gradual impairment of sight, often resulting in blindness.
glau·co·ma·tous (glô-kō′mə-təs, glô-kom′ə-təs), *adj.* of, like, or having glaucoma.
glau·co·nite (glô′kə-nīt′), *n.* [< Gr. *glaukos* (see GLAUCO-); + *-ite*], a greenish silicate of iron and potassium, found in greensand.
glau·cous (glô′kəs), *adj.* [L. *glaucus;* Gr. *glaukos;* see GLAUCO-], 1. green with a grayish-blue cast. 2. in *botany,* covered with a whitish bloom that can be rubbed off, as grapes, plums, cabbage leaves, etc.
glave (glāv), *n.* [Archaic], a glaive.
glaze (glāz), *v.t.* [GLAZED (glāzd), GLAZING], [ME. *glasen* < *glas* (see GLASS); akin to MHG. *glasen*], 1. *a)* to furnish (a building, etc.) with windows. *b)* to furnish (windows, etc.) with glass. 2. to give a hard, smooth, glossy finish to; specifically, *a)* to overlay (pottery, etc.) with a substance which gives a glassy finish when fused. *b)* to make the surface of (leather, etc.) glossy by polishing, etc. *c)* to cover (food) with a coating of sugar sirup, etc. 3. to cover (the eye) with film. *v.i.* to become glassy, glossy, or filmy. *n.* 1. a glassy coating, as on pottery. 2. any substance used to produce this. 3. a coat of semitransparent color applied to a painted surface to modify the effect. 4. a jellylike covering formed or spread on meat. 5. a film or coating, as on the eyes.
gla·zier (glā′zhẽr), *n.* [ME. *glasier;* see GLASS & -IER], 1. a person whose work is cutting glass to the proper size and shape and setting it in windows, etc. 2. a person whose work is glazing pottery.
gla·zier·y (glā′zhẽr-i), *n.* the work done by a glazier.
glaz·ing (glā′ziŋ), *n.* [ME. *glasinge;* see GLASS & -ING], 1. the work of a glazier in fitting windows, etc. with glass. 2. glass set or to be set in frames. 3. a glassy coating; glossy finish. 4. the act of applying a glaze. 5. a substance applied as glaze.
Gla·zu·nov, A·le·ksan·dr Kon·stan·ti·no·vich (å-lyek-sän′dr′ kôn-stän-ti-nô′vich glá-zōō-nôf′), 1865–1936; Russian composer.
gleam (glēm), *n.* [ME. *gleme;* AS. *glæm;* akin to OHG. *gleimo,* MHG. *gleime,* glowworm & Eng. *glimmer;* IE. **ghlei-* < **ĝhel-,* **ghel-,* to shine, gleam; cf. GLASS, GLOW], 1. a momentary brightness; flash or beam of light. 2. a faint light. 3. a reflected brightness, as from a polished surface. 4. a brief, faint manifestation, as of hope, understanding, etc. *v.i.* 1. to shine or reflect with a gleam or gleams. 2. to be manifested briefly; appear or be revealed suddenly. —*SYN.* see **flash.**
glean (glēn), *v.t. & v.i.* [ME. *glenen;* OFr. *glener;* LL. *glennare* < Celt.; cf. OIr. *dīgleinn,* he gleans], 1. to collect (grain left by reapers). 2. to collect the remaining grain from (a field). 3. to collect (facts, etc.) gradually or bit by bit.
glean·ings (glēn′iŋz), *n.pl.* that which is gleaned.
glebe (glēb), *n.* [< Fr. & L.; Fr. *glèbe;* L. *gleba, glaeba,* clod, lump of earth; akin to *globus* (cf. GLOBE)], 1. land belonging to a church, used by the holder of a benefice during his tenure. 2. [Poetic], soil; land; earth; field.
gled (gled), *n.* a glede.
glede (glēd), *n.* [ME.; AS. *glida;* akin to ON. *gletha,* Eng. *glide*], the common kite of Europe, a bird of prey.
glee (glē), *n.* [ME. *gle;* AS. *gleo, gliw,* entertainment, minstrelsy, merriment; akin to (rare) ON. *glȳ;* IE. base **ghleu-,* to be merry, jest], 1. gaiety; mirth; joy; merriment. 2. a part song for three or more solo voices, usually unaccompanied. —*SYN.* see **mirth.**
glee club, [see GLEE, 2], a group formed to sing part songs.
gleed (glēd), *n.* [ME. *glede;* AS. *glæd, gled* < base of *glowan* (see GLOW)], [Dial.], a glowing coal.
glee·ful (glē′fəl), *adj.* full of glee; joyful; merry.
glee·man (glē′mən), *n.* [*pl.* GLEEMEN (-mən)], [ME. *gleeman, gleman, gleoman;* AS. *gleomann;* see GLEE & MAN], [Archaic], a wandering minstrel.
glee·some (glē′səm), *adj.* [see -SOME], gleeful.
gleet (glēt), *n.* [ME. *glete;* OFr. *glete, glette*], 1. [Obs. or Scot.], slimy matter; ooze. 2. formerly, any morbid discharge from the body. 3. a chronic mucous discharge from the urethra in gonorrhea. 4. a chronic discharge from the nasal cavities of horses, etc. *v.i.* to give forth a thin, watery discharge.
gleg (gleg), *adj.* [ME. (northern dial. & Scot.); ON. *gleggr,* clear, clear-sighted], [Scot. & Dial.], quick in perception or action; sharp; keen; alert.
Glen (glen), [Celt.; see GLEN (valley)], a masculine name: variant, *Glenn.*
glen (glen), *n.* [Late MScot. *glen* < Scot. Gael. *glenn* (now *gleann*), mountain valley; akin to W. *glyn*], a narrow, secluded valley.
Glen·dale (glen′dāl), *n.* a city in California, near Los Angeles: pop., 119,000.
Glen·dow·er, Owen (glen′dou′ẽr, glen′dou′ẽr), 1359?–1416?; Welsh chieftain; rebelled against Henry IV.
Glen·gar·ry (glen-gar′i), *n.* [*pl.* GLENGARRIES (-iz)], [< *Glengarry,* valley in Scotland], [sometimes g-], a Scottish cap for men, creased lengthwise across the top and often having short ribbons at the back: also **Glengarry bonnet** (or **cap**).

GLENGARRY

Glenn (glen), a masculine name: see **Glen.**
gle·noid (glē′noid), *adj.* [Gr. *glēnoeides* < *glēnē,* socket of a joint + *eidos,* form], forming a smooth, shallow cavity or socket for a bone; especially, designating the cavity on the head of the scapula which, together with the head of the humerus, forms the shoulder joint.
glib (glib), *adj.* [GLIBBER (-ẽr), GLIBBEST (-ist)], [orig., slippery; cf. D. *glibberig,* slippery, *glibber,* jelly], 1. done in a smooth, offhand fashion. 2. *a)* speaking or spoken in a smooth, easy manner; facile; fluent. *b)* speaking or spoken in a manner too smooth and easy to be convincing.
glide (glīd), *v.i.* [GLIDED (-id), GLIDING], [ME. *gliden;* AS. *glidan;* akin to G. *gleiten;* prob. < IE. **ghlei-dh* (< **ĝhel-,* **ghel-,* to shine; cf. GLAD, GLASS, GLOW, etc.) in basic sense "to move on a shining hence slippery, surface"], 1. to flow or move smoothly and easily, as a skater, sailboat, river, etc. 2. to move by or pass gradually and unnoticed, as time. 3. to descend slowly in an airplane without using an engine. 4. in *music* & *phonetics,* to make a glide. *v.t.* to cause to glide. *n.* 1. a smooth, easy flow. 2. a slow descent in an airplane without using an engine. 3. in *music,* a slur. 4. in *phonetics,* the incidental, indefinite sound made when the speech organs are passing from the position for one sound to that for another, as in the shift from front (ē) to back (ōō) in pronouncing (ū). —*SYN.* see **slide.**
glid·er (glīd′ẽr), *n.* 1. a person or thing that glides. 2. an engineless airplane flown by being manipulated into air currents that keep it aloft: see TYPES OF AIRPLANE, p. 32. 3. a porch seat suspended in an upright frame so that it can swing back and forth.

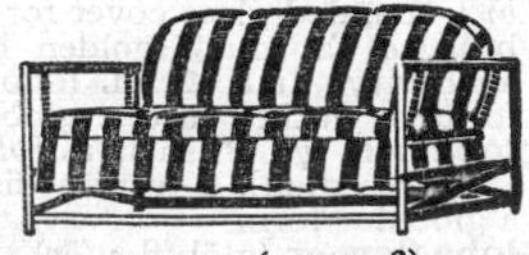
GLIDER (sense 3)

glim (glim), *n.* [ME.; akin to (and in part contracted from) Eng. *glimmer, gleam;* cf. MHG. *glim,* a spark], [Slang], 1. a light; lamp, candle, etc. 2. an eye.
glim·mer (glim′ẽr), *v.i.* [ME. *glemeren, glimeren,* to shine, freq. formation < base of AS. *glæm* (see GLEAM) & *gleomu,* splendor; corresponds in form to AS. **glimorian,* but prob. < MD. or MLG. like the cognate Dan. *glimre;* cf. D. *glimmeren,* G. *glimmern*], 1. to give a faint, flickering light. 2. to appear or be seen faintly or dimly. *n.* 1. a faint, flickering light. 2. a faint manifestation; dim perception; glimpse.
glim·mer·ing (glim′ẽr-iŋ), *n.* a glimmer.
glimpse (glimps), *v.t.* [GLIMPSED (glimpst), GLIMPSING], [ME. *glimsen, glinsen* (with transitional *-p-*; cf. THIMBLE) < base of *gleam, glimmer;* corresponds in form to AS. **glimsian,* **glinsian;* akin to MHG. *glimsen, glinsen*], to catch a brief, quick view of, as in passing; perceive momentarily and incompletely. *v.i.* to look quickly; glance. *n.* 1. a brief, sudden shining; flash. 2. a faint, fleeting appearance; slight trace; inkling. 3. a brief, quick view; passing look.
Glin·ka, Mi·kha·il I·va·no·vich (mi-khä′il i-vä′nô-vich glin′kä; Eng. gliŋ′kə), 1803–1857; Russian composer.
glint (glint), *v.i.* [ME. (chiefly northern) *glinten, glenten;* prob. < ON.; cf. Sw. dial. *glänta* (Norw. dial. *gletta*), akin to G. *glänzen,* to shine, glitter; IE. base **ghlendh-* < **ĝhel-,* etc., to shine (cf. GLASS, GLOW); Eng. literary use < Scot. (Burns)], 1. to gleam; flash. 2. to move quickly; dart. *n.* 1. a gleam. 2. [Dial.], a glimpse.
gli·o·ma (gli-ō′mə), *n.* [*pl.* GLIOMATA (-mə-tə), GLIOMAS (-məz)], [Mod. L. < Gr. *glia,* glue + *-ōma* (see -OMA)], a tumor of the brain, spinal cord, etc., composed of tissue that forms the supporting structure of nerves.
gli·o·ma·tous (gli-ō′mə-təs, gli-om′ə-təs), *adj.* of, like, or having a glioma.
glis·sade (gli-säd′, gli-sād′), *n.* [Fr. < *glisser,* to slide, glide], 1. an intentional slide by a mountain climber down a steep slope covered with snow. 2. in *ballet dancing,* a gliding step to the side. *v.i.* [GLISSADED (-id), GLISSADING], to make a glissade; slide; glide.
glis·san·do (gli-sän′dō), *n.* [*pl.* GLISSANDI (-di)], [formed as if It. ppr., equivalent to Fr. *glissant,* ppr. of *glisser,* to slide], in *music,* 1. a gliding effect achieved by sounding a series of adjacent tones in rapid succession, as by running a finger over the white keys of a piano. 2. a passage having this effect. *adj.* performed with such an effect.
glis·ten (glis′'n), *v.i. & n.* [< ME. *glisnen* (with unhistoric, transitional *-t-*); AS. *glisnian* < base of *glisian,* to shine; IE. base **ghleis-* < **ĝhel-,* etc. as in *glass, glow*], shine; sparkle; gleam; glitter. —***SYN.*** see **flash.**
glis·ter (glis′tẽr), *v.i. & n.* [ME. *glisteren;* prob. < LG. source; cf. MD. *glisteren,* MLG. *glistern;* base as in *glisten*], [Archaic], glitter; sparkle; gleam.
glit·ter (glit′ẽr), *v.i.* [ME. *gliteren, gleteren;* freq. formation; prob. < ON. *glitra;* akin to G. *glitzern;* IE. base **ghleid-* (< **ĝhel-,* etc., to shine; cf. GLASS, GLEAM), seen also in *glide*], 1. to shine with a sparkling light; glisten; sparkle; be bright. 2. to be showy, colorful, and attractive. *n.* 1. a bright, sparkling light; shining brightness. 2. showiness; brilliance; colorful splendor. —***SYN.*** see **flash.**
glit·ter·y (glit′ẽr-i), *adj.* having glitter; glittering.
gloam·ing (glōm′iŋ), *n.* [ME. *glomyng;* AS. *glomung* < *glom,* twilight; akin to *glowan,* to glow (see GLOW); adopted in literature < Scot. dial.], evening dusk; twilight.
gloat (glōt), *v.i.* [prob. via dial. < AS. **glotian* or cognate ON. *glotta,* to grin scornfully; akin to G. *glotzen,* Eng. dial. *glout,* to stare; IE. base **ghlud-* < **ĝhel-,* etc., to shine, as in *glass, glow*], to gaze or meditate with malicious pleasure, exultation, or avarice (often with *over*).
glob·al (glō′b'l), *adj.* 1. globe-shaped. 2. relating to the earth as a whole; world-wide: as, *global* warfare.
glo·bate (glō′bāt), *adj.* [L. *globatus,* pp. of *globare,* to make into a ball < *globus,* a ball, sphere], globe-shaped; spherical.
glo·bat·ed (glō′bā-tid), *adj.* globate.
globe (glōb), *n.* [Fr.; L. *globus,* a ball, sphere; for IE. base see CLOT], 1. any round, ball-shaped thing; sphere; specifically, *a*) the earth; world. *b*) a spherical model of the earth showing the continents, seas, etc. *c*) a similar model of the sky, showing the constellations, etc. 2. anything shaped somewhat like a globe; specifically, *a*) a round glass container, as for goldfish. *b*) a rounded glass cover for a lamp. *c*) an electric light bulb. *d*) a small, golden ball used as a symbol of authority. *v.t. & v.i.* [GLOBED (glōbd), GLOBING], to form or gather into a globe.
globe·fish (glōb′fish′), *n.* [*pl.* GLOBEFISH, GLOBEFISHES (-iz); see FISH], a tropical fish that can puff itself into a globular form.
globe·flow·er (glōb′flou′ẽr), *n.* any of a group of plants of the crowfoot family, with yellow, globe-shaped flowers.
globe-trot·ter (glōb′trot′ẽr), *n.* a person who travels widely about the world, especially one who does so for pleasure or sightseeing.
glo·bin (glō′bin), *n.* [< L. *globus;* + *-in*], the protein component of hemoglobin.
glo·boid (glō′boid), *adj.* somewhat globular; globate. *n.* anything globoid.
glo·bose (glō′bōs), *adj.* [L. *globosus*], globular; spherical or almost spherical.
glo·bos·i·ty (glō-bos′ə-ti), *n.* a globose condition.
glo·bous (glō′bəs), *adj.* [Rare], globose.
glob·u·lar (glob′yoo-lẽr), *adj.* 1. shaped like a globe or ball; spherical; round. 2. made up of globules. —***SYN.*** see **round.**
glob·ule (glob′yool), *n.* [Fr.; L. *globulus,* little ball, dim. of *globus,* a ball], a tiny ball or globe, especially of liquid; very small drop.
glob·u·lif·er·ous (glob′yoo-lif′ẽr-əs), *adj.* [< *globule* + *-ferous*], having or producing globules.
glob·u·lin (glob′yoo-lin), *n.* [< *gobule* + *-in*], any of a group of albuminous proteins, insoluble in water, found in both animal and vegetable tissue.
glock·en·spiel (glok′ən-spēl′; G. glôk′kən-shpēl′), *n.* [G. < *glocke,* a bell + *spiel,* play], in *music,* a percussion instrument with flat metal bars, formerly bells or tubes, set in a frame and chromatically tuned to produce bell-like tones when struck with small hammers.
glom·er·ate (glom′ẽr-it), *adj.* [L. *glomeratus,* pp. of *glomerare,* to wind or make into a ball < *glomus,* a ball, sphere; akin to *globus* (see GLOBE)], formed into a rounded mass; clustered.
glom·er·a·tion (glom′ẽr-ā′shən), *n.* [L. *glomeratio* < *glomeratus;* see GLOMERATE], 1. the act of forming into a rounded mass; agglomeration or conglomeration. 2. something formed into a rounded mass; cluster.
glom·er·ule (glom′ẽr-ōōl′), *n.* [Fr. *glomérule;* Mod.L. *glomerulus,* dim. < L. *glomus, glomeris,* a ball, round knot (in Mod.L., small plexus of blood vessels); see GLOMERATE], a compact cluster, as of a flower head, blood capillaries, etc.
Glom·men (glôm′ən), *n.* a river in eastern Norway, flowing southward into the Skagerrak: length, 375 mi.
glon·o·in (glon′ō-in), *n.* [< *gl*ycerin + *o*xygen + *n*itrogen + *-in*], nitroglycerin, especially a solution of this used in homeopathy.
glon·o·ine (glon′ō-in, glon′ō-ēn′), *n.* glonoin.
gloom (glōōm), *v.i.* [late phonetic sp. (cf. ROOM, COOPER) of ME. *gloum(b)en,* to look morose, with vowel unshifted before the labial *m;* thought to be < AS. **glumian* (cf. LG. *glūm,* muddiness), but more prob. a ME. northern dial. development < AS. *glom,* twilight (see GLOAMING), reborrowed in other dialects; akin to *glum*], 1. to be or look morose, displeased, or dejected. 2. to be or become dark, dim, or dismal. *v.t.* to make dark, dim, or dismal. *n.* [corresponds (see the *v.*) with AS. *glom,* but influenced in sense by the *v.* & *gloomy*], 1. darkness; dimness; obscurity. 2. a dark or dim place. 3. melancholy; sadness; dejection.
gloom·i·ly (glōōm′ə-li), *adv.* in a gloomy manner.
gloom·i·ness (glōōm′i-nis), *n.* the quality or condition of being gloomy.
gloom·y (glōōm′i), *adj.* [GLOOMIER (-i-ẽr), GLOOMIEST (-i-ist)], 1. overspread with or enveloped in darkness or dimness. 2. melancholy; sad; dejected; morose. 3. causing gloom; dismal; depressing. —***SYN.*** see **dark.**
Glo·ri·a (glôr′i-ə, glō′ri-ə), [L., glory], a feminine name. *n.* 1. [also g-], *a*) glory; praise: a word of worship. *b*) any of several Latin hymns in praise of God that begin with this word: see the next two entries. *c*) the music for any of these. 2. [g-], a halo or its representation in art. 3. [g-], a cloth of silk and wool, silk and cotton, etc. with a glossy surface, used for umbrellas, etc.
Gloria in Ex·cel·sis De·o (in ek-sel′sis dē′ō), [L.], glory (be) to God on high: title and first words of the greater doxology.
Gloria Pa·tri (pā′trī), [L.], glory (be) to the Father: title and first words of the lesser doxology: abbreviated **G.P.**
glo·ri·fi·ca·tion (glôr′ə-fi-kā′shən, glō′rə-fi-kā′shən), *n.* [LL. *glorificatio*], 1. a glorifying or being glorified. 2. [Colloq.], a festive occasion; celebration.
glo·ri·fi·er (glôr′ə-fī′ẽr, glō′rə-fī′ẽr), *n.* a person who glorifies.
glo·ri·fy (glôr′ə-fī′, glō′rə-fī′), *v.t.* [GLORIFIED (-fīd′), GLORIFYING], [ME. *glorifien;* OFr. *glorifier;* LL. *glorificare,* to glorify < L. *gloria,* glory + *facere,* to make], 1. to make glorious; give glory to. 2. to exalt and honor in worship. 3. to honor; praise extravagantly; extol. 4. to make, or make seem, better, larger, finer, or more beautiful than is actually the case.
glo·ri·ole (glôr′i-ōl′, glō′ri-ōl′), *n.* [Fr. < L. *gloriola,* dim. of *gloria,* glory], a halo.
glo·ri·ous (glôr′i-əs, glō′ri-əs), *adj.* [ME. & Anglo-Fr.; OFr. *glorios, glorius;* L. *gloriosus*], 1. full of glory; illustrious. 2. giving glory. 3. receiving or deserving glory. 4. splendid; magnificent. 5. [Colloq.], very delightful or enjoyable. —***SYN.*** see **splendid.**
glo·ry (glôr′i, glō′ri), *n.* [*pl.* GLORIES (-iz, -riz)], [ME. & OFr. *glorie* (Fr. *gloire*); L. *gloria*], 1. great honor and admiration won by doing something important or valuable; fame; renown. 2. anything bringing this. 3. worship; adoration; praise. 4. the condition of highest

achievement, splendor, prosperity, etc.: as, Greece in her *glory*. 5. the highest degree of pleasure, satisfaction, pride, etc.: as, the actress was in her *glory* at the stage door. 6. splendor; magnificence; radiance: as, the *glory* of the Rocky Mountains. 7. heaven or the bliss of heaven. 8. a halo or its representation in art. *v.i.* [GLORIED (-id, -rid), GLORYING], to be very proud; rejoice; exult (with *in*).

gone to glory, dead.

gloss (glôs), *n.* [? < ON. *glossi*, a blaze < *gloa*, to glow], 1. the brightness or luster of a smooth, polished surface; sheen: abbreviated **gl.** 2. a deceiving outward appearance; superficial show, as in manners or speech. *v.t.* 1. to give a polished, shiny surface to; make lustrous. 2. to make (an error, inadequacy, fault, etc.) appear right by specious argument or by minimizing (often with *over*). *v.i.* to become shiny.

gloss (glôs), *n.* [ME. & OFr. *glose;* L. *glossa;* Gr. *glōssa*, the tongue, language, word requiring explanation < **glōchia*, pointed object < IE. base **glōgh-*, thorn, point, seen also in OSlav. *glogu*, thorn, Gr. *glōchis*, point], 1. words of explanation or translation inserted between the lines of a text; hence, 2. a note of comment or explanation accompanying a text, as in a footnote or margin. 3. a collection of such notes; glossary. *v.t.* 1. to furnish (a text) with notes of comment or explanation. 2. to interpret falsely. *v.i.* to write notes of explanation for a text; annotate.

glos·sal (glos″'l, glôs″'l), *adj.* [L. *glossa* < Gr. *glōssa*, the tongue; + *-al*], of the tongue.

glos·sar·i·al (glo-sâr′i-əl), *adj.* of, or having the nature of, a glossary.

glos·sar·ist (glos′ẽr-ist, glôs′ẽr-ist), *n.* a person who writes glosses or compiles glossaries.

glos·sa·ry (glos′ẽr-i, glôs′ẽr-i), *n.* [*pl.* GLOSSARIES (-iz)], [L. *glossarium* < *glossa;* see GLOSS (explanation)], a list of foreign, difficult, or technical terms with explanations or translations, as for some particular author, field of knowledge, etc., often included in alphabetical listing at the end of a textbook: abbreviated **gloss.**

glos·sa·tor (glo-sā′tẽr), *n.* [ML.; see GLOSS, *v.* (to explain)], a person who writes glosses.

gloss·er (glôs′ẽr), *n.* a person who writes glosses.

gloss·i·ly (glôs′ə-li), *adv.* in a glossy manner.

gloss·i·ness (glôs′i-nis), *n.* the quality of being glossy.

glos·si·tis (glo-sī′tis), *n.* [*gloss*(*o*)- + *-itis*], in *medicine*, inflammation of the tongue.

glos·so- (glos′ō), [< Gr. *glōssa*, the tongue], a combining form meaning: 1. *of the tongue*, as in *glossoplegia*. 2. *the tongue and*, as in *glossopharyngeal*. 3. *of words or language*, as in *glossology*. Also, before a vowel, **gloss-.**

glos·sog·ra·pher (glo-sog′rə-fẽr), *n.* [Gr. *glōssographos* < *glōssa* (see GLOSS, explanation) + *graphein*, to write], a person who writes or interprets glosses.

gloss·y (glôs′i), *adj.* [GLOSSIER (-i-ẽr), GLOSSIEST (-i-ist)], [*gloss* (luster) + *-y*], 1. having a smooth, shiny, polished surface. 2. smooth and plausible; specious.

-glot (glot), [Gr. *-glōttos* < *glōtta;* see GLOTTIS], a combining form meaning *knowledge of* or *communication in* (a specified number of) *languages*, as in *polyglot, triglot.*

glot·tal (glot″'l), *adj.* of or articulated at the glottis: as, English *h* is produced by a gradual *glottal* narrowing.

glottal stop, a speech sound (IPA symbol [ʔ]) produced by a momentary complete closure of the glottis: it is commonly heard, often as a variant for medial *t* (in *water, bottle*, etc.), in many Scottish and British dialects.

glot·tic (glot′ik), *adj.* [in sense 1, < *glottis;* in sense 2, < Gr. *glōttikos*], 1. glottal. 2. [Obs.], linguistic.

glot·tis (glot′is), *n.* [Mod. L.; Gr. *glōttis* < *glōtta*, Attic var. of *glōssa;* see GLOSS (explanation)], the opening between the vocal cords in the larynx.

Glouces·ter (glos′tẽr, glôs′tẽr), *n.* 1. a city in England, on the River Severn: pop.,68,000. 2. a city in northeastern Massachusetts: pop., 26,000.

Glouces·ter·shire (glos′tẽr-shir′, glôs′tẽr-shir′), *n.* a county of southwestern England: pop., 939,000; county seat, Gloucester.

glove (gluv), *n.* [ME. *glofe;* AS. *glof*, glove, paw (whence ON. *glofi*) < Gmc. **ga-lōfa;* **ga-*, pref., lit., together (AS. *ge-*) + **lōfa* (Goth. *lōfa*, etc.), flat hand, palm of the hand; cf. LUFF], 1. a covering for the hand, made of leather, cloth, etc., with a separate sheath for each finger and the thumb. 2. in *sports*, *a*) a similar covering of padded leather worn by baseball players in the field: see also **mitt.** *b*) a padded mitten worn by boxers: usually **boxing glove.** *v.t.* [GLOVED (gluvd), GLOVING], 1. to supply with gloves. 2. to cover with or as with a glove. 3. to be a glove for.

be hand in glove with, to be closely associated with; be very friendly or intimate with.

handle with (kid) gloves, to deal with gently and tactfully.

put on the gloves, [Colloq.], to box.

glove compartment, a compartment built into the dashboard of an automobile, for miscellaneous articles.

glov·er (gluv′ẽr), *n.* one who makes or sells gloves.

Glov·ers·ville (gluv′ẽrz-vil′), *n.* a city in eastern New York: pop., 22,000.

glove silk, a knitted silk cloth used for gloves, etc.

glow (glō), *v.i.* [ME. *glowen;* AS. *glowan;* akin to G. *glühen;* IE. base **ghlō-* (< **ĝhel-*, **ghel-*, to shine), seen also in Gr. *chlōros*, light green (cf. CHLORINE)], 1. to give off a bright light as a result of great heat; be incandescent or red-hot. 2. to give out a steady, even light without flame or blaze: as, the harbor lights *glowed.* 3. to be or feel hot; give out heat. 4. to radiate health or high spirits. 5. to be elated or enlivened by emotion: as, he *glowed* with pride. 6. to show brilliant, conspicuous colors; be bright; specifically, *a*) to be flushed; show red, as from emotion, enthusiasm, etc.: said of the skin. *b*) to gleam; flash; light up: said of the eyes. *c*) to show great intensity: said of colors. *n.* 1. light given off as a result of great heat; incandescence. 2. steady, even light without flame or blaze; hence, 3. brilliance, vividness, or intensity of color. 4. brightness of skin color; flush, as from health, emotion, etc. 5. a sensation of warmth and well-being. 6. intensity of emotion; ardor, eagerness, animation, etc. —*SYN.* see **blaze.**

glow·er (glou′ẽr), *v.i.* [dial. *glower, glowr*, popularized in literature < Scot.; ME. (northern & Scot.) *gloren;* prob. < ON. (cf. Norw. dial. *glōra*, Sw. dial. *glora*, to stare, gape); Gmc. base **glō-*, IE. **ghlō-*, as in *glow;* senses influenced by *glare*], to stare with sullen anger; scowl. *n.* a sullen, angry, or ill-humored stare; scowl. —*SYN.* see **frown.**

glow·fly (glō′flī′), *n.* a firefly.

glow·worm (glō′wûrm′), *n.* any of a number of wingless insects or insect larvae that give off a phosphorescent light; especially, the wingless female or the larva of the firefly.

glox·in·i·a (glok-sin′i-ə), *n.* [Mod. L.; after Benjamin P. *Gloxin*, 18th-c. G. botanist], a cultivated tropical plant with large, downy leaves and bell-shaped flowers of various colors.

gloze (glōz), *v.t.* [GLOZED (glōzd), GLOZING], [OFr. *gloser* < *glose;* see GLOSS (explanation)], 1. originally, to make glosses, or comments, on; explain. 2. to explain away; gloss (over). *v.i.* [Obs.], 1. to make a gloss or glosses; comment. 2. to fawn or flatter. *n.* [Archaic or Rare], 1. a gloss; comment. 2. flattery. 3. specious talk or insincere action.

glt., in *bookbinding*, gilt.

glu·cin·i·um (gloo-sin′i-əm), *n.* glucinum.

glu·ci·num (gloo-sī′nəm), *n.* [Mod. L. < Fr. *glucine* < Gr. *glykys*, sweet (from the sweet taste of some of its salts)], beryllium, a metallic chemical element: symbol, Gl: the former name.

Gluck, Alma (glook), (born *Reba Fiersohn*), 1884–1938; American operatic soprano, born in Romania.

Gluck, Chris·toph Wil·li·bald (kris′tôf vil′i-bält′), 1714–1787; German composer.

glu·co·pro·tein (gloo′kō-prō′tē-in), *n.* glycoprotein.

glu·cose (gloo′kōs), *n.* [< Gr. *glykys*, sweet; + *-ose*], a crystalline sugar, $C_6H_{12}O_6$, occurring naturally in fruits and honey: also called *dextrose, grape sugar:* the commercial form, containing dextrin and maltose, is prepared as a sweet sirup or, upon desiccation, as a light-colored solid, by the hydrolysis of starch in the presence of dilute acids.

glu·co·sid (gloo′kə-sid), *n.* glucoside.

glu·co·side (gloo′kə-sīd′), *n.* [< *glucose* + *-ide*], any of a class of compounds, either natural or synthetic, which on hydrolysis yield glucose and one or more other substances.

glu·co·sid·ic (gloo′kə-sid′ik), *adj.* of or containing glucosides.

glue (gloo), *n.* [ME. *gly;* OFr. *glu, glus*, birdlime; LL. *glus, glutis*, glue; akin to L. *gluten*, glue, Gr. *gloios*, sticky oil; for IE. base see CLAY], 1. a hard, brittle gelatin made by boiling animal skins, bones, hoofs, etc. to a jelly: when heated in water, it forms a sticky, viscous liquid used to stick things together. 2. any viscous preparation used to stick things together. *v.t.* [GLUED (glood), GLUING], to stick together with or as with glue.

glue·pot (gloo′pot′), *n.* a pot like a double boiler for melting glue.

glue·y (gloo′i), *adj.* [GLUIER (-i-ẽr), GLUIEST (-i-ist)], 1. like glue; sticky. 2. covered with or full of glue.

glum (glum), *adj.* [GLUMMER (-ẽr), GLUMMEST (-ist)], [< ME. *glommen*, var. of *gloum*(*b*)*en;* see GLOOM], gloomy; sullen; morose; depressed. —*SYN.* see **sullen.**

glu·ma·ceous (gloo-mā′shəs), *adj.* 1. having glumes. 2. like glumes.

glume (gloom), *n.* [L. *gluma*, husk < base of *glubere*, to bark], the husk or chafflike bract of grains or grasses.

glut (glut), *v.i.* [GLUTTED (-id), GLUTTING], [ME. *gluten, gloten;* OFr. *glotir, gloutir*, to swallow, gulp down; L. *glutire, gluttire;* ult. < IE. base **gel-*, to devour, seen also in G. *kehle*, AS. *ceole*, throat], to eat like a glutton;

overindulge. *v.t.* 1. to feed, fill, supply, etc. to excess; surfeit. 2. to flood (the market) with certain goods so that the supply is greater than the demand. *n.* [< the *v.*], 1. a glutting or being glutted. 2. a supply of certain goods that is greater than the demand. —*SYN.* see **satiate.**

glu·ta·mine (gloo͞′tə-mēn′, gloo͞′tə-min), *n.* [*gluten* + *-amine*], a crystalline substance, $C_5H_{10}N_2O_3$, found in the leaves and roots of certain plants.

glu·te·al (gloo͞-tē′əl, gloo͞′ti-əl), *adj.* [< *gluteus* + *-al*], of or near the muscles of the buttocks.

glu·ten (gloo͞′t'n), *n.* [L. *gluten*, glue; see GLUE], a gray, sticky, nutritious substance found in wheat flour, which gives dough its tough, elastic quality.

gluten bread, bread made from flour rich in gluten and low in starch: it is eaten by diabetics.

glu·te·nous (gloo͞′t'n-əs), *adj.* 1. like gluten. 2. full of gluten.

glu·te·us (gloo͞-tē′əs), *n.* [*pl.* GLUTEI (-ī)], [Mod. L.; Gr. *gloutos*, rump, buttock; for IE. base see CLOT], any of the three muscles that form each of the buttocks and act to extend, abduct, and rotate the thigh.

glu·ti·nous (gloo͞′ti-nəs), *adj.* [L. *glutinosus* < *gluten*, glue; see GLUE], gluey; sticky.

glut·ton (glut′'n), *n.* [ME. *glutun;* OFr. *gloton, glouton;* L. *gluto, glutto* < *glutire, gluttire*, to devour], 1. a person who eats too much. 2. a person with a great capacity for something: as, a *glutton* for work. 3. [transl. for G. *vielfrass*, lit., great devourer, altered by folk etym. < Norw. *fjeld fross*, lit., mountain bear], a furry, northern animal related to the marten and weasel but larger: the American variety is called *wolverine.* —*SYN.* see **epicure.**

glut·ton·ize (glut′'n-īz′), *v.t. & v.i.* [GLUTTONIZED (-īzd′), GLUTTONIZING], to eat like a glutton; eat greedily or too much.

glut·ton·ous (glut′'n-əs), *adj.* [ME. *glotonous;* see GLUTTON], inclined to eat greedily or too much.

glut·ton·y (glut′'n-i), *n.* [*pl.* GLUTTONIES (-iz)], [ME. *glotonie;* OFr. *gloutonie* < *gloton;* see GLUTTON], the habit or act of eating too much.

gly·cer·ic (gli-ser′ik, glis′ēr-ik), *adj.* [< *glycerin* + *-ic*], 1. of or derived from glycerin. 2. designating or of a colorless, sirupy acid, $CH_2OH{\cdot}CHOH{\cdot}COOH$, obtained by the partial oxidation of glycerin, or glycerol.

glyc·er·id (glis′ēr-id), *n.* glyceride.

glyc·er·ide (glis′ēr-īd′, glis′ēr-id), *n.* an ester of glycerin, or glycerol, either natural or synthetic.

glyc·er·in (glis′ēr-in, glis′rin), *n.* [Fr. *glycérine* < Gr. *glykeros*, sweet < **dlykeros;* IE. base (?) **dlku-*, sweet, seen also in Gr. *glykys*, L. *dulcis*, sweet], an odorless, colorless, sirupy liquid, $C_3H_5(OH)_3$, prepared by the hydrolysis of fats and oils: it is used as a solvent, skin lotion, food preservative, etc., and in the manufacture of explosives: in *chemistry*, called *glycerol.*

glyc·er·ine (glis′ēr-in, glis′rin, glis′ēr-ēn′), *n.* glycerin.

glyc·er·ol (glis′ēr-ōl′, glis′ēr-ol′), *n.* [< *glycerin* + *-ol*], glycerin: the name in chemistry.

glyc·er·yl (glis′ēr-il′), *n.* [*glycerin* + *-yl*], the trivalent radical of glycerin, C_3H_5.

glyceryl tri·ni·trate (trī-nī′trāt), nitroglycerin.

gly·cine (glī′sēn, glī-sēn′), *n.* [< Gr. *glykys*, sweet (see GLYCERIN); + *-ine*], a sweet, crystalline substance, $NH_2CH_2CO_2H$, obtained by hydrolysis from proteins and having the properties of an amino acid.

gly·co- (glī′kō, glī′kə), [Gr. *glyko-* < *glykys;* see GLYCERIN], a combining form meaning *glycerin, glycerol, glycogen*, as in *glycogenesis.*

gly·co·gen (glī′kə-jən), *n.* [*glyco-* + *-gen*], an insoluble, starchlike substance, $(C_6H_{10}O_5)_x$, produced in animal tissues, especially in the liver and muscles, and changed into a simple sugar as the body needs it: also called *animal starch.*

gly·co·gen·e·sis (glī′kə-jen′ə-sis), *n.* [< *glycogen*, after *genesis*], the formation of glycogen.

gly·co·gen·ic (glī′kə-jen′ik), *adj.* of glycogen or glycogenesis.

gly·col (glī′kōl, glī′kol), *n.* [< *glycerin* + *-ol*], 1. a colorless, sirupy liquid, $C_2H_4(OH)_2$, prepared by heating any of certain ethylene compounds with an alkali carbonate and used as an antifreeze: more accurately, **ethylene glycol.** 2. any of a group of alcohols of which this compound is the type.

gly·col·ic (glī-kol′ik), *adj.* 1. of or containing glycol. 2. designating or of a crystalline acid, CH_2OHCO_2H, found naturally in unripe grapes or made by the oxidation of glycol.

gly·co·ne·o·gen·e·sis (glī′kə-nē′ə-jen′ə-sis), *n.* [*glyco-* + *neo-* + *-genesis*], the production of carbohydrates, especially glycogen, from substances not glucosidic.

gly·co·pro·te·id (glī′kə-prō′tē-id), *n.* a glycoprotein.

gly·co·pro·te·in (glī′kə-prō′tē-in), *n.* any of a class of compounds in which a protein is combined with a carbohydrate group: also **glucoprotein.**

gly·co·su·ri·a (glī′kə-syoor′i-ə), *n.* [Mod. L.; see GLYCO- & -URIA], an abnormal condition in which sugar is excreted in the urine.

gly·co·su·ric (glī′kə-syoor′ik), *adj.* of or having glycosuria.

glyph (glif), *n.* [Gr. *glyphē*, a carving < *glyphein*, to carve, cut], 1. a carved figure, either incised or in relief; carved pictograph; hieroglyph. 2. in *architecture*, a vertical channel or groove.

glyph·ic (glif′ik), *adj.* [Gr. *glyphikos*], having to do with a glyph; carved; sculptured.

gly·phog·ra·phy (gli-fog′rə-fi), *n.* [< Gr. *glyphē* (see GLYPH); + *-graphy*], a method of producing a printing plate by engraving on a wax-coated copperplate which is then used to make an electrotype.

glyp·tic (glip′tik), *adj.* [Gr. *glyptikos* < Gr. *glyptos*, fit for carving, carved < *glyphein*, to carve], having to do with carving or engraving, especially on gems.

glyp·tics (glip′tiks), *n.pl.* [construed as sing.], [< *glyptic*], the art of carving or engraving designs on gems, etc.

glyp·to·dont (glip′tə-dont′), *n.* [Mod.L. < Gr. *glyptos*, carved; + *-odont*: so called from its fluted teeth], an extinct South American mammal, related to the armadillo but much larger.

GLYPTODONT (7 ft. long)

glyp·to·graph (glip′tə-graf′, glip′tə-gräf′), *n.* [< Gr. *glyptos*, carved; + *-graph*], 1. a design cut or engraved on a gem, seal, etc. 2. a gem, seal, etc. so engraved.

glyp·tog·ra·phy (glip-tog′rə-fi), *n.* [< Gr. *glyptos*, carved; + *-graphy*], the art or study of engraving on gems.

gm., gram; grams.

G.M., 1. general manager. 2. Grand Master.

G-man (jē′man′), *n.* [*pl.* G-MEN (-men′)], [*Government man*], [Colloq.], an agent of the Federal Bureau of Investigation.

Gmc., Germanic.

G.M.T., Greenwich mean time.

gnarl (närl), *n.* [back-formation < *gnarled*], a knot on the trunk or branch of a tree. *v.t.* to twist; contort; make knotted. *v.i.* to form gnarls.

gnarl (närl), *v.i.* [prob. of echoic origin], to snarl; growl.

gnarled (närld), *adj.* [< ME. *knarre*, knot], knotty, as a tree trunk; contorted; twisted; knobby; rugged.

gnarl·y (närl′i), *adj.* [GNARLIER (-i-ēr), GNARLIEST (-i-ist)], containing or covered with gnarls; gnarled.

gnash (nash), *v.t.* [Early Mod. Eng. for earlier *gnast;* ME. *gnasten, gnaisten;* prob. < ON.; cf. ON. *gnīsta*, to gnash (the teeth); ME. *gnaisten* would correspond to ON. **gneista* < the same IE. base, seen also in Eng. *gnaw*], 1. to grind or strike (the teeth) together. 2. to grind the teeth upon; bite by grinding the teeth. *v.i.* to grind the teeth together in anger or pain.

gnat (nat), *n.* [ME. *gnatte;* AS. *gnæt:* akin to G. dial. *gnatze;* LG. *gnatte;* IE. base **ghnədh-* < **ghen-;* see GNAW], 1. any of a number of small, two-winged insects that bite or sting. 2. [British], a mosquito.

strain at a gnat, to find it hard or impossible to believe or assent to something of trifling importance.

GNAT (1/4 in. long)

gnath·ic (nath′ik), *adj.* [< Gr. *gnathos*, the jaw; + *-ic*], of the jaw.

gnathic index, a measurement of the relative amount of protrusion of the jaw, expressed in terms of the ratio of the distance from the nasion to the basion (arbitrarily taken as 100) to the distance from the basion to the middle point of the alveolar process.

gna·thi·on (nā′thi-on′, nath′i-on′), *n.* [Mod.L. < Gr. *gnathos;* see GNATHIC], the lowest point on the median line of the lower jaw.

gna·thon·ic (na-thon′ik), *adj.* [< *Gnatho*, sycophant in Terence's play *Eunuchus*], fawning; falsely flattering.

-gnathous, [< Gr. *gnathos*], a combining form meaning *having a* (specified kind of) *jaw*, as in *prognathous.*

gnaw (nô), *v.t.* [GNAWED (nôd), GNAWED or GNAWN (nôn), GNAWING], [ME. *gnawen;* AS. *gnagen;* akin to G. *nagen* (OHG. *gnagan*); IE. **ghnēgh* < **ghen-*, to gnaw away, rub away; cf. GNASH, GNAT], 1. to cut, bite, and wear away bit by bit with the teeth. 2. to make by gnawing. 3. to consume; waste away; corrode. 4. to torment, as by constant pain, fear, etc.; harass. *v.i.* 1. to bite repeatedly (with *on, away, at*, etc.). 2. to produce an effect of continual biting, consuming, corroding, etc. (with *on, away, at*, etc.); torment.

gnaw·ing (nô′iŋ), *n.* 1. a sensation of dull, constant pain or suffering. 2. *pl.* pangs, especially of hunger.

gnawn (nôn), alternative past participle of **gnaw.**

gneiss (nīs), *n.* [G. *gneis;* OHG. *gneisto*, a spark (akin to ON. *gneisti*, spark): from the luster of certain of the components], a coarse-grained, metamorphic rock resembling granite, consisting of alternating layers of different minerals, such as feldspar, quartz, mica, and hornblende, and having a banded appearance.

gneiss·ic (nīs′ik), *adj.* of, containing, or like gneiss.

gneiss·oid (nīs′oid), *adj.* like gneiss.

gnome (nōm), *n.* [Fr.; Mod.L. *gnomus* < Gr. *gnōmē;* see GNOME (maxim): so called by Paracelsus, prob. from the belief that gnomes knew of hidden treasures], in *folklore*, any of a race of small, misshapen dwarfs, supposed to dwell in the earth and guard its treasures.

gnome (nōm), ***n.*** [LL. *gnome*, a sentence, maxim; Gr. *gnōmē*, thought, judgment, intelligence < *gignōskein*, to know; cf. KNOW], a wise, pithy saying; maxim.

gno·mic (nō′mik, nom′ik), ***adj.*** [Gr. *gnōmikos* < *gnōmē;* see GNOME (maxim)], 1. wise and pithy; full of aphorisms. 2. designating or of a writer of aphorisms.

gno·mi·cal (nō′mi-k'l, nom′i-k'l), ***adj.*** gnomic.

gnom·ish (nō′mish), ***adj.*** like a gnome, or dwarf.

gno·mon (nō′mon), ***n.*** [Gr. *gnōmōn*, one who knows or examines, index of a sundial < base of *gignōskein*, to know], 1. a column, pin on a sundial, etc. that casts a shadow indicating the time of day: see **sundial**, illus. 2. the part of a parallelogram remaining after a similar parallelogram has been taken from one of its corners.

gno·mon·ic (nō-mon′ik), ***adj.*** 1. of a gnomon, or sundial. 2. of the measurement of time by sundials.

-gnomy, [Gr. *-gnōmia* < *gnōmē;* see GNOME (maxim)], a combining form meaning ***art or science of judging or determining***, as in *physiognomy.*

gno·sis (nō′sis), ***n.*** [Mod.L.; Gr. *gnōsis*, knowledge < *gignōskein*, to know], positive knowledge in spiritual matters, such as was claimed to have been mystically acquired by the Gnostics.

-gnosis, [< Gr. *gnōsis;* see GNOSIS], a combining form meaning ***knowledge, recognition***, as in *diagnosis.*

Gnos·sus (nos′əs), ***n.*** Knossos, an ancient city in Crete.

gnos·tic (nos′tik), ***adj.*** [Gr. *gnōstikos* < *gnōsis;* see GNOSIS], 1. of or having knowledge. 2. [G-], of the Gnostics or Gnosticism. ***n.*** [LL. *gnosticus* < Gr. *gnōstikos*], [G-], a believer in Gnosticism.

-gnostic, [< Gr. *gnōstikos*, knowing < *gnōsis;* see GNOSIS], a combining form meaning ***of knowledge, of recognition***, as in *diagnostic.*

Gnos·ti·cism (nos′tə-siz'm), ***n.*** [*Gnostic* + *-ism*], a system of mystical religious and philosophical doctrines, combining Christianity with Greek and Oriental philosophies, propagated by early Christian sects that were denounced as heretical.

‡**gno·thi se·au·ton** (g'nō′thi se-ou-ton′), [Gr. *gnōthi seauton*], know thyself.

GNP, gross national product (the total value of a nation's annual output of goods and services).

gnu (nōō, nū), ***n.*** [*pl.* GNUS (nōōz, nūz), GNU; see PLURAL, II, D, 1], [< the native (Hottentot) name], a large African antelope with an oxlike head and horns and a horselike mane and tail: also called *wildebeest.*

GNU (4 1/2 ft. high at shoulder)

go (gō), ***v.i.*** [WENT (went), GONE (gôn, gon), GOING], [ME. *go(n)*, *goon;* AS. *gan;* akin to D. *gaan*, G. *gehen*, etc.; IE. base **ghēi-*, orig., to leave behind, go away, prob. seen also in L. *heres* (see HEIR); the p.t. *went* is < *wend*, *v.*, replacing AS. *eode*, ME. *yede*], I. *indicating motion without reference to destination or point of departure* 1. to move along; travel; proceed: as, this car can *go* 90 miles an hour. 2. to be moving: as, who *goes* there? 3. to move; work; operate: as, do you want to see the merry-go-round *go?* 4. to work or operate properly; function in the intended way: as, the motor won't *go.* 5. to behave in a certain way; gesture, act, or make sounds as specified or shown: as, he *went* like this, the balloon *went* "pop." 6. to take or follow a particular course, line of action, etc.; specifically, *a*) to result; turn out: as, the war *went* badly. *b*) to be guided, regulated, or directed by a procedure, method, etc.: as, I shall *go* by what you say. *c*) to take its course; proceed: as, how is the evening *going?* 7. to pass: said of time. 8. to pass from person to person: as, a rumor *went* through the office. 9. to be known or accepted: as, she *goes* by the name of Lindsay. 10. to move about or be in a certain condition or state, usually for some time: as, he *goes* in rags. 11. to pass into a certain condition, state, etc.; become; turn: as, she *went* conservative. 12. to have a certain form, arrangement, etc.; be expressed, phrased, voiced, or sung: as, how does the old story *go?* 13. to be or act in harmony; fit in: as, this hat *goes* well with the dress. 14. to put oneself: as, please don't *go* to any trouble. II. *indicating motion from a point of departure* 1. to move off; leave; depart. 2. to begin to move off, as in a race: used as a command. 3. *a*) originally, to leave a court of justice; hence, *b*) to continue (unpunished, unrewarded, unrequited, etc.). 4. to cease to have an effect; come to an end; pass away: as, the pain has *gone.* 5. to die. 6. to be done away with; be abolished: as, poverty must *go.* 7. to break away; be carried away or broken off: as, the mast *went* in the storm. 8. to fail; give way: as, his eyesight will *go* first. 9. to be given up or sacrificed: as, the country house must *go.* 10. to pass into the hands of someone; come under control of someone; be allotted or given: as, the prize *goes* to Jean. 11. to be sold at: as, it *went* for $20. III. *indicating motion toward a place, point, etc.* 1. to move toward a place or person or in a certain direction: as, when are you *going* to New York? 2. to move out of sight or out of the presence of a person: used as a command. 3. to make regularly scheduled trips to a place or between places: as, this bus *goes* to Canton. 4. *a*) to extend, lead, reach, run, etc. to a place: as, this road *goes* to London. *b*) to be able to extend or reach: as, the belt won't *go* around his waist. 5. to move toward, enter, or attend and then take part in the activities of, engage in, etc.: *a*) additional meaning is conveyed by the use of a noun governed by *to*, or by a participle: as, he *goes* to college, let's *go* swimming. *b*) reason for going is indicated by an infinitive, by *and* with a verb, or by a noun governed by *to*: as, he may *go* hang, I'll *go* and find out, he has *gone* to breakfast. 6. to carry one's case, plan, etc. to an authority: as, you must *go* to the president. 7. to turn to a certain activity; resort to some occupation, etc.: as, do you think they will *go* to war? 8. to carry one's activity to certain lengths; extend or reach so far in behavior, action, etc.: as, how far did he *go* in his protests? 9. to endure; last; hold out. 10. to have a particular or regular place or position: as, the shirts *go* in the second drawer. ***v.t.*** 1. to bet; wager. 2. [Slang], to tolerate; put up with. ***n.*** [*pl.* GOES (gōz)], 1. the act of going. 2. something that operates successfully; a success. 3. [Colloq.], the power of going; animation; energy. 4. [Colloq.], a state of affairs. 5. [Colloq.], fashion; vogue (with *the*). 6. [Colloq.], an agreement; bargain. 7. [Colloq.], a try; attempt; endeavor. 8. [British Colloq.], a quantity given or taken at one time. 9. in *cribbage*, a situation in which a player can lay no card that will not carry the count above 31: the last card played counts one point.

as people (or things) go, in comparison with how other people (or things) are.

go about, 1. to be occupied with; be busy at; do. 2. to move from place to place; circulate. 3. in *nautical usage*, to tack; change direction.

go after, [Colloq.], to try to catch or get; chase; pursue.

go against, to act in opposition to; be contrary to.

go along, 1. to proceed; continue. 2. to agree; cooperate. 3. to accompany (often followed by *with*).

go around, 1. to enclose; surround. 2. to be enough to provide a share for each. 3. to move from place to place; circulate.

go at, to attack or work at.

go back on, [Colloq.], 1. to be faithless or disloyal to, betray. 2. to break (a promise, etc.).

go beyond, to exceed.

go by, 1. to pass. 2. to be overlooked. 3. to be guided or led by. 4. to be known or referred to by.

go down, 1. to descend; sink; set. 2. to suffer defeat; lose. 3. to be perpetuated, as in history.

go for, 1. to be regarded or taken as. 2. to try to get. 3. to advocate; support. 4. [Colloq.], to attack 5. [Slang], to be attracted by; like very much.

go halves (or shares), [Colloq.], to share equally.

go hard with, to cause trouble or pain to.

go in for, [Colloq.], to engage, take part, or indulge in; have a liking for; be given to.

go into, 1. to inquire into. 2. to take up as a study or occupation. 3. to be contained in.

go in with, to share expenses or obligations with; join.

go off, 1. to go away; leave; depart. 2. to explode; detonate; shoot off, as by explosion. 3. to happen.

go on, 1. to move ahead; proceed; continue. 2. to behave. 3. to happen; take place. 4. [Colloq.], to chatter or rant. 5. in the *theater*, to make an entrance.

go (a person) one better, [Colloq.], to outdo or surpass (a person).

go out, 1. to come to an end; specifically, *a*) to be extinguished. *b*) to become outdated. 2. to attend social affairs, the theater, etc. 3. to sympathize. 4. to go on strike.

go over, 1. to examine thoroughly. 2 to do again. 3. to review. 4. [Colloq.], to be successful.

go through, 1. to perform thoroughly. 2. to endure; suffer; experience. 3. to look through; search. 4. to get approval or acceptance. 5. to spend.

go through with, to pursue to the end; complete.

go to! [Archaic], come! indeed!: used to express disapproval, disbelief, etc.

go together, 1. to match; harmonize. 2. [Colloq.], to be sweethearts.

go under, 1. to sink. 2. to be defeated, ruined, etc.

go up, 1. to rise; mount; ascend. 2. to rise in value, price, etc.; increase.

go with, 1. to accompany. 2. to match; harmonize. 3. [Colloq.], to be a sweetheart of.
go without, to manage or do without.
have a go at, [Colloq.], to try; attempt.
let go, 1. to set free; let escape. 2. to release one's hold or grip. 3. to give up; abandon.
let oneself go, to be unrestrained or uninhibited.
no go, [Colloq.], not possible; without use or value.
on the go, [Colloq.], in constant motion or action.
to go, [Slang], to be taken out: said of food in a restaurant.
See also phrases entered under **going.**
SYN.—**go** is the general word indicating motion away from the place where one is; **depart** is a somewhat more formal term and usually suggests a setting out on an expressed or implied journey (he *departed* for France); **leave** stresses the separation from a person or thing (I can't *leave* while she's ill); **quit** emphasizes a getting rid of by leaving (he *quit* his job yesterday); **withdraw** suggests a leaving for a definite, justified, and often unpleasant reason (he *withdrew* from the race because of a strained muscle); **retire,** often equivalent to the preceding, may imply a permanent withdrawal, a retreat, recession, etc. (he *retired* at 65, she *retired* to a nunnery).—***ANT.*** come, arrive.

G.O., g.o., 1. general office. 2. general order.

Go·a (gō'ə), *n.* a Portuguese colony on the southwestern coast of India: area, 1,537 sq. mi.; pop., 601,000; capital, Panjim.

go·a (gō'ə), *n.* [Tibetan *dgoba*], a small antelope of Tibet.

goad (gōd), *n.* [ME. *gode;* AS. *gad;* akin to Lombardic *gaida,* javelin; prob. IE. base *ĝhei-, to throw], 1. a sharp-pointed stick used in driving oxen. 2. any driving impulse; spur. ***v.t.*** to drive with or as with a goad; prod into action; urge on.

go-a·head (gō'ə-hed'), ***adj.*** 1. moving forward; hence, 2. [Colloq.], enterprising; pushing. ***n.*** permission or an order to proceed in an undertaking: usually with *the.*

goal (gōl), *n.* [ME. *gol,* boundary; prob. < AS. **gal,* inferred < *gælan,* to hinder, impede], 1. the line or place at which a race, trip, etc. is ended. 2. an object or end that one strives to attain; aim. 3. in certain games, *a)* the line, crossbar, or net over or into which the ball or puck must be passed to score. *b)* the act of scoring in this way. *c)* the score made. *d)* a goalkeeper. —***SYN.*** see **intention.**

goal·ie (gōl'i), *n.* [Colloq.], a goalkeeper.

goal·keep·er (gōl'kēp'ẽr), *n.* in certain games, a player stationed at a goal to prevent the ball or puck from crossing or entering it: also **goal tender.**

goal line, a line representing the goal in various games; especially, in *football,* either of the two lines, one at each end of the field, across which the ball must be carried or caught for a touchdown.

goal post, either of a pair of upright posts with a crossbar, used as a goal in football, soccer, etc.: in football the ball must be kicked over the crossbar to score a field goal or an extra point after a touchdown.

Goa powder, [first used in *Goa,* India, c. 1852], a bitter, yellowish powder extracted from the wood of the Brazilian araroba tree: it is used in medicine.

goat (gōt), *n.* [*pl.* GOATS (gōts), GOAT; see PLURAL, II, D, 1], [ME. *goot, gote;* AS. *gat;* akin to D. *geit,* G. *geiss,* etc.; IE. base **ghaido-,* he-goat, seen also in L. *haedus,* kid goat], 1. a cud-chewing mammal related to the sheep: it has hollow horns that curve backward, straight hair, and a beardlike tuft on the chin: in medieval folklore the goat was used as the animal representation of lechery; hence, 2. a lecherous man. 3. [Slang], a person forced to take the blame or punishment for others; scapegoat. 4. [G-], the constellation Capricorn.
get one's goat, [Slang], to annoy, anger, or irritate one.

goat·ee (gō-tē'), *n.* [< *goat:* from the resemblance to a goat's beard], a pointed beard on a man's chin.

goat·fish (gōt'fish'), *n.* [*pl.* GOATFISH, GOATFISHES (-iz); see FISH], any of several edible tropical fishes of the mullet family, with large scales, one or more long barbels on the lower jaw, and bright coloration.

goat·herd (gōt'hũrd'), *n.* one who herds or tends goats.

goat·ish (gōt'ish), ***adj.*** 1. like or characteristic of a goat. 2. lustful; lecherous.

goats·beard (gōts'bêrd'), *n.* 1. any of a group of hardy herbs of the rose family, with spikes of white flowers in clusters. 2. a European plant with yellow or purple flower heads: salsify is the root of the purple variety.

goat·skin (gōt'skin'), *n.* 1. the skin of a goat. 2. leather made from this. 3. a container for wine, water, etc. made of this leather.

goat's-rue (gōts'rōō'), *n.* a small, bushy plant with thick clusters of small, whitish flowers.

goat·suck·er (gōt'suk'ẽr), *n.* [transl. of L. *caprimulgus* < *capri,* goat + *mulgere,* to milk: so called from notion that it sucks milk from goats], any of various large-mouthed, nocturnal birds that feed on insects: American species include the whippoorwill and nighthawks.

gob (gob), *n.* [ME. *gobbe;* OFr. *gobe;* see GOBBET], [Colloq.], a lump or mass, as of something slimy.

gob (gob), *n.* [origin doubtful: for hypotheses see H. L. Mencken, *Am. Lang.* (4th ed.), pp. 573 f.], [Slang], a sailor in the United States Navy.

go·bang (gō'bäŋ'), *n.* [Japan. *goban* < Chin. *k'i pan,* chessboard], a Japanese game in which two players in turn place counters on a board divided into many squares, the winner being the first to get five in a row: also spelled **goban.**

gob·bet (gob'it), *n.* [ME. *gobet,* small piece; OFr. *gobet,* mouthful, dim. of *gobe,* mouth], [Archaic or Rare], 1. a fragment or bit, especially of raw flesh. 2. a lump; chunk; mass. 3. a mouthful.

gob·ble (gob''l), *n.* [echoic; var. of *gabble*], the characteristic throaty sound made by a male turkey. ***v.i.*** [GOBBLED (-'ld), GOBBLING], to make this sound.

gob·ble (gob''l), ***v.t.*** & ***v.i.*** [GOBBLED (-'ld), GOBBLING], [prob. echoic freq. formation on base of OFr. *gober,* to swallow < *gobe,* mouth], 1. to eat quickly and greedily. 2. [Slang], to seize eagerly.

gob·ble·dy·gook (gob''l-di-gook'), *n.* [coined by Maury Maverick (1895–1954), U.S. public official; cf. GOBBLE (the sound)], [Slang], talk or writing, especially of officialdom, that is pompous, wordy, involved, and full of long, Latinized words.

gob·bler (gob'lẽr), *n.* [*gobble* (to make a noise) + *-er*], a male turkey.

Gob·e·lin (gob'ə-lin, gō'bə-lin; Fr. gô'blan'), ***adj.*** designating, of, or like a kind of tapestry or upholstery made at the Gobelin works in Paris. *n.* Gobelin tapestry.

go-be·tween (gō'bi-twēn'), *n.* a person who passes back and forth between others with messages, suggestions, etc.; intermediary: often implying shady dealings.

Go·bi (gō'bi), *n.* a large desert in Asia, chiefly in Mongolia: site of archaeological excavations: Chinese name, *Shamo.*

go·bi·oid (gō'bi-oid'), ***adj.*** 1. of the family of gobies. 2. like a goby. *n.* a fish of this family.

gob·let (gob'lit), *n.* [ME. & OFr. *gobelet* < **gobe* (dim., *gobel*) < Bret. *gob, kop* < OFr. *cope,* cup < LL. *cuppa;* see CUP], 1. originally, a bowl-shaped drinking container without handles. 2. now, a drinking glass with a base and stem.

gob·lin (gob'lin), *n.* [ME. & OFr. *gobelin;* ML. *gobelinus;* ? < *cobalus;* Gr. *kobalos,* sprite], in *folklore,* an evil or mischievous spirit, conceived of as ugly or misshapen.

go·by (gō'bi), *n.* [*pl.* GOBIES (-biz), GOBY; see PLURAL, II, D, 1], [L. *gobio, gobius,* gudgeon < Gr. *kōbios*], any of a group of small, spiny-finned fishes, widely distributed throughout warm and temperate seas: the ventral fins are modified to form a suction disk.

go-by (gō'bī'), *n.* [Colloq.], a passing by; especially, an intentional disregard or slight: usually in *give* (or *get*) *the go-by,* to slight (or be slighted).

go·cart (gō'kärt'), *n.* 1. a framework mounted on casters, used to support a child learning to walk. 2. a child's low carriage that can be drawn or pushed by hand. 3. a type of light carriage.

god (god), *n.* [ME. & AS. *god;* akin to G. *gott,* Goth. *guth,* etc.; prob. IE. base **ĝhawa-,* to call out to, invoke], 1. any of various beings conceived of as supernatural, immortal, and having special powers over the lives and affairs of people and the course of nature; deity, especially a male deity. 2. an image that is worshiped; idol. 3. a person or thing deified or excessively honored and admired. 4. [G-], (*also occas.* gôd), in *monotheistic religions,* the creator and ruler of the universe, regarded as eternal, infinite, all-powerful, and all-knowing; Supreme Being; Almighty. Often used in exclamations, as, good *God! God* almighty! my *God!*
God willing, if God is willing.

Go·da·va·ri (gō-dä'və-ri), *n.* a river in southern India, flowing into the Bay of Bengal: length, 900 mi.

god·child (god'chīld'), *n.* [*pl.* GODCHILDREN (-chil'drən)], the person for whom a godparent is sponsor.

god·damned (god'damd'), ***adj.*** strongly cursed or damned: used as a curse or strong intensive, often shortened to **goddamn, goddam.**

god·daugh·ter (god'dô'tẽr), *n.* a female godchild.

god·dess (god'is), *n.* [ME. *godesse, goodesse*], 1. a female god; hence, 2. a woman of very great charm or beauty, or of surpassing goodness.

Go·des·berg (gō'des-berkh'), *n.* a city in the Rhine Province, Germany, on the Rhine: pop., 24,000.

go-dev·il (gō'dev''l), *n.* 1. any of certain kinds of sled, especially one used in logging. 2. a tool for scraping out obstructions from an oil pipe line.

god·fa·ther (god'fäthẽr), *n.* a male godparent.

God-fear·ing (god'fêr'iŋ), ***adj.*** [sometimes g-], 1. fearing God; hence, 2. devout; pious.

God·for·sak·en (god'fẽr-sā'kən), ***adj.*** [sometimes g-], 1. depraved; wicked. 2. [Colloq.], desolate; forlorn.

God·frey (god'fri), [OFr. *Godefrei;* OHG. *Godafrid* < *god, got,* God + *fridu,* peace; hence, lit., peace (of) God], a masculine name: equivalent, G. *Gottfried.*

God-giv·en (god'giv'ən), ***adj.*** [sometimes g-], 1. given by God. 2. very welcome; suitable or opportune.

god·head (god'hed), *n.* [ME. *godhede;* see -HEAD], 1. godhood; divinity. 2. [G-], God.

god·hood (god'hood), *n.* [see -HOOD], the state or quality of being a god; divinity.

Go·di·va (gə-dī'və), *n.* in *English legend,* the 11th-century patroness of Coventry who rode naked through the streets on a white horse so that her husband would abolish a heavy tax, in accordance with their agreement.

god·less (god′lis), ***adj.*** 1. denying the existence of God or a god; irreligious; atheistic. 2. impious; wicked.

god·like (god′līk′), ***adj.*** like or suitable to God or a god; divine.

god·li·ness (god′li-nis), ***n.*** the quality or state of being godly; piety.

god·ling (god′liŋ), ***n.*** [see -LING], a secondary or relatively unimportant god.

god·ly (god′li), ***adj.*** [GODLIER (-li-ẽr), GODLIEST (-li-ist)], [ME.; see GOD & -LY], 1. [Archaic], of or from God; divine. 2. devoted to God; pious; devout; religious.

god·moth·er (god′mu*th*′ẽr), ***n.*** a female godparent.

go·down (gō-doun′), ***n.*** [altered < Malay *godoṅ*, warehouse], in the Far East, a warehouse.

god·par·ent (god′pâr′ənt), ***n.*** a person who sponsors a newborn child and assumes responsibility for its faith; godmother or godfather.

go·droon (gə-drōōn′), ***n.*** a gadroon.

God's acre, a burial ground, especially one in a churchyard; cemetery.

god·send (god′send′), ***n.*** [contr. of *God's send;* ME. *sande*, mission, message; AS. *sand* < *sendan*, to send], anything unexpected and needed or desired that comes at the opportune moment, as if sent by God.

god·ship (god′ship), ***n.*** [see -SHIP], the character or status of a god; deity; divinity.

god·son (god′sun′), ***n.*** a male godchild.

God·speed (god′spēd′), ***n.*** [contr. of *God speed you*], success; good fortune: a wish for the welfare of a person starting on a journey or venture.

Go·du·nov, Bo·ris Fë·do·ro·vich (bô′ris fyô′dô-rô′vich gô-doo-nôf′), 1551?–1605; czar of Russia (1598–1605).

God·ward (god′wẽrd), ***adv. & adj.*** [ME.; see -WARD], 1. toward God. 2. in relation or with reference to God.

God·wards (god′wẽrdz), ***adv.*** Godward.

God·win (god′win), [AS. *Godewine*, lit., friend (of) God; see EDWIN], a masculine name.

God·win, Mary (born *Mary Wollstonecraft*), 1759–1797; English writer; wife of *William* and mother of *Mary Wollstonecraft Shelley.*

Godwin, William, 1756–1836; English philosopher and writer; father of *Mary Wollstonecraft Shelley.*

Godwin Austen, Mount, a mountain of the Karakorum range, Kashmir, India, near the border of Sinkiang: height, 28,250 ft.: second-highest mountain in the world: also called *K2, Dapsang.*

god·wit (god′wit), ***n.*** [parallels D. *rödvitte*, lit., little red thing (< *röd*, red + *vitte*, small thing), but both may be echoic of the cry], any of a group of long-billed wading birds of the snipe family.

Goeb·bels, Jo·seph Paul (yō′zef poul gö′bəls), 1897–1945; German politician and editor; Nazi minister of propaganda (1933–1945).

Goe·ring, Her·mann Wil·helm (her′män vil′helm gö′riŋ), 1893–1946; German politician and Nazi leader; field marshal (1938–1945); convicted of war crimes; committed suicide: also spelled **Göring.**

Goe·thals, George Washington (gō′thəlz), 1858–1928; American engineer and general; chief engineer in charge of building the Panama Canal.

Goe·the, Jo·hann Wolf·gang von (yō′hän vôlf′gäŋ fôn gö′tə; *sometimes Anglicized to* gā′ti, gũr′tə), 1749–1832; German poet and dramatist; wrote *Faust*, etc.

goe·thite (gō′thīt; G. gö′tit), ***n.*** [< *Goethe* + *-ite:* so named in honor of Goethe's studies in geology and mineralogy], a hydrous oxide mineral of iron, $Fe_2O_3 \cdot H_2O$.

gof·fer (gof′ẽr, gôf′ẽr), ***v.t.*** [Fr. *gaufrer*, to crimp < *gaufre*, waffle; D. *wafel*, waffle, honeycomb], to pleat, crimp, or flute (cloth, paper, etc.). ***n.*** 1. a goffering iron. 2. a pleating or fluting. Also **gauffer.**

gof·fer·ing (gof′ẽr-iŋ, gôf′ẽr-iŋ), ***n.*** [see GOFFER], 1. a pleating, crimping, or fluting. 2. a series of pleats, crimps, or flutes.

Gog and Ma·gog (gog′′n mā′gog), [Heb. *gōgh, māgōgh*], 1. in the *Bible*, representations of the nations that are to war against the kingdom of God under the leadership of Satan: Rev. 20:8. 2. [altered, after the Biblical names, from two earlier names, one of which was prob. *Gogmagog* (itself altered after *Gog*) < ML. *Goemagot*, legendary English giant], two huge wooden statues in the Guildhall, London.

go-get·ter (gō′get′ẽr), ***n.*** [Slang], an active and aggressive person who usually gets what he wants.

gog·gle (gog′′l), ***v.i.*** [GOGGLED (-′ld), GOGGLING], [ME. *gogelen*, to look obliquely, freq. formation prob. < Celtic base; cf. Ir. *gog*, a nod, W. *gogi*, to shake, etc.], 1. *a)* to stare with bulging or wide-open eyes. *b)* to roll the eyes. 2. *a)* to bulge; open wide in a stare. *b)* to roll: said of the eyes. ***v.t.*** to roll (the eyes). ***n.*** 1. a bulging or rolling of the eyes. 2. *pl.* large spectacles, especially those fitted with side guards to protect the eyes against dust, wind, etc. ***adj.*** bulging, staring, or rolling: said of the eyes.

gog·gle-eyed (gog′′l-īd′), ***adj.*** having eyes that bulge, stare, or roll, as in amazement.

Gogh, Vincent van (vän′ gokh′; Eng. van gō′, van gôk′), 1853–1890; Dutch painter.

gog·let (gog′lit), ***n.*** [Port. *gorgoleta*], a porous earthenware container with a long neck, for keeping water cool by evaporation: also **gurglet.**

Go·gol, Ni·ko·lai Va·sil·ie·vich (ni-kô-lī′ vä-sil-yā′vich gô′gôl; Eng. gō′gəl), 1809–1852; Russian novelist and dramatist.

Goi·del·ic (goi-del′ik, goi′*th*əl-ik), ***adj.*** [< Ir. *Gaedheal;* OIr. *Góidel;* see GAEL], 1. of the Gaels. 2. designating or of their languages. ***n.*** the subfamily of the Celtic languages that includes Erse (Irish Gaelic), Scottish Gaelic, and Manx: distinguished from *Brythonic.* Also **Gadhelic.**

go·ing (gō′iŋ), ***n.*** 1. a leaving; departure. 2. the condition of the ground or land with reference to the ease with which it can be crossed in traveling; hence, 3. [Colloq.], circumstances affecting progress; working conditions. ***adj.*** 1. moving; running; working. 2. conducting its regular business: as, a *going* concern. 3. in existence or available.

be going to, to be intending to; will or shall.

get going, [Colloq.], to start; begin.

going on, [Colloq.], nearing or nearly (a specified age or time).

goings on, [Colloq.], behavior or actions, especially when regarded with disapproval.

goi·ter, goi·tre (goi′tẽr), ***n.*** [Fr. *goitre* < *goitreux*, having a goiter; LL. **gutturiosus* < L. *guttur*, throat], 1. a diseased condition of the thyroid gland characterized by enlargement of the gland, seen as a swelling in the front of the neck. 2. the enlargement or swelling.

goi·trous (goi′trəs), ***adj.*** 1. of, having the nature of, or having goiter. 2. designating a geographical area where goiter is prevalent.

Gol·con·da (gol-kon′də), ***n.*** 1. an ancient city in Hyderabad, India, famous for diamond cutting in the 16th century. 2. a source of great wealth, as a mine.

gold (gōld), ***n.*** [ME. & AS.; akin to G. *geld;* IE. base **ĝhel-, ghel-*, to shine, gleam, glitter, hence yellow; cf. GLOW, GALL, etc.], 1. a heavy, yellow, metallic chemical element with a high degree of ductility and malleability: it is a precious metal and is used in the manufacture of coins, jewelry, alloys, etc.: symbol, Au; at. wt., 197.2; at. no., 79: abbreviated **G., g.** 2. gold coin; hence, 3. money; riches; wealth. 4. the bright yellow color of the metal. 5. something regarded as having any of the qualities of gold, as great value, luster, splendor, etc.: as, his voice is pure *gold.* ***adj.*** 1. of, made of, like, or containing gold. 2. having the color of gold. 3. secured by or redeemable in gold; based on gold.

gold·beat·er (gōld′bēt′ẽr), ***n.*** a person who pounds gold into thin leaves for use in gilding.

goldbeater's skin, a thin membrane from the intestine of an ox, used by goldbeaters to separate leaves of gold.

gold beetle, any of various gold-colored beetles.

gold·brick (gōld′brik′), ***v.i.*** [Military Slang], to try to avoid work; shirk; loaf.

gold brick, 1. [Colloq.], a worthless metal bar or brick gilded to make it appear solid gold and sold as such by swindlers; hence, 2. [Colloq.], anything worthless passed off as genuine or valuable. 3. [Military Slang], a person who tries to avoid work; shirker; loafer.

gold·bug (gōld′bug′), ***n.*** a gold beetle.

gold certificate, a note of a stated value formerly issued by the United States Treasury as currency and secured by gold coin or bullion payable to the bearer on demand.

Gold Coast, 1. formerly, a British territory in western Africa: it merged with British Togoland (1957) to form the independent state of Ghana. 2. [Colloq.], a district where rich people live: as, the *Gold Coast* of Chicago.

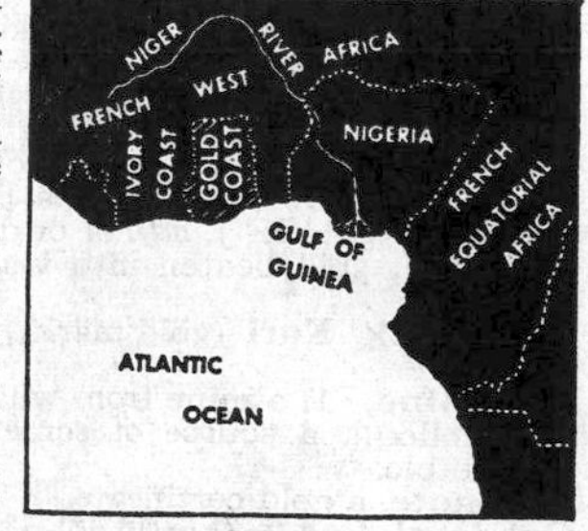

GOLD COAST

Gold Coast Colony, a former British colony in the Gold Coast, Africa: in 1957, it became part of the independent state of Ghana.

gold digger, [Slang], a woman who in her personal relations with men tries to get money and gifts from them.

gold dust, gold in very small bits or as a powder, the normal state in which it is found in placer mining.

gold·en (gōl′d'n), ***adj.*** [ME. *golden* < *gold* (for earlier *gilden, gylden*)], 1. made of, containing, or yielding gold. 2. having the color and luster of gold; bright-yellow. 3. very valuable, favorable, or precious; excellent. 4. prosperous and joyful; flourishing.

Golden Age, [after L. (Ovid) *aurea aetas*], 1. in *Greek & Roman legend*, an imaginary early age in which mankind was ideally happy, prosperous, and innocent. 2. [g- a-], the period of greatest progress, prosperity, or cultural achievement, as in a nation's history.

golden aster, any of a group of hardy plants similar to the daisies, with tall, yellow flower heads.

golden bantam corn, a variety of sweet corn with bright-yellow kernels on small ears.

golden calf, 1. a calf of gold worshiped by the Israelites while Moses was at Mount Sinai: Ex. 32:4; hence, 2. riches regarded as of the greatest importance.

golden eagle, a large, strong eagle found in mountainous districts of the Northern Hemisphere, with brown feathers on the back of its head and neck.

gold·en·eye (gōl'd'n-ī'), *n.* [*pl.* GOLDENEYES (-īz'), GOLDENEYE; see PLURAL, II, D, 1], a wild duck with a dark-green back and a white breast, noted for its expert diving and speed in flying.

Golden Fleece, in *Greek legend*, the fleece of gold that hung in a sacred grove at Colchis guarded by a dragon until taken away by Jason and the Argonauts.

Golden Gate, the strait leading into San Francisco Bay from the Pacific.

golden glow, a tall, hardy North American plant with doubled, yellow, globular flowers.

golden goose, a goose in a Greek fable who laid a golden egg each day: its greedy owner, thinking to get all the gold at once, killed the goose, thus losing everything.

Golden Horde, [so called from the splendors of their leader's camp], the Mongol armies that invaded Europe in 1237 and, under the Khans, ruled over Russia for two centuries.

Golden Horn, an arm of the Bosporus, forming the harbor of Istanbul, Turkey.

Golden Legend, name given by Caxton to his translation from the French (1483) of the Latin collection of saints' lives originally written by Jacobus de Voragine, bishop of Genoa (1230–1298).

golden mean, [transl. of L. (Horace) *aurea mediocritas*], the safe, prudent way between extremes; happy medium; moderation.

golden pheasant, a pheasant of China and Tibet, with brightly colored feathers and a yellow crest.

golden robin, the Baltimore oriole.

gold·en·rod (gōl'd'n-rod'), *n.* any of a group of North American plants of the composite family, typically with long, branching stalks bearing clusters of small, yellow flowers through the late summer and fall.

golden rule, the precept that one should behave toward others as he would want them to behave toward him: see Matt. 7:12, Luke 6:31.

gold·en·seal (gōl'd'n-sēl'), *n.* an American herb of the crowfoot family, with large, round leaves and a thick, yellow rootstock, formerly much used in medicine.

golden warbler, a small, yellow American songbird.

golden wedding, the 50th anniversary of a wedding.

gold-filled (gōld'fild'), *adj.* made of a base metal overlaid with gold.

gold·finch (gōld'finch'), *n.* [ME.; AS. *goldfinc;* see GOLD & FINCH], 1. a European songbird with yellow-streaked wings. 2. a small American songbird the male of which has a yellow body with black markings.

gold·fin·ny (gōld'fin'ni), *n.* [*pl.* GOLDFINNIES (-iz)], 1. a small, bright-yellow European fish. 2. any of several related sea or fresh-water fishes, as the cunner.

gold·fish (gōld'fish'), *n.* [*pl.* GOLDFISH, GOLDFISHES (-iz); see FISH], a small, golden-yellow or orange-colored fish, often kept in ponds or fish bowls.

gold foil, [ME. *goold fuyle*], gold beaten into thin sheets slightly thicker than gold leaf.

gold·i·locks (gōl'di-loks'), *n.* 1. a person with yellow hair. 2. [G-], a little girl in a folk tale who visits the home of three bears. 3. a European plant with clusters of small, yellow flowers. 4. a European buttercup.

gold-leaf (gōld'lēf'), *adj.* of or decorated with gold leaf.

gold leaf, gold beaten into very thin sheets, used for gilding.

Gold·mark, Karl (gōld'märk), 1830–1915; Hungarian composer.

gold mine, 1. a mine from which gold ore is obtained. 2. [Colloq.], a source of something very valuable or profitable.

gold note, a gold certificate.

Gol·do·ni, Car·lo (kär'lō gôl-dô'nē), 1707–1793; Italian dramatist.

gold plate, tableware made of gold.

gold reserve, 1. the gold formerly kept in the United States Treasury for redeeming government notes: most of it is now buried at Fort Knox, Kentucky, as a permanent reserve. 2. the quantity of gold in the central or national bank of a country.

gold rush, a rush of people to territory where gold has recently been discovered, as to California in 1849.

gold·smith (gōld'smith'), *n.* 1. a skilled worker who makes articles of gold. 2. a dealer in such articles.

Gold·smith, Oliver (gōld'smith'), 1728–1774; British poet, playwright, and novelist.

goldsmith beetle, a large, bright-yellow American beetle that feeds on tree foliage.

gold standard, 1. a monetary standard solely in terms of gold, in which the basic currency unit is made equal to and redeemable by a specified quantity of gold. 2. the legal weight and fineness of gold used in United States coins before 1934.

gold star, a small, gold star of cloth, paper, etc. awarded as a mark of honor in school, etc., or displayed to represent a member of the armed forces killed in the line of duty in wartime.

gold-star mother (gōld'stär'), a mother of a member of the armed forces killed in the line of duty in wartime.

gold·stone (gōld'stōn'), *n.* glass containing mineral particles and having a glittering, jewellike appearance.

gold·thread (gōld'thred'), *n.* a small North American plant of the crowfoot family, with white or yellow flowers and yellow roots used in medicine.

go·lem (gō'lim), *n.* [Heb., orig., embryo; later, monster (hence Yid. sense "dolt"); akin to Ar. *ghulām*, lad], in *Jewish legend*, a man artificially created by cabalistic rites; robot; automaton.

golf (gôlf, golf), *n.* [Late ME. (Scot.) *golf, gouff;* usually derived < D. *kolf*, a club (for hitting balls); but all early forms have *g-*, and the *-l-* may be unhistoric; ? directly < Scot. *gowf*, to strike < *gowf*, a blow (with the open hand)], an outdoor game played on a large course with a small, hard rubber ball and a set of clubs with wooden or metal heads, the object being to drive the ball into a series of variously located four-inch holes (usually nine or eighteen) with the fewest possible strokes. *v.i.* to play golf.

GOLF CLUBS
A, driver; B, brassie; C, spoon; D, midiron; E, mashie; F, niblick; G, putter

golf club, 1. any of the various clubs with wooden or metal heads and long, slender handles, used in golf. 2. an organization owning and controlling a golf course, clubhouse, etc., for the use of its members. 3. the golf course, clubhouse, etc. operated by such an organization.

golf course (or **links**), a tract of land for playing golf, with tees, greens, fairways, hazards, etc.

Gol·go·tha (gol'gə-thə), *n.* [LL.; Gr. *Golgotha;* Aram. *gūlgūlthā;* Heb. *gulgōleth*, skull, place of a skull], 1. the place where Jesus was crucified; Calvary: Mark 15:22. 2. [g-], *a*) a burial place. *b*) a place of agony or sacrifice.

gol·iard (gōl'yẽrd), *n.* [OFr., glutton < *gole* (Fr. *gueule*), mouth; L. *gula*, gullet], any of a class of wandering students of the late Middle Ages who wrote satirical Latin verse and often served as minstrels and jesters.

gol·iar·dic (gōl-yär'dik), *adj.* of the goliards or their verse.

Go·li·ath (gə-lī'əth), *n.* [LL.; Heb. *golyāth*], in the *Bible*, the Philistine giant killed by David with a stone shot from a sling: I Sam. 17:4, 49.

gol·li·wog, gol·li·wogg (gol'i-wog'), *n.* [arbitrary formation; ? after *polliwog*], 1. a grotesque black doll used in illustrations by Florence K. Upton for a series of children's books; hence, 2. a grotesque, ugly person.

gol·ly (gol'i), *interj.* an exclamation of surprise, etc.: a euphemism for *God.*

go·losh, go·loshe (gə-losh'), *n.* a galosh.

gom·broon (gom-brōōn'), *n.* [< *Gombroon* (Bandar Abbas), town on the Persian Gulf], a type of white, semitransparent Persian pottery.

Go·mel (gô'mel), *n.* a city in the Byelorussian S.S.R.: pop., 144,000.

gom·er·al, gom·er·el, gom·er·il (gom'ẽr-əl), *n.* [? < obs. *gome*, a man (< AS. *guma*) + *-erel, -rel*, depreciatory suffix < OFr. *-erel*], [Scot. & N. Eng. Dial.], a simpleton; fool; dolt.

Go·mor·rah, Go·mor·rha (gə-môr'ə, gə-mor'ə), *n.* [Gr. *Gomorrha* < Heb.], 1. in the *Bible*, a city destroyed together with a neighboring city, Sodom, by fire from heaven because of the sinfulness of the people: Gen. 19:24; hence, 2. any wicked city or place.

Gom·pers, Samuel (gom'pẽrz), 1850–1924; American labor leader born in England; president of the American Federation of Labor (1886–1895; 1896–1924).

gom·pho·sis (gom-fō'sis), *n.* [Mod.L. < Gr. *gomphōsis*, a nailing together < *gomphos*, a nail, bolt], a form of immovable joint in which a bone or other hard part fits into a socket: teeth fit into the jaw by gomphosis.

go·mu·ti (gō-mōō'ti), *n.* [Malay *gumuti*], 1. a Malayan palm with feathery leaves and a sweet sap from which a crude sugar and palm wine are made: also **gomuti palm.** 2. the wiry fibers from the stalks of its leaves, used in making ropes, etc.

-gon (gon, gən), [Gr. *-gōnon* < *gōnia*, an angle], a combining form used to form nouns meaning *a figure having*

(a specified number of) *angles*, as in *pentagon*.
gon·ad (gon′ad, gō′nad), *n.* [< Gr. *gonē*, a seed, generation; + *-ad*], a gland that produces reproductive cells; ovary or testis.
gon·ad·al (gon′ad-'l, gō′nad-'l), *adj.* of a gonad or gonads.
gon·a·do·trop·ic (gon′ə-dō-trop′ik, gə-nad′ə-trop′ik), *adj.* designating or of any substance acting as a stimulant upon the gonads.
Gon·court, Ed·mond Lou·is An·toine de (ed′mōn′ lwē än′twän′ də gōn′ko͞or′), 1822–1896; French novelist.
Goncourt, Jules Al·fred Hu·ot de (zhül ål′fred′ ü′ō′ də), 1830–1870; brother of *Edmond;* the two collaborated on a number of novels.
Gond (gond), *n.* [< native (Gondi) name], a member of the Dravidian culture group living in Madhya Pradesh, a state in central India.
Gon·di (gon′di), *n.* [< *Gondi*, name of the principal dialect], 1. a group of Dravidian dialects spoken in central India. 2. the principal dialect of this group.
gon·do·la (gon′də-lə), *n.* [It. (Venetian); ult. < Romance base *dond-*, to rock], 1. a long, narrow canalboat with a cabin in the middle and a high, pointed prow and stern, used on the canals of Venice: it is propelled by a pole or one oar at the stern. 2. a flat-bottomed river barge. 3. a gondola car. 4. a cabin suspended under a dirigible or balloon, for holding the motors, instruments, passengers, etc.

GONDOLA

gondola car, a railroad freight car with low sides and no top.
gon·do·lier (gon′də-lêr′), *n.* [It. *gondolier* < *gondola*], a man who rows or poles a gondola.
gone (gôn, gon), [ME. *gon;* AS. *gan*], past participle of **go.** *adj.* 1. moved away; departed. 2. ruined. 3. lost. 4. dying; dead. 5. faint; weak. 6. used up; consumed. 7. ago; past.
far gone, 1. much advanced; deeply involved. 2. very tired.
gone on, [Colloq.] in love with.
gone·ness (gôn′nis, gon′nis), *n.* weakness; exhaustion.
gon·er (gôn′ẽr, gon′ẽr), *n.* [< *gone* + *-er*], [Colloq.], a person or thing that seems certain to die soon, be ruined, etc.; person or thing beyond help.
Gon·er·il (gon′ẽr-il), *n.* in Shakespeare's *King Lear*, the elder of Lear's two wicked daughters.
gon·fa·lon (gon′fə-lən), *n.* [Fr.; It. *gonfalone;* OFr. *gonfanon*, banner; OHG. *gundfano*, battle standard; *gund*, *gunt*, a battle + *fano*, banner], a flag or ensign hanging from a crosspiece instead of an upright staff and usually ending in streamers; especially, such a standard used by any of the medieval republics of Italy.
gon·fa·lon·ier (gon′fə-lə-nêr′), *n.* [< Fr. or It.; Fr. *gonfalonier;* It. *gonfaloniere*], 1. the bearer of a gonfalon. 2. in some medieval republics of Italy, a high official.
gon·fa·non (gon′fə-nən), *n.* [Obs.], a gonfalon.
gong (gôŋ, goŋ), *n.* [Malay *guṅ;* echoic], 1. a slightly convex metallic disk that gives a loud, resonant tone when struck. 2. a saucer-shaped bell with such a tone.
Gon·go·rism (goŋ′gə-riz′m), *n.* 1. the literary style of Gongora y Argote, Spanish poet (d. 1627), characterized by affected metaphor and the use of strained conceits. 2. any style like this.
go·nid·i·al (gō-nid′i-əl), *adj.* of a gonidium or gonidia.
go·nid·i·um (gō-nid′i-əm), *n.* [*pl.* GONIDIA (-ə)], [Mod.L. dim. < Gr. *gonos;* see GONO-], 1. a reproductive cell produced asexually in certain algae. 2. any of the chlorophyll-bearing cells in lichens.
go·ni·o- (gō′ni-ō), [< Gr. *gōnia*, an angle], a combining form meaning *angle*, as in *goniometry*.
go·ni·om·e·ter (gō′ni-om′ə-tẽr), *n.* [Fr. *goniomètre;* see GONIO- & -METER], an instrument for measuring angles, especially of solid bodies.
go·ni·om·e·try (gō′ni-om′ə-tri), *n.* [Fr. *goniométrie;* see GONIO- & -METRY], the theory or science of measuring angles.
go·ni·on (gō′ni-on′), *n.* [*pl.* GONIA (-ə)], [Mod. L. < Gr. *gōnia*, an angle], the point at either angle of the lower jaw.
-go·ni·um (gō′ni-əm), [Mod.L. < Gr. *gonos;* see GONO-], a combining form used to form nouns meaning *a cell* or *structure in which reproductive cells are formed*, as in *sporogonium*.
gon·o- (gon′ə), [< Gr. *gonos, gonē*, procreation, offspring, semen, seed < base of *gignesthai*, to be born], a combining form meaning *reproductive, sexual*, as in *gonococcus, gonophore:* also, before a vowel, **gon-.**
gon·o·coc·cus (gon′ə-kok′əs), *n.* [*pl.* GONOCOCCI (-kok′sī)], [*gono-* + *coccus*], the microorganism that causes gonorrhea.
gon·of, gon·oph (gon′əf), *n.* [see GANOV], a thief.
gon·o·phore (gon′ə-fôr′), *n.* [*gono-* + *-phore*], 1. an extension of the axis of a flower, lifting the pistil and stamens above the floral envelope. 2. an independent animal cell that produces a hydroid colony by fission, budding, or other asexual means.
gon·or·rhe·a, gon·or·rhoe·a (gon′ə-rē′ə), *n.* [LL. *gonorrhoea;* Gr. *gonorrhoia* < *gonos*, a seed, semen (see GONO-) + *rhoia* < *rheein*, to flow], a venereal disease caused by gonococci, characterized by inflammation of the mucous membrane of the genitourinary tract and a discharge of mucus and pus: it is generally transmitted by sexual intercourse and can seriously affect other mucous membranes, especially those of the eye, as in a baby during childbirth.
gon·or·rhe·al, gon·or·rhoe·al (gon′ə-rē′əl), *adj.* of or caused by gonorrhea.
-go·ny (gə-ni), [L. *-gonia;* Gr. *-gonia* < base of *gignesthai*, to be born], a combining form used to form nouns meaning *something generated, produced, descended*, etc., as in *cosmogony, theogony*.
goo (go͞o), *n.* [prob. < baby talk], [Slang], 1. anything sticky, as glue. 2. anything sticky and sweet.
goo·ber (go͞o′bẽr), *n.* [of Afr. origin; said to be < Congo *nguba*], a peanut.
good (good), *adj.* [BETTER (bet′ẽr), BEST (best)], [ME. *gode;* AS. *god;* akin to G. *gut;* IE. base **ghadh-*, to unite, be associated, suitable, etc., seen also in *gather*], I. *a general term of approval or commendation, meaning* "as it should be" or "better than average" **1.** *a*) suitable to a purpose; effective; efficient: as, a jeep is *good* for driving on rough roads. *b*) producing favorable results; beneficial: as, hot lunches are *good* for children. 2. fresh; unspoiled; uncontaminated: as, *good* eggs. 3. valid; genuine; real: as, *good* money. 4. healthy; strong; vigorous; sound: as, *good* eyesight. 5. honorable; worthy: as, one's *good* name. 6. enjoyable, agreeable, happy, etc.: as, life is *good* here. 7. dependable; reliable; right: as, *good* advice. 8. thorough: as, a *good* job of cleaning up. 9. adequate; ample; sufficient; satisfying: as, a *good* meal. 10. morally sound or excellent; specifically, *a*) virtuous. *b*) pious. *c*) kind, benevolent, generous, sympathetic, etc. *d*) well-behaved; dutiful. *e*) proper; becoming: as, *good* manners. **11.** able; skilled; expert: as, a *good* swimmer. II. *a general intensive, meaning* "to a considerable amount, extent, or degree": as, a *good* many, a *good* beating. *n.* something good; specifically, *a*) worth; virtue; merit: as, there is much *good* in him. *b*) something contributing to health, welfare, happiness, etc.; benefit; advantage: as, the greatest *good* of the greatest number. *c*) something desirable or desired. See also **goods.** *interj.* an exclamation of satisfaction, pleasure, agreement, etc. In some exclamatory phrases expressing surprise, consternation, etc. (e.g., good gracious! good grief!) *good* is a euphemism for *God.* *adv.* well, completely, fully, etc.: variously regarded as substandard, dialectal, or colloquial.
as good as, virtually; practically; in effect; nearly.
come to no good, to come to a bad end; end in failure, trouble, etc.
for good, for the last time; for always; finally; permanently: also **for good and all.**
good and, [Colloq.], 1. very. 2. altogether; entirely.
good for, 1. able to survive, endure, or remain in working order for (a specified period of time). 2. worth. 3. able to pay, repay, or give. 4. used to express approval: as, *good for you!*
make good, 1. to give or do something as a substitute for; repay or replace. 2. to fulfill. 3. to succeed in doing; accomplish. 4. to be successful. 5. to prove.
no good, useless; worthless.
the good, 1. those who are good. 2. what is morally good.
to the good, as a profit, benefit, or advantage.
good afternoon, a salutation of greeting or farewell in the afternoon.
Good Book, the Bible (usually with *the*).
good-by, good·by (good′bī′), *interj.* & *n.* [*pl.* GOOD-BYS, GOODBYS (-bīz′)], [contr. of *God be with ye*], farewell.
good-bye, good·bye (good′bī′), *interj.* & *n.* [*pl.* GOOD-BYES, GOODBYES (-bīz′)], good-by.
good cheer, 1. revelry. 2. good food and drink; feasting. 3. courage.
Good Conduct Medal, in the *United States Army*, a bronze medal awarded to enlisted men for exemplary behavior, efficiency, and fidelity.
good day, a salutation of greeting or farewell.
good deal, 1. a large number or quantity; many or much. 2. [Slang], very good!
good evening, a salutation of greeting or farewell in the evening.
good fellow, an agreeable, convivial person.

good-fel·low·ship (good'fel'ō-ship'), *n.* [*good fellow* + *-ship*], hearty, convivial companionship.
good-for-noth·ing (good'fẽr-nuth'iŋ), *adj.* useless or worthless. *n.* a useless or worthless person.
Good Friday, the Friday before Easter Sunday, observed in commemoration of the crucifixion of Jesus.
good-heart·ed (good'här'tid), *adj.* kind, generous, etc.
Good Hope, Cape of, 1. a cape at the southern tip of Africa. 2. a province of the Union of South Africa: area, 276,966 sq. mi.; pop., 3,733,000; capital, Capetown: formerly called *Cape Colony;* also called *Cape Province.*
good humor, a cheerful, agreeable, pleasant mood.
good-hu·mored (good'hū'mẽrd, good'ū'mẽrd), *adj.* having or showing good humor; cheerful and agreeable.
good·ish (good'ish), *adj.* 1. fairly good; rather good. 2. fairly large.
good·li·ness (good'li-nis), *n.* [ME. *goodlinesse*], the quality or condition of being goodly.
good-look·ing (good'look'iŋ), *adj.* pleasing in appearance; beautiful or handsome. —*SYN.* see **beautiful.**
good looks, attractive personal appearance; especially, pleasing facial features.
good·ly (good'li), *adj.* [GOODLIER (-li-ẽr), GOODLIEST (-li-ist)], 1. good-looking. 2. of good quality; pleasing; fine. 3. ample; rather large: as, a *goodly* sum.
good·man (good'mən), *n.* [*pl.* GOODMEN (-mən)], [ME.; see GOOD & MAN], [Obs.], 1. a husband or master of a household. 2. a title equivalent to *Mr.*, applied to a man ranking below a gentleman.
good morning, a salutation of greeting or farewell in the morning.
good nature, a pleasant, agreeable, or kindly disposition; amiability; geniality.
good-na·tured (good'nā'chẽrd), *adj.* having or showing good nature; pleasant; agreeable. —*SYN.* see **amiable.**
Good Neighbor Policy, the policy of encouraging friendly political and economic relations between the United States and Latin America: introduced by President Franklin Roosevelt in 1933.
good·ness (good'nis), *n.* [ME. *goodnesse;* AS. *godnes*], 1. the state or quality of being good; specifically, *a)* virtue; excellence. *b)* kindness; generosity; benevolence. 2. best part, essence, or valuable property of a thing. *interj.* an exclamation of surprise or wonder: used alone or in various phrases, as, for *goodness'* sake!
good night, a salutation of farewell at night, used in parting or going to bed.
goods (goodz), *n.pl.* 1. movable personal property. 2. merchandise; wares. 3. fabric; cloth. 4. [British], freight: often used attributively. Abbreviated **gds.**
deliver the goods, to do or produce the thing required.
get (or have) the goods on, [Slang], to discover (or know) something incriminating about.
the goods, [Slang], what is required, genuine, or valid.
good Samaritan, 1. in the *Bible,* a person who was the only one to pity and help a traveler who had been beaten and robbed: Luke 10:30–37; hence, 2. anyone who pities or helps another or others unselfishly.
Good Shepherd, Jesus: John 10:11.
good-sized (good'sīzd'), *adj.* ample; big or fairly big.
good speed, success; good luck: a farewell denoting a wish for the welfare of a person starting on a journey or venture.
good-tem·pered (good'tem'pẽrd), *adj.* having a good temper; not easily angered or annoyed; amiable.
good turn, a good deed; friendly, helpful act; favor.
good·wife (good'wīf'), *n.* [*pl.* GOODWIVES (-wīvz')], [ME.; see GOOD & WIFE], [Obs.], 1. a wife or mistress of a household. 2. a title equivalent to *Mrs.*, applied to a woman ranking below a lady.
good·will (good'wil'), *n.* good will.
good will, 1. a friendly or kindly attitude; benevolence. 2. cheerful consent; willingness; readiness. 3. the value of a business in patronage, reputation, etc., over and beyond its tangible assets.
good·y (good'i), *n.* [*pl.* GOODIES (-iz)], [Colloq.], 1. *usually in pl.* something considered very good to eat, as a piece of candy. 2. a person who is weakly or cantingly pious; sanctimonious person. *adj.* [Colloq.], weakly or cantingly pious; sanctimonious. *interj.* [Colloq.], a child's exclamation of approval or delight. Often reduplicated as *goody-goody* (for *n.* 2, *adj.* & *interj.*).
good·y (good'i), *n.* [*pl.* GOODIES (-iz)], [< *goodwife*], a woman, especially an old woman or housewife, of lowly social status: formerly used, as in New England, as a title with the surname (e.g., *Goody* Smith).
Good·year, Charles (good'yêr'), 1800–1860; American inventor; originated process for vulcanization of rubber.
goo·ey (gōō'i), *adj.* [< *goo*], [Slang], 1. sticky, as glue. 2. sticky and sweet.
goof (gōōf), *n.* [prob. < or akin to ME. *gofisshe, goofish,* foolish], [Slang], a stupid, silly, or credulous person. *v.i.* [Slang], to err, blunder, fail, etc.
goof·i·ly (gōōf'ə-li), *adv.* [Slang], in a goofy manner.
goof·i·ness (goof'i-nis), *n.* [Slang], the quality or state of being goofy.
goof·y (gōōf'i), *adj.* [GOOFIER (-i-ẽr), GOOFIEST (-i-ist)], [Slang], like or characteristic of a goof; stupid and silly.
goo·gol (gōō'gol), *n.* [arbitrarily coined by Edward Kasner, Am. mathematician], 1. the number 1 followed by 100 zeros. 2. any very large number.
gook (gook, gōōk), *n.* [Military Slang], a Filipino, Japanese, Korean, etc.: a vulgar, offensive term of hostility and contempt.
goon (gōōn), *n.* [after a grotesque comic-strip character invented by E. C. Segar], [Slang], 1. a person who is awkward, grotesque, stupid, etc. 2. a ruffian or thug, especially one used in breaking a strike, etc.
goop, Goop (gōōp), *n.* [after the creatures invented by Gelett Burgess], a silly, ill-mannered, boorish person.
goos·an·der (gōōs-an'dẽr), *n.* [prob. < *goose,* after *bergander,* sheldrake], the merganser, a fish-eating duck.
goose (gōōs), *n.* [ME. *goos, gose;* AS. *gos* < Gmc. **gans* (cf. GANDER); hence akin to D. & G. *gans;* IE. **ĝhans,* seen also in L. *anser* (for **hanser*); cf. ANSERINE; *v.t.* 1 prob. from the fact that geese sometimes attack children from the rear], 1. [*pl.* GEESE (gēs), rarely GOOSE; see PLURAL, II, D, 1], any of a group of long-necked, web-footed, wild or domestic birds that are like ducks but larger; especially, a female of this group: distinguished from *gander.* 2. the flesh of a goose, used for food. 3. [*pl.* GEESE], a silly person. 4. [*pl.* GOOSES (-iz)], a tailor's pressing iron with a long handle curved somewhat like the neck of a goose. 5. [*pl.* GOOSES], [Slang], a goosing; sudden, playful prod in the backside. *v.t.* [GOOSED (gōōst), GOOSING], [Slang], 1. to prod suddenly and playfully in the backside so as to startle; hence, 2. to feed gasoline to (an engine) in irregular spurts.
cook one's goose, [Colloq.], to spoil one's chances, hopes, etc.
goose barnacle, [so called from the fable that geese grew from them], a barnacle that attaches itself to the bottoms of ships, etc. by its long stalk.
goose·ber·ry (gōōs'ber'i, gōōz'bẽr-i), *n.* [*pl.* GOOSEBERRIES (-iz)], [as if < *goose* + *berry;* prob. folk-etym. form for **grose berie;* cf. dial. *grosel, grozel,* gooseberry (< Fr. *groseille*), D. *kruisbezie,* G. *krausbeere,* etc.], 1. a small, sour berry used in making preserves, pies, etc.: it resembles a currant but is larger. 2. the prickly shrub on which it grows.
goose flesh, a roughened condition of the skin in which its papillae are erected, caused by cold, shock, etc.
goose·foot (gōōs'foot'), *n.* [*pl.* GOOSEFOOTS (-foots')], any of a group of plants, including spinach, beets, etc., with large, coarse leaves sometimes shaped like the foot of a goose.
goose·herd (gōōs'hũrd'), *n.* [ME. *gosherde;* see HERD], a person who tends geese.
goose·neck (gōōs'nek'), *n.* any of various mechanical devices shaped like a goose's neck, as an iron joint for pipes, a flexible rod for supporting a desk lamp, etc.
goose pimples (or **skin**), goose flesh.
goose-step (gōōs'step'), *v.i.* to march in goose step: often used figuratively.
goose step, a marching step in which the legs are kept stiff and unbent as they are raised high and lowered: it was used by German infantry as a parade step.
goose·wing (gōōs'wiŋ'), *n.* 1. a studding sail. 2. the lower corner of a foresail or square mainsail when the body of the sail is furled.
goos·y (gōōs'i), *adj.* [GOOSIER (-i-ẽr), GOOSIEST (-i-ist)], 1. like or characteristic of a goose; foolish; stupid. 2. [Slang], *a)* easily upset or disturbed by a sudden, playful prod in the backside; hence, *b)* nervous; jumpy. Also spelled **goosey.**
G.O.P., Grand Old Party (Republican Party).
go·pher (gō'fẽr), *n.* [Fr. *gaufre,* honeycomb (see GOFFER): so called from its habit of burrowing], 1. a burrowing rodent, about the size of a large rat, with wide cheek pouches: also **pocket gopher.** 2. any of a number of striped ground squirrels, related to the chipmunks, found on the prairies of North America. 3. a burrowing land tortoise found in Florida and other southern coastal states. 4. [G-], a native or inhabitant of Minnesota.

GOPHER (9 in. long)

gopher snake, a large, nonpoisonous, burrowing snake of the southern United States.
go·pher·wood (gō'fẽr-wood'), *n.* [Heb. *gōpher*], in the *Bible,* the wood that Noah's ark was made of, believed to be some kind of pine or fir: Gen. 6:14.
go·ral (gō'rəl), *n.* [*pl.* GORALS (-rəlz), GORAL; see PLURAL, II, D, 1], [< native (Himalayan) name], an Asiatic animal like the chamois of Europe, related to the goats and antelopes.
Gor·cha·kov, Prince A·lek·san·dr Mi·khai·lo·vich (ȧ-lyek-sän'dr' mi-khī'lô-vich gôr-chȧ-kôf'), 1798–1883; Russian statesman; chancellor of Russia (1863–1883).
gor·cock (gôr'kok'), *n.* [prob. < *gore* (blood) + *cock,* because of its color], the male red grouse; moor cock.
Gor·di·an knot (gôr'di-ən), 1. in *Greek legend,* a knot tied by King Gordius of Phrygia, which an oracle re-

vealed would be undone only by the future master of Asia: Alexander the Great, failing to untie it, cut the knot with his sword; hence, 2. any perplexing problem. **cut the Gordian knot,** to find a quick, efficient solution for a perplexing problem.

Gor·don (gôr'd'n), [Scot. < surname *Gordon*], a masculine name.

Gordon setter, a large hunting dog of a breed characterized by a black, shaggy coat with tan or brown spots.

gore (gôr, gōr), ***n.*** [ME. *gore,* filth; AS. *gor,* dung, filth; akin to D. *goor,* mud, dirt; IE. base **g(w)her-,* hot, warm, as also in L. *fornax* (cf. FURNACE) & Eng. *warm*], blood shed from a wound; especially, clotted blood.

gore (gôr, gōr), ***v.t.*** [GORED (gôrd, gōrd), GORING], [ME. *goren* (also *gorren*) < or associated with *gore* (AS. *gar*), a spear; cf. GORE (triangle of land)], to pierce with or as with a horn or tusk.

gore (gôr, gōr), ***n.*** [ME. *gore;* AS. *gara,* corner < base of *gar,* a spear (cf. GAR, fish); akin to MD. *gheere,* G. *gehre,* gusset; IE. **ghaisos,* a piercing, a javelin, seen also in G. *geissel,* a whip], 1. [Dial.], a triangular piece of land. 2. a tapering piece of cloth made or inserted in a garment, sail, etc. to give it further width. ***v.t.*** [GORED (gôrd, gōrd), GORING], to make or insert a gore or gores in.

GORE (of skirt)

Gor·gas, William Crawford (gôr'gəs), 1854–1920; American army surgeon; chief sanitary officer, Panama Canal Commission.

gorge (gôrj), ***n.*** [ME.; OFr., throat, gullet; LL. **gorga,* throat, narrow pass; L. *gurges,* whirlpool, stream], 1. the throat; gullet. 2. a gluttonous appetite or meal. 3. the act of eating greedily. 4. what has been swallowed. 5. a feeling of resentment, disgust, anger, etc. 6. the entrance from the rear into a bastion or projecting section of a fortification. 7. a deep, narrow pass between steep heights. 8. a mass that blocks up a passage: as, an ice *gorge.* ***v.i.*** [GORGED (gôrjd), GORGING], to eat gluttonously. ***v.t.*** 1. to fill the gorge of; glut. 2. to swallow greedily. **make one's gorge rise,** to cause one to feel nauseated, disgusted, angry, etc.

gor·geous (gôr'jəs), ***adj.*** [OFr. *gorgias,* beautiful, glorious, also ruff for the neck < *gorge;* see GORGE], 1. brilliantly colored; magnificent; resplendent. 2. [Slang], beautiful; wonderful; delightful. —***SYN.*** see **splendid.**

gor·ger·in (gôr'jẽr-in), ***n.*** [Fr. < *gorgère,* ruff for the throat < *gorge;* see GORGE], in *architecture,* the part of a column just below the top molding or between the shaft and the capital.

gor·get (gôr'jit), ***n.*** [OFr. *gorgete* < *gorge;* see GORGE], 1. a piece of armor to protect the throat: see **armor,** illus.; hence, 2. a collar. 3. an article of clothing covering the neck and breast, formerly worn by women. 4. a patch of color on the throat of a bird.

Gor·gon (gôr'gən), ***n.*** [L. *Gorgo, Gorgonis;* Gr. *Gorgō, Gorgonos* < *gorgos,* terrible, fierce], 1. in *Greek mythology,* any of three sisters with snakes for hair, so horrible that the beholder was turned to stone: Medusa, one of the sisters, was killed by Perseus. 2. [g-], any ugly, terrifying, or repulsive woman.

Gor·go·ni·an (gôr-gō'ni-ən), ***adj.*** of or like a Gorgon.

Gor·gon·zo·la (gôr'gən-zō'lə), ***n.*** [< *Gorgonzola,* town in Italy near Milan], a white Italian pressed cheese like Roquefort in appearance and flavor.

gor·hen (gôr'hen'), ***n.*** [prob. < *gore* (blood) + *hen,* with reference to the color], the female red grouse; moor hen.

go·ril·la (gə-ril'ə), ***n.*** [recorded by Hanno, Carthaginian navigator, as the native name in use in W. Africa in the 5th c. B.C. for a wild creature found there], 1. the largest and most powerful of the manlike apes, native to the jungles of equatorial Africa: the adult male is over five feet high and weighs about 500 pounds. 2. [Slang], *a)* a person regarded as like a gorilla in appearance, strength, etc. *b)* a gangster; thug.

GORILLA (5 ft. high)

gor·i·ly (gôr'ə-li, gō'rə-li), ***adv.*** in a gory manner.

gor·i·ness (gôr'i-nis, gō-ri-nis), ***n.*** the quality or condition of being gory.

Go·ri·zia (gô-rē'tsyä), ***n.*** a city in northeastern Italy, near Yugoslavia: pop., 52,000 (1947).

Gor·ki, Gor·ky (gôr'ki), ***n.*** 1. a region of the R.S.F.S.R., in central European Russia: pop., 3,876,000. 2. its capital, on the Volga: pop., 644,000: formerly called *Nizhni Novgorod.*

Gor·ki, Max·im (mák-sēm' gôr'ki), (pseudonym of *Aleksei Maksimovich Pyeshkov*), 1868–1936; Russian novelist, playwright, etc.: also spelled **Gorky.**

Gör·litz (gör'lits), ***n.*** a city in Silesia, Germany: pop., 94,000.

gor·mand (gôr'mənd), ***n.*** a gourmand.

gor·mand·ize (gôr'mən-dīz'), ***n.*** [< Fr. *gourmandise* < *gourmand;* see GOURMAND], [Now Rare], taste or indulgence in good eating. ***v.i.*** [GORMANDIZED (-dīzd'), GORMANDIZING], [< the *n.*], to eat like a glutton; gorge.

Gor·no-Ba·dakh·shan Autonomous Area (gôr'nō-bá-dákh-shän'), an autonomous area of the Tadzhik S.S.R., in southwest Asiatic Russia: area, 25,784 sq. mi.; pop., 41,800; capital, Khorog.

gorse (gôrs), ***n.*** [ME. & AS. *gorst;* remotely akin to G. *gerste,* barley; IE. base **ghers-,* to stiffen, bristle, as also in L. *horrere,* to stand on end (cf. HORROR)], a low, spiny shrub with yellow flowers; furze.

gors·y (gôr'si), ***adj.*** of, full of, or covered with gorse.

gor·y (gôr'i, gō'ri), ***adj.*** [GORIER (-i-ẽr, -ri-ẽr), GORIEST (-i-ist, -ri-ist)], 1. full of or covered with gore; bloody. 2. characterized by much bloodshed or slaughter: as, a *gory* fight. 3. like gore.

gosh (gosh), ***interj.*** an exclamation of surprise, etc.: a euphemism for *God.*

gos·hawk (gos'hôk', gôs'hôk'), ***n.*** [AS. *goshafoc;* see GOOSE & HAWK], a large, swift, powerful hawk with short wings.

Go·shen (gō'shən), ***n.*** [Heb. *gōshen*], 1. in the *Bible,* the fertile land assigned to the Israelites in Egypt: Gen. 45:10; hence, 2. a land of plenty.

gos·ling (goz'liŋ), ***n.*** [ME. *goslynge* (see GOOSE & -LING), replacing *geslynge* < ON. *gæslingr,* of the same ult. formation], a young goose: sometimes used figuratively.

gos·pel (gos'p'l), ***n.*** [ME. *godspell, gospel* (with assimilated *-d-*); AS. *gōdspel,* orig., good spell, good story, good news; intended as transl. of Gr. *euangelion,* good tidings, but later by shortening of *o* it became *gŏdspel* as if < *god,* God + *spel,* story, history], 1. the teachings of Jesus and the Apostles. 2. the history of the life and teachings of Jesus. 3. [G-], any of the first four books of the New Testament, ascribed to Matthew, Mark, Luke, and John. 4. [G-], an excerpt from any of these books read in a religious service. 5. a belief or body of beliefs proclaimed or accepted as absolutely true. 6. any doctrine or rule of conduct widely maintained.

gos·pel·er, gos·pel·ler (gos'p'l-ẽr), ***n.*** [ME. *gospellere;* AS. *godspellere*], 1. a person who reads the Gospel in church services. 2. a person who claims for himself and his sect the sole possession of gospel truth: formerly applied derisively to Puritans, Nonconformists, etc.

‡Gos·plan (gôs-plän'), ***n.*** [< Russ. Gos*oodarstvennoye* plan*novaya komissiya,* State Planning Commission], the state planning agency of the Soviet Union: see **Five-Year Plan.**

‡gos·po·din (gôs'pô-dēn'), ***n.*** [Russ., lit., lord], a Russian title of respect, equivalent to *Mr.*

gos·sa·mer (gos'ə-mẽr), ***n.*** [ME. *gosesomer,* lit., goose summer: with allusion to the warm period in fall (*St. Martin's summer*) when goose is in season and gossamer is chiefly noticed; cf. G. *mädchensommer,* gossamer, lit., girls' summer], 1. a filmy cobweb floating in the air or spread on bushes or grass. 2. a very thin, soft, filmy cloth. 3. *a)* a lightweight waterproof cloth. *b)* a coat made of this cloth. 4. anything like gossamer. ***adj.*** light, thin, and filmy.

gos·sa·mer·y (gos'ə-mẽr-i), ***adj.*** like gossamer; filmy.

Gosse, Sir **Edmund William** (gôs, gos), 1849–1928; English poet and critic.

gos·sip (gos'əp), ***n.*** [ME. *gossyp* (with assimilated *-d-* as in *gospel*); also *godsip;* Late AS. *godsibbe,* baptismal sponsor, godparent; see GOD & SIB], 1. [Obs. or Dial.], *a)* a godparent. *b)* a close friend. 2. a person who chatters or repeats idle talk and rumors about others. 3. *a)* such talk or rumors. *b)* chatter. ***v.i.*** to be a gossip; indulge in idle talk or rumors about others.

gos·sip·ry (gos'əp-ri), ***n.*** [Rare], 1. gossip. 2. gossips as a group.

gos·sip·y (gos'ə-pi), ***adj.*** 1. inclined to gossip. 2. full of gossip.

gos·soon (go-sōōn'), ***n.*** [altered < Fr. *garçon,* boy, attendant], [Irish], 1. a boy. 2. a servant boy.

got (got), [ME. *gat,* p.t., *geten, goten,* pp.], past tense and alternative past participle of **get.**

Go·ta·ma (gō'tə-mə), ***n.*** Gautama: see **Buddha.**

Gö·te·borg (yö'tə-bôr'y'; Eng. jä'tə-bôrg'), ***n.*** a seaport in southwestern Sweden: pop., 337,000 (1948): also **Gothenburg.**

Goth (goth, gôth), ***n.*** [< LL. *Gothi,* pl. (AS. *Gotan*); Gr. *Gothoi,* pl. < base of Goth. **Gutans,* pl., or *Gut* (*thiuda*), Gothic (people)], 1. any member of a Germanic people that invaded and conquered most of the Roman Empire in the 3d, 4th, and 5th centuries A.D.: see also **Ostrogoth, Visigoth.** 2. an uncouth, uncivilized person; barbarian.

Goth., goth., Gothic.

Go·tha (gō′tä), *n.* a city in Thuringia, Germany: pop., 48,000.

Goth·am (goth′əm, gō′thəm), *n.* 1. (Brit. got′əm), an English village near Nottingham whose inhabitants, the "wise men of Gotham," were, according to legend, very foolish. 2. New York City.

Goth·am·ite (goth′əm-īt′, gō′thəm-īt′), *n.* an inhabitant of Gotham, especially of New York City.

Goth·en·burg (got′ən-bũrg′, goth′ən-bũrg′), *n.* Göteborg.

Goth·ic (goth′ik), *adj.* [LL. *Gothicus;* see GOTH], 1. of the Goths or their language. 2. designating or of a style of architecture developed in western Europe between the 12th and 16th centuries and characterized by the use of ribbed vaulting, flying buttresses, pointed arches, steep roofs, etc.: see TYPES OF ARCHITECTURE, p. 77. 3. [sometimes g-], *a)* medieval. *b)* not classical. *c)* barbarous; uncivilized. 4. in *literature,* using medieval locale, properties, local color, etc., especially to produce an effect of horror and mystery. *n.* 1. the East Germanic language of the Goths: it is known chiefly from the Bible translations of Bishop Ulfilas (4th c. A.D.) and the vocabulary made by van Busbecq in the Crimea (16th c. A.D.). 2. Gothic architecture. 3. in *printing, a)* [often g-], a type characterized by straight lines of even width, and lacking serifs or other extra strokes. This line is in Gothic. *b)* in England, black letter. Abbreviated **Goth., goth.**

Goth·i·cal·ly (goth′i-k′l-i, goth′ik-li), *adv.* in a Gothic manner; like Gothic.

Gothic arch, a pointed arch.

Goth·i·cism (goth′ə-siz′m), *n.* 1. barbarism; rudeness. 2. conformity to Gothic style. 3. a Gothic idiom.

Goth·i·cize (goth′ə-sīz′), *v.t.* [GOTHICIZED (-sīzd′), GOTHICIZING], to make Gothic.

Got·land (got′lənd; Sw. gôt′länd), *n.* a Swedish island, and county, in the Baltic: area, 1,224 sq. mi.; pop., 59,054 (1950); capital, Visby.

got·ten (got′′n), alternative past participle of **get.**

‡**Göt·ter·däm·mer·ung** (göt′ẽr-dem′ẽr-ooŋ), *n.* [G., twilight of the gods], 1. in *Germanic mythology,* the end of the world; time when the gods war with their enemies until all are destroyed. 2. an opera by Richard Wagner on this theme: see **Ring of the Nibelung.**

Göt·ting·en (göt′iŋ-ən), *n.* a city in Hanover, Germany: pop., 47,000.

Gott·wald, Klem·ent (kle′ment gôt′väld), 1896–1953; Czechoslovakian statesman and Communist leader; prime minister of Czechoslovakia (1946–1953).

‡**gouache** (gwäsh), *n.* [Fr.; It. *guazzo,* water color, spray, liquid splashed about, pool; L. *aquatio,* watering, water, watering place < *aqua,* water], 1. a way of painting with opaque colors ground in water and mixed with a preparation of gum. 2. a pigment of this sort. 3. a painting made with such pigments.

Gou·da (gou′də), *n.* [< *Gouda,* Netherlands, city where orig. produced], a mild cheese made from curds: also **Gouda cheese.**

Gou·dy, Frederick William (gou′di), 1865–1947; American designer of printing types.

gouge (gouj), *n.* [Fr.; LL. *gubia, gulbia;* prob. < Celt.; cf. OIr. *gulban,* thorn, goad], 1. a chisel with a curved, hollowed blade, for cutting grooves or holes in wood. 2. [Colloq.], *a)* the act of making a groove or hole with or as with a gouge. *b)* the groove or hole made. 3. [Colloq.], *a)* a trick to rob; fraud; swindle. *b)* a swindler; impostor. *v.t.* [GOUGED (goujd), GOUGING], 1. to make grooves or holes in with or as with a gouge. 2. to scoop out; dig or force out: as, his eye was *gouged* out. 3. [Colloq.], to defraud; swindle.

GOUGE

gou·lash (gōō′läsh, gōō′lash), *n.* [G. *gulasch* < Hung. *gulyás,* lit., a shepherd, hence shepherds' food], a stew made of beef or veal and vegetables seasoned with paprika: also **Hungarian goulash.**

Gould, Jay (jā gōōld), 1836–1892; American financier.

Gou·nod, Charles Fran·çois (shärl frän′swà′ gōō′nō′; Eng. gōō′nō), 1818–1893; French composer.

gourd (gôrd, gōrd, goord), *n.* [ME.; OFr. *gouorde, gougorde* < L. *cucurbita*], 1. any trailing or climbing plant belonging to a family that includes the squash, melon, pumpkin, etc. 2. *a)* the bulb-shaped fruit (*bottle gourd*) of one species of this family. *b)* any of the ornamental, inedible fruits of related plants. 3. any plant producing such a fruit. 4. the dried, hollowed-out shell of such a fruit, used as a drinking cup, dipper, etc.

gourde (gōōrd), *n.* [Fr., fem. of *gourd,* numb, heavy, dull < L. *gurdus,* dull, heavy, stupid], the silver monetary unit of Haiti, having an average value of about 20 cents: originally it was equal to 5 francs.

gour·mand (goor′mənd; Fr. gōōr′män′), *n.* [Fr.; cf. GOURMET], 1. originally, a glutton. 2. a person who likes and is a judge of fine foods; epicure: in this sense, usually *gourmet.* Also **gormand.** —*SYN.* see **epicure.**

gour·met (goor′mā; Fr. gōōr′me′), *n.* [Fr.; OFr. *gourmet, groumet,* servant, wine taster, vintner's assistant; see GROOM], a person who likes and is a judge of fine foods and drinks; epicure. —*SYN.* see **epicure.**

Gour·mont, Re·my de (rə-mē′ də gōōr′mōn′), 1858–1915; French novelist, essayist, playwright, and critic.

gout (gout), *n.* [ME. *goute;* OFr. *goute, goutte,* gout, lit., a drop < L. *gutta,* a drop: so named from being attributed to a defluxion of humors], 1. a disease resulting from a disturbance of the metabolism, characterized by an excess of uric acid in the blood and deposits of uric acid salts in the tissues around the joints, especially of the feet and hands: it causes swelling and severe pain, especially in the big toe. 2. a drop; clot.

‡**goût** (gōō), *n.* [Fr. < L. *gustus*], taste.

gout·i·ly (gout′′l-i), *adv.* in a gouty manner.

gout·i·ness (gout′i-nis), *n.* the quality or condition of being gouty.

gout·y (gout′i), *adj.* [GOUTIER (-i-ẽr), GOUTIEST (-i-ist)], 1. having, or tending to have, gout. 2. of or like gout. 3. resulting from or causing gout. 4. swollen with gout.

gov., Gov., 1. government. 2. governor.

gov·ern (guv′ẽrn), *v.t.* [ME. *governen;* OFr. *gouverner;* L. *gubernare,* to steer or pilot (a ship), direct, guide; Gr. *kybernan,* to steer, govern], 1. to exercise authority over; direct; control; rule; manage. 2. to influence the action or conduct of; guide; sway: as, how is public opinion *governed?* 3. to restrain; hold in check; curb: as, you must *govern* your temper. 4. to regulate the speed (of an automobile, etc.) by means of a governor. 5. to determine; be a rule or law for: as, the scientific principles *governing* a phenomenon. 6. in *grammar, a)* to require (a word) to be in a particular case or mood. *b)* to require (a particular case or mood). In English grammar, the term applies to the relationship between a preposition and a following pronoun. *v.i.* to exercise the function of governing; rule.

SYN.—**govern** implies the exercise of authority in controlling the actions of the members of a body politic and directing the affairs of state, and generally connotes as its purpose the maintenance of public order and the promotion of the common welfare; **rule** now usually signifies the exercise of arbitrary or autocratic power; **administer** implies the orderly management of governmental affairs by executive officials.

gov·ern·a·ble (guv′ẽrn-ə-b′l), *adj.* that can be governed.

gov·ern·ance (guv′ẽr-nəns), *n.* [ME.; OFr. *gouvernance;* ML. *gubernantia* < ppr. of L. *gubernare;* see GOVERN], the act, manner, function, or power of government.

gov·ern·ess (guv′ẽr-nis), *n.* 1. a woman employed in a private home to train and teach a child or children. 2. [Obs.], a woman governor.

gov·ern·ment (guv′ẽr-mənt, guv′ẽrn-mənt), *n.* [OFr. *gouvernement;* see GOVERN & -MENT], 1. *a)* the exercise of authority over an organization, institution, state, district, etc.; direction; control; rule; management. *b)* the right, function, or power of governing. 2. *a)* a system of ruling, controlling, etc. *b)* an established system of political administration by which a state, district, etc. is governed. 3. all the people who administer or control the affairs of a state, institution, etc.; administration. 4. a governed territory. 5. in *grammar,* the influence of one word over the case or mood of another. Abbreviated **govt., gov.**

gov·ern·men·tal (guv′ẽr-men′t′l, guv′ẽrn-men′t′l), *adj.* of or connected with government or a government.

government issue, see **GI, G.I.**

gov·er·nor (guv′ẽr-nẽr; *now often* guv′ə-nẽr), *n.* [ME. *governour;* OFr. *governeor;* L. *gubernator,* a pilot, steersman, governor < *gubernare*], 1. a person who governs; especially, *a)* a person appointed to govern a dependency, province, town, fort, etc. *b)* the elected head of any State of the United States. *c)* a person who directs, manages, or helps to direct or manage an organization or institution. 2. a mechanical device for automatically controlling the speed of an engine or motor by regulating the intake of fuel, steam, etc. Abbreviated **gov.** 3. [Chiefly British Colloq.], a person having authority; especially, one's father: often used as a term of address.

gov·er·nor-gen·er·al (guv′ẽr-nẽr-jen′ẽr-əl, guv′ẽr-nẽr-jen′rəl), *n.* [*pl.* GOVERNORS-GENERAL (-nẽrz-)], [Chiefly British], governor general.

governor general, [*pl.* GOVERNORS GENERAL, GOVERNOR GENERALS], a governor who has subordinate or deputy governors under him, as in the British dominions: abbreviated **Gov. Gen.** (as a title).

gov·er·nor·ship (guv′ẽr-nẽr-ship′; *now often* guv′ə-nẽr-ship′), *n.* [*governor* + *-ship*], the position, function, or term of office of a governor.

Governors Island, an island in New York Bay at the entrance to the East River: site of Fort Jay.

govt., Govt., government.

gow·an (gou′ən), *n.* [< obs. *gollan, golland,* yellow flow-

er; prob. related to *gold*], [Scot.], the English daisy.
Gow·er, John (gō'ẽr, gou'ẽr), 1325?–1408; English poet.
gowk (gouk, gōk), *n.* [ME. *goke, gowk;* ON. *gaukr;* see GAWKY], [Scot.], 1. a cuckoo. 2. a simpleton.
gown (goun), *n.* [ME. *goune;* OFr. *goune, gon;* ML. *gunna*, loose robe], 1. a long, loose outer garment; specifically, *a*) a woman's dress. *b*) a dressing gown. *c*) a nightgown. *d*) a long, flowing robe worn by certain officials, clergymen, scholars, etc., and by students receiving degrees from a university. 2. the members of a college or university, collectively. *v.t.* to dress in a gown, as in an academic, ecclesiastic, or official robe.
gowns·man (gounz'mən), *n.* [*pl.* GOWNSMEN (-mən)], a person wearing a gown as an indication of his profession or office, as a lawyer, judge, clergyman, etc.
‡**goy** (goi), *n.* [Yid.; Heb. *goi*, tribe, nation], [*pl.* GOYIM (-im)], a non-Jew; gentile.
Go·ya, Fran·cis·co Jo·sé de (frän-thēs'kô hô-se' de gô'yä; Eng. *often* goi'ə), 1746–1828; Spanish painter.
G.P., g.p., 1. general paresis. 2. general practitioner.
g.p., in *printing*, great primer.
G.P.O., 1. General Post Office. 2. Government Printing Office: also **GPO** (no period).
G.P.U., Gay-Pay-Oo.
Gr., 1. Grecian. 2. Greece. 3. Greek.
gr., 1. grade. 2. grain; grains. 3. gram; grams. 4. grammar. 5. great. 6. gross. 7. group.
Graaf·i·an follicle (or **vesicle**), (grä'fi-ən), [after Regnier de *Graaf*, 17th-c. D. physician & anatomist], one of the small, round sacs in the ovary of a mammal, each of which contains an ovum.
grab (grab), *v.t.* [GRABBED (grabd), GRABBING], [prob. < MD., MLG. *grabben*], 1. to seize or snatch suddenly; take roughly and quickly. 2. to get possession of by unscrupulous methods. *n.* 1. a grabbing. 2. something grabbed. 3. any of various mechanical devices for clutching something to be hoisted. —*SYN.* see **take**.
grab (grab), *n.* [Anglo-Ind. < Ar. *ghurāb*, lit., raven], an Oriental two-masted ship with triangular sails.
grab bag, a bag or box containing various articles that are sold unseen, the buyer grabbing or drawing any one and paying a fixed price: also used figuratively.
grab·ble (grab''l), *v.i.* [GRABBLED (-'ld), GRABBLING], [D. *grabbelen*, freq. of *grabben*, to grab], 1. to feel about with the hands; grope. 2. to sprawl. *v.t.* to seize.
Grac·chus (grak'əs), *n.* 1. (*Gaius Sempronius Gracchus*), Roman statesman and reformer; 153–121 B.C. 2. (*Tiberius Sempronius Gracchus*), brother of *Gaius;* 163–133 B.C.; Roman statesman and reformer.
Grace (grās), [see next entry], a feminine name.
grace (grās), *n.* [ME.; OFr. *grace* (Fr. *grâce*); L. *gratia*, pleasing quality, favor, good will, thanks, etc. < *gratus*, pleasing; see GRATEFUL, GRATITUDE], 1. beauty or charm of form, composition, movement, or expression. 2. an attractive quality, feature, manner, etc. 3. a sense of what is right and proper; decency. 4. *a*) disposition to grant something freely; favor; good will. *b*) *pl.* the condition or fact of being favored. *c*) a favor or privilege. 5. mercy; clemency. 6. a period of time granted beyond the date set for the performance of an act or the payment of an obligation; temporary exemption. 7. favor shown by granting such a delay. 8. a short prayer in which blessing is asked, or thanks are given, for a meal. 9. [G-], a title of respect or reverence used in speaking to or of an archbishop, duke, or duchess, preceded by *His, Her*, or *Your*. 10. in *music*, one or more grace notes. 11. in *theology*, *a*) the unmerited love and favor of God toward man. *b*) divine influence acting in man to make him pure and morally strong. *c*) the condition of a person thus influenced. *v.t.* [GRACED (grāst), GRACING], 1. to honor; dignify. 2. to give or add grace or graces to; decorate; adorn. 3. in *music*, to add a grace note or notes to.
fall from grace, to do wrong; sin.
have the grace, to be so aware of what is proper as (*to* do something).
in the bad graces of, in disfavor with.
in the good graces of, in favor with.
with bad grace, sullenly or reluctantly.
with good grace, graciously or willingly.
grace cup, 1. a cup from which a toast is drunk at the end of a meal or banquet. 2. the toast.
grace·ful (grās'fəl), *adj.* having grace, or beauty of form, composition, movement, or expression.
grace·less (grās'lis), *adj.* 1. lacking any sense of what is right; reprobate. 2. without grace; clumsy or inelegant.
grace note, in *music*, a note not necessary to the melody, added only for ornamentation: it is usually printed as a small note just before the note that it embellishes, from which its time value is subtracted.
Grac·es (grās'iz), *n.pl.* [transl. of L. *Gratiae* (see GRACE, *n.*), transl. of Gr. *Charites*, pl. of *Charis*, mythological figure personifying grace and beauty], in *Greek mythology*, the three sister goddesses who had control over pleasure, charm, elegance, and beauty in human life and in nature; Aglaia (Brilliance), Euphrosyne (Joy), and Thalia (Bloom).
‡**gra·ci·as** (grä'thē-äs'), *interj.* [Sp.], thanks; thank you.
grac·ile (gras''l), *adj.* [L. *gracilis*, scanty], 1. slender; slim. 2. [by assoc. with *grace*], gracefully slender.
gra·ci·o·so (grā'shi-ō'sō; Sp. grä-thyô'sô), *n.* 1. a clown in Spanish comedies; buffoon. 2. [Archaic], a court favorite.
gra·cious (grā'shəs), *adj.* [ME.; OFr. *gracious;* L. *gratiosus*, in favor, popular, kind < *gratia;* see GRACE, *n.*], 1. having or showing kindness, courtesy, charm, etc. 2. merciful; compassionate. 3. indulgent or polite to supposed inferiors. 4. [Archaic], having pleasing qualities; attractive. *interj.* an expression of surprise.
grack·le (grak''l), *n.* [L. *graculus*, jackdaw: so called from its note], any of various blackbirds somewhat smaller than a crow; especially, the American purple grackle.
grad (grad), *n.* [Colloq.], a graduate.
grad., 1. graduate. 2. graduated.
gra·date (grā'dāt), *v.t.* & *v.i.* [GRADATED (-id), GRADATING], [< L. *gradatus;* see GRADATION], to pass or cause to pass by imperceptible degrees from one to another; shade into one another, as colors.
gra·dat·ed (grā'dāt-id), *adj.* [pp. of *gradate*], in *linguistics*, showing the effects of gradation.
gra·da·tion (grā-dā'shən), *n.* [Fr.; L. *gradatio* < *gradatus*, having steps or grades < *gradus;* see GRADE], 1. the act or process of forming or arranging in grades, stages, or steps. 2. a gradual change by steps or stages from one condition, quality, etc. to another. 3. a gradual shading of one tint, tone, or color into another. 4. a step, stage, or degree in a graded series; transitional stage: as, there are many *gradations* between good and bad. 5. in *geology*, the process of wearing away and building up of land by erosion and deposition. 6. in *linguistics*, the systematic variation seen in the vowels of related bases as conditioned by the presence or absence of stress on the base syllable: as, the vowel variation in *sing, sang, sung* is due to *gradation* in Indo-European.
gra·da·tion·al (grā-dā'shən-'l), *adj.* of or characterized by gradation.
grade (grād), *n.* [Fr.; L. *gradus*, a step, degree, rank < *gradi*, to step, walk], 1. any of the stages in an orderly, systematic progression; step; degree. 2. *a*) a degree in a scale classifying according to quality, rank, worth, etc.: as, these eggs are *grade* A. *b*) a group of people of the same rank, merit, worth, etc. 3. the degree of rise or descent of a sloping surface, as of a highway, railroad, etc. 4. a sloping part. 5. *a*) one of the divisions by years in a school curriculum: most systems include twelve grades after the kindergarten. *b*) the group of pupils in any of these divisions. 6. a mark or rating on an examination, work in a school course, etc. 7. in *animal husbandry*, an animal with one parent of pure breed. 8. in *linguistics*, any of the various forms in which the vowel may appear in the base of a word as a result of gradation. Abbreviated **gr.** *v.t.* [GRADED (-id), GRADING], 1. to arrange or classify by distinct steps or stages; rate according to quality, rank, worth, etc.; sort. 2. to give a grade (sense 6) to. 3. to gradate. 4. to make (ground) level or slope (ground) evenly for a roadway, etc. 5. in *animal husbandry*, to improve by crossing with a better breed (often with *up*). *v.i.* 1. to assume an indicated rank or position in a series; be of a certain grade. 2. to change gradually; go through a series of stages.
at grade, on the same level or degree of rise.
make the grade, 1. to get to the top of a steep incline. 2. to overcome obstacles and reach a desired goal.
the grades, elementary school.
up to grade, with standard quality.
-grade (grād), [< L. *gradi*, to walk], a combining form meaning (a specified manner of) *walking* or *moving*, as in *plantigrade*.
grade crossing, the place where a railroad intersects another railroad or a roadway on the same level.
grad·er (grād'ẽr), *n.* 1. a person or thing that grades. 2. a pupil in a specified grade at school: as, a fifth *grader*.
grade school, elementary school; grammar school.
gra·di·ent (grā'di-ənt, grā'dyənt), *adj.* [L. *gradiens, gradientis*, ppr. of *gradi*, to step, walk], 1. in *zoology*, going forward by taking steps; walking. 2. ascending or descending with a uniform slope. *n.* 1. a slope, as of a road or railroad. 2. the degree of slope. 3. in *physics*, *a*) the rate of change of temperature, pressure, etc. *b*) a diagram or curve representing this.
gra·din (grā'din; Fr. grå'dan'), *n.* [Fr.; It. *gradino*, dim. of *grado* < L. *gradus;* see GRADE], 1. one of a series of steps or seats arranged in tiers. 2. a shelf behind an altar, for candlesticks, etc.
gra·dine (grə-dēn'), *n.* a gradin.

grad·u·al (graj′o͞o-əl), *adj.* [ML. *gradualis* < L. *gradus;* see GRADE], taking place by almost imperceptible steps or degrees; not effected sharply or suddenly; developing or occurring little by little. *n.* [ML. *graduale, gradalis,* book containing hymns and prayers orig. sung on steps of a pulpit < L. *gradus*], in *ecclesiastical usage,* 1. a response sung after the Epistle. 2. a book containing choral responses of the Mass.

grad·u·ate (graj′o͞o-it; *for v.t. & v.i. and occas. for n. & adj.* graj′o͞o-āt′), *n.* [< ML. *graduatus,* pp. of *graduare,* to honor with a degree, graduate < L. *gradus;* see GRADE], 1. a person who has completed a course of study at a school or college and has received a degree or diploma attesting to the fact. 2. a flask, tube, or other container marked with a progressive series of degrees (lines or numbers or both) for measuring liquids or solids: abbreviated **grad.** *v.t.* [GRADUATED (-id), GRADUATING], 1. to give a degree or diploma to in recognition of the completion of a course of study at a school or college. 2. to mark (a flask, tube, gauge, etc.) with degrees for measuring. 3. to arrange or classify into grades according to amount, size, quality, etc.; put into gradations. *v.i.* 1. to receive a degree or diploma in recognition of the completion of a course of study at a school or college. 2. to change by degrees. *adj.* 1. having been graduated from a school, college, etc.; being a graduate. 2. of or for graduates: as, *graduate* courses.

graduate school, a division of a university in which instruction is offered in various fields leading to degrees above the bachelor's.

graduate student, a student working toward an advanced degree at a graduate school.

grad·u·a·tion (graj′o͞o-ā′shən), *n.* [ML. *graduatio* < pp. of *graduare;* see GRADUATE], 1. a graduating or being graduated from a school or college. 2. the ceremony connected with this; graduation exercises; commencement. 3. a marking of a flask, tube, gauge, etc. with a series of degrees for measuring. 4. one or all of the degrees marked; a degree or scale. 5. an arrangement or classification into grades according to amount, size, quality, etc.

grad·u·a·tor (graj′o͞o-ā′tẽr), *n.* 1. an instrument for marking off lines or surfaces into small, regular divisions. 2. a user of such an instrument.

gra·dus (grā′dəs), *n.* [< L. *gradus* (*ad Parnassum*), lit., step (to Parnassus), name for a book on prosody or poetry], 1. a dictionary of prosody for help in writing poetry, especially in Greek or Latin. 2. a collection of piano studies, études, etc. arranged in a progressive order of difficulty.

Grae·ae (grē′ē), *n.pl.* [L.; Gr. *Graiai,* pl. of *graia,* old woman < *grais,* old; akin to *gerōn,* old man], in *Greek mythology,* the three daughters of Phorcus, a sea god: they acted as guards for the Gorgons and had but one eye and one tooth to share among them: also **Graiae.**

Grae·cism (grē′siz'm), *n.* Grecism.

Grae·cize (grē′sīz), *v.t. & v.i.* to Grecize.

Grae·co- (grē′kō), Greco-.

‡**Graf** (gräf), *n.* [*pl.* GRAFEN (-′n)], [G.], a German, Austrian, or Swedish title of nobility corresponding to *earl* or *count.*

graf·fi·to (grə-fē′tō), *n.* [*pl.* GRAFFITI (-ti)], [It., a scribbling < *graffio,* a scratch], an inscription or drawing scratched on pillars, buildings, etc., as in ancient Rome.

graft (graft, gräft), *n.* [with unhistoric *-t* < ME. & OFr. *graffe,* a pencil; L. *graphium;* Gr. *grapheion,* stylus; see GRAPH: so called from resemblance of the scion to a pointed pencil], 1. a shoot or bud of one plant or tree inserted or to be inserted into the stem or trunk of another, where it continues to grow, becoming a permanent part. 2. the act or process of inserting such a bud or shoot. 3. the place on a plant or tree where such a bud or shoot has been inserted. 4. a tree or plant with such a bud or shoot inserted in it. 5. *a*) the act of taking advantage of one's position to gain money, property, etc. dishonestly, as in politics. *b*) anything acquired by such illegal methods, as an illicit profit from government business. 6. in *surgery,* a piece of skin, bone, or other living tissue transplanted or to be transplanted from one body, or place on a body, to another, where it grows and becomes a permanent part. *v.t.* 1. to insert (a graft). 2. to produce (a fruit, flower, etc.) by means of a graft. 3. to obtain (money, etc.) by graft. 4. in *surgery,* to transplant (a graft). *v.i.* 1. to be grafted. 2. to make a graft on a plant. 3. to obtain money or property by graft.

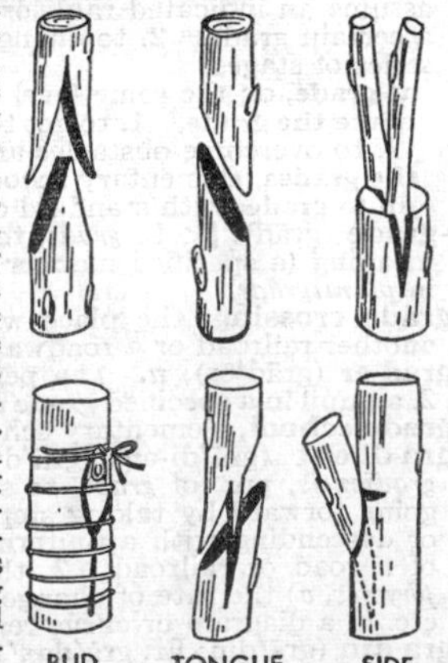

TYPES OF GRAFT

graft·age (graf′tij, gräf′tij), *n.* [see -AGE], 1. the act or science of grafting. 2. the state of being grafted.

gra·ham (grā′əm), *adj.* [< Sylvester *Graham* (1794–1851), Am. physician], designating or made of unsifted, whole-wheat flour: as, *graham* crackers.

Gra·iae (grā′ē, grī′ē), *n.pl.* Graeae.

Grail (grāl), *n.* [OFr. *graal, greal;* ML. *gradalis,* flat dish, cup; ? altered after *cratella,* dim. of L. *crater,* a bowl], in *medieval legend,* the Holy Grail, the cup or platter used by Jesus at the Last Supper, and by Joseph of Arimathea to collect drops of blood from Jesus' body at the Crucifixion: the quest of the Grail, which disappeared because its keepers were morally impure, is the subject of Malory's *Morte d'Arthur,* one of Tennyson's *Idylls of the King,* Wagner's *Parsifal,* etc.

grain (grān), *n.* [ME. *greyne* < OFr. *grein, grain,* a seed, grain (< L. *granum,* a seed, kernel) and *grainne, graine,* seed or grain collectively (< LL. *grana,* fem., orig. pl. of L. *granum*); IE. base **ger-,* **ĝerē-,* to become ripe, seen also in *corn, kernel,* etc.)], 1. a small, hard seed or seedlike fruit, especially that of any cereal plant, as wheat, rice, corn, rye, etc. 2. *a*) cereal seeds in general. *b*) the seeds of a specific cereal. *c*) any plant or plants producing cereal seeds. In Great Britain, commonly called *corn.* 3. a tiny, solid particle, as of salt or sand. 4. a tiny bit; slightest amount: as, a *grain* of sense. 5. [orig. from the weight of a grain of wheat], the smallest unit in the system of weights used in the United States and Great Britain, equal to 0.0648 gram: one pound avoirdupois equals 7,000 grains; one pound troy equals 5,760 grains: abbreviated **gr., G., g.** (*sing. & pl.*). 6. *a*) the arrangement of fibers, layers, or particles of wood, leather, stone, etc. *b*) the markings or texture due to a particular arrangement. *c*) paint or other surface finish imitating such markings or texture. 7. *a*) that side of a piece of leather from which the hair has been removed. *b*) the markings on that side. 8. disposition; nature. 9. [Obs.], *a*) kermes or cochineal. *b*) a red dye made from either. *c*) any fast dye. *v.t.* 1. to form into grains; crystallize. 2. to paint or otherwise finish (a surface) in imitation of the grain of wood, marble, etc. 3. *a*) to remove the hair from (hides). *b*) to put a finish on the grain surface of (leather). *v.i.* to form grains.

against the (or **one's**) **grain,** contrary to one's feelings, nature, wishes, etc.; irritating or displeasing.

grain alcohol, ethyl alcohol, especially when made from grain.

grain elevator, a tall building for storing grain.

grain·field (grān′fēld′), *n.* a field where grain is grown.

Grain·ger, Percy Al·dridge (ôl′drij grān′jẽr), 1882–1961; English composer and pianist, born in Australia.

grains (grānz), *n.pl.* [usually construed as sing.], [ME. *greyne, gran,* forking, branch, bifurcation < ON. *grein,* division, distinction, branch], a metal fish spear with two or more barbed prongs.

grains of paradise, the aromatic, pungent seeds of a tropical West African plant, used as a stimulant and diuretic.

grain·y (grān′i), *adj.* [GRAINIER (-i-ẽr), GRAINIEST (-i-ist)], 1. having a clearly defined grain: said of textures or surfaces, as of wood. 2. full of grain (cereal). 3. consisting of grains; granular.

gral·la·to·ri·al (gral′ə-tôr′i-əl, gral′ə-tō′ri-əl), *adj.* [L. *grallator,* stiltwalker < *grallae,* stilts; + *-ial*], belonging to a group of wading birds including the cranes, herons, etc., characterized by their long legs, neck, and beak.

gram (gram), *n.* [Fr. *gramme* < LL. *gramma,* weight of two oboli, small weight < Gr. *gramma,* what is written or drawn, letter, writing < *graphein,* to write, draw], the basic unit of weight in the metric system, equal to about 1/28 of an ounce (.0022046 pound or 15.4324 grains troy): it was meant to be, and virtually is, the weight of the distilled water at 4° C. contained in a cube whose edge is one hundredth of a meter: also spelled **gramme:** abbreviated **gm., gr., grm., G., g.**

gram (gram), *n.* [Port. *grão;* L. *granum;* see GRAIN], any of certain plants of the pea family, used as fodder; especially, the chick-pea.

-gram (gram), [< Gr. *gramma;* see GRAM (weight)], a combining form used to form nouns meaning: 1. *something written* or *drawn,* as in *telegram, neurogram.* 2. *a*) (a specified number of) *grams,* as in *kilogram.* *b*) (a specified fraction of) *a gram,* as in *centigram.*

gram., 1. grammar. 2. grammarian. 3. grammatical.

gra·ma (grä′mə), *n.* [Sp.; L. *gramen,* grass], any of several pasture grasses grown in the western United States: also **grama grass.**

gram·a·rye, gram·a·ry (gram′ẽr-i), *n.* [ME. *gramery,* grammar, magic; OFr. *gramaire;* see GRAMMAR & GLAMOUR], [Archaic], magic; occult knowledge.

gram atom, in *chemistry,* the quantity of an element having a weight in grams numerically equal to the element's atomic weight: a gram atom of sodium, the atomic weight of which is 23, is a quantity of sodium weighing 23 grams.

gram-a·tom·ic weight (gram'ə-tom'ik), a gram atom.
gram calorie, a small calorie: see **calorie** (sense 1): abbreviated **g-cal.** (*sing. & pl.*).
gra·mer·cy (grə-mũr'si), *interj.* [ME.; OFr. *grant merci*, lit., great thanks], [Archaic], 1. thank you very much; many thanks. 2. an exclamation of surprise.
gra·min·e·ous (grə-min'i-əs), *adj.* [L. *gramineus* < *gramen*, grass], 1. of the grass family. 2. of or like grass; grassy.
gram·i·niv·o·rous (gram'ə-niv'ẽr-əs), *adj.* [< L. *gramen*, grass; + *-vorous*], feeding on grasses; grass-eating.
gram·ma·logue (gram'ə-lôg', gram'ə-log'), *n.* [< Gr. *gramma*, a letter; + *-logue*], a word represented by a single character or symbol, as in shorthand.
gram·mar (gram'ẽr), *n.* [ME. *gramer;* OFr. *gramaire;* L. *grammatica* (*ars*, art); Gr. *grammatikē* (*technē*, art), grammar, learning < *gramma*, something written, letter < *graphein*, to write: in L. & Gr. the term applied to the whole apparatus of literary study, critical and historical as well as linguistic; in the medieval period it came to mean "the study of Latin," hence "all learning as recorded in Latin" (cf. GRAMMAR SCHOOL in Brit. usage), and "the occult sciences as associated with this learning" (cf. GRAMARYE, GLAMOUR); these prestige senses, associated with the then unknown nature of language, are still implicit in the popular usage of the word], 1. that part of the study of language which deals with the forms and structure of words (*morphology*) and with their customary arrangement in phrases and sentences (*syntax*): formerly used to denote all phases of language study (except that of the detailed meaning of words), as centered on morphology and syntax; now often distinguished from the study of pronunciation (*phonology*) and that of word meanings (*semantics, semasiology*). 2. the system of word structures and word arrangements of a given language at a given time. 3. a system of rules for speaking and writing a given language, based on the study of its grammar (sense 2) or on some adaptation of Latin grammar. 4. *a*) a book containing such rules. *b*) a book or treatise on grammar (senses 1 & 2). 5. one's manner of speaking or writing as judged by conventional grammatical rules: as, his *grammar* was poor. 6. *a*) the elementary principles of a field of knowledge. *b*) a book or treatise on these; primer. Abbreviated **gram., gr.**
gram·mar·i·an (grə-mâr'i-ən), *n.* [ME. & OFr. *gramarien*], a specialist or expert in grammar.
grammar school, 1. an elementary school: the term is variously applied to different school levels, especially to that between the fifth and eighth grades. 2. in England, *a*) originally, a school where Latin was taught. *b*) a secondary school corresponding to an academic high school in the United States.
gram·mat·i·cal (grə-mat'i-k'l), *adj.* [L. *grammaticalis* < *grammatica;* see GRAMMAR], 1. of grammar. 2. conforming to or observing the principles or rules of grammar. Abbreviated **gram., gr.**
gram·mat·i·cal·ly (grə-mat'i-k'l-i, grə-mat'ik-li), *adv.* 1. according to the principles or rules of grammar. 2. from the standpoint of grammar.
gramme (gram), *n.* a gram (weight).
gram-mo·lec·u·lar weight (gram'mə-lek'yoo-lẽr), a gram molecule.
gram molecule, in *chemistry*, the quantity of a substance having a weight in grams numerically equal to its molecular weight: also called *mol, mole.*
Gram-neg·a·tive (gram'neg'ə-tiv), *adj.* not forming a color precipitate when treated by Gram's method: said of bacteria or tissues that lose the stain after treatment with alcohol.
gram·o·phone (gram'ə-fōn'), *n.* [< Gr. *gramma*, a letter; + *-phone*], a phonograph: a trade-mark (**Gramophone**).
Gram·pi·an Mountains (or **Hills**), (gram'pi-ən), a mountain system extending across central Scotland, dividing the Highlands from the Lowlands: highest peak, Ben Nevis, 4,405 ft.: also **Grampians.**
Gram-pos·i·tive (gram'poz'ə-tiv), *adj.* forming a color precipitate when treated by Gram's method: said of bacteria or tissues that retain the stain after treatment with alcohol.
gram·pus (gram'pəs), *n.* [*pl.* GRAMPUSES (-iz)], [earlier *graundepose*, altered (after *grand*) < OFr. *graspeis* < L. *crassus pisces; crassus*, fat + *pisces*, fish], 1. a small, black, fierce variety of toothed whale, related to the dolphins. 2. any of several animals related to this. 3. [Colloq.], a person who breathes heavily and loudly.
Gram's method (gramz), [after Hans C. J. *Gram* (1853–1938), Dan. physician], a method of staining bacteria for the purpose of classification.
Gra·na·da (grə-nä'də; Sp. grä-nä'thä), *n.* 1. a district of southern Spain: see **Spain**, map. 2. its capital, noted for the Alhambra: pop., 125,000.
gran·a·dil·la (gran'ə-dil'ə), *n.* [Sp. < dim. of *granada*, pomegranate < L. *granatus*, containing seeds < *granum*, a seed], 1. a vine bearing a species of passionflower. 2. the edible fruit of this vine.
gran·a·ry (gran'ẽr-i; *occas.* grā'nẽr-i), *n.* [*pl.* GRANARIES (-iz)], [L. *granarium* < *granum*, grain], 1. a building for storing grain. 2. a region that produces much grain.
Gran Cha·co (grän chä'kō), plains in Argentina, Paraguay, and Bolivia: area, 300,000 sq. mi.

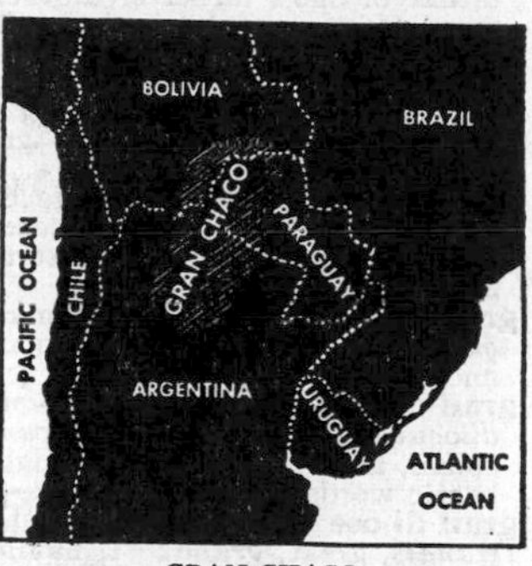

GRAN CHACO

grand (grand), *adj.* [ME.; OFr.; L. *grandis*, full-grown, large, great, etc., replacing *magnus* in LL. & Romance languages], 1. higher in rank, status, or dignity than others having the same title: as, a *grand* duke: abbreviated **gr.** 2. great; chief; most important; main; principal: as, the *grand* ballroom. 3. imposing because of size, beauty, and extent; magnificent: as, *grand* scenery. 4. handsome and luxurious; characterized by splendor and display: as, a *grand* banquet. 5. important; distinguished; illustrious. 6. self-important; pretentious; haughty. 7. complete; over-all; comprehensive: as, the *grand* total. 8. [Colloq.], admirable; delightful; very satisfactory or good: a general term of approval. 9. in *literature, art*, etc., lofty and dignified in expression and treatment. 10. in *music*, full; complete: as, a *grand* chorus. *n.* 1. a grand piano. 2. [Slang], a thousand dollars: abbreviated **G., g.**
SYN.—**grand** is applied to that which makes a strong impression because of its greatness (in size or some favorable quality), dignity, and splendor (the *Grand* Canyon); **magnificent** suggests a surpassing beauty, richness, or splendor, or an exalted or glorious quality (a *magnificent* voice); **imposing** suggests that which strikingly impresses one by its size, dignity, or excellence of character (an *imposing* array of facts); **stately** suggests that which is imposing in dignified grace and may imply a greatness of size (a *stately* dance); **majestic** adds to **stately** the idea of lofty grandeur (the *majestic* Rockies); **august** suggests an exalted dignity or impressiveness such as inspires awe (an *august* personage); **grandiose** is often used disparagingly of a grandeur that is affected or exaggerated (a *grandiose* manner).
grand- (grand), [OFr. (see GRAND), replacing AS. *ealde-*, ME. *olde-* (see OLD)], a combining form meaning, in general, *of the generation older* (or *younger*) *than*, as in *grandfather, grandson.*
gran·dam (gran'dam, gran'dəm), *n.* [ME. *grandame;* Anglo-Fr. *graund dame;* see GRAND- & DAME], [Archaic or Rare], 1. a grandmother. 2. an old woman.
gran·dame (gran'dām, gran'dəm), *n.* a grandam.
Grand Army of the Republic, an association (1866–1949) of men who served in the armed forces of the Union during the Civil War: abbreviated **G.A.R.**
grand·aunt (grand'ant', grand'änt'), *n.* a sister of any of one's grandparents; great-aunt.
Grand Bank, a shoal southeast of Newfoundland: noted fishing grounds: length, 300 miles: also **Grand Banks.**
Grand Canal, 1. a canal in eastern China, connecting Tientsin and Hangchow: length, 850 mi. 2. the main canal in Venice, Italy.
Grand Canyon, 1. the deep gorge of the Colorado River, northern Arizona: length, 217 mi.; width, 4–18 mi.; depth, 1 mi. 2. a national park including the Grand Canyon: area, 1,008 sq. mi.
grand·child (gran'chīld', grand'chīld'), *n.* [*pl.* GRANDCHILDREN (-chil'drən)], a child of one's son or daughter.
grand climacteric, the sixty-third year of one's life.
Grand Cou·lee (kōō'li), a dam on the Columbia River, central Washington: height, 550 ft.
grand·dad, grand-dad (gran'dad'), *n.* [Colloq.], grandfather: an affectionate or children's term: also **grandad.**
grand·daugh·ter (gran'dô'tẽr, grand'dô'tẽr), *n.* a daughter of one's son or daughter.
grand duchess, 1. the wife or widow of a grand duke. 2. a lady whose rank is equivalent to that of a grand duke. 3. in czarist Russia, a princess of the royal family. Abbreviated **G.D.** (as a title).
grand duchy, the territory ruled by a grand duke or a grand duchess: abbreviated **G.D.**
grand duke, 1. in certain European countries, a member of the nobility ranking just below a king and ruling a grand duchy. 2. in czarist Russia, a prince of the royal family. Abbreviated **G.D.** (as a title).
gran·dee (gran-dē'), *n.* [Sp. & Port. *grande;* see GRAND], 1. in Spain or Portugal, a nobleman of the highest rank. 2. a person of high rank; important personage.
gran·deur (gran'jẽr, gran'joor), *n.* [Fr. < *grand;* see

GRAND], 1. greatness of position; eminence. 2. splendor; magnificence. 3. moral and intellectual greatness; nobility; dignity.
Grand Falls, a waterfall of the Hamilton River, Labrador: height, 302 ft.
grand·fa·ther (gran′fä′thẽr, grand′fä′thẽr), *n.* 1. the father of one's father or mother: sometimes used as a term of respectful familiarity to any old man. 2. a male ancestor; forefather.
grand·fa·ther·ly (gran′fä′thẽr-li, grand′fä′thẽr-li), *adj.* 1. of a grandfather. 2. having the characteristics conventionally attributed to a grandfather; kindly; indulgent; benignant.
grandfather's clock, a large clock with a pendulum contained in a tall, upright case.
Grand Forks, a city in eastern North Dakota: pop., 34,000.
gran·dil·o·quence (gran-dil′ə-kwəns), *n.* [< *grandiloquent*], the use of high-flown, pompous, bombastic words and expressions.
gran·dil·o·quent (gran-dil′ə-kwənt), *adj.* [< L. *grandiloquus*, grandiloquent < *grandis*, grand + *loqui*, to speak, after *eloquent*], using high-flown, pompous, bombastic words and expressions. —*SYN.* see **bombastic.**
gran·di·ose (gran′di-ōs′), *adj.* [Fr.; It. *grandioso* < L. *grandis*, great, grand], 1. having grandeur or magnificence; imposing; impressive. 2. affecting grandeur or magnificence; pompous and showy. —*SYN.* see **grand.**
gran·di·os·i·ty (gran′di-os′ə-ti), *n.* a grandiose quality.
‡**gran·dio·so** (grän-dyô′sô), *adj. & adv.* [It.], in *music*, in a grand, noble style: a direction to the performer.
grand jury, a jury of from 12 to 23 citizens that investigates accusations against persons charged with crime and indicts them for trial before a petit jury if there is sufficient evidence.
Grand Lama, the Dalai Lama, head of the Lamaist monks of Tibet and Mongolia: see **Lamaism.**
grand larceny, in *law*, 1. theft in which the property stolen has a value equaling or exceeding a certain amount fixed by law: the amount varies from State to State but is usually between $25 and $50: distinguished from *petty* (or *petit*) *larceny*. 2. in some States, the theft of property of any value directly from the person of the victim, but without the use of force.
grand·ma (gran′mä, gram′mä, gram′ə, grand′mä), *n.* [Colloq.], grandmother.
‡**grand mal** (grän′ mȧl′), [Fr., lit., great ailment], an attack of epilepsy in which there are severe convulsions and loss of consciousness: distinguished from *petit mal*.
Grand Ma·nan (mə-nan′), an island in the Bay of Fundy: part of New Brunswick: pop., 2,000.
grand march, a ceremony in which all the guests at a ball march around the ballroom.
Grand Master, the head of a fraternal order, a military order of knighthood, etc.: abbreviated **G.M.** (as a title).
‡**grand monde** (grän′ mōnd′), [Fr., lit., great world], fashionable society.
grand·moth·er (gran′muth′ẽr, grand′muth′ẽr), *n.* 1. the mother of one's father or mother: sometimes used as a term of respectful familiarity to any old woman. 2. a female ancestor; ancestress.
grand·moth·er·ly (gran′muth′ẽr-li, grand′muth′ẽr-li), *adj.* 1. of a grandmother. 2. having the characteristics conventionally attributed to a grandmother; specifically, *a*) kindly; indulgent. *b*) fussy; interfering.
Grand Mufti, the title of a former Moslem leader of the Arabs in Jerusalem.
grand·neph·ew (gran′nef′ū, grand′nef′ū, grand′nev′ū), *n.* the grandson of one's brother or sister; great-nephew.
grand·niece (gran′nēs′, grand′nēs′), *n.* the granddaughter of one's brother or sister; great-niece.
Grand Old Party, the Republican Party (of the United States): a name given in 1880: abbreviated **G.O.P.**
grand opera, opera, generally on a serious theme, in which the whole text is set to music: distinguished from *operetta*, *comic opera*.
grand·pa (gran′pä, gram′pä, gram′pə, grand′pä), *n.* [Colloq.], grandfather.
grand·par·ent (gran′pâr′ənt, grand′pâr′ənt), *n.* a grandfather or grandmother.
grand piano, a large piano with strings set horizontally in a harp-shaped case.
Grand Pré (gran prā, grand prā; Fr. grän′ prā′), a village in western Nova Scotia, on the Minas Basin, home of the heroine of Longfellow's *Evangeline*.
‡**grand prix** (grän′ prē′), [Fr., lit., great prize], first prize; highest award in a competition.
Grand Rapids, a city in southwestern Michigan, noted for its furniture industry: pop., 177,000.
grand right and left, in *folk dancing*, an interweaving of two concentric circles of dancers, one moving clockwise, one counterclockwise, giving right and left hands alternately to successive partners.
Grand River, 1. a river in southwestern Michigan, flowing into Lake Michigan: length, 275 mi. 2. a river in Iowa and Missouri, flowing southeastward into the Missouri: length, 300 mi.
grand·sir (gran′sẽr, grand′sẽr), *n.* [Archaic], a grandsire.
grand·sire (gran′sīr′, grand′sīr′), *n.* [Archaic], 1. a grandfather. 2. a male ancestor. 3. an old man.
grand slam, 1. in *bridge*, the winning of all the tricks in a deal. 2. in *baseball*, a home run hit when there is a runner on each base.
grand·son (gran′sun′, grand′sun′), *n.* a son of one's son or daughter.
grand·stand (gran′stand′, grand′stand′), *n.* the main seating structure for spectators at a sporting event, etc. *v.i.* [Colloq.], to try to gain the applause of an audience by or as by making grandstand plays.
grandstand play, [Colloq.], an unnecessarily showy play, as in baseball, made to get applause.
Grand Te·ton National Park (tē′ton), a national park in northwestern Wyoming, including a section of the Teton Mountains: area, 150 sq. mi.
grand tour, 1. a tour of continental Europe formerly taken by young men of the British aristocracy to complete their education; hence, 2. any tour like this.
grand·un·cle (grand′uŋ′k'l, grand′uŋ′k'l), *n.* a brother of any of one's grandparents; great-uncle.
grange (grānj), *n.* [ME.; Anglo-Fr. *graunge* (OFr. *grange*); ML. *granica* < L. *granum*; see GRAIN], 1. originally, a granary. 2. a farm with its dwelling house, barns, etc. 3. [G-], the Patrons of Husbandry, an association of farmers organized in the United States in 1867 for mutual welfare and advancement. 4. any local lodge of this association.
grang·er (grān′jẽr), *n.* 1. a member of a grange. 2. [G-], a member of the Grange. 3. a farmer.
grang·er·i·za·tion (grān′jẽr-ə-zā′shən, grān′jẽr-ī-zā′shən), *n.* 1. the act or practice of grangerizing. 2. a grangerized book.
grang·er·ize (grān′jẽr-īz′), *v.t.* [GRANGERIZED (-īzd′), GRANGERIZING], [after James *Granger*, author of a *Biographical History of England* (1769) illustrated by this method], [British], 1. to illustrate (a book already printed) with engravings, prints, etc. obtained elsewhere, often by clipping them from other books. 2. to damage (a book) by clipping such engravings, etc.
gran·i- (gran′i), [< L. *granum*, grain], a combining form meaning *grain*, as in *granivorous*.
Gra·ni·cus (grə-nī′kəs), *n.* a river in northwestern Asia Minor: site of a battle (334 B.C.) in which Alexander the Great defeated the Persians.
gra·nif·er·ous (grə-nif′ẽr-əs), *adj.* [< L. *granifer*; see GRAIN & -FEROUS], bearing grain.
gran·ite (gran′it), *n.* [It. *granito*, granite, lit., grained, pp. of *granire*, to reduce to grains < *grano* < L. *granum*, a seed, grain], a very hard, igneous rock, usually gray or pink, consisting chiefly of crystalline quartz, feldspar, and mica.
Granite City, a city in southwestern Illinois: pop., 40,000.
gran·ite·ware (gran′it-wâr′), *n.* 1. a variety of ironware coated with a hard, gray enamel somewhat resembling granite. 2. a variety of fine, hard pottery.
gra·nit·ic (grə-nit′ik, gra-nit′ik), *adj.* of or like granite.
gran·it·ite (gran′it-īt′), *n.* granite containing biotite.
gran·it·oid (gran′it-oid′), *adj.* like, or having the structure of, granite.
gra·niv·o·rous (grə-niv′ẽr-əs), *adj.* [*grani-* + *-vorous*], feeding on grain and seeds.
gran·ny, gran·nie (gran′i), *n.* [*pl.* GRANNIES (-iz)], [Colloq.], 1. a grandmother. 2. an old woman. 3. any fussy, exacting person. 4. a granny knot.
granny knot, a knot like a square knot but with the ends crossed the wrong way, forming an awkward, insecure knot: also **granny's knot**: see **knot**, illus.
gran·o- (gran′ə), [< L. *granum*, grain], a combining form meaning: 1. *of* or *like granite*, as in *granolithic*. 2. *granular*, as in *granophyre*.
gran·o·lith·ic (gran′ə-lith′ik), *adj.* [*grano-* + *-lithic*], of or made of paving stone consisting of cement and crushed granite.
gran·o·phyre (gran′ə-fīr′), *n.* [*grano-* + *-phyre*; coined (1872) by Vogelsang], a pale-colored igneous rock containing quartz and feldspar.
grant (grant, gränt), *v.t.* [ME. *granten*; OFr. *graanter*, *graunter*, *craanter*, to promise, assure, yield < LL. *credentare*, to promise, yield < L. *credens*, ppr. of *credere*, to believe], 1. to give (what is requested), as permission, etc.; assent to; agree to fulfill. 2. *a*) to give or confer formally or according to legal procedure. *b*) to transfer (property) by a deed. 3. to acknowledge for the sake of argument; admit as true without proof; concede. *n.* 1. a granting. 2. something granted, as property, a tract of land, an exclusive right or power, money from a fund, etc. —*SYN.* see **give.**
take for granted, to consider as true or already settled.
Grant, Ulysses Simp·son (simp′sən grant), (born *Hiram Ulysses Grant*), 1822–1885; eighteenth president of the United States (1869–1877); commander in chief of Union forces in the Civil War.
gran·tee (gran′tē′, grän′tē′), *n.* in *law*, a person to whom a grant is made.
grant·or (gran′tẽr, grän′tôr′), *n.* [Anglo-Fr.], in *law*, a person who makes a grant.
gran·u·lar (gran′yoo-lẽr), *adj.* [< LL. *granulum* (see GRANULE); + *-ar*], 1. containing or consisting of grains

or granules: granular eyelids have an inner surface made rough by disease. 2. like grains or granules; granulated.
gran·u·lar·i·ty (gran'yoo-lâr'ə-ti), *n.* the quality or condition of being granular.
granular snow, snow in small, opaque grains.
gran·u·late (gran'yoo-lāt'), *v.t.* & *v.i.* [GRANULATED (-id), GRANULATING], 1. to form into grains or granules. 2. to make or become rough on the surface by the development of granules or tiny bulges.
gran·u·lat·er (gran'yoo-lāt'ẽr), *n.* a granulator.
gran·u·la·tion (gran'yoo-lā'shən), *n.* 1. formation into granules or grains. 2. in *medicine, a*) the formation of a small, granular mass on a surface, as of a wound that is healing. *b*) the mass itself.
gran·u·la·tive (gran'yoo-lā'tiv), *adj.* of or characterized by granulation.
gran·u·la·tor (gran'yoo-lā'tẽr), *n.* a person or thing that granulates.
gran·ule (gran'yool), *n.* [< LL. *granulum,* dim. of L. *granum,* a grain], 1. a small grain. 2. a small, grainlike particle or spot.
gran·u·lite (gran'yoo-līt'), *n.* [< *granule* + *-ite*], 1. a granular, crystalline rock containing quartz, feldspar, and occasional dark-red garnets. 2. granite containing biotite and muscovite.
gran·u·lit·ic (gran'yoo-lit'ik), *adj.* containing or made of granulite.
gran·u·lose (gran'yoo-lōs'), *n.* the more soluble part of a starch grain, converted into sugar by the action of enzymes. *adj.* granular.
Gran·ville-Bar·ker, Har·ley (här'li gran'vil-bär'kẽr), 1877–1946; English actor, playwright, and critic.
grape (grāp), *n.* [ME. *grap, graap,* replacing earlier *winberie* (cf. WINE & BERRY); OFr. *grape,* dial. *crape* (Fr. *grappe*), bunch of grapes < Frank. *krappo* (OHG. *chrapfo*), hook; prob. via OFr. *graper,* to gather with a hook; cf. GRAPNEL], 1. any of various small, round, smooth-skinned, juicy fruits, generally purple, red, or green, growing in clusters on a woody vine: grapes are eaten raw, used to make wine, or dried to make raisins; they are classified as berries. 2. any of various vines bearing grapes; grapevine. 3. a dark purplish red. 4. grapeshot. 5. *pl. a*) a diseased growth on the fetlock of horses, consisting of a cluster of wartlike lumps. *b*) bovine tuberculosis.
grape·fruit (grāp'frōōt'), *n.* [so named because it grows in clusters], 1. a large, round, edible citrus fruit with a pale-yellow rind, juicy pulp, and a somewhat sour taste. 2. the semitropical evergreen tree that it grows on.
grape hyacinth, any of a group of small, hardy bulbs of the lily family, with spikes of small, bell-shaped flowers of blue or white.
grap·er·y (grāp'ẽr-i), *n.* [*pl.* GRAPERIES (-iz)], a place, especially an enclosed area or building, where grapes are grown.
grape·shot (grāp'shot'), *n.* a cluster of small iron balls formerly fired from a cannon as a dispersing charge.
grape·stone (grāp'stōn'), *n.* a seed of the grape.
grape sugar, a simple sugar occurring in many plants and fruits, especially in ripe grapes; dextrose; glucose.
grape·vine (grāp'vīn'), *n.* 1. any of various woody vines bearing grapes. 2. a secret means of spreading or receiving information: also **grapevine telegraph.** 3. a rumor; unfounded report; hearsay.
graph (graf, gräf), *n.* [short for *graphic formula*], 1. a diagram, as a curve, broken line, series of bars, etc., representing the successive changes in the value of a variable quantity or quantities. 2. in *mathematics,* a curve or surface showing the locus of a function on a series of co-ordinates set at right angles to each other. *v.t.* to put in the form of or represent by a graph.

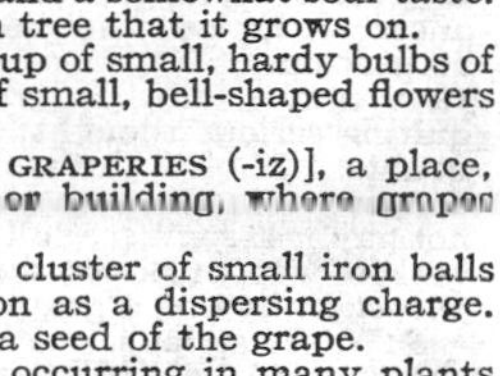

FIRST QUARTER SECOND QUARTER
UNITS SOLD
600
500
400
300
200
100

GRAPH

-graph (graf, gräf), [Gr. *-graphos* < *graphein,* to write], a combining form meaning: 1. *something that writes* or *describes,* as in *telegraph.* 2. *something written,* as in *monograph.*
-grapher, a combining form meaning *a person who writes,* used to form nouns of agent corresponding to nouns ending in *-graph, -graphy,* as *telegrapher, stenographer.*
graph·ic (graf'ik), *adj.* [L. *graphicus;* Gr. *graphikos,* lit., belonging to painting or drawing, picturesque, writing < *graphē,* a drawing, writing < *graphein,* to write], 1. describing or described in realistic and vivid detail; vivid; lifelike. 2. of the graphic arts. 3. *a*) of handwriting; used or expressed in handwriting. *b*) written, inscribed, or recorded in letters, etc. 4. having markings that look like written or printed characters: said of minerals. 5. of graphs or diagrams. 6. shown by a graph or graphs.
SYN.—**graphic** and **pictorial,** with reference to speech or writing, imply description that calls forth a mental image as sharply defined as the visual impression made by a picture; **vivid** implies the bringing of strikingly real or lifelike images to the mind; **picturesque** language is full of beautiful imagery and may achieve interesting pictorial effects at the expense of reality.
-graph·ic (graf'ik), a combining form used to form adjectives from, or corresponding to, nouns ending in *-graph,* as *telegraphic, stenographic:* also **-graphical.**
graph·i·cal (graf'i-k'l), *adj.* graphic.
graphic arts, 1. any form of visual artistic representation; especially, painting, drawing, photography, etc. 2. now, sometimes, only those arts in which impressions are printed from various kinds of blocks or plates, as etching, lithography, dry point, offset, etc.
graph·ics (graf'iks), *n.pl.* [construed as sing.], [< *graphic*], 1. the art of making drawings, as in architecture or engineering, in accordance with mathematical rules. 2. calculation of stresses, etc. from such drawings.
graph·ite (graf'īt), *n.* [G. *graphit* < Gr. *graphein,* to write: so called from use as writing material], a soft, black, lustrous form of carbon used for lead in pencils, for crucibles, lubricants, electrodes, etc.: also called *black lead, plumbago.*
gra·phit·ic (grə-fit'ik), *adj.* of, like, or having the nature of, graphite.
graph·i·tize (graf'ə-tīz'), *v.t.* [GRAPHITIZED (-tīzd'), GRAPHITIZING], 1. to change into graphite by heating or annealing. 2. to put graphite in or on.
graph·o- (graf'ə), [< Gr. *graphē,* a writing < *graphein,* to write], a combining form meaning *writing, drawing,* as in *graphology.*
graph·ol·o·gy (gra-fol'ə-ji), *n.* [*grapho-* + *-logy*], the study of handwriting, especially as it is supposed to indicate character, aptitudes, etc.
graph·o·mo·tor (graf'ə-mō'tẽr), *n.* [*grapho-* + *motor*], in *physiology,* of or affecting the movements made in writing.
graph·o·phone (graf'ə-fōn'), *n.* [*grapho-* + *-phone*], a phonograph: a trade-mark (**Graphophone**).
graph·o·type (graf'ə-tīp'), *n.* [*grapho-* + *-type*], a machine for embossing letters on a thin sheet of metal.
-graphy, [L. *-graphia;* Gr. *-graphia,* writing < *graphein,* to write], a combining form meaning: 1. *a process, method,* or *manner of writing,* or *graphically representing,* as in *calligraphy, photography.* 2. *a descriptive science* or *treatise dealing with such a science,* as in *geography.*
grap·lin, grap·line (grap'lin), *n.* [< *grappling*], a grapnel.
grap·nel (grap'n'l), *n.* [ME. *grapnell,* dim. < OFr. *grapin, grapil;* Pr. *grapin, grapil* < *grapa,* a hook < Frank. *krappo;* see GRAPE], 1. a small anchor with several flukes, or claws. 2. an instrument with a hook or hooks for grasping and holding things; grappling iron.

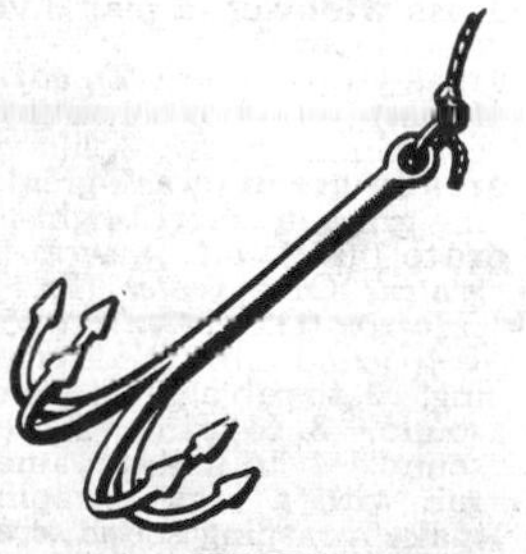

GRAPNEL

grap·ple (grap''l), *n.* [OFr. *grappil, grapil;* see GRAPNEL], 1. a grappling iron or grapnel (sense 2). 2. a seizing; grip or hold, as in wrestling. 3. a close fight in which the fighters grip one another. *v.t.* [GRAPPLED (-'ld), GRAPPLING], to grip and hold; seize. *v.i.* 1. to use a grappling iron. 2. to come to grips, as in wrestling; seize one another.
grap·pler (grap'lẽr), *n.* 1. a person or thing that grapples. 2. [Slang], a hand.
grap·pling (grap'liŋ), *n.* a grappling iron.
grappling iron (or **hook**), a device consisting of an iron bar with claws or hooks at one end for grasping and holding things; grapnel.
grap·y (grāp'i), *adj.* [ME. *grapi*], of or like grapes.
grasp (grasp, gräsp), *v.t.* [ME. *graspen;* by metathesis < *grapsen* (cf. CLASP, WASP); either < MLG. (cf. LG., Fris. *grapsen*) or < AS. **græpsan* < base of AS. *grapian* (see GROPE)], 1. to take hold of firmly with or as with the hand; grip. 2. to take hold of eagerly or greedily; seize. 3. to take hold of mentally; understand; comprehend. *n.* 1. a grasping; grip or clasp of the hand. 2. a firm hold; control; possession. 3. the power to hold or seize; reach. 4. understanding; comprehension; intellectual capacity. —*SYN.* see **take.**
grasp at, 1. to reach for and try to seize. 2. to take eagerly; accept with alacrity.
grasp·ing (gras'piŋ, gräs'piŋ), *adj.* 1. that grasps. 2. greedy; eager for gain; avaricious. —*SYN.* see **greedy.**
grass (gras, gräs), *n.* [ME. *gras;* AS. *gærs, græs;* akin to G. *gras;* IE. **ghrās,* **ghres,* grass, plant growth, etc. (as in L. *gramen,* grass < **ghras-men;* cf. GRAMINIVOROUS) < base **ghrō-,* to grow, become green (seen

also in *grow*)], 1. any of various green plants with bladelike leaves that are eaten by grazing animals: because of their softness and dense growth, grasses are often cultivated for lawns, etc. 2. any of a group of plants with long, narrow leaves, jointed stems, flowers on spikelets, and seedlike fruit, as wheat, rye, barley, oats, sugar cane, etc. 3. ground covered with grass; pasture land or lawn. *v.t.* 1. to pasture or graze (cattle). 2. to grow grass over; cover with grass. 3. to lay (textiles, etc.) on the grass for bleaching by the sun. 4. to bring or throw down, as game by shooting, or an opponent by a blow; fell.

go to grass, 1. to graze. 2. to become worn out, shabby, etc.; decay; go to ruin. 3. to die. 4. to rest.

let the grass grow under one's feet, to waste one's time or neglect one's opportunities.

grass cloth, a cloth made of fibers of grass or ramie.

grass·cut·ter (gras′kut′ẽr, gräs′kut′ẽr), *n.* 1. a machine for cutting grass; lawnmower. 2. [Colloq.], in *baseball*, a batted ball that skims along the ground.

grass·hop·per (gras′hop′ẽr, gräs′hop′ẽr), *n.* [ME. *grashoppere*, modified form, with *-er* suffix (see -ER), of *greshoppe* < AS. *gærshoppe* < *gærs* (see GRASS) + base of *hoppian* (see HOP); akin to D. *græshoppe*, G. *grashüpfer*, etc.], 1. any of a group of leaping insects with two pairs of membranous wings and powerful hind legs adapted for jumping. 2. [Military Slang], a light airplane for scouting and observation.

grass·i·ness (gras′i-nis, gräs′i-nis), *n.* the quality or state of being grassy.

grass·land (gras′land′, gräs′land′), *n.* 1. land with grass growing on it, used for grazing; pasture land. 2. land or region where grass predominates.

grass·plot (gras′plot′, gräs′plot′), *n.* a piece of ground with grass growing on it; lawn.

grass-roots (gras′rōōts′, gräs′roots′), *adj.* [Colloq.], originating among or carried on by the common people: as, a *grass-roots* political movement.

grass snake, any of various small, nonpoisonous snakes that live in swamps and marshes.

grass snipe, a large, grayish-brown sandpiper with a pale, streaked, buff-colored breast; pectoral sandpiper.

grass tree, 1. an Australian woody plant of the lily family, with grasslike leaves and a spike of flowers: some varieties yield resins used commercially. 2. any of various Australasian trees with grasslike foliage.

grass widow, [Early Mod. Eng., discarded mistress; cf. D. *grasweduwe*, G. *strohwittwe* in mod. sense; prob. allusion is to bed of grass or straw], a woman divorced or otherwise separated from her husband.

grass widower, a man divorced or otherwise separated from his wife.

grass·y (gras′i, gräs′i), *adj.* [GRASSIER (-i-ẽr), GRASSIEST (-i-ist)], 1. of or consisting of grass. 2. covered with or containing grass. 3. like grass; grassy-green.

gras·sy-green (gras′i-grēn′, gräs′i-grēn′), *adj.* like growing grass in color; bright-green.

grate (grāt), *v.t.* [GRATED (-id), GRATING], [ME. (rare) *graten*; OFr. *grater* (Fr. *gratter*) < Gmc.; cf. OHG. *chrazzōn* (G. *kratzen*), to scratch; IE. base as in *scratch*], 1. to grind into shreds or particles by rubbing or scraping. 2. to rub against (an object) with a harsh, scraping sound. 3. to grind (the teeth) together with a rasping sound. 4. to irritate; annoy; fret. *v.i.* 1. to grind or rub with a harsh scraping or rasping sound. 2. to make a rasping sound; creak. 3. to have an irritating or annoying effect: as, her voice *grates* on me.

grate (grāt), *n.* [ME. *grate*, trellis, lattice; ML. *grata*, *crata* < L. *cratis*, a hurdle, kind of basket], 1. a framework of parallel or latticed bars set in a window, door, etc. 2. a frame of metal bars for holding fuel in a fireplace, stove, or furnace; hence, 3. a fireplace. 4. in *mining*, a screen for grading crushed ores. *v.t.* [GRATED (-id), GRATING], to provide with a grate or grates.

grate·ful (grāt′fəl), *adj.* [obs. *grate* (< L. *gratus*), pleasing; + *-ful*], 1. feeling or expressing gratitude; thankful; appreciative. 2. causing gratitude; welcome; pleasing.

grat·er (grāt′ẽr), *n.* 1. a person or thing that grates. 2. a utensil with a rough surface on which to grate spices, vegetables, cheese, etc.

Gra·ti·an (grā′shi-ən, grā′shən), *n.* (*Flavius Gratianus*), Roman emperor (375–383 A.D.); lived 359–383 A.D.

grat·i·fi·ca·tion (grat′ə-fi-kā′shən), *n.* [L. *gratificatio*], 1. a gratifying or being gratified. 2. something that gratifies; cause for satisfaction. 3. a voluntary reward for services or benefits; recompense; gratuity.

grat·i·fi·er (grat′ə-fī′ẽr), *n.* a person or thing that gratifies.

grat·i·fy (grat′ə-fī′), *v.t.* [GRATIFIED (-fīd′), GRATIFYING], [Fr. *gratifier*; L. *gratificare*, *gratificari*, to oblige, please, favor < *gratus*, pleasing, agreeable + *facere*, to make], 1. to give pleasure or satisfaction to. 2. to give in to; satisfy; indulge; humor. 3. [Archaic], to reward.

‡**gra·tin** (grȧ′tan′; Eng. grat′′n), *n.* [Fr. < *gratter*, *grater*, to scrape; see GRATE, *v.*], 1. the crust of cheese or buttered crumbs over a casserole dish. 2. the dish itself.

grat·ing (grāt′iŋ), *n.* [*grate* (framework) + *-ing*], 1. a framework of parallel or latticed bars set in a window, door, etc.; grate. 2. in *optics*, an arrangement of parallel wires or very fine, parallel lines etched closely on a smooth, shining surface, used to break up light into spectra by diffraction.

grat·ing (grāt′iŋ), *adj.* [ppr. of *grate* (to rub)], 1. causing a harsh, rasping sound. 2. sounding harsh and rasping; hence, 3. irritating; annoying.

gra·tis (grā′tis, grat′is), *adv. & adj.* [L. < *gratia*, a favor, kindness], without charge or payment; free.

grat·i·tude (grat′ə-tōōd′, grat′ə-tūd′), *n.* [Fr.; LL. *gratitudo* < L. *gratus*, pleasing, thankful], a feeling of thankful appreciation for favors or benefits received; warm, appreciative response to kindness; thankfulness.

Grat·tan, Henry (grat′′n), 1746–1820; Irish statesman and orator.

gra·tu·i·tous (grə-tōō′ə-təs, grə-tū′ə-təs), *adj.* [L. *gratuitus* < *gratus*; see GRACE], 1. given or received without charge or payment; granted without obligation; free. 2. without cause or justification; uncalled-for.

gratuitous contract, in *law*, a contract for the benefit of the person for whom it is made, without a reciprocal promise of benefit to the maker: sometimes called *contract of beneficence*.

gra·tu·i·ty (grə-tōō′ə-ti, grə-tū′ə-ti), *n.* [*pl.* GRATUITIES (-tiz)], [Fr. *gratuité*; ML. *gratuitas* < L. *gratuitus*; see GRATUITOUS], a gift of money, etc., especially one given for a service rendered; tip. —*SYN.* see **present.**

grat·u·lant (grach′oo-lənt), *adj.* [L. *gratulans*, ppr. of *gratulari*; see GRATULATE], expressing joy or gratification; congratulatory.

grat·u·late (grach′oo-lāt′), *v.t.* [GRATULATED (-id), GRATULATING], [< L. *gratulatus*, pp. of *gratulari*, to congratulate, rejoice < *gratus*; see GRACE], [Archaic], to express joy or gratification at the sight of; congratulate.

grat·u·la·tion (grach′oo-lā′shən), *n.* [L. *gratulatio* < *gratulatus*; see GRATULATE], [Archaic], 1. joy; gratification. 2. an expression of this; congratulation.

grat·u·la·to·ry (grach′oo-lə-tôr′i, grach′oo-lə-tō′ri), *adj.* [LL. *gratulatorius*], [Archaic], congratulatory.

Grau·bün·den (grou′bün′dən), *n.* Grisons: the German name.

grau·pel (grou′pəl), *n.* [< G. *graupeln*, to sleet < *graupelein*, dim. of *graupe*, hulled barley, granule of ice, hail < Slav.; cf. Serb. *krupa*, kernel of grain, hail], in *meteorology*, soft sleet or hail.

gra·va·men (grə-vā′men), *n.* [*pl.* GRAVAMENS (-menz), GRAVAMINA (-vam′in-ə)], [LL., lit., a burden, trouble < L. *gravare*, to weigh down < *gravis*, heavy], 1. a grievance. 2. in *law*, the essential part of a complaint or accusation.

grave (grāv), *adj.* [L. *gravis*, heavy, weighty], 1. requiring serious thought; important; weighty: as, *grave* doubts. 2. of a threatening nature; indicating great danger; ominous: as, a *grave* illness. 3. solemn; sedate; not gay. 4. somber; dull: as, *grave* colors. 5. in *music*, low or deep in pitch: distinguished from *acute*. 6. in *phonetics*, having a grave accent. *n.* the grave accent. —*SYN.* see **serious.**

grave (grāv), *n.* [ME. *graf*, *grave*; AS. *græf* (akin to OFris. *gref*; cf. G. *grabe*) < base of *grafan*, to dig; see the *v.t.*], 1. a hole in the ground in which to bury a dead body. 2. a burial mound or monument. 3. any place for receiving something dead: as, his bankruptcy was the *grave* of his hopes. 4. death; extinction: as, he does not fear the *grave*. *v.t.* [GRAVED (grāvd), GRAVEN (-′n) or GRAVED, GRAVING], [ME. *graven*; AS. *grafan*; akin to G. *graben*; IE. base **ghrebh-*, to scratch, scrape], 1. *a*) [Obs.], to dig. *b*) [Archaic], to bury. 2. to shape by carving; carve out; sculpture. 3. to engrave; incise. 4. to impress sharply and clearly; fix permanently.

have one foot in the grave, to be very ill, old, or infirm; be near death.

make one turn in one's grave, to be or do something that would have shocked or strongly displeased one now dead.

grave (grāv), *v.t.* [GRAVED (grāvd), GRAVING], [prob. < OFr. *grave* (Fr. *grève*), beach, coarse sand (see GRAVEL): ships were orig. beached for cleaning the hulls], to clean (the hull of a ship) by removing the barnacles, etc. and coating with pitch or tar.

‡**gra·ve** (grä′ve), *adj. & adv.* [It.], in *music*, slow and with solemnity: a direction to the performer.

grave accent, a mark (\`) used to show: 1. in French, the quality of an open *e* (è), as in *chère*, or a distinction in meaning, as in *où*, where (distinguished from *ou*, or). 2. full pronunciation of an ending or syllable normally elided in speech, as in *lovèd*. 3. secondary or weakened stress, as in *tỳpewrìter*. 4. falling tone or pitch, as in the Chinese language.

grave·clothes (grāv′klōz′, grāv′klōthz′), *n.pl.* the clothes in which a dead body is buried; cerements.

grave·dig·ger (grāv′dig′ẽr), *n.* a person whose work is digging graves.

grav·el (grav′′l), *n.* [ME.; OFr. *gravelle*, dim. of *grave* (Fr. *grève*), coarse sand, shingle, seashore], 1. a loose mixture of pebbles and rock fragments coarser than sand, often mixed with clay, etc. 2. in *medicine*, a deposit of small concretions that form in the kidneys and may pass through the ureters into the bladder;

calculus. *v.t.* [GRAVELED or GRAVELLED (-'ld), GRAVELING or GRAVELLING], 1. to cover (a walk, driveway, etc.) with gravel. 2. to run (a boat or ship) aground on gravel; hence, 3. to embarrass or perplex (a speaker). 4. to lame (a horse), as by pebbles under a shoe. 5. [Colloq.], to irritate or annoy.

grav·el-blind (grav''l-blind'), *adj.* [intens. synonym for *sand-blind*], almost completely blind.

grav·el·ly (grav''l-i), *adj.* 1. full of gravel. 2. consisting of gravel. 3. like gravel.

grave·ly (grāv'li), *adv.* in a grave manner; seriously.

grav·en (grāv''n), alternative past participle of **grave** (to engrave). *adj.* 1. engraved; carved; sculptured. 2. sharply and clearly impressed; permanently fixed.

grave·ness (grāv'nis), *n.* the quality or state of being grave.

graven image, an idol.

Gra·ven·stein (grav''n-stēn', grä'vən-stīn'), *n.* [< *Gravenstein* in Schleswig], a variety of large, yellow, red-striped apple.

grav·er (grāv'ēr), *n.* [ME.; see GRAVE (to engrave) & -ER], 1. a cutting tool used by engravers and sculptors. 2. an engraver; especially, a carver in stone.

Graves, Robert Ran·ke (räŋ'kə grāvz), 1895– ; English poet and novelist.

Graves' disease (grāvz), [after Robert *Graves* (1797–1853), Ir. physician], exophthalmic goiter.

grave·stone (grāv'stōn'), *n.* [ME.], a memorial stone placed at a grave; tombstone.

grave·yard (grāv'yärd'), *n.* a burial ground; cemetery.

grav·id (grav'id), *adj.* [L. *gravidus* < *gravis*, heavy; see GRAVITY], pregnant.

gra·vid·i·ty (grə-vid'ə-ti), *n.* [L. *graviditas* < *gravidus;* see GRAVID], pregnancy.

grav·i·met·ric (grav'i-met'rik), *adj.* [< *gravimetry* + *-ic*], in *chemistry* & *physics*, of or in terms of measurement by weight: distinguished from *volumetric*.

grav·i·met·ri·cal (grav'i-met'ri-k'l), *adj.* gravimetric.

gra·vim·e·try (grə-vim'ə-tri), *n.* [< L. *gravis*, heavy; + *-metry*], the measurement of weight or density.

grav·ing (grāv'iŋ), *n.* [*grave* (to clean a vessel) + *-ing*], the cleaning of a ship's hull by burning or scraping. *adj.* of or for this: as, a *graving* dock.

grav·i·tate (grav'ə-tāt'), *v.i.* [GRAVITATED (-id), GRAVITATING], [< L. *gravitas* (see GRAVITY); + *-ate*], 1. to move or tend to move in accordance with the force of gravity. 2. to sink or fall; tend to settle at a bottom level, as of a liquid. 3. to be attracted or tend to move (*toward* something or someone).

grav·i·ta·tion (grav'ə-tā'shən), *n.* [Mod. L. *gravitatio* < L. *gravitas;* see GRAVITY], 1. the act, process, or fact of gravitating. 2. in *physics*, the force by which every mass or particle of matter attracts and is attracted by every other mass or particle of matter; tendency of these masses or particles toward each other.

grav·i·ta·tion·al (grav'ə-tā'shən-'l), *adj.* of or caused by gravitation.

grav·i·ta·tion·al·ly (grav'ə-tā'shən-'l-i), *adv.* by or according to gravitation.

grav·i·ta·tive (grav'ə-tā'tiv), *adj.* 1. of or caused by gravitation. 2. tending or causing to gravitate.

grav·i·ty (grav'ə-ti), *n.* [*pl.* GRAVITIES (-tiz)], [L. *gravitas*, weight, heaviness < *gravis*, heavy], 1. the state or condition of being grave; especially, *a*) solemnity or sedateness of manner or character; earnestness. *b*) danger or menace; ominous quality: as, the *gravity* of his illness. *c*) seriousness, as of guilt. 2. weight; heaviness, as in specific *gravity*, center of *gravity*. 3. lowness of musical pitch. 4. in *physics*, gravitation; especially, terrestrial gravitation; force that tends to draw all bodies in the earth's sphere toward the center of the earth: the rate of acceleration of gravity is approximately 32 feet per second per second: abbreviated **g** (no period).

gra·vure (grə-vyoor', grā'vyoor), *n.* [Fr., short for *photogravure*], 1. engraving by means of plates made by a photographic process; photogravure. 2. a plate or print so prepared.

gra·vy (grā'vi), *n.* [*pl.* GRAVIES (-viz)], [ME. *grave, gravey*, said to be a misreading of OFr. *grané* < *grain*, apparently used as a name for cooking ingredients], 1. the juice given off by meat in cooking. 2. a sauce made by combining this juice with flour, seasoning, etc. 3. [Slang], easily obtained profit.

gravy boat, a dish for serving gravy: so called from its shape.

gray (grā), *adj.* [ME. *grai, grei;* AS. *græg;* akin to G. *grau;* IE. base **ĝhere-*, to shine, gleam, as also in L. *ravus* (for **gravus*), grayish], 1. of a color that is a mixture or blend of black and white pigments; hence, 2. *a*) darkish; dull. *b*) dreary; dismal. 3. having hair that is gray; hence, 4. old. 5. designating any religious order whose members dress in gray: as, the *Gray* Friars. *n.* 1. a color made by mixing or blending black and white pigments. 2. an animal or thing colored gray; especially, a gray horse. 3. a person dressed in a gray uniform. 4. gray or unbleached fabric or clothing. *v.t.* & *v.i.* to make or become gray. Also spelled **grey.**

Gray, Asa (grā), 1810–1888; American botanist.

Gray, Thomas, 1716–1771; English poet.

gray·back (grā'bak'), *n.* any of certain animals so called because of their coloring, as the hooded crow, scaup duck, etc.: also spelled **greyback.**

gray·beard (grā'bêrd'), *n.* an old man: also spelled **greybeard.**

gray·fish (grā'fish'), *n.* [*pl.* GRAYFISH, GRAYFISHES (-iz); see FISH], the smooth or spiny dogfish: also spelled **greyfish.**

Gray Friar, a Franciscan friar.

gray-head·ed (grā'hed'id), *adj.* 1. having gray hair; hence, 2. old. Also spelled **grey-headed.**

gray·hound (grā'hound'), *n.* a greyhound.

gray·ish (grā'ish), *adj.* somewhat gray: also spelled **greyish.**

gray·lag (grā'lag'), *n.* [said to be *gray* + *lag:* so called from its color and its late migration], the European wild gray goose: also spelled **greylag.**

gray·ling (grā'liŋ), *n.* [*pl.* GRAYLING, GRAYLINGS (-liŋz); see PLURAL, II, D, 2], [*gray* + *-ling*], 1. a fresh-water game fish of the trout family, with a large dorsal fin. 2. any of several varieties of gray or brown butterflies.

gray market, a place or system for selling scarce goods secretly at above prevailing prices, a practice considered unethical although legal: cf. **black market.**

gray matter, 1. grayish nerve tissue of the brain and spinal cord, consisting chiefly of nerve cells, with few nerve fibers: distinguished from *white matter*, which consists chiefly of nerve fibers. 2. [Colloq.], brains; intellectual capacity.

gray mullet, any of a large group of food fishes found mostly in salt water.

Gray's Inn, one of the four Inns of Court in London, the legal societies that admit persons to law practice in England.

gray squirrel, a large, gray or black squirrel native to the United States.

gray·wacke (grā'wak'), *n.* [G. *grauwacke; grau*, gray + *wacke*, wacke], a fine-grained, gray, conglomerate rock resembling sandstone: also spelled **greywacke.**

gray wolf, a large, gray wolf that hunts in packs, native to western North America.

Graz (gräts), *n.* a city in southeastern Austria: pop., 226,000 (1948).

graze (grāz), *v.t.* [GRAZED (grāzd), GRAZING], [ME. *grasen;* AS. *grasian* < base of *græs, gærs*, grass (see GRASS); akin to G. *grasen*], 1. to put (livestock) to feed on growing grass, herbage, etc. 2. to put livestock to feed on (a pasture, growing grass, etc.). 3. to feed on (growing grass, herbage, etc.). 4. to tend (feeding livestock) while in a pasture. *v.i.* to feed on growing grass, etc.

graze (grāz), *v.t.* [GRAZED (grāzd), GRAZING], [prob. < prec. *v.* in orig. sense "to come close to the grass"; cf. G. *grasen*, also in sense "to bound along the ground" (said of cannon balls); some senses influenced by obs. *glace*, to glance off], 1. to touch or rub lightly in passing. 2. to scrape or scratch (the skin) or the skin of in passing: as, a bullet *grazed* his thigh. *v.i.* to scrape, touch, or rub lightly against something in passing. *n.* 1. a grazing. 2. a slight scratch or scrape caused by grazing.

gra·zier (grā'zhēr), *n.* [Chiefly British], a person who grazes beef cattle for sale.

graz·ing (grāz'iŋ), *n.* land for livestock to graze on; pasture.

‡gra·zi·o·so (grä-tsyô'sô), *adj.* & *adv.* [It. < L. *gratiosus;* see GRACIOUS], in *music*, with grace; in a smooth, elegant manner: a direction to the performer.

Gr. Brit., Gr. Br., Great Britain.

grease (grēs), *n.* [ME. *gresse, grese;* OFr. *gresse, graisse* < LL. **crassia* < L. *crassus*, fat, thick; cf. CRASS], 1. the soft fat of game animals: used in hunting with reference to game in the proper condition for killing, as, a stag in prime (or pride) of *grease*. 2. melted animal fat. 3. any thick, oily substance or lubricant. 4. an inflammation of the skin of a horse's fetlocks, accompanied by an oily discharge. 5. *a*) the oily substance in uncleaned wool. *b*) an uncleaned fleece or fur. *v.t.* (grēs, grēz), [GREASED (grēst, grēzd), GREASING], 1. to smear or lubricate with grease; put grease on or in. 2. to influence by giving money to; bribe or tip: often in *grease the hand* (or *palm*).

grease·bush (grēs'boosh'), *n.* greasewood.

grease cup, a small cup over a bearing in machinery, for containing and supplying grease or oil to lubricate the bearing.

grease monkey, [Slang], a mechanic, especially one who works on automobiles or airplanes.

grease paint, a mixture of grease and coloring matter used by actors in making up for the stage.

greas·er (grēs'ēr, grēz'ēr), *n.* 1. a person or device

that greases. 2. [Slang], a Mexican or Latin American: hostile and contemptuous term.
grease·wood (grēs′wood′), *n.* any of a number of shrubby, stiff, prickly plants growing in alkaline soils in the western United States: also **greasebush.**
greas·i·ly (grēs′ə-li, grēz′'l-i), *adv.* in a greasy manner.
greas·i·ness (grēs′i-nis, grēz′i-nis), *n.* the quality or state of being greasy.
greas·y (grēs′i, grēz′i), *adj.* [GREASIER (-i-ẽr), GREASIEST (-i-ist)], 1. smeared or soiled with grease. 2. containing grease; full of grease. 3. like grease; oily; unctuous; slippery. 4. having grease (sense 4).
great (grāt), *adj.* [ME. *grete, gret;* AS. *great;* akin to G. *gross;* IE. base **ghrēu-*, to rub away, grind down, seen also in L. *rudus*, broken stones, rubble & in Eng. *grit;* basic sense "coarse, coarse-grained"; *great* has replaced, and absorbed the senses of, AS. *mycel*, ME. *muchel* (see MICKLE) and is itself now partly replaced by *big;* cf. GRAND], 1. of much more than ordinary size, extent, volume, etc.; especially, *a)* designating a thing or group of things larger than others of the same kind: as, the *great* cats are tigers, lions, etc., the *Great* Lakes. *b)* large in number, quantity, etc.; numerous: as, a *great* company. *c)* long in duration: as, a *great* while. 2. much higher in some quality or degree; much above the ordinary or average; especially, *a)* existing in a high degree; intense: as, a *great* light, *great* pain. *b)* very much of a; acting much as (something specified): as, a *great* reader. *c)* eminent; important; illustrious; superior: as, a *great* playwright. *d)* very impressive or imposing: as, *great* ceremony. *e)* having or showing nobility of mind, purpose, etc.: as, a *great* man. 3. of most importance; highest in its class; main; chief: as, the *Great* War. 4. designating a relationship one generation removed; older or younger by one generation: used in hyphenated compounds, as *great-grandmother*. 5. [Colloq.], clever; expert; skillful (usually with *at*): as, he is *great* at tennis. 6. [Colloq.], excellent; splendid; fine: a generalized epithet of approval. 7. [Archaic], pregnant. *adv.* [Colloq.], very well. *n.* 1. the whole or gross. 2. *pl.* [British Univ. Slang], the final examination for the bachelor's degree: also **great go.** Abbreviated **gt., gr.** —*SYN.* see **large.**
great on, [Colloq.], enthusiastic about.
the great, those who are great.
great auk, a large sea bird of the North Atlantic, that was incapable of flight and is now extinct.
great-aunt (grāt′ant′, grāt′änt′), *n.* a sister of any of one's grandparents; grandaunt.
Great Australian Bight, a part of the Indian Ocean indenting southern Australia.
Great Barrier Reef, a coral reef off the northeastern coast of Queensland, Australia: length, 1,250 mi.
Great Basin, a plateau between the Sierra Nevada and the Wasatch Mountains, covering eastern California, western Utah, and most of Nevada: area, 210,000 sq. mi.: many rivers and streams flow into it, forming lakes with no ultimate outlet to the sea.
Great Bear, the constellation Ursa Major: its seven brightest stars form the Big Dipper.
Great Bear Lake, a lake in Northwest Territories, Canada: area, 11,800 sq. mi.
Great Britain, England, Wales, and Scotland: a division of the United Kingdom and the British Commonwealth of Nations: area, 89,041 sq. mi.; pop., 50,622,000; capital, London: abbreviated **Gt. Brit., Gr. Brit., Gt.Br., Gr.Br., G.B.**
great calorie, see **calorie** (sense 2).
great circle, any circle described on the surface of the earth or other sphere so that its plane passes through the center of the sphere.
great-cir·cle sailing (grāt′sũr′k'l), navigation along any great circle of the earth, as the equator: such a course is the shortest between any two points on the earth's surface.
great·coat (grāt′kōt′), *n.* a heavy overcoat.
Great Commoner, nickname used of William Pitt, Henry Clay, Thaddeus Stevens, and William Jennings Bryan.
great Dane, any of a breed of large, powerful dog with short, smooth hair: also **Great Dane.**
Great Divide, 1. a principal mountain watershed; specifically, the Rocky Mountains. 2. *a)* death. *b)* any important crisis.
Great Dividing Range, a mountain system along the eastern coast of Australia.
great·en (grāt′'n), *v.t. & v.i.* [Archaic], to make or become great or greater.
Great·er (grāt′ẽr), *adj.* designating a large city together with its suburbs: as, *Greater* Cleveland, *Greater* London.
Greater Antilles, a group of islands in the West Indies, including the islands of Cuba, Jamaica, Hispaniola, and Puerto Rico: see **West Indies,** map.
Great Falls, a city in central Montana, on the Missouri River: pop., 55,000.
great go, [British Univ. Slang], the final examination for the bachelor's degree: also **greats.**
great-grand·child (grāt′gran′chīld′, grāt′grand′chīld′), *n.* a child of any of one's grandchildren.
great-grand·daugh·ter (grāt′gran′dô′tẽr, grāt′grand′dô′tẽr), *n.* a daughter of any of one's grandchildren.
great-grand·fa·ther (grāt′gran′fä′*th*ẽr, grāt′grand′fä′*th*ẽr), *n.* the father of any of one's grandparents.
great-grand·moth·er (grāt′gran′mu*th*′ẽr, grāt′grand′mu*th*′ẽr), *n.* the mother of any of one's grandparents.
great-grand·par·ent (grāt′gran′pâr′ənt, grāt′grand′pâr′ənt), *n.* a parent of any of one's grandparents.
great-grand·son (grāt′gran′sun′, grāt′grand′sun′), *n.* a son of any of one's grandchildren.
great-great- (grāt′grāt′), a combining form used with nouns of relationship to indicate *two degrees of removal in an ascending* or *descending scale*, as in *great-great-grandparent, great-great-grandson.* Each additional *great-* indicates one further degree of removal.
great gross, twelve gross: abbreviated **g.gr.**
great·heart·ed (grāt′här′tid), *adj.* 1. brave; fearless; courageous. 2. generous; magnanimous; unselfish.
great horned owl, a large North American owl with two prominent tufts of feathers on its head.
Great Khing·an (khiŋ′än′), a mountain range in western Manchuria.
Great Lakes, a chain of fresh-water lakes in Canada and the United States, emptying into the St. Lawrence River; Lakes Superior, Michigan, Huron, Erie, Ontario, and, sometimes, St. Clair.
great laurel, a large shrub of the rhododendron family, with thick, oblong, dark-green leaves and delicate, pink flowers in cone-shaped clusters.
great·ly (grāt′li), *adv.* 1. in a great manner. 2. very much; highly.
Great Miami, the Miami, a river in western Ohio.
Great Mogul, 1. the title of the ruler of the empire established by the Mongols in India in the 16th century; hence, 2. [g- m-], a person of importance.
great-neph·ew (grāt′nef′ū, grāt′nev′ū), *n.* a grandson of one's brother or sister; grandnephew.
great-niece (grāt′nēs′), *n.* a granddaughter of one's brother or sister; grandniece.
Great Plains, the large area of low valleys and plains east of the Rocky Mountains in the United States and Canada.
great primer, a large size of type, 18 point: abbreviated **g.p.**
Great Russia, central and northeastern European Russia.
Great Salt Lake, a shallow salt lake in northern Utah: area, 2,360 sq. mi.
Great Sandy Desert, 1. a large desert in northwestern Australia. 2. Rub' al Khali, a desert in Arabia.
Great Schism, the division or conflict in the Roman Catholic Church from 1378 to 1417, when there were two rival popes, one at Avignon, the other at Rome.
great seal, 1. the chief seal of a nation, state, etc., with which official papers are stamped as proof of their approval. 2. [G- S-], *a)* the Lord Chancellor of Great Britain, keeper of the great seal. *b)* his position.
Great Slave Lake, a lake in southern Northwest Territories, Canada: area, 11,172 sq. mi.
Great Smoky Mountains, a mountain range of the Appalachians, between Tennessee and North Carolina: highest peak, Clingmans Dome, 6,642 ft.: site of Great Smoky Mountains National Park: area, 715 sq. mi.: also **Smoky Mountains.**
Great Spirit, the chief god of some American Indian tribes.
Great St. Bernard, a mountain pass and hospice in the Pennine Alps, between southwestern Switzerland and Italy: height, 8,110 ft.
great-un·cle (grāt′uŋ′k'l), *n.* a brother of any of one's grandparents; granduncle.
Great Victoria Desert, a large desert in southern Australia.
Great Vowel Shift, the complicated series of sound developments (c. 1450 to c. 1830) which changed the vowel system of Middle English into that of Modern English: the Middle English system was characterized by contrasts of short with long vowels and by values of the vowel symbols roughly resembling those found in Modern French and German; overdifferentiation of the Middle English high vowels caused the long vowels to become diphthongs and the short vowels to be lowered in tongue position: also **Great Sound Shift.**
Great Wall of China, the Chinese Wall.
Great War, World War I.
Great Week, in the *Orthodox Eastern Church*, the week preceding Easter; Holy Week.
Great White Father, the name given by the American Indians to the president of the United States.
Great White Way, the theater district in New York City, on Broadway near Times Square: so called from its bright lights.
great willow herb, a plant of the primrose family, with long leaves and purple flowers in a single spike.
great world, [after Fr. *grand monde*], fashionable society and its way of life.
Great Yarmouth, a city on the eastern coast of England: pop., 51,000: also **Yarmouth.**
greaves (grēvz), *n.pl.* [whaling term < LG. *greven*, pl.,

MD. *grēve* (whence Dan. *grever*); basic sense "coarse elements that will not melt"; base as in *great, grit*], the sediment of skin, etc. formed when animal fat is melted down for tallow; cracklings.

greaves (grēvz), ***n.pl.*** [ME. *greves, grevis;* OFr. *greve,* shin, shin armor; prob. < Gmc.; same base as prec.], armor for the legs from the ankle to the knee: see **armor,** illus.

grebe (grēb), ***n.*** [*pl.* GREBES (grēbz), GREBE; see PLURAL, II, D, 1], [< Fr. *grèbe*], any of a group of diving and swimming birds of the loon family, with partially webbed feet and legs set far back on the body.

Gre·cian (grē'shən), ***adj.*** [< L. *Graecia,* Greece; + *-an*], Greek. ***n.*** 1. a Greek. 2. a scholar of Greek. Abbreviated **Gr.**

Grecian bend, the angle at which women walked, with the body bent forward at the waist, when bustles and the wasp waist were fashionable.

Grecian profile, a profile in which the nose and forehead form a straight line.

Gre·cism (grē'siz'm), ***n.*** [Fr. *grécisme;* ML. *Graecismus* < L. *Graeci,* the Greeks], 1. an idiom of the Greek language. 2. an imitation of this. 3. the spirit of Greek culture; Hellenism. Also spelled **Graecism.**

Gre·cize (grē'sīz), ***v.t.*** [GRECIZED (-sīzd), GRECIZING], [Fr. *gréciser;* L. *Graecizare* < *Graeci,* the Greeks], to make Greek; give a Greek form to; Hellenize. ***v.i.*** to imitate the Greeks in language, manner, etc.; follow Greek custom. Also spelled **Graecize.**

Gre·co- (grē'kō), [< L. *Graecus*], a combining form meaning: 1. *Greek, Greeks.* 2. *Greek and.* Also spelled **Graeco-.**

Gre·co-Ro·man (grē'kō-rō'mən), ***adj.*** of or influenced by both Greece and Rome: as, *Greco-Roman* art.

gree (grē), ***n.*** [ME. *gre;* OFr. *gre, gred* (Fr. *gré,* pleasure, good will) < L. *gratum,* neut. of *gratus;* see GRACE, *n.*], [Archaic], 1. good will. 2. satisfaction for an injury received: only in *do* (or *make*) *gree.*

Greece (grēs), ***n.*** a country in the southern Balkan Peninsula, on the Mediterranean: area, 50,147 sq. mi.; pop., 8,300,000; capital, Athens: abbreviated **Gr.**

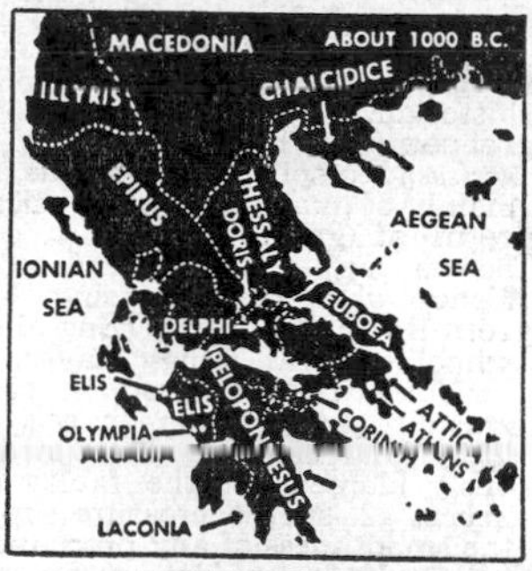

ANCIENT GREECE

greed (grēd), ***n.*** [back-formation < *greedy*], excessive desire for acquiring or having; desire for more than one needs or deserves; greediness; avarice; cupidity.

greed·i·ly (grēd''l-i), ***adv.*** in a greedy manner.

greed·i·ness (grēd'i-nis), ***n.*** the quality of being greedy.

greed·y (grēd'i), ***adj.*** [GREEDIER (-i-ēr), GREEDIEST (-i-ist)], [ME. *gredie;* AS. *grædig* < base of *græd* (in *grædum,* eagerly) + *-ig* (see -Y); akin to Goth. *grēdags,* lit., hungry; IE. base **ĝher-,* to desire, crave], 1. wanting excessively to have or acquire; desiring more than one needs or deserves; avaricious; covetous. 2. wanting to eat and drink too much; gluttonous; voracious.

SYN.—**greedy** implies an insatiable desire to possess or acquire something to an amount inordinately beyond what one needs or deserves and is the broadest of the terms compared here; **avaricious** stresses greed for money or riches and often connotes miserliness; **grasping** suggests an unscrupulous eagerness for gain that manifests itself in a seizing upon every opportunity to get what one desires; **acquisitive** stresses the exertion of effort in acquiring or accumulating wealth or material possessions to an excessive amount; **covetous** implies greed for something that another person rightfully possesses.

Greek (grēk), ***n.*** [ME. & AS. *Grec, Crec;* L. *Graecus;* Gr. *Graikos*], 1. a native or inhabitant of ancient or modern Greece. 2. the Hellenic language of Greece, ancient or modern: see also **Late Greek, Medieval Greek, Modern Greek.** 3. [Slang], a member of a Greek-letter fraternity. 4. [Obs.], a close companion. ***adj.*** [ME. *Grec* < the *n.* & < Fr. *grec* < L. *Graecus*], of ancient or modern Greece, its people, language, or culture. Abbreviated **Gr., Gk.** (in *adj.* & *n.* senses 1 & 2).

be Greek to one, to be incomprehensible or unintelligible to one.

Greek Catholic, 1. a person belonging to an Orthodox Eastern Church. 2. a Uniat Greek or Byzantine.

Greek cross, a cross with four equal arms at right angles: see **cross,** illus.

Greek fire, [so called from its first use by Greeks of Byzantium], an incendiary material used in ancient and medieval warfare, said to have burned in water.

Greek-let·ter fraternity (grēk'let'ēr), any American society, especially a student society, whose name is designated by a combination of Greek letters.

Greek Orthodox Church, 1. the established church of Greece, an autonomous part of the Orthodox Eastern Church. 2. the Orthodox Eastern Church: popularly so called. Also **Greek Church.**

Greek rite, the religious ritual of the Orthodox Eastern Church, as distinguished from that of the Roman Catholic Church.

Gree·ley, Horace (grē'li), 1811–1872; American journalist and politician.

green (grēn), ***adj.*** [ME. & AS. *grene* < same base as *grass, grow;* akin to G. *grün,* D. *groen* (cf. GREENING), etc.], 1. of the color that is characteristic of growing grass. 2. overspread with or characterized by green foliage: as, a *green* field. 3. keeping the green grass of summer; snowless; mild: as, a *green* December. 4. sickly or bilious, as from illness, fear, etc. 5. flourishing; active: as, recollections of his youth were still *green* in his mind. 6. unripe; not mature. 7. inexperienced; not trained. 8. easily imposed on or deceived; simple; naive. 9. not dried, seasoned, or cured; unprocessed. 10. fresh; new. 11. [cf. GREEN-EYED], [Colloq.], jealous. ***n.*** 1. the color of growing grass; any color between blue and yellow in the spectrum: green can be produced by blending blue and yellow pigments. 2. any green pigment or dye. 3. anything colored green, especially clothing: as, the wearing of the *green.* 4. *pl.* green leaves, branches, sprigs, etc., used for ornamentation. 5. *pl.* green leafy vegetables, as kale, spinach, etc. 6. an area of smooth turf set aside for special purposes: as, a village *green,* a bowling *green.* 7. in *golf, a*) the plot of carefully tended turf immediately surrounding each of the holes to facilitate putting. *b*) an entire golf course. ***v.t. & v.i.*** to make or become green.

green with envy, very envious.

the Green, green as the symbol of Irish nationalism; Ireland's national color.

Green, John Richard, 1837–1883; English historian.

Green, Paul Eliot, 1894– ; American playwright.

Green, William, 1873–1952; president of the American Federation of Labor (1924–1952).

green algae, algae in which the chlorophyll predominates.

green·back (grēn'bak'), ***n.*** any piece of United States paper money printed in green ink on the back.

Green·back·er (grēn'bak'ēr), ***n.*** a member of the Greenback Party.

Greenback Party, the Independent Party, a political party in the United States after the Civil War, advocating government paper money as the only currency.

Green Bay, 1. an arm of Lake Michigan indenting northeastern Wisconsin: length, 90 mi. 2. a city in Wisconsin, on this bay: pop., 63,000.

green-blue (grēn'blōō'), ***n.*** the color in the spectrum exactly between primary green and primary blue.

green·bri·er (grēn'brī'ēr), ***n.*** any of various woody, climbing vines of the lily family, with spiny stems.

green corn, unripe ears of sweet corn, used for cooking and eating.

green dragon, an American wild flower of the arum family, similar to the jack-in-the-pulpit but with digitate leaves, a very long spadix, and a greenish spathe.

Greene, Nathanael (grēn), 1742–1786; American general in the Revolutionary War.

Greene, Robert, 1560?–1592; English dramatist and miscellaneous writer.

green·er·y (grēn'ēr-i), ***n.*** [*pl.* GREENERIES (-iz)], 1. green vegetation; verdure. 2. a greenhouse.

green-eyed (grēn'īd'), ***adj.*** 1. having green eyes. 2. [cf. *Othello* III, iii], jealous.

green·finch (grēn'finch'), ***n.*** 1. a finch with olive-green and yellow feathers, native to Europe; green linnet; grosbeak. 2. the Texas sparrow.

green·gage (grēn'gāj'), ***n.*** [after Sir William *Gage,* who introduced it into England from France, c. 1725], a large plum with golden-green skin and flesh.

green glass, coarse, ordinary glass of a greenish color, used for bottles, etc.

green·gro·cer (grēn'grō'sēr), ***n.*** [British], a retail dealer in fresh vegetables and fruit.

green·gro·cer·y (grēn'grō'sēr-i), ***n.*** [*pl.* GREENGROCERIES (-iz)], [British], 1. a retail store where fresh vegetables and fruits are sold. 2. *pl.* things sold by a greengrocer.

green·heart (grēn'härt'), ***n.*** 1. any of various West Indian trees whose wood is valued for its hardness. 2. the wood.

green·horn (grēn'hôrn'), ***n.*** [prob. orig. with reference to a young animal with immature horns], 1. an inexperienced person; beginner; novice. 2. a person easily deceived; dupe. 3. [Colloq.], a recently arrived immigrant. Humorous or patronizing term.

green·house (grēn'hous'), ***n.*** a building whose roof and sides are made largely of glass and in which the temperature and humidity can be regulated for the cultivation of delicate or out-of-season plants; hothouse.

fat, āpe, bâre, cär; ten, ēven, hêre, ovẽr; is, bīte; lot, gō, hôrn, tōōl, look; oil, out; up, ūse, fũr; get; joy; yet; chin; she; thin, *th*en; zh, leisure; ŋ, ring; ə for *a* in *ago, e* in *agent, i* in *sanity, o* in *comply, u* in *focus;* ' as in *able* (ā'b'l); Fr. bål; ë, Fr. coeur; ö, Fr. feu; Fr. mo*n*; ô, Fr. coq; ü, Fr. duc; H, G. ich; kh, G. doch. See pp. x–xii. ‡ foreign; * hypothetical; < derived from.

green·ing (grēn′iŋ), *n.* [MD. *groeninc* < *groen;* see GREEN], any of various apples having greenish-yellow skins when ripe.

green·ish (grēn′ish), *adj.* somewhat green.

Green·land (grēn′lənd), *n.* [orig. so called (ON. *Grönland*, 986 A.D.) to attract settlers], a Danish island northeast of North America: it is the world's largest island: area, 736,518 sq. mi. (ice-free land, 31,284 sq. mi.); pop., 30,000; capital, Godthaab.

Greenland Sea, an extension of the Atlantic, east of Greenland.

green lead ore, pyromorphite, a crystalline mineral found in lead veins.

green·let (grēn′lit), *n.* a small American songbird with greenish feathers; vireo.

green light, 1. the green phase of a traffic light, indicating permission to go ahead; hence, 2. [Colloq.], authorization to proceed with some undertaking: usually in *give* (or *get*) *the green light.*

green·ling (grēn′liŋ), *n.* any of a group of large, flesh-eating fishes with long dorsal fins, living in the North Pacific, especially off the Aleutian Islands.

green manure, 1. a crop of growing plants, as clover, plowed under while still green to fertilize the soil. 2. fresh manure; manure not yet decayed.

green monkey, a small, long-tailed, African monkey with greenish hair; grivet; vervet.

Green Mountain Boys, the Vermont soldiers organized and led by Ethan Allen in the Revolutionary War.

Green Mountains, a mountain range extending the length of Vermont: highest peak, Mt. Mansfield, 4,364 ft.

Green Mountain State, Vermont.

green·ness (grēn′nis), *n.* the quality or state of being green.

Green·ock (grēn′ək, gren′ək), *n.* a seaport in Scotland, on the Firth of Clyde: pop., 78,000.

green·ock·ite (grēn′ək-īt′), *n.* [after C. M. Cathcart, Lord *Greenock* (1783–1859), who found some of the crystals in 1840; + *-ite*], a rare yellow sulfide of cadmium, CdS, occurring usually as a crust on the earth.

green onion, an immature onion with a long stalk and green leaves, eaten raw as a relish or in salads; scallion.

Gree·nough, Horatio (grē′nō), 1805–1852; American sculptor.

green pepper, the green, immature fruit of the sweet red pepper, eaten as a vegetable.

Green River, a river in Wyoming and Utah, flowing into the Colorado: length, 730 mi.

green·room (grēn′rōōm′, grēn′room′), *n.* a waiting room in some theaters, for use by actors and actresses when they are off stage.

green·sand (grēn′sand′), *n.* a green, sandy deposit containing much glauconite.

Greens·bor·o (grēnz′bũr′ō), *n.* a city in north central North Carolina: pop., 120,000.

green·shank (grēn′shaŋk′), *n.* a European sandpiper with greenish legs.

green·sick·ness (grēn′sik′nis), *n.* chlorosis, a kind of anemia, which gives the complexion a greenish tinge.

green soap, a soft soap made of potash, linseed oil, and alcohol, used in treating skin diseases: so called because originally greenish.

green·stone (grēn′stōn′), *n.* 1. any of various dark-green rocks, as diorite. 2. an inferior kind of jade.

green·sward (grēn′swôrd′), *n.* green grass or turf.

green tea, tea prepared from leaves not fermented before drying: distinguished from *black tea.*

green thumb, an apparent talent or skill in growing plants easily.

Green·ville (grēn′vil), *n.* 1. a city in northwestern South Carolina: pop., 66,000. 2. a city in Mississippi: pop., 42,000.

green vitriol, copperas; crystallized ferrous sulfate.

Green·wich (grin′ij, gren′ich), *n.* 1. a borough of London, located on the Prime Meridian: formerly the site of an astronomical observatory: pop., 91,000. 2. (gren′ich, grēn′wich), a town in southwestern Connecticut, on Long Island Sound: pop., 54,000.

Greenwich time, mean solar time of the meridian at Greenwich, England, used as the basis for standard time throughout most of the world.

Green·wich Village (gren′ich), a section of New York City, on the lower west side of Manhattan, noted as a center for artists, authors, etc.: formerly a village.

green·wood (grēn′wood′), *n.* a forest in leaf.

greet (grēt), *v.t.* [ME. *greten;* AS. *gretan, grætan;* akin to D. *groetan*, G. *grüssen;* IE. base **ghrēd-*, to call out], 1. to speak or write to with expressions of friendliness, respect, pleasure, etc., as in meeting or by letter; hail; welcome. 2. to meet, receive, address, or acknowledge (a person, utterance, or event) in a specified way: as, the speech was *greeted* with cheers, he was *greeted* by a rifle shot. 3. to come or appear to; make itself manifest to; meet: as, the aroma of coffee *greeted* us.

greet (grēt), *v.i.* [ME. *greten;* AS. *gretan;* akin to Goth. *gretan*], [Archaic or Dial.], to weep; lament.

greet·ing (grēt′iŋ), *n.* 1. the act or words of a person who greets; salutation; welcome. 2. a message of regards from someone absent.

greg·a·rine (greg′ə-rīn′, greg′ẽr-in), *adj.* [< Mod. L. *Gregarina*, the type genus < L. *gregarius* (see GREGARIOUS); name suggested by the Fr. zoologist Leon Dufour], of a group of parasitic protozoans that live in insects, crustaceans, earthworms, etc.

gre·gar·i·ous (gri-gâr′i-əs), *adj.* [L. *gregarius*, belonging to a flock < *grex, gregis*, a flock, herd], 1. living in herds or flocks. 2. fond of the company of others; sociable. 3. having to do with a herd, flock, or crowd. 4. in *botany*, growing in clusters.

gre·go (grē′gō, grā′gō), *n.* [< It. *Greco* or Port. *Grego*, both < L. *Graecus*, Greek], a short cloak of coarse cloth with an attached hood, worn in the Levant.

Greg·or (greg′ẽr), a masculine name: see **Gregory.**

Gre·go·ri·an (gri-gôr′i-ən, gri-gō′ri-ən), *adj.* of or introduced by Pope Gregory I or Pope Gregory XIII.

Gregorian calendar, a corrected form of the Julian calendar, introduced by Pope Gregory XIII in 1582 and now used in most countries of the world: it provides for an ordinary year of 365 days and a leap year of 366 days every fourth even year, exclusive of century years, which are leap years only if exactly divisible by 400.

Gregorian chant, the ritual plain song introduced by Pope Gregory I and used in the Roman Catholic Church: it is unharmonized, unaccompanied, and without meter.

Greg·o·ry (greg′ẽr-i), [LL. *Gregorius;* Gr. *Grēgorios*, lit., vigilant, hence, watchman < dial. form of *egeirein*, to awaken], a masculine name: diminutive, *Greg;* variant, *Gregor;* equivalents, Fr. *Gregoire*, G. & Scand. *Gregor*, It. & Sp. *Gregorio.*

Gregory I, Saint, 540?–604 A.D.; Pope (590–604 A.D.); introduced the Gregorian Chant: called *the Great.*

Gregory VII, Saint, (born *Hildebrand*), 1020?–1085; Pope (1073–1085): his day is May 25.

Gregory XIII, Saint, (born *Ugo Buoncompagni*), 1502–1585; Pope (1572–1585): see **Gregorian calendar.**

Greg·o·ry, Lady **Augusta** (greg′ẽr-i), (born *Augusta Persse*), 1852–1932; Irish playwright and poet.

Gregory of Nys·sa, Saint (nis′ə), 331?–396? A.D.; brother of Basil the Great; father of the Greek Church.

Gregory of Tours, Saint, 538?–593 A.D.; Frankish historian.

grei·sen (grī′z'n), *n.* [G.; said to be var. of *greiss* < dial. *greissen*, to split], a crystalline, igneous rock consisting mainly of quartz and white mica.

gre·mi·al (grē′mi-əl), *n.* [LL. *gremialis* < L. *gremium*, bosom, lap], a lap cloth placed across the knees of a bishop when he sits during the celebration of Mass.

grem·lin (grem′lin), *n.* [Eng. dial. < Fr. dial. *grimelin*, schoolboy, brat, stingy player, dim < *grimaud*, dunce, scribbler, pedant; prob. < stem of *grimoire*, earlier *gramoire*, Latin grammar; see GRAMMAR], 1. an imaginary small creature whose meddling antics are humorously blamed for the faulty operation of airplanes; hence, 2. such a creature supposed to interfere with the smoothness of any procedure.

Gre·na·da (gri-nā′də), *n.* an island of the Windward group, West Indies Federation: area, 120 sq. mi.; pop., 85,000; capital, St. George's: abbreviated **Gren.**

gre·nade (gri-nād′), *n.* [Fr.; OFr., pomegranate; Sp. *granada*, lit., something containing grains or seeds, grenade < L. *granatus*, grained, having seeds < *granum*, a grain, seed], 1. a small bomb detonated by a fuse and thrown by hand or fired from a rifle. 2. a glass container to be thrown so that it will break and disperse the chemicals inside: used for putting out fires, spreading tear gas, etc.

gren·a·dier (gren′ə-dêr′), *n.* [Fr. < *grenade*], 1. originally, an infantry soldier employed to carry and throw grenades. 2. a member of a special regiment of corps, as of the Grenadier Guards of the British Army. 3. any of a group of deep-sea fishes related to the cod, with a long, tapering tail and soft fins.

gren·a·dine (gren′ə-dēn′, gren′ə-dēn′), *n.* [Fr., dim. of *grenade*, pomegranate], a sirup made from pomegranate juice, used for flavoring some alcoholic drinks.

gren·a·dine (gren′ə-dēn′, gren′ə-dēn′), *n.* [Fr. < *grenade* (see GRENADE): from being spotted with "grains"], a thin, loosely woven cotton, wool, silk, or rayon cloth, used for blouses, dresses, curtains, etc.

Gren·a·dines (gren′ə-dēnz′), *n.* a group of small islands of the Windward group, West Indies Federation: area, 30 sq. mi.; pop., 7,000.

Gren·del (gren′d'l), *n.* the male monster slain by Beowulf: see **Beowulf.**

Gren·fell, Sir **Wilfred Thom·a·son** (tom′ə-s'n gren′-fel), 1865–1940; English physician, writer, and missionary to Labrador.

Gre·no·ble (grə-nō′b'l; Fr. grə-nô′bl′), *n.* a city in southeastern France: pop., 116,000.

Gren·ville, George (gren′vil), 1712–1770; English statesman; prime minister (1763–1765).

Grenville, Sir **Richard,** 1541?–1591; British naval commander and hero.

Gresh·am's law (gresh′əmz), [after the founder of the English Royal Exchange, Sir Thomas *Gresham* (1519-1579), who explained the principle to Queen Elizabeth in 1558], the theory that when two or more kinds of money of equal denomination but unequal intrinsic value are in circulation at the same time, the one of greater value will tend to be hoarded or exported; popularly, the principle that bad money will drive good money out of circulation.

gres·so·ri·al (gre-sôr′i-əl, gre-sō′ri-əl), *adj.* [< L. *gressus*, pp. of *gradi*, to step, go; see GRADE], adapted for walking, as the feet of certain birds and insects.

gres·so·ri·ous (gre-sôr′i-əs, gre-sō′ri-əs), *adj.* gressorial.

Gret·a (gret′ə, grē′tə), [Sw. or < G. *Grete*], a feminine name: see **Margaret.**

Gretch·en (grech′'n), [G.], a feminine name: see **Margaret.**

Gret·na Green (gret′nə), 1. a border village in Scotland where, formerly, many eloping English couples went to be married. 2. any similar village or town.

Greuze, Jean Bap·tiste (zhän bä′tēst′ grëz), 1725–1805; French painter.

grew (grōō), [ME. *greu;* AS. *greow*], past tense of **grow.**

grew·some (grōō′səm), *adj.* gruesome.

grey (grā), *adj., n., v.t. & v.i.* gray: British spelling.

Grey, Charles (grā), second Earl Grey, 1764–1845; English statesman; prime minister (1830–1834).

Grey, Sir Edward, Viscount Grey of Fallodon, 1862–1933; English statesman; foreign secretary (1905–1916); ambassador to the United States (1919–1920).

Grey, Lady **Jane,** 1537–1554; queen of England (July 10–19, 1553); beheaded.

Grey, Zane (zān), 1875–1939; American novelist.

grey·hound (grā′hound′), *n.* [ME. *grihunde, greihund;* AS. *grighund* & ON. *greyhundr;* 1st element (AS. *grig-* for **grieg-*, ON. *grey*, bitch, coward < IE. **ghrū-*, var. of **gher-*, to shine, as in *gray*) prob. means "gray animal," hence "dog"], 1. any of a breed of tall, slender, swift hound with a narrow, pointed head. 2. a swift ocean steamship: in full, **ocean greyhound.** Also (rarely) spelled **grayhound.**

GREYHOUND (28 in. high at shoulder)

grib·ble (grib′'l), *n.* [prob. dim. < base of *grub*], a small sea animal, related to the shrimp, crab, etc., that bores into timber under water and destroys it.

grid (grid), *n.* [short for *gridiron*], 1. a framework of parallel bars; gridiron; grating. 2. in *electricity*, *a)* a lead plate in a storage battery. *b)* an electrode of wire mesh in an electron tube to control the flow of electrons through the tube. *adj.* [Slang], of football.

grid circuit, the part of an electric circuit between the grid and the cathode of an electron tube.

grid condenser, a condenser in series with the grid circuit of an electron tube.

grid current, the flow of electrons between the grid and the cathode of an electron tube.

grid·der (grid′ẽr), *n.* [< *grid, adj.* & *gridiron*], [Slang], a football player.

grid·dle (grid′'l), *n.* [ME. *gredil, gridell;* Anglo-Fr. *gridil* < OFr. **gredil*, var. of *graïl* < L. *craticulum*, var. of *craticula*, small gridiron < *cratis*, wickerwork; see CRATE], a heavy, flat, metal plate or pan for cooking pancakes, etc. *v.t.* [GRIDDLED (-'ld), GRIDDLING], to cook on a griddle.

grid·dle·cake (grid′'l-kāk′), *n.* a thin, flat batter cake cooked on a griddle; pancake.

gride (grīd), *v.t. & v.i.* [GRIDED (-id), GRIDING], [metathesis of ME. *girden*, to pierce (see GIRD), adopted (< Lydgate) & popularized by Spenser], 1. to scrape or grate with a rasping sound. 2. [Obs.], to pierce or wound. *n.* a harsh, rasping sound made by scraping or grating.

grid·i·ron (grid′ī′ẽrn), *n.* [ME. *gridirne, gredirne*, folk etym. on *irne* (see IRON) < *gredire, gridire*, var. of *gredil;* see GRIDDLE], 1. a framework of metal bars or wires for broiling meat or fish; grill. 2. anything suggesting a gridiron in design. 3. a football field.

grid leak, a high resistance in parallel with a grid condenser to prevent an excess of negative charge on the grid.

grief (grēf), *n.* [ME. *gref, greve;* OFr. *grief, gref*, sorrow, grief < *grever;* see GRIEVE], 1. intense emotional suffering caused by loss, disaster, misfortune, etc.; acute sorrow; deep sadness. 2. a cause or the subject of such suffering. 3. [Obs.], *a)* hardship; suffering; pain. *b)* a cause of any of these. —*SYN.* see **sorrow.**

come to grief, to meet with difficulty or failure.

grief-strick·en (grēf′strik′ən), *adj.* stricken with grief; keenly distressed; sorrowful.

Grieg, Ed·vard (ed′värt grig; Eng. grēg), 1843–1907; Norwegian composer.

griev·ance (grēv′əns), *n.* [ME. *grevance;* OFr. *grevance* < *grever;* see GRIEVE], 1. a circumstance or condition thought to be unjust and ground for complaint or resentment. 2. complaint or resentment, or a ground for this, against a wrong, real or imagined. 3. [Obs.], *a)* the inflicting of injury or hardship. *b)* a cause of injury or hardship. —*SYN.* see **injustice.**

grieve (grēv), *v.t.* [GRIEVED (grēvd), GRIEVING], [ME. *greven;* OFr. *grever;* L. *gravare*, to burden, oppress, grieve < *gravis*, heavy, grievous], 1. to cause to feel grief; afflict with deep, acute sorrow; make sad; distress. 2. [Archaic], to harm; injure. *v.i.* to feel deep, acute sorrow or distress; be sad; mourn; lament.

griev·ous (grēv′əs), *adj.* [ME. *grevous;* OFr. *grevous* < *grever;* see GRIEVE], 1. causing grief. 2. showing or characterized by grief: as, a *grievous* cry. 3. causing physical suffering; hard to bear; severe: as, *grievous* pain. 4. deplorable; atrocious: as, a *grievous* crime.

griffe (grif), *n.* [Fr., lit., a claw < *griffer*, to seize < OHG. *grifan*, to grasp; cf. GRIPE], a clawlike ornament at the base of a column.

griffe, griff (grif), *n.* [Fr.; Am. Sp. *grifo*, orig., griffin; see GRIFFIN], [Dial.], 1. the child of a Negro and a mulatto. 2. a mulatto. 3. a person of Negro and American Indian ancestry.

grif·fin (grif′in), *n.* [ME. *griffon, griffyn;* OFr. *grifoun;* < OHG. or It. *grifo;* both < L. *gryphus, gryps;* Gr. *gryps*, griffin < *grypos*, hooked, curved: prob. so called from its hooked beak], 1. a mythical animal with the body and hind legs of a lion, and the head and wings of an eagle. 2. a representation of this used in heraldry. Also **griffon, gryphon.**

GRIFFIN

grif·fin (grif′in), *n.* [prob. < *griffin* (animal), influenced by native word], an Occidental recently arrived in the East, especially India.

Grif·fith (grif′ith), [W. *Gruffydd* < L. *Rufus;* see RUFUS], a masculine name.

Grif·fith, David Wark (wôrk grif′ith), 1875–1948; American motion-picture producer and director.

grif·fon (grif′ən), *n.* [Fr.; prob. a special use of *griffon*, griffin], 1. a griffin. 2. any of a breed of wire-haired European dogs.

grift·er (grif′tẽr), *n.* [prob. altered < *grafter*], [Slang], a person who runs a gambling device at a carnival, resort, etc.; confidence man; petty grafter.

grig (grig), *n.* [ME. *grege*, anything diminutive, dwarf; prob. < ON. (cf. Norw. *krek*, Sw. dial. *krik*, little animal) but influenced by *Grig*, earlier contr. of *Gregory*], 1. a lively, animated person. 2. [Obs. or Dial.], a small eel. 3. [Obs. or Dial.], *a)* a grasshopper. *b)* a cricket.

grill (gril), *v.t.* [Fr. *griller* < the *n.*], 1. to cook on a gridiron; broil. 2. to torture by applying heat; hence, 3. to question relentlessly; cross-examine searchingly. *v.i.* to be subjected to grilling. *n.* [Fr. *gril;* OFr. *graïl;* see GRIDDLE], 1. a framework of metal bars or wires for broiling meat or fish; gridiron. 2. [< the *v.*], grilled food. 3. [short for *grillroom*], a grillroom.

GRILL

grill (gril), *n.* a grille.

gril·lage (gril′ij), *n.* [Fr., wirework, grating, frame < *grille;* see GRILLE], a system of beams laid crosswise to form a foundation for a building in soft soil.

grille (gril), *n.* [Fr. < OFr. *graïlle* < L. *craticula;* see GRIDDLE], an open grating of wrought iron, bronze, wood, etc., forming a screen to a door, window, or the like: sometimes spelled **grill.**

‡gril·lé (grē′yā′), *adj.* [Fr., pp. of *griller;* see GRILL (to cook)], 1. grilled. 2. [Fr., pp. of *griller*, to provide with a grille; see GRILLE], having a background of crossed parallel bars: said of lace.

GRILLE

grilled (grild), *adj.* 1. having a grille. 2. cooked on a grill, or gridiron; broiled.

grill·room (gril′rōōm′, gril′room′), *n.* a restaurant, club, or dining room that makes a specialty of grilled foods.

grill·work (gril′wûrk′), *n.* 1. a grille. 2. something resembling a grille.

grilse (grils), *n.* [*pl.* GRILSE, GRILSES (-iz); see PLURAL, II, D, 2], [? < OFr. *grisle*, dim. < *gris*, gray], a young salmon on its first return from the sea to fresh water.

grim (grim), *adj.* [GRIMMER (-ẽr), GRIMMEST (-ist)], [ME.; AS. *grimm;* akin to G. *grimm;* IE. base **ghrem-*, to make a loud sound, roar angrily, seen also in Gr. *brontē*, thunder (cf. BRONTO-) & Eng. *grumble*], 1. fierce; cruel; savage; merciless. 2. hard and unyielding; relentless; stern; resolute: as, *grim* courage. 3. appearing stern, threatening, forbidding, harsh, etc.: as, a *grim* countenance. 4. repellent; uninviting; hideous: as, a *grim* task. 5. dealing with unpleasant subjects; sinister; frightful; ghastly: as, *grim* humor. —*SYN.* see **ghastly.**

gri·mace (gri-mās′), *n.* [Fr.; prob. adapted < OHG. *grimmiza* < base of *grim* (see GRIM)], a distortion of the face; a wry or ugly smile or facial expression of pain, contempt, etc., sometimes intended to amuse. *v.i.* [GRIMACED (-māst′), GRIMACING], to make grimaces.

gri·mal·kin (gri-mal′kin, gri-môl′kin), *n.* [earlier *gray malkin* as if < *gray* + *malkin*, dim. of *Matilda*, etc., as pet name for cat; prob. < Fr. *grimaud;* see GREMLIN], 1. a cat; especially, an old female cat. 2. a malicious old woman.

grime (grīm), *n.* [Early Mod. Eng. < D. or LG.; cf. Fl. *grijmen*, LG. *grēmen*, to blacken, make dirty], dirt, especially sooty dirt, rubbed into a surface, as of the skin. *v.t.* [GRIMED (grīmd), GRIMING], to make very dirty or grimy.

Grimes Golden (grīmz), [short for *Grimes Golden Pippin*, variety grown (c. 1790) by T. P. *Grimes*, W. Va. fruit grower], an autumn eating apple with a yellow skin: also **Grimes.**

grim·i·ly (grīm′ə-li), *adv.* in a grimy manner.

grim·i·ness (grīm′i-nis), *n.* a grimy quality or state.

Grimm, Ja·kob (yä′kôp grim), 1785–1863; German philologist; collected and wrote fairy tales in collaboration with his brother Wilhelm.

Grimm, Wil·helm (vil′helm), 1786–1859; brother of *Jakob;* German philologist and writer.

Grimm's law (grimz), [after Jakob Grimm's formulation (1822) of parallels noticed by R. K. Rask (1818) & himself], a systematic statement of consonantal correspondences between Germanic words derived from Indo-European bases containing stop consonants and the cognate words of Indo-European languages other than Germanic: Grimm's original formulation has been amplified by the further discoveries of H. Grassmann (1862) and K. Verner (1876). The part of Grimm's statement immediately affecting English may be summarized thus: (1) IE. voiceless stops (p, t, k) = Gmc. voiceless fricatives (f, th, h); hence, L. *p*isc-is (cf. *piscatorial*) = *f*ish, L. *t*en-uis (cf. *tenuous*) = *th*in, Gr. *k*ardia (cf. *cardiac*) = *h*eart. (2) IE. voiced aspirated stops (bh, dh, gh) = Gmc. voiced stops (b, d, g) or equivalent fricatives; hence, Sans. *bh*arā-mi, I bear (Gr. *pherō*, L. *fero;* cf. *feretory*) = *b*ear, Sans. *m*ā*dh*u, honey (Gr. *méthu*, wine; cf. *methyl*) = mea*d*, L. *h*ost-is (IE. **ghost-is;* cf. *hostile*) = *g*uest. (3) IE. voiced stops (b,d, g) = Gmc. voiceless stops (p, t, k); hence, Gr. *b*urse (cf. *bursar*) = *p*urse, L. e*d*-ere (cf. *edible*) = ea*t*, L. a*g*er (cf. *agriculture*) = a*c*re. These correspondences show the kinship, stressed in the etymologies of this dictionary, between various native English words and the English words borrowed from the Classical or Romance languages.

Grims·by (grimz′bi), *n.* a seaport in northeastern England: pop., 89,000 (est. 1946).

grim·y (grīm′i), *adj.* [GRIMIER (-i-ẽr), GRIMIEST (-i-ist)], covered with or full of grime; very dirty. —*SYN.* see **dirty.**

grin (grin), *v.i.* [GRINNED (grind), GRINNING], [ME. *grennien, grennen;* AS. *grennian*, to gnash or bare the teeth; akin to OHG. *grennan*, to mutter, MHG. *grennen*, to grin; < or influenced by the base of AS. *granian*, to howl (see GROAN) or of AS. *granu* (OHG. *grana*), mustache], 1. to smile broadly. 2. to draw back the lips and show the teeth in pain, scorn, foolishness, etc. *v.t.* to express by means of a broad smile: as, he *grinned* his approval. *n.* 1. the act of grinning. 2. a facial expression resulting from grinning. —*SYN.* see **smile.**

grind (grīnd), *v.t.* [GROUND (ground), GRINDING], [ME. *grinden;* AS. *grindan;* akin to (rare) D. *grenden;* IE. base **ghren-*, to rub away, pulverize], 1. to crush into bits or fine particles between two hard surfaces; pulverize. 2. to afflict with cruelty, hardship, etc.; crush; oppress: as, a people *ground* by tyranny. 3. to sharpen, shape, or smooth by friction. 4. to press down or together with a crushing, turning motion; rub harshly or gratingly: as, he *ground* his teeth, she *ground* her heel into the dirt. 5. to operate by turning the crank of: as, *grind* a coffee mill. 6. to make or produce by grinding. 7. [Colloq.], to teach with great effort: as, the boy's teacher had to *grind* the lesson into his head. *v.i.* 1. to perform the act of grinding something. 2. to be capable of being ground: as, some wheats *grind* better than others. 3. to grate. 4. [Colloq.], to work or study hard and steadily. *n.* 1. the act or operation of grinding. 2. a long, difficult, tedious task or study; drudgery. 3. [Colloq.], a student who studies very hard. —*SYN.* see **work.**

grin·de·li·a (grin-dē′li-ə), *n.* [Mod. L., after Hieronymus *Grindel* (1776–1836), professor of botany at Riga], any of a group of coarse plants with large, yellow flowers: the dried stems and leaves are used medicinally in the treatment of bronchitis, asthma, and coughs.

grind·er (grīn′dẽr), *n.* [ME. & AS. *grindere*], 1. a person who grinds; especially, one whose work is sharpening tools, etc. 2. a thing that grinds; specifically, *a*) any of various machines for crushing or sharpening. *b*) a molar tooth. *c*) *pl.* [Colloq.], the teeth.

grind·er·y (grīn′dẽr-i), *n.* 1. [*pl.* GRINDERIES (-iz)], a place where the grinding of tools, etc. is done. 2. [British], leatherworkers' equipment and material.

grind·stone (grīnd′stōn′), *n.* 1. originally, a millstone. 2. a revolving stone disk for sharpening bladed tools or shaping and polishing things.

keep (or **have** or **put**) **one's nose to the grindstone,** to work hard and steadily.

grin·go (griŋ′gō), *n.* [*pl.* GRINGOS (-gōz)], [Mex. Sp.; Sp. gibberish; said to be altered < *Griego*, Greek], in Latin America, a foreigner, especially an American or Englishman: hostile and contemptuous term.

grip (grip), *n.* [ME.; AS. *gripe*, a clutch, *gripa*, handful < var. of the base of AS. *grīpan* (see GRIPE) with a reduced vowel; akin to G. *griff;* some senses < the *v.*], 1. the act of taking firmly and holding fast with the hand, teeth, an instrument, etc.; secure grasp; firm hold. 2. the manner in which this is done. 3. any special manner of clasping hands by which members of a secret or fraternal society identify each other as such. 4. the power of grasping firmly: as, his hand has lost its *grip*. 5. the power of understanding; mental grasp. 6. firm control; mastery: as, in the *grip* of disease, get a *grip* on yourself. 7. a mechanical contrivance for clutching or grasping. 8. the part by which a tool weapon, etc. is grasped in the hand; handle. 9. [prob. < or after D.], a small bag for holding clothes, etc. in traveling; valise. 10. a sudden, intense pain. 11. [Slang], in a motion-picture studio, a stagehand. 12. in *sports*, the manner of holding a bat, club, racket, etc. *v.t.* [GRIPPED or GRIPT (gript), GRIPPING], 1. to take firmly and hold fast with the hand, teeth, an instrument, etc. 2. to give a grip (sense 3) to. 3. to fasten or join firmly (*to*). 4. to get and hold the attention of. 5. to take hold upon; control (the attention, emotions, etc.). *v.i.* to get a grip.

come to grips, 1. to engage in hand-to-hand fighting. 2. to struggle; try to cope (*with*).

grip (grip), *n.* grippe.

gripe (grīp), *v.t.* [GRIPED (grīpt), GRIPING], [ME. *gripen;* AS. *gripan*, to seize, get hold of; akin to G. *greifen;* IE. base **ghreib-*, to grasp], 1. to grasp; pinch; clutch. 2. to distress; oppress; afflict. 3. to cause sudden, sharp pain in the bowels of. 4. [Slang], to annoy; irritate. *v.i.* 1. to feel sharp pains in the bowels. 2. [Archaic], to get a hold. 3. [Slang], to complain; grumble. *n.* 1. a griping; clutching. 2. control; mastery. 3. the pressure or pain of something distressing or afflicting. 4. *pl.* sudden, sharp pains in the bowels. 5. a handle. 6. a device that grips. 7. [Slang], a complaint.

grip·er (grīp′ẽr), *n.* a person or thing that gripes.

grippe (grip), *n.* [Fr., lit., a seizure < Russ. *chripu*, huskiness], a contagious virus disease like a severe cold, characterized by fever, bronchial inflammation, catarrhal discharge, and intestinal disorder; influenza: also spelled **grip.**

grip·per (grip′ẽr), *n.* a person or thing that grips.

grip·ping (grip′iŋ), *adj.* [ppr. of *grip*], that grips; holding the attention.

grip·ple (grip′′l), *adj.* [ME. *gripel;* AS. *gripul* < base of *gripan;* see GRIPE], [Dial.], miserly; avaricious.

grip·py (grip′i), *adj.* [Colloq.], having the grippe.

grip·sack (grip′sak′), *n.* [*grip* (grasp) + *sack*], a small bag for holding clothes, etc. in traveling; valise.

gript (gript), alternative past tense and past participle of **grip.**

grip·y (grīp′i), *adj.* griping; causing or tending to cause gripes.

Gri·qua (grē′kwə, grik′wə), *n.* [altered < *Grigriqua*, name of a group (also named *Bastaards*) of mixed Dutch and Hottentot blood who settled north of the Orange River under Adam Kok in 1803], a South African mulatto.

gri·saille (gri-zāl′; Fr. grē′zä′y′), *n.* [Fr. < *gris*, gray], a style of painting using only gray tints and giving the effect of sculpture in relief.

Gri·sel·da (gri-zel′də, gri-sel′də), [Fr. or It. < G. *Griseldis, Grishilda;* prob. < OHG. *griez*, sand + *hilda* (see HILDA); lit., prob., battle maid (of) sand], a feminine name. *n.* 1. the heroine of various medieval romances, notably the "Clerk's Tale" in Chaucer's *Canterbury Tales*, famous for her meek, long-suffering patience. 2. any patient, meek, long-suffering woman.

gris·e·ous (gris′i-əs, griz′i-əs), *adj.* [ML. *griseus*], gray; mottled gray.

gri·sette (gri-zet′), *n.* [orig., gray woolen cloth used for dresses worn by French working girls < Fr. *gris*, gray;

cf. GRISAILLE], a French working girl or shop girl.
gris·kin (gris′kin), *n.* [prob. < obs. *grice*, pig (ME. *gris*; ON. *griss*, young pig, hog) + *-kin*], [British], the lean section of pork loin.
gris·li·ness (griz′li-nis), *n.* the quality or condition of being grisly.
gris·ly (griz′li), *adj.* [GRISLIER (-li-ẽr), GRISLIEST (-li-ist)], [ME. *grislich, greslie*, etc.; AS. *grislic* (akin to OFris. *grislyk*) < base of *a-grisan*, to shudder with fear], terrifying; horrible; ghastly. —*SYN.* see **ghastly.**
gris·ly (gris′li), *adj.* gristly.
Gri·sons (grē′zôn′), *n.* a canton of eastern Switzerland: pop., 128,000: German name, *Graubünden.*
grist (grist), *n.* [ME.; AS.; akin to OHG. *grist-* in *grist-grimmon*, to gnash the teeth; IE. **ghred-sti* < base **ghren-*, to rub away, grind down; see GRIND], 1. grain that is to be or has been ground; especially, a batch of such grain. 2. [Colloq.], a quantity or lot.
grist to one's mill, anything that one can use profitably.
gris·tle (gris′'l), *n.* [ME. *gristel;* AS. *gristle* (akin to OFris. *gristel*, etc.); sense analogy with OHG. *krustila* (IE. base **greus-*, to crunch) & D. *knarsbeen*, lit., crunch bone (< *knarsen*, to crunch) suggests derivation < base of AS. *grist* (cf. GRIST)], cartilage; tough, elastic tissue.
grist·li·ness (gris′li-nis), *n.* the quality or condition of being gristly.
gris·tly (gris′li), *adj.* [GRISTLIER (-li-ẽr), GRISTLIEST (-li-ist)], [ME. *gristeli*], 1. of or containing gristle. 2. having the nature of gristle. Also spelled **grisly.**
grist·mill (grist′mil′), *n.* a mill for grinding grain, especially for individual customers.
grit (grit), *n.* [with Early Mod. Eng. vowel shortening < ME. *grete;* AS. *greot;* akin to G. *griess;* IE. base **ghrēu-*, to grind down, crush to pieces, seen also in *great, grits*], 1. rough, hard particles of sand, stone, etc. 2. the texture of stone, with regard to the fineness or coarseness of its grain. 3. a hard, coarse sandstone. 4. [orig. < *hard grit*, hard stone], obstinate courage; brave perseverance; pluck. *v.t.* [GRITTED (-id), GRITTING], 1. to cover with grit. 2. to grind (the teeth) in anger or determination. *v.i.* to make a grating or grinding sound. —*SYN.* see **fortitude.**
grith (grith), *n.* [ME.; AS.; ON., orig., home], [Obs.], 1. security, protection, or peace, especially as guaranteed by someone or in some place. 2. a sanctuary.
grits (grits), *n.pl.* [ME. *grytles;* AS. *grytt(e);* akin to G. *grütze;* IE. base as in *great, grit*], grain hulled and coarsely ground; especially, coarse hominy.
grit·ti·ly (grit′'l-i), *adv.* in a gritty manner.
grit·ti·ness (grit′i-nis), *n.* the quality or state of being gritty.
grit·ty (grit′i), *adj.* [GRITTIER (-i-ẽr), GRITTIEST (-i-ist)], 1. of, like, or containing grit; sandy. 2. brave; plucky.
griv·et (griv′it), *n.* [Fr.], a long-tailed, olive-green African monkey: sometimes called *green monkey.*
griz·zle (griz′'l), *n.* [< ME. *grisel;* OFr. *grisel, adj.* < *gris*, gray < OHG. *gris* (G. *greis*), gray], 1. *a*) gray hair. *b*) a gray wig. 2. gray. *v.t.* & *v.i.* [GRIZZLED (-'ld), GRIZZLING], to make or become gray. *adj.* gray.
griz·zle (griz′'l), *v.i.* [GRIZZLED (-'ld), GRIZZLING], [British], to worry; fret; complain.
griz·zled (griz′'ld), *adj.* [< *grizzle, adj.* + *-ed*], 1. gray or streaked with gray. 2. having gray hair.
griz·zly (griz′li), *adj.* [GRIZZLIER (-li-ẽr), GRIZZLIEST (-li-ist)], grayish; grizzled. *n.* [*pl.* GRIZZLIES (-liz)], a grizzly bear.
grizzly bear, [*grizzly* for *grisly*], a large, ferocious, yellow-brown bear, found in western North America from Mexico to Alaska.
gro., gross.
groan (grōn), *v.i.* [ME. *gronen, gronien;* AS. *granian;* akin to G. *greinen*, to weep (cf. GRIN); only Gmc.], 1. to utter a deep sound expressing pain, distress, or disapproval. 2. to make a sound like this: as, the wind *groans.* 3. to suffer deeply from cruelty, oppression, etc. 4. to be loaded or weighed down. *v.t.* to utter with a groan or groans. *n.* a sound made in groaning.
groat (grōt), *n.* [ME. *grote* < MD. *groot* or MLG. *grote* (akin to *great*) in the sense "thick"; the name first applied to a coin circulating in the Low Countries; cf. ML. *grossus*, G. *groschen*, OFr. *gros*], 1. an obsolete English silver coin worth fourpence. 2. a trifling sum.
groats (grōts), *n.pl.* [ME. *grotes;* AS. *grotan*, pl.; IE. base as in *great, grit*], hulled, or hulled and coarsely cracked, grain, especially wheat or oats.
gro·cer (grō′sẽr), *n.* [ME. *grosser;* OFr. *grossier;* ML. *grossarius*, wholesale dealer < *grossus*, great, gross; see GROSS], a storekeeper who sells food and various household supplies.
gro·cer·y (grō′sẽr-i), *n.* [*pl.* GROCERIES (-iz)], [ME. & OFr. *grosserie*], 1. the business of a grocer. 2. a store selling food, household supplies, etc. 3. *pl.* the food and supplies sold by a grocer.
Grod·no (grôd′nô), *n.* a city in the eastern Byelorussian S.S.R., on the Niemen River: pop., 50,000.
grog (grog), *n.* [after Old *Grog*, nickname of Admiral Vernon (1684–1757), Brit. naval officer who introduced the drink about 1745: he was so called because he wore a *grogram* cloak], 1. an alcoholic liquor, originally rum, diluted with water. 2. any alcoholic liquor.
grog·ger·y (grog′ẽr-i), *n.* [*pl.* GROGGERIES (-iz)], a saloon; grogshop.
grog·gi·ly (grog′'l-i), *adv.* [Colloq.], in a groggy manner.
grog·gi·ness (grog′i-nis), *n.* [Colloq.], the quality or condition of being groggy.
grog·gy (grog′i), *adj.* [GROGGIER (-i-ẽr), GROGGIEST (-i-ist)], [< *grog* (rum)], [Colloq.], 1. drunk; tipsy; intoxicated. 2. weak and unsteady; shaky or dizzy, as from a blow, illness, lack of sleep, etc.: the current sense.
grog·ram (grog′rəm), *n.* [earlier *grograin;* OFr. *gros grain; gros*, coarse, gross + *grain*, grain], 1. a coarse fabric made of silk, or of silk, worsted, and mohair, often stiffened with gum. 2. an article of clothing made of this.
grog·shop (grog′shop′), *n.* [*grog* + *shop*], a place where alcoholic drinks are sold; saloon.
groin (groin), *n.* [Early Mod. Eng. phonetic rendering (cf. *boil* for *bile*) of *grine*, var. of *grinde;* ME. *grynde;* said to be < AS. *grynde*, abyss, in sense "depression" (akin to AS. *grund;* see GROUND); but cf. AS. *grin*, region of the groin; varied phonetic history may be due to euphemism], 1. the depressed part or the fold where the abdomen joins either thigh. 2. in *architecture*, *a*) the sharp, curved edge formed at the junction of two intersecting vaults. *b*) the rib of wood, stone, etc. covering this edge. *v.t.* to build or provide with a groin or groins.

GROIN (sense 2)

Gro·li·er (grō′li-ẽr; Fr. grô′lyā′), *adj.* designating a style of bookbinding, with ornamentation in gilt scrolls, bands, or ribbons, designed by Jean Grolier de Servières.
Gro·lier de Ser·vières, Jean (zhän grô′lyā′ də sâr′vyâr′), 1479–1565; French bibliophile.
grom·met (grom′it), *n.* [Fr. *gourmette*, a curb, curb chain; earlier *gromette* < *gourmer*, to curb], 1. a ring of rope or metal used to fasten the edge of a sail to its stay, hold an oar in place, etc. 2. a metal eyelet in cloth, leather, etc. Also **grummet.**
grom·well (grom′wəl), *n.* [ME. *gromylle, gromil;* OFr. *gromil, gremil;* L. *gruinum milium*, kind of millet; *gruinum*, akin to *grus*, a crane + *milium*, millet], any of a group of flowers with hard, stonelike seeds.
Gro·my·ko, An·drei An·drei·e·vich (än-drā′ än-drā′ye-vich grô-mi′kô; Eng. grə-me′ko), 1909– ; Soviet diplomat.
Gro·ning·en (grō′niŋ-ən; D. khrō′niŋ-ən), *n.* 1. a province of the northeastern Netherlands. 2. its capital: pop., 132,000 (1947).
groom (grōōm, groom), *n.* [Early ME. *grome*, boy; connected, either by borrowing or being borrowed, with OFr. *gromet*, servant (see GOURMET, GRUMMET); the parallel development in *bridegroom* (AS. *brydguma*) suggests altered form of obsolescent ME. *gome* (AS. *guma*), man, ? by folk etym. after ME. *growen* (AS. *growan*), to grow (cf. LAD)], 1. a man or boy whose work is tending, feeding, and currying horses. 2. any of a group of officials in charge of particular departments of the British Royal household. 3. a bridegroom. 4. [Archaic], *a*) a man. *b*) a manservant. *v.t.* 1. to tend (horses); feed and curry. 2. to make neat, tidy, and smart. 3. to train or develop (a person) for a particular purpose: as, he was *groomed* for political office.
grooms·man (grōōmz′mən, groomz′mən), *n.* [*pl.* GROOMSMEN (-mən)], a man who attends a bridegroom at the wedding; best man.
groove (grōōv), *n.* [ME. *grofe* < ON. *grof*, a pit, reinforced by MD. *grōve* (D. *groef*), of same ult. origin; akin to G. *grube*, a pit, hole, ditch; for the IE. base see GRAVE (burial place)], 1. a long, narrow furrow or hollow cut in a surface with a tool. 2. any channel like this; rut. 3. a habitual way of doing things; settled routine. 4. in *anatomy*, any narrow furrow, depression, or slit occurring on the surface of an organ, especially of bone. 5. in *printing*, the hollow on the bottom of type: see **type,** illus. *v.t.* [GROOVED (grōōvd), GROOVING], to make a groove or grooves in.
in the groove, [said to be from phonograph recording], [Slang], performing or performed with smooth, effortless skill: said originally of jazz musicians or music.
grope (grōp), *v.i.* [GROPED (grōpt), GROPING], [ME. *gropen, gropien;* AS. *grapian* < base of *grap*, a grasp; akin to G. *greifen*, to grasp; for IE. base see GRIPE], to feel or search about blindly, hesitantly, or un-

certainly; feel one's way. ***v.t.*** to seek or find by groping; feel (one's way). ***n.*** a groping.

gros·beak (grōs'bēk'), ***n.*** [Fr. *grosbec;* see GROSS & BEAK], any of various birds of the finch family, with a thick, strong, conical bill.

gro·schen (grō'shən), ***n.*** [*pl.* GROSCHEN], [G. < 14th-c. dial. *grosch(e)* < Czech *groš* < ML. *grossus*, short for *denarius grossus*, thick denarius, or *grossus Turonensis*, thick (coin of) Tours; see GROSS, GROAT (coin)], 1. in Austria, a bronze coin equal to 1/100 schilling. 2. in Germany, *a)* formerly, a small silver coin of varying value. *b)* [Colloq.], the 10-pfennig coin.

gros·grain (grō'grān'), ***adj.*** [Fr.; see GROGRAM], having heavy, crosswise cords: as, *grosgrain* silk. ***n.*** 1. grosgrain silk. 2. ribbon made of this.

gross (grōs), ***adj.*** [ME. *groos, grose;* OFr. *gros*, big, thick, coarse < LL. *grossus*, thick], 1. too fat; overfed; corpulent; burly. 2. glaring; flagrant; very wrong: as, a *gross* miscalculation. 3. dense; thick. 4. coarse; lacking fineness; not delicate. 5. lacking in refinement or perception; insensitive; dull. 6. vulgar; obscene; rude: as, *gross* language. 7. total; entire; with no deductions: as, one's *gross* income: opposed to *net*. 8. [Archaic], plain; evident; obvious. ***n.*** [ME. *groos;* orig. < OFr. *grosse*, fem. of *gros*], 1. [*pl.* GROSSES (-iz)], the mass or bulk; whole amount. 2. [*pl.* GROSS], twelve dozen: abbreviated **gr., gro.** ***v.t. & v.i.*** [Colloq.], to make (a specified total amount) before expenses are deducted. —***SYN.*** see **coarse, flagrant.**

in the gross, 1. in bulk; as a whole. 2. wholesale.

gross ton, a unit of weight, equal to 2,240 pounds: also called *long ton*.

Gross·war·dein (grōs'vär-dīn'), ***n.*** Oradea, a city in Romania: the German name.

gross weight, the total weight of a commodity or goods, including the weight of the covering material or container: distinguished from *net weight*: abbreviated **gr. wt.**

Grosz, George (grōs), 1893–1959; German painter in America.

grot (grot), ***n.*** [Fr. *grotte;* It. *grotta*], [Poetic], a grotto.

Grote, George (grōt), 1794–1871; English historian.

gro·tesque (grō-tesk'), ***adj.*** [Fr.; It. *grottesco*, odd, extravagant < *grotta*, a grotto: so called from imitating designs found in excavations, etc.], 1. in or of a style of painting, sculpture, etc. in which forms of persons and animals are intermingled with foliage, flowers, fruits, etc. in a fantastic design; hence, 2. characterized by distortions or striking incongruities in appearance, shape, manner, etc.; fantastic; bizarre. 3. ludicrously eccentric or strange; ridiculous; absurd. ***n.*** 1. a grotesque painting, sculpture, etc. 2. grotesque quality, character, or style. 3. a grotesque figure or design. —***SYN.*** see **fantastic.**

gro·tes·quer·ie, gro·tes·quer·y (grō-tes'kẽr-i), ***n.*** [*pl.* GROTESQUERIES (-iz)], [< *grotesque*], 1. a grotesque thing. 2. the quality or state of being grotesque. 3. grotesque paintings, etc. collectively.

Gro·ti·us, Hugo (grō'shi-əs), (born *Huig de Groot*), 1583–1645; Dutch statesman and jurist.

grot·to (grot'ō), ***n.*** [*pl.* GROTTOES, GROTTOS (-ōz)], [It. *grotta* < LL. *grupta;* L. *crypta;* see CRYPT], 1. a cave. 2. a cavelike summerhouse, shrine, etc.

grouch (grouch), ***v.i.*** [prob. < ME. *grouchen*, to murmur, grudge; OFr. *grouchier*], [Colloq.], to grumble or sulk. ***n.*** [Colloq.], 1. a person who grouches. 2. a grumbling or sulky mood. 3. a cause for complaint.

grouch·i·ly (grouch'ə-li), ***adv.*** [Colloq.], in a grouchy manner.

grouch·i·ness (grouch'i-nis), ***n.*** [Colloq.], the quality or state of being grouchy.

grouch·y (grouch'i), ***adj.*** [GROUCHIER (-i-ẽr), GROUCHIEST (-i-ist)], [*grouch* + *-y*], [Colloq.], grumbling; sulky.

ground (ground), ***n.*** [ME. *grounde, grund;* AS. *grund*, sea bottom, etc. (cf. GROUND SWELL); akin to G. *grund;* ? IE. **ghren-to*, what is touched in passing over < base **ghren-*, to rub against, etc.; cf. GRIND], 1. *a)* originally, the lowest part, base, or bottom of anything. *b)* the bottom of the sea. 2. the solid surface of the earth. 3. the soil of the earth; earth; land: as, he tills the *ground*. 4. any particular piece of land; especially, one set aside for a specified purpose: as, a hunting *ground*. 5. any particular area of reference, discussion, work, etc.; topic; subject: as, let us go over the *ground* again. 6. the distance to a goal, objective, position, etc. 7. basis; foundation; groundwork. 8. *often pl.* the logical basis of a conclusion, action, etc.; valid reason, motive, or cause. 9. the background or surface over which other parts are spread or laid, as the main surface of a painting. 10. in *electricity*, the connection of an electrical conductor with the ground: abbreviated **grd.** See also **grounds.** ***adj.*** 1. of, on, or near the ground. 2. growing or living in or on the ground. ***v.t.*** 1. to place or set on the ground; cause to touch the ground. 2. to cause (a ship, etc.) to run aground. 3. to found on a firm basis; establish. 4. to base (a claim, argument, etc.) on: as, *ground* your claims on fact. 5. to instruct (a person) in the elements or first principles of. 6. to provide with a background. 7. in *aviation*, to cause to remain on the ground; keep from flying: as, the plane was *grounded* by bad weather. 8. in *electricity*, to connect (an electrical conductor) with the ground, which becomes part of the circuit. ***v.i.*** 1. to strike or fall to the ground. 2. to strike the bottom or run ashore: said of a ship. 3. in *baseball*, to be put out on a grounder (usually with *out*).

above ground, alive.

break ground, 1. to dig; excavate. 2. to plow. 3. to start building. 4. to start any undertaking. 5. in *nautical usage*, to be hoisted from its bed: said of an anchor.

cover ground, 1. to traverse a certain distance. 2. to travel. 3. to get a certain amount of work done.

cut the ground from under one's feet, to deprive one of effective defense or argument.

from the ground up, from the first or elementary principles, methods, etc. to the last or most advanced; completely; thoroughly.

gain ground, 1. to move forward. 2. to make progress. 3. to gain in strength, extent, popularity, etc.

give ground, to withdraw under attack; retreat; yield.

hold one's ground, to keep one's position against attack or opposition; not withdraw or retreat.

lose ground, 1. to fall behind. 2. to lose in strength, extent, popularity, etc.

on delicate ground, in a situation requiring tact.

on firm ground, in a safe situation.

on one's own ground, 1. in a familiar situation. 2. on a subject that one knows well. 3. at home.

on the ground of, because of.

run into the ground, [Colloq.], to do too long or too often; overdo.

shift one's ground, to shift one's position; change one's argument or defense.

stand one's ground, to maintain one's position against attack or opposition; not withdraw or retreat.

suit down to the ground, [Colloq.], to suit completely.

ground (ground), past tense and past participle of **grind.**

ground·age (groun'dij), ***n.*** [*ground* + *-age*], a fee charged for permitting a ship to remain in a port.

ground bait, bait, often weighted bait, used in fishing close to the bottom of water.

ground bass, in *music*, a short phrase, usually of four to eight measures, played repeatedly in the bass against the melodies and harmonies of the upper parts.

ground beam, in *carpentry*, 1. a groundsel. 2. a sleeper.

ground cherry, any of various plants of the nightshade family, grown for ornamentation: some species have small, edible fruits enclosed in paperlike husks.

ground color, 1. the first coat of paint; base coat. 2. the background color.

ground cover, any of various low, dense-growing plants used for covering the ground, as in places where it is difficult to grow grass.

ground crew, a group of people in charge of the maintenance and repair of aircraft.

ground·er (groun'dẽr), ***n.*** in *baseball, cricket*, etc., a batted ball that rolls or bounces along the ground.

ground floor, that floor of a building which is approximately level with the ground; first floor.

in on the ground floor, [Colloq.], 1. having the same terms and privileges as the original investors: said of someone buying shares of stock after the original issue. 2. in at the beginning (of a business, etc.); hence, 3. in a position of advantage.

ground glass, glass whose surface has been ground so that it diffuses light and is therefore not transparent.

ground hemlock, an evergreen shrub with dark-green foliage and scarlet berries.

ground·hog (ground'hôg', ground'hog'), ***n.*** a ground hog.

ground hog, a woodchuck.

ground-hog (or **groundhog**) **day,** February 2, Candlemas Day, when the ground hog is said to come out of hibernation: if he sees his shadow, he will supposedly return to his hole for another six weeks of winter weather.

ground ivy, a creeping plant of the mint family, with round, toothed leaves and loose clusters of blue flowers.

ground·less (ground'lis), ***adj.*** [see GROUND & -LESS], without reason or cause; unjustified; baseless.

ground·ling (ground'liŋ), ***n.*** 1. *a)* a fish that lives close to the bottom of the water. *b)* an animal that lives on or in the ground. *c)* a plant that grows close to the ground; creeping plant. 2. in the *Elizabethan theater*, a person who watched the performance from the pit, which had only the ground for a floor; hence, 3. a person lacking critical ability or taste.

ground loop, an uncontrollable sharp turn sometimes made by a taxiing airplane in taking off or landing.

ground·mass (ground'mas'), ***n.*** the matrix in which rock crystals are embedded.

ground·nut (ground'nut'), ***n.*** 1. any of various plants with edible tubers or tuberlike parts, as the peanut. 2. the edible tuber or tuberlike part.

ground pine, 1. any of several kinds of club moss, an evergreen with creeping or underground stems and erect, treelike branches. 2. a European plant that smells like resin.

ground plan, 1. a plan of the ground floor or of any

floor of a building, as seen from above: distinguished from *elevation* or *cross section*. 2. a first, fundamental, or basic plan.

ground plate, 1. a groundsel (timber). 2. a metal plate put in the ground to connect an electric circuit with the earth. 3. a bedplate supporting railroad ties.

ground·plot (ground'plot'), *n.* 1. the piece of ground on which a building stands. 2. a ground plan.

ground plum, a small herb with purple flowers and plumlike fruit.

ground rent, rent paid for land on which the occupant can build, make improvements, etc.

grounds (groundz), *n.pl.* [< *ground*], 1. land surrounding or attached to a house or other building; especially, the lawns, gardens, etc. of an estate. 2. the particles that settle to the bottom of a liquid; dregs; sediment: as, coffee *grounds*. 3. basis; foundation; reason: as, *grounds* for divorce.

ground·sel (ground's'l, groun's'l), *n.* [ME. *grundeswylie;* AS. *grundeswylige* < earlier *gundeswelge*, ? lit., pus swallower < *gund*, pus + *swelgan*, to swallow: from use in poultices; AS. *grund-* (see GROUND) < *gund-* by folk etym. referring to the rapid spread of the plant], any of a large group of plants with yellow, rayed flowers, as the golden ragwort.

ground·sel (ground's'l, groun's'l), *n.* [ME. *grondsil, gronsil;* see GROUND & SILL], the bottom horizontal timber in a framework; ground plate; ground beam.

ground·sill (ground'sil), *n.* a groundsel (the timber).

ground speed, the speed with which an aircraft in flight passes over the ground beneath it.

ground squirrel, any of various small, burrowing animals of the squirrel family; especially, the chipmunk or the gopher.

ground swell, a violent swelling or rolling of the ocean, caused by a distant storm or earthquake.

ground water, water found underground in porous rock strata and soils, as in a spring.

ground wire, a wire acting as a conductor from an electric circuit, radio, etc. to the ground.

ground·work (ground'wũrk'), *n.* a foundation; basis. —*SYN.* see **base.**

group (grōōp), *n.* [Fr. *groupe;* It. *gruppo*, a knot, lump, group < Gmc. **kruppa*, round mass; for IE. base see CROP], 1. a number of persons or things gathered closely together and forming a recognizable unit; cluster; aggregation; band: as, a *group* of buildings. 2. a collection of objects or figures forming a design or part of a design. 3. a number of persons or things classified together because of common characteristics, community of interests, etc.; hence, 4. in *biology*, a large number of plants or animals related to each other because of certain similarities. 5. in *chemistry*, a radical. 6. in the *United States Air Force*, a unit consisting of four squadrons of the same kind of aircraft. *v.t.* & *v.i.* to assemble or form into a group or groups. Abbreviated **gr.**

SYN.—**group** is the basic, general word expressing the simple idea of an assembly of persons, animals, or things without further connotation; **herd** is applied to a group of cattle, sheep, or similar large animals feeding, living, or moving together; **flock,** to goats, sheep, or birds; **drove,** to cattle, hogs, or sheep; **pack,** to hounds or wolves; **swarm,** to insects; **school,** to fish, porpoises, whales, or the like; **bevy,** to quails; **covey,** to partridges or quails; **flight,** to birds flying together. In extended applications, **flock** connotes guidance and care, **herd, drove,** and **pack** are used contemptuously of people, **swarm** suggests a thronging, and **bevy** and **covey** are used of girls or women.

group·er (grōōp'ẽr), *n.* [*pl.* GROUPERS (-ẽrz), GROUPER; see PLURAL, II, D, 1], [Port. *garoupa;* prob. of S. Am. origin], a large, tropical food fish related to the sea bass.

group insurance, insurance, especially life insurance, available to a group of employees, etc. at low premium rates, usually regardless of physical condition or age.

group medicine, medical care available to the members of a group, community, state, etc. at a fixed rate, usually annual.

group work, that branch of social work concerned with helping groups or communities of people to advance their individual and collective needs and interests.

grouse (grous), *n.* [*pl.* GROUSE], [Early Mod. Eng.; Weekley suggests confused application of ME. *grewe* (OFr. *grue* < L. *grus*), a crane], any of a group of game birds with a round, plump body, firm, feathered legs, feather-covered nostrils, and mottled feathers, as the ruffed grouse, sage hen, etc.

grouse (grous), *v.i.* [GROUSED (groust), GROUSING], [? akin to *grouch* (< OFr. *groucier*) via the OFr. var. *grousser*], [Slang], to complain; grumble. *n.* [Slang], 1. a complaint. 2. a person who habitually complains.

grout (grout), *n.* [< AS. *grut*, coarse meal, or cognate MD. *gruit, grute;* base as in *grits, groats;* cf. GRUEL], 1. *a*) coarse meal. *b*) *pl.* groats. 2. *usually pl.* [British], sediment; dregs; grounds. 3. a thin mortar used to fill chinks or cracks. 4. a fine plaster for finishing surfaces. *v.t.* to fill or finish with or as with grout.

grout·y (grout'i), *adj.* [*grout* + *-y*], [Dial.], cross; sulky.

grove (grōv), *n.* [ME.; AS. *graf;* akin to *græfa*, thicket; not found outside Eng.], a small wood; group of trees standing together without undergrowth.

grov·el (gruv''l, grov''l), *v.i.* [GROVELED or GROVELLED (-'ld), GROVELING or GROVELLING], [Shakespeare's back-formation < *grovelling, adv.* (ME. *grufelinge*), down on one's face (felt as a ppr.); ME. *grufelinge* actually < *o grufe*, on the face (< ON. *ā grufu*) + *-linge*, adv. suffix], 1. to lie prone or crawl in a prostrate position, especially abjectly; hence, 2. to behave humbly or abjectly, as before authority; debase oneself in a servile fashion. 3. to take pleasure in base or mean things; enjoy what is contemptible.

grov·el·er, grov·el·ler (gruv''l-ẽr, grov''l-ẽr), *n.* a person who grovels.

grow (grō), *v.i.* [GREW (grōō), GROWN (grōn), GROWING], [ME. *growen;* AS. *growan;* akin to D. *groeien;* IE. base **ghrō-*, **ghrē-*, to sprout, spring up, grow green (cf. GRASS, GREEN); the word has largely replaced, and inherited senses from, *wax* (to grow)], 1. to come into being or be produced naturally; sprout; spring up. 2. to exist as living vegetation; thrive: as, orchids do not *grow* in Greenland. 3. to increase in size and develop toward maturity, as a plant or animal does by assimilating food. 4. to increase in size, quantity, or degree, or in some specified manner: as, my troubles are *growing*. 5. to become; turn: as, he *grew* weary. 6. to become attached or united by growth. *v.t.* 1. to cause to grow; raise; cultivate. 2. to cover with a growth: used in the passive. 3. to allow to grow: as, he tried to *grow* a mustache. 4. to develop.

grow on, to have a gradually increasing effect on; come gradually to seem more important, dear, or admirable to.

grow out of, 1. to develop from. 2. to outgrow.

grow up, 1. to reach maturity; become adult; attain full growth. 2. to come to be; develop; arise.

grow·er (grō'ẽr), *n.* 1. a person who grows agricultural products. 2. a plant that grows in a specified way: as, a rapid *grower*.

growing pains, 1. rheumatic pains that sometimes occur in the muscles and joints of growing children: they were formerly attributed to rapid growth. 2. difficulties experienced in the early development of an institution or enterprise.

growl (groul), *v.i.* [ME. *groule(n)*, to rumble; formally corresponds with OFr. *grouler*, to scold, grumble (? < Gmc.; cf. D., G. *grollen*) & Anglo-Fr. *growler*, glossed "to make noise like a crane" (? folk etym. < OFr. *grue*, Anglo-Fr. *grwe*, crane; cf. GROUSE); the modern word may be a later, unconnected echoism], 1. to make a rumbling, throaty, menacing sound in the throat, as a dog does. 2. to complain in an angry or surly manner. 3. to rumble, as thunder, cannon, etc. *v.t.* to express by growling. *n.* 1. a rumbling, throaty, menacing sound made by an angry dog. 2. a sound resembling this; especially, an inarticulate, angry sound made by a person. 3. a complaint muttered angrily.

growl·er (groul'ẽr), *n.* 1. a person, animal, or thing that growls. 2. [Slang], *a*) formerly, a pail or can to carry out beer bought at a saloon, etc. *b*) a keg of beer, equal to 1/8 barrel.

grown (grōn), past participle of **grow.** *adj.* 1. having completed its growth; mature; fully developed. 2. covered with a growth.

grown·up (grōn'up'), *n.* an adult.

grown-up (grōn'up'), *adj.* adult; of, for, or characteristic of an adult or adults. *n.* an adult.

growth (grōth), *n.* [*grow* + *-th*], 1. a growing or developing; specifically, *a*) gradual development toward maturity. *b*) origin and development. 2. *a*) increase in size, weight, power, etc. *b*) the amount of this. 3. something that grows or has grown: as, a thick *growth* of grass. 4. a tumor or other abnormal mass of tissue developed in or on the body.

Groz·ny (grôz'ni), *n.* a city in the northern Caucasus, U.S.S.R.: oil center: pop., 172,000.

grub (grub), *v.i.* [GRUBBED (grubd), GRUBBING], [ME. *grubben*, to dig; prob. < AS. **grybban* (akin to OHG. *grubilōn*, to bore into); cf. GRAVE (burial place)], 1. to dig in the ground. 2. to work hard, especially at something menial or tedious; drudge. 3. to search about, as among records; rummage. 4. [< *n.* 3], [Slang], to eat. *v.t.* 1. to clear (ground) of roots by digging them up. 2. to dig (roots) out of the ground; uproot. 3. [< *n.* 3], [Slang], to feed. *n.* 1. the short, fat, wormlike larva of an insect, especially of a beetle. 2. a person who works hard at some menial or tedious work; drudge. 3. [from notion "what is grubbed for"], [Slang], food.

grub·ber (grub'ẽr), *n.* [ME. *grubbare*], 1. a person who grubs. 2. a tool for grubbing.

grub·bi·ness (grub'i-nis), *n.* the quality or state of being grubby.

grub·by (grub'i), *adj.* [GRUBBIER (-i-ẽr), GRUBBIEST (-i-ist)], 1. infested with grubs, especially with botfly larvae, as cattle or sheep. 2. dirty; messy; untidy.

grubbing hoe, a heavy hoe for grubbing up roots.

grub·stake (grub'stāk'), *n.* [*grub* (food) + *stake*], [Colloq.], 1. money or supplies advanced to a prospector in return for a share in his findings; hence, 2. money advanced for any enterprise. *v.t.* [Colloq.], to provide with a grubstake.

Grub·street (grub'strēt'), *n.* Grub Street. *adj.* [g-], of or like literary hacks or their work.

Grub Street, 1. formerly, a street in London (now Milton Street) where many literary hacks lived. 2. literary hacks.

grudge (gruj), *v.t.* [GRUDGED (grujd), GRUDGING], [Late ME. *grugge*, var. of *grucchen;* cf. GROUCH, GROUSE (to grumble)], 1. to envy (a person) because of his possession or enjoyment of (something): as, he *grudges* John his beautiful wife. 2. to give or allow with ill will or reluctance: as, the miser *grudged* his dog its food. *n.* 1. a strong feeling of resentment or malice held against someone; ill will. 2. a reason, cause, or pretext for this. —*SYN.* see **malice.**

grudg·ing·ly (gruj'iŋ-li), *adv.* in a grudging manner; unwillingly or stingily.

gru·el (grōō'əl), *n.* [ME. & OFr., coarse meal; ML. **grutellum*, dim. of *grutum*, meal, mash < Gmc. **grut*, hulled dried grain; akin to Eng. *groats, grits*], thin, easily digested broth made by cooking meal in water or milk: it is often fed to invalids. *v.t.* [GRUELED or GRUELLED (-əld), GRUELING or GRUELLING], to subject to intense strain; exhaust, as by severe punishment, relentless questioning, etc.

gru·el·ing, gru·el·ling (grōō'əl-iŋ, grōōl'iŋ), *adj.* [ppr. of *gruel*], tormenting; exhausting. *n.* an experience that has a grueling effect.

grue·some (grōō'səm), *adj.* [< obs. *grue*, to shudder (ME. *gruen*) + *-some;* akin to G. *grausam*, horrible], causing fear and loathing; horrifying and revolting; grisly: also spelled **grewsome.** —*SYN.* see **ghastly.**

gruff (gruf), *adj.* [< Early Mod. D. *grof* (akin to G. *grob*, coarse, hence surly); prob. < same IE. base as *grit*], 1. rough or surly in manner, speech, or appearance; rude; unfriendly; bad-tempered. 2. harsh and throaty; hoarse. —*SYN.* see **blunt.**

gruff·y (gruf'i), *adj.* [GRUFFIER (-i-ẽr), GRUFFIEST (-i-ist)], gruff.

gru·gru (grōō'grōō'), *n.* [Sp. *grugrú;* prob. < native Carib name], 1. a tropical American palm with a spiny trunk and feathery leaves: also **grugru palm.** 2. the wormlike, edible larva of a weevil infesting the pith of this palm: also **grugru worm.**

grum·ble (grum'b'l), *v.i.* [GRUMBLED (-b'ld), GRUMBLING], [prob. < D. *grommelen* (akin to G. *grummeln*, Fr. *grommeler*); IE. base as in *grim*], 1. to make low, unintelligible sounds in the throat; growl. 2. to mutter or mumble in discontent; complain in an angry or surly manner. 3. to rumble, as thunder. *v.t.* to express by grumbling. *n.* 1. a grumbling, especially in complaint. 2. a rumble.

grum·bler (grum'blẽr), *n.* a person who grumbles.

grum·ble·to·ni·an (grum'b'l-tō'ni-ən), *n.* [< *grumble*, after 17th-c. *Grindletonian, Muggletonian*, names of religious sects], a grumbler: nickname for an opponent of the policies of William III of England.

grum·bly (grum'bli), *adj.* [GRUMBLIER (-bli-ẽr), GRUMBLIEST (-bli-ist)], that grumbles; complaining.

grume (grōōm), *n.* [OFr., clot; L. *grumus*, little heap], [Rare], 1. a thick, sticky fluid. 2. a clot of blood.

grum·met (grum'it), *n.* a grommet.

gru·mose (grōō'mōs), *adj.* [< L. *grumus*, little heap; + *-ose*], in *botany*, collected in a granular mass.

gru·mous (grōō'məs), *adj.* [< L. *grumus*, little heap; + *-ous*], 1. full of or like grume. 2. grumose.

grump·i·ly (grum'p'l-i), *adv.* in a grumpy manner.

grump·i·ness (grum'pi-nis), *n.* the quality or state of being grumpy.

grump·ish (grum'pish), *adj.* grumpy.

grump·y (grum'pi), *adj.* [GRUMPIER (-pi-ẽr), GRUMPIEST (-pi-ist)], [prob. < *grumble*, after *grunt*, etc.], irritable; peevish; bad-tempered; surly.

Grun·dy, Mrs. (grun'di), a narrow-minded, puritanical neighbor constantly referred to (but never appearing) in Tom Morton's play *Speed the Plough* (1798) with the question "What will Mrs. Grundy say?": used as a personification of prudishness and narrow-minded conventionality.

Grun·dy·ism (grun'di-iz'm), *n.* [< *Mrs. Grundy*], 1. prudish and narrow-minded conventionality. 2. an instance of this.

grun·ion (grun'yən, grōōn-yōn'), *n.* [*pl.* GRUNION, GRUNIONS (-yənz); see PLURAL, II, D, 2], [? < Sp. (colloq.) *gruñón*, grunter], a food fish of the silversides family found off the California coast.

grunt (grunt), *v.i.* [ME. *grunten;* AS. *grunnettan* (akin to G. *grunzen*), freq. of *grunian*, to grunt; origin echoic], 1. to make a deep, gruff sound in the throat: said of a hog. 2. to make a sound like this, as in annoyance, contempt, effort, etc. *v.t.* to express by grunting: as, he *grunted* his disapproval. *n.* 1. the deep, gruff, throaty sound made by a hog. 2. a sound like this, made by a person. 3. any of various related salt-water fishes that grunt when removed from water.

grunt·er (grunt'ẽr), *n.* [ME. *gruntare*], 1. a person or animal that makes a grunting sound; especially, a hog. 2. a grunt (fish).

Grus (grus), *n.* [L., a crane], a southern constellation supposedly resembling a crane in shape: see **constellation,** chart.

Gru·yère (cheese) (grē-yer', grōō-yer'; Fr. grü'yâr'), [orig. made in *Gruyère*, Switzerland], a light-yellow Swiss cheese, very rich in butterfat, or an American cheese resembling this.

gr. wt., gross weight.

gryph·on (grif'ən), *n.* a griffin (mythical monster).

GS, German silver.

G.S., g.s., 1. general secretary. 2. general staff.

G.S.A., Girl Scouts of America.

G.S.C., General Staff Corps.

G string, 1. a loincloth; breechclout. 2. a similar cloth, usually with spangles or tassels, worn by striptease dancers. 3. a string tuned to G, as on a violin.

gt., 1. gilt. 2. great. 3. [*pl.* GTT.], in *pharmacy*, gutta.

Gt. Brit., Gt. Br., Great Britain.

G.T.C., g.t.c., 1. good till canceled. 2. good till countermanded.

g.u., g.-u., genitourinary.

gua·cha·ro (gwä'chä-rō'), *n.* [Sp. *guácharo*, sickly, moaning: ? so named from its cry], a South American night bird of the goatsucker family: the young birds are very plump, and their fat, called *guacharo butter* when rendered, is used for cooking and lighting.

gua·co (gwä'kō), *n.* [S. Am.], any of several aromatic South American plants, used to treat gout, rheumatism, etc.: also believed to be valuable in treating snake bites.

Gua·da·la·ja·ra (gwä'dä-lä-hä'rä), *n.* a city in western Mexico: pop., 590,000.

Gua·dal·ca·nal (gwä'd'l-kə-nal'), *n.* one of the British Solomon Islands, in the South Pacific: pop., 15,000: scene of heavy fighting in World War II.

Gua·dal·quiv·ir (gwä'd'l-kwiv'ẽr; Sp. gwä'*th*äl-kē-vêr'), *n.* a river in southern Spain, flowing into the Atlantic: length, 374 mi.

Gua·da·lupe Hi·dal·go (gwä'd'l-ōōp' hi-dal'gō; Sp. gwä'*th*ä-lōō'pe ē-*th*äl'gô), *n.* a city in Mexico, near Mexico City: pop., 60,000: official name, *Gustavo A. Madero.*

Gua·da·lupe Mountains (gô'd'l-ōōp', gwä'd'l-ōōp'; Sp. gwä'*th*ä-lōō'pe), a mountain range in southern New Mexico and southwestern Texas.

Gua·de·loupe (gô'd'l-ōōp'; Fr. gwȧd'lōōp'), *n.* an overseas department of France consisting of two main islands and five small islands of the Leeward group in the West Indies: area, 688 sq. mi.; pop., 254,000; capital, Basse-Terre.

Gua·di·a·na (gwä'di-ä'nə; Port. gwä-dyä'nə; Sp. gwä-*th*yä'nä), *n.* a river in southern Spain and Portugal, flowing into the Atlantic: length, 515 mi.

guai·ac (gwī'ak), *n.* [< *guaiacum*], 1. guaiacum (senses 2 & 3). 2. the tonka bean, the aromatic seed of a tropical South American tree. 3. the tree yielding this.

guai·a·col (gwī'ə-kōl', gwī'ə-kol'), *n.* [< Mod. L. *guaiacum* (see GUAIACUM); + *-ol*], a white, crystalline solid or colorless, oily liquid, $C_6H_4(OH)OCH_3$, prepared from guaiacum or wood creosote and used in medicine and as a chemical reagent.

guai·a·cum, guai·o·cum (gwī'ə-kəm), *n.* [Mod. L. < Sp. *guayaco* < native Haitian name], 1. any of a group of tropical American trees and shrubs with blue or purple flowers and fruit growing in capsules. 2. the very hard, brownish-green wood of a tree of this group; lignum vitae. 3. a resin obtained from this tree, used to treat rheumatism, gout, etc.

Guam (gwäm), *n.* one of the Marianas Islands, in the Western Pacific, a territory of the United States: area, 209 sq. mi.; pop., 67,000; capital, Agaña.

guan (gwän), *n.* [Sp. < the native (Carib) name], a large game bird of Central and South America.

gua·na·co (gwä-nä'kō), *n.* [*pl.* GUANACOS (-kōz), GUANACO; see PLURAL, II, D, 1], [Sp. < Quechua *huanacu*], a woolly, reddish-brown animal of the Andes, related to the camel but shorter and without humps.

Gua·na·jua·to (gwä'nä-hwä'tô), *n.* 1. a state of central Mexico: pop., 1,566,000. 2. the capital of this state: pop., 24,000.

gua·nay (gwä-nī'), *n.* [Sp. < the native (Quechua) name], a cormorant of Peru: it is a source of guano.

guan·i·din (gwan'ə-din, gwä'nə-din), *n.* guanidine.

guan·i·dine (gwan'ə-dēn', gwä'nə-din), *n.* [< *guanine*], a strongly basic, crystalline substance, $NHC(NH_2)_2$, formed by the oxidation of guanine.

gua·nin (gwä'nin), *n.* guanine.

gua·nine (gwä'nēn), *n.* [< *guano*], an organic base, $C_5H_5N_5O$, found in the liver, pancreas, etc. of animals and obtained commercially from guano.

gua·no (gwä'nō), *n.* [*pl.* GUANOS (-nōz)], [Sp. < Quechua *huanu*, dung], 1. manure of sea birds, found especially on islands off the coast of Peru: it is used as a fertilizer.

2. any manure, artificial or natural, resembling this, especially that of bats.
Guan·tá·na·mo Bay (gwän-tä′nä-mô), a small inlet of the Caribbean, on the southeastern coast of Cuba: site of a United States naval station.
Gua·po·ré (gwä′pô-re′), *n.* a river flowing between Brazil and Bolivia into the Madeira: length, 950 mi.
guar (gwär), *n.* [Hind. *guār*], a leguminous plant of India, now cultivated in the United States for forage.
guar., guaranteed.
Gua·ra·ni (gwä′rä-nē′), *n.* [Guarani, lit., warrior], 1. [*pl.* GUARANIS (-nēz′), GUARANI], a member of a tribe of South American Indians who lived in an area between the Paraguay River and the Atlantic. 2. the Tupian language of this tribe, used as a general native vernacular in Paraguay.
guar·an·tee (gar′ən-tē′), *n.* [prob. < *guaranty*, by analogy with words ending in *-ee*], 1. a guaranty (senses 1 & 3). 2. a pledge or assurance; specifically, *a*) a pledge that something is as represented and will be replaced if it does not meet specifications. *b*) a positive assurance that something will be done in the manner specified. 3. a guarantor. 4. a person who receives a guaranty. 5. something that serves as an assurance of, or promises the happening of, some event: as, the dark clouds were a *guarantee* of rain. ***v.t.*** 1. to give a guarantee or guaranty for: as, they *guarantee* their product. 2. to state with confidence; promise; affirm: as, I *guaranteed* that I'd be there.
guar·an·tor (gar′ən-tẽr, gar′ən-tôr′), *n.* [< *guaranty* + *-or*], one who makes or gives a guaranty or guarantee.
guar·an·ty (gar′ən-ti), *n.* [*pl.* GUARANTIES (-tiz)], [OFr. *garantie* < *garant, guarant, warant*, a warrant, supporter < OHG. *werento*, protector < *weren, warjan*, to protect; cf. WARRANT], 1. a pledge by which a person commits himself to the payment of another's debt or the fulfillment of another's obligation in the event of default. 2. an agreement that secures the existence or maintenance of something: as, the trade pact was a *guaranty* of increased commerce. 3. something given or held as security. ***v.t.*** [GUARANTIED (-tid), GUARANTYING], to guarantee.
guard (gärd), ***v.t.*** [OFr. *guarder* < Gmc. **wardon* (seen in G. *warten*, to wait, OS. *wardon*, to guard, watch over); see WARD], 1. to keep safe from harm; watch over and protect; defend; shield. 2. to watch over; specifically, *a*) to keep from escape or trouble. *b*) to hold in check; control; restrain. *c*) to supervise entrances and exits through (a door, gate, etc.). 3. to cover (a piece of machinery) with a device to protect the operator. 4. [Archaic], to escort. ***v.i.*** 1. to keep watch; take precautions (with *against*). 2. to act as a guard. ***n.*** 1. the act or duty of guarding; careful watch; wariness; defense; protection. 2. caution; precaution; safeguard. 3. a posture of alert readiness for defense, as in fencing, boxing, etc. 4. any device that protects against injury or loss; specifically, *a*) the part of the handle of a sword, knife, or fork that protects the hand. *b*) a chain or cord attached to a watch. *c*) a ring worn to keep a more valuable ring from slipping off the finger. *d*) a safety device, as in machinery. 5. a person or group that guards; specifically, *a*) a sentinel or sentry. *b*) a railway brakeman or gateman. *c*) a person who guards prisoners. *d*) *pl.* a special unit of troops connected with the household of the British sovereign: also extended to other military units. 6. in *basketball*, either of the two players whose special duties are defensive. 7. in *football*, either of the two players at the left and the right of the center. Abbreviated **gd.**
—*SYN.* see **defend.**
mount guard, to go on sentry duty.
on (one's) guard, alert for protection or defense; vigilant.
stand guard, to do sentry duty.
guard·ant (gär′dənt), *adj.* [Fr. *gardant*, ppr. of *garder*; see GUARD], in *heraldry*, designating an animal represented with the face fully turned toward the observer: also spelled **gardant.**
guard·ed (gär′did), *adj.* [pp. of *guard*], 1. kept safe; watched over and protected; defended. 2. kept from escape or trouble; held in check; supervised. 3. cautious; careful; restrained: as, a *guarded* speech.
guard·house (gärd′hous′), *n.* 1. a building used by the members of a military guard when they are not walking a post. 2. a building where military personnel are confined for minor infractions of regulations or while awaiting court-martial.
guard·i·an (gär′di-ən), *n.* [OFr. *guarden, garden* < *guarder*; cf. WARDEN], 1. a person who guards; person who watches over, protects, cares for, or defends another person, property, etc.; custodian. 2. a person legally placed in charge of the affairs of a minor or of someone incapable of managing his own affairs. *adj.* protecting.
guard·i·an·ship (gär′di-ən-ship′), *n.* [*guardian* + *-ship*], the position, duties, or authority of a guardian.
guard·rail (gärd′rāl′), *n.* 1. a protective railing, as on a staircase. 2. an extra rail alongside the main rail of a railroad at a crossing, etc., to keep the cars on the track.
guard·room (gärd′ro͞om′, gärd′room′), *n.* 1. a room used by the members of a military guard when they are not walking a post. 2. a room where military personnel are confined for minor infractions of regulations or while awaiting court-martial.
guard ship, 1. a warship for the protection of the port or harbor in which it is stationed. 2. a ship of a squadron doing guard duty.
guards·man (gärdz′mən), *n.* [*pl.* GUARDSMEN (-mən)], 1. a guard. 2. a member of a National Guard or of any military body called a guard.
Guar·ne·ri, Giu·sep·pe (jo͞o-zep′pe gwär-ne′rē), (Latin name *Guarnerius*), 1687?-1745; Italian violinmaker.
Guar·ner·i·us (gwär-nâr′i-əs), *n.* a violin made by Giuseppe Guarneri or by some other member of the same family.
Gua·te·ma·la (gwä′tə-mä′lə; Sp. gwä′te-mä′lä), *n.* 1. a country in Central America, south and east of Mexico. area, 45,452 sq. mi.; pop., 3,759,000: see **Central America,** map. 2. its capital: pop., 374,000: also **Guatemala City.**
Gua·te·ma·lan (gwä′tə-mä′lən), *adj.* of Guatemala, its people, etc. *n.* a native or inhabitant of Guatemala.
gua·va (gwä′və), *n.* [Sp. *guayaba* < native (prob. Arawakan) name in Brazil], 1. a tropical American tree or shrub bearing a yellowish, pear-shaped, edible fruit. 2. the fruit, used for jelly, preserves, etc.
Guay·a·quil (gwī′ä-kēl′), *n.* a seaport in Ecuador: pop., 296,000.
gua·yu·le (gwä-ū′lā), *n.* [Sp.; Nahuatl *quauholli* < *quauitl*, plant + *olli*, gum], 1. a small shrub of northern Mexico and Texas, cultivated for the rubber obtained from its sap. 2. this rubber: also **guayule rubber.**
gu·ber·na·to·ri·al (go͞o′bẽr-nə-tôr′i-əl, gū′bẽr-nə-tō′ri-əl), *adj.* [L. *gubernator*, helmsman, governor < pp. of *gubernare*, to steer; + *-ial*], of a governor or his office.
gu·ber·ni·ya (goo-ber′ni-yä), *n.* [Russ. < base of L. *gubernare*; see GOVERN], 1. originally, a province of czarist Russia. 2. now, a provincial soviet in the Soviet Union.
gude (güd), *adj.* & *n.* [Scot. & British Dial.], good.
gudg·eon (guj′ən), *n.* [ME. *gojon*; OFr. *goujon*; L. *gobio*; Gr. *kōbios*], 1. a small, European fresh-water fish of the carp family, easily caught, and used for bait. 2. a minnow. 3. a person easily cheated or tricked; dupe; gull. 4. a bait. *v.t.* to cheat; trick; dupe.
gudg·eon (guj′ən), *n.* [ME. *gojon, gojone*; OFr. *gojon*, *goujon*, pivot; ? < *gouge* (a prostitute), with a sexual allusion (cf. PINTLE, FEMALE, *adj.* 5)], 1. a metal pin or shaft at the end of an axle, on which a wheel turns. 2. the socket of a hinge, into which the pin is fitted. 3. the part of a shaft that revolves in a bearing.
Gud·run (good′ro͞on), *n.* [ON. *Guthrūn* < *guthr*, war, battle + *runa*, close friend; see RUNE], in *Norse legend*, the daughter of the Nibelung king: she lured Sigurd away from the Valkyrie Brynhild by a magic drink and married him: also **Guthrun.**
guel·der-rose (gel′dẽr-rōz′), *n.* [after its supposed source *Guelderland*; D. *Gelderland*], 1. a small, cultivated cranberry tree with large, round heads of white flowers: also called *snowball tree*. 2. its flower.
Guelph, Guelf (gwelf), *n.* [It. *Guelfo*, for MHG. *Welf*, a family name < OHG. *welf*, a whelp: used as war cry of the anti-imperial faction at the battle of Weinsberg (1140)], 1. a member of a German royal family from which the present line of British sovereigns is descended. 2. any member of a political party in medieval Italy that supported the authority of the Pope in opposition to the aristocratic party of the Ghibellines.
Guelph·ic, Guelf·ic (gwel′fik), *adj.* of the Guelph family or political party.
Guen·e·ver (gwen′ə-vẽr), a feminine name: see **Guinevere.**
gue·non (gə-nōn′; Fr. gə-nōn′), *n.* [Fr.], any of a large group of long-tailed African monkeys, including the green monkey and grivet.
guer·don (gũr′d'n), *n.* [ME.; OFr.; ML. *widerdonum* < OHG. *widar*, again, against + L. *donum*, gift], [Poetic], a reward; recompense. *v.t.* [Poetic], to reward.
gue·ril·la (gə-ril′ə), *n.* & *adj.* guerrilla.
Guern·sey (gũrn′zi), *n.* [*pl.*, for 2 & 3, GUERNSEYS (-ziz)], 1. a British island in the English Channel: area, 25 sq. mi.; pop., 43,000. 2. any of a breed of dairy cattle, originally from this island: they are usually fawn-colored with white markings. 3. [so called because orig. made on the island; cf. JERSEY], [g-], a close-fitting knitted woolen shirt or sweater, worn by seamen.
guer·ril·la (gə-ril′ə), *n.* [Sp., skirmishing warfare, dim. of *guerra*, war; It. *guerra*; OHG. *werra*, war; see WAR], 1. formerly, warfare carried on by guerrillas. 2. any member of a small defensive force of irregular soldiers, usually volunteers, making surprise raids against supply

lines, etc. behind the lines of an invading enemy army. *adj.* of or by guerrillas.

guess (ges), *v.t. & v.i.* [ME. *gessen*, to think; prob. < ON.; cf. obs. Dan. *getse* (Dan. *gisse*, Sw. *gissa*) in the same senses; akin to MD. *gessen;* extension of the base in *get*], 1. to form a judgment or estimate of (something) without actual knowledge; conjecture; surmise. 2. to judge correctly by doing this. 3. to think or suppose: as, I *guess* you can do it. *n.* 1. a guessing. 2. a judgment or estimate formed by guessing; something guessed; conjecture; surmise.

SYN.—**guess** implies the forming of a judgment or estimate (often a correct one) haphazardly (he *guessed* the number of beans in the jar); to **conjecture** is to infer or predict from incomplete or uncertain evidence (I cannot *conjecture* what his plans are); **surmise** implies a conjecturing through mere intuition or imagination (she *surmised* the truth).

guess-rope (ges'rōp'), *n.* in *nautical usage*, a guest rope.

guess·work (ges'wũrk'), *n.* 1. a guessing; conjecturing. 2. a view, work, etc. based on guessing.

guest (gest), *n.* [ME. *gest, giste, gust;* AS. *giest* (Anglian *gest*); akin to G. *gast*, ON. *gestr* (whence, or < Anglian, the initial *g-*); IE. **ghost-is*, stranger, seen also in L. *hostis*, stranger (cf. HOSTILE)], 1. a person entertained at the home or table of another; visitor. 2. a person paying for his lodgings, meals, etc. at a hotel or boardinghouse. 3. a person receiving the hospitality of a club, institution, etc. of which he is not a member. 4. an insect or other animal living or breeding in the nest, etc. of another animal. *adj.* 1. for guests. 2. performing by invitation: as, a *guest* artist. *v.t.* to treat as a guest. *v.i.* to be a guest. —*SYN.* see **visitor.**

guest rope, 1. a rope in addition to the tow rope, used to steady a vessel being towed. 2. a rope fastened along a ship's side so that vessels coming alongside can be attached. Also **guess-rope.**

guff (guf), *n.* [echoic], [Slang], nonsense; foolish talk.

guf·faw (gə-fô'), *n.* [echoic], a loud, coarse burst of laughter. *v.i.* to laugh in this way. —*SYN.* see **laugh.**

Gug·gen·heim, Daniel (goog'ən-hīm'), 1856–1930; American capitalist and philanthropist.

gug·gle (gug''l), *n., v.i. & v.t.* [GUGGLED (-'ld), GUGGLING], [echoic], gurgle.

Gui·a·na (gi-an'ə, gi-ä'nə), *n.* a region in northern South America, including British Guiana, French Guiana, and Surinam (Dutch Guiana): abbreviated **Gui.**

guid·a·ble (gīd'ə-b'l), *adj.* that can be guided.

guid·ance (gīd''ns), *n.* 1. a guiding; direction; leadership. 2. something that guides.

guide (gīd), *v.t.* [GUIDED (-id), GUIDING], [ME. *giden, guyden;* OFr. *guider*, late var. (< Pr. *guidar* or It. *guidare*) of OFr. *guier* (ME. *gien;* cf. GUY) < Gmc. source; akin to & < same base as AS. *witan*, to guide (cf. WIT)], 1. to point out the way for; direct on a course; conduct; lead. 2. to direct the course or motion of (a person's hand, a vehicle, etc.) by physical action. 3. to give instruction to; train. 4. to direct (the policies, actions, etc.) of; manage; regulate; govern. *v.i.* to act as a guide. *n.* a person or thing that guides; specifically, *a)* a person whose work is conducting strangers or tourists through a region, building, etc. *b)* a part that directs or controls the motion of other parts of a machine. *c)* a guidebook. *d)* a book giving instruction in the elements of some subject: as, a *guide* to mathematics. *e)* in *military usage*, a soldier at the right front of a column, who regulates its pace and alignment and indicates its route. Abbreviated **G., g.**

SYN.—**guide** implies the showing of the way by one who is thoroughly familiar with the course, and connotes his continuous presence or direction along the way (to *guide* a tourist, a mule, one's hand); **lead** implies a going ahead in order to show the way and, figuratively, suggests a taking of the initiative (he *led* them to victory); **steer** suggests a maneuvering of the controls in order to maintain the correct course (to *steer* a ship); **pilot** suggests a guiding over a difficult course, especially one filled with obstacles or intricate twists (he *piloted* us through the maze of tunnels).—*ANT.* follow.

guide·board (gīd'bôrd', gīd'bōrd'), *n.* a sign, as on a guidepost, giving directions for travelers.

guide·book (gīd'book'), *n.* a book containing directions and information for tourists.

guided missile, a military missile whose course is controlled by radio signals, radar devices, etc.

guide·line (gīd'līn'), *n.* a standard or principle by which to make a judgment or determine a policy or course of action: also **guide line.**

guide·post (gīd'pōst'), *n.* a post with a sign and directions for travelers, placed at a roadside or crossroads.

guide rope, a rope attached to another rope lifting or dragging a load, to help steady and direct the load.

Gui·do d'A·rez·zo (gwē'dô dä-ret'tsô), 995?–1050? A.D.; Italian musician and musical theorist: also called *Guido Aretino.*

gui·don (gī'd'n), *n.* [Fr.; It. *guidone* < *guidare;* see GUIDE], 1. formerly, a small flag or pennant carried by the guide of mounted cavalry. 2. in the *United States Army*, *a)* the identification flag of a unit. *b)* a soldier carrying such a flag at the head of the unit: also **guidon bearer.**

Gui·enne (güē'yen'), *n.* Guyenne.

guild (gild), *n.* [ME. *gylde, yelde*, etc.; blend of AS. *gyld, gield*, payment, guild, AS. *gegyld*, association (of paying members), ON. *gildi*, guild, guild-feast; all < base seen in AS. *gieldan*, to pay, make payment; see YIELD], 1. in medieval times, a union of men in the same craft or trade to uphold standards and protect the members. 2. any association for mutual aid and the promotion of common interests. 3. in *plant ecology*, any of four groups of parasitic plants (*parasites, saprophytes, epiphytes*, and *lianas*). Also spelled **gild.**

guil·der (gil'dẽr), *n.* [Early Mod. Eng. *gildren* (ME. *guldren*); altered (with unhistoric *-r-*) < D. *gulden*, florin, lit., golden], 1. a former gold or silver coin of the Netherlands, Germany, or Austria. 2. *a)* the unit of currency in the Netherlands, equal to about $0.26 in 1950. *b)* a silver coin of this value. See also **gulden.**

guild·hall (gild'hôl'), *n.* [AS. *gildheall*], 1. a hall where a guild meets. 2. a town hall; specifically, 3. [G-], the hall of the Corporation of the City of London.

guilds·man (gildz'mən), *n.* [*pl.* GUILDSMEN (-mən)], a member of a guild.

guild socialism, a form of socialism proposed in England in the early 20th century, consisting in government ownership of all industries, each to be managed by a guild of workers.

guile (gīl), *n.* [ME. *gile;* OFr. *guile;* of Gmc. origin; prob. < Frank. *wigila*, guile; see WILE], crafty, deceitful talk or conduct; cunning.

guile·ful (gīl'fəl), *adj.* full of guile; deceitful; tricky.

guile·less (gīl'lis), *adj.* without guile; candid; frank.

guil·le·mot (gil'i-mot'), *n.* [Fr., dim. of *Guillaume*, William; cf. ROBIN], any of various narrow-billed arctic diving birds of the auk family.

guil·loche (gi-lōsh'), *n.* [Fr. *guillochis* < *guillocher*, to ornament with lines < OIt. *ghiocciare*, to drop, drip; LL. **guttiare* < L. *gutta*, a drop], a decorative border design in which two or more lines or bands are interwoven so as to make circular spaces between them.

guil·lo·tine (gil'ə-tēn'), *n.* [Fr., after J. I. *Guillotin*, who advocated its use during the French Revolution in preference to less humane methods], 1. an instrument for beheading, consisting of a heavy blade dropped between two grooved uprights. 2. an instrument, working on a similar principle, for cutting paper, metal, etc. 3. an instrument for removing the tonsils or uvula. *v.t.* (gil'ə-tēn', gil'ə-tēn'), [GUILLOTINED (-tēnd', -tēnd'), GUILLOTINING], [Fr. *guillotiner* < the *n.*], to behead with a guillotine.

GUILLOTINE

guilt (gilt), *n.* [ME. *gilt, gelt, gult;* AS. *gylt*, a sin, offense < Gmc. type **gulti;* found only in Eng.], 1. the act or state of having done a wrong or committed an offense; culpability, legal or ethical. 2. conduct that involves guilt; wrongdoing; crime; sin.

guilt·i·ly (gil'tə-li), *adv.* in a guilty manner.

guilt·i·ness (gil'ti-nis), *n.* the quality or state of being guilty.

guilt·less (gilt'lis), *adj.* 1. free from guilt; innocent. 2. having no knowledge or experience (with *of*).

guilt·y (gil'ti), *adj.* [GUILTIER (-ti-ẽr), GUILTIEST (-ti-ist)], [ME. *gylti, gilti;* AS. *gyltig*], 1. having guilt; deserving blame or punishment; culpable. 2. having one's guilt proved; legally judged an offender. 3. showing or conscious of guilt: as, a *guilty* look. 4. of or involving guilt or a sense of guilt: as, a *guilty* conscience.

guimpe (gimp, gamp), *n.* [Fr.], a short-sleeved blouse worn under a pinafore or jumper.

Guin·ea (gin'i), *n.* 1. a country in western Africa, on the Atlantic: area, 94,925 sq. mi.; pop., 3,000,000; capital, Conakry: formerly *French Guinea*. 2. a region along the western coast of Africa, including Guinea, Portuguese Guinea, and Spanish Guinea. Abbreviated **Guin.**

guin·ea (gin'i), *n.* 1. [so called because the gold of which it was first made came from Guinea], a former English gold coin, last minted in 1813, equal to 21 shillings: the word is still used in England to mean a sum of 21 shillings, as in giving prices of luxury items associated with the aristocracy: abbreviated **G., g.** 2. a guinea fowl. 3. [orig., Negro from Guinea], [Slang], an Italian: hostile and contemptuous term.

guinea fowl, [so called because imported from Guinea in 16th c.], a domestic fowl with a rounded body and dark feathers spotted with white: also **guinea hen.**

guinea grains, grains of paradise.

Guinea, Gulf of, a part of the Atlantic, off western Africa.

guinea hen, 1. a guinea fowl. 2. a female guinea fowl.

Guinea pepper, 1. either of two tropical trees whose seeds are used as spices. 2. the seeds.

guinea pig, [so called prob. from being brought to England by ships plying between England, Guinea, and S. America], 1. a small, fat mammal of the rat family, with short ears and a short tail: it is domesticated and is often used in biological experiments; hence, 2. any person or thing used in an experiment.

GUINEA PIG (7 in. long)

Guinea worm, [so named because frequent in Guinea], a threadlike, parasitic worm of tropical countries, living in the tissues of man, dogs, and horses.

Guin·e·ver (gwin'ə-vẽr), a feminine name: see **Guinevere.** *n.* Guinevere.

Guin·e·vere (gwin'ə-vêr'), [< Celt.; first element prob. W. *gwen,* white], a feminine name: also **Guenever, Guinever.** *n.* in *Arthurian legend,* the wife of King Arthur and mistress of Sir Lancelot.

gui·pure (gi-pyoor'; Fr. gē'pür'), *n.* [Fr. < *guiper,* to cover with silk; of Gmc. origin; prob. < OD. **wipan,* to wind; see WHIP], 1. lace without any ground mesh, having the patterns held together by connecting threads. 2. a kind of gimp or trimming.

guise (gīz), *n.* [ME.; OFr. < OHG. *wisa,* way, manner; cf. WISE, *n.*], 1. [Archaic], customary behavior, manner, or carriage. 2. manner of dress; garb. 3. outward aspect; semblance. 4. a false or deceiving appearance; pretense: as, under the *guise* of friendship he betrayed us. *v.t.* [GUISED (gīzd), GUISING], 1. [Archaic], to dress or arrange (*in* a specified manner). 2. [British Dial.], to disguise. *v.i.* [British Dial.], to go in disguise. —*SYN.* see **appearance.**

Guise, Fran·çois de Lor·raine de (fräṅ'swȧ' də lô'ren' də gēz'), second duc de Guise, 1519–1563; French soldier and statesman.

Guise, Hen·ri I de Lorraine de (äṅ'rē'), third duc de Guise, 1550–1588; son of *François;* French general and statesman; formed the Holy League.

gui·tar (gi tär'), *n.* [Fr. *guitare;* Sp. *guitarra;* Gr. *kithara,* lyre, lute], a musical instrument of the lute family, usually with six strings which are plucked or strummed with the fingers or a plectrum: see also **Hawaiian guitar, Spanish guitar,** electric guitar.

GUITAR

gui·tar·ist (gi-tär'ist), *n.* a person who plays a guitar.

guit·guit (gwit'gwit'), *n.* [echoic of its note], the honey creeper, a small, brightly colored bird of tropical America.

Gui·try, Sa·cha (sȧ'-shȧ' gē'trē'; Eng. sä'-shə gē'tri), 1885–1957; French playwright and actor.

Gui·zot, Fran·çois Pierre Guil·laume (fräṅ'swȧ' pyȧr gē'yōm' gē'zō'), 1787–1874; French statesman and historian; premier of France (1840–1848).

Guj·a·ra·ti (gooj'ä-rä'ti), *n.* the Indo-European, Indic language spoken in the region of the Gujarat States.

Guj·a·rat States (gooj'ä-rät'), native states of western India: area, 7,352 sq. mi.; pop., 1,459,000.

gu·lar (gū'lẽr), *adj.* [< L. *gula,* throat; + *-ar*], of or on the throat.

gulch (gulch), *n.* [prob. < dial. *gulch,* to swallow greedily; ME. *gulchen*], a steep-walled valley cut by a swift stream; deep, narrow ravine.

gul·den (gool'dən), *n.* [D. & G., a florin, lit., golden; orig. applied only to coins of gold], 1. any of various former gold or silver coins of Austria, Germany, or the Netherlands. 2. a guilder (sense 2).

gules (gūlz), *n.* [ME. *goules;* OFr. *goles, goules, gueules,* gules, red-dyed ermine, orig. pl. of *goule, gole,* the mouth < L. *gula,* throat], in *heraldry,* red: indicated in black-and-white engravings by parallel vertical lines.

gulf (gulf), *n.* [Fr. *golfe;* It. *golfo;* Late Gr. *kolphos;* Gr. *kolpos,* a fold, bosom, bay, gulf], 1. a large area of ocean partially enclosed by land, larger than a bay: abbreviated **G., g.** 2. a wide, deep chasm or abyss; hence, 3. a wide or impassable gap or separation; cleavage. 4. an eddy that draws objects down; whirlpool. *v.t.* to swallow up; engulf.

Gulf States, the States on the Gulf of Mexico; Florida, Alabama, Mississippi, Louisiana, and Texas.

Gulf Stream, a warm ocean current flowing from the Gulf of Mexico through the Florida Strait and northward into the Atlantic toward Europe: width, c. 50 mi.

gulf·weed (gulf'wēd'), *n.* a greenish-brown seaweed with berrylike air sacs, found floating in the Gulf Stream and the Sargasso Sea.

gulf·y (gul'fi), *adj.* [*gulf* + *-y*], full of whirlpools.

gull (gul), *n.* [*pl.* GULLS (gulz), GULL; see PLURAL, II, D, 1], [ME. *gull* < Celt.; cf. Corn. *gullan,* W. *gwylan,* Bret. *gwelan* (whence Fr. *goéland*)], any of a large, widely distributed group of sea birds with large wings, slender legs, webbed feet, and feathers of gray, white, and black.

HERRING GULL (18 in. long)

gull (gul), *n.* [prob. < obs. *gull,* to swallow, guzzle; influenced by dial. *gull* (ME. *goll*), unfledged bird], a person easily cheated or tricked; dupe. *v.t.* to cheat; trick; dupe.

gull·a·ble (gul'ə-b'l), *adj.* [Rare], gullible.

Gul·lah (gul'ə), *n.* [altered < *Gola* or *Gora,* names of African tribes living in Liberia], 1. any of a group of Negroes living on the South Carolina and Georgia coast or near-by islands. 2. the English dialect of the Gullahs.

gul·let (gul'it), *n.* [ME. *golet;* OFr. *goulet,* throat, narrow passage, dim. of *gole, goule;* L. *gula,* throat], 1. the tube leading from the mouth to the stomach; esophagus. 2. the throat or neck. 3. a water channel or gully.

gul·li·bil·i·ty (gul'ə-bil'ə-ti), *n.* the state of being or tendency to be gullible.

gul·li·ble (gul'ə-b'l), *adj.* [*gull, v.* + *-ible*], easily cheated or tricked; credulous: also spelled **gullable.**

gul·li·bly (gul'ə-bli), *adv.* in a gullible manner.

Gul·li·ver's Travels (gul'ə-vẽrz), a political and social satire (1726) of 18th-century England by Jonathan Swift, telling of the adventures of the shipwrecked Lemuel Gulliver in four imaginary lands, Lilliput, Brobdingnag, Laputa, and the land of the Houyhnhnms.

gul·ly (gul'i), *n.* [*pl.* GULLIES (-iz)], [Fr. *goulet,* narrow entrance < OFr. *goulet;* see GULLET], a channel or hollow worn by water; narrow ravine. *v.t.* [GULLIED (-id), GULLYING], to make a gully or gullies in.

gulp (gulp), *v.t.* [ME. *gulpen, golpen;* prob. < MD. or MFl.; cf. D. *gulpen,* to gulp down; akin to obs. Dan. *gulpe* (Dan. *gylpe*), to vomit; ult. akin to AS. *gielpan* (see YELP)], 1. to swallow hastily, greedily, or in large amounts. 2. to choke back as if swallowing; repress (a sob, etc.). *v.i.* to catch the breath in or as in swallowing a large amount. *n.* 1. a gulping. 2. a swallow. 3. the amount swallowed at one time.

gum (gum), *n.* [ME. *gumme, gomme;* OFr. *gomme;* L. *gummi;* Gr. *kommi,* gum], 1. a sticky substance given off by certain trees and plants, which dries into an uncrystallized, brittle mass soluble in water. 2. any similar plant secretion, as resin. 3. any plant gum processed for use in industry, art, etc. 4. an adhesive, especially on the back of a postage stamp; glue; mucilage. 5. *a)* any gum tree. *b)* its wood. 6. gum elastic; rubber. 7. *pl.* rubber overshoes. 8. chewing gum. 9. [Dial.], a hollowed gum log used as a trough, etc. *v.t.* [GUMMED (gumd), GUMMING], to coat, unite, or stiffen with gum. *v.i.* 1. to secrete or form gum. 2. to become sticky or clogged.

by gum! [Colloq.], by God!: a euphemism.

gum up, [Slang], to put out of working order; cause to go awry.

gum (gum), *n.* [ME. *gume, gumme, gome;* AS. *goma;* akin to G. *gaum,* roof of the mouth; IE. base **gheu-,* **ghōu-,* to yawn, gape, hence basic sense "revealed in yawning"], the firm flesh covering the jaws on the inside of the mouth and surrounding the base of the teeth.

gum ammoniac, ammoniac, a natural gum resin.

gum arabic, [after L. *gummi Arabicum*], a gum from certain acacia trees, used in medicine, in the manufacture of candy, etc.

gum·bo (gum'bō), *n.* [prob. of Negro origin < ***kingombo,*** native name], 1. the okra plant. 2. the edible, sticky pods of this plant. 3. a soup thickened with unripe okra pods. 4. a fine, silty soil of the Western prairies, which becomes sticky and nonporous when wet: also **gumbo soil.** 5. a French patois spoken by Creoles and Negroes in Louisiana and the French West Indies. Also spelled **gombo.**

gum·boil (gum'boil'), *n.* a small abscess on the gums.

gum·drop (gum'drop'), *n.* a small piece of candy of a firm, jellylike consistency, made of sweetened gum arabic or gelatin, usually colored, flavored, and covered with sugar.

gum elastic, [after Mod. L. *gummi elasticum;* cf. Fr. *gomme élastique*], rubber; caoutchouc.

gum·ma (gum'ə), *n.* [*pl.* GUMMATA (-ə-tə), GUMMAS (-əz)], [Mod. L. < L. *gummi,* gum], a soft, rubbery tumor occurring in tertiary syphilis.

gum·ma·tous (gum'ə-təs), *adj.* of or like a gumma.
gum·mi·ness (gum'i-nis), *n.* the quality or state of being gummy.
gum·mose (gum'ōs), *adj.* gummous.
gum·mo·sis (gə-mō'sis), *n.* [Mod. L. < *gum* + *-osis*], the giving off of gummy substances as a result of cell degeneration: a characteristic of certain plant diseases, especially of stone fruits.
gum·mous (gum'əs), *adj.* [L. *gummosus*], of or like gum.
gum·my (gum'i), *adj.* [GUMMIER (-i-ẽr), GUMMIEST (-i-ist)], 1. having the nature of gum; sticky; viscid. 2. covered with or containing gum. 3. yielding gum.
gump·tion (gump'shən), *n.* [< Scot. dial.; ? < ME. *gome*, heed (< ON. *gaumr*), with jocose Latinate ending], [Colloq.], 1. shrewdness in practical matters; common sense. 2. courage and initiative; enterprise and boldness: the current sense.
gum resin, a mixture of gum and resin, given off by certain trees and plants: ammoniac is a gum resin.
gum·shoe (gum'shōō'), *n.* [*gum* (rubber) + *shoe*], 1. *a*) a rubber overshoe. *b*) *pl.* sneakers. 2. [Slang], a detective. ***v.i.*** [Slang], to go about quietly; sneak.
gum tragacanth, a gum obtained from various Asiatic or East European shrubs and trees of the pea family: also **tragacanth.**
gum tree, any of various trees that yield gum, as the sour gum, sweet gum, eucalyptus, etc.
gum·wood (gum'wood'), *n.* the wood of a gum tree.
gun (gun), *n.* [ME. *gunne, gonne;* prob. < pet name *Gunna*, dim. of *Gunhild, Gunhilda*, fem. name in which both elements mean "war"; *Gunhild* is recorded as name of a ballista, 1330–1331], 1. a weapon consisting of a metal tube from which a projectile is discharged, usually by the explosion of gunpowder: the term is technically restricted to a heavy weapon with a relatively long barrel fixed in a mount, as a cannon or machine gun, but is also applied to rifles and, popularly, to pistols, and revolvers. 2. any similar device not discharged by an explosive: as, an air *gun*. 3. a discharge of a gun in signaling or saluting. 4. anything like a gun in shape or use. 5. [Slang], the throttle of an engine. ***v.i.*** [GUNNED (gund), GUNNING], to shoot or hunt with a gun; go shooting or hunting. ***v.t.*** 1. [Colloq.], to shoot (a person). 2. [Slang], to advance the throttle of (an engine) so as to increase the speed.
big gun, [Slang], 1. an important and influential person. 2. a high-ranking military officer.
give it the gun, [from the resemblance of early airplane accelerators to the trigger of a gun], [Slang], to cause something to start or gain speed.
go great guns, [Slang], to do with speed and efficiency.
gun for, 1. to hunt for with a gun. 2. to look for in order to shoot or harm. 3. [Slang], to try to get; seek.
spike one's guns, to frustrate or defeat one.
stick to one's guns, to hold one's position under attack; not withdraw or retreat; be firm.
gun., gunnery.
gun·boat (gun'bōt'), *n.* a small armed ship of shallow draft, used to patrol rivers, etc.
gun·cot·ton (gun'kot''n), *n.* a highly explosive substance made of cotton treated with nitric and sulfuric acids.
gun dog, a dog trained to help a hunter by finding or retrieving game: pointers, setters, and various hounds are used as gun dogs.
gun·fire (gun'fīr'), *n.* 1. the firing of a gun or guns. 2. the time set for the ceremonial firing of an artillery piece, as at retreat in the evening. 3. the use of firearms or artillery, as distinguished from other military tactics.
gun·flint (gun'flint'), *n.* a piece of flint in the hammer of a flintlock, for striking a spark to set off the charge.
gung ho (guŋ'hō'), [Chin.], work together: slogan of some units of United States Marines in World War II.
gun·lock (gun'lok'), *n.* in some guns, the mechanism by which the charge is set off.
gun·man (gun'mən), *n.* [*pl.* GUNMEN (-mən)], 1. a man armed with a gun, especially for criminal purposes; armed gangster or thug. 2. a person who makes guns.
gun-met·al (gun'met''l), *adj.* dark-gray: also **gun-metal gray.**
gun metal, 1. a kind of bronze formerly used for making cannon. 2. any of several metals or alloys treated to resemble this. 3. dark gray; color like that of tarnished gun metal: also **gun-metal gray.**
gun moll, [Slang], the mistress or female accomplice of a gunman (sense 1).
Gun·nar (goon'är), *n.* [ON. *Gunnarr* < *gunnr*, older form of *guthr*, war, battle; cf. GUDRUN], in *Norse legend*, the brother of Gudrun, husband of Brynhild, and brother-in-law of Sigurd.
gun·nel (gun''l), *n.* [< ?], a small, slimy fish of the blenny family, found in the North Atlantic.
gun·nel (gun''l), *n.* a gunwale.
gun·ner (gun'ẽr), *n.* [ME. *gunnare* < *gunne;* see GUN], 1. a soldier, sailor, etc. who fires or helps fire an artillery piece. 2. a naval warrant officer who has charge of a ship's guns. 3. a hunter who uses a gun.
gun·ner·y (gun'ẽr-i), *n.* 1. heavy guns. 2. the science of making and using heavy guns and projectiles. 3. the use or firing of heavy guns: abbreviated **gun.**
gun·ning (gun'iŋ), *n.* the act of hunting with a gun.
gun·ny (gun'i), *n.* [*pl.* GUNNIES (-iz)], [Hind. *gonī*, gunny bag; Sans. *gonī*, a sack], 1. a coarse, heavy fabric of jute or hemp, used for sacks and bags. 2. a sack or bag made of this: also **gunny sack** (or **bag**).
gun·play (gun'plā'), *n.* an exchange of shots, as between gunmen and police.
gun·pow·der (gun'pou'dẽr), *n.* 1. an explosive powder, especially a mixture of sulfur, saltpeter, and charcoal: it is used as a charge in cartridges, shells, etc., for blasting, and in firecrackers. 2. gunpowder tea.
Gunpowder Plot, see **Fawkes, Guy.**
gunpowder tea, Chinese green tea whose leaves are rolled into pellets.
gun room, 1. on British warships, the junior officers' quarters; originally, the quarters of the gunner and his mates. 2. a room where a collection of guns is kept and displayed.
gun·run·ner (gun'run'ẽr), *n.* a person who engages in gunrunning.
gun·run·ning (gun'run'iŋ), *n.* the smuggling of guns and ammunition into a country.
gun·shot (gun'shot'), *n.* [earlier *gunnes shott*], 1. *a*) shot fired from a gun. *b*) [Rare], the shooting of a gun. 2. the distance that a projectile from a firearm will carry; range of a gun. ***adj.*** caused by a shot from a gun: as, a *gunshot* wound.
gun-shy (gun'shī'), *adj.* easily frightened at the firing of a gun: as, a *gun-shy* dog.
gun·smith (gun'smith'), *n.* a person who makes or repairs small guns.
gun·stock (gun'stok'), *n.* the wooden handle or butt to which the barrel of a gun is attached.
Gun·ter's chain (gun'tẽrz), [after Edmund *Gunter* (1581–1626), Eng. mathematician who invented it], a surveyor's chain 66 feet in length: it consists of 100 links, each 7.92 inches long; ten square chains equal one acre.
Gun·ther (goon'tẽr), *n.* [G. < Gmc. *gund-, gunt-*, battle (seen in ON. *guthr;* cf. GUDRUN) + *har-*, army (cf. AS. *here*)], in the *Nibelungenlied*, a king of Burgundy, brother of Kriemhild and husband of Brunhild.
gun·wale (gun''l), *n.* [Late ME. *gonne walle* (cf. GUN & WALE); first applied to bulwarks supporting a ship's guns], the upper edge of the side of a ship or boat: also spelled **gunnel.**
gup·py (gup'i), *n.* [*pl.* GUPPIES (-iz)], [after R. J. L. *Guppy*, of Trinidad, who first provided specimens for the British Museum], a tiny fresh-water fish found in Barbados, Trinidad, and Venezuela: it is often kept in aquariums because of its brilliant coloring.
gur·gi·ta·tion (gũr'jə-tā'shən), *n.* [< pp. of LL. *gurgitare*, to flood < L. *gurges*, whirlpool], a whirling or surging, as of liquid.
gur·gle (gũr'g'l), *v.i.* [GURGLED (-g'ld), GURGLING], [prob. < LG. (cf. MLG., D. *gorgelen*, akin to G. *gurgeln*) or < cognate OFr. *gorgeler* < L. *gurgulio*, gullet, whence also D. *gorgel*, G. *gurgel*, gullet; IE. base **g(w)her-*, to swallow up], 1. to flow with a bubbling or rippling sound, as water from a narrow-necked bottle. 2. to make a bubbling or rippling sound: as, a baby *gurgles*. ***v.t.*** to utter with a gurgling sound. ***n.*** 1. a gurgling. 2. a gurgling sound.
gur·glet (gũr'glit), *n.* [Port. *gorgoleta*], a goglet.
Gur·kha (goor'kə), *n.* one of a warlike Rajput people, of Hindu faith, living in the mountains of Nepal, Asia.
gur·nard (gũr'nẽrd), *n.* [*pl.* GURNARDS (-nẽrdz), GURNARD; see PLURAL, II, D, 1], [ME.; OFr. *gornart* < *grogner*, to grunt (< L. *grunnire*): from "grunting" when caught; cf. GRUNT, *n.* 3], a spiny-finned sea fish having a large head covered with plates of bone, and large, winglike, pectoral fins, each of which has three fingerlike feelers.
gur·net (gũr'nit), *n.* [*pl.* GURNETS (-nits), GURNET; see PLURAL, II, D, 1], a gurnard.
gush (gush), *v.i.* [ME. *guschen;* prob. for **gussen* < ON. *gusa*, to gush < base of *giosa* (as in G. *giessen*), to pour; IE. **gheus* (cf. GUST, GEYSER) < **gheu-*, to pour], 1. to flow out suddenly and plentifully; pour out; spout. 2. to have a sudden, plentiful flow of blood, tears, etc. (often followed by *with*). 3. [Colloq.], to express oneself with exaggerated enthusiasm or feeling; talk or write effusively. ***v.t.*** to cause to flow out suddenly and plentifully. ***n.*** 1. a gushing; sudden, plentiful outflow. 2. [Colloq.], a display of exaggerated enthusiasm or feeling; effusive talk or writing.
gush·er (gush'ẽr), *n.* 1. a person who gushes. 2. a drilled oil well from which oil spouts without being pumped.
gush·i·ly (gush'ə-li), *adv.* in a gushy manner.
gush·i·ness (gush'i-nis), *n.* the quality of being gushy.
gush·ing (gush'iŋ), *adj.* [ppr. of *gush*], 1. flowing or pouring out suddenly and plentifully. 2. effusive.
gush·y (gush'i), *adj.* [GUSHIER (-i-ẽr), GUSHIEST (-i-ist)], given to or characterized by gush (*n.* 2); effusive. —***SYN.*** see **sentimental.**

gus·set (gus′it), *n.* [ME. *guschet;* OFr. *gousset,* dim. of *gousse,* a husk, pod], 1. a piece of chain mail or a metal plate protecting the opening of a joint in a suit of armor. 2. a triangular or specially shaped piece inserted in a garment, glove, etc. to make it stronger or roomier. 3. a triangular metal brace for reinforcing the corner or angle of something. *v.t.* to furnish with a gusset.

gust (gust), *n.* [ON. *gustr,* gust, blast < *gjosa,* to gush, break out; IE. base as in *gush*], 1. a sudden, strong rush of air or wind. 2. a sudden burst of rain, smoke, fire, sound, etc. 3. an outburst of laughter, rage, etc. —*SYN.* see **wind.**

gust (gust), *n.* [L. *gustis;* see GUSTO], [Archaic], taste; relish; flavor; savor. *v.t.* [Scot.], to taste; relish.

gust·a·ble (gus′tə-b'l), *adj.* [*gust* (to taste) + *-able*], [Rare], 1. that can be tasted. 2. appetizing. 3. gustatory. *n.* [Rare], something gustable.

gus·ta·tion (gus-tā′shən), *n.* [L. *gustatio* < pp. of *gustare,* to taste < *gustus,* a taste], 1. the act of tasting. 2. the sense of taste.

gus·ta·tive (gus′tə-tiv), *adj.* gustatory.

gus·ta·to·ry (gus′tə-tôr′i, gus′tə-tō′ri), *adj.* of tasting or the sense of taste.

Gus·tav V (goos′täf; Eng. gus′täv), see **Gustavus V.**

Gustav VI, 1882– ; king of Sweden (1950–).

Gus·ta·vus (gus-tā′vəs, gus-tä′vəs), [Mod. L. < G. *Gustav* or Sw. *Gustaf,* lit., prob. staff of the Goths], a masculine name: diminutive, *Gus;* equivalents, Fr. *Gustave,* G. *Gustav,* It. & Sp. *Gustavo.*

Gustavus I, (*Gustavus Vasa*), 1496–1560; king of Sweden (1523–1560).

Gustavus II, (*Gustavus Adolphus*), 1594–1632; grandson of Gustavus I; king of Sweden (1611–1632).

Gustavus III, 1746–1792; nephew of Frederick the Great; king of Sweden (1771–1792).

Gustavus IV, (*Gustavus Adolphus*), 1778–1837; son of Gustavus III; king of Sweden (1792–1809); abdicated.

Gustavus V, 1858–1950; king of Sweden (1907–1950): called *Gustav.*

gust·i·ly (gus′tə-li), *adv.* in a gusty manner; in or with gusts.

gust·i·ness (gus′ti-nis), *n.* a gusty quality or state.

gus·to (gus′tō), *n.* [*pl.* GUSTOS (-tōz)], [It. & Sp. < L. *gustus,* taste], 1. taste; liking. 2. keen enjoyment; enthusiastic appreciation; zest; relish. 3. artistic style.

gust·y (gus′ti), *adj.* [GUSTIER (-ti-ẽr), GUSTIEST (-ti-ist)], characterized by gusts; windy or blustery.

gut (gut), *n.* [ME. *gutte;* AS. *guttas,* pl. < base of *geotan,* to pour; IE. base as in *gush*], 1. *pl.* the bowels; entrails: now generally regarded as an indelicate usage. 2. all or part of the alimentary canal; intestine. 3. tough cord made from animal intestines, used for violin strings, surgical sutures, etc.; catgut. 4. the little bag of silk removed from a silkworm before it has spun its cocoon: it is made into strong cord for use in fishing tackle. 5. a narrow passage or gully, as of a stream or path. 6. *pl.* [Slang], *a*) pluck; courage; perseverance. *b*) impudence; presumptuousness; effrontery. *c*) force; power; effectiveness. *v.t.* [GUTTED (-id), GUTTING], 1. to remove the intestines from; eviscerate. 2. to destroy the interior of, as by fire.

‡**gu·ten A·bend** (gōō′t'n ä′bənt), [G.], good evening.

‡**gu·te Nacht** (gōō′tə näkht′), [G.], good night.

Gu·ten·berg, Jo·hann (yō′hän gōō′t'n-bẽrg; G. gōō′tən-berkh′), (born *Johannes Gensfleisch*), 1398?–1468; German printer; reputedly the first European to print with movable type.

Gutenberg Bible, a Latin Bible produced at Mainz sometime before 1456, formerly attributed to Gutenberg: it is generally considered to be the first book printed from movable type.

‡**gu·ten Mor·gen** (gōō′t'n môr′g'n), [G.], good morning.

‡**gu·ten Tag** (gōō′t'n täkh′), [G.], good day.

Guth·rie (guth′ri), [< Scot. surname & place name *Guthrie*], a masculine name.

Guth·run (gooth′rōōn), *n.* Gudrun.

gut·ta (gut′ə), *n.* [< *gutta*-percha], 1. gutta-percha. 2. the main constituent of gutta-percha, a white, amorphous, gummy substance.

gut·ta (gut′ə), *n.* [*pl.* GUTTAE (-ē)], [ME., drop of gum; L.], 1. a drop: abbreviated **gt.** 2. any of a group of small, droplike ornaments on a Doric entablature.

gut·ta-per·cha (gut′ə-pũr′chə), *n.* [Malay *gĕtah,* gum + *pĕrca,* tree from which it is obtained; form influenced by L. *gutta,* a drop], a rubberlike substance formed by the milky juice of certain trees of Malaysia, used in electric insulation, dentistry, golf balls, etc.

gut·tate (gut′āt), *adj.* [L. *guttatus* < *gutta,* a drop], 1. in the form of drops. 2. spotted, as with drops.

gut·tat·ed (gut′ā-tid), *adj.* guttate.

gut·ter (gut′ẽr), *n.* [ME. *gotere;* OFr. *gutiere* < L. *gutta,* a drop], 1. a trough or channel along or under the eaves of a roof, to carry off rain water. 2. a narrow channel or ditch along the side of a road or street, to carry off surface water; hence, 3. a place or state of living characterized by dirt, poverty, and squalor. 4. a channel or groove similar to a gutter, as the grooves on either side of a bowling alley. *v.t.* to furnish with gutters; make gutters in. *v.i.* 1. to flow in a stream. 2. to melt rapidly so that the wax or tallow runs off in channels: said of a candle.

gut·ter·ing (gut′ẽr-iŋ), *n.* 1. the act of making gutters. 2. material for gutters. 3. a system or set of gutters. 4. the melting and running of wax or tallow on a burning candle.

gut·ter·snipe (gut′ẽr-snīp′), *n.* [orig. (Brit. dial.), the common snipe: so called from picking food out of gutters], [Colloq.], a poor, neglected child who spends most of his time in the streets; slum child; street urchin: contemptuous term.

gut·tle (gut′'l), *v.i. & v.t.* [GUTTLED (-'ld), GUTTLING], [prob. < *gut* + *guzzle*], to eat greedily; gormandize.

gut·tur·al (gut′ẽr-'l), *adj.* [L. *guttur,* throat; + *-al*], 1. of the throat. 2. loosely, produced in the throat; rasping: said of sounds. 3. characterized by such sounds: as, a *guttural* language. 4. formed by placing the back of the tongue close to or against the soft palate, as the *k* in *keen;* velar. *n.* 1. a sound produced in this way. 2. a symbol representing such a sound. The term is now seldom used by phoneticians.

Guy (gī), [Fr. *Gui, Guy,* lit., leader; see GUY (rope)], a masculine name: equivalents, It. & Sp. *Guido.*

guy (gī), *n.* [OFr. *guie,* a guide, crane < *guier,* to guide], a rope, chain, or rod attached to something to steady or guide it. *v.t.* to guide or steady with a guy.

guy (gī), *n.* [after *Guy* Fawkes (1570–1606), Eng. conspirator executed for his part in the Gunpowder Plot, an unsuccessful plan to blow up Parliament and King James I on Nov. 5, 1605], 1. in England, an effigy of Guy Fawkes displayed and burned on the anniversary of the Gunpowder Plot. 2. a person whose appearance or dress is odd. 3. [Slang], a boy or man; fellow; chap. *v.t.* [Colloq.], to make fun of; ridicule; josh; tease.

Guy·enne (güē′yen′), *n.* a former province of southwestern France: previously the district of Aquitaine: also spelled **Guienne.**

guz·zle (guz′'l), *v.i. & v.t.* [GUZZLED (-'ld), GUZZLING], [? < OFr. *gosillier* < *gosier,* throat < Gaul. *geusiae,* throat], to drink (or, rarely, eat) greedily or immoderately.

g.v., gravimetric volume.

Gwa·li·or (gwä′li-ôr′), *n.* the chief city in Madhyabharat, India: pop., 22,000.

Gwen·do·len, Gwen·do·line, Gwen·do·lyn (gwen′də-lin), [< Celt.; see GUINEVERE], a feminine name: diminutive, *Gwen.*

Gwin·nett, But·ton (but′'n gwi-net′), 1735?–1777; American patriot; signer of the Declaration of Independence.

Gwyn, Nell (gwin), (born *Eleanor Gwyn*), 1650–1687; English actress; mistress of Charles II.

gybe (jīb), *v.i. & v.t.* [GYBED (jībd), GYBING], *n.* in *nautical usage,* jibe.

gym (jim), *n.* [Colloq.], 1. a gymnasium. 2. a course in gymnastics, athletics, etc., in school or college.

gym·kha·na (jim-kä′nə), *n.* [Anglo-Ind.; prob. comb. of *gymnasium* + Hind. & Urdu *gēd-khānā,* racket court], 1. a place where athletic contests or games are held. 2. a sports meet.

gymn-, gymno-.

gym·na·si·a (jim-nā′zi-ə), alternative plural of **gymnasium.**

gym·na·si·arch (jim-nā′zi-ärk′), *n.* [L. *gymnasiarchus;* Gr. *gymnasiarchos* < *gymnasion,* gymnasium + *archein,* to rule], in ancient Greece, an official who supervised athletic games, contests, and schools, and paid the athletes' trainers.

gym·na·si·ast (jim-nā′zi-ast), *n.* 1. a student in a European Gymnasium. 2. a gymnast.

gym·na·si·um (jim-nā′zi-əm), *n.* [*pl.* GYMNASIUMS (-əmz), GYMNASIA (-ə)], [L.; Gr. *gymnasion,* place for exercising < *gymnazein,* to train naked < *gymnos,* naked, stripped], 1. a room or building equipped for physical training and athletic games and sports. 2. [G-], (G. güm-nä′zi-oom′), in Germany and some other European countries, a secondary school for students preparing to enter a university: name adopted by 15th-century humanists.

gym·nast (jim′nast), *n.* [Gr. *gymnastēs,* trainer of athletes], an expert in gymnastics.

gym·nas·tic (jim-nas′tik), *adj.* [L. *gymnasticus;* Gr. *gymnastikos* < *gymnazein;* see GYMNASIUM], of physical or athletic exercises or activities.

gym·nas·ti·cal (jim-nas′ti-k'l), *adj.* gymnastic.

gym·nas·tics (jim-nas′tiks), *n.pl.* [< *gymnastic*], 1. exercises to develop and train the muscles; especially, exercises that can be done in a gymnasium; calisthenics, tumbling, apparatus work, etc. 2. [construed as sing.], the art or sport of such exercises.

gym·no- (jim′nō, jim′nə), [< Gr. *gymnos,* naked], a

combining form meaning *naked, stripped, bare,* as in *gymnosperm*: also, before a vowel, **gymn-.**

gym·nos·o·phist (jim-nos'ə-fist), *n.* [< L. *gymnosophistae,* pl.; Gr. *gymnosophistai* < *gymnos,* naked + *sophistēs,* philosopher], 1. a member of an ancient Hindu sect of ascetics who wore little or no clothing. 2. a person who practices nudism; nudist.

gym·no·sperm (jim'nə-spũrm'), *n.* [Mod. L. *gymnospermus;* see GYMNOSPERMOUS], any of a large class of plants producing seeds not enclosed in a seed case or ovary, as certain evergreens.

gym·no·sper·mous (jim'nə-spũr'məs), *adj.* [Mod. L. *gymnospermus;* Gr. *gymnospermos* < *gymnos,* naked + *sperma,* a seed], of the gymnosperms; having seeds not enclosed in a seed case or ovary.

gyn- (jin, jin; *sometimes* gīn), gyno-.

gyn·ae·ce·um (jī'ni-sē'əm, jin'i-sē'əm), *n.* [*pl.* GYNAECEA (-ə)], [L.; Gr. *gynaikeion* < *gynaikeios,* of women, feminine < *gynē,* woman], 1. in ancient Greek and Roman houses, the rooms set apart for women. 2. a gynoecium.

gyn·ae·co- (jī'ni-kō, jin'i-kō; *sometimes* gī'ni-kō), gyneco-.

gyn·ae·o- (jī'ni-ō, jin'i-ō), gyneo-.

gy·nan·drous (ji-nan'drəs, ji-nan'drəs, gī-nan'drəs), *adj.* [Gr. *gynandros,* of doubtful sex < *gynē,* a woman + *anēr, andros,* a man], 1. in *botany,* having the stamen, or male organ, and pistil, or female organ, united in one column. 2. characterized by gynandry.

gy·nan·dry (jī-nan'dri, ji-nan'dri, gī-nan'dri), *n.* [*gyn-* + Gr. *anēr, andros,* a man], hermaphroditism.

gyn·arch·y (jī'när-ki, jin'är-ki), *n.* [*pl.* GYNARCHIES (-kiz)], [*gyn-* + *-archy*], government by a woman or women.

gy·ne·ci·um (jī-nē'si-əm, ji-nē'si-əm), *n.* [*pl.* GYNECIA (-ə)], a gynoecium.

gyn·e·co- (jī'ni-kō, jin'i-kō; *sometimes* gī'ni-kō), [Gr. *gynaiko-* < *gynē,* a woman], a combining form meaning *woman, female,* as in *gynecocracy, gynecology*: words beginning with *gyneco-* may also be spelled **gynaeco-.**

gyn·e·coc·ra·cy (jī'ni-kok'rə-si, jin'i-kok'rə-si), *n.* [*pl.* GYNECOCRACIES (-siz)], [Gr. *gynaikokratia* < *gynē, gynaikos,* a woman + *kratein,* to rule], government by a woman or women.

gyn·e·co·log·ic (jī'ni-kə-loj'ik, jin'i-kə-loj'ik, gī'ni-kə-loj'ik), *adj.* of gynecology.

gyn·e·col·o·gist (jī'ni-kol'ə-jist, jin'i-kol'ə-jist, gī'ni-kol'ə-jist), *n.* a specialist in gynecology.

gyn·e·col·o·gy (jī'ni-kol'ə-ji, jin'i-kol'ə-ji, gī'ni-kol'ə-ji), *n.* [*gyneco-* + *-logy*], the branch of medicine dealing with the study and treatment of women's diseases, especially of the genitourinary and rectal tracts.

gyn·e·co·mor·phous (jī-nē'kə-môr'fəs, jin'i-kə-môr'fəs), *adj.* [*gyneco-* + *-morphous*], having the form or structural characteristics of a woman or female.

gyn·e·o- (jī'ni-ō, jin'i-ō), [Gr. *gynaios* < *gynē,* a woman], a combining form meaning *woman*: words beginning with *gyneo-* may also be spelled **gynaeo-.**

gy·ne·pho·bi·a (jī'ni-fō'bi-ə, jin'i-fō'bi-ə), *n.* [*gyne-* + *-phobia*], an abnormal fear of women.

gyn·i·at·rics (jī'ni-at'riks, jin'i-at'riks), *n.pl.* [construed as sing.], [*gyn-* + *-iatrics*], the branch of medicine dealing with the treatment of women's diseases.

gyn·o- (jī'nō, jin'ə), [< Gr. *gynē,* woman], a combining form meaning: 1. *woman, female.* 2. *female reproductive organ, ovary, pistil,* as in *gynoecium, gynophore.* Also, before a vowel, **gyn-,** as in *gynarchy.*

gy·noe·ci·um (jī-nē'si-əm, ji-nē'si-əm), *n.* [*pl.* GYNOECIA (-ə)], [Mod. L. < *gyn-* + Gr. *oikos,* house], the female organ or organs of a flower; pistil or pistils: also spelled **gynaeceum, gynecium.**

gyn·o·phore (jī'nə-fôr', jin'ə-fōr'), *n.* [*gyno-* + *-phore*], a stalk bearing the gynoecium.

-gyn·ous (jin-us), [Mod. L. *-gynus;* Gr. *-gynos* < *gynē,* a woman], a combining form meaning: 1. *woman, female,* as in *polygynous.* 2. *having female organs* or *pistils,* as in *monogynous, androgynous.*

-gyn·y (jin-i), a combining form used to form nouns corresponding to adjectives ending in *-gynous.*

gyp (jip), *n.* [prob. < *gypsy*], [Slang], 1. a swindle; cheat. 2. a swindler. *v.t. & v.i.* [GYPPED (jipt), GYPPING], [Slang], to swindle; cheat. Also spelled **gip.**

gyp (jip), *n.* [? < *gypsy*], [Brit.], a servant at a college.

gyp·se·ous (jip'si-əs), *adj.* [LL. *gypseus* < L. *gypsum*], 1. like gypsum. 2. containing or consisting of gypsum.

gyp·sif·er·ous (jip-sif'ẽr-əs), *adj.* [< *gypsum* + *-ferous*], containing or producing gypsum.

gyp·soph·i·la (jip-sof'ə-lə), *n.* [Mod. L.; see GYPSUM & -PHIL], any of a group of plants bearing clusters of small white or pink flowers with a delicate fragrance, as babies'-breath.

gyp·sum (jip'səm), *n.* [L.; Gr. *gypsos,* chalk, gypsum], a hydrated sulfate of calcium, $CaSO_4 \cdot 2H_2O$, occurring naturally in sedimentary rocks and used for making plaster of Paris, in treating soil, etc.

gyp·sy (jip'si), *n.* [*pl.* GYPSIES (-siz)], [earlier *gypcien,* short for *Egipcien,* Egyptian: so called because thought to have come from Egypt], 1. [often G-], a member of a wandering Caucasian people with dark skin and black hair, found throughout the world and believed to have originated in India: they are known as musicians, fortune-tellers, etc. 2. [G-], their Indo-European, Indic language, probably based on a dialect of northwestern India; Romany. 3. a person whose appearance or habits are like those of a gypsy. *adj.* of or like a gypsy or gypsies. *v.i.* [GYPSIED (-sid), GYPSYING], to wander or live like a gypsy. Also spelled **gipsy.**

gypsy moth, a European moth, brownish or white, now common in the eastern United States: its larvae feed on leaves, doing much damage to trees and plants.

gy·ral (jī'rəl), *adj.* [< *gyre* + *-al*], 1. moving in a circular or spiral path; gyratory. 2. of a gyrus.

gy·rate (jī'rāt, jī-rāt'), *v.i.* [GYRATED (-id), GYRATING], [< L. *gyratus,* pp. of *gyrare,* to turn, whirl < *gyrus;* Gr. *gyros,* a circle], to move in a circular or spiral path; rotate about a center or axis; revolve; whirl. *adj.* (jī'rāt), spiral; coiled; circular; convolute. —*SYN.* see **turn.**

gy·ra·tion (jī-rā'shən), *n.* 1. a gyrating; circular or spiral motion. 2. a whorl.

gy·ra·tor (jī-rā'tẽr), *n.* a person or thing that gyrates.

gy·ra·to·ry (jī'rə-tôr'i, jī'rə-tō'ri), *adj.* moving in a circular or spiral path; whirling; spiraling; gyrating.

gyre (jīr), *n.* [L. *gyrus;* Gr. *gyros,* a circle], 1. a circular or spiral motion; whirl; revolution. 2. a circular or spiral form; vortex. *v.i. & v.t.* [GYRED (jīrd), GYRING], [Rare], to whirl.

gy·rene (jī-rēn', jī'rēn), *n.* [origin unc.], [Slang], a member of the United States Marine Corps.

gyr·fal·con (jũr'fôl'k'n, jũr'fô'k'n), *n.* [ME. & OFr. *gerfaucon;* Frank. **gerfalko* (akin to ON. *geirfalki*) < Gmc. *ger,* spear + *falco,* falcon], a large, fierce, strong falcon of the arctic regions: also spelled **gerfalcon.**

gy·ro (jī'rō), *n.* [Colloq.], 1. an autogiro. 2. a gyroscope. 3. a gyrocompass.

gy·ro- (jī'rō, jī'rə), [< Gr. *gyros,* a circle], a combining form meaning: 1. *gyrating,* as in *gyroscope.* 2. *spiral,* as in *gyroidal.* 3. *gyroscope,* as in *gyrocompass.*

gy·ro·com·pass (jī'rō-kum'pəs), *n.* a compass consisting of a motor-operated gyroscope whose rotating axis, kept in a horizontal plane, takes a position parallel to the axis of the earth's rotation and thus points to the geographic north pole instead of to the magnetic pole.

gy·ro·pi·lot (jī'rō-pī'lət), *n.* [*gyro-* + *pilot*], an instrument that automatically keeps an airplane flying evenly at the same height on a set course: it consists of two vacuum-driven gyroscopes: also called *automatic pilot.*

gy·ro·plane (jī'rə-plān'), *n.* [*gyro-* + *-plane*], an aircraft resembling the autogiro: the pitch of the blades of its horizontal propeller can be changed by rotating the blades around their axes.

gy·ro·scope (jī'rə-skōp'), *n.* [*gyro-* + *-scope*], a wheel mounted in a ring so that its axis is free to turn in any direction: when the wheel is spun rapidly, it will keep its original plane of rotation no matter which way the ring is turned: gyroscopes are used in gyrocompasses and to keep moving ships, airplanes, etc. level.

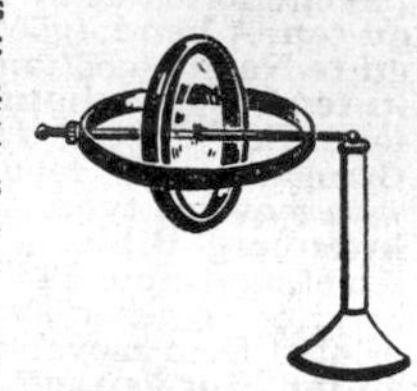

GYROSCOPE

gy·ro·scop·ic (jī'rə-skop'ik), *adj.* of a gyroscope or its characteristic action.

gy·ro·scop·i·cal·ly (jī'rə-skop'i-k'l-i, jī'rə-skop'ik-li), *adv.* by means of a gyroscope.

gy·rose (jī'rōs), *adj.* [< *gyre* + *-ose*], marked with wavy lines or convolutions.

gy·ro·sta·bi·liz·er (jī'rō-stā'bə-līz'ẽr), *n.* a device consisting of a gyroscope spinning in a vertical plane, used to stabilize the side to side rocking of a ship or airplane.

gy·ro·stat (jī'rə-stat'), *n.* [*gyro-* + *-stat*], a gyroscope consisting of a rotating wheel set in a case, used for demonstrating the dynamics of rotating bodies.

gy·ro·stat·ic (jī'rə-stat'ik), *adj.* 1. of a gyrostat. 2. of gyrostatics.

gy·ro·stat·ics (jī'rə-stat'iks), *n.pl.* [construed as sing.], [*gyro-* + *statics*], the branch of physics dealing with rotating bodies and their tendency to maintain their plane of rotation.

gy·rus (jī'rəs), *n.* [*pl.* GYRI (-rī)], [L.; see GYRE, *n.*], in *anatomy,* a convoluted ridge or fold between fissures, or sulci, especially of the cortex of the brain.

gyve (jīv), *n. & v.t.* [GYVED (jīvd), GYVING], [ME. *give;* Anglo-Fr. *guives,* pl.; ? < ME. *withe,* thong, band; cf. WITHY], [Archaic], fetter; shackle.

H

H, h (āch), *n.* [*pl.* H's, h's, Hs, hs (āch'iz)], 1. the eighth letter of the English alphabet: from the Greek *eta*, a borrowing from the Phoenician: see **alphabet**, table. 2. the sound of H or h, phonetically a rough breathing (aspirate): in English, a glottal fricative in which the glottis gradually narrows toward the position for voicing the following vowel while the tongue and lips assume the position for articulating it; in many words originally from French, as *honor*, *honest*, initial *h* is silent. 3. a type or impression for H or h. 4. *a symbol for* the eighth in a sequence or group. *adj.* 1. of H or h. 2. eighth in a sequence or group.

H (āch), *n.* 1. an object shaped like H. 2. a Roman numeral for 200: with a superior bar (H̄), 200,000. 3. in *chemistry, the symbol for* hydrogen. 4. in *music*, the German name for the note B natural. 5. in *physics, the symbol for*: *a*) henry. *b*) the horizontal component of terrestrial magnetism. *adj.* shaped like H.

H., h., 1. harbor. 2. hard. 3. hardness. 4. heavy sea. 5. height. 6. hence. 7. high. 8. hour; hours. 9. hundred. 10. husband. 11. in *music*, horns.

ha (hä), *interj.* [echoic], an exclamation variously expressing wonder, surprise, anger, triumph, etc.: repeated (*ha-ha* or *haw-haw!*) it indicates laughter, derision, etc. *n.* the sound of this exclamation or of a laugh. Also spelled **hah.**

ha., hectare; hectares.

h.a., 1. high-angle (gun). 2. *hoc anno*, [L.], in this year.

haaf (häf), *n.* [ON. *haf*, high sea, ocean; akin to Dan. *hav*], deep-sea fishing waters off the Shetland and Orkney Islands.

Haa·kon VII (hô'koon), 1872–1957; king of Norway (1905–1957).

Haar·lem (här'ləm), *n.* the capital of North Holland, Netherlands: pop., 158,000 (1947).

Ha·bak·kuk (hə-bak'ək, hab'ə-kuk'), *n.* [Heb. *habhaqquq*; prob. < *ḥabaq*, to embrace], in the *Bible*, 1. a Hebrew prophet of about the 7th century B.C. 2. a book of the Old Testament containing his prophecies: abbreviated **Hab.** Also, in the Douay Bible, **Habacuc.**

Ha·ba·na (ä-bä'nä), *n.* Havana: the Spanish name.

ha·ba·ne·ra (hä'bə-nā'rə; Sp. ä'bä-ne'rä), *n.* [Sp., lit., of *Habana* (Havana)], 1. a slow Cuban dance similar to the tango. 2. the music for this.

‡ha·be·as cor·pus (hā'bi-əs kôr'pəs), [L., (that) you have the body], in *law*, a writ or order requiring that a prisoner be brought before a court at a stated time and place to decide the legality of his detention or imprisonment: the right of *habeas corpus* safeguards one against illegal detention or imprisonment.

hab·er·dash·er (hab'ẽr-dash'ẽr), *n.* [ME. *haberdashere*; prob. < Anglo-Fr. *hapertas*, kind of cloth], 1. a person whose work or business is selling men's furnishings, such as hats, shirts, neckties, handkerchiefs, gloves, etc. 2. [Chiefly British], a dealer in various small articles, such as ribbons, lace, thread, needles, etc., or, formerly, caps and hats.

hab·er·dash·er·y (hab'ẽr-dash'ẽr-i), *n.* [*pl.* HABERDASHERIES (-iz)], 1. things sold by a haberdasher. 2. a haberdasher's shop.

hab·er·geon (hab'ẽr-jən), *n.* [OFr. *haubergeon*, dim. of *hauberc*; see HAUBERK], 1. a short, high-necked jacket of mail, usually sleeveless: also **haubergeon.** 2. a hauberk.

hab·ile (hab'il), *adj.* [ME.; OFr.; L. *habilis*; see ABLE], able; skillful; handy; clever.

ha·bil·i·ment (hə-bil'ə-mənt), *n.* [Fr. *habillement* < *habiller*, to clothe, make fit < *habile*; see HABILE], 1. a piece of clothing; garment. 2. *usually in pl.* clothing; dress; attire.

ha·bil·i·tate (hə-bil'ə-tāt'), *v.t.* [HABILITATED (-id), HABILITATING], [< ML. *habilitatus*, pp. of *habilitare*, to make suitable < L. *habilis* (see HABILE); after G. *habilitieren*], 1. to clothe; equip; outfit. 2. in *mining*, to provide (a mine) with money and supplies.

ha·bil·i·ta·tion (hə-bil'ə-tā'shən), *n.* [ML. *habilitatio*], a habilitating or being habilitated.

hab·it (hab'it), *n.* [ME.; OFr.; L. *habitus*, condition, appearance, dress; pp. of *habere*, to have, hold], 1. costume; dress. 2. a particular costume showing rank, status, etc.; specifically, *a*) a distinctive religious costume: as, a monk's *habit*. *b*) a costume worn for certain occasions: as, a woman's riding *habit*. 3. habitual or characteristic condition of mind or body; disposition: as, a man of healthy *habit*. 4. a thing done often and hence, usually, done easily; practice; custom; act that is acquired and has become automatic; hence, 5. a tendency to perform a certain action or behave in a certain way; usual way of doing: as, he does it out of *habit*. 6. an addiction: as, the alcohol *habit*. 7. in *biology*, the tendency of a plant or animal to grow in a certain way; characteristic growth: as, a twining *habit*. *v.t.* 1. to put a habit on; dress; clothe. 2. [Archaic], to inhabit.

SYN.—**habit** refers to an act repeated so often by an individual that it has become automatic with him (his *habit* of tugging at the ear in perplexity); **practice** also implies the regular repetition of an act but does not suggest that it is automatic (the *practice* of reading in bed); **custom** applies to any act or procedure carried on by tradition and often enforced by social disapproval of any violation (the *custom* of dressing for dinner); **usage** refers to custom or practice that has become sanctioned through being long established (*usage* is the only authority in language); **wont** is a literary or somewhat archaic equivalent for **practice** (it was his *wont* to rise early).

hab·it·a·ble (hab'i-tə-b'l), *adj.* [ME.; OFr.; L. *habitabilis* < *habitare*; see HABIT & -ABLE], that can be inhabited; fit to be lived in.

hab·i·tan·cy (hab'i-tən-si), *n.* 1. inhabitancy; dwelling; residing. 2. inhabitants collectively; population.

hab·i·tant (hab'i-tənt; *also, for* 2 & *alternative sp.*, Fr. å'bē'tän'), *n.* [Fr.; L. *habitans*, ppr. of *habitare*; see HABIT], 1. an inhabitant; resident. 2. a farmer in Louisiana or Canada of French descent: also **habitan.**

hab·i·tat (hab'ə-tat'), *n.* [L., it inhabits], 1. the region where a plant or animal naturally grows or lives; native environment. 2. the place where a person or thing is ordinarily found.

hab·i·ta·tion (hab'ə-tā'shən), *n.* [ME. *habitacioun*; OFr. *habitacion*; L. *habitatio*; cf. HABIT], 1. an inhabiting; occupancy. 2. a place in which to live; dwelling; residence; home.

hab·it·ed (hab'it-id), *adj.* [pp. of *habit*], 1. dressed; clothed; attired. 2. [Rare], inhabited.

ha·bit·u·al (hə-bich'ōō-əl), *adj.* [LL. *habitualis*, of habit or dress < L. *habitus*; see HABIT], 1. formed or acquired by continual use; done or caused by habit; customary. 2. being or doing a certain thing by habit; steady; inveterate: as, a *habitual* smoker. 3. usual; frequent; much seen, done, or used. —*SYN.* see **usual.**

ha·bit·u·al·ly (hə-bich'ōō-əl-i, hə-bich'oo-li), *adv.* by habit; regularly; customarily.

ha·bit·u·ate (hə-bich'ōō-āt'), *v.t.* [HABITUATED (-id), HABITUATING], [< LL. *habituatus*, pp. of *habituare*, to bring into a condition or habit of the body < L. *habitus*; see HABIT], 1. to make used (*to*); accustom; familiarize: often used reflexively. 2. [Colloq.], to attend or visit often; frequent.

ha·bit·u·a·tion (hə-bich'ōō-ā'shən), *n.* [ML. *habituatio*], a habituating or being habituated.

hab·i·tude (hab'ə-tōōd', hab'i-tūd'), *n.* [Fr.; L. *habitudo*, condition, habit; see HABIT], 1. habitual or characteristic condition of mind or body; disposition. 2. usual way of doing something; custom.

ha·bit·u·é (hə-bich'ōō-ā', hə-bich'ōō-ā'), *n.* [Fr.; pp. of *habituer*, to accustom], a person who frequents a certain club, restaurant, etc.

Habs·burg (haps'bẽrg; G. häps'boorkh), *n.* Hapsburg.

ha·chure (hə-shoor'; *also, for n.*, hash'oor), *n.* [Fr. < *hacher*, to chop < *hache*, ax], any of a series of short, thin, parallel lines used, especially in map-making, to represent a sloping or elevated surface. *v.t.* [HA-

CHURED (-shoord'), HACHURING], to show by, or shade with, hachures.

ha·cien·da (hä'si-en'də; Sp. ä-syen'dä), *n.* [Sp. < OSp. *facienda*, employment, estate; L. *facienda*, things to be done < *facere*, to do], in Spanish America, 1. a large estate, ranch, plantation, or house in the country. 2. a farm, factory, mine, etc. in the country.

hack (hak), *v.t.* [ME. *hacken*; AS. *haccian*; akin to G. *hacken* & *hacke*, a hoe], 1. to chop or cut crudely, roughly, or irregularly, as with a hatchet; whack at: as, he *hacked* the crate to pieces. 2. to break up (land) with a hoe, mattock, etc. 3. in *Rugby football*, to kick (an opponent) on the shins. *v.i.* 1. to make rough or irregular cuts. 2. to give harsh, dry coughs. *n.* 1. a tool for cutting or hacking; ax, hoe, mattock, etc. 2. a slash, gash, or notch made by a sharp implement. 3. a harsh, dry cough. 4. in *Rugby football*, a cut or bruise made by a kick on the shins.

hack (hak), *n.* [< *hackney*], 1. a horse for hire. 2. a horse for all sorts of work. 3. a saddle-horse. 4. an old, worn-out horse. 5. a person hired to do routine, often dull, writing; literary drudge. 6. a carriage or coach for hire. 7. a taxicab. 8. a hackman. *v.t.* 1. to employ as a hack. 2. to hire out (a horse, etc.). 3. to wear out or make stale by constant use. *v.i.* 1. to ride a horse, especially a hired horse, for pleasure or exercise. 2. [Colloq.], to drive a taxicab. *adj.* 1. employed as a hack: as, a *hack* writer. 2. done by a hack: as, *hack* work. 3. stale; trite; hackneyed.

hack (hak), *n.* [orig., board on which a falcon's meat was put; var. of *hatch*], 1. a grating or rack for drying cheese or fish, holding food for cattle, etc. 2. a pile or row of unburnt bricks set out to dry. *v.t.* to place on a hack for drying.

hack·a·more (hak'ə-môr', hak'ə-mōr'), *n.* [? altered < Sp. *jaquima*, halter], in the Western United States, a rope or rawhide halter, used in breaking horses.

hack·ber·ry (hak'ber'i, hak'bẽr-i), *n.* [*pl.* HACKBERRIES (-iz)], [< Scand.; cf. Dan. *hæggebær*, Norw. *haggebär*, ON. *heggr*; akin to Eng. *hedge*], 1. an American tree of the elm family, with a small fruit resembling a cherry. 2. its fruit. 3. its wood. Also **hagberry.**

hack·but (hak'but), *n.* [Fr. *haquebut*, *haquebute* < obs. D. *hakebus*; *hake*, *haak*, hook + *bus*, a gun, gun barrel, lit., box], an obsolete type of portable firearm with a bent or hooked butt; kind of harquebus: also **hagbut.**

Hack·en·sack (hak''n-sak'), *n.* 1. a river in New York and New Jersey, flowing into Newark Bay: length, 50 mi. 2. a city in northeastern New Jersey, on this river: pop., 31,000.

hack hammer, a tool like an adz with a hammerhead, used in dressing stone.

hack·ing (hak'iŋ), *adj.* [ppr. of *hack* (to cut)], harsh and dry: said of a cough.

hack·le (hak''l), *n.* [orig., *hatchel*; (late) ME. *hakell*, var. of *hechele* (see HATCHEL): so called from resemblance to a *hatchel*], 1. *a*) any of the long, slender feathers at the neck of a rooster, peacock, pigeon, etc. *b*) such feathers, collectively. 2. in *fishing*, *a*) a tuft of feathers from a rooster's neck, used as the legs of an artificial fly. *b*) a hackle fly. 3. *pl.* the hairs on a dog's neck and back that bristle, as when it is in danger. *v.t.* [HACKLED (-'ld), HACKLING], to put feathers from a rooster's neck on (a fishing fly).

hack·le (hak''l), *n.* & *v.t.* [HACKLED (-'ld), HACKLING], hatchel.

hack·le (hak''l), *v.t.* & *v.i.* [HACKLED (-'ld), HACKLING], [freq. of *hack* (to cut)], to hack; cut roughly; mangle.

hackle fly, an artificial fishing fly with a hackle instead of wings.

hack·man (hak'mən), *n.* [*pl.* HACKMEN (-mən)], the driver of a hack or carriage for hire.

hack·ma·tack (hak'mə-tak'), *n.* [Am. Ind. (Algonquian)], 1. the American larch; tamarack. 2. the juniper. 3. the wood of either of these trees. 4. a natural bend in a tamarack used in boatbuilding for the stem or framing of a boat: also **hackmatack joint.**

hack·ney (hak'ni), *n.* [*pl.* HACKNEYS (-niz)], [ME. *hakene*, *hakenei* < *Hackney*, England], 1. a horse for ordinary driving or riding. 2. a carriage for hire. 3. a person hired for dull, monotonous work; drudge. *adj.* 1. hired out. 2. stale; trite; commonplace. *v.t.* 1. to hire out. 2. to make trite by overuse.

hack·neyed (hak'nid), *adj.* [pp. of *hackney*], made trite and commonplace by overuse: as, "raven hair" is a *hackneyed* phrase. —*SYN.* see **trite.**

hack·saw (hak'sô'), *n.* a hack saw.

hack saw, a saw for cutting metal, consisting of a narrow, fine-toothed blade held in a frame.

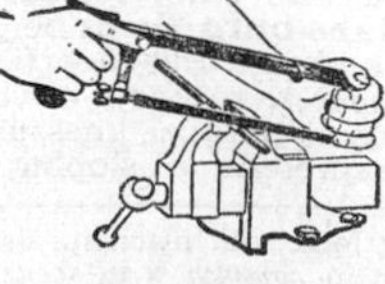

HACK SAW

had (had; *unstressed* həd, əd), [ME. *hadde*, *had*; AS. *hæfde*], past tense and past participle of **have**: also used to indicate preference or necessity, with adverbs, adjectives, and phrases of comparison, such as *rather*, *better*, *as well* (e.g., I *had* better leave).

had·dock (had'ək), *n.* [*pl.* HADDOCK, HADDOCKS (-əks); see PLURAL, II, D, 2], [ME. *hadok*, *haddok*; prob. < OFr. *hadot*, kind of salt fish], a small, edible fish, related to the cod, found off the coasts of Europe and North America.

hade (hād), *n.* [prob. < dial. *hade*, to slope, incline; ? var. of *head*, based on an older pronun.], in *geology*, the angle between the surface of a fault and the vertical plane. *v.i.* [HADED (-id), HADING], in *geology*, to incline from the vertical plane.

Ha·des (hā'dēz), *n.* [Gr. *Haidēs*], 1. in *Greek mythology*, *a*) the home of the dead, beneath the earth. *b*) the ruler of the underworld: also called *Pluto*, *Dis*. 2. in the *Bible*, the state or resting place of the dead: used especially in the Revised Version of the New Testament. 3. [often h-], [Colloq.], hell: a euphemism.

Ha·dhra·maut, Ha·dra·maut (hä'drä-môt'), *n.* a district of southern Arabia, on the Arabian Sea: a part of the Aden Protectorate under Great Britain.

hadj (haj), *n.* [Ar. *hajj* < *hajja*, to set out, go on a pilgrimage], 1. the journey to Mecca that every Moslem is expected to take at least once. 2. a pilgrimage.

hadj·i (haj'ē), *n.* [Ar. *ḥājjī*, form of *ḥājj*, pilgrim; see HADJ], 1. a Moslem who has made his required trip to Mecca: a title of honor. 2. a Christian of the Near East who has visited the shrine of the Holy Sepulcher in Jerusalem.

Had·ley, Henry Kim·ball (kim'bəl had'li), 1871–1937; American composer and conductor.

had·n't (had''nt), had not.

Ha·dri·an (hā'dri-ən), *n.* (*Publius Aelius Hadrianus*), Roman emperor (117–138 A.D.); lived 76–138 A.D.: also **Adrian.**

Hadrian's Wall, a masonry wall from Solway Firth to the Tyne, built (120–123 A.D.) by Hadrian to protect Roman Britain from northern tribes.

hadst (hadst), archaic second person singular, past indicative, of **have**: used with *thou*.

hae (hā, ha), *v.t.* [Scot.], to have.

Haeck·el, Ernst Hein·rich (ernst hīn'riH hek'əl), 1834–1919; German biologist and writer.

haem- (hēm, hem), hem-.

hae·ma- (hē'mə, hem'ə), hema-.

hae·mal (hē'məl), *adj.* hemal.

hae·mat- (hem'at, hē'mat), hemat-.

haem·a·tite (hem'ə-tīt', hē'mə-tīt'), *n.* hematite.

hae·ma·to- (hem'ə-tō, hē'mə-tō), hemato-.

haem·a·tox·y·lon (hē'mə-tok'sə-lon', hem'ə-tok'sə-lon'), *n.* [Mod. L. *haematoxylon*; *haemato-* + Gr. *xylon*, wood], 1. any of a group of tropical trees of the Western Hemisphere, from which logwood is obtained. 2. logwood.

-hae·mi·a (hē'mi-ə), -hemia.

hae·mo- (hē'mə, hem'ə), hemo-.

hae·mo·glo·bin (hē'mə-glō'bin, hem'ə-glō'bin), *n.* hemoglobin.

hae·mo·phil·i·a (hē'mə-fil'i-ə, hem'ə-fil'yə), *n.* hemophilia.

‡**hae·re·des** (hə-rē'dēz), *n.* plural of **haeres.**

‡**hae·res** (hē'rēz), *n.* a heres.

Ha·fiz (hä-fiz'), *n.* (*Shams-ud-Din Mohammed*), Persian lyric poet; lived in the 14th century.

ha·fiz (hä'fiz), *n.* [Ar. *ḥāfiz*, a person who remembers], a Moslem who has memorized the Koran: a title of respect.

haf·ni·um (haf'ni-əm), *n.* [Mod. L. < L. *Hafnia*, ancient name of Copenhagen], a metallic chemical element found with zirconium and somewhat resembling it: symbol, Hf; at. wt., 178.6; at. no., 72.

haft (haft, häft), *n.* [ME.; AS. *hæft*, a handle < base of *habban*, to hold + n. suffix *-t*; see HAVE], a handle or hilt of a knife, sword, etc. *v.t.* to fit with a handle or hilt; fix in a haft.

hag (hag), *n.* [ME. *hagge*, *hegge*, a witch, hag; shortened < AS. *hægtes*, *hægtesse*, a witch, hag < *haga*, a hedge, thicket; akin to G. *hexe* (OHG. *hagazissa*); for sense, cf. ON. *tūnritha*, lit., hedge rider, hence witch, Eng. *hagridden*], 1. originally, a female demon or evil spirit. 2. a witch; enchantress. 3. an ugly, repulsive old woman, especially an evil and malevolent one. 4. a hagfish.

hag (hag), *v.t.* [Scot. < Anglo-N. form of ON. *höggva*, to cut, hack, akin to AS. *heawan* (see HEW)], [Scot. & British dial.], to cut; hack. *n.* [< Anglo-N. form of ON. *högg*, a cutting, chopping < base of the *v.t.*], 1. *a*) a cutting of wood; felling. *b*) a part of a wood marked for felling. *c*) felled trees. 2. *a*) the edge of a cutting in a peat bog. *b*) a marsh or marshy spot. *c*) a place (in a bog or marsh) that is either more or less firm than the surrounding area.

Hag., Haggai.

Ha·gar (hā'gẽr), [Heb. *hāghār* < base prob. akin to Ar. *hajara*, to forsake; cf. HEGIRA], a feminine name. *n.* in the *Bible*, a concubine of Abraham and slave of Abraham's wife Sarah: Hagar fled into the desert with her son Ishmael to escape Sarah's jealous anger: Gen. 16.

hag·ber·ry (hag'ber'i, hag'bẽr-i), *n.* [*pl.* HAGBERRIES (-iz)], the hackberry.

hag·born (hag′bôrn′), *adj.* having a hag, or witch, for a mother.

hag·but (hag′but), *n.* a hackbut.

Ha·gen (hä′gən), *n.* [G.], 1. in the *Nibelungenlied*, Gunther's uncle, who murders Siegfried at the bidding of Brunhild. 2. in Wagner's *Götterdämmerung*, the half-brother of Gunther and Gutrune.

Ha·gers·town (hā′gẽrz-toun′), *n.* a city in northern Maryland: pop., 37,000.

hag·fish (hag′fish′), *n.* [*pl.* HAGFISH, HAGFISHES (-iz); see FISH], [< *hag* (a witch)], any of a number of small, eellike salt-water fishes (*cyclostomes*) with a round, sucking mouth and horny teeth, with which they bore into other fish and devour them.

Hag·ga·da, Hag·ga·dah (hə-gä′də; Heb. hä-gô′dô), *n.* [*pl.* HAGGADOTH (-dōth)], [Heb. *haggadah* < *higgid*, to tell, relate], 1. [often h-], in the *Talmud*, an anecdote or parable that explains or illustrates some point of law; hence, 2. the part of the Talmud devoted to such narratives. 3. the narrative of the Exodus read at the Seder during Passover. 4. a book containing this narrative and the Seder ritual. See also **Halakah.**

hag·gad·ic (hə-gad′ik, hə-gäd′ik), *adj.* of the Haggada.

hag·gad·i·cal (hə-gad′i-k'l, hə-gäd′i-k'l), *adj.* haggadic.

hag·ga·dist (hə-gäd′ist), *n.* a haggadic writer or scholar.

Hag·ga·i (hag′i-ī′, hag′ī), *n.* [Heb. *ḥaggai*, lit., festal], in the *Bible*, 1. a Hebrew prophet who lived c. 500 B.C. 2. a book of the Old Testament attributed to him: abbreviated **Hag.**

hag·gard (hag′ẽrd), *adj.* [MFr. *hagard*, untamed, untamed hawk; prob. < MHG. *hag*, a hedge; see HAG (witch)], 1. in *falconry*, designating a hawk captured after reaching maturity; hence, 2. untamed; unruly; wild. 3. *a*) wild-eyed. *b*) having a wild, wasted, worn look, as from sleeplessness, grief, illness, hunger, etc.; gaunt; drawn. *n.* in *falconry*, a haggard hawk.

Hag·gard, Sir **Henry Ri·der** (rī′dẽr hag′ẽrd), 1856–1925; English novelist.

hag·gis (hag′is), *n.* [ME. *hagas*, kind of pudding; prob. associated with ME. *haggen*, to cut, chop (see HAG, a cutting)], a Scottish dish made of the lungs, heart, etc. of a sheep or calf, mixed with suet, seasoning, and oatmeal and boiled in the animal's stomach.

hag·gish (hag′ish), *adj.* of, like, or characteristic of a hag.

hag·gle (hag′'l), *v.t.* [HAGGLED (-'ld), HAGGLING], [freq. of Scot. *hag* (to chop, cut)], to chop or cut crudely; hack; mangle. *v.i.* to argue about terms, price, etc.; higgle; chaffer; wrangle. *n.* a haggling.

hag·i·arch·y (hag′i-är′ki, hā′ji-är′ki), *n.* [*pl.* HAGIARCHIES (-kiz)], [*hagi-* + *-archy*], 1. government by saints or priests. 2. the hierarchy of saints.

hag·i·o- (hag′i-ō, hā′ji-ō), [< Gr. *hagios*, holy], a prefix meaning *saintly, sacred, holy*, as in *hagiocracy*: also, before a vowel, **hagi-.**

hag·i·oc·ra·cy (hag′i-ok′rə-si, hā′ji-ok′rə-si), *n.* [*pl.* HAGIOCRACIES (-siz)], [*hagio-* + *-cracy*], rule by priests, saints, or others considered holy; theocracy.

Hag·i·og·ra·pha (hag′i-og′rə-fə, hā′ji-og′rə-fə), *n.pl.* [LL.; Gr. *hagiographa* (*biblia*) (transl. of Heb. *kethābhē haqqōdhesh*, lit., writings of holiness) < Gr. *hagios*, holy + *-graphos*, writing], the third and final part of the Jewish Scriptures, those books not in the Law or the Prophets.

hag·i·og·ra·pher (hag′i-og′rə-fẽr, hā′ji-og′rə-fẽr), *n.* 1. any of the authors of the Hagiographa. 2. any sacred or holy writer. 3. an author of lives of the saints.

hag·i·og·ra·phist (hag′i-og′rə-fist, hā′ji-og′rə-fist), *n.* a hagiographer.

hag·i·og·ra·phy (hag′i-og′rə-fi, hā′ji-og′rə-fi), *n.* [*hagio-* + *-graphy*], 1. the writing or study of lives of the saints. 2. a book or books containing such lives.

hag·i·ol·a·ter (hag′i-ol′ə-tẽr, hā′ji-ol′ə-tẽr), *n.* a person given to hagiolatry; saint-worshiper.

hag·i·ol·a·try (hag′i-ol′ə-tri, hā′ji-ol′ə-tri), *n.* [*hagio-* + *-latry*], reverence for or worship of saints.

hag·i·ol·o·gy (hag′i-ol′ə-ji, hā′ji-ol′ə-ji), *n.* [*pl.* HAGIOLOGIES (-jiz)], [*hagio-* + *-logy*], 1. literature about saints' lives and legends, sacred writings, etc. 2. a book or collection of saints' lives and legends. 3. a catalogue or list of saints.

hag·i·o·scope (hag′i-ə-skōp′, hā′ji-ə-skōp′), *n.* [*hagio-* + *-scope*], a narrow opening in an inside wall of a church to let those in a side aisle, or transept, see the main altar.

hag·rid·den (hag′rid′'n), *adj.* 1. originally, ridden by a hag, or witch; hence, 2. obsessed or harassed, as by fears or nightmares.

Hague, The (hāg), the political capital of the Netherlands: pop., 607,000: scene of the first International Peace Conference (1899) and headquarters of the Hague Tribunal: Dutch name, *'s-Gravenhage.*

Hague Tribunal, the Permanent Court of Arbitration founded in 1899: it was succeeded in 1922 by the Permanent Court of International Justice which, since 1945, selects the nominees for election to the United Nations International Court of Justice.

hah (hä), *interj.* & *n.* ha.

ha-ha (hä′hä′), *interj.* & *n.* see **ha,** *interj.* & *n.*

ha-ha, ha·ha (hä′hä′), *n.* [Fr. *haha;* prob. playful extension of *haïe*, a hedge], a fence, wall, etc. set in a ditch around a garden or park so as not to hide the view from within.

Hah·ne·mann, Samuel (hä′nə-mən; G. hä′nə-män′), (*Christian Friedrich Samuel Hahnemann*), 1755–1843; German physician; founder of homeopathy.

Hai·da (hī′də), *n.* 1. any of a tribe of North American Indians of the Queen Charlotte Islands, British Columbia. 2. their (possibly Athapascan) language.

Hai·fa (hī′fə), *n.* a seaport in northern Israel, on the Mediterranean: pop., 170,000.

Haig, Douglas (hāg), first Earl Haig, 1861–1928; British commander in chief, World War I.

haik, haick (hīk, hāk), *n.* [Ar. *ḥayk* < *ḥāka*, to weave], a sheetlike piece of woolen or cotton cloth worn by Arabs as an outer garment.

hai·ku (hī′ko͞o), *n.* [Jap.], 1. a Japanese verse form consisting of three lines totaling 17 syllables, usually on some subject in nature. 2. [*pl.* HAIKU], a poem in this form.

hai·kwan (hī′kwän′), *n.* [Chin., lit., sea gate], Chinese maritime import duties.

hail (hāl), *v.t.* [ME. *hailen, heylen*, to salute, greet; ON. *heilla* < *heill*, whole, sound; akin to AS. *hal* (see HALE, WHOLE): used as a salutation], 1. to shout to in greeting, welcome, etc.; cheer. 2. to name by way of tribute; salute as: as, they *hailed* him their leader. 3. to shout to or after; attract the attention of by calling: as, they *hailed* a taxi. *v.i.* in *nautical usage*, to call out or signal to a ship. *n.* 1. a hailing; greeting; salutation. 2. the distance that a shout will carry: as, he is within *hail. interj.* an exclamation of tribute, greeting, etc.

hail fellow well met, very sociable or friendly to everyone, especially in a superficial manner: also **hail fellow, hail-fellow.**

hail from, to be from; come from (one's birthplace or established residence).

hail (hāl), *n.* [ME. *haile;* AS. *hægel*, var. of *hagol* & hence akin to G. *hagel;* IE. base **kaghlo-*, small pebble], 1. small, rounded pieces of ice that sometimes fall during thunderstorms; frozen raindrops; hailstones; hence, 2. a falling, showering, etc. of hail, or in the manner of hail: as, a *hail* of explosives. *v.i.* [ME. *hailen, hagelen* < AS. *hagalian* < *hagol*, hail; altered after form of *n.*], to drop or pour down hail: usually in an impersonal construction, e.g., it is *hailing. v.t.* to shower, hurl, pour, etc. violently in the manner of hail (often with *on* or *upon*): as, he *hailed* curses upon us.

hail (hāl), *adj.* hale (healthy).

hail Columbia, [euphemism for *hell*], [Slang], 1. a severe beating, punishment, scolding, etc. 2. boisterous activity; racket; rumpus.

Hai·le Se·las·sie (hī′li sə-las′i, sə-lä′si), (*Ras Taffari*), 1891– ; emperor of Ethiopia (1930–).

Hail Mary, Ave Maria.

hail·stone (hāl′stōn′), *n.* a piece of hail.

hail·storm (hāl′stôrm′), *n.* a storm in which hail falls.

Hai·nan (hī′nän′), *n.* an island off southern China: a part of Kwantung province: area, 13,500 sq. mi.; pop., 3,000,000.

Hai·naut (e′nō′), *n.* a province of southwestern Belgium: pop., 1,277,000; capital, Mons.

Hai·phong (hī′foŋ′), *n.* a seaport in North Vietnam: pop., 189,000.

hair (hâr), *n.* [ME. *heer, here;* altered after OFr. *haire*, hair shirt; AS. *hær;* akin to G. *haar;* prob. IE. base **ker-*, bristles], 1. any of the fine, threadlike outgrowths from the skin of an animal or human being. 2. a growth of these; especially, *a*) the growth covering the human head. *b*) the growth covering all or part of the skin of most mammals. 3. material woven from hair. 4. an extremely small space, margin, degree, etc.: as, he missed the target by a *hair*. 5. in *botany*, a threadlike growth on a plant. *adj.* 1. made of or with hair. 2. for the care of the hair: as, *hair* tonic.

get in one's hair, [Slang], to annoy one.

hair of the dog (that bit one), [Colloq.], a drink of alcoholic liquor taken as a supposed cure for a hangover.

let one's hair down, [Slang], to be very informal, relaxed, and free in behavior.

make one's hair stand on end, to terrify or horrify one.

not turn a hair, to show no fear, surprise, embarrassment, etc.; stay calm and unruffled.

split hairs, to make petty distinctions; quibble.

to a hair, exactly; perfectly; right in every detail.

hair·ball (hâr′bôl′), *n.* a rounded mass of hair often found in the stomach of cows, cats, etc.

hair·breadth (hâr′bredth′), *n.* a very short distance; extremely small space. *adj.* very narrow; close: as, a *hairbreadth* escape. Also **hairsbreadth, hair's-breadth.**

hair·brush (hâr′brush′), *n.* a brush for the hair.
hair·cloth (hâr′klôth′), *n.* cloth woven from horsehair or camel's hair: used mainly for covering furniture.
hair·cut (hâr′kut′), *n.* 1. a cutting or clipping of the hair of the head. 2. the style in which the hair is cut.
hair-do (hâr′dōō′), *n.* 1. the style in which (a woman's) hair is arranged; coiffure. 2. a hairdressing.
hair·dress·er (hâr′dres′ẽr), *n.* a person whose work is dressing (women's) hair.
hair·dress·ing (hâr′dres′iŋ), *n.* 1. the business or work of a hairdresser. 2. the action of dressing hair. *adj.* of or for the dressing of hair.
hair·i·ness (hâr′i-nis), *n.* a hairy quality or state.
hair·less (hâr′lis), *adj.* lacking hair; bald.
hair·line (hâr′līn′), *n.* 1. a line, cord, etc. made of hair, as a fishing line of horsehair. 2. a very thin line or stripe. 3. cloth patterned with such stripes. 4. the outline of the hair on the head, especially of the hair above the forehead.
hair net, a net or fine-meshed cap of silk, etc., for keeping a woman's hair in order.
hair·pin (hâr′pin′), *n.* a small, usually U-shaped, piece of wire, shell, etc., for keeping the hair or headdress in place. *adj.* formed like a hairpin: as, a *hairpin* turn.
hair-rais·ing (hâr′rāz′iŋ), *adj.* [Colloq.], causing, or thought of as causing, the hair to stand on end; terrifying; horrifying.
hairs·breadth, hair's-breadth (hârz′bredth′), *n.* & *adj.* hairbreadth.
hair shirt, a shirt or girdle of haircloth, worn for self-punishment by religious ascetics and penitents.
hair space, in *printing,* the narrowest metal space used between words, equal to about 1/2 point.
hair·split·ter (hâr′split′ẽr), *n.* a person who makes overnice or petty distinctions in thought; quibbler.
hair·split·ting (hâr′split′iŋ), *adj.* & *n.* making overnice or petty distinctions; quibbling.
hair·spring (hâr′spriŋ′), *n.* a very slender, hairlike coil that controls the regular movement of the balance wheel in a watch or clock.
hair stroke, a very fine line in writing or printing.
hair-trigger (hâr′trig′ẽr), *adj.* [see next entry], set in motion or operation by a very slight impulse.
hair trigger, a trigger so delicately adjusted that a very slight pressure on it discharges the firearm.
hair·y (hâr′i), *adj.* [HAIRIER (-i-ẽr), HAIRIEST (-i-ist)], 1. covered with hair; hirsute. 2. of or like hair.
Hai·ti (hā′ti), *n.* 1. a republic on the island of Hispaniola, West Indies: area, 10,204 sq. mi.; pop., 3,505,000; capital, Port-au-Prince. 2. Hispaniola: the former name. Abbreviated **Hai.** Also spelled **Hayti.**

HAITI

Hai·ti·an (hā′ti-ən, hā′shən), *adj.* of Haiti, its people, or culture. *n.* 1. a native or inhabitant of Haiti. 2. the French dialect spoken by the Haitians. Also spelled **Haytian.**
haj·i, haj·ji (haj′ē), *n.* hadji.
hake (hāk), *n.* [*pl.* HAKE, HAKES (hāks); see PLURAL, II, D, 2], [prob. < ON. *haki,* a hook (so called from shape of the jaw); cf. Norw. *hakefisk,* trout, salmon, lit., hookfish (so called from shape of lower jaw)], any of various edible sea fishes resembling or related to the cod, as the silver hake, the white hake, etc.
ha·keem (hä-kēm′), *n.* [Ar. *ḥakīm,* wise, learned, hence physician], in Moslem regions, a doctor; physician: also spelled **hakim.**
‡**Ha·ken·kreuz** (hä′k'n-kroits′), *n.* [G., lit., hook-cross], a swastika, especially as the emblem of Nazism.
ha·kim (hä′kim), *n.* [Ar. *ḥākim,* governor], 1. in Moslem regions, a ruler, judge, or governor. 2. (hä-kēm′), [see HAKEEM], a doctor; physician.
Hak·luyt, Richard (hak′lōōt), 1552?–1616; British geographer and travel writer.
Ha·ko·da·te (hä′kô-dä′te), *n.* a city on the southern coast of Hokkaido, Japan: pop., 243,000.
Hal., halogen.
Ha·la·kah, Ha·la·cha (hä′lä-khä′; Heb. hä-lô′khô), *n.* [*pl.* HALAKOTH, HALACHOTH (-khōth′; Heb. -khōth)], [Heb. *halākhāh,* rule by which to go < *halākh,* to go], 1. [often h-], in the *Talmud,* any of the laws or ordinances not written down in the Scriptures but based on an oral interpretation of them. 2. the part of the Talmud devoted to such laws and ordinances. See also **Haggada.**
ha·la·kist, ha·la·chist (hä′lə-kist, hə-lä′kist), *n.* a Hebrew judge or scholar who contributed to the Halakah.
ha·la·tion (hā-lā′shən, hal-ā′shən), *n.* [< *halo* + *-ation*], in *photography,* an undesirable spreading or reflection of light on a negative, appearing like a halo around high lights.

hal·berd (hal′bẽrd; *formerly* hôl′bẽrd, hô′bẽrd), *n.* [Fr. *hallebarde,* earlier *alabarde;* It. *alabarda,* altered < MHG. *helmbarte* (later *halmbarte*); *helm,* handle, helve + *barte,* an ax, lit., a beard], a combination spear and battle-ax used in the 15th and 16th centuries: also **halbert.**

HALBERD

hal·berd·ier (hal′bẽr-dêr′), *n.* [Fr. *hallebardier*], a soldier, guard, etc. armed with a halberd or carrying a halberd as a symbol of office.
hal·bert (hal′bẽrt; *formerly* hôl′bẽrt, hô′bẽrt), *n.* a halberd.
hal·cy·on (hal′si-ən), *n.* [L., earlier *alcyon;* Gr. *alkyōn,* kingfisher; akin to L. *alcedo;* influenced in L. by Gr. *hals,* sea & *kyōn,* conceiving (from popular belief that the bird hatched its young in a nest floating on the sea during the *halcyon days* of the solstice)], 1. in *ancient legend,* a bird, believed to have been the kingfisher, which was supposed to have a peaceful, calming influence on the sea at the time of the winter solstice. 2. in *zoology,* any of a group of Australasian kingfishers. *adj.* 1. of the kingfisher. 2. tranquil; happy; unruffled: usually in *halcyon days.*
Hal·dane, J. B. S. (hôl′dān), (*John Burdon Sanderson Haldane*), 1892– ; British biologist and author.
Haldane, Richard Bur·don (bũr′dən), first Viscount, 1856–1928; British statesman and philosopher; lord chancellor (1912–1915; 1924); uncle of *J.B.S.*
hale (hāl), *adj.* [northern ME. *hal,* same as Midland *hool* (see WHOLE); AS. *hal,* sound, healthy], sound in body; vigorous and healthy, especially as used of an older person: also spelled **hail.** —***SYN.*** see **healthy.**
hale (hāl), *v.t.* [HALED (hāld), HALING], [ME. *halen, halien;* OFr. *haler;* prob. < Gmc.; the word is a var. of *haul*], 1. to pull forcibly; drag; haul; hence, 2. to force (a person) to go: as, he was *haled* into court.
Hale, Edward Everett (hāl), 1822–1909; American clergyman and writer.
Hale, Nathan, 1755–1776; American soldier in the Revolutionary War; hanged by the British as a spy.
Ha·le·a·ka·la (hä′lā-ä′kä-lä′), *n.* a volcano on the island of Maui, Hawaii: height, 10,032 ft.: it has the world's largest extinct crater (area, 19 sq. mi.).
Ha·lé·vy, Jacques Fran·çois Fro·men·tal É·lie (zhäk frän′swȧ′ frô′män′tȧl′ ā′lē′ ȧ′lā′vē′), 1799–1862; French composer.
half (haf, häf), *n.* [*pl.* HALVES (havz, hävz)], [ME.; AS. *healf,* part, half; akin to G. *halb;* IE. *(*s*)*qelep-,* lit., divided < *(*s*)*qel-,* to cut; cf. SCALP, SKILL], 1. either of the two equal parts of something; hence, 2. either of two approximately equal parts; approximately fifty per cent of a mass or number. 3. in *basketball, football,* etc., either of the two equal periods of the game, between which the players rest. Abbreviated **hf.** *adj.* 1. being either of the two equal parts. 2. being approximately fifty per cent of a mass or number; hence, 3. incomplete; fragmentary; partial. *adv.* 1. to an extent approximately or exactly fifty per cent of the whole. 2. [Colloq.], to some extent: as, I was *half* convinced. 3. [Colloq.], by any means; at all: used with *not,* as, he doesn't *half* approve.
by half, considerably; very much.
in half, into halves.
not half bad, not really bad but rather good.
not the half of, only a small part of.
one's better half, [Slang], one's wife or husband.
half-and-half (haf′'nd-haf′, häf′'n-häf′), *n.* 1. something that is half of one thing and half of another; especially, *a*) a mixture of equal parts of milk and cream. *b*) a mixture of equal parts of porter and ale, beer and stout, etc. 2. something considered to be neither one thing nor another; indeterminate mixture of two things. *adj.* combining two things equally. *adv.* in two equal parts.
half·back (haf′bak′, häf′bak′), *n.* in *football,* 1. either of two players whose position is behind the line of scrimmage together with the fullback and the quarterback. 2. the position played by a halfback.
half-baked (haf′bākt′, häf′bākt′), *adj.* 1. only partly baked; hence, 2. not completely planned or thought out: as, a *half-baked* scheme. 3. having or showing little intelligence and experience.
half·beak (haf′bēk′, häf′bēk′), *n.* a small, long-bodied tropical sea fish somewhat like the gar, with an extended lower jaw suggesting a bird's beak.
half binding, a style of binding in which the back, and sometimes the corners, of a book are of leather or other material different from that of the sides.
half-blood (haf′blud′, häf′blud′), *n.* [based on the obsolete notion that the blood is the medium of heredity], 1. a person related to another through one parent only. 2. a person born of parents of different races; half-breed. Also **half blood.** *adj.* half-blooded.
half blood, 1. kinship through one parent only: as, sisters of the *half blood.* 2. a half-blood.

half-blood·ed (haf'blud'id, häf'blud'id), *adj.* 1. having kinship through one parent only. 2. born of parents of different races. 3. in *animal husbandry*, having a sire or dam of poor pedigree in contrast to that of the other parent.

half boot, a boot extending halfway up the lower leg.

half-breed (haf'brēd', häf'brēd'), *n.* a person whose parents are of different races; especially, an offspring of an American Indian and a white person. *adj.* half-blooded; hybrid.

half brother, a brother related through one parent only.

half-caste (haf'kast', häf'käst'), *n.* 1. a person whose parents are of different races; half-breed. 2. an offspring of one European parent and one Asiatic parent. *adj.* of, or having the position of, a half-caste.

half cock, the halfway position of the hammer of a firearm, when the trigger is locked and cannot be pulled.

go off at half cock, 1. to go off too soon: said of a firearm. 2. to speak or act thoughtlessly or too hastily. Also **go off half cocked.**

half crown, a British silver coin equal to two shillings and sixpence (2 1/2 shillings).

half deck, formerly, the deck of a ship below the upper deck, extending from the mainmast to the cabin.

half dollar, 1. a silver coin of the United States and Canada, worth 50 cents. 2. [British Colloq.], a half crown.

half eagle, a gold coin of the United States, worth $5.00: it is no longer current.

half gainer, a back dive made from the stance for a front dive.

half·heart·ed (haf'här'tid, häf'här'tid), *adj.* with little enthusiasm, determination, interest, etc.; spiritless.

half hitch, a knot made by passing the end of the rope around the rope and then through the loop thus made: it is the simplest kind of hitch: see **knot,** illus.

half hose, socks, especially knee-length socks.

half-hour (haf'our', häf'our'), *n.* 1. half of an hour; thirty minutes. 2. the point thirty minutes after any given hour. *adj.* 1. lasting for thirty minutes. 2. occurring every thirty minutes.

half-hour·ly (haf'our'li, häf'our'li), *adj. & adv.* at thirty-minute intervals.

half-length (haf'leŋkth', häf'leŋth'), *adj.* 1. of half the full length. 2. showing a person from the waist up: said of a portrait. *n.* a portrait of this sort.

half life, in *nuclear physics*, the period required for the disintegration of half of the atoms in a sample of some specific radioactive substance: as, plutonium 238 has a *half life* of about 50 years.

half-mast‡ (haf'mast', häf'mäst'), *n.* the position of a flag lowered about halfway down its pole or staff as a sign of mourning or a signal of distress. *adv.* about halfway on the staff. *v.t.* to hang (a flag) at half-mast.

half-moon (haf'mōōn', häf'mōōn'), *n.* 1. the moon between new moon and full moon, when only half its disk is clearly seen. 2. anything shaped like a half-moon or crescent. *adj.* shaped like a half-moon.

half mourning, 1. the second period of mourning, during which black clothes are lightened or replaced by gray, white, or purple. 2. the clothes worn then.

half nelson, in *wrestling*, a hold in which one arm is placed under the opponent's arm from behind with the hand pressed against the back of his neck.

half note, in *music*, a note (𝅗𝅥) having one half the duration of a whole note: also called *minim*.

half·pace (haf'pās', häf'pās'), *n.* [altered < *halpace* < MFr. *hault pas*, lit., high step], 1. a raised platform for a throne, altar, etc., usually at the top of steps. 2. a staircase landing, usually between two half flights.

half·pen·ny (hā'pən-i, hāp'ni), *n.* [*pl.* HALFPENCE (hā'pəns), HALFPENNIES (hā'pən-iz, hāp'niz)], a British bronze coin equal to two farthings or half a penny. *adj.* 1. worth a halfpenny. 2. trifling; insignificant.

half pint, 1. a liquid or dry measure equal to 1/4 quart. 2. [Slang], a small person.

half sister, a sister related through one parent only.

half slip, a woman's slip without a top.

half-sole (haf'sōl', häf'sōl'), *v.t.* to repair (shoes or boots) by attaching new half soles.

half sole, a sole (of a shoe or boot) from the arch to the toe.

half sovereign, a former British gold coin.

half-staff (haf'staf', häf'stäf'), *n.* half-mast.

half step, 1. in *military usage*, a short marching step of fifteen inches (in double time, eighteen inches). 2. in *music*, the difference in pitch between any two adjacent keys on the piano; half tone; semitone.

half tide, the condition or period halfway between flood tide and ebb tide.

half-tim·bered (haf'tim'bẽrd, häf'tim'bẽrd), *adj.* in *architecture*, made of a wooden framework having the spaces filled with plaster, brick, etc.

half title, 1. the title of a book, often abbreviated, appearing on the odd page preceding (or sometimes following) the main title page. 2. the title of a subdivision of a book appearing on the odd page immediately preceding that division.

half-tone (haf'tōn', häf'tōn'), *n.* a half tone. *adj.* designating, of, or producing half tones.

half tone, 1. in *art*, a tone or shading between light and dark. 2. in *music*, a half step. 3. in *photoengraving*, *a*) a technique of representing shadings by dots produced by photographing the object from behind a fine screen. *b*) a photoengraving so made.

half-track (haf'trak', häf'trak'), *n.* an army truck, armored vehicle, etc. with caterpillar treads instead of rear wheels.

half-truth (haf'trōōth', häf'trōōth'), *n.* a statement or account containing only some of the facts, the rest being purposely left out with the intention of deceiving.

half-vol·ley (haf'vol'i, häf'vol'i), *v.t. & v.i.* to return (a ball) with a half volley.

half volley, in *tennis, cricket*, etc., a stroke made by hitting the ball just as it begins to bounce after striking the ground.

half·way (haf'wā', häf'wā'), *adj.* 1. equally distant between two points, states, etc.; midway. 2. incomplete; partial: as, *halfway* measures. *adv.* 1. half the distance; to the midway point. 2. incompletely; partially. 3. [Colloq.], at all; even remotely: as, he'd win if he were *halfway* good.

meet halfway, to be willing to compromise with.

half-wit (haf'wit', häf'wit'), *n.* 1. a person who is feeble-minded, moronic, imbecilic, etc. 2. a stupid, silly person; fool; dolt.

half-wit·ted (haf'wit'id, häf'wit'id), *adj.* 1. feeble-minded, moronic, imbecilic, etc. 2. silly; foolish.

hal·i·but (hal'ə-bət; *occas.* häl'ə-bət), *n.* [*pl.* HALIBUT, HALIBUTS (-bəts); see PLURAL, II, D, 2], [ME. *hali*, holy + *butt*, a flounder: so called because eaten on holidays], a large, edible flatfish found in northern seas: it sometimes weighs hundreds of pounds: also **holibut.**

Hal·i·car·nas·sus (hal'i-kär-nas'əs), *n.* an ancient city in southwestern Asia Minor: site of the Mausoleum, one of the seven wonders of the ancient world.

hal·id (hal'id, hā'lid), *n.* a halide.

hal·ide (hal'īd, hal'id, hā'līd, hā'lid), *n.* [*halo*gen + *-ide*], in *chemistry*, a compound of a halogen with another element or a radical. *adj.* haloid.

hal·i·dom (hal'i-dəm), *n.* [ME.; AS. *haligdom;* see HOLY & -DOM], [Archaic], 1. holiness. 2. a holy place; sanctuary. 3. a thing considered holy; sacred relic.

hal·i·dome (hal'i-dōm'), *n.* [Archaic], halidom.

Hal·i·fax (hal'ə-faks'), *n.* 1. the capital of Nova Scotia, Canada: pop., 93,000. 2. a city in Yorkshire, England: pop., 95,000.

Halifax, first Earl of, (***Edward Frederick Lindley Wood***), 1881–1959; English statesman.

hal·ite (hal'īt, hā'līt), *n.* [< Gr. *hals*, salt; + *-ite*]. native sodium chloride; rock salt.

hal·i·to·sis (hal'ə-tō'sis), *n.* [Mod. L. < L. *halitus*, breath; + *-osis*], bad-smelling breath.

hal·i·tus (hal'i-təs), *n.* [L. < *halare*, to breathe], an exhalation; vapor; breath.

hall (hôl), *n.* [ME. *halle;* AS. *heall* (akin to G. *halle*) lit., that which is covered < base of AS. *helan*, to cover; IE. base **kel-*, to cover, as also in *conceal, color*], 1. originally, *a*) the great central room in the dwelling of a king or chieftain, where banquets, games, etc. took place. *b*) the dwelling itself. 2. the main dwelling on the estate of a baron, squire, etc. 3. [sometimes H-], a building containing public offices or the headquarters of an organization, for transacting business, holding meetings, etc. 4. a large public or semipublic room for gatherings, entertainments, dancing, eating, etc. 5. [sometimes H-], a college dormitory, classroom building, eating center, etc. 6. [sometimes H-], *a*) any of the minor colleges of an English university. *b*) the building that houses such a college. 7. a passageway or room between the entrance and the interior of a building; vestibule. 8. a passageway, corridor, or area onto which rooms open.

Hall, Charles Martin (hôl), 1863–1914; American chemist; discovered electrolytic process for reducing aluminum from bauxite.

Hall, G. Stanley, (*Granville Stanley Hall*), 1846–1924; American educator and psychologist.

Hal·lam, Henry (hal'əm), 1777–1859; English historian.

hall bedroom, a small bedroom off a corridor; especially, a small bedroom at the end of an upstairs corridor.

Hal·le (häl'ə; Eng. hal'i), *n.* a city in southeastern Germany, near Leipzig: pop., 279,000.

Hal·leck, Fitz-Greene (fits'grēn' hal'ək), 1790–1867; American poet.

hal·lel (hə-lāl', häl'el), *n.* [Heb. *hallēl*, praise], a part of the Jewish religious services consisting of *Psalms* 113 to 118 inclusive, recited or sung on certain feast days.

hal·le·lu·jah, hal·le·lu·iah (hal'ə-lōō'yə), *interj.* [Heb. *hallelū-yāh; hallelū*, praise (imperative form) + *yāh*, Jehovah], praise (ye) the Lord! *n.* an exclamation, hymn, or song of praise to God. Also **alleluia.**

Hal·ley, Edmund (hal'i), 1656–1742; English astronomer.

Halley's comet, a famous comet, last seen in 1910, whose periodic reappearance was predicted by Halley: see **comet,** illus.

hal·liard (hal'yẽrd), *n.* a halyard.

hall·mark (hôl'märk'), *n.* 1. the official mark stamped on gold and silver articles at Goldsmiths' Hall in London as a guarantee of genuineness; hence, 2. any mark or symbol of genuineness or high quality. Also **hall mark.** *v.t.* to put a hallmark on.

hal·lo (hə-lō'), *interj., n., v.i. & v.t.* hollo: also spelled **halloa.**

Hall of Fame, a memorial in New York City containing busts and tablets honoring celebrated Americans: five new names are supposed to be chosen every five years.

hal·loo (hə-lōō'), *v.i. & v.t.* [HALLOOED (-lōōd'), HALLOOING], [ME. *halowen* < *halou, interj.;* prob. also < OFr. *halloer*, to follow after with much noise], 1. to shout or call out in order to attract the attention of (a person). 2. to urge on (hounds) by shouting or calling out "halloo." 3. to shout; yell. *interj. & n.* a shout or call, especially one to attract a person's attention or to urge on hounds in hunting.

hal·low (hal'ō), *v.t.* [ME. *halowen, halwen;* AS. *halgian* (used for L. *sanctificare*) < Gmc. base of *halig* (see HOLY); akin to G. *heiligen*], 1. to make holy or sacred; sanctify; consecrate. 2. to regard as holy; honor as sacred; venerate. —*SYN.* see **devote.**

hal·low (hə-lō'; *sometimes, for v & n.,* hal'ō), *v.i. & v.t., interj., n.* halloo.

hal·lowed (hal'ōd; *in poetry or liturgy, often* hal'ō-id), *adj.* [pp. of *hallow*], 1. made holy or sacred. 2. regarded as holy: honored as sacred. —*SYN.* see **holy.**

Hal·low·een, Hal·low·e'en (hal'ō-ēn', häl'ə-wēn'), *n.* [contr. < *all hallow even,* in which *hallow* is < AS. *halga*, definite form of *halig* (see HOLY) in sense "holy person, hence saint"], the evening of October 31, which is followed by All Saints' Day, or Allhallows: Halloween is now generally celebrated with fun-making and masquerading.

Hal·low·mas (hal'ō-məs, hal'ō-mas'), *n.* [< *all hallow mass;* cf. HALLOWEEN], the church festival of All Saints' Day, or Allhallows, November 1: the former name.

hall tree, a stand, usually in an entrance hall, with arms or hooks to hold hats, coats, etc.

hal·lu·ci·nate (hə-lōō'sə-nāt', hə-lū'sə-nāt'), *v.t.* HALLUCINATED (-id), HALLUCINATING], [< L. *hallucinatus, allucinatus*, pp. of *hallucinari, allucinari*, to wander mentally, rave], to cause to have hallucinations.

hal·lu·ci·na·tion (hə-lōō'sə-nā'shən, hə-lū'sə-nā'shən), *n.* [L. *hallucinatio, allucinatio* < *hallucinari, allucinari;* see HALLUCINATE], 1. the apparent perception of sights, sounds, etc. that are not actually present: it may occur in certain mental disorders. 2. the imaginary object apparently seen, heard, etc. Distinguished from *delusion, illusion.* —*SYN.* see **delusion.**

hal·lu·ci·na·to·ry (hə-lōō'sə-nə-tôr'i, hə-lū'sə-nə-tō'ri), *adj.* 1. of or characterized by hallucination. 2. producing hallucination.

hal·lu·ci·no·sis (hə-lōō'sə-nō'sis, hə-lū'sə-nō'sis), *n.* [Mod. L. < *hallucination* + *-osis*], a mental disorder characterized by hallucinations.

hal·lux (hal'əks), *n.* [*pl.* HALLUCES (-yoo-sēz')], [Mod. L.; altered < L. *hallex, allex*, great toe], in *zoology*, 1. the first digit on either of the hind legs of a mammal; especially, in man, the great toe. 2. the hind toe of a bird.

hall·way (hôl'wā'), *n.* 1. a passageway or room between the entrance and the interior of a building; vestibule. 2. a passageway; corridor; hall.

halm (hôm), *n.* haulm.

Hal·ma·he·ra, Hal·ma·hei·ra (häl'mä-hā'rä), *n.* one of the Molucca Islands in the Netherlands Indies: area, 6,500 sq. mi.; pop., 102,000: also called *Gilolo.*

ha·lo (hā'lō), *n.* [*pl.* HALOS, HALOES (-lōz)], [L. *halos* (genit. & acc. *halo*); Gr. *halōs*, threshing floor on which oxen trod in a circular path, round disk of the sun or moon, hence halo around the sun or moon < *halein*, to grind], 1. a ring of light that seems to encircle the sun, moon, or other luminous body: it results from the refraction of light through vapor. 2. a symbolic ring or disk of light shown around the head of a saint, etc., as in pictures; nimbus: often used as a symbol of virtue or innocence. 3. the splendor or glory attributed to a person or thing famed or idealized in legend or history. *v.i.* [HALOED (-lōd), HALOING], to form a halo. *v.t.* to encircle with a halo.

hal·o- (hal'ō, hā'lō), [< Gr. *hals, halos*, salt, hence sea], a combining form meaning: 1. *of the sea.* 2. *having to do with a salt*, as in *halophyte.* 3. *having to do with a halogen.*

hal·o·gen (hal'ə-jən), *n.* [*halo-* + *-gen*], any of the five very active, nonmetallic chemical elements, fluorine, chlorine, bromine, astatine, and iodine: abbreviated **Hal.**

hal·oid (hal'oid, hā'loid), *adj.* [< *halo-* + *-oid*], of or like a binary compound of a halogen with another element or radical. *n.* a halide.

hal·o·phyte (hal'ə-fīt'), *n.* [*halo-* + *-phyte*], a plant that can grow in salty soil.

Hals, Frans (fräns häls; Eng. hals), 1580?–1666; Dutch painter.

Hal·sey, William Frederick (hôl'zi), 1882–1959; American admiral in World War II.

Häl·sing·borg (hel'siŋ-bôr'y'), *n.* a seaport in southwestern Sweden, on The Sound: pop., 70,000 (1948).

halt (hôlt), *n.* [Fr. *halte;* G. *halt*, orig. imperative of *halten;* see HOLD], a temporary stop, as in marching; pause. *v.i. & v.t.* to stop; cease or cause to cease.
call a halt, to order a stop.

halt (hôlt), *v.i.* [ME. *haulten, halten;* AS. *healtian* < *healt* (see the *adj.*); akin to MHG. *halzen*], 1. to walk with a crippled gait; limp; hobble. 2. to be uncertain; waver; hesitate: as, he *halts* in his speech. 3. to have defects; especially, *a)* to be metrically faulty: said of verse. *b)* to be illogical: said of argument. *adj.* [ME. *halte;* AS. *healt, halt;* akin to MHG. *halz;* IE. ***qelā**, to strike, hew; basic sense "lamed by wounding"], [Archaic], halting; limping; crippled; lame. *n.* [Archaic], a halting or limping; lameness.
the halt, those who are lame; cripples.

hal·ter (hôl'tẽr), *n.* [ME.; AS. *hælftre* (akin to G. *halfter*) derived < base of AS. *helfe* (see HELVE); basic sense "that by which something is held"], 1. a rope, cord, strap, etc., usually with a headstall, for tying or leading an animal. 2. a rope for hanging a person; hangman's noose; hence, 3. execution by hanging. 4. a garment for covering the breast, held up by a cord or loop around the neck, and worn by women and girls to bare the shoulders and back. *v.t.* 1. to put a halter on (an animal); tie with a halter. 2. to hang (a person).

HALTER

hal·ter (hal'tẽr), *n.* [*pl.* HALTERES (-têr'ēz)], [Mod. L.; Gr. *haltēr*, pl. *haltēres*, weight held (to give impetus) in leaping], either of a pair of knobbed, threadlike parts serving as balancing organs in two-winged insects.

ha·lutz (khä-lōōts'), *n.* [*pl.* HALUTZIM (-lōō-tsēm')], [Heb. *ḥaluts*, warrior], a Jewish pioneer in the agricultural settlements of Israel: also spelled **chalutz.**

hal·vah (häl-vä'), *n.* [Turk. *helwa;* Ar. *ḥalwa*], a Turkish confection consisting of a paste made of ground sesame seeds and nuts mixed with honey, etc.

halve (hav, häv), *v.t.* [HALVED (havd, hävd), HALVING], [ME. *halven, halfen* < *half;* see HALF], 1. to divide into two equal parts. 2. to share equally (*with* someone): as, he *halved* the winnings with me. 3. to reduce by fifty per cent; reduce to half. 4. in *carpentry*, to fit together (two pieces of wood) by cutting each to half its thickness at its place of joining. 5. in *golf*, to play (a hole, match, etc.) in the same number of strokes as one's opponent.

halves (havz, hävz), *n.* plural of **half.**
by halves, 1. halfway; imperfectly. 2. halfheartedly.
go halves, to share expenses, etc. equally.

hal·yard (hal'yẽrd), *n.* [earlier *halier* < ME. *halien* (see HALE); altered by association with *yard;* cf. LANYARD], a rope or tackle for raising or lowering a flag, sail, etc.: also **halliard.**

Ham (ham), *n.* in the *Bible*, Noah's second son, traditionally the ancestor of African peoples: Gen. 10: 6–20.

ham (ham), *n.* [ME. & AS. *hamm;* akin to G. dial. *hamme;* IE. base ***konāmo-**, shin bone; senses 5 & 6 influenced by *am-* in *amateur*], 1. the part of the leg behind the knee. 2. *a)* the back of the thigh. *b)* the thigh and the buttock together. 3. the hock or hind leg of a four-legged animal. 4. the upper part of a hog's hind leg, or meat from this, salted, dried, smoked, etc.: see **pork,** illus. 5. [< "The *Ham*fat Man," Negro song], [Slang], an incompetent actor or performer, especially one who overacts. 6. [Slang], an amateur radio operator. *v.i. & v.t.* [HAMMED (hamd), HAMMING], [Slang], to act with exaggeration; overact.

Ha·ma·dan (hä'mä-dän'; Eng. ham'ə-dan'), *n.* a city in western Iran: pop., 104,000 (1942).

ham·a·dry·ad (ham'ə-drī'əd, ham'ə-drī'ad), *n.* [L. *Hamadryas, Hamadryadis;* Gr. *Hamadryas* < *hama*, together with + *drys*, a tree], in *Greek mythology*, a dryad; wood nymph whose life was bound up with that of the tree in which she lived.

ha·mal (hə-mäl', hə-môl'), *n.* [< (in part via Turk. *ḥamāl*) Ar. *ḥammāl* < *ḥamala*, to carry], 1. in the Orient, a porter. 2. in India, a man house servant. Also **hammal, hamaul.**

Ha·ma·ma·tsu (hä'mä-mä'tsōō), *n.* a city on the southern coast of Honshu, Japan: pop., 126,000 (1947).

ham·a·me·li·da·ceous (ham'ə-mē'lə-dā'shəs, ham'ə-mel'ə-dā'shəs), *adj.* [< Gr. *hamamēlis*, medlar tree (< *hama*, at the same time + *mēlon*, an apple); + *-aceous*], of the witch-hazel family of trees and shrubs.

Ha·man (hā'mən), *n.* in the *Bible*, a Persian official who sought the destruction of the Jews but was hanged from his own gallows when his scheming was exposed to King Ahasuerus by Esther: Esth. 7.
ha·maul (hə-môl'), *n.* a hamal.
Ham·ble·to·ni·an (ham'b'l-tō'ni-ən), *n.* [name of a famous American stallion (1849–1876)], 1. any of a superior breed of American trotting horses. 2. an annual harness race for three-year-old trotting horses, held at Goshen, New York.
Ham·burg (ham'bẽrg), *n.* 1. (*also* G. häm'boorkh), a city in northern Germany, on the Elbe: pop., 1,808,000. 2. a European variety of small chicken.
ham·burg (ham'bẽrg), *n.* (a) hamburger.
ham·burg·er (ham'bũr'gẽr), *n.* [earlier *Hamburg steak*, after *Hamburg*, Germany], 1. beef ground and, usually, seasoned. 2. a fried, broiled, or baked patty of such meat; Hamburg steak; Salisbury steak. 3. a sandwich made with such a patty, usually in a round bun.
Hamburg steak, hamburger (senses 1 & 2): also called *hamburger steak.*
Ham·den (ham'd'n), *n.* a town in southern Connecticut: pop.,41,000.
hame (hām), *n.* [ME.; AS. *hama*, a cover, skin; akin to OHG. *hamo*, fishing net, fishhook; IE. base **kem-*, **kam-*, a pole; the sense change is unexplained], either of the two rigid pieces along the sides of a horse's collar, to which the traces are attached.
Ham·e·lin (ham'ə-lin), *n.* a city in northwestern Germany: pop., 28,000: cf. **Pied Piper.**
Ha·meln (hä'məln), *n.* Hamelin: the German name.
Ha·mil·car Bar·ca (hə-mil'kär *or* ham''l-kär' bär'kə), 270?–228 B.C.; father of Hannibal; Carthaginian general.
Ham·il·ton (ham'il-t'n), *n.* 1. a river in Labrador, flowing into the Atlantic: length, 600 mi. 2. a city in Ontario, Canada, west of Toronto: pop., 249,000. 3. a city in southwestern Ohio: pop., 72,000. 4. the capital of Bermuda: pop., 3,200.
Hamilton, Alexander, 1757–1804; American statesman; first secretary of the treasury (1789–1795).
Hamilton, Mount, a mountain in western California: height, 4,209 ft.: site of Lick Observatory.
Ham·il·to·ni·an (ham''l-tō'ni-ən), *adj.* of or originated by Alexander Hamilton, or in accord with his federalist doctrines. *n.* a follower of Alexander Hamilton.
Hamilton Inlet, an inlet of the Atlantic, in eastern Canada: length, 150 mi.
Ham·ite (ham'īt), *n.* 1. a person regarded as descended from Ham. 2. a member of any of several dark-skinned peoples native to northern and eastern Africa.
Ham·it·ic (ham-it'ik, hə-mit'ik), *adj.* 1. of Ham or the Hamites. 2. designating or of a group of African languages related to the Semitic languages and including ancient Egyptian (surviving, from 3400 B.C., as Coptic), ancient Libyan, modern Berber dialects, and Cushitic dialects of Ethiopia and eastern Africa.
Ham·let (ham'lit), *n.* 1. a famous tragedy by Shakespeare (c. 1602). 2. the hero of this play, a Danish prince who avenges the murder of his father, the king, by killing his uncle Claudius, the murderer.
ham·let (ham'lit), *n.* [ME. *hamelet;* OFr. *hamelet* (Anglo-Fr. *hamelete*), dim. of *hamel* (Fr. *hameau*), itself dim. of LG. *hām*, home; see HOME], a very small village; small group of houses in the country.
Ham·lin, Hannibal (ham'lin) 1809–1901; vice-president of the United States (1861–1865).
ham·mal (hə-mäl', hə-môl'), *n.* a hamal.
Ham·mar·skjöld, Dag Hjal·mar (dåg yål'mår håm'år-shüld'), 1905–1961; Swedish statesman; secretary-general of the United Nations (1953–1961).
ham·mer (ham'ẽr), *n.* [ME. *hamer;* AS. *hamor;* akin to G. *hammer*, also ON. *hamarr*, crag, cliff; IE. base **ak-m-* < *ak-*, sharp, sharp stone; basic sense, "stone implement or weapon"], 1. a tool for pounding, usually consisting of a metal head and a handle: one end of the head may be a pronged claw for pulling nails. 2. a thing like this tool in shape or use; specifically, *a*) the mechanism that strikes the firing pin or percussion cap in a firearm. *b*) a device for striking a bell or gong. *c*) any of the felt-covered mallets that strike against the strings of a piano. 3. the malleus, one of the bones of the middle ear: see **ear**, illus. 4. an auctioneer's gavel. 5. a metal ball weighing twelve or sixteen pounds, hung from a wire handle and thrown for distance in an athletic competition. 6. a drop hammer; triphammer. *v.t.* 1. to strike repeatedly with or as with a hammer. 2. to make or fasten with a hammer. 3. to drive, force, or shape with or as with hammer blows: as, *hammer* the idea into his head. *v.i.* to strike repeated blows with or as with a hammer.

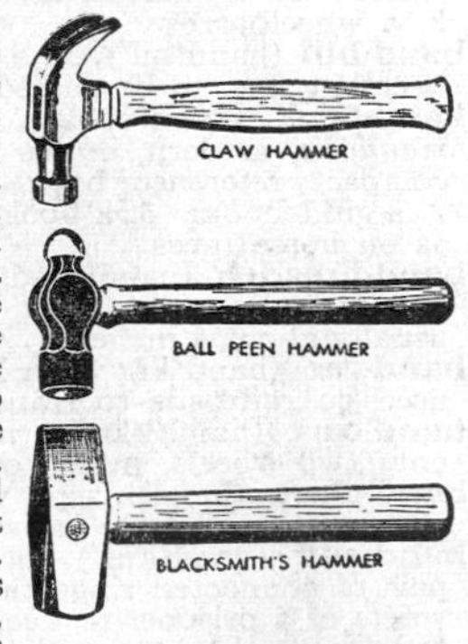

TYPES OF HAMMER

hammer and tongs, [with reference to a blacksmith's work], with all one's might: very vigorously.
hammer (away) at, 1. to work continuously or energetically at. 2. to keep emphasizing or talking about.
hammer out, 1. to shape, construct, or produce by hammering. 2. to make flat by hammering. 3. to take out by or as by hammering. 4. to develop or work out by careful thought or repeated effort.
under the hammer, [cf. *n.* 4], for sale at auction.

hammer and sickle, the emblem of the Communist Party in various countries: it is used on the Soviet flag.
ham·mer·cloth (ham'ẽr-klôth'), *n.* [Late ME. *hamerclothe:* ? so called from its durability], the cloth spread over the driver's seat in a horse-drawn coach.
ham·mered (ham'ẽrd), *adj.* [pp. of *hammer*], shaped or marked by hammer blows: said of metal work.
Ham·mer·fest (ham'ẽr-fest'), *n.* a seaport in northern Norway: pop., 4,000: northernmost city in Europe.
ham·mer·head (ham'ẽr-hed'), *n.* 1. the head of a hammer. 2. a savage shark that has a mallet-shaped head with an eye near the center of each end. 3. any of a group of small sea fishes of the sucker family. 4. an African bat that lives on fruit. 5. an African bird related to the herons and storks; umbrette.
ham·mer·less (ham'ẽr-lis), *adj.* 1. without a hammer. 2. having the hammer or other striking device covered, as some firearms.
hammer lock, in *wrestling*, a hold in which one of the opponent's arms is twisted behind his back.
hammer toe, 1. a condition in which the first joint of a toe is permanently bent downward, resulting in a clawlike deformity. 2. such a toe.
ham·mock (ham'ək), *n.* [Sp. *hamaca;* of Arawakan origin], a length of netting, canvas, etc. swung from ropes at both ends and used as a bed or couch.
ham·mock (ham'ək), *n.* [var. of *hummock*], in the South, a piece of rich land with hardwood trees growing on it.
Ham·mond (ham'ənd), *n.* a city in Indiana, near Chicago: pop., 112,000.
Ham·mu·ra·bi (hä'moo-rä'bi, ham'ə-rä'bi), *n.* king of Babylon (1955?–1913? B.C.); a famous code of laws is attributed to him.
ham·my (ham'i), *adj.* [Slang], like or characteristic of a ham (actor).
Hamp·den, John (hamp'dən, ham'dən), 1594–1643; English statesman; opposed Charles I in fighting for the rights of Parliament.
Hampden, Walter, (born *Walter Hampden Dougherty*), 1879–1955; American actor.
ham·per (ham'pẽr), *v.t.* [northern ME. *hampren;* prob. akin to or < AS. *hamelian*, to mutilate, maim, with freq. *-er* & intrusive *-p-* (cf. Brit. dial. *hamble*); akin to Eng. *hump;* IE. base **qem-*, to press together, as in *hem*], to keep from moving or acting freely; hinder; impede; encumber. *n.* in *nautical usage*, necessary but encumbering articles, as a ship's rigging, etc.
SYN.—**hamper** implies an impeding or encumbering so as to keep from moving or acting freely (*hampered* by a heavy load, by a lack of co-operation); **fetter, shackle,** and **manacle** all imply a checking or restraining so that freedom of movement or progress is curtailed, **fetter,** as if by tying the feet with chains, **shackle,** as if by confining the wrists, ankles, etc. with metal bands, and **manacle,** as if by binding the wrists with handcuffs (a mind *fettered* by superstition, *shackled* to a jealous husband, a *manacled* press).
ham·per (ham'pẽr), *n.* [var. of *hanaper;* ME. *haniper;* OFr. *hanapier* < *hanap*, a cup < Gmc. **hnapp*, a beaker, with usual Fr. intrusive vowel in the consonant cluster (cf. Fr. *canif* < AS. *cnif*, a knife)], a large basket, usually with a cover.
Hamp·shire (hamp'shir), *n.* a county on the southern coast of England, consisting of the administrative divisions of Southampton and the Isle of Wight: pop., 1,197,000: also called (and abbreviated) *Hants.*
Hamp·stead (hamp'sted, hamp'stid), *n.* a borough of London: pop., 95,000.
Hamp·ton (hamp'tən), *n.* a city in southeastern Virginia, on Hampton Roads: pop., 89,000.
Hamp·ton, Wade (wād hamp'tən), 1818–1902; American statesman and Confederate general.
Hampton Roads, a channel of Chesapeake Bay, southeastern Virginia.
ham·ster (ham'stẽr), *n.* [G.], a ratlike, burrowing animal of Europe and Asia, with large cheek pouches in which it carries grain: one variety is used, like the guinea pig, in scientific experiments.

ham·string (ham'striŋ'), *n.* 1. one of the tendons at the back of the human knee. 2. the great tendon at the back of the hock in a four-legged animal. *v.t.* [HAMSTRUNG (-struŋ'), HAMSTRINGING], 1. to disable by cutting a hamstring; hence, 2. to disable; cripple.
Ham·sun, Knut (knōōt häm'soon; Eng. nōōt ham'sən), 1859–1952; Norwegian novelist; received Nobel prize in literature, 1920.
Ham·tramck (ham-tram'ik), *n.* a city in southeastern Michigan, surrounded by Detroit: pop., 34,000.
ham·u·lus (ham'yoo-ləs), *n.* [*pl.* HAMULI (-lī')], [L., dim. of *hamus*, a hook], a small hook or hook-shaped part, as at the ends of some bones, barbicels of feathers, etc.
Han (hän), *n.* [Chin.], 1. a Chinese dynasty (206 B.C.–220 A.D.), characterized by the introduction of Buddhism. 2. a river in central China, flowing southeastward to join the Yangtze River at Hankow: length, 900 mi.
han·a·per (han'ə-pẽr), *n.* [see HAMPER, *n.*], a small hamper in which official papers were formerly kept.
Han Cities (hän), three cities in China: see **Wuhan.**
Han·cock, John (han'kok), 1737–1793; American statesman; president of the Continental Congress (1775–1777); first signer of the Declaration of Independence: see also **John Hancock.**
Hancock, Win·field Scott (win'fēld); 1824–1886; Union general in the Civil War.
hand (hand), *n.* [ME. & AS. *hand;* akin to G. *hand;* prob. < var. of Gmc. base of Goth. *hinthan*, to seize; hence, basic sense "grasper"], I. 1. the part of the human arm below the wrist, including the palm, fingers, and thumb, used for grasping or gripping. 2. the corresponding part in monkeys and some other animals. 3. a side, direction, or position indicated by one hand or the other: as, at one's right *hand.* II. *denoting some function or activity of the hand* 1. the hand as an instrument for making or producing: as, made by *hand.* 2. the hand as a symbol of its grasping or gripping function; specifically, *a*) possession: as, the papers are not in my *hands.* *b*) control; power; authority: as, he rules with an iron *hand.* *c*) care; charge; supervision: as, the child is in good *hands.* *d*) agency; influence: as, one can see his *hand* in the affair. *e*) an active part; share: as, take a *hand* in this work. 3. the hand as a symbol of promise; specifically, *a*) a clasp or handshake as a pledge of agreement, friendship, etc.: as, give me your *hand* on that. *b*) a promise to marry: as, he asked for her *hand.* III. *denoting the manner in which the hand is used* 1. skill; ability; dexterity: as, this work shows a master's *hand.* 2. manner of doing something: as, he plays with a light *hand.* IV. *denoting something produced by the hand* 1. handwriting. 2. a signature. 3. a clapping of hands; applause: as, they gave the singer a *hand.* 4. assistance; aid; help: as, lend me a *hand.* V. *denoting a person as producing or transmitting with the hands* 1. a person whose chief work is with his hands; especially, one of a staff or crew, as a sailor, farm laborer, etc. 2. a person regarded as having some special skill or characteristic: as, she is quite a *hand* at the piano. 3. *a*) a person (or sometimes thing) from or through which something comes: used with an ordinal number: as, he got it at second *hand;* hence, *b*) source; origin; authority. VI. *denoting something like a hand* 1. a conventional drawing of a hand (☛) used on signposts, etc. 2. an indicator; pointer: as, the *hands* of a clock. 3. the breadth of a hand; handbreadth: now usually about 4 inches. VII. *denoting something held in the hand* 1. in *card games*, *a*) the cards held by a player at any one time. *b*) the conventional number of cards dealt to each player. *c*) a player. *d*) a round of play. 2. in *commerce*, *a*) a banana cluster. *b*) a small tied bundle of tobacco leaves, hemp, etc. *adj.* 1. of the hand or hands. 2. controlled by hand; manual. *v.t.* 1. to pass or give with or as with the hand; transfer; transmit; deliver. 2. to help, conduct, steady, etc. by means of the hand: as, *hand* the lady to her car. 3. in *nautical usage*, to make (a sail) snug; furl.
(at) first hand, from the original source; directly.
at hand, 1. near; close by. 2. ready; prepared.
(at) second hand, 1. not from the original source; indirectly. 2. not new; previously used.
at the hand (or **hands**) **of,** through the action of.
bite the hand that feeds one, to turn against one's benefactor.
by hand, not by machines but with the hands.
change hands, to pass into the ownership of another.
eat out of one's hand, to be completely dominated by or devoted to one.
force one's hand, [orig., a whist term], to force one to act, or declare his intentions, before he is ready.
from hand to hand, from one person's possession to another's.
from hand to mouth, spending or consuming immediately what is obtained; with nothing saved for the future.
hand and foot, 1. so that the hands and feet cannot move: as, bound *hand and foot.* 2. constantly and diligently: as, she will wait on him *hand and foot.*
hand down, 1. to give as an inheritance; bequeath. 2. to announce or deliver (a verdict, etc.).
hand in, to give; submit.
hand in (or **and**) **glove,** in intimate association; in close agreement or co-operation.
hand in hand, 1. holding one another's hand. 2. together; in co-operation or correlation.
hand it to, [Slang], to give deserved credit to.
hand on, to pass along; transmit.
hand out, to distribute; deal out.
hand over, to give up; deliver.
hand over fist, [Colloq.], easily and in large amounts.
hands down, easily; without effort.
hands off! don't touch! don't interfere!
hands up! raise your hands over your head!: an order given by a person pointing a gun, etc.
hand to hand, at close quarters: said of fighting.
have one's hands full, to be extremely busy; be doing as much as one can.
hold hands, to hold each other's hand, especially in affection.
in hand, 1. in order or control. 2. in possession. 3. being worked on; in process.
join hands, 1. to become associates; enter into partnership. 2. to become husband and wife.
keep one's hand in, to keep in practice in order to retain one's skill.
lay hands on, 1. to attack, injure, or punish physically. 2. to get hold of; seize; take. 3. to touch with the hands in blessing, ordaining, confirming, etc.
not lift a hand, to do nothing; not even try.
off one's hands, no longer in one's care; out of one's responsibility.
on every hand, on all sides; in all directions.
on hand, 1. near. 2. available; ready. 3. present.
on one's hands, in one's care; being one's responsibility.
on the one hand, from one point of view.
on the other hand, from the opposed point of view.
out of hand, 1. out of control. 2. immediately. 3. over and done with.
shake hands, to clasp each other's (usually the right) hand as a greeting, pledge, etc.
show one's hand, [orig. with reference to card playing], to disclose one's intentions.
take in hand, 1. to take control of or responsibility for. 2. to take up; handle; treat. 3. to try; attempt.
throw up one's hands, to give up in despair.
to hand, 1. near; accessible. 2. in one's possession.
turn (or **put**) **one's hand to,** to undertake; work at.
upper hand, the advantage.
wash one's hands of, to refuse to go on with or take responsibility for.
with a heavy hand, 1. in a heavy manner; without delicacy or grace. 2. with severity or sternness.
with a high hand, with arrogance; in an arbitrary or dictatorial manner.
with clean hands, without guilt; as an innocent person.
hand- (hand; *before consonants other than* r *or* wr, *often* han), an initial combining form meaning *of, with, by,* or *for a hand or hands*, as in *handclasp, handcuff*, etc.
Hand, Lear·ned (lũr'nid hand), 1872–1961; American jurist.
hand·bag (hand'bag'), *n.* 1. a small container for money, toilet articles, keys, etc., carried by women; purse. 2. a small case or satchel for use in traveling.
hand·ball (hand'bôl'), *n.* 1. a game in which a small ball is batted against a wall or walls with the hand: there are usually two or four players. 2. the small rubber ball used in this game.
hand·bar·row (hand'bâr'ō), *n.* 1. a rack or frame carried by a pair of handles attached at each end. 2. a wheelbarrow.
hand·bill (hand'bil'), *n.* a small printed notice, advertisement, etc. to be passed out by hand.
hand·book (hand'book'), *n.* [AS. *handboc*, after L. *manuale;* modern senses after G. *handbuch*], 1. a compact reference book on some subject; manual. 2. a guidebook. 3. a book in which bets are recorded, as on horse races.
hand·breadth (hand'bredth'), *n.* the breadth of the human palm, used as a unit of measurement: now usually about 4 inches.
hand·car (hand'kär'), *n.* a small, hand-powered car used on railroads to transport workers, etc.
hand·cart (hand'kärt'), *n.* a small cart, often with only two wheels, pulled or pushed by hand.
hand·clasp (hand'klasp', hand'kläsp'), *n.* a clasping of hands in greeting, farewell, promise, etc.
hand·cuff (hand'kuf'), *n.* *usually in pl.* either of a pair of connected rings that can be locked about the wrists of a prisoner to keep him from using his hands, or to fasten him to a policeman. *v.t.* to put handcuffs on; fetter; manacle.
hand·ed (han'did), *adj.* 1. having (a specified number or kind of) hands: usually in hyphenated compounds, as *left-handed, two-handed.* 2. involving (a specified number of) players: as, *three-handed* bridge.

Han·del, George Frederick (han'd'l; G. hen'dəl), 1685–1759; English composer, born in Germany: German, **Händel, Georg Friedrich.**

hand·fast (hand'fast', hand'fäst'), *n.* [< the *v.*], [Archaic], 1. a firm hold or grip with or as with the hands. 2. a clasping of hands to bind a bargain; hence, 3. a contract, especially of marriage or betrothal. *adj.* [Archaic], 1. *a*) betrothed. *b*) married. 2. tightfisted. *v.t.* [ME. *handfasten;* AS. *handfæstan,* to make fast, ratify; prob. after ON. *handfesta;* see HAND & FASTEN], [Archaic], 1. to betroth or marry by joining hands. 2. to take hold of with the hand.

hand·fast·ing (hand'fas'tiŋ, hand'fäs'tiŋ), *n.* [see HANDFAST (AS. *handfæstunge,* lit., hand fastening, has the same sense)], [Archaic], 1. a betrothal. 2. an obsolete form of irregular or trial marriage ceremonialized by a joining of hands.

hand·ful (hand'fool'), *n.* [*pl.* HANDFULS (-foolz')], 1. as much or as many as the hand will hold. 2. a relatively small number or amount: as, a mere *handful* of people. 3. enough so that more will be too much; plenty; hence, 4. [Colloq.], someone or something hard to control.

hand glass, 1. a magnifying glass for reading small print, etc. 2. a small mirror with a handle. 3. a protective glass covering for plants.

hand grenade, 1. a small grenade thrown by hand and exploded by a timed fuse or by impact. 2. a glass container full of chemicals, to be thrown at a fire in order to put it out.

hand·grip (hand'grip'), *n.* 1. a handclasp; handshake; specifically, a particular handclasp by which members of a fraternal order or secret society greet or recognize each other. 2. a handle, as on a bicycle handle bar.
come to handgrips, to engage in hand-to-hand fighting.

hand·hold (hand'hold'), *n.* 1. a gripping with the hand or hands. 2. a part or thing to take hold of; hold or support for the hand or hands.

hand·i·cap (han'di-kap'), *n.* [< *hand in cap,* former kind of lottery game in which winners were penalized], 1. a race or other competition in which difficulties are imposed on the superior contestants, or advantages given to the inferior, to make their chances of winning equal. 2. such a difficulty or advantage; hence, 3. something that hampers a person; disadvantage; hindrance. *v.t.* [HANDICAPPED (-kapt'), HANDICAPPING], 1. to give a handicap or handicaps to (contestants). 2. to cause to be at a disadvantage; hinder; impede.

hand·i·cap·per (han'di-kap'ẽr), *n.* an official who assigns handicaps to contestants, as in horse racing.

hand·i·craft (han'di-kraft', han'di-kräft'), *n.* [ME. *handcrafte;* AS. *handcræft;* influenced in form by *handiwork*], 1. expertness with the hands; manual skill. 2. an occupation or art calling for skillful use of the hands, as weaving, pottery, etc.

hand·i·crafts·man (han'di-krafts'mən, han'di-kräfts'mən), *n.* [*pl.* HANDICRAFTSMEN (-mən)], a person who works at handicraft; skilled workman; craftsman.

hand·i·ly (han'd'l-i), *adv.* in a handy manner; deftly or conveniently.

hand·i·ness (han'di-nis), *n.* the quality of being handy.

hand·i·work (han'di-wũrk'), *n.* [ME. *handiwerk;* AS. *handgeweorc; hand* (see HAND) + *geweorc* < *ge-,* collective prefix + *weorc* (see WORK)], 1. handwork; hence, 2. work done by a person himself. 3. the result of one's actions: as, this mess is my *handiwork.*

hand·ker·chief (haŋ'kẽr-chif, haŋ'kẽr-chēf'), *n.* [*pl.* HANDKERCHIEFS (-chivz, -chēfs')], [*hand, n.* + *kerchief*], 1. a small piece of linen, cotton, silk, etc., usually rectangular, for wiping the nose, eyes, or face, or carried or worn for ornament. 2. a larger piece of cloth worn around the neck or the head; kerchief.

hand-knit (hand'nit'), *adj.* knit by hand.

hand-knit·ted (hand'nit'id), *adj.* hand-knit.

han·dle (han'd'l), *n.* [ME. *handel;* AS. *handle* (akin to D. *handel*) < *hand* + *-le*], 1. that part of a utensil, tool, etc. which is to be held, turned, lifted, pulled, etc. with the hand. 2. a thing like a handle. 3. that by which something can be taken advantage of for some purpose; occasion. 4. [Colloq.], any title attached to a person's name. *v.t.* [HANDLED (-d'ld), HANDLING], 1. to touch, lift, etc. with the hand or hands. 2. to manage, operate, or use with the hand or hands; manipulate. 3. to manage; control; direct. 4. to deal with: as, our office *handles* many requests. 5. to write or speak about. 6. to trade in; deal in; do business in. 7. to behave toward; treat. *v.i.* to respond or submit to control: as, the car *handles* well.
fly off the handle, [Colloq.], to become suddenly or violently angry or excited.
SYN.—**handle** implies the possession of sufficient (or a specified degree of) skill in managing or operating with or as with the hands (to *handle* a tool, a problem, etc.); **manipulate** suggests skill, dexterity, or craftiness in handling (to *manipulate* a machine, an account, etc.); **wield** implies skill and control in handling effectively (to *wield* an ax, influence, etc.); **ply** suggests great diligence in operating (to *ply* an oar, one's trade, etc.).

handle bar, *often in pl.* 1. a curved or bent metal bar with handles on the ends, for steering a bicycle, motorcycle, etc. 2. [Colloq.], a long mustache resembling this.

hand·ler (han'dlẽr), *n.* 1. a person or thing that handles. 2. a boxer's trainer, manager, or second.

hand·made (hand'mād'), *adj.* made by hand, not by machine.

hand·maid (hand'mād'), *n.* a woman or girl servant or attendant.

hand·maid·en (hand'mād''n), *n.* [Archaic], a handmaid.

hand-me-down (hand'mi-doun'), *adj.* [Colloq.], 1. *a*) ready-made; hence, *b*) not expensive; not elegant; cheap. 2. used; secondhand. *n.* [Colloq.], a hand-me-down garment.

hand organ, a large music box, similar to a reed organ, played by turning a crank; hurdy-gurdy; barrel organ.

hand·out (hand'out'), *n.* a gift of food, clothing, etc., as to a beggar or tramp.

hand-picked (hand'pikt'), *adj.* 1. picked by hand: said of fruit or vegetables; hence, 2. chosen with care, or for a special purpose: sometimes derogatory, as a *hand-picked* candidate.

hand·rail (hand'rāl'), *n.* a rail serving as a guard or support to be held by the hand, as along a stairway.

hand·saw (hand'sô'), *n.* a saw used with one hand.

hand's-breadth (handz'bredth'), *n.* a handbreadth.

hand screw, 1. a lifting jack operated by hand. 2. in *carpentry,* a wooden clamp tightened by hand.

hand·sel (hand's'l, han's'l), *n.* [ME. *handsel, hansel* < AS. (rare) *handselen,* a giving into hand & ON. *handsal*(*i*), confirmation of bargain by giving one's hand; both < *hand* + base of *sell, sale*], 1. a present for good luck, as on New Year's or on the launching of a new business. 2. [Rare], a first payment; specifically, *a*) a first installment, as a pledge of future payment. *b*) the first money taken in a new business or on any day of business; hence, 3. the first use or specimen of anything, regarded as an indication of what is to follow. *v.t.* [HANDSELED or HANDSELLED (-s'ld), HANDSELING or HANDSELLING], 1. to give a handsel to. 2. to begin or launch with ceremony and gifts; inaugurate. 3. to use, do, etc. for the first time; be the first to use, etc.

hand·set (hand'set'), *n.* a telephone mouthpiece and receiver mounted together on a handle.

hand·shake (hand'shāk'), *n.* a gripping and shaking of each other's hand in greeting, farewell, promise, sealing a bargain, etc.

hand·some (han'səm), *adj.* [orig., easily handled, convenient; ME. *handsom;* see HAND & SOME], 1. *a*) moderately large. *b*) large; impressive; considerable: as, a *handsome* sum. 2. appropriate; fitting; seemly; proper; gracious: as, it was *handsome* of him to say that. 3. good-looking; of pleasing appearance: said especially of attractiveness that is manly, dignified, or impressive rather than delicate and graceful: as, a *handsome* man, a *handsome* book. —*SYN.* see **beautiful.**

hand·spike (hand'spīk'), *n.* [< Early Mod. D. *handspaeke* (D. *handspaak*); *hand,* hand + *spaeke* (MD. *spāke*) rod, pole; influenced by *spike*], a heavy bar used as a lever for shifting heavy objects, especially on ships.

hand·spring (hand'spriŋ'), *n.* a gymnastic feat in which the performer turns over in mid-air with one or both hands touching the ground.

hand-to-hand (hand'tə-hand'), *adj.* in close contact; at close quarters: said of fighting.

hand-to-mouth (hand'tə-mouth'), *adj.* characterized by the immediate spending or consuming of what is obtained; with nothing saved for the future.

hand·work (hand'wũrk'), *n.* work done or made by hand, not by machine.

hand·writ·ing (hand'rīt'iŋ), *n.* 1. writing done by hand, with pen, pencil, chalk, etc. 2. a style or way of forming letters and words in writing: as, I recognize his *handwriting.* 3. [Archaic], something written by hand; manuscript.
see the handwriting on the wall, to see the signs of impending disaster, misfortune, etc.: Dan. 5:5–28.

hand·y (han'di), *adj.* [HANDIER (-di-ẽr), HANDIEST (-di-ist)], 1. close at hand; easily reached; conveniently located; accessible. 2. easily used; convenient; saving time or work: as, a *handy* device. 3. easily managed or handled: said of a ship, etc. 4. clever with the hands; deft; adroit. —*SYN.* see **dexterous.**

handy man, a man employed at various small tasks; doer of odd jobs.

hang (haŋ), *v.t.* [HUNG (huŋ), HANGING; for *v.t.* 3 & *v.i.* 4, HANGED (haŋd) is preferred p.t. & pp.], [ME. *hangen,* with form < AS. *hangian, v.i.* & ON. *hanga, v.i.;* senses < these, also < AS. *hon, v.t.* & ON. *hengja,* *caus. v.;* cf. G. *hangen, v.i., hängen, v.t., henken,* to execute (caus.); IE. base (of all of these verbs) **keg-, *keng-,* hook, etc., for hanging things; hence, basic sense "to hang on a hook"], 1. to attach to something above with no support from below; suspend. 2. to attach so that motion from the point of attachment is possible: as, a door is *hung* on its hinges so that it can swing. 3. to put to death by tying a rope about the neck and suddenly suspending the body so as to snap the neck or cause strangulation. 4. to fasten (pictures, etc.) to a wall by hooks, wires, etc. 5. to ornament or cover (*with* things suspended): as, she *hung* the room with pictures and drapes. 6. to paste (wallpaper) to walls. 7. to exhibit (pictures) in a museum or gallery. 8. to fasten with correct balance, as an ax-head, scythe, etc. 9. to deadlock (a jury), as by withholding one's vote. *v.i.* 1. to be attached to something above with no support from below; be suspended. 2. to swing, as on a hinge. 3. to fall or flow, as cloth, a coat, etc. 4. to die by hanging. 5. to incline; lean; droop; bend. 6. to hesitate; be doubtful or undecided. 7. to exhibit one's pictures in a museum or gallery. *n.* 1. the way that a thing hangs. 2. the way that a thing is done or used. 3. significance; general idea. 4. a pause in motion. 5. [Colloq.], a bit: as, I don't care a *hang* about it.

hang around (or **about**), 1. to cluster around. 2. [Colloq.], to loiter or linger around.

hang back, to be reluctant to advance, as from timidity or shyness.

hang fire, 1. to be slow in firing: said of a gun. 2. to be slow in doing something. 3. to be unsettled or undecided.

hang it! an exclamation of anger or exasperation.

hang on, 1. to keep hold. 2. to go on doing; persevere. 3. to depend on; be contingent on. 4. to lean on; be supported by. 5. to listen attentively to.

hang out, 1. to lean out. 2. [Slang], *a*) to reside. *b*) to spend much of one's time; frequent.

hang over, 1. to project over; overhang. 2. to hover over. 3. to loom over; threaten. 4. to be left from a previous time or state.

hang together, to stick together; be coherent.

hang up, 1. to put on a hanger, hook, etc., especially in the proper place. 2. to put a telephone receiver back on the hook; hence, 3. to end a telephone conversation. 4. to delay or suspend the progress of.

hang·ar (haŋ'ẽr, haŋ'gär), *n.* [Fr., a shed], a shed or other shelter, especially one for aircraft.

hang·bird (haŋ'bûrd'), *n.* the Baltimore oriole or any other bird that builds a hanging nest.

Hang·chow (haŋ'chou'; Chin. häŋ'jō'), *n.* seaport and capital of Chekiang province, China: pop., 518,000.

hang·dog (haŋ'dôg'), *n.* 1. originally, a person considered fit only for hanging dogs, or to be hanged like a dog; hence, 2. a low, skulking person; sneak. *adj.* of low, skulking, abject character or appearance.

hang·er (haŋ'ẽr), *n.* [ME. *hangere*], 1. a person who hangs things: usually in combination, as, a paper *hanger.* 2. a hangman; executioner. 3. a thing that hangs; especially, a short sword hanging from the belt. 4. a thing on which objects are hung, or by which they can be hung; specifically, *a*) a hook, chain, rope, strap, etc. for this purpose. *b*) a small frame on which a garment is hung to keep it in shape. 5. in automobiles, a bracket on the spring shackle to hold it to the chassis.

hang·er-on (haŋ'ẽr-on'), *n.* [*pl.* HANGERS-ON (-ẽrz-on')], a follower or dependent; specifically, *a*) a person who attaches himself to another, to some group, etc. although not wanted. *b*) a favor-seeker; sycophant; parasite. —*SYN.* see **parasite.**

hang·ing (haŋ'iŋ), *adj.* [ppr. of *hang*], 1. attached to something overhead and not supported from below; suspended; pendulous. 2. leaning over; inclining; overhanging. 3. located on a steep slope or slant. 4. unsettled; inconclusive. 5. unhappy; downcast. 6. deserving or causing the death penalty. 7. designating paragraphing in which the first line touches the left margin, the other lines being indented beneath it. *n.* 1. a suspending or being suspended. 2. a putting to death by hanging. 3. *usually in pl.* something hung on a wall, window, etc., as drapery, tapestry, etc.

hang·man (haŋ'mən), *n.* [*pl.* HANGMEN (-mən)], an executioner who hangs convicted criminals.

hang·nail (haŋ'nāl'), *n.* [altered (by popular association with *hang*) < *agnail;* see AGNAIL], a bit of torn or cracked skin hanging at the side or base of a fingernail.

hang-out (haŋ'out'), *n.* [Slang], a place frequented by some person or group.

hang·o·ver (haŋ'ō'vẽr), *n.* 1. something remaining from a previous time or state; a survival. 2. headache, nausea, etc. occurring as an aftereffect of drinking much alcoholic liquor.

hank (haŋk), *n.* [Late ME.; prob. < Anglo-N.; cf. ON. *honk,* a coil, skein, *hanki,* hasp, clasp; IE. base as in *hang*], 1. a loop or coil of something flexible. 2. a specific length of coiled thread or yarn; skein: a hank of worsted yarn contains 560 yards; a hank of cotton contains 840 yards. 3. in *nautical usage,* a ring of wood, metal, or rope on the edge of a staysail, sliding on the controlling stay. *v.t.* [ME. *hanken* < ON. *hanka* < base of the *n.*], to form into a hank or hanks.

hank·er (haŋ'kẽr), *v.i.* [Early Mod. Eng.; prob. < D., LG.; cf. Fl. *hankeren,* to desire, long for, D. *hunkeren;* Eng. dial. *hank* in same sense suggests freq. formation & metaphorical extension < base of *hank* (MLG. *hank,* etc.)], to crave, long, or yearn (followed by *after, for,* or an infinitive).

hank·er·ing (haŋ'kẽr-iŋ), *n.* a craving; yearning.

Han·kow (haŋ'kou'; Chin. häŋ'kō'), *n.* a city on the Yangtze River, Hupeh, China: see **Wuhan.**

hank·y-pank·y (haŋ'ki-paŋ'ki), *n.* [redupl. & dim. formation < *hand* as in *sleight of hand*], [Colloq.], talk, manipulation, etc. used in or as in tricks of illusion or sleight of hand to fool the observer; trickery; jugglery; deception. *adj.* [Colloq.], deceptive; tricky.

Han·na, Mark (han'ə), (born *Marcus Alonzo Hanna*), 1837–1904; American merchant and politician.

Han·nah (han'ə), a feminine name: see **Anna, Joan:** also spelled **Hanna.** *n.* in the *Bible,* the mother of Samuel: I Sam. 1:20.

Han·ni·bal (han'ə-b'l), *n.* 1. Carthaginian general; 247 B.C.–183 B.C.; crossed the Alps to invade Italy in the Second Punic War. 2. a city in northeastern Missouri: pop., 20,000.

Han·no·ver (hä-nō'vẽr, hä-nō'fẽr), *n.* Hanover, Germany: the German name.

Ha·noi (hä'noi'), *n.* the capital of North Vietnam: pop., c. 500,000.

Han·o·ver (han'ō-vẽr), *n.* 1. a former kingdom and duchy in northern Germany and, later, a province of Prussia. 2. a city in north central Germany: pop., 563,000. 3. a ruling family of England (1714–1901), founded by George I, originally Elector of Hanover. 4. a member of this family. 5. a town in western New Hampshire: pop., 6,000.

Han·o·ve·ri·an (han'ō-vêr'i-ən), *adj.* 1. of Hanover, Germany. 2. of the English royal house of Hanover. *n.* 1. a native or inhabitant of Hanover. 2. a supporter of the house of Hanover.

Hans (hans, hanz; G. häns), [G. abbrev. of *Johannes;* equivalent to Eng. *Jack;* see JOHN], a masculine name.

Han·sard (han'sẽrd), *n.* [after Luke *Hansard* (1752–1828) and descendants, by whom the reports were compiled and printed until 1889], the official record of proceedings in the British Parliament.

hanse (hans), *n.* [OFr.; MHG. *hanse,* association of merchants; OHG. *hansa,* band of men; akin to AS. *hos,* a troop], 1. a medieval guild of merchants. 2. the membership fee in this guild. 3. a toll exacted by this guild from nonmembers. 4. [H-], a medieval league of free towns in northern Germany and adjoining countries, formed for economic advancement and protection: the leading members were Bremen, Lübeck, and Hamburg: also called *Hanseatic League.*

Han·se·at·ic (han'si-at'ik), *adj.* [ML. *hanseaticus*], of the Hanse or the towns that formed it.

han·sel (han's'l), *n.* a handsel.

Han·sen's disease (hän's'nz), [after A. *Hansen* (1841–1912), Norw. physician who discovered its causative bacterium], leprosy.

han·som (han'səm), *n.* [after J. A. *Hansom* (1803–1882), Eng. inventor], a two-wheeled covered carriage for two passengers, pulled by one horse: the driver's seat is above and behind the cab: also **hansom cab.**

HANSOM

Han·son, Howard (han's'n), 1896– ; American composer.

Hants (hants), *n.* Hampshire.

Ha·nuk·kah, Ha·nuk·ka (hä'noo-kä'; Heb. khä'noo-kô), *n.* [Heb. *hanūkkāh,* dedication], a Jewish festival commemorating the rededication of the Temple by Judas Maccabeus in 165 B.C.: also **Chanukah:** see **Jewish holidays.**

Han·yang (hän'yäŋ'), *n.* a city on the Yangtze River, China, opposite Hankow: see **Wuhan.**

hap (hap), *n.* [ME. < ON. *happ;* akin to AS. (*ge*)*hæp,* convenient, suitable; IE. base **qob-,* to be fitted to, suit, seen also in OIr. *cob,* victory], [Archaic], 1. chance; fortune; luck. 2. *usually in pl.* an occurrence; happening. *v.i.* [HAPPED (hapt), HAPPING], [ME. *happen* < the *n.* or < (rare) AS. *hæppan,* to go by chance < same base], [Archaic], to occur by chance; happen.

hap·haz·ard (hap'haz'ẽrd; *for adj. & adv.* hap'haz'ẽrd), *n.* [*hap* + *hazard*], mere chance; accident; fortuity. *adj.* not planned; casual; random. *adv.* casually; by chance. —*SYN.* see **random.**

haph·ta·rah (häf'tä-rä', häf'tô'rô), *n.* [*pl.* HAPHTAROTH (-rōth', -rōth)], [Heb. *haphṭārāh,* conclusion], any of the readings from the Prophets included in Jewish synagogue services on the Sabbath and holidays.

hap·less (hap'lis), *adj.* [*hap* + *-less*], unfortunate; unlucky; luckless.

hap·lo- (hap'lō), [< Gr. *haploos*, single, simple], a combining form meaning *single, simple:* also, before a vowel, **hapl-**, as in *haploid*.

hap·loid (hap'loid), *adj.* [*hapl-* + *-oid*], having the number of chromosomes characteristic of the mature germ cell (half the number of the somatic cell). *n.* a haploid cell or gamete. Distinguished from *diploid*.

hap·lo·sis (hap-lō'sis), *n.* [*hapl-* + *-osis*], in *biology*, a lessening of the number of chromosomes through the division of a diploid cell into two haploids.

hap·ly (hap'li), *adv.* [*hap* + *-ly*], [Archaic], by chance or accident; perhaps.

hap·pen (hap''n), *v.i.* [ME. *happenen, hapnen;* see HAP & -EN], 1. to take place; occur; befall. 2. to be or occur by chance or without plan. 3. to have the luck or occasion; chance: as, I *happened* to see it. 4. [Colloq.], to come by chance (*along, by, in,* etc.).
happen on (or **upon**), to meet or find by chance.
happen to, to be done to; befall.
SYN.—**happen** is the general word meaning to take place or come to pass and may suggest either direct cause or apparent accident; **chance**, more or less equivalent to **happen**, always implies apparent lack of cause in the event; **occur** is somewhat more formal and usually suggests a specific event at a specific time (what *happened?*, the accident *occurred* at four o'clock); **transpire** is now frequently used as an equivalent for **happen** or **occur** (what *transpired* at the conference?), apparently by confusion with its sense of to become known, or leak out (reports on the conference never *transpired*).

hap·pen·ing (hap''n-iŋ), *n.* something that happens; occurrence; incident; event.

hap·pen·stance (hap''n-stans'), *n.* [*happen* + circum*stance*], [Colloq.], chance or accidental happening.

hap·pi·ly (hap''l-i), *adv.* 1. by good fortune; luckily. 2. pleasurably; joyfully; contentedly. 3. appropriately; aptly; felicitously: as, the report was *happily* phrased.

hap·pi·ness (hap'i-nis), *n.* 1. good fortune; luck. 2. pleasure; joy; contentment. 3. appropriateness.

hap·py (hap'i), *adj.* [HAPPIER (-i-ēr), HAPPIEST (-i-ist)], [ME. *happi* < *hap;* see HAP], 1. favored by circumstances; lucky; fortunate. 2. having, showing, or causing a feeling of great pleasure, contentment, joy, etc.; joyous; glad; pleased. 3. exactly appropriate to the occasion; suitable and clever; apt; felicitous: as, a *happy* suggestion. 4. [Slang], intoxicated or as if intoxicated: sometimes used in hyphenated combinations, as *slap-happy, flak-happy*.
SYN.—**happy** generally suggests a feeling of great pleasure, contentment, etc. (a *happy* marriage); **glad** implies more strongly an exultant feeling of joy (your letter made her so *glad*), but both **glad** and **happy** are commonly used in merely polite formulas expressing gratification (I'm *glad*, or *happy*, that you could come); **cheerful** implies a steady display of bright spirits, optimism, etc. (he's always *cheerful* in the morning); **joyful** and **joyous** both imply great elation and rejoicing, the former generally because of a particular event, and the latter as a matter of usual temperament (the *joyful* throngs, a *joyous* family). See also **lucky**.—*ANT.* sad.

hap·py-go-luck·y (hap'i-gō-luk'i), *adj.* taking things as they come; easygoing; unworrying; trusting to luck; light-hearted. *adv.* in a haphazard way; by chance.

Haps·burg (haps'bērg; G. häps'boorkh), *n.* the ruling family of Austria (1276–1918), of Spain (1516–1700), and of the Holy Roman Empire (1438–1806): also spelled **Habsburg**.

ha·ra-ki·ri (hä'rä-kêr'i, har'ə-kêr'i), *n.* [Japan. *hara*, belly + *kiri*, a cutting, cut], ritual suicide by disembowelment: it is called *seppuku* by the Japanese, and was practiced by high-ranking Japanese in lieu of execution or to avoid disgrace: also **hari-kari**.

ha·rangue (hə-raŋ'), *n.* [Fr.; ML. *harenga*, assembly, speech; altered < Frank. **hari hring*, gathering of warriors < *hari*, army, host + *hringa*, a ring, assembly, place of justice], a long, blustering, noisy, or pompous speech; tirade. *v.i.* [HARANGUED (-raŋd'), HARANGUING], to give a harangue. *v.t.* to address in a harangue.

Ha·rar (hä'rēr), *n.* a city in eastern Ethiopia: pop., c. 40,000: also spelled **Harrar**.

har·ass (har'əs, hə-ras'), *v.t.* [Fr. *harasser* < OFr. *harer*, to set a dog on], 1. to trouble, worry, or torment, as with cares, debts, repeated questions, etc. 2. in *military usage*, to trouble (the enemy) by constant raids or attacks, continual fire, etc.; harry.

har·ass·ment (har'əs-mənt, hə-ras'mənt), *n.* 1. a harassing or being harassed. 2. a thing that harasses.

Har·bin (här'bin', här'bēn'), *n.* the capital of Heilungkiang province, in northeastern China: pop., 1,552,000.

har·bin·ger (här'bin-jēr), *n.* [ME. *herbergeour* with intrusive *-n-* (cf. PASSENGER); OFr. *herbergeor*, one who provides a lodging < *herbergier; herberge*, a shelter < OHG. *heriberga*, shelter for soldiers; *heri*, army + *berga*, a shelter < *bergan*, to protect], 1. formerly, an advance representative of an army or royal party, who arranged for lodging, entertainment, etc. 2. a person or thing that comes before to announce or give an indication of what follows; herald. *v.t.* to serve as harbinger of; announce; foretell. —*SYN.* see **forerunner**.

har·bor (här'bēr), *n.* [ME. *herberwe*, etc.; AS. *herebeorg* (& ON. *herbergi*), lit., army shelter; *here*, army + *beorg*, a shelter, protection; see HARBINGER], 1. a place of refuge, safety, etc.; retreat; shelter. 2. a protected inlet, or branch of a sea, lake, etc., used as a shelter and anchorage for ships; port; haven: abbreviated **H., h.** *v.t.* 1. to serve as a place of protection to; shelter; house; conceal. 2. to hold in the mind; cherish: as, he *harbors* a grudge. *v.i.* to take shelter, as in a harbor.

har·bor·age (här'bēr-ij), *n.* 1. a shelter for ships; port; anchorage. 2. *a*) shelter. *b*) lodgings.

harbor master, the official in charge of enforcing the regulations governing the use of a harbor.

har·bour (här'bēr), *n., v.t. & v.i.* harbor: British spelling.

hard (härd), *adj.* [ME. *herd, hard;* AS. *heard;* akin to G. *hart;* IE. base **qar-*, hard, seen also in Gr. *kratos*, strength (cf. -CRACY, -CRAT)], 1. not easily dented, pierced, or crushed; resistant to pressure; firm and unyielding to the touch; rigid; solid and compact: opposed to *soft*. 2. made of metal: said of coins. 3. having firm muscles; in good bodily trim; vigorous and robust. 4. showing, or done with, great force or strength; powerful; violent; vigorous: as, a *hard* blow. 5. demanding great physical or mental effort or labor; fatiguing; difficult; specifically, *a*) difficult to do: as, *hard* work. *b*) difficult to understand, explain, or answer: as, a *hard* question. *c*) difficult to deal with; not easily managed or controlled: as, a man *hard* to live with. *d*) firmly fastened or tied: as, a *hard* knot. Opposed to *easy*. 6. not easily moved; unfeeling; callous: as, a *hard* heart. 7. practical and shrewd; severe in business relations: as, a *hard* customer. 8. causing pain or discomfort; specifically, *a*) difficult to endure; trying; exhausting: as, a *hard* life. *b*) harsh; severe; stern: as, a *hard* master, *hard* words. 9. very cold, stormy, etc.; inclement: as, a *hard* winter. 10. too clear, bright, or penetrating to be pleasant: as, a *hard* red. 11. having in solution mineral salts that interfere with the lathering and cleansing properties of soap: said of water. 12. energetic and persistent; steady and earnest: as, a *hard* worker. 13. containing much alcohol; strong: said of alcoholic liquors. 14. in *agriculture*, high in gluten content: as, *hard* wheat. 15. in *commerce*, high and stable: said of a market, prices, etc. 16. in *phonetics*, *a*) popularly, designating *c* and *g* when they are explosive rather than fricative or affricative, as in *cake* and *gun*. *b*) voiceless, as the *th* in *thin*. The term is not used in scientific terminology. Abbreviated **H., h.** (in senses 11, 13, 16). *adv.* 1. energetically and persistently; steadily and earnestly: as, work *hard*. 2. with vigor, strength, or violence: as, hit *hard*. 3. with difficulty: used in hyphenated compounds, as *hard-earned, hard-living*. 4. only after a struggle: as, die *hard*. 5. firmly; tightly: as, hold on *hard*. 6. close; near: as, we live *hard* by. 7. so as to be or make firm, solid, or rigid: as, it will freeze *hard*. 8. in *nautical usage*, with vigor and to the fullest extent: used especially in directions to the helmsman, as, *Hard* alee!
be hard on, 1. to treat severely; be harsh toward. 2. to be difficult, unpleasant, or painful for.
go hard with, to cause pain, trouble, or discomfort to.
hard and fast, 1. invariable; strict: said of rules, etc. 2. firmly grounded: said of a ship on shore.
hard of hearing, partially deaf.
hard put to it, having considerable difficulty or trouble.
hard up, [Colloq.], in great need of something, especially money; in desperate straits.
SYN.—**hard**, in this comparison, is the simple and general word for whatever demands great physical or mental effort (*hard* work, a *hard* problem); **difficult** applies especially to that which requires great skill, intelligence, tact, etc. rather than physical labor (a *difficult* situation); **arduous** implies the need for diligent, protracted effort (the *arduous* fight ahead of us); **laborious** suggests long, wearisome toil (the *laborious* task of picking cotton). See also **firm**.—*ANT.* easy, simple.

hard-bit·ten (härd'bit''n), *adj.* 1. originally, that bites hard; tough in fighting: said of dogs; hence, 2. stubborn; tough; enduring; dogged: as, *hard-bitten* soldiers.

hard-boiled (härd'boild'), *adj.* 1. boiled in water until both the white and yolk solidify: said of eggs. 2. [Colloq.], not affected by sentiment; tough; callous.

hard-bound (härd'bound'), *adj.* designating any book bound in a relatively stiff cover, as of cloth-covered cardboard: distinguished from *paper-backed*.

hard cash, 1. metal coins. 2. ready money; cash.

hard cider, fermented apple juice; alcoholic cider.

hard coal, anthracite coal.

hard-core (härd'kôr'), *adj.* 1. constituting or of a hard core. 2. absolute; unqualified.

hard core, the firm, unyielding, or unchanging central part or group.

hard-cov·er (härd'kuv'ēr), *adj.* hard-bound.

hard·en (här'd'n), *v.t. & v.i.* to make or become hard (in various senses).

hard·en·er (här'd'n-ẽr), *n.* a person or thing that hardens; specifically, *a*) a person who tempers metal tools. *b*) a substance used to give a harder film to paint, varnish, etc.
har·den·ing (här'd'n-iŋ), *n.* 1. a making or becoming hard. 2. a substance used to harden something.
hard-fea·tured (härd'fē'chẽrd), *adj.* having coarse, cruel, stern, or harsh features.
hard·fist·ed (härd'fis'tid), *adj.* selfish; stingy; niggardly: also **closefisted.**
hard·hack (härd'hak'), *n.* [*hard* + (?) *hack*, to chop], an American shrub of the rose family, with clusters of pink, purple, or white flowers and hairy leaves: also called *steeplebush.*
hard·hand·ed (härd'han'did), *adj.* 1. having hands made hard by work. 2. severe; tyrannical; ruthless: said of a ruler or rule.
hard·head (härd'hed'), *n.* 1. a shrewd person, not easily moved. 2. any of various kinds of fish; especially, *a*) the salmon trout. *b*) the menhaden. *c*) the sculpin.
hard·head·ed (härd'hed'id), *adj.* 1. shrewd and unsentimental; practical; matter-of-fact. 2. stubborn.
hard·heart·ed (härd'här'tid), *adj.* unfeeling; pitiless.
har·di·hood (här'di-hood'), *n.* [< *hardy* + *-hood*], 1. resolute boldness; daring. 2. impudence; insolence.
har·di·ly (här'd'l-i), *adv.* in a hardy manner.
har·di·ness (här'di-nis), *n.* the quality of being hardy; specifically, *a*) strength; physical endurance. *b*) hardihood; boldness.
Har·ding, Warren Gamaliel (här'diŋ), 1865–1923; twenty-ninth president of the United States (1921–1923).
hard labor, compulsory and continuous physical labor imposed, together with imprisonment, as a punishment for some crimes.
hard·ly (härd'li), *adv.* [ME. *hardliche;* AS. *heardlice;* see HARD & -LY], 1. with effort or difficulty; not easily. 2. severely; harshly. 3. only just; barely; scarcely: often used ironically or politely to mean "not quite," or "not at all." 4. improbably; not likely.
hard·ness (härd'nis), *n.* the state or quality of being hard (in various senses): abbreviated **H., h.**
hard palate, the bony part of the roof of the mouth, behind the upper teeth.
hard·pan (härd'pan'), *n.* 1. a layer of hard subsoil difficult to work. 2. solid, unplowed ground. 3. the hard, underlying part of anything; solid foundation.
hard rubber, vulcanized rubber that is firm and comparatively inelastic.
hards (härdz), *n.pl.* [ME. *herdes, hyrdys, hardes;* AS. *heordan, pl.*, flax hards; akin to MLG. *herde;* prob. IE. base **qes-*, to scrape, comb], coarse refuse of flax or hemp; tow: also **hurds.**
hard sauce, a sweet, creamy mixture of butter, powdered sugar, and flavoring, served with plum pudding, etc.
hard-set (härd'set'), *adj.* 1. in trouble or difficulty. 2. rigid; fixed; firm. 3. stubborn.
hard-shell (härd'shel'), *adj.* 1. having a hard shell. 2. [Colloq.], strict; uncompromising; strait-laced.
hard-shelled (härd'sheld'), *adj.* having a shell not recently molted: said of crabs.
hard·ship (härd'ship), *n.* [ME. *heardschipe;* see HARD & -SHIP], 1. hard circumstances of life. 2. a thing hard to bear; specific cause of discomfort or suffering, as poverty, pain, etc. —*SYN.* see **difficulty.**
hard-spun (härd'spun'), *adj.* spun with a firm, close twist: said of yarn.
hard·tack (härd'tak'), *n.* [*hard* + *tack* (food)], unleavened bread made in very hard, large wafers: it is traditionally a part of army and navy rations.
hard·top (convertible) (härd'top'), an automobile designed somewhat like a convertible, but with a metal top that cannot be folded back.
hard·ware (härd'wâr'), *n.* articles made of metal, as tools, nails, fittings, utensils, etc.
hard·wood (härd'wood'), *n.* 1. any tough, heavy timber with a compact texture. 2. in *forestry*, wood other than that from a pine, spruce, or other conifer; deciduous timber. 3. a tree yielding hardwood.
har·dy (här'di), *adj.* [HARDIER (-di-ẽr), HARDIEST (-di-ist)], [ME. & OFr. *hardi*, pp. of *hardir*, to make bold < OHG. *hartjan*, to make hard], 1. bold and resolute; daring; courageous. 2. too bold; full of temerity; rash. 3. able to withstand fatigue, privation, etc.; robust; vigorous. 4. in *gardening*, able to survive the winter without special care: said of plants.
har·dy (här'di), *n.* [prob. *hard* + *-y*], a square-shanked chisel used by blacksmiths: it fits into a square hole (*hardy hole*) in the anvil.
Har·dy, Thomas (här'di), 1840–1928; English poet and novelist.
hare (hâr), *n.* [*pl.* HARES (hârz), HARE; see PLURAL, II, D, 1], [ME.; AS. *hara;* akin to G. *hase;* IE. base **kas-*, gray], 1. any of a large group of swift animals of the rodent family, with long ears, soft fur, a cleft upper lip, a short tail, and long, powerful hind legs. 2. the common American rabbit. 3. any of the players chased in the game of hare and hounds.
hare and hounds, a game in which some players, called *hounds*, chase others, called *hares*, who have left a trail of paper scraps along their route.
hare·bell (hâr'bel'), *n.* [ME. *harebelle; hare*, a hare + *belle*, a bell], a slender, delicate plant with clusters of blue, bell-shaped flowers: also called *bluebell.*
hare·brained (hâr'brānd'), *adj.* having no more intelligence than a hare; reckless, flighty, giddy, rash, etc.
ha·reem (hä-rēm'), *n.* a harem.
hare·lip (hâr'lip'), *n.* 1. a congenital deformity of one or both lips, usually only the upper one, consisting of a cleft like that of a hare's lip: it often results in a speech defect. 2. a lip with such a deformity.
ha·rem (hâr'əm), *n.* [Ar. *ḥarīm*, lit., prohibited (place, thing) < *ḥarama*, to forbid], 1. that part of a Moslem's house in which the women live; seraglio. 2. the wives, concubines, women servants, etc. occupying a harem. Also **haram, hareem.**
Har·greaves, James (här'grēvz'), ?–1778; English inventor of the spinning jenny.
har·i·cot (har'i-kō'), *n.* [Fr. < *harigoter*, to cut to pieces; ? < MD. **harigod*, sharp tool < *haren*, to sharpen + *god*, a tool], 1. a highly seasoned stew of lamb or mutton and vegetables. 2. [said to be < Nahuatl *ayecotli*, bean, but ? < name of the stew], *a*) the kidney bean. *b*) its pod or seed.
ha·ri-ka·ri (hä'ri-kä'ri, har'ə-kar'i), *n.* hara-kiri.
hark (härk), *v.i.* [ME. *herkien* (akin to G. *horchen*, etc.); ? < unrecorded AS. **heorcian* or < AS. *heorcnian* (see HEARKEN)], to listen carefully: usually in the imperative, with the effect of an exclamation. *v.t.* [Archaic], to listen to; hear.
hark back, 1. to return to an earlier point so as to pick up the scent or trail again; hence, 2. to go back in thought or speech; revert.
hark·en (här'k'n), *v.i. & v.t.* to hearken.
harl (härl), *n.* [ME. *herle;* prob. < LG. or D.; cf. MLG. *herle, harl*], 1. a filament or filaments, especially of hemp or flax. 2. a barb of a feather: also **herl.**
Har·lan (här'lən), a masculine name.
Har·le·ian Library (här'li-ən), a collection of 8,000 books and 14,000 manuscripts, formed by Robert Harley (1661–1724) and his son Edward (1689–1741), earls of Oxford, and now housed in the British Museum.
Har·lem (här'ləm), *n.* a section of New York City with a large Negro population.
Harlem River, a river northeast of Manhattan Island, New York, connecting the East River with the Hudson.
Har·le·quin (här'lə-kwin, här'lə-kin), *n.* [Fr. *harlequin, arlequin;* It. *arlecchino;* OFr. *harlequin, hierlekin, hellequin*, demon, spirit, orig. demon huntsman], 1. a traditional comic character in pantomime, who wears a mask and gay, spangled tights of many colors, and sometimes carries a wooden wand or sword. 2. [h-], a clown; buffoon. *adj.* [h-], 1. comic; ludicrous. 2. of many colors; colorful. 3. [from the resemblance to the slanting eye holes of the mask], designating eyeglasses with brightly colored frames and slanting, elliptical eyepieces.

HARLEQUIN

har·le·quin·ade (här'lə-kwin-ād'), *n.* [Fr. *arlequinade*], 1. that part of a play or pantomime in which the Harlequin and the clown play leading parts; hence, 2. comic pranks; gay, mischievous antics; buffoonery.
har·lot (här'lət), *n.* [ME.; OFr., rogue, vagabond; orig. used as euphemism for *whore;* akin to Pr. *arlot*, Sp. *arlote;* origin dubious], a prostitute.
har·lot·ry (här'lət-ri), *n.* prostitution.
harm (härm), *n.* [ME. *herm, harm;* AS. *hearm;* akin to G. *harm;* IE. base **kormo-*, pain, torment], 1. hurt; injury; damage; impairment. 2. moral wrong; evil. *v.t.* [ME. *hermen, harmen;* AS. *hearmian* < the *n.*], to do harm to; hurt; damage; impair. —*SYN.* see **injure.**
har·mat·tan (här'mə-tan'), *n.* [Sp. *harmatán* < the native (Fanti) name in W. Africa], a dry, dusty wind that blows across the Atlantic coast of Africa.
harm·ful (härm'fəl), *adj.* causing harm; hurtful.
harm·less (härm'lis), *adj.* 1. [Rare], not harmed. 2. causing no harm; not inflicting hurt; inoffensive.
Har·mo·ni·a (här-mō'ni-ə), *n.* [L.; Gr. *Harmonia* (see HARMONY)], in *Greek mythology*, the daughter of Aphrodite and Ares, and wife of Cadmus: she personified harmony and order.
har·mon·ic (här-mon'ik), *adj.* [L. *harmonicus;* Gr. *harmonikos* < *harmonia;* see HARMONY], 1. harmonious in feeling or effect; agreeing. 2. in *mathematics*, designating or of a series of numbers whose reciprocals are in arithmetical progression. 3. in *music*, *a*) of harmony rather than melody or rhythm. *b*) of or producing a combination of sounds that is pleasing to the ear; consonant. *c*) designating a tone whose rate of vibration is a precise multiple of that of a given fundamental tone. *n.* 1. an overtone, especially one produced by lightly stopping a vibrating string at some specified point. 2. in *electricity*, a voltage or alternating current whose frequency is some integral multiple of the fundamental frequency.

har·mon·i·ca (här-mon′i-kə), *n.* [L., fem. of *harmonicus;* see HARMONIC], 1. a musical instrument consisting of a series of graduated glasses from which tones are produced by rubbing the edges with a wet finger: invented by Benjamin Franklin. 2. a percussion instrument consisting of metal or glass strips which are struck with small mallets. 3. a small wind instrument played with the mouth: it has a series of graduated metal reeds that vibrate and produce tones when air is blown or sucked across them: also called *mouth organ.*

HARMONICA (sense 3)

har·mon·i·cal·ly (här-mon′i-k'l-i), *adv.* 1. [Archaic], harmoniously. 2. in *mathematics*, in a harmonic relation. 3. in *music*, with reference to harmony.
har·mon·i·con (här-mon′i-kən), *n.* [*pl.* HARMONICA (-kə)], [Gr. *harmonikon*, neut. of *harmonikos;* see HARMONIC], 1. a harmonica. 2. an orchestrion.
har·mon·ics (här-mon′iks), *n.pl.* [construed as sing.], [< *harmonic*], the science of musical sounds.
har·mo·ni·ous (här-mō′ni-əs), *adj.* [Fr. *harmonieux;* see HARMONY], 1. having parts combined in a proportionate, orderly, or pleasing arrangement; congruous. 2. having similar or conforming feelings, ideas, interests, etc.; in accord. 3. in *music*, having tones combined to give a pleasing effect; consonant.
har·mo·nist (här′mə-nist), *n.* 1. a musician or composer; especially, an expert in harmony. 2. a poet. 3. a literary scholar who arranges parallel passages of different authors, as in the Scriptures, so as to bring out corresponding ideas, qualities, etc. 4. a person who harmonizes something.
har·mo·ni·um (här-mō′ni-əm), *n.* [Fr. < L. *harmonia;* see HARMONY], a small keyboard organ in which the tones are produced by forcing air through metal reeds by means of a bellows operated by pedals.
har·mon·i·za·tion (här′mən-i-zā′shən, här′mən-ī-zā′shən), *n.* a harmonizing or being harmonized.
har·mo·nize (här′mə-nīz′), *v.i.* [HARMONIZED (-nīzd′), HARMONIZING], [Fr. *harmonizer* < *harmonie*], to be, sing, or play in harmony; accord; agree. *v.t.* 1. to make harmonious; bring into agreement. 2. to add chords to (a melody) so as to form a harmony. —*SYN.* see **agree.**
har·mo·ny (här′mə-ni), *n.* [*pl.* HARMONIES (-niz)], [Fr. *harmonie;* L. *harmonia;* Gr. *harmonia* < *harmos*, a fitting, *harmozein*, to fit together], 1. a combination of parts into a proportionate or orderly whole; congruity. 2. agreement in feeling, action, ideas, interests, etc.; peaceable or friendly relations. 3. agreement or proportionate arrangement of color, size, shape, etc. that is pleasing to the eye; a fitting well together. 4. an arrangement of parallel passages of different authors, the Scriptures, etc., made so as to bring out corresponding ideas, qualities, etc. 5. agreeable sounds; music. 6. in *music*, *a)* the pleasing combination of two or more tones in a chord. *b)* structure in terms of the arrangement, progression, modulation, etc. of chords: distinguished from *melody, rhythm. c)* the study of this structure. —*SYN.* see **symmetry.**
har·ness (här′nis), *n.* [ME. *harneis;* OFr. *harneis, herneis, harnes*, armor], 1. originally, armor and other military equipment for a man or horse. 2. the leather straps and metal pieces by which a horse, mule, etc. is fastened to a vehicle, plow, or load. 3. any trappings or gear similar to this; specifically, *a)* the straps, etc. by which a parachute is fastened to its wearer. *b)* a device for raising and lowering the warp threads on a loom. *v.t.* 1. to put harness on (a horse, etc.). 2. to bring into a condition for working or producing power: as, they *harnessed* the power of the water by building a dam. 3. [Archaic], to put armor on.

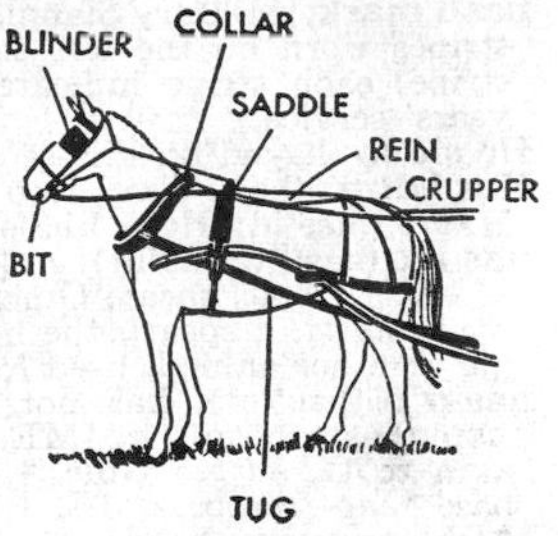

HARNESS

in double harness, 1. in a harness for two animals pulling the same carriage, plow, etc. 2. married.
in harness, in or at one's routine work.
har·nessed antelope (här′nist), any of several striped African antelopes, as the bushbuck.
harness hitch, a kind of knot: see **knot**, illus.
harness race, a horse race between either trotters or pacers, each pulling a sulky and driver.
Har·ney Peak (här′ni), the highest mountain of the Black Hills, western South Dakota: height, 7,242 ft.
Har·old (har′əld), [AS. *Harold, Harald;* ON. *Haraldr;* Gmc. **Hariwald*, lit., ruler, leader of the army < **harja-*, army, host (AS. *here*) + **waldan*, to rule (cf. WIELD)], a masculine name: diminutive, *Hal.*
Harold I, ?–1040; son of Canute II; king of England (1035–1040): called *Harold Harefoot.*
Harold II, 1022?–1066; last Saxon king of England (1066); killed in the Battle of Hastings.
harp (härp), *n.* [ME. *herpe, harpe;* AS. *hearpe;* akin to G. *harfe;* IE. base*(*s*) *qereb*(*h-*), to bend, curve, seen also in Norw. dial. *hurpa*, old, bent crone; the name comes from the shape of the instrument], 1. a musical instrument with strings stretched across an open, triangular frame, played by being plucked with the fingers: the modern harp has forty-six strings and a series of foot pedals which permit the playing of half tones. 2. a harp-shaped object or implement. 3. [H-], Lyra, a northern constellation. 4. [Slang], an Irishman: a vulgar term of prejudice and contempt. *v.i.* 1. to play a harp. 2. to persist in talking or writing tediously or continuously (*on* or *upon* something). *v.t.* [Rare], to give voice to; express.

HARP

Har·pers Ferry, Har·per's Ferry (här′pẽrz), a town in West Virginia, at the juncture of the Potomac and Shenandoah Rivers: site of John Brown's raid in 1859.
harp·ings (här′piŋz), *n.pl.* [prob. < Fr. *harper*, to grip], 1. wooden strips or planks on the bow of a ship to give it added strength. 2. wooden pieces used as supports during the construction of a ship.
harp·ins (här′pinz), *n.pl.* harpings.
harp·ist (här′pist), *n.* a person who plays the harp.
har·poon (här-pōōn′), *n.* [Fr. *harpon*, dim. < *harpe*, a claw, or < MFr. *harper*, to claw, grip < Gmc. **harpan*, to seize], a barbed javelin or spear with a line attached to it, used for spearing whales or other large sea animals. *v.t.* to strike, kill, or catch with a harpoon.
harp·si·chord (härp′si-kôrd′), *n.* [obs. Fr. *harpechorde;* *harpe* (LL. *harpa;* Gmc. *harpa;* see HARP) + *chorde* (see CORD); *-s-* is unexplained], a stringed musical instrument with a keyboard, forerunner of the piano: it somewhat resembles the clavichord, except that when the keys are pressed the strings are plucked by leather-tipped points rather than struck by hammers, and produce short, abrupt tones.

HARPSICHORD

Har·py (här′pi), *n.* [*pl.* HARPIES (-piz)], [OFr. *harpie;* L. *harpyia;* Gr. *harpyiai*, pl., lit., snatchers < *harpazein*, to seize, snatch], 1. in *Greek mythology*, any of several hideous, filthy, winged monsters with the head and trunk of a woman and the tail, legs, and talons of a bird: they carried off the souls of the dead, seized the food of their victims, etc. 2. [h-], a relentless, greedy, or grasping person. 3. [h-], a harpy eagle.

HARPY

harpy eagle, a large, short-winged, tropical American eagle, with a double crest and a powerful bill and claws.
har·que·bus (här′kwi-bəs), *n.* an arquebus, an early type of firearm.
Har·rar (hä′rẽr), *n.* Harar.
har·ri·dan (har′i-dən), *n.* [prob. altered < OFr. *haridelle*, worn-out horse, jade], a haggard, disreputable, shrewish old woman.
har·ri·er (har′i-ẽr), *n.* [< *hare* + *-ier*], 1. any of an English breed of dog, used for hunting hares and rabbits. 2. *pl.* the harriers and hunters in a hunt. 3. a cross-country runner.
har·ri·er (har′i-ẽr), *n.* 1. a person who harries. 2. a hawk that preys on insects and small animals.
Har·ri·et (har′i-ət), [fem. dim. of *Harry*], a feminine name: variants, *Harriot, Harriott;* diminutive, *Hattie.*
Har·ri·man, Edward Henry (har′i-mən), 1848–1909; American capitalist; railroad magnate.
Har·ris, Joel Chand·ler (chand′lẽr har′is), 1848–1908; American writer; wrote the *Uncle Remus* stories.
Har·ris·burg (har′is-bũrg′), *n.* the capital of Pennsylvania, on the Susquehanna: pop., 80,000.
Har·ri·son, Benjamin (har′ə-s'n), 1. 1726?–1791;

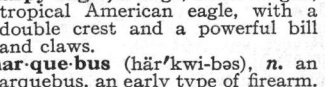

father of *William Henry;* American statesman; signer of the Declaration of Independence. 2. 1833–1901; grandson of *William Henry;* twenty-third president of the United States (1889–1893).

Harrison, William Henry, 1773–1841; American statesman and general; grandfather of *Benjamin* (the president); ninth president of the United States (1841): called *Tippecanoe.*

Harris Tweed, [< *Harris,* island in the Hebrides where the cloth is made], a soft, hand-woven, all-wool tweed in a heather mixture: a trade-mark.

Har·ro·vi·an (ha-rō′vi-ən, hə-rōv′yən), *adj.* of Harrow. *n.* a student or former student of Harrow.

Har·row (har′ō), *n.* a private preparatory school (called *public school* in England) for boys, situated in Harrow-on-the-Hill, a town in Middlesex, near London.

har·row (har′ō), *n.* [ME. *herwe, harwe;* prob. < ON.; cf. ON. *harfr, hervi,* Dan. *harv,* etc.; IE. base possibly *(*s*)*qer-,* to cut], a heavy frame with spikes or sharp-edged disks, drawn by a horse or tractor and used for leveling and breaking up plowed ground, covering seeds, rooting up weeds etc. *v.t.* 1. to draw a harrow over (land). 2. to hurt; cut; wound; lacerate. 3. to make uncomfortable; distress; torment; vex. *v.i.* to take harrowing: as, this ground *harrows* well.

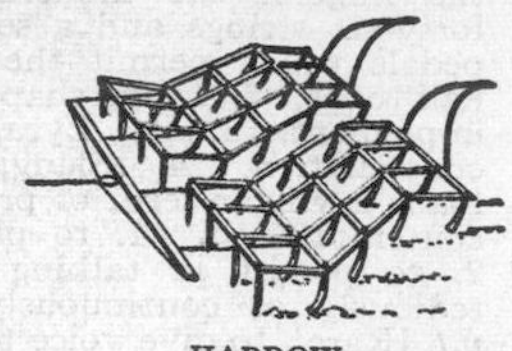
HARROW

Har·ry (har′i), a masculine name: feminine, *Harriet:* see **Henry.** *n.* the Devil; Satan: usually **Old Harry.**

har·ry (har′i), *v.t.* [HARRIED (-id), HARRYING], [ME. *hergien, herien;* AS. *hergian* < base of *here,* army (G. *heer*); see HARBINGER, HERIOT], 1. to raid and destroy or rob; pillage; plunder. 2. to torment; harass.

harsh (härsh), *adj.* [ME. *harsk;* prob. < ON.; cf. Dan. *harsk,* rancid (Norw. *hersk,* Sw. *härsk*); akin to G. *harsch,* rough, raw; prob. IE. base **qars-,* to scratch, comb, seen also in L. *carduus,* thistle, *carrere,* to card (wool)], 1. unpleasantly sharp or rough; specifically, *a*) grating to the ear; discordant. *b*) too bright or vivid to the eye; glaring. *c*) too strong to the taste; bitter. *d*) not smooth to the touch; coarse. 2. unpleasantly crude, abrupt, or strained so as to be offensive to one's mind or feelings. 3. rough, crude, or forbidding in appearance. 4. stern; severe; unfeeling; cruel. —*SYN.* see **rough.**

hars·let (härs′lit), *n.* haslet.

hart (härt), *n.* [*pl.* HARTS (härts), HART; see PLURAL, II, D, 1], [ME. *hert;* AS. *heort, heorot;* akin to G. *hirsch;* IE. base **ker-,* head, what is on the head, horn], a male deer, especially a red deer after its fifth year, when the crown antlers are formed; stag.

Hart, Albert Bush·nell (boosh′n'l härt), 1854–1943; American historian and educator.

Hart, Moss (môs), **1904–1961; American playwright.**

har·tal (här-täl′), *n.* [Hind. *haṛtāl* < *hāt,* a shop, market + *tālā,* a lock], in India, a suspension of work and business, especially as an expression of national mourning or political protest.

hart·beest (härt′bēst′), *n.* [*pl.* HARTBEESTS (-bēsts′), HARTBEEST; see PLURAL, II, D, 1], a hartebeest.

Harte, Bret (bret härt), (*Francis Brett Harte*), 1836–1902; American writer.

har·te·beest (här′tə-bēst′, härt′bēst′), *n.* [*pl.* HARTEBEESTS (-bēsts′), HARTEBEEST; see PLURAL, II, D, 1], [S.Afr. D.; *harte,* hart + *beest,* beast], a large, swift South African antelope, now rare, having a reddish-brown coat with a yellow patch on each haunch, and long horns curved backward at the tips.

Hart·ford (härt′fẽrd), *n.* the capital of Connecticut, on the Connecticut River: pop., 162,000.

harts·horn (härts′hôrn′), *n.* 1. a hart's horn; deer's antler. 2. *a*) ammonia in water solution. *b*) ammonium carbonate, used in smelling salts; sal volatile: so called because formerly obtained from deer's antlers.

hart's-tongue, harts·tongue (härts′tuŋ′), *n.* a fern with long, narrow fronds, found in Europe and Asia.

har·um-scar·um (hâr′əm-skâr′əm), *adj.* [prob. < *hare* + *scare* + *'em*], reckless; rash; wild; irresponsible. *adv.* in a harum-scarum manner. *n.* a harum-scarum person or action.

Ha·run al-Ra·shid (hä-rōōn′ är′rə-shēd′; Eng. har′ōōn-al-rash′id), 764?–809 A.D.; caliph of Bagdad (786–809 A.D.).

ha·rus·pex (hə-rus′peks, har′əs-peks′), *n.* [*pl.* HARUSPICES (hə-rus′pi-sēz′)], [L., lit., inspector of entrails], any of a class of lesser priests and soothsayers in ancient Rome, who professed to foretell the future by interpreting the entrails of sacrificial animals.

ha·rus·pi·cal (hə-rus′pi-k'l), *adj.* of or acting as a haruspex.

Har·vard, John (här′vẽrd), 1607–1638; English clergyman in America; a principal endower of Harvard College.

har·vest (här′vist), *n.* [ME. *hervest, harveste;* AS. *hærfest;* akin to G. *herbst* (OHG. *herbist*); IE. base *(*s*)*qer*(*e*)*p-* (< *(*s*)*qer-,* to cut), seen also in L. *carpere,* to pluck (cf. CARPEL, CARPET); basic sense "time of cutting, plucking"], 1. the time of the year when matured grain, fruit, vegetables, etc. are reaped and gathered in. 2. a season's yield of grain, fruit, etc. when gathered in or ready to be gathered in; crop. 3. the gathering in of a crop. 4. the outcome or consequence of any effort or series of events: as, death is the *harvest* of war. *v.t. & v.i.* 1. to gather in (a crop, etc.). 2. to gather the crop from (a field).

harvest bug (or **mite, tick, louse**), the chigger, a very small, parasitic larva.

har·vest·er (här′vis-tẽr), *n.* 1. a person who gathers in a crop of grain, fruit, etc.; reaper. 2. a harvesting machine; mechanical reaper.

harvest fly, any of various cicadas heard at harvest time.

harvest home, 1. the bringing home of the last harvest load; end of the harvest. 2. a former festival celebrating this. 3. a song sung by harvesters bringing home the last load.

har·vest·man (här′vist-mən), *n.* [*pl.* HARVESTMEN (-mən)], 1. a man who harvests; reaper. 2. any of a group of spiderlike animals with very long, thin legs: often called *daddy-longlegs.*

harvest moon, the full moon at or about the time of the autumnal equinox, September 22 or 23.

harvest mouse, a very small European mouse that builds its nest in the stalks of growing grain.

Har·vey (här′vi), [Fr. *Hervé;* G. *Herwig, Herewig,* lit., army battle < Gmc. **harja,* army (cf. HARRY) + **wig-,* fight, battle], a masculine name. *n.* a city in northeastern Illinois: pop., 29,000.

Har·vey, William (här′vi), 1578–1657; English physician; discovered the circulation of the blood.

Harz (härts), *n.* a mountain range in central Germany: highest peak, Brocken, 3,745 ft.

has (haz; *unstressed* həz, əz), the third person singular, present indicative, of **have.**

Ha·sa, El (el hä′sə), a region in Saudi Arabia, on the Persian Gulf: area, 25,000 sq. mi.

has-been (haz′bin′), *n.* [Colloq.], a person or thing that was formerly popular or effective but is no longer so.

Has·dru·bal (haz′drōō-b'l), *n.* any of various Carthaginian generals; especially, *a*) brother of Hannibal; ?–207 B.C. *b*) brother-in-law of Hannibal; ?–221 B.C.

ha·sen·pfef·fer (hä′s'n-fef′ẽr; G. hä′zən-pfef′ẽr), *n.* [G. < *hase,* rabbit (see HARE) + *pfeffer,* pepper], a German dish of marinated rabbit, seasoned and braised.

hash (hash), *v.t.* [Fr. *hacher,* to chop, mince < *hache,* a hatchet], 1. to chop (meat and vegetables) into small pieces for cooking. 2. [Colloq.], to make a mess or botch of; bungle. *n.* 1. a chopped mixture of cooked meat and vegetables, usually baked or browned. 2. a mixture, as of things used before in different forms; rehash. 3. a hodgepodge; muddle; mess.
make (a) hash of, [Colloq.], 1. to bungle; botch. 2. to destroy or defeat (an opponent, argument, etc.).
settle one's hash, [Colloq.], to overcome or subdue one.

hash·eesh (hash′ēsh), *n.* hashish.

Hash·em·ite Jordan (hash′ə-mīt′), see **Jordan.**

hash house, [Slang], a cheap restaurant.

hash·ish (hash′ēsh, hash′ish), *n.* [Ar. *ḥashīsh,* dried hemp; cf. ASSASSIN], a drug made from the leaves and stalks of Indian hemp, chewed or smoked in the Orient for its intoxicating and narcotic effects.

hash mark, [Military Slang], any of the parallel diagonal stripes worn on the left sleeve of a uniform; service stripe: each stripe indicates the completion of three years' service.

Ha·sid·ic (ha-sid′ik, khä-sē′dik), *adj.* Chassidic.

Has·i·dim (has′i-dim; Heb. khä-sē′dim), *n.pl.* [*sing.* HASID (has′id; Heb. khä′sid)], Chassidim.

has·let (has′lit, hāz′lit), *n.* [ME. *hastelet;* OFr. *hastellet* < *haste,* a spit, spear; Gmc. **harst,* a roast; influenced by L. *hasta,* a spear], the heart, liver, lungs, etc. of a pig or other animal, used for food: also **harslet.**

has·n't (haz′'nt), has not.

hasp (hasp, häsp), *n.* [ME. *haspe, hespe;* AS. *hæpse;* akin to G. *haspe;* Gmc. base **hap-;* prob. < IE. **qab-,* to curve, bend; *n.* senses parallel development of *hank*], 1. a hinged metal fastening for a door, window, lid, book covers, etc.; especially, a metal piece fitted over a staple or into a hole and fastened by a bolt or padlock. 2. a skein of yarn or thread. *v.t.* to fasten with or as with a hasp.

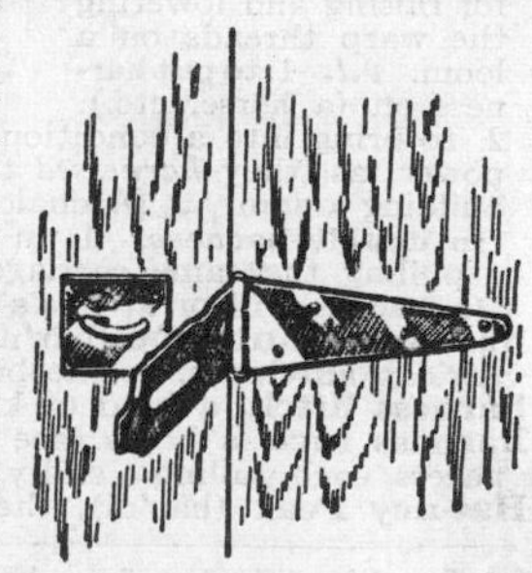
HASP

has·sle, has·sel (has′'l), *n.* [? < dial. *hassle,* to breathe noisily], [Slang], a heated discussion; squabble.

has·sock (has′ək), *n.* [ME.

hassok; AS. *hassuc, hassoc* (clump of) coarse grass; ? < Celtic base + *-ock* (cf. W. *hesg,* sedge, Bret. *hesk,* reed < IE. **seq-,* to cut, as in *sedge*)], 1. a thick clump or tuft of grass; tussock. 2. a firmly stuffed mat or cushion used as a footstool or seat.

hast (hast; *unstressed* həst), archaic second person singular, present indicative, of **have**: used with *thou.*

‡**has·ta la vis·ta** (äs'tä lä vēs'tä), [Sp., lit., until the meeting], good-by.

‡**has·ta ma·ña·na** (äs'tä mä-nyä'nä), [Sp., lit., until tomorrow], good-by.

has·tate (has'tāt), *adj.* [L. *hastatus* < *hasta,* a spear], shaped like a spearhead, as some leaves: see **leaf**, illus.

haste (hāst), *n.* [ME.; OFr. *haste* (Fr. *hâte*) < Gmc.; cf. AS. *hæst,* violence], 1. quickness of motion; hurrying; rapidity: said of voluntary actions. 2. careless hurrying: as, *haste* makes waste. 3. necessity for hurrying; urgency. *v.t. & v.i.* [Rare], to hasten.
  in haste, 1. in a hurry. 2. in too great a hurry; without enough care or thought.
  make haste, to hasten; hurry.
  SYN.—**haste** implies quick or precipitate movement or action, as from the pressure of circumstances or intense eagerness; **hurry**, often interchangeable with **haste**, specifically suggests excitement, bustle, or confusion (the *hurry* of city life); **speed** implies rapidity of movement, operation, etc., suggesting effectiveness and the absence of excitement or confusion (to increase the *speed* of an assembly line); **expedition** adds to **speed** the implication of efficiency and stresses the facilitation of an action or procedure; **dispatch** comes close to **expedition** in meaning but more strongly stresses promptness in finishing something.—*ANT.* slowness, delay.

has·ten (hās''n), *v.t.* [extended form of *haste, v.*], to make hurry; speed up; cause to be or come faster; accelerate. *v.i.* to move swiftly; hurry; be quick.

hast·i·ly (hās't'l-i), *adv.* in a hasty manner.

has·ti·ness (hās'ti-nis), *n.* the quality or condition of being hasty.

Has·tings (hās'tiŋz), *n.* 1. a city in England, on the English Channel: pop., 64,000: site of the decisive battle of the Norman invasion of England (1066). 2. a city in Nebraska: pop., 21,000.

Hastings, Warren, 1732–1818; English statesman; first governor general of India (1773–1785).

hast·y (hās'ti), *adj.* [HASTIER (-ti-ẽr), HASTIEST (-ti-ist)], [ME. *hasti;* OFr. *hasti, hastif;* see HASTE], 1. done or made with haste; quick; hurried. 2. done or made too quickly and with too little thought; rash. 3. short-tempered or impetuous. 4. showing irritation or impatience: as, *hasty* words. —*SYN.* see **fast.**

hasty pudding, [so called because quickly prepared], 1. mush made of corn meal. 2. [British], mush made of flour or oatmeal.

hat (hat), *n.* [ME.; AS. *hætt;* akin to OFris. *hat;* IE. base **kadh-,* to cover, protect, seen also in L. *cassis* (< **kadh-tis*), helmet & Eng. *hood*], 1. a head covering, usually with a brim and a crown: sometimes distinguished from *bonnet, beret, cap,* etc. 2. in the *Roman Catholic Church, a*) the official red hat of a cardinal. *b*) the rank or position of a cardinal. *v.t.* [HATTED (hat'id), HATTING], to cover or provide with a hat.
  pass the hat, to take up a collection, as at a meeting.
  take one's hat off to, to salute; congratulate.
  talk through one's hat, [Colloq.], to make irresponsible or foolish statements; talk nonsense.
  throw one's hat into the ring, 1. to enter a competition. 2. to become a candidate for office.
  under one's hat, [Colloq.], secret; strictly confidential.

hat·a·ble (hāt'ə-b'l), *adj.* hateable.

hat·band (hat'band'), *n.* a band of cloth around the crown of a hat, just above the brim: a band of black cloth is often worn to show mourning.

hat·box (hat'boks'), *n.* a box for carrying or storing a hat or hats.

hatch (hach), *v.t.* [ME. *hacchen;* prob. < unrecorded AS.; akin to G. *hecken,* to breed, bring forth young & AS. *hagan,* the genitals; IE. base **kak-,* male genitalia], 1. to bring forth (young) from an egg or eggs by applying warmth. 2. to bring forth young from (an egg or eggs). 3. *a*) to bring (a plan, idea, etc.) into existence; devise; plan. *b*) to plot. *v.i.* 1. to bring forth young; develop embryos: said of eggs. 2. to come forth from the egg. *n.* 1. the process of hatching. 2. the brood hatched; hence, 3. an outcome; result.

hatch (hach), *n.* [ME. *hacche, hecche;* AS. *hæc,* grating, lattice gate; akin to D., LG. *hek;* prob. IE. base **keg-, *keng-,* hook, etc., for hanging (cf. HANG, HANK)], 1. the lower half of a door, gate, etc. that has two separately movable halves. 2. *a*) an opening in a ship's deck, as one through which cargo can be lowered; hatchway. *b*) a similar opening in the floor or roof of a building. 3. a lid for or as for such an opening; trap door: such lids were originally gratings. 4. a barrier to regulate the flow of water in a stream; floodgate. 5. a kind of fishtrap.

hatch (hach), *v.t.* [OFr. *hacher,* to hack < *hache,* an ax], to mark or engrave with fine, crossed or parallel lines so as to indicate shading. *n.* any of these lines.

hatch·el (hach'əl), *n.* [ME. *hecchel, hechele* (akin to G. *hechel*); AS. **hecel, *hæcel* < base seen in *hook, hang,* etc. + *-le*], a comblike instrument for cleaning and dressing flax, hemp, etc. *v.t.* [HATCHELED or HATCHELLED (-əld), HATCHELING or HATCHELLING], [ME. *hechelen;* akin to D. *hekelen,* to heckle], 1. to clean and dress (flax, hemp, etc.) with a hatchel. 2. [Rare], to heckle; annoy; tease. Also, for *n. & v.* 1, **hackle, heckle.**

hatch·er·y (hach'ẽr-i), *n.* [*pl.* HATCHERIES (-iz)], a place for hatching eggs, especially those of fish or poultry.

hatch·et (hach'it), *n.* [ME. *hachet;* OFr. *hachette,* dim. of *hache,* an ax < Gmc.], 1. a small ax with a short handle, for use with one hand. 2. a tomahawk.
  bury the hatchet, to stop fighting; make peace.
  dig (or **take**) **up the hatchet,** to start fighting; make war.

SHINGLING HATCHET

CLAW HATCHET

LATHING HATCHET

TYPES OF HATCHET

hatchet face, a lean, sharp face, suggesting the cutting edge of a hatchet.

hatch·et-faced (hach'it-fāst'), *adj.* having a hatchet face.

hatch·ing (hach'iŋ), *n.* [*hatch* (to shade) + *-ing*], 1. the drawing or engraving of fine, parallel or crossed lines to show shading. 2. such lines.

hatch·ment (hach'mənt), *n.* [for earlier *atcheament,* altered < *achievement*], in *heraldry,* a square tablet or panel bearing the coat of arms of a man who has just died, hung diagonally for a time at the front of his house and later in church as a sign of his death.

hatch·way (hach'wā'), *n.* 1. a rectangular opening in a ship's deck, through which cargo can be lowered. 2. a similar opening, usually covered with a sliding hatch, at the rear of a deckhouse, etc. 3. a similar opening in the floor or roof of a building. Also **hatch.**

hate (hāt), *v.t.* [HATED (-id), HATING], [ME. *haten, hatien;* AS. *hatian;* akin to G. *hassen;* IE. base **kād-,* bad temper, seen also in W. *cas,* hate], 1. to have strong dislike or ill will for; loathe; despise. 2. to dislike; wish to avoid; shrink from: as, he *hates* to work. *v.i.* to feel hatred. *n.* 1. a strong feeling of dislike or ill will; hatred. 2. a person or thing hated.
  SYN.—**hate** implies a feeling of great dislike or aversion, and, with persons as the object, connotes the bearing of malice; **detest** implies vehement dislike or antipathy; **despise** suggests a looking down with great contempt upon the person or thing one hates; **abhor** implies a feeling of great repugnance or disgust; **loathe** implies utter abhorrence.—*ANT.* love, like.

hate·a·ble (hāt'ə-b'l), *adj.* that deserves to be hated.

hate·ful (hāt'f'l), *adj.* 1. [Rare], feeling or showing hate; malignant; malevolent. 2. causing or deserving hate; loathsome; obnoxious; detestable; odious.
  SYN.—**hateful** is applied to that which provokes extreme dislike or aversion; **odious** stresses a disagreeable or offensive quality in that which is hateful; **detestable** refers to that which arouses vehement dislike or antipathy; **obnoxious** is applied to that which is very objectionable to one and causes great annoyance or discomfort by its presence; that is **repugnant** which is so distasteful or offensive that one offers strong resistance to it; that is **abhorrent** which is regarded with extreme repugnance or disgust; **abominable** is applied to that which is execrably or degradingly offensive or loathsome.

hath (hath), archaic third person singular, present indicative, of **have.**

Hath·a·way, Anne (hath'ə-wā'), 1557–1623; Shakespeare's wife.

Hath·or (hath'ôr), *n.* [Gr. *Hathōr;* Egypt. *Ḥet-Ḥert,* lit., the house above], in *Egyptian mythology,* the goddess of love, mirth, and joy, usually represented as having the head or ears of a cow.

Hathor capital, in *architecture,* a capital with faces of Hathor carved on its sides.

Ha·thor·ic (hə-thor'ik), *adj.* of Hathor or the Hathor capital.

hat·pin (hat'pin'), *n.* a long, ornamental pin for fastening a woman's hat to her hair.

hat·rack (hat'rak'), *n.* a rack, set of pegs or hooks, etc. to hold hats.

ha·tred (hā'trid), *n.* [ME. *hatred, hatreden* < *hate,* hate + *-red, -reden* < AS. *-ræden,* state, condition], strong dislike or ill will; hate.

hat·ter (hat'ẽr), *n.* a person who makes or sells hats, especially men's hats.

Hat·ter·as, Cape (hat'ẽr-əs), a cape on an island off Pamlico Sound, North Carolina: hazardous to ships.

Hat·tie (hat'i), a feminine name: see **Harriet.**

Hat·ties·burg (hat'iz-bũrg'), *n.* a city in southeastern Mississippi: pop., 35,000.

hat tree, a stand with arms or hooks to hold hats, coats, etc.
hau·ber·geon (hô′bẽr-jən), *n.* [Obs.], a habergeon.
hau·berk (hô′bẽrk), *n.* [ME. *hauberk, hauberc;* OFr. *hauberc, halberc* < OHG. *halsberc, halsberge,* protection for the neck, gorget < *hals,* the neck + *bergan,* to protect, save; cf. HARBOR], a medieval coat of armor, usually of chain mail.
haugh·ti·ly (hô′t'l-i), *adv.* in a haughty manner.
haugh·ti·ness (hô′ti-nis), *n.* a haughty quality.
haugh·ty (hô′ti), *adj.* [HAUGHTIER (-ti-ẽr), HAUGHTIEST (-ti-ist)], [ME. *haut,* high, haughty < OFr. *haut,* high < L. *altus* (with *h-* after OHG. *hoh,* high); + *-y;* influenced by ME. *hautein;* OFr. *hautain* < *haut; gh* prob. inserted by analogy with *naughty* (cf. DELIGHT, SPRIGHTLY)], 1. having or showing great pride in oneself and disdain, contempt, or scorn for others; proud; arrogant; supercilious. 2. [Archaic], lofty; noble. —*SYN.* see **proud.**
haul (hôl), *v.t.* [Early Mod. Eng. *haule,* phonetic sp. < ME. *halen* (cf. HALE, *v.t.*); OFr. *haler,* to draw < OFrank. *halōn* (OHG. *halōn*), to fetch; akin to G. *holen,* to fetch; prob. IE. base **kel-,* to cry out; basic sense "to call hither"], 1. to pull with force; move by pulling or drawing; tug; drag. 2. to transport by wagon, truck, etc.: as, he *hauls* coal for a living. 3. in *nautical usage,* to change the course of (a ship) by setting the sails. *v.i.* 1. to pull; tug. 2. to shift direction: said of the wind. 3. to change one's opinion or course of action: as, he *hauled* around to my way of thinking. 4. in *nautical usage,* to change the course of a ship by trimming sail, usually so as to travel closer to the wind. *n.* 1. the act of hauling; pull; tug. 2. the amount gained, won, caught, etc. at one time, as in a net; catch: as, a good *haul* of fish. 3. the distance or route over which something is transported: as, a long *haul.* 4. the load or quantity transported. —*SYN.* see **pull.**
haul off, 1. to change a ship's course so as to draw away from something. 2. to retreat; withdraw. 3. [Colloq.], to draw the arm back before hitting.
haul on (or **to, onto**) **the wind,** to haul in sails until they are nearly parallel with the desired course, in order to sail closer to the wind.
haul up, to sail nearer the direction of the wind.
haul·age (hôl′ij), *n.* [*haul* + *-age*], 1. the act or process of hauling. 2. the force used in hauling something. 3. the charge made for hauling, as by a railroad.
haulm (hôm), *n.* [ME. *halm;* AS. *healm, halm,* straw; akin to G. *halm;* IE. **koləmo-s,* reed, cane, seen also in L. *culmus,* a stalk, straw, *calamus* (< Gr.), a reed, reed pipe], 1. the stalks or stems of cultivated cereals, beans, peas, etc., especially after the crop has been gathered; hence, 2. straw or hay used for thatching roofs, etc. 3. a stem of grass or grain; culm. Also **halm.**
haunch (hônch, hänch), *n.* [ME. *haunche, hanche;* OFr. *hanche, hance, anche* < Gmc.; cf. G. *hanke,* haunch, hip], 1. the part of the body including the hip, buttock, and thickest part of the thigh; hindquarter. 2. an animal's loin and leg together; joint of venison, mutton, etc. 3. in *architecture,* either of the sides of an arch from the point of rising to the vertex.
haunch bone, the ilium; hipbone.
haunt (hônt, hänt), *v.t.* [ME. *haunten, hanten;* OFr. *hanter,* to frequent, resort to], 1. to visit (a place) often or continually; frequent. 2. to annoy or pester (a person) by constant visiting, following, etc. 3. to appear or recur frequently to; obsess: as, memories *haunted* her. 4. to be associated with; fill the atmosphere of; pervade: as, memories of former gaiety *haunt* the house. *Haunt* is often used with a ghost, spirit, etc. as its stated or implied subject. *n.* 1. *a*) a place often visited or stayed in: as, a saloon that was the *haunt* of criminals. *b*) a lair or feeding place of animals. 2. (*also* hant), [Dial.], a ghost.
haunt·ed (hôn′tid, hän′tid), *adj.* [pp. of *haunt*], supposedly frequented by ghosts: as, a *haunted* house.
haunt·ing (hôn′tiŋ, hän′tiŋ), *adj.* [ppr. of *haunt*], often recurring to the mind; not easily forgotten: as, a *haunting* tune.
Haupt·mann, Ger·hart (gär′härt houpt′män), 1862–1946; German dramatist, novelist, and poet; received Nobel prize in literature, 1912.
Hau·sa, Haus·sa (hou′sä), *n.* 1. a Negroid people of Nigeria and the Sudan, numbering over 5,000,000. 2. a member of this people. 3. the language of the Hausa, used as an international trade language in Negro Africa south of the Sahara.
hau·sen (hô′z'n; G. hou′z'n), *n.* [G.], a large sturgeon found in the Black Sea, Caspian Sea, Sea of Azov, etc.
‡**Haus·frau** (hous′frou′), *n.* [G.], a housewife.
haus·tel·lum (hôs-tel′əm), *n.* [*pl.* HAUSTELLA (-ə)], [Mod. L. < L. *haustus,* pp. of *haurire,* to drink, draw water], a tubelike sucking organ, or proboscis, as in various insects.
haus·to·ri·um (hôs-tôr′i-əm, hôs-tō′ri-əm), *n.* [*pl.* HAUSTORIA (-ə)], [Mod. L. < L. *haustus;* see HAUSTELLUM], a rootlike outgrowth in certain parasitic plants, through which food is absorbed from the host

haut·boy (hō′boi, ō′boi), *n.* [Fr. *hautbois; haut,* high (pitch) + *bois,* wood], an oboe.
hau·teur (hō-tũr′; Fr. ō′tër′), *n.* [Fr. < *haut,* high, proud], haughtiness; disdainful pride; snobbery.
‡**haut monde** (ō′mōnd′), [Fr.], high society.
Haut-Rhin (ō′ran′), *n.* a department of France, on the Rhine: area, 1,354 sq. mi.: pop., 510,000: capital, Colmar.
Ha·van·a (hə-van′ə), *n.* 1. the capital of Cuba: pop., 785,000: Spanish name, *Habana.* 2. a cigar made in Havana, or in Cuba, or of Cuban tobacco.
have (hav; *unstressed* həv, əv), *v.t.* [HAD (had; *unstressed* həd, əd), HAVING; the unstressed forms usually occur when the verb is used as auxiliary], [ME. *habben* (pres. t. *ic have,* etc., p.t. *ic hafde, havde, hadde*); AS. *habban,* parallel with Goth. *haban,* ON. *hafa,* OHG. *haben;* IE. base **qap-,* to seize, seen also in L. *capere,* to seize, *capax,* capable of holding (cf. CAPTIVE, CAPACIOUS): primary sense, "to possess"], 1. to hold in the hand or in control; own; possess: as, he *has* money. 2. to possess, hold, or contain as a part, characteristic, attribute, or associated feature: as, the week *has* seven days. 3. to be possessed with; be affected by: as, the children *have* measles. 4. to possess by way of experience; experience; undergo: as, *have* a good time. 5. to possess an understanding of; know: as, Shakespeare is said to have *had* "little Latin and less Greek." 6. to believe, declare, or tell: as, so gossip *has* it. 7. to gain possession, control, or mastery of. 8. to get; take; acquire: as, *have* a drink. 9. to bear or beget (offspring). 10. to perform; carry on; engage in: as, we *had* an argument. 11. to cause to; cause to be: as, please *have* this done at once. 12. to be in a certain relation to: as, we *have* a talkative neighbor beside us. 13. *a*) to permit; tolerate. *b*) to admit. Used in the negative, as I won't *have* this nonsense! 14. [Colloq.], *a*) to hold in a position of disadvantage: as, I *had* my opponent now. *b*) to deceive; take in; cheat: as, they've been *had* in that business deal. *Have* is used **as an auxiliary** with past participles to form phrases expressing completed action, as in the perfect tenses (e.g., I *have* left, I *had* left, I shall *have* left, I would *have* left, etc.), and with infinitives to express obligation or necessity (e.g., we *have* to go). *Have got* often replaces *have*: see **get.** *Have* is conjugated in the present indicative (I) *have,* (he, she, it) *has,* (we, you, they) *have;* in the past indicative (I, he, she, it, we, you, they) *had.* Archaic forms are (thou) *hast, hadst,* (he, she, it) *hath.* The present subjunctive is *have,* the past subjunctive *had.* *n.* [Colloq.], a person or nation with relatively much wealth or rich resources.
have at, to attack; strike.
have done, to stop; get through; finish.
have it in for, [Colloq.], to bear a grudge against.
have it out, to settle an issue, disagreement, etc. by fighting or discussion.
have on, to be wearing; be dressed in.
have to do with, 1. to be related to or connected with. 2. to be associated with; deal with.
to have and to hold, to possess permanently: form used in certain marriage services.
SYN.—**have,** the broadest term here, predicates the relation between a subject and an object (physical or nonphysical) that belongs to it in any of the various senses in which *belong* is understood (he *had* wealth, the poetry *has* charm, you *have* odd notions); **hold** means to have in one's grasp or keeping, or, in extended use, to control as by keeping in a certain place, condition, etc. (to *hold* a book, one's attention, etc.); **own** implies the holding or controlling of something as one's personal property (to *own* lands); **possess** is in its basic sense equivalent to **own,** and in extended senses means to have as an attribute, quality, faculty, etc. (to *possess* wisdom).—*ANT.* lack, want.
have·lock (hav′lok), *n.* [after Sir Henry *Havelock* (1795–1857), Eng. general in India], a light cloth covering for a military cap, falling over the back of the neck for protection against the sun.
ha·ven (hā′v'n), *n.* [ME.; AS. *hæfen;* akin to G. *hafen* (< LG.); for IE. base see HAVE; prob. basic sense "that holds"], 1. a port; harbor; sheltered anchorage. 2. any sheltered, safe place; refuge. *v.t.* 1. to put (a ship) into port. 2. to provide a haven for; shelter.
have-not (hav′not′), *n.* [Colloq.], a person or nation with relatively little wealth or poor resources.
have·n't (hav′'nt), have not.
Hav·er·ford (hav′ẽr-fẽrd), *n.* a township in southeastern Pennsylvania: pop., 54,000.
Ha·ver·hill (hā′vẽr-il), *n.* a city in northeastern Massachusetts: pop., 46,000.
ha·vers (hā′vẽrz), *interj.* [British], rubbish! nonsense!
hav·er·sack (hav′ẽr-sak′), *n.* [Fr. *havresac;* G. *habersack,* lit., sack of oats; *haber, hafer,* oats + *sack,* a sack], a canvas bag worn on the back or over the shoulder by soldiers and hikers for carrying rations, etc.
Ha·ver·sian (hə-vũr′shən), *adj.* [after Clopton *Havers,* Eng. physician (1650–1702)], designating or of the canals through which blood vessels pass in bone.
hav·oc (hav′ək), *n.* [earlier esp. in phrase *cry havoc,* to give (an army) the signal for pillage, taking of booty; ME. & Anglo-Fr. *havok;* OFr. *havot;* prob.

akin to *hef*, a hook, *haver*, to hook, take; of Gmc. origin; cf. Goth. *hafjan*, OHG. *heffen*, to lift up], great destruction and devastation, as that resulting from hurricanes, wars, etc. *v.t.* [HAVOCKED (-əkt), HAVOCKING], [Obs.], to lay waste; devastate. —*SYN.* see **ruin.**
play havoc with, to devastate; destroy; ruin.

Ha·vre (hä′vẽr, häv′rə), *n.* a seaport in northwestern France, on the English Channel: pop., 140,000: French name, *Le Havre.*

haw (hô), *n.* [ME. *hawe;* AS. *haga*, fruit of *haguthorn*, hawthorn, hence, lit., same word as AS. *haga*, a hedge], 1. the berry of the hawthorn. 2. the hawthorn.

haw (hô), *interj. & n.* [? < echoic *geehaw*, as representing a horse's neigh], a word of command to a horse, ox, etc. being driven without reins, meaning "turn to the left!" *v.t. & v.i.* to turn to the left. Opposed to *gee.*

haw (hô), *v.i.* [echoic], to hesitate in speaking; grope for words; falter: usually in *hem and haw. interj. & n.* a conventionalized expression of the sound often made by a speaker when hesitating briefly.

haw (hô), *n.* [?], 1. the third eyelid of certain animals; nictitating membrane. 2. *often pl.* inflammation of the haw.

Ha·wai·i (hə-wä′ē, hə-wä′yə), *n.* 1. a State of the United States, consisting of a group of islands in the North Pacific: a Territory from 1900 to 1959: area, 6,415 sq. mi.; pop., 633,000; capital, Honolulu. 2. the largest of the islands of Hawaii: area, 4,021 sq. mi.; pop., 61,000; chief city, Hilo.

Ha·wai·ian (hə-wä′yən), *adj.* of Hawaii, its people, Polynesian language, etc. *n.* 1. a native or inhabitant of Hawaii, specifically a Polynesian native. 2. the Polynesian language of the Hawaiians: abbreviated **Haw.**

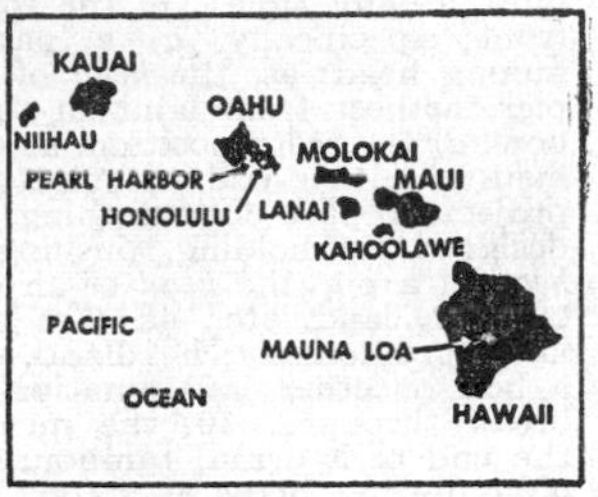

Hawaiian Islands, the islands comprising the State of Hawaii; formerly called *Sandwich Islands.*

Hawaii National Park, a national park consisting of areas on the islands of Hawaii and Maui, containing the Kilauea, Mauna Loa, and Haleakala volcanoes: area, 271 sq. mi.

KAUAI
NIIHAU
OAHU
MOLOKAI
PEARL HARBOR
MAUI
HONOLULU
LANAI
KAHOOLAWE
PACIFIC
MAUNA LOA
OCEAN
HAWAII

HAWAIIAN ISLANDS

haw·finch (hô′finch′), *n.* [*haw* (hawthorn) + *finch*], the common grosbeak of Europe.

haw-haw (hô′hô′), *n. & interj.* see **ha.**

hawk (hôk), *n.* [ME. *hauk, havec;* AS. *hafoc;* akin to G. *habicht;* IE. base **qap-*, to seize, grasp (cf. HAVE)], 1. any of a family of birds of prey characterized by short, rounded wings, a long tail and legs, and a hooked beak and claws; broadly, any such bird active by day except the vultures and eagles: hawks include the falcons, buzzards, harriers, kites, and caracaras; in a more restricted sense, the term is used of birds belonging to a subfamily of falcons typified by the sparrow hawk of Europe and the sharp-shinned hawk and Cooper's hawk of North America. 2. a person regarded as having the preying or grasping nature of a hawk; cheater; swindler. *v.i.* 1. to hunt birds or other small game with the help of falcons or other hawks. 2. to attack by or as by swooping and striking. *v.t.* to attack or prey on as a hawk does.

hawk (hôk), *v.t. & v.i.* [< *hawker* (peddler)], 1. to advertise or peddle (goods) in the streets by shouting. 2. to spread (rumors, etc.).

hawk (hôk), *v.i.* [echoic], to clear the throat audibly. *v.t.* to bring up (phlegm) by coughing. *n.* an audible clearing of the throat.

hawk (hôk), *n.* [? *hawk* (the bird) via a lost *v.* meaning "to grasp, seize"], a small, square board with a handle underneath, used by masons for holding mortar.

hawk·bill (hôk′bil′), *n.* a hawksbill turtle.

hawk·er (hôk′ẽr), *n.* [prob. < MLG. *hoker*, huckster, peddler (D. *heuker*, G. *höker*) < MLG. *hocken*, to crouch (as with a burden, pack, etc.)], a person who hawks goods in the street; peddler; huckster.

hawk·er (hôk′ẽr), *n.* [AS. *hafocere*], a person who uses hawks for hunting; falconer.

Hawk·eye (hôk′ī′), *n.* [Colloq.], a native or inhabitant of Iowa (the *Hawkeye State*).

hawk-eyed (hôk′īd′), *adj.* keen-sighted like a hawk.

hawk·ing (hôk′iŋ), *n.* falconry; hunting with hawks.

Haw·kins, Sir **Anthony Hope** (hô′kinz), see **Hope, Anthony.**

Hawkins (or **Hawkyns**), Sir **John,** 1532–1595; English rear admiral; slave trader.

hawk moth, any of a family of moths with a thick, tapering body, slender wings, and a long feeding tube used for sucking the nectar of flowers: also called *sphinx moth.*

hawk's-beard (hôks′bẽrd′), *n.* any of a number of plants of the composite family, with red, yellow, or orange flowers.

hawks·bill, hawk's-bill (hôks′bil′), *n.* a small turtle found in tropical seas, having a hawklike beak and a horny shell from which tortoise shell is obtained: also **hawksbill turtle.**

Hawk·shaw (hôk′shô′), *n.* [after the character in Tom Taylor's play *The Ticket of Leave Man* (1863)], [Colloq.], a detective: humorous term.

hawk·weed (hôk′wēd′), *n.* any of a group of weedy plants of the composite family, with leaves in flat rosettes and stalks of red, yellow, or orange flowers.

Hawkyns, see **Hawkins.**

hawse (hôz), *n.* [earlier *halse, haulse;* prob. < ON. *hals*, the neck, part of the forecastle or bow of a ship], 1. that part of the bow of a ship containing the hawseholes, through which the cables run; hence, 2. a hawsehole. 3. the space between the bow of a ship and the anchors. 4. the arrangement of a ship's cables when the ship is moored with both a starboard anchor and a port anchor out from forward.

hawse·hole (hôz′hōl′), *n.* any of the holes in a ship's bow through which a hawser or cable is passed.

haw·ser (hô′zẽr), *n.* [earlier *haulser, halser* < ME. *halsen*, to raise, lift; OFr. *haulser, haucier;* LL. **altiare* < L. *altus*, high], a large rope or small cable, often made of steel, by which a ship is anchored, towed, etc.

hawser bend, a kind of knot for tying one hawser to another: see **knot,** illus.

haw·ser-laid (hô′zẽr-lād′), *adj.* cable-laid.

haw·thorn (hô′thôrn′), *n.* [lit., hedge thorn; ME. *hawethorne, hagethorn;* AS. *haguthorn* < *haga*, hedge (cf. HAG, witch) + *thorn;* akin to G. *hagedorn*], any of a group of spiny shrubs and small trees of the rose family, with fragrant flowers of white, pink, or red, and red berries (called *haws*).

Haw·thorne (hô′thôrn′), *n.* a city in southwestern California: suburb of Los Angeles: pop., 33,000.

Haw·thorne, Nathaniel (hô′thôrn′), 1804–1864; American novelist and writer of short stories.

hay (hā), *n.* [ME. *haye, heie;* AS. *hieg, heg* (akin to G. *heu*) < base of AS. *heawan*, to cut (see HEW)], grass, alfalfa, clover, etc. cut and dried for use as fodder. *v.i.* to mow grass, alfalfa, etc., and spread it out to dry. *v.t.* [Rare], 1. to furnish with hay. 2. to grow grass on (land) for hay. 3. to make (grass, etc.) into hay.
hit the hay, [Slang], to go to bed.
make hay, to mow grass, alfalfa, etc., and spread it out to dry.
make hay while the sun shines, to make the most of an opportunity.
not hay, [Slang], not a trifling amount of money; a considerable sum.

hay (hā), *n.* [OFr. *haye*], an old country dance with much winding in and out.

Hay, John Milton (hā), 1838–1905; American statesman and writer; secretary of state (1898–1905).

hay·cock (hā′kok′), *n.* a small heap of hay drying in a field.

Hay·dn, Franz Jo·seph (fränts yō′zef hī′d'n), 1732–1809; Austrian composer.

Hayes, Helen (hāz), (*Mrs. Charles MacArthur*, born *Helen Hayes Brown*), 1900– ; American actress.

Hayes, Roland, 1887– ; American tenor.

Hayes, Ruth·er·ford Bir·chard (ruth′ẽr-fẽrd bũr′chẽrd), 1822–1893; nineteenth president of the United States (1877–1881).

hay fever, an acute inflammation of the eyes and upper respiratory tract, characterized by sneezing and sometimes accompanied by fever and asthma: it is an allergic reaction, caused mainly by the pollen of some grasses and trees; pollinosis.

hay·field (hā′fēld′), *n.* a field of grass, alfalfa, etc. to be made into hay.

hay·fork (hā′fôrk′), *n.* 1. a pitchfork. 2. a mechanically operated device for lifting hay into or out of a hayloft or mow.

hay·loft (hā′lôft′), *n.* a loft, or upper story, in a barn or stable, for storing hay; haymow.

hay·mak·er (hā′māk′ẽr), *n.* 1. a person who tosses cut hay and spreads it out to dry. 2. [Slang], a powerful blow with the fist, intended to cause a knockout.

Hay·mar·ket (hā′mär′kit), *n.* 1. a street in London between Piccadilly Circus and Pall Mall, known as a theater district. 2. a square in Chicago: site of a demonstration (May 4, 1886) for the eight-hour day

hay·mow (hā′mou′), *n.* 1. hay stored in a barn. 2. the place in a barn where hay is stored; hayloft.

hay·rack (hā′rak′), *n.* 1. a rack or frame from which cattle, horses, etc. eat hay. 2. a framework extension on a wagon, to permit carrying larger quantities of hay; hence, 3. a wagon having this.

hay·rick (hā′rik′), *n.* a large heap of hay; haystack.
hay·ride (hā′rīd′), *n.* a pleasure ride in a wagon partly filled with hay, by a group on an outing.
hay·seed (hā′sēd′), *n.* 1. grass seed shaken from mown hay. 2. bits of chaff and straw from hay. 3. [Slang], a person having the awkwardness, simplicity, and lack of sophistication regarded as characteristic of people from the country; rustic: somewhat contemptuous term.
hay·stack (hā′stak′), *n.* a large heap of hay piled up outdoors.
Hay·ti (hā′ti), *n.* Haiti.
Hay·ti·an (hā′ti-ən, hā′shən), *adj. & n.* Haitian.
Hay·ward (hā′wẽrd), *n.* a city in western California: suburb of Oakland: pop., 73,000.
hay·ward (hā′wôrd′, hā′wẽrd), *n.* [ME. *heiward; hei* (obs. Eng. *hay* < AS. *hege*, hedge, OFr. *haie, haye*), a hedge + *ward* (AS. *weard*), a guardian], 1. formerly, an official in charge of fences or hedges around public pastures. 2. an official who impounds stray cattle or other animals.
hay·wire (hā′wīr′), *n.* wire for tying up bales of hay, straw, etc. *adj.* [? < *haywire camp*, Maine term for logging camp with poor or broken equipment that had to be tied up with haywire], [Slang], 1. out of order; disorganized; confused; wrong; hence, 2. crazy: usually in *go haywire*, become, or act as if, crazy.
haz·ard (haz′ẽrd), *n.* [ME.; OFr., game of dice, adventure; ? < Ar. *al-zār*, the die], 1. an early game of chance played with dice, from which craps is derived. 2. chance. 3. risk; peril; danger; jeopardy. 4. [Archaic], something risked. 5. any obstacle on a golf course, including traps, bunkers, ponds, etc. 6. in *court tennis*, any of the openings in the court through which a ball may be sent to win a point. *v.t.* to expose to danger; chance; risk; venture. —*SYN.* see **danger**.
at all hazards, no matter what the risk or danger.
haz·ard·ous (haz′ẽr-dəs), *adj.* [*hazard* + *-ous*], 1. of or involving chance. 2. risky; dangerous; perilous.
haze (hāz), *n.* [prob. < LG. dial. as nautical borrowing; ult. connection with AS. *hasu*, gray, is possible, but prob. via LG. proverb *de hase brouet*, lit., "the hare is brewing," as applied to a mist; cf. HARE], 1. a thin vapor of fog, smoke, dust, etc. in the air. 2. slight confusion or vagueness of mind. —*SYN.* see **mist**.
haze (hāz), *v.t.* [HAZED (hāzd), HAZING], [OFr. *haser*, to irritate, annoy], 1. in *nautical usage*, to oppress, punish, or harass by forcing to do hard and unnecessary work; hence, 2. to initiate or discipline (fellow students) by means of horseplay, practical jokes, and tricks, often in the nature of humiliating or painful ordeals.
Ha·zel (hā′z′l), [Heb. *ḥazā'ēl*, lit., God sees], a feminine name.
ha·zel (hā′z′l), *n.* [ME. *hasel;* AS. *hæsel, hæsl;* akin to G. *hasel;* IE. **qos(e)lo*, hazel, seen also in L. *corulus*, hazel bush, OIr. *coll*, hazel], 1. any of a group of trees or shrubs of the birch family, with edible nuts (called *hazelnuts* or *filberts*). 2. a hazelnut. 3. *a)* the wood of this tree or shrub. *b)* a stick of this wood. 4. the color of a ripened hazelnut; reddish brown. *adj.* 1. of the hazel tree. 2. of its wood. 3. light reddish-brown; yellowish-brown: hazel eyes are usually flecked with green or gray.
ha·zel·ly (hā′z′l-i), *adj.* 1. full of hazels, as a forest. 2. of hazel (the color).
ha·zel·nut (hā′z′l-nut′), *n.* the small, edible, roundish nut of the hazel; filbert.
ha·zi·ly (hā′zi-li), *adv.* in a hazy manner; vaguely.
ha·zi·ness (hā′zi-nis), *n.* a hazy quality or state.
Ha·zle·ton (hā′z′l-tən), *n.* a city in eastern Pennsylvania: pop., 32,000.
Haz·litt, William (haz′lit), 1778–1830; English essayist and critic.
ha·zy (hā′zi), *adj.* [HAZIER (-zi-ẽr), HAZIEST (-zi-ist)], 1. characterized by the presence of haze; somewhat foggy, misty, or smoky. 2. somewhat vague, obscure, confused, or indefinite: as, *hazy* thinking.
Hb, *the symbol for* hemoglobin.
hb., in *football*, halfback.
H.B.M., His (or Her) Britannic Majesty.
H-bomb (āch′bom′), *n.* hydrogen bomb.
H.C., 1. Heralds' College. 2. House of Commons.
H.C.F., h.c.f., highest common factor.
h.c.l., h.c. of l., [Colloq.], high cost of living.
hd., head.
hdqrs., headquarters.
he (hē; *unstressed* hi, ē, i), *pron.* [for *pl.* see THEY], [ME. & AS. (where it contrasts with *heo*, she, *hie*, they < same base); IE. base **ko-, ke-*, this one, this one here, seen also in *here, her, hither;* orig. a demonstrative], 1. the man, boy, or male animal (or, sometimes, the object regarded as male) previously mentioned. 2. the person; the one; anyone: as, *he* who laughs last laughs best. *He* is the nominative case form, *him* the objective, *his* the possessive, and *himself* the intensive and reflexive, of the masculine third personal pronoun. *n.* a man, boy, or male animal: as, our dog is a *he*.
he (hā), *n.* [Heb., lit., window], the fifth letter of the Hebrew alphabet (ה), roughly corresponding to English *h*: see **alphabet**, table.
he- (hē), a combining form meaning *male*, used in hyphenated compounds, as *he-dog*.
He, in *chemistry*, helium.
H.E., 1. His Eminence. 2. His Excellency.
head (hed), *n.* [ME. *hede, heved*, etc.; AS. *heafod;* akin to G. *haupt* (OHG. *houbit*, Goth. *haubith*); IE. base **qap-ut*, orig., cup-shaped (as also in L. *caput;* see CAPITAL) merged in Gmc. with word akin to OHG. *hūba*, a cap, crest (G. *haube*) < IE. **qeu-*, to bend, curve], 1. *a)* the top part of the body in man, the apes, etc., or the front part in most other animals: in higher animals it is a bony structure containing the brain, and including the jaws, eyes, ears, nose, and mouth. *b)* the head exclusive of the face. 2. *a)* the head as the seat of reason, memory, and imagination; mind; intelligence: as, use your *head*. *b)* aptitude; ability: as, he has a *head* for mathematics. 3. the head as a symbol for the individual; person: as, dinner at five dollars a *head*. 4. [*pl.* HEAD], the head as a unit of counting: as, fifty *head* of cattle. 5. a representation of a head, as in painting or sculpture. 6. the side of a coin with such a representation: also called *heads*: opposed to *tail(s)*. 7. the highest or uppermost part or thing; top; specifically, *a)* the top of a page, column of figures, etc. *b)* a printed title at the top of a page, section of writing, etc.; hence, *c)* a chief point of discussion; topic of a section, chapter, etc. in a speech or written work. *d)* a headline or headlines for a newspaper story. *e)* froth floating on newly poured effervescent beverages: as, the *head* on a glass of beer. *f)* that end of a cask or drum which is uppermost at any time. 8. the foremost part of a thing; front; specifically, *a)* a part associated with the human head: as, the *head* of a bed. *b)* the part of a pier farthest from land. *c)* the front part of a ship; bow. *d)* the front position, as of a column of marching men. *e)* either end of something; extremity. 9. the projecting part of something; specifically, *a)* the part designed for holding, pushing, striking, etc.: as, the *head* of a pin, the *head* of an arrow. *b)* a jutting mass of rock, land, etc., as of a mountain. *c)* a point of land; promontory; headland. *d)* a projecting place in a boil or other inflammation where pus is about to break through. 10. the membrane stretched across the end of a drum, tambourine, etc. 11. the source of a flowing body of water; beginning of a stream, river, etc. 12. a source of water kept at some height to supply a mill, etc.; hence, 13. pressure: as, a *head* of steam. 14. a dominant position; position of leadership or first importance: as, the *head* of the class. 15. a foremost person; leader, ruler, chief, etc. 16. a headmaster. 17. a crisis or culmination: as, things may soon come to a *head*. 18. [Nautical Slang], a toilet. 19. in *botany*, *a)* a flat or rounded cluster of little flowers, as in the daisy or clover. *b)* a large, compact bud: as, a *head* of cabbage. *c)* the uppermost part of a plant's foliage: as, the *head* of a tree. 20. in *golf*, the heavy part of the club; striking part at the end of the stick. 21. in *linguistics*, that word in a word group which functions grammatically like the entire group. 22. in *mining*, a heading; drift. 23. in *music*, the rounded part of a note, at the end of the stem. Abbreviated **hd.** *adj.* 1. most important; principal; commanding; first. 2. to be found at the top or front. 3. striking against the front: as, *head* currents. *v.t.* 1. to be chief of; command. 2. to lead; precede: as, she *heads* the list. 3. to supply with a head; shape a head for (a pin, etc.). 4. [Rare], to behead; decapitate. 5. to trim the higher part from (a tree or plant); poll. 6. to go round the head of: as, they *headed* the stream. 7. to turn or cause to go in a specified direction: as, I *headed* the car for home. 8. in *soccer*, to hit (the ball) with one's head. *v.i.* 1. to grow or come to a head. 2. to travel; set out: as, they *headed* eastward. 3. to originate, as a river.
by a head, 1. in *horse racing*, etc., by the length of the animal's head; hence, 2. by a very small margin.
by (or **down by**) **the head**, in *nautical usage*, with the bow deeper in the water than the stern.
come to a head, 1. to be about to suppurate, as a boil. 2. to culminate.
give one his head, to let one do as he likes.
go to one's head, 1. to confuse, excite, or intoxicate one. 2. to make one vain or overconfident.
hang (or **hide**) **one's head**, to lower one's head or conceal one's face in or as in shame.
head and shoulders above, definitely superior to.
head off, to get ahead of and cause to stop or turn away; intercept.
head over heels, 1. tumbling heels over head, as in a somersault. 2. deeply; completely. 3. hurriedly; impetuously; recklessly.
heads up! [Colloq.], look out! be careful!
keep one's head, to keep one's poise, self-control, etc.; not become excited or flustered.
keep one's head above water, 1. to remain afloat; not sink. 2. to keep oneself alive, out of debt, etc.

lay heads together, to consult or scheme together.
lose one's head, to lose one's poise, self-control, etc.; become excited or flustered.
make head, to make headway; go forward; advance.
make head or tail of, to understand: usually in the negative.
on (or **upon**) **one's head,** as one's burden, responsibility, or misfortune.
one's head off, a great deal: preceded by a verb, as, he talked *his head off*.
out of (or **off**) **one's head,** [Colloq.], 1. crazy. 2. delirious; raving.
over one's head, 1. *a*) too difficult for one to understand. *b*) so that one cannot understand. 2. in spite of one's prior claim. 3. without consulting one; to a higher authority.
put heads together, to consult or scheme together.
take it into one's head, to conceive the notion, plan, or intention.
turn one's head, 1. to make one dizzy. 2. to make one vain or overconfident.

-head (hed), -hood, as in *godhead*.
head·ache (hed'āk'), *n.* [ME. *hedake, hevedeche;* AS. *heafodece*], 1. a continuous pain in the head. 2. [Colloq.], a cause of worry, annoyance, or trouble.
head·band (hed'band'), *n.* 1. a band worn around the head. 2. an ornamental printed band at the top of a page or the beginning of a chapter. 3. in *bookbinding*, a cloth band fastened to the top and bottom of the inner back of a book.
head·board (hed'bôrd', hed'bōrd'), *n.* a board or frame that forms the head of a bed, etc.
head·cheese (hed'chēz'), *n.* a loaf of jellied, seasoned meat made from parts of the head and feet of hogs.
head·dress (hed'dres'), *n.* 1. a covering or decoration for the head. 2. the style in which hair is worn or arranged; coiffure.
head·ed (hed'id), *adj.* [ME. *heded*], 1. formed into a head, as cabbage. 2. having a heading.
-head·ed (hed'id), a combining form meaning: 1. *having a* (specified kind of) *head*, as in *clearheaded*. 2. *having* (a specified number of) *heads*, as in *two-headed*.
head·er (hed'ẽr), *n.* 1. a person or device that puts heads on pins, nails, rivets, etc. 2. a machine that takes off the heads of grain and sends them up an inclined plane into a truck or wagon. 3. a pipe, tube, etc. that connects other pieces to permit the flow of a fluid through them. 4. [Colloq.], a headlong fall or dive. 5. in *carpentry*, a wooden beam, as in flooring, placed between two long beams with the ends of short beams resting against it. 6. in *masonry*, a brick or building stone laid across the thickness of a wall with one end toward the face of the wall.
head·first (hed'fũrst'), *adv.* 1. with the head in front; headlong. 2. recklessly; rashly; impetuously.
head·fore·most (hed'fôr'mōst', hed'fōr'məst), *adv.* headfirst.
head gate, a gate that controls the flow of water into a canal lock, sluice, etc.
head·gear (hed'gêr'), *n.* 1. a covering for the head; hat, cap, headdress, etc. 2. the harness for the head of a horse, mule, etc. 3. in *mining*, the lifting apparatus at the opening of a shaft. 4. in *nautical usage*, the rigging on the forward sails.
head-hunt·er (hed'hun'tẽr), *n.* a member of any of certain primitive tribes who remove the heads of slain enemies and preserve them as trophies.
head·i·ly (hed''l-i), *adv.* in a heady manner.
head·i·ness (hed'i-nis), *n.* the quality or condition of being heady.
head·ing (hed'iŋ), *n.* 1. something forming or used to form the head, top, edge, or front; specifically, *a*) an inscription at the top of a paragraph, chapter, page, section, etc., giving the title, topic, etc. *b*) material for the tops or heads of barrels. *c*) a strip of embroidery. 2. in *mining*, *a*) a gallery; drift. *b*) the end of a gallery.
head·land (hed'land'), *n.* [ME. *hedelonde;* AS. *heafod lond*], 1. the unbroken soil at the edge of a plowed field, especially at the ends of the furrows. 2. (hed'lənd), a point of land reaching out into the water; cape; promontory.
head·less (hed'lis), *adj.* [ME. *hevedles;* AS. *heafodleas*], 1. without a head; specifically, *a*) organically without a head; acephalous. *b*) beheaded. 2. without a leader or director. 3. stupid; foolish; brainless.
head·light (hed'līt'), *n.* 1. a light with a reflector and lens, at the front of a locomotive, automobile, etc. 2. a white light at the masthead of a ship.
head·line (hed'līn'), *n.* 1. a line at the top of a page in a book, giving the running title, page number, etc. 2. a line or lines of type at the top of a newspaper article, giving a short statement of its contents: the headline is usually in larger type. 3. a rope tied to the head of a horse, cow, etc. *v.t.* 1. to provide (a news article) with a headline. 2. to give (a performer or performance) featured billing.
head·lin·er (hed'līn'ẽr), *n.* an actor or entertainer advertised as a leading attraction.
head·lock (hed'lok'), *n.* in *wrestling*, a hold in which one contestant's head is locked between the arm and the body of the other.
head·long (hed'lôŋ'), *adv.* [folk-etymologized form, after *-long*, of ME. *hedelinge(s)* < *hede*, head + *-linge*, adv. suffix], 1. with the head first; headforemost. 2. with uncontrolled speed and force. 3. recklessly; rashly; impetuously. *adj.* 1. [Rare & Poetic], steep; dizzy; precipitous: as, a *headlong* height. 2. having the head first. 3. moving with uncontrolled speed and force. 4. reckless; impetuous.
head·man (hed'mən; *also, for 1,* hed'man'), *n.* [*pl.* HEADMEN (-mən; *also, for 1,* -men')], 1. a leader; chief; overseer. 2. [Rare], a headsman; executioner.
head·mas·ter (hed'mas'tẽr, hed'mäs'tẽr), *n.* 1. in certain schools, the man in charge of the school; principal. 2. in some colleges, a faculty member residing in and in charge of a residence hall for men. Also **head master**.
head·mis·tress (hed'mis'tris), *n.* in certain schools, especially schools for girls, the woman in charge of the school; principal: also **head mistress**.
head money, 1. a poll tax. 2. formerly, a reward paid for bringing in the head of an enemy, outlaw, etc., or for his capture.
head·most (hed'mōst'), *adj.* foremost; in the lead.
head-on (hed'on'), *adj. & adv.* with the head or front foremost: as, a *head-on* collision.
head·phone (hed'fōn'), *n.* 1. a telephone or radio receiver held to the ear by a band over the head. 2. *usually pl.* a pair of such receivers.
head·piece (hed'pēs'), *n.* 1. a helmet, cap, or other covering for the head. 2. an apparatus with headphones, fitting over the head. 3. the head; mind; intellect. 4. in *printing*, an ornamental design engraved at the beginning of a book, chapter, etc.
head pin, in *bowling* & *tenpins*, the pin at the front of a triangle of ten pins.
head·quar·ters (hed'kwôr'tẽrz), *n.pl.* [sometimes construed as sing.], 1. the main office, or center of operations and control, of anyone in command, as in an army, police force, etc. 2. the main office or center of control in any organization. 3. all the people working at such a place. Abbreviated **H.Q., Hq., hdqrs.**
head·race (hed'rās'), *n.* the part of a millrace furnishing water to a mill wheel: opposed to *tailrace*.
head register, the upper register of the voice, in which the higher range of tones is produced.
head·rest (hed'rest'), *n.* a support for the head, as on the back of a chair used by dentists, barbers, etc.
head·sail (hed'sāl', hed's'l), *n.* any sail forward of the mast or foremast.
head·set (hed'set'), *n.* an apparatus with headphones, fitting over the head; headpiece.
head·ship (hed'ship'), *n.* [*head* + *-ship*], the position or authority of a chief or leader; leadership; command.
heads·man (hedz'mən), *n.* [*pl.* HEADSMEN (-mən)], [ME. *heddysman* < *heddys, hefdes* (genit. of *hede, heved*, head) + *man*], 1. a person who executes by beheading. 2. [Rare], a leader; chief.
head spin, in *wrestling*, a method of freeing oneself from a half nelson by suddenly kicking one's feet in the air and twisting around on one's head.
head·spring (hed'spriŋ'), *n.* [ME. *hedspring;* see HEAD & SPRING], a fountain; origin; source.
head·stall (hed'stôl'), *n.* [see HEAD & STALL], the part of a bridle or halter that fits over a horse's head.
head·stand (hed'stand'), *n.* the act of supporting oneself upright on the head with the help of the hands.
head start, a start ahead of other contestants or competitors, taken or given as an advantage.
head·stock (hed'stok'), *n.* 1. a bearing for a revolving or moving part of a machine. 2. the part of a lathe supporting the spindle or chuck.
head·stone (hed'stōn'), *n.* 1. the main stone in a foundation; cornerstone. 2. a stone marker placed at the head of a grave.
head·stream (hed'strēm'), *n.* a stream forming the source of another and larger stream.
head·strong (hed'strôŋ'), *adj.* [ME. *heedstronge;* see HEAD & STRONG], 1. determined not to follow orders, advice, etc. but to do as one pleases; self-willed. 2. showing such determination: as, *headstrong* desire.
head tone, in *singing*, any of the tones produced in the head register.
head·wait·er (hed'wāt'ẽr), *n.* a supervisor of waiters, often in charge of table reservations.
head·wa·ters (hed'wô'tẽrz, hed'wä'tẽrz), *n.pl.* the small streams that are the sources of a river.
head·way (hed'wā'), *n.* 1. forward motion; hence, 2. progress or success in work, etc. 3. space or clear-

ance overhead, as in a doorway, tunnel, etc. 4. the difference in time or miles between two trains, ships, etc. traveling in the same direction over the same course.

head wind, a wind blowing in the direction directly opposite the course of a ship or aircraft.

head·work (hed′wûrk′), *n.* 1. mental effort; thinking. 2. an ornament carved on the keystone of an arch.

head·y (hed′i), *adj.* [HEADIER (-i-ẽr), HEADIEST (i-ist)], 1. impetuous; rash; reckless; willful. 2. tending to affect the head; intoxicating: as, *heady* wine.

heal (hēl), *v.t.* [ME. *helen;* AS. *hælan* (akin to G. *heilen*) < base of *hal,* sound, healthy; see HALE, WHOLE], 1. to make sound, well, or healthy again; restore to health: as, *heal* the sick. 2. to cure or get rid of (a disease); restore (a wound, sore, etc.) to a healthy condition. 3. to free from grief, troubles, evil, etc. 4. *a*) to remedy or get rid of (grief, troubles, etc.). *b*) to make up (a breach, differences, etc.); reconcile. *v.i.* 1. to become sound, well, or healthy again; be cured; get well. 2. to become scarred or closed: said of a wound. —***SYN.*** see **cure.**

heal·er (hēl′ẽr), *n.* [ME. *helere*], a person or thing that heals; specifically, *a*) a person who tries to heal through prayer or faith. *b*) a remedy.

heal·ing (hēl′iŋ), *adj.* 1. becoming sound, well, or healthy again. 2. that heals; curative, remedial, etc.

health (helth), *n.* [ME. *helthe;* AS. *hælth* < base of *hal,* sound, healthy (see HALE, HEAL, WHOLE) + *-th*], 1. physical and mental well-being; soundness; freedom from defect, pain, or disease; normality of mental and physical functions. 2. condition of body or mind: as, good or bad *health.* 3. a wish for a person's health and happiness, expressed as in a toast.

health·ful (helth′fəl), *adj.* [ME.], 1. helping to produce, promote, or maintain health; salubrious; salutary; wholesome. 2. [Rare], healthy; sound.

health·i·ly (hel′thə-li), *adv.* in a healthy manner.

health·i·ness (hel′thi-nis), *n.* the quality or condition of being healthy.

health·y (hel′thi), *adj.* [HEALTHIER (-thi-ẽr), HEALTHIEST (-thi-ist)], 1. having good health; well; sound. 2. showing or resulting from good health: as, a *healthy* appetite. 3. healthful. 4. [Colloq.], large, vigorous, etc.: as, a *healthy* yell.

SYN.*—healthy** implies normal physical and mental vigor and freedom from disease, weakness, disorder, etc.; **sound** implies perfectness of health, suggesting a condition in which there is no sign of disease or defect; **hale,** closely synonymous with **sound,** is used especially of vigorous elderly people who are free from the infirmities of old age; **robust** implies a vitality and hardiness that is immediately apparent in muscular build, good color, abundance of energy, etc.; **well** simply implies freedom from illness, without further connotation.—ANT.*** ill, diseased, infirm, frail.

heap (hēp), *n.* [ME. *hepe, heep,* a troop, heap; AS. *heap,* a troop, band, multitude; akin to G. *hauf(en),* D. *hoop* (see FORLORN HOPE); IE. base **qeu-b* < **qeu-,* to bend, curve], 1. many things lying together in a pile; mass; mound. 2. [Colloq.], a large amount; great deal: as, a *heap* of money. *v.t.* 1. to make a heap of; bring together into a pile. 2. to give in large amounts: as, he *heaped* gifts upon me. 3. to fill (a plate, dry measure, etc.) full or to overflowing. *v.i.* to accumulate or rise in a heap, or pile.

hear (hêr), *v.t.* [HEARD (hũrd), HEARING], [ME. *heren;* AS. *hieran, heran;* akin to G. *hören* (Goth. *hausjan*); IE. base **qeu-,* to notice, observe, seen also in L. *cavere,* be on one's guard, take care (cf. CAVEAT, CAUTION)], 1. to become aware of (sounds), especially through the stimulation of auditory nerves in the ear by sound waves. 2. to listen to and consider; specifically, *a*) to take notice of; pay attention to: as, *hear* this piece of news. *b*) to listen to officially; give a formal hearing to: as, he will *hear* your lessons now. *c*) to conduct an examination or hearing of (a law case, etc.); try. *d*) to consent to; grant: as, he *heard* my entreaty. *e*) to be a member of the audience at or of (an opera, radio broadcast, lecture, etc.). *f*) to permit to speak: as, I cannot *hear* you now. 3. to be informed of; be told; learn. *v.i.* 1. to have a normally functioning ear or ears; be able to hear sounds. 2. to listen. 3. to get news; learn; be told (*of* or *about*).

hear from, 1. to get a letter, telegram, etc. from. 2. to get a criticism or reprimand from.

hear! hear! well said! hurrah! bravo!: used to show approval or agreement.

hear out, to listen to until the end.

hear tell, [Dial.], to hear; learn.

not hear of, not listen to or consider; forbid.

hear·ing (hêr′iŋ), *n.* [ME. *heringe;* see HEAR], 1. the act or process of perceiving sounds. 2. the sense by which sounds are perceived. 3. opportunity to speak, sing, etc.; chance to be heard; audience. 4. an investigation or trial before a judge, board of experts, etc. 5. the distance that a sound, especially that of the unaided voice, will carry: as, he is within *hearing.*

heark·en (här′k'n), *v.i.* [ME. *herknien, hercnen;* AS. *heorcnean, hercnian, hyrcnian* < base of *hieran* (see HEAR) & Eng. *hark*], to give careful attention; listen carefully. *v.t.* [Archaic], to hear; pay attention to; heed. Also spelled **harken.**

Hearn, Laf·cad·i·o (laf-kad′i-ō hũrn), (born *Patricio Lafcadio Tessima Carlos Hearn;* Japanese name, *Yakumo Koizumi*), 1850–1904; European-born American writer who became a naturalized Japanese.

hear·say (hêr′sā′), *n.* [< phrase *to hear say;* cf. G. *hörensagen*], common talk or report; rumor; gossip. *adj.* having the nature of or based on hearsay.

hearsay evidence, in *law,* evidence based on something the witness has heard someone else say and, hence, depending on the veracity and competence of someone other than the witness: it is usually inadmissible as testimony.

hearse (hũrs), *n.* [ME. *herce, herse;* OFr. *herce,* a harrow, grated portcullis; L. *hirpex,* a harrow], 1. an automobile, or horse-drawn carriage, for carrying a dead body to a grave. 2. [Rare], *a*) a framelike structure above a coffin or tomb, on which to place candles, hangings, etc. *b*) a framework for holding candles at Tenebrae. 3. [Archaic], a bier.

Hearst, William Randolph (hũrst), 1863–1951; American publisher of newspapers and magazines.

heart (härt), *n.* [ME. *herte;* AS. *heorte;* akin to G. *herz;* IE. base **kẽrd-,* etc., heart, seen also in L. *cor, cordis* (see CORDIAL) & Gr. *kardia* (see CARDIAC)], 1. the hollow, muscular organ that receives blood from the veins and sends it out through the arteries by alternate dilation and contraction. 2. the part of the body thought of as containing the heart; breast; bosom. 3. any place or part like a heart, in that it is near the center; specifically, *a*) the central core of a plant or vegetable: as, *hearts* of celery. *b*) the center or innermost part of a place or region: as, in the *heart* of the city; hence, 4. the central, vital, or main part; essence; real meaning; core. 5. the human heart considered as the center or source of emotions, personality attributes, etc.; specifically, *a*) inmost thoughts and feelings; consciousness or conscience: as, I know in my *heart.* *b*) the source of emotions: contrasted with *head,* the source of intellect. *c*) one's emotional nature; disposition: as, she has a kind *heart.* *d*) any of various humane feelings; love, devotion, sympathy, etc. *e*) mood; feeling: as, I have a heavy *heart.* *f*) energy, spirit, resolution, or courage: as, I lost *heart.* 6. a person, usually one loved or admirable in some specified way: as, he is a valiant *heart.* 7. something like a heart in shape; conventionalized design or representation of a heart, shaped like this (♥). 8. any of a suit of playing cards marked with such symbols in red. 9. *pl.* this suit of cards. 10. *pl.* a card game in which the object is to avoid getting any hearts in the tricks taken. *v.t.* [Rare], to encourage.

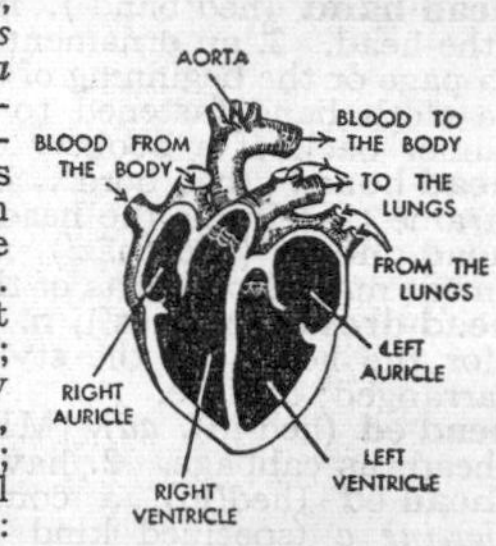

HUMAN HEART

after one's own heart, that suits or pleases one perfectly.

at heart, in one's innermost nature or deepest emotions; fundamentally.

break one's heart, to cause one to be overcome with grief or disappointment.

by heart, 1. by memorizing. 2. from memory.

change of heart, a change of mind, affections, loyalties, etc.

do one's heart good, to make one happy; please one.

eat one's heart out, to be overcome with grief, remorse, or longing; pine away.

from (the bottom of) one's heart, very sincerely or deeply.

have a heart, to be kind, sympathetic, generous, etc.

have one's heart in one's mouth (or **boots**), to be full of fear or nervous anticipation.

have one's heart in the right place, to be well-intentioned or well-meaning.

heart and soul, with all one's effort, enthusiasm, etc.

in one's heart of hearts, in one's innermost nature or deepest feelings; fundamentally.

lay to heart, to remember or consider seriously and try to profit by.

lose one's heart to, to fall in love with.

near one's heart, dear or important to one.

set one's heart at rest, to set aside one's doubts, fears, or worries.

set one's heart on, to have a fixed desire for; long for.

take heart, to have more courage or confidence; cheer up.

take to heart, 1. to consider seriously. 2. to be troubled or grieved by.

to one's heart's content, as much as one desires.

wear one's heart on one's sleeve, to behave so that one's feelings or affections are plainly evident.

with all one's heart, 1. with complete sincerity, devotion, etc. 2. very willingly; with pleasure.
with half a heart, halfheartedly.

heart·ache (härt′āk′), *n.* [AS. *heortece;* see HEART & ACHE], sorrow; distress; grief.

heart·beat (härt′bēt′), *n.* one pulsation, or full contraction and dilation, of the heart; heart throb.

heart·break (härt′brāk′), *n.* overwhelming sorrow, grief, or disappointment.

heart·break·ing (härt′brāk′iŋ), *adj.* causing overwhelming sorrow, grief, or disappointment.

heart·bro·ken (härt′brō′k'n), *adj.* overwhelmed with sorrow, grief, or disappointment.

heart·burn (härt′bũrn′), *n.* 1. a burning sensation in the esophagus and stomach, caused by high acidity of the stomach. 2. jealousy; discontent; envy.

heart·burn·ing (härt′bũrn′iŋ), *n.* jealousy; discontent.

heart cherry, a heart-shaped variety of sweet cherry.

heart·ed (här′tid), *adj.* [ME.], having a (specified kind of) heart: used in compounds, as *downhearted.*

heart·en (här′t'n), *v.t.* [< *heart*], to cheer up; encourage; strengthen.

heart·felt (härt′felt′), *adj.* [*heart* + *felt*, pp. of *feel*], with or expressive of deep feeling; sincere; genuine. —*SYN.* see **sincere.**

heart-free (härt′frē′), *adj.* not in love.

hearth (härth; *occas., esp. poetic,* hũrth), [ME. *herth;* AS. *heorth;* akin to G. *herd;* IE. base **ker-*, to burn, glow, seen also in L. *carbo*, charred wood (see CARBON)], 1. the stone or brick floor of a fireplace, often extending out into the room. 2. *a*) the fireside as the center of family life; hence, *b*) the home; family circle. 3. that part of a furnace, stove, or oven on which the fire rests. 4. the fireplace of a blacksmith's forge. 5. in *metallurgy*, the lowest part of a blast furnace, on which the molten metal and slag are deposited.

hearth·side (härth′sīd′), *n.* 1. the part of a room around a hearth; hence, 2. the home; family circle.

hearth·stone (härth′stōn′), *n.* 1. the stone forming a hearth; hence, 2. fireside; home; family circle. 3. a soft stone or powdered composition used for scouring a hearth, steps, etc.

heart·i·ly (här′t'l-i), *adv.* [ME. *hertili, hertelike;* see HEART & -LY], 1. in a friendly, sincere, cordial way. 2. with zest, enthusiasm, or vigor. 3. with a good appetite and in large amounts: as, he ate *heartily.* 4. completely; fully; very.

heart·i·ness (här′ti-nis), *n.* the quality or state of being hearty.

heart·land (härt′land′), *n.* in *geopolitics*, a political unit dominating an extensive surrounding area that can sustain it agriculturally and industrially and serve as a protective buffer in case of military attack.

heart·less (härt′lis), *adj.* [ME. *herteles;* AS. *heortleas*], 1. lacking in spirit, courage, or enthusiasm; disheartened; spiritless. 2. without kindness; unfeeling; pitiless.

heart point, in *heraldry*, the center point on a shield: also called *fess point.*

heart-rend·ing (härt′ren′diŋ), *adj.* causing much grief or mental anguish.

hearts·ease, heart's-ease (härts′ēz′), *n.* [see HEART & EASE], 1. peace of mind; calmness of emotion. 2. the wild pansy: so called because formerly believed to cure the discomforts of love. 3. any of various other plants, as the wallflower or persicary.

heart·sick (härt′sik′), *adj.* sick at heart; extremely unhappy; in low spirits; despondent.

heart·some (härt′səm), *adj.* [*heart* + *-some*], [Scot.], 1. heartening; cheering. 2. cheerful; lively.

heart·sore (härt′sôr′, härt′sōr′), *adj.* feeling or showing grief.

heart-strick·en (härt′strik″n), *adj.* deeply affected by grief, sorrow, dismay, etc.

heart·string (härt′striŋ′), *n.* 1. a tendon formerly believed to brace and sustain the heart; hence, 2. *usually pl.* deepest feelings or affections.

heart-struck (härt′struk′), *adj.* heart-stricken.

heart-to-heart (härt′tə-härt′), *adj.* intimate and candid; frank.

heart-whole (härt′hōl′), *adj.* 1. not in love; heart-free. 2. sincere; genuine; wholehearted. 3. undismayed; courageous.

heart·wood (härt′wood′), *n.* the hard wood at the core of a tree trunk; duramen: see **alburnum,** illus.

heart·worm (härt′wũrm′), *n.* a nematode worm living as a parasite in the blood stream, especially in the heart, of dogs and certain other animals.

heart·y (här′ti), *adj.* [HEARTIER (-ti-ẽr), HEARTIEST (-ti-ist)], [ME. *herti;* see HEART & -Y], 1. characterized by warmth and friendliness; cordial and sincere; genial: as, a *hearty* welcome. 2. strongly felt; vigorous; not restrained: as, a *hearty* dislike. 3. in or resulting from excellent health; vigorous, strong, and healthy. 4. satisfying and abundant; nourishing: as, a *hearty* meal. 5. needing or liking plenty of food; having a good appetite: as, a *hearty* eater. 6. fertile: said of land. *n.* 1. friend; comrade; fellow: term used especially by sailors (usually preceded by *my*); hence, 2. *usually in pl.* a sailor. —*SYN.* see **sincere.**

heat (hēt), *n.* [ME. *hete;* AS. *hætu* < base of *hat* (see HOT); remotely akin to G. *hitze*], 1. the quality of being hot; hotness: in physics, heat is considered a form of energy whose effect is produced by the accelerated vibration of molecules: theoretically, at -273°C. all molecular vibration would stop and there would be no heat. 2. much hotness; great warmth: as, the *heat* of this room is unbearable. 3. degree of hotness or warmth: as, how much *heat* shall I apply? 4. the perception of heat by the senses, resulting from contact with or nearness to something hot; sensation of hotness or warmth felt through the skin. 5. hot weather or climate. 6. the warming of a room, house, etc., as by a stove or furnace: as, his rent includes *heat*, light, and gas. 7. a burning sensation produced by spices, mustard, etc. 8. fever. 9. color or other appearance as an indication of hotness: as, blue *heat* in metals. 10. strong feeling or intensity of feeling; excitement, ardor, anger, zeal, etc. 11. the period or condition of excitement, intensity, stress, etc.; most violent or intense point or stage: as, in the *heat* of battle. 12. a single effort, round, bout, or trial; especially, any of the preliminary rounds of a race, etc., the winners of which compete in the final round. 13. *a*) sexual excitement. *b*) the period of sexual excitement in animals; rut or estrus. 14. in *metallurgy*, *a*) a single heating of metal, ore, etc. in a furnace or forge. *b*) the amount processed in a single heating. 15. [Slang], *a*) intense activity. *b*) coercion, as by torture. *c*) great pressure, as in criminal investigation. Abbreviated **ht.** (in senses 1, 12, 14). *v.t. & v.i.* 1. to make or become warm or hot. 2. to make or become excited; inflame or become inflamed.

heat·ed·ly (hēt′id-li), *adv.* with anger, vehemence, etc.

heat engine, an engine for changing heat into mechanical energy; steam engine, gas motor, etc.

heat·er (hēt′ẽr), *n.* 1. an apparatus for giving heat or warmth; stove, furnace, radiator, etc.: heaters in automobiles use hot water or gasoline. 2. a person whose work is to heat something. 3. in an electron tube, an element set inside the cathode and heated by an electric current so that it indirectly heats the cathode to the temperature at which it will give off electrons. 4. [Slang], a pistol.

heat exhaustion, a form of heatstroke characterized by low body temperature, collapse, and, in severe cases, coma and death: also called *heat prostration:* cf. **sunstroke.**

heath (hēth), *n.* [ME. *hethe;* AS. *hæth*, heath land, heath plant; akin to G. *heide*, wasteland, heath; IE. base **kaito-*, forested or uncultivated land, seen also in W. *coed*, forest], 1. a tract of open wasteland, especially in the British Isles, covered with heather, low shrubs, etc.; moor. 2. any of various shrubs and plants growing on heaths; especially, heather.
one's native heath, the place of one's birth or childhood.

heath·ber·ry (hēth′ber′i, hēth′bẽr-i), *n.* [*pl.* HEATHBERRIES (-iz)], any of various berries found on heaths; bilberry, crowberry, etc.

heath·bird (hēth′bũrd′), *n.* the black grouse, found on British heaths.

heath cock, a male black grouse; blackcock.

hea·then (hē′*th*ən), *n.* [*pl.* HEATHENS (-*th*ənz), HEATHEN], [ME. *hethen;* AS. *hæthen;* akin to G. *heide;* the word came into the Gmc. languages < Goth. *haithnō*, a mistransl. by Bishop Ulfilas (4th-c. A.D.) of Arm. *hethanos*, heathen, by association with Goth. *haithi*, heath; thence, the folk etym. of *heathen* as "wasteland dwellers" developed in other Gmc. languages], 1. originally, and in the Old Testament, a member of any nation or people not worshiping the God of Israel. 2. anyone not a Jew, Christian, or Moslem; especially, a member of a tribe, nation, etc. worshiping many gods. 3. such people collectively. 4. a person regarded as uncivilized, unenlightened, irreligious, etc. *adj.* 1. of heathen tribes or culture. 2. pagan; hence, 3. irreligious. —*SYN.* see **pagan.**

hea·then·dom (hē′*th*ən-dəm), *n.* [ME.; AS. *hæthendom;* see -DOM], 1. heathen customs and beliefs; paganism. 2. heathen countries or people.

hea·then·ish (hē′*th*ən-ish), *adj.* [prob. *heathen* + *-ish;* but cf. AS. *hædenisc*], 1. of the heathen. 2. like or characteristic of the heathen; uncivilized, unenlightened, etc.

hea·then·ism (hē′*th*ən-iz'm), *n.* 1. heathen customs and beliefs; paganism. 2. behavior or ideas regarded as characteristic of heathens; idolatry, barbarity, etc.

hea·then·ize (hē′*th*ən-īz′), *v.t. & v.i.* [HEATHENIZED (-īzd′), HEATHENIZING], to make or become heathen.

hea·then·ry (hē′*th*ən-ri), *n.* heathenism; heathendom.

heath·er (he*th*′ẽr), ***n.*** [ME. (northern & Scot.) *haddyr,* altered after the unconnected *heath* in the 18th c.; form suggests an AS. **hædre,* parallel with *clofre,* clover, *mædre* madder, etc.], 1. a low-growing plant of the heath family, especially common in the British Isles, with scalelike, overlapping leaves and stalks of small, bell-shaped, purplish-pink flowers. 2. a heath covered with heather. ***adj.*** like heather in color or appearance.

heather bell, the bell-shaped flower of the heather.

heath·er·y (he*th*′ẽr-i), ***adj.*** 1. covered with heather. 2. of or like heather.

heath hen, 1. a female black grouse. 2. a North American grouse related to the prairie chicken.

heath·y (hēth′i), ***adj.*** 1. covered with heath. 2. of or like heath.

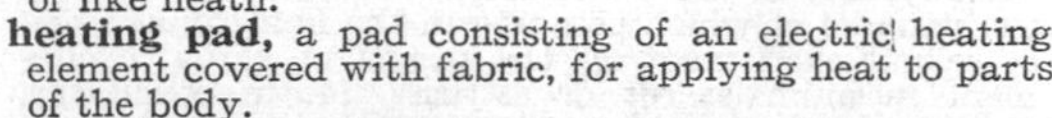

HEATHER

heating pad, a pad consisting of an electric heating element covered with fabric, for applying heat to parts of the body.

heat lightning, lightning without thunder, seen near the horizon, especially on summer evenings: it is believed to be caused by the reflection of distant lightning from clouds.

heat of fusion, the amount of heat needed to melt a unit mass of a solid that has just reached the melting temperature.

heat of vaporization, the amount of heat needed to turn one gram of a liquid into a vapor, without a rise in temperature of the liquid.

heat·stroke (hēt′strōk′), ***n.*** any of several conditions resulting from exposure to excessive heat: see **heat exhaustion, sunstroke.**

heat wave, 1. unusually hot weather, resulting from a slowly moving air mass of relatively high temperature. 2. a period of such weather in a particular place.

heaume (hōm), ***n.*** [Fr.; OFr. *helme;* see HELMET], a heavy helmet worn in the Middle Ages, covering the entire head and often reaching to the shoulders.

heave (hēv), ***v.t.*** [HEAVED (hēvd) or HOVE (hōv), HEAVING], [ME. *heven, hebben;* AS. *hebban;* akin to G. *heben* (Goth. *hafjan*); IE. base **qap-*, to seize, grasp, seen also in *captive, have, hawk,* etc.], 1. to raise or lift, especially with effort. 2. to lift in this way and throw or cast. 3. to make rise or swell; cause to bulge out, as one's chest. 4. to make (a sigh, groan, etc.) with great effort or pain. 5. in *geology,* to displace (a stratum or vein), as by the intersection of another stratum or vein. 6. in *nautical usage, a*) to raise, haul, pull, move, etc. by pulling with a rope or cable. *b*) to cause (a ship) to move in a specified manner or direction. ***v.i.*** 1. to swell up; bulge out. 2. to rise and fall rhythmically: as, his chest *heaved* with sobs. 3. to make strenuous, spasmodic movements of the throat or stomach; specifically, *a*) to retch; vomit or try to vomit. *b*) to pant; breathe hard; gasp. 4. in *nautical usage, a*) to tug or haul (*on* or *at* a cable, rope, etc.). *b*) to proceed; move: as, the ship *heaves* into sight. ***n.*** 1. the act or effort of heaving. 2. in *geology,* the extent of horizontal displacement caused by a fault.

heave ho! pull hard!: a cry of sailors hauling in the anchor, etc.

heave to, 1. in *nautical usage,* to stop forward movement by hauling in or shortening sail and heading into the wind; hence, 2. to stop.

heav·en (hev′′n), ***n.*** [ME. *heven;* AS. *heofon;* akin to OS. *heban;* prob. IE. base **kem-*, to cover, shelter, as also in G. *himmel,* heaven (the AS. *-f-n* < *-bn* by dissimilation of *-mn*), L. *camisia,* shirt (see CAMISADE, CAMISOLE)], 1. *usually pl.* the space surrounding or overarching the earth, in which the sun, moon, and stars appear; visible sky; firmament. 2. [H-], God; Providence. 3. any place of great beauty and pleasure. 4. a state of great happiness. 5. in *theology,* the place where God and his angels are, variously conceived of as the place where the blessed will live after death. Often used in exclamations of surprise, protest, etc.: as, *Heavens!*, for *heaven's* sake!, good *heavens!*

move heaven and earth, to do all that can be done; exert the utmost effort, influence, etc.

heav·en·li·ness (hev′′n-li-nis), ***n.*** the quality or state of being heavenly.

heav·en·ly (hev′′n-li), ***adj.*** [ME. *hevenlich;* AS. *heofonlic*], 1. of the visible heavens: as, the sun is a *heavenly* body. 2. causing or characterized by great happiness, beauty, peace, etc.: a generalized epithet of approval. 3. in *theology,* of or living in heaven; holy; divine.

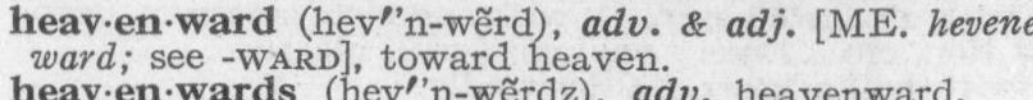

heav·en·ward (hev′′n-wẽrd), ***adv. & adj.*** [ME. *heveneward;* see -WARD], toward heaven.

heav·en·wards (hev′′n-wẽrdz), ***adv.*** heavenward.

heav·er (hēv′ẽr), ***n.*** 1. a person or device that heaves. 2. in *nautical usage,* a short lever for twisting or prying.

heaves (hēvz), ***n.pl.*** [construed as sing.], a respiratory disease of horses, characterized by forced breathing, coughing, heaving of the flanks, etc.: also called *broken wind.*

heav·i·ly (hev′′l-i), ***adv.*** in a heavy manner; specifically, *a*) with a heavy weight: as, *heavily* burdened. *b*) as if with a heavy weight; slowly; clumsily; laboriously. *c*) oppressively; severely: as, *heavily* taxed. *d*) abundantly: as, *heavily* populated.

heav·i·ness (hev′i-nis), ***n.*** a heavy quality or state.

heaving-line bend, a clove hitch: see **knot,** illus.

Heav·i·side layer (hev′i-sīd′), the Kennelly-Heaviside layer.

heav·y (hev′i), ***adj.*** [HEAVIER (-i-ẽr), HEAVIEST (-i-ist)], [ME. *hevi;* AS. *hefig* (akin to OHG. *habig*) < base of *habban* (see HAVE) & *hebban* (see HEAVE) + *-ig* (see -Y); prob. basic sense "containing something, full"], 1. hard to lift or move because of its weight; weighty. 2. of high specific gravity; of concentrated weight for its size. 3. above the usual or defined weight: said of woolens, silks, certain animals, etc. 4. larger, greater, or more intense than usual or normal; specifically, *a*) falling or striking with great force or impact: as, a *heavy* blow. *b*) of more than usual quantity: as, a *heavy* vote. *c*) violent and intense; rough: as, a *heavy* sea. *d*) loud, deep, and resounding: as, *heavy* thunder. *e*) thick; coarse; massive: as, *heavy* features. *f*) to an unusual extent; operating on a large scale: as, a *heavy* drinker, a *heavy* investor. *g*) prolonged and intense: as, *heavy* applause. 5. of great importance; serious; grave; profound: as, a *heavy* responsibility. 6. hard to endure; oppressive; burdensome; distressing: as, *heavy* sorrow. 7. hard to do; difficult: as, *heavy* work. 8. causing grief or sorrow: as, *heavy* news. 9. burdened with grief; sorrowful; depressed: as, a *heavy* heart. 10. burdened with sleep or fatigue: as, *heavy* eyelids. 11. characterized by density, hardness, fullness, etc. suggestive of weight; specifically, *a*) hard to digest: as, a *heavy* meal. *b*) not leavened properly; doughy: as, a *heavy* cake. *c*) remaining in the atmosphere; clinging; penetrating: as, a *heavy* odor. *d*) overcast; cloudy; gloomy; lowering: as, a *heavy* sky. *e*) hard to work or travel because of mud, sand, clay, etc.: as, a *heavy* road, *heavy* soil. 12. tedious; dull. 13. clumsy; unwieldy; physically awkward: as, a *heavy* walk. 14. steeply inclined: as, a *heavy* grade. 15. in *military usage,* heavily armed. 16. in the *theater, a*) somber; tragic. *b*) designating a villain or his role. ***adv.*** heavily: often in hyphenated compounds, as *heavy-laden.* ***n.*** [*pl.* HEAVIES (-viz)], 1. something heavy. 2. in the *theater, a*) a tragic or villainous role. *b*) an actor who plays such roles.

hang heavy, to pass tediously; drag.

heavy with child, pregnant.

SYN.—**heavy** implies relatively great density, quantity, intensity, etc. and figuratively connotes a pressing down on the mind, spirits, or senses (*heavy* water, *heavy*-hearted); **weighty** suggests heaviness as an absolute rather than a relative quality and figuratively connotes great importance or influence (a *weighty* problem); **ponderous** applies to something that is very heavy because of its size or bulk and figuratively connotes a labored or dull quality (a *ponderous* dissertation); **massive** stresses largeness and solidness rather than heaviness and connotes an impressiveness due to great magnitude (*massive* structures); **cumbersome** implies a heaviness and bulkiness that makes for awkward handling and, in extended use, connotes unwieldiness (*cumbersome* formalities).—***ANT.*** light.

heav·y-armed (hev′i-ärmd′), ***adj.*** furnished with heavy weapons or armor.

heav·y-du·ty (hev′i-dōō′ti, hev′i-dū′ti), ***adj.*** 1. that can resist or withstand great strain, weather, wear, etc.; unusually tough. 2. having a high tariff rate.

heavy earth, barium monoxide; baryta.

heav·y-foot·ed (hev′i-foot′id), ***adj.*** heavy or clumsy in or as in walking; plodding.

heav·y-hand·ed (hev′i-han′did), ***adj.*** 1. without a light touch; clumsy; tactless. 2. cruel; oppressive; tyrannical.

heav·y-heart·ed (hev′i-här′tid), ***adj.*** sad; depressed.

heavy hydrogen, the isotope of hydrogen having an atomic weight of slightly more than 2; deuterium: with oxygen it forms heavy water.

heav·y-lad·en (hev′i-lād′′n), ***adj.*** 1. laden, or loaded, heavily. 2. heavily burdened with care and trouble.

heavy nitrogen, the isotope of nitrogen having an atomic weight of 15.

heavy oxygen, either of two isotopes of oxygen of atomic weights 17 and 18.

heavy spar, barium sulfate; barite; barytes.

heavy water, a compound like water, composed of oxygen and the isotope of hydrogen of atomic weight 2; deuterium oxide, D_2O.

heav·y·weight (hev′i-wāt′), ***n.*** 1. a person or animal weighing much more than average. 2. a boxer or wrestler who weighs 176 pounds or more. 3. [Slang], a very intelligent, influential, or important person. *adj.* of heavyweights.

Heb., 1. Hebrew. 2. Hebrews.

Heb·bel, Frie·drich (frē′driH heb′əl), 1813–1863; German dramatist and poet.

heb·do·mad (heb′də-mad′), *n.* [L. *hebdomas, hebdomadis;* Gr. *hebdomas,* the number seven, week < *hebdomos,* seventh < *hepta,* seven], seven days; a week.

heb·dom·a·dal (heb-dom′ə-d'l), *adj.* [L. *hebdomadalis;* see HEBDOMAD], weekly.

He·be (hē′bi), *n.* [L. < Gr. *Hēbē* < *hēbē,* youth], in *Greek mythology,* the goddess of youth, daughter of Hera and Zeus: she was the gods' cupbearer until succeeded by Ganymede.

he·be·phre·ni·a (hē′bi-frē′ni-ə), *n.* [Mod. L. < Gr. *hēbē,* youth + *phrēn,* the mind], a form of dementia praecox developing at the beginning of puberty.

Hé·bert, Jacques Re·né (zhäk rə-nā′ ā′bâr′), 1755–1794; French Revolutionary leader; guillotined.

heb·e·tate (heb′i-tāt′), *v.t.* & *v.i.* [HEBETATED (-id), HEBETATING], [< L. *hebetatus,* pp. of *hebetare,* to make blunt or dull < *hebes,* blunt, dull], to make or become dull or stupid. *adj.* 1. dull; stupid; thick-headed. 2. in *botany,* having a blunt point, as certain leaves.

he·bet·ic (hi-bet′ik), *adj.* [Gr. *hēbētikos,* youthful < *hēbē,* youth], in *physiology,* of or happening at puberty.

heb·e·tude (heb′ə-tōōd′, heb′ə-tūd′), *n.* [LL. *hebetudo* < *hebes, hebetis,* blunt, dull], the quality or condition of being dull or lethargic; obtuseness.

Hebr., 1. Hebrew. 2. Hebrews.

He·bra·ic (hi-brā′ik), *adj.* [LL. *Hebraicus;* Gr. *Hebraïkos*], of or characteristic of the Hebrews, their language, or culture; Hebrew.

He·bra·ism (hē′bri-iz'm), *n.* [Fr. *hébraïsme* < Gr. *Hebraios,* a Hebrew], 1. a Hebrew phrase, idiom, or custom. 2. Hebrew character, thought, or ethical system. 3. Hebrew institutions or practices; Hebrew religion; Judaism.

He·bra·ist (hē′bri-ist), *n.* [Fr. *hébraïste* < Gr. *Hebraios,* a Hebrew], 1. a specialist or expert in the Hebrew language and learning. 2. a follower of Judaism, or the Hebraic ethical system.

He·bra·is·tic (hē′bri-is′tik, hē′brā-is′tik), *adj.* of or characteristic of Hebraists or Hebraism.

He·bra·ize (hē′brə-iz′), *v.t.* [HEBRAIZED (-izd′), HEBRAIZING], to make Hebrew in character, form, etc. *v.i.* to adopt the Hebrew language, customs, ideals, etc.; become Hebrew in character, form, etc.

He·brew (hē′brōō), *n.* [ME. & OFr. *Hebreu, Ebreu;* L. *Hebraeus;* Gr. *Hebraios;* Aram *'ebrai;* Heb. *'ibhri,* lit., one from across (the river)], 1. any member of a group of Semitic peoples tracing descent from Abraham, Jacob, and Isaac; Israelite: in modern usage interchangeable with *Jew.* 2. *a)* the ancient Semitic language of the Israelites, in which most of the Old Testament was written. *b)* the modern form of this language, the official language of Israel. *adj.* 1. of Hebrew or the Hebrews. 2. Jewish. Abbreviated **Heb., Hebr.**

Hebrew calendar, the Jewish calendar.

He·brews (hē′brōōz), *n.pl.* [construed as sing.], in the *Bible,* the Epistle to the Hebrews, a book of the New Testament: abbreviated **Heb., Hebr.**

Heb·ri·des (heb′rə-dēz′), *n.pl.* a group of Scottish islands west of Scotland: area, 2,900 sq. mi.; pop., 62,000.

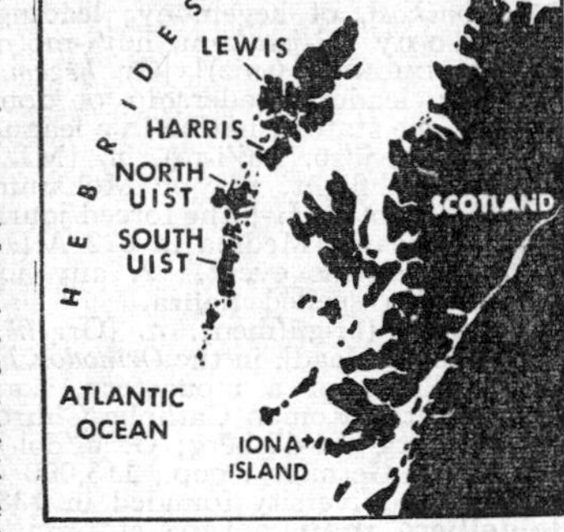

HEBRIDES

He·bron (hē′brən) *n.* a city in southern Palestine: pop., 25,000 (est. 1944).

Hec·a·te (hek′ə-ti; *formerly & still occas.* hek′it), *n.* [L.; Gr. *Hekatē*], in *Greek mythology,* a goddess of the moon, earth, and underground realm of the dead, later regarded as the goddess of sorcery and witchcraft: also spelled **Hekate.**

hec·a·tomb (hek′ə-tōm′, hek′ə-tōōm′), *n.* [L. *hecatombe;* Gr. *hekatombē* < *hekaton,* a hundred + *bous,* ox], 1. in ancient Greece, the slaughter of 100 cattle at one time as an offering to the gods; hence, 2. any large-scale slaughter.

heck (hek), *interj.* [orig. dial. (Lancashire) Eng. (*h*)*eck,* cry of surprise or warning], [Slang], an exclamation used as a euphemism for *hell.*

heck·le (hek′'l), *v.t.* [HECKLED (-'ld), HECKLING], [ME. *hekelin, hechelen* < *hechele;* see HATCHEL], 1. to clean and dress (flax); hackle; hatchel. 2. [orig. Scot.], to annoy or confuse (a speaker) by interrupting with questions or taunts. *n.* a comblike instrument for dressing flax, hemp, etc.; hackle; hatchel. —*SYN.* see **bait.**

heck·ler (hek′lẽr), *n.* one who heckles a speaker, etc.

hect-, hecto-.

hec·tare (hek′târ), *n.* [Fr.; see HECTO- & ARE, *n.*], a metric measure of surface, equal to 10,000 square meters (100 ares or 2.471 acres): abbreviated **ha.** *sing. & pl.*

hec·tic (hek′tik), *adj.* [Fr. *hectique;* LL. *hecticus;* Gr. *hektikos,* habitual, hectic < *hexis,* permanent condition or habit of the body < *echein,* to have], 1. of, affected with, or characteristic of a wasting disease, as tuberculosis; consumptive. 2. designating or of the fever accompanying wasting diseases, especially tuberculosis; hence, 3. feverish; fevered; hot; flushed. 4. characterized by confusion, haste, agitation, etc. *n.* 1. hectic fever. 2. the flush or pink spot on the cheeks of a person suffering from hectic fever. 3. [Rare], a person with tuberculosis.

hec·to- (hek′tō, hek′tə), [Fr., contr. < Gr. *hekaton,* a hundred], a combining form meaning *a hundred,* as in *hectograph:* also **hekto-** or, before a vowel, **hect-, hekt-.**

hec·to·cot·y·lus (hek′tə-kot′i-ləs), *n.* [*pl.* HECTOCOTYLI (-lī′)], [Mod. L. < *hecto-* + Gr. *kotylē,* a cup, hollow object], one of the arms or tentacles of a male octopus, cuttlefish, or other cephalopod, which becomes modified as a sexual organ for impregnating the female.

hec·to·gram, hec·to·gramme (hek′tə-gram′), *n.* [Fr. *hectogramme;* see HECTO- & GRAM], a metric measure of weight, equal to 100 grams (3.527 ounces avoirdupois): abbreviated **hg.** (*sing. & pl.*).

hec·to·graph (hek′tə-graf′, hek′tə-gräf′), *n.* [*hecto-* + *-graph*], a duplicating device by which written or typed matter is transferred to a glycerin-coated sheet of gelatin, from which many copies can be taken. *v.t.* to duplicate by means of a hectograph.

hec·to·li·ter, hec·to·li·tre (hek′tə-lē′tẽr), *n.* [Fr. *hectolitre;* see HECTO- & LITER], a metric measure of capacity, equal to 100 liters (26.418 gallons or 2.8378 bushels): abbreviated **hl.** (*sing. & pl.*), **hectol.**

hec·to·me·ter, hec·to·me·tre (hek′tə-mē′tẽr), *n.* [Fr. *hectomètre;* see HECTO- & METER], a metric measure of length, equal to 100 meters (109.36 yards): abbreviated **hm.** (*sing. & pl.*), **hectom.**

Hec·tor (hek′tẽr), [L.; Gr. *Hēktor,* lit., holding fast < *echein,* to hold, have], a masculine name. *n.* in Homer's *Iliad,* a Trojan hero killed by Achilles to avenge the death of Patroclus: he was Priam's son.

hec·tor (hek′tẽr), *n.* [see prec. entry; in early popular drama, Hector became the type of a braggart and bully], a swaggering fellow; bully; brawler. *v.t.* & *v.i.* 1. to browbeat; bully; threaten. 2. to pester; tease. —*SYN.* see **bait.**

hec·to·stere (hek′tə-stêr′), *n.* [Fr. *hectostère;* see HECTO- & STERE], a metric measure of volume, equal to 100 cubic meters (3,531.44 cubic feet).

Hec·u·ba (hek′yoo-bə), *n.* [L.; Gr. *Hekabē*], in Homer's *Iliad,* the wife of Priam and mother of Hector, Troilus, Paris, and Cassandra.

he'd (hēd), 1. he had. 2. he would.

hed·dle (hed′'l), *n.* [prob. (by metathesis) form of ME. *helde* < AS. *hefeld, hefel* weaving thread (akin to ON. *hafald*) < base of *hebban,* to raise (see HEAVE) + *-eld,* instrumental suffix; for form, cf. ME. *nedel, nelde,* a needle], any of a series of parallel wires or cords in the harness of a loom, equipped with eyes and used for separating and guiding the warp threads. *v.t.* [HEDDLED (-'ld), HEDDLING], to draw (warp thread) through the eyes of the heddles.

hedge (hej), *n.* [ME. *hegge;* AS. *hecg;* akin to G. *hecke;* IE. base **qagh-,* wickerwork, wickerwork pen, seen also in L. *cavea,* enclosure, etc. (see CAGE); basic sense "artificial hedge for defense, enclosure"], 1. a row of closely planted shrubs, bushes, etc. forming a boundary or fence; hence, 2. anything serving as a fence or barrier; restriction or defense. 3. a hedging. *adj.* 1. of, in, or near a hedge; hence, 2. low or disreputable; furtive: as, a *hedge* love affair. *v.t.* [HEDGED (hejd), HEDGING], 1. to place a hedge around or along; border or bound with a hedge. 2. to surround with a barrier; hinder or guard as with a barrier (usually with *in*). 3. to try to avoid or lessen loss in (a bet, risk, etc.) by making counterbalancing bets, investments, etc. *v.i.* 1. to hide or protect oneself, as if behind a hedge. 2. to hide behind words; refuse to commit oneself; shilly-shally. 3. to try to avoid or lessen loss by making counterbalancing bets, investments, etc.

hedge garlic, a tall, white-flowered weed of the mustard family, with heart-shaped leaves, stiff pods, and the odor of garlic.

hedge·hog (hej′hôg′, hej′hog′), ***n.*** [*hedge* + *hog*: from the "hedge" formed by its spines, and from the hoglike snout], 1. a small, insect-eating mammal of Europe, with a shaggy coat and sharp spines on the back, which bristle and form a hedgelike defense when the animal curls up. 2. the porcupine, a similar American animal of a different family.

HEDGEHOG (10 in. long)

hedgehog defense, a method of defensive warfare characterized by the setting up of fortified strong points offering resistance on all sides, thus causing trouble to the enemy even after they have been by-passed: used especially by the Soviet army during the Nazi invasion in World War II.

hedge·hop (hej′hop′), ***v.i.*** [Slang], in *aviation,* to fly very close to the ground, as for spraying insecticide.

hedge hyssop, any of a number of related low-growing plants with golden-yellow flowers.

hedge priest, [cf. parallel D. *haagpreek*], formerly, any English clergyman with little clerical education.

hedg·er (hej′ẽr), ***n.*** 1. a person who plants or trims hedges. 2. a person who hedges in betting, etc.

hedge·row (hej′rō′), ***n.*** a row of shrubs, bushes, etc., forming a hedge.

hedge sparrow, a small European warbler, reddish-brown with white-tipped wings, often found in hedges.

He·din, Sven An·ders (sven än′dẽrs he-dēn′), 1865–1952; Swedish author and explorer in Asia.

He·djaz (he-jäz′, hē-jaz′), ***n.*** Hejaz.

he·don·ic (hē-don′ik), ***adj.*** [Gr. *hēdonikos* < *hēdonē,* pleasure < base of *hedys,* sweet < IE. **swad-,* seen also in *sweet*], 1. having to do with pleasure. 2. of hedonism or hedonists.

he·don·ics (hē-don′iks), ***n.pl.*** [construed as sing.], [< *hedonic*], 1. the branch of ethics dealing with pleasure. 2. the branch of psychology dealing with pleasurable and unpleasurable feelings.

he·don·ism (hē′d′n-iz′m), ***n.*** [< Gr. *hēdonē,* delight, pleasure; + *-ism*], 1. in *philosophy,* the doctrine that pleasure is the principal good and should be the aim of action. 2. in *psychology,* the theory that a person's actions always have pleasure as their purpose. 3. pleasure-seeking as a way of life.

he·don·ist (hē′d′n-ist), ***n.*** 1. a believer in hedonism. 2. a pleasure-seeker; voluptuary. ***adj.*** hedonistic.

he·do·nis·tic (hē′də-nis′tik), ***adj.*** 1. of hedonism or hedonists. 2. living a life of pleasure; self-indulgent.

he·do·nis·ti·cal·ly (hē′də-nis′ti-k′l-i, hē′də-nis′tik-li), ***adv.*** in a hedonistic manner.

-he·dral (hē′drəl), a combining form used to form adjectives corresponding to nouns ending in *-hedron,* as in *hexahedral.*

-he·dron (hē′drən), [Gr. *-edron* < *hedra,* a side, face], a combining form meaning *a geometric figure or crystal with a* (specified) *number of surfaces,* as in *hexahedron.*

hee·bie-jee·bies (hē′bi-jē′biz), ***n.pl.*** [coined by Billy De Beck in his comic strip *Barney Google*], [Slang], an attack of nervousness; jitters.

heed (hēd), ***v.t.*** [ME. *heden;* AS. *hedan* (< **hodjan;* akin to G. *hüten*) < base of *hod* (see HOOD) in the sense "care, keeping, protection"; for IE. base see HAT], to pay close attention to; take careful notice of. ***v.i.*** to pay attention; take notice. ***n.*** close attention; careful notice: as, take *heed* of what I say.

heed·ful (hēd′fəl), ***adj.*** taking heed; careful; attentive.

heed·less (hēd′lis), ***adj.*** not taking heed; careless; inattentive; unmindful.

hee·haw (hē′hô′), ***n.*** [echoic], 1. the sound that a donkey makes; bray; hence, 2. a loud, often silly laugh like a bray. ***v.i.*** 1. to bray. 2. to laugh in a loud, often silly way; guffaw.

heel (hēl), ***n.*** [ME. *hele;* AS. *hela;* akin to D. *hiel;* Gmc. **hanhila* < **hanha;* IE. base **kenk-,* leg joint, heel], 1. the back part of the human foot, under the ankle and behind the instep. 2. the corresponding part of the hind foot of an animal. 3. that part of a stocking, sock, etc. which covers the heel. 4. the built-up part of a shoe, supporting the heel. 5. anything suggesting the human heel in location, shape, or function, as the end of a loaf of bread, the rind on cheese, the lower part of a gunstock, the lower end of a ship's mast, a small quantity of liquor left in a bottle, etc. 6. [Slang], a contemptible or despicable person. ***v.t.*** 1. to furnish with a heel. 2. to follow closely at the rear of; chase. 3. to touch (the floor, etc.) with the heel. 4. [Slang], to equip (a person) with something, especially money. 5. in *cockfighting,* to equip (a gamecock) with metal spurs. 6. in *golf,* to hit (a ball) with the heel of the club. ***v.i.*** 1. to go along at the heels of someone. 2. in *dancing,* to move the heels rhythmically.
at heel, close to one's heels; just behind.
cool one's heels, [Colloq.], to wait or be kept waiting for some time.
down at (the) heel, 1. with the heels of one's shoes in need of repair; hence, 2. shabby; seedy; run-down.
heel in, to cover (plant roots) temporarily with earth in preparation for planting.
kick up one's heels, to be lively or merry; have fun.
lay by the heels, 1. to put in fetters, stocks, or jail. 2. to overcome; frustrate; hinder.
on (or **upon**) **the heels of,** close behind; immediately following.
out at the heels, 1. having holes in the heels of one's shoes or socks; hence, 2. shabby; seedy; run-down.
show one's (or **a clean pair of**) **heels,** to run away.
take to one's heels, to run away.
to heel, 1. close to one's heels; just behind. 2. under discipline or control.

heel (hēl), ***v.i.*** [with assimilated *-d* < ME. *helden,* as also in cognate MLG. *helden, hellen;* AS. *hieldan* (**healdjan*), to incline, slope < base of *heald,* sloping, bent; IE. base **kel-,* to tilt, incline, bow, seen also (via **klei-*) in *incline*], to lean to a side; slant; list; tilt: said especially of a ship. ***v.t.*** to make (a ship) list. ***n.*** 1. the act of heeling. 2. the extent of this.

heel-and-toe (hēl′ən-tō′), ***adj.*** designating or of a walking race or step in which the heel of one foot touches the ground before the toes of the other leave it.

heeled (hēld), ***adj.*** 1. having a heel or heels. 2. [Slang], *a*) having money. *b*) armed or provided, especially with a gun.

heel·er (hēl′ẽr), ***n.*** 1. a person who puts heels on shoes or boots. 2. a fighting cock that uses its heels. 3. [Colloq.], a servile supporter of a politician, serving only for personal gain; hanger-on: as, a ward *heeler.*

heel·less (hēl′lis), ***adj.*** lacking a heel or heels.

heel·piece (hēl′pēs′), ***n.*** 1. a piece forming, or affixed to, the heel of a shoe. 2. any part or piece that by its form, function, etc. suggests a heel.

heel·plate (hēl′plāt′), ***n.*** a thin metal piece put on the bottom of the heel of a shoe to prevent wear.

heel·post (hēl′pōst′), ***n.*** a post forming, or affixed to, the heel or end of something; especially, *a*) the outer post supporting the partition of a stall in a stable. *b*) the post to which a gate or door is hinged.

heel·tap (hēl′tap′), ***n.*** 1. a layer of leather, etc. serving as a lift in the heel of a shoe. 2. a bit of liquor left in a glass after drinking.

Heep, Uriah (hēp), a hypocritically humble, unscrupulous character in Dickens' novel *David Copperfield.*

heft (heft), ***n.*** [< base of *heave*], [Colloq.], 1. weight; heaviness; hence, 2. importance; influence. 3. the larger part or bulk of something. ***v.t.*** [Colloq.], 1. to lift or heave. 2. to try to determine the weight of by lifting. ***v.i.*** [Colloq.], to weigh.

heft (heft), ***n.*** a haft.

heft·y (hef′ti), ***adj.*** [HEFTIER (-ti-ẽr), HEFTIEST (-ti-ist)], [Colloq.], 1. weighty; heavy. 2. large and powerful.

He·gel, Ge·org Wil·helm Frie·drich (gā-ôrkh′ vil′helm frē′driH hā′gəl), 1770–1831; German philosopher.

He·ge·li·an (hā-gā′li-ən, hi-jēl′yən), ***adj.*** of Hegel or Hegelianism. ***n.*** a follower of Hegel or his philosophy.

He·ge·li·an·ism (hā-gā′li-ən-iz′m, hi-jēl′yən-iz′m), ***n.*** the philosophy of Hegel, who maintained that every postulate or affirmation (*thesis*) evokes its natural opposite (*antithesis*), and that these two result in a unified whole (*synthesis*), which in turn reacts upon the original thesis: see **dialectic.**

heg·e·mon·ic (hej′ə-mon′ik, hē′jə-mon′ik), ***adj.*** [Gr. *hēgemonikos*], of hegemony; leading; ruling.

he·gem·o·ny (hi-jem′ə-ni, hej′i-mō′ni, hē′ji-mō′ni), ***n.*** [*pl.* HEGEMONIES (-niz)], [Gr. *hēgemonia,* leadership < *hēgemōn,* leader], leadership or dominance, especially that of one state or nation in a league or confederation.

he·gi·ra (hi-jī′rə, hej′i-rə), ***n.*** [ML.; Ar. *hijrah,* lit., separation, flight, era of Mohammed < *hajara,* to leave], 1. [often H-], the forced journey of Mohammed from Mecca to Medina in 622 A.D.: the Moslem era dates from this event. 2. any journey for safety; flight. Also spelled **hejira.**

he·gu·men (hi-gū′men), ***n.*** [Gr. *hēgoumenos,* ppr. of *hēgeisthai,* to lead], in the *Orthodox Eastern Church,* the elected head of a monastery, corresponding to an abbot in the Roman Catholic Church.

Hei·del·berg (hī′d′l-bẽrg; G. hī′dəl-berkh′), ***n.*** a city in Baden, Germany: pop., 113,000 (est. 1946): site of a famous university founded in 1386.

Heidelberg man, a type of primitive man, inferred from certain fossil remains discovered in 1907 near Heidelberg, Germany: he is believed to have lived between the second and third glacial periods.

heif·er (hef′ẽr), ***n.*** [ME. *hayfre, hayfare;* AS. *heahfore,* lit., full-grown young ox < *heah,* high, hence full-grown (see HIGH) + *fearr,* ox, beast of burden, lit., young animal < IE. base **per-,* to beget (cf. FARROW)], a young cow that has not borne a calf.

Hei·fetz, Ja·scha (yä′shə hī′fits), 1901– ; Russian violinist in America.

heigh (hā, hī), ***interj.*** an exclamation to attract notice, show pleasure, express astonishment, etc.

heigh-ho (hī′hō′, hā′hō′), ***interj.*** an exclamation of mild surprise, boredom, sorrow, fatigue, etc.

height (hīt), *n.* [< earlier *highth;* ME. *heighthe;* AS. *hiehthu* (akin to Goth. *hauhitha*) < *heah* (see HIGH & -TH); pronun. with historical *-th* is still heard colloquially], 1. the topmost point of anything; hence, 2. the highest limit; greatest degree; extreme; climax; culmination: as, the *height* of absurdity. 3. the distance from the bottom to the top. 4. *a)* elevation or distance above a given level, as the earth or sea; altitude. *b)* elevation (of the sun, a star, etc.) above the horizon, measured in degrees. 5. *a)* a relatively great distance from bottom to top. *b)* a relatively great distance above a given level. 6. *often pl.* a point or place considerably above most others; eminence; elevation; hill: abbreviated **hts.** (*pl.*). 7. [Obs.], high rank. Abbreviated **ht., hgt., H., h.** (in senses 3 & 4).

SYN.—**height** refers to distance from bottom to top (a figurine four inches in *height*) or to distance above a given level (he dropped it from a *height* of ten feet); **altitude** and **elevation** refer especially to distance above a given level (usually the surface of the earth) and generally connote great distance (the *altitude* of an airplane, the *elevation* of a mountain); **stature** refers especially to the height of a human being standing erect (drawing himself to his full *stature*).

height·en (hīt''n), *v.t. & v.i.* [< *height*], 1. to bring or come to a high or higher position; raise or rise. 2. to make or become larger, greater, stronger, etc.; increase; intensify. —*SYN.* see **intensify.**

height-to-pa·per (hīt'too-pā'pẽr), *n.* in *printing*, the standard height of type from face to feet, equal to .9186 of an inch.

‡heil (hīl), *interj.* [G.], hail! *v.t.* to say "heil" to.

Heil·bronn (hīl'brôn), *n.* a city in southwestern Germany: pop., 65,000.

Hei·lung·kiang (hā'looŋ'jyäŋ'), *n.* a province of northeastern China: pop., 11,897,000.

Heim·dall (hām'däl'), *n.* [ON. *Heimdallr*], in *Norse mythology*, the watchman of Asgard, city of the gods.

Hei·ne, Hein·rich (hīn'riH hī'nə), 1797–1856; German poet and prose writer.

hei·nie (hī'ni), *n.* [G. *Heine*, dim. of *Heinrich*], [also H-], [Slang], a German soldier: term of contempt used especially in World War I.

hei·nous (hā'nəs), *adj.* [ME. *hainous, heinous;* OFr. *hainös* (Fr. *haineux*) < *haine*, hatred < *hair*, to hate < same LG. base as Eng. *hate*], hateful; odious; extremely wicked; abominable. —*SYN.* see **outrageous.**

heir (âr), *n.* [ME.; OFr. *heir, heyr, eir;* L. *heres;* cf. HEREDITY], 1. a person who inherits or is legally entitled to inherit another's property or title upon the other's death; hence, 2. anyone who inherits any part of another's property, either by the provisions of a will or by the natural action of the law. 3. a person who appears to get some trait from a predecessor or seems to carry on in his tradition.

heir apparent, [*pl.* HEIRS APPARENT], the heir whose right to a certain property or title cannot be denied if he outlives the ancestor: see **heir presumptive.**

heir·dom (âr'dəm), *n.* 1. heirship. 2. an inheritance.

heir·ess (âr'is), *n.* a woman or girl who is an heir; especially, a woman or girl who has inherited or will inherit great wealth.

heir·loom (âr'lo͞om'), *n.* [*heir* + *loom* (tool)], 1. a piece of personal property that goes to an heir along with an estate; hence, 2. any valuable or interesting possession handed down from generation to generation.

heir presumptive, [*pl.* HEIRS PRESUMPTIVE], an heir whose right to a certain property or title will be lost if someone more closely related is born before the ancestor dies: see **heir apparent.**

heir·ship (âr'ship'), *n.* [see -SHIP], the position or rights of an heir; right to inheritance; heirdom.

He·jaz (he-jäz', hē-jaz'), *n.* a former country in western Arabia, along the Red Sea: now a province of Saudi Arabia: area, 150,000 sq. mi.; pop., c. 2,000,000; capital, Mecca: also spelled **Hedjaz.**

he·ji·ra (hi-jī'rə, hej'i-rə), *n.* a hegira.

Hek·a·te (hek'ə-ti; *formerly & still occas.* hek'it), *n.* Hecate.

hek·tare (hek'târ), *n.* a hectare.

hek·to- (hek'tō, hek'tə), hecto-, as in *hektogram:* also, before a vowel, **hekt-**, as in *hektare.*

hek·to·gram (hek'tə-gram'), *n.* a hectogram.

Hel (hel), *n.* [ON.], in *Norse mythology*, 1. Loki's daughter, goddess of death and the underworld. 2. the underworld to which the dead not killed in battle were sent: see also **Valhalla.**

held (held), past tense and past participle of **hold.**

Hel·en (hel'ən), [< Fr. or L.; Fr. *Hélène;* L. *Helena;* Gr. *Helenē*, lit., torch], a feminine name: variants, *Helena, Ellen, Eleanor;* diminutives, *Nell, Nelly, Lena;* equivalents, Fr. *Hélène, Elaine*, It. & Sp. *Elena*, Ir. *Aileen, Eileen.*

Hel·e·na (hel'i-nə; *also, for the fem. name,* he-lē'nə), a feminine name: see **Helen.** *n.* the capital of Montana: pop., 20,000.

Helen of Troy, in *Greek legend*, the beautiful wife of Menelaus, king of Sparta: the Trojan War was started by her elopement with Paris to Troy.

Hel·go·land (hel'gō-länt'; Eng. hel'gō-land'), *n.* a small German island in the North Sea: the British defeated the Germans in a naval battle (Battle of Helgoland Bight) near Helgoland in August, 1914; English name, *Heligoland.*

he·li- (hē'li), helio-.

he·li·ac (hē'li-ak'), *adj.* heliacal.

he·li·a·cal (hi-lī'ə-k'l), *adj.* [Gr. *hēliakos* < *hēlios*, the sun; + *-al*], in *astronomy*, of or near the sun; solar; specifically, *a)* designating the rising of a star when it is first seen again after having been invisible because of its nearness to the sun. *b)* designating the last setting of a star before it becomes invisible again.

he·li·an·thus (hē'li-an'thəs), *n.* [Mod. L. < *heli-* + Gr. *anthos*, a flower], the sunflower.

hel·i·cal (hel'i-k'l), *adj.* [L. *helic-*, base of *helix;* + *-al*], of, or having the form of, a helix; spiral.

hel·i·ces (hel'i-sēz'), *n.* alternative plural of **helix.**

hel·i·cline (hel'i-klīn'), *n.* [*heli-* + *incline*], a curving ramp that ascends gradually.

hel·i·co- (hel'i-kō'), [< Gr. *helix, helikos;* see HELIX], a combining form meaning *spiral, spiral-shaped*, as in *helicopter:* also, before a vowel, **helic-.**

hel·i·coid (hel'i-koid'), *adj.* [Gr. *helikoeidēs* < *helix*, a spiral + *eidos*, form], shaped like a spiral; coiled, as the shell of a snail. *n.* in *geometry*, a surface generated by a straight line moving so that it passes through a fixed helix at all points, as a propeller screw.

hel·i·coi·dal (hel'i-koi'd'l), *adj.* helicoid.

Hel·i·con (hel'i-kon', hel'i-kən), *n.* [L.; Gr. *Helikōn*], 1. a mountain in southern Greece, regarded by the ancient Greeks as the home of the Muses: height, 5,738 ft. 2. the supposed origin of poets' creative impulses. 3. [h-], a brass-wind instrument, similar to a bass tuba, consisting of a long tube bent into a circle so that it can be carried over the shoulder.

HELICON

hel·i·cop·ter (hel'i-kop'tẽr, hē'li-kop'tẽr), *n.* [Fr. *hélicoptère* < Gr. *helix, helikos*, a spiral + *pteron*, wing], a kind of aircraft lifted and moved by a large propeller mounted horizontally above the fuselage: it differs from the autogiro and the gyroplane in that this propeller is turned by motor power and there is no auxiliary vertical propeller for forward motion: see TYPES OF AIRPLANE, p. 32.

Hel·i·go·land (hel'i-gō-land'), *n.* Helgoland: the English name.

he·li·o (hē'li-ō'), *n.* [Colloq.], 1. a heliogram. 2. a heliograph.

he·li·o- (hē'li-ō'), [< Gr. *hēlios*, the sun], a combining form meaning *the sun, bright, radiant*, as in *heliocentric, heliograph:* also **heli-.**

he·li·o·cen·tric (hē'li-ō-sen'trik), *adj.* [*helio-* + *-centric*], 1. calculated from, or viewed as from, the center of the sun. 2. having or taking the sun as the center: as, the *heliocentric* theory of the solar system.

he·li·o·chrome (hē'li-ə-krōm'), *n.* [*helio-* + *-chrome*], a photograph in natural colors.

He·li·o·gab·a·lus (hē'li-ə-gab'ə-ləs), *n.* (born *Varius Avitus Bessianus*), Roman emperor (218–222 A.D.); lived 204–222 A.D.: also **Elagabalus.**

he·li·o·gram (hē'li-ə-gram'), *n.* a message sent by heliograph.

he·li·o·graph (hē'li-ə-graf', hē'li-ə-gräf'), *n.* [*helio-* + *-graph*], 1. formerly, a device for taking photographs of the sun. 2. an instrument for measuring the intensity of sunlight. 3. a photoengraving. 4. a device for sending messages or signaling by flashing the sun's rays from a mirror. *v.t. & v.i.* to signal or communicate by heliograph.

he·li·og·ra·phy (hē'li-og'rə-fi), *n.* [*helio-* + *-graphy*], 1. the study of the sun's surface. 2. the art or process of photoengraving. 3. a signaling or communicating by means of a heliograph.

he·li·o·gra·vure (hē'li-ō'grə-vyoor', hē'li-ə-grā'vyoor), *n.* [Fr. *héliogravure;* see HELIO- & GRAVURE], photoengraving.

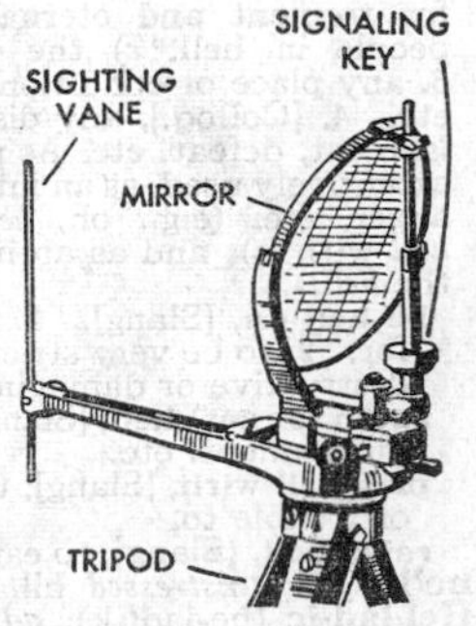

HELIOGRAPH (sense 4)

he·li·ol·a·try (hē'li-ol'ə-tri), *n.* [*helio-* + *-latry*], sun worship.

he·li·om·e·ter (hē'li-om'ə-tẽr), *n.* [Fr. *héliomètre;* see HELIO- & -METER: so called because formerly used in measuring the sun's diameter], an instrument for measuring the angular distance between two stars.

He·li·op·o·lis (hē'li-op'ə-lis), *n.* 1. the ruins of an ancient holy city in Egypt, north of Cairo: Biblical name, *On.* 2. an ancient city in Syria, near Damascus: site of modern Baalbek.

He·li·os (hē'li-os'), *n.* [Gr. *hēlios,* the sun], in *Greek mythology,* the sun god, son of Hyperion: see also **Apollo, Phaëthon, Hyperion.**

he·li·o·scope (hē'li-ə-skōp'), *n.* [*helio-* + *-scope*], a kind of telescope, or a device fitted to a telescope, for looking at the sun without hurting the eye.

he·li·o·stat (hē'li-ə-stat'), *n.* [*helio-* + *-stat*], a device consisting of a mirror slowly revolved by clockwork so as to reflect the sun's rays continuously in a fixed direction.

he·li·o·tax·is (hē'li-ə-tak'sis), *n.* [Mod. L.; see HELIO- & TAXIS], the tendency of certain plants and animals to move or turn under the influence of sunlight.

he·li·o·ther·a·py (hē'li-ō-ther'ə-pi), *n.* [*helio-* + *therapy*], the treatment of disease by exposure to sunlight.

he·li·o·trope (hē'li-ə-trōp', hēl'yə-trōp'), *n.* [Fr. *héliotrope;* L. *heliotropium;* Gr. *hēliotropion* < *hēlios,* the sun + base of *trepein,* to turn], 1. formerly, a sunflower or other plant whose flowers turn to face the sun. 2. any of a group of plants of the borage family, with fragrant clusters of small, reddish-purple or white flowers. 3. reddish purple. 4. a heliograph (sense 4). 5. bloodstone. *adj.* reddish-purple.

he·li·o·trop·ic (hē'li-ə-trop'ik, hēl'yə-trop'ik), *adj.* of, characterized by, or affected by heliotropism.

he·li·ot·ro·pism (hē'li-ot'rə-piz'm), *n.* [< *helio-* + Gr. *tropē,* a turning < *trepein,* to turn; + *-ism*], 1. the tendency of certain plants or other organisms to turn or bend under the influence of light, especially sunlight: ***positive heliotropism*** causes a turning toward the light; ***negative heliotropism*** causes a turning away from the light. 2. positive heliotropism.

he·li·o·type (hē'li-ə-tīp'), *n.* [*helio-* + *-type*], 1. a picture made by printing directly from a gelatin film exposed under a negative and hardened with chrome alum. 2. the process of making such pictures.

he·li·o·typ·y (hē'li-ə-tīp'i), *n.* the art or process of making heliotypes.

he·li·um (hē'li-əm), *n.* [< Gr. *hēlios,* the sun], one of the chemical elements, a very light, inert colorless gas, used for inflating balloons, dirigibles, etc.: it is preferred to hydrogen for such purposes, although it is slightly heavier, because it is not inflammable: symbol, He; at. wt., 4.003; at. no., 2.

he·lix (hē'liks), *n.* [*pl.* HELIXES (-iz), HELICES (hel'i-sēz')], [L., kind of ivy, spiral; Gr. *helix,* a spiral, anything spiral-shaped < *helissein,* to turn round], 1. any spiral, either lying in a single plane or, especially, moving around a cone, cylinder, etc., as the thread of a screw. 2. in *anatomy,* the folded rim of cartilage around the outer ear. 3. in *architecture,* an ornamental spiral, as a volute on a Corinthian or Ionic capital. 4. in *mathematics,* a line so curved around a right circular cylinder that it would become a straight line if the cylinder were unfolded into a plane. 5. in *zoology,* any of a group of spiral-shelled mollusks, including the common snail.

hell (hel), *n.* [ME. *helle;* AS. *hel* (akin to G. *hölle* & ON. *Hel,* name of the underworld goddess; see HEL) < base of AS. *helan,* to cover, conceal, hide; IE. base **kel-,* to hide, cover up, seen also in *conceal, cell, color*], 1. in the *Bible,* the place where the spirits of the dead are: identified with Sheol and Hades. 2. *a)* in *Christianity,* the place where fallen angels, devils, etc. live and to which sinners and unbelievers go after death for torment and eternal punishment; hence, *b)* the people in hell. *c)* the powers of evil or darkness. 3. any place or condition of evil, pain, misery, cruelty, etc. 4. [Colloq.], any disagreeable experience, as punishment, defeat, etc. As profanity *hell* is variously and extensively used, as an interjection expressing irritation, anger, etc. (e.g., oh, *hell!*), as an adverb (e.g., the *hell* with it), and as an intensifier (e.g., *hell,* no!, what the *hell!*).

be hell on, [Slang], 1. to be very difficult or painful for. 2. to be very strict or severe with. 3. to be very destructive or damaging to.

catch (or **get**) **hell,** [Slang], to receive a severe scolding, punishment, etc.

play hell with, [Slang], to cause much damage, injury, or trouble to.

raise hell, [Slang], to cause much trouble, uproar, etc.

he'll (hēl; *unstressed* hil, il), 1. he will. 2. he shall.

Hel·lad·ic (he-lad'ik), *adj.* designating or of the early peoples living on or around the Greek peninsula: as, the Minoans were a *Helladic* people.

Hel·las (hel'əs), *n.* 1. originally, a district and town in northeastern Greece; hence, 2. [Now Poetic], Greece: the ancient name.

hell·bend·er (hel'ben'dẽr), *n.* 1. a large, edible salamander, found especially in the Ohio Valley. 2. [Slang], *a)* a prolonged drunken spree or debauch. *b)* a drunken, rowdy person.

hell·bent (hel'bent'), *adj.* [Slang], firmly resolved to have or do (with *on* or *for*); recklessly determined.

hell·broth (hel'brôth'), *n.* in *legend,* a mixture brewed by witches and soothsayers for performing black magic.

hell·cat (hel'kat'), *n.* 1. a witch. 2. an evil, spiteful, bad-tempered woman.

hell-div·er (hel'dīv'ẽr), *n.* any of several diving birds, as the dabchick.

Hel·le (hel'i), *n.* [L.; Gr. *Hellē*], in *Greek legend,* a girl who, while fleeing with her brother on the ram with the golden fleece, fell off and drowned in the Hellespont.

hel·le·bore (hel'ə-bôr', hel'ə-bōr'), *n.* [OFr. *ellebore;* L. *helleborus, elleborus;* Gr. *helleboros*], 1. any of a group of winter-blooming plants of the crowfoot family, with flowers shaped like buttercups but of various colors: the poisonous roots of the European black variety are used as a heart stimulant. 2. any of a group of plants belonging to the lily family: the white hellebore, or false hellebore, has greenish-white flowers and poisonous roots. 3. these roots when dried and powdered, used as an insecticide.

hel·le·bo·re·in (hel'ə-bôr'i-in, hel'ə-bō'ri-in), *n.* a heart stimulant obtained from certain hellebore roots.

hel·leb·o·rin (he-leb'ə-rin, hel'ə-bôr'in, hel'ə-bō'rin), *n.* a poisonous glucoside, $C_{36}H_{42}O_6$, obtained from certain hellebore roots: it is a strong purgative.

Hel·len (hel'in), *n.* [L.; Gr. *Hellēn*], the legendary ancestor after whom the Hellenes were named.

Hel·lene (hel'ēn), *n.* [Gr. *Hellēn*], a Greek.

Hel·len·ic (he-len'ik, he-lē'nik), *adj.* [Gr. *Hellēnikos* < *Hellēnes,* the Greeks], 1. of the Hellenes; Greek. 2. of the history, language, or culture of the ancient Greeks. *n.* 1. the language of ancient Greece. 2. the branch of the Indo-European family of languages to which Greek, in its various dialects and stages of development, belongs.

Hel·len·ism (hel'ən-iz'm), *n.* [Gr. *Hellēnismos,* imitation of the Greeks < *Hellēnizein,* to speak Greek], 1. a Greek phrase, idiom, or custom. 2. the character, thought, culture, or ethical system of ancient Greece. 3. the adoption of the Greek language, customs, etc., as by the Romans.

Hel·len·ist (hel'ən-ist), *n.* [Gr. *Hellēnistēs,* imitator of the Greeks < *Hellēnizein,* to speak Greek], 1. a non-Greek, especially a Jew of the Diaspora, who adopted the Greek language. 2. a specialist or expert in the Greek language and learning. 3. a great admirer of ancient Greek culture, language, etc. 4. any of the Byzantine Greeks of the 15th century who helped revive classical learning in Europe.

Hel·len·is·tic (hel'ə-nis'tik), *adj.* 1. of or characteristic of Hellenists or Hellenism. 2. of Greek history, language, and culture after the death of Alexander the Great (323 B.C.).

Hel·len·is·ti·cal (hel'ə-nis'ti-k'l), *adj.* Hellenistic.

Hel·len·ize (hel'ə-nīz'), *v.t.* [HELLENIZED (-nīzd'), HELLENIZING], [Gr. *Hellēnizein* < *Hellēnes,* the Greeks], to make Greek, or Hellenistic, in character, form, etc. *v.i.* to adopt the Greek language, customs, ideals, etc.; become Greek in character, form, etc.

hell·er (hel'ẽr), *n.* [Slang], a person who is noisy, wild, reckless, etc.

hel·ler (hel'ẽr), *n.* [*pl.* HELLER], [G.; MHG. *haller, heller,* short for *Haller pfenninc,* penny of Hall: from being first coined (c. 1208) at Hall, Swabia], 1. formerly, *a)* a German copper coin, equal to half a pfennig. *b)* an Austrian bronze coin, equal to 1/100 of a krone. 2. a small Czechoslovakian coin, equal to 1/100 of a koruna.

Hel·les, Cape (hel'is), the southern tip of the Gallipoli Peninsula, Turkey.

Hel·les·pont (hel'əs-pont'), *n.* the Dardanelles: the ancient name.

hell-fire, hell·fire (hel'fīr'), *n.* [ME. *helle fir;* AS. *hellefyr*], the fire, hence punishment, of hell.

Hell Gate, a narrow section of the East River, between Manhattan and Long Island.

hell·gram·mite, hell·gra·mite (hel'grə-mīt'), *n.* [< ?], the dark-brown aquatic larva of the dobson fly, used as fish bait.

hell·hound (hel'hound'), *n.* 1. a dog of hell, as Cerberus; hence, 2. *a)* a fiend. *b)* a fiendish, evil person.

hell·ion (hel'yən), *n.* [*hell* + *-ion,* as in min*ion*], [Colloq.], a person fond of deviltry; mischievous troublemaker.

hell·ish (hel'ish), *adj.* 1. of or from hell. 2. appropriate to hell; infernal; devilish; fiendish. 3. [Colloq.], very unpleasant; detestable.

hell·kite (hel'kīt'), *n.* [*hell* + *kite* (the bird)], a fiendish, cruel, pitiless person.

hel·lo (he-lō', hə-lō'; *variously stressed according to meaning, as* hel'ō, hel'lō', hul'ō), *interj.* [var. of *hollo, holla*], 1. an exclamation of greeting or of response, as in telephoning. 2. an exclamation to attract attention. 3. an exclamation of astonishment or surprise. *n.* a saying or shouting of "hello." *v.i.* to shout or say "hello." *v.t.* to say "hello" to. Cf. **hollo, hullo.**

helm (helm), *n.* & *v.t.* [ME.; AS., protection, helmet; akin to G. *helm*, helmet, AS. *helmian*, to protect; IE. base **kel-*, to cover, hide, seen also in *conceal, cell*, etc.], [Archaic & Poetic], helmet.

helm (helm), *n.* [ME. *helme;* AS. *halma;* akin to G. *helm*, handle; IE. *(*s*)*qel-mo* < base *(*s*)*qel-*, to cut, seen also in *coulter, skill*], 1. *a*) the wheel or tiller by which a ship is steered. *b*) the complete steering gear, including the wheel or tiller, rudder, etc. 2. the control or leadership of an organization, enterprise, etc. *v.t.* to guide; control; steer.

hel·met (hel′mit), *n.* [OFr., dim. of *helme*, helmet; of Gmc. origin; see HELM], 1. a protective covering for the head; specifically, *a*) the hoodlike top part of medieval armor. *b*) the metal head covering worn in modern warfare. *c*) the leather head covering used in football. *d*) the mesh-faced mask used in fencing. *e*) the headpiece of a diver's suit, equipped with air tubes, glass windows, etc. *f*) a fireman's protective hat. *g*) a pith hat with a wide brim, worn as a sunshade in hot countries. 2. something suggesting such a headpiece in appearance or function, as the arched upper part of the corolla or calyx in certain flowers. *v.t.* to cover or equip with a helmet.

TYPES OF HELMET
A, ancient; B, 16th century; C, modern

hel·met·ed (hel′mit-id), *adj.* 1. wearing a helmet. 2. shaped like a helmet.

helmet liner, a plastic or fiber head covering shaped like and worn under a modern military helmet.

Helm·holtz, Her·mann Lud·wig Fer·di·nand von (her′män lōōt′vikh fer′di-nänt′ fôn helm′hōlts′), 1821–1894; German physiologist and physicist.

hel·minth (hel′minth), *n.* [Gr. *helmins, helminthos*], a worm or wormlike parasite, especially of the intestine: tapeworms and roundworms are helminths.

hel·min·thi·a·sis (hel′min-thī′ə-sis), *n.* [Mod. L. < Gr. *helminthiān*, to suffer from worms < *helmins, helminthos*, a worm], a disease caused or characterized by worms in the body.

hel·min·thic (hel-min′thik), *adj.* [< Gr. *helmins, helminthos*, a worm; + *-ic*], of, expelling, or destroying helminths. *n.* a helminthic medicine.

hel·min·thol·o·gy (hel′min-thol′ə-ji), *n.* the scientific study of helminths.

helms·man (helmz′mən), *n.* [*pl.* HELMSMEN (-mən)], the man at the helm; man who steers a ship.

Hel·o·ise (hel′ō-ēz′), a feminine name: see **Eloise.**

Hé·lo·ïse (ā′lô′ēz′), *n.* mistress and, later, wife of her teacher, Pierre Abélard; 1101?–1164?: see **Abélard.**

Hel·ot (hel′ət, hē′lət), *n.* [L. *Helotes* (*Hilotae, pl.*) < Gr. *Heilōtes, pl.*, taken as deriv. of *Helos*, town in Laconia whose inhabitants were enslaved by the Spartans; actually, prob. < base of *helein*, to take, seize], 1. a member of the lowest class of serfs in ancient Sparta; hence, 2. [h-], a serf or slave.

hel·ot·ism (hel′ət-iz'm, hē′lət-iz'm), *n.* the condition of a helot; serfdom or slavery.

hel·ot·ry (hel′ət-ri, hē′lət-ri), *n.* 1. helots as a class; serfs or slaves. 2. serfdom or slavery.

help (help), *v.t.* [HELPED (helpt) or *archaic* HOLP (hōlp), HELPED or *archaic* HOLPEN (hōl′p'n) or *obs.* HOLP, HELPING], [ME. *helpen;* AS. *helpan;* akin to G. *helfen;* IE. base **kelb-*, **kelp-*, to help], 1. to make it easier for (a person) to do something; aid; assist; specifically, *a*) to give (one in need) something necessary, as relief, money, etc. *b*) to do part of the work of; ease or share the labor of: as, will you *help* me do this problem? *c*) to aid in getting (*up, down, in*, etc. or *to, into, out of*, etc.): as, *help* him into his coat. 2. to make it easier for (something) to exist, happen, develop, improve, etc.; specifically, *a*) to make more effective, larger, intense, etc.; aid the growth of; promote: as, ignorance *helps* war. *b*) to cause improvement in; remedy; alleviate; relieve: as, this medicine will *help* your cough. 3. to be responsible for; promote or prevent: as, I can't *help* his bad manners. 4. to keep from; avoid: as, I can't *help* thinking he's wrong. 5. to serve or wait on: said of servants, waiters, clerks, etc. *v.i.* 1. to give assistance; be co-operative, useful, or beneficial. 2. to act as a waiter at table. *n.* [ME. & AS. *help*(*e*) < base of the *v.;* in U.S. sense of "servant," prob. a democratic euphemism to avoid notion of "serve"], 1. a helping; aid; assistance. 2. relief; cure; remedy. 3. a helper. 4. *a*) a hired helper, as a domestic servant, farm hand, etc. *b*) hired helpers; employees. 5. a serving of food; helping.

cannot help but, cannot fail to; be compelled or obliged to.

help oneself to, 1. to serve or provide oneself with (food, etc.). 2. to take without asking or being given.

help out, to help in getting or doing something; help.

so help me God, as God is my witness: used in oaths.

SYN.—**help** is the simplest and strongest of these words meaning to supply another with whatever is necessary to accomplish his ends or relieve his wants; **aid** and **assist** are somewhat more formal and weaker, **assist**, especially, implying a subordinate role in the helper and less need for help (she *assisted* him in his experiments); **succor** suggests timely help to someone in distress (to *succor* a besieged city).—***ANT.*** hinder.

help·er (hel′pẽr), *n.* a person or thing that helps.

help·ful (help′fəl), *adj.* giving help; of service; useful.

help·ing (hel′piŋ), *n.* 1. a giving of aid, assisting. 2. a portion of food served to one person.

help·less (help′lis), *adj.* 1. without power to help oneself; feeble; weak. 2. without help or protection. 3. incompetent; inefficient.

help·mate (help′māt′), *n.* [altered < *help meet;* see HELPMEET], a companion and helper: usually applied to a wife, sometimes to a husband.

help·meet (help′mēt′), *n.* [ghost word; mistakenly read as a single word in "an *help meet* for him" (Gen. 2:18)], a helpmate.

Hel·sing·fors (hel′siŋ-fôrz′; Sw. hel′siŋ-fôrs′), *n.* Helsinki: the Swedish name.

Hel·sing·ör (hel′siŋ-ör′), *n.* a seaport in Denmark: pop., 17,900: English name, *Elsinore.*

Hel·sin·ki (hel′siŋ-ki), *n.* the capital of Finland, on the Gulf of Finland: pop., 328,000 (1943).

hel·ter-skel·ter (hel′tẽr-skel′tẽr), *adv.* [arbitrary formation, prob. on ME. *hele* (see HEEL, back of the foot)], in haste and confusion; in a disorderly, hurried manner. *adj.* hurried and confused; disorderly. *n.* anything helter-skelter.

helve (helv), *n.* [ME. *helfe;* AS. *hielfe, helfe;* akin to MD. *helf;* IE. **sqel*(*e*)-*p* < base *(*s*)*qel-*, to cut (cf. HELM, a tiller)], the handle of a tool, especially of an ax or hatchet. *v.t.* [HELVED (helvd), HELVING], to put a helve on; equip with a helve.

Hel·ve·tia (hel-vē′shə), *n.* 1. an ancient country in Europe: it included most of what is now Switzerland. 2. Switzerland: the Latin name.

Hel·ve·tian (hel-vē′shən), *adj.* 1. of Helvetia or the Helvetii. 2. Swiss. *n.* 1. a native or inhabitant of Helvetia. 2. a Swiss.

Hel·vet·ic (hel-vet′ik), *adj.* Helvetian. *n.* a Swiss Protestant; adherent of Zwingli.

Hel·ve·ti·i (hel-vē′shi-ī′), *n.pl.* [L.], any member of an ancient Celtic people who lived in the western part of what is now Switzerland.

Hel·vé·tius, Claude A·dri·en (klōd å′drē′an′ el′vā′-syüs′; Eng. hel-vē′shi-əs), 1715–1771; French philosopher.

hem (hem), *n.* [ME.; AS. *hem*(*m*); akin to MLG. *ham*, enclosed piece of land; IE. base **qem-*, to compress, impede], 1. the border on a garment or piece of cloth, usually made by folding the edge and sewing it down. 2. any border, edge, or margin. *v.t.* [HEMMED (hemd), HEMMING], 1. to fold back the edge of and sew down; put a hem or hems on. 2. *a*) to encircle; surround. *b*) to confine or restrain: with *in, around*, or *about.*

hem (hem: *conventionalized pronun.*), *interj.* & *n.* a conventionalized expression of the sound made in clearing the throat to attract attention or show doubt. *v.i.* [HEMMED (hemd), HEMMING], 1. to make this sound. 2. to pause or hesitate in speaking.

hem and haw, 1. to pause or hesitate in speaking. 2. to avoid saying something definite.

hem- (hēm, hem), hemo-.

he·ma- (hē′mə, hem′ə), hemo-.

he·ma·chrome (hē′mə-krōm′, hem′ə-krōm′), *n.* [*hema-* + *-chrome*], the red pigment of the blood.

hem·ag·ogue (hē′mə-gôg′, hem′ə-gog′), *n.* [< *hem-* + Gr. *agōgos*, leading < *agein*, to lead], anything that increases the discharge of blood, as in menstruation.

he·mal (hē′məl), *adj.* [< Gr. *haima*, blood; + *-al*], having to do with the blood.

he-man (hē′man′), *n.* [Slang], a strong, virile man.

he·ma·tal (hē′mə-t'l, hem′ə-t'l), *adj.* hemal.

hem·a·te·in (hē′mə-tē′in, hem′ə-tē′in), *n.* [< *hemat*oxylin + *-in*], a reddish-brown, crystalline dye, $C_{16}H_{12}O_6$, obtained from logwood extracts by oxidation: also **hematin.**

he·ma·ther·mal (hē′mə-thũr′m'l, hem′ə-thũr′m'l), *adj.* [*hema-* + *thermal*], in *zoology*, warm-blooded.

he·mat·ic (hi-mat′ik), *adj.* [Gr. *haimatikos*], 1. of, filled with, or colored like blood. 2. in *medicine*, having an effect on the blood. *n.* a hematic medicine.

hem·a·tin (hem′ə-tin, hē′mə-tin), *n.* [*hemat(o)-* + *-in*], 1. formerly, heme. 2. a dark-brown or blackish substance containing iron, obtained by the decomposition of hemoglobin. 3. hematein.

hem·a·tin·ic (hem′ə-tin′ik, hē′mə-tin′ik), *n.* any substance that increases the amount of hemoglobin in the blood. *adj.* 1. of hematin. 2. hematic (sense 1).

hem·a·tite (hem′ə-tīt′, hē′mə-tīt′), *n.* [L. *haematites;* Gr. *haimatitēs*, lit., bloodlike, red iron ore < *haima*, blood], native anhydrous ferric oxide, Fe_2O_3, an important iron ore: it is brownish red when pulverized.

hem·a·tit·ic (hem′ə-tit′ik, hē′mə-tit′ik), *adj.* of hematite.

hem·a·to- (hem′ə-tō, hē′mə-tō), [< Gr. *haima, haimatos*, blood], a combining form meaning *blood*, as in *hematozoon*: also, before a vowel, **hemat-**: words beginning with *hemato-* may also be spelled **haemato-**.

hem·at·o·cyst (hem′ə-tō-sist′, hē′mə-tō-sist′), *n.* a cyst filled with blood.

he·ma·toid (hē′mə-toid′, hem′ə-toid′), *adj.* [*hemat-* + *-oid*], like blood.

hem·a·tol·o·gy (hem′ə-tol′ə-ji, hē′mə-tol′ə-ji), *n.* [*hemato-* + *-logy*], the study of blood and its diseases.

he·ma·to·ma (hē′mə-tō′mə, hem′ə-tō′mə), *n.* [*pl.* HEMATOMATA (-tə), HEMATOMAS (-məz)], [Mod. L.; see HEMAT- & -OMA], a local swelling or tumor filled with effused blood.

hem·a·tose (hem′ə-tōs′, hē′mə-tōs′), *adj.* [*hemat-* + *-ose*], filled or covered with blood.

he·ma·to·sis (hē′mə-tō′sis, hem′ə-tō′sis), *n.* [Mod. L.; Gr. *haimatōsis* < *haimatoein*, to make bloody, turn into blood; see HEMO-], in *physiology*, 1. blood formation. 2. the process by which oxygen is added to the blood in the lungs.

hem·a·to·ther·mal (hem′ə-tō-thũr′m'l, hē′mə-tō-thũr′m'l), *adj.* [*hemato-* + *thermal*], in *zoology*, warm-blooded.

he·ma·tox·y·lin (hē′mə-tok′sə-lin, hem′ə-tok′sə-lin), *n.* [*haematoxylon* + *-in*], a crystalline compound, $C_{16}H_{14}O_6 \cdot 3H_2O$, extracted from logwood and used as an indicator and a stain in microscopy: when oxidized it yields hematein dye.

hem·a·to·zo·on (hem′ə-tō-zō′on, hē′mə-tō-zō′on), *n.* [*pl.* HEMATOZOA (-ə)], [Mod. L.; see HEMATO- & ZOON], any parasitic animal organism in the blood.

heme (hēm), *n.* [shortened < *hematin*], the nonprotein part of the hemoglobin molecule, containing the pigment: formerly called *hematin.*

hem·el·y·tron (hem-el′i-tron′), *n.* [*pl.* HEMELYTRA (-trə)], [Mod. L. < *hemi-* + *elytron*], either of the thickened forewings of certain insects, as the hemipterous insects: also **hemelytrum, hemielytron, hemielytrum.**

hem·el·y·trum (hem-el′i-trəm), *n.* [*pl.* HEMELYTRA (-trə)], a hemelytron.

hem·i- (hem′i), [Gr. *hēmi-*; cf. SEMI-], a prefix meaning *half*, as in *hemisphere.*

-he·mi·a (hē′mi-ə), [var. of *-emia*], -emia: words ending with *hemia-* may also be spelled **-haemia.**

hem·i·al·gi·a (hem′i-al′ji-ə), *n.* [Mod. L.; see HEMI- & -ALGIA], neuralgic pain in only one side or part of the body, especially of the head.

he·mic (hē′mik, hem′ik), *adj.* [*hem-* + *-ic*], of the blood.

hem·i·cra·ni·a (hem′i-krā′ni-ə), *n.* [LL.; Gr. *hēmikrania* < *hēmi-*, half + *kranion*, skull], pain in only one side of the head.

hem·i·cy·cle (hem′i-sī′k'l), *n.* [Fr. *hémicycle;* L. *hemicyclus;* Gr. *hēmikyklon;* see HEMI- & CYCLE], 1. a half circle. 2. a semicircular room, wall, etc.

hem·i·dem·i·sem·i·qua·ver (hem′i-dem′i-sem′i-kwā′-vẽr), *n.* [*hemi-* + *demisemiquaver*], in *music*, a sixty-fourth note (𝅘𝅥𝅱).

hem·i·el·y·tron (hem′i-el′i-tron′), *n.* a hemelytron.

hem·i·el·y·trum (hem′i-el′i-trəm), *n.* a hemelytron.

hem·i·he·dral (hem′i-hē′drəl), *adj.* [< *hemi-* + Gr. *hedra*, base; + *-al*], having half the number of planes required for complete symmetry: said of a crystal.

hem·i·hy·drate (hem′i-hī′drāt), *n.* a hydrate containing half as many molecules of water as of the substance combined with the water.

hem·i·mor·phic (hem′i-môr′fik), *adj.* [*hemi-* + *-morphic*], designating a crystal with unlike planes at the ends of the same axis.

he·min (hē′min), *n.* [< Gr. *haima*, blood; + *-in*], a brown, crystalline chloride of heme obtained when blood is treated with hydrochloric acid or glacial acetic acid and sodium chloride: its production by this reaction is evidence of the presence of blood in fluids, stains, etc.

Hem·ing·way, Ernest (hem′iŋ-wā′), 1899–1961; American novelist and short-story writer; received Nobel prize in literature, 1954.

hem·i·ple·gi·a (hem′i-plē′ji-ə), *n.* [Mod. L.; after Gr. *hēmiplēx, hēmiplēgēs*, stricken on one side; see HEMI- & -PLEGIA], paralysis of one side of the body.

hem·i·pleg·ic (hem′i-plej′ik, hem′i-plē′jik), *adj.* of or having hemiplegia. *n.* a person who has hemiplegia.

he·mip·ter·al (hi-mip′tẽr-əl), *adj.* hemipterous.

he·mip·ter·ous (hi-mip′tẽr-əs), *adj.* [*hemi-* + *-pterous*, after Mod. L. *Hemiptera*, name of the group], belonging to a group of insects, including bedbugs, water bugs, lice, aphids, etc., with piercing and sucking mouth parts: they generally have two pairs of wings, the outer pair thickened toward the base.

hem·i·sphere (hem′ə-sfêr′), *n.* [Fr. & L.; Fr. *hémisphère;* L. *hemisphaerium;* Gr. *hēmisphairion;* cf. ME. *hemisperie* < L.], 1. half of a sphere or globe; specifically, *a)* any of the halves into which the celestial globe is divided by either the celestial equator or the ecliptic. *b)* any of the halves of the earth: the earth is divided by the equator into the Northern and Southern Hemispheres and by a meridian into the Eastern Hemisphere (containing Europe, Asia, Africa, and Australia) and the Western Hemisphere (containing the Americas and Oceania). *c)* a model or map of any of these halves. 2. the countries and peoples of any of the earth's hemispheres. 3. a sphere of action, knowledge, etc. 4. either lateral half of the cerebrum or cerebellum.

hem·i·spher·ic (hem′ə-sfer′ik), *adj.* hemispherical.

hem·i·spher·i·cal (hem′ə-sfer′i-k'l), *adj.* of or shaped like a hemisphere.

hem·i·sphe·roid (hem′ə-sfêr′oid), *n.* a half of a spheroid.

hem·i·stich (hem′i-stik′), *n.* [L. *hemistichium;* Gr. *hēmistichion* < *hēmi-*, half + *stichos*, a row, line, verse], 1. half a line of verse, especially the half preceding or following the chief caesura, or rhythmic pause in the middle of a line. 2. an incomplete line of poetry or one shorter than the metrical pattern calls for.

hem·i·ter·pene (hem′i-tũr′pēn), *n.* [*hemi-* + *terpene*], any of a group of isomeric hydrocarbons with the general formula C_5H_8.

hem·i·trope (hem′i-trōp′), *adj.* [Fr. *hémitrope;* see HEMI- & -TROPE], designating a crystal formed of two other crystals joined so that corresponding faces are directly opposed. *n.* such a crystal.

hem·i·trop·ic (hem′i-trop′ik), *adj.* hemitrope.

hem·lock (hem′lok), *n.* [ME. *hemlok* (< Kentish), *humlok;* AS. *hymlic, hemlic, hymblice;* prob. < AS. *hymele*, hop + *leac*, leek, garden herb (cf. AS. *cerlic*, charlock)], 1. any of a group of poisonous weeds of the carrot family, with small, white flowers and finely divided leaves; poison hemlock: conium, a powerful sedative, is extracted from hemlock. 2. a poison made from such a weed. 3. any of a group of North American and Asiatic evergreen trees of the pine family, with drooping branches and short, flattened needles: the bark is used in tanning. 4. the wood of such a tree.

hem·mer (hem′ẽr), *n.* a person or thing that hems; especially, an attachment (to a sewing machine) for making hems.

he·mo- (hē′mō, hem′ə), [Gr. *haimo-* < *haima*, blood], a combining form meaning *blood*, as in *hemoglobin:* also **hem-, hema-**: words beginning with *hemo-* may also be spelled **haemo-.**

he·mo·flag·el·late (hē′mə-flaj′ə-lāt′, hem′ə-flaj′ə-lit), *n.* any flagellate protozoan parasite in the blood stream.

he·mo·glo·bin (hē′mə-glō′bin, hem′ə-glō′bin, hē′mə-glō′bin), *n.* [shortened (after *hemo-*) < earlier *haematoglobulin;* see HEMATO- & GLOBULIN], the red coloring matter of the red blood corpuscles, a protein yielding heme and globin on hydrolysis: it carries oxygen from the lungs to the tissues, and carbon dioxide from the tissues to the lungs: symbol, Hb (no period).

he·moid (hē′moid), *adj.* [*hem-* + *-oid*], like blood.

he·mo·leu·co·cyte, he·mo·leu·ko·cyte (hē′mə-lōō′kə-sīt′, hem′ə-lōō′kə-sīt′), *n.* [*hemo-* + *leucocyte*], a white blood corpuscle.

he·mo·ly·sin (hē′mə-lī′sin, hem′ə-lī′sin, hi-mol′i-sin), *n.* [< *hemo-* + Gr. *lysis*, a dissolving; + *-in*], a substance in the blood serum that causes the destruction of red corpuscles with liberation of hemoglobin into the surrounding fluid: it is sometimes produced by injecting red corpuscles from another individual of the wrong blood group.

he·mol·y·sis (hi-mol′i-sis), *n.* [*hemo-* + *-lysis*], the destruction of the red corpuscles with liberation of hemoglobin into the surrounding fluid, caused by the presence of hemolysins.

he·mo·lyt·ic (hē′mə-lit′ik, hem′ə-lit′ik), *adj.* of, causing, or characterized by hemolysis.

he·mo·phile (hē′mə-fil′, hem′ə-fil), *n.* [*hemo-* + *-phile*], 1. a hemophiliac. 2. a bacterium that grows well in any medium containing hemoglobin.

he·mo·phil·i·a (hē′mə-fil′i-ə, hem′ə-fil′yə), *n.* [Mod. L.; see HEMO-, -PHIL, -IA], a hereditary condition in which the blood fails to clot quickly enough, causing prolonged, uncontrollable bleeding from even the smallest cut: it occurs in males and is transmitted by females.

he·mo·phil·i·ac (hē′mə-fil′i-ak, hem′ə-fil′yak), *n.* a person who has hemophilia.

he·mo·phil·ic (hē′mə-fil′ik, hem′ə-fil′ik), *adj.* 1. of or having hemophilia. 2. growing well in a medium containing hemoglobin: said of certain bacteria.

he·mop·ty·sis (hi-mop′tə-sis), *n.* [Mod. L. < *hemo* + Gr. *ptysis*, spitting < *ptyein*, to spit out], the spitting or coughing up of blood: usually caused by bleeding of the lungs or bronchi.

hem·or·rhage (hem′ẽr-ij), *n.* [Fr. *hémorrhagie;* L. *haemorrhagia;* Gr. *haimorrhagia* < *haima*, blood + base of *rhēgnynai*, to break, burst], the escape of blood from its vessels; bleeding; especially, heavy bleeding. *v.i.* [HEMORRHAGED (-ijd), HEMORRHAGING], to have a hemorrhage.

hem·or·rhag·ic (hem′ə-raj′ik), *adj.* of or characterized by hemorrhage.

hem·or·rhoid (hem′ə-roid′), *n.* [Fr. pl. *hémorrhoïdes;* L *haemorrhoidae;* Gr. *haimorrhoïdes* (*phlebes*), (veins) discharging blood < *haimorrhoos*, flowing with blood < *haima*, blood + *rhein*, to flow], *usually in pl.* a painful swelling or tumor of a vein in the region of the anus, often with bleeding: also called, in the plural, *piles*.

hem·or·rhoi·dal (hem′ə-roi′d'l), *adj.* of, or having the nature of, hemorrhoids.

hem·or·rhoid·ec·to·my (hem′ə-roi-dek′tə-mi), *n.* [see -ECTOMY], the surgical removal of hemorrhoids.

he·mo·sta·sis (hi-mos′tə-sis), *n.* [Mod. L.; see HEMO- & STASIS], 1. the stoppage of bleeding. 2. the stoppage of the flow of blood in a vein or artery, as with a tourniquet.

he·mo·stat (hē′mə-stat′, hem′ə-stat′), *n.* [< *hemostatic*], anything used to stop bleeding; specifically, a clamplike instrument used in surgery or a chemical applied to a surface wound.

he·mo·stat·ic (hē′mə-stat′ik, hem′ə-stat′ik), *adj.* [see HEMO- & STATIC], capable of stopping the flow of blood; styptic. *n.* a hemostat.

hemp (hemp), *n.* [ME.; AS. *hænep*, *henep* (akin to G. *hanf*, D. *hennep*) corresponding to L. *cannabis*, Gr. *kannabis*, Per. *kanab*, etc.; prob. a very early borrowing < a non-IE. (Semitic?) language], 1. a tall Asiatic plant of the nettle family, grown for its tough fiber. 2. the fiber, used to make rope, sailcloth, etc. 3. a drug, especially hashish, made from the flowers and leaves of this plant.

HEMP
A, plant (10-20 ft. high); B, leaves; C, fruit

hemp agrimony, a European plant of the aster family, with reddish flowers.

hemp·en (hem′pən), *adj.* of, made of, or like hemp.

hemp nettle, any of a number of plants of the mint family; especially, a common prickly weed of the United States.

hemp·seed (hemp′sēd′), *n.* the seed of hemp.

hem·stitch (hem′stich′), *n.* 1. an ornamental stitch, used especially at a hem, made by pulling out several parallel threads and tying the cross threads into small bunches. 2. decorative needlework done with this stitch; hemstitching. *v.t.* to put a hemstitch or hemstitches on.

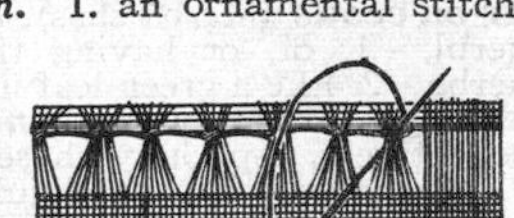

HEMSTITCH

hen (hen), *n.* [ME.; AS. *henn*, fem. of *hana*, rooster; akin to G. *henne* (fem. of *hahn*); IE. base **qan-*, to sing, crow, etc., as also in L. *canere*, to sing (cf. CANTICLE, CHANT, etc.), *carmen* (< **canmen*), song], 1. the female of the chicken, or domestic fowl: the male is called a rooster, or cock. 2. the female of various other birds or of certain other animals, as the lobster. 3. [Slang], a woman.

hen and chickens, any of various plants with many offshoots, as the houseleek.

hen·bane (hen′bān′), *n.* [ME.; see HEN & BANE], a coarse, hairy, foul-smelling plant of the nightshade family, poisonous to animals, especially fowls: it is used in medicine as a narcotic: also called *hyoscyamus*.

hen·bit (hen′bit′), *n.* [*hen* + *bit* (small piece)], a plant of the mint family, with toothed, opposite leaves and purple-red or white flowers.

hence (hens), *adv.* [ME. *hennes* < *henne* (< base of AS. *heonan*(*e*), from here) + -(*e*)*s* adv. genit. suffix (cf. SINCE, THENCE, etc.); IE. base as in *he, here, hither*], 1. from this place; away: as, go *hence*. 2. from this time; after now: as, a year *hence*. 3. from this life: as, departed *hence*. 4. from this origin or source. 5. reasoning from this fact; as a result; therefore: abbreviated **H., h.** *interj.* depart! go away! get out! **hence with!** away with! take away!

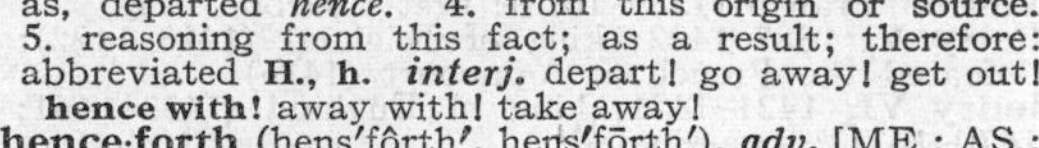

hence·forth (hens′fôrth′, hens′fōrth′), *adv.* [ME.; AS.; see HENCE & FORTH], from this time on; from now on.

hence·for·ward (hens′fôr′wẽrd), *adv.* henceforth.

hench·man (hench′mən), *n.* [*pl.* HENCHMEN (-mən)], [ME. *henxtman*, *hencheman* < AS. *hengest*, male horse (akin to G. *hengst*) + *-man;* orig. sense prob. "horse attendant"], 1. originally, a male attendant; page or squire. 2. a trusted helper or follower. 3. a political supporter who works for his own advantage.

hen·coop (hen′kōōp′, hen′koop′), *n.* a coop for poultry.

hen·dec·a- (hen′dek-ə), [< Gr. *hendeka*, eleven], a combining form meaning *eleven*, as in *hendecagon*.

hen·dec·a·gon (hen-dek′ə-gon′), *n.* [< *hendeca-* + Gr. *gōnia*, an angle], a plane figure with eleven angles and eleven sides.

hen·dec·a·he·dral (hen-dek′ə-hē′drəl), *adj.* of, or having the form of, a hendecahedron.

hen·dec·a·he·dron (hen-dek′ə-hē′drən), *n.* [*pl.* HENDECAHEDRONS (-drənz), HENDECAHEDRA (-drə)], [Mod. L.; see HENDECA- & -HEDRON], a solid figure with eleven plane surfaces.

hen·dec·a·syl·la·ble (hen′dek-ə-sil′ə-b'l), *n.* [L. *hendecasyllabus;* Gr. *hendekasyllabos;* see HENDECA- & SYLLABLE], a line of verse having eleven syllables.

Hen·der·son, Arthur (hen′dẽr-s'n), 1863–1935; British labor leader and politician; received Nobel peace prize, 1934.

hen·di·a·dys (hen-dī′ə-dis), *n.* [ML. < Gr. phrase *hen dia dyoin*, one (thing) by means of two], a figure of speech in which two nouns joined by *and* are used instead of a noun and a modifier: as, *deceit and words* for *deceitful words*.

Hen·don (hen′dən), *n.* a city in southeastern England, near London: pop., 145,000.

hen·e·quen (hen′ə-kin), *n.* [Sp. *henequén*, *jeniquén* < native (Taino) name in Yucatan], 1. fiber obtained from a Central American plant; sisal hemp: it is used for making rope, coarse cloth, etc. 2. this plant, a kind of agave. Also spelled **henequin.**

Hen·gist (heŋ′gist, hen′jist), *n.* ?–488 A.D.; Jute chief; with his brother, Horsa, he is reputed to have led the first Germanic invasion of England and to have founded the kingdom of Kent.

hen·house (hen′hous), *n.* a shelter for poultry.

Hen·ley, William Ernest (hen′li), 1849–1903; English poet, dramatist, and editor.

hen·na (hen′ə), *n.* [Ar. *ḥinnā'*], 1. an ornamental tropical shrub of Asia, with clusters of fragrant flowers of white or rose. 2. a dye extracted from the leaves of this plant, often used to tint the hair auburn. 3. reddish brown. *adj.* reddish-brown. *v.t.* [HENNAED (hen′əd), HENNAING], to tint with henna.

hen·ner·y (hen′ẽr-i), *n.* [*pl.* HENNERIES (-iz)], a place where poultry is kept or raised.

hen·o·the·ism (hen′ō-thi-iz'm), *n.* [< Gr. *heis*, *henos*, one + *theos*, god; + *-ism*], belief in one god, without denying the existence of others.

hen party, [Colloq.], a party for women only.

hen·peck (hen′pek′), *v.t.* [< *henpecked*], to domineer over (one's husband).

hen·pecked (hen′pekt′), *adj.* domineered over by one's wife.

Hen·ri·et·ta (hen′ri-et′ə), [Fr. *Henriette*, dim. of *Henri;* see HENRY], a feminine name: diminutives, *Etta, Hetty, Nettie, Netty*.

Hen·ry (hen′ri), [Fr. *Henri;* G. *Heinrich* < OHG. *Haganrih*, lit., ruler of an enclosure, preserve (< *hag-*, a hedging in, enclosure + *rihhi*, ruler, king) & also altered < OHG. *Heimerich*, lit., home ruler (< *heim*, home, house)], a masculine name: diminutives, *Hal, Hank, Henny;* variant, *Harry;* feminine, *Henrietta;* equivalents, L. *Henricus*, D. *Hendrik*, Fr. *Henri*, G. *Heinrich*, It. *Enrico*, Sp. *Enrique*. *n.* prince of Portugal; lived 1394–1460: called *Henry the Navigator*.

hen·ry (hen′ri), *n.* [*pl.* HENRIES, HENRYS (-riz)], [after J. *Henry* (1797–1878), Am. physicist], in *electricity*, the unit by which inductance is measured, equal to the inductance of a circuit in which the variation of a current at the rate of one ampere per second induces an electromotive force of one volt: abbreviated **H.**

Henry, Cape, a promontory in southeastern Virginia, at the entrance to Chesapeake Bay.

Henry I, 1068–1135; son of William the Conqueror; king of England (1100–1135).

Henry II, 1133–1189; king of England (1154–1189); first Plantagenet king.

Henry III, 1207–1272; king of England (1216–1272).

Henry IV, 1. (*Henry Bolingbroke*), 1367–1413; son of John of Gaunt; king of England (1399–1413); first Lancastrian king. 2. (called *Henry of Navarre*), 1553–1610; as Henry III, king of Navarre (1574–1589);

king of France (1589–1610); first Bourbon king.
Henry V, 1387–1422; king of England (1413–1422); defeated the French at Agincourt (1415).
Henry VI, 1421–1471; king of England (1422–1461; 1470–1471); assassinated.
Henry VII, 1457–1509; king of England (1485–1509); first Tudor king.
Henry VIII, 1491–1547; son of Henry VII; king of England (1509–1547); broke with the papacy and established the Church of England, headed by himself: his six wives were: Catherine (mother of Mary Tudor); Anne Boleyn (mother of Elizabeth I and later beheaded); Jane Seymour (mother of Edward VI); Anne of Cleves; Catherine Howard (beheaded); and Catherine Parr.
Henry, Joseph, 1797–1878; American physicist; first secretary of the Smithsonian Institution (1846–1878).
Henry, O., (pseudonym of *William Sydney Porter*), 1862–1910; American short-story writer.
Henry, Patrick, 1736–1799; American statesman and orator; governor of Virginia (1776–1779; 1784–1786).
Hens·lowe, Philip (henz′lō), ?–1616; English theater manager.
hent (hent), *v.t.* [HENT, HENTING], [ME. *henten;* AS. *hentan;* ? < base of *hand*], [Archaic], to grasp; apprehend. *n.* [Archaic], 1. a grasping. 2. something grasped in the mind; conception; purpose.
hep (hep), *adj.* [? < the drill sergeant's shout (alteration of *step*) marking time for marching troops], [Slang], informed; conversant; having knowledge: often with *to*, as, he's *hep* to our trick.
hep·a·rin (hep′ẽr-in), *n.* [Gr. *hēpar*, the liver; + *-in*], a substance found in various body tissues, especially in the liver, injected into the blood to prevent clotting.
hep·at- (hi-pat′, hep′ət), hepato-.
hep·a·tec·to·my (hep′ə-tek′tə-mi), *n.* [*hepat-* + *-ectomy*], the surgical removal of part or all of the liver.
he·pat·ic (hi-pat′ik), *adj.* [L. *hepaticus;* Gr. *hēpatikos* < *hēpar*, the liver; akin to Sans. *yakrt*, L. *jecur*], 1. of or affecting the liver. 2. like the liver in color or shape. 3. of the liverworts. *n.* 1. a medicine affecting the liver. 2. a liverwort.
he·pat·i·ca (hi-pat′i-kə), *n.* [Mod. L.; see HEPATIC: so named in allusion to its liver-shaped, lobed leaves], a small plant of the crowfoot family, with three-lobed leaves and small flowers of white, pink, blue, or purple that bloom in early spring.
hep·a·ti·tis (hep′ə-tī′tis), *n.* [Mod. L.; see HEPATO- & -ITIS], inflammation of the liver.
hep·a·to- (hep′ə-tō′), [Gr. *hēpato-* < *hēpar*, *hēpatos*, the liver], a combining form meaning *the liver:* also, before a vowel, **hepat-**, as in *hepatectomy*.
hep·cat (hep′kat′), *n.* [*hep* + *cat*, slang for "swing dancer"], [Slang], a jazz expert or enthusiast.
He·phaes·tus (hi-fes′təs), *n.* [Gr. *Hēphaistos*], in *Greek mythology*, the god of fire and the forge, son of Zeus and Hera: he is identified with the Roman god Vulcan.
He·phais·tos (hi-fīs′təs), *n.* Hephaestus.
Hep·ple·white (hep′'l-hwit′), *adj.* designating or of a style of furniture designed by George Hepplewhite (?–1786), English cabinetmaker: it is characterized by the use of graceful curves. *n.* furniture in this style.
hep·ta- (hep′tə), [< Gr. *hepta*], a combining form meaning: 1. *seven*, as in *heptagon*. 2. in *chemistry*, *having seven atoms* (or *radicals*) *of a* (specified) *substance*. Also, before a vowel, **hept-**.
hep·ta·chord (hep′tə-kôrd′), *n.* [< Gr. *heptachordos*, seven-stringed < *hepta*, seven + *chordē*, chord, string], in *music*, 1. the interval of a major seventh. 2. a diatonic scale of seven tones. 3. a musical instrument, especially a lyre, with seven strings.
hep·tad (hep′tad), *n.* [Gr. *heptas*, *heptados* < *hepta*, seven], 1. a series or group of seven. 2. in *chemistry*, an element or radical with a valence of seven.
hep·ta·gon (hep′tə-gon′), *n.* [< Gr. *heptagōnos*, seven-cornered < *hepta*, seven + *gōnia*, a corner, angle], a plane figure with seven angles and seven sides.
hep·tag·o·nal (hep-tag′ə-n'l), *adj.* of, or having the form of, a heptagon.
hep·ta·he·dral (hep′tə-hē′drəl), *adj.* of, or having the form of, a heptahedron.
hep·ta·he·dron (hep′tə-hē′drən), *n.* [*pl.* HEPTAHEDRONS (-drənz), HEPTAHEDRA (-drə)], [Mod. L.; see HEPTA- & -HEDRON], a solid figure with seven plane surfaces.
hep·tam·er·ous (hep-tam′ẽr-əs), *adj.* [*hepta-* + *-merous*], having seven parts in each whorl: said of flowers: also written **7-merous.**
hep·tam·e·ter (hep-tam′ə-tẽr), *n.* [*hepta-* + *-meter*], a line of verse with seven metrical feet. *adj.* containing seven metrical feet.
hep·tarch·y (hep′tär-ki), *n.* [*pl.* HEPTARCHIES (-kiz)], [*hept-* + *-archy*], 1. *a*) government by seven rulers. *b*) a state so governed. 2. [sometimes H-], a group of seven neighboring or allied kingdoms: the seven kingdoms of Anglo-Saxon England from 449 to 828 A.D. (Northumbria, Mercia, Essex, East Anglia, Wessex, Sussex, and Kent) were called *the Heptarchy*.
hep·ta·stich (hep′tə-stik′), *n.* [*hepta-* + Gr. *stichos*, a line, verse], a poem or stanza of seven lines.
Hep·ta·teuch (hep′tə-tōōk′, hep′tə-tūk′), *n.* [L. *Heptateuchos;* Gr. *Heptateuchos* < *hepta*, seven + *teuchos*, a book], the first seven books of the Old Testament.
hep·ta·va·lent (hep′tə-vā′lənt), *adj.* having a valence of seven; septavalent.
her (hũr), *pron.* [ME. *hir, her, hire;* AS. *hire*, dat. sing. of *heo*, she, fem. of *he* (for base see HE); it replaced the orig. AS. accus., *hie*, in ME.], 1. the objective case of **she.** 2. possessive form of **she.** Also used colloquially as a predicate complement with a linking verb (e.g., that's *her*). ***possessive pronominal adj.*** of, belonging to, or done by her (i.e., the female person, animal, etc. previously mentioned).
her., heraldry.
He·ra (hêr′ə), *n.* [L.; Gr. *Hēra, Hērē;* Ionic Gr. *Hērē*], in *Greek mythology*, the sister and wife of Zeus, queen of the gods, and goddess of women and marriage: identified by the Romans with Juno: also **Here.**
Her·a·cle·a (her′ə-klē′ə), *n.* an ancient city of Italy, near the Gulf of Taranto.
Her·a·cles (her′ə-klēz′), *n.* Herakles; Hercules.
Her·a·cli·tus (her′ə-klī′təs), *n.* Greek philosopher; 5th century B.C.: called the *Weeping Philosopher*.
Her·a·cli·us (her′ə-klī′əs, hi-rak′li-əs), *n.* Byzantine emperor (610–641 A.D.); lived 575?–641 A.D.
He·ra·klei·on (i-rä′kli-ôn), *n.* Candia, a city in Crete.
Her·a·kles (her′ə-klēz′), *n.* Hercules: the Greek name.
her·ald (her′əld), *n.* [ME. *herald, herauld;* OFr. *heralt, heraud* < Gmc.; orig., either same word as name *Harold*, or with 1st element < Gmc. base of AS. *herian*, to praise, OHG. *herēn*, to proclaim, etc.], 1. formerly, any of various officials who made proclamations, carried state messages to other sovereigns, took charge of tournaments, arranged ceremonies, etc. 2. in England, an official in charge of genealogies, heraldic arms, etc. 3. a person who proclaims or announces significant news, etc.; messenger: often used as the name of a newspaper. 4. a person or thing that comes before to announce, or give an indication of, what follows; forerunner; harbinger. *v.t.* to introduce; announce; foretell; usher in. —***SYN.*** see **forerunner.**
he·ral·dic (he-ral′dik), *adj.* of heraldry or heralds.
her·ald·ry (her′əld-ri), *n.* [*pl.* HERALDRIES (-riz)], [< *herald*], 1. the art or science having to do with coats of arms, genealogies, etc.: abbreviated **her.** 2. the function of a herald (sense 2). 3. *a*) a coat of arms or heraldic device. *b*) coats of arms collectively; armorial bearings. 4. heraldic ceremony or pomp.
Heralds' College, in England, a royal corporation, appointed in 1483, in charge of granting and recording armorial emblems and coats of arms, keeping records of genealogies, etc.: also called *College of Arms*.
Her·at (he-rät′), *n.* a city in northwestern Afghanistan: pop., 85,000.
herb (ũrb, hũrb), *n.* [ME. & OFr. *erbe, herbe;* L. *herba*, grass, herbage, herb: pronounced after usual ME. form *erbe*, but spelled with initial *h-* after L.], 1. any seed plant whose stem withers away to the ground after each season's growth, as distinguished from a tree or shrub whose woody stem lives from year to year. 2. any such plant used as a medicine, seasoning, or food: mint, thyme, basil, and sage are herbs. 3. vegetative growth; grass; herbage.
her·ba·ceous (hẽr-bā′shəs), *adj.* [L. *herbaceus* < *herba*, herb], 1. of, or having the nature of, an herb or herbs. 2. like a green leaf in texture, color, shape, etc.
herb·age (ũr′bij, hũr′bij), *n.* [Fr.; see -AGE], 1. herbs collectively, especially those used as pasturage; grass. 2. the green foliage and juicy stems of herbs. 3. in *law*, the right of pasturing cattle on another's land.
herb·al (hũr′b'l, ũr′b'l), *adj.* [ML. *herbalis*], of herbs. *n.* formerly, a book about herbs or plants.
herb·al·ist (hũr′b'l-ist, ũr′b'l-ist), *n.* 1. originally, a descriptive botanist; author of an herbal. 2. a person who collects herbs. 3. a dealer in herbs, especially medicinal herbs.
her·bar·i·um (hẽr-bâr′i-əm), *n.* [*pl.* HERBARIUMS (-əmz), HERBARIA (-ə)], [LL. < L. *herba*, herb], 1. a collection of dried plants classified, mounted, and used for botanical study. 2. a room, building, case, etc. for keeping such a collection.
Her·bart, Jo·hann Frie·drich (yō′hän frē′driH her′-bärt; Eng. hũr′bärt), 1776–1841; German philosopher.
Her·bar·ti·an (hẽr-bär′ti-ən), *adj.* of J. F. Herbart or his philosophy of education. *n.* a follower of Herbart or his philosophy.
herb bennet, a plant of the rose family, with yellow flowers and an aromatic, astringent root; avens.
Her·bert (hũr′bẽrt), [AS. *Herebeorht*, lit., bright army < *here*, army + *beorht*, shining], a masculine name: diminutives, *Herb, Bert*.
Her·bert, George (hũr′bẽrt), 1593–1633; English poet and clergyman.
Herbert, Victor, 1859–1924; American composer and conductor, born in Ireland.
her·bif·er·ous (hẽr-bif′ẽr-əs), *adj.* [L. *herbifer* (< *herba*, herb + *ferre*, to bear); + *-ous*], producing herbs: as, a *herbiferous* region.
her·biv·ore (hũr′bi-vôr′, hũr′bi-vōr′), *n.* [Fr. < L.

herba, herb + *vorare*, to devour], a herbivorous animal: opposed to *carnivore*.

her·biv·o·rous (hẽr-biv′ẽr-əs), *adj.* [< L. *herba*, herb; + *-vorous*], feeding chiefly on grass or other plants: opposed to *carnivorous*.

herb Paris, [ML. *herba paris*: ? after the Trojan *Paris*], a plant of the lily family, with a single whorl of leaves below a yellowish-green flower.

herb Robert, [ME. *herbe robert;* ML. *herba Roberti:* said to be so named from being used to cure a disease known as *Robert's plague* (after *Robert*, Duke of Normandy)], a small plant of the geranium family, growing wild in rocky, moist places: it has red stems, red-stained leaves, and purplish-rose flowers.

herb·y (ũr′bi, hũr′bi), *adj.* 1. full of or covered with herbs; grassy. 2. of or like an herb or herbs; herbaceous.

Her·ce·go·vi·na (her′tse-gô′vi-nä), *n.* Herzegovina.

Her·cu·la·ne·um (hũr′kyoo-lā′ni-əm), *n.* an ancient city in Italy, on the Bay of Naples: it was destroyed by an eruption of Mt. Vesuvius (79 A.D.).

Her·cu·le·an (hẽr-kū′li-ən, hũr′kyoo-lē′ən), *adj.* [L. *Herculeus* < *Hercules*, Hercules], 1. of Hercules. 2. [usually h-], having the great size and strength of Hercules; very powerful and courageous. 3. [usually h-], calling for great strength, size, or courage; very difficult to do: as, a *herculean* task.

Her·cu·les (hũr′kyoo-lēz′), *n.* [L.; Gr. *Hēraklees* < *Hēra*, Hera + *kleos*, glory], 1. in *Greek & Roman mythology*, the son of Zeus and Alcmene, renowned for feats of strength, particularly the twelve labors imposed on him by Hera. 2. [h-], any very large, strong man. 3. a northern constellation: see **constellation**, chart.

Her·cu·les'-club (hũr′kyoo-lēz′klub′), *n.* [after the club borne by Hercules], a small, very spiny tree of the ginseng family, found in eastern United States.

herd (hũrd), *n.* [ME.; AS. *heord;* akin to G. *herde;* IE. base **kerdh*(*o*)-, a row, group, seen also in Sans. *çardha-*, a flock, herd, troop], 1. a number of cattle or other large animals feeding, living, or being driven together. 2. the common people; public; crowd: contemptuous term. ***v.t. & v.i.*** to form into a herd, group, crowd, etc. —***SYN.*** see **group**.

herd (hũrd), *n.* [ME. *herde;* AS. *herde, hierde* (akin to G. *hirt*) < same base as prec.], a herdsman: now only in combination, as in *cowherd, shepherd.* ***v.t.*** to tend or drive as a herdsman.

Her·der, Jo·hann Gott·fried von (yō′hän gôt′frēt fôn her′dẽr), 1744–1803; German philosopher and writer.

her·dic (hũr′dik), *n.* [after the inventor, Peter *Herdic* (1824–1888)], a low-hung carriage, usually two-wheeled, with a back entrance and seats along the sides.

herd's-grass (hũrdz′gras′, hũrdz′gräs′), *n.* 1. redtop. 2. timothy. Both are used for hay or pasture.

herds·man (hũrdz′mən), *n.* [*pl.* HERDSMEN (-mən)], 1. a person who tends or drives a herd. 2. [H-], the constellation Boötes.

He·re (hêr′ē), *n.* Hera.

here (hêr), *adv.* [ME.; AS. *her;* akin to G. *hier;* IE. base **ko-*, **ke-*, this one (seen also in *he, her*, etc.) + *-r*, adv. suffix], 1. at or in this place: often used as an intensive, as, John *here* is a good player. 2. toward, to, or into this place; hither: as, come *here.* 3. at this point in action, speech, etc.; now. 4. on earth; in earthly life. Opposed to *there.* ***interj.*** an exclamation used to call attention, introduce a command, answer a roll call, etc. ***n.*** 1. this place; place where the speaker or writer is. 2. the present; this life or time.

here and there, 1. in one place or point and another; at irregular intervals. 2. hither and thither.

here below, on earth; in earthly life.

here goes! an exclamation expressive of decision on starting some action that requires courage, etc.

neither here nor there, beside the point; without significance or importance; irrelevant.

here·a·bout (hêr′ə-bout′), *adv.* in this general vicinity; about or near here.

here·a·bouts (hêr′ə-bouts′), *adv.* hereabout.

here·af·ter (hêr-af′tẽr, hêr-äf′tẽr), *adv.* 1. after this; from now on; in the future. 2. following this, especially in a writing, book, etc. 3. in the state or life after death. ***n.*** 1. the future. 2. the state or life after death.

here·at (hêr-at′), *adv.* 1. at this time; when this occurred. 2. at this; for this reason.

here·by (hêr-bī′, hêr′bī′), *adv.* 1. by or through this; by this means. 2. [Obs.], hereabout.

‡**he·re·des** (hə-rē′dēz), *n.* plural of **heres**.

he·red·i·ta·ble (hə-red′i-tə-b′l), *adj.* [MFr.; ML. *hereditabilis* < LL. *hereditare*, to inherit < L. *hereditas;* see HEREDITY], that can be inherited; heritable.

her·e·dit·a·ment (her′ə-dit′ə-mənt), *n.* [ML. *hereditamentum*], any property that is hereditable.

he·red·i·tar·i·ly (hə-red′ə-ter′ə-li), *adv.* by heredity or inheritance.

he·red·i·tar·i·ness (hə-red′ə-ter′i-nis), *n.* the quality of being hereditary.

he·red·i·tar·y (hə-red′ə-ter′i), *adj.* [L. *hereditarius* < *hereditas;* see HEREDITY], 1. *a*) of, or passed down by, inheritance from an ancestor to a legal heir; ancestral. *b*) having title, etc. by inheritance. 2. of or passed down by heredity; designating or of a characteristic transmitted from generation to generation. 3. being such because of emotional attitudes, etc. passed down from ancestors or predecessors: as, our *hereditary* allies. —***SYN.*** see **innate**.

he·red·i·tist (hə-red′ə-tist), *n.* a person who believes that heredity, rather than environment, determines one's nature and characteristics.

he·red·i·ty (hə-red′ə-ti), *n.* [*pl.* HEREDITIES (-tiz)], [Fr. *hérédité;* L. *hereditas*, heirship < *heres*, heir], 1. the transmission from parent to offspring of certain characteristics; tendency of offspring to resemble parents or ancestors: see **genetics**. 2. the characteristics transmitted in this way: as, a person's *heredity*.

Her·e·ford (her′ə-fẽrd; *also, for n. 3 & adj.*, hũr′fẽrd), *n.* 1. Herefordshire. 2. the county seat of Herefordshire: pop., 24,000. 3. any of a breed of beef cattle originated in Herefordshire, having a white face and a red body with white markings. ***adj.*** of this breed.

Her·e·ford·shire (her′ə-fẽrd-shir′), *n.* a county of west central England: pop., 117,000 (est. 1945); county seat, Hereford.

here·in (hêr-in′), *adv.* 1. in here; in or into this place. 2. in this writing, etc. 3. in this matter, detail, etc.

here·in·af·ter (hêr′in-af′tẽr, hêr′in-äf′tẽr), *adv.* in the part after this part (of this document, speech, etc.).

here·in·be·fore (hêr′in-bi-fôr′, hêr′in-bi-fōr′), *adv.* in the part before this part (of this document, speech, etc.).

here·in·to (hêr-in′tōō), *adv.* 1. into this place. 2. into this matter, condition, etc.

here·of (hêr-uv′, hêr-ov′), *adv.* 1. of this. 2. concerning this. 3. [Archaic], from this; hence.

here·on (hêr-on′), *adv.* hereupon.

‡**he·res** (hē′rēz), *n.* [*pl.* HEREDES (hə-rē′dēz)], [L.; see HEIR], in *law*, an heir: also spelled **haeres**.

here's (hêrz), here is.

he·re·si·arch (hi-rē′si-ärk′, her′ə-si-ärk′), *n.* [LL. *haeresiarcha;* Gr. *hairesiarchēs*, leader of a school < *hairesis* (see HERESY) + *-archēs*, leader < *archein*, to lead], the founder or head of a heresy or heretical sect.

here's to! here's a toast to! I wish success, joy, etc. to!

her·e·sy (her′ə-si), *n.* [*pl.* HERESIES (-siz)], [ME. & OFr. *heresie;* L. *haeresis*, school of thought, sect, heresy; Gr. *hairesis*, a taking, selection, school, sect, heresy < *hairein*, to take], 1. a religious belief opposed to the orthodox doctrines of a church; especially, such a belief specifically denounced by the church and regarded as likely to cause schism. 2. any opinion (in philosophy, politics, etc.) opposed to official or established views or doctrines. 3. the holding of such a belief or opinion.

her·e·tic (her′ə-tik), *n.* [ME. *heretike;* Fr. *herétique;* LL. *haereticus*, of heresy, heretic < Gr. *hairetikos*, able to choose, heretical < *hairein*, to take, choose], a person who professes any heresy; especially, a church member who holds beliefs opposed to the official church doctrines. ***adj.*** heretical.

he·ret·i·cal (hə-ret′i-k′l), *adj.* [ML. *haereticalis*], 1. of heresy or heretics. 2. containing, characterized by, or having the nature of, heresy.

here·to (hêr-tōō′), *adv.* [ME. *her to*], to this; hereunto.

here·to·fore (hêr′too-fôr′, hêr′tə-fōr′), *adv.* [ME. *her* (see HERE) + *toforen*, before < AS. *toforan*], up to now; until the present; before this.

here·un·to (hêr′un-tōō′), *adv.* hereto.

here·up·on (hêr′ə-pon′), *adv.* 1. immediately following this; at once. 2. upon this; concerning this subject, etc.

here·with (hêr-with′, hêr-*with*′), *adv.* 1. along with this. 2. by this method or means.

Her·ges·hei·mer, Joseph (hũr′gəs-hī′mẽr), 1880–1954; American novelist.

her·i·ot (her′i-ət), *n.* [ME. *heriet;* via Anglo-Fr. < AS. *heregeat-* for *heregeatwe*, lit., army equipment < *here*, army (see HARRY, HAROLD) + *geatwe*, earlier *ge-tawe*, equipment, arms < *tawian*, to prepare], in *English feudal law*, a payment in chattels or money (originally, a restoration of arms, equipment, etc.) made to the lord from the possessions of a tenant who had died.

her·it·a·bil·i·ty (her′i-tə-bil′ə-ti), *n.* the quality or state of being heritable.

her·it·a·ble (her′i-tə-b′l), *adj.* [ME.; OFr. < *heriter;* see HERITAGE], 1. that can be inherited; inheritable. 2. that can inherit.

her·it·age (her′ə-tij), *n.* [ME.; OFr. < *heriter* < LL. *hereditare*, to inherit < L. *hereditas;* see HEREDITY], 1. property that is or can be inherited. 2. *a*) something handed down from one's ancestors or the past, as a characteristic, a culture, tradition, etc. *b*) the rights, burdens, or status resulting from being born in a certain time or place; birthright. 3. in the *Bible*, *a*) the chosen people of God; Israelites. *b*) the Christian church.

SYN.—**heritage**, the most general of these words, applies either to property passed on to an heir, or to a tradition, culture, etc. passed on to a later generation (our *heritage* of freedom); **inheritance** applies to property, a characteristic. etc, passed on to an heir; **patrimony** strictly refers to an estate inherited from one's father, but it is also used of anything passed on from an ancestor; **birthright**, in its stricter sense, applies to the property rights of a first-born son.

her·i·tance (her'ə-təns), *n.* [ME.; OFr. < *heriter;* see HERITAGE], [Archaic], inheritance.

her·i·tor (her'ə-tẽr), *n.* [ME. *heriter;* OFr. *heritier;* LL. *herediatarius* (for L. *heres*, heir) < L. *hereditarius;* see HEREDITARY], 1. an inheritor; heir. 2. in *Scottish law*, the holder of heritable land in a parish.

herl (hũrl), *n.* [ME. *herle;* see HARL], 1. the barb or barbs of a feather, with which an artificial fishing fly is trimmed. 2. a fly trimmed with this.

her·ma (hũr'mə), *n.* [*pl.* HERMAE (-mē), HERMAI (-mī)], [L.; Gr. *Hermēs*, Hermes], in ancient Greece, a square pillar of stone topped by a bust or head of Hermes, used as a milestone, signpost, etc.

Her·man (hũr'mən), [G. *Hermann;* OHG. *Hariman* < *heri*, army, host + *man*, man], a masculine name: equivalents, Fr. *Armand*, G. *Hermann*, It. *Ermanno*.

her·maph·rod·ism (hẽr-maf'rə-diz'm), *n.* the quality or condition of a hermaphrodite: also **hermaphroditism**.

her·maph·ro·dite (hẽr-maf'rə-dīt'), *n.* [L. *hermaphroditus;* Gr. *hermaphroditos* < *Hermaphroditos;* see HERMAPHRODITUS], 1. a person or animal with the sexual organs of both the male and the female. 2. a plant having stamens and pistils in the same flower. 3. a hermaphrodite brig. *adj.* hermaphroditic.

hermaphrodite brig, a two-masted ship with a square-rigged foremast and a fore-and-aft-rigged mainmast.

her·maph·ro·dit·ic (hẽr-maf'rə-dit'ik), *adj.* of, or having the nature of, a hermaphrodite.

her·maph·ro·dit·i·cal (hẽr-maf'rə-dit'i-k'l), *adj.* hermaphroditic.

her·maph·ro·dit·ism (hẽr-maf'rə-dīt-iz'm), *n.* hermaphrodism.

Her·maph·ro·di·tus (hẽr-maf'rə-dī'təs), *n.* [L.; Gr. *Hermaphroditos*], in *Greek mythology*, the son of Hermes and Aphrodite: when bathing, he became united in a single body with the nymph Salmacis.

her·me·neu·tic (hũr'mi-nū'tik, hũr'mi-nōō'tik), *adj.* [Gr. *hermēneutikos* < *hermēneuein*, to interpret], of hermeneutics; interpretive, especially of the Biblical text.

her·me·neu·tics (hũr'mi-nū'tiks, hũr'mi-nōō'tiks), *n.* [see HERMENEUTIC & -ICS], the science of interpretation; especially, the branch of theology dealing with the principles of exegesis.

Her·mes (hũr'mēz), *n.* [L.; Gr. *Hermēs*], in *Greek mythology*, a god who served as herald and messenger of the other gods, identified by the Romans with Mercury and generally pictured with winged shoes and hat, carrying a caduceus: he was also the god of science, eloquence, and cunning, the protector of boundaries and commerce, and guide of departed souls to Hades.

Hermes Tris·me·gis·tus (tris'mi-jis'təs), [Gr. *Hermēs trismegistos*, lit., Hermes the thrice greatest], the Greek name for the Egyptian god Thoth, reputed founder of alchemy and other occult sciences: he was, to some extent, identified with Hermes.

her·met·ic (hẽr-met'ik), *adj.* [ML. *hermeticus* < L. *Hermes* < Gr. *Hermēs* (*trismegistos*)], 1. [usually H-], of or derived from Hermes Trismegistus and his lore; hence, 2. magical; alchemical. 3. [from use in alchemy], completely sealed by fusion, soldering, etc. so as to keep air or gas from getting in or out; airtight.

her·met·i·cal (hẽr-met'i-k'l), *adj.* hermetic.

her·met·i·cal·ly (hẽr-met'i-k'l-i, hẽr-met'ik-li), *adv.* in a hermetic way; so as to be airtight.

Her·mi·o·ne (hẽr-mī'ə-ni), *n.* in *Greek legend*, the daughter of Menelaus and Helen of Troy.

her·mit (hũr'mit), *n.* [ME. *hermite, ermite;* OFr. *hermite;* LL. *eremita;* Gr. *erēmitēs* < *erēmia*, solitude, desert place < *erēmos*, desolate, solitary], 1. a person who lives by himself in a lonely or secluded spot, often from religious motives; recluse. 2. a spiced cooky made with nuts and raisins. 3. a tropical hummingbird.

her·mit·age (hũr'mə-tij), *n.* [ME.; OFr.; see -AGE], 1. the place where a hermit lives. 2. a place where a person can live away from other people; secluded retreat. 3. [H-], a full-bodied French wine from a place called *l'Hermitage*, near Valence.

hermit crab, any of various soft-bodied crabs that live in the empty shells of certain mollusks, as snails, etc.

her·mit·ic (hẽr-mit'ik), *adj.* of or fit for a hermit; solitary; secluded.

her·mit·i·cal (hẽr-mit'i-k'l), *adj.* hermitic.

hermit thrush, a North American thrush with a brown body, spotted breast, and reddish-brown tail.

Her·mon, Mount (hũr'mən), a mountain in southwestern Syria: height, 9,200 ft.

hern (hũrn), *n.* [dial. form of *heron*], [Archaic or Dial.], a heron.

her·ni·a (hũr'ni-ə), *n.* [*pl.* HERNIAS (-əz), HERNIAE (-ē')], [L.; for IE. base see YARN], the protrusion of all or part of an organ through a tear in the wall of the surrounding structure; especially, the protrusion of part of the intestine through the abdominal muscles; rupture.

her·ni·al (hũr'ni-əl), *adj.* of hernia.

her·ni·o- (hũr'ni-ō), a combining form meaning *hernia*, as is *herniotomy*.

her·ni·ot·o·my (hũr'ni-ot'ə-mi), *n.* [*pl.* HERNIOTOMIES (-miz)], [*hernio-* + *-tomy*], the surgical repair of a hernia.

He·ro (hêr'ō), *n.* [L.; Gr. *Hērō*], in *Greek legend*, a priestess of Aphrodite at Sestos: her lover, Leander, swam the Hellespont from Abdyos every night to be with her; when he drowned one night, Hero threw herself into the sea.

he·ro (hêr'ō), *n.* [*pl.* HEROES (-ōz)], [L. *heros;* Gr. *hērōs*], 1. in *mythology* & *legend*, a man of great strength and courage, favored by the gods and in part descended from them, often regarded as a half-god and worshiped after his death: as, Aeneas and Hector were *heroes* to the ancients. 2. any man admired for his courage, nobility, or exploits, especially in war: as, Washington is a national *hero*. 3. any person admired for his qualities or achievements and regarded as an ideal or model. 4. the central male character in a novel, play, poem, etc., with whom the reader or audience is supposed to sympathize; protagonist: often opposed to *villain*. 5. the central figure in any important event or period, honored for outstanding qualities.

Her·od (her'əd), *n.* king of Judea (37–4 B.C.); lived 73?–4 B.C.: called *Herod the Great*.

Herod An·ti·pas (an'ti-pas'), ? B.C.–40? A.D., son of Herod the Great; ruler of Galilee (4 B.C.–39 A.D.).

He·ro·di·an (hi-rō'di-ən), *adj.* [L. *Herodianus* < *Herodes;* Gr. *Hērōdēs*, Herod], of or concerning Herod, especially Herod the Great. *n.* a Jewish supporter of Herod, especially of Herod Antipas.

He·ro·di·as (hi-rō'di-əs), *n.* in the *Bible*, the second wife of Herod Antipas: she told her daughter Salome to ask Herod for the head of John the Baptist, thus causing his death: Mark 6: 17–23.

He·rod·o·tus (hi-rod'ə-təs), *n.* Greek historian; 5th century B.C.; called the *Father of History*.

he·ro·ic (hi-rō'ik), *adj.* [L. *heroicus;* Gr. *hērōikos*, of a hero < *hērōs*, hero], 1. of or characterized by men of godlike strength and courage: as, the *heroic* age. 2. like or characteristic of a hero or his deeds; strong, brave, and noble: as, *heroic* conduct. 3. of or about a hero and his deeds; epic: as, a *heroic* poem. 4. exalted; eloquent; high-flown: as, *heroic* words. 5. daring and risky, but used as a last resort: as, *heroic* measures. 6. in *art*, somewhat larger than life-size but less than colossal: as, a *heroic* statue. *n.* 1. *a*) a heroic poem. *b*) *pl.* heroic verse. 2. *pl.* pretentious, extravagant, or melodramatic talk or action, meant to seem heroic.

heroic age, the period when the great heroes of a folk or nation, especially of Greece or Rome, are supposed to have lived.

he·ro·i·cal (hi-rō'i-k'l), *adj.* heroic.

heroic couplet, a pair of rhymed lines in iambic pentameter, a verse form used in the late 14th century by Chaucer, made the dominant form of English neoclassical verse by Waller, Denham, and Dryden, and perfected in the early 18th century by Pope. Example:

"In every work regard the writer's end,
Since none can compass more than they intend."

heroic tenor, 1. a tenor voice with rich, powerful tones. 2. a man with such a voice, especially in opera; dramatic tenor. Distinguished from *lyric tenor*.

heroic verse, the verse form in which epic poetry is traditionally written, as dactylic hexameter in Greek or Latin, the alexandrine in French, and iambic pentameter in English.

her·o·in (her'ō-in, hêr'ō-in), *n.* [G.], a white, crystalline powder, an acetyl derivative of morphine, $C_{21}H_{23}NO_5$: it is a very powerful, habit-forming narcotic whose manufacture and import are now prohibited in the United States: a trade-mark (**Heroin**).

her·o·ine (her'ō-in), *n.* [L. *heroina;* Gr. *hērōinē*, fem. of *hērōs*, hero], 1. a girl or woman hero (in various senses). 2. the central female character in a novel, play, etc., or the one with whom the hero is in love.

her·o·ism (her'ō-iz'm), *n.* [Fr. *héroisme*], 1. the qualities and actions of a hero or heroine. 2. brave, noble action or trait.

Her·on (hêr'on), *n.* (also called *Hero of Alexandria*), Greek geometer and mechanician; c. 3d century.

her·on (her'ən), *n.* [*pl.* HERONS (-ənz), HERON; see PLURAL, II, D, 1], [ME. *heiroun, heroun, hern;* OFr. *hairon* < Frank. **haigiro* (akin to OHG. *heigir*, ON. *hegri*)], any of a large group of wading birds with a long neck, long legs, and a long, tapered bill, living along marshes and river banks.

her·on·ry (her'ən-ri), *n.* [*pl.* HERONRIES (-riz)], a place where many herons gather to breed.

hero worship, exaggerated or excessive reverence or admiration for heroes or other important persons.

her·pes (hũr'pēz), *n.* [L.; Gr. *herpēs*, lit., a creeping, herpes < *herpein*, to creep], an inflammatory virus disease of the skin, characterized by the eruption of small blisters on the skin and mucous membranes, especially (*herpes zoster*) along the course of a nerve.

‡**herpes la·bi·a·lis** (lā'bi-ā'lis), [L.; see LABIAL], a form of herpes; cold sore.
‡**herpes zos·ter** (zos'tẽr), [L.; *herpes* + *zoster*, shingles < Gr. *zōstēr*, a girdle], a form of herpes; shingles.
her·pet·ic (hẽr-pet'ik), *adj.* [Gr. *herpētikos*], of, having, or like herpes.
her·pe·tol·o·gist (hũr'pi-tol'ə-jist), *n.* a student of or specialist in herpetology.
her·pe·tol·o·gy (hũr'pi-tol'ə-ji), *n.* [< Gr. *herpeton*, reptile; + *-logy*], the branch of zoology having to do with the study of reptiles: abbreviated **herpet., herp.**
‡**Herr** (her), *n.* [*pl.* HERREN (-ən)], [G.; orig. compar. of *hehr*, noble, venerable], in Germany, a man; gentleman: also used as a title corresponding to *Mr.* or *Sir.*
‡**Herr·en·volk** (her'ən-fôlk'), *n.* [*pl.* HERRENVÖLKER (-fel'kẽr)], [G.], master race: in Nazi ideology, applied to the German people.
Her·re·ra, Fran·cis·co de (frän-thēs'kô *the* er-re'rä), 1576–1656; Spanish painter and engraver.
Her·rick, Robert (her'ik), 1591–1674; English poet.
her·ring (her'iŋ), *n.* [*pl.* HERRINGS (-iŋz), HERRING; see PLURAL, II, D, 1], [ME. *hering*; AS. *hæring*; akin to G. *häring*], 1. any of a large group of small food fishes of the North Atlantic: the adult fish are eaten cooked, dried, salted, or smoked, and the young are canned as sardines. 2. loosely, any related fish, as the sprat, pilchard, etc. See also **red herring.**
her·ring·bone (her'iŋ-bōn'), *n.* 1. the spine of a herring with the ribs extending from opposite sides in rows of parallel, slanting lines. 2. anything made in this pattern, as a kind of cross-stitch, a twill weave, an arrangement of bricks or tiles, etc. *adj.* having the pattern of a herringbone: as, a *herringbone* stitch. *v.i. & v.t.* [HERRINGBONED (-bōnd'), HERRINGBONING], to use a herringbone stitch or pattern (on).

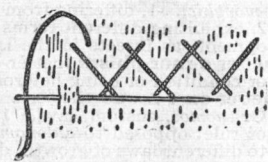

HERRINGBONE STITCH

Her·ri·ot, É·dou·ard (ā'dwȧr' e'ryō'), 1872–1957; premier of France (1924–1925; 1932).
hers (hũrz), *pron.* [Late ME. *hires, hers* < *hire, her(e)*, *poss. adj.* (see HER) + *-s* after *his*], that or those belonging to her: the absolute form of *her*, used without a following noun, often after *of*, as, a friend of *hers*, that book is *hers*, *hers* are better.
Her·schel, Sir **John Frederick William** (hũr'shəl), 1792–1871; son of *Sir William*; English astronomer and chemist.
Herschel, Sir **William,** 1738–1822; English astronomer born in Germany; discovered the planet Uranus.
herse (hũrs), *n.* [Fr.; see HEARSE], 1. a framework on which to dry skins. 2. a portcullis or frame set with spikes, formerly used in warfare to hinder the enemy's advance. 3. a troop formation formerly used in battle.
her·self (hẽr-self'), *pron.* [ME. *hire self*; AS. *hire selfum*, dat. sing. of *hie self*; see HER & SELF], a form of the third person singular, feminine pronoun, used: *a*) as an intensive: as, she went *herself*. *b*) as a reflexive: as, she hurt *herself*. *c*) [Irish], as a subject: as, *herself* will have her tea now. *d*) as a quasi-noun meaning "her real, true, or actual self" (e.g., she is not *herself* when she rages like that): in this construction *her* may be considered a possessive pronominal adjective and *self* a noun, and they may be separated: as, *her* own sweet *self*.
Hert·ford (här'fẽrd, härt'fẽrd), *n.* 1. Hertfordshire. 2. the county seat of Hertfordshire: pop., 11,000.
Hert·ford·shire (här'fẽrd-shir', härt'fẽrd-shir'), *n.* a county of southeastern England: pop., 535,000 (est. 1945); county seat, Hertford.
Hertz, Hein·rich Ru·dolph (hīn'riH rōō'dôlf herts; Eng. *also* hũrts), 1857–1894; German physicist.
Hertz·i·an waves (hert'si-ən, hũrt'si-ən), [after H. R. *Hertz*, G. physicist], [sometimes h-], radio waves or other electromagnetic radiation resulting from the oscillations of electricity in a conductor.
Her·tzog, James Bar·ry Mun·nik (bar'i mun'ək her'tsokh), 1866–1942; Boer general and statesman; prime minister of South Africa (1924–1939).
Her·ze·go·vi·na (her'tsi-gō-vē'nə), *n.* a former province of Austria-Hungary, now a part of Yugoslavia: Serbian spelling, *Hercegovina.*
Herzl, The·o·dor (tā'ô-dôr' her'ts'l), 1860–1904; Austrian-Jewish writer, born in Hungary; founder of Zionism.
he's (hēz), 1. he is. 2. he has.
Hesh·van (hesh'vaŋ; Heb. khesh'vän), *n.* Cheshvan: see **Jewish calendar.**
He·si·od (hē'si-əd, hes'i-əd), *n.* Greek didactic poet; 8th century B.C.
hes·i·tance (hez'ə-təns), *n.* hesitancy.
hes·i·tan·cy (hez'ə-tən-si), *n.* [*pl.* HESITANCIES (-siz)], [L. *haesitantia*, a stammering < *haesitans*, ppr. of *haesitare*], hesitation; indecision; vacillation; doubt.
hes·i·tant (hez'ə-tənt), *adj.* [L. *haesitans*; see HESITANCY], hesitating; undecided; vacillating; doubtful. —*SYN.* see **reluctant.**
hes·i·tate (hez'ə-tāt'), *v.i.* [HESITATED (-id), HESITATING], [< L. *haesitatus*, pp. of *haesitare*, to stick fast, hesitate, intens. of *haerere*, to stick, cleave], 1. to stop in indecision; feel unsure; pause or delay in acting, choosing, or deciding; waver; hence, 2. to pause; stop momentarily. 3. to be reluctant; not be sure that one should: as, I *hesitate* to ask for a loan. 4. to pause continually in speaking; stutter; stammer.
SYN.—**hesitate** implies a pause or delay signifying indecision or reluctance (I *hesitated* to ask him); **waver** suggests especially a holding back or hesitating after a course or decision has been adopted (do not *waver* in your resolution); **vacillate** implies a shifting back and forth in a decision, opinion, etc., resulting in continued hesitation (she *vacillates* in her affection); **falter** suggests a pausing or slowing down, as in fear or irresolution (they never *faltered* in the counterattack).
hes·i·tat·ing·ly (hez'ə-tāt'iŋ-li), *adv.* in a hesitant manner; with hesitation.
hes·i·ta·tion (hez'ə-tā'shən), *n.* [L. *haesitatio*], a hesitating or feeling hesitant; specifically, *a*) indecision; uncertain pausing or delay. *b*) a pausing; momentary delay. *c*) reluctance. *d*) a stammering.
hes·i·ta·tive (hez'ə-tā'tiv), *adj.* characterized by hesitation; hesitating.
Hes·per (hes'pẽr), *n.* [Poetic], Hesperus.
Hes·per·i·a (hes-pêr'i-ə), *n.* [L.; Gr. *Hesperia* < *hesperos*; see HESPERIAN], the Western Land: the ancient Greek name for Italy and the Roman name for Spain.
Hes·pe·ri·an (hes-pêr'i-ən), *adj.* [L. *hesperius*; Gr. *hesperios*, western < *hesperos*, western, evening, *Hesperos*, evening star < **wesperos*; akin to L. *vesper*; see VESPER], 1. of Hesperia; hence, 2. western; occidental. 3. [Poetic], of the Hesperides. *n.* [Rare], an inhabitant of Hesperia or any western land.
Hes·per·i·des (hes-per'ə-dēz'), *n.pl.* [*sing.* HESPERID (hes'pẽr-id)], [L. < Gr. *Hesperides* < *Hesperos*; see HESPERIAN], in *Greek mythology*, 1. the nymphs who guarded the golden apples given as a wedding gift by Gaea to Hera. 2. the garden where the apples grew.
hes·per·i·din (hes-per'ə-din), *n.* [< Mod. L. *hesperidium*, a fruit related to the orange (so named in allusion to the golden apples of the Hesperides); + *-in*], a crystalline glucoside, $C_{22}H_{26}O_{12}$, found in unripe citrus fruits.
Hes·per·us (hes'pẽr-əs), *n.* [L.; Gr. *Hesperos*; see HESPERIAN], the evening star, especially Venus.
Hess, Ru·dolf (rōō'dôlf hes), (*Walther Richard Rudolf Hess*), 1894– ; German Nazi official; sentenced to life imprisonment by Allied War Crimes Commission (1946).
Hesse (hes, hes'i), *n.* 1. a former kingdom and duchy of west central Germany. 2. later, a German state of western Germany: area, 2,969 sq. mi.; pop., 1,470,000 (1939); capital, Darmstadt. 3. a district of the United States zone of occupation, including the former province of Hesse-Nassau: pop., 4,050,000 (est. 1946). German name, *Hessen.*
Hes·sen (hes'ən), *n.* [G.] Hesse.
Hesse-Nas·sau (hes'nas'ô), *n.* a former province of Prussia: capital, Kassel: German name, *Hessen-Nassau.*
Hes·sian (hesh'ən), *adj.* of Hesse or its people. *n.* 1. a native or inhabitant of Hesse. 2. any of the Hessian mercenaries who fought for the British in the Revolutionary War.
Hessian boots, tasseled boots reaching almost to the knee, introduced into England by Hessian troops in the 19th century.
Hessian fly, a small, two-winged fly whose larvae destroy wheat crops.
hess·ite (hes'īt), *n.* [after G. H. *Hess* (1802–1850), Swiss chemist; + *-ite*], in *mineralogy*, silver telluride, Ag_2Te, found in gray, sectile masses.
hes·so·nite (hes'ə-nīt'), *n.* essonite.
hest (hest), *n.* [ME. *hest*; with unhistoric *-t* < AS. *hæs*, command (cf. BEHEST) < base of *hatan*, to call], 1. [Archaic], behest; bidding; order. 2. [Obs.], a pledge.
Hes·ter, Hes·ther (hes'tẽr), a feminine name: see **Esther.**
Hes·ti·a (hes'ti-ə), *n.* [Gr. *Hestia*], in *Greek mythology*, 1. the goddess of the hearth, identified with the Roman Vesta. 2. one of the nymphs guarding the golden apples of the Hesperides.
Hes·y·chast (hes'i-kast'), *n.* [ML. *hesychasta*; Gr. *hēsychastēs*, a quietist, hermit < *hēsychazein*, to be quiet < *hēsychos*, quiet], in *ecclesiastical history*, any member of a sect of mystics begun among the monks at Mt. Athos in the 14th century, dedicated to quietism.
he·tae·ra (hi-têr'ə), *n.* [*pl.* HETAERAE (-ē)], [Gr. *hetaira*, fem. of *hetairos*, companion], in ancient Greece,

a courtesan or concubine, usually an educated slave.
he·tae·rism (hi-têr′iz'm), *n.* [Gr. *hetairismos* < *hetairizein*, to be a hetaera; see HETAERA], 1. concubinage. 2. a system of communal marriage supposed to have been practiced in certain primitive tribes.
he·tai·ra (hi-tī′rə), *n.* [*pl.* HETAIRAI (-rī)], a hetaera.
he·tai·rism (hi-tī′riz'm), *n.* hetaerism.
het·er·o- (het′ēr-ō, het′ēr-ə), [Gr. *hetero-*, other, different < *heteros*, the other (of two), earlier *hateros* < IE. **sm̥-tero-* < base **sem-*, **sm̥-*, one, together (seen also in L. *semper*, *simplus*) + **-tero-*, expressing contrast, comparison], a combining form meaning *other*, *another*, *different*, as in *heterosexual*: opposed to *homo-*: also, before a vowel, **heter-**.
het·er·o·cer·cal (het′ēr-ə-sūr′k'l), *adj.* [< *hetero-* + Gr. *kerkos*, a tail; + *-al*], designating, of, or having a tail fin in which the upper lobe is larger than the lower and contains the upturned end of the spinal column, as in certain fishes.
het·er·o·chro·mat·ic (het′ēr-ə-krō-mat′ik), *adj.* [*hetero-* + *chromatic*], of, having, or consisting of different or contrasting colors; many-colored: opposed to *homochromatic*.
het·er·o·chrome (het′ēr-ə-krōm′), *adj.* heterochromatic.
het·er·o·chro·mo·some (het′ēr-ə-krō′mə-sōm′), *n.* an accessory chromosome, present in some germ cells, which passes over intact to only one of the daughter cells instead of being divided between the two; sex chromosome: it is thought to be the factor that determines the organism's sex.
het·er·o·clite (het′ēr-ə-klit′), *adj.* [Fr. *hétéroclite;* LL. *heteroclitus;* Gr. *heteroklitos*, irregularly inflected < *hetero-* (see HETERO-) + *klinein*, to bend, incline], departing from the standard or norm; abnormal; anomalous. *n.* 1. in *grammar*, a word, especially a noun, inflected irregularly. 2. [Rare], an anomaly.
het·er·o·clit·i·cal (het′ēr-ə-klit′i-k'l), *adj.* deviating from the standard or norm; heteroclite.
het·er·o·cy·clic (het′ēr-ə-sī′klik, het′ēr-ə-sik′lik), *adj.* [*hetero-* + *cyclic*], designating or of a cyclic molecular arrangement of atoms of carbon and other elements.
het·er·o·dox (het′ēr-ə-doks′), *adj.* [Gr. *heterodoxos* < *hetero-*, other + *doxa*, opinion], departing from or opposed to the usual beliefs or established doctrines, especially in religion; inclining toward heresy; unorthodox: opposed to *orthodox*.
het·er·o·dox·y (het′ēr-ə-dok′si), *n.* [*pl.* HETERODOXIES (-siz)], [Gr. *heterodoxia*], 1. the quality or fact of being heterodox. 2. a heterodox belief or doctrine.
het·er·o·dyne (het′ēr-ə-dīn′), *adj.* [*hetero-* + *dyne*], having to do with the combination of radio oscillations of somewhat different frequencies coupled in such a way as to produce beats whose frequency is the difference or sum of the frequencies of the combined oscillations. *v.t.* [HETERODYNED (-dīnd′), HETERODYNING], to combine (a series of waves) with a series of a somewhat different frequency, producing beats.
het·er·oe·cious (het′ēr-ē′shəs), *adj.* [< *hetero-* + Gr. *oikia*, a house, dwelling; + *-ous*], in *biology*, living as a parasite on first one host and then another.
het·er·oe·cism (het′ēr-ē′siz'm), *n.* the parasitism of heteroecious organisms.
het·er·o·ga·mete (het′ēr-ō-gə-mēt′, het′ēr-ō-gam′ēt), *n.* a gamete differentiated sexually or otherwise from another that it unites with, as most male and female gametes: opposed to *isogamete*.
het·er·og·a·mous (het′ēr-og′ə-məs), *adj.* 1. characterized by the uniting of heterogametes. 2. characterized by reproduction in which sexual and asexual generations alternate. 3. characterized by indirect pollination. 4. having flowers in which the stamens and pistils are irregularly arranged.
het·er·og·a·my (het′ēr-og′ə-mi), *n.* 1. the quality or state of being heterogamous. 2. reproduction in which sexual and asexual generations alternate. 3. indirect pollination.
het·er·o·ge·ne·i·ty (het′ēr-ō-jə-nē′ə-ti), *n.* [*pl.* HETEROGENEITIES (-tiz)], [Fr. *hétérogénéité;* ML. *heterogeneitas*], 1. the quality or condition of being heterogeneous; dissimilarity. 2. a heterogeneous element.
het·er·o·ge·ne·ous (het′ēr-ə-jē′ni-əs), *adj.* [ML. *heterogeneus;* Gr. *heterogenēs* < *hetero-*, other, different + *genos*, a race, kind], 1. differing or opposite in structure, quality, etc.; dissimilar; incongruous; foreign. 2. composed of unrelated or unlike elements or parts; varied; miscellaneous. Opposed to *homogeneous*.
het·er·o·gen·e·sis (het′ēr-ō-jen′ə-sis), *n.* [*hetero-* + *genesis*], 1. reproduction in which sexual and asexual generations alternate. 2. reproduction in which the parent bears offspring differing from itself: opposed to *homogenesis*. 3. spontaneous generation.
het·er·o·gen·ic (het′ēr-ō-jen′ik), *adj.* [*hetero-* + *-genic*], of different origin; not from the same source, individual, or species.
het·er·og·e·nous (het′ēr-oj′ə-nəs), *adj.* heterogenic.
het·er·og·o·nous (het′ēr-og′ə-nəs), *adj.* characterized by heterogony.
het·er·og·o·ny (het′ēr-og′ə-ni), *n.* [*hetero-* + *-gony*], 1. reproduction in which sexual and asexual generations alternate. 2. a condition in which two or more kinds of perfect flowers develop on the same plant.
het·er·o·graft (het′ēr-ō-graft′, het′ēr-ə-gräft′), *n.* a graft of skin, bone, etc. taken from another individual.
het·er·o·graph·ic (het′ēr-ō-graf′ik), *adj.* of or characterized by heterography.
het·er·og·ra·phy (het′ēr-og′rə-fi), *n.* [*hetero-* + *-graphy*], 1. spelling that differs from current standard usage. 2. spelling, as in modern English, in which the same letter does not always represent the same sound.
het·er·og·y·nous (het′ēr-oj′i-nəs), *adj.* [*hetero-* + *-gynous*], in *zoology*, having two classes of females, reproductive and nonreproductive: ants and bees are heterogynous.
het·er·ol·o·gous (het′ēr-ol′ə-gəs), *adj.* [< *hetero-* + Gr. *logos*, relation, proportion], consisting of differing elements or the same elements in varying proportions; differing; not corresponding: opposed to *homologous*.
het·er·ol·o·gy (het′ēr-ol′ə-ji), *n.* the state of being heterologous.
het·er·ol·y·sis (het′ēr-ol′ə-sis), *n.* [Mod. L.; see HETERO- & -LYSIS], the destruction of cells of one species by lysins or enzymes derived from cells of a different species.
het·er·om·er·ous (het′ēr-om′ēr-əs), *adj.* [*hetero-* + *-merous*], in *botany*, having a whorl or whorls with a different number of parts than that of the other whorls: opposed to *isomerous*.
het·er·o·mor·phic (het′ēr-ō-môr′fik), *adj.* [*hetero-* + *-morphic*], 1. differing from the standard type or form. 2. exhibiting different forms at various stages of development, as insects in the larval and pupal stages.
het·er·o·mor·phism (het′ēr-ō-môr′fiz'm), *n.* the quality or condition of being heteromorphic.
het·er·on·o·mous (het′ēr-on′ə-məs), *adj.* [< *hetero-* + Gr. *nomos*, custom, law], 1. subject to another's laws or rule: opposed to *autonomous*. 2. in *biology*, subject to different laws of growth; differentiated or specialized, as parts or organs.
het·er·on·o·my (het′ēr-on′ə-mi), *n.* [*hetero-* + *-nomy*], the quality or condition of being heteronomous.
het·er·o·nym (het′ēr-ə-nim′), *n.* [< *heteronymous*, after *synonym*], 1. a word with the same spelling as another but with a different meaning and pronunciation (e.g., *tear*, a drop of water from the eye, *tear*, to pull apart, rip). 2. a name (of something) in one language that is an exact translation of the name in another language (e.g., German *Fernsprecher*, lit., far speaker, English *telephone*).
het·er·on·y·mous (het′ēr-on′ə-məs), *adj.* [Gr. *heterōnymos* < *hetero-*, other, different + *onyma*, name], 1. of, or having the nature of, a heteronym. 2. having different names, as a pair of correlatives: as, *son* and *daughter* are *heteronymous*. 3. in *optics*, designating or of the two crossed images of something seen when the eyes are focused at a point beyond it.
Het·er·o·ou·si·an (het′ēr-ō-ōō′si-ən, het′ēr-ō-ou′si-ən), *adj.* [Gr. *heteroousios* < *hetero-*, different + *ousia*, essence], in *theology & church history*, designating, of, or holding the theory that God the Father and God the Son are different in substance. *n.* an adherent of this theory; Arian. Opposed to *Homoousian*, *Homoiousian*.
het·er·o·phyl·lous (het′ēr-ō-fil′əs), *adj.* [*hetero-* + *-phyllous*], growing leaves of different forms on the same stem or plant.
het·er·o·plas·ty (het′ēr-ō-plas′ti), *n.* [*hetero-* + *-plasty*], plastic surgery in which tissue from one individual is grafted onto another.
het·er·o·sex·u·al (het′ēr-ō-sek′shōō-əl), *adj.* 1. of or characterized by sexual desire for those of the opposite sex. 2. in *biology*, of different sexes. *n.* a heterosexual individual. Opposed to *homosexual*.
het·er·o·sex·u·al·i·ty (het′ēr-ō-sek′shōō-al′ə-ti), *n.* 1. sexual desire for those of the opposite sex. 2. sexual relations between individuals of opposite sex. Opposed to *homosexuality*.
het·er·os·po·rous (het′ēr-os′pēr-əs, het′ēr-ō-spôr′əs, het′ēr-ə-spō′rəs), *adj.* producing more than one kind of asexual spore; especially, producing microspores and megaspores: opposed to *homosporous*.
het·er·o·tax·i·a (het′ēr-ō-tak′si-ə), *n.* [Mod. L. < *hetero-* + Gr. *-taxia* < *taxis*, arrangement], the abnormal position or arrangement of all or some of the internal organs of the body.
het·er·o·tax·is (het′ēr-ō-tak′sis), *n.* heterotaxia.
het·er·o·tax·y (het′ēr-ō-tak′si), *n.* heterotaxia.
het·er·o·to·pi·a (het′ēr-ō-tō′pi-ə), *n.* [Mod. L. < *hetero-* + Gr. *topos*, place], the displacement of an organ or part in the body.
het·er·ot·o·py (het′ēr-ot′ə-pi), *n.* heterotopia.
het·er·o·troph·ic (het′ēr-ō-trof′ik), *adj.* [< *hetero-* + Gr. *trophikos*, nursing < *trephein*, to nourish], obtaining food from organic material; unable to use inorganic matter to form proteins and carbohydrates.
het·er·o·typ·ic (het′ēr-ō-tip′ik), *adj.* [*hetero-* + *typic*], designating or of the first meiotic division of a germ cell.
het·er·o·typ·i·cal (het′ēr-ō-tip′i-k'l), *adj.* heterotypic.
het·er·o·zy·gote (het′ēr-ō-zī′gōt, het′ēr-ō-zig′ōt), *n.* [*hetero-* + *zygote*], in Mendel's theory of heredity, a plant or animal having one or more recessive character-

istics and hence not breeding true to type; hybrid: opposed to *homozygote*.
het·man (het'mən), *n.* [*pl.* HETMANS (-mənz)], [Pol. < G. *hauptmann*, a captain, lit., head man < *haupt*, head + *mann*, man], 1. formerly, a Polish military commander. 2. a Cossack chief or leader; ataman.
Het·ty (het'i), a feminine name: see **Henrietta.**
het up (het), [*het*, dial. p.t. & pp. of *heat*], [Slang], excited.
heu·land·ite (hū'lən-dīt'), *n.* [after Henry *Heuland*, Eng. collector of minerals; + *-ite*], a hydrated silicate of calcium and aluminum, $CaAl_2Si_6O_{16}\cdot5H_2O$, occurring as crystals of various colors with pearly luster.
heu·ris·tic (hyoo-ris'tik), *adj.* [< Gr. *heuriskein*, to invent, discover], helping to discover or learn: sometimes used to designate a method of education in which the pupil is trained to find out things for himself.
hew (hū), *v.t.* [HEWED (hūd), HEWED or HEWN (hūn), HEWING], [ME. *hewen;* AS. *heawan;* akin to G. *hauen;* IE. base **qāu-, *qeu-*, to hew, strike, seen also in L. *caudex, codex* (cf. CODEX, CODICIL), *cudere*, to strike (in Eng. *-cute, -cuss*); cf. HAY], 1. to chop or cut with an ax, knife, etc.; hack; gash. 2. to make or shape by or as by cutting or chopping with an ax, etc. (often with *out*). 3. to chop (a tree) with an ax so as to cause it to fall (usually with *down*). *v.i.* to make cutting or chopping blows with an ax, knife, etc.
hewn (hūn), [ME. *hewen;* AS. *heawen*], alternative past participle of **hew.** *adj.* cut or formed by hewing.
hex (heks), *n.* [G. *hexe*, fem., *hexer*, masc.; OHG. *hagazussa*, akin to AS. *hægtesse;* see HAG (witch)], 1. [Dial.], a witch or sorcerer. 2. [Colloq.], something supposed to bring bad luck; jinx. *v.t.* [Colloq.], to bewitch; jinx.
hex·a- (hek'sə), [< Gr. *hex*, six; see SIX], a combining form meaning *six*, as in *hexagram, hexameter*: also, before a vowel, **hex-.**
hex·a·bas·ic (hek'sə-bās'ik), *adj.* [*hexa-* + *basic*], 1. designating an acid having in each molecule six hydrogen atoms that are replaceable by basic radicals or atoms. 2. containing in each molecule six atoms of a univalent metal or the equivalent in combining capacity.
hex·a·chord (hek'sə-kôrd'), *n.* [< *hexa-* + Gr. *chordē*, a string, chord], in *medieval music*, a diatonic scale of six tones, with a semitone between the third and the fourth.
hex·ad (hek'sad), *n.* [LL. *hexas, hexadis;* Gr. *hexas, hexados*, the number six < *hex*, six; see SIX], 1. a series or group of six. 2. in *chemistry*, an element or radical with a valence of six.
hex·ad·ic (hek-sad'ik), *adj.* of, or having the nature of, a hexad.
hex·a·em·er·on (hek'sə-em'ẽr-on), *n.* [LL.; Gr. *hexaēmeron* < *hexaēmeros*, of or in six days < *hex*, six + *hēmera*, day], 1. in the *Bible*, *a)* the six-day period of the Creation. *b)* a history of this, as in Genesis. 2. a treatise dealing with the Creation. Also **hexahemeron, hexameron.**
hex·a·gon (hek'sə-gon'), *n.* [L. *hexagonum;* Gr. *hexagōnon*, hexagon, neut. of *hexagōnos*, six-cornered < *hex*, six + *gōnia*, a corner, angle], a plane figure with six angles and six sides.
hex·ag·o·nal (hek-sag'ə-n'l), *adj.* 1. of, or having the form of, a hexagon. 2. having a six-sided base or section: said of a solid figure. 3. in *crystallography*, designating or of a system having six-sided forms.
hex·a·gram (hek'sə-gram'), *n.* [*hexa-* + *-gram*], 1. a six-pointed star formed by extending the sides of a regular hexagon, or by placing one equilateral triangle over another so that corresponding sides intersect: see **Star of David.** 2. any figure of six lines.
hex·a·he·dral (hek'sə-hē'drəl), *adj.* of, or having the form of, a hexahedron.
hex·a·he·dron (hek'sə-hē'drən), *n.* [*pl.* HEXAHEDRONS (-drənz), HEXAHEDRA (-drə)], [Mod. L.; see HEXA- & -HEDRON], a solid figure with six plane surfaces.
hex·a·hem·er·on (hek'sə-hem'ẽr-on), *n.* hexaemeron.
hex·a·hy·drate (hek'sə-hī'drāt), *n.* a hydrate containing six gram-molecular weights of water per gram-molecular weight of the substance combined with the water.
hex·a·hy·dric (hek'sə-hī'drik), *adj.* containing six hydroxyl radicals: as, a *hexahydric* alcohol.
hex·am·er·on (hek-sam'ẽr-on), *n.* hexaemeron.
hex·am·er·ous (hek-sam'ẽr-əs), *adj.* [*hexa-* + *-merous*], having six parts in each whorl: said of flowers: also written **6-merous.**
hex·am·e·ter (hek-sam'ə-tẽr), *n.* [ME. *exametron;* L. *hexameter;* Gr. *hexametros;* see HEXA- & METER (rhythm)], 1. a line of verse containing six metrical feet or measures; usually, the six-foot dactylic line of classical verse, the first four feet of which may be either dactyls or spondees, the fifth a dactyl, and the sixth a spondee or trochee. 2. verse consisting of hexameters. *adj.* having six metrical feet or measures.
hex·a·meth·yl·ene·tet·ra·mine (hek'sə-meth'ə-lēn-tet'rə-mēn'), *n.* [*hexamethylene* + *tetramine*], a crystalline compound, $C_6H_{12}N_4$, used to speed up the vulcanization of rubber and, in medicine, as a urinary antiseptic.
hex·a·met·ric (hek'sə-met'rik), *adj.* 1. of hexameter. 2. arranged in hexameters.
hex·ane (hek'sān, hek-sān'), *n.* [*hex-* + *-ane*], any of the five colorless, volatile, liquid hydrocarbons, C_6H_{14}, of the paraffin series.
hex·ang·u·lar (hek-saŋ'gyoo-lẽr), *adj.* [*hex-* + *angular*], having six angles.
hex·a·pla (hek'sə-plə), *n.pl.* [construed as sing.], [Mod. L.; Gr. *hexapla*, neut. pl. of *hexaploos, hexaplous*, sixfold < *hex*, six + base *-plo-*, fold], 1. an edition having six versions arranged in parallel columns. 2. [H-], Origen's edition of the Old Testament.
hex·a·pod (hek'sə-pod'), *n.* [*hexa-* + *-pod*], an invertebrate animal with six feet; especially, any of the true insects. *adj.* having six feet.
hex·ap·o·dous (hek-sap'ə-dəs), *adj.* hexapod.
hex·ap·o·dy (hek-sap'ə-di), *n.* [*pl.* HEXAPODIES (-diz)], a line of verse having six metrical feet; hexameter.
hex·arch·y (hek'sär-ki), *n.* [*pl.* HEXARCHIES (-kiz)], [*hex-* + *-archy*], a group of six friendly or allied states or governments.
hex·a·stich (hek'sə-stik'), *n.* [< L. *hexastichus*, of six lines or rows; Gr. *hexastichos* < *hex*, six + *stichos*, a line, row, verse], a poem or stanza of six lines.
Hex·a·teuch (hek'sə-tōōk', hek'sə-tūk'), *n.* [< *hexa-* + Gr. *teuchos*, book, after *Pentateuch, Heptateuch*], the first six books of the Old Testament.
hex·a·va·lent (hek'sə-vā'lənt), *adj.* 1. having a valence of six. 2. having six valences. Also, esp. for 2, **sexivalent.**
hex·en·be·sen (hek'sən-bā'z'n), *n.* [G. < *hexe* (see HEX) + *besen* (see BESOM)], an abnormal growth of shoots at the ends of branches, usually caused by certain fungi; witches'-broom.
hex·one (hek'sōn), *n.* [*hex-* + *-one*], a colorless liquid, $C_6H_{12}O$, used as a solvent for gums, resins, etc. *adj.* designating a group of organic bases containing six carbon atoms in each molecule, formed by the hydrolysis of proteins.
hex·o·san (hek'sə-san'), *n.* [< *hexose* + *-an*], any of a group of polysaccharides that form hexoses when hydrolyzed.
hex·ose (hek'sōs), *n.* [*hex-* + *-ose*], any of a group of simple sugars containing six carbon atoms in each molecule, as dextrose or fructose.
hex·yl (hek'sil), *n.* [*hex-* + *-yl*], the univalent hydrocarbon radical C_6H_{13}.
hex·yl·res·or·cin·ol (hek'sil-re-zôr'si-nōl'), *n.* [*hexyl* + *resorcinol*], a nonpoisonous, pale-yellow, crystalline substance, $C_6H_{13}C_6H_3(OH)_2$, used as an antiseptic and germicide.
hey (hā), *interj.* [ME. *hei;* echoic formation akin to G. & D. *hei*, etc.], an exclamation used to attract attention, express surprise, etc., or in asking a question.
hey·day (hā'dā'), *n.* [prob. ME. *hey*, high + *day*], the time of greatest health, vigor, beauty, prosperity, etc.; prime. *interj.* [earlier *heyda* < (or akin to) G. & Dan. *heida*, D. *heidaar*, hey there! (see HEY)], an exclamation of surprise, joy, or wonder.
Hey·se, Paul von (poul fôn hī'zə), 1830–1914; German novelist, dramatist, and poet; received Nobel prize in literature, 1910.
Hey·wood, John (hā'wood), 1497?–1580?; English writer of interludes, epigrams, proverbs, etc.
Heywood, Thomas, 1570?–1650?; English dramatist, poet, and actor.
Hez·e·ki·ah (hez'ə-kī'ə), [Heb. *ḥizqīyāh*, lit., God strengthens], a masculine name. *n.* in the *Bible*, any of several persons of the Old Testament; especially, a king of Judah, contemporary with the prophet Isaiah: II Kings 18–20.
Hf, in *chemistry*, hafnium.
hf., half.
H.F., high-frequency.
hf. mor., half-morocco.
Hg, *hydrargyrum*, [L.], in *chemistry*, mercury.
HG., H.G., High German.
hg., hectogram; hectograms.
H.G., 1. His (or Her) Grace. 2. Home Guard.
hgt., height.
H.H., 1. His (or Her) Highness. 2. His Holiness.
hhd., hogshead.
H-Hour, (āch'our'), *n.* in *military usage*, the exact but unspecified hour at which a military operation is to begin: see also **D-Day.**
hi (hī), *interj.* 1. [contr. < *hiya*, contr. < *how are you?*], an exclamation of greeting. 2. an exclamation used to call attention.
H.I., Hawaiian Islands.
Hi·a·le·ah (hī'ə-lē'ə), *n.* a city in southeastern Florida, near Miami: pop., 67,000.
hi·a·tus (hī-ā'təs), *n.* [*pl.* HIATUSES (-iz), HIATUS], [L., pp. of *hiare*, to gape], 1. a break or gap where a part

is missing or lost, as in a manuscript; blank space; lacuna. 2. a slight pause in pronunciation between two successive vowels in adjacent words or syllables, as between the successive *e*'s in *he entered* and *re-enter*.

Hi·a·wa·tha (hī'ə-wô'thə, hē'ə-wä'thə), ***n.*** 1. a Mohawk Indian chief who was responsible for the confederation of the Five Nations (the Iroquois League). 2. the Indian hero of *The Song of Hiawatha*, a long narrative poem (1855) by Longfellow.

hi·ba·chi (hi-bä'chi), ***n.*** [*pl.* HIBACHIS (-chiz)], [Japan. < *hi*, fire + *hachi*, bowl], a charcoal-burning brazier and grill of Japanese design.

Hib·bing (hib'iŋ), ***n.*** a city in northeastern Minnesota: pop., 18,000.

hi·ber·nac·u·lum (hī'bẽr-nak'yoo-ləm), ***n.*** [*pl.* HIBERNACULA (-lə)], [L., winter residence < *hibernare;* see HIBERNATE], any natural covering for protecting an organism during the winter; specifically, *a*) a bud or bulb for protecting a plant in embryo. *b*) a specially modified bud of a fresh-water polyzoan, which can develop into a colony in the spring.

hi·ber·nal (hī-bũr'nəl), ***adj.*** [L. *hibernalis* < *hibernus*, wintry], of winter; wintry.

hi·ber·nate (hī'bẽr-nāt'), ***v.i.*** [HIBERNATED (-id), HIBERNATING], [< L. *hibernatus*, pp. of *hibernare*, to pass the winter < *hibernus*, wintry], 1. to spend the winter. 2. to spend the winter in a dormant state: opposed to *aestivate*.

hi·ber·na·tion (hī'bẽr-nā'shən), ***n.*** the habit or state of hibernating.

Hi·ber·ni·a (hī-bũr'ni-ə), ***n.*** [L.; altered < *Iverna, Juverna* < OCelt. **Iverin*, whence OIr. *Erin;* see ERIN], [Poetic], Ireland.

Hi·ber·ni·an (hī-bũr'ni-ən), ***adj.*** [see prec. entry], [Poetic], Irish. ***n.*** [Poetic], an Irishman.

Hi·ber·ni·cism (hī-bũr'nə-siz'm), ***n.*** [< *Hibernia* + *-ic* + *-ism*], an Irish characteristic, custom, idiom, etc.

hi·bis·cus (hī-bis'kəs, hi-bis'kəs), ***n.*** [L.; Gr. *hibiskos*, marsh mallow], any of a group of plants, shrubs, and small trees of the mallow family, with large, colorful flowers; rose mallow.

hic·cup, hic·cough (hik'əp), ***n.*** [Early Mod. Eng. *hikop, hickock*, vars. of *hicket;* akin to or < Walloon Fr. *hikett* (cf. MD. *huckup*, OFr. *hoquet*) < echoic base **hick-* + dim. suffix; *hiccough* is a late sp. after *cough*], 1. a sudden, involuntary contraction of the diaphragm that closes the glottis at the moment of breathing in. 2. the sharp, quick sound made by this. ***v.i.*** to make a hiccup or hiccups. ***v.t.*** to utter with a hiccup.

‡**hic ja·cet** (hik jā'sit), [L.], 1. here lies: inscribed on tombstones: abbreviated **H.J.** 2. an epitaph.

hick (hik), ***n.*** [altered < *Richard*], [Colloq.], a person having the awkwardness, simplicity, and lack of sophistication regarded as characteristic of people from the country; rustic; hayseed: somewhat contemptuous term. ***adj.*** [Colloq.], of or like a hick or hicks.

hick·ey (hik'i), ***n.*** [orig. U.S. dial., prob. for *doohickey*], a device; gadget; specifically, *a*) a tool used for bending pipe. *b*) a coupling for electrical fixtures.

Hick·ok, James Butler (hik'ok), 1837–1876; American frontier scout and United States marshal: called *Wild Bill Hickok*.

hick·o·ry (hik'ẽr-i), ***n.*** [*pl.* HICKORIES (-iz)], [shortened < 17th-c. *pohickery* (Virginian term) < Am. Ind. *powcohicora*, product made from crushed kernels of the nut], 1. any of a group of American trees of the walnut family, with large leaves, greenish flowers, and smooth-shelled nuts. 2. the hard, tough wood of any of these trees. 3. a switch or cane of this wood. 4. the nut of any of these trees: also **hickory nut**.

hid (hid), [ME.; AS. *hydde*], past tense and alternative past participle of **hide** (conceal).

Hi·dal·go (hi-dal'gō; Mex. Sp. ē-däl'gô), ***n.*** a state of central Mexico: pop., 994,000; capital, Pachuca.

hi·dal·go (hi-dal'gō; Sp. ē-däl'gô), ***n.*** [*pl.* HIDALGOS (-gōz; Sp. -gôs)], [Sp., contr. of *hijo de algo*, son of something; *hijo*, son + *de*, of + *algo*, something], in Spain, a nobleman of secondary rank, below that of a grandee.

hid·den (hid''n), [ME., for AS. *gehydd*], alternative past participle of **hide** (conceal). ***adj.*** concealed; obscure; not seen or known; secret; mysterious.

hid·den·ite (hid''n-īt'), ***n.*** [after W. E. *Hidden*, who discovered it in 1879], an emerald-green variety of spodumene, a semiprecious stone.

hide (hīd), ***v.t.*** [HID (hid), HIDDEN (hid''n) or HID, HIDING (hīd'iŋ)], [ME. *hiden;* AS. *hydan* (< **hūd-jan*); IE. *(*s*)*qeu-dh* < base *(*s*)*qeu-*, to cut, cut off, seen in *hide* (skin); prob. basic sense "to cover (as with skin)"], 1. to put or keep out of sight; secrete; conceal. 2. to conceal from the knowledge of others; keep secret; not reveal. 3. to keep from being seen by covering up, obscuring, etc.; obstruct the view or sight of. 4. to turn away: as, he *hid* his head in shame. ***v.i.*** 1. to be or lie out of sight or concealed. 2. to keep oneself out of sight; conceal oneself.

SYN.—**hide**, the general word, refers to the putting of something in a place where it will not easily be seen or found (the view is *hidden* by the billboard); **conceal**, a somewhat formal equivalent for **hide**, more often connotes intent (to *conceal* one's face, motives, etc.); **secrete** and **cache** suggest a careful hiding in a secret place (they *secreted*, or *cached*, the loot in the cellar), but **cache** now often refers merely to a storing for safekeeping (let's *cache* our supplies in the cave); **bury** implies a covering for, or as if for, concealment (to *bury* treasure, they were *buried* in the landslide).—***ANT.*** reveal, expose.

hide (hīd), ***n.*** [ME.; AS. *hid, hyd* (< **hūdi-*); akin to G. *haut;* IE. *(*s*)*qeu-t* < base *(*s*)*qeu-*, to cut, cut off, seen also in Gr. *kūtos*, L. *cutis*, skin (cf. CUTICLE)], 1. an animal skin or pelt, either raw or tanned. 2. [Colloq.], the human skin: now humorous or contemptuous. ***v.t.*** [HIDED (-id), HIDING], 1. to take the hide off; skin. 2. [Colloq.], to beat severely; thrash; flog. —***SYN.*** see **skin**.

neither hide nor hair, nothing whatsoever.

hide (hīd), ***n.*** [ME.; AS. *hid*, earlier *higid* < base of *higan, hiwan*, members of a household (akin to OHG. *hīwo*, a husband, master of a household); basic sense "enough land to support a family"; IE. base **k̑ei-*, to lie, hence to stay in, settle in (a place), seen also in L. *civis*, citizen (cf. CIVIL, CITY)], an old English measure of land, varying from 80 to 120 acres.

hide-and-seek (hīd'ən-sēk'), ***n.*** a children's game in which some players hide and others then try to find them: also **hide-and-go-seek**.

hide·bound (hīd'bound'), ***adj.*** 1. having the hide tight over the bone and muscle structure of the body: said of animals. 2. obstinately conservative and narrow-minded. 3. having the bark so close that growth is interfered with: said of trees.

hid·e·ous (hid'i-əs), ***adj.*** [ME. & Anglo-Fr. *hidous;* OFr. *hidos, hideus* < *hide, hisde*, fright], horrible to look at, hear, etc.; very ugly; revolting; dreadful.

hid·e·ous·ly (hid'i-əs-li), ***adv.*** 1. in a hideous manner. 2. to a hideous extent.

hide-out (hīd'out'), ***n.*** [Colloq.], a hiding place for gangsters, etc.

hid·ing (hīd'iŋ), ***n.*** [ME. *hidinge*], 1. *a*) the act of one that hides. *b*) the condition of being hidden: usually in the phrase *in hiding*. 2. a place to hide.

hid·ing (hīd'iŋ), ***n.*** [< *hide* (beat)], [Colloq.], a severe beating; thrashing; flogging.

hi·dro·sis (hi-drō'sis), ***n.*** [Mod. L. < Gr. *hidroun*, to perspire, sweat < *hidrōs*, sweat], 1. perspiration; sweating. 2. excessive sweating. 3. any skin condition characterized by excessive sweating.

hi·drot·ic (hi-drot'ik), ***adj.*** [ML. *hidroticus;* Gr. *hidrotikos* < *hidrōs*, sweat], 1. having to do with sweat. 2. causing sweat; sudorific. ***n.*** a sudorific drug.

hie (hī), ***v.i. & v.t.*** [HIED (hīd), HIEING or HYING], [ME. *hien;* AS. *higian*, to strive, hasten; IE. **k̑ei-gh*, to leap, or **k̑ei-g*, to pant, gasp for air (seen also in D. *hijgen*, to strive, Dan. *hige*, to strive for, orig. gasp for air)], to speed; hasten: often used reflexively.

hi·e·mal (hī'i-məl), ***adj.*** [L. *hiemalis*, of winter < *hiems*, winter], of winter; wintry.

hier- (hī'ẽr), hiero-.

hi·er·arch (hī'ẽr-ärk'), ***n.*** [ML. *hierarcha;* Gr. *hierarchēs*, keeper of sacred things < *hieros*, sacred + *archos*, ruler < *archein*, to rule, lead], the leader or chief of a religious group or society; high priest.

hi·er·ar·chal (hī'ẽr-är'k'l), ***adj.*** of a hierarch or hierarchy.

hi·er·ar·chic (hī'ẽr-är'kik), ***adj.*** hierarchical.

hi·er·ar·chi·cal (hī'ẽr-är'ki-k'l), ***adj.*** of a hierarchy.

hi·er·ar·chism (hī'ẽr-är'kiz'm), ***n.*** the principles, practices, or authority of a hierarchy.

hi·er·arch·y (hī'ẽr-är'ki), ***n.*** [*pl.* HIERARCHIES (-kiz)], [Early Mod. Eng. *yerarchy;* ME. *gerarchie;* OFr. *jerarchie;* LL. *ierarchia*, for *hierarchia;* Gr. *hierarchia*, power or rule of a hierarch < *hierarchēs* (see HIERARCH); now spelled after LL. & Gr.], 1. a system of church government by priests or other clergy in graded ranks. 2. the group of officials in such a system. 3. a group of persons or things arranged in order of rank, grade, class, etc. 4. in *theology*, *a*) any of the three divisions of angels. *b*) all the angels.

hi·er·at·ic (hī'ə-rat'ik), ***adj.*** [L. *hieraticus;* Gr. *hieratikos*, of a priest's office, sacerdotal < *hieros*, sacred], 1. of or used by priests; priestly; sacerdotal. 2. designating or of the abridged form of cursive hieroglyphic writing once used by Egyptian priests.

hi·er·at·i·cal (hī'ə-rat'i-k'l), ***adj.*** hieratic.

hi·er·o- (hī'ẽr-ō), [< Gr. *hieros*, sacred, holy], a combining form meaning *sacred, holy*, as in *hierocracy, hierology:* also, before a vowel, **hier-**.

hi·er·oc·ra·cy (hī'ə-rok'rə-si), ***n.*** [*pl.* HIEROCRACIES (-siz)], [*hiero-* + *-cracy*], government by priests or other clergy; a hierarchy.

hi·er·o·crat·ic (hī'ẽr-ə-krat'ik), ***adj.*** of or characterized by hierocracy.

hi·er·o·crat·i·cal (hī'ẽr-ə-krat'i-k'l), ***adj.*** hierocratic.

hi·er·o·dule (hī'ẽr-ə-dūl'), ***n.*** [LL. *hierodulus;* Gr. *hierodoulos* < *hieron*, temple + *doulos*, slave], in ancient Greece, a temple slave, dedicated to the service of a god.

hi·er·o·glyph (hī'ẽr-ə-glif', hī'rə-glif'), ***n.*** [Fr. *hiéroglyphe*], a hieroglyphic.

hi·er·o·glyph·ic (hī'ẽr-ə-glif'ik, hī'rə-glif'ik), *adj.* [Fr. *hiéroglyphique;* LL. *hieroglyphicus;* Gr. *hieroglyphikos* < *hieros,* sacred + *glyphein,* to carve, hollow out], 1. of, or having the nature of, hieroglyphics. 2. written in hieroglyphics. 3. symbolical; emblematic. 4. hard to read or understand. *n.* 1. a picture or symbol representing a word, syllable, or sound, used by the ancient Egyptians and others instead of alphabetic letters. 2. *usually pl.* a method of writing using hieroglyphics; picture writing. 3. a symbol, sign, etc. hard to understand. 4. *pl.* writing hard to decipher.

HIEROGLYPHICS
(Translation: "I sent: I order that you reduce and crush all the high officers of Tsahi. I cast them together with all their possessions at thy feet.")

hi·er·o·glyph·i·cal (hī'ẽr-ə-glif'i-k'l, hī'rə-glif'i-k'l), *adj.* hieroglyphic.

hi·er·og·ly·phist (hī'ẽr-og'li-fist, hī-rog'li-fist), *n.* an expert or specialist in interpreting hieroglyphics.

hi·er·ol·o·gy (hī'ẽr-ol'ə-ji), *n.* [*hiero-* + *-logy*], the religious lore and religious literature of a people.

Hi·er·o·nym·i·an (hī'ẽr-ə-nim'i-ən), *adj.* Hieronymic.

Hi·er·o·nym·ic (hī'ẽr-ə-nim'ik), *adj.* [< L. *Hieronymus,* Jerome; + *-ic*], of or done by Saint Jerome.

Hi·er·on·y·mite (hī'ə-ron'ə-mīt'), *n.* [< L. *Hieronymus,* Jerome; + *-ite*], a member of any of the hermit orders named after Saint Jerome.

Hi·er·on·y·mus (hī'ə-ron'ə-məs), see **Jerome**, Saint.

hi·er·o·phant (hī'ẽr-ə-fant', hī-er'ə-fant'), *n.* [LL. *hierophanta;* Gr. *hierophantēs* < *hieros,* sacred + *phainein,* to show], 1. formerly, a priest who presided at sacred mysteries; especially, the high priest of the Eleusinian mysteries in Greek religion. 2. an interpreter of sacred mysteries or esoteric principles.

hi·er·o·phan·tic (hī'ẽr-ə-fan'tik), *adj.* of or like a hierophant or his acts.

hi-fi (hī'fī'), *adj.* of or having high fidelity of sound reproduction.

Hig·gin·son, Thomas Went·worth (went'wẽrth hig'in-s'n), 1823–1911; American writer and social reformer.

hig·gle (hig''l), *v.i.* [HIGGLED (-'ld), HIGGLING], [prob. weakened form of *haggle*], to argue about terms, price, etc.; haggle; chaffer; wrangle.

hig·gle·dy-pig·gle·dy (hig''l-di-pig''l-di), *adv.* [extension of Early Mod. Eng. *higle-pigle,* redupl. formation, prob. after *pig*], in disorder; in jumbled confusion. *adj.* disorderly; jumbled; confused. *n.* [*pl.* HIGGLEDY-PIGGLEDIES (-diz)], disorder; jumble; confusion.

hig·gler (hig'lẽr), *n.* a person who higgles.

high (hī), *adj.* [ME. *heigh, heh,* & (with loss of final fricative) *hie;* AS. (Anglian) *heh;* akin to G. *hoch;* IE. base **qeu-,* to curve, bend, as also in G. *hügel,* hill], 1. lofty; tall; of more than normal height: not used of persons. 2. extending upward a (specified) distance. 3. *a*) situated far above the ground or some other level. *b*) designating or of highland regions: as, *High* German. 4. reaching to or done from a height: as, a *high* jump, a *high* dive. 5. *a*) above other persons or things in rank, position, etc.; most important. *b*) above other persons or things in quality, character, etc.; superior; excellent. 6. grave; very serious: as, *high* treason. 7. intellectually advanced; complex; profound: usually in the comparative degree, as, *higher* mathematics. 8. main; principal; chief: as, a *high* priest. 9. greater in size, amount, degree, power, intensity, etc. than usual: as, *high* stakes. 10. expensive; costly. 11. luxurious and extravagant: as, *high* living. 12. haughty; overbearing. 13. advanced to its acme or fullness; fully reached: as, *high* noon. 14. designating or producing tones made by relatively fast vibrations; acute in pitch; sharp; shrill. 15. slightly tainted; having a strong smell: as, this meat is *high.* 16. extreme or inflexible in matters of ceremony, doctrine, etc. 17. hilarious; elated: as, *high* spirits; hence, 18. [Slang], drunk; intoxicated. 19. in *geography,* designating a latitude far from the equator. 20. in *machinery,* of, or in adjustment at, the highest transmission ratio: said of gears. 21. in *phonetics,* produced with part of the tongue raised toward the roof of the mouth: said of a vowel. *adv.* 1. in a high manner. 2. in or to a high level, place, degree, rank, etc. *n.* 1. a high level, place, etc. 2. an area of high barometric pressure. 3. an arrangement of gears giving the greatest speed. Abbreviated **H., h.**

fly high, to have high hopes or ambitions.

high and dry, 1. out of the reach of the water. 2. alone and helpless; stranded.

high and low, everywhere.

high and mighty, [Colloq.], arrogant; haughty.

on high, 1. up in space; high above. 2. in heaven.

SYN.—**high** refers to something which has greater extension upward than is normal for its kind, or which is placed at a relatively great distance above the given level (a *high* mountain, *high* clouds), but is never used of persons; **tall** is more or less equivalent to **high** but specifically implies relatively small breadth or width (a *tall* woman); **lofty** and **towering** suggest great, imposing, or conspicuous height (*lofty* peaks, a *towering* castle).—*ANT.* low, short.

high·ball (hī'bôl'), *n.* [sense 1 ? *high* + *ball,* bartender's slang for "whisky glass"; ? influenced by the *v.*], 1. liquor, usually whisky or brandy, mixed with soda water, ginger ale, etc. and served with ice in a tall glass: also **high ball.** 2. a railroad signal, originally a ball hung above the tracks, meaning "go ahead": sometimes used figuratively. *v.i.* [< *n.* 2], [Slang], to proceed at great speed.

high·bind·er (hī'bīn'dẽr), *n.* [< ?], [Slang], 1. a ruffian; gangster. 2. formerly, any of a gang of criminals from the Chinese section of a city who were believed to hire themselves out as assassins.

high blower, a horse, with sound lungs, that blows considerably, as when galloping or under excitement.

high·born (hī'bôrn'), *adj.* of noble birth.

high·boy (hī'boi'), *n.* [*high* + *boy*], a high chest of drawers mounted on legs.

high·bred (hī'bred'), *adj.* 1. of superior stock or breed. 2. showing good breeding; well-mannered; courteous and cultivated.

high-brow, high·brow (hī'brou'), *n.* [Slang], a person having or pretending to have highly cultivated, intellectual tastes; intellectual. *adj.* [Slang], of or fit for such a person. Usually a term of contempt or derision.

high·chair (hī'châr'), *n.* a baby's chair with a tray, mounted on long legs.

High-Church (hī'chûrch'), *adj.* of or like the High Church; stressing formality and ritual in religious observance.

HIGHBOY

High Church, that party of the Anglican Church which emphasizes the importance of the priesthood, rituals, and sacraments, and holds to a more orthodox doctrine than the other Protestant churches: opposed to *Low Church, Broad Church.*

high-class (hī'klas', hī'kläs'), *adj.* of a superior class, rank, quality, etc.: sometimes used colloquially in contempt or derision.

high-col·ored (hī'kul'ẽrd), *adj.* 1. brilliant in color. 2. flushed; florid. 3. vivid. 4. exaggerated; lurid.

high comedy, comedy appealing to, and reflecting the life of, the upper social classes, characterized by witty, and often sophisticated, dialogue; comedy of manners; now often applied to comedy with serious aims, which seeks to provoke thoughtful amusement.

high day, [ME.; cf. HEYDAY, *n.*], a festival day; holiday.

higher education, college or university education.

high·er-up (hī'ẽr-up'), *n.* [Colloq.], a person of higher rank or position.

high-ex·plo·sive (hī'iks-plō'siv), *adj.* of, containing, or having the nature of, a high explosive.

high explosive, any explosive in which the combustion of the particles is so rapid as to be virtually simultaneous throughout the entire mass, so that it has great shattering effect: abbreviated **HE, H.E.**

high·fa·lu·tin, high·fa·lu·ting (hī'fə-lōō't'n, hī'fə-lū't'n), *n.* [? altered < *high-flown* or, more prob., < *high-floating,* with insertion of intrusive vowel in ridicule of oratorical speech], [Colloq.], high-flown, pompous language. *adj.* [Colloq.], high-flown; pretentious.

high fidelity, in radio, sound recording, etc., an approximately exact reproduction of sound achieved by the use of a wide range of sound waves, from 50 to 15,000 (or more) cycles.

high·fli·er, high·fly·er (hī'flī'ẽr), *n.* 1. a person or thing that flies high. 2. a person who acts, talks, or thinks in an extravagant, overly ambitious manner. 3. in the 18th century, an extreme conservative in politics or in religion.

high-flown (hī'flōn'), *adj.* 1. extravagantly ambitious or aspiring. 2. trying to be eloquent; bombastic.

high-fre·quen·cy (hī'frē'kwən-si), *adj.* designating or of an alternating electric current or oscillation with a relatively high frequency, now usually more than 20,000 cycles per second: abbreviated **H.F.**

High German, [after G. *hochdeutsch* (see DEUTSCH, DUTCH)], 1. the Germanic dialects spoken in the high regions of central and southern Germany: distinguished from *Low German.* 2. the official and literary form of the German language, technically called *New High German:* it is based principally on the High German dialects of middle Germany: see also **Old High German, Middle High German.** Abbreviated **HG., H.G.**

high-grade (hī'grād'), *adj.* of fine or superior quality.

high hand, the use of arbitrary, arrogant methods; overbearing or dictatorial ways.
high·hand·ed (hī'han'did), *adj.* overbearing; arbitrary.
high-hat (hī'hat'), *adj.* [Slang], 1. elegant; stylish. 2. snobbish. *n.* [Slang], a snob. *v.t.* [HIGH-HATTED (-id), HIGH-HATTING], [Slang], to treat snobbishly; snub.
high hat, a man's tall, black hat; top hat.
high-hole (hī'hōl'), *n.* [altered (through folk etym.) < earlier *hyghwhele, highwalē;* of echoic origin], [Dial.], the flicker, a kind of woodpecker.
high·jack (hī'jak'), *v.t.* [Colloq.], to hijack.
high·jack·er (hī'jak'ẽr), *n.* [Colloq.], a hijacker.
high jinks, noisy, wild pranks; boisterous merriment.
high jump, an athletic contest in which the contestants jump for height over a horizontal bar set between two upright poles: after each successful trial the bar is raised a little.
high-keyed (hī'kēd'), *adj.* 1. pitched in a high key: said of a piece of music. 2. full of sensitivity and spirit; high-strung.
high·land (hī'lənd), *n.* land well above sea level; region higher than adjacent land and containing many hills or mountains. *adj.* of, in, or from such a region.
the Highlands, the elevated mountainous region in northern and western Scotland: distinguished from *the Lowlands.*
high·land·er (hī'lən-dẽr), *n.* 1. a native or inhabitant of a highland. 2. [H-], *a*) a native or inhabitant of the Highlands. *b*) a soldier of a Highlands regiment.
Highland fling, a lively dance of the Highlands.
Highland Park, 1. a city in southeastern Michigan: pop., 38,000: it is inside the city limits of Detroit. 2. a city in northeastern Illinois: pop., 26,000.
Highland Southern, the variety of American speech typically associated with speakers in the southern Appalachian area but now prevalent throughout the lower and lower middle Mississippi Valley areas and in Kansas, Missouri, southern Illinois, southern and central Indiana, southern Ohio, and southern Pennsylvania: it is characterized by (1) a retained preconsonantal and final *r,* as in *barn, sir;* (2) pitch diphthongization of the checked vowels, as in *bid, bed, bad, bog, bud;* (3) lengthening or diphthongization of these vowels before final *-g;* (4) centralization of the high back vowels, as in *good, moon;* (5) a fronted diphthong (au) in such words as *house, out, crowd;* (6) raising of (e) to (i) before nasals, as in *men, many, tennis* and lowering of (i) to (e) before (ŋ), as in *think, thing.* Highland Southern is spoken at all levels of education and with minor regional modifications of its basic pattern; World War II brought it increasingly into the larger cities of the north central area. Also called *Hill Southern.*
high life, the way of life of fashionable society; luxurious, extravagant way of life.
high·light (hī'līt'), *v.t.* 1. to give a high light or high lights to; hence, 2. to give prominence to.
high light, 1. *a*) a part on which light is brightest: as, the *high lights* on the cheeks. *b*) a part of a painting, photograph, etc. on which light is represented as brightest. *c*) the representation or effect of such light in a painting, photograph, etc. 2. the most important, interesting, or outstanding part, scene, etc.
high-lows (hī'lōz'), *n.pl.* [Archaic], laced shoes that reach to the ankles.
high·ly (hī'li), *adv.* 1. [Rare], in or to a high place. 2. in or to a high office or rank. 3. in or to a high degree; very much; very; extremely. 4. with high approval or esteem; favorably. 5. at a high price.
High Mass, in the *Roman Catholic Church,* a Mass with full ceremonials, music, and incense, celebrated usually at the high altar with a deacon and a subdeacon assisting the celebrant.
high-mind·ed (hī'mīn'did), *adj.* 1. [Rare], haughty. 2. having or showing high ideals, principles, etc.
high-muck-a-muck (hī'muk'ə-muk'), *n.* [prob. < Chinook jargon *hiu muckamuck,* plenty of food], [Slang], a person in a position of importance and authority; especially, one who is always making his authority felt.
high·ness (hī'nis), *n.* 1. the quality or state of being high; height; loftiness. 2. [H-], highest of the nobility: a title used in speaking to or of a member of the royal family, preceded by *His, Her,* or *Your.*
high-oc·tane (hī'ok'tān), *adj.* having a high octane number: said of gasoline.
high-pitched (hī'picht'), *adj.* 1. high in pitch; shrill. 2. lofty; exalted. 3. steep in slope: said of roofs.
high place, in ancient Semitic religions, a temple or other place of worship, usually on a high hill.
High Point, a city in central North Carolina: pop., 62,000.
high-pow·ered (hī'pou'ẽrd), *adj.* very powerful.
high-pres·sure (hī'presh'ẽr), *adj.* 1. having, using, or withstanding relatively high pressure. 2. using or applying energetic or strongly persuasive methods or arguments. *v.t.* [Colloq.], to urge or persuade with such methods or arguments.
high-priced (hī'prīst'), *adj.* costly; expensive.
high priest, [ME.], 1. a chief priest. 2. the chief priest of the ancient Jewish priesthood.
high-proof (hī'prōōf'), *adj.* high in alcohol content: also **high proof.**
high relief, in *sculpture,* etc., relief in which the figures project half or more than half their natural depth from the background; alto-relievo.
high·road (hī'rōd', hī'rōd'), *n.* 1. a main road; highway. 2. an easy or direct way.
high school, 1. in educational systems having no junior high school, a school of four grades offering academic or vocational subjects, attended by students who have completed elementary school. 2. in educational systems having a junior high school, a similar school of three grades. Abbreviated **h.s.**
high seas, ocean waters not under the jurisdiction of any country.
high sign, a signal, often a prearranged one, given secretly, as in warning.
high-sound·ing (hī'soun'diŋ), *adj.* sounding pretentious or imposing.
high-spir·it·ed (hī'spir'it-id), *adj.* 1. having or showing a courageous or noble spirit. 2. spirited; fiery.
high-strung (hī'struŋ'), *adj.* [from the tuning of stringed instruments], highly sensitive; nervous and tense; excitable.
hight (hīt), *adj.* [ME. *highte,* merging AS. *hatte,* pass. p.t. with *hehl,* act. p.t. of *hatan,* to command, call; confused in sense with ME. *hoten,* pp. of same *v.*], [Archaic], named; called: as, a maiden *hight* Elaine.
high tea, [British], a meal somewhat more elaborate and served later than the usual tea.
high-ten·sion (hī'ten'shən), *adj.* having or carrying a high voltage.
high-test (hī'test'), *adj.* 1. passing severe tests; meeting difficult requirements. 2. having a low boiling point: said of gasoline.
high tide, 1. the highest level to which the tide rises; high water. 2. the time when the tide is at this level. 3. any culminating point or time.
high time, 1. time beyond the proper time but before it is too late; none too soon. 2. [Slang], a good time; gay, exciting, enjoyable time.
high-toned (hī'tōnd'), *adj.* 1. high in tone; high-pitched. 2. characterized by dignity, lofty moral or intellectual quality, high principles, etc.: often used ironically or humorously. 3. [Colloq.], stylish; fashionable; modish. 4. [Colloq.], excellent; superior.
high treason, treason against the ruler or government.
high·ty-tigh·ty (hī'ti-tī'ti), *adj., n., interj.* hoity-toity.
high water, 1. high tide. 2. the highest level reached by a body of water.
high-wa·ter mark (hī'wô'tẽr, hī'wä'tẽr), 1. the highest level reached by a body of water in tidal flow, flood, etc. 2. the mark left after high water has receded. 3. a culminating point; highest point.
high·way (hī'wā'), *n.* [ME. *heighwei;* see HIGH & WAY], 1. any road freely open to everyone; public road. 2. a main road; thoroughfare. 3. a main route by land or water. 4. a direct way to some objective.
high·way·man (hī'wā'mən), *n.* [*pl.* HIGHWAYMEN (-mən)], a man who robs travelers on a highway.
H.I.H., His (or Her) Imperial Highness.
Hii·u·maa (hē'oo-mä'), *n.* an Estonian island in the Baltic Sea, west of the Estonian S.S.R.: area, 371 sq. mi.: also called *Dagö.*
hi·jack (hī'jak'), *v.t.* [prob. *hi* (for *high*) + *jack, v.*], [Colloq.], 1. to steal (goods in transit, especially bootlegged liquor) by force. 2. to steal such goods from (a person) by force. Also spelled **highjack.**
hi·jack·er (hī'jak'ẽr), *n.* [Colloq.], a person who hijacks: also spelled **highjacker.**
hike (hīk), *v.i.* [HIKED (hīkt), HIKING], [< dial. *heik;* prob. akin to *hitch*], to take a long, vigorous walk; tramp or march through the country, woods, etc. *v.t.* [Colloq.], 1. to pull up; hoist: as, *hike* up your pants. 2. to raise (prices, etc.). *n.* a hiking; march.
hi·lar·i·ous (hi-lâr'i-əs, hī-lâr'i-əs), *adj.* [L. *hilaris, hilarus;* Gr. *hilaros,* cheerful, glad; akin to *hilēnai,* to be gracious; ? akin to Goth. *sels,* good, kind & Eng. *silly*], very gay; noisily merry; boisterous and cheerful.
hi·lar·i·ty (hi-lar'ə-ti, hī-lar'ə-ti), *n.* [OFr. *hilarité;* L. *hilaritas*], the state or quality of being hilarious; noisy merriment; boisterous gaiety. —*SYN.* see **mirth.**
Hil·a·ry (hil'ẽr-i), [L. *Hilarius,* lit., cheerful; see HILARIOUS], a masculine name; Fr. *Hilaire.*
Hil·da (hil'də), [G. < Gmc. **hild-,* battle, war; often contr. of names containing base (e.g., *Hilde*gunde, Brun*hilde*)], a feminine name.
Hil·de·brand (hil'də-brand'), *n.* 1. in the *Nibelungenlied,* a knight of King Etzel who kills Kriemhild. 2. Pope Gregory VII's name before he was made Pope.
Hil·de·garde (hil'də-gärd'), [G. < Gmc. **hild-,* battle + **gard-,* to enclose, protect (as in Eng. *yard*); hence, lit., battle protector], a feminine name: see **Hilda.**
hil·ding (hil'diŋ), *n.* [prob. < ME. *hilden* (AS. *heldan, hieldan*), to bend down, incline, bow], [Archaic], a low, base person; servile wretch. *adj.* [Archaic], low; base.
hill (hil), *n.* [ME. *hil, hulle, helle;* AS. *hyll;* akin to

MD. *hille, hil, hul;* IE. base **qel-*, to be elevated, rise high, seen also in L. *collis*, hill, *culmen*, peak (cf. CULMINATE)], 1. a natural raised part of the earth's surface, often rounded, smaller than a mountain. 2. a small pile, heap, or mound: as, an ant *hill*. 3. a small mound of soil heaped over and around plants and tubers: as, a *hill* of potatoes. 4. the plant or plants rooted in such a mound. *v.t.* 1. to shape into or like a hill. 2. to cover with a hill (sense 3).

Hill, James Jerome (hil), 1838–1916; American railroad magnate and financier.

hill·bill·y (hil'bil'i), *n.* [*pl.* HILLBILLIES (-iz)], [see BILLY-], [Colloq.], a person who lives in or comes from the mountains or backwoods, especially of the South: somewhat contemptuous term. *adj.* [Colloq.], of or characteristic of hillbillies: as, *hillbilly* music.

hill·i·ness (hil'i-nis), *n.* the quality or state of being hilly.

Hill·man, Sidney (hil'mən), 1887–1946; American labor leader, born in Lithuania.

hill myna, an Asiatic bird resembling the starling: it has the ability to mimic human speech and is often kept as a pet.

hil·lo, hil·loa (hil'ō, hi-lō'), *interj., n., v.i. & v.t.* [Archaic], hollo.

hill·ock (hil'ək), *n.* [ME.; see -OCK], a small hill; mound.

hill of beans, [< *hill, n.* 3], [Colloq.], a very small amount; very little; trifle.

hill·side (hil'sīd'), *n.* the side or slope of a hill.

Hill Southern, Highland Southern.

hill·top (hil'top'), *n.* the top of a hill.

hill·y (hil'i), *adj.* [HILLIER (-i-ẽr), HILLIEST (-i-ist)], 1. full of hills; rugged, uneven, and rolling. 2. like a hill; steep.

Hill·yer, Robert Sil·li·man (sil'ə-mən hil'yẽr), 1895–1961; American poet.

Hi·lo (hē'lō), *n.* seaport and chief city of the island of Hawaii: pop., 26,000.

hilt (hilt), *n.* [ME. & AS. *hilt;* akin to ON. *hjalt;* IE. base **qel-, *qela-*, to strike, hit; cf. HOLT], the handle, or haft, of a sword, dagger, tool, etc. *v.t.* to put a hilt on; set in a hilt.

(up) to the hilt, thoroughly; entirely.

hi·lum (hī'ləm), *n.* [*pl.* HILA (-lə)], [L., little thing], 1. in *anatomy*, a small notch or opening, as where vessels and nerves enter an organ. 2. in *botany, a)* a scar on a seed, marking the place where it was attached to the seed vessel. *b)* the nucleus in a starch grain.

him (him), *pron.* [AS. *him*, dat. of *he*, he, merged in sense with *hine*, acc. of *he*], the objective case of **he**: also used colloquially as a predicate complement with a linking verb (e.g., that's *him*).

H.I.M., His (or Her) Imperial Majesty.

Hi·ma·chal Pra·desh (hi-mä'chəl prä'desh), a state of northern India: area, 10,904 sq. mi.; pop., 1,349,000; capital, Simla.

Hi·ma·la·ya Mountains (hi-mäl'yə, hi-mä'lə-yə, him'ə-lā'ə), the Himalayas.

Hi·ma·la·yan (hi-mäl'yən, hi-mä'lə-yən, him'ə-lā'ən), *adj.* of the Himalayas.

Hi·ma·la·yas (hi-mäl'yəz, hi-mä'lə-yəz, him'ə-lā'əz), *n.pl.* a mountain system between India and Tibet, the highest known: highest peak, Mt. Everest.

hi·mat·i·on (hi-mat'i-ən), *n.* [*pl.* HIMATIA (-ə)], [Gr. *himation*], in ancient Greece, an oblong mantle worn as street dress.

Him·a·vat (him'ə-vat'), *n.* [Hind.], in *Hindu mythology*, the personification of the Himalayan Mountains, the father of Devi.

Hi·me·ji (hē'me-jē'), *n.* a city in southwestern Honshu, Japan: pop., 329,000.

Himm·ler, Hein·rich (hīn'riH him'lẽr), 1900–1945; German Nazi leader; chief of the Gestapo (1936–1945).

him·self (him-self'), *pron.* [AS. *him selfum*, dat. sing. of *he self;* see HIM & SELF], a form of the third person singular, masculine pronoun, used: *a)* as an intensive: as, he went *himself*. *b)* as a reflexive: as, he hurt *himself*. *c)* [Irish], as a subject: as, *himself* will have his dinner now. *d)* as a quasi-noun meaning "his real, true, or actual self" (e.g., he is not *himself* when he rages): in this construction *he* may be considered a possessive pronominal adjective and *self* a noun, and they may be separated: as, *his* own sweet *self*.

Him·yar·ite (him'yə-rīt'), *n.* [< Ar. *Ḥimyar*, a legendary ruler of Yemen; + *-ite*], 1. any member of an ancient Arab tribe that lived in southern Arabia. 2. any Arab descended from this tribe. *adj.* of the Himyarites, their language (an Arabic dialect resembling Ethiopic), their culture, etc.

hind (hīnd), *adj.* [HINDER (-ẽr), HINDMOST (-mōst') or HINDERMOST (-ẽr-mōst')], [ME.; prob. back-formation < *hinder*, influenced by AS. *hindan*, from behind, *behindan, adv.*, behind], back; rear; posterior.

hind (hīnd), *n.* [*pl.* HINDS (hīndz), HIND; see PLURAL, II, D, 1], [ME. & AS. *hind;* akin to G. *hinde;* IE. base **k̑em-*, not having horns (as applied to horned animal species), seen also in Gr. *kemas*, young deer], the female of the red deer, in and after its third year.

hind (hīnd), *n.* [< ME. *hine* (with unhistoric *-d*); AS. *hina*, earlier *higna, hiwna*, generalized < genit. pl. of *higa, hiwa*, member of a household or family; for base see HIDE (piece of land)], 1. in northern England and Scotland, a skilled farm worker or servant. 2. a peasant; rustic.

Hind., 1. Hindi. 2. Hindu. 3. Hindustan. 4. Hindustani.

hind·brain (hīnd'brān'), *n.* the hindmost part of the brain; specifically, *a)* the cerebellum, pons, and medulla oblongata; rhombencephalon. *b)* the cerebellum and pons only; metencephalon. *c)* the cerebellum only.

Hin·de·mith, Paul (poul hin'də-mit; Eng. hin'də-məth), 1895– ; German composer in America.

Hin·den·burg, Paul von (poul fôn hin'dən-boorkh'; Eng. von hin'dən-bẽrg), (*Paul Ludwig Hans Anton von Beneckendorff und von Hindenburg*), 1847–1934; German field marshal and chief of staff, World War I; second president of the German republic (1925–1934).

hin·der (hin'dẽr), *v.t.* [ME. *hindren;* AS. *hindrian*, lit., to keep or hold back (akin to G. *hindern*) < base of AS. *hinder, adv.*, back, behind; see next entry], 1. to keep back; restrain; get in the way of; prevent; stop. 2. to make difficult for; thwart; impede; frustrate.

SYN.*—hinder** implies a holding back of something about to begin and connotes a thwarting of progress (*hindered* by a lack of education); **obstruct** implies a retarding of passage or progress by placing obstacles in the way (to *obstruct* the passage of a bill by a filibuster); **block** implies the complete, but not necessarily permanent, obstruction of a passage or progress (the road was *blocked* by a landslide); **impede** suggests a slowing up of movement or progress by interfering with the normal action (tight garters *impede* the circulation of the blood); **bar** implies an obstructing as if by means of a barrier (he was *barred* forever from the club). See also **delay.**—ANT.*** advance, further.

hind·er (hīn'dẽr), *adj.* [ME. *hindre;* AS. *hinder, adv.*, back, behind (akin to G. *hinter, prep.*, behind) < base of *he* + suffix *-der* (as also in *hither*, ME. *hider*) denoting motion toward; the word is now felt as compar. of *hind*], hind; rear; posterior.

hind·er·most (hīn'dẽr-mōst'), *adj.* [alternative superlative of *hind*], [*hinder, adj.* + *-most*], hindmost.

hind·gut, hind-gut (hīnd'gut'), *n.* the hindmost part of the embryonic alimentary canal, from which the colon is formed.

Hin·di (hin'di), *adj.* [Hind. *hindī* < *Hind;* see HINDU], of or associated with northern India. *n.* the group of Indo-European, Indic languages spoken in northern India, including Assamese, Bengali, Marathi, Punjabi, Hindustani, etc.: abbreviated **Hind.**

hind·most (hīnd'mōst'), *adj.* [alternative superlative of *hind*], [ME.; see HIND, *adj.* & -MOST], farthest back; closest to the rear; last.

Hin·doo (hin'doo), *adj. & n.* [*pl.* HINDOOS (-dooz)], Hindu.

Hin·doo·ism (hin'doo-iz'm), *n.* Hinduism.

Hin·doo·sta·ni (hin'doo-stan'i, hin'doo-stä'ni), *adj. & n.* Hindustani.

hind·quar·ter (hīnd'kwôr'tẽr), *n.* either of the two hind legs and loins of a carcass of veal, beef, lamb, etc.

hin·drance (hin'drəns), *n.* [ME.], 1. a hindering. 2. any person or thing that hinders; obstacle; impediment; obstruction. —***SYN.*** see **obstacle.**

hind·sight (hīnd'sīt'), *n.* 1. the rear sight of a firearm. 2. ability to see, after the event, what should have been done: opposed to *foresight*.

Hin·du (hin'doo), *n.* [Per. *Hindū* < *Hind*, India < OPer. *Hindu*, India, land on the Indus < Sans. *sindhu*, river, the Indus], 1. any member of those peoples of India that speak languages derived from the Indic branch of Indo-European. 2. a follower of Hinduism. 3. popularly, any native of Hindustan. *adj.* 1. of the Hindus, their language, culture, etc. 2. of Hinduism. Also spelled **Hindoo.** Abbreviated **Hind.**

Hin·du-Ar·a·bic numerals (hin'doo-ar'ə-bik), Arabic numerals.

Hin·du·ism (hin'doo-iz'm), *n.* the religion and social system of the Hindus, developed from Brahmanism with elements from Buddhism, etc. added.

Hindu Kush (koosh), a mountain range in northeastern Afghanistan and northwestern India, extending to the Himalayas: highest peak, Tirich Mir, 25,263 ft.

Hin·du·stan (hin'doo-stan', hin'doo-stän'), *n.* 1. the northern part of India where chiefly Hindi is spoken, including the states of Rajasthan, Punjab, and Uttar Pradesh. 2. the Indian peninsula north of the Deccan. 3. popularly, India. Abbreviated **Hind.**

Hin·du·sta·ni (hin'doo-stan'i, hin'doo-stä'ni), *n.* [Hind. *Hindūstānī*, lit., dweller in northern India, Indian < Per. *Hindustan*, lit., country of the Hindus; *Hindu* (see HINDU) + *stan*, a place, country], the most important of the Western Hindi group of languages, used as a trade language throughout India: it contains many words from Persian, Arabic, Turkish, etc., and, as used by Moslems, is also called *Urdu*. *adj.* 1. of Hindustan or its people. 2. of Hindustani. Abbreviated **Hind.**

hinge (hinj), *n.* [ME. *henge* (with late phonetic sp. of vowel raised before the nasal) < ME. *hengen* (ON. *hengja*), to hang; see HANG], 1. a joint on which a door, gate, lid, etc. swings. 2. a natural joint, as of the bivalve shell of a clam or oyster. 3. anything on which matters turn or depend; cardinal point or principle; pivot. *v.t.* [HINGED (hinjd), HINGING], to equip with or attach by a hinge. *v.i.* 1. to hang or swing as on a hinge. 2. to depend; be contingent.

TYPES OF HINGE
A, butt; B, spring; C, strap; D, T hinge

hinged (hinjd), *adj.* [pp. of *hinge*], having a hinge or hinges.

hin·ny (hin'i), *n.* [*pl.* HINNIES (-iz)], [L. *hinnus* < Gr. *ginnos*], the offspring of a male horse and a female donkey: distinguished from *mule.*

hin·ny (hin'i), *v.i.* [HINNIED (-id), HINNYING], [ME.; Fr. *hennir;* L. *hinnire,* to neigh], to whinny; neigh.

hint (hint), *n.* [Early Mod. Eng. < AS. *henten, hinten,* to seize, grasp; see HENT], 1. a slight indication; faint or indirect suggestion; intimation; covert allusion. 2. [Obs.], an occasion; turn; opportunity. *v.t.* to give a hint of; suggest indirectly; intimate. *v.i.* to make a hint or hints. —*SYN.* see **suggest.**

hint at, to suggest indirectly; intimate.

take a hint, to perceive and act on a hint.

hin·ter·land (hin'tẽr-land'), *n.* [G.; *hinter* (cf. HINDER, *adj.*), back + *land,* land], 1. the land or district behind that bordering on a coast or river; inland region. 2. an area far from big cities and towns; back country. 3. the inland trade region served by a port. 4. an inland region claimed by the state that owns the coast.

hip (hip), *n.* [ME. *hipe, hupe;* AS. *hype;* akin to G. *hüfte* (OHG. *huf*); IE. **qeu-b,* to bend, as at a joint (< base **qeu-,* to bend, bend over), as also in *cubit, cubicle*], 1. the part of the human body surrounding and including the joint formed by each thigh bone and the pelvis; especially, the fleshy part of the upper thigh; haunch. 2. the corresponding part of an animal's body. 3. in *architecture,* the angle formed by the meeting of two sloping sides of a roof. *v.t.* [HIPPED (hipt), HIPPING], to make (a roof) with such an angle or angles.

on (or **upon**) **the hip,** in an unfavorable position; at a disadvantage: originally with reference to wrestling.

smite hip and thigh, [Poetic], to attack unsparingly; overwhelm with or as with blows: see Judg. 16:8.

hip (hip), *n.* [with Early Mod. Eng. shortened vowel < ME. *hepe;* AS. *heop;* akin to OHG. *hiufo,* AS. *heope,* briar], the small, fleshy, ripened fruit of a rosebush.

hip (hip), *interj.* an exclamation used in cheers: as, *hip, hip,* hurray!

hip (hip), *adj.* [? < *hep*], [Slang], informed, aware, sophisticated, knowledgeable, etc.

hip·bone (hip'bōn'), *n.* 1. the innominate bone. 2. the ilium. 3. the neck of the femur. Also **hip bone.**

hip·parch (hip'ärk), *n.* [Gr. *hipparchos* < *hippos,* horse + *archein,* to lead, rule], in ancient Greece, a cavalry commander.

Hip·par·chus (hi-pär'kəs), *n.* Greek astronomer of the 2d century B.C.

hipped (hipt), *adj.* 1. having hips (of a specified sort): used in hyphenated compounds, as *broad-hipped.* 2. having the hip dislocated; hipshot. 3. in *architecture,* having a hip or hips: as, a *hipped* roof.

hipped (hipt), *adj.* [< *hyp* in *hypochondria*], [Colloq.], 1. in low spirits; melancholy; depressed. 2. offended. 3. obsessed (with *on*).

hip·po (hip'ō), *n.* [*pl.* HIPPOS (-ōz)], [Colloq.], a hippopotamus.

hip·po- (hip'ō, hip'ə), [< Gr. *hippos,* a horse], a combining form meaning *horse,* as in *hippology:* also, before a vowel, **hipp-.**

hip·po·cam·pal (hip'ə-kam'p'l), *adj.* 1. of or like a hippocampus. 2. having to do with the hippocampus (of the brain).

hip·po·cam·pus (hip'ə-kam'pəs), *n.* [*pl.* HIPPOCAMPI (-pi)], [L., sea horse; Gr. *hippokampos,* hippocampus < *hippos,* a horse + *kampos,* sea monster], 1. in *Greek & Roman mythology,* a sea monster with the head and forequarters of a horse and the tail of a dolphin or fish; hence, 2. a small fish with a horselike head and a grasping tail; sea horse. 3. a ridge along each lateral ventricle of the brain.

hip·po·cras (hip'ə-kras'), *n.* [ME. & OFr. *ypocras* < *Ypocras,* Hippocrates, after ML. *vinum Hippocraticum,* wine of Hippocrates: so named from being filtered through a strainer called "Hippocrates' sleeve" (L. *manica Hippocratis*)], wine highly flavored with spices, formerly drunk as a cordial.

Hip·poc·ra·tes (hi-pok'rə-tēz'), *n.* Greek physician; 460?–377? B.C.: called the *Father of Medicine.*

Hip·po·crat·ic (hip'ə-krat'ik), *adj.* of Hippocrates.

Hippocratic oath, the oath generally taken by students receiving the M.D. degree, attributed to Hippocrates and regarded as setting forth an ethical code for the medical profession.

Hip·po·crene (hip'ə-krēn', hip'ə-krē'ni), *n.* [L.; Gr. *Hippokrēnē* < *hippos,* a horse + *krēnē,* a spring, fountain], in *Greek mythology,* 1. a fountain on Mt. Helicon, sacred to the Muses: it is said to have been opened by the hoof of Pegasus. 2. its waters, supposed to inspire poets.

hip·po·drome (hip'ə-drōm'), *n.* [Fr.; L. *hippodromos;* Gr. *hippodromos* < *hippos,* a horse + *dromos,* a course, running < base of *dramein,* to run], 1. in ancient Greece and Rome, a course for horse races and chariot races, surrounded by tiers of seats built in an oval. 2. an arena or building for a circus, games, etc.

hip·po·griff, hip·po·gryph (hip'ə-grif'), *n.* [Fr. *hippogriffe;* It. *ippogrifo* < Gr. *hippos,* a horse + LL. *gryphus,* griffin], a mythical monster with the body and hindquarters of a horse and the head and wings of a griffin.

Hip·pol·y·tus (hi-pol'i-təs), *n.* [L.; Gr. *Hippolytos*], in *Greek legend,* a son of Theseus: when he rejected the love of his stepmother, Phaedra, she turned Theseus against him by false accusations, and at Theseus' request he was killed by Poseidon, who caused his chariot to overturn.

Hip·pom·e·nes (hi-pom'ə-nēz'), *n.* [L.; Gr. *Hippomenēs*], in *Greek legend,* a youth who won a race against Atalanta: see **Atalanta.**

hip·po·pot·a·mus (hip'ə-pot'ə-məs), *n.* [*pl.* HIPPOPOTAMUSES (-iz), HIPPOPOTAMI (-mī'), HIPPOPOTAMUS; see PLURAL, II, D, 1], [L.; Gr. *hippopotamos,* lit., river horse < *hippos,* a horse + *potamos,* river], a large, plant-eating mammal of the hog family, with a heavy, thick-skinned, almost hairless body and short legs: it lives chiefly in or near rivers in Africa.

-hip·pus (hip'əs), [< Gr. *hippos,* a horse], a combining form meaning *horse,* as in *eohippus.*

hip roof, a roof with sloping ends and sides.

hip·shot (hip'shot'), *adj.* 1. having the hip dislocated. 2. having one hip lower than the other.

HIP ROOF

hip·ster (hip'stẽr), *n.* [Slang], 1. a hip person, especially a devotee of modern jazz. 2. a beatnik, specifically one who professes total indifference to the value or validity of any human activity or experience.

Hi·ram (hī'rəm), [Heb. *ḥīrām;* prob. < *'aḥīrām,* exalted brother], a masculine name: diminutive, *Hi.*

hir·cine (hũr'sīn, hũr'sin), *adj.* [L. *hircinus* < *hircus,* goat], of or like a goat, especially in smell.

hire (hīr), *n.* [ME. *hire, hyre;* AS. *hyr,* wages; akin to D. *huur* (G. dial. *heuer*); ? IE. base **qā-,* to desire, seen also in L. *carus,* dear (in both senses)], 1. the amount paid for getting the services of a person or the use of a thing. 2. a hiring. *v.t.* [HIRED (hīrd), HIRING], 1. to get the services of (a person) or the use of (a thing) in return for payment; employ; engage. 2. to give the use of (a thing) in return for payment.

for hire, available for work or use in return for payment: also **on hire.**

hire out, to give one's work in return for payment.

SYN.—**to hire,** in strict usage, means to get, and **let,** to give, the use of something in return for payment, although **hire,** which is also applied to persons or their services, may be used in either sense (to *hire* a hall, a worker, etc., rooms to *let*); **lease** implies the letting or, in loose usage, the hiring of property (usually real property) by written contract; **rent** implies payment of a specific amount, usually at fixed intervals, for hiring or letting a house, land, or other property; **charter** implies the hiring or leasing of a ship, bus, etc.

hire·ling (hīr'liŋ), *n.* [see HIRE & -LING], a person who works only for the wages he is paid; person who will follow anyone's orders for pay; mercenary. *adj.* of or like a hireling; mercenary.

Hi·ro·hi·to (hêr'ō-hē'tō), *n.* emperor of Japan (1926–); born 1901.

Hi·ro·shi·ge, An·do (än'dō hêr'ō-shē'ge), 1797–1858; Japanese painter.

Hi·ro·shi·ma (hêr′ō-shē′mä), *n.* a city on the southwestern coast of Honshu, Japan: pop., c. 200,000 (1947), 344,000 (1940): on August 6, 1945 it was largely destroyed by an American atomic bomb, the first ever used in warfare.

hir·sute (hũr′sōōt, hẽr-sūt′), *adj.* [L. *hirsutus*], hairy; shaggy; bristly.

hi·ru·di·noid (hi-rōō′də-noid′), *adj.* [< L. *hirudo, hirudinis*, a leech; + *-oid*], of or like a leech.

hi·run·dine (hi-run′din, hi-run′dīn), *adj.* [< L. *hirundo, hirundinis*, a swallow], of or like a swallow (bird).

his (hiz), ***pron.*** [AS. *his*, of him, his, genit. masc. & neut. of *he*], that or those belonging to him: used without a following noun, often after *of*, as, a friend of *his*, that book is *his, his* are better. ***possessive pronominal adj.*** of, belonging to, or done by him.

His·pa·ni·a (his-pā′ni-ə, his-pä′nyə), *n.* [L.], 1. a division of the ancient Roman Empire, including what is now Spain and Portugal. 2. [Poetic], Spain.

His·pan·ic (his-pan′ik), *adj.* [L. *Hispanicus*], Spanish.

His·pan·io·la (his′pən-yō′lə), *n.* an island in the West Indies, between Cuba and Puerto Rico: area, 28,242 sq. mi.; pop., 4,656,000: divided between Haiti and the Dominican Republic: formerly called *Haiti.*

his·pid (his′pid), *adj.* [L. *hispidus*], covered with rough bristles, stiff hairs, or small spines.

his·pid·i·ty (his-pid′ə-ti), *n.* the state of being hispid.

hiss (his), *v.i.* [ME. *hissen;* of echoic origin], 1. to make a sound like that of a prolonged *s*, as of a goose or snake, or of escaping steam, air, etc. 2. to show hatred or disapproval by hissing. ***v.t.*** 1. to say or indicate by hissing. 2. to show hatred or disapproval of by hissing. 3. to force or drive by hissing. ***n.*** a sound like that of a prolonged *s*.

hist (st, hist *is a sp. pronun.*), ***interj.*** an exclamation to attract attention, call for silence, etc., equivalent to "be quiet! listen!"

hist., 1. historian. 2. historical. 3. history.

his·ta·mine (his′tə-mēn′, his′tə-min), *n.* [< *histidine* + *amine*], an amine, $C_3H_3N_2 \cdot CH_2 \cdot CH_2 \cdot NH_2$, produced by the decomposition of histidine and found in all organic matter: it is released by the tissues in allergic reactions, lowers the blood pressure by dilating blood vessels, stimulates gastric secretion, etc.

his·ti·din (his′tə-din), *n.* histidine.

his·ti·dine (his′tə-dēn′, his′tə-din), *n.* [< Gr. *histion*, dim. of *histos* (see HISTO-); + *-ine*], an amino acid, $C_6H_9N_3O_2$, formed by the hydrolysis of proteins.

his·to- (his′tō, his′tə), [< Gr. *histos*, a loom, warp, web, tissue], a combining form meaning *tissue*, as in *histology:* also, before a vowel, **hist-**.

his·toid (his′toid), *adj.* [*hist-* + *-oid*], like the surrounding or normal tissue: as, a *histoid* tumor.

his·to·log·i·cal (his′tə-loj′i-k'l), *adj.* of histology.

his·tol·o·gy (his-tol′ə-ji), *n.* [*histo-* + *-logy*], 1. the branch of biology concerned with the microscopic study of the structure of tissues. 2. the tissue structure of an organism or part.

his·tol·y·sis (his-tol′ə-sis), *n.* [Mod. L.; see HISTO- & -LYSIS], in *biology*, the breaking down and dissolution of organic tissues.

his·ton (his′ton), *n.* histone.

his·tone (his′tōn), *n.* [< Gr. *histos* (see HISTO-); + *-one*], any of a group of simple proteins that yield amino acids on hydrolysis, as the globin of hemoglobin: they are often poisonous when injected into an animal, and prevent the clotting of blood.

his·to·ri·an (his-tôr′i-ən, his-tō′ri-ən), *n.* [Fr. *historien*], 1. a writer of history; chronicler. 2. an authority on or specialist in history. Abbreviated **hist.**

his·tor·ic (his-tôr′ik, his-tor′ik), *adj.* [L. *historicus;* Gr. *historikos*], historical; especially, famous in history.

his·tor·i·cal (his-tôr′i-k'l, his-tor′i-k'l), *adj.* [< L. *historicus;* + *-al*], 1. of or concerned with history as a science: as, the *historical* method. 2. providing evidence for a fact of history; serving as a source of history: as, a *historical* document. 3. based on or suggested by people or events of the past: as, a *historical* novel. 4. established by history; not legendary or fictional; authentic; real; factual. 5. showing the development or evolution in proper chronological order: as, a *historical* account. 6. famous in history: now usually *historic.* Abbreviated **hist.** (in senses 1, 2, 3).

historical linguistics, the branch of linguistics which describes the evolution of language structures.

his·tor·i·cal·ly (his-tôr′i-k'l-i, his-tor′ik-li), *adv.* 1. so as to show the development or evolution in chronological order. 2. according to the facts or principles of history; as history.

historical present, the present tense used in telling about past events: also **historic present.**

his·to·ric·i·ty (his″tə-ris′ə-ti), *n.* historical nature or authenticity.

his·to·ried (his′tə-rid), *adj.* having a history or told about in history.

his·to·ri·og·ra·pher (his-tôr′i-og′rə-fẽr, his-tō′ri-og′rə-fẽr), *n.* [LL. *historiographus;* Gr. *historiographos* < *historia* (see HISTORY) + *graphein*, to write; + *-er*], a historian; especially, one appointed to write the history of some institution, country, etc.

his·to·ri·og·ra·phy (his-tôr′i-og′rə-fi, his-tō′ri-og′rə-fi), *n.* the work of a historiographer; the writing of history.

his·to·ry (his′tə-ri, his′tri), *n.* [*pl.* HISTORIES (-riz, -triz)], [L. *historia;* Gr. *historia*, a learning by inquiry, knowledge, narrative < *histōr*, knowing, learned, wise man < base of *eidenai*, to know], 1. an account of what has happened; narrative; story; tale. 2. *a*) what has happened in the life or development of a people, country, institution, etc. *b*) a systematic account of this, usually with an analysis and explanation. 3. all recorded events of the past. 4. the branch of knowledge that deals systematically with the past; a recording, analyzing, co-ordinating, and explaining of past events: abbreviated **hist.** 5. a known or recorded past: as, this coat has a strange *history.* 6. something that belongs to the past: as, that argument is *history* now. 7. something important enough to be recorded.

make history, to be or do something important enough to be recorded.

his·tri·on·ic (his′tri-on′ik), *adj.* [LL. *histrionicus* < L. *histrio*, actor], 1. of, or having the nature of, acting or actors. 2. overacted or overacting; theatrical; melodramatic; artificial; affected. ***n.*** [Rare], an actor: see also **histrionics.**

his·tri·on·i·cal·ly (his′tri-on′i-k'l-i, his′tri-on′ik-li), *adv.* in a histrionic manner.

his·tri·on·ics (his′tri-on′iks), *n.pl.* 1. [construed as sing.], theatricals; dramatics. 2. an artificial or affected manner, display of emotion, etc.; theatricality.

hit (hit), *v.t.* [HIT, HITTING], [ME. *hitten;* AS. *hittan;* ON. *hitta*, to hit upon, meet with; IE. base **keid-*, to fall, as also in W. *cwydd*, a fall], 1. to come against, usually with force; strike: as, the car *hit* the tree. 2. to give a blow to; strike; knock. 3. to give (a blow): as, she *hit* him a blow. 4. to strike by throwing, shooting, or otherwise sending a missile: as, he fired and *hit* the deer. 5. to cause (something) to knock, bump, or strike, as in falling, moving, etc. (often with *on* or *against*): as, he *hit* his head on the stairs. 6. to affect strongly; distress; injure: as, the Irish were hard *hit* by the potato famine. 7. to come upon by accident or after search; reach; find; light upon: as, he *hit* the right answer. 8. to fall into exact accord with; appeal to; suit: as, the hat *hit* her fancy. 9. in *baseball*, to get (a specified base hit): as, he *hit* a double. ***v.i.*** 1. to give a blow or blows; strike. 2. to knock, bump, or strike (usually with *against*). 3. to come by accident or after search (usually with *upon*). 4. to ignite the combustible mixture in its cylinders: said of an internal-combustion engine. 5. in *baseball*, to get a base hit. ***n.*** 1. a blow that strikes its mark. 2. a collision of one thing with another. 3. an effectively witty or sarcastic remark. 4. a stroke of good fortune. 5. a successful and popular song, book, play, etc. 6. in *backgammon*, a game won by a player after one or more of his opponent's men have been removed from the board. 7. in *baseball*, a base hit. —***SYN.*** see **strike.**

hit it off, to get along well together; be congenial.

hit off, 1. to mimic; imitate. 2. to portray or describe briefly and well.

hit or miss, without regard to success or failure; in a haphazard or aimless way.

hit (out) at, 1. to aim a blow at; try to hit. 2. to attack in words; criticize severely.

hit-and-run (hit″'n-run′), *adj.* hitting and then escaping: usually of an automobile driver who flees from the scene of an accident in which he is involved: also **hit-skip.**

hitch (hich), *v.i.* [ME. *hicchen*, to move jerkily; prob. echoic var. (? via LG. *hicken*) of OFr. *hocier* (Fr. *hocher*), to move jerkily], 1. to move jerkily; walk haltingly; limp; hobble. 2. to become fastened or caught, as by becoming entangled or hooking on to something. 3. to strike the feet together in moving: said of a horse. 4. [Colloq.], to be in harmony; agree. 5. [Slang], to hitchhike. ***v.t.*** 1. to move, pull, or shift with jerks. 2. to fasten with a hook, knot, etc.; unite; tie. 3. [Colloq.], to marry: usually in the passive. ***n.*** 1. a short, sudden movement or pull; tug; jerk. 2. a hobble; limp. 3. a hindrance; obstacle; entanglement. 4. a catching or fastening; thing or part used to connect or join together; catch. 5. [Slang], a ride in hitchhiking. 6. [Military Slang], a period of enlistment. 7. in *nautical usage*, a kind of knot that can be easily undone: see **knot,** illus.

without a hitch, smoothly, easily, and successfully.

hitch·hike (hich′hīk′), *v.i.* [HITCHHIKED (-hīkt′), HITCHHIKING], [*hitch* + *hike*], to travel by asking for rides from motorists along the way.

hith·er (hith'ẽr), *adv.* [ME. & AS. *hider* (akin to Goth. *hidrē*) < base of *he* (see HE) + *-der*, suffix expressing motion toward (see HINDER)], to or toward this place; here. *adj.* on or toward this side; nearer: as, the *hither* horse.

hith·er·most (hith'ẽr-mōst'), *adj.* nearest.

hith·er·to (hith'ẽr-tōō', hith'ẽr-tōō'), *adv.* [see HITHER & TO], 1. until this time; to now. 2. [Obs.], hither.

hith·er·ward (hith'ẽr-wẽrd), *adv.* [AS. *hiderweard;* see -WARD], [Rare], toward this place; hither.

hith·er·wards (hith'ẽr-wẽrdz), *adv.* hitherward.

Hit·ler, A·dolf (ä'dôlf hit'lẽr), 1889–1945; leader of the Nazis and chancellor of Germany (1933–1945); assumed dictatorial power and title *Der Führer;* probably committed suicide during Soviet siege of Berlin in World War II.

Hit·ler·ism (hit'lẽr-iz'm), *n.* the fascist program, ideas, and methods of Hitler and the Nazis.

Hit·ler·ite (hit'lẽr-īt'), *n.* a follower of Hitler; Nazi. *adj.* of or characteristic of Hitler.

hit-or-miss (hit'ẽr-mis'), *adj.* haphazard; random.

hit-skip (hit'skip'), *adj.* hit-and-run.

hit·ter (hit'ẽr), *n.* a person who hits.

Hit·tite (hit'īt), *n.* [< Heb. *ḥittīm*, Hittites], 1. any of an ancient people of Asia Minor and Syria (c. 2000–700 B.C.). 2. the language of the Hittites, considered by most authorities to be associated with Indo-European: it is recorded in divergent cuneiform and hieroglyphic inscriptions. *adj.* of the Hittites, their language, or culture.

hive (hīv), *n.* [ME.; AS. *hyf;* akin to D. *huif*, hive, hood; IE. **qeu-p* (< base **qeu-*, to bend, curve), as also in L. *cupa*, tub, cask; for sense, cf. L. *alveus*, hollow, cavity, hence beehive], 1. a box or other shelter for a colony of domestic bees; beehive: see **beehive**, illus. 2. a colony of bees living in a hive; swarm; hence, 3. a crowd of busy, bustling people. 4. a place of great bustle and activity. *v.t.* [HIVED (hīvd), HIVING], 1. to put or gather (bees) into a hive. 2. to store up (honey) in a hive. 3. to store up for future use; garner. *v.i.* 1. to enter a hive. 2. to live together in or as in a hive.

hives (hīvz), *n.* [orig. Scot. dial.], an allergic skin condition characterized by itching, burning, stinging, and the formation of smooth patches, or wheals, usually red: popular name for urticaria.

H.J., *hic jacet*, [L.], here lies.

hl., hectoliter; hectoliters.

H.L., House of Lords.

h'm (həm: *conventionalized pronun.*), *interj.* hem; hum.

hm., hectometer; hectometers.

H.M., 1. Her Majesty. 2. His Majesty.

H.M.S., 1. His (or Her) Majesty's Service. 2. His (or Her) Majesty's Ship. 3. His (or Her) Majesty's Steamer.

ho (hō), *interj.* [a natural emphatic cry], 1. an exclamation of pleasure, surprise, derision, etc. 2. an exclamation to attract attention: sometimes used after a destination or direction, as, westward *ho!* 3. [ME.; OFr.], whoa! stop! halt!

Ho, in *chemistry*, holmium.

H.O., head office.

ho·ac·tzin (hō-ak'tsin), *n.* hoatzin.

Hoang·ho (hwäŋ'hō'), *n.* the Hwang Ho River.

hoar (hôr, hōr), *adj.* [ME. *hore;* AS. *har;* akin to G. *herr* (OHG. *hērro*, compar.); IE. base **kei-*, seen also in AS. *hæwen*, blue], 1. white, gray, or grayish-white. 2. having white or gray hair because very old; hoary. 3. [Dial.], moldy; stale. *n.* 1. hoariness. 2. hoarfrost.

hoard (hôrd, hōrd), *n.* [< ME. & AS. *hord* with lengthened vowel; akin to G. *hort;* IE. **qeu-s*, what is hidden < base *(*s*)*qeu-*, to hide, conceal, as also in *obscure*], a supply stored up and hidden or kept in reserve. *v.i.* to get and store away money, goods, etc. *v.t.* to accumulate and hide or keep in reserve.

hoard·ing (hôr'diŋ, hōr'diŋ), *n.* 1. the act of a person who hoards. 2. something hoarded.

hoard·ing (hôr'diŋ, hōr'diŋ), *n.* [< obs. *hoard*, hoarding; OFr. *hourde;* Frank. *hurda*, a pen, fold; see HURDLE], [British], 1. a temporary wooden fence around a site of building construction or repair. 2. a billboard.

hoar·frost (hôr'frôst', hōr'frost'), *n.* [ME. *horfrost;* see HOAR & FROST], white, frozen dew on the ground, leaves, etc.; white frost; rime.

hoar·hound (hôr'hound', hōr'hound'), *n.* horehound.

hoar·i·ness (hôr'i-nis, hō'ri-nis), *n.* the quality or condition of being hoary.

hoarse (hôrs, hōrs), *adj.* [ME. *hors, hoos;* AS. *has* (prob. beside lost var. **hars;* cf. Early Mod. D. *heesch, heersch* & ON. *hāss* < Gmc. **hairsa*); akin to G. *heiser* (OHG. *heis*); ? IE. base **qai-*, heat (cf. HOT); ? basic sense "dried out, hence rough"], 1. harsh and grating in sound; sounding rough and husky. 2. having a rough, husky voice, like that of a person with a cold.

hoars·en (hôr's'n, hōr's'n), *v.t. & v.i.* to make or become hoarse.

hoar·y (hôr'i, hō'ri), *adj.* [HOARIER (-i-ẽr, -ri-ẽr), HOARIEST (-i-ist, -ri-ist)], [*hoar, adj.* or *n.* + *-y*], 1. white, gray, or grayish-white; hoar. 2. having white or gray hair because very old. 3. very old; ancient.

hoar·y-head·ed (hôr'i-hed'id, hō'ri-hed'id), *adj.* having white or gray hair because very old.

ho·at·zin (hō-at'sin), *n.* [Sp.; Nahuatl *uatzin*], a crested, olive-colored South American bird: the wings of its young have claws, used in climbing trees: also **hoactzin.**

hoax (hōks), *n.* [altered < *hocus*], a trick or fraud, especially one meant as a practical joke. *v.t.* to deceive with a hoax. —*SYN.* see **cheat.**

hob (hob), *n.* [? var. of *hub*], 1. a projecting ledge at the back or side of a fireplace, for keeping a kettle, saucepan, etc. warm. 2. a peg used as a target in quoits, etc. 3. any game in which such a peg is used.

hob (hob), *n.* [ME., old familiar form for *Robin, Robert*], 1. [Eng. Dial.], a rustic; lout. 2. [H-], Robin Goodfellow, or Puck; hence, 3. an elf; goblin.
play (or **raise**) **hob**, to cause mischief; make trouble.

Ho·bart (hō'bẽrt, hō'bärt), a masculine name: see **Hubert.** *n.* seaport and capital of Tasmania: pop., 109,000.

Hob·be·ma, Mein·dert (mīn'dẽrt hob'ə-mȧ), 1638–1709; Dutch landscape painter.

Hobbes, Thomas (hobz), 1588–1679; English social philosopher; author of *Leviathan.*

Hob·bism (hob'iz'm), *n.* the philosophy of Thomas Hobbes, who believed that a strong government, especially an absolute monarchy, is necessary to control conflicting individual interests and desires.

hob·ble (hob''l), *v.i.* [HOBBLED (-'ld), HOBBLING], [ME. *hobelen;* prob. (? via LG.) < base of *hop* + freq. *-le;* cf. D. *hobbelen*, G. dial. *hobbeln* (G. *hoppeln*) in same sense; see HOP], 1. to go unsteadily, haltingly, etc. 2. to walk lamely or awkwardly; limp. *v.t.* 1. to cause to go haltingly or lamely. 2. to hamper the movement of (a horse, etc.) by tying two legs together. 3. to hamper; hinder. *n.* 1. an awkward, halting walk; limp. 2. a rope, strap, etc. used to hobble a horse; fetter. 3. [Rare], an awkward situation; difficulty.

hob·ble·bush (hob''l-boosh'), *n.* a shrub of the honeysuckle family, with dark, wrinkled leaves, clusters of white flowers, and purple berries.

hob·ble·de·hoy (hob''l-di-hoi'), *n.* [also early vars. *hoberdihoye, hobbedihoy;* prob. based on *hob* (a rustic) with cross associations < *hobble*, Fr. *hober*, to bestir oneself, *hobereau*, a hobby (hawk) & Eng. *hobbyhorse*], 1. a youth between boyhood and manhood; adolescent boy. 2. an awkward, clumsy, gawky youth or boy.

hobble skirt, a woman's long skirt so narrow below the knees as to hinder the wearer's movements: it was popular from 1910 to 1914.

hob·by (hob'i), *n.* [*pl.* HOBBIES (-iz)], [< dim. of *Hob*, familiar form of *Rob*, personal name; cf. HOB (a rustic)], 1. [Obs. or Dial.], a medium-sized, vigorous horse. 2. [Rare], a hobbyhorse; hence, 3. [Rare], a subject that a person constantly talks about or returns to; hence, 4. something that a person likes to do or study in his spare time; favorite pastime or avocation.
ride a hobby, to be excessively devoted to one's favorite pastime or subject.

hob·by (hob'i), *n.* [*pl.* HOBBIES (-iz)], [ME. *hoby;* OFr. *hobé, hobet*, dim. of *hobe*, a hawk], a small European falcon, formerly trained for hawking.

hob·by·horse (hob'i-hôrs'), *n.* 1. *a*) a figure of a horse attached to the waist of a person doing a morris dance so that he seems to be riding it. *b*) the dancer. 2. a children's toy consisting of a stick with a horse's head. 3. a rocking horse. 4. an imitation horse on a merry-go-round.

hob·gob·lin (hob'gob'lin), *n.* [< *Hob*, familiar form of *Rob*, personal name (cf. HOB, a rustic) + *goblin*], 1. [H-], Robin Goodfellow; Puck; hence, 2. an elf; goblin. 3. a frightening apparition; bogy; bugbear.

hob·nail (hob'nāl'), *n.* [*hob* (a peg) + *nail*], 1. a short nail with a broad head, put on the soles of heavy shoes to prevent wear or slipping. 2. a person who wears hobnailed boots; rustic. *v.t.* to put hobnails on.

hob·nob (hob'nob'), *adv.* [earlier *habnab*, lit., to have and not have < ME. *habben*, to have + *nabben* (< *ne habben*), not to have, esp. with reference to alternation in drinking], hit or miss. *v.i.* [HOBNOBBED (-nobd'), HOBNOBBING], 1. to drink together; hence, 2. to be on close terms (*with* someone); associate in a familiar way. *n.* [Rare], a drinking together.

ho·bo (hō'bō), *n.* [*pl.* HOBOS, HOBOES (-bōz)], [19th-c. Americanism; ? < *ho! beau!*, formerly a call of greeting between vagrants], 1. a migratory worker: so used by such workers themselves. 2. a vagrant; tramp: often contemptuous. Sometimes shortened to **bo.** —*SYN.* see **vagrant.**

Ho·bo·ken (hō'bō-kən), *n.* a city in New Jersey, across the Hudson from New York City: pop., 48,000.

Hob·son's choice (hob's'nz), [after Thomas *Hobson* (d. 1631), of Cambridge, England, who owned livery stables and let horses in strict order according to their position near the door], a choice of taking what is offered or nothing at all.

hock (hok), *n.* [southern Brit. var. of Scot. *hough;* ME. & AS. *hoh*, the heel, *hoh-* (in *hohsinu*, lit., hock sinew), hock; Gmc. *hanha (cf. dim. HEEL < *hanhila) with loss of nasal as in *soft, tooth,* etc.; IE. base *kenk-, heel, etc.], 1. the joint bending backward in the hind leg of a horse, ox, etc., corresponding to the human ankle. 2. the corresponding joint in the leg of a fowl. *v.t.* to disable by cutting the tendons of the hock.

hock (hok), *n.* [contr. of *hockamore;* altered < G. *Hochheimer*], [Chiefly British], 1. a white Rhine wine produced at Hochheim, on the Main, in Germany. 2. any white Rhine wine.

hock (hok), *v.t. & n.* [? < *hock,* obs. card game in which the player himself determined the value to be put on certain preferred cards < D. *hok,* prison, debt], [Slang], pawn.

hock·ey (hok′i), *n.* [Early Mod. Eng.; prob. < OFr. *hoquet,* bent stick, crook], 1. a team game played on ice, in which the players, using curved sticks and wearing skates, try to drive a rubber disk (*puck*) into their opponents' goal: also **ice hockey.** 2. a similar game played on a field with a small ball instead of a puck: also **field hockey.**

hockey stick, a stick with a curved end, used in playing hockey.

hock·shop (hok′shop′), *n.* [Slang], a pawnshop.

ho·cus (hō′kəs), *v.t.* [HOCUSED or HOCUSSED (-kəst), HOCUSING or HOCUSSING], [abbrev. of *hocus-pocus*], 1. to play a trick on; dupe; hoax. 2. to drug. 3. to put drugs in (a drink).

ho·cus-po·cus (hō′kəs-pō′kəs), *n.* [imitation L.; ? after L. sacramental blessing, *hoc est corpus. . .*], 1. meaningless words used as a formula by conjurers. 2. a magician's trick or trickery; sleight of hand; legerdemain; hence, 3. any meaningless action or talk meant to draw attention away from some trick or deception. 4. trickery; deception. *v.t. & v.i.* [HOCUS-POCUSED or HOCUS-POCUSSED (-kəst), HOCUS-POCUSING or HOCUS-POCUSSING], [Colloq.], to trick; dupe.

hod (hod), *n.* [earlier *hot* < OFr. *hotte* (< HG.), *hodd* < MD. *hodde;* prob. base as in *hide, v.t.*], 1. a wooden trough with a long handle, used for carrying bricks, mortar, etc. on the shoulder. 2. a coal scuttle.

hod carrier, a worker who carries bricks and mortar in a hod.

hod·den (hod′'n), *n.* [? < northern Eng. form of *holden,* pp. of *hold* (? because it "holds" natural hue)], [Scot.], a coarse, undyed woolen cloth: a gray variety, made by mixing white and black fleece, is called *hodden gray. adj.* [Scot.], dressed in hodden; countrified.

hodge·podge (hoj′poj′), *n.* [ME.; see HOTCHPOTCH], 1. a thick stew of various meats and vegetables; hence, 2. any jumbled mixture; mess; medley.

Hodg·kin's disease (hoj′kinz), [after Dr. Thomas *Hodgkin* (1798–1866), by whom first described], a disease characterized by progressive enlargement of the lymph nodes and inflammation of other lymphoid tissues, especially of the spleen.

hod·man (hod′mən), *n.* [*pl.* HODMEN (-mən)], a hod carrier; bricklayer's helper.

Ho·dur, Ho·der (hō′dẽr), *n.* [ON. *Höthr*], in *Norse mythology,* the blind god who unintentionally killed Balder with a twig of mistletoe given to him by Loki.

hoe (hō), *n.* [ME. *houe;* OFr. *houe;* OHG. *houwa* < *houwan,* to hew, cut; cf. HEW], a tool with a thin blade set across the end of a long handle, used for weeding, loosening soil, etc. *v.t. & v.i.* [HOED (hōd), HOEING], to dig, cultivate, weed, etc. with a hoe.

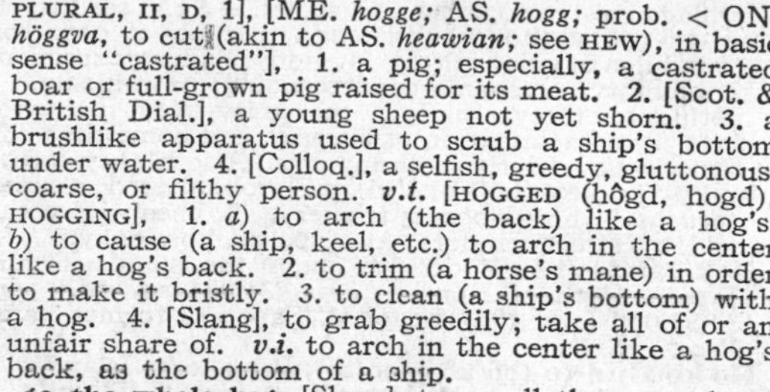

TYPES OF HOE

hoe·cake (hō′kāk′), *n.* a thin bread made of corn meal, originally baked on a hoe at the fire.

hoe·down (hō′doun′), *n.* [prob. of U.S. Negro origin; assoc. with *breakdown* (sense 5)], 1. a lively, rollicking dance, often a square dance. 2. music for this. 3. a party at which hoedowns are danced.

Hoe·nir (hu′nẽr), *n.* [ON.], in *Norse mythology,* the god who, together with Odin and Loki, created the first man and the first woman.

Ho·fer, An·dre·as (än-drā′äs hō′fẽr), 1767–1810; Tyrolese patriot.

Hoff·mann, Ernst The·o·dor Wil·helm (ernst tā′ō-dôr′ vil′helm hôf′män), 1776–1822; German composer, novelist, short-story writer, and painter.

Hof·mann, Josef (hof′mən, hôf′mən), 1876–1957; American pianist and composer, born in Poland.

hog (hôg, hog), *n.* [*pl.* HOGS (hôgz, hogz), HOG; see PLURAL, II, D, 1], [ME. *hogge;* AS. *hogg;* prob. < ON. *höggva,* to cut (akin to AS. *heawian;* see HEW), in basic sense "castrated"], 1. a pig; especially, a castrated boar or full-grown pig raised for its meat. 2. [Scot. & British Dial.], a young sheep not yet shorn. 3. a brushlike apparatus used to scrub a ship's bottom under water. 4. [Colloq.], a selfish, greedy, gluttonous, coarse, or filthy person. *v.t.* [HOGGED (hôgd, hogd), HOGGING], 1. *a*) to arch (the back) like a hog's. *b*) to cause (a ship, keel, etc.) to arch in the center like a hog's back. 2. to trim (a horse's mane) in order to make it bristly. 3. to clean (a ship's bottom) with a hog. 4. [Slang], to grab greedily; take all of or an unfair share of. *v.i.* to arch in the center like a hog's back, as the bottom of a ship.

go the whole hog, [Slang], to go all the way; do or accept something fully.

hog wild, [Colloq.], highly excited; without moderation or restraint.

ho·gan (hō′gôn), *n.* [Navaho *qoghan,* house], the typical dwelling of the Navaho Indians, built of earth walls supported by timbers.

Ho·garth, William (hō′gärth), 1697–1764; English painter and engraver: known for satirical pictures of 18th-century English life.

hog·back (hôg′bak′, hog′bak′), *n.* a ridge with a sharp crest and abruptly sloping sides, often formed by the outcropping edge of tilted rock strata.

hog·fish (hôg′fish′, hog′fish′), *n.* [*pl.* HOGFISH, HOGFISHES (-iz); see FISH], [orig. prob. transl. of OFr. *porpeis;* see PORPOISE], any of several fishes supposedly resembling a hog in some way, as the pigfish.

Hogg, James (hôg, hog), 1770–1835; Scottish poet: called the *Ettrick Shepherd.*

hog·ger·y (hôg′ẽr-i, hog′ẽr-i), *n.* [*pl.* HOGGERIES (-iz)], 1. a place where hogs are kept. 2. a herd of hogs. 3. behavior considered characteristic of hogs, as living in filth, being greedy, etc.

hog·gish (hôg′ish, hog′ish), *adj.* like a hog; very selfish, greedy, gluttonous, coarse, or filthy.

hog·ma·nay (hog′mə-nā′), *n.* [said (by Cotgrave) to be altered < ONorm. Fr. *hoguinané;* altered < OFr. *aguilanneuf;* orig. meaning obscure], [Scot.], New Year's Eve, when young people go around singing and asking for presents.

hog·nose snake (hôg′nōz′, hog′nōz′), a small, harmless North American snake with a flat snout and a thick body.

hog·nut (hôg′nut′, hog′nut′), *n.* 1. the earthnut. 2. the pignut.

hog peanut, a vine of the pea family, with showy flowers and conspicuous pods; earthpea.

hogs·head (hôgz′hed′, hogz′hed′), *n.* [ME. *hogsheved,* lit., hog's head: reason for name uncertain; cf. LG. *bullenkop,* beer barrel, lit., bull's head], 1. a large barrel or cask, especially one holding from 100 to 140 gallons. 2. a liquid measure, especially one equal to 63 gallons (52 1/2 imperial gallons). Abbreviated **hhd.**

hog·tie (hôg′tī′, hog′tī′), *v.t.* [HOGTIED (-tīd′), HOGTYING or HOGTIEING], 1. to tie the four feet or the hands and feet of; hence, 2. [Colloq.], to make incapable of effective action, as if by tying up.

hog·wash (hôg′wôsh′, hog′wäsh′), *n.* 1. refuse fed to hogs; swill; hence, 2. empty talk, writing, etc.

hog·weed (hôg′wēd′, hog′wēd′), *n.* any of several weeds regarded as fit for hogs, as ragweed or knotweed.

Hoh·en·lin·den (hō′ən-lin′dən), *n.* a village near Munich, in Bavaria, where a French army defeated the Austrians in 1800.

Hoh·en·stau·fen (hō′ən-shtou′fən), *n.* the ruling family of Germany and the Holy Roman Empire (1138–1208; 1215–1254) and of Sicily (1194–1268).

Hoh·en·zol·lern (hō′ən-tsôl′ẽrn; Eng. hō′ən-zol′ẽrn), *n.* 1. the ruling family of Prussia and Germany (1701–1918), founded by Frederick I. 2. a former province of Prussia, Germany: area, 440 sq. mi.

hoick (hoik), *interj.* hoicks.

hoicks (hoiks), *interj.* [earlier *hoika;* cf. YOICKS], a hunter's call to the hounds. *v.t. & v.i.* to urge with or as with this call.

hoi·den (hoi′d'n), *n., adj., v.i.* hoyden.

hoi·den·ish (hoi′d'n-ish), *adj.* hoydenish.

‡hoi pol·loi (hoi′pə-loi′), [Gr., the many], the common people; the masses: usually patronizing or contemptuous; popularly and redundantly preceded by *the.*

hoise (hoiz), *v.t.* [HOISED (hoizd) or HOIST (hoist), HOISING], [Early Mod. Eng. phonetic sp. of earlier *hyce, hysse* < D. *hijschen* < LG. *hissen;* apparently of nautical origin], [Obs.], to hoist.

hoist (hoist), *v.t.* [var. of *hoise* with unhistoric *-t* < the pp.], to raise aloft; lift or pull up, especially by means of a cable, pulley, crane, etc. *n.* 1. a hoisting. 2. an apparatus for raising heavy things; elevator or tackle. 3. in *nautical usage, a*) the middle part of a mast. *b*) the perpendicular height of a sail or flag.

c) flags hoisted together as a signal. —*SYN.* see **lift.**

hoi·ty-toi·ty (hoi'ti-toi'ti), *adj.* [redupl. of obs. *hoit*, to indulge in noisy mirth], 1. giddy; flighty; capricious. 2. haughty; arrogant; condescending; patronizing. 3. petulant; fussy; huffy. *n.* hoity-toity behavior. *interj.* an exclamation of surprise and somewhat contemptuous or derisive disapproval. Also **highty-tighty.**

ho·key·po·key (hō'ki-pō'ki), *n.* [prob. altered < *hocus-pocus*], 1. hocus-pocus; trickery. 2. cheap ice cream sold by street vendors. Also spelled **hokypoky.**

Hok·kai·do (hôk'kī-dô'), *n.* one of the islands forming Japan, north of Honshu: area, 34,084 sq. mi.; pop., 3,853,000 (est. 1947); capital, Sapporo: former name, *Yezo.*

Ho·ko Gun·to (hō'kō goon'tō), Pescadores Islands.

ho·kum (hō'kəm), *n.* [altered < *hocus*], [Slang], 1. crudely comic or mawkishly sentimental elements in a play, story, etc., used to gain an immediate emotional response. 2. nonsense; humbug; claptrap; bunk.

Ho·ku·sai, Ka·tsu·shi·ka (kä'tsoo-shē'kä hô'koo-sī'), 1760–1849; Japanese engraver and painter.

Hol·bein, Hans (häns hôl'bīn; Eng. hōl'bīn), 1. 1465?–1524; German painter: called *the Elder.* 2. 1497?–1543; his son; German painter: called *the Younger.*

HOLC, H.O.L.C., Home Owners' Loan Corporation.

hold (hōld), *v.t.* [HELD (held), HOLDING; *archaic* pp. HOLDEN (hōl'd'n)], [ME. *holden;* Anglian AS. *haldan* (W. Sax. *healdan*); akin to G. *halten*, Goth. *haldan*, to tend (sheep); IE. base **qel-*, to drive, as also in L. *celer*, swift (see CELERITY); prob. sense development: drive (cattle, etc.)—tend (cattle, etc.)—possess (cattle, etc.)], 1. to take and keep with the hands, arms, or other means; grasp; clutch; seize. 2. to keep from going away; not let escape: as, *hold* the prisoner, will they *hold* the train till we get there? 3. to keep in a certain place or position, or in a specified condition: as, *hold* your head on one side. 4. to restrain or control as by keeping in a certain place; specifically, *a*) to keep from falling; bear the weight of; support; sustain: as, this pillar *holds* the platform. *b*) to keep from acting; keep back: as, *hold* your tongue. *c*) to keep from advancing or attacking. *d*) to keep from getting an advantage. *e*) to get and keep control of; keep from relaxing: as, the speaker *held* their attention. *f*) to keep (a letter, etc.) for delivery at a later time. *g*) to keep under obligation; bind: as, *hold* him to his word. 5. to have and keep as one's own; be in possession of; own; occupy: as, he *holds* the office of mayor. 6. to keep against an enemy; guard; defend: as, *hold* the fort. 7. to have or conduct together; carry on (a meeting, conversation, etc.); perform (a function, service, etc.): as, the college will *hold* classes today. 8. to call together or preside over: as, the judge will *hold* court. 9. to have or keep within itself; contain; have room or space for: as, this bottle *holds* a quart. 10. to have or keep in the mind. 11. to have an opinion or belief about; regard; consider: as, I *hold* your statement to be untrue. 12. in *law*, *a*) to decide; adjudge; decree. *b*) to bind by contract. *c*) to possess by legal title: as, who *holds* the mortgage? 13. in *music*, to go on sounding (a tone). *v.i.* 1. to go on being firm, loyal, etc.: as, *hold* to your resolution. 2. to remain unbroken or unyielding; not give way: as, the rope *held.* 3. to have right or title (usually with *from* or *of*). 4. to be in effect or in force; be true or valid: as, this principle *holds* in any government. 5. to keep up; continue: as, the wind *held* from the north. 6. to go no further; stop oneself; halt: usually in the imperative. *n.* 1. the act or manner of grasping or seizing; grip. 2. a thing to hold or hold on by. 3. a thing for holding or containing something else. 4. a controlling or dominating force; restraining authority; strong influence: as, his wife has a firm *hold* over him. 5. a means of confinement; prison. 6. [Archaic], a stronghold. 7. [Obs.], the act or fact of guarding, possessing, keeping in custody, etc. 8. in *music*, a symbol for a pause. 9. in *wrestling*, a way of holding or seizing an opponent: as, a scissors *hold.* —*SYN.* see **contain, have.**

catch hold of, to take; seize; grasp.

get hold of, 1. to take; seize; grasp. 2. to acquire.

hold back, 1. to restrain. 2. to refrain. 3. to retain.

hold down, 1. to keep down or under control; restrain. 2. [Colloq.], to have and keep (a job).

hold forth, [after Phil. 2:16], 1. to speak at some length; preach; lecture. 2. to offer; propose.

hold in, 1. to keep in or back. 2. to control oneself or one's impulses.

hold off, 1. to keep away or at a distance. 2. to keep from attacking or doing something.

hold on, 1. to retain one's hold. 2. to continue; persist. 3. [Colloq.], stop! wait!

hold one's own, to keep up; not fall behind.

hold out, 1. to last; endure; continue. 2. to continue resistance; stand firm; not yield. 3. to offer. 4. [Slang], to fail or refuse to give (what is to be given).

hold over, 1. to postpone consideration of or action on. 2. to stay for an additional period or term. 3. to keep as a threat or advantage over.

hold up, 1. to keep from falling; prop up. 2. to show; exhibit. 3. to last; endure; continue. 4. to stop; delay; impede. 5. to stop forcibly and rob; hence, 6. [Colloq.], to overcharge.

hold with, 1. to agree with. 2. to approve of. 3. to side with.

lay (or **take**) **hold of,** 1. to take; seize; grasp. 2. to get control or possession of.

hold (hōld), *n.* [altered (after *hold*, *v.*) < *hole* or < MD. *hol*, a hole, cave, ship's hold], the interior of a ship below decks, especially below the lower deck, in which the cargo is carried.

hold·all (hōld'ôl'), *n.* a large traveling case for carrying clothes, equipment, etc.

hold·back (hōld'bak'), *n.* 1. a thing that holds back; curb; check; hindrance. 2. a strap or iron attached to the shaft of a wagon, carriage, etc. and to the harness, to enable a horse to stop or back the vehicle.

hold·en (hōl'd'n), archaic past participle of **hold.**

hold·er (hōl'dẽr), *n.* [ME. *holdere*], a person or thing that holds; specifically, *a*) a person who holds, and is legally entitled to payment of, a bill, note, or check. *b*) a tenant. *c*) a possessor. *d*) a device for holding something, as a penholder. *e*) a heavy cloth to protect the hands when lifting hot dishes.

hold·fast (hōld'fast', hōld'fäst'), *n.* 1. a holding fast. 2. a device that holds something else in place; hook, nail, clamp, etc.

hold·ing (hōld'iŋ), *n.* [ME. *holdinge;* see HOLD, *v.*], 1. land, especially a farm, rented from another. 2. *usually pl.* property owned, especially stocks or bonds. 3. in certain sports, the act of illegally hindering an opponent, as from using his arms or hands.

holding company, a corporation organized to hold bonds or stocks of other corporations, which it usually controls.

hold·out (hōld'out'), *n.* [Colloq.], in *baseball, football,* etc., a professional player who has not signed a contract at the regular time because he is insisting upon better terms.

hold·o·ver (hōld'ō'vẽr), *n.* [Colloq.], a person or thing staying on from a previous period; specifically, a person, as an officeholder or entertainer, who is held over from one term of office, engagement, etc. to another.

hold·up (hōld'up'), *n.* 1. a stoppage; delay or hindrance. 2. the act of stopping forcibly and robbing; hence, 3. [Colloq.], an overcharging.

hole (hōl), *n.* [ME.; AS. *hol*, orig. neut. of *holh*, *adj.*, hollow; hence akin to G. *hohl*, hollow; IE. base **qaul-*, **qul-*, hollow, hollowed thing, as also in L. *caulis*, stalk, cabbage (cf. COLE, CAULIFLOWER)], 1. a hollow or hollowed-out place; cavity; specifically, *a*) an excavation; pit: as, he dug a *hole* in the ground. *b*) a small bay or inlet; cove: often in place names. *c*) a pool or deep, relatively wide place in a stream: as, a swimming *hole.* *d*) an animal's burrow or lair; den; hence, 2. a small, dingy, squalid place; any dirty, badly lighted room, house, etc. 3. a prison cell. 4. *a*) an opening in or through anything; break; gap: as, a *hole* in the wall. *b*) a tear or rent, as in a garment. 5. a flaw; fault; blemish; defect: as, we found *holes* in his argument. 6. [Colloq.], an embarrassing situation or position; predicament. 7. in *golf*, *a*) a small, round, hollow place into which the ball is to be hit. *b*) the tee, fairway, greens, etc. leading to this: as, 18 *holes* of golf. *v.t.* [HOLED (hōld), HOLING], 1. to make a hole or holes in. 2. to put, hit, or drive into a hole. 3. to create by making a hole: as, they *holed* a tunnel through the mountain.

burn a hole in one's pocket, to make one eager to spend it: said of money.

hole high, in *golf*, as far from the tee as the hole is; even with the hole but not in it.

hole in one, in *golf*, the act of getting the ball into a hole with one drive from the tee.

hole out, in *golf*, to hit the ball into a hole.

hole up, 1. to hibernate, usually in a hole. 2. to shut oneself in.

in the hole, [Colloq.], financially embarrassed or behind: often with a specific sum indicated, as, I'm fifty dollars *in the hole* this month.

make a hole in, to consume a sizable amount of.

pick holes in, to pick out errors or flaws in.

SYN.—**hole** is the general word for an open space in a thing and may suggest a depression in a surface or an opening from surface to surface (a *hole* in the ground, a *hole* in a sock); **hollow** basically suggests an empty space within a solid body, whether or not it extends to the surface, but it may also be applied to a depressed place in a surface (a wooded *hollow*); **cavity**, the Latin-derived equivalent of **hollow**, has special application in formal and scientific usage (the thoracic *cavity*); an **excavation** is a hollow made in or through ground by digging (the *excavations* at Pompeii).

hole·y (hōl'i), *adj.* [ME.], having a hole or holes.

hol·i·but (hol'ə-bət), *n.* [*pl.* HOLIBUT, HOLIBUTS (-bəts); see PLURAL, II, D, 2], a halibut.

hol·i·day (hol'ə-dā'), *n.* [< ME. *holidei*, with shortened first vowel; AS. *hāligdæg*, lit., holy day], 1. a religious festival; holy day: usually **holyday.** 2. a day of freedom from labor; day set aside for leisure and recreation; hence, 3. *often pl.* [Chiefly British], a period of leisure or recreation; vacation. 4. a day set aside by law or custom for the suspension of business, usually in celebration of some event. *adj.* of or suited to a holiday; joyous; gay: as, the *holiday* spirit.

ho·li·ly (hō′lə-li), *adv.* [ME. *holiliche;* AS. *haliglice*], in a holy manner; piously, devoutly, or sacredly.

ho·li·ness (hō′li-nis), *n.* [ME. *holinesse;* AS. *halignesse*], 1. the quality or state of being holy. 2. [H-], a title of the Pope: used with *His* or *Your.*

Hol·ins·hed, Raphael (hol′inz-hed′, hol′in-shed′), ?–c. 1580; English chronicler.

hol·la (hol′ə, hə-lä′), *interj., n., v.t. & v.i.* [< Fr. *holà* < *ho,* ho + *là,* there < L. *illac,* in that place, there], hollo.

Hol·land (hol′ənd), *n.* [D., earlier *Holtland;* prob. < *holt,* wood + *land,* land, but sometimes referred to *hol,* hole, hollow], the Netherlands.

hol·land (hol′ənd), *n.* [< *Holland,* where first made], a linen or cotton cloth, sometimes glazed, used for children's clothing, upholstery, etc.: called *brown holland* when unbleached.

hol·lan·daise sauce (hol′ən-dāz′), [Fr. *hollandaise,* fem. of *hollandais,* of Holland], a creamy sauce for fish or vegetables, made of butter, egg yolks, vinegar, etc.

Hol·land·er (hol′ən-dẽr), *n.* a native or inhabitant of Holland.

Hol·lan·di·a (hô-län′di-ä′; Eng. ho-lan′di-ə), *n.* a city in the former Netherlands New Guinea (now West Irian): now called *Kotabaru.*

Hol·lands (hol′əndz), *n.* [D. *hollandsch* (*genever*)], gin made in Holland: also **Holland gin,** originally **Hollands geneva.**

hol·ler (hol′ẽr), *v.i. & v.t., n.* [var. of *hollo, holla*], shout; yell: considered substandard by some but widely used.

hol·lo (hol′ō, hə-lō′), *interj. & n.* [*pl.* HOLLOS (-ōz, -lōz′)], [var. of *holla, hallo*], 1. a shout or call, especially to attract a person's attention or stop him, or to urge on hounds in hunting. 2. a shout of greeting or surprise. *v.i. & v.t.* [HOLLOED (-ōd, -lōd′), HOLLOING], 1. to shout at or call out in order to attract the attention of (a person). 2. to urge on (hounds) by shouting or calling out "hollo." 3. to shout or call, as in greeting or surprise. Also **hallo, holla, halloa, holloa, hillo, hilloa, hullo.** See **hello.**

hol·loa (hol′ō, hə-lō′), *interj., n., v.t. & v.i.* hollo.

hol·low (hol′ō), *adj.* [ME. *holwe;* AS. *holh;* see HOLE], 1. having an empty space, or only air, within it; having a cavity inside: opposed to *solid.* 2. depressed below the surrounding surface; shaped like a cup or bowl; concave. 3. deeply set; sunken: as, *hollow* cheeks. 4. empty, worthless, or insincere; not real or meaningful. 5. hungry. 6. deep-toned, dull, and muffled, as though resounding from something hollow. *adv.* in a hollow manner. *n.* 1. a hollow formation or place; cavity; hole. 2. a valley. *v.t. & v.i.* to make or become hollow. —*SYN.* see **hole, vain.**
 beat all hollow, [Colloq.], to outdo or surpass by far.
 hollow out, to make by hollowing.

hol·low-eyed (hol′ō-īd′), *adj.* having deep-set eyes or dark areas under the eyes, as from sickness or fatigue.

hol·ly (hol′i), *n.* [*pl.* HOLLIES (-iz)], [ME. *holi, holin;* AS. *holegn;* akin to *hul-* in G. *hulst,* holly; IE. base **qel-,* to prick, as also in W. *celyn,* holly], 1. any of a group of small trees and shrubs with stiff, glossy, sharp-pointed leaves and clusters of bright-red berries. 2. the leaves and berries, used as Christmas ornaments.

hol·ly·hock (hol′i-hok′), *n.* [ME. *holihoc,* lit., holy hock < AS. *halig,* holy + *hoc,* mallow], 1. a tall, hardy plant of the mallow family, with coarse, rounded leaves, a hairy stem, and large, showy flowers of various colors. 2. its flower.

Hol·ly·wood (hol′i-wood′), *n.* 1. a section of Los Angeles, California, regarded as the center of the American motion-picture industry; hence, 2. the American motion-picture industry or its life, world, etc.

Hollywood bed, a bed consisting typically of a mattress on a box spring that rests on a metal frame or has attached legs: it sometimes has a headboard.

holm (hōm), *n.* [ME.; AS., sea; with sense influence < cognate ON. *holmr,* land by water, island; IE. base as in *hill*], 1. a small island in a river or lake, near the mainland or a larger island: often used in place names. 2. [British], low, flat land by a river or stream; bottoms.

holm (hōm), *n.* [altered < *holn,* form of ME. *holin;* see HOLLY], 1. a holm oak. 2. [Dial.], holly.

Hol·man-Hunt, William (hōl′mən-hunt′), 1827–1910; English painter.

Holmes, Oliver Wendell (hōmz), 1. 1809–1894; American writer and physician. 2. 1841–1935; his son; American jurist; associate justice, United States Supreme Court (1902–1932).

Holmes, Sher·lock (shũr′lok), a fictitious British detective, famous for his powers of deduction, the main character in many stories by A. Conan Doyle.

hol·mic (hōl′mik), *adj.* of or containing trivalent holmium.

hol·mi·um (hōl′mi-əm), *n.* [Mod. L. < *Holmia,* Latinized form of *Stockholm*], a metallic chemical element of the rare-earth group: symbol, Ho; at. wt., 164.94; at. no., 67.

holm oak, [see HOLM (holly)], 1. a south European evergreen oak with hollylike leaves. 2. its wood.

hol·o- (hol′ō, hol′ə, hō′lə), [< Gr. *holos,* whole], a combining form meaning *whole, entire,* as in *holomorphic.*

hol·o·blas·tic (hol′ə-blas′tik), *adj.* [*holo-* + *-blast* + *-ic*], in *embryology,* undergoing complete division into segments: said of certain ova, and opposed to *meroblastic.*

hol·o·caine (hol′ə-kān′), *n.* [*holo-* + *cocaine*], 1. an organic, crystalline substance, $C_{18}H_{22}O_2N_2$, derived from the coal tars. 2. its hydrochloride, phenacaine, used as a local anesthetic, especially in eye operations.

hol·o·caust (hol′ə-kôst′), *n.* [ME.; Fr. *holocauste;* LL. *holocaustum;* Gr. *holokauston,* neut. of *holokaustos,* burnt whole < *holos,* whole + *kaustos,* burnt < *kaiein,* to burn], 1. an offering the whole of which is burned; burnt offering. 2. complete destruction of people or animals by fire. 3. great or widespread destruction.

Hol·o·cene (hol′ə-sēn′), *adj.* [*holo-* + *-cene*], designating or of the Recent Epoch of geological time.

Hol·o·fer·nes (hol′ə-fũr′nēz), *n.* the general of Nebuchadnezzar's Assyrian army, killed by Judith to save her people: see **Judith.**

hol·o·graph (hol′ə-graf′, hol′ə-gräf′), *adj.* [Fr. *holographe;* LL. *holographus;* Gr. *holographos* < *holos,* whole, entire + *graphein,* to write], written entirely in the handwriting of the person under whose name it appears. *n.* a holograph document, letter, will, etc.

hol·o·he·dral (hol′ə-hē′drəl), *adj.* [*holo-* + *-hedral*], having the whole number of planes required for complete symmetry: said of a crystal.

hol·o·mor·phic (hol′ə-môr′fik), *adj.* [*holo-* + *-morphic*], having the two ends symmetrical in form.

hol·o·pho·tal (hol′ə-fō′t'l), *adj.* [< *holo-* + Gr. *phōs, phōtos,* light; + *-al*], reflecting or refracting all or most of the light from a source.

hol·o·phote (hol′ə-fōt′), *n.* [see HOLOPHOTAL], an apparatus used in lighthouses, having lenses and reflectors by which almost all the light from a lamp is cast in a desired direction.

hol·o·phras·tic (hol′ə-fras′tik), *adj.* [< *holo-* + Gr. *phrastikos,* suited for expressing < *phrazein,* to speak], expressing an entire sentence or phrase in one word.

hol·o·thu·ri·an (hol′ə-thoor′i-ən), *n.* [< Mod. L. *Holothuria,* generic name < L. *holothuria,* pl. < Gr. *holothouria,* pl. of *holothourion,* kind of water polyp], any of a class of marine animals including organisms with elongated, flexible bodies; sea cucumber or trepang.

holp (hōlp), [ME. *holpe,* southern dial. form of *holpen*], archaic past tense and obsolete past participle of **help.**

hol·pen (hōl′p'n), [ME.], archaic past participle of **help.**

Hol·stein (hōl′stin; G. hôl′shtīn), *n.* 1. a former duchy of Denmark: now a part of Schleswig-Holstein. 2. (hōl′stīn, hōl′stēn), any of a breed of large, black-and-white cattle raised for both milk and beef: so called because originally from Schleswig-Holstein.

HOLSTEIN (1864)

Hol·stein-Frie·sian (hōl′stīn-frē′zhən, hōl′stēn-frē′zhən), *n.* a Holstein.

hol·ster (hōl′stẽr), *n.* [17th-c. borrowing of Sw. *holster* (< ON. *hulstr,* a sheath, akin to AS. *heolstor,* hiding, concealment); prob. via D. *holster,* pistol case; base as in *hall, hell*], a leather pistol case, usually attached to a belt or a saddle.

holt (hōlt), *n.* [ME.; AS.; akin to G. *holz,* wood; IE. **qldos* < base **qel-,* to strike, as also in Gr. *klados,* young sprout, shoot; cf. HALT (lame), HILT], [Archaic], a grove; copse; wooded hill.

ho·lus-bo·lus (hō′ləs-bō′ləs), *adv.* [mock-Latin < Eng. *whole* + *bolus*], all at once; in one lump.

ho·ly (hō′li), *adj.* [HOLIER (-li-ẽr), HOLIEST (-li-ist)], [ME. *holie;* AS. *halig* (akin to G. *heilig*) < base of AS. *hal,* sound, whole, happy (cf. HALE, WHOLE): used as transl. of L. *sacer, sanctus,* etc. in church use], [often H-], 1. dedicated to religious use; belonging to or coming from God; consecrated; sacred. 2. spiritually perfect or pure; untainted by evil or sin; sinless; saintly. 3. deserving reverence or worship. 4. associated with Jesus and his life: as, the *Holy* Rood. 5. [Slang], very much of a: a generalized intensive, as, she's a *holy* terror. *n.* something holy; a sanctuary. *SYN.*—**holy** suggests that which is held in deepest religious reverence or is basically associated with a religion and, in extended use, connotes spiritual purity (the *Holy* Ghost, a *holy* love); **sacred** refers to that which is set apart as holy or is dedicated to some exalted purpose and, therefore, connotes inviolability (Parnassus was *sacred* to Apollo, a *sacred* trust); **consecrated** and **hallowed** describe that which has been made sacred or holy, **consecrated**, in addition connoting solemn devotion or dedication (a life *consecrated* to art), and **hallowed**, inherent or intrinsic holiness (*hallowed* ground); **divine** suggests that which is of the nature of, is associated with, or is derived from God or a god (the *divine* right of kings), and, in extended use, connotes supreme greatness (the *Divine* Duse).—*ANT.* profane, unholy.

Holy Alliance, an alliance formed in 1815 by the rulers of Russia, Austria, and Prussia to suppress the democratic revolutionary movement in Europe.

Holy Bible, the Bible.

Holy City, 1. a city regarded as sacred by the believers of some religion: as, Jerusalem, Mecca, and Rome are *Holy Cities.* 2. Heaven.

Holy Communion, any of various church rites in which bread and wine are consecrated and received as (symbols of) the body and blood of Jesus; sacrament of the Eucharist, or the Lord's Supper.

Holy Cross, Mount of the, a peak in central Colorado, bearing a cross formed by snow: height, 13,996 ft.

ho·ly·day (hō'li-dā'), *n.* a religious festival: also **holy day.**

Holy Father, a title of the Pope: also **Most Holy Father.**

Holy Ghost, the third person of the Trinity; spirit of God: also called *Holy Spirit.*

Holy Grail, see **Grail.**

Holy Innocents' Day, Childermas.

Holy Land, Palestine.

Holy Mother, Mary, mother of Jesus.

Holy Office, in the *Roman Catholic Church,* a tribunal for the protection of faith and morals, the suppression of heresy, etc.: formerly called *the Inquisition.*

holy of holies, [a Hebraism], 1. the innermost part of the Jewish tabernacle and Temple, where the ark of the covenant was kept. 2. any most sacred place.

Hol·yoke (hōl'yōk), *n.* a city in central Massachusetts, on the Connecticut River: pop., 53,000.

holy orders, 1. the sacrament or rite of ordination. 2. the rank of an ordained Christian minister or priest. 3. three higher ranks or orders of Christian ministers or priests; specifically, *a)* in the *Roman Catholic Church,* priests, deacons, and subdeacons. *b)* in the *Anglican Church,* bishops, priests, and deacons.
 take holy orders, to be ordained as a Christian minister or priest.

Holy Roller, a member of a minor religious sect that expresses religious emotion by making violent movements and sounds during services of worship: humorous or contemptuous term.

Holy Roman Empire, the central European empire, chiefly of German-speaking peoples, established with the crowning of Otto I as emperor by the Pope in 962 A.D. (or, according to some, with the papal crowning of Charlemagne in 800 A.D.) and ending with the resignation of the title by Francis II of Austria in 1806: it was regarded as the re-embodiment of the Roman Empire as a universal political unity over which the Pope had spiritual control.

HOLY ROMAN EMPIRE

Holy Rood, holy rood, 1. the cross on which Jesus was crucified. 2. any representation of this; cross or crucifix symbolizing Christianity, placed over the entrance to the chancel of a church, etc.

Holy Saturday, the Saturday before Easter.

Holy Scripture, the Bible.

Holy See, the position, authority, or court of the Pope; Apostolic See.

Holy Sepulcher, the sepulcher at Jerusalem in which the body of Jesus was placed after the Crucifixion.

Holy Spirit, the Holy Ghost.

ho·ly·stone (hō'li-stōn'), *n.* [said to be from use for cleaning decks for Sunday; ? for *holey stone*], a large, flat piece of sandstone used for scouring a ship's wooden decks. *v.t.* to scour or scrub with a holystone.

Holy Synod, the administrative council of any Orthodox church.

Holy Thursday, 1. the day before Good Friday, in Holy Week; Maundy Thursday. 2. in the *Anglican Church,* Ascension Day, the 40th day after Easter.

ho·ly·tide (hō'li-tīd'), *n.* [*holy* + *tide, n.*], a holy season; day or longer period spent in religious rites or worship.

holy water, water blessed by a priest.

Holy Week, the week before Easter.

Holy Writ, the Bible.

hom- (hōm, hom), homo-.

hom·age (hom'ij, om'ij), *n.* [ME.; OFr.; ML. *hominaticum,* vassal's service, homage < L. *homo,* a man], 1. originally, *a)* a public avowal of allegiance by a vassal to his lord. *b)* an act done or thing given to show the relationship between lord and vassal. 2. anything given or done to show the reverence, honor, or respect in which a person is held: usually with *do* or *pay,* as, the town paid *homage* to the great man. —*SYN.* see **allegiance, honor.**

hom·bre (ôm'brā, om'bri), *n.* [*pl.* HOMBRES (-brās, -briz)], [Sp. < L. *homo,* man], [Slang], a man; fellow.

hom·bre (om'bẽr), *n.* omber, a card game.

Hom·burg (hom'bẽrg), *n.* [< *Homburg,* Prussia, where first worn], 1. a man's felt hat with a crown dented from front to back and a stiffened brim turned up slightly at the sides. 2. a woman's hat like this.

home (hōm), *n.* [ME. *home, hoom;* AS. *ham;* akin to G. *heim;* IE. base **kei-,* to lie, remain, seen also in Gr. *keimai,* to lie down, rest, L. *civis,* townsman (cf. CIVIL, CIVIC); cf. HIDE (piece of land); basic sense "place where one lies; dwelling"], 1. the place where a person (or family) lives; one's dwelling place; specifically, *a)* the house, apartment, etc. where one lives or is living temporarily; living quarters. *b)* the region, city, state, etc. where one lives. 2. the place where one was born or reared; one's own city, state, or country. 3. a place thought of as home; specifically, *a)* a place where one likes to be; place thought of as the center of one's affections; restful or congenial place. *b)* the grave. 4. the members of a family; household: as, the depression ruined many *homes.* 5. a place or institution for orphans, people who are blind, old, poor, sick, etc. 6. *a)* the place that is the natural environment of an animal, plant, etc. *b)* the place where something is or has been founded, developed, etc.: as, Paris is the *home* of women's fashions. 7. in many games, the base or goal; especially, the home plate in baseball. *adj.* 1. of home or a home; specifically, *a)* of the family, household, etc.; domestic. *b)* of one's country, government, etc.; domestic: opposed to *foreign. c)* of or at the center of activity; of or at headquarters: as, a *home* office. 2. reaching its goal; effective; forceful; to the point. 3. played in the city where the team originates: as, a *home* game. *adv.* [orig. the *n.* as acc. of direction], 1. at, to, or in the direction of home or a home. 2. to the place where it belongs; to the point aimed at: as, he drove the nail *home.* 3. to the center or heart of a matter; closely; directly; deeply. *v.i.* [HOMED (hōmd), HOMING], 1. to go to one's home. 2. to have a home. *v.t.* to send to, put into, or provide with a home.
 at home, 1. in one's own house, neighborhood, city, or country. 2. as if in one's own home; comfortable; at ease; familiar. 3. willing to receive visitors. 4. a reception at one's home.
 bring home to, 1. to impress upon or make clear to. 2. to fasten the blame for (something) on (someone).
 come home, 1. to return, as to one's home. 2. in *nautical usage,* to fail to hold, as an anchor.
 see a person home, to escort a person to his home.

home-bred (hōm'bred'), *adj.* 1. bred or reared at home; domestic; native. 2. not cultivated; not polished; not sophisticated; crude.

home-brew (hōm'brōō'), *n.* any alcoholic liquor, especially beer, made at home.

home·com·ing (hōm'kum'iŋ), *n.* 1. a coming or returning to one's home. 2. in many colleges and universities, an annual celebration attended by alumni.

home economics, the science and art of homemaking, including nutrition, clothing, budgeting, and child care.

home-grown (hōm'grōn'), *adj.* grown for local consumption: said of fruits and vegetables.

home·land (hōm'land'), *n.* the country in which one was born or makes one's home.

home·less (hōm'lis), *adj.* without a home.

home·like (hōm'līk'), *adj.* having qualities usually associated with home; comfortable, familiar, friendly, cozy, etc.

home·li·ness (hōm'li-nis), *n.* a homely quality or state.

home·ly (hōm'li), *adj.* [HOMELIER (-li-ẽr), HOMELIEST (-li-ist)], [ME. *homli*], 1. originally, *a)* of the home; domestic. *b)* familiar; intimate. *c)* fond of home. 2. *a)* characteristic of or suitable for home or home life; simple; unpretentious; plain; everyday: as, *homely* virtues. *b)* crude; unpolished. 3. not good-looking; not attractive; plain; ugly.

home·made (hōm'mād'), *adj.* 1. made, or as if made, at home; hence, 2. plain; simple; crude.

home·mak·er (hōm'māk'ẽr), *n.* a woman who manages a home; housewife.

home·mak·ing (hōm'māk'iŋ), *n.* the work of a homemaker; management of a home.

ho·me·o- (hō'mi-ə, hom'i-ə), [Gr. *homoio-* < *homos,* same], a combining form meaning *like, the same,* *similar*, as in *homeomorphism*: also **home-**, **homoio-**: words beginning with *homeo-* may also be spelled **homoeo-**.

Home Office, the department of government in Great Britain corresponding to the Department of the Interior in the United States.

ho·me·o·mor·phism (hō'mi-ə-môr'fiz'm, hom'i-ə-môr'-fiz'm), *n.* [< *homeo-* + Gr. *morphē*, form; + *-ism*], a close similarity of crystalline forms between substances of different chemical composition.

ho·me·o·path (hō'mi-ə-path', hom'i-ə-path'), *n.* a person who practices or believes in homeopathy.

ho·me·o·path·ic (hō'mi-ə-path'ik, hom'i-ə-path'ik), *adj.* 1. of, like, according to, or practicing homeopathy. 2. containing a very small amount of a drug or other active substance.

ho·me·op·a·thist (hō'mi-op'ə-thist, hom'i-op'ə-thist), *n.* a homeopath.

ho·me·op·a·thy (hō'mi-op'ə-thi, hom'i-op'ə-thi), *n.* [*homeo-* + *-pathy*, after G. *homöopathie*, lit., likeness of feeling; adopted (c. 1800) by S. Hahnemann, G. physician], a system of medical treatment based on the theory that certain diseases can be cured by giving very small doses of drugs which in a healthy person and in large doses would produce symptoms like those of the disease: opposed to *allopathy*.

ho·me·o·ther·a·py (hō'mi-ə-ther'ə-pi, hom'i-ə-ther'ə-pi), *n.* [*homeo-* + *therapy*], the treatment of a disease by giving a substance similar to the agent that caused the disease.

ho·me·o·typ·ic (hō'mi-ə-tip'ik, hom'i-ə-tip'ik), *adj.* [*homeo-* + *typic*], designating the second division of the nuclei of germ cells in meiosis.

home plate, in *baseball*, the slab that the batter stands beside, across which the pitcher must throw the ball for a strike: it is the last of the four bases that a runner must touch in succession to score a run.

Ho·mer (hō'mẽr), [L. *Homerus;* Gr. *Homēros;* identical in form with *homēros*, a pledge, hostage, but said in ancient folk etymologies to be a Cumaean word meaning "blind"], a masculine name. *n.* Greek epic poet; c. 8th century B.C.; according to legend, the author of the *Iliad* and the *Odyssey*.

ho·mer (hō'mẽr), *n.* [Heb. *ḥomer*, homer, mound < *ḥāmar*, to surge up, swell up], an early Hebrew measure, equal to about 11 2/3 bushels.

hom·er (hōm'ẽr), *n.* [Colloq.], in *baseball*, a home run.

Ho·mer, Wins·low (winz'lō hō'mẽr), 1836–1910; American painter.

Ho·mer·ic (hō-mer'ik), *adj.* of, like, or characteristic of the legendary Homer, his poems, or the Greek civilization that they describe (c. 1200–800 B.C.).

Ho·mer·i·cal (hō-mer'i-k'l), *adj.* Homeric.

Homeric laughter, loud, unrestrained laughter.

home·room (hōm'rōōm', hōm'room'), *n.* 1. the room where a class in school meets every day to be checked for attendance, receive school bulletins, etc. 2. the students in a specific homeroom. Also **home room.**

home rule, the administration of the affairs of a country, colony, district, city, etc. by the citizens who live in it; local self-government: abbreviated **H.R.**

home run, in *baseball*, a hit driving the ball safely beyond the reach of the opponent fielders and permitting the batter to make a circuit of the bases to score a run.

home·sick (hōm'sik'), *adj.* [back-formation < *homesickness*, 18th-c. rendering of Swiss *heimweh*], unhappy or depressed at being away from home and family; longing for home.

home·spun (hōm'spun'), *n.* 1. cloth made of yarn spun at home. 2. coarse, loosely woven cloth like this. *adj.* 1. spun or made at home. 2. made of homespun. 3. plain; unpretentious; homely: as, *homespun* virtues.

Home·stead (hōm'sted', hōm'stid), *n.* a borough in Pennsylvania, near Pittsburgh: pop., 8,000: scene of famous steel strike (1892).

home·stead (hōm'sted'), *n.* [AS. *hamstede;* see HOME & STEAD], 1. a place where a family makes its home, including the land, house, and outbuildings. 2. in *law*, such a place occupied by the owner and his family and exempted from seizure or forced sale to meet general debts. 3. a 160-acre tract of public land granted by the United States government to a settler to be developed as a farm. *v.i.* to become a settler on a homestead.

home·stead·er (hōm'sted'ẽr), *n.* 1. a person who has a homestead. 2. a settler who holds a homestead granted by the United States government.

homestead law, 1. a law exempting a homestead from seizure or forced sale to meet general debts. 2. a United States law granting each settler a 160-acre tract of public land to be developed as a farm.

home·stretch (hōm'strech'), *n.* 1. the part of a race track between the last turn and the finish line; hence, 2. the final part of any undertaking.

home·ward (hōm'wẽrd), *adv. & adj.* [ME. *hamward;* AS. *hamweard*], toward home.

home·wards (hōm'wẽrdz), *adv.* homeward.

home·work (hōm'wũrk'), *n.* 1. work done at home. 2. lessons to be studied or schoolwork to be done outside the classroom.

home·y (hōm'i), *adj.* [HOMIER (-i-ẽr), HOMIEST (-i-ist)], [Colloq.], having qualities usually associated with home; comfortable, familiar, friendly, cozy, etc.: also spelled **homy.**

hom·i·cid·al (hom'ə-sīd''l), *adj.* 1. of, having the nature of, or characterized by homicide. 2. having a tendency to homicide; murderous.

hom·i·cide (hom'ə-sīd'), *n.* [ME.; OFr.; LL. *homicidium*, manslaughter, murder < L. *homicida*, murderer < *homo*, a man + *caedere*, to cut, kill], 1. any killing of one human being by another: *justifiable homicide* is homicide committed in the performance of duty, in self-defense, etc.: see also **murder, manslaughter.** 2. [OFr.; L. *homicida*], a person who kills another.

hom·i·let·ic (hom'ə-let'ik), *adj.* [Gr. *homilētikos*, of or for conversation < *homilein*, to be in company, converse < *homilos;* see HOMILY], 1. having the nature of or characteristic of a homily. 2. of homiletics.

hom·i·let·i·cal (hom'ə-let'i-k'l), *adj.* homiletic.

hom·i·let·ics (hom'ə-let'iks), *n.pl.* [construed as sing.], [< *homiletic*], 1. the art of writing and preaching sermons. 2. the study of sermons.

hom·i·list (hom''l-ist), *n.* a person who writes or delivers homilies.

hom·i·ly (hom''l-i), *n.* [*pl.* HOMILIES (-iz)], [ME. *omelye;* OFr. *omelie;* LL. *homilia*, sermon < Gr. *homilia*, converse, instruction < *homilos*, assembly < *homos*, the same + *ile*, a crowd], 1. a sermon, especially one about something in the Bible. 2. a solemn moral talk or writing; tedious, moralizing lecture.

hom·ing (hōm'iŋ), *adj.* [ppr. of *home*], 1. going home; homeward bound. 2. longing for home.

homing pigeon, a pigeon trained to find its way home from distant places, probably by a capacity for response to the earth's magnetism, and hence used to carry messages; carrier pigeon.

hom·i·ny (hom'ə-ni), *n.* [Am. Ind. (Algonquian) *rockahominie*, parched corn], dry corn (maize) hulled and coarsely ground or broken: it is boiled for food.

ho·mo (hō'mō), *n.* [*pl.* HOMINES (hom'ə-nēz')], [L.], 1. man. 2. [H-], the genus of primates comprising modern man (*Homo sapiens*) and several extinct species of man.

ho·mo- (hō'mə, hom'ə), [Gr. *homo-* < *homos*, the same], a combining form meaning *same, equal, like*, as in *homogenize:* also, before a vowel, **hom-.**

ho·mo·cen·tric (hō'mə-sen'trik, hom'ə-sen'trik), *adj.* [Mod. L. *homocentricus* < Gr. *homokentros* < *homos*, the same + *kentron*, a center], having the same center.

ho·mo·cer·cal (hō'mə-sũr'k'l, hom'ə-sũr'k'l), *adj.* [< *homo-* + Gr. *kerkos*, a tail; + *-al*], designating, of, or having a tail fin in which the upper and lower lobes are symmetrical and the spine ends at or near the center of the base.

ho·mo·chro·mat·ic (hō'mə-krō-mat'ik), *adj.* [*homo-* + *chromatic*], of or having one or the same color: opposed to *heterochromatic*.

ho·mo·chro·mous (hō'mə-krō'məs), *adj.* homochromatic.

ho·moe·o- (hō'mi-ə, hom'i-ə), homeo-.

ho·mo·e·rot·ic (hō'mō-i-rot'ik), *adj.* of or characterized by homoerotism.

ho·mo·er·o·tism (hō'mō-er'ə-tiz'm), *n.* [*homo-* + *erotism*], sexual desire for a person of the same sex.

ho·mog·a·mous (hō-mog'ə-məs), *adj.* [*homo-* + *-gamous*], 1. having flowers all of one sex or all two-sexed. 2. having stamens and pistils that mature at the same time.

ho·mog·a·my (hō-mog'ə-mi), *n.* 1. a homogamous condition. 2. interbreeding in an isolated group of individuals of the same species.

ho·mo·ge·ne·i·ty (hō'mə-jə-nē'ə-ti, hom'ə-jə-nē'ə-ti), *n.* [ML. *homogeneitas*], the quality or condition of being homogeneous.

ho·mo·ge·ne·ous (hō'mə-jē'ni-əs, hom'ə-jē'ni-əs), *adj.* [ML. *homogeneus;* Gr. *homogenēs*, of the same race, family, or kind < *homos*, the same + *genos*, a race, family, kind], 1. the same in structure, quality, etc.; similar or identical. 2. composed of similar or identical elements or parts; uniform. Opposed to *heterogeneous*. 3. in *mathematics*, *a*) of the same kind and therefore capable of being compared in size. *b*) having all terms of the same dimensions.

ho·mo·gen·e·sis (hō'mə-jen'ə-sis, hom'ə-jen'ə-sis), *n.* [*homo-* + *genesis*], reproduction in which successive generations are alike: opposed to *heterogenesis*.

ho·mo·gen·ize (hə-moj'ə-nīz', hō'mə-jə-nīz'), *v.t.* [HOMOGENIZED (-nīzd'), HOMOGENIZING], 1. to make homogeneous. 2. to make more uniform throughout in texture, mixture, quality, etc., by breaking down and blending the particles.

ho·mo·gen·ized milk (*usually* hə-moj′ə-nīzd′), milk in which the fat particles are so finely divided and emulsified that the cream does not separate on standing.

ho·mog·e·nous (hō-moj′ə-nəs), *adj.* [*homo-* + *-genous*], in *biology*, having similarity in structure because of common descent.

ho·mog·e·ny (hō-moj′ə-ni), *n.* [Gr. *homogeneia*, community of birth < *homogenēs*], the quality of being homogenous.

ho·mog·o·nous (hō-mog′ə-nəs), *adj.* characterized by homogony.

ho·mog·o·ny (hō-mog′ə-ni), *n.* [< Gr. *homogonos*, of the same kind < *homos*, the same + *gonos*, offspring], the state of having flowers of one kind with stamens and pistils of equal length: opposed to *heterogony*.

ho·mo·graft (hō′mə-graft′, hom′ə-gräft′), *n.* a graft of skin, bone, etc. taken from an individual of the same species.

hom·o·graph (hom′ə-graf′, hō′mə-gräf′), *n.* [< Gr. *homographos*, with the same letters, identically worded < *homos*, the same + *graphein*, to write], a word with the same spelling as another but with a different meaning and origin (e.g., *bow*, a tie, *bow*, to bend).

ho·moi·o- (hō-moi′ō), homeo-.

Ho·moi·ou·si·an (hō′moi-ōō′si-ən, hō′moi-ou′si-ən), *adj.* [< Gr. *homoiousios*, of like substance < *homoios*, like + *ousia*, essence], in *theology & church history*, designating, of, or holding the theory that God the Father and God the Son are neither identical nor different in substance, but similar. *n.* an adherent of this theory. Opposed to *Homoousian*, *Heteroousian*.

ho·mol·o·gate (hō-mol′ə-gāt′), *v.t.* [HOMOLOGATED (-id), HOMOLOGATING], [< ML. *homologatus*, pp. of *homologare* < Gr. *homologein*, to agree, assent < *homos*, the same + *legein*, say, speak], in *law*, to approve; confirm; ratify. *v.i.* to agree.

ho·mo·log·i·cal (hō′mə-loj′i-k′l, hom′ə-loj′i-k′l), *adj.* homologous.

ho·mol·o·gize (hō-mol′ə-jīz′), *v.t.* [HOMOLOGIZED (-jīzd′), HOMOLOGIZING], 1. to make homologous. 2. to demonstrate homology in. *v.i.* to be homologous.

ho·mol·o·gous (hō-mol′ə-gəs), *adj.* [Gr. *homologos*, agreeing, assenting < *homos*, the same + *legein*, to speak], 1. matching in structure, position, character, etc.; corresponding: opposed to *heterologous*. 2. in *biology*, corresponding in type of structure and deriving from a common primitive origin: as, the wing of a bat and the foreleg of a mouse are *homologous*. 3. in *chemistry*, *a*) designating or of a series of compounds each member of which has a structure differing regularly by some radical from that of the adjacent members. *b*) having this relation with another or other compounds of such a series. 4. in *immunology & medicine*, having the relationship of a serum and the bacterium from which it is made.

hom·o·lo·graph·ic (hom′ə-lə-graf′ik), *adj.* [altered (after *homo-*) < *homalographic* < Gr. *homalos*, even, level; + *-graphic*], keeping the parts in proper relative size and form.

hom·o·logue (hom′ə-lôg′, hom′ə-log′), *n.* [Fr. < Gr. *homologos*], a homologous part, thing, organ, etc.

ho·mol·o·gy (hō-mol′ə-ji), *n.* [*pl.* HOMOLOGIES (-jiz)], [Fr. *homologie;* Gr. *homologia*, agreement, conformity < *homologos*], 1. the quality or state of being homologous. 2. a homologous correspondence or relationship, as of animal organs, chemical compounds, etc.

ho·mol·o·sine projection (hə-mol′ə-sin, hə-mol′ə-sīn′), [< Gr. *homalos*, even; + *sine*], a map of the earth's surface with land areas shown in their proper relative size and form, with a minimum of distortion: it is made by combining two homolographic projections.

HOMOLOSINE PROJECTION

ho·mo·mor·phic (hō′mə-môr′fik, hom′ə-môr′fik), *adj.* 1. of or characterized by homomorphism. 2. similar in form and size, as certain chromosomes.

ho·mo·mor·phism (hō′mə-môr′fiz′m, hom′ə-môr′fiz′m), *n.* [< *homo-* + Gr. *morphē*, form; + *-ism*], 1. similarity in form. 2. homomorphy. 3. the possession of perfect flowers of a single type or kind. 4. similarity between an insect's larva and its matured form.

ho·mo·mor·phous (hō′mə-môr′fəs, hom′ə-môr′fəs), *adj.* homomorphic.

ho·mo·mor·phy (hō′mə-môr′fi, hom′ə-môr′fi), *n.* [< *homo-* + Gr. *morphē*, form], in *biology*, external resemblance without actual relationship in structure or origin: said of organs or organisms.

hom·o·nym (hom′ə-nim′, hō′mə-nim′), *n.* [Fr. *homonyme* < L. *homonymus;* Gr. *homōnymos*, having the same name < *homos*, the same + *onyma*, *onoma*, name], 1. a word with the same pronunciation as another but with a different meaning, origin, and, usually, spelling (e.g., *bore* and *boar*); homophone. 2. either of two people with the same name; namesake.

hom·o·nym·ic (hom′ə-nim′ik, hō′mə-nim′ik), *adj.* homonymous.

ho·mon·y·mous (hō-mon′ə-məs), *adj.* [L. *homonymus*], 1. of, or having the nature of, a homonym. 2. having the same name.

ho·mon·y·my (hō-mon′ə-mi), *n.* [L. *homonymia;* Gr. *homōnymia*], the quality or condition of being homonymous.

Ho·mo·ou·si·an (hō′mō-ōō′si-ən, hō′mō-ou′si-ən), *adj.* [< Gr. *homoousios*, consubstantial < *homos*, the same + *ousia*, essence], in *theology & church history*, designating, of, or holding the theory that God the Father and God the Son are identical in substance. *n.* an adherent of this theory. Opposed to *Heteroousian*, *Homoiousian*.

hom·o·phone (hom′ə-fōn′), *n.* [< Gr. *homophōnos;* see HOMOPHONIC], 1. any of two or more letters having a sound in common, as *c* and *s*. 2. a homonym.

hom·o·phon·ic (hom′ə-fon′ik), *adj.* [< Gr. *homophōnos*, of the same sound (< *homos*, same + *phōnē*, sound); + *-ic*], 1. in *music*, *a*) formerly, sounding alike; having the same pitch; in unison. *b*) having a single voice carrying the melody; monodic; monophonic: opposed to *polyphonic*. 2. homonymous.

ho·moph·o·nous (hō-mof′ə-nəs), *adj.* homophonic.

ho·moph·o·ny (hō-mof′ə-ni), *n.* [*pl.* HOMOPHONIES (-niz)], [Gr. *homophōnia* < *homophōnos;* see HOMOPHONIC], 1. in *music*, *a*) formerly, unison, or music written, sung, or played in unison. *b*) music in which a single voice carries the melody, often with an accompaniment in chords; monody; monophony: opposed to *polyphony*. 2. in *phonetics*, the quality of a homophone or homophones.

ho·mop·ter·ous (hō-mop′tēr-əs), *adj.* [*homo-* + *-pterous*] belonging to a group of insects with sucking mouth parts and wings of uniform thickness throughout, as aphids, cicadas, scale insects, etc.

Ho·mo sa·pi·ens (hō′mō sā′pi-enz′), [L.; see HOMO & SAPIENT], man; human being: the scientific name for the only living species of the genus *Homo*.

ho·mo·sex·u·al (hō′mə-sek′shōō-əl), *adj.* of or characterized by sexual desire for those of the same sex. *n.* a homosexual individual. Opposed to *heterosexual*.

ho·mo·sex·u·al·i·ty (hō′mə-sek′shōō-al′ə-ti), *n.* 1. sexual desire for those of the same sex. 2. sexual relations between individuals of the same sex. Opposed to *heterosexuality*.

ho·mos·po·rous (hō-mos′pēr-əs, hō′mə-spôr′əs, hō′mə-spō′rəs), *adj.* in *botany*, producing only one kind of asexual spore: opposed to *heterosporous*.

ho·mo·tax·is (hō′mə-tak′sis, hom′ə-tak′sis), *n.* [Mod. L. < *homo-* + *-taxis*], in *geology*, a similarity in the arrangement of layers, or in the fossil content, between noncontemporaneous strata of different regions.

ho·mo·zy·go·sis (hō′mə-zi-gō′sis, hom′ə-zi-gō′sis), *n.* the producing of a homozygote by the union of two gametes of the same strain.

ho·mo·zy·gote (hō′mə-zī′gōt, hom′ə-zig′ōt), *n.* [*homo-* + *zygote*], in Mendel's theory of heredity, a plant or animal resulting from the union of gametes with similar characteristics, and hence breeding true to type: opposed to *heterozygote*.

Homs (hôms), *n.* a city in west central Syria: pop., 146,000.

ho·mun·cu·lus (hō-muŋ′kyoo-ləs), *n.* [*pl.* HOMUNCULI (-li′)], [L., dim. of *homo*, a man], 1. a little man; dwarf. 2. a model of a human being, used for demonstrating anatomy.

hom·y (hōm′i), *adj.* [HOMIER (-i-ēr), HOMIEST (-i-ist)], [Colloq.], homey.

Hon., hon., 1. honorable. 2. honorary.

Ho·nan (hō′nän′), *n.* a province of eastern China: area, 63,843 sq. mi.; pop., 44,215,000; capital, Kaifeng.

Hond., Honduras.

Hon·do (hon′dō), *n.* Honshu.

Hon·du·ran (hon-door′ən, hon-dyoor′ən), *adj.* of Honduras, its people, or culture. *n.* a native or inhabitant of Honduras.

Hon·du·ras (hon-door′əs, hon-dyoor′əs), *n.* a country in Central America, on the Caribbean and the Pacific: area, 59,160 sq. mi.; pop., 1,950,000; capital, Tegucigalpa: see **Central America**, map.

hone (hōn), *n.* [ME. *hoone;* AS. *han*, a stone; akin to ON. *hein*, a hone; IE. base **kōi-*, to sharpen, whet, as also in L. *cos*, whetstone, *cotes*, sharp rock], a whetstone used to sharpen cutting tools, especially razors. *v.t.* [HONED (hōnd), HONING], to sharpen on a hone.

hone (hōn), *v.i.* [HONED (hōnd), HONING], [ME. *honen;* OFr. *hogner*, to mutter, murmur, repine], [Dial.], 1. to yearn; long. 2. to grumble; moan.

Ho·neg·ger, Arthur (hō′neg-ēr; Fr. ô′ne′gâr′), 1892–1955; French composer.

hon·est (on′ist), *adj.* [ME.; OFr. *honeste* (Fr. *honnête;*) L. *honestus* < *honor*, honor], 1. originally, *a*) honorable; held in respect. *b*) respectable, creditable, commendable, seemly, etc.: a generalized epithet of commendation. 2. that will not lie, cheat, or steal; truthful; trustworthy: as, an *honest* man. 3. *a*) showing fairness and sincerity; straightforward; free from deceit: as, an *honest* effort. *b*) gained or earned by fair methods, not by cheating, lying, or stealing: as, an *honest* living. 4. being what it seems; genuine; pure: as, *honest* wool. 5. frank and open: as, an *honest* face. 6. [Archaic], virtuous; chaste. —*SYN.* see **upright.**

hon·est·ly (on′ist-li), *adv.* 1. in an honest manner. 2. truly; really: an intensive, as, *honestly*, I'll do it.

hon·es·ty (on′is-ti), *n.* [ME. & OFr. *honeste;* L. *honestas* < *honestus*], 1. the state or quality of being honest; specifically, *a*) originally, honor. *b*) a refraining from lying, cheating, or stealing; a being truthful, trustworthy, or upright. *c*) sincerity; fairness; straightforwardness. *d*) [Archaic], chastity. 2. a common garden plant with large purple flowers: so called because of its semitransparent pods.

SYN.—**honesty,** the most general of these terms, implies freedom from lying, stealing, cheating, etc. (*honesty* is the best policy); **honor** implies faithful adherence to the moral or ethical principles that are expected of one in his social class, profession, position, etc. (*honor* among thieves); **integrity** implies an incorruptible soundness of moral character, especially as displayed in fulfilling trusts (elect men of *integrity*); **probity** suggests honesty or rectitude that is tried and proved; **veracity** specifically stresses honesty as displayed in habitual truthfulness (a witness of unquestioned *veracity*).—*ANT.* dishonesty, deceitfulness.

hone·wort (hōn′wûrt′), *n.* [obs. *hone*, a swelling + *wort:* from being used to cure such swellings], any of certain plants of the carrot family, as the stone parsley.

hon·ey (hun′i), *n.* [*pl.* HONEYS (-iz)], [ME. *honi, hunig;* AS. *hunig;* akin to G. *honig* (OHG. *honang*); IE. base **q(e)nəgó-*, gold-colored, seen also in Sans. *kāñcana-*, golden], 1. a thick, sweet, sirupy substance that bees make as food from the nectar of flowers. 2. anything like honey in quality or nature; sweetness. 3. sweet one; darling; dear. *adj.* 1. of or like honey; hence, 2. sweet; dear. *v.t.* [HONEYED or HONIED (-id), HONEYING], 1. to make sweet or pleasant with or as with honey. 2. to speak sweetly or lovingly to. 3. to flatter. *v.i.* to speak sweetly or lovingly; be very affectionate, attentive, or coaxing.

hon·ey·bee (hun′i-bē′), *n.* a bee that makes honey; common hive bee.

hon·ey·comb (hun′i-kōm′), *n.* [ME. *hunicomb;* AS. *hunigcamb; hunig*, honey + *camb*, comb], 1. the structure of six-sided wax cells made by bees to hold their honey, eggs, etc. 2. anything like this in structure or appearance. *v.t.* 1. to fill with holes like a honeycomb; riddle; hence, 2. to permeate or undermine: as, *honeycombed* with intrigue. *v.i.* to become full of holes like a honeycomb. *adj.* of, like, or patterned after a honeycomb.

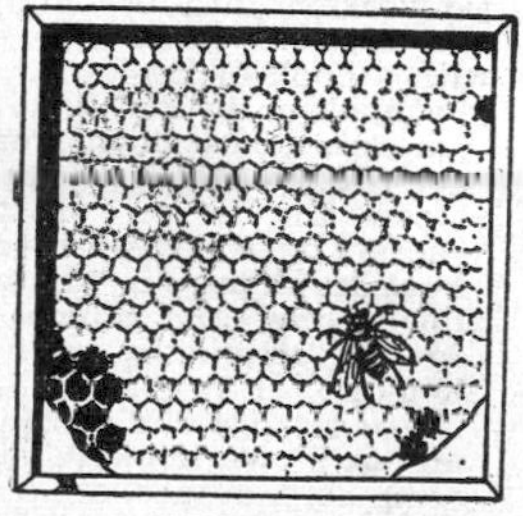

HONEYCOMB

honey creeper, any of a large group of bright-colored singing birds of tropical and subtropical America.

hon·ey·dew (hun′i-dōō′, hun′i-dū′), *n.* 1. a sweet fluid exuded from the leaves of some plants in summer. 2. a sweet substance secreted by aphids and other juice-sucking plant insects. 3. a honeydew melon.

honeydew melon, a greenish-white variety of muskmelon with a smooth rind and sweet, green flesh.

honey eater, any of a large family of Australasian birds that feed on insects and on honey from flowers: also **honeysucker.**

hon·eyed (hun′id), [ME.], alternative past tense and past participle of **honey.** *adj.* 1. sweetened, covered, or filled with honey. 2. sweet as honey; flattering or affectionate: as, *honeyed* words.

honey guide, a member of either of two groups of small, heavily built, plain-colored birds of Africa, Asia, and the East Indies: they are said to lead men and animals to bees' nests in order to eat the grubs when the honeycombs are taken.

honey locust, a North American tree of the pea family, with strong, spiny branches, featherlike foliage, and glossy, flat pods.

hon·ey·moon (hun′i-mōōn′), *n.* [orig. with reference, not to the period of a month, but to the mutual affection of newlyweds, regarded as waning like the moon; cf. G. *flitterwochen*, lit., tinsel weeks], 1. formerly, the first month of marriage. 2. the holiday or vacation spent together by a newly married couple. *v.i.* to have or spend a honeymoon.

hon·ey·suck·er (hun′i-suk′ẽr), *n.* the honey eater.

hon·ey·suck·le (hun′i-suk′'l), *n.* [ME. *honisocle, hunisuccle*, dim. (see -LE) < AS. *hunigsuce, hunigsuge* (Brit. dial. *honeysuck*) < *hunig*, honey + *sucan*, to suck: orig. applied to clover flowers, which are particularly rich in honey], 1. any of a group of climbing, twining vines with small, fragrant flowers of red, yellow, or white. 2. any of several similar plants with fragrant flowers. 3. [Obs.], clover.

honeysuckle ornament, a floral design resembling the honeysuckle, used in painting and relief sculpture; anthemion.

hong (hoŋ, hôŋ), *n.* [Chin. *hang, hong*, a row, series, factory], a warehouse or factory for foreign trade, in China or Japan.

Hong Kong (hoŋ′ koŋ′, hôŋ′ kôŋ′), 1. a British crown colony in southeastern China, on the South China Sea, including Hong Kong island, Kowloon peninsula, and a section of the Chinese mainland: area, 391 sq. mi.; pop., 2,806,000. 2. Victoria, its capital. Also **Hongkong.**

hon·ied (hun′id), alternative past tense and past participle of **honey.** *adj.* honeyed.

‡ho·ni soit qui mal y pense (ô′nē′ swå′ kē′ mål′ ē′ päns′), [Fr.], shamed be (anyone) who thinks evil of it: motto of the Order of the Garter.

honk (hôŋk, hoŋk), *n.* [echoic], 1. the call of a wild goose. 2. any similar sound, as of an automobile horn. *v.i.* to make any such sound. *v.t.* 1. to express by honking. 2. [Colloq.], to sound (an automobile horn).

hon·ky-tonk (hôŋ′ki-tôŋk′, hoŋ′ki-toŋk′), *n.* [prob. echoic], [Slang], a cheap, disreputable saloon, cabaret, etc.; dive.

Hon·o·lu·lu (hon′ə-lōō′lōō), *n.* the chief city of Oahu and capital of the State of Hawaii: pop., 294,000: see **Hawaiian Islands,** map.

hon·or (on′ẽr), *n.* [ME.; OFr. *honur, honeur;* L. *honor, honos*, official dignity, repute, esteem], 1. high regard or great respect given, received, or enjoyed; especially, *a*) glory; fame; renown. *b*) credit; good reputation: opposed to *dishonor, disgrace.* 2. a keen sense of right and wrong; adherence to action or principles considered right; integrity: as, he conducts himself with *honor.* 3. *a*) chastity; purity. *b*) reputation for chastity. 4. high rank or position; distinction; dignity: as, it is a great *honor* to be president. 5. [H-], a title of respect given to certain officials, as judges (preceded by *His, Her,* or *Your*). 6. something done or given as a token or act of respect; specifically, *a*) [Obs.], a curtsy; bow. *b*) a social courtesy: as, will you do me the *honor* of attending my wedding? *c*) a badge, token, or decoration given to a person. *d*) *pl.* public acts or ceremonies of respect: as, funeral *honors*. *e*) *pl.* special distinction or credit given to students who graduate or pass examinations with unusually high marks. *f*) in British universities, an award for scholarly distinction, based on a specialized examination more difficult than that required for an ordinary (pass) degree. 7. a source or cause of respect and fame; person or thing that brings respect and fame to a school, country, etc. 8. in *bridge*, etc., any of the four or five highest cards of the trump suit; in a no-trump hand, any of the four aces. 9. in *golf*, the privilege of driving first from the tee. *v.t.* 1. to respect greatly; regard highly; esteem. 2. to show great respect or high regard for; treat with deference and courtesy. 3. to worship. 4. to confer an honor on; exalt; ennoble. 5. to accept and pay when due: as, will you *honor* this check?

do honor to, 1. to show great respect for. 2. to bring or cause honor to.

do the honors, 1. to act as host or hostess. 2. to perform certain formal acts of courtesy, such as making introductions, proposing toasts, etc.

on (or **upon**) **one's honor,** staking one's good name on the truth of one's statement or the fulfillment of one's promises.

SYN.—**honor,** as compared here, implies popular acknowledgment of one's right to great respect as well as any expression of such respect (in *honor* of the martyred dead); **homage** suggests great esteem shown in praise, tributes, or obeisance (to pay *homage* to the genius of Milton); **reverence** implies deep respect together with love (he held her memory in *reverence*); **deference** suggests a display of courteous regard for a superior, or for one to whom respect is due, by yielding to his claims or wishes (in *deference* to his age). See also **honesty.**

hon·or·a·ble (on′ẽr-ə-b'l), *adj.* [ME. *honourable;* OFr. *honorable;* L. *honorabilis* < *honorare*], 1. worthy of being honored; specifically, *a*) of, or having a position of, high rank or worth: used as a title of courtesy for certain officials. *b*) noble; illustrious. *c*) of good reputation; respectable. 2. having or showing a sense of right and wrong; characterized by honesty and integrity; upright. 3. bringing honor to the owner or doer: as, *honorable* mention. 4. doing honor; accompanied with marks of respect: as, an *honorable* burial. Abbreviated **hon., Hon.** —*SYN.* see **upright.**

hon·or·a·bly (on'ẽr-ə-bli), *adv.* [ME. *honourabilli*], in an honorable manner: abbreviated **hon.**

hon·o·ra·ri·um (on'ə-râr'i-əm), *n.* [*pl.* HONORARIUMS (-əmz), HONORARIA (-ə)], [LL. *honorarium* (*donum*, gift), neut. of *honorarius*, honorary], a payment to a professional man for services on which no fee is set or legally obtainable.

hon·or·ar·y (on'ə-rer'i), *adj.* [L. *honorarius*, of or conferring honor], 1. done or given as an honor: as, an *honorary* degree. 2. designating an office or position held as an honor only, without service or pay. 3. holding such a position or office. 4. depending on one's honor; that cannot be legally enforced or collected: said of debts, etc. Abbreviated **hon., Hon.**

hon·or·if·ic (on'ə-rif'ik), *adj.* [L. *honorificus* < *honor* + *facere*, to make], conferring honor; showing respect: as, an *honorific* epithet, title, etc. *n.* a complimentary form or phrase for describing or addressing a person or thing that commands respect: used grammatically in Japanese and some other Oriental languages.

hon·or·if·i·cal (on'ə-rif'i-k'l), *adj.* honorific.

honor point, in *heraldry*, the point between the center and the top of an escutcheon: also called *color point.*

honors of war, special privileges granted to a defeated army, especially that of bearing arms and flags as they march out to surrender.

honor system, in various schools and colleges, a system whereby students are trusted to do their work, take examinations, etc. without supervision.

hon·our (on'ẽr), *n.* & *v.t.* honor: British spelling.

Hon·shu (hon'shōō'), *n.* the largest of the islands forming Japan: area, 91,278 sq. mi.; pop., 48,681,000; chief city, Tokyo: also called *Hondo.*

hooch (hōōch), *n.* [contr. of Alaskan Ind. *hoochinoo*, crude alcoholic liquor; ? var. of *Hutanuwu*, name of a Tlingit tribe], [Slang], alcoholic liquor; especially, liquor made or obtained surreptitiously, as during prohibition.

Hooch, Pie·ter de (pē'tẽr də hōH), 1629–1677?; Dutch painter: also spelled **Hoogh.**

hood (hood), *n.* [ME.; AS. *hod;* akin to G. *hut*, hat; for IE. base see HAT, HEED], 1. a covering for the head and neck, worn separately or as part of a robe or cloak: as, a monk's cowl is a *hood.* 2. anything resembling a hood in shape or use; specifically, *a*) a fold of cloth worn over the back of the academic gown by a graduate of a college or university: it has distinguishing colors to indicate the wearer's degree or degrees. *b*) the metal cover over the engine of an automobile. *c*) the folding cover of a carriage, beach chair, etc. *d*) the cowl of a chimney. *e*) in *falconry*, the covering for a falcon's head when it is not chasing game. 3. in *zoology*, a bird's crest. *v.t.* to cover with or as with a hood; provide a hood for.

hood (hood), *n.* [< *hoodlum*], [Slang], a hoodlum; gangster.

-hood (hood) [ME. *-had, -hod* < AS. *had*, order, condition, quality, rank; akin to G. *-heit;* IE. *(*s*)*qāi-t*, bright, gleaming; basic sense "appearance by which known"], a suffix used to form nouns, meaning: 1. *state, quality, condition*, as in *childhood.* 2. *the whole group of* (a specified class, profession, etc.), as in *priesthood.* Also **-head.**

Hood, John Bell (hood), 1831–1879; Confederate general in the Civil War.

Hood, Mount, a volcanic mountain of the Cascade Range, in northern Oregon: height, 11,245 ft.

Hood, Robin, see **Robin Hood.**

Hood, Thomas, 1799–1845; English poet and humorist.

hood·ed (hood'id), *adj.* 1. having or covered with a hood. 2. shaped like a hood. 3. in *botany*, rolled into a cone shape, as the spathe of the jack-in-the-pulpit; cucullate. 4. in *zoology*, *a*) having the head different in color from the body. *b*) having a crest like a hood: as, the *hooded* crow. *c*) capable of expanding the skin at each side of the neck by movements of the ribs, as the cobra and puffing adder.

hood·lum (hōōd'ləm), *n.* [orig. used in San Francisco of gangs of toughs employed to beat up the Chinese; said to be < *huddle 'em*, as used by gangs; ? < *noodlum*, back slang for *Muldoon*, name of gang leader], [Colloq.], a young rowdy, often a member of a gang; street tough; hooligan.

hood·man-blind (hood'mən-blīnd'), *n.* [Archaic], blindman's buff.

hoo·doo (hōō'dōō), *n.* [*pl.* HOODOOS (-dōōz)], [var. of *voodoo*], 1. voodoo. 2. [Colloq.], a person or thing that causes bad luck. 3. [Colloq.], bad luck. *v.t.* [Colloq.], to bring bad luck to; bewitch.

hood·wink (hood'wiŋk'), *v.t.* [*hood* + *wink*], 1. to blindfold. 2. to prevent from seeing the truth; hence, 3. to play a deceiving trick on; deceive.

hoo·ey (hōō'i), *interj.* & *n.* [echoic], [Slang], nonsense; bunk.

hoof (hoof, hōōf), *n.* [*pl.* HOOFS (hoofs, hōōfs), rarely HOOVES (hōōvz, hoovz)], [ME. *hoof;* AS. *hof;* akin to G. *huf;* IE. base **kāpho-* hoof, as also in Sans. *çapha-*, hoof, claw], 1. the horny covering on the feet of cattle, deer, swine, etc. 2. the entire foot of such animals. 3. [Slang], the human foot. *v.t.* & *v.i.* 1. to trample with the hoofs. 2. [Colloq.], to walk; tramp. 3. [Slang], to dance.

on the hoof, not butchered; alive.

hoof·beat (hoof'bēt', hōōf'bēt'), *n.* the sound made by the hoof of an animal when it stamps, walks, etc.

hoof·bound (hoof'bound', hōōf'bound'), *adj.* having a condition of dryness and contraction of the hoof, which causes pain and lameness.

hoofed (hooft, hōōft), *adj.* having hoofs; ungulate.

hoof·er (hoof'ẽr, hōōf'ẽr), *n.* [Slang], a professional dancer, especially a tap dancer.

Hoogh, Pieter de (hōH), see **Hooch, Pieter de.**

Hoogh·ly (hōōg'li), *n.* the westernmost channel of the Ganges, in India: also spelled **Hugli.**

hook (hook), *n.* [ME. *hook, hok;* AS. *hoc;* akin to D. *hoeck*, Eng. *hake;* IE. base **keg-*, peg for hanging, etc.; cf. HACK, HANK], 1. a curved or bent piece of metal, wood, etc. used to catch, hold, or pull something; specifically, *a*) a curved piece of wire or bone with a barbed end, for catching fish. *b*) a curved piece of metal, wood, etc. fastened to a wall or chain at one end, used to hang things on, raise things up, etc.: as, a coat *hook.* *c*) a small metal catch inserted in a loop, or eye, to fasten clothes together: part of a hook and eye. *d*) [Nautical Slang], an anchor. 2. a curved metal implement for cutting grain, etc.; sickle. 3. something shaped like a hook; specifically, *a*) a curving cape or headland: used in place names, as, Sandy *Hook.* *b*) a bend in a stream. 4. a trap; snare. 5. the stationary part of a hinge, used to hold the pin. 6. in *baseball*, a curve. 7. in *boxing*, a short blow delivered with the arm bent at the elbow. 8. in *golf*, a stroke in which the ball curves to the left of the direction intended. 9. in *music*, one of the lines at the end of a stem, indicating whether a note is an eighth, sixteenth, etc. *v.t.* 1. to attach or fasten with or as with a hook or hook and eye. 2. to take hold of with a hook. 3. to catch with or as with a hook. 4. to catch or deceive by a trick; swindle. 5. to steal; snatch. 6. to attack or pierce with the horns, as a bull; gore. 7. to make into the shape of a hook. 8. to work (canvas) by drawing yarn through it with a hook. 9. in *baseball*, to throw (a ball) so that it curves. 10. in *boxing*, to hit with a hook. 11. in *cricket*, to pull. 12. in *golf*, to drive (a ball) so that it curves to the left of the direction intended. 13. [Labor Union Slang], to trap (a worker) into becoming a labor spy or informer. *v.i.* 1. to curve as a hook does; bend. 2. to be fastened with a hook or hooks. 3. to be caught by a hook.

by hook or by crook, in any way whatever; by any means, honest or dishonest.

get the hook, [Slang], to be discharged or dismissed: from the former practice of pulling incompetent actors off the stage by means of a long hooked pole.

hook it, [Slang], to run away.

hook, line, and sinker, [Colloq.], completely; altogether: originally, a fisherman's expression.

hook up, 1. to connect or attach with a hook or hooks. 2. to arrange and connect the parts of (a radio, etc.).

on one's own hook, [Colloq.], by oneself; without getting help, advice, etc.

hook·ah, hook·a (hook'ə), *n.* [Ar. *huqqah*, pipe for smoking, vase], an Oriental pipe with a long, flexible tube by means of which the smoke is drawn through water so as to be cooled.

HOOKAH

hook and eye, a device for fastening clothes, etc., consisting of a small loop and a hook that catches on it.

Hooke, Robert (hook), 1635–1703; English physicist, inventor, and mathematician.

hooked (hookt, hook'id), *adj.* 1. curved like a hook. 2. having a hook or hooks. 3. made with a hook: as, a *hooked* rug.

hooked rug, a rug made by drawing strips of cloth or yarn back and forth through a canvas or burlap backing.

hook·er (hook'ẽr), *n.* [D. *hoeker* < *hoek*, a hook; sense 4 < *hook, v.t.* 13], 1. a small Dutch fishing ship with two masts. 2. an Irish or English fishing smack with one mast. 3. any clumsy, old ship: sailor's term of contempt or affection. 4. [Labor Union Slang], an undercover operative employed by a labor spy agency, etc. to trap workers into becoming labor spies.

Hook·er, Joseph (hook'ẽr), 1814–1879; Union general in the Civil War.

Hooker, Richard, 1554?–1600; English clergyman and writer.

Hooker, Thomas, 1586?–1647; English Puritan clergyman; one of the founders of the colony of Connecticut.

hook·nose (hook'nōz'), *n.* a nose curved downward somewhat like a hook; aquiline nose.

hook-nosed (hook′nōzd′), ***adj.*** having a hooknose.
hook·up (hook′up′), ***n.*** [< *hook up*], 1. the arrangement and connection of parts, circuits, etc. in a radio, telephone system, network of radio stations, etc. 2. [Colloq.], a connection or alliance between two governments, parties, etc.
hook·worm (hook′wũrm′), ***n.*** a small, parasitic roundworm with hooks around the mouth, infesting the small intestine of man and other animals, especially in tropical climates.
hookworm disease, a disease caused by hookworms in the small intestine, characterized by anemia, fever, weakness, and abdominal pain: the larvae enter the body through the skin of the feet, or in contaminated food or drinking water: also called *ancylostomiasis.*
hooky, ***n.*** see **play hooky.**
hoo·li·gan (hōō′li-gən), ***n.*** [< *Hooligan,* name of an Irish family in Southwark, London], a young ruffian, especially a member of a street gang; hoodlum.
hoo·li·gan·ism (hōō′li-gən-iz′m), ***n.*** the behavior or character of a hooligan; rowdiness; vandalism.
hoop (hōōp, hoop), ***n.*** [ME.; AS. *hop;* akin to D. *hoep;* prob. IE. **qeu-b* (< base **qeu-,* to bend, curve), as also in *cubicle, cubit;* hence, basic sense "curved around"], 1. a circular band or ring for holding together the staves of a barrel, cask, etc. 2. anything like a hoop; specifically, *a)* a large, circular band rolled along the ground by children. *b) usually in pl.* a ring of whalebone, steel, etc. for spreading out a woman's skirt. *c)* a finger ring. 3. in *croquet,* any of the arches through which the balls are hit. ***v.t.*** to bind or fasten with a hoop or hoops; encircle.
hoop·er (hōōp′ẽr, hoop′ẽr), ***n.*** a person whose work is putting hoops on barrels, casks, etc.; cooper.
Hoo·per rating (hōō′pẽr), [< name of the Am. deviser of the method], a rating of the popularity of a radio or television performer or broadcast, determined by a sample telephone poll of listeners taken during the time of the broadcast, and expressed in terms of millions of estimated listeners.
hoop·la (hōōp′lä), ***n.*** [orig., stage driver's exclamation], [Colloq.], great excitement; furor; bustle.
hoo·poe (hōō′pōō), ***n.*** [earlier *houpe, hoopoop;* Fr. *huppe, hupe;* L. *upupa;* prob. echoic of its cry], a brightly colored European bird with a long, curved bill and an erectile crest.
hoop skirt, 1. a framework of hoops fastened together with tapes, worn to spread out a woman's skirt. 2. a skirt worn over this.

HOOP SKIRT

hoo·ray (hoo-rā′, hə-rā′, hōō-rā′), ***interj., n., v.i. & v.t.*** hurrah.
hoose·gow, hoos·gow (hōōs′gou), ***n.*** [prob. < Sp. *juzgado,* sentenced < *juzgar,* to judge; L. *judicare* < *judex,* a judge], [Slang], a jail or guardhouse.
Hoo·sier (hōō′zhẽr), ***n.*** [prob. specialization of dial. *hoosier,* mountaineer; extension of dial. *hoojee, hoojin,* dirty person, tramp: southern Indiana was largely settled by Kentucky mountaineers], a native or inhabitant of Indiana: a nickname.
hoot (hōōt), ***v.i.*** [ME. *hoten, houten,* to utter the exclamation "hoot!"; ? < ON. (cf. Sw., Norw. *huta*); orig. echoic], 1. to utter its characteristic hollow sound: said of an owl. 2. to utter a sound like this. 3. to shout or cry out, especially in scorn or disapproval. ***v.t.*** 1. to express (scorn, disapproval, etc.) by hooting. 2. to express scorn or disapproval of by hooting. 3. to drive or chase away by hooting: as, they *hooted* him out of the room. ***n.*** 1. the sound that an owl makes. 2. any sound like this. 3. a loud shout or cry of scorn or disapproval. 4. something of no worth: as, he doesn't give a *hoot* for your opinion.
hoot (hōōt, ōōt), ***interj.*** [var. of *hoot, n.*], [Scot. & North Eng.], an exclamation of objection, irritation, or impatience: also **hoots.**
hoot·en·an·ny (hōōt′'n-an′i), ***n.*** [*pl.* HOOTENANNIES (-iz)], [orig. in sense of "dingus," "thingumajig"; a fanciful coinage, used also as derogatory epithet; assimilated in form to *Hootin' Annie*], [Slang], a meeting of folk singers, especially for public entertainment.
hoot owl, any of various owls that hoot; especially, the great horned owl.
hoots (hōōts, ōōts), ***interj.*** [Scot. & North Eng.], hoot.
Hoo·ver, Herbert Clark (hōō′vẽr), 1874– ; thirty-first president of the United States (1929–1933).
Hoover Dam, a very high dam, at the Black Canyon, Colorado River, between Nevada and Arizona: height, 727 ft.: formerly called *Boulder Dam.*
Hoo·ver·ville (hōō′vẽr-vil), ***n.*** [after Herbert *Hoover*], any of the collections of ramshackle huts at the outskirts of a city, for housing the unemployed during the depression of the early 1930's.
hooves (hōōvz, hoovz), ***n.*** rare plural of **hoof.**
hop (hop), ***v.i.*** [HOPPED (hopt), HOPPING], [ME. *hoppen;* AS. *hoppian;* akin to G. *hüpfen;* IE. **qeu-b* (cf. HOOP) < base **qeu-,* to bend, curve; basic sense "to bend forward"; cf. HOBBLE], 1. to make a short leap or leaps on one foot. 2. to move by leaping or springing on both (or all) feet at once, as a bird, frog, etc. 3. [Colloq.], to dance. 4. [Slang], to go. ***v.t.*** 1. to jump over: as, *hop* the hedge. 2. to jump onto: as, *hop* a train. 3. [Colloq.], to fly over in an airplane. ***n.*** 1. a hopping. 2. [Colloq.], a dance, especially an informal one. 3. [Colloq.], a flight in an airplane. ***—SYN.*** see **skip.**
hop off, [Colloq.], in *aviation,* to leave the ground; take off.
hop (hop), ***n.*** [Late ME. *hoppe* < MD. *hoppe;* akin to G. *hopfen*], 1. a climbing vine with cone-shaped female flowers, differentiated in form from the male flowers. 2. *pl.* the dried ripe cones of the female flowers, used for flavoring beer, ale, etc., and in medicine. ***v.t.*** [HOPPED (hopt), HOPPING], to flavor or treat with hops.
hop clover, any of a group of clovers with yellow flowers resembling hops.
Hope (hōp), a feminine name.
hope (hōp), ***n.*** [ME.; AS. *hopa;* akin to D. *hoop;* see the *v.*], 1. a feeling that what is wanted will happen; desire accompanied by anticipation or expectation. 2. the object of this. 3. a person or thing from which something may be hoped. 4. [Archaic], trust; reliance. ***v.t.*** [HOPED (hōpt), HOPING], [ME. *hopen;* AS. *hopian,* to expect, look for; akin to G. *hoffen;* for suggested IE. base see HOOP, HOP, *v.i.*; sense development "bend to spring on—spring on—expect to get (by springing)," paralleling that of L. *cupere,* to desire (cf. CUPIDITY)], 1. to want and expect. 2. to want very much. ***v.i.*** 1. to have hope (*for*). 2. [Archaic], to trust or rely. ***—SYN.*** see **expect.**
hope against hope, to go on having hope though it seems to be baseless.
Hope, Anthony (hōp), (pseudonym of *Sir Anthony Hope Hawkins*), 1863–1933; English novelist.
hope chest, a chest in which a young woman collects linen, clothing, etc. in anticipation of getting married.
hope·ful (hōp′fəl), ***adj.*** [ME.], 1. feeling or showing hope; expecting to get what one wants. 2. inspiring or giving hope: as, a *hopeful* sign. ***n.*** a young person who seems likely to succeed: used humorously.
Ho·pei, Ho·peh (hō′pā′), ***n.*** a province on the eastern coast of China: area, 56,116 sq. mi.; pop., 28,730,000 (1947); capital, Peking: formerly called *Chihli.*
hope·less (hōp′lis), ***adj.*** 1. without hope. 2. arousing no hope; despaired of: as, a *hopeless* situation.
SYN.*—hopeless** means having no expectation of, or showing no sign of, a favorable outcome (a *hopeless* situation); **despondent** implies a being in very low spirits due to a loss of hope and a sense of futility about continuing one's efforts (her rejection of his suit left him *despondent*); **despairing** implies utter loss of hope and may suggest the extreme dejection that results (the *despairing* lover spoke of suicide); **desperate** implies such despair as makes one resort to extreme measures (hunger makes men *desperate*).—ANT.*** hopeful, optimistic.
hop·head (hop′hed′), ***n.*** [*hop* (underworld slang for *drug*) + *head*], [Slang], a drug addict.
Ho·pi (hō′pi), ***n.*** [Hopi *Hópitu,* lit., peaceful ones], 1. a member of a Pueblo tribe of Shoshonean Indians in northeastern Arizona: also called *Moki, Moqui.* 2. their language.
Hop·kins, Gerard Man·ley (man′li hop′kinz), 1844–1889; English Jesuit and poet.
Hopkins, Harry Lloyd, 1890–1946; American statesman; adviser to President Roosevelt.
Hopkins, Mark 1802–1887; American educator.
Hop·kin·son, Francis (hop′kin-sən), 1737–1791; American poet and jurist.
hop·lite (hop′līt), ***n.*** [Gr. *hoplitēs* < *hoplon,* a tool], a heavily armed foot soldier of ancient Greece.
hop-o'-my-thumb (hop′ə-mi-thum′), ***n.*** [earlier *hop on my thombe* (< *hop, v.*)], a very small person; midget.
hopped up, [Slang], 1. stimulated by or as by a drug. 2. supercharged: said of an automobile engine, etc.
hop·per (hop′ẽr), ***n.*** [ME. *hoppere*], 1. a person or thing that hops. 2. any hopping insect. 3. [so called from making material *hop*], a box, tank, or other container for loose material or liquid that is passed or fed into something else: as, the *hopper* of an automatic coal stoker. 4. a device on the back of a piano key, for lifting the hammer.
hopper car, a freight car with an open top and a collapsible bottom through which freight can be unloaded.
hop·ple (hop′'l), ***v.t. & n.*** [var. of *hobble*], hobble (fetter).

hop·scotch (hop′skoch′), *n.* [*hop* (to jump) + *scotch*, a line, scratch], a children's game in which each player tosses a small stone into one of several compartments of a figure drawn on the ground or pavement and then hops from one compartment to another, picking the stone up or kicking it.

hor., 1. horizon. 2. horizontal. 3. horology.

Hor·ace (hôr′is, hor′is), [Fr.; L. *Horatius*], a masculine name: see **Horatio.** *n.* (*Quintus Horatius Flaccus*), Roman poet; 65–8 B.C.; known for his odes.

Hor·ae (hō′rē), *n.pl.* [L.; Gr. *Hōrai*], in *Greek mythology*, the Hours.

ho·ral (hō′rəl), *adj.* [LL. *horalis* < L. *hora*, hour], of an hour or hours.

ho·ra·ry (hō′rə-ri), *adj.* [ML. *horarius* < L. *hora*, hour], 1. of an hour or hours. 2. indicating the hours. 3. occurring once every hour; hourly. 4. lasting an hour.

Ho·ra·ti·an (hə-rā′shən, hō-rā′shi-ən), *adj.* [L. *Horatianus* < *Horatius*, Horace], of, like, or characteristic of Horace or his poetry.

Ho·ra·ti·o (hə-rā′shō, hō-rā′shi-ō), [< L. *Horatius* (with ending after It. *Orazio*, of same origin), name of a Roman gens], a masculine name: variant, *Horace*.

Ho·ra·ti·us (hə-rā′shəs, hō-rā′shi-əs), *n.* in *Roman legend*, the hero who defended a bridge over the Tiber against the Etruscan army until the Romans had destroyed the bridge, and then swam across the river to safety.

horde (hôrd, hōrd), *n.* [Fr.; G. *horde*, earlier *horda; Pol. horda;* Turk. *ordū*, a camp; Tatar *urdu*, a camp, lit., something put up, erected < *urmak*, to pitch (a camp); see URDU], 1. a nomadic tribe or clan of Mongols; hence, 2. any wandering tribe or group. 3. a crowd; pack; swarm. *v.i.* [HORDED (hôr′did, hōr′did), HORDING], to form a horde; live together in large tribes or groups. —*SYN.* see **crowd.**

Ho·reb (hō′reb), *n.* in the *Bible*, a mountain usually identified with Mt. Sinai: Ex. 3:1.

hore·hound (hôr′hound′, hōr′hound′), *n.* [ME. *horehune;* AS. *harhune; har*, hoar, white + *hune*, horehound], 1. a bitter plant of the mint family, with white, downy leaves. 2. a bitter juice extracted from its leaves. 3. cough medicine or candy made with this juice. 4. any of various other mints. Also spelled **hoarhound.**

ho·ri·zon (hə-rī′z′n), *n.* [ME. *orizont;* OFr. *orizonte;* L. *horizon;* Gr. *horizōn* (*kyklos*), the bounding (circle), horizon, properly ppr. of *horizein*, to bound, limit < *horos*, boundary, limit], 1. the line where the sky seems to meet the earth: called *visible* or *apparent horizon*. 2. the limit of one's mental outlook, experience, interest, knowledge, etc. 3. in *astronomy*, *a*) the plane extending at right angles to the direction of gravity from the eye of the observer to the celestial sphere: called *sensible horizon*. *b*) the plane parallel to this plane, passing through the center of the earth; also, the great circle of the celestial sphere whose plane this is: called *astronomical*, *celestial*, or *true horizon*. 4. in *geology*, a deposit of rock characterized by specific fossils and hence known to have been formed in some particular period. Abbreviated **hor.**

hor·i·zon·tal (hôr′ə-zon′t'l, hor′ə-zon′t'l), *adj.* [< L. *horizon*, *horizontis*, horizon; + *-al*], 1. of or near the horizon. 2. parallel to the plane of the horizon: opposed to *vertical*. 3. placed, operating, or acting chiefly in a horizontal direction. 4. flat and even; level. *n.* anything horizontal; horizontal line, plane, etc. Abbreviated **hor.**

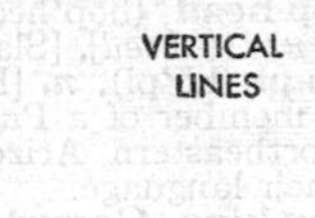

horizontal bar, in *gymnastics*, a metal bar fixed in a horizontal position for chinning and other exercises.

hor·i·zon·tal·ly (hôr′ə-zon′tə-li, hor′ə-zon′tə-li), *adv.* in a horizontal manner or direction.

horizontal union, a labor union whose members all work at the same trade but not necessarily in the same industry; craft union: opposed to *vertical union*.

hor·mo·nal (hôr-mō′n'l), *adj.* of, or having the nature of, a hormone.

hor·mone (hôr′mōn), *n.* [< Gr. *hormōn*, ppr. of *hormaein*, to stimulate, excite < *hormē*, impulse], 1. a chemical substance formed in some organ of the body, as the adrenal glands, the pituitary, etc., and carried to another organ or tissue, where it has a specific effect. 2. a similar substance in plants.

hor·mon·ic (hôr-mon′ik), *adj.* hormonal.

Hor·muz, Strait of (hôr′muz), the strait joining the Persian Gulf and the Gulf of Oman: also **Strait of Ormuz.**

horn (hôrn), *n.* [ME.; AS.; akin to G. *horn;* IE. base **ker-*, upper part of the body, head, etc., as also in L. *cornu* (cf. CORNET), Gr. *kĕras*, horn (cf. KERATIN); see HART], 1. *a*) a hard, bonelike, permanent projection that grows on the heads of cattle, sheep, and some other hoofed animals. *b*) either of a pair of branched, bonelike projections that grow on the head of a deer and are shed annually. 2. anything that protrudes naturally from the head of an animal, as one of the tentacles of a snail, the tuft of feathers of the horned owl, etc. 3. *usually pl.* the symbol of a cuckold: cuckolds are spoken of as wearing horns. 4. *a*) the substance that horns are made of. *b*) any similar substance. 5. *a*) a container made by hollowing out a horn: as, a powder *horn*, drinking *horn*. *b*) a drink contained in a horn. 6. a horn of plenty; cornucopia. 7. anything shaped like or suggesting a horn; specifically, *a*) a peninsula or cape. *b*) the end of a crescent. *c*) the beak of an anvil. *d*) the pommel of a saddle. *e*) one of the branches of a river at its delta. 8. *a*) an instrument made of horn and sounded by blowing. *b*) any brass-wind instrument; specifically, the French horn: abbreviated **H., h.** 9. a horn-shaped loud-speaker. 10. a device sounded to give a warning: as, a fog-*horn*, an automobile *horn*. 11. in the *Bible*, an emblem of glory, strength, or honor. 12. in *geology*, a jagged mountain peak resulting from the erosion of several cirques against one headland, as the Matterhorn in the Alps. *v.t.* 1. to furnish with horns. 2. to make hornlike in shape. 3. to strike or butt with the horns; gore. 4. [Archaic], to cuckold. *adj.* made of horn: as, *horn*-rimmed glasses.

blow one's own horn, [Colloq.], to praise oneself; boast.

horn in, [Slang], to enter without being asked; intrude or meddle.

on the horns of a dilemma, having to make a choice between two things, both usually unpleasant.

pull (or **draw** or **haul**) **in one's horns,** 1. to hold oneself back; restrain one's impulses, efforts, etc. 2. to withdraw; recant.

Horn, Cape, the southernmost point of South America, on Horn Island, Tierra del Fuego, Chile.

horn·beam (hôrn′bēm′), *n.* [*horn* + *beam* (tree)], 1. any of a group of small, hardy trees of the birch family, with smooth, gray bark and large clusters of light-green nuts. 2. the very hard, white wood of this tree, which takes a hornlike polish; ironwood.

horn·bill (hôrn′bil′), *n.* any of a family of large tropical birds with partly united toes and a huge, curved bill, often with a bony protuberance on it.

horn·blende (hôrn′blend′), *n.* [G.; *horn*, horn + *blende*, blende, ore of zinc < *blenden*, to blind, dazzle, deceive], a black, blackish-green, or dark-brown silicate of calcium and magnesium, usually with iron, manganese, etc.: it is a common mineral found in granite and other igneous rocks.

horn·book (hôrn′book′), *n.* 1. a sheet of parchment with the alphabet, table of numbers, etc. on it, mounted on a small board with a handle and protected by a thin, transparent plate of horn: it was formerly used as a child's primer; hence, 2. an elementary treatise.

horned (hôrnd; *poetic* hôr′nid), *adj.* 1. having a horn or horns: as, a *horned* cow, a one-*horned* animal. 2. having a hornlike projection: as, the *horned* toad, the *horned* moon. 3. [Archaic], cuckolded.

horned pout, a catfish or other bullhead: also **horn pout, hornpout.**

horned toad, any of several small, scaly, insect-eating lizards with a short tail and hornlike spines.

horned viper, a poisonous African snake with a hornlike spine above each eye; cerastes.

hor·net (hôr′nit), *n.* [ME. *harnette;* AS. *hyrnet;* akin to G. *hornisse;* Gmc. **hurznata* < IE. base **ker-*, upper part of body, horns (cf. HORN); basic sense "horned," prob. with reference to the antennae; cf. OS. *horn-bero*, lit., horn bearer, hornet], a large wasp whose sting is very painful.

Horn·ie (hôr′ni), *n.* [Scot.], Satan.

hor·ni·ness (hôr′ni-nis), *n.* the quality of being horny.

hor·ni·to (hôr-nē′tō; Sp. ôr-nē′tô), *n.* [Sp., dim. of *horno*, oven < L. *furnus;* see FURNACE], a low, oven-shaped mound, usually giving off smoke and vapor, common in the volcanic districts of South America.

horn-mad (hôrn′mad′), *adj.* 1. maddened enough to gore: said of horned animals; hence, 2. furious; mad. 3. [Archaic], mad with jealousy because cuckolded.

horn of plenty, 1. in *Greek mythology*, the horn of the goat that suckled Zeus: see **Amalthaea.** 2. a representation in painting, sculpture, etc. of a horn overflowing with fruits, flowers, and grains; cornucopia; hence, 3. an overflowing fullness; abundance.

horn·pipe (hôrn′pīp′), *n.* [ME.], 1. an obsolete wind instrument with a bell and mouthpiece made of horn. 2. a lively dance to the music of the hornpipe, formerly popular with sailors. 3. music for this.

horn·pout (hôrn′pout′), *n.* the horned pout.

horn silver, native chloride of silver; cerargyrite.

horn·stone (hôrn′stōn′), *n.* [transl. of G. *hornstein:* so named because of its appearance], a flintlike rock.

horn·swog·gle (hôrn′swog′'l), *v.t.* [HORNSWOGGLED (-'ld), HORNSWOGGLING], [fanciful coinage, orig. prob. associated with cuckoldry], [Slang], to swindle; humbug; bamboozle.

horn·tail (hôrn′tāl′), *n.* a four-winged insect related to the sawfly: in the adult female the organ for depositing eggs is modified with a horny, taillike extension for cutting into tree trunks, where the eggs are deposited.

horn·worm (hôrn'wūrm'), *n.* the larval caterpillar of various hawk moths, with a horny growth on the last segment.

horn·wort (horn'wūrt'), *n.* [*horn* + *wort*, after Mod. L. *Ceratophyllum*], any of a group of plants growing entirely submerged in lakes and slow-moving streams, with whorls of finely divided leaves.

horn·y (hôr'ni), *adj.* [HORNIER (-ni-ẽr), HORNIEST (-ni-ist)], [ME.], 1. made of horn or a hornlike substance. 2. having horns or hornlike growths. 3. hard like horn; callous and tough.

horn·y-hand·ed (hôr'ni-han'did), *adj.* having hands toughened and calloused by hard work.

horol., horology.

ho·ro·loge (hôr'ə-lōj', hor'ə-loj'), *n.* [ME.; OFr.; L. *horologium;* Gr. *hōrologion* < *hōra*, hour + *legein*, to tell], a timepiece; clock, watch, hourglass, sundial, etc.

ho·rol·o·ger (hô-rol'ə-jẽr, hō-rol'ə-jẽr), *n.* a horologist.

hor·o·log·ic (hôr'ə-loj'ik, hor'ə-loj'ik), *adj.* [L. *horologicus*], of horology or horologes.

hor·o·log·i·cal (hôr'ə-loj'i-k'l, hor'ə-loj'i-k'l), *adj.* horologic.

ho·rol·o·gist (hô-rol'ə-jist, hō-rol'ə-jist), *n.* an expert in horology; a maker of or dealer in timepieces.

Hor·o·lo·gi·um (hôr'ə-lō'ji-əm, hor'ə-lō'ji-əm), *n.* [L.; see HOROLOGE], a southern constellation: see **constellation**, chart.

ho·rol·o·gy (hô-rol'ə-ji, hō-rol'ə-ji), *n.* [< Gr. *hōra*, hour; + *-logy*], the science or art of measuring time or making timepieces: abbreviated **horol.**, **hor.**

hor·o·scope (hôr'ə-skōp', hor'ə-skōp'), *n.* [Fr.; L. *horoscopus;* Gr. *hōroskopos*, one who observes the hour of birth < *hōra*, hour + *skopos*, watcher < *skopein*, to view], in *astrology*, 1. the position of the planets and stars with relation to one another at a given time, especially at the time of a person's birth, regarded as determining his destiny. 2. a chart of the zodiacal signs and the positions of the planets, etc., by which astrologers profess to tell a person's future.

cast a horoscope, to draw up a horoscope so as to calculate the supposed influence of the stars and planets on a person's life.

ho·ros·co·py (hô-ros'kə-pi, hō-ros'kə-pi), *n.* 1. the art of casting horoscopes. 2. the aspect of the heavens at a given time, especially at one's birth.

hor·ren·dous (hô-ren'dəs, ho-ren'dəs), *adj.* [L. *horrendus* < ppr. of *horrere*, to bristle], horrible; frightful.

hor·rent (hôr'ənt, hor'ənt), *adj.* [L. *horrens*, *horrentis*, ppr. of *horrere*, to bristle], 1. standing up like bristles; bristling. 2. [Rare], horrified; shuddering.

hor·ri·ble (hôr'i-b'l, hor'i-b'l), *adj.* [ME.; OFr.; L. *horribilis* < *horrere*, to bristle, be afraid], 1. causing a feeling of horror; terrible; dreadful; frightful. 2. [Colloq.], very bad, ugly, shocking, unpleasant, etc.

hor·ri·bly (hôr'i-bli, hor'i-bli), *adv.* 1. in a horrible manner. 2. to a horrible degree.

hor·rid (hôr'id, hor'id), *adj.* [L. *horridus* < *horrere*, to bristle], 1. originally, bristling; shaggy; rough. 2. causing a feeling of horror; terrible; revolting; detestable. 3. [Colloq.], very bad, ugly, unpleasant, etc.: the current sense.

hor·rif·ic (hô-rif'ik, ho-rif'ik), *adj.* [Fr. or L.; Fr. *horrifique;* L. *horrificus* < *horrere*, to bristle, be afraid + *facere*, to make], causing horror; horrifying; horrible.

hor·ri·fi·ca·tion (hôr'ə-fi-kā'shən, hor'ə-fi-kā'shən), *n.* 1. a horrifying or being horrified. 2. something horrifying.

hor·ri·fy (hôr'ə-fī', hor'ə-fī'), *v.t.* [HORRIFIED (-fīd'), HORRIFYING], [L. *horrificare* < *horrificus;* see HORRIFIC], 1. to cause to feel horror. 2. [Colloq.], to shock greatly. —*SYN.* see **dismay.**

hor·rip·i·late (hô-rip'ə-lāt', ho-rip'ə-lāt'), *v.t.* [HORRIPILATED (-id), HORRIPILATING], [< L. *horripilatus*, pp. of *horripilare*, to bristle with hairs < *horrere*, to bristle + *pilus*, hair], to produce horripilation. *v.i.* to experience horripilation; bristle or shudder.

hor·rip·i·la·tion (hô-rip'ə-lā'shən, ho-rip'ə-lā'shən), *n.* [LL. *horripilatio;* see HORRIPILATE], the erection of hair of the head or body as a result of fear, disease, or cold; goose flesh.

hor·ror (hôr'ẽr, hor'ẽr), *n.* [ME. *orrour*, *horrour;* OFr. *orror*, *horror*, *horrour;* L. *horror* < *horrere*, to bristle, shake, be afraid < IE. **ĝhṛs-eyō*, to bristle < base **ĝhers-*, bristle, be rigid; cf. GORSE], 1. originally, *a)* a bristling. *b)* a shuddering. 2. the strong feeling caused by something frightful or shocking; shuddering fear and disgust; terror and repugnance. 3. strong dislike or aversion; loathing. 4. the quality of causing horror. 5. something that causes horror. 6. [Colloq.], something very bad, ugly, disagreeable, etc.

Hor·sa (hôr'sə), *n.* brother of Hengist; ?–455 A.D.: see **Hengist.**

‡**hors de com·bat** (ôr' də kōn'bä'), [Fr., out of combat], put out of action; disabled.

hors d'oeu·vre (ôr'dūrv'; ôr'duv'; Fr. ôr'dö'vr'), [*pl.* HORS D'OEUVRES (-dūrvz', -duvz'; Fr. -dö'vr')], [Fr., lit., outside of work < *hors*, outside (< L. *foris*) + *de*, of (see DE-) + *oeuvre*, work (< L. *opera*, works)], *usually in pl.* an appetizer, as olives, anchovies, etc., served usually at the beginning of a meal.

horse (hôrs), *n.* [*pl.* HORSES (-iz), HORSE; see PLURAL, II, D, 1], [ME. *hors;* AS. *hors*, *hros;* akin to G. *ross* (OHG. *hros*); prob. IE. base *(*s*)*ker-*, to leap, as also in L. *scurra*, buffoon, entertainer, joker (cf. SCURRILOUS)], 1. a large, strong animal with four legs, solid hoofs, and flowing mane and tail, long ago domesticated for drawing or carrying loads, carrying riders, etc. 2. the full-grown male of the horse; gelding or stallion, as distinguished from a mare. 3. anything like a horse in that a person sits, rides, or is carried on it. 4. a frame on legs to support something; specifically, *a)* a sawing frame. *b)* a clotheshorse. 5. a man: a joking, friendly, or insolent term. 6. [Colloq.], in *chess*, a knight. 7. [Slang], a translation used illegitimately by students in the preparation of their work: also called *trot*, *pony*. 8. in *gymnastics*, a padded block on legs, used for jumping or vaulting. 9. in *military usage*, mounted troops; cavalry. 10. in *mining*, a mass of earth or rock inside a vein. 11. in *zoology*, any of the horse species, as the zebra, tapir, etc. *v.t.* [HORSED (hôrst), HORSING], 1. to supply with a horse or horses; put on horseback. 2. to place on a man's back or a wooden horse for flogging; hence, 3. to flog. 4. [Slang], to subject (a person) to horseplay; make fun of. *v.i.* to mount or go on horseback. *adj.* 1. of a horse or horses. 2. mounted on horses. 3. large, strong, or coarse of its kind: as, *horse*radish.

a horse on one, [cf. HORSELAUGH], [Slang], a joke at one's expense.

back the wrong horse, 1. to bet on a horse that loses the race; hence, 2. to uphold the losing side.

be on one's high horse, [Colloq.], to behave in an arrogant, haughty, or disdainful manner.

hold one's horses, [Slang], to curb one's impatience.

horse around, [Slang], to engage in horseplay.

horse of another (or **different**) **color**, an entirely different matter.

to horse! get on your horse! mount!

horse·back (hôrs'bak'), *n.* 1. the back of a horse. 2. a ridge of earth; hogback. *adv.* on horseback.

horse·car (hôrs'kär'), *n.* 1. a streetcar drawn by horses, formerly used in the United States. 2. a car for transporting horses.

horse chestnut, [so called because orig. thought of as fodder for horses], 1. a tree with large palmate leaves, clusters of white flowers, and glossy brown nuts growing in burs. 2. its nut. 3. any of various related shrubs or trees.

horse·cloth (hôrs'klôth', hôrs'kloth'), *n.* a blanketlike covering for a horse's back and loins.

horse·flesh (hôrs'flesh'), *n.* 1. the flesh of the horse, especially as food. 2. horses collectively.

horse·fly (hôrs'flī'), *n.* [*pl.* HORSEFLIES (-flīz')], [ME. *hors flevgis*, *pl.*], 1. any of a number of related large flies the female of which sucks the blood of horses, cattle, etc.; gadfly. 2. any of various other flies troublesome to horses, as the botfly.

horse gentian, any of a number of weedy plants of the honeysuckle family, with opposite leaves, inconspicuous flowers, and leathery fruit.

Horse Guards, 1. a body of cavalry; especially, the cavalry brigade forming the household guard of the English sovereign. 2. [Colloq.], the building opposite Whitehall, London, housing this guard and certain departments of the War Office.

horse·hair (hôrs'hâr'), *n.* [ME. *horsher*], 1. hair from the mane or tail of a horse. 2. the stiff fabric made from this hair; haircloth. *adj.* 1. of horsehair. 2. covered or stuffed with horsehair.

horse·hide (hôrs'hīd'), *n.* 1. the hide of a horse. 2. leather made from this.

horse latitudes, [reason for name obscure; said to be < Sp. *golfo de las yeguas*, mare's gulf, so named from the fickle wind conditions], either of two belts of calms, light winds, and high barometric pressure, situated at about 30° N. and 30° S. latitude.

horse·laugh (hôrs'laf', hôrs'läf'), *n.* a loud, boisterous laugh, usually derisive; guffaw.

horse·leech (hôrs'lēch'), *n.* 1. a large European leech said to attach itself to the mouths of horses while they are drinking. 2. [Archaic], a veterinary surgeon.

horse·less (hôrs'lis), *adj.* 1. without a horse. 2. not requiring a horse; self-propelled: as, an automobile was formerly called a *horseless* carriage.

horse mackerel, 1. the largest fish of the mackerel family, the tuna, or tunny. 2. any of various other fishes, as the saurel, cavally, etc.

horse·man (hôrs'mən), *n.* [*pl.* HORSEMEN (-mən)], 1. a man who rides on horseback. 2. a cavalryman. 3. a man skilled in the riding, managing, or care of horses.
horse·man·ship (hôrs'mən-ship'), *n.* [*horseman* + *-ship*], the art of riding a horse; skill in handling horses.
horse marine, 1. a member of an imaginary corps of marine cavalry. 2. anyone as much out of his element as a mounted marine would be on shipboard.
horse·mint (hôrs'mint'), *n.* [ME. *horsminte*], 1. any of a group of North American plants of the mint family, with clusters of showy flowers, usually red or purplish. 2. any of certain European mints.
horse nettle, a weed of the nightshade family, with yellow prickles, white or blue flowers, and yellow berries.
horse opera, [Slang], a motion picture or play about cowboys, cattle rustlers, etc., especially in the western United States.
horse pistol, a large pistol formerly carried by men on horseback.
horse·play (hôrs'plā'), *n.* [orig., play involving spectacular horsemanship], rough, boisterous fun.
horse·pow·er (hôrs'pou'ẽr), *n.* [said to have been first adopted by James Watt, inventor of the steam engine], 1. the power exerted by a horse in pulling. 2. a unit for measuring the power of motors or engines, equal to a rate of 33,000 foot-pounds per minute (the force required to raise 33,000 pounds at the rate of one foot per minute): abbreviated **H.P., HP, h.p., hp.**
horse·pox (hôrs'poks'), *n.* an acute infectious disease of horses: it is a modified form of smallpox.
horse·rad·ish (hôrs'rad'ish), *n.* 1. a plant of the mustard family, grown for its pungent, white, fleshy root. 2. a relish made of the grated root of this plant.
horse rake, a horse-drawn rake.
horse sense, [Colloq.], plain common sense.
horse·shoe (hôr'shōō', hôrs'shōō'), *n.* [ME. *horscho*, contr. of *horsissho*, *horsis sho*], 1. a flat, U-shaped metal plate nailed to a horse's hoof for protection. 2. anything shaped like this. 3. *pl.* a game in which the players toss horseshoes at a stake driven in the ground, the object being to encircle the stake or come as close to it as possible: the stakes in regulation horseshoes are 40 feet apart. *v.t.* to fit with a horseshoe or horseshoes.
horseshoe crab, any of a group of horseshoe-shaped sea animals with a long, spinelike tail; king crab.
horse·tail (hôrs'tāl'), *n.* 1. a horse's tail. 2. a horse's tail as a former Turkish ensign denoting the rank of pasha. 3. any of a number of related rushlike, flowerless plants with hollow, jointed stems and scalelike leaves.
horse·weed (hôrs'wēd'), *n.* 1. any of a group of strong-smelling, weedy plants of the mint family, with clusters of small, yellow flowers. 2. a common weed of the composite family.
horse·whip (hôrs'hwip'), *n.* a whip for driving or managing horses. *v.t.* to lash with a horsewhip.
horse·wom·an (hôrs'woom'ən), *n.* [*pl.* HORSEWOMEN (-wim'in)], 1. a woman who rides on horseback. 2. a woman skilled in the riding or managing of horses.
hors·i·ly (hôr's'l-i), *adv.* in a horsy manner.
hors·i·ness (hôr'si-nis), *n.* the quality of being horsy.
horst (hôrst), *n.* [G., orig., thicket, aerie], in *geology*, a raised rock mass between two faults.
hors·y (hôr'si), *adj.* [HORSIER (-si-ẽr), HORSIEST (-si-ist)], 1. of, having the nature of, or suggesting a horse or horses. 2. connected with or fond of horses, fox hunting, or horse racing; dressing, talking, etc. in the manner of people who are fond of horses, hunting, etc.
hort., 1. horticultural. 2. horticulture.
hor·ta·tive (hôr'tə-tiv), *adj.* [L. *hortativus*], hortatory.
hor·ta·to·ry (hôr'tə-tôr'i, hôr'tə-tō'ri), *adj.* [L. *hortatorius* < pp. of *hortari*, to incite, encourage, freq. of *horiri*, to urge, encourage; IE. base **ĝher-*, to desire, enjoy, seen also in *yearn*], 1. serving to encourage or urge to good deeds. 2. exhorting; giving advice.
Hor·tense (hôr-tens', hôr'tens), [Fr.; L. *Hortensia*, fem. of *Hortensius*, of a Roman gens, lit., gardener < *hortensius*, of a garden < *hortus*, a garden], a feminine name: variant, *Hortensia*. *n.* (Fr. ôr'täns'), (*Hortense de Beauharnais*), mother of Louis Napoleon; 1783–1837; queen of Holland.
Hor·ten·si·a (hôr-ten'shi-ə, hôr-ten'si-ə), a feminine name: see **Hortense.**
Hor·thy von Nagy·bá·nya, Mik·lós (mik'lôsh hôr'ti fôn nä'dy'-bä'nyä), 1868–1957; Hungarian admiral; regent of Hungary (1920–1944).
hor·ti·cul·tur·al (hôr'ti-kul'chẽr-əl), *adj.* of horticulture: abbreviated **hort., hortic.**
hor·ti·cul·ture (hôr'ti-kul'chẽr), *n.* [< L. *hortus*, a garden + *cultura;* see CULTURE], the cultivation of a garden or orchard; art or science of growing flowers, fruit, and vegetables: abbreviated **hort., hortic.**
hor·ti·cul·tur·ist (hôr'ti-kul'chẽr-ist), *n.* a specialist or expert in horticulture.
hor·tus sic·cus (hôr'təs sik'əs), [L.; *hortus*, a garden + *siccus*, dry], a classified collection of dried plants; herbarium.
Ho·rus (hō'rəs), *n.* [L.; Gr. *Hōros;* Egypt. *Ḥeru*, hawk], the ancient Egyptian god of the sun, represented as having the head of a hawk: he was the son of Osiris and Isis.
Hos., Hosea.
ho·san·na (hō-zan'ə), *n.* & *interj.* [LL.; Gr. *hōsanna* < Heb. *hōshī'āh nnā*, lit., save, we pray], an exclamation or shout of praise to God.
hose (hōz), *n.* [*pl.* HOSE, *archaic* HOSEN (hō'z'n)], [ME.; AS. *hosa*, leg covering; akin to G. *hose;* IE. *(*s*)*qeu-s* (in the extension **qudh-* or **qut-so*) < base *(*s*)*qeu-*, to cover, hide, conceal; cf. HOARD, HOUSE], 1. formerly, a tight-fitting outer garment covering the hips, legs, and feet, attached to the doublet by cords or ribbons (called *points*), but sometimes extended only to the knees or ankles. 2. *pl.* *a*) stockings. *b*) socks. 3. [*pl.* HOSE, HOSES (-iz)], [prob. influenced by D. *hoos*, water pipe, of same origin], *a*) a flexible pipe or tube, used to convey fluids, especially water from a hydrant. *b*) such a pipe equipped with a nozzle and attachments. *c*) a sheath or sheathing part resembling such a pipe. *v.t.* [HOSED (hōzd), HOSING], 1. to put water on with a hose; drench or soak with a hose. 2. [Slang], to beat with a hose.
Ho·se·a (hō-zē'ə, hō-zā'ə), [Heb. *hōshēa'* lit., salvation], a masculine name. *n.* 1. a Hebrew prophet who lived in the 8th century B.C. 2. a book of the Old Testament containing his writings. Abbreviated **Hos.**
ho·sen (hō'z'n), archaic plural of **hose.**
ho·sier (hō'zhẽr), *n.* [ME.], a person who makes or sells hosiery or similar knitted or woven goods.
ho·sier·y (hō'zhẽr-i), *n.* [< *hosier*], 1. *a*) hose; stockings and socks. *b*) other similar knitted or woven goods. 2. the business of a hosier.
hosp., hospital.
hos·pice (hos'pis), *n.* [Fr.; L. *hospitium*, hospitality, inn, lodging < *hospes*, host, guest], 1. a place of refuge for travelers, especially that belonging to the monks of Saint Bernard in the Alps. 2. a home for the sick or poor.
hos·pi·ta·ble (hos'pi-tə-b'l; *occas.* hos-pit'ə-b'l), *adj.* [MFr. < L. *hospitare*, to receive as a guest < *hospes*, host, guest], 1. entertaining, or fond of entertaining, guests in a friendly, generous manner. 2. caused or characterized by generosity and friendliness to guests: as, a *hospitable* act. 3. liberal and generous in disposition and mind; receptive or open, as to new ideas.
hos·pi·ta·bly (hos'pi-tə-bli; *occas.* hos-pit'ə-bli), *adv.* in a hospitable manner.
hos·pi·tal (hos'pi-t'l), *n.* [ME.; OFr.; ML. *hospitale*, a house, inn < L. *hospitalia*, strangers' apartments, neut. pl. of *hospitalis*, of a guest < *hospes*, host, guest], 1. originally, *a*) a place of shelter and rest for travelers, etc. *b*) a charitable institution for providing and caring for the aged, infirm, orphaned, etc.: now only in names. 2. an institution where the ill or injured may receive medical, surgical, or psychiatric treatment, nursing, food and lodging, etc. during illness.
hos·pi·tal·er (hos'pi-t'l-ẽr), *n.* [ME.; OFr. *hospitalier;* ML. *hospitalarius* < *hospitale*], 1. [Rare], a person receiving the care of a hospital. 2. [usually H-], a member of one of the charitable societies organized during the Middle Ages to care for the sick, needy, etc., especially a member of a military religious order called the Knights Hospitaler of St. John of Jerusalem. Also spelled **hospitaller.**
hos·pi·tal·i·ty (hos'pi-tal'ə-ti), *n.* [*pl.* HOSPITALITIES (-tiz)], [L. *hospitalitas* < *hospitalis;* see HOSPITAL], the act, practice, or quality of being hospitable; friendly and generous entertainment of guests.
hos·pi·tal·i·za·tion (hos'pi-t'l-ə-zā'shən, hos'pi-t'l-ī-zā'shən), *n.* 1. a hospitalizing or being hospitalized. 2. [Colloq.], hospitalization insurance.
hospitalization insurance, insurance providing hospitalization for the subscriber and, usually, members of his immediate family.
hos·pi·tal·ize (hos'pi-t'l-īz'), *v.t.* [HOSPITALIZED (-īzd'), HOSPITALIZING], to send or admit to, put in, or cause to be put in a hospital.
hos·pi·ti·um (hos-pish'i-əm), *n.* [*pl.* HOSPITIA (-ə)], [L.], [Archaic], a hospice; inn.
hos·po·dar (hos'pô-där'), *n.* [Romanian; ult. < OSlav. *gospodĭ*, lord; for IE. base see HOST, GUEST], a title formerly given to the princes or governors of Moldavia and Wallachia.
Host, host (hōst), *n.* [ME. *hoste;* OFr. *oiste, hoiste;* L. *hostia*, animal sacrificed, victim; prob. < *hostire*, to recompense, requite], the bread of the Eucharist.
host (hōst), *n.* [ME. *hoste, oste;* OFr. (*h*)*oste* (Fr. *hôte*), host, guest; L. *hospes* (*hospit-*) < **hosti-potis*, guest lord; IE. **ghosti-s*, stranger, guest, seen also in Eng. *guest*, L. *hostis*, enemy, orig., stranger (cf. HOSTILE)], 1. a man who entertains guests in his own home or at his own expense; person who initiates or presides over any social gathering. 2. a man who keeps an inn or hotel; innkeeper, landlord, etc. 3. any organism on or in which another (called a *parasite*) lives for nourishment or protection.
reckon without one's host, to make plans or decisions

without considering some important factor or factors.

host (hōst), *n.* [ME. *host, ost;* OFr. (*h*)*ost;* ML. *hostis,* hostile thing, invading army < L. *hostis;* see prec.], 1. an army. 2. a multitude; great number. —*SYN.* see **crowd.**

hos·tage (hos'tij), *n.* [ME.; OFr., apparently a merging of two words, *hostage,* lodging (< ML. *hospitagium;* ult. < L. *hospes,* host) + *ostage,* hostage, state of a hostage (< ML. **obsidaticum* < L. *obsidatus* < *obses, obsidis,* hostage, pledge < *ob-,* at + *sedere,* to sit)], 1. a person kept or given as a pledge for the fulfillment of certain agreements. 2. the state of the person thus kept or given. —*SYN.* see **pledge.**

give hostages to fortune, to get, be responsible for the care of, or be liable to lose, a wife, children, etc.

hos·tel (hos't'l), *n.* [ME.; OFr.; ML. *hospitale;* see HOSPITAL], a lodging place; inn; hostelry; especially, one of a series of supervised shelters (*youth hostels*) used by young people on hikes, etc.

hos·tel·er (hos't'l-ẽr), *n.* [ME.; OFr. *hostelier*], [Archaic], the keeper of a hostel; innkeeper.

hos·tel·ry (hos't'l-ri), *n.* [*pl.* HOSTELRIES (-riz)], [ME. & OFr. *hostellerie* < *hostel;* see HOSTEL], a lodging place; inn; hotel.

host·ess (hōs'tis), *n.* [ME.; OFr. *hostesse,* fem. of *hoste;* see HOST], 1. a woman who entertains guests in her own home or at her own expense; often, the wife of a host. 2. *a*) a woman who keeps an inn or hotel. *b*) a woman married to an innkeeper and sharing some of his duties. 3. *a*) a woman whose work is seeing that guests or travelers are comfortable, entertained, etc., as on an airplane. *b*) a woman employed in a restaurant to supervise the waitresses, assign guests to tables, etc. *c*) a woman who serves as a paid partner at a public dance hall.

hostess gown, a long, dresslike negligee worn for lounging and entertaining at home.

hos·tile (hos't'l; Brit. hos'tīl), *adj.* [L. *hostilis* < *hostis,* foreigner, enemy; see HOST], 1. of or characteristic of an enemy; warlike. 2. having or showing ill will; unfriendly; adverse; antagonistic.

hos·til·i·ty (hos-til'ə-ti), *n.* [*pl.* HOSTILITIES (-tiz)], [Fr. *hostilité;* LL. *hostilitas* < L. *hostilis;* see HOSTILE], 1. a feeling of enmity, ill will, unfriendliness, etc.; antagonism. 2. *a*) expression of enmity and ill will; active opposition; hostile act. *b*) *pl.* a state of war; acts of war; warfare. —*SYN.* see **enmity.**

hos·tler (hos'lẽr, os'lẽr), *n.* [contr. of *hosteler*], 1. a person who takes care of horses at an inn, stable, etc.; groom. 2. a person who services a railroad engine at the end of a run. 3. [Obs.], an innkeeper. Also **ostler.**

hot (hot), *adj.* [HOTTER (-ẽr), HOTTEST (-ist)], [with shortened vowel < ME. *hoot;* AS. *hat;* akin to G. *heiss,* Goth. *heito,* fever; IE. base **qāi-,* heat, seen also in *hoarse*], 1. *a*) having much heat; characterized by a temperature higher than that of the human body. *b*) characterized by a relatively or abnormally high temperature; very warm: opposed to *cold.* 2. producing a burning sensation in the mouth, throat, etc.: as, *hot* pepper. 3. full of or characterized by any very strong feeling or violent activity; specifically, *a*) impetuous; fiery; excitable: as, a *hot* temper. *b*) violent; raging; angry: as, a *hot* battle, *hot* words. *c*) full of enthusiasm; eagerly intent; ardent. *d*) inflamed with sexual desire; lustful. *e*) very controversial. 4. *a*) following or pressing closely: as, *hot* pursuit. *b*) close to what is being sought: said of the seeker. 5. as if heated by friction; specifically, *a*) in constant use: as, the news kept the wires *hot.* *b*) thrown or batted hard or with great speed: said of a ball. *c*) electrically charged, especially with a current of high voltage: as, a *hot* wire. *d*) radioactive. 6. [Slang], that has not had time to lose heat, freshness, currency, etc.; specifically, *a*) recently issued or announced; new: as, *hot* news. *b*) just arrived: as, *hot* from the front. *c*) clear; intense; strong: said of the scent in hunting. *d*) recent and seemingly valid: as, a *hot* tip. *e*) recently stolen. *f*) contraband. 7. [Slang], excellent; good. 8. in *jazz music, a*) designating or of playing characterized by exciting rhythmic and tonal effects, imaginative improvisation, and, often, a fast, driving tempo. *b*) designating or of music played in this way. *adv.* in a hot manner; hotly.

get hot, [Slang], to act, perform, etc. with great spirit or enthusiasm.

make it hot for, [Colloq.], to make things disagreeable, difficult, or uncomfortable for.

hot air, [Slang], empty or pretentious talk or writing.

hot·bed (hot'bed'), *n.* 1. a bed of earth covered with glass and heated by manure, for forcing plants. 2. any place that fosters rapid growth or extensive activity.

hot-blood·ed (hot'blud'id), *adj.* easily excited; excitable, ardent, passionate, reckless, etc.

hot·box (hot'boks'), *n.* an overheated bearing on an axle or shaft.

hot cake, a griddlecake.

sell like hot cakes, [Colloq.], to be sold rapidly and in large quantities.

hotch·pot (hoch'pot'), *n.* [ME. & OFr. *hochepot* < Walloon *hosepot,* kind of stew < OD. *hutspot,* stew of beef or mutton, hodgepodge], in *English law,* a pooling of property for equal redistribution.

hotch·potch (hoch'poch'), *n.* [< *hotchpot*], 1. a thick stew of various meats and vegetables; hence, 2. a jumbled mixture; medley; mess. 3. a hotchpot. In senses 1 & 2, now usually **hodgepodge.**

hot cockles, formerly, a game in which a blindfolded player tried to guess who hit him.

hot cross bun, a bun marked with a cross, eaten especially during Lent.

hot dog, [Colloq.], 1. a frankfurter or wiener. 2. a sandwich made of a hot frankfurter or wiener, usually in a soft roll, often served with mustard, catsup, etc.

ho·tel (hō-tel'), *n.* [18th c. < Fr. *hôtel;* OFr. *hostel* < LL. *hospitale;* see HOSPITAL], 1. an establishment or building providing a number of bedrooms, baths, etc., and usually food, for the accommodation of travelers, semipermanent residents, etc. 2. [Fr.], the mansion of a person of wealth or rank.

‡hô·tel de ville (ō-tel' də vēl'), [Fr.], a town hall.

hot·foot (hot'foot'), *adv.* [ME. *hot fot*], [Colloq.], in great haste. *v.i.* [Colloq.], to hurry; hasten.

hot-foot (hot'foot'), *n.* the prank of secretly inserting a match between the sole and upper of a victim's shoe and then lighting it.

hot·head (hot'hed'), *n.* a hotheaded person.

hot·head·ed (hot'hed'id), *adj.* 1. quick-tempered; easily made angry. 2. hasty; impetuous; rash.

hot·house (hot'hous'), *n.* a building with the roof and sides of glass, artificially heated for growing plants; greenhouse.

Ho·tien (hō'tyen'), *n.* Khotan, a city in western China.

hot·ly (hot'li), *adv.* in a hot manner; with heat; fierily.

hot·ness (hot'nis), *n.* the quality or state of being hot.

hot plate, a small gas or electric stove for cooking.

hot pot, meat and potatoes cooked together in a tightly covered pot.

hot-press (hot'pres'), *v.t.* to produce a gloss on (paper or cloth) by heat and pressure. *n.* a machine for doing this.

hot rod, [Slang], an automobile, usually a jalopy, whose motor has been supercharged for high speed.

Hot Springs, a city in southwestern Arkansas: pop., 29,000: Hot Springs National Park, containing 46 boiling springs, is near by (area, 1 1/2 sq. mi.).

hot·spur (hot'spũr'), *n.* [nickname of Henry Percy: cf. Shakespeare's *Henry IV*], a rash, hotheaded person.

hot-tem·pered (hot'tem'pẽrd), *adj.* having a fiery temper; easily made angry.

Hot·ten·tot (hot''n tot'), *n.* [S. Afr. D., lit., *hot & tot,* syllables used to imitate clicks characteristic of their language], 1. a member of a Negroid race living in South Africa. 2. the language of the Hottentots, the chief dialect of which is Nama: regarded as forming, together with Bushman, a separate linguistic family. *adj.* of the Hottentots or their language.

hot water, 1. water that is hot, especially when continuously provided as a utility in an apartment, etc. 2. [Colloq.], trouble; difficulty (preceded by *in*).

Hou·dan (hōō'dan), *n.* [< *Houdan,* France where it originated], one of a French breed of crested, five-toed chickens with white or black-and-white feathers.

Hou·din·i, Harry (hōō-dē'ni), (born *Ehrich Weiss*), 1874–1926; American stage magician.

Hou·don, Jean An·toine (zhän än'twån' ōō'dôn'; Eng. hōō'don), 1741–1828; French sculptor.

hough (hok; Scot. hokh), *n.* [see HOCK (joint)], [Chiefly Scot.], the joint bending backward in the hind leg of a horse, ox, etc., corresponding to the human ankle.

hound (hound), *n.* [ME.; AS. *hund,* a dog (generic term); akin to G. *hund;* IE. base **kuon-,* dog, seen also in *canine, cynic;* sense 1 shows specialization, accompanied by generalization of AS. *dogga* (see DOG)], 1. any of several breeds of large hunting dogs characterized by long, drooping ears, short hair, and a deep-throated bark. 2. any dog. 3. a contemptible person. *v.t.* 1. to hunt or chase with or as with hounds; chase or follow continually; nag: as, bill collectors *hound* him. 2. to urge on; incite to pursuit. —*SYN.* see **bait.**

follow the (or **ride to**) **hounds,** to hunt (a fox, etc.) on horseback with hounds.

hound (hound), *n.* [< ME. *houn* < ON. *hūnn,* knob, with unhistoric *-d* after prec. *hound*], 1. in *shipbuilding,* a projection at the masthead for supporting the heel of the topmast and the upper parts of the lower rigging. 2. a side bar in a vehicle, for increasing the rigidity of the parts connected.

hound's-tongue (houndz'tuŋ'), *n.* any of a group of plants of the borage family, with blue flowers and hairy leaves shaped somewhat like a hound's tongue.

hour (our), *n.* [ME. *houre, oure, our;* OFr. *hore, hure, ore, ure;* L. *hora;* Gr. *hōra*, hour, time, period, season; akin to OSlav. *jare*, year, Goth. *jer;* for IE. base see YEAR], 1. *a)* a division of time, one of the twenty-four parts of a day; sixty minutes. *b)* one of the twelve points marking the beginning or end of such a division: as, the ninth *hour.* 2. a point or period of time; specifically, *a)* a fixed point or period of time for a particular activity, occasion, etc.: as, the dinner *hour.* *b)* an indefinite period of time: as, he spent his happiest *hours* in Paris. *c)* the period of time in a classroom: as, the *hour* lasts fifty minutes. *d) pl.* a special period for work, receiving patients, etc.: as, his office *hours* are 2–5. *e) pl.* the usual times for getting up and going to bed: as, he keeps late *hours.* 3. the time of day as indicated by a timepiece, expressed in hours and minutes: as, the *hour* is 2:30. 4. a measure of distance set by the normal amount of time passed in traveling it: as, it is two *hours* from New York to Philadelphia by rail. 5. in *astronomy*, a sidereal hour; angular unit of right ascension equaling 15° measured along the equinoctial circle. 6. in *ecclesiastical usage,* *a)* the seven times of the day set aside for prayers. *b)* the prayers said at these times. See also **Hours.** Abbreviated **hr., H., h.** (*sing & pl.*), **hrs.** (*pl.*).
after hours, after the regular hours for business, school, etc.
hour after hour, every hour.
hour by hour, each hour.
of the hour, of this time; of the present.
one's hour, the time of one's death.
the small (or **wee**) **hours,** the hours just after midnight.

hour circle, in *astronomy*, any of the twelve great imaginary circles passing through the celestial poles at right angles to the equator.

hour·glass (our'glas', our'gläs'), *n.* an instrument for measuring time by the trickling of sand, mercury, water, etc. through a small opening in one glass bulb to another below it: the shift of contents takes one hour.

HOURGLASS

hour hand, the short hand of a clock or watch, which indicates the hours and moves around the dial once every twelve hours.

hou·ri (hoo'ri, hou'ri), *n.* [*pl.* HOURIS (-riz)], [Fr.; Per. *ḥūri* < Ar. *ḥūrīyah*, black-eyed woman, ult. < *ḥawira*, to be dark-eyed], 1. a nymph of the Moslem Paradise, thought of as always young and beautiful; hence, 2. a seductively beautiful woman.

hour·ly (our'li), *adj.* 1. done or happening every hour; at intervals of an hour. 2. done or happening in the course of an hour: as, the *hourly* output. 3. done or happening very often; frequent; continual. *adv.* 1. at intervals of an hour; once an hour; every hour. 2. hour by hour; at any hour. 3. often; frequently; continually.

Hours (ourz), *n.pl.* [see HOUR], 1. in *Greek mythology,* the goddesses of the seasons, justice, order, and peace. 2. in the *Roman Catholic Church*, a book containing prayers for certain times of the day.

house (hous; *for v.*, houz), *n.* [*pl.* HOUSES (houz'iz)], [ME. *hous;* AS. *hus;* akin to G. *haus* (OHG. *hūs*); IE. *(*s*)*qeu-s* < base *(*s*)*qeu-*, to cover, hide; cf. HIDE, HOSE], 1. a building for human beings to live in; specifically, *a)* the building or part of a building occupied by one family or tenant; dwelling place. *b)* a college in a university. *c)* an inn; tavern; hotel. *d)* a building where a group of people live as a unit: as, a fraternity *house.* *e)* a monastery, nunnery, or similar religious establishment. 2. the people who live in a house, considered as a unit; social group; especially, a family or household. 3. a family as including kin, ancestors, and descendants, especially a royal or noble family: as, the *House* of Tudor. 4. something regarded as a house; place that provides shelter, living space, etc.; specifically, *a)* the habitation of an animal, as the shell of a mollusk. *b)* a building or shelter where animals are kept: as, the monkey *house* in a zoo. *c)* a building where things are kept when not in use: as, a carriage *house.* *d)* a deckhouse. 5. any place where something is thought of as living, resting, etc. 6. *a)* a theater. *b)* the audience in a theater. 7. *a)* a place of business. *b)* a business firm; commercial establishment. 8. a church, temple, or synagogue. 9. *a)* the building or rooms where a legislature or branch of a legislature meets. *b)* a legislative assembly or governing body: as, the *House* of Representatives. 10. in *astrology, a)* one of the twelve parts into which the heavens are divided by great circles through the north and south points of the horizon: used by astrologers in casting horoscopes. *b)* a sign of the zodiac considered as the seat of a planet's greatest influence. *v.t.* [HOUSED (houzd), HOUSING], 1. to provide a house or lodgings for. 2. to store in a house. 3. to cover, harbor, or shelter by or as if by putting in a house. *v.i.* 1. to take shelter. 2. to reside; live.
bring down the house, [Colloq.], to receive enthusiastic applause from the audience.
clean house, 1. to clean and put a house in order. 2. to do away with undesirable conditions.
keep house, to take care of the affairs of a home; run a house; be a housekeeper.
on the house, given free, at the expense of the establishment.
play house, [Colloq.], to pretend to be grown-up people with the customary household duties and routine: a children's phrase.
set (or **put**) **one's house in order,** to put one's affairs in order.

House, Edward Man·dell (man'dəl hous), 1858–1938; American statesman and diplomat: called *Colonel House.*

house·boat (hous'bōt'), *n.* 1. a large, flat-bottomed boat with a superstructure resembling a house, usually moored and used as a residence. 2. a motor yacht with particularly commodious living quarters aboard.

house·break·er (hous'brāk'ẽr), *n.* 1. a person guilty of housebreaking; burglar. 2. [British], a person who dismantles houses.

house·break·ing (hous'brāk'iŋ), *n.* 1. the act of breaking into another's house to commit theft or some other felony: it is itself a felony. 2. [British], the dismantling of houses.

house·bro·ken (hous'brō'k'n), *adj.* trained to live in a house (i.e., to defecate and urinate in the proper place): said of a dog, cat, etc.

house·carl (hous'kärl'), *n.* [Late AS. *huscarl;* ON. *hūskarl*, lit., houseman; see HOUSE & CHURL], a member of the bodyguard or household troops of a Danish or English king or nobleman in late Anglo-Saxon times.

house·coat (hous'kōt'), *n.* a woman's long, loose garment for informal wear about the house.

house·dress (hous'dres'), *n.* any relatively inexpensive dress, as of printed cotton, worn in the home while doing housework, etc.

house·fly (hous'flī'), *n.* [*pl.* HOUSEFLIES (-flīz')], a two-winged fly found in and around houses: it feeds on garbage, manure, and food, and is a carrier of typhoid and some other diseases.

house·ful (hous'fool'), *n.* as much or as many as a house will hold or accommodate.

house·hold (hous'hōld'), *n.* [ME. *houshold;* see HOUSE & HOLD, *n.*], 1. all the persons who live in one house; family, or family and servants. 2. the home and its affairs. 3. [H-], the royal household. *adj.* of a household or home; domestic.

household arts, home economics.

house·hold·er (hous'hōl'dẽr), *n.* [ME. *housholdere*], 1. a person who owns or maintains a house as his own. 2. the head of a household or family.

household word, a very familiar word or saying; byword.

house·keep·er (hous'kēp'ẽr), *n.* 1. a woman who runs a home, takes care of the housework, etc. 2. a woman hired to run a home, supervise the servants, etc.

house·keep·ing (hous'kēp'iŋ), *n.* the work of a housekeeper; management of a house.

hou·sel (hou'z'l), *n.* [ME.; AS. *husl, husel;* akin to Goth. *hunsl*, a sacrifice; Gmc. **kun-s-lo* < IE. base **kwen-*, to make holy], [Obs.], the Eucharist. *v.t.* [Obs.], to administer the Eucharist to.

house·leek (hous'lēk'), *n.* [ME. *houslek;* see HOUSE & LEEK], 1. a plant with pink or red flowers and rosettes of thick, fleshy leaves, often found on walls and roofs. 2. any related plant.

house·line (hous'līn'), *n.* in *nautical usage*, a small line of three strands laid counterclockwise, used for seizing.

house·maid (hous'mād'), *n.* a girl or woman servant who does housework.

housemaid's knee, an inflammation of the saclike cavity covering the kneecap, caused by much kneeling.

house·moth·er (hous'muth'ẽr), *n.* [transl. of G. *hausmutter*], a woman who heads a group of people living together or has charge of a dormitory, sorority house, etc. as chaperon and, often, housekeeper.

House of Assembly, the lower branch of the legislature of South Africa.

House of Burgesses, the lower branch of the colonial legislature of Virginia or Maryland.

house of cards, any flimsy, insubstantial structure, plan, etc.

House of Commons, the lower branch of the legislature of Great Britain or Canada: abbreviated **H.C.**

house of correction, a place of short-term confinement for persons convicted of minor offenses and regarded as capable of being reformed.

House of Delegates, the lower branch of the legislature of Maryland, Virginia, or West Virginia.

House of Keys (kēz), the lower, elective branch of the legislature of the Isle of Man: also **Keys.**

House of Lords, the upper branch of the legislature of Great Britain, made up of the nobility and high-ranking clergy: abbreviated **H.L.**

House of Peers, the upper branch of the legislature of Japan.

House of Representatives, the lower branch of the legislature of: *a)* the United States. *b)* most of the States of the United States. *c)* Australia. *d)* New Zealand. *e)* Mexico. Abbreviated **H.R.**

house organ, a periodical published by a business firm for its employees, etc.

house party, 1. the entertainment of guests overnight or over a period of a few days in a home, usually a country home, or fraternity house, etc. 2. the guests.

house physician, a resident physician of a hospital, hotel, etc.

house·rais·ing (hous'rāz'iŋ), *n.* a gathering of the members of a rural community to help a neighbor build his house or its framework.

house·room (hous'rōōm', hous'room'), *n.* room or space in a house; accommodation.

house·top (hous'top'), *n.* the top of a house; roof. **from the housetops,** publicly and widely.

house·wares (hous'wârz'), *n.pl.* articles, as kitchenware, dishes, glassware, etc., for household use.

house·warm·ing (hous'wôr'miŋ), *n.* a party given by or for someone moving into a new home.

house·wife (hous'wīf'; *for 2, usually* huz'if), *n.* [*pl.* HOUSEWIVES (-wīvz'; *for 2,* -ivz)], [ME. *houswif, huswif*], 1. *a)* a woman who runs a home and takes care of domestic affairs. *b)* a woman who runs her own household. 2. a small sewing kit: also called *hussy*.

house·wife·ly (hous'wīf'li), *adj.* of or characteristic of a housewife; thrifty, orderly, and managing well. *adv.* in the manner of a good housewife.

house·wif·er·y (hous'wīf'ẽr-i, hous'wif'ri), *n.* the work of a housewife; housekeeping.

house·work (hous'wũrk'), *n.* the work involved in housekeeping; washing, cleaning, cooking, etc.

hous·ing (houz'iŋ), *n.* [ME. *husing*], 1. the act of providing shelter or lodging. 2. shelter or lodging; accommodation in houses, apartments, etc.: often used attributively, as, the *housing* problem. 3. houses collectively. 4. a shelter; covering. 5. in *architecture,* a space or recess made in a solid part to receive the end of a beam, etc. 6. in *mechanics,* a frame, box, etc. for containing some part. 7. in *nautical usage,* the part of the mast below decks.

hous·ing (houz'iŋ), *n.* [< Early Mod. Eng. *house,* housing < OFr. *huche, houce;* ML. *hultia* < Frank. **hulfti*], 1. an ornamental blanket or covering for a horse. 2. *pl.* trappings.

Hous·man, A. E. (hous'mən), (*Alfred Edward Housman*), 1859–1936; English poet and classical scholar.

Hous·ton (hūs'tən), *n.* a city in southeastern Texas: pop., 938,000: a port on a ship canal.

Hous·ton, Samuel (hūs'tən), 1793–1863; American general, president of the Republic of Texas (1836 1838; 1841–1844); United States senator (1846–1859).

hous·to·ni·a (hōōs-tō'ni-ə), *n.* [Mod. L., after Wm. *Houston* (d. 1733), Eng. botanist], any of a group of small plants of the madder family, with blue, white, or purple flowers.

Hou·yhn·hnm (hōō-in'əm, hwin'əm), *n.* in Swift's *Gulliver's Travels,* any of a race of horses with reasoning power and human virtues: see also **Yahoo.**

hove (hōv), alternative past tense and past participle of **heave.**

hov·el (huv''l, hov''l), *n.* [ME.; ? < OFr. **huvel,* dim. < *huve,* a hood < Frank. *huba,* a hood; cf. OFr. *huvelet,* penthouse], 1. a low, open shed for sheltering animals, storing supplies or equipment, etc. 2. any small, miserable dwelling; hut. *v.t.* [HOVELED OR HOVELLED (-'ld), HOVELING or HOVELLING], 1. to shelter in a hovel. 2. to make in the form of a hovel.

hov·er (huv'ẽr, hov'ẽr), *v.i.* [ME. *hoveren,* freq. (see -ER) of ME. *hoven* (to stay, stay suspended), which it superseded], 1. to stay suspended or flutter in the air near one place (often with *over* or *about*). 2. to linger or wait close by; move around (with *near* or *about*). 3. to be in an uncertain condition; waver (with *between*). *n.* a hovering. —*SYN.* see **fly.**

how (hou), *adv.* [ME. & AS. *hu;* also AS. *hwu* for **hwo;* akin to OHG. *hweo* (G. *wie*), Goth. *hwai-wa;* IE. interrogative base **qwo-,* **qwe-,* as also in *who, why,* etc.], 1. in what manner or way; by what means. 2. in what state or condition. 3. for what reason or purpose; why: as, *how* is it that you don't know? 4. by what name. 5. with what meaning; to what effect. 6. to what extent, degree, amount, etc. 7. at what price. 8. [Colloq.], what: usually a request to repeat something said. *How* is also used in exclamations and relative constructions, and as an intensive. *n.* the way of doing; manner; method.
how now? how is that? what is the meaning of this?
how so? how is it so? why?
how then? 1. what is the meaning of this? 2. how else?

how (hou), *interj.* an exclamation of greeting attributed to, and still used humorously in imitation of, American Indians.

How., howitzer.

How·ard (hou'ẽrd), [< the surname *Howard*], a masculine name.

How·ard, Catherine (hou'ẽrd) 1520?–1542; fifth wife of Henry VIII; beheaded.

Howard, Roy Wilson, 1883– ; American editor and newspaper magnate.

Howard, Sidney Coe (kō), 1891–1939; American playwright.

how·be·it (hou-bē'it), *adv.* [*how* + *be* + *it*], 1. [Archaic], however it may be; nevertheless. 2. [Obs.], although.

how·dah (hou'də), *n.* [Hind. *haudah* < Ar. *haudaj*], a canopied seat for riding on the back of an elephant or camel: also spelled **houdah.**

HOWDAH

how-do-you-do, how-d'-ye-do (hou'də-yə-dōō', hou'dyə-dōō'), *n.* [Colloq.], an annoying or awkward situation: usually preceded by *fine, pretty, nice,* etc.

How do you do? How is your health?: a conventionalized expression of greeting, used when meeting a person or being introduced.

how·dy (hou'di), *interj.* [contr. < *how do you* (*do*)?], [Dial. or Colloq.], an expression of greeting.

Howe, Elias (hou), 1819–1867; American inventor of the sewing machine.

Howe, Julia Ward, 1819–1910; American social reformer, lecturer, and poet.

Howe, Sir **William,** fifth Viscount Howe, 1729–1814; commander in chief of the British forces in the American Revolution.

how·e'er (hou-er'), *adv. & conj.* however.

How·ells, William Dean (dēn hou'əlz), 1837–1920; American novelist and editor.

how·ev·er (hou-ev'ẽr), *adv.* [ME. *hou-ever*], 1. no matter how; by whatever means; in whatever manner. 2. to whatever degree or extent. *conj.* nevertheless; yet; in spite of that; all the same: used in a clause or sentence that could properly begin with *but.*

how·itz·er (hou'it-sẽr), *n.* [G. *haubitze* < Czech *haufnice,* howitzer, orig., a sling], a short cannon with a low muzzle velocity, firing shells in a relatively high trajectory: abbreviated **How.**

HOWITZER

howl (houl), *v.i.* [ME. *houlen;* prob. echoic; cf. G. *heulen,* D. *hiulen,* etc.], 1. to utter the long, loud, wailing cry of wolves, dogs, etc. 2. to utter a similar cry of pain, anger, grief, etc. 3. to make a sound like this: as, the wind *howled.* 4. to shout or laugh in scorn, mirth, etc. *v.t.* 1. to utter with a howl or howls. 2. to drive or effect by howling. *n.* 1. a long, loud, wailing cry of a wolf, dog, etc. 2. any similar sound.
howl down, to drown out the voice or words of with shouts of scorn, anger, etc.

How·land Island (hou'lənd), a small equatorial island in the mid-Pacific, belonging to the United States.

howl·er (houl'ẽr), *n.* 1. a person or thing that howls. 2. a howling monkey. 3. [Colloq.], a foolish blunder.

howl·et (hou'lit), *n.* [prob. < Fr. *hulotte,* ? dim. of **hule,* owl < OHG. *huwela,* owl], [Archaic], an owl.

howl·ing (houl'iŋ), *adj.* [ppr. of *howl*], 1. that howls. 2. [cf. Deut. 32:10], filled with howls; mournful; dreary. 3. [Slang], great: as, a *howling* success.

howling monkey, any of a group of long-tailed monkeys with a loud, howling cry, found in Central and South America.

How·rah (hou'rä), *n.* a city in northeastern India, on the Hooghly River, opposite Calcutta: pop., 434,000.

how·so·ev·er (hou'sō-ev'ẽr), *adv.* [ME. *hou so evere*], 1. to whatever degree or extent. 2. by whatever means; in whatever manner.

hoy (hoi), *n.* [ME. *hoye;* MD. *hoei;* ? < Fl. *hui,* a hoy, *hui,* hoy!], 1. a small fore-and-aft rigged vessel resembling a sloop, no longer used. 2. a heavy barge.

hoy (hoi), *interj.* [natural shout; cf. Fl. *hui, interj.*], an exclamation to attract attention, drive hogs, etc. *n.* a shout of "hoy."

hoy·den (hoi'd'n), *n.* [Early Mod. Eng., orig., awkward man; ? phonetic sp. of D. *heiden,* heathen; cf. phrase *little heathen*], a bold, boisterous girl; tomboy. ***adj.*** bold and boisterous; tomboyish. ***v.i.*** to behave like a hoyden. Also spelled **hoiden.**

hoy·den·ish (hoi′d'n-ish), ***adj.*** of or like a hoyden; bold and boisterous; tomboyish: also spelled **hoidenish.**

Hoyle (hoil), ***n.*** a book of rules and instructions for card games, originally compiled and edited by Edmond Hoyle (1672–1769), English authority on card games and chess.

according to Hoyle, according to the rules and regulations; in the prescribed, fair, or correct way.

H.P., HP, h.p., hp., 1. high pressure. 2. horsepower.

H.Q., Hq., Headquarters.

hr., [*pl.* HRS.], hour; hours.

H.R., 1. Home Rule. 2. House of Representatives.

Hr·dlič·ka, A·leš (ȧ′lesh hũr′dlich-kȧ), 1869–1943; American anthropologist born in Bohemia; curator of the United States National Museum (1910–1943).

H.R.H., 1. Her Royal Highness. 2. His Royal Highness.

Hrolf (rolf), see **Rollo.**

H.S.H., His (or Her) Serene Highness.

Hsin·king (shin′kiŋ′; Chin. shin′jiŋ′), ***n.*** Changchun, a city in Manchuria: name during Japanese occupation.

H.S.M., 1. Her Serene Majesty. 2. His Serene Majesty.

ht., 1. heat. 2. [*pl.* HTS.], height; heights.

H.T., Hawaiian Territory.

hua·ra·ches (hə-rä′chiz; Sp. wä-rä′ches), ***n.pl.*** [pl. of Am. Sp. *huarache*, prob. < *huaraca, guaraca*, leather thong < Quechua *huaraca*], Mexican sandals, usually made of straps or woven leather strips.

Huás·car (wäs′kär), ***n.*** Inca ruler; lived c. 1495–1533; deposed by his half-brother Atahualpa.

Huas·ca·rán (wäs′kä-rän′), ***n.*** a mountain of the Andes, in western Peru: height, 22,180 ft.

Huas·tek (wäs′tek), ***n.*** [< native name], an American Indian language of Mexico that constitutes, with its dialect, a branch of the Mayan family of languages.

hub (hub), ***n.*** [prob. var. of *hob* (a peg)], 1. the center part of a wheel. 2. a center of interest, importance, or activity.

the Hub, Boston.

Hub·bard, Elbert Green (hub′ẽrd), 1856–1915; American writer.

Hubbard squash, a hard winter squash with a green or yellow rind and firm, yellow flesh: also **Hubbard.**

hub·ble (hub′'l), ***n.*** [dim. of *hub*], a small hump.

hub·ble-bub·ble (hub′'l-bub′'l), ***n.*** [echoic], 1. a smoking pipe in which the smoke is drawn through water, causing a bubbling sound; simple type of hookah. 2. a bubbling sound. 3. hubbub; uproar.

hub·bly (hub′li), ***adj.*** full of bubbles; uneven; rough.

hub·bub (hub′ub), ***n.*** [said to be < Ir. cry], a confused sound of many voices; uproar; tumult; turmoil. —***SYN.*** see **noise.**

hub·by (hub′i), ***n.*** [*pl.* HUBBIES (-iz)], [Colloq.], a husband: familiar diminutive.

Hu·bert (hū′bẽrt), [Fr.; OHG. *Huguberht*, lit., bright (in) spirit < *hugu*, mind, spirit + *beraht*, bright], a masculine name: equivalent, It. *Uberto.*

Hu·ber·tus·burg (hoo-ber′təs-boorkh′), ***n.*** a town in the north central part of Germany: a treaty signed there by Austria and Prussia in 1763 ended the Seven Years' War.

hu·bris (hū′bris), ***n.*** [Gr. *hybris*], wanton insolence or arrogance resulting from excessive pride or from passion.

huck (huk), ***n.*** [Colloq.], huckaback.

huck·a·back (huk′ə-bak′), ***n.*** [Early Mod. Eng. *hugaback, hagabag* suggest association with *back* or *bag*], a coarse linen or cotton cloth with a rough surface, used for toweling.

huck·le (huk′'l), ***n.*** [dim. (see -LE) of obs. *huck* in same sense; ? < or akin to ON. *hūka*, to crouch], [Rare], the hip or haunch.

huck·le·ber·ry (huk′'l-ber′i), ***n.*** [*pl.* HUCKLEBERRIES (-iz)], [said to be altered < *hurtleberry, whortleberry* < AS. *wyrtil*, small shrub + *berie*, a berry], 1. any of a number of related shrubs having dark-blue berries resembling blueberries. 2. the fruit of any of these shrubs. 3. loosely, a blueberry.

huck·le·bone (huk′'l-bōn′), ***n.*** [see HUCKLE], 1. the hipbone. 2. the anklebone; talus.

huck·ster (huk′stẽr), ***n.*** [ME. *hokestere* < or akin to MD. *hokester, hoekster;* prob. < *hoek, hoke*, a corner; see HOOK], 1. a peddler or hawker of wares, especially of fruits, vegetables, etc. 2. a mean, haggling tradesman; tricky, mercenary peddler. 3. [Colloq.], an advertising man. ***v.t.*** 1. to peddle; sell. 2. to bargain in or haggle over.

Hud·ders·field (hud′ẽrz-fēld′), ***n.*** a city in southwestern Yorkshire, England: pop., 124,000 (est. 1946).

hud·dle (hud′'l), ***v.i.*** [HUDDLED (-'ld), HUDDLING], [orig., (16th c.), to put out of sight; ? var. of ME. *hoderen* in same sense (< base of *hide*)], 1. to crowd close together; nestle together in a heap: as, animals *huddle* together from fear or for warmth. 2. to draw or hunch oneself up in a heap. 3. in *football*, to gather in a huddle. ***v.t.*** 1. to crowd close together. 2. to hunch or draw (oneself) up. 3. to do, put, or make hastily and carelessly. 4. to push or thrust in a hurried or disordered manner: as, he *huddled* the children into the automobile. ***n.*** 1. a confused crowd or heap of persons or things. 2. confusion; muddle; jumble. 3. in *football*, a grouping of a team behind the line of scrimmage to receive signals before a play; hence, 4. [Slang], a private conference; secret discussion.

go into a huddle, [Slang], to have a private conference or secret discussion.

Hu·di·bras·tic (hū′di-bras′tik), ***adj.*** like, or in the style of, Samuel Butler's *Hudibras*, a mock-heroic satirical poem (1663–1678) in tetrameter couplets, ridiculing the Puritans.

Hud·son (hud′s'n), ***n.*** a river in eastern New York, flowing southward into New York Bay: length, 306 mi.

Hudson, Henry, ?–1611; English navigator and explorer; discovered the river and the bay named for him.

Hudson, William Henry, 1841–1922; English naturalist and writer, born in Argentina.

Hudson Bay, a part of the Atlantic extending into central Canada: area, 400,000 sq. mi.

Hudson's Bay Company, a British joint-stock company chartered in 1670 to carry on fur trading with the North American Indians: abbreviated **H.B.C.**

Hudson seal, muskrat fur dyed and plucked to resemble seal.

HUDSON BAY

Hudson Strait, the strait connecting Hudson Bay with the Atlantic: length, c. 450 mi.

Hu·é (ü′ā′), ***n.*** a city on the coast of South Viet-Nam: pop., 28,000.

hue (hū), ***n.*** [ME. *hew;* AS. *heow, hiw;* akin to Goth. *hiwi*, appearance, form; prob. IE. **ki-wo* < base **kei-*, (dark-)colored, seen also in AS. *hæwen*, blue; cf. HOAR], 1. color. 2. a particular variety of a color; shade; tint. —***SYN.*** see **color.**

hue (hū), ***n.*** [ME. & OFr. *hu*, hunting cry], a shouting; outcry: now only in ***hue and cry.***

hue and cry, [Anglo-Norm. *hu e cri*], 1. originally, *a)* a loud shout or cry by those pursuing a felon: all who heard were obliged to join in the pursuit. *b)* the pursuit itself; hence, 2. any loud outcry or clamor.

hued (hūd), ***adj.*** [ME. *hewed;* AS. *-hiwod;* see HUE (color)], having some (specified) shade or intensity of color or (a specified number of) colors: used in hyphenated compounds, as *rosy-hued, many-hued.*

huff (huf), ***v.t.*** [prob. echoic], 1. [Obs.], to blow, swell, or puff up. 2. to treat insolently; bully; hector. 3. to make angry; offend. ***v.i.*** 1. to blow; puff. 2. [Obs.], to swell with pride or arrogance. 3. to become angry; take offense. ***n.*** a burst of anger or resentment.

huff·i·ly (huf′'l-i), ***adv.*** in a huffy manner.

huff·i·ness (huf′i-nis), ***n.*** the quality or condition of being huffy.

huff·ish (huf′ish), ***adj.*** [*huff* + *-ish*], 1. peevish; petulant; sulky. 2. [Obs.], inclined to be arrogant.

huff·y (huf′i), ***adj.*** [HUFFIER (-i-ẽr), HUFFIEST (-i-ist)], [see HUFF], 1. easily offended; touchy. 2. angered or offended. 3. [Obs.], arrogant.

hug (hug), ***v.t.*** [HUGGED (hugd), HUGGING], [prob. via dial. < ON. *hugga*, to comfort, console; akin to AS. *hycgan*, to think], 1. to put the arms around and hold closely and fondly; embrace tightly and affectionately. 2. *a)* to squeeze tightly between the forelegs: said of a bear. *b)* to squeeze tightly with the arms. 3. to cling to or cherish (a belief, opinion, etc.). 4. to keep close to: as, the automobile *hugged* the curb. ***v.i.*** to clasp or embrace one another closely. ***n.*** 1. a close, affectionate embrace. 2. a tight clasp or hold with the arms, as in wrestling. 3. a bear's squeeze.

huge (hūj), ***adj.*** [ME. *huge, hoge;* OFr. *ahuge, ahoge;* prob. < Gmc. base of OHG. *hōh* (G. *hoch*), high], very large; gigantic; immense. —***SYN.*** see **enormous.**

huge·ly (hūj′li), ***adv.*** to a huge extent; very much.

hug·ger·mug·ger (hug′ẽr-mug′ẽr), ***n.*** [earlier also *hoker-moker*, apparently rhyming compound based on ME. *mokeren*, to hoard, conceal, whence the basic sense "secrecy"], 1. a confusion; muddle; jumble. 2. [Archaic], secrecy. ***adj.*** 1. confused; muddled; jumbled. 2. [Archaic], secret. ***adv.*** 1. in a confused or jumbled manner. 2. [Archaic], secretly.

Hugh (hū), [OFr. *Hue;* OHG. *Hugo;* prob. < *hugu*, the mind], a masculine name: variant, *Hugo.*

Hughes, Charles Evans (hūz), 1862–1948; American statesman and jurist; chief justice, United States Supreme Court (1930–1941).

Hughes, Lang·ston (laŋ′stən), (*James Langston Hughes*), 1902– ; American poet and writer.

Hughes, Thomas, 1822–1896; English lawyer and writer.

Hug·li (hoog′li), ***n.*** the Hooghly.

Hu·go (hū′gō), a masculine name: see **Hugh.**

Hu·go, Victor Marie (hū′gō; Fr. ü′gō′), 1802–1885; French poet, novelist, and dramatist.
Hu·gue·not (hū′gə-not′), *n.* [Fr.; earlier *eiguenot, eydguenot* < G. *eidgenosse*, sworn companion, confederate; influenced by Besançon *Hugues*, a Geneva reformer], any French Protestant of the 16th or 17th century.
huh (hu), *interj.* an exclamation used to express contempt, derision, surprise, etc., or to ask a question.
Hui·la, Mount (wē′lä), a volcanic mountain of the Andes, in southwestern Colombia: height, 18,700 ft.
hu·la-hu·la (hōō′lə-hōō′lə), *n.* [Haw.], a native Hawaiian dance performed by women: also **hula**.
hulk (hulk), *n.* [ME.; AS. *hulc;* akin to G. *holk;* said to be < ML. *hulcus* < Gr. *holkas*, towed vessel < *hēlkein*, to drag], 1. *a)* originally, any ship. *b)* a big, unwieldy ship. 2. the body of a ship, especially if old and dismantled. 3. *usually pl.* an old, dismantled ship or one specially built and not intended to be seagoing, formerly used as a prison. 4. a big, clumsy person or thing. *v.i.* 1. to rise bulkily (usually with *up*). 2. [Dial.], to slouch or lounge about in a heavy, clumsy manner.
hulk·ing (hul′kiŋ), *adj.* [ppr. of *hulk*], bulky and unwieldy; big and clumsy.
hulk·y (hul′ki), *adj.* hulking.
Hull (hul), *n.* 1. a seaport in Yorkshire, England, on the River Humber: pop., 287,000 (est. 1946): officially called *Kingston-upon-Hull.* 2. a city in southwestern Quebec, Canada, on the Ottawa River: pop., 35,000 (est. 1944).
hull (hul), *n.* [ME. *hule, holl, hole;* AS. *hulu;* akin to G. *hülle*, covering; for IE. base see HALL], 1. the outer covering of a seed or fruit, as the husk of grain, pod of peas, shell of nuts, etc. 2. the calyx of some fruits, as the raspberry, strawberry, etc. 3. any outer covering. *v.t.* to take the hull or hulls off.
hull (hul), *n.* [special use of *hull* (seed covering); prob. influenced by D. *hol*, ship's hold], 1. the frame or body of a ship, excluding the spars, sails, and rigging. 2. the frame or main body of a flying boat or amphibian, on which it floats when in the water. *v.t.* to put a shell, torpedo, etc. through the hull of a ship.
hull down, far enough away so that the hull is below the horizon.
Hull, Cor·dell (kôr′del hul), 1871–1955; American statesman; secretary of state (1933–1944).
hul·la·ba·loo (hul′ə-bə-lōō′, hul′ə-bə-lōō′), *n.* [echoic duplication based on *hullo, hallo*], loud noise and confusion; clamor; uproar; hubbub.
Hull House, a social settlement house founded in Chicago in 1889 by Jane Addams.
hul·lo (hə-lō′), *interj., n., v.t. & v.i.* 1. hollo. 2. hello.
hum (hum), *v.i.* [HUMMED (humd), HUMMING], [ME. *hummen;* echoic], 1. to make a low, continuous, murmuring sound like that of a bee, a revolving electric fan, etc. 2. to sing with closed lips, not saying the words. 3. to give forth a confused, droning sound: as, the room *hummed* with voices. 4. [Colloq.], to be busy or full of activity. *v.t.* 1. to sing (a tune, etc.) with the lips closed, not saying the words. 2. to produce an effect on by humming: as, *hum* a child to sleep. *n.* 1. a humming. 2. a continuous, murmuring sound.
hum (həm: *conventionalized pronun.*), *interj.* 1. a conventionalized expression of the sound made when clearing the throat to attract attention or show doubt. 2. a conventionalized expression of a sound made with closed lips to express contempt, surprise, pleasure, etc. *v.i.* [HUMMED (humd), HUMMING], 1. to make either of these sounds. 2. to pause or hesitate in speaking: usually in the phrase *hum and haw*.
hu·man (hū′mən), *adj.* [ME. *humayne;* OFr. *humaine;* L. *humanus;* akin to *homo*, a man, *humus*, soil (see HUMUS)], 1. of or characteristic of a person or persons; such as people have. 2. having the form or nature of a person; that is a person; consisting of people. 3. having or showing the qualities characteristic of people. *n.* a person: usually **human being**.
hu·mane (hyoo-mān′), *adj.* [earlier var. of *human;* now usually associated directly with L. *humanus*], 1. having what are considered the best qualities of mankind; kind, tender, merciful, considerate, etc. 2. civilizing; refining; humanizing: as, *humane* learning.
hu·man·ism (hū′mən-iz′m), *n.* 1. the quality of being human; human nature. 2. any system or way of thought or action concerned with the interests and ideals of people. 3. the study of the humanities. 4. [H-], the intellectual and cultural movement that stemmed from the study of classical Greek and Latin literature and culture during the Middle Ages and was one of the factors giving rise to the Renaissance: it was characterized by an emphasis on human interests rather than on the natural world or religion.
hu·man·ist (hū′mən-ist), *n.* [Fr. *humaniste*], 1. a student of human nature and human affairs. 2. a student of the humanities. 3. [H-], a student of Latin and Greek culture; especially, any Renaissance scholar who was a follower of Humanism. *adj.* of humanism or the humanities; humanistic.
hu·man·is·tic (hū′mə-nis′tik), *adj.* of humanism or humanists.
hu·man·is·ti·cal·ly (hū′mə-nis′ti-k'l-i, hū′mə-nis′tik-li), *adv.* in a humanistic manner.
hu·man·i·tar·i·an (hyoo-man′ə-târ′i-ən), *n.* 1. a person devoted to promoting the welfare of humanity, especially through the elimination of pain and suffering; philanthropist. 2. an adherent of humanitarianism (senses 2 & 3). *adj.* 1. helping humanity. 2. of humanitarianism. —*SYN.* see **philanthropic**.
hu·man·i·tar·i·an·ism (hyoo-man′ə-târ′i-ən-iz′m), *n.* 1. the beliefs or actions of humanitarians (sense 1). 2. in *ethics*, *a)* the doctrine that man's obligations are limited to the welfare of mankind. *b)* the doctrine that man may perfect his own nature without the aid of divine grace. 3. in *theology*, the doctrine that denies the divinity of Jesus.
hu·man·i·ty (hyoo-man′ə-ti), *n.* [*pl.* HUMANITIES (-tiz)], [ME. & OFr. *humanite;* L. *humanitas*], 1. the fact or quality of being human; human nature. 2. *pl.* human qualities; characteristics of human beings, especially those considered desirable. 3. the human race; mankind; people. 4. the fact or quality of being humane; kindness; mercy, sympathy, etc.
the humanities, 1. languages and literature, especially the classical Greek and Latin. 2. the branches of learning concerned with human thought and relations, as distinguished from the sciences; especially, literature and philosophy, and, often, the fine arts, history, etc.
hu·man·i·za·tion (hū′man-i-zā′shən, hū′mən-ī-zā′shən), *n.* a humanizing or being humanized.
hu·man·ize (hū′mə-nīz′), *v.t.* [HUMANIZED (-nīzd′), HUMANIZING], 1. to make human; give a human nature or character to. 2. to make humane; make kind, merciful, considerate, etc.; civilize; refine. *v.i.* to become human or humane.
hu·man·kind (hū′mən-kīnd′), *n.* the human race; mankind; people.
hu·man·ly (hū′mən-li), *adv.* 1. in a human manner. 2. within human ability or knowledge; by human means. 3. according to the experience or knowledge of human beings; from a human viewpoint.
‡hu·ma·num est er·ra·re (hū-mā′nəm est e-rā′ri), [L.], it is human to err.
Hum·ber (hum′bẽr), *n.* the estuary of the Ouse and the Trent, in eastern England: length, 37 mi.
Hum·bert I (hum′bẽrt), 1844–1900; son of Victor Emmanuel II; king of Italy (1878–1900).
hum·ble (hum′b'l; *occas.* um′b'l), *adj.* [HUMBLER (-blẽr), HUMBLEST (-blist)], [ME.; OFr.; L. *humilis*, low, small, slight; akin to *humus*, soil, earth (see HUMUS)], 1. having or showing a consciousness of one's defects or shortcomings; not proud; not self-assertive; modest. 2. low in condition, rank, or position; lowly; unimportant; unpretentious: as, a *humble* home. *v.t.* [HUMBLED (-b'ld), HUMBLING], 1. to lower in condition, rank, or position; abase. 2. to lower in pride; make modest or humble in mind.
SYN.—**humble**, in a favorable sense, suggests an unassuming character in which there is an absence of pride and assertiveness (a *humble* genius) and, unfavorably, connotes an almost abject lack of self-respect; **lowly** is an older equivalent for **humble** but never carries the unfavorable connotation of abjectness (he answered in *lowly* terms); **meek** stresses a mildness and patience of disposition which is not easily stirred to anger or resentment and, in an unfavorable sense, connotes spineless submissiveness; **modest** implies the absence of pretensions, boastfulness, conceit, etc. (to be *modest* about one's achievements). See also **degrade**.—*ANT.* proud, conceited.
hum·ble·bee (hum′b'l-bē′), *n.* [ME. *humbylbee* < *hum-(b)len*, to keep on humming (< *hummen*, to hum + *-le*, freq. suffix) + *bee*], a bumblebee.
humble pie, [earlier *umble pie* < *umbles*, entrails of a deer; ME. & OFr. *nombles* < L. *lumbulus*, dim. of *lumbus*, loin], formerly, a pie made of the inner parts of a deer, served to the servants after a hunt.
eat humble pie, to undergo humiliation, especially that of admitting one's error and apologizing.
hum·bly (hum′bli; *occas.* um′bli), *adv.* in a humble manner.
Hum·boldt, Baron **A·le·xan·der von** (ä′lek-sän′dẽr fôn hoom′bôlt; Eng. hum′bōlt), (*Friedrich Heinrich Alexander von Humboldt*), 1769–1859; German scientist and explorer.
Humboldt, Baron **Karl Wil·helm von** (kärl vil′helm), 1767–1835; brother of *Alexander;* German philologist and statesman.
hum·bug (hum′bug′), *n.* [18th-c. slang; orig. reference lost], 1. *a)* something made or done to cheat or

deceive; fraud; sham; hoax. *b)* misleading, dishonest, or empty talk. 2. a dishonest person; person who does not live up to his claims; impostor. 3. a spirit of trickery, deception, etc. ***v.t.*** [HUMBUGGED (-bugd'), HUMBUGGING], to dupe; cheat; deceive; hoax.

hum·bug·ger (hum'bug'ẽr), ***n.*** a humbug; impostor.

hum·bug·ger·y (hum'bug'ẽr-i), ***n.*** [*pl.* HUMBUGGERIES (-iz)], the practices of a humbug; fraud; deception; pretense; sham.

hum·ding·er (hum'diŋ'ẽr), ***n.*** [prob. fanciful coinage], [Slang], a person or thing considered excellent of its kind.

hum·drum (hum'drum'), ***adj.*** [echoic extension of *hum*], having no variety; dull; monotonous; commonplace. ***n.*** 1. a humdrum person. 2. humdrum talk, routine, etc.; monotony; commonplaceness.

Hume, David (hūm), 1711–1776; Scottish philosopher and historian.

hu·mer·al (hū'mẽr-əl), ***adj.*** [Mod. L. *humeralis* < L. *humerus*], 1. of or near the humerus. 2. of or near the shoulder or shoulders.

hu·mer·us (hū'mẽr-əs), ***n.*** [*pl.* HUMERI (-ī')], [L. *humerus, umerus*, the shoulder, upper arm; IE. **om(e)so-s*, the shoulder, seen also in Sans. *anisa-h*, Gr. *ōmos*], the bone of the upper arm or forelimb, extending from the shoulder to the elbow: see **skeleton**, illus.

hu·mic (hū'mik), ***adj.*** of or derived from humus.

hu·mid (hū'mid), ***adj.*** [Fr. *humide;* L. *humidus, umidus*, < *humere, umere*, to be moist], damp; moist; specifically, containing much water vapor. —***SYN.*** see **wet.**

hu·mid·i·fi·ca·tion (hyoo-mid'ə-fi-kā'shən), ***n.*** a humidifying or being humidified.

hu·mid·i·fi·er (hyoo-mid'ə-fī'ẽr), ***n.*** anything that humidifies; specifically, a device for keeping air moist.

hu·mid·i·fy (hyoo-mid'ə-fī'), ***v.t.*** [HUMIDIFIED (-fīd'), HUMIDIFYING], to make humid; moisten; dampen.

hu·mid·i·ty (hyoo-mid'ə-ti), ***n.*** [ME. *humidytee;* OFr. *humidite;* L. *humiditas* < *humidus;* see HUMID], 1. moistness; dampness. 2. the amount or degree of moisture in the air.

relative humidity, the amount of moisture in the air as compared with the amount that the air could contain at the same temperature, expressed as a percentage.

hu·mi·dor (hū'mi-dôr'), ***n.*** [< *humid*], 1. a device for keeping the air moist in a tobacco jar, case, etc.: it is often a tube containing moistened sponges. 2. a jar, case, etc. equipped with such a device.

hu·mil·i·ate (hyoo-mil'i-āt'), ***v.t.*** [HUMILIATED (-id), HUMILIATING], [< LL. *humiliatus*, pp. of *humiliare*, to humiliate < L. *humilis*, humble, lowly], to lower the pride or dignity of; hurt the feelings of by causing to be or seem foolish or contemptible; mortify. —***SYN.*** see **degrade.**

hu·mil·i·a·tion (hyoo-mil'i-ā'shən), ***n.*** a humiliating or being humiliated.

hu·mil·i·a·to·ry (hyoo-mil'i-ə-tôr'i, hyoo-mil'i-ə-tō'ri), ***adj.*** humiliating or tending to humiliate.

hu·mil·i·ty (hyoo-mil'ə-ti), ***n.*** [*pl.* HUMILITIES (-tiz)], [ME. & OFr. *humilite;* L. *humilitas* < *humilis*, lowly, humble], 1. the state or quality of being humble of mind or spirit; absence of pride or self-assertion. 2. *pl.* acts of self-abasement.

hum·mer (hum'ẽr), ***n.*** 1. a person or thing that hums. 2. a hummingbird.

hum·ming (hum'iŋ), ***adj.*** [ppr. of *hum*], 1. buzzing; droning. 2. [Colloq.], having great activity or intensity; active; spirited; agitated; brisk.

hum·ming·bird (hum'iŋ-bũrd'), ***n.*** any of a group of very small, brightly colored birds with a long, slender bill and narrow wings that vibrate rapidly and make a humming sound in flight.

hum·mock (hum'ək), ***n.*** [earlier also *hammock;* orig. naut.; ? < base of *hump* + nautical *-ock* (cf. HAMMOCK)], 1. a low, rounded hill; knoll; hillock. 2. a ridge or bump in an ice field. 3. a tract of wooded land, higher than a near-by swamp or marsh.

hum·mock·y (hum'ək-i), ***adj.*** 1. having hummocks. 2. like a hummock.

hu·mor (hū'mẽr, ū'mẽr), ***n.*** [ME.; OFr.; L. *humor, umor*, moisture, fluid, akin to *humere, umere*, to be moist; IE. base **wegw-*, **ugw-*, moist, moisten, seen also in Gr. *hygros*, moist, fluid, Eng. *wake* (of a boat), D. *wak*, moist, wet], 1. originally, any fluid or juice of an animal or plant; especially, any of the four fluids (*cardinal humors*) formerly considered responsible for one's health and disposition; blood, phlegm, choler (yellow bile), or melancholy (black bile); hence, 2. *a)* a person's disposition or temperament. *b)* a mood; state of mind. 3. whim; fancy; caprice. 4. the quality that makes something seem funny, amusing, or ludicrous; comicality. 5. *a)* the ability to perceive, appreciate, or express what is funny, amusing, or ludicrous. *b)* the expression of this in speech, writing, or action. Usually distinguished from *wit.* 6. any chronic disease of the skin, supposedly caused by a bad blood condition. 7. any fluid or fluidlike substance of the body; blood, lymph, bile, etc.: as, the aqueous *humor.* ***v.t.*** 1. to comply with the mood or whim of (another); indulge. 2. to act in agreement with the nature of; adapt oneself to. —***SYN.*** see **indulge, mood, wit.**

out of humor, not in a good mood; cross; disagreeable; displeased; out of sorts.

hu·mor·al (hū'mẽr-əl), ***adj.*** [Fr. < L. *humor*], of the humors of the body.

hu·mor·esque (hū'mə-resk'), ***n.*** [G. *humoreske* < L. *humor;* see HUMOR & -ESQUE], a light, fanciful, playful, or humorous musical composition; caprice.

hu·mor·ist (hū'mẽr-ist, ū'mẽr-ist), ***n.*** [Fr. *humoriste;* ML. *humorista*], 1. a person with a well-developed sense of humor. 2. a person skilled in the literary or artistic expression of humor; professional writer or teller of amusing stories, jokes, etc.

hu·mor·is·tic (hū'mə-ris'tik), ***adj.*** 1. of humor. 2. of or like a humorist or humorists.

hu·mor·ous (hū'mẽr-əs, ū'mẽr-əs), ***adj.*** [LL. *humorosus*, moist; also Eng. *humor* + *-ous*], 1. having or expressing humor; funny; amusing; comical; droll. 2. [Archaic], whimsical; capricious. 3. [Obs.], *a)* moist. *b)* humoral. —***SYN.*** see **witty.**

hu·mour (hū'mẽr, ū'mẽr), ***n.*** **&** ***v.t.*** humor: British spelling.

hump (hump), ***n.*** [17th c.; prob. < international naut. usage; cf. LG. *humpe*, Norw. *hump* in same senses; IE. **qum-b* (< base **qeu-*, to bend, curve), as also in Sans. *kumba-ḥ*, thick end of a bone], 1. a rounded, protruding lump, as the fleshy mass on the back of a camel: in man, a hump is caused by a deformity of the spine. 2. a hummock; mound. 3. [British Slang], a fit of melancholy. ***v.t.*** 1. to cause to assume the shape of a hump; arch; hunch: as, the cat ***humped*** its back. 2. [Slang], to exert (oneself).

the Hump, the Himalayas: a term used by Allied airmen in World War II.

hump·back (hump'bak'), ***n.*** 1. a humped, deformed back. 2. a person having a humped back; hunchback. 3. a large whale with long flippers and a dorsal fin resembling a humpback.

hump·backed (hump'bakt'), ***adj.*** having a humped back.

humped (humpt), ***adj.*** having a hump or humps; humpbacked.

Hum·per·dinck, Eng·el·bert (eŋ'gəl-bert' hoom'pẽr-diŋk'; Eng. hum'pẽr-diŋk'), 1854–1921; German composer.

humph (*usually uttered as a voiced snort with the mouth closed; conventionalized pronun.* humf), ***interj.*** **&** ***n.*** a snorting or grunting sound expressing doubt, surprise, disdain, disgust, etc.

Hum·phrey, Hum·phry (hum'fri), [AS. *Hunfrith* < Gmc. **hun*, strength + AS. *frith*, peace], a masculine name: equivalents, G. *Humfried*, It. *Onfredo.*

Hump·ty Dump·ty (hump'ti dump'ti), the personified egg of a well-known nursery rhyme, represented as a short, squat person.

hump·y (hump'i), ***adj.*** [HUMPIER (-i-ẽr), HUMPIEST (-i-ist)], 1. having humps. 2. like a hump.

hu·mus (hū'məs), ***n.*** [L., earth, ground, soil; IE. base **ĝhthem-*, **ĝhth(o)m-*, earth, soil, seen also in Gr. *chthōn*, soil, Sans. *kṣam*], a brown or black substance resulting from the partial decay of leaves and other vegetable matter; organic part of the soil.

Hun (hun), ***n.*** [ME. *Hunne;* AS. *Hune* (akin to ON. *Hunar*) < native name; cf. Chin. *Hiong-nu, Han*], 1. a member of a savage Asiatic people who, led by Attila, invaded eastern and central Europe in the 4th and 5th centuries A.D. 2. [h-], any savage or destructive person; vandal: term of contempt applied to German soldiers in World War I.

Hu·nan (hōō'nän'), ***n.*** a province of southeastern China: area, 83,921 sq. mi.; pop., 25,949,000 (1947); capital, Changsha.

hunch (hunch), ***v.t.*** [< *hunchback*], to draw (one's body, etc.) into the shape of a hump; form into a hump: as, don't *hunch* your back so. ***v.i.*** to move forward jerkily; push; shove. ***n.*** 1. a hump. 2. a chunk; lump; hunk. 3. [Colloq.], a feeling that something is going to happen; premonition or suspicion: from the superstition that it brings good luck to touch the back of a hunchback.

hunch·back (hunch'bak'), ***n.*** 1. a humped, deformed back. 2. a person having a humped back; humpback.

hunch·backed (hunch'bakt'), ***adj.*** humpbacked.

hund., hundred; hundreds.

hun·dred (hun'drid; *still often* hun'dẽrd), ***n.*** [ME. *hondred, honderd;* Late AS. *hundred;* prob. < ON. *hundrath*, lit., the 100 reckoning < *hund-*, 100 (akin to AS. *hund*) + *-rath*, reckoning, number (akin to Goth. *rathjan*, to reckon; cf. READ, RIDDLE)]; the IE. base of *hund-* is **kṃtōm* (for orig. **dekṃtōm* < **dekṃ*, ten; see DECADE), seen also in L. *centum*, Gr. *(he)katōn*, Sans. *śatām*, OSlav. *seto*, etc.], 1. the cardinal number next above ninety-nine; ten times ten; 100; C: abbreviated **H., h., hund.** 2. a division of an English county: originally, probably, 100 hides of land. 3. a corresponding division in the early United States, still surviving in Delaware. ***adj.*** ten times ten.

Hundred Days, the days from March 15 to June 28,

1815, the period between Napoleon's return to France from Elba and his final defeat and abdication.

hun·dred·fold (hun′drid-fōld′), *adj.* [see -FOLD], 1. having a hundred parts. 2. having a hundred times as much or as many. *adv.* a hundred times as much or as many: with *a* (or, British, *an*). *n.* a number or an amount a hundred times as great.

hun·dredth (hun′dridth), *adj.* [*hundred* + *-th*], 1. preceded by ninety-nine others in a series; 100th. 2. designating any of the hundred equal parts of something. *n.* 1. the one following the ninety-ninth. 2. any of the hundred equal parts of something; 1/100.

hun·dred·weight (hun′drid-wāt′), *n.* a unit of weight, equal to 100 pounds in the United States and 112 pounds in England: abbreviated **cwt.**, **c.**, **C.**

Hundred Years' War, a series of wars between England and France from 1339 to 1453, in which England lost all her possessions in France except Calais.

Hun·e·ker, James Gibbons (hun′ə-kẽr), 1860–1921; American writer and critic.

hung (huŋ), past tense and past participle of **hang**: see **hang**.

Hung., 1. Hungarian. 2. Hungary.

Hun·gar·i·an (huŋ-gâr′i-ən), *adj.* of Hungary, its people, their language, or culture. *n.* 1. a native or inhabitant of Hungary, especially one of Magyar stock. 2. the Finno-Ugric language of the Magyars.

Hun·ga·ry (huŋ′gẽr-i), *n.* a country in central Europe: area, 35,872 sq. mi.; pop., 9,977,000; capital, Budapest: Hungarian name, *Magyarország*.

hun·ger (huŋ′gẽr), *n.* [ME.; AS. *hungor;* akin to G. *hunger;* IE. base **kenk-*, to burn, dry up], 1. the discomfort, pain, or weakness caused by a need for food. 2. a desire, need, or appetite for food; hence, 3. any strong desire; craving. *v.i.* 1. to feel hunger; be hungry; need food. 2. to crave; desire eagerly (with *for* or *after*). *v.t.* to subject to hunger or starvation; starve.

hunger strike, a refusal of a prisoner, political leader, etc. to eat until the authorities grant certain demands.

hun·gri·ly (huŋ′grə-li), *adv.* in a hungry manner.

hun·gri·ness (huŋ′gri-nis), *n.* the quality of being hungry; hunger.

hun·gry (huŋ′gri), *adj.* [HUNGRIER (-gri-ẽr), HUNGRIEST (-gri-ist)], [ME. *houngrie, hungre;* AS. *hungrig*], 1. feeling, having, or showing hunger; specifically, *a*) wanting or needing food. *b*) craving; eager: as, a *hungry* glance. 2. [Rare], producing hunger. 3. not fertile; barren: said of soil.

SYN.—**hungry** is the general word expressing any degree of wanting or needing food; **ravenous** implies a greedy or gluttonous hunger (he seized the bait with *ravenous* appetite); **famished** suggests hunger to the point of actual weakness or suffering; **starved** implies a continued lack or inadequacy of food resulting in emaciation or death. Both **famished** and **starved** are often used colloquially as hyperbolic equivalents of **hungry**.—*ANT.* sated, satiated.

hunk (huŋk), *n.* [prob. < Fl. *hunke*, hunk], [Colloq.], a large piece, lump, or slice of bread, meat, etc.; chunk.

hunks (huŋks), *n.* [*pl.* HUNKS], [prob. akin to D. *hondsch*, lit., doggish, stingy, G. *hündisch;* cf. HOUND], a stingy, disagreeable, surly person; miser.

hunk·y (huŋ′ki), *n.* [*pl.* HUNKIES (-kiz)], [< *Hungarian;* cf. BOHUNK], [Slang], a person from east central Europe; especially, a person of Hungarian extraction: also **hunkie, hunkey, hunk**: vulgar term of prejudice and contempt.

hunk·y (huŋ′ki), *adj.* [HUNKIER (-ki-ẽr), HUNKIEST (-ki-ist)], [< U.S. local *hunk*, goal, home (in tag and similar games), hence safe place, all right < D. *honk*, a post, station, goal], [Slang], 1. all right; giving satisfaction. 2. even; square.

hunk·y-do·ry (huŋ′ki-dôr′i, huŋ′ki-dō′ri), *adj.* [extended < *hunky* (all right)], [Slang], to one's satisfaction; as it should be.

Hun·nish (hun′ish), *adj.* 1. of or like the Huns; hence, 2. barbarous; savage and destructive.

hunt (hunt), *v.t.* [ME. *hunten;* AS. *huntian;* prob. < base of *hentan*, to seize; see HENT], 1. to chase (game) for food or sport. 2. to search eagerly or carefully for; try to find. 3. *a*) to pursue; chase; drive. *b*) to hound; harry; persecute. 4. *a*) to go through (a tract of country) in pursuit of game. *b*) to search (a place) carefully. 5. to use (dogs or horses) in chasing game. 6. in *bell ringing*, to change the order of (a bell) in a hunt. *v.i.* 1. to go out after game; take part in the chase. 2. to search; seek. 3. in *bell ringing*, to change the order of bells in a hunt. *n.* 1. a hunting; the chase. 2. a group of people who hunt together. 3. a district covered in hunting. 4. a search. 5. in *bell ringing*, a series of regularly varying sequences in ringing a group of from five to twelve bells.

hunt down, 1. to pursue until successful in catching or killing. 2. to search for until successful in finding.

hunt up, 1. to hunt for; search for. 2. to find by searching.

Hunt, Leigh (hunt), (*James Henry Leigh Hunt*), 1784–1859; English critic, essayist, and poet.

Hunt, William Holman, see **Holman-Hunt, William.**

hunt·er (hun′tẽr), *n.* [ME. *huntere;* AS. *hunta*], 1. a person who hunts. 2. a horse or dog trained for hunting. 3. a watch with a hunting case.

Hun·ter, John (hunt′ẽr), 1728–1793; Scottish physiologist and surgeon.

hunter's moon, the full moon after the harvest moon.

hunt·ing (hunt′iŋ), *n.* [ME. *huntinge;* AS. *huntung*], 1. the act of a person or animal that hunts. 2. in *electricity*, the periodic increase and decrease in the speed of a synchronous motor with respect to the current. *adj.* of or for hunting.

hunting case, a watchcase with a hinged cover to protect the crystal: so called from use by foxhunters.

Hunt·ing·don·shire (hun′tiŋ-dən-shir′), *n.* a county of east central England: pop., 69,000; county seat, Huntingdon.

hunting ground, a tract of country used for hunting.

hunting horn, a horn used to give signals during a hunt.

hunting knife, a large, sharp knife used by hunters to skin and cut up game.

Hunt·ing·ton (hun′tiŋ-tən), *n.* a city in western West Virginia, on the Ohio: pop., 84,000.

Hun·ting·ton, Samuel (hun′tiŋ-tən), 1731–1796; American statesman; governor of Connecticut (1786–1796); signer of the Declaration of Independence.

Huntington Park, a city in southwestern California: pop., 30,000.

hunting watch, a watch with a hunting case; hunter.

hunt·ress (hun′tris), *n.* 1. a woman (or goddess) who hunts. 2. a mare used for hunting.

hunts·man (hunts′mən), *n.* [*pl.* HUNTSMEN (-mən)], [Chiefly British], 1. a hunter. 2. the manager of a hunt.

hunts·man's-cup (hunts′mənz-kup′), *n.* a pitcher plant with large, cuplike leaves and purple or greenish flowers.

hunt's-up (hunts′up′), *n.* [contr. < *the hunt is up* (i.e., the hunt is starting)], a rousing tune played on a hunting horn to get the hunters out.

Hunts·ville (hunts′vil), *n.* a city in northern Alabama: pop., 72,000.

Hu·nya·di, Já·nos (yä′nôsh hoo′nyä-di), c.1387–1456; Hungarian general and national hero.

Hu·on pine (hū′on), [after the *Huon*, river in Tasmania], a large Tasmanian tree with bright-green, scalelike leaves and close-grained wood.

Hu·pa (hoo̅′pə), *n.* 1. any member of a tribe of North American Indians of northwestern California. 2. their Athapascan language.

Hu·peh, Hu·pei (hoo̅′pe′), *n.* a province of east central China: area, 71,234 sq. mi.; pop., 27,790,000; capital, Wuchang.

hur·dle (hũr′d'l), *n.* [ME. *hurdel, hirdel;* AS. *hyrdel* < base **hurd-*, wickerwork, hurdle (cf. HOARDING); IE. base **qert-*, to plait, twist together, seen also in *crate*], 1. a portable frame made of interlaced twigs, etc., used for temporary fences or enclosures. 2. a kind of frame or sled on which prisoners in England were drawn through the streets to execution. 3. a movable, framelike barrier for horses or runners to jump over in a race. 4. an obstacle; difficulty to be overcome. *v.t.* [HURDLED (-d'ld), HURDLING], 1. to enclose or fence off with hurdles. 2. to jump over (a hurdle) in a race. 3. to overcome (an obstacle).

HURDLES

the hurdles, a race in which the contestants must jump over a series of hurdles.

hur·dler (hũr′dlẽr), *n.* a runner who takes part in the hurdles.

hurds (hũrdz), *n.pl.* [ME. *herdes* < AS. *heordan* (akin to MD. *heerde, herde*)], the refuse of flax, jute, hemp, etc.; tow: also **hards**.

hur·dy-gur·dy (hũr'di-gũr'di), *n.* [*pl.* HURDY-GURDIES (-diz)], [prob. echoic], 1. a boxed, lutelike instrument played by turning a crank attached to a resined wheel that scrapes the strings and produces sound: it is used by street musicians. 2. any musical instrument played by turning a crank; barrel organ.

HURDY-GURDY

hurl (hũrl), *v.t.* [ME. *hurlen;* prob. of ON. echoic origin; cf. Dan. *hurle,* to whirr, Norw. *hurla,* to buzz; cf. HURRY, WHIRL], 1. to throw or fling with force or violence. 2. to cast down; overthrow. 3. to utter vehemently. *v.i.* 1. to throw or fling something (at a person or thing). 2. [Archaic], to move with force or violence; rush. 3. [Slang], in *baseball,* to pitch. *n.* a hurling; violent throw. —*SYN.* see **throw.**

hurl·ing (hũr'liŋ), *n.* [< *hurl, v.*], an Irish game like field hockey.

hurl·y (hũr'li), *n.* [*pl.* HURLIES (-liz)], [< *hurl, v.*], [Archaic], uproar; turmoil; confusion.

hurl·y-burl·y (hũr'li-bũr'li), *n.* [*pl.* HURLY-BURLIES (-liz)], [prob. extended < *hurly*], a turmoil; uproar; hubbub; confusion. *adj.* disorderly and confused.

Hu·ron (hyoor'ən; *also, for n. 1 & adj.,* hyoor'on), *n.* [Fr., coarse fellow, ruffian < *hure,* unkempt head], 1. a member of a confederation of Iroquoian Indian tribes that lived between Georgian Bay and Lake Ontario, Canada: also called *Wyandot.* 2. the second largest of the Great Lakes, between Michigan and Ontario, Canada: area, 23,010 sq. mi.: usually **Lake Huron.** *adj.* of the Hurons.

hur·rah (hoo-rô', hə-rä'), *interj. & n.* [prob. < D. *hoera* or G. *hurra* as 17th-c. replacement of earlier *huzza;* echoic], a shout of joy, triumph, approval, etc. *v.i.* to cheer; shout "hurrah." *v.t.* to greet, encourage, or applaud with shouts of "hurrah."

hur·ray (hoo-rā', hə-rā'), *interj., n., v.t. & v.i.* hurrah.

hur·ri·cane (hũr'i-kān'), *n.* [Sp. *huracán;* W. Ind. (Taino) *huracan*], 1. a violent cyclonic storm with winds moving at 73 or more miles per hour, originating in the tropics, especially the West Indian region: winds of hurricane force sometimes occur in the absence of a hurricane system. 2. anything like a hurricane in force and speed; violent outburst.

hurricane deck, the top deck of a passenger ship plying inland waters.

hur·ried (hũr'id), *adj.* [pp. of *hurry*], 1. forced to do, move, act, etc. in a hurry. 2. done, carried on, etc. in a hurry; hasty: as, a *hurried* meal.

hur·ry (hũr'i), *v.t.* [HURRIED (-id), HURRYING], [prob. < echoic base seen in *hurl;* but cf. ON. *hurra,* to whir, whirl around; the word may be < ON. via ME. dial.], 1. to cause to move or act more rapidly or too rapidly; drive, move, send, force, or carry with haste. 2. to cause to occur or be done more rapidly or too rapidly; accelerate the preparation or completion of; urge on. 3. to urge or cause to act soon or too soon. *v.i.* to move or act with haste; move faster than is comfortable or natural. *n.* [*pl.* HURRIES (-iz)], 1. a hurrying or being hurried; rush; urgency. 2. eagerness to do, act, go, etc. quickly. —*SYN.* see **haste.**

hur·ry-scur·ry, hur·ry-skur·ry (hũr'i-skũr'i), *n.* an agitated, confused rushing about; disorderly confusion. *v.i.* to hurry and scurry about; act hurriedly and confusedly. *adj.* hurried and confused. *adv.* in a hurried, confused manner.

Hurst, Fannie (hũrst), 1889– ; American novelist.

hurt (hũrt), *v.t.* [HURT, HURTING], [ME. *hurten, hirten,* to knock, hit, hurt; OFr. *hurter,* to push, thrust, hit; prob. < Frank. **hurt,* a thrust, blow (as by a ram); akin to ON. *hrutr,* a ram], 1. to cause physical pain or injury to; wound. 2. to harm or damage in some way; be bad for. 3. to cause mental distress or pain to; wound the feelings of; offend. *v.i.* 1. to cause injury, damage, or pain. 2. to give or have the sensation of pain; be sore: as, my leg *hurts.* *n.* 1. a hurting; pain, injury, or wound. 2. harm; damage. 3. something that wounds the feelings. —*SYN.* see **injure.**

hurt·ful (hũrt'fəl), *adj.* causing hurt; harmful.

hur·tle (hũr't'l), *v.i.* [HURTLED (-t'ld), HURTLING], [ME. *hurtlen;* prob. < *hurten* (see HURT); + *-le*], 1. to come with a crash; clash; collide; dash violently (with *against* or *together*). 2. to make a crashing sound when or as when colliding; clatter: as, the noise of battle *hurtled* in the air. 3. to move noisily with a crashing or clattering sound; move violently and swiftly. *v.t.* 1. to throw, shoot, fling, or cast with violence; hurl. 2. [Archaic], to dash against; come into collision with. *n.* [Poetic], a hurtling; collision; clash.

hur·tle·ber·ry (hũr't'l-ber'i), *n.* [*pl.* HURTLEBERRIES (-iz)], [see HUCKLEBERRY], 1. a whortleberry. 2. a huckleberry.

hurt·less (hũrt'lis), *adj.* 1. causing no hurt. 2. unhurt.

Hus, Jan (yän hoos), see **Huss, John.**

hus·band (huz'bənd), *n.* [ME. *husbonde,* householder, husband; Late AS. *husbonda;* ON. *hūsbondi,* lit., householder; *hūs,* house + *-bondi,* freeholder, yeoman < earlier *būandi,* ppr. of *būa,* to dwell], 1. a man to whom a woman is married; married man: the correlative of *wife:* abbreviated **H., h.** 2. [Archaic], a manager, as of a household. *v.t.* 1. to marry (a woman); become, or act as, the husband of. 2. to manage economically; conserve. 3. [Archaic], to provide with a husband. 4. [Obs.], to cultivate (soil or plants).

hus·band·man (huz'bənd-mən), *n.* [*pl.* HUSBANDMEN (-mən)], [ME.; see HUSBAND], [Archaic or Poetic], a farmer; person whose occupation is husbandry.

hus·band·ry (huz'bənd-ri), *n.* [ME. *husbonderie;* see HUSBAND], 1. originally, management of domestic affairs, resources, etc. 2. careful, thrifty management; thrift; frugality. 3. farming.

hush (hush), *v.t.* [ME. *huschen* < *huscht,* quiet, mistaken as pp.; of echoic origin], 1. to stop from making noise; make quiet or silent. 2. to soothe; calm; lull. *v.i.* to stop making noise; be or become quiet or silent. *adj.* [Archaic], silent; hushed. *n.* absence of noise; quiet; silence. *interj.* an exclamation calling for silence.

hush up, 1. to keep quiet. 2. to keep from being told; suppress the report or discussion of.

hush·a·by (hush'ə-bī'), *interj.* [see HUSH & LULLABY], an exclamation used to hush infants.

hush money, money paid to a person to keep him from telling something.

hush puppy, [? because orig. used to hush the hunger cries of hunting dogs], in the southern United States, a small, fried ball of corn-meal dough.

husk (husk), *n.* [ME. *huske;* prob. < MD. *huuskijn,* dim. of *huus,* a house], 1. the dry outer covering of various fruits or seeds, as of an ear of corn. 2. the dry, rough, or useless outside covering of anything. *v.t.* to remove the husk or husks from.

husk·i·ly (hus'k'l-i), *adv.* in a husky voice; hoarsely.

hus·ki·ly (hus'k'l-i), *adv.* in a husky manner; with strength or force.

husk·i·ness (hus'ki-nis), *n.* the quality of being husky, or hoarse.

hus·ki·ness (hus'ki-nis), *n.* the quality of being husky, or big and strong.

husk·ing (bee) (hus'kiŋ), a cornhusking.

Hus·kis·son, William (hus'ki-sən), 1770–1830; English statesman and financier.

Hus·ky (hus'ki), *n.* [*pl.* HUSKIES (-kiz)], [? altered < *Eskimo*], 1. an Eskimo. 2. the Eskimo language. 3. [sometimes h-], an Eskimo dog; hardy dog used for pulling sleds in the Arctic.

husk·y (hus'ki), *adj.* [HUSKIER (-ki-ẽr), HUSKIEST (-ki-ist)], 1. *a)* full of, containing, or consisting of husks. *b)* like a husk. 2. dry in the throat; hoarse.

hus·ky (hus'ki), *adj.* [HUSKIER (-ki-ẽr), HUSKIEST (-ki-ist)], [< *husk* (outer covering)], big and strong; robust; burly. *n.* [*pl.* HUSKIES (-kiz)], a husky person.

Huss, John (hus), (*Jan Hus*), 1369?–1415; Bohemian religious reformer and martyr.

hus·sar (hoo-zär'), *n.* [Hung. *huszár;* Serb. *husar, gusar;* MGr. *koursarios;* LL. *cursarius;* see CORSAIR], 1. originally, a member of the light cavalry of Hungary or Croatia. 2. now, a member of any European regiment of light-armed cavalry, usually with brilliant dress uniforms.

Huss·ite (hus'īt), *n.* a follower of John Huss. *adj.* of John Huss or his religious ideas.

hus·sy (huz'i, hus'i), *n.* [*pl.* HUSSIES (-iz)], [contr. < ME. *huswife,* housewife], 1. a woman, especially one of low morals: contemptuous or playful term. 2. a saucy, pert girl; minx. 3. [Dial.], a small sewing kit.

hust·ings (hus'tiŋz), *n.pl.* [usually construed as sing.], [ME. & AS. *husting;* ON. *hūsthing,* lit., house council; *hūs,* a house + *thing,* assembly: orig. applied to a lord's household assembly as distinct from a general assembly], [British], 1. originally, *a)* a deliberative assembly. *b)* a court held in various English cities: it survives in London. *c)* the platform in London Guildhall where such a court was formerly held. *d)* the temporary platform where candidates for Parliament formerly stood for nomination and spoke; hence, 2. the proceedings at an election. 3. any place where political campaign speeches are made.

hus·tle (hus''l), *v.t.* [HUSTLED (-'ld), HUSTLING], [D. *hutseln, husselen,* to shake up (coins, lots, etc.) < MD. *hutsen,* to shake + *-el,* -le], 1. to push or knock about; shove or jostle in a rude, rough manner. 2. to force in a rough, hurried manner: as, he *hustled* the unwelcome visitors out of the house. 3. [Colloq.], to cause to be done quickly or too quickly; hurry. *v.i.* 1. to push one's way; move hurriedly. 2. [Colloq.], to work or act rapidly or energetically. *n.* 1. a hustling; rough jostling, pushing, or shoving. 2. [Colloq.], energetic action; drive; push.

hus·tler (hus'lẽr), *n.* one who hustles (esp. *v.i.* 2).

hut (hut), ***n.*** [Fr. *hutte* (in 17th-c. military usage); OHG. *hutta* < base of *hide, hat*], a small, shedlike house; hovel; roughly made little cabin. ***v.t.*** [HUTTED (-id), HUTTING], to put in or furnish with a hut or huts. ***v.i.*** to live in a hut or huts.

hutch (huch), ***n.*** [ME. *hucche, huche, hoche;* OFr. *huche,* bin, kneading trough < LL. *hutica,* a chest], 1. a bin, chest, or box for storage. 2. a pen or coop for animals or poultry. 3. a hut. 4. a mining trough for washing ore. 5. a car or truck for carrying ore out of a mine. ***v.t.*** to store or put in or as in a hutch.

Hutch·ins, Robert May·nard (mā′nẽrd huch′inz), 1899– ; American educator; president (1929–1945) and chancellor (1945–1951) of the University of Chicago.

Hutch·in·son (huch′in-sən), ***n.*** a city in central Kansas, on the Arkansas River: pop., 38,000.

Hutchinson, Anne, 1591–1643; American religious leader; one of the founders of Rhode Island.

Hux·ley, Al·dous Leonard (ôl′dəs huks′li), 1894– ; grandson of *T. H.;* English novelist, poet, and essayist.

Huxley, Julian Sor·rell (sôr′əl), 1887– ; grandson of *Thomas Henry;* English biologist and writer.

Huxley, Thomas Henry, 1825–1895; English biologist and writer.

Huy·gens, Christian (hī′gənz; D. hoi′gəns), 1629–1695; Dutch physicist, astronomer, and mathematician: also spelled **Huyghens.**

Huys·mans, Jo·ris Karl (yō′ris kärl hois′mäns; Fr. ü-ēs′mäns′), 1848–1907; French novelist of Dutch descent.

huz·za (hə-zä′, hoo-zä′), ***interj. & n.*** [echoic; but cf. G. *hussa*], a shout of joy, triumph, approval, etc. ***v.i.*** to cheer; shout "huzza." ***v.t.*** to greet, encourage, or applaud with shouts of "huzza." Replaced in current usage by ***hurrah.***

H.V., h.v., high voltage.

Hwang Hai (hwäŋ′ hī′), the Yellow Sea: Chinese name.

Hwang Ho (hwäŋ′ hō′), a river in China, flowing into the Yellow Sea: length, 2,700 mi.: also **Hwangho, Hoangho:** also called *Yellow River.*

hy·a·cinth (hī′ə-sinth′), ***n.*** [Fr. *hyacinthe;* L. *hyacinthus;* Gr. *hyakinthos*], 1. a gem; specifically, *a*) among the ancients, a blue gem, probably the sapphire. *b*) any of the reddish-orange varieties of zircon, garnet, or topaz; jacinth. 2. any of a group of plants of the lily family, with long, narrow leaves and spikes of fragrant, bell-shaped flowers. 3. *a*) the bulb of any of these plants. *b*) the flower. 4. a water bird with purple feathers. 5. bluish purple.

hy·a·cin·thine (hī′ə-sin′thin, hī′ə-sin′thīn), ***adj.*** [L. *hyacinthinus;* Gr. *hyakinthinos* < *hyakinthos,* hyacinth], 1. of or like the hyacinth (gem or flower); made of or adorned with hyacinths. 2. blue or bluish-purple. 3. red-orange. 4. [H-], of or like Hyacinthus.

Hy·a·cin·thus (hī′ə-sin′thəs), ***n.*** [L.; Gr. *Hyakinthos*], in *Greek mythology,* a youth loved and accidentally slain by Apollo, who caused to grow from his blood a flower bearing the letters AI AI (a Greek cry of sorrow).

Hy·a·des (hī′ə-dēz′), ***n.pl.*** [L. *Hyades;* Gr. *Hyades*], 1. in *Greek mythology,* the daughters of Atlas, placed in the sky by Zeus; hence, 2. a cluster of five stars forming a V in the constellation Taurus: when the Hyades rose with the sun, they were considered by the ancients to be a sign of rain.

Hy·ads (hī′adz), ***n.pl.*** the Hyades.

hy·ae·na (hī-ē′nə), ***n.*** a hyena.

hy·al- (hī′əl), hyalo-.

hy·a·lin (hī′ə-lin), ***n.*** [*hyal-* + *-in*], any of various translucent, albuminoid substances; especially, such a substance forming the walls of hydatid cysts.

hy·a·line (hī′ə-lin, hī′ə-līn′), ***adj.*** [L. *hyalinus;* Gr. *hyalinos,* glassy < *hyalos,* glass], transparent as glass; glassy. ***n.*** 1. anything transparent or glassy, as the smooth sea or clear sky. 2. hyalin.

hy·a·lite (hī′ə-līt′), ***n.*** [*hyal-* + *-ite*], a colorless variety of opal, sometimes transparent, sometimes whitish and translucent.

hy·a·lo- (hī′ə-lō, hī′ə-lə), [< Gr. *hyalos,* glass], a combining form meaning ***glass, glassy, transparent,*** as in *hyaloid:* also, before a vowel, **hyal-.**

hy·al·o·gen (hī-al′ə-jən′), ***n.*** [*hyalo-* + *-gen*], any of the various insoluble, mucoidlike substances found in animal tissue and producing hyalins upon hydrolysis.

hy·a·loid (hī′ə-loid′), ***adj.*** [Gr. *hyaloeidēs* < *hyalos,* glass + *eidos,* appearance], in *anatomy,* glassy, vitreous, or transparent; hyaline.

hy·a·lo·plasm (hī′ə-lə-plaz′m), ***n.*** [*hyalo-* + *-plasm*], the ground substance of the protoplasm of a cell: it is clear and fluid, as distinguished from the granular and reticulate parts.

hy·brid (hī′brid), ***n.*** [L. *hybrida, hibrida,* offspring of tame sow and wild boar], 1. the offspring of two animals or plants of different races, varieties, species, etc. 2. anything of mixed origin. 3. in *linguistics,* a word made up of elements from different languages (e.g., *hydroplane, sociology*). ***adj.*** of, or having the nature of, a hybrid.

hy·brid·ism (hī′brid-iz′m), ***n.*** 1. the production of hybrids; crossbreeding; interbreeding. 2. the quality, condition, or fact of being hybrid.

hy·brid·i·ty (hī-brid′ə-ti), ***n.*** the quality or condition of being hybrid.

hy·brid·i·za·tion (hī′brid-ə-zā′shən, hī′brid-ī-zā′shən), ***n.*** the producing of a hybrid or hybrids; crossing of different races, species, varieties, etc.

hy·brid·ize (hī′bri-dīz′), ***v.t. & v.i.*** [HYBRIDIZED (-dīzd′), HYBRIDIZING], to produce or cause to produce hybrids; interbreed; cross.

hyd., 1. hydraulics. 2. hydrostatics.

hy·da·tid (hī′də-tid), ***n.*** [Gr. *hydatis, hydatidos,* watery vesicle < base of *hydōr,* water], a cyst containing watery fluid and the larvae of a tapeworm, sometimes found in the body of both animals and man. ***adj.*** of or like such a cyst.

Hyde, Douglas (hīd), 1860–1949; Irish statesman and writer; president of Eire (1938–1945).

Hyde, Mr., see **Jekyll, Dr.**

Hyde Park, 1. a park in London, where public meetings often take place. 2. a village in southern New York, on the Hudson: the estate and burial place of Franklin D. Roosevelt is near by.

Hy·der·a·bad (hī′dẽr-ə-bad′, hī′drə-bäd′), ***n.*** 1. a city in south central India: pop., 1,086,000: capital of former Hyderabad state. 2. a former state of south central India. 3. a city in West Pakistan, on the Indus River: pop., 242,000.

hyd·no·car·pate (hid′nə-kär′pāt), ***n.*** a salt or ester of hydnocarpic acid.

hyd·no·car·pic (hid′nə-kär′pik), ***adj.*** [< Mod. L. *Hydnocarpus,* name of the genus of trees (< Gr. *hydnon,* edible fungus + *karpos,* fruit: so named in reference to the fruit of one species); + *-ic*], designating or of an acid, $C_{15}H_{27}COOH$, found in the oil of a tree that grows in India and Malaysia, used in treating leprosy.

hydr-, hydro-

Hy·dra (hī′drə), ***n.*** [*pl.,* for 2 & 4, HYDRAS (-drəz), HYDRAE (-drē)], [ME. & OFr. *ydre;* also ME. *ydra;* both < L.; Gr. *hydra,* water serpent], 1. in *Greek mythology,* the nine-headed serpent slain by Hercules: when any one of its heads was cut off, it was replaced by two others; hence, 2. [h-], any persistent or ever-increasing evil with many sources and causes. 3. a southern constellation outlining a serpent: see **constellation,** chart. 4. [h-], any of a group of very small fresh-water animals, with a tube-like body and a mouth surrounded by tentacles.

HYDRA

hy·drac·id (hī-dras′id), ***n.*** an acid that does not contain oxygen, as HCl, H_2S, HCN, etc.

hy·dra·gogue (hī′drə-gôg′, hī′drə-gog′), ***adj.*** [Fr.; L. *hydragogus,* carrying off water; Gr. *hydragōgos* < *hydōr,* water + *agein,* to lead], causing a discharge of water, especially from the intestine. ***n.*** any cathartic or other substance causing such a discharge.

hy·dran·ge·a (hī-drān′jə, hī-dran′ji-ə), ***n.*** [Mod. L. < *hydr-* + Gr. *angeion,* vessel], any of a group of shrubs of the saxifrage family, with opposite leaves and large, showy clusters of white, blue, or pink flowers.

hy·drant (hī′drənt), ***n.*** [< Gr. *hydōr,* water], a large discharge pipe with a valve for drawing water from a water main; fireplug.

hy·dranth (hī′dranth), ***n.*** [< *hydra* + Gr. *anthos,* a flower], in *zoology,* any of the feeding branches (*zooids*) of a hydroid colony.

hy·drar·gyr·ic (hī′drär-jir′ik), ***adj.*** [< L. *hydrargyrus* (see HYDRARGYRUM); + *-ic*], of or containing mercury; mercuric.

hy·drar·gy·rism (hī-drär′ji-riz′m), ***n.*** [< *hydrargyrum* + *-ism*], poisoning with mercury; mercurialism.

hy·drar·gy·rum (hī-drär′ji-rəm), ***n.*** [Mod. L.; L. *hydrargyrus;* Gr. *hydrargyros* < *hydōr,* water + *argyros,* silver], mercury: symbol, Hg (no period).

hy·dras·tin (hī-dras′tin), ***n.*** hydrastine.

hy·dras·tine (hī-dras′tēn, hī-dras′tin), ***n.*** [< Mod. L. *Hydrastis,* name of the genus of herbs (< Gr. *hydōr,* water); + *-ine*], a bitter, crystalline alkaloid, $C_{21}H_{21}O_6N$, extracted from the rootstalk of the goldenseal and used in treating dyspepsia, constipation, etc.

hy·drate (hī′drāt), ***n.*** [*hydr-* + *-ate*], a compound formed by the chemical combination of water and some other substance: as, plaster of Paris, $2CaSO_4{\cdot}H_2O$, is a *hydrate.* ***v.t. & v.i.*** [HYDRATED (-id), HYDRATING], 1.

to become or cause to become a hydrate. 2. to combine with water.

hy·drat·ed (hī′drāt-id), *adj.* [pp. of *hydrate*], formed by chemical combination with water.

hy·dra·tion (hī-drā′shən), *n.* a hydrating; especially, chemical combination with water to form a hydrate.

hy·drau·lic (hī-drô′lik), *adj.* [Fr. *hydraulique;* L. *hydraulicus;* Gr. *hydraulikos*, of a water organ < *hydraulis, hydraulos*, water organ, water pipe < *hydōr*, water + *aulos*, tube, pipe], 1. of hydraulics. 2. operated by the movement and force of liquid: as, a *hydraulic* brake or press. 3. setting or hardening under water: as, *hydraulic* mortar.

PISTONS FORCED BY FLUID TO APPLY BRAKE PRESSURE — BRAKE SHOE — BRAKE SHOE — SPRING RELEASE FOR BRAKE

HYDRAULIC BRAKE

hy·drau·li·cal·ly (hī-drô′li-k'l-i, hī-drô′lik-li), *adv.* by hydraulic power.

hy·drau·lics (hī-drô′liks), *n.pl.* [construed as sing.], [< *hydraulic*], the branch of physics having to do with the mechanical properties of water and other liquids and with the application of these properties in engineering: abbreviated **hyd., hydraul.**

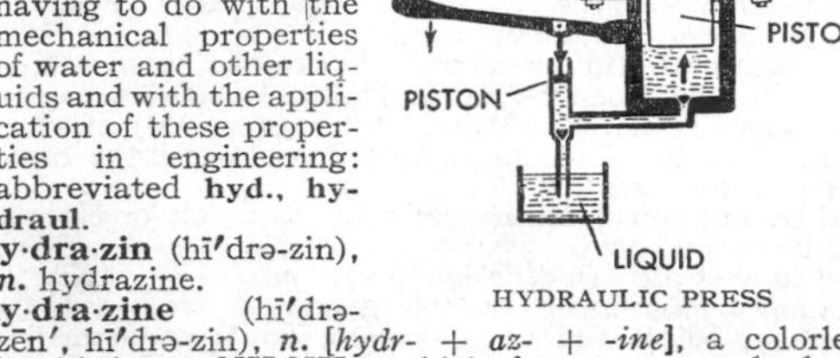

HYDRAULIC PRESS

hy·dra·zin (hī′drə-zin), *n.* hydrazine.

hy·dra·zine (hī′drə-zēn′, hī′drə-zin), *n.* [*hydr-* + *az-* + *-ine*], a colorless liquid base, NH_2NH_2, which forms a monohydrate ($NH_2NH_2 \cdot H_2O$) and a series of salts: it is used as a jet and rocket fuel.

hy·dra·zo·ate (hī′drə-zō′āt), *n.* any salt of hydrazoic acid.

hy·dra·zo·ic (hī′drə-zō′ik), *adj.* [*hydr-* + *azo-* + *-ic*], designating or of a colorless, volatile acid, HN_3, from which the hydrazoates are derived.

hy·dric (hī′drik), *adj.* [*hydr-* + *-ic*], of or containing hydrogen.

-hy·dric (hī′drik), [see HYDRIC], a combining form used to indicate *the presence of* (a specified number of) *hydroxyl radicals* or *replaceable hydrogen atoms in the molecule,* as in *monohydric.*

hy·drid (hī′drid), *n.* a hydride.

hy·dride (hī′drīd, hī′drid), *n.* [*hydr-* + *-ide*], a compound of hydrogen with another element or a radical.

hy·dri·od·ic (hī′dri-od′ik), *adj.* [*hydr-* + *iodic*], designating or of an acid, HI, produced by the direct combination of hydrogen and iodine or by the hydrolysis of phosphorus tri-iodide: it is a colorless gas, readily soluble in water, and forms salts called iodides.

hy·dro- (hī′drō, hī′drə), [< Gr. *hydōr*, water], a combining form meaning: 1. *water,* as in *hydrostatic, hydrometer.* 2. in *chemistry, the presence of hydrogen,* as in *hydrocyanic.* Also, before a vowel, **hydr-.**

hy·dro·bro·mic (hī′drə-brō′mik), *adj.* [*hydro-* + *bromic*], designating or of an acid, HBr, produced by the direct combination of hydrogen and bromine or by the hydrolysis of phosphorus tribromide: it is a colorless gas, readily soluble in water, and forms salts called bromides.

hy·dro·car·bon (hī′drə-kär′bən), *n.* any compound containing only hydrogen and carbon: benzene and methane are hydrocarbons.

hy·dro·cele (hī′drə-sēl′), *n.* [L.; Gr. *hydrokēlē* < *hydōr*, water + *kēlē*, tumor], a collection of watery fluid in a cavity of the body, especially in the scrotum or along the spermatic cord.

hy·dro·ceph·a·loid (hī′drə-sef′ə-loid′), *adj.* of or like hydrocephalus.

hy·dro·ceph·a·lous (hī′drə-sef′ə-ləs), *adj.* hydrocephaloid.

hy·dro·ceph·a·lus (hī′drə-sef′ə-ləs), *n.* [Mod. L.; Gr. *hydrokephalon* < *hydōr*, water + *kephalē*, head], a condition characterized by an abnormal increase in the amount of fluid in the cranium, causing enlargement of the head and wasting away of the brain.

hy·dro·ceph·a·ly (hī′drə-sef′ə-li), *n.* hydrocephalus.

hy·dro·chlo·ric (hī′drə-klôr′ik, hī′drə-klō′rik), *adj.* [*hydro-* + *chloric*], designating or of an acid, HCl, produced by the combination of hydrogen and chlorine or by the reaction of salt and sulfuric acid, and existing as a colorless gas or as a colorless solution of this gas in water: it forms salts called chlorides.

hy·dro·chlo·ride (hī′drə-klôr′īd, hī′drə-klō′rīd), *n.* a compound of hydrochloric acid and an organic base.

hy·dro·cy·an·ic (hī′drō-sī-an′ik), *adj.* [*hydro-* + *cyanic*], designating or of a weak, highly poisonous acid, HCN (also called *prussic acid*), produced by the combination of hydrogen and cyanogen, and existing as a colorless liquid with the odor of peach blossoms or bitter almonds.

hy·dro·dy·nam·ic (hī′drō-dī-nam′ik), *adj.* 1. having to do with hydrodynamics. 2. of, derived from, or operated by, the action of water, etc. in motion.

hy·dro·dy·nam·ics (hī′drō-dī-nam′iks), *n.pl.* [construed as sing.], the branch of physics having to do with the motion and action of water and other liquids; dynamics of liquids: abbreviated **hydrodyn.**

hy·dro·e·lec·tric (hī′drō-i-lek′trik), *adj.* producing, or having to do with the production of, electricity by water power or by the friction of water or steam.

hy·dro·e·lec·tric·i·ty (hī′drō-i-lek′tris′ə-ti), *n.* electricity produced by water power or by the friction of water or steam.

hy·dro·flu·or·ic (hī′drō-flo͞o-ôr′ik, hī′drō-flo͞o-or′ik), *adj.* [*hydro-* + *fluoric*], designating or of an acid, H_6F_6, H_4F_4, H_2F_2, or HF (depending on the temperature), produced by the reaction of concentrated sulfuric acid with solid fluorides, and existing as a colorless, fuming, corrosive liquid: it reacts with silicates and is therefore used in etching glass.

hy·dro·foil (hī′drə-foil′), *n.* [*hydro-* + air*foil*], 1. any of the winglike structures attached to the hull of some watercraft: at a certain speed the hull is lifted above the water and the craft skims along on the hydrofoils at great speeds. 2. a craft with hydrofoils.

hy·dro·gen (hī′drə-jən), *n.* [Fr. *hydrogène;* see HYDRO- & -GEN: coined in 1787 by the Fr. chemist G. de Morveau, in reference to the generation of water from the combustion of hydrogen], an inflammable, colorless, odorless, gaseous chemical element, the lightest of all known substances: symbol, H; at. wt., 1.0080; at. no., 1.

hy·dro·gen·ate (hī′drə-jə-nāt′), *v.t.* [HYDROGENATED (-id), HYDROGENATING], to combine with, treat with, or expose to the action of, hydrogen: as, oil is *hydrogenated* to produce a solid fat.

hy·dro·gen·a·tion (hī′drə-jə-nā′shən), *n.* the process of hydrogenating.

hydrogen bomb, an extremely destructive kind of atom bomb operating on the principle of nuclear fusion, in which the atoms of a heavy isotope of hydrogen are fused into helium under the extraordinarily intense heat and pressure created by explosion of a nuclear-fission unit in the bomb: the first hydrogen bomb was reported to have been exploded in November, 1952, by the United States: also **H-bomb, fusion bomb:** cf. **nuclear fusion.**

hydrogen ion, the positively charged ion in all acids: symbol, H^+.

hy·dro·gen·ize (hī′drə-jə-nīz′), *v.t.* [HYDROGENIZED (-nīzd′), HYDROGENIZING], to hydrogenate.

hy·drog·en·ous (hī-droj′ə-nəs), *adj.* of or containing hydrogen.

hydrogen peroxide, an unstable compound, H_2O_2, existing as a slightly blue, sirupy liquid, often used in dilute solution as a bleaching or disinfecting agent.

hydrogen sulfide, an inflammable, poisonous gas, H_2S, with the characteristic odor of rotten eggs.

hy·drog·ra·pher (hī-drog′rə-fēr), *n.* an expert or specialist in hydrography.

hy·dro·graph·ic (hī′drə-graf′ik), *adj.* having to do with hydrography.

hy·drog·ra·phy (hī-drog′rə-fi), *n.* [Fr. *hydrographie;* see HYDRO- & -GRAPHY], 1. the study, description, and mapping of oceans, lakes, and rivers, especially with reference to their navigational and commercial uses. 2. the parts of a map that represent surface waters.

hy·droid (hī′droid), *adj.* [< *hydra* + *-oid*], 1. like a hydra or polyp. 2. of or related to the group of hydrozoans of which the hydra is the typical member. *n.* any member of this group; especially, any of the polyps, which reproduce by budding.

hy·dro·ki·net·ic (hī′drō-ki-net′ik), *adj.* [*hydro-* + *kinetic*], of the motions of fluids or the forces producing or influencing such motions.

hy·dro·ki·net·ics (hī′drō-ki-net′iks), *n.pl.* [construed as sing.], [*hydro-* + *kinetics*], the branch of physics having to do with the motions of fluids.

hy·dro·log·ic (hī′drə-loj′ik), *adj.* of hydrology.

hy·drol·o·gist (hī-drol′ə-jist), *n.* an expert in hydrology.

hy·drol·o·gy (hī-drol′ə-ji), *n.* [Mod. L. *hydrologia;* see HYDRO- & -LOGY], the science of water, its properties, laws, and distribution; especially, the study of underground sources of water.

hy·drol·y·sis (hī-drol′ə-sis), *n.* [*pl.* HYDROLYSES (-sēz′)], [*hydro-* + *-lysis*], a chemical reaction in which a compound reacts with the ions of water (H^+ and OH^-) to produce a weak acid, a weak base, or both.

hy·dro·lyte (hī′drə-līt′), *n.* any substance undergoing hydrolysis.

hy·dro·lyt·ic (hī′drə-lit′ik), *adj.* of or causing hydrolysis.

hy·dro·lyze (hī′drə-līz′), *v.t. & v.i.* [HYDROLYZED (-līzd′), HYDROLYZING], to undergo or cause to undergo hydrolysis.

hy·dro·man·cy (hī′drə-man′si), *n.* [ME. *idromancie;* L. *hydromantia;* Gr. *hydromanteia;* see HYDRO- & -MANCY], divination by the observation of water.

hy·dro·me·chan·i·cal (hī′drō-mi-kan′i-k'l), *adj.* of hydromechanics.

hy·dro·me·chan·ics (hī′drō-mi-kan′iks), *n.pl.* [construed as sing.], [*hydro-* + *mechanics*], the branch of

physics having to do with the laws governing the motion and equilibrium of fluids.
hy·dro·me·du·sa (hī'drō-mə-dōō'sə, hī'drō-mə-dū'sə), *n.* [*pl.* HYDROMEDUSAE (-sē)], [Mod. L.; see HYDRA & MEDUSA], a jellyfish (*medusa*) formed from a budding growth on a hydroid.
hy·dro·mel (hī'drə-mel'), *n.* [ME. *ydromel* (cf. OFr. *ydromelle*) < L. *hydromeli;* Gr. *hydromeli* < *hydōr,* water + *meli,* honey], a mixture of honey and water that becomes mead when fermented.
hy·dro·met·al·lur·gy (hī'drə-met''l-ũr'ji), *n.* [*hydro-* + *metallurgy*], the reduction of ores by washing out the insoluble matter with various liquid reagents.
hy·drom·e·ter (hī-drom'ə-tẽr), *n.* [*hydro-* + *-meter*], an instrument for determining the specific gravity of liquids: it is a graduated, weighted tube that sinks in the liquid up to a point set by the specific gravity.
hy·dro·met·ric (hī'drə-met'rik), *adj.* 1. of hydrometry. 2. of or according to a hydrometer.
hy·dro·met·ri·cal (hī'drə-met'ri-k'l), *adj.* hydrometric.
hy·drom·e·try (hī-drom'ə-tri), *n.* measurement of the specific gravity of liquids by the use of a hydrometer.
hy·dron·ic (hī-dron'ik), *adj.* of or having to do with hydronics.
hy·dron·ics (hī-dron'iks), *n.pl.* [construed as sing.], [*hydr-* + electr*onics*], the science dealing with electrically controlled systems for heating, cooling, etc. by the forced circulation of liquids or vapors.
hy·dro·path·ic (hī'drə-path'ik), *adj.* of, by, or using hydropathy.
hy·drop·a·thist (hī-drop'ə-thist'), *n.* a person who practices or advocates hydropathy.
hy·drop·a·thy (hī-drop'ə-thi), *n.* [*hydro-* + *-pathy*], the treatment of disease by the use of water; specifically, a method of treatment that attempts to cure all diseases by the external or internal use of much water.
hy·dro·phane (hī'drə-fān'), *n.* [*hydro-* + *-phane*], an opaque variety of opal that becomes translucent or transparent when wet.
hy·droph·a·nous (hī-drof'ə-nəs), *adj.* [< *hydrophane* + *-ous*], translucent or transparent when wet.
hy·dro·pho·bi·a (hī'drə-fō'bi-ə), *n.* [LL.; Gr. *hydrophobia;* see HYDRO- & -PHOBIA], 1. an abnormal fear of water. 2. [from the symptomatic aversion to, and inability to swallow, water and other liquids], rabies (especially in man).
hy·dro·pho·bic (hī'drə-fō'bik, hī'drə-fob'ik), *adj.* of or having hydrophobia.
hy·dro·phone (hī'drə-fōn'), *n.* [*hydro-* + *-phone*], 1. an instrument for detecting, and registering the distance and direction of, sound transmitted through water. 2. an instrument for detecting the flow of water in a pipe.
hy·dro·phyte (hī'drə-fīt'), *n.* [*hydro-* + *-phyte*], any plant growing only in water or very wet earth.
hy·drop·ic (hī-drop'ik), *adj.* [ME. *ydropike;* OFr. *idropique;* L. *hydropicus;* Gr. *hydropikos* < *hydrops;* see DROPSY], of or having dropsy; dropsical.
hy·dro·plane (hī'drə-plān'), *n.* [*hydro-* + *plane*], 1. a small, light motorboat with a flat bottom rising in steps to the stern so that it can skim along the water's surface at high speeds. 2. a seaplane. 3. an attachment for an airplane that enables it to glide along on the water. 4. a horizontal rudder used to submerge or raise a submarine. *v.i.* 1. to drive or ride in a hydroplane. 2. to skim along like a hydroplane.
hy·dro·pon·ic (hī'drə-pon'ik), *adj.* of or grown by hydroponics.
hy·dro·pon·ics (hī'drə-pon'iks), *n.pl.* [construed as sing.], [< *hydro-* + Gr. *ponos,* labor; + *-ics*], the science of growing plants in solutions containing the necessary minerals, instead of in soil.
hy·dro·quin·ol (hī'drə-kwin'ōl, hī'drə-kwin'ol), *n.* hydroquinone.
hy·dro·qui·none (hī'drō-kwi-nōn', hī'drə-kwin'ōn), *n.* [*hydro-* + *quinone*], a white, crystalline substance, $C_6H_4(OH)_2$, used in medicine and photography.
hy·dro·scope (hī'drə-skōp'), *n.* [*hydro-* + *-scope*], a device for seeing things far below the surface of water.
hy·dro·sol (hī'drə-sol', hī'drə-sōl'), *n.* [*hydro-* + *solu*tion], a colloidal dispersion in which water is the dispersing medium: also **hy·dro·sole** (hī'drə-sōl').
hy·dro·sphere (hī'drə-sfēr'), *n.* [*hydro-* + *-sphere*], 1. all the water on the surface of the earth. 2. the moisture in the atmosphere surrounding the earth.
hy·dro·stat (hī'drə-stat'), *n.* [*hydro-* + *-stat*], 1. an electrical device for showing or regulating the level of water in a reservoir, etc. 2. an apparatus for preventing the explosion of a steam boiler.
hy·dro·stat·ic (hī'drə-stat'ik), *adj.* of hydrostatics.
hy·dro·stat·ics (hī'drə-stat'iks), *n.pl.* [construed as sing.], the branch of physics having to do with the pressure and equilibrium of water and other liquids; statics of liquids: abbreviated **hydros., hyd.**
hy·dro·sul·fide (hī'drə-sul'fīd), *n.* a compound containing the HS radical and some other radical or element, produced by the partial replacement of the hydrogen in hydrogen sulfide: also called *bisulfide.*
hy·dro·sul·fite (hī'drə-sul'fīt), *n.* 1. any salt of hydrosulfurous acid; hyposulfite. 2. loosely, sodium hyposulfite, a bleaching agent.
hy·dro·sul·fu·rous (hī'drō-sul-fyoor'əs, hī'drə-sul'fẽr-əs), *adj.* hyposulfurous.
hy·dro·ther·a·peu·tic (hī'drə-ther'ə-pū'tik), *adj.* of hydrotherapeutics, or hydrotherapy.
hy·dro·ther·a·peu·tics (hī'drə-ther'ə-pū'tiks), *n.pl.* [construed as sing.], hydrotherapy.
hy·dro·ther·a·py (hī'drə-ther'ə-pi), *n.* [*hydro-* + *therapy*], the treatment of disease by the internal or external use of water.
hy·dro·ther·mal (hī'drə-thũr'məl), *adj.* [*hydro-* + *thermal*], having to do with hot water; especially, having to do with the action of hot water in dissolving, shifting, and otherwise changing the distribution of minerals in the earth's crust.
hy·dro·tho·rax (hī'drə-thôr'aks, hī'drə-thō'raks), *n.* [Mod. L.; *hydro* + *thorax*], a condition marked by an abnormal amount of watery fluid in the pleural cavity.
hy·dro·trop·ic (hī'drə-trop'ik), *adj.* of or showing hydrotropism.
hy·drot·ro·pism (hī-drot'rə-piz'm), *n.* [*hydro-* + *-tropism*], the tendency of a plant to grow or turn in the direction of moisture.
hy·drous (hī'drəs), *adj.* [*hydr-* + *-ous*], 1. containing water; watery. 2. containing water, especially water of crystallization, in chemical combination.
hy·drox·ide (hī-drok'sīd, hī-drok'sid), *n.* [*hydr-* + *oxide*], a compound consisting of an element or radical combined with the hydroxyl radical (OH).
hy·drox·y (hī-drok'si), *adj.* hydroxyl.
hy·drox·y- (hī-drok'si), a combining form meaning *hydroxyl* (in organic chemistry): preferred to *oxy-.*
hydroxy acid, an organic acid, as lactic acid, in which both the hydroxyl and carboxyl radicals occur.
hy·drox·y·ke·tone (hī-drok'si-kē'tōn), *n.* a ketone containing the hydroxyl radical.
hy·drox·yl (hī-drok'sil), *n.* [*hydr-* + *oxygen* + *-yl*], the monovalent radical OH, present in all hydroxides.
hy·drox·yl·a·mine (hī-drok'sil-ə-mēn', hī-drok-sil'ə-min), *n.* [*hydroxyl* + *amine*], a colorless, odorless base, NH_2OH, used as a reducing agent.
hy·dro·zo·an (hī'drə-zō'ən), *adj.* [< *hydra* + Gr. *zōion,* an animal], of a class of water animals having a saclike body consisting of two layers of cells, and a mouth that opens directly into the body cavity. *n.* any animal of this class, as a hydra, polyp, etc.
Hy·drus (hī'drəs), *n.* [L. < Gr. *hydros,* water snake], a southern constellation: see **constellation,** chart.
hy·e·na (hī-ē'nə), *n.* [L. *hyaena;* Gr. *hyaina,* lit., a sow, hence, from its hoglike mane, *hyaina* < *hys,* a hog], any of a group of wolflike, flesh-eating animals of Africa and Asia, with a bristly mane, short hind legs, and a characteristic shrill cry: hyenas feed on carrion and are considered cowardly: also spelled **hyaena.**
hy·e·to- (hī'i-tō, hī'i-tə), [< Gr. *hyetos,* rain < *hyein,* to rain], a combining form meaning *rain, rainfall,* as in *hyetograph, hyetology:* also, before a vowel, **hyet-.**
hy·e·to·graph (hī'i-tə-graf', hī'i-tə-gräf'), *n.* [*hyeto-* + *-graph*], a chart showing the average annual rainfall.
hy·e·to·graph·ic (hī'i-tə-graf'ik), *adj.* of hyetography.
hy·e·tog·ra·phy (hī'i-tog'rə-fi), *n.* [*hyeto-* + *-graphy*], the branch of meteorology having to do with the geographical distribution of rainfall.
hy·e·to·log·i·cal (hī'i-tə-loj'i-k'l), *adj.* of hyetology.
hy·e·tol·o·gy (hī'i-tol'ə-ji), *n.* [*hyeto-* + *-logy*], the branch of meteorology dealing with rain, snow, etc.
Hy·ge·ia (hī-jē'ə), *n.* [L. *Hygea;* Gr. *Hygeia, Hygieia* < *hygiēs,* healthy], the ancient Greek goddess of health.
hy·giene (hī'jēn, hī'ji-ēn'), *n.* [Fr. *hygiène* < Gr. *hygieinē* (*technē*), (art) of health < *hygiēs,* healthy, sound], the science of health and its maintenance; system of principles for the preservation of health and prevention of disease.
hy·gi·en·ic (hī'ji-en'ik, hī-jē'nik), *adj.* 1. of hygiene or health. 2. promoting health; healthful; sanitary.
hy·gi·en·i·cal (hī'ji-en'i-k'l, hī-jē'ni-k'l), *adj.* hygienic.
hy·gi·en·ics (hī'ji-en'iks, hī-jē'niks), *n.pl.* [construed as sing.], the science of health; hygiene.
hy·gi·en·ist (hī'ji-ən-ist), *n.* an expert in hygiene.
hy·gro- (hī'grə), [< Gr. *hygros,* wet, moist], a combining form meaning *wet, moisture,* as in *hygrometer, hygroscope;* also, before a vowel, **hygr-.**
hy·grom·e·ter (hī-grom'ə-tẽr), *n.* [*hygro-* + *-meter*], an instrument for measuring humidity.
hy·gro·met·ric (hī'grə-met'rik), *adj.* 1. of hygrometry. 2. attracting or absorbing moisture from the air.
hy·grom·e·try (hī-grom'ə-tri), *n.* [*hygro-* + *-metry*], the branch of physics having to do with measuring the amount of moisture in the air.
hy·gro·scope (hī'grə-skōp'), *n.* [*hygro-* + *-scope*], an

instrument for recording changes in atmospheric humidity.

hy·gro·scop·ic (hī'grə-skop'ik), *adj.* 1. of, measurable by, or according to a hygroscope. 2. attracting or absorbing moisture from the air; hygrometric.

hy·ing (hī'iŋ), alternative present participle of **hie.**

Hyk·sos (hik'sōs, hik'sos), *n.pl.* [Gr. *Hyksōs* < Egypt. *Hiq shasu,* chief of the nomadic tribes], foreign kings of Egypt who formed the XVth and XVIth dynasties (1750?–1580? B.C.): also called *Shepherd Kings.*

hy·la (hī'lə), *n.* [Mod. L. < Gr. *hylē,* wood], a tree frog: loosely called *tree toad.*

hy·lo- (hī'lō, hī'lə), [< Gr. *hylē,* wood, matter], a combining form meaning: 1. *wood,* as in *hylophagous.* 2. *matter, substance,* as in *hylozoism.* Also, before a vowel, **hyl-.**

hy·loid membrane (hī'loid), a delicate membrane containing the vitreous humor of the eye.

hy·loph·a·gous (hī-lof'ə-gəs), *adj.* [*hylo-* + *-phagous*], wood-eating, as some insects.

hy·lo·zo·ic (hī'lə-zō'ik), *adj.* of or believing in hylozoism.

hy·lo·zo·ism (hī'lə-zō'iz'm), *n.* [< *hylo-* + Gr. *zōē,* life; + *-ism*], the doctrine that all matter has life, or that life is inseparable from matter.

Hy·men (hī'mən), *n.* [L.; Gr. *Hymēn*], 1. the ancient Greek god of marriage. 2. [h-], *a*) marriage. *b*) a wedding song or poem.

hy·men (hī'mən), *n.* [Gr. *hymēn,* skin; for IE. base see SEAM], the thin mucous membrane that usually covers part of the opening of the vagina in a virgin.

hy·me·ne·al (hī'mə-nē'əl), *adj.* [< L. *hymenaeus;* Gr. *hymenaios* (see HYMEN); + *-al*], of a wedding or marriage. *n.* a wedding song or poem.

hy·me·ne·an (hī'mə-nē'ən), *adj.* hymeneal.

hy·me·no- (hī'mə-nō), [< Gr. *hymēn;* see HYMEN (membrane)], a combining form meaning *membrane,* as in *hymenopter:* also, before a vowel, **hymen-.**

hy·me·nop·ter (hī'mə-nop'tẽr), *n.* a hymenopterous insect.

hy·me·nop·ter·an (hī'mə-nop'tẽr-ən), *adj.* hymenopterous. *n.* a hymenopterous insect.

hy·me·nop·ter·on (hī'mə-nop'tẽr-on), *n.* [*pl.* HYMENOPTERA (-ə)], a hymenopterous insect.

hy·me·nop·ter·ous (hī'mə-nop'tẽr-əs), *adj.* [Gr. *hymenopteros,* membrane-winged < *hymēn,* membrane + *pteron,* a wing], belonging to a large, highly specialized group of insects, including wasps, bees, ants, etc., which have a biting or sucking mouth and, when winged, four membranous wings.

Hy·met·tus (hī-met'əs), *n.* a mountain in southeastern Greece, near Athens: height, 3,370 ft.: famous for the honey produced there.

hymn (him), *n.* [ME. *ympne* < AS. & OFr.; AS. *ymen* (pl. *ymnas*); OFr. *ymne;* both < LL. *hymnus;* Gr. *hymnos,* a hymn, festive song, ode], 1. a song in praise or honor of God, a god, or gods. 2. any song of praise or glorification. *v.t. & v.i.* to praise in a hymn.

hym·nal (him'nəl), *n.* [ME. < L. *hymnus*], a collection of hymns; hymnbook. *adj.* of or using hymns.

hymn·book (him'book'), *n.* a book of hymns; hymnal.

hym·nist (him'nist), *n.* a composer of hymns.

hym·no·dist (him'nə-dist), *n.* an expert in hymnody.

hym·no·dy (him'nə-di), *n.* [Gr. *hymnōidia;* see HYMN & ODE], 1. the singing of hymns. 2. the study of hymns, their use, history, etc. 3. hymns collectively.

hym·nol·o·gist (him-nol'ə-jist), *n.* 1. an expert in hymnology. 2. a person who composes hymns.

hym·nol·o·gy (him-nol'ə-ji), *n.* [Gr. *hymnologia;* see HYMN & -LOGY], 1. the study of hymns, their use, history, etc. 2. hymns collectively. 3. the writing or composition of hymns. Abbreviated **hymnol.**

hy·oid (hī'oid), *adj.* [Fr. *hyoïde;* Gr. *hyoeidēs,* shaped like the letter Υ (upsilon) < name of this letter + *eidos,* form], designating or of a bone or bones at the base of the tongue, U-shaped in man. *n.* the hyoid bone or bones.

hy·os·cy·a·min (hī'ə-sī'ə-min), *n.* hyoscyamine.

hy·os·cy·a·mine (hī'ə-sī'ə-mēn', hī'ə-sī'ə-min), *n.* [< L. *hyoscyamus,* henbane (< Gr. *hyoskyamos* < *hys,* pig + *kyamos,* bean); + *-ine*], a colorless, crystalline, very poisonous alkaloid, $C_{17}H_{23}NO_3$, obtained from henbane and other plants of the nightshade family: it is used in medicine as a sedative, hypnotic, etc.

hy·os·cy·a·mus (hī'ə-sī'ə-məs), *n.* [L.; see HYOSCYAMINE], henbane.

hyp (hip), *n.* [Obs.; formerly Colloq.], *often pl.* a fit of melancholy; hypochondria (usually with *the*).

hyp- (hīp, hip), hypo-.

hyp., 1. hypotenuse. 2. hypothesis. 3. hypothetical.

hyp·a·byss·al (hip'ə-bis''l), *adj.* [*hyp-* + *abyssal*], in *geology,* consolidated or partly crystalline from fusion at moderate depths underground.

hy·pae·thral (hi-pē'thrəl, hī-pē'thrəl), *adj.* [< L. *hypaethrus,* uncovered, in the open air (< Gr. *hypaithros* < *hypo,* under + *aithēr,* ether, clear sky); + *-al*], open to the sky; roofless: said of buildings and courts in classical architecture: also spelled **hypethral.**

hy·per- (hī'pẽr), [Gr. < *hyper,* over, above, concerning], a prefix meaning: 1. *over, above, more than the normal, excessive,* as in *hypercritical, hyperopia.* 2. in *chemistry,* formerly, *per-,* as in *hyperoxide.* Opposed to *hypo-.*

hy·per·ac·id (hī'pẽr-as'id), *adj.* excessively acid.

hy·per·ac·id·i·ty (hī'pẽr-ə-sid'ə-ti), *n.* excessive acidity, especially of the gastric juice.

hy·per·a·cu·si·a (hī'pẽr-ə-kū'zhi-ə), *n.* [Mod. L. < *hyper-* + Gr. *akousis,* a hearing], an abnormally keen sense of hearing, often with pain in the ears.

hy·per·a·cu·sis (hī'pẽr-ə-kū'sis), *n.* hyperacusia.

hy·per·al·ge·si·a (hī'pẽr-al-jē'zi-ə, hī'pẽr-al-jē'si-ə), *n.* [Mod. L. < *hyper-* + Gr. *algēsis,* sense of pain], abnormally high sensitiveness to pain.

hy·per·al·ge·sic (hī'pẽr-al-jē'sik), *adj.* of or characterized by hyperalgesia.

hy·per·al·ge·sis (hī'pẽr-al-jē'sis), *n.* hyperalgesia.

hy·per·bo·la (hī-pũr'bə-lə), *n.* [*pl.* HYPERBOLAS (-ləz)], [Mod. L. < Gr. *hyperbolē,* a throwing beyond, excess, < *hyperballein,* to throw beyond; *hyper-,* over, beyond + *ballein,* to throw], a curve formed by the section of a cone cut by a plane that makes a greater angle with the base than the side of the cone makes.

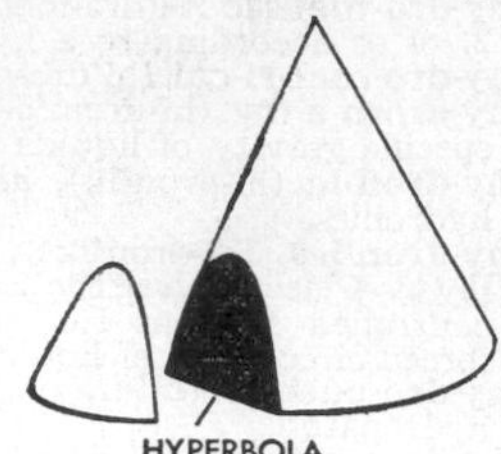

HYPERBOLA

hy·per·bo·le (hī-pũr'bə-li), *n.* [L.; Gr.; see HYPERBOLA], exaggeration for effect, not meant to be taken literally. Example: This story is as old as time.

hy·per·bol·ic (hī'pẽr-bol'ik), *adj.* [L. *hyperbolicus;* Gr. *hyperbolikos* < *hyperbolē*], 1. of, having the nature of, or using hyperbole; exaggerated. 2. of, or having the form of, a hyperbola.

hy·per·bol·i·cal·ly (hī'pẽr-bol'i-k'l-i, hī'pẽr-bol'ik-li), *adv.* in a hyperbolic manner.

hy·per·bo·lism (hī-pũr'bə-liz'm), *n.* 1. the use of hyperbole. 2. a hyperbolic statement.

hy·per·bo·lize (hī-pũr'bə-līz'), *v.t. & v.i.* [HYPERBOLIZED (-līzd'), HYPERBOLIZING], to express with hyperbole.

hy·per·bo·re·an (hī'pẽr-bôr'i-ən, hī'pẽr-bō'ri-ən), *adj.* [LL. *Hyperboreanus* < L. *Hyperboreus;* Gr. *hyperboreos,* beyond the north wind < *hyper-,* over, beyond + *boreas,* north wind], 1. of the far north; hence, 2. very cold; frigid. 3. [H-], of the Hyperboreans. *n.* 1. [H-], in *Greek legend,* an inhabitant of a northern region of sunshine and everlasting spring, beyond the mountains of the north wind. 2. a person living in a far northern region.

hy·per·cat·a·lec·tic (hī'pẽr-kat'ə-lek'tik), *adj.* [L. *hypercatalecticus;* Gr. *hyperkatalēktikos;* see HYPER- & CATALECTIC], having one or two extra syllables following the last regular measure: said of a line of verse.

hy·per·crit·ic (hī'pẽr-krit'ik), *n.* a hypercritical person.

hy·per·crit·i·cal (hī'pẽr-krit'i-k'l), *adj.* too critical; too severe in judgment; hard to please. —*SYN.* see **critical.**

hy·per·du·li·a (hī'pẽr-doo-lī'ə, hī'pẽr-dyoo-lī'ə), *n.* [*hyper-* + *dulia*], in the *Roman Catholic Church,* the special homage paid to the Virgin Mary as a holier and nobler creature than any angel or saint.

hy·per·e·mi·a (hī'pẽr-ē'mi-ə), *n.* [Mod. L.; see HYPER- & -EMIA], a greatly increased blood flow; congestion of blood anywhere in the body.

hy·per·e·mic (hī'pẽr-ē'mik, hī'pẽr-em'ik), *adj.* of or characterized by hyperemia.

hy·per·es·the·si·a (hī'pẽr-es-thē'zhə, hī'pẽr-es-thē'zhi-ə), *n.* [Mod. L.; see HYPER- & ESTHESIA], an abnormal sensitivity of the skin or some sense organ.

hy·per·es·thet·ic (hī'pẽr-es-thet'ik), *adj.* of or having hyperesthesia.

hy·per·eu·tec·tic (hī'pẽr-yoo-tek'tik), *adj.* containing more of the lesser component than is present in a eutectic solution or alloy.

Hy·pe·ri·on (hī-pêr'i-ən), *n.* [L.; Gr. *Hyperiōn*], in *Greek mythology,* 1. a Titan, son of Uranus and Gaea, and father of the sun god Helios. 2. Helios himself.

hy·per·ki·ne·si·a (hī'pẽr-ki-nē'si-ə, hī'pẽr-ki-nē'zi-ə), *n.* [Mod. L. < *hyper-* + Gr. *kinēsis,* motion], a condition of abnormally increased muscular movement.

hy·per·ki·ne·sis (hī'pẽr-ki-nē'sis), *n.* hyperkinesia.

hy·per·ki·net·ic (hī'pẽr-ki-net'ik), *adj.* of or characterized by hyperkinesia.

hy·per·met·ric (hī'pẽr-met'rik), *adj.* [< Gr. *hypermetros,* beyond measure; see HYPER- & METRIC], in *prosody,* having an extra syllable or syllables.

hy·per·met·ri·cal (hī'pẽr-met'ri-k'l), *adj.* hypermetric.

hy·per·me·tro·pi·a (hī'pẽr-mi-trō'pi-ə), *n.* [Mod. L. < Gr. *hypermetros,* excessive + *ōps, ōpos,* eye], the condition of being farsighted; abnormal vision in which the rays of light are focused behind the retina so that distant objects are seen more clearly than near ones.

hy·per·me·trop·ic (hī'pẽr-mi-trop'ik), *adj.* of or having hypermetropia; farsighted.

Hy·perm·nes·tra (hī'pẽrm-nes'trə), *n.* [L.; Gr. *Hypermnēstrē*], in *Greek mythology,* the only one of the Danaïdes, the fifty daughters of King Danaüs, who did not kill her husband at her father's command.

hy·per·o·pi·a (hī'pĕr-ō'pi-ə), *n.* [Mod. L.; see HYPER- & -OPIA], hypermetropia.
hy·per·op·ic (hī'pĕr-op'ik), *adj.* hypermetropic.
hy·per·os·to·sis (hī'pĕr-os-tō'sis), *n.* [*pl.* HYPEROSTOSES (-sēz)], [Mod. L.; see HYPER- & OSTOSIS], an abnormal increase or thickening of bony tissue.
hy·per·os·tot·ic (hī'pĕr-os-tot'ik), *adj.* of or having hyperostosis.
hy·per·phys·i·cal (hī'pĕr-fiz'i-k'l), *adj.* 1. beyond the physical; supernatural. 2. separate from the physical.
hy·per·pi·tu·i·ta·rism (hī'pĕr-pi-tōō'i-tə-riz'm, hī'pĕr-pi-tū'i-tə-riz'm), *n.* 1. excessive activity of the pituitary gland or its anterior lobe. 2. the condition of excessive skeletal growth caused by this.
hy·per·pla·si·a (hī'pĕr-plā'zhi-ə, hī'pĕr-plā'zi-ə), *n.* [Mod. L.; see HYPER- & -PLASIA], an abnormal increase in the number of cells composing a tissue or organ.
hy·per·plas·tic (hī'pĕr-plas'tik), *adj.* of or characterized by hyperplasia.
hy·perp·ne·a, hy·perp·noe·a (hī'pĕrp-nē'ə), *n.* [*hyper-* + Gr. *pnoē*, breathing < *pnein*, to breathe], abnormally rapid breathing; panting.
hy·per·py·ret·ic (hī'pĕr-pi-ret'ik), *adj.* of or having hyperpyrexia.
hy·per·py·rex·i·a (hī'pĕr-pi-rek'si-ə), *n.* [Mod. L.; *hyper-* + *pyrexia*], an abnormally high fever.
hy·per·sen·si·tive (hī'pĕr-sen'sə-tiv), *adj.* abnormally or excessively sensitive.
hy·per·son·ic (hī'pĕr-son'ik), *adj.* designating, of, or traveling at a speed equal to about five times the speed of sound or greater: see **sonic.**
hy·per·sthene (hī'pĕr-sthēn'), *n.* [< *hyper-* + Gr. *sthenos*, strength], a lustrous, greenish-black or dark-brown mineral of the pyroxene group, a silicate of iron and magnesium.
hy·per·sthen·ic (hī'pĕr-sthen'ik), *adj.* of or containing hypersthene.
hy·per·ten·sion (hī'pĕr-ten'shən), *n.* 1. any abnormally high tension. 2. abnormally high blood pressure, especially in the arteries, or a diseased condition of which this is the chief symptom.
hy·per·ten·sive (hī'pĕr-ten'siv), *adj.* of or having high blood pressure. *n.* a hypertensive person.
hy·per·thy·roid (hī'pĕr-thī'roid), *adj.* of, characterized by, or having hyperthyroidism. *n.* a person having hyperthyroidism.
hy·per·thy·roid·ism (hī'pĕr-thī'roid-iz'm), *n.* 1. excessive activity of the thyroid gland. 2. the condition caused by this or by taking too much thyroid extract, characterized by a rapid pulse, sleeplessness, etc.
hy·per·ton·ic (hī'pĕr-ton'ik), *adj.* 1. having abnormally high tension or tone, especially of the muscles 2. having an osmotic pressure higher than that of an isotonic solution.
hy·per·troph·ic (hī'pĕr-trof'ik), *adj.* of or characterized by hypertrophy.
hy·per·tro·phy (hī-pũr'trə-fi), *n.* [*hyper-* + *-trophy*], an abnormal increase in the size of an organ or tissue, caused by enlargement of its cellular components. *v.i. & v.t.* [HYPERTROPHIED (-fid), HYPERTROPHYING], to increase abnormally in size.
hyp·es·the·si·a (hip'es-thē'zhə, hip'es-thē'zhi-ə), *n.* [Mod. L.; see HYP- & ESTHESIA], impaired power of sensation; especially, diminished sensitivity to touch.
hy·pe·thral (hi-pē'thrəl, hī-pē'thrəl), *adj.* hypaethral.
hy·pha (hī'fə), *n.* [*pl.* HYPHAE (-fē)], [Mod. L. < Gr. *hyphē*, a web], any of the threadlike parts making up the mycelium of a fungus.
hy·phen (hī'f'n), *n.* [LL.; Gr. *hyphen* (for *hyph' hen*), a hyphen, lit., under one, together, in one < *hypo-*, under + *hen*, neut. acc. of *heis*, one], a mark (-) used between the parts of a compound word or the syllables of a divided word, as at the end of a line. *v.t.* to hyphenate.
hy·phen·ate (hī'f'n-āt'), *v.t.* [HYPHENATED (-id), HYPHENATING], 1. to connect or separate by a hyphen. 2. to write or print with a hyphen. *adj.* hyphenated.
hy·phen·a·tion (hī'f'n-ā'shən), *n.* 1. a hyphenating or being hyphenated. 2. a hyphen.
hyp·no- (hip'nō, hip'nə), [< Gr. *hypnos*, sleep], a combining form meaning: 1. *sleep*, as in *hypnology*. 2. *hypnotism*, as in *hypnotherapy*. Also, before a vowel, **hypn-.**
hyp·no·gen·e·sis (hip'nō-jen'ə-sis), *n.* [Mod. L.; see HYPNO- & GENESIS], the inducing of hypnosis.
hyp·noid (hip'noid), *adj.* resembling hypnosis.
hyp·noi·dal (hip-noi'd'l), *adj.* hypnoid.
hyp·nol·o·gy (hip-nol'ə-ji), *n.* [*hypno-* + *-logy*], the science dealing with sleep and hypnotism.
Hyp·nos (hip'nos), *n.* [Mod. L.; Gr. *Hypnos* < *hypnos*, sleep; IE. **sup-no-s*, seen also in L. *somnus*, sleep], in *Greek mythology*, the god of sleep; identified by the Romans with Somnus: also **Hypnus.**
hyp·no·sis (hip-nō'sis), *n.* [*pl.* HYPNOSES (-sēz)], [Mod. L. < Gr. *hypnos* (see HYPNOS); + *-osis*], a sleeplike condition psychically induced, usually by another person, in which the subject loses consciousness but responds, with certain limitations, to the suggestions of the hypnotist.
hyp·no·ther·a·py (hip'nō-ther'ə-pi), *n.* [*hypno-* + *therapy*], the treatment of disease by hypnotism.
hyp·not·ic (hip-not'ik), *adj.* [Fr. or L.; Fr. *hypnotique;* L. *hypnoticus;* Gr. *hypnōtikos*, tending to sleep < *hypnos;* see HYPNOS], 1. causing sleep; soporific. 2. of, having the nature of, or inducing hypnosis. 3. easily hypnotized. 4. under the influence of hypnosis. *n.* 1. any drug causing sleep; soporific. 2. a hypnotized person or one easily hypnotized.
hyp·not·i·cal·ly (hip-not'i-k'l-i, hip-not'ik-li), *adv.* 1. in a hypnotic manner. 2. by hypnotism.
hyp·no·tism (hip'nə-tiz'm), *n.* 1. the act or practice of inducing hypnosis. 2. the science of hypnosis.
hyp·no·tist (hip'nə-tist), *n.* a person who induces hypnosis.
hyp·no·tiz·a·ble (hip'nə-tīz'ə-b'l), *adj.* that can be hypnotized.
hyp·no·tize (hip'nə-tīz'), *v.t.* [HYPNOTIZED (-tīzd'), HYPNOTIZING], 1. to put into a state of hypnosis. 2. [Colloq.], to entrance, as by eloquent speech.
Hyp·nus (hip'nəs), *n.* Hypnos.
hy·po (hī'pō), *n.* [*pl.* HYPOS (-pōz)], 1. (Colloq.], a hypodermic. 2. [Slang], a hypochondriac.
hy·po (hī'pō), *n.* [contr. < *hyposulfite*], sodium thiosulfate, $Na_2S_2O_3 \cdot 5H_2O$, a colorless, crystalline salt used in solution as a fixing agent in photography.
hy·po- (hī'pō, hip'ə), [Gr. *hypo-* < *hypo*, under, less than], a prefix meaning: 1. *under, beneath, below*, as in *hypodermic, hypocycloid*. 2. *less than, subordinated to*, as in *hypotaxis*. 3. in *chemistry, having a lower state of oxidation*, as in *hypophosphorous*. Also, before a vowel, **hyp-**. Opposed to *hyper-*.
hy·po·blast (hī'pə-blast', hip'ə-bläst'), *n.* [*hypo-* + *-blast*], the inner or lower layer of the blastoderm.
hy·po·caust (hip'ə-kôst', hī'pə-kôst'), *n.* [L. *hypocaustum;* Gr. *hypokauston* < *hypo-*, under + *kaiein*, to burn], a space below the floor in some ancient Roman buildings, into which hot air was piped from a furnace to warm the rooms.
hy·po·chlo·rite (hī'pə-klôr'īt, hī'pə-klō'rīt), *n.* any salt of hypochlorous acid.
hy·po·chlo·rous (hī'pə-klôr'əs, hī'pə-klō'rəs), *adj.* [*hypo-* + *chlorous*], designating or of an unstable acid, HClO, known only in solution and used as a bleaching and oxidizing agent.
hy·po·chon·dri·a (hī'pə-kon'dri-ə, hip'ə-kon'dri-ə), *n.* [LL., *pl.*, abdomen < pl. of Gr. *hypochondrion*, soft part of the body below the cartilage and above the navel < *hypo-*, under + *chondros*, cartilage: so called because the condition was supposed to have its seat in this region], abnormal anxiety over one's health, often with imaginary illnesses and severe melancholy.
hy·po·chon·dri·ac (hī'pə-kon'dri-ak', hip'ə-kon'dri-ak'), *adj.* [Fr. *hypocondriaque;* ML. *hypochondriacus* < LL. *hypochondria*], 1. designating or of the region of the hypochondrium. 2. of or having hypochondria. *n.* a person who has hypochondria.
hy·po·chon·dri·a·cal (hī'pə-kən-drī'ə-k'l, hip'ə-kən-drī'ə-k'l), *adj.* hypochondriac.
hy·po·chon·dri·a·sis (hī'pə-kən-drī'ə-sis, hip'ə-kən-drī'ə-sis), *n.* hypochondria.
hy·po·chon·dri·um (hī'pə-kon'dri-əm, hip'ə-kon'dri-əm), *n.* [*pl.* HYPOCHONDRIA (-ə)], [Mod. L.; see HYPOCHONDRIA], either side of the abdomen just below the lowest rib.
hyp·o·co·ris·tic (hip'ə-kô-ris'tik, hī'pə-kō-ris'tik), *adj.* [< Gr. *hypokoristikos* < *hypo-*, under + *korizesthai*, to pet], of, or having the nature of, a pet name, as a diminutive or term of endearment.
hy·po·cot·yl (hī'pə-kot''l, hip'ə-kot''l), *n.* [< *hypo-* + *cotyledon*], the part of the axis, or stem, below the cotyledons in the embryo of a plant.
hy·poc·ri·sy (hi-pok'rə-si), *n.* [*pl.* HYPOCRISIES (-siz)], [ME. & OFr. *ipocrisie* < L. *hypocrisis*, mimicry (in LL., hypocrisy); Gr. *hypokrisis*, a reply, acting a part, feigning < *hypokrinesthai*, to play a part, pretend; *hypo-*, under + *krinesthai*, to contend, dispute], a pretending to be what one is not, or to feel what one does not feel; especially, a pretense of virtue, etc.
hyp·o·crite (hip'ə-krit), *n.* [ME. & OFr. *ipocrite;* L. *hypocrita*, actor (in LL., hypocrite); Gr. *hypokritēs*, one who plays a part, pretender < *hypokrinesthai;* see HYPOCRISY], a person who pretends to be what he is not; one who pretends to be better than he really is, or pious, virtuous, etc. without really being so.
hyp·o·crit·i·cal (hip'ə-krit'i-k'l), *adj.* of or characterized by hypocrisy; like a hypocrite; not sincere.
hy·po·cy·cloid (hī'pə-sī'kloid, hip'ə-sī'kloid), *n.* [*hypo-* + *cycloid*], in *geometry*, the curve traced by a point on the circumference of a circle that rolls around the inner circumference of another circle.

hy·po·der·ma (hī'pə-dũr'mə), *n.* [Mod. L.; see HYPO- & DERMA], 1. in *botany*, a layer of strengthening tissue under the epidermis. 2. in *zoology*, the hypodermis.

hy·po·der·mal (hī'pə-dũr'm'l), *adj.* 1. of the hypoderma or hypodermis. 2. lying under the epidermis.

hy·po·der·mic (hī'pə-dũr'mik), *adj.* [< *hypoderma* + *-ic*], 1. of the parts under the skin. 2. injected under the skin. 3. of the hypodermis. *n.* 1. a hypodermic injection. 2. a hypodermic syringe or needle.

hy·po·der·mi·cal·ly (hī'pə-dũr'mi-k'l-i, hī'pə-dũr'mik-li), *adv.* (by injection) under the skin.

hypodermic injection, the injection of a medicine or drug under the skin.

hypodermic syringe, a glass syringe attached to a hollow needle (*hypodermic needle*), used for giving hypodermic injections.

hy·po·der·mis (hī'pə-dũr'mis), *n.* [Mod. L.; see HYPO- & DERMIS], a layer of cells that lies beneath, and secretes, the cuticle of annelids, arthropods, etc.

hy·po·eu·tec·tic (hī'pō-yoo-tek'tik, hip'ō-yoo-tek'tik), *adj.* containing less of the secondary component than is present in the eutectic mixture of the same components.

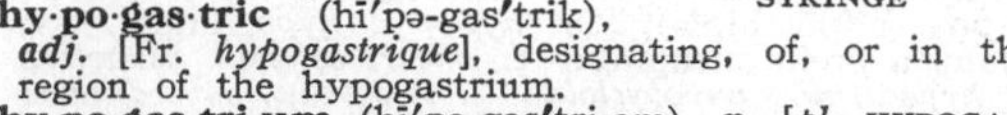

HYPODERMIC SYRINGE

hy·po·gae·ous (hī'pə-jē'əs, hip'ə-jē'əs), *adj.* hypogeous.

hy·po·gas·tric (hī'pə-gas'trik), *adj.* [Fr. *hypogastrique*], designating, of, or in the region of the hypogastrium.

hy·po·gas·tri·um (hī'pə-gas'tri-əm), *n.* [*pl.* HYPOGASTRIA (-ə)], [Mod. L.; Gr. *hypogastrion*, lower belly, neut. of *hypogastrios*, abdominal < *hypo-*, under + *gastēr*, the belly], the lower, middle part of the abdomen.

hy·po·ge·al (hī'pə-jē'əl, hip'ə-jē'əl), *adj.* [< LL. *hypogeus*, *hypogaeus* (Gr. *hypogaios*, under the earth, underground < *hypo-*, under + *gē*, *gaia*, earth); + *-al*], 1. of, or occurring in, the region below the surface of the earth. 2. hypogeous.

hyp·o·gene (hip'ə-jēn', hī'pə-jēn'), *adj.* [< *hypo-* + Gr. *-genēs* (see -GEN)], originating or formed below the surface of the earth, as certain rocks.

hy·pog·e·nous (hī-poj'i-nəs, hi-poj'i-nəs), *adj.* [*hypo-* + *-genous*], growing on the lower surface of something, as spores on the underside of some fern leaves.

hy·po·ge·ous (hī'pə-jē'əs, hip'ə-jē'əs), *adj.* [< L. *hypogeus*; see HYPOGEAL], growing or maturing underground, as peanuts, truffles, some insect larvae, etc.: also spelled **hypogaeous.**

hy·po·glos·sal (hī'pə-glos''l, hip'ə-glos''l), *adj.* [< *hypo-* + Gr. *glōssa*, tongue; + *-al*], under the tongue; especially, designating or of the motor nerves of the tongue. *n.* a hypoglossal nerve.

hy·po·gly·ce·mi·a (hī'pō-glī-sē'mi-ə), *n.* [Mod. L.; see HYPO- & GLYCEMIA], a deficiency of sugar in the blood.

hy·pog·na·thous (hī-pog'nə-thəs, hi-pog'nə-thəs), *adj.* [*hypo-* + *-gnathous*], having a protruding lower jaw.

hy·pog·y·nous (hī-poj'ə-nəs, hi-poj'ə-nəs), *adj.* [*hypo-* + *-gynous*], 1. growing attached to the receptacle, below and free from the pistil: said of the parts of some flowers. 2. having the parts so arranged: as, *hypogynous* flowers.

hy·pog·y·ny (hī-poj'ə-ni, hi-poj'ə-ni), *n.* the state of being hypogynous.

hy·po·nas·ty (hī'pə-nas'ti, hip'ə-nas'ti), *n.* [< *hypo-* + Gr. *nastos*, pressed; + *-y*], in *botany*, a state in which the more rapid growth of the undersurface of a part causes it to curve upward.

hy·po·ni·trous (hī'pə-nī'trəs), *adj.* [*hypo-* + *nitrous*], designating or of a nitrogenous dibasic acid, $H_2N_2O_2$, an active reducing and oxidizing agent.

hy·po·phos·phate (hī'pə-fos'fāt), *n.* a salt of hypophosphoric acid.

hy·po·phos·phite (hī'pə-fos'fīt), *n.* a salt of hypophosphorous acid.

hy·po·phos·phor·ic (hī'pō-fos-fôr'ik, hī'pō-fos-for'ik), *adj.* designating or of an acid, $H_4P_2O_6$, obtained when phosphorus is slowly oxidized in moist air.

hy·po·phos·pho·rous (hī'pə-fos'fẽr-əs), *adj.* designating or of a monobasic acid of phosphorus, H_3PO_2: it is a strong reducing agent.

hy·poph·y·sis (hī-pof'ə-sis), *n.* [*pl.* HYPOPHYSES (-sēz')], [Mod. L.; Gr. *hypophysis*, undergrowth, process < *hypophyein*; *hypo-*, under + *phyein*, to cause to grow], the pituitary gland.

hy·po·pi·tu·i·ta·rism (hī'pō-pi-tōō'i-tə-riz'm, hī'pō-pi-tū'i-tə-riz'm), *n.* 1. deficient activity of the pituitary gland. 2. the condition caused by this, characterized by excessive fat, loss of the sexual urge, wasting away of the external sex organs, and loss of hair.

hy·po·pla·si·a (hī'pə-plā'zhi-ə), *n.* [Mod. L. < *hypo-* + *-plasia*], a condition of decreased or arrested growth of an organ or tissue of the body.

hy·po·plas·tic (hī'pə-plas'tik), *adj.* of or characterized by hypoplasia.

hy·po·po·di·um (hī'pə-pō'di-əm), *n.* [*pl.* HYPOPODIA (-ə)], [Mod. L.; see HYPO- & -PODIUM], the base of a leaf, including the stalk.

hy·po·py·on (hī-pō'pi-on', hi-pō'pi-on'), *n.* [Mod. L.; Gr. *hypopyon*, kind of ulcer, neut. sing. of *hypopyos*, tending to suppurate < *hypo-*, under + *pyon*, pus], an accumulation of pus in the cavity between the cornea and the lens of the eye.

hy·pos·ta·sis (hī-pos'tə-sis, hi-pos'tə-sis), *n.* [*pl.* HYPOSTASES (-sēz')], [Gr. *hypostasis*, a supporting, foundation < *hyphistanai*, to set under, pass, stand under < *hypo-*, under + *histanai*, to stand, cause to stand], 1. in *medicine*, *a*) a deposit; sediment. *b*) a settling of blood in the lower parts of the body as a result of a slowing down of the blood flow. 2. in *philosophy*, the underlying principle or nature; essence; substance. 3. in *theology*, *a*) originally, the unique essence or nature of the Godhead and, therefore, of the three persons of the Trinity. *b*) any of the three persons of the Trinity. *c*) the personality of Christ as distinguished from his two natures, human and divine.

hy·po·stat·ic (hī'pə-stat'ik, hip'ə-stat'ik), *adj.* [Gr. *hypostatikos*], 1. having to do with substance or essence; essential; elemental. 2. *a*) having to do with distinct personality; distinctly personal. *b*) having to do with divine personality. 3. masked or suppressed by another factor that is not an allelomorph: said of certain factors in heredity. 4. in *medicine*, due to hypostasis, or deposition.

hy·pos·ta·ti·za·tion (hī-pos'tə-ti-zā'shən, hī-pos'tə-tī-zā'shən), *n.* 1. a hypostatizing or being hypostatized. 2. something hypostatized.

hy·pos·ta·tize (hī-pos'tə-tīz', hi-pos'tə-tīz'), *v.t.* [HYPOSTATIZED (-tīzd'), HYPOSTATIZING], [< *hypostasis* + *-ize*], 1. to make into or consider as a distinct substance; attribute substantial or personal existence to. 2. to regard as a reality; assume to be actual.

hyp·o·style (hip'ō-stīl', hī'pə-stīl'), *adj.* [Gr. *hypostylos*, resting on pillars; *hypo-*, under + *stylos*, a pillar], having a roof supported by rows of pillars or columns.

hy·po·sul·fite (hī'pə-sul'fīt), *n.* 1. a salt of hyposulfurous acid. 2. sodium hyposulfite, $Na_2S_2O_4$. 3. formerly, and still popularly but incorrectly, sodium thiosulfate, $Na_2S_2O_3$, used as a fixing agent in photography: also called *hypo.*

hy·po·sul·fu·rous (hī'pə-sul-fyoor'əs, hī'pə-sul'fẽr-əs), *adj.* designating or of a dibasic acid, $H_2S_2O_4$, produced by the reduction of sulfurous acid and used as a bleaching and reducing agent.

hy·po·tax·is (hī'pə-tak'sis, hip'ə-tak'sis), *n.* [Mod. L. < Gr.; see HYPO- & -TAXIS], in *grammar*, the dependent relation of a clause or construction on another: opposed to *parataxis*.

hy·pot·e·nuse (hī-pot''n-ōōs', hi-pot''n-ūs'), *n.* [L. *hypotenusa*; Gr. *hypoteinousa*, lit., subtending, properly fem. of ppr. of *hypoteinein*, to subtend, stretch under; *hypo-*, under + *teinein*, to stretch], the side of a right-angled triangle opposite the right angle: also **hypothenuse:** abbreviated **hyp.**

HYPOTENUSE

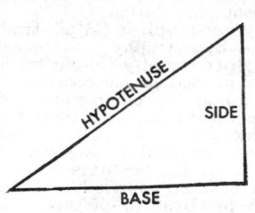

hypoth., 1. hypothesis. 2. hypothetical.

hy·poth·ec (hī-poth'ik), *n.* [< Fr. & L.; Fr. *hypothèque*; L. *hypotheca*, a pledge, security; Gr. *hypothēkē*, something put under (obligation), pledge < *hypotithenai*, to put under, pledge; see HYPOTHESIS], in *law*, security or right given to a creditor over a debtor's property without transfer of possession or title.

hy·poth·e·car·y (hī-poth'ə-ker'i, hi-poth'ə-ker'i), *adj.* [LL. *hypothecarius*], of or secured by a hypothec.

hy·poth·e·cate (hī-poth'ə-kāt', hi-poth'ə-kāt'), *v.t.* [HYPOTHECATED (-id), HYPOTHECATING], [< ML. *hypothecatus*, pp. of *hypothecare*, to hypothecate < L. *hypotheca*; see HYPOTHEC], to pledge (property) to another as security without transferring possession or title; mortgage.

hy·poth·e·ca·tion (hī-poth'ə-kā'shən, hi-poth'ə-kā'shən), *n.* 1. a hypothecating or being hypothecated. 2. a claim against hypothecated property.

hy·poth·e·ca·tor (hī-poth'ə-kā'tẽr, hi-poth'ə-kā'tẽr), *n.* a person who hypothecates.

hy·poth·e·nuse (hī-poth''n-ōōs', hi-poth''n-ūs'), *n.* a hypotenuse.

hy·po·ther·mal (hī'pə-thũr'm'l, hip'ə-thũr'm'l), *adj.* 1. tepid. 2. of or characterized by hypothermia.

hy·po·ther·mi·a (hī'pə-thũr'mi-ə, hip'ə-thũr'mi-ə), *n.* [Mod. L. < *hypo-* + Gr. *thermē*, heat], a subnormal body temperature.

hy·poth·e·sis (hī-poth'ə-sis, hi-poth'ə-sis), *n.* [*pl.* HYPOTHESES (-sēz')], [Mod. L.; Gr. *hypothesis*, groundwork, foundation, supposition < *hypotithenai*, to place under; *hypo-*, under + *tithenai*, to place], an unproved theory, proposition, supposition, etc. tentatively accepted to explain certain facts or (*working hypothesis*) to provide a basis for further investigation, argument,

etc.: abbreviated **hypoth., hyp.** —*SYN.* see **theory.**
hy·poth·e·size (hī-poth'ə-sīz', hi-poth'ə-sīz'), *v.i.* [HYPOTHESIZED (-sīzd'), HYPOTHESIZING], to make a hypothesis. *v.t.* to assume; suppose.
hy·po·thet·ic (hī'pə-thet'ik), *adj.* hypothetical.
hy·po·thet·i·cal (hī'pə-thet'i-k'l), *adj.* [Gr. *hypothetikos* < *hypothesis*], 1. based on, involving, or having the nature of, a hypothesis; assumed; supposed. 2. given to the use of hypotheses: as, a *hypothetical* mind. 3. in *logic*, conditional: as, a *hypothetical* proposition. Abbreviated **hypoth., hyp.**
hy·po·thet·i·cal·ly (hī'pə-thet'i-k'l-i, hī'pə-thet'ik-li), *adv.* in a hypothetical manner; as (a) hypothesis.
hy·po·thy·roid (hī'pō-thī'roid), *adj.* of or characterized by hypothyroidism. *n.* a hypothyroid person.
hy·po·thy·roid·ism (hī'pō-thī'roid-iz'm), *n.* 1. deficient activity of the thyroid gland. 2. the abnormal condition caused by this, often characterized by sluggishness, goiter, etc.
hy·po·ton·ic (hī'pə-ton'ik), *adj.* 1. having abnormally low tension or tone, especially of the muscles. 2. having an osmotic pressure lower than that of an isotonic solution. See **hypertonic.**
hy·po·xan·thine (hī'pə-zan'thēn, hī'pə-zan'thin), *n.* a nitrogenous compound, $C_5H_4N_4O$, found with xanthine in the muscles, spleen, etc.
hyp·so- (hip'sō, hip'sə), [< Gr. *hypsi*, on high], a combining form meaning *height*, as in *hypsometer.*
hyp·sog·ra·phy (hip-sog'rə-fi), *n.* [*hypso-* + *-graphy*], 1. the configuration of a land surface with respect to its different heights; topographic relief. 2. the observation, representation, or description of this. 3. the parts of a map that show this. 4. hypsometry.
hyp·som·e·ter (hip-som'ə-tẽr), *n.* [*hypso-* + *-meter*], a device for measuring heights of land surfaces by the boiling point of a liquid.
hyp·som·e·try (hip-som'ə-tri), *n.* [*hypso-* + *-metry*], the measurement of heights on the surface of the earth, especially with reference to sea level.
hy·ra·coid (hī'rə-koid'), *n.* [< Mod. L. *Hyracoidea*, name of the genus; see HYRAX & -OID], any of a group of small hoofed mammals of Africa and southwest Asia, resembling the rodents. *adj.* of this group.
hy·rax (hī'raks), *n.* [*pl.* HYRAXES (-rak-siz), HYRACES (-rə-sēz')], [Mod. L.; Gr. *hyrax*, shrew mouse], a hyracoid; rock rabbit: the cony of the Bible.
Hyr·ca·ni·a (hẽr-kā'ni-ə), *n.* an ancient district of Asia, on the southern shores of the Caspian.
Hyr·ca·ni·an (hẽr-kā'ni-ən), *adj.* of Hyrcania.
hy·son (hī's'n), *n.* [Chin. *hsi-tchun*, lit., blooming spring, first crop], a variety of Chinese green tea: the early crop is called *young hyson*, and the inferior leaves are called *hyson skin.*
hys·sop (his'əp), *n.* [ME. & AS. *ysope*, OFr. *ysope*, *hyssope*; L. *hysopum*, *hyssopum*; Gr. *hyssōpos*, *hyssōpon* < Heb. *ēzōb*, aromatic plant], 1. a fragrant, blue-flowered plant of the mint family, used in medicine as a tonic, stimulant, etc. 2. its flowers. 3. any of several American thistle plants. 4. in the *Bible*, a plant whose twigs were used for sprinkling water in certain ancient Jewish religious rites: Psalms 51:7.
hys·ter- (his'tẽr), hystero-.
hys·ter·ec·to·my (his'tẽr-ek'tə-mi), *n.* [*pl.* HYSTERECTOMIES (-miz)], [*hyster-* + *-ectomy*], surgical removal of the uterus or part of the uterus.
hys·ter·e·sis (his'tə-rē'sis), *n.* [Mod. L.; Gr. *hysterēsis*, a coming short, deficiency < *hysterein*, to be behind, come short < *hysteros*, later, behind], in *physics*, a lag of the effect in a body when the force acting on it is changed; especially, a lag in the changes of magnetization behind the varying magnetizing force.
hys·ter·et·ic (his'tə-ret'ik), *adj.* of, characterized by, or caused by hysteresis.
hysteretic constant, the hysteretic loss in ergs per cubic centimeter per cycle.
hysteretic loss, a loss of power in operating electrical devices, caused by magnetic hysteresis.
hys·te·ri·a (his-têr'i-ə, his-ter'i-ə), *n.* [Mod. L. < *hysterical*], 1. a psychiatric condition variously characterized by emotional excitability, excessive anxiety, sensory and motor disturbances, and the simulation of organic disorders, such as blindness, deafness, etc. 2. any outbreak of wild, uncontrolled excitement or feeling, such as fits of laughing and crying; hysterics. —*SYN.* see **mania.**
hys·ter·ic (his-ter'ik), *adj.* hysterical. *n.* 1. *usually pl.* [occas. construed as sing.], a hysterical fit; hysteria (sense 2). 2. a person subject to hysteria.
hys·ter·i·cal (his-ter'i-k'l), *adj.* [L. *hystericus*; Gr. *hysterikos*, of or suffering in the uterus, hysterical < *hystera*, uterus; + *-al*: because women seemed to be hysterical more than men, hysteria was attributed by the ancients to disturbances of the uterus], 1. of or characteristic of hysteria. 2. like or suggestive of hysteria; emotionally uncontrolled and wild. 3. having or subject to hysteria.
hys·ter·o- (his'tẽr-ō, hist'ẽr-ə), [< Gr. *hystera*, uterus, womb; see HYSTERICAL], a combining form meaning: 1. *uterus, womb*, as in *hysterotomy*. 2. *hysteria*, *hysteria and*, as in *hysterocatalepsy*. Also, before a vowel, **hyster-.**
hys·ter·o·cat·a·lep·sy (his'tẽr-ə-kat'ə-lep'si), *n.* hysteria with catalepsy.
hys·ter·o·gen·ic (his'tẽr-ə-jen'ik), *adj.* [*hystero-* + *-genic*], causing hysteria.
hys·ter·oid (his'tẽr-oid'), *adj.* [*hyster-* + *-oid*], like hysteria.
hys·ter·on pro·te·ron (his'tẽr-on' prot'ẽr-on'), [LL.; Gr. *hysteron*, neut. of *hysteros*, latter, following + *proteron*, neut. of *proteros*, former], 1. a figure of speech in which the logical order of ideas is reversed. Example: "I die, I faint, I fail." 2. in *logic*, the fallacy of assuming as true, and using as an argument, what is to be proved; begging the question.
hys·ter·ot·o·my (his'tə-rot'ə-mi), *n.* [*hystero-* + *-tomy*], 1. a Caesarean operation. 2. an incision of the uterus.
hys·tri·co·mor·phic (his'tri-kə-môr'fik), *adj.* [< Mod. L. *Hystricomorpha*, name of the division (< L. *hystrix*, porcupine; Gr. *hystrix* + *morphē*, form); + *-ic*], designating or of a group of rodents including the porcupines, chinchillas, cavies, agoutis, etc.

I

I, i (ī), *n.* [*pl.* I's, i's, Is, is (īz)], 1. the ninth letter of the English alphabet: via Latin from the Greek *iota*, a modification of the Phoenician (Semitic *yodh*, a hand): see **alphabet**, chart. This letter, first dotted in the 11th century, was not distinguished from *j* until the 17th century. 2. a sound of I or i: in most European languages the letter primarily represents a high front unrounded vowel, IPA [i]; in English, because of sound changes during the Late Middle English and Early Modern periods, it represents both a lowered high front unrounded vowel, IPA [ɪ], and a diphthong, typically IPA [aɪ]. 3. a type or impression for I or i. 4. *a symbol for* the ninth in a sequence or group. *adj.* 1. of I or i. 2. ninth in a sequence or group.
I (ī), *n.* 1. an object shaped like I. 2. a Roman numeral for 1: when it is placed after another numeral, a unit is to be added (e.g., VI = V + I, or 6), and when it is placed before another numeral, a unit is to be subtracted (e.g., IV = 4). 3. in *astronomy*, the inclination of an orbit to the ecliptic. 4. in *chemistry*, *the symbol for* iodine. 5. in *education*, a mark of *incomplete*, given in a course not completed by the student. 6. in *logic*, a particular affirmative proposition. 7. in *physics*, *the symbol for a*) density of current. *b*) intensity of magnetization. *c*) the moment of inertia. 8. in *zoology*, *the symbol for* incisor. *adj.* shaped like I.
I (ī), *pron.* [for *pl.* see WE], [ME. *i*, *ich*, *ih*; AS. *ic*; akin to G. *ich*, Goth. *ik*, etc.; IE. base *eĝ(h)om-, orig. prob. neut. n. meaning "(my) presence here," seen also in L. *ego*, Gr. *egō*, Sans. *ahám*, etc.; cf. EGO], the person speaking or writing: *I* is the nominative case form, *me* the objective, *my* and *mine* the possessive, and *myself* the intensive and reflexive, of the first personal singular pronoun. *n.* [*pl.* I's], 1. this pronoun thought of as a

word: as, he uses too many "*I*'s" in writing. 2. the ego.
i-, (i), [Archaic], y-.
I., 1. Idaho. 2. Independent. 3. Iowa.
i., 1. incisor. 2. interest. 3. intransitive.
I., i., 1. imperator. 2. island; islands. 3. isle; isles.
-i·a (i-ə, yə), [for 1, 2, (sometimes) 4, 7, 8, L. *-ia* & Gr. *-ia* < *-i-*, thematic vowel + *-a*, noun suffix of 1st declension; for 3, (sometimes) 4, 5, 6, L. *-ia* & Gr. *-ia*, neut. pl. ending of L. nouns in *-ium* & Gr. nouns in *-ion; -i-*, thematic vowel + *-a*, suffix], a noun-forming suffix used in: 1. the names of countries, as in *India*. 2. the names of diseases, as in *pneumonia*. 3. the names of classic festivals, as in *Lupercalia*. 4. Greek and Latin words carried over into English, as in *militia*. 5. English plurals of Greek and Latin words, as in *paraphernalia*. 6. in *biology*, the names of classes, as in *Reptilia*. 7. in *botany*, the generic names of plants, as in *zinnia*. 8. in *chemistry*, the names of alkaloids, as in *strychnia:* see **-ine**.
Ia., Iowa.
i.a., *in absentia*, [L.], in absence; absent.
I·a·go (i-ä'gō), *n.* the villain in Shakespeare's *Othello:* see **Othello**.
-i·al (yəl, i-əl), [L. *-ialis, -iale*], an adjective-forming suffix, as in *magisterial, artificial*.
I.A.M., International Association of Machinists: a labor union.
i·amb (ī'amb), *n.* [Fr. *iambe;* L. *iambus;* Gr. *iambos*], a metrical foot of two syllables, the first unaccented and the other accented, as in English verse, or the first short and the other long, as in Greek and Latin verse. Example: "Tŏ strívе, | tŏ séek, | tŏ fínd, | ănd nót | tŏ yíeld."
i·am·bic (ī-am'bik), *adj.* [< Fr. or L.; Fr. *iambique;* L. *iambicus;* Gr. *iambikos*], of or made up of iambs. *n.* 1. an iamb. 2. an iambic verse. 3. a piece of satirical verse written in iambs.
i·am·bus (ī-am'bəs), *n.* [*pl.* IAMBUSES (-iz), IAMBI (-bī)], [L.], an iamb.
-i·an (i-ən, yən), [Fr. or L.; Fr. *-ien;* L. *-ianus* < *-i-* stem ending + *-anus;* see -AN], -an, as in *Grecian, Hamiltonian, reptilian*, etc.
-i·an·a (i-an'ə), -ana.
iar·o·vize (yär'ə-vīz'), *v.t.* [IAROVIZED (-vīzd'), IAROVIZING], to jarovize.
Ia·si (yäsh), *n.* Jassy: the Romanian name.
-i·a·sis (ī'ə-sis), [Mod. L.; Gr. *-iasis*], a combining form meaning: 1. *process* or *condition*. 2. *pathological* or *morbid condition*, as in *hypochondriasis, elephantiasis*.
i·at·ric (ī-at'rik), *adj.* [Gr. *iatrikos* < *iatros*, physician < *iasthai*, to cure, heal], of medicine or medical doctors; medical; medicinal.
i·at·ri·cal (ī-at'ri-k'l), *adj.* iatric.
-i·at·rics (i-at'riks), [see IATRIC], a combining form meaning *treatment of disease*, as in *pediatrics*.
i·a·tro- (ī-at'rō, ī-at'rə), [Gr. *iatro-* < *iatros;* see IATRIC], a combining form meaning *medical, medicinal*, as in *iatrology*.
i·a·trol·o·gy (ī'ə-trol'ə-ji), *n.* [*iatro-* + *-logy*], the science of medicine.
-i·a·try (ī'ə-tri), [< Gr. *iatreia*, healing], a combining form meaning *medical treatment*, as in *psychiatry*.
ib., *ibidem*, [L.], in the same place.
I·ba·dan (ē-bä'dän), *n.* a city in southwestern Nigeria, Africa: pop., 327,000 (1945).
Ibáñez, see **Blasco-Ibáñez**.
I-beam (ī'bēm'), *n.* a steel beam shaped like an **I** in cross section.
I·be·ri·a (ī-bêr'i-ə), *n.* 1. the Spanish-Portuguese peninsula: the ancient Latin name. 2. an ancient region in the Caucasus, between the Black Sea and the Caspian.
I·be·ri·an (ī-bêr'i-ən), *adj.* of Iberia (either region), its people, etc. *n.* 1. any member of an ancient people in Caucasian Iberia, believed to be the ancestors of the Georgians. 2. a native or inhabitant of Iberia (sense 1). 3. the language spoken there in ancient times, from which Basque is believed to be derived.
i·bex (ī'beks), *n.* [*pl.* IBEXES (-bek-siz), IBICES (ib'ə-sēz', ī'bə-sēz'), IBEX; see PLURAL, II, D, 1], [L.], any of several varieties of wild goat of Europe, Asia, or Africa, especially that found in the Alps, Apennines, and Pyrenees: the male has large, backward-curved horns.
‡i·bi·dem (i-bī'dem), *adv.* [L.], in the same place: used in writing to show further reference to the book, chapter, etc. cited just before: abbreviated **ibid., ib.**
-i·bil·i·ty (ə-bil'ə-ti), [*pl.* -IBILITIES (-tiz)], [L. *-ibilitas; -i-*, thematic vowel + *-bilitas;* see -ABILITY], a suffix used to form nouns from adjectives ending in *-ible*, as in *sensibility*.
i·bis (ī'bis), *n.* [*pl.* IBISES (-iz), IBIS; see PLURAL, II, D, 1], [L.; Gr. *ibis*], any of several large wading birds related to the herons, with long legs and a long, slender, curved bill, found chiefly in tropical regions: the sacred ibis of the Nile is the most common.
-i·ble (i-b'l), [L. *-ibilis*], -able: used in forming adjectives derived directly from Latin verbs ending in *-ire* or *-ere*, as *divisible, legible*.
ib·n- (ib''n), [Ar., son (of)], a combining form used as the first element in many hyphenated Arabic names, as in *ibn-Saud*.
ibn-Sa·ud, Ab·dul-A·ziz (əb-dool'ä-zēz' ib''n-sä-ōōd'), 1880?–1953; king of Saudi Arabia (1932–1953).
I·bo (ē'bō), *n.* [< the native name], 1. [*pl.* IBO], a member of a Negroid people living in Nigeria, Africa. 2. the group of West Sudanic dialects spoken by the Ibo.
Ib·sen, Hen·rik (hen'rik ib's'n), 1828–1906; Norwegian dramatist and poet.
Ib·sen·ism (ib's'n-iz'm), *n.* the ideas, aims, and principles of playwriting, etc. characteristic of Ibsen and his followers.
I.B.T.C.W.H., International Brotherhood of Teamsters, Chauffeurs, Warehousemen, and Helpers of America.
-ic (ik), [< Fr. or L. or Gr.; Fr. *-ique;* L. *-icus;* Gr. *-ikos;* akin to G. *-isch*, AS. *-ig* (see -Y)], a suffix: 1. used to form adjectives meaning: *a*) *of, having to do with*, as in *volcanic, Germanic*. *b*) *like, having the nature of, characteristic of*, as in *angelic, classic*. *c*) *produced by, caused by*, as in *photographic, symphonic*. *d*) *made up of, consisting of, containing*, as in *dactylic, alcoholic*. *e*) in *chemistry, having a higher valence than is indicated by the suffix -ous*, as in *nitric, phosphoric*. 2. [< ME. or L. or Gr.; ME. *-ike;* L. *-icus;* Gr. *-ikos:* from substantive use of respective adjectives], used to form nouns, through the substantive use of adjectives in *-ic*, as in *magic, cosmetic*. Adverbs corresponding to adjectives in *-ic* are formed by adding *-ally* or, less often, *-ly*.
I.C., *Iesus Christus*, [L.], Jesus Christ.
I·ça (ē'sä), *n.* Putumayo River: the Brazilian name.
-i·cal (i-k'l), [LL. *-icalis* < *-icus, -ic* + *-alis, -al*], a suffix corresponding to *-ic*, used to form adjectives from nouns ending in *-ic*, as in *physical, polemical*, or from other adjectives ending in *-ic*, as in *poetical, comical:* such adjectives sometimes have special or differentiated meanings (e.g., *historical, economical*), further removed from the base than those of the corresponding *-ic* forms.
I·car·i·an (i-kâr'i-ən, ī-kâr'i-ən), *adj.* [L. *Icarius;* Gr. *Ikarios*, of Icarus], 1. of, like, or characteristic of Icarus; hence, 2. too daring; foolhardy; rash.
Icarian Sea, the southern part of the Aegean Sea: the ancient name.
Ic·a·rus (ik'ə-rəs, ī'kə-rəs), *n.* [L.; Gr. *Ikaros*], in *Greek legend*, the son of Daedalus: escaping from Crete by flying with wings made by Daedalus, Icarus flew so high that the sun's heat melted the wax by which his wings were fastened, and he fell to his death in the sea.
ICBM, intercontinental ballistic missile
I.C.C., ICC, Interstate Commerce Commission.
ice (īs), *n.* [ME. & AS. *is;* akin to G. *eis* (OHG. *īs*); prob. akin to Avestan *isu*, cold; hence < IE. base **eis-*], 1. the glassy, brittle, crystalline form of water made solid by cold; frozen water. 2. a piece, layer, or sheet of this. 3. anything like frozen water in appearance, structure, etc. 4. a frozen dessert, usually made of water, fruit juice, egg white, and sugar. 5. icing; frosting. 6. [Slang], a diamond or diamonds. *v.t.* [ICED (īst), ICING], 1. to change into ice; freeze. 2. to cover with ice; apply ice to. 3. to cool by putting ice on, in, or around. 4. to cover (cake, etc.) with icing, or frosting. *v.i.* to freeze (often with *up* or *over*).
break the ice, 1. to make a start by getting over initial difficulties. 2. to make a start toward getting better acquainted and less formal, as by talking to someone just met.
cut no ice, [Colloq.], to have no influence or effect.
on thin ice, [Colloq.], in a risky, unsafe situation.
-ice (is), [ME. *-ice, -ise, -is;* OFr. *-ice;* L. *-itius*, masc., *-itia*, fem., *-itium*, neut.], a suffix meaning *the condition, state*, or *quality of*, as in *justice, malice*.
Ice., 1. Iceland. 2. Icelandic.
ice age, the glacial epoch.
ice bag, an ice pack (sense 2).
ice·berg (īs'bŭrg'), *n.* [prob. < D. *ijsberg*, lit., ice mountain], a great mass of ice broken off from a glacier and floating in the sea.
ice·blink (īs'blink'), *n.* [*ice* + *blink*, after D. *ijsblink* or Dan. *isblink*], a luminosity in the sky near the horizon, caused by the reflection of light from an expanse of ice.
ice·boat (īs'bōt'), *n.* 1. originally, a light skiff mounted on runners and propelled over ice by sails. 2. now, a light, boatlike frame, often triangular, equipped with runners resembling the blades of skates and propelled by a sail. 3. an icebreaker.
ice·bound (īs'bound'), *adj.* 1. held fast or surrounded by ice, as a boat. 2. blocked up or made inaccessible by ice, as a coast.
ice·box (īs'boks'), *n.* a refrigerator, especially one in which ice is used for cooling foods, beverages, etc.
ice·break·er (īs'brāk'ēr), *n.* 1. a sturdy boat for breaking a channel through ice. 2. a wedgelike structure for protecting a pier, etc. from floating ice.
ice·cap (īs'kap'), *n.* a large, permanent ice sheet with a raised center, especially one covering the top of a mountain, plateau, etc.
ice-cream (īs'krēm', īs'krēm'), *adj.* made of or with ice cream. *n.* ice cream.
ice cream, [orig., *iced cream*], a food consisting of cream,

butterfat, or milk, and sometimes eggs, sweetened, flavored, beaten to a uniform consistency, and frozen.
ice-cream cone, a cone-shaped wafer holding a scoop of ice cream.
iced (īst), *adj.* 1. having ice on, in, or around it; cooled by ice: as, *iced* coffee. 2. covered with icing; frosted.
iced fruits, preserved fruits coated with sugar.
ice field (or **floe**), a large sheet of ice floating in the sea.
ice foot, [*ice* + *foot*, after Dan. *isfod*], a wall of ice along a shore in polar regions, formed between the high and low watermarks by the tide.
ice-free (īs′frē′), *adj.* 1. without ice; not frozen. 2. always without ice; never frozen: as, an *ice-free* harbor.
ice hockey, the game of hockey played on ice by players wearing skates.
ice·house (īs′hous′), *n.* 1. a building where ice is stored. 2. a place where artificial ice is made.
Ice·land (īs′lənd), *n.* an island republic in the North Atlantic, between Norway and Greenland: area, 39,758 sq. mi.; pop., 174,000; capital Reykjavik: abbreviated **Ice., Icel.**
Ice·land·er (īs′lan′dẽr, īs′lən-dẽr), *n.* a native or inhabitant of Iceland.
Ice·lan·dic (īs-lan′dik), *adj.* of Iceland, its people, their language, or culture. *n.* 1. the North Germanic language of the Icelanders, considered the most conservative of Germanic languages. 2. loosely, Old Icelandic, the language of the Icelandic sagas. Abbreviated **Ice., Icel.** See also **Norse.**
Iceland moss, an arctic lichen, sometimes used as a food and in medicine.
Iceland spar, a transparent, colorless calcite, found especially in Iceland: it is used by opticians for making double-refracting prisms.
ice·man (īs′man′, īs′mən), *n.* [*pl.* ICEMEN (-men′, -mən)], a person who sells or delivers ice.
ice needle, in *meteorology*, a thin piece of ice, so light that it floats in the air in clear, cold weather.
I·ce·ni (ī-sē′nī), *n.pl.* [L.], an ancient British people who, led by their queen Boadicea, rebelled against the Romans in 61 A.D.
ice pack, 1. a large, floating expanse of broken ice masses pressed and frozen together. 2. a bag holding ice, applied to a part of the body to reduce swelling, ease pain, etc.
ice pick, a pointed metal tool used to break up pieces of ice.
ice plant, a plant growing in Mediterranean regions, South Africa, and southern California, having leaves covered with sparkling particles like ice crystals.
ice rain, 1. rain that forms a glaze of ice. 2. sleet.
ice sheet, a thick layer of ice covering an extensive area for a long period, as in the ice age.
ice water, 1. melted ice. 2. water cooled with or as with ice.
Ich·a·bod (ik′ə-bod′), [Heb. *ī-khābhōdh*, lit., according to pop. etym., no glory; real meaning unknown], a masculine name.
I·chang (ē′chäŋ′), *n.* a city on the Yangtze River, Hupeh province, China: pop., 110,000.
‡ich dien (iH′dēn′), [G.], I serve: motto on the coat of arms of the Prince of Wales.
ich·neu·mon (ik-nū′mən, ik-nōō′mən), *n.* [L.; Gr. *ichneumōn*, ichneumon, lit., tracker < *ichneuein*, to track out, hunt after < *ichnos*, a track, footstep: from its supposed practice of locating and destroying crocodile eggs], 1. a small, weasellike animal of India and Africa; mongoose. 2. the ichneumon fly.
ichneumon fly, any of a large group of wasplike but stingless insects having wormlike larvae that live as parasites in or on the larvae of other insects.
ich·no- (ik′nō), [< Gr. *ichnos*, footprint], a combining form meaning *track, footprint, trace*, as in *ichnology*.
ich·nog·ra·phy (ik-nog′rə-fi), *n.* [< Fr. or L.; Fr. *ichnographie;* L. *ichnographia;* Gr. *ichnographia*, a tracing out, ground plan; see ICHNO- & -GRAPHY], 1. a scale drawing of the ground plan of a building; floor plan. 2. the art of drawing such plans.
ich·no·log·i·cal (ik′nə-loj′i-k′l), *adj.* of ichnology.
ich·nol·o·gy (ik-nol′ə-ji), *n.* [*ichno-* + *-logy*], the scientific study of fossil footprints.
i·chor (ī′kôr, ī′kẽr), *n.* [Mod. L.; Gr. *ichōr*], 1. in *Greek mythology*, the ethereal fluid flowing instead of blood in the veins of the gods. 2. a thin, acrid, watery discharge from a wound or ulcer.
i·chor·ous (ī′kẽr-əs), *adj.* of, or having the nature of, ichor.
ich·thy- (ik′thi), ichthyo-.
ich·thy·ic (ik′thi-ik), *adj.* [< Gr. *ichthys*, a fish; + *-ic*], of or characteristic of a fish or fishes.
ich·thy·o- (ik′thi-ō, ik′thi-ə), [Gr. *ichthyo-* < *ichthys*, a fish], a combining form meaning *fish* or *like a fish*, as in *ichthyology*: also, before a vowel, **ichthy-.**
ich·thy·og·ra·phy (ik′thi-og′rə-fi), *n.* [*ichthyo-* + *-graphy*], a treatise on fishes.
ich·thy·oid (ik′thi-oid′), *adj.* [Gr. *ichthyoeidēs* < *ichthys*, a fish + *-eidēs*, form], like a fish. *n.* formerly, a fishlike vertebrate.
ich·thy·o·lite (ik′thi-ə-līt′), *n.* [*ichthyo-* + *-lite*], a fossil of a fish or of part of a fish.
ich·thy·o·log·ic (ik′thi-ə-loj′ik), *adj.* ichthyological.
ich·thy·o·log·i·cal (ik′thi-ə-loj′i-k′l), *adj.* of ichthyology.
ich·thy·ol·o·gist (ik′thi-ol′ə-jist), *n.* an expert or specialist in ichthyology.
ich·thy·ol·o·gy (ik′thi-ol′ə-ji), *n.* [*ichthyo-* + *-logy*], 1. the branch of zoology dealing with fishes, their structure, classification, and life history: abbreviated **ichth., ich.** 2. [*pl.* ICHTHYOLOGIES (-jiz)], a treatise on fishes.
ich·thy·oph·a·gous (ik′thi-of′ə-gəs), *adj.* [Gr. *ichthyophagos;* see ICHTHYO- & -PHAGOUS], living on fish; fish-eating.
ich·thy·or·nis (ik′thi-ôr′nis), *n.* [Mod. L.; *ichthy-* + Gr. *ornis*, bird], any of a group of prehistoric birds, now extinct, which had well-developed teeth set in sockets.
ich·thy·o·saur (ik′thi-ə-sôr′), *n.* [Mod. L. < *ichthyo-* + Gr. *sauros*, lizard], any of a group of prehistoric marine reptiles, now extinct, which had a fishlike body, four paddle-shaped flippers, and a dolphinlike head.
ich·thy·o·sau·rus (ik′thi-ə-sôr′əs), *n.* [*pl.* ICHTHYOSAURI (-ī)], an ichthyosaur.
ich·thy·o·sis (ik′thi-ō′sis), *n.* [Mod. L.; see ICHTHY- & -OSIS], a skin disease characterized by roughening and thickening of the horny layer of the skin, producing dryness and scaling: also called *fishskin disease, xeroderma.*
ich·thy·ot·ic (ik′thi-ot′ik), *adj.* of, like, or having ichthyosis.
-i·cian (ish′ən), [Fr. *-icien;* see -IC & -IAN], a suffix used to form nouns meaning *a person engaged in, practicing, or specializing in* (a specified field), as in *beautician.*
i·ci·cle (ī′si-k′l), *n.* [ME. *isikel;* AS. *isgicel* (akin to ON. *isjökull*) < *is*, ice + *gicel*, piece of ice, icicle (Brit. dial. *ickle*); akin to ON. *jökull*, icicle, glacier, *jaki*, lump of ice], a tapering, pointed, hanging piece of ice, formed by the freezing of dripping or falling water.
i·ci·cled (ī′si-k′ld), *adj.* covered with icicles.
i·ci·ly (ī′sə-li), *adv.* in an icy manner; very coldly.
i·ci·ness (ī′si-nis), *n.* the quality or state of being icy.
ic·ing (īs′iŋ), *n.* a mixture of sugar, water or other liquid, flavoring, and, sometimes, whites of eggs, etc., for covering a cake; frosting.
‡i·ci on parle fran·çais (ē′sē′ ōn′ pârl′ frän′se′), [Fr.], French is spoken here.
Ick·es, Harold L. (ik′əs, ik′iz), 1874–1952; American lawyer, writer, and public official.
i·con (ī′kon), *n.* [*pl.* ICONS (-konz), ICONES (-kə-nēz′)], [L.; Gr. *eikōn*, an image, figure, likeness], 1. an image; figure; representation; picture. 2. in the *Orthodox Eastern Church*, a sacred image or picture of Jesus, Mary, a saint, etc. Also spelled **ikon, eikon.**
i·con·ic (ī-kon′ik), *adj.* [L. *iconicus;* Gr. *eikonikos* < *eikōn*, an image], 1. of, or having the nature of, an icon. 2. conventional; of a fixed style: said of some statues and busts.
i·con·i·cal (ī-kon′i-k′l), *adj.* iconic.
i·con·o- (ī-kon′ō, ī-kon′ə), [< Gr. *eikōn*, a figure, image], a combining form meaning *image, likeness, figure*, as in *iconoclast, iconolatry*: also, before a vowel, **icon-.**
i·con·o·clasm (ī-kon′ə-klaz′m), *n.* [< *icono-* + Gr. *klasma*, broken thing < *klaein*, to break], 1. the breaking of images; hence, 2. the attacking or ridiculing of traditional or venerated institutions or ideas.
i·con·o·clast (ī-kon′ə-klast′), *n.* [ML. *iconoclastes;* MGr. *eikonoklastēs* < Gr. *eikōn*, an image + *klaein*, to break]. 1. a member of a group in the Orthodox Eastern Church in the 8th and 9th centuries who denounced the use of icons. 2. a member of a group who engaged in or advocated the destruction of church images in the Netherlands in the 16th and 17th centuries. 3. a person who attacks or ridicules traditional or venerated institutions or ideas regarded by him as erroneous or based on superstition.
i·con·o·clas·tic (ī-kon′ə-klas′tik), *adj.* of or characteristic of iconoclasts or iconoclasm.
i·con·o·graph·ic (ī-kon′ə-graf′ik), *adj.* of iconography; showing by pictures, images, etc.
i·con·o·graph·i·cal (ī-kon′ə-graf′i-k′l), *adj.* iconographic.
i·co·nog·ra·phy (ī′kə-nog′rə-fi), *n.* [ML. *iconographia;* Gr. *eikonographia*, a sketch, description; see ICONO- & -GRAPHY], 1. the art of representing or illustrating by pictures, figures, images, etc. 2. the study or description of pictures, images, etc.; especially, the study of the portraits of a specific person.
i·co·nol·a·try (ī′kə-nol′ə-tri), *n.* [*icono-* + *-latry*], the worship of images.
i·co·nol·o·gy (ī′kə-nol′ə-ji), *n.* [*icono-* + *-logy*], 1. the study of icons, images, etc. 2. icons collectively. 3. symbolic representation; symbolism.

i·con·o·scope (ī-kon'ə-skōp'), *n.* [*icono-* + *-scope*], an electronic device in a television transmitter, consisting of a vacuum tube enclosing a photosensitive plate on which the image is projected and an electron gun that scans the image with a narrow focused beam: a trademark (**Iconoscope**).

i·con·o·stas (ī-kon'ə-stas'), *n.* an iconostasis.

i·con·o·sta·si·on (ī-kon'ə-stā'si-ən), *n.* an iconostasis.

i·co·nos·ta·sis (ī'kə-nos'tə-sis), *n.* [*pl.* ICONOSTASES (-sēz')], [Mod. L.; Mod. Gr. *eikonostasis* < Gr. *eikōn*, an image + *stasis*, a standing], in the *Orthodox Eastern Church*, a partition or screen, decorated with icons, separating the sanctuary from the rest of the church.

i·co·sa·he·dral (ī'kō-sə-hē'drəl), *adj.* of, or having the form of, an icosahedron.

i·co·sa·he·dron (ī'kō-sə-hē'drən), *n.* [*pl.* ICOSAHEDRA (-drə)], [Gr. *eikosaedron* < *eikosi*, twenty + *hedra*, a seat, base], a solid figure with twenty plane surfaces.

i·co·si- (ī'kō-si), [Gr. *eikosi-* < *eikosi*, twenty; IE. base **wi-kṃti*, twenty (**wi*, two + **kṃti*, ten), seen also in L. *viginti*, OIr. *fiche*], a combining form meaning *twenty*, as in *icositetrahedron:* also, before a vowel, **icos-**.

i·co·si·tet·ra·he·dron (ī'kō-si-tet'rə-hē'drən), *n.* [*icosi-* + *tetra-* + *-hedron*], a solid figure with twenty-four plane surfaces.

-ics (iks), [see -IC], a suffix used to form plural nouns meaning: 1. (a specified) *art* or *science*, as in *mathematics:* such nouns are construed as singular. 2. (specified) *activities, practice, system, properties*, as in *statistics:* such nouns are usually construed as plural.

I.C.S., International Correspondence School.

ic·ter·ic (ik-ter'ik), *adj.* [L. *ictericus;* Gr. *ikterikos* < *ikteros*, jaundice], 1. of jaundice. 2. having jaundice. 3. used in treating jaundice. *n.* a remedy for jaundice.

ic·ter·i·cal (ik-ter'i-k'l), *adj.* icteric.

ic·ter·us (ik'tẽr-əs), *n.* [Mod. L.; L.; Gr. *ikteros*, jaundice], 1. jaundice. 2. a plant disease in which the leaves become yellow.

Ic·ti·nus (ik-tī'nəs), *n.* Greek architect of the 5th century B.C.; designed the Parthenon.

ic·tus (ik'təs), *n.* [*pl.* ICTUSES (-iz), ICTUS], [L., a blow, stroke, metrical stress; pp. of *icere*, to strike, hit, beat], 1. rhythmical or metrical stress, or accent. 2. in *medicine*, a stroke, fit, or sudden attack.

i·cy (ī'si), *adj.* [ICIER (-si-ẽr), ICIEST (-si-ist)], [AS. *isig*], 1. having much ice; full of or covered with ice. 2. of ice. 3. like ice; specifically, *a)* slippery. *b)* very cold; frigid. 4. cold in manner or attitude; unfriendly; aloof.

id (id), *n.* [L., it; neut. sing. of *is*, he; used as transl. of G. *es*, it], in *psychoanalysis*, that part of the psyche which is regarded as the reservoir of the libido and the source of instinctive energy: it is dominated by the pleasure principle and impulsive wishing, and its impulses are controlled through the development of the ego and superego: distinguished from *ego, superego*.

-id (id), a suffix of various origins and meanings: 1. [< L. *-is*, pl. *-ides;* Gr. *-is*, pl. *-idēs*, patronymic suffix], used to form nouns meaning *a thing belonging to or connected with;* specifically, *a) a meteor that seems to radiate from a* (specified) *constellation*, as in *Leonid*. *b) an epic poem about* (a specified subject), as in *Aeneid*. *c)* [< Fr. or Mod. L.; Fr. *-ide;* Mod. L. *-idae* (see -IDAE)], *an animal belonging to a* (specified) *group*, as in *arachnid*. 2. [L. *-idus*], used in many words of Latin origin as *felid, tepid, fluid*. 3. [Fr. *-ide;* L. *-is, -idis;* Gr. *-is, -idos;* also directly < L. or Gr.], used in certain words of Greek origin, as *pyramid, orchid*. 4. in *chemistry*, *-ide*.

I'd (īd), 1. I had. 2. I would. 3. I should.

Id., Idaho.

id., *idem*, [L.], the same.

I.D., Intelligence Department.

I·da (ī'də), [ML.; OHG.; ? akin to ON. *Ithunn*, goddess of youth], a feminine name.

Ida., Idaho.

Ida, Mount, 1. a mountain in Asia Minor, near the site of ancient Troy: height, 5,750 ft. 2. Mount Psiloriti in Crete: the ancient name.

-i·dae (i-dē'), [Mod. L., pl. of L. *-ides;* Gr. *-idēs*, patronymic suffix], a suffix used in forming the scientific names of zoological families, as *Canidae* (the dog family).

I·da·ho (ī'də-hō'), *n.* a Northwestern State of the United States: area, 83,557 sq. mi.; pop., 667,000; capital, Boise: abbreviated **I., Ida., Id.**

I·da·ho·an (ī'də-hō'ən), *adj.* of Idaho. *n.* a native or inhabitant of Idaho.

-ide (īd, id), [< ox*ide*], a suffix added to part of the name of one of the elements in a binary compound, as in sodium *chloride*, hydrogen *sulfide*.

i·de·a (ī-dē'ə), *n.* [L.; Gr. *idea*, a form, look, or appearance of a thing as opposed to its reality; IE. **wids-wo* < base **wid-*, **weid-*, **woid-*, seen also in L. *videre*, to see, Gr. *idein*, to see, AS. *witan*, to know (cf. WIT)], 1. a thought; mental conception; mental image; notion. 2. an opinion or belief. 3. a plan; scheme; project; intention; aim; design. 4. a hazy perception; vague impression; fanciful notion; fancy; inkling. 5. in *philosophy*, according to Plato, a model or archetype of which all real things are but imperfect imitations and from which their existence derives: in modern philosophy, the term is used variously to mean absolute truth, the immediate object of thought, one of the ultimate principles apprehended by reason, etc.
SYN.—**idea**, the most general of these terms, may be applied to anything existing in the mind as an object of knowledge or thought; **concept** refers to a generalized idea of a class of objects, based on knowledge of particular instances of the class (his *concept* of a republic); **conception**, often equivalent to **concept**, specifically refers to something conceived in the mind, or imagined (my *conception* of how the role should be played); **thought** is used of any idea, whether or not expressed, that occurs to the mind in reasoning or contemplation (she rarely speaks her *thoughts*); **notion** implies vagueness or incomplete intention (I had a *notion* to go); **impression** also implies vagueness of an idea provoked by some external stimulus (I have the *impression* that she's unhappy).

i·de·al (ī-dē'əl; *also, for adj. 2 & 4, n. 1 & 2*, ī-dēl'), *adj.* [Fr. *idéal;* LL. *idealis*, existing in idea, ideal < L. *idea*, an idea], 1. existing as an idea, model, or archetype; consisting of ideas (sense 5). 2. thought of as perfect or as a perfect model; exactly as one would desire; of a perfect kind. 3. of, or having the nature of, an idea or conception; identifying or illustrating an idea or conception; conceptual. 4. existing only in the mind as an image, fancy, or concept; visionary; imaginary: distinguished from *real, material*. 5. in *philosophy*, of idealism; idealistic. *n.* 1. a conception of something in its most excellent or perfect form. 2. a person or thing regarded as fulfilling this conception; perfect model. 3. something that exists only in the mind.

i·de·al·ism (ī-dē'əl-iz'm), *n.* [< Fr. *idéalisme* or G. *idealismus*], 1. behavior or thought based on a conception of things as they should be or as one would wish them to be; idealization. 2. a striving to achieve one's ideals. 3. in *art & literature*, imaginative treatment that seeks to show the artist's or author's conception of perfection; representation of imagined types, or ideals: opposed to *realism*. 4. in *philosophy*, any of various theories which hold that the objects of perception are actually ideas of the perceiving mind and that it is impossible to know whether reality exists apart from the mind: opposed to *materialism*.

i·de·al·ist (ī-dē'əl-ist), *n.* 1. a person whose behavior or thought is based on ideals: often used contemptuously to mean an impractical visionary or dreamer. 2. an adherent or practitioner of idealism in art, literature, or philosophy. *adj.* idealistic.

i·de·al·is·tic (ī'dē-ə-lis'tik, ī-dē'ə-lis'tik), *adj.* 1. of or characteristic of an idealist. 2. of, characterized by, or based on idealism.

i·de·al·is·ti·cal (ī'dē-ə-lis'ti-k'l, ī-dē'ə-lis'ti-k'l), *adj.* idealistic.

i·de·al·i·ty (ī'di-al'ə-ti), *n.* [*pl.* IDEALITIES (-tiz)], 1. the state or quality of being ideal. 2. *usually in pl.* something that is only ideal and has no reality. 3. the ability to conceive ideals.

i·de·al·i·za·tion (ī-dē'əl-i-zā'shən, ī-dē'əl-i-zā'shən), *n.* 1. an idealizing or being idealized. 2. the result of idealizing.

i·de·al·ize (ī-dē'ə-līz'), *v.t.* [IDEALIZED (-līzd'), IDEALIZING], to make ideal; think of or represent as ideal; regard or show as perfect or more nearly perfect than is true. *v.i.* 1. to form an ideal or ideals. 2. to represent things in the manner of an idealist.

i·de·al·ly (ī-dē'əl-i), *adv.* 1. in accordance with an ideal or ideals; in an ideal manner; perfectly. 2. in theory.

i·de·ate (ī-dē'āt), *v.t. & v.i.* [IDEATED (-id), IDEATING], to form an idea (of); imagine or conceive. *n.* (ī-dē'it), in *philosophy*, the external object correlative with an idea.

i·de·a·tion (ī'di-ā'shən), *n.* the formation of ideas.

i·de·a·tion·al (ī'di-ā'shən-'l), *adj.* of ideation.

‡**i·dée fixe** (ē'dā'fēks'), [Fr.], a fixed idea; obsession.

‡**i·dem** (ī'dem), *pron. & adj.* [L.], the same; the same as that previously mentioned: abbreviated **id.**

i·den·tic (ī-den'tik), *adj.* identical; especially, having exactly the same wording, form, etc.: said of diplomatic messages or action by two or more governments.

i·den·ti·cal (ī-den'ti-k'l), *adj.* [ML. *identicus* < L. *identidem*, repeatedly < *idem*, the same; + *-al*], 1. the very same. 2. exactly alike or equal. —*SYN.* see **same**.

identical proposition, in *logic*, a proposition whose subject and predicate are identical in content and extent (e.g., that which is mortal is not immortal).

identical twins, a pair of twins who were developed from a single fertilized ovum: they are always of the same sex and show great similarity in physical appearance.

i·den·ti·fi·a·ble (ī-den'tə-fī'ə-b'l), *adj.* that can be identified.

i·den·ti·fi·ca·tion (ī-den'tə-fi-kā'shən), *n.* 1. an identifying or being identified. 2. anything by which a person or thing can be identified: as, he used his driver's license as *identification*. 3. in *psychoanalysis*, an emotional tie unconsciously causing a person to think, feel, and act as he imagines the person with whom he has the tie does.

i·den·ti·fi·er (ī-den'tə-fī'ẽr), *n.* a person or thing that identifies.

i·den·ti·fy (ī-den'tə-fī'), *v.t.* [IDENTIFIED (-fīd'), IDENTIFYING], [ML. **identificare;* see IDENTICAL & -FY], 1. to make identical; consider or treat as the same: as, *identify* your interests with ours. 2. to show to be a certain person or thing; fix the identity of; show to be the same as something or someone assumed, described, or claimed. 3. to join or associate closely: as, he has become *identified* with the labor movement. 4. in *psychoanalysis*, to make identification of (oneself) with someone else: often used absolutely.

i·den·ti·ty (ī-den'tə-ti), *n.* [*pl.* IDENTITIES (-tiz)], [Fr. *identité;* ML. *identitas* < *identicus;* see IDENTICAL], 1. the condition or fact of being the same in all qualities under consideration; sameness; oneness. 2. *a*) the condition or fact of being some specific person or thing; individuality. *b*) the condition of being the same as something or someone assumed, described, or claimed.

id·e·o- (id'i-ə, ī'di-ə), [< Fr. or Gr.; Fr. *ideo-* < Gr. *idea*], a combining form meaning *idea*, as in *ideogram.*

id·e·o·gram (id'i-ə-gram', ī'di-ə-gram'), *n.* [*ideo-* + *-gram*], 1. a graphic symbol representing an object or idea without expressing, as in a phonetic system, the sounds that form its name. 2. a symbol representing an idea rather than a word (e.g., 5, +, =, φ, ¢, ÷).

id·e·o·graph (id'i-ə-graf', ī'di-ə-gräf'), *n.* an ideogram.

id·e·o·graph·ic (id'i-ə-graf'ik, ī'di-ə-graf'ik), *adj.* of, or having the nature of, an ideogram or ideography.

id·e·og·ra·phy (id'i-og'rə-fi, ī'di-og'rə-fi), *n.* 1. the use of ideograms to express ideas; graphic representation without the use of names. 2. the study of ideograms.

id·e·o·log·ic (ī'di-ə-loj'ik, id'i-ə-loj'ik), *adj.* ideological.

id·e·o·log·i·cal (ī'di-ə-loj'i-k'l, id'i-ə-loj'i-k'l), *adj.* of or concerned with ideology.

id·e·ol·o·gist (ī'di-ol'ə-jist, id'i-ol'ə-jist), *n.* 1. a student of or expert in ideology. 2. a person occupied mainly with ideas; idle theorist or visionary. 3. an exponent of a specified ideology; theorist.

id·e·ol·o·gy (ī'di-ol'ə-ji, id'i-ol'ə-ji), *n.* [*pl.* IDEOLOGIES (-jiz)], [Fr. *idéologie;* see IDEO- & -LOGY], 1. the study of ideas, their nature and source. 2. the theory that all ideas arise from sensations. 3. thinking or theorizing of an idealistic, abstract, or impractical nature; fanciful speculation. 4. the doctrines, opinions, or way of thinking of an individual, class, etc.

id·e·o·mo·tor (id'i-ə-mō'tēr, ī'di-ə-mō'tēr), *adj.* [*ideo-* + *motor*], in *psychology*, designating or of an unconscious movement made in response to an idea.

ides (īdz), *n.pl.* [Fr.; L. *idus*], in the ancient Roman calendar, the fifteenth day of March, May, July, or October, or the thirteenth of the other months.

‡**id est** (id est), [L.], that is (to say): abbreviated **i.e.**

Idg., Indo-Germanic.

id·i·o- (id'i-ō, id'i-ə), [Gr. *idio-* < *idios*, one's own], a combining form meaning *one's own, personal, distinct,* as in *idiocrasy, idiograph.*

id·i·o·blast (id'i-ə-blast'), *n.* [*idio-* + *-blast*], in *biology*, any of the hypothetical units of which a cell is ultimately composed.

id·i·oc·ra·sy (id'i-ok'rə-si), *n.* [*pl.* IDIOCRASIES (-siz)], [Gr. *idiokrasia;* cf. IDIOSYNCRASY], an idiosyncrasy.

id·i·o·cy (id'i-ə-si), *n.* [*pl.* IDIOCIES (-siz)], [< *idiot* + *-cy* (as *prophecy* < *prophet*); but cf. Gr. *idiōteia*, uncouthness, lack of training], 1. the state of being an idiot. 2. behavior like that of an idiot; great foolishness or stupidity. 3. an idiotic act or remark.

id·i·o·e·lec·tric (id'i-ō-i-lek'trik), *adj.* [*idio-* + *electric*], that can be electrified by friction.

id·i·o·graph (id'i-ə-graf', id'i-ə-gräf'), *n.* [Gr. *idiographos*, written in one's own hand; see IDIO- & -GRAPH], a characteristic or distinguishing mark or signature; trademark.

id·i·om (id'i-əm), *n.* [< Fr. & LL.; Fr. *idiome;* LL. *idioma;* Gr. *idiōma*, peculiarity, peculiar phraseology, idiom < *idios*, one's own, private, peculiar], 1. the language or dialect of a people, region, class, etc. 2. the usual way in which the words of a language are joined together to express thought. 3. an accepted phrase, construction, or expression contrary to the usual patterns of the language or having a meaning different from the literal. 4. the style of expression characteristic of an individual: as, the *idiom* of Carlyle. 5. a characteristic style, as in art or music.

id·i·o·mat·ic (id'i-ə-mat'ik), *adj.* [Gr. *idiōmatikos*, peculiar, characteristic], 1. in accordance with the individual nature of a language; characteristic of a particular language. 2. using or having many idioms. 3. of, or having the nature of, an idiom or idioms.

id·i·o·mat·i·cal·ly (id'i-ə-mat'i-k'l-i, id'i-ə-mat'ik-li), *adv.* in an idiomatic manner.

id·i·o·mor·phic (id'i-ə-môr'fik), *adj.* [*idio-* + *-morphic*], 1. having its own proper form; having a form of its own. 2. in *mineralogy*, having its usual form: said of crystals.

id·i·o·path·ic (id'i-ə-path'ik), *adj.* of, or having the nature of, an idiopathy.

id·i·op·a·thy (id'i-op'ə-thi), *n.* [*pl.* IDIOPATHIES (-thiz)], [Gr. *idiopatheia*, feeling for oneself alone; see IDIO- & -PATHY], a disease not following or caused by another disease; spontaneous or primary disease.

id·i·o·phone (id'i-ə-fōn'), *n.* [*idio-* + *-phone*], any of a class of musical instruments that consist of some elastic material, as wood or metal, capable in itself of producing sound, as the triangle, chimes, or celesta.

id·i·o·syn·cra·sy (id'i-ə-siŋ'krə-si, id'i-ə-sin'krə-si), *n.* [*pl.* IDIOSYNCRASIES (-siz)], [Gr. *idiosynkrasia* < *idio-*, one's own, peculiar + *synkrasis*, a mixing together, tempering < *synkerannynai*, to mix together; *syn-*, together + *kerannynai*, to mix], 1. the temperament or mental constitution peculiar to a person or group. 2. any personal peculiarity, mannerism, etc.

***SYN.*—idiosyncrasy** refers to any personal mannerism or peculiarity and connotes strong individuality (the *idiosyncrasies* of a writer's style); **eccentricity** implies considerable deviation from what is normal or customary and connotes whimsicality or even mental aberration (his *eccentricity* of wearing overshoes in the summer).

id·i·o·syn·crat·ic (id'i-ō-sin-krat'ik), *adj.* of, characterized by, or resulting from idiosyncrasy.

id·i·o·syn·crat·i·cal·ly (id'i-ō-sin-krat'i-k'l-i, id'i-ō-sin-krat'ik-li), *adv.* in an idiosyncratic manner.

id·i·ot (id'i-ət), *n.* [ME. *idiote;* OFr. *idiot;* L. *idiota*, ignorant and common person; Gr. *idiōtēs*, one without professional knowledge, ignorant and common person < *idios*, one's own, peculiar], 1. a mentally deficient person with an intelligence quotient of less than 25; person mentally equal or inferior to a child two years old: *idiot* is the lowest classification of mental deficiency, below *imbecile* and *moron.* 2. loosely, a very foolish or stupid person.

id·i·ot·ic (id'i-ot'ik), *adj.* [L. *idioticus*, uneducated, ignorant; Gr. *idiōtikos*, private, peculiar, rude], of, having the nature of, or characteristic of an idiot; very foolish or stupid.

id·i·ot·i·cal·ly (id'i-ot'i-k'l-i, id'i-ot'ik-li), *adv.* in an idiotic manner.

id·i·ot·ism (id'i-ət-iz'm), *n.* [Fr. *idiotisme* (cf. -ISM); in sense 3 < LL. *idiotismus*, popular way of speaking < Gr. *idiōtismos*, popular manners], 1. [Rare], idiocy. 2. idiotic action or behavior. 3. [Obs.], idiom.

i·dle (ī'd'l), *adj.* [IDLER (ī'dlēr), IDLEST (ī'dlist)], [ME. & AS. *idel*, empty; akin to G. *eitel*, vain, empty; prob. IE. base **ai-dh*, to burn, shine; basic sense, either "only apparent, seeming" or "burnt out"], 1. *a*) having no value, use, or significance; worthless; useless; hence, *b*) ineffective; vain; futile; pointless: as, an *idle* wish. 2. baseless; unfounded: as, *idle* rumors. 3. *a*) unemployed; not busy: as, *idle* men. *b*) inactive; not used: as, *idle* machines. *c*) not filled with activity: as, *idle* hours. 4. not inclined to work; lazy. *v.i.* [IDLED (ī'd'ld), IDLING], [< the *adj.;* parallel with AS. *idlian*, to come to nothing, be useless], 1. to move slowly or aimlessly; loaf; hence, 2. to spend time unprofitably; be unemployed or inactive. 3. to operate slowly without transmitting power: said of machinery, as, the windmill *idled* in the breeze. *v.t.* 1. to waste; squander (usually with *away*): as, he *idled* away his youth. 2. to cause (a motor, etc.) to idle. —***SYN.*** see **inactive, loiter, vain.**

i·dle·ness (ī'd'l-nis), *n.* the quality or state of being idle.

idle pulley, a pulley riding loosely on a shaft, pressing against a belt to guide it or take up the slack.

i·dler (ī'dlēr), *n.* 1. a person who wastes time and does no work; lazy person. 2. in *mechanics*, an idle wheel or idle pulley.

idle wheel, a gear wheel placed between two others to transfer motion from one to the other without changing their direction or speed.

IDLE WHEEL

IDLE WHEEL

i·dly (ī'dli), *adv.* [ME. *idelliche;* AS. *idellice*], in an idle manner; specifically, *a*) lazily. *b*) uselessly; ineffectively.

I·do (ē'dō), *n.* [an Esperanto affix used as a complete word, meaning "offspring"], an artificial, international auxiliary language, a modified form of Esperanto.

i·do·crase (ī'dō-krās', id'ō-krās'), *n.* [Fr. < Gr. *eidos*, form + *krasis*, mixture], vesuvianite.

i·dol (ī'd'l), *n.* [ME. & OFr. *idole;* L. *idolum*, an image, form, specter, apparition; Gr. *eidōlon*, an image, phantom < *eidos*, form], 1. an image of a god, used as an object or instrument of worship: sometimes said of any heathen deity. 2. any object of ardent or excessive devotion or admiration. 3. [Obs.], *a*) an image; effigy. *b*) anything that has no substance but can be seen, as a shadow or an image in a mirror. 4. in *logic*, a fallacy.

i·dol·a·ter (ī-dol′ə-tẽr), *n.* [ME. & OFr. *idolatre;* LL. *idololatres;* Gr. *eidōlolatrēs* < *eidōlon,* an image, idol + *latris,* one hired to serve, servant < *latron,* pay, hire], 1. a person who worships an idol or idols. 2. a devoted admirer; adorer.

i·dol·a·tress (ī-dol′ə-tris), *n.* a woman who is an idolater.

i·dol·a·trize (ī-dol′ə-trīz′), *v.t.* [IDOLATRIZED (-trīzd′), IDOLATRIZING], to make an idol of; idolize. *v.i.* to worship idols.

i·dol·a·trous (ī-dol′ə-trəs), *adj.* 1. of, or having the nature of, idolatry. 2. worshiping an idol or idols. 3. having or showing excessive admiration or devotion.

i·dol·a·try (ī-dol′ə-tri), *n.* [*pl.* IDOLATRIES (-triz)], [ME. & OFr. *idolatrie;* LL. *idolatria;* Gr. *eidōlolatreia* < *eidōlon,* idol + *latreia,* service], 1. worship of idols. 2. excessive devotion to or reverence for some person or thing.

i·dol·ism (ī′d'l-iz'm), *n.* 1. idolatry. 2. a fallacious notion; false reasoning.

i·dol·ist (ī′d'l-ist), *n.* an idolater.

i·dol·i·za·tion (ī′d'l-i-zā′shən, ī′d'l-ī-zā′shən), *n.* an idolizing or being idolized.

i·dol·ize (ī′d'l-īz′), *v.t.* [IDOLIZED (-īzd′), IDOLIZING], 1. to make an idol of. 2. to love or admire excessively; adore. *v.i.* to worship idols.

I·dom·e·neus (ī-dom′ə-nūs′, ī-dom′ə-nōōs′), *n.* in *Greek legend,* a king of Crete who led his subjects against Troy in the Trojan War.

Id·u·mae·a, Id·u·me·a (id′yoo-mē′ə, ī′dyoo-mē′ə), *n.* Edom, an ancient kingdom: the Greek name.

I·dun (ē′doon), *n.* Ithunn.

i·dyl, i·dyll (ī′d'l), *n.* [L. *idyllium;* Gr. *eidyllion,* dim. of *eidos,* a form, figure, image], 1. a short poem or prose work describing a simple, pleasant scene of rural, pastoral, or domestic life: the literary tradition of the term goes back to Theocritus, who described pastoral life in Sicily for sophisticated readers of Alexandria. 2. a scene or incident suitable for such a work. 3. an extended narrative poem: as, "The *Idylls* of the King." 4. in *music,* a simple, pastoral composition.

i·dyl·ist, i·dyll·ist (ī′d'l-ist), *n.* a writer or composer of idyls.

i·dyl·lic (ī-dil′ik), *adj.* 1. of, or having the nature of, an idyl; hence, 2. pleasing and simple; pastoral or picturesque.

i·dyl·li·cal·ly (ī-dil′i-k'l-i, ī-dil′ik-li), *adv.* in an idyllic manner.

-ie (i), [earlier form of *-y;* revitalized in back-formation *movie*], a suffix meaning *small, little,* as in *lassie, doggie:* often used to express affection.

IE., I.E., Indo-European.

i.e., *id est,* [L.], that is.

Ie·per·en (ē′pẽr-ən), *n.* Ypres, Belgium: Flemish name.

-ier (êr, ẽr, i-ẽr), [< various sources: *1.* ME. & OFr.; L. *-arius.* *2.* Fr. < OFr. as in *1,* with the primary stress in Eng. on the suffix. *3.* ME. var. of *-er.* *4.* ME. < *-i-* ending of prec. stem + *-er*], a suffix used to form nouns meaning *a person concerned with* (a specified action or thing), as in *bombardier, collier, glazier.*

if (if), *conj.* [ME.: AS. *gif;* akin to G. *ob* (OHG. *oba, ibu,* Goth. *ibai*); ult. source doubtful], 1. *expressing a condition, supposition, or hypothesis:* on condition that; in case that; supposing that: as, *if* I come, I'll see him; *if* I were you, I wouldn't do that. 2. *expressing concession:* although; allowing that; granting that: as, *if* it was wrong, it was at least meant well. 3. *introducing an indirect question:* whether: as, he asked *if* the train had arrived. 4. *introducing an exclamation expressing a) a wish:* as, *if* I had only known! *b) surprise, annoyance,* etc.: as, well, *if* he didn't do it anyway! *n.* 1. the word *if;* hence, 2. a supposition; condition.
as if, as the situation would be if; as though.

I.F.L.W.U., International Fur and Leather Workers' Union: a labor union.

If·ni (ēf′ni), *n.* a Spanish colony on the northwestern coast of Africa: area, 965 sq. mi.; pop., 20,000.

I.F.S., Irish Free State.

I.G., 1. Indo-Germanic: also **I.-G.** 2. Inspector General.

Ig·dra·sil, Ig·dra·syl, Igg·dra·sil (ig′drə-sil′), *n.* in *Norse mythology,* Yggdrasill, the tree of the universe.

ig·loo (ig′lōō), *n.* [*pl.* IGLOOS (-lōōz)], [Esk. *igdlu,* snow house], an Eskimo house or hut, dome-shaped and usually built of blocks of packed snow: also spelled **iglu.**

IGLOO

ign., 1. ignition. 2. *ignotus,* [L.], unknown.

Ig·na·ti·us (ig-nā′shəs, ig-nā′shi-əs), [L.; Gr. *Ignatios;* ? akin to L. *ignis,* a fire, hence, lit., fiery], a masculine name.

Ignatius, Saint, 1. ?–107? A.D.; Christian martyr; bishop of Antioch: his day is February 1. 2. 799?–878 A.D.; patriarch of Constantinople (846–858 A.D.; 867–878 A.D.): called *Nicetas;* his day is October 23.

Ignatius (of) Loy·o·la, Saint (loi-ō′lə), (*Iñigo de Oñez y Loyola*), 1491–1556; Spanish founder of the Society of Jesus (the Jesuit Order): his day is July 31.

ig·ne·ous (ig′ni-əs), *adj.* [L. *igneus* < *ignis,* a fire], 1. of, containing, or having the nature of, fire; fiery. 2. produced by the action of fire; specifically, formed by volcanic action or great heat: as, *igneous* rock.

ig·nes·cent (ig-nes′'nt), *adj.* [L. *ignescens,* ppr. of *ignescere,* to take fire, burn < *ignis,* a fire], 1. bursting into flame. 2. giving off sparks when struck with steel. *n.* an ignescent substance.

‡**ig·nis fat·u·us** (ig′nis fach′ōō-əs), [*pl.* IGNES FATUI (ig′nēz fach′ōō-ī′)], [ML. or Mod. L. < L. *ignis,* a fire + *fatuus,* foolish], 1. a light seen at night moving over swamps or marshy places, believed to be caused by the combustion of gases arising from rotting organic matter: popularly called *will-o'-the-wisp, jack-o'-lantern.* 2. a deceptive hope, goal, or influence; delusion.

ig·nit·a·ble (ig-nī′tə-b'l), *adj.* that can be ignited.

ig·nite (ig-nīt′), *v.t.* [IGNITED (-id), IGNITING], [< L. *ignitus,* pp. of *ignire,* to set on fire < *ignis,* a fire], 1. to set fire to; cause to burn. 2. to heat to a great degree; make glow with heat. 3. to excite: as, his speech *ignited* the crowd. *v.i.* to catch on fire; start burning.

ig·nit·er (ig-nīt′ẽr), *n.* 1. a person or thing that ignites. 2. a device used to set off explosives, as a time exploder for igniting the powder of a torpedo.

ig·nit·i·ble (ig-nī′tə-b'l), *adj.* that can be ignited.

ig·ni·tion (ig-nish′ən), *n.* [Fr. < pp. of L. *ignire,* to set on fire], 1. a setting on fire or catching on fire. 2. the means by which a thing is ignited. 3. in an internal-combustion engine, *a)* the igniting of the explosive mixture in the cylinder. *b)* the device for doing this: abbreviated **ign.** 4. in *chemistry,* the heating of a compound or mixture to the point of complete combustion or complete chemical change.

ig·ni·tor (ig-nīt′ẽr), *n.* an igniter.

ig·ni·tron (ig-nī′trən, ig′ni-tron′), *n.* [*ignite* + *electron*], a type of mercury-arc rectifier tube having a mercury-pool cathode and a single graphite anode: when a current is passed through an igniter rod into the pool, the mercury vapor is ionized and an arc starts between the cathode and anode: it is used chiefly in high resistance welders.

ig·no·ble (ig-nō′b'l), *adj.* [Fr.; L. *ignobilis,* unknown, obscure < *in-,* not + *nobilis,* OL. *gnobilis,* known], 1. [Rare], not noble in birth or position; of low origin or humble condition. 2. not noble in character or quality; dishonorable; base; mean. —*SYN.* see **base.**

ig·no·bly (ig-nō′bli), *adv.* in an ignoble manner.

ig·no·min·i·ous (ig′nə-min′i-əs), *adj.* [Fr. *ignominieux;* L. *ignominiosus*], 1. characterized by or bringing on ignominy; shameful; dishonorable; disgraceful. 2. contemptible; despicable. 3. degrading; humiliating.

ig·no·min·y (ig′nə-min′i), *n.* [*pl.* IGNOMINIES (-iz)], [Fr. *ignominie;* L. *ignominia* < *in-,* without, not + *nomen,* name, renown], 1. loss of one's reputation; shame and dishonor; infamy. 2. disgraceful, shameful, or contemptible quality, behavior, or act. —*SYN.* see **disgrace.**

ig·no·ra·mus (ig′nə-rā′məs; *now often* ig′nə-ram′əs), *n.* [*pl.* IGNORAMUSES (-iz)], [L., lit., we take no notice; 1st pers. pl., pres. indic., of *ignorare,* to take no notice, be ignorant], 1. originally, the word written by a grand jury on a bill of indictment thrown out for lack of evidence. 2. an ignorant person.

ig·no·rance (ig′nẽr-əns), *n.* [ME.; OFr.; L. *ignorantia*], 1. the condition or quality of being ignorant; lack of knowledge, education, etc. 2. unawareness (*of*).

ig·no·rant (ig′nẽr-ənt), *adj.* [ME.; OFr.; L. *ignorans,* ppr. of *ignorare;* see IGNORE], 1. lacking knowledge, education, or experience; uneducated; inexperienced. 2. caused by or showing lack of knowledge, education, or experience. 3. uninformed (*in*) or unaware (*of*).
SYN.—**ignorant** implies a lack of knowledge, either generally (an *ignorant* man) or on some particular subject (*ignorant* of the reason for their quarrel); **illiterate** implies a failure to conform to some standard of knowledge, especially, an inability to read or write; **unlettered,** sometimes a milder term for **illiterate,** often implies unfamiliarity with fine literature (although a graduate engineer, he is relatively *unlettered*); **uneducated** and **untutored** imply a lack of formal or systematic education, as of that acquired in schools (his brilliant, though *uneducated,* mind); **unlearned** suggests a lack of learning, either generally or in some specific subject (*unlearned* in science).—*ANT.* educated, erudite, learned.

ig·nore (ig-nôr′, ig-nōr′), *v.t.* [IGNORED (-nôrd′, nōrd′), IGNORING], [Fr. *ignorer;* L. *ignorare,* to have no knowledge of, ignore < *in-,* not + base of *gnarus,* knowing; IE. base **ĝnā-,* **ĝnē-,* to know, seen also in Gr. *gnōrizein,* to make known, Eng. *know*], 1. to disregard deliberately; pay no attention to; refuse to consider. 2. in *law,* to reject (a bill of indictment) for lack of evidence. —*SYN.* see **neglect.**

I·go·rot (ig′ə-rōt′, ē′gə-rōt′), *n.* [*pl.* IGOROT, IGOROTS (-rōts′)], [Sp. *Igorrote,* prob. < *Igolot,* name used in certain older records; of Tagalog origin], 1. a member of any of the Malayan tribes of head-hunters living in Luzon, in the Philippines. 2. their Indonesian language.

I·graine (i-grān′), *n.* [cf. OFr. *Iguerne, Igerne;* ? < Celt.], in *Arthurian legend,* the mother of King Arthur.

i·gua·na (i-gwä′nə), ***n.*** [Sp. < native Haitian name], any of several large tropical American lizards, usually living in trees.

i·guan·o·don (i-gwan′ə-don′), ***n.*** [Mod. L. < *iguana* + Gr. *-odōn*, -toothed < *odōn*, *odontos*, a tooth], any of a group of very large two-footed lizards, now extinct.

I·guas·sú (ē′gwä-sōō′), ***n.*** a river in southern Brazil, flowing into the Paraná River: length, 380 mi.: Spanish name, *Iguazú*.

Iguassú Falls, a waterfall of the Iguassú River: height, 210 ft.

IGY, International Geophysical Year.

IH., I.H., Indo-Hittite.

i.h.p., I.H.P., indicated horse power.

ih·ram (i-räm′), ***n.*** [Ar. *iḥrām*, a prohibiting < *ḥarama*, to forbid], 1. a costume consisting of one piece of white cotton around the waist and another over the shoulder, worn by Moslem pilgrims to Mecca: while wearing it they are under certain restrictions and rules. 2. a pilgrim who has put on this costume. 3. the restrictions and rules that he must observe.

IHS, [< L. misreading of ΙΗΣ, for which the proper L. form would be IES], a contraction derived from the Greek word ΙΗ(ΣΟΥ)Σ, Jesus, used as a symbol or monogram.

I.H.S., 1. *Iesus Hominum Salvator*, Jesus, Savior of Men. 2. *In Hoc Signo* (*Vinces*), in this sign (thou shalt conquer). 3. *In Hoc* (*Cruce*) *Salus*, in this (cross) salvation.

Ijs·sel (ī′səl), ***n.*** a river in the Netherlands, flowing into the Zuider Zee: length, 70 mi.: Dutch spelling, *IJssel*.

Ijs·sel·meer (ī′səl-mâr′), ***n.*** the Zuider Zee, an arm of the North Sea, in the Netherlands: Dutch spelling, *IJsselmeer*: also called *Ijssel Lake*.

Ikh·na·ton (ik-nä′tən), ***n.*** see **Amenhotep IV.**

i·kon (ī′kon), ***n.*** an icon.

il- (il), 1. in- (not). 2. in- (in). Used before *l*.

-il (il), -ile.

i·lang-i·lang (ē′läŋ-ē′läŋ), ***n.*** [Tagalog], 1. an East Indian tree with fragrant, greenish-yellow flowers. 2. the oil obtained from these flowers, used in perfumes. Also spelled **ylang-ylang.**

‡Il Du·ce (ēl dōō′che), see **duce.**

-ile (il), [< Fr. or L.; Fr. *-il*, *-ile*; L. *-ilis*], a suffix meaning *of, having to do with, that can be, like, suitable for*, as in *docile, missile*: sometimes also **-il**, as in *civil, fossil*.

il·e·ac (il′i-ak′), ***adj.*** of the ileum.

il·e·ac (il′i-ak′), ***adj.*** of an ileus.

Île de France (ēl′ də fräns′), a former province in northern France, surrounding Paris.

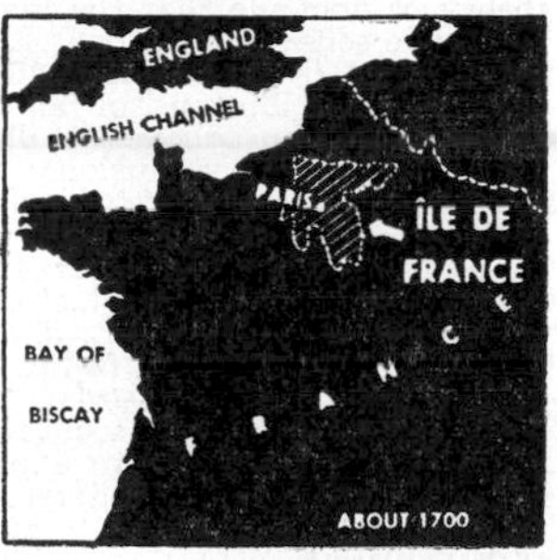

ÎLE DE FRANCE

Île du Dia·ble (ēl′ dü′ dyȧ′bl′), Devil's Island, one of the Safety Islands: the French name.

il·e·i·tis (il′i-ī′tis), ***n.*** inflammation of the ileum.

il·e·o- (il′i-ō, il′i-ə), a combining form meaning: 1. *of the ileum*, as in *ileostomy*. 2. *ileac and*. Also, before a vowel, **ile-**.

il·e·os·to·my (il′i-os′tə-mi), ***n.*** the surgical operation of making an opening in the ileum.

il·e·um (il′i-əm), ***n.*** [L. *ile, ilium, ileum*, usually in pl. *ilia*, the flank, groin; form *ileum* by association with *ileus*; see next entry], the lowest part of the small intestine, opening into the large intestine.

il·e·us (il′i-əs), ***n.*** [Mod. L.; L. *ileus, ileos*; Gr. *eileos*, colic < *eilein*, to twist, turn, roll], an abnormal condition caused by obstruction of the intestines, resulting in severe constipation and pain.

i·lex (ī′leks), ***n.*** [*pl.* ILEXES (ī′lek-siz)], [L., holm oak], 1. the evergreen oak; holm oak. 2. any tree or shrub of the holly family.

Il·ford (il′fẽrd), ***n.*** a city in Essex, England, near London: pop., 180,000 (est. 1946).

I.L.G.W.U., ILGWU, International Ladies' Garment Workers Union: an AFL-CIO labor union.

il·i·ac (il′i-ak′), ***adj.*** [Fr. *iliaque*, in form < LL. *iliacus*, relating to colic < L. *ileus* (see ILEUS), but with meaning as if < L. *ileum*], 1. of or near the ilium. 2. [Obs.], of the ileum; ileac.

Il·i·ad (il′i-əd), ***n.*** [L. *Ilias, Ilidis*; Gr. *Ilias, Iliados* (*poiēsis*) < *Ilios, Ilion*, Ilium, Troy < *Ilos*, Ilus, legendary founder of Troy], a long Greek epic poem, in twenty-four books, about the siege of Troy by the Greeks in the Trojan War: it is ascribed to Homer.

il·i·o- (il′i-ō, il′i-ə), a combining form meaning: 1. *of the ilium*. 2. *iliac and*, as in *iliosacral*.

Il·i·on (il′i-ən), ***n.*** [Gr.; see ILIAD], [Obs.], ancient Troy.

il·i·o·sa·cral (il′i-ō-sā′krəl), ***adj.*** of the ilium and the sacrum.

-il·i·ty (il′ə-ti), [Fr. *-ilité*; L. *-ilitas*], a suffix used to form nouns from adjectives (and their derived nouns) ending in *-ile, -il, -able, -ible*, as in *imbecility, civility, ability, sensibility*.

Il·i·um (il′i-əm), ***n.*** [see ILIAD], ancient Troy.

il·i·um (il′i-əm), ***n.*** [*pl.* ILIA (-ə)], [see ILEUM], the uppermost of the three sections of the hipbone: see **skeleton,** illus.

ilk (ilk), ***adj.*** [Scot. dial.; ME. *ilke*; AS. *ilca*, same; prob. < **ī-līca* < *ī-*, lit., the, orig. a pronominal prefix + *-līca*, like (see LIKE)], [Obs.], same; like. ***pron.*** [Obs.], the same. ***n.*** [Colloq.], a family; kind; sort; class: from a misunderstanding of the phrase *of that ilk*.

of that ilk, 1. in Scotland, of the same name (as the place he owns or from which he comes) as, MacDonald *of that ilk* (i.e., MacDonald of MacDonald); hence, 2. of the same sort or class.

ill (il), ***adj.*** [WORSE (wũrs), WORST (wũrst)], [ME.; ON. *illr* (replacing AS. *yfel*, evil, in many senses); prob. < Gmc. **ilhila*, **elhila* < IE. base **elk-*, hungry, bad, seen also in OIr. *elc*, bad], 1. characterized by, causing, or tending to cause harm or evil; specifically, *a*) morally bad or wrong; evil: as, *ill* repute. *b*) causing pain, discomfort, etc.; adverse: as, *ill* fortune. *c*) harsh; cruel; not kind or friendly: as, *ill* will. *d*) unfavorable; unfortunate; unpropitious; promising trouble: as, *ill* news. 2. not healthy; not well; having a disease; sick; indisposed. 3. not according to rule, custom, desirability, etc.; faulty; incomplete; imperfect; improper: as, *ill* breeding. ***n.*** anything ill; anything causing harm, trouble, wrong, pain, unhappiness, etc.; an evil or a disease. ***adv.*** [WORSE, WORST], 1. in an ill manner; specifically, *a*) badly; wrongly; improperly; imperfectly. *b*) harshly; cruelly; unkindly. 2. with difficulty; scarcely: as, he can *ill* afford to refuse. —***SYN.*** see **bad, sick.**

go ill with, to be unfortunate for or unfavorable to.

ill at ease, uneasy; uncomfortable.

take ill, to be annoyed or offended at.

I'll (īl), 1. I shall. 2. I will.

Ill., Illinois.

ill., 1. illustrated. 2. illustration.

ill-ad·vised (il′əd-vīzd′), ***adj.*** showing or resulting from lack of proper consideration or sound advice; unwise.

Il·lam·pu, Mount (ē-yäm′pōō), a mountain of the Andes, in west central Bolivia: height, 21,489 ft.: also called *Sorata*.

il·la·tion (i-lā′shən), ***n.*** [L. *illatis* < *illatus* (used as pp. of *inferre*, to bring in) < *in-*, in + *latus* (used as pp. of *ferre*, to bring) < earlier **tlatus* < base seen also in L. *tolerare* (see TOLERATE), Gr. *tlenai*, to bear], 1. the act of drawing a conclusion or making an inference from premises. 2. the conclusion drawn; inference.

il·la·tive (il′ə-tiv, i-lā′tiv), ***adj.*** [L. *illativus*; see ILLATION], 1. expressing or introducing an inference: said of words, as *therefore*. 2. of, or having the nature of, an illation; inferential. 3. expressing movement inward: as, the Uralic languages have an *illative* case.

ill-be·ing (il′bē′iŋ), ***n.*** an unhealthy, unhappy, or evil condition: opposed to *well-being*.

ill-bod·ing (il′bōd′iŋ), ***adj.*** boding evil; ominous; inauspicious.

ill-bred (il′bred′), ***adj.*** badly brought up; lacking good manners; rude; impolite.

ill breeding, the quality or state of being ill-bred.

ill-con·sid·ered (il′kən-sid′ẽrd), ***adj.*** not properly considered; not suitable; not wise.

ill-de·fined (il′di-fīnd′), ***adj.*** poorly defined; not clear or definite.

ill-dis·posed (il′dis-pōzd′), ***adj.*** 1. having a bad disposition; malicious or malevolent. 2. unfriendly or unfavorable (*toward*).

il·le·gal (i-lē′gəl), ***adj.*** [< Fr. *illégal* or ML. *illegalis*; see IN- (not) & LEGAL], prohibited by law; against the law; unlawful; illicit; not authorized or sanctioned.

il·le·gal·i·ty (il′ē-gal′ə-ti), ***n.*** 1. the state or quality of being illegal. 2. [*pl.* ILLEGALITIES (-tiz)], an illegal action.

il·leg·i·bil·i·ty (il′ej-ə-bil′ə-ti, i-lej′ə-bil′ə-ti), ***n.*** the quality or state of being illegible.

il·leg·i·ble (i-lej′ə-b'l), ***adj.*** [*il-* (not) + *legible*], very difficult or impossible to read because badly written or printed, obscured by age, etc.

il·leg·i·bly (i-lej′ə-bli), ***adv.*** in an illegible manner; so as to be illegible.

il·le·git·i·ma·cy (il′i-jit′ə-mə-si), ***n.*** [*pl.* ILLEGITIMACIES (-siz)], the fact, condition, or quality of being illegitimate; specifically, bastardy.

il·le·git·i·mate (il′i-jit′ə-mit), ***adj.*** [< L. *illegitimus*, not lawful; see IN- (not) & LEGITIMATE], 1. born of parents not married to each other; bastard. 2. incorrectly deduced or concluded; not logical. 3. contrary to law or rules; illegal; unlawful. 4. not in keeping with accepted usage: said of words or phrases.

ill fame, bad reputation: as, a house of prostitution is sometimes called a house of *ill fame.*

ill-fat·ed (il'fāt'id), *adj.* 1. having or certain to have an evil fate or unlucky end. 2. causing misfortune; unlucky.

ill-fa·vored (il'fā'vẽrd), *adj.* 1. of unpleasant or evil appearance; ugly. 2. unpleasant; offensive.

ill-found·ed (il'foun'did), *adj.* not supported by facts or sound reasons.

ill-got·ten (il'got''n), *adj.* obtained by evil, unlawful, or dishonest means: as, *ill-gotten* gains.

ill-hu·mor (il'hū'mẽr), *n.* a disagreeable, cross, or sullen mood or state of mind: also **ill humor.**

ill-hu·mored (il'hū'mẽrd), *adj.* having or showing ill-humor; disagreeable, cross, or sullen.

il·lib·er·al (i-lib'ẽr-əl), *adj.* [Fr. *illibéral;* L. *illiberalis;* see IN- (not) & LIBERAL], 1. lacking a liberal education or training; without culture; ill-mannered. 2. intolerant; bigoted; narrow-minded. 3. miserly; stingy.

il·lib·er·al·i·ty (i-lib'ə-ral'ə-ti), *n.* the quality of being illiberal.

il·lic·it (i-lis'it), *adj.* [Fr. *illicite;* L. *illicitus,* not allowed; see IN- (not) & LICIT], not allowed by law, custom, etc.; unlawful; prohibited; unauthorized; improper.

Il·li·ma·ni, Mount (ē'yē-mä'nē), a mountain of the Andes, in western Bolivia: height, 21,280 ft.

il·lim·it·a·ble (i-lim'i-tə-b'l), *adj.* [*il-* (not) + *limitable*], without limit or boundary; immeasurable; endless.

il·lin·i·um (i-lin'i-əm), *n.* [Mod. L., after the University of *Illinois,* where research on it was done], a former name for chemical element 61: see **promethium.**

Il·li·nois (il'ə-noi', il'ə-noiz'), *n.* 1. [*pl.* ILLINOIS], a member of a confederation of Algonquian Indian tribes that lived in Illinois. 2. a Middle Western State of the United States: area, 56,400 sq. mi.; pop., 10,081,000; capital, Springfield: abbreviated **Ill.** 3. a river in Illinois, flowing southward into the Mississippi: length, 273 mi.

Il·li·nois·an (il'ə-noi'ən, il'ə-noiz'ən), *adj.* of Illinois. *n.* a native or inhabitant of Illinois.

il·lit·er·a·cy (i-lit'ẽr-ə-si), *n.* 1. the state or quality of being illiterate; lack of education or culture; especially, inability to read or write. 2. [*pl.* ILLITERACIES (-siz)], a mistake (in writing or speaking) resulting from ignorance.

il·lit·er·ate (i-lit'ẽr-it), *adj.* [L. *illiteratus,* unlettered; see IN- (not) & LITERATE], 1. ignorant; uneducated; especially, unable to read or write. 2. having or showing limited knowledge, experience, or culture, especially in some particular field: as, he is musically *illiterate.* *n.* an illiterate person; especially, one unable to read or write. Abbreviated **illit.** —*SYN.* see **ignorant.**

ill-look·ing (il'look'iŋ), *adj.* 1. ugly. 2. of evil or sinister appearance.

ill-man·nered (il'man'ẽrd), *adj.* having bad manners; rude; impolite. —*SYN.* see **rude.**

ill nature, an unpleasant, disagreeable disposition; peevishness; sullenness.

ill-na·tured (il'nā'chẽrd), *adj.* having or showing ill nature; cross; sullen; peevish; disagreeable.

ill·ness (il'nis), *n.* an unhealthy condition of the body or mind; sickness; disease.

il·log·i·cal (i-loj'i-k'l), *adj.* [*il-* (not) + *logical*], not logical or reasonable; using, based on, or caused by faulty reasoning.

ill-o·mened (il'ō'mənd), *adj.* having bad omens; ill-fated; inauspicious.

ill-spent (il'spent'), *adj.* misspent; spent wastefully.

ill-starred (il'stärd'), *adj.* born or conceived under an evil star; unlucky: from astrological notions.

ill-suit·ed (il'sōōt'id, il'sūt'id), *adj.* not well-suited; not appropriate.

ill-tem·pered (il'tem'pẽrd), *adj.* having or showing a bad temper; quarrelsome; cross; sullen; peevish.

ill-timed (il'tīmd'), *adj.* unsuitable at the time; inappropriate: as, an *ill-timed* remark.

ill-treat (il'trēt'), *v.t.* to treat unkindly, cruelly, or unfairly; harm; abuse; maltreat.

ill-treat·ment (il'trēt'mənt), *n.* unkind, cruel, or unfair treatment; abuse: also **ill treatment.**

ill turn, 1. an unfriendly, unkind, or malevolent act. 2. a decline in health, wealth, etc.

il·lume (i-lōōm', i-lūm'), *v.t.* [ILLUMED (-lōōmd', -lūmd'), ILLUMING], [Poetic], to illuminate.

il·lu·mi·na·ble (i-lōō'mən-ə-b'l, i-lū'mən-ə-b'l), *adj.* that can be illuminated.

il·lu·mi·nant (i-lōō'mə-nənt, i-lū'mə-nənt), *adj.* [L. *illuminans,* ppr. of *illuminare*], giving light; illuminating. *n.* something that illuminates, or gives light.

il·lu·mi·nate (i-lōō'mə-nāt', i-lū'mə-nāt'), *v.t.* [ILLUMINATED (-id), ILLUMINATING], [< L. *illuminatus,* pp. of *illuminare,* to light up < *in-,* in + *luminare,* to light < *lumen, luminis,* a light < IE. **leuq-s-men* < base **leuq-;* see ILLUSTRATE], 1. to give light to; light up. 2. *a*) to make clear; explain; elucidate. *b*) to inform; instruct; enlighten. 3. to make famous; make illustrious. 4. to decorate with lights: as, they *illuminated* the city for the holiday. 5. *a*) to decorate (an initial letter or word) with designs, tracings, etc. of gold, silver, or bright colors. *b*) to decorate (a manuscript, page border, etc.) with such initial letters, miniature pictures, etc. *v.i.* to light up.

il·lu·mi·na·ti (i-lōō'mə-nä'tī, i-lū'mə-nä'ti), *n.pl.* [*sing.* ILLUMINATO (-tō)], [pl. of L. *illuminatus* or It. *illuminato;* see ILLUMINATE], 1. people who have or profess to have special intellectual or spiritual enlightenment. 2. formerly, baptized persons: during baptism, a lighted taper was handed to them to symbolize their spiritual enlightenment.

il·lu·mi·na·tion (i-lōō'mə-nā'shən, i-lū'mə-nā'shən), *n.* [ME. *illumynacyon;* OFr. *illumination;* LL. *illuminatio*], 1. an illuminating or being illuminated; specifically, *a*) a lighting up; supplying of light. *b*) clarification; explanation. *c*) enlightenment; instruction. *d*) decoration with lights. *e*) decoration of initial letters, manuscripts, etc. with designs, colors, etc. 2. light; intensity of light per unit of area. 3. the designs, tracings, etc. used in decorating manuscripts. 4. the lights used in decorating a city, etc.

il·lu·mi·na·tive (i-lōō'mə-nā'tiv, i-lū'mə-nā'tiv), *adj.* illuminating or tending to illuminate.

il·lu·mi·na·tor (i-lōō'mə-nā'tẽr, i-lū'mə-nā'tẽr), *n.* [LL.], a person or thing that illuminates; specifically, *a*) any apparatus or device for giving, concentrating, or reflecting light. *b*) one who decorates manuscripts, etc.

il·lu·mine (i-lōō'min, i-lū'min), *v.t. & v.i.* [ILLUMINED (-mind), ILLUMINING], [ME. *illuminen;* Fr. *illuminer;* L. *illuminare*], to illuminate or be illuminated; light up.

illus., 1. illustrated. 2. illustration.

ill-us·age (il'ūs'ij, il'ūz'ij), *n.* unfair, unkind, or cruel treatment; abuse: also **ill usage.**

ill-use (il'ūz'; *for n.,* il'ūs'), *v.t.* to use badly; treat unfairly, unkindly, or cruelly; abuse. *n.* ill-usage.

il·lu·sion (i-lōō'zhən, i-lū'zhən), *n.* [L. *illusio,* a mocking, jeering < *illusus,* pp. of *illudere,* to mock, play with < *in-,* on + *ludere,* to play], 1. a false idea or conception; belief or opinion not in accord with the facts. 2. an unreal, deceptive, or misleading appearance or image. 3. a false perception, conception, or interpretation of what one sees, where one is, etc.: in psychology, an abnormal illusion is a ***hallucination.*** 4. a delicate, gauzy cloth used for veils, etc.; tulle. —*SYN.* see **delusion.**

il·lu·sion·al (i-lōō'zhən-'l, i-lū'zhən-'l), *adj.* of, or having the nature of, an illusion.

il·lu·sion·ism (i-lōō'zhən-iz'm, i-lū'zhən-iz'm), *n.* the theory or doctrine that the material world exists only in illusive sense impressions.

il·lu·sion·ist (i-lōō'zhən-ist, i-lū'zhən-ist), *n.* 1. a person subject to illusions, or false impressions; visionary. 2. a person who believes in illusionism. 3. an entertainer who produces illusions; sleight-of-hand artist.

il·lu·sive (i-lōō'siv, i-lū'siv), *adj.* producing, based on, or having the nature of, illusion; deceptive; unreal.

il·lu·so·ry (i-lōō'sẽr-i, i-lū'sẽr-i), *adj.* illusive; unreal.

il·lus·trate (il'əs-trāt', i-lus'trāt), *v.t.* [ILLUSTRATED (-id), ILLUSTRATING], [< L. *illustratus,* pp. of *illustrare,* to light up, illuminate < *in-,* in + *lustrare,* to illuminate < *lustrum* < IE. **leuqs-trom,* **louqs-trom,* illumination < base **leuq-,* to light, seen also in L. *lux,* light, AS. *lieg,* fire, flame], 1. *a*) to explain; make clear. *b*) to make clear or easily understood by examples, comparisons, etc.; exemplify. 2. *a*) to furnish (books, etc.) with explanatory or decorative drawings, designs, or pictures. *b*) to explain or decorate: said of pictures, etc. 3. [Obs.], *a*) to make luminous; illuminate. *b*) to make bright; adorn. *c*) to make illustrious.

il·lus·tra·tion (il'əs-trā'shən), *n.* [ME. *illustracione* < OFr. or L.; OFr. *illustration;* L. *illustratio*], 1. an illustrating or being illustrated. 2. an example, story, analogy, etc. used to help explain or make something clear. 3. a picture, design, diagram, etc. used to decorate or explain something: abbreviated **illus., illust., ill.** —*SYN.* see **instance.**

il·lus·tra·tive (i-lus'trə-tiv, il'əs-trā'tiv), *adj.* illustrating or tending to illustrate; serving as an example.

il·lus·tra·tor (il'əs-trā'tẽr, i-lus'trā'tẽr), *n.* a person or thing that illustrates; especially, an artist who makes illustrations for books, magazines, etc.

il·lus·tri·ous (i-lus'tri-əs), *adj.* [< ME. *illustre* (< L. *illustris,* clear, conspicuous, distinguished < *illustrare;* see ILLUSTRATE); + *-ous*], 1. originally, lustrous; shining; bright; hence, 2. very distinguished; famous; eminent; celebrated. —*SYN.* see **famous.**

ill will, unfriendly feeling; enmity; hate; dislike. —*SYN.* see **malice.**

ill-wish·er (il'wish'ẽr), *n.* a person who wishes evil or misfortune to another.

il·ly (il'li), *adv.* badly; ill: regularly formed from *ill,* but now generally regarded as substandard or dialectal.

Il·lyr·i·a (i-lẽr'i-ə), *n.* an ancient country on the east coast of the Adriatic: see **Roman Empire,** map.

Il·lyr·i·an (i-lẽr'i-ən), *adj.* of Illyria, its people, or culture. *n.* 1. a native or inhabitant of Illyria. 2. the ancient language of the Illyrians: it is regarded as a distinct branch of the Indo-European family of lan-

guages, possibly represented today by Albanian.
Il·lyr·i·cum (i-lêr'i-kəm), *n.* a Roman province in ancient Illyria: see **Etruria**, map.
il·men·ite (il'mən-īt'), *n.* [< the *Ilmen* Mountains in the southern Urals], a lustrous black mineral, an oxide of iron and titanium.
I.L.O., International Labor Organization.
I·lo·i·lo (ē'lō-ē'lō), *n.* a seaport in southern Panay, in the Philippines.
I.L.W.U., International Longshoremen's and Warehousemen's Union.
I'm (im), I am.
im- (im), 1. in- (not). 2. in- (in).
I.M., Isle of Man.
im·age (im'ij), *n.* [ME.; OFr.; L. *imago*, imitation, copy, image < base of *imitari*, to imitate], 1. *a*) an imitation or representation of a person or thing, drawn, painted, etc.; especially, a statue. *b*) a sculptured figure used as an idol. 2. the visual impression of something produced by reflection from a mirror, refraction through a lens, etc. 3. a person or thing very much like another; copy; counterpart; likeness. 4. a mental picture of something; conception; idea; impression. 5. a type; typical example; symbol; embodiment: as, he is the *image* of laziness. 6. a vivid representation; graphic description: as, this play is the *image* of life. 7. a figure of speech, especially a metaphor or simile. 8. in *psychoanalysis*, a picture or likeness of a person, as of a parent, constructed in the unconscious and remaining there. *v.t.* [IMAGED (-ijd), IMAGING], [< the *n.*; also < Fr. *imager* < the *n.*], 1. to make a representation or imitation of; figure; portray; delineate. 2. to reflect; mirror. 3. to picture in the mind; imagine. 4. to be a symbol or type of; typify. 5. to describe graphically or vividly; describe with figures of speech.
im·age·ry (im'ij-ri, im'ij-ẽr-i), *n.* [*pl.* IMAGERIES (-riz, -iz)], [ME. & OFr. *imagerie*], 1. images generally; especially, statues. 2. mental images, as produced by memory or imagination. 3. descriptions and figures of speech: as, Shakespeare's poetry is rich in *imagery*.
im·ag·i·na·ble (i-maj'i-nə-b'l), *adj.* [ME. *ymaginable;* LL. *imaginabilis*], that can be imagined.
im·ag·i·na·bly (i-maj'i-nə-bli), *adv.* in an imaginable manner; conceivably.
im·ag·i·nal (i-maj'i-n'l), *adj.* in *zoology*, of an imago.
im·ag·i·nar·y (i-maj'i-ner'i), *adj.* 1. existing only in the imagination; fanciful; unreal. 2. in *mathematics*, designating or of the square root of a negative quantity or any expression involving such a root.
SYN.*—imaginary** applies to that which exists in the imagination only and is, therefore, unreal (*imaginary* enemies); **fanciful** refers to that which has been conceived in the fancy and usually connotes quaintness or whimsicality (*fanciful* tales); **visionary** refers to something unreal conceived of in, or as in, a vision and usually connotes impracticality (the airplane was once a *visionary* dream); **fantastic** applies to something which seems to be so highly fanciful or odd as to be beyond belief (a *fantastic* scheme for storing energy).—ANT.*** real, actual.
im·ag·i·na·tion (i-maj'i-nā'shən), *n.* [ME. *ymaginacioun;* L. *imaginatio* < pp. of *imagniari;* see IMAGINE], 1. *a*) the act or power of forming mental images of what is not actually present. *b*) the act or power of creating mental images of what has never been actually experienced, or of creating new images or ideas by combining previous experiences; creative power. *Imagination* is often regarded as the more seriously and deeply creative faculty, which perceives the basic resemblances between things, as distinguished from *fancy*, the lighter and more decorative faculty, which perceives superficial resemblances. 2. anything imagined; mental image; creation of the mind; fancy. 3. a foolish notion; empty fancy. 4. the ability to understand and appreciate imaginative creations of others, especially works of art and literature.
im·ag·i·na·tion·al (i-maj'i-nā'shən-'l), *adj.* of or caused by the imagination.
im·ag·i·na·tive (i-maj'i-nā'tiv, i-maj'i-nə-tiv), *adj.* [ME. & OFr. *imaginatif* < L. *imaginatus*, pp. of *imaginari*, to imagine], 1. having, using, or showing imagination; having creative or productive talent; able to imagine or fond of imagining. 2. of or resulting from imagination: as, *imaginative* literature.
im·ag·ine (i-maj'in), *v.t.* [IMAGINED (-ind), IMAGINING], [ME. *imaginen;* OFr. *imaginer;* L. *imaginari* < *imago*, an image, likeness], 1. to make a mental image of; form an idea or notion of; conceive in the mind; create by the imagination. 2. to suppose; guess; think. *v.i.* 1. to use the imagination. 2. to suppose; guess; think.
im·ag·ism (im'əj-iz'm), *n.* [< *Des imagistes*, title of the first anthology of imagist poetry (1914)], a movement that arose in modern poetry during the years before the end of World War I as a revolt against romanticism: its principles included the use of precise, concrete images, freedom from convention in theme and form, the extensive use of free verse, subject matter drawn from modern life, and the use of suggestion rather than complete statement.
im·ag·ist (im'əj-ist), *n.* any of a group of poets who believed in and practiced imagism (c. 1912–1924). *adj.* of imagism or the imagists.
im·ag·is·tic (im'ə-jis'tik), *adj.* imagist.
i·ma·go (i-mā'gō), *n.* [*pl.* IMAGOS (-gōz), IMAGINES (i-maj'ə-nēz')], [L., an image, likeness; adopted by Linnaeus], 1. *a*) the final, adult, reproductive stage in the development of an insect. *b*) an insect in this stage. 2. in *psychoanalysis*, an image.
i·mam (i-mäm'), *n.* [Ar. *imām*, a guide, chief, leader < *amma*, to walk before, precede], 1. a Moslem priest. 2. [often I-], any of various Moslem leaders with this title, as the Caliph, etc. Also **i·maum** (i-môm').
i·ma·ret (i-mä'ret), *n.* [Turk. *'imārat* < Ar. *'imārah*, building], in Turkey, an inn.
im·bal·ance (im-bal'əns), *n.* lack of balance, as in proportion, force, functioning, etc.
im·balm (im-bäm'), *v.t.* to embalm.
im·bark (im-bärk'), *v.t. & v.i.* to embark.
im·be·cile (im'bə-s'l), *adj.* [Fr. *imbécile;* L. *imbecilis*, *imbecillus*, feeble, weak], 1. of or showing feeble intellect; mentally deficient. 2. very foolish or stupid. *n.* 1. a mentally deficient person with an intelligence quotient ranging from 25 to 50; person mentally equal to a child between three and eight years old: *imbecile* is the second-lowest classification of mental deficiency, above *idiot* and below *moron*. 2. loosely, a very foolish or stupid person.
im·be·cil·i·ty (im'bə-sil'ə-ti), *n.* [*pl.* IMBECILITIES (-tiz)], [Fr. *imbécillité;* L. *imbecillitas*], 1. the state of being an imbecile. 2. behavior like that of an imbecile; great foolishness or stupidity. 3. an imbecile act or remark.
im·bed (im-bed'), *v.t.* to embed.
im·bibe (im-bīb'), *v.t.* [IMBIBED (-bībd'), IMBIBING], [ME. *enbiben;* OFr. *imbiber;* L. *imbibere* < *in-*, in + *bibere*, to drink], 1. to drink or drink in; hence, 2. *a*) to absorb (moisture). *b*) to inhale. 3. to take into the mind and keep, as ideas, principles, etc. *v.i.* to drink.
im·bit·ter (im-bit'ẽr), *v.t.* to embitter.
im·bod·y (im-bod'i), *v.t.* to embody.
im·bold·en (im-bōl'd'n), *v.t.* to embolden.
im·bos·om (im-booz'əm, im-bōō'zəm), *v.t.* to embosom.
im·bow·er (im-bou'ẽr), *v.t. & v.i.* to embower.
im·bri·cate (im'bri-kāt'; *also, for adj.*, im'bri-kit), *adj.* [L. *imbricatus*, pp. of *imbricare*, to cover with gutter tiles < *imbrex*, gutter tile < *imber*, rain], 1. overlapping evenly, as tiles or fish scales. 2. ornamented with overlapping scales or a pattern resembling these. *v.t.* [IMBRICATED (-id), IMBRICATING], to place (tiles, shingles, etc.) in overlapping order. *v.i.* to overlap.
im·bri·cat·ed (im'bri-kāt'id), *adj.* imbricate.
im·bri·ca·tion (im'bri-kā'shən), *n.* [see IMBRICATE], 1. an overlapping, as of tiles, scales, etc. 2. an ornamental pattern resembling this.
im·bro·glio (im-brōl'yō), *n.* [*pl.* IMBROGLIOS (-yōz)], [It. < *broglio*, confusion; cf. BROIL], 1. [Rare], a confused heap. 2. an involved and confusing situation; state of confusion and complication. 3. a confused misunderstanding or disagreement; entanglement.
im·brown (im-broun'), *v.t.* to embrown.
im·brue (im-brōō'), *v.t.* [IMBRUED (-brōōd'), IMBRUING], [ME. *enbrowen*, to soil; OFr. *embreuver*, *embreuvrer*, to moisten; LL. **imbiberare*, for L. *imbibere;* see IMBIBE], to wet, soak, or stain, especially with blood.
im·brute (im-brōōt'), *v.t. & v.i.* [IMBRUTED (-id), IMBRUTING], [*im-* (in) + *brute*], to make or become brutal.
im·bue (im-bū'), *v.t.* [IMBUED (-būd'), IMBUING], [L. *imbuere*, to wet, soak], 1. to fill with moisture; saturate; imbrue. 2. to fill with color; dye; stain; tinge. 3. to fill (the mind, etc.); permeate; pervade; inspire (*with* principles, feelings, emotions, etc.).
im·id·az·ole (im'id-az'ōl, im'id-ə-zōl'), *n.* [< *imide* + *azole*], a colorless, crystalline base, $C_3H_4N_2$.
im·ide (im'id, im'īd), *n.* [arbitrary alteration of *amide*], an organic compound having the divalent radical NH combined with two acid radicals: also **im·id** (im'id).
i·mi·do (i-mē'dō, im'i-dō'), *adj.* of an imide or imides.
i·mi·do- (i-mē'də, im'i-dō), [< *imide*], a combining form meaning *of or containing the divalent radical NH combined with two acid radicals.*
i·mid·o·gen (i-mid'ə-jen', i-mē'də-jen'), *n.* [*imido-* + hydro*gen*], [Rare], the divalent radical NH.
i·mine (i-mēn', im'in), *n.* [arbitrary alteration of *amine*], a compound containing the divalent radical NH united to alkyl or other nonacid radicals.
i·mi·no (i-mē'nō, im'i-nō), *adj.* of an imine or imines.
i·mi·no- (i-mē'nə, im'i-nō), [< *imine*], a combining form meaning *of or containing the divalent radical NH united to alkyl or other nonacid radicals.*
im·i·ta·ble (im'i-tə-b'l), *adj.* [Fr.; L. *imitabilis*], that can be imitated.
im·i·tate (im'ə-tāt'), *v.t.* [IMITATED (-id), IMITATING], [< L. *imitatus*, pp. of *imitari*, to imitate], 1. to try to

act or be the same as; follow the example of: as, one should *imitate* the wise. 2. to act the same as; mimic. 3. to reproduce in form, color, etc.; make a duplicate of; copy; counterfeit. 4. to be or become like in appearance; look like; resemble: as, glass is made to *imitate* diamonds. 5. to use as a model or pattern.

SYN.—**imitate** implies the following of something as an example or model but does not necessarily connote exact correspondence with the original (the child *imitates* the father's mannerisms); **copy** implies as nearly exact imitation or reproduction as is possible (to *copy* a painting); **mimic** suggests close imitation, often in fun or ridicule (to *mimic* the speech peculiarities of another); **mock** implies imitation with the intent to deride or affront ("I can't," she echoed *mockingly*); **ape** implies close imitation either in mimicry or in servile emulation (she *aped* the fashions of the court ladies).

im·i·ta·tion (im'ə-tā'shən), ***n.*** [L. *imitatio*], 1. an imitating. 2. *a*) the result or product of imitating; artificial likeness; copy. *b*) a counterfeit. 3. in *biology*, mimicry. 4. in *music*, the repetition of a theme in different parts of a composition, with or without slight changes in rhythm, intervals, etc. ***adj.*** made to resemble something else, usually something superior or genuine; not real; sham; bogus: as, *imitation* leather. Abbreviated **imit.**

im·i·ta·tive (im'ə-tā'tiv), ***adj.*** [L. *imitativus*], 1. formed from a model; reproducing the qualities of an original or another. 2. given to imitating; inclined to imitate others. 3. not genuine or real; imitation. 4. approximating in sound the thing signified; echoic: said of words (e.g., *hiss, ripple, clang*): abbreviated **imit.**

im·i·ta·tor (im'ə-tā'tẽr), ***n.*** [L.], a person or animal that imitates.

im·mac·u·late (i-mak'yoo-lit), ***adj.*** [ME.; L. *immaculatus* < *in-*, not + *maculatus*, pp. of *maculare*, to spot, soil < *macula*, a spot], 1. perfectly clean; without a spot or stain; unsoiled. 2. perfectly correct; without a flaw, fault, or error. 3. pure; innocent; without sin.

Immaculate Conception, in the *Roman Catholic Church*, the doctrine that the Virgin Mary, though conceived naturally, was from the moment of conception free from any stain of original sin: sometimes confused with ***virgin birth.***

im·ma·nence (im'ə-nəns), ***n.*** [< *immanent*], the fact or condition of being immanent.

im·ma·nen·cy (im'ə-nən-si), ***n.*** immanence.

im·ma·nent (im'ə-nənt), ***adj.*** [LL. *immanens*, ppr. of *immanere*, to remain in or near < *in-*, in + *manere*, to remain], 1. living, remaining, or operating within; inherent. 2. in *theology*, present throughout the universe: said of God.

Im·man·u·el (i-man'ū-əl), [Heb. *'immānūēl* < *'im*, with + *ānū*, us + *ēl*, God, hence, lit., God with us], a masculine name: variants, *Emmanuel, Manuel.* ***n.*** a name given by Isaiah to the Messiah of his prophecy (Is. 7:14), often applied to Jesus (Matt. 1:23).

im·ma·te·ri·al (im'ə-têr'i-əl), ***adj.*** [ME. *immateriel;* ML. *immaterialis;* see IN- (not) & MATERIAL], 1. not consisting of matter; without substance; incorporeal; spiritual. 2. that does not matter; unimportant.

im·ma·te·ri·al·ism (im'ə-têr'i-əl-iz'm), ***n.*** the theory or doctrine that material things do not exist objectively but only as mental perceptions.

im·ma·te·ri·al·ist (im'ə-têr'i-əl-ist), ***n.*** a believer in immaterialism.

im·ma·te·ri·al·i·ty (im'ə-têr'i-al'ə-ti), ***n.*** 1. the state or quality of being immaterial. 2. [*pl.* IMMATERIALITIES (-tiz)], something immaterial.

im·ma·te·ri·al·ize (im'ə-têr'i-ə-līz'), ***v.t.*** [IMMATERIALIZED (-līzd'), IMMATERIALIZING], to make immaterial.

im·ma·ture (im'ə-tyoor', im'ə-toor; *now often* im'ə-choor'), ***adj.*** [L. *immaturus*], 1. not mature; not completely grown or developed; not ripe. 2. not finished or perfected; incomplete.

im·ma·tu·ri·ty (im'ə-tyoor'ə-ti, im'ə-toor'ə-ti; *now often* im'ə-choor'ə-ti), ***n.*** an immature quality or state.

im·meas·ur·a·bil·i·ty (i-mezh'ẽr-ə-bil'ə-ti), ***n.*** the quality of being immeasurable.

im·meas·ur·a·ble (i-mezh'ẽr-ə-b'l), ***adj.*** that cannot be measured; boundless; vast; immense.

im·meas·ur·a·bly (i-mezh'ẽr-ə-bli), ***adv.*** to an immeasurable degree or extent.

im·med·i·a·cy (i-mē'di-ə-si), ***n.*** the quality or state of being immediate.

im·me·di·ate (i-mē'di-it), ***adj.*** [ML. *immediatus;* see IN- (not) & MEDIATE], having nothing coming between; with no intermediary; specifically, *a*) not separated in space; in direct contact; closest; nearest; also, near; close; adjoining; adjacent. *b*) not separated in time; acting or happening at once; instant; of the present. *c*) next in order, succession, etc.; next in line; directly or closely related: as, one's *immediate* family. *d*) directly affecting; direct; first-hand: as, an *immediate* cause. *e*) understood or perceived directly or intuitively: as, an *immediate* inference.

im·me·di·ate·ly (i-mē'di-it-li), ***adv.*** in an immediate manner; specifically, *a*) without intervening agency or cause; directly. *b*) without delay; at once; instantly. ***conj.*** [Chiefly British], at the very moment that; as soon as: as, please return *immediately* you are done.

im·med·i·ca·ble (i-med'i-kə-b'l), ***adj.*** [L. *immedicabilis;* see IN- (not) & MEDICABLE], that cannot be healed; incurable.

Im·mel·mann turn (im'əl-män'), [after Max *Immelmann*, G. ace (1890–1916)], a maneuver in which an airplane is half looped to an upside-down position and then half rolled back to normal, upright flight: used to gain altitude while making a 180-degree change in direction.

im·me·mo·ri·al (im'ə-môr'i-əl, im'mə-mō'ri-əl), ***adj.*** [ML. *immemorialis;* see IN- (not) & MEMORIAL], extending back beyond memory or record; very old; ancient.

im·mense (i-mens'), ***adj.*** [Fr.; L. *immensus* < *in-*, not + *mensus*, pp. of *metiri*, to measure], 1. originally, unmeasured; limitless; infinite. 2. very large; vast; huge. 3. [Slang], very good; excellent. —***SYN.*** see **enormous.**

im·men·si·ty (i-men'sə-ti), ***n.*** [*pl.* IMMENSITIES (-tiz)], [Fr. *immensité;* L. *immensitas*], the state or quality of being immense; specifically, *a*) vastness; great size or limitless extent. *b*) infinite space or being; infinity.

im·men·su·ra·ble (i-men'shoor-ə-b'l), ***adj.*** [< Fr. or L.; Fr. *immensurable;* LL. *immensurabilis;* see IN- (not) & MENSURABLE], immeasurable.

im·merge (i-mũrj'), ***v.t.*** [IMMERGED (-mũrjd'), IMMERGING], [L. *immergere;* see IMMERSE], to immerse. ***v.i.*** to plunge or disappear, as in a liquid.

im·merse (i-mũrs'), ***v.t.*** [IMMERSED (-mũrst'), IMMERSING], [< L. *immersus*, pp. of *immergere*, to dip, plunge into; see IN- (in) & MERGE], 1. to plunge, drop, or dip into or as if into a liquid, especially so as to cover completely. 2. to baptize by dipping under water. 3. to plunge into a specified state; absorb or involve deeply; engross: as, he was *immersed* in thought.

im·mersed (i-mũrst'), ***adj.*** [pp. of *immerse*], 1. plunged into or as if into a liquid. 2. baptized by immersion. 3. in *biology*, embedded in another organ or part. 4. in *botany*, growing completely under water.

im·mer·sion (i-mũr'shən, i-mũr'zhən), ***n.*** [LL. *immersio*], 1. an immersing or being immersed. 2. baptism in which the person's whole body is dipped under water. 3. in *astronomy*, the concealment of one heavenly body behind, or in the shadow of, another.

im·mesh (im-mesh'), ***v.t.*** to enmesh.

im·me·thod·i·cal (im'mə-thod'i-k'l), ***adj.*** not methodical.

im·mi·grant (im'ə-grənt), ***n.*** [< L. *immigrans*, ppr.], a person who immigrates. ***adj.*** immigrating. —***SYN.*** see **alien.**

im·mi·grate (im'ə-grāt'), ***v.i.*** [IMMIGRATED (-id), IMMIGRATING], [< L. *immigratus*, pp. of *immigrare*, to go or remove into; see IN- (in) & MIGRATE], to come into a new country, region, or environment in order to settle there: opposed to *emigrate.* ***v.t.*** to bring in as an immigrant or immigrants. —***SYN.*** see **migrate.**

im·mi·gra·tion (im'ə-grā'shən), ***n.*** 1. an immigrating. 2. the number of immigrants during a specified period.

im·mi·nence (im'ə-nəns), ***n.*** [L. *imminentia* < *imminens*], 1. the quality or fact of being imminent. 2. something imminent; impending evil, danger, etc.

im·mi·nen·cy (im'ə-nən-si), ***n.*** imminence.

im·mi·nent (im'ə-nənt), ***adj.*** [L. *imminens*, ppr. of *imminere*, to project over, overhang, threaten < *in-*, on + *minere*, to project], 1. [Rare], overhanging. 2. likely to happen without delay; impending; threatening: said of danger, evil, misfortune, etc.

im·min·gle (im-miŋ'g'l), ***v.t. & v.i.*** to mix or mingle thoroughly; blend.

im·mis·ci·ble (i-mis'ə-b'l), ***adj.*** [*im-* (not) + *miscible*], that cannot be mixed or blended.

im·mit·i·ga·ble (i-mit'i-gə-b'l), ***adj.*** [L. *immitigabilis*], that cannot be mitigated.

im·mit·i·ga·bly (i-mit'i-gə-bli), ***adv.*** 1. in an immitigable manner. 2. to an immitigable degree.

im·mix (im-miks'), ***v.t. & v.i.*** [< *immixt*, mixed in with (< L. *immixtus*, pp. of *immiscere* < *in-*, in + *miscere*, to mix), assumed to be Eng. pp.], to mix thoroughly.

im·mix·ture (im-miks'chẽr), ***n.*** 1. an immixing. 2. the state or fact of being immixed or involved.

im·mo·bile (i-mō'b'l, im-mō'bēl), ***adj.*** [ME. *inmobill;* OFr. *immobile;* L. *immobilis;* see IN- (not) & MOBILE], 1. not movable; firmly set or placed; stable. 2. not moving or changing; motionless.

im·mo·bil·i·ty (im'ō-bil'ə-ti, im'mō-bil'ə-ti), ***n.*** [< Fr. or L.; Fr. *immobilité;* L. *immobilitas*], the state or quality of being immobile.

im·mo·bi·li·za·tion (i-mō'b'l-ə-zā'shən, im'mō-b'l-ī-zā'shən), ***n.*** an immobilizing or being immobilized.

im·mo·bi·lize (i-mō'b'l-īz', im-mō'b'l-īz'), ***v.t.*** [IMMOBILIZED (-īzd'), IMMOBILIZING], [Fr. *immobiliser*], 1. to make immobile; prevent the movement of; keep in place. 2. to take out of circulation and hold as security for bank notes: said of coin. 3. to prevent the movement of (a limb or joint) with splints or a cast.

im·mod·er·a·cy (i-mod'ẽr-ə-si), ***n.*** [Rare], immoderation.

im·mod·er·ate (i-mod'ẽr-it), ***adj.*** [ME.; L. *immoderatus*], 1. not moderate; without restraint; too much; unreasonable; excessive; extravagant: as, *immoderate* spending. 2. [Obs.], boundless. —***SYN.*** see **excessive.**

im·mod·er·a·tion (i-mod'ẽr-ā'shən), ***n.*** [< Fr. or L.; Fr. *immodération;* L. *immoderatio*], lack of moderation; excess.

im·mod·est (i-mod'ist), ***adj.*** not modest; specifically, *a)* not decorous; indecent. *b)* bold; forward; impudent.

im·mod·es·ty (i-mod'is-ti), ***n.*** [L. *immodestia*], the quality of being immodest.

im·mo·late (im'ə-lāt'), ***v.t.*** [IMMOLATED (-id), IMMOLATING], [< L. *immolatus,* pp. of *immolare,* to sprinkle a victim with sacrificial meal < *in-,* on + *mola,* meal], to sacrifice; especially, to offer or kill as a sacrifice.

im·mo·la·tion (im'ə-lā'shən), ***n.*** [L. *immolatio* < *immolare;* see IMMOLATE], 1. a sacrificing or being sacrificed. 2. something sacrificed.

im·mo·lat·or (im'ə-lāt'ẽr), ***n.*** [L.], one who immolates.

im·mor·al (i-môr'əl, i-mor'əl), ***adj.*** [*im-* (not) + *moral*], not in conformity with accepted principles of right and wrong behavior; contrary to the moral code of the community; wicked; especially, not in conformity with the accepted standards of proper sexual behavior; unchaste; lewd; licentious; obscene.

im·mo·ral·i·ty (im'ə-ral'ə-ti), ***n.*** 1. the state or quality of being immoral. 2. immoral behavior. 3. [*pl.* IMMORALITIES (-tiz)], an immoral act or practice; vice.

im·mor·tal (i-môr't'l), ***adj.*** [ME.; L. *immortalis*], 1. not mortal; deathless; living forever. 2. of immortal beings or immortality; divine; heavenly: as, an *immortal* vision. 3. lasting as long as this world; enduring; unfading; constant. 4. having lasting fame; remembered forever. ***n.*** an immortal being; specifically, *a) pl.* the gods of ancient Greece or Rome. *b)* a person having lasting fame.

im·mor·tal·i·ty (im'ôr-tal'ə-ti), ***n.*** [ME. *immortalite;* OFr. *immortalité;* L. *immortalitas*], the quality or state of being immortal; specifically, *a)* endless existence. *b)* lasting fame.

im·mor·ta·lize (i-môr't'l-īz'), ***v.t.*** [IMMORTALIZED (-īzd'), IMMORTALIZING], to make immortal; especially, to give lasting fame to.

im·mor·telle (im'ôr-tel'), ***n.*** [Fr. fem. of *immortel,* undying], any of various plants whose blossoms keep their color and shape when dried; an everlasting.

im·mo·tile (im-mō't'l), ***adj.*** not motile; unable to move.

im·mov·a·bil·i·ty (i-mōōv'ə-bil'ə-ti), ***n.*** the quality or state of being immovable.

im·mov·a·ble (i-mōōv'ə-b'l), ***adj.*** [ME. *immouable*], 1. that cannot be moved; firmly fixed; not capable of movement. 2. not moving; immobile; motionless; stationary. 3. that cannot be changed; unyielding; steadfast. 4. unemotional; impassive. 5. in *law,* not liable to be removed. ***n. pl.*** in *law,* immovable possessions or property, as land, trees, buildings, etc.

im·mov·ab·ly (i-mōōv'ə-bli), ***adv.*** in an immovable manner.

im·mune (i-mūn'), ***adj.*** [ME. *immuin;* OFr. *immune;* L. *immunis,* free from public service, exempt < *in-,* without + *munus,* duty, burden, tax], having immunity; exempt from or protected against something disagreeable or harmful; especially, not susceptible to some specified disease; protected as by inoculation.

immune body, a substance giving immunity to a specific disease, produced in the blood and lymph of individuals exposed to or inoculated with the antigen causing the disease; antibody.

im·mu·ni·ty (i-mū'nə-ti), ***n.*** [*pl.* IMMUNITIES (-tiz)], [ME. *ynmunite;* OFr. *immunité;* L. *immunitas,* freedom from public service < *immunis;* see IMMUNE], 1. exemption or release from taxes, military service, etc. 2. resistance to or protection against a specified disease; power to resist infection. —***SYN.*** see **exemption.**

im·mu·ni·za·tion (im'yoo-ni-zā'shən, im-ū'nī-zā'shən), ***n.*** an immunizing or being immunized.

i·mmu·nize (im'yoo-nīz'), ***v.t.*** [IMMUNIZED (-nīzd'), IMMUNIZING], to make immune; give immunity to, as by inoculation.

im·mu·no- (i-mū'nō), a combining form meaning *immune, immunity.*

im·mu·nol·o·gy (im'yoo-nol'ə-ji), ***n.*** [*immuno-* + *-logy*], the branch of medicine dealing with immunity to disease: abbreviated **immun.**

im·mu·no·re·ac·tion (i-mū'nō-ri-ak'shən), ***n.*** the reaction between an antigen and its antibody in the establishment of immunity.

im·mure (i-myoor'), ***v.t.*** [IMMURED (-myoord'), IMMURING], [OFr. *emmurrer;* ML. *immurrare* < L. *in-,* in + *murus,* wall], 1. to shut up within or as within walls; imprison; confine. 2. to seclude or isolate (oneself): as, he *immured* himself in his books.

im·mure·ment (i-myoor'mənt), ***n.*** an immuring or being immured.

im·mu·ta·bil·i·ty (i-mū'tə-bil'ə-ti), ***n.*** [L. *immutabilitas*], the quality or state of being immutable.

im·mu·ta·ble (i-mū'tə-b'l), ***adj.*** [ME.; L. *immutabilis;* see IN- (not) & MUTABLE], never changing or varying; unchangeable.

im·mut·ab·ly (i-mū'tə-bli), ***adv.*** in an immutable manner.

Im·o·gen (im'ə-jən), [first recorded in Shakespeare's *Cymbeline* (First Folio); ? misprint for Holinshed's *Innagon*], a feminine name.

Im·o·gene (im'ə-jēn'), a feminine name: see **Imogen.**

imp (imp), ***n.*** [ME. *impe;* AS. *impa* < *impian,* to imp, graft in < LL. *impotus,* a shoot; Gr. *emphytos* < *emphyein,* to implant; *em-,* in + *phyein,* to produce], 1. originally, a child; offspring. 2. a devil's offspring; young demon. 3. a mischievous child. ***v.t.*** [Archaic], 1. to implant, especially by grafting; hence, 2. to repair (the wing or tail of a falcon) by grafting on a feather or feathers. 3. to furnish with wings; hence, 4. to help out by adding, increasing, enlarging, etc.

imp., 1. imperative. 2. imperfect. 3. imperial. 4. impersonal. 5. import. 6. imported. 7. importer. 8. imprimatur. 9. imprint.

im·pact (im-pakt'; *for n.,* im'pakt), ***v.t.*** [< L. *impactus,* pp. of *impingere,* to press or drive firmly together; see IMPINGE], to force tightly together; pack; wedge. ***n.*** 1. a striking together; violent contact; collision. 2. the force of a collision; shock.

im·pact·ed (im-pak'tid), ***adj.*** [pp. of *impact*], pressed tightly together; driven firmly in; wedged in; especially, firmly lodged in the jaw: said of a tooth unable to erupt because of its abnormal position.

im·pac·tion (im-pak'shən), ***n.*** [L. *impactio*], an impacting or being impacted.

im·pair (im-pâr'), ***v.t.*** [ME. *empaire, empeire;* OFr. *empeirer* < L. *in-,* intens. + LL. *pejorare,* to make worse < L. *pejor,* worse], to make worse, less, weaker, etc.; damage; reduce; deteriorate. —***SYN.*** see **injure.**

im·pair·ment (im-pâr'mənt), ***n.*** 1. an impairing or being impaired. 2. damage; deterioration; injury.

im·pale (im-pāl'), ***v.t.*** [IMPALED (-pāld'), IMPALING], [Fr. *empaler;* L. *impalare* < *in-,* on + *palus,* a pole, stake], 1. [Rare], to surround with or as with a palisade; fence in. 2. *a)* to pierce through with, or fix on, something pointed; transfix. *b)* to punish or torture by fixing on a stake thrust through the body; hence, 3. to make helpless, as if fixed on a stake: as, her glance *impaled* him. 4. in *heraldry,* to join (two coats of arms) side by side on one shield. Also spelled **empale.**

im·pale·ment (im-pāl'mənt), ***n.*** [Fr. *empalement*], an impaling or being impaled.

im·pal·pa·bil·i·ty (im'pal-pə-bil'ə-ti, im-pal'pə-bil'ə-ti), ***n.*** the quality of being impalpable.

im·pal·pa·ble (im-pal'pə-b'l), ***adj.*** [Fr.; see IN- (not) & PALPABLE], 1. not perceptible to the touch; that cannot be felt. 2. too slight or subtle to be grasped easily by the mind; inappreciable: as, *impalpable* variations.

im·pal·pa·bly (im-pal'pə-bli), ***adv.*** in an impalpable manner; imperceptibly.

im·pa·na·tion (im'pə-nā'shən), ***n.*** [ML. *impanatio* < pp. of *impanare,* to embody in bread < L. *in-,* in + *panis,* bread], the doctrine that the body of Christ is present in the bread and wine of the Eucharist after consecration by the priest, with no actual change in their substance: distinguished from *transubstantiation.*

im·pan·el (im-pan''l), ***v.t.*** to empanel.

im·par·a·dise (im-par'ə-dīs'), ***v.t.*** [IMPARADISED (-dīst') IMPARADISING], 1. to make as happy as though in paradise; transport; enrapture. 2. to make into a paradise.

im·par·i·ty (im-par'ə-ti), ***n.*** [*pl.* IMPARITIES (-tiz)], [LL. *imparitas*], [Rare], disparity; lack of equality.

im·park (im-pärk'), ***v.t.*** [OFr. *enparquer*], 1. to shut up (animals) in a park. 2. to enclose (land) for a park.

im·part (im-pärt'), ***v.t.*** [OFr. *empartir;* L. *impartire;* see IN- (in) & PART], 1. to give a share or portion of; give. 2. to make known; tell; reveal; communicate.

im·par·ta·tion (im'pär-tā'shən), ***n.*** an imparting or being imparted.

im·par·tial (im-pär'shəl), ***adj.*** [*im-* (not) + *partial*], favoring no one side or party more than another; without prejudice or bias; fair; just. —***SYN.*** see **fair.**

im·par·ti·al·i·ty (im'pär-shi-al'ə-ti, im-pär'shi-al'ə-ti), ***n.*** freedom from favoritism, bias, or prejudice; impartial attitude or treatment; fairness; justice.

im·part·i·bil·i·ty (im-pär'tə-bil'ə-ti), ***n.*** the quality or condition of being impartible.

im·part·i·ble (im-pär'tə-b'l), ***adj.*** [LL. *impartibilis;* see IN- (not) & PARTIBLE], that cannot be partitioned or divided; indivisible: said of an estate.

im·part·i·ble (im-pär'tə-b'l), ***adj.*** that can be imparted, or communicated.

im·part·i·bly (im-pär'tə-bli), ***adv.*** in an impartible manner.

im·pass·a·bil·i·ty (im-pas'ə-bil'ə-ti), ***n.*** the quality or state of being impassable.

im·pass·a·ble (im-pas'ə-b'l), ***adj.*** that cannot be passed, crossed, or traveled over: as, an *impassable* highway.

im·passe (im'pas, im-pas'; Fr. aṅ'päs'), ***n.*** [*pl.* IMPASSES

(-iz; Fr. aṅ'päs')], [Fr.], 1. a passage open only at one end; blind alley; hence, 2. a situation from which there is no escape; difficulty without solution; deadlock.

im·pas·si·bil·i·ty (im-pas'ə-bil'ə-ti), *n.* [LL. *impassibilitas*], the quality or state of being impassible.

im·pas·si·ble (im-pas'ə-b'l), *adj.* [ME.; OFr.; LL. *impassibilis;* see IN- (not) & PASSIBLE], 1. that cannot feel pain; incapable of suffering. 2. that cannot be injured; invulnerable. 3. that cannot be moved or aroused emotionally; unfeeling.

im·pas·si·bly (im-pas'ə-bli), *adv.* in an impassible manner.

im·pas·sion (im-pash'ən), *v.t.* [It. *impassionare*], to fill with passion; arouse emotionally.

im·pas·sioned (im-pash'ənd), *adj.* [pp. of *impassion*], filled with passion; having or showing strong feeling; passionate; fiery; ardent. —*SYN.* see **passionate.**

im·pas·sive (im-pas'iv), *adj.* [*im-* (not) + *passive*], 1. not feeling pain; not suffering; insensible. 2. that cannot be injured; invulnerable. 3. not feeling or showing emotion; placid; calm; serene.

SYN.—**impassive** means not having or showing any feeling or emotion, although it does not necessarily connote an incapability of being affected (his *impassive* face did not betray his anguish); **apathetic** stresses an indifference or listlessness from which one cannot easily be stirred to feeling (an *apathetic* electorate); **stoic** implies an austere indifference to pleasure or pain and specifically suggests the ability to endure suffering without flinching (he received the bad news with *stoic* calm); **stolid** suggests dullness, obtuseness, or stupidity in one who is not easily moved or excited; **phlegmatic** is applied to one who by temperament is not easily disconcerted or aroused.

im·pas·siv·i·ty (im'pa-siv'ə-ti), *n.* the quality or state of being impassive.

im·paste (im-pāst'), *v.t.* [It. *impastare*], 1. to enclose or crust over with paste or a pasty substance. 2. to make a paste or crust of. 3. to apply a thick coat or coats of paint to.

im·pas·to (im-päs'tō), *n.* [It. < *impastare;* see IN- (in) & PASTE], 1. painting in which the paint is laid on thickly. 2. paint so laid on.

im·pa·tience (im-pā'shəns), *n.* [ME. & OFr. *impacience;* L. *impatientia*], lack of patience; specifically, *a*) annoyance because of delay, opposition, etc. *b*) restless eagerness to do something, go somewhere, etc.

im·pa·ti·ens (im-pā'shi-enz), *n.* [L.; see IMPATIENT], any of a group of flowers of the balsam family, with spurred flowers and pods that burst and scatter their seeds when ripe: also called *touch-me-not, jewelweed.*

im·pa·tient (im-pā'shənt), *adj.* [ME. & OFr. *impacient;* L. *impatiens;* see IN- (not) & PATIENT], feeling or showing a lack of patience; specifically, *a*) feeling or showing annoyance because of delay, opposition, etc. *b*) feeling or showing restless eagerness to do something, go somewhere, etc.

impatient of, not willing to bear or tolerate; showing dislike for.

im·pav·id (im-pav'id), *adj.* [L. *impavidus* < *in-*, not + *pavidus*, timid], [Rare], not afraid; fearless.

im·pawn (im-pôn'), *v.t.* to put in pawn; pledge as security.

im·peach (im-pēch'), *v.t.* [ME. *empechen;* OFr. *empechier, empescher,* to hinder; LL. *impedicare,* to fetter, catch, entangle < L. *in-*, in + *pedica,* a fetter < *pes, pedis,* foot], 1. to challenge or discredit (a person's honor, reputation, etc.). 2. to challenge the practices or honesty of; accuse; especially, to bring (a public official) before the proper tribunal on a charge of wrongdoing. *n.* [Rare], impeachment. —*SYN.* see **accuse.**

im·peach·a·bil·i·ty (im-pēch'ə-bil'ə-ti), *n.* the quality of being impeachable.

im·peach·a·ble (im-pēch'ə-b'l), *adj.* 1. liable to be impeached. 2. making one liable to be impeached: as, an *impeachable* act.

im·peach·ment (im-pēch'mənt), *n.* [ME. *empeschement*], an impeaching or being impeached.

im·pearl (im-pũrl'), *v.t.* & *v.i.* [*im-* (in) + *pearl,* after Fr. *emperler*], 1. to form into pearls or pearllike drops. 2. to decorate with or as with pearls. 3. to make pearly.

im·pec·ca·bil·i·ty (im-pek'ə-bil'ə-ti), *n.* the quality of being impeccable.

im·pec·ca·ble (im-pek'ə-b'l), *adj.* [LL. *impeccabilis* < L. *in-*, not + *peccare,* to sin], 1. not liable to sin or wrongdoing. 2. without defect or error; faultless; flawless. *n.* an impeccable person.

im·pec·cab·ly (im-pek'ə-bli), *adv.* in an impeccable manner.

im·pec·cance (im-pek'əns), *n.* impeccancy.

im·pec·can·cy (im-pek'ən-si), *n.* [LL. *impeccantia*], the quality of being impeccant.

im·pec·cant (im-pek'ənt), *adj.* [< L. *in-*, not + *peccans,* ppr. of *peccare,* to sin], free from sin or wrong; blameless.

im·pe·cu·ni·os·i·ty (im'pi-kū'ni-os'ə-ti), *n.* the quality or state of being impecunious; poverty.

im·pe·cu·ni·ous (im'pi-kū'ni-əs), *adj.* [< Fr. or L.; Fr. *impécunieux* < L. *in-*, not + *pecuniosus,* wealthy < *pecunia,* money; see PECUNIARY], having no money; poor; especially, constantly poor. —*SYN.* see **poor.**

im·ped·ance (im-pēd''ns), *n.* [< *impede* + *-ance*], 1. the apparent resistance in an alternating electrical current, corresponding to the true resistance in a direct current. 2. the ratio of the force per unit area to the volume displacement of a given surface across which sound is being transmitted.

im·pede (im-pēd'), *v.t.* [IMPEDED (-id), IMPEDING], [L. *impedire,* to entangle, ensnare, lit., to hold the feet < *in-*, in + *pes, pedis,* foot], to bar or hinder the progress of; obstruct; retard. —*SYN.* see **delay, hinder.**

im·ped·i·ment (im-ped'ə-mənt), *n.* [ME.; L. *impedimentum,* hindrance], 1. an impeding or being impeded. 2. anything that impedes; specifically, *a*) a speech defect; stutter, lisp, stammer, etc. *b*) anything preventing the making of a legal contract, especially of a marriage contract. —*SYN.* see **obstacle.**

im·ped·i·men·ta (im-ped'ə-men'tə, im'ped-ə-men'tə), *n.pl.* [L., pl. of *impedimentum;* see IMPEDIMENT], things hindering progress, as on a trip; encumbrances; specifically, *a*) baggage; equipment carried while traveling. *b*) the supplies or baggage carried along with an army.

im·ped·i·men·tal (im-ped'ə-men't'l), *adj.* of or like an impediment; obstructive.

im·ped·i·tive (im-ped'ə-tiv), *adj.* impedimental.

im·pel (im-pel'), *v.t.* [IMPELLED (-peld'), IMPELLING], [L. *impellere* < *in-*, in + *pellere,* to drive], 1. to push, drive, or move forward; propel. 2. to force, compel, or urge; incite; constrain.

im·pel·lent (im-pel'ənt), *adj.* [L. *impellens,* ppr. of *impellere*], impelling or tending to impel. *n.* anything that impels; motive, inducement, etc.

im·pel·ler (im-pel'ẽr), *n.* a person or thing that impels.

im·pend (im-pend'), *v.i.* [L. *impendere,* to overhang, threaten < *in-*, in + *pendere,* to hang], 1. to hang or be suspended (*over*). 2. to be about to happen; be near at hand; be imminent: as, an *impending* disaster.

im·pend·ence (im-pen'dəns), *n.* the quality or state of being impendent; imminence.

im·pen·den·cy (im-pen'dən-si), *n.* impendence.

im·pend·ent (im-pen'dənt), *adj.* [L. *impendens,* ppr. of *impendere*], impending; about to happen.

im·pend·ing (im-pen'diŋ), *adj.* [ppr. of *impend*], 1. hanging above; overhanging. 2. about to happen; imminent or threatening.

im·pen·e·tra·bil·i·ty (im-pen'i-trə-bil'ə-ti), *n.* the quality or condition of being impenetrable.

im·pen·e·tra·ble (im-pen'i-trə-b'l), *adj.* [Fr.; L. *impenetrabilis*], 1. that cannot be penetrated or pierced; impervious. 2. that cannot be solved or understood; unfathomable; inscrutable. 3. unreceptive to ideas, impressions, influences, etc. 4. in *physics,* having the property by which two bodies are prevented from occupying the same space at the same time.

im·pen·e·tra·bly (im-pen'i-trə-bli), *adv.* in an impenetrable manner.

im·pen·i·tence (im-pen'i-təns), *n.* [LL. *impaenitentia*], the quality or condition of being impenitent.

im·pen·i·ten·cy (im-pen'i-tən-si), *n.* impenitence.

im·pen·i·tent (im-pen'i-tənt), *adj.* [LL. *impaenitens*], without regret, shame, or remorse; not penitent; unrepentant. *n.* an impenitent person.

im·pen·nate (im-pen'āt), *adj.* [*im-* (not) + *pennate*], of a group of nonflying, swimming birds, with very short wings covered with scalelike feathers, as the penguins.

im·per·a·tive (im-per'ə-tiv), *adj.* [LL. *imperativus,* commanding < pp. of L. *imperare,* to command, order < *in-*, in + *parare,* to prepare, order], 1. having the nature of, or indicating, authority or command: as, an *imperative* gesture. 2. absolutely necessary; urgent; compelling: as, it is *imperative* that I go at once. 3. in *grammar,* designating or of the mood of a verb that expresses a command, strong request, or exhortation. *n.* 1. a command; order. 2. in *grammar, a*) the imperative mood. *b*) a verb in this mood. Abbreviated **imper., imp., impv.**

im·pe·ra·tor (im'pə-rā'tẽr, im'pə-rā'tôr), *n.* [L. < pp. of *imperare,* to command; see EMPEROR], in ancient Rome, a title of honor given originally to generals and later to emperors: abbreviated **I., i.**

im·per·a·to·ri·al (im-pẽr'ə-tôr'i-əl, im-pẽr'ə-tō'ri-əl), *adj.* [< L. *imperatorius;* + *-al*], of or suitable for an imperator.

im·per·cep·ti·bil·i·ty (im'pẽr-sep'tə-bil'ə-ti), *n.* the quality of being imperceptible.

im·per·cep·ti·ble (im'pẽr-sep'tə-b'l), *adj.* [Fr.; ML. *imperceptibilis;* see IN- (not) & PERCEPTIBLE], not plain or distinct to the senses or the mind; especially, so slight, gradual, subtle, etc. as not to be easily perceived.

im·per·cep·ti·bly (im'pẽr-sep'tə-bli), *adv.* in an imperceptible manner; not noticeably.

im·per·cep·tive (im'pẽr-sep'tiv), *adj.* not perceiving; lacking perception.

im·per·fect (im-pũr'fikt), *adj.* [ME. & OFr. *imparfit;* L. *imperfectus;* see IN- (not) & PERFECT], 1. not finished or complete; lacking in something. 2. not perfect; having a defect, fault, or error. 3. in the grammar of certain inflected languages, designating or of the tense of a verb that indicates a past action or state as incomplete, continuous, customary, or going on at the same time as another: "was writing" and "used to write" are forms corresponding to the imperfect tense in languages having such a tense. 4. in *music,* diminished. ***n.*** in *grammar,* 1. the imperfect tense. 2. a verb in this tense. Abbreviated **imperf., impf., imp.**

imperfect flower, a flower in which either the stamens or pistil are lacking; unisexual flower.

im·per·fec·tion (im'pẽr-fek'shən), ***n.*** [ME. *imperfecioun;* OFr. *imperfection;* LL. *imperfectio*], 1. the quality or condition of being imperfect. 2. a shortcoming; defect; fault; blemish. —***SYN.*** see **defect.**

im·per·fec·tive (im'pẽr-fek'tiv), ***adj.*** in *grammar,* designating or of an aspect of verbs, as in Russian and other Slavonic languages, expressing incompletion, or continued repetition, of the action. ***n.*** 1. the imperfective aspect. 2. a verb in this aspect.

im·per·fo·rate (im-pũr'fẽr-it), ***adj.*** [*im-* (not) + *perforate*], 1. having no holes or openings; unpierced. 2. having a straight edge without perforations: said of a postage stamp, etc. 3. in *anatomy,* lacking the normal opening. ***n.*** an imperforate stamp. Abbreviated **imperf.**

im·per·fo·rat·ed (im-pũr'fə-rā'tid), ***adj.*** imperforate.

im·per·fo·ra·tion (im-pũr'fə-rā'shən), ***n.*** the state, or an instance, of being imperforate.

im·pe·ri·al (im-pêr'i-əl), ***adj.*** [ME.; OFr.; L. *imperialis* < *imperium,* empire, command; see EMPIRE], 1. of an empire. 2. of a country having control or sovereign rights over other countries or colonies. 3. of, or having the rank of, an emperor or empress. 4. having supreme authority; sovereign. 5. majestic; august; magnificent. 6. of great size or superior quality. 7. according to the standard of weights and measures fixed by British law. ***n.*** 1. [I-], *a)* a supporter of the Holy Roman emperor. *b)* a soldier of his troops. 2. a gold coin of the former Russian Empire. 3. *a)* the roof or top of a coach. *b)* a case or trunk carried on this. 4. an article of great size or superior quality: often a trade name. 5. a size of writing paper measuring 23 by 31 inches (in England, 22 by 30 or 32 inches). 6. [after Napoleon III, who set this fashion], a pointed tuft of beard on the lower lip and chin. Abbreviated **imp.**

IMPERIAL (beard)

imperial gallon, the standard British gallon, equal to 277.42 cubic inches or about 1 1/5 United States gallons: abbreviated **imp. gal.**

im·pe·ri·al·ism (im-pêr'i-əl-iz'm), ***n.*** 1. imperial state, authority, spirit, or system of government. 2. the policy and practice of forming and maintaining an empire: in modern times, it is characterized by a struggle for the control of raw materials and world markets, the subjugation and control of territories, the establishment of colonies, etc.

im·pe·ri·al·ist (im-pêr'i-əl-ist), ***n.*** [*imperial* + *-ist,* after Fr. *impérialiste*], 1. [I-], *a)* a supporter of the Holy Roman emperor. *b)* a soldier of his troops. 2. a supporter of any emperor. 3. a person favoring imperialism. ***adj.*** imperialistic.

im·pe·ri·al·is·tic (im-pêr'i-əl-is'tik), ***adj.*** 1. of or characteristic of imperialism or imperialists. 2. favoring imperialism.

im·pe·ri·al·is·ti·cal·ly (im-pêr'i-əl-is'ti-k'l-i, im-pêr'i-əl-is'tik-li), ***adv.*** in an imperialistic manner.

imperial moth, a large American moth having yellow wings with dark markings.

Imperial Valley, a productive agricultural region in southeastern California, reclaimed from the Colorado Desert by irrigation.

im·per·il (im-per'əl), ***v.t.*** [IMPERILED or IMPERILLED (-əld), IMPERILING or IMPERILLING], to put in peril; endanger.

im·pe·ri·ous (im-pêr'i-əs), ***adj.*** [L. *imperiosus* < *imperium,* empire, command; see EMPIRE], 1. overbearing; arrogant; domineering; dictatorial. 2. urgent; imperative. —***SYN.*** see **masterful.**

im·per·ish·a·bil·i·ty (im-per'ish-ə-bil'ə-ti), ***n.*** the quality of being imperishable.

im·per·ish·a·ble (im-per'ish-ə-b'l), ***adj.*** not perishable; that will not decay; indestructible; immortal.

im·per·ish·ab·ly (im-per'ish-ə-bli), ***adv.*** in an imperishable manner.

im·pe·ri·um (im-pêr'i-əm), ***n.*** [*pl.* IMPERIA (-ə)], [L.; see EMPIRE], 1. supreme power; absolute authority or rule; imperial sovereignty; empire. 2. in *law,* the right of a state to use force in maintaining the law.

im·per·ma·nent (im-pũr'mə-nənt), ***adj.*** not permanent; not lasting; fleeting; temporary.

im·per·me·a·bil·i·ty (im-pũr'mi-ə-bil'ə-ti), ***n.*** the condition or quality of being impermeable.

im·per·me·a·ble (im-pũr'mi-ə-b'l), ***adj.*** [LL. *impermeabilis*], not permeable; not permitting passage, especially of fluids; impenetrable.

im·per·me·a·bly (im-pũr'mi-ə-bli), ***adv.*** in an impermeable manner.

im·per·mis·si·ble (im'pẽr-mis'ə-b'l), ***adj.*** not permissible.

im·per·son·al (im-pũr's'n-əl), ***adj.*** [LL. *impersonalis*], 1. not personal; specifically, *a)* without connection or reference to any particular person: as, an *impersonal* attitude. *b)* not existing as a person: as, time is an *impersonal* force. 2. in *grammar,* designating or of a verb occurring only in the third person singular, in English generally with *it* as the indefinite subject (e.g., "it is snowing"). ***n.*** 1. [Rare], an impersonal thing. 2. an impersonal verb. Abbreviated **imp., impers.**

im·per·son·al·i·ty (im'pẽr-sə-nal'ə-ti, im-pũr'sə-nal'ə-ti), ***n.*** 1. the condition or quality of being impersonal. 2. [*pl.* IMPERSONALITIES (-tiz)], an impersonal thing.

im·per·son·al·ize (im-pũr's'n-əl-īz'), ***v.t.*** to make impersonal.

im·per·son·al·ly (im-pũr's'n-əl-i), ***adv.*** in an impersonal manner.

im·per·son·ate (im-pũr'sə-nāt'), ***v.t.*** [IMPERSONATED (-id), IMPERSONATING], 1. to represent in the form of a person; personify; embody: as, he *impersonates* the spirit of the people. 2. to act the part of; take the character of: as, Edwin Booth *impersonated* many of Shakespeare's heroes. 3. to mimic the appearance, behavior, manner, etc. of (a person) for purposes of entertainment. ***adj.*** embodied in a person; personified.

im·per·son·a·tion (im'pẽr-sə-nā'shən, im-pũr'sə-nā'shən), ***n.*** an impersonating or being impersonated; specifically, *a)* personification; embodiment. *b)* an imitation of another's character or personality.

im·per·son·a·tor (im-pũr'sə-nā'tẽr), ***n.*** a person who impersonates; especially, an actor or entertainer who mimics other persons.

im·per·ti·nence (im-pũr't'n-əns), ***n.*** [Fr.], 1. the quality or fact of being impertinent; specifically, *a)* lack of pertinence; irrelevance; pointlessness. *b)* unsuitability; inappropriateness; incongruity. *c)* insolence; impudence. 2. an impertinent act, remark, etc.

im·per·ti·nen·cy (im-pũr't'n-ən-si), ***n.*** [*pl.* IMPERTINENCIES (-siz)], impertinence.

im·per·ti·nent (im-pũr't'n-ənt), ***adj.*** [ME.; OFr.; L. *impertinens*], 1. not pertinent; having no meaning, importance, or relationship to a given matter; irrelevant; pointless. 2. not suitable to the circumstances; inappropriate; incongruous. 3. not showing proper respect or manners; saucy; insolent; impudent.

SYN.—**impertinent** implies a forwardness of speech or action that is disrespectful and oversteps the bounds of propriety or courtesy; **impudent** implies a shameless or brazen impertinence; **insolent** implies defiant disrespect as displayed in openly insulting and contemptuous speech or behavior; **saucy** implies a flippancy and provocative levity toward one to whom respect should be shown.

im·per·turb·a·bil·i·ty (im'pẽr-tũr'bə-bil'ə-ti), ***n.*** the condition or quality of being imperturbable.

im·per·turb·a·ble (im'pẽr-tũr'bə-b'l), ***adj.*** [LL. *imperturbabilis;* see IN- (not), PERTURB, -ABLE], that cannot be disconcerted, disturbed, or excited; impassive.

im·per·turb·a·bly (im'pẽr-tũr'bə-bli), ***adv.*** in an imperturbable manner.

im·per·tur·ba·tion (im'pẽr-tẽr-bā'shən), ***n.*** [LL. *imperturbatio* (see IN- (not) & PERTURBATION), used as transl. of Gr. *apatheia* (see APATHY)], freedom from excitement; serenity; calmness.

im·per·vi·a·ble (im-pũr'vi-ə-b'l), ***adj.*** [< *impervious* + *-able*], impervious; impermeable.

im·per·vi·ous (im-pũr'vi-əs), ***adj.*** [L. *impervius;* see IN- (not) & PERVIOUS], 1. incapable of being passed through or penetrated: as, a fabric *impervious* to moisture. 2. not affected or influenced by (with *to*): as, a man *impervious* to reason.

im·pe·tig·i·nous (im'pi-tij'ə-nəs), ***adj.*** [L. *impetiginosus*], 1. of or like impetigo. 2. having impetigo.

im·pe·ti·go (im'pi-tī'gō), ***n.*** [L. < *impetere,* to attack < *in-,* in + *petere,* to rush at, assault], any of certain skin diseases characterized by the eruption of pustules; especially, a contagious disease of this kind, caused by staphylococci.

im·pe·trate (im'pi-trāt'), ***v.t.*** [IMPETRATED (-id), IMPETRATING], [< L. *impetratus,* pp. of *impetrare,* to accomplish < *in-,* intens. + *patrare,* to accomplish], 1. to get by request or entreaty. 2. [Rare], to implore.

im·pe·tra·tion (im'pi-trā'shən), ***n.*** an impetrating.

im·pe·tra·tive (im'pi-trā'tiv), ***adj.*** impetrating.

im·pe·tra·tor (im'pi-trā'tẽr), ***n.*** one who impetrates.

im·pet·u·os·i·ty (im'pech-ōō-os'ə-ti, im-pech'ōō-os'ə-ti), ***n.*** [Fr. *impétuosité;* LL. *impetuositas* < L. *impetuosus*], 1. the quality of being impetuous. 2. [*pl.* IMPETUOSITIES (-tiz)], an impetuous action or feeling.

im·pet·u·ous (im-pech'ōō-əs), ***adj.*** [Fr. *impétueux;* L. *impetuosus* < *impetus;* see IMPETUS], 1. moving with great force or violence; having great impetus; rushing;

furious: as, *impetuous* winds. 2. acting suddenly with little thought; rash; impulsive. —*SYN.* see **sudden.**

im·pe·tus (im′pə-təs), *n.* [*pl.* IMPETUSES (-iz)], [L. < *impetere*, to rush upon < *in-*, in + *petere*, to rush at, seek], 1. the force with which a body moves against resistance, resulting from its mass and the velocity at which it is set in motion. 2. anything that stimulates activity; driving force or motive; incentive; impulse.

impf., imperfect.

imp. gal., imperial gallon.

Imp·hal (imp′hul), *n.* the capital of Manipur state, India, near the border of Burma: pop., 86,000.

im·pi (im′pi), *n.* [Zulu], a large band of Zulu or Kaffir warriors.

im·pi·e·ty (im-pī′ə-ti), *n.* [ME. *impietie* < OFr. or L.; OFr. *impiété*; L. *impietas*], 1. a lack of piety; specifically, *a*) lack of reverence for God. *b*) disrespect for persons or things to which one should be devoted. 2. [*pl.* IMPIETIES (-tiz)], an impious act or behavior.

im·pinge (im-pinj′), *v.i.* [IMPINGED (-pinjd′), IMPINGING], [L. *impingere* < *in-*, in + *pangere*, to strike], 1. to strike, hit, or dash (*on*, *upon*, or *against* something). 2. to make inroads or encroach (*on* or *upon* the property or rights of another).

im·pinge·ment (im-pinj′mənt), *n.* an impinging.

im·ping·er (im-pinj′ẽr), *n.* a person or thing that impinges.

im·pi·ous (im′pi-əs), *adj.* [L. *impius*], not pious; specifically, *a*) lacking reverence for God. *b*) [Rare], disrespectful toward persons or things to which one should be devoted.

imp·ish (imp′ish), *adj.* of or like an imp; mischievous.

im·pla·ca·bil·i·ty (im′plā-kə-bil′ə-ti, im-plak′ə-bil′ə-ti), *n.* the condition or quality of being implacable.

im·pla·ca·ble (im-plā′kə-b′l, im-plak′ə-b′l), *adj.* [Fr.; L. *implacabilis*], 1. not placable; not to be appeased or pacified; relentless; inexorable. 2. [Obs.], that cannot be eased, lessened, or allayed. —*SYN.* see **inflexible.**

im·plac·ab·ly (im-plā′kə-bli, im-plak′ə-bli), *adv.* in an implacable manner.

im·pla·cen·tal (im′plə-sen′t′l), *adj.* [*im-* (not) + *placental*], having no placenta: said of a division of mammals that includes the marsupials and monotremes. *n.* a mammal having no placenta.

im·pla·cen·tate (im′plə-sen′tāt, im-plas′′n-tāt′), *adj.* implacental.

im·plant (im-plant′, im-plänt′), *v.t.* [Fr. *implanter*], 1. to plant firmly or deeply; embed. 2. to fix firmly in the mind; instill; inculcate. 3. in *medicine*, to insert (a piece of living tissue) in grafting. *n.* (im′plant′, im′plänt′), in *medicine*, 1. an implanted piece of tissue; graft. 2. a small tube containing a radioactive substance, implanted in an organ or tissue in the treatment of cancer, etc. —*SYN.* see **instill.**

im·plan·ta·tion (im′plan-tā′shən), *n.* an implanting or being implanted.

im·plau·si·ble (im-plô′zə-b′l), *adj.* not plausible.

im·plau·si·bly (im-plô′zə-bli), *adv.* in an implausible manner.

im·plead (im-plēd′), *v.t. & v.i.* [ME. *enpleden*; Anglo-Fr. *empleder*; OFr. *emplaidier*; see IN- (in) & PLEAD], 1. to sue in a law court. 2. to plead (a cause, etc.).

im·ple·ment (im′plə-mənt; *for v.*, im′plə-ment′), *n.* [LL. *implementum*, a filling up < L. *implere*, to fill up < *in-*, in + *plere*, to fill], something used or needed in a given activity; tool, instrument, utensil, etc. *v.t.* 1. to carry into effect; fulfill; accomplish. 2. to provide with the means for carrying into effect or fulfilling; give practical effect to. 3. to provide with implements.

SYN.—**implement** applies to any device used to carry on some work or effect some purpose (agricultural *implements*); **tool** is commonly applied to manual implements such as are used in carpentry, plumbing, etc.; **instrument** specifically implies use for delicate work or for scientific or artistic purposes (surgical *instruments*) and may also be applied, as is **tool**, to a thing or person serving as a means to an end; **appliance** specifically suggests a mechanical or power-driven household device, usually one that is in some way controlled by the hands; **utensil** is used of any implement or container for domestic use, especially a pot, pan, etc.

im·ple·men·tal (im′plə-men′t′l), *adj.* of, or having the nature of, an implement; instrumental.

im·ple·men·ta·tion (im′plə-men-tā′shən), *n.* an implementing or being implemented.

im·ple·tion (im-plē′shən), *n.* [LL. *impletio* < pp. of L. *implere*; see IMPLEMENT], a filling or being filled.

im·pli·cate (im′pli-kāt′), *v.t.* [IMPLICATED (-id), IMPLICATING], [< L. *implicatus*, pp. of *implicare*, to enfold, involve < *in-*, in + *plicare*, to fold], 1. to twist or fold together; intertwine; entangle. 2. to imply. 3. to show to be a party to a crime, fault, etc.; involve.

im·pli·ca·tion (im′pli-kā′shən), *n.* [ME. *implicacioun*; L. *implicatio*], 1. an implicating or being implicated. 2. an implying or being implied. 3. something implied, from which an inference may be drawn.

im·pli·ca·tive (im′pli-kā′tiv), *adj.* tending to imply or implicate.

im·pli·ca·to·ry (im′pli-kə-tôr′i, im′pli-kə-tō′ri), *adj.* implicating.

im·plic·it (im-plis′it), *adj.* [< Fr. or L.; Fr. *implicite*; L. *implicitus*, pp. of *implicare*; see IMPLICATE], 1. formerly, implicated; entangled. 2. suggested or to be understood though not plainly expressed; implied: distinguished from *explicit*. 3. necessarily or naturally involved though not plainly apparent or expressed; essentially a part or condition; inherent. 4. without reservation or doubt; unquestioning; absolute.

im·plied (im-plīd′), *adj.* [pp. of *imply*], involved, suggested, or understood without being openly or directly expressed.

im·plode (im-plōd′), *v.t. & v.i.* [IMPLODED (-id), IMPLODING], [< *im-*, in + L. *plodere*, *plaudere*; see EXPLODE], 1. to burst inward. 2. to pronounce by implosion.

im·plore (im-plôr′, im-plōr′), *v.t.* [IMPLORED (-plôrd′, -plōrd′), IMPLORING], [L. *implorare*, to beseech, entreat < *in-*, intens. + *plorare*, to cry out, weep], 1. to ask or beg earnestly for; beseech. 2. to ask or beg (a person) to do something; entreat. —*SYN.* see **beg.**

im·plo·sion (im-plō′zhən), *n.* [< *implode*, after *explosion*], an imploding; specifically, *a*) a bursting inward. *b*) the abrupt cutting off of the breath stream in beginning to pronounce certain consonants, as *p*, *t*, and *k*.

im·plo·sive (im-plō′siv), *adj.* formed by implosion. *n.* an implosive sound or consonant.

im·ply (im-plī′), *v.t.* [IMPLIED (-plīd′), IMPLYING], [ME. *implien*; OFr. *emplier*; L. *implicare* < *in-*, in + *plicare*, to fold], 1. to have as a necessary part, condition, or effect; contain, include, or involve naturally or necessarily: as, drama *implies* conflict. 2. to indicate without saying openly or directly; hint; suggest; intimate: as, his attitude *implied* boredom. 3. [Obs.], to enfold; entangle. —*SYN.* see **suggest.**

im·pol·i·cy (im-pol′ə-si), *n.* [*pl.* IMPOLICIES (-siz)], [*im-* (not) + *policy*], an unwise policy; anything impolitic.

im·po·lite (im′pə-līt′), *adj.* [L. *impolitus*, unpolished], not polite; ill-mannered; discourteous. —*SYN.* see **rude.**

im·pol·i·tic (im-pol′ə-tik), *adj.* not politic; unwise; injudicious; inexpedient.

im·pon·der·a·bil·i·ty (im-pon′dẽr-ə-bil′ə-ti), *n.* the condition or quality of being imponderable.

im·pon·der·a·ble (im-pon′dẽr-ə-b′l), *adj.* not ponderable; that cannot be weighed or measured. *n.* anything imponderable.

im·pone (im-pōn′), *v.t.* [IMPONED (-pōnd′), IMPONING], [L. *imponere*, to set upon < *in-*, in, on + *ponere*, to put, place], [Obs.], to wager; stake.

im·port (im-pôrt′, im′pōrt; *for n.*, im′pôrt, im′pōrt), *v.t.* [ME. *importen*; L. *importare*, to bring in, introduce, bring about < *in-*, in + *portare*, to carry; *v.t.* 2, 3 & *v.i.* < ML. *importare*, to imply, mean, be of importance < L.], 1. *a*) to bring in from the outside; introduce. *b*) to bring (goods) into one country from another in commerce: opposed to *export*. 2. to mean; signify: as, this action *imports* trouble. 3. to be of importance to; concern. *v.i.* to be of importance; matter. *n.* 1. the act or business of importing (goods). 2. something imported: abbreviated **imp.** 3. meaning; signification: as, the *import* of his statement. 4. importance. —*SYN.* see **meaning.**

im·por·tance (im-pôr′t′ns), *n.* [Fr.; ML. *importantia*], 1. the state or quality of being important; significance; consequence; value. 2. [Obs.], *a*) a matter of consequence. *b*) import. *c*) importunity.

SYN.—**importance**, the broadest of these terms, implies greatness of worth, meaning, influence, etc. (news of *importance*); **consequence**, often interchangeable with the preceding, more specifically suggests importance with regard to outcome or result (a disagreement of no *consequence*); **moment** expresses this same idea of importance in effect with somewhat stronger force (affairs of great *moment*); **weight** implies an estimation of the relative importance of something (his word carries great *weight* with us); **significance** implies an importance or momentousness because of a special meaning that may or may not be immediately apparent (an event of *significance*).

im·por·tant (im-pôr′t′nt), *adj.* [Fr.; ML. *importans*, ppr. of *importare*; see IMPORT], 1. meaning a great deal; having much significance, consequence, or value. 2. having, or acting as if having, power, authority, influence, high position, etc. 3. [Obs.], importunate.

im·por·ta·tion (im′pôr-tā′shən, im′pōr-tā′shən), *n.* 1. an importing or being imported. 2. something imported.

im·port·er (im-pôr′tẽr, im-pōr′tẽr), *n.* a person or firm in the business of importing goods: abbreviated **imp.**

im·por·tu·na·cy (im-pôr′chə-nə-si), *n.* importunity.

im·por·tu·nate (im-pôr′chə-nit), *adj.* [ML. *importunatus*, pp. of *importunari*, to vex, be troublesome < L. *importunus*; see IMPORTUNE], 1. urgent or persistent in asking or demanding; insistent; refusing to be denied; annoyingly urgent or persistent. 2. [Obs.], troublesome; annoying.

im·por·tune (im′pôr-tōōn′, im′pôr-tūn′, im-pôr′choon), *v.t.* [IMPORTUNED (-tōōnd′, -tūnd′, -choond), IMPORTUNING], [Fr. *importuner*; ML. *importunari*, to be troublesome, vex < L. *importunus*, without access, troublesome < *in-*, not, without + *portus*, a port, harbor, entrance, access; cf. PORTAL], 1. to trouble with requests or demands; urge or entreat persistently or repeatedly. 2. [Rare], to ask for urgently; demand. 3. [Obs.], *a)* to trouble; annoy. *b)* to impel. ***v.i.*** to be importunate. ***adj.*** importunate. —***SYN.*** see **beg, urge.**

im·por·tu·ni·ty (im'pôr-tōō'nə-ti, im'pôr-tū'nə-ti), ***n.*** [*pl.* IMPORTUNITIES (-tiz)], [Fr. *importunité;* L. *importunitas*], an importuning or being importunate; persistence in requesting or demanding.

im·pose (im-pōz'), ***v.t.*** [IMPOSED (-pōzd'), IMPOSING], [Fr. *imposer;* see IN- (in) & POSE], 1. to place (a burden, tax, etc. *on* or *upon*); inflict; force: as, the king *imposed* a tax on the people. 2. to force (oneself, one's presence, etc.) on another or others without right or invitation; obtrude. 3. to pass off; palm off; foist, especially by deception: as, he *imposed* his doctrines upon the confused nation. 4. to arrange (pages of type) in a frame in the proper order of printing. 5. [Archaic], to place; put; deposit. 6. in *ecclesiastical usage,* to lay on (the hands), as in ordination or confirmation.

impose on (or **upon**), 1. [Rare], to make an impression on; have influence with because of prestige, etc. 2. to take liberties with; take advantage of. 3. to get the better of by deceiving; cheat; defraud.

im·pos·ing (im-pōz'iŋ), ***adj.*** [ppr. of *impose*], making a strong impression because of great size, strength, dignity, etc.; impressive. —***SYN.*** see **grand.**

im·po·si·tion (im'pə-zish'ən), ***n.*** [ME.; OFr.; L. *impositio,* a laying upon, application], 1. an imposing or imposing on; specifically, *a)* the forcing of oneself, one's presence, etc. on another or others without right or invitation; obtrusion. *b)* a taking advantage of friendship, etc.: as, it is an *imposition* to ask him to help. *c)* in *ecclesiastical usage,* the laying on of hands, as in ordination or confirmation. 2. something imposed; specifically, *a)* a tax, fine, etc. *b)* an unjust burden, requirement, etc. *c)* a deception; fraud.

im·pos·si·bil·i·ty (im-pos'ə-bil'ə-ti), ***n.*** [OFr. *impossibilite;* LL. *impossibilitas*], 1. the fact or quality of being impossible. 2. [*pl.* IMPOSSIBILITIES (-tiz)], something impossible.

im·pos·si·ble (im-pos'ə-b'l), ***adj.*** [ME.; OFr.; L. *impossibilis;* see IN- (not) & POSSIBLE], 1. not capable of being, being done, or happening. 2. not capable of being done easily or conveniently: as, it was *impossible* for me to come yesterday. 3. [Colloq.], not capable of being endured, used, etc., because disagreeable or unsuitable: as, an *impossible* person.

im·pos·si·bly (im-pos'ə-bli), ***adv.*** 1. in an impossible manner. 2. to an impossible extent.

im·post (im'pōst), ***n.*** [OFr.; LL. *impositus* (in L., pp. of *imponere*); see IN- (in) & POSE], a tax; especially, a duty on imported goods; customs duty. ***v.t.*** to classify (imported goods) in order to assess the proper taxes.

im·post (im'pōst), ***n.*** [Fr. *imposte;* It. *imposta* < L. *impositus;* see IMPOST (a tax)], the top part of a pillar supporting an arch.

im·pos·tor (im-pos'tẽr), ***n.*** [Fr. *imposteur;* LL. *impostor* < pp. of L. *imponere;* see IMPOSE], a cheat or fraud; especially, a person who deceives by pretending to be someone or something that he is not. —***SYN.*** see **quack.**

im·pos·ture (im-pos'chẽr), ***n.*** [Fr.; LL. *impostura*], the act or practice of an impostor; fraud; deception.

im·po·tence (im'pə-təns), ***n.*** [ME.; OFr.; L. *impotentia*], the quality or condition of being impotent; specifically, *a)* lack of physical strength; weakness. *b)* lack of effectiveness; helplessness. *c)* lack of ability to engage in sexual intercourse: said of males.

im·po·ten·cy (im'pə-tən-si), ***n.*** [*pl.* IMPOTENCIES (-siz)], impotence.

im·po·tent (im'pə-tənt), ***adj.*** [ME.; OFr.; L. *impotens;* see IN- (not) & POTENT], 1. lacking physical strength; hence, 2. ineffective, powerless, or helpless: as, *impotent* rage. 3. unable to engage in sexual intercourse: said of males. —***SYN.*** see **sterile.**

im·pound (im-pound'), ***v.t.*** 1. to shut up (an animal) in a pound; hence, 2. to take into legal custody. 3. to gather and enclose (water) for irrigation, etc.

im·pov·er·ish (im-pov'ẽr-ish), ***v.t.*** [OFr. *empovrir* < L. *in,* in + *pauper,* poor], 1. to make poor; reduce to poverty. 2. to deprive of strength, resources, etc.

im·pov·er·ish·ment (im-pov'ẽr-ish-mənt), ***n.*** [OFr. *empoverissement*], 1. an impoverishing or being impoverished. 2. something that impoverishes.

im·pow·er (im-pou'ẽr), ***v.t.*** to empower.

im·prac·ti·ca·bil·i·ty (im'prak-ti-kə-bil'ə-ti, im-prak'ti-kə-bil'ə-ti), ***n.*** 1. the quality of being impracticable. 2. [*pl.* IMPRACTICABILITIES (-tiz)], something impracticable.

im·prac·ti·ca·ble (im-prak'ti-kə-b'l), ***adj.*** [*im-* (not) + *practicable*], 1. not capable of being carried out in practice: as, an *impracticable* plan. 2. not capable of being used: as, an *impracticable* road. 3. not capable of being managed or dealt with; intractable: as, an *impracticable* person.

im·prac·ti·ca·bly (im-prak'ti-kə-bli), ***adv.*** 1. in an impracticable manner. 2. to an impracticable degree.

im·prac·ti·cal (im-prak'ti-k'l), ***adj.*** not practical.

im·prac·ti·cal·i·ty (im'prak-ti-kal'ə-ti, im-prak'ti-kal'ə-ti), ***n.*** 1. the quality of being impractical. 2. [*pl.* IMPRACTICALITIES (-tiz)], something impractical.

im·pre·cate (im'pri-kāt'), ***v.t.*** [IMPRECATED (-id), IMPRECATING], [< L. *imprecatus,* pp. of *imprecari,* to invoke, pray to < *in-,* in, on + *precari,* to pray < *prex,* prayer], 1. to pray for (evil, misfortune, etc.); invoke (a curse). 2. [Rare], to invoke evil upon; curse. —***SYN.*** see **curse.**

im·pre·ca·tion (im'pri-kā'shən), ***n.*** [L. *imprecatio*], 1. the act of imprecating evil, etc. on someone. 2. a curse.

im·pre·ca·tor (im'pri-kā'tẽr), ***n.*** one who imprecates.

im·pre·ca·to·ry (im'pri-kə-tôr'i, im'pri-kə-tō'ri), ***adj.*** of, like, or uttering an imprecation.

im·preg·na·bil·i·ty (im'preg-nə-bil'ə-ti, im-preg'nə-bil'ə-ti), ***n.*** the quality or condition of being impregnable.

im·preg·na·ble (im-preg'nə-b'l), ***adj.*** [ME. & OFr. *imprenable;* see IN- (not) & PREGNABLE], 1. not capable of being captured or entered by force. 2. unshakable; unyielding; firm: as, an *impregnable* belief.

im·preg·na·ble (im-preg'nə-b'l), ***adj.*** [< *impregnate*], that can be impregnated.

im·preg·na·bly (im-preg'nə-bli), ***adv.*** so as to be impregnable: as, *impregnably* defended.

im·preg·nate (im-preg'nāt), ***v.t.*** [IMPREGNATED (-id), IMPREGNATING], [< LL. *impraegnatus,* pp. of *impraegnare,* to make pregnant < L. *in-,* in + *praegnans,* pregnant], 1. to fertilize (an ovum). 2. to make pregnant. 3. to fertilize (land); make fruitful. 4. to fill or saturate; cause to be permeated: as, they *impregnated* their clothing with insecticide. 5. to indoctrinate or imbue (*with* ideas, feelings, principles, etc.). ***adj.*** (im-preg'nit), impregnated. —***SYN.*** see **soak.**

im·preg·na·tion (im'preg-nā'shən), ***n.*** 1. an impregnating or being impregnated. 2. something that impregnates.

im·preg·na·tor (im-preg'nā-tẽr), ***n.*** a person or thing that impregnates.

im·pre·sa·ri·o (im'pri-sä'ri-ō'), ***n.*** [*pl.* IMPRESARIOS (-ōz')], [It. < *impresa,* enterprise], the organizer, manager, or director of an opera or ballet company, concert series, etc.

im·pre·scrip·ti·ble (im'pri-skrip'tə-b'l), ***adj.*** [Fr.; see IN- (not) & PRESCRIPTIBLE], that cannot rightfully be taken away, lost, or revoked; inviolable.

im·pre·scrip·ti·bly (im'pri-skrip'tə-bli), ***adv.*** in an imprescriptible manner; inviolably.

im·press (im-pres'; *for n.,* im'pres), ***v.t.*** [*im-* (in) + *press* (to force into service)], 1. to draft or force (men) to serve in an army or, especially, a navy. 2. to levy, seize, or requisition (money, property, etc.) for public use. 3. to introduce and make use of (a fact, etc.). ***n.*** impressment.

im·press (im-pres'; *for n.,* im'pres), ***v.t.*** [ME. *impressen;* OFr. *empresser* < L. *impressus,* pp. of *imprimere;* see IN- (in) & PRESS (to squeeze)], 1. to use pressure on so as to leave a mark: as, he *impressed* the clay with a die. 2. to mark by using pressure; stamp; imprint. 3. to apply with pressure: as, he *impressed* the die in the clay. 4. to have a considerable effect on the mind or emotions of. 5. to implant firmly on the mind or fix in the memory. ***n.*** 1. an impressing. 2. any mark, imprint, etc. made by pressure; stamp; impression. 3. an effect produced on the mind or feelings by some strong influence. —***SYN.*** see **affect.**

im·press·i·bil·i·ty (im-pres'ə-bil'ə-ti), ***n.*** the quality of being impressible.

im·press·i·ble (im-pres'ə-b'l), ***adj.*** that can be impressed; impressionable.

im·pres·sion (im-presh'ən), ***n.*** [ME. *impressioun;* OFr. *impression;* L. *impressio*], 1. an impressing. 2. a result or effect of impressing; specifically, *a)* a mark, imprint, etc. made by physical pressure. *b)* an effect produced on the mind or senses by some force or influence: as, his music makes little *impression* on me. *c)* the effect produced by any effort or activity: as, our attempt at cleaning made no *impression* on the dirt. 3. a vague notion or feeling; inkling: as, I have the *impression* that he was there. 4. in *dentistry,* the imprint of the teeth and surrounding tissues in wax or plaster, used as a mold in making dentures. 5. in *printing, a)* the pressing of type or plates on paper, etc.; printing. *b)* a printed copy. *c)* all the copies printed as a single edition. —***SYN.*** see **idea.**

im·pres·sion·a·bil·i·ty (im-presh'ən-ə-bil'ə-ti), ***n.*** the quality or state of being impressionable.

im·pres·sion·a·ble (im-presh'ən-ə-b'l), ***adj.*** [Fr.], easily affected by impressions; capable of being influenced intellectually, emotionally, or morally; sensitive.

im·pres·sion·al (im-presh'ən-'l), ***adj.*** of, or having the nature of, an impression.

im·pres·sion·ism (im-presh'ən-iz'm), ***n.*** [cf. Fr. *impressionnisme*], a theory and school of art, exemplified by the work of Manet, Monet, Renoir, Degas, Pissarro, etc., whose chief aim is to reproduce only the immediate and over-all impression made by the subject on the artist, without much attention to detail: the term has been extended to literature that similarly seeks to express the immediate impressions of reality on the writer, and to music, as by Debussy and Ravel, which seeks to produce atmospheric effects and suggest impressions by various characteristic devices.

im·pres·sion·ist (im-presh'ən-ist), ***n.*** a painter, writer, composer, etc. who practices impressionism. ***adj.*** of or characteristic of impressionism or impressionists.

im·pres·sion·is·tic (im-presh'ən-is'tik), ***adj.*** 1. impressionist. 2. conveying a quick or over-all impression.

im·pres·sive (im-pres'iv), ***adj.*** impressing or tending to impress the mind or emotions.

im·press·ment (im-pres'mənt), ***n.*** [*impress* (to force into service) + *-ment*], the practice or act of impressing men or property for the use or service of the public.

im·pres·sure (im-presh'ẽr), ***n.*** [< *impress* (to use pressure)], impression.

im·prest (im'prest), ***n.*** [It. *impresto*, a loan < phr. (*dare*) *in prestito*, (to give) in loan; *in*, in + *prestito*, a loan < *prestare*, to lend < L. *praestare*, to become surety for, lit., to stand before; *prae-*, before + *stare*, to stand (see STAND)], a loan or advance of money; especially, money advanced to a person from government funds to enable him to carry on some work for the government. ***adj.*** lent; advanced as a loan.

im·pri·ma·tur (im'pri-mā'tẽr), ***n.*** [Mod. L., lit., let it be printed, 3d pers. sing., pres. subj. pass., of L. *imprimere* < *in-*, in, on + *premere*, to press], 1. license to publish or print a book, article, etc.; especially, sanction given by the Roman Catholic Church: abbreviated **imp.** 2. any sanction or approval.

‡im·pri·mis (im-prī'mis), ***adv.*** [L., for *in primis*, lit., among the first; *in*, among + *primis*, abl. pl. of *primus*, first], first; in the first place.

im·print (im-print'; *for n.*, im'print), ***v.t.*** [ME. *empreynten;* OFr. *empreinter* < pp. of LL. **impremere*, for L. *imprimere;* see IN- (in) & PRESS (to squeeze)], 1. to mark by pressing or stamping; impress: as, he *imprinted* the paper with his seal. 2. to reproduce (a mark, letters, etc.) by pressing. 3. to press: as, she *imprinted* a kiss on my forehead. 4. to implant firmly on the mind or fix in the memory. ***n.*** [OFr. *empreinte* < the *v.*], 1. a mark made by imprinting. 2. a characteristic effect or result: as, the *imprint* of starvation. 3. a publisher's or printer's note on the title page or at the end of a book, giving his name, the time and place of publication, etc.: abbreviated **imp.**

im·pris·on (im-priz''n), ***v.t.*** 1. to put or keep in prison; jail. 2. to restrict, limit, or confine in any way.

im·pris·on·ment (im-priz''n-mənt), ***n.*** an imprisoning or being imprisoned.

im·prob·a·bil·i·ty (im'prob-ə-bil'ə-ti, im-prob'ə-bil'ə-ti), ***n.*** 1. the quality of being improbable. 2. [*pl.* IMPROBABILITIES (-tiz)], something improbable.

im·prob·a·ble (im-prob'ə-b'l), ***adj.*** [L. *improbabilis*], not probable; not likely to happen or be true; unlikely.

im·prob·ab·ly (im-prob'ə-bli), ***adv.*** with little or no probability: now only in *not improbably*.

im·pro·bi·ty (im-prō'bə-ti), ***n.*** [*pl.* IMPROBITIES (-tiz)], [L. *improbitas*], lack of probity; dishonesty.

im·promp·tu (im-promp'tōō, im-promp'tū), ***adj. & adv.*** [Fr.; L. *in promptu*, in readiness; *in*, in + *promptu*, abl. of *promptus*, readiness < *promptus*, brought out, ready, prompt], without preparation or advance thought; offhand; extempore: see **extemporaneous.** ***n.*** an impromptu speech, performance, etc.

SYN.—**impromptu** is applied to that which is spoken, made, or done on the spur of the moment to suit the occasion and stresses spontaneity; **extemporaneous, extempore** (more commonly used as an adverb), and **extemporary** may express the same idea but are now more often used of a speech that has received some preparation, but has not been written out or memorized; **improvised** applies to something composed or devised without any preparation and, with reference to things other than music, suggests the ingenious use of whatever is at hand to fill an unforeseen and immediate need.

im·prop·er (im-prop'ẽr), ***adj.*** [ME.; OFr. *impropre;* L. *improprius;* see IN- (not) & PROPER], 1. not suitable for or consistent with the purpose or circumstances; ill-adapted; unfit. 2. not in accordance with the truth, fact, or rule; wrong; incorrect. 3. contrary to good taste or decency; indecorous. Abbreviated **improp.**

SYN.—**improper**, the word of broadest application in this list, refers to anything that is not proper or suitable, especially to that which does not conform to conventional standards; **unseemly** applies to that which is improper or inappropriate to the particular situation (her *unseemly* laughter at my remarks); **unbecoming** applies to that which is inappropriate to a particular person (his rigid views are most *unbecoming* in a teacher); **indecorous** refers to that which violates propriety or good taste in behavior, speech, etc. (his *indecorous* interruption of their chat); **indelicate** implies a lack of propriety or tact and connotes immodesty or coarseness (an *indelicate* anecdote); **indecent** is used of that which is regarded as highly offensive to morals or modesty (*indecent* exposure).—*ANT.* proper, decorous.

improper fraction, a fraction in which the denominator is less than the numerator (e.g., 5/3).

im·pro·pri·ate (im-prō'pri-āt'), ***v.t.*** [IMPROPRIATED (-id), IMPROPRIATING], [< ML. *impropriatus*, pp. of *impropriare*, to take as one's own < L. *in*, in + *proprius*, one's own], 1. to transfer (church income or property) to private individuals. 2. [Obs.], to appropriate. ***adj.*** (im-prō'pri-it), having been impropriated.

im·pro·pri·a·tion (im-prō'pri-ā'shən), ***n.*** 1. an impropriating. 2. anything impropriated.

im·pro·pri·a·tor (im-prō'pri-ā'tẽr), ***n.*** a person who makes or receives an impropriation.

im·pro·pri·e·ty (im'prə-prī'ə-ti), ***n.*** [*pl.* IMPROPRIETIES (-tiz)], [Fr. *impropriété;* L. *improprietas;* see IN- (not) & PROPRIETY], 1. the quality of being improper. 2. improper action or behavior. 3. an improper use of a word or phrase (e.g., "borrow" for "lend"): see also **barbarism, solecism.**

im·prov·a·bil·i·ty (im-prōōv'ə-bil'ə-ti), ***n.*** the quality of being improvable.

im·prov·a·ble (im-prōōv'ə-b'l), ***adj.*** that can be improved.

im·prove (im-prōōv'), ***v.t.*** [IMPROVED (-prōōvd'), IMPROVING], [earlier *improw, emprou* < Anglo-Fr. *emprower* < *en-*, in + *prou, pro*, gain, advantage < base of L. *prodesse*, to profit], 1. to use profitably or to good advantage: as, he *improved* his leisure by studying. 2. to raise to a better quality or condition; make better. 3. to make (land) more valuable by cultivation, etc. ***v.i.*** to become better in quality or condition.

improve on (or **upon**), to do or make better than.

SYN.—**improve** and **better** both imply a correcting or advancing of something that is not in itself necessarily bad, the former by supplying a lack or want (to *improve* a method) and the latter by seeking something more satisfying (he's left his job to *better* himself); **ameliorate** implies a bad, oppressive, or intolerable condition to begin with (they sought to *ameliorate* working conditions).—*ANT.* worsen, impair.

im·prove·ment (im-prōōv'mənt), ***n.*** [Anglo-Fr. *emprowement*], 1. an improving or being improved; especially, *a*) betterment. *b*) an increase in value or in excellence of quality or condition. *c*) profitable use. 2. *a*) an addition or change that improves something. *b*) a person or thing representing a higher degree of excellence. 3. a change or addition to land, property, etc. to make it more valuable.

im·prov·i·dence (im-prov'ə-dəns), ***n.*** [L. *improvidentia;* see IN- (not), PROVIDE, -ENCE], failure to provide for the future; lack of foresight or thrift.

im·prov·i·dent (im-prov'ə-dənt), ***adj.*** [*im-* (not) + *provident*, after *improvidence*], failing to provide for the future; lacking foresight or thrift.

im·pro·vi·sa·tion (im-prov'ə-zā'shən, im'prov-ə-zā'shən, im'prə-vī-zā'shən), ***n.*** 1. an improvising. 2. something improvised.

im·prov·i·sa·tor (im-prov'ə-zā'tẽr, im'prə-vī-zā'tẽr), ***n.*** a person who improvises.

im·prov·i·sa·to·ri·al (im-prov'i-zə-tôr'i-əl, im-prov'i-zə-tō'ri-əl), ***adj.*** of, or having the nature of, an improvisator or improvisation.

im·prov·i·sa·to·ry (im'prə-vī'zə-tôr'i, im'prə-viz'ə-tō'ri), ***adj.*** improvisatorial.

im·pro·vise (im'prə-vīz', im'prə-vīz'), ***v.t. & v.i.*** [IMPROVISED (-vīzd', -vīzd'), IMPROVISING], [Fr. *improviser;* It. *improvisare* < *improviso*, unprepared; L. *improvisus*, unforeseen < *in-*, not + *provisus*, pp. of *providere*, to foresee, anticipate; see PROVIDE], 1. to compose, or simultaneously compose and perform, sing, etc., on the spur of the moment and without any preparation; extemporize. 2. to make, provide, or do with the tools and materials at hand, usually to fill an unforeseen and immediate need: as, he *improvised* a bed out of leaves.

‡im·prov·vi·sa·to·re (ēm'prô-vē'zä-tô're), ***n.*** [*pl.* IMPROVVISATORI (-rē)], [It.], a performer who improvises poems or songs.

im·pru·dence (im-prōō'd'ns), ***n.*** 1. the quality of being imprudent. 2. imprudent action or behavior.

im·pru·dent (im-prōō'd'nt), ***adj.*** [ME.; L. *imprudens*], not prudent; without thought of the consequences; lacking in judgment or caution; rash; indiscreet.

im·pu·dence (im'pyoo-dəns), ***n.*** [ME.; OFr.; L. *impudentia*], 1. the quality of being impudent. 2. impudent speech or behavior.

im·pu·den·cy (im'pyoo-dən-si), ***n.*** [*pl.* IMPUDENCIES (-siz)], impudence.

im·pu·dent (im'pyoo-dənt), ***adj.*** [ME.; Fr.; L. *impudens* < *in-*, not + *pudens*, modest, orig. ppr. of *pudere*, to feel shame], 1. originally, immodest; shameless. 2. shamelessly bold; saucy; insolent. —*SYN.* see **impertinent.**

im·pu·dic·i·ty (im'pyoo-dis'ə-ti), ***n.*** [Fr. *impudicité;* LL. **impudicitas*, for L. *impudicitia* < *in-*, not + *pudicus*, modest], immodesty; shamelessness.

im·pugn (im-pūn'), ***v.t.*** [OFr. *impugner;* L. *impugnare* < *in-*, on, against + *pugnare*, to fight], to attack by argument or criticism; call in question; oppose or challenge as false. —*SYN.* see **deny.**

im·pug·na·tion (im'pəg-nā'shən), ***n.*** an impugning or being impugned.

im·pu·is·sance (im-pū'i-s'ns, im-pwis''ns), ***n.*** [Fr.; see IN- (not) & PUISSANCE], lack of power; weakness.

im·pu·is·sant (im-pū'i-s'nt, im-pwis''nt), ***adj.*** [Fr.; see IN- (not) & PUISSANT], lacking power; weak; impotent.

im·pulse (im'puls), ***n.*** [L. *impulsus*, pp. of *impellere;* see IMPEL], 1. *a)* an impelling, or driving forward with sudden force. *b)* an impelling force; sudden, driving force; push; thrust; impetus. *c)* the motion or effect caused by such a force. 2. *a)* incitement to action arising from a state of mind or some external stimulus. *b)* a sudden inclination to act, without conscious thought. *c)* a motive or tendency coming from within. 3. in *mechanics*, the change in momentum effected by a force, measured by multiplying the average value of the force by the time during which it acts. 4. in *physiology*, a stimulus transmitted in a muscle or nerve, which causes or inhibits activity in the body.

im·pul·sion (im-pul'shən), ***n.*** [L. *impulsio* < *impulsus;* see IMPULSE], 1. an impelling or being impelled. 2. an impelling force. 3. movement or tendency to move resulting from this force; impetus. 4. impulse (sense 2).

im·pul·sive (im-pul'siv), ***adj.*** [< OFr. or ML.; OFr. *impulsif;* ML. *impulsivus* < L. *impulsus;* see IMPULSE], 1. impelling; driving forward. 2. *a)* acting or given to acting on impulse: as, an *impulsive* person. *b)* produced by or resulting from impulse: as, an *impulsive* remark. 3. in *mechanics*, acting briefly and as a result of impulse. —***SYN.*** see **spontaneous.**

im·pu·ni·ty (im-pū'nə-ti), ***n.*** [Fr. *impunité;* L. *impunitas* < *impunis*, free from punishment < *in-*, without + *poena*, punishment], freedom from punishment, penalty, harm, or loss. —***SYN.*** see **exemption.**

im·pure (im-pyoor'), ***adj.*** [L. *impurus*], not pure; specifically, *a)* unclean; dirty. *b)* unclean according to religious ritual; defiled. *c)* immoral; obscene; unchaste. *d)* mixed with foreign matter; adulterated. *e)* mixed; having more than one color, tone, style, etc. *f)* not idiomatic or grammatical.

im·pu·ri·ty (im-pyoor'ə-ti), ***n.*** [OFr. *impurité;* L. *impuritas*], 1. the state or quality of being impure. 2. [*pl.* IMPURITIES (-tiz)], an impure thing or element.

im·put·a·bil·i·ty (im-pūt'ə-bil'ə-ti), ***n.*** the quality or state of being imputable.

im·put·a·ble (im-pūt'ə-b'l), ***adj.*** [ML. *imputabilis*], that can be imputed; ascribable.

im·put·a·bly (im-pūt'ə-bli), ***adv.*** in an imputable manner.

im·pu·ta·tion (im'pyoo-tā'shən), ***n.*** [LL. *imputatio*], 1. an imputing or being imputed; charge of a fault or crime. 2. a fault or crime imputed.

im·put·a·tive (im-pūt'ə-tiv), ***adj.*** [LL. *imputativus*], of, inclined to, or characterized by imputation.

im·pute (im-pūt'), ***v.t.*** [IMPUTED (-id), IMPUTING], [ME. *inputen;* OFr. *emputer* (Fr. *imputer*); L. *imputare* < *in-*, in, to + *putare*, to estimate, charge, think], 1. to attribute (something, especially a crime or fault) to another; charge with; ascribe. 2. in *theology*, to ascribe (good or evil) to a person as coming from another. —***SYN.*** see **ascribe.**

impv., imperative.

in (in), ***prep.*** [ME.; AS.; akin to G. *in;* IE. base **en-*, seen also in Gr. *en*, L. *in* (OL. *en*), OIr. *in*, OSlav. *on-*, Sans. *an-*, etc.], 1. contained or enclosed by; inside; within: as, *in* the room, *in* the envelope. 2. wearing; clothed by: as, the lady *in* red. 3. during the course of: as, it was done *in* a day. 4. at, before, or after the end of: as, I'll be with you *in* an hour. 5. perceptible to (a specified sense): as, he is *in* sight. 6. limited by the scope of: as, *in* my opinion. 7. being a member of or worker at: as, he is *in* business. 8. amidst; surrounded by: as, *in* a storm. 9. affected by; having: as, he is *in* trouble. 10. engaged or occupied by: as, *in* a search for truth. 11. with regard to; as concerns: as, weak *in* faith, they vary *in* size. 12. so as to form: as, arranged *in* curls. 13. with; by; using: as, he paints *in* oil, written *in* English. 14. made of: as, it was done *in* wood. 15. because of; for: as, he cried *in* pain. 16. by way of: as, do this *in* my defense. 17. as a part of the capacity or function of; belonging to: as, he didn't have it *in* him. 18. into: as, come *in* the house: *into* is generally preferred in this sense. *In* expresses inclusion with relation to space, place, time, state, circumstances, manner, quality, substance, a class, a whole, etc. ***adv.*** 1. from a point outside to one inside: as, he went *in*, the ring of hunters closed *in*. 2. so as to be contained by a certain space, condition, or position: as, labor's vote put him *in*. 3. so as to be agreeing with: as, he fell *in* with our plans. 4. so as to form a part of: as, mix cream *in* the sauce. ***adj.*** 1. that is in power: as, the *in* group. 2. inner; inside. 3. coming or going inside; inward: as, the *in* door, the *in* boat. 4. [Colloq.], profiting to the extent of: as, he is *in* a hundred dollars. ***n.*** 1. *usually in pl.* a person or thing that is in power, as a team at bat, a party holding office, etc. 2. [Colloq.], a place or means of entrance; introduction; hence, 3. [Colloq.], special influence or favor; pull. ***v.t.*** [INNED (ind), INNING], [Dial.], 1. to collect; gather in: as, *in* the hay before it rains. 2. to enclose.

have it in for, [Colloq.], to hold a grudge against.

in for, certain to have or get (usually an unpleasant experience).

ins and outs, 1. all the complex physical details of a place; hence, 2. all the details and intricacies.

in that, because; since.

in with, associated with in partnership, friendship, etc.

in- (in), [< the prep. *in;* in words of L. origin < the L. prep. *in*], a prefix used: 1. to mean *in, into, within, on, toward*, as in *inbreed, infer, induct.* 2. as an intensifier in some words of Latin origin, as in *instigate.* Assimilated in words of Latin origin to *il-* before *l*, as in *illuminate*, *ir-* before *r*, as in *irrigate*, and *im-* before *m*, *p*, and *b*, as in *immigrate, impeach, imbibe.*

in- (in), [L. *in-*], a prefix meaning *no, not, without, non-*, as in *insignificant:* assimilated to *il-* before *l*, as in *illiterate*, *ir-* before *r*, as in *irresponsible*, and *im-* before *m*, *p*, and *b*, as in *immaterial, impossible, imbecile.*

-in (in), in *chemistry*, -ine.

In, in *chemistry*, indium.

in., [*pl.* IN., INS.], inch; inches.

-i·na (ē'nə), [L., fem. of *-inus*], a suffix used primarily to form feminine names, titles, occupational designations, etc., as in *Christina, czarina, ballerina.*

in·a·bil·i·ty (in'ə-bil'ə-ti), ***n.*** [*in-* (not) + *ability*], the quality or state of being unable; lack of ability, capacity, means, or power.

‡in ab·sen·ti·a (in ab-sen'shi-ə, in əb-sen'shə), [L.], in absence; although not present: as, she received her college degree *in absentia:* abbreviated **i.a.**

‡in ab·strac·to (in ab-strak'tō), [L.], in the abstract.

in·ac·ces·si·bil·i·ty (in'ək-ses'ə-bil'ə-ti, in'ak-ses'ə-bil'ə-ti), ***n.*** the quality or state of being inaccessible.

in·ac·ces·si·ble (in'ək-ses'ə-b'l, in'ak-ses'ə-b'l), ***adj.*** not accessible; specifically, *a)* impossible to reach or enter. *b)* that cannot be seen, talked to, influenced, etc.; inapproachable. *c)* not obtainable.

in·ac·ces·si·bly (in'ək-ses'ə-bli, in'ak-ses'ə-bli), ***adv.*** so as to be inaccessible.

in·ac·cu·ra·cy (in-ak'yoo-rə-si), ***n.*** 1. the quality of being inaccurate; lack of accuracy. 2. [*pl.* INACCURACIES (-siz)], something inaccurate; error; mistake.

in·ac·cu·rate (in-ak'yoo-rit), ***adj.*** not accurate; not correct; not exact; in error.

in·ac·tion (in-ak'shən), ***n.*** absence of action or motion; inertness or idleness.

in·ac·ti·vate (in-ak'tə-vāt'), ***v.t.*** [INACTIVATED (-id), INACTIVATING], 1. to make inactive. 2. to cause (a military unit, governmental bureau, etc.) to go out of existence; dissolve. 3. in *biochemistry*, to destroy the activity of (a serum) by heat.

in·ac·tive (in-ak'tiv), ***adj.*** 1. not active or moving; inert. 2. not inclined to act; idle; dull. 3. not affecting the plane of polarized light: said of some isomers of certain optically active crystalline substances.

SYN.**—inactive** is a general word applied to any person or thing that is not active, operating, working, in force, etc. (an *inactive* machine, ballplayer, contract, etc.); **idle** is used especially of persons who are not at the moment occupied, either voluntarily, as through indolence, or of necessity (the shutdown left 2000 workers *idle*); **inert** is applied to anything which has no inherent power of motion or action (*inert* matter) or to any person who seems inherently indisposed to action (the *inert* electorate); **passive** refers to something that is acted upon but does not act in return and, hence, often connotes submissiveness or failure to resist (*passive* compliance).—***ANT.*** active, lively, dynamic.

in·ac·tiv·i·ty (in'ak-tiv'ə-ti), ***n.*** the quality or state of being inactive.

in·ad·e·qua·cy (in-ad'i-kwə-si), ***n.*** [*pl.* INADEQUACIES (-siz)], quality, state, or instance of being inadequate.

in·ad·e·quate (in-ad'i-kwit), ***adj.*** not adequate; not sufficient; not equal to what is required.

in·ad·mis·si·bil·i·ty (in'əd-mis'ə-bil'ə-ti), ***n.*** the quality of being inadmissible.

in·ad·mis·si·ble (in'əd-mis'ə-b'l), ***adj.*** not admissible; not to be admitted, allowed, granted, or conceded.

in·ad·mis·si·bly (in'əd-mis'ə-bli), ***adv.*** 1. in an inadmissible manner. 2. to an inadmissible degree.

in·ad·vert·ence (in'əd-vũr't'ns), ***n.*** [ML. *inadvertentia*], 1. the quality of being inadvertent. 2. an instance of this; oversight; mistake.

in·ad·ver·ten·cy (in'əd-vũr't'n-si), ***n.*** [*pl.* INADVERTENCIES (-siz)], inadvertence.

in·ad·vert·ent (in'əd-vũr't'nt), ***adj.*** [*in-* (not) + obs. *advertent*, heeding < L. *advertens*, ppr. of *advertere*, to heed; see ADVERT], 1. not attentive or observant; negligent; heedless. 2. due to oversight; unintentional.

in·ad·vis·a·ble (in'əd-vīz'ə-b'l), ***adj.*** not advisable; not wise or prudent.

-i·nae (ī'nē), [L., fem. pl. of adjectives in *-inus* (in agreement with understood *bestiae*, animals)], a suffix used in zoology to form the names of subfamilies, as in *Felinae*.

‡**in ae·ter·num** (in ē-tũr′nəm), [L.], to eternity; forever.

in·al·ien·a·bil·i·ty (in-āl′yən-ə-bil′ə-ti), *n.* the quality of being inalienable.

in·al·ien·a·ble (in-āl′yən-ə-b'l), *adj.* [*in-* (not) + *alienable*], that cannot be taken away or transferred: as, *inalienable* rights.

in·al·ien·a·bly (in-āl′yən-ə-bli), *adv.* so as to be inalienable.

in·al·ter·a·bil·i·ty (in-ôl′tẽr-ə-bil′ə-ti), *n.* the quality of being inalterable.

in·al·ter·a·ble (in-ôl′tẽr-ə-b'l), *adj.* that cannot be altered; unchangeable.

in·al·ter·a·bly (in-ôl′tẽr-ə-bli), *adv.* in an inalterable manner.

in·am·o·ra·ta (in-am′ə-rä′tə, in′am-ə-rä′tə), *n.* [It., fem. of *innamorato*, lover, orig. pp. of *innamorare*, to fall in love], a woman loved; one's sweetheart or mistress.

in·am·o·ra·to (in-am′ə-rä′tō, in′am-ə-rä′tō), *n.* [see INAMORATA], a man loved; a woman's lover.

in-and-in (in′ənd-in′), *adj. & adv.* repeatedly with individuals of the same or closely related stocks: as, *in-and-in* breeding.

in·ane (in-ān′), *adj.* [L. *inanis* < *in-*, not + unexplained base], 1. empty; vacant. 2. lacking sense or meaning; foolish; silly. *n.* that which is inane, especially the void of infinite space.

in·an·i·mate (in-an′ə-mit), *adj.* [LL. *inanimatus*], 1. not animate; not endowed with (animal) life. 2. not animated; dull; spiritless. —*SYN.* see **dead.**

in·a·ni·tion (in′ə-nish′ən), *n.* [ME. *in-anisioun;* OFr.; LL. *inanitio* < L. *inanitus*, pp. of *inanire*, to empty < *inanis;* see INANE], 1. the quality or condition of being empty; emptiness. 2. exhaustion from lack of food or an inability to assimilate it.

in·an·i·ty (in-an′ə-ti), *n.* [Fr. *inanité;* L. *inanitas*, emptiness], 1. the quality or condition of being inane; specifically, *a*) emptiness. *b*) lack of sense or meaning; silliness. 2. [*pl.* INANITIES (-tiz)], something inane; senseless or silly act, remark, etc.

in·ap·peas·a·ble (in′ə-pēz′ə-b'l), *adj.* that cannot be appeased.

in·ap·pe·tence (in-ap′ə-təns), *n.* [*in-* (not) + *appetence*], lack of appetite or desire.

in·ap·pe·ten·cy (in-ap′ə-tən-si), *n.* inappetence.

in·ap·pe·tent (in-ap′ə-tənt), *adj.* having or showing inappetence.

in·ap·pli·ca·bil·i·ty (in′ap-li-kə-bil′ə-ti, in-ap′li-kə-bil′ə-ti), *n.* the quality or condition of being inapplicable.

in·ap·pli·ca·ble (in-ap′li-kə-b'l), *adj.* not applicable; not suitable; inappropriate.

in·ap·pli·ca·bly (in-ap′li-kə-bli), *adv.* in an inapplicable manner.

in·ap·po·site (in-ap′ə-zit), *adj.* not apposite; irrelevant; inappropriate.

in·ap·pre·ci·a·ble (in′ə-prē′shi-ə-b'l, in′ə-prē′shə-b'l), *adj.* [*in-* (not) + *appreciable*], too small to be observed or have any value; negligible.

in·ap·pre·ci·a·bly (in′ə-prē′shi-ə-bli, in′ə-prē′shə-bli), *adv.* to an inappreciable degree.

in·ap·pre·ci·a·tive (in′ə-prē′shi-ā′tiv, in′ə-prē′shi-ə-tiv), *adj.* lacking appreciation.

in·ap·pre·hen·si·ble (in′ap-ri-hen′sə-b'l), *adj.* that cannot be apprehended, or understood.

in·ap·pre·hen·sion (in′ap-ri-hen′shən), *n.* lack of apprehension.

in·ap·pre·hen·sive (in′ap-ri-hen′siv), *adj.* 1. lacking the ability to apprehend, or understand. 2. not perceiving danger, trouble, etc.

in·ap·proach·a·bil·i·ty (in′ə-prōch′ə-bil′ə-ti), *n.* the quality or condition of being inapproachable.

in·ap·proach·a·ble (in′ə-prōch′ə-b'l), *adj.* that cannot be approached.

in·ap·proach·a·bly (in′ə-prōch′ə-bli), *adv.* so as to be inapproachable.

in·ap·pro·pri·ate (in′ə-prō′pri-it), *adj.* not appropriate; not suitable, fitting, or proper.

in·apt (in-apt′), *adj.* 1. not apt; not suitable; inappropriate. 2. lacking skill or aptitude; awkward.

in·apt·i·tude (in-ap′tə-tōōd′, in-ap′tə-tūd′), *n.* lack of aptitude; specifically, *a*) lack of suitability. *b*) lack of skill.

in·arch (in-ärch′), *v.t.* [*in-* (in) + *arch, v.*], to graft by uniting (a shoot) to another plant while both are growing on their own roots.

in·arm (in-ärm′), *v.t.* to surround with or as with the arms; embrace.

in·ar·tic·u·late (in′är-tik′yoo-lit), *adj.* [LL. *inarticulatus*; see IN- (not) & ARTICULATE], 1. produced without the normal articulation of understandable speech: said of vocal sounds, as, an *inarticulate* cry. 2. *a*) not able to speak; mute; dumb. *b*) not able to speak understandably or expressively. 3. unexpressed: as, *inarticulate* passion. 4. in *zoology*, without joints, segments, hinges, or valves.

‡**in ar·ti·cu·lo mor·tis** (in är-tik′yoo-lō′ môr′tis), [L.], at the point of death.

in·ar·ti·fi·cial (in-är′tə-fish′′l), *adj.* 1. not artificial; natural. 2. inartistic; unskillful. 3. unaffected; simple.

in·ar·tis·tic (in′är-tis′tik), *adj.* not artistic; specifically, *a*) not conforming to the standards or principles of art. *b*) lacking artistic taste.

in·ar·tis·ti·cal·ly (in′är-tis′ti-k'l-i, in′är-tis′tik-li), *adv.* in an inartistic manner.

in·as·much (in′əz-much′), *conj.* because; since; seeing that (followed by *as*).

in·at·ten·tion (in′ə-ten′shən), *n.* 1. failure to give attention; negligence. 2. a heedless or negligent act.

in·at·ten·tive (in′ə-ten′tiv), *adj.* not attentive; heedless; negligent. —*SYN.* see **absent-minded.**

in·au·di·bil·i·ty (in′ô-də-bil′ə-ti, in-ô′də-bil′ə-ti), *n.* the quality or condition of being inaudible.

in·au·di·ble (in-ô′də-b'l), *adj.* [LL. *inaudibilis*], not audible; that cannot be heard.

in·aud·i·bly (in-ô′də-bli), *adv.* so as to be inaudible.

in·au·gu·ral (in-ô′gyoo-rəl), *adj.* [Fr.], of an inauguration. *n.* a speech made at an inauguration.

in·au·gu·rate (in-ô′gyoo-rāt′), *v.t.* [INAUGURATED (-id), INAUGURATING], [< L. *inauguratus*, pp. of *inaugurare*, to practice augury, consecrate by augury; see IN- (in) & AUGUR], 1. to induct (an official) into office with a formal ceremony. 2. to make a formal beginning of; enter with ceremony: as, the company is *inaugurating* a new policy. 3. to celebrate formally the first public use of; dedicate: as, the mayor *inaugurated* the new library. —*SYN.* see **begin.**

in·au·gu·ra·tion (in-ô′gyoo-rā′shən), *n.* [LL. *inauguratio*], an inaugurating or being inaugurated.

Inauguration Day, the day on which a newly elected president of the United States is inaugurated: before 1934, March 4, now, January 20, of the year following the election.

in·au·gu·ra·tor (in-ô′gyoo-rā′tẽr), *n.* a person who inaugurates.

in·aus·pi·cious (in′ôs-pish′əs), *adj.* not auspicious; unfavorable; unlucky; ill-omened.

in·be·ing (in′bē′iŋ), *n.* 1. inherent existence. 2. essence; basic nature.

in·board (in′bôrd′, in′bōrd′), *adv. & adj.* [< *in board;* see BOARD (ship)], 1. inside the hull or bulwarks of a ship or boat. 2. in *mechanics*, toward the inside. *n.* a marine motor mounted inboard.

in·born (in′bôrn′), *adj.* [AS. *inboren*], present in the organism at birth; innate; natural. —*SYN.* see **innate.**

in·bound (in′bound′), *adj.* bound toward the place where one is: opposed to *outbound.*

in·breathe (in-brēth′), *v.t.* [ME. *inbrethen;* after L. *inspirare*], [Rare], 1. to breathe in. 2. to inspire.

in·bred (in′bred′; *for 2, often* in′bred′), *adj.* [pp. of *inbreed*], 1. inborn. 2. bred from closely related parents; resulting from inbreeding. —*SYN.* see **innate.**

in·breed (in′brēd′, in′brēd′), *v.t.* [INBRED (-bred′, -bred′), INBREEDING], 1. to form or develop within. 2. to breed by continual mating of individuals of the same or closely related stocks.

in·burst (in′bũrst′), *n.* 1. a bursting in, inward, or into. 2. something that bursts in.

in·by, in·bye (in′bi′), *adv.* [*in-* (in) + *by*], [Scot.], toward the center or interior; inward. *adj.* [Scot.], located near by. *prep.* [Scot.], near to.

inc., 1. inclosure. 2. included. 3. including. 4. inclusive. 5. income. 6. incorporated. 7. increase.

In·ca (iŋ′kə), *n.* [Sp. < Peruvian native (Quechua) *ynca*, prince of the royal family], 1. any member of a group of Quechuan Indian tribes that dominated ancient Peru until the Spanish conquest: the Incas had a highly developed civilization. 2. a king or other member of the ruling family of these tribes.

in·cage (in-kāj′), *v.t.* to encage.

in·cal·cu·la·bil·i·ty (in′kal-kyoo-lə-bil′ə-ti, in-kal′kyoo-lə-bil′ə-ti), *n.* 1. the quality or state of being incalculable. 2. [*pl.* INCALCULABILITIES (-tiz)], something incalculable.

in·cal·cu·la·ble (in-kal′kyoo-lə-b'l), *adj.* 1. that cannot be calculated; too great or too many to be counted. 2. too uncertain to be counted on; unpredictable.

in·cal·cu·la·bly (in-kal′kyoo-lə-bli), *adv.* so as to be incalculable.

in·ca·les·cent (in′kə-les′′nt), *adj.* [L. *incalescens;* see IN- (intens.) & CALESCENT], [Rare], becoming hotter.

in cam·er·a (in kam′ẽr-ə), [L., in chamber], 1. in a judge's private office rather than in open court. 2. in closed session, as a committee meeting or hearing not open to the public; secretly.

In·can (iŋ′kən), *adj.* of the Incas, their empire, or civilization. *n.* 1. an Inca. 2. Quechua.

in·can·desce (in′kən-des′), *v.i. & v.t.* [INCANDESCED (-dest′), INCANDESCING], [L. *incandescere*], to become or make incandescent.

in·can·des·cence (in′kən-des′′ns), *n.* a being or becoming incandescent.

in·can·des·cen·cy (in′kən-des′ən-si), *n.* incandescence.

in·can·des·cent (in′kən-des′′nt), *adj.* [L. *incandescens*, ppr. of *incandescere;* see IN- (in) & CANDESCENT], 1. glowing with intense heat; red-hot or, especially, white-hot. 2. very bright; shining brilliantly; gleaming.

incandescent lamp, a lamp in which the light is produced by a filament of conducting material contained in a vacuum and heated to incandescence by an electric current.

INCANDESCENT LAMP

in·can·ta·tion (in'kan-tā'shən), *n.* [ME. *incantacion;* LL. *incantatio* < pp. of L. *incantare; in-*, in + *cantare*, to sing, chant], 1. the chanting of magical words or a formula in casting a spell or performing other magic. 2. the words or formula so chanted. 3. any magic or sorcery.

in·ca·pa·bil·i·ty (in'kā-pə-bil'ə-ti, in-kā'pə-bil'ə-ti), *n.* the quality or state of being incapable; incapacity.

in·ca·pa·ble (in-kā'pə-b'l), *adj.* 1. not capable; lacking the necessary ability, competence, strength, etc. 2. in *law*, not legally qualified or eligible.

incapable of, 1. not allowing or admitting; not able to accept or experience: as, *incapable of* change. 2. lacking the ability or fitness for: as, *incapable of* sustained thought. 3. not legally qualified for.

in·ca·pa·bly (in-kā'pə-bli), *adv.* in an incapable manner.

in·ca·pa·cious (in'kə-pā'shəs), *adj.* [< LL. *incapax*, incapable; + *-ious*], 1. not capacious; lacking capacity. 2. lacking mental capacity; mentally deficient.

in·ca·pac·i·tate (in'kə-pas'ə-tāt'), *v.t.* [INCAPACITATED (-id), INCAPACITATING], [< *incapacity* + *-ate*], 1. to make unable or unfit; especially, to make incapable of normal activity; disable. 2. in *law*, to make ineligible; disqualify.

in·ca·pac·i·ta·tion (in'kə-pas'ə-tā'shən), *n.* an incapacitating or being incapacitated.

in·ca·pac·i·ty (in'kə-pas'ə-ti), *n.* [*pl.* INCAPACITIES (-tiz)], 1. lack of capacity, power, or fitness; disability. 2. legal ineligibility or disqualification.

in·car·cer·ate (in-kär'sə-rāt'), *v.t.* [INCARCERATED (-id), INCARCERATING], [< ML. *incarceratus*, pp. of *incarcerare*, to imprison < L. *in*, in + *carcer*, prison], 1. to imprison; jail. 2. to shut up; confine. *adj.* (in-kär'sẽr-it), [Archaic], confined.

in·car·cer·a·tion (in-kär'sə-rā'shən), *n.* [ML. *incarceratio*], an incarcerating or being incarcerated.

in·car·cer·a·tor (in-kär'sə-rā'tẽr), *n.* a person who incarcerates.

in·car·di·nate (in-kär'də-nāt'), *v.t.* [INCARDINATED (-id), INCARDINATING], [< pp. of ML. *incardinare;* see IN- (in) & CARDINAL], in the *Roman Catholic Church*, 1. to install (a priest, deacon, etc.) in a specified diocese, etc. 2. to make (a person) a cardinal.

in·car·na·dine (in-kär'nə-dīn', in-kär'nə-din), *adj.* [Fr. *incarnadin;* It. *incarnatino* < *incarnato;* LL. *incarnatus;* see INCARNATE], 1. flesh-colored; pink. 2. red; especially, blood-red. *n.* the color of either flesh or blood. *v.t.* [INCARNADINED (-dīnd', -dind), INCARNADINING], to make incarnadine.

in·car·nate (in-kär'nit; *also, and for v. always*, in-kär'nāt), *adj.* [ME.; LL. *incarnatus*, pp. of *incarnari*, to be made flesh < *in-*, in + *caro, carnis*, flesh], 1. endowed with a human body; in human form; personified: as, he is evil *incarnate.* 2. *a)* flesh-colored; pink. *b)* red; rosy. *v.t.* [INCARNATED (-id), INCARNATING], 1. to provide with flesh or a body; embody. 2. to give actual form to; make real. 3. to be the type or embodiment of (a quality or concept): as, he *incarnates* the courage of the whole race.

in·car·na·tion (in'kär-nā'shən), *n.* [ME. *incarnacion;* OFr. *incarnatiun;* LL. *incarnatio* < pp. of *incarnari;* see INCARNATE], 1. endowment with a human body; appearance in human form. 2. [I-], the taking on of human form and nature by Jesus conceived of as the Son of God. 3. any person or animal serving as the embodiment of a god or spirit. 4. any person or thing serving as the type or embodiment of a quality or concept: as, he is the *incarnation* of courage.

in·case (in-kās'), *v.t.* to encase.

in·case·ment (in-kās'mənt), *n.* 1. an incasing or being incased. 2. something that incases.

in·cau·tion (in-kô'shən), *n.* lack of caution.

in·cau·tious (in-kô'shəs), *adj.* not cautious; not careful or prudent; reckless; rash.

in·cen·di·a·rism (in-sen'di-ə-riz'm), *n.* [< *incendiary* + *-ism*], 1. the willful destruction of property by fire. 2. the willful stirring up of strife, riot, rebellion, etc.

in·cen·di·ar·y (in-sen'di-er'i), *adj.* [L. *incendiarius*, setting on fire, an incendiary < *incendium*, a fire < *incendere;* see INCENSE (to anger)], 1. having to do with the willful destruction of property by fire. 2. causing or designed to cause fires, as certain substances, bombs, etc. 3. willfully stirring up strife, riot, rebellion, etc. *n.* [*pl.* INCENDIARIES (-iz)], 1. a person who willfully destroys property by fire. 2. a person who willfully stirs up strife, riot, rebellion, etc. 3. an incendiary bomb, substance, etc.

in·cense (in'sens), *n.* [ME. *ansens, encenz;* OFr. *encens;* LL. *incensum*, incense, neut. of L. *incensus*, pp. of *incendere;* see INCENSE (to anger)], 1. any substance producing a pleasant odor when burned: used in some religious ceremonies. 2. the smoke or fragrance from such a substance; hence, 3. any pleasant odor. 4. pleasing attention, praise, or admiration. *v.t.* [INCENSED (-senst), INCENSING], 1. to make fragrant with or as with incense; perfume. 2. to burn or offer incense to. *v.i.* to burn incense.

in·cense (in-sens'), *v.t.* [INCENSED (-senst'), INCENSING], [OFr. *incenser, encenser* < L. *incensus*, pp. of *incendere*, to set on fire, inflame < *in-*, in, on + *candere*, to shine, glow, burn], to make very angry; fill with wrath; enrage.

in·cense·ment (in-sens'mənt), *n.* 1. an incensing, or making angry. 2. a being incensed.

in·cen·tive (in-sen'tiv), *adj.* [ME. *incentiue;* L. *incentivus* < pp. of *incinere*, to sing < *in-*, in, on + *canere*, to sing], influencing to action; encouraging; stimulating; motivating. *n.* something that influences to action; stimulus; encouragement. —*SYN.* see **motive.**

in·cept (in-sept'), *v.t.* [L. *inceptare*, to begin, freq. of *incipere;* see INCIPIENT], 1. to begin or undertake. 2. to take in; receive; specifically, to ingest; intussuscept: as, amoebas *incept* food particles.

in·cep·tion (in-sep'shən), *n.* [L. *inceptio* < *inceptus*, pp. of *incipere;* see INCIPIENT], a beginning or being begun; start; commencement. —*SYN.* see **origin.**

in·cep·tive (in-sep'tiv), *adj.* [OFr. *inceptif* < L. *inceptus*, pp. of *incipere;* see INCIPIENT], 1. beginning; introductory; initial. 2. in *grammar*, expressing the beginning of an action. *n.* an inceptive verb or phrase.

in·cer·ti·tude (in-sũr'tə-tōōd', in-sũr'tə-tūd'), *n.* [Fr.; ML. *incertitudo* < L. *incertus*, uncertain], 1. an uncertain state of mind; doubt. 2. insecurity.

in·ces·san·cy (in-ses''n-si), *n.* the state or quality of being incessant.

in·ces·sant (in-ses''nt), *adj.* [Fr.; LL. *incessans;* L. *in-*, not + *cessans*, ppr. of *cessare*, to cease], not stopping; never ceasing; continuing or being repeated without interruption; constant. —*SYN.* see **continual.**

in·cest (in'sest), *n.* [ME.; L. *incestum*, unchastity, incest, neut. of *incestus*, unchaste < *in-*, not + *castus*, chaste], 1. sexual intercourse between persons too closely related to marry legally. 2. in *ecclesiastical usage*, spiritual incest.

in·ces·tu·ous (in-ses'chōō-əs), *adj.* [L. *incestuosus*], 1. guilty of incest. 2. of, or having the nature of, incest.

inch (inch), *n.* [ME. *inche;* AS. *ynce;* L. *uncia*, twelfth part, inch, ounce], 1. a measure of length, equal to 1/12 foot (2.54 centimeters): symbol, ″ (e.g., 10″); abbreviated **in.** (*sing. & pl.*): *square inch* is a measure of surface area; *cubic inch* is a measure of volume or cubic content. 2. a fall (of rain, snow, etc.) equal to the amount that would cover a surface to the depth of one inch. 3. a unit of pressure as measured by a barometer or manometer, equal to the pressure balanced by the weight of a one-inch column of liquid, usually mercury, in the instrument. 4. a very small amount, degree, or distance; trifle; bit. *v.t. & v.i.* to move by inches or degrees; move very slowly.

by inches, gradually; slowly; by degrees.

every inch, in all respects; thoroughly.

inch by inch, gradually; slowly; by degrees.

within an inch of, not far from; almost to; very near.

within an inch of one's life, almost to one's death; very near to losing one's life.

inch (inch), *n.* [Gael. *innis*, island], in Scotland and Ireland, an isolated piece of land, as an island or hill.

inch·meal (inch'mēl'), *adv.* [*inch* + *meal;* cf. PIECEMEAL], gradually; inch by inch: also **by inch-meal.**

in·cho·ate (in-kō'it, in'kō-āt'), *adj.* [L. *inchoatus, incohatus*, pp. of *inchoare, incohare*, to begin], just begun; in the early stages; incipient; rudimentary.

in·cho·a·tion (in'kō-ā'shən), *n.* [L. *inchoatio, incohatio;* see INCHOATE], a beginning; early stage.

in·cho·a·tive (in-kō'ə-tiv, in'kō-ā'tiv), *adj.* 1. [Rare], inchoate. 2. in *grammar*, inceptive; expressing the beginning of an action. *n.* an inceptive verb. Abbreviated **incho., inch.**

inch·worm (inch'wũrm'), *n.* a measuring worm; larva of a geometrid moth.

in·ci·dence (in'si-dəns), *n.* [ME. (North); OFr. < *incident;* see INCIDENT] 1. the act, fact, or manner of falling upon or influencing. 2. the degree or range of occurrence or effect; extent of influence. 3. in *geometry*, partial coincidence between two figures, as of a line and a point contained in it. 4. in *physics*, *a)* the falling of a line, or a ray of light, projectile, etc. moving in a line, on a surface. *b)* the direction of such falling. See also **angle of incidence.**

in·ci·dent (in'si-dənt), *adj.* [Fr.; L. *incidens*, ppr. of *incidere*, to fall upon < *in-*, on + *cadere*, to fall], 1. likely to happen in connection with; naturally attaching to; attendant on: as, the cares *incident* to leadership. 2. falling upon, striking, or affecting: as, *incident* rays. 3. in *law*, dependent upon or involved in something else: as, his maintenance of the estate was *incident* to his inheritance. ***n.*** [ME. *incydente*], 1. something that happens; event; occurrence. 2. something that happens as a result of or in connection with something more important; minor event or episode, especially one in a novel, play, etc. 3. in *law*, something incident to something else. —***SYN.*** see **occurrence.**

in·ci·den·tal (in'si-den't'l), ***adj.*** [*incident* + *-al*], 1. happening or likely to happen as a result of or in connection with something more important; being an incident; casual; hence, 2. secondary or minor, but usually associated: as, the *incidental* costs of education. ***n.*** 1. something incidental. 2. *pl.* miscellaneous items or expenses. 3. in *music*, a grace note, etc. immediately preceding, or included in, a chord to which it does not properly belong. —***SYN.*** see **accidental.**

in·ci·den·tal·ly (in'si-den't'l-i), ***adv.*** 1. in an incidental manner; by chance; accidentally. 2. by the way: an expression used in introducing a new but related topic.

incidental music, music played in connection with the presentation of a play, motion picture, poem, etc. in order to heighten the mood or effect on the audience; mood music.

in·cin·er·ate (in-sin'ə-rāt'), ***v.t. & v.i.*** [INCINERATED (-id), INCINERATING], [< ML. *incineratus*, pp. of *incinerare*, to burn to ashes < L. *in*, in, to + *cinis*, *cineris*, ashes], to burn to ashes; burn up; cremate.

in·cin·er·a·tion (in-sin'ə-rā'shən), ***n.*** [Fr.; ML. *incineratio*], an incinerating or being incinerated.

in·cin·er·a·tor (in-sin'ə-rā'tẽr), ***n.*** a person or thing that incinerates; specifically, *a*) a furnace or other device for burning trash. *b*) a crematory.

in·cip·i·ence (in-sip'i-əns), ***n.*** the fact or condition of being incipient; a beginning; first stage.

in·cip·i·en·cy (in-sip'i-ən-si), ***n.*** incipience.

in·cip·i·ent (in-sip'i-ənt), ***adj.*** [L. *incipiens*, ppr. of *incipere*, to begin, lit., take up < *in-*, in, on + *capere*, to take], in the first stage of existence; just beginning to exist or to come into notice: as, an *incipient* tumor.

‡**in·ci·pit** (in'sip-it), [L.], (here) begins: a word sometimes placed at the beginning of medieval manuscripts; hence, ***n.*** a beginning.

in·cise (in-sīz'), ***v.t.*** [INCISED (-sīzd'), INCISING], [Fr. *inciser* < L. *incisus*, pp. of *incidere*, to cut into < *in-*, into + *caedere*, to cut], 1. to cut into with a sharp tool. 2. to make (figures, inscriptions, etc.) by cutting; engrave; carve.

in·cised (in-sīzd'), ***adj.*** [pp. of *incise*], 1. *a*) cut into. *b*) engraved or carved. 2. having the edges deeply notched, as a leaf.

in·ci·sion (in-sizh'ən), ***n.*** 1. an incising. 2. a result of incising; cut; gash. 3. incisive quality. 4. in *surgery*, a cut made into a tissue or organ.

in·ci·sive (in-sī'siv), ***adj.*** [ML. *incisivus* < L. *incisus*; see INCISE], 1. cutting into; hence, 2. sharp; keen; penetrating; piercing; acute: as, an *incisive* mind, *incisive* language. 3. of an incisor.

SYN.—**incisive** is applied to speech or writing that seems to penetrate directly to the heart of the matter, resulting in a clear and unambiguous statement (an *incisive* criticism); **trenchant** implies clean-cut expression that results in sharply defined categories, differences, etc. (a *trenchant* analysis); **cutting** implies incisive qualities but also connotes such harshness or sarcasm as to hurt the feelings (his *cutting* allusion to her inefficiency); **biting** implies a caustic or stinging quality that makes a deep impression on the mind (his *biting* satire).

in·ci·sor (in-sī'zẽr), ***n.*** [Mod. L. < L. *incisus* (see INCISE); + *-or*], a cutting tooth; any of the front teeth between the canines in either jaw: symbol, I: abbreviated **i.**: see **tooth,** illus.

in·ci·so·ry (in-sī'sẽr-i), ***adj.*** [*incisor* + *-y*], capable of or designed for cutting.

in·ci·ta·tion (in'sī-tā'shən, in'si-tā'shən), ***n.*** [Fr.; L. *incitatio*], an inciting.

in·cite (in-sīt'), ***v.t.*** [INCITED (-id), INCITING], [Fr. *inciter*; L. *incitare*; *in-*, in, on + *citare*, to set in motion, urge], to urge to action; stimulate; stir up; rouse.

SYN.—**incite** implies an urging or stimulating to action, either in a favorable or unfavorable sense (she *incited* him to heroic deeds); **instigate** always implies responsibility for initiating the action and usually connotes a bad or evil purpose (Iago *instigated* Othello to murder); **arouse,** in this connection, means little more than a bringing into being or action (it *aroused* my suspicions); **foment** suggests continued incitement over an extended period of time (the unjust taxes *fomented* rebellion).—***ANT.*** restrain, inhibit.

in·cite·ment (in-sīt'mənt), ***n.*** 1. an inciting. 2. something that incites; stimulus; incentive.

in·ci·vil·i·ty (in'si-vil'ə-ti), ***n.*** [*pl.* INCIVILITIES (-tiz)], [Fr. *incivilité*; LL. *incivilitas* < L. *incivilis*, uncivil], 1. a lack of courtesy or politeness; rudeness. 2. a rude or discourteous act.

in·ci·vism (in'si-viz'm), ***n.*** [Fr. *incivisme*; see IN- (not) & CIVISM], lack of loyalty to one's country or government.

incl., 1. inclosure. 2. including. 3. inclusive.

in·clem·en·cy (in-klem'ən-si), ***n.*** [*pl.* INCLEMENCIES (-siz)], [L. *inclementia*], quality, condition, or instance of being inclement.

in·clem·ent (in-klem'ənt), ***adj.*** [L. *inclemens*; see IN- (not) & CLEMENT], 1. unfavorable; rough; severe; stormy. 2. lacking mercy or leniency; harsh.

in·clin·a·ble (in-klīn'ə-b'l), ***adj.*** 1. inclined; favorably disposed. 2. that can be inclined.

in·cli·na·tion (in'klə-nā'shən), ***n.*** [ME.; L. *inclinatio* < pp. of *inclinare*; see INCLINE], 1. a bending, leaning, or sloping. 2. bend; lean; slope; slant. 3. the extent or degree of incline from a horizontal or vertical position, course, etc. 4. the difference in direction of two lines, planes, or surfaces as measured by the angle between them. 5. *a*) a particular disposition or bent of mind; bias; tendency. *b*) a liking or preference. 6. any action, practice, or thing toward which one is inclined.

SYN.—**inclination** refers to a more or less vague mental disposition toward some action, practice, or thing (he had an *inclination* to refuse); **leaning** suggests a general inclination toward something but implies only the direction of attraction and not the final choice (Dr. Green had always had a *leaning* toward the study of law); **bent** and **propensity** imply a natural or inherent inclination, the latter also connoting an almost uncontrollable attraction (she has a *bent* for art, he has a *propensity* for getting into trouble); **proclivity** usually suggests strong inclination as a result of habitual indulgence, usually toward something bad or wrong (a *proclivity* to falsehood).

in·cli·na·to·ry (in-klī'nə-tôr'i, in-klī'nə-tō'ri), ***adj.*** of or characterized by inclination; leaning.

in·cline (in-klīn'), ***v.i.*** [INCLINED (-klīnd'), INCLINING], [ME. *enclinen*; OFr. *encliner*; L. *inclinare*; *in-*, on, to + *clinare*, to lean], 1. to deviate from a horizontal or vertical position, course, etc.; lean; slope; slant. 2. to bend or bow the body or head. 3. to have a particular disposition or bent of mind, body, etc.; have a tendency; hence, 4. to have a preference or liking. ***v.t.*** 1. to cause to lean, slope, slant, etc.; bend. 2. to give a tendency to; make willing; dispose; influence. ***n.*** (in'-klīn, in-klīn'), an inclined plane or surface; slope; grade; slant.

incline one's ear, to pay heed; listen willingly.

in·clined (in-klīnd'), ***adj.*** [pp. of *incline*], 1. having an inclination; specifically, *a*) sloping; leaning. *b*) disposed; willing; tending. 2. forming an angle with another line, plane, or body.

inclined plane, any plane surface set at an angle against a horizontal surface; sloping plane.

INCLINED PLANE

in·cli·nom·e·ter (in'kli-nom'ə-tẽr), ***n.*** [< *incline* + *-meter*], 1. a magnetic needle free to swing in a vertical plane, used to indicate the direction of the earth's magnetic force. 2. an instrument measuring the angle of inclination of a surface; clinometer. 3. a turn-and-bank indicator of an airplane.

in·close (in-klōz'), ***v.t.*** [INCLOSED (-klōzd'), INCLOSING], [ME. *inclosen*, *enclosen*; see ENCLOSE], 1. to shut in all around; surround; hem in; fence in. 2. to put into a receptacle. 3. to insert in an envelope, etc. together with a letter. 4. to contain. Also spelled **enclose.**

in·clo·sure (in-klō'zhẽr), ***n.*** [var. of *enclosure*], 1. an inclosing or being inclosed. 2. something that incloses, as a fence, wall, etc. 3. something inclosed; specifically, *a*) an inclosed place or area. *b*) a document, money, etc. inclosed in an envelope with a letter. Abbreviated **inc., incl.** Also spelled **enclosure.**

in·clud·a·ble (in-klōōd'ə-b'l), ***adj.*** that can be included.

in·clude (in-klōōd'), ***v.t.*** [INCLUDED (-id), INCLUDING], [ME. *includen*; L. *includere* < *in-*, in + *claudere*, to shut, close], 1. to enclose; shut up or in. 2. to have as part of a whole; contain; comprise; hence, 3. to take into account; consider as part of a whole; put in a total, category, etc.: as, I *include* the five dollars you owe me.

SYN.—**include** implies a containing as part of a whole; **comprise,** in discriminating use, means to consist of and takes as its object the various parts that make up the whole (his library *comprises* 2000 volumes and *includes* many first editions); **comprehend** suggests that the object is contained within the total scope or range of the subject, sometimes by implication (the word "beauty" *comprehends* various concepts); **embrace** stresses the variety of objects comprehended (he had *embraced* a number of hobbies); **involve** implies inclusion of an object because of its connection with the subject as a consequence or antecedent (acceptance of the office *involves* responsibilities). —***ANT.*** exclude.

in·clud·ed (in-klōōd'id), ***adj.*** [pp. of *include*], 1. enclosed, contained, or involved. 2. in *botany*, with stamens and pistils wholly contained within the petals, sheath, etc.: opposed to *exserted*. Abbreviated **inc., incl.**

in·clud·i·ble (in-klōōd'ə-b'l), ***adj.*** includable.

in·clu·sion (in-klōō'zhən), ***n.*** [L. *inclusio*], 1. an including or being included. 2. something included; especially, a foreign body encased in mineral or rock.

inclusion body, any of various small particles occurring in the leucocytes in various diseases, especially in scarlet fever.

in·clu·sive (in-klōō′siv), *adj.* [ML. *inclusivus* < L. *inclusus*, pp. of *includere*], 1. including or tending to include; especially, taking everything into account; reckoning everything. 2. including the terms, limits, or extremes mentioned: as, a vacation from the first to the tenth *inclusive* is a vacation of ten days. Abbreviated **incl., inc.**

inclusive of, including; taking into account.

in·co·er·ci·ble (in′kō-ũr′sə-b′l), *adj.* 1. that cannot be coerced. 2. in *physics*, incapable of being reduced to a liquid by pressure: said of a gas.

in·cog (in-kog′), *adj., adv., n.* [Colloq.], incognito.

in·cog·i·ta·ble (in-koj′ə-tə-b′l), *adj.* [L. *incogitabilis;* see IN- (not) & COGITABLE], unthinkable.

in·cog·i·tant (in-koj′ə-tənt), *adj.* [L. *incogitans; in-*, not + *cogitans*, ppr. of *cogitare*, to cogitate, think], unthinking; thoughtless.

in·cog·ni·ta (in-kog′ni-tə), *n. & adj.* [*pl.* INCOGNITAS (-təz)], [It.], feminine of **incognito.**

in·cog·ni·to (in-kog′ni-tō′, in′kəg-nē′tō), *adv. & adj.* [It. < L. *incognitus*, unknown; *in-*, not + *cognitus*, pp. of *cognoscere*, to know], with true identity unrevealed or disguised; under an assumed name, rank, etc.: as, the duke traveled *incognito*. *n.* [*pl.* INCOGNITOS (-tōz′)], 1. a person who is incognito. 2. *a*) the state of being incognito. *b*) the disguise assumed. Abbreviated **incog.** —*SYN.* see **pseudonym.**

in·cog·ni·zant (in-kog′ni-zənt, in-kon′i-zənt), *adj.* not cognizant (*of*).

in·co·her·ence (in′kō-hêr′əns), *n.* 1. lack of coherence; a being incoherent. 2. incoherent speech, thought, etc.

in·co·her·en·cy (in′kō-hêr′ən-si), *n.* [*pl.* INCOHERENCIES (-siz)], incoherence.

in·co·her·ent (in′kō-hêr′ənt), *adj.* not coherent; specifically, *a*) lacking cohesion; not sticking together. *b*) not logically connected; disjointed; rambling. *c*) characterized by incoherent speech, thought, etc.

in·com·bus·ti·bil·i·ty (in′kəm-bus′tə-bil′ə-ti), *n.* the quality or state of being incombustible.

in·com·bus·ti·ble (in′kəm-bus′tə-b′l), *adj.* not combustible; that cannot be burned; fireproof. *n.* an incombustible substance.

in·come (in′kum), *n.* [ME. < AS. *in*, in + *cuman*, to come], 1. a coming in. 2. the money or other gain periodically received by an individual, corporation, etc., for labor or services, or from property, investments, operations, etc.: abbreviated **inc.**

in·com·er (in′kum′ẽr), *n.* a person or thing that comes in or follows another.

income tax, a tax on income or on that part of income which exceeds a certain amount.

in·com·ing (in′kum′iŋ), *adj.* [ME. < *incomen* to come in; AS. *incuman*], coming in or about to come in: as, *incoming* profits. *n.* 1. a coming in. 2. what comes in.

in·com·men·su·ra·bil·i·ty (in′kə-men′shoor-ə-bil′ə-ti, in′kə-men′sẽr-ə-bil′ə-ti), *n.* the quality or state of being incommensurable.

in·com·men·su·ra·ble (in′kə-men′shoor-ə-b′l, in′kə-men′sẽr-ə-b′l), *adj.* [ML. *incommensurabilis;* see IN- (not) & COMMENSURABLE], 1. that cannot be measured or compared by the same standard or measure; without a common standard of comparison: as, coins and trees are *incommensurable*. 2. not worthy of comparison: as, your belief is *incommensurable* with truth. 3. having no common divisor: said of two or more numbers or quantities. *n.* an incommensurable thing, quantity, etc.

in·com·men·su·ra·bly (in′kə-men′shoor-ə-bli, in′kə-men′sẽr-ə-bli), *adv.* 1. in an incommensurable manner. 2. to an incommensurable degree.

in·com·men·su·rate (in′kə-men′shoor-it, in′kə-men′sẽr-it), *adj.* not commensurate; specifically, *a*) not equal in measure or size. *b*) not proportionate; not adequate: as, his ability is *incommensurate* to his work. *c*) that cannot be measured or compared by the same standard or measure; incommensurable.

in·com·mode (in′kə-mōd′), *v.t.* [INCOMMODED (-id), INCOMMODING], [Fr. *incommoder;* L. *incommodare* < *incommodus*, inconvenient; *in-*, not + *commodus*, convenient], to inconvenience; bring discomfort to; put out; bother.

in·com·mo·di·ous (in′kə-mō′di-əs), *adj.* [*in-* (not) + *commodious*], 1. causing inconvenience; uncomfortable; troublesome. 2. inconveniently small, narrow, etc.

in·com·mod·i·ty (in′kə-mod′ə-ti), *n.* [*pl.* INCOMMODITIES (-tiz)], [Fr. *incommodité;* L. *incommoditas;* see INCOMMODE], inconvenience; discomfort.

in·com·mu·ni·ca·ble (in′kə-mū′ni-kə-b′l), *adj.* [LL. *incommunicabilis*], that cannot be communicated or told.

in·com·mu·ni·ca·bly (in′kə-mū′ni-kə-bli), *adv.* in an incommunicable manner.

in·com·mu·ni·ca·do (in′kə-mū′ni-kä′dō), *adj.* [Sp.], unable or not allowed to communicate; cut off from means of communication: as, the prisoners were held *incommunicado*.

in·com·mu·ni·ca·tive (in′kə-mū′ni-kā′tiv, in′kə-mū′ni-kə-tiv), *adj.* not communicative; not inclined to talk; reserved; reticent.

in·com·mut·a·ble (in′kə-mū′tə-b′l), *adj.* [L. *incommutabilis;* see IN- (not) & COMMUTABLE], that cannot be changed or exchanged.

in·com·mut·a·bly (in′kə-mū′tə-bli), *adv.* in an incommutable manner.

in·com·pact (in′kəm-pakt′), *adj.* not compact; loosely assembled; not solid.

in·com·pa·ra·bil·i·ty (in′kom-pẽr-ə-bil′ə-ti, in-kom′prə-bil′ə-ti), *n.* the quality or state of being incomparable.

in·com·pa·ra·ble (in-kom′pẽr-ə-b′l, in-kom′prə-b′l), *adj.* that cannot be compared; specifically, *a*) having no basis of comparison; having no characteristics in common; incommensurable. *b*) beyond comparison; unequaled; matchless; peerless: as, *incomparable* skill.

in·com·pa·ra·bly (in-kom′pẽr-ə-bli, in-kom′prə-bli), *adv.* in an incomparable manner; beyond comparison.

in·com·pa·ti·bil·i·ty (in′kəm-pat′ə-bil′ə-ti), *n.* [Fr. *incompatibilité*], 1. the quality of being incompatible; inability to live together harmoniously or get along well with each other; disagreement. 2. [*pl.* INCOMPATIBILITIES (-tiz)], something incompatible.

in·com·pat·i·ble (in′kəm-pat′ə-b′l), *adj.* [ML. *incompatibilis*], 1. not compatible; not in harmony or agreement; incongruous (often followed by *with*). 2. that cannot be held at one time by the same person: said of positions, ranks, etc. 3. in *medicine & pharmacy*, not suitable for being mixed or used together: said of substances having an undesirable action on each other or on the body. *n. usually in pl.* an incompatible person or thing.

in·com·pat·i·bly (in′kəm-pat′ə-bli), *adv.* in an incompatible manner.

in·com·pe·tence (in-kom′pə-təns), *n.* [Fr. *incompétence*], the quality, state, or fact of being incompetent.

in·com·pe·ten·cy (in-kom′pə-tən-si), *n.* incompetence.

in·com·pe·tent (in-kom′pə-tənt), *adj.* [Fr. *incompétent;* LL. *incompetens;* see IN- (not) & COMPETENT], 1. without adequate ability, knowledge, fitness, etc.; failing to meet requirements; incapable; unskillful. 2. not legally qualified. *n.* an incompetent person; especially, one who is mentally deficient.

in·com·plete (in′kəm-plēt′), *adj.* [LL. *incompletus;* see IN- (not) & COMPLETE], 1. lacking a part or parts; not whole; not full. 2. unfinished; not concluded. 3. not perfect; not thorough. 4. designating or of a chemical reaction that is reversible.

in·com·plete·ly (in′kəm-plēt′li), *adv.* not completely; not entirely; imperfectly.

in·com·ple·tion (in′kəm-plē′shən), *n.* the state of being incomplete.

in·com·pli·ance (in′kəm-plī′əns), *n.* a being incompliant.

in·com·pli·an·cy (in′kəm-plī′ən-si), *n.* incompliance.

in·com·pli·ant (in′kəm-plī′ənt), *adj.* not compliant; not yielding; not pliant.

in·com·pre·hen·si·bil·i·ty (in′kom-pri-hen′sə-bil′ə-ti, in-kom′pri-hen′sə-bil′ə-ti), *n.* the quality or fact of being incomprehensible.

in·com·pre·hen·si·ble (in′kom-pri-hen′sə-b′l, in-kom′pri-hen′sə-b′l), *adj.* 1. not comprehensible; that cannot be understood; unintelligible. 2. [Archaic], illimitable.

in·com·pre·hen·si·bly (in′kom-pri-hen′sə-bli, in-kom′pri-hen′sə-bli), *adv.* in an incomprehensible manner; beyond comprehension.

in·com·pre·hen·sive (in′kom-pri-hen′siv, in-kom′pri-hen′siv), *adj.* 1. not inclusive; including little. 2. not able to comprehend well; understanding little.

in·com·press·i·bil·i·ty (in′kəm-pres′ə-bil′ə-ti), *n.* the quality or state of being incompressible.

in·com·press·i·ble (in′kəm-pres′ə-b′l), *adj.* that cannot be compressed.

in·com·put·a·bil·i·ty (in′kəm-pūt′ə-bil′ə-ti), *n.* the quality of being incomputable.

in·com·put·a·ble (in′kəm-pūt′ə-b′l), *adj.* that cannot be computed.

in·con·ceiv·a·bil·i·ty (in′kən-sēv′ə-bil′ə-ti), *n.* the quality of being inconceivable.

in·con·ceiv·a·ble (in′kən-sēv′ə-b′l), *adj.* that cannot be conceived; that cannot be thought of, understood, imagined, or believed.

in·con·ceiv·a·bly (in′kən-sēv′ə-bli), *adv.* 1. in an inconceivable manner. 2. to an inconceivable degree.

in·con·clu·sive (in′kən-klōō′siv), *adj.* not conclusive; not decisive; not final; ineffective.

in·con·den·sa·bil·i·ty, in·con·den·si·bil·i·ty (in′kən-den′sə-bil′ə-ti), *n.* the quality of being incondensable.

in·con·den·sa·ble, in·con·den·si·ble (in′kən-den′sə-b′l), *adj.* that cannot be condensed.

in·con·dite (in-kon'dit), *adj.* [L. *inconditus; in-*, not + *conditus*, pp. of *condere*, to put together; see CONDITION], 1. poorly constructed: said of literary works. 2. lacking finish or refinement; unpolished; crude.

in·con·form·i·ty (in'kən-fôr'mə-ti), *n.* lack of conformity.

in·con·gru·ent (in-koŋ'grōō-ənt), *adj.* [L. *incongruens*], not congruent; incongruous.

in·con·gru·i·ty (in'kən-grōō'ə-ti), *n.* [ML. *incongruitas* < L. *incongruus*], 1. the condition, quality, or fact of being incongruous; specifically, *a*) lack of harmony or agreement. *b*) lack of fitness or appropriateness. 2. [*pl.* INCONGRUITIES (-tiz)], something incongruous.

in·con·gru·ous (in-koŋ'grōō-əs), *adj.* [L. *incongruus*], not congruous; not congruent; specifically, *a*) lacking harmony or agreement; incompatible. *b*) having inconsistent or inharmonious parts, elements, etc. *c*) not corresponding to what is right, proper, or reasonable; unsuitable; inappropriate.

in·con·sec·u·tive (in'kən-sek'yoo-tiv), *adj.* not consecutive.

in·con·se·quence (in-kon'si-kwens', in-kon'si-kwəns), *n.* quality or instance of being inconsequent; absence of logic, logical sequence, or relevance.

in·con·se·quent (in-kon'si-kwent', in-kon'si-kwənt), *adj.* [L. *inconsequens*], not consequent; specifically, *a*) not following as a result. *b*) not following as a logical inference or conclusion; irrelevant. *c*) not proceeding in logical sequence; characterized by lack of logic.

in·con·se·quen·tial (in'kon-si-kwen'shəl, in-kon'si-kwen'shəl), *adj.* 1. inconsequent; illogical. 2. of no consequence; unimportant; trivial. *n.* something inconsequential.

in·con·sid·er·a·ble (in'kən-sid'ẽr-ə-b'l), *adj.* not worth consideration; unimportant; trivial; small.

in·con·sid·er·a·bly (in'kən-sid'ẽr-ə-bli), *adv.* 1. in an inconsiderable manner. 2. to an inconsiderable degree.

in·con·sid·er·ate (in'kən-sid'ẽr-it), *adj.* 1. insufficiently considered; ill-advised. 2. without thought or consideration for others; thoughtless; heedless.

in·con·sid·er·a·tion (in'kən-sid'ə-rā'shən), *n.* [LL. *inconsideratio*], lack of consideration; inconsiderate act.

in·con·sist·ence (in'kən-sis'təns), *n.* inconsistency.

in·con·sist·en·cy (in'kən-sis'tən-si), *n.* 1. the quality or state of being inconsistent. 2. [*pl.* INCONSISTENCIES (-siz)], something inconsistent; inconsistent act, remark, etc.

in·con·sis·tent (in'kən-sis'tənt), *adj.* not consistent; specifically, *a*) lacking agreement in kind, nature, form, etc.; not in harmony or accord; incompatible: as, practice *inconsistent* with belief. *b*) not uniform; not holding together; self-contradictory: as, an *inconsistent* narrative. *c*) not holding to the same principles or practice; changeable: as, *inconsistent* behavior.

in·con·sol·a·bil·i·ty (in'kən-sōl'ə-bil'ə-ti), *n.* the condition of being inconsolable.

in·con·sol·a·ble (in'kən-sōl'ə-b'l), *adj.* that cannot be consoled; disconsolate; brokenhearted.

in·con·sol·a·bly (in'kən-sōl'ə-bli), *adv.* in an inconsolable manner.

in·con·so·nance (in-kon'sə-nəns), *n.* the quality or state of being inconsonant.

in·con·so·nant (in-kon'sə-nənt), *adj.* not consonant; not in harmony or agreement; discordant.

in·con·spic·u·ous (in'kən-spik'ū-əs), *adj.* [LL. *inconspicuus*], not conspicuous; hard to see or perceive; attracting little attention; not striking.

in·con·stan·cy (in-kon'stən-si), *n.* [L. *inconstantia*], the state or quality of being inconstant; especially, *a*) lack of firmness in mind or purpose. *b*) unsteadiness or fickleness in affections or loyalties. *c*) lack of uniformity in nature, value, etc.; irregularity.

in·con·stant (in-kon'stənt), *adj.* not constant; changeable; specifically, *a*) not remaining firm in mind or purpose. *b*) unsteady in affections or loyalties; fickle. *c*) not uniform in nature, value, etc.; irregular.
SYN.**—inconstant** implies an inherent tendency to change or a lack of steadfastness (an *inconstant* lover); **fickle** suggests an even greater instability or readiness to change, especially in affection (spurned by a *fickle* public); **capricious** implies an instability or irregularity that seems to be the product of whim or erratic impulse (a *capricious* climate); **unstable,** in this connection, applies to one who is emotionally unsettled or variable (an *unstable* person laughs and cries easily).—***ANT.*** constant, reliable.

in·con·sum·a·ble (in'kən-sōōm'ə-b'l, in'kən-sūm'ə-b'l), *adj.* that cannot be consumed.

in·con·test·a·bil·i·ty (in'kən-tes'tə-bil'ə-ti), *n.* the quality of being incontestable.

in·con·test·a·ble (in'kən-tes'tə-b'l), *adj.* [Fr.], not to be contested; indisputable; unquestionable.

in·con·test·a·bly (in'kən-tes'tə-bli), *adv.* without doubt; unquestionably; certainly.

in·con·ti·nence (in-kon'tə-nəns), *n.* quality, state, or instance of being incontinent.

in·con·ti·nent (in-kon'tə-nənt), *adj.* [ME.; OFr.; L. *incontinens;* see IN- (not) & CONTINENT], 1. without self-restraint, especially in regard to sexual activity. 2. incapable of containing, holding, keeping, etc.: as, *incontinent* of information. 3. unable to restrain a natural discharge, as of urine, from the body.

in·con·ti·nent (in-kon'tə-nənt), *adv.* [ME. *incontynent;* OFr.; L. *in continenti* (*tempore*), in continuous (time); see CONTINENT], [Archaic], immediately; without delay.

in·con·trol·la·ble (in'kən-trōl'ə-b'l), *adj.* uncontrollable.

in·con·tro·vert·i·bil·i·ty (in'kon-trə-vũr'tə-bil'ə-ti, in-kon'trə-vũr'tə-bil'ə-ti), *n.* the quality of being incontrovertible.

in·con·tro·vert·i·ble (in'kon-trə-vũr'tə-b'l, in-kon'trə-vũr'tə-b'l), *adj.* that cannot be controverted; not disputable or debatable; undeniable.

in·con·tro·vert·i·bly (in'kon-trə-vũr'tə-bli, in-kon'trə-vũr'tə-bli), *adv.* undeniably.

in·con·ven·ience (in'kən-vēn'yəns), *n.* [ME.; OFr.; LL. *inconvenientia*], 1. the quality or state of being inconvenient; lack of comfort, ease, etc.; bother; trouble. 2. anything inconvenient. *v.t.* [INCONVENIENCED (-yənst), INCONVENIENCING], to cause inconvenience to; cause trouble or bother to; incommode.

in·con·ven·ien·cy (in'kən-vēn'yən-si), *n.* inconvenience.

in·con·ven·ient (in'kən-vēn'yənt), *adj.* not convenient; specifically, *a*) not favorable to one's comfort; difficult to do, use, or get to; causing trouble, bother, work, etc.; unhandy. *b*) [Obs.], not appropriate.

in·con·vert·i·bil·i·ty (in'kən-vũr'tə-bil'ə-ti), *n.* the quality or condition of being inconvertible.

in·con·vert·i·ble (in'kən-vũr'tə-b'l), *adj.* that cannot be converted; that cannot be changed or exchanged: as, some paper money is *inconvertible* into silver or gold.

in·con·vin·ci·ble (in'kən-vin'sə-b'l), *adj.* that cannot be convinced.

in·con·vin·ci·bly (in'kən-vin'sə-bli), *adv.* so as to be inconvincible.

in-co-or·di·nate (in'kō-ôr'də-nit, in'kō-ôr'də-nāt'), *adj.* not co-ordinate.

in-co-or·di·na·tion (in'kō-ôr'də-nā'shən), *n.* lack of co-ordination.

incorp., incor., incorporated.

in·cor·po·ra·ble (in-kôr'pẽr-ə-b'l), *adj.* that can be incorporated.

in·cor·po·rate (in-kôr'pẽr-it; *for v.,* in-kôr'pə-rāt'), *adj.* [ME. *incorporat;* LL. *incorporatus*, pp. of *incorporare;* see IN- (in) & CORPORATE], 1. formed or combined into one body or unit; intimately united, joined, or blended. 2. formed into, or combined as part of, a corporation; incorporated. *v.t.* [INCORPORATED (-id), INCORPORATING], 1. to combine or join with something already formed; make part of another thing; include; embody. 2. to bring together into a single whole; mix or combine completely; merge. 3. to admit into a corporation or association as a member. 4. to form (individuals or units) into a legally organized group that acts as one individual; form into a corporation. 5. to give substantial, material, or physical form to. *v.i.* to unite or combine into one group or substance; be combined or merged; form a corporation.

in·cor·po·rate (in-kôr'pẽr-it), *adj.* [L. *incorporatus;* see IN- (not) & CORPORATE], incorporeal.

in·cor·po·rat·ed (in-kôr'pə-rāt'id), *adj.* [pp. of *incorporate*], 1. combined; united. 2. organized as a legal corporation: as, an *incorporated* town: abbreviated **inc., incorp., incor.**

in·cor·po·ra·tion (in-kôr'pə-rā'shən), *n.* [ME. *incorporacion;* OFr.; LL. *incorporatio*], 1. an incorporating or being incorporated. 2. a corporation.

in·cor·po·ra·tive (in-kôr'pə-rā'tiv), *adj.* characterized by incorporation; tending to incorporate.

in·cor·po·ra·tor (in-kôr'pə-rā'tẽr), *n.* 1. a person who incorporates. 2. any of the original members of a corporation, whose names appear in its charter.

in·cor·po·re·al (in'kôr-pôr'i-əl, in'kôr-pō'ri-əl), *adj.* [L. *incorporeus;* see IN- (not) & CORPOREAL], 1. not consisting of matter; without material body or subs nce. 2. of spirits or angels. 3. in *law*, without physical existence in itself but belonging as a right to a material thing or property, as a patent, copyright, etc.

in·cor·po·re·i·ty (in'kôr-pə-rē'ə-ti), *n.* [ML. *incorporeitas* < L. *incorporeus*], 1. the quality or state of being incorporeal. 2. [*pl.* INCORPOREITIES (-tiz)], an incorporeal entity or attribute.

in·cor·rect (in'kə-rekt'), *adj.* [L. *incorrectus*], not correct; specifically, *a*) improper. *b*) untrue; inaccurate; wrong; faulty. Abbreviated **incorr.**

in·cor·ri·gi·bil·i·ty (in-kôr'i-jə-bil'ə-ti, in-kor'i-jə-bil'ə-ti), *n.* the quality of being incorrigible.

in·cor·ri·gi·ble (in-kôr'i-jə-b'l, in-kor'i-jə-b'l), *adj.* [ME. *incorygibile;* OFr.; LL. *incorrigibilis*], not corrigible; that cannot be corrected, improved, or reformed, especially because firmly established, as a habit, or set in bad habits, as a child. *n.* an incorrigible person.

in·cor·ri·gi·bly (in-kôr'i-jə-bli, in-kor'i-jə-bli), *adv.* in an incorrigible manner; so as to be incorrigible.

in·cor·rupt (in'kə-rupt'), *adj.* [L. *incorruptus*], not corrupt; specifically, *a*) sound; uncontaminated; not rotten. *b*) morally sound; not depraved, evil, impure, or perverted. *c*) not taking bribes; upright; honest.

d) containing no errors, alterations, or foreign admixtures: said of languages, texts, etc.

in·cor·rupt·i·bil·i·ty (in'kə-rup'tə-bil'ə-ti), *n.* the quality or state of being incorruptible.

in·cor·rupt·i·ble (in'kə-rup'tə-b'l), *adj.* that cannot be corrupted; specifically, *a*) that cannot be bribed. *b*) not liable to decay or destruction.

in·cor·rupt·i·bly (in'kə-rup'tə-bli), *adv.* in an incorruptible manner; so as to be incorruptible.

in·cor·rup·tion (in'kə-rup'shən), *n.* [Archaic], the quality or state of being incorrupt or incorruptible.

incr., 1. increase. 2. increased. 3. increasing.

in·cras·sate (in-kras'āt), *v.t. & v.i.* [INCRASSATED (-id), INCRASSATING], [< L. *incrassatus*, pp. of *incrassare*, to make thick; *in-*, in + *crassare*, to thicken < *crassus*, thick], to make or become thick or thicker; specifically, to thicken, as by evaporation: said of fluids. *adj.* thickened; swollen; incrassated.

in·cras·sa·tion (in'kra-sā'shən), *n.* [< *incrassate*], 1. a thickening or being thickened. 2. a thickened growth or formation.

in·creas·a·ble (in-krēs'ə-b'l), *adj.* that can be increased.

in·crease (in-krēs'; *for n.*, in'krēs), *v.i.* [INCREASED (-krēst'), INCREASING], [ME. *encresen;* OFr. *encreistre;* L. *increscere; in-*, in, on + *crescere*, to grow], 1. to become greater in size, amount, degree, etc.; grow. 2. to become greater in numbers by producing offspring; multiply. *v.t.* to cause to become greater in size, amount, degree, etc.; add to; augment. *n.* [ME. *encrese*], 1. an increasing or becoming increased; multiplication, as of offspring. 2. the result or amount of an increasing: as, the population showed an *increase* of 10 per cent. Abbreviated **inc., incr.**

on the increase, increasing.

SYN.—**increase**, the general word in this list, means to make or become greater in size, amount, degree, etc. (to *increase* one's weight, one's power, debts, etc.); **enlarge** specifically implies a making or becoming greater in size, volume, extent, etc. (to *enlarge* a house, a business, etc.); **augment**, a more formal word, generally implies increase by addition, often of something that is already of a considerable size, amount, etc. (to *augment* one's income); **multiply** suggests increase in number, specifically by procreation (rabbits *multiply* rapidly). —*ANT.* decrease, diminish, lessen.

in·creas·ing·ly (in-krēs'iŋ-li), *adv.* more and more; to an ever-increasing degree.

in·cre·ate (in'kri-āt', in'kri-āt'), *adj.* [ME. *increat;* ML. *increatus*], not created; existing eternally: as, a divine being is considered to be *increate.*

in·cred·i·bil·i·ty (in-kred'ə-bil'ə-ti), *n.* [L. *incredibilitas*], the quality or state of being incredible.

in·cred·i·ble (in-kred'ə-b'l), *adj.* not credible; unbelievable; seeming too unusual or improbable to be possible.

in·cred·i·bly (in-kred'ə-bli), *adv.* 1. in an incredible manner. 2. to an incredible degree.

in·cre·du·li·ty (in'krə-dōō'lə-ti, in'krə-dū'lə-ti), *n.* [ME. *incredulite;* Late OFr. *incrédulité;* L. *incredulitas;* see IN- (not) & CREDULITY], unwillingness or inability to believe; doubt; skepticism. —*SYN.* see **unbelief.**

in·cred·u·lous (in-krej'oo-ləs), *adj.* [L. *incredulus;* see IN- (not) & CREDULOUS], 1. unwilling or unable to believe; doubting; skeptical. 2. showing doubt or disbelief: as, an *incredulous* look.

in·cre·ment (in'krə-mənt, iŋ'krə-mənt), *n.* [ME.; L. *incrementum* < base of *increscere*, to increase; see INCREASE], 1. a becoming greater or larger; increase; gain; growth. 2. amount of increase. 3. in *mathematics*, any of several small changes in a variable quantity.

in·cre·men·tal (in'krə-men't'l), *adj.* of or resulting from an increment or increments.

in·cres·cent (in-kres''nt), *adj.* [L. *increscens*, ppr. of *increscere*, to increase; see INCREASE], increasing; growing; waxing: said especially of the moon.

in·cre·tion (in-krē'shən), *n.* [*in* + *secretion*], in *physiology*, 1. secretion into the body. 2. a substance, as a hormone, internally secreted.

in·crim·i·nate (in-krim'ə-nāt'), *v.t.* [INCRIMINATED (-id), INCRIMINATING], [< ML. *incriminatus*, pp. of *incriminare;* see IN- (in) & CRIMINATE], 1. to charge with a crime; accuse. 2. to involve in, or make appear guilty of, a crime or fault.

in·crim·i·na·tion (in-krim'ə-nā'shən), *n.* an incriminating or being incriminated.

in·crim·i·na·tor (in-krim'ə-nā'tẽr), *n.* a person who incriminates.

in·crim·i·na·to·ry (in-krim'ə-nə-tôr'i, in-krim'ə-nə-tō'ri), *adj.* incriminating or likely to incriminate.

in·crust (in-krust'), *v.t.* [OFr. *encrouster;* L. *incrustare;* see IN- (in) & CRUST], 1. to cover with or as with a crust, or hard outer layer. 2. to decorate elaborately, especially with gems.

in·crus·ta·tion (in'krus-tā'shən), *n.* [LL. *incrustatio*], 1. an incrusting or being incrusted. 2. a crust; hard outer layer or coating. 3. an elaborate decorative coating, inlay, etc.

in·cu·bate (in'kyoo-bāt', iŋ'kyoo-bāt'), *v.t.* [INCUBATED (-id), INCUBATING], [< L. *incubatus*, pp. of *incubare*, to lie in or upon; *in-*, in, on + *cubare*, to lie], 1. to sit on and hatch (eggs). 2. to keep (eggs, embryos, bacteria, etc.) in a favorable environment for hatching or developing. *v.i.* to go through the process of incubation.

in·cu·ba·tion (in'kyoo-bā'shən, iŋ'kyoo-bā'shən), *n.* [L. *incubatio*], 1. an incubating or being incubated. 2. the phase in the development of a disease between the infection and the first appearance of symptoms.

in·cu·ba·tion·al (in'kyoo-bā'shən-'l, iŋ'kyoo-bā'shən-'l), *adj.* of incubation.

in·cu·ba·tive (in'kyoo-bā'tiv, iŋ'kyoo-bā'tiv), *adj.* of or characterized by incubation.

in·cu·ba·tor (in'kyoo-bā'tẽr, iŋ'kyoo-bā'tẽr), *n.* [L.], a person or thing that incubates; specifically, *a*) an artificially heated container for hatching eggs. *b*) a similar apparatus in which premature babies are kept for a period. *c*) an apparatus for developing bacterial cultures.

in·cu·bus (in'kyoo-bəs, iŋ'kyoo-bəs), *n.* [*pl.* INCUBUSES (-iz), INCUBI (-bī')], [ME.; LL., nightmare (in ML., demon supposed to cause nightmare) < L. *incubare;* see INCUBATE], 1. a spirit or demon thought in medieval times to lie on sleeping persons, especially women, with whom it sought sexual intercourse: see also **succubus.** 2. a nightmare. 3. anything oppressive; burden.

in·cu·des (in-kū'dēz), *n.* plural of **incus.**

in·cul·cate (in-kul'kāt, in'kul-kāt'), *v.t.* [INCULCATED (-id), INCULCATING], [< L. *inculcatus*, pp. of *inculcare*, to tread in, tread down < *in-*, in, on + *calcare*, to trample underfoot < *calx*, *calcis*, heel], to impress upon the mind by frequent repetition or insistent urging (often with *on* or *upon*). —*SYN.* see **instill.**

in·cul·ca·tion (in'kul-kā'shən), *n.* an inculcating or being inculcated.

in·cul·ca·tor (in-kul'kāt'ẽr, in'kul-kāt'ẽr), *n.* a person who inculcates.

in·culp·a·ble (in-kul'pə-b'l), *adj.* not culpable.

in·cul·pate (in-kul'pāt, in'kul-pāt'), *v.t.* [INCULPATED (-id), INCULPATING], [< ML. *inculpatus*, pp. of *inculpare*, to blame < L. *in*, in, on + *culpa*, fault, blame], to incriminate (in both senses).

in·cul·pa·tion (in'kul-pā'shən), *n.* an inculpating.

in·cul·pa·to·ry (in-kul'pə-tôr'i, in-kul'pə-tō'ri), *adj.* inculpating or likely to inculpate.

in·cult (in-kult'), *adj.* [L. *incultus;* see IN- (not) & CULT], [Rare], 1. uncultivated: said of land. 2. unrefined.

in·cum·ben·cy (in-kum'bən-si), *n.* [*pl.* INCUMBENCIES (-siz)], 1. the quality or condition of being incumbent. 2. something incumbent; specifically, *a*) a duty or obligation. *b*) an overlying weight or mass. 3. *a*) the holding and administering of a position; especially, the holding of a church benefice. *b*) tenure of office.

in·cum·bent (in-kum'bənt), *adj.* [L. *incumbens*, ppr. of *incumbere*, to recline or rest on < *in-*, on + *cubare*, to lie down], 1. lying, resting, or pressing with its weight on something else; hence, 2. [Poetic], impending; imminent. *n.* the holder of a benefice or office.

incumbent on (or **upon**), resting or coming upon as a duty or obligation.

in·cum·ber (in-kum'bẽr), *v.t.* to encumber.

in·cum·brance (in-kum'brəns), *n.* encumbrance.

in·cu·nab·u·la (in'kyoo-nab'yoo-lə), *n.pl.* [*sing.* INCUNABULUM (-ləm)], [L., neut. pl., swaddling clothes, cradle, origin, beginning; *in-*, in + *cunabula*, neut. pl., a cradle, dim. of *cunae*, fem. pl., a cradle], 1. the very first stages of anything; infancy; beginnings. 2. early printed books; especially, books printed before 1500.

in·cu·nab·u·lar (in'kyoo-nab'yoo-lẽr), *adj.* of incunabula.

in·cur (in-kũr'), *v.t.* [INCURRED (-kũrd'), INCURRING], [ME. *incurren;* L. *incurrere*, to run into or toward, attack; *in-*, in, toward + *currere*, to run], to come into, acquire, or meet with (something undesirable), especially through one's own actions; bring upon oneself.

in·cur·a·bil·i·ty (in'kyoor-ə-bil'ə-ti, in-kyoor'ə-bil'ə-ti), *n.* the state or quality of being incurable.

in·cur·a·ble (in-kyoor'ə-b'l), *adj.* not curable; that cannot be remedied or corrected. *n.* a person having an incurable disease or disorder.

in·cur·a·bly (in-kyoor'ə-bli), *adv.* in an incurable manner; without possibility of cure; beyond remedy or correction.

in·cu·ri·ous (in-kyoor'i-əs), *adj.* 1. not curious; not eager to find out; uninterested; indifferent. 2. not interesting; lacking novelty. —*SYN.* see **indifferent.**

in·cur·rence (in-kũr'əns), *n.* an incurring.

in·cur·rent (in-kũr'ənt), *adj.* [L. *incurrens*, ppr. of *incurrere;* see INCUR], flowing in; especially, characterized by the flowing in of water: as, the *incurrent* canals of sponges.

in·cur·sion (in-kũr'zhən, in-kũr'shən), *n.* [ME.; L. *incursio* < *incurrere;* see INCUR], 1. a running in or coming in. 2. an unfriendly entry; invasion; raid.

in·cur·sive (in-kũr′siv), *adj.* making or tending to make an incursion; attacking; invasive.
in·cur·vate (in-kũr′vit; *also, and for v. always,* in-kũr′vāt), *adj.* [L. *incurvatus,* pp. of *incurvare;* see INCURVE], bent or curving inward. *v.t. & v.i.* [INCURVATED (-id), INCURVATING], to bend or curve inward.
in·cur·va·tion (in′kẽr-vā′shən), *n.* [L. *incurvatio*], an incurvating or being incurvated.
in·curve (in-kũrv′), *v.t. & v.i.* [L. *incurvare*], to curve inward. *n.* (in′kũrv′), 1. an incurving. 2. [*in-* (in) + *curve, n.*], in *baseball,* a pitched ball that curves toward the batter. Also, for *n.*, **in-curve.**
in·cus (iŋ′kəs), *n.* [*pl.* INCUDES (in-kū′dēz)], [L., anvil < *incusus;* see INCUSE], the central, somewhat anvil-shaped one of the three small bones in the middle ear: also called *anvil.*
in·cuse (in-kūz′), *adj.* [L. *incusus,* pp. of *incudere,* to forge with a hammer, lit., to pound upon; *in-*, in, on + *cudere,* to strike, hit], hammered or pressed in: said of the design on a coin, etc. *n.* such a design.
Ind (ind), *n.* [ME. & OFr. *Inde;* L. *India*], 1. [Poetic], India. 2. [Obs.], the Indies.
Ind., 1. India. 2. Indian. 3. Indiana. 4. Indies.
ind., 1. independent. 2. index. 3. indicative. 4. indigo. 5. industrial.
I.N.D., *in nomine Dei,* [L.], in the name of God.
in·da·ba (in-dä′bä), *n.* [Zulu *in-daba,* subject, matter], a council or conference among South African tribes.
in·da·min (in′də-min), *n.* indamine.
in·da·mine (in′də-mēn′, in′də-min), *n.* [prob. < *indigo* + *amine*], any of a group of organic dyes containing the NH group; especially, phenylene blue, $NH{:}C_6H_4{:}N{\cdot}C_6H_4{\cdot}NH_2$.
in·debt (in-det′), *v.t.* [back-formation < *indebted*], [Rare], to make indebted or obligated.
in·debt·ed (in-det′id), *adj.* [ME. *endetted,* pp. of *endetten,* to put in debt; OFr. *endetter* < *en-* (L. *in-*) + *dette;* see DEBT], 1. in debt or under legal obligation to repay something received. 2. obliged; owing gratitude, as for a favor received.
in·debt·ed·ness (in-det′id-nis), *n.* 1. the state of being indebted. 2. the amount owed; all one's debts.
in·de·cen·cy (in-dē′s′n-si), *n.* [L. *indecentia*], 1. the state or quality of being indecent; lack of modesty, taste, or propriety. 2. [*pl.* INDECENCIES (-siz)], an indecent act, statement, etc.
in·de·cent (in-dē′s′nt), *adj.* [< Fr. or L.; Fr. *indécent;* L. *indecens*], not decent; specifically, *a*) not proper and fitting; unseemly; improper. *b*) morally offensive; immodest; obscene. —*SYN.* see **improper.**
in·de·cid·u·ous (in′di-sij′ōō-əs), *adj.* not deciduous.
in·de·ci·pher·a·bil·i·ty (in′di-sī′fẽr-ə-bil′ə-ti), *n.* the quality or state of being indecipherable.
in·de·ci·pher·a·ble (in′di-sī′fẽr-ə-b′l), *adj.* that cannot be deciphered; illegible.
in·de·ci·sion (in′di-sizh′ən), *n.* [Fr. *indécision*], lack of decision; inability to decide or a tendency to change the mind frequently; hesitation or vacillation.
in·de·ci·sive (in′di-sī′siv), *adj.* 1. not decisive; not conclusive or final. 2. characterized by indecision; hesitating or vacillating.
in·de·clin·a·ble (in′di-klīn′ə-b′l), *adj.* not declinable; having no case inflections: abbreviated **indecl.**
in·de·com·pos·a·ble (in′dē-kəm-pōz′ə-b′l), *adj.* that cannot be decomposed.
in·dec·o·rous (in-dek′ə-rəs, in′di-kôr′əs, in′di-kō′rəs), *adj.* not decorous; lacking decorum, propriety, good taste, etc.; unseemly. —*SYN.* see **improper.**
in·de·co·rum (in′di-kôr′əm, in′di-kō′rəm), *n.* [L., neut. of *indecorus*], 1. lack of decorum; lack of propriety, good taste, etc. 2. an indecorous act, remark, etc.
in·deed (in-dēd′), *adv.* [ME. *indede;* see IN, *prep.* & DEED], certainly; truly; admittedly: often used to give emphasis, as, it is *indeed* warm. *interj.* an exclamation of surprise, bitterness, doubt, sarcasm, etc.
indef., indefinite.
in·de·fat·i·ga·bil·i·ty (in′di-fat′i-gə-bil′ə-ti), *n.* the quality of being indefatigable.
in·de·fat·i·ga·ble (in′di-fat′i-gə-b′l), *adj.* [MFr. *indéfatigable;* L. *indefatigabilis* < *in-*, not + *defatigare,* to tire out, weary; see DE- & FATIGUE], that cannot be tired out; tireless; untiring.
in·de·fat·i·ga·bly (in′di-fat′i-gə-bli), *adv.* in an indefatigable manner.
in·de·fea·si·bil·i·ty (in′di-fē′zə-bil′ə-ti), *n.* the quality of being indefeasible.
in·de·fea·si·ble (in′di-fē′zə-b′l), *adj.* not defeasible; that cannot be undone or made void.
in·de·fea·si·bly (in′di-fē′zə-bli), *adv.* so as to be indefeasible.
in·de·fect·i·ble (in′di-fek′tə-b′l), *adj.* [*in-* (not) + *defect* + *-ible*], 1. not likely to fail, decay, become imperfect, etc. 2. without a fault or blemish; perfect.
in·de·fec·tive (in′di-fek′tiv), *adj.* not defective.
in·de·fen·si·bil·i·ty (in′di-fen′sə-bil′ə-ti), *n.* the quality or state of being indefensible.
in·de·fen·si·ble (in′di-fen′sə-b′l), *adj.* 1. that cannot be defended or protected. 2. that cannot be justified.
in·de·fen·si·bly (in′di-fen′sə-bli), *adv.* in an indefensible manner; so as to be indefensible.
in·de·fin·a·ble (in′di-fīn′ə-b′l), *adj.* that cannot be defined.
in·de·fin·a·bly (in′di-fīn′ə-bli), *adv.* in an indefinable manner.
in·def·i·nite (in-def′ə-nit), *adj.* [L. *indefinitus*], not definite; specifically, *a*) having no exact limits. *b*) not precise or clear in meaning; vague. *c*) not sharp or clear in outline; blurred; indistinct. *d*) not certain or positive; unsure. *e*) in *botany,* of no fixed number, or too many to count: said of the stamens, etc. of certain flowers. *f*) in *grammar,* not limiting or specifying: as *a* and *an* are *indefinite* articles, *any* is an *indefinite* pronoun. Abbreviated **indef.**
in·de·his·cence (in′di-his′′ns), *n.* the quality of being indehiscent.
in·de·his·cent (in′di-his′′nt), *adj.* not dehiscent; not opening at maturity to discharge its seeds: as, the apple is an *indehiscent* fruit.
in·del·i·bil·i·ty (in′del-ə-bil′ə-ti, in-del′ə-bil′ə-ti), *n.* the quality of being indelible.
in·del·i·ble (in-del′ə-b′l), *adj.* [L. *indelibilis; in-*, not + *delibilis,* perishable < *delere,* to destroy], 1. that cannot be erased, blotted out, washed out, etc.; permanent; lasting. 2. leaving an indelible mark: as, *indelible* ink.
in·del·i·bly (in-del′ə-bli), *adv.* so as to be indelible.
in·del·i·ca·cy (in-del′i-kə-si), *n.* 1. the quality of being indelicate. 2. [*pl.* INDELICACIES (-siz)], something indelicate.
in·del·i·cate (in-del′i-kit), *adj.* not delicate; coarse; crude; rough; especially, lacking, or offensive to, propriety or modesty; gross. —*SYN.* see **coarse, improper.**
in·dem·ni·fi·ca·tion (in-dem′nə-fi-kā′shən), *n.* 1. an indemnifying or being indemnified. 2. something that indemnifies; recompense. —*SYN.* see **reparation.**
in·dem·ni·fi·er (in-dem′nə-fi′ẽr), *n.* a person or company that indemnifies.
in·dem·ni·fy (in-dem′nə-fī′), *v.t.* [INDEMNIFIED (-fīd′), INDEMNIFYING], [< L. *indemnis,* unhurt < *in-*, not + *damnum,* hurt, harm, damage; + *-fy*], 1. to protect against or keep free from loss, damage, etc.; insure. 2. *a*) to repay for what has been lost or damaged; compensate for a loss, etc.; reimburse. *b*) to redeem or make good (a loss). —*SYN.* see **pay.**
in·dem·ni·tor (in-dem′nə-tẽr), *n.* a person who provides indemnity.
in·dem·ni·ty (in-dem′nə-ti), *n.* [*pl.* INDEMNITIES (-tiz)], [Fr. *indemnité;* LL. *indemnitas* < L. *indemnis;* see INDEMNIFY], 1. protection or insurance against loss, damage, etc. 2. legal exemption from penalties or liabilities incurred by one's actions. 3. repayment or reimbursement for loss, damage, etc.; compensation.
in·de·mon·stra·ble (in′di-mon′strə-b′l, in-dem′ən-strə-b′l), *adj.* not demonstrable; that cannot be proved.
in·dene (in′dēn), *n.* [< *indole* + *-ene*], a colorless, oily hydrocarbon, C_9H_8, obtained from coal tar.
in·dent (in-dent′; *for n., usually* in′dent), *v.t.* [ME. *endent;* OFr. *endenter;* ML. *indentare* < L. *in,* in + *dens, dentis,* tooth], 1. *a*) to cut toothlike points into (an edge or border); notch; hence, *b*) to make jagged or zigzag in outline. 2. to sever (a written contract, etc.) along an irregular line, so that the parts may be identified. 3. to write out (a contract, etc.) in duplicate. 4. to indenture. 5. *a*) to space (the beginning of a paragraph, the edge of a column of figures, etc.) in from the regular margin. *b*) to make an indention in (a paragraph, etc.). 6. *a*) to request or order goods from. *b*) to make an order for (goods). *v.i.* 1. to form or be marked by notches, points, or a jagged border. 2. to enter into an indenture, or contract. 3. to space in from the margin; make an indention. 4. to draw up an order or requisition in duplicate. *n.* 1. a notch or cut in an edge. 2. an indenture, or written contract. 3. a space in from the margin; indention. 4. an indented line, paragraph, etc. 5. an official requisition or order for goods.
in·dent (in-dent′; *for n., usually* in′dent), *v.t.* [*in-* (in) + *dent* (slight hollow)], 1. to make a dent, or slight hollow, in. 2. to apply (a mark, etc.) with pressure; impress; stamp in. *n.* a dent.
in·den·ta·tion (in′den-tā′shən), *n.* [*indent* (to cut) or *indent* (to make a dent in) + *-ation*], 1. an indenting or being indented. 2. a result of indenting; specifically, *a*) a notch or cut. *b*) a dent, or slight hollow. *c*) an indention; space in from a margin.
in·den·tion (in-den′shən), *n.* [*indent* (to cut) or *indent* (to make a dent in) + *-ion*], 1. a spacing in from the margin. 2. an empty or blank space left by this. 3. *a*) a dent, or slight hollow. *b*) the making of a dent.
in·den·ture (in-den′chẽr), *n.* [ME. & OFr. *endenture;* ML. *indentura* < *indentare;* see INDENT (to cut); now used also as if < *indent* (to make a dent in)], 1. indentation. 2. a written contract or agreement: originally, it was in duplicate, the two copies having correspondingly notched edges. 3. *usually pl.* a contract binding one person to work for another for a given length of time, as an apprentice to a master, or an immigrant to service in a colony. 4. an official, authen-

ticated list, inventory, etc. *v.t.* [INDENTURED (-chẽrd), INDENTURING], 1. to bind by indenture. 2. to indent.

In·de·pend·ence (in'di-pen'dəns), *n.* a city in western Missouri, near Kansas City: pop., 62,000.

in·de·pend·ence (in'di-pen'dəns), *n.* 1. the state or quality of being independent; freedom from the influence, control, or determination of another or others. 2. an income sufficient for a livelihood.

Independence Day, the Fourth of July, the anniversary of the adoption of the Declaration of Independence on July 4, 1776: a legal holiday in the United States.

in·de·pend·en·cy (in'di-pen'dən-si), *n.* [*pl.* INDEPENDENCIES (-siz)], 1. independence. 2. an independent nation, province, etc.

in·de·pend·ent (in'di-pen'dənt), *adj.* [*in-* (not) + *dependent*], 1. free from the influence, control, or determination of another or others; specifically, *a*) free from the rule of another; controlling or governing oneself; self-governing. *b*) free from influence, persuasion, or bias; self-determined, self-confident, or self-reliant: as, *independent* thinking. *c*) not connected with any political party or organization: as, an *independent* voter. *d*) not connected or related to another, to each other, or to a group; separate: as, an *independent* grocer. 2. *a*) not depending on another for financial support. *b*) large enough to enable one to live without working: said of an income, a fortune, etc. *c*) having an independent income; not needing to work for living. 3. [I-], of or having to do with the Independents. *n.* 1. a person who is independent in thinking, action, etc.; specifically [often I-], a person not an adherent of any political party; one who votes as he wishes, without regard to party labels. 2. [I-], *a*) a person who believes that a local organized Christian church is or should be self-sufficient and not dependent on external ecclesiastical authority. *b*) in England, a Congregationalist. Abbreviated **ind., I.**
  independent of, apart from; regardless of.

independent clause, in *grammar*, a main clause.

in·de·scrib·a·bil·i·ty (in'di-skrīb'ə-bil'ə-ti), *n.* the quality or state of being indescribable.

in·de·scrib·a·ble (in'di-skrīb'ə-b'l), *adj.* that cannot be described; beyond the power of description.

in·de·scrib·a·bly (in'di-skrīb'ə-bli), *adv.* in an indescribable manner; so as to be indescribable.

in·de·struct·i·bil·i·ty (in'di-struk'tə-bil'ə-ti), *n.* the quality or state of being indestructible.

in·de·struct·i·ble (in'di-struk'tə-b'l), *adj.* not destructible; that cannot be destroyed.

in·de·struct·i·bly (in'di-struk'tə-bli), *adv.* so as to be indestructible.

in·de·ter·mi·na·ble (in'di-tũr'mi-nə-b'l), *adj.* [LL. *indeterminabilis*], not determinable; specifically, *a*) that cannot be decided or settled. *b*) that cannot be definitely set down or ascertained.

in·de·ter·mi·na·cy (in'di-tũr'mə-nə-si), *n.* the state or quality of being indeterminate.

in·de·ter·mi·nate (in'di-tũr'mə-nit), *adj.* 1. not determinate; specifically, *a*) having inexact limits; indefinite; indistinct; vague: as, an *indeterminate* result. *b*) unsettled; undecided; inconclusive. *c*) irresolute. 2. in *botany*, *a*) racemose. *b*) having the floral leaves separate and not overlapping in the bud.

in·de·ter·mi·na·tion (in'di-tũr'mə-nā'shən), *n.* 1. the state or quality of being indeterminate. 2. lack of determination.

in·de·ter·min·ism (in'di-tũr'min-iz'm), *n.* [*in-* (not) + *determinism*], the doctrine that the will is to some degree free, or that one's actions and choices are not altogether determined by a sequence of causes independent of his will.

in·de·ter·min·ist (in'di-tũr'min-ist), *n.* a person who believes in indeterminism. *adj.* of indeterminism or indeterminists.

in·de·ter·min·is·tic (in'di-tũr'mi-nis'tik), *adj.* indeterminist.

in·dex (in'deks), *n.* [*pl.* INDEXES (-iz), INDICES (-də-sēz')], [L., informer, that which points out < *indicare;* see INDICATE], 1. the index finger; forefinger. 2. a pointer or indicator, as the needle on a dial; hence, 3. a thing that points out; indication; sign; representation: as, performance is an *index* of ability. 4. *a*) an alphabetical list of names, subjects, etc. together with page numbers, usually placed at the end of a book or other publication. *b*) a list describing the items of a collection and where they may be found; catalogue: as, a library *index*. 5. the relation or proportion of one amount or dimension to another. 6. [I-], *a*) the *Index Librorum Prohibitorum*. *b*) the *Index Expurgatorius*. 7. [Obs.], a table of contents, preface, prologue, or statement of subject. 8. in *mathematics*, an exponent. 9. in *printing*, a sign (☛) calling special attention to certain information; fist. Abbreviated **ind.** *v.t.* 1. *a*) to make an index of or for. *b*) to include in an index. 2. to indicate or give a sign of.

‡In·dex Ex·pur·ga·to·ri·us (in'deks eks-pũr'gə-tō'ri-əs), [Mod. L., expurgatory index], formerly, a list of books that the Roman Catholic Church forbade its members to read unless certain passages condemned as dangerous to faith, morality, etc. were deleted or changed.

index finger, the finger next to the thumb; forefinger.

‡In·dex Lib·ro·rum Pro·hib·i·to·rum (in'deks lī-brō'-rəm prō-hib'i-tō'rəm), [L., index of prohibited books], a list of books that the Roman Catholic Church condemns and forbids its members to read (except by special permission) as dangerous to faith, morality, etc.

index (number), a number used to measure change in prices, wages, employment, production, etc.: it shows percentage variation from an arbitrary standard, usually 100, representing the status at some earlier time.

In·di·a (in'di-ə), *n.* [L.; Gr. *India* < *Indos*, the Indus < OPer. *Hindu*, India; see HINDU], 1. a large peninsula of southern Asia, between the Bay of Bengal and the Arabian Sea: area, c. 1,500,000 sq. mi.; formerly divided into British India and the Indian States and Agencies, it now contains India (sense 2), Pakistan, Nepal, Bhutan, and the small enclaves of Portuguese India: abbreviated **Ind.** 2. a republic in central and southern India, a member of the British Commonwealth of Nations: formerly a dominion (1947–1950): area, 1,260,000 sq. mi.; pop. (not including Jammu and Kashmir), 356,879,000; capital, New Delhi: figures include the protectorate of Sikkim: Hindi name (of the republic of India), *Bharat*.

India ink, 1. a black pigment of lampblack mixed with a gelatinous substance, used in writing, painting, etc. 2. a liquid ink made from this.

In·di·a·man (in'di-ə-mən), *n.* [*pl.* INDIAMEN (-mən)], a merchant ship traveling regularly between England and India; especially, a large ship of this sort belonging to the English East India Company.

In·di·an (in'di-ən), *adj.* [LL. *Indianus* < L. *India*], 1. of India or the East Indies, their people, or culture. 2. of the American aboriginal races (American Indians) or the West Indies, or their cultures. 3. of a type used or made by Indians. 4. made of maize, or Indian corn. *n.* 1. a native of India or the East Indies. 2. a member of any of the aboriginal races of North America, South America, or the West Indies: originally so named from the belief, held by early explorers, that these regions were part of Asia. 3. popularly, any of the languages spoken by the American Indians. Abbreviated **Ind.**

In·di·an·a (in'di-an'ə), *n.* a Middle Western State of the United States: area, 36,291 sq. mi.; pop., 4,662,000; capital, Indianapolis: abbreviated **Ind.**: nicknamed *Hoosier State*.

In·di·an·ap·o·lis (in'di-ən-ap''l-is), *n.* the capital of Indiana, in the central part of the State: pop., 476,000.

Indian bread, 1. bread made from corn meal. 2. a fungus eaten by the American Indians; tuckahoe.

Indian club, a wooden or metallic club shaped like a tenpin, swung in the hand for exercise.

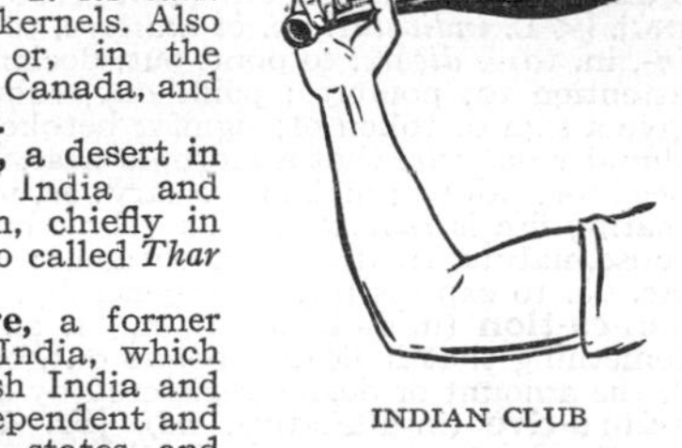

INDIAN CLUB

Indian corn, 1. a kind of grain that grows in kernels on large ears. 2. its ears. 3. its seeds or kernels. Also called *maize* or, in the United States, Canada, and Australia, *corn*.

Indian Desert, a desert in northwestern India and West Pakistan, chiefly in Rajasthan: also called *Thar Desert*.

Indian Empire, a former federation in India, which included British India and a number of dependent and semidependent states and agencies: area, 1,575,187 sq. mi.; capital, New Delhi: abbreviated **IE.**

Indian file, single file; (in a) single line, one behind the other: it was the American Indians' way of walking a trail.

Indian giver, [Colloq.], a person who gives something and then asks for it back: from the belief that American Indians expected an equivalent in return when giving something.

Indian hemp, 1. the American dogbane, a plant with a tough bark formerly used in ropemaking: the root is used in medicine. 2. the common hemp.

In·di·an·i·an (in'di-an'i-ən), *adj.* of Indiana. *n.* a native or inhabitant of Indiana; Hoosier.

Indian licorice, an Indian shrub of the pea family, with licoricelike roots and poisonous, red and black seeds used for beads, as a weight, and in medicine: also called *jequirity*.

Indian mallow, a tall weed with small, yellow flowers and large, velvety leaves.

Indian meal, meal made from Indian corn; corn meal.
Indian millet, a tall grass whose varieties include durra and broomcorn; grain sorghum.
Indian Mutiny, an uprising of native troops in India against British colonial policy (1857–1858).
Indian Ocean, an ocean south of Asia, between Africa and Australia: area, 28,357,000 sq. mi.
Indian paintbrush, the painted cup, a plant of the figwort family.
Indian pipe, a leafless wild herb native to Asia and the United States, with one waxy, pipe-shaped flower on each stem: it is a saprophyte.
Indian pudding, a pudding containing chiefly corn meal, milk, and molasses.
Indian red, 1. a yellowish-red iron ore, originally from an island in the Persian Gulf, used in early times as a pigment. 2. a native iron (ferric) oxide used by North American Indians as war paint, and by early American painters.
Indian States and Agencies, formerly, a number of semidependent native states and agencies of India: in 1947, they became independent states or affiliated with the republics of India or Pakistan.
Indian summer, [? so named in sense of "bogus summer"; cf. INDIAN GIVER; for other surmises see H. L. Mencken, *Am. Lang., Suppl. I*, pp. 181–184], 1. a period of mild, warm, hazy weather following the first frosts of late autumn, especially on the North American continent; hence, 2. the final years of a person's life, regarded as being serene, tranquil, reminiscent, etc.
Indian Territory, a former territory of the United States, reserved for the settlement of Indians: now a part of Oklahoma.
Indian tobacco, a hardy weed with spikes of light-blue flowers, growing in the northwestern United States.
Indian turnip, 1. the jack-in-the-pulpit. 2. its root.
India paper, [< former use of *India* in sense "Far Eastern"], 1. a thin, absorbent paper made in China and Japan from vegetable fiber, used in taking prints from engraved plates. 2. a thin, tough, opaque printing paper, originally made in the Orient, used for Bibles, etc.
In·di·a-rub·ber (in'di-ə-rub'ẽr), ***adj.*** [sometimes i-], of, or having the characteristics of, India rubber.
India rubber, india rubber, natural rubber; especially, caoutchouc, crude rubber obtained from latex.
In·dic (in'dik), ***adj.*** [L. *Indicus;* Gr. *Indikos*], 1. of India. 2. designating or of a branch of the Indo-European languages, including many of the languages spoken, or formerly spoken, in India: cf. **Indo-Iranian.**
indic., 1. indicating. 2. indicative. 3. indicator.
in·di·can (in'di-kan'), ***n.*** [< L. *indicum*, indigo; + *-an*], 1. a glucoside, $C_{14}H_{17}NO_6$, found in a natural state in the indigo plant: it is converted by water and oxygen into indigo. 2. an indigo-forming substance, C_8H_6NO-SO_2OH, the potassium salt of which is present in animal urine.
in·di·cant (in'di-kənt), ***adj.*** [L. *indicans*], indicating; pointing out. ***n.*** something that indicates or points out.
in·di·cate (in'də-kāt'), ***v.t.*** [INDICATED (-id), INDICATING], [< L. *indicatus*, pp. of *indicare*, to indicate, show; *in-*, in, to + *dicare*, to point out, declare], 1. to direct attention to; point to; point out; show. 2. to be or give a sign or token of; signify; betoken; intimate: as, thunder *indicates* that a storm is near. 3. to show the need for; call for; make necessary: as, in this weather a roaring fire is *indicated.* 4. to show or point out as a cause, nature, treatment, or outcome: said of a disease, etc. 5. to express briefly or generally.
in·di·ca·tion (in'də-kā'shən), ***n.*** 1. an indicating. 2. something that indicates, points out, or signifies; sign. 3. the amount or degree registered by an indicator.
in·dic·a·tive (in-dik'ə-tiv), ***adj.*** [Fr. *indicatif;* L. *indicativus*], 1. giving an indication, suggestion, or intimation; showing; signifying; pointing out. 2. designating or of that mood of a verb used to express an act, state, or occurrence as actual, or to ask a question of fact: it is the usual form of the verb: distinguished from *subjunctive, imperative.* ***n.*** 1. the indicative mood. 2. a verb in this mood. Abbreviated **indic., ind.**
in·di·ca·tor (in'də-kā'tẽr), ***n.*** [LL.], 1. a person or thing that indicates; specifically, *a)* any device, as a gauge, dial, register, or pointer, that measures or records and visibly indicates. *b)* an apparatus that diagrams the varying fluid pressure of an engine in operation. 2. any of various substances used to indicate the acidity or alkalinity of a solution, the beginning or end of a chemical reaction, the presence of certain substances, etc., by changes in color. Abbreviated **indic.**
in·di·ca·to·ry (in'di-kə-tôr'i, in'di-kə-tō'ri), ***adj.*** indicating; indicant.
in·di·ces (in'də-sēz'), ***n.*** alternative plural of **index.**
in·di·ci·a (in-dish'i-ə), ***n.pl.*** [*sing.* INDICIUM (-əm)], [L., pl. of *indicium*, a notice, information < *index, indicis;* see INDEX], signs; characteristic marks; indications; tokens; especially, printed markings substituted for the stamps, cancellations, or postmarks, on bulk mail.
in·dict (in-dīt'), ***v.t.*** [ME. *enditen*, to write down, accuse; Anglo-Fr. & OFr. *enditer*, to inform, point out < LL. **indictare* < L. *in*, against + *dictare;* see DICTATE], to charge with the commission of a crime; especially, to make formal accusation against on the basis of positive legal evidence: usually said of the action of a grand jury. —***SYN.*** see **accuse.**
in·dict·a·ble (in-dīt'ə-b'l), ***adj.*** 1. liable to be indicted. 2. making indictment possible, as an offense.
in·dic·tion (in-dik'shən), ***n.*** [ME. *indictioun* (? via OFr.) < L. *indictio* < pp. of *indicere*, to declare, announce; *in-*, in + *dicere*, to say, tell; see DICTION], 1. the edict of a Roman emperor fixing the valuation of property for tax purposes at the beginning of each fifteen-year period: it was first made by Constantine in 312 A.D. 2. the tax so levied. 3. *a)* a cycle of fifteen years. *b)* a particular year in such a cycle.
in·dict·ment (in-dīt'mənt), ***n.*** [ME. & Anglo-Fr. *enditement*], 1. an indicting or being indicted. 2. a charge; accusation; specifically, a formal written accusation charging one or more persons with the commission of a crime, presented by a grand jury to the court when the jury has found, after examining the prosecutor's statement of the charge (*bill of indictment*), that there is a valid case.
In·dies (in'dēz), ***n.pl.*** 1. the East Indies. 2. the East Indies, India, and Indo-China. 3. the West Indies. Abbreviated **Ind.**
in·dif·fer·ence (in-dif'ẽr-əns, in-dif'rəns), ***n.*** [Fr.; L. *indifferentia*], the quality, state, or fact of being indifferent; specifically, *a)* lack of concern, interest, or feeling; apathy. *b)* lack of importance, meaning, or worth.
in·dif·fer·ent (in-dif'ẽr-ənt, in-dif'rənt), ***adj.*** [ME.; OFr.; L. *indifferens;* see IN- (not) & DIFFERENT], 1. having or showing no partiality, bias, or preference; neutral. 2. having or showing no interest, concern, or feeling; uninterested; apathetic. 3. of no consequence or importance; immaterial. 4. not particularly good or bad, large or small, etc.; fair; average; hence, 5. not particularly good; rather poor or bad. 6. inactive; neutral in quality, as a chemical, magnet, etc.; chiefly in scientific use. 7. in *biology*, undifferentiated.
SYN.—**indifferent** implies either apathy or neutrality, especially with reference to choice (to remain *indifferent* in a dispute); **unconcerned** implies a lack of concern, solicitude, or anxiety, as because of callousness, ingenuousness, etc. (to remain *unconcerned* in a time of danger); **incurious** suggests a lack of interest or curiosity (*incurious* about the details); **detached** implies an impartiality or aloofness resulting from a lack of emotional involvement in a situation (he viewed the struggle with *detached* interest); **disinterested** strictly implies a commendable impartiality resulting from a lack of selfish motive or desire for personal gain (a *disinterested* journalist), but it is now often used colloquially to mean not interested, or indifferent.
in·dif·fer·ent·ism (in-dif'ẽr-ənt-iz'm, in-dif'rənt-iz'm), ***n.*** the state of being indifferent; especially, systematic indifference to religion.
in·dif·fer·ent·ist (in-dif'ẽr-ənt-ist, in-dif'rənt-ist), ***n.*** a person who believes in or practices indifferentism.
in·di·gence (in'di-jəns), ***n.*** [ME.; OFr.; L. *indigentia*], the condition of being indigent. —***SYN.*** see **poverty.**
in·di·gene (in'di-jēn'), ***n.*** [Fr. *indigène;* L. *indigena* < OL. *indu* (L. *in*), in + *gignere*, to be born], a native animal or plant.
in·dig·e·nous (in-dij'ə-nəs), ***adj.*** [LL. *indigenus* < L. *indigena;* see INDIGENE], 1. born, growing, or produced naturally in a region or country; native. 2. innate; inherent; inborn. —***SYN.*** see **native.**
in·di·gent (in'di-jənt), ***adj.*** [Fr.; L. *indigens*, ppr. of *indigere*, to be in need < OL. *indu* (L. *in*), in + *egere*, to need], 1. poor; needy; destitute; in poverty. 2. [Archaic], lacking; destitute (*of*). —***SYN.*** see **poor.**
in·di·gest·ed (in'də-jes'tid), ***adj.*** [*in-* (not) + *digested*], 1. not well considered; not ordered in the mind. 2. confused; chaotic. 3. not digested; undigested.
in·di·gest·i·bil·i·ty (in'də-jes'tə-bil'ə-ti), ***n.*** the quality of being indigestible.
in·di·gest·i·ble (in'də-jes'tə-b'l), ***adj.*** [L. *indigestibilis*], that cannot be digested; not easily digested.
in·di·ges·tion (in'də-jes'chən), ***n.*** [Fr.; LL. *indigestio*], inability to digest, or difficulty in digesting, food.
in·di·ges·tive (in'də-jes'tiv), ***adj.*** 1. having indigestion. 2. likely to cause indigestion.
in·dign (in-dīn'), ***adj.*** [Fr. *indigne;* L. *indignus; in-*, not + *dignus*, worthy], [Obs. or Poetic], 1. undeserving; unworthy. 2. disgraceful.
in·dig·nant (in-dig'nənt), ***adj.*** [L. *indignans*, ppr. of *indignari*, to consider as unworthy or improper, be displeased at; *in-*, not + *dignari*, to deem worthy < *dignus*, worthy], feeling or expressing anger or scorn, especially at unjust, mean, or ungrateful action or treatment.
in·dig·na·tion (in'dig-nā'shən), ***n.*** [ME. *indignacioun;* OFr. *indignacion;* L. *indignatio* < pp. of *indignari;* see INDIGNANT], anger or scorn resulting from injustice, ingratitude, or meanness; righteous anger. —***SYN.*** see **anger.**
in·dig·ni·ty (in-dig'nə-ti), ***n.*** [*pl.* INDIGNITIES (-tiz)], [L.

indignitas, unworthiness, vileness; see IN- (not) & DIGNITY], 1. something that humiliates, insults, or injures the dignity or self-respect; affront. 2. [Obs.], *a*) the quality or state of being unworthy or disgraceful. *b*) unworthy or disgraceful conduct. *c*) indignation.

in·di·go (in′di-gō′), *n.* [*pl.* INDIGOS, INDIGOES (-gōz′)], [earlier also *indico;* Sp. *indigo, indico;* L. *indicum;* Gr. *indikon* (*pharmakon*), lit., Indian (dye) < *Indikos*, Indian < *India*, India], 1. a blue dye obtained from certain plants or made synthetically, usually from aniline. 2. any of a group of plants of the pea family that yield indigo. 3. a deep violet-blue, designated by Newton as one of the seven prismatic or primary colors. *adj.* of this color. Abbreviated **ind.**

in·di·go-blue (in′di-gō′blōō′), *n.* indigo blue. *adj.* of indigo blue.

indigo blue, 1. the coloring matter of indigo; indigotin. 2. the color indigo.

indigo bunting (or **bird**), a small finch native to the eastern United States: the male is indigo-blue, the female brown.

in·di·goid (in′di-goid′), *adj.* [< *indigo* + *-oid*], of a class of dyes that produce a color resembling indigo. *n.* a dye of this class.

in·dig·o·tin (in-dig′ə-tin, in′di-gō′tin), *n.* [*indigo* + *-t-* + *-in*], a dark-blue powder with a coppery luster, $C_{16}H_{10}N_2O_2$, the coloring matter and chief ingredient of indigo; indigo blue.

in·di·rect (in′də-rekt′), *adj.* [ME. *indyrect*], not direct; specifically, *a*) not straight; deviating; roundabout. *b*) not straight to the point, or to the person or thing aimed at: as, an *indirect* reply. *c*) not straightforward; not fair and open; dishonest: as, *indirect* dealing. *d*) not immediate; secondary: as, an *indirect* result.

indirect discourse, statement of what a person said, without quoting his exact words (e.g., *she said that she could not go*).

in·di·rec·tion (in′də-rek′shən), *n.* [< *indirect*, after *direction*], 1. roundabout act, procedure, or means. 2. deceit; dishonesty.

indirect lighting, lighting reflected, as from a ceiling, or diffused so as to provide an even illumination without glare or shadows.

indirect object, the word or words denoting the person or thing indirectly affected by the action of the verb: it generally names the person or thing to which something is given or for which something is done (e.g., *him* in *give him the ball, do him a favor*).

indirect tax, a tax on manufactured goods, imports, etc. that is paid indirectly by the consumer because it is added to the price.

in·dis·cern·i·ble (in′di-zũr′nə-b'l, in′di-sũr′nə-b'l), *adj.* that cannot be discerned; imperceptible.

in·dis·cern·i·bly (in′di-zũr′nə-bli, in′di-sũr′nə-bli), *adv.* so as to be indiscernible; imperceptibly.

in·dis·creet (in′dis-krēt′), *adj.* not discreet; lacking prudence, as in speech or action; unwise.

in·dis·crete (in′dis-krēt′), *adj.* [L. *indiscretus*], not discrete; not separated; compact.

in·dis·cre·tion (in′dis-kresh′ən), *n.* [L. *indiscretio*], 1. lack of discretion, or good judgment; imprudence. 2. an indiscreet act or remark.

in·dis·crim·i·nate (in′dis-krim′ə-nit), *adj.* 1. confused; random. 2. not discriminating; making no distinctions.

in·dis·crim·i·na·tion (in′dis-krim′ə-nā′shən), *n.* the condition of being indiscriminate; lack of discrimination.

in·dis·crim·i·na·tive (in′dis-krim′ə-nā′tiv), *adj.* not discriminating.

in·dis·pen·sa·bil·i·ty (in′dis-pen′sə-bil′ə-ti), *n.* the quality or state of being indispensable.

in·dis·pen·sa·ble (in′dis-pen′sə-b'l), *adj.* not dispensable; absolutely necessary or required. *n.* an indispensable person or thing. —*SYN.* see **essential.**

in·dis·pen·sa·bly (in′dis-pen′sə-bli), *adv.* to an indispensable degree; essentially.

in·dis·pose (in′dis-pōz′), *v.t.* [*in-* (not) + *dispose*], 1. to make unfit or unable; disqualify. 2. to make unwilling or disinclined. 3. to make slightly ill.

in·dis·posed (in′dis-pōzd′), *adj.* [ME. *indisposid*], 1. slightly ill. 2. unwilling; disinclined. —*SYN.* see **sick.**

in·dis·po·si·tion (in′dis-pə-zish′ən), *n.* the condition of being indisposed; specifically, *a*) slight illness. *b*) unwillingness; disinclination.

in·dis·pu·ta·bil·i·ty (in′dis-pū′tə-bil′ə-ti, in-dis′pyoo-tə-bil′ə-ti), *n.* the quality or state of being indisputable.

in·dis·pu·ta·ble (in′dis-pū′tə-b'l, in-dis′pyoo-tə-b'l), *adj.* [LL. *indisputabilis*], that cannot be disputed or doubted; unquestionable.

in·dis·pu·ta·bly (in′dis-pū′tə-bli, in-dis′pyoo-tə-bli), *adv.* in an indisputable manner; unquestionably.

in·dis·sol·u·bil·i·ty (in′di-sol′yoo-bil′ə-ti), *n.* the quality or state of being indissoluble.

in·dis·sol·u·ble (in′di-sol′yoo-b'l), *adj.* [L. *indissolubilis*], that cannot be dissolved, decomposed, disintegrated, or destroyed; firm; stable; lasting.

in·dis·sol·u·bly (in′di-sol′yoo-bli), *adv.* in an indissoluble manner.

in·dis·tinct (in′di-stiŋkt′), *adj.* [Late ME.; L. *indistinctus*], not distinct; specifically, *a*) not seen or heard clearly; faint; dim; obscure. *b*) not separate or separable; not clearly marked off; not plainly defined.

in·dis·tinc·tive (in′di-stiŋk′tiv), *adj.* 1. not distinctive; lacking distinction. 2. making no distinction; incapable of distinguishing.

in·dis·tin·guish·a·ble (in′di-stiŋ′gwish-ə-b'l), *adj.* that cannot be distinguished; not separable; imperceptible.

in·dis·tin·guish·a·bly (in′di-stiŋ′gwish-ə-bli), *adv.* so as to be indistinguishable.

in·dite (in-dīt′), *v.t.* [INDITED (-id), INDITING], [ME. *enditen;* see INDICT], 1. [Archaic], to express or describe in prose or verse. 2. to put in writing; compose and write. 3. [Obs.], to prompt; dictate.

in·dite·ment (in-dīt′mənt), *n.* 1. an inditing. 2. something indited.

in·di·um (in′di-əm), *n.* [Mod. L. < L. *indicum*, indigo; + *-ium*: from the two indigo lines in its spectrum], a rare metallic chemical element, soft, ductile, and silver-white, occurring in some zinc ores: symbol, In; at. wt., 114.76; at. no., 49.

in·di·vert·i·ble (in′di-vũr′tə-b'l), *adj.* that cannot be diverted or turned aside.

in·di·vid·u·al (in′də-vij′ōō-əl), *adj.* [ML. *individualis* < L. *individuus;* see IN- (not) & DIVISIBLE], 1. originally, not divisible; not separable. 2. existing as a single, separate thing or being; single; separate; particular. 3. of, for, or by a single person or thing. 4. relating to or characteristic of a single person or thing. 5. distinguished from others by special characteristics; of a peculiar or striking character: as, an *individual* style. *n.* 1. a single thing or being, or a single group when taken as a unit. 2. a person. —*SYN.* see **characteristic.**

in·di·vid·u·al·ism (in′də-vij′ōō-əl-iz'm), *n.* [*individual* + *-ism*; or < Fr. *individualisme*], 1. the leading of one's life in one's own way without regard for others. 2. individual character; individuality. 3. an individual peculiarity. 4. the doctrine that individual freedom in economic enterprise should not be restricted by governmental or social regulation; laissez-faire. 5. the doctrine that the state exists for the individual and not the individual for the state. 6. in *philosophy*, egoism.

in·di·vid·u·al·ist (in′də-vij′ōō-əl-ist), *n.* a person who practices or believes in individualism (in various senses). *adj.* individualistic.

in·di·vid·u·al·is·tic (in′də-vij′ōō-ə-lis′tik), *adj.* of individualism or individualists.

in·di·vid·u·al·i·ty (in′də-vij′ōō-al′ə-ti), *n.* [*pl.* INDIVIDUALITIES (-tiz)], 1. the sum of the characteristics or qualities that set one person or thing apart from others; individual character. 2. the condition of existing as an individual; separate existence; oneness. 3. a single person or thing; individual. 4. [Obs.], indivisibility; inseparability.

in·di·vid·u·al·i·za·tion (in′də-vij′ōō-əl-i-zā′shən, in′də-vij′ōō-əl-ī-zā′shən), *n.* an individualizing or being individualized.

in·di·vid·u·al·ize (in′də-vij′ōō-ə-līz′), *v.t.* [INDIVIDUALIZED (-līzd′), INDIVIDUALIZING], 1. to make individual; mark as different from other persons or things. 2. to consider individually; specify; particularize.

in·di·vid·u·al·ly (in′də-vij′ōō-əl-i), *adv.* 1. as an individual or individuals; separately; one at a time. 2. showing individual characteristics; distinctively.

in·di·vid·u·ate (in′də-vij′ōō-āt′), *v.t.* [INDIVIDUATED (-id), INDIVIDUATING], [< ML. *individuatus*, pp. of *individuare* < L. *individuus;* see INDIVIDUAL], 1. to give individuality to; make individual or distinct. 2. to distinguish from others of the same species.

in·di·vid·u·a·tion (in′də-vij′ōō-ā′shən), *n.* [ML. *individuatio*], 1. an individuating or being individuated. 2. the condition of existing as an individual.

in·di·vis·i·bil·i·ty (in′də-viz′ə-bil′ə-ti), *n.* the quality or state of being indivisible.

in·di·vis·i·ble (in′də-viz′ə-b'l), *adj.* [ME. *indyvysible;* LL. *indivisibilis;* see IN- (not) & DIVISIBLE], 1. that cannot be divided. 2. in *mathematics*, that cannot be divided without leaving a remainder. *n.* anything indivisible.

in·di·vis·i·bly (in′də-viz′ə-bli), *adv.* so as to be indivisible.

In·do- (in′dō), [Gr. < *Indos;* see INDIA], a combining form meaning: 1. *of India, of Indian* (*Hindu*) *stock.* 2. *of India and.*

In·do-Ar·yan (in′dō-âr′i-ən, in′dō-âr′yən), *adj.* [cf. ARYAN], 1. of the Indo-Aryans. 2. designating or of the Indo-European languages of India; Indic. *n.* a native of India who speaks such a language. The term is now seldom used.

In·do·chi·na, In·do-Chi·na (in'dō-chī'nə), ***n.*** 1. the large peninsula south of China, including Burma, Thailand, Malaya, North Vietnam, South Vietnam, Laos, and Cambodia: also called *Farther India.* 2. a former region in the eastern part of this peninsula, consisting of Vietnam, Laos, and Cambodia: also *French Indochina.*

In·do·chi·nese, In·do-Chi·nese (in'dō-chī-nēz'), ***adj.*** 1. of Indochina, its Mongoloid people, or their culture. 2. Sino-Tibetan: term now seldom used.

in·doc·ile (in-dos''l), ***adj.*** [Fr.; L. *indocilis*], not docile; not easy to teach or discipline.

in·do·cil·i·ty (in'dō-sil'ə-ti), ***n.*** the quality of being indocile.

in·doc·tri·nate (in-dok'tri-nāt'), ***v.t.*** [INDOCTRINATED (-id), INDOCTRINATING], [< ML. *in-*, in + pp. of *doctrinare*, to instruct < L. *doctrina*], 1. to instruct in doctrines, principles, theories, or beliefs. 2. to instruct; teach.

in·doc·tri·na·tion (in-dok'tri-nā'shən, in'dok-tri-nā'shən), ***n.*** an indoctrinating or being indoctrinated.

in·doc·tri·na·tor (in-dok'tri-nā'tẽr), ***n.*** a person who indoctrinates.

In·do-Eu·ro·pe·an (in'dō-yoor'ə-pē'ən), ***adj.*** designating or of a family of languages that includes most of those spoken in Europe and many of those spoken in southwestern Asia and India. ***n.*** 1. the Indo-European family of languages: its principal branches are Indic, Iranian, Armenian, Tokharic, Hellenic, Illyrian, Albanian, Italic, Celtic, Germanic, Baltic, and Slavic. 2. the hypothetical language, reconstructed by modern linguists, from which these languages are thought to have descended. See **Indo-Hittite.** Abbreviated **IE., I.E.** See the table on the back end paper of this book.

In·do-Ger·man·ic (in'dō-jẽr-man'ik), ***adj. & n.*** Indo-European: term now chiefly used by German-trained scholars: abbreviated **Idg., I.G.**

In·do-Hit·tite (in'dō-hit'īt), ***n.*** according to recent research, the hypothetical language from which the Indo-European and Hittite languages descended: it is divided into two branches, pre-Indo-European and pre-Anatolic, from which are derived the Indo-European languages on the one hand and such languages as Hittite, hieroglyphic Hittite, and Luwian on the other.

In·do-I·ra·ni·an (in'dō-ī-rā'ni-ən), ***adj.*** designating or of the Indic and Iranian branches of the Indo-European family of languages as spoken or formerly spoken in India, Afghanistan, Iran, etc.: the term is now chiefly applied to the status of these languages before Indic and Iranian became dialectically distinct.

in·dol (in'dōl, in'dol), ***n.*** indole.

in·dole (in'dōl), ***n.*** [< *indigo* + *phenol*], a white, crystalline compound, C_8H_7N, obtained from indigo and formed as a product of the intestinal putrefaction of proteins: it is used in perfumery, etc.

in·do·lence (in'də-ləns), ***n.*** [< Fr. or L.; Fr. *indolence;* L. *indolentia*], quality, condition, or instance of being indolent; idleness; laziness.

in·do·lent (in'də-lənt), ***adj.*** [Fr.; LL. *indolens;* L. *in-*, not + *dolens*, ppr. of *dolere*, to feel pain], 1. disliking or avoiding work; idle; lazy. 2. in *medicine*, causing little or no pain: as, an *indolent* cyst.

in·dom·i·ta·ble (in-dom'i-tə-b'l), ***adj.*** [LL. *indomitabilis* < L. *indomitus*, untamed, ungoverned; *in-*, not + *domitus*, pp. of *domitare*, to tame, intens. < *domere*, to tame, subdue], not easily discouraged, defeated, or subdued; unyielding; unconquerable.

in·dom·i·ta·bly (in-dom'i-tə-bli), ***adv.*** 1. in an indomitable manner. 2. to an indomitable degree.

In·do·ne·si·a (in'dō-nē'zhə, in'dō-nē'shə), ***n.*** 1. the Malay Archipelago; East Indies. 2. a republic established in 1949 (from 1946–1949, an independent commonwealth under the Netherlands crown), consisting of Java, Sumatra, Borneo (the southern part), Celebes, and other islands in the Malay Archipelago: area, 575,893 sq. mi.; pop., 92,600,000; capital, Jakarta: these islands and Netherlands New Guinea formerly constituted the Netherlands Indies.

In·do·ne·sian (in'dō-nē'zhən, in'dō-nē'shən), ***adj.*** 1. of Indonesia, its people, etc. 2. designating or of a group of some two hundred Austronesian languages spoken in Indonesia, the Philippines, Java, etc., including Malay, Tagalog, Javanese, etc. ***n.*** 1. a member of a light-brown, non-Malay race of Indonesia, the Philippines, Java, etc., apparently of mixed Polynesian and Mongoloid stock. 2. an inhabitant of Indonesia. 3. the Indonesian languages.

in·door (in'dôr', in'dōr'), ***adj.*** [for earlier *within-door*], 1. of the inside of a house or building. 2. living, belonging, or carried on in a house or building.

indoor baseball, 1. the game of baseball, adapted for playing in a gymnasium or on a small field: the ball is larger and softer and the base lines shorter than those in baseball proper: also called *softball.* 2. this ball.

in·doors (in'dôrz', in'dōrz'), ***adv.*** [*indoor* + adv. genit. *-s*], in or into a house or building.

in·do·phe·nol (in'dō-fē'nōl, in'dō-fē'nol), ***n.*** [*indigo* + *phenol*], any of a series of synthetic blue dyes derived from quinonimines.

In·dore (in-dôr', in-dōr'), ***n.*** 1. a city in Madhya Pradesh, central India: capital of former state of Madhya Bharat: pop., 311,000. 2. a former state of Central India Agency.

in·dors·a·ble (in-dôr'sə-b'l), ***adj.*** endorsable.

in·dorse (in-dôrs'), ***v.t.*** [INDORSED (-dôrst'), INDORSING], [var. of *endorse*, after ML. *indorsare*], to endorse.

in·dor·see (in-dôr'sē', in'dôr-sē'), ***n.*** an endorsee.

in·dorse·ment (in-dôrs'mənt), ***n.*** an endorsement.

in·dox·yl (in-dok'sil), ***n.*** [*ind*igo + hydr*oxyl*], a compound, C_8H_7NO, produced by the hydrolysis of indican and synthesized by several methods: it is important in the synthesis of indigo.

In·dra (in'drə), ***n.*** [Sans.], the chief god of the early Hindu religion, associated with rain and thunderbolts: he is later treated as a god of the second rank.

in·draft, in·draught (in'draft', in'dräft'), ***n.*** 1. a drawing in; inward pull or attraction. 2. an inward flow, stream, or current.

in·drawn (in'drôn'), ***adj.*** drawn in; introspective.

in·dri (in'dri), ***n.*** [Fr.; false use of Malagasy *indry*, behold, mistaken for the name of the animal], a large lemur of Madagascar.

INDRA

in·du·bi·ta·ble (in-do͞o'bi-tə-b'l, in-dū'bi-tə-b'l), ***adj.*** [L. *indubitabilis;* see IN- (not) & DUBITABLE], that cannot be doubted; unquestionable.

in·du·bi·ta·bly (in-do͞o'bi-tə-bli, in-dū'bi-tə-bli), ***adv.*** in an indubitable manner; without doubt; surely.

in·duce (in-do͞os', in-dūs'), ***v.t.*** [INDUCED (-do͞ost', -dūst'), INDUCING], [ME. *enducen;* L. *inducere; in-*, in + *ducere*, to lead], 1. to lead on to some action, condition, belief, etc.; prevail on; persuade. 2. to bring on; bring about; cause; effect: as, indigestion is *induced* by overeating. 3. to draw (a general rule or conclusion) from particular facts; infer by induction. 4. in *physics*, to bring about (an electric or magnetic effect) in a body by exposing it to the influence or variation of a field of force. —***SYN.*** see **persuade.**

in·duce·ment (in-do͞os'mənt, in-dūs'mənt), ***n.*** 1. an inducing or being induced. 2. anything that induces; motive; incentive. 3. in *law*, an explanatory introduction in a pleading. —***SYN.*** see **motive.**

in·duc·i·ble (in-do͞os'ə-b'l, in-dūs'ə-b'l), ***adj.*** that can be induced.

in·duct (in-dukt'), ***v.t.*** [ME. *inducten* < L. *inductus*, pp. of *inducere;* see INDUCE], 1. to bring in; introduce. 2. to place in a benefice or official position with formality or ceremony; install. 3. *a*) to bring formally into a society or organization; initiate. *b*) to bring formally into the armed forces. 4. in *physics*, to induce.

in·duct·ance (in-duk'təns), ***n.*** [*induct* + *-ance*], 1. the property of an electric circuit by which a varying current in it produces a varying magnetic field that induces voltages in the same circuit or in a near-by circuit: it is measured in henrys. 2. the capacity of an electric circuit for reacting to a current produced in this way. 3. a circuit, condenser, etc. having inductance.

in·duct·ee (in-duk'tē'), ***n.*** a person inducted or being inducted.

in·duc·tile (in-duk't'l), ***adj.*** not ductile; specifically, *a*) that cannot be stretched, drawn, or hammered thin without breaking. *b*) not easily molded; not pliant. *c*) not easily led; intractable.

in·duc·til·i·ty (in'duk-til'ə-ti), ***n.*** the quality or condition of being inductile.

in·duc·tion (in-duk'shən), ***n.*** [ME. *induccion;* OFr. *induction;* L. *inductio*], 1. an inducting or being inducted; installation, initiation, etc. 2. *a*) reasoning from particular facts or individual cases to a general conclusion. *b*) the conclusion reached by such reasoning. 3. [Archaic], an introduction; preface or prelude. 4. an inducing, or bringing about. 5. in *physics*, the act or process by which an electric or magnetic effect is produced in an electrical conductor or magnetizable body when it is exposed to the influence or variation of a field of force. Abbreviated **induc.**

induction coil, a coiled apparatus made up of two coupled circuits: interruptions in the direct current in one circuit produce an alternating current of high potential in the other.

in·duc·tive (in-duk'tiv), ***adj.*** [LL. *inductivus*], 1. inducing; attractive; persuasive. 2. of, or proceeding by methods of, logical induction: as, *inductive* reasoning. 3. produced by induction. 4. of inductance or electrical or magnetic induction. 5. introductory. 6. in *physiology*, producing a change or response in an organism.

in·duc·tiv·i·ty (in'duk-tiv'ə-ti), ***n.*** 1. the property of a substance which determines its capacity for electrical or magnetic induction; inductance. 2. specific inductive capacity.

in·duc·tor (in-duk'tẽr), ***n.*** [L., one who stirs up, lit., one who leads or brings in], 1. a person who inducts.

2. a thing that inducts; specifically, a part of an electrical apparatus that acts on another, or is acted upon, by induction.

in·due (in-dōō′, in-dū′), *v.t.* [INDUED (-dōōd′, -dūd′), INDUING], [L. *induere*, to put on, dress oneself < OL. *indu* (L. *in*), in, on + base seen also in L. *exuere*, to strip off (cf. EXUVIAE)], to endue.

in·dulge (in-dulj′), *v.t.* [INDULGED (-duljd′), INDULGING], [L. *indulgere*, to be kind to, yield to; ? < IE. base **delē-gh-*, long, seen also in Sans. *dīrgha*, long, Goth. *tulgus*, firm, constant; ? hence, orig., to be long-suffering, patient], 1. to yield to or satisfy (a desire); give oneself up to. 2. to gratify the wishes of; be very lenient with; humor. 3. to grant an ecclesiastical indulgence or dispensation to. 4. [Obs.], to grant as a kindness, favor, or privilege. 5. in *business*, to grant (a person) an extension of time to make payment on a bill or note. *v.i.* to give way to one's own desires; indulge oneself (*in* something).

SYN.—**indulge** implies a yielding to the wishes or desires of oneself or another, as because of a weak will or an amiable nature; **humor** suggests compliance with the mood or whim of another (they *humored* the dying man); **pamper** implies overindulgence or excessive gratification; **spoil** emphasizes the harm done to the personality or character by overindulgence or excessive attention (grandparents often *spoil* children); **baby** suggests the sort of pampering and devoted care lavished on infants and connotes a potential loss of self-reliance (because he was sickly, his mother continued to *baby* him).—***ANT.*** discipline, restrain.

in·dul·gence (in-dul′jəns), *n.* [ME.; OFr.; L. *indulgentia*], 1. an indulging or being indulgent. 2. what is indulged in. 3. an indulging oneself; giving way to one's own desires. 4. a favor or privilege. 5. in *business*, an extension of time to make payment on a bill or note, granted as a favor. 6. [sometimes I-], in *English history*, the grant of certain religious liberties to Dissenters and Roman Catholics by Charles II and James II. 7. in the *Roman Catholic Church*, a remission of temporal or purgatorial punishment still due for a sin after the guilt has been forgiven in the sacrament of penance. *v.t.* [INDULGENCED (-jənst), INDULGENCING], to apply an indulgence to.

in·dul·gent (in-dul′jənt), *adj.* [L. *indulgens*], indulging or inclined to indulge; kind or lenient, often to excess.

in·du·lin (in′dyoo-lin), *n.* induline.

in·du·line (in′dyoo-lēn′, in′dyoo-lin), *n.* [*indigo* + *-ule* + *-ine*], any of a series of blue or black aniline dyes.

in·dult (in-dult′), *n.* [< Fr. or LL.; Fr. *indult*; LL. *indultum*, neut. of L. *indultus*, pp. of *indulgere*; see INDULGE], in *canon law*, a privilege or special permission to do something otherwise prohibited, granted by ecclesiastical authority, as by the Pope to a bishop, for a specified or unspecified period of time.

in·du·na (in-dōō′nə), *n.* [Zulu], a Zulu leader.

in·du·pli·cate (in-dōō′plə-kit, in-dū′plə-kit), *adj.* [*in-* (in) + *duplicate*], having the edges folded or rolled in, but not overlapping: said of the arrangement of leaves in a leaf bud or of the calyx or corolla in a flower bud.

in·du·rate (in′doo-rāt′, in′dyoo-rāt′), *v.t.* [INDURATED (-id), INDURATING], [< L. *induratus*, pp. of *indurare*, to make hard; *in-*, in + *durare*, to harden < *durus*, hard], 1. to make hard; harden. 2. to make callous, unfeeling, or stubborn. *v.i.* to become indurated. *adj.* 1. hardened. 2. made callous, unfeeling, or stubborn.

in·du·ra·tion (in′doo-rā′shən, in′dyoo-rā′shən), *n.* [ME. *induracion*; OFr.; ML. *induratio*], 1. an indurating or being indurated. 2. a hardened mass or formation.

in·du·ra·tive (in′doo-rā′tiv, in′dyoo-rā′tiv), *adj.* indurating or tending to indurate.

In·dus (in′dəs), *n.* a river in northwestern India, flowing into the Arabian Sea: length, 2,000 mi.

In·dus (in′dəs), *n.* a southern constellation: see **constellation**, chart.

in·du·si·a (in-dōō′zi-ə, in-dū′zhi-ə), *n.* plural of **indusium**.

in·du·si·al (in-dōō′zi-əl, in-dū′zhi-əl), *adj.* of or characterized by an indusium or indusia.

in·du·si·ate (in-dōō′zi-it, in-dū′zhi-it), *adj.* [L. *indusiatus*], having an indusium.

in·du·si·um (in-dōō′zi-əm, in-dū′zhi-əm), *n.* [*pl.* INDUSIA (-ə)], [L., undergarment, tunic; associated with *induere*, to put on (see INDUE), but prob. < Gr. *endysis*, dress, clothing < *endyein*, to go into, put on], 1. in *anatomy & zoology*, *a*) any covering membrane, as the amnion. *b*) a case enclosing an insect larva. 2. in *botany*, an outgrowth of the leaf epidermis in ferns, covering the sporangia.

in·dus·tri·al (in-dus′tri-əl), *adj.* [< Fr. & ML.; Fr. *industriel*; ML. *industrialis*], 1. having the nature of or characterized by industry or industries. 2. of, connected with, or resulting from industry or industries. 3. working in industries. 4. of or concerned with people working in industries. 5. for use by industries: said of products. *n.* 1. a person working in industry. 2. a stock, bond, etc. of an industrial corporation or enterprise. Abbreviated **ind.**

industrial arts, the technical arts used in industry, especially as a subject for study in schools.

industrial disease, any disease commonly occurring in a particular industry.

in·dus·tri·al·ism (in-dus′tri-əl-iz′m), *n.* social and economic organization characterized by large industries, machine production, concentration of workers in towns and cities, etc.

in·dus·tri·al·ist (in-dus′tri-əl-ist), *n.* a person who owns, controls, or has an important position in the management of an industrial enterprise.

in·dus·tri·al·i·za·tion (in-dus′tri-əl-i-zā′shən, in-dus′-tri-əl-ī-zā′shən), *n.* an industrializing or being industrialized.

in·dus·tri·al·ize (in-dus′tri-əl-īz′), *v.t.* [INDUSTRIALIZED (-īzd′), INDUSTRIALIZING], 1. to make industrial; establish or develop industrialism in. 2. to organize as an industry.

in·dus·tri·al·ly (in-dus′tri-əl-i), *adv.* in an industrial manner; as concerns industry.

industrial relations, relations between employers and employees.

Industrial Revolution, [often i- r-], the change in social and economic organization resulting from the replacement of hand tools by machine and power tools and the development of large-scale industrial production: applied to this development in England from about 1760 and to later changes in other countries.

industrial school, a technical school offering instruction in the manual or industrial arts; especially, such a school to which neglected youths are sent for training.

industrial union, a labor union to which all the workers in a given industry can belong, no matter what their occupation or trade: distinguished from *craft* (or *horizontal*) *union*: also called *vertical union*.

in·dus·tri·ous (in-dus′tri-əs), *adj.* [< Fr. or L.; Fr. *industrieux*; L. *industriosus* < *industria*; see INDUSTRY], 1. originally, characterized by or showing intelligent work; skillful; clever. 2. characterized by earnest, steady effort; hard-working; diligent. —***SYN.*** see **busy.**

in·dus·try (in′dəs-tri), *n.* [*pl.* INDUSTRIES (-triz)], [Fr. *industrie*; L. *industria* < *industrius*, active, industrious], 1. originally, *a*) intelligent work; skill; cleverness. *b*) an application of this; device; contrivance. 2. earnest, steady effort; constant diligence in or application to work. 3. systematic work; habitual employment. 4. any branch of trade, business, production, or manufacture: as, the paper *industry*, the motion-picture *industry*. 5. *a*) manufacturing productive enterprises as distinguished from agriculture. *b*) the owners and managers of industry. —***SYN.*** see **business.**

in·dwell (in′dwel′), *v.i.* [INDWELT (-dwelt′), INDWELLING], to dwell, or live (*in*). *v.t.* to dwell in; inhabit.

In·dy, Vin·cent d' (van′sän′ dan′dē′), 1851–1931; French composer.

-ine (*variously* īn, in, ēn), a suffix meaning *of*, *having the nature of*, *like*: 1. [Fr. *-in*, *-ine*; L. *-inus*, masc., *-ina*, fem., *-inum*, neut.], added to bases of Latin origin to form adjectives, and nouns derived from them, as in *aquiline*, *divine*, *marine*. 2. [L. *-inus*; Gr. *-inos*], used to form adjectives, as in *adamantine*, *crystalline*.

-ine (*variously* in, īn, ēn), a suffix of various sources, used to form feminine nouns: 1. [< L. *-ina* < Gr. *-inē*], as in *heroine*. 2. [< L. *-ina*], as in *Clementine*. 3. [< G. *-in*, after Fr. *-ine*], as in *landgravine* and some other German feminine titles.

-ine (in), [Fr.; L. *-ina*, suffix of fem. abstract nouns], a suffix used to form certain abstract nouns, as in *medicine*, *doctrine*.

-ine (ēn, in, īn), [arbitrary use of L. *-inus*, masc., *-ina*, fem., n. & adj. ending], 1. a suffix used to form the commercial names of certain products, as in *vaseline*. 2. a suffix used to form the chemical names of *a*) *halogens*, as in *bromine*, *iodine*. *b*) *alkaloids or nitrogen bases*, as in *morphine*: also **-in**. The names of neutral substances, as carbohydrates, glucosides, proteins, etc., are formed with *-in* (e.g., *inulin*, *amygdalin*, *albumin*).

in·earth (in-ũrth′), *v.t.* [Poetic], to put into the earth; bury; inter.

in·e·bri·ant (in-ē′bri-ənt), *adj.* [L. *inebrians*, ppr. of *inebriare*], inebriating; intoxicating. *n.* something that inebriates; intoxicant.

in·e·bri·ate (in-ē′bri-āt′; *for adj. & n.*, *usually* in-ē′bri-it), *v.t.* [INEBRIATED (-id), INEBRIATING], [< L. *inebriatus*, pp. of *inebriare*, to intoxicate; *in-*, intens. + *ebriare*, to make drunk < *ebrius*, drunk], 1. to make drunk; intoxicate; hence, 2. to excite; exhilarate. *adj.* drunk; intoxicated. *n.* a drunken person, especially a habitual drunkard.

in·e·bri·at·ed (in-ē′bri-āt′id), *adj.* [pp. of *inebriate*], drunk; intoxicated. —***SYN.*** see **drunk.**

in·e·bri·a·tion (in-ē′bri-ā′shən), *n.* [LL. *inebriatio*], an inebriating or being inebriated; drunkenness.

in·e·bri·e·ty (in'i-brī'ə-ti), ***n.*** [< *inebriate*], drunkenness; intoxication.

in·ed·i·bil·i·ty (in'ed-ə-bil'ə-ti, in-ed'ə-bil'ə-ti), ***n.*** the quality or state of being inedible.

in·ed·i·ble (in-ed'ə-b'l), ***adj.*** not edible; not fit to be eaten.

in·ed·it·ed (in-ed'it-id), ***adj.*** not edited or published.

in·ef·fa·bil·i·ty (in'ef-ə-bil'ə-ti, in-ef'ə-bil'ə-ti), ***n.*** the quality of being ineffable.

in·ef·fa·ble (in-ef'ə-b'l), ***adj.*** [Fr.; L. *ineffabilis; in-*, not + *effabilis*, utterable < *effari*, to speak out < *ex-*, out + *fari*, to speak], 1. too overwhelming to be expressed or described in words; inexpressible. 2. too awesome or sacred to be spoken: as, God's *ineffable* name.

in·ef·fa·bly (in-ef'ə-bli), ***adv.*** so as to be ineffable.

in·ef·face·a·ble (in'i-fās'ə-b'l), ***adj.*** that cannot be effaced; impossible to wipe out or erase; indelible.

in·ef·face·a·bly (in'i-fās'ə-bli), ***adv.*** so as to be ineffaceable.

in·ef·fec·tive (in'ə-fek'tiv), ***adj.*** 1. not effective; not producing the desired effect; ineffectual. 2. not capable of performing satisfactorily; incompetent; inefficient: as, he is *ineffective* in an emergency.

in·ef·fec·tu·al (in'ə-fek'choo-əl), ***adj.*** not effectual; not producing or not able to produce the desired effect.

in·ef·fi·ca·cious (in'ef-i-kā'shəs), ***adj.*** not efficacious; unable to produce the desired effect: said of medicines, treatments, etc.

in·ef·fi·ca·cy (in-ef'i-kə-si), ***n.*** [LL. *inefficacia*], lack of efficacy; inability to produce the desired effect.

in·ef·fi·cien·cy (in'ə-fish'ən-si), ***n.*** the quality, condition, or fact of being inefficient; lack of efficiency.

in·ef·fi·cient (in'ə-fish'ənt), ***adj.*** not efficient; specifically, *a*) not producing the desired effect with a minimum use of energy, time, etc.; ineffective. *b*) lacking the necessary ability; unskilled; incapable.

in·e·las·tic (in'i-las'tik), ***adj.*** not elastic; inflexible, rigid, unyielding, unadaptable, etc. —***SYN.*** see **stiff.**

in·e·las·tic·i·ty (in'i-las-tis'ə-ti), ***n.*** the quality or condition of being inelastic.

in·el·e·gance (in-el'ə-gəns), ***n.*** 1. lack of elegance; quality of being inelegant. 2. something inelegant.

in·el·e·gan·cy (in-el'ə-gən-si), ***n.*** [*pl.* INELEGANCIES (-siz)], inelegance.

in·el·e·gant (in-el'ə-gənt), ***adj.*** not elegant; lacking refinement, good taste, grace, etc.; coarse; crude.

in·el·i·gi·bil·i·ty (in-el'i-jə-bil'ə-ti), ***n.*** the quality, state, or fact of being ineligible; lack of eligibility.

in·el·i·gi·ble (in-el'i-jə-b'l), ***adj.*** not eligible; not legally or morally qualified for office, etc.; not suitable. ***n.*** a person who is ineligible.

in·el·o·quence (in-el'ə-kwəns), ***n.*** lack of eloquence.

in·el·o·quent (in-el'ə-kwənt), ***adj.*** not eloquent; not fluent, forceful, and persuasive.

in·e·luc·ta·bil·i·ty (in'i-luk'tə-bil'ə-ti), ***n.*** the quality or state of being ineluctable.

in·e·luc·ta·ble (in'i-luk'tə-b'l), ***adj.*** [L. *ineluctabilis; in-*, not + *eluctabilis*, that can be resisted by struggling < *eluctari*, to struggle], not to be avoided or escaped; certain; inevitable: as, *ineluctable* fate.

in·e·luc·ta·bly (in'i-luk'tə-bli), ***adv.*** so as to be ineluctable.

in·e·lud·i·ble (in'i-lood'ə-b'l, in'i-lūd'ə-b'l), ***adj.*** that cannot be eluded.

in·ept (in-ept'), ***adj.*** [< Fr. or L.; Fr. *inepte;* L. *ineptus* < *in-*, not + *aptus*, suitable, fit], 1. not suitable to the purpose; unfit. 2. unreasonable; foolish; absurd. 3. awkward; clumsy; inefficient. —***SYN.*** see **awkward.**

in·ept·i·tude (in-ep'tə-tood', in-ep'tə-tūd'), ***n.*** [L. *ineptitudo*], 1. the quality of being inept. 2. an inept act, remark, etc.

in·e·qual·i·ty (in'i-kwäl'ə-ti, in'i-kwôl'ə-ti), ***n.*** [*pl.* INEQUALITIES (-tiz)], [MFr. *inequalité;* L. *inaequalitas*], 1. the quality of being unequal; lack of equality. 2. an instance of lack of equality; specifically, *a*) difference or variation in size, amount, rank, quality, social position, etc. *b*) unevenness in surface; lack of levelness. *c*) lack of proper proportion; unequal distribution. 3. in *mathematics*, the relation between two unequal quantities, or an expression of this relationship: also **inequation.** Examples: $a \neq b$ (a is not equal to b), $4 < 7$ (4 is less than 7), $3a > 2b$ (3a is greater than 2b).

in·e·qua·tion (in'i-kwā'zhən, in'i-kwā'shən), ***n.*** [< L. *inaequatus*, unequal, after Eng. *equation*], in *mathematics*, an inequality.

in·e·qui- (in'ē-kwi), [*in-* (not) + *equi-*], a combining form meaning *not equal, not equally*, as in *inequilateral*.

in·e·qui·lat·er·al (in'ē-kwi-lat'ẽr-əl), ***adj.*** not equilateral.

in·eq·ui·ta·ble (in-ek'wi-tə-b'l), ***adj.*** not equitable; unfair; unjust.

in·eq·ui·ty (in-ek'wi-ti), ***n.*** [*in-* (not) + *equity*], 1. lack of justice; unfairness. 2. [*pl.* INEQUITIES (-tiz)], an instance of this.

in·e·rad·i·ca·ble (in'i-rad'i-kə-b'l), ***adj.*** that cannot be eradicated; too firmly fixed to be rooted out or done away with.

in·e·rad·i·ca·bly (in'i-rad'i-kə-bli), ***adv.*** so as to be ineradicable.

in·e·ras·a·ble (in'i-rās'ə-b'l), ***adj.*** that cannot be erased.

in·er·ra·bil·i·ty (in-er'ə-bil'ə-ti, in-ũr'ə-bil'ə-ti), ***n.*** the quality or state of being inerrable.

in·er·ra·ble (in-er'ə-b'l, in-ũr'ə-b'l), ***adj.*** [L. *inerrabilis*], not erring; infallible.

in·er·ra·bly (in-er'ə-bli, in-ũr'ə-bli), ***adv.*** in an inerrable manner; infallibly.

in·er·ran·cy (in-er'ən-si, in-ũr'ən-si), ***n.*** the state or quality of being inerrant.

in·er·rant (in-er'ənt, in-ũr'ənt), ***adj.*** [L. *inerrans*, not wandering, fixed; see IN- (not) & ERRANT], not erring; making no mistakes; infallible.

in·er·rat·ic (in'ə-rat'ik), ***adj.*** not erratic.

in·ert (in-ũrt'), ***adj.*** [L. *iners*, without skill or art, idle < *in-*, not + *ars, artis*, skill, art], 1. having inertia; without power to move or to resist an opposing force. 2. tending to be physically or mentally inactive; dull; slow. 3. with few or no active properties; neutral: as, the *inert* ingredients of a medicine. —***SYN.*** see **inactive.**

in·er·tia (in-ũr'shə), ***n.*** [L., lack of art or skill, ignorance < *iners;* see INERT], 1. in *physics*, the tendency of matter to remain at rest if at rest, or, if moving, to keep moving in the same direction, unless affected by some outside force: symbol, I; hence, 2. a tendency to remain in a fixed condition without change; disinclination to move or act.

in·er·tial (in-ũr'shəl), ***adj.*** of, or having the nature of, inertia.

in·es·cap·a·ble (in'ə-skāp'ə-b'l), ***adj.*** that cannot be escaped; unavoidable; inevitable.

‡**in es·se** (in es'i), [L.], in being; in existence.

in·es·sen·tial (in'ə-sen'shəl), ***adj.*** 1. [Rare], without essence or existence; immaterial. 2. not essential; not really necessary or important; unessential. ***n.*** something inessential.

in·es·ti·ma·ble (in-es'ti-mə-b'l), ***adj.*** that cannot be estimated or measured; especially, too great or valuable to be properly measured or appreciated; invaluable.

in·es·ti·ma·bly (in-es'ti-mə-bli), ***adv.*** to an inestimable degree.

in·ev·i·ta·bil·i·ty (in'ev-i-tə-bil'ə-ti, in-ev'i-tə-bil'ə-ti), ***n.*** the state, quality, or fact of being inevitable.

in·ev·i·ta·ble (in-ev'i-tə-b'l), ***adj.*** [ME.; L. *inevitabilis;* see IN- (not) & EVITABLE], that cannot be avoided or evaded; certain to happen.

in·ev·i·ta·bly (in-ev'i-tə-bli), ***adv.*** so as to be inevitable; unavoidably; certainly.

in·ex·act (in'ig-zakt'), ***adj.*** not exact; not accurate or precise.

in·ex·act·i·tude (in'ig-zak'tə-tood', in'ig-zak'tə-tūd'), ***n.*** [Fr.], lack of exactitude; inexactness.

in·ex·cus·a·bil·i·ty (in'ik-skūz'ə-bil'ə-ti), ***n.*** the quality of being inexcusable.

in·ex·cus·a·ble (in'ik-skūz'ə-b'l), ***adj.*** that cannot or should not be excused; unpardonable; unjustifiable.

in·ex·cus·a·bly (in'ik-skūz'ə-bli), ***adv.*** in an inexcusable manner; so as to be inexcusable.

in·ex·e·cu·tion (in-ek'sə-kū'shən), ***n.*** lack of execution; failure to do something.

in·ex·er·tion (in'ig-zũr'shən), ***n.*** lack of exertion; failure to exert oneself.

in·ex·haust·i·bil·i·ty (in'ig-zôs'tə-bil'ə-ti), ***n.*** the quality or state of being inexhaustible.

in·ex·haust·i·ble (in'ig-zôs'tə-b'l), ***adj.*** that cannot be exhausted; specifically, *a*) that cannot be used up or emptied. *b*) indefatigable; tireless.

in·ex·haust·i·bly (in'ig-zôs'tə-bli), ***adv.*** 1. in an inexhaustible manner. 2. to an inexhaustible degree.

in·ex·ist·ent (in'ig-zis'tənt), ***adj.*** [LL. *inexistens*], not existent; not in or having being.

in·ex·o·ra·bil·i·ty (in-ek'sẽr-ə-bil'ə-ti), ***n.*** the quality of being inexorable.

in·ex·o·ra·ble (in-ek'sẽr-ə-b'l), ***adj.*** [L. *inexorabilis;* see IN- (not) & EXORABLE], that cannot be moved or influenced by persuasion or entreaty; unrelenting; inflexible.

in·ex·o·ra·bly (in-ek'sẽr-ə-bli), ***adv.*** in an inexorable manner.

in·ex·pe·di·ence (in'ik-spē'di-əns), ***n.*** inexpediency.

in·ex·pe·di·en·cy (in'ik-spē'di-ən-si), ***n.*** the quality or condition of being inexpedient.

in·ex·pe·di·ent (in'ik-spē'di-ənt), ***adj.*** not expedient; not suitable or practicable for a given situation; inadvisable; unwise.

in·ex·pen·sive (in'ik-spen'siv), ***adj.*** not expensive; costing relatively little; low-priced; cheap. —***SYN.*** see **cheap.**

in·ex·pe·ri·ence (in'ik-spêr'i-əns), ***n.*** [Fr. *inexpérience;* LL. *inexperientia*], lack of experience or of the knowledge or skill resulting from experience.

in·ex·pe·ri·enced (in'ik-spêr'i-ənst), ***adj.*** lacking experience or the knowledge or skill resulting from experience.

in·ex·pert (in'ik-spũrt', in-ek'spẽrt), ***adj.*** [MFr.; L. *inexpertus*], not expert; unskillful; amateurish.

in·ex·pi·a·ble (in-ek'spi-ə-b'l), ***adj.*** [L. *inexpiabilis*], 1. that cannot be expiated or atoned for: as, an *inexpiable* sin. 2. [Archaic], that cannot be appeased; implacable.

in·ex·pi·a·bly (in-ek'spi-ə-bli), ***adv.*** in an inexpiable manner.
in·ex·plain·a·ble (in'iks-plān'ə-b'l), ***adj.*** that cannot be explained; inexplicable.
in·ex·pli·ca·bil·i·ty (in-eks'pli-kə-bil'ə-ti), ***n.*** the quality or state of being inexplicable.
in·ex·pli·ca·ble (in-eks'pli-kə-b'l; *sometimes* in'ik-splik'-ə-b'l), ***adj.*** [Fr.; L. ***inexplicabilis***], not explicable; that cannot be explained, understood, or accounted for.
in·ex·pli·ca·bly (in-eks'pli-kə-bli; *sometimes* in'ik-splik'-ə-bli), ***adv.*** in an inexplicable manner.
in·ex·plic·it (in'iks-plis'it), ***adj.*** [L. ***inexplicitus***], not explicit; vague; indefinite; general.
in·ex·plo·sive (in'iks-plō'siv), ***adj.*** not explosive.
in·ex·press·i·bil·i·ty (in'iks-pres'ə-bil'ə-ti), ***n.*** the quality of being inexpressible.
in·ex·press·i·ble (in'iks-pres'ə-b'l), ***adj.*** that cannot be expressed; indescribable or unutterable.
in·ex·press·i·bly (in'iks-pres'ə-bli), ***adv.*** in an inexpressible manner; so as to be inexpressible.
in·ex·pres·sive (in'iks-pres'iv), ***adj.*** 1. [Archaic], inexpressible. 2. not expressive; lacking meaning or expression.
in·ex·pug·na·ble (in'ik-spug'nə-b'l), ***adj.*** [Fr.; L. ***inexpugnabilis; in-***, not + ***expugnabilis***, that can be taken by storm < ***expugnare***, to take by storm; ***ex-***, intens. + ***pugnare***, to fight < ***pugna***, a fight], that cannot be defeated by force; unconquerable; unyielding.
in·ex·pug·na·bly (in'ik-spug'nə-bli), ***adv.*** so as to be inexpugnable.
in·ex·ten·si·ble (in'ik-sten'sə-b'l), ***adj.*** not extensible.
‡in ex·ten·so (in ik-sten'sō), [L.], at full length; unabridged.
in·ex·tin·guish·a·ble (in'ik-stiŋ'gwish-ə-b'l), ***adj.*** not extinguishable; that cannot be quenched, put out, or stopped.
in·ex·tin·guish·a·bly (in'ik-stiŋ'gwish-ə-bli), ***adv.*** so as to be inextinguishable.
in·ex·tir·pa·ble (in'ik-stũr'pə-b'l), ***adj.*** [L. ***inextirpabilis***], that cannot be extirpated.
‡in ex·tre·mis (in iks-trē'mis), [L., in extremity], at the point of death.
in·ex·tri·ca·bil·i·ty (in-eks'tri-kə-bil'ə-ti), ***n.*** the quality or state of being inextricable.
in·ex·tri·ca·ble (in-eks'tri-kə-b'l), ***adj.*** [Fr.; L. ***inextricabilis***], 1. that one cannot extricate himself from. 2. that cannot be disentangled or untied. 3. so complicated or involved as to be insolvable.
in·ex·tri·ca·bly (in-eks'tri-kə-bli), ***adv.*** so as to be inextricable.
I·nez (ī'niz, ī'nez'), [Sp. ***Iñez***], a feminine name: see **Agnes.**
Inf., inf., infantry.
inf., 1. infinitive. 2. information. 3. *infra*, [L.], below.
in f., *in fine*, [L.], finally; at the end.
in·fal·li·bil·i·ty (in-fal'ə-bil'ə-ti), ***n.*** the state or quality of being infallible.
in·fal·li·ble (in-fal'ə-b'l), ***adj.*** [ML. ***infallibilis***; see IN- (not) & FALLIBLE], 1. incapable of error; never wrong. 2. not liable to fail, go wrong, make a mistake, etc.; dependable; reliable. 3. in the *Roman Catholic Church*, incapable of error in setting forth doctrine on faith and morals: said especially of the Pope speaking ***ex cathedra*** (i.e., in his official capacity). ***n.*** an infallible person or thing.
in·fal·li·bly (in-fal'ə-bli), ***adv.*** in an infallible manner.
in·fa·mous (in'fə-məs), ***adj.*** [ME.; OFr. ***infameux;*** ML. ***infamosus*** < L. ***infamis;*** see IN- (not) & FAMOUS], 1. having a very bad reputation; notorious; in disgrace or dishonor. 2. causing or deserving a bad reputation; scandalous; outrageous. 3. in *law*, *a*) punishable by imprisonment in a penitentiary: said of certain crimes. *b*) guilty of such a crime. —***SYN.*** see **vicious.**
in·fa·my (in'fə-mi), ***n.*** [*pl.* INFAMIES (-miz)], [Fr. ***infamie;*** L. ***infamia*** < ***infamis;*** see INFAMOUS], 1. very bad reputation; notoriety; disgrace; dishonor. 2. the quality of being infamous; great wickedness. 3. an infamous act. 4. in *law*, loss of character and of certain civil rights sustained by a person convicted of an infamous crime. —***SYN.*** see **disgrace.**
in·fan·cy (in'fən-si), ***n.*** [*pl.* INFANCIES (-siz)], [L. ***infantia***, inability to speak], 1. the state or period of being an infant; babyhood; very early childhood. 2. the beginning or earliest stage of anything. 3. in *law*, the state or period of being a minor; period before the age of legal majority, usually twenty-one; minority.
in·fant (in'fənt), ***n.*** [ME. ***enfaunt;*** OFr. ***enfant;*** L. ***infans, infantis,*** *adj.* not speaking, *n.* a child, infant; ***in-***, not + ***fans, fantis,*** ppr. of ***fari***, to speak], 1. a very young child; baby. 2. a person in the state of legal infancy; minor. ***adj.*** 1. of or for infants or infancy. 2. in a very early stage.
in·fan·ta (in-fan'tə), ***n.*** [Sp. & Port., fem. of ***infante***, child, infant], 1. any daughter of a king of Spain or Portugal. 2. the wife of an infante.
in·fan·te (in-fan'tā), ***n.*** [Sp. & Port.; L. ***infans;*** see INFANT], any son of a king of Spain or Portugal, except the heir to the throne.
in·fan·ti·cide (in-fan'tə-sīd'), ***n.*** [Fr.; LL. ***infanticidium*** < ***infanticida***, one who kills an infant < L. ***infans***, infant + ***caedere***, to kill], 1. the murder of a baby. 2. [Fr.; LL. ***infanticida***], a person guilty of this.
in·fan·tile (in'fən-tīl', in'fən-til), ***adj.*** [L. ***infantilis***], 1. of infants or infancy. 2. like or characteristic of an infant; babyish; childish or childlike. 3. in the earliest stage of development.
infantile paralysis, an acute infectious disease, especially of children, caused by a virus inflammation of the gray matter of the spinal cord: it is accompanied by paralysis of various muscle groups that atrophy, resulting, usually, in permanent deformities: also called (*acute anterior*) *poliomyelitis.*
in·fan·ti·lism (in-fan'tə-liz'm), ***n.*** an abnormal state in which infantile, or childish, characteristics persist into adult life: it is marked by retarded mental and physical growth and a lack of sexual development.
in·fan·tine (in'fən-tīn', in'fən-tin), ***adj.*** [Fr. ***infantin***, ***enfantin***], infantile; babyish; childish or childlike.
in·fan·try (in'fən-tri), ***n.*** [*pl.* INFANTRIES (-triz)], [Fr. ***infanterie;*** Sp. ***infanteria*** < Sp. & Port. ***infante***, very young person, knight's page, foot soldier < L. ***infans;*** see INFANT], foot soldiers collectively; especially, that branch of an army consisting of soldiers trained and equipped to fight on foot: abbreviated **Inf., inf.**
in·fan·try·man (in'fən-tri-mən), ***n.*** [*pl.* INFANTRYMEN (-mən)], a soldier in the infantry.
in·farct (in-färkt'), ***n.*** [ML. ***infarctus***, for L. ***infartus***, pp. of ***infarcire; in-***, in + ***farcire***, to stuff], an area of dying or dead tissue resulting from obstruction of the blood vessels normally supplying the part.
in·fat·u·ate (in-fach'o͞o-āt'), ***v.t.*** [INFATUATED (-id), INFATUATING], [< L. ***infatuatus***, pp. of ***infatuare***, to make a fool of < ***in-***, intens. + ***fatuus***, foolish], 1. to make foolish; cause to lose sound judgment. 2. to inspire with unreasoning passion or attraction. ***adj.*** infatuated. ***n.*** a person who is infatuated.
in·fat·u·at·ed (in-fach'o͞o-āt'id), ***adj.*** [pp. of ***infatuate***], 1. foolish; lacking sound judgment. 2. completely carried away by unreasoning passion or attraction.
in·fat·u·a·tion (in-fach'o͞o-ā'shən), ***n.*** 1. an infatuating. 2. the fact or state of being infatuated; unreasoning passion or attraction. —***SYN.*** see **love.**
in·fea·si·bil·i·ty (in-fē'zə-bil'ə-ti), ***n.*** the quality or state of being infeasible.
in·fea·si·ble (in-fē'zə-b'l), ***adj.*** not feasible; not easily done or put to use; impracticable.
in·fect (in-fekt'), ***v.t.*** [ME. ***enfecten;*** OFr. ***infecter*** < L. ***infectus***, pp. of ***inficere***, to put or dip into, tinge, stain < ***in-***, in + ***facere***, to do, make], 1. to contaminate with a disease-producing organism or matter. 2. to cause to become diseased by bringing into contact with such an organism or matter. 3. to affect or imbue with one's feelings or beliefs; especially, to affect in a harmful or undesirable way; corrupt.
in·fec·tion (in-fek'shən), ***n.*** [ME. ***infeccioun;*** OFr.; LL. ***infectio***], 1. an infecting; specifically, *a*) the act of causing to become diseased. *b*) the act of affecting with one's feelings or beliefs. 2. the fact or state of being infected. 3. something resulting from an infecting; specifically, *a*) a disease resulting from the presence of certain microorganisms or matter in the body. *b*) a feeling, belief, influence, etc. transmitted from one person to another. 4. anything that infects.
in·fec·tious (in-fek'shəs), ***adj.*** 1. likely to cause infection; containing disease-producing organisms or matter. 2. designating a disease caused by infection: see **infectious disease.** 3. tending to spread or to affect others; catching: as, an *infectious* laugh. 4. [Obs.], infected with disease.
infectious disease, any disease caused by the presence in the body of bacteria, protozoa, viruses, or other parasites: it may or may not be contagious, i.e., transmitted directly from person to person.
in·fec·tive (in-fek'tiv), ***adj.*** [ME. ***infectyve;*** OFr. ***infectif;*** L. ***infectivus***], likely to cause infection; infectious.
in·fec·tor (in-fek'tẽr), ***n.*** a person or thing that infects.
in·fe·cund (in-fē'kənd, in-fek'ənd), ***adj.*** [ME. ***infecunde;*** L. ***infecundus***], not fecund; not fertile; barren.
in·fe·cun·di·ty (in'fi-kun'də-ti), ***n.*** [L. ***infecunditas***], the quality or state of being infecund.
in·fe·lic·i·tous (in'fə-lis'ə-təs), ***adj.*** not felicitous; specifically, *a*) not happy; unfortunate. *b*) not appropriate; unsuitable.
in·fe·lic·i·ty (in'fə-lis'ə-ti), ***n.*** [L. ***infelicitas***], 1. the quality or condition of being infelicitous. 2. [*pl.* INFELICITIES (-tiz)], something infelicitous; unsuitable or inappropriate remark, action, etc.
in·felt (in'felt'), ***adj.*** inwardly and deeply felt.
in·fer (in-fũr'), ***v.t.*** [INFERRED (-fũrd'), INFERRING], [L. ***inferre***, to bring or carry in, infer; ***in-***, in + ***ferre***, to

bring, carry], 1. originally, to bring on or about; cause; induce. 2. to conclude or decide from something known or assumed; derive by reasoning; draw as a conclusion. 3. to lead to as a conclusion; indicate; imply: generally regarded as a loose usage. *v.i.* to draw inferences.

SYN.—**infer** suggests the arriving at a decision or opinion by reasoning from known facts or evidence (from your smile, I *infer* that you're pleased); **deduce**, in strict discrimination, implies inference from a general principle by logical reasoning (the method was *deduced* from earlier experiments); **conclude** strictly implies an inference that is the final logical result in a process of reasoning (I must, therefore, *conclude* that you are wrong); **judge** stresses the careful checking and weighing of premises, etc. in arriving at a conclusion; **gather** is an informal substitute for **infer** or **conclude** (I *gather* that you don't care).

in·fer·a·ble (in-fũr'ə-b'l), *adj.* that can be inferred: also spelled **inferrible.**

in·fer·ence (in'fẽr-əns), *n.* [ML. & LL. *inferentia*], 1. an inferring. 2. something inferred; logical conclusion; deduction.

in·fer·en·tial (in'fə-ren'shəl), *adj.* [< ML. *inferentia;* + *-al*], based on or having to do with inference.

in·fe·ri·or (in-fêr'i-ẽr, in-fêr'yẽr), *adj.* [ME.; L., compar. of *inferus*, low, below], 1. lower in space; placed lower down. 2. low or lower in order, status, rank, etc.; subordinate. 3. lower in quality or value than (with *to*). 4. poor in quality; below average; mediocre. 5. in *anatomy*, located below or directed downward: opposed to *superior*. 6. in *astronomy*, *a*) between the earth and the sun. *b*) below the celestial pole. 7. in *botany*, growing below another part or organ. 8. in *printing*, placed below the type line, as 2 in NO_2. *n.* an inferior person or thing.

in·fe·ri·or·i·ty (in-fêr'i-ôr'ə-ti, in'fêr-i-or'ə-ti), *n.* the quality or condition of being inferior.

inferiority complex, 1. in *psychology*, a neurotic condition resulting from various feelings of inferiority, such as derive from physical inadequacy or situations of early childhood, and often manifested in excessive aggressiveness, a domineering attitude, etc.: so used by Adler. 2. popularly, any feeling of inferiority, inadequacy, etc. whether or not a neurotic condition exists. Cf. **superiority complex.**

in·fer·nal (in-fũr'n'l), *adj.* [ME.; OFr.; LL. *infernalis* < L. *infernus*, underground, lower, infernal < *inferus*, below], 1. *a*) of the ancient mythological world of the dead. *b*) of hell. 2. hellish; diabolical; fiendish; inhuman. 3. [Colloq.], hateful; abominable; outrageous.

infernal machine, any hidden or disguised device designed to explode or to cause injury or destruction.

in·fer·no (in-fũr'nō), *n.* [*pl.* INFERNOS (-nōz)], [It. < L. *infernus;* see INFERNAL], 1. hell. 2. any place suggesting hell, usually characterized by great heat or flames. 3. [I-], that section of Dante's *Divine Comedy* which describes hell and the sufferings of the damned.

in·fe·ro- (in'fẽr-ō), [< L. *inferus*, below], a combining form meaning *below, in the lower part, on the lower side*, as in *inferoanterior*.

in·fe·ro·an·te·ri·or (in'fẽr-ō-an-têr'i-ẽr), *adj.* [*infero-* + *anterior*], lying below and in front.

in·fer·rer (in-fũr'ẽr), *n.* a person who infers.

in·fer·ri·ble (in-fũr'ə-b'l), *adj.* inferable.

in·fer·tile (in-fũr't'l), *adj.* 1. not fertile; not productive; barren. 2. not fertilized, as an egg. —*SYN.* see **sterile.**

in·fer·til·i·ty (in'fẽr-til'ə-ti), *n.* the quality or state of being infertile.

in·fest (in-fest'), *v.t.* [Fr. *infester;* L. *infestare*, to attack, disturb, trouble < *infestus*, hostile < base seen also in *manifestus* (cf. MANIFEST), and prob. in Sans. *dhṛṣṇō-ti*, he is bold, brave, Eng. *dare*], to overrun or inhabit in large numbers, usually so as to be harmful or bothersome; swarm in or about.

in·fes·ta·tion (in'fes-tā'shən), *n.* [LL. *infestatio*], an infesting or being infested.

in·feu·da·tion (in'fyoo-dā'shən), *n.* [ML. *infeudatio* < pp. of *infeudare*, to enfeoff < *in-*, in + *feudum;* see FEE], 1. the granting of an estate in fee; enfeoffment. 2. the granting of tithes to laymen.

in·fi·del (in'fə-d'l), *adj.* [Fr. *infidèle;* L. *infidelis*, unfaithful (LL., unbelieving); *in-*, not + *fidelis*, faithful], 1. *a*) not believing in religion. *b*) not believing in a certain religion or the prevailing religion, especially Christianity; heathen; pagan. 2. of infidels or infidelity. *n.* 1. a person who does not believe in a certain religion or the prevailing religion; non-Christian, non-Moslem, etc. 2. a person who does not believe in any religion. 3. a person who does not accept some particular belief. —*SYN.* see **atheist.**

in·fi·del·i·ty (in'fə-del'ə-ti), *n.* [*pl.* INFIDELITIES (-tiz)], [Fr. *infidélité;* L. *infidelitas* < *infidelis;* see INFIDEL], 1. lack of belief in all religion or in any one religion, especially Christianity. 2. lack of faith, trust, or loyalty. 3. unfaithfulness of a husband or wife; adultery. 4. an unfaithful or disloyal act.

in·field (in'fēld'), *n.* [*in, adv.* + *field*], 1. the land of a farm nearest the farmhouse. 2. *a*) the square area enclosed by the four base lines on a baseball field. *b*) the infielders collectively. Distinguished from *outfield*.

in·field·er (in'fēl'dẽr), *n.* in *baseball*, a player whose position is in the infield; shortstop, first baseman, second baseman, or third baseman: the pitcher and the catcher are considered infielders when fielding the ball: distinguished from *outfielder*.

in·fil·trate (in-fil'trāt; *also, esp. for v. 2,* in'fil-trāt'), *v.t. & v.i.* [INFILTRATED (-id), INFILTRATING], [*in-* (in) + *filtrate*], 1. to pass, or cause (a fluid) to pass, through small gaps or openings; filter. 2. to pass through, as in filtering; specifically, in *military usage*, to pass, or cause (individual troops) to pass, through weak places in the enemy's lines in order to attack the enemy's flanks or rear. *n.* something that infiltrates.

in·fil·tra·tion (in'fil-trā'shən), *n.* 1. an infiltrating or being infiltrated. 2. something that infiltrates.

infin., infinitive.

in·fi·nite (in'fə-nit), *adj.* [ME.; L. *infinitus;* see IN- (not) & FINITE], 1. lacking limits or bounds; extending beyond measure or comprehension; endless; immeasurable; hence, 2. very great; vast; immense; inexhaustible. 3. in *mathematics*, of a greater value (*positively infinite*) or a lesser value (*negatively infinite*) than any assigned number. *n.* 1. something infinite, as space or time. 2. in *mathematics*, an infinite quantity.
the Infinite (Being), God.

in·fi·nite·ly (in'fə-nit-li), *adv.* to an infinite degree.

in·fin·i·tes·i·mal (in'fin-ə-tes'ə-m'l), *adj.* [< Mod. L. *infinitesimus* < L. *infinitus* (see INFINITE), after *centesimus*, hundredth < *centum*, one hundred], 1. in *mathematics*, continually diminishing and approaching zero as its limit: said of a variable. 2. too small to be measured; infinitely small. *n.* an infinitesimal quantity.

in·fin·i·ti·val (in'fin-ə-tī'v'l, in-fin'ə-tī'v'l), *adj.* having to do with the infinitive.

in·fin·i·tive (in-fin'ə-tiv), *adj.* [LL. *infinitivus* < *infinitus;* see INFINITE], in *grammar*, 1. of or connected with an infinitive. 2. not defined or limited. *n.* the simple, uninflected form of the verb, expressing existence or action without reference to person, number, or tense: in English, it is preceded by *to*, as, *to go, to think*, or by another verb form, as, *can he go, make us think:* abbreviated **inf., infin.**

in·fin·i·tude (in-fin'ə-tōōd', in-fin'ə-tūd'), *n.* [< L. *infinitus*, infinite], 1. the quality of being infinite. 2. an infinite quantity, number, or extent.

in·fin·i·ty (in-fin'ə-ti), *n.* [*pl.* INFINITIES (-tiz)], [ME. *infinite;* OFr. *infinité;* L. *infinitas*], 1. the quality of being infinite. 2. anything infinite; endless or unlimited space, time, distance, quantity, etc. 3. an indefinitely large number or amount. 4. in *geometry*, a point or space infinitely distant from the point or space being considered. 5. in *mathematics*, an infinite quantity, indicated by ∞. 6. in *photography*, a distance so great that rays of light originating there may be considered as parallel.
to infinity, without limit or end.

in·firm (in-fũrm'), *adj.* [ME.; OFr. *infirm, enferm;* L. *infirmus*], 1. not firm or strong physically; weak; feeble, as from old age. 2. not firm in mind or purpose; unstable; vacillating. 3. [Rare], not stable, firm, or sound; frail; shaky, as a structure. 4. not secure or valid: as, an *infirm* title to property. —*SYN.* see **weak.**

in·fir·ma·ry (in-fũr'mə-ri), *n.* [*pl.* INFIRMARIES (-riz)], [OFr. *enfermerie;* ML. *infirmaria, infirmarium* < L. *infirmus*], a place for the care of the sick, injured, or infirm; hospital; especially, the building or room in a school, etc. that serves as a hospital or dispensary.

in·fir·mi·ty (in-fũr'mə-ti), *n.* [ME. *infirmite;* OFr. *enfermeté;* L. *infirmitas*], 1. the quality or state of being infirm; feebleness; weakness. 2. [*pl.* INFIRMITIES (-tiz)], an instance of this; specifically, *a*) a physical weakness or defect; frailty or ailment, as from old age. *b*) a moral weakness; defect.

in·fix (in-fiks'; *for n.,* in'fiks'), *v.t.* [ME. *inficchen;* OFr. *infixer* < L. *infixus*, pp. of *infigere*, to fix, thrust, or drive in; see IN- (in) & FIX], 1. to fasten or set firmly in or on, especially by inserting or piercing. 2. to instill; teach; implant. 3. to place (an infix) within the body of a word. *n.* in *linguistics*, an element consisting of one or more sounds or syllables placed within the body of a word to modify its meaning: it corresponds in function to a suffix or prefix. Example: Arabic *-ta-* in *iq-ta-riba*, to cause oneself to come near (< *qariba*, to come near).

‡**in fla·gran·te de·lic·to** (in flə-gran'ti di-lik'tō), [L.], in the very act of committing the offense; red-handed.

in·flame (in-flām'), *v.t.* [INFLAMED (-flāmd'), INFLAMING], [ME. *enflamen;* OFr. *enflammer;* L. *inflammare;* see IN- (in) & FLAME], 1. to set on fire. 2. to arouse passion, desire, or violence in; excite intensely, especially with anger. 3. to increase the intensity of (passion, desire, violence, etc.). 4. to cause to be hot, feverish, swollen, red, sore, etc.; cause inflammation in. *v.i.* 1. to become roused, excited, stimulated, etc. 2. to catch fire. 3. to become hot, feverish, swollen, red, sore, etc.

in·flam·ma·bil·i·ty (in-flam'ə-bil'ə-ti), *n.* the quality or condition of being inflammable; specifically, *a*) a tendency to burn readily or the degree of this tendency. *b*) excitability.

in·flam·ma·ble (in-flam'ə-b'l), *adj.* [Fr. < L. *inflammare;* see INFLAME], 1. easily set on fire; that will burn readily or quickly; combustible. 2. easily roused, provoked, or excited. *n.* anything inflammable.

in·flam·ma·bly (in-flam'ə-bli), *adv.* in an inflammable manner; so as to be easily inflamed.

in·flam·ma·tion (in'flə-mā'shən), *n.* [Fr.; L. *inflammatio*], 1. an inflaming. 2. a being inflamed; specifically, in *medicine,* a diseased condition of some part of the body, resulting from injury, infection, irritation, etc. and characterized by redness, pain, heat, and swelling.

in·flam·ma·to·ry (in-flam'ə-tôr'i, in-flam'ə-tō'ri), *adj.* [< L. *inflammatus,* pp. of *inflammare* (see INFLAME); + *-ory*], 1. rousing or likely to rouse excitement, anger, violence, rioting, etc., as a speech. 2. in *medicine,* of, caused by, or characterized by inflammation.

in·flat·a·ble (in-flāt'ə-b'l), *adj.* that can be inflated.

in·flate (in-flāt'), *v.t.* [INFLATED (-id), INFLATING], [< L. *inflatus,* pp. of *inflare,* to blow into, inflate; *in-,* in + *flare,* to blow], 1. to blow full or swell out with air or gas; distend; expand; dilate. 2. to raise in spirits; make proud or elated. 3. to increase or raise beyond normal or valid proportions. 4. to increase the amount of (currency in circulation): see **inflation.** *v.i.* to become inflated; swell. Opposed to *deflate.* —*SYN.* see **expand.**

in·flat·ed (in-flāt'id), *adj.* [pp. of *inflate*], 1. swollen; puffed out. 2. pompous; bombastic; high-flown. 3. increased or raised beyond normal or valid proportions.

in·flat·er (in-flāt'ẽr), *n.* a person or thing that inflates.

in·fla·tion (in-flā'shən), *n.* [ME. *inflacioun;* L. *inflatio*], 1. an inflating or being inflated. 2. an increase in the amount of currency in circulation, resulting in a relatively sharp and sudden fall in its value and rise in prices: it may be caused by an increase in the volume of paper money issued or of gold mined, or a relative increase in expenditures, as when the supply of goods fails to meet the demand. Opposed to *deflation.*

in·fla·tion·ar·y (in-flā'shən-er'i), *adj.* of, causing, or characterized by inflation.

in·fla·tion·ist (in-flā'shən-ist), *n.* a person who favors inflation.

in·fla·tor (in flā'tẽr), *n.* an inflater.

in·flect (in-flekt'), *v.t.* [ME. *inflecte(n);* L. *inflectere; in-,* in + *flectere,* to bend], 1. to turn, bend, or curve, usually inward. 2. to vary or change the tone or pitch of (the voice); modulate. 3. to change the form of (a word) by inflection, as in conjugating or declining.

in·flec·tion (in-flek'shən), *n.* [L. *inflexio* < *inflexus,* pp. of *inflectere;* see INFLECT], 1. a turning, bending, or curving. 2. a turn, bend, or curve. 3. a change in the tone or pitch of the voice; modulation. 4. *a)* the change of form by which some words indicate certain grammatical relationships, as number, case, gender, tense, etc. *b)* an inflected form. *c)* an inflectional element, as those used in English to form the plural and possessive case of nouns (ship*s,* ship'*s*) and the past tense and third person singular, present indicative, of verbs (he shipp*ed,* ship*s*). 5. a change of a curve or arc from convex to concave or the reverse.

in·flec·tion·al (in-flek'shən-'l), *adj.* of, having, or showing grammatical inflection.

inflectional language, a language in which inflection is the principal grammatical device; specifically, a language in which the subject-object relation is indicated by inflection: Greek and Latin are inflectional languages, whereas English is syntactically analytical.

in·flec·tive (in-flek'tiv), *adj.* 1. that can bend or curve; tending to bend or curve. 2. inflectional.

in·flexed (in-flekst'), *adj.* [< L. *inflexus,* pp. (see INFLECT); + *-ed*], in *botany* & *zoology,* bent inward; turned toward the axis.

in·flex·i·bil·i·ty (in-flek'sə-bil'ə-ti, in'flek-sə-bil'ə-ti), *n.* the quality or condition of being inflexible.

in·flex·i·ble (in-flek'sə-b'l), *adj.* [ME.; L. *inflexibilis;* see IN- (not) & FLEXIBLE], 1. that cannot be bent or curved; stiff; rigid. 2. firm in mind or purpose; stubborn; unyielding; unshakeable. 3. that cannot be changed; fixed; unalterable: as, an *inflexible* rule.
SYN.—**inflexible** implies an unyielding or unshakeable firmness in mind or purpose, sometimes connoting stubbornness (his *inflexible* attitude); **adamant** implies a firm or unbreakable resolve that remains unaffected by temptation or pleading (*adamant* to her entreaties); **implacable** suggests the impossibility of pacifying or appeasing (*implacable* in his hatred); **obdurate** implies a hardheartedness that is not easily moved to pity, sympathy, or forgiveness (her *obdurate* refusal to help). See also **stiff.**—*ANT.* flexible, yielding, compliant.

in·flex·i·bly (in-flek'sə-bli), *adv.* in an inflexible manner.

in·flex·ion (in-flek'shən), *n.* inflection: chiefly British spelling.

in·flict (in-flikt'), *v.t.* [< L. *inflictus,* pp. of *infligere,* to strike or beat against, strike on; *in-,* on, against + *fligere,* to strike], 1. to give or cause (pain, wounds, blows, etc.) by or as by striking; cause to be borne. 2. to impose (a punishment, disagreeable task, etc.).

in·flic·tion (in-flik'shən), *n.* [LL. *inflictio*], 1. an inflicting. 2. something inflicted, as pain or punishment.

in·flic·tive (in-flik'tiv), *adj.* of or characterized by infliction.

in·flo·res·cence (in'flô-res''ns, in'flō-res''ns), *n.* [Mod. L. *inflorescentia* < LL. *inflorescens,* ppr. of *inflorescere,* to begin to blossom; see IN- (in) & FLORESCENCE], in *botany,* 1. a flowering. 2. the arrangement of flowers on a stem or axis. 3. a flower cluster on a common axis. 4. flowers collectively. 5. a single flower.

in·flo·res·cent (in'flô-res''nt, in'flō-res''nt), *adj.* [LL. *inflorescens;* see INFLORESCENCE], in flower; flowering.

in·flow (in'flō'), *n.* 1. a flowing in or into. 2. anything that flows in.

in·flu·ence (in'flōō-əns), *n.* [ME.; OFr.; ML. *influentia,* a flowing in < L. *influens,* ppr. of *influere,* to flow in; *in-,* in + *fluere,* to flow], 1. originally, the supposed flowing of an ethereal fluid or power from the stars, thought to affect the characters and actions of people. 2. *a)* the power of persons or things to affect others, seen only in its effects. *b)* the action or effect of such power. 3. the power of a person or group to produce effects without the exertion of physical force or authority, based on wealth, social position, ability, etc. 4. a person or thing that has influence. 5. in *electricity,* induction. *v.t.* [INFLUENCED (-ənst), INFLUENCING], to exert or have influence on; have an effect on the nature or behavior of; affect the action or thought of; modify.
SYN.—**influence** implies the power of persons or things (whether or not exerted consciously or overtly) to affect others (he owed his position to *influence*); **authority** implies the power to command acceptance, belief, obedience, etc., based on strength of character, expertness of knowledge, etc. (a statement made on good *authority*); **prestige** implies the power to command esteem or admiration, based on brilliance of achievement or outstanding superiority; **weight** implies influence that is more or less preponderant in its effect (he threw his *weight* to the opposition). See also **effect.**

in·flu·ent (in'flōō-ənt), *adj.* [L. *influens;* see INFLUENCE], flowing in. *n.* anything flowing in, as a tributary.

in·flu·en·tial (in'flōō-en'shəl), *adj.* [< ML. *influentia* (see INFLUENCE); + *-al*], 1. having or exerting influence. 2. having great influence; powerful; effective.

in·flu·en·za (in'flōō-en'zə), *n.* [It., lit., an influence: so called because formerly attributed by astrologers to the influence of the stars < LL. *influentia;* see INFLUENCE], an acute, contagious, infectious disease, caused by any of several viruses and characterized by inflammation of the respiratory tract, fever, muscular pain, and, often, intestinal disorders: also called *grippe, flu.*

in·flu·en·zal (in'flōō-en'z'l), *adj.* of influenza.

in·flux (in'fluks'), *n.* [Fr.; LL. *influxus,* properly pp. of *influere;* see INFLUENCE], 1. *a)* a flowing in; inpouring; inflow, as of a liquid, gas, etc. *b)* a continual coming in of persons or things: as, an *influx* of customers. 2. the point where a river joins another body of water.

in·fold (in-fōld'), *v.t.* 1. to wrap in folds; wrap up. 2. to embrace. Also spelled **enfold.**

in·form (in-fôrm'), *v.t.* [ME. *informen;* OFr. *enformer;* L. *informare;* see IN- (in) & FORM], 1. *a)* to give form or character to; be the formative principle of. *b)* to give, imbue, or inspire with some specific quality or character; animate. 2. [Rare], to form or shape (the mind); teach. 3. to give knowledge of something to; tell; acquaint with a fact, etc. *v.i.* to give information, especially information laying blame or accusation upon another. —*SYN.* see **notify.**

in·form (in-fôrm'), *adj.* [Fr. *informe;* L. *informis*], without form; formless.

in·for·mal (in-fôr'm'l), *adj.* not formal; specifically, *a)* not according to prescribed or fixed customs, rules, ceremonies, etc. *b)* casual, easy, unceremonious, or relaxed. *c)* designed for use or wear on everyday occasions. *d)* not requiring formal dress. *e)* colloquial.

in·for·mal·i·ty (in'fôr-mal'ə-ti), *n.* 1. the quality or state of being informal; absence of formality. 2. [*pl.* INFORMALITIES (-tiz)], an informal act.

in·form·ant (in-fôr'mənt), *n.* [< L. *informans,* ppr. of *informare,* to inform], 1. a person who gives information. 2. a native speaker who repeats the forms, correct sounds, etc. of his language for the benefit of linguists, teachers, translators, etc.

in·for·ma·tion (in'fẽr-mā'shən), *n.* [ME. & OFr. *enformacion;* L. *informatio,* a representation, outline, sketch], 1. an informing or being informed; especially, a telling or being told of something. 2. something told; news; intelligence; word. 3. knowledge acquired in any manner; facts; data; learning; lore. 4. a person or agency answering questions as a service to others. 5. in *law,* an accusation of criminal offense, not by indictment of a grand jury, but by a public officer, such as a prosecutor. Abbreviated **inf.**
SYN.—**information** applies to facts that are gathered in any way, as by reading, observation, hearsay, etc. and does not

necessarily connote validity (inaccurate *information*); **knowledge** applies to any body of facts gathered by study, observation, etc. and to the ideas inferred from these facts, and connotes an understanding of what is known (man's *knowledge* of the universe); **learning** is knowledge acquired by study, especially in languages, literature, philosophy, etc.; **erudition** implies profound or abstruse learning beyond the comprehension of most people; **wisdom** implies superior judgment and understanding based on broad knowledge.—*ANT.* ignorance.

in·for·ma·tion·al (in'fẽr-mā'shən-'l), *adj.* of or giving information.

in·form·a·tive (in-fôr'mə-tiv), *adj.* [ML. *informativus* < L. *informatus*, pp. of *informare* (see INFORM)], giving information; educational; instructive.

in·form·a·to·ry (in-fôr'mə-tôr'i, in-fôr'mə-tō'ri), *adj.* informative.

in·formed (in-fôrmd'), *adj.* [pp. of *inform*], having much information, knowledge, or education.

in·form·er (in-fôr'mẽr), *n.* a person who informs; informant; especially, a person who makes an accusation against, or gives evidence of the guilt of, another.

in·fra- (in'frə), [<L. *infra, adv. & prep.*, below], a prefix meaning *below, beneath*, as in *infrared, infracostal.*

in·fra·cos·tal (in'frə-kos'təl), *adj.* [< *infra-* + L. *costa*, a rib; + *-al*], situated beneath the ribs.

in·fract (in-frakt'), *v.t.* [< L. *infractus*, pp. of *infringere;* see INFRINGE], to break or violate (a law, pledge, etc.).

in·frac·tion (in-frak'shən), *n.* [L. *infractio;* see IN- (in) & FRACTION], a breaking of a law, pact, etc.; violation; infringement.

‡in·fra dig·ni·ta·tem (in'frə dig'ni-tā'təm), [L.], beneath (one's) dignity: abbreviated **infra dig.**

in·fra·lap·sar·i·an (in'frə-lap-sâr'i-ən), *n.* [< *infra-* + L. *lapsus*, a fall; + *-arian* as in *Unitarian*, etc.], any of a group of Calvinists who held that God's plan of salvation for some people followed and was a consequence of the fall of man from grace: opposed to *supralapsarian. adj.* of this doctrine.

in·fra·me·di·an (in'frə-mē'di-ən), *adj.* [*infra-* + *median*], designating those areas of the ocean bottom ranging in depth from 300 to 600 feet.

in·fran·gi·bil·i·ty (in-fran'jə-bil'ə-ti), *n.* the quality or state of being infrangible.

in·fran·gi·ble (in-fran'jə-b'l), *adj.* [*in-* (not) + *frangible*], 1. that cannot be broken or separated. 2. that cannot be violated or infringed.

in·fra·red (in'frə-red'), *adj.* designating or of those invisible rays just beyond the red of the visible spectrum: their waves are longer than those of the spectrum colors but shorter than radio waves, and have a penetrating heating effect.

in·fre·quence (in-frē'kwəns), *n.* infrequency.

in·fre·quen·cy (in-frē'kwən-si), *n.* [L. *infrequentia*], the condition or fact of being infrequent.

in·fre·quent (in-frē'kwənt), *adj.* [L. *infrequens*], not frequent; not occurring often; happening seldom or at long intervals; rare; uncommon. —*SYN.* see **rare.**

in·fringe (in-frinj'), *v.t.* [INFRINGED (-frinjd'), INFRINGING], [L. *infringere*, to break off, break, impair, violate < *in-*, in + *frangere*, to break], to break (a law or agreement); fail to observe the terms of; violate.

infringe on (or **upon**), to break in on; encroach or trespass on (the rights, patents, etc. of others).

in·fringe·ment (in-frinj'mənt), *n.* an infringing; violation or encroachment.

in·fun·dib·u·lar (in'fən-dib'yoo-lẽr), *adj.* 1. having the shape of a funnel. 2. of or having an infundibulum.

in·fun·dib·u·late (in'fən-dib'yoo-lāt', in'fən-dib'yoo-lit), *adj.* infundibular.

in·fun·dib·u·lum (in'fən-dib'yoo-ləm), *n.* [*pl.* INFUNDIBULA (-lə)], [L., a funnel < *infundere;* see INFUSE], in *anatomy*, any of various funnel-shaped organs or passages; specifically, *a)* the extension of the third ventricle of the brain to the pituitary body. *b)* the bronchiole endings in the lungs.

in·fu·ri·ate (in-fyoor'i-it; *for v.*, in-fyoor'i-āt'), *adj.* [< ML. *infuriatus*, pp. of *infuriare*, to enrage; L. *in-*, in + *furiare*, to enrage < *furia*, rage, anger], furious; very angry; enraged. *v.t.* [INFURIATED (-id), INFURIATING], to cause to become very angry; enrage.

in·fu·ri·a·tion (in-fyoor'i-ā'shən), *n.* an infuriating or being infuriated.

in·fus·cate (in-fus'kit), *adj.* [L. *infuscatus*, pp. of *infuscare*, to make dark, obscure; *in-*, in + *fuscare*, to darken < *fuscus*, dark], darkened or tinged with brown, as the wings of an insect.

in·fus·cat·ed (in-fus'kā-tid), *adj.* infuscate.

in·fuse (in-fūz'), *v.t.* [INFUSED (-fūzd'), INFUSING], [ME. *enfusen* < L. *infusus*, pp. of *infundere*, to pour in; *in-*, in + *fundere*, to pour], 1. to pour (a liquid) in, into, or upon. 2. to put (qualities, etc.) in, as by pouring; instill; impart. 3. to fill; pervade; imbue; inspire. 4. to steep or soak so as to extract certain qualities: as, tea is *infused* in hot water. —*SYN.* see **instill.**

in·fu·si·bil·i·ty (in-fū'zə-bil'ə-ti), *n.* the quality of being infusible.

in·fu·si·ble (in-fū'zə-b'l), *adj.* [*in-* (not) + *fusible*], that cannot be fused or melted.

in·fu·si·ble (in-fū'zə-b'l), *adj.* that can be infused.

in·fu·sion (in-fū'zhən), *n.* [< Fr. or L.; Fr. *infusion;* L. *infusio*], 1. the act or process of infusing. 2. something infused; tincture; admixture. 3. the liquid extract that results when a substance is infused in water.

in·fu·sion·ism (in-fū'zhən-iz'm), *n.* the doctrine that the human soul enters the body by divine infusion at conception or birth.

in·fu·sive (in-fū'siv), *adj.* having the quality or power of infusing.

In·fu·so·ri·a (in'fyoo-sôr'i-ə, in'fyoo-sō'ri-ə), *n.pl.* [Mod. L. < L. *infusus;* see INFUSE: so called from their occurrence in infusions exposed to the air], 1. formerly, a large group consisting of most of the microscopic organisms found in decayed organic matter and stagnant water. 2. a class of very small one-celled animals (*Protozoa*) characterized by cilia which permit free movement, found especially in exposed bodies of water.

in·fu·so·ri·al (in'fyoo-sôr'i-əl, in'fyoo-sō'ri-əl), *adj.* of, consisting of, containing, or having the nature of, Infusoria.

infusorial earth, a loose, slightly coherent earth formed of the skeletons of diatoms, a type of algae, and used as an absorbent for nitroglycerin in dynamite: also called *kieselguhr.*

in·fu·so·ri·an (in'fyoo-sôr'i-ən, in'fyoo-sō'ri-ən), *n.* any member of the Infusoria. *adj.* of this class.

‡in fu·tu·ro (in fyoo-tyoor'ō), [L.], in the future.

-ing (iŋ; *in context often* 'ŋ, ən, 'n), a suffix of various origins and meanings: 1. [ME.; AS.], used primarily to form nouns, meaning *related to, made of, descended from*, as in *farthing, atheling:* also used to form diminutives. 2. [ME. *-ing, -yng*, orig. *-end, -and, -ind* < AS. *-ende*, suffix of ppr. of verbs], used to form the present participle, as in *hearing, noticing.* 3. [ME. *-ing, -yng;* AS. *-ung*], added to verbs or, sometimes, nouns, to form verbal nouns meaning: *a) the act* or *an instance of* (a specified verb), as in *talking, digging. b) something produced by the action of* (a specified verb), as in a *painting. c) something that does the action of* (a specified verb), as in a *covering* for her head. *d) material used for* (a specified thing), as in *blanketing, carpeting.*

in·gath·er (in-gath'ẽr), *v.t. & v.i.* to gather in; harvest.

Inge, William Ralph (iŋ), 1860–1954; English theologian and author; dean of St. Paul's, London (1911–1934).

in·gem·i·nate (in-jem'ə-nāt'), *v.t.* [INGEMINATED (-id), INGEMINATING], [< L. *ingeminatus*, pp. of *ingeminare*, to redouble, repeat; see IN- (in) & GEMINATE], to stress or make more forceful by repeating; reiterate.

in·gem·i·na·tion (in-jem'ə-nā'shən), *n.* an ingeminating; repetition.

in·gen·er·ate (in-jen'ẽr-it), *adj.* [L. *ingeneratus*, pp. of *ingenerare;* see ENGENDER], innate; inborn. *v.t.* (in-jen'ə-rāt'), [INGENERATED (-id), INGENERATING], to produce or create within; engender.

in·gen·er·ate (in-jen'ẽr-it), *adj.* [< L. *in-*, not + *generatus;* see GENERATE], not generated or produced, but originating and existing in itself.

in·gen·ious (in-jēn'yəs), *adj.* [Fr. *ingénieux;* L. *ingeniosus*, of good capacity, gifted with genius, ingenious < *ingenium*, innate or natural quality, inclination, ability < *in-*, in + *gignere*, to produce], 1. originally, having genius; having great mental ability. 2. clever, resourceful, original, and inventive. 3. cleverly or originally made or done; characterized by originality, inventiveness, and skill. —*SYN.* see **clever.**

in·gé·nue (an'zhi-nōō'; Fr. an'zhā'nü'), *n.* [*pl.* INGÉNUES (-nōōz'; Fr. -nü')], [Fr., fem. of *ingenu;* L. *ingenuus*, ingenuous], 1. an innocent, inexperienced, unworldly young woman. 2. in the *theater, a)* the role of such a character. *b)* an actress playing such a role.

in·ge·nu·i·ty (in'jə-nōō'ə-ti, in'jə-nū'ə-ti), *n.* [L. *ingenuitas* < *ingenuus* (see INGENUOUS); sense 1 affected by association with *ingenious*], 1. the quality of being ingenious; cleverness, originality, skill, etc. 2. [Rare], the quality of being ingenuous.

in·gen·u·ous (in-jen'ū-əs), *adj.* [L. *ingenuus*, native, inborn, freeborn, noble, frank < *ingignere*, to ingenerate; *in-*, in + *gignere*, to produce], 1. originally, of honorable birth, nature, or character; noble. 2. frank; open; candid; straightforward. 3. simple; artless; innocent; naive; without guile. —*SYN.* see **naive.**

In·ger·soll, Robert Green (iŋ'gẽr-səl, iŋ'gẽr-sôl'), 1833–1899; American lawyer and lecturer; exponent of agnosticism.

in·gest (in-jest'), *v.t.* [< L. *ingestus*, pp. of *ingerere*, to carry, put into; *in-*, into + *gerere*, to carry], to take or put (food, drugs, etc.) into the body for digestion.

in·ges·ta (in-jes'tə), *n.pl.* [L., neut. pl. of *ingestus;* see INGEST], things ingested: sometimes used figuratively.

in·ges·tion (in-jes'chən), *n.* [LL. *ingestio*], the act or process of ingesting.

in·ges·tive (in-jes'tiv), *adj.* serving or tending to ingest.

in·gle (iŋ'g'l), *n.* [Scot.; Gael. *aingeal*, fire], 1. a fire or blaze, especially on a hearth. 2. a fireplace.

in·gle·nook (iŋ'g'l-nook'), *n.* [Chiefly British], a corner by a fireplace; chimney corner: also **ingle nook.**

In·gle·wood (iŋ'g'l-wood'), *n.* a city in southwestern California: pop., 63,000.

in·glo·ri·ous (in-glôr′i-əs, in-glō′ri-əs), *adj.* [L. *inglori-osus;* see IN- (not) & GLORIOUS], 1. not giving, receiving, or deserving glory; shameful; disgraceful; dishonorable. 2. without glory; not famous; little-known; obscure.
in·go·ing (in′gō′iŋ), *adj.* going in; entering.
in·got (iŋ′gət), *n.* [ME., lit., that which is poured in, mold for molten metal < *in,* in + *goten,* pp. of *yeten, geten* (AS. *geotan*), to pour; akin to G. *giessen;* IE. base *ĝheu-, to pour], 1. originally, a mold for casting metal into a bar. 2. a mass of metal cast into a bar or other convenient shape.
in·graft (in-graft′, in-gräft′), *v.t.* to engraft.
in·grain (in-grān′; *also for adj., and for n., always,* in′grān′), *v.t.* [see ENGRAIN], 1. to dye in grain; dye in the fiber before manufacture. 2. to work into the grain or fiber; infuse deeply: chiefly in a figurative sense, and in the past participle. Also **engrain.** *adj.* 1. dyed in grain; dyed before manufacture; thoroughly dyed. 2. made of fiber or yarn dyed before weaving: said of rugs, carpeting, etc. *n.* yarn, carpeting, etc. dyed before manufacture.
in·grained (in-grānd′), *adj.* 1. worked into the grain or fiber; deeply infused or imbued; firmly established: as, *ingrained* principles. 2. inveterate; thoroughgoing: as, an *ingrained* liar.
In·gram (iŋ′grəm), [< Gmc.; cf. AS. *Ing,* OHG. *Inc,* name of a Gmc. sea god, usually identified with Frey & OHG. *hramn,* raven; hence, lit., Ing's raven], a masculine name.
in·grate (in′grāt), *adj.* [ME. & OFr. *ingrat;* L. *ingratus,* unpleasant, disagreeable, ungrateful; *in-,* not + *gratus,* grateful], [Obs.], ungrateful. *n.* an ungrateful person.
in·gra·ti·ate (in-grā′shi-āt′), *v.t.* [INGRATIATED (-id), INGRATIATING], [prob. via It. *ingratiare* (now *ingraziare*) < L. phr. *in gratiam,* for the favor of < *in,* in + *gratia,* favor, agreeableness], to bring (oneself) into another's favor or good graces.
in·gra·ti·a·tion (in-grā′shi-ā′shən), *n.* an ingratiating.
in·gra·ti·a·to·ry (in-grā′shi-ə-tôr′i, in-grā′shi-ə-tō′ri), *adj.* ingratiating or serving to ingratiate.
in·grat·i·tude (in-grat′ə-tōōd′, in-grat′ə-tūd′), *n.* lack of gratitude; ungratefulness.
in·gra·ves·cent (in′grə-ves″nt), *adj.* [L. *ingravescens,* ppr. of *ingravescere,* to become heavier, grow worse < *in-,* in + *gravis,* heavy, severe], becoming more and more severe: said of a disease.
in·gre·di·ent (in-grē′di-ənt), *n.* [Fr. *ingrédient* < L. *ingrediens,* ppr. of *ingredi;* see INGRESS], 1. any of the things that a mixture is made of: as, the *ingredients* of ice cream. 2. a component part, or constituent, of anything. —*SYN.* see **element.**
In·gres, Jean Au·guste Do·mi·nique (zhän ô′güst′ dô′mē′nēk′ *an*′gr′), 1780–1867; French painter.
in·gress (in′gres), *n.* [ME. < L. *ingressus,* pp. of *ingredi,* to step or go into, enter in < *in-,* into + *gradi,* to go], 1. the act of entering. 2. the right or permission to enter. 3. a place or means of entering; entrance.
in·gres·sion (in-gresh′ən), *n.* [L. *ingressio*], the act of entering; ingress.
in·gres·sive (in-gres′iv), *adj.* 1. having to do with ingress. 2. in *grammar,* inceptive.
Ing·rid (iŋ′grid), [< Scand.; ult. < ON. *Ingvi,* name of a Gmc. god (cf. AS. *Ing;* see INGRAM) + *rida,* ride], a feminine name.
in-group (in′grōōp′), *n.* any group of people regarded from the point of view of any of its members as contrasted to all outside groups (*out-groups*).
in·grow·ing (in′grō′iŋ), *adj.* growing within, inward, or into; especially, growing into the flesh: as, an *ingrowing* hair.
in·grown (in′grōn′), *adj.* 1. grown within, inward, or into; especially, grown into the flesh: as, an *ingrown* toenail. 2. inborn; native; innate.
in·growth (in′grōth′), *n.* 1. a growing inward. 2. something ingrowing or ingrown.
in·gui·nal (iŋ′gwi-n′l), *adj.* [L. *inguinalis* < *inguen, inguinis,* the groin], of or near the groin.
in·gui·no- (iŋ′gwi-nō, iŋ′gwi-nə), a combining form meaning *inguinal* or *inguinal and:* also, before a vowel, **inguin-.**
in·gulf (in-gulf′), *v.t.* to engulf.
in·gur·gi·tate (in-gũr′jə-tāt′), *v.t. & v.i.* [INGURGITATED (-id), INGURGITATING], [< L. *ingurgitatus,* pp. of *ingurgitare,* to pour in like a flood, gormandize; see IN- (in) & GURGITATION], to swallow up greedily or in large amounts; gulp; gorge.
in·gur·gi·ta·tion (in-gũr′jə-tā′shən), *n.* [LL. *ingurgitatio*], an ingurgitating or being ingurgitated.
Ing·win·i·an (iŋ-gwin′i-ən), *adj.* [< AS. *Ingwine,* lit., friend of *Ing;* see INGRAM], 1. designating or of a group of Low German peoples whose tutelary deity was *Ing* and who inhabited the Jutland Peninsula and adjacent regions during the Dark Ages: the Angles, Saxons, Jutes, and Frisians were Ingwinian. 2. designating or of the group of closely associated Low German dialects spoken by these peoples. *n.* the Ingwinian language, regarded as the immediate ancestor of Anglo-Saxon and Old Frisian: also called *Anglo-Frisian.*
in·hab·it (in-hab′it), *v.t.* [ME. *enhabiten;* OFr. *enhabiter;* L. *inhabitare; in-,* in + *habitare,* to dwell], to dwell or live in; occupy (a region, house, etc.). *v.i.* [Archaic], to dwell; live.
in·hab·it·a·bil·i·ty (in-hab′i-tə-bil′ə-ti), *n.* the fact or quality of being inhabitable, or habitable.
in·hab·it·a·bil·i·ty (in′hab′i-tə-bil′ə-ti), *n.* [Rare], the fact or quality of being inhabitable, or not habitable.
in·hab·it·a·ble (in-hab′i-tə-b′l), *adj.* that can be inhabited; fit to live in; habitable.
in·hab·it·a·ble (in′hab′i-tə-b′l), *adj.* [Rare], not habitable.
in·hab·it·ance (in-hab′i-təns), *n.* [Obs.], inhabitancy.
in·hab·it·an·cy (in-hab′i-tən-si), *n.* [*pl.* INHABITANCIES (-siz)], [< L. *inhabitans*], 1. an inhabiting or being inhabited. 2. place of residence; home; dwelling.
in·hab·it·ant (in-hab′i-tənt), *n.* [Anglo-Fr.; OFr. < L. *inhabitans,* ppr. of *inhabitare;* see INHABIT], a person or animal that inhabits some specified region, house, etc.; permanent resident.
in·hab·i·ta·tion (in-hab′i-tā′shən), *n.* [ME. *inhabitacioun;* Anglo-Fr. *enhabitacion;* LL. *inhabitatio*], an inhabiting or being inhabited.
in·hab·it·ed (in-hab′i-tid), *adj.* having inhabitants; lived in.
in·hal·ant (in-hāl′ənt), *adj.* [< L. *inhalans*], used in inhalation; inhaling. *n.* 1. a medicine to be inhaled. 2. an inhaler.
in·ha·la·tion (in′hə-lā′shən), *n.* [< pp. of L. *inhalare*], 1. an inhaling. 2. a medicine to be inhaled.
in·hale (in-hāl′), *v.t.* [INHALED (-hāld′), INHALING], [L. *inhalare; in-,* in + *halare,* to breathe], to breathe in; draw into the lungs. *v.i.* to breathe a substance into the lungs; especially, to breathe in tobacco smoke.
in·hal·er (in-hāl′ẽr), *n.* 1. a person who inhales. 2. any apparatus for filtering smoke, dust, etc. out of the air. 3. an apparatus for administering medicinal vapors by inhalation.
in·har·mon·ic (in′här-mon′ik), *adj.* not harmonic; out of harmony; discordant.
in·har·mon·i·cal (in′här-mon′i-k′l), *adj.* inharmonic.
in·har·mo·ni·ous (in′här-mō′ni-əs), *adj.* not harmonious; specifically, *a*) having a disagreeable sound; discordant. *b*) not in accord; in conflict.
in·haul (in′hôl′), *n.* a rope used to haul in a sail.
in·haul·er (in′hôl′ẽr), *n.* an inhaul.
in·here (in-hêr′), *v.i.* [INHERED (-hêrd′), INHERING], [L. *inhaerere,* to stick in, adhere to; *in-,* in + *haerere,* to stick], to be inherent; exist as a quality, characteristic, or right; be innate.
in·her·ence (in-hêr′əns), *n.* the fact or state of inhering or being inherent; specifically, in *philosophy,* the relation of an attribute to its subject.
in·her·en·cy (in-hêr′ən-si), *n.* [*pl.* INHERENCIES (-siz)], 1. inherence. 2. something inherent.
in·her·ent (in-hêr′ənt; *now often* in-her′ənt), *adj.* [L. *inhaerens,* ppr. of *inhaerere;* see INHERE], existing in someone or something as a natural and inseparable quality, characteristic, or right; innate; basic; inborn.
in·her·ent·ly (in-hêr′ənt-li), *adv.* by virtue of its inherent qualities; basically.
in·her·it (in-her′it), *v.t.* [ME. *enheriten;* OFr. *enheriter* < LL. *inhereditare,* to appoint as heir, inherit < L. *in,* in + *heres,* heir], 1. [Obs.], to transfer property to (an heir). 2. to receive (property) by the laws of inheritance. 3. to have (certain characteristics) by heredity. *v.i.* to receive an inheritance; become an heir.
in·her·it·a·bil·i·ty (in-her′i-tə-bil′ə-ti), *n.* the quality or state of being inheritable.
in·her·it·a·ble (in-her′i-tə-b′l), *adj.* [Anglo-Fr. & OFr. *enheritable, inheritable*], 1. capable of inheriting; having the rights of an heir. 2. capable of being inherited.
in·her·it·ance (in-her′i-təns), *n.* [ME. *inheritauns;* Anglo-Fr. & OFr. *enheritance*], 1. the action of inheriting. 2. something inherited or to be inherited; legacy; bequest. 3. ownership by virtue of birthright; right to inherit. 4. any blessing or possession coming as a gift. 5. any characteristic passed on by heredity. —*SYN.* see **heritage.**
inheritance tax, a tax on inherited property.
in·her·i·tor (in-her′i-tẽr), *n.* one that inherits; heir.
in·her·i·tress (in-her′i-tris), *n.* a woman or girl who inherits; heiress.
in·her·i·trix (in-her′i-trix), *n.* [see -TRIX], an inheritress.
in·he·sion (in-hē′zhən), *n.* [LL. *inhaesio* < pp. of L. *inhaerere;* see INHERE], inherence.
in·hib·it (in-hib′it), *v.t.* [< L. *inhibitus,* pp. of *inhibere,* to hold back, restrain, curb < *in-,* in, on + *habere,* to have, hold], 1. to prohibit; forbid; especially, to forbid (a priest, etc.) to perform church functions. 2. to suppress; withhold; check. —*SYN.* see **restrain.**
in·hi·bi·tion (in′hi-bish′ən, in′i-bish′ən), *n.* 1. an in-

fat, āpe, bâre, cär; ten, ēven, hêre, ovẽr; is, bīte; lot, gō, hôrn, tōōl, look; oil, out; up, ūse, fũr; get; joy; yet; chin; she; thin, *th*en; zh, leisure; ŋ, ring; ə for *a* in *ago, e* in *agent, i* in *sanity, o* in *comply, u* in *focus;* ′ as in *able* (ā′b′l); Fr. bål; ë, Fr. coeur; ö, Fr. feu; Fr. mon; ô, Fr. coq; ü, Fr. duc; H, G. ich; kh, G. doch. See pp. x–xii. ‡ foreign; * hypothetical; < derived from.

hibiting or being inhibited. 2. anything that inhibits; especially, a mental or psychological process that restrains or suppresses an action, emotion, or thought.

in·hib·i·tive (in-hib'i-tiv), *adj.* inhibitory.

in·hib·i·tor (in-hib'i-tẽr), *n.* a person or thing that inhibits; especially, any substance that slows or prevents a chemical or organic reaction: also spelled **inhibiter.**

in·hib·i·to·ry (in-hib'ə-tôr'i, in-hib'ə-tō'ri), *adj.* [ML. *inhibitorius* < L. *inhibitus*], of, or having the nature of, inhibition; inhibiting.

‡in hoc sig·no vin·ces (in hok sig'nō vin'sēz), [L.], in this sign (i.e., the Cross) you will conquer: motto of Constantine the Great: abbreviated **I.H.S.**

in·hos·pi·ta·ble (in-hos'pi-tə-b'l; *occas.* in'hos-pit'ə-b'l), *adj.* 1. not hospitable; not offering hospitality to visitors or guests. 2. not offering protection or refuge; barren; forbidding: said of a country, region, etc.

in·hos·pi·ta·bly (in-hos'pi-tə-bli; *occas.* in'hos-pit'ə-bli), *adv.* in an inhospitable manner.

in·hos·pi·tal·i·ty (in'hos-pə-tal'ə-ti, in-hos'pə-tal'ə-ti), *n.* lack of hospitality; inhospitable treatment.

in·hu·man (in-hū'mən), *adj.* [Fr. *inhumain;* L. *inhumanus*], not human; not having the characteristics considered normal to human beings; especially, unfeeling, hard-hearted, cruel, barbarous, etc. —*SYN.* see **cruel.**

in·hu·mane (in'hyoo-mān'), *adj.* [*in-* (not) + *humane;* also older sp. for *inhuman*], not humane; unmoved by the suffering of others; cruel, brutal, unkind, etc.

in·hu·man·i·ty (in'hyoo-man'ə-ti), *n.* [< Fr or L.; Fr. *inhumanité;* L. *inhumanitas*], 1. the quality or condition of being inhuman or inhumane. 2. [*pl.* INHUMANITIES (-tiz)], an inhuman act or remark.

in·hu·ma·tion (in'hyoo-mā'shən), *n.* [< *inhume* + *-ation*], burial; interment.

in·hume (in-hūm'), *v.t.* [INHUMED (-hūmd'), INHUMING], [L. *inhumare* < *in-*, in + *humus*, earth, ground], to bury (a dead body); inter.

in·im·i·cal (in-im'i-k'l), *adj.* [LL. *inimicalis* < L. *inimicus*, hostile, enemy < *in-*, not + *amicus*, friend], 1. like an enemy; hostile; unfriendly. 2. in opposition; adverse; unfavorable: as, acts *inimical* to peace.

in·im·i·ta·bil·i·ty (in-im'i-tə-bil'ə-ti), *n.* the quality or state of being inimitable.

in·im·i·ta·ble (in-im'i-tə-b'l), *adj.* [L. *inimitabilis;* see IN- (not) & IMITABLE], that cannot be imitated or matched; too good to be equaled or copied.

in·im·i·ta·bly (in-im'i-tə-bli), *adv.* so as to be inimitable.

in·i·on (in'i-ən), *n.* [Mod. L.; Gr. *inion*, the back of the head < *is, inos*, sinew, muscle, lit., strength], the bulging part at the rear of the human skull.

in·iq·ui·tous (in-ik'wə-təs), *adj.* showing iniquity; wicked; unjust. —*SYN.* see **vicious.**

in·iq·ui·ty (in-ik'wə-ti), *n.* [ME. *iniquite;* OFr. *iniquité;* L. *iniquitas* < *iniquus*, unequal < *in-*, not + *aequus*, level, equal], 1. lack of righteousness or justice; wickedness; sin. 2. [*pl.* INIQUITIES (-tiz)], a wicked, unjust, or unrighteous act.

in·i·tial (i-nish'əl), *adj.* [< Fr. or L.; Fr. *initial;* L. *initialis* < *initium*, a beginning < *inire*, to go into, enter upon, begin; *in-*, into, in + *ire*, to go], 1. having to do with, indicating, or occurring at the beginning: as, the *initial* stage of a disease. 2. designating the first letter or syllable of a word. *n.* a letter beginning a word; specifically, *a*) an extra-large capital letter at the start of a printed paragraph, chapter, etc. *b*) the first letter of a name. *v.t.* [INITIALED or INITIALLED (-əld), INITIALING or INITIALLING], to mark or sign with one's initial or initials. Abbreviated **init.**

in·i·tial·ly (i-nish'əl-i), *adv.* at the beginning; at first.

in·i·ti·ate (i-nish'i-āt'; *for adj. & n., usually* i-nish'i-it), *v.t.* [INITIATED (-id), INITIATING], [< L. *initiatus*, pp. of *initiare*, to enter upon, initiate < *initium;* see INITIAL], 1. to bring into practice or use; introduce by first doing or using. 2. to teach the fundamentals of some subject to; help (someone) to begin doing something. 3. to admit as a member into a fraternity, club, etc., especially through use of secret ceremony or rites. *adj.* 1. initiated. 2. beginning; commenced; in the first stage. *n.* a person who has recently been, or is about to be, initiated. —*SYN.* see **begin.**

in·i·ti·a·tion (i-nish'i-ā'shən), *n.* [L. *initiatio*], 1. an initiating or being initiated. 2. the ceremonies or rites by which a person is initiated into a fraternity, etc.

in·i·ti·a·tive (i-nish'i-ə-tiv, i-nish'ə-tiv, i-nish'i-ā'tiv), *adj.* of, or having the nature of, initiation; introductory; initial. *n.* 1. the action of taking the first step or move; responsibility for beginning or originating. 2. the characteristic of originating new ideas or methods; ability to think and act without being urged; enterprise. 3. *a*) the right of a legislature to introduce new legislation on some specified matter. *b*) the right of a group of citizens to introduce a matter for legislation either to the legislature or directly to the voters. *c*) the procedure by which such matters are introduced, usually a petition signed by a specified percentage of the voters.

in·i·ti·a·tor (i-nish'i-ā'tẽr), *n.* [LL.], a person or thing that initiates.

in·i·ti·a·to·ry (i-nish'i-ə-tôr'i, i-nish'i-ə-tō'ri), *adj.* 1. beginning; introductory; initial. 2. of or used in an initiation: as, *initiatory* ceremonies.

in·ject (in-jekt'), *v.t.* [< L. *injectus*, pp. of *injicere*, to throw, cast, or put in < *in-*, in + *jacere*, to throw], 1. to force or drive (a fluid) into some passage or cavity; especially, to introduce or force (a liquid) into some part of the body by means of a syringe, hypodermic needle, etc. 2. to fill (a cavity, etc.) by injection. 3. to introduce or throw in a remark, etc.; interject.

in·jec·tion (in-jek'shən), *n.* [L. *injectio*], 1. an injecting. 2. something injected; especially, a liquid injected into the body. 3. congestion.

in·jec·tor (in-jek'tẽr), *n.* a person or thing that injects; especially, a device for injecting water into a steam boiler.

in·ju·di·cious (in'jōō-dish'əs), *adj.* [*in-* (not) + *judicious*], showing poor judgment; not discreet, wise, or prudent.

in·junc·tion (in-juŋk'shən), *n.* [LL. *injunctio;* see IN- (in) & JUNCTION], 1. an enjoining; bidding; command. 2. something enjoined; command; order. 3. a legal order from a court prohibiting a person or group from carrying out a given action, or ordering a given action to be done.

in·jure (in'jẽr), *v.t.* [INJURED (-jẽrd), INJURING], [Fr. *injurier;* L. *injuriari* < *injuria;* see INJURY], 1. to do physical harm or damage to; hurt. 2. to wrong or offend deeply; be unjust to.

SYN.—**injure** implies the marring of the appearance, health, soundness, etc. of a person or thing (*injured* pride); **harm** more strongly suggests the pain or distress caused (he wouldn't *harm* a fly); **damage** stresses the loss, as in value, usefulness, etc., resulting from an injury (*damaged* goods); **hurt** implies a wounding physically or emotionally or a causing of any kind of harm or damage (the rumors *hurt* his business); to **impair** something is to cause it to deteriorate in quality or to lessen in value, strength, etc. (*impaired* hearing); **spoil** implies such serious impairment of a thing as to destroy its value, usefulness, etc. (the canned food was *spoiled*).

in·ju·ri·ous (in-joor'i-əs), *adj.* 1. injuring or likely to cause injury; harmful; damaging. 2. offensive; insulting; abusive; slanderous or libelous.

in·ju·ry (in'jẽr-i), *n.* [*pl.* INJURIES (-iz)], [ME. & Anglo-Fr. *injurie;* OFr. *injure;* L. *injuria* < *injurius*, wrongful, unjust < *in-*, not + *jus, juris*, right, justice], 1. physical harm or damage to a person, property, etc. 2. unjust treatment; violation of rights; offense. 3. an injurious act. 4. [Obs.], insult. —*SYN.* see **injustice.**

in·jus·tice (in-jus'tis), *n.* [ME.; OFr.; L. *injustitia*], 1. the quality of being unjust or unfair; lack of justice; wrong. 2. an unjust act; injury.

SYN.—**injustice** implies unjust treatment of another or a violation of his rights; **injury** and **wrong** have special application to injustices for the redress or punishment of which legal action can be taken, both applying to a violation of the private rights of an individual, and **wrong** alone, to crimes and misdemeanors which affect the whole community; a **grievance** is a circumstance considered by the person affected to be unjust and ground for complaint or resentment.—*ANT.* justice.

ink (iŋk), *n.* [ME. *enke;* OFr. *enque;* LL. *encaustum;* Gr. *enkauston*, purple or red ink < *enkaustos*, burnt in < *enkaiein*, to burn in; *en-*, in + *kaiein*, to burn], 1. a colored liquid used for writing, drawing, etc. 2. a sticky, colored paste used in printing; printer's ink. 3. a dark, liquid secretion squirted out by cuttlefish, etc. to cloud the water for protection. *v.t.* 1. to cover with ink; spread ink on. 2. to mark or color with ink.

ink·ber·ry (iŋk'ber'i), *n.* [*pl.* INKBERRIES (-iz)], 1. an evergreen holly growing in eastern North America. 2. the pokeweed. 3. the dark-purple or black fruit of either of these plants.

ink·er (iŋk'ẽr), *n.* a person or thing that inks; specifically, in *printing*, a roller for spreading ink on type.

ink·horn (iŋk'hôrn'), *n.* a small container made of horn or other material, formerly used to hold ink.

ink·i·ness (iŋk'i-nis), *n.* 1. the condition of being covered with ink. 2. blackness; darkness.

in·kle (iŋ'k'l), *n.* [prob. < obs. D. *inckel* (D. *enkel*), single (with reference to the narrow width)], 1. a kind of braided linen tape. 2. the thread or yarn from which this is made.

ink·ling (iŋk'liŋ), *n.* [< ME. *inclen*, to give an inkling of], 1. a hint; suggestion; slight indication. 2. a vague idea or notion; suspicion.

ink·stand (iŋk'stand'), *n.* 1. a small stand holding an inkwell, pens, etc. 2. an inkwell.

ink·well (iŋk'wel'), *n.* a container for holding ink, usually set in a desk, inkstand, etc.

ink·wood (iŋk'wood'), *n.* a tropical tree of the soapberry family, having dark wood and growing in Florida and the West Indies.

ink·y (iŋ'ki), *adj.* [INKIER (-ki-ẽr), INKIEST (-ki-ist)], 1. like ink in color; dark; black. 2. colored, marked, stained, or covered with ink.

in·lace (in-lās'), *v.t.* to enlace.

in·laid (in'lād', in-lād'), *adj.* [pp. of *inlay*], 1. set in a surface so as to form a decoration, usually level with the surface. 2. decorated with material set in the surface.

in·land (in′lənd; *for n. & adv., also* in′land′), *adj.* [*in, adv.* + *land*], 1. of, located in, or confined to the interior of a country or region; away from the coast or border. 2. carried on or operating within the borders of a country; domestic. *n.* [ME.; AS. *in-lande*], the interior of a country or region; inland areas. *adv.* into or toward the interior; away from the coast or border.
in·land·er (in′lən-dẽr), *n.* a person living inland.
Inland Sea, the body of water surrounded by the Japanese islands of Honshu, Shikoku, and Kyushu.
in·law (in-lô′), *v.t.* [ME. *inlawen; AS. inlagian;* see IN & LAW], to restore the benefits and protection of the law to (an outlaw): opposed to *outlaw.*
in-law (in′lô′), *n.* [contr. < *mother-in-law,* etc.], [Colloq.], a relative by marriage.
in·lay (in-lā′; *also, and for n., always,* in′lā′), *v.t.* [INLAID (in-lād′, in′lād′), INLAYING], [*in-* (in) + *lay, v.*], 1. to set (pieces of wood, gold, etc.) in a surface so as to form a decoration, usually level with the surface. 2. to decorate with pieces of wood, gold, etc. set in the surface. *n.* [*pl.* INLAYS (-lāz′)], 1. inlaid decoration or material. 2. a filling for a tooth, consisting of a solid mass of metal, porcelain, etc., made to fit into a cavity and then cemented in.
in·let (in-let′; *for n.,* in′let), *v.t.* [INLET, INLETTING], [ME. *inletan;* see IN- (in) & LET (to leave)], to inlay or insert. *n.* [ME. *inlate* < the *v.*], 1. *a)* a narrow strip of water extending into a body of land from a river, lake, ocean, etc.; small bay or creek. *b)* a narrow strip of water between islands. 2. an entrance or opening, as to a culvert. 3. something let in, inlaid, or inserted.
in·li·er (in′lī′ẽr), *n.* [*in-* (in) + *lie* (to recline) + *-er*], an older rock formation entirely surrounded in outcrop by younger rock.
‡**in loc.cit.,** *in loco citato,* [L.], in the place cited.
‡**in lo·co pa·ren·tis** (in lō′kō pə-ren′tis), [L.], in the place of a parent: said of a person acting temporarily with parental authority.
in·ly (in′li), *adj.* [ME. *inliche;* AS. *inlice;* see IN- (in) & -LY], [Obs.], inward; felt within. *adv.* [Poetic], 1. inwardly; within. 2. deeply; intimately.
in·mate (in′māt′), *n.* [*in-* (in) + *mate;* 1st element ? < *inn*], 1. a person living with others in the same building; occupant. 2. a person lodged with others, and often confined, in an institution, asylum, etc. 3. an inhabitant.
‡**in me·di·as res** (in mē′di-əs rēz), [L.], into the midst of things; in the middle of the action rather than at the beginning, as in commencing an epic.
in me·mo·ri·am (in′ mə-môr′i-əm, in′ mi-mō′ri-am′), [L.], in memory (of): put on tombstones, in obituary notices, etc.
in·mesh (in-mesh′), *v.t.* to enmesh.
in-mi·grant (in′mī′grənt), *adj.* coming in from another region of the same country: as, *in-migrant* workers. *n.* an in-migrant person or animal.
in-mi·grate (in′mī′grāt), *v.i.* [IN-MIGRATED (-id), IN-MIGRATING], to come in from another region of the same country.
in-mi·gra·tion (in′mī-grā′shən), *n.* an in-migrating.
in·most (in′mōst′, in′məst), *adj.* [ME. *innemest;* AS. *innemest;* see IN- (in) & -MOST], 1. located farthest within; deepest in from the edge or outside; innermost. 2. most intimate or secret: as, *inmost* thoughts.
Inn (in), *n.* a river flowing through Switzerland, Austria, and Germany into the Danube: length, 320 mi.
inn (in), *n.* [AS. *inn* (akin to ON. *inni*) < *inn, inne, adv.,* within; cf. IN], 1. originally, any dwelling or lodging. 2. *a)* an establishment or building providing food, drink, bedrooms, etc. for travelers; hotel, especially one in the country or along a highway. *b)* a restaurant or tavern. Now usually only in the names of such places. 3. formerly, a house providing board and lodging for students: as, an *Inn of Court.* *v.t. & v.i.* to lodge at an inn.
in·nards (in′ẽrdz), *n.pl.* [altered < *inwards*], [Dial.], 1. the internal organs of the body; viscera; entrails. 2. the inner parts of anything.
in·nate (in′āt, i-nāt′), *adj.* [L. *innatus,* pp. of *innasci,* to be born in, originate in; *in-,* in + *nasci,* to be born], natural; inborn; not acquired.
SYN.—**innate** and **inborn** are often interchangeable, but **innate** has more extensive connotations, describing that which belongs to something as part of its nature or constitution, and **inborn,** the simpler term, more specifically suggesting qualities so much a part of one's nature as to seem to have been born in or with one (*inborn* modesty); **inbred** refers to qualities which are deeply ingrained by breeding (an *inbred* love of learning); **congenital** implies existence at or from one's birth, specifically as a result of prenatal environment (*congenital* blindness); **hereditary** implies acquirement of characteristics by transmission genetically from parents or ancestors (*hereditary* blondness).
in·ner (in′ẽr), *adj.* [ME.; AS. *innerra,* compar. of *inne,* within, in], 1. located farther within; interior; internal. 2. of the mind or spirit. 3. more intimate or secret: as, *inner* emotions. *n.* 1. the inside. 2. the circle of a target next to the bull's-eye. 3. a shot that hits this.
inner circle, a small group of people who control or influence customs, thought, etc.; ruling coterie.
Inner City, the old walled section of Peking, China, containing the Forbidden City and the foreign legations.
Inner Light, in Quaker doctrine, a guiding influence resulting from the presence of God in the soul of the individual: also **Inner Word.**
inner man, 1. originally, one's spiritual being; mind or soul. 2. humorously, one's stomach or palate.
Inner Mongolia, a region in Mongolia, made up of the Chinese provinces of Jehol, Chahar, Suijuan, and Ningsia: it is southeast of Outer Mongolia.
in·ner·most (in′ẽr-mōst′, in′ẽr-məst), *adj.* [< *inmost,* after *inner*], inmost; farthest in.
in·ner·spring mattress (in′ẽr-spriŋ′), a mattress with built-in coil springs for continued resilience.
Inner Temple, an Inn of Court.
in·ner·vate (i-nũr′vāt, in′ẽr-vāt′), *v.t.* [INNERVATED (-id), INNERVATING], [< *in-* (in) + *nerve* + *-ate*], 1. to supply (a part of the body) with nerves. 2. to stimulate to movement or action.
in·ner·va·tion (in′ẽr-vā′shən), *n.* [< *innervate* + *-ion*], 1. the distribution of nerves to a part of the body. 2. the sending out of necessary nerve impulses to some part of the body.
in·nerve (i-nũrv′, in-nũrv′), *v.t.* to innervate.
In·ness, George (in′is), 1825–1894; American painter.
in·ning (in′iŋ), *n.* [ME. *inninge;* AS. *innung,* gerund of *innian,* to get in, put in], 1. *a)* a taking in, enclosing, or reclaiming, as of wasteland. *b) pl.* lands reclaimed, as from the sea. 2. in *baseball* and (*often pl.*) *cricket, a)* the period of play in which a team has a turn at bat, completed in baseball by three outs. *b)* a numbered round of play in which both teams have a turn at bat: a baseball game normally consists of nine innings. 3. *often pl.* the time a person or political party is in power; period of or opportunity for action, expression, etc.: as, the election gave him his *inning.*
inn·keep·er (in′kēp′ẽr), *n.* the proprietor of an inn.
in·no·cence (in′ə-s′ns), *n.* [ME.; OFr.; L. *innocentia*], 1. the quality or state of being innocent; specifically, *a)* freedom from sin, evil, or guilt. *b)* freedom from knowledge of evil. *c)* freedom from guile or cunning; simplicity. *d)* silliness; foolishness. *e)* incapability of harming, injuring, or corrupting. 2. an innocent person. 3. the bluet, a meadow plant with bluish or white flowers, common in the United States.
in·no·cen·cy (in′ə-s′n-si), *n.* 1. innocence (senses 1 & 2). 2. [*pl.* INNOCENCIES (-siz)], an instance of this.
in·no·cent (in′ə-s′nt), *adj.* [ME.; OFr.; L. *innocens; in-,* not + *nocens,* ppr. of *nocere,* to do wrong to], 1. free from sin, evil, or guilt; specifically, *a)* doing or thinking nothing morally wrong; pure. *b)* not guilty of a specific crime or offense; guiltless. *c)* free from evil or harmful effect or cause; that cannot harm, injure, or corrupt; hence, *d)* not malignant; benign: as, an *innocent* tumor. 2. *a)* knowing no evil. *b)* without guile or cunning; artless; simple. *c)* foolish; ignorant. *n.* 1. a person knowing no evil or sin, as a child. 2. a simple-minded person; fool. 3. *pl.* bluets.
In·no·cent II (in′ə-s′nt), (born *Gregorio Papareschi*), ?–1143; Pope (1130–1143).
Innocent III, (born *Giovanni Lotario de' Conti*), 1161–1216; Pope (1198–1216).
Innocent IV, (born *Sinibaldo de' Fieschi*), ?–1254; Pope (1243–1254).
Innocent XI, (born *Benedetto Odescalchi*), 1611–1689; Pope (1676–1689).
in·noc·u·ous (i-nok′ū-əs), *adj.* [L. *innocuus; in-,* not + *nocuus,* harmful < *nocere,* to harm, injure], that cannot injure or harm; without bad effect; harmless.
Inn of Court, [cf. INN, 3], 1. one of the four London legal societies having the exclusive right to admit persons to practice at the bar. 2. one of the four groups of buildings (*Inner Temple, Middle Temple, Lincoln's Inn,* and *Gray's Inn*) belonging to these societies.
in·nom·i·nate (i-nom′ə-nit, in-nom′ə-nit), *adj.* [LL. *innominatus;* see IN- (not) & NOMINATE], 1. not named; anonymous. 2. having no specific name.
innominate bone, either of the two large, flat bones that, together with the sacrum, make up the pelvis; hipbone: it is formed of three bones, the ilium, ischium, and pubis, which become fused in the adult.
in·no·vate (in′ə-vāt′), *v.i.* [INNOVATED (-id), INNOVATING], [< L. *innovatus,* pp. of *innovare,* to renew; *in-,* in + *novare,* to alter, make new < *novus,* new], to introduce new methods, devices, etc.; make changes; bring in innovations. *v.t.* [Rare], to bring in as an innovation.
in·no·va·tion (in′ə-vā′shən), *n.* [LL. *innovatio*], 1. the act or process of innovating. 2. something newly introduced; new method, custom, device, etc.; change in the way of doing things.

in·no·va·tion·al (in'ə-vā'shən-'l), ***adj.*** of or characterized by innovation.

in·no·va·tion·ist (in'ə-vā'shən-ist), ***n.*** a person who believes in and supports innovations.

in·no·va·tive (in'ə-vā'tiv), ***adj.*** causing, or characterized by, innovation.

in·no·va·tor (in'ə-vā'tẽr), ***n.*** a person who innovates; maker of changes or introducer of new methods, etc.

in·nox·ious (i-nok'shəs, in-nok'shəs), ***adj.*** [L. *innoxius*], not noxious; harmless; innocuous.

Inns·bruck (inz'brook; G. ins'brook), ***n.*** a city in the Tyrol, Austria: pop., 99,000 (est. 1948).

in·nu·en·do (in'ū-en'dō), [L., by nodding to, abl. of gerund of *innuere*, to nod to, intimate, hint; *in-*, in + *-nuere* (in comp.), to nod], meaning; that is to say: Latin formula for introducing explanatory material in legal documents; hence, ***n.*** [*pl.* INNUENDOES (-dōz)], 1. in *law*, the explanatory material so introduced; especially, that part of a complaint in an action for libel or slander which explains the expressions alleged to be libelous or slanderous. 2. an indirect remark, gesture, or reference, usually implying something derogatory; hint; insinuation.

in·nu·mer·a·ble (i-nōō'mẽr-ə-b'l, in-nū'mẽr-ə-b'l), ***adj.*** [ME.; L. *innumerabilis;* see IN- (not) & NUMERABLE], too numerous to be counted; very many; countless. —***SYN.*** see **many.**

in·nu·mer·a·bly (i-nōō'mẽr-ə-bli, in-nū'mẽr-ə-bli), ***adv.*** so as to be innumerable; in very great numbers.

in·nu·mer·ous (i-nōō'mẽr-əs, in-nū'mẽr-əs), ***adj.*** [Poetic], innumerable.

in·nu·tri·tion (in'nōō-trish'ən, in'ū-trish'ən), ***n.*** lack of nutrition.

in·nu·tri·tious (in'nōō-trish'əs, in'ū-trish'əs), ***adj.*** not nutritious; providing little or no nourishment.

in·ob·serv·ance (in'əb-zũr'vəns), ***n.*** 1. lack of attention; disregard. 2. failure to observe a custom, rule, etc.

in·ob·serv·ant (in'əb-zũr'vənt), ***adj.*** showing inobservance.

in·oc·u·la·bil·i·ty (in-ok'yoo-lə-bil'ə-ti), ***n.*** the quality or state of being inoculable.

in·oc·u·la·ble (in-ok'yoo-lə-b'l), ***adj.*** [< *inoculate* + *-able*], 1. that can be communicated by inoculation. 2. that can be infected with a disease by inoculation. 3. that may be used in inoculation.

in·oc·u·lant (in-ok'yoo-lənt), ***n.*** an inoculum.

in·oc·u·late (in-ok'yoo-lāt'), ***v.t.*** [INOCULATED (-id), INOCULATING], [ME. *enoculate(n)* < L. *inoculatus*, pp. of *inoculare*, to engraft an eye or bud from one plant to another, inoculate < *in-*, in + *oculus*, an eye, bud], 1. originally, *a*) to insert (a bud or shoot of one plant) into the stem or trunk of another. *b*) to insert a bud or shoot of one plant into (the stem or trunk of another). 2. *a*) to inject a serum, vaccine, etc. into, especially in order to prevent, cure, or experiment with disease, usually so as to make immune. *b*) to inject (a disease virus, etc.) into by inoculation. 3. to put or implant bacteria, etc. into (soil, a culture medium, etc.). 4. to introduce ideas, etc. into the mind of; imbue; infect.

in·oc·u·la·tion (in-ok'yoo-lā'shən), ***n.*** [Late ME. *inoculacion;* L. *inoculatio*], an inoculating; especially, *a*) the injection of a disease virus into the body, usually to cause a mild form of the disease and build up immunity to it. *b*) the putting of bacteria, serum, etc. into soil, a culture medium, etc.

in·oc·u·la·tive (in-ok'yoo-lā'tiv), ***adj.*** of or characterized by inoculation.

in·oc·u·la·tor (in-ok'yoo-lā'tẽr), ***n.*** a person or thing that inoculates.

in·oc·u·lum (in-ok'yoo-ləm), ***n.*** [Mod. L.], material used in making an inoculation, as bacteria, viruses, spores, etc.: also **inoculant.**

in·o·dor·ous (in-ō'dẽr-əs), ***adj.*** [L. *inodorus*], not odorous; having no odor.

in·of·fen·sive (in'ə-fen'siv), ***adj.*** not offensive; not objectionable; causing no harm, discomfort, or annoyance.

in·of·fi·cious (in'ə-fish'əs), ***adj.*** [L. *inofficiosus*, undutiful; see IN- (not) & OFFICIOUS], 1. without office or function; inoperative. 2. [Obs.], disobliging. 3. in *law*, showing neglect of or opposition to moral duty.

‡**in om·ni·a pa·ra·tus** (in om'ni-ə pə-rā'təs), [L.], prepared for all things; ready for anything.

I·nö·nü, Is·met (is-met' ē'nö-nü), 1884– ; Turkish statesman; president of Turkey (1938–1950).

in·op·er·a·ble (in-op'ẽr-ə-b'l), ***adj.*** not operable; specifically, *a*) not practicable. *b*) in *surgery*, not suitable to be operated on: as, an *inoperable* cancer.

in·op·er·a·tive (in-op'ə-rā'tiv, in-op'ẽr-ə-tiv), ***adj.*** not operative; not working; not functioning; without effect.

in·op·por·tune (in-op'ẽr-tōōn', in'op-ẽr-tūn'), ***adj.*** [L. *inopportunus*], not opportune; coming or happening at a poor time; not appropriate.

in·or·di·na·cy (in-ôr'd'n-ə-si), ***n.*** 1. the quality or condition of being inordinate. 2. [*pl.* INORDINACIES (-siz)], an inordinate act or practice.

in·or·di·nate (in-ôr'd'n-it), ***adj.*** [ME. *inordinat;* L. *inordinatus;* see IN- (not) & ORDINATE], 1. disordered; not regulated. 2. without restraint or moderation; excessive; immoderate. —***SYN.*** see **excessive.**

in·or·di·nate·ly (in-ôr'd'n-it-li), ***adv.*** to an inordinate degree; excessively.

in·or·gan·ic (in'ôr-gan'ik), ***adj.*** not organic; specifically, *a*) designating or composed of matter that is not animal or vegetable; not characterized by vital processes; not having the organized structure of living things. *b*) not like an organism in structure; without design, relation, and co-ordination of parts. *c*) designating or of any chemical compound not classified as organic: most inorganic compounds do not contain carbon and are derived from mineral sources. *d*) designating or of the branch of chemistry dealing with these compounds. Abbreviated **inorg.**

in·or·gan·i·cal·ly (in'ôr-gan'i-k'l-i, in'ôr-gan'ik-li), ***adv.*** so as to be inorganic.

in·or·gan·i·za·tion (in-ôr'gən-i-zā'shən, in-ôr'gən-ī-zā'shən), ***n.*** lack of organization.

in·os·cu·late (in-os'kyoo-lāt'), ***v.t. & v.i.*** [INOSCULATED (-id), INOSCULATING], [*in-* (in) + *osculate*], 1. *a*) to join together by openings at the ends: said of arteries, ducts, etc. *b*) to intertwine: said of vines, etc. 2. to join, blend, or unite in an intimate manner.

in·os·cu·la·tion (in-os'kyoo-lā'shən), ***n.*** an inosculating or being inosculated.

in·o·site (in'ə-sīt'), ***n.*** inositol.

in·o·si·tol (i-nō'si-tōl', i-nō'si-tol'), ***n.*** [< Gr. *is*, *inos*, muscle, fiber; + *-ite* + *-ol*], a crystalline alcohol, $C_6H_6(OH)_6$, existing in several isomeric forms and found in both plant and animal tissues: one of the B complex vitamins, sometimes erroneously called *muscle sugar.*

in·ox·i·dize (in-ok'sə-dīz'), ***v.t.*** to prevent oxidation in.

in·pa·tient (in'pā'shənt), ***n.*** a person who is lodged and fed, as well as given treatment, in a hospital, clinic, etc.: opposed to *outpatient.*

‡**in per·pe·tu·um** (in pẽr-pet'ū-əm), [L.], forever.

‡**in per·so·nam** (in pẽr-sō'nam), [L., against the person], in *law*, designating an action or judgment against a person, as distinguished from one against property (*in rem*).

‡**in pet·to** (ēn pet'tô), [It.], 1. literally, in the breast; in the heart. 2. secretly; not revealed: said of cardinals appointed by the Pope but not named in consistory.

in·phase (in'fāz'), ***adj.*** in *electricity*, being of the same phase: said of currents.

‡**in pos·se** (in pos'i), [L.], in possibility; only potentially.

in·pour (in-pôr', in-pōr'), ***v.i. & v.t.*** to pour in.

in·put (in'poot'), ***n.*** what is put in, as electric current or other power put into a machine.

in·quest (in'kwest), ***n.*** [ME. & OFr. *enqueste;* LL. **inquaesita*, fem. of **inquaesitus*, pp. of **inquaerere;* see INQUIRE], 1. a judicial inquiry, especially when held before a jury, as a coroner's investigation of a death. 2. the jury or group holding such an inquiry. 3. the verdict of such an inquiry. —***SYN.*** see **investigation.**

in·qui·et (in-kwī'ət), ***adj.*** not quiet; uneasy; disturbed.

in·qui·e·tude (in-kwī'ə-tōōd', in-kwī'ə-tūd'), ***n.*** [Fr. *inquiétude;* LL. *inquietudo*], restlessness; uneasiness.

in·qui·line (in'kwi-lin', in'kwi-lin), ***n.*** [L. *inquilinus*, inhabitant < *in-*, in + *colere*, to dwell], an animal, usually an insect, that lives in the nest or abode of another; commensal.

in·quire (in-kwīr'), ***v.i.*** [INQUIRED (-kwīrd'), INQUIRING], [ME. *enquere;* OFr. *enquerre;* LL. **inquaerere;* L. *inquirere* < *in-*, into + *quaerere*, to seek], 1. to seek information; ask a question or questions. 2. to carry out an examination or investigation (usually with *into*). ***v.t.*** to seek information about: as, he *inquired* the way. Also spelled **enquire.** —***SYN.*** see **ask.**

inquire after, to pay respects by asking about the health of (someone).

inquire for, 1. to ask to see (someone). 2. to try to get by asking.

in·quir·y (in-kwīr'i, in'kwə-ri), ***n.*** [*pl.* INQUIRIES (-iz, -riz)], [earlier *enquery* < ME. *enquere*], 1. the act of inquiring. 2. an investigation or examination. 3. a question; query. Also **enquiry.**

in·qui·si·tion (in'kwə-zish'ən), ***n.*** [ME. *inquicisioun;* OFr.; L. *inquisitio* < *inquisitus*, pp. of *inquirere*], 1. an inquiring; inquiry; investigation. 2. in *law*, an inquest. 3. [I-], in the *Roman Catholic Church*, *a*) a search for and punishment of nonbelievers or heretics. *b*) the general tribunal established in the 13th century for the discovery and suppression of heresy and the punishment of heretics: also called the *Holy Office.* *c*) the activities of this tribunal. 4. any strict or arbitrary suppression or punishment of those believed to be dangerous to the ruling powers. —***SYN.*** see **investigation.**

in·qui·si·tion·al (in'kwə-zish'ən-'l), ***adj.*** of, like, or characterized by an inquisition.

in·qui·si·tion·ist (in'kwə-zish'ən-ist), ***n.*** an inquisitor.

in·quis·i·tive (in-kwiz'ə-tiv), ***adj.*** [OFr. *inquisitif;* LL. *inquisitivus* < L. *inquisitus*, pp. of *inquirere;* see INQUIRE], 1. inclined to ask many questions or seek information; eager to learn. 2. asking more questions than is necessary or proper; unnecessarily curious; prying. ***n.*** an inquisitive person. —***SYN.*** see **curious.**

in·quis·i·tor (in-kwiz'ə-tẽr), ***n.*** [OFr. *inquisiteur;* L. *inquisitor* < *inquisitus*, pp.; see INQUIRE], 1. an official whose work is examining, or making an inquisition;

investigator. 2. [I-], an official of the Inquisition.
in·quis·i·to·ri·al (in-kwiz'ə-tôr'i-əl, in'kwiz-ə-tō'ri-əl), *adj.* [< ML. *inquisitorius*], 1. of, or having the nature of, an inquisitor or an inquisition. 2. inquisitive; unnecessarily or unpleasantly curious.
‡**in re** (in rē'), [L.], in the matter (of); concerning.
‡**in rem** (in rem), [L., against the thing], *in law*, designating an action or judgment against property, as distinguished from one against a person (*in personam*).
‡**I.N.R.I.**, *Iesus Nazarenus, Rex Iudaeorum*, [L.], Jesus of Nazareth, King of the Jews.
in·road (in'rōd'), *n.* [*in-* (in) + *road* (in obs. sense of "riding")], 1. a sudden invasion or raid. 2. *usually in pl.* any injurious or wasting encroachment: as, these long hours will make *inroads* on your health.
in·rush (in'rush'), *n.* a rushing in; inflow; influx.
INS, I.N.S., International News Service: see **United Press International.**
ins., 1. inches. 2. inscribed. 3. insulated. 4. insurance.
‡**in sae·cu·la sae·cu·lo·rum** (in sek'ū-lə sek'ū-lō'rəm), [L., into ages of ages], for ever and ever; for all eternity.
in·sal·i·vate (in-sal'ə-vāt'), *v.t.* [INSALIVATED (-id), INSALIVATING], [*in-* (in) + *salivate*], to mix (food) with saliva in chewing.
in·sal·i·va·tion (in-sal'ə-vā'shən), *n.* an insalivating.
in·sa·lu·bri·ous (in'sə-lōō'bri-əs, in'sə-lū'bri-əs), *adj.* [L. *insalubris*], not salubrious; not healthful; unwholesome.
in·sa·lu·bri·ty (in'sə-lōō'brə-ti, in'sə-lū'brə-ti), *n.* [Fr. *insalubrité*], the quality or state of being insalubrious.
in·sane (in-sān'), *adj.* [L. *insanus*], 1. not sane; mentally ill or deranged; demented; mad; crazy. 2. for insane people: as, an *insane* asylum. 3. very foolish, impractical, extravagant, etc.; senseless.
the insane, insane people.
in·san·i·tar·y (in-san'ə-ter'i), *adj.* not sanitary; unhealthful; likely to cause disease.
in·san·i·ta·tion (in-san'ə-tā'shən), *n.* absence of sanitation; unhealthfulness.
in·san·i·ty (in-san'ə-ti), *n.* [*pl.* INSANITIES (-tiz)], [L. *insanitas* < *insanus*], 1. the state of being insane; mental illness or derangement, usually excluding amentia; madness: not a scientific term; specifically, in *law*, any form or degree of mental derangement or unsoundness, permanent or temporary, that makes a person incapable of what is regarded legally as normal, rational conduct or judgment: it usually implies a need for hospitalization. 2. great folly; extreme senselessness.
SYN.—**insanity**, current in popular and legal language but not used technically in medicine (see definition above), implies mental derangement in one who formerly had mental health; **lunacy** specifically suggests periodic spells of insanity, but is now most commonly used in its extended sense of extreme folly; **dementia** is the general term for an acquired mental disorder, now generally one of organic origin, as distinguished from *amentia* (congenital mental deficiency); **psychosis** is the psychiatric term for any of various specialized mental disorders, functional or organic, in which the personality is seriously disorganized.—***ANT.*** sanity.
in·sa·ti·a·bil·i·ty (in-sā'shə-bil'ə-ti, in-sā'shi-ə-bil'ə-ti), *n.* the quality or state of being insatiable.
in·sa·ti·a·ble (in-sā'shə-b'l, in-sā'shi-ə-b'l), *adj.* [see IN- (not) & SATIATE], constantly wanting more; that cannot be satisfied or appeased; very greedy.
in·sa·ti·a·bly (in-sā'shə-bli, in-sā'shi-ə-bli), *adv.* 1. in an insatiable manner. 2. to an insatiable degree.
in·sa·ti·ate (in-sā'shi-it), *adj.* [L. *insatiatus*], insatiable.
in·scrib·a·ble (in-skrīb'ə-b'l), *adj.* that can be inscribed.
in·scribe (in-skrīb'), *v.t.* [INSCRIBED (-skrībd'), INSCRIBING], [L. *inscribere;* see IN- (in) & SCRIBE], 1. to mark or engrave (words, symbols, etc.) on some surface. 2. to mark or engrave (a surface) with words, symbols, etc. 3. to add the name of (someone) to a list; enroll. 4. to dedicate (a book, song, etc.) briefly and informally. 5. to fix or impress deeply or lastingly in the mind, memory, etc. 6. in *geometry*, to draw (a figure) inside another figure so that their boundaries touch at as many points as possible.
in·scrip·tion (in-skrip'shən), *n.* [ME. *inscripcioun;* L. *inscriptio* < *inscriptus*, pp. of *inscribere*], 1. an inscribing. 2. something inscribed or engraved, as ancient markings on stones or the information on a coin. 3. a brief or informal dedication in a book, etc.
in·scrip·tion·al (in-skrip'shən-'l), *adj.* inscriptive.
in·scrip·tive (in-skrip'tiv), *adj.* of or like an inscription.
in·scroll (in-skrōl'), *v.t.* to record on a scroll.
in·scru·ta·bil·i·ty (in-skrōō'tə-bil'ə-ti), *n.* 1. the quality or state of being inscrutable. 2. [*pl.* INSCRUTABILITIES (-tiz)], something inscrutable.
in·scru·ta·ble (in-skrōō'tə-b'l), *adj.* [LL. *inscrutabilis* < L. *in-*, not + *scrutari*, to search carefully, examine], that cannot be learned or understood; completely obscure or mysterious; incomprehensible; unfathomable; enigmatic. —***SYN.*** see **mysterious.**
in·scru·ta·bly (in-skrōō'tə-bli), *adv.* in an inscrutable manner; so as to be inscrutable.
in·sect (in'sekt), *n.* [L. *insectum*, neut. of *insectus*, pp. of *insecare*, to cut into; *in-*, into + *secare*, to cut, divide: from the segmented bodies], 1. any of a large group of small invertebrate animals characterized, in the adult state, by division of the body into head, thorax, and abdomen, three pairs of legs, and, usually, two pairs of membranous wings: beetles, bees, flies, wasps, mosquitoes, etc. are insects. 2. popularly, any of a group of small animals, usually wingless, including spiders, centipedes, wood lice, ticks, mites, etc. 3. a small, unimportant, contemptible person.

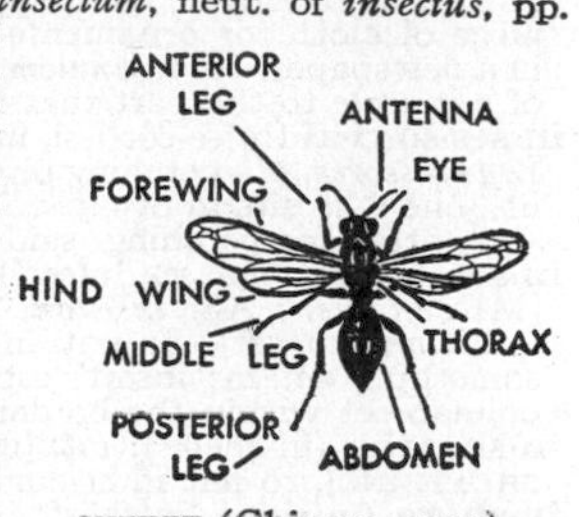

INSECT (Chinese wasp)

in·sec·tar·i·um (in'sek-târ'i-əm), *n.* [*pl.* INSECTARIA (-ə)], [Mod. L.], 1. a place where insects are raised, especially for study. 2. the insects so raised.
in·sec·tar·y (in'sek-ter'i), *n.* [*pl.* INSECTARIES (-iz)], an insectarium.
in·sec·ti·cide (in-sek'tə-sīd'), *n.* [< L. *insectum*, insect; + *-cide*], any substance used to kill insects.
in·sec·tile (in-sek'til), *adj.* [Rare], 1. of or like an insect. 2. consisting of insects.
in·sec·ti·val (in'sek-tī'v'l, in-sek'tə-v'l), *adj.* of or like an insect.
In·sec·tiv·o·ra (in'sek-tiv'ə-rə), *n.pl.* [Mod. L. < L. *insectum* (see INSECT) + *vorare*, to eat greedily, devour], an order of mammals that feed principally on insects: moles, shrews, and hedgehogs are members of it.
in·sec·ti·vore (in-sek'tə-vôr', in-sek'tə-vōr'), *n.* [Fr.], any animal or plant that feeds on insects; especially, any of the Insectivora.
in·sec·tiv·o·rous (in'sek-tiv'ẽr-əs), *adj.* [< L. *insectum* (see INSECT); + *-vorous*], 1. feeding chiefly on insects. 2. of the Insectivora.
in·sec·tol·o·gy (in'sek-tol'ə-ji), *n.* [Fr. *insectologie;* see INSECT & -LOGY], the study of insects, especially of their economic effects in agriculture and industry.
in·se·cure (in'si-kyoor'), *adj.* not secure; specifically, *a)* not safe from danger. *b)* feeling more anxiety than seems warranted. *c)* not firm or dependable; unreliable.
in·se·cu·ri·ty (in'si-kyoor'ə-ti), *n.* [ML. *insecuritas*], 1. the quality or state of being insecure. 2. [*pl.* INSECURITIES (-tiz)], something insecure.
in·sem·i·nate (in-sem'ə-nāt'), *v.t.* [INSEMINATED (-id), INSEMINATING], [< L. *inseminatus*, pp. of *inseminare*, to sow in; *in-*, in + *seminare*, to sow < *semen*, seed], to sow seeds in; especially, to impregnate by sexual intercourse or by artificially injecting semen. —***SYN.*** see **instill.**
in·sem·i·na·tion (in-sem'ə-nā'shən, in'sem-e-nā'shən), *n.* an inseminating or being inseminated.
in·sen·sate (in-sen'sāt, in-sen'sit), *adj.* [LL. *insensatus; in-*, not + *sensatus*, gifted with sense < *sensus*, sense], 1. lacking sensation; not feeling or incapable of feeling sensation; **inanimate.** 2. without sense or reason; foolish; stupid. 3. lacking sensibility; without regard or feeling; cold; hardened.
in·sen·si·bil·i·ty (in-sen'sə-bil'ə-ti), *n.* [LL. *insensibilitas*], the quality or condition of being insensible.
in·sen·si·ble (in-sen'sə-b'l), *adj.* [ME. *incensible;* LL. *insensibilis;* see IN- (not) & SENSIBLE], 1. lacking sensation; not having the power to perceive with the senses. 2. having lost sensation; unconscious. 3. not recognizing or realizing; unaware; indifferent. 4. so small, slight, or gradual as to be virtually imperceptible.
in·sens·i·bly (in-sen'sə-bli), *adv.* [see prec. & -LY], by degrees so slight as to be virtually imperceptible.
in·sen·si·tive (in-sen'sə-tiv), *adj.* not sensitive; incapable of being impressed or influenced; insensate.
in·sen·ti·ent (in-sen'shi-ənt, in-sen'shənt), *adj.* not sentient; without life, consciousness, or perception.
in·sep·a·ra·bil·i·ty (in'sep-ẽr-ə-bil'ə-ti, in-sep'ẽr-ə-bil'ə-ti), *n.* the quality or state of being inseparable.
in·sep·a·ra·ble (in-sep'ẽr-ə-b'l), *adj.* not separable; that cannot be separated or parted: abbreviated **insep.** *n. pl.* inseparable persons or things.
in·sep·a·ra·bly (in-sep'ẽr-ə-bli), *adv.* in an inseparable manner; so as to be inseparable.
in·sert (in-sũrt'; *for n.*, in'sẽrt), *v.t.* [< L. *insertus*, pp. of *inserere; in-*, into + *serere*, to join], to put or fit (something) into something else; put in; introduce: as, *insert* a coin in a slot machine. *n.* anything inserted or for insertion; especially, an extra leaf or section inserted in a newspaper, etc. —***SYN.*** see **introduce.**
in·sert·ed (in-sũr'tid), *adj.* [pp. of *insert*], in *biology*, joined by natural growth.
in·ser·tion (in-sũr'shən), *n.* [L. *insertio*], 1. an inserting or being inserted. 2. something inserted; specifically,

a) a piece of lace or embroidery that can be set into a piece of cloth for ornamentation. *b*) an advertisement in a newspaper. 3. in *anatomy*, the point of attachment of a muscle to the part that it moves.

in·ses·so·ri·al (in'se-sôr'i-əl, in'se-sō'ri-əl), *adj.* [< Mod. L. *Insessores*, *pl.*, perching birds < L. *insessor*, occupant, lit., one who sits in or on < *insidere* (see INSIDIOUS); + *-ial*], fitted for perching: said of certain birds.

in·set (in-set'; *for n.*, in'set'), *v.t.* [INSET, INSETTING], [ME. *insetten;* AS. *insettan*, to set in, appoint; *in-*, in + *settan*, to set], to put into something; insert. *n.* something set in; insert; especially, a smaller picture or map set within the border of a larger one.

in·sheathe (in-shēth'), *v.t.* [INSHEATHED (-shēthd'), INSHEATHING], to put in or cover with a sheath.

in·shore (in'shôr', in'shōr'), *adv. & adj.* 1. in toward the shore. 2. near the shore.

inshore of, nearer than (something else) to the shore.

in·side (in'sīd', in'sīd'; *for prep., usually* in'sīd'), *n.* 1. the part lying within; inner side, surface, or part; interior. 2. the part of a sidewalk or path lying farthest from the road. 3. *pl.* [Colloq.], the internal organs of the body, as the stomach and intestines. *adj.* 1. lying on or in the inside; internal. 2. of or suited for the inside. 3. working or used indoors; indoor. 4. known only to insiders; secret or private: as, the *inside* story. *adv.* 1. on or in the inside of; within. 2. indoors. *prep.* inside of; in; within.

inside of, [Colloq.], in less than (a specified time); within the space of.

inside out, with the inside where the outside should be; showing the inside; reversed.

in·sid·er (in'sid'ẽr), *n.* 1. a person inside a given place or group; hence, 2. a person having or likely to have secret or confidential information.

inside track, 1. the inner, shorter way around a race track; hence, 2. a favorable position or advantage.

in·sid·i·ous (in-sid'i-əs), *adj.* [Fr. *insidieux;* L. *insidiosus* < *insidiae*, an ambush, plot < *insidere*, to sit in or on, lie in wait for < *in-*, in + *sedere*, to sit], 1. characterized by treachery or slyness; crafty; wily. 2. operating in a slow or not easily apparent manner; more dangerous than seems evident: as, an *insidious* disease.

in·sight (in'sīt'), *n.* [ME. *insiht;* see IN- (in) & SIGHT], 1. the ability to see and understand clearly the inner nature of things. 2. a clear understanding of the inner nature of some specific thing.

in·sig·ni·a (in-sig'ni-ə), *n.pl.* [*sing.* INSIGNE (-nē); now sometimes INSIGNIA], [L., pl. of *insigne*, neut. of *insignis*, distinguished by a mark, striking, eminent < *in-*, in + *signum*, a mark, sign], badges, emblems, or other distinguishing marks, as of rank, membership, etc.

in·sig·nif·i·cance (in'sig-nif'ə-kəns), *n.* [< *insignificant*], the quality or condition of being insignificant; specifically, *a*) unimportance; triviality. *b*) meaninglessness.

in·sig·nif·i·can·cy (in'sig-nif'ə-kən-si), *n.* 1. insignificance. 2. [*pl.* INSIGNIFICANCIES (-siz)], an insignificant person or thing.

in·sig·nif·i·cant (in'sig-nif'ə-kənt), *adj.* [*in-* (not) + *significant*], 1. meaningless. 2. unimportant; trivial. 3. small; unimposing.

in·sin·cere (in'sin-sêr'), *adj.* not sincere; deceptive or hypocritical; not to be trusted.

in·sin·cer·i·ty (in'sin-ser'ə-ti), *n.* 1. the quality of being insincere. 2. [*pl.* INSINCERITIES (-tiz)], an insincere action, remark, etc.

in·sin·u·ate (in-sin'ū-āt'), *v.t.* [INSINUATED (-id), INSINUATING], [< L. *insinuatus*, pp. of *insinuare*, to introduce by windings and turnings, insinuate < *in-*, in + *sinus*, curved surface], 1. to get in, push, or introduce slowly, indirectly, and skillfully. 2. to hint or suggest (something) indirectly; imply: as, he *insinuated* his doubt of her ability. —*SYN.* see **introduce, suggest.**

in·sin·u·a·tion (in-sin'ū-ā'shən), *n.* [L. *insinuatio*], 1. the act of insinuating. 2. something insinuated; specifically, *a*) a sly hint or suggestion, especially against someone. *b*) an act or remark intended to win favor; ingratiating action.

in·sin·u·a·tive (in-sin'ū-ā'tiv), *adj.* 1. insinuating or tending to insinuate. 2. using or containing an insinuation; subtly suggestive.

in·sin·u·a·tor (in-sin'ū-ā'tẽr), *n.* a person or thing that insinuates.

in·sip·id (in-sip'id), *adj.* [< Fr. & L.; Fr. *insipide;* LL. *insipidus* < L. *in-*, not + *sapidus*, savory < *sapere*, to taste], 1. without flavor; tasteless. 2. not exciting or interesting; dull; lifeless.

SYN.—**insipid** implies a lack of taste or flavor and is, hence, figuratively applied to anything that is lifeless, dull, etc. (*insipid* table talk); **vapid** and **flat** apply to that which once had, but has since lost, freshness, sharpness, tang, zest, etc. (the *vapid*, or *flat*, epigrams that had once so delighted him); **banal** is used of that which is so trite or hackneyed as to seem highly vapid or flat (her *banal* compliments).—*ANT.* zestful, spicy, pungent.

in·si·pid·i·ty (in'si-pid'ə-ti), *n.* 1. an insipid quality or state. 2. [*pl.* INSIPIDITIES (-tiz)], something insipid.

in·sip·i·ence (in-sip'i-əns), *n.* [ME. *insipiens;* OFr. *insipience;* L. *insipientia* < *insipiens*, unwise, foolish < *in-*, not + *sapiens*, wise], lack of wisdom or intelligence; stupidity.

in·sip·i·ent (in-sip'i-ənt), *adj.* not wise; stupid.

in·sist (in-sist'), *v.i.* [Fr. *insister;* L. *insistere*, to stand on, tread on, pursue diligently, persist; *in-*, in, on + *sistere*, to stand, cause to stand], to take and maintain a stand; make a firm demand (often with *on* or *upon*): as, he *insists* on the rights of the minorities. *v.t.* to demand strongly: as, I *insist* that you come.

in·sist·ence (in-sis'təns), *n.* 1. the quality of being insistent. 2. the act or an instance of insisting.

in·sist·en·cy (in-sis'tən-si), *n.* [*pl.* INSISTENCIES (-siz)], insistence.

in·sist·ent (in-sis'tənt), *adj.* [L. *insistens*], 1. insisting or demanding; persistent in demands or assertions. 2. compelling the attention: as, an *insistent* rhythm.

‡**in si·tu** (in sī'tū), [L.], in position; in its original place.

in·snare (in-snâr'), *v.t.* to ensnare.

in·so·bri·e·ty (in'sə-brī'ə-ti, in'sō-brī'ə-ti), *n.* lack of sobriety; intemperance, especially in drinking.

in·so·far (in'sō-fär', in'sə-fär'), *adv.* to the degree that (with *as*): as, *insofar* as I can say now, I shall come: often **in so far.**

in·so·late (in'sō-lāt'), *v.t.* [INSOLATED (-id), INSOLATING], [< L. *insolatus*, pp. of *insolare*, to expose to the sun < *in-*, in + *sol*, the sun], to put out in the sun for drying, bleaching, etc.

in·so·la·tion (in'sō-lā'shən), *n.* [L. *insolatio*], 1. an insolating. 2. the treatment of disease by exposure to the sun's rays. 3. sunstroke. 4. in *meteorology*, *a*) the radiation from the sun received by a surface, especially the earth's surface. *b*) the rate of such radiation per unit of surface.

in·sole (in'sōl'), *n.* 1. the inside sole of a shoe. 2. an extra, removable inside sole put in for comfort or waterproofing.

in·so·lence (in'sə-ləns), *n.* [ME.; OFr.; L. *insolentia* < *insolens*], 1. the quality of being insolent; impudence; arrogance. 2. insolent behavior, action, or speech.

in·so·lent (in'sə-lənt), *adj.* [ME.; OFr.; L. *insolens; in-*, not + *solens*, ppr. of *solere*, to be accustomed], disrespectful of custom or established authority; impertinent; impudent. —*SYN.* see **impertinent, proud.**

in·sol·u·bil·i·ty (in'sol-yoo-bil'ə-ti, in-sol'yoo-bil'ə-ti), *n.* the quality or state of being insoluble.

in·sol·u·ble (in-sol'yoo-b'l), *adj.* [ME. *insolible;* OFr.; L. *insolubilis*], 1. that cannot be solved; unsolvable. 2. that cannot be dissolved; not soluble.

in·sol·u·bly (in-sol'yoo-bli), *adv.* in an insoluble manner.

in·solv·a·ble (in-sol'və-b'l), *adj.* that cannot be solved.

in·sol·ven·cy (in-sol'vən-si), *n.* [*pl.* INSOLVENCIES (-siz)], the fact or condition of being insolvent; bankruptcy.

in·sol·vent (in-sol'vənt), *adj.* 1. not solvent; unable to pay debts; bankrupt. 2. not enough to pay all debts: as, an *insolvent* inheritance. 3. of insolvents or insolvency. *n.* an insolvent person.

in·som·ni·a (in-som'ni-ə), *n.* [L. < *insomnis*, sleepless < *in-*, without + *somnus*, sleep], prolonged or abnormal inability to sleep.

in·som·ni·ac (in-som'ni-ak'), *n.* a person who has insomnia.

in·som·ni·ous (in-som'ni-əs), *adj.* having insomnia.

in·so·much (in'sō-much', in'sə-much'), *adv.* 1. to such a degree or extent; so (usually with *as* or *that*): as, he worked very fast, *insomuch* that he was through in an hour. 2. inasmuch (with *as*).

in·sou·ci·ance (in-sōō'si-əns; Fr. an'sōō'syäns'), *n.* [Fr. < *insouciant*], the quality or fact of being insouciant.

in·sou·ci·ant (in-sōō'si-ənt; Fr. an'sōō'syän'), *adj.* [Fr.; *in-*, not + *souciant*, ppr. of *soucier*, to regard, care < L. *sollicitare;* see SOLICIT], calm and unbothered; carefree; indifferent.

in·soul (in-sōl'), *v.t.* to ensoul.

insp., inspector.

in·span (in-span'), *v.t. & v.i.* [INSPANNED (-spand'), INSPANNING], [D. *inspannen;* see IN- (in) & SPAN], in South Africa, to harness or yoke (animals) to a wagon, etc.

in·spect (in-spekt'), *v.t.* [L. *inspectare*, freq. < *inspectus*, pp. of *inspicere*, to look into, examine < *in-*, in, at + *specere*, to look at], 1. to look at carefully; examine critically. 2. to examine or review officially: as, the captain will *inspect* Company B. —*SYN.* see **scrutinize.**

in·spec·tion (in-spek'shən), *n.* [ME. *inspeccioun;* OFr.; L. *inspectio* < *inspectus;* see INSPECT], 1. careful investigation; critical examination. 2. official examination or review, as of troops.

in·spec·tor (in-spek'tẽr), *n.* [L.], 1. a person who inspects; official examiner; overseer. 2. an officer on a police force, ranking next below a superintendent. Abbreviated **insp., ins.**

in·spec·to·ral (in-spek'tẽr-əl), *adj.* of an inspector.

in·spec·tor·ate (in-spek'tẽr-it), *n.* 1. the position or duties of an inspector. 2. inspectors collectively. 3. the district supervised by an inspector.

in·spec·to·ri·al (in'spek-tôr'i-əl, in'spek-tō'ri-əl), *adj.* of an inspector or an inspectorate.

in·spec·tor·ship (in-spek'tẽr-ship'), *n.* [see -SHIP], the position or tenure of an inspector.

in·sphere (in-sfêr'), *v.t.* to ensphere.

in·spir·a·ble (in-spīr′ə-b'l), *adj.* that can be inspired.

in·spi·ra·tion (in′spə-rā′shən), *n.* [ME. *inspiracioun;* OFr.; LL. *inspiratio*], 1. a breathing in; drawing of air into the lungs; inhaling: opposed to *expiration.* 2. an inspiring or being inspired mentally or emotionally. 3. an inspiring influence; any stimulus to creative thought or action. 4. an inspired idea, action, etc. 5. a prompting of something written or said; suggestion. 6. in *theology*, a divine influence upon human beings resulting in writing, as of the Scriptures, or in action, as of a saint.

in·spi·ra·tion·al (in′spə-rā′shən-'l), *adj.* 1. of or giving inspiration; inspiring. 2. produced, influenced, or stimulated by inspiration; inspired.

in·spir·a·to·ry (in-spīr′ə-tôr′i, in-spīr′ə-tō′ri), *adj.* [< L. *inspiratus* (see INSPIRATION); + *-ory*], of, for, or characterized by inspiration, or inhalation.

in·spire (in-spīr′), *v.t.* [INSPIRED (-spīrd′), INSPIRING], [ME. *inspiren;* OFr. *inspirer;* L. *inspirare; in-*, in, on + *spirare*, to breathe], 1. originally, *a)* to breathe or blow upon or into. *b)* to infuse (life, etc. *into*) by breathing. 2. to draw (air) into the lungs; inhale: opposed to *expire.* 3. to have an animating effect upon; influence, stimulate, or impel; especially, to stimulate or impel to some creative or effective effort. 4. to cause, guide, communicate, or motivate by divine influence: as, God *inspired* the Scriptures. 5. to arouse or produce (a thought or feeling): as, kindness *inspires* love. 6. to affect with a specified feeling or thought: as, it *inspired* us with fear. 7. to occasion, cause, or produce. 8. to prompt, or cause to be written or said, by influence, without acknowledgment of the real authorship. *v.i.* 1. to inhale. 2. to give inspiration.

in·spir·it (in-spir′it), *v.t.* to put spirit into; give life or courage to; cheer; exhilarate.

in·spis·sate (in-spis′āt), *v.t. & v.i.* [INSPISSATED (-id), INSPISSATING], [< LL. *inspissatus*, thick; *in-*, in + *spissatus*, pp. of *spissare*, to thicken < *spissus*, thick], to thicken by evaporation, etc.; condense.

in·spis·sa·tion (in′spi-sā′shən), *n.* [ML. *inspissatio*], an inspissating or being inspissated.

Inst., 1. Institute. 2. Institution.

inst., 1. instant (the present month). 2. instrumental.

in·sta·bil·i·ty (in′stə-bil′ə-ti), *n.* [*pl.* INSTABILITIES (-tiz)], lack of stability; unstableness; specifically, *a)* lack of firmness or steadiness. *b)* lack of determination; irresolution; inconstancy.

in·sta·ble (in-stā′b'l), *adj.* [L. *instabilis*], unstable.

in·stall (in-stôl′), *v.t.* [Fr. *installer;* ML. *installare* < *in-*, in + *stallum* < OHG. *stal*, a place, seat, stall], 1. to place (a person) in an office, rank, etc., with formality or ceremony. 2. to establish in a place or condition; settle: as, we *installed* ourselves in the balcony. 3. to fix in position for use: as, we *installed* new light fixtures.

in·stal·la·tion (in′stə-lā′shən), *n.* 1. an installing or being installed. 2. a complete mechanical apparatus fixed in position for use: as, a heating *installation.* 3. any military establishment, including the plant, equipment, etc.

in·stall·ment, in·stal·ment (in-stôl′mənt), *n.* [earlier *estallment* < *estall*, to arrange payments for < OFr. *estaler*, to stop, fix < *estal*, a halt, place < OHG. *stal;* see INSTALL], 1. any of the parts of a debt or other sum of money to be paid at regular times over a specified period. 2. any of several parts appearing at intervals: as, the story was published in *installments.*

in·stall·ment, in·stal·ment (in-stôl′mənt), *n.* [*install* + *-ment*], an installing or being installed; installation.

installment plan, a credit system by which debts, as for purchased articles, are paid in installments.

in·stance (in′stəns), *n.* [ME. *instaunce;* OFr.; L. *instantia*, a standing upon or near, being present < *instans;* see INSTANT], 1. originally, an urgent plea; persistent solicitation. 2. a request; suggestion; instigation: as, his case was reviewed by the dean at the *instance* of the student council. 3. an example; case; illustration. 4. a step in proceeding; occasion: as, in the first *instance.* 5. [Obs.], a motive; cause. 6. in *law*, a process or proceeding in a court; suit. *v.t.* [INSTANCED (-stənst), INSTANCING], 1. to show by an instance; exemplify: as, the game was exciting, as was *instanced* by the score. 2. to give as an example; cite.

for instance, as an example; by way of illustration.

SYN.—**instance** refers to a person, thing, or event that is adduced to prove or support a general statement (here is an *instance* of his sincerity); **case** is applied to any happening or condition that demonstrates the general existence or occurrence of something (a *case* of mistaken identity); **example** is applied to something that is cited as typical of the members of its group (his novel is an *example* of romantic literature); **illustration** is used of an instance or example that helps to explain or clarify something (this sentence is an *illustration* of the use of a word).

in·stan·cy (in′stən-si), *n.* [L. *instantia*], the quality or condition of being instant; specifically, *a)* urgency; pressure; insistence. *b)* [Rare], imminence; immediateness. *c)* [Rare], instantaneousness.

in·stant (in′stənt), *adj.* [OFr. < L. *instans*, ppr. of *instare*, to stand upon or near, press; *in-*, in, upon + *stare*, to stand], 1. urgent; pressing. 2. of the current month: as, yours of the 13th *instant* received: abbreviated **inst.** 3. soon to happen; imminent. 4. without delay; immediate: as, I demand *instant* obedience. 5. designating coffee, tea, cocoa, etc. in readily soluble form, prepared by adding water or other liquid. *adv.* [Poetic], at once; instantly. *n.* 1. a point or very short space of time; moment. 2. a particular moment.

on the instant, without delay; immediately.

the instant, as soon as.

in·stan·ta·ne·ous (in′stən-tā′ni-əs), *adj.* [< *instant*, after *momentaneous*], 1. done, made, or happening in an instant. 2. done or made without delay; immediate: as, an *instantaneous* response.

in·stan·ter (in-stan′tẽr), *adv.* [L., earnestly, pressingly < *instans;* see INSTANT], without delay; immediately.

in·stant·ly (in′stənt-li), *adv.* 1. in an instant; without delay; immediately. 2. [Archaic], urgently; pressingly. *conj.* as soon as; the instant that: as, I came *instantly* I saw the need.

in·star (in′stär), *n.* [L., a shape, form], any of the various forms of an insect or other arthropod between molts.

in·star (in-stär′), *v.t.* [INSTARRED (-stärd′), INSTARRING], 1. to set as a star. 2. to stud or adorn as with stars.

in·state (in-stāt′), *v.t.* [INSTATED (-id), INSTATING], [*in-* (in) + *state*], 1. to put in a particular status, position, or rank; install. 2. [Obs.], *a)* to endow; invest. *b)* to confer (with *on* or *upon*).

‡in sta·tu quo (in stā′tū kwō′, in stach′oo kwō′), [L., in the state in which], in the existing, or same, condition.

in·stau·ra·tion (in′stô-rā′shən), *n.* [L. *instauratio* < *instauratus*, pp. of *instaurare*, to renew, repeat], restoration; repair; renewal; renovation.

in·stead (in-sted′), *adv.* [*in* + *stead*], in place of the person or thing mentioned; as an alternative or substitute: as, since we had no sugar, we used honey *instead.*

instead of, in place of; rather than.

in·step (in′step′), *n.* [prob. *in-* (in) + *step*], 1. the upper surface of the arch of the foot, between the ankle and the toes. 2. the part of a shoe or stocking that covers this surface. 3. the front surface of the hind leg of a horse, between the hock and the pastern joint.

in·sti·gate (in′stə-gāt′), *v.t.* [INSTIGATED (-id), INSTIGATING], [< L. *instigatus*, pp. of *instigare*, to stimulate, incite; *in-*, in + *-stigare* (in comp.), to prick; IE base **steig-*, to prick, seen also in *sting, stick*, Gr. *stigma*], 1. to urge on, spur on, or incite to some action or course of action: as, Mephistopheles *instigated* Faust to sin. 2. to cause by inciting; foment: as, they *instigated* a rebellion. —*SYN.* see **incite.**

in·sti·ga·tion (in′stə-gā′shən), *n.* [ME. *instigacioun;* L. *instigatio*], an instigating; incitement.

at the instigation of, instigated by.

in·sti·ga·tive (in′stə-gā′tiv), *adj.* instigating or tending to instigate.

in·sti·ga·tor (in′stə-gā′tẽr), *n.* a person who instigates.

in·still, in·stil (in-stil′), *v.t.* [INSTILLED (-stild′), INSTILLING], [Fr. *instiller;* L. *instillare; in-*, in + *stillare*, to drop < *stilla*, a drop], 1. to put in drop by drop. 2. to put (a notion, principle, feeling, etc.) *in* or *into* little by little; impart gradually.

SYN.—**instill,** in this figurative connection, implies a gradual imparting of knowledge over an extended period of time (he had *instilled* honesty in his children); **implant** suggests the imparting of knowledge as if by planting it in the mind, with the implication that it will develop there; **inculcate** implies frequent or insistent repetition so as to impress upon the mind (prejudice is *inculcated* in one during childhood); **infuse** suggests the imparting of qualities as if by pouring (he *infused* life into the play); **inseminate** implies the spreading of ideas throughout a group, nation, etc. as if by sowing seeds.

in·stil·la·tion (in′sti-lā′shən), *n.* [L. *instillatio*], 1. an instilling. 2. anything instilled.

in·still·ment, in·stil·ment (in-stil′mənt), *n.* an instilling or being instilled.

in·stinct (in′stiŋkt; *for adj.*, in-stiŋkt′), *n.* [< L. *instinctus*, pp. of *instinguere*, to impel, instigate; *in-*, in + **stinguere*, to prick; for IE. base see INSTIGATE], 1. (an) inborn tendency to behave in a way characteristic of a species; natural, unacquired mode of response to stimuli: as, suckling is an *instinct* in mammals. 2. a natural or acquired tendency, aptitude, or talent; bent; knack; gift: as, she has an *instinct* for doing the right thing. *adj.* filled or charged (*with*): as, the speech was *instinct* with emotion.

in·stinc·tive (in-stiŋk′tiv), *adj.* 1. of, or having the nature of, instinct. 2. caused, prompted, or done by instinct. —*SYN.* see **spontaneous.**

in·stinc·tu·al (in-stiŋk′choo-əl), *adj.* having to do with instinct.

in·sti·tute (in′stə-toot′, in′stə-tūt′), *v.t.* [INSTITUTED

(-id), INSTITUTING], [< L. *institutus*, pp. of *instituere*, to set up, erect, construct < *in-*, in, on + *statuere*, to cause to stand, set up, place], 1. to set up; establish; found; introduce. 2. to start; initiate: as, the city council *instituted* an investigation. 3. to appoint to or install in an office, position, benefice, etc. *n.* [L. *institutum*, arrangement, plan, intention < the *v.*], something instituted; specifically, *a*) an established principle, law, custom, or usage. *b*) *pl.* a summary or digest of established principles, especially in law. *c*) an organization for the promotion of art, science, education, etc. *d*) the building in which such an organization is housed. *e*) a type of school for higher education in technical subjects: it may be part of a university. *f*) an institution for advanced study, research, and instruction in a restricted field, organized in connection with a university. *g*) a short teaching program established for a special group concerned with some special field of work. Abbreviated **Inst.** (in senses *c, d, e, f, g*).

in·sti·tu·tion (in'stə-tōō'shən, in'stə-tū'shən), *n.* [ME.; OFr.; L. *institutio*], 1. an instituting or being instituted; establishment. 2. an established law, custom, practice, system, etc. 3. an organization having a social, educational, or religious purpose, as a school, church, hospital, reformatory, etc. 4. the building housing such an organization. 5. [Colloq.], a familiar person or thing. 6. in *ecclesiastical usage*, *a*) the establishment of a sacrament by Jesus. *b*) the establishment of a clergyman in a benefice. 7. in *law*, a collection of established principles or fundamental rules. Abbreviated **Inst., instn.** (in senses 3 & 4).

in·sti·tu·tion·al (in'stə-tōō'shən-'l, in'stə-tū'shən-'l), *adj.* 1. of, or having the nature of, an institution. 2. organized so as to function in social, charitable, and educational activities: as, *institutional* religion. 3. in *advertising*, intended primarily to gain prestige and good will rather than to increase immediate sales.

in·sti·tu·tion·al·ism (in'stə-tōō'shən-'l-iz'm, in'stə-tū'shən-'l-iz'm), *n.* a belief in and support of the usefulness or sanctity of established institutions.

in·sti·tu·tion·al·ize (in'stə-tōō'shən-'l-īz', in'stə-tū'shən-'l-īz'), *v.t.* [INSTITUTIONALIZED (-īzd'), INSTITUTIONALIZING], 1. to make into or consider as an institution. 2. to make institutional. 3. [Colloq.], to put (a person) into an institution.

in·sti·tu·tion·ar·y (in'stə-tōō'shən-er'i, in'stə-tū'shən-er'i), *adj.* 1. of legal institutes. 2. of clerical institution. 3. of institutions; institutional.

in·sti·tu·tive (in'stə-tōō'tiv, in'stə-tū'tiv), *adj.* 1. instituting or tending to institute; of institution. 2. sanctioned by law, custom, or usage; established.

in·sti·tu·tor (in'stə-tōō'tẽr, in'stə-tū'tẽr), *n.* [L.], 1. a person who institutes; founder; organizer. 2. in the *Episcopal Church*, the bishop, or a person acting for him, who installs a clergyman in a parish or church.

instr., 1. instructor. 2. instrument. 3. instrumental.

in·struct (in-strukt'), *v.t.* [< L. *instructus*, pp. of *instruere*, to pile upon, put in order, erect; *in-*, in, upon + *struere*, to pile up, arrange, build], 1. to communicate knowledge to; teach; educate. 2. to give the facts of the matter to; inform: as, a judge *instructs* the jury. 3. to give directions or orders to: as, the officer *instructed* the sentry to shoot. —*SYN.* see **command, teach.**

in·struc·tion (in-struk'shən), *n.* [ME. *instruccioun;* OFr. *instruccion;* L. *instructio*], 1. an instructing; education. 2. knowledge, information, etc. given or taught; any teaching; lesson. 3. *pl.* directions; orders.

in·struc·tion·al (in-struk'shən-'l), *adj.* of or for instruction; educational.

in·struc·tive (in-struk'tiv), *adj.* instructing; giving knowledge; used to inform.

in·struc·tor (in-struk'tẽr), *n.* [L.], 1. a person who instructs; teacher. 2. a college teacher ranking below an assistant professor. Abbreviated **instr.**

in·struc·tor·ship (in-struk'tẽr-ship'), *n.* [see -SHIP], the position of an instructor.

in·struc·tress (in-struk'tris), *n.* a woman instructor.

in·stru·ment (in'stroo-mənt), *n.* [ME.; OFr.; L. *instrumentum*, a tool or tools, stock in trade, furniture, dress < *instruere;* see INSTRUCT], 1. *a*) a thing by means of which something is done; means. *b*) a person used by another to bring something about. 2. a tool or implement, especially one used for delicate work or for scientific or artistic purposes. 3. any of various devices producing musical sound, as a piano, violin, oboe, etc.: abbreviated **instr.** 4. in *law*, a formal document, as a deed, contract, etc. *v.t.* 1. in *law*, to write an instrument. 2. in *music*, to arrange (a composition) for instruments; orchestrate. —*SYN.* see **implement.**

in·stru·men·tal (in'stroo-men't'l), *adj.* [ME.; OFr.; ML. *instrumentalis*], 1. serving as a means; helpful. 2. of or performed with an instrument or tool. 3. of, performed on, or written for a musical instrument or instruments. 4. in *grammar*, designating or of a case showing means or agency: the instrumental case is found in Anglo-Saxon, Sanskrit, Slavonic, etc. Abbreviated **instr., inst.** (in senses 3 & 4).

in·stru·men·tal·ism (in'stroo-men't'l-iz'm), *n.* in *philosophy*, the pragmatic doctrine that ideas are plans for action which serve as instruments for adjusting the organism to its environment.

in·stru·men·tal·ist (in'stroo-men't'l-ist), *n.* 1. a person who performs on a musical instrument. 2. a person who believes in instrumentalism.

in·stru·men·tal·i·ty (in'stroo-men-tal'ə-ti), *n.* [*pl.* INSTRUMENTALITIES (-tiz)], the condition, quality, or fact of being instrumental, or serving as a means; means; agency.

in·stru·men·ta·tion (in'stroo-men-tā'shən), *n.* [Fr.], 1. the composition or arrangement of music for instruments; orchestration. 2. the use of, or work with, scientific instruments.

instrument flying, the navigation of an aircraft completely by the use of instruments.

instrument panel (or **board**), a panel or board with instruments, gauges, etc. mounted on it, as in an automobile or airplane.

in·sub·or·di·nate (in'sə-bôr'd'n-it), *adj.* [*in-* (not) + *subordinate*], not submitting to authority; disobedient. *n.* an insubordinate person.

in·sub·or·di·na·tion (in'sə-bôr'd'n-ā'shən), *n.* the condition or fact of being insubordinate; disobedience.

in·sub·stan·tial (in'səb-stan'shəl), *adj.* [ML. *insubstantialis*], not substantial; specifically, *a*) unreal; imaginary. *b*) not solid or firm; weak or flimsy.

in·sub·stan·ti·al·i·ty (in'səb-stan'shi-al'ə-ti), *n.* the quality or state of being insubstantial.

in·suf·fer·a·ble (in-suf'ẽr-ə-b'l), *adj.* not sufferable; intolerable; unbearable.

in·suf·fer·a·bly (in-suf'ẽr-ə-bli), *adv.* 1. in an insufferable manner. 2. to an insufferable degree.

in·suf·fi·cience (in'sə-fish'əns), *n.* [ME. & OFr. *insuffisance* < LL.], [Rare], insufficiency.

in·suf·fi·cien·cy (in'sə-fish'ən-si), *n.* [LL. *insufficientia*], 1. lack of sufficiency; deficiency; inadequacy. 2. failure of an organ or tissue to perform its normal function: said especially of a heart valve or muscle.

in·suf·fi·cient (in'sə-fish'ənt), *adj.* not sufficient; not enough; inadequate.

in·suf·flate (in-suf'lāt, in'sə-flāt'), *v.t.* [INSUFFLATED (-id), INSUFFLATING], [< L. *insufflatus*, pp. of *insufflare*, to blow or breathe into; *in-*, in + *sufflare*, to blow from below < *sub-*, under + *flare*, to blow], 1. to blow or breathe into or on. 2. to breathe on (baptismal waters or a person being baptized). 3. in *medicine*, *a*) to blow (a powder, vapor, air, etc.) into a cavity of the body, especially the lungs. *b*) to blow such a substance into (the lungs, etc.).

in·suf·fla·tion (in'sə-flā'shən), *n.* [LL. *insufflatio*], an insufflating or being insufflated.

in·suf·fla·tor (in'sə-flā'tẽr), *n.* a device for insufflating.

in·su·lar (in'sə-lẽr, in'syoo-lẽr), *adj.* [L. *insularis* < *insula*, island], 1. of, or having the form of, an island. 2. living or situated on an island. 3. like an island; detached; insulated. 4. of, like, or characteristic of islanders; hence, 5. narrow-minded; not liberal; prejudiced. 6. in *medicine*, *a*) characterized by isolated spots. *b*) of the islands of Langerhans or other islands of tissue.

in·su·lar·i·ty (in'sə-lar'ə-ti, in'syoo-lar'ə-ti), *n.* [*insular* + *-ity*], 1. the state of being an island. 2. the state of living on an island; hence, 3. narrow-mindedness; prejudice.

in·su·late (in'sə-lāt', in'syoo-lāt'), *v.t.* [INSULATED (-id), INSULATING], [< L. *insulatus*, made like an island < *insula*, island], 1. to set apart; detach from the rest; isolate. 2. to separate or cover with a nonconducting material in order to prevent the passage or leakage of electricity, heat, or sound.

in·su·la·tion (in'sə-lā'shən, in'syoo-lā'shən), *n.* 1. an insulating or being insulated. 2. any material used to insulate.

in·su·la·tor (in'sə-lā'tẽr, in'syoo-lā'tẽr), *n.* anything that insulates; especially, a device, usually of glass or porcelain, for insulating and supporting electric wires: abbreviated **ins.**

in·su·lin (in'sə-lin, in'syoo-lin), *n.* [< L. *insula*, island; + *-in*: after the islands of Langerhans, in the pancreas], 1. a secretion of the islands of Langerhans, in the pancreas, which helps the body use sugar and other carbohydrates. 2. a product extracted from the pancreas of sheep or oxen and used hypodermically in the treatment of diabetes mellitus: a trade-mark (**Insulin**).

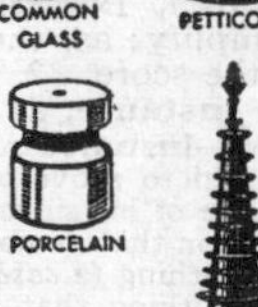

TYPES OF INSULATOR

insulin shock, an abnormal condition caused by an overdose or excess secretion of insulin, resulting in a sudden reduction in the sugar content of the blood: it is characterized by tremors, cold sweat, convulsions, and coma.

in·su·lize (in'sə-līz', in'syoo-līz'), *v.t.* [INSULIZED (-līzd'), INSULIZING], to treat with insulin.

in·sult (in'sult; *for v.,* in-sult'), *n.* [Fr.; LL. *insultus*, lit., a leaping upon, pp. of L. *insilire*, to leap upon < *in-*, on, upon + *salire*, to leap], 1. originally, an attack; onset. 2. an act, remark, etc. meant to hurt the feelings or self-respect of another; affront; indignity. ***v.t.*** 1. to subject to an insult; treat with scorn or insolence; affront. 2. [Obs.], to attack; assail. ***v.i.*** [Archaic], to behave insolently. —***SYN.*** see **offend.**

in·su·per·a·bil·i·ty (in-sōō'pẽr-ə-bil'ə-ti, in-sū'pẽr-ə-bil'ə-ti), ***n.*** the quality or state of being insuperable.

in·su·per·a·ble (in-sōō'pẽr-ə-b'l, in-sū'pẽr-ə-b'l), ***adj.*** not superable; that cannot be overcome or passed over.

in·su·per·a·bly (in-sōō'pẽr-ə-bli, in-sū'pẽr-ə-bli), ***adv.*** 1. in an insuperable manner. 2. to an insuperable degree.

in·sup·port·a·ble (in'sə-pôr'tə-b'l, in'sə-pōr'tə-b'l), ***adj.*** not supportable; intolerable; unbearable; unendurable.

in·sup·port·a·bly (in'sə-pôr'tə-bli, in'sə-pōr'tə-bli), ***adv.*** 1. in an insupportable manner. 2. to an insupportable degree.

in·sup·press·i·ble (in'sə-pres'ə-b'l), ***adj.*** not suppressible; that cannot be suppressed.

in·sup·press·i·bly (in'sə-pres'ə-bli), ***adv.*** in an insuppressible manner; so as to be insuppressible.

in·sur·a·bil·i·ty (in-shoor'ə-bil'ə-ti), ***n.*** the quality or condition of being insurable.

in·sur·a·ble (in-shoor'ə-b'l), ***adj.*** that can be insured.

in·sur·ance (in-shoor'əns), ***n.*** [earlier *ensurance;* OFr. *enseurance;* see ENSURE], 1. an insuring or being insured against loss; a system of protection against loss in which a number of individuals agree to pay certain sums for a guarantee that they will be compensated for any specified loss by fire, accident, death, etc. 2. a contract whereby, in return for a fixed payment (*premium*), the insurer guarantees the insured that a certain sum will be paid for a specified loss: usually called *insurance policy.* 3. the fixed payment made by the insured; premium. 4. the amount for which life, property, etc. is insured. 5. the business of insuring against loss. Abbreviated **insur., ins.**

in·sur·ant (in-shoor'ənt), ***n.*** a person who is insured.

in·sure (in-shoor'), ***v.t.*** [INSURED (-shoord'), INSURING], [ME. *ensuren;* OFr. *enseurer;* see IN- (in) & SURE], 1. to make sure; ensure; guarantee: as, please *insure* the accuracy of your reports. 2. to get as a certainty; secure: as, your degree will *insure* you a job. 3. to make safe; guard against injury, damage, etc.; protect: as, care *insures* one against error. 4. to assure against loss; contract to be paid or to pay money in the case of loss of (life, property, etc.); take out or issue insurance on (something or someone). ***v.i.*** to give or take out insurance. Also spelled **ensure.**

in·sured (in-shoord'), ***n.*** [< pp. of *insure*], a person whose life, property, etc. is insured against loss.

in·sur·er (in-shoor'ẽr), ***n.*** a person or company that insures others against loss or damage; underwriter.

in·sur·gence (in-sũr'jəns), ***n.*** [< *insurgent*], a rising in revolt; uprising; insurrection.

in·sur·gen·cy (in-sũr'jən-si), ***n.*** 1. the quality, state, or fact of being insurgent. 2. insurgence.

in·sur·gent (in-sũr'jənt), ***adj.*** [L. *insurgens*, ppr. of *insurgere*, to rise up, rise up against; *in-*, in, upon + *surgere*, to rise], rising up against political or governmental authority; rebellious. ***n.*** an insurgent person.

in·sur·mount·a·bil·i·ty (in'sẽr-moun'tə-bil'ə-ti), ***n.*** the quality or state of being insurmountable.

in·sur·mount·a·ble (in'sẽr-moun'tə-b'l), ***adj.*** not surmountable; that cannot be passed over or overcome; insuperable.

in·sur·mount·a·bly (in'sẽr-moun'tə-bli), ***adv.*** 1. in an insurmountable manner. 2. to an insurmountable degree.

in·sur·rec·tion (in'sə-rek'shən), ***n.*** [Late ME.; LL. *insurrectio* < pp. of L. *insurgere;* see INSURGENT], a rising up against established authority; rebellion; revolt. —***SYN.*** see **rebellion.**

in·sur·rec·tion·al (in'sə-rek'shən-'l), ***adj.*** of or like an insurrection.

in·sur·rec·tion·ar·y (in'sə-rek'shən-er'i), ***adj.*** of or engaged in insurrection. ***n.*** [*pl.* INSURRECTIONARIES (-iz)], an insurgent; rebel.

in·sur·rec·tion·ist (in'sə-rek'shən-ist), ***n.*** a person who aids or takes part in an insurrection; insurgent.

in·sus·cep·ti·bil·i·ty (in'sə-sep'tə-bil'ə-ti), ***n.*** the fact, state, or quality of being insusceptible.

in·sus·cep·ti·ble (in'sə-sep'tə-b'l), ***adj.*** not susceptible; not easily affected or influenced; unimpressible.

in·swathe (in-swāth'), ***v.t.*** to enswathe.

in·swept (in'swept'), ***adj.*** tapering at the front: said of an automobile frame.

int., 1. interest. 2. interim. 3. interior. 4. interjection. 5. internal. 6. international. 7. intransitive.

in·tact (in-takt'), ***adj.*** [L. *intactus; in-*, not + *tactus*, pp. of *tangere*, to touch], untouched or uninjured; kept or left whole; sound; unimpaired. —***SYN.*** see **complete.**

in·tagl·io (in-tal'yō, in-täl'yō), ***n.*** [*pl.* INTAGLIOS (-yōz)], [It. < *intagliare*, to cut in, engrave; *in-*, in + *tagliare*, to cut], 1. a design or figure carved or engraved below the surface. 2. a gem or stone ornamented with such a design or figure: opposed to *cameo.* 3. the art or process of making such designs or figures: usually in phrase *in intaglio.* 4. a die cut to produce a design in relief. ***v.t.*** 1. to engrave a design on. 2. to cut (a design) in a surface.

in·take (in'tāk'), ***n.*** 1. a taking in. 2. the amount or thing taken in: as, a small pipe has little *intake.* 3. the place in a pipe, channel, etc. where a fluid is taken in: as, the sewer *intake* was too small. 4. a narrowing; an abrupt lessening in breadth. 5. in *mechanics*, the amount of energy taken in. 6. in *mining*, an air shaft.

in·tan·gi·bil·i·ty (in-tan'jə-bil'ə-ti), ***n.*** 1. the quality or state of being intangible. 2. [*pl.* INTANGIBILITIES (-tiz)], something intangible.

in·tan·gi·ble (in-tan'jə-b'l), ***adj.*** [ML. *intangibilis;* see IN- (not) & TANGIBLE], 1. that cannot be touched; incorporeal; impalpable. 2. that cannot be easily defined, formulated, or grasped; vague. ***n.*** something intangible, as good will or a similar asset.

in·tan·gi·bly (in-tan'jə-bli), ***adv.*** in an intangible manner; vaguely; impalpably.

in·tar·si·a (in-tär'si-ə), ***n.*** [It. *intarsio* < *intarsiare*, to inlay, incrust < *in-*, in + Ar. *tarṣi*, incrustation], a surface decoration made by inlaying small pieces of wood in patterns; mosaic woodwork.

in·te·ger (in'tə-jẽr), ***n.*** [L., untouched, whole, entire < *in-*, not + base of *tangere*, to touch], 1. anything complete in itself; entity; whole. 2. a whole number (e.g., 5, 10, 748, etc.): distinguished from *fraction.*

‡in·te·ger vi·tae (in'tə-jẽr vī'tē), [L., lit., unblemished in life], blameless; upright: from Horace, *Odes*, I.

in·te·gra·ble (in'tə-grə-b'l), ***adj.*** that can be integrated.

in·te·gral (in'tə-grəl), ***adj.*** [LL. *integralis* < L. *integer;* see INTEGER], 1. necessary for completeness; essential. 2. whole or complete. 3. in *mathematics, a)* of or having to do with an integer or integers; not fractional. *b)* of or having to do with integrals or integration. ***n.*** 1. a whole. 2. in *mathematics*, the result of integrating a function or an equation.

integral calculus, the branch of calculus dealing with the theory, application, functions, etc. of integrals.

in·te·gral·i·ty (in'tə-gral'ə-ti), ***n.*** the quality or state of being integral; wholeness.

in·te·grand (in'tə-grand'), ***n.*** [< L. *integrandus*, gerundive of *integrare*], in *mathematics*, the function or equation to be integrated.

in·te·grant (in'tə-grənt), ***adj.*** [L. *integrans*, ppr. of *integrare;* see INTEGRATE], integral. ***n.*** an integral part; constituent.

in·te·grate (in'tə-grāt'), ***v.t.*** [INTEGRATED (-id), INTEGRATING], [< L. *integratus*, pp. of *integrare*, to make whole, renew < *integer;* see INTEGER], 1. to make whole or complete by adding or bringing together parts. 2. to put or bring (parts) together into a whole; unify. 3. to give or indicate the whole, sum, or total of. 4. to remove the legal and social barriers imposing segregation upon (racial groups). 5. in *mathematics, a)* to calculate the integral or integrals of (a function, equation, etc.). *b)* to perform the process of integration upon. ***v.i.*** to unite or become whole.

in·te·gra·tion (in'tə-grā'shən), ***n.*** [L. *integratio*], 1. an integrating or being integrated. 2. in *mathematics*, the process of finding the quantity or function of which a given quantity or function is the derivative or differential: opposed to *differentiation.* 3. in *psychoanalysis*, the organization of various traits or tendencies into one harmonious personality.

in·te·gra·tive (in'tə-grā'tiv), ***adj.*** 1. of integration. 2. integrating.

in·te·gra·tor (in'tə-grā'tẽr), ***n.*** [L.], 1. a person or thing that integrates. 2. a mechanical device for calculating integrals.

in·teg·ri·ty (in-teg'rə-ti), ***n.*** [L. *integritas* < *integer;* see INTEGER], 1. the quality or state of being complete; unbroken condition; wholeness; entirety. 2. the quality or state of being unimpaired; perfect condition; soundness. 3. the quality or state of being of sound moral principle; uprightness, honesty, and sincerity. —***SYN.*** see **honesty.**

in·teg·u·ment (in-teg'yoo-mənt), ***n.*** [L. *integumentum*, a covering < *integere*, to cover; *in-*, in, upon + *tegere*, to cover], an outer covering, as of the body or of a plant; skin, shell, hide, husk, rind, etc.

in·teg·u·men·ta·ry (in-teg'yoo-men'tẽr-i), ***adj.*** of, like, or forming an integument.

in·tel·lect (in'tə-lekt', in't'l-ekt'), ***n.*** [ME.; L. *intellectus*, a perceiving, understanding < *intellegere, intelligere*, to perceive, understand < *inter-*, between, among + *legere*, to gather, pick, choose; cf. INTELLIGENT], 1. the ability to reason, perceive, or understand; ability to perceive relations, differences, etc.: distinguished from *will, feeling.* 2. great mental ability; high intelligence. 3. *a*) a mind or intelligence, especially a superior one. *b*) a person of intelligence. *c*) minds or intelligent persons, collectively.

in·tel·lec·tion (in'tə-lek'shən), ***n.*** [ML. *intellectio*], 1. the process of using the intellect; thinking; cognition. 2. an act of the intellect; a thought or perception.

in·tel·lec·tive (in'tə-lek'tiv), ***adj.*** [Fr. *intellectif;* LL. *intellectivus*], of or characterized by intellect; intellectual.

in·tel·lec·tu·al (in'tə-lek'chōō-əl), ***adj.*** [ME.; L. *intellectualis*], 1. of or done by the intellect. 2. appealing to the intellect. 3. requiring or using intelligence. 4. having or showing a high degree of intelligence; having superior mental powers. ***n.*** 1. a person with intellectual interests or tastes. 2. a person who does intellectual work. 3. a member of the intelligentsia. —***SYN.*** see **intelligent.**

in·tel·lec·tu·al·ism (in'tə-lek'chōō-əl-iz'm), ***n.*** 1. the quality of being intellectual; devotion to intellectual pursuits. 2. in *philosophy*, the theory that knowledge comes wholly from pure reason, without aid from the senses; rationalism.

in·tel·lec·tu·al·ist (in'tə-lek'chōō-əl-ist), ***n.*** 1. a person who tends to overemphasize intellectual pursuits. 2. in *philosophy*, a believer in intellectualism.

in·tel·lec·tu·al·i·ty (in'tə-lek'chōō-al'ə-ti), ***n.*** [LL. *intellectualitas*], 1. intellectual ability or nature. 2. the quality of being intellectual.

in·tel·lec·tu·al·ize (in'tə-lek'chōō-əl-īz'), ***v.t.*** [INTELLECTUALIZED (-īzd'), INTELLECTUALIZING], to make intellectual; give an intellectual quality to. ***v.i.*** to reason; think.

in·tel·lec·tu·al·ly (in'tə-lek'chōō-əl-i), ***adv.*** 1. in an intellectual manner. 2. as concerns the intellect.

in·tel·li·gence (in-tel'ə-jəns), ***n.*** [ME.; OFr.; L. *intelligentia*, perception, discernment < *intelligens*, ppr. of *intelligere;* see INTELLECT], 1. *a*) the ability to learn or understand from experience; ability to acquire and retain knowledge; mental ability. *b*) the ability to respond quickly and successfully to a new situation; use of the faculty of reason in solving problems, directing conduct, etc. effectively. *c*) in *psychology*, measured success in using these abilities to perform certain tasks. 2. news; tidings; information. 3. the gathering of secret information, as for military or police purposes. 4. the persons or agency employed at this; secret service. 5. intelligence personified; an intelligent spirit or being.

intelligence department (or **bureau**), a division of a government gathering information for the use of a country's navy and army in military operations, or for the guidance of a state department or foreign office in its formation of foreign policy: abbreviated **I.D.**

intelligence office, 1. an intelligence department: abbreviated **I.O.** 2. [Obs.], an employment office or agency for domestic help.

intelligence quotient, a number indicating a person's level of intelligence: it is the mental age (as shown by intelligence tests) multiplied by 100 and divided by the chronological age: abbreviated **IQ, I.Q.**

in·tel·li·genc·er (in-tel'ə-jən-sẽr), ***n.*** [< *intelligence* (sense 2) + *-er*], 1. a person who supplies news or information; especially, a spy or secret agent. 2. formerly, a newsletter or newspaper.

intelligence test, a standardized series of problems progressively graded in difficulty, intended to test the intelligence of an individual.

in·tel·li·gent (in-tel'ə-jənt), ***adj.*** [L. *intelligens*, ppr. of *intelligere;* see INTELLECT], 1. having or using intelligence. 2. having or showing a high intelligence; quick to learn. 3. having knowledge, understanding, or awareness (*of* something).

SYN.—**intelligent** implies the ability to learn or understand from experience or to respond successfully to a new experience; **clever** implies quickness in learning or understanding, but sometimes connotes a lack of thoroughness or depth; **alert** emphasizes quickness in sizing up a situation; **bright** and **smart** are somewhat informal, less precise equivalents for any of the preceding; **brilliant** implies an unusually high degree of intelligence; **intellectual** suggests keen intelligence coupled with interest and ability in the more advanced fields of knowledge.—***ANT.*** stupid, dull.

in·tel·li·gen·tial (in-tel'ə-jen'shəl), ***adj.*** 1. of, like, or having to do with intelligence or intellect. 2. conveying intelligence or information: as, *intelligential* channels.

in·tel·li·gent·si·a (in-tel'ə-jent'si-ə, in-tel'ə-gent'si-ə), ***n.*** [Russ. *intelligentsiya;* It. *intelligenza*, lit., intelligence < L. *intelligentia;* see INTELLIGENCE], the people regarded as, or regarding themselves as, the educated and enlightened class; intellectuals collectively.

in·tel·li·gi·bil·i·ty (in-tel'i-jə-bil'ə-ti), ***n.*** 1. the quality or fact of being intelligible; capability of being understood; clarity. 2. [*pl.* INTELLIGIBILITIES (-tiz)], something intelligible.

in·tel·li·gi·ble (in-tel'i-jə-b'l), ***adj.*** [ME.; L. *intelligibilis*, *intellegibilis* < *intelligere;* see INTELLECT], 1. that can be understood; clear; comprehensible. 2. in *philosophy*, understandable by the intellect only; conceptual.

in·tel·li·gi·bly (in-tel'i-jə-bli), ***adv.*** in an intelligible manner; so as to be intelligible.

in·tem·er·ate (in-tem'ẽr-it), ***adj.*** [L. *intemeratus; in-*, not + *temeratus*, pp. of *temerare*, to defile, pollute], undefiled; unpolluted; pure.

in·tem·per·ance (in-tem'pẽr-əns), ***n.*** 1. a lack of temperance or restraint; immoderation; excess. 2. excessive drinking of alcoholic liquor.

in·tem·per·ate (in-tem'pẽr-it), ***adj.*** 1. not temperate; specifically, *a*) not moderate; excessive; going to extremes. *b*) severe or violent; inclement: as, an *intemperate* wind. 2. drinking too much alcoholic liquor.

in·tend (in-tend'), ***v.t.*** [ME. *entende;* OFr. *entendre;* L. *intendere*, to stretch out for, aim at; *in-*, in, at + *tendere*, to stretch], 1. to have in mind as a purpose; plan; purpose. 2. to mean (something) to be or be used for; design; destine: as, the cake was *intended* for the party. 3. to mean or take to mean; signify. 4. [Archaic], to direct; turn; bend: as, they *intend* their thoughts homeward. 5. in *law*, to construe or interpret legally. ***v.i.*** to have a purpose or intention.

SYN.—**intend** implies a having in mind of something to be done, said, etc. (I *intended* to write you); **mean**, a more general word, does not connote so clearly a specific, deliberate purpose (he always *means* well); **design** suggests careful planning in order to bring about a particular result (their delay was *designed* to forestall suspicion); **propose** implies a clear declaration, openly or to oneself, of one's intention (I *propose* to speak for an hour); **purpose** adds to **propose** a connotation of strong determination to effect one's intention (he *purposes* to become a doctor).

in·tend·ance (in-ten'dəns), ***n.*** [Fr. < *intendant;* see INTENDANT], 1. superintendence; supervision. 2. intendancy. 3. an administrative department, as in France. 4. an intendant's official quarters.

in·tend·an·cy (in-ten'dən-si), ***n.*** [*pl.* INTENDANCIES (-siz)], 1. the position or duties of an intendant. 2. intendants collectively. 3. [Sp. *intendencia* < *intendente*, intendant], in South America, the district supervised by an intendant.

in·tend·ant (in-ten'dənt), ***n.*** [Fr. < L. *intendens*, ppr. of *intendere;* see INTEND], a director, manager of a public business, superintendent, etc.: term applied to certain foreign officials, as to the supervisors of any of certain districts in South America.

in·tend·ed (in-ten'did), ***adj.*** [pp. of *intend*], 1. meant; planned; intentional; purposed. 2. prospective; future: as, an *intended* wife. ***n.*** [Colloq.], one's prospective wife or husband.

in·tend·ment (in-tend'mənt), ***n.*** [ME. & OFr. *entendement;* see INTEND], 1. [Archaic], intention, purpose, or design. 2. in *law*, the meaning (of a word, etc.) as used in law; legal meaning.

intens., 1. intensified. 2. intensifier. 3. intensive.

in·tense (in-tens'), ***adj.*** [ME.; Late OFr.; L. *intensus*, pp. of *intendere;* see INTEND], 1. occurring or existing in a high degree; very strong; violent, excessive, or vivid: as, an *intense* light. 2. strained to the utmost; strenuous; earnest; fervent; zealous: as, *intense* thought. 3. having or showing strong emotion, firm purpose, great seriousness, etc.: as, an *intense* person. 4. characterized by much action, emotion, etc. 5. in *photography*, dense or opaque.

in·tense·ly (in-tens'li), ***adv.*** 1. in an intense manner; with strong feeling. 2. in a high degree; extremely.

in·ten·si·fi·ca·tion (in-ten'sə-fi-kā'shən), ***n.*** an intensifying or being intensified.

in·ten·si·fi·er (in-ten'sə-fī'ẽr), ***n.*** 1. something that intensifies. 2. in *photography*, any of several solutions used to increase the printing density of a negative.

in·ten·si·fy (in-ten'sə-fī'), ***v.t.*** [INTENSIFIED (-fīd'), INTENSIFYING], 1. to make intense or more intense; increase; strengthen. 2. in *photography*, to make (a film, etc.) dense or opaque by treating with an intensifier. ***v.i.*** to become intense or increase in intensity.

SYN.—**intensify** implies an increasing in the degree of force, vehemence, vividness, etc. (his absence only *intensified* her longing); **aggravate** implies a making more serious, unbearable, etc. and connotes something that is unpleasant or troublesome in itself (your insolence only *aggravates* the offense); to **heighten** is to make greater, stronger, more vivid, etc. so as to raise above the ordinary or commonplace (music served to *heighten* the effect); **enhance** implies the addition of something so as to make more attractive or desirable (she used cosmetics to *enhance* her beauty).—***ANT.*** diminish, mitigate.

in·ten·sion (in-ten'shən), ***n.*** [L. *intensio* < *intensus*, pp. of *intendere;* see INTEND], 1. intentness; determination. 2. intensification. 3. the quality of being intense; intensity; extreme degree. 4. in *logic*, all the qualities or properties which a term or concept signifies; connotation: opposed to *extension.*

in·ten·si·ty (in-ten'sə-ti), ***n.*** [*pl.* INTENSITIES (-tiz)], 1. the quality of being intense; specifically, *a*) extreme degree of anything. *b*) great energy or vehemence of emotion, thought, or activity. 2. in *photography*, the density or opaqueness of an image. 3. in *physics*, the amount of force or energy of heat, light, sound, electric current, etc. per unit area, volume, charge, etc.

in·ten·sive (in-ten'siv), ***adj.*** [Fr. *intensif* < L. *intensus;* see INTEND], 1. increasing or causing to increase in degree or amount. 2. of or characterized by intensity; thorough, profound, and intense; not broad or extensive; concentrated or exhaustive. 3. of or characterized by logical intension. 4. in *agriculture*, designating a system of farming which aims at the increase of crop yield per unit area. 5. in *grammar*, giving force or emphasis; emphasizing: as, *oneself* is frequently *intensive*. *n.* 1. anything that intensifies. 2. in *grammar*, an intensive word, prefix, etc. Abbreviated **intens.**

in·tent (in-tent′), *adj.* [L. *intentus*, pp. of *intendere*; see INTEND], 1. firmly directed or fixed; earnest; intense: as, an *intent* look. 2. *a)* having the mind or attention firmly directed or fixed; engrossed: as, he was *intent* on his studies. *b)* strongly resolved: as, he was *intent* on going. *n.* [ME. *entent, intent*; OFr. *entent*; L. *intentus*, a stretching out < *intendere*; see INTEND; also ME. *entente*; OFr. *entente* < L. *intendere*], 1. an intending. 2. something intended; specifically, *a)* a purpose; object. *b)* [Obs.], meaning. —*SYN.* see **intention.**
to all intents and purposes, in almost every respect; practically; virtually.

in·ten·tion (in-ten′shən), *n.* [ME. *entencioun*; OFr. *entencion, intention*; L. *intentio* < pp. of *intendere*], 1. an intending; determination to do a specified thing or act in a specified manner. 2. *a)* anything intended; ultimate end or purpose: as, what is your *intention*? *b) pl.* purpose in regard to marriage. 3. [Archaic], intentness. 4. [Archaic or Rare], meaning or intent. 5. in *logic*, the general concept of a thing. 6. in *surgery*, the manner or process by which a wound heals: the three degrees (*first, second*, and *third intention*) are distinguished by the relative amounts and types of granulation that occur.
SYN.—**intention** is the general word implying a having something in mind as a plan or design or referring to the plan had in mind; **intent**, a somewhat formal term now largely in legal usage, connotes more deliberation (assault with *intent* to kill); **purpose** connotes greater resolution or determination in the plan (I have a *purpose* in writing you); **aim** refers to a specific intention and connotes a directing of all efforts toward this (his *aim* is to become a doctor); **goal** suggests laborious effort in striving to attain something (the presidency was the *goal* of his ambition); **end** emphasizes the final result one hopes to achieve as distinct from the process of achieving it (is this *end* justified by the means used?); **object** is used of an end that is the direct result of a need or desire (the *object* of the discussion was to arouse controversy); **objective** refers to a specific end that is capable of being reached (her immediate *objective* is to pass the course).

in·ten·tion·al (in-ten′shən-'l), *adj.* [ML. *intentionalis*], 1. [Rare], having to do with intention or purpose. 2. done purposely; intended. —*SYN.* see **voluntary.**

in·ten·tion·al·ly (in-ten′shən-'l-i), *adv.* with intention; purposely.

in·ten·tioned (in-ten′shənd), *adj.* having (specified) intentions: as, a generously *intentioned* person: often in hyphenated compounds, as *well-intentioned*.

in·ter (in-tũr′), *v.t.* [INTERRED (-tũrd′), INTERRING], [ME. *enteren*; OFr. *enterrer*; LL. *interrare*, to put in the earth < L. *in*, in + *terra*, earth], to put (a dead body) into the ground or a tomb; bury.

in·ter- (in′tẽr), [L. < *inter*, between, among; IE. **enter*, **nter* (compar. of **en*, in), seen also in Sans. *antár*, within, AS. *under*, G. *unter*, among], a combining form meaning: 1. *between, among*, as in *interborough*. 2. *with* or *on each other* (or *one another*), *together, mutual, reciprocal, mutually, reciprocally*, as in *interact*.

inter., interrogation.

in·ter·act (in′tẽr-akt′), *v.i.* to act on each other; act reciprocally.

in·ter·ac·tion (in′tẽr-ak′shən), *n.* action on each other; reciprocal action or effect.

in·ter·ac·tive (in′tẽr-ak′tiv), *adj.* interacting.

‡in·ter a·li·a (in′tẽr ā′li-ə), [L.], among other things.

‡in·ter a·li·os (in′tẽr ā′li-ōs′), [L.], among other persons.

in·ter-A·mer·i·can (in′tẽr-ə-mer′ə-kən), *adj.* between or among nations of North, South, and Central America.

in·ter·bor·ough (in′tẽr-bũr′ō), *adj.* between or among boroughs.

in·ter·breed (in′tẽr-brēd′), *v.t.* to cross different varieties of (animals or plants) in breeding. *v.i.* to breed in this way.

in·ter·ca·lar·y (in-tũr′kə-ler′i), *adj.* [L. *intercalarius, intercalaris* < *intercalare*; see INTERCALATE], 1. added to the calendar: said of a day, month, etc. added as in leap year to make the calendar correspond to the solar year. 2. having such a day, month, etc. added: said of a year. 3. interpolated or inserted.

in·ter·ca·late (in-tũr′kə-lāt′), *v.t.* [INTERCALATED (-id), INTERCALATING], [< L. *intercalatus*, pp. of *intercalare*, to insert; *inter-*, between + *calare*, to call, proclaim], 1. to add (a day, month, etc.) to the calendar. 2. to interpolate or insert.

in·ter·ca·la·tion (in-tũr′kə-lā′shən), *n.* 1. an intercalating; interpolation. 2. something intercalated.

in·ter·cede (in′tẽr-sēd′), *v.i.* [INTERCEDED (-id), INTERCEDING], [L. *intercedere*; *inter-*, between + *cedere*, to go], 1. to plead or make a request in behalf of another or others: as, his colleagues *interceded* with the president for a hearing. 2. to intervene for the purpose of producing agreement; mediate. 3. in ancient Rome, to interpose a veto: said of a tribune or other magistrate. —*SYN.* see **interpose.**

in·ter·cel·lu·lar (in′tẽr-sel′yoo-lẽr), *adj.* located between or among cells.

in·ter·cept (in′tẽr-sept′; *for n.*, in′tẽr-sept′), *v.t.* [< L. *interceptus*, pp. of *intercipere*, to take between, interrupt < *inter-*, between + *capere*, to take], 1. to seize or stop on the way, before arrival at the intended place; stop or interrupt the course of; cut off. 2. to stop, hinder, or prevent: as, he *intercepted* the escape of the thief. 3. to cut off communication with, sight of, etc. 4. in *mathematics*, to cut off, mark off, or bound between two points, lines, or planes. *n.* in *mathematics*, the part of a line, plane, etc. intercepted.

in·ter·cept·er (in′tẽr-sep′tẽr), *n.* an interceptor.

in·ter·cep·tion (in′tẽr-sep′shən), *n.* an intercepting or being intercepted.

in·ter·cep·tive (in′tẽr-sep′tiv), *adj.* intercepting or tending to intercept.

in·ter·cep·tor (in′tẽr-sep′tẽr), *n.* a person or thing that intercepts; especially, a fast-climbing military airplane used in fighting off enemy attacks.

in·ter·ces·sion (in′tẽr-sesh′ən), *n.* [L. *intercessio* < *intercessus*, pp. of *intercedere*], an interceding; mediation, pleading, or prayer in behalf of another or others.

in·ter·ces·sion·al (in′tẽr-sesh′ən-'l), *adj.* of or characterized by intercession.

in·ter·ces·sor (in′tẽr-ses′ẽr, in′tẽr-ses′ẽr), *n.* [L. < *intercessus*, pp. of *intercedere*], a person who intercedes.

in·ter·ces·so·ry (in′tẽr-ses′ẽr-i), *adj.* [ML. *intercessorius*], of or serving as intercession; interceding.

in·ter·change (in′tẽr-chānj′; *for n.*, in′tẽr-chānj′), *v.t.* [INTERCHANGED (-chānjd′), INTERCHANGING], [ME. *entrechangen*; OFr. *entrechangier*; see INTER- & CHANGE], 1. to give and take mutually; exchange: as, they *interchanged* presents. 2. to put (each of two things) in the other's place. 3. to alternate; cause to follow in succession: as, he *interchanged* work with play. *v.i.* to make an interchange. *n.* 1. an interchanging; specifically, *a)* a mutual giving in exchange. *b)* alternation. 2. any of the places on a freeway where traffic can enter or depart, usually by means of a cloverleaf.

in·ter·change·a·bil·i·ty (in′tẽr-chān′jə-bil′ə-ti), *n.* the quality or condition of being interchangeable.

in·ter·change·a·ble (in′tẽr-chān′jə-b'l), *adj.* [OFr. *entrechangeable*], that can be interchanged; especially, that can be put or used in place of each other.

in·ter·change·a·bly (in′tẽr-chān′jə-bli), *adv.* so as to be interchangeable.

in·ter·class (in′tẽr-klas′, in′tẽr-kläs′), *adj.* between or among classes: as, *interclass* debates.

in·ter·clav·i·cle (in′tẽr-klav′ə-k'l), *n.* a bone situated between the clavicles and in front of the sternum in certain vertebrates.

in·ter·cla·vic·u·lar (in′tẽr-klə-vik′yoo-lẽr), *adj.* situated between the clavicles.

in·ter·col·le·gi·ate (in′tẽr-kə-lē′jit, in′tẽr-kə-lē′ji-it), *adj.* between or among colleges and universities.

in·ter·co·lo·ni·al (in′tẽr-kə-lō′ni-əl), *adj.* between or among colonies: as, *intercolonial* commerce.

in·ter·co·lum·nar (in′tẽr-kə-lum′nẽr), *adj.* situated between columns.

in·ter·co·lum·ni·a·tion (in′tẽr-kə-lum′ni-ā′shən), *n.* in *architecture*, 1. the space between two columns, measured from their axes. 2. the system of placing columns with reference to their spacing.

in·ter·com (in′tẽr-kom′), *n.* [Slang], an intercommunication system, as between the pilot and the bombardier in an airplane.

in·ter·com·mu·ni·cate (in′tẽr-kə-mū′ni-kāt′), *v.t. & v.i.* to communicate with or to each other or one another.

in·ter·com·mu·ni·ca·tion (in′tẽr-kə-mū′ni-kā′shən), *n.* communication with or to each other or one another.

in·ter·com·mun·ion (in′tẽr-kə-mūn′yən), *n.* mutual communion, as among religious groups.

in·ter·com·mu·ni·ty (in′tẽr-kə-mū′nə-ti), *n.* the quality of being common to two or more; a sharing of something in common.

in·ter·con·nect (in′tẽr-kə-nekt′), *v.t. & v.i.* to connect or be connected with each other or one another.

in·ter·con·nec·tion (in′tẽr-kə-nek′shən), *n.* connection with each other or one another.

in·ter·con·ti·nen·tal (in′tẽr-kon′tə-nen′t'l), *adj.* between or among continents.

in·ter·cos·tal (in′tẽr-kos′t'l), *adj.* [Mod. L. *intercostalis*; see INTER- & COSTAL], between the ribs.

in·ter·course (in′tẽr-kôrs′, in′tẽr-kōrs′), *n.* [OFr. *entrecours*; L. *intercursus*; see INTER- & COURSE], 1. communication or dealings between or among people, countries, etc.; interchange of products, services, ideas, feelings, etc. 2. the sexual joining of two individuals; coitus; copulation: usually **sexual intercourse.**

in·ter·crop (in′tẽr-krop′), *v.t. & v.i.* [INTERCROPPED

(-kropt′), INTERCROPPING], [*inter-* + *crop*], to cultivate (land) by planting different crops in alternate rows. *n.* (in′tẽr-krop′), any such crop.

in·ter·cross (in′tẽr-krôs′), *v.t.* & *v.i.* 1. to cross (one another). 2. to interbreed. *n.* (in′tẽr-krôs′), 1. an interbreeding. 2. the hybrid resulting from this.

in·ter·cur·rent (in′tẽr-kũr′ənt), *adj.* [L. *intercurrens*, ppr. of *intercurrere; inter-*, between + *currere*, to run], 1. running between; intervening. 2. occurring during another disease and modifying it.

in·ter·de·nom·i·na·tion·al (in′tẽr-di-nom′ə-nā′shən-'l), *adj.* between, among, shared by, or involving different religious denominations.

in·ter·den·tal (in′tẽr-den′t'l), *adj.* 1. situated between the teeth. 2. in *phonetics*, pronounced with the tip of the tongue between the teeth, as *th* in *think*.

in·ter·de·part·men·tal (in′tẽr-di-pärt′men′t'l, in′tẽr-dē′pärt-men′t'l), *adj.* between or among departments.

in·ter·de·pend·ence (in′tẽr-di-pen′dəns), *n.* dependence on each other or one another; mutual dependence.

in·ter·de·pend·en·cy (in′tẽr-di-pen′dən-si), *n.* interdependence.

in·ter·de·pend·ent (in′tẽr-di-pen′dənt), *adj.* dependent on each other or one another; mutually dependent.

in·ter·dict (in′tẽr-dikt′; *for n.*, in′tẽr-dikt′), *v.t.* [ME. *entrediten* < *entredit*, *n.* (< OFr. *entredit*), remodeled after L. *interdictus*, pp. of *interdicere*, to speak between, forbid, prohibit (*inter-*, between + *dicere*, to speak, say), which is also source of the OFr. word], 1. to prohibit (an action) or the use of (a thing); forbid with authority. 2. to restrain from doing or using something. 3. in the *Roman Catholic Church*, to exclude (a person, parish, etc.) from certain church offices, sacraments, or privileges. *n.* [L. *interdictum* < the *v.*], an official prohibition or restraint; specifically, *a*) in *Scottish law*, an injunction. *b*) in the *Roman Catholic Church*, an interdicting of a person, parish, etc. —***SYN.*** see **forbid**.

in·ter·dic·tion (in′tẽr-dik′shən), *n.* [L. *interdictio*], an interdicting or being interdicted.

in·ter·dic·tive (in′tẽr-dik′tiv), *adj.* interdictory.

in·ter·dic·to·ry (in′tẽr-dik′tẽr-i), *adj.* [LL. *interdictorius*], of, or having the nature of, an interdict.

in·ter·dig·i·tal (in′tẽr-dij′i-t'l), *adj.* [*inter-* + *digital*], between or joining the fingers or toes.

in·ter·est (in′tẽr-ist, in′trist; *also, for v.*, in′tə-rest′), *n.* [ME. *interesse;* ML. *interesse*, usury, compensation (in L., to be between, be different or important; *inter-*, between + *esse*, to be); modified by OFr. *interest* < L. *interest*, it interests, concerns, is to the advantage, 3d pers. sing., pres. indic., of *interesse*], 1. a right or claim to something. 2. a share or participation in something. 3. anything in which one participates or has a share. 4. *often pl.* profit; welfare; benefit. 5. a group of people having a common concern in some industry, occupation, cause, etc.: as, the steel *interest*. 6. social or political influence. 7. *a*) a feeling of intentness, concern, or curiosity about something. *b*) the power of causing this feeling. *c*) something causing this feeling. 8. importance; consequence: as, a matter of little *interest*. 9. *a*) money paid for the use of money. *b*) the rate of such payment, expressed as a percentage per unit of time; hence, 10. an increase or addition over what is owed: as, he repaid her kindness with *interest*. Abbreviated **int.**, **i.** (in senses 9 *a* & *b*). *v.t.* [prob. < ME. *interressed* < *interesse* + *-ed*], 1. to involve the interest, or concern, of; have an effect upon. 2. to cause to have an interest, or share, in: as, can I *interest* you in joining our club? 3. to excite the attention or curiosity of.

in the interest (or **interests**) **of**, for the sake of; in order to promote.

in·ter·est·ed (in′tẽr-is-tid, in′tris-tid, in′tə-res′tid), *adj.* [pp. of *interest*], 1. having an interest or share; concerned. 2. influenced by personal interest; biased or prejudiced. 3. feeling or showing interest, or curiosity.

in·ter·est·ing (in′tẽr-is-tiŋ, in′tris-tiŋ, in′tə-res′tiŋ), *adj.* exciting curiosity or attention; of interest.

in·ter·face (in′tẽr-fās′), *n.* a surface that lies between two parts of matter or space and forms their common boundary.

in·ter·fa·cial (in′tẽr-fā′shəl), *adj.* designating the angle between any two faces of a crystal or a crystal form.

in·ter·fen·es·tra·tion (in′tẽr-fen′is-trā′shən), *n.* [*inter-* + *fenestration*], the spacing of the windows of a building.

in·ter·fere (in′tẽr-fêr′), *v.i.* [INTERFERED (-fêrd′), INTERFERING], [OFr. *s'entreferir*, to strike (each other) < L. *inter*, between, among + *ferire*, to strike], 1. to knock one foot or leg against the other: said of a horse. 2. to strike against each other; come into collision or opposition; clash; collide. 3. *a*) to come in or between for some purpose; intervene. *b*) to meddle. 4. in *football*, to effect an interference. 5. in *patent law*, to claim priority for an invention, as when two or more applications for its patent are pending. 6. in *physics*, to affect each other by interference: said of two waves or streams of vibration. 7. in *radio*, to create interference in reception. —***SYN.*** see **interpose**.

interfere with, 1. to hinder; prevent. 2. to annoy.

in·ter·fer·ence (in′tẽr-fêr′əns), *n.* 1. an interfering. 2. in *football*, *a*) the obstruction of opposing tacklers in order to make the way clear for the ball carrier. *b*) the illegal hindering of the receiving of a pass. 3. in *physics*, the mutual action of two waves or streams of vibration, as of sound, light, etc., in reinforcing or neutralizing each other according to their relative phases on meeting. 4. in *radio*, static, unwanted signals, etc., producing a confusion of sounds and preventing good reception.

run interference for, in *football*, to accompany (the ball carrier) in order to obstruct opposing tacklers.

in·ter·fe·ren·tial (in′tẽr-fə-ren′shəl), *adj.* in *physics*, of or working by interference.

in·ter·fer·om·e·ter (in′tẽr-fêr-om′ə-tẽr), *n.* [< *interfere* + *-meter*], an instrument for measuring wave lengths of light and for analyzing small parts of a spectrum by means of the interference phenomena of light.

in·ter·fold (in′tẽr-fōld′), *v.t.* & *v.i.* to fold together or inside each other.

in·ter·fuse (in′tẽr-fūz′), *v.t.* [< L. *interfusus*, pp. of *interfundere*, to pour between; see INTER- & FUSE, *v.*], 1. to combine by mixing, blending, or fusing together. 2. to cause to pass into or through a substance; infuse. 3. to spread itself through; pervade. *v.i.* to fuse; blend.

in·ter·fu·sion (in′tẽr-fū′zhən), *n.* [LL. *interfusio*], an interfusing or being interfused.

in·ter·gla·cial (in′tẽr-glā′shəl), *adj.* formed or occurring between two glacial epochs.

in·ter·gra·da·tion (in′tẽr-grā-dā′shən), *n.* an intergrading.

in·ter·grade (in′tẽr-grād′), *v.i.* [INTERGRADED (-id), INTERGRADING], to pass into another form or kind by a series of intermediate grades. *n.* (in′tẽr-grād′), an intermediate grade; transitional form.

in·ter·im (in′tẽr-im), *n.* [L. < *inter*, between], the period of time between; meantime. *adj.* for or during an interim; temporary; provisional: as, an *interim* council.

in·te·ri·or (in-têr′i-ẽr), *adj.* [OFr.; L., compar. of *inter*, between, within], 1. situated within; on the inside; inner. 2. away from the coast, border, or frontier; inland. 3. of the internal, or domestic, affairs of a country: opposed to *foreign*. 4. of the inner nature of a person or thing; private, secret, etc. *n.* 1. the interior part of anything; specifically, *a*) the inside of a room or building. *b*) the inland part of a country or region. *c*) the inner nature of a person or thing. 2. a picture, view, etc. of the inside of a room or building. 3. the internal, or domestic, affairs of a country: as, the United States Department of the *Interior;* hence, 4. [I-], the Department of the Interior. Abbreviated **int.**

interior angle, 1. any of the four angles formed on the inside of two straight lines by a straight line cutting across them. 2. the angle formed inside a polygon by two adjacent sides. Cf. **exterior angle**.

interior decoration, 1. the decorating and furnishing of the interior of a room, house, etc. 2. the art or business of decorating and furnishing such interiors.

in·te·ri·or·i·ty (in-têr′i-ôr′ə-ti, in-têr′i-or′ə-ti), *n.* 1. the quality or state of being interior. 2. inner nature or character.

in·te·ri·or·ly (in-têr′i-ẽr-li), *adv.* 1. in, or with respect to, the interior; on the inside; internally. 2. in, or with respect to, the inner nature of a person or thing.

interj., interjection.

in·ter·ja·cent (in′tẽr-jā′sənt), *adj.* [L. *interjacens*, ppr. of *interjacere*, to lie between; *inter-*, between + *jacere*, to lie], lying between; situated between; intervening.

in·ter·ject (in′tẽr-jekt′), *v.t.* [< L. *interjectus*, pp. of *interjicere*, *interjacere*, to throw between < *inter-*, between + *jacere*, to throw], to throw in between; interrupt with; insert; interpose: as, she *interjected* a question. *v.i.* [Obs.], to come between. —***SYN.*** see **introduce**.

in·ter·jec·tion (in′tẽr-jek′shən), *n.* [Fr.; L. *interjectio*], 1. an interjecting. 2. something interjected; exclamation. 3. in *grammar*, an exclamation thrown in without grammatical connection (e.g., ah! lo! pshaw! good-by!): abbreviated **interj.**, **int.**

in·ter·jec·tion·al (in′tẽr-jek′shən-'l), *adj.* 1. of, or having the nature of, an interjection. 2. interjected. 3. containing an interjection.

in·ter·ject·or (in′tẽr-jek′tẽr), *n.* a person or thing that interjects.

in·ter·jec·to·ry (in′tẽr-jek′tẽr-i), *adj.* interjectional.

in·ter·knit (in′tẽr-nit′), *v.t.* & *v.i.* to knit together; intertwine.

in·ter·lace (in′tẽr-lās′), *v.t.* & *v.i.* [INTERLACED (-lāst′), INTERLACING], [ME. *entrelacen;* OFr. *entrelacier;* see INTER- & LACE], 1. to unite by passing over and under each other; weave together. 2. to connect intricately.

in·ter·lace·ment (in′tẽr-lās′mənt), *n.* 1. an interlacing or being interlaced. 2. something interlaced in arrangement or structure.

In·ter·la·ken (in′tẽr-lä′kən), *n.* a resort between Lakes Thun and Brienz in central Switzerland: pop., 3,800.

in·ter·lam·i·nate (in′tẽr-lam′ə-nāt′), *v.t.* [INTERLAMINATED (-id), INTERLAMINATING], 1. to put between laminae. 2. to place in alternate laminae.

in·ter·lam·i·na·tion (in′tẽr-lam′ə-nā′shən), *n.* 1. an interlaminating. 2. an interlaminated formation.

in·ter·lard (in′tẽr-lärd′), *v.t.* [Fr. *entrelarder;* see INTER-

& LARD], 1. to put strips or pieces of fat, bacon, etc. in with (meat to be cooked). 2. to intersperse; diversify: as, the professor *interlarded* his lecture with quotations. 3. to be intermixed in: said of things.
in·ter·lay (in'tẽr-lā'), ***v.t.*** [INTERLAID (-lād'), INTERLAYING], 1. to lay or put between or among. 2. to ornament with something laid or put between.
in·ter·leaf (in'tẽr-lēf'), ***n.*** [*pl.* INTERLEAVES (-lēvz')], 1. a leaf, usually blank, bound between the other leaves of a book, for notes, etc. 2. what is written or printed on such a leaf.
in·ter·leave (in'tẽr-lēv'), ***v.t.*** [INTERLEAVED (-lēvd'), INTERLEAVING], to put an interleaf or interleaves in.
in·ter·line (in'tẽr-līn'), ***v.t.*** [ME. *enterlynen;* OFr. *entreligner;* ML. *interlineare;* see INTER- & LINE], 1. to write or print between the lines of (a text, document, etc.). 2. to insert between the lines: as, he *interlined* notes on the pages.
in·ter·line (in'tẽr-līn'), ***v.t.*** [INTERLINED (-līnd'), INTERLINING], to put an inner lining between the outer material and the ordinary lining of (a garment).
in·ter·lin·e·al (in'tẽr-lin'i-əl), ***adj.*** 1. interlinear. 2. arranged in alternate lines.
in·ter·lin·e·ar (in'tẽr-lin'i-ẽr), ***adj.*** [ML. *interlinearis*], 1. written or printed between the lines: as, *interlinear* notes. 2. having the same text in different languages printed in alternate lines: as, an *interlinear* Bible.
in·ter·lin·e·ate (in'tẽr-lin'i-āt'), ***v.t.*** [< ML. *interlineatus*, pp.], [Rare], to interline (insert between lines).
in·ter·lin·e·a·tion (in'tẽr-lin'i-ā'shən), ***n.*** [< *interlineate*], 1. the insertion of a word or words between the lines of written or printed matter. 2. the word or words thus inserted.
in·ter·lin·ing (in'tẽr-līn'iŋ), ***n.*** 1. an inner lining put between the outer material and the ordinary lining of a garment. 2. any fabric used as an interlining.
in·ter·link (in'tẽr-liŋk'), ***v.t.*** to link together.
in·ter·lock (in'tẽr-lok'), ***v.t. & v.i.*** 1. to lock together; join with one another. 2. to connect or be connected so that neither part can be operated independently.
interlocking directorates, boards of directors having some members in common, so that the corporations concerned are more or less under the same control.
interlocking signals, railroad signals interlocked with each other so that when one has been lowered the others cannot be changed until the train has passed.
in·ter·lo·cu·tion (in'tẽr-lō-kū'shən), ***n.*** [L. *interlocutio;* see INTER- & LOCUTION], talk between two or more people; interchange of speech; conversation; dialogue.
in·ter·loc·u·tor (in'tẽr-lok'yoo-tẽr), ***n.*** [< pp. of L. *interloqui;* see INTERLOCUTION], 1. a person taking part in a conversation or dialogue. 2. an entertainer in a minstrel show who asks questions of the end men.
in·ter·loc·u·to·ry (in'tẽr-lok'yoo-tôr'i, in'tẽr-lok'yoo-tō'ri), ***adj.*** [< *interlocution* + *-ory*], 1. of, having the nature of, or occurring in dialogue; conversational. 2. interjected: as, *interlocutory* wit. 3. in *law*, pronounced during the course of a suit, pending final decision; not final: as, an *interlocutory* divorce decree.
in·ter·loc·u·tress (in'tẽr-lok'yoo-tris), ***n.*** a woman or girl interlocutor.
in·ter·lope (in'tẽr-lōp'), ***v.i.*** [INTERLOPED (-lōpt'), INTERLOPING], [< *interloper*], 1. originally, to intrude on another's trading rights or privileges; hence, 2. to intrude or meddle in others' affairs. —***SYN.*** see **intrude.**
in·ter·lop·er (in'tẽr-lōp'ẽr), ***n.*** [prob. < D. *enterlooper*, coasting vessel, smuggler < Fr. *entre*, between + D. *loopen*, to run (akin to *lope* & *leap*)], 1. *a)* originally, an unauthorized trading vessel in areas assigned to monopolies or chartered companies; hence, *b)* any unauthorized trader. 2. a person who meddles in others' affairs.
in·ter·lude (in'tẽr-lōōd', in'tẽr-lūd'), ***n.*** [ME. *enterlude;* OFr. *entrelude;* ML. *interludium* < L. *inter*, between + *ludus*, play], 1. a type of short humorous play, usually with two characters, formerly presented between the parts of miracle plays or moralities, at entertainments, etc. 2. any performance given between the acts of a play. 3. a short play, either farcical or moralistic in tone, as presented in the hall of a Tudor noble before an aristocratic audience by professional players: the typical interlude, as written by John Heywood and others, draws its plot from French farce, the morality play, or the Latin school play: regarded as the earliest form of modern English drama. 4. instrumental music played between the parts of a song, church liturgy, play, etc. 5. anything that fills time between two events: as, *interludes* of waiting between trains.
in·ter·lu·nar (in'tẽr-lōō'nẽr, in'tẽr-lū'nẽr), ***adj.*** [*inter-* + *lunar*], between the old moon and the new moon; of the period of about four days between old and new moon, when the moon cannot be seen because it is too close to the sun.
in·ter·mar·riage (in'tẽr-mar'ij), ***n.*** 1. marriage between persons of different families, clans, tribes, races, castes, etc. 2. marriage between closely related persons.
in·ter·mar·ry (in'tẽr-mar'i), ***v.i.*** 1. to become connected by or unite in marriage: said of different families, clans, tribes, races, castes, etc. 2. to marry: said of closely related persons.
in·ter·med·dle (in'tẽr-med''l), ***v.t.*** [ME. *entremedlen;* Anglo-Fr. *entremedler;* see INTER- & MEDDLE], [Obs.], to mix together. ***v.i.*** to meddle in the affairs of others.
in·ter·me·di·a·cy (in'tẽr-mē'di-ə-si), ***n.*** the state of being intermediate.
in·ter·me·di·ar·y (in'tẽr-mē'di-er'i), ***adj.*** [< L. *intermedius* (see INTERMEDIATE); + *-ary*], 1. acting between two persons; acting as mediator. 2. being or happening between; intermediate. ***n.*** [*pl.* INTERMEDIARIES (-iz)], 1. a go-between; mediator. 2. a medium; means; agency. 3. an intermediate form, phase, etc.
in·ter·me·di·ate (in'tẽr-mē'di-it), ***adj.*** [ML. *intermediatus* < L. *intermedius; inter-*, between + *medius*, middle], being or happening between; in the middle. ***n.*** 1. anything intermediate. 2. an intermediary. ***v.i.*** (in'tẽr-mē'di-āt'), [INTERMEDIATED (-id), INTERMEDIATING], to act as an intermediary; mediate.
in·ter·me·di·a·tion (in'tẽr-mē'di-ā'shən), ***n.*** an intermediating.
in·ter·me·di·a·tor (in'tẽr-mē'di-ā'tẽr), ***n.*** a person who intermediates.
in·ter·ment (in-tũr'mənt), ***n.*** an interring; burial.
in·ter·mez·zo (in'tẽr-met'sō, in'tẽr-med'zō), ***n.*** [*pl.* INTERMEZZOS (-sōz, -zōz), INTERMEZZI (-si, -zi)], [It. < L. *intermedius;* see INTERMEDIATE], 1. a short, light dramatic, musical, or ballet entertainment between the acts of a play or opera. 2. in *music, a)* a short movement connecting the main parts of a composition. *b)* any of certain short instrumental pieces similar to this.
in·ter·mi·na·ble (in-tũr'mi-nə-b'l), ***adj.*** [ME. *intermynable;* OFr.; LL. *interminabilis;* see IN- (not) & TERMINABLE], without, or apparently without, end; lasting, or seeming to last, forever; endless.
in·ter·mi·na·bly (in-tũr'mi-nə-bli), ***adv.*** without end.
in·ter·min·gle (in'tẽr-miŋ'g'l), ***v.t. & v.i.*** to mix together; mingle; blend.
in·ter·mis·sion (in'tẽr-mish'ən), ***n.*** [L. *intermissio* < *intermissus*, pp. of *intermittere*], 1. an intermitting or being intermitted; interruption. 2. an interval of time between periods of activity: as, *intermissions* between acts of a play.
in·ter·mis·sive (in'tẽr-mis'iv), ***adj.*** of, or having the nature of, an intermission; intermittent.
in·ter·mit (in'tẽr-mit'), ***v.t. & v.i.*** [INTERMITTED (-id), INTERMITTING], [L. *intermittere; inter-*, between + *mittere*, to send], to stop for a time; cease at intervals; make or be intermittent; discontinue.
in·ter·mit·tence (in'tẽr-mit''ns), ***n.*** the state or fact of being intermittent.
in·ter·mit·ten·cy (in'tẽr-mit''n-si), ***n.*** intermittence.
in·ter·mit·tent (in'tẽr-mit''nt), ***adj.*** [L. *intermittens*, pp. of *intermittere;* see INTERMIT], stopping and starting again at intervals; pausing from time to time; periodic.
SYN.—**intermittent** and **recurrent** both apply to something that stops and starts, or disappears and reappears, from time to time, but the former usually stresses the breaks or pauses, and the latter, the repetition or return (an *intermittent* fever, *recurrent* attacks of the hives); **periodic** refers to something that recurs at more or less regular intervals (*periodic* economic crises); **alternate** is usually used of two recurrent things that follow each other in regular order (a life of *alternate* sorrow and joy).—***ANT.*** continued, continuous.
intermittent current, an electric current interrupted at intervals but always flowing in the same direction.
intermittent fever, a fever characterized by periodic intervals when the body temperature returns to normal.
in·ter·mit·ter (in'tẽr-mit'ẽr), ***n.*** a person or thing that intermits.
in·ter·mix (in'tẽr-miks'), ***v.t. & v.i.*** to mix together; blend; intermingle.
in·ter·mix·ture (in'tẽr-miks'chẽr), ***n.*** 1. an intermixing or being intermixed. 2. a mixture. 3. an added ingredient; admixture.
in·ter·mon·tane (in'tẽr-mon'tān), ***adj.*** [< *inter-* + L. *montanus*, of a mountain < *mons, montis*, mountain], between or among mountains.
in·tern (in'tẽrn; *for v.t.*, in-tũrn'), ***n.*** [Fr. *interne*, resident within < L. *internus*, inward, internal], a doctor serving as an assistant resident in a hospital generally just after his graduation from medical school: also spelled **interne.** ***v.i.*** to be, or act as, an intern. ***v.t.*** 1. to detain and confine within a country or a definite area: as, countries often *intern* aliens in time of war. 2. to detain (ships) in port.
in·ter·nal (in-tũr'n'l), ***adj.*** [ML. *internalis* < L. *internus;* see INTERN], 1. of or on the inside; inward; inner; interior: opposed to *external.* 2. having to do with or belonging to the inner nature of a thing; intrinsic: as, *internal* evidence. 3. having to do with or belonging to the inner nature of man; subjective. 4. domestic: as, *internal* wars, *internal* revenue: opposed to *foreign.*

5. to be taken or applied inside the body: as, *internal* remedies. 6. in *anatomy*, situated toward the inside of the body or closer to its center. Abbreviated **int.** *n.* 1. *pl.* the internal organs of the body; entrails. 2. inner, intrinsic, or essential quality or attribute.
in·ter·nal-com·bus·tion engine (in-tũr′n'l-kəm-bus′chən), an engine, used in airplanes, automobiles, etc., in which the power is produced by the explosion of a fuel-and-air mixture within the cylinder or cylinders.
internal ear, that part of the ear in the temporal bone, consisting of the labyrinth and semicircular canals.
in·ter·nal·i·ty (in′tẽr-nal′ə-ti), *n.* the quality or state of being internal.
in·ter·nal·ly (in-tũr′n'l-i), *adv.* 1. with respect to or as concerns the inside or interior of anything; in or on the inside. 2. inwardly; subjectively or intrinsically. 3. inside the body: as, apply the medicine *internally*.
internal medicine, the branch of medicine that deals with the diagnosis and nonsurgical treatment of diseases of the internal organs and systems.
internal revenue, governmental income from taxes on income, profits, amusements, luxuries, etc.
in·ter·na·tion·al (in′tẽr-nash′ən-'l), *adj.* 1. between or among nations: as, an *international* treaty. 2. concerned with the relations between nations: as, an *international* court. 3. for the use of all nations. Abbreviated **internat., int.** *n.* 1. a person having connections with two different countries, as a resident alien, etc. 2. [I-], any of several international socialist organizations: see **First International, Second International, Comintern (Third International), Vienna International, Labor and Socialist International.** 3. [I-], the Internationale.
international candle, a unit of measure of the intensity of light, equal to the light given off by the flame of a sperm candle 7/8 inch in diameter burning at the rate of 7.776 grams per hour.
international date line, the date line (sense 2).
In·ter·na·tio·nale (in′tẽr-nash′ən-'l; Fr. aṅ′ter′nȧ′syô′nȧl′), *n.* a revolutionary socialist hymn written in 1871 by Eugène Pottier, with music by Adolphe Degeyter.
International Geophysical Year, a period (July, 1957–December, 1958) set aside for intensive geophysical and astronomical observations by scientists from many co-operating nations.
in·ter·na·tion·al·ism (in′tẽr-nash′ən-'l-iz'm), *n.* 1. the principle of international co-operation for the common good. 2. international character, quality, etc.
in·ter·na·tion·al·ist (in′tẽr-nash′ən-'l-ist), *n.* 1. a person who believes in internationalism. 2. a specialist in international law and relations.
in·ter·na·tion·al·i·ty (in′tẽr-nash′ən-al′ə-ti), *n.* the quality or state of being international.
in·ter·na·tion·al·i·za·tion (in′tẽr-nash′ən-'l-i-zā′shən, in′tẽr-nash′ən-'l-ī-zā′shən), *n.* an internationalizing or being internationalized.
in·ter·na·tion·al·ize (in′tẽr-nash′ən-'l-īz′), *v.t.* [INTERNATIONALIZED (-īzd′), INTERNATIONALIZING], to make international; bring under international control.
international law, the rules generally observed and regarded as binding in the relations between states or nations.
in·ter·na·tion·al·ly (in′tẽr-nash′ən-'l-i), *adv.* in an international manner; between or among nations.
International News Service, see **United Press International.**
International Phonetic Alphabet, a phonetic alphabet sponsored by the International Phonetic Association, a society founded in 1886 for the advancement of the study of phonetics: this alphabet, used in one form or other by most phoneticians and linguists, consists of letters to symbolize the position of the articulating organs, and thus has the same symbol for the same sound irrespective of the language, or period in the development of a language, in which the sound occurs: abbreviated **IPA** (no period). Example: ðɪs ˈsɛntṇs ɪz ˈrɪtn ɪn ðə ˈsɪmblz əv ðəˌɪntəˈnæʃṇḷ fəˈnɛtɪk ˈælfəˌbɛt. (This sentence is written in the symbols of the International Phonetic Alphabet.) See **Introduction,** p. x–xi, xvi, xviii–xix.
in·terne (in′tẽrn), *n.* an intern.
in·ter·ne·cine (in′tẽr-nē′sin, in′tẽr-nē′sīn), *adj.* [L. *internecinus* < *internecare*, to kill, destroy; *inter-*, between + *necare*, to kill], 1. deadly; destructive; with great slaughter. 2. deadly to both sides; mutually destructive.
in·tern·ee (in′tẽr-nē′), *n.* [*intern* + *-ee*], a person interned as a prisoner of war or enemy alien.
in·ter·nist (in-tũr′nist), *n.* a doctor who specializes in internal medicine.
in·tern·ment (in-tũrn′mənt), *n.* an interning or being interned.
in·ter·nod·al (in′tẽr-nōd′'l), *adj.* 1. of an internode. 2. between two nodes.
in·ter·node (in′tẽr-nōd′), *n.* [L. *internodium*], 1. in *anatomy & zoology*, the part between two nodes, as a segment of a nerve fiber. 2. in *botany*, the section of a plant stem between two successive nodes or joints.
‡in·ter nos (in′tẽr nōs′), [L.], between (or among) ourselves.
in·tern·ship (in′tẽrn-ship′), *n.* [see -SHIP], 1. the position of an intern. 2. the period of service as an intern.
in·ter·nun·ci·o (in′tẽr-nun′shi-ō′), *n.* [*pl.* INTERNUNCIOS (-ōz′)], [It. *internunzio;* L. *internuntius;* see INTER- & NUNCIO], 1. a messenger between two parties; envoy. 2. a papal representative ranking below a nuncio.
in·ter·o·ce·an·ic (in′tẽr-ō′shi-an′ik), *adj.* between oceans.
in·ter·o·cep·tive (in′tẽr-ə-sep′tiv), *adj.* of or arising from an interoceptor.
in·ter·o·cep·tor (in′tẽr-ə-sep′tẽr), *n.* [Mod. L.; see INTERNAL & RECEPTOR], a specialized cell or end organ that responds to and transmits stimuli from the internal organs, muscles, blood vessels, and the ear labyrinth.
in·ter·os·cu·late (in′tẽr-os′kyoo-lāt′), *v.i.* [INTEROSCULATED (-id), INTEROSCULATING], [*inter-* + *osculate*], 1. to intermix; intermingle. 2. in *biology*, to have some common characteristics: said of species.
in·ter·os·cu·la·tion (in′tẽr-os′kyoo-lā′shən), *n.* an interosculating.
in·ter·pel·lant (in′tẽr-pel′ənt), *adj.* [L. *interpellans*, ppr.], interpellating. *n.* a person who interpellates.
in·ter·pel·late (in′tẽr-pel′āt, in-tũr′pi-lāt′), *v.t.* [INTERPELLATED (-id), INTERPELLATING], [< L. *interpellatus*, pp. of *interpellare*, to interrupt in speaking; *inter-*, between + *-pellare* < *pellere*, to drive, urge], to ask (a person) formally for an explanation of his action or policy: a form of political challenge to governmental officials, etc. in legislative bodies of certain countries.
in·ter·pel·la·tion (in′tẽr-pe-lā′shən, in-tũr′pi-lā′shən), *n.* [L. *interpellatio*], an interpellating; formal calling to account of a minister, etc. by a legislative body.
in·ter·pen·e·trate (in′tẽr-pen′ə-trāt′), *v.t.* to penetrate thoroughly; pervade; permeate. *v.i.* 1. to penetrate each other. 2. to penetrate between parts, etc.
in·ter·pen·e·tra·tion (in′tẽr-pen′ə-trā′shən), *n.* an interpenetrating; thorough or mutual penetration.
in·ter·pen·e·tra·tive (in′tẽr-pen′ə-trā′tiv), *adj.* interpenetrating or tending to interpenetrate.
in·ter·phone (in′tẽr-fōn′), *n.* a telephone system for communication between the members of the crew of an airplane, tank, etc.
in·ter·plan·e·tar·y (in′tẽr-plan′ə-ter′i), *adj.* 1. between planets; in the planetary region. 2. within the solar system but outside the atmosphere of any planet or the sun.
in·ter·play (in′tẽr-plā′), *n.* action, effect, or influence on each other or one another; interaction. *v.i.* (in′tẽr-plā′), to exert influence reciprocally.
in·ter·plead (in′tẽr-plēd′), *v.i.* [Anglo-Fr. *entrepleder;* see INTER- & PLEAD], in *law*, to go to trial with each other in order to settle a dispute in which a third party is concerned; initiate an interpleader.
in·ter·plead·er (in′tẽr-plēd′ẽr), *n.* [< Anglo-Fr. *entrepleder*, to interplead; substantive use of inf.], a legal proceeding by which a person sued by two others having the same claim against him may compel them to go to trial with each other to arrive at a settlement.
in·ter·po·late (in-tũr′pə-lāt′), *v.t.* [INTERPOLATED (-id), INTERPOLATING], [< L. *interpolatus*, pp. of *interpolare*, to polish, dress up, corrupt < *interpolis*, altered by furbishing, repaired < *inter-*, between + *polire*, to polish], 1. to alter, enlarge, or corrupt (a book, manuscript, etc.) by putting in new words, subject matter, etc. 2. to insert between or among others. 3. in *mathematics*, to supply (intermediate terms) in a series of terms. *v.i.* to make interpolations. —*SYN.* see **introduce.**
in·ter·po·la·tion (in-tũr′pə-lā′shən), *n.* [< Fr. or L.; Fr. *interpolation;* L. *interpolatio*], 1. an interpolating or being interpolated. 2. something interpolated. 3. in *surgery*, the transfer of tissue in a plastic operation.
in·ter·po·la·tor (in-tũr′pə-lā′tẽr), *n.* [LL.], a person who interpolates.
in·ter·pos·al (in′tẽr-pōz′'l), *n.* interposition.
in·ter·pose (in′tẽr-pōz′), *v.t.* [INTERPOSED (-pōzd′), INTERPOSING], [Fr. *interposer;* see INTER- & POSE], 1. to place or put between; insert. 2. to introduce by way of intervention; put forward as interference. 3. to introduce (a remark, opinion, etc.) into a conversation, debate, etc.; put in as an interruption. *v.i.* 1. to be or come between. 2. to intervene. 3. to interrupt.
SYN.—**interpose,** in this comparison, is the general word meaning no more than to introduce action, a remark, etc. in some conversation or affair, with no further implication of motive or effect; **intervene** implies an interposing in order to modify action, adjust differences, etc. (to *intervene* in the internal affairs of another country); **interfere** implies an interposing actively in order to hinder action or effect certain results (don't *interfere* in their decision to move); **intercede** suggests an intervening in order to plead or argue on behalf of another (he *interceded* for the accused); **mediate** implies intervention in order to reconcile, or effect a compromise between opposing parties (to *mediate* a labor dispute). See also **introduce.**
in·ter·po·si·tion (in′tẽr-pə-zish′ən), *n.* [Fr.; L. *interpositio* < pp. of *interponere;* see INTERPOSE], 1. an interposing or being interposed. 2. a thing interposed.
in·ter·pret (in-tũr′prit), *v.t.* [Fr. *interpréter;* L. *interpretari* < *interpres*, agent between two parties, broker, negotiator, interpreter], 1. to explain the meaning of

make understandable, as by translating; elucidate. 2. to have or show one's own understanding of the meaning of; construe: as, he *interpreted* the silence as contempt. 3. to bring out the meaning of, especially to give one's own conception of, in performing, criticizing, or producing a work of art: as, the theatrical company *interpreted* Shakespeare's *Julius Caesar* in the light of modern political conflicts. *v.i.* to act as an interpreter; explain or translate. —*SYN.* see **explain.**

in·ter·pre·ta·tion (in-tũr'pri-tā'shən), *n.* [ME. *interpretacioun;* OFr. *interpretation, entrepretation;* L. *interpretatio*], 1. an interpreting. 2. the result of this; explanation; meaning; translation; exposition. 3. the expression of a person's conception of a work of art, subject, etc. through acting, playing, writing, criticizing, etc.: as, the pianist's *interpretation* of the sonata.

in·ter·pre·ta·tive (in-tũr'pri-tā'tiv), *adj.* [< L. *interpretatus,* pp. of *interpretari;* + *-ive*], used to interpret; explanatory.

in·ter·pret·er (in-tũr'pri-tẽr), *n.* [ME. & Anglo-Fr. *interpretour;* OFr. *interpreteur;* LL. *interpretator*], a person who interprets; specifically, a person whose work is translating a foreign language orally, as in a conversation between people speaking different languages.

in·ter·pre·tive (in-tũr'pri-tiv), *adj.* interpretative.

in·ter·ra·cial (in'tẽr-rā'shəl), *adj.* 1. between, among, or involving different races. 2. of or for persons of different races.

in·ter·ra·di·al (in'tẽr-rā'di-əl), *adj.* situated between rays or radii.

in·ter·re·ges (in'tẽr-rē'jēz), *n.* plural of **interrex.**

in·ter·reg·num (in'tẽr-reg'nəm), *n.* [*pl.* INTERREGNUMS (-nəmz), INTERREGNA (-nə)], [L.; *inter-,* between + *regnum,* reign, rule], 1. an interval between two successive reigns, when the country has no sovereign. 2. a suspension of governmental or administrative functions; period without the usual ruler, governor, etc. 3. any break in a series or in a continuity; pause or interval.

in·ter·re·lat·ed (in'tẽr-ri-lā'tid), *adj.* having a close connection with each other or one another; mutually related.

in·ter·re·la·tion (in'tẽr-ri-lā'shən), *n.* the state or fact of being interrelated; mutual relationship.

in·ter·rex (in'tẽr-reks'), *n.* [*pl.* INTERREGES (in'tẽr-rē'jēz)], [L.; *inter-,* between + *rex, regis,* king], a person who acts as the ruler during an interregnum.

interrog., 1. interrogation. 2. interrogative.

in·ter·ro·gate (in-ter'ə-gāt'), *v.t.* [INTERROGATED (-id), INTERROGATING], [< L. *interrogatus,* pp. of *interrogare,* to ask; *inter-,* between + *rogare,* to ask], to ask questions of formally; examine by questioning: as, he *interrogated* the witness. *v.i.* to ask questions. —*SYN.* see **ask.**

in·ter·ro·ga·tion (in-ter'ə-gā'shən), *n.* 1. an interrogating; a questioning or examination. 2. a question. 3. an interrogation mark. Abbreviated **interrog., inter.**

interrogation mark (or **point**), a mark of punctuation (?) used to indicate that the sentence preceding it is a direct question, and also to show doubt, uncertainty, etc.: also called *question mark.*

in·ter·rog·a·tive (in'tə-rog'ə-tiv), *adj.* [L. *interrogativus;* see INTERROGATE], 1. asking, or having the form of, a question. 2. used in asking a question. *n.* an interrogative word, construction, or element (e.g., what? where?). Abbreviated **interrog.**

in·ter·ro·ga·tor (in-ter'ə-gā'tẽr), *n.* [LL.], a person who interrogates; questioner.

in·ter·rog·a·to·ri·ly (in'tə-rog'ə-tôr'i-li, in'tə-rog'ə-tō'ri-li), *adv.* in an interrogative manner.

in·ter·rog·a·to·ry (in'tə-rog'ə-tôr'i, in'tə-rog'ə-tō'ri), *adj.* [LL. *interrogatorius*], expressing or implying a question. *n.* [*pl.* INTERROGATORIES (-iz, -riz)], an interrogating; formal question or set of questions.

in·ter·rupt (in'tə-rupt'), *v.t.* [ME. *interrupte(n)* < L. *interruptus,* pp. of *interrumpere,* to break apart, break off; *inter-,* between + *rumpere,* to break], 1. to break into or in upon (a discussion, train of thought, etc.); break in upon (a person) while he is speaking, singing, etc.; hinder; stop temporarily. 2. to make a break in the continuity of; get in the way of; cut off; obstruct. *v.i.* to break in upon an action, talk, etc.; make an interruption.

in·ter·rupt·ed (in'tə-rup'tid), *adj.* [pp. of *interrupt*], 1. broken by interruptions or discontinuity; not continuous. 2. in *botany,* asymmetrical; irregular.

interrupted screw, a device for closing the breech of certain guns in which the breech and the block have alternate threads and slots that permit the block to be locked or released by giving it a partial turn.

in·ter·rupt·er (in'tə-rup'tẽr), *n.* 1. a person or thing that interrupts. 2. in *electricity,* a mechanism used to interrupt, or open and close, a circuit.

in·ter·rup·tion (in'tə-rup'shən), *n.* [ME. *interrupcion;* OFr.; L. *interruptio*], 1. an interrupting or being interrupted. 2. anything that interrupts. 3. the interval during which something is interrupted; intermission.

in·ter·scho·las·tic (in'tẽr-skə-las'tik), *adj.* between or among schools: as, an *interscholastic* debate.

‡in·ter se (in'tẽr sē'), [L.], between (or among) themselves.

in·ter·sect (in'tẽr-sekt'), *v.t.* [< L. *intersectus,* pp. of *intersecare,* to cut between, cut off; *inter-,* between + *secare,* to cut], to divide into two parts by passing through or across; cut across: as, a line *intersects* the angle. *v.i.* to cross each other: as, the roads *intersect* at the railroad.

in·ter·sec·tion (in'tẽr-sek'shən), *n.* [L. *intersectio*], 1. an intersecting. 2. a place of intersecting; specifically, *a*) the point or line where two lines or surfaces meet or cross. *b*) the place where two streets cross.

in·ter·space (in'tẽr-spās'), *n.* a space between. *v.t.* (in'tẽr-spās'), [INTERSPACED (-spāst'), INTERSPACING], 1. to make spaces between. 2. to fill spaces between.

in·ter·sperse (in'tẽr-spũrs'), *v.t.* [INTERSPERSED (-spũrst'), INTERSPERSING], [< L. *interspersus,* pp. of *interspergere* < *inter-,* between, among + *spargere,* to scatter], 1. to scatter among other things; put here and there. 2. to decorate or diversify with things scattered here and there.

in·ter·sper·sion (in'tẽr-spũr'zhən, in'tẽr-spũr'shən), *n.* an interspersing or being interspersed.

in·ter·state (in'tẽr-stāt'), *adj.* between or among states of a federal government: as, *interstate* commerce.

Interstate Commerce Commission, a United States Federal commission created in 1887 to regulate the commerce between the States: it has eleven members, appointed by the President: abbreviated **ICC, I.C.C.**

in·ter·stel·lar (in'tẽr-stel'ẽr), *adj.* [*inter-* + *stellar*], between or among the stars: as, *interstellar* space.

in·ter·stice (in-tũr'stis), *n.* [*pl.* INTERSTICES (-iz)], [Fr. < L. *interstitium* < *inter-,* between + *sistere,* to set < *stare,* to stand], a small or narrow space between things or parts of things; crevice; chink; crack.

in·ter·sti·tial (in'tẽr-stish'əl), *adj.* 1. of, forming, or occurring in interstices. 2. in *anatomy,* situated between the cellular components of an organ or structure.

in·ter·tex·ture (in'tẽr-teks'chẽr), *n.* [< L. *intertextus,* pp. of *intertexere,* to interweave (*inter-,* between + *texere,* to weave); + *-ure*], 1. the act or process of interweaving. 2. something formed by interweaving.

in·ter·trib·al (in'tẽr-tri'bəl), *adj.* between or among tribes.

in·ter·trop·i·cal (in'tẽr-trop'i-k'l), *adj.* within or between the tropics (of Cancer and Capricorn).

in·ter·twine (in'tẽr-twin'), *v.t.* & *v.i.* to twine together; intertwist: as, the strands of a rope are *intertwined.*

in·ter·twist (in'tẽr-twist'), *v.t.* & *v.i.* to twist together; intertwine.

in·ter·ur·ban (in'tẽr-ũr'bən), *adj.* [*inter-* + *urban*], between cities or towns: as, an *interurban* railway. *n.* 1. an interurban railway, trolley route, etc. 2. an interurban train, railway car, trolley car, etc.

in·ter·val (in'tẽr-v'l), *n.* [ME. *enterval, intervalle;* OFr. *entreval;* L. *intervallum,* lit., space between two palisades or walls; *inter-,* between + *vallum,* palisade, wall], 1. a space between two things; gap; distance. 2. a period of time between two points of time, events, etc.; intervening period. 3. the extent of difference between two qualities, conditions, etc. 4. in *music,* the difference in pitch between two tones.

at intervals, 1. once in a while. 2. here and there.

in·ter·vale (in'tẽr-vāl'), *n.* [a blending of *interval* + *vale*], low, flat land between hills or along a river or stream: also **intervale** (or **interval**) **land.**

in·ter·vene (in'tẽr-vēn'), *v.i.* [INTERVENED (-vēnd'), INTERVENING], [L. *intervenire; inter-,* between + *venire,* to come], 1. to come, be, or lie between. 2. to take place between two points of time, events, etc. 3. to come or be in between as something unnecessary or irrelevant. 4. to come between as an influencing force; come in to modify, settle, or hinder some action, argument, etc. 5. in *law,* to come in as a third party to a suit, for the protection of one's own interests. —*SYN.* see **interpose.**

in·ter·ven·er (in'tẽr-vēn'ẽr), *n.* a person who intervenes.

in·ter·ven·ient (in'tẽr-vēn'yənt), *adj.* [L. *interveniens,* ppr.], intervening. *n.* an intervening person or thing.

in·ter·ven·tion (in'tẽr-ven'shən), *n.* [LL. *interventio* < L. *intervenire*], 1. an intervening. 2. any interference in the affairs of others; especially, interference of one state in the affairs of another.

in·ter·ven·tion·ist (in'tẽr-ven'shən-ist), *n.* a person who favors or practices intervention, especially in international affairs. *adj.* 1. of intervention or interventionists. 2. favoring or practicing intervention.

in·ter·view (in'tẽr-vū'), *n.* [Fr. *entrevue;* see INTER- & VIEW], 1. a meeting of people face to face to confer about something: as, an *interview* between an employer and an applicant for a job. 2. a meeting between a reporter and a person whose activities, views, etc. are to be the subject of a published article. 3. a journalistic article giving such information. ***v.t.*** to have an interview with.

in·ter·volve (in'tẽr-volv'), ***v.t. & v.i.*** [INTERVOLVED (-volvd'), INTERVOLVING], [< *inter-* + L. *volvere*, to roll], 1. to wind or roll up together; coil up. 2. to involve or be involved with one another.

in·ter·weave (in'tẽr-wēv'), ***v.t. & v.i.*** 1. to weave together; interlace; intertwine. 2. to connect closely or intricately; intermingle; blend.

in·ter·wo·ven (in'tẽr-wō'vən), ***adj.*** [pp. of *interweave*], 1. woven together. 2. intermixed.

in·tes·ta·cy (in-tes'tə-si), ***n.*** the fact or state of dying intestate.

in·tes·tate (in-tes'tāt, in-tes'tit), ***adj.*** [ME.; OFr. *intestat;* L. *intestatus; in-*, not + *testatus*, pp. of *testari*, to make a will], 1. having made no will. 2. not disposed of by a will. ***n.*** a person who has died intestate.

in·tes·ti·nal (in-tes'ti-n'l), ***adj.*** of or in the intestines.

intestinal fortitude, courage and perseverance; grit; pluck: a euphemism for *guts*, in the same sense.

in·tes·tin·al·ly (in-tes'ti-n'l-i), ***adv.*** in, through, or by the intestines.

in·tes·tine (in-tes'tin), ***adj.*** [L. *intestinus*, inward, internal < *intus*, within < *in*, in], internal, especially with regard to a country or community; domestic. ***n.*** [L. *intestinum*, neut. sing. of *intestinus*], *usually pl.* the lower part of the alimentary canal, extending from the stomach to the anus and consisting of a convoluted upper part (*small intestine*) and a lower part of greater diameter (*large intestine*); bowel(s): food passes from the stomach into the intestines for further digestion.

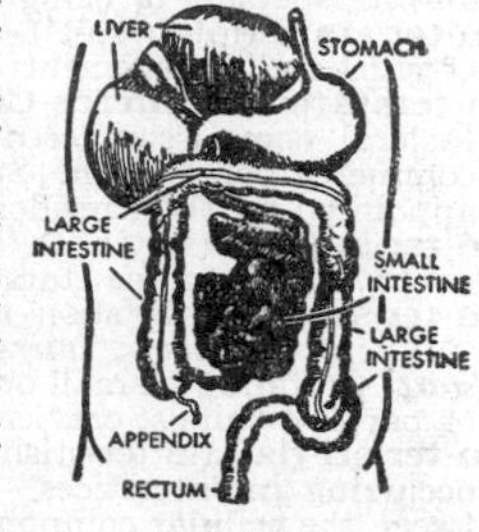

INTESTINES

in·thrall, in·thral (in-thrôl'), ***v.t.*** [INTHRALLED (-thrôld'), INTHRALLING], to enthrall.

in·throne (in-thrōn'), ***v.t.*** [INTHRONED (-thrōnd'), INTHRONING], to enthrone.

in·ti·ma (in'ti-mə), ***n.*** [*pl.* INTIMAE (-mē')], [Mod. L. < L. *intimus;* see INTIMATE], 1. the innermost layer of the walls of an artery, vein, or lymphatic. 2. the lining membrane of an insect's trachea.

in·ti·ma·cy (in'tə-mə-si), ***n.*** [*pl.* INTIMACIES (-siz)], 1. the state or fact of being intimate; intimate association; familiarity. 2. an intimate act; especially, illicit sexual intercourse: a euphemism.

in·ti·mate (in'tə-mit; *for v.*, in'tə-māt'), ***adj.*** [Fr. *intime* < L. *intimus*, superl. of *intus*, within; + *-ate* (by association with the *v.*)], 1. inmost; most inward; essential: as, the *intimate* structure of the atom. 2. most private or personal: as, one's *intimate* feelings. 3. closely acquainted or associated; very familiar: as, an *intimate* friend. 4. *a*) resulting from careful study or investigation. *b*) very close. 5. having illicit sexual relations: a euphemism. ***n.*** an intimate friend or companion. ***v.t.*** [INTIMATED (-id), INTIMATING], [< L. *intimatus*, pp. of *intimare*, to announce < *intimus*], 1. to make known formally; announce. 2. to make known indirectly; hint or imply. —***SYN.*** see **familiar, suggest.**

in·ti·ma·tion (in'tə-mā'shən), ***n.*** [Fr.; LL. *intimatio*], 1. an intimating. 2. a formal announcement or notice; declaration. 3. a hint; indirect suggestion.

in·tim·i·date (in-tim'ə-dāt'), ***v.t.*** [INTIMIDATED (-id), INTIMIDATING], [< ML. *intimidatus*, pp. of *intimidare*, to make afraid < L. *in-*, in + *timidus*, afraid, fearful], 1. to make timid; make afraid; overawe. 2. to force or deter with threats or violence; cow.

in·tim·i·da·tion (in-tim'ə-dā'shən), ***n.*** an intimidating or being intimidated.

in·tim·i·da·tor (in-tim'ə-dā'tẽr), ***n.*** one who intimidates.

in·tinc·tion (in-tiŋk'shən), ***n.*** [LL. *intinctio*, a dipping in, baptizing < L. *intinctus*, pp. of *intingere*, to dip in; *in-*, in + *tingere*, to tinge, dye], the act of dipping the bread or wafers of the Eucharist into the consecrated wine, so that the communicant can receive both together.

in·ti·tle (in-tī't'l), ***v.t.*** [INTITLED (-t'ld), INTITLING], to entitle.

in·tit·ule (in-tit'ūl), ***v.t.*** [INTITULED (-ūld), INTITULING], [Fr. *intituler;* LL. *intitulare;* see ENTITLE], to give a name or title to (a legislative act, etc.).

in·to (in'tōō, in'too, in'tə; *occas., in rhetoric & poetry,* in-tōō'), ***prep.*** [ME.; AS.; see IN & TO], 1. from the outside to the inside of; toward and within: as, *into* a house. 2. advancing or continuing to the midst of (a period of time): as, they danced far *into* the night. 3. to the form, substance, or condition of: as, turned *into* a swan, divided *into* parts. 4. in *mathematics*, *a*) [Rare], (multiplied) by; times: as, 7 (multiplied) *into* 3 is 21. *b*) *used as an indication of division:* as, 3 *into* 21 is 7.

in·tol·er·a·bil·i·ty (in-tol'ẽr-ə-bil'ə-ti), ***n.*** the quality of being intolerable.

in·tol·er·a·ble (in-tol'ẽr-ə-b'l), ***adj.*** not tolerable; unbearable; too severe, painful, cruel, etc. to be endured.

in·tol·er·a·bly (in-tol'ẽr-ə-bli), ***adv.*** in an intolerable manner; so as to be intolerable; unbearably.

in·tol·er·ance (in-tol'ẽr-əns), ***n.*** 1. lack of tolerance, especially in matters of religion; bigotry. 2. inability to endure: as, an *intolerance* for sulfa drugs.

in·tol·er·ant (in-tol'ẽr-ənt), ***adj.*** not tolerant; unwilling to tolerate others' opinions, religious beliefs, etc.; bigoted; illiberal. ***n.*** an intolerant person.
intolerant of, not able or willing to tolerate.

in·tomb (in-tōōm'), ***v.t.*** to entomb.

in·to·nate (in'tō-nāt'), ***v.t.*** [INTONATED (-id), INTONATING], [< ML. *intonatus*, pp. of *intonare;* see INTONE], 1. to intone. 2. [Rare], in *phonetics*, to voice.

in·to·na·tion (in'tō-nā'shən), ***n.*** [< *intonate* + *-ion*], 1. an intoning. 2. the manner of producing or uttering tones with regard to rise and fall in pitch. 3. the manner of applying final pitch to a spoken sentence or phrase: as, he spoke the words with a rising *intonation.* 4. *a*) the opening phrase of a Gregorian chant. *b*) the reciting of this by a priest or a few choristers.

in·tone (in-tōn'), ***v.t.*** [INTONED (-tōnd'), INTONING], [ML. *intonare;* see IN- (in) & TONE], 1. to utter or recite in a singing tone or in prolonged monotones; chant. 2. to give a particular intonation to. 3. to sing the opening phrase of (a chant, canticle, etc.). ***v.i.*** 1. to speak or recite in a singing tone or in prolonged monotones; chant. 2. to utter a long, drawn-out sound: as, dogs *intone* to the moon.

in·tor·sion (in-tôr'shən), ***n.*** [Fr.; L. *intortio* < *intortus*], an intorting, as in plant stems.

in·tort (in-tôrt'), ***v.t.*** [< L. *intortus*, pp. of *intorquere*, to twist; *in-*, in + *torquere*, to twist], to twist inward; curl or twine.

‡in to·to (in tō'tō), [L.], in the whole; as a whole.

in·tox·i·cant (in-tok'sə-kənt), ***n.*** [< ML. *intoxicans*, ppr. of *intoxicare*], something that intoxicates; specifically, *a*) a drug that intoxicates. *b*) alcoholic liquor. ***adj.*** intoxicating.

in·tox·i·cate (in-tok'sə-kāt'), ***v.t.*** [INTOXICATED (-id), INTOXICATING], [< ML. *intoxicatus*, pp. of *intoxicare*, to poison, drug; L. *in-*, in + *toxicare*, to smear with poison < *toxicum*, poison; see TOXIC], 1. to make drunk; inebriate. 2. to excite greatly, to a point beyond self-control; elate to a frenzy. 3. in *medicine*, to poison or have a poisonous effect on. ***adj.*** (*usually* in-tok'sə-kit), [Archaic], intoxicated.

in·tox·i·ca·tion (in-tok'sə-kā'shən), ***n.*** 1. an intoxicating or becoming intoxicated; specifically, *a*) a making or becoming drunk. *b*) in *medicine*, a poisoning or becoming poisoned. 2. great excitement; rapture; frenzy.

intr., intransitive.

in·tra- (in'trə), [L. < *intra*, within, inside < **intera;* akin to *interior, inter*], a combining form meaning *within, inside of*, as in *intramural, intravenous.*

in·trac·ta·bil·i·ty (in-trak'tə-bil'ə-ti), ***n.*** the quality or state of being intractable.

in·trac·ta·ble (in-trak'tə-b'l), ***adj.*** not tractable; specifically, *a*) hard to manage; unruly or stubborn. *b*) hard to work, manipulate, cure, treat, etc. —***SYN.*** see **unruly.**

in·trac·ta·bly (in-trak'tə-bli), ***adv.*** in an intractable manner.

in·trac·tile (in-trak't'l), ***adj.*** not tractile; not ductile.

in·tra·dos (in-trā'dos), ***n.*** [Fr.; L. *intra*, within + Fr. *dos* < L. *dorsum*, the back], the inside curve or surface of an arch or vault.

in·tra·mo·lec·u·lar (in'trə-mə-lek'yoo-lẽr), ***adj.*** acting, existing, or taking place within a molecule or molecules.

in·tra·mu·ral (in'trə-myoor'əl), ***adj.*** [*intra-* + *mural*], 1. within the walls or limits of a city, college, etc.; hence, 2. limited to the members of a particular school, college, etc.: as, *intramural* athletics. 3. in *anatomy*, etc., within the substance of the walls of an organ.

in·tra·mus·cu·lar (in'trə-mus'kyoo-lẽr), ***adj.*** located or injected within the substance of a muscle.

intrans., intransitive.

in trans., *in transitu*, [L.], on the way; during passage.

‡in·tran·si·geance (aṅ'träṅ'zē'zhäṅs'), ***n.*** [Fr.], intransigence.

‡in·tran·si·geant (aṅ'träṅ'zē'zhäṅ'), ***n.*** [Fr. < Sp. *intransigente* < L. *in-*, not + *transigens*, ppr. of *transigere*, to come to a settlement; see TRANSACT], an intransigent. ***adj.*** intransigent.

in·tran·si·gence (in-tran'si-jəns), ***n.*** quality, state, or instance of being intransigent.

in·tran·si·gen·cy (in-tran'si-jən-si), ***n.*** intransigence.

in·tran·si·gent (in-tran'si-jənt), ***adj.*** [Fr. *intransigeant* < Sp. (*los*) *intransigentes*, the intransigents, term applied to the extreme Left (Republicans); see INTRANSIGEANT], refusing to compromise, come to an agreement, or be reconciled; uncompromising. ***n.*** a person who is intransigent, especially in politics.

in·tran·si·tive (in-tran'sə-tiv), ***adj.*** [LL. *intransitivus*], not transitive; not used with an object to complete its meaning: said of certain verbs. ***n.*** an intransitive verb or construction. Abbreviated **i., intr., intrans., int.**

in·trant (in'trənt), ***n.*** [< L. *intrans*, ppr. of *intrare*, to enter; see ENTER], a person who enters a public office.

holy orders, membership in a club, etc. *adj.* entering.

in·tra·nu·cle·ar (in'trə-nōō'kli-ẽr, in'trə-nū'kli-ẽr), *adj.* within the nucleus, as of an atom, cell, etc.

in·tra·state (in'trə-stāt'), *adj.* within a state; especially, within a State of the United States.

in·tra·tel·lu·ric (in'trə-tel-yoor'ik), *adj.* [*intra-* + *telluric*], 1. formed, located, or occurring deep inside the earth: used especially to refer to the minerals of igneous rocks before eruption. 2. designating or of the period when rocks crystallize, before eruption.

in·trav·a·sa·tion (in-trav'ə-sā'shən), *n.* [*intra-* + extra-*vasation*], the entry of a foreign substance into a blood or lymph vessel.

in·tra·ve·nous (in'trə-vē'nəs), *adj.* [*intra-* + *venous*], in, into, or within a vein or veins: as, an *intravenous* injection: abbreviated **i.v.**

in·treat (in-trēt'), *v.t. & v.i.* to entreat.

in·trench (in-trench'), *v.t.* 1. to cut a trench or furrow in. 2. to surround or fortify with a trench or trenches. 3. to establish securely. *v.i.* to encroach (with *upon*). Also spelled **entrench** (except *v.t.*, sense 1).

intrenching tool, any of various small tools, as a spade or pickax, carried by a combat soldier, for digging foxholes, etc.

in·trench·ment (in-trench'mənt), *n.* 1. an intrenching or being intrenched. 2. a trench or system of trenches, usually fortified with mounds of earth, rubble, etc.; hence, 3. any fortification or defense. Also spelled **entrenchment.**

in·trep·id (in-trep'id), *adj.* [L. *intrepidus; in-*, not + *trepidus*, alarmed, anxious], not alarmed; unafraid; bold fearless; dauntless; very brave. —*SYN.* see **brave.**

in·tre·pid·i·ty (in'trə-pid'ə-ti), *n.* the quality of being intrepid; fearlessness; boldness; great courage.

Int. Rev., internal revenue.

in·tri·ca·cy (in'tri-kə-si), *n.* 1. the quality or state of being intricate; complexity. 2. [*pl.* INTRICACIES (-siz)], something intricate; involved matter, proceeding, etc.; complication.

in·tri·cate (in'tri-kit), *adj.* [L. *intricatus*, pp. of *intricare*, to entangle, perplex, embarrass < *in-*, in + *tricae*, vexations, perplexities], hard to follow or understand because entangled, involved, complicated, or perplexing: as, an *intricate* path, *intricate* directions. —*SYN.* see **complex.**

in·tri·gant (in'tri-gənt; Fr. aɴ'trē'gäɴ'), *n.* [*pl.* INTRIGANTS (-gənts; Fr. -gäɴ')], [Fr.; It. *intrigante* < *intrigare*], a man given to or involved in intrigue.

in·tri·gante (in'tri-gant'; Fr. aɴ'trē'gäɴt'), *n.* [*pl.* INTRIGANTES (-gants'; Fr. -gäɴt')], [Fr., fem. of *intrigant*], a woman given to or involved in intrigue.

in·trigue (in-trēg'; *for n., also* in'trēg), *v.i.* [INTRIGUED (-trēgd'), INTRIGUING], [Fr. *intriguer;* It. *intrigare;* L. *intricare;* see INTRICATE], 1. to carry on a secret love affair. 2. to plot or scheme secretly or underhandedly. *v.t.* 1. to bring on or get by secret or underhanded plotting. 2. to excite the interest or curiosity of; fascinate: as, the puzzle *intrigued* her. 3. [Rare], to perplex. *n.* 1. an intriguing; secret or underhanded plotting. 2. a secret or underhanded plot or scheme; machination. 3. a secret love affair. —*SYN.* see **plot.**

in·trin·sic (in-trin'sik), *adj.* [Fr. *intrinsèque;* ML. *intrinsicus* < L. *intrinsecus*, inwardly < *intra-*, within + *secus*, otherwise, beside], 1. belonging to the real nature of a thing; not dependent on external circumstances; essential; inherent. 2. in *anatomy*, located within, or exclusively of, a part. Opposed to *extrinsic.*

in·trin·si·cal (in-trin'si-k'l), *adj.* intrinsic; inherent.

in·trin·si·cal·ly (in-trin'si-k'l-i, in-trin'sik-li), *adv.* [*intrinsical* + *-ly*], naturally; essentially; inherently.

in·tro- (in'trō), [L. < *intro*, inwardly, on the inside < **intero;* akin to *inter, interior*], a combining form meaning *into, within, inward*, as in *introvert, introspective.*

introd., intro., 1. introduction. 2. introductory.

in·tro·duce (in'trə-dōōs', in'trə-dūs'), *v.t.* [INTRODUCED (-dōōst', -dūst'), INTRODUCING], [L. *introducere; intro-*, within, in + *ducere*, to lead], 1. to lead or bring into a given place or position; conduct in. 2. to bring (a person) into society or a group. 3. to put in or within; insert: as, he *introduced* an electric wire into the conduit. 4. to bring in or add as a new feature; bring or put in to some action, composition, etc.: as, he *introduced* some humor into his play. 5. to bring into use, knowledge, or fashion; give currency to; institute: as, the war *introduced* many new words. 6. to offer (a new product) for sale. 7. *a*) to bring to and make known to; make acquainted with; present to: as, please *introduce* me to your friend. *b*) to give knowledge or experience of: as, they *introduced* him to city life. 8. to bring forward; bring to notice formally: as, *introduce* a bill into Congress. 9. to start; open; begin: as, he *introduced* his speech with a joke.

SYN.—**introduce** implies the bringing or putting of someone or something into a place, position, notice, etc., sometimes stressing this as an innovation (to *introduce* a new song to the public); **insert** suggests the putting of something into a hole or gap or between two things (*insert* the candle into the holder); **insinuate** implies the slow, indirect, but skillful introduction of something (he *insinuated* the coins into her hand); **interpolate** refers to the introduction of new words or passages, especially of spurious copy, into a writing (many of Shakespeare's plays have been *interpolated*); **interpose,** in this connection, and **interject** imply the introduction of a comment or opinion that serves to interrupt (if I may *interpose*, or *interject*, a few remarks at this point).—*ANT.* withdraw, remove.

in·tro·duc·tion (in'trə-duk'shən), *n.* [ME. *introduccion;* Late OFr.; L. *introductio*], 1. an introducing or being introduced. 2. anything introduced, or brought into use, knowledge, or fashion. 3. anything that introduces, or prepares the way for; specifically, *a*) the preliminary section of a book, speech, etc., usually explaining or defining the subject matter; preface or foreword, often by someone other than the author. *b*) an opening section of a musical composition. *c*) a preliminary guide or text. 4. the formal presentation of one person to another, to an audience, to society, etc. Abbreviated **introd., intro.**

SYN.—**introduction,** in strict usage, refers to the preliminary section of a book, etc. that explains and leads into the subject proper; **preface** strictly refers to a statement preliminary to, and distinct from, a book, etc. written by the author or someone else and explaining the purpose, plan, or preparation of the work; **foreword** is usually used for a very brief or simple preface; **preamble** refers to a formal, but usually brief, introduction to a constitution, treaty, etc.; **prologue** applies to the preliminary section of a play, poem, etc., serving as an introduction and, in the play, frequently spoken by one of the characters.—*ANT.* conclusion, epilogue.

in·tro·duc·tive (in'trə-duk'tiv), *adj.* introductory.

in·tro·duc·to·ri·ly (in'trə-duk'tẽr-ə-li), *adv.* in an introductory manner; as an introduction.

in·tro·duc·to·ry (in'trə-duk'tẽr-i), *adj.* [LL. *introductorius*], used as an introduction; serving to introduce; preliminary: abbreviated **introd., intro.**

in·tro·it (in-trō'it), *n.* [Fr. *introït;* L. *introitus*, a going in, entrance < *introire; intro-*, within + *ire*, to go], 1. in the *Anglican Church*, a psalm or hymn sung or played at the opening of the Communion service. 2. [I-], in the *Roman Catholic Church*, the first variable part of the Mass, consisting of a psalm verse and an antiphon followed by the *Gloria Patri.*

in·tro·jec·tion (in'trə-jek'shən), *n.* [*intro-* + pro*jection*], in *psychiatry*, the incorporating of external events into the psyche and reacting to them as though they were internal, as when a person suffers the same pains as another, without physical cause: opposed to *projection.*

in·tro·mis·sion (in'trə-mish'ən), *n.* [< L. *intromissus*, pp. of *intromittere*], an intromitting or being intromitted.

in·tro·mit (in'trə-mit'), *v.t.* [INTROMITTED (-id), INTROMITTING], [L. *intromittere; intro-*, within + *mittere*, to send], 1. to cause to enter; put in; insert. 2. to allow to enter; let in; admit.

in·tro·mit·tent (in'trə-mit''nt), *adj.* that intromits or can intromit.

in·tro·mit·ter (in'trə-mit'ẽr), *n.* a person or thing that intromits.

in·trorse (in-trôrs'), *adj.* [L. *introrsus*, contr. of *introversus; intro-*, within + *versus*, turned], in *botany*, facing inward, or toward the center.

in·tro·spect (in'trə-spekt'), *v.t.* [L. *introspectare*, freq. < *introspectus*, pp. of *introspicere*, to look within; *intro-*, within + *specere*, to look], [Rare], to look into (one's own mind, feelings, reactions, etc.). *v.i.* to look into one's own mind, etc.; practice introspection.

in·tro·spec·tion (in'trə-spek'shən), *n.* [*introspect* + *-ion*], a looking into one's own mind, feelings, reactions, etc.; observation and analysis of oneself.

in·tro·spec·tive (in'trə-spek'tiv), *adj.* of, based on, inclined toward, or characterized by introspection.

in·tro·ver·sion (in'trə-vũr'zhən, in'trə-vũr'shən), *n.* [Mod. L. *introversio* (after *introvert*) < *intro-* + L. *versus*, pp. of *vertere*, to turn], 1. an introverting or being introverted. 2. in *psychology*, a tendency to direct one's interest upon oneself rather than upon external objects or events.

in·tro·ver·sive (in'trə-vũr'siv), *adj.* of or tending to introversion.

in·tro·vert (in'trə-vũrt'; *for n. & adj.*, in'trə-vũrt'), *v.t.* [< *intro-* + L. *vertere*, to turn], 1. to direct (one's interest, mind, or attention) upon oneself; introspect. 2. to bend (something) inward. 3. in *zoology*, etc., to draw (a tubular organ or part) inward upon itself. *v.i.* to practice introversion; become introverted. *n.* 1. a thing that is or can be introverted. 2. in *psychology*, a person characterized by introversion: opposed to *extrovert.* *adj.* of or characterized by introversion.

in·tro·ver·tive (in'trə-vũr'tiv), *adj.* introversive.

in·trude (in-trōōd'), *v.t.* [INTRUDED (-id), INTRUDING], [L. *intrudere; in-*, in + *trudere*, to thrust, push], 1. to push or force (something) in or upon. 2. to force (oneself) upon others without being asked or welcomed. 3. in *geology*, to force (melted rock) into another stratum: usually in the passive. *v.i.* to intrude oneself. *SYN.*—**intrude** implies the forcing of oneself or something upon another without invitation, permission, or welcome (to *intrude* upon another's privacy); **obtrude** connotes even more strongly the distractive nature or the undesirability of the invasion (side issues keep *obtruding*); **interlope** implies an intrusion upon the rights or privileges of another to the disadvantage or harm of the latter (the *interloping* merchants have ruined our trade); **butt in** (or **into**) is a slang term implying intrusion in a meddling or officious way (stop *butting into* my business). See also **trespass**.

in·tru·sion (in-tro͞o′zhən), *n.* [ME. *intrucioun;* OFr.; ML. *intrusio* < L. *intrudere*], 1. an intruding; specifically, in *law*, the illegal entering or taking of another's property. 2. intrusive rock.

in·tru·sive (in-tro͞o′siv), *adj.* [< L. *intrusus*, pp. of *intrudere;* + *-ive*], 1. intruding or tending to intrude. 2. in *geology*, *a*) forced into another stratum while in a molten state: said of rock. *b*) formed of such rock.

in·trust (in-trust′), *v.t.* to entrust.

in·tu·bate (in′tyoo-bāt′, in′too-bāt′), *v.t.* [INTUBATED (-id), INTUBATING], to treat by intubation.

in·tu·ba·tion (in′tyoo-bā′shən, in′too-bā′shən), *n.* [< *in-* (in) + *tube* + *-ation*], the insertion of a tube into an orifice or hollow organ, as into the larynx to permit air to enter in severe cases of diphtheria.

in·tu·it (in′tū-it, in-to͞o′it), *v.t.* & *v.i.* [< L. *intuitus*], to know or learn by intuition.

in·tu·i·tion (in′to͞o-ish′ən, in′tū-ish′ən), *n.* [ML. < L. *intuitus*, pp. of *intueri*, to look at, regard, contemplate; *in-*, in + *tueri*, to look at, view], 1. the immediate knowing or learning of something without the conscious use of reasoning; instantaneous apprehension. 2. something known or learned in this way.

in·tu·i·tion·al (in′to͞o-ish′ən-'l, in′tū-ish′ən-'l), *adj.* of, having the nature of, or resulting from intuition.

in·tu·i·tion·al·ism (in′to͞o-ish′ən-'l-iz'm, in′tū-ish′ən-'l-iz'm), *n.* the philosophical doctrine that absolute truth or any given truth can be perceived by intuition: also called *intuitionism.*

in·tu·i·tion·ism (in′to͞o-ish′ən-iz'm, in′tū-ish′ən-iz'm), *n.* 1. intuitionalism. 2. the doctrine that the reality of perceived objects is known by intuition. 3. in *ethics*, the doctrine that moral principles are acquired by intuition; intuitivism.

in·tu·i·tive (in-to͞o′i-tiv, in-tū′i-tiv), *adj.* [ML. *intuitivus* < L. *intuitus*], 1. knowing, learning, acting, or characterized by intuition. 2. that is or can be perceived by intuition: as, an *intuitive* truth.

in·tu·i·tive·ly (in-to͞o′i-tiv-li, in-tū′i-tiv-li), *adv.* in an intuitive manner; by intuition.

in·tu·i·tiv·ism (in-to͞o′i-tiv-iz'm, in-tū′i-tiv-iz'm), *n.* in *ethics*, intuitionism.

in·tu·mesce (in′to͞o-mes′, in′tyoo-mes′), *v.i.* [INTUMESCED (-mest′), INTUMESCING], [L. *intumescere; in-*, intens. + *tumescere*, inceptive of *tumere*, to swell], to swell, enlarge, expand, or bubble up, as with heat.

in·tu·mes·cence (in′to͞o-mes″ns, in′tyoo-mes″ns), *n.* 1. an intumescing or being intumesced. 2. a swollen or enlarged organ or part, as a tumor; swelling.

in·tu·mes·cent (in′to͞o-mes″nt, in′tyoo-mes″nt), *adj.* [L. *intumescens*, ppr.], intumescing; swelling; swollen.

in·turn (in′tũrn′), *n.* a bending or turning inward, especially of the toes.

in·tus·sus·cept (in′təs-sə-sept′), *v.t.* [< L. *intus*, within + *susceptus*, pp. of *suscipere;* see INTUSSUSCEPTION], to receive within itself or into another part; specifically, to telescope (one section of the intestines) into another; invaginate; introvert.

in·tus·sus·cep·tion (in′təs-sə-sep′shən), *n.* [< L. *intus*, within + *susceptio*, a taking up < pp. of *suscipere*, to take up < *sub-*, under + *capere*, to take], 1. an intussuscepting or being intussuscepted. 2. the process of taking in food or other foreign matter and converting it into tissue.

in·tus·sus·cep·tive (in′təs-sə-sep′tiv), *adj.* of, characterized by, or caused by intussusception.

in·twine (in-twīn′), *v.t.* & *v.i.* to entwine.

in·twist (in-twist′), *v.t.* to entwist.

in·u·lase (in′yoo-lās′), *n.* [< *inulin* + *-ase*], an enzyme that converts inulin into levulose.

in·u·lin (in′yoo-lin), *n.* [< Mod. L. *Inula*, genus of plants including the elecampane < L. *inula*, elecampane; + *-in*], a white polysaccharide found in the roots of many plants, which yields levulose when hydrolyzed.

in·unc·tion (in-uŋk′shən), *n.* [L. *inunctio;* see IN- (in) & UNCTION], 1. an anointing or being anointed. 2. the rubbing of ointment, etc. into the skin. 3. an ointment, liniment, etc.

in·un·dant (in-un′dənt), *adj.* [L. *inundans*, ppr. of *inundare;* see INUNDATE], overflowing.

in·un·date (in′ən-dāt′, in-un′dāt′), *v.t.* [INUNDATED (-id), INUNDATING], [< L. *inundatus*, pp. of *inundare*, to overflow; *in-*, in, on + *undare*, to move in waves, flood < *unda*, a wave], to cover with or as with a flood; deluge; flood; overflow or overwhelm.

in·un·da·tion (in′ən-dā′shən), *n.* [ME. *inundacion;* L. *inundatio*], an inundating or being inundated; flood.

in·un·da·tor (in′ən-dā′tẽr, in-un′dā-tẽr), *n.* something that inundates.

in·un·da·to·ry (in-un′də-tôr′i, in-un′də-tō′ri), *adj.* of, characterized by, or like an inundation.

in·ur·bane (in′ũr-bān′), *adj.* [L. *inurbanis*], not urbane; crude; unpolished; impolite.

in·ur·ban·i·ty (in′ũr-ban′ə-ti), *n.* an inurbane quality.

in·ure (in-yoor′), *v.t.* [INURED (-yoord′), INURING], [*in-*, in + obs. *ure*, work < OFr. *eure, ovre* < L. *opera*, work], to cause to become used to something difficult, painful, etc.; habituate. *v.i.* to come into use or take effect; as, compensation benefits *inure* from the first day of disability. Also spelled **enure**.

in·ure·ment (in-yoor′mənt), *n.* an inuring or being inured.

in·urn (in-ũrn′), *v.t.* 1. to put (ashes of the dead) into an urn; hence, 2. to bury; entomb.

in·u·tile (in-ū′t'l), *adj.* [Fr.; L. *inutilis; in-*, not + *utilis*, useful], useless; unprofitable.

in·u·til·i·ty (in′yoo-til′ə-ti), *n.* [Fr. *inutilité;* L. *inutilitas*], 1. the quality of being inutile; uselessness. 2. [*pl.* INUTILITIES (-tiz)], a useless person or thing.

inv., 1. *invenit*, [L.], he (or she) designed it. 2. invented. 3. inventor. 4. invoice.

‡**in va·cu·o** (in vak′ū-ō′), [L.], in a vacuum.

in·vade (in-vād′), *v.t.* [INVADED (-id), INVADING], [L. *invadere; in-*, in + *vadere*, to come, go], 1. to enter forcibly or hostilely; come into as an enemy; hence, 2. to crowd into; throng: as, the children *invaded* the kitchen. 3. to intrude upon; infringe; violate: as, he *invaded* my privacy. 4. to enter and spread through with harmful effects: as, disease *invades* tissue. *v.i.* to make an invasion. —*SYN.* see **trespass.**

in·vad·er (in-vād′ẽr), *n.* a person or thing that invades.

in·vag·i·nate (in-vaj′ə-nāt′), *v.t.* [INVAGINATED (-id), INVAGINATING], [< *in-*, in + L. *vagina*, a sheath; + *-ate*], 1. to place or receive into a sheath. 2. to intussuscept. *v.i.* to become invaginated.

in·vag·i·na·tion (in-vaj′ə-nā′shən), *n.* 1. an invaginating or being invaginated. 2. an invaginated part.

in·va·lid (in′və-lid), *adj.* [Fr. *invalide* < L. *invalidus; in-*, not + *validus*, strong], 1. not well; weak and sickly; infirm. 2. of or for invalids: as, an *invalid* home. *n.* a weak, sickly person; especially, one who is chronically ill or disabled. *v.t.* 1. to make invalid; disable or weaken. 2. to put (a soldier, sailor, etc.) on a sick list or dismiss from active service because of injury or illness. *v.i.* 1. to become an invalid. 2. to retire from the army, navy, etc. because of ill health.

in·val·id (in-val′id), *adj.* [L. *invalidus*], not valid; having no force; null or void.

in·val·i·date (in-val′ə-dāt′), *v.t.* [INVALIDATED (-id), INVALIDATING], [*invalid* + *-ate*, after Fr. *invalider*], to make invalid; deprive of legal force. —*SYN.* see **nullify.**

in·val·i·da·tion (in-val′ə-dā′shən), *n.* an invalidating or being invalidated.

in·va·lid·ism (in′və-lid-iz'm), *n.* the state of being an invalid; chronic ill health or disability.

in·va·lid·i·ty (in′və-lid′ə-ti), *n.* lack of validity.

in·val·id·ly (in-val′id-li), *adv.* without validity.

in·val·u·a·ble (in-val′ū-ə-b'l), *adj.* extremely valuable; having a greater value than can be measured; priceless; precious. —*SYN.* see **costly.**

in·val·u·a·bly (in-val′ū-ə-bli), *adv.* so as to be invaluable.

in·var (in-vär′), *n.* [< *invariable*], a steel alloy containing 36 per cent nickel, used in the manufacture of precision instruments because of its low coefficient of expansion: a trade-mark (**Invar**).

in·var·i·a·bil·i·ty (in-vâr′i-ə-bil′ə-ti), *n.* the quality or condition of being invariable.

in·var·i·a·ble (in-vâr′i-ə-b'l), *adj.* not variable; not changing; constant; uniform.

in·var·i·a·bly (in-vâr′i-ə-bli), *adv.* in an invariable manner; without change or exception; constantly; always.

in·var·i·ant (in-vâr′i-ənt), *adj.* not varying; constant. *n.* in *mathematics*, an invariable quantity.

in·va·sion (in-vā′zhən), *n.* [Fr.; LL. *invasio* < L. *invasus*, pp. of *invadere*], an invading or being invaded; specifically, *a*) an entering or being entered by an attacking army. *b*) an intrusion or infringement. *c*) in *medicine*, the onset (*of* a disease).

in·va·sive (in-vā′siv), *adj.* [Fr.; LL. *invasivus*], of, like, or having the nature of, invasion.

in·vec·tive (in-vek′tiv), *adj.* [ME. *invectiff;* Late OFr. *invectif;* L. *invectivus* < *invectus*, pp. of *invehere;* see INVEIGH], inveighing; using, inclined to use, or characterized by invective. *n.* 1. a violent verbal attack; strong denunciation; vituperation. 2. *often in pl.* an abusive word: as, a volley of *invectives.*

in·veigh (in-vā′), *v.i.* [L. *invehere*, to bring in, attack with words, scold; *in-*, in, to + *vehere*, to carry], to make a violent verbal attack; make strong denunciations; utter invective; rail (usually with *against*): as, he *inveighed* against the existing order.

in·vei·gle (in-vē′g'l, in-vā′g'l), *v.t.* [INVEIGLED (-g'ld), INVEIGLING], [prob. altered < Fr. *aveugler*, to blind, delude < LL. *aboculus*, blind; L. *ab*, from + *oculus*, an eye], to lead on with deception; entice or trick into doing something, going somewhere, etc. —*SYN.* see **lure.**

in·vei·gle·ment (in-vē'g'l-mənt, in-vā'g'l-mənt), ***n.*** an inveigling or being inveigled.

in·vent (in-vent'), ***v.t.*** [ME. *inventen;* OFr. *inventer* < L. *inventus,* pp. of *invenire,* to come upon, meet with, discover; *in-,* in, on + *venire,* to come], 1. to think up; devise or fabricate in the mind: as, try to *invent* an alibi. 2. to think out or produce (a new device, process, etc.); originate, as by experiment; devise for the first time: as, Edison *invented* the phonograph. 3. [Archaic], to find; come upon; discover.

in·vent·er (in-vent'ẽr), ***n.*** an inventor.

in·ven·tion (in-ven'shən), ***n.*** [ME. *inuencioun;* OFr. *invencion;* L. *inventio*], 1. an inventing or being invented. 2. the power of inventing; ingenuity. 3. something invented; specifically, *a*) something thought up or mentally fabricated; falsehood. *b*) something originated by experiment, etc.; new device or contrivance. 4. in *music,* a short piano composition developing a single theme in two-part counterpoint; especially, any of a group of these by Bach.

in·ven·tion·al (in-ven'shən-'l), ***adj.*** of or like an invention.

in·ven·tive (in-ven'tiv), ***adj.*** [OFr. *inventif*], 1. of invention. 2. skilled or resourceful in inventing. 3. indicating an ability to invent: as, *inventive* powers.

in·ven·tor (in-ven'tẽr), ***n.*** [L.], a person who invents; especially, one who makes or introduces a new contrivance, device, etc.: also spelled **inventer**: abbreviated **inv.**

in·ven·to·ri·al (in'ven-tôr'i-əl, in'ven-tō'ri-əl), ***adj.*** of, having the nature of, or characterized by an inventory.

in·ven·to·ry (in'vən-tôr'i, in'vən-tō'ri), ***n.*** [*pl.* INVENTORIES (-iz, -riz)], [ML. *inventorium;* L. *inventarium* < *inventus;* see INVENT], 1. an itemized list or catalogue of goods, property, etc.; especially, such a list of the stock of a business, taken annually. 2. the store of goods, etc., which are or may be so listed; stock. Abbreviated **invt.** ***v.t.*** [INVENTORIED (-id, -rid), INVENTORYING], 1. to make an inventory of. 2. to place on an inventory. —*SYN.* see **list.**

In·ver·ness (in'vẽr-nes'), ***n.*** 1. Inverness-shire. 2. the county seat of Inverness-shire: pop., 30,000. 3. [often i-], *a*) a kind of overcoat with a long, removable, sleeveless cape. *b*) the cape: also **Inverness cape.**

In·ver·ness-shire (in'vẽr-nes'shir), ***n.*** a county of northern Scotland: pop., 83,000; county seat, Inverness.

in·verse (in-vũrs'; *also, for adj.,* in'vũrs'), ***adj.*** [L. *inversus,* pp. of *invertere*], 1. inverted; reversed in order or relation; directly opposite. 2. in *mathematics,* designating or of a relation between variables in which one increases as the other decreases: as, an *inverse* proportion: opposed to *direct.* ***n.*** any inverse thing; direct opposite: as, love is the *inverse* of hate. ***v.t.*** [INVERSED (-vũrst'), INVERSING], to invert; reverse.

in·ver·sion (in-vũr'zhən, in-vũr'shən), ***n.*** [L. *inversio* < *inversus,* pp. of *invertere*], 1. an inverting or being inverted. 2. something inverted; reversal. 3. in *chemistry,* a chemical change in which an optically active substance is converted into another substance having no effect, or the opposite rotatory effects, on the plane of polarization: as, sucrose yields dextrose and levulose by *inversion.* 4. in *grammar & rhetoric,* a reversal of the normal order of words in a sentence. 5. in *mathematics, a*) the process of using an opposite rule or method. *b*) an interchange of the terms of a ratio. 6. in *medicine & pathology,* introversion. 7. in *music,* the reversal of the position of the tones in an interval, chord, etc., as by raising the lower tone by an octave, etc. 8. in *phonetics,* a position of the tongue in which the tip is turned upward and backward. 9. in *psychiatry,* homosexuality.

in·ver·sive (in-vũr'siv), ***adj.*** showing or causing inversion.

in·vert (in-vũrt'; *for adj. & n.,* in'vũrt'), ***v.t.*** [L. *invertere; in-,* in, to, toward + *vertere,* to turn], 1. to turn upside down. 2. to change to the direct opposite; reverse the order, position, direction, etc. of. 3. to subject to inversion (in various senses). ***adj.*** in *chemistry,* inverted: as, *invert* sugar. ***n.*** 1. an inverted person or thing. 2. in *psychiatry,* a homosexual. —*SYN.* see **reverse.**

in·vert·ase (in-vũr'tās), ***n.*** [*invert* + *-ase*], an enzyme, present in certain plants and in animal intestines, which changes sucrose into dextrose and levulose.

in·ver·te·brate (in-vũr'tə-brit, in-vũr'tə-brāt'), ***adj.*** [Mod. L. *invertebratus* (neut. pl. *invertebrata,* invertebrates)], 1. not vertebrate; having no backbone, or spinal column. 2. of invertebrates. 3. having no moral backbone; lacking courage, resolution, etc. ***n.*** any animal without a backbone, or spinal column: the classification includes all animals except fishes, amphibians, reptiles, birds, and mammals.

inverted commas, [British], quotation marks.

in·vert·er (in-vũr'tẽr), ***n.*** in *electricity,* a device for transforming direct current to alternating current.

invert sugar, a mixture of dextrose and levulose in approximately equal proportions, found in fruits and produced artificially by the inversion of sucrose.

in·vest (in-vest'), ***v.t.*** [L. *investire; in-,* in + *vestire,* to clothe < *vestis,* clothing], 1. [Rare], to clothe; array; adorn. 2. *a*) to cover, surround, or envelop like, or as if with, a garment: as, fog *invests* the city. *b*) to endue. 3. to install in office with ceremony. 4. to furnish with power, privilege, or authority. 5. [Rare], *a*) to vest or settle (a power or right) in a person, legislative body, etc. *b*) to put on; don. 6. to put (money) into business, real estate, stocks, bonds, etc., for the purpose of obtaining an income or profit. 7. to spend (time, effort, etc.) with the expectation of some satisfaction. 8. in *military usage,* to hem in or besiege (a town, port, etc.). ***v.i.*** to invest money; make an investment.

in·ves·ti·ga·ble (in-ves'ti-gə-b'l), ***adj.*** [LL. *investigabilis*], that can be investigated.

in·ves·ti·gate (in-ves'tə-gāt'), ***v.t.*** [INVESTIGATED (-id), INVESTIGATING], [< L. *investigatus,* pp. of *investigare,* to trace out; *in-,* in + *vestigare,* to track < *vestigium,* a track], to search into; examine in detail; inquire into systematically. ***v.i.*** to make an investigation.

in·ves·ti·ga·tion (in-ves'tə-gā'shən), ***n.*** [ME. *investigacioun;* Late OFr.; L. *investigatio*], an investigating; careful search or examination; systematic inquiry.

SYN.—**investigation** refers to a detailed examination or search, often formal or official, to uncover facts and determine the truth (the *investigation* of a crime); **probe** applies to an extensive, searching investigation, as by an appointed committee, of alleged corrupt practices, etc.; **inquest** now refers to a judicial inquiry, especially one conducted by a coroner to determine the cause of a suspicious death; **inquisition** strictly refers to any penetrating investigation, but because of its application to the ecclesiastical inquiries for the suppression of heresy, it now usually connotes ruthless, hounding persecution; **research** implies careful, patient study and investigation from original sources of information, as by scientists or scholars.

in·ves·ti·ga·tive (in-ves'tə-gā'tiv), ***adj.*** 1. of or characterized by investigation. 2. inclined to investigate.

in·ves·ti·ga·tor (in-ves'tə-gā'tẽr), ***n.*** [L.], a person who investigates.

in·ves·ti·ga·to·ry (in-ves'ti-gə-tôr'i, in-ves'ti-gə-tō'ri), ***adj.*** investigative.

in·ves·ti·tive (in-ves'tə-tiv), ***adj.*** [< L. *investitus,* pp. (see INVEST); + *-ive*], 1. that invests or can invest authority, etc. 2. of such investing.

in·ves·ti·ture (in-ves'tə-chẽr), ***n.*** [ME.; ML. *investitura* < L. *investire*], 1. a formal investing with an office, power, authority, etc. 2. anything that clothes or covers; vesture. 3. in *feudal law,* the livery of seizin: a ceremonial conveyance of land.

in·vest·ment (in-vest'mənt), ***n.*** 1. an investing or being invested. 2. clothing; covering. 3. an investiture. 4. *a*) the investing of money. *b*) the amount of money invested. *c*) anything in which money is or may be invested.

investment fund, a trust or corporation that invests in securities the funds obtained from the sale of its own shares and distributes a return to its shareholders from the income.

in·ves·tor (in-ves'tẽr), ***n.*** a person who invests money.

in·vet·er·a·cy (in-vet'ẽr-ə-si), ***n.*** 1. the state or quality of being inveterate. 2. [*pl.* INVETERACIES (-siz)], an enmity or prejudice of long standing.

in·vet·er·ate (in-vet'ẽr-it), ***adj.*** [L. *inveteratus,* pp. of *inveterare,* to make or become old < *in-,* in + *vetus,* old], 1. firmly established over a long period; of long standing; deep-rooted. 2. settled in a habit, practice, prejudice, etc.; habitual. —*SYN.* see **chronic.**

in·vid·i·ous (in-vid'i-əs), ***adj.*** [L. *invidiosus* < *invidia;* see ENVY], 1. *a*) such as to excite ill will, odium, or envy; giving offense. *b*) giving offense by discriminating unfairly: as, *invidious* comparisons. 2. [Obs.], envious.

in·vig·i·late (in-vij'ə-lāt'), ***v.i.*** [INVIGILATED (-id), INVIGILATING], [< L. *invigilatus,* pp. of *invigilare; in-,* in, on + *vigilare,* to watch; cf. VIGIL], [Chiefly British], to keep watch over students during a written examination.

in·vig·or·ant (in-vig'ẽr-ənt), ***n.*** a thing that invigorates.

in·vig·or·ate (in-vig'ə-rāt'), ***v.t.*** [INVIGORATED (-id), INVIGORATING], [L. *in,* in + *vigor* (see VIGOR); + *-ate*], to give vigor to; fill with energy; strengthen; enliven. —*SYN.* see **animate.**

in·vig·or·a·tion (in-vig'ə-rā'shən), ***n.*** an invigorating or being invigorated.

in·vig·or·a·tive (in-vig'ə-rā'tiv), ***adj.*** invigorating or tending to invigorate.

in·vig·or·a·tor (in-vig'ə-rā'tẽr), ***n.*** a person or thing that invigorates.

in·vin·ci·bil·i·ty (in-vin'sə-bil'ə-ti), ***n.*** the quality or state of being invincible.

in·vin·ci·ble (in-vin'sə-b'l), ***adj.*** [ME. *invyncyble;* Late OFr.; L. *invincibilis;* see IN- (not) & VINCIBLE], that cannot be overcome; unconquerable.

in·vin·ci·bly (in-vin'sə-bli), ***adv.*** in an invincible manner; so as to be invincible.

in·vi·o·la·bil·i·ty (in-vī'ə-lə-bil'ə-ti), ***n.*** the quality or state of being inviolable.

in·vi·o·la·ble (in-vī'ə-lə-b'l), ***adj.*** [L. *inviolabilis*], 1. not to be violated; not to be profaned or injured; sacred: as, an *inviolable* promise. 2. that cannot be violated; indestructible: as, the *inviolable* heavens.

in·vi·o·la·cy (in-vī'ə-lə-si), ***n.*** the state or quality of being inviolate.

in·vi·o·late (in-vī'ə-lit, in-vī'ə-lāt'), ***adj.*** [ME.; L. *inviolatus;* see IN- (not) & VIOLATE], not violated; kept sacred or unbroken.

in·vis·i·bil·i·ty (in'viz-ə-bil'ə-ti, in-viz'ə-bil'ə-ti), ***n.*** [LL. *invisibilitas*], the state or quality of being invisible.

in·vis·i·ble (in-viz'ə-b'l), ***adj.*** [ME.; OFr.; L. *invisibilis*], 1. not visible; that cannot be seen. 2. out of sight; not apparent. 3. too small or too faint to be seen; imperceptible; indistinct. 4. kept hidden: as, *invisible* assets. ***n.*** an invisible thing or being.
the Invisible, 1. God. 2. the unseen world.

invisible ink, a colorless ink that cannot be seen on paper until it is treated with heat, vapor, or a chemical reagent: also called *sympathetic ink.*

in·vis·i·bly (in-viz'ə-bli), ***adv.*** in an invisible manner; so as to be invisible.

in·vi·ta·tion (in'və-tā'shən), ***n.*** [L. *invitatio* < pp. of *invitare*], 1. an inviting to come somewhere or do something. 2. the message or note used in inviting. 3. enticement or allurement.

in·vi·ta·to·ry (in-vī'tə-tôr'i, in-vī'tə-tō'ri), ***adj.*** [ML. *invitatorius*], containing an invitation. ***n.*** [*pl.* INVITATORIES (-iz, -riz)], a form of invitation used in worship to call to prayer or praise.

in·vite (in-vīt'), ***v.t.*** [INVITED (-id), INVITING], [Fr. *inviter* < L. *invitare*, to ask, treat as a guest, entertain], 1. to ask (a person) courteously to come somewhere or do something; request the presence or participation of. 2. to make a request for: as, the speaker *invited* questions. 3. to tend to bring on; give occasion for: as, such talk *invites* scandal. 4. to tempt; allure; entice. ***n.*** (in'vīt), [Slang], an invitation. —***SYN.*** see **call.**

in·vit·ing (in-vīt'iŋ), ***adj.*** [ppr. of *invite*], tempting; alluring; enticing.

in·vo·cate (in'və-kāt'), ***v.t. & v.i.*** [INVOCATED (-id), INVOCATING], [< L. *invocatus*, pp. of *invocare;* see INVOKE], [Rare], to speak or ask in invocation.

in·vo·ca·tion (in'və-kā'shən), ***n.*** [ME.; OFr.; L. *invocatio* < pp. of *invocare;* see INVOKE], 1. the act of calling on God, a saint, the Muses, etc. for blessing, help, inspiration, protection, etc. 2. *a*) a formal prayer used in invoking, as at the beginning of a church service. *b*) a formal plea for aid from a Muse, god, etc., at the beginning of an epic or similar poem. 3. *a*) a conjuring of evil spirits. *b*) an incantation used in conjuring. 4. in *law*, a formal request from the bench for the papers or evidence pertaining to a case other than that under trial.

in·voc·a·to·ry (in-vok'ə-tôr'i, in-vok'ə-tō'ri), ***adj.*** of, having the nature of, or used in invocation.

in·voice (in'vois), ***n.*** [earlier *invoyes, pl.;* Fr. *envois*, pl. of *envoi*, a sending, conveyance < *envoyer*, to send; see ENVOY], 1. an itemized list of goods shipped to a buyer, stating quantities, prices, shipping charges, etc. 2. a shipment of invoiced goods. Abbreviated **inv.** ***v.t.*** [INVOICED (-voist), INVOICING], to make an invoice of; enter in an invoice.

in·voke (in-vōk'), ***v.t.*** [INVOKED (-vōkt'), INVOKING], [Fr. *invoquer;* L. *invocare; in-*, in, on + *vocare*, to call], 1. to call on (God, a saint, the Muses, etc.) for blessing, help, inspiration, protection, etc. 2. to summon (evil spirits) by incantation; conjure. 3. to ask solemnly for; beg for; implore; entreat.

in·vol·u·cel (in-vol'yoo-sel'), ***n.*** [Mod. L. *involucellum*, dim. < L. *involucrum*], a secondary involucre; ring of small leaves, or bracts, at the base of each flower of a cluster.

in·vo·lu·cral (in'və-lo͞o'krəl, in'və-lū'krəl), ***adj.*** of or like an involucre.

in·vo·lu·crate (in'və-lo͞o'krit, in'və-lū'krāt), ***adj.*** having an involucre.

in·vo·lu·cre (in'və-lo͞o'kẽr, in'və-lū'kẽr), ***n.*** [Fr.; L. *involucrum*, wrapper, case, envelope < *involvere;* see INVOLVE], 1. in *anatomy*, a membranous covering or envelope. 2. in *botany*, a ring of small leaves, or bracts, at the base of a flower, flower cluster, or fruit: involucres often resemble calyxes and are found in all composite plants.

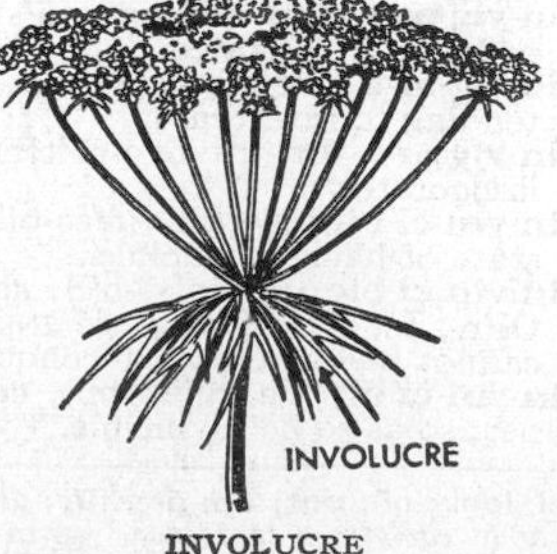

INVOLUCRE

in·vo·lu·crum (in'və-lo͞o'krəm, in'və-lū'krəm), ***n.*** [*pl.* INVOLUCRA (-krə)], an involucre.

in·vol·un·tar·i·ly (in-vol'ən-ter'ə-li), ***adv.*** in an involuntary manner.

in·vol·un·tar·i·ness (in-vol'ən-ter'i-nis), ***n.*** the quality or state of being involuntary.

in·vol·un·tar·y (in-vol'ən-ter'i), ***adj.*** [LL. *involuntarius*], not voluntary; specifically, *a*) not done of one's own free will; not done by choice. *b*) unintentional; accidental. *c*) not consciously controlled; automatic: as, digestion is *involuntary.* —***SYN.*** see **spontaneous.**

in·vo·lute (in'və-lo͞ot', in'və-lūt'), ***adj.*** [L. *involutus*, pp. of *involvere*], 1. intricate; involved. 2. rolled up or curled in a spiral; having the whorls wound closely around the axis: as, *involute* shells. 3. in *botany*, rolled inward at the edges: as, *involute* leaves. ***n.*** 1. [Rare], anything intricate or involved. 2. in *geometry*, the curve traced by the end of a taut string when it is wound upon or unwound from a fixed curve on the same plane with it: correlative to *evolute.*

INVOLUTE (of leaf)

in·vo·lut·ed (in'və-lo͞o'tid, in'və-lū'tid), ***adj.*** involute.

in·vo·lu·tion (in'və-lo͞o'shən, in'və-lū'shən), ***n.*** [L. *involutio* < *involutus*, pp. of *involvere*], 1. an involving or being involved; entanglement. 2. anything that is involved; complication; intricacy. 3. in *anatomy*, a part formed by rolling or curling inward. 4. in *biology*, a retrograde or degenerative change. 5. in *grammar*, an involved construction, especially one created by a clause separating a subject from its predicate 6. in *mathematics*, the raising of a quantity to any given power. 7. in *medicine*, *a*) the return of an organ to its normal size after distention: as, the *involution* of the womb after childbirth. *b*) a decline in the normal functions of the body or an organ; especially, the changes occurring at the menopause.

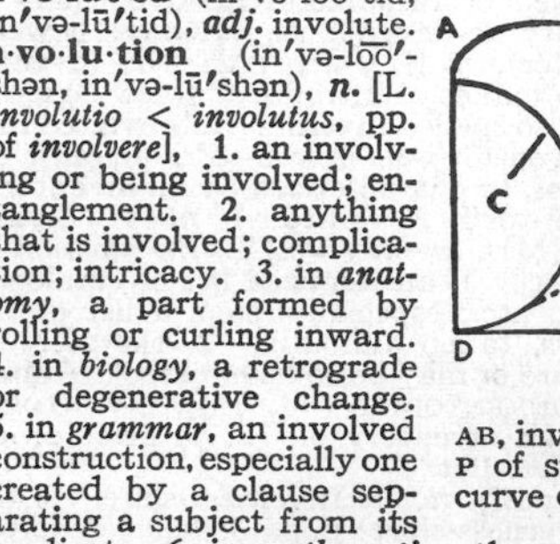

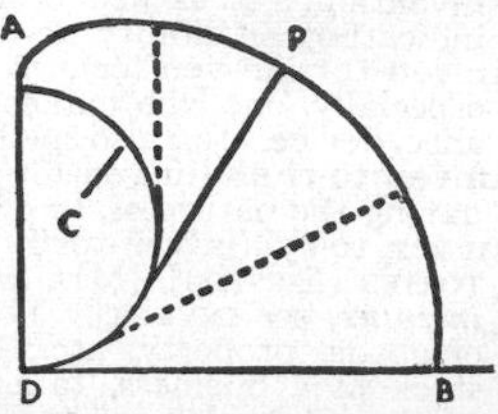

INVOLUTE

AB, involute made by point P of string unrolled from curve C

in·vo·lu·tion·al (in'və-lo͞o'shən-'l, in'və-lū'shən-'l), ***adj.*** of or resulting from involution.

in·vo·lu·tion·ar·y (in'və-lo͞o'shən-er'i, in'və-lū'shən-er'i), ***adj.*** of or characterized by involution.

in·volve (in-volv'), ***v.t.*** [INVOLVED (-volvd'), INVOLVING], [ME. *enuoluen;* OFr. *involver;* L. *involvere; in-*, in + *volvere*, to roll], 1. to roll up; wrap; enfold; envelop: as, fog *involved* the shoreline. 2. to wind spirally; coil up: as, the serpent *involved* its body. 3. to make intricate or tangled; complicate. 4. to entangle in trouble, difficulty, danger, etc.; implicate. 5. to roll up within itself; include: as, the procession *involved* thousands as it moved toward the Bastille. 6. to bring into connection; require: as, expansion in business *involves* expenditure. 7. to occupy the attention of: as, he was *involved* in working out a solution to the problem. 8. in *mathematics*, to raise (a quantity) to a given power. —***SYN.*** see **include.**

in·volved (in-volvd'), ***adj.*** [pp. of *involve*], not easily understood; intricate; complicated.—***SYN.*** see **complex.**

in·volve·ment (in-volv'mənt), ***n.*** 1. an involving or being involved. 2. anything that is involved; complicated state of affairs.

invt., inventory.

in·vul·ner·a·bil·i·ty (in-vul'nẽr-ə-bil'ə-ti), ***n.*** the quality or state of being invulnerable.

in·vul·ner·a·ble (in-vul'nẽr-ə-b'l), ***adj.*** not vulnerable; specifically, *a*) that cannot be wounded or injured. *b*) proof against attack; unassailable.

in·vul·ner·a·bly (in-vul'nẽr-ə-bli), ***adv.*** in an invulnerable manner; so as to be invulnerable.

in·wall (in-wôl'), ***v.t.*** to surround by or as by a wall. ***n.*** (in'wôl'), an inner wall.

in·ward (in'wẽrd), ***adj.*** [ME. *inneward;* AS. *inweard, inneweard;* see IN- (in) & -WARD], 1. situated within; being on the inside; internal: as, the *inward* organs of the body. 2. of or belonging to the inner nature of a person; mental or spiritual. 3. directed toward the inside; ingoing: as, the *inward* pull of a centrifuge. 4. of the inside or inner part, as of the body. 5. inland: as, *inward* Asia. 6. inherent; intrinsic. 7. [Archaic], domestic. 8. [Obs.], *a*) intimate; familiar. *b*) private; secret. ***n.*** 1. the inside; inward part; hence, 2. *pl.* the entrails. 3. [British], *pl.* imported articles, or dues on these. ***adv.*** 1. toward the inside, interior, or center. 2. into the mind, thoughts, or soul. 3. [Obs.], internally.

in·ward·ly (in'wẽrd-li), ***adv.*** [ME. *inwardlich;* AS. *inweardlic;* see INWARD & -LY], 1. in or on the inside; internally. 2. in the mind or spirit: as, to be *inwardly* resentful. 3. toward the inside or center.

in·ward·ness (in′wẽrd-nis), *n.* 1. the inner nature, essence, or meaning. 2. the quality or state of being inward; spirituality. 3. depth of thought or feeling; sincerity.
in·wards (in′wẽrdz), *adv.* inward.
in·weave (in-wēv′), *v.t.* to weave in; interweave.
in·wind (in-wīnd′), *v.t.* to wind in; wind about; entwine.
in·wrap (in-rap′), *v.t.* to enwrap.
in·wreathe (in-rēth′), *v.t.* to enwreathe.
in·wrought (in′rôt′, in-rôt′), *adj.* [*in-* (in) + *wrought*], 1. worked into a fabric: said of a pattern, etc.; inwoven; interwoven. 2. having a decoration worked in. 3. closely blended with other things.
I·o (ī′ō), *n.* [L.; Gr. *Iō*], in *Greek mythology*, a maiden loved by Zeus and changed into a heifer by jealous Hera or, in some tales, by Zeus, to protect her: she was watched by hundred-eyed Argus and was driven to Egypt, where she regained her natural form.
Io, in *chemistry*, ionium.
Io., Iowa.
Io·an·ni·na (yô-ä′nē-nä′, yä′nē-nä′), *n.* a city in northwestern Greece: pop., 32,000: Serbian name, *Janina, Yanina.*
iod-, iodo-.
i·o·date (ī′ə-dāt′), *v.t.* [IODATED (-id), IODATING], [*iod-* + *-ate*], to treat with iodine. *n.* any salt of iodic acid.
i·o·da·tion (ī′ə-dā′shən), *n.* an iodating or being iodated.
i·od·ic (ī-od′ik), *adj.* 1. of or containing iodine. 2. caused by iodine: as, *iodic* poisoning. 3. designating or of a chemical compound in which iodine has a valence of five; specifically, designating or of an oxygen acid of iodine, HIO_3, also called *hydrogen iodate.*
i·o·did (ī′ə-did), *n.* an iodide.
i·o·dide (ī′ə-dīd′, ī′ə-did), *n.* [*iod-* + *-ide*], a compound of iodine with another element, as in sodium iodide, NaI, or with a radical, as in methyl iodide, CH_3I.
i·o·din (ī′ə-din), *n.* iodine.
i·o·dine (ī′ə-dīn′, ī′ə-din; *in chemistry, often* ī′ə-dēn′), *n.* [Fr. *iode*, iodine < Gr. *iōdēs*, violetlike (< *ion*, a violet + *eidos*, form); + *-ine*], 1. a nonmetallic chemical element belonging to the halogen family and consisting of grayish-black crystals that volatilize into a violet-colored vapor: used as an antiseptic, in the manufacture of dyes, in photography, etc.: symbol, I; at. wt., 126.92; at. no., 53. 2. [Colloq.], tincture of iodine, used as an antiseptic.
i·o·dism (ī′ə-diz′m), *n.* a diseased condition caused by the excessive use of iodine; iodine poisoning.
i·o·dize (ī′ə-dīz′), *v.t.* [IODIZED (-dīzd′), IODIZING], [*iod-* + *-ize*], to treat (a wound, photographic plate, etc.) with iodine or an iodide.
iodized salt, common table salt to which a small amount of sodium iodide or potassium iodide has been added.
i·o·do- (ī-ō′də, ī′ə-dō), [< Mod. L. *iodum*, iodine], a combining form meaning *iodine* or *a compound of iodine*, as in *iodoform:* also, before a vowel, **iod-.**
i·o·do·form (ī-ō′də-fôrm′, ī-od′ə-fôrm′), *n.* [*iodo-* + *formyl*], a yellowish, crystalline compound of iodine, CHI_3, used as an antiseptic in surgical dressings.
i·o·dol (ī′ə-dōl′, ī′ə-dol′), *n.* [*iod-* + *pyrrole*], a brownish, crystalline compound of iodine, C_4HI_4N, used as an antiseptic, etc.
i·o·do·met·ric (ī′ə-dō-met′rik), *adj.* of iodometry.
i·o·dom·e·try (ī′ə-dom′ə-tri), *n.* quantitative determination of iodine, or of substances that will react with it or liberate it, by volumetric analytical methods.
i·o·dous (ī-ō′dəs, ī-od′əs), *adj.* 1. of or containing iodine. 2. designating or of a chemical compound in which iodine has a valence of less than five. 3. designating or of a hypothetical acid, HIO_2, in which iodine has a valence of three: sodium hypoiodite, NaIO, is a salt of this acid.
i·o·lite (ī′ə-līt′), *n.* [< Gr. *ion*, violet; + *-lite*], a bluish or violet, crystalline mineral, a silicate of aluminum, iron, and magnesium; cordierite: it is used as a gem.
I.O.M., Isle of Man.
I·o moth (ī′ō), a large American moth with an eyelike spot on each hind wing.
i·on (ī′ən, ī′on), *n.* [Gr. *ion*, ppr. of *ienai*, to go], an electrically charged atom or group of atoms, the electrical charge of which results when a neutral atom or group of atoms loses or gains one or more electrons: the loss of electrons results in a positively charged ion (*cation*), the gain of electrons in a negatively charged ion (*anion*): such loss or gain occurs during chemical reactions in which electrons are transferred from one atom to another, by the action on matter of X rays, ultraviolet light, and certain other forms of radiant energy, or by the impact of alpha and beta particles, protons, deuterons, etc. on atoms and molecules.
-ion, [< Fr. or L.; Fr. *-ion;* L. *-io*, nom., *-ionis*, genit.], a noun-forming suffix meaning *a* ——*ing, a being* ——*ed*, or *the result of* ——*ing*, as in *fusion, translation, conscription, correction.*
Ion., Ionic.
I·o·ni·a (ī-ō′ni-ə), *n.* an ancient district on the western coast of Asia Minor, colonized by the Greeks in the 11th century B.C.
I·o·ni·an (ī-ō′ni-ən), *adj.* 1. of Ionia, its people, or their culture. 2. of an ancient Greek people who settled in eastern Greece and Ionia. 3. in *music*, *a*) designating or of one of the ancient Greek modes. *b*) designating or of the six medieval church modes, corresponding to the modern major diatonic scale. *n.* an Ionian Greek.
Ionian Islands, a group of seven Greek islands along the west coast of Greece: area, 963 sq. mi.; pop., 229,000.
Ionian Sea, that part of the Mediterranean between southern Italy and Greece.
I·on·ic (ī-on′ik), *adj.* [L. *Ionicus;* Gr. *Iōnikos*], 1. of Ionia or its people; Ionian. 2. designating or of a branch of the ancient Greek language, including that of Attica. 3. designating or of a Greek style of architecture characterized by ornamental scrolls on the capitals. 4. of the Ionic of Greek and Latin prosody. *n.* 1. in *Greek & Latin prosody*, *a*) either of two feet consisting of four syllables, the first two long and the second two short (- - ⌣ ⌣) (*greater Ionic*) or the first two short and the second two long (⌣ ⌣ - -) (*smaller* or *lesser Ionic*). *b*) verse or meter of such feet. 2. in *printing*, a kind of heavy-faced type that is easy to read. 3. the Ionic dialect. Abbreviated **Ion.**

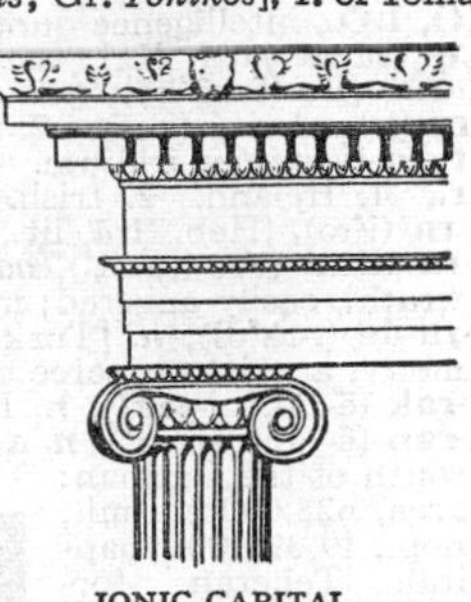
IONIC CAPITAL

i·on·ic (ī-on′ik), *adj.* of, or being in the form of, an ion or ions.
i·o·ni·um (ī-ō′ni-əm), *n.* [*ion* + *uranium*], a radioactive isotope of thorium, resulting from the disintegration of uranium: symbol, Io; at. wt., 230; at. no., 90.
i·on·i·za·tion (ī′ən-i-zā′shən, ī′ən-ī-zā′shən), *n.* an ionizing or being ionized; dissociation into ions.
i·on·ize (ī′ə-nīz′), *v.t. & v.i.* [IONIZED (-nīzd′), IONIZING], to change or be changed into ions; dissociate into ions, as a salt dissolved in water, or become electrically charged, as a gas under the influence of radiation.
i·on·o·gen (ī-on′ə-jən), *n.* a substance that can be ionized or that produces ions.
i·o·none (ī′ə-nōn′), *n.* [Gr. *ion*, violet; + *-one*], a colorless liquid, $C_{13}H_{20}O$, made from citral and acetone and used in perfume manufacture for its violetlike odor.
i·on·o·sphere (ī-on′ə-sfêr′, ī-ō′nə-sfêr′), *n.* [< *ion* + *sphere*], the outer part of the earth's atmosphere, extending far beyond the stratosphere and consisting of a series of constantly changing layers of heavily ionized molecules: cf. **Kennelly-Heaviside layer.**
i·o·ta (ī-ō′tə), *n.* [Gr. *iōta*], 1. the ninth letter of the Greek alphabet (Ι, ι), corresponding to English *I, i:* see **alphabet**, table. 2. a very small quantity; jot.
i·o·ta·cism (ī-ō′tə-siz′m), *n.* [LL. *iotacismus;* Gr. *iōtakismos*], 1. excessive use of *i* (Gr. *iota*). 2. a tendency to give the sound of this letter to other vowels.
IOU, I.O.U. (ī′ō′ū′), 1. I owe you. 2. a paper bearing these letters, acknowledging a specified debt and signed by the debtor.
-i·ous (i-əs, yəs, əs), [*-i-*, thematic vowel + *-ous*], a suffix used to form adjectives corresponding to nouns ending in *-ion*, as in *rebellious, religious*, or to form analogous adjectives meaning *having, characterized by*, as in *furious, anxious.*
I·o·wa (ī′ə-wə; *occas., esp. locally*, ī′ə-wā′), *n.* 1. a Middle Western State of the United States: area, 56,280 sq. mi.; pop., 2,758,000; capital, Des Moines: abbreviated **Ia., I., Io.** 2. a river flowing from northern Iowa to the Mississippi: length, 350 mi.
Iowa City, a city in eastern Iowa: pop., 33,000.
I·o·wan (ī′ə-wən), *adj.* of Iowa. *n.* a native or inhabitant of Iowa.
IPA, 1. International Phonetic Alphabet. 2. International Phonetic Association.
ip·e·cac (ip′i-kak′), *n.* [contr. < *ipecacuanha*], 1. a tropical South American creeping plant of the madder family, with small, drooping flowers. 2. the dried roots of this plant. 3. a preparation from the dried roots, used in the treatment of laryngitis, bronchitis, and chronic diarrhea.
ip·e·cac·u·an·ha (ip′i-kak′ū-an′ə), *n.* [Port. < Tupi *ipe-kaa-guêne*, small emetic plant], ipecac.
Iph·i·ge·ni·a (if′ə-ji-nī′ə), *n.* [L.; Gr. *Iphigeneia*], in *Greek mythology*, a daughter of Agamemnon, offered by him as a sacrifice to Artemis and saved by the goddess, who made her a priestess: subject of tragedies by Euripides and Goethe and of two operas by Gluck.
ip·o·moe·a (ip′ə-mē′ə, ī′pə-mē′ə), *n.* [Mod. L. < Gr. *ips, ipos*, a worm + *homoios*, like], any of a group of

twining or creeping plants, including the morning-glory, with showy leaves and trumpet-shaped flowers.
Ip·po·li·tov-I·va·nov, Mi·kha·il Mi·khai·lo·vich (mü-khä-ēl' mü-khīl'ô-vich ē'pô-lü'tôf-i-vä'nôf), 1859–1935; Russian composer.
‡**ip·se dix·it** (ip'si dik'sit), [L.], literally, he himself has said (it); hence, an arbitrary or dogmatic statement.
‡**ip·sis·si·ma ver·ba** (ip-sis'i-mə vũr'bə), [L.], the very words.
‡**ip·so fac·to** (ip'sō fak'tō), [L.], by the fact (or act) itself; by that very fact.
‡**ip·so ju·re** (ip'sō jōō'ri), [L.], by the law itself.
Ips·wich (ips'wich), *n.* a city in eastern England: pop., 115,000.
IQ, I.Q., intelligence quotient.
i.q., *idem quod,* [L.], the same as.
I·qui·que (ē-kē'ke), *n.* a city in Chile: pop., 40,000.
ir- (ir), 1. in- (not). 2. in- (in). Used before *r*.
Ir, in *chemistry,* iridium.
Ir., 1. Ireland. 2. Irish.
I·ra (ī'rə), [Heb. *'īrā,* lit., watchful], a masculine name.
i·ra·cund (ī'rə-kund'), *adj.* [L. *iracundus* < *ira,* anger, wrath], easily angered; irascible.
i·ra·de (i-rä'di), *n.* [Turk; Ar. *irādah,* will, desire], formerly, a written decree of the Sultan of Turkey.
I·rak (ē-räk', i-rak'), *n.* Iraq.
I·ran (ē-rän', ī-ran'), *n.* a country in southwestern Asia, south of the Caspian: area, 628,000 sq. mi.; pop., 19,395,000; capital, Teheran: formerly (officially until March, 1935) called *Persia.*

IRAN AND IRAQ

Iran., Iranian.
I·ra·ni (ē-rä'ni), *adj.* Iranian.
I·ra·ni·an (ī-rā'ni-ən), *adj.* of Iran, its people, their language, or culture. *n.* 1. one of the people of Iran; Persian. 2. a branch of the Indo-European family of languages that includes languages now spoken in the Iranian Plateau and a small area of the Caucasus: among the extant languages of the group are Persian, Kurdish, and Afghan (Pushtu). Abbreviated **Iran.**
Iranian Plateau, a plateau mostly in Iran, extending from the Tigris River to the Indus River.
I·ran·ic (ī-ran'ik), *adj. & n.* Iranian (language).
I·raq (ē-räk', i-rak'), *n.* a country in southwestern Asia, on the Persian Gulf: area, 116,600 sq. mi.; pop., 6,538,000; capital, Bagdad: formerly called *Mesopotamia:* also spelled **Irak.**
I·ra·qi (ē-rä'ki), *n.* 1. a native of Iraq. 2. the dialect of Arabic spoken by the Iraqis. *adj.* of Iraq, its people, their language, or culture.
i·ras·ci·bil·i·ty (i-ras'ə-bil'ə-ti, ī-ras'ə-bil'ə-ti), *n.* the fact or quality of being irascible; irritability.
i·ras·ci·ble (i-ras'ə-b'l, ī-ras'ə-b'l), *adj.* [ME. *irascibel;* Late OFr.; LL. *irascibilis* < L. *irasci;* see IRATE], easily angered; quick-tempered. —*SYN.* see **irritable.**
i·ras·ci·bly (i-ras'ə-bli, ī-ras'ə-bli), *adv.* in an irascible manner.
i·rate (ī'rāt, ī-rāt'), *adj.* [L. *iratus* < *irasci,* to be angry < *ira;* see IRE], angry; wrathful; incensed.
I·ra·zú, Mount (ē'rä-zōō'), a volcanic mountain in central Costa Rica: height, 10,525 ft.
IRBM, intermediate range ballistic missile.
ire (īr), *n.* [ME.; OFr.; L. *ira*], anger; wrath. —*SYN.* see **anger.**
ire·ful (īr'fəl), *adj.* full of ire; angry; wrathful; incensed.
Ire·land (īr'lənd), *n.* 1. one of the British Isles, comprising Ireland (sense 2) and Northern Ireland: formerly part of the United Kingdom: area, 31,839 sq. mi.; pop., 4,301,000; chief cities, Dublin and Belfast. 2. a country comprising the southern provinces of Ireland (Leinster, Munster, and Connaught) and three counties (Cavan, Donegal, and Monaghan) of Ulster province: it was established as a republic in December, 1925, associated (until 1949) with the British Commonwealth of Nations: area, 26,601 sq. mi.; pop., 2,898,000; capital, Dublin: former names, *Irish Free State, Eire.* Abbreviated **Ire., Ir.**
I·rene (ī-rēn'), [< Fr. or L.; Fr. *Irène;* L. *Irene;* Gr. *Eirēnē,* lit., peace], a feminine name. *n.* (ī-rē'nē), in *Greek mythology,* the goddess of peace, daughter of Zeus and Themis: identified by the Romans with Pax.
i·ren·ic (ī-ren'ik, ī-rē'nik), *adj.* [Gr. *eirēnikos* < *eirēnēs,* peace], promoting peace; peaceful; pacific.
i·ren·i·cal (ī-ren'i-k'l, ī-rē'ni-k'l), *adj.* irenic.
i·ren·ics (ī-ren'iks, ī-rē'niks), *n.pl.* [construed as sing.], [< *irenic*], the doctrine or practice of promoting peace among Christian churches in relation to theological differences; irenic theology.
ir·id- (ir'id, ī'rid), irido-.
i·ri·da·ceous (ī'ri-dā'shəs, ir'i-dā'shəs), *adj.* [< Mod. L. *Iris,* iris genus (see IRIS); + *-aceous*], of the iris family of perennial plants, including the iris and crocus.
ir·i·dec·to·my (ir'i-dek'tə-mi, ī'ri-dek'tə-mi), *n.* [*pl.* IRIDECTOMIES (-miz)], [*irid-* + *-ectomy*], the surgical removal of part of the iris of the eye.
ir·i·des (ī'rə-dēz'), alternative plural of **iris.**
ir·i·des·cence (ir'ə-des''ns), *n.* the quality or fact of being iridescent; interplay of rainbowlike colors.
ir·i·des·cent (ir'ə-des''nt), *adj.* [< L. *iris, iridis,* rainbow; Gr. *iris,* rainbow; + *-escent*], having or showing an interplay of rainbowlike colors.
i·rid·ic (i-rid'ik, ī-rid'ik), *adj.* 1. of or containing iridium. 2. designating or of a chemical compound in which iridium has a valence of four.
i·rid·i·um (i-rid'i-əm, ī-rid'i-əm), *n.* [< L. *iris, iridis;* Gr. *iris,* rainbow: so called because of the changing color of some of its salts], a white, heavy, brittle, metallic chemical element found in platinum ores: alloys of iridium are used for pen points, contact points in telegraphy, and bearings of watches and scientific instruments: symbol, Ir; at. wt., 193.1; at. no., 77.
ir·i·do- (ir'i-dō, ī'ri-də), [< Gr. *iris, iridos,* iris], a combining form meaning *the iris* (of the eye): also, before a vowel, **irid-,** as in *iridectomy.*
ir·i·dos·mine (ir'i-doz'min, ī'ri-dos'min), *n.* [< *iridium* + *osmium*], osmiridium.
ir·i·dos·mi·um (ir'i-doz'mi-em, ī'ri-dos'mi-əm), *n.* iridosmine; osmiridium.
I·ris (ī'ris), [L.; Gr. *Iris;* see IRIDESCENT], a feminine name. *n.* in *Greek mythology,* the goddess of the rainbow: in the *Iliad,* she is the messenger of the gods.
i·ris (ī'ris), *n.* [*pl.* IRISES (-iz), IRIDES (ī'rə-dēz')], [see prec.], 1. a rainbow. 2. a rainbowlike show or play of colors. 3. the round, pigmented membrane surrounding the pupil of the eye, having muscles that adjust the size of the pupil to regulate the amount of light entering the eye: see **eye,** illus. 4. any of a large group of plants with sword-shaped leaves and a conspicuous flower composed of three petals and three drooping sepals of widely varying color. 5. the flower of this plant. Also called *flag* (in senses 4 & 5).
iris diaphragm, a device consisting of thin, overlapping metal plates that can be adjusted to form an aperture of varying size for camera lenses, etc.
I·rish (ī'rish), *adj.* [ME. *Irisch, Irisc* < base of AS. *Iras,* the Irish < OIr. *Eriu,* Ireland; cf. EIRE], of Ireland, its people, their language, or culture. *n.* 1. the Goidelic, Celtic language spoken by some of the Irish; Erse. 2. the English dialect of Ireland. 3. [Colloq.], temper: chiefly in *get one's Irish up,* to arouse one's temper. Abbreviated **Ir.**
the Irish, the Irish people.
Irish Free State, Ireland (sense 2): especially so called from 1922 to 1937: abbreviated **I.F.S.**
I·rish·ism (ī'rish-iz'm), *n.* an Irish idiom, custom, etc.
I·rish·man (ī'rish-mən), *n.* [*pl.* IRISHMEN (-mən)], 1. a native or inhabitant of Ireland, especially a man. 2. a person of Irish ancestry, especially a man.
Irish moss, carrageen, a seaweed dried and bleached for use as a medicine, a thickening agent in food, etc.
Irish potato, the common white potato: so called because extensively cultivated in Ireland.
Irish Republican Army, a secret organization founded to work for Irish independence from England: it continued to exist after the establishment of the Irish Free State, which declared it illegal in 1936.
Irish Sea, the part of the Atlantic between Ireland and England.
Irish setter, any of a breed of setter with a coat of long, silky, reddish-brown hair.
Irish stew, meat, potatoes, carrots, onions, and other vegetables cooked with a small amount of water.
Irish terrier, any of a breed of small, lean, active dog with a wiry, reddish-brown coat.
Irish wolfhound, any of a breed of very large, heavy, powerful dog with a hard, rough coat, formerly used in hunting wolves.
I·rish·wom·an (ī'rish-woom'ən), *n.* [*pl.* IRISHWOMEN (-wim'in)], 1. a woman who is a native or inhabitant of Ireland. 2. a woman of Irish ancestry.

IRISH TERRIER
(18 in. high)

i·ri·tis (ī-rī'tis), *n.* [Mod. L.; cf. IRIS & -ITIS], inflammation of the iris of the eye.
irk (ũrk), *v.t.* [ME. *irken,* to loathe, be weary of; prob. < northern & north Midland adj. *irk, yrk,* weary, troubled, bored], to make tired; disgust; annoy; trouble; vex; bore. —*SYN.* see **annoy.**
irk·some (ũrk'səm), *adj.* [ME. *irksum;* see IRK & -SOME], tiresome; troublesome; tedious.
Ir·kutsk (êr-kootsk'), *n.* a city in the southern Asiatic U.S.S.R., near Lake Baikal: pop., 365,000.
Ir·ma (ũr'mə), [G., orig. contr. of *Irmenberta, Irmintrud, Irmgard,* and other names with first component *Irm-,*

Irmen- < OHG. *Irmin*, cognomen of the Gmc. deity Tiu], a feminine name.

i·ron (ī′ẽrn), *n.* [see PLURAL, II, D, 3], [ME. *iren;* AS. *iren* (chiefly poetic & prob. dissimilated), beside *isern, isen* (akin to Goth. *eisarn, isarn*); Gmc. **īsarna;* said to be borrowed < Celt. with *ī-* by transmission through Illyrian; prob. < IE. **ajos*, metal, seen also in Sans. *ayas-*, metal, iron, L. *aes*, copper (cf. ORE), etc.; some authorities derive IE. **ajos* < *Al′as(ja)*, orig. name of the island of Cyprus (cf. COPPER)], 1. a metallic chemical element, white, malleable, and ductile, the most common and most useful of all the metals: symbol, Fe; at. wt., 55.85; at. no., 26. 2. *a)* any tool, implement, device, apparatus, etc. made of iron. *b)* such a device with a flat, smooth undersurface, used, when heated, for pressing clothes or cloth. 3. *pl.* iron shackles or chains. 4. firm strength; power. 5. [Slang], a shooting iron; small firearm. 6. in *golf*, a club having a metal head. 7. in *medicine*, a tonic or other preparation containing iron. *adj.* 1. of or consisting of iron. 2. like iron; strong, firm, or unyielding: as, an *iron* temperament. 3. cruel; merciless. *v.t.* 1. to furnish or cover with iron. 2. to put (a prisoner) in irons. 3. to press (clothes or cloth) flat with a hot iron. *v.i.* to iron clothes or cloth.

have irons in the fire, to have or be engaged in activities, enterprises, etc.

in irons, 1. shackled with irons; imprisoned. 2. in *nautical usage*, failing to come about or fill away: said of a sailing vessel.

iron out, to smooth out; eliminate.

strike while the iron is hot, to act at an opportune time.

Iron Age, 1. a period of civilization (c. 1000 B.C.–100 A.D.) characterized by the introduction and development of iron tools and weapons: it followed the Bronze Age. 2. [i- a-], in *classical mythology*, the last and worst age of the world, characterized by wickedness, selfishness, and degeneracy.

i·ron·bark (ī′ẽrn-bärk′), *n.* any of several Australian eucalyptus trees with hard wood and hard, gray bark: also **ironbark tree.**

i·ron·bound (ī′ẽrn-bound′), *adj.* 1. bound with iron. 2. hard; rigid; unyielding; inflexible. 3. edged with rocks or cliffs, as a coast.

i·ron·clad (ī′ẽrn-klad′), *adj.* 1. covered or protected with iron. 2. difficult to change or break: as, an *ironclad* lease. *n.* a warship armored with thick iron plates: 19th-century term.

Iron Cross, a silver-edged Maltese cross of iron, awarded by Germany for conspicuous service in warfare: instituted in 1813.

iron curtain, a term popularized by Winston Churchill in a speech (1946) to connote the secrecy and censorship forming a Soviet-made barrier around the Soviet Union and some other countries regarded as in its sphere.

I·ron·de·quoit (i-run′di-kwoit′), *n.* a town in western New York: pop., 55,000.

i·ron-gray (ī′ẽrn-grā′), *adj.* of the color iron gray.

iron gray, a gray like that of freshly broken cast iron.

Iron Guard, a Romanian fascist organization active before World War II.

iron hand, firm, rigorous, severe control.

i·ron·hand·ed (ī′ẽrn-han′did), *adj.* [cf. prec.], firm and rigorous; strict and severe: as, an *ironhanded* king.

i·ron·heart·ed (ī′ẽrn-här′tid), *adj.* unfeeling; cruel.

iron horse, [Colloq.], 1. a locomotive. 2. a bicycle or tricycle.

i·ron·ic (ī-ron′ik), *adj.* ironical.

i·ron·i·cal (ī-ron′i-k'l), *adj.* [< L. *ironicus;* Gr. *eirōnikos* < *eirōneia* (see IRONY); + *-al*], 1. meaning the contrary of what is expressed. 2. using, or given to the use of, irony. 3. having the quality of irony; directly opposite to what is or might be expected. —*SYN.* see **sarcastic.**

ironing board, a cloth-covered board on which clothes are ironed.

iron lung, a large metal respirator which encloses all of the body but the head, used for maintaining artificial respiration in a person who has difficulty in breathing as a result of infantile paralysis, gas poisoning, etc.

IRON LUNG

i·ron·mas·ter (ī′ẽrn-mas′tẽr, ī′ẽrn-mäs′tẽr), *n.* a manufacturer of iron.

iron mold, [earlier *iron mole;* cf. MOLE (spot, mark)], a brownish stain made on cloth by iron rust or ink.

i·ron·mon·ger (ī′ẽrn-muŋ′gẽr), *n.* [ME. *irenmonger*, beside earlier *irmonger, ismonger;* see IRON & MONGER], [British], a dealer in articles made of iron and other metals; hardware dealer.

i·ron·mon·ger·y (ī′ẽrn-muŋ′gẽr-i), *n.* [British], 1. iron goods; hardware. 2. an ironmonger's shop. 3. an ironmonger's business.

iron pyrites, a gold-colored ore of iron; fool's gold: see **pyrite.**

i·ron·side (ī′ẽrn-sīd′), *n.* 1. a courageous, resolute man. 2. [I-], Oliver Cromwell: also **Ironsides.**

I·ron·sides (ī′ẽrn-sīdz′), *n.pl.* 1. [construed as sing.], Oliver Cromwell. 2. *a)* the regiment that he led in the English Civil War. *b)* his whole army. 3. [i-], [construed as sing.], an ironclad.

i·ron·smith (ī′ẽrn-smith′), *n.* an ironworker or blacksmith.

i·ron·stone (ī′ẽrn-stōn′), *n.* any of various hard iron ores.

i·ron·ware (ī′ẽrn-wâr′), *n.* things made of iron; hardware.

i·ron·weed (ī′ẽrn-wēd′), *n.* [so named from its hard stem], a plant of the aster family, with clusters of red, purple, or white tubular flowers.

i·ron·wood (ī′ẽrn-wood′), *n.* 1. any of various trees with extremely hard, heavy wood. 2. the wood.

i·ron·work (ī′ẽrn-wũrk′), *n.* articles or parts made of iron.

i·ron·work·er (ī′ẽrn-wũr′kẽr), *n.* 1. a person who makes iron or articles of iron. 2. a worker who builds the framework of steel bridges, etc.

i·ron·works (ī′ẽrn-wũrks′), *n.pl.* [also construed as sing.], a place where iron is smelted or heavy iron goods are made.

i·ro·ny (ī′rə-ni), *n.* [*pl.* IRONIES (-niz)], [Fr. *ironie;* L. *ironia;* Gr. *eirōneia* < *eirōn*, dissembler in speech < *eirein*, to speak], 1. a method of humorous or sarcastic expression in which the intended meaning of the words used is the direct opposite of their usual sense: as, the speaker was using *irony* when he said that the stupid plan was "very clever." 2. an instance of this. 3. a combination of circumstances or a result that is the opposite of what might be expected or considered appropriate: as, it was an *irony* of fate that the fireboat burned and sank. 4. the feigning of ignorance in argument: more frequently **Socratic irony** (after Socrates, who uses this device in Plato's *Dialogues*). —*SYN.* see **wit.**

i·ron·y (ī′ẽr-ni), *adj.* of, like, or containing iron.

Ir·o·quoi·an (ir′ə-kwoi′ən), *adj.* [< *Iroquois* + *-an*], of an important linguistic family of North American Indians, including speakers of Huron (Wyandot), Seneca, Mohawk, Tuscarora, Oneida, Cayuga, Onondaga, and Cherokee. *n.* 1. a member of an Iroquoian tribe. 2. the Iroquoian languages collectively.

Ir·o·quois (ir′ə-kwoi′, ir′ə-kwoiz′), *n.* [*pl.* IROQUOIS], [Fr. < Algonquian *Irinakoiw*, lit., real adders], a member of a confederation of Iroquoian Indian tribes that lived in western and northern New York: see **Five Nations.** *adj.* of the Iroquois or their tribes.

ir·ra·di·ance (i-rā′di-əns), *n.* an irradiating; radiance.

ir·ra·di·an·cy (i-rā′di-ən-si), *n.* the fact or quality of being irradiant.

ir·ra·di·ant (i-rā′di-ənt), *adj.* [L. *irradians*, ppr.; see IRRADIATE], radiating light; shining brightly.

ir·ra·di·ate (i-rā′di-āt′), *v.t.* [IRRADIATED (-id), IRRADIATING], [< L. *irradiatus*, pp. of *irradiare*, to beam upon, illumine; see IN- (in) & RADIATE], 1. to shine or throw light upon; light up; make bright. 2. to make clear; illuminate intellectually; enlighten. 3. to radiate; diffuse; spread; give out. 4. to treat by exposing to X rays, ultraviolet rays, radium, or some other form of radiant energy. 5. to heat with radiant energy. *v.i.* 1. to emit rays; shine. 2. to become radiant. *adj.* (*usually* i-rā′di-it), irradiated.

ir·ra·di·a·tion (i-rā′di-ā′shən, ir′rā-di-ā′shən), *n.* [Fr.; ML. *irradiatio*], 1. an irradiating or being irradiated. 2. something irradiated; specifically, *a)* a ray of light, etc. *b)* intellectual enlightenment. 3. in *optics*, the apparent enlargement of a brightly lighted object seen against a dark background.

ir·ra·di·a·tive (i-rā′di-ā′tiv), *adj.* having the power to irradiate.

ir·ra·tion·al (i-rash′ən-'l), *adj.* [L. *irrationalis;* see IN- (not) & RATIONAL], 1. lacking the power to reason. 2. contrary to reason; senseless; unreasonable; absurd. 3. in *Greek & Latin prosody*, *a)* designating a syllable which is long when it should be short according to the normal meter. *b)* a foot with such a syllable. 4. in *mathematics*, not capable of being expressed as an integer or as a quotient of an integer.

SYN.—**irrational** implies mental unsoundness or may be used to stress the utterly illogical nature of that which is directly contrary to reason (an *irrational* belief that everybody was his enemy); **unreasonable** implies bad judgment, willfulness, prejudice, etc. as responsible for that which is not justified by reason (*unreasonable* demands).—*ANT.* rational, reasonable.

ir·ra·tion·al·ism (i-rash′ən-'l-iz'm), *n.* irrational thought, belief, or action.

ir·ra·tion·al·i·ty (i-rash'ə-nal'ə-ti), ***n.*** 1. the quality or state of being irrational. 2. [*pl.* IRRATIONALITIES (-tiz)], an instance of this.

Ir·ra·wad·dy (ir'ə-wä'di, ir'ə-wô'di), ***n.*** a river in eastern Asia, flowing southward through central Burma into the Bay of Bengal: length, 1,250 mi.

ir·re·claim·a·bil·i·ty (ir'i-klām'ə-bil'ə-ti, ir'ri-klām'ə-bil'ə-ti), ***n.*** the quality or state of being irreclaimable.

ir·re·claim·a·ble (ir'i-klām'ə-b'l, ir'ri-klām'ə-b'l), ***adj.*** that cannot be reclaimed.

ir·re·claim·a·bly (ir'i-klām'ə-bli, ir'ri-klām'ə-bli), ***adv.*** in an irreclaimable manner; so as to be irreclaimable.

ir·rec·on·cil·a·bil·i·ty (i-rek'ən-sīl'ə-bil'ə-ti), ***n.*** the quality or state of being irreconcilable.

ir·rec·on·cil·a·ble (i-rek'ən-sīl'ə-b'l, ir'rek-ən-sīl'ə-b'l), ***adj.*** that cannot be reconciled; that cannot be brought into agreement; incompatible; conflicting; inconsistent: as, *irreconcilable* foes. ***n.*** 1. a person who is irreconcilable and refuses to make any compromise. 2. *pl.* ideas, beliefs, etc. that cannot be brought into agreement with each other.

ir·rec·on·cil·a·bly (i-rek'ən-sīl'ə-bli, ir'rek-ən-sīl'ə-bli), ***adv.*** in an irreconcilable manner; so as to be irreconcilable.

ir·re·cov·er·a·ble (ir'i-kuv'ẽr-ə-b'l, ir'ri-kuv'ẽr-ə-b'l), ***adj.*** that cannot be recovered, regained, rectified, or remedied; irretrievable.

ir·re·cov·er·a·bly (ir'i-kuv'ẽr-ə-bli, ir'ri-kuv'ẽr-ə-bli), ***adv.*** in an irrecoverable manner; beyond recovery.

ir·re·cu·sa·ble (ir'i-kū'zə-b'l, ir'ri-kū'zə-b'l), ***adj.*** [< Fr. or LL.; Fr. *irrécusable;* LL. *irrecusabilis* < *in-*, not + *recusabilis,* that should be rejected < *recusare,* to refuse], that cannot be refused or rejected.

ir·re·cu·sa·bly (ir'i-kū'zə-bli, ir'ri-kū'zə-bli), ***adv.*** in an irrecusable manner.

ir·re·deem·a·ble (ir'i-dēm'ə-b'l, ir'ri-dēm'ə-b'l), ***adj.*** [see IN- (not) & REDEEMABLE], 1. that cannot be bought back. 2. that cannot be converted into coin, as certain kinds of paper money. 3. that cannot be changed; hopeless. 4. that cannot be reformed; beyond redemption.

ir·re·deem·a·bly (ir'i-dēm'ə-bli, ir'ri-dēm'ə-bli), ***adv.*** in an irredeemable manner; so as to be irredeemable.

ir·re·den·ta (ir'i-den'tə), ***adj.*** [It.], unredeemed: said of territory inhabited chiefly by the natives of a specified country which formerly held it and seeks to recover it (especially *Italia irredenta*).

Ir·re·den·tism (ir'i-den'tiz'm), ***n.*** the program or policy of the Irredentists.

Ir·re·den·tist (ir'i-den'tist), ***n.*** [It. *irredentista* < (*Italia*) *irredenta,* unredeemed (Italy) < L. *in-*, not + *redemptus;* see REDEMPTION], 1. any member of an Italian political party, organized in 1878, seeking to recover for Italy adjacent regions inhabited largely by Italians and under foreign control. 2. any person who advocates a similar policy with regard to territory formerly a part of his country.

ir·re·duc·i·ble (ir'i-dōōs'ə-b'l, ir'ri-dūs'ə-b'l), ***adj.*** that cannot be reduced.

ir·re·duc·i·bly (ir'i-dōōs'ə-bli, ir'ri-dūs'ə-bli), ***adv.*** in an irreducible manner; so as to be irreducible.

ir·ref·ra·ga·bil·i·ty (i-ref'rə-gə-bil'ə-ti), ***n.*** the quality or state of being irrefragable.

ir·ref·ra·ga·ble (i-ref'rə-gə-b'l), ***adj.*** [LL. *irrefragabilis* (cf. *in-*, not & obs. *refragable,* refutable) < L. *refragari,* to oppose], that cannot be refuted; indisputable.

ir·ref·ra·ga·bly (i-ref'rə-gə-bli), ***adv.*** in an irrefragable manner; so as to be irrefragable.

ir·re·fran·gi·ble (ir'i-fran'jə-b'l, ir'ri-fran'jə-b'l), ***adj.*** [*ir-* (not) + *refrangible*], 1. that cannot be broken or violated. 2. that cannot be refracted.

ir·ref·u·ta·bil·i·ty (i-ref'yoo-tə-bil'ə-ti, ir'ri-fū'tə-bil'ə-ti), ***n.*** the state or quality of being irrefutable.

ir·ref·u·ta·ble (i-ref'yoo-tə-b'l, ir'ri-fū'tə-b'l), ***adj.*** that cannot be refuted; incapable of being disproved.

ir·ref·u·ta·bly (i-ref'yoo-tə-bli, ir'ri-fū'tə-bli), ***adv.*** in an irrefutable manner; so as to be irrefutable.

ir·re·gard·less (ir'i-gärd'lis, ir'ri-gärd'lis), ***adj.* & *adv.*** regardless: a substandard or humorous redundancy.

ir·reg·u·lar (i-reg'yoo-lẽr), ***adj.*** [ME. *irreguler;* OFr. *irregulier;* ML. *irregularis;* see IN- (not) & REGULAR], 1. not conforming to established rule, method, usage, etc.; out of the ordinary; anomalous. 2. not conforming or having conformed to legal or moral requirements; lawless; disorderly. 3. not straight or even; not symmetrical; not uniform in shape, design, or proportion. 4. uneven in occurrence or succession. 5. in *botany,* not uniform in shape, size, etc., as the petals of flowers. 6. in *grammar,* not inflected in the normal or usual manner: as, *go* is an *irregular* verb. 7. in *military usage,* not belonging to the regularly established army. ***n.*** 1. a person or thing that is irregular. 2. *usually in pl.* a soldier who belongs to an irregular military force. Abbreviated **irreg.**

SYN.—**irregular** implies deviation from the customary or established rule, procedure, etc. (an *irregular* marriage); **abnormal** and **anomalous** imply deviation from the normal condition or from the ordinary type, **abnormal** stressing atypical form or character (a man of *abnormal* height), and **anomalous,** an exceptional condition or circumstance (in the *anomalous* position of a leader without followers); **unnatural** applies to that which is contrary to the order of nature or to natural laws (her *unnatural* hatred for her baby).—***ANT.*** regular, normal, natural.

ir·reg·u·lar·i·ty (i-reg'yoo-lar'ə-ti, ir'reg-yoo-lar'ə-ti), ***n.*** 1. the quality or state of being irregular; lack of regularity. 2. [*pl.* IRREGULARITIES (-tiz)], something irregular.

ir·rel·a·tive (i-rel'ə-tiv), ***adj.*** 1. not relative; having no relation; unrelated. 2. irrelevant.

ir·rel·e·vance (i-rel'ə-vəns), ***n.*** 1. the quality or state of being irrelevant. 2. something irrelevant.

ir·rel·e·van·cy (i-rel'ə-vən-si), ***n.*** [*pl.* IRRELEVANCIES (-siz)], irrelevance.

ir·rel·e·vant (i-rel'ə-vənt), ***adj.*** not relevant; not pertinent; not to the point; not relating to the subject.

ir·re·liev·a·ble (ir'i-lēv'ə-b'l, ir'ri-lēv'ə-b'l), ***adj.*** that cannot be relieved.

ir·re·li·gion (ir'i-lij'ən, ir'ri-lij'ən), ***n.*** [< Fr. or L.; Fr. *irréligion;* L. *irreligio*], lack of, or indifference or hostility to, religion; state of being irreligious.

ir·re·li·gious (ir'i-lij'əs, ir'ri-lij'əs), ***adj.*** [L. *irreligiosus*], 1. not religious; indifferent or hostile to religion. 2. not in accord with religious principles; profane; impious.

ir·rem·e·a·ble (i-rem'i-ə-b'l, ir-rē'mi-ə-b'l), ***adj.*** [L. *irremeabilis* < *in-*, not + *remeabilis,* returning < *remeare,* to go back; *re-*, back + *meare,* to go], from which there is no return.

ir·re·me·di·a·ble (ir'i-mē'di-ə-b'l, ir'ri-mē'di-ə-b'l), ***adj.*** [L. *irremediabilis*], that cannot be remedied or corrected; incurable or irreparable.

ir·re·me·di·a·bly (ir'i-mē'di-ə-bli, ir'ri-mē'di-ə-bli), ***adv.*** so as to be irremediable.

ir·re·mis·si·ble (ir'i-mis'ə-b'l, ir'ri-mis'ə-b'l), ***adj.*** not remissible; that cannot be excused or pardoned.

ir·re·mov·a·bil·i·ty (ir'i-mōōv'ə-bil'ə-ti, ir'ri-mōōv'ə-bil'ə-ti), ***n.*** the quality or state of being irremovable.

ir·re·mov·a·ble (ir'i-mōōv'ə-b'l, ir'ri-mōōv'ə-b'l), ***adj.*** that cannot be removed.

ir·re·mov·a·bly (ir'i-mōōv'ə-bli, ir'ri-mōōv'ə-bli), ***adv.*** so as to be irremovable.

ir·rep·a·ra·bil·i·ty (i-rep'ẽr-ə-bil'ə-ti), ***n.*** the quality or condition of being irreparable.

ir·rep·a·ra·ble (i-rep'ẽr-ə-b'l), ***adj.*** not reparable; that cannot be repaired, mended, remedied, etc.

ir·rep·a·ra·bly (i-rep'ẽr-ə-bli), ***adv.*** in an irreparable manner; so as to be irreparable.

ir·re·peal·a·ble (ir'i-pēl'ə-b'l, ir'ri-pēl'ə-b'l), ***adj.*** that cannot be repealed.

ir·re·place·a·ble (ir'i-plās'ə-b'l, ir'ri-plās'ə-b'l), ***adj.*** that cannot be replaced.

ir·re·plev·i·a·ble (ir'i-plev'i-ə-b'l, ir'ri-plev'i-ə-b'l), ***adj.*** [ML. *irrepleviabilis*], that cannot be replevied.

ir·re·press·i·bil·i·ty (ir'i-pres'ə-bil'ə-ti, ir'ri-pres'ə-bil'ə-ti), ***n.*** the quality or state of being irrepressible.

ir·re·press·i·ble (ir'i-pres'ə-b'l, ir'ri-pres'ə-b'l), ***adj.*** that cannot be repressed or restrained.

ir·re·press·i·bly (ir'i-pres'ə-bli, ir'ri-pres'ə-bli), ***adv.*** in an irrepressible manner; so as to be irrepressible.

ir·re·proach·a·ble (ir'i-prōch'ə-b'l, ir'ri-prōch'ə-b'l), ***adj.*** [Fr. *irréprochable*], not reproachable; above reproach; blameless; faultless.

ir·re·proach·a·bly (ir'i-prōch'ə-bli, ir'ri-prōch'ə-bli), ***adv.*** in an irreproachable manner; faultlessly.

ir·re·sist·i·bil·i·ty (ir'i-zis'tə-bil'ə-ti, ir'ri-zis'tə-bil'ə-ti), ***n.*** the state or quality of being irresistible.

ir·re·sist·i·ble (ir'i-zis'tə-b'l, ir'ri-zis'tə-b'l), ***adj.*** that cannot be resisted; too strong, fascinating, compelling, etc. to be withstood; overpowering.

ir·re·sist·i·bly (ir'i-zis'tə-bli, ir'ri-zis'tə-bli), ***adv.*** in an irresistible manner.

ir·res·o·lu·ble (i-rez'ə-lyoo-b'l), ***adj.*** 1. that cannot be resolved; insoluble. 2. that cannot be relieved.

ir·res·o·lute (i-rez'ə-lōōt', i-rez'ə-lūt'), ***adj.*** [L. *irresolutus*], not resolute; wavering in decision, purpose, or opinion; indecisive; vacillating.

ir·res·o·lu·tion (i-rez'ə-lōō'shən, ir'rez-ə-lū'shən), ***n.*** lack of resolution; state of being irresolute; indecision; vacillation.

ir·re·solv·a·ble (ir'i-zol'və-b'l, ir'ri-zol'və-b'l), ***adj.*** 1. that cannot be resolved into elements or parts. 2. that cannot be solved.

ir·re·spec·tive (ir'i-spek'tiv, ir'ri-spek'tiv), ***adj.*** [*ir-* (not) + *respective*], [Rare], characterized by a disregard for persons or consequences.

irrespective of, regardless of; independent of.

ir·re·spir·a·ble (ir'ri-spīr'ə-b'l, i-res'pi-rə-b'l), ***adj.*** [*ir-* (not) + *respirable*], not suitable to be breathed.

ir·re·spon·si·bil·i·ty (ir'i-spon'sə-bil'ə-ti, ir'ri-spon'sə-bil'ə-ti), ***n.*** the fact or state of being irresponsible.

ir·re·spon·si·ble (ir'i-spon'sə-b'l, ir'ri-spon'sə-b'l), ***adj.*** 1. not responsible; not liable to be called to account or made to answer for actions. 2. lacking a sense of responsibility. ***n.*** an irresponsible person.

ir·re·spon·si·bly (ir'i-spon'sə-bli, ir'ri-spon'sə-bli), ***adv.*** in an irresponsible manner.

ir·re·spon·sive (ir'i-spon'siv, ir'ri-spon'siv), ***adj.*** not responsive.

ir·re·ten·tive (ir'i-ten'tiv, ir'ri-ten'tiv), *adj.* not retentive.

ir·re·triev·a·bil·i·ty (ir'i-trēv'ə-bil'ə-ti, ir'ri-trēv'ə-bil'ə-ti), *n.* the state or quality of being irretrievable.

ir·re·triev·a·ble (ir'i-trēv'ə-b'l, ir'ri-trēv'ə-b'l), *adj.* that cannot be retrieved, recovered, restored, or recalled.

ir·re·triev·a·bly (ir'i-trēv'ə-bli, ir'ri-trēv'ə-bli), *adv.* so as to be irretrievable.

ir·rev·er·ence (i-rev'ēr-əns), *n.* 1. lack of reverence; disrespect. 2. an act or statement showing this. 3. the condition of not being treated with reverence.

ir·rev·er·ent (i-rev'ēr-ənt), *adj.* [OFr.; L. *irreverens*], not reverent; showing disrespect.

ir·re·vers·i·bil·i·ty (ir'i-vūr'sə-bil'ə-ti, ir'ri-vūr'sə-bil'ə-ti), *n.* the state or quality of being irreversible.

ir·re·vers·i·ble (ir'i-vūr'sə-b'l, ir'ri-vūr'sə-b'l), *adj.* that cannot be reversed; specifically, *a)* that cannot be repealed or annulled. *b)* that cannot be turned inside out, run backward, etc.

ir·re·vers·i·bly (ir'i-vūr'sə-bli, ir'ri-vūr'sə-bli), *adv.* in an irreversible manner.

ir·rev·o·ca·bil·i·ty (i-rev'ə-kə-bil'ə-ti), *n.* the state or quality of being irrevocable.

ir·rev·o·ca·ble (i-rev'ə-kə-b'l), *adj.* that cannot be revoked, recalled, or undone; unalterable.

ir·rev·o·ca·bly (i-rev'ə-kə-bli), *adv.* in an irrevocable manner.

ir·ri·ga·ble (ir'i-gə-b'l), *adj.* that can be irrigated.

ir·ri·gate (ir'ə-gāt'), *v.t.* [IRRIGATED (-id), IRRIGATING], [< L. *irrigatus*, pp. of *irrigare*, to bring water to or upon < *in-*, in, to, upon + *rigare*, to water, moisten], 1. to supply with water; refresh by or as by watering. 2. to supply (land) with water by means of artificial ditches or channels. 3. in *medicine*, to wash out or flush (a cavity or canal) with water or other fluid.

ir·ri·ga·tion (ir'ə-gā'shən), *n.* [L. *irrigatio*], an irrigating or being irrigated.

ir·ri·ga·tion·al (ir'ə-gā'shən-'l), *adj.* of irrigation.

ir·ri·ga·tive (ir'ə-gā'tiv), *adj.* irrigating.

ir·ri·ga·tor (ir'ə-gā'tēr), *n.* [LL.], a person or thing that irrigates.

ir·rig·u·ous (i-rig'ū-əs), *adj.* [L. *irriguus* < *in-*, in + *riguus*, watered < *rigare*; see IRRIGATE], 1. moist; well-watered. 2. irrigative.

ir·ri·ta·bil·i·ty (ir'ə-tə-bil'ə-ti), *n.* [*pl.* IRRITABILITIES (-tiz)], [L. *irritabilitas* < *irritabilis*; see IRRITABLE], 1. the quality or state of being easily annoyed or provoked to anger; impatience; fretfulness. 2. in *medicine*, an excessive responsiveness of an organ or part to a mild stimulation. 3. in *physiology*, the property of living matter to react when stimulated.

ir·ri·ta·ble (ir'ə-tə-b'l), *adj.* [L. *irritabilis* < *irritare*, to irritate], 1. easily annoyed or provoked; impatient; fretful. 2. in *medicine*, excessively sensitive to a stimulus. 3. in *physiology*, able to respond to a stimulus.

SYN.—**irritable** implies quick excitability to annoyance or anger, usually resulting from emotional tension, restlessness, physical indisposition, etc.; **irascible** and **choleric** are applied to persons who are hot-tempered and can be roused to a fit of anger at the slightest irritation; **splenetic** suggests a peevish moroseness in one quick to vent his malice or spite; **touchy** applies to one who is acutely irritable or sensitive and is too easily offended; **cranky** and **cross** suggest moods in which one cannot be easily pleased or satisfied, **cranky** because of stubborn notions or whims, and **cross**, because of ill-humor.

ir·ri·ta·bly (ir'ə-tə-bli), *adv.* in an irritable manner.

ir·ri·tan·cy (ir'ə-tən-si), *n.* [< *irritant*], an irritating condition or quality; irritation.

ir·ri·tant (ir'ə-tənt), *adj.* [L. *irritans*, ppr. of *irritare*], causing irritation or inflammation. *n.* something that causes irritation.

ir·ri·tate (ir'ə-tāt'), *v.t.* [IRRITATED (-id), IRRITATING], [< L. *irritatus*, pp. of *irritare*, to excite, stimulate, irritate], 1. to excite to impatience or anger; provoke; annoy; exasperate. 2. to cause to be inflamed or sore: as, harsh soap *irritates* the skin. 3. in *physiology*, to excite (an organ, muscle, etc.) to a characteristic action or function by a stimulus.

SYN.—**irritate**, the broadest in scope of these terms, may suggest passing, superficial impatience, constant annoyance, or an outburst of anger in the person stirred to feeling (their smugness *irritated* him); to **provoke** is to arouse strong annoyance or resentment, or, sometimes, vindictive anger (*provoked* by an insult); **nettle** implies irritation that stings or piques rather than infuriates (sly, *nettling* remarks); **exasperate** implies intense irritation such as exhausts one's patience or makes one lose his self-control (*exasperating* impudence); **peeve**, an informal word, means to cause to be annoyed, cross, or fretful (he seems *peeved* about something).

ir·ri·ta·tion (ir'ə-tā'shən), *n.* 1. the act or process of irritating. 2. the fact or condition of being irritated. 3. something that irritates. 4. in *medicine*, an excessive response to stimulation in an organ or part.

ir·ri·ta·tive (ir'ə-tā'tiv), *adj.* 1. causing irritation; irritating. 2. attended with or caused by irritation.

ir·rup·tion (i-rup'shən), *n.* [L. *irruptio* < *irruptus*, pp. of *irrumpere*, to break in, burst in < *in-*, in + *rumpere*, to break, burst], 1. a bursting or breaking in. 2. a swift, violent invasion.

ir·rup·tive (i-rup'tiv), *adj.* [< L. *irruptus* (see IRRUPTION); + *-ive*], 1. bursting or rushing in; tending to sudden, violent invasion. 2. in *geology*, intrusive.

Ir·tish (êr-tish'), *n.* a river in western Siberia, flowing into the Ob River: length, 2,250 mi.

Ir·ving (ũr'viŋ), [north Brit. surname; prob. orig. a place name], a masculine name.

Ir·ving, Sir **Henry** (ũr'viŋ), (born *John Henry Brodribb*), 1838–1905; English actor.

Irving, Washington, 1783–1859; American writer.

Ir·ving·ton (ũr'viŋ-tən), *n.* a city in northeastern New Jersey, near Newark: pop., 59,000.

Ir·win (ũr'win), a masculine name: see **Erwin**.

is (iz), [ME.; AS.; akin to G. *ist* (with lost *-t*); IE. **es-ti* (seen also in Sans. *as-tī*, Gr. *es-ti*, L. *est*), in which *-ti* is an enclitic pron.], the third person singular, present indicative, of **be**.

as is, as it now is; without change from its present condition.

is- (īs), iso-.

Is., Isa., Isaiah.

is., 1. island. 2. isle.

I·saac (ī'zək), [LL. *Isaacus*; Heb. *yitsḥāq*, lit., laughter], a masculine name: diminutive, *Ike*. *n.* in the *Bible*, one of the patriarchs, son of Abraham and Sarah, and father of Jacob and Esau: Gen. 21:3.

Is·a·bel (iz'ə-bel', iz'ə-b'l), [Sp.; said to be an alteration of *Elizabeth*], a feminine name: diminutive, *Bel*; variants, *Isabelle*, *Isabella*.

Is·a·bel·la (iz'ə-bel'ə), [It.], a feminine name: diminutive, *Bella*: see **Isabel**.

Isabella I, 1451–1504; wife of Ferdinand V; queen of Castile (1474–1504); queen of Castile and León (1479–1504); gave help to Columbus in his expedition.

Is·a·belle (iz'ə-bel'), [Fr.], a feminine name: diminutive, *Belle*: see **Isabel**.

is·a·cous·tic (īs'ə-kōōs'tik), *adj.* [*is-* + *acoustic*], of or having to do with equal intensity of sound.

Is·a·dor, Is·a·dore (iz'ə-dôr', iz'ə-dōr'), a masculine name: feminine, *Isadora*: see **Isidore**.

Is·a·dor·a (iz'ə-dôr'ə, iz'ə-dō'rə), [var. of Gr. *Isidōra*; see ISIDORE], a feminine name.

i·sa·go·ge (ī'sə-gō'ji), *n.* [L.; Gr. *eisagōgē* < *eisagein*, to lead in, introduce; *eis-*, into + *agein*, to lead], an introduction, as to a branch of study.

i·sa·gog·ic (ī'sə-goj'ik), *adj.* [LL. *isagogicus*; Gr. *eisagōgikos*; see ISAGOGE], introductory.

i·sa·gog·ics (ī'sə-goj'iks), *n.pl.* [construed as sing.], [see ISAGOGIC & -ICS], introductory study; especially, the study of the literary history of the Bible, considered as introductory to the study of Bible interpretation.

I·sa·iah (i-zā'ə, i-zī'ə), [Heb. *yĕsha 'yah*, lit., God is salvation], a masculine name. *n.* 1. a Hebrew prophet of the 8th century B.C. 2. a book of the Old Testament containing his teachings. Abbreviated **Isa., Is.**

I·sai·as (ī-zā'əs, i-zī'əs), *n.* [L.; see prec.], Isaiah: form used in the Douay Bible.

i·sal·lo·bar (ī-sal'ə-bär'), *n.* [< *is-* + *allo-* + Gr. *baros*, weight], a line on a weather map connecting places having an equal change of barometric pressure over a given period.

I·sar (ē'zär), *n.* a river flowing through western Austria and southern Germany into the Danube: length, 219 mi.

i·sa·tin (ī'sə-tin), *n.* [< L. *isatis*, variety of herb (< Gr. *isatis*, woad); + *-in*], a reddish-orange, crystalline compound, $C_8H_5NO_2$, produced by the oxidation of indigo and used in making dyes.

i·sa·tine (ī'sə-tin, ī'sə-tēn'), *n.* isatin.

Is·car·i·ot (is-kar'i-ət), *n.* [L. *Iscariota*; Gr. *Iskariōtēs*; Heb. *īsh-qĕrīyōth*, man of Kerioth (town in Palestine)], 1. in the *Bible*, the surname of the disciple Judas, who betrayed Jesus: Luke 22:3; hence, 2. a traitor.

is·che·mi·a, is·chae·mi·a (is-kē'mi-ə), *n.* [Mod. L. < Gr. *ischein*, to hold + *haima*, blood], a temporary lack of blood supply in an organ or tissue; local anemia.

is·che·mic (is-kē'mik, is-kem'ik), *adj.* of or having ischemia.

is·chi·ad·ic (is'ki-ad'ik), *adj.* ischiatic.

is·chi·al (is'ki-əl), *adj.* of the ischium.

is·chi·at·ic (is'ki-at'ik), *adj.* [< L. *ischiadicus*; Gr. *ischiadikos*, relating to gout in the hip < *ischion*, hip; + *-atic*], of the ischium.

is·chi·um (is'ki-əm), *n.* [*pl.* ISCHIA (-ə)], [L.; Gr. *ischion*, hip, hip joint], the lowermost of the three sections of the hipbone; bone on which the body rests when sitting: see **skeleton**, illus.

-ise (īz), -ize.

I·seult (i-sōōlt'), *n.* [Fr.], Isolde.

Is·fa·han (is'fä-hän'), *n.* a city in west central Iran: pop., 205,000 (1942): the capital of Persia in the 17th century: also **Ispahan**.

-ish (ish), [ME. *-ish, -issh, -isch;* AS. *-isc;* akin to G. *-isch*], 1. a suffix meaning: *a*) *of* or *belonging to* (a specified nation or people), as in *Spanish, Irish. b*) *like* or *characteristic of,* as in *devilish, boyish. c*) *tending to, verging on,* as in *bookish, knavish. d*) *somewhat, rather,* as in *tallish, bluish. e*) [Colloq.], *approximately, about,* as in *thirtyish.* 2. [ME. *-ishen, -ischen, -issen;* OFr. *-iss-, -is-,* stem element in pres. tense of some Fr. verbs; L. *-isc-,* stem element in inceptive verbs], a suffix used in verbs of French origin or in verbs similarly formed, as in *finish, punish.*

Ish·ma·el (ish′mi-əl), *n.* [LL. *Ismaël;* Heb. *yishmā'ēl,* lit., God hears], 1. in the *Bible,* the son of Abraham and Hagar: at Sarah's insistence, he and his mother were made outcasts: Gen. 16:12; hence, 2. an outcast.

Ish·ma·el·ite (ish′mi-əl-īt′), *n.* 1. a descendant of Ishmael. 2. an outcast. 3. an Arab: the Arabs claim to be descended from Ishmael.

Ish·ma·el·it·ish (ish′mi-əl-īt′ish), *adj.* of or like the Ishmaelites.

Ish·tar (ish′tär), *n.* [Assyr.-Bab.], the Babylonian and Assyrian goddess of love and fertility.

Is·i·dore, Is·i·dor (iz′ə-dôr′, iz′ə-dōr′), [G. *Isidor;* Fr. *Isidore;* L. *Isidorus;* Gr. *Isidōros* < *Isis* + *dōron,* gift; hence, lit., gift of Isis], a masculine name: diminutive, *Izzy;* variants, *Isador, Isadore.*

Isidore of Seville, Saint, (*Isidorus Hispalensis*), 560?–636 A.D.; Spanish archbishop and encyclopedist.

i·sin·glass (ī′ziŋ-glas′, ī′z′n-gläs′), *n.* [prob. altered < MD. *huizenblas,* lit., sturgeon bladder; *huizen,* sturgeon + *blas,* bladder], 1. a form of gelatin prepared from the internal membranes of fish bladders: it is used as a clarifying agent and adhesive. 2. mica, especially when it occurs in thin sheets.

I·sis (ī′sis), *n.* [L.; Gr. *Isis*], the Egyptian goddess of fertility, sister and wife of Osiris, represented with a cow's horns and the sun's disk as a crown.

ISIS

Is·kan·da·ri·ya, El (el is-kän′dä-rē′yä), Alexandria, a city in Egypt: the Arabic name.

Is·ken·der·un (is-ken′də-rōōn′), *n.* Alexandretta, a city in Turkey: the Turkish name.

isl., [*pl.* ISLS.], 1. island. 2. isle.

Is·lam (is′ləm, is-läm′, iz′ləm), *n.* [Ar. *islām,* lit., submission (to God's will) < *salama,* to be resigned], 1. the Moslem religion, a monotheistic religion whose supreme deity is called Allah and whose chief prophet and founder is Mohammed. 2. Moslems collectively. 3. all the lands in which the Moslem religion predominates.

Is·lam·ic (is-lam′ik, is-läm′ik, iz-lam′ik), *adj.* of Islam; Moslem.

Is·lam·ism (is′ləm-iz′m, iz′ləm-iz′m), *n.* the religion, doctrines, customs, etc. of Islam.

Is·lam·ite (is′ləm-īt′, iz′ləm-īt′), *n.* a Moslem.

Is·lam·it·ic (is′lə-mit′ik, iz′lə-mit′ik), *adj.* Islamic.

Is·lam·ize (is′ləm-īz′, iz′ləm-īz′), *v.i. & v.t.* [ISLAMIZED (-īzd′), ISLAMIZING], to bring into or be in conformity with Islam.

is·land (ī′lənd), *n.* [< ME. *iland* (respelled after unrelated *isle*) < AS. *igland, iegland,* lit., island land & *ealand,* lit., water land; *ig, ieg,* isle & *ea,* water < IE. **aqwā,* water, as also in L. *aqua*], 1. a land mass not as large as a continent, surrounded by water: abbreviated **I., i.** (*sing & pl.*), **is., isl.** 2. anything like an island in position or isolation. 3. in *anatomy,* a tissue or cluster of cells differing from surrounding tissue in formation, etc. *v.t.* 1. to make into or like an island; isolate. 2. to intersperse with or as with islands: as, a prairie *islanded* with wooded tracts.

is·land·er (ī′lən-dẽr), *n.* a native or inhabitant of an island.

islands (or **islets**) **of Lang·er·hans** (läŋ′ẽr-häns′), [after Paul *Langerhans* (1847–1888), G. histologist], irregular groups of cells in the pancreas that produce the hormone insulin: their degeneration is believed to be a cause of diabetes mellitus.

Islands of the Blessed, in *Greek & Roman mythology,* the islands of bliss in the Western Ocean, where heroes went after death.

island universe, any of the large number of galaxies of stars like the one containing the earth.

isle (īl), *n.* [ME. & OFr. *isle, ile;* LL. *iscla* for L. *insula;* prob. < (*terra*) *in salo,* (land) in the sea < *salum,* sea: the form *isle* became general in the Renaissance after L. *insula*], an island, especially a small island: abbreviated **I., i.** (*sing. & pl.*), **is., isl.** *v.t.* [ISLED (īld), ISLING], to island. *v.i.* to live on an isle.

Isle Roy·ale (roi′əl), an island in northern Lake Superior: it is part of the State of Michigan and comprises the Isle Royale National Park: area, 209 sq. mi.

is·let (ī′lit), *n.* [OFr. *islet, islette,* dim. of *isle;* see ISLE & -LET], a very small island.

Is·ling·ton (iz′liŋ-tən), *n.* a borough of London: pop., 322,000.

isls., 1. islands. 2. isles.

ism (iz′m), *n.* [< *-ism*], any doctrine, theory, system, etc. whose name ends in *-ism:* usually disparaging.

-ism (iz′m), [L. *-ismus;* Gr. *-ismos*], a noun-forming suffix meaning: 1. *the act, practice,* or *result of,* as in *terrorism.* 2. *the condition of being,* as in *barbarism, pauperism.* 3. *action, conduct,* or *qualities characteristic of,* as in *scoundrelism, patriotism, Americanism.* 4. *the doctrine, theory,* or *principle of,* as in *atomism, socialism.* 5. *devotion to,* as in *nationalism.* 6. *an instance, example,* or *peculiarity of,* as in *Gallicism, witticism.* 7. *an abnormal condition caused by,* as in *alcoholism.*

Is·ma·e·li·an (is′mə-ē′li-ən), *n.* an Ismailian.

Is·ma·il (is-mä-ēl′), *n.* the elder son of the sixth imam of the Moslems; died 760 A.D., five years before his father: see **Ismailian.**

Is·ma·il·i·an (is′mə-il′i-ən), *n.* any member of a sect of the Shiite branch of Moslems which holds that the office of imam should have gone to the descendant of Ismail at the death of his father, the imam Jafar, in 765 A.D.

is·n't (iz′′nt), is not.

i·so- (ī′sō, ī′sə), [< Gr. *isos,* equal], a combining form meaning *equal, similar, alike, identical,* as in *isomeric:* also, before a vowel, **is-.**

i·so·ag·glu·ti·na·tion (ī′sō-ə-glōō′tə-nā′shən), *n.* [*iso-* + *agglutination*], the clumping of the red blood cells of an individual by the blood serum of another member of the same species.

i·so·ag·glu·ti·nin (ī′sō-ə-glōō′tə-nin), *n.* [*iso-* + *agglutinin*], a substance in the blood that is capable of clumping the red cells of other members of the same species.

i·so·bar (ī′sə-bär′), *n.* [< *iso-* + Gr. *baros,* weight], 1. a line on a map connecting points on the earth's surface having equal barometric pressure over a given period or at a given time. 2. any of two or more forms of an atom having the same atomic weight (or mass number) but different atomic numbers and representing different chemical elements: distinguished from *isotope.*

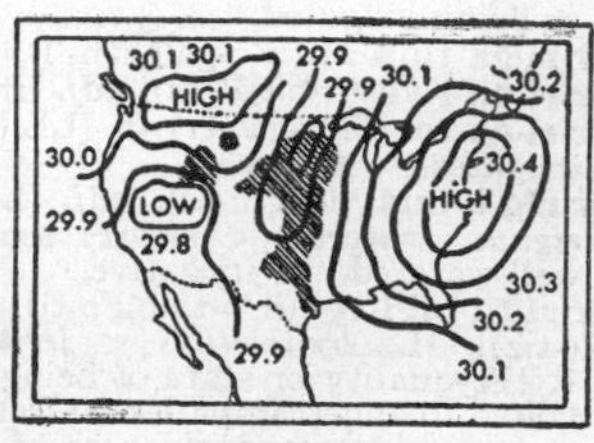

ISOBARS

i·so·bar·ic (ī′sə-bar′ik), *adj.* 1. of or having isobars. 2. having or showing equal barometric pressure.

isobaric isotope, any of two or more forms of radioactive atoms having the same atomic weight (or mass number) and the same atomic number and representing different chemical elements because of differences in the nature of their radioactive disintegration: such isotopes are produced artificially: see **isobar, isotope.**

i·so·cheim (ī′sə-kīm′), *n.* [< *iso-* + Gr. *cheima,* winter], a line on a map connecting points on the earth's surface that have the same mean winter temperature.

i·so·chei·mal (ī′sə-kī′m′l), *adj.* 1. of or having isocheims. 2. having or showing the same mean winter temperature.

i·so·chei·me·nal (ī′sə-kī′mi-n′l), *adj.* isocheimal. *n.* an isocheim.

i·so·chor, i·so·chore (ī′sə-kôr′), *n.* [< *iso-;* + Gr. *chōra,* a place], in *thermodynamics,* a line on a graph representing the parallel changes in pressure and temperature of something whose volume remains constant.

i·so·chro·mat·ic (ī′sə-krō-mat′ik), *adj.* [*iso-* + *chromatic*], 1. in *optics,* having the same color: said of lines or curves in figures formed by interfering light waves from biaxial crystals. 2. in *photography,* orthochromatic.

i·soch·ro·nal (ī-sok′rə-n′l), *adj.* [< Mod. L. *isochronus;* Gr. *isochronos* < *isos,* equal + *chronos,* time; + *-al*], 1. equal in length of time. 2. occurring at equal intervals of time.

i·soch·ro·nism (ī-sok′rə-niz′m), *n.* the quality, condition, or fact of being isochronal.

i·soch·ro·nize (ī-sok′rə-nīz′), *v.t.* [ISOCHRONIZED (-nīzd′), ISOCHRONIZING], to make isochronal.

i·soch·ro·nous (ī-sok′rə-nəs), *adj.* isochronal.

i·soch·ro·ous (ī-sok′rō-əs), *adj.* [*iso-* + *-chroous*], having the same color in every part.

i·so·cli·nal (ī′sə-klī′n′l), *adj.* [< *iso-* + Gr. *kleinein,* to slope; + *-al*], 1. of equal inclination or dip. 2. connecting or showing points on the earth's surface having equal magnetic inclination or dip: as, *isoclinal* lines on a map. 3. in *geology,* dipping in the same direction: said of strata. *n.* an isoclinal line.

i·so·cline (ī′sə-klīn′), *n.* [see ISOCLINAL], a fold of rock in which the strata have the same angle of dip on each side.

i·so·clin·ic (ī′sə-klin′ik), *adj.* isoclinal.

i·soc·ra·cy (ī-sok′rə-si), *n.* [Gr. *isokratia;* see ISO- &

-CRACY], a system of government in which everybody has equal political power.
I·soc·ra·tes (ī-sok′rə-tēz′), *n.* Greek orator and rhetorician; lived 436–338 B.C.
i·so·cy·a·nin (ī′sə-sī′ə-nin), *n.* isocyanine.
i·so·cy·a·nine (ī′sə-sī′ə-nēn′, ī′sə-sī′ə-nin), *n.* [*iso-* + *cyanine*], any of a group of quinoline dyes used in sensitizing photographic plates and films.
i·so·di·a·met·ric (ī′sə-dī′ə-met′rik), *adj.* having equal diameters.
i·so·di·mor·phism (ī′sō-dī-môr′fiz'm), *n.* a similarity of crystalline structure between the two forms of two dimorphous substances.
i·so·di·mor·phous (ī′sō-dī-môr′fəs), *adj.* of or characterized by isodimorphism.
i·so·dy·nam·ic (ī′sō-dī-nam′ik), *adj.* [*iso-* + *dynamic*], 1. of or having equal force. 2. connecting or showing points on the earth's surface having equal magnetic intensity: as, *isodynamic* lines on a map.
i·so·dy·nam·i·cal (ī′sō-dī-nam′i-k'l), *adj.* isodynamic.
i·so·e·lec·tric (ī′sō-i-lek′trik), *adj.* having equal electric potential.
i·so·ga·mete (ī′sō-gə-mēt′, ī′sō-gam′ēt), *n.* a gamete not differentiated sexually or otherwise from another that it unites with: opposed to *heterogamete*.
i·sog·a·mous (ī-sog′ə-məs), *adj.* characterized by the uniting of isogametes.
i·sog·a·my (ī-sog′ə-mi), *n.* reproduction by the uniting of isogametes.
i·sog·e·nous (ī-soj′ə-nəs), *adj.* [*iso-* + *-genous*], in *biology*, of the same origin.
i·sog·e·ny (ī-soj′ə-ni), *n.* [*iso-* + *-geny*], in *biology*, the condition of being isogenous; identity of origin.
i·so·ge·o·therm (ī′sə-jē′ə-thũrm′), *n.* [< *iso-* + *geo-* + Gr. *thermē*, heat], an imaginary line or surface connecting points beneath the earth's surface having the same average temperature.
i·so·ge·o·ther·mal (ī′sə-jē′ə-thũr′məl), *adj.* of, or having the nature of, an isogeotherm.
i·so·ge·o·ther·mic (ī′sə-jē′ə-thũr′mik), *adj.* isogeothermal.
i·so·gloss (ī′sə-glôs′, ī′sə-glos′), *n.* [< *iso-*; + Gr. *glōssa*, tongue, speech], in *linguistics*, an imaginary line of demarcation between regions differing in some feature of pronunciation, syntax, etc.
i·so·gon (ī′sə-gon′), *n.* [*iso-* + *-gon*], a polygon with all angles equal.
i·sog·o·nal (ī-sog′ə-n'l), *adj.* having equal angles; isogonic.
i·so·gon·ic (ī′sə-gon′ik), *adj.* [*iso-* + *-gon* + *-ic*], 1. of or having equal angles. 2. connecting or showing points on the earth's surface having the same magnetic declination, as lines on a map. *n.* an isogonic line.
i·so·la·ble (ī′sə-lə-b'l, is′ə-lə-b'l), *adj.* that can be isolated.
i·so·late (ī′sə-lāt′, is′ə-lāt′), *v.t.* [ISOLATED (-id), ISOLATING], [back-formation < *isolated*; It. *isolato*, pp. of *isolare*, to isolate < *isola* < L. *insula*, island; see ISLE], 1. to set apart from others; place alone. 2. in *bacteriology*, to grow a pure culture of (a specific bacterium). 3. in *chemistry*, to separate (an element or compound) in pure form from substances with which it is combined or mixed. 4. in *medicine*, to place (a patient with a contagious disease) apart from others to prevent the spread of infection.
i·so·la·tion (ī′sə-lā′shən, is′ə-lā′shən), *n.* [Fr.], an isolating or being isolated. —*SYN.* see **solitude.**
i·so·la·tion·ism (ī′sə-lā′shən-iz'm, is′ə-lā′shən-iz'm), *n.* the policy advocated by isolationists.
i·so·la·tion·ist (ī′sə-lā′shən-ist, is′ə-lā′shən-ist), *n.* a person who believes in or advocates isolation; person who wants his country to take no part in international alliances, etc. *adj.* of isolationists or isolationism.
I·solde (i-sōld′, i-sōl′də; G. ē-zôl′də), *n.* [G.; OFr. *Isolt*, *Iseut;* OHG. *Isold;* prob. < *is*, ice + *waltan*, to rule], in *medieval legend*, 1. the Irish princess married to King Mark of Cornwall and beloved by Tristram. 2. the daughter of the king of Brittany, married to Tristram. Also **Iseult.** See **Tristram.**
i·sol·o·gous (ī-sol′ə-gəs), *adj.* [< *iso-* + Gr. *logos*, proportion; + *-ous*], 1. designating or of any of two or more chemical compounds of similar structure but consisting of different atoms of the same valence and usually of the same periodic group. 2. designating or of a series formed by such compounds.
i·so·mag·net·ic (ī′sə-mag-net′ik), *adj.* 1. of equality of magnetic force. 2. connecting or showing points on the earth's surface having the same magnetic intensity, as lines on a map. *n.* an isomagnetic line.
i·so·mer (ī′sə-mẽr), *n.* [< Gr. *isomerēs*, equally divided < *isos*, equal + *meros*, a part, share], any of two or more chemical compounds having the same constituent elements in the same proportion by weight but differing in physical or chemical properties because of differences in the structure of their molecules.
i·so·mer·ic (ī′sə-mer′ik), *adj.* of or indicating isomerism.
i·som·er·ism (ī-som′ẽr-iz'm), *n.* the state or relation of isomers.
i·som·er·ous (ī-som′ẽr-əs), *adj.* [*iso-* + *-merous*], 1. having the same number of parts, markings, etc. 2. in *botany*, having the same number of parts in each whorl: opposed to *heteromerous*. 3. isomeric.
i·so·met·ric (ī′sə-met′rik), *adj.* [< Gr. *isometros* < *isos*, equal + *metron*, measure; + *-ic*], 1. of, indicating, or having equality of measure. 2. designating a crystalline form that has three equal axes at right angles to one another. *n.* in *thermodynamics*, a line indicating changes of pressure or temperature at constant volume.
i·so·met·ri·cal (ī′sə-met′ri-k'l), *adj.* isometric.
isometric projection, a method of drawing figures and maps so that three dimensions are shown not in perspective but in their actual measurements.
i·so·me·tro·pi·a (ī′sə-mi-trō′pi-ə), *n.* [Mod. L. < *iso-* + Gr. *metron*, measure; + *-opia*], the condition of being equal in refraction: said of the two eyes.
i·som·e·try (ī-som′ə-tri), *n.* [*iso-* + *-metry*], 1. equality of measure. 2. in *geography*, equality of height above sea level.
i·so·morph (ī′sə-môrf′), *n.* [*iso-* + *-morph*], a substance or organism isomorphic with another or others.
i·so·mor·phic (ī′sə-môr′fik), *adj.* 1. having similar or identical structure or appearance. 2. in *biology* & *mineralogy*, showing isomorphism; isomorphous.
i·so·mor·phism (ī′sə-môr′fiz'm), *n.* [< *isomorphic* + *-ism*], 1. in *biology*, a similarity in the appearance or structure of organisms of different species or races. 2. in *chemistry* & *mineralogy*, an identity or close similarity in the crystalline form of substances of similar composition.
i·so·mor·phous (ī′sə-môr′fəs), *adj.* designating or of compounds that crystallize in the same or closely related forms; isomorphic.
-i·son (ə-s'n), [OFr. *-ison, -eson, -eison, -aison;* L. *-atio, -ationis;* see -ATION], a formative suffix seen in nouns derived from Old French, corresponding to *-ation*, as in *comparison*.
i·so·ni·a·zid (ī′sə-nī′ə-zid), *n.* [*iso-* + *ni*cotinic + hydr*azine* + *-id*], an antibacterial drug used in treating tuberculosis.
i·son·o·my (ī-son′ə-mi), *n.* [Gr. *isonomia* < *isos*, equal + *nomos*, law], equality of laws, rights, or privileges.
i·so·pi·es·tic (ī′sə-pī-es′tik), *adj.* [*iso-* + Gr. *piezein*, to press; + *-ic*], indicating equal pressure. *n.* an isobar.
i·so·pleth (ī′sə-pleth′), *n.* [< Gr. *isoplēthēs*, equal in number or quantity < *isos*, equal + *plēthos*, number, quantity], 1. a graph plotting the occurrence or frequency of a phenomenon in meteorology, etc. as a function of two variables, time and space. 2. the line connecting points on a graph that have equal or corresponding values with regard to certain variables.
i·so·pod (ī′sə-pod′), *n.* [*iso-* + *-pod*], a crustacean with a flat, oval body and seven pairs of legs of similar size and form, each pair attached to a segment of the thorax. *adj.* of an isopod or the isopods.
i·sop·o·dan (ī-sop′ə-dən), *adj.* & *n.* isopod.
i·so·prene (ī′sə-prēn′), *n.* [apparently arbitrarily coined by C. G. Williams; see -ENE], a colorless, volatile liquid, C_5H_8, prepared by the dry distillation of raw rubber or synthetically: when heated with sodium it polymerizes to form a substance closely resembling natural rubber.
i·so·pro·pyl (ī′sə-prō′pil), *n.* the univalent radical $(CH_3)_2CH$, an isomer of the univalent propyl radical, C_3H_7.
i·so·pyre (ī′sə-pīr′), *n.* [< *iso-* + Gr. *pyr*, fire], a kind of opal containing iron or other impurities.
i·sos·ce·les (ī-sos′ə-lēz′), *adj.* [L.; Gr. *isoskelēs* < *isos*, equal + *skelos*, a leg], designating a triangle with two equal sides.
i·so·seis·mal (ī′sə-sīz′m'l, ī′sə-sīs′m'l), *adj.* [< *iso-* + Gr. *seismos*, earthquake; + *-al*], 1. of equal intensity of earthquake shock. 2. connecting or showing points of such intensity on the earth's surface: as, *isoseismal* lines on a map. *n.* an isoseismal line.
i·so·seis·mic (ī′sə-sīz′mik, ī′sə-sīs′mik), *adj.* isoseismal.

ISOSCELES TRIANGLES

i·sos·ta·sy (ī-sos′tə-si), *n.* [< *iso-* + Gr. *stasis*, a standing still], 1. the state or quality of being isostatic. 2. in *geology*, universal equilibrium in the earth's crust, the maintenance of which is supposedly due to gravitational yielding of rocks beneath the earth's surface.
i·so·stat·ic (ī′sə-stat′ik), *adj.* [*iso-* + *static*], 1. denoting a condition in which there is equal pressure on every side. 2. in hydrostatic equilibrium.

i·soth·er·al (ī-soth′ẽr-əl), *adj.* 1. of or having isotheres. 2. having or showing the same mean summer temperature. *n.* an isothere.

i·so·there (ī′sə-thêr′), *n.* [< *iso-* + Gr. *theros*, summer], a line on a map connecting points on the earth's surface that have the same mean summer temperature.

i·so·therm (ī′sə-thũrm′), *n.* [*iso-* + Gr. *thermē*, heat < *thermos*, hot], 1. a line on a map connecting points on the earth's surface having the same mean temperature or the same temperature at a given time. 2. a line representing changes of volume or pressure at constant temperature.

i·so·ther·mal (ī′sə-thũr′m'l), *adj.* [*iso-* + *thermal*], 1. of or indicating equality of temperature. 2. of or indicating changes of volume or pressure at constant temperature: as, an *isothermal* line. 3. of an isotherm or isotherms. *n.* an isotherm.

i·so·ton·ic (ī′sə-ton′ik), *adj.* [< Gr. *isotonos* (< *isos*, equal + *tonos*, a stretching); + *-ic*], 1. having equal tension. 2. having the same osmotic pressure; especially, designating or of a salt solution having the same osmotic pressure as blood, so that it will not destroy the red corpuscles when injected into the blood stream.

i·so·to·nic·i·ty (ī′sə-tō-nis′ə-ti), *n.* the property of being isotonic.

i·so·tope (ī′sə-tōp′), *n.* [< *iso-* + Gr. *topos*, place], any of two or more forms of an element having the same or very closely related properties and the same atomic number but different atomic weights (or mass numbers): as, U 235, U 238, and U 239 are three *isotopes* of uranium: distinguished from *isobar*.

i·so·top·ic (ī′sə-top′ik), *adj.* of, or having the nature of, an isotope.

i·sot·o·py (ī-sot′ə-pi), *n.* the state or relation of isotopes.

i·so·trop·ic (ī′sə-trop′ik, ī′sə-trō′pik), *adj.* [*iso-* + *-tropic*], having physical properties, as conductivity, elasticity, etc., that are the same regardless of the direction of measurement.

i·sot·ro·pous (ī-sot′rə-pəs), *adj.* isotropic.

i·sot·ro·py (ī-sot′rə-pi), *n.* the state or quality of being isotropic.

Is·pa·han (is′pə-hän′), *n.* Isfahan.

Is·ra·el (iz′ri-əl), [L.; Gr. *Israēl*; Heb. *yisrā'ēl*, lit., contender with God < *sārāh*, to wrestle + *ēl*, God], a masculine name: diminutive, *Izzy*. *n.* 1. in the *Bible*, Jacob: he was so named after wrestling with the angel: Gen. 32:28. 2. the Jewish people: so named because regarded as descendants of Jacob. 3. the kingdom in the northern part of ancient Palestine formed by the ten tribes of Israel that broke with Judah and Benjamin: I Kings 11:31. 4. a republic comprising parts of Palestine, established as a Jewish state in 1948, in conformity with the United Nations plan of 1947 to partition Palestine into separate Jewish and Arab states: area, 7,993 sq. mi.; pop., 2,128,000; capital, Jerusalem.

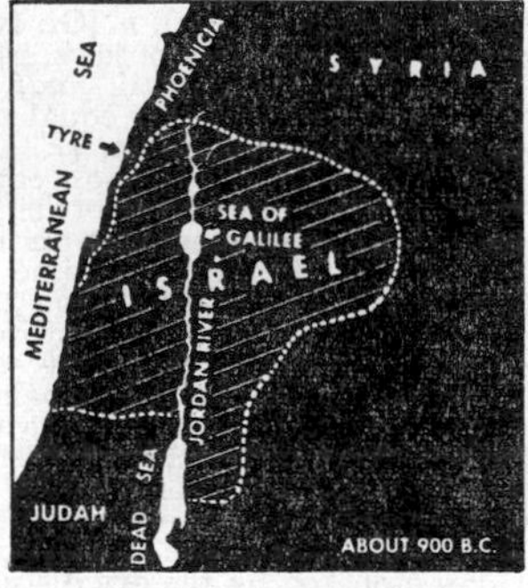

ANCIENT ISRAEL

Is·ra·el·i (iz-rā′li), *adj.* of Israel (sense 4) or its people. *n.* a native or inhabitant of Israel (sense 4).

Is·ra·el·ite (iz′ri-əl-īt′), *n.* 1. any of the people of Israel or their descendants; Jew; Hebrew. 2. [Rare], any member of a group regarded by others or itself as chosen by God. *adj.* of Israel or the Israelites; Jewish.

Is·ra·el·it·ic (iz′ri-əl-it′ik), *adj.* Israelitish.

Is·ra·el·it·ish (iz′ri-əl-īt′ish), *adj.* of the Israelites.

is·sei (ēs′sā′), *n.* [*pl.* ISSEI, ISSEIS (-sāz′)], [Japan., lit., first generation], [also I-], a Japanese who emigrated to the United States after the Oriental exclusion proclamation of 1907 and was thus ineligible by law, until 1952, to become an American citizen: cf. *nisei*, *kibei*.

is·su·a·ble (ish′ōō-ə-b'l, ish′ū-ə-b'l), *adj.* 1. that can issue or be issued. 2. that can be raised as an issue at law.

is·su·ance (ish′ōō-əns, ish′ū-əns), *n.* an issuing; issue.

is·su·ant (ish′ōō-ənt, ish′ū-ənt), *adj.* 1. issuing. 2. in *heraldry*, denoting an animal of which the upper part only is visible.

is·sue (ish′ōō, ish′ū), *n.* [ME. < OFr. *issue*, *eissue*, pp. of *issir*, *eisser*, to go out; L. *exire*; *ex-*, out + *ire*, to go], 1. an outgoing; outflow; passing out; exit. 2. a place or means of going out; exit; outlet. 3. a result; consequence; upshot. 4. offspring; a child or children. 5. profits from lands, estates, or fines; produce; proceeds. 6. a point, matter, or question to be disputed or decided. 7. a sending or giving out; putting forth. 8. the thing or set of things issued; the entire amount put forth and circulated at one time: as, the January *issue* of a magazine, an *issue* of bonds. 9. in *medicine*, *a*) a discharge of blood, pus, etc. *b*) an incision or artificial ulcer made so that pus may be discharged. *v.i.* [ISSUED (-ōōd, -ūd), ISSUING], 1. to go, come, pass, or flow out; emerge. 2. to be descended; be born. 3. to be derived; result, as from a cause. 4. to end (*in*); result, as in an effect or consequence. 5. to come as revenue; accrue. 6. to be published; be put forth and circulated. *v.t.* 1. to let out; discharge. 2. to give or deal out: as, a quartermaster *issues* supplies. 3. to publish; put forth and circulate; give out publicly or officially: as, a government *issues* bonds. —*SYN.* see **effect, rise.**

at issue, 1. in dispute; to be decided. 2. at variance; in disagreement.

join issue, 1. to enter into conflict, argument, etc. with another or each other. 2. to join in submitting an issue for decision at law.

take issue, to disagree; differ.

Is·sus (is′əs), *n.* an ancient town in southeastern Asia Minor: Alexander defeated Darius there (333 B.C.).

Is·syk-Kul (is′ik-kool′), *n.* a lake in the Kirghiz S.S.R., Asia: area, 2,230 sq. mi.

-ist (ist), [Fr. *-iste*; L. *-ista*; Gr. *-istēs* < verbs ending in *-izein*], a suffix forming nouns corresponding to verbs ending in *-ize* or nouns ending in *-ism*, meaning: 1. *a person who does* or *practices*, as in *moralist*, *satirist*. 2. *a person skilled in* or *occupied with*, as in *chemist*, *violinist*. 3. *an adherent of*, *believer in*, as in *anarchist*.

Is·tan·bul (is′tan-bōōl′, is′tän-bōōl′; Turk. is-täm′-bool), *n.* a city in Turkey, on the European side of the Bosporus: pop., 1,215,000: also called *Constantinople*, *Stamboul*: ancient name, *Byzantium*.

Isth., isth., isthmus.

isth·mi·an (is′mi-ən), *adj.* [< L. *isthmius* (Gr. *isthmios* < *isthmos*; see ISTHMUS); + *-an*], 1. of an isthmus. 2. [I-], of the Isthmus of Panama. 3. [I-], of the Isthmus of Corinth or the games held there in ancient times. *n.* a native or inhabitant of an isthmus.

isth·mus (is′məs; *the sp. pronun.* isth′məs *is rare*), *n.* [*pl.* ISTHMUSES (-iz), ISTHMI (-mī)], [L.; Gr. *isthmos*, a neck, narrow passage, isthmus], 1. a narrow strip of land having water on either side and connecting two larger bodies of land. 2. in *anatomy*, *a*) a narrow strip of tissue connecting two larger parts of an organ: as, the *isthmus* of the thyroid or prostate. *b*) a narrow passage between two larger cavities: as, the *isthmus* of the Fallopian tubes. Abbreviated **Isth., isth.** (in sense 1).

the Isthmus, 1. the Isthmus of Panama. 2. the Isthmus of Suez.

-is·tic (is′tik), [Fr. *-istique*; L. *-isticus*; Gr. *-istikos*; also formed in Eng. < *-ist* + *-ic*], a suffix forming adjectives corresponding to nouns ending in *-ism* and *-ist*, as in *artistic*, *altruistic*.

is·tle (ist′li), *n.* [Mex.], the fiber of certain tropical American plants, used for cordage, nets, baskets, etc.

Is·tri·a (is′tri-ə), *n.* a peninsula in northeastern Italy: formerly Austrian territory.

Is·tri·an (is′tri-ən), *adj.* of Istria. *n.* a native or inhabitant of Istria.

it (it), *pron.* [for *pl.* see THEY], [ME. *hit*, *it*; AS. *hit*; akin to D. *het*, Goth. *hita*, this, etc.; IE. base as in *he*; basic sense "this one"], the animal or thing previously mentioned or under discussion. *It* is used as: *a*) the subject of an impersonal verb without reference to agent: as, *it* is snowing. *b*) the grammatical subject of a clause of which the actual subject is another clause or phrase following: as, *it* is clear that he wants to go. *c*) an object of indefinite sense in certain idiomatic expressions: as, to lord *it* over someone. *d*) the antecedent to a relative pronoun from which it is separated by a predicate: as, *it* is your car that we want. *e*) a term of reference to something indefinite but understood, as the state of affairs: as, *it*'s all right, I didn't hurt myself. *f*) [Colloq.], an emphatic predicate pronoun referring to the person, thing, situation, etc. which is ultimate or final: as, zero hour is here; this is *it*. *n.* in the game of "tag," etc., the player who must try to touch or find another.

it·a·col·u·mite (it′ə-kol′yoo-mīt′), *n.* [< *Itacolumi*, mountain in Brazil, where found], a kind of quartzite readily split into thin, flexible layers; flexible sandstone.

Ital., 1. Italian. 2. Italic. 3. Italy. Also **It.**

ital., italic; italics. Also **it.**

I·tal·ia (ē-täl′yä), *n.* Italy: the Italian name.

‡**Italia ir·re·den·ta** (ē′re-den′tä), an Italian-speaking district under foreign rule: cf. **irredenta.**

I·tal·ian (i-tal′yən), *adj.* [< L. *Italia*, Italy; Gr. *Italia*], of Italy, its people, their language, or culture. *n.* 1. a native or inhabitant of Italy. 2. the Romance language of the Italians. Abbreviated **It., Ital.**

I·tal·ian·ate (i-tal′yən-āt′; *also, for adj.*, i-tal′yən-it), *adj.* [It. *Italianato*], of Italian form, appearance, or character. *v.t.* [ITALIANATED (-id), ITALIANATING], [It. *italianare*], to Italianize.

Italian East Africa, a former Italian colony in eastern Africa, consisting of Ethiopia, Eritrea, and Italian Somaliland.

I·tal·ian·ism (i-tal′yən-iz′m), *n.* 1. an Italian expression, idiom, or custom. 2. Italian spirit, quality, etc. 3. fondness for Italian customs, ideas, etc.

I·tal·ian·i·za·tion (i-tal′yən-i-zā′shən, i-tal′yən-ī-zā′-shən), *n.* an Italianizing or being Italianized.

I·tal·ian·ize (i-tal′yən-īz′), *v.t. & v.i.* [ITALIANIZED (-izd′), ITALIANIZING], [Fr. *italianiser*], to make or become Italian in character, form, etc.

Italian Somaliland, a former Italian colony in eastern Africa: a United Nations trust territory from 1950 to 1960, when it merged with British Somaliland to form the independent country of Somalia.

Italian sonnet, a Petrarchan sonnet.

I·tal·ic (i-tal′ik), *adj.* [L. *Italicus;* Gr. *Italikos*], 1. of ancient Italy, its people, etc. 2. designating or of the subfamily of the Indo-European languages that includes Latin, the Italian dialects contemporary with Old Latin, and the languages descended from Latin, as Italian, French, Spanish, Portuguese, Romanian, etc. *n.* the Italic languages collectively. Abbreviated **Ital., It.**

i·tal·ic (i-tal′ik), *adj.* [see prec.: so called because first used in an Italian edition of Virgil, printed in Venice in 1501], designating a type in which the letters slant upward to the right, used to give emphasis to words, to indicate foreign words and phrases, etc.: *this is italic type. n.* italic type or print: also **italics,** *pl.* (sometimes construed as sing.). Abbreviated **ital., it.**

I·tal·i·cism (i-tal′ə-siz′m), *n.* Italianism.

i·tal·i·cize (i-tal′ə-sīz′), *v.t.* [ITALICIZED (-sīzd′), ITALICIZING], 1. to print in italics. 2. to underscore (written matter) with a straight line to indicate that it is to be printed in italics.

It·a·ly (it″l-i), *n.* a country in southern Europe, including the islands of Sicily and Sardinia: area, 119,768 sq. mi.; pop., 49,052,000; capital, Rome: Italian name, *Italia*: abbreviated **It., Ital.**

I·tas·ca, Lake (ī-tas′kə), a lake in northern Minnesota: area, 2 sq. mi.: it is the source of the Mississippi.

itch (ich), *v.i.* [ME. *yicchen, yitchen, icchen;* AS. *giccan;* akin to G. *jucken*], 1. to feel an irritating sensation on the skin, with the desire to scratch the affected part. 2. to have a restless desire or hankering. *n.* 1. an irritating sensation on the skin that causes a desire to scratch the affected part. 2. a contagious skin disease caused by a parasitic mite and accompanied by intense irritation of the skin; scabies (with *the*). 3. a restless desire; hankering: as, an *itch* to travel.

itch·i·ness (ich′i-nis), *n.* the condition of being itchy.

itch·y (ich′i), *adj.* [ITCHIER (-i-ẽr), ITCHIEST (-i-ist)], itching; like, feeling, or causing an itch.

-ite (īt), [< Fr. or L. or Gr.; Fr. *-ite;* L. *-ita, -ites;* Gr. *-itēs,* fem. *-itis*], a noun-forming suffix meaning: 1. *a native, inhabitant,* or *citizen of,* as in *Brooklynite.* 2. *an adherent of, believer in,* as in *Buchmanite.* 3. *a commercially manufactured product,* as in *lucite, dynamite, vulcanite.* 4. *a fossil,* as in *ammonite.* 5. *a part of a body* or *bodily organ,* as in *somite.* 6. *a salt* or *ester of an acid whose name ends in -ous,* as in *nitrite, sulfite.* 7. *a* (specified) *mineral* or *rock,* as in *anthracite, dolomite.*

-ite (īt), [L. *-itus,* ending of some past participles], a suffix, appearing in words derived from Latin past participles in *-itus,* used to form: 1. adjectives, as in *finite, partite.* 2. nouns derived from such adjectives, as in *favorite.* 3. verbs, as in *unite.*

i·tem (ī′təm), *adv.* [ME.; L.], also: used before each article in a series being enumerated. *n.* 1. originally, an admonition; hint. 2. an article; unit; separate thing; particular; entry in an account. 3. a bit of news or information. *v.t.* to set down as an item or by items.

SYN.—**item** applies to each separate article or thing entered or included in a list, inventory, record, etc.; **detail** applies to any single thing or small section that is part of a whole structure, design, etc. (an architectural *detail,* the *details* of a plot, one's life, etc.); **particular** stresses the distinctness of a thing as an individual unit in a whole (to go into *particulars*).

i·tem·ize (ī′təm-īz′), *v.t.* [ITEMIZED (-īzd′), ITEMIZING], to specify the items of; set down by items: as, *itemize* my bill of purchases.

item veto, the power of the governors of some States to veto a section of an appropriation bill, without vetoing the bill as a whole.

it·er·ance (it′ẽr-əns), *n.* iteration; repetition.

it·er·ant (it′ẽr-ənt), *adj.* iterating; repeating.

it·er·ate (it′ə-rāt′), *v.t.* [ITERATED (-id), ITERATING], [< L. *iteratus,* pp. of *iterare,* to repeat < *iterum,* again], to utter or do again or repeatedly. —*SYN.* see **repeat.**

it·er·a·tion (it′ə-rā′shən), *n.* [L. *iteratio*], 1. an iterating or being iterated; repetition. 2. something iterated.

it·er·a·tive (it′ə-rā′tiv, it′ẽr-ə-tiv), *adj.* [Fr. *itératif* < L. *iteratus*], 1. characterized by iteration; repetitious; repeating or repeated. 2. in *grammar,* frequentative.

Ith·a·ca (ith′ə-kə), *n.* 1. one of the Ionian Islands, off the west coast of Greece: legendary home of Odysseus. 2. a city in south central New York: pop., 29,000.

I·thunn, I·thun (ē′thōōn), *n.* [ON. *Ithunn*], in *Norse mythology,* the goddess of youth and spring, wife of Bragi and guardian of the golden apples that the gods ate to keep their youth: also **Idun.**

I·thu·ri·el (i-thyoor′i-əl), *n.* [Heb. *yithūrī′ēl,* lit., superiority of God], an angel in Milton's *Paradise Lost,* who restored Satan to his proper shape.

ith·y·phal·lic (ith′i-fal′ik), *adj.* [L. *ithyphallicus;* Gr. *ithyphallikos* < *ithyphallos,* erect phallus < *ithys,* straight + *phallos,* phallus], 1. of the phallus carried in the rites of Bacchus; hence, 2. lewd; obscene; lascivious. 3. in the meter of the Bacchic hymns. *n.* an ithyphallic poem, written in lines of three trochees.

i·tin·er·a·cy (ī-tin′ẽr-ə-si, i-tin′ẽr-ə-si), *n.* [< L. *iter, itineris,* a walk, journey; + *-acy*], itinerancy.

i·tin·er·an·cy (ī-tin′ẽr-ən-si, i-tin′ẽr-ən-si), *n.* 1. *a)* an itinerating; traveling from place to place. *b)* the state of being itinerant. 2. a group of itinerant preachers or judges. 3. official work requiring constant travel from place to place or frequent change of residence, as preaching or presiding over courts in a circuit.

i·tin·er·ant (ī-tin′ẽr-ənt, i-tin′ẽr-ənt), *adj.* [LL. *itinerans,* ppr. of *itinerari,* to travel < L. *iter, itineris,* a walk, journey], traveling from place to place or on a circuit. *n.* a person who travels from place to place.

SYN.—**itinerant** applies to persons whose work or profession requires them to travel from place to place (*itinerant* laborers, an *itinerant* preacher); **ambulatory** specifically implies ability to walk about (an *ambulatory* patient); **peripatetic** implies a walking or moving about in carrying on some activity and is applied humorously to persons who are always on the go; **nomadic** is applied to tribes or groups of people who have no permanent home, but move about constantly in search of food for themselves, pasture for the animals they herd, etc.; **vagrant** is applied to individuals, specifically hobos or tramps, who wander about without a fixed home, and implies shiftlessness, disorderliness, etc.

i·tin·er·ar·y (ī-tin′ə-rer′i, i-tin′ə-rer′i), *adj.* [LL. *itinerarius* < *itinerans,* ppr. of *itinerari;* see ITINERANT], of traveling, journeys, routes, or roads. *n.* [*pl.* ITINERARIES (-iz)], [LL. *itinerarium,* neut. of *itinerarius*], 1. a route. 2. a record of a journey. 3. a guidebook; roadbook. 4. a plan or outline of a journey or route.

i·tin·er·ate (ī-tin′ə-rāt′, i-tin′ə-rāt′), *v.i.* [ITINERATED (-id), ITINERATING], [< LL. *itineratus,* pp. of *itinerari;* see ITINERANT], to travel from place to place or on a circuit.

i·tin·er·a·tion (ī-tin′ə-rā′shən, i-tin′ə-rā′shən), *n.* 1. an itinerating. 2. a circuit; tour.

-i·tion (ish′ən), [< Fr. or L.; Fr. *-ition;* L. *-itio, -itionis* < *-i-,* thematic vowel + *-tio, -tionis*], a noun-forming suffix corresponding to *-ation,* as in *nutrition.*

-i·tious (ish′əs), [L. *-icius, -itius*], a suffix meaning *of, having the nature of, characterized by,* used to form adjectives corresponding to nouns ending in *-ition,* as in *nutritious, seditious.*

-i·tis (ī′tis), [Gr. *-itis,* orig. fem. of adjs. ending in *-itēs,* used to modify *nosos,* disease (later understood, but omitted)], a noun-forming suffix meaning *inflammatory disease* or *inflammation of* (a specified part or organ), as in *neuritis, bronchitis.*

it'll (it″l), 1. it will. 2. it shall.

-i·tol (i-tōl′, i-tol′), [< *-ite* + *-ol*], a suffix used in forming the names of certain alcohols with more than one hydroxyl group, as in *mannitol.*

its (its), *pron.* [Early Mod. Eng. analogical formation < *it* + *'s;* written *it's* until early 19th c.; the ME. & AS. form was *his*], that or those belonging to it. ***possessive pronominal adj.*** of, belonging to, or done by it.

it's (its), 1. it is. 2. it has.

it·self (it-self′), *pron.* a form of the third person singular, neuter pronoun, used: *a)* as an intensive: as, the picture frame *itself* is a work of art. *b)* as a reflexive: as, the dog scratched *itself.*

I.T.U., International Typographical Union.

-i·ty (ə-ti, i-ti), [< Fr. or L.; Fr. *-ité;* L. *-itas; -i-,* ending of stem, or thematic vowel + *-tas, -ty*], a suffix meaning *state, character, condition,* as in *chastity, adversity.*

-i·um (i-əm), a suffix used in forming Modern Latin names for chemical elements, as in *sodium.*

i.v., 1. initial velocity. 2. intravenous.

I·van (ī′vən; Russ. i-vän′), [Russ. < Gr. *Iōannēs;* see JOHN], a masculine name.

Ivan III, 1440–1505; grand duke of Muscovy (1462–1505): called *the Great.*

I·van IV, 1530–1584; grandson of Ivan III; duke of Muscovy (1533–1584); first czar of Russia (1547–1584): called *the Terrible.*

I·va·no·vo (i-vä′nô-vô), *n.* 1. a region of the R.S.F.S.R., in central European Russia: pop., 1,306,000. 2. its capital: pop., 332,000.

I've (īv), I have.

-ive (iv), [< Fr. or L.; Fr. *-if,* fem. *-ive;* L. *-ivus*], a suffix meaning: 1. *of, relating to, belonging to, having the nature* or *quality of,* as in *native, substantive.* 2. *tending to, given to,* as in *creative, destructive.*

i·vied (ī′vid), *adj.* covered or overgrown with ivy.
i·vo·ry (ī′vẽr-i), *n.* [*pl.* IVORIES (-iz)], [ME. *ivory, ivorie;* OFr. *ivurie, yvoire;* L. *ebur, eboris*], 1. the hard, white substance forming the tusks of elephants, walruses, etc.: it is a form of dentine. 2. *a*) any form of dentine. *b*) any substance like ivory in appearance, use, etc. 3. the color of ivory; creamy white. 4. a tusk of an elephant, walrus, etc. 5. *pl.* things made of, resembling, or suggesting ivory; specifically, [Slang], *a*) piano keys. *b*) teeth. *c*) dice. *d*) billiard balls. *adj.* 1. of, made of, or like ivory. 2. creamy-white.
ivory black, a fine black pigment prepared from burnt ivory.
Ivory Coast, 1. a country in west central Africa, on the Gulf of Guinea: a former French colony, it is now a member of the French Community: area, 124,500 sq. mi.; pop., 3,410,000; capital, Abidjan. 2. formerly, the African coast in this region.
ivory nut, the seed of a certain tropical palm tree, resembling ivory when dried: it is used for buttons, etc.
ivory tower, figuratively, a place of mental withdrawal from reality and action: used as a symbol of escapist tendencies, especially in art and literature.
i·vo·ry·type (ī′vẽr-i-tīp′), *n.* a photographic picture in which a natural-color effect is produced by superimposing a light print, tinted on the back and made translucent by varnishing, on a stronger print.
i·vor·y-white (ī′vẽr-i-hwīt′), *adj.* creamy-white.
I·vy (ī′vi), [< *ivy* (the plant)], a femine name. *adj.* of or characteristic of the Ivy League.
i·vy (ī′vi), *n.* [*pl.* IVIES (-viz)], [ME. *ivi;* AS. *ifig, ifegn;* akin to G. *efeu* (OHG. *ebawi, ebah*), D. *ei-* in *eiloof*, ivy leaf (MLG. *īflōf, ilōf, eilōf*); by some authorities derived < IE. base **ibhewo-* (Gmc. **ibahs*) with basic sense "the climber"], 1. a variety of climbing vine with a woody stem and evergreen leaves, grown as ornamentation on buildings, walls, etc.: also **English ivy.** 2. any of various similar climbing plants: as, poison *ivy.*
Ivy League, a group of colleges in the northeastern United States forming a league for intercollegiate sports: often used to describe the fashions, standards, attitudes, etc. associated with students at these colleges.
ivy vine, 1. an American woody vine of the grape family, with heart-shaped leaves. 2. the Virginia creeper.
i·wis (i-wis′), *adv.* [ME. *iwis, iwisse;* AS. *gewis, gewisse,* certain(ly), used as ME. adv., later misunderstood by Romantic poets as *I wis,* I know; akin to G. *gewiss*], [Archaic], certainly; assuredly: also spelled **ywis.**
I·wo Ji·ma (ē′wō jē′mä, ē′wə jē′mə), a small island of the Volcano Islands in the western Pacific: scene of heavy fighting (1945) in World War II.
I.W.W., Industrial Workers of the World.
I.X., *Iēsous Khristos,* [Gr.], Jesus Christ.
ix·i·a (ik′si-ə), *n.* [Mod. L. < Gr. *ixos,* birdlime: so called from the viscid nature of some of the species], any of a group of South African plants of the iris family.
Ix·i·on (ik-sī′ən), *n.* [L.; Gr. *Ixiōn*], in *Greek legend,* a Thessalian king and father of the Centaurs, who was bound to a constantly revolving wheel in Tartarus because he sought the love of Hera.
Ix·ta·ci·huatl (ēs′tä-sē′wät-′l), *n.* a volcanic mountain in Mexico, southeast of Mexico City: height, 16,960 ft.
ix·tle (iks′tli, is′tli), *n.* istle.
I·yar (ē′yär), *n.* [Heb.], the eighth month of the Jewish year: see **Jewish calendar.**
-i·za·tion (ə-zā′shən, ī-zā′shən), a compound suffix forming nouns from verbs in *-ize,* as in *realization.*
-ize (īz), [Fr. *-ise;* LL. *-izare;* Gr. *-izein*], a verb-forming suffix meaning: 1. *to cause to be* or *become, make conform with* or *resemble, make,* as in *democratize, Americanize, sterilize.* 2. *to become, become like,* as in *crystallize.* 3. *to subject to, treat with, combine with,* as in *oxidize, galvanize.* 4. *to engage in, act in a specified way,* as in *theorize, soliloquize.* Sometimes spelled **-ise.**
I·zhevsk (i-zhevsk′), *n.* a city in European R.S.F.S.R.: pop., 283,000.
Iz·mir (iz′mir), *n.* Smyrna, Turkey: Turkish name.
iz·zard (iz′ẽrd), *n.* [earlier *ezed, ezod;* OFr. *ezed;* Pr. *izedo* < Gr. *zēta;* see ZED], [Archaic or Dial.], the letter Z.

J

J, j (jā), *n.* [*pl.* J's, j's, Js, js (jāz)], 1. the tenth letter of the English alphabet: formerly a variant of I, i, in the seventeenth century it became established as a consonant only, as in *Julius,* originally spelled *Iulius:* see **alphabet,** table. 2. the usual sound of this letter in English, phonetically a voiced affricate (IPA dʒ or ǰ). 3. a type or impression for J or j. 4. *a symbol for* the tenth in a sequence or group. *adj.* 1. of J or j. 2. tenth in a sequence or group.
J (jā), *n.* an object shaped like J. *adj.* shaped like J.
J, in *physics,* joule.
j, [Rare], the Roman numeral i, as in *vij* (vii).
J., 1. James. 2. Judge. 3. Justice.
‡**ja** (yä), *adv.* [G.], yes.
Ja., 1. James. 2. January.
J.A., 1. Joint Agent. 2. Judge Advocate.
jab (jab), *v.t. & v.i.* [JABBED (jabd), JABBING], [var. of *job* (to poke, stab); ME. *jobben,* to peck], 1. to poke or thrust, as with a sharp instrument. 2. to punch with short, straight blows. *n.* a quick thrust or blow.
jab·ber (jab′ẽr), *v.i. & v.t.* [prob. echoic], to speak or say quickly, incoherently, or nonsensically; chatter; gibber. *n.* fast, incoherent, nonsensical talk; gibberish.
jab·i·ru (jab′i-rōō′), *n.* [Sp. *jabirú* < Tupi *jabirú*], a large wading bird of the stork family, found in Africa and tropical America; the wood ibis.
jab·o·ran·di (jab′ə-ran′di), *n.* [Port. < Tupi], the dried leaves of a South American plant, from which a poisonous drug is obtained.
ja·bot (zha′bō′; Fr. zhȧ′bō′), *n.* [*pl.* JABOTS (-bōz′; Fr. -bō′)], [Fr., bird's crop; hence, jabot], 1. a trimming or frill, usually of lace, attached to the neck of a woman's blouse or bodice. 2. formerly, a similar ruffle or frill on a man's shirt front.
ja·ça·na (zhä′sə-nä′), *n.* [Port. < Tupi *jaçanam, jassanam*], a bird of South America and India, with long toes that enable it to walk on the leaves of water plants.
ja·cinth (jā′sinth, jas′inth), *n.* [ME. *jacinte, jacinct;* OFr. *iacinte, iacinct;* L. *hyacinthus;* see HYACINTH], 1. a reddish-orange precious stone, a variety of zircon; hyacinth. 2. a reddish-orange color.
jack (jak), [J-], [ME. *Jacke, Jake;* OFr. *Jaque, Jaques;* LL. *Jacobus;* Gr. *Iakōbos;* Heb. *ya'aqob,* Jacob, lit., seizing by the heel, a supplanter], a nickname for John, and, sometimes, for James or Jacob. *n.* [*pl.,* for 9, 10, 11, 12 JACKS (jaks), JACK; see PLURAL, II, D, 1], [< nickname], 1. [often J-], originally, a common fellow or boy assistant. 2. [often J-], a man or boy; fellow. 3. [often J-], a sailor; jack-tar. 4. a lumberjack. 5. [sometimes J-], a worker at odd jobs; jack-of-all-trades. 6. a bootjack. 7. a device for turning a roast; kitchen jack. 8. any of various machines used to lift, hoist, or move something heavy a short distance: as, a *jack*screw, hydraulic *jack,* automobile *jack,* etc. 9. a male donkey; jackass. 10. a jack rabbit. 11. a jackdaw. 12. a male salmon. 13. [Slang], money. 14. in *games,* *a*) a playing card with a page boy's picture on it; knave. *b*) a small ball used as the center mark in bowling. *c*) one of the small metal pieces or stones used in playing jackstones. 15. in *hunting,* *a*) a torch or light used to attract game or fish at night. *b*) the container holding the lighting fuel. 16. in *navigation,* a small flag flown on a ship's bow as a signal or to show nationality; union jack. 17. in *electricity,* a plug-in receptacle used to make electric contact. *v.t.* 1. to raise by means of a jack. 2. to hunt or fish for with a light. *adj.* male: of some animals.

AXLE
JACK

JACK

every man jack, every man; everyone.
jack up, 1. to raise by means of a jack. 2. [Colloq.], to raise (prices, salaries, etc.). 3. [Colloq.], to reproach for misbehavior or neglect; encourage to duty.
jack (jak), *n.* [ME. *jakke;* OFr. *jaque;* Sp. *jaco;* prob. < Ar. *shakk*], 1. a sleeveless coat, usually of leather, worn by a medieval foot soldier. 2. a drinking mug of leather.

jack (jak), *n.* [Port. *jaca;* Malay *chakka*], 1. an East Indian tree like the breadfruit. 2. its large, heavy fruit, which has tasteless pulp and edible seeds. 3. its wood.

jack- (jak), [see JACK (a man, boy, etc.)], a combining form meaning: 1. *male,* as in *jackass, jackdaw.* 2. *large* or *strong,* as in *jackboot, jackknife.* 3. *boy, fellow:* used in hyphenated compounds, as *jack-in-the-box.*

jack·al (jak'ôl, jak'əl), *n.* [*pl.* JACKALS (-ôlz, -əlz), JACKAL; see PLURAL, II, D, 1], [Turk. *chaqāl;* Per. *shagāl;* Sans. *s'rgala*], 1. a yellowish-gray, meat-eating wild dog of Asia and northern Africa, smaller than the wolf: it runs in packs and hunts its prey at night. 2. a person who does low or dishonest work for another: from the notion that the jackal hunts game for the lion and eats the leavings. 3. a person who cheats or swindles in a mean, underhanded way.

JACKAL
(15 in. high at shoulder)

jack·a·napes (jak'ə-nāps'), *n.* [earlier *Jack a Napes,* as if *Jack of Naples;* refashioning of *Jack Napes,* nickname of William de la Pole, Duke of Suffolk (d.1450), whose badge was a clog and a chain like a tame ape's and who favored a royal alliance with the House of Naples], 1. formerly, a monkey; hence, 2. a conceited, insolent, presumptuous fellow. 3. a pert, monkeylike, mischievous child.

jack·ass (jak'as'), *n.* [*jack-* + *ass*], 1. a male donkey. 2. a stupid or foolish person; nitwit.

jack·boot (jak'bōōt'), *n.* [*jack-* + *boot*], a heavy, sturdy boot that reaches above the knee: also **jack boot.**

jack·daw (jak'dô'), *n.* [*jack-* + *daw*], a European black bird like the crow, but smaller.

jack·et (jak'it), *n.* [OFr. *jaquette,* dim. of *jaque;* see JACK (coat)], 1. a short coat, usually with sleeves. 2. an outer coating or covering, such as the removable paper cover of a book, the metal covering of a bullet, the insulating casing on a pipe or boiler, the skin of a potato, etc. *v.t.* 1. to put a jacket, or coat, on. 2. to cover with a casing, wrapper, etc.

Jack Frost, frost or cold weather personified.

jack-in-a-box (jak'in-ə-boks'), *n.* [*pl.* JACK-IN-A-BOXES (-bok'siz)], [see JACK-], 1. a tropical tree having pulpy fruit which rattles when dry. 2. a jack-in-the-box.

jack-in-the-box (jak'in-*th*ə-boks'), *n.* [*pl.* JACK-IN-THE-BOXES (-bok'siz)], [see JACK-], a toy consisting of a box from which a grotesque little figure on a spring jumps up when the lid is lifted.

jack-in-the-pul·pit (jak'in-*th*ə-pool'pit), *n.* [*pl.* JACK-IN-THE-PULPITS], [see JACK-], an American plant of the lily family, with a flower spike partly arched over by a hoodlike covering.

Jack Ketch (kech), [after famous public executioner in England, ?-1686], [British], an official hangman.

jack·knife (jak'nīf'), *n.* [*pl.* JACKKNIVES (-nīvz')], [*jack-* + *knife*], 1. a large pocketknife. 2. a dive in which the diver keeps his legs straight and touches his feet with his hands just before plunging into the water. *v.t.* to cut or stab with a jackknife. *v.i.* to bend at the middle, as in a dive.

jack-of-all-trades (jak'əv-ôl'trādz'), *n.* [*pl.* JACKS-OF-ALL-TRADES], [see JACK-, 3], [often J-], a person who can do many kinds of work acceptably; handy man.

jack-o'-lan·tern (jak'ə-lan'tẽrn), *n.* [*pl.* JACK-O'-LANTERNS], [see JACK-, 3], 1. a shifting, elusive light seen over marshes at night; will-o'-the-wisp. 2. a hollow pumpkin, real or artificial, cut to look like a face and used as a lantern.

jack·pot (jak'pot'), *n.* [*jack,* the playing card + *pot;* ? influenced by *jack-,* 2], 1. cumulative stakes in a poker game, which can be played for only when some player has a pair of jacks or better with which to open. 2. any cumulative stakes, as in a bingo game or a slot machine. 3. [Colloq.], the highest stakes that can be won in any enterprise. Also **jack pot.**
  hit the jackpot, [Slang], 1. to win the jackpot. 2. to attain the highest success.

jack rabbit, [see JACK, *adj.*], a large hare of western North America, with long ears and strong hind legs.

jacks (jaks), *n.pl.* [construed as sing.], the game of jackstones.

jack·screw (jak'skrōō'), *n.* [*jack-* + *screw*], a machine for raising heavy things a short distance, operated by turning a screw.

jack·snipe (jak'snīp'), *n.* [*pl.* JACKSNIPES (-snīps'), JACKSNIPE; see PLURAL, II, D, 1], [*jack-* + *snipe*], 1. a species of small European snipe. 2. the American sandpiper.

Jack·son (jak's'n), *n.* 1. the capital of Mississippi, on the Pearl River: pop., 144,000. 2. a city in southern Michigan: pop., 51,000. 3. a city in western Tennessee: pop., 34,000.

Jack·son, Andrew (jak's'n), 1767–1845; American general and statesman; seventh president of the United States (1829–1837): called *Old Hickory.*

Jackson, Helen Hunt, (pseudonym *H. H.*), 1830–1885; American novelist and poet.

Jackson, Robert Hough·wout (how'ət), 1892–1954; American jurist; associate justice, United States Supreme Court (1941–1954).

Jackson, Thomas Jonathan, 1824–1863; Confederate general in the Civil War: called *Stonewall Jackson.*

Jack·son·ville (jak's'n-vil'), *n.* 1. a city of northeastern Florida, on the St. Johns River: pop., 201,000. 2. a city in western Illinois: pop., 22,000.

jack·stay (jak'stā'), *n.* [*jack-* + *stay, n.*], 1. a rope or staff along a ship's yard, to which the sail is fastened. 2. a rope or rod that runs up and down a ship's mast, on which the yard moves.

jack·stone (jak'stōn'), *n.* [for dial. *checkstone, chackstone* < *check, chuck,* pebble], 1. *pl.* [construed as sing.], a children's game of tossing, catching, or picking up pebbles or small metal pieces, played in various ways: often shortened to *jacks.* 2. a pebble or small metal piece used in this game.

jack·straw (jak'strô'), *n.* [*jack-* + *straw*], 1. a straw man. 2. a narrow strip of wood, bone, etc. used in a game played by tossing a number of such strips into a jumbled heap and trying to remove them one at a time without moving any of the others. 3. *pl.* [construed as sing.], this game.

jack-tar (jak'tär'), *n.* [see JACK (nickname)], [often J-], a sailor.

jack towel, a roller towel.

Ja·cob (jā'kəb), [LL. *Jacobus;* see JACK (nickname)], a masculine name: diminutives, *Jake, Jack;* variant, *James;* equivalents, Fr. *Jacques,* It. *Giacomo.* *n.* in the *Bible,* a son of Isaac and father of the founders of the twelve tribes of Israel: also called *Israel:* Gen. 25–50.

Jac·o·be·an (jak'ə-bē'ən), *adj.* [Mod. L. & LL. *Jacobaeus* < *Jacobus,* Latinized form of the name of James I; see JACK (nickname)], 1. of James I of England. 2. of the period in England when he was king (1603–1625). *n.* a poet, diplomat, etc. of this period.

Jac·o·bin (jak'ə-bin), *n.* [OFr. *Jacobin* < LL. *Jacobinus* < *Jacobus;* see JACK (nickname)], 1. a French Dominican friar: so called because the Dominicans were established in a convent at the Church of St. Jacques (St. James of Compostella) in Paris. 2. any member of a society of revolutionary democrats in France during the Revolution of 1789: so called because their meetings were held in the Jacobin friars' convent; hence, 3. a political radical. 4. [j-], a kind of pigeon with hoodlike neck feathers resembling a Dominican cowl. *adj.* Jacobinic.

Jac·o·bin·ic (jak'ə-bin'ik), *adj.* of the Jacobins or Jacobinism.

Jac·o·bin·i·cal (jak'ə-bin'i-k'l), *adj.* Jacobinic.

Jac·o·bin·ism (jak'ə-bin-iz'm), *n.* 1. the political doctrines of the Jacobins. 2. political radicalism.

Jac·o·bite (jak'ə-bīt'), *n.* [< LL. *Jacobus;* see JACK (nickname)], in *English history,* a supporter of James II after his abdication, or of his descendants' claims to the throne.

Ja·cob's-lad·der (jā'kəbz-lad'ẽr), *n.* a small plant with blue or white flowers and leaf formation somewhat like a ladder.

Jacob's ladder, 1. in the *Bible,* the ladder from earth to heaven that Jacob saw in a dream: Gen. 28:12. 2. a ladder made of rope, wire, etc., used on ships.

jac·o·net (jak'ə-net'), *n.* [< *Jagannath,* India, where it was manufactured], 1. a soft, white, lightweight cotton textile. 2. cotton cloth glazed on one side and dyed. Also spelled **jacconet, jacconot.**

Jac·quard loom (jə-kärd'), [after the French inventor, J.M. *Jacquard* (1752–1834)], a loom for weaving patterns into fabrics: it has an endless belt of cards with holes in them arranged to produce the desired pattern.

Jacquard (weave), the figured weave produced by a Jacquard loom.

Jac·que·line (jak'wə-lin), [Fr., fem. of *Jacques;* see JACK (nickname)], a feminine name.

Jacque·mi·not (jak'mi-nō'; Fr. zhák'mē'nō'), *n.* [after J. F. *Jacqueminot* (1787–1865), Fr. general], a deep-red, hybrid perennial rose.

‡Jac·que·rie (zhák'rē'), *n.* [Fr. < *Jacques Bonhomme,* name applied to a peasant by the nobles], 1. a French peasants' revolt of 1358; hence, 2. [often j-], any peasants' revolt.

jac·ta·tion (jak-tā'shən), *n.* [L. *jactatio,* a throwing, boasting < *iactare;* see JACTITATION], 1. bragging. 2. in *medicine,* jactitation.

jac·ti·ta·tion (jak'ti-tā'shən), *n.* [ML. *jactitatio* < L. *jactitare,* to utter, tell in public < *jactare,* to throw, flourish < *jacere,* to throw], 1. bragging. 2. in *law,* a false boast or false statement that causes harm to another person. 3. in *medicine,* a restless tossing or twitching of the body, a muscle, etc.

jade (jād), *n.* [Fr.; Sp. < *piedra de ijada,* stone of the side, colic stone: so called because of the notion that it cured pains in the side], 1. a hard ornamental stone, either jadeite (true jade) or nephrite, usually green or white. 2. the green color of this stone. *adj.* 1. made of jade. 2. green like jade.

jade (jād), *n.* [ME.; ? < ON. *jalda,* a mare], 1. a horse, especially a worn-out, worthless one. 2. a loose or disreputable woman. 3. any woman: a playful or ironic usage. *v.t. & v.i.* [JADED (-id), JADING], to make or become tired, weary, or worn-out.

jad·ed (jād'id), *adj.* [pp. of *jade, v.*], 1. tired; worn-out; wearied. 2. dulled or satiated, as from overuse.

jade·ite (jād'īt), *n.* a complex silicate, hard, tough, and translucent, usually green or white; true jade.

jae·ger (yā'gẽr), *n.* 1. a jäger. 2. (*also* jā'gẽr), a robber bird of the gull family, which forces other weaker birds to leave or give up their prey: also spelled **jäger.**

Ja·el (jā'əl), *n.* [Heb. *yā'el,* lit., mountain goat], in the *Bible,* the woman who killed Sisera by hammering a spike through his head while he slept: Judg. 4:17-22.

Ja·én (hä-en'), *n.* 1. a province of southern Spain: pop., 736,000. 2. its capital: pop., 65,000.

Jaf·fa (jaf'ə, yä'fä), *n.* a seaport in Israel: pop., with Tel-Aviv, 387,000: ancient name, *Joppa.*

Jaff·na (jaf'nə), *n.* a seaport in northern Ceylon: pop., 77,000.

jag (jag), *n.* [ME. *jagge,* projecting point; prob. < dial. var. < AS. *sceacga;* cf. SHAG], 1. a notch or pointed tear, as in cloth. 2. a sharp, toothlike projection or similar indentation. *v.t.* [JAGGED (jagd), JAGGING], [ME. *jaggen, joggen* < the *n.*], 1. to cut jags in; notch; pink (cloth, etc.). 2. to cut unevenly; tear raggedly.

jag (jag), *n.* [prob. special use of *jag* (a notch) with sense "load of scrub wood"], 1. [Colloq.], a small load or amount, as of wood, hay, etc. 2. [Slang], an intoxicated condition due to alcoholic liquor or drugs. 3. [Slang], a drunken celebration; spree.

J.A.G., Judge Advocate General.

Jag·an·nath (jug'ə-nät', jug'ə-nôt'), *n.* a Hindu god: see **Juggernaut.**

Jag·a·tai (jag'ə-tī'), *n.* a dialect of Turkish spoken in southern Turkestan and parts of the southwestern Asiatic U.S.S.R.

jä·ger (yā'gẽr), *n.* [G., huntsman < *jagen,* to hunt], 1. a hunter. 2. [often J-], a rifleman in the old Austrian and German armies. 3. (*also* jā'gẽr), a jaeger. Also spelled **yager.**

jag·ged (jag'id), *adj.* [pp. of *jag, v.*], having sharp projecting points or notches; ragged. —*SYN.* see **rough.**

jag·ger·y (jag'ẽr-i), *n.* [Anglo-Ind.; Hind. *jagri* < Sans. *sarkarā,* sugar], a dark, crude sugar, specifically that made from the sap of East Indian palm trees.

jag·gy (jag'i), *adj.* [JAGGIER (-i-ẽr), JAGGIEST (-i-ist)], jagged.

jag·uar (jag'wär, jag'ū-är'), *n.* [*pl.* JAGUARS (-wärz, -ärz'), JAGUAR; see PLURAL, II, D, 1], [Port. < Tupi], a wild animal of the cat family, yellowish with black spots, found in Central and South America: it is like the leopard, but larger.

Jah·veh, Jah·ve (yä've), *n.* Jehovah.

Jah·weh (yä'we), *n.* Jehovah.

jai-a·lai (hī'ə-lī'), *n.* [Sp. < Basque *jai,* celebration + *alai,* merry], a game like handball, played with a basketlike racket fastened to the arm: it is popular in Latin America.

jail (jāl), *n.* [ME. *jaile, gaile, gayhol;* OFr. *jaiole, jaole, gaole,* a cage, prison; LL. *caveola,* dim. of L. *cavea,* a cage, coop], a building for the confinement of people who have broken the law or are awaiting trial; prison, especially for those convicted of minor offenses. *v.t.* to put or keep in jail; imprison. Also, British, **gaol.**

jail·bird (jāl'bũrd'), *n.* [Colloq.], 1. a person sentenced to jail; prisoner. 2. a person often put in jail; habitual lawbreaker.

jail delivery, 1. escape from jail; liberation of prisoners by force. 2. in *English law,* the act of clearing a jail by bringing the prisoners to trial.

jail·er, jail·or (jāl'ẽr), *n.* a person in charge of a jail or of prisoners.

Jain (jīn), *n.* [Hind. *Jaina* < Sans. *jina,* saint, lit., conqueror], a believer in Jainism. *adj.* of the Jains or Jainism.

Jai·na (jī'nə), *n. & adj.* Jain.

Jain·ism (jīn'iz'm), *n.* a Hindu religious creed resembling Buddhism, founded about 500 B.C.: it teaches reverence of wise and good men and respect for animals.

Jai·pur (jī'poor, jī-poor'), *n.* 1. a former native Indian state, attached to the Rajputana agency until 1948: since 1950, included in Rajasthan state. 2. the capital of Rajasthan: pop., 403,000.

Ja·kar·ta (jä-kär'tä), *n.* the capital of Indonesia, on the northwestern coast of Java: pop., c. 3,000,000: former, Dutch name, *Batavia.*

jake (jāk) *adj.* [prob. < *Jake,* abbrev. of *Jacob;* sense development unknown], [Slang], just right; satisfactory.

jakes (jāks), *n.* [< *Jacques;* cf. JOHN], [Archaic or Dial.], an outdoor toilet; privy.

jal·ap (jal'əp), *n.* [Fr.; Sp. *jalapa* < *Jalapa,* city in Mexico from which it is imported], 1. the dried root of a Mexican plant, used as a purgative. 2. the plant.

Ja·la·pa (hä-lä'pä), *n.* the capital of Veracruz, Mexico: pop., 51,000.

jal·a·pin (jal'ə-pin), *n.* a glucoside contained in jalap.

Ja·lis·co (hä-lēs'kô), *n.* a state of western Mexico, on the Pacific: area, 31,149 sq. mi.; pop., 2,443,000; capital, Guadalajara.

ja·lop·y (jə-lop'i), *n.* [*pl.* JALOPIES (-iz)], [earlier *jaloupy,* prob. altered < Fr. *chaloupe,* lit., a shallop, skiff], [Slang], an old, ramshackle automobile or airplane.

jal·ou·sie (jal'oo-sē', zhal'oo-zē'), *n.* [Fr. < OFr. *jalousie, gelosie,* jealousy; see JEALOUSY], a window, shade, door, or wall formed of wooden, metal, or glass slats arranged somewhat as in a Venetian blind, for regulating the air and light coming through.

jam (jam), *v.t.* [JAMMED (jamd), JAMMING], [earlier *jambe,* as if from Fr. *jambe,* leg, support, supporting layer], 1. to squeeze or wedge into or through a confined space. 2. to bruise; crush. 3. to push; shove; crowd. 4. to fill or block (a passageway, etc.) by crowding or squeezing into it. 5. to cause to become wedged so that it cannot move: as, the door was *jammed.* 6. in *radio,* to make (broadcasts or signals) unintelligible by sending out others on the same wave length. *v.i.* 1. *a*) to become wedged or stuck fast. *b*) to become unworkable through such jamming of parts. 2. to push against one another in a confined space. 3. [Slang], in *jazz,* to improvise. *n.* 1. a jamming or being jammed: as, a traffic *jam.* 2. [Colloq.], a difficult situation; predicament.

jam (jam), *n.* [as if from *jam, v.;* but note *Jameco,* early sp. of *Jamaica,* source of cane sugar], a food made by boiling fruit with sugar to a thick mixture: distinguished from *preserve, jelly.*

Ja·mai·ca (jə-mā'kə), *n.* a country on an island in the West Indies, south of Cuba: formerly a British dependency, since 1962 a member of the British Commonwealth of Nations: area, 4,411 sq. mi.; pop., 1,652,000; capital, Kingston: see **West Indies,** map.

Ja·mai·can (jə-mā'kən), *adj.* of Jamaica, its people, or culture. *n.* a native or inhabitant of Jamaica.

jamb, jambe (jam), *n.* [Fr. *jambe;* OFr. *jambe,* a leg, shank, pier, side post of a door < LL. *gamba,* a leg, hoof], 1. a side post of a doorway, window frame, fireplace, etc. 2. a jambeau.

jam·beau (jam'bō), *n.* [*pl.* JAMBEAUX (-bōz)], [ME. < OFr. *jambe;* see JAMB], a piece of armor for the leg.

jam·bo·ree (jam'bə-rē'), *n.* [coined word; prob. < *jam, v.* by analogy with *corroboree, charivari*], 1. [Colloq.], a hilarious party; noisy revel. 2. a large, especially international, assembly of boy scouts.

James (jāmz), [Fr. < LL. *Jacobus;* see JACK (nickname)], a masculine name: diminutives, *Jamie, Jim, Jimmy, Jem:* see **Jacob.** *n.* 1. in the *Bible, a*) a Christian apostle, Zebedee's son: called *the Greater. b*) a Christian apostle, Alphaeus' son: sometimes called *the Less. c*) a brother of Jesus: Gal. 1:19. *d*) one of the books of the New Testament. Abbreviated **Ja., Jas., J.** 2. a river of Virginia flowing eastward into Chesapeake Bay: length, 340 mi. 3. a river of North and South Dakota, flowing southward into the Missouri: length, 710 mi.

James I, 1566-1625; son of *Mary, Queen of Scots;* king of England (1603-1625); as James VI, king of Scotland (1567-1625).

James II, 1633-1701; son of *Charles I;* king of England (1685-1688); deposed.

James, Henry (jāmz), 1843-1916; brother of *William;* American novelist and essayist in England.

James, Jesse, 1847-1882; American outlaw.

James, William, 1842-1910; American psychologist and philosopher; exponent of pragmatism.

James Bay, the southward extension of Hudson Bay.

James Edward, (*James Francis Edward Stuart*), 1688-1766; son of *James II:* called *The Old Pretender.*

James Range, a mountain range of central Australia.

James·town (jāmz'toun'), *n.* 1. a colonial settlement (1607) at the mouth of the James River, Virginia. 2. a city in southwestern New York: pop., 42,000.

Jam·mu and Kashmir (jum'ōō), see **Kashmir.**

jam session, [Slang], an informal gathering of jazz musicians to play improvisations.

Jam·shid, Jam·shyd (jam-shēd'), *n.* [Per.], in *Persian mythology,* the king of the peris: because he boasted that he was immortal, he had to live as a human being on earth, where he became a famous ruler.

Jan., January.

Ja·ná·ček, Le·oš (le'ôsh yá'nä-chek'), 1854-1928; Czech composer.

Jane (jān), [Fr. *Jeanne;* ML. *Joanna;* see JOANNA], a feminine name: diminutives, *Janet, Jenny.*

Janes·ville (jānz'vil), *n.* a city in southern Wisconsin: pop., 35,000.

Jan·et (jan'it, jə-net'), a feminine name: see **Jane.**

jan·gle (jaŋ'g'l), *v.i.* [JANGLED (-g'ld), JANGLING], [ME. *janglen, jangelen;* OFr. *jangler,* to jangle, prattle, wrangle], 1. to make a harsh, inharmonious sound, as a bell out of tune. 2. to quarrel; bicker. *v.t.* 1. to utter in a harsh, inharmonious manner. 2. to cause to make a harsh sound. *n.* 1. noisy talk. 2. a harsh sound; discordant ringing. 3. bickering; quarrel.

Jan·ice (jan′is), [< *Jane, Janet*], a feminine name.

Ja·ni·na (yä′nē-nä′), *n.* Ioannina, a city in Greece: the Serbian name: also **Yanina.**

Jan·is·sar·y, jan·is·sar·y (jan′ə-ser′i), *n.* a Janizary.

jan·i·tor (jan′i-tẽr), *n.* [L., doorkeeper < *janua*, door], 1. a doorman; house porter. 2. a person who takes care of a building, apartment house, etc.

jan·i·tress (jan′i-tris), *n.* a woman janitor.

Jan·i·zar·y, jan·i·zar·y (jan′ə-zer′i), *n.* [*pl.* JANIZARIES (-iz)], [Fr. *janissaire* < Turk. *yeñicheri*, lit., new troops; *yeñi*, new + *cheri*, soldiery], 1. a soldier (originally a slave) in the Turkish sultan's guard, established in the 14th century and abolished in 1826. 2. any soldier in the Turkish army.

Jan·sen, Cor·ne·lis (kôr-nā′lis yän′sən; Eng. jan′s'n), (*Cornelius Jansenius*), 1585–1638; Dutch theologian; bishop of Ypres.

Jan·sen·ism (jan′s'n-iz'm), *n.* the teaching of Cornelis Jansen, who believed in predestination, denied free will, and held that man, though depraved in nature, is unable to resist God's grace.

Jan·sen·ist (jan′s'n-ist), *n.* a believer in Jansenism. *adj.* of Jansen or Jansenism.

Jan·sen·is·tic (jan′s'n-is′tik), *adj.* Jansenist.

Jan·u·ar·i·us, Saint (jan′ū-âr′i-əs), 272?–305? A.D.; Christian prelate and martyr; patron saint of Naples.

Jan·u·ar·y (jan′ū-er′i), *n.* [*pl.* JANUARIES (-iz)], [L. *Januarius* (*mensis*), (the month) of Janus, to whom it was sacred], the first month of the year, having 31 days: abbreviated **Jan., Ja.**

Ja·nus (jā′nəs), *n.* [L.], in *Roman mythology*, the god who was guardian of portals and patron of beginnings and endings: he is shown as having two faces, one in front, the other at the back of his head, symbolizing his powers.

Ja·nus-faced (jā′nəs-fāst′), *adj.* two-faced; deceiving.

Jap (jap), *n.* & *adj.* Japanese: a shortened form often expressing contempt, hostility, etc.

Jap., 1. Japan. 2. Japanese.

Ja·pan (jə-pan′), *n.* an island country east of Asia, including Hokkaido, Honshu, Shikoku, Kyushu, and smaller islands: area, 147,700 sq. mi.; pop., 89,275,000; capital, Tokyo: Japanese names, *Nippon, Nihon*: Marco Polo's name, *Zipangu;* hence, poetic name, *Cipango.*

ja·pan (jə-pan′), *n.* [< *Japan*], 1. a hard lacquer or varnish giving a glossy finish: it was originally from Japan. 2. a liquid mixture used as a paint drier. 3. objects decorated and lacquered in the Japanese style. *v.t.* [JAPANNED (-pand′), JAPANNING], to varnish with japan or a similar lacquer.

Japan., Japanese.

Japan, Sea of, an extension of the Pacific, between Korea and Japan: area, 389,000 sq. mi.

Japan clover, a cloverlike plant of the bean family, used for fodder.

Japan current, a warm current in the Pacific, flowing east of Taiwan and northeast past Japan.

Jap·a·nese (jap′ə-nēz′), *adj.* of Japan, its people, language, culture, etc. *n.* 1. [*pl.* JAPANESE], a native of Japan. 2. the language of Japan. Abbreviated **Japan., Jap.**

Japanese beetle, a green-and-brown beetle, originally from Japan, which eats leaves, fruits, and grasses, and is damaging to crops.

Japanese ivy, a woody vine of China and Japan, bearing three-lobed leaves: also called *Boston ivy.*

Japanese persimmon, 1. an Asiatic tree of the ebony family, bearing large, soft, edible, red or orange-colored fruit. 2. its fruit. Also called *kaki, date plum.*

Japanese quince, 1. a spiny shrub with large pink or red flowers and hard, fragrant, greenish-yellow fruit sometimes used for jelly: also called *flowering quince.* 2. the fruit.

Jap·a·nesque (jap′ə-nesk′), *adj.* in the Japanese manner.

jape (jāp), *v.i.* [JAPED (jāpt), JAPING], [ME. *japen*], 1. to joke; jest. 2. to play tricks. *v.t.* 1. to make fun of; mock. 2. to play tricks on; fool. *n.* 1. a joke; jest. 2. a trick.

jap·er·y (jāp′ẽr-i), *n.* [*pl.* JAPERIES (-iz)], [see JAPE], [Archaic], 1. japing; joking; trickery. 2. ribaldry.

Ja·pheth (jā′fith), *n.* [L.; Gr. *Iapheth;* Heb. *yepheth*, lit., enlargement], in the *Bible*, the youngest of Noah's three sons: Gen. 5:32.

Ja·phet·ic (jə-fet′ik), *adj.* 1. of or from Japheth. 2. formerly, in *linguistics*, Indo-European: distinguished from *Hamitic* and *Semitic.*

ja·pon·i·ca (jə-pon′i-kə), *n.* [Mod. L., of Japan < Fr. *Japon*, Japan: used as n. through mistaken understanding of use as adj. in scientific names of plants originating in Japan], the Japanese quince, camellia, or any of several other unrelated plants.

Jap·o·nism (jap′ə-niz'm), *n.* [Fr. *Japon*, Japan; + *-ism*], any characteristic of the Japanese; Japanese idiom, principle of art, mannerism, etc.

Ja·pu·ra (zhä′po͞o-rä′), *n.* a river of southern Colombia and northwestern Brazil, flowing into the Amazon: length, 1,750 mi.

Ja·ques (jā′kwēz, jā′kwiz), *n.* [OFr.; see JACK (nick-name)], a character in Shakespeare's *As You Like It*, a cynically philosophic nobleman who is one of the attendants of the exiled duke.

jar (jär), *v.i.* [JARRED (järd), JARRING], [ME. *jarren* < OFr. borrowing of Gmc. echoic base seen in AS. *gierran*, MHG. *garren*, to creak, grate, grunt; earlier forms like *charre* suggest confusion with the base of *ajar, chore*, etc.], 1. to make a harsh sound or a discord; grate. 2. to have a harsh, irritating effect (*on* one). 3. to shake or vibrate from a sudden impact. 4. to clash; conflict; quarrel. *v.t.* 1. to make vibrate or shake by sudden impact. 2. to cause to give a harsh, grating sound or discord. 3. to jolt or shock. *n.* 1. a harsh, grating sound; discord. 2. a vibration due to a sudden impact. 3. a jolt or shock. 4. a clash; conflict; petty quarrel.

jar (jär), *n.* [Fr. *jarre;* Sp. *jarra* < Ar. *jarrah*, earthen water container], 1. a container made of glass, stone, or earthenware, usually cylindrical, with a large opening and no spout: some jars have handles. 2. as much as a jar will hold.

jar (jär), *n.* [see AJAR], a turn or turning: now used only in the phrase, *on the jar*, ajar; partially open.

jar·di·niere (jär′d'n-êr′; Fr. zhȧr′dē′nyâr′), *n.* [Fr., a flower stand, orig. fem. of *jardinier*, gardener < *jardin*, a garden], an ornamental bowl, pot, or stand for flowers or plants.

Jar·ed (jâr′id), [L.; Gr. *Iared;* Heb. *yeredh*, lit., descent], a masculine name.

jar·gon (jär′gən, jär′gon), *n.* [ME. *jargoun;* OFr. *jargon, gergon*, a chattering (of birds) < Gmc. base **jarg-*, **garg-*, as in AS. *gierran* (see JAR, *v.*); an IE. echoic base **gher-* is seen in Sans. *gharghara-h*, gurgling (see GARGLE)], 1. incoherent speech; gibberish. 2. a language or dialect that is incomprehensible, outlandish, etc. to one. 3. a mixed or hybrid language or dialect. 4. the specialized vocabulary and idioms of those in the same work, way of life, etc., as journalism or social work: somewhat derogatory term, implying unintelligibility: see **slang.** *v.i.* to talk jargon; talk in an unintelligible way. —*SYN.* see **dialect.**

jar·gon (jär′gon), *n.* [Fr.; It. *giargone;* Ar. *zarqūn;* Per. *zargūn;* see ZIRCON], a colorless or smoky variety of zircon: also **jargoon.**

jar·go·nelle, jar·go·nel (jär′gə-nel′), *n.* [Fr. *jargonelle*, dim. of *jargon*, zircon: so called from the hardness of the fruit], an early harvest pear.

jar·gon·ize (jär′gən-īz′), *v.i.* [JARGONIZED (-īzd′), JARGONIZING], to talk or write in jargon. *v.t.* to express in jargon; make jargon of.

jar·goon (jär-go͞on′), *n.* jargon (zircon).

jarl (yärl), *n.* [ON.; parallel with AS. *eorl* (see EARL, *n.*); IE. base **er-*, **or-*, eagle, hence man of eminence], an ancient Scandinavian chieftain or nobleman.

jar·o·vize (yär′ə-vīz′), *v.t.* [JAROVIZED (-vīzd′), JAROVIZING], [Russ. *yar'*, spring grain], to bring about early maturing of (a plant) by retarding the germination of the seed, as through exposure to low temperature and darkness for a time; vernalize: also spelled **yarovize.**

Jar·row (jar′ō), *n.* a city in northeastern England, on the Tyne River: pop., 29,000.

jar·vey (jär′vi), *n.* [*pl.* JARVEYS (-viz)], [< surname *Jarvis*], [British Colloq.], a driver of a hackney coach.

Jar·vis (jär′vis), [older *Gervas* < Norm. var. of Fr. *Gervais;* LL. *Gervasius*, name of an early Christian saint and martyr], a masculine name: variant, *Jervis.*

Jas., James.

jas·mine, jas·min (jas′min, jaz′min), *n.* [Fr. *jasmin;* Ar. *yās(a)mīn;* Per. *yāsamīn*], 1. a tropical and subtropical shrub of the olive family, with fragrant flowers of yellow, red, or white: also called *jessamine.* 2. any of several other similar plants with fragrant flowers, as cape jasmine, yellow jasmine, etc.

Ja·son (jā′s'n), [L. *Iāson;* Gr. *Iāson*, lit., healer], a masculine name. *n.* in *Greek legend*, a prince who led the Argonauts, and, with Medea's help, got the Golden Fleece in spite of the fire-breathing bulls and the dragon guarding it.

Jas·per (jas′pẽr), [OFr. *Jaspar;* said to be < Per. base meaning, lit., "lord of the treasure"], a masculine name: equivalents, Fr. *Gaspard*, G. *Kaspar*, Sp. *Gaspar.*

jas·per (jas′pẽr), *n.* [ME. *jaspe, jaspre;* OFr. *jaspe, jaspre;* L. *iaspis;* Gr. *iaspis*, a green precious stone], 1. an opaque variety of colored quartz, usually reddish, yellow, or brown. 2. in the *Bible*, probably a green ornamental stone.

Jas·per Park (jas′pẽr), a Canadian national park and

game preserve in western Alberta: area, 4,200 sq. mi.
Jas·sy (yä'si), *n.* a city in the northeastern part of Romania: pop., 121,000: Romanian name, *Iași*: also spelled **Yassy.**
Jat (jät, jôt), *n.* [Hind.], a member of a large race or caste in India, living largely in the Punjab district.
JATO, jato (jā'tō), jet-assisted take-off.
jaun·dice (jôn'dis, jän'dis), *n.* [ME. *jaundis, jandis;* OFr. *jaunisse* < *jaune, jalne,* yellow; L. *galbinus,* greenish yellow < *galbus,* yellow], 1. a diseased condition in which the eyeballs, the skin, and the urine become abnormally yellow, caused by the presence of bile pigments in the blood. 2. a soured state of mind, caused by jealousy, envy, etc., in which judgment is distorted. *v.t.* [JAUNDICED (-dist), JAUNDICING], 1. to cause to have jaundice. 2. to make soured or prejudiced through jealousy, envy, etc.
jaunt (jônt, jänt), *v.i.* [as if from OFr. *jante,* inner rim of a wheel], to take a short trip for pleasure. *n.* a short trip for pleasure; excursion. —*SYN.* see **trip.**
jaun·ti·ly (jôn't'l-i, jän't'l-i), *adv.* in a jaunty manner.
jaun·ti·ness (jôn'ti-nis, jän'ti-nis), *n.* the quality or state of being jaunty.
jaunting car, a light, topless, two-wheeled cart used in Ireland, with seats on both sides, back to back.
jaun·ty (jôn'ti, jän'ti), *adj.* [JAUNTIER (-ti-ẽr), JAUNTIEST (-ti-ist)], [earlier *janty, genty* < Fr. *gentil,* genteel], 1. stylish; chic. 2. easy and careless; gay and swaggering; sprightly; perky.
Jau·rès, Jean Lé·on (zhän lā'ōn' zhô'res'), 1859–1914; French Socialist leader and writer; assassinated.
Jav., Javanese.
Ja·va (jä'və, jav'ə), *n.* 1. a large island of Indonesia, between the Malay Peninsula and Australia: area, 48,504 sq. mi.; pop., with Madura, 56,800,000. 2. any of a breed of chickens with black or mottled black plumage. 3. a kind of coffee grown in Java and the islands near it. 4. [often j-], [Slang], any coffee.
Java cotton, kapok.
Java man, a type of primitive man known from fossil remains found in Java in 1891: also called *Pithecanthropus* (*erectus*).
Jav·a·nese (jav'ə-nēz'), *adj.* of Java, its people, their language, or culture. *n.* 1. [*pl.* JAVANESE], a native of Java, especially a member of a group of tribes occupying the main part of Java. 2. the Malay language of these tribes. 3. a group of Malayo-Polynesian languages spoken in Java, Bali, and near-by islands. Abbreviated **Jav.**
Ja·va·ry, Ja·va·rí (zhä'vä-rē'), *n.* a river flowing between northeastern Peru and Brazil into the Amazon: length, 650 mi.
Java Sea, a part of the Pacific, between Java and Borneo.
Java sparrow, a white, pink, and gray weaverbird resembling a finch: it is used as a cage bird.
Ja·vel (or **Ja·velle**) **water** (zhə-vel'), a solution of sodium hypochlorite, NaOCl, in water, used as a bleaching agent or disinfectant.
jave·lin (jav'lin, jav'ə-lin), *n.* [Fr. *javeline,* fem. dim. < *javelot,* a spear; akin to AS. *gafeluc,* ON. *gaflac,* a light spear; ult. < Celt. **gablach;* IE. base **ghabholo,* fork of a twig, fork, as in AS. *geafol,* G. *gabel,* a fork], 1. a light spear for throwing. 2. a pointed wooden shaft, about 8 1/2 feet long, thrown for distance in a contest.
jaw (jô), *n.* [ME. *jowe;* OFr. *joue,* cheek < L. *gabata,* dish; form influenced by *jowl;* for the sense development see CHEEK], 1. either of the two bones or bony parts that hold the teeth and frame the mouth: the lower jaw is called the *mandible,* the upper the *maxilla.* 2. either of two mechanical parts that open and close to grasp or crush something, as in a monkey wrench or vise. 3. *pl.* the entrance of (a canyon, valley, etc.). 4. [Slang], talk; especially, offensive or abusive talk. *v.i.* [Slang], to talk. *v.t.* [Slang], to scold or reprove.
jaw·bone (jô'bōn'), *n.* 1. a bone of a jaw. 2. either of the two bones of the lower jaw.
jaw·break·er (jô'brāk'ẽr), *n.* [Slang], 1. a word that is hard to pronounce. 2. a kind of hard candy.
Jax·ar·tes (jak-sär'tēz), *n.* Syr Darya, a river in Asia: the ancient name.
jay (jā), *n.* [ME.; OFr. *gai;* LL. *gaius,* a jay, prob. echoic, but sp. influenced by the L. proper name *Gaius*], 1. any of several birds of the crow family. 2. a bluejay. 3. [Slang], a stupid, foolish, or talkative person.
Jay, John (jā), 1745–1829; American jurist and statesman; first chief justice, United States Supreme Court (1789–1795).
jay·hawk·er (jā'hôk'ẽr), *n.* [prob. < *jayhawk,* variety of hawk noted for its ferocity; prob. of Australian origin], 1. [Slang], an abolitionist guerrilla soldier of Missouri and Kansas in Civil War days. 2. [J-], [Colloq.], a native or inhabitant of Kansas.
jay·walk (jā'wôk'), *v.i.* [*jay,* stupid person + *walk*], [Colloq.], to walk in or across a street without regard to traffic rules and signals.
jazz (jaz), *n.* [< Creole patois *jass,* sexual term applied to the Congo dances (New Orleans); present use from Chicago, c. 1914, but ? from earlier similar use in the vice district of New Orleans], 1. a kind of music, originally improvised but now also arranged, characterized by syncopation, rubato, heavily accented 4/4 time, dissonances, melodic variations, and unusual tonal effects on the saxophone, clarinet, trumpet, trombone, etc.: it originated among New Orleans Negro musicians: see also **swing.** 2. any popular dance music. 3. [Slang], a quality reminiscent of jazz music; lively spirit. *adj.* of, in, or like jazz. *v.t.* to play or arrange as jazz.
jazz up, [Slang], to fill with jazz qualities; enliven.
jazz·i·ly (jaz''l-i), *adv.* in a jazzy manner.
jazz·y (jaz'i), *adj.* 1. characterized by the qualities of jazz music. 2. [Slang], lively.
J.C., 1. Jesus Christ. 2. Julius Caesar. 3. jurisconsult.
J.C.D., *Juris Civilis Doctor,* [L.], Doctor of Civil Law.
jct., junction.
J.D., *Jurum Doctor,* [L.], Doctor of Laws.
Je., June.
jeal·ous (jel'əs), *adj.* [ME. *jelous, gelos;* OFr. *gelos;* LL. *zelosus;* see ZEAL], 1. watchful or solicitous in guarding or keeping: as, a man is *jealous* of his rights. 2. resentfully suspicious of a rival or a rival's influence: as, her husband was *jealous* of the other man. 3. resulting from such a feeling: as, a *jealous* rage. 4. demanding exclusive loyalty: as, the Lord is a *jealous* God. 5. resentfully envious.
jeal·ous·y (jel'əs-i), *n.* [*pl.* JEALOUSIES (-iz)], [ME. *jalousie, gelousy;* OFr. *gelosie, jalousie* < *gelos;* see JEALOUS], 1. the quality of being jealous; jealous state of mind or feeling. 2. an instance of this.
Jean (jēn), 1. a masculine name: see **John.** 2. a feminine name: see **Joanna.**
jean (jēn, jān), *n.* [< OFr. *Janne;* LL. *Janua;* L. *Genua,* Genoa], 1. a durable cotton cloth in a twill weave, used for work clothes. 2. *pl.* trousers or overalls of this material.
Jeanne (jēn), a feminine name: diminutive, *Jeannette:* see **Joanna.**
Jean·nette (jə-net'), a feminine name: diminutives, *Nettie, Netty:* see **Jeanne.**
Jeans, Sir James Hop·wood (hop'wood' jēnz), 1877–1946; English mathematician, astronomer, physicist, and writer.
Jeb·el Mu·sa (jeb'əl mōō'sȧ), a mountain in northern Morocco, opposite Gibraltar: height, 2,800 ft.
Jed·da (jed'ə), *n.* Jidda.
jee (jē), *interj., n., v.t. & v.i.* gee.
jeep (jēp), *n.* [orig. military slang < sound made by droll little animal (Eugene the Jeep) with extraordinary powers, in comic strip by E. C. Segar (1894–1938); supposedly suggested by *G.P., General Purpose* Car], 1. a small, rugged automotive vehicle with a 1/4-ton capacity and a four-wheel drive: first used by U.S. armed forces in World War II: also called *peep.* 2. a similar vehicle for civilian use. 3. in many military units, a larger vehicle with a 3/4-ton capacity, used as a reconnaissance and command car: distinguished from *peep.*
jeer (jêr), *v.i. & v.t.* [? altered form of *cheer*], to make fun of (a person or thing) in a rude, sarcastic manner; mock; taunt; scoff (at). *n.* a jeering remark; sarcastic or derisive comment; gibe. —*SYN.* see **scoff.**
jeer·ing·ly (jêr'iŋ-li), *adv.* in a jeering manner; derisively.
jeers (jêrz), *n.pl.* [? altered form of *gears*], the tackle by which the lower yards of a sailing vessel are hoisted or lowered.
Jef·fer·son, Thomas (jef'ẽr-s'n), 1743–1826; American statesman; third president of the United States (1801–1809); drew up the Declaration of Independence.
Jefferson City, the capital of Missouri, on the Missouri River: pop., 28,000.
Jef·fer·so·ni·an (jef'ẽr-sō'ni-ən), *adj.* 1. of or characteristic of Thomas Jefferson. 2. of or like his ideas and principles; democratic. *n.* a follower of Thomas Jefferson; believer in Jefferson's democratic ideas.
Jeff·rey (jef'ri), a masculine name: diminutive, *Jeff:* see **Geoffrey.**
Jef·fries, Jim (jim jef'riz), (*James J. Jeffries*), 1875–1953; American prize fighter; heavyweight champion (1899–1905).
je·had (ji-häd'), *n.* a jihad.
Je·hol (jə-hol', re-hō'), *n.* 1. a former province of northeastern China. 2. a city in northeastern China: pop., 60,000: also called *Chengteh.*
Je·hosh·a·phat (ji-hosh'ə-fat', ji-hos'ə-fat'), *n.* [Heb. *yehōshāphāt,* lit., God has judged], in the *Bible,* a king of Judah in the 9th century B.C., noted for his righteousness: II Chron. 17 ff.
Je·ho·vah (ji-hō'və), *n.* [modern transliteration of the Heb. sacred name for God, the so-called tetragrammaton, YHWH; the vowels appear through arbitrary transference of the vowel points of *adōnāi,* my Lord; see YAHWEH], God; (the) Lord.
Jehovah's Witnesses, a Christian sect founded by Charles T. Russell (1852–1916) and led after 1916 by

Joseph F. ("Judge") Rutherford (1869–1942): its members are opposed to war and refuse to accept the authority of any government in matters of religious conscience: formerly called *International Bible Students Association* or *Russellites*.

Je·ho·vic (ji-hō'vik), *adj.* of Jehovah.

Je·ho·vist (ji-hō'vist), *n.* 1. a person holding the opinion that the correct transliteration of the Hebrew sacred name for God is *Jehovah:* see **Jehovah.** 2. the author of those parts of the Old Testament in which *Jehovah* (*Yahweh*) is used as the name of God; Yahwist: cf. **Elohist.**

Je·ho·vis·tic (jē'hō-vis'tik), *adj.* 1. of a Jehovist or his views. 2. using *Jehovah* (*Yahweh*) as the name of God; Yahwistic.

Je·hu (jē'hū), *n.* [Heb.], 1. in the *Bible*, a king of Israel in the 9th century B.C., described as a furious charioteer: II Kings 9:6 & 20; hence, 2. [j-], a fast, reckless driver or coachman: humorous term.

je·june (ji-jōōn'), *adj.* [L. *jejunus*, empty, dry, barren], 1. not nourishing; barren. 2. not satisfying; not interesting; dull and flat; as, a *jejune* story.

je·ju·nec·to·my (ji'jōō-nek'tə-mi), *n.* [*jejun*um + *-ectomy*], the surgical removal of all or part of the jejunum.

je·ju·num (ji-jōō'nəm), *n.* [Mod. L. < L. *jejunus;* see JEJUNE], the middle part of the small intestine, between the duodenum and the ileum: so named because formerly thought to be empty after death.

Je·kyll, Dr. (jē'k'l, jek''l), a doctor in Robert Louis Stevenson's story *Dr. Jekyll and Mr. Hyde*, who discovers drugs that enable him to change back and forth between his own pleasant personality and a vicious, brutal one named Mr. Hyde.

jell (jel), *v.i. & v.t.* [< *jelly*], [Colloq.], 1. to become or cause to become jelly. 2. to take or cause to take definite form; crystallize: as, our plans haven't *jelled* yet. *n.* [Colloq.], jelly.

Jel·li·coe, John Rush·worth (rush'wẽrth jel'i-kō'), first Earl Jellicoe, 1859–1935; English admiral.

jel·lied (jel'id), *adj.* [pp. of *jelly*], 1. changed into jelly. 2. served in or with jelly. 3. coated with jelly.

jel·li·fy (jel'ə-fī'), *v.t. & v.i.* [JELLIFIED (-fīd'), JELLIFYING], to change into jelly.

jel·ly (jel'i), *n.* [*pl.* JELLIES (-iz)], [ME. *gely, gelē;* OFr. *gelée*, a frost, jelly, properly fem. pp. of *geler* < L. *gelare*, to freeze], 1. a soft, resilient, partially transparent, semisolid, gelatinous food resulting from the cooling of fruit juice boiled with sugar, or of meat juice cooked down. 2. any substance like this; gelatinous substance. *v.t.* [JELLIED (-id), JELLYING], 1. to make into jelly. 2. to put jelly on. *v.i.* to become jelly.

jel·ly·bean (jel'i-bēn'), *n.* a small, gelatinous candy shaped like a bean.

jel·ly·fish (jel'i-fish'), *n.* [*pl.* JELLYFISH, JELLYFISHES (-iz); see FISH], 1. any of a number of related sea animals with a body made up largely of jellylike substance and shaped like an umbrella; medusa: it has long, hanging tentacles with stinging hairs on them. 2. [Colloq.], a weak-willed person.

JELLYFISH (16 in. long)

jel·ly·roll (jel'i-rōl'), *n.* a thin sheet of sponge cake spread with jelly and rolled so as to form layers.

jem·a·dar (jem'ə-där'), *n.* [Hind. < Per. *jemā'at*, body of men + *dar*, one who holds], formerly, a native officer in the army of India, second in rank in a sepoy company.

Je·mappes (zhə-màp'), *n.* a city in western Belgium: pop., 15,000.

Je·mi·ma (jə-mī'mə), [Heb. *yemīmāh*, lit., a dove], a feminine name.

jem·my (jem'i), *n.* [*pl.* JEMMIES (-iz)], [< dim. of *James*], 1. a jimmy. 2. [Obs.], a sort of riding boot. 3. [British Slang], a sheep's head used as food. *v.t.* [JEMMIED (-id), JEMMYING], to jimmy.

Je·na (yā'nä), *n.* city in Thuringia, Germany: pop., 58,000: site of a battle (1806) in which Prussian troops were routed by Napoleon.

‡**je ne sais quoi** (zhə nə sā' kwà'), [Fr.], 1. I know not what; hence, 2. a thing hard to describe or express.

Jenghiz Khan see **Genghis Khan.**

Jen·ner, Edward (jen'ẽr), 1749–1823; English physician; introduced vaccination.

Jenner, Sir **William,** 1815–1898; English physician.

jen·net (jen'it), *n.* [OFr. *genette;* Sp. *jinete*, horseman, mounted soldier; prob. < Ar. *Zenāta*, a tribe of Barbary], 1. any of a breed of small Spanish horses. 2. a female donkey.

Jen·ni·fer (jen'i-fẽr), [adaptation of *Winifred*], a feminine name.

Jen·ny (jen'i), a feminine name: see **Jane.**

jen·ny (jen'i), *n.* [*pl.* JENNIES (-iz)], [< *Jenny*], 1. a spinning machine with a number of spindles; spinning jenny. 2. the female of some animals: as, a *jenny* wren.

jeop·ard (jep'ẽrd), *v.t.* to jeopardize.

jeop·ard·ize (jep'ẽr-dīz'), *v.t.* [JEOPARDIZED (-dīzd'), JEOPARDIZING], to put in jeopardy; risk loss, damage, or failure of; endanger.

jeop·ard·y (jep'ẽr-di), *n.* [*pl.* JEOPARDIES (-diz)], [ME. *juperdi, jeuparti;* OFr. *ieu parti*, lit., a divided game, game with even chances; LL. *jocus partitus*, an even chance, an alternative < L. *jocus*, a joke, play, game + pp. of *partire*, to divide], 1. risk; danger; peril. 2. in *criminal law*, exposure to conviction; situation of an accused person when being tried. —*SYN.* see **danger.**

Jeph·thah (jef'thə, jep'thə), *n.* [Heb.], in the *Bible*, the judge who killed his only daughter because he had vowed that if he won in battle he would sacrifice to God whatever he first met coming from his house on his return, and this turned out to be his daughter: Judg. 11:30–40.

je·quir·i·ty (ji-kwir'ə-ti), *n.* [Fr. *jéquirity* < Tupi-Guarani], 1. the poisonous, red and black seed of the Indian licorice plant, used for beads, as a weight, and in medicine. 2. the plant it grows on. Also **jequirity bean.**

Jer., Jeremiah.

jer·bo·a (jẽr-bō'ə), *n.* [Mod. L. < Ar. *yarbū*, an oblique, descending muscle: the animal is so called because of the strong muscles of its hind legs], a small, leaping rodent of northern Africa and Asia, with long hind legs.

JERBOA (15 in. long, including tail)

je·reed (je-rēd'), *n.* [Ar. *jerīd, jarīd*, rod, shaft, javelin], 1. a blunted javelin used by Turks, Arabs, etc. in warlike games. 2. a mock battle with such javelins. Also spelled **jerid, jerreed, jerrid.**

jer·e·mi·ad (jer'ə-mī'əd), *n.* [Fr. *jérémiade* < *Jérémie*, Jeremiah], a lamentation or tale of woe: in allusion to the *Lamentations of Jeremiah* in the Bible.

Jer·e·mi·ah (jer'ə-mī'ə), [LL. *Jeremias;* Heb. *yirmeyāhū*, lit., the Lord loosens (i.e., from the womb)], a masculine name: diminutive, *Jerry;* variant, *Jeremy.* *n.* in the *Bible*, 1. a Hebrew prophet of the 6th and 7th centuries B.C. 2. a book of the Old Testament containing his prophecies. Abbreviated **Jer.**

Jer·e·mi·as (jer'ə-mī'əs), *n.* Jeremiah: form used in the Douay Bible.

Jer·e·my (jer'ə-mi), a masculine name: see **Jeremiah.**

Je·rez (he-reth'), *n.* a city in southwestern Spain: noted for the making of sherry: pop., 93,000 (est. 1946): former name, *Xeres;* also **Jerez de la Frontera.**

Jerez de la Fron·te·ra (*th*e lä frôn-te'rä), Jerez.

Jer·i·cho (jer'ə-kō'), *n.* a village in western Jordan: site of an ancient city whose walls were miraculously destroyed when trumpets were sounded: Josh. 6.

je·rid (je-rēd'), *n.* a jereed.

Je·ri·tza, Ma·ri·a (mä-rē'ä ye'ri-tsä'), 1887?– ; Austrian operatic soprano.

jerk (jũrk), *v.t.* [var. of archaic *yerk* < ?], 1. to pull at, twist, push, thrust, or throw with a sudden, sharp movement. 2. to utter in quick, sharp ejaculations or gasps (with *out*). *v.i.* 1. to move with a jerk or in jerks. 2. to twitch. *n.* 1. a sharp, abrupt movement; quick pull, twist, push, etc. 2. a sudden muscular contraction caused by a reflex action. 3. [Slang], a person regarded as stupid, dull, eccentric, etc.

jerk (jũrk), *v.t.* [altered < Sp. *charqui*, dried meat < Peruv. *ccharqui*, meat dried in strips], to preserve (meat) by slicing it into strips and drying these in the sun or over a fire. *n.* jerked meat, especially beef.

jerk·i·ly (jũr'k'l-i), *adv.* in a jerky manner; with abrupt starts and stops.

jer·kin (jũr'kin), *n.* [? < OFr. *Joire, Jour*, familiar form of *George* + *-kin*, dim. suffix; cf. OFr. *georget* (< *George*), *jergot*, doublet], 1. a short, close-fitting coat or jacket, often sleeveless, worn in the 16th and 17th centuries. 2. a short, sleeveless vest worn by women and girls.

jerk·i·ness (jũr'ki-nis), *n.* the quality of moving jerkily.

jerk·wa·ter (jũrk'wô'tẽr, jũrk'wät'ẽr), *n.* [*jerk, v.*, to pull + *water*], a train on an early branch railroad. *adj.* [Colloq.], small, unimportant, etc.: as, a *jerkwater* town.

jerk·y (jũr′ki), ***adj.*** [JERKIER (-ki-ẽr), JERKIEST (-ki-ist)], 1. characterized by jerks; making sudden starts and stops. 2. making convulsive or spasmodic movements.

jerk·y (jũr′ki), ***n.*** [< Sp. *charqui;* see JERK (to preserve)], jerked beef.

Jer·o·bo·am (jer′ə-bō′əm), ***n.*** [Heb. *yārobh'ām,* lit., prob., the people increases], in the *Bible,* 1. the first king of the northern kingdom, Israel, after the death of Solomon and the division into the kingdoms of Israel and Judah: I Kings 11:26–14:20. 2. a rich king of Israel: II Kings 14:23–29. 3. [often j-], a large bottle for champagne, usually one holding about .7 gallon.

Je·rome (jə-rōm′; *chiefly* Brit. jer′əm), [Fr. *Jérôme;* L. *Hieronymus;* Gr. *Hierōnymos* < *hieros,* holy + *onyma,* name], a masculine name: diminutive, *Jerry;* equivalents, L. *Hieronymus,* It. *Geronimo,* Sp. *Jeronimo.*

Je·rome, Saint (jə-rōm′, jer′əm), (*Eusebius Hieronymus*), 340?–420 A.D.; monk and church scholar; author of the Vulgate: his day is September 30.

jer·reed, jer·rid (je-rēd′), ***n.*** a jereed.

Jer·ry (jer′i), ***n.*** [*pl.* JERRIES (-iz)], [< *German*], [Chiefly British Slang], a German, especially a German soldier.

jer·ry-built (jer′i-bilt′), ***adj.*** [originated in Liverpool, England, c. 1860; prob. < name *Jerry,* reinforced by nautical term *jury*], built poorly, of cheap materials.

Jer·sey (jũr′zi), ***n.*** 1. one of the Channel Islands off the French coast: area, 45 sq. mi.; pop., 55,000. 2. [*pl.* JERSEYS (-ziz)], any of a breed of small, reddish-brown dairy cattle, originally from Jersey: its milk has a high butterfat content.

jer·sey (jũr′zi), ***n.*** [*pl.* JERSEYS (-ziz)], [< *Jersey,* the Channel island], 1. a soft, elastic, knitted cloth of wool, cotton, silk, or rayon. 2. a close fitting pull-on sweater or shirt worn by athletes, sailors, etc. 3. any close-fitting, knitted upper garment.

Jersey City, a seaport of northeastern New Jersey, across the Hudson from New York City: pop., 276,000.

Je·ru·sa·lem (jə-ro͞o′sə-ləm), ***n.*** a city divided between Israel and Jordan: pop., 231,000: the Israeli part is the capital of Israel, pop., 156,000: a holy city, it has been at various times under the control of the Hebrews, Romans, Persians, Arabs, Crusaders, Turks, and British.

Jerusalem artichoke, [altered < It. *girasole,* sunflower < L. *girare,* to turn + *sol,* sun], 1. a kind of sunflower with coarse hairy leaves, small flowers, and potatolike tubers used as a vegetable. 2. such a tuber.

Jer·vis (jũr′vis; Brit. jär′vis), a masculine name: see **Jarvis.**

Jes·per·sen, Jens Ot·to Har·ry (yens ot′ō hä′ri yes′pẽr-s'n), 1860–1943; Danish linguist.

jess (jes), ***n.*** [ME. *ges;* OFr. *gies, ges, gets,* pl.; see JET (a gush): so called from its use in letting a hawk fly], a strap for fastening around a falcon's leg, with a ring at one end for attaching a leash. ***v.t.*** to fasten a jess on.

Jes·sa·mine (jes′ə-min), [< MFr. *jessemin;* see JASMINE], a feminine name. ***n.*** [j-], jasmine.

Jes·se (jes′i), [L.; Gr. *Iessai;* Heb. *yīshay;* meaning ?], a masculine name: diminutive, *Jess.* ***n.*** in the *Bible,* the father of David: I Sam. 16.

Jes·si·ca (jes′i-kə), [see JESSE], a feminine name.

Jes·sie (jes′i), a feminine name: variant of **Jessica.**

jest (jest), ***n.*** [ME. *geste, jeste;* OFr. *geste,* an exploit, tale of exploits; L. *gesta,* neut. pl. pp. of *gerere,* to perform, carry out], 1. a mocking or bantering remark; jibe; taunt. 2. a joke; witticism. 3. joking; fun; ridicule. 4. something to be laughed at or joked about. 5. [Obs.], *a)* a notable deed. *b)* a story of exploits. *c)* an unfounded tale. ***v.i.*** 1. to jeer; mock; banter. 2. to be playful in speech and actions; joke. —***SYN.*** see **joke.**

jest·er (jes′tẽr), ***n.*** a person who jests; especially, a professional fool employed by a ruler in the Middle Ages to amuse him with antics, tricks, and jokes.

Je·su (jē′zū, jē′zo͞o, jē′sū, jē′so͞o), ***n.*** [Poetic], Jesus.

Jes·u·it (jezh′o͞o-it, jez′ū-it), ***n.*** [Fr. *Jésuite* < Mod. L. *Jesuita* < L. *Iesus, Jesus,* Jesus; + *-ite, -it*], 1. a member of the Society of Jesus, a Roman Catholic religious order founded by Ignatius Loyola in 1534: abbreviated **S.J.** 2. [j-], a crafty schemer; cunning dissembler; casuist: hostile term, as used by anti-Jesuits. ***adj.*** 1. of the Jesuits. 2. [j-], jesuitic.

Jes·u·it·ic (jezh′o͞o-it′ik, jez′ū-it′ik), ***adj.*** 1. of or like the Jesuits or their doctrines, practices, etc. 2. [j-], crafty; cunning; equivocal: hostile term, as used by anti-Jesuits.

Jes·u·it·i·cal (jezh′o͞o-it′i-k'l, jez′ū-it′i-k'l), ***adj.*** 1. Jesuitic. 2. [j-], jesuitic.

Jes·u·it·ism (jezh′o͞o-it-iz'm, jez′ū-it-iz'm), ***n.*** 1. the teachings or practice of the Jesuits. 2. [j-], craftiness; duplicity; intrigue: hostile term, as used by anti-Jesuits.

Jes·u·it·ry (jezh′o͞o-it-ri, jez′ū-it-ri), ***n.*** Jesuitism.

Je·sus (jē′zəs), [L. *Iesus;* Gr. *Iēsous;* Heb. *yēshū'a,* contr. of *yĕhōshu'a,* help of Jehovah < *yāh,* Jehovah + *hōshīa,* to help], a masculine name. ***n.*** 1. the founder of the Christian religion: 4? B.C.–29? A.D. (the birth date is the result of later revision of the calendar): often **Jesus Christ, Jesus of Nazareth:** see also **Christ.** 2. the author of *Ecclesiasticus,* one of the books of the Apocrypha.

jet (jet), ***v.t. & v.i.*** [JETTED (-id), JETTING], [Fr. *jeter;* LL. *jectare;* L. *jactare,* to throw < *jacere,* to throw], to spout, gush, or shoot out in a stream, as liquid or gas. ***n.*** [ME. *jet, jette, get;* OFr. *get, giet, ject,* a throw, cast, gush, spurt < L. *jactus,* a throw, cast, properly pp. of *jacere,* to throw], 1. a stream of water or other liquid suddenly emitted, as from a spout; gush. 2. a similar stream of gas. 3. a spout or nozzle for emitting a stream of water or gas. 4. a jet-propelled airplane: also **jet (air)plane.** ***adj.*** jet-propelled.

jet (jet), ***n.*** [ME. *jete, geet;* OFr. *jaiet;* L. *gagates;* Gr. *gagatēs,* jet < *Gagas,* town and river of Lycia in Asia Minor], 1. a hard, black mineral like coal, a kind of lignite: used in jewelry when polished. 2. a lustrous black. ***adj.*** 1. made of jet. 2. black, like jet.

jet·black (jet′blak′), ***adj.*** glossy black, like jet.

jet-pro·pelled (jet′prə-peld′), ***adj.*** driven by jet propulsion.

jet propulsion, a method of propelling airplanes, boats, and bombs by causing gases to be emitted under pressure through a vent at the rear: abbreviated **JP** (no period).

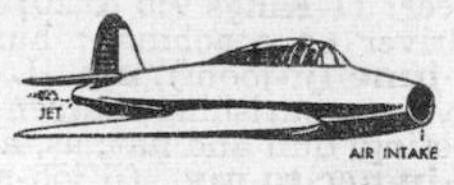

JET-PROPELLED PLANE

jet·sam (jet′səm), ***n.*** [OFr. *jetaison, getaison;* see JETTISON], 1. that part of the cargo thrown overboard to lighten a ship in danger: distinguished from *flotsam.* 2. such discarded cargo washed ashore. 3. discarded things.

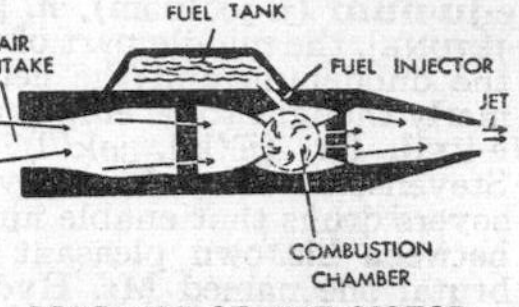

DIAGRAM OF JET MOTOR

jet stream, 1. a stream of very strong wind moving around either of the earth's poles, usually from west to east, at altitudes between 10,000 and 50,000 feet. 2. the stream of exhaust that trails behind a jet plane, rocket, etc.

jet·ti·son (jet′ə-s'n, jet′ə-z'n), ***n.*** [OFr. *getaison, gettaison,* a throwing, jetsam < L. *jactatio,* a throwing < *jactare,* to throw], 1. a throwing overboard of goods to lighten a ship, airplane, etc. in an emergency. 2. jetsam. ***v.t.*** 1. to throw (goods) overboard. 2. to throw (something) away as useless or a burden.

jet·ty (jet′i), ***n.*** [*pl.* JETTIES (-iz)], [ME. *jettey;* OFr. *jetée,* jetty, jutty; orig. pp. of *jeter;* see JET, *v.*], 1. a kind of wall built out into the water to restrain currents, protect a harbor or the end of a pier, etc. 2. a landing pier.

jet·ty (jet′i), ***adj.*** very black, like jet.

‡**jeu** (zhö), ***n.*** [*pl.* JEUX (zhö)], [Fr.], a game; diversion.

‡**jeu de mots** (zhö′də-mō′), [Fr.], a play on words; pun.

‡**jeu d'es·prit** (zhö′des′prē′), [Fr., lit., play of intellect], a witticism; clever turn of phrase.

‡**jeune fille** (zhön′fē′y'), [Fr.], a young girl.

‡**jeu·nesse do·rée** (zhë′nes′ dô′rā′), [Fr., gilded youth], rich, fashionable young people.

Jev·ons, William Stanley (jev′ənz), 1835–1882; English political economist and logician.

Jew (jo͞o), ***n.*** [ME. *Jewe, Jui, Gui;* OFr. *giu, jueu* < L. *Judaeus;* Gr. *Ioudaios;* Heb. *yehūdi,* citizen or subject of the tribe or kingdom of Judah; see JUDAH], 1. a person descended, or regarded as descended, from the ancient Hebrews of Biblical times. 2. a person whose religion is Judaism. ***adj.*** Jewish: in this sense used vulgarly, as by anti-Semites. ***v.t.*** [j-], [Colloq.], to get the better of in bargaining, as by sharp practices, or haggle with in order to get a lower price or a better bargain (usually with *down*): vulgar and offensive expression, in allusion to methods attributed to Jewish merchants by anti-Semites. See also **Hebrew.**

Jew-bait·ing (jo͞o′bā′tiŋ), ***n.*** persecution of Jews, as a manifestation of anti-Semitism.

jew·el (jo͞o′əl), ***n.*** [ME. *jewel, jouel, jowel;* OFr. *jouel, joel;* ML. **jocale* < L. *jocus,* a trifle, joke; see JOKE], 1. a valuable ornament, often set with gems. 2. a precious stone; gem. 3. any person or thing very dear to one. 4. a small gem or gemlike object used as one of the bearings in a watch. ***v.t.*** [JEWELED or JEWELLED (-əld), JEWELING or JEWELLING], to decorate or set with jewels.

jew·el·er, jew·el·ler (jo͞o′əl-ẽr), ***n.*** [ME. *jueler;* OFr. *joieleor* < *joel, jouel;* see JEWEL], a person who makes, deals in, or repairs jewelry, watches, etc.

jew·el·ler·y (jo͞o′əl-ri), ***n.*** jewelry: British spelling.

jew·el·ry (jo͞o′əl-ri), ***n.*** jewels collectively.

jew·el·weed (jo͞o′əl-wēd′), ***n.*** any of a number of related plants bearing yellow or orange-yellow flowers with three sepals and a spur, and seed pods that curl at the touch when ripe; touch-me-not.

Jew·ess (jo͞o′is), ***n.*** a Jewish woman or girl: often a patronizing or contemptuous term.

Jew·ett, Sarah Orne (ôrn jo͞o′it), 1849–1909; American short-story writer.

jew·fish (jo͞o′fish′), ***n.*** [*pl.* JEWFISH, JEWFISHES (-iz); see FISH], [?*Jew* + *fish*], 1. the giant black sea bass. 2. any of several species of large fish found in warm seas.

Jew·ish (jōō′ish), *adj.* of, belonging to, or characteristic of the Jews: abbreviated **Jew.** *n.* popularly, Yiddish.

Jewish calendar, a calendar used by the Jews in calculating Jewish history, holidays, etc., based on the lunar month and reckoned from 3761 B.C., the traditional date of the Creation.

Months of the Jewish Calendar

1. ***Tishri*** (30 days)	7. ***Nisan*** (30 days)
2. ***Cheshvan*** (29 or 30 days)	8. ***Iyar*** (29 days)
3. ***Kislev*** (29 or 30 days)	9. ***Sivan*** (30 days)
4. ***Tebet*** (29 days)	10. ***Tammuz*** (29 days)
5. ***Shebat*** (30 days)	11. ***Ab*** (30 days)
6. ***Adar*** (29 or 30 days)	12. ***Elul*** (29 days)

N.B. About once every three years (seven times in each nineteen years) an extra month, ***Veadar*** (29 days), falls between *Adar* and *Nisan*, as the Jewish year has only 354 days. The first month, *Tishri*, begins in late September or early October. Alternative names of the months are: for ***Tishri, Ethanim;*** for ***Cheshvan, Marcheshvan*** or ***Bul;*** for ***Nisan, Abib;*** for ***Iyar, Zif;*** for ***Veadar, Adar Sheni.*** The Jewish day is from sunset to sunset.

Jewish holidays, the holidays of the Jewish religion, including:
1. ***Rosh Hashana,*** New Year (*Tishri* 1, 2)
2. ***Yom Kippur,*** Day of Atonement (*Tishri* 10)
3. ***Sukkoth,*** Feast of Tabernacles (*Tishri* 15–22)
4. ***Simchath Torah,*** Rejoicing in the Law (*Tishri* 23)
5. ***Hanukkah,*** Feast of the Dedication, Festival of Lights (*Kislev* 25–*Tebet* 2)
6. ***Purim,*** Feast of Lots (*Adar* 14)
7. ***Pesach,*** the Passover (*Nisan* 15–22)
8. ***Lag b'Omer,*** 33d day from the 2d of Passover (*Iyar* 18)
9. ***Shabuoth,*** Feast of Weeks, Pentecost (*Sivan* 6, 7)
10. ***Tishah b'Ab,*** day of fasting (*Ab* 9), in commemoration of the destruction of the Temple.

Jewish National Autonomous Region, an autonomous region of the R.S.F.S.R., in far eastern Siberia north of the Amur River, set aside for Jewish colonization: area, 14,204 sq. mi.; pop., 114,000: also called *Birobijan.*

Jew·ry (jōō′ri), *n.* [*pl.* JEWRIES (-riz)], [ME. *jewerie;* OFr. *juerie* < *Jui, Giu;* see JEW], 1. a district inhabited only or mainly by Jews; ghetto. 2. the Jewish people; Jews collectively: as, American *Jewry.* 3. [Obs.], Judea.

jew's-harp, jews'-harp (jōōz′härp′), *n.* a small musical instrument made of metal, held between the teeth and played by plucking a projecting bent piece with the finger: it produces twanging tones.

JEW'S-HARP

Jez·e·bel (jez′ə-b'l), *n.* [Heb.], 1. in the *Bible,* the wicked woman who married Ahab, king of Israel: I Kings 16, 19; II Kings 9:7–10, 30–37. 2. any woman regarded as shameless, wicked, etc.

Jez·re·el, Plain of (jez′ri-əl, jez-rēl′), Esdraelon, a plain in northern Israel.

j.g., jg., junior grade: designation of the lower rank of lieutenant in the United States Navy.

Jhe·lum (jā′ləm), *n.* a river in southern Kashmir, flowing into the Chenab River: length, 450 mi.

JHS, Jesus: see **IHS.**

JHVH, JHWH, see **Tetragrammaton.**

jib (jib), *n.* [prob. < *gibbet*], the projecting arm of a crane; boom of a derrick.

jib (jib), *v.i. & v.t.* [JIBBED (jibd), JIBBING], [var. of former *gibe;* cf. Dan. *gibbe*], in *nautical usage,* to jibe; shift: also spelled **jibb.** *n.* [prob. < the *v.*, because the sail is "easily jibbed"], a triangular sail projecting ahead of the foremast: see **mainmast,** illus.

cut of one's jib, [prob. influenced by Fr. *guibre,* cutwater, figurehead], [Colloq.], one's appearance or way of dressing.

jib (jib), *v.i.* [JIBBED (jibd), JIBBING], [prob. < ME. *regibben, regiber,* to kick; OFr. *regibber* (Fr. *regimber*), to kick back, be obstinate < *giber,* to shake, shock < *gibet;* see GIBBET; form and meaning influenced by nautical *jib, jibe*], 1. to stop and refuse to go forward; balk. 2. to move backward or sideways instead of ahead. 3. to start or shy (*at* something). *n.* [prob. < *v.*], 1. a jibbing. 2. an animal that jibs, as a horse.

jib boom, a spar fixed to and extending beyond the bowsprit of a ship: the jib is attached to it.

jibe (jīb), *v.i.* [JIBED (jībd), JIBING], [< D. *gijpen,* to shift over (of sails); orig., to gasp for air], 1. to shift from one side of a ship to the other: said of a fore-and-aft sail or its boom when the course is changed in a following or quartering wind. 2. to change the course of a ship so that the sails shift thus; change tack without going about. 3. [Colloq.], to be in harmony, agreement, or accord: as, our views don't *jibe.* *v.t.* in *nautical usage,* to cause to jibe. *n.* 1. a shift of sail or boom from one side of a ship to another. 2. a change of course brought about by jibing. Also, in nautical senses, spelled **gibe, gybe.**

jibe (jīb), *v.i. & v.t.* [JIBED (jībd), JIBING], [var. of *gibe*], to jeer; scoff (at). *n.* a jeer; taunt. Also spelled **gibe.**

jib-head·ed (jib′hed′id), *adj.* 1. cut like a jib; triangular: said of fore-and-aft sails; hence, 2. rigged with sails (especially the mainsail) so cut.

Ji·bu·ti (jē-bōō′ti, jē′bōō′tē′), *n.* Djibouti, the capital of French Somaliland.

Jid·da (jid′ə), *n.* a city in Arabia, on the Red Sea, near Mecca: pop., 40,000: also spelled **Jedda.**

jiff (jif), *n.* [Colloq.], a jiffy.

jif·fy (jif′i), *n.* [*pl.* JIFFIES (-iz)], [early 18th-c. slang], [Colloq.], a very short time; instant: as, done in a *jiffy.*

jig (jig), *n.* [merging of two words ult. akin: *a*) OFr. *gigue* < OHG. **gigan* (G. dial. *geigen*), to move back and forth, whence OHG. *giga,* G. *geige,* fiddle; *b*) ON. base of Dan. *gig,* spinning top, Eng. *gig,* carriage, boat, top; base sense of both, "erratic movement"; IE. base **ĝhei-*, to yawn, split open, as also in Eng. *giggle;* cf. MLG. *geck,* of same origin, similar senses], 1. a fast, gay, springy sort of dance, usually in triple time. 2. the music for such a dance. 3. any of several kinds of fishhook, sometimes arranged in sets, having a spoonlike part that twirls in trolling so as to attract fish. 4. any of several mechanical devices operated in a jerky manner, as a sieve for separating ores, a pounding machine, or a drill. 5. a device, often with metal surfaces, used as a guide for a tool or as a template. *v.i. & v.t.* [JIGGED (jigd), JIGGING], [? < OFr. *giguer;* see the *n.*], 1. to dance or perform (a jig or in jig style). 2. to move jerkily and quickly up and down or to and fro. 3. to use a jig (on) in working or fishing.

the jig is up, [Slang], that ends it; all chances for a successful completion are gone: said of enterprises involving risk or danger.

jig·ger (jig′ẽr), *n.* [altered < *chigoe*], 1. a small tropical flea. 2. a mite larva or tick that burrows into the skin. See **chigoe, chigger.**

jig·ger (jig′ẽr), *n.* 1. a person who jigs. 2. a small cup or glass used to measure liquor, containing usually 1 1/2 fluid ounces. 3. the quantity of liquor in a jigger. 4. any thing, device, or contraption whose name does not occur to one; gadget. 5. in *billiards,* a support or bridge for the cue. 6. in *fishing,* a jig, or kind of hook. 7. in *golf,* a short club with an iron head and narrow face, used for approach shots: it is like a midiron. 8. in *mechanics,* any of several devices with a jerky motion in operation. 9. in *mining,* a jig, or kind of sieve. 10. in *nautical usage, a*) a small tackle. *b*) a small sail. *c*) a small boat with such a sail. *d*) a jigger mast. 11. in *printing,* a compositor's guide mark. 12. in *radio,* an oscillation transformer.

jigger mast, 1. a small mast in the stern of a ship. 2. the mast nearest the stern in a ship with four masts.

jig·gle (jig′'l), *v.t. & v.i.* [JIGGLED (-'ld), JIGGLING], [dim. or freq. of *jig, v.*], to move in a succession of quick, slight jerks; rock lightly. *n.* a jiggling movement.

jig·saw (jig′sô′), *n.* [*jig, v.* + *saw, n.*], a saw with a narrow blade set in a frame, used with a vertical motion for cutting along wavy or irregular lines, as in scroll work: also **jig saw.**

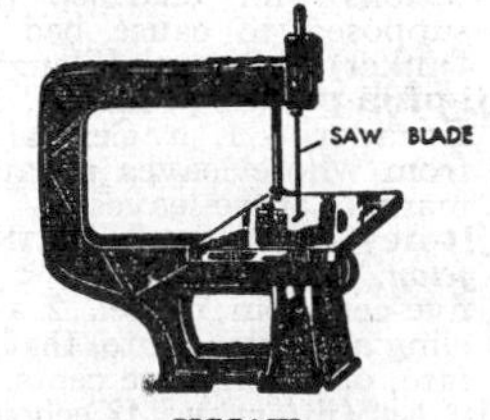

JIGSAW

jigsaw puzzle, a toy consisting of irregularly cut pieces of pasteboard, wood, etc. which when correctly fitted together form a picture, etc.

ji·had (ji-häd′), *n.* [Ar., a contest, war], 1. a Moslem holy war; campaign against unbelievers or enemies of Islam; hence, 2. a campaign for or against an idea, etc.; crusade. Also spelled **jehad.**

Jill (jil), a feminine name. *n.* [often j-], 1. a girl or young woman. 2. a sweetheart.

jilt (jilt), *n.* [? dim. of *Jill,* sweetheart], a woman who rejects (a lover or suitor) after accepting or encouraging him. *v.t.* to reject or cast off (a previously accepted lover or sweetheart).

Jim-Crow (jim′krō′), *adj.* discriminating against or segregating Negroes: as, *Jim-Crow* laws, schools, etc.

Jim Crow (jim′ krō′), [name of an early Negro minstrel song], 1. [Colloq.], discrimination against or segregation of Negroes: the current sense. 2. [Slang], a Negro: hostile term, now seldom used in this sense.

jim-crow (jim′krō′), [Colloq.], *adj.* Jim-Crow. *n.* Jim

Crow (sense 1). *v.t.* to subject to Jim-Crow practices.
jim·jams (jim′jamz′), *n.pl.* [arbitrary echoic formation], [Slang], 1. delirium tremens. 2. a nervous feeling: also called *the jitters*.
jim·my (jim′i), *n.* [*pl.* JIMMIES (-iz)], [dim. of *James*], a short crowbar, used by burglars to pry open windows, etc. *v.t.* [JIMMIED (-id), JIMMYING], to use a jimmy on; pry open with a jimmy or similar tool. Also **jemmy.**
jim·son weed, Jim·son weed (jim′s'n), [altered < *Jamestown weed* < *Jamestown*, Virginia], a poisonous plant of the nightshade family, with bad-smelling leaves, prickly fruit, and white or purplish, trumpet-shaped flowers; thorn apple; stinkweed.
jin·gal (jin′gôl), *n.* [Hind. *janjāl*], a light, swivel-mounted cannon or a large musket fired from a rest, formerly used in central Asia: also **gingal, gingall.**
jin·gle (jiŋ′g'l), *v.i.* [JINGLED (-g'ld), JINGLING], [ME. *gingelen, ginglen;* origin echoic], 1. to make a succession of light, ringing sounds, as small bells or bits of metal striking together; tinkle. 2. to have obvious, easy rhythm, simple repetitions of sound, etc., as some poetry and music. *v.t.* to cause to jingle. *n.* 1. a jingling sound. 2. a verse that jingles; jingling arrangement of words or syllables.
jin·gly (jiŋ′gli), *adj.* of or like a jingle; jingling.
jin·go (jiŋ′gō), *n.* [*pl.* JINGOES (-gōz)], [< phr. *by jingo* in the refrain of a patriotic British music-hall song (1878)], a person who boasts of his patriotism and favors an aggressive, threatening, warlike foreign policy; chauvinist. *adj.* of jingoes; jingoistic.
by jingo! [Colloq.], a meaningless exclamation used to indicate strong assertion, surprise, etc.
jin·go·ism (jiŋ′gō-iz'm), *n.* the ideas, policies, actions, etc. of jingoes.
jin·go·is·tic (jiŋ′gō-is′tik), *adj.* of jingoes or jingoism.
jink (jiŋk), *v.i.* [Scot. < name of 17th-c. dance, *Hey-Jinks*], [Scot.], to move swiftly or with sudden turns, as in dodging a pursuer. *n.* 1. [Scot.], an eluding, as by a quick, sudden turn. 2. *pl.* lively pranks; boisterous fun; horseplay: in full, usually, **high jinks.**
jinn (jin), *n.* 1. plural of **jinni.** 2. [*pl.* JINNS], popularly, a jinni.
Jin·nah, Mohammed A·li (ä′lē jin′ə), 1876–1948; Moslem leader in India; first governor-general of Pakistan (1947–1948).
jin·ni (ji-nē′), *n.* [*pl.* JINN (jin)], [Ar., pl. *jinn*], in *Moslem legend*, a supernatural being that can take human or animal form and influence human affairs: also **jinnee, jinn, genie.**
jin·rik·i·sha (jin-rik′shə, jin-rik′shô), *n.* [Japan.; *jin*, a man + *riki*, power + *sha*, carriage], a small, two-wheeled oriental carriage with a hood, pulled by one or two men: also spelled **jinricksha, jinriksha, jinrickshaw.**

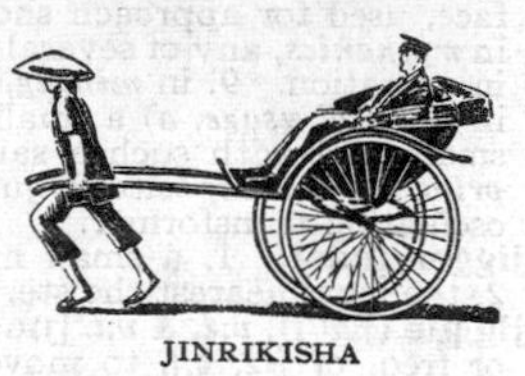

JINRIKISHA

Jin·sen (jin′sen′), *n.* Chemulpho, a seaport of Korea: the Japanese name.
jinx (jiŋks), *n.* [? < L. *iynx*, Gr. *iynx*, the wryneck, bird used in incantations and charms], [Slang], a person or thing supposed to cause bad luck; hoodoo. *v.t.* [JINXED (jiŋkst), JINXING], [Slang], to cause bad luck to.
ji·pi·ja·pa (hē′pi-hä′pä), *n.* [Sp. < *Jipijapa*, place in Ecuador], 1. a Central and South American plant from whose leaves panama hats are made. 2. a hat made of these leaves.
jit·ney (jit′ni), *n.* [*pl.* JITNEYS (-niz)], [c. 1903; ? < Fr. *jeton*, a token, counter < *jeter*, to throw], [Slang], 1. a five-cent coin; nickel. 2. a bus or car, especially one traveling a regular route, that carries passengers for a small fare, originally five cents.
jit·ter (jit′ẽr), *v.i.* [? echoic], [Slang], 1. to be nervous; have the jitters; fidget. 2. to jitterbug.
the jitters, [Slang], a nervous feeling; fidgets.
jit·ter·bug (jit′ẽr-bug′), *n.* [*jitter* + *bug*], [Slang], 1. a person who dances in a fast, acrobatic manner to jazz music. 2. a person who shows enthusiasm for jazz music, often by extravagant gestures, shouts, etc. *v.i.* [JITTERBUGGED (-bugd′), JITTERBUGGING], [Slang], to dance in the manner of a jitterbug.
jit·ter·y (jit′ẽr-i), *adj.* [Slang], having the jitters.
jiu·jit·su (jōō-jit′sōō), *n.* jujitsu.
jiu·jut·su (jōō-jit′sōō, jōō-jōō′sōō), *n.* jujitsu.
jive (jiv), *n.* [? coinage, after *jibe*], [Slang], 1. in *jazz*, talking or joking while playing; hence, 2. the jargon of jazz musicians and jazz devotees. 3. loosely, jazz.
jj., 1. judges. 2. justices.
Jl., July.
Jno., John.
jo, joe (jō), *n.* [*pl.* JOES (jōz)], [Scot.], a sweetheart.
Jo., Joel.
Jo·ab (jō′ab), [L.; Gr. *Iōab;* Heb. *yō′ābh*, lit., the Lord is (his) father], a masculine name. *n.* in the *Bible*, the commander of David's army.
Jo·a·chim, Jo·seph (yō′zef yō-ä′khim; Eng. yō′ə-kim′), 1831–1907; Hungarian violinist in Germany.
Joan (jōn, jō′ən, jō-an′), a feminine name: see **Joanna.**
Jo·an·na (jō-an′ə), [ML., fem. of *Joannes;* see JOHN], a feminine name: variants, *Joan, Jane, Jean, Jeanne, Johanna;* equivalents, L. & G. *Johanna*, D. *Hanna*, Fr. *Jeanne*, It. *Giovanna*, Sp. *Juana.*
Joan of Arc, Saint (ärk), (Fr. *Jeanne d'Arc*), 1412–1431; French heroine; defeated the English at Orléans (1429); burned at the stake for witchcraft; canonized in 1920: called the *Maid of Orleans.*
Job (jōb), [L.; Gr. *Iōb;* Heb. *iyyōbh*, lit., prob., afflicted], a masculine name. *n.* in the *Bible*, 1. a man who endured much suffering but did not lose his faith in God. 2. a book of the Old Testament telling of him.
job (job), *n.* [ME. *gobbe*, a lump, portion; orig., mouthful < Celt. *gob, gop*, the mouth], 1. a piece of work; definite piece of work, as in one's trade, or done by agreement for pay. 2. anything one has to do; task; chore; duty. 3. the thing or material being worked on. 4. a thing done supposedly in the public interest but actually for private gain; dishonest piece of official business. 5. a position of employment; situation; work. 6. [Colloq.], a criminal act or deed, as a theft, etc. 7. [Colloq.], any happening, affair, etc. *adj.* hired or done by the job: see also **job lot.** *v.i.* [JOBBED (jobd), JOBBING], 1. to do odd jobs. 2. to act as a jobber or broker. 3. to do public or official business dishonestly for private gain. *v.t.* 1. to buy (goods) in quantity from importers or manufacturers and sell to dealers; handle as middleman. 2. to let or sublet (work, contracts, etc.). 3. to transact (public business) dishonestly for private gain. 4. to hire or let for hire, as a horse or carriage. —*SYN.* see **position, task.**
odd jobs, miscellaneous pieces of work.
on the job, 1. [Colloq.], while working at one's job. 2. [Slang], attentive to one's task or duty.
job (job), *n., v.t. & v.i.* [JOBBED (jobd), JOBBING], [ME. *jobben*, to peck; see JAB], jab.
job analysis, a study of a specific job, as in industry, with respect to operations and hazards involved, qualifications required of the worker, etc.
job·ber (job′ẽr), *n.* 1. a person who jobs; one who buys goods in quantity from manufacturers or importers and sells them to dealers. 2. a person who works by the job; also, one who does piecework or hack work. 3. a person who does public or official business dishonestly for his own gain. 4. [British], a person who deals in stock-exchange securities: distinguished from *broker.*
job·ber·y (job′ẽr-i), *n.* [< *jobber*], the carrying on of public or official business dishonestly for private gain.
job lot, goods, often of various sorts, brought together for sale as one quantity.
job printer, a printer who does various kinds of printing, such as letterheads, circulars, posters, etc.
Job's comforter (jōbz), a person who aggravates one's misery while pretending to comfort: see Job 4–6.
Job's-tears (jōbz′têrz′), *n.pl.* [see JOB], 1. a tall grass with hard, droplike, gray or whitish seeds. 2. its seeds, used as a cereal in the Orient, or as beads.
Jo·cas·ta (jō-kas′tə), *n.* [L.; Gr. *Iokastē*], in *Greek legend*, the woman who unwittingly married her own son, Oedipus: she killed herself when she found out.
Joc·e·lin, Joc·e·line, Joc·e·lyn (jos′ə-lin, jos′lin), [prob. ult. < L. *jocus*, a jest, trifle], a feminine name.
jock·ey (jok′i), *n.* [*pl.* JOCKEYS (-iz)], [< *Jocky, Jockie*, northern Eng. and Scot. form of *Jacky*, dim. of *Jack*, masculine name], a person whose job is to ride a horse in a race. *v.t. & v.i.* [JOCKEYED (-id), JOCKEYING], 1. to ride (a horse) in a race. 2. to cheat; swindle. 3. to maneuver for position or advantage.
jock·o (jok′ō), *n.* [Fr., earlier *engeco* < *ncheko*, the native name in W. Africa], 1. a chimpanzee. 2. any monkey.
jock·strap (jok′strap′), *n.* [*jock*, male genital organs < *Jock*, Scot. form of *Jack* (see JACK, nickname); + *strap*], an elastic belt with a groin pouch, worn for support by male athletes: also called *athletic supporter.*
jo·cose (jō-kōs′), *adj.* [L. *jocosus* < *jocus*, a joke, jest], humorous; joking; facetious; playful. —*SYN.* see **witty.**
jo·cos·i·ty (jō-kos′ə-ti), *n.* 1. the quality or state of being jocose. 2. [*pl.* JOCOSITIES (-tiz)], a jocose action or remark.
joc·u·lar (jok′yoo-lẽr), *adj.* [L. *jocularis* < *jocus*, a joke, jest], 1. joking; humorous; full of fun. 2. said as a joke. —*SYN.* see **witty.**
joc·u·lar·i·ty (jok′yoo-lar′ə-ti), *n.* 1. the quality or state of being jocular. 2. [*pl.* JOCULARITIES (-tiz)], a jocular action or remark.
joc·und (jok′ənd, jō′kənd), *adj.* [ME.; OFr. *jocond;* LL. *jocundus;* L. *jucundus*, pleasant, agreeable, helpful < *juvare*, to help; form influenced by L. *jocus*, a joke, jest], cheerful; genial; gay.
jo·cun·di·ty (jō-kun′də-ti), *n.* [L. *jucunditas* < *jucundus*], 1. the quality or state of being jocund. 2. [*pl.* JOCUNDITIES (-tiz)], a jocund action or remark.
Jodh·pur (jōd-poor′, jōd′poor), *n.* 1. a native state of northwest India in Rajputana: area, 36,071 sq. mi.; pop., 2,126,000: also called *Marwar.* 2. its capital: pop., 95,000.

jodh·purs (jod′pẽrz, jōd′pẽrz), *n.pl.* [after *Jodhpur*, state in India], riding breeches made loose and full above the knees and closefitting below them.

joe (jō), *n.* [Scot.], a jo.

Jo·el (jō′əl), [L.; Gr. *Iōēl;* Heb. *yō'ēl*, lit., the Lord is God], a masculine name. *n.* in the *Bible*, 1. an ancient Hebrew prophet, probably of the 5th century B.C. 2. the book of his preachings, in the Old Testament: abbreviated **Jo.**

joe-pye weed (jō′pī′), [? < the name of an Indian doctor said to have used the plant as medicine], any of three kinds of eupatorium, a tall plant of the composite family, with clusters of pink or purplish flowers.

jo·ey (jō′i), *n.* [Australian native name, *joè*], [Australian], 1. a young kangaroo. 2. any young animal.

Jof·fre, Jo·seph Jacques Cé·saire (zhô′zef′ zhäk sā′zâr′ zhô′fr′), 1852–1931; French general; commander in chief of the French and Allied armies, World War I.

jog (jog), *v.t.* [JOGGED (jogd), JOGGING], [ME. *joggen;* prob. of echoic origin, after *shog*], 1. to give a little shake, shove, or jerk to. 2. to nudge. 3. to shake up or revive (a person's memory). *v.i.* 1. to move along at a slow, steady, jolting pace or trot. 2. to go on in a steady, slow, heavy manner (with *on* or *along*). *n.* [< the *v.*], 1. a little shake, shove, or nudge. 2. a slow, steady, jolting motion or trot: also **jog trot.**

jog (jog), *n.* [var. of *jag*], a projecting or notched part, especially one at right angles, in a surface or line: as, a *jog* in the wall. *v.i.* [JOGGED (jogd), JOGGING], to form or make a jog: as, turn left where the road *jogs.*

jog·gle (jog′'l), *v.t. & v.i.* [JOGGLED (-'ld), JOGGLING], [freq. of *jog*], to shake or jolt slightly. *n.* a joggling.

jog·gle (jog′'l), *n.* [? < *jog*, a projection], 1. a joint made between two surfaces of wood, stone, etc. by cutting a notch in one and making a projection in the other to fit into it. 2. a notch or projection for such a joint. *v.t.* [JOGGLED (-'ld), JOGGLING], [< the *n.*], to fasten or join by joggles.

joggle post, 1. a post made of pieces joined by joggles. 2. a post with shoulders to receive the feet of struts.

jog trot, 1. a slow, steady trot. 2. a routine, monotonous, or leisurely way of doing something.

Jo·han·na (jō-han′ə), a feminine name: see **Joanna.**

jo·han·nes (jō-han′ēz), *n.* [*pl.* JOHANNES], [Mod. L. < *John* V of Portugal; see JOHN], a Portuguese gold coin of the 18th and 19th centuries, worth about $9.00.

Jo·han·nes·burg (jō-han′is-bũrg′, yō-hän′is-bũrg′), *n.* a city in the Transvaal, Union of South Africa: pop., 1,097,000: gold-mining center.

John (jon), [ML. *Johannes, Joannes;* Gr. *Iōannēs;* Heb. *yōḥānān*, contr. < *yehōḥānān*, lit., the Lord is gracious], a masculine name: diminutives, *Jack, Johnny;* feminine, *Jane, Jean, Jeanne, Joan, Joanna, Johanna;* equivalents, Fr. *Jean*, G. *Johann, Johannes, Hans*, It. *Giovanni*, Pol. *Jan*, Russ. *Ivan*, Sp. *Juan*. *n.* 1. in the *Bible*, *a*) a Christian apostle, credited with having written the Gospel of Saint John, the three Epistles of John, and the Book of Revelation: called *the Evangelist* and *the Divine*. *b*) the fourth book of the New Testament. *c*) any of the three Epistles of John. *d*) John the Baptist. 2. son of Henry II; 1167?–1216; king of England (1199–1216); forced by his barons to sign the Magna Charta (1215). Abbreviated **Jno.**

john (jon), *n.* [Slang], a toilet.

John III, 1624–1696; king of Poland (1674–1696).

John XXIII, 1881–1963; Pope (1958–1963).

John, Augustus Edwin, 1878–1961; English painter.

John Barleycorn, [see BARLEYCORN], a personification of corn liquor, malt liquor, etc.

John Bull (bool), England, or an Englishman, personified.

John Doe (dō), [see DOE], a fictitious name used in legal papers, etc. for that of a person who is not known.

John Do·ry (dôr′i, dō′ri), [*pl.* JOHN DORYS (-iz, -riz)], [*John* + *dory*, the fish], an edible salt-water fish with a yellow-ringed black spot on each side of its flat body: also spelled **John Doree.**

John Han·cock (han′kok), [Colloq.], a person's signature: so called because John Hancock's signature on the Declaration of Independence is bold and legible.

John·nie, John·ny (jon′i), a masculine name: see **John.** *n.* [*pl.* JOHNNIES (-iz)], [Slang], 1. [cf. JACK (nickname)], any man or boy. 2. a fop; dandy.

john·ny·cake (jon′i-kāk′), *n.* [altered < *Shawnee-cake*, kind of bread made by Shawnee Indians], a kind of corn bread baked on a griddle.

John·ny-jump-up (jon′i-jump′up′), *n.* 1. any early spring violet. 2. the wild pansy. Also **Johnny jumper.**

John·ny-on-the-spot (jon′i-on′*th*ə-spot′), *adj.* [Colloq.], ready and at hand whenever needed. *n.* [Colloq.], a person who is Johnny-on-the-spot.

John of Gaunt (gônt), Duke of Lancaster, 1340–1399; son of Edward III.

John·son, Andrew (jon′s'n), 1808–1875; seventeenth president of the United States (1865–1869).

Johnson, James Wel·don (wel′d'n), 1871–1938; American writer and diplomat.

Johnson, Lyn·don Baines (lin′dən bānz), 1908– ; thirty-sixth president of the United States (1963–).

Johnson, Samuel, 1709–1784; English writer, critic, and lexicographer; known as *Dr. Johnson.*

Johnson City, a city in northeastern Tennessee: pop., 31,000.

John·son·ese (jon′s'n-ēz′), *n.* 1. the literary style of Samuel Johnson. 2. a literary style like Johnson's, heavy, pompous, erudite, etc.: a derogatory term.

John·so·ni·an (jon-sō′ni-ən), *adj.* 1. of or like Samuel Johnson or his writings. 2. full of Johnsonese. *n.* 1. an imitator or admirer of Johnson. 2. a person who makes a special study of Johnson and his work.

John·ston, Albert Sidney (jon′stən, jon′s'n), 1803–1862; Confederate general.

Johnston, Joseph Eggleston, 1807–1891; Confederate general.

Johns·town (jonz′toun′), *n.* a city in southwestern Pennsylvania, on the Conemaugh River: pop., 54,000: a disastrous flood occurred there in 1889.

John the Baptist, in the *Bible*, the forerunner and baptizer of Jesus: he was killed by Herod: Matt. 3.

Jo·hore (jə-hôr′), *n.* a state of the Federation of Malaya, at the tip of the Malay Peninsula: area, 7,330 sq. mi.; pop., 1,026,000.

‡joie de vi·vre (zhwȧ′də-vē′vr′), [Fr.], joy of living; zestful enjoyment of life.

join (join), *v.t.* [ME. *joynen, joignen;* OFr. *joindre, juindre* < L. *jungere*, to bind together, yoke], 1. to place together; bring together; connect; fasten; combine. 2. to make into one; unite: as, *join* forces, *join* people in marriage. 3. to become a part or member of; enter into association with: as, he *joined* a labor union. 4. to go to and combine with: as, the path *joins* the highway. 5. to enter into the company of; accompany: as, *join* me in a walk, *join* us soon. 6. to go and take one's proper place in: as, a soldier must *join* his regiment when his leave is over. 7. [Colloq.], to adjoin. 8. in *geometry*, to connect with a straight line or curve. *v.i.* 1. to come together; meet. 2. to enter into association. 3. to participate (*in* a conversation, singing, etc.). *n.* [< the *v.*], 1. a joining or being joined. 2. a place of joining: as, a seam in a coat is a *join.*

join battle, to start fighting or competing.

SYN.—**join** is the general term implying a bringing or coming together of two or more things and may suggest direct contact, affiliation, etc.; **combine** implies a mingling together of things, often with a loss of distinction of elements that completely merge with one another (to *combine* milk and water); **unite** implies a joining or combining of things to form a single whole (the *United* States); **connect** implies attachment by some fastening or relationship (roads *connected* by a bridge, the duties *connected* with a job); **link** stresses firmness of a connection (*linked* together in a common cause); **associate** implies a joining with another or others as a companion, partner, etc. and, in extended use, suggests a logical connection made in the mind (to *associate* Freud's name with psychoanalysis); **consolidate** implies a merger of distinct and separate units into a single whole for resulting compactness, strength, efficiency, etc. (to *consolidate* one's debts).—*ANT.* separate, part.

join·der (join′dẽr), *n.* [Fr. *joindre*, a use of inf. as *n.;* see JOIN], 1. a joining; act of meeting or coming together. 2. in *law*, *a*) a joining of causes. *b*) a joining of parties as co-plaintiffs or co-defendants. *c*) a uniting on facts or procedure. *d*) an accepting of an issue offered.

join·er (join′ẽr), *n.* [ME. *joinour;* OFr. *joignour* < *joindre;* see JOIN], 1. a person or thing that joins. 2. a carpenter, especially one who finishes interior woodwork, as doors, molding, stairs, etc. 3. [Colloq.], a person given to joining various organizations.

join·er·y (join′ẽr-i), *n.* 1. the work, trade, or skill of a joiner. 2. the things made by a joiner.

joint (joint), *n.* [ME.; OFr. *joint, joinct;* L. *junctus*, pp. of *jungere*, to join, yoke], 1. a place or part where two things or parts are joined. 2. the way in which two things are joined at such a part. 3. one of the parts or sections of a jointed whole. 4. a large cut of meat with the bone still in it, as for a roast. 5. in *anatomy*, *a*) a place or part where two bones or corresponding structures are joined, usually so that they can move. *b*) the way in which they are joined. 6. in *botany*, a point where a branch or leaf grows out of the stem. 7. in *geology*, a fissure in a rock mass, without displacement of strata. 8. [Slang], a saloon, cheap restaurant, etc. 9. [Slang], any house, building, etc. *adj.* [OFr. *joint, jointe*, pp. of *joindre;* see JOIN], 1. joined as to time; concurrent. 2. common to two or more persons, governments, etc. as to ownership or action: as, a *joint* declaration, *joint* property. 3. sharing with someone else: as, a *joint* owner. *v.t.* 1. to fasten together by a joint or joints. 2. to give a joint or joints to. 3. to cut (meat) into joints; separate at the joints.

out of joint, 1. not in place at the joint; dislocated. 2. disordered.

joint account, a bank account in the name of two or more persons, each of whom may withdraw funds.
joint committee, a committee with members from both houses of a legislative body, or from two or more organizations.
joint·ed (join'tid), *adj.* having joints.
joint·er (join'tẽr), *n.* 1. a person or machine that joints. 2. a long plane used in dressing boards. 3. a triangular device with an edge, fastened to a plow beam. 4. a bent iron bar for holding stones together.
joint·ly (joint'li), *adv.* in a joint manner; together.
joint resolution, a resolution passed by both houses of a bicameral legislature: it has the force of an act if signed by the chief executive or passed over his veto.
joint·ress (join'tris), *n.* a woman with a jointure.
joint return, a single income tax return filed by a married couple, combining their individual incomes.
joint stock, stock or capital held in a common fund.
joint-stock company (joint'stok'), a business firm with a joint stock, owned by the stockholders in shares which each may sell or transfer independently.
join·ture (join'chẽr), *n* [ME.; OFr.; L. *junctura*, a joining < *jungere;* see JOIN]. 1. [Obs.], a joining. 2. in *law*, *a*) an arrangement by which a husband settles property on his wife for her use after his death. *b*) the property thus settled; widow's portion. *c*) [Obs.], the holding of property jointly.
joint·weed (joint'wēd'), *n.* a plant of the buckwheat family, with threadlike leaves, jointed stems, and clusters of small, white flowers.
joint·worm (joint'wũrm'), *n.* any of the larvae of various small flies, which produce gall-like swellings in the joints of grain stems.
Join·ville, Jean de (zhän' də zhwan'vēl'), 1224?–1317; French historian.
joist (joist), *n.* [ME. *giste, gyste*, a joist, beam; OFr. *giste*, a bed, couch, beam < *gesir*, to lie < L. *jacere*, to lie], any of the parallel timbers that hold up the planks of a floor or the laths of a ceiling. *v.t.* to provide with joists.

JOISTS

Jó·kai, Mau·rus (mou'roos yō'koi), 1825–1904; Hungarian writer.
joke (jōk), *n.* [L. *jocus*, a joke, game], 1. anything said or done to arouse laughter; funny anecdote; witty, amusing remark; amusing trick played on someone. 2. something not meant to be taken seriously; thing done or said in fun. 3. a person or thing to be laughed at, not to be taken seriously. *v.i.* [JOKED (jōkt), JOKING], [< the *n.* or L. *jocari*, to joke], 1. to make jokes; say or do things meant to amuse. 2. to say something not meant to be taken seriously. *v.t.* to make fun of; make (a person) the object of jokes or teasing.
no joke, a serious matter.
SYN.—**joke** is the simple, basic word for anything said or done in fun or to excite laughter and may apply to remarks, anecdotes, pranks, etc.; **jest**, the more formal equivalent, usually is applied to joking language and suggests banter or light, good-natured ridicule; **quip** and **sally** suggest a smart, neatly turned jest; a **witticism** is a witty or amusingly clever saying or remark; **wisecrack**, a slang term, applies to a witty remark that is flippant or facetious.
jok·er (jōk'ẽr), *n.* 1. a person who jokes. 2. a hidden or cunningly worded provision put into a law, legal document, etc. to make it different from what it seems to be; hence, 3. any hidden, unsuspected difficulty. 4. an extra playing card, used in some games to represent the highest trump or any card the holder desires.
Jok·ja·kar·ta (jok'yä-kär'tä), *n.* a city in central Java: pop., 289,000: also spelled **Djokjakarta, Jokyakarta.**
jole (jōl), *n.* a jowl.
Jo·li·et (jō'li-et', jō'li-et', jol'i-et'), *n.* a city in northeastern Illinois: pop., 67,000.
Jo·li·et, Louis (jō'li-et', jo'li-et'; Fr. zhô'lye'), 1645–1700; French-Canadian explorer of the Mississippi: also spelled **Jolliet.**
Jo·liot-Cu·rie, Fré·dé·ric (frā'dā'rēk' zhô'lyō'kü'rē'), (born *Frédéric Joliot*), 1900–1958; husband of *Irène;* French chemist; shared Nobel prize in chemistry, 1935, with his wife.
Joliot-Curie, I·rène (ē'ren'), 1897–1956; daughter of *Pierre* and *Marie Curie;* French chemist: see **Joliot-Curie, Frédéric.**
jol·li·er (jol'i-ẽr), *n.* [Colloq.], a person who jollies others.
jol·li·fi·ca·tion (jol'ə-fi-kā'shən), *n.* [Colloq.], a jollifying; merrymaking; revel.
jol·li·fy (jol'ə-fī'), *v.t. & v.i.* [JOLLIFIED (-fīd'), JOLLIFYING], [Colloq.], to make or be jolly or merry.
jol·li·ly (jol''l-i), *adv.* in a jolly manner.
jol·li·ness (jol'i-nis), *n.* jollity.
jol·li·ty (jol'ə-ti), *n.* [ME. & OFr. *jolite, jolivete* < *joli;* see JOLLY], 1. the quality or state of being jolly; fun; gaiety. 2. [*pl.* JOLLITIES (-tiz)], [British], a jolly occasion; festive gathering. —*SYN.* see **mirth.**
jol·ly (jol'i), *adj.* [JOLLIER (-i-ẽr), JOLLIEST (-i-ist)], [ME. & OFr. *ioli, jolif*, joyful, merry; prob. < Gmc. base of *Yule*], 1. full of high spirits and good humor; merry; gay; convivial. 2. [Colloq.], enjoyable; pleasant. *adv.* [British Colloq.], very; altogether. *v.t. & v.i.* [JOLLIED (-id), JOLLYING], [Colloq.], 1. to try to make (a person) feel good or agreeable by coaxing, flattering, joking, etc. (often with *along*). 2. to make fun of (someone). *n.* [British Slang], a British marine.
jol·ly-boat (jol'i-bōt'), *n.* [prob. < D. *jolle* or Dan. *jolle*, yawl], a ship's small boat: also **jolly boat, jolly.**
Jol·ly Rog·er (jol'i roj'ẽr), [*jolly* + *Roger*, pirate flag < the proper name *Roger*], a black flag with white skull and crossbones, emblem of piracy.
Jo·lo (hô-lô'), *n.* the largest island of the Sulu Archipelago, Philippine Islands: area, 326 sq. mi.; pop., 116,000.
jolt (jōlt), *v.t.* [earlier *jot*, *v.*, influenced by *jowl*], to shake up or jar, as a vehicle running on a rough surface. *v.i.* to move along in a bumpy, jerky manner. *n.* 1. a sudden jerk, bump, or shake, as from a blow; hence, 2. a shock or surprise: as, the news gave us all a *jolt.*
jol·ty (jōl'ti), *adj.* jolting; bumpy.
Jo·nah (jō'nə), [L. *Jonas;* Gr. *Iōnas;* Heb. *yōnāh*, lit., a dove], a masculine name: variant, *Jonas*. *n.* 1. in the *Bible*, a Hebrew prophet: thrown overboard in a storm sent because he had disobeyed God, he was swallowed by a big fish, but three days later was cast up on the shore unharmed. 2. a book of the Old Testament telling Jonah's story. 3. any person said to bring bad luck just by being present: from the fact that Jonah brought bad luck to the sailors.
Jo·nas (jō'nəs), *n.* Jonah: form used in the Douay Bible.
Jon·a·than (jon'ə-thən), [Heb. *yōnāthān*, contr. < *yehōnāthān*, lit., the Lord has given], a masculine name. *n.* 1. in the *Bible*, Saul's oldest son, a close friend of David: I Sam. 18–20. 2. a late fall variety of apple.
Jones, Daniel (jōnz), 1881– ; English phonetician.
Jones, Henry Arthur, 1851–1929; English dramatist.
Jones, In·i·go (in'i-gō'), 1573–1652; English architect and stage designer.
Jones, John Paul, (born *John Paul*), 1747–1792; American naval officer in the Revolutionary War, born in Scotland.
jon·gleur (joŋ'glẽr; Fr. zhōn'glẽr'), *n.* [Fr.; see JUGGLER], a wandering minstrel in medieval France and England, who entertained by reciting or singing.
jon·quil (joŋ'kwil, jon'kwil), *n.* [Fr. *jonquille;* Sp. *junquillo*, dim. of *junco*, a reed; L. *juncus*, a rush], 1. a variety of narcissus resembling a daffodil, with small, fragrant, yellow or white flowers and long, slender leaves. 2. its bulb or flower.
Jon·son, Ben (ben jon's'n), 1573?–1637; English dramatist and poet.
Jop·lin (jop'lin), *n.* a city in southwestern Missouri: pop., 39,000.
Jop·pa (jop'ə), *n.* Jaffa: the ancient name.
Jor·daens, Ja·cob (yȧ'kop yôr'dȧns), 1593–1678; Flemish painter.
Jor·dan (jôr'd'n), *n.* 1. a river in the Near East, flowing southward through the Sea of Galilee, through Jordan, into the Dead Sea: length, 200 mi. 2. an Arab kingdom in the Near East, east of Israel: British mandate (1921–1946): area, c. 37,000 sq. mi.; pop., c. 1,600,000; capital, Amman: official name *Hashemite Kingdom of Jordan;* former names, *Trans-Jordan, Transjordania.*
jor·dan (jôr'd'n), *n.* [ME. *jurdan* < name *Jordan, Jourdain*], [Obs. or Dial.], a chamber pot.
Jor·dan, David Starr (stär jôr'd'n), 1851–1931; American educator and naturalist.
Jordan almond, [altered, after the proper name *Jordan*, < ME. *jardyne almaunde;* prob. < OFr. *jardin*, garden; hence, a garden (cultivated) almond], a variety of large Spanish almond much used in confections.
jo·rum (jō'rəm, jôr'əm), *n.* [prob. < *Joram* (II Sam. 8:10), bringer of silver vessels], 1. a large drinking bowl. 2. the amount of liquor that it holds.
Jo·seph (jō'zəf), [L. *Joseph, Josephus;* Gr. *Iōsēph;* Heb. *yōsēph*, lit., may he add], a masculine name: diminutives, *Jo, Joe;* feminine, *Josepha, Josephine;* equivalents, L. *Josephus*, It. *Giuseppe*, Sp. *José*. *n.* in the *Bible*, 1. one of Jacob's sons, who was sold into slavery in Egypt by his jealous brothers but became a high official there: Gen. 37, 39–41. 2. the husband of Mary, mother of Jesus: Matt. 1:18–25.
jo·seph (jō'zəf), *n.* [< *Joseph;* prob. in allusion to the "coat of many colors"], a woman's long riding coat, with a cape, worn in the 18th century.
Jo·se·phine (jō'zə-fēn'), [Fr. *Joséphine* < *Joseph;* see JOSEPH], a feminine name: diminutives, *Jo, Josie;* variant, *Josepha*. *n.* wife of *Napoleon I;* 1763–1814; empress of France (1804–1809).
Joseph of Arimathea, in the *Bible*, a wealthy disciple who provided a tomb for Jesus' body: Matt. 27: 57–60.
Jo·se·phus (jō-sē'fəs), a masculine name: see **Joseph.**
Josephus, Fla·vi·us (flā'vi-əs), (born *Joseph ben Mat-thias*), 37 A.D.–100? A.D.; Jewish historian.

josh (josh), *v.t. & v.i.* [said to merge *joke* and *bosh*], [Slang], to ridicule in a good-humored way; tease jokingly; banter.

Josh·u·a (josh′oo-ə), [Heb. *yehōshū'a*, lit., help of Jehovah], a masculine name: diminutive, *Josh.* *n.* in the *Bible*, 1. Moses' successor, and leader of the Israelites into the Promised Land. 2. a book of the Old Testament telling about him. Abbreviated **Josh.**

Jo·si·ah (jō-sī′ə), [Heb. *yōshīyāh*, lit., the Lord supports], a masculine name. *n.* in the *Bible*, a king of Judah in the 7th century B.C.: II Kings 22, 23.

Jo·si·as (jō-sī′əs), a masculine name: see **Josiah.**

joss (jos), *n.* [Pid. Eng.; var. of Port. *deos*, L. *deus*, a god], a figure of a Chinese god; Chinese idol.

joss house, a Chinese temple.

joss stick, a thin stick of dried paste made of fragrant wood dust, burned by the Chinese as incense.

jos·tle (jos′'l), *v.t. & v.i.* [JOSTLED (-'ld), JOSTLING], [earlier *justle*, freq. < ME. *justen;* see JOUST], to bump or push, as in a crowd; elbow or shove roughly. *n.* a jostling; rough bump or shove.

Jos·u·e (jos′ū-ē′), *n.* Joshua: form used in the Douay Bible.

jot (jot), *n.* [L. *iota;* Gr. *iōta*, *i*, the smallest letter, very small thing], a very small or trifling amount: as, she doesn't care a *jot* for him. *v.t.* [JOTTED (-id), JOTTING], [prob. < the *n.*], to make a brief note of (usually with *down*).

Jo·tunn, Jo·tun (yô′toon, yō′toon), *n.* [ON. *jötunn*], in *Norse mythology*, a giant.

Jö·tunn (yö′toon), *n.* a Jotunn.

Jo·tunn·heim, Jo·tun·heim (yô′toon-hām′, yō′toon-hām′), *n.* [ON. *jötunheimar*, n. pl.], in *Norse mythology*, the home of the giants, at the northwestern edge of the world: also **Jotunnheimr, Jötunnheim.**

joule (joul, jōōl), *n.* [after J.P. *Joule*], in *physics*, a unit of work or energy equal to 10,000,000 ergs; practically, the energy expended in one second by a current of one ampere at a potential of one volt: abbreviated **J** (no period).

Joule, James Prescott (joul), 1818–1889; English physicist.

jounce (jouns), *v.t. & v.i.* [JOUNCED (jounst), JOUNCING], [prob. dial. var. of *jaunce*, altered form of *jaunt*], to shake, jolt, or bounce, as in riding. *n.* a bounce or jolt.

jour., 1. journal. 2. journeyman.

jour·nal (jũr′n'l), *n.* [OFr. *journal, jornal, jurnal;* L. *diurnalis*, daily < *dies*, day], 1. a daily record of happenings. 2. a diary. 3. a record of the transactions of a legislature, committee, club, etc. 4. a ship's log book. 5. a daily newspaper; hence, 6. any newspaper or periodical; magazine. 7. in *bookkeeping*, *a)* a daybook. *b)* a book of original entry, used, in the double-entry system, for recording all transactions with an indication of the special accounts to which they belong. 8. [orig. Scot.], in *mechanics*, the part of a rotatory axle or shaft that turns in a bearing: see **crankshaft**, illus.

journal box, in *mechanics*, 1. a bearing for a journal. 2. a casing or housing for a journal.

jour·nal·ese (jũr′n'l-ēz′, jũr′n'l-ēs′), *n.* a style of writing and diction characteristic of many newspapers, magazines, etc.; facile style, with hackneyed expressions and effects.

jour·nal·ism (jũr′n'l-iz'm), *n.* [Fr. *journalisme* < *journal;* see JOURNAL], 1. the work of gathering news for, writing for, editing, or directing the publication of a newspaper or other periodical. 2. journalistic writing. 3. newspapers and magazines collectively.

jour·nal·ist (jũr′n'l-ist), *n.* 1. a person whose occupation is journalism; reporter, editor, etc. of a newspaper or other periodical. 2. a person who keeps a diary.

jour·nal·is·tic (jũr′n'l-is′tik), *adj.* of or characteristic of journalism or journalists.

jour·nal·is·ti·cal·ly (jũr′n'l-is′ti-k'l-i), *adv.* 1. in a journalistic manner. 2. from the standpoint of journalism.

jour·nal·ize (jũr′n'l-īz′), *v.t. & v.i.* [JOURNALIZED (-īzd′), JOURNALIZING], to enter (records) in a journal, as in bookkeeping.

jour·ney (jũr′ni), *n.* [*pl.* JOURNEYS (-niz)], [ME. *journee, jorney;* OFr. *journee, jornee;* LL. **diurnata*, day's journey, day's work < L. *diurnus*, daily < *dies*, day], a traveling from one place to another; trip. *v.i.* [JOURNEYED (-nid), JOURNEYING], to go on a trip; travel. —*SYN.* see **trip.**

jour·ney·man (jũr′ni-mən), *n.* [*pl.* JOURNEYMEN (-mən)], [archaic *journey*, day's work + *man*], 1. originally, a worker for a daily wage. 2. formerly, a worker who had served his apprenticeship and thus qualified himself to work at his trade. 3. now, a worker who has learned his trade. Distinguished from *apprentice, master workman.* Abbreviated **jour.**

jour·ney·work (jũr′ni-wũrk′), *n.* work of a journeyman.

joust (just, joust, jōōst), *n.* [ME. *jouste, juste;* OFr. *jouste* < *jouster;* see the *v.*], 1. a combat or mock combat with lances, between two knights on horseback. 2. *pl.* a tournament. *v.i.* [ME. *justen, justien;* OFr. *juster, joster, jouster;* LL. *juxtare*, to approach, tilt < L. *juxta*, close to], to engage in a joust. Also **just.**

Jove (jōv), *n.* [< L. *Jovis*, genit. of *Jupiter*, Jupiter], [Poetic], Jupiter (in both senses).

by Jove! an exclamation expressing astonishment, emphasis, etc.

jo·vi·al (jō′vi-əl), *adj.* [Fr.; LL. *Jovialis*, of Jupiter < L. *Jovis;* see JOVE], 1. of Jove, the god or the planet. 2. full of hearty, playful good humor; genial and gay; jolly: from the astrological notion that people born under the influence of the planet Jupiter are joyful.

jo·vi·al·i·ty (jō′vi-al′ə-ti), *n.* [Fr. *jovialité;* see JOVIAL], 1. the quality or state of being jovial. 2. [*pl.* JOVIALITIES (-tiz)], a jovial act or remark.

Jo·vi·an (jō′vi-ən), *adj.* 1. of or like Jove (the god Jupiter); majestic. 2. of the planet Jupiter.

Jow·ett, Benjamin (jou′it), 1817–1893; English translator of Plato, Thucydides, and Aristotle.

jowl (joul, jōl), *n.* [ME. *chaul, chavel;* influenced by *jowe* (see JAW); AS. *ceafl*, jaw, cheek], 1. a jawbone or jaw, especially the lower jaw with the chin and cheeks. 2. the cheek.

jowl (joul, jōl), *n.* [ME. *chol, cholle;* AS. *ceolc*, throat (G. *kehle*)], 1. the fleshy, hanging part under the lower jaw. 2. *a)* the dewlap of cattle. *b)* the wattle of fowl. 3. the head and adjacent parts of a fish.

joy (joi), *n.* [ME. *joye, joie;* OFr. *joie, joye;* LL. *gaudia* < L. *gaudium*, joy], 1. a very glad feeling; happiness; great pleasure; delight. 2. anything causing this feeling. 3. the expression of this feeling. *v.i.* to be full of joy; rejoice. *v.t.* 1. to make joyful; gladden. 2. [Archaic], to enjoy. —*SYN.* see **pleasure.**

joy·ance (joi′əns), *n.* [Archaic], joy; rejoicing.

Joyce (jois), [< older *Jocosa;* L. *jocosa*, fem. of *jocosus*, merry < *jocus*, jest, trifle], a feminine name.

Joyce, James (jois), 1882–1941; Irish novelist and poet.

joy·ful (joi′fəl), *adj.* 1. full of joy. 2. feeling, expressing, or causing joy; glad; happy. —*SYN.* see **happy.**

joy·less (joi′lis), *adj.* without joy; unhappy; sad.

joy·ous (joi′əs), *adj.* [OFr. < *joie;* see JOY], joyful; happy; gay; glad. —*SYN.* see **happy.**

joy-ride (joi′rīd′), *v.i.* [Colloq.], to take a joy ride.

joy ride, [Colloq.], an automobile ride merely for pleasure, often with reckless speed, rowdy behavior, etc.

joy stick, [Slang], the control stick of an airplane.

JP, jet propulsion.

J.P., Justice of the Peace.

Jr., jr., junior.

Ju., June.

Ju·an de Fu·ca Strait (jōō′ən də fū′kə), a strait between Washington and Vancouver Island: length, 100 mi.

Juan Fer·nán·dez Islands (hwän fer-nän′deth; Eng. jōō′ən fẽr-nan′dez), two islands in the South Pacific, about 500 mi. west of, and belonging to, Chile: area, 70 sq. mi.

Jua·rez, Be·ni·to Pa·blo (be-nē′tô pä′blô hwä′res), 1806–1872; Mexican statesman; president of Mexico (1857–1863; 1863–1867, in exile; 1867–1872).

Ju·ba (jōō′bä), *n.* a river in eastern Africa, flowing into the Indian Ocean: length, 1,000 mi.: also spelled **Giuba.**

ju·ba (jōō′bə), *n.* [? < Bantu; ? back-formation < *jubilee*], a Southern Negro dance, characterized by a lively rhythm marked by clapping the hands.

Ju·bal (jōō′b'l), *n.* [Heb. *yūbhāl*], in the *Bible*, one of Cain's descendants, a musician or inventor of musical instruments: Gen. 4:19–21.

jub·bah (joob′bə), *n.* [Ar.], a long outer garment worn by both men and women in some Moslem countries.

Jub·bul·pore (jub′əl-pôr′), *n.* a city in Madhya Pradesh state, India: pop., 124,000.

ju·be (jōō′bi), *n.* [Fr. < imperative of L. *jubere*, to bid, command: so called from a prayer that begins *Jube*, spoken from this gallery], a loft or gallery over the rood screen in a church.

ju·bi·lance (jōō′b'l-əns), *n.* jubilant feeling; rejoicing.

ju·bi·lant (jōō′b'l-ənt), *adj.* [L. *jubilans*, ppr. of *jubilare;* see JUBILATE, *v.*], joyful and triumphant; elated.

Ju·bi·la·te (jōō′bə-lā′tē, jōō′bə-lä′tē), *n.* [< imperative of L. *jubilare;* see JUBILATE, *v.*], 1. in the *Bible*, the 100th Psalm (99th in the Vulgate and Douay versions). 2. the third Sunday after Easter: so called because the Introit for the day begins *Jubilate.*

ju·bi·late (jōō′b'l-āt′), *v.i.* [JUBILATED (-id), JUBILATING], [< L. *jubilatus*, pp. of *jubilare*, to shout for joy < *jubilum*, wild shout], to rejoice, as in triumph; exult.

ju·bi·la·tion (jōō′b'l-ā′shən), *n.* 1. a jubilating; rejoicing. 2. a happy celebration, as of victory.

ju·bi·lee (jōō′b'l-ē′), *n.* [OFr. *jubile;* LL. *jubilaeus;* Gr. *iōbēlaios* < Heb. *yōbēl*, a ram, ram's horn used as a trumpet to announce the sabbatical year; influenced by L. *jubilum*, wild shout], 1. in *Jewish history*, a year-long celebration held every fifty years in which all bondmen were freed, mortgaged lands were restored to the original owners, and land was left fallow: Lev. 25:8-17. 2. a fiftieth or twenty-fifth anniversary, or a celebration of this. 3. a time or occasion of rejoicing. 4. jubilation; rejoicing. 5. in the *Roman Catholic Church*, a year of plenary indulgence or remission of punishment for sin, on certain conditions: *ordinary jubilees* occur every twenty-five years.

Jud., 1. Judges. 2. Judith.

Ju·dae·a (jo͞o-dē′ə), *n.* Judea.

Ju·dae·an (jo͞o-dē′ən), *adj.* & *n.* Judean.

Ju·dah (jo͞o′də), [Heb. *yehūdhāh*, lit., praised (by the Lord)], a masculine name: diminutive, *Jude;* feminine, *Judith. n.* in the *Bible*, 1. one of Jacob's sons. 2. the tribe descended from him, strongest of the twelve tribes of Israel. 3. the kingdom in the southern part of ancient Palestine formed by the tribes of Judah and Benjamin after they broke with the other ten tribes: I Kings 11:31, 12:17-21.

Ju·da·ic (jo͞o-dā′ik), *adj.* [L. *Judaicus;* Gr. *Ioudaikos* < *Ioudaios;* see JEW], 1. of Judah. 2. of the Jews, their culture, etc.; Jewish. 3. of Judaism.

Ju·da·ism (jo͞o′di-iz′m), *n.* [LL. *Judaismus;* Gr. *Ioudaismos* < *Ioudaios;* see JEW], 1. the Jewish religion. 2. observance of Jewish customs, ceremonies, rules, etc.

Ju·da·ize (jo͞o′di-iz′), *v.i.* [JUDAIZED (-izd′), JUDAIZING], [LL. *Judaizare;* Gr. *Ioudaizein* < *Ioudaios;* see JEW], to conform to Jewish customs, beliefs, etc. *v.t.* to bring into conformity with Judaism.

Ju·das (jo͞o′dəs), *n.* [LL.; Gr. *Ioudas;* Heb. *yehūdhah*, Judah], 1. Judas Iscariot, the disciple who betrayed Jesus for pay: Matt. 26:14, 48. 2. a person who behaves like Judas Iscariot; betrayer. 3. Jude, the apostle. 4. a brother of Jesus and James: Mark 6:3, Matt. 13:55.

Ju·das, Saint (jo͞o′dəs), see **Jude.**

Judas Maccabaeus, see **Maccabaeus, Judas.**

Judas tree, [so called because Judas Iscariot is said to have hanged himself on one], any of a number of related shrubs or trees of the pea family, with clusters of rose-pink or purplish flowers; redbud.

Jude (jo͞od), a masculine name: see **Judah.** *n.* in the *Bible*, 1. a Christian apostle and saint: also called *Judas* (not Iscariot): John 14:22, Luke 6:13-16. 2. a book of the New Testament, the Epistle of Jude. 3. its author, perhaps the Judas called Jesus' brother. See **Judas.**

Ju·de·a (jo͞o-dē′ə), *n.* a part of southern Palestine that was under Roman rule: also spelled **Judaea.**

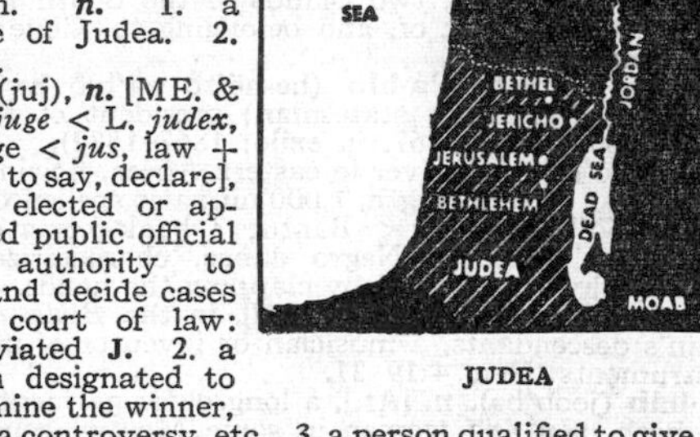

JUDEA

Ju·de·an (jo͞o-dē′ən), *adj.* [L. *Judaeus;* see JEW], 1. of Judea or its people. 2. Jewish. *n.* 1. a native of Judea. 2. a Jew.

judge (juj), *n.* [ME. & OFr. *juge* < L. *judex*, a judge < *jus*, law + *dicere*, to say, declare], 1. an elected or appointed public official with authority to hear and decide cases in a court of law: abbreviated **J.** 2. a person designated to determine the winner, settle a controversy, etc. 3. a person qualified to give an opinion or decide on the relative worth of anything: as, a good *judge* of music, a poor *judge* of books. 4. in *Jewish history*, any of the governing leaders of the Israelites before the time of the kings: judges ruled for over four centuries after Joshua died. *v.t.* & *v.i.* [JUDGED (jujd), JUDGING], [ME. *juggen;* OFr. *juger* < L. *judicare*, to judge, declare the law < *judex;* see the *n.*], 1. to hear and pass judgment on (persons or cases) in a court of law. 2. to determine the winner of (a contest); settle (a controversy). 3. to decree. 4. to form an idea or opinion about (any matter). 5. to criticize or censure. 6. to think or suppose. 7. in *Jewish history*, to govern.

SYN.—**judge** is applied to one who, by the authority vested in him or by expertness of knowledge, is qualified to settle a controversy or decide on the relative merit of things (a *judge* of a beauty contest); **arbiter** emphasizes the authoritativeness of decision of one whose judgment in a particular matter is considered indisputable (an *arbiter* of the social graces); **referee** and **umpire** both apply to a person to whom anything is referred for decision or settlement (a *referee* in bankruptcy) and, in sports, to officials charged with the regulation of a contest, ruling on the plays in game, etc. (a *referee* in boxing, basketball, etc., an *umpire* in baseball, cricket, etc.). See also **infer.**

judge advocate, [*pl.* JUDGE ADVOCATES], a military legal officer; especially, an officer designated to act as prosecutor at a court-martial: abbreviated **J.A.**

judge-made (juj′mād′), *adj.* made by judges or by their decisions taken as precedent.

Judg·es (juj′iz), *n.pl.* [construed as sing.], a book of the Old Testament telling the history of the Jews from the death of Joshua to the birth of Samuel: abbreviated **Judg., Jud.**

judge·ship (juj′ship), *n.* the position, functions, or term of office of a judge.

judg·mat·ic (juj-mat′ik), *adj.* [< *judge* + *-matic* as in *dogmatic*], [Colloq.], discerning; judicious.

judg·ment (juj′mənt), *n.* [ME. *jugement;* OFr. *jugement;* LL. *judicamentum* < L. *judicare;* see JUDGE, *v.*], 1. a judging; deciding. 2. a legal decision; order or sentence given by a judge or law court. 3. a debt resulting from a court order. 4. a misfortune looked on as a punishment from God. 5. an opinion or estimate. 6. criticism or censure. 7. the ability to come to opinions of things; power of comparing and deciding; understanding; good sense. 8. in the *Bible*, justice; right. 9. [J-], in *theology*, *a)* God's final sentence as judge of all things. *b)* the time of this: often called *the Last Judgment.* Also spelled **judgement.**

judgment day, Judgment Day, in *theology*, the day of God's final judgment of all people; end of the world.

ju·di·ca·ble (jo͞o′di-kə-b'l), *adj.* [LL. *judicabilis* < L. *judicatus*, pp. of *judicare;* see JUDGE, *v.*], 1. that can be judged. 2. liable to be judged.

ju·di·ca·tive (jo͞o′di-kā′tiv, jo͞o′di-kə-tiv), *adj.* [L. *judicatus*, pp. of *judicare* (see JUDGE, *v.*); + *-ive*], judging; judicial.

ju·di·ca·to·ry (jo͞o′di-kə-tôr′i, jo͞o′di-kə-tō′ri), *adj.* [LL. *judicatorius* < L. *judicatus*, pp. of *judicare;* see JUDGE, *v.*], judging; having to do with administering justice. *n.* [*pl.* JUDICATORIES (-iz, -riz)], [LL. *judicatorium;* see the *adj.*], 1. a court of law; tribunal. 2. the system of administration of justice; law courts collectively.

ju·di·ca·ture (jo͞o′di-kə-chẽr), *n.* [Fr.; ML. *judicatura* < L. *judicare;* see JUDGE, *v.*], 1. the administering of justice. 2. the position, functions, or legal power of a judge. 3. the extent of legal power of a judge or court of law; jurisdiction. 4. a court of law. 5. judges or courts of law collectively.

ju·di·cial (jo͞o-dish′əl), *adj.* [L. *judicialis* < *judex;* see JUDGE], 1. of judges, law courts, or their functions. 2. allowed, enforced, or set by order of a judge or law court. 3. administering justice. 4. like or befitting a judge; hence, 5. fair; unbiased; carefully considering the facts, arguments, etc., and reasoning to a decision.

ju·di·ci·ar·y (jo͞o-dish′i-er′i, jo͞o-dish′ẽr-i), *adj.* [L. *judiciarius* < *judicium*, judgment, court of justice < *judex;* see JUDGE], of judges, law courts, or their functions. *n.* [*pl.* JUDICIARIES (-iz)], 1. the part of government whose work is the administration of justice; system of law courts. 2. judges collectively.

ju·di·cious (jo͞o-dish′əs), *adj.* [Fr. *judicieux* < L. *judicium*, judgment < *judex;* see JUDGE], having, applying, or showing sound judgment; wise and careful. —***SYN.*** see **wise.**

Ju·dith (jo͞o′dith), [L.; Gr. *Ioudith;* Heb. *yehūdhīth*, woman of Judah, lit., praised (by the Lord)], a feminine name: diminutive, *Judy. n.* 1. a book of the Apocrypha and the Douay Bible. 2. the Jewish woman told about in this book, who saved her people by killing the Assyrian general Holofernes. Abbreviated **Jud.**

ju·do (jo͞o′dō), *n.* jujitsu.

Ju·dy (jo͞o′di), a feminine name: see **Judith.** *n.* Punch's wife in the puppet show *Punch and Judy.*

jug (jug), *n.* [echoic], a sound meant to imitate a nightingale's note. *v.i.* [JUGGED (jugd), JUGGING], to make a nightingale's sound or a sound imitating this.

jug (jug), *n.* [apparently a pet form of *Judith* or *Joan;* corresponds to ME. *jubbe* < *Job*], 1. an earthenware, glass, or metal container for liquids, usually with a small opening and a handle. 2. [Slang], a jail. *v.t.* [JUGGED (jugd), JUGGING], 1. to put into a jug. 2. to cook in a jug. 3. [Slang], to jail.

ju·gal (jo͞o′gəl), *adj.* [L. *jugalis* < *jugum*, a yoke], 1. designating or of a bone of the side of the face, under the eye. 2. of the cheek.

ju·gate (jo͞o′git, jo͞o′gāt), *adj.* [L. *jugatus*, pp. of *jugare*, to yoke, connect < *jugum*, a yoke], 1. in *biology*, paired. 2. in *botany*, having paired leaflets.

Jug·ger·naut (jug′ẽr-nôt′), *n.* [altered < Hind. *Jagannāth;* Sans. *Jagannātha*, lord of the world < *jagat*, world + *nātha*, lord], 1. an incarnation of the Hindu god Vishnu, whose idol, it is said, so excited his worshipers when it was hauled along on a large car during religious rites that they threw themselves under the wheels and were crushed: also **Jagannath.** 2. [often j-], anything that exacts blind devotion or terrible sacrifice. 3. [often j-], any terrible, irresistible force.

jug·gle (jug′'l), *v.t.* [JUGGLED (-'ld), JUGGLING], [ME. *jogelen;* OFr. *jogler*, *jugler*, to juggle, play false < L. *joculari*, to joke < *joculus*, dim. of *jocus*, a joke], 1. to perform skillful tricks of sleight of hand with (balls, knives, etc.). 2. to manipulate or practice trickery on (a thing or a person) so as to deceive or cheat: as, the cashier *juggled* the figures to show a profit. *v.i.* to toss up a number of balls, knives, etc. and keep them continuously in the air. **n.** 1. an act of juggling. 2. a clever trick or deception.

jug·gler (jug′lẽr), *n.* 1. a person who juggles; expert in tricks of sleight of hand. 2. a person who practices trickery to deceive or cheat.

jug·gler·y (jug′lẽr-i), *n.* [*pl.* JUGGLERIES (-iz)], [ME. & OFr. *jogelerie, juglerie*], 1. the art or act of juggling; sleight of hand. 2. trickery; deception.

ju·glan·da·ceous (jōō′glan-dā′shəs), *adj.* [< Mod. L. *Juglandaceae*, walnut family < L. *juglans*, walnut], in *botany*, of the walnut family.

Ju·go·slav, Ju·go-Slav (ū′gō-släv′, ū′gō-slav′), *n.* & *adj.* Yugoslav.

Ju·go·sla·vi·a, Ju·go-Sla·vi·a (ū′gō-slä′vi-ə), *n.* Yugoslavia.

Ju·go·sla·vi·an (ū′gō-slä′vi-ən), *adj.* & *n.* Yugoslavian.

Ju·go·slav·ic (ū′gō-släv′ik), *adj.* Yugoslavic.

jug·u·lar (jug′yoo-lẽr, jōō′gyoo-lẽr), *adj.* [Mod. L. *jugularis* < L. *jugulum*, collarbone, neck, throat, dim. of *jugum*, a yoke], 1. of the neck or throat. 2. of a jugular vein. 3. in *zoology*, of or having ventral fins in front of the pectoral, under the throat. *n.* a jugular vein.

jugular vein, either of two large veins in the neck carrying blood back from the head to the heart.

ju·gu·late (jōō′gyoo-lāt′), *v.t.* [JUGULATED (-id), JUGULATING], [L. *jugulatus*, pp. of *jugulare* < *jugulum*; see JUGULAR], 1. to cut the throat of or strangle; hence, 2. in *medicine*, to halt (a disease) by severe measures.

Ju·gur·tha (jōō-gũr′thə), *n.* a king of Numidia (113–104 B.C.); lived ?–104 B.C.

juice (jōōs), *n.* [ME. *juis, juce, jus;* OFr. *jus;* L. *jus*, broth, soup, juice], 1. the liquid part of a plant, fruit, or vegetable. 2. a liquid in or from animal tissue: as, gastric *juice*, meat *juice*. 3. the essence of anything. 4. [Slang], electricity. 5. [Slang], gasoline, oil, or any other liquid that supplies power. *v.t.* [JUICED (jōōst), JUICING], [Colloq.], to extract juice from.

juic·i·ly (jōō′s′l-i), *adv.* in a juicy manner.

juic·i·ness (jōō′si-nis), *n.* the quality of being juicy.

juic·y (jōō′si), *adj.* [JUICIER (-si-ẽr), JUICIEST (-si-ist)], 1. full of juice; containing much juice. 2. full of interest, as a joke or story; piquant; lively; racy; spicy.

ju·jit·su (jōō-jit′sōō), *n.* [Japan. *jū-jutsu*, lit., soft art; *jū*, soft, pliant + *jutsu*, art], a Japanese system of wrestling in which the strength and weight of an opponent are used against him by means of anatomical knowledge and the principle of leverage: also **jujutsu, jiujitsu, jiujutsu, judo.**

ju·ju (jōō′jōō), *n.* [W. Afr.; ? < Fr. *joujou*, a toy], 1. a magic charm or fetish used by some West African tribes. 2. its magic. 3. a taboo connected with its use.

ju·jube (jōō′jōōb), *n.* [Fr.; ML. *jujuba* < L. *zizyphum;* Gr. *zizyphon* < Per. *zīzafūn*], 1. the edible, datelike fruit of any of a number of trees and shrubs of the buckthorn family growing in warm climates. 2. a tree or shrub bearing this fruit. 3. a jelly made from this fruit. 4. a lozenge of gelatinous candy flavored with or like this fruit.

ju·jut·su (jōō-jit′sōō, jōō-joot′sōō), *n.* jujitsu.

juke box (jōōk), [Negro Gullah *jook-house*, roadhouse; orig., house of prostitution; akin to W. Afr. *dzug, dzog, dzugu*], [Colloq.], an electric phonograph used in some restaurants, saloons, etc., operated by dropping a coin in a slot and pushing a button to choose the record.

Jukes, the (jōōks), *the fictitious name of* a New York family whose case history over several generations, compiled by 19th-century sociologists, shows an abnormally high incidence of poverty, disease, criminality, etc.: a similar study was made of a New Jersey family (fictitious name, *the Kallikaks*).

Jul., July.

ju·lep (jōō′lip), *n.* [Fr.; Ar. *julāb;* Per. *gulāb*, julep, rose water; *gul*, rose + *āb*, water], 1. a cool drink containing aromatic herbs. 2. a cold drink made of whisky or brandy flavored with sugar and fresh mint: also **mint julep.** 3. a mixture of water with sirup or sugar for administering medicine.

Jul·ia (jōōl′yə), [L., fem. of *Julius;* see JULIUS], a feminine name: diminutive, *Juliet;* equivalents, Fr. & G. *Julie*, It. *Giulia.*

Jul·ian (jōōl′yən), [L. *Julianus* < *Julius;* see JULIUS], a masculine name: diminutive, *Jule;* feminine, *Juliana;* equivalents, Fr. *Julien*, It. *Giuliano.* *n.* (*Flavius Claudius Julianus*), nephew of *Constantine the Great;* Roman statesman and general; emperor of Rome (361–363 A.D.); lived 331–363 A.D.: called *Julian the Apostate.* *adj.* of Julius Caesar.

Ju·li·an·a (jōō′li-an′ə), [L., fem. of *Julian*], a feminine name: equivalents, Fr. *Julienne*, It. *Giuliana.* *n.* (D. yü′li-ä′nȧ), queen of the Netherlands (1948–); born 1909.

Julian Alps, a range of the Alps, between Italy and Yugoslavia: highest peak, Triglav, 9,394 ft.

Julian calendar, the calendar introduced by Julius Caesar in 46 B.C., in which the ordinary year had 365 days and every fourth year (leap year) had 366 days: the months were the same as in the Gregorian or New Style calendar now used.

ju·li·enne (jōō′li-en′; Fr. zhü′lyen′), *n.* [Fr.; named after *Julien*, a French caterer of Boston], a clear soup containing vegetables cut into strips or bits. *adj.* in *cooking*, cut into strips: said of vegetables.

Ju·li·et (jōōl′yət, jōō′li-ət, jōō′li-et′), [Fr. *Juliette*, dim. < L. *Julia*], a feminine name: see **Julia.** *n.* the heroine of Shakespeare's tragedy *Romeo and Juliet:* see **Romeo.**

Juliet cap, a girl's small cap, worn usually on the back of the head.

Jul·ius (jōōl′yəs), [L., name of a Roman gens], a masculine name: diminutive, *Jule;* feminine, *Julia;* equivalents, Fr. *Jules*, It. *Giulio*, Sp. *Julio.*

Julius Caesar, see **Caesar, Julius.**

Jul·lun·dur (jul′ən-dẽr), *n.* a city in Punjab, India: pop., 169,000.

Ju·ly (jōō-li′), *n.* [*pl.* JULIES (-līz′)], [Anglo-Fr. *Julie;* L. *Julius* < *mensis Julius*, the month of Julius (Caesar)], the seventh month of the year, having 31 days: abbreviated **Jul., Jl., Jy.**

jum·ble (jum′b'l), *n.* [prob. OFr. *jumel, gemel* (Fr. *jumeau*), twin; see GIMBAL], a kind of cooky shaped like a ring: also spelled **jumbal.**

jum·ble (jum′b'l), *v.t.* [JUMBLED (-b'ld), JUMBLING], [portmanteau merging of *jump* with *tumble, fumble*, etc.], 1. to mix in a confused, disorderly heap. 2. to confuse mentally. *v.i.* to be jumbled. *n.* 1. a confused mixture or heap. 2. a muddle. —***SYN.*** see **confusion.**

jum·bo (jum′bō), *n.* [*pl.* JUMBOS (-bōz)], [after *Jumbo*, the famous elephant exhibited by P. T. Barnum; prob. < *mumbo jumbo*], a large, clumsy person, animal, or thing; unusually large thing of its kind. *adj.* very large; larger than usual of its kind: sometimes used as a trade classification of size, as of olives.

Jum·na (jum′nə), *n.* a river in northern India, joining the Ganges at Allahabad: length, 850 mi.

jump (jump), *v.i.* [? It. loan word (16th c.) < orig. Gmc. source; cf. North It. *tzumpa*, Dan. *gumpe* (G. dial. *gumpen*) < *gump*, buttocks], 1. to move oneself suddenly from the ground, etc. by using the leg muscles; leap; spring. 2. to be moved with a jerk; bob; bounce. 3. to start in sudden surprise. 4. to pass suddenly from one thing or topic to another. 5. to rise suddenly: as, prices have *jumped*. 6. in *checkers*, to move a piece over an opponent's piece, thus capturing it. *v.t.* 1. to leap over. 2. to cause to leap: as, he *jumped* his horse over the fence. 3. *a*) to leap upon; spring aboard. *b*) to leap from (a moving train, etc.). 4. to cause (prices, etc.) to rise. 5. to break in continuity of action, as a motion-picture image, because of faulty alignment of the film. 6. [Slang], to attack suddenly. 7. [Slang], to leave suddenly; flee: as, he *jumped* town. 8. in *bridge*, to raise (a partner's bid) or, in contract, to make an unnecessarily high bid in (a partner's suit). 9. in *checkers*, to capture (an opponent's piece). 10. in *journalism*, to continue (a story) on another page. *n.* 1. a jumping; leap; bound; spring. 2. a distance jumped. 3. a thing to be jumped over. 4. a sudden transition. 5. a sudden rise, as in prices. 6. a sudden, nervous start or jerk; twitch; hence, 7. *pl.* [Slang], chorea; also, delirium tremens (usually with *the*). 8. in *athletics*, a contest in jumping: as, the high *jump*, the broad *jump*. 9. in *checkers*, a move by which an opponent's piece is captured. 10. in *journalism*, a line telling on what page a story is continued. *adj.* designating or of a style of jazz music characterized by the constant mechanical repetition of short riffs and a strong, steady beat.

get (or **have**) **the jump on,** [Slang], to get (or have) an earlier start than and thus have an advantage over.

jump a claim, to seize mining rights or land claimed by someone else.

jump at, 1. to reach (a conclusion) hastily, without careful consideration. 2. to accept hastily and eagerly.

jump bail, to forfeit one's bail by running away.

jump off, [Military Slang], to start an attack.

jump on, [Slang], to scold; censure.

jump the gun, [Slang], 1. to begin a race before the signal has been given; hence, 2. to begin anything before the proper time.

jump the track, to go suddenly off the rails.

on the jump, [Colloq.], busily moving about; busy.

jump ball, in *basketball*, a ball tossed by the referee between two opposing players, as in beginning or resuming play.

jump bid, in *bridge*, a bid that is higher than is necessary to increase the previous bid.

jump·er (jum′pẽr), *n.* 1. a person or thing that jumps. 2. a kind of sled. 3. a watch pawl. 4. a short wire to close a break in, or cut out part of, a circuit. 5. a man or boy who delivers packages from a delivery truck. 6. in *mining*, a boring tool that is operated with an up-and-down jumping motion.

jump·er (jum′pẽr), *n.* [< earlier dial. *jump*, short coat; prob. < Fr. *juppe, jupe;* Sp. *aljuba*, Moorish garment; Ar. *al jubbah; al*, the + *jubbah*, loose outer garment], 1. a loose jacket or blouse, worn by workmen and sailors to protect clothing. 2. a sleeveless dress for wearing over a blouse or sweater. 3. a hooded fur jacket. 4. *pl.* rompers.

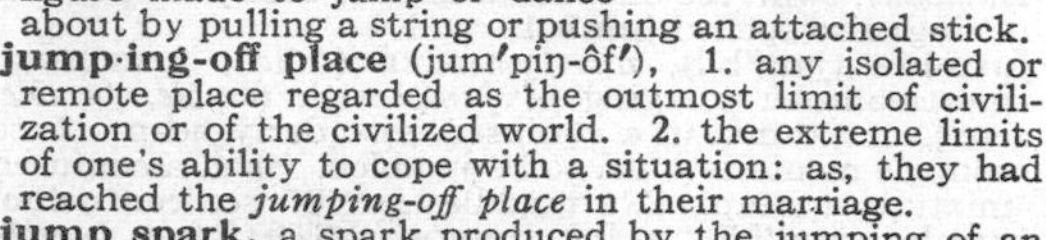

JUMPER

jump·i·ly (jum′p'l-i), *adv.* in a jumpy manner.
jump·i·ness (jum′pi-nis), *n.* the quality or state of being jumpy.
jumping bean, the seed of any of several related Mexican plants, which is caused to jump and roll about by the movements of a moth larva inside it.
jumping jack, a child's toy consisting of a little jointed figure made to jump or dance about by pulling a string or pushing an attached stick.
jump·ing-off place (jum′piŋ-ôf′), 1. any isolated or remote place regarded as the outmost limit of civilization or of the civilized world. 2. the extreme limits of one's ability to cope with a situation: as, they had reached the *jumping-off place* in their marriage.
jump spark, a spark produced by the jumping of an electric current across a space between permanently fixed poles, as in the ignition system of some engines.
jump·y (jum′pi), *adj.* [JUMPIER (-pi-ẽr), JUMPIEST (-pi-ist)], 1. moving in jumps, jerks, or abrupt variations. 2. easily made nervous; apprehensive.
Jun., 1. June. 2. Junior.
jun·ca·ceous (juŋ-kā′shəs), *adj.* [< Mod. L. *Juncaceae*, the rush family < L. *juncus*, a rush], in *botany*, of the rush family.
jun·co (juŋ′kō), *n.* [*pl.* JUNCOS (-kōz)], [prob. < Sp. *junco*, a rush; L. *juncus*, a rush], any of a number of American finches found from the Arctic regions to Central America; snowbird.
junc·tion (juŋk′shən), *n.* [L. *junctio* < *jungere*, to join], 1. a joining or being joined. 2. a place or point of joining or crossing, as of highways or railroads: abbreviated **jct., junc.**
junc·ture (juŋk′chẽr), *n.* [L. *junctura* < *jungere*, to join], 1. a joining or being joined. 2. a point or line of joining or connection; joint, as of two bones, or seam. 3. a point of time. 4. a particular or critical moment in the development of events; crisis. 5. a state of affairs.
June (jo͞on), a feminine name: see **Junius.** *n.* [Fr. *juin;* L. *Junius* < *mensis Junius*, the month of Junius (a Roman family name)], the sixth month of the year, having 30 days: abbreviated **Je., Ju., Jun.**
Ju·neau (jo͞o′nō), *n.* the capital of Alaska, on the southeastern coast: pop., 7,000.
June·ber·ry (jo͞on′ber′i, jo͞on′bẽr-i), *n.* [*pl.* JUNEBERRIES (-iz)], 1. any of a number of related plants of the rose family, with white flowers, purple-black berries, and leaves usually covered with white, wooly hairs; shadbush; shadblow. 2. its fruit.
June bug, 1. any of several large, brownish beetles of the cockchafer group, found in the northern United States: they begin to appear in early June. 2. the figeater, a large, green beetle of the southern United States. Also called *June beetle.*
Jung, Carl Gus·tav (kärl goos′täf yooŋ), 1875–1961; Swiss psychologist.
Jung·frau (yooŋ′frou′), *n.* a mountain of the Bernese Alps, southern Switzerland: height, 13,667 ft.
jun·gle (juŋ′g'l), *n.* [Hind. *jangal*, desert, forest, jungle < Sans. *jangala*, wasteland, desert], 1. land covered with dense growth of trees, tall vegetation, vines, etc., typically in tropical regions, and inhabited by predatory animals. 2. any thick, tangled growth. 3. [Slang], a hoboes' camp.
jungle fever, a severe malarial fever.
jungle fowl, any of several game birds native to Malaysia and India, having combs and throat wattles: the red Indian species is regarded as the ancestor of the present-day domestic fowl.
jung·ly (jun′gli), *adj.* covered with, or like, a jungle.
jun·ior (jo͞on′yẽr), *adj.* [L., contr. of *juvenior*, compar. of *juvenis*, young], 1. the younger: written *Jr.* after the name of a son who bears the same name as his father: opposed to *senior.* 2. of more recent position or lower status: as, a *junior* partner, a *junior* lien. 3. of later date. 4. made up of younger members. 5. relating to a third-year student or class in a high school or college. *n.* 1. a younger person. 2. a person of lower standing or rank. 3. a member of a third-year class in a high school or college. Abbreviated **jr., jun.**
one's junior, a person younger than oneself.
junior college, a school giving training in only the first one or two years of the standard college course.
junior high school, a school intermediate between elementary school and senior high school: it usually has the seventh, eighth, and ninth grades.
jun·ior·i·ty (jo͞on-yôr′ə-ti, jo͞on-yor′ə-ti), *n.* the quality or state of being junior, as in age or rank.
Junior League, any of the local branches of the Association of the Junior Leagues of America, Inc. (founded 1921), the members of which are young women of leisure and the upper social class organized to engage in volunteer welfare work.
Junior Leaguer, a member of a Junior League.
ju·ni·per (jo͞o′nə-pẽr), *n.* [L. *juniperus*], 1. a small evergreen shrub or tree of the pine family, with scale-like foliage and berrylike cones that yield an oil used for medicinal and other purposes. 2. any of several similar trees that bear cones.
Jun·ius (jo͞on′yəs, jo͞o′ni-əs), [L., name of a Roman gens], a masculine name: feminine, *June.* *n.* the pseudonym of the unknown writer of a series of public letters (1768–1772) criticizing the policies of the British ministry.
junk (juŋk), *n.* [in 15th-c. nautical language, worthless rope; ? < Port. *junco*, a reed, rush; L. *juncus*, a rush], 1. old cable or rope used for making oakum, mats, etc. 2. old metal, glass, paper, rags, etc. 3. a piece or chunk. 4. [Colloq.], useless stuff; trash; rubbish. 5. in *nautical usage*, hard salted meat. *v.t.* [Colloq.], to throw away as worthless; discard; scrap.

JUNK

junk (juŋk), *n.* [Sp. & Port. *junco* < Malay *dgong*], a Chinese flat-bottomed ship with battened sails.
Jun·ker, jun·ker (yooŋ′kẽr), *n.* [G. < MHG. *junc herre*, young nobleman; OHG. *jung*, young + *herro*, lord, orig. compar. of *her*, august, venerable, orig. old, gray], 1. a member of the privileged land-owning class in Germany; Prussian aristocrat. 2. formerly, a member of a reactionary political party in Prussia, made up of aristocrats seeking to keep their privileged position. *adj.* of or like the Junkers.
jun·ket (juŋ′kit), *n.* [formerly also *juncate* < It. *giuncata*, a sweetmeat, cream cheese < L. *juncus*, a rush: so called because originally brought to market in rush baskets], 1. curds with cream. 2. milk sweetened, flavored, and thickened into curd with rennet. 3. a feast or picnic. 4. an excursion for pleasure. 5. an excursion paid for out of public funds. *v.i.* to go on a junket or excursion, especially one paid for out of public funds. *v.t.* to entertain, as on a junket.
junk·man (juŋk′man′), *n.* [*pl.* JUNKMEN (-men′)], a dealer in old metal, glass, paper, rags, etc.
junk·yard (juŋk′yärd′), *n.* a place where old metal, paper, etc. is kept, sorted, and sold.
Ju·no (jo͞o′nō), *n.* [L.], 1. in *Roman mythology*, the goddess of marriage, Jupiter's wife and queen of the gods: identified with the Greek Hera. 2. [*pl.* JUNOS (-nōz)], a stately, regal woman.
Ju·no·esque (jo͞o′nō-esk′), *adj.* stately and regal like Juno.
jun·ta (jun′tə; Sp. hoon′tä), *n.* [Sp. < L. *juncta*, fem. of *junctus*, pp. of *jungere*, to join], 1. an assembly or council, particularly a Spanish or Latin-American legislative or administrative body. 2. a junto.
jun·to (jun′tō), *n.* [*pl.* JUNTOS (-tōz)], [altered form of *junta*], a group of political intriguers; faction; cabal.
Ju·pi·ter (jo͞o′pə-tẽr), *n.* [L.; orig. a vocative < bases of *Jovis*, Jove & *pater*, father], 1. in *Roman mythology*, the god ruling over all other gods and all people: identified with the Greek Zeus. 2. the largest planet in the solar system and the fifth in distance from the sun: diameter, 87,000 mi.; period of revolution, 11.86 yrs.; symbol, ♃.
Jupiter Plu·vi·us (plo͞o′vi-əs), [L., lit., Jupiter who brings rain; *pluvius*, rainy < *pleure*, to rain], Jupiter regarded as the giver of rain.
ju·pon (jo͞o′pon, jo͞o-pon′; Fr. zhü-pōn′), *n.* [OFr. < *jupe;* obs. It. *giuppa* (later *giubba*); Ar. *jubbah*, outer garment with long sleeves], a jacket or tunic formerly worn over or under armor: also **gipon.**
Ju·ra (joor′ə), *n.* the Jurassic period or rocks.
‡**ju·ra** (jo͞o′rə), *n.* [L.], plural of **jus, law.**
ju·ral (joor′əl), *adj.* [< L. *jus, juris*, right, law; + *-al*], 1. of law; legal. 2. relating to rights and duties.
Jura Mountains, a mountain range between Switzerland and France: highest peak, 5,654 ft.
ju·rant (joor′ənt), *adj.* [L. *jurans*, ppr. of *jurare*, to swear < *jus;* see JURAL], in *law*, taking oath; swearing. *n.* a person who takes oath.

Ju·ras·sic (joo-ras′ik), ***adj.*** [Fr. *jurassique* < *Jura*], designating or of the second period of the Mesozoic Era, immediately following the Triassic and preceding the Cretaceous, characterized by the dominance of dinosaurs and the appearance of flying reptiles and birds.
the Jurassic, the Jurassic Period or its rocks: see **geology,** chart.

ju·rat (joor′at), ***n.*** [Fr. < LL. *juratus*, lit., one sworn < L. *juratus*, pp. of *jurare*, to swear], 1. [Obs. except in historical usage], a person legally sworn. 2. a municipal officer or magistrate in certain French towns and the Channel Islands. 3. [< L. *juratum*, neut. pp. of *jurare*, to swear], in *law*, a statement added to an affidavit, telling when and before whom (also, in British usage, where) the affidavit was made.

ju·ra·to·ry (joor′ə-tôr′i, joor′ə-tō′ri), ***adj.*** [LL. *juratorius* < L. *jurator*, sworn witness < *jurare*, to swear], in *law*, of or expressed in an oath.

‡ju·re di·vi·no (jōō′ri di-vī′nō), [L.], by divine law.

‡ju·re hu·ma·no (jōō′ri hū-mā′nō), [L.], by human law.

ju·rel (hōō-rel′), ***n.*** [Sp.], any of a number of edible fishes of warm seas, having typically narrow bodies and widely forked tails.

ju·rid·ic (joo-rid′ik), ***adj.*** juridical.

ju·rid·i·cal (joo-rid′i-k′l), ***adj.*** [L. *juridicus* < *jus, juris*, right, law + *dicere*, to point out, declare; + *-al*], of judicial proceedings, jurisprudence, or law.

juridical days, the days on which courts are in session.

ju·ris·con·sult (joor′is-kən-sult′, joor′is-kon′sult), ***n.*** [L. *jurisconsultus*, lawyer; *jus, juris*, law + *consultus*; see CONSULT], a jurist: abbreviated **J.C.**

ju·ris·dic·tion (joor′is-dik′shən), ***n.*** [L. *jurisdictio*, *juris dictio*, administration of the law; *jus, juris*, right, law + *dictio* < *dicere*, to speak, declare], 1. the administering of justice; authority or legal power to hear and decide cases. 2. authority or power in general. 3. the range of authority. 4. the territorial range of authority. 5. a law court or system of law courts. —***SYN.*** see **power.**

ju·ris·dic·tion·al (joor′is-dik′shən-′l), ***adj.*** of jurisdiction.

ju·ris·pru·dence (joor′is-prōō′d′ns), ***n.*** [L. *jurisprudentia; jus, juris*, right, law + *prudentia*, a foreseeing, knowledge, skill], 1. the science or philosophy of law. 2. a system of laws. 3. a part or division of law.

ju·ris·pru·dent (joor′is-prōō′d′nt), ***n.*** [Fr. < *jurisprudence;* see JURISPRUDENCE], a student of jurisprudence; jurist. ***adj.*** skilled in the law.

ju·ris·pru·den·tial (joor′is-prōō-den′shəl), ***adj.*** of jurisprudence.

ju·rist (joor′ist), ***n.*** [Fr. *juriste;* ML. *jurista* < L. *jus, juris*, right, law], an expert in law; scholar or writer in the field of law.

ju·ris·tic (joo-ris′tik), ***adj.*** of jurists or jurisprudence; having to do with law; legal.

ju·ris·ti·cal·ly (joo-ris′ti-k′l-i), ***adv.*** in a juristic manner.

ju·ror (joor′ẽr), ***n.*** [ME. *jurour;* OFr. *jureur, jureor* < L. *jurator*, taker of an oath < *jurare*, to swear], a member of a jury or jury panel; juryman.

Ju·ru·á (zhōō′rōō-ä′), ***n.*** a river in western Brazil, flowing northeastward to the Amazon: length, c. 1,200 mi.

ju·ry (joor′i), ***n.*** [*pl.* JURIES (-iz)], [OFr. *jurée*, oath, judicial inquest < ML. *jurata*, a jury, properly fem. pp. of L. *jurare*, to take an oath, swear < *jus, juris*, law], 1. a group of people sworn to hear the evidence and inquire into the facts in a law case, and to give a decision in accordance with their findings. 2. a group of people, often experts, selected to decide the winners and award the prizes in a competition or contest.

ju·ry (joor′i), ***adj.*** [? < OFr. *ajurie*, relief < L. *adjutare*, to help; see ADJUTANT], for temporary or emergency use on a ship: as, a *jury* mast.

ju·ry·man (joor′i-mən), ***n.*** [*pl.* JURYMEN (-mən)], a juror.

ju·ry-rigged (joor′i-rigd′), ***adj.*** [see JURY, *adj.*], rigged for temporary use on a ship.

‡jus (zhü), ***n.*** [Fr.], juice; gravy: as, *au jus*, with gravy.

jus (jus), ***n.*** [*pl.* JURA (jōō′rə)], [L.], 1. (a or the) law. 2. a legal principle, right, or power.

‡jus ca·no·ni·cum (jus kə-non′i-kəm), [L.], canon law.

‡jus ci·vi·le (jus si-vī′li, jus siv′ə-li), [L.], civil law.

‡jus di·vi·num (jus di-vī′nəm), [L.], divine law.

‡jus gen·ti·um (jus jen′shi-əm), [L., law of nations], 1. ancient Roman law for aliens. 2. international law.

‡jus na·tu·rae (jus nə-tū′rē), [L.], law of nature; natural law.

Jus·se·rand, Jean Jules (zhän′ zhül′ zhüs′rän′), 1855–1932; French diplomat and literary historian.

jus·sive (jus′iv), ***adj.*** [< L. *jussus*, a command (< *jubere*, to command); + *-ive*], in *grammar*, expressing a command. ***n.*** in *grammar*, a jussive word, form, or mood.

just (just), ***adj.*** [ME.; OFr. *juste;* L. *justus*, lawful, rightful, proper < *jus*, right, law], 1. right or fair; equitable; impartial: as, a *just* decision. 2. righteous; upright: as, a *just* man. 3. deserved; merited: as, a *just* rebuke. 4. legally right; lawful; rightful. 5. right; proper. 6. well-founded: as, a *just* suspicion. 7. correct; true. 8. accurate; exact. ***adv.*** 1. exactly; precisely: as, *just* one o'clock. 2. almost exactly. 3. only; no more than: as, *just* a simple soul. 4. by a very little; barely: as, he *just* missed the train. 5. a very short time ago: as, she has *just* left. 6. [Colloq.], quite; really: as, it's *just* beautiful. —***SYN.*** see **fair, upright.**
just now, a moment ago.
just the same, [Colloq.], nevertheless.

just (just), ***n.*** & ***v.i.*** joust.

jus·tice (jus′tis), ***n.*** [ME. *justise;* OFr. *justice;* L. *justitia* < *justus;* see JUST, *adj.*], 1. the quality of being righteous. 2. impartiality; fairness. 3. the quality of being right or correct. 4. sound reason; rightfulness; validity. 5. reward or penalty as deserved; just deserts. 6. the use of authority and power to uphold what is right, just, or lawful. 7. the administration of law; procedure of a law court. 8. a judge: abbreviated **jus., just., j.** 9. a justice of the peace.
bring to justice, to cause (a wrongdoer) to be tried in court and duly punished.
do justice to, 1. to treat fitly or fairly. 2. to treat with due appreciation; enjoy properly.
do oneself justice, 1. to do something in a manner worthy of one's abilities. 2. to be fair to oneself.

justice of the peace, a magistrate with jurisdiction over a small district or part of a county, authorized to decide minor cases, commit persons to trial in a higher court, perform marriages, etc.: abbreviated **J.P.**

jus·tice·ship (jus′tis-ship′), ***n.*** the position, functions, or term of office of a justice.

jus·ti·ci·a·ble (jus-tish′i-ə-b′l), ***adj.*** [OFr. < *justice;* see JUSTICE], 1. liable for trial in court. 2. subject to court jurisdiction.

jus·ti·ci·ar (jus-tish′i-ẽr), ***n.*** a justiciary.

jus·ti·ci·ar·y (jus-tish′i-er′i), ***n.*** [*pl.* JUSTICIARIES (-iz)], [ML. *justitiarius* < L. *justitia;* see JUSTICE], 1. in *English history*, the chief political and judicial officer under the Norman and early Plantagenet kings. 2. an officer of justice, especially a judge of a superior court. 3. the jurisdiction of a justiciar. ***adj.*** relating to the administration of justice or the office of a judge.

jus·ti·fi·a·bil·i·ty (jus′tə-fī′ə-bil′ə-ti), ***n.*** the quality or state of being justifiable.

jus·ti·fi·a·ble (jus′tə-fī′ə-b′l), ***adj.*** [Fr. < *justifier;* see JUSTIFY], that can be justified or defended as correct.

jus·ti·fi·a·bly (jus′tə-fī′i-bli), ***adv.*** in a justifiable manner; with good reason.

jus·ti·fi·ca·tion (jus′tə-fi-kā′shən), ***n.*** [Fr.; LL. *justificatio* < *justificare;* see JUSTIFY], 1. a justifying or being justified. 2. a fact that justifies or vindicates. 3. in *printing*, the adjustment of type by proper spacing.

justification by faith, in *theology*, the act by which a sinner is freed through faith from the penalty of his sin and is accepted by God as righteous or worthy of being saved.

jus·ti·fi·ca·to·ry (jus-tif′ə-kə-tôr′i, jus-tif′ə-kə-tō′ri, jus′tə-fi-kā′tə-ri), ***adj.*** [LL. *justificatus*, justified < *justificare* (see JUSTIFY); + *-ory*], justifying; serving to uphold or vindicate.

jus·ti·fi·er (jus′tə-fī′ẽr), ***n.*** a person or thing that justifies.

jus·ti·fy (jus′tə-fī′), ***v.t.*** [JUSTIFIED (-fīd′), JUSTIFYING], [ME. *justifien;* OFr. *justifier;* LL. *justificare*, to act justly toward, justify < L. *justus*, just + *-ficare* < *facere*, to do, make], 1. to show to be just, right, or in accord with reason. 2. to free from blame; declare guiltless; acquit; absolve. 3. to supply good or lawful grounds for; warrant. 4. in *printing*, to adjust (type) by spacing so that the lines will be of the correct length. ***v.i.*** 1. in *law*, *a)* to show an adequate reason for something done. *b)* to prove qualified as surety. 2. in *printing*, to fit; be in line or flush, as type.

Jus·tin (jus′tin), [L. *Justinus* < *justus;* see JUST], a masculine name: variant, *Justus;* feminine, *Justina.*

Justin, Saint, 2d century A.D.; Christian apologist: called *Justin Martyr.*

Jus·ti·na (jus-tī′nə), [L., fem. of *Justinus;* see JUSTIN], a feminine name: variant, *Justine.*

Jus·tin·i·an I (jus-tin′i-ən), 483–565 A.D.; Byzantine emperor (527–565 A.D.); known for the **Justinian Code,** the codification of the Roman law by his jurists: called *the Great.*

jus·tle (jus′′l), ***v.t.*** & ***v.i.*** to jostle.

just·ly (just′li), ***adv.*** 1. in a just manner. 2. rightly. 3. deservedly.

Jus·tus (jus′təs), a masculine name: see **Justin.**

jut (jut), ***v.i.*** [JUTTED (-id), JUTTING], [var. of *jet, v.*], to stick out; project; protrude. ***n.*** a part that juts.

Jute (jōōt), ***n.*** [AS. *Iote, Yte;* L. *Iuta*], a member of any of several Germanic tribes that lived long ago in Jutland: Jutes invading southeastern England in the 5th century A.D. spearheaded the Anglo-Saxon conquest.

jute (jōōt), *n.* [E. Ind. *jhuto;* Sans. *juṭa*, matted hair, *jaṭa*, braid of hair, fibrous roots], 1. a strong, glossy fiber used for making burlap, sacks, mats, rope, etc. 2. either of two East Indian plants from which this fiber is obtained. *adj.* of jute.

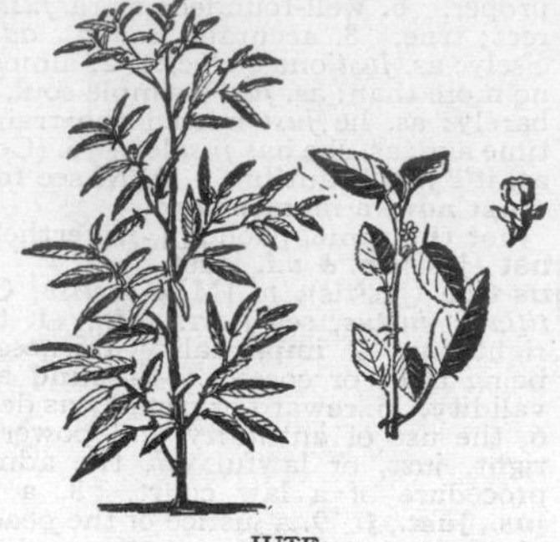

JUTE plant (5–10 ft. high); branch; flower

Jut·ish (jōōt′ish), *adj.* of the Jutes.
Jut·land (jut′lənd), *n.* the peninsula of northern Europe which forms the mainland of Denmark: Danish name, *Jylland*: a naval battle between the Germans and the British was fought in the Skagerrak, a strait near Jutland, in 1916.
jut·ty (jut′i), *n.* [*pl.* JUTTIES (-iz)], [prob. a form of *jetty*, influenced by *jut*], [Obs.], 1. a projecting part, as of a wall. 2. a pier; mole; jetty. *v.i. & v.t.* [Obs.], to project; overhang.
Ju·ve·nal (jōō′və-n′l), *n.* (*Decimus Junius Juvenalis*), Roman satirical poet; lived 60?–140? A.D.
ju·ve·nes·cence (jōō′və-nes′′ns), *n.* [< *juvenescent*], a becoming young or youthful.
ju·ve·nes·cent (jōō′və-nes′′nt), *adj.* [L. *juvenescens*, ppr. of *juvenescere*, to become young < *juvenis*, young], becoming young; growing youthful.
ju·ven·ile (jōō′və-n′l, jōō′və-nīl′), *adj.* [L. *juvenilis* < *juvenis*, young], 1. young; youthful; immature. 2. of, characteristic of, or suitable for children or young persons. *n.* 1. a young person; child. 2. an actor who takes youthful rolès. 3. a book for children. Abbreviated **juv.** —*SYN.* see **young.**
juvenile court, a law court for cases involving children under a fixed age.
ju·ve·nil·i·a (jōō′və-nil′i-ə, jōō′və-nil′yə), *n.pl.* [L., neut. pl. of *juvenilis;* see JUVENILE], writings, paintings, etc. done in childhood or youth.
ju·ve·nil·i·ty (jōō′və-nil′ə-ti), *n.* [*pl.* JUVENILITIES (-tiz)], 1. the quality or state of being juvenile. 2. a childish action, manner, or characteristic. 3. juveniles collectively.
jux·ta- (juks′tə), [< L. *juxta*, near, beside], a combining form meaning *near, beside, close by*, as in *juxtaposition.*
jux·ta·pose (juks′tə-pōz′), *v.t.* [JUXTAPOSED (-pōzd′), JUXTAPOSING], [*juxta-* + *pose, v.*], to put side by side; place close together.
jux·ta·po·si·tion (juks′tə-pə-zish′ən), *n.* [Fr.; L. *juxta*, near to + Fr. *position;* see POSITION], 1. a putting side by side or close together. 2. the position of being side by side or close together.
J.W.V., Jewish War Veterans (of the United States).
Jy., July.
Jyl·land (yül′län), *n.* Jutland: the Danish name.

K

K, k (kā), *n.* [*pl.* K's, k's, Ks, ks (kāz)], 1. the eleventh letter of the English alphabet: from the Greek *kappa*, a borrowing from the Phoenician: see **alphabet**, table. 2. the sound of K or k, normally an unvoiced, back-tongue stop consonant, IPA [k]: when used as the first letter of a word and followed by *n*, it is usually not pronounced (e.g., *knee, knife*). 3. a type or impression for K or k. 4. *a symbol for* the eleventh in a sequence or group (or the tenth if J is omitted). *adj.* 1. of K or k. 2. eleventh in a sequence or group (or tenth if J is omitted).
K (kā), *n.* 1. an object shaped like K. 2. a Roman numeral for 250: with a superior bar ($\overline{K}$), 250,000. 3. in *assaying, the symbol for* carat. 4. *kalium*, [Mod. L.], in *chemistry, the symbol for* potassium. 5. in *mathematics, a symbol for* constant. 6. in *meteorology, a symbol for* smoke. *adj.* shaped like K.
K, 1. knit. 2. in *chess*, king.
K., k., 1. karat (carat). 2. kilo. 3. kilogram. 4. king. 5. knight. 6. kopeck; kopecks. 7. krona; kronor. 8. krone; kronen; kroner. 9. in *electricity*, capacity. 10. in *nautical usage*, knot.
K2, the Godwin Austen, a mountain in India.
ka (kä), *n.* [Egypt.], in *ancient Egyptian religion*, the soul, regarded as dwelling in a person's body or in an image and continuing after death.
Kaa·ba (kä′bə, kä′ə-bə), *n.* [Ar. *ka'bah*, lit., square building < *ka'b*, a cube], the sacred Moslem shrine at Mecca, toward which believers turn when praying: it is a small stone structure in the court of the great mosque and contains a black stone supposedly given to Abraham by the angel Gabriel: also spelled **Caaba.**
kab (kab), *n.* a cab (measure).
kab·a·la, kab·ba·la (kab′ə-lə, kə-bä′lə), *n.* cabala.
Ka·bar·di·no-Bal·kar Autonomous Soviet Socialist Republic (kä′bär-dē′nô-bål-kär′), a division of the R.S.F.S.R., in the Caucasus: area, 4,747 sq. mi.; pop., 377,000; capital, Nalchik.
ka·bobs (kə-bobz′), *n.pl.* cabobs.
Ka·bul (kä′bool), *n.* the capital of Afghanistan: pop., c. 120,000.
Ka·byle (kə-bīl′), *n.* [Fr. < Ar. *qabā'il*, pl. of *qabīlah*], 1. a member of the Algerian or Tunisian Berber tribes. 2. the Berber dialect of the Kabyles, belonging to the Hamitic family of languages.
kad·dish (käd′ish), *n.* [Aram. *qaddīsh*, holy], in *Judaism*, a hymn in praise of God, recited as a mourners' prayer.
Ka·desh (kā′desh), *n.* an ancient city in Syria.
ka·di (kä′di, kā′di), *n.* a cadi.
Kaf·fir (kaf′ẽr), *n.* [Ar. *kāfir*, infidel < *kafara*, to be skeptical about religion], 1. a South African Bantu. 2. the language of the Kaffirs. 3. a Kafir.
kaf·fir (kaf′ẽr), *n.* [< *Kaffir*], any of a group of grain sorghums grown in dry regions for grain and fodder: also **kaffir corn.**
Kaf·fra·ri·a (kə-frâr′i-ə), *n.* the region of the Kaffirs, in eastern Cape Province, Union of South Africa.
Ka·fir (käf′ẽr, kaf′ẽr), *n.* [Ar. *kāfir;* see KAFFIR], 1. a member of an Indo-Iranian people of Kafiristan. 2. a non-Moslem: term of contempt used by Moslems. 3. a Kaffir.
ka·fir (kä′fẽr, kaf′ẽr), *n.* kaffir.
Ka·fi·ri·stan (kä′fi-ri-stän′), *n.* a mountainous region in eastern Afghanistan, south of the Hindu Kush Mountains.
Kaf·ka, Franz (fränts käf′kä), 1883–1924; Austrian writer.
kaf·tan (kaf′tən, käf′tän′), *n.* a caftan.
Ka·ga·wa, To·yo·hi·ko (tô′yô-hē′kô kä′gä-wä′), 1888–1960; Japanese writer and social reformer.
ka·go (kä′gō), *n.* [Japan.], a Japanese palanquin: it is carried on a pole over the shoulders of two bearers.
Ka·go·shi·ma (kä′gô-shē′mä), *n.* a city on the southern coast of Kyushu, Japan: pop., 170,000 (est. 1947).
Kahn test (kän), [after R. L. *Kahn* (1887–), Am. immunologist, who developed it], a modified form of the Wassermann test for the diagnosis of syphilis.
Ka·hoo·la·we (kä′hōō-lä′wē), *n.* one of the Hawaiian Islands, southwest of Maui: area, 45 sq. mi.: see **Hawaiian Islands,** map.
kai·ak (kī′ak), *n.* a kayak.
Kai·e·teur Falls (kī′e-tōōr′), a waterfall in central British Guiana: height, 741 ft.
Kai·feng (kī′fuŋ′), *n.* the capital of Honan province, China, on the Yellow River: pop., 200,000.
kail (kāl), *n.* kale; cole.
kail·yard (kāl′yärd′), *n.* [Scot.], a kaleyard: applied to fiction by J. M. Barrie and others (the *kailyard school*) treating Scottish life and using much Scottish dialect.
ka·i·nite (kä-ī-nīt′, kī′nīt), *n.* [G. *kainit* < Gr. *kainos*, new; cf. RECENT], a mineral, $MgSO_4 \cdot MgCl_2 \cdot K_2SO_4 \cdot 6H_2O$, much used in fertilizers as a source of potassium.
Kair·ouan (ker′wän′), *n.* a city in northeastern Tunisia: holy city of the Moslems: pop., 23,000.
kai·ser (kī′zẽr), *n.* [ME. *kaiser, cayser* < AS. *casere*, ON. *keisari*, etc. < L. *Caesar*, family name of first Roman emperors; reinforced, esp., in senses *b* & *c*, by

MD. *keiser* & G. *kaiser* (in 17th c.)], emperor: the title [K-] of *a*) the rulers of the Holy Roman Empire, 962–1806. *b*) the rulers of Austria, 1804–1918. *c*) the rulers of Germany, 1871–1918.

Kai·ser, Henry J. (kī'zẽr), 1882– ; American industrialist.

Kai·sers·lau·tern (kī'zẽrs-lou'tẽrn), *n.* a city in southwestern Germany: pop., 63,000.

ka·ka (kä'kə), *n.* [Maori; echoic of the bird's cry], a New Zealand parrot having an olive-brown body with markings of various other colors.

ka·ka·po (kä'kä-pō'), *n.* [Maori; *kaka*, parrot + *po*, night], the nocturnal parrot of New Zealand, having a green body with brown and yellow markings.

ka·ke·mo·no (kä'ke-mô'nō), *n.* [Japan.; *kake*, to hang + *mono*, thing], a Japanese hanging or scroll made of silk or paper with an inscription or picture on it and a roller at the bottom.

ka·ki (kä'kē), *n.* [*pl.* KAKIS (-kēz)], [Japan.], **1.** the Japanese persimmon, or date plum, an Asiatic tree of the ebony family. **2.** its edible fruit.

kal., kalends.

ka·la-a·zar (kä'lä-ä-zär', kä'lä-az'ẽr), *n.* [Hind. *kālā-āzār*, lit., black disease], an infectious disease caused by a protozoan parasite and characterized by an enlarged spleen and liver, irregular fever, anemia, etc.: also called *black fever, visceral leishmaniasis.*

Ka·la·ha·ri (kä'lä-hä'ri), *n.* a desert plateau in Bechuanaland, southern Africa: area, c. 400,000 sq. mi.

Kal·a·ma·zoo (kal'ə-mə-zōō'), *n.* a city in southwestern Michigan: pop., 82,000.

Ka·lat (kə-lät'), *n.* **1.** a former state in western India and Pakistan: now a division of West Pakistan. **2.** the former capital of Kalat state.

Kalb, Johann, see **De Kalb, Johann.**

kale (kāl), *n.* [Scot. *kale, kail*, var. of *cole*], **1.** a hardy, nonheading cabbage with loose, spreading, curled leaves; cole or colewort. **2.** [Scot.], *a*) any cabbage or greens. *b*) a broth made of cabbage or other greens. **3.** [Slang], money; especially, paper money.

ka·lei·do·scope (kə-lī'də-skōp'), *n.* [< Gr. *kalos*, beautiful + *eidos*, form; + *-scope*], **1.** a tubelike instrument containing loose bits of colored glass reflected by mirrors so that various symmetrical patterns appear as the instrument is rotated. **2.** anything that constantly changes, as in color and pattern.

ka·lei·do·scop·ic (kə-lī'də-skop'ik), *adj.* **1.** of a kaleidoscope. **2.** constantly changing, as in pattern.

ka·lei·do·scop·i·cal·ly (kə-lī'də-skop'i-k'l-i), *adv.* in a kaleidoscopic manner.

kal·en·dar (kal'ən-dẽr), *n.* a calendar.

kal·ends (kal'əndz), *n.pl.* calends: abbreviated **kal.**

Ka·le·va·la (kä'li-vä'lä), *n.* [Finn.; *kaleva*, heroic + *-la*, abode, hence, lit., land of heroes], a Finnish epic poem in unrhymed trochaic verse, compiled by Elias Lönnrot from the oral transmission of folklore and mythology and first published in 1835.

kale·yard (kāl'yärd'), *n.* [Scot.], a vegetable garden; especially, a cabbage garden: see **kailyard.**

Kal·gan (kål'gän'), *n.* a city in northeastern China, formerly in Inner Mongolia: pop., 151,000.

kal·i (kal'i, kā'li), *n.* [Ar. *qalīy*; see ALKALI], the glasswort; saltwort: when burned it yields soda ash.

Ka·li·da·sa (kä'li-dä'sä), *n.* Hindu poet and dramatist; fl. 5th century A.D.

ka·lif (kā'lif, kal'if), *n.* a caliph.

Ka·li·nin (kä-lē'nin), *n.* **1.** a region of the R.S.F.S.R., in western European Russia: pop., 1,802,000. **2.** its capital: pop., 261,000: formerly called *Tver.*

Ka·li·nin, Mi·kha·il I·va·no·vich (mē'khä-ēl' i-vän'ô-vich kä-lē'nin), 1875–1946; Russian statesman; president of the Soviet Union (1923–1946).

Ka·lin·in·grad (kä-lē'nin-grät'), *n.* a city in western U.S.S.R.: former capital of East Prussia: pop., 202,000: former, German name, *Königsberg.*

ka·liph (kā'lif, kal'if), *n.* a caliph.

Ka·lisz (kä'lish), *n.* a city in central Poland: pop., 48,000.

Kal·li·kaks, the (kal'ə-kaks'), see **Jukes, the.**

Kal·mar (käl'mär), *n.* a seaport in southeastern Sweden: pop., 30,000.

kal·mi·a (kal'mi-ə), *n.* [Mod. L., after Peter *Kalm* (1715–1779), Swed. botanist], any of a group of North American evergreen shrubs of the heath family, as the mountain laurel, with flowers of white or rose.

Kal·muck (kal'muk), *n.* [Turk. *kalmuk*, lit., that part (of the tribe) remaining (at home), orig. pp. of *kalmak*, to remain], **1.** a member of a group of Mongol peoples living chiefly in the Kalmuck A.S.S.R. and northern Sinkiang. **2.** the Altaic, western Mongolic language of the Kalmucks. Also **Kalmyk.**

Kalmuck Autonomous Soviet Socialist Republic, a former division of the R.S.F.S.R., in the northeastern Caucasus: area, 28,641 sq. mi.: abolished 1945.

Kal·myk (kal'mik), *n.* Kalmuck.

ka·long (kä'loŋ), *n.* [Jav. *kaloṅ*], a large, long-muzzled, fruit-eating bat of Malaysia and near-by regions.

kal·pak (kal'pak), *n.* a calpac.

kal·so·mine (kal'sə-mīn', kal'sə-min), *n.* & *v.t.* calcimine.

Ka·ma (kä'mə), *n.* [Sans. *kāma*, desire, love, god of love], in *Hindu mythology*, the god of love.

Ka·ma (kä'mä), *n.* a river flowing from the Ural mountain region of the R.S.F.S.R. into the Volga: length, 1,100 mi.

ka·ma·la (kə-mā'lə, kam'ə-lə), *n.* [Sans.], **1.** a powder obtained from an East Indian tree, used as the base of an orange-red dye for silk and wool. **2.** the tree.

Kam·chat·ka (kam-chat'kə; Russ. käm-chät'kä), *n.* a peninsula in northeastern Siberia, between the Sea of Okhotsk and the Bering Sea: length, c. 800 mi.; area, c. 105,000 sq. mi.

kame (kām), *n.* [north Brit. dial. var. of *comb, coomb*], a hill or short, high ridge of stratified glacial material.

‡Ka·me·rad (kä'mə-rät'), *n.* [*pl.* KAMERADEN (-räd''n)], [G.], comrade: a German soldiers' cry of surrender.

Ka·me·run (kam'ə-rōōn'; G. kä'mə-rōōn'), *n.* Cameroun or Cameroons: the German name.

‡ka·mi·ka·ze (kä'mi-kä'zi), *n.* [Japan., lit., divine wind < *kami*, (Shinto) god or goddess + *kaze*, the wind], **1.** a suicide attack by a Japanese airplane pilot in World War II. **2.** the airplane or pilot in such an attack.

kam·seen (kam-sēn'), *n.* a khamsin.

kam·sin (kam'sin), *n.* a khamsin.

Kan., Kansas.

Kan·a·ka (kə-nak'ə, kan'ə-kə), *n.* [Haw., man], **1.** a Hawaiian. **2.** a native of the South Sea Islands.

Ka·na·ra (kun'ə-rə; Eng. kə-nä'rə), *n.* a region in western and southern India: area, c. 8,000 sq. mi.: also spelled **Canara.**

Ka·na·rese (kä'nə-rēz'), *adj.* of Kanara, its people, or their language. *n.* **1.** [*pl.* KANARESE], any of a group of Dravidian people living chiefly in Kanara. **2.** their language, a dialect belonging to the Dravidian family of languages. Also spelled **Canarese.**

Ka·na·za·wa (kä'nȧ-zä'wȧ), *n.* a city on the western coast of Honshu, Japan: pop., 277,000.

Kan·chen·jun·ga, Mount (kän'chən-joon'gə), a mountain of the Himalayas, on the Nepal-Sikkim border: height, 28,146 ft.: also **Kinchinjunga.**

Kan·da·har (kən-də-här'), *n.* a city in southeastern Afghanistan: pop., 77,000.

Kan·dy (kan'di, kän'di), *n.* a city in central Ceylon: pop., 57,000: site of famous Buddhist temples.

kan·ga·roo (kaŋ'gə-rōō'), *n.* [*pl.* KANGAROOS (-rōōz'), KANGAROO; see PLURAL, II, D, 1], [prob. < former native Australian name in Queensland], any of a group of leaping, plant-eating mammals native to Australia and neighboring islands, with short forelegs, strong, large hind legs, and a long, thick tail: the female has a pouch, or marsupium, in front, in which she carries her young.

kangaroo court, [said to be so named because its justice progresses by leaps and bounds], [Colloq.], an unauthorized, irregular court, usually disregarding normal legal procedure, as an irregular court in a frontier region or a mock court set up by prison inmates.

kangaroo rat, **1.** a small Australian marsupial somewhat resembling a rat. **2.** any of various small mouselike rodents living in desert regions of the United States and Mexico.

Kan·ka·kee (kaŋ'kə-kē'), *n.* a city in northeastern Illinois: pop., 28,000.

Ka·no (kä'nō), *n.* a city in northern Nigeria: pop., 130,000.

Kan·san (kan'zən), *adj.* of Kansas. *n.* a native or inhabitant of Kansas.

Kan·sas (kan'zəs), *n.* **1.** a Middle Western State of the United States: area, 82,276 sq. mi.; pop., 2,179,000; capital, Topeka: abbreviated **Kan., Kans., Kas.**: nicknamed *Sunflower State.* **2.** a river flowing from northeastern Kansas into the Missouri at Kansas City: length, 169 mi.

Kansas City, **1.** a city in western Missouri, on the Missouri River: pop., 476,000. **2.** a city in Kansas, on the Missouri and Kansas Rivers, opposite Kansas City, Missouri: pop., 122,000.

Kan·su (kän'sōō'; Chin. gän'sōō'), *n.* a province of northwestern China: area, c. 250,000 sq. mi.; pop., 12,928,000; capital, Lanchow.

Kant, Im·ma·nu·el (i-mä'nōō-el känt; Eng. kant), 1724–1804; German philosopher.

kan·tar (kän-tär'), *n.* [Ar. *qinṭār* < L. *quintarius*, containing five < *quintus*, a fifth; see QUINT], an Egyptian weight equal to 99.05 pounds: it corresponds to the hundredweight.

Kant·i·an (kan'ti-ən), *adj.* of Kant or Kantianism. *n.* a follower of Kant or Kantianism.

Kant·i·an·ism (kan'ti-ən-iz'm), *n.* the philosophy of

Kant, who held that the content of knowledge comes a posteriori from sense perception, but that its form is determined by a priori categories of the mind: he also declared that God, freedom, and immortality cannot be denied and must necessarily be presupposed, although they cannot be proved.

Kant·ism (kant′iz'm), *n.* Kantianism.

ka·o·li·ang (kä′ō-li-aŋ′), *n.* [Chin., lit., tall grain], any of a group of grain-bearing sorghums of eastern Asia: some are now grown in the United States.

ka·o·lin, ka·o·line (kā′ə-lin), *n.* [Fr.; Chin., lit., high hill: name of the hill where it was found], a fine white clay used in making porcelain, as a filler in textiles, paper, rubber, etc., and in medicine.

ka·o·lin·ite (kā′ə-lin-īt′), *n.* in *mineralogy,* hydrous aluminum silicate, the main constituent of kaolin.

‡Ka·pell·meis·ter (kä-pel′mīs′tẽr), *n.* [*pl.* KAPELLMEISTER], [G., lit., chapel master < *kapelle,* chapel (hence the choir or orchestra in a court chapel) + *meister,* a master], the conductor of a choir or orchestra.

kaph (käf, kôf), *n.* [Heb.], the eleventh letter of the Hebrew alphabet (כ, ך), corresponding to English *K, k:* see **alphabet**, table.

ka·pok (kā′pok), *n.* [Malay *kapoq*], the silky fibers around the seeds of the tropical silk-cotton tree (*kapok tree*), used for stuffing pillows, mattresses, etc.: also called *Java cotton.*

kap·pa (kap′ə), *n.* [Gr.], the tenth letter of the Greek alphabet (Κ, κ), corresponding to English *K, k*: it often appears as *c* in English words derived from Greek, as in *center, cosmetic:* see **alphabet**, table.

ka·put (kə-po͞ot′; G. kä-poot′), *adj.* [via soldiers' slang < G. *kaput,* lost, spoiled, done for], [Colloq.], ruined, destroyed, defeated, etc.

Ka·ra·chi (kə-rä′chi), *n.* a city in West Pakistan, on the Arabian Sea: pop., 2,153,000: the former capital.

Ka·ra·fu·to (kä′rȧ-fo͞o′tô), *n.* 1. Sakhalin island: the Japanese name. 2. the southern part of this island: annexed by Japan, 1905; returned to U.S.S.R., 1945.

Ka·ra·gan·da (kä′rä-gän′dä), *n.* a city in central Kazakh S.S.R.: pop., 398,000.

Ka·ra-Kal·pak (kä-rä′käl-päk′), *n.* 1. a member of a Turkic people living in the Uzbek S.S.R. 2. the language of this people.

Kara-Kalpak Autonomous Soviet Socialist Republic, a part of the Uzbek S.S.R., in central Asia: area, 79,631 sq. mi.; pop., 544,000; capital, Nukus.

Ka·ra·ko·ram (kä′rä-kō′rəm), *n.* a mountain range in northern India, near the Chinese border: highest peak, Godwin Austen, 28,250 ft.: also called *Mustagh.*

kar·a·kul (kar′ə-kəl), *n.* [< *Kara Kul,* lit., black lake, lake in Bokhara], 1. a sheep of central Asia. 2. the loosely curled, usually black fur made from the fleece of its newborn lambs. Also spelled **caracul, karakule.**

Ka·ra Kum (kä-rä′ ko͝om′), a desert in western Asia, chiefly in the Turkmen S.S.R.: also spelled **Qara Qum.**

Ka·ra Sea (kä′rä), an arm of the Arctic Ocean, between Novaya Zemlya and western Siberia.

kar·at (kar′ət), *n.* a carat: abbreviated **K., k.**

ka·ra·te (kä-rä′tē), *n.* [Japan., lit., open hand < *kara,* empty + *te,* hand], a Japanese system of self-defense characterized by chopping blows delivered with the side of the open hand.

Ka·re·li·a (kə-rē′li-ə, kə-rēl′yə), *n.* an autonomous republic of the R.S.F.S.R.: officially, *Karelian Autonomous Soviet Socialist Republic:* see **Karelo-Finnish S.S.R.**

Ka·re·li·an (kə-rē′li-ən, kə-rēl′yən), *adj.* of Karelia, its people, etc. *n.* 1. a member of a branch of the Finnish people living in Karelia and eastern Finland. 2. the Finnish dialect of the Karelians.

Karelian Isthmus, an isthmus in the U.S.S.R., between Lake Ladoga and the Gulf of Finland.

Ka·re·lo-Fin·nish Soviet Socialist Republic (kə-rē′lō-fin′ish), a former republic of the U.S.S.R., east of Finland, composed of Karelia and territory ceded by Finland in 1940.

Kar·en (kar′ən), a feminine name: see **Catherine.**

Kar·lo·vy Var·y (kär′lô-vi vä′ri), Karlsbad.

Karls·bad (kärls′bät; Eng. kärlz′bad), *n.* a town in northwestern Bohemia, Czechoslovakia, famous for its hot springs: pop., 43,000: also spelled **Carlsbad;** Czech name, *Karlovy Vary.*

Karls·ruh·e (kärls′ro͞o′ə; Eng. kärlz′ro͞o′ə), *n.* a city in southwestern Germany: pop., 240,000.

kar·ma (kär′mə, kũr′mə), *n.* [Sans., a deed, act], 1. in *Buddhism* & *Hinduism,* the totality of a person's actions in one of the successive states of his existence, thought of as determining his fate in the next; hence, 2. loosely, fate; destiny.

Kar·nak (kär′nak), *n.* a village on the Nile, Egypt: site of ancient Thebes: see **Egypt**, map.

kar·roo, ka·roo (kə-ro͞o′, ka-ro͞o′), *n.* [*pl.* KARROOS, KAROOS (-ro͞oz′)] ,[Hottentot; ? < *karusa,* dry, hard], in South Africa, a dry tableland.

the Great Karroo, the karroo in Cape of Good Hope province, 350 miles long, 40 to 80 miles wide, and 2,000 to 3,000 feet above sea level.

kar·y·o- (kar′i-ō, kar′i-ə), [< Gr. *karyon,* a nut, kernel], a combining form meaning: 1. *nut, kernel.* 2. in *biology, the nucleus of a cell,* as in *karyoplasm.* Also spelled **caryo-.**

kar·y·o·plasm (kar′i-ə-plaz'm), *n.* [*karyo-* + *-plasm*]. nuclear protoplasm: distinguished from *cytoplasm.*

kar·y·o·some (kar′i-ə-sōm′), *n.* [*karyo-* + *-some* (body)], in *biology,* 1. an aggregation of chromatin in a resting nucleus. 2. a chromosome. 3. the nucleus of a cell.

kar·y·o·tin (kar′i-ō′tin), *n.* [*karyo-* + chroma*tin*], chromatin: also spelled **caryotin.**

Kas., Kansas.

Kas·bah (käz′bä), *n.* the native quarter of Algiers: also spelled **Casbah.**

ka·sher (kä′shẽr), *adj. & n.* kosher. *v.t.* (*also* Heb. kä-shâr′), to make or declare kosher: also **kosher.**

Kash·gar (käsh′gär′), *n.* a city in northwesternmost China: pop., 91,000: also called *Shufu.*

Kash·mir (kash-mêr′), *n.* a state of northern India: area, 85,861 sq. mi.; pop., 4,410,000; capital, Srinagar: control of this region is disputed by Pakistan: also spelled **Cashmere:** name in full, **Jammu and Kashmir.**

Kash·mir·i (kash-mêr′i), *n.* 1. the Indic, Indo-European language of the Kashmirians. 2. [*pl.* KASHMIRI], a Kashmirian.

Kash·mir·i·an (kash-mêr′i-ən), *adj.* of Kashmir, its people, their language, or culture. *n.* a native or inhabitant of Kashmir.

Kas·sel (käs′əl), *n.* a city in west central Germany: pop., 206,000. also spelled **Cassel.**

kat·a- (kat′ə), cata-: also, before a vowel, **kat-.**

ka·tab·a·sis (kə-tab′ə-sis), *n.* [*pl.* KATABASES (-sēz′)], [Gr. < *katabainein,* to go down; *kata-,* down + *bainein,* to go], 1. literally, a going down; hence, 2. [K-], the retreat to the sea made by the Greek mercenaries who followed Cyrus against Artaxerxes, as described by Xenophon in the *Anabasis.* 3. any similar retreat.

Ka·tah·din, Mount (kə-tä′din), the highest mountain in Maine: height, 5,268 ft.

Kate (kāt), a feminine name: see **Catherine.**

Kath·a·rine, Kath·er·ine (kath′ẽr-in, kath′rin), a feminine name: diminutives, *Kate, Kay, Kit, Kitty*: also **Kathryn:** see **Catherine.**

ka·thar·sis (kə-thär′sis), *n.* catharsis.

Kath·leen (kath′lēn, kath-lēn′), [Ir.], a feminine name: see **Catherine.**

kath·ode (kath′ōd), *n.* a cathode: abbreviated **ka.**

Kath·ryn (kath′rin), a feminine name: see **Katherine.**

kat·i·on (kat′ī′ən), *n.* a cation.

Kat·mai (kat′mī′), *n.* 1. a national monument in the Aleutian Range, southwestern Alaska. 2. an active volcano in this monument: height, 6,970 ft.

Kat·man·du (kät′män-do͞o′), *n.* the capital of Nepal: pop., 195,000.

Ka·to·wi·ce (kä′tô-vē′tse), *n.* a city in southern Poland: pop., 269,000: German name, *Kattowitz.*

Kat·rine, Loch (kat′rin; Scot. kät′rin), a lake in central Scotland, celebrated in Scott's *Lady of the Lake:* length, 8 mi.

Kat·te·gat (kat′i-gat′), *n.* an arm of the North Sea, between Sweden and Denmark: width, 40–70 mi.

Kat·to·witz (kä′tô-vits), *n.* Katowice.

ka·ty·did (kā′ti-did′), *n.* any of several large, green, tree insects resembling and related to the grasshopper: so called from the shrill sound made by the males.

Ka·u·a·i (kä′o͞o-ä′ē), *n.* one of the Hawaiian Islands, northwest of Oahu: area, 551 sq. mi.; pop., 28,000.

Kauf·man, George S. (kôf′mən), 1889–1961; American playwright.

Kau·nas (kou′näs), *n.* a city in the Lithuanian S.S.R.: pop., 214,000: Russian name, *Kovno.*

kau·ri, kau·ry (kou′ri), *n.* [Maori], 1. a tall pine tree of New Zealand. 2. its wood. 3. a resin (*kauri resin, kauri gum*) from this tree, used in varnish.

ka·va (kä′vä), *n.* [Maori *kawa,* lit., bitter], 1. either of two shrubs of the pepper family, growing in the South Sea Islands. 2. an intoxicating drink made from the roots of either of these.

ka·va·ka·va (kä′vä-kä′vä), *n.* kava.

Ka·vir Desert (kə-vêr′), a large desert in north central Iran: Persian name, *Dasht-i-Kavir.*

Ka·wa·sa·ki (kä′wȧ-sä′ki), *n.* a city in Japan, near Tokyo: pop., 633,000.

Kay, Sir (kā), in *Arthurian legend,* one of the knights of the Round Table, the boastful, rude, malicious seneschal and foster brother of King Arthur.

kay·ak (kī′ak), *n.* [Esk.], 1. an Eskimo canoe made of skins, especially sealskins, stretched over a frame of wood so as to cover it completely except for an opening in the middle for the paddler. 2. any similar canoe. Also spelled **kaiak, kyak.**

KAYAK

kay·o (kā′ō′), *v.t.* [KAYOED (-ōd′), KAYOING], [< *k*nock *o*ut], [Slang], in *boxing,* to knock out. *n.* [Slang], in *boxing*, a knockout. Often written **K.O., KO, k.o.**

Kay·se·ri (kī'se-rē'), *n.* a city in central Turkey: pop., 81,000: ancient name, *Caesarea*.

Ka·zak, Ka·zakh (kȧ-zäk'), *n.* a member of a Kirghiz people living chiefly in the Kazak S.S.R.

Kazak Soviet Socialist Republic, a republic of the U.S.S.R., in western Asia: area, 1,059,700 sq. mi.; pop., 9,301,000; capital, Alma-Ata.

Ka·zak·stan (kä'zäk-stän'), *n.* the Kazak S.S.R.

Ka·zan (kä-zän'; Russ. kȧ-zän'y'), *n.* the capital of the Tatar A.S.S.R., on the Volga: pop., 643,000.

Kaz·bek, Mount (kȧz-bek'), a volcanic mountain of the Caucasus, U.S.S.R.: height, 16,547 ft.

ka·zoo (kə-zōō'), *n.* [arbitrary or echoic], a toy musical instrument consisting of a small tube containing a membrane or piece of paper that vibrates and produces a buzzing sound when one hums into the tube.

K.B., 1. King's Bench. 2. Knight Bachelor. 3. Knight of the Bath.

K.B.E., Knight Commander of the British Empire.

Kč., koruna.

kc., kilocycle; kilocycles.

K.C., 1. King's Counsel. 2. Knight Commander. 3. Knight (or Knights) of Columbus.

K.C.B., Knight Commander of the Bath.

K.D., in *commerce*, knocked down (not assembled).

ke·a (kā'ä, kē'ə), *n.* [Maori], a large, green, mountain parrot of New Zealand, which kills sheep by tearing at their backs to eat the fat there.

Kean, Edmund (kēn), 1787–1833; English actor.

Kear·ny (kär'ni), *n.* a town in New Jersey, across the Passaic from Newark: pop., 37,000.

Keats, John (kēts), 1795–1821; English poet.

keb·buck, keb·bock (keb'ək), *n.* [Gael. *ceapag*, a cheese, wheel], [Scot. & Irish Dial.], a cheese.

Ke·ble, John (kē'b'l), 1792–1866; English clergyman and poet; a founder of the Oxford Movement.

Kech·ua (kech'wä), *n.* Quechua.

Kech·uan (kech'wən), *adj. & n.* Quechuan.

keck (kek), *v.i.* [echoic], 1. to retch or heave, as if about to vomit. 2. to feel or show great disgust.

Kecs·ke·mét (kech'ke-māt'), *n.* a city in central Hungary: pop., 67,000.

Ke·dah (kā'dä), *n.* a state of the Federation of Malaya: area, 3,660 sq. mi.; pop., 702,000.

ked·dah (ked'ə), *n.* [Hind. *khedā*], an elephant trap: also spelled **khedah**.

kedge (kej), *n.* [earlier also *cagger, kaggyng anker;* hence prob. form of *cadge*, var. of *catch*, in the sense "that which catches"], a light anchor, used especially in warping a ship or freeing it when ashore: also **kedge anchor.** *v.t.* [KEDGED (kejd), KEDGING], to warp or pull (a ship) along by means of a rope fastened to an anchor dropped at some distance. *v.i.* 1. to move a ship by kedging. 2. to move by being kedged.

Ke·dron (kē'drən), *n.* a little ravine east of Jerusalem: formerly a stream flowing into the Dead Sea: II Sam. 15:23: also **Kidron.**

keek (kēk), *v.i.* [ME. *kiken;* prob. < MD. or MLG. *kiken*], [Scot. & North Eng. Dial.], to peep; spy.

keel (kēl), *n.* [ME. *kele* < ON. *kjölr* (prob. influenced in sense by L. *carina*, a keel, hull); IE. base **geu-l*, bent, rounded, curved (with reference to the curved stem of a ship's keel)], 1. the chief timber or steel piece extending along the entire length of the bottom of a boat or ship and supporting the frame; hence, 2. [Poetic], a ship. 3. anything resembling a ship's keel. 4. the assembly of beams, girders, etc. at the bottom of a rigid or semirigid airship to prevent sagging or buckling. 5. in *biology*, a ridgelike part. *v.t.* 1. to furnish with a keel. 2. to turn (a ship) over on its side; turn up the keel of. *v.i.* to turn up the keel.

keel over, [Colloq.], 1. to turn over; turn upside down; upset; capsize. 2. to fall over suddenly, as in a faint.

on an even keel, 1. in an upright, level position, without dipping to either side. 2. with an even, smooth, steady motion.

keel (kēl), *n.* [ME. *kele* < MD. *kiel* or MLG. *kēl;* akin to AS. *ceol*, ship of burthen, ON. *kjöll*], 1. a flat-bottomed ship; especially, a low, flat-bottomed coal barge or lighter, used on the Tyne. 2. a barge load of coal; hence, 3. a British unit of weight for coal, equal to 21.2 long tons.

keel (kēl), *v.t.* [ME. *kelen;* AS. *celan* (akin to G. *kühlen*) < base of *col;* see COOL], [Obs. or Dial.], to cool (a hot liquid) by stirring, skimming, etc.

keel (kēl), *n.* [prob. < Ir. or Gael. *cīl*, ruddle], a red stain used for marking lumber, etc.; ruddle.

keel·haul (kēl'hôl'), *v.t.* [D. *kielhalen; kiel*, keel + *halen*, to haul], 1. to haul (a person) through the water under the keel of a ship from one side to the other: a former method of punishment or torture. 2. to scold or rebuke harshly.

Kee·ling Islands (kē'liŋ), the Cocos Islands.

keel·son (kel's'n, kēl's'n), *n.* [prob. < Sw. *kölsvin; köl*, a keel + *svin*, swine], a longitudinal beam or set of timbers or metal plates fastened over and along a ship's keel to add structural strength: also **kelson.**

keen (kēn), *adj.* [ME. *kene;* AS. *cene*, wise, learned; akin to G. *kühn*, bold; IE. base **ĝen-*, to know, understand, in the sense "knowing, expert," the material senses spring from the basic notion "capable"], 1. having a sharp edge or point; that can cut well: as, a *keen* knife, a *keen* edge. 2. sharp; cutting; piercing: as, *keen* appetite, *keen* wind. 3. very sensitive; very perceptive; penetrating; acute: as, *keen* eyes, a *keen* intelligence. 4. sharp-witted; mentally acute; shrewd. 5. eager; enthusiastic; much interested. 6. intense; strong; vivid; pungent. 7. [Slang], good; excellent: a generalized term of approval. —*SYN.* see **eager, sharp.**

keen (kēn), *n.* [Ir. *caoine* < *caoinim*, I wail], [Irish], a wailing for the dead; dirge. *v.t. & v.i.* [Irish], to lament or wail for (the dead). —*SYN.* see **cry.**

keep (kēp), *v.t.* [KEPT (kept), KEEPING], [ME. *kepen;* AS. *cepan*, to behold, watch out for, lay hold of; ? akin, via **kōpjan*, to ON. *kōpa*, to stiffen, gape, MLG. *kapen*, to gape, stare at, AS. *capian up*, to look up at; ? IE. base **ĝab-*, to look at or for], 1. to observe or pay regard to; specifically, *a)* to observe with due or prescribed acts, ceremonies, etc.; celebrate or solemnize: as, they *kept* the Sabbath. *b)* to fulfill (a promise, etc.). *c)* [Archaic], to show observance by regularly attending (church, etc.). 2. to take care of, or have and take care of; specifically, *a)* to protect; guard; defend. *b)* to look after; watch over; tend. *c)* to raise (livestock). *d)* to maintain in good order or condition; preserve. *e)* to supply with food, shelter, etc.; provide for; support. *f)* to supply with food or lodging for pay: as, she *keeps* boarders. *g)* to have or maintain in one's service or for one's use: as, they *keep* servants. *h)* to set down regularly in writing; maintain (a continuous written report or record): as, he *keeps* an account of sales in the store. *i)* to make regular entries in; maintain a continuous record of transactions, accounts, or happenings in: as, businessmen *keep* books, she *keeps* a diary. *j)* to carry on; conduct; manage. 3. to maintain, or cause to stay or continue, in a specified condition, position, etc.: as, *keep* your engine running. 4. to have or hold; specifically, *a)* to have or hold for future use or for a long time. *b)* to have usually in stock for sale. 5. to have or hold and not let go; specifically, *a)* to hold in custody; prevent from escaping. *b)* to prevent from leaving; detain. *c)* to hold back; restrain: as, the rain *kept* us from going out. *d)* to withhold. *e)* to conceal; not tell (a secret, etc.). *f)* to continue to have or hold; not lose or give up. *g)* to stay in or at; not leave (a path, course, or place). *v.i.* 1. to stay or continue in a specified condition, position, etc. 2. to continue; go on; persevere (often with *on*): as, *keep* on talking. 3. to hold oneself back; refrain: as, she can't *keep* from telling us. 4. to stay in good condition; not become spoiled, sour, stale, etc.; last. 5. [Colloq.], to continue in session: as, will school *keep* all day? 6. [Colloq.], to reside; live; stay. *n.* 1. originally, care, charge, or custody. 2. *a)* the strongest, innermost part or central tower of a medieval castle; donjon. *b)* a stronghold; fort; castle. 3. [Rare], a keeping or being kept. 4. what is needed to keep a person or animal; food and shelter; support; livelihood.

for keeps, [Colloq.], 1. with the agreement that the winner will keep what he wins. 2. permanently.

keep in with, [Colloq.], to remain on good terms with.

keep to oneself, 1. to avoid the company of others. 2. to treat (information, etc.) as confidential; not tell.

keep up, 1. to maintain in good order or condition. 2. to continue; not stop or end. 3. to maintain the pace; not lag behind. 4. to remain informed about (with *on* or *with*).

SYN.—**keep,** a general word of broad application, in its simplest sense implies merely a continuing to have or hold; **retain,** a more formal equivalent, often stresses the possibility of loss or seizure (he has managed to *retain* most of his fortune); **withhold** implies a keeping or holding back and connotes refusal to release (to *withhold* information); **reserve** implies a keeping or holding back for some time or for some future use (is this table *reserved* for us?). See also **celebrate.**—*ANT.* relinquish, release.

keep·er (kēp'ẽr), *n.* a person or thing that keeps; specifically, *a)* a guard, as of prisoners, animals, etc. *b)* a guardian or protector. *c)* a custodian; caretaker. *d)* [British], a gamekeeper. *e)* any of several devices for keeping something in place; lock nut, clasp, etc. *f)* something that keeps, or lasts (well or poorly).

keep·ing (kēp'iŋ), *n.* 1. observance (of a rule, holiday, promise, etc.). 2. care; custody; charge. 3. maintenance or means of maintenance; keep. 4. the condition in which something is kept. 5. retention. 6. reservation for future use; preservation. 7. agreement; conformity: as, in *keeping* with his character.

keep·sake (kēp′sāk′), *n.* something kept, or to be kept, for the sake of, or in memory of, the giver; memento.

Kee·wa·tin (kē-wä′tin), *n.* a district of Northwest Territories, on Hudson Bay: area, 228,160 sq. mi. *adj.* in *geology*, designating or of the older of two series of rocks of the Archaean system: cf. **Laurentian.**
the Keewatin, the Keewatin series of rocks.

kef (kāf), *n.* [colloq. form of Ar. *kaif*, well-being], 1. a drowsy, dreamy condition, produced by smoking narcotics. 2. Indian hemp or other narcotic smoked to produce this.

keg (keg), *n.* [var. of Brit. dial. *cadge* < ME. *cagge;* ON. *-kaggr* in *vinkaggr*, wine barrel (cf. Sw. & Norw. *kagge*, keg); IE. base *ĝog(h)-, ĝeg(h)-, branch, stake], 1. a small barrel, usually one holding less than ten gallons: abbreviated **kg.** (*sing. & pl.*). 2. a unit of weight for nails, equal to 100 pounds.

keg·ler (keg′lẽr), *n.* [G. < *kegel*, (nine)pin, (ten)pin], [Colloq.], a person who bowls; bowler.

Kei·jo (kā′jō′), *n.* Seoul: the Japanese name.

keir (kêr), *n.* a kier.

Keith (kēth), [Scot. < Gael. base meaning "the wind"], a masculine name.

Keith, Sir **Arthur** (kēth), 1866–1955; Scottish anthropologist in England.

keit·lo·a (kīt′lō-ə, kāt′lō-ə), *n.* [Sechuana *kgetlwa*], a large, black, two-horned rhinoceros of southern Africa.

Ke·lan·tan (kə-län′tän′), *n.* a state of the Federation of Malaya: area, 5,720 sq. mi.; pop., 506,000.

kel·ep (kel′ep), *n.* [native name in Guatemala], a Central American stinging ant that feeds on insects.

Kel·ler, Helen Adams (kel′ẽr), 1880– ; American writer and lecturer; blind and deaf from infancy, she was taught to speak and read.

Kel·logg, Frank Bil·lings (bil′iŋz kel′əg, kel′og), 1856–1937; American statesman and diplomat.

ke·loid (kē′loid), *n.* [Fr. *kéloïde*, *chéloïde* < Gr. *chēlē*, crab's claw; + *-oid*], a fibrous tumor arising from connective tissue of the skin, generally an excessive growth of scar tissue: also spelled **cheloid.**

kelp (kelp), *n.* [ME. *culp*, *culpe*], 1. any of various large, coarse, brown seaweeds. 2. ashes of seaweed, from which iodine is obtained.

kel·pie, kel·py (kel′pi), *n.* [*pl.* KELPIES (-piz)], [Scot.], in *Gaelic folklore*, a water spirit, supposed to take the form of a horse and drown people or warn them that they will be drowned.

kel·son (kel′s'n), *n.* a keelson.

Kelt (kelt), *n.* a Celt.

kel·ter (kel′tẽr), *n.* [Colloq.], kilter.

Kel·tic (kel′tik), *adj. & n.* Celtic.

Kel·vin (kel′vin), [< Eng. surname], a masculine name.

Kel·vin, first Baron (kel′vin), (*William Thomson*), 1824–1907; British physicist and mathematician.

Kelvin scale, [after Baron *Kelvin*], in *physics*, a scale of temperature measured in degrees centigrade from absolute zero, -273.18°C.

Ke·mal A·ta·turk, Mus·ta·fa (moos-tä-fä′ ke-mäl′ ä-tä-türk′), (*Mustafa Kemal*), 1881–1938; Turkish military leader; president of Turkey (1923–1938).

Kem·ble, Fanny (kem′b'l), (*Frances Anne Kemble*), 1809–1893; English actress.

Kemble, John Philip, 1757–1823; uncle of *Fanny;* English tragedian.

Kempis, Thomas à, see **Thomas à Kempis.**

ken (ken), *v.t.* [KENNED (kend), KENNING], [ME. *kennen;* AS. *cennan*, lit., to cause to know < **kannjan* < base of *can* (see CAN); akin to G. *kennen*, to know], 1. [Scot.], to know. 2. [Archaic], to see; look at; descry. 3. [Archaic or Dial.], to recognize. *v.i.* [Scot.], to know (*of* or *about*). *n.* [abbrev. < earlier *kenning* < the *v.t.*], 1. [Rare], range of vision or sight. 2. mental perception or recognition; range of knowledge.

Ken., Kentucky.

kench (kench), *n.* [also *kinch;* ? var. of Brit. dial. *canch*], a box or bin in which fish or skins are salted.

Ken·dal green (ken′d'l), 1. a coarse, green woolen cloth, originally woven and dyed at Kendal, Westmorland, England. 2. its color. Also **Kendal.**

Ken·il·worth (ken′'l-wûrth′), *n.* an urban district in Warwickshire, England: site of a ruined castle.

Ken·ne·bec (ken′ə-bek′), *n.* a river in Maine, flowing southward to the Atlantic: length, 164 mi.

Ken·ne·dy, John Fitzgerald (ken′ə-di), 1917– ; thirty-fifth president of the United States (1961–).

ken·nel (ken′'l), *n.* [ME. *kenel, kenell;* OFr. **kenil;* LL. *canile* < L. *canis*, a dog], 1. a doghouse. 2. *often pl.* a place where dogs are bred or kept. 3. a pack of dogs. *v.t.* [KENNELED or KENNELLED (-'ld), KENNELING or KENNELLING], to place or keep in a kennel. *v.i.* to live or take shelter in a kennel.

ken·nel (ken′'l), *n.* [ME. *canel;* OFr. *canel*, *chanel*, a channel], an open drain or sewer; gutter.

ken·nel (ken′'l), *n.* [Obs.], cannel.

Ken·nel·ly-Heav·i·side layer (ken′'l-i-hev′i-sīd′), [after A. E. *Kennelly* (1861–1939), Am. electrical engineer & Oliver *Heaviside* (1850–1925), Eng. physicist], a highly ionized layer of the upper atmosphere, variously estimated as being from 30 to 200 miles above the earth's surface and believed to reflect radio waves so that they travel parallel to the earth's surface: also **Heaviside layer:** cf. **ionosphere.**

Ken·ne·saw Mountain (ken′ə-sô′), a peak in northwestern Georgia: height, 1,809 ft.: scene of a Civil War battle.

Ken·neth (ken′ith), [Scot.; Gael. *Caioneach*, lit., handsome], a masculine name: diminutive, *Ken.*

ken·ning (ken′iŋ), *n.* [ME.; see KEN], 1. [Scot.], *a)* knowledge or recognition. *b)* a small or recognizable quantity. 2. [< ON. *kennungar*, *pl.*, lit., symbols], in early Germanic poetry, a metaphorical name for something (e.g., *sea-stead* for *ship*): in Anglo-Saxon most kennings are compounds; they are called *true kennings* when neither element is a true name for the object, *half-kennings* when one element is.

Ken·ny method (or **treatment**), (ken′i), [after Elizabeth *Kenny* (1886–1952), Australian nurse who developed it], a method of treating poliomyelitis by relaxing and stimulating the affected muscles with hot applications, etc., and then bringing the muscles back into use by moving them and helping the patient to learn again how to co-ordinate them.

ke·no (kē′nō), *n.* [prob. < Fr. *quine*, five winners < L. *quini*, five each < *quinque*, five], a gambling game resembling lotto.

Ke·no·sha (ki-nō′shə), *n.* a city in southeastern Wisconsin, on Lake Michigan: pop., 68,000.

ke·no·sis (ki-nō′sis), *n.* [Mod. L.; Gr. *kenōsis*, an emptying < *kenos*, empty], in *theology*, Jesus' humbling himself by taking on the form of man.

Ken·sing·ton (ken′ziŋ-tən), *n.* a borough in the western part of London: pop., 168,000.

Kent (kent), *n.* 1. a former Anglo-Saxon kingdom. 2. a county of southeastern England: pop., 1,564,000; county seat, Maidstone.

Kent·ish (ken′tish), *adj.* of Kent or its people. *n.* the dialect of Kent, especially in its Anglo-Saxon and Middle English stages of development.

kent·ledge (kent′lij), *n.* [Fr. *quintelage* < *quintal* (see QUINTAL) + *-age* (see -AGE)], pig iron used as permanent ballast in a ship.

Ken·tuck·i·an (kən-tuk′i-ən, ken-tuk′i-ən), *adj.* of Kentucky. *n.* a native or inhabitant of Kentucky.

Ken·tuck·y (kən-tuk′i, ken-tuk′i), *n.* 1. an East Central State of the United States: area, 40,395 sq. mi.; pop., 3,038,000; capital, Frankfort: abbreviated **Ky., Ken.:** nicknamed *Bluegrass State.* 2. a river in Kentucky, flowing northwest into the Ohio: length, 259 mi.

Kentucky coffee tree, a large North American tree with brown, curved pods containing seeds sometimes used as a substitute for coffee.

Kentucky colonel, an unofficial honorary title commonly conferred in Kentucky.

Kentucky Der·by (dũr′bi *or, in imitation of the Brit. pron.*, där′bi), an annual horse race run at Churchill Downs in Louisville, Kentucky.

Ken·ya (ken′yə, kēn′yə), *n.* a British colony and protectorate in east central Africa, on the Indian Ocean: area, 224,960 sq. mi.; pop., 6,450,000; capital, Nairobi.

Kenya, Mount, a mountain in central Kenya, Africa: height, 17,040 ft.

Ken·yon, John Samuel (ken′yən), 1874–1959; American educator and phonetician.

Ke·o·kuk (kē′ə-kuk′), *n.* a city in southeastern Iowa, on the Mississippi: pop., 16,000.

Ke·os (ke′ôs), *n.* one of the Cyclades Islands, in the Aegean: area, 67 sq. mi.: also called *Zea.*

Ke·phal·le·ni·a (ke′fä-li-nē′ä), *n.* Cephalonia, one of the Ionian Islands: the Greek name.

kep·i (kep′i), *n.* [Fr. *képi;* G. dial. *käppi*, dim. of *kappe*, a cap], a cap with a flat, round top and stiff visor, worn by French soldiers.

Kep·ler, Jo·han·nes (yō-hä′nəs kep′lẽr), 1571–1630; German astronomer and mathematician.

kept (kept), past tense and past participle of **keep.**

Ker·ak, El (el ker′äk), *n.* a city in Jordan, near the Dead Sea.

ke·ram·ic (ki-ram′ik), *adj.* ceramic.

ke·ram·ics (ki-ram′iks), *n.pl.* ceramics.

ker·at- (ker′ət), kerato-.

ker·a·tec·to·my (ker′ə-tek′tə-mi), *n.* [*kerat-* + *-ectomy*], the surgical removal of part or all of the cornea.

ker·a·tin (ker′ə-tin), *n.* [*kerat-* + *-in*], an albuminous substance forming the principal matter of hair, nails, horn, etc.

ke·rat·i·nous (ke-rat′ə-nəs), *adj.* of, or having the nature of, keratin; horny.

ker·a·ti·tis (ker′ə-tī′tis), *n.* [*kerat-* + *-itis*], inflammation of the cornea.

ker·a·to- (ker′ə-tō, ker′ə-tə), [< Gr. *keras*, *keratos*, horn], a combining form meaning: 1. *horn, hornlike, horny tissue*, as in *keratogenous.* 2. *the cornea*, as in *keratotomy.* Also, before a vowel, **kerat-.**

ker·a·tode (ker′ə-tōd′), *n.* keratose.

ker·a·tog·e·nous (ker′ə-toj′ə-nəs), *adj.* [*kerato-* + *-genous*], causing the growth of horn or horny tissue.

ker·a·toid (ker′ə-toid′), *adj.* [Gr. *keratoeidēs;* see KERATO- & -OID], hornlike; horny.

ker·a·to·plas·ty (ker′ə-tō-plas′ti), *n.* [*pl.* KERATOPLASTIES (-tiz)], [*kerato-* + *-plasty*], the surgical operation of grafting new corneal tissue onto an eye.

ker·a·tose (ker′ə-tōs′), *n.* [*kerat-* + *-ose*], a horny substance in the skeleton of some sponges and other invertebrates; keratode. *adj.* of or like keratose.

ker·a·to·sis (ker′ə-tō′sis), *n.* [Mod. L. < *kerat-* + *-osis*], 1. a horny growth of the skin, as a wart. 2. any disease characterized by horny growths.

ker·at·ot·o·my (ker′ə-tot′ə-mi), *n.* [*kerato-* + *-tomy*], surgical incision of the cornea.

kerb (kũrb), *n.* curb (of a pavement): British spelling.

Kerch (kerch), *n.* a seaport in the Crimea, U.S.S.R., on Kerch Strait: pop., 99,000.

ker·chief (kũr′chif), *n.* [ME. *kerchef, coverchef;* OFr. *covrechef, couvrechef* < *covrir,* to cover + *chef, chief,* the head], 1. a piece of cloth, usually square, worn over the head or around the neck. 2. a handkerchief.

ker·chiefed, ker·chieft (kũr′chift), *adj.* wearing a kerchief; covered with a kerchief.

Kerch Strait, a narrow strait connecting the Black Sea and the Sea of Azov.

Ke·ren·sky, A·le·ksan·dr Fe·o·do·ro·vich (ä′lyek-sän′-dr′ fyô′də-rô′vich kye-ryen′ski; Eng. kə-ren′ski), 1881– ; Russian Social Democratic statesman in the United States; prime minister of Russia (July-November, 1917); overthrown by Bolshevik Revolution.

kerf (kũrf, kärf), *n.* [ME. *kerf, kurf, kirf;* AS. *cyrf* (akin to ON. *kurfr,* a cutting, chip) < pp. base of *ceorfan,* to cut, carve; see CARVE], 1. a cutting or cut; especially, a cut or notch made by an ax, saw, etc. 2. a strip, piece, or quantity cut off.

Ker·gue·len (kũr′gə-lən), *n.* a French island in the southern Indian Ocean: area, 1,400 sq. mi.

Ker·ky·ra (ker′kē-rä′), *n.* Corfu: the Greek name.

Ker·man (kũr′män, ker-män′), *n.* a city in eastern Iran: pop., 62,000.

Ker·man·shah (ker′män-shä′), *n.* a city in western Iran: pop., 125,000.

ker·mes (kũr′mēz), *n.* [Fr. *kermès;* Ar. & Per. *qirmiz;* see CRIMSON], 1. the dried bodies of the females of certain scale insects found in Mediterranean regions. 2. a red dye made from these bodies. 3. the oak (*kermes oak*) on which these insects are found.

ker·mis, ker·mess (kũr′mis), *n.* [D. *kermis,* orig. *kerkmis; kerk, kirk,* a church + *mis,* Mass; orig. applied to the annual celebration of the feast day of the local patron saint, then to fairs or carnivals held on the same day], 1. an annual outdoor fair or carnival, held in the Netherlands, Belgium, etc. 2. in the United States, a somewhat similar fair or entertainment held indoors, usually for charity. Also spelled **kirmess.**

kern (kũrn), *n.* [Fr. *carne,* projecting angle, hinge < dial. form of OFr. *charne,* a hinge, corner, edge < L. *cardo, cardinis,* a hinge], that part of the face of a letter of type which projects beyond the body. *v.t.* to make (type) with a kern; put a kern on (type).

kern, kerne (kũrn), *n.* [ME. < Ir. *ceatharn,* band of soldiers, soldier], 1. [Archaic], a medieval Irish or Scottish foot soldier armed with light weapons. 2. an Irish peasant.

Kern, Jerome David (kũrn), 1885–1945; American composer.

ker·nel (kũr′n'l), *n.* [ME. *kernel, kirnel, curnel,* etc.; AS. *cyrnel* < base of *corn,* seed (see CORN) + *-el,* dim. suffix], 1. a grain or seed, as of corn, wheat, etc. 2. the inner, softer part of a nut, fruit stone, etc. 3. the central, most important part of something; core; essence. *v.t.* [KERNELED or KERNELLED (-n'ld), KERNELING or KERNELLING], to enclose as a kernel.

ker·o·sene (ker′ə-sēn′, ker′ə-sēn′), *n.* [Gr. *kēros,* wax; + *-ene*], a thin oil distilled from petroleum, coal, etc., used in lamps, stoves, etc.; coal oil: also, especially in scientific and industrial usage, spelled **kerosine.**

Ker·ry (ker′i), *n.* 1. a county of southwestern Ireland, in Munster province: pop., 134,000 (1946). 2. [*pl.* KERRIES (-iz)], any of a breed of small, black dairy cattle, originally from this county.

ker·sey (kũr′zi), *n.* [*pl.* KERSEYS (-ziz)], [ME. < *Kersey,* village in Suffolk, England], a coarse, lightweight woolen cloth, usually ribbed and with a cotton warp.

ker·sey·mere (kũr′zi-mêr′), *n.* [altered after *kersey* < *cassimere*], cassimere, a fine, twilled woolen cloth.

kes·trel (kes′trəl), *n.* [ME. *castrel;* OFr. *cresserelle, quercerelle;* origin echoic], a small European falcon that can hover in the air against the wind; windhover.

ketch (kech), *n.* [said to be var. of 15th-c. *cache* < ME. *cacchen,* to catch, in the sense "to hunt"; cf. YACHT], a fore-and-aft rigged sailing vessel with a mainmast toward the bow and a relatively tall mizzenmast, forward of the rudder post, toward the stern; distinguished from *yawl.*

Ketch·i·kan (kech′i-kan′), *n.* a seaport in southwestern Alaska: pop., 6,500.

ketch·up (kech′əp), *n.* [Malay *kēchap,* taste < Chin. *ke-tsiap*], a sauce for meat, fish, etc., especially a thick sauce (*tomato ketchup*) made of tomatoes flavored with onion, salt, sugar, and spice: also **catsup, catchup.**

ke·ten (kē′ten), *n.* ketene.

ke·tene (kē′tēn), *n.* [*ket-* + *-ene*], 1. a colorless gas, $H_2C:CO$, with a penetrating odor: it combines with water to form acetic acid. 2. any of a series of related organic compounds of which ketene is the simplest.

ke·to- (kē′tō, kē′tə), a combining form meaning *ketone, of ketones,* as in *ketogenesis*: also, before a vowel, **ket-.**

ke·to·gen·e·sis (kē′tə-jen′ə-sis), *n.* [*keto-* + *-genesis*], the formation of ketones, such as acetone, in the body.

ke·to·gen·ic (kē′tə-jen′ik), *adj.* convertible into ketones.

ke·tone (kē′tōn), *n.* [G. *keton,* arbitrary var. of Fr. *acétone;* see ACETONE], an organic chemical compound containing the divalent carbonyl group, CO, in combination with two hydrocarbon radicals: when these radicals are alike, the ketone is called *simple,* when unlike, *mixed.*

ketone body, any of three related substances, including acetone, important in human metabolism: also called *acetone body.*

ke·ton·ic (ki-ton′ik), *adj.* of or like ketones.

ke·to·nu·ri·a (kē′tə-nyoor′i-ə), *n.* [Mod. L.], the presence of ketone bodies in the urine.

ke·to·sis (ki-tō′sis), *n.* [Mod. L. < *ket-* + *-osis*], a condition in which there is excessive formation of ketones in the body, occurring as a complication of diabetes mellitus, etc.

Ket·ter·ing (ket′ẽr-iŋ), *n.* a city in southwestern Ohio: suburb of Dayton: pop., 54,000.

ket·tle (ket′'l), *n.* [ME. *ketel, kettell;* AS. *cetel;* akin to G. *kessel* (Goth. *katils*); prob. a loan word < L. *catillus,* dim. of *catinus,* container for food], 1. a metal container for boiling liquids, etc. 2. a teakettle. 3. a kettledrum. 4. in *geology,* a deep hollow with no outlet, resulting from glacial action: also **kettle hole.**
kettle of fish, a difficult or embarrassing situation.

ket·tle·drum (ket′'l-drum′), *n.* a drum consisting of a hollow hemisphere of copper or brass and a parchment top that can be tightened or loosened to change the pitch; timpano.

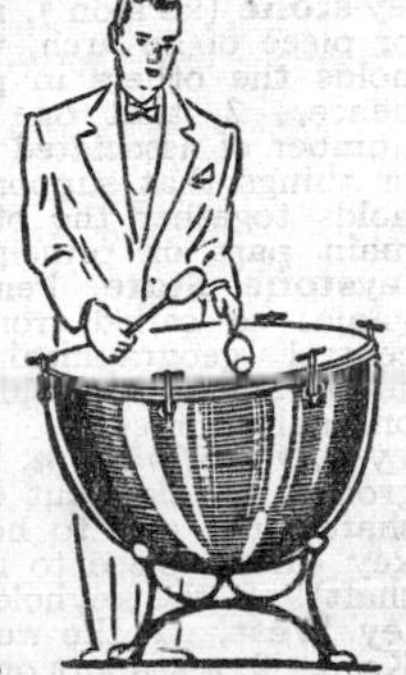
KETTLEDRUM

kettle hole, in *geology,* a kettle.

kev·el (kev′'l), *n.* [ME. *keuil, kyuil;* ONorm.Fr. *keville;* L. *clavicula,* small key (in LL., a bar, bolt for a door), dim. of *clavis,* key], a cleat or peg for fastening the heavy lines of a ship.

Kev·in (kev′in), [Ir. *Caomghin;* OIr. *Coemgen,* lit., comely birth], a masculine name.

Kew (kū), *n.* a village in Surrey, England: pop., 4,400: suburb of London and site of botanical gardens.

key (kē), *n.* [*pl.* KEYS (kēz)], [ME. *keye, kai, keige,* etc.; AS. *cæge;* akin to OFris. *kei, kēia,* to secure, guard; not known outside Anglo-Fris.; the mod. pronun. is north Brit. dial.], 1. an instrument, usually of metal, for moving the bolt of a lock and thus locking or unlocking something. 2. any of several instruments or mechanical devices somewhat resembling or suggesting this in form or use; specifically, *a*) a device to turn a bolt, etc.: as, a skate *key,* a watch *key. b*) a pin, bolt, wedge, cotter, or similar device put into a hole or space to lock or hold parts together. *c*) something that completes or holds together the parts of another thing, as the keystone of an arch or that part of the first coat of plaster which passes between the laths and forms a secure base for later coats. *d*) any of a set of levers, or the disks, buttons, etc. connected to them, pressed down in operating a piano, accordion, clarinet, typewriter, linotype, etc. *e*) a device for opening or closing an electric circuit. *f*) a small metal piece for fastening a wheel, pulley, etc. to a shaft. 3. something regarded as like a key in opening or closing a way, revealing or concealing, etc.; specifically, *a*) a place so located as to give access to or control of a region: as, Vicksburg was the *key* to the lower Mississippi. *b*) a thing that explains or solves something else, as a book of answers, the explanations on a map, the code to a system of pronunciation, etc. *c*) a controlling or essential person or thing. 4. tone of voice; pitch; hence, 5. tone or style of thought or expression: as, he wrote and spoke in a cheerful *key.* 6. in *botany,* a key fruit. 7. in *music, a*) [Obs.], the keynote of a scale. *b*) a system of related notes or tones based on and named after a certain note (*keynote, tonic*) and forming a given scale; tonality. *c*) the main tonality of a composition. ***adj.*** controlling; essential; important: as, he has a *key* position in the department. ***v.t.*** [KEYED (kēd), KEYING], 1. to fasten or lock with a key or wedge. 2. to furnish with a key; specifically, *a*) to put the keystone in (an arch). *b*) to provide with an explanatory key. 3. to regulate the tone or pitch of. 4. to bring into harmony, as in style of expression.

key up, 1. to raise the key of; hence, 2. to bring into a state of nervous tension, as in anticipation.

key (kē), ***n.*** [*pl.* KEYS (kēz)], [Sp. *cayo;* sp. influenced by *key* (instrument) *& key* (quay)], a reef or low island.

Key, Francis Scott (kē), 1780–1843; American lawyer; wrote "The Star-Spangled Banner."

key·board (kē'bôrd', kē'bōrd'), ***n.*** the row or rows of keys of a piano, typewriter, linotype, etc.

keyed (kēd), ***adj.*** 1. having keys, as some musical instruments. 2. fastened or reinforced with a key. 3. pitched in a specified key. 4. made with a keystone.

key fruit, a dry, winged fruit, as of the maple, ash, or sycamore, containing the seed or seeds; samara.

key·hole (kē'hōl'), ***n.*** an opening (in a lock) into which a key is inserted.

Key Lar·go (lär'gō), a large island in the Florida Keys, off the coast of southeastern Florida.

Keynes, John Maynard (kānz), 1st Baron Keynes; 1883–1946; English economist and author.

key·note (kē'nōt'), ***n.*** 1. the lowest, basic note or tone of a musical scale, or key; tonic. 2. the basic idea or ruling principle, as of a speech, policy, etc. ***v.t.*** to give the keynote of (a political platform, etc.).

key·not·er (kē'nōt'ēr), ***n.*** a person who delivers a keynote speech, as at a political convention.

keynote speech, a speech, as at the convention of a political party, that sets forth the main line of policy.

key punch, a machine, operated from a keyboard, that records data by punching holes in cards that can then be fed into machines for sorting, accounting, etc.

key ring, a metal ring for holding keys.

Key·ser·ling, Her·mann (her'män kī'sēr-liŋ; Eng. kī'zēr-liŋ), Count, 1880–1946; German philosopher.

key signature, in *music,* one or more sharps or flats placed after the clef on the staff to indicate the key.

key·stone (kē'stōn'), ***n.*** 1. the central, topmost stone or piece of an arch, which holds the others in place; hence, 2. that one of a number of associated parts or things that supports or holds together the others; main part or principle.

KEYSTONE

Keystone State, Pennsylvania: so called from its central geographical position among the thirteen original colonies.

key·way (kē'wā'), ***n.*** 1. a groove or slot cut in a shaft, hub, etc. to hold a key (metal piece to fasten a wheel or pulley to the shaft). 2. the keyhole in a lock worked by a flat key.

Key West, 1. the westernmost island in the Florida Keys. 2. a seaport on this island: pop., 34,000.

kg., 1. keg; kegs. 2. kilogram; kilograms.

K.G., Knight of the Garter.

Kha·ba·rovsk Territory (khä-bä'rôfsk), a territory of the R.S.F.S.R., in eastern Siberia, extending from China to the Arctic Ocean: area, 901,000 sq. mi.; pop., 1,143,000; capital, Khabarovsk (pop., 322,000): also called *Far Eastern Region.*

Khai·bar, Khai·ber (kī'bēr), ***n.*** the Khyber Pass.

Kha·kass Autonomous Region (khä-käs'), a division of the R.S.F.S.R., in south central Siberia: area, 19,161 sq. mi.; pop., 414,000; capital, Abakan.

kha·ki (kak'i, kä'ki), ***adj.*** [Hind. *khākī,* dusty, dust-colored < Per. *khāk,* dust, earth], 1. dull yellowish-brown. 2. made of khaki cloth. ***n.*** [*pl.* KHAKIS (-kiz)], 1. a dull yellowish brown. 2. strong, twilled wool or, especially, cotton cloth of this color, used for military uniforms. 3. *often pl.* a khaki uniform or uniforms.

kha·lif (kā'lif, kal'if), ***n.*** a caliph.

Khal·ki·di·ke (khäl'kē-*thē*'kē), ***n.*** Chalcidice, Greece.

kham·seen (kam-sēn'), ***n.*** a khamsin.

kham·sin (kam'sin, kam-sēn'), ***n.*** [Ar. *khamsīn* < *khamsūn,* fifty], a hot south wind that blows in Egypt from late March until early May (about 50 days).

khan (kän, kan), ***n.*** [Turki *khān,* lord, prince; of Tatar origin], 1. a title given to Genghis Khan and his successors, who ruled over Turkish, Tatar, and Mongol tribes and dominated most of Asia during the Middle Ages. 2. a title given to various officials and dignitaries in Central Asia, Iran, Afghanistan, etc.

khan (kän, kan), ***n.*** [ME.; Ar. *khān*], in Turkey and other Eastern countries, a public inn; caravansary.

khan·ate (kän'āt, kan'āt), ***n.*** 1. a region ruled by a khan. 2. the position, authority, or tenure of a khan.

Kha·ni·a (khän-yä'; Eng. kä-nē'ə), ***n.*** Canea, a city in Crete: the Greek name.

khaph (khäf, khôf), ***n.*** [Heb.], a variant of the eleventh letter (*kaph*) of the Hebrew alphabet (כ, ך), corresponding to Scottish *ch,* as in *loch*: see **alphabet,** table.

Khar·kov (khär'kôf; Eng. kär'kôf, kär'kov), ***n.*** a city in the Ukrainian S.S.R.: pop., 930,000.

Khar·toum, Khar·tum (kär-to͞om'), ***n.*** the capital of Sudan, on the Nile: pop., 93,000.

Khayyám, Omar, see **Omar Khayyám.**

khed·ah (ked'ə), ***n.*** a keddah.

khe·dive (kə-dēv'), ***n.*** [Fr. *khédive;* Turk. *khidīv;* Per. *khidīw, khadīw,* prince, ruler], the title of the Turkish viceroys of Egypt, from 1867 to 1914.

Kher·son (kher-sôn'), ***n.*** a city in the Ukrainian S.S.R., on the lower Dnepr: pop., 157,000.

kheth (kheth, khes), ***n.*** the eighth letter of the Hebrew alphabet (ח), a velar fricative equivalent to Scottish *ch,* as in *loch:* also spelled **cheth**: see **alphabet,** table.

Khi·os (khē'ôs; Eng. kī'os), ***n.*** Chios: Greek name.

Khi·va (khē'vä; Eng. kē'və), ***n.*** 1. a former khanate in western Asia: now in the U.S.S.R. 2. a city in the Uzbek S.S.R.: pop., 24,000.

Khmer (k'mer), ***n.*** [< the Khmer name], 1. one of a native people of Cambodia: they had a highly developed civilization in the Middle Ages. 2. their language: see **Mon-Khmer.**

Khond (kond), ***n.*** [< Dravidian name], a member of a group of Dravidian tribes of east central India.

Kho·tan (khō'tän'), ***n.*** a city in westernmost China: pop., 50,000: also called *Hotien.*

Khrush·chev, Ni·ki·ta Ser·gey·e·vich (ni-kē'tä syer-gā'ye-vich khro͞os'chyôf; Eng. kro͞os'chev), 1894– ; premier of the U.S.S.R. (1958–).

Khu·fu (ko͞o'fo͞o), ***n.*** Cheops, an ancient king of Egypt.

Khu·zis·tan (kho͞o'zis-tän'), ***n.*** a province of Iran, on the Persian Gulf: area, 38,500 sq. mi.; pop., 1,800,000.

Khy·ber Pass (kī'bēr), a mountain pass between West Pakistan and Afghanistan: length, c. 33 mi.: also spelled **Khaibar Khaiber.**

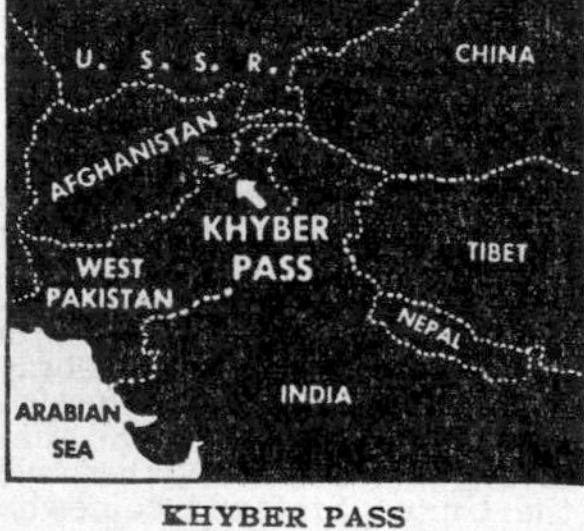

KHYBER PASS

Ki., Kings (book of the Old Testament).

Kiang·si (kyaŋ'sē'; Chin. jyäŋ'sē'), ***n.*** a province of southeastern China: area, 67,300 sq. mi.; pop., 16,773,000; capital, Nanchang.

Kiang·su (kyaŋ'so͞o'; Chin. jyäŋ'so͞o'), ***n.*** a province on the coast of eastern China: area, 39,100 sq. mi.; pop., 41,252,000; capital, Nanking.

Kiao·chow (kyou'chou'; Chin. jyou'jō'), ***n.*** a district of Shantung province, China: area, 200 sq. mi.

kib·butz (ki-bo͞ots'), ***n.*** [*pl.* KIBBUTZIM (kē'bo͞o-tsēm')], [Heb.], a collective farm settlement in Israel.

kibe (kīb), ***n.*** [ME.; prob. < W. *cibi, cibwst,* chilblains], a chapped or ulcerated chilblain, especially on the heel.

ki·bei (kē'bā'), ***n.*** [*pl.* KIBEI, KIBEIS (-bāz')], [Japan.], [also K-], a native American citizen born of immigrant Japanese parents but educated largely in Japan: distinguished from *issei, nisei.*

kib·itz (kib'its), ***v.i.*** [Colloq.], to act as a kibitzer.

kib·itz·er (kib'it-sēr), ***n.*** [Yid. < colloq. G. *kiebitzen,* to look on (at cards) < *kiebitz,* orig., plover, meddlesome onlooker], [Colloq.], 1. an onlooker at a card game, especially one who volunteers advice; hence, 2. a giver of unwanted advice; meddler.

kib·lah (kib'lä), ***n.*** [Ar. *qiblah,* something placed opposite < *qabala,* to be opposite], the point toward which Moslems turn when praying, the location of the black stone at Mecca: see **kaaba.**

ki·bosh (kī'bosh, ki-bosh'), ***n.*** [earlier also *kyebosh, kybosh,* prob. < Yid.; ? ult. < prov. G. *kaib* < MHG. *keibe,* carrion; influenced in Eng. by association with *bosh*], [Slang], nonsense: now usually in *put the kibosh on,* to put an end to; squelch; veto.

kick (kik), ***v.i.*** [ME. *kiken, kyken* (late 14th c.); ? < or akin to ON. *kika,* to bend at the knee, *kikna,* to bend from the knees; ? IE. base **gei-,* to bend], 1. to strike out with the foot or feet, as in anger, or in swimming, soccer, etc. 2. to spring back suddenly, as a gun when fired; recoil. 3. [Colloq.], to object strongly; complain; grumble. ***v.t.*** 1. to strike or shove suddenly with the foot or feet. 2. to drive or move (a ball, etc.) by striking with the foot. 3. to spring back against suddenly, as a gun when fired. 4. to make or force (one's way, etc.) by kicking. 5. to score (a goal or point in football) by kicking. ***n.*** 1. *a*) a blow with the foot. *b*) the act of doing this. 2. a sudden recoil, as of a gun when fired. 3. [Colloq.], an objection; complaint. 4. [Colloq.], *a*) a stimulating or intoxicating effect, especially of alcoholic liquor. *b*) pleasurable excitement; thrill. 5. in *football, a*) a kicking of the ball. *b*) the kicked ball. *c*) the distance that it travels. *d*) one's turn at kicking.

kick around (or **about**), [Colloq.], 1. to treat roughly. 2. to move from place to place. 3. to go about unnoticed or neglected. 4. to think about or discuss.
kick back, 1. [Colloq.], to recoil suddenly and in an unexpected way. 2. [Slang], *a)* to give back (stolen goods). *b)* to give back (part of money received as pay, commission, etc.), often as a result of coercion or a previous understanding.
kick in, [Slang], 1. to pay (one's share). 2. to die.
kick off, 1. to put a football into play with a kickoff. 2. [Slang], to die.
kick out, 1. [Colloq.], to get rid of; eject; dismiss. 2. in *football*, to make a kick out of bounds.
kick up, 1. to raise by kicking. 2. [Slang], to make or cause (trouble, confusion, etc.).

kick (kik), *n.* [prob. < prec. *kick;* ? with reminiscence of basic sense via dial.], an indentation at the bottom of a glass bottle, which reduces its capacity.

Kick·a·poo (kik'ə-pōō'), *n.* 1. [*pl.* KICKAPOOS (-pōōz')], any member of a tribe of Algonquian Indians who lived in northern Illinois and southern Wisconsin. 2. the Algonquian language of the Kickapoos.

kick·back (kik'bak'), *n.* 1. [Colloq.], a sharp, violent reaction. 2. [Slang], *a)* a giving back of stolen goods. *b)* a giving back of part of money received as payment, commission, etc., often as a result of coercion or a previous understanding. *c)* the money so returned.

kick·off (kik'ôf'), *n.* in *football*, a place kick from the forty-yard line of the kicking team, that puts the ball into play at the beginning of each half or after a touchdown.

kick·shaw (kik'shô'), *n.* [properly *kickshaws* < Fr. *quelque chose*, something], 1. a fancy food or dish; delicacy; tidbit. 2. a trinket; trifle; gewgaw.

kick·shaws (kik'shôz'), *n.* a kickshaw.

kick·up (kik'up'), *n.* [Colloq.], a fuss; row.

kid (kid), *n.* [ME. *kide;* prob. < Anglo-N.; cf. ON. *kith*, Dan. & Sw. *kid;* akin to G. *kitze;* the Gmc. base may be echoic of the animal's bleat], 1. a young goat or, occasionally, antelope. 2. its flesh, used as a food. 3. leather made from the skin of young goats, used for gloves, shoes, etc. 4. *pl.* gloves or shoes made of this leather. 5. [Colloq.], *a)* a child. *b)* any young person. 6. [Slang], a hoax. *adj.* 1. made of kidskin. 2. [Colloq.], younger: as, my *kid* sister. *v.t. & v.i.* [KIDDED (-id), KIDDING], 1. to give birth to (a kid or kids): said of goats or antelopes. 2. [Slang], *a)* to try to make (a person) believe what is not true; deceive; fool; delude; hoax. *b)* to tease or ridicule playfully with jokes, banter, misleading talk, etc.

kid (kid), *n.* [? var. of *kit* (tub)], a small wooden tub in which rations were formerly served to sailors.

Kidd, Captain (kid), (*William Kidd*), 1645?–1701; Scottish privateer and pirate; hanged.

kid·der (kid'ẽr), *n.* [Slang], a person who kids, or deceives, teases, etc.

Kid·der·min·ster (kid'ẽr-min'stẽr), *n.* a kind of ingrain or reversible carpet, originally made at Kidderminster, England.

kid·dy, kid·die (kid'i), *n.* [*pl.* KIDDIES (-iz)], [dim. of *kid* (child)], [Colloq.], a child.

kid gloves, soft, smooth gloves made of kidskin.
handle with kid gloves, [Colloq.], to handle or treat with care, tact, etc.

kid·nap (kid'nap), *v.t.* [KIDNAPED or KIDNAPPED (-napt), KIDNAPING or KIDNAPPING], [*kid*, child + *nap*, dial. var. of *nab*, to snatch], 1. to steal (a child). 2. to seize and hold or carry off (a person) against his will, by force or fraud, often for ransom.

kid·nap·er, kid·nap·per (kid'nap'ẽr), *n.* a person who kidnaps.

kid·ney (kid'ni), *n.* [*pl.* KIDNEYS (-niz)], [ME. *kidenei* < *kiden-*, ? genit. pl. of *kid* (young goat) + *ei, ey*, an egg (? in the sense of "testicle"; cf. similar use of G. *eier*)], 1. either of a pair of glandular organs in the upper abdominal cavity of vertebrates, which separate water and waste products of metabolism from the blood and excrete them as urine through the bladder. 2. an animal's kidneys, used as food. 3. *a)* disposition; temperament. *b)* class; kind; sort.

KIDNEY KIDNEY

KIDNEYS

kidney bean, 1. a bean shaped like a kidney. 2. the scarlet runner bean.

kidney stone, a hard, mineral deposit (*renal calculus*) formed in the kidney from phosphates, urates, etc.

Ki·dron (kē'drən, kid'rən), *n.* Kedron.

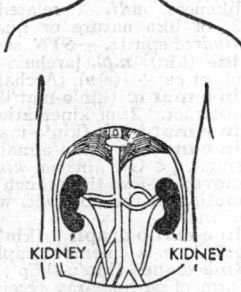

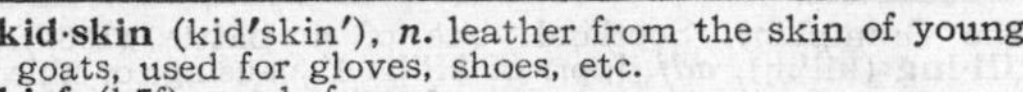

kid·skin (kid'skin'), *n.* leather from the skin of young goats, used for gloves, shoes, etc.

kief (kēf), *n.* kef.

Kiel (kēl), *n.* seaport and capital of Schleswig-Holstein, Germany, on the Kiel Canal: pop., 213,000 (est. 1946).

Kiel Canal, a ship canal in Germany, connecting the North Sea with the Baltic: length, 61 mi.

Kiel·ce (kyel'tse), *n.* a city in southwestern Poland: pop., 50,000 (1946).

kier (kêr), *n.* [prob. < ON. *ker*, tub, transmitted orally via northwestern Brit. dial.], a large vat to hold cloth for bleaching, boiling, etc.

Kier·ke·gaard, So·ren Aa·bye (sö'rən ô'bü kêr'kə-gôr'), 1813–1855; Danish philosopher and theologian.

kie·sel·guhr, kie·sel·gur (kē'z'l-goor'), *n.* [G. < *kiesel*, flint + *guhr, gur*, earthy sediment < *gären*, to ferment], diatomite.

kie·ser·ite (kē'zẽr-it'), *n.* [after D. G. *Kieser*, G. scientist], hydrous magnesium sulfate, $MgSO_4 \cdot H_2O$.

Ki·ev (kē'yef; Eng. kē-ev', kē'ev), *n.* the capital of the Ukrainian S.S.R., on the Dnepr: pop., 846,000.

kike (kik), *n.* [? extension of *-(s)ky* or *-(s)ki* ending of names of some Eastern European Jews; for other hypotheses see H. L. Mencken, *Am. Lang. Suppl. I*, pp. 613–616], [Slang], a Jew: vulgar, offensive term of hostility and contempt, as used by anti-Semites.

kil., kilometer; kilometers.

Ki·lau·e·a (kē'lou-ā'ə), *n.* the active crater of Mauna Loa, on the island of Hawaii: width, 2 mi.

Kil·dare (kil-dâr'), *n.* a county of eastern Ireland, Leinster province: pop., 65,000 (1943).

kil·der·kin (kil'dẽr-kin), *n.* [ME. *kylderkin;* altered < MD. *kinderkin*, quarter tun; prob. < Fr. *quintal* (see QUINTAL) + D. *-kin*, -kin], 1. a cask; small barrel. 2. an old English liquid measure equal to 18 gallons.

kil·erg (kil'ũrg'), *n.* [< *kilo-* + *erg*], in *physics*, a unit of work, equal to 1,000 ergs.

Kil·i·man·ja·ro, Mount (kil'i-män-jä'rō), a volcanic mountain in northern Tanganyika Territory, Africa: height, 19,321 ft.

Kil·ken·ny (kil-ken'i), *n.* 1. a county of southern Ireland, Leinster province: pop., 68,000 (1943). 2. its county seat: pop., 10,000.

kill (kil), *v.t.* [ME. *kullen, killen, kellen;* prob. < AS. **cyllan*, special late phonetic development of *cwellan*, to kill (see QUELL), with *w-* rounding of the vowel and assimilation of *-w*], 1. to cause the death of; put to death; slay. 2. *a)* to destroy the vital or active qualities of. *b)* to destroy; put an end to; ruin. 3. to prevent the passage of (legislation); defeat or veto. 4. to spend (time) on matters of little or no importance. 5. to cause (an engine, etc.) to stop. 6. to prevent publication of: as, the editor *killed* the story. 7. to spoil the effect of; destroy by contrast: said of colors, etc. 8. [Colloq.], to overcome, as with laughter or embarrassment. 9. in *printing*, to mark as not to be used; score out; cancel. 10. in *tennis*, to return (the ball) with such force that it cannot be played back; smash. *v.i.* 1. to destroy life. 2. to be killed: as, these plants *kill* easily. *n.* 1. the act of killing. 2. an animal or animals killed.
in at the kill, 1. present when the hunted animal is killed. 2. present at the end of some action or undertaking.
SYN.—**kill** is the general word in this list, meaning to cause the death of in any way and may be applied to persons, animals, or plants; **slay**, now largely a literary word, implies deliberate and violent killing; **murder** applies to an unlawful and malicious or premeditated killing; **assassinate** implies specifically the sudden killing of a politically important person by someone hired or delegated to do this; **execute** denotes a killing in accordance with a legally imposed sentence; **dispatch** suggests a killing by direct action, such as stabbing or shooting, and emphasizes speed or promptness.

kill (kil), *n.* [D. *kil;* MD. *kille;* ? akin to ON. *kīll*, inlet], a stream; channel; creek: used especially in place names.

Kil·lar·ney (ki-lär'ni), *n.* a town in southwestern Ireland: pop., 5,300.

Killarney, Lakes of, three lakes near Killarney, Ireland: the largest is Lough Leane.

kill·dee (kil'dē'), *n.* [*pl.* KILLDEES (-dēz'), **KILLDEE**; see PLURAL, II, D, 1], a killdeer.

kill·deer (kil'dêr'), *n.* [*pl.* KILLDEERS (-dêrz'), KILLDEER; see PLURAL, II, D, 1], [echoic of its cry], a small, North American wading bird of the plover family.

kill·er (kil'ẽr), *n.* 1. a person, animal, or thing that kills; especially, one that kills habitually. 2. a killer whale.

killer whale, a fierce dolphin that hunts in large packs and preys on large fish, seals, and whales.

kil·lick (kil'ik), *n.* [New England dial.], a small anchor; often, an anchor weighted with a stone, or a stone used for an anchor: also **killock.**

Kil·lie·cran·kie (kil'i-kraŋ'ki), *n.* a mountain pass in the Grampians, Scotland: site of a battle (1689).

kill·ing (kil′iŋ), *adj.* [ppr. of *kill*], 1. causing, or able to cause, death; destructive; deadly. 2. exhausting; fatiguing. 3. [Colloq.], very attractive. 4. [Colloq.], very funny; very comical. *n.* 1. slaughter; murder. 2. [Colloq.], a sudden great profit or success.

kill-joy (kil′joi′), *n.* a person who destroys or lessens other people's enjoyment.

kil·lock (kil′ək), *n.* a killick.

Kil·mar·nock (kil-mär′nək), *n.* a city in southwestern Scotland: pop., 41,000 (1946).

Kil·mer, Joyce (kil′mẽr), 1886–1918; American poet.

kiln (kil, kiln), *n.* [ME. *kylne; kulne;* also *kylle;* AS. *cylene, cylne;* L. *culina,* cookstove, kitchen (cf. CULINARY)], a furnace or oven for drying, burning, or baking something, as bricks, grain, or lime. *v.t.* to dry, burn, or bake in a kiln.

kiln-dry (kil′drī′, kiln′drī′), *v.t.* to dry in a kiln.

ki·lo (kē′lō, kil′ō), *n.* [*pl.* KILOS (-lōz, -ōz)], [Fr.: abbreviated form], 1. a kilogram. 2. a kilometer. Abbreviated **K., k.**

kil·o- (kil′ō, kil′ə), [Fr. < Gr. *chilioi,* thousand], a combining form used in the metric system, meaning *one thousand,* as in *kilogram, kilowatt.*

kilo., 1. kilogram. 2. kilometer.

kil·o·cal·o·rie (kil′ə-kal′ẽr-i), *n.* [see KILO- & CALORIE], the amount of heat needed to raise the temperature of one kilogram of water one degree centigrade; 1,000 calories; great calorie.

kil·o·cy·cle (kil′ə-sī′k'l), *n.* 1. 1,000 cycles. 2. 1,000 cycles per second: used in radio to express the frequency of electromagnetic waves. Abbreviated **kc.** (*sing. & pl.*).

kil·o·gram, kil·o·gramme (kil′ə-gram′), *n.* [Fr. *kilogramme;* see KILO- & GRAM], a unit of weight and mass, equal to 1,000 grams (2.2046 pounds): abbreviated **kg.** (*sing. & pl.*), **k., kilo., kilog.**

kil·o·gram-me·ter, kil·o·gram-me·tre (kil′ə-gram-mē′tẽr), *n.* a unit of energy or work, being the amount needed to raise one kilogram one meter: it is equal to 7.2334 foot-pounds.

kil·o·li·ter, kil·o·li·tre (kil′ə-lē′tẽr), *n.* [Fr. *kilolitre;* see KILO- & LITER], a unit of capacity, equal to 1,000 liters, or one cubic meter (264.17 gallons, or 1.308 cubic yards): abbreviated **kilol., kl.** (*sing. & pl.*).

kil·o·me·ter, kil·o·me·tre (kil′ə-mē′tẽr, ki-lom′ə-tẽr), *n.* [Fr. *kilomètre;* see KILO- & METER], a unit of length or distance, equal to 1,000 meters (3,280.8 feet, or about 5/8 mile): abbreviated **kil., km., kilo., kilom.**

kil·o·met·ric (kil′ə-met′rik), *adj.* 1. of a kilometer. 2. marking, or measured in, kilometers.

kil·o·watt (kil′ə-wot′, kil′ə-wôt′), *n.* a unit of electrical power, equal to 1,000 watts: abbreviated **kw.**

kil·o·watt-hour (kil′ə-wot′our′, kil′ə-wôt′our′), *n.* a unit of electrical energy or work, equal to that done by one kilowatt acting for one hour: abbreviated **kwh., K.W.H., kw-h, kw-hr** (no period).

kilt (kilt), *v.t.* [ME. (northern) *kilte;* prob. < ON. **kilta* (cf. ON. *kilting,* a skirt, Dan. *kilte,* to tuck)], 1. [Scot.], to tuck up (skirts); fasten up (often with *up*). 2. to pleat. *n.* a short, pleated skirt reaching to the knees, worn by men of the Scottish Highlands.

KILT

kil·ter (kil′tẽr), *n.* [Colloq.], good condition; proper order: also **kelter:** now always preceded by *in* or *out of.*

kilt·ing (kil′tiŋ), *n.* [*kilt, v.* + *-ing*], flat pleats, each folded so as to half cover the one before it.

Kim·ber·ley (kim′bẽr-li), *n.* a city in Cape Province, Union of South Africa: pop., 40,200: large diamond mines are located near by.

ki·mo·no (kə-mō′nə, ki-mō′nō), *n.* [*pl.* KIMONOS (-nəz, -nōz)], [Japan.], 1. a loose outer garment with short, wide sleeves and a sash, worn by both men and women in Japan. 2. a woman's loose dressing gown like this.

kin (kin), *n.* [ME. *kyn, kun, ken(ne); AS. cynn;* akin to D. *kunne,* Goth. *kuni,* etc.; IE. base **ĝen-,* to produce, as also in L. *genus* (cf. GENUS, GENERATE, etc.), Eng. *kind*], 1. relatives; family; kinsfolk; kindred. 2. family relationship; connection by birth or, sometimes, by marriage. *adj.* related, as by blood; kindred.
near of kin, closely related.
of kin, related.

-kin (kin), [ME.; prob. < MD. *-ken, -kijn,* dim. suffix; akin to G. *-chen*], a suffix meaning *little,* added to nouns to form the diminutive, as in *lambkin, manikin.*

Kin·a·ba·lu, Mount (kin′ä-bä′lōō), a mountain in British North Borneo: height, 13,451 ft.

kin·aes·the·si·a (kin′is-thē′zhə, kin′is-thē′zhi-ə), *n.* kinesthesia.

kin·aes·the·sis (kin′is-thē′sis), *n.* kinesthesis.

kin·aes·thet·ic (kin′is-thet′ik), *adj.* kinesthetic.

Kin·car·dine (kin-kär′din), *n.* a county on the eastern coast of Scotland: pop., 28,000 (est. 1946); county seat, Stonehaven.

Kin·chin·jun·ga, Mount (kin′chin-jooŋ′gə), Mount Kanchenjunga.

kind (kīnd), *n.* [ME. *kynde, kund, kende;* AS. *cynd* < base of *cynn* (see KIN); IE. extended base **ĝn̥ti-,* seen also in L. *gens, gentis,* family (cf. GENS, GENTILE, GENTLE)], 1. [Rare or Archaic], *a*) origin. *b*) nature. *c*) manner; way. 2. a natural group or division; race: as, the rodent *kind.* 3. sort; variety; class. *adj.* [ME. *kinde, kynde, kunde;* AS. *gecynde, cynde*], 1. sympathetic, friendly, gentle, tender-hearted, generous, etc. 2. cordial: as, *kind* regards. 3. [Obs.], *a*) natural; native. *b*) rightful. *c*) well-born.
after one's (or **its**) **kind,** [Archaic], in agreement with one's (or its) nature; with one's (or its) natural group.
in kind, 1. in goods or produce instead of money. 2. with something like that received; in the same way.
kind of, [Colloq.], somewhat; rather; almost.
of a kind, 1. of the same kind; alike. 2. of poor quality; makeshift; mediocre: as, entertainment *of a kind.*
SYN.*—kind** implies the possession of sympathetic or generous qualities, either habitually or specifically, or is applied to actions manifesting these (he is ***kind only to his mother, your ***kind*** remarks); **kindly** usually implies a characteristic nature or general disposition marked by such qualities (his ***kindly*** old uncle); **benign** suggests a mild or kindly nature and is applied especially to a gracious superior (a ***benign*** employer); **benevolent** implies a charitable or altruistic inclination to do good (his ***benevolent*** interest in orphans). See also **type.—*ANT.*** unkind, unfeeling, cruel.

kin·der·gar·ten (kin′dẽr-gär′t'n), *n.* [G., lit., garden of children; *kinder,* genit. pl. of *kind,* child (see KIND, *n.*) + *garten,* garden], a school or class for young children, usually four to six years old, that develops basic skills and social behavior by games, exercises, toys, simple handicraft, etc.

kin·der·gart·ner, kin·der·gar·ten·er (kin′dẽr-gärt′nẽr), *n.* 1. a kindergarten teacher. 2. a child who attends kindergarten.

kind·heart·ed (kīnd′här′tid), *adj.* having or resulting from a kind heart; sympathetic; generous; kindly.

kin·dle (kin′d'l), *v.t.* [KINDLED (-d'ld), KINDLING], [ME. *kindlen;* freq. of ON. *kynda,* to set on fire], 1. to set on fire; ignite. 2. to light (a fire). 3. to arouse or excite (interest, feelings, etc.). 4. to cause to light up; make bright. *v.i.* 1. to catch fire; start burning. 2. to become aroused or excited. 3. to light up; become bright: as, her eyes *kindled* with joy.

kin·dle (kin′d'l), *v.t. & v.i.* [KINDLED (-d'ld), KINDLING], [ME. *kindlen, cundlen;* see KIND, *n.*], [Dial.], to give birth to (young).

kind·less (kīnd′lis), *adj.* 1. [Poetic], lacking kindness. 2. [Obs.], lacking natural feeling; unnatural.

kind·li·ness (kīnd′li-nis), *n.* 1. the quality of being kindly. 2. a kindly act.

kin·dling (kin′dliŋ), *n.* [ME.; see KINDLE (ignite)], 1. bits of wood or other easily lighted material for starting a fire. 2. the act of one who kindles.

kind·ly (kīnd′li), *adj.* [KINDLIER (-li-ẽr), KINDLIEST (-li-ist)], [ME. *cyndelich;* AS. *cyndelic,* natural < *cynde;* see KIND], 1. kind; gracious; benign; benevolent. 2. agreeable; pleasant; genial: as, a ***kindly*** climate. 3. [*Archaic*], natural; native; innate. *adv.* 1. in a kind, gracious manner. 2. agreeably; favorably. 3. please: as, *kindly* shut the door. 4. [Obs.], naturally: now only in *take kindly to.* —***SYN.*** see **kind.**
take kindly to, to be naturally attracted to.

kind·ness (kīnd′nis), *n.* [ME. *kyndeness*], 1. the state, quality, or habit of being kind. 2. kind act or treatment. 3. [Rare], kind feeling; affection; good will.

kin·dred (kin′drid), *n.* [with intrusive *-d-* < ME. *kinrede, kinreden* < AS. *cynn,* kin + *-ræden,* state, condition], 1. relationship by birth or, sometimes, by marriage; family relationship; kinship. 2. relatives or family; kin; kinsfolk. 3. resemblance in qualities; likeness. *adj.* 1. related by birth or common origin. 2. of like nature or qualities; similar: as, they are *kindred* spirits. —***SYN.*** see **related.**

kine (kīn), *n.pl.* [archaic double pl. of *cow* < AS. *cy,* pl. of *cu* + *-(e)n*], [Archaic or Dial.], cows; cattle.

kin·e·mat·ic (kin′ə-mat′ik), *adj.* 1. of motion in the abstract. 2. of kinematics.

kin·e·mat·i·cal (kin′ə-mat′i-k'l), *adj.* kinematic.

kin·e·mat·ics (kin′ə-mat′iks), *n.pl.* [construed as sing.], [< Gr. *kinēma, kinēmatos,* motion < *kinein,* to move; + *-ics*], the branch of mechanics that deals with motion in the abstract, without reference to the force or mass.

kin·e·mat·o·graph (kin′ə-mat′ə-graf′, kin′ə-mat′ə-gräf′), *n.* a cinematograph.

kin·e·scope (kin′ə-skōp′), *n.* [*kineto-* + *-scope*], a form of cathode-ray receiving tube used in television: it has a luminescent screen at one end, on which the images are reproduced: a trade-mark (**Kinescope**).

kin·es·the·si·a (kin′is-thē′zhə, kin′is-thē′zhi-ə), *n.* [Mod. L. < Gr. *kinein,* to move + *aisthēsis,* perception], the sensation of position, movement, tension, etc. of parts of the body, perceived through nerve end organs in muscles, tendons, and joints: also spelled **kinaesthesia.**

kin·es·the·sis (kin'is-thē'sis), *n.* kinesthesia.
kin·es·thet·ic (kin'is-thet'ik), *adj.* of kinesthesia.
ki·net·ic (ki-net'ik, kī-net'ik), *adj.* [Gr. *kinētikos* < *kinein*, to move], of or resulting from motion.
kinetic energy, that energy of a body which results from its motion: it is equal to half the product of its mass and the square of its velocity $\left(\frac{mv^2}{2}\right)$: opposed to *potential energy.*
ki·net·ics (ki-net'iks, kī-net'iks), *n.pl.* [construed as sing.], [< *kinetic*], the science that deals with the motion of masses in relation to the forces acting on them.
kinetic theory, the theory that the minute particles of all matter are in constant motion and that the temperature of a substance is dependent on the velocity of this motion, increased motion being accompanied by increased temperature: according to the kinetic theory of gases, the elasticity, diffusion, pressure, and other physical properties of a gas are due to the rapid motion in straight lines of its molecules, to their impacts against each other and the walls of the container, to weak cohesive forces between molecules, etc.
ki·ne·to- (ki-nē'tō, kī-net'ə), [< Gr. *kinētos*, movable < *kinein*, to move], a combining form meaning *moving, motion,* as in *kinetograph.*
ki·ne·to·graph (ki-nē'tə-graf', kī-net'ə-gräf'), *n.* [*kineto-* + *-graph*], a motion-picture camera.
kin·folk (kin'fōk'), *n.pl.* [Dial.], kinsfolk.
king (kiŋ), *n.* [ME. *kynge;* AS. *cyning* < base of *cynn* (see KIN) + *-ing*, patronymic suffix; akin to D. *koning*, ON. *konungr*, etc.; prob. basic sense, either "head of a kin" or "son of noble kin"], 1. a male ruler of a nation or state usually called a kingdom; male sovereign, limited or absolute; monarch. 2. a man who is supreme or highly successful in some field: as, an oil *king.* 3. something supreme in its class. 4. in *card games*, a playing card with a conventionalized picture of a king on it. 5. in *checkers*, a piece that has moved across the board to the opponent's base and been crowned, so that it can move both forward and backward. 6. in *chess*, the chief piece, which can move one square in any direction: the game is ended when either player's king is checkmated. Abbreviated **K, K., k.** *adj.* chief (in size, importance, etc.): often in combination.
King, William Lyon Mac·ken·zie (mə-ken'zi), 1874–1950; Canadian statesman and economist; prime minister (1921–June 1926; Sept. 1926–1930; 1935–1948).
King apple, a large winter apple with red stripes.
King Arthur, a real or legendary king of Britain: see **Arthur.**
king·bird (kiŋ'bũrd'), *n.* any of several American birds called tyrant flycatchers, especially a species known as the bee martin or common kingbird.
king bolt (kiŋ'bōlt'), *n.* a vertical bolt connecting the front axle of a wagon, etc., or the truck of a railroad car, with the body; kingpin: it acts as a pivot when the vehicle turns.
King Charles spaniel, a small English spaniel with long, silky fur, usually black and tan, and drooping ears: so called because made fashionable by Charles II.
king cobra, a large, very poisonous snake native to India.
king crab, a horseshoe crab.
king·craft (kiŋ'kraft', kiŋ'kräft'), *n.* the art of ruling as a monarch; royal statecraft.
king·cup (kiŋ'kup'), *n.* 1. a buttercup. 2. a marsh marigold.
king·dom (kiŋ'dəm), *n.* [ME.; AS. *cynedom, cyningdom;* see KING & -DOM], 1. a government or country headed by a king or queen; monarchy: abbreviated **km.** 2. a realm; domain: as, the *kingdom* of poetry. 3. one of the three great divisions into which all natural objects have been classified (the animal, vegetable, and mineral kingdoms). 4. [Archaic], the position, rank, or power of a king. 5. the spiritual realm of God.
kingdom come, [< "thy kingdom come," in the Lord's Prayer], the next world; the hereafter; heaven.
king·fish (kiŋ'fish'), *n.* 1. [*pl.* KINGFISH, KINGFISHES (-iz); see FISH], any of several large food fishes found along the Atlantic or Pacific coast, including the California whiting, the opah, and the pintado. 2. [Colloq.], the acknowledged head or dictator of some group, lawmaking body, place, etc.
king·fish·er (kiŋ'fish'ẽr), *n.* [orig. (ME.) *king's fisher;* cf. Fr. *martin-pêcheur*], any of a large family of birds, usually bright-colored and having a large, crested head, a large, strong beak, and a short tail: many kingfishers eat fish.
King Horn (hôrn), the hero of an English metrical romance of the same name (c. 1225), and of various other romances in English, Scottish, and French.
King James Version, the Authorized Version of the Bible, a revised English translation published in 1611 with the authorization of King James I.
King Lear (lêr), 1. a famous tragedy by Shakespeare (1606?). 2. the main character of this play, a legendary British king who divides his kingdom between his two older daughters, Goneril and Regan, and disinherits his youngest, Cordelia. Goneril and Regan prove wicked and ungrateful, driving Lear insane by their mistreatment; when Cordelia tries to rescue him she is caught and hanged, and Lear dies of grief.
king·let (kiŋ'lit), *n.* [see -LET], 1. a petty, unimportant king, as of a small country. 2. any of several small, greenish songbirds with bright-colored crowns, as the golden-crowned kinglet and the ruby-crowned kinglet.
king·li·ness (kiŋ'li-nis), *n.* the quality or condition of being kingly.
king·ly (kiŋ'li), *adj.* [KINGLIER (-li-ẽr), KINGLIEST (-li-ist)], [ME.], of, like, or fit for a king or kings; royal; regal; noble. *adv.* [Archaic], in the manner of a king.
king-of-arms (kiŋ'əv-ärmz'), *n.* in Great Britain, any of the chief officers who decide questions of heraldry: also **king of arms.**
king of beasts, the lion.
king of the forest, the oak.
king·pin (kiŋ'pin'), *n.* 1. a kingbolt. 2. the pin at the apex (or the one in the center) in bowling, tenpins, etc. 3. [Colloq.], the main or essential person or thing.
king post, in *carpentry*, a vertical supporting post between the apex of a triangular truss and the base, or tie beam, as at the ridge of a roof.

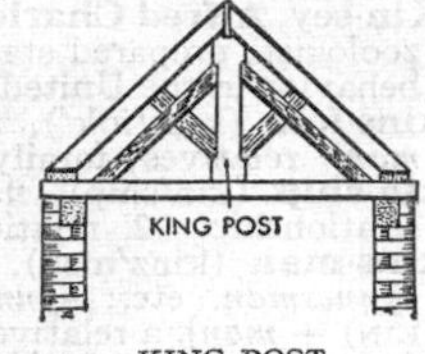

KING POST

Kings (kiŋz), *n.pl.* 1. the two books (I Kings, II Kings) in the Old Testament which give the history of the reigns of the Jewish kings after David. 2. four books in the Roman Catholic Old Testament (Douay Version) which include I & II Samuel and I & II Kings (of the Protestant Version). Abbreviated **Ki.**
King's (or **Queen's**) **Bench** (kiŋz), [so called because the sovereign used to sit there on a raised bench], a former court of record and the highest court of common law in England; King's Bench Division of the High Court of Justice: abbreviated **K.B.**
King's (or **Queen's**) **Counsel,** a senior member of the bar in England, appointed to his honorary office by the Crown on the Lord Chancellor's nomination: abbreviated **K.C.**
king's (or **queen's**) **English, the,** standard (especially British) English; accepted English usage in speech or writing: so called from the notion of royal sanction.
king's (or **queen's**) **evidence,** in *English law*, state's evidence.
king's evil, [after ML. *regius morbus*], scrofula: so called from the old notion that a king's touch could cure it.
king·ship (kiŋ'ship), *n.* [see -SHIP], 1. the position, rank, dignity, or dominion of a king. 2. the rule of a king; monarchical government. 3. majesty: a title sometimes used (with *his*) in referring to a king.
king-size (kiŋ'sīz'), *adj.* [Colloq.], of greater than normal size: as, a *king-size* cigarette.
king-sized (kiŋ'sīzd'), *adj.* [Colloq.] king-size.
Kings·ley, Charles (kiŋz'li), 1819–1875; English clergyman, poet, and novelist.
Kingsley, Sidney, 1906– ; American playwright.
king snake, a large, harmless snake found in the southern United States: it eats mice, rats, and lizards and kills other snakes.
Kings·port (kiŋz'pôrt), *n.* a city in northeastern Tennessee: pop., 26,000.
king's ransom, a large sum of money.
Kings·ton (kiŋz'tən, kiŋ'stən), *n.* 1. seaport and capital of Jamaica: pop., 126,000. 2. a city in Ontario, Canada, at the outlet of Lake Ontario into the St. Lawrence: pop., 33,000. 3. a city in southern New York, on the Hudson River: pop., 29,000. 4. a city in eastern Pennsylvania: pop., 20,000.
Kings·ton-up·on-Hull (kiŋz'tən-ə-pon'hul', kiŋ'stən-ə-pon'hul'), *n.* Hull, a seaport in eastern England.
king truss, in *carpentry*, a truss, or braced structure to support a roof, framed with a king post.
king·wood (kiŋ'wood'), *n.* 1. a hard, fine-grained, violet-tinted wood from a certain tree that grows in Brazil. 2. the tree.
kink (kiŋk), *n.* [prob. < D. or Sw. *kink*, twist or curl in a rope; akin to G. *kink*, ult. to ON. *kikna*, to bend at the knees; cf. KICK], 1. a short twist, curl, or bend in a thread, rope, hair, wire, etc. 2. a painful muscle spasm or cramp in the neck, back, etc.; crick. 3. *a*) a mental twist; queer notion; whim; crotchet; eccentricity. *b*) a quirk; peculiarity. *v.i. & v.t.* to form or cause to form a kink or kinks.

kin·ka·jou (kiŋ′kə-jōō′), *n.* [Fr. *quincajou;* Sp. *quincajú;* Port. *kinkaju* < native Brazilian (Tupi) name], a flesh-eating mammal of Central and South America, somewhat like a raccoon, with soft, yellowish-brown fur, large eyes, and a long prehensile tail: lives in trees and moves about at night.

KINKAJOU (about 3 ft. long including tail)

kink·i·ness (kiŋ′ki-nis), *n.* the quality or state of being kinky.

kink·y (kiŋ′ki), *adj.* [KINKIER (-ki-ēr), KINKIEST (-ki-ist)], full of kinks; tightly curled: as, *kinky* hair.

kin·ni·ki·nick, kin·ni·kin·nic (kin′i-kə-nik′), *n.* [Am. Ind. (Algonquian), lit., that which is mixed], a mixture, commonly of dried sumac leaves and bark, formerly smoked by certain American Indians.

ki·no (kē′nō), *n.* [< W. African (Mandingo) native name], a dark-red or reddish-brown gum obtained from certain tropical trees, used chiefly in tanning and as an astringent in medicine: also **kino gum.**

Kin·ross (kin-rôs′), *n.* 1. Kinrossshire. 2. the county seat of Kinrossshire: pop., 2,400.

Kin·ross·shire (kin-rôs′shir, kin-rô′shir), *n.* a county of central Scotland: pop., 7,000.

Kin·sey, Alfred Charles (kin′zi), 1894–1956; American zoologist; prepared statistical surveys of human sexual behavior in the United States.

kins·folk (kinz′fōk′), *n.pl.* [< *kin* + *folk*, after *kinsman*], relatives; family; kin; kindred.

kin·ship (kin′ship), *n.* [see KIN & -SHIP], 1. family relationship. 2. relationship; close connection.

kins·man (kinz′mən), *n.* [*pl.* KINSMEN (-mən)], [ME. *kynnesman*, etc.; *kynnes-*, genit. sing. of *kynne* (see KIN) + *man*], a relative; especially, a male relative.

kins·wom·an (kinz′woom′ən), *n.* [*pl.* KINSWOMEN (-wim′in)], [see KINSMAN], a female relative.

ki·osk (ki-osk′; *also, for 2,* ki′osk), *n.* [Fr. *kiosque* < Turk. *kiūshk*, pavilion < Per. *kūshk*, palace], 1. in Turkey and Persia, a summerhouse or pavilion of open construction. 2. a somewhat similar small structure open at one or more sides, used as a newsstand, bandstand, covering for the entrance to a subway, etc.

kip (kip), *n.* [earlier *kippe;* prob. < D. *kip*, *kijp* (in sense 2)], 1. the untanned hide of a calf, lamb, or other young or small animal. 2. a set of such hides.

kip (kip), *n.* [corresponds in sense with MLG. *kiffe*, hovel, in form with Dan. *kippe*, low alehouse], 1. [Slang], *a*) a rooming house. *b*) a lodging or bed there. *c*) any bed. 2. [Obs.], a brothel.

Kip·ling, Rud·yard (rud′yērd kip′liŋ), 1865–1936; British poet, short-story writer, and novelist; received Nobel prize in literature, 1907.

kip·per (kip′ēr), *v.t.* [? < the *n.*], to cure (herring, salmon, etc.) by cleaning, salting, and drying or smoking. *n.* [ME. *kypre;* AS. *cypera*], 1. a male salmon or sea trout during or shortly after the spawning season: at this time, the male salmon grows a hook of cartilage (dialectally called a *kip*) on its lower jaw, used in fighting. 2. a kippered herring, salmon, etc.

Kirch·hoff, Gus·tav Ro·bert (goos′täf rō′bert kērH′-hôf), 1824–1887; German physicist.

Kir·ghiz (kir-gēz′), *n.* [native name: said to be after a legendary chief of the same name], 1. [*pl.* KIRGHIZ, KIRGHIZES (-iz)], a member of a Mongolian people in west central Asia. 2. their Turko-Tatar language.

Kirghiz Soviet Socialist Republic, a republic of the U.S.S.R., in south central Asia: area, 75,950 sq. mi.; pop., 1,533,000; capital, Frunze.

Ki·rin (kē′rin′), *n.* 1. a province of central Manchuria: area, 105,000 sq. mi.; pop., 6,465,000 (est. 1947). 2. its capital, on the Sungari River: pop., 174,000.

kirk (kũrk; Scot. kirk), *n.* [Scot.; ME. *kirke* < AS. *circe* (influenced by the cognate ON. *kirkja*); see CHURCH], [Scot. & North Eng.], a church.

the Kirk, the (Presbyterian) Church of Scotland: so used in England.

Kirk·cud·bright (kẽr-kōō′bri), *n.* 1. Kirkcudbrightshire. 2. its county seat: pop., 2,300.

Kirk·cud·bright·shire (kẽr-kōō′bri-shir′), *n.* a county of southwestern Scotland, on Solway Firth: pop., 30,400; county seat, Kirkcudbright.

kirk·man (kũrk′mən), *n.* [*pl.* KIRKMEN (-mən)], [*kirk* + *man*], 1. [Scot.], a church member or clergyman. 2. a member or supporter of the (Presbyterian) Church of Scotland.

kir·mess (kũr′mis), *n.* a kermis.

kirn (kũrn; Scot. *also* kirn), *n.* [? var. of *churn;* from the use of a churnful of cream at the feast], in Scotland, 1. a feast to celebrate the end of the harvest; harvest home. 2. the last sheaf of the harvest.

Ki·rov (kē′rôf), *n.* 1. a region of the R.S.F.S.R., in east central European Russia. 2. its capital: pop., 86,000: formerly called *Vyatka.*

Ki·rov·a·bad (kē′rô-vä-bät′), *n.* a city in the Azerbaijan S.S.R., in Transcaucasia: pop., 99,000: formerly called *Elisavetpol, Gandzha.*

Ki·rov·o·grad (kē′rô-vô-gräd′), *n.* a city in the central Ukrainian S.S.R.: pop., 91,000: formerly called *Elisavetgrad, Zinoviersk.*

kirsch (kêrsh), *n.* kirschwasser.

kirsch·was·ser (kêrsh′väs′ēr), *n.* [G. < *kirsche*, cherry + *wasser*, water], an alcoholic drink distilled from the fermented juice of black cherries.

kir·tle (kũr′t'l), *n.* [ME. *kirtel*, etc.; AS. *cyrtel;* prob. < L. *curtus*, short + *-el*, dim. suffix; akin to ON. *kyrtill*], [Archaic], 1. a man's tunic or coat. 2. a woman's dress or skirt.

Ki·shi·nev (kish′i-nef′; Russ. ki-shi-nyôf′), *n.* the capital of the Moldavian S.S.R.: pop., 114,000: Romanian name, *Chişinău.*

Kis·ka (kis′kə), *n.* one of the western Aleutian Islands.

Kis·lev, Kis·lew (kis′lef), *n.* [Heb.], the third month of the Jewish year: see **Jewish calendar.**

kis·mat (kiz′mət, kis′mət), *n.* kismet.

kis·met (kiz′met, kis′met), *n.* [Turk. *qismet;* Ar. *qismah*, a portion, lot, fate < *qasama*, to divide], fate; destiny.

kiss (kis), *v.t. & v.i.* [ME. *kyssen, kissen;* AS. *cyssan* < Gmc. **kuss-*, base of AS. *coss*, a kiss; akin to G. *küssen;* IE. base **qu-*, **qus-*, found also by some authorities in Sans. *cūšati*, sucks], 1. to give a kiss to (a person, a thing, or one another); touch or caress with the lips. 2. to touch lightly or gently. *n.* [ME. *kisse* < the *v.*, replacing *cosse* < AS. *coss*], 1. a touch or caress with the lips, often with some pressure and suction, as an act of affection, desire, greeting, etc. 2. a light, gentle touch or slight contact, as of billiard balls in motion. 3. *a*) any of various candies. *b*) a baked confection of egg white and powdered sugar.

kiss·er (kis′ēr), *n.* 1. a person who kisses. 2. [Slang], *a*) the mouth or lips. *b*) the face.

kissing bug, any of various poisonous, bloodsucking insects that bite the face, lips, etc.

kist (kist), *n.* [ME. *kist, kiste;* ON. *kista;* L. *cista;* see CHEST], [Chiefly Scot. & North Eng. Dial.], a chest, box, or locker, as for holding money.

kist (kist), *n.* a cist.

Kist·na (kist′nə), *n.* a river in southern India, flowing eastward into the Bay of Bengal: length, 800 mi.

Kit (kit), 1. a masculine name: see **Christopher.** 2. a feminine name: see **Catherine.**

kit (kit), *n.* [ME. *kyt;* prob. < MD. *kitte*, container made of hooped staves; cf. KID], 1. a small wooden tub or bucket for holding fish, butter, etc. 2. *a*) a soldier's equipment, exclusive of arms: now called *pack. b*) personal equipment, especially as packed for travel. *c*) a set of tools or implements. *d*) equipment for some particular activity, sport, etc. 3. a box, bag, or other container for carrying such equipment or tools. 4. [Colloq.], a set; lot; collection.

the whole kit and caboodle, [Colloq.], the whole lot; everybody or everything.

kit (kit), *n.* a kitten.

kit (kit), *n.* [Early Mod. Eng.; prob. abbrev. < *cithara* or one of its derivative forms], [Rare], a small violin.

kitch·en (kich′ən), *n.* [ME. *kychene;* AS. *cycene* < LL. *cucina* < L. *coquina* < *coquere*, to cook], 1. a room or place for the preparation and cooking of food. 2. the cooking department; cuisine. 3. a portable outfit for cooking: as, an army field *kitchen.*

kitch·en·er (kich′ən-ēr), *n.* 1. a person who works in or has charge of a kitchen, especially in a monastery. 2. [British], a stove or range for cooking.

Kitch·e·ner of Khartoum (kich′ən-ēr), first Earl, (*Horatio Herbert Kitchener*), 1850–1916; British statesman and field marshal.

kitch·en·ette, kitch·en·et (kich′ən-et′), *n.* a small, compact kitchen or part of a room arranged as a kitchen, as in some apartments.

kitchen garden, a garden in which vegetables and, sometimes, fruit are grown, usually for home use.

kitch·en·maid (kich′ən-mād′), *n.* a domestic worker who helps the cook.

kitchen midden, [after Dan. *kökkenmödding*], a mound of shells, animal bones, and other refuse such as often marks the location of a prehistoric settlement: also **midden.**

kitchen police, 1. soldiers detailed to assist the cooks in an army kitchen. 2. this duty. Abbreviated **KP, K.P.**

kitch·en·ware (kich′ən-wâr′), *n.* kitchen utensils; pots, pans, etc.

kite (kīt), *n.* [ME.; AS. *cyta*], 1. any of various birds of the hawk family, with long, pointed wings. 2. a greedy, grasping person; sharper; rogue. 3. a light frame, usually of wood, covered with paper or cloth, to be flown in the wind at the end of a string. 4. *pl.* the highest sails of a ship, used in a light breeze. 5. in *business*, a bad check or similar fictitious or worthless commercial paper used to raise money or maintain credit temporarily. *v.i.* [KITED (-id), KITING], 1. [Colloq.], to fly like a kite; move lightly and rapidly; soar or glide. 2. in *business*, to get money or credit by using bad checks, etc. *v.t.* in *business*, to issue (a bad check, etc.) as a kite.

kith (kith), *n.* [ME.; AS. *cyth*, earlier *cyththu;* prob. < base of *cuth*, known; see UNCOUTH], [Archaic], friends, acquaintances, or neighbors: now only in *kith and kin.* **kith and kin**, friends, acquaintances, and relatives: now often restricted to mean only relatives, or kin.

‡**kitsch** (kich), *n.* [G.], gaudy trash; specifically, art, writing, etc. of a pretentious, but shallow kind, calculated to have popular appeal.

kit·ten (kit''n), *n.* [ME. *kitoun;* OFr. *chitoun*, var. of *chaton*, dim. of *chat;* see CAT], a young cat: occasionally applied to the young of some other small animals. *v.i. & v.t.* to give birth to (kittens).

kit·ten·ish (kit''n-ish), *adj.* like a kitten; playful; frisky; often, playfully coy.

kit·ti·wake (kit'i-wāk'), *n.* [*pl.* KITTIWAKES (-wāks'), KITTIWAKE; see PLURAL, II, D, 1], [echoic of its cry], any of several sea gulls of the Arctic and North Atlantic, having a short or rudimentary hind toe.

kit·tle (kit''l), *v.t.* [KITTLED (-'ld), KITTLING], [Late ME. *kytylle;* Late AS. *citelian* < ON. *killa;* akin to G. *kitzeln;* prob. echoic in origin], [Scot.], 1. to tickle. 2. to puzzle. *adj.* [Scot. or Obs.], ticklish; hard to deal with; troublesome; skittish.

Kit·tredge, George Ly·man (lī'mən kit'rij), 1860–1941; American educator, scholar, and author.

Kit·ty (kit'i), a feminine name: see **Catherine.**

kit·ty (kit'i), *n.* [*pl.* KITTIES (-iz)], 1. a kitten. 2. a pet name for a cat of any age.

kit·ty (kit'i), *n.* [*pl.* KITTIES (-iz)], [as if < *kit* (tub) + *-y;* orig. in sense of "jail"], 1. the stakes or pool in a poker game. 2. money pooled by card players, etc. for some particular purpose, as to pay for the cards. 3. in certain card games, an extra hand or part of a hand, dealt to the table, etc.

kit·ty-cor·nered (kit'i-kôr'nẽrd), *adj. & adv.* catercornered: also **kitty-corner.**

Kitty Hawk, a place in northeastern North Carolina near where the first controlled and sustained airplane flight was made by Orville and Wilbur Wright in 1903.

Kiung·shan (kyoon'shän'; Chin. jyooŋ'shän'), *n.* a seaport in China, on Hainan Island: pop., 46,000.

Kiu·shu (kū'shōō'), *n.* Kyushu.

ki·va (kē'və), *n.* [Hopi], in a Pueblo Indian dwelling, a large room used for religious and other purposes.

Ki·wa·ni·an (kə-wä'ni-ən, kə-wô'ni-ən), *n.* a member of a Kiwanis Club. *adj.* of Kiwanis Clubs or Kiwanians.

Ki·wa·nis (kə-wä'nis, kə-wô'nis), *n.* [< Am. Ind. *keewanis*, to make (oneself) known], an international group of clubs of business and professional men, organized at Detroit in 1915 for civic service, the promotion of ideals of fair dealing, fellowship, etc.

ki·wi (kē'wi), *n.* [*pl.* KIWIS (-wiz)], [Maori: echoic of its cry], the apteryx, a bird of New Zealand.

Kiz·il Ir·mak (kiz'il ir-mäk'), a river flowing through central Turkey into the Black Sea: length, 600 mi.

Kiz·il Kum (kiz'il koom), a desert in the Asiatic U.S.S.R., east of Lake Aral: also spelled **Kyzil Kum, Qizil Qum.**

Kjö·len (chö'lən), *n.* a mountain range in northern Norway and Sweden: highest peak, 6,965 ft.

K.K.K., KKK, Ku Klux Klan.

kl., kiloliter; kiloliters.

Kla·gen·furt (klä'gən-foort'), *n.* a city in southwestern Austria: pop., 63,000.

Klam·ath (klam'əth), *n.* a river in southern Oregon and northern California, flowing into the Pacific: length, 275 mi.

Klamath Falls, a city in southwestern Oregon: pop., 17,000.

Klan (klan), *n.* 1. the Ku Klux Klan. 2. any of its chapters.

Klans·man (klanz'mən), *n.* [*pl.* KLANSMEN (-mən)], a member of the Ku Klux Klan.

Klau·sen·burg (klou'zən-boorkh'), *n.* Cluj, a city in Transylvania: the German name.

klea·gle (klē'g'l), *n.* [? *klan* + *eagle*], an official in the Ku Klux Klan.

Klé·ber, Jean Bap·tiste (zhän' bà'tēst' klā'bâr'), 1753–1800; French general.

Klebs-Löff·ler bacillus (klebz'lef'lẽr), [after Edwin *Klebs* (1834–1913) & Friedrich *Löffler* (1853–1915), G. bacteriologists who identified it], the bacillus that causes diphtheria.

Klee, Paul (klā), 1879–1940; Swiss abstract painter.

kleig light (klēg), a klieg light.

klepht (kleft), *n.* [Mod. Gr. *klephtēs*, robber; Gr. *kleptēs*, thief], 1. a member of the Greek patriot bands who held out in the mountains after the Turkish conquest of Greece. 2. a brigand.

klep·to·ma·ni·a (klep'tə-mā'ni-ə), *n.* [Mod. L. < Gr. *kleptēs*, thief; + *mania*], an abnormal, persistent impulse or tendency to steal.

klep·to·ma·ni·ac (klep'tə-mā'ni-ak'), *n.* a person who has kleptomania.

klieg light (klēg), [after the brothers A. and J. *Kliegl*, the inventors], a very bright, hot arc light used to light motion-picture sets: also spelled **kleig.**

Kline test (klīn), [after Benjamin S. *Kline*, Am. pathologist by whom it was developed], a modified form of the Kahn test for the diagnosis of syphilis.

Kling·sor (kliŋ'zôr, kliŋ'zōr), *n.* [G.], in Wagner's *Parsifal*, a magician who is the main enemy of the Knights of the Holy Grail.

klip·spring·er (klip'spriŋ'ẽr), *n.* [*pl.* KLIPSPRINGERS (-ẽrz), KLIPSPRINGER; see PLURAL, II, D, 1], [S. Afr. D.; *klip*, a rock, cliff + *springer*, springer], a small, agile mountain antelope of southern and eastern Africa, somewhat like the chamois.

Klon·dike (klon'dīk), *n.* 1. a region in northwestern Canada, in the Yukon Territory, celebrated for its gold fields. 2. a river in this region, flowing west to the Yukon River.

‡**kloof** (klōōf), *n.* [D. < *klooven*, to cleave; akin to Eng. *cleave*], in South Africa, a deep, narrow valley; gorge.

Klop·stock, Frie·drich Gott·lieb (frē'driH gôt'lēp klôp'shtôk), 1724–1803; German poet.

klys·tron (klis'tron, klī'strən), *n.* [Gr. *klys-* (as in *clyster*); + *electron*], an electron tube, used in television, etc., for converting a stream of electrons into ultra high-frequency waves which it transmits as a pencil-like radio beam.

km., 1. kilometer; kilometers. 2. kingdom.

kn., 1. krona; kronor. 2. krone; kronen; kroner.

knack (nak), *n.* [ME. *knak*, sharp blow; prob. echoic in origin], 1. *a)* a trick; device. *b)* a clever expedient or way of doing something. 2. ability to do something easily; particular skill: dexterity. 3. [Rare], a knick-knack; trinket; trifle. —***SYN.*** see **talent.**

knack·er (nak'ẽr), *n.* [Early Mod. Eng., harness maker; ? < *knack* in the sense "knack maker" (cf. *knack*, 1 *a* or 3)], 1. in England, a person who buys and slaughters worn-out horses and sells their flesh as dog's meat, etc. 2. a person who buys and wrecks old houses, etc. and sells their materials.

knag·gy (nag'i), *adj.* [< ME. *knag*, a knot; prob. < ON. (cf. LG. *knagge*); + *-y*], knotty; rough.

knap (nap), *v.t. & v.i.* [KNAPPED (napt), KNAPPING], [MScot.; of direct echoic origin or < MLG. or MD. *knappen*, of echoic origin], [Dial.], 1. to knock, rap, or snap. 2. to break or shape (stones or flints) by a quick, hard blow. 3. to bite sharply; snap; nibble. *n.* [Dial.], a sudden blow or stroke; rap.

knap (nap), *n.* [ME.; AS. *cnæp*, *cnæpp*, top, knob, button], [Chiefly Dial.], the top of a hill; summit.

knap·sack (nap'sak'), *n.* [D. *knapzak* < *knappen*, to snap, eat + *zak*, a sack], a leather or canvas bag or case for carrying equipment or supplies on the back: used by soldiers, hikers, etc.

knap·weed (nap'wēd'), *n.* [earlier *knopweed;* see KNOP & WEED], a weed of the composite family, with knob-like heads of light-purple flowers.

knar (när), *n.* [ME. *knarre;* prob. < MLG. or MD. (cf. LG. *knarre*, D. *knar*, a stump, knob, knot)], a knot in wood; especially, a bark-covered protuberance on a tree trunk or root.

knarred (närd), *adj.* full of knars.

knave (nāv), *n.* [ME. *knaue;* AS. *cnafa*, boy, male child (cf. sense 3); akin to G. *knabe;* IE. base **gnebh-*, **gnobh-*, a stick, peg, piece of wood (cf. G. dial. *knabe* in this sense); for sense development cf. LAD], 1. [Archaic], *a)* a serving boy or male servant; hence, *b)* a man of humble birth or status. 2. a dishonest, deceitful person; tricky rascal; rogue. 3. in *card games*, a playing card with a page's picture on it; jack.

knav·er·y (nāv'ẽr-i), *n* [*pl.* KNAVERIES (-iz)], 1. behavior or act characteristic of a knave; rascality; dishonesty. 2. [Obs.], roguishness; mischievous quality.

knav·ish (nāv'ish), *adj.* like or characteristic of a knave; especially, dishonest; tricky.

knead (nēd), *v.t.* [ME. *kneden;* AS. *cnedan;* akin to G. *kneten;* IE. base **gnet-*, to press together, etc.], 1. to mix and work into a plastic mass by folding over, pressing, and squeezing, usually with the hands: said of dough, clay, etc. 2. to press, rub, or squeeze with the hands; massage. 3. to make by kneading.

knee (nē), *n.* [ME. *kne*, etc.; AS. *cneow;* akin to G. *knie;* IE. base **ĝeneu-*, seen also in Sans. *jánu*, Gr. *gōnu*, L. *genu*, a knee], 1. *a)* the joint between the thigh and the lower part of the human leg. *b)* the front part of the leg about this joint. 2. a joint regarded as corresponding or similar to the human knee, as in the hind limb of a vertebrate, in the forelimb of a hoofed, four-footed animal (*carpal joint*), or the tarsal joint of a bird. 3. anything resembling or suggesting a knee, especially a bent knee, as a bent piece of wood used as a brace. 4. the part of a stocking, trouser leg, etc. covering the knee. *v.t.* [KNEED (nēd), KNEEING], 1. to hit or touch with the knee. 2. in *carpentry*, to fasten with a knee or knees (sense 3). **bring to one's knees,** to force to submit or give in.

knee action, a type of suspension for the front wheels of an automobile, that permits their independent vertical movement.
knee breeches, breeches reaching to the knees or just below them.
knee·cap (nē′kap′), ***n.*** 1. the patella, a movable bone at the front of the human knee; kneepan. 2. a protective covering or padding for the knee.
knee-deep (nē′dēp′), ***adj.*** 1. sunk to the knees: as, they stood *knee-deep* in water. 2. so deep as to reach to the knees, as water.
knee-high (nē′hī′), ***adj.*** so high or tall as to reach to the knees.
knee·hole (nē′hōl′), ***n.*** a space for the knees in a desk, etc.
kneel (nēl), ***v.i.*** [KNELT (nelt) or KNEELED (nēld), KNEELING], [ME. *knelen*, etc.; AS. *cneowlian* < *cneow;* see KNEE], to bend or rest on one's knee or knees.
knee·pad (nē′pad′), ***n.*** a protective pad worn around the knee, as by basketball players.
knee·pan (nē′pan′), ***n.*** the kneecap; patella.
knee·piece (nē′pēs′), ***n.*** a piece of armor to protect the knee: see **armor,** illus.
knee-sprung (nē′spruŋ′), ***adj.*** having the knees bent forward as a result of a shortening of the flexor tendons: said of a horse.
knell (nel), ***v.i.*** [ME. *knyllen* & (with echoic vowel change) *knellen;* AS. *cnyllan;* akin to MHG. *(er)knellen;* prob. echoic], 1. to ring in a slow, solemn way; toll. 2. to sound ominously or mournfully. ***v.t.*** 1. to call or announce by or as by a knell. 2. [Obs.], to ring or toll (a bell). ***n.*** 1. the sound of a bell, especially of a bell rung slowly, as at a funeral. 2. an omen of death, extinction, failure, etc. 3. a mournful sound.
knelt (nelt), alternative past tense and past participle of **kneel.**
Knes·set (knes′et), ***n.*** [Heb.], the unicameral legislature of (modern) Israel.
knew (nōō, nū), past tense of **know.**
Knick·er·bock·er (nik′ẽr-bok′ẽr), ***n.*** [< Diedrich *Knickerbocker*, fictitious D. author of Washington Irving's *History of New York* (1809)], 1. a descendant of the early Dutch settlers of New York; hence, 2. any New Yorker. 3. [k-], *pl.* short, loose trousers gathered in at or just below the knees; knickers, as those worn by Dutch settlers of New York.
knick·ers (nik′ẽrz), ***n.pl.*** 1. knickerbockers. 2. a bloomerlike undergarment worn by women or girls.
knick·knack (nik′nak′), ***n.*** [redupl. of *knack*], a small ornamental article or contrivance; gimcrack; trinket: also spelled **nicknack.**
knife (nīf), ***n.*** [*pl.* KNIVES (nīvz)], [ME. *knif, kniue;* AS. *cnif;* akin to G. *kneif*, MD. *cnijf*, etc. (Gmc. word borrowed, with intrusive vowel, in Fr. *canif*); IE. **gn-eibh* (as also in Lith. *gnaibis*, a pinching) < base **gen-*, to press together, pinch, etc.], 1. a cutting instrument with one or more sharp-edged blades, often pointed, set in a handle. 2. a cutting blade, as in a machine. ***v.t.*** [KNIFED (nīft), KNIFING], 1. to cut or stab with a knife. 2. [Colloq.], to use underhand methods in order to hurt, defeat, or betray.
under the knife, [Colloq.], undergoing surgery.
knife-edge (nīf′ej′), ***n.*** 1. the edge of a knife. 2. any very sharp edge. 3. a metal wedge whose fine edge serves as the fulcrum for a scale beam, pendulum, etc.
knife switch, an electrical switch in which the hinged, knifelike contact blade is pressed down between the contact clips.
knight (nīt), ***n.*** [ME. *kniht;* AS. *cniht, cneoht*, boy, retainer; akin to G. *knecht*, lad, servant; IE. base **gnegh-* < **gen-* as in *knife;* for sense cf. KNAVE, LAD], 1. in the Middle Ages, *a)* a military servant of the king or other feudal superior; tenant holding land on condition that he serve his superior as a mounted man-at-arms. *b)* later, a man, usually one of high birth, who after serving as page and squire was formally raised to honorable military rank by the king or other qualified lord and pledged to chivalrous conduct. 2. in Great Britain, a man who for some achievement or service to his country is given honorary nonhereditary rank next below a baronet, entitling him to use *Sir* before his given name. 3. an ancient Roman, Athenian, etc. whose status is regarded as equivalent to that of a knight. 4. a member of any order or society that officially calls its members *knights.* 5. [Poetic], *a)* a lady's devoted champion or attendant. *b)* a devoted follower of some cause, person, etc. 6. in *chess*, a piece shaped like a horse's head: in a single move it is advanced one square, whether occupied or unoccupied, in any vertical or horizontal direction, and then one square diagonally, coming to rest on a different color from that on which it started. Abbreviated **K., k., Kt** (no period). ***v.t.*** to make (a man) a knight.
knight bachelor, [*pl.* KNIGHTS BACHELORS], a member of the oldest and lowest class of British knights: abbreviated **K.B., Kt. Bach.**
knight-er·rant (nīt′er′ənt), ***n.*** [*pl.* KNIGHTS-ERRANT], 1. a medieval knight wandering in search of adventures, especially those in which to redress wrongs or show his prowess. 2. a chivalrous or quixotic person.
knight-er·rant·ry (nīt′er′ən-tri), ***n.*** [*pl.* KNIGHT-ERRANTRIES (-triz)], the behavior, character, or action of a knight-errant; quixotic behavior or act.
knight·hood (nīt′hood), ***n.*** [see -HOOD], 1. the rank or status of a knight. 2. the profession or vocation of a knight. 3. knightliness. 4. knights collectively.
knight·li·ness (nīt′li-nis), ***n.*** the quality of being like a knight; chivalry.
knight·ly (nīt′li), ***adj.*** 1. of, characteristic of, like, or befitting a knight; chivalrous, brave, etc. 2. consisting of knights. ***adv.*** [Archaic], in a knightly manner.
Knights of Columbus, an international fraternal and benevolent society of Roman Catholic men, founded in 1882: abbreviated **K. of C., K.C.** (*sing. & pl.*).
Knights of Pythias, a secret fraternal society, founded in 1864: abbreviated **K. of P., K.P.** (*sing. & pl.*).
Knight Templar, [*pl.* KNIGHTS TEMPLARS for 1, KNIGHTS TEMPLAR for 2], 1. a member of a military and religious order established among the Crusaders early in the 12th century to protect pilgrims to the Holy Land: it was suppressed in 1312. 2. a member of a certain order of Masons. Abbreviated **K.T.**
knit (nit), ***v.t.*** [KNITTED (-id) or KNIT, KNITTING], [ME. *knitten;* AS. *cnyttan* (Gmc. **knuttjan*) < base of *cnotta* (see KNOT); akin to G. *knütten*], 1. to make (cloth or a piece of clothing) by looping together yarn or thread by means of special needles: abbreviated K (no period). 2. to form into cloth in this way instead of by weaving. 3. to fasten together closely and firmly; unite. 4. to draw (the brows) together; contract in wrinkles. 5. [Archaic & Dial.], to tie or fasten in or with a knot. ***v.i.*** 1. to make cloth or a piece of clothing by looping together yarn or thread. 2. to be fastened together closely and firmly; grow together, as a broken bone. 3. to become drawn together in wrinkles: as, his brows *knit* in thought.
knit·ting (nit′iŋ), ***n.*** 1. the action of a person or thing that knits. 2. knitted work.
knitting needle, an eyeless, usually long, needle of metal, bone, etc., with a blunt point at one or both ends, used in pairs, etc. in knitting by hand.
knives (nīvz), ***n.*** plural of **knife.**
knob (nob), ***n.*** [ME. *knobbe;* prob. < MLG. *knobbe*, a knot, knob, bud, etc.; IE. **gn-eu-bh* < base **gen-*, to press together; cf. KNEAD], 1. a rounded lump or protuberance. 2. a handle, usually round, of a door, drawer, etc. 3. a rounded hill or mountain; knoll.
knobbed (nobd), ***adj.*** having a knob or knobs.
knob·by (nob′i), ***adj.*** [KNOBBIER (-i-ẽr), KNOBBIEST (-i-ist)], 1. covered with knobs. 2. like a knob.
knob·ker·rie (nob′ker′i), ***n.*** [S. Afr. D. *knopkerie, knopkirie* < D. *knobbe*, knob + Hottentot *kirri, kerri*, a club, stick], a short club with a knobbed end, used by some South African tribes as a throwing and striking weapon.
knob·stick (nob′stik′), ***n.*** a knobkerrie.
knock (nok), ***v.i.*** [ME. *knokken;* AS. *cnocian, cnucian;* akin to ON. *knoka*, AS. *cnycled*, bent, crooked; IE. **gn-eu-ĝ* (as also in *knuckle*) < base **gen-*, to press together; basic sense "to hit with the knuckles of the clenched fist"], 1. to strike a blow or blows with the fist or some hard object; especially, to rap on a door. 2. to bump; collide; clash. 3. to make a thumping, pounding, or rattling noise: said of an engine, etc. 4. [Colloq.], to find fault; criticize adversely. 5. in *gin rummy*, to end a deal by exposing one's hand and showing a surplus of not more than ten points in unmatched cards. ***v.t.*** 1. to hit; strike. 2. to hit so as to cause to fall (with *down* or *off*). 3. to make by hitting or striking: as, he *knocked* a hole in the screen. 4. [Colloq.], to find fault with; criticize adversely. ***n.*** 1. a knocking. 2. a hit; sharp or resounding blow; rap, as on a door. 3. a thumping or rattling noise in an engine, etc., as because of faulty combustion. 4. [Colloq.], an adverse criticism. —***SYN.*** see **strike.**
knock about (or **around**), [Colloq.], 1. to wander about; roam. 2. to treat roughly.
knock down, 1. to take apart for convenience in shipping. 2. to indicate the sale of (an article) at an auction, as by a blow of the auctioneer's hammer.
knock off, 1. [Colloq.], *a)* to stop working. *b)* to leave off (work). 2. [Colloq.], to deduct. 3. [Colloq.], to do; accomplish. 4. [Slang], to kill, overcome, etc.
knock out, 1. in *boxing*, to defeat (an opponent) by knocking him to the ground so that he cannot rise within a specified time. 2. to make unconscious or exhausted. 3. to defeat. 4. [Colloq.], to do; make.
knock out of the box, in *baseball*, to make so many hits against (an opposing pitcher) as to cause his removal.
knock together, to make or compose hastily or crudely.
knock up, 1. [British Colloq.], to tire out; exhaust. 2. [Slang], to make pregnant.
knock·a·bout (nok′ə-bout′), ***n.*** a small, one-masted yacht with a mainsail, a jib, and a centerboard or keel, but no bowsprit. ***adj.*** 1. rough; noisy; boisterous. 2. made or suitable for knocking about or rough use.
knock·down (nok′doun′), ***adj.*** 1. so severe as to knock down; overwhelming. 2. made so as to be easily taken

apart: as, a *knockdown* table. *n.* 1. a knocking down; felling. 2. a blow, stroke, etc. that knocks one down. 3. [Slang], an introduction (to a person).

knocked down, in *commerce,* not assembled: said of furniture, etc.: abbreviated **K.D.**

knock·er (nok'ẽr), *n.* a person or thing that knocks; specifically, *a)* a small metal ring, hammer, etc. attached by a hinge to a door, for use in knocking for admittance. *b)* [Colloq.], a faultfinder.

knock-knee (nok'nē'), *n.* 1. a condition in which the legs bend inward so that the knees knock together or touch each other in walking. 2. *pl.* such knees.

knock-kneed (nok'nēd'), *adj.* having knock-knee.

knock·out (nok'out'), *adj.* that knocks out: said of a blow, etc. *n.* 1. a knocking out or being knocked out. 2. a blow that knocks out; blow that causes a boxer to fall and fail to resume the fight before the referee has counted ten: cf. **technical knockout.** 3. [Slang], a person or thing that is very attractive or striking. Abbreviated (in *boxing*) **K.O., KO, k.o.**

knockout drops, [Slang], a drug put into a drink to cause the drinker to become stupefied or unconscious.

knoll (nōl), *n.* [ME.; AS. *cnoll;* akin to G. *knollen,* lump, clod; IE. base as in *knot*], a hillock; mound.

knop (nop), *n.* [ME. *knoppe, knappe;* prob. < ON. *knappr* or MD. *cnoppe;* akin to *knob*], a knob; especially, a knoblike architectural ornament.

Knos·sos (nos'əs), *n.* the chief city of ancient Crete: also **Cnossus, Gnossus.**

knot (not), *n.* [ME. *knotte;* AS. *cnotta* (cf. KNIT); akin to D. *knot,* G. *knoten,* etc.; IE. **gn-eu-t* < base **gen-,* to press together; cf. KNOB, KNEAD], 1. a lump or knob in a thread, cord, etc., formed by passing one free end through a loop and drawing it tight, or by a tangle drawn tight. 2. a fastening made by intertwining or tying together pieces of string, cord, rope, etc. 3. an ornamental bow of ribbon or twist of braid; cockade; epaulet. 4. a small group or cluster. 5. something that ties or fastens closely or intricately; bond of union; especially, the bond of marriage. 6. a problem; difficulty; entanglement. 7. a knotlike part; node or lump: as, a *knot* sometimes forms in a tense muscle; specifically, *a)* a hard lump on a tree where a branch grows out. *b)* a cross section of such a lump, appearing as cross-grained in a board or log. *c)* a joint on a plant stem where leaves grow out. *d)* a fungous disease of trees, in which abnormal protuberances appear. 8. in *nautical usage, a)* a division of the log line, by which a ship's rate of speed is measured; hence, *b)* a unit of speed of one nautical mile (6,076.10 feet) an hour: as, the ship can easily make a speed of 10 *knots:* abbreviated **K., k.** *c)* loosely, a nautical mile. *v.t.* [KNOTTED (-id), KNOTTING], 1. to tie, fasten, or intertwine in or with a knot or knots; make a knot or knots in. 2. to tie or unite closely or intricately; entangle. 3. to make (fringe) by tying knots. *v.i.* 1. to form a knot or knots; become entangled. 2. to make knots for fringe.

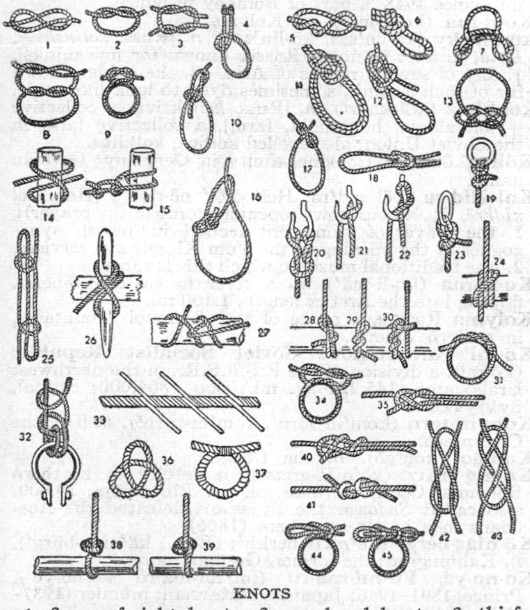

KNOTS

1. figure-of-eight knot; 2. overhand knot; 3. thief knot; 4. half hitch; 5. stevedore's knot; 6. loop knot; 7. harness hitch; 8. reef knot; 9. granny knot; 10. bowline knot; 11. bowline on a bight; 12. bowline with a bight; 13. prolonge knot; 14. clove hitch; 15. round turn and two half hitches; 16. running bowline; 17. slide knot; 18. slipknot; 19. fisherman's bend; 20. cat's-paw; 21. single Blackwall hitch; 22. double Blackwall hitch; 23. studding-sail tack bend; 24. magnus hitch; 25. sheepshank; 26. half hitch over pin; 27. rolling hitch; 28. studding-sail halyard bend; 29. timber hitch; 30. timber hitch and a half hitch; 31. surgeon's knot; 32. anchor knot; 33. long splice; 34. surgeon's knot; 35. sheet bend; 36. trefoil knot; 37. throat seizing; 38. outside clinch; 39. inside clinch; 40. double sheet bend; 41. Englishman's tie; 42. single carrick bend; 43. double carrick bend; 44. single bowknot; 45. double bowknot.

knot (not), *n.* [rare ME. *knotte;* also (17th c.) *gnat;* ? analogical sp., after prec. *knot,* for partly assimilated *gn-*], a small, red-breasted sandpiper that breeds in arctic regions and then migrates.

knot·grass (not'gras', not'gräs'), *n.* 1. a common weed with jointed or knotty stems. 2. oat grass or any of various similar grasses with bent stems.

knot·hole (not'hōl'), *n.* a hole in a board, etc. where a knot has fallen out.

knot·ted (not'id), *adj.* 1. tied or fastened in or with a knot or knots. 2. having or full of knots. 3. tangled; intricate. 4. puzzling; knotty.

knot·ter (not'ẽr), *n.* 1. a person or thing that ties knots. 2. a remover of knots.

knot·ti·ness (not'i-nis), *n.* the quality of being knotty.

knot·ting (not'iŋ), *n.* fringe made of knotted threads.

knot·ty (not'i), *adj.* [KNOTTIER (-i-ẽr), KNOTTIEST (-i-ist)], [ME.], 1. having or full of knots; knotted: as, a *knotty* board. 2. hard to solve or explain; puzzling: as, a *knotty* problem.

knot·weed (not'wēd'), *n.* 1. knapweed. 2. knotgrass.

knout (nout), *n.* [Russ. *knut;* prob. < Sw. *knut,* a knot], a leather whip formerly used in Russia to flog criminals. *v.t.* to flog with a knout.

know (nō), *v.t.* [KNEW (nōō, nū), KNOWN (nōn), KNOWING], [ME. *knowen;* AS. *cnawan;* akin to OHG. *-cnāhan;* IE. base **ĝenē-,* **ĝenō-,* to know, apprehend, seen also in L. *gno-scere,* to know, Gr. *(gi)gnō-skein,* etc.; cf. CAN, KEN, GNOMON, GNOSTIC, etc.], 1. to have a clear perception or understanding of; be sure of or well informed about: as, we *know* the facts. 2. to be aware or cognizant of; have perceived or learned: as, he *knew* that we were home. 3. to have a firm mental grasp of; have securely in the memory: as, the actor *knows* his lines. 4. to be acquainted or familiar with. 5. to have understanding of or skill in as a result of study or experience: as, she *knows* music. 6. to recognize: as, I'd *know* that face anywhere. 7. to recognize as distinct; distinguish: as, it's not always easy to *know* right from wrong. 8. in *Biblical & legal usage,* to have sexual intercourse with. *v.i.* 1. to have knowledge. 2. to be sure, informed, or aware.

in the know, [Colloq.], having confidential information.

know·a·ble (nō'ə-b'l), *adj.* that can be known.

know-all (nō'ôl'), *n.* [Colloq.], a know-it-all.

know-how (nō'hou'), *n.* [Colloq.], knowledge of how to do something; technical skill.

know·ing (nō'iŋ), *adj.* [ppr. of *know*], 1. having knowledge or information. 2. shrewd; clever; worldly-wise. 3. implying shrewd understanding or possession of secret or inside information: as, a *knowing* look. 4. deliberate; intentional.

know·ing·ly (nō'iŋ-li), *adv.* 1. in a knowing manner. 2. with knowledge of what one is doing; on purpose.

know-it-all (nō'it-ôl'), *adj.* [Colloq.], pretending or claiming to know much about almost everything. *n.* [Colloq.], a know-it-all person.

knowl·edge (nol'ij), *n.* [ME. *knoweleche, knowlege,* acknowledgment, confession; Late AS. *cnawlæc* < *cnawan* (see KNOW), prob. via **cnawleccian,* to acknowledge, seen in Early ME. *cnawlechien*], 1. the act, fact, or state of knowing; specifically, *a)* acquaintance or familiarity (with a fact, place, etc.). *b)* awareness. *c)* understanding. 2. acquaintance with facts; range of information, awareness, or understanding. 3. all that has been perceived or grasped by the mind; learning; enlightenment. 4. the body of facts accumulated by mankind. 5. [Archaic], sexual intercourse: generally preceded by *carnal.* —*SYN.* see **information.**

to (the best of) one's knowledge, as far as one knows; within the range of one's information.

knowl·edge·a·ble (nol'ij-ə-b'l), *adj.* [Colloq.], having or showing knowledge or intelligence.

known (nōn), past participle of **know.**

know-noth·ing (nō'nuth'iŋ), *n.* 1. an ignorant person; ignoramus. 2. an agnostic. 3. [K- N-], a member of a secret political party that flourished in the United States from 1853 to 1856, with a program of keeping out of governmental office anyone not a native-born American: so called because members professed ignorance of the party's activities.

known quantity, an algebraic quantity whose value is given: usually represented by *a*, *b*, etc.

Knox, John (noks), 1505–1572; Scottish Protestant preacher and religious reformer.

Knox·ville (noks′vil), ***n.*** a city in eastern Tennessee, on the Tennessee River: pop., 112,000.

knt., knight.

knuck·le (nuk′'l), ***n.*** [ME. *knokyl;* prob. < LG.; cf. MLG. *knokel*, dim. of *knoke*, bone; AS., however, has the cognate *cnycled*, bent (see KNOCK); basic sense "bent, clenched"; IE. **gn-eu-ĝ* < base **gen-*, to press together; cf. KNOB, KNOT, etc.], 1. *a)* a joint of the finger; especially, any of the joints connecting the fingers to the rest of the hand. *b)* the rounded knob formed by the bones at such a joint. 2. the knee or hock joint and near-by parts of a pig or other animal, used as food. 3. something resembling a knuckle, as the joint of a hinge. 4. *pl.* a knuckle-duster. 5. in *shipbuilding*, an angular fitting of timbers rather than a continuously curved one. ***v.i.*** [KNUCKLED (-'ld), KNUCKLING], to rest the knuckles on the ground in shooting a marble (often with *down*). ***v.t.*** to strike, press, or touch with the knuckles.

knuckle down, 1. to work energetically; apply oneself seriously. 2. to yield; give in: also **knuckle under.**

knuckle ball, in *baseball*, a slow ball pitched with the two middle fingers tucked under and pressing against the top of the ball.

knuck·le·bone (nuk′'l-bōn′), ***n.*** 1. any bone of a human knuckle. 2. *a)* an animal's limb bone with a rounded knob at the joint end. *b)* the knob. 3. *pl.* an old game played with the knucklebones of sheep.

knuck·le-dust·er (nuk′'l-dus′tẽr), ***n.*** linked metal rings or a metal bar with holes for the fingers, worn for rough fighting: now usually **brass knuckles.**

knuckle joint, 1. any articulation, or point of movement, between two bones forming a knuckle. 2. a hinged joint formed by a projection between two others.

knur (nũr), ***n.*** [ME. *knorre, knurre;* prob. < MD. or MLG.], a knot, as on the trunk or branch of a tree.

knurl (nũrl), ***n.*** [as if dim. of *knur;* prob. phonetic var. of *gnarl* suggested by the parallel assimilations of *gn-*, *kn-*], 1. a knot, knob, nodule, etc. 2. a ridge or any of a series of small beads or ridges on a metal surface, as on the edge of a coin or nut. 3. [Scot.], a short, thickset person. ***v.t.*** to make knurls on the edge of; mill.

knurl·y (nũr′li), ***adj.*** [KNURLIER (-li-ẽr), KNURLIEST (-li-ist)], full of knurls, as wood; gnarled.

Knut II (k'nōōt), see **Canute II.**

KO (kā′ō′), ***v.t.*** [KO'D (-ōd′), KO'ING], [Slang], in *boxing*, to knock out. ***n.*** [*pl.* KO's (-ōz′)], [Slang], in *boxing*, a knockout. Also **kayo, K.O., k.o.**

ko·a (kō′ə), ***n.*** [Haw.], a Hawaiian acacia tree valued for its wood, used in building and cabinetmaking, and its bark, used in tanning.

ko·a·la (kō-ä′lə), ***n.*** [< the native name in Australia], an Australian tree-dwelling animal with thick, gray fur and large, tufted ears, which carries its young in a pouch: it is about two feet long and looks somewhat like a small bear.

KOALA (24 in. long)

Ko·be (kô′be′; Eng. kō′bi), ***n.*** a city on the southern coast of Honshu, Japan: pop., 979,000.

Kö·ben·havn (kö′p'n-houn′), ***n.*** Copenhagen: the Danish name.

Ko·blenz (kō′blents), ***n.*** Coblenz, a city in Germany: the German spelling.

ko·bold (kō′bold, kō′bōld), ***n.*** [G.], in *German folklore*, 1. a helpful or mischievous sprite in households; brownie. 2. a gnome in mines and other underground places.

Koch, Robert (kōk; G. kôkh), 1843–1910; German bacteriologist and physician; received Nobel prize in physiology, 1905.

Ko·dak (kō′dak), ***n.*** [arbitrary formation], a small, portable camera for taking photographs on a roll of film: a trade-mark.

ko·di·ak bear (kō′di-ak′), a large, brown bear found on Kodiak Island: it can attain a weight of 1,500 pounds.

Ko·di·ak Island (kō′di-ak′), an island off the southwestern coast of Alaska, considered part of Alaska: pop., 7,200.

Ko·dok (kō′dok), ***n.*** a town in the Sudan, on the White Nile: formerly called *Fashoda.*

ko·el (kō′əl), ***n.*** [Hind. < Sans. *kokila;* origin echoic], any of various cuckoos found in India, the East Indies, and Australia.

K. of C., Knight (or Knights) of Columbus.

Koff·ka, Kurt (koort kôf′kä), 1886–1941; German psychologist in America.

K. of P., Knight (or Knights) of Pythias.

Ko·hel·eth (kō-hel′ith), ***n.*** [Heb. *qōheleth;* see ECCLESIASTES], in the *Bible*, 1. the book of Ecclesiastes. 2. Solomon: so called in this book.

Koh-i-noor, Koh-i-nur, Koh·i·noor (kō′i-noor′, kō′i-noor′), ***n.*** [Per. *kōh-i-nūr*, lit., mountain of light], a famous large Indian diamond, now one of the British crown jewels.

kohl (kōl), ***n.*** [Ar. *kuḥl;* cf. ALCOHOL], a cosmetic preparation, usually powdered antimony sulfide, used in certain Eastern countries to darken the eyelids.

kohl·ra·bi (kōl′rä′bi, kōl′rä′bi), ***n.*** [*pl.* KOHLRABIES (-biz)], [G. < It. *cavoli rape*, pl. of *cavolo rapa*, cole rape; cf. COLE (kale) & RAPE (herb)], a kind of cabbage with an edible, bulbous stem that looks somewhat like a turnip.

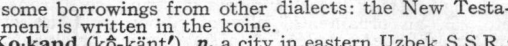

KOHLRABI

koi·ne, Koi·ne (koi-nā′, koi′ni), ***n.*** [Gr. (*hē*) *koinē* (*dialektos*), (the) common (dialect)], the language used throughout the Greek world, from Syria to Gaul, during the Hellenistic and Roman periods: its spoken form consisted of colloquial Attic, supplemented by numerous Ionic words and some borrowings from other dialects: the New Testament is written in the koine.

Ko·kand (kô-känt′), ***n.*** a city in eastern Uzbek S.S.R.: pop., 105,000.

Ko·ko·mo (kō′kə-mō′), ***n.*** a city in central Indiana: pop., 47,000.

Ko·ko Nor (kō′kō′nôr′), 1. a lake in northeastern Chinghai province, China: area, 2,200 sq. mi. 2. Chinghai, a province of China.

kok-sa·gyz (kōk′sa-gēz′), ***n.*** [Russ. < Turk. *kök*, a root + East Turk. *sagiz*, rubber, gum], a dandelion grown in parts of the Soviet Union for the rubber obtained from its roots.

ko·la (kō′lə), ***n.*** [see COLA], 1. the kola nut. 2. the tree that it grows on. 3. an extract or stimulant made from kola nuts. Also spelled **cola.**

kola nut, the brown, bitter nut of either of two tropical trees: it contains some caffeine and theobromine and is used in making certain soft drinks.

Ko·la Peninsula (kô′lȧ), a peninsula in northwestern U.S.S.R., between the White and Barents Seas.

Kol·ha·pur and Deccan States (kōl′hä-poor′), formerly, a group of individual Indian states: area, 10,870 sq. mi.: since 1948, a part of Bombay province.

Ko·li·ma (ko-li-mä′), ***n.*** Kolyma.

ko·lin·sky (kə-lin′ski, kō-lin′ski), ***n.*** [Russ. *kolinski* < *Kola*, district in north Russia known for fine minks], 1. any of several minks of Asia. 2. the golden-brown fur of such a mink, sometimes dyed to look like sable.

kol·khoz (kôl-khôz′), ***n.*** [Russ. *kol*lektivnoe, collective + *khoz*aĭstvo, household, farm], a collective farm in the Soviet Union: also spelled **kolhoz, kolkhos.**

Köln (köln), ***n.*** Cologne, a city in Germany: German name.

Kol Nid·re (kōl nid′rə; Heb. kôl′ nē-drā′), [Heb. *kōl nidhrē*, lit., all our vows (opening words of the prayer)], 1. the prayer of atonement recited in Jewish synagogues at the opening of the Yom Kippur eve services. 2. the traditional music to which this is sung.

Ko·ly·ma (ko-li-mä′), ***n.*** a river in eastern Siberia, flowing into the Arctic: length, 1,100 mi.

Kolyma Range, a range of the Stanovoi Mountains, in eastern Siberia.

Ko·mi Autonomous Soviet Socialist Republic (kō′mi), a division of the R.S.F.S.R., in the northwest Urals: area, 145,221 sq. mi.; pop., 804,000; capital, Syktyvkar.

Kom·in·tern (kom′in-tũrn′, kom′in-tũrn′), ***n.*** [G.], the Comintern.

Kon·go (koŋ′gō), ***n.*** the Congo.

Kö·nig·grätz (kö′niH-grets′), ***n.*** a city in northern Bohemia, Czechoslovakia, on the Elbe: pop., 19,000: also called *Sadowa:* the Prussians defeated the Austrians in a battle near here (1866).

Kö·nigs·berg (kö′niHs-berkh′; Eng. kā′nigz-bũrg′), ***n.*** Kaliningrad: the former, German name.

Ko·no·ye, Fu·mi·ma·ro (foo′mi-mä′rô kô′nô-ye′), Prince, 1891–1946; Japanese statesman; premier (1937–1939; 1940–1941).

Ko·ny·a (kôn′yä), ***n.*** a city in southern Turkey: pop., 93,000: also spelled **Konia.**

Koo, Wel·ling·ton (wel′iŋ-tən kōō; Chin. gōō), (*Ku Wei-chün*), 1887– ; Chinese statesman and diplomat.

koo·doo (kōō′dōō), ***n.*** a kudu.

kook·a·bur·ra (kook′ə-bur′ə, kook′ə-bur′ə), *n.* [< native name in Australia], a large kingfisher of Australia and New Guinea: also called *laughing jackass.*
koo·ra·jong (ko͞o′rə-joŋ′), *n.* a kurrajong.
Koord (kürd, ko͝ord), *n.* a Kurd.
Koo·te·nay, Koo·te·nai (ko͞o′t'n-ā′), *n.* 1. a lake in British Columbia, Canada: area, 221 sq. mi. 2. a river flowing through Montana, Idaho, and British Columbia, into this lake: length, 400 mi. 3. [*pl.* KOOTENAY, KOOTENAI], a small group of Indian tribes living in Montana, Idaho, and British Columbia. 4. their language. Also spelled **Kutenai, Kutenay.**
‡kop (kop), *n.* [S. Afr. D. < D. *kop*, a head], in South Africa, a hill or mountain.
ko·peck, ko·pek (kō′pek), *n.* [Russ. *kopeika* < *kopye*, a lance], a small Russian coin of bronze or copper (originally silver), equal to 1/100 ruble: abbreviated **k., kop.**; also spelled **copeck.**
koph (kôf), *n.* [Heb. *qoph*], the nineteenth letter of the Hebrew alphabet (ק), corresponding to English *K, k:* also spelled **qoph**: see **alphabet**, table.
‡kop·je (kop′i), *n.* [S. Afr. D., dim. of *kop;* see KOP], in South Africa, a small hill; hillock.
kor (kôr, kōr), *n.* [Heb. *kōr*, lit., round vessel], an old Hebrew measure of capacity; homer.
Ko·ran (kō-rän′, kō′ran), *n.* [Ar. *qur'ān*, lit., book, reading, recitation < *qara'a*, to read], the sacred book of the Moslems, written in Arabic: its contents are reported revelations made to Mohammed by Allah.
Kor·do·fan (kôr′dō-fän′), *n.* a province of central Sudan: formerly a country: area, 147,100 sq. mi.; pop., 2,052,000; capital, El Obeid.
Ko·re·a (kō-rē′ə, kô-rē′ə), *n.* a country on a peninsula in eastern Asia, west of Japan: area, 85,228 sq. mi.; pop., 36,089,000: occupied by Japan (1910–1945): since 1948 divided into two republics: capitals, Seoul (South), Pyongyang (North): Japanese name, *Chosen:* war between North and South (June, 1950) with the UN supporting South Korea: truce signed (July, 1953).
Ko·re·an (kō-rē′ən, kô-rē′ən), *adj.* of Korea, its people, their language, or culture. *n.* 1. a native of Korea. 2. the language of the Koreans.
Korea Strait, the strait between Japan and Korea, connecting the Sea of Japan with the Yellow Sea.

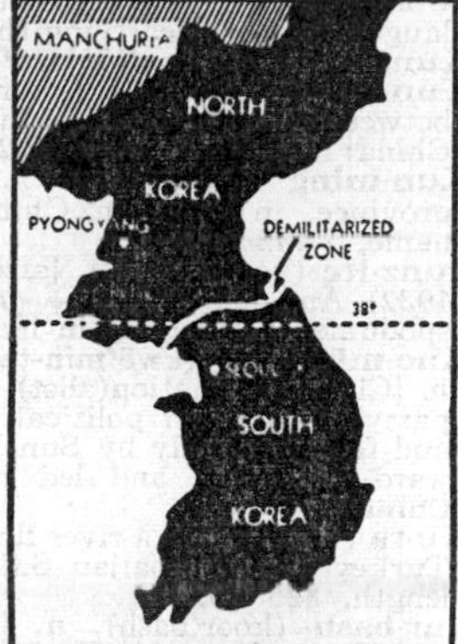

KOREA (July, 1953)

ko·ru·na (kô-ro͞o′nä), *n.* [*pl.* KORUNY (-ni), KORUN (-ro͞on′)], [Czech < L. *corona;* see CROWN (coin)], the monetary unit and a coin of Czechoslovakia, valued at about two cents in 1946: abbreviated **Kč.**
Kos (kos, kôs), *n.* one of the Dodecanese Islands.
kos (kōs), *n.* [Hind. < Sans. *krósa*, lit., a shout], [*pl.* KOS], in India, a measure of distance whose value varies in different localities from 1.5 to 3 miles.
Kos·ci·us·ko, Thaddeus (kos′i-us′kō; Pol. kôsh-cho͞osh′kô), (*Tadeusz Kościuszko*), 1746–1817; Polish hero, statesman, and general; served in the American army during the American Revolution.
Kosciusko, Mount, a mountain of the Australian Alps, southern New South Wales: height, 7,352 ft.
ko·sher (kō′shẽr), *adj.* [Heb. *kāshēr*, fit, right, proper], 1. in *Judaism, a)* clean or fit to eat according to the dietary laws: Lev. 11. *b)* serving or dealing in such food: as, a *kosher* kitchen. 2. [Slang], fit; proper. *n.* kosher food. *v.t.* (kosh′ẽr), to make kosher. Also **kasher.**
Ko·ši·ce (kô′shi-tse), *n.* a city in eastern Slovakia, Czechoslovakia: pop., 81,000.
Kos·suth, Louis (kos′o͞oth, ko-so͞oth′; Hung. kô′shoot), 1802–1894; Hungarian patriot and statesman.
Ko·stro·ma (kô-strô-mä′), *n.* a city in the R.S.F.S.R., on the Volga: pop., 171,000.
Ko·ta·ba·ru (kō′tä-bä′ro͞o), *n.* capital of West Irian: pop., 14,000: former name, *Hollandia.*
ko·to (kō′tō), *n.* [Japan.], a Japanese musical instrument consisting of an oblong box with thirteen silk strings stretched over it, plucked with the fingers.
ko·tow (kō′tou′), *n.* & *v.i.* kowtow.
Kot·ze·bue, Au·gust Fried·rich Fer·di·nand von (ou′goost frēd′riH fer′di-nänt fôn kôt′sə-bo͞o′), 1761–1819; German dramatist.
kou·mis, kou·miss, kou·myss (ko͞o′mis), *n.* kumiss.
Kous·se·vitz·ky, Serge (sûrj *or* serzh ko͞o′sə-vits′ki), (*Sergei Alexandrovich Koussevitzky*), 1874–1951; Russian orchestral conductor in America.
Kov·no (kôv′nô), *n.* Kaunas: the Russian name.
Kow·loon (kou′lo͞on′), *n.* 1. a peninsula opposite Hong Kong island: it is part of the British colony of Hong Kong. 2. a city on this peninsula: pop., 1,350,000.
kow·tow (kou′tou′, kō′tou′), *n.* [Chin. *k'o-t'ou*, lit., knock head], the act of kneeling and touching the ground with the forehead to show great deference, submissive respect, homage, etc.: a Chinese form of salutation to a superior. *v.i.* 1. to make a kowtow; hence, 2. to show submissive respect (*to* a person).
KP, K.P., kitchen police.
Kr, in *chemistry*, krypton.
kr., 1. kreutzer. 2. krona; kronor. 3. krone; kronen. 4. kroner.
Kra, Isthmus of (krä), a narrow strip of land in Thailand, connecting the Malay Peninsula with the peninsula of Indochina.
kraal (kräl), *n.* [S. Afr. D., village, pen, enclosure; prob. < Port. *curral*, pen for cattle], 1. a village of South African natives, surrounded by a stockade for protection. 2. a fenced enclosure for cattle or sheep in South Africa; pen. *v.t.* to shut up in a kraal.
Krafft-E·bing, Baron **Rich·ard von** (riH′ärt fôn kräft′ā′biŋ), 1840–1902; German neurologist.
kraft (kraft, kräft), *n.* [G., strength], strong wrapping paper, usually brown, made from sulfate pulp: also **kraft paper.**
krait (krīt), *n.* [Hind. *karait*], a very poisonous snake of India.
Kra·ka·ta·o (krä′kä-tou′), *n.* an island in Indonesia, between Java and Sumatra.
kra·ken (krä′k'n, krā′k'n), *n.* [Norw.], a legendary sea monster of northern seas.
Kra·ków (krak′ou, krā′kō; Pol. krä′koof), *n.* Cracow, a city in Poland: the Polish name.
Kras·no·dar (kräs′nô-där′), *n.* the capital of Krasnodar Territory: pop., 312,000: former name, *Ekaterinodar.*
Krasnodar Territory, a division of the R.S.F.S.R., in the north Caucasus: pop., 3,766,000.
Kras·no·yarsk (kräs′nô-yärsk′), *n.* a city in southern Krasnoyarsk Territory, on the Yenisei River: pop., 409,000.
Krasnoyarsk Territory, a division of the R.S.F.S.R., extending from the southern border of Siberia to the Arctic: pop., 2,614,000.
K ration, a United States Army field ration consisting of a small can of meat or cheese, hard crackers, powdered beverage, confection, and a few cigarettes, compactly boxed so as to be protected from moisture, gas, etc.: three boxes constitute one day's ration.
Kre·feld (krā′felt), *n.* a city in western Germany: pop., 211,000; also **Crefeld.**
Kreis·ler, Fritz (frits krīs′lẽr), 1875–1962; Austrian violinist and composer in America.
Krem·en·chug (krem-en-chook′), *n.* a city in the central Ukrainian S.S.R., on the Dnepr: pop., 86,000.
krem·lin (krem′lin), *n.* [Fr. < Russ. *kreml'*], in Russia, the citadel of a city.
the Kremlin, 1. the citadel of Moscow, formerly housing government offices of the Soviet Union; hence, 2. the government of the Soviet Union.
Kre·te (krē′ti), *n.* Crete: the Greek name.
kreut·zer, kreu·zer (kroit′sẽr), *n.* [G. *kreuzer* < *kreuz*, a cross: so called because the coin had the figure of a cross on it], a former copper coin of Germany and Austria, valued at about half a cent: abbreviated **kr.**
Kreym·borg, Alfred (krām′bôrg), 1883– ; American poet.
krieg·spiel (krēg′spēl′), *n.* [G. *kriegsspiel; kriegs* (genit. of *krieg*, war) + *spiel*, game], a game for teaching or practicing military tactics by the use of small figures representing troops, tanks, etc. moved about on a large map or representation of the terrain.
Kriem·hild (krēm′hild; G. krēm′hilt), *n.* [G.; MHG. *Kriemhilt* < Gmc. **grim-*, a mask, face, visor (cf. GRIMACE) + **hild-*, battle], in the *Nibelungenlied*, the wife of Siegfried: after he was killed at her brother's command, she married Etzel (Attila), king of the Huns, and with his help avenged the murder.
krim·mer (krim′ẽr), *n.* [G. < *Krim*, Crimea], a grayish fur similar to astrakhan, made from the pelts of Crimean lambs: also spelled **crimmer.**
kris (krēs), *n.* a creese, a Malay dagger.
Krish·na (krish′nə), *n.* [Sans. *Kṛṣṇa*], an important Hindu god, an incarnation of Vishnu, second god of the Hindu trinity.
Krish·na·ism (krish′nə-iz'm), *n.* the worship or cult of Krishna.
Kriss Krin·gle (kris kriŋ′g'l), [G. *Christkindel; Christ*, Christ + *kindel*, dim. of *kind*, child], Santa Claus.
Kri·vo·i Rog (kri-voi′ rôg′), a city in the south central Ukrainian S.S.R.: pop., 386,000.
kro·na (krō′nə; Sw. kro͞o′nə), *n.* [*pl.* KRONOR (-nôr)],

[Sw. < L. *corona;* see CROWN (coin)], the monetary unit and a silver coin of Sweden, valued at about 19 cents in 1950: abbreviated **kr., K., k., kn.** (*sing. & pl.*): also called *crown.*

kro·ne (krō′nə), *n.* [*pl.* KRONEN (-nən)], [G. < L. *corona;* see CROWN (coin)], 1. a former German gold coin, worth ten marks (c. $2.38). 2. the former monetary unit or a silver coin of Austria, worth about twenty cents. Abbreviated **kr., K., k., kn.** (*sing. & pl.*). Also called *crown.*

kro·ne (krō′ne), *n.* [*pl.* KRONER (-ner)], [Dan. < L. *corona;* see CROWN (coin)], the monetary unit and a silver coin of Denmark or Norway, valued at about 14 cents in 1950: abbreviated **kr., K., k., kn.** (*sing. & pl.*): also called *crown.*

Kron·stadt (krôn-shtät′), *n.* a fortified port in the northern European U.S.S.R., on an island in the Gulf of Finland, near Leningrad.

Kron·stadt (krōn′shtät), *n.* Brașov: the German name.

kroon (kro͞on), *n.* [*pl.* KROONS (kro͞onz), KROONI (kro͞o′ni)], [Estonian *kron;* see KRONA], the monetary unit of Estonia, equivalent to the krona of Sweden.

Kro·pot·kin, Prince **Pëtr A·le·kse·ye·vich** (pyô′-tr′ ä′lyek-syā′ə-vich krô-pôt′kin; Eng. krə-pot′kin), 1842–1921; Russian anarchist.

Kru·ger, Paul (kro͞o′gẽr), (*Stephanus Johannes Paulus Kruger*), 1825–1904; Dutch South African statesman; president of Transvaal (1883–1900): called *Oom Paul.*

Kru·gers·dorp (kro͞o′gẽrz-dôrp′), *n.* a city in the Transvaal, Union of South Africa: pop., 76,000.

krul·ler (krul′ẽr), *n.* a cruller.

Krupp, Alfred (krup; G. kroop), 1812–1887; German armaments manufacturer.

kryp·ton (krip′ton), *n.* [Mod. L. < Gr. *krypton,* neut. of *kryptos,* hidden < *kryptein,* to hide], a rare chemical element, an inert gas present in very small quantities in air: symbol, Kr; at. wt., 83.7; at. no., 36.

Kshat·ri·ya (kshat′ri-yə), *n.* [Sans. *kṣatriya* < *kṣatra,* rule], among the Hindus, a member of the military caste, second of the four great castes.

Kt, in *chess,* knight.

kt., carat.

K.T., 1. Knight of the (Order of the) Thistle. 2. Knight (or Knights) Templar.

Kua·la Lum·pur (kwä′lə loom-poor′), a city in the Malay Peninsula: capital of the Federation of Malaya: pop., 316,000.

Ku·ban (koo-bän′y′), *n.* a river in the Caucasus, U.S.S.R., flowing into the Sea of Azov: length, 550 mi.

Ku·ban·go River (koo-bän′gō), a river in South Africa, flowing from central Angola to Bechuanaland: length, 1,000 mi.: also called *Okavango.*

Ku·be·lik, Ján (yȧn koo′bə-lik), 1880–1940; Bohemian-Hungarian violinist.

Ku·blai Khan (ko͞o′blī kän′), 1216?–1294; grandson of Genghis Khan; Mongol emperor (1259–1294); founder of the Mongol dynasty in China.

ku·chen (ko͞o′khən), *n.* [G., cake; see CAKE], a kind of German coffeecake, made of yeast dough covered with sugar and spices, and often containing raisins, nuts, etc.

ku·dos (kū′dos), *n.* [Gr. *kydos,* glory, fame], [Colloq.], credit for an achievement; glory; fame; prestige.

ku·du (ko͞o′do͞o), *n.* [*pl.* KUDUS (-do͞oz), KUDU; see PLURAL, II, D, 1], [Hottentot], a large, grayish-brown African antelope with white markings: also spelled **koodoo.**

Ku·fic (kū′fik), *adj.* [< *Kufa* (Ar. *al-Kūfah*), town on the Euphrates, south of Babylon + *-ic*], designating or of an early Arabic alphabet used in a region south of Babylon: also spelled **Cufic.**

Kui·by·shev (kwē′bi-shef′), *n.* 1. a region of the R.S.F.S.R., in east central European Russia: pop., 2,257,000. 2. its capital, on the Volga: pop., 806,000: formerly called *Samara.*

Ku-Klux, Ku·klux (kū′kluks′), *n.* [< Gr. *kyklos,* a circle (cf. CYCLE), after *circle* in names of various secret organizations sympathetic to the Confederacy (e.g., Knights of the Golden Circle)], 1. the Ku Klux Klan. 2. a member of the Ku Klux Klan.

Ku Klux Klan (kū′kluks′klan′), [for *Ku-Klux Clan:* sp. altered for alliteration], 1. a secret society of white men founded in the Southern States after the Civil War to re-establish and maintain white supremacy. 2. a secret society organized in Atlanta, Georgia, in 1915 as "the Invisible Empire, Knights of the Ku Klux Klan": it is anti-Negro, anti-Semitic, anti-Catholic, etc., and uses terrorist methods. Abbreviated K.K.K.

Ku Klux Klan·ner (klan′ẽr), a member of the Ku Klux Klan.

ku·lak (ko͞o-läk′), *n.* [Russ., lit., fist, hence, tight-wad < Estonian], a well-to-do farmer in Russia who profited from the labor of poorer peasants: the kulaks as a class opposed Soviet policies, especially the collectivization of the land.

‡Kul·tur (kool-to͝or′), *n.* [G.], civilization; social organization; especially, the highly systematized social organization of Hohenzollern or Nazi Germany: now usually ironic in application, with reference to chauvinism, militarism, terrorism, etc.

Kul·tur·kampf (kool-to͝or′kämpf′), *n.* [G.; *kultur* (see KULTUR) + *kampf,* a battle], the struggle between the Roman Catholic Church and the German government from 1873 to 1887, mainly over the government's efforts to control education, civil marriage, church appointments, etc.

Ku·lun (ko͞o′lo͞on′), *n.* Ulan Bator, capital of the Mongolian People's Republic: the Chinese name.

Ku·ma·mo·to (ko͞o′mä-mô′tô), *n.* a city on the western coast of Kyushu, Japan: pop., 332,000.

Ku·mas·i (koo-mȧs′i), *n.* the capital of Ashanti, Ghana: pop., 78,000.

ku·miss (ko͞o′mis), *n.* [G.; Russ. *kumis* < Tatar *kumiz*], 1. mare's or camel's milk fermented (or distilled) and used as a drink by Tatar nomads of Asia. 2. a similar drink made from cow's milk, used in certain special diets. Also spelled **koumis, koumiss, koumyss.**

Kum·ka·le·si (ko͞om′kä-le′si), *n.* a town in Asiatic Turkey, at the western end of the Dardanelles.

küm·mel (kim″l; G. küm′əl), *n.* [G.; OHG. *kumil, kumin;* L. *cuminum;* see CUMIN], a liqueur flavored with caraway seeds, anise, cumin, etc.

kum·mer·bund (kum′ẽr-bund′), *n.* a cummerbund.

kum·quat (kum′kwot), *n.* [< dial. pronun. of Chin. *chin-chü,* lit., golden orange], 1. an orange-colored, oval fruit about the size of a small plum, with a sour pulp and a sweet rind, used in preserves and confections. 2. the tree that it grows on. Also spelled **cumquat.**

Kun, Bé·la (bā′lä koon), 1885–193?; Hungarian Communist leader.

Kun·dry (koon′dri), *n.* [G.], in Wagner's *Parsifal,* a woman doomed to eternal punishment because she had laughed at Jesus carrying the Cross.

Kung Fu-tse (kooŋ′fo͞o′dsu′), see **Confucius.**

Kun·lun Mountains (koon′loon′), mountain ranges between Tibet and Sinkiang, extending to central China: highest peaks, over 20,000 ft.

Kun·ming (koon′miŋ′), *n.* the capital of Yunnan province, in southern China: pop., 300,000: former name, *Yunnan.*

kunz·ite (koonts′īt), *n.* [after George F. *Kunz* (1856–1932), Am. gem expert; + *-ite*], a transparent variety of spodumene, occurring in lilac crystals used as a gem.

Kuo·min·tang (kwō′min-taŋ′; Chin. gwō′min′däŋ′), *n.* [Chin. *kuo,* nation(alist) + *min,* people('s) + *tang,* party], nationalist political party of China, organized and formed chiefly by Sun Yat-sen in 1911 and afterward controlled and led by Chiang Kai-shek: see **China.**

Ku·ra (ko͞o-rä′), *n.* a river flowing through northeastern Turkey and Azerbaijan S.S.R. into the Caspian Sea: length, 825 mi.

kur·bash (koor′bash), *n.* [Turk. *qirbāch*], a leather whip formerly used in Turkey, Egypt, etc. for punishing offenders. *v.t.* to flog with a kurbash.

Kurd (kũrd, koord), *n.* [Turk. & Ar.], any of a nomadic Moslem people living chiefly in Kurdistan and the southern Caucasus.

Kurd·ish (kũr′dish, koor′dish), *adj.* of the Kurds, their language, culture, etc. *n.* the Iranian language of the Kurds.

Kur·di·stan (kũr′di-stan′, koor′di-stän′), *n.* 1. a region in southeastern Turkey, northern Iraq, and northwestern Iran inhabited chiefly by Kurds. 2. any of various rugs made by Kurds, especially in Iran.

Ku·re (ko͞o′re), *n.* a city on the southwestern coast of Honshu, Japan: pop., 199,000.

Kurg (koorg), *n.* Coorg.

Ku·rile Islands (ko͞o′ril, ko͞o-rēl′), one of the chains of islands, north of Hokkaido, between Japan and Kamchatka: ceded to the U.S.S.R. in 1945: area, 6,150 sq. mi.: Japanese name, *Chishima.*

Kur·land (ko͝or′lənd), *n.* a former Russian province, on the Baltic Sea: now a part of the Latvian S.S.R.: also spelled **Courland.**

kur·ra·jong (kũr′ə-joŋ′), *n.* [< native name in Australia], any of several Australian trees and shrubs of the mallow family, which yield fibers used by the natives for weaving nets, mats, etc.: also **koorajong, currajong,** etc.

Kursk (ko͞orsk), *n.* 1. a region of the R.S.F.S.R., in south central European Russia: pop., 1,481,000. 2. its capital: pop., 203,000.

Kush (kush), *n.* Cush.

Kush·it·ic (kush-it′ik), *adj. & n.* Cushitic.

Ku·te·nai, Ku·te·nay (ko͞o′t'n-ā′), *n.* Kootenay.

Ku·tu·zov, Mi·kha·il I·la·ri·o·no·vich (mē′khä-ēl′ ē′lä-ri-ô′nô-vich koo-to͞o′zôf), 1745–1813; Russian field marshal; defeated Napoleon at Smolensk (1812).

Ku·wait (koo-wīt′), koo-wät′), *n.* 1. an independent Arab sheikdom in eastern Arabia, on the Persian Gulf: under British protection until 1961: area, 6,000 sq. mi.; pop., 206,000. 2. its capital: pop., 105,000.

Kuyp, Aalbert, see **Cuyp, Aalbert.**

Kuz·netsk Basin (ko͞oz-netsk′), an industrial region in south central R.S.F.S.R.

kvass, kvas (kväs, kvas), *n.* [Russ. *kvas*], a Russian fermented drink like sour beer, made from rye, barley, rye bread, etc.: also spelled **quass.**

kw., kilowatt.

Kwang·chow (kwäŋ'chō'; Chin. gwäŋ'jō'), *n.* Canton, China: the Chinese name.

Kwang·cho·wan (kwäŋ'chō'wän'; Chin. gwäŋ'jō'wän'), *n.* a territory on the coast of Kwangtung province, China, leased to France (1898–1945): area, 325 sq. mi.; pop., 250,000; chief city, Fort Bayard: official name, *Chankiang.*

Kwang·si (kwaŋ'sē'; Chin. gwäŋ'sē'), *n.* a province of southern China: area, 80,972 sq. mi.; pop., 14,603,000 (est. 1947); capital, Nanning.

Kwang·tung (kwaŋ'tooŋ'; Chin. gwäŋ'dooŋ'), *n.* a province of southern China, on the South China Sea: area, 90,247 sq. mi.; pop., 27,736,000 (est. 1947); capital, Canton.

Kwan·tung (kwan'tooŋ'; Chin. gwän'dooŋ'), *n.* a region in Manchuria leased to Japan (1905–1945).

Kwei·chow (kwā'chou'; Chin. gwā'jō'), *n.* 1. a province of southern China: area, 72,058 sq. mi.; pop., 10,490,000 (est. 1947); capital, Kweiyang. 2. a city in eastern Szechwan province, China, on the Yangtze River: also called *Fengkieh.*

Kwei·hwa·cheng (kwā'hwä'chuŋ'; Chin. gwā'hwä'-juŋ'), *n.* Kweihwating.

Kwei·hwa·ting (kwā'hwä'tiŋ'; Chin. gwā'hwä'tiŋ'), *n.* a city in northern Shansi province, China: pop., 100,000.

Kwei·lin (kwā'lin'; Chin. gwā'lin'), *n.* a city in southern China, Kwangsi province: pop., 100,000.

Kwei·yang (kwā'yäŋ'; Chin. gwā'yäŋ'), *n.* the capital of Kweichow province, China: pop., 117,000.

kwh., K.W.H., kw-h, kw-hr, kilowatt-hour.

Ky., Kentucky.

ky·ack (kī'ak), *n.* [?], in the western United States, a packsack swung on either side of a packsaddle.

ky·ak (kī'ak), *n.* a kayak.

ky·a·nite (kī'ə-nīt'), *n.* cyanite.

ky·an·ize (kī'ə-nīz'), *v.t.* [KYANIZED (-nīzd'), KYANIZING], [after J. H. *Kyan* (1774–1850), Ir. inventor of the process], to make (wood) resistant to decay by treatment with a solution of corrosive sublimate.

Kyd, Thomas (kid), 1558–1594; English dramatist.

ky·mo·graph (kī'mə-graf', kī'mə-gräf'), *n.* [< Gr. *kyma*, a wave; + *-graph*], an apparatus consisting of a rotating drum for recording wavelike motions, variations, or modulations, such as muscular contractions, the pulse, etc.: also **cymograph.**

ky·mo·graph·ic (kī'mə-graf'ik), *adj.* of or recorded by a kymograph.

Kym·ric (kim'rik), *adj.* & *n.* Cymric; Welsh.

Kym·ry, Kym·ri (kim'ri), *n.* [*pl.* KYMRY or KYMRI, KYMRIES (-riz)], Cymry; the Welsh.

Kyo·to, Kio·to (kyō'tō'), *n.* a city in southern Honshu, Japan: pop., 1,000,000 (est. 1947).

ky·phos (kī'fos), *n.* [Gr. *kyphos*, a hump, hunch], the hump in the spine of a humpback.

ky·pho·sis (kī-fō'sis), *n.* [Mod. L.; Gr. *kyphōsis* < *kyphos*, humpbacked, bent], abnormal curvature of the spine resulting in a hump; humpback.

ky·phot·ic (kī-fot'ik), *adj.* of or having kyphosis.

Kyr·i·e e·le·i·son (kir'i-ē' ə-lā'i-s'n), [LL.; Gr. *Kyrie eleēson*, Lord, have mercy (upon us)], 1. a brief prayer of the Orthodox Eastern Church. 2. *a*) a part of the Roman Catholic service after the introit in the Mass. *b*) the music for this. 3. a response in the Anglican service of Holy Communion.

Ky·the·ra (kē'thē-rä'), *n.* Cerigo Island: Greek name.

Kyu·shu (kū'shōō'), *n.* one of the islands forming Japan: area, 14,719 sq. mi.; pop., 9,646,000; chief city, Nagasaki: also spelled **Kiushu.**

Kyz·il Kum (kiz'il koom), Kizil Kum.

L

L, l (el), *n.* [*pl.* L's, l's, Ls, ls (elz)], **1.** the twelfth letter of the English alphabet: from the Greek *lambda*, a borrowing from the Phoenician: see **alphabet**, table. 2. the sound of L or l: in English, it is normally a voiced alveolar continuant formed by the tongue apex, IPA [l]; in many words, *l* preceding *f, k, m,* and *v* is silent (e.g., *half, balk, calm,* and *salve*); in most varieties of American speech, final and preconsonantal *l* (e.g., *feel, field*) has the cavity friction, and hence the sonority, associated with vowels. 3. a type or impression for L or l. 4. *a symbol for* the twelfth (or the eleventh if J is omitted) in a sequence or group. ***adj.*** 1. of L or l. 2. twelfth (or eleventh if J is omitted) in a sequence or group.

L (el), *n.* 1. an object shaped like L; especially, an extension of a house or building that gives the whole a shape resembling L. 2. a Roman numeral for 50: with a superior bar ($\bar{L}$), 50,000. 3. in *geodesy, the symbol for* longitude. 4. in *physics, the symbol for* latent heat. ***adj.*** shaped like L.

L (el), *n.* [for *el*, short for *elevated*], in certain American cities, an elevated railroad: also spelled **el.**

L-, liaison: followed by a number to designate a specific model of United States Army airplane designed for reconnaissance and liaison work.

L., l., 1. lady. 2. lake. 3. land. 4. latitude. 5. law. 6. leaf. 7. league. 8. left. 9. length. 10. liberal. 11. [L.], *libra*, pound; *librae*, pounds. 12. licentiate. 13. [*pl.* LL.], line. 14. link. 15. lira; lire. 16. liter; liters. 17. locus. 18. lodge. 19. lord. 20. low.

L., Latin.

la (lä, lô), ***interj.*** [cf. LO], [Dial. or Archaic], oh! look!: an exclamation of surprise or emphasis.

la (lä), *n.* [said to be < *la*bii, word of a Latin hymn; see GAMUT], in *music*, a syllable representing the sixth tone of the diatonic scale: see **solfeggio.**

La, in *chemistry*, lanthanum.

La., Louisiana.

L.A., 1. Legislative Assembly. 2. [Colloq.], Los Angeles.

laa·ger (lä'gẽr), *n.* [S.Afr.D. < D. *leger*, a camp], in South Africa, a temporary camp within an encircling barricade of wagons, etc. *v.t.* to form into a laager. *v.i.* to camp in a laager. Also spelled **lager.**

lab (lab), *n.* [Colloq.], a laboratory.

Lab., 1. Laborite. 2. Labrador.

lab., 1. labial. 2. labiate. 3. laboratory.

La·ban (lā'bən), *n.* [Heb. *lābhān*, lit., white], in the *Bible*, the father of Rachel and Leah: Gen. 29:16.

lab·a·rum (lab'ə-rəm), *n.* [*pl.* LABARA (-rə)], [LL.; Gr. *labaron*], the royal cavalry standard carried before the Roman emperors in war, especially that first carried by Constantine, the first emperor to adopt Christianity: it usually bore the first two letters (XP) of the Greek *Khristos* (Christ).

lab·da·num (lab'də-nəm), *n.* [ML.; L. *ladanum, ledanum;* Gr. *ladanon, lēdanon* < *lēdon*, mastic; Ar. *lādan;* Per. *lādan*], a dark resin obtained from certain varieties of the rockrose: also **ladanum.**

La·be (lä'be), *n.* the Elbe: the Czech name.

lab·e·fac·tion (lab'ə-fak'shən), *n.* [< L. *labefactus*, pp. of *labefacere*, to cause to totter < *labare*, to totter + *facere*, to make], a weakening, ruining, etc.; downfall; deterioration.

la·bel (lā'b'l), *n.* [ME.; OFr., a rag, strip, tatter < OHG. *lappa*, a rag, shred], 1. a narrow band of cloth, etc.; fillet. 2. a narrow strip of ribbon attached to a document to hold the seal. 3. a card, strip of paper, etc. marked and attached to an object to indicate its nature, contents, ownership, destination, etc. 4. a descriptive word or phrase applied to a person, group, theory, etc. as a convenient generalized classification. 5. in *architecture*, a projecting molding over a door, window, etc. 6. in *heraldry*, a horizontal bar with several dependent points on the coat of arms of an eldest son. ***v.t.*** [LABELED or LABELLED (-b'ld), LABELING or LABELLING], 1. to attach a label to; mark with a label. 2. to classify as; call; name; describe.

la·bel·er, la·bel·ler (lā'b'l-ẽr), *n.* a person who labels.

la·bel·lum (lə-bel'əm), *n.* [*pl.* LABELLA (-ə)], [L., dim. of *labrum*, a lip], the lowest of the three petals forming the corolla of an orchid, usually larger than the other two petals, and often spurred.

la·bi·a (lā'bi-ə), *n.* plural of **labium.**

la·bi·al (lā'bi-əl), *adj.* [ML. *labialis* < L. *labium*, a lip; see LIP], 1. of the labia, or lips. 2. in *phonetics*, formed mainly with the lips: said especially of *b, m,* and *p.* *n.* 1. an organ pipe whose tone is produced by the action of an air current against a liplike edge. 2. a labial sound. Abbreviated **lab.**

la·bi·al·ism (lā'bi-əl-iz'm), *n.* 1. the quality of being labial. 2. the tendency to labialize sounds; especially, a speech defect characterized by this.

la·bi·al·i·za·tion (lā'bi-əl-i-zā'shən, lā'bi-əl-ī-zā'shən), *n.* a labializing or being labialized.

la·bi·al·ize (lā'bi-əl-iz'), *v.t.* [LABIALIZED (-īzd'), LABIALIZING], [*labial* + *-ize*], in *phonetics*, 1. to pronounce (a sound or sounds) by using the lips, sometimes excessively. 2. to round (a vowel).

labia ma·jo·ra (mə-jō'rə), [L., lit., greater lips], the outer folds of skin on either side of the vulva.

labia mi·no·ra (mi-nō'rə), [L., lit., lesser lips], the folds of mucous membrane within the labia majora.

la·bi·ate (lā'bi-āt', lā'bi-it), *adj.* [Mod. L. *labiatus* < L. *labium*, a lip; see LIP], 1. formed or functioning like a lip. 2. having a lip or lips; lipped. 3. in *botany*, having the calyx or corolla so divided that one part overlaps the other like a lip: abbreviated **lab.**

LABIATE COROLLA (of nettle)

La·biche, Eu·gène Ma·rin (ö'zhen' mȧ'ran' lȧ'bēsh'), 1815–1888; French comic dramatist.

la·bile (lā'b'l, lā'bil), *adj.* [L. *labilis* < *labi*, to slip, fall], 1. liable to change; unstable: as, certain chemical compounds are *labile.* 2. in *electrotherapy*, passing over or gliding across: said of the application of an electric current by passing an electrode over the diseased part.

la·bi·o- (lā'bi-ō), [< L. *labium;* see LIP], a combining form meaning *the lips, the lips and,* as in *labiodental.*

la·bi·o·den·tal (lā'bi-ō-den't'l), *adj.* [*labio-* + *dental*], in *phonetics*, formed by placing the lower lip against the upper teeth and forcing the breath through them: said of *f* and *v.* *n.* a labiodental sound.

la·bi·o·na·sal (lā'bi-ō-nā'z'l), *adj.* [*labio-* + *nasal*], in *phonetics*, formed with the lips but having nasal resonance: said of *m.* *n.* a labionasal sound.

la·bi·o·ve·lar (lā'bi-ō-vē'lẽr), *adj.* [*labio-* + *velar*], in *phonetics*, formed by rounding and half closing the lips and placing the back of the tongue against or near the velum, or soft palate: said of *w.* *n.* a labiovelar sound.

la·bi·um (lā'bi-əm), *n.* [*pl.* LABIA (-ə)], [L., a lip; see LIP], a lip or liplike organ; especially, *a*) *pl.* the outer folds of skin (*labia majora*) or the inner folds of mucous membrane (*labia minora*) of the vulva. *b*) the lower, liplike part of the corolla of certain flowers. *c*) the lower lip of an insect.

la·bor (lā'bẽr), *n.* [ME. *labour;* OFr. *labour, labor;* L. *labor*, labor, hardship, pain], 1. physical or mental exertion; work; toil. 2. a specific task; piece of work. 3. *a*) all wage-earning workers: distinguished from *capital* or *management.* *b*) all manual workers whose work is characterized largely by physical exertion: distinguished from *white-collar* or *professional workers.* 4. the work accomplished or the part played in society by all workers. 5. in *medicine*, the process of childbirth; parturition; especially, the muscular contractions of giving birth. *v.i.* [ME. *laboren;* OFr. *laborer;* L. *laborare* < the *n.*], 1. to work; toil. 2. to work hard; exert oneself to get or do something; strive. 3. *a*) to move slowly and with difficulty: as, the old car *labored* up the hill. *b*) to pitch and roll heavily: as, the ship *labored* in the rough sea. 4. to undergo, and suffer the pains of, childbirth. *v.t.* [earlier *elabour* < Fr. *élaborer;* see ELABORATE], to spend too much time and effort on; develop in too great detail: as, do not *labor* the point. —*SYN.* see **work.**

labor under, to be subjected to or suffer from: as, he is *laboring under* a false impression.

Labor and Socialist International, an association formed in Hamburg in 1923 by a merging of the Second International and the Vienna International.

lab·o·ra·to·ry (lab'rə-tôr'i, lab'ẽr-ə-tō'ri), *n.* [*pl.* LABORATORIES (-iz, -riz)], [ML. *laboratorium* < L. *laborare;* see LABOR, *v.i.*], 1. a room or building for scientific experimentation or research. 2. a place for preparing chemicals, drugs, etc. *adj.* of or performed in, or as in, a laboratory. Abbreviated **lab.**

Labor Day, in most States of the United States, the first Monday in September, set aside as a legal holiday in honor of labor.

la·bored (lā'bẽrd), *adj.* [pp. of *labor, v.t.*], made or done with great effort; not effortless and natural.

la·bor·er (lā'bẽr-ẽr), *n.* [ME.; OFr. *laboreor, laborier* < *laborer;* see LABOR, *v.*], a person who labors; especially, a wage-earning worker, skilled or semiskilled, whose work is characterized largely by physical exertion.

la·bo·ri·ous (lə-bôr'i-əs, lə-bō'ri-əs), *adj.* [ME.; OFr. *laborios;* L. *laboriosus* < *labor*, labor], 1. involving or calling for much hard work; difficult. 2. industrious; hard-working. —*SYN.* see **hard.**

la·bor·ite (lā'bẽr-īt'), *n.* 1. a member or supporter of a labor party. 2. [L-], a member or supporter of the British Labor Party: abbreviated **Lab.**

labor of love, [after I Thess. 1:3], work that one enjoys doing.

‡la·bor om·ni·a vin·cit (lā'bôr om'ni-ə vin'sit), [L.], labor conquers all.

labor party, 1. a political party organized to protect and further the rights of workers, or professing to do so. 2. [L- P-], such a party in Great Britain: British spelling, **Labour Party.**

la·bor-sav·ing (lā'bẽr-sāv'iŋ), *adj.* lessening the amount of work required: as, *labor-saving* appliances.

labor union, an association of workers to promote and protect the welfare, interests, and rights of its members, primarily by collective bargaining.

la·bour (lā'bẽr), *n., v.t. & v.i.* labor: British spelling.

la·bra (lā'brə, lab'rə), *n.* plural of **labrum.**

Lab·ra·dor (lab'rə-dôr'), *n.* 1. a peninsula in northeastern North America, between the Atlantic and Hudson Bay: area, c. 530,000 sq. mi. 2. the eastern part of this peninsula, constituting part of Newfoundland: area, 112,400 sq. mi.; pop., 5,000 (est. 1947). Abbreviated **Lab.**

Labrador Current, an icy arctic current flowing southward past Labrador and Newfoundland.

lab·ra·dor·ite (lab'rə-dôr-īt', lab'rə-dôr'īt), *n.* [after *Labrador*, where excellent specimens have been found], a variety of feldspar showing a play of colors.

la·bret (lā'bret), *n.* [dim. of L. *labrum*, a lip; see LIP], an ornament of wood, bone, etc. worn (by some primitive tribes) in a hole pierced through the lip.

lab·roid (lab'roid), *adj.* [< Mod. L. *Labrus*, type genus of the family *Labridae* < L. *labrus, labros*, kind of fish; + *-oid*], belonging to a large group of sea fishes related to the sea perches, including the wrasses and parrot fishes. *n.* a fish of this group.

la·brum (lā'brəm, lab'rəm), *n.* [*pl.* LABRA (-brə, -rə)], [L.; see LIP], a lip or liplike edge; especially, in *zoology*, *a*) the upper or front lip of insects and other arthropods. *b*) the outer edge of a univalve shell.

La Bru·yère, Jean de (zhän də lȧ brü'yâr'), 1645–1696; French essayist and moralist.

La·bu·an (lä-bōō-än'), *n.* a British island north of Borneo: area, 29 sq. mi.; pop., 8,000.

la·bur·num (lə-bûr'nəm), *n.* [L.], any of a group of small trees and shrubs of the pea family, with three-part leaves and drooping clusters of yellow flowers.

lab·y·rinth (lab'ə-rinth'), *n.* [L. *labyrinthus;* Gr. *labyrinthos*], 1. an intricate structure or enclosure containing a series of winding passages hard to follow without losing one's way; maze; 2. [L-], in *Greek legend*, such a structure built by Daedalus for King Minos of Crete, to house the Minotaur. 3. a complicated, perplexing arrangement, course of affairs, etc. 4. in *anatomy*, the inner ear: see **ear.**

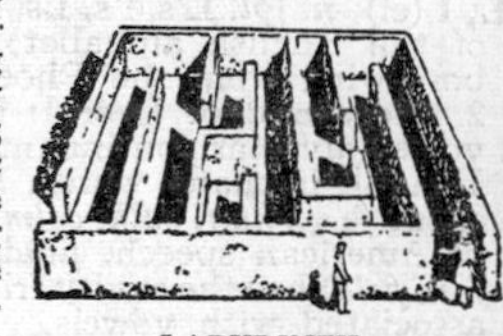
LABYRINTH

lab·y·rin·thi·an (lab'ə-rin'thi-ən), *adj.* labyrinthine.

lab·y·rin·thic (lab'ə-rin'thik), *adj.* labyrinthine.

lab·y·rin·thine (lab'ə-rin'thin), *adj.* 1. of or constituting a labyrinth. 2. like a labyrinth; intricate; complicated; puzzling.

lac (lak), *n.* [Hind. *lākh;* Sans. *lākshā*], a resinous substance formed on certain trees in southern Asia by a variety of scale insect: when melted, strained, and rehardened, it forms shellac.

lac (lak), *n.* [Hind. *lākh;* Sans. *laksha*, a mark, sign, hundred thousand], in India, 1. the sum of 100,000: said specifically of rupees (written Rs. 1,00,000: sums of one lac or over are written with a comma after the number of lacs). 2. any indefinitely large number. Also spelled **lakh.**

Lac·ca·dive Islands (lak'ə-dīv'), a group of islands off the southwest coast of India, belonging to Madras province: area, 80 sq. mi.; pop., 16,000.

lac·co·lite (lak'ə-līt'), *n.* a laccolith.

lac·co·lith (lak'ə-lith), *n.* [< Gr. *lakkos*, a cistern; + *-lith*], an irregular formation of igneous rock intruded between the layers of sedimentary rock so as to cause them to bulge upward.

lace (lās), *n.* [ME. *las;* OFr. *laz, las;* L. *laqueus*, a noose, snare, trap], 1. a string, ribbon, etc. used to draw together and fasten the parts of a shoe, corset, etc. by being drawn through eyelets or over hooks. 2. an ornamental braid of gold or silver, for trimming uniforms, hats, etc. 3. a fine netting or openwork fabric of linen, cotton, silk, etc., woven in ornamental designs. 4. a dash of some alcoholic liquor added to coffee, tea, etc. *v.t.* [LACED (lāst), LACING], 1. to draw the ends of (a garment, shoe, etc.) together and fasten with a lace. 2. to compress the waist of by lacing a corset, etc. (often with *up*). 3. to weave together; intertwine. 4. to decorate with lace. 5. to streak, as with color. 6. to thrash; whip. 7. to add a dash of alcoholic liquor to (a beverage). *v.i.* to be fastened with a lace: as, she wants shoes that *lace.*

lace into, [Colloq.], 1. to attack physically; assail. 2. to attack verbally; criticize sharply; scold.

Lac·e·dae·mon (las'ə-dē'mən), *n.* ancient Sparta.

Lac·e·dae·mo·ni·an (las'ə-di-mō'ni-ən), *adj.* & *n.* Spartan.

lace pillow, a pillow held in the lap or on the knees and used as a support for lace being made by hand.

lac·er·a·ble (las'ẽr-ə-b'l), *adj.* that can be lacerated.

lac·er·ate (las'ə-rāt'), *v.t.* [LACERATED (-id), LACERATING], [< L. *laceratus,* pp. of *lacerare,* to tear < *lacer,* lacerated], 1. to tear jaggedly; mangle (something soft, as flesh). 2. to wound or hurt (one's feelings, etc.); distress. *adj.* (las'ẽr-it), 1. torn; mangled. 2. in *botany,* having jagged edges: said of a leaf.

lac·er·a·tion (las'ə-rā'shən), *n.* 1. a lacerating. 2. the result of lacerating; jagged tear or wound.

la·cer·ti·an (lə-sũr'shi-ən), *adj.* & *n.* lacertilian.

la·cer·til·i·an (las'ẽr-til'i-ən), *adj.* [< Mod. L. *Lacertilia,* name of the division < L. *lacertus, lacerta,* a lizard; + *-an*], belonging to a group of reptiles comprising the ordinary lizards, geckos, chameleons, etc. *n.* any reptile of this group.

lace·wing (lās'wiŋ'), *n.* any of a large group of insects with four delicate, gauzy wings.

lace·work (lās'wũrk'), *n.* 1. lace. 2. any openwork decoration like lace.

La Chaise, Fran·çois d'Aix de (frän'swȧ' deks' də lä shez'), 1624–1709; French Jesuit; confessor to Louis XIV.

lach·es (lach'iz), *n.* [ME. *lacchesse, lachesse;* OFr. *laschesse* < *lasche,* lax, negligent < *laschier,* to slack; LL. **lascare,* for **laxicare* < L. *laxare* < *laxus,* lax], in *law,* failure to do the required thing at the proper time (e.g., inexcusable delay in forwarding a claim).

Lach·e·sis (lak'ə-sis), *n.* [L. < Gr. *lachesis,* lit., lot < *lanchanein,* to obtain by lot or fate, happen], in *Greek & Roman mythology,* that one of the three Fates who determines the length of the thread of life.

lach·ry·mal (lak'rə-m'l), *adj.* [ML. *lacrimalis, lachrymalis* < L. *lacrima,* a tear], of, for, or producing tears. *n.* 1. any of a number of small vases found in ancient Roman sepulchers, popularly supposed to have been a receptacle for the tears of mourners; lachrymatory. 2. *pl.* the lachrymal glands, which produce tears. Also spelled **lacrimal.**

lach·ry·ma·tor (lak'rə-mā'tẽr), *n.* [< L. *lacrima,* a tear; + *-ator*], a substance that irritates the eyes and produces tears, as tear gas: also spelled **lacrimator.**

lach·ry·ma·to·ry (lak'rə-mə-tôr'i, lak'rə-mə-tō'ri), *n.* [*pl.* LACHRYMATORIES (-iz, -riz)], [ML. *lacrimatorium,* neut. of *lacrimatorius,* of tears < *lacrima,* a tear], a lachrymal vase. *adj.* of, causing, or producing tears. Also spelled **lacrimatory.**

lach·ry·mose (lak'rə-mōs'), *adj.* [L. *lacrimosus* < *lacrima,* a tear], 1. inclined to shed many tears; mournful. 2. causing to cry and shed tears; sad. Also spelled **lacrimose.**

lac·i·ly (lās'ə-li), *adv.* in a lacy manner or pattern.

lac·i·ness (lās'i-nis), *n.* a lacy quality or state.

lac·ing (lās'iŋ), *n.* 1. the act of a person who laces. 2. a thrashing. 3. a cord or lace, as a shoelace. 4. gold or silver braid used to trim a uniform, etc.

la·cin·i·ate (lə-sin'i-āt', lə-sin'i-it), *adj.* [< L. *lacinia,* a flap; + *-ate*], 1. having a fringe; fringed. 2. cut deeply into narrow, jagged segments: said of a leaf.

la·cin·i·at·ed (lə-sin'i-ā'tid), *adj.* laciniate.

lack (lak), *n.* [Early ME. *lac;* prob. < MLG., MD. *lak,* lack; IE. base as in *slack, lax*], 1. the fact or condition of not having enough; shortage; deficiency. 2. the fact or condition of not having any; complete absence. 3. the thing that is lacking or needed. *v.i.* [ME. *lacen, lakyn;* prob. < MD. *laken,* to be wanting, with sense influence < the *n.*], 1. to be wanting or missing; show a deficiency. 2. *a*) to be short (with *of* or *in*). *b*) to be in need. *v.t.* 1. to be deficient in or entirely without. 2. to want; need.

supply the lack, to provide with whatever is needed.

SYN.—**lack** implies an absence or insufficiency of something essential or desired (she *lacks* experience); **want** (in this sense, chiefly British) and **need** stress the urgency of supplying what is lacking (this matter *needs,* or *wants,* immediate attention); **require** emphasizes even more strongly imperative need, connoting that what is needed is indispensable (his work *requires* great powers of concentration).—***ANT.*** have, possess.

lack·a·dai·si·cal (lak ə-dā'zi-k'l), *adj.* [< *lackadaisy* (altered < *alackaday*)], showing lack of interest or spirit; listless; spiritless; languid.

lack·a·day (lak'ə-dā'), *interj.* [contr. < *alackaday*], [Archaic], an exclamation of regret, sorrow, pity, etc.

Lack·a·wan·na (lak'ə-wä'nə, lak'ə-wô'nə), *n.* a city in western New York, near Lake Erie: pop., 30,000.

lack·er (lak'ẽr), *n.* & *v.t.* [Obs.], lacquer.

lack·ey (lak'i), *n.* [*pl.* LACKEYS (-iz)], [Fr. *laquais,* a lackey, soldier; Sp. *lacayo,* a lackey, footman; ? < Ar. *al-kaid,* the captain], 1. a male servant of low rank, usually in some sort of livery or uniform. 2. a follower who has no will of his own; toady. *v.t.* & *v.i.* to serve as a lackey. Formerly, also spelled **lacquey.**

lack·lus·ter, lack·lus·tre (lak'lus'tẽr), *adj.* lacking brightness; dull: as, *lackluster* eyes. *n.* [Rare], absence of brightness; dullness.

La·co·ni·a (lə-kō'ni-ə), *n.* an ancient country in southeastern Peloponnesus: capital, Sparta: see **Greece,** map.

La·co·ni·an (lə-kō'ni-ən), *adj.* of Laconia, its people, or their culture; Spartan. *n.* a native or inhabitant of Laconia; Spartan.

la·con·ic (lə-kon'ik), *adj.* [L. *Laconicus;* Gr. *Lakōnikos,* Laconian < *Lakōn,* a Laconian, Spartan], expressing much in few words; pithy; concise. —***SYN.*** see **concise.**

la·con·i·cal·ly (lə-kon'i-k'l-i, lə-kon'ik-li), *adv.* in a laconic manner; in few words; concisely.

la·con·i·cism (lə-kon'ə-siz'm), *n.* laconism.

lac·o·nism (lak'ə-niz'm), *n.* [Gr. *Lakōnismos* < *Lakōnizein,* to imitate the Laconians], 1. brevity of speech or expression. 2. a laconic speech or expression.

La Co·ru·ña (lä kô-rōō'nyä), Corunna: Spanish name.

lac·quer (lak'ẽr), *n.* [Fr. & Port. *lacre* < *laca,* gum lac < Hind. *lākh;* see LAC (resin)], 1. a clear varnish consisting of shellac or gum resins dissolved in alcohol and other quick-drying solvents, with or without nitrocellulose: pigments may be added to lacquers to form lacquer enamels. 2. a resinous varnish obtained from certain trees in China and Japan, used to give a hard, smooth, highly polished finish to wood. 3. a decorative article or articles made of wood and coated with this lacquer. *v.t.* to coat with lacquer. Formerly, also spelled **lacker.**

lac·quey (lak'i), *n., v.t.* & *v.i.* [Obs.], lackey.

lac·ri·mal (lak'rə-m'l), *adj.* & *n.* lachrymal.

lac·ri·ma·tor (lak'rə-mā'tẽr), *n.* a lachrymator.

lac·ri·ma·to·ry (lak'rə-mə-tôr'i, lak'rə-mə-tō'ri), *adj.* & *n.* [*pl.* LACRIMATORIES (-iz, -riz)], lachrymatory.

lac·ri·mose (lak'rə-mōs'), *adj.* lachrymose.

la·crosse (lə-krôs', lə-kros'), *n.* [Fr. *la crosse; la,* the + *crosse,* a crutch, hockey stick, cross], a ball game in which two teams of ten men each, using long-handled, webbed rackets, try to advance the ball across the field into the opponents' goal: the game was first played by North American Indians.

LACROSSE

La Crosse (lə krôs', lə kros'), a city in western Wisconsin, on the Mississippi: pop., 48,000.

lact-, lacto-.

lac·tam (lak'tam), *n.* [*lactone* + *amino*], any of a group of organic cyclic compounds containing the -NH-CO- group in the ring, formed by the elimination of water from the amino and carboxyl groups; inner anhydride of an amino acid.

lac·ta·rene (lak'tə-rēn'), *n.* [< L. *lactarius, adj.;* see LACTARY], a preparation of casein or milk curds, used in calico printing to set the colors.

lac·ta·rine (lak'tə-rin, lak'tə-rēn'), *n.* lactarene.

lac·ta·ry (lak'tə-ri), *adj.* [L. *lactarius* < *lac, lactis,* milk], of or for milk. *n.* [*pl.* LACTARIES (-riz)], a dairy.

lac·tase (lak'tās), *n.* [*lact-* + dias*tase*], an enzyme, present in certain yeasts and in the intestines of animals, which splits lactose into glucose and galactose.

lac·tate (lak'tāt), *v.i.* [LACTATED (-id), LACTATING], [< L. *lactatus,* pp. of *lactare* < *lac, lactis,* milk], 1. to secrete milk. 2. to suckle young. *n.* any salt or ester of lactic acid.

lac·ta·tion (lak-tā'shən), *n.* [< pp. of L. *lactare;* see prec.], 1. the secretion of milk by a mammary gland. 2. the period during which milk is secreted. 3. the suckling of young.

lac·te·al (lak'ti-əl), *adj.* [< L. *lacteus,* milky < *lac, lactis,* milk; + *-al*], 1. of or like milk; milky. 2. containing or carrying chyle, the milky fluid that is a product of digestion. *n.* any of the lymphatic vessels that take up this fluid from the small intestine and carry it to the thoracic duct.

lac·te·ous (lak'ti-əs), *adj.* [< L. *lacteus* (see LACTEAL); + *-ous*], milky; like milk.

lac·tes·cence (lak-tes''ns), *n.* [< L. *lactescens;* see LACTESCENT], 1. the act or process of becoming milky. 2. milkiness. 3. the flow of a milky fluid or sap from

fat, āpe, bâre, cär; ten, ēven, hêre, ovẽr; is, bīte; lot, gō, hôrn, tōōl, look; oil, out; up, ūse, fũr; get; joy; yet; chin; she; thin, *th*en; zh, leisure; ŋ, ring; ə for *a* in *ago, e* in *agent, i* in *sanity, o* in *comply, u* in *focus;* ' as in *able* (ā'b'l); Fr. bål; ë, Fr. coeur; ö, Fr. feu; Fr. mo*n*; ô, Fr. coq; ü, Fr. duc; H, G. ich; kh, G. doch. See pp. x–xii. ‡ foreign; * hypothetical; < derived from.

certain plants when they are gashed or wounded.

lac·tes·cen·cy (lak-tes'ən-si), *n.* lactescence.

lac·tes·cent (lak-tes''nt), *adj.* [L. *lactescens,* ppr. of *lactescere,* to turn into milk < *lactare;* see LACTATE], 1. becoming milky. 2. milky. 3. secreting or forming milk or a milky fluid.

lac·tic (lak'tik), *adj.* [*lact-* + *-ic*], 1. of or obtained from milk. 2. designating or of a clear, sirupy acid, $CH_3CHOHCOOH$, formed by the fermentation of lactose when milk sours, or produced from sucrose and some other carbohydrates by the action of certain microorganisms.

lac·tif·er·ous (lak-tif'ẽr-əs), *adj.* [LL. *lactifer* < L. *lac, lactis,* milk + *ferre,* to bear; + *-ous*], yielding or conveying milk.

lac·to- (lak'tō, lak'tə), [< L. *lac, lactis,* milk], a combining form meaning: 1. *milk,* as in *lactoscope.* 2. in *chemistry, lactic* or *lactate,* as in *lactone.* Also, before a vowel, **lact-**.

lac·to·ba·cil·lus (lak'tō-bə-sil'əs), *n.* [Mod. L.; *lacto-* + *bacillus*], any of a group of bacteria that ferment milk, carbohydrates, etc. to produce lactic acid.

lac·to·fla·vin (lak'tō-flā'vin), *n.* [*lacto-* + *flavin*], riboflavin; vitamin B_2.

lac·tom·e·ter (lak-tom'ə-tẽr), *n.* [*lacto-* + *-meter*], an instrument for determining the specific gravity, and hence the richness, of milk.

lac·tone (lak'tōn), *n.* [*lact-* + *-one*], any of a group of organic compounds formed by the elimination of a molecule of water from the -OH and -COOH groups of a molecule of a hydroxy acid.

lac·to·pro·te·id (lak'tō-prō'tē-id), *n.* a lactoprotein.

lac·to·pro·te·in (lak'tō-prō'tē-in, lak'tō-prō'tēn), *n.* [*lacto-* + *protein*], any of the proteins found in milk.

lac·to·scope (lak'tə-skōp'), *n.* [*lacto-* + *-scope*], an instrument for determining the amount of cream in milk by the difference in opacity of the two fluids.

lac·tose (lak'tōs), *n.* [*lact-* + *-ose*], a white, crystalline sugar, $C_{12}H_{22}O_{11}$, found in milk and prepared by evaporation of the whey and the subsequent crystallization of the sugar: used in infant foods, etc.: also called *milk sugar, sugar of milk.*

La Cum·bre (lä ko͝om'bre), Uspallata Pass, in the Andes.

la·cu·na (lə-kū'nə), *n.* [*pl.* LACUNAS (-nəz), LACUNAE (-nē)], [L., a ditch, hole, pool < *lacus;* see LAKE (water)], 1. a space where something has been omitted or has come out; gap; hiatus. 2. in *anatomy & biology,* a space or cavity; specifically, any of the very small cavities in bone that are filled with bone cells.

la·cu·nal (lə-kū'n'l), *adj.* lacunar.

la·cu·nar (lə-kū'nẽr), *adj.* of or having a lacuna or lacunae. *n.* [*pl.* LACUNARS (-nẽrz), LACUNARIA (lak'yoo-nâr'i-ə)], [L. < *lacuna*], in *architecture,* a ceiling made up of sunken panels.

lac·u·nar·y (lak'yoo-ner'i), *adj.* lacunar.

la·cu·nose (lə-kū'nōs), *adj.* [L. *lacunosus*], full of lacunae.

la·cus·trine (lə-kus'trin), *adj.* [< L. *lacus,* lake], 1. of a lake or lakes. 2. found in or on lakes.

lac·y (lās'i), *adj.* [LACIER (-i-ẽr), LACIEST (-i-ist)], 1. of lace. 2. like lace; having a delicate open pattern.

lad (lad), *n.* [ME. *ladde;* Late AS. *-ladda,* byname & place-name element; prob. < ON.; akin to Goth. *-lauths* (in *juggalauths,* young man < *liudan,* to grow), AS. *-led* (in name *Sumerled,* lit, summer sprout, shoot); prob. basic sense "young sprout"], 1. a boy; young man. 2. a man of any age: familiar term.

lad·a·num (lad'ə-nəm), *n.* [L.], labdanum.

lad·der (lad'ẽr), *n.* [ME. *laddre, leddre;* AS. *hlæd(d)er;* akin to G. *leiter;* IE. base **klei-,* to incline, lean, seen also in *incline, decline, climax, lean,* etc.], 1. a framework consisting of two parallel sidepieces connected by rungs, or narrow crosspieces, on which a person steps in climbing up or down. 2. anything by means of which a person climbs or rises: as, the *ladder* of success.

lad·der-back chair (lad'ẽr-bak'), a chair with a back consisting of two upright posts connected by horizontal slats.

ladder stitch, an embroidery stitch with parallel crossbars in a ladderlike design.

lad·die (lad'i), *n.* [Scot., dim. of *lad*], [Chiefly Scot.], a lad.

lade (lād), *v.t. & v.i.* [LADED (-id), LADEN (-'n) or LADED, LADING], [ME. *laden;* AS. *hladan;* akin to G. *laden;* IE. base **qlā-,* to set down, lay, place, as also in OSlav. *klasti-,* to load & Eng. *ladle*], 1. to load. 2. to dip or draw out (water, etc.) with a ladle; bail; ladle. Also **laden.**

lad·en (lād''n), alternative past participle of **lade.** *adj.* 1. loaded. 2. burdened; afflicted: as, *laden* with pain.

lad·en (lād''n), *v.t. & v.i.* to lade.

la-di-da (lä'di-dä'), *adj.* [imitation of affected speech, popularized through music halls (c. 1870)], [Slang], characterized by affectation; foppish. *n.* [Slang], an affected, foppish person. *interj.* an exclamation of derision at affectation, foppishness, etc. Also spelled **la-de-da.**

La·din (lə-dēn'), *n.* [Rhaeto-Romanic < L. *Latinus,* Latin], 1. a group of Romance dialects spoken in southeastern Switzerland and contiguous regions of northern Italy and the Tyrol; Rhaeto-Romanic; Romansh: they form a distinct Romance language. 2. a native of these regions who speaks this dialect.

lad·ing (lād'iŋ), *n.* [Late ME.; see LADE], 1. a loading. 2. a load; cargo; freight.

La·di·no (lä-dē'nō; Sp. lä-*thē*'nô), *n.* [*pl.* LADINOS (-nōz; Sp. -nôs)], [Sp., wise, cunning, learned, lit., Latin < L. *Latinus*], 1. the mixed Spanish and Hebrew dialect spoken by Sephardic Jews in Turkey and some other countries. 2. in Spanish America, a person of mixed blood; mestizo.

la·dle (lā'd'l), *n.* [ME. *ladel;* AS. *hlædel,* a ladle < *hladan,* to draw water; see LADE & -LE], a long-handled, cuplike spoon for dipping out liquids. *v.t.* [LADLED (-d'ld), LADLING], 1. to dip out with or as with a ladle. 2. to lift out and carry in a ladle.

la·dle·ful (lā'd'l-fool'), *n.* [*pl.* LADLEFULS (-foolz')], as much as a ladle will hold.

La·do·ga, Lake (lä'dô-gȧ), a lake in the Karelo-Finnish S.S.R., near Leningrad: area, 7,000 sq. mi.

la·drone (lə-drōn'), *n.* [Sp. *ladrón* < L. *latro,* hired servant, mercenary soldier, freebooter], a robber; bandit: used with reference to Spanish-speaking regions.

La·drone Islands (lə-drōn'), the Marianas Islands, in the Pacific: the former name.

la·dron·ism (lə-drōn'iz'm), *n.* [see LADRONE & -ISM], in the Philippines, organized banditry.

la·dy (lā'di), *n.* [*pl.* LADIES (-diz)], [ME. *lavedi, levedy;* AS. *hlæfdige,* lady, mistress < *hlaf,* loaf + *-dige* < base of *dæge,* (bread) kneader; see DOUGH], 1. the mistress of a household: now obsolete except in the phrase *the lady of the house.* 2. a woman who has the rights, rule, or authority of a lord. 3. a woman of good breeding or some social position: corresponding to *gentleman.* 4. any woman: used in polite reference or [*pl.*], in addressing a group of women. 5. a woman loved by a man; sweetheart. 6. a wife. 7. [L-], the Virgin Mary (usually with *Our*). 8. [L-], in the British Empire, the title of respect given to a marchioness, countess, viscountess, or baroness, to the daughter of a duke, marquis, or earl, or to the wife of a baronet, knight, or holder of a courtesy title of *Lord.* *adj.* 1. female: as, a *lady* barber. 2. of or suitable for a lady or ladies. Abbreviated **L., l.** —***SYN.*** see **woman.**

la·dy·bird (lā'di-bũrd'), *n.* [short for *Our Lady's bird;* see LADY, 7], a ladybug.

Lady Bountiful, 1. a wealthy, charitable lady in Farquhar's comedy *The Beaux' Stratagem* (1707); hence, 2. any charitable woman.

la·dy·bug (lā'di-bug'), *n.* any of certain small, roundish beetles with spotted backs, often brightly colored: both larvae and adults feed on insect pests and their eggs: also **ladybird, lady beetle.**

Lady chapel, a chapel, as in a cathedral or parish church, dedicated to the Virgin Mary: it is usually built east of the high altar.

Lady Day, the church festival on March 25 commemorating the angel Gabriel's announcement to Mary that she was to give birth to Jesus; Annunciation Day: in England it is now the spring quarter day; originally, the term was applied to any of various days celebrated in honor of the Virgin Mary.

la·dy·fin·ger (lā'di-fiŋ'gẽr), *n.* a cooky made of sponge-cake dough and shaped somewhat like a finger: also **lady's-finger.**

lady in waiting, a woman attending, or waiting upon, a queen or princess.

la·dy-kill·er (lā'di-kil'ẽr), *n.* [Slang], a man to whom women are supposed to be irresistibly attracted.

la·dy·kin (lā'di-kin), *n.* [*lady* + *-kin*], a little lady.

la·dy·like (lā'di-līk'), *adj.* like, characteristic of, or suitable for a lady; refined; well-bred.—***SYN.*** see **female.**

la·dy·love (lā'di-luv'), *n.* a sweetheart.

Lady of the Lake, in *Arthurian legend,* Vivian, mistress of Merlin: she lived in a castle surrounded by a lake.

la·dy's-fin·ger (lā'diz-fiŋ'gẽr), *n.* a ladyfinger.

la·dy·ship (lā'di-ship'), *n.* [see -SHIP], 1. the rank or position of a lady. 2. [often L-], the form used in speaking to or of a woman having the title of *Lady:* always preceded by *your* or *her.* Abbreviated **Lp.**

la·dy-slip·per (lā'di-slip'ẽr), *n.* a lady's-slipper.

lady's (or **ladies'**) **man,** a man very fond of the company of women and very attentive and gallant to them.

la·dy's-slip·per (lā'diz-slip'ẽr), *n.* any of certain wild orchids whose flowers somewhat resemble a slipper.

la·dy's-smock (lā'diz-smok'), *n.* the cuckooflower, a variety of cress: also **lady smock.**

la·dy's-trac·es (lā'diz-trās'iz), *n.* lady's-tresses.

la·dy's-tress·es (lā'diz-tres'iz), *n.* any of a group of native orchids with small, white flowers arranged spirally on spikes.

La·er·tes (lā-ũr'tēz, li-ũr'tēz), *n.* [L.; Gr. *Laertēs*], 1. in *Greek legend,* the father of Odysseus. 2. in Shakespeare's *Hamlet,* the brother of Ophelia.

lae·vo- (lē'vō, lē'və), levo-.

La Farge, John (lə färzh', lə färj'), 1835–1910; Ameri-

can painter, writer, and worker in stained glass.
La·fa·yette (laf′i-yet′), *n.* 1. a city in western Indiana: pop., 42,000. 2. a city in south central Louisiana: pop., 40,000.
La·fa·yette, Marquis **de** (də lä′fi-yet′, laf′i-yet′; Fr. là′fà′yet′), (*Marie Joseph Paul Yves Roch Gilbert du Motier*), 1757–1834; French statesman and general; served as volunteer in the Continental army in the American Revolution.
La Fol·lette, Robert Marion (lə fol′it), 1855–1925; American statesman and Progressive political leader; United States senator (1906–1925).
La Fon·taine, Jean de (zhän də là′fōn′ten′; Eng. lə fon-tān′), 1621–1695; French poet and fabulist.
lag (lag), *v.i.* [LAGGED (lagd), LAGGING], [prob. specialized form of *lack, v.t.*, with variant final consonant; cf. MDan. *lakke*, to go slowly (of same origin)], 1. to fall behind; move slowly; loiter; linger. 2. in *billiards*, to strike the cue ball with the cue so that it rebounds from the end rail and returns toward the head rail: done to decide the order of play, the winner being the player whose stroke brings the ball nearest to the head rail. 3. in *marbles*, to toss one's shooting marble, or taw, toward a line marked on the ground (*lag line*) in order to decide the order of play. *n.* 1. a falling behind or being retarded in motion, development, etc. 2. the amount of such falling behind. 3. in *billiards & marbles*, a lagging. 4. in *electricity*, the delay in the phase of current peak behind the corresponding voltage peak in an alternating-current circuit. 5. in *physiology*, the time interval between a stimulus and the response.
lag (lag), *n.* [prob. < Anglo-N.; cf. ON. *lögg*, rim of a tub, Sw. *lagg*, barrel stave; IE. base **leu-*, to cut off, as also in L. *luere*, to cleanse, purge, *solvere* (**soluere*), to loosen (cf. SOLVE, SOLUTION)], 1. a barrel stave. 2. any of the narrow strips of insulating material used for covering boilers, cylinders, etc. *v.t.* [LAGGED (lagd), LAGGING], to cover with lags.
lag (lag), *v.t.* [LAGGED (lagd), LAGGING], [? < prec. *lag* via thieves' slang], [Slang], 1. to send to penal servitude or transport as a criminal. 2. to arrest. *n.* [Slang], 1. a person transported or sentenced to penal servitude; convict. 2. a term of transportation or penal servitude.
lag·an (lag′ən), *n.* [ML. & OFr. *lagan;* prob. < base of ON. *leggja*, to lie, lag; cf. LAW], in *maritime law*, goods cast overboard, as in a storm, but with a buoy attached to identify the owner: also **ligan, lagend.**
lag bolt, a bolt with a square head.
Lag b'O·mer (läg′ bō′mẽr), [Heb. *lag b'ōmer*, 33d (day) of the omer (the count of 49 days from the second day of Passover to the first day of Shabuoth)], a Jewish holiday: see **Jewish holidays.**
lag·end (lag′ənd), *n.* lagan.
la·ger (lä′gẽr), *n.* a laager.
la·ger beer (lä′gẽr, lô′gẽr), [G. *lagerbier*, lit., store beer; *lager*, storehouse (cf. LAIR) + *bier*, beer], a beer, originally made in Germany, which is aged for several months after it has been brewed: also **lager.**
La·ger·löf, Sel·ma (sel′mà lä′gẽr-löf′), 1858–1940; Swedish novelist; received Nobel prize in literature, 1909.
lag·gard (lag′ẽrd), *n.* [< *lag* (to loiter) + *-ard*], a slow person, especially one who is always falling behind; loiterer. *adj.* backward; slow; hanging back.
lag·ger (lag′ẽr), *n.* a person or thing that lags.
lag·ging (lag′iŋ), *n.* [< *lag* (barrel stave) + *-ing*], 1. the strips of wood or other nonconducting material with which a boiler, cylinder, wall, etc. is covered. 2. the act of covering with lags. 3. an open frame woodwork to support an arch while it is being built.
la·gniappe, la·gnappe (lan-yap′, lan′yap), *n.* [Creole < Fr. *la*, the + Sp. *ñapa*, lagniappe < Peruv. (Quechuan) *yapa*], [Dial.], a small present given to a customer with a purchase.
lag·o·morph (lag′ə-môrf′), *n.* [< Gr. *lagōs*, hare; + *-morph*], any of a group of rodent mammals characterized by two pairs of upper incisors, one behind the other, as the rabbits, hares, and pikas.
la·goon (lə-gōōn′), *n.* [< Fr. *lagune* & It. *laguna;* L. *lacuna;* see LACUNA], 1. a shallow lake or pond, especially one connected with a larger body of water. 2. the area of water enclosed by a circular coral reef, or atoll. 3. an area of shallow salt water separated from the sea by sand dunes. Also spelled **lagune.**
Lagoon Islands, the Ellice Islands: the former name.
La·gos (lä′gōs, lā′gos), *n.* the capital of Nigeria, on the Gulf of Guinea: pop., 350,000.
La Grange (lə grānj′), a city in western Georgia: pop., 24,000.
La·grange, Jo·seph Lou·is (zhô′zef′ lwē là′gränzh′), 1736–1813; French mathematician and astronomer.
Lag·ting, Lag·thing (läg′tiŋ), *n.* [Norw. *lagthing, lagting; lag*, society, law (cf. LAW) + *t(h)ing*, parliament], the upper house of the Norwegian parliament.
La Guar·di·a, Fi·o·rel·lo Henry (fē′ə-rel′ō lə gwär′di-ə), 1882–1947; American political leader.
la·gune (lə-gōōn′), *n.* a lagoon.
La·hore (lə-hôr′; lä-hōr′), *n.* the capital of West Pakistan: pop., 850,000.
Lai·bach (lī′bäkh), *n.* Ljubljana: the German name.
la·ic (lā′ik), *adj.* [LL. *laicus;* Gr. *laikos* < *laos*, the people], of the laity; secular; lay. *n.* a layman.
la·i·cal (lā′i-k'l), *adj.* laic.
la·i·cize (lā′ə-sīz′), *v.t.* [LAICIZED (-sīzd′), LAICIZING], [*laic* + *-ize*], to cause to be lay (nonclerical); open (an office or position) to laymen; secularize.
laid (lād), past tense and past participle of **lay.**
laid up, 1. *a)* stored away. *b)* dismantled and out of use, as a ship. 2. [Colloq.], so ill or injured as to be confined or disabled.
laid paper, paper having evenly spaced parallel lines watermarked in it.
lain (lān), past participle of **lie** (to recline).
lair (lâr), *n.* [ME. *leir, leyre;* AS. *leger*, lit., lying place, hence bed, couch, etc. < Gmc. base (**leg-*) of *licgan*, to lie (see LIE); akin to MD. *leger*, Eng. *leaguer, lager*, etc.], a bed or resting place, especially of a wild animal; den. *v.i.* to go to, rest in, or have a lair. *v.t.* 1. to place in or provide with a lair. 2. to serve as a lair for.
laird (lârd), *n.* [Scot. form of *lord;* MScot. *lard*], in Scotland, a landowner, especially a wealthy one.
lais·sez-faire (les′ā-fâr′), *adj.* of or based on laissez faire.
lais·sez faire (les′ā fâr′), [Fr., let (people) do (as they please)], noninterference; letting people do as they please; especially, noninterference in matters of economics and business; letting the owners of industry and business fix the rules of competition, the conditions of labor, etc. as they please, without governmental regulation or control: also **laisser faire** (les′ā-fâr′).
la·i·ty (lā′ə-ti), *n.* [*pl.* LAITIES (-tiz)], [< *lay, adj.*], 1. all the people not included among the clergy; laymen collectively. 2. all the people not belonging to any given profession.
La·ius (lā′yəs), *n.* [L.; Gr. *Laios*], in *Greek legend*, a king of Thebes and the father of Oedipus: see **Oedipus.**
lake (lāk), *n.* [ME. *lak, laake*, etc.; merging of AS. *lacu*, a stream, pool, pond (IE. base **leg-*, to drip, trickle, flow slowly; cf. LACK) with OFr. *lac* (L. *lacus*, basin, tank, pond; IE. base **lagu-*, water in a depression, as also in OIr. *loch;* cf. LOCH)], 1. an inland body of water, usually fresh water, formed by glaciers, river drainage, etc., larger than a pool or pond: abbreviated **L., l.** 2. a pool of oil or other liquid. 3. a place where a river widens out greatly.
lake (lāk), *n.* [see LAC (resin)], 1. a dark-red pigment prepared from cochineal. 2. its color. 3. an insoluble coloring compound precipitated from a solution of a dye by adding a metallic salt, which acts as a mordant: used in the application of certain dyes to cloth.
Lake Charles, a city in southwestern Louisiana: pop., 63,000.
Lake District (or **Country**), a section of mountain and lake country in the counties of Cumberland, Westmorland, and Lancashire, England.
lake dweller, an inhabitant of a lake dwelling.
lake dwelling, a dwelling built on wooden piles rising above the surface of a lake; especially, such a structure built in prehistoric times.
lake herring, a variety of cisco of the Great Lakes.
Lake·hurst (lāk′hũrst′), *n.* a town in central New Jersey: pop., 2,800: site of a U.S. Naval Air Station.
Lake·land (lāk′lənd), *n.* a city in central Florida: pop., 41,000.
Lake of the Woods, a lake in southern Canada and Minnesota: area, 1,850 sq. mi.: a summer resort.
Lake poets, the English poets Wordsworth, Coleridge, and Southey, who lived in the Lake District.
Lake Success, a village on Long Island, New York: early site of meetings of the United Nations.
lake trout, any of several varieties of trout and salmon found in lakes; especially, the namaycush of the northern United States, and Canada.
Lake·wood (lāk′wood′), *n.* 1. a city in northeastern Ohio: suburb of Cleveland: pop., 66,000. 2. a city in southwestern California, near Los Angeles: pop., 67,000.
lakh (lak), *n.* a lac (one hundred thousand).
lak·y (lāk′i), *adj.* of or like a lake.
lak·y (lāk′i), *adj.* of the color of the pigment lake; specifically, in *medicine*, designating blood in which the red corpuscles have been partially destroyed.
Lal·lan (lal′ən), *adj.* [Scot.], of the Lowlands of Scotland. *n.* the dialect of the Lowlands.
lal·la·tion (la-lā′shən), *n.* [< pp. of L. *lallare*, to sing a lullaby], the pronunciation of *r* so that it sounds like *l;* lambdacism.
La·lo, É·dou·ard Vic·tor An·toine (ā′dwàr′ vēk′tôr′ än′twàn′ là′lō′), 1823–1892; French composer.
lam (lam), *v.t.* [LAMMED (lamd), LAMMING], [? < ON.

lemja, to thrash, beat, flog, lit., to lame; see LAME], [Slang], to beat; thrash; flog.

lam (lam), *n.* [? < prec. *lam;* cf. slang BEAT IT], [Slang], headlong flight, usually to escape punishment for a crime. *v.i.* [LAMMED (lamd), LAMMING], [Slang], to flee; escape.

on the lam, [Slang], in headlong flight.

take it on the lam, [Slang], to make a getaway; escape.

Lam., Lamentations.

la·ma (lä′mə), *n.* [Tibetan *blama*, a chief, high priest], a Buddhist priest or monk in Tibet, Mongolia, and the extreme western part of China: cf. **Dalai Lama.**

La·ma·ism (lä′mə-iz′m), *n.* the religious system of the lamas, a form of Buddhism characterized by elaborate ritual and strong hierarchal organization.

La·ma·is·tic (lä′mə-is′tik), *adj.* of Lamaism or its followers.

La·marck, Chevalier **de** (də là′màrk′; Eng. lə-märk′), (*Jean Baptiste Pierre Antoine de Monet*), 1744–1829; French naturalist: see **Lamarckism.**

La·marck·i·an (lə-mär′ki-ən), *adj.* of Lamarck or Lamarckism. *n.* an adherent of Lamarckism.

La·marck·ism (lə-märk′iz′m), *n.* the theory of organic evolution advanced by Lamarck; theory that acquired characteristics can be inherited: see **acquired characteristic.**

La·mar·tine, Al·phonse Ma·rie Lou·is de Prat de (àl′fōns′ mà′rē′ lwē də prà′ də là′màr′tēn′), 1790–1869; French poet.

la·ma·ser·y (lä′mə-ser′i), *n.* [*pl.* LAMASERIES (-iz)], [Fr. *lamaserie*], a monastery of lamas.

lamb (lam), *n.* [ME. *lam(b);* AS. *lamb;* akin to G. *lamm* (OHG. *lamb*); IE. **l-on-bho-s*, var. of **el-n̥-bho-s* < base **el-*, horned animal, seen also in *elk*, *eland*], 1. a young sheep. 2. the flesh of a young sheep, used as food. 3. lambskin. 4. a gentle or innocent person, particularly a child. 5. a person easily tricked or outwitted, as an inexperienced speculator. *v.i.* to give birth: said of a ewe.

like a lamb, 1. with gentleness or mildness; timidly. 2. innocent and easily tricked.

the Lamb, Jesus.

Lamb, Charles (lam), 1775–1834; English essayist, poet, and critic; pen name, *Elia*.

Lamb, Mary Ann, 1764–1847; sister of *Charles;* co-author with him of *Tales from Shakespeare*.

lam·bast (lam-bast′), *v.t.* [Dial.], to lambaste.

lam·baste (lam-bāst′), *v.t.* [LAMBASTED (-id), LAMBASTING], [*lam* (to beat) + *baste*], [Slang], 1. to beat soundly; thrash. 2. to scold or denounce severely.

lamb·da (lam′də), *n.* [Gr. < Phoen.; cf. Heb. *lāmedh*], the eleventh letter of the Greek alphabet (Λ, λ), corresponding to English *L*, *l:* see **alphabet**, table.

lamb·da·cism (lam′də-siz′m), *n.* [LL. *lambdacismus;* Gr. *lambdakismos* < *lambdakizein*, to pronounce *l* imperfectly < *lambda*, lambda], lallation.

lamb·doid (lam′doid), *adj.* [Gr. *lambdoeidēs;* see LAMBDA & -OID], shaped like the Greek lambda (Λ); specifically, in *anatomy*, designating the suture that connects the occipital and the parietal bones of the skull.

lamb·doi·dal (lam-doi′d'l), *adj.* lambdoid.

lam·ben·cy (lam′bən-si), *n.* 1. the fact, quality, or state of being lambent. 2. [*pl.* LAMBENCIES (-siz)], something lambent.

lam·bent (lam′bənt), *adj.* [L. *lambens*, ppr. of *lambere*, to lick, lap], 1. playing lightly over a surface without burning it; flickering: said of a flame, etc. 2. giving off a soft radiance. 3. playing lightly and gracefully over a subject: said of wit, humor, etc.

Lam·bert (lam′bẽrt), [Fr.; G. *Lambert, Lambrecht;* OHG. *Lambreht, Landberht* < *lant*, land + *beraht*, bright; hence, lit., brightness (of the) country, or ? illustrious with land (possessions)], a masculine name.

lam·bert (lam′bẽrt), *n.* [after Johann Heinrich *Lambert* (1728–1777), G. physicist, astronomer, and mathematician], the C.G.S. unit of brightness, equal to the brightness of a perfectly diffusing surface that radiates or reflects light at the rate of one lumen per square centimeter.

Lam·beth (lam′bəth), *n.* a borough of London: pop., 296,000.

Lambeth Palace, the official London residence of the archbishops of Canterbury since 1197.

lamb·kin (lam′kin), *n.* a little lamb: sometimes applied to a child or young person as a term of affection.

lamb·like (lam′līk′), *adj.* like, or having qualities attributed to, a lamb; gentle, meek, innocent, etc.

Lamb of God, Jesus: so called by analogy with the paschal lamb: John 1:29,36.

lam·bre·quin (lam′bẽr-kin, lam′brə-kin), *n.* [Fr.; D. *lamperkin; lamper*, a veil + *-kin*, -kin], a drapery hanging from a shelf or covering the upper part of a window or doorway.

lamb·skin (lam′skin′), *n.* 1. the skin of a lamb, especially with the fleece left on it. 2. leather or parchment made from the skin of a lamb.

lamb's wool, 1. the wool of lambs. 2. a cloth made from this.

lame (lām), *adj.* [ME. *lam, lame;* AS. *lama;* akin to G. *lahm;* IE. base **lem-*, to break; cf. LAM], 1. crippled; disabled; especially, having an injured leg or foot; unable to use a limb or limbs properly. 2. stiff and very painful: as, a *lame* back. 3. poor; halting; unconvincing; ineffectual: as, a *lame* excuse. *v.t. & v.i.* [LAMED (lāmd), LAMING], to make or become lame.

lame (lām; Fr. làm), *n.* [Fr. < L. *lamina, lamna;* see LAMINA], 1. a thin plate, usually of metal. 2. *pl.* the thin, overlapping metal plates in a piece of armor.

la·mé (la-mā′), *n.* [Fr., laminated < *lame*, metal plate or sheet, metallic thread or wire, esp. of gold or silver; see prec. entry], a cloth made of metal threads, especially of gold or silver, sometimes interwoven with silk, wool, or cotton.

la·medh, la·med (lä′mid), *n.* [Heb., lit., a whip, or club], the twelfth letter of the Hebrew alphabet (ל), corresponding to English *L*, *l:* see **alphabet**, table.

lame duck, 1. a disabled, inefficient, ineffectual, or helpless person or thing. 2. a speculator, especially on the stock exchange, who is unable to fulfill his obligations. 3. a member of a legislative body, especially (formerly) of Congress, whose term extends beyond the time of the election at which he was not re-elected.

Lame Duck Amendment, the Twentieth Amendment to the Constitution of the United States: it eliminated the short Congressional session (*Lame Duck Session*) following the November elections.

la·mel·la (lə-mel′ə), *n.* [*pl.* LAMELLAE (-ē), LAMELLAS (-əz)], [L., dim. of *lamina;* see LAMINA], 1. a thin plate, scale, leaf, or layer, as of bone or animal tissue. 2. a platelike part or organ; especially, any of the vertical, platelike parts (*gills*) on the underside of the cap of a mushroom, or agaric.

la·mel·lar (lə-mel′ẽr, lam′ə-lẽr), *adj.* lamellate.

lam·el·late (lam′ə-lāt′, lə-mel′āt), *adj.* [LL. *lamellatus*], having, consisting of, arranged in, or resembling a lamella or lamellae.

lam·el·lat·ed (lam′ə-lā′tid), *adj.* lamellate.

la·mel·li- (lə-mel′i), a combining form meaning *of, like,* or *consisting of a lamella* or *lamellae*, as in *lamelliform, lamellibranch.*

la·mel·li·branch (lə-mel′i-braŋk′), *n.* [< Mod. L. *Lamellibranchia*, name of the class; see LAMELLI- & BRANCHIA], any of a group of mollusks, including the clams, oysters, etc., with platelike gills and compressed bodies enclosed in bivalve shells.

la·mel·li·bran·chi·ate (lə-mel′i-braŋ′ki-āt′, lə-mel′i-braŋ′ki-it), *adj.* [Mod. L. *lamellibranchiatus*], of the lamellibranchs. *n.* a lamellibranch.

la·mel·li·corn (lə-mel′i-kôrn′), *adj.* [Mod. L. *lamellicornis* < *lamelli-* + L. *cornu*, a horn], 1. ending in flattened plates: said of the antennae of some beetles. 2. having such antennae: said of a large group of beetles, including the cockchafers and scarabs. *n.* a lamellicorn beetle.

la·mel·li·form (lə-mel′i-fôrm′), *adj.* having the form of a lamella; platelike or scalelike.

la·mel·li·ros·tral (lə-mel′i-ros′trəl), *adj.* [< Mod. L. *lamellirostris;* see LAMELLI- & ROSTRAL], of a group of water birds, as ducks, geese, and swans, with fringes of lamellae on each side of the tongue and bill.

la·mel·li·ros·trate (lə-mel′i-ros′trāt), *adj.* lamellirostral.

la·mel·lose (lə-mel′ōs, lam′ə-lōs′), *adj.* lamellate.

la·ment (lə-ment′), *v.i.* [Fr. *lamenter;* L. *lamentari* < *lamentum*, a mourning, wailing], to feel or express deep sorrow; mourn; grieve. *v.t.* 1. to feel or express deep sorrow for; mourn or grieve for. 2. to regret deeply. *n.* 1. an outward expression of sorrow; lamentation; wail. 2. a literary or musical composition, as an elegy or dirge, mourning some loss or calamity.

lam·en·ta·ble (lam′ən-tə-b'l), *adj.* [ME.; L. *lamentabilis*], 1. to be lamented; grievous; deplorable; distressing. 2. expressing sorrow; mournful. 3. of poor quality; wretched: as, a *lamentable* piece of acting.

lam·en·ta·bly (lam′ən-tə-bli), *adv.* in a lamentable manner; so as to be lamentable.

lam·en·ta·tion (lam′ən-tā′shən), *n.* a lamenting; outward expression of grief; wailing.

Lamentations, a book of the Old Testament attributed to Jeremiah: abbreviated **Lam.**

la·ment·ed (lə-men′tid), *adj.* [pp. of *lament*], mourned for: usually said of someone dead.

la·mi·a (lā′mi-ə), *n.* [ME. *lamya;* L. *lamia;* Gr. *lamia;* akin to *lamos*, abyss; basic notion "gaping mouth"], 1. in *Greek & Roman mythology*, one of a class of man-devouring monsters, represented with a woman's head and breasts and a serpent's body, supposed to lure children in order to suck their blood; hence, 2. a vampire; female demon; sorceress.

la·mi·a·ceous (lā′mi-ā′shəs), *adj.* [< Mod. L. *Lamium*, genus of herbs < L. *lamium*, dead nettle < Gr. **lamion* < base of *lamia*, lamia; + *-aceous*], of the mint family of plants, mainly aromatic herbs and shrubs, including mint, rosemary, and bergamot.

lam·i·na (lam′ə-nə), *n.* [*pl.* LAMINAE (-nē′), LAMINAS (-nəz)], [L., thin piece of metal or wood; ? < IE. **(s)tlamen*, a spreading out < base **stela-*, to spread], 1. a thin flake, scale, or layer, as of metal, animal tissue, etc. 2. the flat, expanded part of a leaf; blade, as distinguished from the stem.

lam·i·na·ble (lam′ə-nə-b'l), *adj.* that can be formed or pressed into a lamina or separated into laminae.

lam·i·nal (lam′ə-n'l), *adj.* laminate.

lam·i·nar (lam′ə-nẽr), *adj.* laminate.

lam·i·na·ri·a·ceous (lam′ə-nâr′i-ā′shəs), *adj.* [< Mod. L. *Laminaria*, family of brown algae (< L. *lamina;* see LAMINA); + *-aceous*], of a group of brown algae containing many giant kelps and seaweeds.

lam·i·nate (lam′ə-nāt′; *for adj., usually* lam′ə-nit), *v.t.* [LAMINATED (-id), LAMINATING], [< Mod. L. *laminatus* < L. *lamina;* see LAMINA], 1. to form or press into a thin sheet or layer. 2. to separate into thin sheets or layers. 3. to cover with thin layers. 4. to make by building up in layers, as plywood. *v.i.* to split into thin layers. *adj.* laminated; composed of or arranged in thin sheets or layers.

lam·i·na·tion (lam′ə-nā′shən), *n.* 1. a laminating or being laminated. 2. a laminated structure; something built up in layers. 3. a lamina; thin layer; ply.

lam·i·ni·tis (lam′ə-nī′tis), *n.* [Mod. L.; see -ITIS], an inflammation of laminae, especially in a horse's hoof.

lam·i·nose (lam′ə-nōs′), *adj.* laminate.

lam·i·nous (lam′ə-nəs), *adj.* laminate.

Lam·mas (lam′əs), *n.* [ME. *lammasse;* AS. *hlammæsse*, for *hlafmæsse*, lit., loaf mass, bread feast; *hlaf*, loaf + *mæsse*, mass, festival], 1. a harvest festival formerly held in England on the first day of August, when bread baked from the first crop of wheat was consecrated at Mass; hence, 2. a Roman Catholic festival (also observed on August 1) to commemorate St. Peter's deliverance from prison.

Lam·mas·tide (lam′əs-tīd′), *n.* the season or period of Lammas.

lam·mer·gei·er, lam·mer·gey·er (lam′ẽr-gī′ẽr), *n.* [G. *lämmergeier; lämmer*, pl. of *lamm*, lamb + *geier*, vulture], a large, fierce European and Asiatic bird of the vulture family, with grayish-black plumage streaked with white: also called *bearded vulture*.

lam·mer·geir (lam′ẽr-gîr′), *n.* a lammergeier.

lamp (lamp), *n.* [ME. & OFr. *lampe;* L. *lampas;* Gr. *lampas* < *lampein*, to shine], 1. a container with a wick for burning oil, alcohol, etc. to produce light or heat: the wick is often enclosed in a glass tube, or chimney, to protect the flame. 2. any device for producing light or therapeutic rays, as a gas jet, electric light, or sun-ray lamp. 3. a source of knowledge or wisdom. 4. [Rare or Poetic], the sun, moon, a star, etc. 5. *pl.* [Slang], the eyes. *v.t.* [Slang], to look at.

lam·pas (lam′pəs), *n.* [Fr.; OFr. *lampas*, throat; ? akin to *lamper*, to guzzle (nasalized form of *laper*, to lap)], an inflammatory disease of horses, in which the roof of the mouth becomes swollen: also **lampers.**

lam·pas (lam′pəs), *n.* [Fr.], an ornamentally designed cloth; especially, a silk cloth like damask.

lamp·black (lamp′blak′), *n.* [*lamp* + *black*], fine soot produced by the incomplete combustion of tars, oils, and other forms of carbon: used as a pigment.

Lam·pe·du·sa (läm′pe-dōō′zä), *n.* an Italian island in the Mediterranean, between Malta and Tunisia.

lam·per eel (lam′pẽr), [dial. *lamper*, var. of *lamprey*], a lamprey.

lam·pers (lam′pẽrz), *n.* lampas (the disease).

lam·pi·on (lam′pi-ən), *n.* [Fr.; It. *lampione* < *lampa*, a lamp; L. *lampas;* see LAMP], a small oil lamp, usually with a colored glass chimney, for decorative outdoor illumination.

lamp·light (lamp′līt′), *n.* light given off by a lamp.

lamp·light·er (lamp′līt′ẽr), *n.* 1. a person whose work is lighting and extinguishing gas street lamps. 2. a roll of paper, wood splinter, etc. used to light lamps.

lam·poon (lam-pōōn′), *n.* [Fr. *lampon* < *lampons*, let us drink (refrain in a drinking song) < *lamper*, to drink; cf. LAMPAS (disease)], a piece of strongly satirical writing, usually attacking or ridiculing someone. *v.t.* to attack or ridicule by means of a lampoon. —*SYN.* see **caricature.**

lam·poon·er (lam-pōōn′ẽr), *n.* a lampoonist.

lam·poon·er·y (lam-pōōn′ẽr-i), *n.* 1. the writing of lampoons. 2. the satirical quality of lampoons.

lam·poon·ist (lam-pōōn′ist), *n.* a writer of lampoons.

lamp·post (lamp′pōst′), *n.* a post supporting a street lamp.

lam·prey (lam′pri), *n.* [*pl.* LAMPREYS (-priz)], [ME. & OFr. *lampreie;* ML. *lampreda, lampetra* < L. *lambere*, to lick + *petra*, a rock: said to be so called from their habit of clinging to rocks with their mouths], any of a group of eellike water animals with a funnel-shaped, jawless, sucking mouth: also called *lamper eel.*

La·na·i (lä-nä′ē), *n.* one of the Hawaiian Islands, west of Maui: area, 141 sq. mi.; pop., 2,100: see **Hawaiian Islands,** map.

‡**la·na·i** (lä-nä′ē), *n.* [Haw.], in Hawaii, a porch.

Lan·ark (lan′ẽrk), *n.* 1. Lanarkshire. 2. the county seat of Lanarkshire: pop., 6,000.

Lan·ark·shire (lan′ẽrk-shir′), *n.* a county of south central Scotland: pop., 1,628,000; county seat, Lanark.

la·nate (lā′nāt), *adj.* [L. *lanatus*, woolly < *lana*, wool], having a woolly or hairy covering: said especially of the leaves of certain plants.

Lan·ca·shire (laŋ′kə-shir′), *n.* a county on the northwestern coast of England: pop., 5,118,000; county seat, Lancaster.

Lan·cas·ter (laŋ′kə-stẽr; *also, for 3 & 4,* lan′kas′tẽr), *n.* 1. the ruling family of England (1399–1461): founded by Henry IV. 2. seaport and county seat of Lancashire, England: pop., 49,000. 3. a city in southeastern Pennsylvania: pop., 61,000. 4. a city in southern Ohio: pop., 30,000.

Lan·cas·tri·an (laŋ-kas′tri-ən), *adj.* 1. of the English royal house of Lancaster. 2. from Lancaster or Lancashire. *n.* 1. a member or follower of the house of Lancaster, especially in the Wars of the Roses. 2. a native or inhabitant of Lancaster or Lancashire.

lance (lans, läns), *n.* [ME. *launce, lance;* OFr.; L. *lancea*, light spear, lance, orig., Spanish lance < Celt. cognate of Eng. *fling* (IE. base **plāq-*, to hit, strike; cf. FLAW, a squall)], 1. a thrusting weapon consisting of a long wooden shaft with a sharp metal spearhead. 2. a soldier, especially a cavalry soldier, armed with a lance; lancer. 3. any sharp instrument resembling a lance, as a fish spear. 4. a lancet. *v.t.* [LANCED (lanst, länst), LANCING], 1. to attack or pierce with a lance. 2. to cut open with a lancet.

lance (lans, läns), *n.* a launce.

lance corporal, [after obs. *lance-pesade;* OFr. *lance-pessade;* It. *lancia spezzata*, lit., broken lance], in the *British Army*, a private acting temporarily as a corporal, without the extra pay.

lance·let (lans′lit, läns′lit), *n.* [*lance* + *-let*], any of a group of small, fishlike sea animals, closely related to the vertebrates: also called *amphioxus.*

Lan·ce·lot (lan′sə-lot′, län′sə-lot′, län′sə-lət), *n.* [Fr., double dim. < *Lance* < OHG. *Lanzo* < *lant*, land], in *Arthurian legend*, the bravest and most celebrated of the Knights of the Round Table: he was Guinevere's lover.

lan·ce·o·late (lan′si-ə-lit, lan′si-ə-lāt′), *adj.* [LL. *lanceolatus* < *lanceola*, dim.; see LANCE (spear)], narrow and tapering like the head of a lance: said of certain leaves: see **leaf,** illus.

lanc·er (lan′sẽr, län′sẽr), *n.* [Fr. *lancier*], a soldier, especially a cavalry soldier, armed with a lance.

lanc·ers (lan′sẽrz, län′sẽrz), *n.pl.* [construed as sing.], [< *lancer*], 1. a form of 19th-century square dance, or quadrille. 2. music for this. Also spelled **lanciers.**

lance sergeant, in the *British Army*, a corporal acting temporarily as a sergeant, without the extra pay.

lan·cet (lan′sit, län′sit), *n.* [ME. *lawnsetys, pl.;* OFr. *lancette*, dim. of *lance;* see LANCE (spear)], 1. a small, pointed surgical knife, usually two-edged. 2. a lancet arch or window.

lancet arch, a narrow, sharply pointed arch.

lan·cet·ed (lan′sə-tid, län′sə-tid), *adj.* having lancet arches or windows.

lancet window, a narrow, sharply pointed window without tracery, set in a lancet arch.

lance·wood (lans′wood′, läns′wood′), *n.* 1. a tough, elastic wood used for lance shafts, fishing rods, etc. 2. any of various tropical American trees yielding this wood.

LANCET ARCH

Lan·chow (län′chō′), *n.* the capital of Kansu province, China, on the Yellow River: pop., 204,000.

lan·ciers (lan′sẽrz, län′sẽrz), *n.pl.* [construed as sing.], lancers.

lan·ci·form (lan′sə-fôrm′), *adj.* [< *lance* + *-form*], narrow and pointed, like the head of a lance.

lan·ci·nate (lan′sə-nāt′), *v.t.* [LANCINATED (-id), LANCINATING], [< L. *lancinatus*, pp. of *lancinare*, to tear < *lacer*, lacerated], to pierce or tear: especially figuratively, as, he was *lancinated* with pain.

lan·ci·na·tion (lan′sə-nā′shən), *n.* [< *lancinate* + *-ion*], a piercing pain.

land (land), *n.* [ME.; AS.; akin to G. *land;* IE. base **lendh-*, unoccupied land, heath, steppe, seen also in Bret. *lann*, heath (whence Fr. *lande*, moor), W. *llan*, enclosure, yard, etc.], 1. the solid part of the earth's surface: distinguished from *sea.* 2. a specific part of the earth's surface: as, the *land* of the Seminoles; hence, 3. *a*) a country, region, etc. *b*) the inhabitants of such an area; nation's people. 4. ground or soil in terms of its quality, location, etc.: as, rich *land*,

high *land*. 5. ground considered as property; estate: as, *land* is a good investment. 6. *pl.* specific holdings in land. 7. rural regions as distinguished from urban regions: as, let us go back to the *land*. 8. that part of a grooved surface which is not indented, as any of the ridges between the grooves in the bore of a rifle. 9. the Lord: a euphemism, as in the phrase *for land's sake!* 10. in *economics*, natural resources: abbreviated L., l. *v.t.* [*landen, londen* < the *n.*; replacing AS. *lendan* < **land-jan*], 1. to put, or cause to go, on shore from a ship. 2. to bring into: as, this train will *land* you in Denver tomorrow morning. 3. to cause to enter or become confined in a particular place: as, this fight *landed* them both in jail. 4. to set (an aircraft) down on land or water. 5. to draw successfully onto land or into a boat; catch: as, he *lands* the fish which she hooks. 6. [Colloq.], to get, win, or secure: as, he *landed* a job. 7. [Colloq.], to deliver (a blow). *v.i.* 1. to leave a ship and go on shore; disembark. 2. to come to a port or to shore: said of a ship. 3. to arrive at a specified place; end up. 4. to alight or come to rest, as after a flight, jump, or fall.
make land, to see or reach the shore.

-land (land, lənd), a combining form meaning: 1. *a kind* or *quality of land*, as in *grassland, highland*. 2. *a particular territory* or *country*, as in *England*. 3. figuratively, *a place having a* (specified) *character* or *quality*, as in *cloudland*.

lan·dau (lan′dô, lan′dou), *n.* [< *Landau*, German town where made], 1. a four-wheeled covered carriage with the top in two sections, either of which can be lowered independently. 2. a former style of automobile with a somewhat similar top.

lan·dau·let, lan·dau·lette (lan′dô-let′), *n.* 1. a small landau. 2. a former style of small automobile, with a top whose back could be folded down.

land bank, a bank that finances transactions in real estate.

land breeze, a breeze blowing seaward from the land.

land·ed (lan′did), *adj.* 1. owning land: as, *landed* gentry. 2. consisting of, or having the nature of, land or real estate: as, a *landed* estate.

land·fall (land′fôl′), *n.* [*land* + *fall* (a happening)], 1. a sighting of land from a ship at sea. 2. the land sighted. 3. a landing by ship or airplane.

land-grab·ber (land′grab′ẽr), *n.* a person who gets possession of land unfairly or fraudulently.

land-grant (land′grant′, land′gränt′), *adj.* designating any of a number of colleges and universities originally given federal land on condition that they offer instruction in agriculture and the mechanical arts: they are now supported by the individual States with supplementary funds from the Federal government.

land grant, an appropriation of public land by the government for a State college, railroad, etc.

land·grave (land′grāv′), *n.* [G. *landgraf; land*, land + *graf*, a count], 1. in medieval Germany, a count having jurisdiction over a specified territory. 2. later, the title of any of certain German princes.

land·gra·vi·ate (land-grā′vi-it), *n.* the rank, territory, or authority of a landgrave or landgravine.

land·gra·vine (land′grə-vēn′), *n.* [G. *landgräfin* or D. *landgravin*], 1. the wife of a landgrave. 2. a woman having the rank of a landgrave in her own right.

land·hold·er (land′hōl′dẽr), *n.* an owner or occupant of land.

land·hold·ing (land′hōl′diŋ), *adj.* owning or occupying land. *n.* the act of owning or occupying land.

land·ing (lan′diŋ), *n.* [ME. *londyng;* see LAND & -ING], 1. the act of coming to shore or of going or putting ashore. 2. the place where a ship is unloaded or loaded. 3. a platform at the end of a flight of stairs. 4. the act of alighting, or coming to the ground, as after a flight, jump, or fall.

landing field, a field provided with a smooth surface to enable airplanes to land and take off easily.

landing gear, the undercarriage of an aircraft, including wheels, pontoons, etc., for support on land or water: see **airplane**, illus.

landing net, a small, baglike net attached to a long handle, for taking a hooked fish from the water.

landing stage, a pier or platform, often a floating platform, on which persons and goods can be unloaded from a ship.

Lan·dis, Ken·e·saw Moun·tain (ken′ə-sô′ moun′t'n lan′dis), 1866–1944; American jurist; commissioner of professional baseball (1920–1944).

land·la·dy (land′lā′di), *n.* [*pl.* LANDLADIES (-diz)], [orig. parallel with *landlord*], 1. a woman who leases land, houses, etc. to others. 2. a woman who keeps a rooming house, inn, etc.

‡Länd·ler (lent′lẽr), *n.* [G. *ländler* < dial. *Landl*, upper Austria, dim. < *land*, land], 1. an Austrian country dance in slow rhythm and triple time. 2. music for this.

land·less (land′lis), *adj.* not owning land.

land·locked (land′lokt′), *adj.* 1. entirely or almost entirely surrounded by land, as a bay or a country. 2. cut off from the sea and confined to fresh water by a geographical barrier: said of certain fishes: as, the *landlocked* salmon.

land·lop·er (land′lō′pẽr), *n.* [D. *landlooper* < *land*, land + *loopen*, to run (akin to *leap*)], a person who wanders about the country; vagabond.

land·lord (land′lôrd′), *n.* [ME. *londelorde;* AS. *landhlaford;* see LAND & LORD; cf. LANDLADY], 1. a man who leases land, houses, etc. to others. 2. a man who keeps a rooming house, inn, etc.

land·lord·ism (land′lôrd′iz′m), *n.* the principles and practices of landlords collectively; especially, the economic system under which land is privately owned and rented to tenants.

land·loup·er (land′loup′ẽr, land′lo͞op′ẽr), *n.* [Dial. or Archaic], a landloper.

land·lub·ber (land′lub′ẽr), *n.* [*land* + *lubber*], a person who has had little experience at sea, and is therefore awkward aboard a ship: a sailor's term of contempt.

land·man (land′mən), *n.* [*pl.* LANDMEN (-mən)], a man who lives, works, or serves on land.

land·mark (land′märk′), *n.* 1. any fixed object used to mark the boundary of a piece of land. 2. any prominent feature of the landscape, as a tree or house, marking a particular locality. 3. an event considered as a high point or turning point of a period.

land measure, 1. a system of square measure for finding the area of a piece of land. 2. any unit of measurement in such a system, as an acre, hectare, etc.

land mine, an explosive charge hidden under the surface of the ground and discharged by the pressure of troops or vehicles upon it.

Land of Beulah, see **Beulah**.

land office, a government office that handles and records the sales and transfers of public lands.

land-of·fice business (land′ôf′is), [with reference to Western U. S. land offices in the 19th c.], [Colloq.], a booming business.

Land of Nod (nod), 1. in the *Bible*, the country to which Cain journeyed after slaying Abel: Gen. 4:16. 2. sleep.

Land of Promise, 1. in the *Bible*, Canaan, promised by God to Abraham and his descendants: Gen. 15:18, 17:8; hence, 2. [l- p-], a place where one expects to improve his lot. Also **Promised Land**.

Land of the Midnight Sun, Norway.

Land of the Rising Sun, Japan.

Lan·dor, Walter Sav·age (sav′ij lan′dẽr, lan′dôr), 1775–1864; English writer.

land·own·er (land′ōn′ẽr), *n.* a person who owns land.

land·own·er·ship (land′ōn′ẽr-ship′), *n.* [see -SHIP], the state of being a landowner.

land·own·ing (land′ōn′iŋ), *adj.* 1. owning land. 2. of landowners or landownership. *n.* landownership.

land patent, a legal document granting ownership of a piece of public land.

land plaster, finely ground gypsum, used as a fertilizer.

land-poor (land′poor′), *adj.* owning land, often much land, but poor because of high taxes, etc.

land power, 1. military strength on land. 2. a nation having great military strength on land.

land·scape (land′skāp′), *n.* [17th-c. art borrowing (cf. EASEL, LAY FIGURE) < D. *landschap; land*, land + *-schap*, -ship; earlier also *landskip;* akin to AS. *landscipe* (*landsceap*), G. *landschaft*], 1. a picture representing a section of natural, inland scenery, as of prairie, woodland, mountains, etc. 2. the branch of painting, photography, etc. dealing with such pictures. 3. an expanse of natural scenery seen by the eye in one view. *v.t.* [LANDSCAPED (-skāpt′), LANDSCAPING], to change the natural features of (a plot of ground) so as to make it more attractive, as by adding lawns, trees, bushes, etc. *v.i.* to work as a landscape architect or gardener.

landscape architect, a person skilled in landscape architecture.

landscape architecture, the art of changing the natural scenery of a place so as to produce the most attractive or desirable effect.

landscape gardener, a person skilled in landscape gardening.

landscape gardening, the art or work of placing or arranging lawns, trees, bushes, etc. on a plot of ground to make it more attractive.

land·scap·ist (land′skāp′ist), *n.* a painter of landscapes.

Land·seer, Sir **Edwin Henry** (land′sêr), 1802–1873; English painter of animal pictures.

Land's End, a cape at the southwesternmost point of England.

land·skip (land′skip), *n.* [Obs.], landscape.

land·slide (land′slīd′), *n.* 1. the sliding of a mass of loosened rocks or earth down a hillside or slope. 2. the mass of loosened material sliding down. 3. an overwhelming majority of votes for one candidate or party in an election. 4. any overwhelming victory.

land·slip (land′slip′), *n.* [Chiefly British], a landslide (senses 1 & 2).

lands·man (landz′mən), *n.* [*pl.* LANDSMEN (-mən)], 1. a person who lives on land: distinguished from *seaman*. 2. a new, inexperienced sailor.

Land·stei·ner, Karl (land'stī'nẽr; G. länt'shtīn'ẽr), 1868–1943; American pathologist, immunologist, and bacteriologist, born in Austria; received Nobel prize in physiology, 1930.

Lands·ting, Lands·thing (läns'tiŋ'), ***n.*** [Dan. < *land* (poss. *lands*), land + *thing*, parliament], formerly, the upper house of the Danish Parliament: see **Rigsdag.**

Land·sturm (länt'shtoorm'), ***n.*** [G., lit., land-storm; orig. Swiss G., after Fr. *levée en masse*], 1. in Germany and, later, other countries, a general levy in time of war of men under sixty not already in the armed services or in the reserve, as for home defense. 2. the force so called out or subject to such levy.

‡Land·tag (länt'täkh'), ***n.*** [G.; *land*, land + *tag*, day, day of meeting, hence meeting, council; see DAY; cf. DIET (assembly)], formerly, the legislative assembly of a German state, especially of Prussia.

land·ward (land'wẽrd), ***adv.*** toward the land. ***adj.*** situated or facing toward the land.

land·wards (land'wẽrdz), ***adv.*** landward.

Land·wehr (länt'vâr'), ***n.*** [G.; *land*, country + *wehr*, defense < *wehren*, to defend], in Germany, and later, other countries, the military reserve of trained men.

land wind, a wind blowing seaward from the land.

lane (lān), ***n.*** [ME.; AS. *lanu, lane;* akin to D. *laan;* IE. base **elā-*, to be in motion, go], 1. a narrow way between hedges, walls, buildings, etc.; narrow country road or city street. 2. any narrow way, as an opening in a crowd of people. 3. a path or course designated, for reasons of safety, for ships, aircraft, automobiles, etc. 4. a path or course marked off for each contestant in a race, etc.

Lang, Andrew (laŋ), 1844–1912; Scottish writer.

lang., language.

Langerhans islands (or **islets**), see **islands of Langerhans.**

Lang·land, William (laŋ'lənd), 1332?–1400?; English poet.

‡lang·lauf (läŋ'louf'), ***n.*** [G.; *lang*, long + *lauf*, a course < *laufen*, to run], in *skiing*, a cross-country run.

‡lang·läuf·er (läŋ'loi'fẽr), ***n.*** [G.; see LANGLAUF], in *skiing*, a participant in a cross-country run.

Lang·ley, Samuel Pier·pont (pẽr'pont laŋ'li), 1834–1906; American physicist, astronomer, and inventor; pioneer in airplane construction.

Lang·muir, Irving (laŋ'myoor), 1881–1957; U.S. chemist; received Nobel prize in chemistry, 1932.

lan·grage, lan·gridge (laŋ'grij), ***n.*** [? for earlier *langrel*, after *cartridge;* cf. Scot. dial. *langrel*, lanky], a type of irregularly shaped shot formerly used in naval battles to damage the enemy's rigging and sails.

lan·grel (laŋ'grəl), ***n.*** langrage.

lang·syne (laŋ'sīn'; *occas.* laŋ'zīn'), ***adv.*** [Scot.; *lang*, long + *syne*, since], [Scot.], long since; long ago. ***n.*** [Scot.], the long ago, bygone days. Also **lang syne.**

Lang·try, Lily (laŋ'tri), (*Mrs. Edward Langtry, Lady Hugo Gerald de Bathe*), 1852–1929; English actress.

lan·guage (laŋ'gwij), ***n.*** [ME. & OFr. *langage* < *langue*, tongue < L. *lingua*, tongue, language; altered (by association with *lingere*, to lick) < OL. *dingua* < IE. **dn̥ghwa*, seen also in AS. *tunge;* cf. TONGUE], 1. *a)* the expression or communication of thoughts and feelings by means of vocal sounds, and combinations of such sounds, to which meaning is attributed; human speech. *b)* the ability to express or communicate by this means. *c)* the vocal sounds so used, or the written symbols for them. 2. any means of expressing or communicating, as gestures, signs, animal sounds, etc. 3. all the vocal sounds, words, and the ways of combining them common to a particular nation, tribe, or other group: as, the English *language*. 4. *a)* the particular form or manner of selecting and combining words characteristic of a person, group, etc.; form, style, or kind of expression in words: as, the *language* of poetry. *b)* the particular words and phrases of a profession, group, etc.: as, the *language* of the army. 5. the study of language in general or of some particular language or languages; linguistics. Abbreviated **lang.**

Langue·doc (läng'dôk'), ***n.*** a former province of southern France, between the Pyrenees and the Loire River: capital, Toulouse.

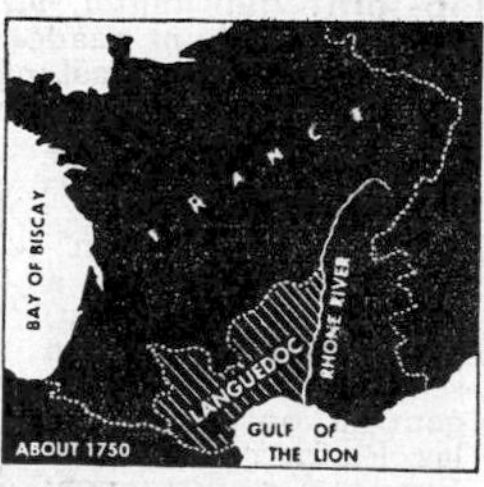

LANGUEDOC

‡langue d'oc (läng'dôk'), [Fr., lit., language of *oc* (Pr. *oc*, yes < L. *hoc*, this thing): from characteristic use of *oc* for affirmation (in contrast to the *langue d'oïl*)], a group of French dialects spoken in southern France in the Middle Ages and surviving in the Provençal language.

‡langue d'o·il (läng'dô'ēl', läng'dô'y'), [Fr., lit., language of *oïl* (OFr. *oïl*, yes < LL. *hoc illi* < L. *hoc*, this + *ille*, that): from characteristic use of *oïl* (Fr. *oui*) for affirmation; cf. prec.], a group of French dialects spoken in most of central and northern France in the Middle Ages: it is the Old French from which modern French is derived.

lan·guet, lan·guette (laŋ'gwet), ***n.*** [ME.; Late OFr., dim. of *langue* < L. *lingua*, tongue], a thing or part resembling the tongue in shape or use.

lan·guid (laŋ'gwid), ***adj.*** [< Fr. or L.; Fr. *languide;* L. *languidus* < *languere*, to be faint or listless], 1. without vigor or vitality; drooping; weak. 2. without interest or spirit; listless; indifferent. 3. sluggish; dull; slow.

lan·guish (laŋ'gwish), ***v.i.*** [ME. *languishen;* OFr. *languir;* L. *languescere* < *languere*, to be weary, languish], 1. to lose vigor or vitality; fail in health; become weak; droop. 2. to live under unfavorable or dispiriting conditions; continue in a state of suffering: as, he *languished* in poverty many years. 3. to become slack or dull; lose intensity. 4. to suffer with longing; pine. 5. to put on an air of sentimental tenderness or wistful melancholy.

lan·guish·ing (laŋ'gwish-iŋ), ***adj.*** [ppr. of *languish*], that languishes; specifically, *a)* becoming weak; drooping. *b)* lingering. *c)* slow; not intense. *d)* pining; longing. *e)* tender; sentimental; wistfully amorous.

lan·guish·ment (laŋ'gwish-mənt), ***n.*** 1. a languishing. 2. the state of being weak or drooping. 3. a languishing look, expression, or feeling.

lan·guor (laŋ'gẽr), ***n.*** [ME. *langour;* OFr. *langueur;* L. *languor* < *languere*, to be weary], 1. a lack of vigor or vitality; weakness. 2. a lack of interest or spirit; listlessness; indifference. 3. tenderness of mood or feeling. 4. a lack of or lull in activity; sluggishness; dullness. 5. heaviness; oppressiveness; stillness: used with reference to the atmosphere. —***SYN.*** see **lethargy.**

lan·guor·ous (laŋ'gẽr-əs), ***adj.*** 1. characterized by or feeling languor; languid. 2. causing or tending to cause languor.

lan·gur (lun-goor'), ***n.*** [Hind. *laṅgūr;* Sans. *lāṅgūlin*, lit., having a tail], any of a large group of monkeys of southeastern Asia, with a very long tail, bushy eyebrows, and a chin tuft.

lan·i- (lan'i), [< L. *lana*, wool], a combining form meaning *wool.*

lan·iard (lan'yẽrd), ***n.*** a lanyard.

la·ni·ar·y (lā'ni-er'i, lan'i-er'i), ***adj.*** [L. *laniarius*, of a butcher < *lanius*, a butcher; of Etruscan origin], adapted for tearing; canine: said of teeth. ***n.*** a canine tooth.

La·nier, Sidney (lə-nêr'), 1842–1881; American poet.

la·nif·er·ous (lə-nif'ẽr-əs), ***adj.*** [L. *lanifer* (< *lana*, wool + *ferre*, to bear); + *-ous*], bearing wool or fine hairs resembling wool; fleecy.

la·nig·er·ous (lə-nij'ẽr-əs), ***adj.*** [L. *laniger* (< *lana*, wool + *gerere*, to bear, carry, wear); + *-ous*], laniferous.

lan·i·tal (lan'i-t'l), ***n.*** [It. *lana* (< L. *lana*), wool + *Italia*, Italy], a synthetic fabric resembling wool, made originally in Italy from casein.

lank (laŋk), ***adj.*** [ME.; AS. *hlanc;* basic sense "flexible"; IE. base **qleng-*, to bend, seen also in G. *lenken*, to bend, OHG. *(h)lanca*, hip], 1. long and slender; lean. 2. straight and flat; not curly: said of hair.

lank·i·ly (laŋ'kə-li), ***adv.*** in a lanky form.

lank·i·ness (laŋ'ki-nis), ***n.*** a lanky quality or state.

lank·y (laŋ'ki), ***adj.*** [LANKIER (-ki-ẽr), LANKIEST (-ki-ist)], [*lank* + *-y*], awkwardly tall and lean or long and slender. —***SYN.*** see **lean.**

lan·ner (lan'ẽr), ***n.*** [Fr. *lanier;* LL. **lanarius* for L. *laniarius;* see LANIARY], a falcon of southern and eastern Europe; especially, the female of this falcon, used in falconry.

lan·ner·et (lan'ẽr-et'), ***n.*** [Fr. *laneret*, dim.], the male of the lanner: it is smaller than the female.

lan·o·lin (lan'ə-lin), ***n.*** [< L. *lana*, wool + *oleum*, oil; + *-in*], a fatty substance obtained from wool and used as a base for ointments, cosmetics, etc.

lan·o·line (lan'ə-lin, lan'ə-lēn'), ***n.*** lanolin.

la·nose (lā'nōs), ***adj.*** [L. *lanosus* < *lana*, wool], woolly.

lans·downe (lanz'doun), ***n.*** [? < *Lansdown*, town in England, or the title Earl of *Lansdowne*], a finely woven silk and wool dress fabric.

Lan·sing (lan'siŋ), ***n.*** the capital of Michigan: pop., 108,000.

Lan·sing, Robert (lan'siŋ), 1864–1928; American statesman and diplomat; secretary of state (1915–1920).

lans·que·net (lans'kə-net'), ***n.*** [Fr.; G. *landsknecht*, foot soldier < *land*, country + *knecht*, servant (see KNIGHT), with Fr. intrusive vowel], 1. a German mercenary foot soldier of the 16th and 17th centuries. 2. a card game of German origin.

lan·ta·na (lan-tā'nə, lan-tä'nə), ***n.*** [Mod. L., viburnum], any of a group of shrubby plants resembling verbena, growing in tropical and subtropical America.

lan·tern (lan′tẽrn), *n.* [ME. & Fr. *lanterne;* L. *lanterna;* Gr. *lamptēr* < *lampein,* to shine], 1. a transparent case for holding a light and protecting it from wind and weather: it usually has a handle on its framework so that it can be carried. 2. the room containing the lamp at the top of a lighthouse. 3. an open structure on the roof of a building or in the upper part of a tower or the like, to admit light and air. 4. a magic lantern.

KEROSENE LANTERN

lantern fly, any of a group of large, brightly colored South American insects having a long head with a hollow part formerly supposed to give off light.
lantern jaw, [from resemblance to the early lantern with long sides of thin, concave horn], 1. a projecting lower jaw. 2. *pl.* long, thin jaws that give the face a lean appearance.
lan·tern-jawed (lan′tẽrn-jôd′), *adj.* [see prec.], having long, thin jaws and sunken cheeks.
lantern pinion, an old type of gearwheel consisting of two circular disks connected by projecting bars.
lantern slide, a photographic slide for projection, as, originally, by a magic lantern.
lantern wheel, a lantern pinion.
lan·tha·nide series (lan′thə-nīd′), [< *lanthanum,* first in the series], the rare-earth metals.
lan·tha·num (lan′thə-nəm), *n.* [Mod. L. < Gr. *lanthanein,* to be concealed], a silvery, lustrous metallic chemical element of the rare-earth group: symbol, La; at. wt., 138.92; at. no., 57.
lant·horn (lan′tẽrn), *n.* [altered < *lantern* after *horn,* material once used for the sides], [Archaic], a lantern.
Lan·tsang (län′tsäŋ′), the Mekong: Chinese name.
la·nu·gi·nose (lə-nōō′ji-nōs′, lə-nū′ji-nōs′), *adj.* lanuginous.
la·nu·gi·nous (lə-nōō′ji-nəs, lə-nū′ji-nəs), *adj.* [L. *lanuginosus* < *lanugo,* down < *lana,* wool], covered with fine, soft hair or down; downy.
la·nu·go (lə-nōō′gō, lə-nū′gō), *n.* [L., down < *lana,* wool], a thick, soft, downy growth; especially, the soft, downy hair covering the human fetus.
lan·yard (lan′yẽrd), *n.* [ME. *lanyer;* Fr. *lanière;* OFr. *lasniere* < *lasne,* noose; altered after *yard* (spar)], 1. a short rope or cord used on board ship for holding or fastening something. 2. a cord used by sailors to hang a knife around the neck. 3. a cord with attached hook, for firing certain types of cannon. Also spelled **laniard.**
La·o (lä′ō), *n.* a member of a Buddhist Siamese (Thai) people living in Laos.
La·oag (lä-wäg′), *n.* a city in northwestern Luzon, in the Philippines: pop., 47,000.
La·oc·o·ön (lā-ok′ə-won′, lā-ok′ō-on′), *n.* [L.; Gr. *Laokoōn*], 1. in *Greek legend,* a priest of Troy who, with his two sons, was destroyed by two huge sea serpents after he had warned the Trojans against the wooden horse. 2. a sculpture in the Vatican, representing Laocoön and his sons in the coils of the serpents.
La·od·i·ce·a (lā′ə-də-sē′ə, lā-od′ə-sē′ə), *n.* the city of Latakia: the ancient name.
La·od·i·ce·an (lā′ə-də-sē′ən, lā-od′ə-sē′ən), *adj.* 1. of Laodicea. 2. indifferent or lukewarm in religion, as the early Christians of that city: Rev. 3:14-16. 3. lacking strong feeling on any subject; indifferent; lukewarm. *n.* 1. a native or inhabitant of Laodicea. 2. a person who is Laodicean.
La·om·e·don (lā-om′ə-don′), *n.* [L.; Gr. *Laomedōn*], in *Greek legend,* father of Priam and founder of Troy.
La·os (lä′ōs), *n.* a kingdom in the northwestern part of the Indochinese peninsula: area, 91,500 sq. mi.; pop., 1,760,000; capital, Vientiane.
Lao-tse (lou′dzu′), *n.* Chinese philosopher and moralist; 604–531 B.C.; founder of Taoism: also spelled **Lao-tzu.**
lap (lap), *n.* [ME. *lappe;* AS. *læppa, lappa,* fold or hanging part of a garment, skin, etc.; akin to G. *lappen;* IE. base **leb-,* etc., to hang down, hang loosely, seen also in L. *labi* (< **lab-*), to fall, sink, *lapsus* (see LAPSE)], 1. the loose lower part of a garment, which may be doubled or folded over; skirt of a coat or gown. 2. the front part of the skirt when held up to form a hollow place in which things can be carried. 3. *a)* the front part from the waist to the knees of a person in a sitting position. *b)* the part of the clothing covering this. 4. anything hollow like a lap: as, the *lap* of a green valley. 5. that in which a person or thing rests or is cared for, sheltered, or coddled. 6. a part extending over another part; overlapping part. 7. *a)* such extension; overlapping. *b)* amount or place of this. 8. a turn or loop, as of a rope around a post. 9. a revolving disk for cutting and polishing glass, gems, etc. 10. one complete circuit of a race track, in a race consisting of more than one. 11. a lapping. *v.t.* [LAPPED (lapt), LAPPING], [ME. *lappen* < the *n.*], 1. to fold (*over* or *on*). 2. to wrap; enfold. 3. to hold in or as in the lap; envelop: as, he was *lapped* in luxury. 4. to place partly upon something else: as, you must *lap* the second board over the first. 5. to lie partly upon: as, the second board *laps* the first. 6. to cut or polish with a lap, as glass or gems. 7. to get a lap ahead of (an opponent) in a race. *v.i.* 1. to be folded: as, rough edges must *lap* under. 2. to lie partly upon something or upon one another; overlap. 3. to project beyond something in space, or extend beyond something in time (with *over*).
in the lap of luxury, surrounded by luxury.
in the lap of the gods, beyond human control or power.
lap (lap), *v.i. & v.t.* [LAPPED (lapt), LAPPING], [ME. *lapen, lappen* (the latter prob. via OFr. < Gmc.); AS. *lapian;* akin to MD. *lapen;* IE. echoic base **lăb-,* to lick loudly, seen also in L. (nasalized) *lambere,* to lick (cf. LAMBENT)], 1. to drink (a liquid) by dipping it up with the tongue in the manner of a dog. 2. to move or strike gently with a light, splashing sound such as a dog makes in lapping: said of waves, etc. *n.* 1. a lapping. 2. the sound of lapping. 3. something that is, or is intended to be, lapped up.
lap up, 1. to take up (liquid or liquid food) by lapping. 2. [Colloq.], to eat or drink greedily; hence, 3. [Colloq.], to take in eagerly.
lap·a·ro- (lap′ə-rə), [< Gr. *lapara,* the flank], a combining form meaning *the flank, the abdominal wall,* as in *laparotomy:* also, before a vowel, **lapar-.**
lap·a·rot·o·my (lap′ə-rot′ə-mi), *n.* [*pl.* LAPAROTOMIES (-miz)], [*laparo-* + *-tomy*], a surgical incision into the abdomen at the flanks or, less precisely, at any point.
La Paz (lä päs′), the actual seat of government of Bolivia (the nominal capital is Sucre): pop., 339,000.
lap·board (lap′bôrd′, lap′bōrd′), *n.* a flat board placed on or over the lap and used as a table.
lap dissolve, in *motion pictures,* a dissolving view in which a new scene is blended in with a scene being faded out, as by lapping two exposures on one film.
lap dog, any pet dog small enough to be held in the lap.
la·pel (lə-pel′), *n.* [dim. of *lap* (a fold)], the front part of a coat, jacket, etc., folded back on the chest and forming a continuation of the collar.
lap·ful (lap′fool′), *n.* as much as a lap can hold.
lap·i·dar·y (lap′ə-der′i), *n.* [*pl.* LAPIDARIES (-iz)], [ME. *lapidarie;* L. *lapidarius* < *lapis,* a stone], 1. a workman who cuts, polishes, and engraves precious stones. 2. an expert in precious stones; collector of or dealer in gems. *adj.* 1. of or connected with the art of cutting and engraving precious stones. 2. engraved on stone.
lap·i·date (lap′ə-dāt′), *v.t.* [LAPIDATED (-id), LAPIDATING], [< L. *lapidatus,* pp. of *lapidare,* to stone < *lapis,* a stone], 1. to throw stones at. 2. to stone to death.

LAPELS

lap·i·da·tion (lap′ə-dā′shən), *n.* a lapidating.
la·pid·i·fi·ca·tion (lə-pid′ə-fi-kā′shən), *n.* a lapidifying or being lapidified.
la·pid·i·fy (lə-pid′ə-fī′), *v.t. & v.i.* [LAPIDIFIED (-fīd′), LAPIDIFYING], [Fr. *lapidifier;* ML. *lapidificare* < L. *lapis, lapidis,* a stone + *facere,* to make], to turn into stone; petrify.
la·pil·lus (lə-pil′əs), *n.* [*pl.* LAPILLI (-ī)], [L., dim. of *lapis,* a stone], a small, glassy igneous rock, about the size of a walnut, ejected from a volcano.
lap·in (lap′in; Fr. lȧ′pan′), *n.* [Fr., rabbit], rabbit fur, generally dyed in imitation of more valuable skins.
‡la·pis (lā′pis, lap′is), *n.* [*pl.* LAPIDES (lap′ə-dēz′)], [L.], a stone: used chiefly in Latin expressions.
lap·is laz·u·li (lap′is laz′yoo-lī′), [Mod. L.; L. *lapis,* a stone + ML. *lazuli,* genit. of *lazulus,* azure < Ar. *lāzaward;* see AZURE], 1. an azure-blue, opaque, semiprecious stone, a mixture of various minerals. 2. its color.
lap-joint (lap′joint′), *v.t.* to join by a lap joint.
lap joint, a joint made by lapping one piece or part over another and fastening them together.
Lap·land (lap′land′), *n.* a region in northern Norway, Sweden, Finland, and the U.S.S.R., inhabited by the Lapps.
Lap·land·er (lap′lan′dẽr, lap′lən-dẽr), *n.* a Lapp.
La Pla·ta (lä plä′tä), a seaport in eastern Argentina, on the Rio de la Plata, capital of Buenos Aires Province: pop., 357,000.
Lapp (lap), *n.* [Sw.], 1. a member of a people living in Lapland, having short stature, short,

LAPLAND

broad heads, high cheekbones, flat noses, and other Mongoloid characteristics: before 1900 they were completely nomadic. 2. their Finno-Ugric language.

lap·per (lap'ẽr), *n.* a person or thing that laps.

lap·pet (lap'it), *n.* [dim. of *lap* (a fold)], 1. a small, loose flap or fold of a garment. 2. any fleshy or membranous part hanging loosely or in a fold, as the dewlap of a cow, the lobe of the ear, etc.

lap robe, a heavy blanket, fur covering, etc. laid over the lap and knees for warmth when riding in an automobile, watching outdoor sports, etc.

laps·a·ble (lap'sə-b'l), *adj.* liable to lapse: also spelled **lapsible.**

lapse (laps), *n.* [Late ME.; L. *lapsus*, a fall, pp. of *labi*, to slip, fall; cf. COLLAPSE, RELAPSE], 1. a slip of the tongue, pen, or memory; small error; fault. 2. a falling away from a moral standard; moral slip. 3. a falling or slipping into a lower condition. 4. a falling into ruin. 5. a gliding or passing away, as of time or of anything continuously flowing. 6. in *law*, *a*) the termination or forfeiture of a right or privilege through disuse or through failure to meet stated obligations within a stated time. *b*) the failure of a bequest to take effect because of the death of the person who was intended to receive it. *v.i.* [LAPSED (lapst), LAPSING], [L. *lapsare* < *labi*], 1. to slip or fall; especially, to slip into a specified state: as, he *lapsed* into unconsciousness. 2. to slip or deviate from virtue; fall back into former unregenerate ways. 3. to pass away; elapse. 4. to become forfeit or void because of the holder's failure to pay his premium at the stipulated time: said of an insurance policy. 5. in *law*, to pass to another proprietor by reason of negligence or death.

lapse rate, the rate of decrease of atmospheric temperature with increase of altitude.

laps·i·ble (lap'sə-b'l), *adj.* lapsable.

lap·strake (lap'strāk'), *adj.* [*lap* (a fold) + *strake*], having an outer shell constructed of planks overlapping and riveted together; clinker-built: said of a boat. *n.* a boat so constructed.

lap·streak (lap'strēk'), *adj.* & *n.* lapstrake.

‡lap·sus (lap'səs), *n.* [L.], a slip; error; lapse.

‡lap·sus lin·guae (lap'səs liŋ'gwē), [L.], a slip of the tongue.

‡lap·sus me·mo·ri·ae (lap'səs me-mō'ri-ē'), [L.], a slip of the memory.

Lap·tev Sea (läp'tef), the Nordenskjöld Sea.

La·pu·ta (lə-pū'tə), *n.* in Swift's *Gulliver's Travels*, a flying island inhabited by impractical, visionary philosophers, who do various absurd things.

lap·wing (lap'wiŋ'), *n.* [ME. *lapwinge*, *lapwink*; AS. *hleapewince* < *hleapan*, to leap + *wince* (prob. < *wincan*, to totter): prob. so called from its irregular flight; cf. Fris. *liap*, lapwing; the form *-wing* is due to folk etym.], an Old World crested plover noted for its irregular, wavering flight: also called *pewit.*

lar (lär), *n.* singular of **lares.**

Lar·a·mie (lar'ə-mi), *n.* a city in southeastern Wyoming: pop., 18,000.

Laramie Range, a mountain range in southeastern Wyoming: highest point, Laramie Peak, 9,020 ft.

lar·board (lär'bẽrd, lär'bôrd', lär'bōrd'), *n.* [ME. *laddeborde*, lit., prob. lading side < AS. *hladan*, to lade + *bord*, side; sp. influenced by *starboard*], the left-hand side of a ship when facing the front end, or bow; port. *adj.* & *adv.* on or toward this side. Now largely replaced by *port* and *left-rudder* because of possible confusion in sound with *starboard.*

lar·ce·ner (lär'sə-nẽr), *n.* a person guilty of larceny.

lar·ce·nist (lär'sə-nist), *n.* a larcener.

lar·ce·nous (lär'sə-nəs), *adj.* 1. of, or having the nature of, larceny. 2. guilty of larceny.

lar·ce·ny (lär'sə-ni), *n.* [*pl.* LARCENIES (-niz)], [OFr. *larrecin*; L. *latrocinium* < *latrocinari*, to rob, plunder < *latro*, freebooter, mercenary soldier, robber], in *law*, the unlawful taking away of another's property without his consent and with the intention of depriving him of it; theft: see also **grand larceny, petty larceny.** —*SYN.* see **theft.**

larch (lärch), *n.* [G. *lärche*; L. *larix*], 1. any of a group of trees of the pine family, found throughout the northern hemisphere, bearing cones and needlelike leaves that are shed annually. 2. the tough wood of this tree.

lard (lärd), *n.* [ME.; OFr.; L. *lardum*, *laridum*, bacon fat, lard; akin to Gr. *larinos*, fattened, fat, L. *largus*, large], the fat of hogs, melted down and clarified; especially, the inner abdominal fat. *v.t.* 1. to cover or smear with lard or other fat; grease. 2. to stuff (meat or poultry) with bits of bacon or fat pork before cooking. 3. to enrich; garnish; interlard: as, his speech was *larded* with picturesque oaths.

lar·da·ceous (lär-dā'shəs), *adj.* of or like lard.

lard·er (lär'dẽr), *n.* [ME.; OFr. *lardier*, orig., storehouse for bacon; ML. *lardarium* < L. *lardum*, lard], 1. a place where the food supplies of a household are kept; pantry. 2. a household's supply of food; provisions.

Lard·ner, Ring (riŋ lärd'nẽr), (*Ringgold Wilmer Lardner*), 1885–1933; American humorist and writer.

lard oil, an oil made from lard, used as a lubricant and lighting fluid.

lar·don (lär'dən), *n.* [Fr. < *lard*; see LARD], a strip of bacon or pork used to lard meat.

lar·doon (lär-dōōn'), *n.* a lardon.

lard·y (lär'di), *adj.* [LARDIER (-di-ẽr), LARDIEST (-di-ist)], 1. containing or covered with lard. 2. like lard.

La·re·do (lə-rā'dō), *n.* a city in southern Texas, on the Rio Grande: pop., 61,000.

la·res (lâr'ēz, lā'rēz), *n.pl.* [*sing.* LAR (lär)], [L., pl. of *lar*; cf. LARVA], in ancient Rome, guardian spirits; especially, the deified spirits of ancestors, who watched over and protected the households of their descendants.

lares and penates, 1. the household gods of the ancient Romans: see **lares, penates.** 2. the treasured belongings of a family or household.

‡lar·gan·do (lär-gän'dô), *adj.* & *adv.* [It.], in *music*, gradually slower and louder: a direction to the performer.

large (lärj), *adj.* [ME.; OFr.; L. *largus*], 1. [Archaic or Rare], liberal; generous. 2. big; great; specifically, *a*) taking up much space; bulky. *b*) enclosing much space; spacious: as, a *large* office. *c*) of great extent or amount: as, a *large* sum of money. 3. big as compared with others of its kind; of more than usual size, extent, or amount. 4. comprehensive; far-reaching: as, he has *large* views on the subject. 5. operating on a big scale: as, a *large* manufacturer. 6. in *nautical usage*, fair or favorable: said of a wind. *adv.* 1. in a large way; so as to be large: as, do not write so *large*. 2. in *nautical usage*, with a favoring wind. *n.* liberty: now only in the following phrase.

at large, 1. free; not confined; not in jail. 2. fully; in complete detail. 3. in general; taken altogether. 4. representing an entire State or other district rather than only one of its subdivisions: as, a congressman *at large.*

SYN.—**large, big,** and **great** are often interchangeable in meaning of more than usual size, extent, etc. (a *large*, *big*, or *great* tree), but in strict discrimination, **large** is used with reference to dimensions or quantity (a *large* studio, amount, etc.), **big,** to bulk, weight, or extent (a *big* baby, *big* business), and **great,** to size or extent that is impressive, imposing, surprising, etc. (a *great* river, success, etc.).—*ANT.* small, little.

large·heart·ed (lärj'här'tid), *adj.* generous; kindly.

large intestine, the relatively large part of the intestines between the small intestine and the anus, including the caecum, colon, and rectum.

large·ly (lärj'li), *adv.* 1. much; in great amounts. 2. for the most part; mainly.

large-mind·ed (lärj'mīn'did), *adj.* liberal in one's views; tolerant; broad-minded.

large-scale (lärj'skāl'), *adj.* 1. drawn to a large scale: said of a map, etc. 2. of wide scope; over a large area; extensive: as, *large-scale* business operations.

lar·gess, lar·gesse (lär'jis, lär'jes), *n.* [ME. & OFr. *largesse* < LL. **largitia* < L. *largus*, large], 1. generous giving. 2. a gift or gifts generously given.

lar·ghet·to (lär-get'ō), *adj.* & *adv.* [It. < *largo*; see LARGO], in *music*, relatively slow, but faster than largo: a direction to the performer. *n.* [*pl.* LARGHETTOS (-ōz)], a larghetto movement or passage.

larg·ish (lär'jish), *adj.* rather large.

lar·go (lär'gō), *adj.* & *adv.* [It., large, slow < L. *largus*, large], in *music*, slow and stately: a direction to the performer. *n.* [*pl.* LARGOS (-gōz)], a largo movement or passage.

lar·i·at (lar'i-ət), *n.* [Sp. *la reata*; *la*, the + *reata*, a rope], 1. a rope used for tethering grazing horses, etc. 2. a lasso. *v.t.* to tie or catch with a lariat.

lar·ine (lar'in, lā'rīn), *adj.* [< LL. *larus*, a gull; Gr. *laros*; + *-ine*], 1. designating or of a group of sea birds comprising the gulls. 2. of or like a gull.

lark (lärk), *n.* [ME. *larke*, *laverke* (cf. LAVEROCK); AS. *laferce*, older *læwerce*; akin to G. *lerche* (OHG. *lērahha*), ON. *lævirki* (Dan. *lerke*), etc.], 1. any of a large group of songbirds found throughout the world; especially, the English skylark. 2. any of a number of similar birds, as the wagtail, pipit, and meadow lark.

lark (lärk), *v.i.* [S. Eng. alteration (after prec.) of northern dial. *lake*; ME. *laike*, to play < ON. *leika* & cognate AS. *lacan*; akin to Goth. *laikan*, to hop, leap; IE. base **leig-*, **loig-*, to hop, seen also in Sans. *rējatē*, (he) hops, quivers, etc.], [Colloq.], to play or frolic; have a merry time. *v.t.* [Colloq.], 1. to make fun of; tease. 2. to hurdle (a fence, etc.), especially on horseback. *n.* [northern dial. *lake*; ME. *laik*; AS. *lac* & ON. *leikr* (akin to G. *leich*, song, *laich*, spawn) < base of *v.i.*], a frolic or spree; merry prank.

lark·spur (lärk'spũr'), *n.* any of a group of plants with green, feathery leaves and spurred flowers of blue or, occasionally, white or pink; delphinium.

La Roche·fou·cauld, Duc Fran·çois de (fräṅ′swȧ′ də lȧ′rôsh′fōō′kō′), 1613–1680; French moralist and writer of maxims.

La Ro·chelle (lȧ′ rô′shel′), a seaport in western France: pop., 59,000.

La·rousse, Pierre A·tha·nase (pyâr ȧ′tȧ′näz′ lȧ′rōōs′), 1817–1875; French grammarian and lexicographer.

lar·ri·gan (lar′ə-gən), *n.* [prob. of Canad. origin], a high moccasin made of oiled leather, worn by lumbermen and trappers.

lar·ri·kin (lar′ə-kin), *n.* [Australian, c.1870; said to be < Ir. pronun. *larikin'* of *larking;* prob. fanciful coinage < *Larry*, nickname for *Laurence* (name common among the Irish)], a rough, disorderly person; rowdy; hoodlum. *adj.* rough and disorderly.

lar·rup (lar′əp), *v.t.* [East Anglian dial.; prob., with intrusive vowel, for **lerp, *larp;* akin to or < D. *larpen*, to thrash], [Colloq.], to whip; flog; beat.

Lar·ry (lar′i), a masculine name: see **Laurence**.

lar·va (lär′və), *n.* [*pl.* LARVAE (-vē)], [L. *larva, larua*, ghost, specter; akin to *lar*, household spirit], 1. an insect in the earliest stage of development, after it is hatched and before it is changed into a pupa; caterpillar, maggot, or grub. 2. the early form of any animal that changes structurally when it becomes an adult: as, the tadpole is the *larva* of the frog.

lar·val (lär′v'l), *adj.* 1. of or like a larva or larvae. 2. in the form of a larva.

la·ryn·gal (lə-riŋ′gəl), *adj.* produced in the larynx.

la·ryn·ge·al (lə-rin′ji-əl), *adj.* 1. of, in, or near the larynx. 2. used for treating the larynx.

lar·yn·git·ic (lar′in-jit′ik), *adj.* of or having laryngitis.

lar·yn·gi·tis (lar′in-jī′tis), *n.* [Mod. L.; *laryng-* + *-itis*], an inflammation of the larynx, characterized by hoarseness and, often, a temporary loss of voice.

la·ryn·go- (lə-riŋ′gō, lə-riŋ′gə), [< Gr. *larynx, laryngos*, larynx], a combining form meaning: 1. *the larynx*, as in *laryngoscope*. 2. *laryngeal and*, as in *laryngopharyngeal*. Also, before a vowel, **laryng-**.

lar·yn·gol·o·gy (lar′iŋ-gol′ə-ji), *n.* [*laryngo-* + *-logy*], the branch of medicine having to do with the study and treatment of the larynx and adjacent parts.

la·ryn·go·pha·ryn·ge·al (lə-riŋ′gō-fə-rin′ji-əl), *adj.* of both the larynx and the pharynx.

la·ryn·go·scope (lə-riŋ′gə-skōp′), *n.* [*laryngo-* + *-scope*], an instrument for examining the larynx, consisting of mirrors attached to a rod.

la·ryn·gos·co·py (lar′iŋ-gos′kə-pi), *n.* examination of the larynx by means of a laryngoscope.

lar·yn·got·o·my (lar′iŋ-got′ə-mi), *n.* [*laryngo-* + *-tomy*], a surgical incision of the larynx, especially to prevent suffocation in cases of laryngeal obstruction.

lar·ynx (lar′iŋks), *n.* [*pl.* LARYNGES (lə-rin′jēz), LARYNXES (-iz)], [Mod. L.; Gr. *larynx, laryngos*], 1. the structure of muscle and cartilage at the upper end of the human trachea, containing the vocal cords, and serving as the organ of voice: see **pharynx**, illus. 2. a similar structure in other animals: in birds there is a larynx at each end of the trachea.

la·sa·gna (lə-zän′yə), *n.* [It. < L. *lasanum*, a pot; Gr. *lasanon*, pot with feet], macaroni in broad strips, often baked in a dish with ground meat, cheeses, etc.

La Salle, Sieur Ro·bert Ca·ve·lier de (rô′bâr′ kȧ′və-lyā′ də lȧ′sȧl′; Eng. lə sal′), 1643–1687; French explorer in America.

las·car (las′kẽr), *n.* [Hind. *lashkar*, army, camp (used with sense of *lashkarī*, belonging to the army, soldier) < Per. *lashkar*, army < Ar. *al-'askar*, army], 1. an East Indian sailor. 2. a low-ranking East Indian artilleryman in the British Army.

las·civ·i·ous (lə-siv′i-əs), *adj.* [ME. *lascyuyous;* ML. *lasciviosus* < L. *lascivia*, wantonness < *lascivus*, wanton], 1. characterized by or expressing lust or lewdness; wanton. 2. tending to excite lustful desires.

la·ser (lā′zẽr), *n.* [*l*ight *a*mplification by *s*timulated *e*mission of *r*adiation], a device, usually containing a crystal, such as a synthetic ruby, in which atoms, when stimulated by focused light waves, amplify and concentrate these waves, then emit them in a narrow, very intense beam: also called *optical maser*.

lash (lash), *n.* [ME. *lassche;* prob. merging of MLG. *lasch*, flap, with OFr. *laz* (see LACE) & with cross influence < OFr. *lachier* (see LASH, to fasten)], 1. a whip, especially the flexible striking part as distinguished from the handle. 2. a stroke with or as with a whip; switch. 3. a sharp remark, censuring, rebuking, or ridiculing. 4. an eyelash. *v.t.* [ME. *laschen;* prob. < the *n.*], 1. to strike or drive with or as with a lash; flog. 2. to fling quickly; switch energetically or angrily: as, the cat *lashed* her tail. 3. to strike with great force; dash against: as, the waves *lashed* the white cliffs. 4. to attack violently in words; censure, rebuke, or ridicule. 5. to incite by appealing to the emotions: as, he *lashed* the crowd into a frenzy of anger. *v.i.* 1. to move quickly or violently; switch: as, the lion's tail *lashed* back and forth. 2. to make strokes with or as with a whip (with *at*): as, he *lashed* at everything that came near.

lash out, 1. to strike out violently. 2. to speak angrily or bitterly; rebuke violently.

lash (lash), *v.t.* [OFr. *lachier, lacier;* see LACE, *v.*], to fasten or tie with a rope, etc.

lash·ing (lash′iŋ), *n.* the act of a person or thing that lashes; specifically, *a)* a whipping. *b)* a strong rebuke: as, he got a tongue *lashing*.

lash·ing (lash′iŋ), *n.* 1. the act of lashing, or fastening or tying with a rope, etc. 2. a rope, etc. so used.

Lash·io (läsh′yō), *n.* a town in east central Burma: pop., 4,600: the Burmese terminus of the Burma Road.

Lash·kar (lush′kẽr), *n.* a city in northcentral India: pop., 301,000.

Las·ki, Harold Joseph (las′ki), 1893–1950; British political scientist and Socialist leader.

Las Pal·mas (läs päl′mäs), a seaport in the Canary Islands: pop., 194,000.

La Spe·zia (lä spe′tsyä), *n.* a seaport in northwestern Italy, on the Ligurian Sea: pop., 112,000.

lass (las), *n.* [north ME. *lasce, lasse;* distribution in ME. suggests N. origin & derivation < Anglo-N. **lasqa* (ON. *lösk-r*, weak, idle) in the sense "not bound"], 1. a young woman; girl. 2. a sweetheart. 3. [Scot.], a girl servant; maid.

Las·salle, Ferdinand (lə-sal′; G. lä-säl′), (*Ferdinand Johann Gottlieb Lasalle*), 1825–1864; German socialist.

Las·sen Peak (las′'n), an active volcano in Lassen Volcanic National Park: height, 10,453 ft.

Lassen Volcanic National Park, a national park in northern California: area, 163 sq. mi.

las·sie (las′i), *n.* [dim. of *lass*], [Scot.], 1. a young girl. 2. a sweetheart.

las·si·tude (las′ə-tōōd′, las′ə-tūd′), *n.* [Fr.; L. *lassitudo* < *lassus*, faint, weary], a state or feeling of being tired or weak; weariness; languor. —*SYN.* see **lethargy.**

las·so (las′ō), *n.* [*pl.* LASSOS, LASSOES (-ōz)], [Sp. *lazo* < L. *laqueus*, noose, snare], a long rope or leather thong with a sliding noose at one end, thrown over the head or leg of a wild horse, etc. to catch it. *v.t.* to catch with a lasso.

last (last, läst), *adj.* [alternative superlative of *late*], [ME. *laste*, earlier *latest, latst;* AS. *latost*, superl. of *læt, adj., late, adv.;* see LATE], 1. being or coming after all others in place; furthest from the first; hindmost. 2. *a)* coming after all others in time; furthest from the beginning; latest; final. *b)* only remaining. 3. most recent; directly before the present: as, *last* month. 4. furthest from what is expected; least likely: as, she was the *last* person that they would have suspected. 5. utmost; greatest: usually in the phrase *of the last importance*. 6. coming after all others in importance; lowest in rank: said especially of a prize. 7. newest: as, the *last* thing in topcoats. 8. conclusive; authoritative: as, the *last* word in scientific research. *adv.* [alternative superlative of *late*], 1. after all others in place or time; at the end. 2. at the most recent time or occasion. 3. finally; in conclusion. *n.* 1. someone or something which comes last: as, this is the *last* of the apples. 2. the final or concluding part; end: as, he remained a cynic to the *last*.

at last, at the end of a long time; finally.

breathe one's last, to die.

see the last of, to see for the last time; never see again.

SYN.—**last** implies a coming after all others in a series or sequence and connotes that nothing else follows (he was the *last* one to enter); **final** implies a coming at the end so as to terminate or conclude and connotes decisiveness (that's my *final* offer); **terminal** applies to that which marks an end, limit, or extremity (the *terminal* outpost of a settlement); **ultimate** applies to a concluding point or result beyond which it is impossible to go (his *ultimate* fate is death).—*ANT.* first.

last (last, läst), *v.i.* [ME. *lasten, lesten;* AS. *læstan;* akin to G. *leisten, v.t.*, to perform, carry out, Goth. *laistjan*, lit., to follow in the track of; IE. base **leis-*, a track, spoor, seen also in L. *lira* (**leisa*), furrow, *delirus*, lit., off the track, hence mad (cf. DELIRIOUS); sense development: to follow—to be following—to go on, continue], 1. to remain in existence or operation; continue; go on; endure. 2. to remain in good condition; wear well. 3. to be enough (*for*); continue unconsumed, unspent, etc. —*SYN.* see **continue.**

last (last, läst), *n.* [ME. *laste;* AS. *læst*, a boot, *læst*, shoemaker's last < base of *last*, footstep, track, furrow < same base as prec.], 1. a block or form shaped like a person's foot, used by shoemakers in building or repairing shoes and boots. 2. a particular form or shape of shoe. *v.t.* to form with a last.

stick to one's last, to attend to one's own business.

last (last, läst), *n.* [ME. *laste;* AS. *hlæst* (akin to G. *last*, OHG. *hlast*) < base of *hladan* (see LADE); basic sense "that which is loaded, weight as cargo"], a measure or weight that varies for different things and in different places: often considered as 4,000 pounds.

las·tex (las′teks), *n.* [coined word; cf. ELASTIC, TEXTILE], a fine, round rubber thread wound with cotton, rayon, silk, etc. and woven into cloth or knitted into other fabrics: a trade-mark (**Lastex**).

last·ing (las′tiŋ, läs′tiŋ), *adj.* that lasts a long time; enduring; durable; permanent; as, a *lasting* peace. *n.* 1. endurance; permanence. 2. a strong twilled cloth used for shoe uppers, covering buttons, etc.

Last Judgment, in *theology,* 1. the final judgment of mankind by God or Jesus, at the end of the world. 2. the time of this.

last·ly (last′li, läst′li), *adv.* in conclusion; finally.

last offices, final rites and prayers for a dead person.

last quarter, 1. the period when the moon's apparent shape is changing from half-moon to new moon. 2. the moon's apparent shape when this period begins.

last sleep, death.

last straw, [from the last straw that broke the back of the overburdened camel in the fable], the last of a sequence of annoyances or troubles that results in a breakdown, defeat, etc.

Last Supper, 1. the last supper eaten by Jesus with his disciples before the Crucifixion, on the night of his betrayal by Judas: cf. **Lord's Supper.** 2. a famous painting by Leonardo da Vinci depicting this supper.

last word, 1. the final word or speech, regarded as settling the argument. 2. something regarded as incapable of improvement. 3. [Colloq.], the very latest style, model, development, etc.

Las Ve·gas (läs vā′gəs), a city in southeastern Nevada: pop., 64,000.

lat (lät), *n.* [*pl.* LATS (läts), LATU (lä′too)], [Lett. *lats,* pl. *lati* < *Lat*via], former monetary unit of Latvia.

Lat., Latin.

lat., latitude.

La·ta·ki·a (lä′tä-kē′ä), *n.* 1. a district of Syria, on the Mediterranean: area, 2,800 sq. mi. 2. its capital, a seaport: pop., 59,000: ancient name, *Laodicea.* 3. (lat′ə-kē′ə), a fine grade of Turkish smoking tobacco: so called because produced near the port of Latakia.

latch (lach), *n.* [ME. *lacche* < *lacchen,* to seize, catch hold of; AS. *læccan, læccean*], 1. a fastening for a door or gate, especially one capable of being worked from either side by means of a lever and consisting of a bar that falls into a notch in a piece attached to the doorjamb or gatepost: sometimes said of a spring lock on a door. 2. a fastening for a window, etc. *v.t. & v.i.* [< the *n.*], to fasten or close with a latch.
latch on to, [Slang], to get or obtain.
on the latch, fastened by the latch but not bolted.

latch·et (lach′it), *n.* [ME. *lachet;* OFr. *lachet,* dial. var. of *lacet,* dim. of *laz;* see LACE], [Archaic], a strap or lace for fastening a sandal or shoe to the foot.

latch·key (lach′kē′), *n.* a key for drawing back or unfastening the latch of a door, especially of an outer door, from the outside.

latch·string (lach′striŋ′), *n.* a cord fastened to the bar of a latch and passed through a hole in the door so that the latch can be raised from the outside.

late (lāt), *adj.* [LATER (lāt′ēr) or LATTER (lat′ēr), LATEST (lāt′ist) or LAST (last, läst)], [ME. *late, lat;* AS. *læt,* slow, sluggish, tardy; akin to D. *laat,* G. *lass,* slow, lazy, etc.; IE. base **lēid-* (< **lēi-,* to neglect, discontinue), seen also in *lassitude, let, n.*], 1. happening, coming, etc. after the usual, proper, or expected time; tardy; behindhand. 2. *a*) happening, being, continuing, etc. far on in the day, night, year, etc.: as, the *late* afternoon, a *late* party. *b*) happening, being, continuing, etc. toward the end; far advanced in a period, development, etc.: as, the *late* Middle Ages. 3. happening, etc. just previous to the present time; recent: as, *late* years. 4. that was recently but not now; specifically, *a*) recently dead. *b*) recently gone out of office. *adv.* [LATER, LATEST or LAST], [ME.; AS. < base of the *adj.*], 1. after the usual, proper, or expected time; tardily. 2. at or until an advanced time of the day, night, year, etc. 3. toward the end of a given period, development, etc.: as, mammals appeared *late* in the Mesozoic Era. 4. recently; lately: as, I saw him as *late* as yesterday. —***SYN.*** see **dead, tardy.**
of late, lately; recently.

lat·ed (lāt′id), *adj.* [Poetic], belated.

la·teen (la-tēn′), *adj.* [Fr. *latine,* fem. of *latin,* Latin (for *voile latine,* Latin sail) < L. *Latinus,* Latin], 1. designating or of a triangular sail attached to a long yard suspended obliquely from a short mast: used formerly by Portuguese explorers and now on Mediterranean vessels. 2. having such a sail. *n.* a vessel with such a sail.

LATEEN SAIL

la·teen-rigged (la-tēn′-rigd′), *adj.* having a lateen sail.

Late Greek, the Greek language of the period after classical Greek: term applied chiefly to the written language seen in patristic writings and texts from the early Byzantine Empire, from 200–300 A.D. to about 600 A.D.: abbreviated **Late Gr.**

Late Latin, the Latin language of the period after classical Latin, seen chiefly in late Western Roman Empire and patristic writings from 200–300 A.D. to about 600 A.D.: abbreviated **LL., L.Lat.:** cf. **Low Latin.**

late·ly (lāt′li), *adv.* [see LATE & -LY], recently; during a recent period; a short while ago.

la·ten·cy (lā′t'n-si), *n.* the quality or condition of being latent.

la·tent (lā′t'nt), *adj.* [L. *latens,* ppr. of *latere,* to lie hidden or concealed, lurk], 1. lying hidden and undeveloped within a person or thing, as a quality or power; as yet concealed; unrevealed. 2. in *biology,* dormant but capable of normal development under the best conditions: said of buds, spores, cocoons, etc. 3. in *law,* not appearing on the face of a thing; hidden: as, a *latent* ambiguity.
SYN.—**latent** applies to that which exists but is as yet concealed or unrevealed (his *latent* ability); **potential** applies to that which exists in an undeveloped state but which can be brought to development in the normal course of events (a *potential* concert pianist); **dormant** suggests a lack of visible activity, as of something asleep (a *dormant* volcano); **quiescent** implies a stopping of activity, usually only temporarily (the raging sea had become *quiescent*).—***ANT.*** active, actual, operative.

latent heat, additional heat required to change the state of a substance from solid to liquid at its melting point, or from liquid to gas at its boiling point, after the temperature of the substance has reached either of these points.

latent period, 1. the interval in the course of a disease between the time of the infection and the first appearance of the symptoms; incubation period. 2. the interval between a stimulus and its response.

lat·er (lāt′ēr), *adj.* alternative comparative of **late.** *adv.* [comparative of *late*], at a later time; after some time; subsequently.
later on, subsequently.

lat·er·al (lat′ēr-əl), *adj.* [L. *lateralis* < *latus, lateris,* a side], 1. of, at, from, or toward the side; sideways: as, *lateral* movement. 2. descended from a brother or sister of a person: as, the *lateral* branch of a family. 3. in *phonetics,* formed in such a manner that the breath can escape along the side or sides of the tongue, as English *l.* *n.* 1. anything located, done, etc., to the side; lateral part, growth, branch, etc. 2. in *football,* a lateral pass. 3. in *mining,* a drift off to the side of and parallel to a main drift. 4. in *phonetics,* a lateral sound.

lat·er·al·ly (lat′ēr-əl-i), *adv.* in a lateral manner; especially, *a*) in a lateral direction; sideways. *b*) from a lateral branch (of a family, etc.).

lateral pass, in *football,* a short pass parallel to the goal line or in a slightly backward direction: distinguished from *forward pass.*

Lat·er·an (lat′ēr-ən), *n.* [< L. *Lateranus,* pl. *Laterani,* name of a Roman family (the *Plautii Laterani*) whose palace once occupied the same site], 1. the church of St. John Lateran, the cathedral church of the Pope as bishop of Rome. 2. the palace adjoining this church: it is now a museum. *adj.* of this church or palace; specifically, designating or of certain Catholic general councils held there in 1123, 1139, 1179, 1215, and 1512–1517.

lat·er·ite (lat′ēr-īt′), *n.* [L. *later,* brick, tile; + *-ite*], in *geology,* a red, porous deposit containing large amounts of aluminum and ferric hydroxides, formed by the decomposition of certain rocks.

la·tes·cence (lə-tes′'ns), *n.* [< *latescent*], the quality or condition of becoming latent.

la·tes·cent (lə-tes′'nt), *adj.* [L. *latescens,* ppr. of *latescere,* to lie hidden < *latere,* to lurk, lie hidden], becoming latent, or hidden.

lat·est (lāt′ist), *adj. & adv.* [alternative superlative of *late*], 1. most recent; newest. 2. [Archaic & Poetic], last.
at the latest, no later than (the time specified).
the latest, the most recent thing, development, etc.

la·tex (lā′teks), *n.* [LATEXES (-tek-siz), LATICES (lat′ə-sēz′)], [L. *latex, laticis,* a fluid, liquid; Gr. *latax,* a drop, wine lees; IE. base **lat-,* wet, as also in MIr. *laith,* beer], a milky liquid in certain plants and trees, as the rubber tree, milkweed, and poppy: the basis of various commercial products, notably rubber.

lath (lath, läth), *n.* [*pl.* LATHS (lathz, läths)], [ME. *laththe, latt;* the former < AS. **læth(th)* < Gmc. **laththō-,* as also in OHG. *latta;* the latter < AS. *lætt* < Gmc. **lattō,* as also in ON. *latta;* IE. base **lat-,* lath, seen also in W. *llath,* which may have influenced the 1st ME. form & suggested the AS. forms], 1. any of the thin, narrow strips of wood used in building lattices or nailed to two-by-fours, rafters, etc. as a groundwork for plastering, tiling, etc. 2. light sheet metal with holes (or wire cloth) designed for similar uses. 3. lathing. *v.t.* to cover with laths.

lathe (lā*th*), *n.* [ME., turning lathe, supporting stand; prob. < MD. *lade* in the same senses (whence also Dan. *dreielad*, turning lathe); IE. base as in *lath;* the final *-th* may be from *lath*, since lathes were formerly actuated by spring laths], 1. a machine for shaping an article of wood, metal, etc. by holding and turning it rapidly against the edge of a cutting tool. 2. a variety of potter's wheel. *v.t.* [LATHED (lā*th*d), LATHING], to shape on a lathe.

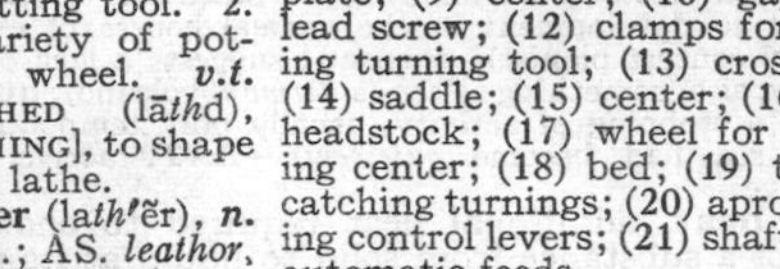

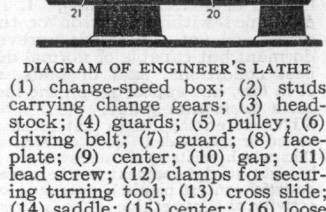

DIAGRAM OF ENGINEER'S LATHE
(1) change-speed box; (2) studs carrying change gears; (3) headstock; (4) guards; (5) pulley; (6) driving belt; (7) guard; (8) faceplate; (9) center; (10) gap; (11) lead screw; (12) clamps for securing turning tool; (13) cross slide; (14) saddle; (15) center; (16) loose headstock; (17) wheel for adjusting center; (18) bed; (19) tray for catching turnings; (20) apron holding control levers; (21) shaft giving automatic feeds

lath·er (la*th*'ẽr), *n.* [ME.; AS. *leathor*, washing soda or soap; akin to ON. *lauthr*, washing soda, foam; IE. *lou-tro < base *lou-, wash, seen also in L. *lavare, lavere*, to wash, bathe (cf. LAVE, LAVATORY)], 1. the foam or froth formed by soap and water. 2. foamy sweat, as that on a race horse. *v.t.* 1. to cover with lather. 2. [Colloq.], to flog soundly. *v.i.* to form or become covered with lather.

lath·er·y (la*th*'ẽr-i), *adj.* made of, covered with, or capable of forming lather.

lath·ing (lath'iŋ, läth'iŋ), *n.* 1. laths collectively, especially when serving as a foundation for plastering, etc.; lathwork. 2. the putting up of laths on walls, etc.

lath·work (lath'wũrk', läth'wũrk'), *n.* lathing.

lath·y (lath'i, läth'i), *adj.* [LATHIER (-i-ẽr), LATHIEST (-i-ist)], like a lath; tall and thin.

lat·i·ces (lat'ə-sēz'), *n.* alternative plural of **latex**.

lat·i·cif·er·ous (lat'ə-sif'ẽr-əs), *adj.* [see LATEX & -FEROUS], producing, containing, or secreting latex.

lat·i·fun·di·um (lat'ə-fun'di-əm), *n.* [*pl.* LATIFUNDIA (-ə)], [L. < *latus*, broad + *fundus*, estate], a large landed estate, as in ancient Rome.

Lat·i·mer, Hugh (lat'ə-mẽr), 1485?–1555; English Protestant churchman and religious reformer; burned at the stake.

Lat·in (lat''n), *adj.* [L. *Latinus* < *Latium*, Latium (in which Rome was included)], 1. of ancient Latium or its people. 2. of ancient Rome or its people. 3. of or in the language of ancient Latium and ancient Rome. 4. designating or of the languages derived from Latin, the peoples who speak them, their countries, cultures, etc. 5. of the Roman Catholic Church, especially as distinguished from the Orthodox Eastern Church. *n.* 1. a native or inhabitant of ancient Latium or ancient Rome. 2. the Italic language of ancient Latium and ancient Rome: see also **Old Latin, Late Latin, Low Latin, Medieval Latin, Modern Latin.** 3. a person, as a Spaniard or an Italian, whose language is derived from Latin. 4. a Roman Catholic: so called especially by Eastern Christians. Abbreviated **L., Lat.**

Latin America, the countries in North America, South America, Central America, and the West Indies where Spanish, Portuguese, and French are spoken; all of the Western Hemisphere excluding the United States and its possessions, Canada, and the British possessions.

Lat·in-A·mer·i·can (lat''n-ə-mer'i-k'n), *adj.* of Latin America, its people, or their culture.

Latin American, a native or inhabitant of a Latin-American country.

Lat·in·ate (lat''n-āt'), *adj.* of or derived from Latin.

Latin Church, that part of the Catholic Church which adheres to the Latin Rite; Roman Catholic Church.

Latin cross, a plain, right-angle cross whose lowest limb is longer than any of the other three.

La·tin·ic (la-tin'ik), *adj.* of Latin.

Lat·in·ism (lat''n-iz'm), *n.* a Latin idiom or expression, used in another language.

Lat·in·ist (lat''n-ist), *n.* a scholar in Latin.

La·tin·i·ty (la-tin'ə-ti), *n.* [L. *latinitas*], the manner of speaking or writing Latin; use of Latin.

Lat·in·i·za·tion (lat''n-ə-zā'shən, lat''n-i-zā'shən), *n.* a Latinizing or being Latinized.

Lat·in·ize (lat''n-īz'), *v.t.* [LATINIZED (-īzd'), LATINIZING], [LL. *latinizare*, to translate into Latin < L. *Latinus*, Latin], 1. to translate into Latin. 2. to give Latin form or characteristics to. 3. to transliterate into the Latin alphabet; Romanize. 4. to make conform to the rites, practices, etc. of the Roman Catholic Church. *v.i.* to use Latin expressions, forms, etc.

Latin Quarter, [transl. of Fr. *Quartier Latin*], a section of Paris, south of the Seine, where many artists and students live.

Latin Rite, 1. the Latin liturgies used in the Latin Church. 2. the Latin Church.

lat·ish (lāt'ish), *adj. & adv.* somewhat late.

lat·i·tude (lat'ə-tōōd', lat'ə-tūd'), *n.* [ME.; OFr.; L. *latitudo* < *latus*, wide], 1. [Rare], breadth; width. 2. extent; scope; range of applicability. 3. freedom from narrow restrictions; allowed freedom of opinion, conduct, or action. 4. a region considered with reference to its distance north or south of the equator: as, in this *latitude* we rarely see the northern lights. 5. in *astronomy*, the angular distance of a heavenly body from the plane in which the earth moves around the sun. 6. in *geography*, angular distance, measured in degrees, north or south from the equator: as, the ship gave its position as forty degrees north *latitude*. Cf. **longitude.** Abbreviated **L., l., lat.**

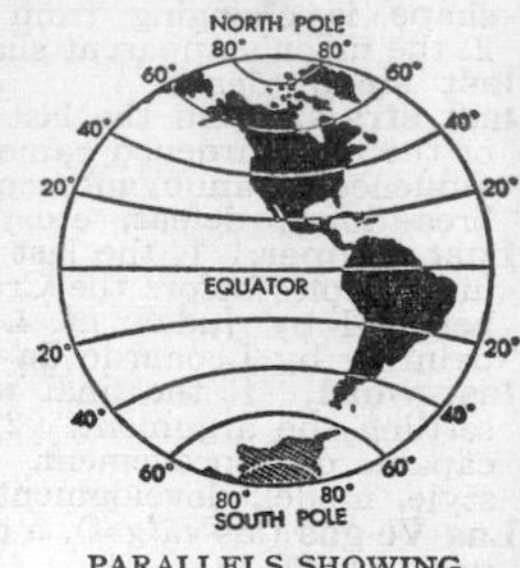

PARALLELS SHOWING LATITUDE

lat·i·tu·di·nal (lat'ə-tōō'd'n-əl, lat'ə-tū'd'n-əl), *adj.* of latitude.

lat·i·tu·di·nar·i·an (lat'ə-tōō'd'n-âr'i-ən, lat'ə-tū'd'n-âr'i-ən), *adj.* [< L. *latitudo* (see LATITUDE); + *-arian*], liberal in one's views; permitting free thought, especially in religious matters; very tolerant of the differing opinions of others. *n.* 1. a person who is very liberal in his views and, in religion, cares little about particular creeds and forms. 2. any of a group of Anglican churchmen of the 17th century who favored freedom of belief and were not opposed to varying forms of worship or doctrine.

lat·i·tu·di·nar·i·an·ism (lat'ə-tōō'd'n-âr'i-ən-iz'm, lat'ə-tū'd'n-âr'i-ən-iz'm), *n.* [*latitudinarian* + *-ism*], broadness and tolerance, especially in religion; liberal interpretation of doctrines, creeds, etc.

La·ti·um (lā'shi-əm), *n.* an ancient country in central Italy, southeast of Rome.

La·to·na (lə-tō'nə, lā-tō'nə), *n.* [L.], in *Roman mythology*, the mother of Apollo and Diana: identified with the Greek Leto.

LATIUM

la·tri·a (lə-trī'ə), *n.* [LL.; Gr. *latreia*, service, worship < *latreuein*, to serve, worship < *latris*, hired servant], in the *Roman Catholic Church*, that worship which is due to God alone.

la·trine (lə-trēn'), *n.* [Fr.; L. *latrina*, contr. of *lavatrina*, bath < *lavare*, to wash; see LATHER], a toilet, or privy, for the use of a large number of people, as in a camp, barracks, etc.

-la·try (lə-tri), [Gr. *-latreia* < *latreia;* see LATRIA], a combining form meaning *worship of* or *excessive devotion to*, as in *idolatry*.

lat·ten (lat''n), *n.* [ME. *laton, latoun;* OFr. *laton, laiton;* prob. < MHG. *latte*, thin plate, lath; see LATH], 1. brass or a brasslike alloy hammered into thin sheets, formerly used for making church vessels. 2. any metal, especially tin, in thin sheets.

lat·ter (lat'ẽr), *adj.* [alternative comparative of *late*], [ME. *lattre;* AS. *lætra*, compar. of *læt:* it represents the orig. compar. form; *later* is a new formation], 1. *a)* later; more recent. *b)* nearer the end or close; as, in the *latter* part of the year. 2. last mentioned of two: opposed to *former;* often used absolutely (with *the*).

lat·ter-day (lat'ẽr-dā'), *adj.* of recent or present time; modern.

Lat·ter-day Saint (lat'ẽr-dā'), a Mormon: abbreviated **L. D. S.** (in *pl.*).

lat·ter·ly (lat'ẽr-li), *adv.* lately; of late; recently.

lat·ter·most (lat'ẽr-mōst'), *adj.* last in succession; farthest toward the rear.

lat·tice (lat'is), *n.* [ME. *latis;* OFr. *lattis* < *latte* < MHG. *latte*, a lath; see LATH], 1. an openwork structure of crossed strips or bars of wood, metal, etc., used as a screen, support, etc. 2. something resembling or suggesting such a structure, as a heraldic bearing of crossed vertical and horizontal bars. 3. a window, door, gate, etc. screened by such a structure. *v.t.* [LATTICED (-ist), LATTICING], 1. to arrange like a lattice; make a lattice of. 2. to furnish or cover with a lattice or latticework.

lat·tice·work (lat′is-wũrk′), *n.* 1. a lattice. 2. lattices collectively; trelliswork.

lat·tic·ing (lat′is-iŋ), *n.* 1. the act of making, or furnishing with, a lattice or latticework. 2. a lattice or latticework.

la·tu (lä′too), *n.* alternative plural of **lat.**

Lat·vi·a (lat′vi-ə), *n.* a country in northeastern Europe annexed as the Latvian Soviet Socialist Republic in August, 1940.

Lat·vi·an (lat′vi-ən), *adj.* 1. of Latvia or its people; Lettish. 2. of the group of Baltic dialects spoken in Latvia. *n.* 1. a native or inhabitant of Latvia. 2. the Lettish language: with Lithuanian and Old Prussian it represents the Baltic branch of the Indo-European family of languages.

Latvian Soviet Socialist Republic, a republic of the U.S.S.R., on the Baltic Sea: area, 24,700 sq. mi.; pop., 1,951,000; capital, Riga.

laud (lôd), *n.* [ME. & OFr. *laude;* L. *laus, laudis,* glory, praise], 1. praise. 2. any song or hymn of praise. 3. *pl. a)* [often L-], an early morning church service that includes the singing of psalms of praise to God. *b)* [L-], in the *Roman Catholic Church,* the service of dawn which constitutes the second (or, when said together with matins, the first) of the canonical hours. *v.t.* [ME. *lauden;* L. *laudare* < the *n.*], to praise; extol. —*SYN.* see **praise.**

Laud, William (lôd), 1573–1645; English clergyman; archbishop of Canterbury; executed for treason.

laud·a·bil·i·ty (lôd′ə-bil′ə-ti), *n.* [L. *laudabilitas* < *laudabilis*], the quality of being laudable; praiseworthiness.

laud·a·ble (lôd′ə-b′l), *adj.* [L. *laudabilis*], 1. worthy of being lauded; praiseworthy; commendable. 2. [Obs.], in *medicine,* such as indicates an improving condition; healthy: said of pus.

laud·a·bly (lôd′ə-bli), *adv.* in a laudable manner.

laud·a·num (lôd′′n-əm, lôd′nəm), *n.* [altered use (by Paracelsus) of ML. var. of L. *ladanum;* Gr. *lēdanon,* resinous juice from the shrub *lēdon,* mastic; Per. *ladan*], 1. formerly, any of various preparations containing opium. 2. a solution of opium in alcohol; tincture of opium.

lau·da·tion (lô-dā′shən), *n.* [L. *laudatio*], a lauding or being lauded; praise; commendation.

laud·a·tive (lôd′ə-tiv), *adj.* [L. *laudativus*], laudatory.

laud·a·to·ry (lôd′ə-tôr′i, lôd′ə-tō′ri), *adj.* [LL. *laudatorius* < L. *laudare;* see LAUD], expressing praise; eulogistic; commendatory.

Lau·der, Sir **Harry** (lô′dẽr), (*Harry MacLennan*), 1870–1950; Scottish comedian, singer, and song writer.

Lau·en·burg (lou′′n-bẽrg), *n.* a former duchy of Denmark, now a part of Schleswig-Holstein: see **Holstein,** map.

laugh (laf, läf), *v.i.* [ME. *laughen, lahen,* etc.; AS. *hleahhan;* akin to G. *lachen* (OHG. *hlahhan*); IE. base **qlēg-,* etc., to cry out, sound, seen also in *clangor*], 1. to make the characteristic sounds of the voice and movements of the features and body that express mirth, amusement, ridicule, etc. 2. to feel or suggest joyousness; appear bright and gay. *v.t.* 1. to express or say with laughter. 2. to bring about, effect, or influence by means of laughter: as, she *laughed* the child into a better humor. *n.* 1. the act or sound of laughing. 2. anything that provokes or is fit to provoke laughter.

have the last laugh, to win after apparent defeat and discomfiture.

laugh at, 1. to be amused by. 2. to make fun of; ridicule; deride. 3. to be indifferent to or contemptuous of; disregard.

laugh away, to get rid of (something unpleasant or embarrassing) by laughter.

laugh down, to silence or suppress by laughing.

laugh in one's sleeve, to laugh secretly or inwardly.

laugh off, to scorn, avoid, or reject by laughter or ridicule.

laugh out of (or **on**) **the other** (or **wrong**) **side of the mouth,** to change from joy to sorrow, from amusement to annoyance, etc.

no laughing matter, a matter that is not to be taken lightly; serious matter.

SYN.—**laugh** is the general word for the sounds or exhalation made in expressing mirth, amusement, etc.; **chuckle** implies soft laughter in low tones, expressive of mild amusement or inward satisfaction; **giggle** and **titter** both refer to a half-suppressed laugh consisting of a series of rapid, high-pitched sounds, suggesting embarrassment, silliness, etc., but **titter** is also used of a laugh of mild amusement suppressed in affected politeness; **snicker** is used of a sly, half-suppressed laugh, as at another's discomfiture or a bawdy story; **guffaw** refers to loud, coarse laughter.

laugh·a·ble (laf′ə-b′l, läf′ə-b′l), *adj.* of such a nature as to cause laughter; amusing or ridiculous. —*SYN.* see **funny.**

laugh·a·bly (laf′ə-bli, läf′ə-bli), *adv.* so as to be laughable.

laugh·ing (laf′iŋ, läf′iŋ), *adj.* 1. that laughs; showing amusement or happiness by laughter: as, a *laughing* face. 2. causing laughter: as, a *laughing* matter.

laughing gas, nitrous oxide, N_2O, used as an anesthetic, especially in dentistry: so called from the reaction of laughter and exhilaration that inhaling it may produce.

laughing jackass, an Australian kingfisher with a harsh cry suggestive of loud laughter; kookaburra.

laugh·ing·ly (laf′iŋ-li, läf′iŋ-li), *adv.* with laughter.

laugh·ing·stock (laf′iŋ-stok′, läf′iŋ-stok′), *n.* a person or thing made the object of ridicule.

laugh·ter (laf′tẽr, läf′tẽr), *n.* [ME. *lahter, lauhter;* AS. *hleahtor* (akin to G. *gelächter*) < base of *hleahhan* (see LAUGH) + suffix *-tor* (Gmc. **-tro-;* cf. SLAUGHTER)], 1. the action of laughing or the sound resulting. 2. a matter for or cause of laughter.

launce (lans, läns), *n.* [ME. *launce, lance,* lance; see LANCE], any of a small group of sea fishes with a pointed snout and a long, slender body, found in American coastal waters: also **sand launce:** also spelled **lance.**

launch (lônch, länch), *v.t.* [ME. *lanchen, launchen;* OFr. *lanchier, lancier* < *lance;* see LANCE], 1. to hurl, discharge, or send off (a weapon, blow, etc.). 2. to send forth with some force: as, the catapult *launched* the plane into the air. 3. to cause (a newly built vessel) to slide from the land into the water; set afloat. 4. to set in operation; start: as, the army *launched* an attack. 5. to start (a person) on some course or career. *v.i.* 1. to put to sea (often with *out* or *forth*). 2. to start on some new course or enterprise. 3. to throw oneself (*into*) with vigor; rush; plunge: as, she *launched* into a tirade. *n.* the movement of a vessel in sliding from the land into water.

launch out, 1. to put to sea. 2. to begin something new. 3. to be reckless in action or thought.

launch (lônch, länch), *n.* [Sp. or Port. *lancha;* prob. < Malay *lanca,* three-masted boat < *lancār,* speedy, quick], 1. the largest boat carried by a warship. 2. a large, open motorboat.

launching pad (or **platform**), the platform from which a rocket, guided missile, etc. is launched or fired.

laun·der (lôn′dẽr, län′dẽr), *n.* [ME. *lavender,* washerwoman; OFr. *lavandier;* LL. *lavandarius,* masc., *lavandaria,* fem., washer < L. *lavare,* to wash; see LATHER], a water trough, especially one used in mining for washing dirt from the ore. *v.t.* to wash (clothes, etc.); wash and iron. *v.i.* 1. to withstand washing: as, this fabric *launders* well. 2. to do laundry.

laun·dress (lôn′dris, län′dris), *n.* a woman whose work is washing clothes, ironing, etc.; washerwoman.

laun·dry (lôn′dri, län′dri), *n.* [*pl.* LAUNDRIES (-driz)], [ME. & OFr. *lavenderie;* L. *lavandaria*], 1. a laundering. 2. a place where laundering is done. 3. clothes, etc., ready for, at, or returned from such a place.

laun·dry·man (lôn′dri-mən, län′dri-mən), *n.* [*pl.* LAUNDRYMEN (-mən)], a man who works in or for a laundry, especially one who collects and delivers clothes, etc. for laundering service.

laun·dry·wom·an (lôn′dri-woom′ən, län′dri-woom′ən), *n.* [*pl.* LAUNDRYWOMEN (-wim′in)], a laundress.

Lau·ra (lô′rə), [It.; prob. < L. *laurus,* laurel], a feminine name: variants, *Laurinda, Lorinda.*

lau·ra·ceous (lô-rā′shəs), *adj.* [< Mod. L. *Lauraceae,* laurel family (< L. *laurus,* laurel; + *-aceae*); + *-ous*], of the laurel family of aromatic trees and shrubs, including the laurel, avocado, nutmeg, camphor, etc.

lau·re·ate (lô′ri-it; *for v.,* lô′ri-āt′), *adj.* [ME. *laureat;* L. *laureatus* < *laurea,* laurel tree < *laurus,* laurel], 1. woven of sprigs of laurel: said of a crown or wreath. 2. crowned with a laurel wreath as a mark of honor or distinction. 3. worthy of honor; distinguished; pre-eminent, especially among poets. *n.* 1. a person crowned with laurel. 2. a poet laureate. *v.t.* [LAUREATED (-id), LAUREATING], 1. to honor or confer distinction upon by crowning with laurel. 2. to appoint to the poet laureateship.

lau·re·ate·ship (lô′ri-it-ship′), *n.* [see -SHIP], 1. the position of poet laureate. 2. the time during which a poet holds this position.

lau·rel (lô′rəl, lär′əl), *n.* [ME. *lorer, laurer, lorel;* OFr. *laurier, lorier;* L. *laurus*], 1. any of a group of evergreen trees or shrubs, native to southern Europe and widely cultivated in the United States, with large, glossy, aromatic leaves, greenish-yellow flowers, and black berries: also called *bay tree.* 2. the foliage of this tree, especially as woven into wreaths such as those used by the ancient Greeks to crown the victors in various contests; hence, 3. *pl. a)* fame; honor. *b)* victory. 4. any of various trees and shrubs resembling the true laurel, as the azaleas, rhododendrons, mountain laurel, etc. *v.t.* [LAURELED or LAURELLED (-rəld, -əld), LAURELING or LAURELLING], 1. to crown with laurel; hence, 2. to honor.

look to one's laurels, to beware of having one's achievements or record surpassed.

rest on one's laurels, to be satisfied with what one has already achieved or accomplished.
Lau·rence (lôr′əns, lär′əns), [L. *Laurentius;* prob. < *laurus,* laurel (or ? < *Laurentus,* town in Latium)], a masculine name: diminutive, *Larry;* variant, *Lorenzo;* feminine, *Laura;* equivalents, Fr. *Laurent,* G. *Lorenz,* It. & Sp. *Lorenzo:* also spelled **Lawrence.**
Lau·ren·cin, Ma·rie (mȧ′rē′ lō′rän′san′), 1885–1956; French painter.
Lau·ren·ti·an (lô-ren′shi-ən, lä-ren′shən), *adj.* [< L. *Laurentius,* Lawrence; + *-an*], 1. of or connected with the St. Lawrence River. 2. in *geology,* designating or of the younger of two series of rocks of the Archaean system: cf. **Keewatin.**
the Laurentian, the Laurentian series of rocks.
Laurentian Mountains, a mountain range in Canada, between Hudson Bay and the St. Lawrence River.
Lau·ri·er, Sir **Wilfrid** (lô′ri-ā′, lä′ri-ā′), 1841–1919; Canadian statesman; prime minister (1896–1911).
Lau·rin·da (lô-rin′də), a feminine name: see **Laura.**
lau·rus·tine (lô′rəs-tin), *n.* [Mod. L. *laurustinus* < L. *laurus,* laurel + *tinus,* the laurustine], a tall evergreen shrub grown in the Mediterranean regions of Europe for its fragrant, white or pinkish flowers.
Lau·sanne (lō-zan′; Fr. lō′zȧn′), *n.* a city in western Switzerland, near Lake Geneva: pop., 93,000.
‡**laus De·o** (lôs dē′ō), [L.], praise (be) to God.
Lau·wine (lô′win; G. lou-vē′nə), *n.* a Lawine.
la·va (lä′və, lav′ə), *n.* [It. < *lavare;* L. *lavare,* to wash; see LATHER], 1. melted rock issuing from a volcano. 2. such rock when solidified by cooling.
la·va·bo (lə-vā′bō), *n.* [*pl.* LAVABOES (-bōz)], [L., I will wash; see LATHER], [sometimes L-], in the *Roman Catholic Church,* 1. the ritual of washing the celebrant's hands after the offertory, accompanied by the repetition of verses 6-12 of Psalm 25 (26 in the Authorized and Revised Versions), beginning with *lavabo:* a similar ritual is used in some Episcopal churches. 2. these verses. 3. *a*) the washbowl or basin used. *b*) in monasteries, the room containing this. 4. the small towel for drying the celebrant's hands.
lav·age (lav′ij; Fr. lȧ′vȧzh′), *n.* [Fr. < *laver;* L. *lavare,* to wash; see LATHER], 1. a washing. 2. in *medicine,* the washing out of an organ, especially the stomach or intestinal tract.
La·val, Pierre (pyâr lȧ′vȧl′; Eng. lə-val′), 1883–1945; French politician; premier and minister of foreign affairs (1931–1932; 1935–1936); executed for treason.
la·va-la·va (lä′vä-lä′vä), *n.* [Samoan], a calico loincloth or waistcloth worn by Samoans and other South Sea islanders.
lav·a·liere, lav·a·lier (lav′ə-lêr′), *n.* [Fr. *lavallière,* kind of tie < Duchesse de *La Vallière* (1644–1710), mistress of Louis XIV], an ornament hanging from a chain, worn around the neck.
la·val·lière (lav′ə-lêr′; Fr. lȧ′vȧ′lyâr′), *n.* [Fr.], a lavaliere.
la·va·tion (la-vā′shən), *n.* [L. *lavatio* < *lavare,* to wash; see LATHER], 1. a washing. 2. water for washing.
lav·a·to·ry (lav′ə-tôr′i, lav′ə-tō′ri), *n.* [*pl.* LAVATORIES (-iz, -riz)], [LL. *lavatorium* < L. *lavare,* to wash; see LATHER], 1. a bowl or basin for washing the face and hands. 2. a room equipped with such a basin or basins: now often a euphemism for *toilet.* 3. in *ecclesiastical usage,* the ritual washing of the celebrant's hands at the offertory: cf. **lavabo.**
lave (lāv), *v.t. & v.i.* [LAVED (lāvd), LAVING], [ME. *laven;* OFr. *laver;* L. *lavare* (see LATHER); prob. merged with *lave* (to dip)], [Poetic], 1. to wash; bathe. 2. to flow along or against.
lave (lāv), *v.t.* [LAVED (lāvd), LAVING], [ME. *laven;* AS. *lafian;* prob. < L. *lavare;* see prec.], to dip or pour with or as with a ladle.
lave (lāv), *n.* [AS. *laf;* see LEAVE (to let remain)], [Scot.], what is left over; the remainder.
lav·en·der (lav′ən-dẽr), *n.* [ME.; Anglo-Fr. *lavendre;* ML. *livendula, lavendula* (whence G. *lavandel,* Fr. *lavande,* etc.); associated with L. *lavare,* to wash (cf. LAVE, *v.*), from use as bath perfume, but prob. of different origin; ? < L. *livere,* to be bluish, or *lividus,* blue (cf. LIVID)], 1. any of a group of fragrant European plants of the mint family, having spikes of pale-purplish flowers and yielding an aromatic oil (*oil of lavender*). 2. the dried flowers, leaves, and stalks of this plant, used to fill sachets and to perfume clothes, linens, etc. 3. a pale purple, the color of the flowers of this plant. *adj.* pale-purple. *v.t.* to perfume with lavender.
lavender water, a perfume or toilet water made from flowers of the lavender plant.
la·ver (lā′vẽr), *n.* [ME. *laver, lavour;* OFr. *laveoir, lavur;* L. *lavatorium* < *lavare,* to wash; see LATHER], 1. [Archaic], a large basin to wash in; especially, the brass basin of the ancient Jewish Temple in which the priests washed their hands and feet. 2. anything that cleanses spiritually; especially, the water of baptism or the font containing this.
la·ver (lā′vẽr), *n.* [L., water plant], any of various large, edible, purple seaweeds.
lav·er·ock (lav′ẽr-ək, lāv′rək), *n.* [Late ME. *laveroc,* var. of *laverke;* see LARK], [Archaic or Scot.], the lark.
La·vin·i·a (lə-vin′i-ə, lə-vin′yə), [L.], a feminine name.
lav·ish (lav′ish), *adj.* [orig. n. < OFr. *lavasse, lavache,* torrent of rain; Pr. *lavaci;* L. *lavatio;* see LAVATION], 1. very generous or liberal in giving or spending, often extravagantly so; prodigal. 2. more than enough; very abundant; unstinted: as, *lavish* entertainment. *v.t.* to give or spend generously or liberally: as, he *lavished* his love on the child. —*SYN.* see **profuse.**
La·voi·sier, An·toine Lau·rent (än′twȧn′ lō′rän′ lȧ′vwȧ′zyā′), 1743–1794; French chemist; founder of modern chemistry; died on the guillotine.
law (lô), *n.* [ME. *lawe, laghe;* Late AS. *lagu* < Anglo-N. **lagu* (ON. *lög*), pl. of *lag,* something laid down or settled < base of Eng. *lie, lay* (IE. base **legh-*); not connected with L. *lex* (< IE. base **leĝ-,* to bring together, collect) but influenced in various senses by this word, L. *jus* (cf. JUSTICE), & Fr. *loi;* for sense development cf. G. *gesetz,* Eng. *doom,* & L. *statutum* (cf. STATUTE); the Norse word replaced the native AS. *æ* (akin to G. *ehe,* marriage)], 1. all the rules of conduct established and enforced by the authority, legislation, or custom of a given community or other group: as, a basic tenet of English *law.* 2. any one of such rules. 3. the condition existing when obedience to such rules is general: as, they have established *law* and order. 4. the branch of knowledge dealing with such rules; jurisprudence. 5. the system of courts in which such rules are referred to in defending one's rights, securing justice, etc.: as, they had to resort to *law* to settle the matter. 6. all such rules having to do with a particular sphere of human activity: as, business *law.* 7. in England, common law, as distinguished from equity. 8. the profession of lawyers, judges, etc. (often with *the*). 9. knowledge of the law (sense 1): as, his *law* is sound. 10. *a*) a sequence of events in nature or in human activities that has been observed to occur with unvarying uniformity under the same conditions: often **law of nature.** *b*) the formulation in words of such a sequence: as, the *law* of gravitation, the *law* of diminishing returns. 11. any rule or principle expected to be observed: as, the *laws* of health, a *law* of grammar. 12. inherent tendency; instinct: as, the *law* of self-preservation. 13. in *ecclesiastical usage, a*) a divine commandment. *b*) all divine commandments collectively. 14. in *mathematics,* a general principle to which all applicable cases must conform: as, the *laws* of exponents. 15. [Chiefly British], in *sports,* an allowance in distance or time, as in a race; handicap. Abbreviated **L., l.**
go to law, to take a problem or dispute to a law court for settlement.
lay down the law, 1. to give explicit orders in an authoritative manner. 2. to give a scolding (*to*).
read law, to study to become a lawyer.
the Law, 1. the Mosaic code, or the part of the Old Testament containing it; hence, 2. the Old Testament. 3. [l-], [Colloq.], a policeman, or the police.
SYN.—**law,** in its specific application, implies prescription and enforcement by a ruling authority (the *law* of the land); a **rule** may not be authoritatively enforced, but it is generally observed in the interests of order, uniformity, etc. (the *rules* of golf); **regulation** refers to a rule of a group or organization, enforced by authority (military *regulations*); a **statute** is a law enacted by a legislative body; an **ordinance** is a local, generally municipal, law; a **canon** is, strictly, a law of a church, but the term is also used of any rule or principle regarded as true or in conformity with good usage (the *canons* of taste). See also **theory.**
law-a·bid·ing (lô′ə-bīd′iŋ), *adj.* obeying the law; abiding by the law.
law·book (lô′book′), *n.* a book containing or discussing laws; especially, such a book used as a textbook for students of law.
law·break·er (lô′brāk′ẽr), *n.* one who violates the law.
law·break·ing (lô′brāk′iŋ), *n.* violation of the law. *adj.* violating the law.
law court, a court for the administration of justice under the law; judicial tribunal.
law·ful (lô′f'l), *adj.* 1. in conformity with the principles of the law; permitted by law: as, a *lawful* act: see also **legal** (sense 2). 2. recognized by law; just: as, *lawful* debts. —*SYN.* see **legal.**
law·giv·er (lô′giv′ẽr), *n.* a person who draws up, introduces, or enacts a code of laws for a nation or people; lawmaker; legislator.
‡**La·wi·ne** (lä-vē′nə), *n.* [*pl.* LAWINEN (-nən)], [G. < LL. *labina;* see AVALANCHE], an avalanche.
law·less (lô′lis), *adj.* 1. without law; not regulated by the authority of law: as, a *lawless* city. 2. not in conformity with law; illegal: as, *lawless* practices. 3. not obeying the law; unruly; disorderly.
law·mak·er (lô′māk′ẽr), *n.* a person who makes or helps to make laws; especially, a member of a legislature; legislator.
law·mak·ing (lô′māk′iŋ), *n.* the making of laws; legislation. *adj.* making laws; legislative.
Law·man (lô′mən), *n.* Layamon.

law merchant, all the rules and usages originating in the customs of merchants and now applied to dealings in trade and commerce.

lawn (lôn), *n.* [ME. & OFr. *launde,* heath < Bret. *lann,* territory, country; akin to W. *llan,* open space; IE. base as in *land*], 1. land covered with grass kept closely mown, especially in front of or around a house. 2. [Archaic], an open space in a forest; glade.

lawn (lôn), *n.* [earlier *laune lynen,* for *Laon linen* < *Laon,* city in France, where made], a fine, sheer cloth of linen or cotton, used for handkerchiefs, blouses, curtains, etc.

lawn mower, a hand-propelled or power-driven machine for cutting the grass of a lawn, typically with spiral steel blades rotating on a horizontal bar set between wheels.

lawn tennis, see **tennis.**

lawn·y (lôn′i), *adj.* 1. [Rare], having many lawns. 2. resembling a lawn.

lawn·y (lôn′i), *adj.* of or like lawn (cloth).

Law of Moses, the first five books of the Old Testament (Genesis, Exodus, Leviticus, Numbers, Deuteronomy); Pentateuch; Torah.

law of nations, international law.

law of the Medes and Persians, unchangeable law.

Law·rence (lôr′əns, lär′əns), a masculine name: see **Laurence.** *n.* 1. a city in northeastern Massachusetts, on the Merrimack River: pop., 71,000. 2. a city in eastern Kansas: pop., 33,000.

Lawrence, Saint, 3d century A.D.; Christian martyr.

Law·rence, D. H. (lôr′əns, lär′əns), (*David Herbert Lawrence*), 1885–1930; English novelist and poet.

Lawrence, Ernst Orlando, 1901–1958; American physicist; received Nobel prize in physics, 1939.

Lawrence, T. E., (name legally changed, 1927, to *Thomas Edward Shaw*), 1888–1935; British adventurer and writer: called *Lawrence of Arabia.*

Lawrence, Sir **Thomas,** 1769–1830; English portrait painter.

law·ren·ci·um (lô-ren′si-əm, lä-ren′si-əm), *n.* [after E. O. *Lawrence*], a radioactive chemical element produced by bombarding californium with boron nuclei: symbol, Lw; at. wt., 257?; at. no., 103?

law·suit (lô′sōōt′, lô′sūt′), *n.* a suit at law or in equity; case presented before a civil court for decision.

law·yer (lô′yẽr), *n.* [ME. *lawyere;* see LAW & -IER], a person who has been trained in the law, especially one whose profession is advising others in matters of law or representing them in lawsuits: abbreviated **law.**
SYN.—**lawyer** is the general term for a person trained in the law and authorized to advise or represent others in legal matters; **counselor** and its British equivalent, **barrister,** refer to a lawyer who conducts cases in court; **attorney,** generally, and its British equivalent, **solicitor,** always, refer to a lawyer legally empowered to act for a client, as in drawing up a contract or will, settling property, etc.; **counsel,** often equivalent to **counselor,** is frequently used collectively for a group of counselors.

lax (laks), *adj.* [ME.; L. *laxus;* IE. base **(s)lēg-, *(s)lĕg-,* to be loose, lax, seen also in *languid, languish, slack, lease*], 1. *a)* loose; emptying easily: said of the bowels. *b)* having lax bowels. 2. slack; of a loose texture; not rigid or tight. 3. not strict or exact; careless: as, *lax* morals. 4. in *botany,* loose; open: said of a flower cluster. 5. in *phonetics,* pronounced with the jaw and tongue relatively relaxed: said of certain vowels, as *e* in *met, i* in *hill.* *n.* a lax vowel. —*SYN.* see **remiss.**

lax·a·tion (lak-sā′shən), *n.* [ME. *laxacion;* L. *laxatio*], the act or process of making or being made lax.

lax·a·tive (lak′sə-tiv), *adj.* [ME. & Late OFr. *laxatif;* L. *laxativus*], tending to make lax; specifically, making the bowels loose and relieving constipation. *n.* any laxative medicine; mild cathartic. —*SYN.* see **physic.**

lax·i·ty (lak′sə-ti), *n.* [Fr. *laxité;* L. *laxitas*], the quality or condition of being lax.

lay (lā), *v.t.* [LAID (lād), LAYING], [ME. *leyen, leien;* new formation < 3d pers. sing. of earlier *leggen;* AS. *lecgan,* lit., to make lie (akin to Goth. *lagjan,* G. *legen*) < p.t. base of AS. *licgan,* to lie; cf. LIE (recline)], 1. to cause to come down or fall with force; knock down, as from an erect position: as, he *laid* his opponent low with one punch. 2. to cause to lie; place or put so as to be in a resting or recumbent position; deposit (with *on* or *in*): as, *lay* the pencil on the table. 3. *a)* to put down in the correct position for a specific purpose, as bricks, carpeting, etc. *b)* to cause to be situated in a particular place or condition: as, the scene is *laid* in France. 4. to place; put; set: of something abstract, as, he *lays* great emphasis on accuracy. 5. to produce and deposit (an egg or eggs): said of a bird, etc. 6. *a)* to cause to subside or settle: as, *lay* the dust. *b)* to allay, suppress, overcome, or appease: as, this *laid* the ghost, his doubts were *laid.* 7. to press or smooth down: as, she *laid* the nap of the cloth. 8. to bet (a specified sum, etc.). 9. to impose (a tax, penalty, etc.). 10. to work out; devise: as, *lay* your plans carefully. 11. to prepare (a table) for a meal; set with silverware, plates, etc. 12. to advance, present, or assert: as, he *laid* claim to the property. 13. to attribute; ascribe; charge; impute: as, the murder was *laid* to Jones. 14. *a)* to form (the strands of a rope) by twisting yarn. *b)* to form (a rope) by arranging and twisting the strands. 15. [Slang], to have sexual intercourse with. *v.i.* 1. to lay an egg or eggs. 2. to bet; wager. 3. to lie; recline: substandard usage. 4. to apply oneself with energy: as, the sailors *lay* to their oars. 5. in *nautical usage,* to station oneself in a required or specified position: as, they *lay* aft. *n.* 1. the way or position in which something is situated or arranged: as, the *lay* of the land. 2. a share in the profits of some enterprise, especially of a whaling expedition. 3. the direction or amount of twist of the strands of a rope, cable, etc.

lay about (one), 1. to deliver blows on all sides; strike out in every direction. 2. to act energetically.

lay a course, 1. in *nautical usage,* to proceed in a certain direction without tacking; hence, 2. to make plans to do something.

lay aside, 1. to put to one side; lay out of the way. 2. to save; lay away.

lay away, 1. to set aside for future use; save. 2. to set (merchandise) aside for future delivery. 3. to bury (usually in the passive).

lay before, to present to for consideration.

lay by, to save; lay away.

lay down, 1. to sacrifice or give up (one's life). 2. to assert or declare. 3. to bet; wager. 4. to store away, as wine in a cellar.

lay (fast) by the heels, 1. to put in chains or fetters; imprison. 2. to deprive of freedom of movement.

lay for, [Colloq.], to be waiting to attack.

lay in, to get and store away.

lay into, [Slang], 1. to attack and hit repeatedly; beat. 2. to attack with words; scold.

lay it on, [Colloq.], 1. to exaggerate. 2. to flatter; give effusive compliments.

lay off, 1. to put aside, as a garment. 2. to discharge (employees), especially temporarily. 3. to mark off the boundaries of. 4. [Slang], *a)* to cease. *b)* to stop criticizing, teasing, etc.

lay on, 1. to spread on. 2. to attack with force; strike repeatedly.

lay oneself open, to expose oneself to attack, blame, etc.

lay oneself out, [Colloq.], to try very hard.

lay open, 1. to open up; cut open. 2. to expose.

lay out, 1. to spend. 2. to arrange according to a plan. 3. to spread out (clothes, equipment, etc.) ready for wear, inspection, etc. 4. to make (a dead body) ready for burial; hence, 5. [Slang], to knock down or make unconscious.

lay over, to stop a while in a place before going on.

lay to, 1. to attribute to; credit to or blame on. 2. to apply oneself with vigor. 3. in *nautical usage, a)* to check the motion of a ship and cause it to become stationary. *b)* to lie more or less stationary with the bow to the wind: said of a ship.

lay up, 1. to store for future use; hoard. 2. to disable; confine to bed or the sickroom. 3. to put (a ship) in dock, as for repairs.

lay (lā), past tense of **lie** (to recline).

lay (lā), *adj.* [ME. & OFr. *lai;* L. *laicus;* Gr. *laikos* < *laos,* the people], 1. of the laity, or ordinary people, as distinguished from the clergy. 2. not belonging to or connected with a given profession; nonprofessional: as, no *lay* reader will understand this medical text.

lay (lā), *n.* [ME. & OFr. *lai;* prob. < Gmc. word represented by AS. *lac,* play, sport & OHG. *leich* (G. *leiche*), song, melody (see LARK, to play)], 1. a short poem, especially a narrative poem, for singing: originally applied to a short narrative poem for performance by a minstrel and with a story of Arthurian or Breton tradition. 2. [Archaic or Poetic], a song or melody.

Lay·a·mon (lā′ə-mən, lä′yə-mən), *n.* English priest and poet; fl. c. 1200; author of the Middle English verse chronicle *Brut:* also **Lawman** (form preferred by most modern scholars.

lay brother, 1. a member of a monastery who has taken vows and wears a distinctive habit but is not in holy orders: lay brothers are generally employed in manual labor. 2. a layman.

lay day, [short for *delay day*], 1. in *commerce,* any of the days allowed for loading or unloading a ship without payment of extra charge. 2. in *nautical usage,* any of the days that a ship is delayed in port.

lay·er (lā′ẽr), *n.* 1. a person or thing that lays. 2. a single thickness, coat, fold, or stratum. 3. a shoot or twig (of a living plant) bent down and partly covered with earth so that it may take root. *v.t. & v.i.* to grow (plants) by layering.

lay·er·age (lā'ẽr-ij), *n.* [see -AGE], the growing of plants by layering.

layer cake, a cake baked in two or more layers, which are placed one on the other, usually with icing, etc. in between.

lay·er·ing (lā'ẽr-iŋ), *n.* [*layer, v.* + *-ing*], a method of growing plants and shrubs by bending a shoot or twig and covering it with earth until it has rooted.

lay·ette (lā-et'), *n.* [Fr., dim. of *laie*, packing box, drawer; Fl. *laeye;* MD. *lade*, a chest, trunk < Gmc. **hlatho-*, container < base of Eng. *lade* (to load), G. *laden*], a complete outfit for a newborn baby, including clothes, bedding, and accessories.

lay figure, [earlier *layman;* D. *leeman* < MD. *led*, limb, joint + *man*, man], 1. an artist's jointed model of the human form, on which drapery is arranged to get the proper effect. 2. a mere puppet; figurehead.

lay·man (lā'mən), *n.* [*pl.* LAYMEN (-mən)], [*lay* (of the laity) + *man*], 1. a member of the laity; person not a clergyman. 2. a person not belonging to or skilled in a given profession: as, this medical textbook is not for the *layman*.

lay·off (lā'ôf'), *n.* [< phr. *lay off*], 1. a putting out of work or being put out of work, especially temporarily. 2. the period of such unemployment.

lay of the land, 1. the way the land is situated; arrangement of the terrain. 2. the existing state or disposition of affairs. Also **lie of the land.**

lay·out (lā'out'), *n.* 1. the act of laying something out. 2. the manner in which anything is laid out; arrangement; specifically, the plan or make-up of a newspaper, book, page, advertisement, etc. 3. the thing laid out. 4. an outfit or set, as of tools.

lay·o·ver (lā'ō'vẽr), *n.* [< phr. *lay over*], a stopping for a while in some place during a journey: as, we had a two-hour *layover* at Ogden.

la·zar (lā'zẽr, laz'ẽr), *n.* [ME. *lazar, lazer;* OFr. *lazar;* ML. *lazarus*, leper < L. *Lazarus;* Gr. *Lazaros*, Lazarus, beggar spoken of in Luke 16:19-31 < Heb. *el'āzār;* see LAZARUS], [Rare], an impoverished, diseased beggar, especially a leper.

laz·a·ret, laz·a·rette (laz'ə-ret'), *n.* [Fr. *lazaret* < It.], a lazaretto.

laz·a·ret·to (laz'ə-ret'ō), *n.* [*pl.* LAZARETTOS (-ōz)], [It.; Venetian *lazareto, nazareto* < Venetian church of Santa Madonna di *Nazaret*, used as a plague hospital during the 15th c.; initial *l-* by analogy with *lazzaro*, leper; see LAZAR], 1. a public hospital for poor people having contagious diseases, especially for lepers. 2. a building or ship used as a quarantine station. 3. in certain ships, a space between decks, used for storing provisions.

Laz·a·rus (laz'ə-rəs), [L.; Gr. *Lazaros* < Heb. *el'āzār*, lit., God has helped; cf. LAZAR, ELEAZAR], a masculine name. *n.* 1. in the *Bible*, *a*) the brother of Mary and Martha, raised from the dead by Jesus: John 11. *b*) the diseased beggar in Jesus' parable of the rich man and the beggar: Luke 16:19-31; hence, 2. [often l-], any horribly diseased beggar, especially a leper.

Laz·a·rus, Emma (laz'ə-rəs), 1849–1887; American poet and essayist.

laze (lāz), *v.i.* [LAZED (lāzd), LAZING], [back-formation < *lazy*], to be lazy or idle; loaf. *v.t.* to spend (time, etc.) in idleness (often with *away*).

La·zear, Jesse William (lə-zêr'), 1866–1900; American physician; known for his work on yellow fever.

la·zi·ly (lā'z'l-i), *adv.* in a lazy manner.

la·zi·ness (lā'zi-nis), *n.* a lazy quality or state.

lazuli, see **lapis lazuli.**

laz·u·lite (laz'yoo-lit'), *n.* [< ML. *lazulum*, azure; + *-ite*], a glassy, azure-blue mineral, hydrous aluminum phosphate, with varying amounts of iron and magnesium.

la·zy (lā'zi), *adj.* [LAZIER (-zi-ẽr), LAZIEST (-zi-ist)], [Early Mod. Eng.; prob. < MLG. or MD.; cf. MLG. *lasich*, slack, loose; for IE. base see LATE], 1. not eager or willing to work or exert oneself; indolent; slothful. 2. slow and heavy; sluggish: as, a *lazy* motion. 3. tending to cause laziness: as, a *lazy* day.

la·zy·bones (lā'zi-bōnz'), *n.* [Colloq.], a lazy person.

Lazy Susan, a large revolving tray for food.

lazy tongs, a device consisting of a series of jointed bars crossing each other: it can be extended to pick up small objects at a slight distance from the person using it.

LAZY TONGS

laz·za·ro·ne (laz'ə-rō'nā), *n.* [*pl.* LAZZARONI (-ni)], [It. < *lazzaro*, leper; see LAZAR], any of a class of homeless beggars formerly common on the streets of Naples.

lb., [L.], *libra*, pound; *librae*, pounds.

L.B., 1. *Lit(t)erarum Baccalaureus*, [L.], Bachelor of Letters; Bachelor of Literature. 2. Local Board.

L bar (or beam), a steel bar or beam made in the shape of an L.

lbs., pounds.

L/C, l/c, letter of credit.

L.C., 1. Library of Congress. 2. Lower Canada.

l.c., 1. left center (of the stage). 2. *loco citato*, [L.], in the place cited. 3. in *typography*, lower case.

L.C.D., l.c.d., lowest (or least) common denominator.

L.C.F., l.c.f., lowest (or least) common factor.

LCI, Landing Craft, Infantry.

L.C.L., l.c.l., in *commerce*, less than carload lot.

L.C.M., l.c.m., lowest (or least) common multiple.

LD, L.D., Low Dutch.

Ld., 1. Limited. 2. Lord.

Ldp., Lordship.

L.D.S., 1. Latter-day Saints. 2. Licentiate in Dental Surgery.

-le ('l), an old suffix of various origins and meanings: 1. [ME. n. suffix *-el, -le;* AS. *-ol, -ul, -el*], *a*) *small*, as in *icicle*. *b*) *a person that does* (something specified), as in *beadle*. *c*) *a thing used for doing* (something specified), as in *girdle, handle*. 2. [ME. adj. suffix *-el* < AS. *-ol*], *having a tendency toward*, as in *brittle, fickle*. 3. [ME. v. suffix *-len;* AS. *-lian*], used with a frequentative force, as in *babble, prattle*. 4. [ME. n. suffix *-el* < OFr. *-el* (see MANTLE), *-aille* (see BATTLE), or *-eille* (see BOTTLE)], various other meanings.

le., in *football*, left end.

lea (lē), *n.* [ME. *ley, lee;* AS. *leah*, orig., open ground in a wood; akin to D. *-loo* (in *Waterloo*, etc.), G. *-loh*, grove; IE. base **leuq-*, light, shine, seen also in L. *lucus*, grove, orig., clearing, glade, *lux*, light, *lucere*, to shine (cf. LUCID)], [Chiefly Poetic], a meadow, grassy field, or pasture; grassland.

lea (lē), *n.* [? taken as sing. < *leas* < OFr. *lesse, laisse;* see LEASH], a measure of yarn varying from 80 to 300 yards, according to the kind of yarn (usually 80 yards for wool, 120 yards for silk and cotton, 300 yards for linen).

lea., 1. league. 2. leather. 3. leave.

leach (lēch), *v.t.* [prob. < AS. *leccan*, to water, irrigate < same base as *lacu*, a stream, pond; see LAKE (body of water)], 1. to cause (a liquid) to filter down through some material. 2. to subject to the washing action of a filtering liquid: as, wood ashes are *leached* to extract lye. 3. to extract (a soluble substance) from some material by causing water to filter down through the material: as, lye is *leached* from wood ashes. *v.i.* 1. to lose soluble matter as a result of the filtering through of water: as, this soil has *leached* badly. 2. to dissolve and be washed away: as, much of the mineral content of this soil has *leached* out. *n.* 1. a leaching. 2. a sievelike container used in leaching. 3. the substance through which a liquid is leached.

leach·y (lēch'i), *adj.* [*leach* + *-y*], porous, as soil.

Lea·cock, Stephen Butler (lē'kok), 1869–1944; Canadian political economist, humorist, and educator.

lead (lēd), *v.t.* [LED (led), LEADING], [ME. *leden;* AS. *lædan*, caus. of *lithan*, to travel, go; akin to G. *leiten*], 1. to show the way to, or direct the course of, by going before or along with; conduct; guide. 2. to guide, or cause to follow one, by physical contact, holding the hand, pulling a rope, etc.: as, he *led* the horse by the bridle. 3. to show (the way, etc.) by traveling a course or path: as, *lead* the way! 4. to show the way to; mark the way for: as, the lights *led* me to the shore. 5. to guide the course or direction of (water, steam, rope, etc.); conduct in a certain direction, channel, etc. 6. *a*) to guide by persuasion; induce to a course of action or thought; direct by influence: as, a teacher *leads* his pupils to think clearly. *b*) to cause; prompt: as, his troubles *led* him to drink. 7. to be the head of; specifically, *a*) to act as chief officer of; command the operations of (a military unit). *b*) to direct the operations of (an expedition, etc.). *c*) to direct, conduct, or serve as the leader or conductor of (an orchestra, ballet, etc.). 8. to be the first or foremost among; be at the head of: as, she *leads* the class. 9. to live; spend; pass: as, he *leads* a strenuous life. 10. to cause to live or spend: as, she *leads* him a dog's life. 11. to begin or open. 12. in *card games*, to begin the play with (a card or suit); lay down as the first card or suit of a hand or round. 13. in *hunting*, to aim a rifle, etc. just ahead of (a moving target). *v.i.* 1. to show the way by going before or along; act as guide; guide; conduct. 2. to submit to being led; be tractable. 3. to be or form a way; tend in a certain direction; go (with *to, from, under*, etc.). 4. to bring as a result (with *to*): as, one thing *led* to another. 5. to be first, chief, or head; act as leader. 6. to begin. 7. in *boxing*, to strike a first blow or one designed to test an opponent's defense: as, never *lead* with your right. 8. in *card games*, to play, or have the right to play, the first card of a hand or round. *n.* 1. the part of director or leader; leadership: as, in community projects he always took the *lead*. 2. example: as, we will follow your *lead*. 3. first or front place; precedence: as, he took the *lead* at the first turn. 4. the extent of distance ahead or precedence: as, we now hold a safe *lead*. 5. anything that leads or serves as a clue. 6. in *boxing*, a leading, or the blow used. 7. in *card games*, act or right of playing first, as in a hand, or the card or suit played. 8. in *electricity*, *a*) a wire carrying current from one point to another in a circuit.

b) a wire or cable carrying current to or from a piece of apparatus. 9. in the *theater*, a) the principal role, or a leading role, in a play or other production. b) the actor or actress who plays such a role. 10. in *journalism*, the opening paragraph of a news story, containing all the essential facts of the story. 11. in *mining*, a stratum of ore in an old river bed; lode. 12. in *nautical usage*, the course of a rope. *adj.* acting as leader: as, the *lead* horse. —*SYN.* see **guide.**

lead off, to begin.

lead on, 1. to conduct further. 2. to encourage to continue; lure.

lead one a chase (or **dance**), to cause a person trouble by luring him into a vain pursuit.

lead out, 1. to begin. 2. to take a partner to begin dancing.

lead up to, to prepare the way for.

lead (led), *n.* [ME. *lede;* AS. *lead;* akin to D. *lood,* G. *lot,* plummet; prob. Celt. word (cf. MIr. *luiade,* lead) borrowed in Gmc. with basic sense "easily melted"], 1. a heavy, soft, malleable, bluish-gray metallic chemical element used for piping and in numerous alloys and compounds: symbol, Pb; at. wt., 207.21; at. no., 82. 2. anything made of this metal; specifically, a) a weight for sounding depths at sea, etc.: it is attached to a line and tossed over the side of the ship. b) *usually in pl.* any of the strips of lead used to hold the individual panes in ornamental windows. c) *pl.* [British], sheets of lead used for covering a roof. d) in *printing*, a thin strip of type metal inserted to increase the space between lines of type. 3. bullets. 4. a thin stick of graphite, used in pencils. *adj.* made of or containing lead. *v.t.* 1. to cover, line, weight, or fasten with lead or leads. 2. in *ceramics*, to glaze (pottery) with a glaze made primarily of lead. 3. in *printing*, to increase the space between (lines of type) by inserting thin strips of type metal. *v.i.* to become covered with lead.

heave the lead, to take soundings, or depth measurements, in the sea.

lead acetate, a poisonous, colorless, crystalline compound, $Pb(C_2H_3O_2)_2 \cdot 3H_2O$, used as a mordant in dyeing, and in making varnishes; sugar of lead.

lead arsenate, a very poisonous, colorless, crystalline compound, $Pb_3(AsO_4)_2$, used as an insecticide.

lead·en (led′'n), *adj.* 1. made of lead. 2. having the inert heaviness of lead; hard to move or lift. 3. sluggish; dull; heavy in action, feeling, etc. 4. depressed; dispirited; gloomy. 5. of a dull gray.

lead·er (lēd′ẽr), *n.* 1. a person or thing that leads; directing, commanding, or guiding head, as of a group or activity. 2. a horse harnessed before all others in the same hitch or as one of the two horses in the foremost span. 3. a pipe for carrying water, etc. 4. a tendon. 5. a featured article of trade, especially one offered at an attractively low price. 6. in *fishing*, a short piece of catgut, etc. often used to attach the hook, lure, etc. to the fishline proper. 7. in *journalism*, one of the main editorials or articles, as in a newspaper. 8. in *music*, a) a conductor, especially the conductor of a dance band. b) the main performer in an instrumental or vocal section, generally given the solo passages. 9. in *nautical usage*, a wooden block or metal piece with holes in it for leading lines to their proper places. 10. *pl.* in *printing*, dots, dashes, etc. in a line, used to direct the eye across the page, as in a table of contents.

lead·er·ship (lēd′ẽr-ship′), *n.* [see -SHIP], 1. the position or guidance of a leader. 2. the ability to lead.

lead-in (lēd′in′), *n.* the wire leading from the aerial to a radio receiver or transmitter.

lead-in (lēd′in′), *adj.* leading in: as, a *lead-in* wire or cable for a radio.

lead·ing (led′iŋ), *n.* 1. a covering or being covered with lead. 2. strips or sheets of lead, collectively.

lead·ing (lēd′iŋ), *n.* the action of one that leads; guidance; direction; leadership. *adj.* 1. that leads; guiding. 2. principal; chief. 3. playing the lead in a play, motion picture, etc. —*SYN.* see **chief.**

leading article, a principal editorial or article in a newspaper.

leading edge, 1. in *aeronautics*, the front edge of a propeller blade or airfoil. 2. in *nautical usage*, that edge of the sail which first encounters the wind.

leading light, 1. a light used to guide ships into and out of a harbor. 2. [Slang], one of the most important members of a club, community, etc.

leading question, a question put in such a way as to suggest the answer sought.

leading strings, 1. strings or straps used to guide and support a young child learning to walk; hence, 2. guidance; especially, excessive guidance or control.

leading tone, in *music*, the seventh tone of a scale, a half tone below the tonic.

lead line (led), in *nautical usage*, a sounding line.

lead·off (lēd′ôf′), *n.* a beginning; especially, in certain sports, the first blow, play, or turn.

lead-off (lēd′ôf′), *adj.* that leads off, or begins.

lead pencil (led), a pencil consisting of a slender stick of graphite encased in wood, etc.; common pencil.

lead poisoning, an acute or chronic poisoning caused by the absorption of lead or any of its salts into the body: it may result in anemia, constipation, colic, paralysis, or muscular cramps.

leads·man (ledz′mən), *n.* [*pl.* LEADSMEN (-mən)], in *nautical usage*, a man who heaves a lead to take soundings.

lead tet·ra·eth·yl (tet′rə-eth′əl), tetraethyl lead.

lead time (lēd), in *manufacturing*, the period of time required from the decision to make a product to the beginning of actual production.

lead·y (led′i), *adj.* resembling lead; leaden.

leaf (lēf), *n.* [*pl.* LEAVES (lēvz)], [ME. *lefe;* AS. *leaf;* akin to D. *loof,* G. *laub;* IE. base **leub(h)-*, to peel off, pull off, etc., seen also in Lith. *lupù*, to skin, pare off], 1. any of the flat, thin, expanded organs, usually green, growing from the stem or twig of a plant: it usually consists of a broad blade, a petiole, or stalk, and stipules: see LEAF FORMS, p. 832. 2. in popular usage, a) the blade of a leaf. b) a petal: as, a tulip *leaf.* 3. leaves collectively: as, a consignment of choice tobacco *leaf.* 4. a sheet of paper, especially as part of a book, with a page on each side. 5. a) a very thin sheet of metal; lamina. b) such sheets collectively: as, a frame covered with gold *leaf.* 6. a) a hinged section of a table top, forming an extension when raised into place. b) a board inserted into a table top to increase its surface. 7. a flat, hinged or movable part of a folding door, shutter, etc. 8. one of a number of metal strips laid one upon another to make a leaf spring. Abbreviated **L., l.** *v.i.* to put forth or bear leaves; leave (often with *out*). *v.t.* to turn the pages of (a book, etc.), as in looking through it quickly (often with *through*).

in leaf, having leaves grown; with foliage.

take a leaf from one's book, to follow one's example.

turn over a new leaf, to make a new start.

leaf·age (lēf′ij), *n.* [*leaf* + *-age*], leaves collectively; foliage.

leaf fat, fat built up in flakes or layers around the kidneys of a pig.

leaf hopper, an insect that leaps from one plant to another, sucking the juices and causing destruction.

leaf·i·ness (lēf′i-nis), *n.* the state of being leafy.

leaf lard, lard made from leaf fat.

leaf·less (lēf′lis), *adj.* having no leaves.

leaf·let (lēf′lit), *n.* [*leaf* + *-let*], 1. one of the divisions of a compound leaf. 2. a small or young leaf. 3. a separate sheet of printed matter, often folded but not stitched; folder: as, propaganda *leaflets.*

leaf mold, a rich soil consisting largely of decayed leaves.

leaf spring, a spring built up of curved strips of metal: see **spring,** illus.

leaf·stalk (lēf′stôk′), *n.* a supporting stem by which a leaf is attached to a twig or larger branch; petiole.

leaf·y (lēf′i), *adj.* [LEAFIER (-i-ẽr), LEAFIEST (-i-ist)], 1. of, covered with, consisting of, or like a leaf or leaves. 2. having many leaves. 3. having broad leaves: as, lettuce and spinach are *leafy* vegetables.

league (lēg), *n.* [ME. *ligg;* OFr. *ligue;* It. *liga, lega* < *legare;* L. *ligare*, to bind], 1. a compact or covenant made by nations, groups, or individuals for promoting common interests, assuring mutual protection, etc. 2. an association or alliance of individuals, groups, or nations, formed by such a covenant. *v.t. & v.i.* [LEAGUED (lēgd), LEAGUING], to form into a league. —*SYN.* see **alliance.**

in league, associated for a common purpose; allied.

the League, the League of Nations.

league (lēg), *n.* [ME. *lege;* OFr. *legue;* LL. *leuga, leuca,* Gallic mile; of Celt. origin], a measure of distance varying in different times and countries: in English-speaking countries it is usually about 3 statute miles or 3 nautical miles: abbreviated **L., l., lea.**

League of Nations, an association of nations, established January 10, 1920, by the Versailles treaty, to promote international co-operation and peace: it was dissolved in April, 1946, and was succeeded by the United Nations after World War II.

lea·guer (lē′gẽr), *n.* [D. *leger*, a camp, bed; see LAIR], [Archaic], 1. a siege; beleaguering. 2. a besieging army. 3. the camp of such an army. *v.t.* [Archaic], to besiege.

lea·guer (lē′gẽr), *n.* a member of a league.

Le·ah (lē′ə), [Heb. *lē'āh*, lit., gazelle, wild cow], a feminine name. *n.* in the *Bible*, the elder daughter of Laban, given in marriage to Jacob after Jacob had served Laban seven years believing he would receive Rachel, the younger daughter: Gen. 29:13-30.

LEAF FORMS

Kinds

SIMPLE

ABRUPTLY PINNATE

ODD-PINNATE

TWICE ODD-PINNATE

PINNATELY DECOMPOUND

PALMATE

Margins

DENTATE

CRENATE

ENTIRE

SERRATE

DOUBLY SERRATE

PINNATELY LOBED

PALMATELY LOBED

UNDULATE

Shapes

OVAL

OBLONG

LINEAR

KIDNEY-SHAPED

WEDGE-SHAPED

AWL-SHAPED

SPATULATE

ELLIPTICAL

SAGITTATE

PELTATE

ACEROSE

OVATE

OBOVATE

ORBICULAR

LANCEOLATE RUNCINATE

DELTOID

Bases

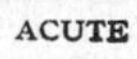
ACUTE

OBLIQUE

ROUNDED

ACUMINATE

SAGITTATE

HASTATE

CORDATE

AURICULATE

Tips

ACUTE

OBTUSE

OBCORDATE

MUCRONATE

EMARGINATE

ARISTATE

ACUMINATE

TRUNCATE

Venation

BASE TO MARGIN

MIDRIB TO MARGIN

PARALLEL FROM BASE TO TIP

PINNATE

PALMATE

Lea·hy, William Daniel (lā′hi, lā′i), 1875–1959; American admiral and diplomat.

leak (lēk), *v.i.* [ME. *leken* < ON. *leka*, to drip; akin to AS. *leccan*, to water, moisten; see LEACH, LAKE], 1. to let a fluid substance out or in accidentally: as, the ship *leaks*. 2. to enter or escape accidentally from an object or container (often with *in* or *out*). 3. to become known little by little, by accident, carelessness, or treachery: as, the truth *leaked* out. *v.t.* 1. to permit (water, air, etc.) to pass accidentally in or out; allow to leak. 2. to allow to become known: as, to *leak* secrets or information. *n.* 1. an accidental hole or crack that lets something out or in. 2. any means of escape for something that ought not to be let out, lost, etc. 3. the fact of leaking; leakage. 4. *a)* a loss of electrical charge through faulty insulation. *b)* the point where this occurs.

leak·age (lēk′ij), *n.* [see -AGE], 1. a leaking in or out; leak. 2. something that leaks in or out. 3. the amount that leaks in or out. 4. in *commerce*, an allowance for a partial loss by leaking, as of liquids in shipment.

leak·i·ness (lēk′i-nis), *n.* a leaky quality or state.

leak·y (lēk′i), *adj.* [LEAKIER (-i-ēr), LEAKIEST (-i-ist)], 1. allowing the accidental entrance or escape of a fluid substance; having a leak or leaks. 2. [Colloq.], not able to keep a secret.

leal (lēl), *adj.* [north Brit. dial. form of *loyal* < OFr. *leal*; L. *legalis*], [Archaic or Scot.], loyal; true.

lean (lēn), *v.i.* [LEANED (lēnd) or LEANT (lent), LEANING], [ME. *lenen*; AS. *hlinian*, to lean, *hlænan*, to cause to lean; akin to G. *lehnen*; IE. base **klei-*, to incline, lean, seen also in *incline, decline, climax, ladder*, etc.], 1. to bend or deviate from an upright position; stand slanting; incline. 2. to bend or incline the body so as to rest part of one's weight upon or against something: as, he *leaned* on the desk. 3. to rely; depend for encouragement, advice, etc. (with *upon* or *on*). 4. to tend; favor slightly: as, you *lean* toward state control of education. *v.t.* 1. to cause to bend from an upright position: as, the storm *leaned* the telephone poles over. 2. to place (something) so that it rests against something else: as, *lean* the ladder against the house. *n.* a bend or deviation from the upright; incline; slant.

lean over backward, [Colloq.], to counterbalance a tendency, prejudice, etc. by an extreme effort in the opposite direction.

lean (lēn), *adj.* [ME. *lene*; AS *hlæne*; usually derived < *lean*, *v.* in sense "leaning, drooping," hence "thin, slender"], 1. with little flesh or fat; thin; spare: opposed to *fat*. 2. containing little or no fat: said of meat. 3. lacking in richness, profit, productiveness, etc.; meager. *n.* meat containing little or no fat.

***SYN.*—lean** implies a healthy, natural absence of fat or fleshiness; **spare** suggests a sinewy frame without any superfluous flesh; **lanky** implies an awkward tallness and leanness, and, often, loose-jointedness; **skinny** and **scrawny** imply extreme thinness that is unattractive and indicative of a lack of vigor; **gaunt** implies a bony thinness such as that caused by a wasting away of the flesh from hunger or suffering. See also **thin.**—*ANT.* fleshy, fat, stout.

Le·an·der (li-an′dēr), [L.; Gr. *Leiandros, Leandros*; ? < *leōn*, lion + *anēr, andros*, a man], a masculine name. *n.* in *Greek legend*, the lover of Hero: see **Hero.**

lean·ing (lēn′iŋ), *n.* 1. the act of a person or thing that leans. 2. tendency; inclination; penchant; predilection. —*SYN.* see **inclination.**

Leaning Tower of Pisa, a tower in Pisa, Italy, which leans more than 16 feet from the perpendicular.

leant (lent), alternative past tense and past participle of **lean.**

lean-to (lēn′to͞o′), *n.* [*pl.* LEAN-TOS (-to͞oz′)], 1. a roof with a single slope, its upper edge abutting a wall or building. 2. a shed with a one-slope roof, the upper end of the rafters resting against an external support, such as trees or the wall of a building. 3. a structure, as the wing of a building, whose roof is a lean-to. *adj.* having or characterized by such construction.

leap (lēp), *v.i.* [LEAPED (lēpt) or LEAPT (lept, lēpt), LEAPING], [ME. *lepen*; AS. *hleapan*; akin to MD. *lopen* (cf. LOPE), G. *laufen*; prob. IE. base **klou-b-*, < **klou-*, to bend (the legs, etc.), as also in Lith. *šlubúoti*, to hobble, limp], 1. to move oneself suddenly from the ground, etc. by using one's leg muscles; jump; spring. 2. to move suddenly or swiftly, as if by jumping; bound. *v.t.* 1. to pass over by a jump. 2. to cause or force to leap: as, he *leaped* his horse over the wall. *n.* 1. the act of leaping; jump; spring. 2. the distance covered in a jump. 3. a place that is, or is to be, leaped over or from. 4. a sudden transition.

leap in the dark, an act that is risky because its consequences cannot be foreseen.

leap·frog (lēp′frôg′, lēp′frog′), *n.* a game in which each of the players takes a turn jumping, with legs spread wide, over the bent backs of the other players.

leapt (lept, lēpt), alternative past tense and past participle of **leap.**

leap year, a year of 366 days, occurring every fourth year: the additional day, given to February, makes up for the time lost annually when the approximate 365 1/4-day cycle is computed as 365 days: a leap year is a year whose number is exactly divisible by four, or, in the case of century years, by 400.

Lear (lêr), *n.* King Lear.

Lear, Edward (lêr), 1812–1888; English humorist and painter.

learn (lũrn), *v.t.* [LEARNED (lũrnd) or LEARNT (lũrnt), LEARNING], [ME. *lernen*, to learn, teach; AS. *leornian* (akin to G. *lernen*) < base of *lar*, learning, knowledge; see LORE], 1. to get knowledge of (a subject) or skill in (an art, trade, etc.) by study, experience, instruction, etc.; get and keep in the mind. 2. to come to know: as, I *learned* that he had been sick. 3. to come to know how: as, we are *learning* to swim. 4. to fix in mind; memorize. 5. to acquire as a habit or attitude: as, you have *learned* humility. 6. to teach: now substandard or dialectal. *v.i.* 1. to gain knowledge or skill. 2. to be informed; hear (*of*).

***SYN.*—learn**, as considered here, implies a finding out of something without conscious effort (I *learned* of his marriage from a friend); **ascertain** implies a finding out with certainty by careful inquiry, experimentation, research, etc. (he *ascertained* the firm's credit rating): **determine** stresses intention to establish the facts exactly, often so as to settle something in doubt (to *determine* the exact denotation of a word); **discover** implies a finding out, by chance, exploration, etc., of something already existing or known to others (to *discover* a plot, a star, etc.); **unearth**, in its figurative sense, implies a bringing to light, as by diligent search, of something that has been concealed, lost, forgotten, etc. (to *unearth* old documents, a secret, etc.).

learn·ed (lũr′nid), *adj.* [orig. pp. of *learn* in obs. sense of "teach"], 1. *a)* having or showing much learning; well-informed; erudite. *b)* having or showing much learning in some special field: as, a *learned* doctor. 2. of scholarship and study: as, a *learned* society. 3. characterized by, resulting from, or requiring study and learning.

learn·ing (lũr′niŋ), *n.* [ME. *lerning*; AS. *leornung* < *leornian*, to learn], 1. the acquiring of knowledge or skill. 2. acquired knowledge or skill; especially, much knowledge in a special field. —*SYN.* see **information.**

learnt (lũrnt), alternative past tense and past participle of **learn.**

lear·y (lêr′i), *adj.* [Colloq.], leery.

leas·a·ble (lēs′ə-b'l), *adj.* that can be leased.

lease (lēs), *n.* [OFr. *lais, leis, lez* < *laissier, lesser* < L. *laxare*, to loosen, relax < *laxus*, loose; see LAX], 1. a contract by which one party (landlord, or lessor) gives to another (tenant, or lessee) the use and possession of lands, buildings, etc. for a specified time and for fixed payments. 2. the document in which this contract is written. 3. the period of time for which such a contract is in force: as, during his *lease* the property was well kept up. *v.t.* [LEASED (lēst), LEASING], [OFr. *laissier, lesser*], 1. to give by a lease; let. 2. to get by a lease; take a lease on. —*SYN.* see **hire.**

new lease on life, a chance to live better or more happily because of a recovery of health, position, money, etc.

lease·hold (lēs′hōld′), *n.* 1. a holding by lease. 2. lands, buildings, etc. held by lease. *adj.* held by lease.

lease·hold·er (lēs′hōl′dēr), *n.* a tenant who holds a lease; lessee.

leash (lēsh), *n.* [ME. *leesshe, lese, lees*; OFr. *lesse*; L. *laxa*, fem. of *laxus*, loose; see LAX], 1. a cord, strap, etc. by which a dog or other animal is held in check. 2. in *hunting*, a set of three, as of hounds; brace and a half. *v.t.* to attach a leash to; check as by a leash.

hold in leash, to control; curb; restrain.

strain at the leash, to be eager to do as one pleases without restraint; be impatient to have freedom.

leas·ing (lēz′iŋ), *n.* [ME. *lesinge*; AS. *leasung*, falsehood < *leas*, lacking, false < base of *leosan*, to lose; see LOSE], [Obs.], lying; lies; a lie.

least (lēst), *adj.* [alternative superlative of *little*], [ME. *leste, lest*; AS. *læsest, læst*, superl. of *læssa*, less], 1. smallest in size, degree, extent, importance, etc.; slightest: as, the *least* movement. 2. [Dial.], smallest or youngest: as, her *least* child is sick. *adv.* [superlative of *little*], in the smallest degree. *n.* the smallest in size, amount, importance, etc.

at (the) least, 1. at the very lowest figure, amount, etc.; with no less. 2. at any rate; in any event.

not in the least, not at all; not in the smallest degree.

least common multiple, the lowest number that exactly contains each of two or more given numbers: as, the *least common multiple* of 4, 5, and 10 is 20: abbreviated **L.C.M., l.c.m.**

least·ways (lēst′wāz′), *adv.* [< phr. *at the least ways*, at least], [Chiefly Dial.], leastwise.

least·wise (lēst′wīz′), *adv.* [Colloq.], at least; anyway.

leath·er (leth'ẽr), *n.* [ME. *leder, lether;* AS. *lether-;* akin to G. *leder,* ON. *lethr;* not known outside Gmc.], 1. a material consisting of animal skin prepared for use by removing the hair and tanning. 2. any of various articles or parts made of this material. *adj.* of or made of leather. Abbreviated **lea.** *v.t.* 1. to cover or furnish with leather. 2. [Colloq.], to whip or thrash with or as with a leather strap.

leath·er·back (leth'ẽr-bak'), *n.* a nonedible tropical sea turtle covered with a tough, dark-brown, leathery upper shell spotted with yellow: it is the largest of the turtle family, weighing up to 1,500 pounds.

leath·er·ette, leath·er·et (leth'ẽr-et'), *n.* [see -ETTE], imitation leather made of paper or cloth.

leath·er·i·ness (leth'ẽr-i-nis), *n.* the quality or condition of being leathery.

leath·ern (leth'ẽrn), *adj.* [ME. & AS. *letheren;* cf. BEECHEN, OAKEN], 1. made of or consisting of leather. 2. like leather.

leath·er·neck (leth'ẽr-nek'), *n.* [Slang], a United States marine.

leath·er·oid (leth'ẽr-oid'), *n.* imitation leather made of chemically treated paper stock or the like.

leath·er·wood (leth'ẽr-wood'), *n.* a small American tree with a tough, fibrous bark and tough, flexible shoots.

leath·er·y (leth'ẽr-i), *adj.* like leather in appearance or texture; tough and flexible.

leave (lēv), *v.t.* [LEFT (left), LEAVING], [ME. *leven;* AS. *læfan,* lit., to let remain (**lafjan* < base of AS. *laf,* remnant, what remains); akin to AS. (*be*)*lifan,* to remain (G. *bleiben;* OHG. *belīban*); IE. base **leip-,* to stick to, adhere; cf. LIVE, LIFE], 1. to cause or allow to remain; not take away: as, the pickers *left* much fruit on the trees. 2. to make, place, deposit, etc., and cause to remain behind one: as, the invaders *left* a trail of destruction. 3. to have remaining after one: as, the deceased *leaves* a widow and two children. 4. to bequeath: as, she *left* her fortune to charity. 5. to commit; entrust (with *to* or *up to*): as, he *leaves* such decisions up to me. 6. to allow to remain unremoved or unchanged: as, ten minus two *leaves* eight. 7. to reject: as, here is my proposal—take it or *leave* it. 8. to go away from. 9. to go away from and let remain in a certain condition: as, I *left* him alone in the building. 10. to give up; abandon; forsake. 11. to stop living in, working for, or belonging to. 12. [Slang], to let: as, *leave* us go now. *v.i.* to go away, depart, or set out: abbreviated **lv.** —*SYN.* see **go.**

leave in, in *bridge,* to let the declared suit of (one's partner) stand by refusing to bid further.

leave off, 1. to stop; cease. 2. to stop doing, using, or wearing.

leave one alone, not to bother or disturb one.

leave out, 1. to omit. 2. to fail to consider; ignore.

leave (lēv), *n.* [ME. *leve;* AS. *leaf,* permission; akin to obs. G. *laube,* permission, *erlauben,* to allow, permit; IE. base **leubh-,* to like, desire, seen also in L. *libido* (cf. LIBIDO, LIBIDINOUS), Eng. *believe, lief*], 1. permission. 2. permission to be absent from duty or work; especially, in *military usage,* such permission given to officers in any of the armed services or to enlisted personnel in the navy. 3. the period for which such permission is granted. Abbreviated **lv., lea.**

beg leave, to ask permission.

by your leave, with your permission.

on leave, absent from duty with permission.

take leave of, to say good-by to.

take one's leave, to go away; depart.

leave (lēv), *v.i.* [LEAVED (lēvd), LEAVING], [ME. *leven;* see LEAF], to put forth, or bear, leaves; leaf.

leaved (lēvd), *adj.* 1. in leaf. 2. having (a specified number or kind of) leaves: usually in hyphenated compounds, as *narrow-leaved.*

leav·en (lev''n), *n.* [ME. *levain, levein;* OFr. *levain* < L. *levamen,* alleviation, mitigation, solace < *levare,* to make light, relieve, raise], 1. *a*) a substance, such as yeast, used to produce fermentation, especially in dough. *b*) a small piece of fermenting dough put aside for this use. 2. any influence spreading through something and working on it to bring about a gradual change; tempering quality or thing. *v.t.* 1. to produce fermentation in by means of yeast or other ferment; make (dough) rise. 2. to spread through, causing a gradual change.

leav·en·ing (lev''n-iŋ), *n.* 1. a causing to ferment by leaven. 2. a thing that leavens; leaven.

Leav·en·worth (lev''n-wũrth'), *n.* 1. a city in northeastern Kansas: pop., 22,000. 2. a Federal prison located there.

leave of absence, a leave (*n.* sense 2).

leaves (lēvz), *n.* plural of **leaf.**

leave-tak·ing (lēv'tāk'iŋ), *n.* the act of taking leave, or saying good-by.

leav·ing (lēv'iŋ), *n.* [< *leave* (to cause to remain)], 1. *usually in pl.* a thing left; leftover; remnant. 2. *pl.* refuse; offal.

leav·y (lēv'i), *adj.* [LEAVIER (-i-ẽr), LEAVIEST (-i-ist)], [Poetic], leafy.

Leb·a·nese (leb'ə-nēz'), *adj.* of Lebanon or its people. *n.* [*pl.* LEBANESE], a native or inhabitant of Lebanon.

Leb·a·non (leb'ə-nən), *n.* 1. a country in western Asia, on the Mediterranean: area, 3,600 sq. mi.; pop., 1,652,000; capital, Beirut. 2. a city in southeastern Pennsylvania: pop., 30,000.

Lebanon Mountains, a mountain range in Lebanon: highest peak, Dahr el Quadib, 10,060 ft.

‡Le·bens·raum (lā'bəns-roum'), *n.* [G.], living space; territory for political and economic expansion: term of German imperialism.

Le·brun, Al·bert (ål'bâr' lə-brön'), 1871–1950; French statesman; president of France (1932–1940).

lech·er (lech'ẽr), *n.* [ME. *lechoure, lichour;* OFr. *leicheor,* debauchee < OHG. *leccōn* (G. *lecken*), to lick; cf. LICK], a man who indulges his sexual desires excessively and without restraint; lewd, grossly sensual man.

lech·er·ous (lech'ẽr-əs), *adj.* [ME.; OFr. *lecheros*], given to, characterized by, or stimulating to lechery; lustful.

lech·er·y (lech'ẽr-i), *n.* [ME. *lecherie;* OFr. *lecherie, licherie* < *lecheor;* see LECHER], unrestrained, excessive indulgence of sexual desires; gross sensuality; lewdness.

lec·i·thin (les'ə-thin), *n.* [< Gr. *lekithos,* yolk of an egg; + *-in*], a nitrogenous, fatty substance found in nerve tissue, blood, milk, egg yolk, and some vegetables: it is used in medicine, foods, etc.

Leck·y, William Edward Hart·pole (härt'pōl' lek'i), 1838–1903; Irish essayist and historian.

Le·conte de Lisle, Charles Ma·rie (shårl' må'rē' lə-kōnt' də lēl'), 1818–1894; French poet.

Le Cor·bu·sier (lə kôr'bü'zyā'), (born *Charles Édouard Jeanneret*), 1887–; Swiss architect in France.

lect., 1. lecture. 2. lecturer.

lec·tern (lek'tẽrn), *n.* [ME. & OFr. *lettrun;* LL. *lectrum* < L. *lectus,* pp. of *legere,* to read], 1. a reading desk in a church; especially, such a desk from which a part of the Scriptures is read in a church service. 2. a small stand for holding the notes, written speech, etc., as of a lecturer.

lec·tion (lek'shən), *n.* [L. *lectio* < *lectus;* see LECTERN], 1. a reading, as found in a particular text. 2. a part of the Scriptures read in a church service.

lec·tion·ar·y (lek'shən-er'i), *n.* [*pl.* LECTIONARIES (-iz)], [ML. *lectionarium* < L. *lectio*], a sequence or list of lections to be read in church services during the year.

lec·tor (lek'tẽr), *n.* [Late ME.; L., reader < *lectus,* pp. of *legere,* to read], 1. a person who reads the Scripture lessons in a church service. 2. a foreign lecturer in a German, Swiss, or Scandinavian university.

lec·ture (lek'chẽr), *n.* [ME. *letture,* act of reading; L. *lectura* < pp. of *legere,* to read], 1. *a*) an informative talk given before an audience, class, etc., and usually prepared beforehand. *b*) the text of such a talk. 2. a lengthy scolding. *v.i.* [LECTURED (-chẽrd), LECTURING], to give a lecture or lectures. *v.t.* 1. to give a lecture to. 2. to scold at length. —*SYN.* see **speech.**

lec·tur·er (lek'chẽr-ẽr), *n.* a person who gives lectures, especially by profession or in connection with teaching duties, as at a college or university: sometimes used as an academic title for one who teaches at a college or university but does not have the rank or tenure of a regular faculty member: abbreviated **lect.**

lec·ture·ship (lek'chẽr-ship'), *n.* [*lecture* + *-ship*], the position or rank of a lecturer.

led (led), past tense and past participle of **lead** (to guide).

Le·da (lē'də), *n.* [L.; Gr. *Lēda*], in *Greek mythology,* a Spartan queen, wife of Tyndareus: she was the mother of Clytemnestra (by Tyndareus) and (by Zeus, who visited her in the form of a swan) of Helen of Troy and Castor and Pollux.

ledge (lej), *n.* [ME. *legge;* prob. < base of *leggen,* to lay; see LAY (to put down)], 1. a shelf or shelflike projection. 2. *a*) a projecting ridge of rocks. *b*) such a ridge under the surface of the water near the shore. 3. in *mining,* a layer of ore-bearing rock; vein.

ledg·er (lej'ẽr), *n.* [earlier *leger, lidger, ligger;* prob. < ME. *leggen* or *liggen* after MD.; see LAY (to put down), LIE (to recline)], 1. a large flat stone placed over a tomb. 2. a large horizontal timber in a scaffold. 3. [< ME. sense "large volume kept in one place in church"], in *bookkeeping,* the book of final entry, in which a record of debits, credits, and all money transactions is kept. 4. in *fishing,* ledger bait. *adj.* that lies or remains where it is placed; stationary: now only in a few expressions.

ledger bait, fishing bait hooked to a floating line fastened to the bank of a stream, etc.

ledger board, a board forming the topmost rail of a fence, balustrade, or the like.

ledger line, in *music,* a short line written above or below the staff, for notes beyond the range of the staff.

ledger paper, writing paper for use in ledgers.

ledger tackle, fishing tackle arranged so that the bait lies on the bottom of the water.

ledg·y (lej'i), *adj.* having ledges.

Lee (lē), [var. of *Leigh*], a masculine name.

lee (lē), *n.* [ME. *le;* AS. *hleo,* shelter; akin to ON. *hle,* D. *lij,* G. *lee* (in sense 3); prob. IE. base **kleu-* <

*kel-, warm], 1. shelter; protection. 2. a sheltered place, especially one on that side of anything away from the wind. 3. in *nautical usage*, the side or part of a ship, etc. farthest from the side from which the wind blows; side or part away from the wind. *adj.* 1. of or on the side sheltered from the wind. 2. of or in the direction toward which the wind is blowing: opposed to *weather*.

Lee, Charles (lē), 1731–1782; English-born American general in the Revolutionary War; court-martialed and relieved of command.

Lee, Fitz·hugh (fits′hū′), 1835–1905; nephew of *Robert E.*; Confederate general in the Civil War and American major general in the Spanish-American War.

Lee, Henry, 1756–1818; American general in the Revolutionary War; governor of Virginia (1792–1795): called *Light-Horse Harry*.

Lee, Richard Henry, 1732–1794; American statesman; signer of the Declaration of Independence.

Lee, Robert Edward, 1807–1870; son of *Henry*; commander in chief of the Confederate army in the Civil War.

lee·board (lē′bôrd′, lē′bōrd′), *n.* a large flat board or piece of metal let down into the water on the lee side of a sailboat to lessen its drift to that side.

leech (lēch), *n.* [ME. *leche;* AS. *læce;* akin to OHG. *lâhhi*, Goth. *lêkeis*, magician, healer, AS. *lacnian*, to heal; IE. base disputed, but ? *leĝ-, to collect, gather together, seen also in L. *lex* (see LAW); sense 2 is supposedly same word (from use in medicine), but AS. *lyce*, ME. *liche*, MD. *lieke* suggest different word assimilated by folk etym.], 1. formerly, a physician. 2. any of a number of bloodsucking worms living in water or wet earth and used in medicine, especially in former times, to bleed patients. 3. a person who clings to another to get some gain out of him; parasite. 4. in *medicine*, a suction apparatus for drawing blood. *v.t.* 1. formerly, to heal. 2. to apply leeches to; bleed with leeches. —*SYN.* see **parasite**.

LEECH (2–4 in. long)

leech (lēch), *n.* [Early Mod. Eng. phonetic sp. of ME. *lich;* akin to ON. *lík*, D. *lijk*, leech line, boltrope; prob. from international language of the sea; prob. IE. base *leiĝ-, to bind, fasten, as also in L. *ligare* (cf. LIGAMENT), with reference to the roping], the free or outside edge of a sail: distinguished from *luff*.

Leeds (lēdz), *n.* a city in Yorkshire, England: pop., 482,000 (est. 1946).

leek (lēk), *n.* [ME. *lek*, *lik;* AS. *leac;* akin to G. *lauch;* IE. base *leue-, to bend, prob. seen also in *luxuriance*: so named from the flexible leaves], a vegetable related to the onion but of milder flavor, with a cylindrical bulb and long, broad, succulent leaves: it is the national emblem of Wales.

LEEK

leer (lêr), *n.* [< ME. *lere*, cheek; AS. *hleor*: in sense "look over one's cheek, look askance"], a sly, sidelong look showing ill will, lustfulness, malicious triumph, etc. *v.i.* to look with a leer.

leer·y (lêr′i), *adj.* [prob. *leer*, *v.* + *-y*], [Colloq.], 1. knowing. 2. wary; suspicious. Also spelled **leary**.

lees (lēz), *n.pl.* [pl. of *lee* (obs. in sing.); ME. & OFr. *lie;* ML. *lia;* Gaul. *ligja;* akin to OIr. *lige*, a bed, layer], dregs; grounds; sediment, as of wine.

lee shore, the shore on the lee side of a ship; shore toward which the wind is blowing and driving a ship.

leet (lēt), *n.* [ME. & Anglo-Fr. *lete;* ? akin to AS. *læth*, land division, esp. in southeast England], in England, formerly, a manorial court or its jurisdiction.

lee tide, a leeward tide.

Leeu·wen·hoek, An·ton van (än′tôn vän lā′vən-hook′), 1632–1723; Dutch microscopist and naturalist.

lee·ward (lē′wẽrd; *in nautical usage* lōō′ẽrd, lū′ẽrd), *adj.* in the direction toward which the wind blows; of the lee part or side: opposed to *windward*. *n.* the lee part or side. *adv.* toward the lee.

Lee·ward Islands (lē′wẽrd), 1. the northern group of islands in the Lesser Antilles, in the West Indies. 2. a British colony made up of some of these islands: area, 422 sq. mi.; pop., 109,000 (est. 1947). See **West Indies**, map.

lee·way (lē′wā′), *n.* 1. the leeward drift of a ship or aircraft from the true course. 2. [Colloq.], *a*) margin of time, money, etc. *b*) room for freedom of action.

left (left), *adj.* [ME. (Kent.) var. of *lift*, *luft;* prob. < AS. *lyft;* akin to *lyft*, sky, *lyften*, aerial, etc. (see LIFT, *v.*); cf. MD. *lucht*, sky, left hand, LG. *luchter*, etc.; basic sense "raised hand," with reference to use in greeting], 1. *a*) of or designating that side of one's body which is toward the west when one faces north, usually the side of the less-used hand. *b*) of or designating the corresponding side of anything. *c*) closer to the left side of a person directly before and facing the thing mentioned or understood: as, the top *left* drawer of a desk. 2. of the political left; liberal or radical. Opposed to *right*. *n.* 1. *a*) all or part of the left side. *b*) what is on the left side. 2. in *boxing*, *a*) the left hand. *b*) a blow delivered with the left hand. 3. [often L-], in *politics*, a liberal or radical position, party, or group (often with *the*): so called from the position of the seats occupied in some European legislatures. *adv.* on or toward the left hand or side. Abbreviated **L.**, **l.** —*SYN.* see **liberal**.

left (left), past tense and past participle of **leave** (to go away).

get left, [Slang], 1. to be left behind. 2. to be outdone or frustrated.

left field, in *baseball*, the left-hand part of the outfield (as viewed from home plate).

left-hand (left′hand′), *adj.* 1. being on or directed toward the left. 2. of, for, or with the left hand.

left-hand·ed (left′han′did), *adj.* 1. using the left hand more skillfully than, and in preference to, the right. 2. done with the left hand. 3. clumsy; awkward. 4. insincere; dubious: as, a *left-handed* compliment. 5. morganatic: from the former custom in which the groom gave the left hand to the bride in the ceremony of such marriages. 6. made for use with the left hand. 7. turning from right to left; worked by counterclockwise motion. *adv.* with the left hand: as, he writes *left-handed*.

left·ism (lef′tiz′m), *n.* [see LEFT, *n.*], in *politics*, liberal or radical ideas or actions.

left·ist (lef′tist), *n.* in *politics*, a person whose political position is liberal or radical; member of the left. *adj.* in *politics*, liberal or radical.

left·o·ver (left′ō′vẽr), *n.* something left over, as from a meal. *adj.* remaining unused, uneaten, etc.

left-wing (left′wiŋ′), *adj.* of the left wing; leftist.

left wing, [see LEFT, *n.* 3], in *politics*, the more liberal or radical section of a party, group, etc.

left·y (lef′ti), *n.* [*pl.* LEFTIES (-tiz)], [Slang], a left-handed person: often used as a nickname.

leg (leg), *n.* [ME.; ON. *leggr*, a leg, limb; IE. base *leq-, limb, seen also in L. *lac-ertus*, muscle, *lac-erta*, hedgehog], 1. one of the parts of the body by means of which men and animals stand and walk. 2. the part of a garment covering the leg. 3. anything that resembles a leg in shape or use; specifically, *a*) a bar or pole used as a support or prop. *b*) one of the supports of a piece of furniture. *c*) one of the branches of a forked or jointed object. 4. the run made by a sailing vessel on one tack. 5. one of the stages of a journey or other course. 6. in *bridge*, the first game of a rubber, for either side. 7. in *cricket*, that part of the field which lies to the left and back of the batsman. 8. in *mathematics*, either of the sides of a triangle other than its base or, in a right-angled triangle, its hypotenuse. *v.i.* [LEGGED (legd), LEGGING], [Colloq.], to walk or run (usually with *it*): as, we had to *leg* it back.

give a leg up, [Colloq.], to help to mount or advance.

have not a leg to stand on, [Colloq.], to have absolutely no defense, excuse, or justification.

on one's last legs, [Colloq.], not far from exhaustion, death, failure, etc.

pull one's leg, [Colloq.], to make fun of or fool a person by playing on his credulity.

shake a leg, [Slang], 1. to hurry. 2. to dance.

stretch one's legs, to walk, especially after sitting a long time.

leg., 1. legal. 2. legate. 3. legato. 4. legend. 5. legislative. 6. legislature.

leg·a·cy (leg′ə-si), *n.* [*pl.* LEGACIES (-siz)], [ME. & OFr. *legacie;* ML. *legatia* < L. *legatus;* see LEGATE], 1. money or property left to someone by a will; bequest. 2. anything handed down from, or as from, an ancestor to a descendant.

le·gal (lē′g'l), *adj.* [Fr. *légal;* L. *legalis* < *lex*, *legis*, law; see LAW], 1. of, based upon, or authorized by law. 2. in conformity with the positive rules of law; permitted by law: as, a *legal* act: see also **lawful**, sense 2. 3. that can be enforced in a court of law: as, *legal* rights: distinguished from *equitable*. 4. of or applicable to lawyers: as, *legal* ethics. 5. in terms of the law: as, a *legal* offense. 6. in *theology*, *a*) of the Mosaic law. *b*) of the doctrine of salvation by good works rather than free grace. Abbreviated **leg.** *n.pl.* investments that savings banks and certain other fiduciaries are legally authorized to make.

SYN.—**legal** implies literal connection or conformity with statute law or its administration (*legal* rights); **lawful**, a more

fat, āpe, bâre, cär; ten, ēven, hêre, ovẽr; is, bīte; lot, gō, hôrn, tōōl, look; oil, out; up, ūse, fũr; get; joy; yet; chin; she; thin, *th*en; zh, leisure; ŋ, ring; ə for *a* in *ago*, *e* in *agent*, *i* in *sanity*, *o* in *comply*, *u* in *focus*; ′ as in *able* (ā′b'l); Fr. bál; ë, Fr. coeur; ö, Fr. feu; Fr. mon; ô, Fr. coq; ü, Fr. duc; H, G. ich; kh, G. doch. See pp. x–xii. ‡ foreign; * hypothetical; < derived from.

general word, may suggest conformity to the principle rather than to the letter of the law or may broadly refer to that which is not contrary to the law (a *lawful* but shady enterprise); **legitimate** implies legality of a claim to a title or right (a *legitimate* heir) or accordance with what is sanctioned or accepted as lawful, reasonable, etc. (a *legitimate* argument); **licit** implies strict conformity to the law, especially in trade, commerce, or personal relations (*licit* marriage).—***ANT.*** illegal, unlawful.

legal cap, a kind of writing paper, varying in size from 8 1/2 by 14 inches to 13 by 16 inches, with the fold at the top, made for use by lawyers.

le·gal·ism (lē′g'l-iz'm), *n.* 1. strict, often too strict and literal, adherence to law. 2. in *theology*, the doctrine of salvation by good works.

le·gal·ist (lē′g'l-ist), *n.* 1. a person who practices legalism. 2. a person skilled in law.

le·gal·is·tic (lē′g'l-is′tik), *adj.* of or characterized by legalism.

le·gal·i·ty (li-gal′ə-ti), *n.* [*pl.* LEGALITIES (-tiz)], 1. quality, condition, or instance of being legal or lawful; conformity with the law. 2. the spirit or a characteristic of the legal profession.

le·gal·i·za·tion (lē′g'l-i-zā′shən, lē′g'l-ī-zā′shən), *n.* a legalizing or being legalized.

le·gal·ize (lē′g'l-īz′), *v.t.* [LEGALIZED (-īzd′), LEGALIZING], to make legal or lawful.

Le Gal·lienne, Eva (lə gal′yən, lə gal-yen′), 1899– ; American actress, theatrical producer, and director.

le·gal·ly (lē′g'l-i), *adv.* 1. in a legal manner. 2. according to law: as, he was declared *legally* dead.

legal reserve, the sum of money that a bank is required by law to have for covering deposits.

legal separation, in *law*, a separation of husband and wife so that they do not live together but are not divorced: also called *judicial separation.*

legal tender, money which the law requires a creditor to accept in payment of a debt: as, dimes are *legal tender* for any sum up to ten dollars.

leg·ate (leg′it), *n.* [ME. & OFr. *legat;* L. *legatus*, pp. of *legare*, to send as ambassador < *lex, legis*, law; cf. LEECH (physician)], 1. an envoy or ambassador, especially one officially representing the Pope. 2. in ancient Rome, *a*) an assistant or deputy of the governor of a province. *b*) after 31 B.C., the governor of a province. Abbreviated **leg.**

leg·a·tee (leg′ə-tē′), *n.* [< L. *legatus*, pp. of *legare*, to bequeath, appoint (see LEGATE); + *-ee*], one to whom a legacy is bequeathed.

leg·ate·ship (leg′it-ship′), *n.* [see -SHIP], the position, authority, or tenure of office of a legate.

leg·a·tine (leg′ə-tin, leg′ə-tīn′), *adj.* of a legate.

le·ga·tion (li-gā′shən), *n.* [Fr. *légation;* L. *legatio*], 1. *a*) the act of sending a legate on a mission. *b*) the mission on which he is sent. 2. a legate and his staff collectively, representing their government in a foreign country and ranking just below an embassy. 3. the building or buildings housing such a legation. 4. the position or authority of such a legation.

le·ga·to (li-gä′tō; It. le-gä′tô), *adj. & adv.* [It., pp. of *legare;* L. *ligare*, to tie, bind], in *music*, in a smooth, even style, with no noticeable interruption between the notes: a direction to the performer: abbreviated **leg.**: opposed to *staccato.*

leg·end (lej′ənd), *n.* [ME. & OFr. *legende;* ML. *legenda*, things read, neut. pl. of L. *legendus*, gerundive of *legere*, to read], 1. [Obs.], *a*) a story of the life of a saint. *b*) a collection of such stories. 2. a story of some wonderful event, handed down for generations among a people and popularly believed to have a historical basis, although not verifiable: distinguished from *myth.* 3. all such stories belonging to a particular group of people: as, a name famous in Irish *legend.* 4. an inscription on a coin, coat of arms, etc. 5. a title, brief description, or key accompanying an illustration or map. Abbreviated **leg.**

leg·end·ar·y (lej′ən-der′i), *adj.* of, based on, or presented in a legend or legends; traditional. *n.* a collection of saints' lives. —***SYN.*** see **fictitious.**

leg·end·ry (lej′ən-dri), *n.* legends collectively.

leg·er (lej′ẽr), *n. & adj.* ledger.

leg·er·de·main (lej′ẽr-di-mān′), *n.* [Fr. *léger de main*, lit., light of hand; *léger* < LL. **levarius* < L. *levis*, light; *de* < L. *de*, of, from; *main* < L. *manus*, hand], 1. sleight of hand; tricks of a stage magician; hence, 2. trickery of any sort; deceit.

‡**le·ges** (lē′jēz), *n.* plural of **lex.**

leg·ged (leg′id, legd), *adj.* having (a specified number or kind of) legs: usually in hyphenated compounds, as *long-legged, four-legged.*

leg·ging (leg′iŋ), *n. usually in pl.* a covering of canvas, leather, etc. for protecting the leg below the knee.

leg·gy (leg′i), *adj.* 1. having long legs. 2. having long and awkward legs: as, a *leggy* colt.

Leg·horn (leg′hôrn′; *for 2 & 3, usually* leg′ẽrn), *n.* 1. a city in western Italy, on the Ligurian Sea: pop., 135,000: Italian name, *Livorno.* 2. [sometimes l-], any of a breed of small chicken originally developed in the Mediterranean region. 3. [l-], *a*) a plaiting made of an Italian wheat straw, cut green and bleached when dry. *b*) a wide-brimmed hat made of this straw.

leg·i·bil·i·ty (lej′ə-bil′ə-ti), *n.* the quality or state of being legible.

leg·i·ble (lej′ə-b'l), *adj.* [ME. (northern) *legeable;* LL. *legibilis* < *legere*, to read], 1. that can be read or deciphered. 2. that can be read or deciphered easily.

leg·i·bly (lej′ə-bli), *adv.* in a legible manner; so as to be legible.

le·gion (lē′jən), *n.* [ME. & OFr. *legiun;* L. *legio* < *legere*, to choose, select], 1. in ancient Rome, a military division varying at times from 3,000 to 6,000 foot soldiers, with additional cavalrymen. 2. a large group of soldiers; army. 3. a large number; multitude: as, his honors are *legion.* 4. [L-], the American Legion.

le·gion·ar·y (lē′jən-er′i), *adj.* [L. *legionarius*], of or constituting a legion or legions. *n.* [*pl.* LEGIONARIES (-iz)], a member of a legion.

le·gion·naire (lē′jən-âr′), *n.* [Fr. *légionnaire*], 1. a member of a legion. 2. [often L-], a member of the American Legion.

Legion of Honor, a French honorary society founded in 1802 by Napoleon for recognition of distinguished military or civil service.

Legion of Merit, a United States military decoration given to officers, enlisted men, and soldiers of allies for extraordinary fidelity and essential service.

Legis., Legislature.

leg·is·late (lej′is-lāt′), *v.i.* [LEGISLATED (-id), LEGISLATING], [back-formation < *legislator*], to make or pass a law or laws. *v.t.* to cause to become, go, etc. by making laws.

leg·is·la·tion (lej′is-lā′shən), *n.* [LL. *legislatio* < L. *lex, legis*, law + *latio*, a bringing, proposing < *latus*, pp. of *ferre*, to bring], 1. the act or process of making a law or laws. 2. the law or laws made.

leg·is·la·tive (lej′is-lā′tiv), *adj.* 1. of legislation: as, *legislative* powers. 2. having the power to make laws: as, a *legislative* assembly. 3. brought about or enforced by legislation. *n.* the lawmaking branch of a government; legislature. Abbreviated **leg.**

leg·is·la·tor (lej′is-lā′tẽr), *n.* [L. *legis lator; legis*, genit. sing. of *lex*, law + *lator*, proposer of a law < *latus*, pp. of *ferre*, to bring], a member of a legislative assembly; lawmaker.

leg·is·la·ture (lej′is-lā′chẽr), *n.* [< *legislator* + *-ure*], a body of persons given the responsibility and power to make laws for a country or state; specifically, the lawmaking body of a State, corresponding to the Congress of the United States: abbreviated **leg., Legis.**

le·gist (lē′jist), *n.* [Fr. *légiste;* ML. *legista* < L. *lex, legis*, law], a person trained in the law.

le·git (li-jit′), *n.* [Slang], the legitimate theater, drama, stage, etc. *adj.* [Slang], legitimate.

le·git·i·ma·cy (li-jit′ə-mə-si), *n.* the quality or state of being legitimate.

le·git·i·mate (li-jit′ə-mit; *for v.*, li-jit′ə-māt′), *adj.* [ML. *legitimatus*, pp. of *legitimare*, to make lawful < L. *legitimus*, lawful < *lex, legis*, law], 1. conceived or born of parents legally married to each other. 2. sanctioned by law or custom; lawful; allowed: as, a *legitimate* claim. 3. ruling by the rights of heredity: as, a *legitimate* king. 4. reasonable; logically correct: as, a *legitimate* inference. 5. in the *theater*, *a*) formerly, of recognized literary merit; in conformity with certain literary standards: as, the *legitimate* drama. *b*) designating or of stage plays, as distinguished from motion pictures, burlesque, vaudeville, etc. *v.t.* [LEGITIMATED (-id), LEGITIMATING], 1. to make or declare legitimate; hence, 2. to justify or authorize. —***SYN.*** see **legal.**

le·git·i·ma·tion (li-jit′ə-mā′shən), *n.* [ML. *legitimatio*], a legitimating or being legitimated.

le·git·i·ma·tize (li-jit′ə-mə-tīz′), *v.t.* [LEGITIMATIZED (-tīzd′), LEGITIMATIZING], to legitimate.

le·git·i·mism (li-jit′ə-miz'm), *n.* [Fr. *légitimisme*], the principles of a legitimist.

le·git·i·mist (li-jit′ə-mist), *n.* [Fr. *légitimiste*], a supporter of legitimate authority or, especially, of claims to monarchy based on the rights of heredity.

le·git·i·mi·za·tion (li-jit′ə-mi-zā′shən, li-jit′ə-mī-zā′shən), *n.* legitimation.

le·git·i·mize (li-jit′ə-mīz′), *v.t.* [LEGITIMIZED (-mīzd′), LEGITIMIZING], to legitimate.

leg·less (leg′lis), *adj.* having no legs.

leg-of-mut·ton (leg′ə-mut′'n, leg′əv-mut′'n), *adj.* shaped somewhat like a leg of mutton; much larger at one end than at the other: said of a sleeve, sail, etc.

Le·gree, Simon (li-grē′), 1. the cruel slave dealer in Harriet Beecher Stowe's *Uncle Tom's Cabin;* hence, 2. any cruel or exacting master, overseer, etc.

leg·ume (leg′ūm, li-gūm′), *n.* [Fr. *légume;* L. *legumen, leguminis*, lit., anything that can be gathered < *legere*, to gather; cf. LEECH (physician)], 1. any of a large group of plants of the pea family, characterized by true pods enclosing seeds: because of their ability to store up nitrates, legumes are often plowed under to fertilize the soil. 2. the fruit of any plant of the pea family, often used as food; pod. 3. the seed of such a plant, contained in the pod.

le·gu·min (li-gū'min), *n.* a globulin present in legumes.
le·gu·mi·nous (li-gū'mi-nəs), *adj.* 1. of, having the nature of, or bearing a legume or legumes. 2. of the group of plants bearing legumes, or pods, to which peas and beans belong.
leg work, [Colloq.], walking; especially, much walking or traveling as the necessary, but routine, part of a job, as of a newspaper reporter, etc.
Le·hár, Franz (fränts le'här; Eng. lā'här), 1870–1948; Hungarian composer of operettas.
Le Ha·vre (lə å'vr'; Eng. lə hä'vẽr), Havre, a seaport in France: the French name.
Le·high (lē'hī), *n.* a river in eastern Pennsylvania, flowing into the Delaware at Easton: length, 100 mi.
Leh·man, Herbert Henry (lē'man, lā'man), 1878–; American banker and statesman.
Leh·mann, Lil·li (li'li lā'män; Eng. lā'mən), (*Mme. Paul Kalisch*), 1848–1929; German operatic soprano.
Lehmann, Lot·te (lôt'ə), 1893?– ; American operatic soprano, born in Germany.
le·hu·a (lā-hōō'ä), *n.* [Haw.], 1. a tropical tree of the myrtle family, with clusters of bright-red flowers and hard wood: it grows in Hawaii and other Pacific Islands. 2. its wood. 3. its flower.
le·i (lā, lā'i), *n.* [*pl.* LEIS (lāz, lā'iz)], [Haw.], in Hawaii, a garland or wreath of flowers and leaves, generally worn about the neck.
lei (lā), *n.* plural of **leu.**
Leib·nitz, Baron **Gott·fried Wil·helm von** (gôt'frēt vil'helm fôn lip'nits), 1646–1716; German philosopher and mathematician.
Leices·ter (les'tẽr), *n.* 1. Leicestershire. 2. the county seat of Leicestershire, England: pop., 275,000 (est. 1946). 3. any of a breed of long-wooled sheep originally developed in Leicestershire.
Leicester, Earl of, (*Robert Dudley*), 1532?–1588; English courtier; favorite of Queen Elizabeth.
Leices·ter·shire (les'tẽr-shir'), *n.* a county of central England: pop., 565,000 (est. 1945); county seat, Leicester: also **Leicester.**
Lei·den (lī'd'n), *n.* a university city in the western Netherlands: pop., 88,000 (1947): also spelled **Leyden.**
Leif (lēf), [ON. *Leifr;* akin to *ljufr,* beloved; cf. LIEF], a masculine name.
Leif Ericsson, see **Ericsson, Leif.**
Leigh (lē), [< surname *Leigh* < ME. *lei;* see LEA], a masculine name.
Lei·la, Lei·lah (lē'lə), [Ar. *layla,* lit., darkness, night], a feminine name.
Lein·ster (len'stẽr), *n.* a province of eastern Ireland: area, 7,580 sq. mi.; pop., 1,260,000 (1943).
Leip·zig (līp'sig, līp'sik; G. līp'tsikh), *n.* a city in the state of Saxony, Germany: pop., 702,000.
leish·man·i·as·is (lish'mən-ī'ə-sis), *n.* [Mod. L. < *Leishmania,* name of the parasitic genus; after Gen. Sir William Boog *Leishman* (1865–1926), Brit. army surgeon], any of various diseases caused by a variety of protozoan parasite; especially, kala-azar.
leis·ter (lēs'tẽr), *n.* [< ON. *ljoster* < *ljosta,* to strike], a kind of fish spear, usually with three prongs. *v.t.* to spear (fish) with a leister.
lei·sure (lē'zhẽr, lezh'ẽr), *n.* [ME. *leisere, leiser;* OFr. *leisir* < L. *licere,* to be permitted], free, unoccupied time during which a person may indulge in rest, recreation, etc. *adj.* 1. free and unoccupied; spare: as, *leisure* time. 2. having much leisure; not working for a living: as, the *leisure* class.
at leisure, 1. having free or spare time. 2. with no hurry. 3. not occupied or engaged.
at one's leisure, when one has time or opportunity; when it is convenient for one.
lei·sured (lē'zhẽrd, lezh'ẽrd), *adj.* 1. having leisure. 2. without haste; leisurely.
lei·sure·li·ness (lē'zhẽr-li-nis, lezh'ẽr-li-nis), *n.* the quality of being leisurely; freedom from haste.
lei·sure·ly (lē'zhẽr-li, lezh'ẽr-li), *adj.* characterized by or having leisure; without haste; deliberate; slow: as, we made a *leisurely* inspection of the old ruin. *adv.* in an unhurried manner.
Leith (lēth), *n.* a former burgh in Scotland: now a part of Edinburgh.
leit·mo·tiv, leit·mo·tif (līt'mō-tēf'), *n.* [G. *leitmotiv* < *leiten,* to lead, guide (see LEAD) + *motiv* (see MOTIVE)], a short musical phrase representing and recurring with a given character, situation, or emotion in an opera: first developed by Richard Wagner.
Le·ly, Sir **Peter** (lē'li; D. lā'li), (born *Pieter Van der Faes*), 1618–1680; Dutch portrait painter in England.
lem·an (lem'ən, lē'mən), *n.* [ME. *lemman, lefman* < *lef, leve,* dear (see LIEF) + *man*], [Archaic], a sweetheart or lover (man or woman); especially, a mistress.
Le·man, Lake (lē'mən), Lake Geneva.
Lem·berg (lem'berkh; Eng. lem'bẽrg), *n.* Lwów, a city in Poland: the German name.
lem·ma (lem'ə), *n.* [*pl.* LEMMAS (-əz), LEMMATA (-ə-tə)], [L.; Gr. *lēmma,* something taken or received, something taken for granted, assumed premise < *lambanein,* to take, assume], a secondary proposition assumed to be true and used in demonstrating the primary one.
lem·ming (lem'iŋ), *n.* [*pl.* LEMMINGS (-iŋz), LEMMING; see PLURAL, II, D, 1], [Norw.], any of various small arctic rodents resembling mice but having short tails and fur-covered feet.
lem·nis·cus (lem-nis'kəs), *n.* [*pl.* LEMNISCI (-nis'ī)], [Mod. L.; L., hanging ribbon; Gr. *lēmniskos,* ribbon], a band of sensory nerve fibers in the central nervous system.
Lem·nos (lem'nos), *n.* a Greek island in the Aegean: area, 175 sq. mi.; pop., 25,000.
lem·on (lem'ən), *n.* [ME. *lymon;* Late OFr. *limon;* Sp. *limón;* Ar. *laimūn;* Per. *līmūn*], 1. a small, egg-shaped, edible citrus fruit with a pale-yellow rind and a juicy, sour pulp, rich in vitamin C. 2. the small, spiny, semitropical evergreen tree that it grows on. 3. [Slang], something or someone undesirable or inadequate. *adj.* 1. of the pale-yellow color of lemon rind. 2. made with or from lemons. 3. having a flavor more or less like that of lemons.
lem·on·ade (lem'ən-ād'), *n.* [Fr. *limonade*], a drink made of lemon juice, sugar, and water.
lemon drop, a small, hard, lemon-flavored candy.
lemon verbena, a Chilean shrub of the verbena family, with white flowers and whorls of narrow, lemon-scented leaves.
lem·pi·ra (lem-pē'rä), *n.* [Am. Sp., after *Lempira,* native chief who resisted the Spaniards], the gold monetary unit of Honduras, equal to 50 cents in 1947.
Lem·u·el (lem'ū-əl), [Heb. *lemū'ēl,* lit., belonging to God], a masculine name: diminutive, *Lem.*
le·mur (lē'mẽr), *n.* [< L. *lemures,* ghosts, specters (akin to Gr. *lamia;* see LAMIA): so called from its nocturnal habits], any of a group of small mammals related to the monkeys, with large eyes, a pointed muzzle, and soft, woolly fur: it is found mainly in Madagascar and is active mostly at night.
lem·u·res (lem'yoo-rēz'), *n.pl.* [L.; see LEMUR], in *Roman mythology,* the night-walking spirits of the dead.
Le·mur·i·a (li-myoor'i-ə), *n.* [Mod. L.: so called from Haeckel's idea that it was the original home of lemuroid primates], a hypothetical continent thought by some to have existed long ago, now supposedly covered by the Indian Ocean.
lem·u·rine (lem'yoo-rīn', lem'yoo-rin), *adj.* lemuroid.
lem·u·roid (lem'yoo-roid'), *adj.* of or like a lemur or lemurs. *n.* a lemur.
Le·na (lē'nə; *also, for n.,* Russ. lye'nä), a feminine name: see **Helena, Magdalene.** *n.* a river in the Yakut A.S.S.R., eastern Siberia, flowing into the Arctic Ocean: length, 2,800 mi.
Len·a·pe (len'ə-pē'), *n.* [*pl.* LENAPE], [short for Lenape *Leni-lenape,* lit., real man; *leni,* real + *lenape,* man], 1. a member of the Delaware Indians. 2. their Algonquian language. Also **Leni-Lenape, Lenni-Lenape.** *adj.* of the Lenape or their language.
lend (lend), *v.t.* [LENT (lent), LENDING], [< ME. *lenen* with unhistoric *-d* < p.t.; AS. *lænan* < *læn,* a loan; see LOAN], 1. to let another use or have (a thing) temporarily and on condition that it, or the equivalent, is to be returned: opposed to *borrow.* 2. to let out (money) at interest. 3. to give; impart: as, a fire *lends* cheer to a room. *v.i.* to make a loan or loans.
lend itself (or **oneself**) **to,** to be adapted to, useful for, or open to.
lending library, a library from which books may be borrowed, usually for a fee.
lend-lease (lend'lēs'), *n.* in World War II, material aid in the form of airplanes, munitions, tools, food, etc., granted to foreign countries whose defense was deemed vital to the defense of the United States, under the provisions of the Lend-Lease Act of March 11, 1941. *adj.* authorized by or authorizing lend-lease. *v.t.* [LEND-LEASED (-lēst'), LEND-LEASING], to grant (material aid) to a foreign country in accordance with the Lend-Lease Act.
L'En·fant, Pierre Charles (pyâr shårl län'fän'), 1754–1825; French engineer and architect who served in the American Revolutionary army and drew up plans for Washington, D.C.
length (leŋkth, leŋth), *n.* [ME. *lengthe;* AS. *lengthu* (*langitha) < base of *lang, long* (see LONG) + *-th*], 1. the measure of how long a thing is; measurement of anything from end to end; the greatest of the two or three dimensions of anything: opposed to *width* or *breadth.* 2. extent in space; distance anything extends. 3. extent in time; duration. 4. a long stretch or extent. 5. the quality, state, or fact of being long: opposed to *shortness.* 6. a piece of a certain or standardized length: as, a *length* of stove pipe. 7. a unit of measure consisting of the length of an object or animal

competing in a race: as, his boat won by two *lengths*. 8. in *phonetics*, *a*) the duration of the pronunciation of a vowel: as, the *i* in *bride* has greater *length* than the *i* in *bright*. *b*) popularly, the quality of a vowel. 9. in *prosody*, syllabic quantity. Abbreviated **L., l., lgth.**

at full length, stretched out; completely extended.

at length, 1. after a long time; finally. 2. in or to the whole extent; in full.

go to any length, to do whatever is necessary; scruple at nothing.

keep at arm's length, to act coldly toward.

length·en (leŋk'th'n, leŋ'th'n), *v.t. & v.i.* to make or become longer. —*SYN.* see **extend.**

length·i·ly (leŋk'thə-li, leŋ'thə-li), *adv.* in a lengthy manner.

length·i·ness (leŋk'thi-nis, leŋ'thi-nis), *n.* the quality of being lengthy.

length·ways (leŋkth'wāz', leŋth'wāz'), *adv. & adj.* lengthwise.

length·wise (leŋkth'wīz', leŋth'wīz'), *adv. & adj.* in the direction of the length.

length·y (leŋk'thi, leŋ'thi), *adj.* [LENGTHIER (-thi-ẽr), LENGTHIEST (-thi-ist)], 1. having length; long; especially, too long; so long as to be tiresome: said of speeches, writings, etc. 2. [Colloq.], tall: of a person.

le·ni·ence (lē'ni-əns, lēn'yəns), *n.* leniency.

le·ni·en·cy (lē'ni-ən-si, lēn'yən-si), *n.* 1. the quality or condition of being lenient. 2. [*pl.* LENIENCIES (-siz)], a lenient act.

le·ni·ent (lē'ni-ənt, lēn'yənt), *adj.* [L. *leniens*, ppr. of *lenire*, to soften, alleviate < *lenis*, smooth, soft, mild], 1. not harsh or severe; mild; merciful; gentle; clement. 2. [Archaic], softening; soothing; relaxing.

Len·i-Len·a·pe (len'i-len'ə-pē'), *n. sing. & pl.* Lenape.

Len·in, V. I. (len'in; Russ. lyen'in), (born *Vladimir Ilich Ulianov*), 1870–1924; Russian revolutionary; leader of Bolshevik (Communist) party; directed revolution of 1917; premier of Soviet Union (1918–1924): also **Nikolai Lenin.**

Len·i·na·kan (lyen'i-nä-khän'), *n.* a city in the Armenian S.S.R., in the Transcaucasus: pop., 108,000.

Len·in·grad (len'in-grad'; Russ. lyen'in-grät'), *n.* 1. a region of the R.S.F.S.R., in northwestern European Russia: pop., 4,561,000. 2. its capital, a seaport on the Gulf of Finland: pop., 3,300,000: formerly called *Petrograd, St. Petersburg.*

Len·in·ism (len'in-iz'm), *n.* the communist theories, doctrines, policies, and methods of Lenin, including especially his theory of the dictatorship of the proletariat and analysis of imperialism: a development of Marxism.

Len·in·ist (len'in-ist), *n.* a follower of Lenin; believer in Leninism. *adj.* of Lenin or Leninism.

Len·in·ite (len'in-īt'), *n. & adj.* Leninist.

le·nis (lē'nis), *adj.* [L., gentle, smooth, soft, mild], in *phonetics*, weakly articulated: as, a *lenis* stop. *n.* [*pl.* LENES (-nēz)], a weakly articulated speech sound, especially a stop. Opposed to *fortis.*

len·i·tive (len'ə-tiv), *adj.* [Late ME.; ML. *lenitivus* < L. *lenitus*, pp. of *lenire*, to soften, assuage], 1. softening, soothing, lessening pain, etc. 2. formerly, acting as a mild laxative. *n.* anything that soothes; especially, a lenitive medicine.

len·i·ty (len'ə-ti), *n.* [OFr. *lenité*; L. *lenitas* < *lenis*, smooth, soft, mild], 1. the quality or condition of being lenient; mildness; gentleness; mercifulness. 2. [*pl.* LENITIES (-tiz)], a lenient act. —*SYN.* see **mercy.**

Len·ni-Len·a·pe (len'i-len'ə-pē'), *n. sing. & pl.* Lenape.

le·no (lē'nō), *n.* [Fr. *linon* < *lin*, flax; cf. LINEN], 1. a type of weave in which the warp yarns are paired and twisted. 2. a soft, light fabric of this weave.

lens (lenz), *n.* [L., lentil: from the resemblance of a double-convex lens to a lentil], 1. a piece of glass, or other transparent substance, with two curved surfaces, or one plane and one curved, regularly bringing together or spreading rays of light passing through it: a lens or combination of lenses is used in optical instruments to form an image: for kinds of lenses, see **concave, convex,** illus. 2. a combination of two or more such pieces. 3. in *anatomy*, a transparent, biconvex body situated between the iris and the vitreous humor of the eye: its function is to focus upon the retina light rays entering the pupil: see **eye,** illus.

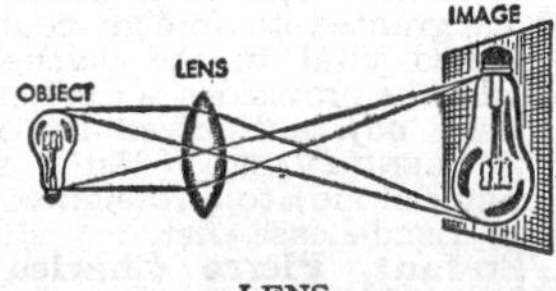

LENS

Lent (lent), *n.* [ME. *lenten, lente*; AS. *lencten, lengten*, the spring < base of *lang*, long (see LONG, *adj.*): so called from the lengthening of the days in the spring; akin to G. *lenz*, spring: cognates in other Gmc. languages mean merely "spring"], 1. the period of forty weekdays from Ash Wednesday to Easter, observed in Christian churches by fasting and penitence to commemorate Jesus' fasting in the wilderness. 2. in the Middle Ages, the period from Martinmas (November 11) to Christmas: in full, **St. Martin's Lent.**

lent (lent), past tense and past participle of **lend.**

-lent (lənt), [L. *-lentus*, -ful], a suffix meaning *full of, characterized by*, as in *virulent, fraudulent, pestilent.*

‡**len·ta·men·te** (len'tä-men'te), *adv.* [It. < *lento*, slow < L. *lentus*], in *music*, slowly: a direction to the performer.

‡**len·tan·do** (len-tän'dô), *adv. & adj.* [It. < *lentare*, to make slow < *lento*; see prec.], in *music*, slowing down by degrees: a direction to the performer.

Lent·en, lent·en (len'tən), *adj.* [ME. *lenten*; AS. *lencten*, full forms of *Lent*; now felt as *Lent* + *-en*], 1. of, connected with, or suitable for Lent. 2. meager; cheerless: as, *Lenten* fare.

len·ti·cel (len'ti-səl), *n.* [Fr. *lenticelle*; Mod. L. *lenticella*, dim. < L. *lens, lentis*, lentil], a ventilating pore in the bark of woody plants.

len·tic·u·lar (len-tik'yoo-lẽr), *adj.* [L. *lenticularis* < *lenticula*, dim. of *lens*; see LENS], 1. shaped like a lentil or double-convex lens. 2. of a lens. 3. of the lens of the eye. 4. in *motion pictures*, lenticulated.

len·tic·u·lat·ed (len-tik'yoo-lā'tid), *adj.* 1. lenticular. 2. in *motion pictures*, designating a film having microscopic lenses embossed on its base side and used with a special color filter to produce pictures in natural color.

len·tig·i·nous (len-tij'ə-nəs), *adj.* [LL. *lentiginosus* < L. *lentigo*, freckly eruption < *lens*, lentil], freckly.

len·ti·go (len-tī'gō), *n.* [*pl.* LENTIGINES (-tij'ə-nēz')], [L. < *lens*, lentil], 1. a freckle. 2. a freckly condition of the skin.

len·til (len't'l, len'til), *n.* [ME. & Fr. *lentille*; L. *lenticula*, dim. of *lens, lentis*, lentil], 1. a plant of the pea family, with small, edible seeds shaped like double-convex lenses. 2. the seed of this plant.

‡**len·tis·si·mo** (len-tēs'sē-mô'; Eng. len-tis'ə-mō'), *adv. & adj.* [It., superl. of *lento* (< L. *lentus*), slow], in *music*, very slow: a direction to the performer.

len·to (len'tō), *adv. & adj.* [It. < L. *lentus*, slow], in *music*, slow: a direction to the performer.

len·toid (len'toid), *adj.* [< L. *lens, lentis* (see LENS); + *-oid*], lens-shaped.

l'en·voi, l'en·voy (len'voi, len-voi'; Fr. län'vwå'), *n.* [Fr. *l'envoi* < *le*, the + *envoi*, a sending; see ENVOY], 1. originally, a dedication or postscript to a poem, essay, or book, directing it to a specific person's attention. 2. a concluding stanza added to a ballade and some other forms, customarily a direct address to a prince, princess, lord, lady, etc. Also **envoy.**

Le·o (lē'ō), [L.; see LION], a masculine name: variant, *Leon*; feminine, *Leona*. *n.* 1. a northern constellation between Cancer and Virgo, supposedly outlining a lion: see **constellation,** chart. 2. the fifth sign of the zodiac (♌), entered by the sun about July 22: see **zodiac,** illus.

Leo I, Saint, 390?–461 A.D.; Pope (440–461 A.D.): his day is April 11: called *the Great.*

Leo III, Saint, 750?–816 A.D.; Pope (795–816 A.D.).

Leo XIII, 1810–1903; Pope (1878–1903).

Leom·in·ster (lem'in-stẽr), *n.* a city in northern Massachusetts: pop., 28,000.

Le·on (lē'on), a masculine name: see **Leo.**

Le·ón (le-ôn'), *n.* a former province of northwestern Spain.

Le·o·na (lē-ō'nə), a feminine name: see **Leo.**

Leon·ard (len'ẽrd), [Fr. *Léonard*; OFr. *Leonard*; OHG. **Lewenhart*, lit., strong as a lion < *lewo*, lion (< L. *leo*; see LION) + *hart*, strong, hard], a masculine name.

Leon·ard, William El·ler·y (el'ẽr-i len'ẽrd), 1876–1944; American poet, scholar, and teacher.

Le·o·nar·desque (lē'ə-när-desk'), *adj.* of or resembling the style of Leonardo da Vinci.

Leonardo da Vinci, see **Vinci, Leonardo da.**

Le·on·ca·val·lo, Rug·gie·ro (rōōd-je'rô le-ôn'kä-väl'lô; Eng. lā'ən-kə-vä'lō), 1858–1919; Italian composer.

Le·o·nid (lē'ə-nid), *n.* [*pl.* LEONIDS (-nidz), LEONIDES (li-on'ə-dēz')], [Fr. < L. *Leo, Leonis*; see LEO & -ID], any of a shower of meteors visible yearly about November 15, appearing to radiate from the constellation Leo.

Le·on·i·das (lē-on'ə-dəs), *n.* king of Sparta; lived ?–480 B.C.; defeated and killed by the Persians at Thermopylae.

le·o·nine (lē'ə-nīn'), *adj.* [ME. & OFr. *leonin*; L. *leoninus* < *leo*], of, characteristic of, or like a lion.

Le·o·no·ra (lē'ə-nôr'ə, lē'ə-nō'rə), a feminine name: diminutive, *Nora*: see **Eleanor.**

Le·o·nore (lē'ə-nôr', lē'ə-nōr'), a feminine name: variant of *Leonora.*

leop·ard (lep'ẽrd), *n.* [*pl.* LEOPARDS (-ẽrdz), LEOPARD; see PLURAL, II, D, 1], [ME. *leoparde, leparde, libbard*; OFr. *leopard, lebard*; LL. *leopardus*; Gr. *leopardos, leontopardos* < *leōn*, lion + *pardos*, pard, panther], 1. a large, ferocious animal of the cat family, usually having a tawny coat spotted with black, found in Africa and southern Asia: also called *panther*. 2. the jaguar, or American leopard. 3. in *heraldry*, a lion represented in side view, with one foreleg raised and the head facing to the front.

leop·ard·ess (lep'ẽr-dis), *n.* a female leopard.

Le·o·par·di, Conte **Gia·co·mo** (jä′kô-mô′ le′ô-pär′dē), 1798–1837; Italian poet.

Le·o·pold (lē′ə-pōld′), [G.; OHG. *Liutbalt* < *liut,* people (orig., prob., free man; cf. AS. *leod,* man, king) + *balt,* bold, strong]; a masculine name.

Leopold I, 1. 1640–1705; emperor of the Holy Roman Empire (1658–1705). 2. 1790–1865; uncle of Victoria; king of the Belgians (1831–1865).

Leopold II, 1. 1747–1792; son of Maria Theresa; emperor of the Holy Roman Empire (1790–1792). 2. 1835–1909; son of Leopold I; king of the Belgians (1865–1909); founder of the Congo Free State.

Leopold III, 1901–; son of Albert I; king of the Belgians (1934–1951); exiled, 1945–1950.

Lé·o·pold·ville (lā′ô′pôld′vēl′; Eng. lē′ə-pōld-vil′), *n.* the capital of the Belgian Congo, on the Congo River: pop., 116,000.

le·o·tard (lē′ə-tärd′), *n.* [after *Léotard,* 19th-c. French aerial performer], a one-piece, sleeveless, tight-fitting garment, worn by acrobats, dancers, etc.

Le·pan·to, Gulf of (li-pan′tō), the Gulf of Corinth.

Lepanto, Strait of, a narrow strait between the Ionian Sea and the Gulf of Corinth: site of a naval battle (1571) in which the European powers defeated Turkey.

lep·er (lep′ẽr), *n.* [ME. *lepre,* leprosy; OFr. *lepre, liepre;* L. *lepra, leprae;* Gr. *lepra,* leprosy < *lepros,* rough, scaly < *lepos,* a scale < *lepein,* to peel], a person having leprosy.

lep·id- (lep′id), lepido-.

lep·i·do- (lep′ə-dō′), [< Gr. *lepis, lepidos,* a scale, husk], a combining form meaning *scaly,* as in *lepidolite.*

le·pid·o·lite (li-pid′ə-līt′, lep′ə-dō-līt′), *n.* [*lepido-* + *-lite*], mica that contains lithia, commonly occurring in scaly masses.

lep·i·dop·ter·al (lep′ə-dop′tẽr-əl), *adj.* lepidopterous.

lep·i·dop·ter·an (lep′ə-dop′tẽr-ən), *adj.* lepidopterous. *n.* a lepidopterous insect.

lep·i·dop·ter·on (lep′ə-dop′tẽr-on′), *n.* [*pl.* LEPIDOPTERA (-ə)], a lepidopterous insect.

lep·i·dop·ter·ous (lep′ə-dop′tẽr-əs), *adj.* [< Mod. L. *Lepidoptera,* name of the order; see LEPIDO- & -PTEROUS], of a large group of insects, including the butterflies and moths, characterized by two pairs of broad, membranous wings covered with very fine scales, often brightly colored.

lep·i·do·si·ren (lep′ə-dō-sī′rən), *n.* [*lepido-* + *siren*], an eel-shaped fish found in the swamps of the Amazon.

lep·i·dote (lep′ə-dōt′), *adj.* [Gr. *lepidōtos* < *lepis, lepidos,* a scale], in *botany,* covered with flakes or scales; scurfy.

Lep·i·dus (lep′i-dəs), *n.* (*Marcus Aemilius Lepidus*), Roman triumvir; lived ?–13 B.C.

Le·pon·tine Alps (li-pon′tin), that part of the Alps between Switzerland and Italy: highest peak, Monte Leone, 11,684 ft.

lep·o·rid (lep′ə-rid), *n.* [*pl.* LEPORIDAE (li-por′ə-dē′)], [< ML. *Leporidae,* name of the family < L. *lepus, leporis,* a hare; see -ID], any of a family of animals consisting of the hares and rabbits. *adj.* of this family.

lep·o·ride (lep′ə-rid), *n.* [< L. *lepus, leporis,* a hare], a cross between a European hare and European rabbit; Belgian hare.

lep·o·rine (lep′ə-rīn′, lep′ə-rin), *adj.* [L. *leporinus* < *lepus, leporis,* a hare], of or like a hare or hares.

lep·re·chaun (lep′rə-kôn′; Ir. lep′rə-khôn′), *n.* [Ir. *lupracān;* OIr. *luchorpan* < *lu,* little + *corpān,* dim. of *corp,* body < L. *corpus,* body], in *Irish folklore,* a fairy in the form of a little old man who can reveal hidden treasure to anyone who catches him.

lep·ro·sa·ri·um (lep′rə-sâr′i-əm), *n.* [Mod. L. < *leprosy* + *sanitarium*], a hospital or colony for lepers.

lep·rose (lep′rōs), *adj.* [LL. *leprosus;* see LEPROUS], in *botany,* scaly; scurfy.

lep·ro·sy (lep′rə-si), *n.* [OFr. *leprosie;* prob. < ML. *leprosus;* see LEPROUS], a chronic infectious disease that attacks the skin, tissues, or nerves: it is characterized by nodules, ulcers, white scaly scabs, deformities, and wasting of body parts, and is apparently communicated only after long and close contact.

lep·rous (lep′rəs), *adj.* [OFr. *leprous, lepros;* LL. *leprosus* < L. *lepra;* Gr. *lepra,* leprosy; see LEPER], 1. of or like leprosy. 2. having leprosy. 3. leprose.

-lep·si·a (lep′si-ə), -lepsy.

-lep·sy (lep′si), [Mod. L. *-lepsia;* Gr. *-lēpsia*], a combining form meaning *a fit, attack,* as in *catalepsy.*

lep·to- (lep′tō, lep′tə), [Gr. *lepto-* < *leptos,* slender, thin], a combining form meaning *thin, fine, slender,* as in *leptodactylous:* also, before a vowel, **lept-.**

lep·to·dac·ty·lous (lep′tə-dak′ti-ləs), *adj.* [*lepto-* + *dactyl* + *-ous*], having slender toes, as some birds.

lep·ton (lep′ton), *n.* [*pl.* LEPTA (-tə)], [Gr. < *leptos,* thin, small], 1. a small coin of ancient Greece. 2. the smallest Greek coin, worth 1/100 of a drachma.

lep·tus (lep′təs), *n.* [Mod. L. < Gr. *leptos,* small, thin], the six-legged larva of certain mites.

Le·pus (lē′pəs), *n.* [L., a hare], a southern constellation supposedly outlining a hare: see **constellation,** chart.

Ler·mon·tov, Mi·kha·il Yur·ie·vich (mē′khå-ēl′ ūr′-yə-vich lyâr′mon-tôf′), 1814–1841; Russian poet and novelist.

‡le roi est mort, vive le roi (lə rwä′ e′ môr′ vēv′ lə rwä), [Fr.], the king is dead, (long) live the (new) king!

Le·roy (lə-roi′, lē′roi), [< Fr. *le roi,* the king], a masculine name.

Le·sage, A·lain Re·né (å′lan′ rə-nā′ lə såzh′), 1668–1747; French novelist and dramatist.

Les·bi·an (lez′bi-ən), *adj.* [L. *Lesbius;* Gr. *Lesbios*], 1. of Lesbos, its people, etc. 2. *a*) homosexual: only of women, from the homosexuality attributed to Sappho and her followers in Lesbos. *b*) [Rare], erotic. *n.* 1. a native or inhabitant of Lesbos. 2. a homosexual woman.

Les·bi·an·ism (lez′bi-ən-iz′m), *n.* the sexual practices of Lesbians; homosexuality between women.

Les·bos (lez′bəs, lez′bos), *n.* Mytilene, an island in the Aegean: the ancient name.

Le·sche·tiz·ky, Theodore (le′she-tits′ki), 1830–1915; Polish pianist and composer.

‡lèse-ma·jes·té (lez′må′zhes′tā′), *n.* [Fr.], lese majesty.

lese maj·es·ty (lēz′ maj′is-ti), [Fr. *lèse-majesté;* L. *laesa majestas; laesa,* fem. of *laesus,* pp. of *laedere,* to hurt, injure + *majestas,* majesty], a crime against the sovereign; offense against a ruler's dignity as head of the state; treason: also **leze majesty.**

le·sion (lē′zhən), *n.* [Fr. *lésion;* L. *laesio* < *laesus,* pp. of *laedere,* to harm, injure], 1. an injury; hurt; damage. 2. an injury or other change of an organ or tissue of the body tending to result in impairment or loss of function.

Les·lie (les′li, lez′li), [orig. surname, said to be < *less lee* (*lea*), i.e., smaller meadow, dell], a masculine or feminine name.

less (les), *adj.* [alternative comparative of *little*], [ME. *les, lesse;* AS. *læs, adv., læssa, adj.,* used as compar. of *lytel* (cf. LITTLE); akin to OFris. *lēs, lēssa;* not found outside Anglo-Fris. & prob. not connected with the *lyt-* of AS. *lytel*], not so much; not so great, so many, etc.; smaller; fewer. *adv.* [comparative of *little*], not so much; to a smaller extent. *n.* a smaller amount. *prep.* with the deduction of; minus: as, total income *less* earned income.

no less a person than, a person of no lower importance, rank, etc. than.

-less (lis), [ME. *-les, -leas;* AS. *-leas* < *leas,* free, loose; cf. LOOSE, LOSE], a suffix meaning: 1. *without, lacking,* as in *pitiless, valueless.* 2. *not* _____*ing,* as in *relentless, tireless.* 3. *not capable of being* _____*ed,* as in *dauntless.*

les·see (les-ē′), *n.* [OFr. *lessé,* pp. of *lesser;* see LEASE & -EE], a person to whom a lease is given; tenant.

less·en (les′'n), *v.t.* 1. to make less; decrease. 2. to belittle; depreciate; minimize; disparage. *v.i.* to become less. —*SYN.* see **decrease.**

Les·seps, Vicomte **Fer·di·nand Ma·rie de** (fer′dē′nän′ må′rē′ də le′seps′; Eng. les′əps), 1805–1894; French diplomat; builder of the Suez Canal.

less·er (les′ẽr), *adj.* [alternative (double) comparative of *little*], [*less* + *-er;* cf. parallel OFris. *lēssera*], smaller, less, or less important.

Lesser Antilles, a group of islands in the West Indies, southeast of Puerto Rico, including the Leeward Islands, the Windward Islands, and the islands north of Venezuela: see **West Indies,** map.

Lesser Bear, the constellation Ursa Minor.

Les·sing, Gott·hold E·phra·im (gôt′hôlt ā′frä-im les′iŋ), 1729–1781; German dramatist and critic.

les·son (les′'n), *n.* [ME. *lessoun;* OFr. *leçon* < L. *lectio;* see LECTION], 1. something to be learned; specifically, *a*) an exercise or assignment that a student is to prepare or learn within a given time; unit of instruction. *b*) the instruction given during one class or instruction period. *c*) something that needs to be learned (or the event through which it is learned) for the sake of one's safety, well-being, etc.: as, breaking through thin ice has taught many a skater a *lesson.* *d*) *pl.* course of instruction: as, music *lessons.* 2. a selection from the Bible, read as part of a church service. 3. a lecture; rebuke. *v.t.* 1. to give a lesson or lessons to. 2. to rebuke; reprove.

les·sor (les′ôr, les-ôr′), *n.* [Anglo-Fr. < *lesser;* see LEASE], a person who gives a lease; landlord.

lest (lest), *conj.* [ME. *leste;* AS. *the læste* < *thy læs the,* lit., by the less that; based on *læs* (cf. LESS) with *thy,* instrumental of the def. art.], 1. for fear that; in case; so that. . .not: as, we spoke very low *lest* we should be overheard. 2. that: used only after an expression denoting fear, as, I was afraid *lest* he should fall.

Les·ter (les′tẽr), [orig. surname < *Leicester* (city)], a masculine name.

let (let), *v.t.* [LET or *obs.* LETTED (-id), LETTING], [ME. *leten;* AS. *lætan;* to leave behind; akin to G. *lassen;*

IE. base *lēid- (< *lēi-, to neglect; leave behind, etc.), seen also in L. *lassus* (*ləd-to), tired, worn out, etc. (cf. LASSITUDE), Eng. *late, last*, etc.], 1. to leave; forsake; abandon: now only in phrases *let alone, let be*. 2. *a*) to give temporary use of (a house, room, etc.) to a tenant in return for rent; rent; hire out. *b*) to give out (work); assign (a contract). 3. to allow or cause to escape; cause to flow or come out, as by shedding, emitting, etc.: as, *let* blood. 4. to allow to pass, come, or go. 5. to allow; permit: *a*) followed by an infinitive, often without *to*: as, will you *let* me smoke? *b*) with the following verb understood: as, don't *let* me down. 6. to cause: usually with *know* or *hear*, as, *let* me hear from you. 7. to suppose; assume; regard as. When used in commands or suggestions with a noun or pronoun as object, *let* serves as an auxiliary: as, *let* us give generously. ***v.i.*** to be rented or leased: as, this place *lets* for $150 a month.

let alone, 1. to refrain from bothering, disturbing, touching, etc.; not interfere with; have nothing to do with. 2. not to mention; much less: as, we couldn't even hold our ground, *let alone* advance.

let be, to refrain from bothering, disturbing, touching, etc.; have nothing to do with.

let down, 1. to lower. 2. to slow up; relax; slacken. 3. to disappoint or disillusion.

let drive at, to strike a powerful blow at.

let in, to allow to come, pass, or flow in; admit.

let off, 1. to give forth, as steam. 2. to excuse from work for a short time. 3. to deal leniently with; release with light punishment or none.

let on, [Colloq.], 1. to pretend. 2. to indicate one's awareness of a fact (usually used in the negative).

let out, 1. to allow to flow, run, etc. away; release. 2. to give forth; emit. 3. to lease or rent out. 4. to reveal (a secret, etc.). 5. to make a garment larger by reducing (the seams, hem, etc.). 6. [Colloq.], to dismiss or be dismissed, as school.

let up, 1. to slacken; relax. 2. to cease.

let up on, [Colloq.], to ease up; stop dealing harshly or severely with.

SYN.—**let** may imply positive consent but more often stresses the offering of no opposition or resistance, sometimes connoting negligence, lack of power, etc. (don't *let* this happen again); **allow** and **permit** imply power or authority to give or deny consent, **allow** connoting a refraining from the enforcement of usual requirements (honor students were *allowed* to miss the examinations), and **permit** more positively suggesting formal consent or authorization (he was *permitted* to talk to the prisoner); **suffer,** now somewhat rare in this sense, is closely synonymous with **allow** and may connote passive consent or reluctant tolerance. See also **hire.**

let (let), ***v.t.*** [LETTED (-id), or LET, LETTING], [ME. *letten;* AS. *lettan*, lit., to make late (akin to Goth. *latjan*, to delay) < base of AS. *læt*, late; hence ult. < same IE. base as prec. *let*], [Archaic], to hinder; obstruct; prevent. ***n.*** 1. an obstacle; hindrance: usually in the legal phrase *without let or hindrance.* 2. in *tennis*, etc., an interference with the course of the ball in some way specified in the rules, making it necessary to play the point over again.

-let (lit), [< Fr. *-el* (< L. *-ellus*) + *-et*, both dim. suffixes], a noun suffix, generally meaning *small*, as in *ringlet, hamlet:* used in some words (e.g., *anklet, armlet*) meaning *small object worn as a band on* (a specified part of the body).

‡**l'é·tat, c'est moi** (lā'tȧ' se' mwȧ'), [Fr., lit., the state, it is I], I am the state: a saying attributed to Louis XIV of France.

let·down (let'doun'), ***n.*** 1. a slowing up, relaxing, or slackening, as after great excitement, effort, etc. 2. [Colloq.], a disappointment or disillusionment.

le·thal (lē'thəl), ***adj.*** [L. *letalis, lethalis* < *letum, lethum*, death], 1. causing death; fatal; deadly. 2. of or suggestive of death. —***SYN.*** see **fatal.**

lethal chamber, 1. a room where persons may be painlessly executed by gases. 2. a similar room for killing dogs and cats.

le·thar·gic (li-thär'jik), ***adj.*** [ME. *litargik;* L. *lethargicus;* Gr. *lēthargikos*], 1. of or producing lethargy. 2. having lethargy; abnormally drowsy; dull; sluggish.

le·thar·gi·cal·ly (li-thär'ji-k'l-i, li-thär'jik-li), ***adv.*** in a lethargic manner.

leth·ar·gize (leth'ẽr-jīz'), ***v.t.*** [LETHARGIZED (-jīzd'), LETHARGIZING], to make lethargic.

leth·ar·gy (leth'ẽr-ji), ***n.*** [*pl.* LETHARGIES (-jiz)], [ME. *letharge;* OFr. *litarge, lethargie;* LL. *lethargia;* Gr. *lēthargia* < *lēthargos*, forgetful < *lēthē;* see LETHE], 1. *a*) an abnormal drowsiness; great lack of energy; inertness. *b*) a prolonged and unnatural sleep. 2. total indifference; apathy.

SYN.—**lethargy** implies a dull, sluggish state brought on by illness, great fatigue, overeating, etc.; **languor** now generally suggests an inertia or limpness that results from indolence, enervating weather, a dreamy, tender mood, etc.; **lassitude** suggests a listlessness or spiritlessness resulting from overwork, dejection, etc.; **stupor** suggests a state in which the faculties and senses are deadened, as by emotional shock, alcohol, or narcotics; **torpor** implies a temporary loss of all or part of the power of sensation or motion.

Le·the (lē'thi), ***n.*** [L. < Gr. *lēthē*, forgetfulness, oblivion], 1. in *Greek & Roman mythology*, the river of forgetfulness, flowing through Hades, whose water produced loss of memory in those who drank of it; hence, 2. oblivion; forgetfulness.

Le·the·an (lē-thē'ən), ***adj.*** 1. of Lethe or its water. 2. causing forgetfulness or oblivion.

le·thif·er·ous (li-thif'ẽr-əs), ***adj.*** [L. *letifer, lethifer* < *letum*, death + *ferre*, to bring], bringing destruction and death; deadly.

Le·ti·ti·a (li-tish'i-ə, li-tish'ə), [< L. *laetitia*, gladness < *laetus*, gay, glad], a feminine name.

Le·to (lē'tō), ***n.*** [Gr. *Lētō*], in *Greek mythology*, the mother of Apollo and Artemis: identified by the Romans with Latona.

‡**le tout en·sem·ble** (lə tōō'tän'sän'bl'), [Fr.], the whole (taken) together.

let's (lets), let us.

Lett (let), ***n.*** 1. a member of a people living in Latvia and adjacent Baltic regions. 2. Lettish.

Lett., Lettish.

let·ted (let'id), 1. obsolete past tense and past participle of **let** (to allow). 2. alternative past tense and past participle of **let** (to hinder).

let·ter (let'ẽr), ***n.*** [ME. *lettre, letre;* OFr. *lettre;* L. *littera*, letter of the alphabet, (in pl.) a letter, epistle], 1. a symbol or character employed, theoretically, to represent a speech sound: in English, many words contain letters that are no longer pronounced. 2. a written or printed personal or business message, usually sent by mail in an envelope. 3. an official document giving certain authorities or privileges. 4. strict interpretation of the literal meaning, or the literal meaning itself; exact wording. 5. the first letter of the name of a school or college, awarded and worn for superior activity in sports, etc. 6. in *printing*, *a*) a type or impression of a character of the alphabet. *b*) a particular style of type. ***v.t.*** 1. to make hand-printed letters on; mark with letters: as, the poster was artistically *lettered.* 2. to set down in hand-printed letters: as, on the blank page he *lettered* his name. ***v.i.*** to make hand-printed letters: as, she learned to *letter* in art school.

letters, 1. literature generally. 2. learning; knowledge, especially of literature. 3. the profession of a writer.

to the letter, just as written or directed; precisely.

letter box, a box to hold mail being sent or delivered; mailbox.

letter carrier, a postman; mail carrier.

let·tered (let'ẽrd), ***adj.*** 1. able to read and write; literate. 2. very well educated; learned. 3. inscribed or marked with letters.

let·ter·gram (let'ẽr-gram'), ***n.*** [*letter* + tele*gram*], a day letter or night letter (kind of telegram).

let·ter·head (let'ẽr-hed'), ***n.*** 1. the name, address, etc. of a person or firm printed as a heading on a sheet of letter paper. 2. a sheet of letter paper with such a heading printed on it.

let·ter·ing (let'ẽr-iŋ), ***n.*** 1. the act of making letters or of inscribing in or with letters, especially by hand-printing, drawing, or painting. 2. a series of letters so made or inscribed.

letter of advice, a letter notifying the receiver of a special fact, as that a bill of exchange has been drawn on him or that a consignment of goods has been sent to him.

letter of credit, a letter from a bank asking that the holder of the letter be allowed to draw specified sums of money from other banks or agencies, to be charged to the account of the writer of the letter: abbreviated **L/C, l/c** (no period).

let·ter-per·fect (let'ẽr-pũr'fikt), ***adj.*** 1. correct in all its letters, or in every respect. 2. knowing one's lines, part, or lesson perfectly: said of an actor, etc.

let·ter·press (let'ẽr-pres'), ***n.*** printed words; especially, reading matter, as distinguished from illustrations.

letter press, a device for making copies of letters.

letters of administration, in *law*, a document by which an administrator is authorized to administer the goods or property of a dead person.

letters (or **letter**) **of credence,** a formal document which a country's diplomatic representative carries as his credentials to a foreign government: also **letters credential.**

letters (or **letter**) **of marque,** 1. originally, a governmental document authorizing an individual to make reprisals on the subjects or citizens of an enemy nation for injuries done him by enemy troops; hence, 2. later, a governmental document authorizing an individual to arm a ship and capture the merchant ships and property of an enemy nation: also **letters** (or **letter**) **of marque and reprisal.**

letters pat·ent (pat''nt), [cf. PATENT, *adj.*], a document issued by a government to a person, authorizing him to perform some act or to enjoy some privilege, such as exclusive right to an invention: so called because the document is not sealed but open.

letters testamentary, in *law*, a document granted

after probate of a will by the probate court or some officer who has authority, directing the person named as executor in the will to act in that capacity.

Let·tic (let'ik), *adj.* 1. designating or of a branch of the Baltic languages, including Lettish and Lithuanian. 2. Lettish. *n.* the Lettic language.

Let·tish (let'ish), *adj.* of the Letts or their language. *n.* the Baltic language of the Letts. Abbreviated **Lett.**

‡let·tre de ca·chet (let'r' də kȧ'shā'), [Fr.], a sealed letter; especially, a letter containing a royal warrant for the imprisonment without trial of a specified person, common in France before the Revolution.

let·tuce (let'is), *n.* [ME. *letuse;* OFr. *laituës,* pl. of *laituë;* L. *lactuca* < *lac, lactis,* milk: so called from its milky juice], 1. any of a number of varieties of a plant of the composite family; especially, head lettuce or leaf lettuce. 2. the crisp, green leaves of such a plant, much used for salads. 3. [Slang], paper money.

let·up (let'up'), *n.* [< phr. *let up*], [Colloq.], 1. a slackening; lessening. 2. a stop; pause; cessation.

le·u (le'oo), *n.* [*pl.* LEI (lā)], [Romanian, lit., lion < L. *leo;* see LION], the monetary unit and a silver coin of Romania: also **ley.**

Leu·cas, Leu·kas (lōō'kəs, lū'kəs), *n.* Levkas.

leu·ce·mi·a, leu·cae·mi·a (lōō-sē'mi-ə, lyoo-sē'mi-ə), *n.* leukemia.

leu·cin (lōō'sin, lū'sin), *n.* leucine.

leu·cine (lōō'sēn, lū'sin), *n.* [< Gr. *leukos,* white; + *-ine*], an amino acid, $C_6H_{13}NO_2$, produced by the hydrolysis of proteins by pancreatic enzymes during digestion and by the putrefaction of nitrogenous organic matter.

leu·cite (lōō'sīt, lū'sīt), *n.* [G. *leukit* < Gr. *leukos,* white], a white or gray mineral, $KAl(SiO_3)_2$, found in igneous rocks.

leu·co- (lōō'kō, lū'kə), [< Gr. *leukos,* white], a combining form meaning *white* or *colorless,* as in *leucocyte, leucorrhea*: also, before a vowel, **leuc-**: words beginning with *leuc-* or *leuco-* are now often spelled **leuk-** or **leuko-**, as in *leukemia,* especially in medical and biological usage.

leu·co·cyte (lōō'kə-sīt', lū'kə-sīt'), *n.* [*leuco-* + *-cyte*], any of the small, colorless cells in the blood, lymph, and tissues, which move like amoebae and destroy organisms that cause disease; white blood corpuscle.

leu·co·cyt·ic (lōō'kə-sit'ik, lū'kə-sit'ik), *adj.* 1. of leucocytes. 2. having an excess of leucocytes.

leu·co·cy·to·sis (lōō'kō-sī-tō'sis, lū'kō-sī-tō'sis), *n.* [Mod. L. < *leucocyte* + *-osis*], an increase in the number of leucocytes in the blood: it is a normal occurrence in digestion and during pregnancy but a pathological condition in infections, anemia, and certain fevers.

leu·co·cy·tot·ic (lōō'kō-sī-tot'ik, lū'kō-sī-tot'ik), *adj.* of or having leucocytosis.

leu·co·der·ma (lōō'kə-dūr'mə, lū'kə-dūr'mə), *n.* [Mod. L.; see LEUCO- & DERM], a congenital lack of pigmentation in the skin, resulting in abnormal white patches.

leu·co·ma (lōō-kō'mə, lyoo-kō'mə), *n.* [Mod. L.; Gr. *leukōma* < *leukos,* white], a dense, white opacity of the cornea, caused by ulceration.

leu·co·ma·ine (lōō-kō'mə-ēn', lyoo-kō'mə-in), *n.* [*leuco-* + *-maine* as in pto*maine*], any of a large group of basic substances present in the body as normal products of protein metabolism.

leu·co·me·lan·ic (lōō'kō-mi-lan'ik, lū'kō-mi-lan'ik), *adj.* leucomelanous.

leu·co·mel·a·nous (lōō'kō-mel'ə-nəs, lū'kō-mel'ə-nəs), *adj.* having a light complexion and dark hair (and, sometimes, dark eyes).

leu·co·plast (lōō'kə-plast', lū'kə-plast'), *n.* [*leuco-* + *-plast*], any of the colorless granules found in the protoplasm of vegetable cells, constituting points about which starch forms.

leu·cor·rhe·a, leu·cor·rhoe·a (lōō'kə-rē'ə, lū'kə-rē'ə), *n.* [Mod. L.; see LEUCO- & -RRHEA], a morbid whitish discharge from the vagina and uterus, usually resulting from chronic infection: also called *whites.*

leuk-, leuko-, see **leuco-.**

leu·ke·mi·a, leu·kae·mi·a (lōō-kē'mi-ə, lyoo-kē'mi-ə), *n.* [Mod. L.; see LEUCO- & -EMIA], a disease of the blood-forming tissues, characterized by an abnormal and persistent increase in the number of leucocytes and the amount of bone marrow, with enlargement of the spleen and lymph glands.

leu·ko·pe·ni·a (lōō'kə-pē'ni-ə, lū'kə-pē'ni-ə), *n.* [Mod. L. < *leuco-* + Gr. *penia,* poverty], a decrease in the number of leucocytes in the blood.

leu·ko·pe·nic (lōō'kə-pē'nik, lū'kə-pē'nik), *adj.* of or having leukopenia.

lev (lef), *n.* [*pl.* LEVA (le'və)], [Bulg., lit., lion; OSlav. *livu,* ult. < Gr. *leōn,* lion; cf. LEU], the monetary unit and a copper coin of Bulgaria, valued at about one third of a cent in 1947.

Lev., Leviticus.

Le·vant (lə-vant'), *n.* [Fr. *levant;* It. *levante* (< L. *levans,* rising, raising < *levare,* to raise), *se levare,* to rise; cf. LEVER: applied to the East, from the "rising" of the sun], 1. the regions on the eastern Mediterranean and the Aegean, from Greece to Egypt, including Syria, Lebanon, and Palestine. 2. [l-], Levant morocco. 3. [l-], levanter.

Levant dollar, see **dollar.**

le·vant·er (lə-van'tẽr), *n.* [< *Levant* + *-er*], 1. a strong wind that blows over the Mediterranean area from the east. 2. [L-], a Levantine.

Le·van·tine (lə-van'tin, lev'ən-tīn', lev'ən-tēn'), *adj.* [Fr. *levantin*], of the Levant. *n.* 1. a native or inhabitant of the Levant. 2. a ship of the Levant. 3. [l-], [Fr. *levantine*: from being made in the Levant], a strong, twilled, black silk cloth.

Levant morocco, a fine morocco leather with a large, irregular grain, used especially in bookbinding.

le·va·tor (lə-vā'tẽr), *n.* [*pl.* LEVATORES (lev'ə-tôr'ēz, lev'ə-tō'rēz)], [Mod. L. < pp. of L. *levare,* to raise], 1. a muscle that raises a limb or other part of the body. 2. a surgical instrument for lifting depressed fragments of bone in a skull fracture.

lev·ee (lev'i), *n.* [Fr. *levée,* fem. pp. of *lever,* to raise; see LEVANT], 1. an embankment built alongside a river to prevent high water from flooding bordering land. 2. a landing place along the bank of a river; quay. *v.t.* [LEVEED (-id), LEVEEING], to build a levee or levees along.

lev·ee (lev'i, lə-vē'), *n.* [Fr. *levé* < *lever,* to raise, *se lever,* to rise; see LEVANT], 1. a morning reception held by a sovereign or person of high rank when rising from bed. 2. a reception held by the President or other high official. 3. [British], a court assembly held in the early afternoon, attended only by men.

lev·el (lev''l), *n.* [ME. & OFr. *level, livel;* L. *libella,* dim. of *libra,* a balance, level], 1. an instrument for determining whether a surface is on an even horizontal plane or for adjusting a surface to such a plane: it has a glass tube partly filled with ether or alcohol so as to leave an air bubble that moves to the exact center of the tube when the instrument is on an even horizontal plane. 2. a measuring of differences in height, or altitude, with such an instrument. 3. a horizontal plane or line; especially, such a plane taken as a basis for the measurement of elevation: as, sea *level.* 4. a relatively flat and even area of land or other surface; horizontal area. 5. the same horizontal plane: as, the tops of the pictures should be on a *level.* 6. height; altitude: as, water boils more quickly at this *level.* 7. usual or normal position or height: as, water seeks its *level.* 8. position or elevation considered as one of the planes in a scale of values: as, few can rise to the *level* of a great man. 9. a horizontal walk or passageway, as between tiers of seats. *adj.* 1. having no part higher than any other; perfectly flat and even; conforming to the surface of still water. 2. conforming to the plane of the horizon; not sloping. 3. being of the same height or being in the same plane; even (*with*). 4. even with the top of the container; not heaping: as, a *level* teaspoonful. 5. *a*) equal in importance, rank, degree, etc. *b*) equally advanced in development. *c*) even or uniform in tone, color, pitch, volume, etc. 6. not having or showing sudden differences or inequalities; well balanced; equable. *adv.* on a level line. *v.t.* [LEVELED or LEVELLED (-'ld), LEVELING or LEVELLING], 1. to make level; specifically, *a*) to make perfectly horizontal by means of a level. *b*) to make even; give a flat, horizontal surface to (often with *off*). *c*) to equalize in height, rank, quality, etc. (often with *down* or *up*). *d*) to make even in tone, color, pitch, etc. 2. to knock to the ground; demolish; lay low: as, the storm *leveled* the tree. 3. to raise (a gun, etc.) to a level position for firing; hence, 4. to aim. 5. in *surveying,* to determine the differences in altitude in (a plot of ground). *v.i.* 1. to aim a gun or other weapon (with *at*). 2. to select some person or thing as a target or goal. 3. to bring people or things to an equal rank, condition, etc. (usually with *down* or *up*). 4. [Slang], to be frank and honest (*with* someone).

LEVEL (*n.* 1)

find one's (or **its**) **level,** to reach one's proper or natural place according to one's qualities, capacity, etc.

level off, 1. to give a flat, horizontal surface to; make even with the surfaces immediately surrounding. 2. in *aviation,* to come, or bring, to a horizontal position just before landing.

one's level best, [Colloq.], the best one can do.

on the level, [Slang], honest(ly) and fair(ly).

SYN.—**level** is applied to a surface that is parallel to, or conforms with, the horizon; **flat** implies the absence to any marked degree of depressions or elevations in a surface, in whatever direction it lies; **plane** describes a real or imaginary surface that is absolutely flat and wholly contains every straight line joining any two points lying in it; **even** is applied to a surface that is uniformly level or flat, or to a surface that is in the same or a parallel plane with another; a **smooth** surface has no roughness or projections, often as a result of wear, planing, polishing, etc.

level crossing, a place where a road crosses one or more railroads on the same level.

lev·el·er (lev′'l-ẽr), *n.* 1. a person or thing that levels. 2. a person who wishes to abolish social inequalities. 3. [L-], [British], a member of a party that arose in the army of the Long Parliament (c. 1647) and advocated the leveling of all ranks and establishment of a more democratic government. Also spelled **leveller.**

lev·el-head·ed (lev′'l-hed′id), *adj.* having or showing an even temper and sound judgment; sensible.

leveling rod (or **staff**), in *surveying,* a graduated rod used in determining the difference in elevation between two points.

lev·er (lev′ẽr, lē′vẽr), *n.* [ME. *lever, levour,* OFr. *leveour* < *lever;* L. *levare,* to raise < *levis,* light], 1. a bar used as a pry. 2. in *mechanics,* a device consisting of a bar turning about a fixed point, the fulcrum, using power or force applied at a second point to lift or sustain a weight at a third point. *v.t.* 1. to move, lift, etc. with or as with a lever. 2. to use as a lever. *v.i.* to use a lever.

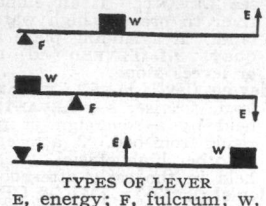

TYPES OF LEVER
E, energy; F, fulcrum; W, weight

Le·ver, Charles James (lē′vẽr), 1806–1872; Irish novelist.

lev·er·age (lev′ẽr-ij, lē′vẽr-ij), *n.* [see -AGE], 1. the action of a lever. 2. the mechanical power resulting from this. 3. increased means of accomplishing some purpose.

lev·er·et (lev′ẽr-it), *n.* [Late ME.; Anglo-Fr.; OFr. *levrete,* dim. of *levre,* hare < L. *lepus, leporis*], a hare during its first year.

Le·vi (lē′vī), [Heb. *lēwī,* lit., joining], a masculine name: diminutive, *Lev. n.* in the *Bible,* the third son of Jacob and Leah: Gen. 29:34: see also **Levite.**

lev·i·a·ble (lev′i-ə-b'l), *adj.* 1. that can be levied upon; taxable; assessable. 2. that can be levied.

le·vi·a·than (lə-vī′ə-thən), *n.* [ME. *leuyethan;* LL.; Heb. *liwyāthān*], 1. in the *Bible,* a sea monster, variously thought of as a reptile or a whale. 2. anything huge of its kind. 3. [L-], a political treatise by Thomas Hobbes (1651), upholding the supreme authority of the sovereign.

lev·i·er (lev′i-ẽr), *n.* a person who levies taxes, etc.

lev·i·gate (lev′ə-gāt′), *v.t.* [LEVIGATED (-id), LEVIGATING], [< L. *levigatus,* pp. of *levigare,* to make smooth, polish < *levis,* smooth + *agere,* to make], to make smooth; specifically, *a)* to grind to a fine, smooth powder. *b)* to make a smooth paste of; mix thoroughly. *adj.* smooth or smoothed, as if polished.

lev·i·ga·tion (lev′ə-gā′shən), *n.* a levigating or being levigated.

lev·in (lev′in), *n.* [ME. *levene* (revived by Scott); prob. representing Gmc. **lauh-ubni* via ON. (cf. *lȳvna,* lightning) or AS.; IE. base **leuq-,* to shine, light, seen also in L. *lux, lumen,* light], [Archaic], lightning.

lev·i·rate (lev′ə-rāt′, lē′vẽr-it), *n.* [L. *levir,* husband's brother, brother-in-law < **daiwer* (IE. **dāiwẽr,* seen also in Sans. *dēvár,* Gr. *daẽr,* AS. *tacor*); + *-ate*], a custom of the ancient Jews by which a dead man's brother was obligated to marry the widow if there were no sons: Deut. 25:5-10.

lev·i·rat·i·cal (lev′ə-rat′i-k'l, lē′və-rat′i-k'l), *adj.* of the levirate.

lev·is (lē′vīz), *n.pl.* [after *Levi* Strauss, the Am. maker], overalls; especially, bibless overalls, worn by cowboys, reinforced at the seams, etc. with small copper rivets: a trade-mark (**Levis**).

lev·i·tate (lev′ə-tāt′), *v.t.* [LEVITATED (-id), LEVITATING], [< L. *levis,* light; by analogy with *gravitate*], [Rare], to cause to rise and float in the air. *v.i.* to rise and float in the air because of, or as if because of, lightness and buoyancy.

lev·i·ta·tion (lev′ə-tā′shən), *n.* 1. a levitating or being levitated. 2. the illusion of raising and keeping a heavy body in the air with little or no physical support.

Le·vite (lē′vīt), *n.* [LL. *Levites;* Gr. *Leuitēs* < Heb. *lēwī;* see LEVI], in the *Bible,* any member of the tribe of Levi, chosen to assist the Jewish priests.

Le·vit·i·cal (lə-vit′i-k'l), *adj.* [< LL. *Leviticus;* + *-al*], 1. of the Levites. 2. of Leviticus or its laws.

Le·vit·i·cus (lə-vit′i-kəs), *n.* [LL. *Leviticus* (*liber*); Gr. *Leuitikon* (*biblion*), lit., the Levitical book], the third book of the Old Testament, containing the laws relating to priests and Levites: abbreviated **Lev., Levit.**

lev·i·ty (lev′ə-ti), *n.* [*pl.* LEVITIES (-tiz)], [OFr. *levité;* L. *levitas* < *levis,* light], 1. [Rare], lightness of weight; buoyancy. 2. lightness or gaiety of disposition, conduct, or speech; especially, improper or unbecoming gaiety or flippancy; lack of seriousness; frivolity. 3. fickleness; instability.

Lev·kas (lef-käs′), *n.* one of the Ionian Islands, off the western coast of Greece: also **Leucas, Leukas.**

le·vo- (lē′vō, lē′və), [< L. *laevus,* left < earlier **laiwos;* IE. **laiwos* (seen also in Gr. *laios*) < base **lēi-,* **lĕi-,* to bend, curve], a combining form meaning: 1. *on* or *to the left,* as in *levoduction.* 2. *levorotatory.* Words beginning with *levo-* may also be spelled **laevo-.**

le·vo·duc·tion (lē′və-duk′shən), *n.* [< *levo-* + L. *ductio,* a leading < pp. of *ducere,* to lead], motion toward the left, as of an eye.

le·vo·gy·rate (lē′və-jī′rāt), *adj.* [*levo-* + *gyrate, adj.*], turning toward the left, or counterclockwise; levorotatory.

le·vo·gy·rous (lē′və-jī′rəs), *adj.* levogyrate.

le·vo·ro·ta·tion (lē′və-rō-tā′shən), *n.* [*levo-* + *rotation*], rotation to the left; counterclockwise rotation: usually said of the plane of polarization of light.

le·vo·ro·ta·to·ry (lē′və-rō′tə-tôr′i, lē′və-rō′tə-tō′ri), *adj.* [*levo-* + *rotatory*], 1. turning or circling to the left, in a counterclockwise direction. 2. that turns the plane of polarized light to the left, or in a counterclockwise direction: said of certain crystals, etc. Opposed to *dextrorotatory.*

lev·u·lin (lev′yoo-lin), *n.* [*levulose* + *-in*], a colorless, starchlike carbohydrate, $C_6H_{10}O_5$, which hydrolyzes to form levulose.

lev·u·lose (lev′yoo-lōs′), *n.* [< L. *laevus,* left; + *-ule* + *-ose:* so called because levorotatory], fructose.

lev·y (lev′i), *n.* [*pl.* LEVIES (-iz)], [ME. *leve(e);* Late OFr. *levée,* fem. pp. of *lever,* to raise; see LEVER], 1. an imposing and collecting of a tax or other payment. 2. the amount collected. 3. the compulsory enlistment of personnel, as for military service. 4. a group so enlisted. *v.t.* [LEVIED (-id), LEVYING], 1. to impose (a tax, tribute, fine, etc.). 2. to enlist (troops) for military service, usually by force. 3. to wage (war). *v.i.* 1. to make a levy. 2. in *law,* to seize property in order to satisfy a judgment (often with *on*).

levy in mass, [after Fr. *levée en masse*], a levy of all men able to bear arms when their country is attacked suddenly.

lewd (lōōd, lūd), *adj.* [ME. *lewed;* AS. *læwede,* lay, unlearned; ? borrowing < base of L. *laicus* (cf. LAY, *adj.*) merged in form with AS. *læwan,* to betray], 1. indecent; lustful; unchaste; lascivious. 2. [Obs.], *a)* unlearned; ignorant. *b)* base; unprincipled; vicious.

Lew·es, George Henry (lōō′is, lū′is), 1817–1878; English literary critic and writer on philosophy.

Lew·is (lōō′is, lū′is), a masculine name: diminutives, *Lew, Lewie:* see **Louis.**

lew·is (lōō′is, lū′is), *n.* [? < the name *Lewis;* cf. DAVIT & var. LEWISSON], an attachment for lifting heavy stones: it consists of a dovetailed iron piece made in sections that fit into a dovetailed opening in the stone to be lifted: also **lewisson.**

Lewis, John Llewellyn, 1880– ; American labor leader; president of the C.I.O. (1935–1940) and of the United Mine Workers of America (1920–1960).

Lewis, Mer·i·weth·er (mer′i-weth′ẽr), 1774–1809; American explorer; co-leader of the Lewis and Clark expedition (1804–1806).

Lewis, Sinclair, 1885–1951; American novelist; received Nobel prize in literature, 1930.

lew·is·ite (lōō′is-īt′, lū′is-īt′), *n.* [after W. L. *Lewis* (1878–1943), Am. chemist], an arsenical compound, $ClCH=CHAsCl_2$, used as a blistering poison gas.

Lewis machine gun, [after the Am. inventor, Col. I. N. *Lewis* (1858–1931) of the U.S. Army], an air-cooled, automatic firearm having a circular cartridge drum and designed to be held and fired by one man: also **Lewis gun, Lewis automatic rifle.**

Lewis Mountains, a mountain range in western Montana and Alberta, Canada.

Lew·i·sohn, Lud·wig (lud′wig lōō′i-zən, lōō′i-sōn′), 1882–1955; American novelist and literary critic, born in Germany.

lew·is·son (lōō′i-sən, lū′i-sən), *n.* a lewis.

Lew·is·ton (lōō′is-tən, lū′is-tən), *n.* a city in southwestern Maine: pop., 40,000.

‡**lex** (leks), *n.* [*pl.* LEGES (lē′jēz)], [L.], law.

lex., lexicon.

lex·i·cal (lek′si-k'l), *adj.* [Mod. L. *lexicalis* < Gr. *lexikon,* lexicon], 1. of a vocabulary, or stock of words, as of a language. 2. of, or having the nature of, a lexicon or lexicography.

lexicog., 1. lexicographer. 2. lexicographical. 3. lexicography.

lex·i·cog·ra·pher (lek′sə-kog′rə-fẽr), *n.* [Late Gr. *lexikographos* < Gr. *lexikon,* lexicon + *graphein,* to write], a person who writes or compiles a dictionary.

lex·i·co·graph·ic (lek′si-kə-graf′ik), *adj.* lexicographical.

lex·i·co·graph·i·cal (lek′si-kə-graf′i-k'l), *adj.* of lexicography.

lex·i·cog·ra·phy (lek′sə-kog′rə-fi), *n.* [< Gr. *lexikon*, lexicon; + *-graphy*], the act, process, art, or work of writing or compiling a dictionary or dictionaries.

lex·i·con (lek′si-kən), *n.* [Gr. *lexikon*, neut. of *lexikos*, of words < *lexis*, a saying, phrase, word < *legein*, to say, speak], 1. a dictionary, especially of an ancient language. 2. a special vocabulary, as of an author, science, etc. 3. in *linguistics*, the total stock of morphemes in a language. Abbreviated **lex.**

Lex·ing·ton (lek′siŋ-tən), *n.* 1. a town in eastern Massachusetts: pop., 28,000: site of the first battle (April 19, 1775) of the American Revolution. 2. a city in north central Kentucky: pop., 63,000.

‡lex lo·ci (leks lō′sī), [L.], the law of the place.

‡lex non scrip·ta (leks non skrip′tə), [L., lit., unwritten law], common law.

‡lex scrip·ta (leks skrip′tə), [L., lit., written law], statute law.

‡lex ta·li·o·nis (leks tal′i-ō′nis), [L.], the law of retaliation.

ley (lā), *n.* a leu.

Ley·den (lī′d'n), *n.* Leiden.

Ley·den, Lu·cas van (lü′käs vän lī′d'n), (born *Lucas Hugensz*), 1494–1533; Dutch painter and engraver.

Leyden jar (or **vial**), [< *Leiden*, Netherlands city where it was invented], a glass jar coated outside and inside with tin foil and having a metallic rod connecting with the inner lining and passing through the lid: it acts as a condenser for static electricity.

METAL ROD
POSITIVE CHARGE
NEGATIVE CHARGE
TIN FOIL
TIN FOIL
TIN FOIL
WIRE

LEYDEN JAR

Ley·te (lā′tā; *now often* lā′-ti), *n.* one of the Philippine Islands, between Samar and Cebu: area, 2,799 sq. mi.; pop., 1,210,000: see **Philippine Islands**, map.

Ley·ton (lā′t'n), *n.* a city in Essex, England: pop., 98,000.

leze maj·es·ty (lēz maj′is-ti), lese majesty.

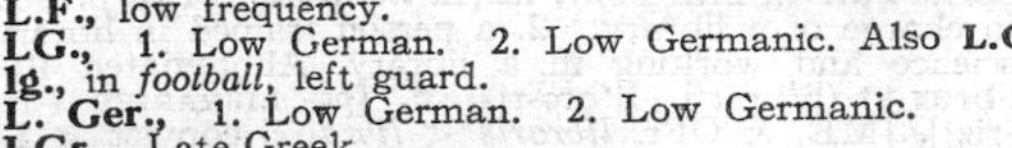

lf., in *baseball*, 1. left field. 2. left fielder.

L.F., low frequency.

LG., 1. Low German. 2. Low Germanic. Also **L.G.**

lg., in *football*, left guard.

L. Ger., 1. Low German. 2. Low Germanic.

LGr., Late Greek.

lgth., length.

lg. tn., long ton.

l.h., in *music*, left hand.

Lha·sa (lä′sə), *n.* the capital of Tibet: pop., 50,000: it is a Buddhist holy city.

L.H.D., *Litterarum Humaniorum Doctor*, [L.], Doctor of the Humanities: an honorary degree.

Lhe·vinne, Jo·sef (jō′zif lā-vēn′), 1874–1944; Russian pianist.

li (lē), *n.* [arbitrary modification of *la*], in *music*, a syllable representing the tone intermediate between la and ti of the diatonic scale: see **solfeggio.**

li (lē), *n.* [*pl.* LI], [Chin.], a Chinese measure of distance, equal to about one third of a mile.

Li, in *chemistry*, lithium.

L.I., 1. Light Infantry. 2. Long Island.

li·a·bil·i·ty (lī′ə-bil′ə-ti), *n.* [*pl.* LIABILITIES (-tiz)], 1. the state of being liable. 2. anything for which a person is liable. 3. *usually in pl.* a debt: as, accounts payable, surplus, losses, and capital stock are *liabilities* of a corporation: opposed to *asset.* 4. something that works to one's disadvantage.

li·a·ble (lī′ə-b'l), *adj.* [< Fr. *lier*, to bind < L. *ligare*, to bind; + *-able*], 1. legally bound, as to make good any loss or damage that occurs in a transaction; answerable; responsible. 2. likely to have, suffer from, etc.; exposed to or subject to: as, he is *liable* to heart attacks. 3. *a*) subject to the possibility of; disagreeably likely: used with the infinitive. *b*) [Colloq.], likely: as, I am *liable* to be there. —*SYN.* see **likely.**

li·ai·son (lē′ā-zōn′; Fr. lye′zōn′; *also, esp. in military usage,* lē′ə-zon′, lī′ə-z'n, li-ā′z'n), *n.* [Fr. < L. *ligatio* < *ligare*, to bind], 1. a linking up or connecting of the parts of a whole, intended to bring about proper co-ordination of activities; especially, intercommunication between units of a military force. 2. an illicit love affair. 3. in spoken French, the linking of words, under certain conditions, by pronouncing the final consonant of one word as though it were the initial consonant of a following word, as in the phrase *chez elle* (pronounced shā′zel′); sandhi. 4. in *cookery*, a thickening, as of flour and butter or beaten eggs and cream, for sauces, soups, etc.

liaison officer, a staff officer whose function is to insure proper co-ordination between parts of an army, allied armies, etc. involved in a military operation.

li·a·na (li-ä′nə, li-an′ə), *n.* [Norm. Fr. *liane* < *lierne*, *liorne*, altered (after *lier*, to bind) < *viorne* < L. *viburnum*, wayfaring tree; cf. VIBURNUM], any luxuriantly growing, woody, tropical vine that roots in the ground and climbs, as around tree trunks.

li·ane (li-än′), *n.* liana.

Liao (lyou), *n.* a river in northeastern China, flowing into the Yellow Sea: length, 700 mi.

Liao·ning (lyou′niŋ′), *n.* a province of northeastern China: pop., 18,545,000: former name, *Fengtien.*

Liao·tung Peninsula (lyou′dooŋ′), a peninsula in northeastern China.

Liao·yang (lyou′yäŋ′), *n.* a city in Liaoning province: pop., 102,000.

li·ar (lī′ẽr), *n.* [ME. *lier, leier;* AS. *leogere, legere* < base of *leogan*, to tell lies + *-er;* akin to OHG. *liugari*], a person who states that something is true which he knows is untrue; person who tells lies.

Li·ard (li-är′, lē′ärd), *n.* a river in western Canada, flowing into the Mackenzie River: length, 550 mi.

Li·as (lī′əs), *n.* [ME. *lyas;* OFr. *liois* (Fr. *liais*), kind of limestone; ? < MHG. *lei*, rock], an important series of bluish rocks, the oldest strata of the Jurassic system, occurring principally in England.

Lib., 1. Liberal. 2. Liberia.

lib., 1. *liber*, [L.], book. 2. librarian. 3. library.

li·ba·tion (lī-bā′shən), *n.* [ME. *libacioun;* L. *libatio* < *libare*, to taste, pour out], 1. the ritual of pouring out wine or oil upon the ground, or upon a victim for sacrifice in honor of a god. 2. the liquid poured out. 3. an alcoholic drink: used humorously.

Li·bau (lē′bou), *n.* a city in the Latvian S.S.R., on the Baltic Sea: pop., 71,000: Lettish name, *Liepāja.*

li·bel (lī′b'l), *n.* [ME., little book; OFr.; L. *libellus*, little book, writing, lampoon, dim. of *liber*, a book; see LIBRARY], 1. any written or printed statement, or any sign, picture, or effigy, not made in the public interest, tending to expose a person to public ridicule or contempt or to injure his reputation in any way: cf. **slander.** 2. the act of publishing such a thing. 3. anything that gives an unflattering or damaging picture of the subject with which it is dealing. 4. in *admiralty & ecclesiastical law*, the plaintiff's written statement of the wrongs he has suffered. *v.t.* [LIBELED or LIBELLED (-b'ld), LIBELING or LIBELLING], 1. to publish or make a libel against. 2. to give an unflattering or damaging picture of; say or print unfavorable or false things about. 3. in *admiralty & ecclesiastical law*, to bring suit against by presenting a written statement of grievances.

li·bel·ant, li·bel·lant (lī′b'l-ənt), *n.* a person who sues by filing a libel (sense 4).

li·bel·ee, li·bel·lee (lī′b'l-ē′), *n.* the defendant in a suit by libel (sense 4).

li·bel·er, li·bel·ler (lī′b'l-ẽr), *n.* a person who libels.

li·bel·ous, li·bel·lous (lī′b'l-əs), *adj.* 1. of the nature of a libel; involving a libel. 2. given to writing and publishing libels; slanderous; vilifying; defamatory.

‡li·ber (lī′bẽr), *n.* [*pl.* LIBRI (-brī)], [L.; see LIBRARY], a book; especially, a book of public records, as of mortgages or deeds: abbreviated **lib.**

lib·er·al (lib′ẽr-əl, lib′rəl), *adj.* [ME.; OFr.; L. *liberalis* < *liber*, free], 1. originally, suitable for a freeman; not restricted: now obsolete except in *the liberal arts, liberal education*, etc. 2. giving freely; generous. 3. large or plentiful; ample; abundant: as, a *liberal* reward. 4. not restricted to the literal meaning; free and unconfined: as, a *liberal* interpretation of the Constitution. 5. tolerant of views differing from one's own; broad-minded. 6. of democratic or republican forms of government, as distinguished from monarchies, aristocracies, etc. 7. favoring reform or progress, as in religion, education, etc.; specifically, favoring political reforms tending toward democracy and personal freedom for the individual; progressive: now sometimes distinguished from *progressive*, as connoting somewhat more conservatism. 8. [L-], designating or of a political party upholding liberal principles, especially such a party in England that developed from a coalition of the Whigs and Radicals in the first half of the 19th century. 9. [Obs.], excessively free or indecorous in behavior; licentious. *n.* 1. a person favoring liberalism. 2. [L-], a member of a liberal political party, especially that of England. Abbreviated **Lib., L., l.**

SYN.—**liberal** implies tolerance of others' views as well as open-mindedness to ideas that challenge tradition, established institutions, etc.; **progressive**, a relative term as opposed to *reactionary* or *conservative*, is applied to persons favoring progress and reform in politics, education, etc. and connotes an inclination to more direct action than **liberal**; **advanced** specifically implies a being ahead of the times, as in science, the arts, philosophy, etc.; **radical** implies a favoring of fundamental or extreme change, specifically of the social structure; **left**, originally referring to the position in legislatures of the seats occupied by parties holding such views, implies political liberalism or radicalism. The terms **radical** and **left** frequently connote varying degrees of disapproval as used by conservatives and reactionaries.

liberal arts, [transl. of L. *artes liberales*, lit., arts befitting a freeman: so named in contrast to *artes serviles*, lower (lit., servile) arts, and because open to study only by freemen (L. *liberi*); in later use understood as "arts becoming a gentleman"], the subjects of an academic college course, including literature, philosophy, languages, history, etc., as distinguished from professional or technical subjects; primarily cultural studies: sometimes referred to as *arts* (e.g., Bachelor of *Arts*, as distinguished from Bachelor of *Science*).

liberal education, an education mainly in the liberal arts, not necessarily preparing the student for any specific profession.

lib·er·al·ism (lib′ẽr-əl-iz'm, lib′rəl-iz'm), ***n.*** 1. the quality or state of being liberal, especially in politics or religion. 2. liberal principles and ideals.

lib·er·al·ist (lib′ẽr-əl-ist, lib′rəl-ist), ***adj.*** liberalistic. ***n.*** a person who upholds the principles of liberalism.

lib·er·al·is·tic (lib′ẽr-ə-lis′tik, lib′rə-lis′tik), ***adj.*** of or inclined to liberalism.

lib·er·al·i·ty (lib′ə-ral′ə-ti), ***n.*** [*pl.* LIBERALITIES (-tiz)], [ME. & OFr. *liberalite;* L. *liberalitas*], 1. the quality or state of being liberal; especially, generosity. 2. a gift, etc. indicating generosity. 3. absence of narrowness or prejudice in thinking; broad-mindedness.

lib·er·al·i·za·tion (lib′ẽr-əl-i-zā′shən, lib′rəl-ī-zā′shən), ***n.*** a liberalizing or being liberalized.

lib·er·al·ize (lib′ẽr-ə-līz′, lib′rə-līz′), ***v.t. & v.i.*** [LIBERALIZED (-līzd′), LIBERALIZING], to make or become liberal.

lib·er·ate (lib′ə-rāt′), ***v.t.*** [LIBERATED (-id), LIBERATING], [< L. *liberatus*, pp. of *liberare*, to set free, release < *liber*, free], 1. to release from slavery, enemy occupation, etc. 2. in *chemistry*, to free from combination in a compound. 3. [Military Slang], to appropriate or steal from an enemy or an occupied country; loot. —***SYN.*** see **free.**

lib·er·a·tion (lib′ə-rā′shən), ***n.*** [L. *liberatio*], a liberating or being liberated.

lib·er·a·tor (lib′ə-rā′tẽr), ***n.*** [L.], a person who liberates; especially, one who frees his country from an enemy or tyranny.

Li·ber·i·a (lī-bêr′i-ə), ***n.*** a country on the western coast of Africa, founded in 1847 by freed American Negro slaves: area, 43,000 sq. mi.; pop., c. 2,500,000; capital, Monrovia: abbreviated **Lib.**

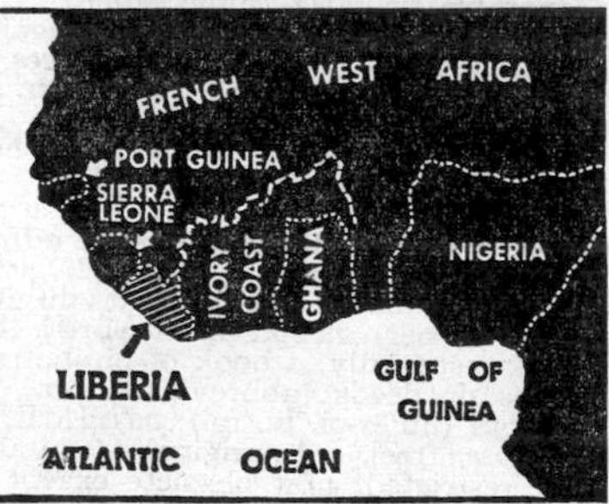

LIBERIA

Li·ber·i·an (lī-bêr′i-ən), ***adj.*** of Liberia, its people, or their culture. ***n.*** a native or inhabitant of Liberia.

lib·er·tar·i·an (lib′ẽr-târ′i-ən), ***n.*** [< *liberty* + *-arian*], 1. a person who believes in the doctrine of the freedom of the will. 2. a person who advocates full civil liberties. ***adj.*** of or upholding either of these principles.

‡**li·ber·té, é·ga·li·té, fra·ter·ni·té** (lē′ber′tā′ ā′gȧ′lē′tā′ frȧ′ter′nē′tā′), [Fr.], liberty, equality, fraternity: the motto of the French Revolution of 1789.

li·ber·ti·cid·al (li-bũr′tə-sī′d'l), ***adj.*** [< *liberticide* + *-al*], tending to destroy liberty.

li·ber·ti·cide (li-bũr′tə-sīd′), ***n.*** [< *liberty* + *-cide*, after Fr. *liberticide*], 1. the destruction of liberty. 2. a destroyer of liberty. ***adj.*** destroying liberty.

lib·er·tin·age (lib′ẽr-tin-ij), ***n.*** [see -AGE], libertinism.

lib·er·tine (lib′ẽr-tēn′, lib′ẽr-tin), ***n.*** [ME. *libertyn;* L. *libertinus* < *libertus*, freedman < *liber*, free], 1. in ancient Rome, a person who had been freed from slavery. 2. [prob. via Fr. *libertin*], a man who leads an unrestrained, immoral life; rake. 3. [Rare], a freethinker; skeptic. ***adj.*** morally unrestrained; licentious.

lib·er·tin·ism (lib′ẽr-tin-iz'm), ***n.*** the behavior of a libertine; licentiousness.

lib·er·ty (lib′ẽr-ti), ***n.*** [*pl.* LIBERTIES (-tiz)], [ME. & OFr. *liberte;* L. *libertas* < *liber*, free], 1. freedom or release from slavery, imprisonment, captivity, or any other form of arbitrary control. 2. the sum of rights and exemptions possessed in common by the people of a community, state, etc.: see also **civil liberties, political liberty.** 3. a particular right, franchise, or exemption from compulsion: as, he has the *liberty* of coming with us. 4. *usually pl.* unnecessary or excessive freedom or familiarity. 5. a place or area in which certain privileges or immunities prevail. 6. the limits within which a certain amount of freedom may be exercised: as, you may have the *liberty* of the third floor. 7. *a)* permission given to a sailor to go ashore. *b)* the period of forty-eight hours or less for which it is given. 8. in *philosophy*, freedom to choose; absence of the control of necessity. —***SYN.*** see **freedom.**

at liberty, 1. not confined; free. 2. permitted (to do or say something); allowed. 3. not busy or in use.

take liberties, to be too free or familiar in action or speech.

Liberty Bell, the bell of Independence Hall in Philadelphia, rung on July 4, 1776 to proclaim the independence of the United States: it cracked in 1835.

Liberty bond, a United States government bond issued to help finance the costs of World War I.

liberty cap, a soft, close-fitting, visorless cap, adopted by the French Revolutionists as a symbol of liberty.

Liberty Island, an island in New York Bay: site of the Statue of Liberty: formerly called *Bedloe's Island.*

Liberty Ship, a United States merchant ship carrying about 10,000 gross tons, built in large numbers during World War II.

Li·bia (lē′byä), ***n.*** Libya: the Italian name.

li·bid·i·nal (li-bid′'n-əl), ***adj.*** of the libido.

li·bid·i·nous (li-bid′'n-əs), ***adj.*** [Fr. *libidineux;* L. *libidinosus, lubidinosus* < *libido, lubido;* see LIBIDO], full of or characterized by lust; lewd; lascivious.

li·bi·do (li-bī′dō, li-bē′dō), ***n.*** [L. *libido, lubido*, pleasure, wantonness < *libet, lubet*, it pleases; cf. LIEF, LOVE], 1. the sexual urge or instinct. 2. in *psychoanalysis*, psychic energy generally; driving force behind all human action.

Li·bra (lī′brə), ***n.*** [L., a balance, Roman pound], 1. a southern constellation between Virgo and Scorpio, supposedly resembling a pair of scales in shape: see **constellation,** chart. 2. the seventh sign of the zodiac (♎), entered by the sun at the autumnal equinox, about September 23: see **zodiac,** illus.

li·bra (lī′brə; *for 3*, lē′brä), ***n.*** [*pl.* LIBRAE (-brē)], [L.], 1. pound: abbreviated **lb., L., l.** (*sing. & pl.*): the British symbol for the monetary unit (£) is derived from the first letter of this word. 2. an ancient Roman unit of weight, equal to about 12 ounces. 3. [Sp.; cf. POUND (coin)], a former gold coin of Peru, valued at about $4.87: now called *sol.*

li·brar·i·an (lī-brâr′i-ən), ***n.*** [L. *librarius*], 1. a person in charge of a library. 2. a person trained in library science and working in a library. Abbreviated **lib.**

li·brar·y (lī′brer′i, lī′brə-ri), ***n.*** [*pl.* LIBRARIES (-iz, -riz)], [ME. & OFr. *librarie* < *libraire*, copyist < L. *librarius, n.*, transcriber of books, *adj.*, of books < *liber*, a book, orig. inner bark or rind of a tree (which was written on); IE. base **leub*(*h*)-, to peel off, seen also in Gr. *lepein*, to strip off rind, Eng. *leaf*, etc.], 1. a room or building where a collection of books, etc. is kept for reading or reference. 2. *a)* a public or private institution in charge of the care and circulation of such a collection. *b)* a commercial establishment that rents books. 3. a collection of books, especially a large, systematically arranged collection for reading or reference. 4. a set or series of books issued in the same format by a publishing house. Abbreviated **lib.**

Library of Congress, the large public library in Washington, D. C., established in 1800 and rebuilt in 1815: abbreviated **L.C.**

li·brate (lī′brāt), ***v.i.*** [LIBRATED (-id), LIBRATING], [< L. *libratus*, pp. of *librare*, to weigh, balance < *libra*, a balance], 1. to move back and forth slowly like the beam of a balance before it comes to rest; oscillate. 2. to poise; hover; remain balanced.

li·bra·tion (lī-brā′shən), ***n.*** 1. a librating; oscillating or poising. 2. in *astronomy*, an actual or apparent irregularity in the movement of the moon, a planet, etc.

li·bra·to·ry (lī′brə-tôr′i, lī′brə-tō′ri), ***adj.*** librating; oscillating or poising.

li·bret·tist (li-bret′ist), ***n.*** a writer of librettos.

li·bret·to (li-bret′ō), ***n.*** [*pl.* LIBRETTOS (-ōz), LIBRETTI (-i)], [It., dim. of *libro* (< L. *liber*), a book; see LIBRARY], 1. the words, or text, of an opera, oratorio, or other long choral work. 2. a book containing these words.

‡**li·bri** (lī′brī), ***n.*** plural of **liber.**

li·bri·form (lī′bri-fôrm′), ***adj.*** [L. *liber, libri*, inner bark of a tree (see LIBRARY); + *-form*], like bast in form or substance; resembling the inner bark of certain trees.

Lib·y·a (lib′i-ə, lib′yə), ***n.*** 1. northern Africa west of Egypt: the ancient Greek and Roman name. 2. a country in northern Africa, on the Mediterranean: area, 679,358 sq. mi.; pop., 1,172,000; capital, Tripoli: Italian name, *Libia.*

Lib·y·an (lib′i-ən, lib′yən), ***adj.*** of Libya or its people. ***n.*** 1. a native or inhabitant of Libya. 2. a group of Berber languages of the Hamitic group, spoken especially in ancient Libya: they are known from inscriptions found chiefly in Numidia but also in scattered localities from Sinai to the Canary Islands.

Libyan Desert, a large desert in northeastern Africa.

lice (līs), ***n.*** plural of **louse.**

li·cense (lī′s'ns), *n.* [ME.; OFr.; L. *licentia* < *licens*, ppr. of *licere*, to be permitted], 1. a formal permission to do something; especially, authorization by law to do some specified thing: as, *license* to marry, practice medicine, hunt, etc. 2. a document indicating that such permission has been granted. 3. *a*) freedom to deviate from strict conduct, rule, or practice, generally permitted by common consent: as, poetic *license*. *b*) an instance of such deviation. 4. excessive, undisciplined freedom, constituting an abuse of liberty. *v.t.* [LICENSED (-s'nst), LICENSING], to give license or a license to or for; permit formally. Also spelled **licence.** —*SYN.* see **authorize, freedom.**

li·cen·see (lī′s'n-sē′), *n.* a person to whom a license is granted: also spelled **licencee.**

li·cens·er (lī′s'n-sēr), *n.* a person with authority to grant licenses: also spelled **licencer.**

li·cen·sor (lī′s'n-sēr), *n.* in *law*, a licenser.

li·cen·ti·ate (lī-sen′shi-it, lī-sen′shi-āt′), *n.* [ME. *licenciat;* ML. *licentiatus*, pp. of *licentiare*, to license < L. *licentia;* see LICENSE], 1. a person licensed to practice a specified profession. 2. in certain European universities, an academic degree between that of bachelor and that of doctor: abbreviated **L., l.**

li·cen·tious (lī-sen′shəs), *adj.* [Fr. *licencieux;* L. *licentiosus* < *licentia;* see LICENSE], 1. [Rare], disregarding accepted rules and standards. 2. morally unrestrained; dissolute; lascivious; libertine.

‡**li·cet** (lī′set), [L.], it is allowed; it is legal.

lich (lich), *n.* [ME.; AS. *lic;* akin to G. *leiche*, corpse; IE. base **līg-*, figure, shape; also similar, like (cf. LIKE)], [Scot. & Eng. Dial.], a dead body; corpse.

li·chee (lē′chē′), *n.* a litchi.

li·chen (lī′kən), *n.* [L.; Gr. *leichēn* < *leichein*, to lick], 1. any of a large group of mosslike plants, consisting of algae and fungi growing in close association in patches on rocks and tree trunks. 2. any of various eruptive skin diseases.

li·chen·in (lī′kən-in), *n.* [*lichen* + *-in*], a carbohydrate having the same empirical formula as starch, $(C_6H_{10}O_5)_n$, obtained from Iceland moss and other lichens.

li·chen·ol·o·gy (lī′kən-ol′ə-ji), *n.* the study of lichens.

li·chen·ose (lī′kən-ōs′), *adj.* lichenous.

li·chen·ous (lī′kən-əs), *adj.* of, like, or covered with lichens.

Lich·field (lich′fēld′), *n.* a city in central England: birthplace of Samuel Johnson: pop., 11,000.

lich gate, a roofed gate at the entrance to a churchyard, where a coffin can be set down to await the arrival of the clergyman.

licht (likht), *adj., n., v.i. & v.t.* [Scot.], light (in all senses).

lic·it (lis′it), *adj.* [Fr. *licite;* L. *licitus*, pp. of *licere*, to be permitted], permitted; lawful. —*SYN.* see **legal.**

lick (lik), *v.t.* [ME. *licken;* AS. *liccian;* akin to G. *lecken* (cf. LECHER); IE. base **leiĝh-*, to lick, seen also in Gr. *leikhein*, L. *ligurrire*, to lick, *lingere*, to lick up, etc.], 1. to pass the tongue over: as, dogs *lick* their wounds. 2. to bring into a certain condition by passing the tongue over: as, the child *licked* his fingers clean. 3. to pass lightly over like a tongue: as, the flames are *licking* the ends of the logs. 4. [Colloq.], *a*) to whip; thrash. *b*) to overcome (a person or thing); vanquish. *v.i.* to move lightly and quickly, as a flame: as, the waves *licked* about her feet. *n.* 1. the act of licking with the tongue. 2. a small quantity. 3. a deposit of natural salt cropping out at the surface of the earth, where animals come to lick the salt. 4. [Colloq.], *a*) a sharp blow. *b*) a short, rapid burst of activity, often careless, as in cleaning up, etc.; spurt of energy. *c*) a fast pace; clip; spurt of speed. 5. [Slang], a phrase of jazz music, especially an interpolated ornamentation. 6. *often in pl.* [Slang], chance; turn: as, I'll get my *licks* in later.

lick into shape, [Colloq.], to bring into proper condition by careful, persistent work.

lick up, to consume by or as by licking or lapping.

lick·er·ish (lik′ēr-ish), *adj.* [< Anglo-Fr. form of OFr. *lecheros*], 1. lecherous; lustful; lewd. 2. greedy or eager, especially to eat or taste. 3. [Obs.], tempting the appetite; appetizing. Also spelled **liquorish.**

lick·e·ty-split (lik′ə-ti-split′), *adv.* [fanciful formation based on *lick, n.* 4 *c*], [Slang], at great speed.

lick·ing (lik′iŋ), *n.* 1. the act of a person or thing that licks. 2. [Colloq.], a whipping; thrashing.

lick·spit (lik′spit′), *n.* a lickspittle.

lick·spit·tle (lik′spit″'l), *n.* a servile flatterer; toady.

lic·o·rice (lik′ēr-is, lik′ēr-ish, lik′rish), *n.* [ME. *licorys;* OFr. *licoresse;* LL. *liquiritia;* altered < L. *glycyrrhiza;* Gr. *glycyrrhiza* < *glykys*, sweet + *rhiza*, root], 1. a European plant of the pea family, with spikes of blue flowers and short, flat pods. 2. the dried root of this plant or the black extract made from it, used in medicine. 3. candy flavored with or as with this extract. Also spelled **liquorice.**

lic·tor (lik′tēr), *n.* [ME. *littour;* L.; prob. < base of *ligare*, to bind, in allusion to the bundles of bound rods which he bore], any of a group of minor Roman officials who carried the fasces and went before the chief magistrates to clear the way.

lid (lid), *n.* [ME. *lidd;* AS. *hlid* (akin to G. *-lid* in *augenlid*, eyelid) < base seen in AS. *hlidan*, to cover; IE. base **klei-*, to lean, slope, incline, as in *lean, v., ladder, climax*], 1. a movable cover, hinged or unattached, as for a box, trunk, pot, etc.; top. 2. an eyelid. 3. [Colloq.], a curb or restraint: as, the police put the *lid* on vice. 4. [Slang], a cap, hat, etc.

lid·ded (lid′id), *adj.* 1. covered with or as with a lid. 2. having (a specified kind of) eyelids: usually in hyphenated compounds, as *heavy-lidded*.

Li·di·ce (lē′di-tse; Eng. lid′ə-si), *n.* a town in Czechoslovakia, near Prague: totally destroyed by the Nazis in 1942, rebuilding started in 1946.

lid·less (lid′lis), *adj.* 1. without a lid. 2. without eyelids; hence, 3. [Poetic], watchful; not sleeping.

Li·do (lē′dō), *n.* an island resort in Italy, near Venice.

lie (lī), *v.i.* [LAY (lā), LAIN (lān), LYING (lī′iŋ)], [ME. *lien* < 2d & 3d pers. sing. of earlier *liggen*, AS. *licgan*, to lie (cf. LAY, *v.*); akin to G. *liegen;* IE. base **legh-*, to lie, lay oneself down, seen also in L. *lectus* & Gr. *lēkhos*, bed, *lōkhos*, lair, etc.], 1. to be or put oneself in a reclining position along a relatively horizontal surface. 2. to be in a more or less horizontal position on some supporting surface: said of inanimate things. 3. to be or remain in a specified condition: as, his motives *lie* hidden. 4. to be situated: as, Canada *lies* to the north of us. 5. to extend; stretch: as, the road *lies* straight across the prairie. 6. to be; exist; be found: as, the remedy *lies* within yourself. 7. to be buried or entombed. 8. [Archaic], to stay overnight or for a short while; lodge. 9. in *law*, to be maintainable or admissible: as, this action will not *lie*. *n.* 1. the way in which something is situated or arranged; lay: as, the *lie* of the land. 2. an animal's lair. 3. in *golf*, the relative situation of a ball with reference to the advantage it offers the player: as, a good *lie*.

lie down on the job, [Colloq.], to put forth less than one's best efforts.

lie in, to be in confinement for childbirth.

lie over, to stay and wait until some future time.

lie to, in *nautical usage*, to lie stationary with the head to the wind: said of a ship.

lie with, [Archaic], to have sexual intercourse with.

take lying down, [Colloq.], to submit to without protest or opposition.

lie (lī), *v.i.* [LIED (līd), LYING (lī′iŋ)], [ME. *lien, leien, legen*, etc.; AS. *leogan;* akin to G. *lügen* (Goth. *liugan*); IE. base **leugh-*, to tell lies], 1. *a*) to make a statement that one knows is false, especially with intent to deceive. *b*) to make such statements habitually. 2. to give a false impression; deceive one: as, mirages *lie*. *v.t.* to bring, put, accomplish, etc. by lying: as, he *lied* himself into office. *n.* 1. a false statement or action, especially one made with intent to deceive: see also **white lie.** 2. anything that gives or is meant to give a false impression. 3. the charge of lying.

give the lie to, 1. to charge with telling a lie. 2. to prove to be false; belie.

lie in one's throat, to tell a great or outrageous lie.

lie out of, to get out of (trouble, etc.) by lying.

SYN.—**lie** is the simple direct word meaning to make a deliberately false statement; **prevaricate** strictly means to quibble or confuse the issue in order to evade the truth, but it is loosely used as a formal or affected substitute for **lie; equivocate** implies the deliberate use of ambiguity in order to deceive or mislead; **fabricate** suggests the invention of a false story, excuse, etc. intended to deceive and is, hence, sometimes used as a somewhat softer equivalent for **lie; fib** implies the telling of a falsehood about something unimportant and is sometimes used as a euphemism for **lie.**

Lie, Jonas (lē), 1. 1833–1908; Norwegian novelist. 2. 1880–1940; his nephew; American painter.

Lie, Tryg·ve Halv·dan (trig′və hälv′dän lē), 1896– ; Norwegian statesman; secretary-general of the United Nations (1946–1953).

Lie·big, Baron Jus·tus von (yoos′toos fôn lē′biH), 1803–1873; German chemist.

Lieb·knecht, Karl (kärl lēp′kneHt′), 1871–1919; son of *Wilhelm;* German socialist; leader of Spartacist uprising (1919); arrested and murdered.

Liebknecht, Wil·helm (vil′helm), 1826–1900; German socialist and newspaper editor.

Liech·ten·stein (lēH′tən-shtīn′), *n.* a country in west central Europe, between Switzerland and Austria: area, 65 sq. mi.; pop., 16,000; capital, Vaduz.

lied (lēd; G. lēt), *n.* [*pl.* LIEDER (lē′dēr)], [G.], a German lyric or song.

‡**Lie·der·kranz** (lē′dēr-kränts′), *n.* [G., lit., garland of songs; see prec.], 1. a group of songs. 2. a men's singing society. 3. a soft cheese having a strong odor and flavor: a trade-mark.

lie detector, a polygraph (sense 2) used by law enforcement officials on persons suspected of not telling the truth in connection with a crime: it records certain bodily changes of the subject as he responds to questions: the results of such tests are usually not legally acceptable.

lief (lēf), *adj.* [ME. *lef, leve;* AS. *leof,* beloved, dear; akin to G. *lieb;* IE. base **leubh-,* to be fond of, desire; cf. LIBIDO, LEAVE (permission), LOVE, etc.], [Obs.], 1. valued; dear; beloved. 2. willing. *adv.* [Rare], willingly; gladly: only in *would* (or *had*) *as lief,* etc.

Li·ège (li-āzh′; Fr. lyezh), *n.* 1. a province of eastern Belgium: pop., 964,000. 2. its capital, on the Meuse River: pop., 156,000. Flemish name *Luik.*

liege (lēj), *adj.* [ME. *leyge, liege;* OFr. *liege, lige;* prob. < OHG. *ledig,* free (G. *ledig,* not occupied), but influenced by L. *ligare,* to bind; in a charter of 1253 a MHG. *ledighman* glosses ML. *ligius homo,* liegeman], 1. in *feudal law, a*) entitled to the service and allegiance of his vassals: as, a *liege* lord. *b*) bound to give service and allegiance to the lord: as, *liege* subjects; hence, 2. loyal; faithful. *n.* in *feudal law,* 1. a lord or sovereign. 2. a subject or vassal.

liege lord, a feudal lord.

liege·man (lēj′mən), *n.* [*pl.* LIEGEMEN (-mən)], 1. a vassal; hence, 2. a loyal follower. Also **liege man.**

Lieg·nitz (lēg′nits), *n.* a city in southwestern Poland: formerly in Germany: pop., 24,000 (1946): Polish name, *Lignica.*

li·en (lēn, lē′ən), *n.* [Fr.; L. *ligamen,* a band < *ligare,* to bind, tie], in *law,* a claim on the property of another as security against the payment of a just debt.

li·en·ec·to·my (lī′ən-ek′tə-mi), *n.* [L. *lien,* the spleen; + *-ectomy*], the surgical removal of the spleen: also called *splenectomy.*

li·en·ter·ic (lī′ən-ter′ik), *adj.* of or having lientery.

li·en·ter·y (lī′ən-ter′i), *n.* [Fr. *lienterie;* Mod. L. *lienteria;* Gr. *leienteria* < *leios,* smooth + *entera,* bowels], diarrhea in which incompletely digested food is discharged.

Li·e·pā·ja (lē′e′pä-yä), *n.* Libau: the Lettish name.

li·er (lī′ẽr), *n.* one who lies (reclines).

li·erne (li-ûrn′), *n.* [Fr.; see LIANA], in *architecture,* a short rib used in Gothic vaulting to connect the bosses and intersections of the main ribs.

lieu (lōō, lū), *n.* [ME. *liue* (in *in liue of*); OFr. *lieu* (in *au lieu de*) < L. *locus,* place], place; stead.
 in lieu of, instead of; in place of.

Lieut., Lieutenant.

Lieut. Col., Lieutenant Colonel.

Lieut. Comdr., Lieutenant Commander.

lieu·ten·an·cy (lōō-ten′ən-si, lū-ten′ən-si), *n.* [*pl.* LIEUTENANCIES (-siz)], the rank, commission, status, or authority of a lieutenant.

lieu·ten·ant (lōō-ten′ənt, lū-ten′ənt; Brit., *esp. army,* lef-ten′ənt), *n.* [ME. *lutenand, lutenaunt, luftenand;* Late OFr. < *lieu, luef* (see LIEU) + *tenant,* holding, ppr. of *tenir,* to hold < L. *tenere,* to hold], 1. a person who acts for a superior, as during the latter's absence; aide; deputy. 2. a military officer normally commanding a platoon and ranking below a captain: see also **first lieutenant, second lieutenant.** 3. a naval officer ranking below a lieutenant commander and above a lieutenant junior grade. Abbreviated **Lieut., Lt.** (as a title in senses 2 & 3).

lieutenant colonel, a military officer ranking below a colonel and above a major: abbreviated **Lieut. Col., Lt. Col.** (as a title).

lieutenant commander, a naval officer ranking below a commander and above a lieutenant: abbreviated **Lieut. Comdr., Lt. Comdr., Lt.-Comm.** (as a title).

lieutenant general, a military officer normally commanding a corps and ranking below a general and above a major general: abbreviated **Lieut. Gen., Lt. Gen.** (as a title).

lieutenant governor, 1. an elected official of a State who ranks below and substitutes for the governor in case of the latter's absence or death. 2. in certain countries, an official substituting for the governor general of a province or district. Abbreviated **Lt. Gov., Lieut. Gov.**

lieutenant junior grade, a naval officer ranking below a lieutenant and above an ensign: abbreviated **Lt. (j.g.), Lieut. (j.g.).**

life (līf), *n.* [*pl.* LIVES (līvz)], [ME. & AS. *lif;* akin to G. *leib,* body; sense "body" for all other Gmc. cognates; prob. IE. base **leip-,* to stick, stick to, adhere (seen also in Gr. *leipein,* to leave, remain, Eng. *leave*), whence sense development: what adheres—what remains—body—life], 1. that property of plants and animals which makes it possible for them to take in food, get energy from it, grow, adapt themselves to their surroundings, and reproduce their kind: it is the quality that distinguishes a living animal or plant from inorganic matter or a dead organism. 2. the state of possessing this property: as, we tried to bring the drowned child back to *life.* 3. a living being, especially a human being: as, the cyclone took a heavy toll of *lives.* 4. living things collectively, often of a specified kind: as, plant *life.* 5. the time a person or thing is alive, or a specific portion of such time: as, Shakespeare's *life* in London. 6. one's manner of living: as, his was a *life* of poverty. 7. the activities of a given time or in a given setting, and the people who take part in them: as, military *life.* 8. lives considered together as belonging to a certain class or type: as, low *life.* 9. *a*) an individual's animate existence. *b*) an account of this; biography. 10. the existence of the soul: as, the eternal *life.* 11. something essential to the continued existence of something else: as, freedom of speech is the *life* of democracy. 12. the source of vigor or liveliness: as, she was the *life* of the party. 13. vigor; liveliness; animation; vivacity. 14. the period of flourishing, usefulness, etc.; period during which anything lasts: as, most fashions have a short *life.* 15. in the *fine arts, a*) a lifelike quality or appearance. *b*) representation from living models: as, a class in *life.*
 a matter of life and death, 1. something whose outcome determines whether a person lives or dies; hence, 2. an extremely important matter.
 as large (or **big**) **as life,** life-size.
 bring to life, 1. to bring back to consciousness. 2. to make lively; animate.
 come to life, 1. to recover consciousness. 2. to become lively or animated.
 for dear life, to, or as if to, save one's life; with a desperate intensity.
 for life, 1. for the duration of one's life. 2. in order to save one's life.
 for the life of me, [Colloq.], even though my life were at stake on it; by any means: used in negative expressions.
 from life, from a living model.
 not on your life, [Colloq.], by no means; certainly not.
 see life, to have a wide variety of social experiences.
 take life, to kill.
 take one's own life, to commit suicide.
 to the life, like the living original; exactly.
 true to life, corresponding to what happens or exists in real life; true to reality.

life belt, a life preserver in the form of a belt, worn around a person's chest.

life·blood (līf′blud′), *n.* 1. the blood necessary to life. 2. the vital part or animating influence of anything.

life·boat (līf′bōt′), *n.* 1. a strong, seaworthy boat kept in readiness on the shore for use in rescuing people in danger of drowning: it is usually built with air chambers, etc. for more buoyancy. 2. one of the small boats carried by a ship for use in case the ship has to be abandoned.

life buoy, a life preserver (sense 1).

life cycle, the series of changes in form undergone by an organism in development from its earliest stage to the recurrence of the same stage in the next generation.

life expectancy, the average number of years that an individual of a given age may expect to live.

life-giv·er (līf′giv′ẽr), *n.* a life-giving person or thing.

life-giv·ing (līf′giv′iŋ), *adj.* 1. that gives or can give life. 2. strengthening; refreshing; inspiring.

life·guard (līf′gärd′), *n.* an expert swimmer employed at bathing beaches, pools, etc. to prevent drownings.

Life Guards, [earlier also *liefguard;* prob. after obs. D. *lijfgarde,* bodyguard; *lijf,* body (cf. LIFE) + *garde* (see GUARD)], two regiments of British cavalry which act as a bodyguard for the king and queen.

life history, 1. the history of the changes undergone by an organism in development from the egg, spore, etc. to its death as an adult. 2. one series of such changes.

life insurance (or **assurance**), insurance in which a stipulated sum is paid to the beneficiary or beneficiaries at the death of the insured, or to the insured when he reaches a specified age.

life interest, interest (in property) that is payable to a person during his lifetime but cannot be passed on by him to another or others at his death.

life·less (līf′lis), *adj.* 1. without life; specifically, *a*) inanimate. *b*) dead. 2. dull; listless. —***SYN.*** see **dead.**

life·like (līf′līk′), *adj.* 1. resembling actual life: as, a *lifelike* picture of early America. 2. closely resembling a real person or thing: as, a *lifelike* portrait.

life line, 1. a rope shot to a ship in distress near the shore in order that connection may be established between it and the shore. 2. any rope fastened where it may be clutched by persons in danger of being swept away and drowned. 3. the rope by means of which a diver is raised and lowered, used by him for signaling. 4. a line in the palm of the hand, curving about the base of the thumb, supposed (in palmistry) to reveal facts about the person's life. 5. a commercial, especially maritime, route of great importance. 6. a route that is the only one over which supplies can be transported to a certain place.

life·long (līf′lôŋ′), *adj.* lasting, or remaining as such, for all one's life: as, a *lifelong* defender of liberty.

life net, a strong net used by firemen, etc. to catch people jumping from a height, as to escape from a burning building.
life of Riley, [Slang], a life of ease and pleasure.
life preserver, 1. a device for saving a person from drowning by keeping his body afloat: it is usually a ring or sleeveless jacket of canvas-covered cork. 2. a walking stick loaded with lead, carried for self-defense.

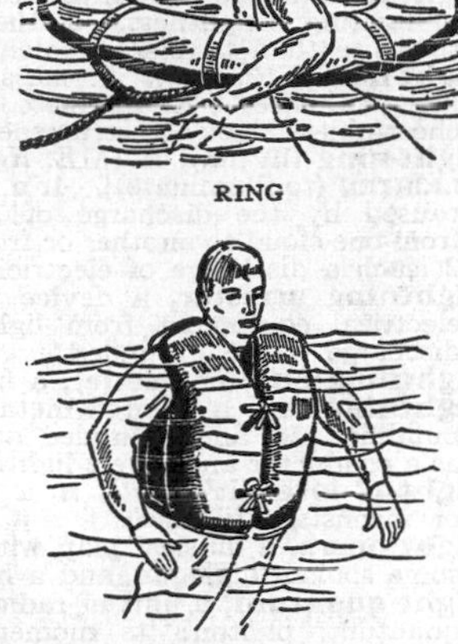
RING

JACKET
TYPES OF LIFE PRESERVER

lif·er (līf'ẽr), *n.* [Slang], a person sentenced to imprisonment for life.
life·sav·er (līf'sāv'ẽr), *n.* 1. a person or thing that saves people from drowning. 2. a lifeguard. 3. [Colloq.], a person or thing that is essential to one's work, welfare, etc.
life·sav·ing (līf'sāv'iŋ), *adj.* designed for or connected with the saving of human life. *n.* the saving of human life, especially through the prevention of drowning.
life-size (līf'sīz'), *adj.* as big as the person or thing represented: said of a picture, sculpture, etc.
life-sized (līf'sīzd'), *adj.* life-size.
life·time (līf'tīm'), *n.* the time during which the life of an individual lasts. *adj.* lasting for such a period: as, a *lifetime* job.
life·work (līf'wûrk'), *n.* the work to which a person devotes his life; most important work of one's life.
lift (lift), *v.t.* [ME. *liften, leften* < ON. *lypta* (akin to G. *lüften*) < base of AS. *lyft* (G. *luft*), air, cloud, sky; cf. LOFT], 1. to bring up to a higher position; raise. 2. to pick up and set: as, to *lift* a baby down from its high chair. 3. to hold up; support high in the air. 4. to raise in rank, condition, dignity, spirits, etc.; bring to a higher level; elevate; exalt. 5. to cancel (a mortgage) by paying it off. 6. to change (a person's face) by means of a surgical operation intended, ordinarily, to remove wrinkles and give a more youthful appearance. 7. [Colloq.], to plagiarize: as, he *lifted* a passage from Milton. 8. [Slang], to steal. 9. in *agriculture*, to loosen and remove (seedlings) from a seed bed in preparation for transplanting. 10. in *golf*, *a*) to hit (a ball) unusually high by means of an upward stroke. *b*) to pick (a ball) up in one's hand, as from an unplayable position. *v.i.* 1. to exert strength in raising or trying to raise something. 2. to rise and vanish; be dispelled: as, the gloom *lifted*. 3. to become raised or elevated; go up. *n.* 1. a lifting, raising, or rising; upward movement. 2. the amount lifted at one time. 3. *a*) the distance through which something is lifted. *b*) the extent of rise or elevation. 4. lifting power or influence. 5. elevation of spirits or mood. 6. elevated position or carriage: as, the proud *lift* of her head. 7. a ride in the direction in which one is going. 8. help of any kind. 9. a swell or rise in the ground. 10. the means by which something is lifted; specifically, *a*) any layer of leather in the heel of a shoe. *b*) [British], an elevator. 11. in *aeronautics*, the upward pull resulting from the force of the air against an airfoil passing through it.
lift a cry (or **one's voice**), to call, cry, or speak out loudly.
SYN.—**lift,** in its general literal sense, implies the use of some effort in bringing something up to a higher position (help me *lift* the table); **raise,** often interchangeable with **lift,** specifically implies a bringing into an upright position by lifting one end (to *raise* a flagpole); **elevate** is now a less frequent synonym for **lift** or **raise** (the balloon had been *elevated* 500 feet); **rear** is a literary equivalent of **raise** (the giant trees *reared* their trunks to the sky); **hoist** implies the lifting of something heavy, usually by some mechanical means, as a block and tackle, crane, etc. (to *hoist* bales of cotton into a ship); **boost** is a colloquial term implying a lifting by or as by a push from behind or below (*boost* me into the tree). All these terms are used figuratively to imply a bringing into a higher or better state (to *lift*, or *hoist*, one's spirits, to *raise* one's hopes, to *elevate* one's mind, to *rear* children, to *boost* sales). See also **steal.**—*ANT.* lower.
lift-drag ratio (lift'drag'), in *aeronautics*, the ratio of the lift of a body to its drag.
lift pump, a suction pump that raises a column of liquid to the level of a spout out of which the liquid runs of its own accord: opposed to *force pump*.
lig·a·ment (lig'ə-mənt), *n.* [L. *ligamentum* < *ligare*, to tie, bind; cf. LEECH (of a sail)], 1. a bond or tie serving to connect one thing with another. 2. in *anatomy*, a band of tough tissue connecting bones or holding organs in place.
lig·a·men·tal (lig'ə-men't'l), *adj.* of, having the nature of, or forming a part of a ligament.
lig·a·men·ta·ry (lig'ə-men'tẽr-i), *adj.* ligamental.
lig·a·men·tous (lig'ə-men'təs), *adj.* ligamental.
li·gan (lī'gən), *n.* a lagan.
li·gate (lī'gāt), *v.t.* [LIGATED (-id), LIGATING], [< L. *ligatus*, pp. of *ligare*, to bind, tie], to tie or bind with a ligature, as a bleeding artery.
li·ga·tion (lī-gā'shən), *n.* [L. *ligatio* < pp. of *ligare*, to bind], 1. a binding or being bound. 2. a thing that binds; tie; bond; ligature.
lig·a·ture (lig'ə-chẽr), *n.* [ME.; Late OFr.; LL. *ligature* < pp. of L. *ligare*, to bind; IE. base **leiĝ-*, to bind, seen also in MLG. *lik*, a tie, MHG. *geleich*, joint], 1. a tying or binding together. 2. a thing used in tying or binding together; tie, bond, bandage, etc. 3. in *music*, *a*) a curved line indicating that the notes which it connects are to be sung or played as one phrase; slur. *b*) the notes so connected. 4. in *surgery*, a thread or wire used to tie up an artery, etc. 5. in *writing* & *printing*, *a*) a character containing two or more letters united, as *æ*, *ﬁ*, *ﬂ*. *b*) a curved line connecting such letters in writing. *v.t.* [LIGATURED (-chẽrd), LIGATURING], to tie or bind together with a ligature; ligate.
li·geance (lī'jəns, lē'jəns), *n.* [ME. *legeaunce;* OFr. *ligeance, legeance* < *lige;* see LIEGE], 1. [Archaic], allegiance. 2. in *law*, the power or territory of a ruler.
light (līt), *n.* [ME. *liht;* AS. *leoht;* akin to G. *licht;* IE. base **leuq-*, to shine, bright, seen also in L. *lucere*, to shine, *lux, lumen*, light (cf. LUCID, LUMINOUS), *luna*, moon (cf. LUNAR), etc.], 1. *a*) that which makes it possible to see: opposed to *darkness;* form of radiant energy that acts upon the retina of the eye, optic nerve, etc., making sight possible: this energy is transmitted at a velocity of about 186,000 miles per second by wavelike or vibrational motion. *b*) a form of radiant energy similar to this, but not acting on the normal retina, as ultraviolet and infrared radiation. 2. the rate of flow of light radiation with respect to the sense of sight: it is measured in *lumens*. 3. the sensation that light stimulates in the organs of sight. 4. brightness; illumination: usually with reference to a particular case. 5. the thing from which light comes; source of light, as a lamp, the sun, etc. 6. the light from the sun; daylight or dawn. 7. a thing by means of which something can be started burning: as, a *light* for a cigarette. 8. the means by which light is let in; window or windowpane. 9. knowledge; enlightenment; mental illumination: as, early writings shed *light* on our past. 10. public knowledge or view: as, every day new facts are brought to *light*. 11. the way in which something is seen; appearance due to what is presented to view; aspect: as, he put the matter in an unfavorable *light*. 12. facial expression showing a mental or emotional state: as, a *light* of recognition came into his eyes. 13. a person whose brilliant record makes him an example for others; outstanding figure: as, a shining *light*. 14. in the *fine arts*, *a*) the quality suggestive of light. *b*) the part of a picture upon which light is represented as falling. *adj.* [ME. *liht;* AS. *leoht*], 1. having light; not dark; bright. 2. pale in color; whitish; fair. *adv.* [< the *adj.*], palely: as, the ribbon is *light* blue. *v.t.* [LIGHTED (-id) or LIT (lit), LIGHTING], 1. to set on fire; ignite: as, let's *light* a bonfire. 2. to cause to give off light: as, she *lit* the lamp. 3. to give light to; furnish with light: as, lamps *light* the streets. 4. to brighten; animate. 5. to show the way to by or as by giving light: as, the beacon *lighted* the planes safely to the airport. *v.i.* 1. to catch fire: as, the fuse *lighted* at once. 2. to be lighted; brighten (usually with *up*).
according to one's lights, as one's opinions, information, or abilities may direct.
bring to light, to reveal; disclose.
come to light, to be revealed or disclosed.
in the light of, with knowledge of; considering.
light up, 1. to make or become light. 2. to make or become bright, cheerful, etc. 3. [Colloq.], to begin smoking (a cigar, etc.).
see the light (of day), 1. to come into existence. 2. to come to public view. 3. to understand.
shed (or **throw**) **light on,** to give facts about; clarify.
stand in one's own light, to harm oneself or one's reputation by acting foolishly, thoughtlessly, or unwisely.
strike a light, to make a flame, as with a match.
light (līt), *adj.* [ME. *lighte;* AS. *leoht* (< *Gmc. *liŋxta*); akin to G. *leicht*, not heavy, not difficult; IE. base

*lengwh-to < *legwh-, light in weight or motion (cf. LIGHTS, LUNG)], 1. having little weight; not heavy. 2. having little weight for its size; of low specific gravity. 3. below the usual or defined weight: as, a *light* coin. 4. less than usual or normal in amount, extent, intensity, force, etc.; specifically, *a*) falling or striking with little force or impact: as, a *light* blow. *b*) of less than the usual quantity or density: as, a *light* vote, a *light* rain. *c*) not thick, coarse, or massive; delicate and graceful in structure: as, *light* tracery, *light* architecture. *d*) not violent or intense; mild: as, a *light* wind. *e*) soft, muted, or muffled: as, a *light* sound. *f*) not prolonged or intense: as, *light* applause. 5. of little importance; not serious or profound: as, *light* conversation. 6. easy to bear; not burdensome: as, a *light* tax. 7. easy to do; not difficult: as, *light* work. 8. not burdened with grief or sorrow; gay; happy; buoyant: as, *light* spirits. 9. flighty; frivolous; fickle; capricious. 10. loose in morals; wanton. 11. dizzy; giddy. 12. of an amusing or nonserious nature: as, *light* entertainment, *light* reading. 13. containing little alcohol: as, *light* wine. 14. characterized by qualities suggestive of little weight; not dense, hard, full, etc.; specifically, *a*) not as full as usual; moderate: as, a *light* meal. *b*) easy to digest. *c*) well leavened; soft and spongy: as, a *light* cake. *d*) loose in consistency; easily crumbled; porous: as, *light* sand. 15. moving with ease and nimbleness: as, she is *light* on her feet. 16. carrying little weight: as, we shall travel *light*. 17. unstressed or slightly stressed: said of a syllable in phonetics, prosody, etc. 18. having light weapons, armor, equipment, etc.: as, a *light* tank. 19. in *meteorology*, designating a condition (*light air*) in which the speed of the wind is from 1 to 3 miles per hour. *adv.* lightly. *v.i.* [LIGHTED (-id) or LIT (lit), LIGHTING], [ME. *lihten;* AS. *lihtan, lyhtan;* also aphetic for *alight*], 1. [Rare], to get down from a horse or vehicle; dismount; alight. 2. to come to rest after traveling through the air: as, we waited for the ducks to *light*. 3. to come by chance; happen (with *on* or *upon*). 4. to fall or strike suddenly, as a blow.

light in the head, 1. dizzy. 2. simple; foolish.
light into, [Slang], 1. to attack. 2. to scold; berate.
light out, [Slang], to depart suddenly.
make light of, to treat as trifling or unimportant; pay little or no attention to.

light-armed (līt′ärmd′), *adj.* bearing light weapons.

light·en (līt′'n), *v.t.* [ME. *lihtnen* < *lihten*], 1. to make light; illuminate. 2. to shed knowledge or spiritual light on; enlighten. 3. to cause to flash in or as in lightning (with *out* or *forth*). *v.i.* 1. to become light; grow brighter. 2. to shine brightly; flash. 3. to give off flashes of lightning.

light·en (līt′'n), *v.t.* [ME. *lihtnen* < *lihten*], 1. *a*) to make lighter in weight. *b*) to make less heavy; reduce the load of. 2. to make less severe, harsh, troublesome, etc. 3. to make more cheerful; gladden. *v.i.* to become lighter in weight. —*SYN.* see **relieve.**

light·er (līt′ẽr), *n.* a person or thing that lights something or starts it burning: as, a cigarette *lighter*.

light·er (līt′ẽr), *n.* [D. *lichter* < *licht*, light], a large, open barge used chiefly in loading or unloading larger ships wherever shallow water prevents these from coming in to the shore. *v.t. & v.i.* to transport (goods) in a lighter.

light·er·age (līt′ẽr-ij), *n.* [see -AGE], 1. the loading or unloading of a ship, or transportation of goods, by means of a lighter, or barge. 2. the charge for this.

light·face (līt′fās′), *n.* in *printing*, type having thin, light lines: distinguished from *standard, boldface, extrabold*. *adj.* having thin, light lines.

light-fin·gered (līt′fiŋ′gẽrd), *adj.* 1. having a light, delicate touch. 2. skillful at stealing, especially by picking pockets; thievish.

light-foot (līt′foot′), *adj.* [Poetic], light-footed.

light-foot·ed (līt′foot′id), *adj.* stepping lightly and gracefully; nimble of foot.

light-hand·ed (līt′han′did), *adj.* 1. having a light, delicate touch. 2. having little to carry.

light·head (līt′hed′), *n.* a lightheaded person.

light·head·ed (līt′hed′id), *adj.* 1. delirious. 2. giddy; dizzy. 3. thoughtless; flighty; frivolous.

light·heart·ed (līt′här′tid), *adj.* free from care; gay.

light heavyweight, a boxer or wrestler who weighs between 161 and 175 pounds.

light horse, light-armed cavalry.

Light-Horse Harry (līt′hôrs′), see **Lee, Henry.**

light-horse·man (līt′hôrs′mən), *n.* [*pl.* LIGHT-HORSEMEN (-mən)], a light-armed cavalryman.

light·house (līt′hous′), *n.* [Early Mod. Eng., replacing earlier *pharos, phare*], a tower located at some place important or dangerous to navigation: it has a very bright light at the top, by which ships are guided and warned at night.

light infantry, infantry carrying light weapons and equipment: abbreviated **L.I., Lt. Inf.**

light·ing (līt′iŋ), *n.* 1. a giving light or being lighted; illumination; ignition. 2. the distribution of light and shade in a painting. 3. in the *theater*, *a*) the art, practice, or manner of using and arranging lights on the stage. *b*) the stage lights collectively.

light·ly (līt′li), *adv.* 1. with little weight or pressure. 2. gently. 3. to a small degree or amount: as, to spend *lightly*. 4. nimbly; deftly. 5. cheerfully; merrily. 6. with indifference or neglect. 7. with little or no reason. 8. wantonly; shamelessly. 9. [Archaic], with ease; readily.

light-mind·ed (līt′mīn′did), *adj.* flighty; thoughtless; frivolous.

light·ness (līt′nis), *n.* 1. the state, quality, or intensity of lighting; brightness. 2. the state of being nearer to white than to black; paleness; whitishness.

light·ness (līt′nis), *n.* 1. the state of being light, not heavy; hence, 2. mildness, nimbleness, delicacy, cheerfulness, lack of seriousness, etc.

light·ning (līt′niŋ), *n.* [ME. *lightninge* < *lightnen;* see LIGHTEN (to illuminate)], 1. a flash of light in the sky caused by the discharge of atmospheric electricity from one cloud to another or from a cloud to the earth. 2. such a discharge of electricity.

lightning arrester, a device that protects radio or electrical equipment from lightning by causing the discharge to be grounded.

lightning bug (or **beetle**), a firefly.

lightning rod, a pointed metal rod placed high on a building, etc. and grounded at the lower end to act as a conductor and divert lightning from the structure.

light-o'-love (līt′ə-luv′), *n.* a woman who is wanton or inconstant in love.

light opera, a musical play with humorous situations, some spoken dialogue, and a happy ending; operetta.

light quantum, a unit of radiant energy equal to the quantum; photon: its momentum is equal to the energy divided by the velocity of light.

lights (līts), *n.pl.* [ME. *lihte, lihtes* < *liht* (see LIGHT, *adj.*): so called from being lighter in weight than the rest of the body; cf. Russ. *lyogkii*, light, *lyogkoye*, lung & Eng. *lung* < same base], the lungs of animals, as sheep, hogs, cattle, etc., used as food.

light·ship (līt′ship′), *n.* a ship moored in a place dangerous to navigation and bearing a bright light at the masthead to warn pilots away from the spot.

light·some (līt′səm), *adj.* [ME. *lihtsum;* see LIGHT, *adj.* & -SOME], 1. nimble, buoyant, graceful, or lively. 2. lighthearted; cheerful; gay. 3. frivolous.

light·some (līt′səm), *adj.* [ME. *lyghtesum;* see -SOME], 1. giving light; luminous. 2. well-lighted; bright.

lights out, a signal, as in a military camp, etc., to extinguish lights at bedtime.

light-struck (līt′struk′), *adj.* in *photography*, injured or fogged by exposure to light.

light·weight (līt′wāt′), *n.* 1. one below normal weight. 2. [Colloq.], a person of low mentality or little importance. 3. a boxer or wrestler who weighs between 127 and 135 pounds. *adj.* 1. light in weight. 2. of lightweights.

light·wood (līt′wood′), *n.* wood, especially southern pine, which burns readily and makes a bright light.

light-year (līt′yêr′), *n.* a unit of astronomical distance, equal to the distance that light travels in one year, approximately 6,000,000,000,000 miles.

lign·al·oes (līn′al′ōz, lig-nal′ōz), *n.* [ME. *ligne Aloes;* OFr.; L. *lignum aloës*, wood of aloe], 1. the resinous wood of the aloes tree, native to the East Indies, burnt for its pleasant aroma. 2. aloes, the drug.

lig·ne·ous (lig′ni-əs), *adj.* [L. *ligneus* < *lignum*, wood], of, or having the nature of, wood; woody.

lig·ni- (lig′ni), [< L. *lignum*, wood], a combining form meaning *wood*, as in *lignify*: also **ligno-** or, before a vowel, **lign-.**

Lig·ni·ca (lēg-nē′tsä), *n.* Liegnitz: the Polish name.

lig·ni·fi·ca·tion (lig′nə-fi-kā′shən), *n.* a lignifying.

lig·ni·fy (lig′nə-fī′), *v.t.* [LIGNIFIED (-fīd′), LIGNIFYING], [*ligni-* + *-fy*], to make into wood. *v.i.* to become wood or like wood as a result of the depositing of lignin in the cell walls.

lig·nin (lig′nin), *n.* [*lign-* + *-in*], an organic substance forming the essential part of woody fiber.

lig·nite (lig′nīt), *n.* [Fr.; see LIGNI- & -ITE], a soft, brownish-black coal in which the texture of the original wood can still be seen: it is denser and contains more carbon than peat: also called *brown coal*.

lig·nit·ic (lig-nit′ik), *adj.* relating to lignite.

lig·no- (lig′nō, lig′nə), ligni-.

lig·no·cel·lu·lose (lig′nō-sel′yoo-lōs′), *n.* [*ligno-* + *cellulose*], any of several combinations of lignin and cellulose: it forms the essential part of woody tissue.

lig·nose (lig′nōs), *n.* [*lign-* + *-ose*], 1. lignin. 2. an explosive containing nitroglycerin and wood fiber.

lig·num vi·tae (lig′nəm vī′tē), [L. *lignum*, wood + *vitae*, genit. of *vita*, life], 1. any of several related tropical American trees and shrubs with leathery leaves, small purple flowers, and very hard, heavy, greenish-brown wood. 2. the wood of these trees.

lig·ro·in, lig·ro·ine (lig′rō-in), *n.* an inflammable distillate of petroleum, used as a solvent and illuminant.

lig·u·la (lig′yoo-lə), *n.* [*pl.* LIGULAE (-lē′), LIGULAS (-ləz)], a ligule.

lig·u·late (lig'yoo-lāt', lig'yoo-lit), *adj.* 1. of or having ligules. 2. shaped like a strap or bandage.

lig·u·lat·ed (lig'yoo-lā'tid), *adj.* ligulate.

lig·ule (lig'ūl), *n.* [L. *ligula*, a spoon, tongue of a shoe, shoe strap; IE. base **leigh-*, to lick, seen also in MIr. *liag*, Cymric *llwy*, spoon, Eng. *lick;* affected by association with L. *lingua*, tongue, *ligare*, to bind], 1. a strap-shaped corolla in certain composite flowers. 2. a thin membrane attached to a leaf of grass, etc. at the point where the blade meets the leafstalk.

lig·ure (lig'yoor), *n.* [LL. *ligurius;* LGr. *ligyrion*], in the *Bible*, one of the twelve precious stones worn in the breastplate of the Jewish high priest: it is believed by some to be the yellow jacinth: Ex. 28:19.

Li·gu·ri·a (li-gyoor'i-ə), *n.* a department of Italy, along the northwestern coast: chief city, Genoa.

Li·gu·ri·an (li-gyoor'i-ən), *adj.* 1. of Liguria, its people, etc. 2. of the dialect of Italian spoken there. *n.* 1. a native or inhabitant of Liguria. 2. the Ligurian dialect of Italian.

Ligurian Republic, a republic set up by Napoleon in 1797 under French control: previously the Republic of Genoa.

Ligurian Sea, a part of the Mediterranean, between Corsica and northern Italy.

Li Hung-chang (lē' hooŋ'jäŋ'), 1823–1901; Chinese statesman and diplomat; prime minister (1895–1898).

lik·a·ble (līk'ə-b'l), *adj.* having qualities that inspire liking; worthy of being liked; attractive, pleasant, genial, etc.: also spelled **likeable.**

like (līk), *adj.* [ME. *lik, lich* < AS. type **lic*, shortened < *gelic*, similar, equal, lit., of the same form or shape; akin to G. *gleich* (OHG. *gilīh*), AS. *lic*, body, form (see LICH)], 1. having almost or exactly the same qualities, characteristics, etc.; similar; equal: as, a cup of sugar and a *like* amount of flour. 2. [Rare], alike. 3. [Dial.], likely. *adv.* 1. in the manner of one that is: as, he works *like* mad. 2. [Colloq.], likely: as, *like* as not, he is already there. *prep.* 1. similar to; somewhat resembling: as, she is *like* a bird. 2. in a manner characteristic of; similarly to: as, she sings *like* a bird. 3. in accord with the nature of; characteristic of: as, it was not *like* him to forget her birthday. 4. in the mood for; desirous of: as, I feel *like* sleeping. 5. indicative or prophetic of: as, it looks *like* a clear day tomorrow. *Like* was originally an adjective in senses 1, 3, 4, 5, and an adverb in sense 2, and is still considered so by conservative grammarians. *conj.* [Colloq.], 1. as: as, it was just *like* you said. 2. as if: as, it looks *like* he is signaling to us. *n.* a person or thing regarded as the equal or counterpart of another or of the person or thing being discussed: as, I have never seen the *like* of it. *v.t.* [LIKED (līkt), LIKING], [Obs.], to compare; liken. *v.i.* [Dial.], to come near (*to* doing something): in this use the verb is equal to the adverb *almost.*
and the like, and others of the same kind.
like anything (or **blazes, crazy, the devil, mad,** etc.), [Colloq. or Slang], with furious energy, speed, etc.
nothing like, not at all like; completely different from.
something like, almost like; about.
the like (or **likes**) **of,** [Colloq.], any person or thing like.

like (līk), *v.i.* [LIKED (līkt), LIKING], [ME. *liken;* AS. *lician* (akin to G. *leikan*) < base of *lic*, body, form (cf. LIKE, *adj.*); sense development: to be of like form—be like—be suited to—be pleasing to], 1. [Obs.], to please; be agreeable to: with the dative, as, it *likes* me not. 2. to be so inclined; choose: as, you may leave whenever you *like.* *v.t.* 1. to have a taste or fondness for; be pleased with; have a preference for; enjoy. 2. to wish: as, I should *like* to go there. *n. pl.* preferences, tastes, or affections: as, we know nothing of his *likes* and dislikes.

-like (līk), [AS. *-lic* < *gelic;* see LIKE, *adj.*, -LY], a suffix added to nouns: 1. to form adjectives meaning *like, characteristic of, suitable for*, as in *doglike, manlike, homelike.* 2. to form adverbs meaning *in the manner of.* Words formed with *-like* are usually written as one word, but are hyphenated if three *l's* fall together (e.g., *ball-like*).

like·a·ble (līk'ə-b'l), *adj.* likable.

like·li·hood (līk'li-hood'), *n.* [ME. *liklihode;* see LIKELY & -HOOD], 1. probability. 2. something that is likely to happen; a probability.

like·ly (līk'li), *adj.* [LIKELIER (-li-ẽr), LIKELIEST (-li-ist)], [ME. *likly, likliche*, after AS. *geliclic* or cognate ON. *likligr;* see LIKE, *adj.* & -LY], 1. apparently true to the facts; credible; probable: as, a *likely* account of the brawl. 2. seeming as if it would happen or make happen; reasonably to be expected; apparently destined: as, it is *likely* to leave at any minute. 3. such as will probably be satisfactory or rewarding; suitable: as, a *likely* place to find deer. 4. promising: as, a *likely* lad. *adv.* probably: as, he will very *likely* go.
SYN.—**likely** suggests probability or an eventuality that can reasonably be expected (he's not *likely* to win); **liable** and **apt** are loosely or informally used as equivalents of **likely,** but in strict discrimination, **liable** implies exposure or susceptibility to something undesirable (he's *liable* to be killed playing with firearms) and **apt** suggests a natural or habitual inclination or tendency (such people are always *apt* to become frightened); **prone** also suggests a propensity or predisposition to something that seems almost inevitable (he's *prone* to suspect others' motives). See also **probable.**—*ANT.* unlikely, indisposed.

like-mind·ed (līk'mīn'did), *adj.* having the same ideas, plans, tastes, etc.; agreeing mentally.

lik·en (līk''n), *v.t.* to represent as like, or similar; compare.

like·ness (līk'nis), *n.* 1. the state or quality of being like; similarity. 2. (the same) form; shape; semblance: as, Jupiter appeared in the *likeness* of a swan. 3. something that is like; copy; facsimile; portrait; picture.
SYN.—**likeness** implies close correspondence in appearance, qualities, nature, etc. (his remarkable *likeness* to his brother); **similarity** suggests only partial correspondence (your problem bears a certain *similarity* to mine); **resemblance** usually implies correspondence in appearance or in superficial aspects (the *resemblance* between a diamond and zircon); **analogy** refers to a correspondence between attributes or circumstances of things that are basically unlike (the *analogy* between a calculating machine and the human brain).—*ANT.* unlikeness, difference.

like·wise (līk'wīz'), *adv.* [short for *in like wise*], 1. in the same manner. 2. also; too; moreover.

li·kin (lē'kēn'), *n.* [Chin. *li-chin* < *li*, a Chinese weight, coin of this weight + *chin*, money], a Chinese provincial tax on articles being transported.

lik·ing (līk'iŋ), *n.* [ME.; AS. *licung* < *lician;* see LIKE, *v.*], 1. fondness; affection. 2. preference; taste; pleasure; predilection: as, not to my *liking.*

li·lac (lī'lək), *n.* [OFr.; Sp.; Ar. *laylak, līlak;* Per. *līlak, nīlak*, bluish < *nīl*, indigo; Sans. *nīla*, dark blue, indigo], 1. any of a group of hardy shrubs or trees with large clusters of tiny, fragrant flowers ranging in color from white, through many shades of lavender, to deep crimson. 2. the flower or flower cluster of this plant. 3. the pale-purple color often characteristic of this flower. *adj.* of a pale-purple color.

lil·i·a·ceous (lil'i-ā'shəs), *adj.* [LL. *liliaceus* < L. *lilium*, lily], 1. of or characteristic of lilies. 2. of the lily family, which includes many flowers and several vegetable species, such as the onion, leek, etc.

Lil·i·an (lil'i-ən), [prob. < L. *lilium*, lily], a feminine name: diminutives, *Lil, Lily:* also spelled **Lillian.**

lil·ied (lil'id), *adj.* 1. having many lilies; decorated or covered with lilies. 2. like a lily; fair.

Lil·ien·thal, David Eli (lil'yən-thäl', lil'yən-thôl'), 1899– ; American lawyer and administrator; chairman of U. S. Atomic Energy Commission, 1947–1950.

Li·li·en·thal, Ot·to (ôt'ō lē'li-ən-täl'), 1848–1896, German aeronautical inventor.

Lil·ith (lil'ith), *n.* [Heb. *līlīth;* Assyr.-Bab. *lilītu*, lit., of the night], 1. in *early Semitic folklore*, a female demon or vampire believed to live in ruins and other desolate places. 2. in *medieval Jewish folklore*, the first wife of Adam, before the creation of Eve. 3. in *medieval folklore*, a witch believed to menace little children.

Li·li·u·o·ka·la·ni, Lydia Ka·me·ke·ha (kä'mā-kā'hä li-lē'ōō-ō-kä-lä'ni), 1838–1917; queen of the Hawaiian Islands (1891–1893).

Lille (lēl), *n.* a city in northern France: pop., 189,000 (1946): formerly called *Lisle.*

Lil·li·an (lil'i-ən), a feminine name: see **Lilian.**

lil·li·bul·le·ro (lil'i-bə-lêr'ō), *n.* [< *lilli burlero*: arbitrary formation], 1. part of the refrain of a song popular in England during the revolution of 1688, ridiculing the Irish Catholics; hence, 2. this song.

Lil·li·put (lil'ə-put', lil'ə-pət), *n.* in Swift's *Gulliver's Travels*, a land inhabited by tiny people about six inches tall.

Lil·li·pu·tian (lil'ə-pū'shən), *adj.* 1. of Lilliput or its people; hence, 2. tiny; very small; dwarfed. *n.* 1. an inhabitant of Lilliput. 2. a very small person.

Lil·ly (lil'i), a feminine name: see **Lilian.**

lilt (lilt), *v.t. & v.i.* [ME. *lilten, lulten;* prob. < echoic base seen in *lull, Lollard*], to sing, speak, or play with a light, graceful rhythm or swing. *n.* 1. a gay song or tune with a light, swingy, and graceful rhythm. 2. a light, swingy, and graceful rhythm or movement.

Lil·y (lil'i), [dim. of *Lilian* or < *lily*], a feminine name.

lil·y (lil'i), *n.* [*pl.* LILIES (-iz)], [ME. & AS. *lilie;* L. *lilium;* Gr. *leirion*, lily], 1. any of a large group of plants grown from a bulb and having typically trumpet-shaped flowers, white or colored. 2. the flower or the bulb of any of these plants. 3. any of several plants related or similar to the true lily: as, the water *lily.* 4. the flower of any of these plants. 5. the heraldic fleur-de-lis, as in the royal arms of France. *adj.* like a lily, as in whiteness, delicacy, purity, etc.

lily iron, a harpoon with a detachable barbed head.

lil·y-liv·ered (lil′i-liv′ẽrd), *adj.* [after Shakespeare, *Macbeth*, V, iii], cowardly.

lily of the valley, [*pl.* LILIES OF THE VALLEY], [after Vulg. L. *lilium convallium* in *Song of Solomon*], a low-growing plant with a single, one-sided spike of very fragrant, small, white, bell-shaped flowers.

lily pad, one of the large, flat, floating leaves of the water lily.

Li·ma (lē′mə), *n.* 1. the capital of Peru: pop., 1,186,000. 2. (lī′mə), a city in northwestern Ohio: pop., 51,000.

Li·ma bean (lī′mə), [after *Lima*, Peru: from being native to tropical America], 1. a common variety of bean plant with creamy flowers and broad pods. 2. the broad, flat, nutritious bean of this plant.

lim·a·cine (lim′ə-sīn′, lī′mə-sin), *adj.* [< L. *limax, limacis*, a slug; + *-ine*], of or like slugs or shell-less snails.

limb (lim), *n.* [with unhistoric *-b* < ME. & AS. *lim;* akin to ON. *limr*, limb; IE. base **lei-*, to bend, seen also in *limit;* basic sense "bending, flexible"], 1. an arm, leg, or wing. 2. a large branch of a tree. 3. any projecting part like an arm or leg or forming an outgrowth or extension from a larger body. 4. a person or thing regarded as a branch, part, agent, or representative: as, a policeman is a *limb* of the law. 5. a naughty child. *v.t.* to dismember; disjoint.
out on a limb, [Colloq.], in a precarious or vulnerable position or situation.

limb (lim), *n.* [Fr. *limbe;* L. *limbus;* see LIMBO], a border, margin, or edge; specifically, *a)* the graduated edge of a quadrant. *b)* in *astronomy*, the outer edge of a heavenly body. *c)* in *botany*, the spreading outer portion of the corolla of certain flowers as distinguished from the lower, tubelike part.

lim·bate (lim′bāt), *adj.* [LL. *limbatus* < *limbus;* see LIMBO], having a distinct border or edging.

limbed (limd), *adj.* having (a specified number or kind of) limbs: usually in hyphenated compounds, as *crooked-limbed.*

lim·ber (lim′bẽr), *adj.* [prob. < *limb* (bodily member)], 1. easily bent; flexible; pliant. 2. able to bend the body easily; supple; lithe. *v.t.* to make limber: as, exercise *limbers* the fingers. *v.i.* to make oneself limber: as, the dancers were *limbering* up.

lim·ber (lim′bẽr), *n.* [earlier *lymor;* prob. < Fr. *limonière* < *limon*, a shaft], the two-wheeled, detachable front part of a gun carriage, usually supporting an ammunition chest. *v.t.* to attach the limber to (a gun carriage). *v.i.* to fasten the two parts of a gun carriage together, as in preparing to move off (often with *up*).

lim·bers (lim′bẽrz), *n.pl.* [prob. < Fr. *lumière*, a hole, aperture, lit., light], in *nautical usage*, holes or channels made near a ship's keel or keelson to drain water into the pump well.

lim·bo (lim′bō), *n.* [L., abl. of *limbus*, edge, border (in *in limbo*, in or on the border); akin to Sans. *lambatē*, hangs down, falls, Eng. *limp*], 1. in some Christian theologies, a region bordering upon hell, the abode after death of unbaptized children and righteous people who lived before Jesus. 2. a prison or imprisonment. 3. a place or condition of neglect or oblivion to which unwanted things or persons are relegated.

Lim·bourg (laṉ′bo͞or′; Eng. lim′bẽrg), *n.* a province of northeastern Belgium: pop., 555,000; capital, Hasselt: also called *Limburg.*

Lim·burg (lim′bẽrg), *n.* 1. a province of the southeastern Netherlands: pop., 869,000; capital, Maastricht. 2. Limbourg.

Lim·burg·er (or **Limburg**) **cheese** (lim′bẽr-gẽr), a soft, white brick cheese with a strong odor, originally made at Limburg (Limbourg), Belgium: also **Limburger.**

lim·bus (lim′bəs), *n.* [L.; see LIMBO], in *botany* & *zoology*, a distinct border or edging.

lime (līm), *n.* [ME. & AS. *lim;* akin to G. *leim;* IE. base **lei-*, slimy, wet and sticky, etc., seen also in L. *limus*, slime, AS. *lam* (see LOAM)], 1. [Rare], birdlime. 2. a white substance, calcium oxide, CaO, obtained by the action of heat on limestone, shells, and other material containing calcium carbonate, and used in making mortar and cement and in neutralizing acid soil: also called *quicklime, burnt lime, caustic lime. v.t.* [LIMED (līmd), LIMING], 1. to cement. 2. to smear with birdlime. 3. to catch with or as with birdlime. 4. to apply lime to; treat with lime.

lime (līm), *n.* [Fr.; Sp. *lima;* Ar. *limah;* Pers. *līmūn*, lemon, citron; cf. LEMON], 1. a small, lemon-shaped, greenish-yellow fruit with a juicy, sour pulp, rich in vitamin C. 2. the small, thorny, semitropical tree that it grows on, originally native to southern Asia but now widely cultivated. *adj.* 1. made with or of limes. 2. having a flavor like that of limes.

lime (līm), *n.* [< earlier *line;* ME. *lind;* see LINDEN], the linden tree.

lime·ade (līm′ād′), *n.* [*lime* + *-ade*], a drink of lime juice, sugar, and water.

lime burner, a person who burns limestone to make lime.

Lime·house (līm′hous′), *n.* a district in the East End of London, on the Thames, inhabited largely by sailors and dock workers.

lime·kiln (līm′kil′, līm′kiln′), *n.* a furnace in which limestone, shells, etc. are reduced to lime by burning.

lime·light (līm′līt′), *n.* 1. a brilliant light created by the oxidation of lime and formerly used in theaters to throw an intense beam of light upon a particular part of the stage, a certain actor, etc. 2. the part of a stage where a limelight or spotlight is cast. 3. a prominent or conspicuous position before the public.

li·men (lī′men), *n.* [L. *limen, liminis*, threshold; akin to *limus* (see LIMES, LIMB, a border): used as transl. of G. *schwelle*], in *psychology* & *physiology*, the least degree of stimulation that produces a response: also called *threshold.*

Lim·er·ick (lim′ẽr-ik), *n.* 1. a county of central Munster province, Ireland: pop., 138,000. 2. its capital: pop., 51,000. 3. [l-], [prob. < Ir. refrain containing the name], a nonsense poem of five anapestic lines, usually with the rhyme scheme aabba, the first, second, and fifth lines having three stresses, the third and fourth, two: the form was popularized by Edward Lear. Example:

A flea and a fly in a flue
Were imprisoned, so what could they do?
Said the flea, "Let us fly!"
Said the fly, "Let us flee!"
So they flew through a flaw in the flue.

li·mes (lī′mēz), *n.* [L., border, boundary, limit; akin to *limus*, aslant, oblique; IE. base **lēi-, *lĕi-*, seen also in AS. *lim;* see LIMB (bodily member)], 1. originally, a Roman frontier fortification: as, the *Limes* Germanicus protected the southern German provinces. 2. [L-], a series of German defenses built to oppose the French Maginot line: also called *Siegfried line.*

lime·stone (līm′stōn′), *n.* rock consisting mainly of calcium carbonate, from which building stones, lime, etc. are made: when crystallized by heat and pressure it becomes marble.

lime sulfur, a mixture made by boiling together sulfur, water, and lime: used as an insecticide and fungicide, especially in the form of a spray.

lime tree, 1. the linden or basswood tree. 2. the sour or black gum tree of southern United States; tupelo.

lime twig, 1. a twig smeared with birdlime to snare birds. 2. any kind of snare.

lime·wa·ter (līm′wô′tẽr, līm′wat′ẽr), *n.* a solution of lime in water, used to neutralize acids.

lim·ey (līm′i), *n.* [from the *lime* juice formerly served to the crew on British ships to prevent scurvy], [Slang], 1. an English soldier or sailor. 2. any Englishman. A generally patronizing or contemptuous term.

li·mic·o·line (lī-mik′ə-lin′), *adj.* [< L. *limicola*, mud dweller < *limus*, mud + *colere*, to dwell; + *-ine*], inhabiting the shore; specifically, designating or of a group of wading birds that live along the shore, as the plovers, curlews, killdeers, snipes, sandpipers, etc.

li·mic·o·lous (lī-mik′ə-ləs), *adj.* [< L. *limicola* (see LIMICOLINE); + *-ous*], living in mud.

lim·i·nal (lim′i-n'l, lī′mi-n'l), *adj.* of or at the limen.

lim·it (lim′it), *n.* [ME. & OFr. *limite;* L. *limes;* see LIMES], 1. the point, line, or edge where something ends or must end; boundary or border beyond which something ceases to be or to be possible. 2. *pl.* bounds; boundary lines. 3. the greatest number or amount allowed: as, they soon caught the *limit* for one day of trout fishing. 4. in *mathematics*, a fixed quantity or value which a varying quantity is regarded as approaching indefinitely. 5. in *poker*, etc., the maximum amount by which a bet may be raised at one time. *v.t.* [ME. *limiten;* OFr. *limiter;* L. *limitare*], to confine within bounds; set a limit to; restrict; curb.
the limit, [Colloq.], any person or thing regarded as almost or completely unbearable, remarkable, etc.
SYN.—**limit** implies the prescribing of a point in space, time, extent, etc. beyond which it is impossible or forbidden to go (*limit* your slogan to 25 words); **bound** implies an enclosing in boundaries or borders (a meadow *bounded* by hills); **restrict** implies a boundary that completely encloses and connotes a restraining within these bounds (the soldier was *restricted* to the camp area); **circumscribe** emphasizes more strongly the cutting off or isolation of that which is within the bounds (he leads the *circumscribed* life of a monk); **confine** stresses the restraint or hampering of enclosing limits (*confined* in jail).—***ANT.*** widen, expand.

lim·i·tar·y (lim′ə-ter′i), *adj.* [L. *limitaris*], 1. serving as a limit or boundary; restrictive. 2. limited; restricted.

lim·i·ta·tion (lim′ə-tā′shən), *n.* [ME. *limitacioun;* OFr. *limitacion;* L. *limitatio*], 1. a limiting or being limited. 2. something that limits, as some lack in a person's make-up which restricts the scope of his activity or accomplishment; qualification; restriction. 3. in *law*, a period of time, fixed by statute, during which legal action can be brought, as for settling a claim.

lim·i·ta·tive (lim′ə-tā′tiv), *adj.* [Fr. *limitatif;* ML. *limitativus*], limiting; restrictive.

lim·it·ed (lim′it-id), *adj.* [pp. of *limit*], 1. confined within bounds; restricted; circumscribed; narrow. 2.

accommodating a restricted number of passengers or making a restricted number of stops, and often charging extra fare: said of a train, bus, etc. 3. exercising governmental powers under constitutional restrictions; not having absolute power: as, a *limited* monarch. 4. restricting the liability of each partner or shareholder to the amount of his actual investment in the business: as, a *limited* company. ***n.*** a limited train, bus, etc. Abbreviated **Ltd., ltd., Lim., Ld.**

limited edition, a special, finely bound edition of a book, of which only a predetermined number of copies are printed.

lim·it·ing (lim′it-iŋ), ***adj.*** in *grammar*, designating or of any of a class of adjectives that limit or restrict the words modified (e.g., *several, these, four*, etc.).

lim·it·less (lim′it-lis), ***adj.*** without limits; unbounded; infinite; vast.

limn (lim), ***v.t.*** [LIMNED (limd), LIMNING (lim′iŋ, lim′niŋ)], [ME. *limnen*, contr. of *luminen*, for *enluminen;* OFr. *enluminer;* L. *illuminare*, to make light; see ILLUMINE], 1. to paint or draw. 2. to portray in words; describe. 3. [Obs.], to illuminate (manuscripts).

limn·er (lim′ẽr, lim′nẽr), ***n.*** a person who limns.

lim·nol·o·gy (lim-nol′ə-ji), ***n.*** [< Gr. *limnē*, marsh; + *-logy*], the scientific study of the biological, chemical, geographical, and physical features of fresh waters, especially lakes and ponds.

Li·moges (lē′mōzh′), ***n.*** 1. a city in central France: pop., 106,000. 2. fine chinaware or porcelain made there: also **Limoges ware.**

lim·o·nene (lim′ə-nēn′), ***n.*** [< Mod. L. *Limonum* (Fr. *limon*), lemon; + *-ene*], any of three isomeric terpenes, $C_{10}H_{16}$, present in many plant products such as lemon peel, orange oil, pine needles, peppermint, etc.

li·mo·nite (lī′mə-nīt′), ***n.*** [< Gr. *leimōn*, meadow; + *-ite*], a yellowish-brown iron ore, $2Fe_2O_3{\cdot}3H_2O$, responsible for the yellowish-brown color of many rocks and of clay.

li·mo·nit·ic (lī′mə-nit′ik), ***adj.*** of or like limonite.

Li·mou·sin (lē′mo͞o′zaṅ′), ***n.*** a former province of central France.

lim·ou·sine (lim′ə-zēn′, lim′ə-zēn′), ***n.*** [Fr., lit., a hood: from the costume worn in *Limousin*], 1. an automobile with a closed compartment seating three or more passengers: the top is extended forward over the driver's seat, which is open at the sides. 2. any large, luxurious sedan, usually with back and front seats separated by a glass partition.

limp (limp), ***v.i.*** [< AS. *limpan*, to befall, occur (in a specialized sense, to walk lamely); cf. AS. *lempheallt*, lame, MHG. *limpfen*, to walk with a limp, OHG. *limfan*, to befall, happen; IE. base **lemb-* < **leb-*, etc., to hang down, be limp (cf. LAPSE, LUMP)], 1. to walk with or as with a lame or partially disabled leg; hence, 2. to move unevenly, jerkily, or laboriously. ***n.*** a halt or lameness in walking.

limp (limp), ***adj.*** [< base of *limp, v.;* akin to MHG. *lampen*, to hang limply, Swiss G. dial. *lampe*, belly (both < var., IE. **lemb-*, of same base)], 1. lacking or having lost starch or stiffness; wilted; flexible. 2. lacking firmness, energy, or vigor.

limp·et (lim′pit), ***n.*** [ME. *lempet;* AS. *lempedu;* LL. *lempreda*, limpet, lamprey; cf. LAMPREY], any of several varieties of shellfish with a single, low, cone-shaped shell and a thick fleshy foot, by means of which it clings to rocks and timbers.

lim·pid (lim′pid), ***adj.*** [Fr. *limpide;* L. *limpidus*], perfectly clear; transparent; not roiled up.

lim·pid·i·ty (lim-pid′ə-ti), ***n.*** [Fr. *limpidité;* LL. *limpiditas*], the quality or state of being limpid; clearness.

limp·kin (limp′kin), ***n.*** [prob. *limp, v.* + *-kin:* from its walk], the American courlan, a bird found in Florida, Central America, and the West Indies.

Lim·po·po River (lim-pō′pō), a river in southern Africa, flowing into the Indian Ocean: length, 1,000 mi.: also called *Crocodile River*.

lim·u·loid (lim′yoo-loid′), ***adj.*** [< Mod. L. *limulus*, a crab < L. *limulus*, somewhat askance, dim. of *limus*, sidelong; + *-oid*], of or like the king crab. ***n.*** the king crab.

lim·u·lus (lim′yoo-ləs), ***n.*** [*pl.* LIMULI (-lī′)], [Mod. L.; see prec.], a king crab.

lim·y (lim′i), ***adj.*** [LIMIER (-i-ẽr), LIMIEST (-i-ist)], 1. covered with, consisting of, or like birdlime; sticky. 2. of, like, or containing lime.

lin., 1. lineal. 2. linear.

lin·age (līn′ij), ***n.*** [see -AGE], 1. alignment. 2. the number of written or printed lines on a page. 3. payment based on the number of lines produced by a writer. Also spelled **lineage.**

lin·al·o·öl (lin-al′ə-ōl′, lin′ə-lo͞ol′), ***n.*** [< *linaloa*, an aromatic Mexican wood (< Sp. *lináloe;* cf. Eng. *lignaloes*); + *-ol*], a terpene alcohol, $C_{10}H_{17}OH$, present in several essential oils.

linch·pin (linch′pin′), ***n.*** [ME. *lynspin;* AS. *lynis-* (akin to G. *lünse*) < base of *linnan*, to lose, desist, *alynnan*, to release (with reference to the movable nature of the pin); IE. base as in *lithe*], a pin that goes through the end of an axle outside the wheel to keep the wheel from coming off.

Lin·coln (liŋ′kən), ***n.*** 1. the capital of Nebraska: pop., 129,000. 2. Lincolnshire. 3. the county seat of Lincolnshire: pop., 73,000. 4. a breed of sheep having long wool: originally from Lincoln, England.

Lincoln, Abraham, 1809–1865; sixteenth president of the United States (1861–1865); assassinated: called the *Great Emancipator*.

Lincoln green, a bright-green cloth made at Lincoln, England: associated especially with Sherwood Forest.

Lincoln Park, a city in southeastern Michigan: suburb of Detroit: pop., 54,000.

Lin·coln·shire (liŋ′kən-shir′), ***n.*** a county on the eastern coast of England: pop., 706,000; county seat, Lincoln: also called *Lincoln*.

Lincoln's Inn, see **Inn of Court.**

Lind, Jenny (lind), (*Mme. Otto Goldschmidt*), 1820–1887; Swedish soprano: called the *Swedish Nightingale*.

Lin·da (lin′də), a feminine name: see **Belinda.**

Lind·bergh, Charles Augustus (lind′bẽrg), 1902– ; American aviator; made the first nonstop solo flight from New York to Paris (1927).

Lin·den (lin′dən), ***n.*** a city in eastern New Jersey: pop., 40,000.

lin·den (lin′dən), ***n.*** [ME.; AS., *adj.* (*lind* + *-en*), popularized as *n.* via G. *linden*, pl. of *linde;* cf. LIME (tree), LITHE], any of a group of trees with dense, heart-shaped leaves and fragrant, yellowish flowers, widely cultivated throughout the North Temperate Zone: the American variety is also called *basswood*.

Lind·say, Va·chel (vā′chəl lin′zi, lind′zi), (*Nicholas Vachel Lindsay*), 1879–1931; American poet.

line (līn), ***n.*** [ME. *line*, merging AS. *line*, a cord, with OFr. *ligne* (both < L. *linea*, lit., linen thread, n. use of fem. of *lineus*, of flax < *linum*, flax); akin to G. *leine*, a cord], 1. *a*) a cord, rope, wire, or string. *b*) a long, fine, strong cord with a hook or hooks, used in fishing. *c*) a cord, steel tape, etc. used in measuring or leveling. *d*) *often pl.* a rein, especially when long. 2. *a*) a wire or wires connecting stations in a telephone or telegraph system. *b*) the whole system of such wires. *c*) effective contact between stations: as, hold the *line*, please. 3. any wire, pipe, system of pipes or wires, etc. conducting fluid, electricity, etc. from one place to another. 4. a very thin threadlike mark; specifically, *a*) a long, thin mark made by a pencil, pen, chalk, etc. *b*) a similar mark cut in a hard surface. *c*) a thin crease in the palm or on the face. 5. a mark made on the ground in certain sports; specifically, *a*) one of the straight, narrow marks dividing a football field, tennis court, etc. *b*) a mark indicating a starting point or a limit not to be crossed. 6. a border or boundary: as, the State *line*. 7. a division between conditions, qualities, classes, etc.; limit; demarcation. 8. outline; contour; lineament. 9. *pl.* conditions or circumstances of life; one's fate. 10. *usually pl.* a plan of construction; plan of making or doing. 11. a row or series of persons or things, especially when more or less alike, as in shape, size, etc.; specifically, *a*) a row of written or printed characters extending across or part way across a page. *b*) a straight row of persons waiting in turn to buy something, enter a room, etc. 12. agreement; conformity; harmony: as, he brought the troublemakers into *line*. 13. a connected series of persons or things following each other in time or place; succession: as, a *line* of Democratic presidents. 14. lineage. 15. *a*) a transportation system or service consisting of regular trips by buses, ships, etc. between two or more points. *b*) a company operating such a system. *c*) one branch or division of such a system: as, the main *line* of a railroad. *d*) a single track of a railroad. 16. the course or direction anything moving takes; path: as, the *line* of fire. 17. a course of conduct, action, explanation, etc.: as, what was the *line* of his argument? 18. a person's trade or occupation, or the things he deals in: as, his *line* is leather goods. 19. a stock of goods of a particular type considered with reference to quality, quantity, variety, etc. 20. the field of one's special knowledge, interest, or ability: as, debating was right in his *line*. 21. a short letter, note, or card: as, drop me a *line* when you get to Portland. 22. *a*) a single metrical unit consisting of a specified number of feet; verse of poetry. *b*) a verse which in its form is typical of a poet or style: as, Marlowe's mighty *line*. 23. *pl.* all the speeches in a play; especially, all the speeches of any one character in a play. 24. 1/12 of an inch. 25. in *bridge*, the horizontal line dividing trick scores from honor scores: as, a game is based only on the score below the *line*. 26. in *football*, *a*) the players arranged in a row even with the ball at the start of each play, or those directly opposite them; centers, guards, tackles, ends. *b*) the line of scrimmage. 27. in *geography*, an imaginary circle or arc used for convenience of division: as, the date *line*. 28. in *mathematics*, *a*) the path of a moving point, thought of as having length but not breadth, whether straight or curved. *b*) such a path when considered perfectly straight. 29. in *military usage*, *a*) a formation of ships, troops, etc. in which elements are abreast of each other: distinguished from *column* in which elements are one behind the other. *b*) the area or position in closest contact with the enemy during combat. *c*) the troops in this area. *d*) those troops that do the actual fighting on the ground; combatant troops: sometimes distinguished from *staff*. *e*) the officers in immediate command of fighting ships. 30. in *music*, any of the long parallel marks forming the staff. Abbreviated **L., l.** *v.t.* [LINED (lind), LINING], 1. to draw lines on or in. 2. to bring or cause to come into a straight row or into conformity; bring into alignment (often with *up*). 3. to form a line along: as, great elms *line* the streets. 4. to place objects along the edge of: as, *line* the walk with flowers. *v.i.* to form a line (usually with *up*).

all along the line, 1. everywhere. 2. at every turn of events.

bring into line, to bring or cause to come into a straight row or into conformity; bring into alignment.

come into line, 1. to become part of a straight row; become straight. 2. [Colloq.], to correspond; agree; harmonize. 3. [Colloq.], to behave properly.

draw the (or **a**) **line,** to set a limit.

get a line on, [Colloq.], to find out about.

hard lines, [Slang], misfortune; bad luck.

hit the line, 1. in *football*, to try to carry the ball through the opposing line; hence, 2. to try boldly or firmly to do something.

hold the line, to stand firm; not permit a breakthrough or retreat: often used figuratively.

in line, 1. in a straight row; in alignment. 2. in harmony or agreement. 3. in readiness; prepared.

in line of duty, in the performance of authorized or prescribed duty: a military term used with reference to sickness, injury, or death of someone resulting from no fault or neglect of his.

line out, in *baseball*, 1. to get (a hit) by batting the ball in a straight, nearly horizontal line. 2. to be put out by batting a liner straight to a fielder.

line up, 1. to form a line. 2. to bring into a line; hence, 3. to organize effectively, secure a pledge of support from, etc. 4. to take a position (*against* a competitor or rival).

on a line, in the same plane; level.

out of line, 1. not in a straight line; not in alignment; hence, 2. not in agreement or conformity.

read between the lines, to discover a hidden meaning or purpose in something written, said, or done.

toe the line, to do exactly what has been commanded.

line (līn), *v.t.* [LINED (līnd), LINING], [ME. *lynen* < *lin*, long fiber flax, linen cloth < AS. *lin* < L. *linum*, flax: linen was orig. used for lining clothes], 1. to put a layer or lining on the inside of. 2. to fill with money: chiefly in *line one's pockets*. 3. to be used as a lining in: as, strong cloth *lined* the trunk.

lin·e·age (lin'i-ij), *n.* [ME. *linage;* OFr. *lignage* < *ligne;* see LINE, *n.*], 1. direct descent from an ancestor; hence, 2. ancestry; family.

line·age (līn'ij), *n.* linage.

lin·e·al (lin'i-əl), *adj.* [Fr. *linéal;* LL. *linealis* < L. *linea;* see LINE, *n.*], 1. in the direct line of descent from an ancestor. 2. hereditary. 3. of or composed of a line or lines; linear: abbreviated **lin.**

lin·e·al·ly (lin'i-əl-i), *adv.* by or in the direct line of descent.

lin·e·a·ment (lin'i-ə-mənt), *n.* [ME. *liniamente* < L. *lineamentum* < *lineare*, to fashion to a straight line < *linea*, a line; see LINE, *n.*], *usually in pl.* 1. any of the features of the face, especially with regard to its outline. 2. a distinctive feature or characteristic.

lin·e·ar (lin'i-ẽr), *adj.* [L. *linearis*], 1. of a line or lines. 2. made of or using lines: as, *linear* design. 3. having length only; extended in a line. 4. in *botany*, narrow and uniform in width, as the leaves of certain willows: see **leaf**, illus. Abbreviated **lin.**

linear equation, an algebraic equation whose variable quantity or quantities are in the first power only. Example: a + b − 5 = 0.

linear measure, 1. measurement of length, as distinguished from volume, weight, etc. 2. a system of measuring length; especially, the system in which
12 inches = 1 foot
3 feet = 1 yard
5 1/2 yards = 1 rod
40 rods = 1 furlong
8 furlongs (1,760 yards or 5,280 feet) = 1 mile.

lin·e·ate (lin'i-it, lin'i-āt'), *adj.* [L. *lineatus*, pp. of *lineare*, to fashion to a straight line < *linea*, a line; see LINE, *n.*], having or marked with lines; streaked.

lin·e·a·tion (lin'i-ā'shən), *n.* [ME. *lyneacion;* L. *lineatio*], 1. *a*) a marking with lines. *b*) a system or series of lines. 2. a dividing into lines.

line·back·er (līn'bak'ẽr), *n.* in *football*, any of the players stationed directly behind the line in a defensive formation.

line-breed (līn'brēd'), *v.t.* to use line breeding among.

line breeding, the producing of desired characteristics in animals by inbreeding through several successive generations.

line engraving, 1. a kind of engraving in which the effect is produced by lines of varying thickness and nearness to each other. 2. a plate engraved in this way. 3. a print from such a plate.

line·man (līn'mən), *n.* [*pl.* LINEMEN (-mən)], 1. a man who carries a surveying line, tape, or chain. 2. a man whose work is setting up and repairing telephone wires or other lines conducting electricity. 3. a man whose work is inspecting railroad tracks. 4. in *football*, one of the players in the line; center, tackle, guard, or end: distinguished from a *back*.

lin·en (lin'ən), *n.* [see PLURAL, II, D, 3], [ME. *lynnen;* AS. *linen* (akin to G. *leinen*) < *lin*, flax; see LINE (to put lining in)], 1. yarn, thread, or cloth made of flax. 2. articles made of linen, as tablecloths and sheets. 3. similar articles made of cotton or other cloth like linen, as shirts, underwear, etc. 4. fine stationery originally made from linen rags. *adj.* 1. spun from flax: as, *linen* thread. 2. made of linen.

linen closet, a closet for sheets, towels, table linen, etc.

line of battle, troops or ships in a position ready to fight.

line of fire, 1. the course of a bullet, shell, etc. that has been, or is to be, fired; hence, 2. a position open to attack of any kind.

line of force, a line in a field of electrical or magnetic force that shows the direction taken by the force at any point.

line of vision, the straight line from the point of clearest vision at the center of the eye to the point upon which the vision is fixed.

lin·e·o·late (lin'i-ə-lāt'), *adj.* [< L. *lineola*, dim. of *linea* (see LINE, *n.*); + *-ate*], in *botany & zoology*, marked with fine, usually parallel, lines.

lin·er (līn'ẽr), *n.* 1. a person or thing that traces lines or stripes. 2. a steamship, passenger airplane, etc. in regular service for a specific line. 3. in *baseball*, a batted ball that travels in a nearly horizontal line not high above the ground: also called *line drive*.

lin·er (līn'ẽr), *n.* 1. a person who makes or attaches linings. 2. a lining or something which suggests a lining by fitting inside something else: as, a helmet *liner*.

lines·man (līnz'mən), *n.* [*pl.* LINESMEN (-mən)], 1. a lineman. 2. in *football*, an official who measures and records the gains or losses in ground and determines where the ball goes out of bounds. 3. in *tennis*, an official who watches one or more lines on the court and reports faults involving his line or lines.

line squall, the line of thunderstorms or windstorms that marks the progress of a cold front.

line-up, line·up (līn'up'), *n.* an arrangement of persons or things in or as in a line; specifically, *a*) a group of suspected criminals lined up for inspection and identification by the police. *b*) in *football, baseball*, etc., the list of a team's players arranged according to the positions they play, their order at bat, etc.

line·y (līn'i), *adj.* liny.

ling (liŋ), *n.* [*pl.* LING, LINGS (liŋz); see PLURAL, II, D, 2], [ME. *lenge, lienge;* prob. < MLG. or MD.; cf. earlier D. *lenghe, linghe* (D. *ling*), prob. < base of Eng. *long*], 1. any of a large group of edible fish of the cod family, found in the North Atlantic from Greenland to Norway. 2. any of various other fishes, especially the burbot.

ling (liŋ), *n.* [ME.; ON. *lyng*], heather.

-ling (liŋ), [ME. *-ling, -lyng;* AS. *-ling*, combining the bases of *-le* & *-ing*], a suffix added to nouns, meaning, 1. *small*, as in *duckling*. 2. *unimportant* or *contemptible*: as in *princeling, hireling*.

-ling (liŋ), [ME. *-linge, -linges;* AS. *-ling, -lang, -lunga* < base of *lang* (see LONG)], [Archaic or Dial.], a suffix used to form adverbs meaning *direction, extent*, or *condition*, as in *darkling*.

lin·ga (liŋ'gə), *n.* a lingam.

lin·gam (liŋ'gəm), *n.* [Sans. *liṅgam*, lit., symbol], the phallic symbol used in the worship of the Hindu god Siva.

Lin·ga·yen Gulf (liŋ'gä-yen'), an arm of the South China Sea in Luzon Island, Philippines.

lin·ger (liŋ'gẽr), *v.i.* [North ME. *lenger*, freq. of *lengen*, to delay, stay (cf. -ER) < base of *long*], 1. to continue to stay, especially through reluctance to leave: as, he *lingered* before the fire. 2. to continue to live or exist although very close to death or the end. 3. to be unnecessarily slow in doing something; delay; loiter. *v.t.* to spend (time) lingeringly. —*SYN.* see **stay**.

lin·ge·rie (län'zhə-rē'; Fr. lan'zh'-rē'), *n.* [Fr. < *linger*, dealer in linen < *linge*, linen; L. *lineus*, linen < *linum*, flax, linen], 1. formerly, articles made of linen. 2. women's underwear of linen, silk, rayon, etc.

lin·go (liŋ'gō), *n.* [*pl.* LINGOES (-gōz)], [Pr. *lingo, lengo;* L. *lingua*, tongue, language], language; especially, a dialect, jargon, or special vocabulary that one is not familiar with: as, the *lingo* of medical men: a humorous or disparaging term. —*SYN.* see **dialect.**

-lings (liŋz), -ling (adverbial suffix).

lin·gua (liŋ'gwə), *n.* [*pl.* LINGUAE (-gwē)], [L.], a tongue or an organ resembling a tongue, as the proboscis of a butterfly or moth.

lin·gua fran·ca (liŋ'gwə fraŋ'kə), [It., lit., Frankish language], 1. a hybrid language of Italian, Spanish, French, Greek, Arabic, and Turkish elements, spoken in certain Mediterranean ports; hence, 2. any hybrid language used for communication between different peoples, as pidgin English. 3. any mixture of dialects similarly used: as, the East Anglian *lingua franca.*

lin·gual (liŋ'gwəl), *adj.* [ML. *lingualis* < L. *lingua*, the tongue; see LANGUAGE], 1. of the tongue. 2. pronounced by using the tongue. *n.* in *phonetics*, a sound, or a letter representing it, pronounced by using the tongue especially: as, *l* and *t* are *linguals.*

lin·gui·form (liŋ'gwi-fôrm'), *adj.* [< L. *lingua*, the tongue; + *-form*], shaped like a tongue.

lin·guist (liŋ'gwist), *n.* [< L. *lingua*, the tongue; + *-ist*], 1. a person who can speak, read, and write several languages; polyglot. 2. a specialist in linguistics: cf. **philologist.**

lin·guis·tic (liŋ-gwis'tik), *adj.* 1. of language. 2. of linguistics.

lin·guis·ti·cal·ly (liŋ-gwis'ti-k'l-i, liŋ-gwis'tik-li), *adv.* as regards language or linguistics; from a linguistic viewpoint.

linguistic form, any speech unit having meaning; base, word, affix, phrase, sentence, etc.

lin·guis·tics (liŋ-gwis'tiks), *n. pl.* [construed as sing.], [< *linguistic*], 1. the science of language, including phonology, morphology, syntax, and semantics: often **general linguistics:** usually subdivided into *descriptive, historical, comparative,* and *geographical linguistics.* 2. the study of the structure, development, etc. of a particular language and of its relationship to other languages: as, English *linguistics.*

linguistic stock, 1. a parent language and all the languages and dialects derived from it. 2. all the native speakers of any of these languages or dialects.

lin·gu·late (liŋ'gyoo-lāt'), *adj.* [L. *lingulatus* < *lingula*, dim. of *lingua*, the tongue], shaped like a tongue.

lin·i·ment (lin'ə-mənt), *n.* [ME. *lynyment;* LL. *linimentum* < L. *linere*, to smear], a medicated liquid to be rubbed on the skin for soothing sore or inflamed areas.

li·nin (lī'nin), *n.* [< L. *linum*, flax; + *-in*], 1. the achromatic substance constituting the netlike structure that connects the granules of chromatin in the nucleus of a cell. 2. a white, bitter cathartic obtained from a variety of flax.

lin·ing (lin'iŋ), *n.* [see LINE (to cover on the inside) & -ING], 1. the act of covering the inner surface of something. 2. the material used or suitable for this purpose; hence, 3. the contents of something.

link (liŋk), *n.* [ME. *linke* < Anglo-N.; cf. Ice. *hlekkr*, Dan. *lænke*, Sw. *länk*, in same senses; akin to (? combined with) AS. *hlence*, link of a chain < base of *hlencan*, to twist (MHG. *lenken*, to bend, twist); IE. base **qleng-*, to bend, etc.], 1. any of the series of rings or loops making up a chain or chain armor. 2. *a*) a section of something resembling a chain: as, a *link* of sausage. *b*) a point or stage in a series of circumstances: as, a weak *link* in the evidence. 3. a cuff link. 4. anything serving to connect or tie: as, a *link* with the past. 5. one length in a surveyor's chain, equal to 7.92 inches: abbreviated **L., l.** 6. in *mechanics*, a short connecting rod for transmitting power or motion. *v.t.* to join together with or as with a link or links. *v.i.* to join; be or become connected: as, each clue *links* up with the next. —*SYN.* see **join.**

link (liŋk), *n.* [? < prec., as being made in links], a torch, especially one made of tow and pitch.

link·age (liŋk'ij), *n.* [see -AGE], 1. a linking or being linked. 2. a series or system of links; especially, a series of connecting rods for transmitting power or motion. 3. in *biology*, the tendency of some genes to remain together and act as a unit (*linkage group*) in inheritance, generally in the same chromosome, without segregation throughout maturation. 4. in *electricity*, the product of a magnetic flux by the number of turns in the coil surrounding it.

link·boy (liŋk'boi'), *n.* in the days before street lighting, a boy or man hired to carry a torch to light the way for people at night: also **linkman.**

linking verb, a verb that functions chiefly as a connection between a subject and a predicate complement (e.g., *be, appear, seem, become,* etc.).

link·man (liŋk'mən), *n.* [*pl.* LINKMEN (-mən)], a linkboy.

link motion, a valve gear that reverses the motion in steam engines: it operates by a slotted bar linked with the eccentric rods.

links (liŋks), *n.pl.* [AS. *hlinc*, a slope < base of *link* (a ring)], 1. [Scot.], flat or slightly rolling land, especially along a seashore. 2. a golf course.

Link trainer (liŋk), [after Edward A. *Link* (1904–), Am. inventor], an apparatus for training student airplane pilots under simulated conditions of flight: it consists of a hooded cockpit containing the necessary instruments, and is pneumatically operated on a grounded turntable.

link·work (liŋk'wũrk'), *n.* 1. anything made in links, as a chain. 2. a gear system operating by links.

Lin·lith·gow (lin-lith'gō), *n.* West Lothian, a county of Scotland: the former name.

linn (lin), *n.* the American linden or a related tree.

linn (lin), *n.* [< AS. *hlynn*, torrent, or Gael. *linne*, a pond], 1. a waterfall. 2. a pool of water, especially one at the base of a waterfall. 3. a steep ravine.

Lin·nae·an, Lin·ne·an (li-nē'ən), *adj.* of Linnaeus; especially, designating or of his system of classifying plants and animals by using a double name, the first word naming the genus, and the second the species: abbreviated **Linn.**

Lin·nae·us, Car·o·lus (kar'ə-ləs li-nē'əs), (born *Karl von Linné*), 1707–1778; Swedish botanist.

lin·net (lin'it), *n.* [OFr. *linette* < *lin*, flax (L. *linum*; cf. LINEN): so called because it feeds on the seed of flax], a small songbird of the finch family, found in Europe, Asia, and Africa.

lin·o·le·ic (lin'ə-lē'ik, li-nō'li-ik), *adj.* [< L. *linum*, flax + *oleum*, oil; + *-ic*], designating or of an unsaturated fatty acid, $C_{18}H_{32}O_2$, found as a glyceryl ester in linseed oil and other drying oils.

li·no·le·um (li-nō'li-əm), *n.* [< L. *linum*, flax + *oleum*, oil], 1. linseed oil hardened by oxidizing; hence, 2. a hard, smooth, washable floor covering made of a mixture of ground cork and oxidized linseed oil spread over a burlap or canvas backing.

lin·o·type (līn'ə-tīp'), *n.* [< *line of type*], a typesetting machine that casts an entire line of type in one bar: it is operated from a keyboard like that of a typewriter: a trade-mark (**Linotype**). *v.t. & v.i.* [LINOTYPED (-tīpt'), LINOTYPING], to set (matter) with this machine.

lin·o·typ·er (līn'ə-tīp'ẽr), *n.* a person who operates a linotype.

lin·o·typ·ist (līn'ə-tīp'ist), *n.* a linotyper.

lin·sang (lin'saŋ), *n.* [Jav. *linsaṅ, wlinsaṅ*], a long-tailed, catlike animal about the size of a weasel, found in Australia and the East Indies.

lin·seed (lin'sēd'), *n.* [ME. *linsed*, AS. *linsæd*, *lin*, flax (see LINE, to put a lining in) + *sæd* (see SEED)], the seed of flax.

linseed cake, a solid cake of linseed from which the oil has been extracted: used to feed cattle.

linseed meal, meal made from ground linseed cake.

linseed oil, a yellowish oil extracted from flaxseed, and used, because of its drying qualities, in making oil paints, printer's ink, linoleum, etc.

lin·sey (lin'zi), *n.* [*pl.* LINSEYS (-ziz)], linsey-woolsey.

lin·sey-wool·sey (lin'zi-wool'zi), *n.* [*pl.* LINSEY-WOOLSEYS (-ziz)], [ME. < *lin*, flax (see LINE, to put a lining in) + *wool* with jingling suffix *-sey*], 1. a coarse cloth made of linen and wool or cotton and wool. 2. [Obs.], jargon; nonsense.

lin·stock (lin'stok'), *n.* [altered < D. *lontstok; lont*, a match, lunt + *stok*, a stick], a long stick formerly used to hold a lighted match for firing a cannon.

lint (lint), *n.* [ME. *linnet, lynete, lynt;* L. *linteum*, linen cloth < *linum*, flax; see LINEN], 1. scraped and softened linen formerly used as a dressing for wounds. 2. bits of thread, ravelings, or fluff from cloth or yarn. 3. the fiber surrounding the seed of unginned cotton.

lin·tel (lin't'l), *n.* [ME.; OFr.; LL. **limitellus, lintellus* < L. *limes;* see LIMES], the horizontal crosspiece over a door or window, carrying the weight of the structure above it.

lint·er (lin'tẽr), *n.* 1. a machine for removing the short fibers which remain stuck to cotton seeds after ginning. 2. *pl.* these fibers, used in making cotton batting.

lint·white (lint'hwīt'), *n.* [ME. *lynkwhitte;* AS. *lynetuige*, lit., flax-plucker; ME. form ? < AS. *lynece*, linnet], the linnet.

lint·y (lin'ti), *adj.* [LINTIER (-ti-ẽr), LINTIEST (-ti-ist)], of, like, or covered with lint.

lin·y (līn'i), *adj.* [LINIER (-i-ẽr), LINIEST (-i-ist)], 1. like a line; thin. 2. marked with, or full of, lines or streaks. Also spelled **liney.**

Linz (lints), *n.* a city in northern Austria, on the Danube: pop., 184,000 (est. 1948).

li·on (lī′ən), *n.* [*pl.* LIONS (-ənz), LION; see PLURAL, II, D, 1], [ME.; OFr.; L. *leo, leonis;* Gr. *leōn, leontos*], 1. a large, powerful mammal of the cat family, found in Africa and southwest Asia, with a tawny coat, a tufted tail, and, in the adult male, a shaggy mane: in folklore and fable the lion is considered king of the beasts; it is also the symbol of Great Britain. 2. a person of great courage or strength. 3. a person who arouses great interest and is invited to many social affairs; celebrity. 4. [L-], *a*) the constellation Leo. *b*) the fifth sign of the zodiac.

beard the lion in his den, to visit and defy or oppose a person in his own home, etc.

twist the lion's tail, to make statements against Great Britain.

Lion, Gulf of the, a bay of the Mediterranean, on the southern coast of France, from Toulon to Spain.

Li·o·nel (lī′ə-n'l, lī′ə-nel′), [Fr., dim. of *lion;* see LION; cf. LEO], a masculine name.

li·on·ess (lī′ən-is), *n.* [ME. *lionesse;* OFr. *lionnesse,* fem. of *lion,* lion], a female lion.

li·on·et (lī′ən-et′), *n.* [OFr., dim. of *lion*], a small or young lion.

li·on·heart (lī′ən-härt′), *n.* 1. a lionhearted person. 2. [L-], Richard I of England, called *Coeur de Lion.*

li·on·heart·ed (lī′ən-här′tid), *adj.* very brave.

li·on·ism (lī′ən-iz'm), *n.* a lionizing or being lionized.

li·on·i·za·tion (lī′ən-i-zā′shən, lī′ən-ī-zā′shən), *n.* a lionizing or being lionized.

li·on·ize (lī′ən-īz′), *v.t.* [LIONIZED (-īzd′), LIONIZING], [in sense 1, < *lion,* 3; in sense 2, from the practice of showing visitors the celebrities and celebrated places], 1. to treat as a celebrity. 2. [Now Rare], to visit or explore the interesting sights of (a place).

lion's share, the biggest or best portion.

lip (lip), *n.* [ME. *lippe;* AS. *lippa;* akin to G. *lippe* (< LG.); IE. base **leb-,* prob., what is licked (var. of **lāb-, *lebh-,* etc., to lick with gusto), prob. seen also in L. *labium* (cf. LABIAL)], 1. either of the two fleshy folds, normally pink or reddish in color, forming the edges of the mouth and important in speech. 2. anything like a lip; specifically, *a*) the edge of a wound. *b*) the projecting rim of a pitcher, cup, etc. *c*) the mouthpiece of a wind instrument. *d*) the cutting edge of any of certain tools. *e*) in *anatomy,* a labium. *f*) in *botany,* a labellum. 3. [Slang], impertinent or insolent talk. 4. the position of the lips in playing a wind instrument. *v.t.* [LIPPED (lipt), LIPPING], 1. to touch with the lips; specifically, *a*) to kiss. *b*) to place the lips in the proper position for playing (a wind instrument). 2. in *golf,* to hit the ball just to the edge of (the cup). *adj.* 1. merely spoken or superficial; not genuine, sincere, or heartfelt: as, *lip* service. 2. formed with a lip or the lips; labial: as, a *lip* consonant.

bite one's lips, to keep back one's anger, annoyance, etc.

hang on the lips of, to listen to with close attention.

keep a stiff upper lip, [Colloq.], to fail to become frightened or discouraged under difficulties.

smack one's lips, to express great satisfaction in anticipating or remembering something pleasant.

Li·pa·ri Islands (lē′pä-rē′; Eng. lip′ēr-i), a group of volcanic islands north of Sicily: area, 45 sq. mi.; pop., 14,000.

lip·a·roid (lip′ə-roid′), *adj.* [< Gr. *liparos,* oily < *lipos,* fat; + *-oid*], fatty; like fat.

li·pase (lī′pās, lip′ās), *n.* [< Gr. *lipos,* fat], an enzyme that aids in digestion by changing fats into fatty acids and glycerin.

lip·id (lī′pid, lip′id), *n.* a lipide.

lip·ide (lī′pid, lip′id), *n.* [*lip-* + *-ide*], any of a group of organic compounds consisting of the fats and other substances of similar properties: they are insoluble in water, soluble in fat solvents and alcohol, and greasy to the touch: also **lipoid.**

Li Po (lē pō), ?–762 A.D.; Chinese poet.

lip·o- (lip′ō, lip′ə), [< Gr. *lipos,* fat], a combining form meaning *of or like fat, fatty,* as in *lipolysis*: also, before a vowel, **lip-.**

lip·oid (lip′oid, lī′poid), *adj.* [*lip*(*o*)- + *-oid*], in *biochemistry,* resembling fat. *n.* a lipide.

li·pol·y·sis (li-pol′ə-sis), *n.* [Mod. L.; *lipo-* + *-lysis*], the decomposition of fat, as during digestion.

lip·o·lyt·ic (lip′ə-lit′ik), *adj.* [< *lipolysis*], that can decompose fats.

li·po·ma (li-pō′mə), *n.* [*pl.* LIPOMATA (-tə), LIPOMAS (-məz)], [Mod. L.; *lip-* + *-oma*], a tumor made up of fat tissue.

Lip·pe (lip′ə), *n.* a division of northwestern Germany: formerly a principality, duchy, and republic: area, 469 sq. mi.; pop., 189,000; capital, Detmold.

lipped (lipt), *adj.* 1. having a lip or lips: often in compounds, as *tight-lipped.* 2. having a spoutlike projection in the rim: said of a pitcher, cup, etc. 3. in *botany & zoology,* labiate.

lip·per (lip′ēr), *n.* [North Eng. & Scot.; prob. < base of *lap* (of waves)], 1. a gentle ruffling movement of the surface of the sea. 2. light spray caused by this.

Lip·pi, Fi·lip·pi·no (fē′lēp-pē′nô lēp′pē; Eng. lip′i), 1457?–1504?; Florentine painter; son of *Filippo.*

Lippi, Fra Fi·lip·po (fi-lēp′pô), 1406?–1469; Florentine painter: also called *Fra Filippo del Carmine* and *Fra Lippo Lippi.*

Lipp·mann, Walter (lip′mən), 1889– ; American journalist and author.

lip-read (lip′rēd′), *v.t. & v.i.* to recognize (a speaker's words) by watching the movements of his lips.

lip reader, a person skilled in lip reading.

lip reading, the art of recognizing a speaker's words by watching the movement of his lips: it is often taught to the deaf.

lip service, insincere expression of affection, respect, loyalty, etc.

lip·stick (lip′stik′), *n.* 1. a small stick of rouge for coloring the lips. 2. a similar stick of colorless pomade for softening and protecting the lips.

liq., 1. liquid. 2. liquor.

li·quate (lī′kwāt), *v.t.* [LIQUATED (-id), LIQUATING], [< L. *liquatus,* pp. of *liquare,* to melt], in *metallurgy,* to heat (a metal, etc.) in order to separate a fusible substance from one less fusible.

li·qua·tion (lī-kwā′shən), *n.* [L. *liquatio*], a liquating.

liq·ue·fac·tion (lik′wə-fak′shən), *n.* a liquefying or being liquefied.

liq·ue·fi·a·ble (lik′wə-fī′ə-b'l), *adj.* that can be liquefied.

liq·ue·fi·er (lik′wə-fī′ēr), *n.* an apparatus for liquefying gases.

liq·ue·fy (lik′wə-fī′), *v.t. & v.i.* [LIQUEFIED (-fīd′), LIQUEFYING], [Fr. *liquefier* < L. *liquefacere* < *liquere,* to be liquid + *facere,* to make], to change into a liquid. —*SYN.* see **melt.**

li·ques·cence (li-kwes′'ns), *n.* a liquescent condition.

li·ques·cent (li-kwes′'nt), *adj.* [L. *liquescens,* ppr. of *liquescere,* to become liquid < *liquere,* to be liquid], becoming liquid; melting.

li·queur (li-kũr′), *n.* [Fr.], any of certain strong, sweet, sirupy alcoholic liquors, variously flavored.

liq·uid (lik′wid), *adj.* [ME. & OFr. *liquide;* L. *liquidus* < *liquere,* to be liquid], 1. readily flowing; fluid. 2. clear; transparent: said especially of the air. 3. flowing smoothly and musically: as, *liquid* verse. 4. readily convertible into cash. 5. nonfrictional and vowellike: term sometimes used in nonscientific context to describe certain consonants, especially *l* and *r.* *n.* 1. a substance that, unlike a solid, flows readily but, unlike a gas, does not tend to expand indefinitely. 2. a liquid consonant. Abbreviated **liq.**

SYN.—**liquid** refers to a substance that flows readily and assumes the form of its container but retains its independent volume (water that is neither ice nor steam is a *liquid*); **fluid** applies to any substance that flows (all liquids, gases, and viscous substances are *fluids*).—*ANT.* solid.

liquid air, air brought to a liquid state by being subjected to great pressure and then cooled by its own expansion to a temperature below the boiling point of its constituents, nitrogen and oxygen: it is used as a refrigerant.

liq·uid·am·bar (lik′wid-am′bēr), *n.* [< Mod. L. *Liquidambar,* name of the genus; see LIQUID & AMBER], 1. a variety of tree with star-shaped leaves yielding a fragrant balsam used in medicine: also called *sweet gum.* 2. this balsam.

liq·ui·date (lik′wi-dāt′), *v.t.* [LIQUIDATED (-id), LIQUIDATING], [< ML. *liquidatus,* pp. of *liquidare,* to make liquid or clear < L. *liquidus,* liquid], 1. to settle by agreement or legal process the amount of (indebtedness, damages, etc.). 2. to clear up the affairs of (a bankrupt business firm that is closing, etc.); settle the accounts of, by apportioning assets and debts. 3. to pay (a debt). 4. to convert into cash. 5. to dispose of; get rid of, as by killing. *v.i.* to liquidate one's debts.

liq·ui·da·tion (lik′wi-dā′shən), *n.* a liquidating or being liquidated.

go into liquidation, to close one's business by gathering in assets and settling all debts.

liq·ui·da·tor (lik′wi-dā′tēr), *n.* a person who liquidates, especially one legally in charge of liquidating a company, estate, etc.

liquid crystal, a liquid that has certain characteristics of crystals, as interference colors and double refraction.

liquid fire, an inflammable chemical composition which can be shot in a jet for a considerable distance: used in war against tanks and fortified positions.

li·quid·i·ty (li-kwid′ə-ti), *n.* [L. *liquiditas*], the quality or state of being liquid.

liquid measure, 1. the measurement of liquids. 2. a system of measuring liquids; especially, the system in which

4 gills = 1 pint
2 pints = 1 quart
4 quarts = 1 gallon
31 1/2 gallons = 1 barrel
2 barrels = 1 hogshead.

liq·uor (lik′ēr), *n.* [repatterned after L. < ME. *licour;* OFr. *licor, licur, likeur;* L. *liquor*], 1. any liquid or juice: as, meat *liquor.* 2. an alcoholic drink, especially one made by distilling, as whisky or rum. 3. in *pharmacy*, a solution of some substance in water: abbreviated **liq.** *v.t.* [Slang], to give alcoholic liquor to (usually with *up*). *v.i.* [Slang], to drink alcoholic liquor, especially in large quantities (usually with *up*).

liq·uo·rice (lik'ẽr-is, lik'ẽr-ish, lik'rish), *n.* licorice.

liq·uor·ish (lik'ẽr-ish), *adj.* 1. lickerish. 2. fond of liquor.

li·ra (lêr'ə), *n.* [*pl.* LIRE (-ā), LIRAS (-əz)], [It. < L. *libra*, a balance, pound], 1. the monetary unit and a silver coin of Italy, originally equal to 19.3 cents but valued at one seventh of a cent in 1950. 2. the monetary unit and a gold coin of Turkey, valued at 36 cents in 1950. Abbreviated **L., l.** (*sing. & pl.*).

lir·i·o·den·dron (lir'i-ə-den'drən), *n.* [*pl.* LIRIODENDRA (-drə)], [Mod. L. *Liriodendron*, name of the genus < Gr. *leirion*, lily + *dendron*, tree], any of a variety of Asiatic and North American trees of the magnolia family, as the tulip tree or whitewood.

lir·i·pipe (lir'i-pīp'), *n.* [ML. *liripipium;* ? altered < LL. *cleri ephippium*, cleric's caparison; *cleri*, genit. of *clerus*, cleric + *ephippium* < Gr. *ephippion*, saddlecloth], in early academic costume, a long tail to a hood.

Lis·bo·a (lēzh-bô'ȧ), *n.* Lisbon.

Lis·bon (liz'bən), *n.* the capital of Portugal: pop., 709,000: Portuguese name, *Lisboa*.

Lisle (lēl; Fr. lēl), *n.* Lille: the former name.

lisle (līl), *n.* [< *Lisle*, earlier sp. of *Lille*, France], 1. a fine, hard, extra-strong cotton thread: in full, **lisle thread.** 2. a fabric, stockings, gloves, etc., knit or woven of lisle. *adj.* made of lisle.

lisp (lisp), *v.i.* [ME. *lyspen*, earlier *wlispen;* AS. *-wlyspian* < *wlisp, wlips*, a lisping; akin to G. *lispeln*, MLG. *wlispen, wilspen*, etc.; origin prob. echoic], 1. to substitute the sounds (th) and (*th*) for the sounds of *s* and *z:* a person who pronounces *sing* as though it were *thing* is lisping. 2. to speak imperfectly or like a child. *v.t.* to utter with a lisp or in an imperfect or childlike way. *n.* 1. the act or habit of lisping. 2. the sound of lisping, or a sound like this.

‡lis pen·dens (lis pen'denz), [L.], literally, a pending suit: with reference to the legal doctrine that a court acquires jurisdiction over property involved in a suit.

lis·some, lis·som (lis'əm), *adj.* [altered < *lithesome*], 1. supple; limber; flexible. 2. nimble; agile.

list (list), *n.* [ME. *liste*, merging AS. *liste*, a hem, border (cf. sense 2) & Anglo-Fr. *liste* < Gmc.; akin to G. *leiste;* IE. base **leizd-*, edge, border], 1. a narrow strip of cloth; especially, the selvage cut from a wide piece of goods. 2. a stripe of color. 3. a slender strip of wood, as one cut from a board. 4. a boundary. 5. a ridge of earth between two furrows. 6. [from the idea of a narrow slip of paper], a series of names, words, numbers, etc. set forth in order, usually in writing; catalogue; roll. *v.t.* 1. to edge with a strip or strips of cloth. 2. to arrange in stripes or bands. 3. *a*) to set forth (a series of names, words, etc.) in order. *b*) to enter in a list, directory, catalogue, etc.: as, no such name is *listed* here. 4. *a*) to plow (ground) with a lister. *b*) to plant (corn) with a lister having a seed drill attached to it. *v.i.* 1. [Rare], to enlist in the armed forces. 2. to plow with a lister.

SYN.—**list**, the broadest in scope of these terms, applies to a series of items of any kind, no matter what the arrangement or purpose; **catalogue** implies methodical arrangement, usually alphabetical, and is used of lists of articles for sale or on exhibit, library card files, etc.; an **inventory** is an itemized list of goods, property, etc., especially one made annually in business; a **register** is a book, etc. in which names, events, or other items are formally or officially recorded (a *register* of voters); a **roll** is an official list of the members of an organization, especially as used for checking attendance.

list (list), *v.i.* [ME. *listen, lusten, lesten;* AS. *lystan* < base of *lust*, desire, appetite; see LUST], [Archaic], 1. to be pleasing (*to* someone). 2. to wish; like; choose.

list (list), *v.t. & v.i.* [same word as prec. in basic etym. sense "to incline, bend toward"], to tilt to one side, as a ship. *n.* a tilting or inclining to one side.

list (list), *v.t. & v.i.* [ME. *listen;* AS. *hlystan* < base of *hlyst*, hearing; akin to G. *lauschen*, dial. *laustern;* IE. base **kleu-*, to hear, seen also in L. *cluere*, to be called; cf. LOUD], [Archaic], to listen (to).

lis·ten (lis''n), *v.i.* [ME. *listnen*, felt as freq. of *listen* (see prec.); AS. *hlysnan* (akin to MHG. *lüsenen*) < Gmc. base **hlus-*, as in AS. *hlyst*, hearing], 1. to make a conscious effort to hear; attend closely, so as to hear. 2. to give heed; take advice. *n.* a listening.

listen in, to be a listener to a telephone conversation of others, a radio program, etc.

listening post, 1. in *military usage*, an advanced, concealed position near the enemy's lines, for detecting the enemy's movements by listening; hence, 2. any position for securing information unobserved.

list·er (lis'tẽr), *n.* [*list* (a strip) + *-er:* from the ridges and furrows formed], a plow with a double moldboard, which heaps the earth on both sides of the furrow: it is sometimes combined with a drill that plants seed in the same operation.

Lis·ter, Joseph (lis'tẽr), first Baron Lister, 1827–1912; English surgeon; introduced antiseptic surgery.

Lis·ter·ism (lis'tẽr-iz'm), *n.* the general principles and practice of antisepsis and aseptic surgery.

list·ing (lis'tiŋ), *n.* 1. the act of making a list. 2. the fact of being listed, as in a directory.

list·less (list'lis), *adj.* [*list* (var. of *lust*) + *less*], 1. feeling only indifference to what is going on about one, as a result of illness, weariness, dejection, etc.; spiritless; languid. 2. characterized by such a feeling.

list price, price shown in a list or catalogue: dealers usually receive a discount from it.

lists (lists), *n.pl.* [ME. *listes*, specialized use of *liste*, border, hedging, boundary (cf. LIST, strip of cloth, etc.); prob. influenced by OFr. *lisse* (Fr. *lice*) in same sense], 1. in the Middle Ages, a high fence of stakes enclosing the area in which a tournament was held; hence, 2. this area itself or the tournament held there. 3. in modern usage, an arena or place of combat.

enter the lists, to enter a contest or struggle.

Liszt, Franz (fränts list), 1811–1886; Hungarian pianist and composer.

lit (lit), 1. alternative past tense and past participle of **light** (to illuminate). 2. alternative past tense and past participle of **light** (to alight).

lit (lit), *n.* [Lith. < *Litva*, Lithuanians], formerly, the monetary unit and a silver coin of Lithuania, valued at about 10 cents: replaced by the ruble.

lit., 1. liter; liters. 2. literal. 3. literally. 4. literary. 5. literature.

lit·a·ny (lit''n-i), *n.* [*pl.* LITANIES (-iz)], [ME. & OFr. *letanie;* LL. *litania;* Gr. *litaneia*], 1. a form of prayer in which the clergy and the congregation take part alternately, with recitation and response. 2. [L-], a special form of service of this kind in the Book of Common Prayer (with *the*).

li·tas (lē'täs), *n.* [*pl.* LITAI (-tā), LITU (-to͞o)], a lit.

Lit.B., Lit.D., see **Litt.B., Litt.D.**

li·tchi (lē'chē'), *n.* [Chin. *li-chih*], 1. a Chinese evergreen tree of the soapberry family, cultivated in warm climates for its fruit. 2. the fruit of this tree (**litchi nut**) eaten dried or preserved: it consists of a single seed surrounded by a sweet, edible, raisinlike pulp, enclosed in a rough, brown, papery shell. Also spelled **lichee.**

-lite (līt), [Fr., for *-lithe;* see -LITH], a combining form, meaning *stone*, used in the names of minerals and rocks, as in *chrysolite, cryolite:* also **-lyte.**

li·ter (lē'tẽr), *n.* [Fr. *litre* < *litron*, obs. unit of measure; ML. *litra;* Gr. *litra*, a pound], the basic unit of capacity in the metric system, equal to 1 cubic decimeter or 61.025 cubic inches (1.0567 liquid quarts or .906 dry quarts): it is the volume of a kilogram of distilled water at 4° C.: also spelled **litre:** abbreviated **L., l., lit.** (*sing. & pl.*).

lit·er·a·cy (lit'ẽr-ə-si), *n.* the state or quality of being literate; ability to read and write.

lit·er·al (lit'ẽr-əl), *adj.* [ME.; OFr.; LL. *litteralis, literalis* < L. *littera, litera*, a letter; see LETTER], 1. of, involving, or expressed by a letter or letters of the alphabet: as, a *literal* grade. 2. following or representing the exact words of the original; word-for-word: as, a *literal* translation. 3. *a*) based on the actual words in their ordinary meaning; not figurative or symbolical: as, the *literal* meaning of a passage. *b*) giving the actual denotation of the word: said of the senses of words. *c*) giving the original or earlier meaning of a word; etymological: as, the *literal* meaning of *ponder* is *weigh.* 4. habitually interpreting statements or words according to their actual denotation; prosaic; matter-of-fact: as, a *literal* mind. 5. real; not going beyond the actual facts; accurate; unvarnished: as, the *literal* truth. 6. [Colloq.], virtual: used as an intensive: see **literally.** Abbreviated **lit.** (in senses 2 & 3).

lit·er·al·ism (lit'ẽr-əl-iz'm), *n.* 1. the tendency or disposition to take words, statements, etc. in their literal sense. 2. in *art*, thoroughgoing realism.

lit·er·al·ist (lit'ẽr-əl-ist), *n.* one given to literalism.

lit·er·al·is·tic (lit'ẽr-ə-lis'tik), *adj.* of, based on, or favoring literalism.

lit·er·al·i·ty (lit'ẽr-al'ə-ti), *n.* 1. the state or quality of being literal. 2. [*pl.* LITERALITIES (-tiz)], a literal meaning or interpretation.

lit·er·al·ize (lit'ẽr-ə-līz'), *v.t.* [LITERALIZED (-līzd'), LITERALIZING], 1. to make literal, as a translation. 2. to interpret according to the literal sense.

lit·er·al·ly (lit'ẽr-əl-i), *adv.* in a literal manner or sense; specifically, *a*) word for word; not imaginatively, figuratively, or freely: as, translate this passage *literally.* *b*) [Colloq.], virtually: used as an intensive, in a sense opposite to that above, as, he *literally* flew into the room: regarded by many as an erroneous usage. Abbreviated **lit.**

lit·er·al-mind·ed (lit'ẽr-əl-mīn'did), *adj.* unimaginative; prosaic.
lit·er·ar·i·ness (lit'ə-rer'i-nis), *n.* a literary quality.
lit·er·ar·y (lit'ə-rer'i), *adj.* [L. *litterarius, literarius*], 1. of, having the nature of, or dealing with literature. 2. appropriate to literature: as, he has a *literary* style. 3. *a*) skilled in learning and literature. *b*) making literature a profession. Abbreviated **lit.**
lit·er·ate (lit'ẽr-it), *adj.* [ME. *litterate;* L. *litteratus, literatus* < *littera, litera,* a letter; see LETTER], 1. educated; especially, able to read and write. 2. having or showing extensive knowledge, experience, or culture. 3. of or skilled in literature. *n.* a literate person.
lit·e·ra·ti (lit'ə-rā'tī, lit'ə-rä'ti), *n.pl.* [L. *litterati, literati,* learned, pl. of *litteratus, literatus;* see LITERATE], men of letters; scholarly or learned people.
‡lit·e·ra·tim (lit'ə-rā'tim), *adv.* [L. < *littera, litera,* a letter; see LETTER], letter for letter; literally.
lit·er·a·ture (lit'ẽr-ə-chẽr, lit'rə-choor'), *n.* [ME. *literature;* OFr. (Fr. *littérature*); L. *litteratura, literatura* < *littera, litera,* a letter; see LETTER], 1. the profession of an author; production of writings, especially of imaginative prose, verse, etc. 2. *a*) all writings in prose or verse, especially those of an imaginative or critical character, without regard to their excellence: often distinguished from scientific writing, news reporting, etc. *b*) all the writings of a particular time, country, region, etc.: as, American *literature. c*) all of such writings considered as having permanent value, excellence of form, great emotional effect, etc. *d*) all the writings dealing with a particular subject. 3. all the compositions for a specific musical instrument or ensemble. 4. [Colloq.], printed matter of any kind, as advertising, campaign leaflets, etc. Abbreviated **lit.**
-lith (lith), [Fr. *-lithe* < Gr. *lithos,* stone; cf. -LITE], a combining form meaning *stone,* as in *eolith, monolith.*
Lith., 1. Lithuania. 2. Lithuanian.
lith., 1. lithograph. 2. lithography.
li·thae·mi·a (li-thē'mi-ə), *n.* lithemia.
li·thae·mic (li-thē'mik), *adj.* lithemic.
lith·arge (lith'ärj, li-thärj'), *n.* [ME. & OFr. *litarge;* L. *lithargyrus;* Gr. *lithargyros,* spume or foam of silver < *lithos,* a stone + *argyros,* silver], a yellowish-red oxide of lead, PbO, made by heating lead in a current of air and used in the manufacture of glass, enamel, varnishes, paints, and insecticides.
lithe (līth), *adj.* [ME.; AS. *lithe,* soft, mild (< **linthi-*); akin to OHG. *lindi;* IE. base **lento-,* flexible, bendable, seen also in L. *lentus,* pliant, flexible, slow, Eng. *lime* (the tree) < AS. *lind* (cf. LINDEN); see LISSOME], bending easily; flexible; supple; limber.
li·the·mi·a (li-thē'mi-ə), *n.* [< *lithic* acid, uric acid + *-emia*], a condition in which there is an excess of uric acid or its salts in the blood, resulting from an incomplete metabolism of the nitrogen-containing compounds: also spelled **lithaemia.**
li·the·mic (li-thē'mik), *adj.* of or having lithemia.
lithe·some (līth'səm), *adj.* lithe; lissome.
lith·i·a (lith'i-ə), *n.* [Mod. L. < Gr. *lithos,* stone], lithium oxide, Li_2O, a white, crystalline compound. *adj.* containing a compound of lithium: as, *lithia* water.
li·thi·a·sis (li-thī'ə-sis), *n.* [Mod. L.; Gr. *lithiasis* < *lithos,* stone], the formation of calculi, or mineral concretions, in the body.
lithia water, a mineral water containing lithium salts, used as a diuretic and in the treatment of rheumatism.
lith·ic (lith'ik), *adj.* [Gr. *lithikos* < *lithos,* a stone], 1. of stone. 2. in *medicine,* of calculi, or uric-acid stones, formed in the bladder.
lith·ic (lith'ik), *adj.* in *chemistry,* of lithium.
-lith·ic (lith'ik), a combining form meaning *of a* (specified) *stage in the use of stone,* as in *neolithic.*
lith·i·um (lith'i-əm), *n.* [Mod. L. < Gr. *lithos,* a stone], a soft, silver-white, metallic chemical element, the lightest known metal: symbol, Li; at. wt., 6.940; at. no., 3.
lith·o- (lith'ə), [< Gr. *lithos,* a stone], a combining form meaning *stone, rock, calculus,* as in *lithosphere, lithograph:* also, before a vowel, **lith-.**
lith·o·graph (lith'ə-graf', lith'ə-gräf'), *n.* a print made by lithography. *v.i.* to make prints by this process. *v.t.* to reproduce (a picture, writing, etc.) by this process: abbreviated **lith., litho., lithog.**
li·thog·ra·pher (li-thog'rə-fẽr), *n.* a person who makes lithographs.
lith·o·graph·ic (lith'ə-graf'ik), *adj.* 1. of a lithograph or lithographs. 2. of, used in, or made by lithography.
lith·o·graph·i·cal (lith'ə-graf'i-k'l), *adj.* lithographic.
lith·o·graph·i·cal·ly (lith'ə-graf'i-k'l-i, lith'ə-graf'ik-li), *adv.* by lithography.
li·thog·ra·phy (li-thog'rə-fi), *n.* [*litho-* + *-graphy*], the art or process of printing from a flat stone or metal plate by a method based on the repulsion between grease and water: the design is put on the surface with a greasy material, and then water and printing ink are successively applied; the greasy parts, which repel water, absorb the ink, but the wet parts do not: abbreviated **lith., litho., lithog.**
lith·oid (lith'oid), *adj.* [Gr. *lithoeidēs;* see LITHO- & -OID], having the nature of a stone; stonelike.
li·thoi·dal (li-thoi'd'l), *adj.* lithoid.
li·thol·o·gy (li-thol'ə-ji), *n.* [*litho-* + *-logy*], the scientific study of rocks.
lith·o·marge (lith'ə-märj'), *n.* [< *litho-* + L. *marga,* marl], a smooth, closely packed clay, a variety of kaolin.
lith·o·phyte (lith'ə-fīt'), *n.* [*litho-* + *-phyte*], 1. a plantlike organism, as a coral, that is stony in structure. 2. a plant that grows on rock or stone.
lith·o·pone (lith'ə-pōn'), *n.* [< *litho-* + (?) L. *ponere,* to place, put: from being put on stone as paint], a white pigment made by mixing barium sulfate with zinc sulfide, used in paints, linoleum, etc.
lith·o·print (lith'ə-print'), *v.t.* & *v.i.* to lithograph. *n.* a lithographed book.
lith·o·sphere (lith'ə-sfêr'), *n.* [*litho-* + *sphere*], the solid, rocky part of the earth; earth's crust: distinguished from *atmosphere, hydrosphere.*
lith·o·tom·ic (lith'ə-tom'ik), *adj.* of lithotomy.
lith·o·tom·i·cal (lith'ə-tom'i-k'l), *adj.* lithotomic.
li·thot·o·my (li-thot'ə-mi), *n.* [LL. *lithotomia;* Gr. *lithotomia;* see LITHO- & -TOMY], in *surgery,* the surgical removal of a calculus, or mineral concretion, by cutting into the bladder.
li·thot·ri·ty (li-thot'ri-ti), *n.* [< *litho-* + L. *tritus,* pp. of *terere,* to grind, crush], the process of crushing a calculus in the bladder into very small pieces so that it can be eliminated in the urine.
Lith·u·a·ni·a (lith'oo-wā'ni-ə, lith'ū-ān'yə), *n.* a country in northeastern Europe annexed as the Lithuanian S.S.R. in August, 1940: abbreviated **Lith.**
Lith·u·a·ni·an (lith'oo-wā'ni-ən, lith'ū-ān'yən), *adj.* of Lithuania, its people, or their language. *n.* 1. a native or inhabitant of Lithuania. 2. the Baltic language of the Lithuanians. Abbreviated **Lith.**
Lithuanian Soviet Socialist Republic, a republic of the U.S.S.R., on the Baltic Sea: area, 22,800 sq. mi.; pop., 3,134,000; capital, Vilna.
lit·i·ga·ble (lit'i-gə-b'l), *adj.* that can be litigated, or contested in law.
lit·i·gant (lit'ə-gənt), *adj.* [Fr.; L. *litigans*], engaged in or inclined to litigation. *n.* a party to a lawsuit.
lit·i·gate (lit'ə-gāt'), *v.t.* [LITIGATED (-id), LITIGATING], [< L. *litigatus,* pp. of *litigare,* to dispute, carry on a suit < *lis, litis,* dispute (cf. LOATH) + *agere,* to do], to contest in a lawsuit. *v.i.* to carry on a lawsuit.
lit·i·ga·tion (lit'ə-gā'shən), *n.* 1. the act or process of carrying on a lawsuit; litigating. 2. a lawsuit.
lit·i·ga·tor (lit'ə-gā'tẽr), *n.* a person who litigates.
li·ti·gious (li-tij'əs), *adj.* [ME.; Late OFr. *litigieux;* L. *litigiosus* < *litigium,* strife < *litigare;* see LITIGATE], 1. given to carrying on lawsuits; quarrelsome. 2. disputable at law. 3. of lawsuits.
lit·mus (lit'məs), *n.* [Anglo-Fr. *lytemoise;* ON. *litmose,* lichen used in dyeing < *litr,* color + *mosi,* moss; cf. D. *lakmoes* (< base of *lēken,* to drip + *moes,* pulp), litmus], a purple coloring matter obtained from various lichens and used as an acid-base indicator in chemical analysis: it turns blue in bases and red in acids.
litmus paper, absorbent paper treated with litmus and used as an acid-base indicator.
li·to·tes (lī'tə-tēz'), *n.* [Mod. L.; Gr. *litotēs* < *litos,* smooth, simple, plain], a figure of speech in which something is expressed by a negation of the contrary. Examples: not a few (meaning "many"), no rare occurrence (meaning "a frequent occurrence").
li·tre (lē'tẽr), *n.* a liter.
Litt.B., *Lit(t)erarum Baccalaureus,* [L.], Bachelor of Letters; Bachelor of Literature: also **Lit.B.**
Litt.D., *Lit(t)erarum Doctor,* [L.], Doctor of Letters; Doctor of Literature: also **Lit.D.**
lit·ten (lit''n), *adj.* [falsely assumed pp. of *light, v.*], [Poetic], lighted: usually in compounds.
lit·ter (lit'ẽr), *n.* [ME. *liter, litere;* OFr. *litiere;* ML. *lectaria* < L. *lectus,* a couch], 1. a framework having long horizontal shafts near the bottom and enclosing a couch on which a person can be carried. 2. a stretcher for carrying the sick or wounded. 3. straw, hay, leaves, etc. used as bedding for animals, as a protective covering for plants, as scratch material for fowl, etc. 4. the young borne at one time by a dog, cat, or other animal which normally produces several young at birth. 5. things lying about in disorder; rubbish. 6. untidiness; disorder. 7. in *forestry,* the surface layer of the forest floor, in which the leaves are slightly decomposed. *v.t.* 1. to supply with a bed, covering, etc. of straw, hay, etc. 2. to bring forth (a number of young) at one time: said of certain animals. 3. to make untidy (often with *up*): as, he *littered* (*up*) the floor with peanut hulls. 4. to scatter about in a careless manner. *v.i.* to bring forth a number of young at one time: said of certain animals.
lit·té·ra·teur (lit'ẽr-ə-tũr'; Fr. lē'tā'rȧ'tẽr'), *n.* [Fr.], a literary man; man of letters: also written **litterateur.**
lit·ter·bug (lit'ẽr-bug'), *n.* a person who litters highways or other public places with waste paper, garbage, etc.
lit·ter·y (lit'ẽr-i), *adj.* 1. serving as or serviceable for litter, or bedding. 2. covered with litter; untidy.

lit·tle (lit′'l), ***adj.*** [LITTLER (-ẽr, lit′lẽr) or LESS (les) or LESSER (les′ẽr), LITTLEST (-ist, lit′list) or LEAST (lēst)], [ME. *littel, lutil;* AS. *lytel* (akin to G. dial. *lützel*) < base of AS. *lyt,* small; IE. base **leud-*, to stoop, seen also in AS. *lutan,* to stoop, bend (see LOUT), but prob. with cross influence of IE. base **leid-*, to joke, play, seen in Goth. *leitils* (ON. *lītill,* etc.), little], **1.** small in size; not big, large, or great. **2.** small in amount, number, or degree; not much. **3.** short in duration or distance; brief; not long. **4.** small in importance or power: as, the rights of the *little* man. **5.** small in force, intensity, etc.; weak. **6.** trivial; trifling. **7.** lacking in breadth of vision; narrow-minded; illiberal: as, a *little* mind. **8.** young: of children or animals. Sometimes used with implications of pleasing or endearing qualities, as, bless your *little* heart. ***adv.*** [LESS (les), LEAST (lēst)], **1.** in a small degree; to a slight extent; only slightly; not much. **2.** not in the least: as, he *little* suspects the plot. ***n.*** **1.** a small amount, degree, etc.: as, *little* will be done about it. **2.** a short time or distance. —***SYN.*** see **small.**

in little, on a small scale; in miniature.
little by little, by slow degrees or small amounts; gradually.
make little of, to consider or treat as not very important; pay little attention to; depreciate.
not a little, very much; very.
think little of, 1. to consider as not very important or valuable. **2.** to have no hesitancy about.

Little America, the operational base used by the Admiral Byrd expeditions in the Antarctic.
Little Bear, the constellation Ursa Minor.
Little Corporal, Napoleon Bonaparte.
Little Dipper, a group of stars in the constellation Ursa Minor (the Little Bear), supposed to outline a dipper.
little finger, the finger farthest from the thumb; smallest finger.
Little Fox, Vulpecula, a small northern constellation.
Little Horn, a river in southern Montana, flowing into the Big Horn River: at the junction of the two rivers, a battle (Battle of Little Big Horn, 1876) was fought in which Custer's troops were massacred by Sioux Indians led by Sitting Bull.
little hours, in the *Roman Catholic Church,* the hours of prime, tierce, sext, and none.
Little John, in *English legend,* a famous member of Robin Hood's band.
lit·tle·neck (lit′'l-nek′), [< *Little Neck,* Long Island], ***n.*** the young of the quahog, a round, thick-shelled clam, usually eaten raw: also **littleneck clam.**
little office, in the *Roman Catholic Church,* an office similar to but shorter than the breviary; especially, such an office in honor of the Virgin Mary.
little people, the fairies.
Little Rock, the capital of Arkansas, on the Arkansas River: pop., 108,000.
Little Russia, southwestern European Russia; the Ukraine and regions near it.
Little Russian, Ukrainian.
little slam, in *bridge,* the winning of all but one trick.
Little St. Bernard, a mountain pass in the Alps, between France and Italy.
little theater, 1. a theater of a small community, college, or art group, usually noncommercial and amateur, that produces experimental or low-cost drama. **2.** experimental drama, or drama of limited audience appeal, as produced by such theaters.
lit·tlish (lit′'l-ish, lit′lish), ***adj.*** rather little.
lit·to·ral (lit′ə-rəl), ***adj.*** [Fr.; L. *littoralis, litoralis* < *littus, litus,* seashore, coast], of, on, or along the shore. ***n.*** the region along the shore.
li·tu (lē′tōō), ***n.*** plural of **litas.**
li·tur·gic (li-tũr′jik), ***adj.*** liturgical.
li·tur·gi·cal (li-tũr′ji-k'l), ***adj.*** [Gr. *leitourgikos*], of or connected with liturgies or public worship.
li·tur·gics (li-tũr′jiks), ***n.pl.*** [construed as sing.], the science of public worship; study of liturgies.
lit·ur·gist (lit′ẽr-jist), ***n.*** **1.** a person who uses, or advocates the use of, a liturgy. **2.** an authority on or compiler of liturgies.
lit·ur·gy (lit′ẽr-ji), ***n.*** [*pl.* LITURGIES (-jiz)], [Fr. *liturgie;* ML. *liturgia;* Gr. *leitourgia;* ult. < *leōs, laos,* people + *ergon,* work], **1.** prescribed forms or ritual for public worship in any of various Christian churches. **2.** the Eucharistic service: called *Divine Liturgy* in the Orthodox Eastern Church and *Mass* in the Roman Catholic Church.
Lit·vi·nov, Max·im (mák-sēm′ lit-vē′nôf), 1876–1951; Soviet Russian statesman.
liv·a·ble (liv′ə-b'l), ***adj.*** **1.** fit or pleasant to live in; habitable: said of a house, room, etc. **2.** that can be lived through; endurable: said of life or of a specified sort of existence. **3.** ‡agreeable to live with (often followed by *with*): said of a person. Also spelled **liveable.**

live (liv), ***v.i.*** [LIVED (livd), LIVING], [ME. *liven, livien;* AS. *lifian, libban* < base of *lif* (see LIFE); akin to G. *leben,* Goth. *liban,* etc.], **1.** to be alive; have life. **2.** *a)* to remain alive. *b)* to last; endure. **3.** *a)* to pass life in a specified manner: as, they *lived* wretchedly. *b)* to regulate or conduct one's life; govern one's way of life: as, the Spartans *lived* by a rigorous discipline. **4.** to enjoy a full and varied life. **5.** to maintain life; support oneself: as, she *lives* on twenty dollars a week. **6.** to feed; subsist; have as one's usual food: as, bats *live* on insects and fruit. **7.** to make one's dwelling; reside. **8.** to remain in the memory of man: as, their evil deeds *live* after them. **9.** to remain afloat under trying conditions: said of a ship. ***v.t.*** **1.** to practice or carry out in one's life: as, he *lives* his faith. **2.** to spend; pass: as, she *lived* a useful life.

live and let live, to do as one pleases and let other people do the same; be tolerant.
live down, to live in such a way as to wipe out the memory or shame of (some fault, misdeed, etc.).
live high, to live in luxury.
live in, in domestic service, to sleep at one's place of work.
live out, 1. to live until the end of; last through. **2.** in domestic service, to sleep away from one's place of work.
live through, to experience and survive; endure.
live up to, 1. to live or act in accordance with (one's ideals, reputation, etc.). **2.** to fulfill (something expected).
live well, 1. to live in luxury. **2.** to lead a virtuous life.
live with, 1. to dwell with; be a lodger at the home of. **2.** to cohabit with.

live (līv), ***adj.*** [short for *alive*], **1.** having life; not dead. **2.** of the living state or living beings. **3.** energetic; wide-awake: as, the company needs a *live* executive. **4.** of immediate or present interest: as, a *live* campaign issue. **5.** still burning or glowing: as, a *live* spark. **6.** not burned; unstruck: as, a *live* match. **7.** unexploded: as, a *live* shell. **8.** unused; unexpended: as, *live* steam. **9.** bright; vivid: as, a *live* color. **10.** carrying electrical current: as, a *live* wire. **11.** in the native state; not quarried or mined: as, *live* rocks. **12.** stirring or swarming with living beings. **13.** fresh; pure: said of the air. **14.** involving an appearance or performance in person, rather than a filmed or recorded one: as, a *live* concert broadcast from New York. **15.** in *mechanics,* imparting motion or power. **16.** in *printing,* set up ready to be printed.
live·a·ble (liv′ə-b'l), ***adj.*** livable.
live center, the center in the revolving spindle of a lathe or other machine on which work is turned.
-lived (livd; *occas., by mistaken etym.,* līvd), [< *life* + *-ed*], a combining form used in hyphenated compounds, meaning *having* (a specified kind or duration of) *life or* (a specified number of) *lives,* as in *short-lived.*
live-for·ev·er (liv′fẽr-ev′ẽr), ***n.*** an evergreen plant that grows by attaching itself to rocks and walls and is much used in rock gardens.
live·li·hood (līv′li-hood′), ***n.*** [ME. *livelode;* AS. *liflad* (**lifgelad*), course of life; *lif* (see LIFE) + *-lad,* course (see LODE); akin to OHG. *libleita;* modern form due to confusion with *lively* & *-hood*], means of living or of supporting life; subsistence.
live·li·ly (līv′lə-li), ***adv.*** in a lively manner.
live·li·ness (līv′li-nis), ***n.*** the quality or condition of being lively.
live load, any moving load, not constant in its application, which a bridge or other structure carries in addition to its own weight.
live·long (liv′lôŋ′), ***adj.*** [ME. *lefe longe,* lit., lief long (cf. LIEF), phr. in which the first word is merely intens.; cf. G. *die liebe lange nacht,* lit., the lief long night; the ME. phr. has been confused with *live* & *long*], long or tediously long in passing; whole; entire: as, the *livelong* day.
live·ly (līv′li), ***adj.*** [LIVELIER (-li-ẽr), LIVELIEST (-li-ist)], [ME. *liflich;* AS. *liflic;* see LIFE & -LY], **1.** [Rare], lifelike. **2.** full of life; active; vigorous. **3.** full of spirit; exciting; animated: as, a *lively* session of the council. **4.** showing or inspiring liveliness; gay; cheerful. **5.** moving quickly and lightly, as a dance. **6.** brisk: as, a *lively* breeze. **7.** vivid; keen; intense: as, *lively* colors. **8.** bounding back with, or having, great resilience: as, a *lively* ball. ***adv.*** in a lively manner.

SYN.—**lively** implies a being full of life and energy and suggests an active or vigorous quality in something (a *lively* dance, talk, etc.); **animated** is applied to that which is made alive or bright and suggests a spirited quality (an *animated* face, discussion, etc.); **vivacious** and, more emphatically, **sprightly** suggest buoyancy of spirit or sparkling brightness (a *vivacious* manner, a *sprightly* tune); **gay** suggests lightheartedness and unrestrained good spirits (a *gay* life).—***ANT.*** dull.

liv·en (līv′ən), ***v.t.*** & ***v.i.*** [< *live, adj.* + *-en*], to make or become lively or gay; cheer (often with *up*).

Li·ven·za (lē-ven'tsä), *n.* a river in northeastern Italy, flowing from the Alps to the Adriatic: length, 70 mi.
live oak, 1. a wide-spreading, evergreen oak native to the southeastern United States. 2. the hard wood of this tree, used in shipbuilding and other construction.
liv·er (liv'ẽr), *n.* [ME. *livere, livre; AS. lifer;* akin to G. *leber;* prob. < IE. **liperos,* fat (cf. Gr. *lipos*), with reference to fattened livers as food], 1. the largest glandular organ in vertebrate animals, located in the upper part of the abdomen: it secretes bile, has an important function in carbohydrate, fat, and protein metabolism, and contains a substance essential to the normal production of red blood cells. 2. the flesh of this organ in cattle, fowl, etc., used as food. 3. a similar organ or tissue in invertebrate animals. 4. the liver thought of as the seat of emotion or desire.

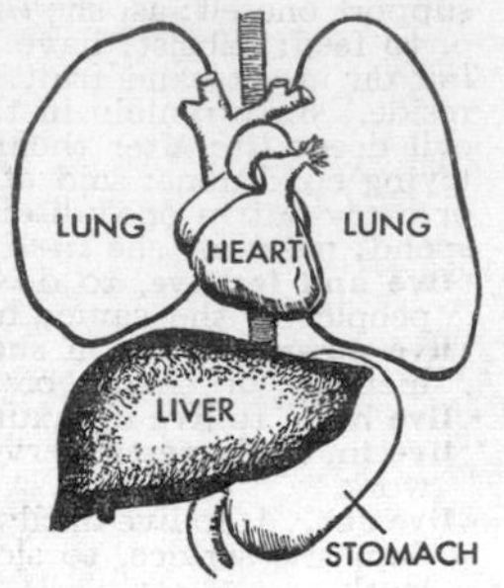

LIVER

liv·er (liv'ẽr), *n.* a person who lives (in a specified way or place): as, a plain *liver.*
liv·er-col·ored (liv'ẽr-kul'ẽrd), *adj.* reddish-brown to purplish-brown.
liver extract, an extract consisting of the water-soluble, nonprotein constituents of fresh mammalian liver, used in treating pernicious anemia.
liv·er·ied (liv'ẽr-id), *adj.* wearing a livery.
liv·er·ish (liv'ẽr-ish), *adj.* [Colloq.], 1. having a disordered liver; bilious; hence, 2. having or displaying a sour disposition; peevish; cross.
Liv·er·pool (liv'ẽr-po͞ol'), *n.* a seaport in Lancashire, England, on the River Mersey: pop., 752,000 (est. 1947).
liver spot, a yellowish-brown spot or patch on the skin, especially one caused by faulty functioning of the liver.
liv·er·wort (liv'ẽr-wũrt'), *n.* [ME.; see LIVER & WORT: so called from having liver-shaped parts], 1. any of a group of green, red, purple, or yellow-brown plants, undifferentiated as to stems and leaves: they somewhat resemble the mosses, together with which they constitute the bryophytes. 2. a hepatica.
liv·er·wurst (liv'ẽr-wũrst'), *n.* [*liver* + G. *wurst,* sausage], a sausage containing ground liver.
liv·er·y (liv'ẽr-i), *n.* [*pl.* LIVERIES (-iz)], [ME. *livere,* allowance of food, gift of clothes to a servant, thing delivered; OFr. *livree,* pp. of *livrer,* to deliver; L. *liberare,* to free], 1. an identifying uniform such as was formerly worn by feudal retainers or is now worn by servants or those in some particular group, trade, etc. 2. the people wearing such uniforms. 3. characteristic dress or appearance. 4. the keeping and feeding of horses for a fixed charge. 5. the keeping of horses, vehicles, or both, for hire. 6. a livery stable. 7. in *law,* the legal delivery of property, especially landed property, into the hands of the new owner.
livery company, any of the London city companies that grew out of earlier trade guilds, characterized by a distinctive dress.
liv·er·y·man (liv'ẽr-i-mən), *n.* [*pl.* LIVERYMEN (-mən)], 1. formerly, a liveried retainer or servant. 2. a member of any of the London city companies. 3. a person who owns or works in a livery stable.
livery stable, a stable where horses and carriages can be had for hire, or where horses are kept and fed for a fixed charge.
lives (līvz), *n.* plural of **life.**
live steam, steam that comes directly from the boiler, before its expansion in work, as distinguished from exhaust steam.
live·stock (līv'stok'), *n.* domestic animals kept for use on a farm or raised for sale and profit.
live wire, 1. a wire carrying an electric current. 2. [Colloq.], a person who is alert and energetic.
liv·id (liv'id), *adj.* [< Fr. or L.; Fr. *livide;* L. *lividus,* akin to *livere,* to be black and blue; IE. base *(*s*)*līweyō-,* seen also in AS. *slah,* sloe, OSlav. *sliva,* plum], 1. discolored by a bruise; black-and-blue: said of the flesh. 2. grayish-blue; lead-colored: as, *livid* with rage. —*SYN.* see **pale.**
li·vid·i·ty (li-vid'ə-ti), *n.* a livid quality or state.
liv·ing (liv'iŋ), *adj.* 1. alive; having life; not dead. 2. full of vigor; in active operation or use: as, a *living* institution. 3. of persons alive: as, within *living* memory. 4. gushing forth; flowing: as, a *living* stream. 5. still spoken as a native tongue: said of a language. 6. true; lifelike; exact: now mainly in the phrase *the living image.* 7. *a*) of life or the sustaining of life: as, *living* conditions. *b*) enough to maintain a reasonable standard of existence: as, a *living* wage. *n.* 1. the state of being alive. 2. the means of sustaining life; livelihood: as, he must work for a *living.* 3. the manner of existence: as, a higher standard of *living.* 4. in England, a church benefice.
the living, those that are still alive.
SYN.—**living** and **alive,** the latter usually a predicate adjective, are the simple basic terms for organisms having life or existence, **living** figuratively connoting continued existence or activity (a *living* faith) and **alive,** full force or vigor (prejudices kept *alive* by ignorance); **animate,** opposed to *inanimate,* is applied to living organisms as distinguished from lifeless ones or inorganic objects; **animated** is applied to inanimate things to which life or, in extended use, motion has been imparted (*animated* cartoons); **vital** is applied to that which is essential to organic life (*vital* functions) or to the energy, force, etc. manifested by living things.
living death, a life of unrelieved misery.
living picture, a tableau vivant.
living room, a room (in a home) furnished with sofas, chairs, etc., used as for conversation, reading, or entertaining guests, etc.: also called *parlor, sitting room.*
Livingston, Robert R., 1746–1813; American statesman; helped draft the Declaration of Independence.
Liv·ing·stone, David (liv'iŋ-stən), 1813–1873; Scottish missionary and explorer in Africa.
living wage, a wage sufficient to enable a person to maintain himself and his family in reasonable comfort.
Li·vo·ni·a (li-vō'ni-ə), *n.* a former province of the Russian Empire, on the Gulf of Riga: now part of the Latvian and Estonian republics of the U.S.S.R.
Li·vo·ni·an (li-vō'ni-ən), *n.* 1. a native or inhabitant of Livonia. 2. the High Lettish Baltic dialect spoken by some Livonians. *adj.* 1. of Livonia or its people. 2. of Livonian.
Li·vor·no (lē-vôr'nô), *n.* Leghorn, Italy.
li·vre (lē'vẽr; Fr. lē'vr'), *n.* [Fr. < L. *libra,* a pound], a former French money of account and a silver coin, originally equivalent in value to a pound of silver: it was gradually reduced in value and was replaced by the franc: abbreviated **lv.** (*sing. & pl.*).
Liv·y (liv'i), *n.* (*Titus Livius*), Roman historian; 59 B.C.–17 A.D.
lix·iv·i·ate (lik-siv'i-āt'), *v.t.* [LIXIVIATED (-id), LIXIVIATING], [see LIXIVIUM & -ATE], to leach.
lix·iv·i·a·tion (lik-siv'i-ā'shən), *n.* [< *lixiviate*], the process of leaching.
lix·iv·i·um (lik-siv'i-əm), *n.* [L. < *lix,* ashes, lye], a solution obtained by lixiviation, as lye.
liz·ard (liz'ẽrd), *n.* [ME. *lesarde;* OFr. *lesard* < L. *lacertus, lacerta,* lizard; cf. LEG], 1. any of a large group of reptiles with long slender bodies and tails, a scaly skin, and four legs, sometimes merely vestigial: most species live in hot, dry regions, as the gecko, horned lizard, chameleon, and iguana. 2. loosely, any of various similar animals, as the salamanders.
lizard fish, 1. any of a group of brightly-colored, tropical sea fishes with slender bodies, lizardlike heads, and large mouths. 2. in Australia, the saury.

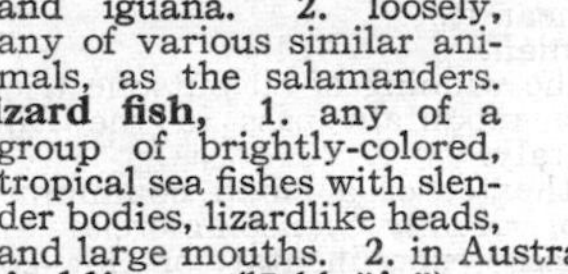

LIZARD (12 in. long)

Lju·blja·na (lū-blyä'nä), *n.* a city in northwestern Yugoslavia: pop., 60,000: German name, *Laibach.*
'll, contraction of **will** or **shall:** as, she'*ll* sing, I'*ll* go.
LL., L.L., 1. Late Latin. 2. Low Latin.
ll., lines.
l.l., *loco laudato,* [L.], in the place cited.
lla·ma (lä'mə), *n.* [*pl.* LLAMAS (-məz), LLAMA; see PLURAL, II, D, 1], [Sp. < Peruv. native name], 1. any of a group of South American animals related to the camel but smaller and without humps: it is used as a beast of burden and as a source of wool, meat, and milk. 2. cloth made from the woolly hair of this animal.
Llan·e·lly (lä-nel'i), *n.* a seaport in southern Wales: pop., 37,000.
lla·no (lä'nō; Sp. lyä'nô), *n.* [*pl.* LLANOS (-nōz; Sp. -nôs)], [Sp. < L. *planus,* plain], any of the level, grassy plains covering large areas in Spanish America.

LLAMA (3 ft. high at shoulder)

Lla·no Es·ta·ca·do (lä'nō es'tə-kä'dō; Sp. lyä'nô es'tä-kä'dô), [Sp., staked plain], a large plateau in southeastern New Mexico and western Texas: height, 1,000 to 5,000 ft.
L. Lat., 1. Late Latin. 2. Low Latin.
LL.B., *Legum Baccalaureus,* [L.], Bachelor of Laws.
LL.D., *Legum Doctor,* [L.], Doctor of Laws.

Llew·el·lyn (lōō-el′in), [W. *Llewelyn*, lit., prob., lionlike], a masculine name.
LL.M., *Legum Magister*, [L.], Master of Laws.
Lloyd (loid), [W. *Llwyd*, lit., gray], a masculine name.
Lloyd George, David (loid jôrj), 1863–1945; British statesman; prime minister (1916–1922); created Earl of Dwyfor in 1945.
Lloyd's (loidz), *n.* [< *Lloyd's* coffeehouse, meeting place of the original association], an association of insurance underwriters in London formed in the early 18th century to subscribe marine insurance policies and to publish shipping news: it now handles many kinds of insurance.
Lloyd's Register, an annual list of the seagoing vessels of all countries, stating their age, tonnage, classification as to seaworthiness, etc.: it is published by Lloyd's.
L.M., 1. Licentiate in Medicine. 2. Lord Mayor.
lo (lō), *interj.* [ME.; AS. *la*], look! see!: now mainly in *lo and behold!*
loach (lōch), *n.* [ME. & OFr. *loche* < Celt.], any of a group of small European fresh-water fishes of the carp family.
load (lōd), *n.* [ME. *lode; AS. lad*, a course, way, journey < base of *lædan*, to guide, direct (cf. LEAD, *v.*); influenced in sense by *lade;* akin to G. *leite* (cf. LIVELIHOOD)], 1. something carried or to be carried at one time or in one trip; burden; hence, 2. a measure of weight or quantity, varying with the type of conveyance: as, a *load* of wood. 3. something carried with difficulty; specifically, *a*) a heavy burden or weight. *b*) a great mental or spiritual burden: as, that's a *load* off my mind. 4. the weight borne up by a structure. 5. a single charge, as of powder and bullets, for a firearm. 6. *often in pl.* [Colloq.], a great amount or quantity: as, she has *loads* of friends. 7. the amount of time or work that an employee, especially a teacher, has contracted to carry: as, thirty hours a week is a heavy teaching *load*. 8. in *electricity*, the amount of current supplied by a dynamo or other source of electric power. 9. in *mechanics*, the amount of work performed by an engine, etc.; specifically, the external resistance offered to an engine by the machine that it is operating. *v.t.* 1. to put something to be carried into or upon; especially, to fill or cover with as much as can be carried: as, they *loaded* the boxcars with wheat. 2. to put into or upon a carrier: as, they *loaded* the wheat into the boxcars. 3. to weigh down with or as with a heavy load; burden; oppress. 4. to supply in large quantities; give much of something to: as, they *loaded* him with honors. 5. to put a charge of ammunition into (a firearm, etc.). 6. to put a roll of film or a plate into (a camera). 7. to add weight to, especially so as to make one end or one side heavier: as, he *loaded* the dice. 8. to add a foreign substance to; adulterate; doctor: as, they *loaded* the wine. 9. to phrase (a question or questions) in such a way that the desired answer cannot easily be evaded. *v.i.* 1. to put a charge of ammunition into a firearm. 2. to receive a charge of ammunition: as, these mortars *load* at the muzzle.
get a load of, [Slang], 1. to listen to or hear. 2. to look at or see.
have a load on, [Slang], to be intoxicated.
load displacement, the displacement of a completely loaded ship.
load·ed (lōd′id), *adj.* [pp. of *load*], 1. carrying a load. 2. having a charge of ammunition in it. 3. weighted; specifically, weighted on certain sides so as to fall with the desired sides up: said of fraudulent dice. 4. [Slang], intoxicated. 5. [Slang], well supplied with money.
load factor, in *electricity*, the ratio of average load to greatest load.
loading coil, a coil placed in an electric circuit to increase its inductance.
load line, the line along the sides of a ship marking the level to which the ship sinks when fully loaded.
load·star (lōd′stär′), *n.* a lodestar.
load·stone (lōd′stōn′), *n.* [*load, lode* + *stone*], 1. a strongly magnetic variety of the mineral magnetite. 2. something that attracts as with magnetic force. Also spelled **lodestone.**
loaf (lōf), *n.* [*pl.* LOAVES (lōvz)], [ME. *lof, loof;* AS. *hlaf;* akin to G. *laib;* IE. base **kloibho-*, prob., bread baked in a pan; widely borrowed < Gmc. in Baltic & Slavic languages], 1. a portion of bread baked in one piece, commonly in a standardized size convenient for table use. 2. a fairly large cake baked in one piece: also called *loaf cake*: opposed to *layer cake*. 3. any mass of food shaped somewhat like a loaf of bread and baked: as, a salmon *loaf*. 4. a piece of loaf sugar, usually shaped like a cone.
loaf (lōf), *v.i.* [prob. back-formation < *loafer*], 1. to loiter or lounge about doing nothing; idle. 2. to work in a lazy way, accomplishing little: as, he *loafs* on the job. *v.t.* to spend (time) idly (often with *away*). *n.* the act of loafing.
loaf·er (lōf′ẽr), *n.* [18th-c. Western New England dial., "one who owns but does not actively work his farm"; prob. < Hudson Valley D.; akin to LG. *lofen*, G. *laufen*, to run, as in G. *landläufer* (cf. LANDLOPER)], 1. a person who loafs; lounger; idler. 2. a moccasin-like sport shoe for informal wear.
loam (lōm), *n.* [ME. *lome;* AS. *lam;* for IE. base see LIME], 1. a rich soil composed of clay, sand, and some organic matter. 2. a mixture of clay, sand, and straw used in making foundry molds, plastering, etc. 3. popularly, any rich, dark soil. *v.t.* to fill or cover with loam.
loam·y (lōm′i), *adj.* [LOAMIER (-i-ẽr), LOAMIEST (-i-ist)], like or consisting of loam.
loan (lōn), *n.* [ME. *lone, lane* < ON. *lān* (akin to AS. *læn*, lending, loan, *lænan*, to lend); cf. LEND; the *v.* is chiefly < the *n.*, but ME. *lanen* (< ON. *lāna*) occurs occasionally], 1. the act of lending: as, thanks for the *loan* of your pen. 2. something lent; especially, a sum of money lent, often for a specified period and repayable with interest. *v.t.* & *v.i.* to lend.
loan collection, a collection of pictures, curios, etc. lent for temporary public exhibition.
Lo·an·da (lō-än′də), *n.* Luanda: former name.
loan office, 1. an office where loans are made. 2. a pawnshop. 3. a public office for receiving subscriptions to government loans, as formerly established in some States by the Revolutionary Continental government.
loan shark, [Colloq.], a person who lends money at exorbitant or illegal rates of interest.
loan society, a group of people who pay various sums into a fund which is then used as a source of loans to them and, sometimes, to others.
loan word, [after G. *lehnwort*], a word of one language adopted into another and naturalized. English examples: *kindergarten* (< German), *depot* (< French).
loath (lōth), *adj.* [ME. *loth(e);* AS. *lath*, hostile, hateful, loathsome; akin to G. *leid*, sorrow (orig. *adj.*); IE. base **leit-*, to detest, abhor, seen also by some authorities in L. *lis* (< **lit-s*), strife, dispute (cf. LITIGATE)], unwilling; reluctant (usually followed by an infinitive): as, they were *loath* to depart: sometimes spelled **loth.** —*SYN.* see **reluctant.**
nothing loath, not reluctant(ly); willing(ly).
loathe (lōth), *v.t.* [LOATHED (lōthd), LOATHING], [ME. *lothen, lothien;* AS. *lathian*, to be hateful < base of *lath;* see LOATH], to feel intense dislike, disgust, or hatred for; abhor; detest. —*SYN.* see **hate.**
loath·ful (lōth′fəl), *adj.* [Rare], loathsome.
loath·ing (lōth′iŋ), *n.* [< *loathe* + *-ing*], intense dislike, disgust, or hatred; abhorrence. —*SYN.* see **aversion.**
loath·ly (lōth′li; *also, formerly,* lōth′li), *adv.* [ME. *lothlie, lothliche,* AS. *lathlice;* see LOATH & -LY], [Rare], unwillingly; reluctantly.
loath·ly (lōth′li), *adj.* [ME. *lothli, lothelich;* AS. *lathlic;* see LOATHE & -LY], [Rare], loathsome.
loath·some (lōth′səm), *adj.* [ME. *lothsum;* see -SOME], causing loathing; disgusting; abhorrent; detestable.
loaves (lōvz), *n.* plural of **loaf.**
lob (lob), *n.* [ME. *lobbe, lob-* (& *Lobbe*, pers. name), lit., "heavy, hanging, thick" (cf. *lobbe*, pollack, spider, *lobfisch, lobkeling*, coalfish); prob. < LG. or ON.; akin to E.Fris., MLG. *lobbe*, hanging lump of flesh, hanging lip, etc.; IE. base **leubh-*, **leup-*, to hang limply], 1. [Dial.], a big, slow, clumsy person. 2. in *cricket*, a slow underhand throw. 3. in *tennis*, a stroke in which the ball is sent high into the air, usually with the intention of dropping it into the back of the opponent's court. *v.t.* [LOBBED (lobd), LOBBING], to throw, toss, etc. slowly and in a high curve; send (a ball) in a lob. *v.i.* 1. to move heavily and clumsily (often with *along*). 2. to lob a ball.
lo·bar (lō′bẽr), *adj.* [Mod. L. *lobaris*], of a lobe or lobes: as, *lobar* pneumonia.
lo·bate (lō′bāt), *adj.* [Mod. L. *lobatus*], having or formed into a lobe or lobes.
lo·bat·ed (lō′bā-tid), *adj.* lobate.
lo·ba·tion (lō-bā′shən), *n.* 1. lobate formation. 2. a lobe.
lob·ber (lob′ẽr), *n.* a person or thing that lobs.
lob·by (lob′i), *n.* [*pl.* LOBBIES (-iz)], [ML. *lobium, lobia;* see LODGE], 1. a hall or large anteroom; waiting room or vestibule, as of an apartment house, hotel, theater, etc. 2. a large hall adjacent to the assembly hall of a legislature and open to the public. 3. a group of lobbyists representing the same special interest: as, a cotton *lobby*. *v.i.* [LOBBIED (-id), LOBBYING], to act as a lobbyist. *v.t.* to get or try to get legislators to vote for (a measure) by acting as a lobbyist (often with *through*).
lob·by·ism (lob′i-iz′m), *n.* the practice of lobbying.
lob·by·ist (lob′i-ist), *n.* [*lobby* + *-ist*], a person who tries to get legislators to introduce or vote for measures favorable to a special interest that he represents.

lobe (lōb), *n.* [Fr.; LL. *lobus;* Gr. *lobos*], a rounded projecting part; specifically, *a*) the fleshy lower end of the human ear. *b*) any of the main divisions of an organ separated by fissures, etc.: as, a *lobe* of the brain, lung, or liver. *c*) any of the rounded divisions of the leaves of certain trees.

lo·bec·to·my (lō-bek'tə-mi), *n.* [< *lobe* + *-ectomy*], the surgical removal of a lobe, as of the brain, etc.

lobed (lōbd), *adj.* having a lobe or lobes; lobate; specifically, in *botany*, having lobes, or divisions, that extend less than halfway from the margin to the middle of the base: said of leaves.

lo·be·li·a (lō-bē'li-ə, lō-bēl'yə), *n.* [< Mod. L., after Matthias de *Lobel* (1538–1616), Fl. botanist, physician to James I], any of a large group of plants with long clusters of blue, red, or white flowers.

lob·lol·ly (lob'lol'i), *n.* [*pl.* LOBLOLLIES (-iz)], [16th-c.; prob. < *lob*, in basic sense "heavy, thick" + dial. *lolly*, broth, soup], 1. [Obs.], a thick gruel. 2. [Colloq.], a mudhole; muddy puddle. 3. *a*) any of various thick-barked pines of the southern United States. *b*) the wood of any of these trees: also **loblolly pine.**

loblolly boy, [*loblolly* in nautical sense of "stiff medicine"], [Obs.], the attendant of a ship's doctor.

lo·bo (lō'bō), *n.* [Sp.; L. *lupus*], the large, gray timber wolf of the western United States.

lo·bot·o·my (lō-bot'ə-mi), *n.* [< *lobe* + *-tomy*], a surgical operation in which a lobe of the brain, especially the frontal lobe of the cerebrum, is cut into or across, as in the treatment of certain psychoses.

lob·scourse (lob'skôrs', lob'skōrs'), *n.* lobscouse.

lob·scouse (lob'skous'), *n.* [*lob* in basic sense of "heavy, thick" + dial. *scouse*, stew], a sailor's stew of meat, vegetables, and ship's biscuit.

lob·ster (lob'stẽr), *n.* [*pl.* LOBSTERS (-stẽrz), LOBSTER; see PLURAL, II, D, 1], [ME. *lobstere, loppester;* AS. *loppestre, lopustre;* altered < L. *locusta*, locust, marine shellfish, after AS. *loppe*, spider (from the external resemblance); cf. G. *meerespinne*, lit., sea spider, lobster], 1. any of a group of edible sea crustaceans, with compound eyes, long antennae, and five pairs of legs, the first pair of which are modified into large, powerful pincers: lobsters are greenish or dark gray in color when alive, but turn bright red when boiled. 2. the flesh of this animal used as food. 3. the spiny lobster.

lobster pot, a basketlike trap for lobsters.

lobster ther·mi·dor (thũr'mi-dôr'), [cf. THERMIDOR], a dish consisting of lobster flesh, mushrooms, etc. in a sauce, served in half of a lobster shell.

lob·u·lar (lob'yoo-lẽr), *adj.* of or like a lobule or lobules.

lob·ule (lob'ūl), *n.* [Fr.; Mod. L. *lobulus*, dim.], 1. a small lobe. 2. a subdivision of a lobe.

lob·worm (lob'wũrm'), *n.* a lugworm.

lo·cal (lō'k'l), *adj.* [Fr.; LL. *localis* < L. *locus*, a place], 1. relating to place. 2. of, characteristic of, or confined to a particular place: as, items of *local* interest. 3. restricted; narrow; confined: as, *local* outlook. 4. of or for a particular part or specific area of the body. 5. making all stops along its run: as, a *local* train. *n.* 1. a local train, bus, etc. 2. a newspaper item relating to a particular community and having interest only to the residents of it. 3. a chapter or branch of a larger organization, especially of a labor union.

local color, customs and other features characteristic of a certain region or time, introduced into a novel, play, etc. to supply realism.

lo·cale (lō-kal', lō-käl'), *n.* [Fr. *local*], a place; locality, especially with reference to events or circumstances connected with it.

local government, 1. government of the affairs of a town, district, etc. by the people living there. 2. the people chosen to administer this government.

lo·cal·ism (lō'k'l-iz'm), *n.* 1. a way of acting or speaking peculiar to one locality; local custom. 2. a word, meaning, expression, pronunciation, etc. peculiar to one locality. 3. attachment to a particular locality. 4. provincialism.

lo·cal·i·ty (lō-kal'ə-ti), *n.* [*pl.* LOCALITIES (-tiz)], [Fr. *localité;* LL. *localitas;* see LOCAL], 1. position with regard to surrounding objects, landmarks, etc.: as, a sense of *locality*. 2. a place; district; neighborhood.

lo·cal·i·za·tion (lō'k'l-i-zā'shən, lō'k'l-ī-zā'shən), *n.* a localizing or being localized.

lo·cal·ize (lō'k'l-īz'), *v.t.* [LOCALIZED (-īzd'), LOCALIZING], 1. to make local; limit or confine to a particular place, area, or locality. 2. to determine the specific local origin of, as a tradition.

lo·cal·ly (lō'k'l-i), *adv.* 1. in a local way; with respect to place. 2. within a given area or areas: as, the tornado did much damage *locally*.

local option, the right of determining by a vote of the residents whether something, especially the sale of intoxicating liquors, shall be permitted, restricted, or forbidden in their locality.

Lo·car·no (lō-kär'nō), *n.* a town in southern Switzerland, on Lake Maggiore: pop., 6,600: a series of peace pacts was signed there in 1925 by Germany and six Allied nations of World War I.

lo·cate (lō'kāt, lō-kāt'), *v.t.* [LOCATED (-id), LOCATING], [< L. *locatus*, pp. of *locare*, to place < *locus*, a place], 1. to mark off or designate the site of, as a mining claim. 2. to establish in a certain place: as, his offices are *located* on the third floor. 3. to discover the position of after a search: as, he *located* the seat of the trouble. 4. to show the position of: as, *locate* Guam for me on this map. 5. to assign to a particular place, function, occupation, etc. *v.i.* [Colloq.], to settle: as, he *located* in Cleveland.

lo·ca·tion (lō-kā'shən), *n.* [L. *locatio*], 1. a locating or being located. 2. position in space; place where a factory, house, etc. is; situation. 3. an area marked off or designated for a specific purpose. 4. an outdoor set, away from the studio, where scenes for a motion picture are photographed.

loc·a·tive (lok'ə-tiv), *adj.* [< pp. of L. *locare* (see LOCATE) after L. *vocativus*, vocative], in *grammar*, designating or of a case expressing place at which or in which, as in Latin, Greek, Sanskrit, etc. *n.* 1. the locative case. 2. a word in the locative case.

loc. cit., *loco citato*, [L.], in the place cited.

loch (lok, lokh), *n.* [Gael. & OIr.; for IE. base see LAKE], [Scot.], 1. a lake. 2. an arm of the sea, especially when narrow and nearly surrounded by land.

lo·chi·a (lō'ki-ə, lok'i-ə), *n.* [Mod. L. < Gr. *lochia*, neut. pl. of *lochios*, of childbirth < *lochos*, childbirth], the discharge from the vagina for several weeks after childbirth.

Loch·in·var (lok'in-vär', lokh'in-vär'), *n.* the hero of a ballad in Scott's *Marmion*, who boldly rides off with his sweetheart just as she is about to be married to another.

lo·ci (lō'sī), *n.* plural of **locus.**

lock (lok), *n.* [ME. *lokke;* AS. *loc*, a bolt, bar, enclosure, prison; akin to G. *loch*, a hole, ON. *lok*, a lid; prob. IE. base **leug-*, to bend, seen also in AS. *lucan*, to close (cf. LEEK)], 1. a mechanical device furnished with a spring and bolt, for fastening a door, strongbox, etc. by means of a key or combination. 2. anything that fastens something else and prevents it from opening, turning, etc. 3. a locking together; jam. 4. an enclosed part of a canal, waterway, etc. equipped with gates so that the level of the water can be changed to raise or lower boats from one level to another. 5. the mechanism of a firearm used to explode the ammunition charge. 6. in *engineering*, an airtight room opening into a compartment where the air is under compression. 7. in *wrestling*, any of several holds: as, an arm *lock*. *v.t.* 1. to fasten (a door, trunk, etc.) by means of a lock. 2. to shut (*up*, *in*, or *out*); confine: as, he was *locked* in the closet. 3. to fit; link; intertwine: as, we *locked* arms. 4. to embrace tightly. 5. to jam together so as to make immovable: as, the gears are *locked*. 6. to equip (a canal, etc.) with a lock or locks. 7. to move or pass (a ship) through a lock. *v.i.* 1. to become locked. 2. to be capable of being locked. 3. to intertwine or interlock; link together. 4. to close tightly and firmly: as, his jaws *locked*. 5. to jam, as gears.

LOCK IN CANAL

lock away, to store or safeguard in a locked box, container, etc.

lock out, 1. to shut out by or as by locking the door against. 2. to keep (workers) from a place of employment in an attempt to make them accept the employer's terms.

lock, stock, and barrel, [Colloq.], completely.

lock up, 1. to fasten the doors of (a house, etc.) by means of locks. 2. to enclose or store in a locked container. 3. to put in jail.

under lock and key, locked up; safely put away.

lock (lok), *n.* [ME. *lokke;* AS. *loc* (akin to G. *locke*); basic sense "a bend, twist"; IE. base as in prec. *lock*], 1. a curl of hair; ringlet; hence, 2. *pl.* [Poetic], the hair of the head. 3. a tuft of wool, cotton, etc.

lock·age (lok'ij), *n.* [see -AGE], 1. the act of moving a ship from one water level to another by means of a lock. 2. the charge for such service. 3. the construction or operation of locks in a canal, etc. 4. the amount of rise and fall effected by a lock or locks in a canal, etc.

Locke, David Ross (lok), (pseudonym *Petroleum V. Nasby*), 1833–1888; American humorist.

Locke, John, 1632–1704; English empirical philosopher.

lock·er (lok'ẽr), *n.* 1. a person or thing that locks. 2. a chest, closet, compartment, drawer, etc., usually of metal, which can be fastened with a lock, especially such a container for individual use. 3. a chest or compartment in a ship's cabin to store things in.

locker room, a room equipped with lockers, especially one used as a place for changing and storing one's clothes, as in a gymnasium, club, etc.

lock·et (lok′it), *n.* [ME. *loket;* OFr. *locquet, loquet,* dim. of *loc,* a latch, lock < Frank. *lok, akin to AS. *loc;* see LOCK], a small, hinged case of gold, silver, or other metal, for holding a picture, lock of hair, etc.: it is usually worn suspended from a necklace.

lock·jaw (lok′jô′), *n.* [short for earlier *locked jaw*], a form of the disease tetanus, in which the jaws become firmly closed because of spasmodic muscular contraction.

lock·nut (lok′nut′), *n.* a lock nut.

lock nut, 1. a thin nut screwed down hard on an ordinary nut to prevent the latter from working loose. 2. a specially designed nut that locks itself when screwed down tight.

lock·out (lok′out′), *n.* the refusal by an employer to allow his employees to come in to work unless they agree to his terms.

Lock·port (lok′pôrt′, lok′pōrt′), *n.* a city in western New York, on the New York State Barge Canal: pop., 26,000.

lock·smith (lok′smith′), *n.* a person whose work is making or repairing locks and keys.

lock step, a method of marching in such close file that the corresponding legs of the marchers must keep step precisely.

lock stitch, a stitch, as by a sewing machine, in which two threads are interlocked at short intervals.

lock·up (lok′up′), *n.* 1. a locking up. 2. a being locked up, as in jail. 3. a jail.

lo·co (lō′kō), *n.* [Sp., insane, mad], 1. the locoweed. 2. loco disease. *v.t.* [LOCOED (-kōd), LOCOING], 1. to poison with locoweed. 2. [Slang], to craze. *adj.* [Slang], crazy; demented.

lo·co- (lō′kō, lō′kə), [< L. *locus,* a place], a combining form meaning *from place to place,* as in *locomotive.*

‡lo·co ci·ta·to (lō′kō si-tā′tō), [L.], in the place cited or quoted: used in footnotes to refer to a previously cited passage: abbreviated **l.c., loc. cit.**

loco disease, a chronic nervous disease of horses, cattle, and sheep, caused by locoweed poisoning.

lo·co·fo·co (lō′kō-fō′kō), *n.* [*pl.* LOCOFOCOS (-kōz)], [said to be from a self-lighting cigar (c. 1834), called by the inventor (John Marck, of New York) a *locofoco* cigar, after *locomotive* interpreted as "self-moving" (as if *loco-* = "self"); hence, *loco-,* "self" + It. *fuoco,* fire; see LOCO- & FOCUS], 1. originally, a friction cigar or match. 2. *a)* [L-], a faction of the Democratic Party (c. 1835), called the Equal Rights party. *b)* a member of this faction. 3. formerly, any Democrat.

lo·co·mo·bile (lō′kə-mō′bil), *adj.* [*loco-* (cf. prec.) + *mobile*], [Rare], moving by its own power; self-propelling.

lo·co·mo·tion (lō′kə-mō′shən), *n.* [*loco-* + *motion*], motion, or the power of moving, from one place to another: as, walking is a form of *locomotion.*

lo·co·mo·tive (lō′kə-mō′tiv), *adj.* [< *loco-* + LL. *motivus,* moving], 1. of locomotion. 2. moving or capable of moving from one place to another; not stationary. 3. of engines that move under their own power: as, *locomotive* design. *n.* an engine that can move about by its own power; especially, an electric, steam, or diesel engine on wheels, designed to push or pull a railroad train.

lo·co·mo·tor (lō′kə-mō′tēr), *n.* [*loco-* + L. *motor,* mover], a person or thing with power of locomotion. *adj.* of locomotion.

locomotor ataxia, a chronic disease of the nervous system, usually caused by syphilis: it is characterized at first by intense pain, and later by disturbances of sensations, loss of reflexes and of muscular co-ordination, functional disorders of organs, etc.

‡lo·co pri·mo ci·ta·to (lō′kō prī′mō sī-tā′tō), [L.], in the place first cited: abbreviated **loc. primo cit.**

lo·co·weed (lō′kō-wēd′), *n.* any of a number of plants of the pea family, with dense clusters of small flowers resembling sweet peas: it grows on western prairies and causes loco disease in sheep, horses, or cattle that have eaten it.

Lo·cris (lō′kris), *n.* a district of ancient Greece, on the Gulf of Corinth.

loc·u·lar (lok′yoo-lẽr), *adj.* in *botany* & *zoology,* of, having the nature of, or consisting of cells, or loculi.

loc·u·late (lok′yoo-lit, lok′yoo-lāt′), *adj.* locular.

loc·u·lat·ed (lok′yoo-lā′tid), *adj.* loculate.

loc·u·lus (lok′yoo-ləs), *n.* [*pl.* LOCULI (-lī′)], [L., dim. of *locus,* place], any small cavity, cell, or chamber in plant or animal tissue.

lo·cum te·nens (lō′kəm tē′nənz), [ML., holding the place; *locum,* acc. of *locus,* a place + *tenens,* ppr. of *tenere,* to hold; cf. LIEUTENANT], [Chiefly British], a person taking another's place for the time being; temporary substitute, as for a doctor or clergyman.

lo·cus (lō′kəs), *n.* [*pl.* LOCI (-sī)], [L.], 1. a place. 2. in *mathematics, a)* any system of points, lines, etc. which satisfies one or more given conditions. *b)* a line, plane, etc. every point of which satisfies a given condition and which contains no point that does not satisfy this condition. Abbreviated **L., l.**

‡lo·cus clas·si·cus (lō′kəs klas′i-kəs), [*pl.* LOCI CLASSICI (lō′sī klas′i-sī′)], [L.], a passage generally recognized as authoritative or illustrative of its subject and hence often cited.

‡lo·cus in quo (lō′kəs in kwō′), [L.], the place in which.

lo·cust (lō′kəst), *n.* [ME. & OFr. *locuste;* L. *locusta;* cf. LOBSTER], 1. any of various large winged insects related to the grasshoppers and crickets: certain locusts travel in large swarms destroying nearly all vegetation in their path. 2. a cicada. 3. a tree of the pulse family, common throughout the eastern United States: it has a compound leaf and clusters of fragrant white flowers: also called *black locust.* 4. the yellowish, exceedingly hard and durable wood of this tree. 5. the honey locust.

LOCUST (3 in. long)

lo·cu·tion (lō-kū′shən), *n.* [ME. *locucion;* L. *locutio,* a speaking < pp. of *loqui,* to speak], 1. a word, phrase, or expression. 2. a particular style of speech.

loc·u·to·ry (lok′yoo-tôr′i, lok′yoo-tō′ri), *n.* [ML. *locutorium* < L. *locutor,* speaker < pp. of *loqui,* to speak], a room set aside for conversation, as in a monastery.

lode (lōd), *n.* [sp. var. of *load* (ME. *lode,* AS. *lad*) retaining etym. senses "course, way," etc.], in *mining,* 1. a vein containing metallic ore and filling a well-defined fissure in the rock. 2. any deposit of ore separated from the adjoining rock.

lode·star (lōd′stär′), *n.* [ME. *lodesterre;* see LODE & STAR], 1. a star by which one directs his course; especially, the North Star. 2. a guiding ideal; model for imitation. Also spelled **loadstar.**

lode·stone (lōd′stōn′), *n.* a loadstone.

lodge (loj), *n.* [ME. *loge, logge,* hut, masons' workshop (whence sense 2); OFr. *loge,* summerhouse, arbor (cf. LOGE) < OHG. *louba, loupa,* upper roof, upper story, hut, etc. (G. *laube*); IE. base as in *leaf, loft;* cf. LOBBY], 1. a small house, especially one for a servant, or one for use during a special season: as, a caretaker's *lodge,* hunting *lodge.* 2. *a)* the place where members of a local chapter of an association, especially of a secret fraternal organization, hold their meetings. *b)* the local chapter itself. *c)* a meeting of such a chapter. Abbreviated **L., l.** 3. the den of a wild animal, particularly of a beaver. 4. *a)* the hut or tent of an American Indian. *b)* those who live in it. *v.t.* [LODGED (lojd), LODGING], 1. to provide with a place of temporary residence; house. 2. to rent rooms to; take as a paying guest. 3. to place or deposit for safekeeping. 4. to put or send into a place or position by shooting, thrusting, etc.; place; land (with *in*): as, he *lodged* an arrow in the deer's back. 5. to bring (an accusation, complaint, etc.) before legal authorities. 6. to confer (powers) upon (with *in*). 7. to beat down (growing crops), as rain. *v.i.* 1. to live in a certain place for a time. 2. to live (*with* another or *in* his home) as a paying guest. 3. to come to rest or be placed and remain firmly fixed (with *in*): as, the bullet *lodged* in her spine.

Lodge, Henry Cabot (loj), 1850–1924; American statesman and writer; United States senator (1893–1924).

Lodge, Sir Oliver Joseph, 1851–1940; English physicist and writer.

lodge·ment (loj′mənt), *n.* lodgment.

lodg·er (loj′ẽr), *n.* a person or thing that lodges; especially, one who lives in a rented room or rooms in another's home.

lodg·ing (loj′iŋ), *n.* [ME. *loggyng;* see LODGE, *v.*], 1. a place to live in, especially temporarily; quarters. 2. *pl.* a room or rooms rented in a private home.

lodging house, a rooming house.

lodg·ment (loj′mənt), *n.* [Fr. *logement*], 1. a lodging or being lodged. 2. a lodging place. 3. an accumulation of deposited material, often in the nature of an obstruction. 4. in *military science,* a foothold gained in territory held by the enemy. Also spelled **lodgement.**

Lo·di (lô′dē), *n.* a city in northern Italy: pop., 31,000.

Łódź (lodz; Pol. looj), *n.* a city in central Poland: pop., 698,000.

lo·ess (lō′is, lös), *n.* [G. *löss* < *lösen,* to loosen, dissolve], a fine-grained, yellowish-brown, extremely fertile loam deposited by the wind.

Löff·ler, Frie·drich Au·gust Jo·han·nes (frē′driH ou′goost yō-hän′is löf′lẽr), 1852–1915; German bacteriologist.

Lo·fo·ten Islands (lō′foo-t'n, lō-fō′t'n), a group of Norwegian islands northwest of Norway: area, 475 sq. mi.

loft (lôft, loft), *n.* [ME. *lofte;* Late AS. *loft* < ON. *lopt,* upper room, air, sky (akin to AS. *lyft,* air, sky); IE. base **leup-,* **leubh-,* to peel off (cf. LEAF, LEFT); basic sense "roof of peeled-off bark"], 1. *a*) an attic or atticlike space, usually not partitioned off into rooms, immediately below the roof of a house, barn, etc. *b*) any of the upper stories of a warehouse or factory. 2. a gallery: as, the choir *loft* in a church. 3. in *golf, a*) the slope given to the face of a club to aid in knocking the ball in a high curve. *b*) a stroke that knocks the ball in a high curve. *v.t.* 1. to store in a loft. 2. to provide with a loft. 3. in *golf, a*) to strike (a ball) in such a way as to knock it in a high curve. *b*) to hold (a club) so that the face slants back. *v.i.* in *golf,* to knock a ball in a high curve.

loft·er (lôf′tẽr, lof′tẽr), *n.* a golf club with a sloping face to aid in lofting the ball: also called *lofting iron.*

loft·i·ly (lôf′t'l-i, lof′t'l-i), *adv.* in a lofty manner.

loft·i·ness (lôf′ti-nis, lof′ti-nis), *n.* the quality or state of being lofty.

Lof·ting, Hugh (lôf′tiŋ), 1886–1948; English author and illustrator, especially of children's books.

loft·ing iron (lôf′tiŋ, lof′tiŋ), a lofter.

loft·y (lôf′ti, lof′ti), *adj.* [LOFTIER (-ti-ẽr), LOFTIEST (-ti-ist)], 1. very high: as, a *lofty* peak in the Alps. 2. elevated; noble; sublime; grand. 3. haughty; overproud; arrogant. —*SYN.* see **high.**

log (lôg, log), *n.* [ME. *logge;* prob. < MScand. dial. via the timber trade; akin to ON. *lāg* (Dan. *laag*), felled tree < base of *lie* (to recline)], 1. a section of the trunk of a felled tree, either in its natural state or cut up for use in building, as firewood, etc. 2. [so called because it was orig. a quadrant of wood], a device for measuring the speed of a ship: see also **log chip, log line, log reel.** 3. a daily record of a ship's speed and progress; logbook: in it are usually entered the ship's position and any notable events of the trip. 4. *a*) a record of the operating history of an aircraft or of its engines. *b*) a record of a pilot's flying time, experience, etc. 5. any record of progress, as on a journey, in an experiment, etc. *adj.* made of a log or logs. *v.t.* [LOGGED (lôgd, logd), LOGGING], 1. to saw (trees) into logs. 2. to cut down the trees of (a region). 3. to enter in a ship's log. 4. to sail (a specified distance) as indicated by a log. *v.i.* to cut down trees and transport the logs to a sawmill.

log- (lôg, log), logo-.

log, logarithm.

log., logic.

Lo·gan (lō′gən), *n.* 1. a city in northern Utah: pop., 19,000. 2. a mountain of the St. Elias Range, Yukon, Canada: height, 19,850 ft.

lo·gan·ber·ry (lō′gən-ber′i), *n.* [*pl.* LOGANBERRIES (-iz)], [after Judge J. H. *Logan,* of California, who developed it in 1881], 1. a hybrid bramble developed from the blackberry and the red raspberry and extensively grown for its fruit. 2. the highly acid, purplish-red fruit of this shrub.

Lo·gans·port (lō′gənz-pôrt′, lō′gənz-pōrt′), *n.* a city in northern Indiana: pop., 21,000.

log·a·oe·dic (lôg′ə-ē′dik, log′ə-ē′dik), *adj.* [L. *logaoedicus;* Gr. *logaoidikos* < *logos,* discourse, prose + *aoidē,* song: so named because the rhythm stands between that of prose and that of poetry], having a meter of combined dactyls and trochees or anapests and iambics. *n.* a logaoedic verse.

log·a·rithm (lôg′ə-rith'm, log′ə-rith'm), *n.* [Mod. L. *logarithmus* < Gr. *logos,* a word, proportion, ratio + *arithmos,* number], in *mathematics,* the exponent of the power to which a fixed number (the *base*) must be raised in order to produce a given number (the *antilogarithm*): logarithms are normally computed to the base of 10 and are used for shortening mathematical calculations: abbreviated **log** (no period).

log·a·rith·mic (lôg′ə-rith′mik, log′ə-rith′mik), *adj.* of a logarithm or logarithms.

log·a·rith·mi·cal·ly (lôg′ə-rith′mi-k'l-i, log′ə-rith′mik-li), *adv.* by means of logarithms.

log·book (lôg′book′, log′book′), *n.* a log (senses 3 & 4).

log chip, a flat piece of wood attached to a line and reel and thrown into the water to measure a ship's rate of speed.

loge (lōzh), *n.* [Fr.; see LODGE], any of a series of compartments in a theater, etc.; box.

log·ger (lôg′ẽr, log′ẽr), *n.* 1. a person whose work is logging; lumberjack. 2. a machine for loading logs on flat cars.

log·ger·head (lôg′ẽr-hed′, log′ẽr-hed′), *n.* [< *log* + *head*], 1. a stupid fellow; blockhead. 2. a long-handled tool with a ball, or bulb, at the end, used when heated to melt tar, heat liquids, etc. 3. a tropical sea turtle with a hard shell and a large head: also **loggerhead turtle.** 4. a post on a whaling ship around which a harpoon line is turned to keep it from running out too fast.

at loggerheads, in disagreement; in a quarrel.

loggerhead shrike, any of a variety of birds of the eastern United States, white below with black markings on the upper parts; common shrike.

log·gia (loj′i-ə, lô′jə; It. lôd′jä), *n.* [*pl.* LOGGIAS (-əz, -jəz), It. LOGGIE (-je)], [It.; see LODGE], an arcaded or roofed gallery built into or projecting from the side of a building, particularly one overlooking an open court.

LOGGIA

log·ging (lôg′iŋ, log′iŋ), *n.* the occupation of cutting down trees, cutting them into logs, and transporting them to the sawmill.

log·i·a (log′i-ə), *n.pl.* [*sing.* LOGION (-on′)], [Gr., *pl.,* sayings < *logos,* a word], maxims attributed to a religious leader; especially, [L-], sayings attributed to Jesus but not recorded in the Gospels.

log·ic (loj′ik), *n.* [ME. *logike,* OFr. *logique;* L. *logica;* Gr. *logikē* (*technē*), logical (art) < *logikos,* of speaking or reasoning < *logos,* a word, speech, reckoning, calculation, thought < *legein,* to speak], 1. the science of correct reasoning; science which deals with the criteria of valid thought. 2. a book dealing with this science. 3. correct reasoning; valid induction or deduction: as, *logic* shows us a better course. 4. way of reasoning, whether correct or incorrect: as, at this point our *logic* was at fault. 5. the system of principles underlying any art or science. 6. necessary connection or outcome, as through the working of cause and effect: as, the *logic* of events. Abbreviated **log.**

-log·ic (loj′ik), -logical.

log·i·cal (loj′i-k'l), *adj.* 1. of or used in the science of logic. 2. according to the principles of logic, or correct reasoning. 3. necessary or to be expected because of what has gone before; that follows as reasonable. 4. using or accustomed to use correct reasoning.

-log·i·cal (loj′i-k'l), [Gr. *-logikos* < *logikos;* see LOGIC], a suffix used to form adjectives corresponding to nouns ending in *-logy,* as in *biological, pathological.*

log·i·cal·i·ty (loj′i-kal′ə-ti), *n.* the quality of being logical; logical nature.

logical positivism, a movement in philosophy concerned with the unification of the sciences, especially by an analysis of the language of science and the consequent development of a vocabulary applicable to all sciences: also called *logical empiricism.*

lo·gi·cian (lō-jish′ən), *n.* an expert in logic.

log·i·on (log′i-on′), *n.* singular of **logia.**

lo·gis·tic (lə-jis′tik), *adj.* [< *logistics*], of logistics.

lo·gis·tic (lə-jis′tik), *adj.* [ML. *logisticus;* Gr. *logistikos,* skilled in calculation < *logizesthai,* to calculate < *logos,* a word, reckoning, calculation], of calculation. *n.* [Rare], the art of calculation; common arithmetic.

lo·gis·tics (lə-jis′tiks), *n.pl.* [construed as sing.], [Fr. *logistique* < *loger,* to quarter; see LODGE], the branch of military science having to do with moving, supplying, and quartering troops.

log line, a graduated line attached to a log chip.

log·o- (lôg′ō, log′ə), [< Gr. *logos;* see LOGIC], a combining form meaning *word, speech, discourse,* as in *logogram:* also, before a vowel, **log-.**

log·o·gram (lôg′ə-gram′, log′ə-gram′), *n.* [*logo-* + *-gram*], a letter, character, or symbol used to represent an entire word (e.g., $ for *dollar*).

log·o·gram·mat·ic (lôg′ə-grə-mat′ik, log′ə-grə-mat′ik), *adj.* of or using logograms.

log·o·graph (lôg′ə-graf′, log′ə-gräf′), *n.* a logogram.

log·o·graph·ic (lôg′ə-graf′ik, log′ə-graf′ik), *adj.* of logography.

lo·gog·ra·phy (lō-gog′rə-fi), *n.* [Gr. *logographia;* see LOGO- & -GRAPHY], 1. the use of logotypes in printing. 2. a system of longhand reporting in which several reporters take down a few words each in succession.

log·o·griph (lôg′ə-grif′, log′ə-grif′), *n.* [< *logo-* + Gr. *griphos,* fishing basket, riddle], 1. an anagram. 2. a kind of word puzzle in which it is required to discover a certain word by combining the letters of various given words.

lo·gom·a·chy (lō-gom′ə-ki), *n.* [*pl.* LOGOMACHIES (-kiz)], [Gr. *logomachia* < *logos,* a word + *machē,* a fight, battle], 1. strife or contention in words only or an argument about words. 2. the game of anagrams.

Log·os (log′os, lô′gos), *n.* [L. *logos;* Gr. *logos,* a word, etc.; see LOGIC], 1. [sometimes l-], in *Greek philosophy,* reason, thought of as constituting the controlling principle of the universe and as being manifested by speech. 2. in *Christian theology,* the Word; Jesus as the second person of the Trinity: John 1.

log·o·type (lôg′ə-tīp′, log′ə-tip′), *n.* [*logo-* + *-type*], in *typography,* several letters, often making up a short word, cast in one piece but not united as in a ligature.

log reel, a reel for winding and unwinding a log line.

log·roll (lôg′rōl′, log′rōl′), *v.i.* [back-formation < *logrolling*], to take part in logrolling. *v.t.* to get passage of (a bill) by logrolling.

log·roll·er (lôg′rōl′ẽr, log′rōl′ẽr), *n.* 1. a person who logrolls. 2. a device used in sawmills to load logs.

log·roll·ing (lôg′rōl′iŋ, log′rōl′iŋ), *n.* 1. the act of rolling logs, as when a group of neighbors help to clear off land by rolling logs into some spot for burning, etc. 2. *a*) a giving of help, praise, etc. in return for help, praise, etc. *b*) in *politics*, mutual aid among politicians, as by reciprocal voting for each other's bills. 3. the sport of birling.

-logue (lôg, log), [Fr.; L. *-logus;* Gr. *-logos* < *logos;* see LOGIC], a combining form meaning *a* (specified kind of) *speaking or writing*, as in *monologue*: also **-log.**

log·wood (lôg'wood', log'wood'), *n.* [so called from being imported in logs], 1. the hard, brownish-red wood of a tropical tree native to Central America and the West Indies, used in dyeing. 2. this tree.

lo·gy (lō'gi), *adj.* [LOGIER (-gi-ẽr), LOGIEST (-gi-ist)], [? < D. *log*, heavy, dull], [Colloq.], dull or sluggish, as from overeating.

-lo·gy (lə-ji), [replacing earlier *-logie* (< Fr. *-logie*); both ult. < Gr. *-logia* < *logos;* see LOGIC], a combining form meaning: 1. *a* (specified kind of) *speaking*, as in *eulogy*. 2. *science, doctrine, theory of*, as in *geology*.

Lo·hen·grin (lō'ən-grin'), *n.* in *German legend*, a knight of the Holy Grail, son of Parsifal: title character of an opera (1850) by Richard Wagner.

loin (loin), *n.* [ME. *loine;* OFr. *loigne, logne* < ML. **lumbea;* L. *lumbus;* cf. LUMBAR], 1. *usually in pl.* the lower part of the back on either side of the backbone between the hipbones and the ribs. 2. the front part of the hindquarters of beef, lamb, mutton, veal, etc. with the flank removed: see **beef**, illus. 3. *pl.* the hips and the lower abdomen regarded as a part of the body to be clothed or as the region of strength and procreative power.

gird up one's loins, to get ready to do something difficult or strenuous.

loin·cloth (loin'klôth', loin'kloth'), *n.* a cloth worn about the loins, as by some tribes in warm climates.

Loire (lwär), *n.* a river in southern France, flowing into the Bay of Biscay: length, 625 mi.

Lo·is (lō'is), [L.; Gr. *Lōis*], a feminine name.

loi·ter (loi'tẽr), *v.i.* [ME. *loitren;* MD. *loteren*], 1. to spend time idly (often with *about*); linger; dawdle. 2. to walk or move slowly and indolently, with frequent stops and pauses: as, he *loitered* on the way. ***v.t.*** to spend (time) idly.

SYN.—**loiter** implies aimlessness or slowness of movement and may suggest a wasting of time in lingering or lagging (to *loiter* around street corners); **dawdle** implies a wasting of time over trifles or a frittering away of time that makes for slow progress (to *dawdle* over a cup of tea); **dally** suggests a spending of time in trifling or frivolous pursuits; **idle** suggests habitual avoidance of work, or inactivity, indolence, etc. (to *idle* away the hours).

Lo·ki (lō'ki), *n.* [ON.], in *Norse mythology*, the god who constantly created discord and mischief: he caused the death of Balder.

loll (lol), *v.i.* [ME. & MD. *lollen*], 1. to lean or lounge about in a relaxed or lazy manner. 2. to hang in a relaxed manner; droop: as, their heads *lolled* forward in their sleep. ***v.t.*** to let hang loosely, as the tongue. ***n.*** the act of lolling.

Lol·land (lôl'än), *n.* a Danish island, south of Zealand Island.

lol·la·pa·loo·za, lol·la·pa·loo·sa (lol'ə-pə-lōō'zə), *n.* [< ?; but cf. LOLLIPOP], [Slang], something very striking or excellent: also **lollypalooza**, etc.

Lol·lard (lol'ẽrd), *n.* [MD. *lollaerd*, lit., mutterer (of prayers, psalms) < *lollen*, to mumble, doze, loll; cf. LULL, LILT], a member of a group of political and religious reformers of 14th- and 15th-century England, followers of John Wycliffe, whose doctrines anticipated many points in the later Protestant Reformation.

lol·li·pop, lol·ly·pop (lol'i-pop'), *n.* [child's word; prob. after dial. *lolly*, the tongue + *pop*], a piece of hard candy attached to the end of a small stick, etc.: also called *sucker*.

Lom·bard (lom'bẽrd, lum'bẽrd, lom'bärd'), *n.* [OFr.; It. *Lombardo;* LL. *Longobardus;* ? < OHG. *lang*, long + *bart*, a beard; cf. LOMBARDY], 1. a native or inhabitant of Lombardy. 2. a member of a Germanic tribe that settled in the Po Valley. ***adj.*** of Lombardy or the Lombards.

Lom·bar·dic (lom-bär'dik, ləm-bär'dik), *adj.* [ML. *Lombardicus*], 1. of Lombardy or the Lombards. 2. of the medieval architecture of northern Italy. 3. of the Renaissance painters in Lombardy.

Lombard Street, 1. the street in London where many banks and financial houses are located; hence, 2. the London financial market or financiers.

Lom·bar·dy (lom'bẽr-di, lum'bẽr-di), *n.* [so called because the region was invaded and settled by the Lombards in the 6th c. A.D.], a department of northern Italy: pop., 5,836,300.

Lombardy poplar, a tall, slender variety of the black poplar tree, with upward-curving branches.

Lom·bok (lom-bok'), *n.* an island of Indonesia, between Bali and Sumbawa: area, 1,811 sq. mi.; pop., 600,000.

Lom·bro·si·an School (lom-brō'zi-ən), a school of criminologists adhering to the theories and methods of Lombroso, who regarded the criminal as a distinct and atavistic type of person.

Lom·bro·so, Ce·sa·re (che'zä-re' lôm-brô'sô), 1836–1909; Italian criminologist and physician.

lo·ment (lō'ment), *n.* [L. *lomentum*, bean meal < pp. of *lavare*, to wash: Roman women used it in a cosmetic wash], a legume that separates at its constrictions into one-seeded capsules when ripe.

lo·men·ta·ceous (lō'mən-tā'shəs), *adj.* 1. like a loment. 2. having loments.

lo·men·tum (lō-men'təm), *n.* [L.], a loment.

Lo·mond, Loch (lō'mənd), a lake in west central Scotland: area, c. 27 sq. mi.

Lon·don (lun'dən), *n.* 1. an administrative county of southeastern England, consisting of the City of London and 28 metropolitan boroughs: area, 117 sq. mi.; pop., 2,601,000 (est. 1946): it is the capital of the United Kingdom and the British Empire. 2. this county with its suburbs (*Greater London*): pop., 6,785,000 (est. 1946). 3. a city in southeastern Ontario, Canada: pop., 95,000. Abbreviated **Lon., Lond.**

City of London, the ancient center of the county of London: area, 677 acres; pop., 11,000.

London, Jack, (*John Griffith London*), 1876–1916; American novelist and short-story writer.

Lon·don·der·ry (lun'dən-der'i), *n.* a city in Northern Ireland, on the River Foyle: pop., 45,000.

Lon·dres (lon'dres), *n.* [Fr., London], a medium-sized or large cigar of cylindrical shape.

lone (lōn), *adj.* [< *alone*], 1. by oneself; alone; solitary. 2. lonesome. 3. unmarried or widowed: a humorous usage. 4. *a*) standing apart from others of its kind; isolated. *b*) unfrequented. —***SYN.*** see **alone.**

lone hand, 1. in *card games*, a hand played without help from a partner. 2. a person who operates alone.

lone·li·ness (lōn'li-nis), *n.* a lonely state or quality.

lone·ly (lōn'li), *adj.* [LONELIER (-li-ẽr), LONELIEST (-li-ist)], [*lone* + *-ly*], 1. alone; solitary. 2. *a*) standing apart from others of its kind; isolated. *b*) unfrequented. 3. unhappy at being alone; longing for friends, company, etc. 4. giving such a feeling. —***SYN.*** see **alone.**

lone·some (lōn'səm), *adj.* [see LONE & -SOME], 1. having or causing a lonely feeling. 2. unfrequented; desolate. —***SYN.*** see **alone.**

lone wolf, a person who by choice plays a solitary role in his ventures.

long (lôŋ), *adj.* [ME.; AS. *long, lang;* akin to G. *lang;* IE. *(*d*)*longho-s* (< base **del-*, long), seen also in L. *longus* (cf. LONGITUDE)], 1. measuring much from end to end in space or time; not short or brief. 2. measured from end to end: as, the *long* dimension. 3. of a specified extent in length: as, the parade was a mile *long*. 4. of greater than usual or standard length, quantity, etc.: as, a *long* dozen, a *long* game. 5. containing many items or members: said of a series, list, etc. 6. overextended in length; hence, 7. tedious; slow. 8. extending to what is distant in space or time; far-reaching: as, he took a *long* view of the matter. 9. large; big: as, a bet at the *long* odds of 100 to 1, he's taking a *long* chance. 10. having an abundance of (with *of* or *on*): as, he was *long* on excuses. 11. in *finance*, holding a large supply of a commodity or stock in anticipation of a scarcity and rise in price. 12. in *phonetics*, *a*) held for a relatively long time: said of a pronounced vowel or consonant. *b*) popularly, having the quality determined by its relative back position as compared with other vowel variants: said of a vowel. 13. in *prosody*, *a*) requiring a relatively long time to pronounce: said of syllables in quantitative verse. *b*) stressed: said of syllables in accentual verse. ***adv.*** 1. for a long time. 2. for the duration of; from the beginning to the end: as, he lay awake all night *long*. 3. at a much earlier or a much later time than the time indicated; remotely: as, it happened *long* ago. ***n.*** 1. in *finance*, a person who buys or is on the long side of the market. 2. in *phonetics* & *prosody*, a long vowel, consonant, or syllable.

as (or so) long as, 1. during the time that. 2. seeing that; since. 3. provided that.

before long, soon.

the long and the short of, the whole story of in a few words; gist or point of.

long (lôŋ), *v.i.* [ME. *longen;* AS. *langian* (akin to G. *langen*, to reach, extend) < base of *lang* (see LONG, *adj.*); sense < ME. impers. *me longeth*, lit., to me it seems long (for, etc.)], to feel a strong yearning; desire greatly; wish earnestly: as, we *long* to go home.

long (lôŋ), *v.i.* [ME. *longen* < *long*, aphetic form of AS. *gelang*, dependent on], 1. [Archaic & Poetic], to be fitting or appropriate. 2. [Obs.], to belong.

long., longitude.

lon·ga·nim·i·ty (loŋ'gə-nim'ə-ti), *n.* [LL. *longanimitas* < L. *longus*, long + *animus*, mind], patient endurance of injuries; forbearance.

Long Beach, a city in Los Angeles County, California, on the Pacific: pop., 334,000.

long·boat (lôŋ'bōt'), *n.* the largest boat carried on a merchant sailing ship.

long·bow (lôŋ'bō'), *n.* a bow drawn by hand and shooting a long, feathered arrow: cf. *crossbow.*
draw (or **pull**) **the longbow,** to exaggerate in telling something.

Long Branch, an ocean resort in New Jersey: pop., 26,000.

long·cloth (lôŋ'klôth', lôŋ'kloth'), *n.* [so called because made in long pieces], a soft cotton fabric of fine quality.

long-dis·tance (lôŋ'dis'təns), *adj.* to or from a distant place or places: as, *long-distance* telephone calls.

long distance, a telephone exchange or operator that puts through long-distance calls.

long division, the process of dividing a number by another number containing, ordinarily, two or more figures and of putting the steps down in full.

long dozen, thirteen.

long-drawn (lôŋ'drôn'), *adj.* continuing for a long or very long time; prolonged.

longe (lunj), *n.* [Fr., back-formation < *allonge*, extension < *allonger* < LL. *elongare;* see ELONGATE], 1. a long rope fastened to a horse's head and held by the trainer, who causes the horse to move around in a circle. 2. the use of the longe in training horses. *v.t.* [LONGED (lunjd), LONGING], to put (a horse) through his paces, using a longe. Also spelled **lunge.**

‡**lon·ge·ron** (lon'jẽr-ən; Fr. lōn'zh'-rōn'), *n.* [Fr.], a main structural member along the length of an airplane body, or fuselage.

lon·gev·i·ty (lon-jev'ə-ti), *n.* [L. *longaevitas* < *longaevus;* see LONGEVOUS], long life; great span of life.

lon·ge·vous (lon-jē'vəs), *adj.* [L. *longaevus* < *longus*, long + *aevum*, age], [Rare], long-lived.

long-faced (lôŋ'fāst'), *adj.* 1. having a long face; hence, 2. glum; disconsolate.

Long·fel·low, Henry Wads·worth (wädz'wẽrth lôŋ'-fel'ō), 1807–1882; American poet.

long green, [Slang], paper money.

long·hair (lôŋ'hâr'), *adj.* [Colloq.], designating or of intellectuals or intellectual tastes; specifically, playing or preferring classical music rather than jazz or popular tunes. *n.* [Colloq.], an intellectual; specifically, a longhair musician.

long·hand (lôŋ'hand'), *n.* ordinary handwriting, in which the words are written out in full: cf. *shorthand.*

long·head (lôŋ'hed'), *n.* 1. a head with a cephalic index of less than 80. 2. a person having such a head; dolichocephalic person.

long head, much foresight; shrewdness; good sense.

long-head·ed, long·head·ed (lôŋ'hed'id), *adj.* 1. having a longhead. 2. having much foresight; shrewd.

long·horn (lôŋ'hôrn'), *n.* any of a breed of long-horned cattle formerly raised in great numbers in the southwestern United States: also **Texas longhorn.**

long house, a communal home or council hall among the Iroquois and other Indian tribes.

long hundredweight, the British hundredweight, equal to 112 pounds.

lon·gi- (lon'ji), [L. < *longus*], a combining form meaning *long*, as in *longicorn.*

lon·gi·corn (lon'ji-kôrn'), *adj.* [< *longi-* + L. *cornu*, horn], in *zoology*, having long feelers, or antennae. *n.* a longicorn beetle.

long·ing (lôŋ'iŋ), *n.* [*long* (to yearn) + *-ing*], strong desire; yearning. *adj.* feeling or showing a yearning.

Lon·gi·nus, Dionysius Cassius (lon-ji'nəs), 213?–273 A.D.; Greek Platonic philosopher and rhetorician.

long·ish (lôŋ'ish), *adj.* somewhat long.

Long Island, an island in New York State, between Long Island Sound and the Atlantic: it includes Kings, Queens, Nassau, and Suffolk Counties: area, 1,411 sq. mi.; pop., 6,404,000.: abbreviated **L.I.**

Long Island Sound, the arm of the Atlantic between Connecticut and Long Island: length, 110 mi.

lon·gi·tude (lon'jə-to͞od', lon'jə-tūd'), *n.* [ME.; L. *longitudo* < *longus*, long; cf. LONG, *adj.*], 1. length: now used humorously. 2. angular distance east or west on the earth's surface, measured by the angle (expressed in degrees up to 180° in either direction) which the meridian passing through a particular place makes with a standard or prime meridian, usually the one passing through Greenwich, England, or by the difference in time between the two meridians. 3. in *astronomy*, the arc of the ecliptic measured eastward from the vernal equinox to the point where the ecliptic is intersected by the great circle through the star, planet, etc. and the poles of the ecliptic: also called *celestial longitude.* Abbreviated **long., lon.**

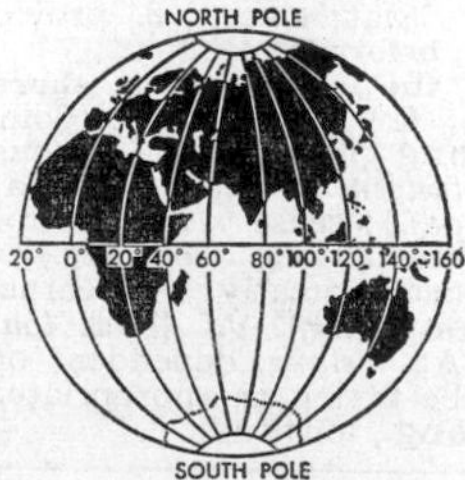

MERIDIANS SHOWING LONGITUDE

lon·gi·tu·di·nal (lon'jə-to͞o'di-n'l, lon'jə-tū'di-n'l), *adj.* 1. of or in length. 2. running lengthwise; placed lengthwise: opposed to *transverse.* 3. of longitude.

long jump, the broad jump.

long·leaf, long-leaf (lôŋ'lēf'), *n.* Georgia pine: also **longleaf pine, longleaf yellow pine.**

long-leaved (**pitch**) **pine** (lôŋ'lēvd'), a longleaf.

long-lived (lôŋ'līvd'; *occas.* lôŋ'livd'), *adj.* [*long* + *-lived*], having or tending to have a long life span or existence.

long measure, linear measure.

long moss, a moss forming long, hanging tufts on tree trunks and branches in southern United States.

Lon·go·bar·di (loŋ'gə-bär'di), *n.pl.* [LL., pl. of *Longobardus;* see LOMBARD], the Lombards.

Long Parliament, the English Parliament that met in 1640, was expelled by Cromwell in 1653, reconvened in 1659, and was dissolved in 1660.

long pig, human flesh or a human body as food for cannibals: from the Maori and Polynesian term.

long prim·er (prim'ẽr), a size of type, 10 point: abbreviated **L.P., l.p.** This line is in long primer.

long-range (lôŋ'rānj'), *adj.* 1. designed to shoot over a great distance: as, *long-range* guns. 2. taking the future into consideration: as, *long-range* plans.

long·shore (lôŋ'shôr', lôŋ'shōr'), *adj.* [< *alongshore*], existing, occurring, employed, or working along the shore or water front. *adv.* along the shore.

long·shore·man (lôŋ'shôr'mən, lôŋ'shōr'mən), *n.* [*pl.* LONGSHOREMEN (-mən)], [*longshore* + *man*], a person who works on a water front loading and unloading ships.

long shot, 1. [Colloq.], in betting, a choice that has only a slight chance of winning and, hence, carries great odds. 2. in *motion pictures*, a scene photographed with the camera at some distance from the action.
not by a long shot, [Colloq.], absolutely not; not at all.

long-sight·ed (lôŋ'sīt'id), *adj.* farsighted.

Longs Peak, (lôŋz), a peak in Rocky Mountain National Park, Colorado: height, 14,255 ft.

long·spur (lôŋ'spũr'), *n.* [*long* + *spur*], any of a group of birds related to the sparrows and finches and distinguished by their long hind claws: they breed in the arctic regions and winter over a wide expanse of the United States.

long-stand·ing (lôŋ'stan'diŋ), *adj.* having continued for a long time.

Long·street, James (lôŋ'strēt'), 1821–1904; Confederate general in the Civil War.

long-suf·fer·ance (lôŋ'suf'ẽr-əns), *n.* [Archaic], long-suffering.

long-suf·fer·ing (lôŋ'suf'ẽr-iŋ), *adj.* bearing injuries, insults, trouble, etc. patiently for a long time. *n.* long and patient endurance of injuries, insults, trouble, etc.

long suit, 1. in *card games*, the suit in which a player holds the most cards; hence, 2. something at which one excels.

long ton, a unit of weight, equal to 2,240 pounds avoirdupois: abbreviated **l.t., lg. tn.:** cf. **ton.**

long-tongued (lôŋ'tuŋd'), *adj.* 1. having a long tongue; hence, 2. talkative; tattling; gossipy.

Long·view (lôŋ'vū'), *n.* a city in northeastern Texas: pop., 40,000.

long-wave (lôŋ'wāv'), *adj.* of, by, or for long waves.

long wave, a radio wave more than 545 meters in length: frequencies of long waves are lower than 550 kilocycles.

long·ways (lôŋ'wāz'), *adv.* lengthwise.

long-wind·ed (lôŋ'win'did), *adj.* 1. capable of considerable exertion without getting out of breath. 2. *a*) speaking or writing at great, often tiresome length. *b*) tiresomely long: said of a speech, writing, etc.

long·wise (lôŋ'wīz'), *adv.* lengthwise.

loo (lo͞o), *n.* [abbrev. of *lanterloo* < Fr. *lanturelu*, name of the game], 1. a card game played for a pool made up of stakes and forfeits. 2. a stake or forfeit in the game. *v.t.* to cause to pay a forfeit at loo.

loo·by (lo͞o'bi), *n.* [*pl.* LOOBIES (-biz)], [ME. *loby;* prob. akin to *lob, lubber;* ? influenced by OFr. *lubin*, nickname for a friar, said to be < L. *lupus*, a wolf], a big, clumsy fellow; lout; lubber.

loo·fah (lo͞o'fə), *n.* [Ar. *lūfah*], the fibrous substance of the pod of a tropical gourd, used as a sponge.

loo·ie, loo·ey (lo͞o'i), *n.* [Military Slang], a lieutenant.

look (look), *v.i.* [ME. *loken, lokien;* AS. *locian;* akin to OS. *lōkōn*, OHG. *luogēn* (G. dial. *lugen*), to spy after, look for; IE. base **lak-*, to see, as also in Bret. *lagad*, W. *llygad*, eye], 1. to make use of the sense of sight; see. 2. *a*) to direct one's eyes in order to see. *b*) to direct one's attention mentally upon something. 3. to try to see or find something; search. 4. to appear; seem. 5. to be facing or turned in a specified direction. 6. to expect (followed by an infinitive). *v.t.* 1. to direct one's eyes on: as, he couldn't *look* us in the face. 2. to express by one's looks, or appearance: as, he *looked* his despair. 3. [Rare], to bring to a certain condition by looking. 4. to appear as having attained (some age): as, she scarcely *looks* her years. *n.* 1. the act of looking; glance. 2. appearance; aspect. 3. *pl.* [Colloq.], *a*) appearance: as, I don't like the *looks* of things. *b*) personal appearance, especially of a pleasing nature: as, she has *looks* and youth. *interj.* 1. see! 2. pay attention!

it looks like, 1. it seems that there will be. 2. [Colloq.], it seems as if.

look after, to take care of; watch over.

look alive, [Colloq.], to be alert; act or move quickly: usually in the imperative.

look back, to recall the past; recollect.

look daggers, to look with anger; glare.

look down on (or **upon**), 1. to regard as an inferior. 2. to regard with contempt; despise.

look for, 1. to search or hunt for. 2. to expect; anticipate.

look forward to, to anticipate, especially eagerly.

look in (on), to pay a brief visit (to).

look into, to examine carefully; investigate.

look on, 1. to be an observer or spectator. 2. to consider; regard.

look oneself, to seem in normal health, spirits, etc.

look out, to be on the watch; be careful.

look over, to examine; inspect.

look to, 1. to take care of; give attention to. 2. to rely upon; resort to. 3. to look forward to; expect.

look up, 1. to search for in a book of reference, etc. 2. [Colloq.], to pay a visit to; call on. 3. [Colloq.], to get better; improve.

look up and down, 1. to search everywhere. 2. to examine with an appraising eye; scrutinize.

look up to, to regard with great respect; admire.

***SYN.*—look** is the general term meaning to direct the eyes in order to see (don't *look* now); **gaze** implies a looking intently and steadily, as in wonder, delight, or interest (to *gaze* at the stars); to **stare** is to look fixedly with wide-open eyes, as in surprise, curiosity, abstraction, etc. (it is rude to *stare* at people); to **gape** is to stare with the mouth open in ignorant or naive wonder or curiosity (the child stood *gaping* at the elephant); to **glare** is to stare fiercely or angrily (he *glared* at her for talking); to **peek** is to take a quick, furtive look, as through a hole or from behind a barrier, at something not supposed to be seen; to **peer** is to look searchingly with the eyes narrowed (she *peered* down the well). See also **appearance.**

look·er (look′ẽr), *n.* 1. a person who looks. 2. [Slang], a handsome person; especially, a pretty woman.

look·er-on (look′ẽr-on′), *n.* [*pl.* LOOKERS-ON (-ẽrz-on′)], an observer or spectator.

look-in (look′in′), *n.* 1. a hasty glance. 2. a brief visit.

looking glass, a (glass) mirror.

look·out (look′out′), *n.* 1. a careful watching for someone or something. 2. *a*) a place for keeping watch, usually one at a height affording an extensive view. *b*) in *nautical usage*, a crow's nest. 3. a person detailed to watch. 4. outlook; prospect. 5. [Colloq.], concern; worry: as, that is none of my *lookout.*

Lookout Mountain, a mountain ridge in Tennessee, Georgia, and Alabama: highest point, 2,126 ft.: the part of this ridge near Chattanooga, Tennessee was the site of a Civil War battle (1863) in which the Union forces defeated the Confederates.

look-see (look′sē′), *n.* [Slang], a quick look; brief inspection.

loom (lōōm), *n.* [ME. *lome;* AS. (*ge*)*loma,* tool, utensil; connected with AS. *gelome,* frequent, in basic sense "often used thing"]. 1. a machine for weaving thread or yarn into cloth. 2. the art of weaving. 3. the part of an oar between the handle and the blade.

loom (lōōm), *v.i.* [earlier *lome, loam;* prob. < a LG. or Scand. source via naut. language; cf. E.Fris. *lōmen,* Sw. *loma,* to come slowly (akin to Eng. *lame*); conjectured sense "to come slowly toward"], to appear, take shape, or come in sight indistinctly as through a mist, especially in a large, portentous, or threatening form (often with *up*): as, the peak *loomed* up before us; also used figuratively, as, the specter of revolution *loomed* ahead. *n.* a looming appearance, as of land or a ship in the fog.

loom (lōōm), *n.* a loon (bird).

loon (lōōn), *n.* [earlier *loom* < ON. *lomr*], any of a group of fish-eating, diving birds somewhat like ducks but with a pointed bill and a weird cry, found mainly in subarctic regions: also called *loom, great northern diver.*

loon (lōōn), *n.* [Scot. *lown, loun, loon;* ? < D. *loen,* stupid fellow], 1. a clumsy, stupid person; lout; dolt. 2. [Scot.], a boy. 3. [Archaic], a servant or other person of low rank. 4. [Archaic], a rogue; scamp.

loon·y (lōōn′i), *adj.* [LOONIER (-i-ẽr), LOONIEST (-i-ist)], [< *lunatic*], [Slang], crazy; demented. *n.* [*pl.* LOONIES (-iz)], [Slang], a loony person. Also spelled **luny.**

loop (lōōp), *n.* [ME. *loup, lope* < Anglo-N. forms corresponding to ON. *hlaup,* a leap, *hlaupa,* to run (cf. LEAP); cf. Dan. *löb-knude,* lit., running knot; the form *loop* represents a borrowed northernism or an eastern dial. form based on Anglo-Dan.; cf. LOOSE], 1. the more or less circular figure formed by a line, thread, wire, etc. that crosses itself. 2. anything having or forming this figure: as, a written *l* can be described as a lengthened *loop.* 3. a sharp bend, as in a mountain road, which almost comes back upon itself. 4. a ring-shaped fastening or ornament: as, staples, eyelets, and various sewing stitches are *loops.* 5. in *aeronautics,* a movement in which an airplane describes a closed curve or circle in the vertical plane: it is an *inside loop* when the top of the airplane is toward the center of the circle, and an *outside loop* when it faces away from the center. 6. in *electricity,* a complete circuit. 7. in *physics,* the part of a vibrating string, air column, etc. between the nodes; antinode. *v.t.* 1. to make a loop or loops in or of. 2. to wrap around one or more times: as, *loop* the wire around that post. 3. to fasten with a loop or loops: as, she *looped* back the draperies from the window. 4. in *electricity,* to join (conductors) so as to complete a circuit. *v.i.* 1. to form into a loop or loops. 2. to progress as a measuring worm does by alternately straightening the body and drawing it up into a loop. 3. in *aeronautics,* to perform a loop or loops.

loop the loop, to make a vertical loop in the air, as in an airplane or roller coaster.

the Loop, the main business, shopping, and theater district in downtown Chicago: so called because the elevated railway makes a loop around this area.

loop (lōōp), *n.* [ME. *loupe;* prob. < MD. *lupen,* to peer; but cf. LOOPHOLE], [Archaic], a narrow opening or loophole.

loop·er (lōōp′ẽr), *n.* a person or thing that loops; specifically, *a*) a device (on a sewing machine) for making loops. *b*) a measuring worm.

loop·hole (lōōp′hōl′), *n.* [*loop* (loophole) + *hole;* orig. sense "hole in a *loup*" (i.e., penthouse for ventilation)], 1. a hole or narrow slit in the wall of a fort, etc. for looking or shooting through. 2. a means of escaping or evading something unpleasant.

loop knot, a knot tied in a doubled rope so that a loop extends beyond it: see **knot,** illus.

loop stitch, a sewing stitch that forms connecting loops.

loose (lōōs), *adj.* [ME. *los, lous* < Anglo-N.; cf. ON. *lauss,* akin to AS. *leas* (see -LESS)], 1. not confined or restrained; free; unbound. 2. not put up in a container: as, *loose* salt. 3. readily available; not put away under lock and key: as, *loose* cash. 4. not firmly fastened down or in: as, the leg of this table is *loose.* 5. not tight; giving enough room: as, *loose* clothing. 6. not compact or compactly constructed: as, a *loose* frame, *loose* soil. 7. not restrained; irresponsible: as, *loose* talk. 8. not precise or close; inexact: as, a *loose* translation. 9. sexually immoral; lewd. 10. moving freely or excessively: as, *loose* bowels. *adv.* loosely; in a loose manner. *v.t.* [LOOSED (lōōst), LOOSING], 1. to make loose; specifically, *a*) to set free; unbind. *b*) to make less tight. *c*) to make less compact. *d*) to free from restraint; make less rigid; relax. *e*) to free from an obligation or responsibility; absolve. 2. to let fly; release: as, he *loosed* the arrow into the air. *v.i.* to loose something or become loose.

break loose, 1. to free oneself by force. 2. to shake off restraint.

cast loose, to untie or unfasten; become or set free.

cut loose, 1. to break or cut from a connecting tie; make or become unfastened. 2. to become free; escape. 3. [Colloq.], to have fun in a free, unrestrained manner.

let loose (with), to set free or give out; release.

on the loose, 1. not confined or bound; free. 2. [Colloq.], having fun in a free, unrestrained manner.

set (or **turn**) **loose,** to make free; release.

loose ends, [from the ends of a spliced rope], final, relatively minor matters still to be taken care of.

loose-joint·ed (lōōs′join′tid), *adj.* 1. having loose joints; hence, 2. limber; moving freely and flexibly.

loose-leaf (lōōs′lēf′), *adj.* having or designed to have leaves which can easily be removed or inserted: as, a *loose-leaf* notebook.

loos·en (lōōs′'n), *v.t.* & *v.i.* to make or become loose or looser (in various senses).

loose sentence, a sentence in which the grammatical form and essential meaning are complete before the end: distinguished from *periodic sentence.*

loose·strife (lōōs′strīf′), *n.* [*loose, v.* + *strife;* used as transl. of L. *lysimachia* < Gr. *lysimachion* < *lyein,* to loose + *machē,* battle], 1. any of various plants of the primrose family, with leafy stems and loose spikes of white, rose, or yellow flowers. 2. a variety of this plant with whorls of yellow flowers on fringed petioles. 3. any of a number of related plants with whorled leaves and spikes of purple flowers: also **purple loosestrife.**

loose-tongued (lo͞os′tuŋd′), *adj.* talking too much; careless or irresponsible in speech.

loot (lo͞ot), *n.* [Hind. *lūt* < Sans. *luṇṭ*, to rob], goods stolen or taken by force, as from a captured enemy city in wartime or by a corrupt official; plunder; spoils. *v.t.* 1. to plunder; strip of everything valuable; despoil. 2. to take or carry off as plunder. *v.i.* to engage in plundering. —*SYN.* see **spoil.**

lop (lop), *v.t.* [LOPPED (lopt), LOPPING], [ME. *loppen;* Late AS. **loppian* (inferred < pp. adj. *loppede*); prob. < ON. (cf. Norw. *loppa*)], 1. to trim (a tree, etc.) by cutting off branches, twigs, or stems. 2. to remove by or as by cutting off (usually with *off*). *n.* 1. the act of lopping. 2. something lopped off.

lop (lop), *v.i.* [LOPPED (lopt), LOPPING], [< same base as (& prob. var. of) *lob*], to hang down loosely. *v.t.* to let hang down loosely. *adj.* hanging down loosely.

lope (lōp), *v.i.* [LOPED (lōpt), LOPING], [ME. *lopen;* ON. *hlaupa*, to leap, run], to move with a long, swinging stride, as in galloping. *v.t.* to cause to lope. *n.* a long, swinging stride.

lop-eared (lop′êrd′), *adj.* having drooping or hanging ears.

Lope de Vega, see **Vega, Lope de.**

lop·er (lōp′ẽr), *n.* a horse that lopes, especially one whose normal gait is a lope.

lo·pho·branch (lō′fə-braŋk′, lof′ə-braŋk′), *adj.* [< Mod. L. *Lophobranchii*, name of the suborder < Gr. *lophos*, crest, tuft + *branchion*, gill], of a group of fishes, including the pipefishes and sea horses, having gills arranged in tufts along the branchial arches. *n.* a fish of this group.

lop·per (lop′ẽr), *n.* a person or thing that lops, or trims trees, etc.

lop·py (lop′i), *adj.* hanging down loosely; drooping.

lop·sid·ed (lop′sīd′id), *adj.* noticeably heavier, bigger, or lower on one side; not symmetrical.

loq., [L.], *loquitur*.

lo·qua·cious (lō-kwā′shəs), *adj.* [< L. *loquax, loquacis* < *loqui*, to speak; + *-ous*], very talkative; fond of talking. —*SYN.* see **talkative.**

lo·quac·i·ty (lō-kwas′ə-ti), *n.* [L. *loquacitas* < *loquax;* see LOQUACIOUS], talkativeness, especially when excessive.

lo·quat (lō′kwät, lō′kwat), *n.* [< dial. pronun. of Chin. *lu chü*, lit., rush orange], 1. a small evergreen tree of the rose family, native to China and Japan. 2. the small, yellow, edible, plumlike fruit of this tree.

‡**lo·qui·tur** (lok′wi-tẽr), [L.], he (or she) speaks.

Lo·rain (lô-rān′), *n.* a city in northern Ohio, on Lake Erie: pop., 69,000.

Lor·an, lor·an (lôr′an, lō′ran), *n.* [< *Lo*ng *Ra*nge *N*avigation], a system by which a ship or aircraft can determine its position by radio signals sent from known stations.

Lor·ca (lôr′kä), *n.* a city in southeastern Spain: pop., 68,000.

lord (lôrd), *n.* [ME. *lorde, laverde;* AS. *hlaford* < earlier *hlafweard; hlaf* (cf. LOAF) + *weard* (cf. WARD, WARDEN); basic sense "loaf keeper" (i.e., one who feeds dependents); cf. AS. *hlaf-æta*, lit., loaf eater, hence servant; cf. MD. *brotherr* (G. *brotherr*), lord < *brot*, bread + *herr*, master; many senses influenced by L. *dominus*], 1. a person having great power and authority; ruler; master. 2. the owner and head of a feudal estate. 3. a husband: now humorous. 4. [L-], *a*) God (with *the* except in direct address). *b*) Jesus Christ (often with *Our*). 5. in Great Britain, *a*) a nobleman holding the rank of baron, viscount, earl, or marquis; member of the House of Lords. *b*) a man who by courtesy or because of his office is given the title of Lord, as a bishop, the son of a duke, or a lord mayor. 6. [L-], *pl.* the House of Lords in the British Parliament (usually with *the*). 7. [L-], in Great Britain, the title of a lord, variously used: as Earl of Leicester, John Doe would be called *Lord* Leicester; as a baron, John, *Lord* Doe; as the son of a marquis or duke, *Lord* John Doe: abbreviated **L., l., Ld.** *v.i.* to act like a lord; rule: chiefly in the phrase *lord it* (*over*), to act in an overbearing, dictatorial manner (toward). *v.t.* to make a lord of.

Lord Chief Justice, the highest judicial officer of England.

Lord (High) Chancellor, the highest officer of state of Great Britain, Keeper of the Great Seal, privy councilor, presiding officer of the House of Lords, etc.: abbreviated **L.H.C., L.C.**

lord·ing (lôrd′iŋ), *n.* 1. a petty or minor lord; lordling: usually contemptuous. 2. [Archaic], a lord. 3. *pl.* [Archaic], gentlemen; lords: a term of address.

lord·li·ness (lôrd′li-nis), *n.* the quality of being lordly.

lord·ling (lôrd′liŋ), *n.* a petty or minor lord: usually contemptuous.

lord·ly (lôrd′li), *adj.* [LORDLIER (-li-ẽr), LORDLIEST (-li-ist)], of, like, characteristic of, or suitable to a lord; specifically, *a*) noble; magnificent. *b*) haughty; overbearing. *adv.* in the manner of a lord.

Lord Mayor, the title of the mayor of London and of the mayor of any of several other English cities.

Lord of hosts, Jehovah; God.

Lord of Misrule, formerly, in England, a person who presided over revels and games, as at Christmas.

lor·do·sis (lôr-dō′sis), *n.* [Mod. L.; Gr. *lordōsis* < *lordos*, bent backward], forward curvature of the spine, producing a hollow in the back.

lor·dot·ic (lôr-dot′ik), *adj.* of or having lordosis.

Lord's day, [transl. of L. *dies Dominica*, Gr. *hē kyriakē hēmera* (cf. Rev. 1:10): from being the day of the resurrection of Christ], Sunday.

lord·ship (lôrd′ship), *n.* [AS. *hlafordscipe;* see -SHIP], 1. the rank or authority of a lord; hence, 2. rule; dominion. 3. a title used in speaking of or to a lord, preceded by *his* or *your*. Abbreviated **Ldp., Lp.**

Lord's Prayer, the prayer beginning *Our Father*, which Jesus taught his disciples: Matt. 6:9-13.

lords spiritual, the archbishops and bishops who are members of the British House of Lords: distinguished from *lords temporal*.

Lord's Supper, 1. the Last Supper; final supper of Jesus with his disciples before the Crucifixion. 2. Holy Communion; Eucharist: so called because it commemorates the Last Supper.

lords temporal, those members of the British House of Lords who are not clergy: distinguished from *lords spiritual*.

lore (lôr, lōr), *n.* [ME. *loor, lore;* AS. *lar*, learning, teaching; akin to G. *lehre*, teaching; see LEARN], 1. [Archaic], *a*) a teaching or being taught; instruction. *b*) something taught. 2. knowledge or learning; specifically, all the knowledge of a particular group or having to do with a particular subject, especially that of a traditional nature.

lore (lôr, lōr), *n.* [L. *lorum*, thong], the space between the eye and the upper edge of the bill of a bird or between the eye and the nostril of a snake.

Lor·e·lei (lôr′ə-lī′; G. lō′rə-lī′), *n.* [G.], in *German legend*, a siren whose singing on a rock in the Rhine lured sailors to shipwreck on the reefs: also **Lurlei.**

Lo·rentz, Hen·drik An·toon (hen′drik än′tōn lō′rents), 1853–1928; Dutch physicist; received Nobel prize in physics, 1902.

Lo·ren·zo (lô-ren′zō, lə-ren′zō), a masculine name: see **Laurence.**

Lo·ret·ta (lô-ret′ə, lə-ret′ə), [dim. of *Laura*], a feminine name.

lor·gnette (lôr-nyet′), *n.* [Fr. < *lorgner*, to spy, peep, quiz < OFr. *lorgne*, squinting], 1. a pair of eyeglasses attached to a handle. 2. an opera glass similarly mounted.

‡**lor·gnon** (lôr′nyōn′), *n.* [Fr. < *lorgner;* see LORGNETTE], 1. a single or double eyeglass, as a monocle or pince-nez. 2. a lorgnette.

lo·ri·ca (lō-rī′kə), *n.* [*pl.* LORICAE (-sē)], [L., orig., corselet of thongs < *lorum*, a thong; akin to Gr. *eulēra*, reins], 1. in ancient Rome, the leather corselet, or cuirass, worn by a Roman legionary. 2. in *zoology*, a hard, protective shell or other covering.

lor·i·cate (lôr′ə-kāt′, lor′ə-kāt′), *adj.* [L. *loricatus*, pp. of *loricare*, to harness, clothe in mail < *lorica*], having, covered with, or resembling a lorica.

lor·i·cat·ed (lôr′ə-kā′tid, lor′ə-kā′tid), *adj.* loricate.

lor·i·keet (lôr′ə-kēt′, lor′ə-kēt′), *n.* [< *lory* + *parrakeet*], any of several small, brightly colored birds of the lory family, found in Australia and the East Indies.

Lo·rin·da (lô-rin′də, lə-rin′də), a feminine name: see **Laura.**

lo·ris (lôr′is, lō′ris), *n.* [*pl.* LORIS], [Fr. < D. *loeres*, a clown < *loer*, a clown], either of two kinds of small, slow-moving, Asiatic lemurs that live in trees and are active at night.

lorn (lôrn), *adj.* [ME.; pp. of *losen, lesen*, to lose (see LOSE); the change of *s* to *r* is due to Verner's phenomenon], 1. [Obs.], lost, ruined, or undone. 2. [Archaic], forsaken, forlorn, bereft, or desolate.

Lor·na (lôr′nə), [prob. of AS. origin; akin to Eng. *lorn*], a feminine name.

Lor·rain, Claude (lô-rān′, lō-rān′; Fr. lô′ran′), (born *Claude Gelée*), 1600–1682; French landscape painter.

Lor·raine (lô-rān′, lō-rān′; Fr. lô′ren′), [Fr.], a feminine name. *n.* a former province of northeastern France: see **Alsace-Lorraine.**

Cross of Lorraine, a cross having two horizontal arms, the lower one longer than the upper.

lor·ry (lôr′i, lor′i), *n.* [*pl.* LORRIES (-iz)], [prob. < dial. *lurry, lorry*, to tug, pull], 1. a low, flat wagon without sides. 2. any of various trucks fitted to run on rails. 3. [British], a motor truck.

lo·ry (lō′ri, lôr′i), *n.* [*pl.* LORIES (-riz, -iz)], [Malay *lūrī*], any of a number of small, brightly colored parrots, native to Australia and near-by islands and characterized by a fringed, brushlike tip of the tongue.

los·a·ble (lo͞oz′ə-b'l), *adj.* that can be lost.

Los Al·a·mos (lôs al′ə-mōs′), a town in north central New Mexico near Santa Fe, established as the site of an atomic-bomb laboratory: pop., 13,000.

Los An·gel·es (lôs aŋ′gəl-əs, lôs an′j'l-əs, los an′jə-lēz′), a city on the southwestern coast of California: area, 442 sq. mi.; pop., 2,479,000; with suburbs, 6,743,000.

lose (lo͞oz), *v.t.* [LOST (lôst), LOSING], [ME. *losen, lesen,* merged form of AS. *losian,* to be lost, *leosan,* to lose; influenced by *loose;* cf. LYSIS], 1. to bring to ruin or destruction. 2. to become unable to find; mislay: as, he *lost* his keys. 3. to have taken from one by negligence, accident, death, removal, separation, etc.; suffer the loss of; be deprived of. 4. to fail to keep (a state of mind or body, one's position, etc.): as, he *loses* his temper easily. 5. *a*) to fail to see, hear, or understand: as, she did not *lose* a word of his lecture. *b*) to fail to keep in sight, mind, or existence. 6. to fail to have, get, take advantage of, etc.; miss: as, he *lost* a good opportunity. 7. to fail to win or gain: as, we *lost* the game. 8. to cause the loss of: as, his negligence *lost* him his job. 9. to wander from and not be able to find (one's way, the right track, etc.). 10. to spend unprofitably or uselessly; waste; squander: as, we can't afford to *lose* any time. 11. to outdistance in a race. 12. to engross or preoccupy: usually in the passive, as, he was *lost* in reverie. *v.i.* 1. to undergo or suffer loss. 2. to be defeated in a contest, etc.

lose oneself, 1. to lose one's way; go astray; become bewildered. 2. to become absorbed.

lo·sel (lō′z'l, lo͞o′z'l, loz′'l), *n.* [ME. *losel, lorel* < MD.; influenced by ME. *losen, lesen,* to lose (cf. LOSE); cf. MD. *lose,* loose conduct, lechery], [Archaic or Dial.], a worthless person. *adj.* [Archaic or Dial.], worthless.

los·er (lo͞oz′ẽr), *n.* 1. a person or thing that loses. 2. a person who reacts to loss or defeat in a specified way: as, a bad *loser.*

los·ing (lo͞oz′iŋ), *n.* 1. the act of a person or thing that loses. 2. *pl.* losses by gambling. *adj.* 1. that loses: as, the *losing* team. 2. resulting in loss: as, a *losing* proposition.

loss (lôs), *n.* [ME. *los* < pp. of *losen, lesen,* to lose (cf. LOSE, LOST); AS. had *los,* ruin, dissolution < base of *leosan*], 1. a losing or being lost. 2. an instance of this. 3. the damage, trouble, disadvantage, deprivation, etc. caused by losing something. 4. the person, thing, or amount lost. 5. in *electricity,* any reduction of voltage, current, or power between parts of a circuit or between different circuits, due to resistance of the elements. 6. in *insurance,* death, injury, damage, etc. that is the basis for a valid claim for indemnity under the terms of the policy. 7. in *military usage, a*) the losing of soldiers in battle by death, injury, or capture. *b*) *pl.* soldiers lost in this way.

at a loss, puzzled; in an uncertain or perplexed state.

at a loss to, not able to; uncertain how to.

loss leader, any article that a store sells cheaply or below cost in order to attract customers.

loss ratio, the ratio between the losses incurred and the premiums earned by an insurance company during a specified time.

lost (lôst), past tense and past participle of **lose.** *adj.* 1. ruined; destroyed. 2. not to be found; missing. 3. no longer held or possessed; parted with. 4. no longer seen, heard, or known: as, a person *lost* in a crowd. 5. not gained or won; attended with defeat. 6. having wandered from the way. 7. bewildered; perplexed. 8. not spent profitably or usefully; wasted. 9. spent away from one's place of work, as because of illness: as, he made up all his *lost* time.

lost in, absorbed in; engrossed in.

lost on, without effect on; failing to influence.

lost to, 1. no longer in the possession or enjoyment of. 2. no longer available to. 3. having no sense of (shame, right, etc.); insensible to.

lost cause, an undertaking or movement that has failed or is certain to fail.

lost motion, the difference in the rate of motion of driving and driven parts of a machine, due to faulty fittings, etc.

lost tribes, the ten tribes making up the kingdom of Israel that were carried off into Assyrian captivity about 722 B.C.: II Kings 17:6.

Lot (lot), *n.* [Heb. *lōṭ*], in the *Bible,* Abraham's nephew, who, warned by two angels, fled from the doomed city of Sodom: his wife, who glanced back to behold the destruction, was turned into a pillar of salt: Gen. 19:1-26.

Lot (lôt), *n.* a river in southern France, flowing into the Garonne River: length, c. 300 mi.

lot (lot), *n.* [ME. *lotte;* AS. *hlot;* akin to G. *los;* IE. base **qlēu-,* **qlāu-,* a hook, forked branch, twig, etc., seen also in L. *clavis* (cf. CLAVICLE); prob. basic sense "piece of twig as used in drawing lots"], 1. an object used in deciding a matter by chance, a number of these being placed in a container and then drawn or cast out at random one by one. 2. the use of such an object or objects in determining a matter: as, ten men were chosen by *lot.* 3. the decision or choice arrived at by this means, regarded as the verdict of chance. 4. what a person receives as the result of such a decision; share; hence, 5. one's portion in life; fortune: as, her *lot* was not a happy one. 6. a plot of ground; specifically, *a*) a subdivision of a block in a town or city. *b*) a parcel of land in a cemetery. 7. a number of persons or things regarded as a group. 8. *often pl.* [Colloq.], a great number or amount: as, we saw a *lot* of wild ducks. 9. [Colloq.], sort (of person): as, he's a bad *lot.* 10. in *motion pictures,* a studio with the surrounding area belonging to it. *adv.* a great deal; very much: as, she is a *lot* happier. *v.t.* [LOTTED (-id), LOTTING], 1. to divide into lots. 2. [Rare], to allot. *v.i.* to draw or cast lots. —*SYN.* see **fate.**

cast (or **throw**) **in one's lot with,** to take one's chances in association with; share the fortunes of.

draw (or **cast**) **lots,** to decide an issue by using lots.

the lot, [Colloq.], the whole of a quantity or number.

loth (lōth), *adj.* loath.

Lo·thar·i·o (lō-thâr′i-ō′), *n.* [*pl.* LOTHARIOS (-ōz′)], [name of young rake in Nicholas Rowe's play *The Fair Penitent* (1703)], a gay seducer of women; rake.

Lo·thi·ans, The (lō′*th*i-ənz, lō′thi-ənz), a district of Scotland made up of three counties (*East Lothian, Midlothian,* and *West Lothian*), south of the Firth of Forth.

Lo·ti, Pierre (pyâr′ lô′tē′), (pseudonym of *Louis Marie Julien Viaud*), 1850–1923; French novelist.

lo·tion (lō′shən), *n.* [ME. *loscion;* L. *lotio, lotionis* < *lotus, lavatus,* pp. of *lavare,* to wash, bathe], a liquid preparation used, as on the skin, for washing, soothing, healing, etc.

lo·tos (lō′təs), *n.* the lotus.

Lot·ta (lot′ə), a feminine name: see **Charlotte.**

lot·ter·y (lot′ẽr-i), *n.* [*pl.* LOTTERIES (-iz)], [It. *lotteria* < *lotto,* lot < Fr. *lot* < Gmc. **laut;* see LOT], a game of chance, often sponsored by a civic or other organization for the purpose of raising funds: subscribers buy numbered chances on the prizes offered, the winning numbers being chosen by lot.

Lot·tie, Lot·ty (lot′i), a feminine name: see **Charlotte.**

lot·to (lot′ō), *n.* [It.; see LOTTERY], a game of chance played with cards having squares numbered in rows, no two cards being numbered alike: counters are used to cover the numbered squares corresponding to the numbered disks drawn by lot from a bag or box and the player who first gets one row, etc. on his card covered is the winner: see also **bingo, keno,** etc.

lo·tus (lō′təs), *n.* [L.; Gr. *lōtos*], 1. in *Greek legend, a*) the fruit eaten by the lotus-eaters, which was supposed to induce a dreamy languor and forgetfulness. *b*) the plant bearing this fruit. 2. any of several tropical water lilies, especially the blue African lotus, a similar species from India, and the white lotus of Egypt. 3. a representation of any of these plants in ancient, especially Egyptian, sculpture and architecture. 4. any of various kinds of shrubs and herbs of the pea family, with irregular, pinnate leaves and pealike flowers of yellow, purple, or white. Also spelled **lotos.**

LOTUS

lo·tus-eat·er (lō′təs-ēt′ẽr), *n.* 1. in *Greek legend,* one of the inhabitants of a land described in the *Odyssey* (Bk. 9), who ate the fruit of the lotus and consequently became indolent, dreamy, and forgetful; hence, 2. anyone thought of as living a life of indolence and ease, forgetful of reality and duty.

loud (loud), *adj.* [ME.; AS. *hlud;* akin to G. *laut;* IE. base **kleu-,* to hear, listen; cf. LISTEN], 1. striking with force on the organs of hearing; of great intensity; strongly audible: said of sound. 2. making a sound or sounds of great intensity: as, a *loud* bell. 3. noisy. 4. clamorous; emphatic; insistent: as, *loud* denials. 5. [Colloq.], too vivid; showy; flashy: as, a *loud* pattern in clothes. 6. [Colloq.], unrefined; vulgar. *adv.* in a loud manner; loudly.

loud·en (loud′'n), *v.t.* & *v.i.* to make or become loud or louder.

loud·ish (loud′ish), *adj.* somewhat loud.

loud·mouthed (loud′mouthd′, loud′moutht′), *adj.* talking in a loud, irritating voice; blatant.

loud-speak·er (loud′spēk′ẽr), *n.* in *radio,* etc., a device for converting electrical energy to sound and for amplifying this sound to the desired volume.

lough (lokh), *n.* [ME.; Gael. & OIr. *loch;* see LOCH], [Irish], 1. a lake. 2. an arm of the sea.

Lou·is (lōō′is, lōō′i; Fr. lwē), [Fr.; OFr. *Loeis;* prob. via ML. *Ludovicus* < OHG. *Hluodowig* < Gmc. base **hluda-*, famous (< base of *loud*) + **wiga-*, war; hence, lit., famous in war; in the form *Lewis*, sometimes an adaptation of W. *Llewelyn*], a masculine name: diminutives, *Lou, Louie;* feminine, *Louise;* equivalents, L. *Ludovicus*, G. *Ludwig*, It. *Luigi*, Sp. *Luis*: also **Lewis.**

lou·is (lōō′i), *n.* [*pl.* LOUIS (lōō′iz)], a louis d'or.

Louis I, 778–840 A.D.; son and successor of Charlemagne; king of France and emperor of the Holy Roman Empire (814–840 A.D.): called *le Débonnaire, the Pious.*

Louis II de Bourbon, see **Condé,** Prince **de.**

Louis IX, 1214–1270; king of France (1226–1270): also **Saint Louis.**

Louis XI, 1423–1483; son of Charles VII; king of France (1461–1483).

Louis XII, 1462–1515; king of France (1498–1515): called *Father of the People.*

Louis XIII, 1601–1643; king of France (1610–1643); acted under advice of Richelieu.

Louis XIV, 1638–1715; son of Louis XIII; king of France (1643–1715); his reign encompassed a great period of French culture: called *the Great.*

Louis XV, 1710–1774; great-grandson of Louis XIV; king of France (1715–1774); reign marked by War of the Austrian Succession and Seven Years' War.

Louis XVI, 1754–1793; grandson of Louis XV; king of France (1774–1792); reign marked by French Revolution; guillotined.

Louis XVII, 1785–1795; son of Louis XVI; titular king of France.

Louis XVIII, (*Louis Xavier Stanislas*), 1755–1824; grandson of Louis XV and brother of Louis XVI; king of France (1814–1815; 1815–1824).

Lou·is, Joe (lōō′is), (*born Joseph Louis Barrow*), 1914– ; American prize fighter; world heavyweight champion (1937–1949).

Lou·i·sa (loo-wē′zə), [It.], a feminine name: see **Louise.**

lou·is d'or (lōō′i dôr′), [Fr., gold louis: so called after various French kings], 1. an old French gold coin of varying value, issued through the reigns of Louis XIII–Louis XVI. 2. a later French gold coin worth 20 francs.

Lou·ise (loo-wēz′), [Fr., fem. of *Louis*], a feminine name: diminutives, *Lou, Lulu;* variants, *Louisa, Eloise.*

Louise, Lake, a small lake in Banff National Park, Alberta, Canada: altitude, 5,670 ft.

Lou·i·si·an·a (lōō′i-zi-an′ə, loo-wē′zi-an′ə), *n.* a Southern State of the United States, on the Gulf of Mexico: area, 48,523 sq. mi.; pop., 3,257,000; capital, Baton Rouge: abbreviated **La.**

Lou·i·si·an·an (lōō′i-zi-an′ən, loo-wē′zi-an′ən), *adj.* & *n.* Louisianian.

Louisiana Purchase, the land bought by the United States from France in 1803 for $15,000,000: it extended from the Gulf of Mexico to Canada and from the Mississippi to the Rocky Mountains.

LOUISIANA PURCHASE (1803)

Lou·i·si·an·i·an (lōō′i-zi-an′i-ən, loo-wē′zi-an′i-ən), *adj.* of Louisiana. *n.* a native or inhabitant of Louisiana.

Louis Napoleon, (born *Charles Louis Napoleon Bonaparte*), 1808–1873; nephew of Napoleon; as Napoleon III, emperor of France (1852–1870); deposed.

Lou·is Phi·lippe (lwē fē′lēp′; Eng. lōō′i fi-lēp′), 1773–1850; king of France (1830–1848); abdicated in Revolution of 1848: called *Roi citoyen* (*Citizen King*).

Louis Qua·torze (kȧ′tôrz′), designating or of the style of furniture, architecture, etc. of the time of Louis XIV of France, characterized by massive, baroque forms and lavish ornamentation.

Louis Quinze (kanz), designating or of the style of furniture, architecture, etc. of the time of Louis XV of France, characterized by rococo treatment with emphasis on curved lines and highly decorative forms based on shells, flowers, etc.

Louis Seize (sez), designating or of the style of furniture, architecture, etc. of the time of Louis XVI of France, characterized by a return to straight lines, symmetry, and classic ornamental details.

Louis Treize (trez), designating or of the style of furniture, architecture, etc. of the time of Louis XIII of France, characterized by Renaissance forms, rich inlays, deep moldings, etc.

Lou·is·ville (lōō′i-vil′), *n.* a city in northern Kentucky, on the Ohio: pop., 391,000.

lounge (lounj), *v.i.* [LOUNGED (lounjd), LOUNGING], [15th-c. Scot. dial.; ? < *lungis*, laggard, drowsy person < OFr. *longis* < L. *Longinus*, supposed name of soldier who lanced Jesus in the side, merged with L. *longus*], 1. to stand, move, sit, lie, etc. in a relaxed or lazy way; loll. 2. to spend time in idleness. *v.t.* to spend by lounging: as, they *lounged* the summer away. *n.* 1. an act or time of lounging. 2. a lounging gait or stroll. 3. a room, as in a hotel, equipped with comfortable furniture for lounging. 4. a couch or sofa, especially a backless one with a headrest at one end.

loung·er (loun′jẽr), *n.* a person who lounges; idler.

‡**loup-ga·rou** (lōō′gȧ′rōō′), *n.* [*pl.* LOUPS-GAROUS (lōō′-gȧ′rōō′)], [Fr.; *loup*, wolf (L. *lupus*) + *garou*, werewolf; OFr. *garous, garoul* < Frank. **wari-wulf;* see WEREWOLF], a werewolf.

lour (lour), *v.i.* & *n.* lower (scowl).

Lourdes (loord; Fr. lōōrd), *n.* a town in southwestern France: pop., 14,000: site of a famous shrine.

Lou·ren·ço Mar·ques (lō-ren′sō mär′kes; Port. lô-ren′soo mär′kezh), the capital of Mozambique: pop., 93,000.

louse (lous; *for v.,* louz), *n.* [*pl.* LICE (līs)], [ME.; AS. *lus;* akin to G. *laus;* IE. **lōus*, seen also in W. *lleuen*, Bret. *laouen*, etc.], 1. any of several small, flat, wingless parasitic insects, with either biting or sucking mouth parts, that infest the hair or skin of man and other warm-blooded animals. 2. any of various other small insects, arachnids, and crustaceans, parasitic on plants or animals. 3. [*pl.* LOUSES (-iz)], [Slang], a person regarded as mean, contemptible, etc. *v.t.* [LOUSED (louzd), LOUSING], [Rare], to delouse.
 louse up (lous), [Slang], to botch; bungle; spoil; ruin.

louse·wort (lous′wũrt′), *n.* [so called because sheep feeding on the plants were said to become infested with vermin], any of a group of plants of the figwort family, with soft, hairy, fernlike leaves and spiked clusters of reddish and yellowish flowers: also called *wood betony.*

lous·i·ness (louz′i-nis), *n.* the condition of being lousy.

lous·y (lou′zi), *adj.* [LOUSIER (-zi-ẽr), LOUSIEST (-zi-ist)], 1. infested with lice; hence, 2. [Slang], dirty, disgusting, or contemptible. 3. [Slang], poor; inferior: a generalized epithet of disapproval or condemnation. 4. [Slang], well supplied or oversupplied (*with*).

lout (lout), *n.* [prob. < or connected with ME. *lowt*, a rag (for **lowd*), hence akin to MLG. *lūder*, lappet, rag, ragged fellow; prob. influenced by *lout*, to bow], a clumsy, stupid fellow; boor. *v.t.* [Obs.], to treat with contempt; flout.

lout (lout), *v.i.* & *v.t.* [ME. *louten;* AS. *lutan;* akin to ON. *luta;* IE. base **leud-*, to stoop (cf. LITTLE), seen also in Ir. *lūda*, little finger], [Archaic & Dial.], to bow or curtsy; bend; stoop.

lout·ish (lout′ish), *adj.* like or characteristic of a lout; clumsy and stupid; boorish.

Lou·vain (lōō′van′; Eng. lōō-vān′), *n.* a city in central Belgium: pop., 34,000.

lou·ver (lōō′vẽr), *n.* [ME. *luver, lover;* OFr. *lover, lovier* < base of OHG. *louba, loupa*, upper story gallery, upper roof, etc.; for IE. base see LEAF, LOFT], 1. in *medieval architecture*, an open turret or lantern on the roof of a building. 2. *a)* a window or opening in a turret, etc. furnished with louver boards. *b)* a louver board. 3. any ventilating slit, as in the side of an automobile hood.

louver board, any of a series of sloping slats set in a window or other opening to provide air and light but to shed rainwater outward: also **louver boarding.**

LOUVER BOARDS

L'Ouverture, Toussaint, see **Toussaint L'Ouverture.**

Lou·vre (lōō′vrə, lōōv, lōō′vẽr; Fr. lōō′vr′), *n.* an ancient royal palace in Paris, converted into a museum in the 18th century: it contains many of the world's great art treasures.

lov·a·bil·i·ty (luv′ə-bil′ə-ti), *n.* the quality of being lovable.

lov·a·ble (luv′ə-b'l), *adj.* inspiring love; endearing: also spelled **loveable.**

lov·a·bly (luv′ə-bli), *adv.* in a lovable manner; so as to be lovable: also spelled **loveably.**

lov·age (luv′ij), *n.* [ME. *loveache;* altered (after *love* & *ache*) < OFr. *levesche, luvesche;* LL. *levisticum* for L. *ligusticum*, lovage plant native to Liguria < *Ligusticus*, Ligurian < *Liguria*, country in Cisalpine Gaul], a European herb of the carrot family, formerly cultivated for use as a home medicine.

love (luv), *n.* [ME. *love, luve;* AS. *lufu;* akin to OHG. *luba* &, more remotely, G. *liebe;* IE. base **leubh-*, to be fond of; cf. LIBIDO, LIBIDINOUS, LIEF, LUST], 1. a strong affection for or attachment or devotion to a person or persons. 2. a strong liking for or interest in something: as, her *love* of acting. 3. a strong, usually passionate, affection for a person of the opposite sex. 4. the person who is the object of such an affection;

sweetheart; lover. 5. sexual passion or its gratification. 6. [L-], *a)* Cupid, or Eros, as the god of love. *b)* [Rare], Venus. 7. [< phr. *play for love,* i.e., play for nothing], in *tennis,* a score of zero. 8. in *theology, a)* God's benevolent concern for mankind. *b)* man's devout attachment to God. *c)* the feeling of benevolence and brotherhood that people should have for each other. ***v.t.*** [LOVED (luvd), LOVING], 1. to feel love for. 2. to show love for by embracing, fondling, kissing, etc. 3. to delight in; take pleasure in: as, she *loves* good music. ***v.i.*** to feel the emotion of love; be in love.

fall in love, to begin to love; feel a strong, usually passionate, affection.

for love, as a favor or for pleasure; without payment.

for the love of, for the sake of; with loving regard for.

in love, feeling love; enamored.

make love, to woo or embrace, kiss, etc. as lovers do.

no love lost between, no liking or affection existing between.

***SYN.*—love** implies intense fondness or deep devotion and may apply to various relationships or objects (sexual *love,* brotherly *love, love* of one's work, etc.); **affection** suggests warm, tender feelings, usually not as powerful or deep as those implied by **love** (he has no *affection* for children); **attachment** implies connection by ties of affection, attraction, devotion, etc. and may be felt for inanimate things as well as for people (an *attachment* to an old hat); **infatuation** implies a foolish or unreasoning passion or affection, often a transient one (an elderly man's *infatuation* for a young girl).

love·a·ble (luv'ə-b'l), ***adj.*** lovable.

love·a·bly (luv'ə-bli), ***adv.*** lovably.

love affair, an amorous or romantic relationship or episode between two people not married to each other.

love apple, [cf. Fr. *pomme d'amour,* G. *liebesapfel;* orig. prob. folk etym. for earlier It. *pomi dei Mori,* lit., apples of the Moors], the tomato: former name.

love·bird (luv'bũrd'), ***n.*** any of various small birds of the parrot family, originally from Africa or South America, often kept as cage birds: so called because mates appear to be greatly attached to each other.

love feast, 1. among the early Christians, a meal eaten together as a symbol of affection and brotherhood. 2. in certain modern religious denominations, a feast or gathering imitating this. 3. any feast or gathering characterized by friendliness and good feeling.

love game, in *tennis,* a game in which the losing player or team scores no points.

love-in-a-mist (luv'in-ə-mist'), ***n.*** any of a group of European plants of the crowfoot family, with finely cut leaves and blue flowers.

love-in-i·dle·ness (luv'in-ī'd'l-nis), ***n.*** the wild pansy.

love knot, a knot of ribbon, etc. that serves as a token between lovers.

Love·lace, Richard (luv'lās'), 1618–1658; English Cavalier poet.

love·less (luv'lis), ***adj.*** without love; specifically, *a)* feeling no love. *b)* receiving no love; unloved.

love-lies-bleed·ing (luv'līz'blēd'iŋ), ***n.*** a variety of amaranth with drooping spikes of small, red flowers.

love·li·ness (luv'li-nis), ***n.*** the quality of being lovely.

love·lock (luv'lok'), ***n.*** [cf. Fr. *accroche-coeur*], a lock of hair lying apart from the rest of the hair; specifically, such a long lock as formerly worn by courtiers.

love·lorn (luv'lôrn'), ***adj.*** [see LORN], deserted by or pining for one's sweetheart; pining from love.

love·ly (luv'li), ***adj.*** [LOVELIER (-li-ẽr), LOVELIEST (-li-ist)], [ME. *luvelich;* AS. *luflic*], having those qualities that inspire love, affection, or admiration; specifically, *a)* beautiful; exquisite. *b)* morally or spiritually attractive; gracious. *c)* [Colloq.], highly enjoyable: as, a *lovely* party. —***SYN.*** see **beautiful.**

love-mak·ing (luv'māk'iŋ), ***n.*** the act of making love; wooing or embracing, fondling, kissing, etc.

love match, a marriage for love only, not for wealth, social status, etc.

love potion, a magic drink supposed to arouse love for a certain person in the drinker.

lov·er (luv'ẽr), ***n.*** a person who loves; specifically, *a)* a sweetheart. *b) pl.* a man and a woman in love with each other. *c)* a paramour: now usually applied only to a man. *d)* a person who greatly enjoys some (specified) thing: as, a *lover* of good music.

lov·er·ly (luv'ẽr-li), ***adj. & adv.*** like, or in the manner of, a lover.

love seat, a double chair or small sofa seating two persons.

love set, in *tennis,* a set in which the loser wins no games.

love·sick (luv'sik'), ***adj.*** 1. so much in love as to be incapable of carrying on in a normal fashion. 2. expressive of such a condition: as, a *lovesick* song.

lov·ing (luv'iŋ), ***adj.*** [ppr. of *love*], 1. feeling love; devoted. 2. expressing love: as, a *loving* act.

loving cup, a large drinking cup of silver, etc., with two or more large handles by which it was formerly passed from guest to guest at banquets: now often given as a prize in sporting events, etc.

lov·ing-kind·ness (luv'iŋ-kīnd'nis), ***n.*** kindness or affectionate behavior resulting from or expressing love.

low (lō), ***adj.*** [ME. *lowe, louh,* etc.; AS. *lah* (akin to ON. *lagr,* MD. *lage*); for base see LIE (to recline) & LAY, *v.*], 1. of little height or elevation; not high or tall. 2. depressed below the surrounding surface or normal elevation: as, water stood in the *low* places. 3. of little depth; shallow: as, the river is *low.* 4. of little quantity, degree, intensity, value, etc.: as, a *low* cost, *low* pressure. 5. of less than normal height, elevation, depth, quantity, degree, etc. 6. near the horizon: as, the sun was *low.* 7. near the equator: as, a *low* latitude. 8. cut so as to expose the neck or part of the shoulders, chest, or back; décolleté: as, a dress with a *low* neckline. 9. *a)* prostrate or dead: as, he was laid *low.* *b)* in hiding or obscurity: as, I must stay *low* until the trial is over. 10. deep: as, a *low* bow. 11. lacking energy; enfeebled; weak. 12. depressed in spirits; melancholy. 13. not of high rank; humble; plebeian: as, his *low* origin did not hamper him. 14. vulgar; coarse; debased; undignified. 15. poor; slight; unfavorable: as, she has a *low* opinion of him. 16. not rich or nourishing; simple; plain: as, a *low* diet. 17. not advanced in evolution, development, complexity, etc.; inferior: as, a *low* form of plant life. 18. relatively recent: as, a manuscript of a *low* date. 19. designating the gear ratio of a motor vehicle, etc., producing the lowest speed and the greatest power. 20. *a)* not well supplied with; short of (with *on*): as, to be *low* on ammunition. *b)* [Colloq.], not having any or much money; short of ready cash. 21. of little intensity; not loud: said of a sound. 22. designating or producing tones made by relatively slow vibrations; deep in pitch. 23. in the *Anglican Church,* relating to the Low Church or its doctrines. 24. in *phonetics,* pronounced with the tongue depressed in the mouth: said of certain vowels, such as the *a* in *calm.* ***adv.*** 1. in, to, or toward a low position, direction, etc.: as, hit them *low.* 2. in a low manner. 3. quietly; softly: as, talk *low* so as not to disturb the others. 4. with a deep pitch. 5. in a low rank or humble position. 6. cheaply: as, sell high and buy *low.* 7. so as to be near the horizon or near the equator. ***n.*** something low; specifically, *a)* that gear of a motor vehicle, etc., producing the lowest speed and the greatest power. *b)* [Colloq.], a low level of accomplishment: as, her performance represents a new *low* in acting. *c)* in certain card games, the lowest trump. *d)* in certain sports, games, etc., the lowest score or number, or the person or team having this. *e)* in *meteorology,* a low-pressure area. Abbreviated **L., l.** —***SYN.*** see **base.**

lay low, 1. to cause to fall by hitting. 2. to overcome or kill.

lie low, to keep oneself hidden or inconspicuous.

low (lō), ***v.i.*** [ME. *lowen;* AS. *hlowan;* akin to ON. *hloa,* to roar; IE. base **kel-,* to cry, cry out, seen also in L. *clamor,* cry (cf. CLAMOR)], to make the characteristic sound of a cow; moo. ***v.t.*** to express by lowing. ***n.*** the characteristic sound of a cow.

Low Archipelago, the Tuamotu Archipelago.

low·born (lō'bôrn'), ***adj.*** born into a low, or humble, rank or position.

low·boy (lō'boi'), ***n.*** a chest of drawers mounted on short legs to about the height of a table: distinguished from *highboy.*

LOWBOY

low·bred (lō'bred'), ***adj.*** 1. of inferior stock; poorly born. 2. ill-mannered; vulgar; crude; coarse.

low-brow (lō'brou'), ***n.*** [Slang], a person lacking or considered to lack highly cultivated and intellectual tastes. ***adj.*** [Slang], of or for a low-brow. Usually a term of contempt or of false humility.

Low-Church (lō'chũrch'), ***adj.*** of or like the Low Church; stressing simplicity in religious observance.

Low Church, that party of the Anglican Church which attaches little importance to rituals, sacraments, etc., and holds to a more evangelical doctrine than the High Church.

low comedy, comedy that gets its effect mainly from action and situation, as burlesque, farce, slapstick, and horseplay, rather than from witty dialogue and characterization; broadly humorous comedy.

low-cost (lō'kôst'), ***adj.*** available at a low cost.

Low Countries, the Netherlands, Belgium, and Luxemburg.

low-coun·try (lō′kun′tri), *adj.* of the Low Countries.
low-down (lō′doun′), *n.* [Slang], the pertinent facts; especially, secret information (with *the*). *adj.* (lō′-doun′), [Colloq.], mean; contemptible; despicable.
Low·ell (lō′əl), *n.* a city in northeastern Massachusetts: pop., 92,000.
Lowell, Abbott Lawrence, 1856–1943; American educator and lawyer; president of Harvard (1909–1933).
Lowell, Amy, 1874–1925; sister of *Abbott Lawrence;* American poet and critic.
Lowell, James Russell, 1819–1891; American poet, essayist, editor, and diplomat.
low·er (lō′ẽr), *adj.* [comparative of *low*], 1. in a place or physical condition below another. 2. inferior in rank, authority, dignity, etc. 3. [L-], in *geology*, earlier: used of a division of a period, as, *Lower* Devonian. *n.* something below another similar thing; specifically [Colloq.], a lower berth. *v.t.* 1. to let or put down: as, he *lowered* the window. 2. to reduce in height, amount, value, etc.: as, he will *lower* his prices. 3. to weaken or lessen: as, a cold had *lowered* his resistance. 4. to cause to be less respected: as, such acts *lowered* him in our eyes. 5. to reduce (a sound) in volume or in pitch. *v.i.* to become lower; sink, fall, become reduced, etc.
low·er (lou′ẽr), *v.i.* [ME. *louren, luren;* cf. G. *lauern,* to lurk], 1. to scowl or frown. 2. to appear black and threatening: as, a *lowering* sky or clouds. *n.* a frowning or threatening look. Also **lour.**
Lower Alsace, the part of Alsace that is now Bas-Rhin.
Lower Austria, a province of northeastern Austria: pop., 1,400,000.
Lower California, a peninsula in Mexico, between the Pacific and the Gulf of California: area, 55,629 sq. mi.; pop., 538,000; capital of northern territory, Mexicali; of southern territory, La Paz: Mexican name, *Baja California.*
Lower Canada, Quebec, a province of Canada: the former name: abbreviated **L.C.**
low·er-case (lō′ẽr-kās′), *adj.* in *printing,* designating, of, or in small letters as distinguished from capital (*upper-case*) letters. *v.t.* [LOWER-CASED (-kāst′), LOWER-CASING], to set up in, or to change to, small letters.
lower case, [from their being kept in the lower of two cases of type], small-letter type used in printing as distinguished from capital letters (*upper case*): abbreviated **l.c.**
low·er·class·man (lō′ẽr-klas′mən), *n.* [*pl.* LOWERCLASSMEN (-mən)], a student in either of the first two years of a four-year course in a school or college; freshman or sophomore.
Lower House, [sometimes l- h-], the popular and, usually, larger and more representative branch of a legislature having two branches, as the House of Representatives of the United States Congress.
low·er·ing (lou′ẽr-iŋ, lour′iŋ), *adj.* [ppr. of *lower* (to scowl)], 1. scowling; frowning darkly. 2. dark, as if about to rain or snow; overcast.
low·er·most (lō′ẽr-mōst′), *adj.* lowest.
Lower Silurian, in *geology,* the Ordovician.
lower world, 1. the supposed abode of the dead; hell; Hades; Sheol. 2. the earth.
Lowes, John Liv·ing·ston (liv′iŋ-stən lōz), 1867–1945; American scholar, critic, and teacher.
lowest common multiple, the lowest number exactly divisible by each of two or more numbers: abbreviated **L.C.M., l.c.m.**
Lowes·toft (lōs′toft, lōs′təft), *n.* 1. a port on the eastern coast of England: pop., 42,000. 2. a variety of china made there.
low-fre·quen·cy (lō′frē′kwən-si), *adj.* in *electricity,* designating or of an alternating current or oscillation with a relatively low frequency, now usually less than 10,000 cycles per second.
Low German, 1. *a*) the German dialects spoken in the northern lowlands of Germany, the Netherlands, etc. *b*) Plattdeutsch. 2. that branch of the Germanic subfamily of the Indo-European family of languages which includes English, Frisian, Dutch, Flemish, Old Saxon, Plattdeutsch, etc.: distinguished from *High German.* Abbreviated **LG., L.G., L.Ger.**
low-grade (lō′grād′), *adj.* of inferior quality.
low·land (lō′lənd; *also, for n.,* lō′land′), *n.* land that is below the level of the surrounding land. *adj.* of or from such a region.
the Lowlands, lowlands of southern and eastern Scotland: distinguished from *the Highlands.*
low·land·er (lō′lən-dẽr), *n.* a native or inhabitant of a lowland or of the Lowlands.
Low Latin, the Latin language from 200–300 A.D. to the time when Latin disappeared as a vernacular distinct from the various Romance languages: abbreviated **LL., L.Lat.:** cf. **Late Latin, Medieval Latin, Vulgar Latin.**
low·li·ness (lō′li-nis), *n.* a lowly state or condition.
low·ly (lō′li), *adj.* [LOWLIER (-li-ẽr), LOWLIEST (-li-ist)], 1. of or suited to a low position or rank. 2. humble; meek. 3. low. *adv.* 1. humbly; meekly. 2. in a low manner, position, etc. —*SYN.* see **humble.**
Low Mass, a Mass said without music and with less ceremonialism than High Mass: it is conducted by one priest with, usually, only one server, or altar boy.
low-mind·ed (lō′mīn′did), *adj.* having or showing a coarse, vulgar mind.
low-necked (lō′nekt′), *adj.* having a low neckline; décolleté: said of a dress, etc.
low-pitched (lō′picht′), *adj.* 1. having a low tone or a low range of tone: as, a *low-pitched* voice. 2. having little pitch, or slope: said of a roof.
low-pres·sure (lō′presh′ẽr), *adj.* having or using relatively low pressure: abbreviated **l.p.**
low relief, bas-relief.
low-spir·it·ed (lō′spir′i-tid), *adj.* in low spirits; sad.
Low Sunday, the first Sunday after Easter.
low-ten·sion (lō′ten′shən), *adj.* in *electricity,* having, or carrying a current of, low potential.
low-test (lō′test′), *adj.* having a high boiling point: said of gasoline.
low tide, 1. the lowest level reached by the ebbing tide. 2. the time when this point is reached. 3. the lowest point reached by something.
low water, 1. water at its lowest level, as in a stream. 2. low tide.
low-wa·ter mark (lō′wô′tẽr, lō′wät′ẽr), 1. a mark showing low water. 2. the lowest point reached by something. Abbreviated **L.W.M.**
lox (loks), *n.* [via Yid. < G. *lachs,* salmon; akin to AS. *leax,* salmon, Tocharian *laks,* fish], a variety of salty smoked salmon.
lox (loks), *n.* [< *l*iquid *ox*ygen], oxygen in a liquid state, used in a fuel mixture for rockets.
lox·o·drom·ic (lok′sə-drom′ik), *adj.* [< Gr. *loxos,* oblique + *dromos,* a running], having to do with sailing on rhumb lines; of oblique sailing.
lox·o·drom·ics (lok′sə-drom′iks), *n.pl.* [construed as sing.], the art or practice of oblique sailing.
loy·al (loi′əl), *adj.* [Fr.; OFr. *loial, leial* < L. *legalis;* see LEGAL], 1. faithful to the constituted authority of one's country. 2. faithful to those persons, ideals, etc. that one is under obligation to defend or support. 3. relating to or indicating loyalty. —*SYN.* see **faithful.**
loy·al·ist (loi′əl-ist), *n.* 1. a person who is loyal; especially, one who supports the established government of his country during times of revolt. 2. [often L-], in the American Revolution, a colonist who was loyal to the British government. 3. [L-], in the Spanish Civil War, one who remained loyal to the elected government of the Republic in opposition to the insurrection led by Franco.
loy·al·ty (loi′əl-ti), *n.* [*pl.* LOYALTIES (-tiz)], [ME. *loyaltee, loyaulte;* OFr. *loialte*], quality, state, or instance of being loyal; faithfulness or faithful adherence to a person, government, cause, duty, etc. —*SYN.* see **allegiance.**
Loyola, Saint **Ignatius of,** see **Ignatius of Loyola.**
loz·enge (loz′inj), *n.* [OFr. *losenge;* prob. < Pr. *lausa,* stone slab], 1. a plane figure with four equal sides and two obtuse angles; diamond. 2. a cough drop, candy, etc., originally in this shape.
LP, *adj.* [*L*ong *P*laying], designating or of a phonograph record marked with microgrooves and designed to be played at 33 1/3 revolutions per minute. *n.* an LP record: a trade-mark.
L.R., Lloyd's Register.
L.S., 1. Licentiate in Surgery. 2. Linnaean Society. 3. *locus sigilli,* [L.], place of the seal.
l.s.c., *loco supra citato,* [L.], in the place cited above.
L.S.D., £.s.d., l.s.d., *librae, solidi, denarii,* [L.], pounds, shillings, pence.
Lt., Lieutenant.
lt., in *football,* left tackle.
l.t., long ton.
Lt. Col., Lieutenant Colonel.
Lt. Comdr., Lt.-Comm., Lieutenant Commander.
Ltd., ltd., limited.
Lt. Gen., Lieutenant General.
Lt. Gov., Lieutenant Governor.
Lu, in *chemistry,* lutetium.
Lu·an·da (lōō-ān′də), *n.* seaport and capital of Angola, Africa: pop., 142,000: formerly called *Loanda, São Paolo de Loanda.*
lu·au (lōō-ou′, lōō′ou′), *n.* [Haw.], a Hawaiian feast, usually with entertainment.
Lu·bang Islands (lōō-bäŋ′), a small group of islands in the Philippines, near Manila Bay: pop., 15,000.
lub·ber (lub′ẽr), *n.* [ME. *lobre, lobur* < *lobbe* (see LOB); basic sense prob. "sexually impotent"], 1. a big, slow, clumsy person. 2. an inexperienced, clumsy sailor; landlubber. *adj.* big and clumsy.
lub·ber·li·ness (lub′ẽr-li-nis), *n.* a lubberly quality.
lub·ber·ly (lub′ẽr-li), *adj.* big and clumsy. *adv.* in the manner of a lubber.
Lub·bock (lub′ək), *n.* a city in northwestern Texas: pop., 129,000.
lube (lōōb, lūb), *n.* [short for *lubricating oil*], a lubricating oil for machinery: also **lube oil.**
Lü·beck (lōō′bek; G. lü′bek), *n.* a city in northern Germany: pop., 231,000.

Lu·blin (lōō′blin; Pol. lyōō′blēn), ***n.*** a city in southeastern Poland: pop., 99,000 (1946): site of Maidenek, a Nazi extermination camp: Russian name, *Lyublin.*

lu·bri·cant (lōō′bri-kənt, lū′bri-kənt), ***adj.*** [L. *lubricans*], reducing friction by providing a smooth film as a covering over parts that move against each other; lubricating. ***n.*** a substance for reducing friction in this way, as oil or grease. Abbreviated **lubric.**

lu·bri·cate (lōō′bri-kāt′, lū′bri-kāt′), ***v.t.*** [LUBRICATED (-id), LUBRICATING], [< L. *lubricatus*, pp. of *lubricare*, to make smooth or slippery < *lubricus*, smooth], 1. to make slippery or smooth. 2. to apply a lubricant to (machinery, etc.) in order to reduce friction in operation. ***v.i.*** to serve as a lubricant.

lu·bri·ca·tion (lōō′bri-kā′shən, lū′bri-kā′shən), ***n.*** a lubricating or being lubricated.

lu·bri·ca·tive (lōō′bri-kā′tiv, lū′bri-kā′tiv), ***adj.*** lubricating or able to lubricate.

lu·bri·ca·tor (lōō′bri-kā′tẽr, lū′bri-kā′tẽr), ***n.*** a person or thing that lubricates; specifically, *a)* a lubricant. *b)* an oil cup or similar device for lubricating machinery.

lu·bric·i·ty (lōō-bris′ə-ti, lū-bris′ə-ti), ***n.*** [*pl.* LUBRICITIES (-tiz)], [Fr. *lubricité;* LL. *lubricitas*], 1. slipperiness; smoothness; especially, effectiveness as a lubricant as indicated by this quality. 2. trickiness. 3. lewdness.

lu·bri·cous (lōō′bri-kəs, lū′bri-kəs), ***adj.*** [L. *lubricus*], having or characterized by lubricity.

Lu·can (lōō′kən, lū′kən), ***n.*** (*Marcus Annaeus Lucanus*), Roman poet, born in Spain; 39–65 A.D.

Lu·ca·ni·a (lōō-kā′ni-ə, lū-kā′ni-ə), ***n.*** 1. an ancient region in southern Italy. 2. a department of southern Italy. 3. a mountain of the St. Elias Range, in Yukon Territory, Canada: height, 17,147 ft.

Luc·ca (lōōk′kä), ***n.*** a city in northwestern Italy: pop., 86,000 (1947).

luce (lōōs, lūs), ***n.*** [OFr. *lus, luis;* L. *lucius*, kind of fish], a pike (fish); especially, a full-grown pike.

lu·cen·cy (lōō′s'n-si, lū′s'n-si), ***n.*** the quality or state of being lucent.

lu·cent (lōō′s'nt, lū′s'nt), ***adj.*** [L. *lucens*, ppr. of *lucere*, to shine], 1. giving off light; shining. 2. translucent.

Lu·cerne (lōō-sũrn′, lū-sũrn′; Fr. lü′sern′), ***n.*** 1. a canton of central Switzerland: pop., 207,000. 2. its capital, on the Lake of Lucerne: pop., 55,000: German name, *Luzern.*

lu·cerne, lu·cern (lōō-sũrn′, lū-sũrn′), ***n.*** [Fr. *luzerne* < OFr. *luiserne*, light, luminous object (< L. *lucerna*, a lamp < *lucere*, to shine): ? so named because the seed has a glowing appearance], alfalfa: the common name in Australia and New Zealand.

Lucerne, Lake of, a lake in central Switzerland: area, 44 sq. mi.

lu·ces (lōō′sēz, lū′sēz), ***n.*** alternative plural of **lux.**

Lu·cia (lōō′shə, lū′shə), [It.; L.; see LUCIUS, LUCY], a feminine name.

Lucia, Saint, see **Lucy,** Saint.

Lu·cian (lōō′shən, lū′shən), [L. *Lucianus*, lit., of Lucius], a masculine name: equivalent, Fr. *Lucien.* ***n.*** Greek satirist; 2d century A.D.

Lucian, Saint, ?–290 A.D.; Roman Christian martyr; missionary in Gaul: his day is January 7.

lu·cid (lōō′sid, lū′sid), ***adj.*** [L. *lucidus* < *lucere*, to shine; cf. LIGHT], 1. [Poetic], bright; shining. 2. transparent. 3. sane; mentally sound. 4. clear; readily understood: as, a *lucid* talk. 5. clearheaded; rational: as, a *lucid* thinker.

lu·ci·da (lōō′si-də, lū′si-də), ***n.*** [*pl.* LUCIDAE (-dē′)], [Mod. L. < L. *lucida* (*stella*), bright (star); see LUCID], the brightest star in a constellation.

lu·cid·i·ty (lōō-sid′ə-ti, lū-sid′ə-ti), ***n.*** the quality or state of being lucid.

Lu·ci·fer (lōō′sə-fẽr, lū′sə-fẽr), ***n.*** [L., Lucifer, lit., light-bringing < *lux, lucis*, light + *ferre*, to bear], 1. [Poetic], the planet Venus when it is the morning star. 2. Satan, especially as the leader of the revolt of the angels before his fall. 3. [l-], an early type of match ignited by friction.

lu·cif·er·in (loo-sif′ẽr-in, lyoo-sif′ẽr-in), ***n.*** [*lucifer* + *-in*], a substance in the blood of fireflies, some sea mollusks, etc. that combines with an enzyme in their bodies to produce light.

lu·cif·er·ous (lōō-sif′ẽr-əs, lū-sif′ẽr-əs), ***adj.*** [L. *lucifer* (see LUCIFER); + *-ous*], 1. providing light. 2. providing mental light or insight.

Lu·cile, Lu·cille (lōō-sēl′, lū-sēl′), a feminine name: see **Lucy.**

Lu·cin·da (lōō-sin′də, lū-sin′də), a feminine name: see **Lucy.**

lu·cite (lōō′sīt, lū′sīt), ***n.*** [< L. *lux, lucis*, light; + *-ite*], a crystal-clear synthetic resin, plastic under heat: it is used for airplane windshields, store fronts, light panels, etc.: a trade-mark (**Lucite**).

Lu·cius (lōō′shəs, lū′shəs), [L. < *lux*, light], a masculine name: feminine, *Lucia.*

luck (luk), ***n.*** [ME. *luk, lukke;* prob. < D. *luk, geluk* < OD. **gilukki* (whence G. *glück*, fortune, good luck); IE. base **leug-*, to bend (cf. LEEK, LOCK); basic sense "what bends together," hence, "what occurs, what is fitting, lucky occurrence"], 1. the seemingly chance happening of events which affect one; fortune; lot; fate. 2. good fortune; success, prosperity, advantage, etc. 3. an object believed to bring good luck.

down on one's luck, in misfortune; unlucky.

in luck, fortunate; lucky.

out of luck, unfortunate; unlucky.

try one's luck, try to do something without being sure of one's ability or of the outcome.

worse luck, unfortunately; unhappily.

luck·i·ly (luk′'l-i), ***adv.*** by or with good luck; fortunately.

luck·i·ness (luk′i-nis), ***n.*** a lucky quality or state.

luck·less (luk′lis), ***adj.*** having no good luck; unlucky.

Luck·now (luk′nou), ***n.*** the capital of Uttar Pradesh, a state of northern India: pop., 387,000.

luck·y (luk′i), ***adj.*** [LUCKIER (-i-ẽr), LUCKIEST (-i-ist)], 1. having good luck; fortunate. 2. happening or resulting fortunately: as, a *lucky* change. 3. bringing or believed to bring good luck: as, a *lucky* coin.

SYN.—**lucky** implies a favorable or advantageous event happening by mere chance, often unexpectedly, and not as the result of effort or merit (a *lucky* find, guess, etc.); **fortunate,** a more formal word, is usually used of more important or serious matters (a *fortunate* choice of profession); **providential** connotes the intervention of God or some higher agency in bringing about the favorable event (a *providential* escape from death); **happy** emphasizes the pleasure felt by the person affected by the lucky event (marriage resulted from that *happy* encounter). —***ANT.*** unlucky, disastrous.

lu·cra·tive (lōō′krə-tiv, lū′krə-tiv), ***adj.*** [L. *lucrativus* < pp. of *lucrari*, to gain < *lucrum*, gain, riches], producing wealth or profit; profitable; remunerative: as, a *lucrative* investment.

lu·cre (lōō′kẽr, lū′kẽr), ***n.*** [ME.; OFr. < L. *lucrum*, gain, riches], riches; money: now chiefly in a humorously derogatory sense, as in *filthy lucre.*

Lu·cre·tia (lōō-krē′shə, lū-krē′shə), [L., fem. of *Lucretius;* prob. < *lucrum*, gain, riches], a feminine name: equivalents, Fr. *Lucrèce*, It. *Lucrezia.*

Lu·cre·tius (lōō-krē′shəs, lū-krē′shəs), ***n.*** (*Titus Lucretius Carus*), Roman poet and philosopher; 96?–55 B.C.

lu·cu·brate (lōō′kyoo-brāt′, lū′kyoo-brāt′), ***v.i.*** [LUCUBRATED (-id), LUCUBRATING], [< L. *lucubratus*, pp. of *lucubrare*, to work by candlelight < *lux, lucis*, light], 1. to work, study, or write laboriously, especially late at night. 2. to write in a scholarly manner.

lu·cu·bra·tion (lōō′kyoo-brā′shən, lū′kyoo-brā′shən), ***n.*** [L. *lucubratio*], 1. a lucubrating; laborious work, study, or writing, especially that done late at night. 2. something produced by such work, study, or writing; especially, a learned or carefully elaborated production; hence, 3. *often in pl.* any literary composition: humorous usage suggesting pedantry.

lu·cu·bra·tor (lōō′kyoo-brā′tẽr, lū′kyoo-brā′tẽr), ***n.*** a person who lucubrates.

lu·cu·lent (lōō′kyool-ənt, lū′kyool-ənt), ***adj.*** [ME.; L. *luculentus* < *lux, lucis*, light], 1. [Rare], bright; shining. 2. clear; readily understood; lucid.

Lu·cul·lan (lōō-kul′ən, lū-kul′ən), ***adj.*** of or like Lucullus or the banquets given by him; rich and luxurious.

Lu·cul·le·an (lōō′kə-lē′ən, lū′kə-lē′ən), ***adj.*** Lucullan.

Lu·cul·li·an (lōō-kul′i-ən, lū-kul′i-ən), ***adj.*** Lucullan.

Lu·cul·lus (lōō-kul′əs, lū-kul′əs), ***n.*** (*Lucius Licinius Lucullus*), Roman consul and general, proverbial for his wealth and luxury; 110?–57? B.C.

Lu·cy (lōō′si, lū′si), [prob. via Fr. *Lucie* < L. *Lucia*, fem. of *Lucius;* see LUCIUS], a feminine name: variants, *Lucile, Lucille, Lucinda*: equivalents, It. & Sp. *Lucia.*

Lucy Ston·er (stōn′ẽr), [see STONE, LUCY], a person who advocates the keeping of their own names by married women.

Lud·dite (lud′īt), ***n.*** [said to be after Ned *Lud*, feebleminded man who smashed two frames belonging to a Leicestershire employer (c. 1779)], any of a group of workers in England between 1811 and 1816 who smashed new labor-saving textile machinery in protest against reduced wages and unemployment attributed to its introduction.

Lu·den·dorff, E·rich Frie·drich Wil·helm (ā′riH frē′driH vil′helm lōō′dən-dôrf′), 1865–1937; German general in World War I.

lu·di·crous (lōō′di-krəs, lū′di-krəs), ***adj.*** [L. *ludicrus* < *ludus*, a play, game], causing laughter because absurd or ridiculous; laughably absurd. —***SYN.*** see **absurd.**

Lud·wig, E·mil (ā′mēl lōōt′viH, lōōd′viH; Eng. lud′wig), (born *Emil Cohn*); 1881–1948; German biographer in America.

Lud·wigs·ha·fen (loot′viHs-hä′fən, lōōd′viHs-hä′fən),

n. a city on the Rhine, in Rhineland-Palatinate, Germany: pop., 108,000 (est. 1947).

lu·es (lo͞o′ēz, lū′ēz), *n.* [L., a plague, discharge < *luere*, to flow], syphilis.

lu·et·ic (lo͞o-et′ik, lū-et′ik), *adj. & n.* [see LUES], syphilitic.

luff (luf), *n.* [ME. *lof, loof*, a leeboard; prob. (as OFr. *lof*, G. *luv*, etc.) < OD.; akin to ON. *lōfi*, palm of the hand (cf. L. *palma*, flat hand, oar blade); IE. base *lēp-, *lōp-, flat object, flat hand, seen also in OHG. *lappo*, flat hand, rudder blade, Russ. *lopata*, a shovel, rudder blade, etc.], 1. a sailing close to the wind. 2. [from indicating a luff by its shaking], the forward edge of a fore-and-aft sail. 3. [orig., from location of leeboard], the fullest part of a ship's bow. *v.i.* 1. to turn the bow of a ship toward the wind; sail near or nearer the wind. 2. to cause a sail to shake by turning too close to the wind.

luff the helm, turn the bow of a ship toward the wind: a call to the helmsman.

‡**Luft·waf·fe** (looft′vä′fə), *n.* [G. < *luft*, air (akin to AS. *lyft*, air & ON. *lopt*, whence Eng. *loft*) + *waffe*, weapon (akin to Eng. *weapon*)], the Nazi air force in World War II.

lug (lug), *v.t.* [LUGGED (lugd), LUGGING], [ME. *luggen;* prob. < ON.; cf. Sw. *lugga*, to pull, lit., pull by the hair < *lugg*, forelock], 1. to carry or drag (something heavy). 2. to introduce (a topic, story, etc.) without good reason into a conversation, discourse, etc. *n.* [cf. Sw. *lugg*, forelock], 1. [Scot.], an ear. 2. an earlike projection by which a thing is held or supported. 3. the act of lugging. 4. [Slang], money exacted for political purposes: chiefly in *put the lug on*, to exact a contribution from. 5. [Slang], a stupid fellow.

lug (lug), *n.* a lugsail.

lug (lug), *n.* [< *lug*, *v.*], a lugworm.

Lu·gansk (loo-gänsk′), *n.* Voroshilovgrad, a city in the U.S.S.R.: the former name.

lug·gage (lug′ij), *n.* [< *lug*, *v.* + *-age*], 1. suitcases, valises, trunks, etc.; baggage. 2. reddish brown or tan. *adj.* designating or of such a color.

lug·ger (lug′ẽr), *n.* a small vessel equipped with a lugsail or lugsails.

lug·sail (lug′s'l, lug′sāl′), *n.* [prob. < *lug*, *v.*, with reference to hauling sail around the mast in changing course], a four-cornered sail without boom, or lower yard: it is attached to an upper yard which hangs obliquely on the mast.

LUGSAIL

lu·gu·bri·ous (loo-go͞o′bri-əs, lyoo-gū′bri-əs), *adj.* [L. *lugubris* < *lugere*, to mourn], very sad; mournful; dismal; doleful: usually implying ridiculously excessive grief.

lug·worm (lug′wũrm′), *n.* [*lug*, lugworm + *worm*], any of a group of bristly, segmented worms that burrow in muddy sand along the shore and are used for bait.

Lu·i·an (lo͞o′i-ən), *n. & adj.* Luwian.

Luik (loik, lük), *n.* Liége: the Flemish name.

Lu·ish (lo͞o′ish), *n. & adj.* Luwian.

Luke (lo͝ok, lūk), [L. *Lucas;* Gr. *Loukas;* prob. contr. of *Loukanos*], a masculine name. *n.* in the *Bible*, 1. one of the four Evangelists, a physician and companion of the Apostle Paul and the reputed author of the third book of the New Testament and the Acts of the Apostles: he was probably a Gentile: also **Saint Luke.** 2. the third book of the New Testament, telling the story of Jesus' life.

luke·warm (lo͝ok′wôrm′, lūk′wôrm′), *adj.* [< ME. *louke, leuke*, tepid + *warm;* ME. forms < base of, or akin to, LG. *luk*, D. *leuk*, tepid; IE. base *kleu- (< *kel-, warm), seen also in AS. *hleow*, warm, sheltered, sunny (cf. LEE & dial. var. *lew warm*)], 1. barely warm; moderately warm: said of liquids. 2. lacking warmth of feeling or enthusiasm: as, he was *lukewarm* in his support of the bill.

lull (lul), *v.t.* [ME. *lullen, lollen;* origin echoic; cf. LILT], 1. to calm or soothe by gentle sound or motion or both: chiefly in *lull to sleep*. 2. to bring (a person) into a specified condition by soothing and reassuring him. 3. to make less intense; mitigate; allay. *v.i.* to become calm. *n.* a short period of quiet or of comparative calm.

lull·a·by (lul′ə-bī′), *n.* [*pl.* LULLABIES (-bīz′)], [orig., *lulla!* < *lull*, *v.* + *by!*], 1. a song for lulling a baby to sleep; cradlesong. 2. music for this. 3. [Obs.], good night or good-by: a farewell. *v.t.* [LULLABIED (-bīd′), LULLABYING], to lull with or as with a lullaby.

Lul·ly, Jean Bap·tiste (zhän bȧ′tēst′ lü′lē′), (born *Giovanni Battista Lulli*), 1632–1687; Italian composer in France.

Lu·lu (lo͞o′lo͞o), a feminine name: see **Louise.** *n.* [l-], [Slang], any person or thing outstanding for some quality, as a beautiful girl, a difficult course, etc.

lum·ba·go (lum-bā′gō), *n.* [LL. < L. *lumbus*, loin], rheumatic pain in the joints of the lumbar region; backache, especially in the lower part of the back.

lum·bar (lum′bẽr), *adj.* [Mod. L. *lumbaris* < L. *lumbus*, loin], of or near the loins. *n.* a lumbar nerve, artery, vertebra, etc.

lum·ber (lum′bẽr), *n.* [< *Lombard*: orig., pawnbroker's shop or storeroom, hence pawned articles in storage, hence stored articles, hence lumber], 1. miscellaneous discarded household articles, furniture, etc. stored away or taking up room. 2. timber sawed into beams, planks, boards, etc. of convenient sizes. *v.t.* 1. to fill or obstruct with useless articles or rubbish; clutter. 2. to remove (timber) from an area; cut down (trees). *v.i.* to cut down timber and saw it into lumber.

lum·ber (lum′bẽr), *v.i.* [ME. *lomeren* < ON.; cf. Sw. *lomra*, to resound, *loma*, to walk heavily], 1. to move heavily, clumsily, and, often, noisily: as, the tanks *lumbered* up the steep incline. 2. to rumble. *n.* a rumbling sound.

lum·ber·ing (lum′bẽr-iŋ), *n.* the occupation and business of cutting trees and preparing lumber.

lum·ber·ing (lum′bẽr-iŋ), *adj.* 1. moving heavily, clumsily, or noisily. 2. rumbling.

lum·ber·jack (lum′bẽr-jak′), *n.* [*lumber* + *jack* (man, boy, etc.)], 1. a man whose work is cutting down timber and preparing it for the sawmill. 2. a short, straight coat or jacket of leather, wool, etc., originally made to resemble those worn by lumberjacks.

lum·ber·man (lum′bẽr-mən), *n.* [*pl.* LUMBERMEN (-mən)], 1. a lumberjack (sense 1). 2. a person who deals in lumber or timber.

lum·ber·yard (lum′bẽr-yärd′), *n.* a place where lumber is kept for sale.

lum·bo- (lum′bō, lum′bə), [< L. *lumbus*, loin], a combining form meaning *loin* or *lumbar*: also **lumb-.**

lum·bri·cal (lum′bri-k'l), *adj.* [Mod. L. *lumbricalis*], designating or of the lumbricales.

lum·bri·ca·lis (lum′bri-kā′lis), *n.* [*pl.* LUMBRICALES (-lēz)], [Mod. L. < L. *lumbricus*, intestinal worm, earthworm: from the shape of the muscles], any of four small muscles in the palm of the hand and in the sole of the foot.

lum·bri·coid (lum′bri-koid′), *adj.* [< L. *lumbricus*, intestinal worm, earthworm; + *-oid*], 1. like an earthworm. 2. designating a particular variety of roundworm. *n.* a parasitic roundworm that infests the human intestine.

lu·men (lo͞o′mən, lū′mən), *n.* [*pl.* LUMINA (-mi-nə), LUMENS (-mənz)], [L., light], 1. a unit of measure for the flow of light, equal to the amount of flow through a unit solid angle from a uniform point source of one international candle. 2. in *anatomy*, the passage within a tubular organ.

lu·min·al (lo͞o′mə-nəl, lū′mə-nal′), *n.* phenobarbital, a sedative and hypnotic: a trade-mark **(Luminal).**

lu·mi·nar·y (lo͞o′mə-ner′i, lū′mə-ner′i), *n.* [*pl.* LUMINARIES (-iz)], [OFr. *luminarie;* ML. *luminarium* for L. *luminare* < *lumen, luminis*, light], 1. a body that gives off light, such as the sun or moon. 2. a person who sheds light on some subject or enlightens mankind; famous intellectual.

lu·mi·nesce (lo͞o′mə-nes′, lū′mə-nes′), *v.i.* [LUMINESCED (-nest′), LUMINESCING], [back-formation < *luminescent*], to be or become luminescent.

lu·mi·nes·cence (lo͞o′mə-nes′'ns, lū′mə-nes′'ns), *n.* [< L. *lumen*, a light; + *-escence*], any giving off of light caused by the absorption of radiant or corpuscular energy and not by incandescence; any cold light.

lu·mi·nes·cent (lo͞o′mə-nes′'nt, lū′mə-nes′'nt), *adj.* [< L. *lumen*, a light; + *-escent*], of, exhibiting, or capable of exhibiting luminescence.

lu·mi·nif·er·ous (lo͞o′mə-nif′ẽr-əs, lū′mə-nif′ẽr-əs), *adj.* [< L. *lumen*, a light; + *-ferous*], giving off or transmitting light.

lu·mi·nos·i·ty (lo͞o′mə-nos′ə-ti, lū′mə-nos′ə-ti), *n.* [< L. *luminosus* (see LUMINOUS); + *-ity*], 1. the quality or condition of being luminous. 2. [*pl.* LUMINOSITIES (-tiz)], something luminous.

lu·mi·nous (lo͞o′mə-nəs, lū′mə-nəs), *adj.* [ME. *luminose;* L. *luminosus* < *lumen*, a light; cf. LIGHT], 1. giving off light; bright. 2. flooded with light. 3. clear; readily understood. 4. intellectually brilliant. —*SYN.* see **bright.**

luminous energy, light.

luminous flux, the rate of flow of light radiation.

lum·mox (lum′əks), *n.* [also dial. *lummix, lommix;* corresponds with common pronun. of pers. name *Lomax* (ME. *lumhalghs* < *lumb*, a pool + *halgh*, AS. *halh*, corner, recess, valley + *-s*) and may refer to a specific clumsy person; cf. RIBALD], [Colloq.], a clumsy or stupid person.

lump (lump), *n.* [ME. *lompe, lumpe;* prob. < Anglo-N. or MLG.; cf. earlier Dan. *lompe*, a mass, lump, Sw. dial. *lump*, a block, stump; IE. base *lemb- (< *leb-, *lab-, etc., to hang limply), seen also in L. *limbus*, dress trimming, edge of cloth, etc.; cf. LIMP], 1. an indefinitely shaped mass of something, usually small enough to be taken up in the hand. 2. a small cube, domino, etc.: only in *lump of sugar*. 3. a swelling. 4. aggregate; collection. 5. a dull, clodlike person.

6. soft coal in pieces ranging from the size of a goose egg to several times as large. *adj.* forming or formed into a lump or lumps: as, *lump* sugar. *v.t.* 1. to put together in a lump or lumps. 2. to put together; treat or deal with in a mass; include in one group. 3. to make lumps in. *v.i.* 1. to become lumpy. 2. to move heavily and laboriously (usually with *along*).
in the lump, in the mass or aggregate; all together.
lump (lump), *v.t.* [Early Mod. Eng., to look sour; prob. < *lump* in etym. sense, but influenced by echoic *grump, dump, mump,* etc.], [Colloq.], to put up with (something disagreeable): as, if you don't like it, you can *lump* it.
lump·er (lump'ẽr), *n.* [*lump* (to put together) + *-er*], a laborer who helps to load and unload ships; stevedore.
lump·fish (lump'fish'), *n.* [*pl.* LUMPFISH, LUMPFISHES (-iz); see FISH], [prob. so called from its bulkiness], a plump, clumsily shaped fish found on both sides of the North Atlantic, with a thick, greenish skin studded with bony tubercles, or knobs: its pelvic fins unite to form a sucker: also **lumpsucker.**
lump·i·ly (lump'ə-li), *adv.* so as to form lumps.
lump·i·ness (lump'i-nis), *n.* a lumpy quality or state.
lump·ish (lump'ish), *adj.* 1. like a lump; hence, 2. heavy; dull; stupid.
lump sum, a gross, or total, sum paid at one time.
lump·y (lump'i), *adj.* [LUMPIER (-i-ẽr), LUMPIEST (-i-ist)], 1. full of lumps: as, *lumpy* pudding. 2. covered with lumps; having an uneven surface. 3. rough: said of water. 4. like a lump; heavy; clumsy.
lumpy jaw, actinomycosis, a disease of cattle, etc.
Lu·na (lōō'nə, lū'nə), *n.* [ME.; L., the moon], 1. in *Roman mythology,* the goddess of the moon, identified with the Greek Selene. 2. the moon personified. 3. [l-], in *alchemy,* silver.
lu·na·cy (lōō'nə-si, lū'nə-si), *n.* [*pl.* LUNACIES (-siz)], [*lunatic* + *-cy*], 1. *a*) originally, intermittent insanity, formerly supposed to change in intensity with the phases of the moon. *b*) mental unsoundness; insanity. 2. great folly; utter foolishness. —*SYN.* see **insanity.**
Luna moth, a large North American moth with crescent-marked, pastel-green wings, the hind pair of which end in elongated tails.
lu·nar (lōō'nẽr, lū'nẽr), *adj.* [L. *lunaris* < *luna,* the moon; cf. LIGHT], 1. of the moon. 2. like the moon; specifically, *a*) pale; pallid. *b*) round or crescent-shaped. 3. measured by the moon's revolutions: as, a *lunar* year. 4. of or containing silver.
lunar caustic, fused silver nitrate, used in medicine for cauterizing.
lunar distance, the distance of the moon from the sun, a planet, or a fixed star: calculated to determine longitude at sea.
lu·nar·i·an (lōō-nâr'i-ən, lū-nâr'i-ən), *n.* [< L. *lunaris* (see LUNAR); + *-ian*], 1. a supposed inhabitant of the moon. 2. one who makes a study of the moon.
lunar month, the interval from one new moon to the next, equal to about 29 1/2 days; time in which the moon completes one full revolution about the earth.
lunar year, a period of 12 lunar months, or about 354 1/3 days.
lu·nate (lōō'nāt, lū'nit), *adj.* [L. *lunatus* < *luna,* the moon], crescent-shaped.
lu·nat·ed (lōō'nā-tid, lū'nā-tid), *adj.* lunate.
lu·na·tic (lōō'nə-tik, lū'nə-tik), *adj.* [ME. *lunatik;* OFr.; LL. *lunaticus* < L. *luna,* the moon], 1. suffering from lunacy; insane. 2. of or characterized by lunacy. 3. of or for insane persons. 4. utterly foolish. *n.* an insane person.
lu·nat·i·cal (lōō-nat'i-k'l, lū-nat'i-k'l), *adj.* lunatic.
lunatic asylum, a hospital for the mentally ill: term no longer in good usage.
lunatic fringe, the minority considered foolishly extremist, fanatical, etc. in any political, social, religious, or other movement.
lu·na·tion (lōō-nā'shən, lū-nā'shən), *n.* [ME. *lunacyon;* ML. *lunatio* < L. *luna,* the moon], the interval from one new moon to the next, equal to about 29 1/2 days; lunar month.
lunch (lunch), *n.* [earlier, a piece, thick piece; first appears as rendering of Sp. *lonja,* slice of ham, which it formerly paralleled in pronun.; a transitional form, N.Brit. dial. *lounge,* lump of bread and cheese, seems to confirm this derivation], 1. any light meal; especially, the regular midday meal between breakfast and dinner. 2. the food prepared for such a meal: as, the children took their *lunches* to school. *v.i.* to eat lunch. *v.t.* to provide lunch for.
lunch·eon (lun'chən), *n.* [earlier *lunchion, lunshin* < *lunch;* prob. after *puncheon, truncheon,* etc.], a lunch; especially, a formal lunch.
lunch·eon·ette (lun'chən-et'), *n.* [see -ETTE], 1. a place where light lunches can be had, usually in connection with soda fountain service. 2. a light lunch.
lunch·room (lunch'rōōm', lunch'room'), *n.* a restaurant where light, quick meals, as lunches, are served.
Lun·dy's Lane (lun'diz lān), a road near Niagara Falls, Ontario, Canada: site of a battle (1814) between the British and the Americans.
lune (lōōn, lūn), *n.* [Fr.; L. *luna,* the moon], a crescent-shaped figure on a plane or spherical surface; geometrical figure bounded by two arcs: also called *lunula.*
lune (lōōn, lūn), *n.* [var. of *loyn;* OFr. *loigne*], a leash for a hawk.
lunes (lōōnz, lūnz), *n.pl.* [see LUNATIC], fits of lunacy.
lu·nette (lōō-net', lū-net'), *n.* [Fr., dim. of *lune,* the moon], 1. a crescent-shaped opening in a vaulted roof to admit light. 2. a semicircular space, often containing a windowpane or a mural, above a door or window. 3. in *military science,* a projecting fieldwork consisting of two faces and two flanks. Formerly also **lunet.**
Lu·né·ville (lü'nā'vēl'), *n.* a city in northeastern France: pop., 20,000 (1946): a treaty signed here (1801) by France and Austria marked the virtual end of the Holy Roman Empire.
lung (luŋ), *n.* [ME. *lunge, lungene;* AS. *lungen;* akin to G. *lunge;* IE. base **legwh-,* light in weight and movement: the lungs were so named because of their lightness; cf. LIGHTS < same base], 1. either of the two spongelike respiratory organs in the thorax of vertebrates, that oxygenate the blood and remove carbon dioxide from it. 2. any analogous organ in invertebrates.
at the top of one's lungs, in one's loudest voice.

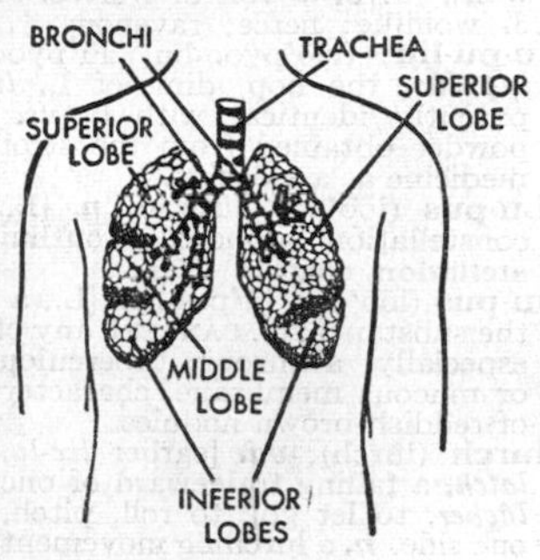

LUNGS

lunge (lunj), *n.* [short for *allonge;* Fr. *allonge,* lit., a lengthening < *allonger,* to lengthen, thrust < *a-* (L. *ad*), to + *long* (L. *longus*), long], 1. a sudden thrust with a sword or other weapon. 2. a sudden plunge forward. *v.i.* [LUNGED (lunjd), LUNGING], [< the *n.*], 1. to make a lunge. 2. to move with a lunge. *v.t.* to cause to lunge.
lunge (lunj), *n.* & *v.t.* [LUNGED (lunjd), LUNGING], longe.
lun·gee (luŋ'gē), *n.* a lungi.
lung·er (luŋ'ẽr), *n.* [Slang], a person who has tuberculosis of the lungs.
lung·fish (luŋ'fish'), *n.* [*pl.* LUNGFISH, LUNGFISHES (-iz); see FISH], any of a group of fishes having lungs as well as gills; dipnoan: also called *mudfish.*
lun·gi (luŋ'gē), *n.* [Hind. & Per. *lungī*], in India, *a*) a long cloth used for loincloths, scarves, turbans, etc. *b*) a loincloth. Also spelled **lungee.**
Lung·ki (looŋ'kē'), *n.* Changchow, a city in China.
Lung·kiang (looŋ'jyäŋ'), *n.* a city in northern Manchuria: pop., 133,000: Japanese name, *Tsitsihar.*
lung·wort (luŋ'wûrt'), *n.* [AS. *lungenwyrt* (see LUNG & WORT): from a fancied resemblance to human lungs], 1. any of a number of plants of the borage family, with large, spotted leaves and clusters of blue or purple flowers. 2. a species of lichen.
lu·ni- (lōō'ni, lū'ni), [< L. *luna,* the moon], a combining form meaning: 1. *moon,* as in *lunitidal.* 2. *of the moon and,* as in *lunisolar.*
lu·ni·so·lar (lōō'ni-sō'lẽr, lū'ni-sō'lẽr), *adj.* [*luni-* + *solar*], involving the mutual relationship or combined attraction of the moon and sun: as, *lunisolar* tides.
lu·ni·tid·al (lōō'ni-tī'd'l, lū'ni-tī'd'l), *adj.* [*luni-* + *tidal*], of a tide or tidal movement caused by the moon's attraction.
lunitidal interval, the interval by which the lunar high tide lags behind the transit of the moon.
lunk·head (luŋk'hed'), *n.* [prob. echoic alteration of *lump-* after *hunk-,* etc.], [Colloq.], a stupid person.
lunt (lunt, loont), *n.* [D. *lont,* a match, earlier lamp wick], [Scot.], 1. *a*) a slow-burning match. *b*) a torch. 2. smoke. *v.t.* & *v.i.* [Scot.], to kindle or smoke.
lu·nu·la (lōō'nyoo-lə, lū'nyoo-lə), *n.* [*pl.* LUNULAE (-lē')], [L., dim. of *luna,* the moon], 1. a lunule. 2. a lune (crescent-shaped figure).
lu·nu·lar (lōō'nyoo-lẽr, lū'nyoo-lẽr), *adj.* of, or having the nature of, a lunule; crescent-shaped.
lu·nu·late (lōō'nyoo-lit, lū'nyoo-lāt'), *adj.* [< L. *lunula* (see LUNULA); + *-ate*], 1. crescent-shaped. 2. having crescent-shaped markings.
lu·nu·lat·ed (lōō'nyoo-lā'tid, lū'nyoo-lā'tid), *adj.* lunulate.
lu·nule (lōō'nyool, lū'nyool), *n.* [Fr.; L. *lunula,* dim. of *luna,* the moon], in *anatomy,* any structure or marking

in the shape of a crescent, as the whitish half-moon at the base of a fingernail.

lun·y (lo͞on'i), *adj.* [LUNIER (-i-ẽr), LUNIEST (-i-ist)], *& n.* [*pl.* LUNIES (-iz)], loony.

Lu·per·cal (lo͞o'pẽr-kal', lū'pẽr-k'l), *n.* [Rare], Lupercalia.

Lu·per·ca·li·a (lo͞o'pẽr-kā'li-ə, lū'pẽr-kāl'yə), *n.pl.* [L. < *Lupercalis*, of Lupercus < *Lupercus* < *lupus*, a wolf; orig. meaning obscure], an ancient Roman festival with fertility rites, held on February 15 in honor of Lupercus, a pastoral god sometimes identified with Faunus.

Lu·per·ca·li·an (lo͞o'pẽr-kā'li-ən, lū'pẽr-kāl'yən), *adj.* of or connected with the Lupercalia.

lu·pine (lo͞o'pin, lū'pin), *n.* [ME. *lupyne;* L. *lupinus* < *lupus*, a wolf; reason for name uncertain], 1. any of a group of plants of the pea family, with long spikes of white, rose, yellow, or blue flowers and pods containing white, beanlike seeds. 2. the seed of this plant, used in some parts of Europe as food.

lu·pine (lo͞o'pīn, lū'pīn), *adj.* [L. *lupinus* < *lupus*, a wolf], 1. of a wolf or wolves. 2. related to the wolf. 3. wolflike; fierce; ravenous.

lu·pu·lin (lo͞o'pyoo-lin, lū'pyoo-lin), *n.* [Mod. L. *lupulus*, the hop, dim. of L. *lupus*, hop plant (apparently identical with *lupus*, a wolf)], a resinous powder obtained from the strobiles of hops, used in medicine as a sedative.

Lu·pus (lo͞o'pəs, lū'pəs), *n.* [L., a wolf], a southern constellation supposedly outlining a wolf: see **constellation**, chart.

lu·pus (lo͞o'pəs, lū'pəs), *n.* [L., a wolf: from eating into the substance; cf. CANCER], any of various skin diseases; especially, a chronic tuberculous disease of the skin or mucous membrane, characterized by the formation of reddish-brown nodules.

lurch (lũrch), *v.i.* [earlier *lee-lurch* < *lee-larch* < *lee-latch*, a falling to leeward of one's course; prob. < Fr. *lâcher*, to let go], to roll, pitch, or sway suddenly to one side. *n.* a lurching movement; sudden rolling, pitching, etc.

lurch (lũrch), *v.i.* [ME. *lorchen;* var. of *lurk*], [Obs.], to remain furtively near a place; lurk. *v.t.* [Archaic], 1. to prevent (a person) from getting his share of something by getting ahead of him; hence, 2. to cheat; trick; rob. *n.* [Obs.], a lurching or lurking.

lurch (lũrch), *n.* [Fr. *lourche*, name of a game like backgammon; prob. < OFr. *lourche*, deceived, duped < MD. *lurz*, left (hand), hence unlucky; akin to MHG. *lërz*, left, *lürzen*, to deceive], 1. in *cribbage*, the condition of a player who fails to score a specified number of points in losing to his opponent. 2. a game lost in this way.

leave in the lurch, to leave in a difficult situation; leave (a person) in trouble and needing help.

lurch·er (lũr'chẽr), *n.* 1. a person that lurches, or lurks. 2. a thief; poacher. 3. [British], a crossbred dog trained to hunt silently, used by poachers.

lur·dan, lur·dane (lũr'd'n), *n.* [OFr. *lourdin* < *lourd*, heavy, dull, stupid], [Archaic or Dial.], a lazy, dull person. *adj.* [Archaic or Dial.], lazy and dull.

lure (loor, lyoor), *n.* [ME.; OFr. *leurre;* prob. < Gmc.; cf. OHG. *luoder*, G. *luder*, bait], 1. a device consisting of a bunch of feathers on the end of a long cord, often baited with food: it is used in falconry to recall the hawk. 2. anything that attracts, tempts, or entices; attraction: as, the *lure* of the stage. 3. a bait, especially an artificial one, used in fishing. *v.t.* [LURED (loord, lyoord), LURING], 1. to recall (a falcon) with a lure. 2. to attract; tempt; entice (often with *on*).

SYN.—**lure** suggests an irresistible force, as desire, greed, curiosity, etc., in attracting someone, especially to something harmful or evil (*lured* on by false hopes); **entice** implies a crafty or skillful luring (he *enticed* the squirrel to eat from his hand); **inveigle** suggests the use of deception or cajolery in enticing someone (they *inveigled* him with false promises); **decoy** implies the use of deceptive appearances in luring into a trap (artificial birds are used to *decoy* wild ducks); **beguile** suggests the use of subtly alluring devices in leading someone on (*beguiled* by her sweet words); **tempt** suggests the influence of a powerful attraction that tends to overcome scruples or judgment (I'm *tempted* to accept your offer); **seduce** implies enticement to a wrongful or unlawful act, especially to loss of chastity. —***ANT.*** repel.

lu·rid (loor'id, lyoor'id), *adj.* [L. *luridus*], 1. [Rare], deathly pale. 2. glowing through a haze, as flames enveloped by smoke. 3. *a*) vivid in a harsh or shocking way; startling; sensational. *b*) characterized by violent passion or crime: as, a *lurid* tale.

lurk (lũrk), *v.i.* [ME. *lurken, lorken;* said to be freq. of *louren* (see LOWER, to scowl); cf. Norw. *lurka*, to sneak off], 1. to stay hidden, ready to spring out, attack, etc.; lie in wait. 2. to be concealed; exist secretly or unobserved. 3. to move furtively.

SYN.—**lurk** implies a waiting in concealment or in the background, especially with sinister or menacing intentions; **skulk** implies a lurking or moving about in a stealthy, sinister way, and also connotes cowardliness; **sneak** and **slink** suggest stealthy movement to avoid being seen or heard, but **sneak** more often implies an underhand or cowardly purpose and **slink** suggests merely fear, guilt, etc.; **prowl** suggests a furtive, watchful roaming about, as in searching for prey or loot.

Lur·lei (loor'lī), *n.* Lorelei.

Lu·sa·ti·a (lo͞o-sā'shi-ə, lū-sā'shə), *n.* a former region in eastern Germany, between the Elbe and Oder Rivers.

lus·cious (lush'əs), *adj.* [ME. *lucius*, thought to be var. of *licious*, aphetic form of *delicious;* prob. influenced by *lush*], 1. highly gratifying to taste or smell, especially because of a rich sweetness; delicious. 2. delighting any of the senses. 3. sickeningly sweet or full-flavored; cloying.

lush (lush), *adj.* [ME. *lusch*, echoic var. of *lassch*, soft, flaccid; OFr. *lasche*, lax, loose < *laschier*, to loosen; LL. **lascare* < L. **laxicare* < *laxare*, to slacken, expand < *laxus;* see LAX], 1. tender and full of juice. 2. of luxuriant growth: as, *lush* vegetation. 3. characterized by a rich growth of vegetation: as, *lush* fields. 4. [Colloq.], characterized by rich and extravagant ornamentation, invention, etc. often tending to excess: as, *lush* writing. —***SYN.*** see **profuse.**

lush (lush), *n.* [prob. shortened < (*City of*) *Lushington*, name of actors' club at the Harp Tavern in London, dissolved 1895], [Slang], 1. alcoholic liquor. 2. a drunken person. *v.i. & v.t.* [Slang], to drink (liquor).

Lu·si·ta·ni·a (lo͞o'si-tā'ni-ə, lū'si-tā'ni-ə), *n.* 1. an ancient region in the Iberian Peninsula, corresponding to what is now Portugal. 2. a British steamship that was torpedoed by a German submarine off Ireland on May 7, 1915, with the loss of 1,198 lives.

lust (lust), *n.* [ME. *luste;* AS. *lust*, pleasure, delight, appetite; akin to G. *lust*, pleasure; IE. base **las-*, to be eager, etc., seen also in L. *lascivus*, playful, sportive, etc. (cf. LASCIVIOUS), *larva*, specter, ghost (cf. LARVA); sexual senses only in Eng. < rendering Vulgate *concupiscentia carnis* (I John 2:16) as *lusts of the flesh*], 1. a desire to gratify the senses; bodily appetite. 2. *a*) sexual desire. *b*) excessive sexual desire, especially as seeking unrestrained gratification. 3. overmastering desire: as, a *lust* for power. 4. [Obs.], *a*) pleasure. *b*) inclination. *v.i.* to feel an intense desire, especially sexual desire (often with *after* or *for*).

lus·ter (lus'tẽr), *n.* [Fr. *lustre;* It. *lustro* < *lustrare;* L. *lustrare*, to light, illumine < *lustrum;* see LUSTRUM], 1. the quality, condition, or fact of shining by reflected light; gloss; sheen. 2. brightness; radiance; brilliance. 3. brilliant beauty or fame; distinction; glory. 4. one of the glass pendants on a chandelier. 5. a chandelier adorned with such pendants. 6. a substance used for polishing. 7. a glossy dress fabric of cotton and wool. 8. the reflecting quality and brilliance of the surface of a mineral. 9. a metallic, sometimes iridescent, appearance given to pottery by a glaze. *v.t.* to give a lustrous finish or gloss to. *v.i.* to be or become lustrous. Also spelled **lustre.**

lus·ter (lus'tẽr), *n.* a lustrum.

lus·ter·ware (lus'tẽr-wâr'), *n.* highly glazed earthenware decorated by the application of metallic oxides to the glaze: also spelled **lustreware.**

lust·ful (lust'fəl), *adj.* 1. filled with or characterized by lust. 2. [Archaic], lusty.

lust·i·hood (lus'ti-hood'), *n.* [see -HOOD], [Archaic], lustiness.

lust·i·ly (lus'tə-li), *adv.* in a lusty manner; vigorously.

lust·i·ness (lus'ti-nis), *n.* the quality or state of being lusty; vigor.

lus·tral (lus'trəl), *adj.* [L. *lustralis* < *lustrum;* see LUSTRUM], 1. of, used in, or connected with ceremonial purification. 2. of a lustrum, or five-year period.

lus·trate (lus'trāt), *v.t.* [LUSTRATED (-id), LUSTRATING], [< L. *lustratus*, pp. of *lustrare*, to purify by means of a propitiatory sacrifice; see LUSTRUM], to purify by means of certain ceremonies.

lus·tra·tion (lus-trā'shən), *n.* [L. *lustratio*], a lustrating or being lustrated.

lus·tra·tive (lus'trə-tiv), *adj.* of lustration; purifying.

lus·tre (lus'tẽr), *n., v.t. & v.i.* [LUSTRED (-tẽrd), LUSTRING], luster.

lus·tre·ware (lus'tẽr-wâr'), *n.* lusterware.

lus·tring (lus'triŋ), *n.* [Fr. *lustrine;* It. *lustrino* < *lustro*, luster], a glossy silk cloth: also **lutestring.**

lus·trous (lus'trəs), *adj.* having luster; shining; bright. —***SYN.*** see **bright.**

lus·trum (lus'trəm), *n.* [*pl.* LUSTRUMS (-trəmz), LUSTRA (-trə)], [L., orig., prob. illumination < IE. **leuqs-trom*, **louqs-trom*, illumination < base **leuq-*, to light, shine, seen also in AS. *lieg*, fire, flame, OSlav. *luča*, ray (of light); cf. LIGHT], 1. in ancient Rome, a purification of all the people by means of certain ceremonies held every five years, after the census. 2. a five-year period.

lust·y (lus'ti), *adj.* [LUSTIER (-ti-ẽr), LUSTIEST (-ti-ist)], [see LUST & -Y], full of youthful vigor; strong; robust.

‡**lu·sus na·tu·rae** (lo͞o'səs nə-tyoor'ē, lū'səs nə-toor'ē), [L.], a sport of nature; freak of nature.

lu·ta·nist (lo͞ot''n-ist, lūt''n-ist), *n.* [ML. *lutanista* < *lutana*, a lute], a player on or composer for the lute: also spelled **lutenist.**

Lut Desert (lo͞ot), a large desert in east central Iran: Persian name, *Dasht-i-lut.*

lute (lo͞ot, lūt), *n.* [ME.; OFr. *leüt;* Sp. *laúd;* Ar. *al'ūd,* lit., the wood], an old stringed instrument related to the guitar, with a body shaped like half of a pear and six to thirteen strings stretched along the fretted neck, which is often bent to form a sharp angle.

LUTE

lute (lo͞ot, lūt), *n.* [OFr. *lut;* L. *lutum,* mud, clay < *luere,* to wash], a clayey cement used for making the joints of pipes airtight and as a sealing agent generally. *v.t.* [LUTED (-id), LUTING], to seal with lute.
lu·te·ci·um (lo͞o-tē'shi-əm, lū-tē'shi-əm), *n.* lutetium: the former spelling.
lu·te·nist (lo͞ot''n-ist, lūt''n-ist), *n.* a lutanist.
lu·te·o (lo͞o'ti-ō, lū'ti-ə), [< L. *luteus;* see LUTEOUS], a combining form meaning *yellow* or *yellowish,* as in *luteolin.*
lu·te·o·lin (lo͞o'ti-ə-lin, lū'ti-ə-lin), *n.* [Fr. *lutéoline* < Mod. L. *(Reseda) luteola,* lit., yellowish (reseda); L. *luteolus,* yellowish, dim. of *luteus,* yellow], a yellow crystalline compound, $C_{15}H_{10}O_6$, used for dyeing cloth.
lu·te·ous (lo͞o'ti-əs, lū'ti-əs), *adj.* [L. *luteus,* golden-yellow < *lutum,* weed used in dyeing yellow], orange-yellow or reddish-yellow.
lute·string (lo͞ot'striŋ', lūt'striŋ'), *n.* [altered (after *lute & string*) < *lustring*], lustring.
Lu·te·tia (lo͞o-tē'shə, lū-tē'shə), *n.* Paris: the ancient name.
lu·te·ti·um (lo͞o-tē'shi-əm, lū-tē'shi-əm), *n.* [Mod. L. < L. *Lutetia,* city in Gaul (now Paris)], a metallic chemical element of the rare-earth group: symbol, Lu; at. wt., 174.99; at. no., 71: formerly spelled **lutecium.**
Lu·ther (lo͞o'thẽr, lū'thẽr), [G.; OHG. *Chlothar, Hludher* < Gmc. base **hluda-,* famous (akin to *loud*) + OHG. *hari,* army, host; hence, lit., famous fighter], a masculine name: equivalents, Fr. *Lothaire,* It. *Lotario.*
Lu·ther, Martin (lo͞o'thẽr, lū'thẽr), 1483–1546; German theologian; leader of the German Reformation; translated Old and New Testaments into German.
Lu·ther·an (lo͞o'thẽr-ən, lū'thẽr-ən), *adj.* 1. of Martin Luther. 2. of the Protestant denomination founded by Luther, or of its doctrines, etc. *n.* a member of the Lutheran Church. Abbreviated **Luth.**
Lu·ther·an·ism (lo͞o'thẽr-ən-iz'm, lū'thẽr-ən-iz'm), *n.* the beliefs and practices of the Lutheran Church.
lu·thern (lo͞o'thẽrn, lū'thẽrn), *n.* [? altered < Fr. *lucarne*], a dormer window.
lut·ing (lo͞ot'iŋ, lūt'iŋ), *n.* lute (cement).
lut·ist (lo͞ot'ist, lūt'ist), *n.* 1. a lute player. 2. a maker of lutes.
Lu·vi·an (lo͞o'vi-ən), *n. & adj.* Luwian.
Lu·wi·an (lo͞o'i-ən), *n.* [< the native name], an extinct Anatolic language of the Indo-Hittite language family, recorded in scanty inscriptions discovered in Asia Minor: it is now regarded as closely related to cuneiform and hieroglyphic Hittite. *adj.* of this language. Also **Luian, Luvian, Luish,** etc.
lux (luks), *n.* [*pl.* LUXES (-iz), LUCES (lo͞o'sēz, lū'sēz)], [L., light; cf. LIGHT], a unit of illumination, equal to one lumen per square meter or the illumination of a surface uniformly one meter distant from a point source of one international candle.
Lux., Luxemburg.
lux·ate (luk'sāt), *v.t.* [LUXATED (-id), LUXATING], [< L. *luxatus,* pp. of *luxare,* to dislocate < *luxus,* dislocated; Gr. *loxos,* slanting], to put (a joint) out of position; dislocate.
lux·a·tion (luk-sā'shən), *n.* [LL. *luxatio* < *luxare;* see LUXATE], a dislocating or being dislocated.
luxe (looks, luks; Fr. lüks), *n.* [Fr.; L. *luxus;* see LUXURY], special quality; richness; elegance: usually in *de luxe*: see **de luxe.**
Lux·em·bourg (luk'səm-bũrg'; Fr. lük'sän'bo͞or'), *n.* 1. a province of southeastern Belgium: area, 1,706 sq. mi.; pop., 217,000; capital, Arlon. 2. Luxemburg.
Luxembourg Palace, a former palace in Paris, now used as the assembly place of the Senate of France.
Lux·em·burg (luk'səm-bũrg'; G. look'səm-boorkh'), *n.* 1. a grand duchy in western Europe, bounded by Belgium, Germany, and France: area, 999 sq. mi.; pop., 325,000. 2. its capital: pop., 70,000. 3. Luxembourg. Abbreviated **Lux.**
Luxemburg, Rosa, 1870–1919; German socialist; leader of Spartacist uprising (1919); arrested and murdered.
Lux·or (luk'sôr, look'sôr), *n.* a town in Egypt on the Nile, near the ruins of ancient Thebes: see **Egypt,** map.
lux·u·ri·ance (lug-zhoor'i-əns, luk-shoor'i-əns), *n.* the quality or condition of being luxuriant.
lux·u·ri·an·cy (lug-zhoor'i-ən-si, luk-shoor'i-ən-si), *n.* luxuriance.
lux·u·ri·ant (lug-zhoor'i-ənt, luk-shoor'i-ənt), *adj.* [L. *luxurians,* ppr. of *luxuriare;* see LUXURIATE], 1. [Rare], very productive; fertile: as, *luxuriant* soil. 2. growing with vigor and in great abundance; lush; teeming. 3. characterized by rich and extravagant ornamentation, invention, etc., often tending to excess: as, a *luxuriant* imagination. —*SYN.* see **profuse.**
lux·u·ri·ate (lug-zhoor'i-āt', luk-shoor'i-āt'), *v.i.* [LUXURIATED (-id), LUXURIATING], [< L. *luxuriatus,* pp. of *luxuriare,* to be too fruitful, be rank < *luxuria;* see LUXURY], 1. to grow with vigor and in great abundance. 2. to live in great luxury. 3. to take great pleasure; revel (with *in*).
lux·u·ri·a·tion (lug-zhoor'i-ā'shən, luk-shoor'i-ā'shən), *n.* a luxuriating.
lux·u·ri·ous (lug-zhoor'i-əs, luk-shoor'i-əs), *adj.* [ME.; OFr. *luxurius;* L. *luxuriosus*], 1. fond of or indulging in luxury. 2. constituting or contributing to luxury; splendid, rich, comfortable, etc. —*SYN.* see **sensuous.**
lux·u·ry (luk'shə-ri; *occas.* lug'zhə-ri), *n.* [*pl.* LUXURIES (-riz)], [ME. & OFr. *luxurie;* L. *luxuria* < *luxus,* extravagance, luxury], 1. the use and enjoyment of the best and most costly things that offer the most physical comfort and satisfaction. 2. anything contributing to such enjoyment, usually something considered unnecessary to life and health. 3. *a)* the unusual intellectual or emotional pleasure derived from some specified thing: as, she can't do without the *luxury* of tears. *b)* something producing this pleasure.
Lu·zern (lo͞o-tsern'), *n.* Lucerne: the German name.
Lu·zon (lo͞o-zon'), *n.* the main island of the Philippine Islands: area, 40,420 sq. mi.; pop., 8,090,000; chief city, Manila: see **Philippine Islands,** map.
lv., 1. leave; leaves. 2. livre; livres.
Lvov (lvôf), *n.* Lwów: the Russian name.
Lw, in *chemistry,* lawrencium.
Lwów (lvo͞of), *n.* a city in the western Ukrainian S.S.R.: formerly in Poland: pop., 410,000: German name, *Lemberg;* Russian name, *Lvov.*
LWS., Late West Saxon.
LXX, Septuagint.
-ly (li), [ME. *-ly, -lich, -liche;* AS. *-lic*], an adjective-forming suffix meaning: 1. *like, characteristic of, suitable to,* as in *fatherly, manly.* 2. *happening (once) every* (specified period of time), as in *hourly, monthly.*
-ly (li), [ME. *-ly, -lich, -liche;* AS. *-lice* < *-lic*], an adverb-forming suffix meaning: 1. *in* (a specified) *manner, to* (a specified) *extent or direction, in or at* (a specified) *time or place,* as in *harshly, outwardly, hourly.* 2. *in the* (specified) *order of sequence,* as in *secondly, thirdly.*
ly·can·thrope (lī'kən-thrōp', lī-kan'thrōp), *n.* [Gr. *lykanthrōpos* < *lykos,* a wolf + *anthrōpos,* a man], 1. a person having lycanthropy. 2. a werewolf.
ly·can·throp·ic (lī'kən-throp'ik), *adj.* of lycanthropy.
ly·can·thro·py (lī-kan'thrə-pi), *n.* [Gr. *lykanthrōpia;* see LYCANTHROPE], 1. a form of mental disorder in which the patient imagines himself to be a wolf. 2. in *folklore,* the power to transform oneself or another into a wolf by the use of magic.
Ly·ca·on (lī-kā'ən), *n.* [L.; Gr. *Lykaōn* (cf. Gr. *lykos,* a wolf)], in *Greek mythology,* a king of Arcadia who was turned into a wolf by Zeus because he tested the divinity of the disguised god by offering him human flesh as food.
Lyc·a·o·ni·a (lik'ā-ō'ni-ə), *n.* an ancient province of central Asia Minor.
‡ly·cée (lē'sā'), *n.* [Fr. < L. *lyceum;* see LYCEUM], in France, a secondary school maintained by the government for preparing students for a university.
ly·ce·um (lī-sē'əm, lī'si-əm), *n.* [L.; Gr. *Lykeion,* the Lyceum: so called from the neighboring temple of *Apollōn Lykeios*], 1. [L-], the grove at Athens where Aristotle taught. 2. a lecture hall. 3. an organization providing public lectures, concerts, etc. 4. a lycée.
lych gate (lich), a lich gate.
lych·nis (lik'nis), *n.* [L.; Gr. *lychnis*], any of a large group of plants of the pink family, with red, pink, or white flowers.
Ly·ci·a (lish'i-ə), *n.* an ancient country in southern Asia Minor.
Lyc·i·an (lish'i-ən), *adj.* of Lycia, its people, or their language. *n.* 1. a native or inhabitant of Lycia. 2. the language of the Lycians, probably akin to cuneiform Hittite.
ly·co·pod (lī'kə-pod'), *n.* [see LYCOPODIUM], any of a group of erect or creeping, flowerless, evergreen plants with scalelike leaves: also called *club moss.*
ly·co·po·di·um (lī'kə-pō'di-əm), *n.* [Mod. L. < Gr. *lykos,* a wolf; + *-podium*: so named because the root resembles a claw], a lycopod.
Ly·cur·gus (lī-kũr'gəs), *n.* Spartan lawgiver; 9th? century B.C.
lydd·ite (lid'īt), *n.* [< *Lydd,* in Kent, England +

-*ite*: first made and tested at Lydd], a powerful explosive containing picric acid, used in shells.

Lyd·gate, John (lid′gāt′, lid′git), 1370?–1451?; English poet and translator.

Lyd·i·a (lid′i-ə), [L.; Gr. *Lydia*, fem. of *Lydios*, Lydian], a feminine name. *n.* an ancient country in western Asia Minor: capital, Sardis.

Lyd·i·an (lid′i-ən), *adj.* 1. of Lydia, its people, or their language. 2. *a)* soft; gentle; effeminate. *b)* voluptuous; sensual. *n.* 1. a native or inhabitant of Lydia. 2. their language, probably Anatolic.

lye (lī), *n.* [ME. *lige, lihe, lege, leih,* etc.; AS. *leag;* akin to G. *lauge;* IE. base **lou-*, to wash, seen also in L. *lavare, lavere,* to wash (cf. LAVE, LAVATORY); see LATHER], 1. originally, a strong, alkaline solution obtained by leaching wood ashes. 2. any strongly alkaline substance. Lye is used in cleaning and in making soap. 3. any substance obtained by leaching.

Ly·ell, Sir **Charles** (lī′əl), 1797–1875; British geologist.

ly·ing (lī′iŋ), present participle of **lie** (to tell lies). *adj.* false; not truthful. *n.* the telling of a lie or lies. —*SYN.* see **dishonest.**

ly·ing (lī′iŋ), present participle of **lie** (to recline).

ly·ing-in (lī′iŋ-in′), *n.* confinement in childbirth. *adj.* of or for childbirth: as, a *lying-in* hospital.

Lyle (līl), [< Brit. place name & surname], a masculine name.

Lyl·y, John (lil′i), 1554?–1606; English author and dramatist: see **euphuism.**

Ly·man (lī′mən), [< Brit. surname], a masculine name.

lymph (limf), *n.* [L. *lympha*, spring water, a respelling of **limpa*, **lumpa* through erroneous association with Gr. *nymphē;* see NYMPH], 1. [Poetic or Obs.], a spring of clear water. 2. a clear, yellowish, alkaline fluid found in the lymphatic vessels of the body: it resembles blood plasma but contains only colorless corpuscles. 3. any of various colorless liquids similar to this; especially, the clear liquid given off from inflamed body tissue.

lymph-, lympho-.

lym·phad·e·ni·tis (lim-fad′ə-nī′tis, lim′fə-də-nī′tis), *n.* [Mod. L.; *lymph-* + *aden-* + *-itis*], inflammation of the lymph glands.

lym·phan·gi·al (lim-fan′ji-əl), *adj.* [< *lymph-* + Gr. *angeion*, vessel; + *-al*], of the lymphatic vessels.

lym·phan·gi·i·tis (lim-fan′ji-ī′tis), *n.* lymphangitis.

lym·phan·gi·o- (lim-fan′ji-ə), a combining form meaning *lymphangial*: also, before a vowel, **lymphangi-.**

lym·phan·gi·tis (lim′fan-jī′tis), *n.* [Mod. L.; *lymphangi-* + *-itis*], inflammation of the lymphatic vessels.

lym·phat·ic (lim-fat′ik), *adj.* [< *lymph*, after L. *lymphaticus*, distracted, panic-stricken, frenzied, transl. of Gr. *nympholēptos*, caught by nymphs; cf. LYMPH], 1. of, containing, or conveying lymph. 2. of, or caused by improper functioning of, the lymph glands. 3. sluggish; without energy: a sluggish condition was formerly thought to be due to too much lymph in the body. *n.* a lymphatic vessel.

lymphatic gland, a lymph gland.

lym·pha·to- (lim′fə-tō, lim′fə-tə), a combining form meaning *lymphatic*, as in *lymphatolysis.*

lym·pha·tol·y·sis (lim′fə-tol′ə-sis), *n.* [*lymphato-* + *-lysis*], the destruction of lymphatic tissue.

lymph gland, any of the many glandlike structures lying in groups along the course of the lymphatic vessels and producing lymphocytes: also **lymph node.**

lym·pho- (lim′fō, lim′fə), a combining form meaning *of lymph* or *the lymphatics*, as in *lymphocyte:* also, before a vowel, **lymph-.**

lym·pho·cyte (lim′fə-sīt′), *n.* [*lympho-* + *-cyte*], a variety of colorless corpuscle formed in the tissue of the lymph glands and passed from the lymph into the blood.

lym·pho·cy·to·sis (lim′fə-sī-tō′sis), *n.* [Mod. L.; see –OSIS], a condition characterized by an abnormal increase in the number of lymphocytes in the blood.

lymph·oid (lim′foid), *adj.* [*lymph-* + *-oid*], of or like lymph or the tissue of the lymph glands.

lyn·ce·an (lin-sē′ən), *adj.* [< L. *lynceus* (< Gr. *lynkeios* < *lynx*, lynx); + *-an*], of or like a lynx; especially, having the keenness of sight attributed to the lynx.

lynch (linch), *v.t.* [< *lynch law*], to kill (an accused person) by mob action and without lawful trial, as by hanging, usually in defiance of local authority.

Judge Lynch, lynch law personified.

Lynch·burg (linch′bērg), *n.* a city in central Virginia, on the James River: pop., 55,000.

lynch law, [formerly *Lynch's law;* after Capt. William *Lynch* (1742–1820), member of a vigilance committee in Pittsylvania, Virginia, in 1780], the practice of killing by lynching.

Lynn (lin), [prob. < Brit. place name *Lynn* < Britannic *lindo-* (W. *llyn*), a lake], a masculine or feminine name. *n.* a city in northeastern Massachusetts, on Massachusetts Bay: pop., 94,000.

Lyn·wood (lin′wood′), *n.* a city in southwestern California: suburb of Los Angeles: pop., 32,000.

lynx (liŋks), *n.* [*pl.* LYNXES (-iz), LYNX; see PLURAL, II, D, 1], [ME.; L.; Gr. *lynx*], 1. any of a group of wildcats found throughout the northern hemisphere and characterized by a ruff on each side of the face, long legs, a short tail, long, tufted ears, and keen vision: the North American species are the *Canada lynx* and the *Bay lynx*, or *bobcat.* 2. the long, silky, tawny fur of the lynx, sometimes dyed black. 3. [L-], a northern constellation lying between Auriga and Ursa Major.

LYNX (3 ft. long)

lynx-eyed (liŋks′īd′), *adj.* having very keen sight.

Lyon (lyōn), *n.* a city in southeastern France, on the Rhone: pop., 471,000: English name, *Lyons.*

Ly·on·nais, Ly·o·nais (lē′ô′ne′), *n.* a former province of east central France.

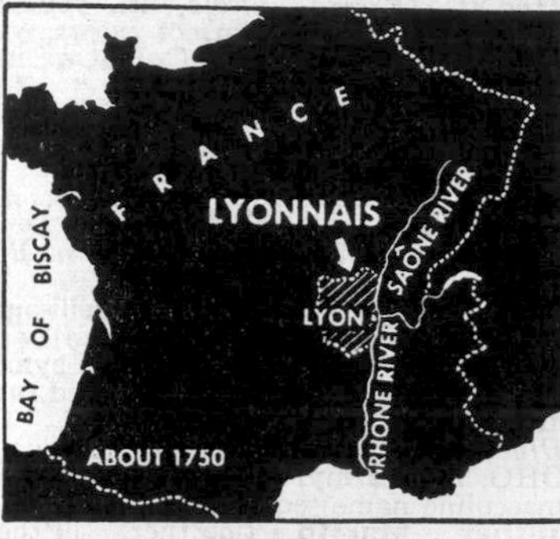

LYONNAIS

ly·on·naise (lī′ə-nāz′; Fr. lyô′nez′), *adj.* [Fr., fem. of *Lyonnais*, of Lyon], prepared with finely sliced onions; especially, designating potatoes prepared with fried onions.

Ly·on·nesse (lī′ə-nes′), *n.* [OFr. *Leonois*, earlier *Loonois*, orig. *Lothian*, former division of Scotland], in *Arthurian legend*, a region in southwest England, apparently near Cornwall, supposed to have sunk beneath the sea.

Ly·ons (lī′ənz), *n.* Lyon: the English name.

Ly·ra (lī′rə), *n.* [L.; Gr. *Lyra;* see LYRE], a northern constellation lying between Hercules and Cygnus, supposedly resembling the harp of Orpheus in outline: it contains the star Vega: see **constellation,** chart.

ly·rate (lī′rāt), *adj.* [Mod. L. *lyratus*], shaped like or suggestive of a lyre.

ly·rat·ed (lī′rā-tid), *adj.* lyrate.

lyre (līr), *n.* [L. *lyra;* Gr. *lyra;* prob. < IE. base **lu-*, **lēu-*, seen also in L. *laus, laudis,* praise, AS. *leothian*, to sing], a small stringed instrument of the harp family, used by the ancient Greeks to accompany singers and reciters.

LYRE

lyre·bird (līr′būrd′), *n.* any of several species of Australian songbirds: the long tail feathers of the males resemble a lyre when spread.

lyr·ic (lir′ik), *adj.* [< Fr. or L.; Fr. *lyrique;* L. *lyricus;* Gr. *lyrikos*], 1. of a lyre. 2. suitable for singing, as to the accompaniment of a lyre; songlike; specifically, designating poetry or a poem expressing the poet's personal emotion or sentiment rather than telling of external events: sonnets, elegies, odes, hymns, etc. are lyric poems. 3. writing or having written lyric poetry. 4. in *music, a)* characterized by a relatively high compass and a light, flexible quality: as, a voice of *lyric* quality. *b)* having such a voice: as, a *lyric* tenor. Opposed to *dramatic.* *n.* 1. a lyric poem. 2. *usually pl.* the words of a song, as distinguished from the music.

lyr·i·cal (lir′i-k′l), *adj.* 1. lyric. 2. expressing feelings of enthusiasm, etc. in strong, emotional language: as, he became *lyrical* in his account of the performance.

lyr·i·cism (lir′i-siz′m), *n.* 1. lyric quality, style, or character: as, Shelley's *lyricism.* 2. emotional and poetic expression of enthusiasm, etc.

lyr·i·cist (lir′i-sist), *n.* a writer of lyrics, especially lyrics for popular songs.

lyr·i·co- (lir′i-kō, lir′i-kə), [< L. *lyricus*], a combining form meaning *lyric and.*

ly·ri·form (lī′rə-fôrm′), *adj.* shaped like a lyre.

lyr·ism (lir′iz′m; *also, and for 2 always,* lir′iz′m), *n.* [Fr. *lyrisme;* Gr. *lyrismos*], 1. the act of playing on a lyre. 2. lyricism.

lyr·ist (lir′ist; *also, and for 2 always,* lir′ist), *n.* [L. *lyristes;* Gr. *lyristēs* < *lyrizein*, to play on a lyre], 1. a player on a lyre. 2. a lyric poet.

Ly·san·der (lī-san'dẽr), *n.* Spartan admiral and general; ?–395 B.C.

-lyse (līz), -lyze.

ly·si- (lī'si, lis'i), [Gr. *lysi-*, *lys-* < *lysis;* see LYSIS], a combining form meaning *freeing, relieving, loosening, dissolving*, as in *lysimeter:* also, before a vowel, **lys-**.

Ly·sim·a·chus (lī-sim'ə-kəs), *n.* Macedonian general; lived 361–281 B.C.; king of Thrace.

ly·sim·e·ter (lī-sim'ə-tẽr), *n.* [*lysi-* + *-meter*], a device for determining the solubility of substances.

ly·sin (lī'sin), *n.* [< Gr. *lysis* (see LYSIS); + *-in*], 1. any antibody dissolving bacteria, blood corpuscles, etc. 2. lysine.

ly·sine (lī'sēn, lī'sin), *n.* [*lys-* + *-in*], an amino acid, $C_6H_{14}N_2O_2$, obtained synthetically or by the hydrolysis of certain proteins in digestion.

Ly·sip·pus (lī-sip'əs), *n.* Greek sculptor; 4th century B.C.

ly·sis (lī'sis), *n.* [Mod. L.; Gr. *lysis*, a loosening < *lyein*, to loose; IE. base **lu-*, **lēu-*, to cut, loosen, seen also in L. *luere*, to release (from debt), Eng. *lose*, etc.], 1. the gradual and successful ending of a disease. 2. the process of cell destruction through the action of specific lysins.

-lysis, [< Gr. *lysis;* see LYSIS], a combining form meaning *a loosing, dissolution, dissolving, destruction*, as in *catalysis, paralysis.*

ly·sol (lī'sol, lī'sôl), *n.* [< Gr. *lysis* (see LYSIS); + *-ol*], a brown liquid mixture of soap and cresol, used as an antiseptic and disinfectant: a trade-mark (**Lysol**).

lys·so·pho·bi·a (lis'ə-fō'bi-ə), *n.* [< Gr. *lyssa*, rabies; + *-phobia*], an abnormal fear of becoming insane.

-lyte (līt), [< Gr. *lytos;* see LYSIS], a combining form meaning *a substance subjected to a process of decomposition* (indicated by the corresponding noun in *-lysis*), as in *hydrolyte.*

-lyte (līt), -lite.

lyt·ic (lit'ik), *adj.* [see -LYTIC], 1. of a lysin. 2. of or causing lysis.

-lyt·ic (lit'ik), [Gr. *-lytikos* < *lytikos*, able to loose; see LYSIS], 1. a suffix used to form adjectives corresponding to nouns ending in *-lysis*, as in *catalytic, hydrolytic.* 2. in *biochemistry*, a suffix meaning *undergoing hydrolysis by enzymes.*

lyt·ta (lit'ə), *n.* [*pl.* LYTTAE (-ē)], [L., worm said to grow under the tongues of dogs and to cause madness < Gr. *lytta, lyssa*, madness], a band of cartilage lying along the underside of the tongue of dogs and certain other flesh-eating animals.

Lyt·ton (lit'ən), see **Bulwer-Lytton.**

Lyu·blin (lyoo'blin), *n.* Lublin: the Russian name.

-lyze (līz), [Fr. *-lyser* < nouns ending in *-lysis* + *-er*, inf. ending], a combining form used to form verbs corresponding to nouns ending in *-lysis*, as in *paralyze, electrolyze:* also spelled **-lyse.**

M

M, m (em), *n.* [*pl.* M's, m's, Ms, ms (emz)], 1. the thirteenth letter of the English alphabet, from the Greek *mu*, derived ultimately from the Phoenician: see **alphabet**, table. 2. the sound of M or m: in English, it is usually a voiced bilabial nasal, IPA [m]. 3. a type or impression for M or m. 4. *a symbol for* the thirteenth in a sequence or group (or the twelfth if J is omitted). 5. in *printing*, an em. *adj.* 1. of M or m. 2. thirteenth (or twelfth if J is omitted) in a sequence or group.

M (em), *n.* 1. an object shaped like M. 2. a Roman numeral for 1,000: with a superior bar ($\overline{M}$), 1,000,000. 3. in *chemistry, the symbol for* an element in electrolysis. 4. in *electricity, the symbol for* mutual inductance (in henrys). 5. in *logic, the symbol for* the middle term of a syllogism. *adj.* shaped like M.

m-, in *chemistry*, meta-.

M'-, (mə, mi), Mac-, as in *M'Coy.*

M., 1. Manitoba. 2. Marshal. 3. Master. 4. Medieval. 5. Monday. 6. [*pl.* MM.], Monsieur.

M., m., 1. majesty. 2. male. 3. manual. 4. mark (a coin). 5. marquis. 6. married. 7. masculine. 8. medicine. 9. medium. 10. meridian. 11. *meridies*, [L.], noon, as in *A.M., P.M.* 12. meter; meters. 13. middle. 14. mile; miles. 15. mill; mills. 16. minim. 17. minute; minutes. 18. month. 19. moon. 20. morning. 21. mountain. 22. in *dentistry, a)* molar. *b)* mouth. 23. in *mathematics*, modulus. 24. in *mechanics*, mass.

ma (mä; *dial. often* mô), *n.* [Colloq.], mamma; mother.

Ma, in *chemistry*, masurium.

M.A., 1. *Magister Artium*, [L.], Master of Arts: also **A.M.** 2. Military Academy. 3. Mountain Artillery.

ma'am (mam, mäm; *unstressed* məm, 'm), *n.* [Colloq.], madam: used in direct address.

Maas (mäs), *n.* the Meuse: the Dutch name.

Maas·tricht (mäs'triHt), *n.* a city in the Netherlands, on the Maas River: pop., 75,000 (1947): also spelled **Maestricht.**

Mab (mab), *n.* Queen Mab.

Ma·bel (mā'b'l), [< *Amabel* < L. *amabilis*, lovable < *amare*, to love], a feminine name: diminutive, *Mab.*

Mac- (mak, mək, mə), [< Ir. & Gael. *mac*, son < OCelt. **makkos*, akin to **makwos*, son, seen in OW. *map*, W. *mab, ap*, son; for IE. base see MAIDEN], a prefix meaning *son of*, used in Scottish and Irish family names: also **Mc-, Mc-, M'**: in alphabetizing, all these forms are sometimes placed together.

Mac., Maccabees.

ma·ca·ber (mə-kä'bẽr), *adj.* macabre.

ma·ca·bre (mə-kä'brə, mə-kä'bẽr), *adj.* [Fr.; OFr. (*danse*) *Macabré*, (dance) of death, prob. altered < *Maccabeus*, Maccabee; said to be the name of a character in a morality play], gruesome; grim and horrible; ghastly. —*SYN.* see **ghastly.**

ma·ca·co (mə-kā'kō), *n.* [*pl.* MACACOS (-kōz)], [Port.; Braz. (Tupi) *macaco, macaca*], 1. any of several African and Asiatic lemurs; especially, the black lemur. 2. [< African (Congo) native name], a macaque.

mac·ad·am (mə-kad'əm), *n.* [after John L. *MacAdam* (1756–1836), Scot. engineer who invented the process], 1. small broken stones, used in making roads: see **macadamize.** 2. a road made with layers of such stones.

mac·ad·am·ize (mə-kad'əm-īz'), *v.t.* [MACADAMIZED (-īzd'), MACADAMIZING], 1. to make (a road) by rolling successive layers of small broken stones (*macadam*) on a dry earth roadbed, often with tar or asphalt for binding. 2. to repair or cover (a road) by this process.

Ma·ca·o (mə-kou', mə-kä'ō), *n.* 1. an island at the mouth of the Canton River, China, opposite Hong Kong. 2. a seaport on this island. 3. a Portuguese colony including Macao Island and two near-by islands: area, 6 sq. mi.; pop., 374,700: Portuguese name, *Macáu.*

ma·caque (mə-käk'), *n.* [Fr.; Port. *macaco;* see MACACO], any of a large group of short-tailed monkeys of Asia, Africa, and the East Indies.

mac·a·ro·ni (mak'ə-rō'ni), *n.* [*pl.* MACARONIS, MACARONIES (-niz)], [It. *maccaroni, maccheroni*, pl. of *maccherone* < LGr. *makaria*, food composed of broth and barley groats, in Gr., bliss (semantic development obscure) < *makar*, blessed], 1. long, thin, hollow tubes made of dried flour paste, to be cooked and used as food. 2. an 18th-century English dandy who affected foreign mannerisms and fashions. Also spelled **maccaroni.**

mac·a·ron·ic (mak'ə-ron'ik), *adj.* [Fr. *macaronique* or It. *maccaronico* < *maccaroni*, lit., macaroni], 1. involving or characterized by a mixture of languages; especially, designating or of burlesque verse in which real or coined words from two or more languages are mixed, or vernacular words of a modern language or languages are given Latin case endings and mixed with Latin words and hybrid forms. 2. [Obs.], having the nature of a medley; mixed; jumbled. *n.* 1. *usually in pl.* macaronic verse. 2. [Obs.], a jumble; medley. Also spelled **maccaronic.**

mac·a·ron·i·cal (mak'ə-ron'i-k'l), *adj.* macaronic.

mac·a·roon (mak'ə-ro͞on'), *n.* [Fr. *macaron* < It. *maccaroni;* see MACARONI], a small cooky made chiefly of egg white, crushed almonds or coconut, and sugar.

Mac·Ar·thur, Douglas (mək-är′thẽr), 1880– ; American general; commander in chief of Allied forces in the southwest Pacific, World War II.

Ma·cas·sar (mə-kas′ẽr), *n.* 1. a city on the southwestern coast of Celebes, in the Netherlands Indies: pop., 85,000. 2. a member of a Malay tribe living in the region of Macassar. 3. the language of this tribe. Also spelled **Makassar.**

Macassar, Strait of, the strait between Borneo and Celebes: site of a naval battle between the Allies and the Japanese, January, 1942.

Ma·cá·u (mə-kä′oo), *n.* Macao: the Portuguese name.

Ma·cau·lay, Thomas Bab·ing·ton (bab′iŋ-tən mə-kô′li), first Baron Macaulay, 1800–1859; English historian, essayist, poet, and statesman.

ma·caw (mə-kô′), *n.* [Port. *macao;* prob. < the Braz. native name], any of a group of large, bright-colored, harsh-voiced parrots of Central and South America.

Mac·beth (mək-beth′, mak-beth′), *n.* 1. a famous tragedy by Shakespeare (1606?). 2. the main character of this play, who, urged by his ruthlessly ambitious wife, murders his king, Duncan, and becomes king himself, but is finally killed by the patriot Macduff.

Macc., Maccabees.

Mac·ca·bae·us, Judas (mak′ə-bē′əs), 2nd century B.C.; Jewish military leader of the successful Jewish revolt against the Syrians.

Mac·ca·be·an (mak′ə-bē′ən), *adj.* of Judas Maccabaeus or the Maccabees.

Mac·ca·bees (mak′ə-bēz′), *n.pl.* [LL. *Machabaei,* pl. of *Machabaeus,* surname of Judas; Gr. *Makkabaios;* prob. < Aram. *maqqābā,* hammer: hence, lit., the hammerer, prob. because of his zealous attacks against the Syrians], 1. a family of Jewish patriots who headed a successful revolt against Antiochus IV of Syria (175–164 B.C.). 2. in the *Bible,* two books of the Old Testament Apocrypha that tell of this revolt: called *Machabees* in the Douay Version: abbreviated **Macc., Mac.**

mac·ca·boy (mak′ə-boi′), *n.* [Fr. *macouba;* Sp. *macuba* < *Macouba,* district in Martinique where it is made], a kind of snuff, usually perfumed: also spelled **maccoboy.**

mac·ca·ro·ni (mak′ə-rō′ni), *n.* macaroni (both senses).

mac·ca·ro·nic (mak′ə-ron′ik), *adj.* macaronic.

Mac·Don·ald, James Ram·say (ram′zi mək-don′əld), 1866–1937; British statesman and Labor leader; prime minister (1924; 1929–1935).

Mac·Dow·ell, Edward Alexander (mək-dou′əl), 1861–1908; American composer and pianist.

mace (mās), *n.* [ME.; OFr. < LL. **mattea,* a club], 1. a heavy, armor-breaking club with a metal head, often spiked, used in the Middle Ages. 2. any similar weapon. 3. a staff used as a symbol of authority by certain officials. 4. a person who carries a mace. 5. a light, flat-headed stick formerly used in billiards instead of a cue, for certain types of shots.

mace (mās), *n.* [ME., assumed as sing. of *macis,* mace; OFr. *macis;* L. *macir;* Gr. *maker,* spicy bark from India], a spice, usually ground, made from the dried outer covering of the nutmeg.

mace-bear·er (mās′bâr′ẽr), *n.* a person who carries a mace in ceremonial processions.

ma·cé·doine (mas′ā-dwän′; Fr. må′sā′dwån′), *n.* [Fr., orig., kind of parsley; OFr. (*perresil*) *macidoine;* L. (*petroselinon*) *macedonicum,* lit., Macedonian (parsley)], 1. a mixture of vegetables or fruits served as a salad, cocktail, etc., often in jelly. 2. a medley.

Mac·e·don (mas′ə-don′), *n.* ancient Macedonia.

Mac·e·do·ni·a (mas′ə-dō′ni-ə), *n.* 1. an ancient kingdom north of Greece: now part of Greece, Bulgaria, and Yugoslavia: see **Roman Empire,** map. 2. a district of northern Greece. Abbreviated **Maced.**

Mac·e·do·ni·an (mas′ə-dō′ni-ən), *adj.* of Macedonia, its people, their language, etc. *n.* 1. a native or inhabitant of Macedonia. 2. the ancient Indo-European language of the Macedonians, akin either to Greek or to Illyrian. Abbreviated **Maced.**

Ma·ce·ió (mä′sā-yô′), *n.* a seaport in eastern Brazil: pop., 80,000.

mac·er (mās′ẽr), *n.* [ME. *macere;* OFr. *massier;* see MACE (club) & -ER], a mace-bearer; specifically, in Scotland, an official in a law court.

mac·er·ate (mas′ə-rāt′), *v.t.* [MACERATED (-id), MACERATING], [< L. *maceratus,* pp. of *macerare,* to make soft or tender, weaken, harass; akin to Gr. *massein,* to knead], 1. *a*) to soften by soaking in liquid for some time. *b*) to separate the parts of by soaking; specifically, to soften (food) in the digestive system. 2. to cause to waste away or grow thin. 3. to torment. *v.i.* to undergo maceration; waste away; grow thin.

mac·er·at·er, mac·er·a·tor (mas′ə-rā′tẽr), *n.* a person or thing that macerates; specifically, a device for converting fibrous matter into pulp, as in making paper.

mac·er·a·tion (mas′ə-rā′shən), *n.* [L. *maceratio*], a macerating or being macerated.

mach., 1. machine. 2. machinery. 3. machinist.

Ma·cha·do, Ge·rar·do (he-rär′thô mä-chä′thô), 1871–1939; Cuban statesman; president of Cuba (1925–1933).

‡ma chère (må′ shâr′), [Fr.], my dear (girl or woman).

ma·che·te (mä-chā′tā, mə-shet′, mə-shet′i), *n.* [Sp., dim. of *macho,* an ax, hammer < L. *marculus,* dim. of *marcus,* hammer], a large, heavy-bladed knife used as a tool for cutting sugar cane, etc., or as a weapon, in Central and South America, etc.

MACHETE

Mach·i·a·vel·li, Nic·co·lo (nē′kô-lô′ mä′kyä-vel′lē; Eng. mak′i-ə-vel′i, mak′yə-vel′i), 1469–1527; Italian (Florentine) statesman and writer on government.

Mach·i·a·vel·li·an, Mach·i·a·vel·i·an (mak′i-ə-vel′i-ən, mak′yə-vel′yən), *adj.* 1. of Machiavelli. 2. of, like, or characterized by his political principles and proposed methods of craftiness and duplicity; crafty, deceitful, etc. *n.* a follower of such principles and methods.

Mach·i·a·vel·lism (mak′i-ə-vel′iz′m, mak′yə-vel′iz′m), *n.* the political principles and methods of craftiness and duplicity advocated by Machiavelli.

ma·chi·co·late (mə-chik′ə-lāt′), *v.t.* [MACHICOLATED (-id), MACHICOLATING], [< ML. *machicolatus,* pp. of *machicolare* < MFr. *machicoler* < Pr. *machacol,* balcony < *macar,* to beat + *col,* neck: from the dropping of stones, etc.], to put machicolations in (a parapet, etc.).

ma·chic·o·la·tion (mə-chik′ə-lā′shən), *n.* [< *machicolate*], 1. an opening in the floor of a projecting gallery or parapet, between the supports or corbels, or in the roof over an entrance, through which hot liquids, heavy stones, etc. could be dropped by the defenders of a fortress. 2. a gallery, parapet, etc. with such openings.

mach·i·nate (mak′ə-nāt′), *v.i. & v.t.* [MACHINATED (-id), MACHINATING], [< L. *machinatus,* pp. of *machinari,* to devise, plan, plot < *machina;* see MACHINE], to devise, plan, or plot artfully, especially with evil intent.

mach·i·na·tion (mak′ə-nā′shən), *n.* [L. *machinatio*], 1. [Rare], a machinating; plotting; scheming. 2. *usually in pl.* an artful or secret plot, scheme, or intrigue, especially one with evil intent. —*SYN.* see **plot.**

mach·i·na·tor (mak′ə-nā′tẽr), *n.* [L.; see MACHINATE], a plotter; schemer; intriguer.

ma·chine (mə-shēn′), *n.* [Fr.; L. *machina;* Gr. *mēchanē,* a machine, engine, device < *mēchos,* a contrivance], 1. [Rare or Archaic], a structure or built-up fabric of any kind; specifically, the human or animal frame. 2. *a*) a vehicle, as, formerly, a carriage, cart, etc. *b*) a vehicle operated mechanically; specifically, an automobile. 3. a structure consisting of a framework and various fixed and moving parts, for doing some kind of work; mechanism: as, a sewing *machine.* 4. a person or organization regarded as acting like a machine, without thought or will. 5. *a*) the members of a political party or group who control policy and confer patronage. *b*) the party organization generally. 6. a device or apparatus, as in the ancient theater, for producing stage effects: see **deus ex machina;** hence, 7. a literary device for dramatic presentation, as a supernatural agent or agency introduced into a poem. 8. in *mechanics,* a device that transmits, or changes the application of, energy: the lever, wheel, and screw are called *simple machines.* *adj.* 1. of a machine or machines. 2. made or done by machinery; hence, 3. standardized; stereotyped. *v.t.* [MACHINED (-shēnd′), MACHINING], to make, shape, etc. by machinery. Abbreviated **mach.**

machine bolt, a bolt or screw with a square or hexagonal head and no threads on the upper parts.

ma·chine-gun (mə-shēn′gun′), *v.t.* [MACHINE-GUNNED (-gund′), MACHINE-GUNNING], to fire at with, or hit by fire from, a machine gun.

machine gun, an automatic gun, usually mounted and with a cooling apparatus, firing a rapid and continuous stream of bullets fed into it by a belt, clip, or disk.

ma·chine-made (mə-shēn′mād′), *adj.* made by or as by machinery, not by hand.

ma·chin·er·y (mə-shēn′ẽr-i, mə-shēn′ri), *n.* [*pl.* MACHINERIES (-iz, -riz)], 1. machines collectively. 2. the working parts of a machine. 3. any combination of things or persons by which something is kept in action or a desired result is obtained: as, the *machinery* of government. Abbreviated **mach.**

machine screw, a machine bolt: see **screw,** illus.

machine shop, a workshop, factory, or part of a factory for making or repairing machines or machine parts.

ma·chine-tool (mə-shēn′tōōl′), *adj.* of, for, or by a machine tool.

machine tool, an automatic or semiautomatic power-driven tool, as an electric lathe, drill, or planer: machine tools are used in making machines or machine parts.

ma·chin·ist (mə-shēn′ist), *n.* 1. a person who makes or repairs machinery. 2. a worker skilled in using machine tools. 3. a worker who operates a machine.

Mach (number) (mäk), [after Ernst *Mach* (1838–1916), Austrian physicist], in *aerodynamics,* a number representing the ratio of the air speed of an object to the speed of sound in the same region of the atmosphere.

ma·chree (mə-krē′, mə-khrē′), *n.* [< Ir. *mo,* my + *croidhe* (OIr. *cride*), heart], literally, my heart: Anglo-Irish term of endearment, as, Mother *machree.*

-ma·chy (mə-ki), [< Gr. *machē,* a battle], a combining form meaning *struggle, contest of,* as in *gigantomachy.*

mac·in·tosh (mak′in-tosh′), *n.* a mackintosh.
Mack·en·sen, Au·gust von (ou′goost fôn mäk′ən-zən), 1849–1945; German field marshal in World War I.
Mac·ken·zie (mə-ken′zi), *n.* 1. a river in northwestern Canada, flowing into the Beaufort Sea: length, 2,500 mi. 2. a district of Northwest Territories, Canada: area, 527,490 sq. mi.
mack·er·el (mak′ẽr-əl), *n.* [*pl.* MACKEREL, MACKERELS (-əlz); see PLURAL, II, D, 2], [OFr. *makerel, maquerel* (Fr. *maquereau*); ML. *macarellus*], 1. an edible fish of the North Atlantic, with a greenish, blue-striped back and a silvery belly. 2. any of various other related fishes.
mackerel sky, a sky covered with rows of small, fleecy clouds, suggesting the streaks on a mackerel's back.
Mack·i·nac, Strait of (mak′ə-nô′), the strait connecting Lake Huron and Lake Michigan: width, 4 mi.
Mackinac Island, a small island in the Strait of Mackinac: it is a State park of Michigan.
Mack·i·naw (mak′ə-nô′), *adj.* [Canad. Fr. *Mackinac* < *Michilimackinac,* Mackinac Island < Am. Ind. (Ojibway) *mitchimakinak,* large turtle], of or from Mackinac Island, formerly a center of trade with the Indians of the Northwest. *n.* [m-], 1. a Mackinaw blanket. 2. a Mackinaw coat. 3. a Mackinaw boat.
Mackinaw blanket, a thick woolen blanket, often woven in bars of bright colors, much used by Indians, lumbermen, etc. in the American Northwest.
Mackinaw boat, a rowboat or sailboat with a flat bottom, sharp bow, and square or pointed stern, used on and around the upper Great Lakes.
Mackinaw coat, a short, double-breasted coat made of heavy woolen cloth, often plaid.
Mackinaw trout, the namaycush.
mack·in·tosh (mak′in-tosh′), *n.* [after Charles *Macintosh* (1766–1843), the Scot. inventor], 1. a waterproof outer coat; raincoat. 2. the fabric used for this, made waterproof by cementing layers of cloth with rubber.
mack·le (mak′'l), *n.* [Fr. *macule;* L. *macula,* a spot, stain], in ‡*printing,* 1. a blot or blur. 2. a blurred sheet. *v.t.* & *v.i.* [MACKLED (-'ld), MACKLING], in *printing,* to blot; blur; print blurred or double.
ma·cle (mak′'l), *n.* [Fr.; OFr. *mascle;* ML. *mascula,* mesh of a net, metal plate in a coat of mail < L. *macula,* a spot, stain], 1. a twin crystal, as of a diamond. 2. a dark spot in certain minerals.
Mac·Leish, Archibald (mək-lēsh′), **1892–** ; American poet.
Mac·leod, John James Rick·ard (rik′ərd mək-loud′), 1876–1935; Scottish physiologist; co-discoverer of insulin; shared Nobel prize in medicine, 1923.
Mac·Ma·hon, Ma·rie Ed·me Pa·trice Mau·rice de (må′rē′ ed′mə på′trēs′ mō′rēs′ də måk′må′ôn′), Count, Duke of Magenta, 1808–1893; French marshal and statesman; president of France (1873–1879).
Mac·Mil·lan, Donald Bax·ter (baks′tẽr mak-mil′ən, mək-mil′ən), 1874– ; American explorer of the Arctic.
Mac·mil·lan, (Maurice) Harold (mək-mil′ən), 1894– ; British prime minister (1957–).
Mac·Mon·nies, Frederick William (mək-mon′iz), 1863–1937; American sculptor.
Ma·con (mā′kən, mā′kon), *n.* a city in central Georgia: pop., 70,000.
Mac·pher·son, James (mək-fũr′sən), 1736–1796; Scottish poet: see **Ossian.**
Mac·quar·ie (mə-kwôr′i, mə-kwär′i), *n.* a river in southeastern Australia, flowing into the Darling River: length, 750 mi.
mac·ra·mé (mak′rə-mā′), *n.* [Turk. *maqramah,* napkin, towel < Ar. *miqramah,* a veil], a coarse fringe or lace of thread or cord knotted in designs, used for decorating furniture, etc.: also **macramé lace.**
Mac·rea·dy, William Charles (mək-rē′di), 1793–1873; English actor.
mac·ro- (mak′rō, mak′rə), [< Gr. *makros,* long], a combining form meaning *long* (*in extent* or *duration*), *large, enlarged* or *elongated* (in a specified part), as in *macrocosm:* also, before a vowel, **macr-:** opposed to *micro-.*
mac·ro·ce·phal·ic (mak′rō-sə-fal′ik), *adj.* macrocephalous.
mac·ro·ceph·a·lous (mak′rə-sef′ə-ləs), *adj.* of or having macrocephaly.
mac·ro·ceph·a·ly (mak′rə-sef′ə-li), *n.* [*macro-* + *cephal-* + *-y*], a condition in which the head or cranial capacity is abnormally large: opposed to *microcephaly.*
mac·ro·cosm (mak′rə-koz'm), *n.* [Fr. *macrocosme;* see MACRO- & COSMOS], the great world; the universe: opposed to *microcosm.*
mac·ro·cos·mic (mak′rə-koz′mik), *adj.* of or like the macrocosm.
mac·ro·cyst (mak′rə-sist′), *n.* [*macro-* + *-cyst*], a large or enlarged cyst; especially, in *botany,* a large reproductive cyst in certain fungi.
mac·ro·cyte (mak′rə-sīt′), *n.* [*macro-* + *-cyte*], an abnormally large red blood corpuscle occurring especially in pernicious anemia.
mac·ro·dome (mak′rə-dōm′), *n.* [*macro-* + *dome*], in *crystallography,* a dome with its planes parallel to the longer lateral axis.
mac·ro·dont (mak′rə-dont′), *adj.* having large teeth.
ma·cro·ga·mete (mak′rō-gə-mēt′, mak′rə-gam′ēt), *n.* [*macro-* + *gamete*], the larger of two conjugating cells or spores, usually considered to be female.
mac·ro·graph (mak′rə-graf′, mak′rə-gräf′), *n.* [*macro-* + *-graph*], a drawing or photograph of an object as seen with little or no magnification.
ma·crog·ra·phy (mə-krog′rə-fi), *n.* [*macro-* + *-graphy*], 1. examination of an object with the naked eye instead of with a microscope: opposed to *micrography.* 2. large handwriting, often a sign of nervous disorder.
ma·cron (mā′krən, mak′ron), *n.* [Gr. *makron,* neut. of *makros,* long], a short, straight mark (¯) placed horizontally over a vowel to indicate that it is long or is to be pronounced in a certain way.
mac·ro·phys·ics (mak′rə-fiz′iks), *n.* [*macro-* + *physics*], the branch of physics that deals with masses large enough to be directly observed and measured.
mac·ro·scop·ic (mak′rə-skop′ik), *adj.* [*macro-* + *-scopic*], visible to the naked eye: opposed to *microscopic.*
mac·ro·spo·ran·gi·um (mak′rō-spə-ran′ji-əm), *n.* [*pl.* MACROSPORANGIA (-ə)], a megasporangium.
mac·ro·spore (mak′rə-spôr′, mak′rə-spōr′), *n.* [*macro-* + *spore*], 1. a large spore. 2. a megaspore.
ma·cru·ral (mə-kroor′əl), *adj.* [Mod. L. *Macrura,* name of the suborder (< *macr-* + Gr. *oura,* tail); + *-al*], of a group of ten-legged, stalk-eyed crustaceans, comprising the lobsters, prawns, shrimps, etc.
ma·cru·ran (mə-kroor′ən), *n.* a macrural animal. *adj.* macrural.
mac·u·la (mak′yoo-lə), *n.* [*pl.* MACULAE (-lē′)], [L., a spot, stain, etc.], a spot, stain, blotch, etc.; especially, *a*) a discolored spot on the skin. *b*) a spot on the sun.
mac·u·lar (mak′yoo-lẽr), *adj.* 1. of or constituting a macula. 2. characterized by maculae.
mac·u·late (mak′yoo-lāt′; *for adj.,* mak′yoo-lit), *v.t.* [MACULATED (-id), MACULATING], [< L. *maculatus,* pp. of *maculare,* to spot, speckle < *macula,* a spot, stain], to spot; stain; blemish; defile. *adj.* 1. spotted; blotched; hence, 2. defiled; impure.
mac·u·la·tion (mak′yoo-lā′shən), *n.* [LL. *maculatio;* see MACULATE], 1. a spotting. 2. a spot; stain; blemish. 3. the pattern of spots on an animal or plant.
mac·ule (mak′ūl), *n.* [Fr.], a macula or mackle. *v.t.* & *v.i.* [MACULED (-ūld), MACULING], to mackle; blur.
mad (mad), *adj.* [MADDER (-ẽr), MADDEST (-ist)], [ME. *madde, medde* (aphetic form) < AS. *gemædd, gemæded,* pp. of (*ge*)*mædan,* to make mad, drive mad; akin to Goth. *gamaiths,* crippled, OS. *gimēd,* foolish; IE. base **mait-,* to cut down < **mai-,* to hew, cut off; prob. sense development: castrated, crippled—mentally deficient], 1. mentally ill; insane; crazy. 2. frenzied; wildly excited; frantic: as, *mad* with fear. 3. showing or resulting from lack of reason; foolish and rash; senseless; unwise. 4. blindly and foolishly enthusiastic or fond; infatuated: as, she's *mad* about him. 5. wildly gay; hilarious. 6. having rabies: as, a *mad* dog. 7. [Colloq.], angry; enraged; wrathful; furious (often with *at*). *v.t* & *v.i.* [MADDED (-id), MADDING], [Rare], to madden.
  have a mad on, [Colloq.], to be angry.
  like mad, 1. in the manner of a madman. 2. with furious energy, speed, enthusiasm, etc.
  mad as a hatter (or **March hare**), completely crazy.
Mad·a·gas·can (mad′ə-gas′kən), *adj.* of Madagascar or its people. *n.* a native or inhabitant of Madagascar.
Mad·a·gas·car (mad′ə-gas′kẽr), *n.* a large island off the southeastern coast of Africa: formerly belonging to France, it is now coextensive with the republic of Malagasy.

MADAGASCAR

mad·am (mad′əm), *n.* [*pl.* MADAMS (-əmz); *for 1, usually* MESDAMES (mā-dām′; Fr. mā′dåm′)], [Fr. *madame,* orig. *ma dame;* L. *mea domina,* my lady], 1. a woman; lady: a polite title used in speaking to or of a woman: often **ma'am.** 2. the mistress of a household. 3. a woman in charge of a brothel. Abbreviated **Mdm., Mad., Madm.**
mad·ame (mad′əm; Fr. må′dåm′), *n.* [*pl.* MESDAMES (mā-dām′; Fr. mā′dåm′)], [Fr.; see MADAM], a married woman: French title equivalent to *Mrs.;* generally used of all foreign married women, in American and British usage: abbreviated **Mme., Mdme.**
Ma·da·ria·ga, Sal·va·dor de (säl′vä-*th*ôr′ *the* mä′*th*ä-ryä′gä), 1886– ; Spanish writer and diplomat.
mad·cap (mad′kap′), *n.* [*mad* + *cap,* fig. for head],

a reckless, impulsive person, especially a girl. *adj.* reckless and impulsive.

mad·den (mad''n), *v.t.* & *v.i.* to make or become mad; make or become insane, angry, or wildly excited.

mad·der (mad'ẽr), *n.* [ME. *mader;* AS. *mædere, mæddre;* akin to ON. *mathra,* Norw. *modra,* etc.; IE. base **modhro-*, dye plant], 1. any of a number of related plants that yield medicines and dyes; especially, a vine with small, yellow flowers and berries. 2. *a)* the red root of this plant. *b)* a red dye made from this: the term is also applied to a synthetic coal-tar dye, alizarin. 3. bright red; crimson.

mad·der (mad'ẽr), *adj.* comparative of **mad.**

mad·ding (mad'iŋ), *adj.* [Rare], 1. raving; frenzied: as, "the *madding* crowd." 2. maddening; making mad.

mad·dish (mad'ish), *adj.* somewhat mad.

made (mād), past tense and past participle of **make.** *adj.* 1. constructed; shaped; formed: as, a well-*made* play. 2. produced artificially; not natural: as, *made* ground. 3. invented; contrived: as, a *made* word. 4. specially prepared: as, a *made* dish. 5. sure of success or fortune; successful: as, a *made* man.

Ma·deir·a (mə-dêr'ə; Port. mä-de'rə), *n.* 1. a group of five Portuguese islands, off the coast of Morocco: area, 314 sq. mi.; pop., 267,000; capital, Funchal. 2. the chief island of this group. 3. a river in Brazil, flowing into the Amazon: length, c. 2,000 mi. 4. [also m-], a strong white wine made on the island of Madeira.

Mad·e·line (mad'ə-lin', mad''l-in), a feminine name: see **Magdalene.**

ma·de·moi·selle (mad'ə-mə-zel'; *popularly, often* mam'-zel'; Fr. måd'mwå'zel'), *n.* [Fr. *pl.* MESDEMOISELLES (mād'mwå'zel')], [Fr.; *ma,* my + *demoiselle,* young lady; see DAMSEL], an unmarried woman or girl: French title equivalent to *Miss:* abbreviated **Mlle., Mdlle.**

Ma·de·ro, Fran·cis·co In·da·le·cio (frän-sēs'kô ēn'dä-le'syô mä-de'rô), 1873–1913; Mexican revolutionist and statesman; president of Mexico (1911–1913).

made-to-or·der (mād'tə-ôr'dẽr), *adj.* made to conform to the customer's specifications or measurements; custom-made: opposed to *ready-made.*

made-up (mād'up'), *adj.* 1. put together; arranged: as, a *made-up* page of type. 2. invented; fabricated; false: as, a *made-up* story. 3. with cosmetics applied.

Madge (maj), a feminine name: see **Margaret, Margery.**

mad·house (mad'hous'), *n.* 1. a place of confinement for the mentally ill; insane asylum; hence, 2. any place of turmoil, noise, and confusion.

Mad·hya Bha·rat (mud'hyə bu'rut), a former state of central India: now in Madhya Pradesh.

Mad·hya Pra·desh (mud'hyə prä'desh), a state of central India: area, 171,200 sq. mi.; pop., 26,072,000; capital, Bhopal: former name, *Central Provinces and Berar.*

Mad·i·son (mad'i-s'n), *n.* the capital of Wisconsin: pop., 127,000.

Madison, James, 1751–1836; fourth president of the United States (1809–1817).

Madison Avenue, 1. a street in New York City, regarded as the center of the American advertising industry. 2. this industry, its practices, influence, etc.

mad·ly (mad'li), *adv.* 1. insanely. 2. wildly; furiously. 3. foolishly.

mad·man (mad'man', mad'mən), *n.* [*pl.* MADMEN (-men', -mən)], a demented person; lunatic; maniac.

mad·ness (mad'nis), *n.* 1. dementia; insanity; lunacy. 2. great anger; fury. 3. great folly. 4. wild excitement or enthusiasm. 5. rabies.

Ma·doe·ra (mä-do͞o'rä), *n.* **Madura,** an island in Indonesia: the Dutch spelling.

Ma·don·na (mə-don'ə), *n.* [It., my lady; *ma,* my (L. *mea*) + *donna,* lady (L. *domina,* fem. of *dominus,* lord; see DOMINATE)], 1. [m-], a former Italian title for a woman, equivalent to *madam.* 2. *a)* Mary, mother of Jesus. *b)* a picture or statue of Mary.

Ma·dras (mə-dras', mə-dräs'), *n.* 1. a state of southeastern India: area, 50,172 sq. mi.; pop., 29,970,000. 2. its capital, on the Bay of Bengal: pop., 1,416,000.

ma·dras (mad'rəs, mə-dras', mə-dräs'), *n.* [< *Madras,* India], 1. a fine, firm cotton cloth, usually striped, used for shirts, dresses, etc. 2. a durable silk cloth, usually striped. 3. a figured cotton or rayon cloth in leno weave, used for draperies. 4. a large, bright-colored kerchief of silk or cotton. *adj.* made of madras.

Madras States, a former agency of British India, including the native states of Travancore, Cochin, and Pudukottai: area, 10,334 sq. mi.

‡ma·dre (mä'dre), *n.* [Sp.], mother.

Ma·dre de Dios (mä'dre de' dyôs'), a river in southeastern Peru and northwestern Bolivia, flowing into the Beni: length, 900 mi.

mad·re·pore (mad'ri-pôr', mad'ri-pōr'), *n.* [Fr. *madrépore;* It. *madrepora,* lit., mother-stone (from its rapid production) < *madre* (< L. *mater*), mother + *poro,* a pore (or Gr. *pōros,* soft stone)], any of a group of corals, usually branching, which form coral reefs and islands in tropical seas.

Ma·drid (mə-drid'; Sp. mä-*thrē*'), *n.* the capital of Spain, in the central part: pop., 1,899,000.

mad·ri·gal (mad'ri-g'l), *n.* [It. *madrigale, mandrigale;* prob. parallel with *madregal,* feverfew, a perennial herb < LL. (*herba*) *matricalis,* feverfew < *matricalis,* of the womb (see MATRIX); form affected by association with It. *mandra,* flock (< L. *mandra,* stall, herd < Gr. *mandra,* fold, stable), as if "pastoral song"; prob. orig. sense "invented song"], 1. a short poem, usually a love poem, which can be set to music. 2. a contrapuntal song with parts for several voices, sung without accompaniment, popular in the 15th, 16th, and 17th centuries. 3. loosely, any song, especially a part song.

mad·ri·gal·ist (mad'ri-g'l-ist), *n.* 1. a composer of madrigals. 2. a singer of madrigals.

ma·dro·na (mə-drō'nə), *n.* [< *madroño,* the Sp. name], 1. an evergreen found on the Pacific coast of North America. 2. its edible red berry: also **madrona apple.**

ma·dro·no (mə-drō'nō), *n.* a madrona.

Ma·du·ra (mä-do͞o'rä), *n.* an island of Indonesia, northeast of Java: area, 1,726 sq. mi.; pop., 1,954,000: Dutch spelling, *Madoera.*

Mad·u·ra (maj'oo-rə), *n.* a city in southern India: pop., 362,000.

ma·du·ro (mə-door'ō), *adj.* [Sp., mature < L. *maturus*], dark and strong: said of cigars.

mad·wo·man (mad'woom'ən), *n.* [*pl.* MADWOMEN (-wim'ən)], a demented, or insane, woman.

mad·wort (mad'wũrt'), *n.* [*mad* + *wort* (plant): so named because supposed remedy for rabies], any of a group of plants or shrubs of the mustard family, with grayish leaves and small, pale flowers; alyssum.

Mae (mā), a feminine name: see **Mary.**

Mae·an·der (mi-an'dẽr), *n.* the Menderes River (sense 1): the ancient name: also spelled **Meander.**

Mae·ce·nas (mi-sē'nəs), *n.* 1. (*Gaius Cilnius Maecenas*), Roman statesman and patron of literature, friend of Horace and Virgil; 70?–8 B.C. 2. any wealthy, generous patron, especially of literature or art.

mael·strom (māl'strəm), *n.* [Early Mod. D. (now *maalstroom*) < *malen,* to grind, whirl round + *stroom,* a stream; first applied by 16th-c. D. geographers], 1. [M-], a famous and dangerous whirlpool off the west coast of Norway; hence, 2. any large or violent whirlpool. 3. a violently confused, turbulent, or dangerously agitated state of mind, emotions, affairs, etc.

mae·nad (mē'nad), *n.* [*pl.* MAENADS (-nadz), MAENADES (men'ə-dēz')], [L. *Maenas, Maenadis;* Gr. *mainas, mainados* < *mainesthai,* to rave], 1. in *Greek & Roman mythology,* a nymph who attended Dionysus; female participant in the cult of Bacchus; bacchante; hence, 2. a frenzied or raging woman. Also spelled **menad.**

mae·nad·ic (mi-nad'ik), *adj.* of, like, or characteristic of a maenad.

‡ma·es·to·so (mä'es-tô'sô), *adj.* & *adv.* [It.], in *music,* with majesty or dignity: a direction to the performer.

Maes·tricht (mäs'triHt), *n.* Maastricht.

ma·es·tro (mis'trō, mä-es'trō), *n.* [*pl.* MAESTROS (-trōz), MAESTRI (-tri)], [It.; L. *magister,* a master], a master in any art; especially, a great composer, conductor, or teacher of music.

Mae·ter·linck, Count **Maurice** (mā'tẽr-liŋk', met'ẽr-liŋk'), 1862–1949; Belgian dramatist, poet, and essayist; awarded Nobel prize in literature, 1911.

Mae West (mā west), [after *Mae West,* shapely American actress], an inflated life preserver vest worn by aviators downed at sea.

Maf·e·king (mäf'ə-kiŋ'), *n.* a town in the northern part of the Union of South Africa: pop., 6,000: it was besieged during the Boer War (1899–1900).

maf·fi·a, ma·fi·a (mä'fi-ä'), *n.* [It. *maffia*], 1. in Sicily, popular hostility to law and government. 2. [M-], an alleged secret society of Sicilians or Italians in the United States and other countries, for purposes of vengeance, reprisal, and blackmail; Black Hand.

‡ma foi (må' fwä'), [Fr.], 1. literally, my faith; hence, 2. my goodness! really!

mag., 1. magazine. 2. magnetic. 3. magnitude.

Ma·gal·la·nes (mä'gä-yä'nes), *n.* a seaport in southern Chile, on the Strait of Magellan: pop., 69,000: southernmost city in the world: former name, *Punta Arenas.*

mag·a·zine (mag'ə-zēn', mag'ə-zēn'), *n.* [Fr. *magasin;* OFr. *magazin;* It. *magazzino;* Ar. *makhāzin,* pl. of *makhzan,* a storehouse, granary < *khazana,* to store up], 1. a place of storage, as a warehouse, storehouse, or military supply depot. 2. a space in which explosives are stored, as a building or room in a fort, or a section of a warship. 3. a supply chamber, as the space in a rifle or pistol from which the cartridges are fed, the space in a camera from which the plates or rolls of film are fed, or the part of a stove in which the fuel is stored. 4. the things kept in a magazine, as munitions or supplies. 5. [from the idea of "storehouse of information"], a publication, usually paper-backed and sometimes illustrated, that appears at regular intervals and contains stories, articles, etc. by various writers and, usually, advertisements. Abbreviated **mag.**

Mag·da·len (mag'də-lin, mag'də-lən), *n.* 1. Magdalene. 2. (môd'lin), Magdalen College, Oxford.

Mag·da·le·na (mäg'dä-le'nä), *n.* a river in western

Colombia, flowing into the Caribbean; length, 950 mi.

Mag·da·lene (mag′də-lēn′), [LL.; Gr. *Magdalēnē*, lit., of Magdala < *Magdala*, town on the Sea of Galilee], a feminine name: variants, *Magdalen, Madeline;* diminutive, *Lena.* ***n.*** 1. (*also* mag′də-lē′ni), Mary Magdalene (preceded by *the*): Luke 8:2 (identified with the repentant woman in Luke 7:37). 2. [m-], *a*) a reformed and repentant prostitute. *b*) a reformatory for prostitutes. 3. (môd′lin), Magdalene College, Cambridge.

Mag·da·le·ni·an (mag′də-lē′ni-ən), ***adj.*** [Fr. *magdalenien*, after *La Madeleine*, in west central France, where many of the artifacts were found], designating or of a late period of the Old Stone Age, characterized by cave art and tools of polished stone and bone.

the Magdalenian, the Magdalenian period.

Mag·de·burg (mag′də-bûrg′; G. mäg′də-boorkh′), ***n.*** a city in the province of Saxony, Germany: pop., 306,000.

mage (māj), ***n.*** [Fr.; L. *magus;* see MAGI], [Archaic], a magician; wizard.

Ma·gel·lan, Ferdinand (mə-jel′ən), 1480?–1521; Portuguese navigator; discoverer of the Strait of Magellan and the Philippine Islands.

Magellan, Strait of, a strait between the South American mainland and Tierra del Fuego: length, 370 mi.

Mag·el·lan·ic (maj′ə-lan′ik), ***adj.*** having to do with Ferdinand Magellan.

Magellanic cloud, [after Ferdinand *Magellan*], in *astronomy*, 1. either of two large, cloudlike phenomena containing star clusters, in the Milky Way in the southern hemisphere. 2. a dark area in the Milky Way, near the Southern Cross.

ma·gen·ta (mə-jen′tə), ***n.*** [< *Magenta*, town in Italy: so called because discovered about the time (1859) of the battle fought there], 1. fuchsin, a purplish-red aniline dye. 2. purplish red. ***adj.*** purplish-red.

Mag·gie (mag′i), a feminine name: see **Margaret.**

Mag·gio·re, Lake (mə-jôr′i; It. mäd-jô′re), a lake in Switzerland and northwestern Italy: area, 82 sq. mi.

mag·got (mag′ət), ***n.*** [ME. *magotte;* prob. < earlier *mathek*, flesh worm (< ON. *mathkr* or AS. *matha*, a worm, maggot; cf. MAWKISH) after *Magot*, form of *Margaret*], 1. a wormlike insect larva, as the legless larva of the housefly: maggots are usually found in filth and decaying matter. 2. an odd notion; whim.

mag·got·y (mag′ət-i), ***adj.*** 1. full of maggots. 2. full of odd notions or whims.

Ma·gi (mā′jī), ***n.pl.*** [*sing.* MAGUS (mā′gus)], [L., pl. of *magus;* Gr. *magos;* OPer. *magu*, member of a priestly caste, magician], 1. the priestly caste in ancient Media and Persia, supposedly having occult powers. 2. in the *Bible*, the wise men from the East (in later tradition, three in number) who came bearing gifts to the infant Jesus: Matt. 2:1–13.

Ma·gi·an (mā′ji-ən), ***n.*** 1. one of the Magi. 2. an adherent of the Magi. 3. [m-], a magician; wizard. ***adj.*** 1. of the Magi. 2. [m-], [Rare], magical.

mag·ic (maj′ik), ***n.*** [ME. *magike;* OFr. *magique;* LL. *magica* (*ars*); L. *magice;* Gr. *magikē* (*technē*), magic (art), sorcery < *magikos*, of the Magi; see MAGI], 1. the pretended art of producing effects or controlling events by charms, spells, and rituals supposed to govern certain natural or supernatural forces; sorcery; witchcraft. 2. any mysterious, seemingly inexplicable, or extraordinary power or influence: as, the *magic* of love. 3. the art of producing baffling effects or illusions by sleight of hand, concealed apparatus, etc. ***adj.*** [L. *magicus;* Gr. *magikos*], 1. of, produced by, used in, or using magic. 2. producing extraordinary results, as if by magic or supernatural means.

SYN.—**magic** is the general term for any of the supposed arts of producing marvelous effects by supernatural or occult power and is figuratively applied to any extraordinary, seemingly inexplicable power; **sorcery** implies magic in which spells are cast or charms are used, usually for a harmful or sinister purpose; **witchcraft** (of women) and **wizardry** (of men) imply the possession of supernatural power by compact with evil spirits, **witchcraft** figuratively suggesting the use of womanly wiles, and **wizardry,** remarkable skill, cleverness, etc.

mag·i·cal (maj′i-k'l), ***adj.*** magic (especially in sense 2): used predicatively as well as attributively, whereas *magic* tends to be attributive only.

ma·gi·cian (mə-jish′ən), ***n.*** [ME. & OFr. *magicien*], an expert in magic; specifically, *a*) a sorcerer; wizard. *b*) a performer skilled in magic (sense 3).

magic lantern, an optical instrument with an arrangement of lenses and a light for projecting on a screen a magnified image of a picture on a small slide or card.

ma·gilp (mə-gilp′), ***n.*** megilp.

ma·gilph (mə-gilf′), ***n.*** megilp.

Ma·gin·da·na·o (mä-gēn′dä-nä′ō), ***n.*** 1. a member of the chief Moro people of Mindanao. 2. their Malay language; Moro.

Ma·gi·not line (mazh′ə-nō′; Fr. mȧ′zhē′nō′), [after André *Maginot* (1877–1932), Fr. minister of war], a system of heavily fortified pillboxes, tank traps, etc. on the eastern frontier of France, built before World War II: though considered impregnable, it failed to prevent invasion by the Nazi armies.

mag·is·te·ri·al (maj′is-têr′i-əl), ***adj.*** [ML. *magisterialis* < LL. *magisterius* < L. *magister*, a master], 1. of or suitable for a magistrate or master. 2. authoritative. 3. domineering; pompous. —***SYN.*** see **masterful.**

mag·is·tra·cy (maj′is-trə-si), ***n.*** [*pl.* MAGISTRACIES (-siz)], 1. the position, office, function, or term of a magistrate. 2. magistrates collectively. 3. the district under a magistrate; magistrate's jurisdiction.

mag·is·tral (maj′is-trəl), ***adj.*** [L. *magistralis*], 1. magisterial; authoritative or imperious. 2. guiding; main: as, a *magistral* line in fortification. 3. in *pharmacy*, prepared for a particular case: said of a prescription: opposed to *officinal.* ***n.*** in *fortification*, a magistral line.

mag·is·trate (maj′is-trāt′, maj′is-trit), ***n.*** [ME.; L. *magistratus* < *magister;* see MASTER], 1. a civil officer empowered to administer and enforce the law: the President of the United States is sometimes called the *first* (or *chief*) *magistrate.* 2. a minor official with certain limited judicial and executive powers, as a justice of the peace or judge of a police court.

mag·ma (mag′mə), ***n.*** [*pl.* MAGMAS (-məz), MAGMATA (-mə-tə)], [L.; Gr. *magma* < *massein*, to knead], 1. a thin paste composed of crude mixed mineral or organic matter. 2. in *geology*, molten rock deep in the earth, from which igneous rock is formed. 3. in *pharmacy*, a suspension of precipitated matter in a watery substance.

mag·mat·ic (mag-mat′ik), ***adj.*** of, like, or produced by magma.

Mag·na Char·ta, Mag·na Car·ta (mag′nə kär′tə), [ML., lit., great charter], 1. the great charter that King John of England was forced by the English barons to grant at Runnymede, June 15, 1215: it guaranteed certain civil and political liberties to the English people. 2. any basic constitution that guarantees civil and political liberties.

‡**mag·na cum lau·de** (mag′nə kum lô′di, mäg′nä koom lou′de), [L.], with great praise: phrase used to signify graduation with high honors from a university or college: cf. **cum laude, summa cum laude.**

mag·na·nim·i·ty (mag′nə-nim′ə-ti), ***n.*** 1. the quality or state of being magnanimous. 2. [*pl.* MAGNANIMITIES (-tiz)], a magnanimous act.

mag·nan·i·mous (mag-nan′ə-məs), ***adj.*** [L. *magnanimus* < *magnus*, great + *animus*, mind, soul], noble in mind; high-souled; generous in overlooking injury or insult; rising above pettiness or meanness.

mag·nate (mag′nāt), ***n.*** [ME.; LL. *magnas*, pl. *magnates*, great man, nobleman < L. *magnus*, great], 1. a very important or influential person in any field of activity, especially in a large business. 2. formerly, in Hungary and Poland, a member of the upper branch of the Diet.

mag·ne·sia (mag-nē′shə, mag-nē′zhə), ***n.*** [ME.; ML. < Gr. *Magnēsia lithos*, stone of Magnesia (district in Thessaly)], 1. magnesium oxide, MgO, a white, tasteless powder, used as a mild laxative and antacid, and as an insulating substance, in firebrick, etc. 2. hydrated magnesium carbonate, also used as a laxative.

mag·ne·sian (mag-nē′shən, mag-nē′zhən), ***adj.*** of or containing magnesium.

mag·ne·sic (mag-nē′sik), ***adj.*** of or containing magnesium or one of its compounds.

mag·ne·site (mag′nə-sīt′), ***n.*** native magnesium carbonate, $MgCO_3$, a mineral occurring usually in white, compact masses, but sometimes granular or crystalline: used for furnace linings, etc.

mag·ne·si·um (mag-nē′shi-əm, mag-nē′zhi-əm), ***n.*** [Mod. L. < *magnesia*], a light, silver-white metallic chemical element, malleable and ductile: used in making several alloys and, because it burns with a hot, white light, in photographic flash bulbs, incendiary bombs, etc.: symbol, Mg; at. wt., 24.32; at. no., 12.

mag·net (mag′nit), ***n.*** [ME. & OFr. *magnete;* L. *magnes*, *magnetis* < Gr. *Magnētis lithos*, stone of Magnesia (district in Thessaly)], 1. any piece of iron, steel, or, originally, magnetite (*loadstone*) that has the property of attracting iron or steel, etc.: this property may be naturally present or artificially induced, as by passing an electric current through a coil of wire wrapped around the metal. 2. a person or thing that attracts.

mag·net·ic (mag-net′ik), ***adj.*** 1. having the properties of a magnet: as, *magnetic* iron. 2. of, producing, caused by, or operated by magnetism. 3. of the earth's magnetism: as, the *magnetic* meridian. 4. that can be magnetized. 5. powerfully attractive: said of a person, personality, etc. 6. mesmeric. Abbreviated **mag.**

mag·net·i·cal·ly (mag-net′i-k'l-i, mag-net′ik-li), ***adv.*** in a magnetic manner; by magnetism.

magnetic axis, the straight line joining the two poles of a magnet: if the magnet is freely suspended, the magnetic axis will parallel the lines of magnetic force.

magnetic circuit, a closed path through which magnetic lines of force pass.

magnetic compass, an instrument for indicating geographical directions by the action of the earth's magnetic field on a bar magnet (*magnetic needle*) suspended so as to swing freely on a pivot.
magnetic equator, the aclinic line, an imaginary line around the earth near the equator, where the magnetic needle does not dip.
magnetic field, the space occupied by magnetic lines of force; space around a magnet in which the magnetic force exerted is appreciable.
magnetic flux, the total flow of magnetism or magnetic lines of force through a magnetic circuit.
magnetic induction, the power of a magnet to induce magnetism in a piece of iron, steel, etc. brought into its magnetic field.
magnetic meridian, that circle of the celestial sphere passing through the zenith and the Magnetic Poles.
magnetic mine, a naval mine designed to explode when the metal hull of a ship passing near it deflects a magnetic needle, closing an electric circuit and thus detonating the charge.
magnetic needle, a slender bar of magnetized steel which, when mounted so as to swing freely on a pivot, will point along the line of the magnetic meridian toward the Magnetic Poles, approximately north and south: it is the essential part of a magnetic compass.
magnetic north, the direction toward which a magnetic needle points: in most places it is not true north.
magnetic pickup, a pickup, often used in electric phonographs, in which the varying movements of the needle produce corresponding variations in electrical output to the amplifier through an arrangement of a magnet and coils: distinguished from *crystal pickup*.
magnetic pole, 1. either pole of a magnet, where the magnetic lines of force seem to be concentrated. 2. [M- P-], either point on the earth's surface toward which the needle of a magnetic compass points: the North and South Magnetic Poles do not precisely coincide with the geographical poles.
magnetic tape, a thin strip of metal, plastic, etc. coated with magnetic particles on which sound, a television program, computer data, etc., in the form of electric signals, can be recorded as magnetic variations: these variations can be reconverted into electric signals to reproduce the original sound, etc.
mag·net·ics (mag-net′iks), ***n.pl.*** [construed as sing.], the branch of physics dealing with magnets and magnetic phenomena.
magnetic storm, a noticeable disturbance of the earth's magnetism.
mag·net·ism (mag′nə-tiz′m), ***n.*** 1. the property, quality, or condition of being magnetic: as, a loadstone has *magnetism*. 2. the force to which this is due. 3. the branch of physics dealing with magnets and magnetic phenomena; magnetics. 4. power to attract; personal charm or allure. 5. mesmerism. Abbreviated **mag.**
mag·net·ite (mag′nə-tīt′), ***n.*** [G. *magnetit;* see MAGNET & -ITE], a black iron oxide, Fe_3O_4, an important iron ore: called *loadstone* when magnetic.
mag·net·iz·a·ble (mag′nə-tīz′ə-b'l), ***adj.*** that can be magnetized.
mag·net·i·za·tion (mag′nə-ti-zā′shən, mag′nə-tī-zā′-shən), ***n.*** a magnetizing or being magnetized.
mag·net·ize (mag′nə-tīz′), ***v.t.*** [MAGNETIZED (-tīzd′), MAGNETIZING], 1. to make into a magnet; give magnetic properties to (steel, iron, etc.). 2. to attract or charm (a person): often with a suggestion of sense 3. 3. [Rare], to mesmerize. ***v.i.*** to become magnetic.
mag·ne·to (mag-nē′tō), ***n.*** [*pl.* MAGNETOS (-tōz)], a dynamo in which one or more permanent magnets produce the magnetic field; especially, a small machine of this sort connected with and run by an internal-combustion engine, used to generate the electric current providing a spark for the ignition: in full, **magnetoelectric machine:** also **magnetogenerator.**

MAGNET
ROTATING ARMATURE
CIRCUIT BREAKER

MAGNETO

mag·ne·to- (mag-nē′tō, mag-net′ə), [see MAGNET], a combining form meaning: 1. *magnetism, magnetic force,* as in *magnetoelectric.* 2. *magnetoelectric.*
mag·ne·to·dy·na·mo (mag-nē′tō-dī′nə-mō′, mag-nət′ə-dī′nə-mō′), ***n.*** a dynamo with permanent field magnets.
mag·ne·to·e·lec·tric (mag-nē′tō-i-lek′trik, mag-net′ō-i-lek′trik), ***adj.*** of or characterized by electricity produced by magnets.
mag·ne·to·e·lec·tric·i·ty (mag-nē′tō-i-lek′tris′ə-ti, mag-net′ō-ē′lek-tris′ə-ti), ***n.*** electricity produced by the relative movement of electric conductors and magnets.
mag·ne·to·gen·er·a·tor (mag-nē′tō-jen′ə-rā′tẽr, mag-net′ə-jen′ə-rā′tẽr), ***n.*** a magneto.
mag·ne·tom·e·ter (mag′nə-tom′ə-tẽr), ***n.*** [*magneto-* + *-meter*], an instrument for measuring magnetic forces.
mag·ne·to·mo·tive (mag-nē′tō-mō′tiv, mag′ni-tə-mō′-tiv), ***adj.*** [*magneto-* + *motive*], designating or of a force (abbreviated **m.m.f.**) that gives rise to magnetic flux.
mag·ne·to·scope (mag-nē′tə-skōp′, mag-net′ə-skōp′), ***n.*** [*magneto-* + *-scope*], an instrument for detecting magnetic force.
mag·ne·tron (mag′nə-tron′), ***n.*** [*magnet* + *electron*], a vacuum tube in which the flow of ions from the heated cathode to the anode is controlled by a magnetic field externally applied and perpendicular to the electric field by which they are propelled: used to produce very short radio waves.
mag·ni- (mag′ni), [< L. *magnus*, great, big], a combining form meaning *great, big, large,* as in *magnificent, magniloquence;* also, in *zoology, long.*
mag·ni·fic (mag-nif′ik), ***adj.*** [Fr. *magnifique;* L. *magnificus*], [Archaic], 1. magnificent. 2. imposing in size, dignity, etc. 3. *a*) pompous. *b*) grandiloquent. 4. eulogistic.
mag·nif·i·cal (mag-nif′i-k'l), ***adj.*** [Archaic], magnific.
Mag·nif·i·cat (mag-nif′i-kat′), ***n.*** [L.], 1. *a*) the hymn of the Virgin Mary in Luke 1:46–55, beginning *Magnificat anima mea Dominum,* "My soul doth magnify the Lord." *b*) any musical setting for this. 2. [m-], any song, poem, or hymn of praise.
mag·ni·fi·ca·tion (mag′nə-fi-kā′shən), ***n.*** [LL. *magnificatio*], 1. a magnifying or being magnified. 2. the power of magnifying. 3. a magnified image, model, or representation.
mag·nif·i·cence (mag-nif′ə-s'ns), ***n.*** [ME.; OFr.; L. *magnificentia* < *magnificus*, noble < *magnus*, great + *facere*, to do], richness and splendor; stately or imposing beauty; grandeur.
mag·nif·i·cent (mag-nif′ə-s'nt), ***adj.*** [OFr.; LL. *magnificens;* see MAGNIFICENCE], 1. splendid; stately; imposingly beautiful; grand; rich or sumptuous, as in construction, decoration, etc. 2. exalted: said of ideas, etc., and also of some former rulers, as, Lorenzo the *Magnificent.* —***SYN.*** see **grand.**
mag·nif·i·co (mag-nif′ə-kō′), ***n.*** [*pl.* MAGNIFICOES (-kōz′)], [It. < L. *magnificus;* see MAGNIFICENCE], 1. a nobleman of ancient Venice; hence, 2. a person of high rank or great importance.
mag·ni·fi·er (mag′nə-fī′ẽr), ***n.*** 1. a person who magnifies. 2. a thing that magnifies; specifically, a lens or combination of lenses for magnifying.
mag·ni·fy (mag′nə-fī′), ***v.t.*** [MAGNIFIED (-fīd′), MAGNIFYING], [ME. *magnifien;* OFr. *magnifier;* L. *magnificare* < *magnus*, great + *facere*, to make], 1. [Rare], to make greater in size, status, or importance; enlarge. 2. to cause (a person or thing) to seem greater, more important, etc. than is really so; exaggerate: as, she *magnified* her sufferings in telling about them. 3. to cause to seem larger than is really so; increase the apparent size of (an object), especially by means of a lens or lenses. 4. [Archaic], to glorify; praise; extol. ***v.i.*** to have the power of increasing the apparent size of an object: as, telescopes and microscopes *magnify.*
magnifying glass, a lens or combination of lenses that increases the apparent size of an object seen through it.
mag·nil·o·quence (mag-nil′ə-kwəns), ***n.*** [L. *magniloquentia*], magniloquent quality, style, or expression.
mag·nil·o·quent (mag-nil′ə-kwənt), ***adj.*** [< L. *magnus*, great + *loquens*, ppr. of *loqui*, to speak], 1. lofty, pompous, or grandiose in speech or style of expression. 2. boastful; bombastic; talking big.
Mag·ni·to·gorsk (mäg′ni-tô-gôrsk′), ***n.*** a city on the Ural River, in western Siberia, U.S.S.R.: pop., 311,000.
mag·ni·tude (mag′nə-to͞od′, mag′nə-tūd′), ***n.*** [L. *magnitudo* < *magnus*, great], 1. greatness; specifically, *a*) of size. *b*) of extent. *c*) of importance or influence. *d*) [Obs.], of character. 2. *a*) size or measurable quantity: as, the *magnitude* of a velocity. *b*) importance or influence. 3. in *astronomy*, *a*) any of the classes into which fixed stars are arranged according to degree of brightness with reference to the polestar as the standard: the brightest stars are of the first magnitude; stars just visible to the unaided eye are of the sixth magnitude. *b*) a number expressing brightness. 4. in *mathematics*, a number given to a quantity for purposes of comparison with other quantities of the same class. Abbreviated **mag.**
of the first magnitude, of the greatest importance.
mag·no·li·a (mag-nō′li-ə, mag-nōl′yə), ***n.*** [Mod. L. < Pierre *Magnol* (1638–1715), Fr. botanist], 1. any of a group of trees or shrubs with large, fragrant flowers of white, pink, or purple. 2. the flower.
mag·no·li·a·ceous (mag-nō′li-ā′shəs), ***adj.*** of the magnolia family of trees and shrubs.
mag·num (mag′nəm), ***n.*** [L. *magnum*, neut. sing. of *magnus*, great; cf. also earlier *magnum bonum* in this sense], 1. a bottle holding two quarts, used for wine or liquor. 2. the amount that such a bottle holds.
‡mag·num o·pus (mag′nəm ō′pəs), [L.], 1. a great work, especially of art or literature; masterpiece. 2. a person's greatest work or undertaking.
Mag·nus effect (mag′nəs; G. mäg′noos), [after H. G. *Magnus* (1802–1870), G. scientist], the sideways thrust on a rotating cylinder with its axis perpendicular to an air current, used to propel rotor ships, etc.

mag·nus hitch (mag′nəs), [prob. < L. *magnus*, large], a kind of knot: see **knot**, illus.
Magog, see **Gog and Magog**.
mag·pie (mag′pī′), *n.* [< *Mag*, dim. of *Margaret* + *pie*, magpie; cf. Fr. *margot*], 1. any of a number of birds of the crow family, related to the jays and characterized by black-and-white coloring, a long, tapering tail, and a habit of noisy chattering. 2. a person who chatters.
M. Agr., Master of Agriculture.
mag·uey (mag′wā; Sp. mä-ge′ē), *n.* [Sp.], any of a number of related fleshy-leaved or fiber-yielding plants of the southwestern United States, Mexico, and Central America; agave or related plant; especially, the century plant; American aloe.
Ma·gus (mā′gəs), *n.* [*pl.* MAGI (mā′jī)], [L.; see MAGI], 1. one of the Magi (in either sense). 2. [m-], a magician, sorcerer, or ancient astrologer; especially, Simon Magus (Acts 8:9–24).
Mag·yar (mag′yär, Hung. môd′yär), *n.* [Hung.], 1. a member of the people constituting the main ethnic group in Hungary. 2. their Ugrian language; Hungarian. *adj.* of the Magyars, their language, or culture.
Ma·gyar·or·szág (môd′yär-ôr′säg), *n.* Hungary: the Hungarian name.
Ma·ha·bha·ra·ta (mə-hä′bä′rə-tə), *n.* [Sans. *Mahābhārata*, lit., the great story], one of the two great epics of India, written in Sanskrit about 200 B.C.: it combines stories and poems with history and mythology: cf. **Ramayana.**
Ma·ha·bha·ra·tam (mə-hä′bä′rə-təm), *n.* the Mahabharata.
Ma·han, Alfred Thay·er (thā′ẽr mə-han′), 1840–1914; American naval officer and historian.
ma·ha·ra·jah, ma·ha·ra·ja (mä′hə-rä′jə; Hind. mə-hä′rä′jə), *n.* [Sans. *mahārāja; maha*, great + *rājā*, king], in India, a sovereign prince, especially the prince of any of the chief native states: a title higher than *rajah.*
ma·ha·ra·ni, ma·ha·ra·nee (mä′hə-rä′nē; Hind. mə-hä′rä′nē), *n.* [Hind. *mahārānī; maha*, great + *rānī*, queen], in India, 1. the wife of a maharajah. 2. a sovereign queen or princess of this rank in her own right.
ma·hat·ma (mə-hat′mə, mə-hät′mə), *n.* [Sans. *mahātman* < *maha*, great + *ātman*, soul], in *theosophy* & *esoteric Buddhism*, one of a class of wise and holy persons supposed to have unusual powers: Mohandas Gandhi was often called *the Mahatma.*
Mah·di (mä′di), *n.* [Ar. *mahdīy*, one guided aright < *hadā* to lead aright], a leader and prophet expected by Moslems to appear on earth before the world ends; Moslem Messiah: the title has been assumed by various leaders, especially Mohammed Ahmed, who led a revolt in the Egyptian Sudan in 1883.
Mah·dism (mä′diz'm), *n.* the doctrine of the coming of the Mahdi.
Mah·dist (mä′dist), *n.* 1. a believer in Mahdism. 2. a follower of a person calling himself the Mahdi.
Ma·hi·can (mə-hē′kən), *n.* [Am. Ind. (Algonquian), lit., a wolf; cf. MOHEGAN], 1. a confederacy or tribe of Algonquian Indians that lived chiefly in the upper Hudson Valley. 2. an Indian of this confederacy. 3. Mohegan. *adj.* of this confederacy. Also **Mohican.**
mah-jongg, mah·jong (mä′jôŋ′, mä′joŋ′), *n.* [< dial. form of Chin. *ma-ch'iao*, lit., house sparrow: from the figure on one of the tiles], a game of Chinese origin, played, usually by four persons, with 136 or 144 pieces resembling dominoes, marked in suits and called *tiles:* the object is to build combinations or sets by drawing, discarding, and exchanging these.
Mah·ler, Gus·tav (goos′täf mä′lẽr), 1860–1911; Bohemian conductor and composer.
mahl·stick (mäl′stik′, môl′stik′), *n.* a maulstick.
ma·hog·a·ny (mə-hog′ə-ni, mə-hôg′ə-ni), *n.* [*pl.* MAHOGANIES (-niz)], [obs. Sp. *mahogani* < the native W. Ind. name; adopted (1702) by Linnaeus < Eng.], 1. *a)* the hard wood of a tropical American tree, much used‡for furniture: it varies in color from reddish brown to yellow. *b)* the tree. 2. *a)* any of various woods of similar properties and color: as, Philippine *mahogany.* *b)* a tree from which such wood is obtained. 3. reddish brown. *adj.* 1. made of mahogany. 2. reddish-brown.
Ma·hom·et (mə-hom′it), *n.* Mohammed.
Ma·hom·et·an (mə-hom′ə-tən), *adj.* & *n.* Mohammedan.
Ma·hom·et·an·ism (mə-hom′ə-tən-iz'm), *n.* Mohammedanism.
Ma·hound (mə-hound′, mə-hōōnd′), *n.* [ME. *Mahun, Mahoun;* OFr. *Mahon, Mahum* < *Mahomet*], 1. [Archaic], Mohammed. 2. [Scot.], the Devil.
ma·hout (mə-hout′), *n.* [Hind. *mahāut, mahāvat;* Sans. *mahāmātra*, lit., great in measure, hence high officer], in India and the East Indies, an elephant driver or elephant keeper.
Mah·rat·ta (mə-rat′ə), *n.* a Maratha.
Mah·rat·ti, Mah·ra·ti (mə-rat′i), *n.* Marathi.
Mäh·ren (me′rən), *n.* Moravia: the German name.
Mäh·risch-Os·trau (me′rish-ôs′trou), *n.* Moravská Ostrava: the German name.
mah·zor (mäkh′zẽr; Heb. mäkh-zôr′), *n.* [*pl.* MAHZORS (-zẽrz); Heb. MAHZORIM (-zôr′im)], [Heb., cycle], the Jewish prayer book that contains the liturgy for festivals and holy days: distinguished from *siddur.*
Ma·ia (mā′yə, mī′ə), *n.* [L.; Gr. *Maia*], 1. in *Greek mythology*, the eldest and loveliest of the Pleiades, mother of Hermes by Zeus. 2. in *Roman mythology*, an earth goddess, sometimes identified with the Greek Maia: the month of May was named in her honor.
maid (mād), *n.* [< *maiden*], 1. *a)* a girl or young unmarried woman. *b)* a virgin. 2. an unmarried woman; spinster: now **old maid.** 3. a girl or woman servant: often in compounds, as *barmaid, housemaid*, etc.
the Maid, Joan of Arc.
Mai·da·nek (mī′də-nek′), *n.* a Nazi concentration camp near Lublin, Poland: notorious as an extermination center.
maid·en (mād′'n), *n.* [ME. *mayden, meiden;* AS. *mægden* < base of *mægeth* (Goth. *magaths*), maid, virgin, *magu*, young man, etc.; IE. base **maghu-*, youngster, unmarried, seen also in OIr. *macc*, son (cf. MAC-)], 1. *a)* a girl or young unmarried woman. *b)* a virgin. 2. a race horse that has never won a race. 3. [M-], a device like the guillotine, formerly used in Scotland for beheading criminals. 4. in *cricket*, an over in which no runs are scored: in full, **maiden over.** *adj.* 1. of, characteristic of, or suitable for a maiden. 2. *a)* unmarried. *b)* virgin. 3. inexperienced; untried; unused; new; fresh. 4. first or earliest: as, a *maiden* speech, a *maiden* voyage. 5. *a)* never having won a race: as, a *maiden* horse. *b)* for such horses: as, a *maiden* race.
maid·en·hair (mād′'n-hâr′), *n.* 1. any of a group of ferns with delicate fronds and slender stalks: also **maidenhair fern.** 2. the ginko: also **maidenhair tree.**
maid·en·head (mād′'n-hed′), *n.* 1. [Archaic], maidenhood; virginity. 2. the hymen.
maid·en·hood (mād′'n-hood′), *n.* [see -HOOD], the state or time of being a maiden.
maid·en·li·ness (mād′'n-li-nis), *n.* the quality of being maidenly.
maid·en·ly (mād′'n-li), *adj.* 1. of a maiden or maidenhood. 2. like, characteristic of, or suitable for a maiden; modest, gentle, etc. *adv.* in a maidenly manner.
maiden name, the surname that a woman had when not yet married.
maiden over, a maiden (sense 4).
maid·hood (mād′hood′), *n.* maidenhood.
maid in waiting, [*pl.* MAIDS IN WAITING], an unmarried woman, usually of noble birth, attending a queen or princess.
Maid Marian, 1. a character in old May-day games and morris dances, variously a May queen, a boy dressed as a girl, or a buffoon. 2. Robin Hood's sweetheart.
maid of honor, 1. an unmarried woman acting as chief attendant to the bride at a wedding: cf. **matron of honor.** 2. an unmarried woman, usually of noble birth, attending a queen or princess.
Maid of Orleans, Joan of Arc.
maid·ser·vant (mād′sũr′vənt), *n.* a girl or woman servant.
Maid·stone (mād′stən, mād′stōn′), *n.* the county seat of Kent, England: pop., 50,000 (est. 1946).
ma·ieu·tic (mā-ū′tik), *adj.* [Gr. *maieutikos* < *maia*, midwife], designating or of the Socratic method of helping a person to bring forth and become aware of his latent ideas or memories.
ma·ieu·ti·cal (mā-ū′ti-k'l), *adj.* maieutic.
mai·gre (mā′gẽr), *adj.* [Fr.; see MEAGER], not made from flesh or its juices: said of food permissible to Roman Catholics, etc. on fast days.
mai·hem (mā′hem), *n.* mayhem.
mail (māl), *n.* [ME. & OFr. *male* (Fr. *malle*); OHG. *malaha, malha*, wallet], 1. *a)* [Obs. except Scot.], a bag or piece of baggage. *b)* [Archaic], a bag or packet of letters, etc. to be transported by post. 2. *a)* letters, papers, packages, etc. handled, transported, and delivered by the post office. *b)* letters, papers, etc. received by, or for, a person: as, my *mail* is full of bills. 3. a person or, especially, boat, train, etc. that transports letters, packages, etc. 4. the system of collection, transportation, and delivery of letters, packages, etc.; postal system. 5. the collection or delivery of letters, packages, etc. at a certain time: as, the morning *mail* is late. *adj.* of mail; carrying, or used in the handling of, mail. *v.t.* to send by mail; put into a mailbox or give to the post office for transmission; post.
mail (māl), *n.* [ME. & OFr. *maile, maille*, a link, mesh < L. *macula*, a spot, mesh of a net], 1. a flexible body armor made of small, overlapping metal rings, loops of chain, or scales. 2. any defensive armor. 3. the hard protective covering of some animals, as turtles or lobsters. *v.t.* to cover or protect with or as with mail.
mail·bag (māl′bag′), *n.* a large bag for carrying mail.

mail·boat (māl′bōt′), *n.* a boat that transports mail: also **mail boat.**
mail·box (māl′boks′), *n.* 1. a box or compartment into which mail is put when delivered, as at one's home. 2. a box, as on a street corner, into which mail is put for collection. Also **mail box.**
mail car, a railroad car equipped for handling mail.
mail·catch·er (māl′kach′ẽr), *n.* a device for transferring bags of mail to or from a railroad train in motion: also **mail catcher.**
mailed (māld), *adj.* covered with or clad in mail or a maillike outer layer, as of scales.
mailed fist, the use or threat of force, as between nations.
mail·er (māl′ẽr), *n.* 1. a person who mails or addresses letters, etc. 2. a mailing machine. 3. a mailboat.
mailing machine, a machine for stamping or addressing letters, cards, etc.
mailing tube, a pasteboard cylinder in which printed matter or fragile objects are inserted for mailing.
mail·lot (mī-yō′), *n.* [Fr., dim. < *maille,* knitted material, lit. mail: see MAIL (armor)], 1. a swimming suit; especially, a one-piece swimming suit. 2. a garment like this, worn by gymnasts, etc.
mail·man (māl′man′, māl′mən), *n.* [*pl.* MAILMEN (-men′, -mən)], a man whose work is carrying or delivering mail; postman.
mail-or·der (māl′ôr′dẽr), *adj.* having to do with ordering and delivering goods by mail.
mail order, an order for goods to be sent by mail.
mail-order house, a business establishment that takes mail orders and sends goods by mail.
mail·plane (māl′plān′), *n.* an airplane that transports mail: also **mail plane.**
maim (mām), *v.t.* [ME. *maime, maine;* OFr. *mahaigner, mayner*], to deprive of the use of some necessary part of the body; cripple; mutilate; disable. *n.* [ME. *maheym;* OFr. *mahaing, main*], [Obs.], an injury causing the loss or crippling of some necessary part of the body; mutilation; disablement: see **mayhem.**
SYN.—**maim** implies an injuring of a person's body so as to deprive him of some member or its use (*maimed* in an auto accident); to **cripple** is to cause to be legless, armless, or lame in any member (*crippled* by rheumatism); to **mutilate** is to remove or severely damage a part of a person or thing essential to his or its completeness (a speech *mutilated* by censors); **mangle** implies mutilation or disfigurement by or as by repeated tearing, hacking, or crushing (his arm was *mangled* in the press); to **disable** is to make incapable of normal physical activity, as by crippling (*disabled* war veterans).
Mai·mon·i·des (mī-mon′ə-dēz′), 1135–1204; Spanish rabbi, theologian, and philosopher: also called *Moses ben Maimon.*
Main (mīn; Eng. mān), *n.* a river in northern Bavaria, Germany, flowing westward into the Rhine: length, 305 mi.
main (mān), *n.* [ME. *mein, maine;* AS. *mægen;* akin to ON. *magn;* IE. base as in *may, might*], 1. physical strength; force; power: now only in *with might and main,* with all one's strength. 2. [< the *adj.*], the principal or most important part or point: usually in the phrase *in the main,* mostly, chiefly. 3. a principal pipe, conduit, or line in a distributing system for water, gas, electricity etc. 4. a railroad trunk line. 5. [Poetic], the high, or open, sea; ocean. 6. in *nautical usage, a*) mainmast. *b*) mainsail, 7. [Archaic], the mainland: see **Spanish main.** 8. [Obs.], any broad expanse. *adj.* [< AS. *mægen-* (in comp.) & ON. *meginn,* strong], 1. originally, strong; powerful. 2. chief in size, extent, importance, etc.; principal; leading. 3. designating a broad expanse of land, sea, or space. 4. of, near, or connected with the mainmast or mainsail. 5. [British Dial.], remarkable; considerable. 6. [Obs.], very essential, important, high in rank, etc. —*SYN.* see **chief.**
by main force (or **strength**), by sheer or utter force (or strength).
main (mān), *n.* [prob. < *main, adj.*, as in *main chance*], 1. in *dice playing, a*) a number called by a player before he throws. *b*) a throw or match. *c*) a stake played for. 2. in *cockfighting,* a match between two birds.
main clause, in a complex sentence, a clause that can function syntactically as a complete sentence by itself; independent clause: distinguished from *subordinate* (or *dependent*) clause. Example: *She will visit us* if she can.
main course, the mainsail of a square-rigged vessel.
main deck, the principal deck of a vessel; specifically, *a*) in a warship, the topmost deck, from stem to stern. *b*) in a merchantman, the part of the upper deck between the forecastle and the poop.
main drag, [Slang], the principal street of a city or town.
Maine (mān), *n.* 1. a New England State of the United States: area, 33,215 sq. mi.; pop., 969,000; capital, Augusta: abbreviated **Me.** 2. a United States battleship blown up in the harbor of Havana, Cuba, February 15, 1898.
Main·land (mān′lənd), *n.* 1. Pomona, the largest of the Orkney Islands. 2. the largest of the Shetland Islands: pop., 15,000.
main·land (mān′land′, mān′lənd), *n.* the principal land or largest part of a continent, as distinguished from a relatively small island or peninsula.
main·ly (mān′li), *adv.* 1. chiefly; principally; in the main. 2. [Archaic], *a*) strongly. *b*) very much.
main·mast (mān′məst, mān′mast′, mān′mäst′), *n.* the principal mast of a vessel: in a schooner, brig, bark, etc., the mast second from the bow; in a ketch or yawl, the mast nearer the bow.

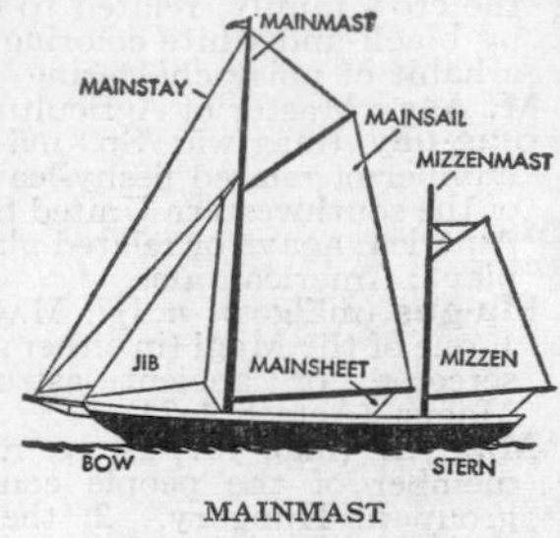

MAINMAST

main·sail (mān′s'l, mān′sāl′), *n.* 1. in a square-rigged vessel, the sail set from the main yard: also called *main course.* 2. in a fore-and-aft-rigged vessel, the large sail set from the mainmast.
main·sheet (mān′shēt′), *n.* the sheet of a mainsail; line controlling the angle at which a mainsail is set: see **mainmast,** illus.
main·spring (mān′spriŋ′), *n.* 1. the principal spring in a clock, watch, or other mechanism; driving spring, by the steady uncoiling of which the mechanism is kept going; hence, 2. the chief motive, incentive, or impelling cause: as, profit is the *mainspring* of business.
main·stay (mān′stā′), *n.* 1. the stay of the mainmast; line extending forward from the mainmast, supporting it and holding it in position: see **mainmast,** illus.; hence, 2. a chief support: as, her son is her *mainstay.*
main stem, [Slang], the principal street of a city or town.
Main Street, 1. the principal street of any small town. 2. the typical inhabitants of a small town or rural community.
main·tain (mān-tān′), *v.t.* [ME. *mainteinen;* OFr. *maintenir* < L. *manu tenere,* to hold in the hand; *manu,* abl. of *manus,* hand + *tenere,* to hold], 1. to keep or keep up; continue in or with; carry on. 2. *a*) to keep in existence or continuance: as, food *maintains* life. *b*) to keep in a certain condition or position, especially of efficiency, good repair, etc.; preserve: as, the state *maintains* the roads. 3. to keep or hold (a place, position, etc.) against attack; defend. 4. to uphold or defend, as by argument; declare to be true; affirm: as, he *maintains* his contentions. 5. to support by aid, influence, protection, etc. 6. to support by providing means of existence; bear the expenses of: as, he can't *maintain* his family. —*SYN.* see **support.**
main·te·nance (mān′tə-nəns), *n.* [ME. *maintenaunce;* OFr.], 1. a maintaining or being maintained; upkeep, support, defense, etc. 2. means of support or sustenance; livelihood: as, her job provided a mere *maintenance.* 3. in *common law,* support or assistance that a person is legally bound to give to another or others. 4. in *criminal law,* the act of interfering unlawfully in a suit between others by helping either party, as by giving money, etc., to carry it on.
maintenance of membership, in some union contracts, a provision by which all employees who are already members of the union, and all who join during the time covered by the contract, must remain members and pay dues or be discharged by the employer.
Main·te·non, Marquise **de** (də mant′nōn′), (*Françoise d'Aubigné*), 1635–1719; second wife of Louis XIV.
main·top (mān′top′), *n.* a platform at the head of the lower section of the mainmast.
main·top·gal·lant (mān′tə-gal′'nt, mān′top′gal′'nt), *n.* the mast, sail, or yard above a ship's maintopmast.
main·top·mast (mān′top′məst), *n.* the section of the mainmast above the maintop.
main·top·sail (mān′top′s'l, mān′top′sāl), *n.* the sail above the mainsail on the mainmast.
main-trav·eled, main-trav·elled (mān′trav′'ld), *adj.* much traveled on: said of roads, etc.
main yard, the lower yard on the mainmast; yard from which the mainsail is set.
Mainz (mīnts), *n.* a city in western Germany, on the Rhine: pop., 127,000: French name, *Mayence.*
mair (mâr), *adj.* [Scot.], more.
‡**mai·son de san·té** (mā′zōn′ də sän′tā′), [Fr., lit., house of health], a hospital or sanitarium.
maist (māst), *adj.* [Scot.], most.
Mait·land, Frederic William (māt′lənd), 1850–1906; English historian and jurist.
‡**maî·tre d'hô·tel** (me′tr′ dō′tel′), [Fr., lit., master of the house], 1. a butler or steward; major-domo. 2. a hotel manager. 3. a headwaiter. 4. (with) a sauce of melted butter, parsley, and lemon juice or vinegar.
maize (māz), *n.* [Sp. *maíz;* W. Ind. (Taino) *mahiz*], 1. *a*) a kind of grain that grows in kernels on large ears. *b*) its ears. *c*) its seeds or kernels. Also called *Indian corn* or, in the United States, Canada, and Australia, *corn.* 2. its color (when ripe); yellow. *adj.* yellow.
Maj., Major.

ma·jes·tic (mə-jes′tik), ***adj.*** having or characterized by majesty; stately; noble; august. —***SYN.*** see **grand.**
ma·jes·ti·cal (mə-jes′ti-k'l), ***adj.*** majestic.
maj·es·ty (maj′is-ti), ***n.*** [*pl.* MAJESTIES (-tiz)], [ME. *majeste;* OFr. *majesté;* L. *majestas* < *majus*, old compar. < base of *magnus*, great], 1. *a)* the dignity or power of a sovereign. *b)* sovereign power: as, the *majesty* of the law. *c)* a sovereign; hence, 2. [M-], a title used in speaking to or of a sovereign, preceded by *His, Her,* or *Your.* 3. grandeur; dignity; stateliness; nobility. Abbreviated **M., m.**
Maj. Gen., Major General.
ma·jol·i·ca (mə-jol′i-kə, mə-yol′i-kə), ***n.*** [It. *maiolica;* prob. < the earlier name of *Majorca*, whence the first specimens came], 1. a kind of Italian pottery, enameled, glazed, and richly colored and decorated. 2. pottery made in imitation of this.
ma·jor (mā′jẽr), ***adj.*** [L., compar. of *magnus*, great], 1. *a)* greater in size, amount, number, or extent. *b)* greater in importance or rank. Opposed to *minor.* 2. of full legal age. 3. constituting the majority: said of a part, etc. 4. in *education*, designating a field of study in which a student specializes and receives his degree. 5. in *logic*, broader; more inclusive: see **major premise, major term.** 6. in *music*, *a)* designating an interval higher than the minor by a half tone. *b)* designating a tone distant by a major interval from another tone. *c)* characterized by major intervals, scales, or tones: as, the *major* mode or key. *d)* based on the scale pattern of the major mode: see **major scale.** ***v.i.*** in *education*, to pursue a principal subject or field of study; specialize (with *in*): as, he will *major* in physics. ***n.*** 1. [< the *adj.*], a superior in some class or group. 2. [Fr. < the L. *adj.*], a military officer ranking above a captain and below a lieutenant colonel: abbreviated **Maj.** (as a title). 3. in *education*, *a)* a major subject or field of study. *b)* a person specializing in a (specified) subject: as, he's a history *major.* 4. in *law*, a person who has reached his majority (full legal age). 5. in *logic*, a major term or premise. 6. in *music*, a major interval, key, mode, etc.
Ma·jor·ca (mə-jôr′kə), ***n.*** the largest of the Balearic Islands; area, 1,352 sq. mi.; pop., 290,000; Spanish name, *Mallorca.*
ma·jor-do·mo (mā′jẽr-dō′mō), ***n.*** [*pl.* MAJOR-DOMOS (-mōz)], [Sp. *mayordomo* or It. *maggiordomo;* ML. *major domus;* L. *major*, greater, an elder + genit. of *domus*, house], 1. a man in charge of a great, royal, or noble household; chief steward; hence, 2. a steward or butler: humorous usage.
major general, [*pl.* MAJOR GENERALS], a military officer normally commanding a division, and ranking above a brigadier general and below a lieutenant general: abbreviated **Maj. Gen., M.G.** (as a title).
ma·jor·i·ty (mə-jôr′ə-ti, mə-jor′ə-ti), ***n.*** [*pl.* MAJORITIES (-tiz)], [Fr. *majorité;* ML. *majoritas* < L. *major;* see MAJOR], 1. the greater part or larger number; more than half of a total: opposed to *minority.* 2. the excess of the larger number of votes cast for one candidate, bill, etc. over all the rest of the votes: if candidate A gets 100 votes, candidate B, 200, and candidate C, 350, C has a majority of 50: cf. **plurality.** 3. the group, party, or faction with the larger number of votes. 4. the full legal age, at which one is legally no longer a minor: as, he reached his *majority* at the age of 21. 5. the military rank or position of a major. 6. [Obs.], the state, quality, or fact of being greater; superiority.
 join the (great) majority, to die.
ma·jor-league (māj′ẽr-lēg′), ***adj.*** of, in, or suitable to a major league or leagues.
major leagues, the two main leagues of professional baseball clubs in the United States, the National League and the American League.
major premise, the premise (in a syllogism) that contains the major term.
major scale, one of the two standard diatonic musical scales, consisting of eight tones with half steps instead of whole steps after the third and seventh tones: distinguished from *minor scale.*
major suit, in *bridge*, spades or hearts: so called from their higher value in scoring.
major term, the predicate of the conclusion of a syllogism.
ma·jus·cu·lar (mə-jus′kyoo-lẽr), ***adj.*** 1. of, or having the nature of, a majuscule. 2. written in majuscules.
ma·jus·cule (mə-jus′kūl), ***n.*** [Fr.; L. *majuscula*, fem. of *majusculus*, somewhat larger, dim. < *major;* see MAJOR], 1. a large letter, capital or uncial, as in medieval manuscripts. 2. writing in which such letters are used. ***adj.*** majuscular. Cf. *minuscule.*
Ma·kas·sar (mə-kas′ẽr), ***n.*** Macassar.
make (māk), ***v.t.*** [MADE (mād), MAKING], [ME. *maken;* AS. *macian;* akin to G. *machen;* IE. base **mag̑-*, to knead, press, stretch, etc., seen also in Gr. *magis*, kneaded mass, paste, dough, *mageus*, kneader, etc.; Gmc. senses with orig. reference to mud-wall constructions], 1. to bring into being; specifically, *a)* to form by shaping or putting parts or ingredients together, physically or mentally; build, construct, fabricate, fashion, create, compose, devise, formulate, etc. *b)* to cause; bring about; produce: as, what *made* this sudden change? 2. to bring into a specified condition; specifically, *a)* to cause to be or become: as, they *made* him president. *b)* to cause to seem: as, this portrait *makes* her an old woman. Sometimes used reflexively, as, *make* yourself comfortable. 3. to prepare for use; arrange: as, *make* the beds. 4. *a)* to amount to; add up to; form as a total: as, four quarts *make* a gallon. *b)* to count as; constitute: as, this *made* the tenth and last of his novels. 5. to turn out to be; have, or prove to have, the essential qualities of: as, he will *make* a good doctor. 6. to set up; establish: as, we *made* a rule that only members might attend. 7. *a)* to get or acquire, as by one's behavior: as, he *made* many friends. *b)* to get by earning, etc.: as, we all want to *make* money. 8. to cause the success of: as, this lucky venture *made* him. 9. to understand or regard as the meaning (*of*): as, what do you *make* of his queer actions? 10. to estimate to be; regard as: as, I *make* the distance about 500 miles. 11. *a)* to do or perform (the action indicated by the object); execute; accomplish: as, she *made* a quick movement. *b)* to engage in; carry on: as, *make* war. 12. to deliver (a speech) or utter (remarks, etc.). 13. to cause or force to: followed by an infinitive without *to*, as, *make* the machine work, *make* him behave. 14. *a)* to arrive at; reach: as, the ship *made* port. *b)* to arrive at in time: as, he *made* the train. *c)* to arrive at and do business in: as, the salesman *made* six towns on this trip. 15. *a)* to go; travel; traverse: as, they *made* the distance in five hours. *b)* to go or travel at (a specified speed): as, my car can *make* 90 miles an hour. 16. [Colloq.], to succeed in getting membership in, a position on, the status of, recognition in, etc.: as, he *made* the team, she *made* the headlines. 17. [Slang], to succeed in becoming the lover of. 18. in *card playing*, *a)* to win (tricks). *b)* to take a trick with (a card). *c)* to name (the trump or a bid). *d)* to shuffle (the cards). 19. in *electricity*, to close (a circuit); effect (a contact). 20. in *games*, to score; get as a score. 21. in *law*, *a)* to perform, execute, or sign (a will or other legal instrument). *b)* to do (what one has bound himself to do). To *make oath* is to swear in the legally prescribed form; to *make default* is to fail in a prescribed or accepted duty. ***v.i.*** 1. to start (to do something): as, she *made* to go. 2. *a)* to go; proceed: as, he *made* for the door. *b)* to tend, extend, or point (*to, toward*, etc.). 3. to behave in a specified manner: with a following adjective, as, *make* bold, *make* merry, etc. 4. to cause something to be in a specified condition: as, *make* ready, *make* fast, etc. 5. to increase in depth or volume; rise or accumulate, as tide, snow, water in a ship, etc. 6. to mature: said of hay, etc. *Make* is widely and variously used in idiomatic phrases, many of which are entered in this dictionary under the key word, as *make fun of, make faces, make good*, etc. ***n.*** 1. the act or process of making; especially, manufacture. 2. the amount made; output, especially of manufacture. 3. the way in which something is made; style; build. 4. type, sort, or brand: with reference to the maker or the place, time, etc. of making, as, an automobile of English *make.* 5. disposition; character; nature: as, a man of this *make.* 6. in *bridge*, the declaration. 7. in *electricity*, the closing of a circuit by making contact.
 make a fool (or **ass,** etc.) **of,** to cause to seem a fool (or ass, etc.).
 make after, to chase or follow.
 make a meal on (or **of**), to eat as a meal.
 make as if (or **as though**), to behave as if.
 make away with, 1. to steal. 2. to get rid of. 3. to eat all of. 4. to kill.
 make believe, to pretend; act a part.
 make for, 1. to head for; go toward. 2. to charge at; attack. 3. to tend toward; help effect.
 make heavy weather, in *nautical usage*, to pitch and roll, as in rough water.
 make it, [Colloq.], to do or achieve a certain thing.
 make like, [Slang], to imitate; impersonate.
 make off, to go away; run away.
 make off with, to steal.
 make or break, to cause the success or failure of.
 make out, 1. to see with some difficulty; descry. 2. to understand. 3. to write out. 4. to fill out (a blank form, etc.). 5. to show or prove to be. 6. to try to show, affirm, or imply to be. 7. to succeed; get along.
 make over, 1. to change; renovate. 2. to transfer the ownership of by or as by signing a legal document. 3. [Colloq.], to be demonstrative toward or about.
 make up, 1. to put together; compose; compound. 2. to form; constitute. 3. to invent; create. 4. to complete by providing what is lacking. 5. to compensate (*for*). 6. to arrange. 7. *a)* to become friendly

again after a disagreement or quarrel. *b*) to settle (an argument or differences) in a friendly manner. 8. *a*) to put on the required costume, cosmetics, etc. for a role in a play. *b*) to put cosmetics on. 9. to resolve or decide (one's mind). 10. to select and arrange type, illustrations, etc. for (a book, magazine, page, etc.). 11. in *education*, to take again (an examination or course that one has failed) or to take (an examination that one has missed).

make up to, to flatter, or try to be agreeable to, in order to become friendly or intimate with.

make with, [Slang], to use, or do something with, in the way indicated or implied.

on the make, 1. [Colloq.], trying to succeed financially, socially, etc.: usually derogatory, implying pushing behavior and neglect of other values. 2. [Slang], trying to get a lover.

SYN.—**make** is the general term meaning to bring into being and may imply a producing of something physically or mentally; **form** suggests a definite contour, structure, design, etc. in the thing made; **shape** suggests the imparting of a specific form as by molding, cutting, hammering, etc.; **fashion** implies inventiveness, cleverness of design, the use of skill, etc.; **construct** implies a putting of parts together systematically according to some design; **manufacture** implies a producing from raw materials, now especially by machinery and on a large scale; **fabricate** implies a building or manufacturing, often by assembling standardized parts, and, in extended use, connotes fictitious invention.

make (māk), *n.* [ME.; AS. *gemaca* (akin to G. *gemach*, fitting, suitable) + cognate ON. *maki;* base as in prec. *make*], [Obs. or British Dial.], 1. an equal; peer. 2. a mate, companion, consort, or spouse.

make and break, a device for alternately making, or closing, and breaking, or opening, an electric circuit.

make-be·lieve (māk′bə-lēv′), *n.* 1. pretense; feigning. 2. a pretender. *adj.* pretended; feigned; sham.

make·fast (māk′fast′, māk′fäst′), *n.* a buoy, post, pile, etc. to which a boat is fastened.

make-peace (māk′pēs′), *n.* a peacemaker.

mak·er (māk′ẽr), *n.* 1. a person or thing that makes (in various senses). 2. [M-], God. 3. [Archaic], a poet. 4. in *law*, the signer of a promissory note.

make-read·y (māk′red′i), *n.* in *printing*, the operation of leveling a type form by the use of overlays and underlays to obtain a clean impression.

make·shift (māk′shift′), *n.* a thing that will do for a while as a substitute; temporary expedient. *adj.* that will do for a while as a substitute. —*SYN.* see **resource.**

make-up (māk′up′), *n.* 1. the way in which something is put together; composition; construction. 2. nature; disposition; constitution: as, he has a stolid *make-up*. 3. *a*) the way in which an actor is costumed, painted, etc. for a role. *b*) the costumes, cosmetics, etc. used. 4. *a*) cosmetics generally; rouge, lipstick, mascara, etc. *b*) the way in which these are applied or worn. 5. the arrangement of type, illustrations, etc. in a book, newspaper, page, etc. 6. [Colloq.], a special test taken by a student to make up for a test that he has missed or failed to pass. *adj.* of or for making up.

make·weight (māk′wāt′), *n.* 1. anything added to a scale to complete the required weight. 2. an unimportant person or thing added to make up some lack.

mak·ing (māk′iŋ), *n.* 1. the act of one that makes or the process of being made; formation, construction, creation, production, composition, manufacture, development, performance, etc. 2. the cause or means of success or advancement: as, this experience will be the *making* of him. 3. *a*) something made. *b*) the quantity made at one time. *c*) *pl.* earnings; profits. 4. *a*) *often pl.* the material or qualities needed for the making or development of something: as, he has the *making(s)* of a good doctor. *b*) *pl.* [Colloq.], tobacco and paper for making cigarettes.

mal- (mal), [Fr.; L. *male-* < *male*, badly < *malus*, bad, evil], a prefix meaning *bad* or *badly, wrong, ill*, as in *malfeasance, maladjustment:* also **male-.**

Mal., 1. Malachi. 2. Malay. 3. Malayan.

Mal·a·bar (mal′ə-bär′), *n.* a coastal region in southwestern India, extending inland to the Western Ghats: also **Malabar Coast.**

Ma·lac·ca (mə-lak′ə), *n.* 1. a state in the Federation of Malaya, on the west coast of the Malay Peninsula: area, 640 sq. mi.; pop., 291,000. 2. its chief city: pop., 55,000.

Malacca, Strait of, the strait between the Malay Peninsula and Sumatra: width, 35–185 mi.

Malacca cane, [< *Malacca* (the city)], a lightweight walking stick of rattan, often mottled brown.

ma·la·ceous (mə-lā′shəs), *adj.* [< L. *malum*, an apple; + *-aceous*], of the apple family of plants and trees.

Mal·a·chi (mal′ə-kī′), *n.* [Heb. *malākhī*, lit., my messenger], 1. a Hebrew prophet of the 5th century B.C.: the last of the minor prophets. 2. a book of the Old Testament attributed to him: abbreviated **Mal.**

mal·a·chite (mal′ə-kīt′), *n.* [Fr.; OFr. *melochite* < L. *malache*, mallow; Gr. *malachē, molochē*, mallow: so called because its color is like that of mallow leaves], native basic copper carbonate, $CuCO_3 \cdot Cu(OH)_2$, a green mineral used as an ore of copper or for ornamental objects: it takes a high polish.

mal·a·co- (mal′ə-kə), [< Gr. *malakos*, soft], a combining form meaning: 1. *soft*, as in *malacopterygian*. 2. *mollusks*, as in *malacology*.

mal·a·col·o·gy (mal′ə-kol′ə-ji), *n.* [*malaco-* + *-logy*], the branch of zoology dealing with mollusks.

mal·a·cop·ter·yg·i·an (mal′ə-kop′tə-rij′i-ən), *adj.* [< *malaco-* + Gr. *pteryx, pterygos*, a wing, fin], designating or of a group of bony fishes with soft fin rays.

mal·a·cos·tra·can (mal′ə-kos′trə-kən), *adj.* [< Mod. L. *Malacostraca*, name of the subclass (< Gr. *malakostrakos*, soft-shelled < *malakos*, soft + *ostrakon*, shell); + *-an*], of a group of crustaceans comprising the lobsters, shrimps, crabs, etc. *n.* such a crustacean.

mal·a·cos·tra·cous (mal′ə-kos′trə-kəs), *adj.* of or characteristic of the malacostracans.

mal·ad·just·ed (mal′ə-jus′tid), *adj.* poorly adjusted.

mal·ad·just·ment (mal′ə-just′mənt), *n.* poor adjustment, especially to the environment.

mal·ad·min·is·ter (mal′əd-min′ə-stẽr), *v.t.* to administer badly; conduct without efficiency or honesty.

mal·ad·min·is·tra·tion (mal′əd-min′ə-strā′shən), *n.* bad administration; inefficient or corrupt conduct of affairs, especially public affairs.

mal·a·droit (mal′ə-droit′), *adj.* [Fr.; see MAL- & ADROIT], awkward; clumsy; bungling. —*SYN.* see **awkward.**

mal·a·dy (mal′ə-di), *n.* [*pl.* MALADIES (-diz)], [ME. & OFr. *maladie* < OFr. *malade*, sick < L. *male habitus*, badly kept, out of condition; *male*, badly + *habitus*, held, pp. of *habere*, to hold], an ailment; disease; illness; sickness: often used figuratively. —*SYN.* see **disease.**

‡**ma·la fi·de** (mā′lə fī′di), [L.], in bad faith; with intent to deceive: opposed to *bona fide*.

Má·la·ga (mä′lä-gä′; Eng. mal′ə-gə), *n.* 1. a seaport in southern Spain: pop., 283,000. 2. a province of southern Spain.

Mal·a·ga (mal′ə-gə), *n.* [after *Málaga*, Spain], 1. a large, white, oval, firm-fleshed grape. 2. a white wine, originally from Málaga.

Mal·a·gas·y (mal′ə-gas′i), *n.* [*pl.* MALAGASY, MALAGASIES (-iz)], [< native name; var. of the base *Madagas-* in *Madagascar*], 1. a native of Madagascar. 2. the Indonesian language of the Malagasy. 3. a country coextensive with the island of Madagascar: formerly a French colony, it is now a member of the French Community: area, 230,000 sq. mi.; pop., 5,071,000; capital, Tananarive: French name, *Malgache*. *adj.* of the Malagasy or their language.

ma·laise (ma-lāz′; Fr. mȧ′lez′), *n.* [Fr.; *mal*, bad + *aise*, ease], a vague feeling of physical discomfort or uneasiness, as before an illness.

ma·la·mute (mä′lə-mūt′), *n.* [< native name], a large, strong Alaskan dog with a thick coat of gray or black-and-white fur: also spelled **malemute, malemiut.**

mal·an·ders (mal′ən-dẽrz), *n.pl.* [Late ME.; Fr. *malandres;* L. *malandria*, blisters or pustules on the neck, esp. of horses], a variety of eczema about the knee of a horse's foreleg: also spelled **mallanders.**

mal·a·pert (mal′ə-pũrt′), *adj.* [ME.; OFr. < *mal*, badly (< L. *malus*, bad) + *appert*, var. of *espert*, experienced, deft (see EXPERT); influenced by *apert*, open, bold (< L. *apertus;* see APERTURE)], [Archaic], saucy; impudent; pert. *n.* [Archaic], a saucy, impudent person.

Mal·a·prop, Mrs. (mal′ə-prop′), [< *malapropos*], a character in Sheridan's play *The Rivals*, who makes ridiculous blunders in her use of words.

mal·a·prop·ism (mal′ə-prop-iz′m), *n.* [< Mrs. *Malaprop*], 1. ridiculous misuse of words, especially through confusion caused by resemblance in sound. 2. an instance of this (e.g., *progeny* for *prodigy*).

mal·ap·ro·pos (mal′ap-rə-pō′), *adj.* [Fr. *mal à propos;* see MAL- & APROPOS], at an awkward or improper time or place; inopportune; inappropriate. *adv.* in an inopportune or inappropriate manner.

ma·lar (mā′lẽr), *adj.* [< L. *mala*, the cheek; + *-ar*], of the cheek, cheekbone, or side of the head. *n.* the cheekbone: see **skull**, illus.

Mäl·ar, Lake (mel′är), *n.* a lake in eastern Sweden: area, 449 sq. mi.

ma·lar·i·a (mə-lâr′i-ə), *n.* [It., contr. of *mala aria*, bad air; see MAL- & ARIA], 1. unwholesome or poisonous air, as from marshy ground; miasma. 2. [from the former notion that it was caused by the bad air of swamps], an infectious disease, generally intermittent and recurrent, caused by any of various protozoa that are parasitic in the red blood corpuscles and are transmitted to man by the bite of an infected anopheles mosquito: it is characterized by severe chills and fever.

ma·lar·i·al (mə-lâr′i-əl), *adj.* 1. of, having the nature of, or caused by malaria. 2. having malaria.

ma·lar·i·an (mə-lâr′i-ən), *adj.* malarial.

ma·lar·i·ous (mə-lâr′i-əs), *adj.* malarial.

ma·lar·key, ma·lar·ky (mə-lär′ki), *n.* [? < Irish pers. name], [Slang], insincere or meaningless talk; nonsense; buncombe.

mal·as·sim·i·la·tion (mal′ə-sim′ə-lā′shən), *n.* incomplete assimilation of food materials.

mal·ate (mal′āt, mā′lāt), *n.* a salt or ester of malic acid.

mal·a·thi·on (mal'ə-thī'ən), *n.* an organic phosphate, $C_{10}H_{19}O_6PS_2$, of relatively low toxicity for mammals, used as an insecticide.

Ma·lay (mā'lā, mə-lā'), *n.* [Malay *malāyu*], 1. a member of a large group of brown-skinned, short, black-haired peoples living in the Malay Peninsula, the Malay Archipelago, and near-by islands. 2. their Indonesian language, widely used in the Far East as a trade language. 3. one of an oriental breed of game fowls. *adj.* of the Malays, their country, language, culture, etc. Abbreviated **Mal.**

Ma·lay·a (mə-lā'ə), *n.* the Malay Peninsula.

Malaya, Federation of, a former country in the lower Malay Peninsula: see **Malaysia, Federation of.**

Mal·a·ya·lam (mal'ə-yä'ləm), *n.* [Malayalam *malayālam*], a Dravidian language spoken on the Malabar Coast, southeastern India, dialectally related to Tamil.

Ma·lay·an (mə-lā'ən), *adj.* & *n.* Malay.

Malay Archipelago, a chain of islands extending from the Malay Peninsula to a point north of eastern Australia.

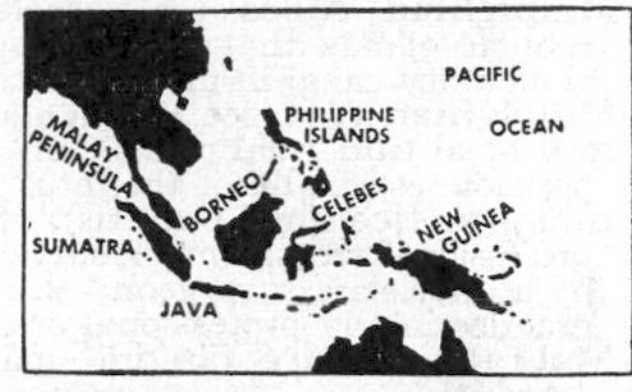

MALAY ARCHIPELAGO

Ma·lay·o- (mə-lā'ō), a combining form meaning *Malay, Malay and.*

Ma·lay·o-Pol·y·ne·sian (mə-lā'ō-pol'ə-nē'zhən, mə-lā'ō-pol'ə-nē'shən), *adj.* Austronesian.

Malay Peninsula, a peninsula in southeastern Asia, including Federation of Malaya and part of Thailand.

Ma·lay·sia (mə-lā'zhə, mə-lā'shə), *n.* 1. the Malay Archipelago. 2. Federation of Malaysia.

Malaysia, Federation of, a federation in southeast Asia, in the British Commonwealth of Nations: it comprises the former country of Malaya and the former British territories of North Borneo, Sarawak, and Singapore: area, 128,562 sq. mi.; pop., 10,074,000; capital, Kuala Lumpur.

Ma·lay·sian (mə-lā'zhən, mə-lā'shən), *adj.* of Malaysia, its peoples, or their culture. *n.* a native of Malaysia.

Mal·colm (mal'kəm), [Celt. *Maolcolm*, lit., servant of (St.) Columba], a masculine name.

mal·con·tent (mal'kən-tent'), *adj.* [Fr.; see MAL- & CONTENT], discontented; dissatisfied; rebellious. *n.* a discontented, dissatisfied, or rebellious person: applied especially to critics of the government.

‡**mal de mer** (mål' də mâr'), [Fr.], seasickness.

Mal·den (môl'dən), *n.* a city in Massachusetts, near Boston: pop., 58,000.

Mal·dive Islands (mal'dīv), a group of islands, southwest of India: sultanate under British protection: area, 115 sq. mi.; pop., 90,950.

male (māl), *adj.* [ME.; OFr. *male, masle* < L. *masculus*, dim. of *mas, maris*, a male, man; ? akin to Sans. *marya*, youth, Gr. *meirax*, boy], 1. designating or of the sex that fertilizes the ovum and begets offspring: opposed to *female*: biological symbol, ♂. 2. of, characteristic of, or suitable for members of this sex; masculine; virile; hence, 3. strong; vigorous. 4. consisting of men or boys. 5. in *botany*, *a)* designating or of fertilizing bodies, organs, or parts: as, *male* gametes. *b)* designating plants with such organs; having stamens but no pistil. 6. in *mechanics*, designating or having a part shaped to fit into a corresponding hollow part (called *female*): said of a gauge, etc. *n.* a male person, animal, or plant. Abbreviated **M., m.**
SYN.—**male** is the basic term applied to members of the sex that is biologically distinguished from the female sex and is used of animals and plants as well as of human beings; **masculine** is applied to qualities, such as strength, vigor, etc., characteristic of men, or to things appropriate to men; **manly** suggests the noble qualities, such as courage, independence, etc., that one associates with a man who has maturity of character; **mannish**, used chiefly of women, implies imitation of the traits, dress, etc. of a man; **virile** stresses qualities such as robustness, vigor, and, specifically, sexual potency, that belong to a physically mature man.

Male·branche, Nich·o·las de (nē'kô'lä' də mål'bränsh'), 1638–1715; French metaphysical philosopher.

mal·e·dict (mal'ə-dikt'), *adj.* [L. *maledictus*, pp. of *maledicere*; see MALEDICTION], [Archaic], accursed.

mal·e·dic·tion (mal'ə-dik'shən), *n.* [OFr.; L. *maledictio* < pp. of *maledicere; male*, evil + *dicere*, to speak], 1. a calling down of evil on someone; curse: opposed to *benediction*. 2. evil talk about someone; slander.

mal·e·dic·to·ry (mal'ə-dik'tēr-i), *adj.* of, having the nature of, or expressing a malediction.

mal·e·fac·tion (mal'ə-fak'shən), *n.* [L. *malefactio* < pp. of *malefacere;* see MALEFACTOR], wrongdoing; crime.

mal·e·fac·tor (mal'ə-fak'tēr), *n.* [L. < pp. of *malefacere; male*, evil + *facere*, to do], an evildoer; criminal.

mal·e·fac·tress (mal'ə-fak'tris), *n.* a woman malefactor.

ma·lef·ic (mə-lef'ik), *adj.* [L. *maleficus* < *malefacere;* see MALEFACTOR], causing disaster; harmful; evil.

ma·lef·i·cence (mə-lef'ə-s'ns), *n.* maleficent quality or action; evil; mischief; harm.

ma·lef·i·cent (mə-lef'ə-s'nt), *adj.* [see MALEFIC], harmful; hurtful; evil.

ma·le·ic (mə-lē'ik), *adj.* [< Fr. *maléique* < L. *malum*, apple], designating or of a white, crystalline acid, $C_4H_4O_4$, an isomer of fumaric acid, used as a dye, etc.

ma·le·mute, ma·le·miut (mä'lə-mūt'), *n.* a malamute.

‡**mal·en·ten·du** (mål'än'tän'dü'), *adj.* [Fr.], misunderstood; poorly conceived. *n.* a misunderstanding.

ma·lev·o·lence (mə-lev'ə-ləns), *n.* [L. *malevolentia*], the quality or state of being malevolent; malice; spitefulness; ill will: opposed to *benevolence.* —***SYN.*** see **malice.**

ma·lev·o·lent (mə-lev'ə-lənt), *adj.* [OFr. *malivolent;* L. *malevolens, malevolentis; male*, evil + *volens*, ppr. of *velle*, to wish], wishing evil or harm to others; having or showing ill will; malicious: opposed to *benevolent.*

mal·fea·sance (mal-fē'z'ns), *n.* [obs. Fr. *malfaisance* < *malfaisant; mal*, evil + *faisant*, ppr. of *faire* (L. *facere*), to do], wrongdoing or misconduct, especially in handling public affairs: as, an official who takes graft is guilty of *malfeasance*: cf. **misfeasance, nonfeasance.**

mal·fea·sant (mal-fē'z'nt), *adj.* & *n.* [Fr. *malfaisant;* see MALFEASANCE], criminal.

mal·for·ma·tion (mal'fôr-mā'shən), *n.* faulty, irregular, or abnormal formation or structure of a body or part.

mal·formed (mal-fôrmd'), *adj.* faultily or abnormally formed; misshapen.

mal·func·tion (mal-fuŋk'shən), *v.i.* [*mal-* + *function*], to fail to function as it should. *n.* the act or an instance of malfunctioning.

Mal·gache (mål'gåsh'), *n.* Malagasy: the French name.

‡**mal·gré lui** (mål'grā'lwē'), [Fr.], in spite of oneself.

Ma·li (mä'li), *n.* a country in western Africa, south and east of Mauritania: area, 464,873 sq. mi.; pop., 4,300,000; capital, Bamako: formerly, *French Sudan.*

mal·ic acid (mal'ik, mā'lik), [Fr. *malique* < L. *malum* < Gr. *mēlon*, apple], a colorless, crystallizable acid, $C_4H_6O_5$, occurring in apples and some other fruits.

mal·ice (mal'is), *n.* [ME.; OFr. < L. *malitia* < *malus*, bad], 1. active ill will; desire to harm others or do mischief; spite. 2. in *law*, evil intent; state of mind shown by intention to do, or intentional doing of, something unlawful.

malice aforethought (or **prepense**), a deliberate intention and plan to do something unlawful, as murder.
SYN.—**malice** implies a deep-seated animosity that delights in causing others to suffer or in seeing them suffer; **ill will** and the more formal **malevolence** imply hostile or unfriendly feelings such as dispose one to wish evil to others; **spite** suggests a mean desire to hurt, annoy, or frustrate others, usually as displayed in petty, vindictive acts; **rancor** implies an intensely bitter ill will that rankles; **malignity** suggests extreme and virulent malevolence that is relentless in expressing itself; **grudge** implies ill will inspired by resentment over a grievance.

ma·li·cious (mə-lish'əs), *adj.* [ME.; OFr. *malicios, malicius* (Fr. *malicieux*) < L. *malitiosus* < *malitia*], having, showing, or caused by malice; spiteful; intentionally mischievous or harmful.

ma·lign (mə-līn'), *v.t.* [ME. *malignen;* OFr. *malignier, maliner*, to plot, deceive; LL. *malignare* < L. *malignus*, wicked, malicious < *male*, ill + base of *genus*, born], to speak evil of; defame; slander; traduce. *adj.* 1. malevolent; malicious. 2. evil; baleful: as, a *malign* influence. 3. very harmful; malignant. —***SYN.*** see **sinister.**

ma·lig·nance (mə-lig'nəns), *n.* malignancy.

ma·lig·nan·cy (mə-lig'nən-si), *n.* the quality or condition of being malignant.

ma·lig·nant (mə-lig'nənt), *adj.* [LL. *malignans, malignantis*, ppr. of *malignare;* see MALIGN], 1. having an evil influence; malign. 2. wishing evil; very malevolent or malicious. 3. very harmful. 4. very dangerous or virulent; causing or likely to cause death; not benign: as, a cancer is a *malignant* tumor. 5. [Obs.], malcontent; rebellious; disaffected. *n.* [Obs.], a malcontent.

ma·lig·ni·ty (mə-lig'nə-ti), *n.* [ME. *malignitee;* OFr. *malignité;* L. *malignitas;* see MALIGN], 1. persistent, intense ill will or desire to harm others; great malice. 2. the quality of being very harmful or dangerous; malignancy. 3. [*pl.* MALIGNITIES (-tiz)], a malignant act, event, or feeling. —***SYN.*** see **malice.**

Ma·lines (må'lēn'), *n.* a city in north central Belgium: pop., 64,000: English name, *Mechlin.*

ma·lines (mə-lēn'; Fr. må'lēn'), *n.* [Fr. < *Malines*, Mechlin], 1. Mechlin (lace). 2. a thin, somewhat stiff, silk net used in dressmaking, etc.: also spelled **maline.**

ma·lin·ger (mə-liŋ'gēr), *v.i.* [< Fr. *malingre*, sickly, infirm < *mal* (L. *malus*), bad + OFr. *heingre*, lean, haggard; prob. < Frank. form akin to ME. *hagger;* see HAGGARD], to pretend to be ill or otherwise incapac-

itated in order to escape duty or work; shirk.
Ma·li·now·ski, Bron·is·law Kas·per (brô-nē′släf käs′-per mä′li-nôf′ski), 1884–1942; Polish anthropologist in America.
mal·i·son (mal′ə-z'n, mal′ə-s'n), ***n.*** [ME. *malisun;* OFr. *maleison, maleiçon* < L. *maledictio*], [Archaic], a curse.
mal·kin (mô′kin; *occas.* môl′kin, mal′kin), ***n.*** [ME. *malkyn,* dim. of *Malde,* Maud, itself dim. of *Matilda;* cf. MAUD], [Obs. or British Dial.], 1. a slovenly or lewd woman. 2. a mop. 3. a scarecrow. 4. [Chiefly Scot.], a hare. 5. a cat. Also **maukin, mawkin.**
mall (môl; *occas.* mal; *cf.* PALL MALL), ***n.*** [var. of *maul,* mallet; esp. associated in 17th c. with senses < cognate Fr. *mail*], 1. originally, *a)* a large, heavy mallet, used in the game of pall-mall; hence, *b)* the game itself. *c)* a lane or alley where the game was played; hence, 2. a shaded walk or public promenade.
mall (môl), ***n. & v.t.*** maul.
mal·lan·ders (mal′ən-dẽrz), ***n.pl.*** malanders.
mal·lard (mal′ẽrd), ***n.*** [*pl.* MALLARDS (-ẽrdz), MALLARD; see PLURAL, II, D, 1], [ME.; OFr. *malart, mallart* < **maslart* < *masle;* see MALE], 1. *a)* the male, or drake, of the common wild duck. *b)* [Obs.], any drake. 2. the common wild duck (male or female), from which the domestic duck is descended: the male has a green or bluish-black head and a band of white around the neck.
Mal·lar·mé, Sté·phane (stā′fán′ má′lár′mā′), 1842–1898; French symbolist poet.
mal·le·a·bil·i·ty (mal′i-ə-bil′ə-ti), ***n.*** the quality or condition of being malleable.
mal·le·a·ble (mal′i-ə-b'l), ***adj.*** [ME. *malliable;* OFr. < L. *malleare;* see MALLEATE], 1. that can be hammered, pounded, or pressed into various shapes without breaking or returning to its original shape: said of metals. 2. yielding; amenable; adaptable. —***SYN.*** see **pliable.**
malleable iron, 1. cast iron made from a kind of pig iron by a special process of long heating at a high temperature: it is especially strong and malleable: also **malleable pig iron.** 2. wrought or forged iron.
mal·le·ate (mal′i-āt′), ***v.t.*** [MALLEATED (-id), MALLEATING], [< L. *malleatus,* pp. of *malleare,* to beat with a hammer < *malleus,* a hammer], to shape into a leaf or plate by pounding.
mal·lee (mal′i), ***n.*** [native name in Australia], 1. any of several species of Australian eucalyptus. 2. in Australia, a dense thicket formed by such plants.
mal·le·muck (mal′i-muk′), ***n.*** [D. *mallemok* < *mal,* foolish + *mok,* a gull], any of several large ocean birds, as the petrel, fulmar, or albatross.
mal·le·o·lar (mə-lē′ə-lẽr), ***adj.*** of a malleolus.
mal·le·o·lus (mə-lē′ə-ləs), ***n.*** [*pl.* MALLEOLI (-lī′)], [L. *malleolus,* dim. of *malleus,* a hammer], a rounded bony protuberance on each side of the ankle joint.
mal·let (mal′it), ***n.*** [Fr. *maillet,* dim. of *mail;* see MAUL], 1. a kind of hammer, usually with a heavy wooden head and a short handle, for driving a chisel, etc. 2. *a)* a long-handled hammer with a cylindrical wooden head, used in playing croquet. *b)* a similar but lighter instrument used in playing polo.
mal·le·us (mal′i-əs), ***n.*** [*pl.* MALLEI (-ī′)], [L., a hammer], the largest and outermost of the three small bones of the middle ear, shaped somewhat like a hammer: also called *hammer.*
Mal·lor·ca (mäl-yôr′kä), ***n.*** Majorca: the Spanish name.
mal·low (mal′ō), ***n.*** [ME. *malewe, malwe;* AS. *mealuwe* < L. *malva* (whence also G. *malve,* Fr. *mauve,* etc.); cf. MAUVE], 1. any of a family of plants, including the hollyhock, cotton, marsh mallow, and okra, typically with large, showy flowers and a sticky juice in their stems, leaves, and roots. 2. any of a certain genus of plants in this family; especially, the wild mallow, a plant with purplish, pink, or white flowers and hairy leaves and stems.
mallow rose, 1. any of several mallows with large pink or white flowers. 2. the flower. Also **rose mallow.**
malm (mäm), ***n.*** [ME.; AS. *mealm,* sand; for the base see MEAL (ground grain)], 1. a soft, crumbly, grayish-white limestone. 2. [British Dial.], a soft, chalky loam found in southern England; marl.
Malmes·bur·y, William of (mämz′ber′i, mämz′bẽr-i), 1095?–1143; English historian.
Malm·ö (mälm′ö; Eng. mal′mō), ***n.*** a seaport in southern Sweden: pop., 226,000.
malm·sey (mäm′zi), ***n.*** [ME. *malmesey;* ML. *malmasia* < Gr. *Monembasia,* Monemvasia, or Malvasia, small town on the coast of Laconia, Greece, formerly noted for exporting wine], 1. a strong, full-flavored, sweet white wine. 2. the grape from which this is made.
mal·nu·tri·tion (mal′nōō-trish′ən, mal′nū-trish′ən), ***n.*** faulty or inadequate nutrition; undernourishment resulting from insufficient food, improper diet, etc.
mal·oc·clu·sion (mal′ə-klōō′zhən), ***n.*** in *dentistry,* faulty occlusion.
mal·o·dor (mal-ō′dẽr), ***n.*** a bad odor; stench.
mal·o·dor·ous (mal-ō′dẽr-əs), ***adj.*** having a bad odor; stinking. —***SYN.*** see **stinking.**
Ma·lone, Edmond, (mə-lōn′), 1741–1812; Irish scholar; editor of Shakespeare's works.
ma·lo·nic acid (mə-lon′ik, mə-lō′nik), [Fr. *malonique*], a colorless, crystalline, dibasic acid, $CH_2(CO_2H)_2$, obtained from malic acid by oxidation.
Mal·o·ry, Sir Thomas (mal′ə-ri), fl. 1470; English writer and translator: compiler of the final version of *Morte d'Arthur,* Arthurian tales translated from French.
Mal·pi·ghi, Mar·cel·lo (mär-chel′ô mäl-pē′gē), 1628–1694; Italian physiologist and anatomist.
mal·pigh·i·a·ceous (mal-pig′i-ā′shəs), ***adj.*** [< Mod. L. *Malpighiaceae,* name of the family (after Marcello *Malpighi*); + *-ous*], of a family of tropical plants with leaves set oppositely and red or yellow flowers.
Mal·pigh·i·an (mal-pig′i-ən), ***adj.*** of or discovered by Marcello Malpighi.
Malpighian body (or **corpuscle**), 1. any nodule of lymphatic tissue in the spleen. 2. any of a number of small masses of blood vessels (*Malpighian tufts*) in the kidney, enclosed by a capsule that is an enlargement of the end of a tubule through which urine passes.
Malpighian layer, the soft, lowest layer of the epidermis, from which the other layers are derived.
Malpighian tubes (or **vessels**), a group of small, tubular glands that open into the hind part of the alimentary canal in most insects.
Malpighian tuft, see **Malpighian body.**
mal·po·si·tion (mal′pə-zish′ən), ***n.*** faulty or abnormal position, especially of the fetus in the uterus.
mal·prac·tice (mal-prak′tis), ***n.*** 1. injurious or unprofessional treatment or culpable neglect of a patient by a physician or surgeon. 2. misconduct or improper practice in any professional or official position.
Mal·raux, An·dré (än′drā′ mál′rō′), 1901– ; French novelist.
malt (môlt), ***n.*** [ME. *malte;* AS. *mealt;* akin to G. *malz;* IE. **mel-d,* prob., what is softened, ground down, etc. (< base **mel-,* to grind down), seen also in L. *mollis,* soft, yielding, Eng. *melt, smelt,* etc.], 1. barley or other grain softened by soaking in water until it sprouts and then kiln-dried, for brewing and distilling certain alcoholic liquors. 2. such liquor; beer, ale, etc. ***adj.*** made with malt. ***v.t.*** 1. to change (barley, etc.) into malt or something maltlike. 2. to treat or prepare (milk, etc.) with malt or malt extract. ***v.i.*** 1. to be changed into malt or something maltlike. 2. to change barley, etc. into malt; germinate grain artificially in order to change the starch into a sugar.
Mal·ta (môl′tə), ***n.*** 1. a British island in the Mediterranean, south of Sicily. 2. a British colony consisting of this island and two others: area, 122 sq. mi.; pop., 327,000; chief city, Valletta.

MALTA

Malta fever, [so named because prevalent in Malta and other Mediterranean areas], undulant fever: also called *Mediterranean fever.*
malt·ase (môl′tās), ***n.*** [*malt* + *-ase*], an enzyme, occurring in animals, plants, bacteria, etc., that changes maltose into dextrose.
malted milk, 1. a powdered preparation of dried milk and malted cereals. 2. a drink made by mixing this with milk and, usually, ice cream and flavoring.
Mal·tese (môl′tēz′), ***adj.*** 1. of Malta, its inhabitants, their language, etc. 2. of the medieval Knights of Malta. ***n.*** 1. [*pl.* MALTESE], a native or inhabitant of Malta. 2. the language spoken in Malta, a mixture of Arabic and Italian. 3. a Knight of Malta. 4. a Maltese cat or dog.
Maltese cat, a variety of domestic cat with bluish-gray fur.
Maltese cross, [so called from its use as an emblem by the medieval Knights of Malta], a cross whose arms look like arrowheads pointing inward: see **cross,** illus.
Maltese dog, a variety of small spaniel with long, silky, white hair, originated in Malta.
malt extract, a sticky, sugary substance obtained from malt soaked in water: it is used as a medicinal food.
mal·tha (mal′thə), ***n.*** [L.; Gr. *maltha,* mixture of wax and pitch], 1. any of several cements of varying consistencies. 2. any of several black, semisolid bitumens between petroleum and asphalt in consistency. 3. any of several hydrocarbon mixtures, as ozocerite.
Mal·thus, Thomas Robert (mal′thəs), 1766–1834; English clergyman and political economist; known for his theory that the population of the world tends to increase faster than the food supply, and that unless birth is controlled, poverty and war must serve as a natural restriction of the increase.
Mal·thu·sian (mal-thōō′zhən, mal-thū′zi-ən), ***adj.*** of Malthus or his theory. ***n.*** an adherent of Malthus.
malt liquor, beer, ale, or other fermented liquor made with malt or barley.
malt·ose (môl′tōs), ***n.*** a white, crystalline, dextro-

tatory sugar, $C_{12}H_{22}O_{11}$, obtained by the action of the diastase of malt on starch; malt sugar.

mal·treat (mal-trēt′), ***v.t.*** [Fr. *maltraiter;* see MAL- & TREAT], to treat roughly, unkindly, or brutally; abuse.

mal·treat·ment (mal-trēt′mənt), ***n.*** rough, unkind, or brutal treatment; abuse; mistreatment.

malt·ster (môlt′stẽr), ***n.*** one who makes or sells malt.

malt sugar, maltose.

malt·y (môl′ti), ***adj.*** 1. of, like, or containing malt. 2. fond of malt liquor. 3. [Slang], drunk.

mal·va·ceous (mal-vā′shəs), ***adj.*** [< L. *malva*, mallow; + *-aceous*], of the mallow family of plants.

mal·va·si·a (mal′və-sē′ə), ***n.*** [It.; see MALMSEY], 1. the grape from which malmsey is made. 2. malmsey.

mal·va·si·an (mal′və-sē′ən), ***adj.*** of malvasia.

Mal·vern Hill (mal′vẽrn), a plateau near Richmond, Virginia: site of a battle (1862) of the Civil War.

mal·ver·sa·tion (mal′vẽr-sā′shən), ***n.*** [Fr. < *malverser*, to commit malpractices < L. *male*, badly + *versari*, to turn, occupy oneself], corrupt conduct or fraudulent practices in public office or other position of trust.

mal·voi·sie (mal′voi-zi, mal′və-zi), ***n.*** [Fr.], [Archaic], malmsey (wine or grape).

ma·ma (mä′mə; *now less freq.* mə-mä′), ***n.*** mamma; mother.

mam·ba (mäm′bə), ***n.*** [Zulu *im-amba*], any of several poisonous snakes of southern Africa, related to the cobras but not hooded; especially, a common green or black snake of this sort.

mamb·o (mäm′bō), ***n.*** [Am. Sp.; musicians' slang term equivalent to "riff"], 1. a rhythmic musical form, of Cuban Negro origin, in 4/4 syncopated time and with a heavy accent on the second and fourth beats. 2. an American ballroom dance to such music. ***v.i.*** to dance the mambo.

Mam·e·luke (mam′ə-lo͞ok′, mam′ə-lūk′), ***n.*** [Fr. *mameluk;* Ar. *mamlūk*, slave, lit., one possessed < *malaka*, to possess], 1. a member of a military force, originally made up of slaves, that seized power in Egypt in about 1250, ruled there until 1517, and remained powerful until destroyed in 1811. 2. [m-], in Moslem countries, a slave: sometimes figurative.

ma·mey (mä-mā′, mä-mē′), ***n.*** a mammee.

mam·ma (mä′mə; *now less freq.* mə-mä′), ***n.*** [like L. *mamma*, mother, Sans. *mā*, Gr. *mammē* < baby talk; sp. prob. affected by association with next entry], mother: a child's word, corresponding to *papa* for *father:* also **mama, ma, mom, maw,** etc.

mam·ma (mam′ə), ***n.*** [*pl.* MAMMAE (-ē)], [AS.; L., breast; associated with *mamma*, mother, but prob. < IE **mandma* < base **mand-*, to suck, breast, **mad-*, to be moist, drip, seen also in Gr. *mastos*, breast, L. *madere*, to flow], a gland for secreting milk, present in the female of all mammals; mammary gland: in the male it is usually rudimentary and does not function.

mam·mal (mam′əl), ***n.*** [< *Mammalia*], any of a group of vertebrates the females of which have milk-secreting glands for feeding their offspring.

Mam·ma·li·a (ma-mā′li-ə), ***n.pl.*** [Mod. L. < LL. *mammalis*, of the breasts < L. *mamma;* see MAMMA (milk gland)], in *zoology*, mammals as a class.

mam·ma·li·an (ma-mā′li-ən), ***adj.*** of a mammal or mammals. ***n.*** a mammal.

mam·mal·o·gy (ma-mal′ə-ji), ***n.*** the branch of zoology dealing with mammals.

mam·ma·ry (mam′ə-ri), ***adj.*** designating or of the milk-secreting glands; of the mammae.

mam·mee (mä-mā′, mä-mē′), ***n.*** [Sp. *mamey* < Taino], 1. any of three tropical American trees with large, edible, yellow or brown fruit; marmalade tree (*mammee sapota, mammee colorado*), mammee apple tree, or sapodilla. 2. the fruit. Also spelled **mamey.**

mam·met (mam′it), ***n.*** a maumet.

mam·mif·er·ous (ma-mif′ẽr-əs), ***adj.*** [see -FEROUS], having mammae, or breasts.

mam·mil·la (ma-mil′ə), ***n.*** [*pl.* MAMMILLAE (-ē)], [L. *mam(m)illa*, dim. of *mamma*, a breast, teat], a nipple.

mam·mil·lar·y (mam′ə-ler′i), ***adj.*** [L. *mamillaris*], of or like a mammilla.

mam·mil·late (mam′ə-lāt′), ***adj.*** 1. having mammillae, or nipples. 2. shaped like a nipple.

mam·mock (mam′ək), ***n.*** [prob. < echoic base *mam-*, symbolistic of smacking the lips, enjoyable chewing, etc. + *-ock*], [Archaic or Dial.], a fragment; shred; scrap. ***v.t.*** to break or tear into fragments or shreds.

mam·mon (mam′ən), ***n.*** [ME. *mammon(as);* LL. *mammon, mammona, mammonas;* Gr. *mammōnas;* Aram. *māmōnā*, riches; prob. < *mā′mon*, that which is made secure or deposited < *'āman*, to trust], 1. [usually M-], the false god of riches and avarice. 2. riches regarded as an object of worship and greedy pursuit; wealth as an evil, more or less personified.

mam·mon·ism (mam′ən-iz′m), ***n.*** worship of mammon.

mam·moth (mam′əth), ***n.*** [Russ. *mammot′, mamant′*], a huge extinct elephant with a hairy skin and long tusks curving upward: remains have been found in North America, Europe, and Asia. ***adj.*** very big; huge; gigantic; enormous. —***SYN.*** see **enormous.**

Mammoth Cave National Park, a national park in southwestern Kentucky, containing enormous caverns and underground rivers: area, 78 sq. mi.

mam·my (mam′i), ***n.*** [*pl.* MAMMIES (-iz)], [dial. var. of *mamma* (mother)], 1. mamma; mother: a child's word. 2. a Negro woman who takes care of white children or is an old family servant: so used especially in the southern States.

Ma·mo·ré (mä′mô-re′), ***n.*** a river in Bolivia, joining the Beni to form the Madeira: length, 1,200 mi.

man (man), ***n.*** [*pl.* MEN (men)], [ME.; AS. *mann;* akin to G. *mann*, Goth. *manna*, etc.; prob. IE. base **men-*, to think, seen also in L. *mens*, mind (cf. MENTAL), *mentio* (cf. MENTION), *monere*, to admonish (cf. MONITOR, etc.), *commentus* (cf. COMMENT), etc.; hence, basic sense "the one that thinks"], 1. a human being; person, whether male or female. 2. the human race; mankind: used without *the* or *a*. 3. *a)* an adult male human being. *b)* sometimes, a boy. 4. *a)* an adult male servant, follower, attendant, or subordinate. *b)* a male employee; workman: as, the employer talked to the *men*. *c) usually in pl.* a soldier, sailor, etc.; especially, one of the rank and file: as, officers and *men*. *d)* [Archaic], a vassal. 5. *a)* a husband: as, they are *man* and wife. *b)* a lover. 6. a person with qualities conventionally regarded as manly, such as strength, courage, etc. 7. manly qualities; virility. ‡ 8. a player on a team 9. one of the pieces used in chess, checkers, etc. 10. in *nautical usage*, a ship: used in compounds, as *man-of-war, merchantman. Man* is also used as a term of address. ***v.t.*** [MANNED (mand), MANNING], 1. to furnish with men for work, defense, etc.: as, they *manned* the ship. 2. to take assigned places in, on, or at for work or defense: as, *man* the guns! 3. to strengthen; brace; fortify; nerve: as, he *manned* himself for the ordeal. 4. in *falconry*, to tame or accustom (a hawk) to the presence of men. ***interj.*** [Slang], an exclamation of pleasure, surprise, etc. ***adj.*** male.

as a (or **one**) **man,** in unison; unanimously.

be one's own man, 1. to be free and independent. 2. to be in full control of one's powers, senses, etc.

man and boy, first as a boy and then as a man.

to a man, with no one as an exception; every one.

-man (mən, man), a combining form meaning *man* or *person;* specifically, *a) a member of a* (specified) *nation*, as in *Frenchman*. *b) a person engaged in a* (specified) *kind of work*, as in *laundryman*. *c) a person operating a* (specified) *device*, as in *motorman*.

Man., 1. Manila (paper). 2. Manitoba.

man., manual.

Man, Isle of, one of the British Isles, between Northern Ireland and England: area, 221 sq. mi.; pop., 51,000; capital, Douglas: abbreviated **I.M., I.O.M.**

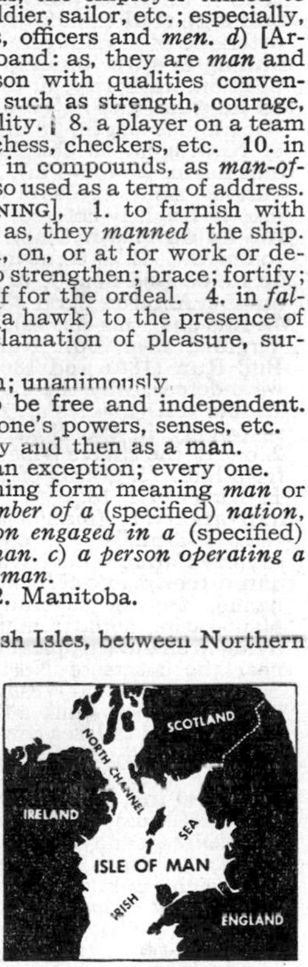

ISLE OF MAN

ma·na (mä′nä), ***n.*** [native Polynesian term], the impersonal supernatural force to which certain primitive peoples attribute good fortune, magical powers, etc.

man about town, a man who spends much time in fashionable restaurants, clubs, bars, etc.

man·a·cle (man′ə-k'l), ***n.*** [ME. & OFr. *manicle;* L. *manicula*, dim. of *manus*, hand], *usually in pl.* 1. a handcuff; fetter or shackle for the hand; hence, 2. any restraint. ***v.t.*** [MANACLED (-k'ld), MANACLING], 1. to put handcuffs on; fetter. 2. to restrain; hamper. —***SYN.*** see **hamper.**

man·age (man′ij), ***v.t.*** [MANAGED (-ijd), MANAGING], [It. *maneggiare;* LL. **manidiare* < L. *manus*, hand], 1. originally, to train (a horse) in his paces; cause to do the exercises of the manège; hence, 2. *a)* to handle; wield (a weapon, instrument, etc.). *b)* to control, guide, or work (a vehicle, boat, etc.). 3. to have charge of; direct; conduct; administer: as, she *manages* the household. 4. [Rare], to handle or use (money, supplies, etc.) carefully. 5. to get (a person) to do what one wishes, especially by skill, tact, flattery, etc.; make docile or submissive to control. 6. to bring about by contriving; contrive; succeed in accomplishing: often used ironically, as, I *managed* to make a mess of it. ***v.i.*** 1. to conduct or direct affairs; carry on business. 2. to contrive to get along; succeed in handling matters. ***n.*** [It. *maneggio* < *maneggiare;* influenced by Fr. *ménage;* see MÉNAGE], [Archaic], 1. manège. 2. management. —***SYN.*** see **conduct.**

man·age·a·bil·i·ty (man′ij-ə-bil′ə-ti), ***n.*** the state or quality of being manageable.

man·age·a·ble (man′ij-ə-b'l), *adj.* that can be managed; controllable, tractable, contrivable, etc.
man·age·a·bly (man′ij-ə-bli), *adv.* so as to be manageable.
man·aged currency (man′ijd), currency whose buying power is arbitrarily stabilized, as by varying the gold value of the basic monetary unit, to control price fluctuations.
man·age·ment (man′ij-mənt), *n.* 1. *a*) the act, art, or manner of managing, or handling, controlling, directing, etc. *b*) a being managed. 2. skillful managing; careful, tactful treatment. 3. skill in managing; executive ability. 4. *a*) the person or persons managing a business, institution, etc.: as, labor and *management* failed to agree on wages. *b*) such persons collectively, regarded as a distinct social group with special interests, characteristic economic views, etc.
man·ag·er (man′ij-ẽr), *n.* 1. a person who manages; especially, a person who manages a business, institution, etc.: abbreviated **Mgr.** 2. a person who manages affairs or expenditures, as of a household, skillfully and carefully.
man·ag·er·ess (man′ij-ẽr-is, man′ij-ris; Brit. man′ij-ẽr-es′), *n.* [Chiefly British], a woman manager.
man·a·ge·ri·al (man′ə-jêr′i-əl), *adj.* 1. of, like, or characteristic of a manager. 2. of management.
man·ag·er·ship (man′ij-ẽr-ship′), *n.* [see -SHIP], the position, authority, or duties of a manager.
Ma·na·gua (mä-nä′gwä), *n.* 1. a lake in western Nicaragua: length, 38 mi.; width, 16 mi. 2. the capital of Nicaragua, on this lake: pop., 184,000.
man·a·kin (man′ə-kin), *n.* [see MANIKIN], 1. any of various small birds of Central and South America, mostly brightly colored. 2. a manikin.
‡ma·ña·na (mä-nyä′nä), *n.* [Sp.], tomorrow. *adv.* 1. tomorrow. 2. at some indefinite time in the future.
Ma·ná·os (mä-nous′), *n.* a city in north central Brazil, on the Amazon: pop., 111,000: also spelled **Manaus.**
Ma·nas·sas (mə-nas′əs), *n.* a town in northeastern Virginia, near Bull Run: site of the two battles of Bull Run (1861 and 1862), in which the Union forces were defeated by the Confederates.
Ma·nas·seh (mə-nas′ə), *n.* [Heb. *mĕnaşşeh*, lit., causing to forget], in the *Bible*, 1. the elder son of Joseph. 2. one of the twelve tribes of Israel, said to be descended from him. 3. a king of Judah in the 7th century B.C.: II Kings 21:1–18.
man-at-arms (man′ət-ärmz′), *n.* [*pl.* MEN-AT-ARMS (men′ət-ärmz′)], 1. a soldier. 2. a heavily armed cavalryman in a medieval army.
man·a·tee (man′ə-tē′), *n.* [Sp. *manati* < native (Carib) name], any of several large, plant-eating aquatic mammals living in shallow tropical waters near the coasts of North and South America and West Africa, having flippers and a broad, flat, rounded tail; sea cow.

MANATEE
(about 13 ft. long)

Ma·naus (mä-nous′), *n.* Manáos.
ma·nav·el·ins, ma·nav·il·ins (mə-nav′′l-inz), *n.pl.* [for *manarvelings* < naval slang *manarvel*, to steal small stores; ult. origin unknown], [Slang], in *nautical usage*, leftovers; odds and ends.
Man·ches·ter (man′ches′tẽr, man′chis-tẽr), *n.* 1. a city and canal port in Lancashire, England: pop., 672,000: a textile manufacturing center. 2. a city in southern New Hampshire, on the Merrimack River: pop., 88,000. 3. a town in north central Connecticut: pop., 42,000.
man·chet (man′chit), *n.* [ME. *manchete;* use of ME. *maine* (in same sense) & Caxton's form *maynchet* suggest derivation < OFr. *paindemaine* (L. *panis dominicus*), lit., lord's bread], [Archaic or British Dial.], 1. white bread made of the finest wheat flour. 2. a roll or small loaf of such bread.
man-child (man′chīld′), *n.* [*pl.* MAN-CHILDREN (-chil′drən)], a male child; boy.
man·chi·neel (man′chi-nēl′), *n.* [Fr. *mancenille;* Sp. *manzanillo* < *manzana*, apple < L. (*mala*) *matiana*, (apples) of Matius < *Matius*, name of a Roman gens and of the author of a manual on cookery], 1. a tropical American tree with poisonous, yellowish-green, applelike fruit and milky juice. 2. its wood.
Man·chu, Man·choo (man-chōō′, man′chōō), *n.* [Manchu, lit., pure], 1. a member of a Mongolian people of Manchuria: the Manchus conquered China in 1643–1644 and set up a dynasty that ruled until 1912. 2. the Tungus language of the Manchus. *adj.* of Manchuria, the Manchus, their language, etc.
Man·chu·kuo, Man·chou·kuo (man′chōō-kwō′, man-chōō′kwō; Chin. män′jō′kwō′), *n.* a former state in eastern Asia, including Manchuria, Jehol province, and part of Chahar, set up by Japan in 1932, abolished in 1945 as a result of World War II: area, 460,000 sq. mi.: abbreviated **Manch.**
Man·chu·ri·a (man-choor′i-ə), *n.* a region in northeastern China, on the Yellow Sea: formerly an administrative unit, it is now divided into the provinces of Heilungkiang, Kirin, and Liaoning: area, c. 364,000 sq. mi.: abbreviated **Manch.** Cf. **Manchukuo.**

MANCHURIA

Man·chu·ri·an (man-choor′i-ən), *adj.* of Manchuria or its people. *n.* a native or inhabitant of Manchuria.
man·ci·ple (man′si-p'l), *n.* [OFr. *manciple, mancipe;* L. *mancipium* < *manceps*, buyer, contractor < *manus*, a hand + base of *capere*, to take], a steward or buyer of provisions, as for an English college, a monastery, etc.
Man·cu·ni·an (man-kū′ni-ən), *adj.* [< ML. *Mancunium*, Manchester], of Manchester, England. *n.* a native or inhabitant of Manchester, England.
-man·cy (man′si), [OFr. or LL.; OFr. *-mancie;* LL. *-mantia* < Gr. *manteia*, divination], a combining form meaning *divination*, as in *necromancy, chiromancy.*
Man·dae·an (man-dē′ən), *n.* & *adj.* Mandean.
Man·da·lay (man′də-lā′, man′də-lā′), *n.* a city in central Burma, on the Irrawaddy River: pop., 182,000.
man·da·mus (man-dā′məs), *n.* [L., we command; 1st pers. pl., pres. indic., of *mandare*, to command], in *law*, a writ, or written order, requiring that a specified thing be done, issued by a higher court to a lower one, or to a corporation, city, official, etc.: originally, in England, it was a writ of royal prerogative. *v.t.* [Colloq.], to serve with or command by such a writ.
Man·dan (man′dan), *n.* [*pl.* MANDAN, MANDANS (-danz)], 1. a member of a tribe of Siouan Indians who lived in the Missouri River Valley. 2. their language. *adj.* of or developed by the Mandan: as, *Mandan* corn.
man·da·rin (man′də-rin), *n.* [Port. *mandarim* < Malay *mantrī*, minister of state < Hind. *mantrī* < Sans. *mantrin*, counselor < *mantra*, counsel; IE. base **men-*, to think; cf. MAN], 1. a high official of China under the Empire: the nine classes of mandarin were distinguished from one another by a certain kind of jeweled button worn on the cap. 2. [M-], the dialect of Chinese spoken by officials and the educated classes; official or main dialect of Chinese. 3. *a*) a small, sweet orange with a loose rind; tangerine. *b*) the tree that it grows on. *c*) any of several related trees. 4. a deep-orange dye. 5. *a*) a long, brocaded Chinese coat with loose sleeves, worn by mandarins. *b*) a woman's evening coat like this: also **mandarin coat.**
mandarin duck, a bright-colored, crested Asiatic duck.
man·da·tar·y (man′də-ter′i), *n.* [*pl.* MANDATARIES (-iz)], [LL. *mandatarius*], 1. [Rare], a person to whom a mandate has been given. 2. a country to which a mandate has been given. Also **mandatory.**
man·date (man′dāt; *also, for n.,* man′dit), *n.* [L. *mandatum*, neut. pp. of *mandare*, lit., to put into one's hand, command, entrust < *manus*, a hand + pp. of *dare*, to give], 1. an authoritative order or command, especially a written one. 2. *a*) formerly, a commission from the League of Nations to a country (called the *mandatary*) to administer some region, colony, etc. *b*) the area so administered: cf. **trusteeship, trust territory.** 3. the wishes of constituents expressed to a representative, legislature, etc. as an order, or regarded as an order. 4. in *law, a*) an order from a higher court or official to a lower one: a *mandate on remission* is a mandate from an appellate court to the lower court, communicating its decision in a case appealed. *b*) in *canon law*, a papal rescript, especially one having to do with preferment to a benefice. *c*) in *English law*, a bailment of personal property with no consideration. *d*) in *Roman law*, a commission or contract by which a person undertakes to do something for another, without recompense but with indemnity against loss. *e*) any contract of agency. *v.t.* [MANDATED (-id), MANDATING], to assign (a region, etc.) as a mandate.
man·da·tor (man-dā′tẽr), *n.* [L.], one that gives a mandate.
man·da·to·ry (man′də-tôr′i, man′də-tō′ri), *adj.* [L. *mandatorius*], 1. of, having the nature of, or containing a mandate. 2. authoritatively commanded or required; obligatory. 3. having received a mandate

over some territory; being a mandatary. ***n.*** a mandatary.
Man·de·an (man-dē′ən), ***n.*** [< Mandean *mandayyā*, lit., having knowledge (used as transl. of Gr. *gnōstikoi*, Gnostics) < *mandā*, knowledge; + *-an*], 1. a member of an ancient Gnostic sect (*Christians of St. John*), still extant in southern Iraq. 2. the Eastern Aramaic dialect used in Mandean writings: it was spoken along the Euphrates from the 7th to the 9th centuries A.D. ***adj.*** 1. of the Mandeans, their doctrines, etc. 2. of Mandean. Also spelled **Mandaean.**
Man·de·ville, Bernard (man′də-vil′), 1670?–1733; English satirical writer and philosopher, born in the Netherlands.
Mandeville, Sir **John,** fictitious British author of a 14th-century book of travels, originally written in French, probably by John de Bourgogne, a physician who died at Liège in 1372.
man·di·ble (man′də-b'l), ***n.*** [OFr.; LL. *mandibula* < *mandibulum*, a jaw < L. *mandere*, to chew], the jaw, especially the lower jaw, or any part corresponding to this; specifically, *a*) either part of a bird's beak. *b*) either of the pair of outermost, biting jaws of an insect or other arthropod.
man·dib·u·la (man-dib′yoo-lə), ***n.*** [LL.], the mandible.
man·dib·u·lar (man-dib′yoo-lẽr), ***adj.*** of or like a mandible. ***n.*** the mandible; lower jawbone.
man·dib·u·late (man-dib′yoo-lit), ***adj.*** 1. having a mandible or mandibles, as some insects. 2. adapted for chewing. ***n.*** a mandibulate insect.
Man·din·ga (man-diŋ′gə), ***n.*** **& *adj.*** Mandingo.
Man·din·gan (man-diŋ′gən), ***adj.*** of the Mandingos or their language. ***n.*** Mandingo.
Man·din·go (man-diŋ′gō), ***n.*** [*pl.* MANDINGOS, MANDINGOES (-gōz)], [< the native name], 1. a member of a group of Negro peoples of western Africa. 2. a language or dialect spoken by the Mandingos. ***adj.*** of the Mandingos or Mandingo. Also **Mandinga.**
man·do·lin (man′d'l-in′, man′də-lin′), ***n.*** [Fr. *mandoline;* It. *mandolino*, dim. of *mandola*, *mandora* < LL. *pandura*, kind of lute; Gr. *pandoura*], a musical instrument with eight, ten, or twelve metal strings, usually paired, stretched over a deep, rounded sound box: it is played with a plectrum, which is moved rapidly back and forth to give a tremolo effect.

MANDOLIN

man·drag·o·ra (man-drag′ə-rə), ***n.*** mandrake.
man·drake (man′drāk), ***n.*** [ME. *mondrake*, altered by folk etym. (after *man* + *drake*, dragon) < *mandrag(g)e;* AS. *mandragora;* LL. *mandragora;* L. *mandragoras;* Gr. *mandragoras*], 1. a poisonous plant of the nightshade family, found in Mediterranean regions: it has a short stem, purple or white flowers, and a thick root, often forked, used in medicine for its narcotic and emetic properties. 2. the root, formerly thought to resemble the human shape. 3. the May apple.
man·drel, man·dril (man′drəl), ***n.*** [earlier *manderil;* prob. < Fr. *mandrin*], 1. a tight-fitting metal spindle or bar, often cone-shaped, inserted into something to hold it while it is being machined or turned on a lathe, etc. 2. a metal rod or bar used as a core around which metal, glass, etc. is cast, molded, or shaped, as in forging, or wire is wound. 3. a form that metalwork is pressed against in spinning.
man·drill (man′dril), ***n.*** [*man* + *drill* (baboon)], a large, fierce, strong baboon of western Africa: the male has blue and scarlet patches on the face and rump.
man·du·cate (man′joo-kāt′), ***v.t.*** [MANDUCATED (-id), MANDUCATING], [< L. *manducatus*, pp. of *manducare;* see MANGER], [Rare], to chew; masticate.
mane (mān), ***n.*** [ME. *mane, maane;* AS. *manu;* akin to G. *mähne* (with unexplained vowel); IE. base **mono-*, neck, seen also in L. *monile*, a collar, necklace, mane, AS. *mene*, necklace], 1. the long hair growing from the top or sides of the neck of certain animals, as the horse, bison, lion, etc. 2. long, thick human hair.
man-eat·er (man′ēt′ẽr), ***n.*** 1. a cannibal. 2. an animal that eats, likes to eat, or is thought to eat, human flesh; specifically, *a*) a certain shark of tropical waters. *b*) a lion, tiger, etc. with a taste for human flesh.
maned (mānd), ***adj.*** having a mane.
ma·nège, ma·nege (ma-nezh′, mə-nāzh′), ***n.*** [Fr. < It. *maneggio;* see MANAGE], 1. the art of riding and training horses; horsemanship. 2. the paces and exercises of a trained horse. 3. a school for training horses and teaching riders; riding academy.
Ma·nes (mā′nēz), ***n.*** Persian prophet; 216?–276? A.D.; founder of Manicheism: also called *Manicheus.*
ma·nes, Ma·nes (mā′nēz), ***n.pl.*** [ME.; L.; IE. base **māni-*, anger; inferred basic sense "the angry ones"], 1. in *ancient Roman religion*, the souls of the dead, especially of dead ancestors, regarded as gods. 2. [construed as sing. or pl.], the soul or shade of some dead person.
Ma·net, É·dou·ard (ā′dwȧr′ má′ne′; Eng. mə-nā′), 1832–1883; French impressionist painter.
ma·neu·ver (mə-nōō′vẽr, mə-nū′vẽr), ***n.*** [Fr. *manœuvre* < LL. *manuopera* < L. *manu operare*, to work by hand < *manus*, a hand + *opera*, pl. of *opus*, a work], 1. a planned and controlled tactical or strategic movement of troops, warships, etc. 2. *pl.* large-scale practice movements and exercises of troops, warships, etc. under conditions resembling those of combat. 3. any movement or procedure intended as a skillful or shrewd step toward some objective; stratagem; artifice; scheme: as, the child tried various *maneuvers* to get his own way. ***v.i.* & *v.t.*** 1. to perform or cause to perform a maneuver or maneuvers. 2. to manage or plan skillfully or shrewdly; manipulate or scheme. 3. to move, get, put, make, compel, etc. (a person or thing) by some stratagem or scheme: as, he *maneuvered* his way to victory, she *maneuvered* herself out of an embarrassing position. Also spelled **manoeuvre.** —***SYN.*** see **trick.**
ma·neu·ver·a·bil·i·ty (mə-nōō′vẽr-ə-bil′ə-ti, mə-nū′vẽr-ə-bil′ə-ti), ***n.*** the quality or state of being maneuverable.
ma·neu·ver·a·ble (mə-nōō′vẽr-ə-b'l, mə-nū′vẽr-ə-b'l), ***adj.*** that can be maneuvered.
man Friday, 1. in Defoe's *Robinson Crusoe*, the hero's devoted servant: so named because rescued from cannibals on a Friday; hence, 2. a loyal and devoted or servile follower or servant.
man·ful (man′fəl), ***adj.*** manly; brave, resolute, etc.
man·ga·nate (maŋ′gə-nāt′), ***n.*** a salt of manganic acid: as, potassium *manganate*, K_2MnO_4.
man·ga·nese (maŋ′gə-nēs′, maŋ′gə-nēz′), ***n.*** [Fr. *manganèse;* It. *manganese;* by metathesis < ML. *magnesia;* see MAGNESIA], a grayish-white metallic chemical element, usually hard and brittle, which rusts like iron but is not magnetic: it is used in the manufacture of alloys of iron, aluminum, and copper: symbol, Mn; at. wt., 54.93; at. no., 25.
manganese bronze, 1. a bronze-colored dye. 2. an alloy of copper and zinc strengthened with a small percentage of manganese.
manganese spar, rhodonite.
manganese steel, a hard, malleable and ductile steel containing 12 to 14 per cent of manganese.
man·gan·ic (man-gan′ik, maŋ-gan′ik), ***adj.*** 1. designating or of chemical compounds in which manganese has a higher valence than in the corresponding manganous compounds. 2. designating or of an acid, H_2MnO_4, existing only as salts, the manganates.
man·ga·nin (maŋ′gə-nin), ***n.*** [< *manganese* + *-in*], an alloy consisting mainly of copper with some manganese and nickel: it is used in electrical heating elements, rheostats, etc.
man·ga·nite (maŋ′gə-nīt′), ***n.*** 1. hydrous manganese trioxide, $Mn_2O_3 \cdot H_2O$, a steel-gray or black, crystalline mineral with a metallic luster. 2. any of a series of salts that may be considered as derivatives of manganous acid, the hydroxide of tetravalent manganese.
man·gan·ous (maŋ′gə-nəs, man-gan′əs, maŋ-gan′əs), ***adj.*** designating or of chemical compounds in which manganese has a lower valence than in the corresponding manganic compounds.
mange (mānj), ***n.*** [ME. *manjewe;* OFr. *mangeue, manjue*, an itch, eating < *manjuer, mangier* (Fr. *manger*); L. *manducare;* see MANGER], any of various skin diseases of domestic animals, and occasionally of man, especially one caused by a parasitic mite and characterized by a loss of hair.
man·gel-wur·zel (maŋ′g'l-wũr′z'l, maŋ′g'l-wũrt′s'l), ***n.*** [G. < *mangoldwurzel; mangold*, beet + *wurzel*, a root], a variety of large beet, used as food for cattle, especially in Europe: also **mangel.**
man·ger (mān′jẽr), ***n.*** [ME.; OFr. *mangeoire, mangeure* < LL. **manducatoria*, feeding trough < pp. of L. *manducare*, to eat < *mandere*, to chew], a box or trough to hold hay, etc. for horses or cattle to eat.
man·gi·ly (mān′ji-li), ***adv.*** in a mangy manner.
man·gi·ness (mān′ji-nis), ***n.*** the quality or condition of being mangy.
man·gle (maŋ′g'l), ***v.t.*** [MANGLED (-g'ld), MANGLING], [Anglo-Fr. *mangler, mahangler*, freq. of OFr. *mehaigner*, to maim; see MAIM], 1. to mutilate or disfigure by repeatedly and roughly cutting, tearing, hacking, or crushing; lacerate and bruise badly: as, the body was *mangled* beyond recognition. 2. to spoil; botch; mar; garble: as, the text was *mangled.* —***SYN.*** see **maim.**
man·gle (maŋ′g'l), ***n.*** [D. *mangel* < *mangelen*, to mangle < MD. *mange*, a mangle; It. *mangano;* LL. *manganum;* Gr. *manganon*, pulley, war machine, orig. device for deceiving; IE. base **mang-*, to embellish (in deceptive

fashion), seen also in MIr. *meng*, deceit, craft, L. *mango*, dealer who falsifies his wares; prob. nazalized form of IE. base **mag̑-*; see MAKE], a machine for pressing and smoothing cloth, especially sheets and other flat pieces, between rollers. *v.t.* [MANGLED (-g'ld), MANGLING], to press in a mangle.

man·gler (maŋ'glẽr), *n.* a person or thing that mangles, or mutilates.

man·gler (maŋ'glẽr), *n.* a person who presses sheets, etc. in a mangle.

man·go (maŋ'gō), *n.* [*pl.* MANGOES, MANGOS (-gōz)], [Port. *manga;* Malay *mañga* < Tamil *mān-kāy; mān*, mango tree + *kāy*, fruit], 1. a yellow-red, oblong tropical fruit with a thick rind, somewhat acid and juicy pulp, and a hard stone: it is eaten when ripe, or preserved or pickled when unripe. 2. the tree that it grows on. 3. pickled muskmelon or cucumber.

man·go·nel (maŋ'gə-nel'), *n.* [OFr., dim. < LL. *manganum;* see MANGLE (machine)], an obsolete military apparatus for hurling heavy stones and other missiles.

man·go·steen (maŋ'gə-stēn'), *n.* [Malay *mangustan*], 1. an edible East Indian fruit somewhat like an orange, with a thick, reddish-brown rind and sweet, white, juicy, segmented pulp. 2. the tree that it grows on.

man·grove (man'grōv), *n.* [< Port. *mangue* or Sp. *mangle* < the W. Ind. (Taino) name; sp. influenced by Eng. *grove;* earlier forms, *mangrowe, mangrave*], any of a group of tropical trees or shrubs growing in swampy ground along river banks, with branches that spread and send down roots, thus forming more trunks and causing a thick growth over a large area.

man·gy (mān'ji), *adj.* [MANGIER (-ji-ẽr), MANGIEST (-ji-ist)], 1. having, infected with, resembling, or caused by the mange. 2. shabby and filthy; sordid; squalid. 3. mean and low; despicable.

man·han·dle (man'han'd'l, man'han'd'l), *v.t.* [MANHANDLED (-d'ld), MANHANDLING], 1. [Rare], to move or do by human strength only, without mechanical aids. 2. to handle roughly.

Man·hat·tan (man-hat'ən), *n.* 1. an island between the Hudson and East rivers, forming part of New York City: length, 13 mi.; greatest width, 2 1/4 mi.; area, with small near-by islands, 22 sq. mi.: also **Manhattan Island.** 2. a borough of New York City consisting of this island: pop., 1,698,000. Manhattan contains the chief business district, theatrical center, etc. of New York City. 3. any member of a tribe of Algonquian Indians who lived on Manhattan Island. 4. a cocktail made of whisky and vermouth, usually with a dash of bitters and a maraschino cherry.

Manhattan District, a division of the U.S. Army Corps of Engineers, established in 1942, which produced the atomic bomb.

man·hole (man'hōl'), *n.* a hole through which a man can get into a sewer, pipe, conduit, etc. for repair work or inspection.

man·hood (man'hood), *n.* [see -HOOD], 1. the state or time of being a man (human being or, especially, adult male human being). 2. manly character or qualities; virility; courage, resolution, etc. 3. men collectively.

man-hour (man'our'), *n.* a unit of work, equal to that done by one man in one hour.

man·hunt (man'hunt'), *n.* a hunt for a man, especially for a fugitive: also **man hunt.**

ma·ni·a (mā'ni-ə), *n.* [ME.; L.; Gr. *mania*, madness < *mainesthai*, to rage], 1. wild or violent insanity; specifically, the manic phase of manic-depressive psychosis, characterized generally by abnormal excitability, exaggerated feelings of well-being, flight of ideas, excessive activity, etc. 2. an excessive, persistent enthusiasm, liking, craving, or interest; obsession; craze: as, a *mania* for collecting stamps.

SYN.—**mania** in its basic sense (see definition above) describes the phase of manic-depressive psychosis that is distinguished from *melancholia;* **delirium** denotes a temporary state of extreme mental disturbance (marked by restlessness, incoherence, and hallucinations) that occurs during fevers, in alcoholic psychosis, etc.; **frenzy**, not used technically in psychiatry, implies extreme emotional agitation in which self-control is lost; **hysteria** is applied in psychiatry to certain psychogenic disorders characterized by excitability, anxiety, sensory and motor disturbances, and the involuntary simulation of blindness, deafness, etc. In extended use, **mania** suggests a craze for something (a *mania* for dancing), **delirium**, rapturous excitement (a *delirium* of joy), and **hysteria**, an outburst of wild, uncontrolled feeling (she laughed and cried in her *hysteria*).

-ma·ni·a (mā'ni-ə), [see MANIA], a combining form meaning: 1. *a* (specified) *type of mental disorder* or *manic state*, as in **kleptomania.** 2. *an excessive, persistent enthusiasm, craving,* or *liking for, obsession with,* or *craze for* (a specified thing), as in **bibliomania.**

ma·ni·ac (mā'ni-ak'), *adj.* [ML. *maniacus*], of, having, or showing mania; wildly insane; raving. *n.* a wildly or violently insane person; madman; lunatic.

-ma·ni·ac (mā'ni-ak'), a combining form used to form adjectives and nouns (referring to persons) from corresponding nouns ending in *-mania*, as in **kleptomaniac.**

ma·ni·a·cal (mə-nī'ə-k'l), *adj.* of, having, or showing mania; wildly insane; raving.

man·ic (man'ik, mā'nik), *adj.* in *psychiatry*, 1. having or characterized by mania. 2. of or like mania.

man·ic-de·pres·sive (man'ik-di-pres'iv, mā'nik-di-pres'iv), *adj.* designating, of, or having a psychosis characterized by alternating periods of mania and melancholia, or mental depression. *n.* a person who has this psychosis.

Man·i·che·an, Man·i·chae·an (man'ə-kē'ən), *n.* an adherent of Manicheism; Manichee. *adj.* of the Manicheans or Manicheism.

Man·i·che·an·ism, Man·i·chae·an·ism (man'ə-kē'ən-iz'm), *n.* Manicheism.

Man·i·chee (man'ə-kē'), *n.* [Late ME.], a Manichean.

Man·i·che·ism, Man·i·chae·ism (man'ə-kē'iz'm), *n.* a religious philosophy taught from the 3d century to the 7th century A.D. by the Persian Manes, or Manicheus, and his followers, combining Zoroastrian, Gnostic Christian, and pagan elements, and based on the doctrine of the two contending principles of good (light, God, the soul) and evil (darkness, Satan, the body).

Man·i·che·us, Man·i·chae·us (man'ə-kē'əs), *n.* Manes (Persian prophet).

man·i·cure (man'ə-kyoor'), *n.* [Fr. < L. *manus*, a hand + *cura*, care], 1. the care of the hands; especially, trimming, polishing, etc. of the fingernails. 2. [Rare], a manicurist. *v.t. & v.i.* [MANICURED (-kyoord'), MANICURING], to take care of (the hands and fingernails); do the work of a manicurist for (a person or persons).

man·i·cur·ist (man'ə-kyoor'ist), *n.* a person, usually a woman, whose work is manicuring.

man·i·fest (man'ə-fest'), *adj.* [ME.; OFr. *manifeste;* L. *manifestus*, earlier *manufestus*, lit., struck by the hand, near at hand, palpable, evident < *manus*, a hand + base akin to *-fendere*, to strike], apparent to the senses, especially that of sight, or to the mind; evident; obvious; clear; plain; patent. *v.t.* 1. to make clear or evident; show plainly; reveal; evince. 2. to prove; be evidence of. 3. *a)* to enter in a ship's manifest. *b)* to show the manifest of (cargo). *v.i.* to appear to the senses; show itself. *n.* 1. *a)* an itemized list of a ship's cargo, telling the place of lading, destination, etc., to be shown to customs officials. *b)* a waybill of lading. 2. perishable goods carried by fast freight. 3. [Obs.], *a)* a manifestation. *b)* a manifesto. —*SYN.* see **evident.**

man·i·fes·tant (man'ə-fes'tənt), *n.* a person who takes part in a manifestation, or public demonstration.

man·i·fes·ta·tion (man'ə-fes-tā'shən), *n.* [LL. *manifestatio*], 1. a manifesting or being manifested. 2. something that manifests: as, his silence was a *manifestation* of cowardice. 3. a public demonstration, as by a government, party, etc., for political effect.

Manifest Destiny, the 19th-century doctrine that it is the destiny of the Anglo-Saxon nations, especially of the United States, to dominate the entire Western Hemisphere.

man·i·fes·to (man'ə-fes'tō), *n.* [*pl.* MANIFESTOES (-tōz)], [It. < L. *manifestus*], a public declaration of motives and intentions by a government or by a person or group regarded as having some public importance.

man·i·fold (man'ə-fōld'), *adj.* [ME. *manifold, manifald;* AS. *manigfeald;* see MANY & -FOLD], 1. having many and various forms, features, parts, etc.: as, *manifold* wisdom. 2. of many sorts; many and varied; multifarious: used with a plural noun, as, *manifold* duties. 3. being such in many and various ways or for many reasons: as, a *manifold* villain. 4. comprising, consisting of, or operating several units or parts of one kind: said of certain devices. *n.* 1. what is manifold. 2. any of many copies made by manifolding. 3. a pipe with one inlet and several outlets or with one outlet and several inlets, for connecting with other pipes, as, in an automobile, for conducting exhausts from each cylinder into a single exhaust pipe. *v.t.* 1. to make manifold; multiply. 2. to make more than one copy of: as, she will *manifold* the letter with carbon paper. —*SYN.* see **many.**

MANIFOLD PIPE

man·i·fold·er (man'ə-fōl'dẽr), *n.* a person or thing that manifolds; specifically, a machine for making copies of documents, etc.

man·i·hot (man'i-hot'), *n.* [Mod. L.; Fr. < Braz. (Tupi) *mandioca*], any of a group of tropical American plants found mainly in Brazil, including the cassava, or manioc, from which tapioca is obtained, and others that yield a kind of rubber.

man·i·kin (man'ə-kin), *n.* [D. *manneken* < *man*, man + dim. suffix *-ken*], 1. a little man; dwarf. 2. an anatomical model of the human body, usually with movable and detachable parts, used in medical schools, etc. 3. a mannequin. Also spelled **manakin, mannikin.**

Ma·nil·a (mə-nil'ə), *n.* 1. the principal city and former capital of the Philippine Islands, on Luzon: pop., 1,200,000: see **Quezon City.** 2. [often m-], *a)* Manila hemp. *b)* Manila paper: abbreviated **Man.** *c)* Manila rope. *d)* a kind of cigar made in Manila. Sometimes spelled **Manilla.**

Manila Bay, an arm of the South China Sea, off Manila: site of an American naval victory (1898).

Manila hemp, a strong fiber from the leafstalk of a Philippine tree related to the banana; abacá: it is used for making rope, paper, etc.

Manila paper, a strong, brownish wrapping paper, originally made of Manila hemp, now of various fibers.

Manila rope, strong rope made of Manila hemp.

Ma·nil·la (mə-nil'ə), *n.* Manila.

ma·nil·la (mə-nil'ə), *n.* [< Fr. & Sp.; Fr. *manille;* Sp. *malilla* (*carta*) < *malillo*, dim. of *malo*, bad (L. *malus*)], in ombre, quadrille, and some other card games, the second-highest trump: also **manille** (mə-nil').

man in the street, the average man; ordinary person.

man·i·oc (man'i-ok', mā'ni-ok'), *n.* [Fr. < Braz. (Tupi) *mandioca;* cf. MANIHOT], 1. a cassava, a tropical plant with edible starchy roots. 2. the starch from these roots, used in making bread and tapioca.

man·i·ple (man'ə-p'l), *n.* [ME.; OFr. (Fr. *manipule*); L. *manipulus*, handful < *manus*, a hand + base of *plere*, to fill], 1. a subdivision of the ancient Roman legion; one third of a cohort, consisting of either 60 or 120 men. 2. a silk band worn hanging over the left forearm as a eucharistic vestment.

ma·nip·u·lar (mə-nip'yoo-lẽr), *adj.* [L. *manipularis*], 1. of a maniple (in the ancient Roman army). 2. of manipulation. *n.* a soldier of a maniple.

ma·nip·u·late (mə-nip'yoo-lāt'), *v.t.* [MANIPULATED (-id), MANIPULATING], [back-formation < *manipulation*], 1. to work or operate with or as with the hand or hands; handle or use, especially with skill: as, the pilot of an airplane must *manipulate* various controls. 2. to manage or control artfully or by shrewd use of influence, especially in an unfair or fraudulent way: as, the political boss *manipulated* the voting. 3. to change or falsify (figures, accounts, etc.) for one's own purposes or profit; juggle; rig; specifically, to cause (prices of stocks, etc.) to fall or rise, as by wash sales, etc. —***SYN.*** see **handle.**

ma·nip·u·la·tion (mə-nip'yoo-lā'shən), *n.* [Fr.; as if < L. **manipulatio* < pp. of **manipulare* < *manipulus;* see MANIPLE, MANIPULATE], 1. a handling or being handled; especially, skillful handling or operation. 2. artful management or control, as by shrewd use of influence, especially in an unfair or fraudulent way. 3. change or falsification (of figures, prices, etc.) for one's own purposes or profit.

ma·nip·u·lat·ive (mə-nip'yoo-lā'tiv), *adj.* of or done by manipulation.

ma·nip·u·la·tor (mə-nip'yoo-lā'tẽr), *n.* a person or thing that manipulates.

ma·nip·u·la·to·ry (mə-nip'yoo-lə-tôr'i, mə-nip'yoo-lə-tō'ri), *adj.* manipulative.

Man·i·pur (mun'i-poor'), *n.* a state of eastern India: area, 8,620 sq. mi.; pop., 578,000; capital, Imphal.

Ma·ni·sa, Ma·nis·sa (mä'ni-sä'), *n.* a city in western Turkey: pop., 38,000: site of a battle (190 B.C.) in which the Romans defeated Antiochus the Great.

man·i·to (man'ə-tō'), *n.* [Am. Ind. (Massachusetts) *manitto*, he is a god], in *Algonquian Indian religion*, a spirit or force underlying the world and life, understood as a nature spirit of both good and evil influence: also **manitou, manitu.**

Man·i·to·ba (man'ə-tō'bə, man'ə-tō-bä'), *n.* 1. a province of south central Canada: area, 246,512 sq. mi.; pop., 850,000; capital, Winnipeg: abbreviated **Man., Manit., M.** 2. a lake in southern Manitoba: area, 1,711 sq. mi.

Man·i·to·ban (man'ə-tō'bən), *adj.* of Manitoba. *n.* a native or inhabitant of Manitoba.

man·i·tou, man·i·tu (man'ə-tōō'), *n.* a manito.

Man·i·tou·lin Island (man'ə-tōō'lin), a Canadian island in Lake Huron, south of Ontario, Canada: length, 80 mi.

Man·i·to·woc (man'i-tə-wok'), *n.* a city in central Wisconsin, on Lake Michigan: pop., 32,000.

Man·ka·to (man-kā'tō), *n.* a city in southern Minnesota: pop., 24,000.

man·kind (man'kīnd'; *also, and for 2 always,* man'kīnd'), *n.* [see MAN & -KIND], 1. all human beings; the human race. 2. all human males; the male sex.

man·like (man'līk'), *adj.* 1. like or characteristic of a man or men. 2. fit for a man; masculine.

man·li·ness (man'li-nis), *n.* the quality or state of being manly; virility.

man·ly (man'li), *adj.* [MANLIER (-li-ẽr), MANLIEST (-li-ist)], 1. having the qualities generally regarded as those that a man should have; virile; strong, resolute, honorable, etc. 2. fit for a man; masculine: as, *manly* sports. *adv.* in a manly way. —***SYN.*** see **male.**

Mann, Hein·rich (hīn'riH män), 1871–1950; German writer in America: brother of *Thomas.*

Mann, Horace (man), 1796–1859; American educator.

Mann, Tho·mas (tō'mäs män), 1875–1955; German novelist in America, etc.; received Nobel prize in literature, 1929.

man·na (man'ə), *n.* [AS.; LL.; Gr. *manna;* Aram. *mannā;* Heb. *mān*], 1. in the *Bible*, food miraculously provided for the Israelites in the wilderness: Ex. 16: 14–36. 2. anything thought of as like this; any needed sustenance that seems miraculously supplied, comforting words, spiritual food, etc. 3. a sweet, gummy juice obtained from certain European ash trees, used as a laxative.

Mann Act (man), [after James Robert *Mann* (1856–1922), U.S. Congressman], an act of Congress (June, 1910) prohibiting the interstate transportation of women for immoral purposes (*white slavery*).

man·ne·quin (man'ə-kin), *n.* [Fr. < D. *manneken;* see MANIKIN], 1. a model of the human body, used by tailors, window dressers, artists, etc. 2. a woman whose work is exhibiting new clothes in stores, etc. by wearing them.

man·ner (man'ẽr), *n.* [ME. *manere;* OFr. *maniere;* LL. **manaria* < L. *manuarius*, of the hand < *manus*, a hand], 1. a way or method of doing something; way in which something is done or happens; mode or fashion of procedure. 2. *a)* a way of acting; personal behavior or bearing: as, his *manner* showed his anger. *b)* distinguished bearing or behavior: as, she has *manner.* 3. a usual way of acting; customary behavior; habit: as, it is his *manner* to be sarcastic. 4. *pl. a)* ways of social life; prevailing social conditions or customs: as, a comedy of *manners. b)* ways of social behavior; deportment, especially with reference to polite conventions: as, good *manners*, bad *manners. c)* polite ways of social behavior; deportment conforming with polite conventions: as, the child really has *manners.* 5. *a)* characteristic style or method in art, music, literature, etc. *b)* mannerism. 6. [Archaic or Literary], *a)* kind; sort: as, what *manner* of man is he? *b)* kinds; sorts: as, all *manner* of things. —***SYN.*** see **bearing, method.**

by all manner of means, of course; surely.

by no manner of means, in no way; definitely not.

in a manner of speaking, so to speak; in a certain sense or way.

to the manner born, 1. accustomed from birth to the way or usage spoken of. 2. naturally fitted for a certain thing.

man·nered (man'ẽrd), *adj.* 1. having manners of a specified sort: as, ill-*mannered*, well-*mannered.* 2. affected: as, a *mannered* literary style.

Man·ner·heim, Baron **Carl Gus·taf E·mil von** (kärl goos'tȧf e'mil fon mȧn'ẽr-hām'; Eng. man'ẽr-hīm'), 1867–1951; Finnish field marshal and statesman.

man·ner·ism (man'ẽr-iz'm), *n.* 1. excessive use of some distinctive, often affected, manner or style in art, literature, speech, or behavior. 2. a peculiarity of manner in behavior, speech, etc. —***SYN.*** see **pose.**

man·ner·ist (man'ẽr-ist), *n.* a person characterized by mannerism; especially, an artist or writer whose work shows a persistent or excessive adherence to some style or method.

man·ner·less (man'ẽr-lis), *adj.* lacking good manners; impolite; unmannerly.

man·ner·li·ness (man'ẽr-li-nis), *n.* the quality or state of being mannerly.

man·ner·ly (man'ẽr-li), *adj.* having or showing good manners; well-behaved; polite. *adv.* politely.

Mann·heim (man'hīm; G. män'hīm), *n.* a city in southwestern Germany, on the Rhine: pop., 300,000.

man·ni·kin (man'ə-kin), *n.* a manikin.

man·nish (man'ish), *adj.* characteristic of, of, like, or imitating a man; masculine. —***SYN.*** see **male.**

man·nite (man'īt), *n.* [< *manna* + *-ite*], mannitol.

man·nit·ic (mə-nit'ik), *adj.* of or obtained from mannitol.

man·ni·tol (man'ə-tōl', man'ə-tol'), *n.* [< *mannite* + *-ol*], a colorless, crystalline alcohol, $C_6H_8(OH)_6$, occurring in various plants and animals, as the flowering ash, sponges, etc.

man·nose (man'ōs), *n.* [*manni*tol + *-ose*], a sugar, $C_6H_{12}O_6$, formed by the oxidation of mannitol.

ma·noeu·vre (mə-nōō'vẽr, mə-nū'vẽr), *n., v.i. & v.t.* [MANOEUVRED (-vẽrd), MANOEUVRING], maneuver.

Man of Destiny, Napoleon I: self-applied term.

Man of Galilee, Jesus.

man of God, 1. a holy man; saint, hermit, etc. 2. a clergyman; minister, priest, rabbi, etc.

Man of Sorrows, Jesus: cf. Isa. 53:3.

man of the world, a man familiar with and tolerant of various sorts of people and their ways; sophisticate.

man-of-war (man'əv-wôr', man'ə-wôr'), *n.* [*pl.* MEN-OF-WAR (men'əv-wôr', men'ə-wôr')], [see MAN, *n.*, 10], an armed naval vessel; warship.

man-of-war bird (or **hawk**), a frigate bird.

ma·nom·e·ter (mə-nom'ə-tẽr), *n.* [Fr. *manomètre* < Gr. *manos*, rare + Fr. *-mètre*, -meter], 1. an instrument, usually a U-shaped tube, for measuring the pressure of gases or vapors. 2. an instrument for measuring blood pressure by measuring the pressure of compressed air necessary to equalize the tension in the blood vessels.

man on horseback, a military man with such influence and power over the people as to threaten the current regime or administration.

man·or (man′ẽr), *n.* [ME. *maner;* OFr. *manoir* < *manoir, maneir,* to stay, dwell < L. *manere,* to remain], 1. in England, *a*) in feudal times, the district over which a lord held authority, subject to the jurisdiction of his court; land belonging to a lord and partly divided among his peasants in return for rent of some kind, or land reserved by him for his own use. *b*) more recently, a landed estate, usually with a main residence, the owner of which still holds some feudal rights over the land. 2. in the United States during colonial times, a district granted as a manor and leased to tenants at a set rental. 3. [Obs.], *a*) a mansion. *b*) the main residence on an estate. *c*) a lord's mansion with its land.

manor house, the house of the lord of a manor.

ma·no·ri·al (mə-nôr′i-əl, ma-nō′ri-əl), *adj.* of, like, or constituting a manor.

man·pow·er (man′pou′ẽr), *n.* 1. power furnished by human physical strength. 2. the normal rate at which a man is able to work, equal to 1/10 horsepower. 3. the collective strength or availability for work of the people in any given area, nation, etc. Also **man power.**

‡**man·qué** (män′kā′), *adj.* [Fr. < pp. of *manquer,* to fail; be lacking], that has failed or falls short of the goal; defective: placed after the noun it modifies, as, a poet *manqué.*

man·rope (man′rōp′), *n.* a rope serving as a handrail along a gangway, ladder, etc.

man·sard (man′särd), *n.* [after François *Mansard* (1598–1666), Fr. architect, who revived the use of such roofs: they had been in use about 100 years earlier], 1. a roof with two slopes on each of the four sides, the lower steeper than the upper: also **mansard roof.** 2. a garret; attic; story under such a roof.

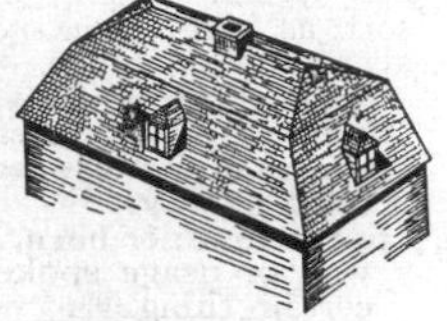
MANSARD ROOF

manse (mans), *n.* [ML. *mansus* (or *mansum, mansa*), a dwelling < pp. of L. *manere,* to remain, dwell; cf. MANOR], 1. a parsonage; residence of a minister, especially a Scottish Presbyterian minister. 2. [Obs.], *a*) a mansion. *b*) enough land to support a family.

man·ser·vant (man′sũr′vənt), *n.* [*pl.* MENSERVANTS (men′sũr′vənts)], a male servant: also **man servant.**

Mans·field (manz′fēld′, mans′fēld′), *n.* 1. a city in north central Ohio: pop., 47,000. 2. a city in Nottinghamshire, England: pop., 53,000. 3. the highest peak of the Green Mountains, in northern Vermont: height, 4,393 ft.: in full, **Mount Mansfield.**

Mans·field, Katherine (mans′fēld′, manz′fēld′), (pseudonym of *Kathleen Beauchamp, Mrs. John Middleton Murry*), 1888–1923; English short-story writer.

Mansfield, Richard, 1857–1907; English actor in America.

man·sion (man′shən), *n.* [ME.; OFr.; L. *mansio,* a sojourn, dwelling < pp. of *manere,* to remain, dwell; cf. MANSE, MANOR], 1. formerly, a manor house; hence, 2. a large, imposing house; stately residence. 3. [Obs.], a stay; sojourn. 4. [Archaic], *a*) a dwelling place. *b*) *usually pl.* [Chiefly British], an apartment house. 5. in *astrology, a*) a house. *b*) one of the 28 parts of the moon's course occupied on successive days.

man-sized (man′sīzd′), *adj.* [Colloq.], of a size fit for a man; large; big.

man·slaugh·ter (man′slô′tẽr), *n.* the killing of a human being by another; especially, such killing when unlawful but without malice: see also **murder, homicide.**

man·slay·er (man′slā′ẽr), *n.* a person who commits homicide or manslaughter.

man·sue·tude (man′swi-tood′, man′swi-tūd′), *n.* [L. *mansuetudo* < pp. of *mansuescere,* to tame < *manus,* a hand + *suescere,* to accustom], gentleness; tameness.

man·ta (man′tə; Sp. män′tä), *n.* [Sp. < LL. *mantum,* a cloak; back-formation < *mantellum;* see MANTLE], 1. coarse cotton cloth used for cheap shawls, capes, etc. in Latin America. 2. a shawl, cape, etc. made of this. 3. a kind of horse blanket or cloth for covering a pack-animal's load. 4. [Obs.], a mantelet. 5. in *zoology,* a very large ray; devilfish: also **manta ray.**

man·teau (man′tō; Fr. män′tō′), *n.* [*pl.* MANTEAUS (-tōz), Fr. MANTEAUX (-tō′)], [Fr. < OFr. *mantel;* see MANTLE], 1. *a*) a woman's cloak or mantle. *b*) any mantle. 2. [Obs.], a mantua, or woman's loose gown.

Man·te·gna, An·dre·a (än-dre′ä män-te′nyä), 1431–1506; Italian painter and engraver.

man·tel (man′t'l), *n.* [see MANTLE], 1. the facing of stone, marble, etc. about a fireplace, including a projecting shelf or slab above it. 2. the shelf or slab.

man·tel·et (man′t'l-et′, mant′lit), *n.* [OFr., dim. of *mantel;* see MANTLE], 1. a short mantle, cape, or cloak. 2. a movable or stationary protective shelter or screen; especially, *a*) a movable roof or screen formerly used in war to protect besiegers from the enemy. *b*) a bulletproof shield or screen, as about a gun to protect the gun crew. *c*) a bulletproof enclosure for observation in target shooting. Also (for 2) **mantlet.**

Man·tell, Robert Bruce (man-tel′), 1854–1928; Scottish actor in America.

man·tel·let·ta (man′tə-let′ə), *n.* [It., dim < *mantello;* see MANTLE], a sleeveless vestment worn by cardinals, bishops, etc. of the Roman Catholic Church.

man·tel·piece (man′t'l-pēs′), *n.* a mantel (sense 2).

man·tel·tree (man′t'l-trē′), *n.* 1. a beam, stone, or arch above the opening of a fireplace, supporting the masonry above. 2. [Archaic], a mantelpiece.

man·tic (man′tik), *adj.* [Gr. *mantikos* < *mantis,* seer, soothsayer; see MANTIS], of, or having powers of, divination; prophetic.

-man·tic (man′tik), [< Gr. *mantikos;* see MANTIC], a combining form used to form adjectives corresponding to nouns ending in *-mancy,* as in *necromantic.*

man·til·la (man-til′ə), *n.* [Sp., dim. of *manta;* see MANTA], 1. a woman's veil or scarf worn over the hair and shoulders, as in Spain, Mexico, etc. 2. a short mantle, cape, or cloak.

MANTILLA

man·tis (man′tis), *n.* [*pl.* MANTISES (-iz), MANTES (-tēz)], [Mod. L.; Gr. *mantis,* prophet, seer, kind of insect; IE. base **men-,* to think; see MAN], any of various related insects that hold their forelegs folded as if praying, and feed on other insects: often **praying mantis.**

mantis crab (or **shrimp**), a squilla.

man·tis·sa (man-tis′ə), *n.* [L., (useless) addition, makeweight; ? < Etruscan], the decimal part of a logarithm: so called because added to the integral part (called the *characteristic*).

MANTIS (2.5–3 in. long)

man·tle (man′t'l), *n.* [ME. *mantel, mentel* < AS. *mentel* & OFr. *mantel;* both < L. *mantellum, mantelum,* a cloth, napkin, cloak, mantle; origin obscure], 1. a loose, sleeveless cloak or cape; hence, 2. anything that cloaks, envelops, covers, or conceals: as, hidden under the *mantle* of night. 3. a small hood or cap, usually cylindrical, of a meshwork substance, such as a thorium or cerium compound, which when placed over a flame becomes white-hot and gives off light. 4. the outer covering of a wall. 5. the outer wall and casing of a blast furnace, above the hearth. 6. a covering of clay put over a wax model so as to form a mold when the wax is melted out. 7. a mantel. 8. in *anatomy,* the cortex of the cerebrum. 9. in *geology,* the soil, sand, and other loose material covering the solid bedrock of the earth. 10. in *zoology, a*) the membranous flap or folds of the body wall of a mollusk or similar organism, containing glands that secrete a shell-forming fluid. *b*) the soft outer body wall of a tunicate or barnacle. *c*) the back and folded wings of a bird. ***v.t.*** [MANTLED (-t'ld), MANTLING], 1. to cover with a mantle. 2. to cover; envelop; cloak; conceal. ***v.i.*** 1. to be or become covered, as a surface with scum or froth. 2. to form a covering; spread like a mantle, as a blush over the face. 3. to blush or flush: as, her cheeks *mantled* at the praise. 4. in *falconry, a*) to spread first one wing, then the other, over the outstretched legs: said of a perched hawk. *b*) to spread out: said of the wings.

mant·let (mant′lit), *n.* a mantelet.

Man·to·va (män′tô-vä′), *n.* Mantua: the Italian name.

Man·tu·a (man′choo-ə, man′too-ə), *n.* a city in northern Italy: birthplace of Virgil: pop., 54,000.

man·tu·a (man′choo-ə, man′too-ə), *n.* [altered < Fr. *manteau,* a mantle; sp. influenced by *Mantua,* Italy], a mantle or loose gown or cloak formerly worn by women.

Man·tu·an (man′choo-ən, man′too-ən), *adj.* of Mantua. *n.* a native or inhabitant of Mantua.
the Mantuan, Virgil.

man·u·al (man′ū-əl), *adj.* [ME. & OFr. *manuel;* L. *manualis* < *manus,* a hand; IE. **mə-n-és,* a hand; akin to **mn̥tos,* seen in ON. & AS. *mund,* a hand, etc.], 1. of a hand or the hands; made, done, worked, or used by the hands. 2. of the nature of a manual, or handbook. 3. in *law,* in actual possession. *n.* 1. a handy book for use as a guide, reference, etc.; handbook. 2. a hand-operated keyboard on an organ. 3. prescribed drill in the handling of a weapon, especially a rifle: also **manual of arms.** Abbreviated **man., M., m.**

man·u·al·ly (man′ū-ə-li), *adv.* 1. with the hand or hands; by hand. 2. as regards work with the hands.

manual training, training in woodwork, sewing, metalworking, and similar arts and crafts, as in a school.

ma·nu·bri·um (mə-noo′bri-əm, mə-nū′bri-əm), *n.* [*pl.* MANUBRIA (-ə), MANUBRIUMS (-əmz)], [L., a handle, hilt, haft < *manus*, a hand], a handlelike structure, process, or part; especially, the uppermost of the three bony segments constituting the sternum, or breastbone.

Man·u·el (man'ū-əl, man'ū-el'), a masculine name: see **Emmanuel.**

manuf., manufac., 1. manufacture. 2. manufacturer. 3. manufacturing.

man·u·fac·to·ry (man'yoo-fak'tẽr-i), *n.* [*pl.* MANUFACTORIES (-iz)], [< *manufacture*, after *factory*], a factory.

man·u·fac·ture (man'yoo-fak'chẽr), *n.* [Fr.; ML. *manufactura;* L. *manu*, abl. of *manus*, a hand + L. *factura*, a making < *factus*, pp. of *facere*, to make], 1. the making of goods and articles by hand or, especially, by machinery, often on a large scale and with division of labor. 2. anything so made; manufactured product. 3. the making of something in any way, especially when regarded as merely mechanical. *v.t.* [MANUFACTURED (-chẽrd), MANUFACTURING], 1. to make by hand or, especially, by machinery, often on a large scale and with division of labor. 2. to work (wool, steel, etc.) into usable form. 3. to produce (art, literature, etc.) in a way regarded as mechanical. 4. to make up (excuses, evidence, etc.); invent; fabricate; concoct. Abbreviated **mfr., manuf., manufac.** —*SYN.* see **make.**

man·u·fac·tur·er (man'yoo-fak'chẽr-ẽr), *n.* a person in the business of manufacturing; especially, a factory owner: abbreviated **mfr., manuf., manufac.**

man·u·mis·sion (man'yoo-mish'ən), *n.* [L. *manumissio* < pp. of *manumittere;* see MANUMIT], a freeing or being freed from slavery; liberation; emancipation.

man·u·mit (man'yoo-mit'), *v.t.* [MANUMITTED (-id), MANUMITTING], [L. *manumittere*, lit., to let go from the hand, free; *manu*, abl. of *manus*, a hand + *mittere*, to send], to free from slavery; liberate (a slave, serf, etc.).

ma·nure (mə-nyoor', mə-noor'), *v.t.* [MANURED (-nyoord', -noord'), MANURING], [ME. *manouren*, orig., to farm (land); Anglo-Fr. *maynoberer;* OFr. *manouvrer*, to cultivate, lit. to work with the hands; see MANEUVER], to put manure on or into; fertilize (soil). *n.* [< the *v.*], animal excrement or other substance put on or into the soil to fertilize it.

ma·nus (mā'nəs), *n.* [*pl.* MANUS], [L.], 1. the terminal part of the forelimb of a vertebrate, as the hand of a person or the forefoot of a four-legged animal. 2. in *Roman law*, the authority of a husband over his wife.

man·u·script (man'yoo-skript'), *adj.* [L. *manu scriptus*, written by hand; *manu*, abl. of *manus*, a hand + *scriptus*, pp. of *scribere*, to write], written by hand or with a typewriter, not printed. *n.* [ML. *manuscriptum* < L. *manu scriptus*], 1. a book or document written by hand, especially before the invention of printing: see **codex.** 2. a written or typewritten document or paper, especially an author's copy of his work, as submitted to an editor or publisher. Abbreviated **Ms., ms.**

Ma·nu·ti·us, Al·dus (ôl'dəs *or* al'dəs mə-nū'shi-əs), (born *Teobaldo Mannucci*), 1450–1515; Italian printer; inventor of italic type: cf. **Aldine.**

man·ward (man'wẽrd), *adj. & adv.* toward man; in relation to man.

man·wards (man'wẽrdz), *adv.* manward.

man·wise (man'wīz'), *adv.* [see -WISE], as a man would do; like a man.

Manx (maŋks), *adj.* [for *Mansk* < ON. *manskr* < *Man-*, inflectional base of *Mǫn*, Isle of Man < Celtic name; cf. MW. *Manau*, OIr. *Manu*], of the Isle of Man, its people, or their language. *n.* the Gaelic language spoken on the Isle of Man, now almost extinct.

the Manx, the people of the Isle of Man.

manx cat, Manx cat, a variety of domestic cat with a rudimentary tail.

Manx·man (maŋks'mən), *n.* [*pl.* MANXMEN (-mən)], a native or inhabitant of the Isle of Man.

man·y (men'i), *adj.* [MORE (môr, mōr), MOST (mōst)], [ME. *meni, mani, moni;* AS. *manig, mænig, monig;* akin to G. *manch* (OHG. *manag*); IE. base **menegh-*, etc., many, richly, seen also in Sans. *maghā-*, gift], 1. consisting of some large, indefinite number (of persons or things); numerous. 2. relatively numerous (preceded by *as, too*, etc.). *n.* a large number (of persons or things). *pron.* many persons or things. *Many a* (or *an, another*) followed by a singular noun or pronoun is equivalent to *many* followed by the corresponding plural (e.g., many a man has tried).

a good many, [construed as pl.], a relatively large number (of persons or things).

a great many, [construed as pl.], an extremely large number (of persons or things).

be one too many for, to defeat; overwhelm.

the many, 1. the majority of people. 2. the people; the multitude; the masses.

SYN.—**many** is the simple, common word implying a relatively large number of units (*many* children, excuses, bacteria, etc.); **numerous,** a more formal equivalent for **many,** sometimes connotes a crowding of one unit upon another (*numerous* complaints have come in); **manifold** adds the connotation of great variety (*manifold* problems) or, in modifying a singular noun, great complexity in the component parts of the whole (her *manifold* sorrow); **multifarious** adds the connotation of great diversity, or even incongruity, in the variety (*multifarious* interests); **innumerable** implies a number too great to count and is often used hyperbolically (*innumerable* instances of his kindness).—*ANT.* few.

man·y·plies (men'i-plīz'), *n.* [*many, adj.* + pl. of *ply* (a fold)], the third stomach of a cud-chewing animal; omasum.

man·y-sid·ed (men'i-sīd'id), *adj.* 1. having many sides or faces. 2. having many possibilities, qualities, interests, or accomplishments: as, a *many-sided* woman.

Man·za·nil·lo (män'sä-nē'yô), *n.* a seaport in southern Cuba: pop., 36,000.

man·za·ni·ta (man'zə-nē'tə), *n.* [Sp., dim. of *manzana*, apple; see MANCHINEEL], any of several evergreen shrubs or small trees of the western United States.

Man·zo·ni, A·les·san·dro (ä'les-sän'drô män-dzô'nē), 1785–1873; Italian poet and novelist.

Ma·o·ri (mä'ō-ri, mou'ri), *n.* [< Maori; said to mean "native, of the usual kind"], 1. [*pl.* MAORIS (-riz)], a member of a brown-skinned people native to New Zealand, of Polynesian origin. 2. their Polynesian language. *adj.* of the Maoris, their language, etc.

Mao Tse-tung (mä'ō dzu'dooŋ'), 1893– ; Chinese Communist leader; chairman of Chinese People's Republic (1949–1959).

map (map), *n.* [OFr. *mappe*, in *mappemonde;* ML. *mappa (mundi)*, map (of the world); L. *mappa*, napkin, cloth (on which maps were painted)], 1. a drawing or other representation, usually on a flat surface, of all or part of the earth's surface, ordinarily showing countries, bodies of water, cities, mountains, etc. 2. a similar representation of part of the sky, showing the relative position of the stars, planets, etc. 3. any maplike representation or delineation. 4. [Slang], the face. *v.t.* [MAPPED (mapt), MAPPING], 1. to make a map or maps of; represent or chart on or as on a map. 2. to arrange or plan in detail (often with *out*): as, he *mapped* out his working time. 3. to survey or explore for the purpose of making a map.

put on the map, [Colloq.], to make well known.

Map, Walter (map), 1140?–1209?; Welsh writer.

Mapes, Walter (māps, mā'pēz,) Walter Map: Latinized name.

ma·ple (mā'p'l), *n.* [ME. *mapil;* AS. *mapel (treow)*, maple (tree)], 1. any of a large group of trees with dry, two-winged fruits and opposite leaves, grown for wood, sap, or shade. 2. the hard, close-grained, light-colored wood of such a tree, used for furniture, flooring, etc. 3. the reddish-yellow or yellowish color of the finished wood. 4. the flavor of maple sirup or of the sugar made from this. *adj.* 1. of or made of maple. 2. flavored with maple.

maple sirup, sirup made by boiling down the sap of a certain variety of maple.

maple sugar, sugar made by boiling down maple sirup.

ma·qui (mä'kē), *n.* [Sp. < Chilean (Araucan) name], an ornamental evergreen shrub of Chile: its bark gives a fiber used for stringing native musical instruments, and its purple berries are made into a medicinal wine.

ma·quis (mä-kē'; *also, for 2,* Fr. må'kē'), *n.* [Fr. < It. *macchia*, a thicket, orig. a spot < L. *macula*, a spot, stain], 1. a zone of shrubby plants, chiefly evergreens, growing in the area around the Mediterranean, known as a hiding place for fugitives, guerrilla fighters, etc.; hence, 2. [often M-], [*pl.* MAQUIS (-kē')], a French guerrilla fighter against the Nazis in World War II; member of the military branch of the French underground movement (French Forces of the Interior).

mar (mär), *v.t.* [MARRED (märd), MARRING], [ME. *merren, marren;* AS. *merran, mierran*, to hinder, spoil, impair; akin to D. *marren*, to tie up; IE. base **mer-*, to rub, rub off, seen also in L. *mortarium*, mortar (cf. MORTAR), Eng. *marble*], to injure or damage so as to make imperfect, less attractive, etc.; spoil; impair; disfigure. *n.* something that mars; an injury or blemish.

Mar., March.

mar., 1. marine. 2. maritime. 3. married.

mar·a·bou (mar'ə-bōō'), *n.* [Fr.; Port. *marabute;* Ar. *murābit*, hermit], 1. any of several large storks, especially one of a kind found in Africa. 2. the adjutant, a bird of India. 3. soft feathers from the wing coverts and tail of the marabou, used in millinery. 4. a delicate, white raw silk that can be dyed even though the natural gum has not been taken out.

mar·a·bout (mar'ə-bōōt'), *n.* [Fr.; Port. *marabuto;* Ar. *murābit*, hermit], 1. a Moslem hermit or holy man, especially among the Berbers and Moors. 2. the tomb or shrine of such a man. 3. marabou.

ma·ra·ca (mə-rä'kə; Port. mä-rä'kä), *n.* [Port. *maracá* < the Braz. native name], a percussion instrument consisting of a dried gourd or a gourd-shaped rattle with loose pebbles in it.

Mar·a·cai·bo (mar'ə-kī'bō; Sp. mär'ä-kī'bô), *n.* 1. a seaport in western Venezuela: pop., 236,000. 2. a lake formed by an extension of the Gulf of Maracaibo: area, 6,300 sq. mi.

Maracaibo, Gulf of, an arm of the Caribbean, off western Venezuela.

Mar·a·can·da (mar'ə-kan'də), *n.* Samarkand, a city in central Asia: the ancient name.

Ma·ra·jó (mä-rä-zhô'), *n.* an island between the estuaries of the Amazon and Pará Rivers, Brazil: area, 16,000 sq. mi.

mar·a·nath·a (mar'ə-nath'ə), *n.* [ME. < Aram. *māran atha*, the Lord has come, or O Lord, come], an invocation to the Lord, sometimes regarded as forming, with the preceding ***anathema*** (in I Cor. 16:22), an intensified curse or malediction.

Ma·ra·ñón (mä'rä-nyôn'), *n.* a river in Peru that joins the Ucayali to form the Amazon: sometimes called the *Upper Amazon*: length, 750 mi.

ma·ras·ca (mə-ras'kə), *n.* [It.; see MARASCHINO], a wild cherry from which maraschino is made: the fruit is small, black, and bitter.

mar·a·schi·no (mar'ə-skē'nō), *n.* [It. < *marasca, amarasca*, kind of cherry < *amaro* (L. *amarus*), bitter], a strong, sweet liqueur or cordial made from the fermented juice of the marasca.

maraschino cherries, cherries in a sirup flavored with maraschino.

ma·ras·mic (mə-raz'mik), *adj.* of or having marasmus.

ma·ras·mus (mə-raz'məs), *n.* [Mod. L.; Gr. *marasmos*, a wasting away < *marainein*, to put out, quench, cause to waste away], a condition of progressive emaciation, especially in children; wasting away of the body.

Ma·rat, Jean Paul (zhän pôl mà'rà'), 1743–1793; one of the leaders of the French Revolution; assassinated by Charlotte Corday.

Ma·ra·tha (mə-rä'tə), *n.* [Marathi *Marathā* (Hind. *Marhaṭā*); Sans. *Mahārāṣṭra*, lit., great country], a member of a people of Bombay state, in south central India: also **Mahratta.**

Ma·ra·thi (mə-rä'ti, mə-rat'i), *n.* the Indic language of the Marathas: also **Mahratti.**

Mar·a·thon (mar'ə-thon'), *n.* 1. an ancient Greek village on the eastern coast of Attica. 2. a plain near by: site of a battle (490 B.C.), in which the Athenians under Miltiades defeated the Persians under Darius.

mar·a·thon (mar'ə-thon', mar'ə-thən), *n.* 1. a foot race of 26 miles, 385 yards, run over an open course: so called in allusion to the story of the Greek runner who went from Marathon to Athens to tell of the victory over the Persians (490 B.C.), and then dropped dead. 2. any long-distance or endurance contest: as, a dance *marathon.*

ma·raud (mə-rôd'), *v.i.* [Fr. *marauder* < *maraud*, vagabond; OFr. *marault*; prob. < pers. name *Marault* < OHG. *Mari-wald*, lit., fame-wielder], to rove in search of plunder; make raids. *v.t.* to raid; plunder; pillage. *n.* a marauding; raid; foray.

mar·a·ve·di (mar'ə-vā'di), *n.* [Sp. < Ar. *Murābiṭīn*, name of a Moorish dynasty at Córdoba (1086–1147) < *murābiṭ*; see MARABOUT], 1. a gold coin used by the Moors in Spain in the 11th and 12th centuries. 2. an obsolete Spanish copper coin worth about 1/3 cent.

mar·ble (mär'b'l), *n.* [ME. & OFr. *marble, marbre* < L. *marmor*; Gr. *marmaros*, white glistening stone, orig. stone, boulder, hard object (meaning affected by association with *marmairein*, to shine); IE. base **mer-*, to rub; cf. MAR], 1. a hard, crystalline or granular, metamorphic limestone, white or variously colored and sometimes streaked or mottled, which can take a high polish: it is much used in building and sculpture. 2. a piece or slab of this stone, used as a monument, inscribed record, etc. 3. anything resembling or suggesting marble in hardness, smoothness, coldness, coloration, etc. 4. a little ball of stone, glass, or clay, used in games. 5. *pl. a*) [construed as sing.], a children's game in which a marble is propelled by the thumb to hit other marbles, usually to drive them out of a marked circle. *b*) a group of sculptures in marble. 6. a marbled pattern; marbling. *adj.* 1. made or consisting of marble. 2. like marble in some way; hard, cold, smooth, white, etc., or streaked, mottled, etc. *v.t.* [MARBLED (-b'ld), MARBLING], to make (paper, book edges, etc.) look mottled or streaked like marble.

marble cake, a cake made of light and dark batter mixed to give a streaked, marblelike appearance.

Mar·ble·head (mär'b'l-hed'), *n.* a resort town on the coast of Massachusetts: pop., 19,000.

mar·ble·ize (mär'b'l-īz'), *v.t.* [MARBLEIZED (-īzd'), MARBLEIZING], to make, color, grain, or streak in imitation of marble.

mar·bling (mär'bliŋ), *n.* 1. the art or process of staining or veining like marble. 2. a streaked, veined, or mottled appearance like that of marble. 3. in *bookbinding*, the decoration of paper, book edges, etc. in marblelike patterns.

mar·bly (mär'bli), *adj.* like marble; cold, hard, etc.

Mar·burg (mär'bûrg; G. mär'boorkh), *n.* a city in western Germany: pop., 40,000.

marc (märk; Fr. màr), *n.* [Fr.; prob. < *marcher*, to tread, trample, march, press, etc.; see MARCH (to walk)], 1. refuse of grapes, seeds, fruits, etc. after pressing. 2. a brandy distilled from this. 3. any insoluble matter left after treating a substance with a solvent.

Marc An·to·ny (märk an'tə-ni), see **Antonius, Marcus.**

mar·ca·site (mär'kə-sīt'), *n.* [Fr. *marcassite*; ML. *marcasita*; Ar. *marqashīṭā*], 1. formerly, crystallized iron pyrites, used in the 18th century for ornaments. 2. a piece of this, especially as an ornament. 3. iron disulfide, FeS_2, a mineral resembling iron pyrites.

Mar·cel (mär-sel'), a masculine name: see **Marcellus.**

mar·cel (mär-sel'), *n.* [after M. *Marcel*, 19th-c. Fr. hairdresser], a series of even waves or tiers put in the hair: also **marcel wave.** *v.t.* [MARCELLED (-seld'), MARCELLING], to put such waves in (hair).

Mar·cel·la (mär-sel'ə), [L.], a feminine name: see **Marcellus.**

Mar·cel·lus (mär-sel'əs), [L., dim. of *Marcus*], a masculine name: variant, *Marcel*; feminine, *Marcella*. *n.* (*Marcus Claudius Marcellus*), Roman general and statesman; lived 268?–208 B.C.

mar·ces·cent (mär-ses''nt), *adj.* [L. *marcescens*, ppr. of *marcescere*, to wither, decay < *marcere*, to wither], in *botany*, withering but not falling off. *n.* a plant with marcescent parts.

March (märch), *n.* [ME.; OFr. *march, marz*; L. *Martius* (*mensis*), (month) of Mars < ***Mars***, Mars], the third month of the year, having 31 days: abbreviated **Mar.**

March (märH), *n.* the Morava River, in Czechoslovakia: the German name.

march (märch), *v.i.* [Fr. *marcher* (cf. MARC) < LL. **marcare*, to trample < L. *marcus*, a hammer], 1. to walk with regular, steady steps of equal length, usually in a group or military formation. 2. to walk in a grave, stately way. 3. to go or advance steadily; progress or proceed regularly. *v.t.* 1. to cause (troops, etc.) to march. 2. to cause or force to go. *n.* 1. a marching. 2. a regular forward movement; steady advance; progress: as, the ***march*** of events. 3. a regular, steady step or pace. 4. the distance covered in a period of marching: as, a day's ***march.*** 5. a long, tiring walk. 6. a piece of music for marching.

on the march, marching.

steal a march on, to get an advantage over without being perceived.

march (märch), *n.* [ME. & Late OFr. *marche* < Gmc. base of *mark* (OHG. *marca*, etc.)], 1. a boundary, border, or frontier, as of a country. 2. a borderland, especially one disputed between countries. *v.i.* [Rare], to border.

the Marches, 1. the borderlands between England and Scotland, or between England and Wales. 2. Le Marche: the English name.

March., Marchioness.

Mar·che, Le (le mär'ke), a former department of central Italy, on the Adriatic.

‡Mär·chen (mâr'Hən), *n.* [*pl.* MÄRCHEN], [G.], a story; tale; especially, a fairy tale or folk tale.

march·er (mär'chẽr), *n.* a person who marches, or walks with regular, steady steps.

march·er (mär'chẽr), *n.* 1. a person who lives in a march, or borderland. 2. an officer governing or defending a border or borderland.

‡mar·che·sa (mär-ke'zä), *n.* [*pl.* MARCHESE (-ze)], [It.], the wife or widow of a marchese; Italian marchioness.

‡mar·che·se (mär-ke'ze), *n.* [*pl.* MARCHESI (-zē)], [It.; see MARQUIS], an Italian nobleman ranking just above a count and just below a prince; marquis.

Mar·chesh·van (mär-khesh'vən), *n.* [Heb.], Cheshvan: see **Jewish calendar.**

March hare, a hare in breeding time, proverbially regarded as an example of madness.

marching orders, orders to march, go, or leave.

mar·chion·ess (mär'shən-is, mär'shə-nes'), *n.* [ML. *marchionissa, marcionissa*, fem. of *marchio*, prefect of the marches; see MARCH (border)], 1. the wife or widow of a marquis. 2. a lady whose rank in her own right equals that of a marquis. Abbreviated **March.** See also **marquise.**

march·land (märch'land'), *n.* [*march* (border) + *land*], borderland.

march·pane (märch'pān'), *n.* [It. *marzapane*, marchpane, confection; earlier, the small box containing it, small dry measure, certain weight < ML. *matapanus*, Venetian coin with the figure of Christ seated on a throne, one tenth < Ar. *mauthaban*, seated king, coin (< *wathaba*, to sit); G. *marzipan* is < the It.], a confection of ground almonds, sugar, and egg white made into a paste and variously shaped: also **marzipan.**

Mar·cia (mär'shə), [L., fem. of *Marcius*, name of a Roman gens < *Marcus*; see MARCUS], a feminine name.

Mar·co·ni, Gu·gliel·mo (gōō-lyel'mō mär-kô'nē; Eng. mär-kō'ni), Marchese, 1874–1937; Italian physicist; known for his development of wireless telegraphy; received Nobel prize in physics, 1909.

mar·co·ni·gram (mär-kō'ni-gram'), *n.* a message sent by wireless telegraphy; radiogram: formerly so called.

Marco Polo, see **Polo, Marco.**

Mar·cus (mär′kəs), [L. < *Mars*], a masculine name: variant, *Mark;* feminine, *Marcia.*

Mar·cus Au·re·li·us (mär′kəs ô-rē′li-əs), (*Marcus Aurelius Antoninus*), 121–180 A.D.; Roman statesman and Stoic philosopher; emperor of Rome (161–180 A.D.).

Mar·cy, Mount (mär′si), a mountain of the Adirondacks, in northern New York: height, 5,344 ft.

Mar·di gras (mär′di grä′), [Fr., lit., fat Tuesday], Shrove Tuesday, the last day before Lent: it is a day of merrymaking and carnival in New Orleans, Paris, and some other cities.

Mar·duk (mär′dook), *n.* [Bab.], the chief god of the ancient Babylonian religion, originally a local sun god.

mare (mâr), *n.* [ME. *mare, mere;* AS. *mere*, fem. of *mearh;* akin to G. *mähre*, jade; inferred IE. base **marko-*, horse, seen otherwise only in Celt. (Ir. *marc*, W. *march*, horse, etc.)], a female horse, mule, donkey, burro, etc.

ma·re (mâr′i), *n.* [*pl.* MARIA (mâr′i-ə)], [L., sea; akin to Goth. *marei*, sea, AS. *mere*, sea, lake; see MERE (lake)], 1. a sea. 2. a dark area on the moon's surface, formerly supposed to be a sea.

mare (mâr), *n.* [ME.; AS.; akin to G. dial. *mahr*, ON. *mar*, etc.; for IE. base see MAR; OFr. *mare*, seen in Fr. *cauchemar*, nightmare, is < Gmc.], [Obs.], the spirit or goblin formerly believed to produce nightmares.

‡ma·re clau·sum (mâr′i klô′səm), [L., closed sea], a sea under the jurisdiction of a single nation and not open to all others.

Mare Island (mâr), an island in San Pablo Bay, northern California: site of a U. S. navy yard and arsenal.

‡ma·re li·be·rum (mâr′i li′bĕr-əm), [L., free sea], a sea open to all nations.

ma·rem·ma (mə-rem′ə), *n.* [*pl.* MAREMME (mə-rem′i)], [It. < L. *maritimus;* see MARITIME], low, unhealthy, but fertile marshy land near the sea, especially in Italy.

Ma·ren·go (mə-reŋ′gō), *n.* a village in Piedmont, northwestern Italy, where Napoleon's army defeated the Austrians in 1800.

‡ma·re nos·trum (mâr′i nos′trəm), [L.], our sea: Roman name for the Mediterranean.

mare's-nest (mârz′nest′), *n.* something supposed to be a wonderful discovery but turning out to be a hoax or a delusion: earlier called *horse-nest.*

mare's-tail (mârz′tāl′), *n.* 1. long, narrow formations of cirrus cloud somewhat like a horse's tail in shape, supposed to be a sign of bad weather. 2. a water plant with tiny flowers and narrow, hairlike leaves growing in thick whorls around the slender, erect stems. 3. the horsetail, a plant with jointed, hollow stems.

marg., 1. margin. 2. marginal.

Mar·ga·ret (mär′grit, mär′gə-rit), [OFr. *Margarete* < L. *margarita*, a pearl; Gr. *margaritēs* < *margaron*, a pearl; of Oriental origin], a feminine name: diminutives, *Greta, Madge, Maggie, Marge, Meg, Peg, Peggy;* variants, *Margery, Margot, Marjory;* equivalents, Fr. *Marguerite*, G. *Margarete, Gretchen*, It. *Margherita*, Sp. *Margarita.*

Margaret of Anjou, 1430–1482; queen of Henry VI of England (1445–1461; 1470–1471).

Margaret of Navarre, 1492–1549; queen of Navarre (1544–1549); writer and poet; author of the *Heptaméron*: also **Margaret of Angoulême.**

Margaret of Valois, 1553–1615; queen of Henry IV of France (1589–1599): also called *Queen Margot.*

mar·gar·ic (mär-gar′ik, mär-gär′ik), *adj.* [Fr. *margarique* < Gr. *margaron*, a pearl (see MARGARET): so called from the pearly luster of its crystals], designating a white, crystalline fatty acid, $C_{16}H_{33}CO_2H$, obtained from lichens or synthetically.

mar·ga·rin (mär′jə-rin; *occas.* mär′gə-rin), *n.* [Fr. *margarine* < *margarique;* see MARGARIC], 1. a fatty compound found in certain animal and vegetable oils, consisting of a mixture of stearin and palmitin. 2. the glyceride of margaric acid. 3. margarine.

mar·ga·rine (mär′jə-rin, mär′jə-rēn′; *occas.* mär′gə-rēn′), *n.* [Fr., orig., a mistaken use of the chemical term (see MARGARIN), from the belief that margaric acid was contained in all fats and oils], a blend of refined, edible vegetable oil or meat fat or both, churned with cultured skim milk to the consistency of butter and generally fortified with a minimum of 9,000 U.S.P. units of vitamin A per pound: it is used like butter: cf. **oleomargarine.**

mar·ga·rite (mär′gə-rīt′), *n.* [ME.; OFr.; L. *margarita;* see MARGARET], 1. a hydrated silicate of calcium and aluminum, found as scales with a pearly luster. 2. tiny, round crystals forming a beadlike design in glassy igneous rocks. 3. [Obs.], a pearl.

Mar·gate (mär′git), *n.* a seaport and summer resort in Kent, southeastern England: pop., 39,000.

mar·gay (mär′gā), *n.* [Fr. < Port. *maracajá* < Braz. (Tupi) *mbaracaïa*], a spotted wild cat of Central and South America, like the ocelot but smaller.

marge (märj), *n.* [Fr.; L. *margo;* see MARGIN], [Archaic or Poetic], a border; edge; margin.

mar·gent (mär′jənt), *n.* [< *margin*, with unhistoric *-t*], [Archaic], 1. a margin. 2. marginal comment in a book.

Mar·ger·y (mär′jĕr-i), [OFr. *Margerie* < L. *margarita;* see MARGARET], a feminine name: also spelled **Marjorie.**

mar·gin (mär′jin), *n.* [ME. *margine;* L. *margo, marginis*], 1. a border; edge; brink; verge: as, the *margin* of the pond. 2. the blank space around the printed or written area on a page or sheet. 3. a limit. 4. an amount of money, supplies, etc. reserved or allowed beyond what is needed; extra amount for contingencies or emergencies: as, we allow a *margin* of $35 a month in our budget. 5. provision for increase, addition, or advance. 6. in *business*, *a*) the difference between the cost and the selling price of merchandise, stocks, etc. *b*) money or collateral deposited with a broker to insure him against loss on contracts which he undertakes for the actual buyer or seller of stocks, etc. *c*) speculation in which the broker advances part of the money, with reservations to protect him against loss, and the buyer deposits the rest, taking the profit and loss on fluctuations in value. *d*) a customer's equity if his account is closed at the prevailing prices. 7. in *economics*, *a*) the minimum return, below which activities are not profitable enough to be continued. *b*) the difference between selling price and cost of production. 8. in *psychology*, the fringe of consciousness. *v.t.* [L. *marginare*], 1. to provide with a margin; be a margin to; border. 2. to enter, place, or summarize in the margin of a page or sheet. 3. in *business*, *a*) to deposit a margin upon. *b*) to hold by depositing or adding to a margin upon. Abbreviated **marg.** —*SYN.* see **border.**

mar·gin·al (mär′ji-n′l), *adj.* [Mod. L. *marginalis*], 1. written or printed in the margin of a page or sheet. 2. of or constituting a margin. 3. at, on, or close to the margin. 4. in *economics*, designating land capable of providing an economic return at existing prices but so low in productivity that it tends to remain unused until better land is very scarce. Abbreviated **marg.**

mar·gi·na·li·a (mär′jə-nā′li-ə, mär′jə-nāl′yə), *n.pl.* [Mod. L. < *marginalis*, marginal], marginal notes.

marginal utility, in *economics*, the minimum degree of utility, below which activity is not profitable enough to be continued.

mar·gin·ate (mär′jə-nāt′), *v.t.* [MARGINATED (-id), MARGINATING], [< L. *marginatus*, pp. of *marginare*], to provide with a margin. *adj.* (*also* mär′jə-nit), having a distinct margin.

mar·gin·at·ed (mär′jə-nāt′id), *adj.* marginate.

mar·gin·a·tion (mär′jə-nā′shən), *n.* a marginating or being marginated.

Mar·got (mär′gō, mär′gət), [Fr.], a feminine name: see **Margaret.**

mar·gra·vate (mär′grə-vāt′), *n.* margraviate.

mar·grave (mär′grāv), *n.* [MD. *markgrave* < MHG. *marcgrave* < *mark* (see MARCH, boundary), a march, border + *graf*, a count, earl (cf. REEVE, SHERIFF)], 1. originally, a military governor of a march, or border province, in Germany. 2. the hereditary title of certain princes of the Holy Roman Empire or Germany.

mar·gra·vi·ate (mär-grā′vi-it), *n.* [as if < ML. **margraviate*], the territory ruled over by a margrave.

mar·gra·vine (mär′grə-vēn′), *n.* [D. *markgravin*, fem. of *markgraaf*], the wife of a margrave.

Mar·gue·rite (mär′gə-rēt′), [see next entry], a feminine name.

mar·gue·rite (mär′gə-rēt′), *n.* [Fr., a pearl, daisy; see MARGARET], 1. a daisy with a yellow center and white petals; oxeye daisy or common garden daisy. 2. any of several chrysanthemums with a single flower.

Ma·ri·a (mə-rī′ə, mə-rē′ə), a feminine name: see **Mary.**

‡ma·ri·age de con·ve·nance (må′ryåzh′ də kōnv′näns′), [Fr.], a marriage of convenience; marriage entered into from calculated self-interest or expediency.

Mar·i·an (mâr′i-ən), [var. of *Marion* but spelled as if < *Mary* + *Ann, Anne, Anna*], a feminine name: variants, *Marianne, Marianna.* *adj.* 1. of the Virgin Mary. 2. of Queen Mary of England. 3. of Mary, Queen of Scots. *n.* 1. a worshiper or devotee of the Virgin Mary. 2. a follower or defender of Mary, Queen of Scots.

Ma·ri·a·nas Islands (mä′rē-ä′näs), a chain of islands in the Pacific, east of the Philippines: area, c. 450 sq. mi.; pop., 48,000: (except Guam) formerly a Japanese mandate, now under United States trusteeship: also called *Ladrone Islands, Ladrones.*

Mar·i·anne (mâr′i-an′), a feminine name: see **Marian.** *n.* a personification of the French Republic, as on coins.

Maria Theresa, 1717–1780; queen of Hungary and Bohemia (1740–1780); archduchess of Austria and wife of Francis I of the Holy Roman Empire; mother of Marie Antoinette.

Ma·ri Autonomous Soviet Socialist Republic (mä′rē), a division of the R.S.F.S.R., in the middle Volga region: area, 8,994 sq. mi.; pop., 608,000; capital, Ioshkar-Ola.

Ma·rie (mə-rē′), a feminine name: see **Mary.** ***n.*** queen of Romania (1914–1927); lived 1875–1938.

Marie An·toi·nette (an′twə-net′, an′tə-net′; Fr. må′rē′ än′twå′net′), 1755–1793; wife of Louis XVI; queen of France (1774–1792); guillotined.

Marie Byrd Land (bũrd′), a region in Antarctica, southeast of the Ross Sea.

Ma·rie de Mé·di·cis (må′rē′ də mā′dē′sēs′), 1573–1642; second wife of Henry IV; queen consort of France (1600–1610); queen regent (1610–1617): also **Maria de' Medici.**

Ma·rie Ga·lante (må′rē′ gå′länt′), a French island of the Leeward group, in the West Indies: area, 60 sq. mi.; pop., 30,000.

Marie Louise, 1791–1847; second wife of Napoleon I.

Mar·i·et·ta (mâr′i-et′ə), a feminine name: see **Mary.** ***n.*** a town in southeastern Ohio, on the Ohio River: pop., 17,000: first settlement (1788) in the Northwest Territory.

mar·i·gold (mar′i-gōld′), ***n.*** [< *Mary* (prob. the Virgin Mary) + *gold*], 1. any of several plants of the composite family, with red, yellow, or orange flowers. 2. the flower of any of these plants.

ma·ri·jua·na, ma·ri·hua·na (mâr′i-wä′nə, mä′ri-hwä′nə), ***n.*** [Am. Sp. *marihuana, mariguana;* ? native word blended with pers. name *Maria Juana,* Mary Jane], 1. the hemp plant. 2. a narcotic obtained from its dried leaves and flowers, smoked in cigarettes by addicts.

Mar·i·lyn (mar′ə-lin), a feminine name: see **Mary.**

ma·rim·ba (mə-rim′bə), ***n.*** [< Afr. (Bantu) *marimba, malimba,* pl. of *limba,* kind of musical instrument], a musical instrument somewhat like a xylophone, consisting of a series of hard wooden bars, usually with resonators beneath, played by being struck with small hammers.

MARIMBA

ma·ri·na (mə-rē′nə), ***n.*** [It. & Sp., seacost < L. *marinus;* see MARINE], a small harbor or boat basin providing dockage, supplies, and services for small pleasure craft.

mar·i·nade (mar′ə-nād′), ***n.*** [Fr. < Sp. *marinada* < *marinar,* to pickle in brine < *marino* < L. *marinus;* see MARINE], 1. vinegar or wine, usually spiced, in which meats and fish are pickled. 2. meat or fish pickled in this. ***v.t.*** (mar′ə-nād′), [MARINADED (-id), MARINADING], to marinate.

mar·i·nate (mar′ə-nāt′), ***v.t.*** [MARINATED (-id), MARINATING], [< *marinade* + *-ate*], 1. to soak (meat or fish) in marinade; steep in brine. 2. to let (salad ingredients, etc.) steep in oil and vinegar.

Ma·rin·du·que (mä′rin-dōō′ke), ***n.*** one of the Philippine Islands, south of Luzon: area, 356 sq. mi.; pop., 86,000.

ma·rine (mə-rēn′), ***adj.*** [ME. *maryn(e);* Late OFr. *marin;* L. *marinus* < *mare,* the sea; see MARE (sea)], 1. of the sea or ocean; inhabiting, found in, or formed by the sea. 2. *a*) of navigation on the sea; nautical. *b*) of naval affairs; naval. *c*) of shipping by sea; maritime. 3. used, or to be used, at sea: as, a *marine* engine. 4. trained for service at sea, etc., as certain troops. 5. of such troops; of the marines. ***n.*** 1. one of a class of troops trained for service at sea, etc.; specifically, [often M-], a member of the Marine Corps. 2. naval or merchant ships collectively; seagoing ships of a nation; fleet: as, the merchant *marine.* 3. in some countries, the department of government in charge of naval affairs. 4. a picture of a ship or sea scene.

Marine Corps, a branch of the United States armed forces, established by the Continental Congress in 1775, equipped and trained for land, sea, and aerial combat: the Commandant of the Marine Corps is responsible to the Secretary of the Navy.

mar·i·ner (mar′ə-nẽr), ***n.*** [ME. *marinere;* Anglo-Fr. *mariner* (OFr. *marinier*); ML. *marinarius* < L. *marinus;* see MARINE], a sailor; seaman.

Mar·i·ol·a·try (mâr′i-ol′ə-tri), ***n.*** [< Gr. *Maria,* Mary; + *-latry*], worship of the Virgin Mary, regarded as carried to an idolatrous extreme: opprobrious term.

Mar·i·on (mâr′i-ən), [Fr.; cf. MARIONETTE], 1. a masculine name. 2. a feminine name: see **Mary.** ***n.*** 1. a city in central Ohio: pop., 37,000. 2. a city in central Indiana: pop., 38,000.

Marion, Francis, 1732?–1795; American general in the Revolutionary War: called the *Swamp Fox.*

mar·i·o·nette (mar′i-ə-net′), ***n.*** [Fr., dim. of *Marion;* or ? < **mariolette,* dim. of *mariole,* a doll, figurine (orig., of the Virgin Mary), dim. of *Marie;* see MARY], a puppet or little jointed doll moved by strings or wires, often on a miniature stage.

Mar·i·po·sa lily (or **tulip**) (mar′ə-pō′sə, mar′ə-pō′zə), [Sp. *mariposa,* butterfly: from the appearance of the blossoms], 1. any of a group of plants of the lily family, found in the western United States and Mexico, with tuliplike flowers of white, red, yellow, or violet. 2. the flower of any of these plants.

mar·ish (mar′ish), ***n.*** [ME. *mareis;* OFr. *marais;* see MORASS, MARSH], [Archaic, Poetic, or Dial.], a marsh; swamp. ***adj.*** [Archaic, Poetic, or Dial.], marshy.

Mar·ist (mâr′ist), ***adj.*** in the *Roman Catholic Church,* 1. of or dedicated to the Virgin Mary. 2. of the Society of Mary (*Marist Fathers*), a congregation of missionary priests founded in 1824, or the Little Brothers of Mary (*Marist Brothers of the Schools*), an institute of teaching brothers founded in 1817. ***n.*** a member of either of these groups.

Ma·ri·tain, Jacques (zhåk må′rē′tan′), 1882– ; French philosopher and diplomat.

mar·i·tal (mar′ə-t'l), ***adj.*** [L. *maritalis* < *maritus,* married, a husband], 1. of a husband. 2. of marriage; matrimonial; connubial.

mar·i·time (mar′ə-tīm′), ***adj.*** [Fr.; L. *maritimus* < *mare,* the sea], 1. on, near, or living near the sea: as, *maritime* provinces, a *maritime* people. 2. of the sea in relation to navigation, shipping, etc.: as, *maritime* law. 3. characteristic of sailors; nautical. Abbreviated **mar.**

Maritime Alps, a range of the Alps in northwestern Italy and southeastern France.

Maritime Provinces, the Canadian provinces of Nova Scotia, New Brunswick, and Prince Edward Island.

Ma·ri·u·pol (mä′ri-ōō′pôl), ***n.*** a city in the Ukrainian S.S.R., on the Sea of Azov: pop., 284,000.

Mar·i·us, Gai·us (gā′yəs *or* gī′əs mâr′i-əs), 155?–86 B.C.; Roman general and statesman; consul.

mar·jo·ram (mär′jẽr-əm), ***n.*** [ME. *majoran;* OFr. *majorane;* ML. *majorana;* prob. ult. < L. *amaracus,* marjoram; Gr. *amarakos*], any of a number of plants of the mint family; especially, a fragrant plant (*sweet marjoram*) used for flavoring in cooking.

Mar·jo·rie, Mar·jo·ry (mär′jẽr-i), a feminine name: see **Margaret:** also spelled **Margery.**

Mark (märk), a masculine name: see **Marcus.** ***n.*** in the *Bible,* 1. one of the four Evangelists (*John Mark*), the reputed author of the second book of the New Testament: also **Saint Mark.** 2. the second book of the New Testament, telling the story of Jesus' life.

Mark (märk), ***n.*** [G. *marke,* a label, brand], a name for a model of tank, or other weapon, machine, etc., used by the Germans in World War II: the Mark VI (called the *Tiger*) was a heavy tank carrying an 88mm. gun.

mark (märk), ***n.*** [ME. *merke, marke;* AS. *mearc,* orig., boundary, hence boundary sign, hence sign, etc. (cf. MARCH, boundary); akin to G. *mark,* boundary, boundary stone, landmark, etc., *marke,* a token, mark; IE. base **mareg-,* seen also in L. *margo,* an edge, border (cf. MARGIN); basic idea either "extending" or "visible boundary"], 1. a visible trace or impression on a surface, as a line, dot, spot, stain, scratch, blemish, mar, bruise, dent, etc.; distinctive feature produced by drawing, coloring, stamping, etc. 2. a sign, symbol, or indication; specifically, *a*) a printed or written sign or stroke: as, punctuation *marks. b*) a brand, label, seal, or tag put on an article to show the owner, maker, etc.: as, a trade-*mark. c*) a sign or indication of some quality, character, etc.: as, politeness and consideration for others are *marks* of a good upbringing. *d*) a letter or figure used in schools, etc. to show quality of work or behavior; grade; rating: as, a *mark* of B in history. *e*) a cross or other sign made on a document as a substitute for a signature by a person unable to write. 3. a standard of quality, proficiency, propriety, etc.: as, this novel doesn't come up to the *mark.* 4. importance; distinction; eminence: as, a man of *mark.* 5. impression; influence: as, good teachers leave their *mark* on their students. 6. a visible object of known position, serving as a guide or point of reference: as, the tower was a *mark* for fliers. 7. a line, dot, notch, etc. used to indicate position, as on a graduated scale. 8. *a*) an object aimed at; target. *b*) an object desired or worked for; end; aim; goal. 9. an observing; a taking notice; heed. 10. [Archaic], *a*) a boundary, border, or borderland; march. *b*) among Germanic peoples in earlier times, land held or worked in common by a community. 11. in *nautical usage, a*) one of the knots, bits of leather, or colored cloth placed at intervals on a sounding line to indicate depths in fathoms. *b*) the Plimsoll mark. 12. in *sports, a*) the starting line of a race. *b*) the jack in the game of bowls. ***v.t.*** 1. to put or make a mark or marks on. 2. to identify or designate by or as by a mark or marks: as, his abilities *marked* him for success. 3. to trace, make, or produce by or as by marks; draw, write, etc. 4. to show or indicate by a mark or marks. 5. to show plainly; manifest; make clear or perceptible: as, her smile *marked* her happiness. 6. to distinguish; set off; characterize: as, great scientific discoveries *marked* the 19th century. 7. to observe; note; pay attention to; take notice of; heed: as, *mark* my words. 8. to give a grade or grades to; rate: as, the teacher *marked* the examination papers. 9. to put price tags on (merchandise). 10. to keep (score, etc.); record. ***v.i.*** 1. to make a mark or marks. 2. to observe; take note. 3. in *games,* to keep score. —***SYN.*** see **sign.**

beside the mark, 1. not striking the point aimed at. 2. not to the point; irrelevant.

hit the mark, 1. to achieve one's aim; be successful

in one's attempt. 2. to be accurate; be right.
make one's mark, to achieve success or fame.
mark down, 1. to make a note of; write down; record. 2. to mark for sale at a reduced price.
mark off (or **out**), to mark the limits of; demarcate.
mark out for, to select for or note as selected for.
mark time, 1. to keep time while at a halt by lifting the feet alternately as if marching. 2. to suspend progress for a time, as while awaiting developments. 3. to perform the motions of action without really getting anything done.
mark up, 1. to cover with marks. 2. to mark for sale at an increased price. 3. to add overhead and profit to the cost of in order to arrive at the selling price.
miss the mark, 1. to fail in achieving one's aim; be unsuccessful in one's attempt. 2. to be inaccurate.
save the mark! an exclamation of humorous astonishment, irony, contempt, etc.: originally used with reference to skillful marksmanship, later applied ironically to unskillful.
wide of the mark, 1. not striking the point aimed at. 2. not to the point; irrelevant.

mark (märk), *n.* [ME. *marke;* AS. *marc;* prob. < LL. *marca;* ult. etymon may be Gmc. < prec.], 1. an old European unit of weight for gold and silver, equal to about eight ounces. 2. a coin or money of account, originally equivalent in value to about eight ounces of silver; specifically, *a)* an obsolete Scottish silver coin worth 13 shillings, 4 pence. *b)* a silver coin and the gold monetary unit of the old German Empire, valued at 23.8 cents: it was superseded in 1924 by the reichsmark: see also **Deutschemark, Ostmark.** 3. a markka. Abbreviated **M., m., mk.**

Mark An·to·ny (märk an′tə-ni), see **Antonius, Marcus.**

mark·down (märk′doun′), *n.* 1. a marking for sale at a reduced price. 2. the amount of reduction in price.

marked (märkt), *adj.* 1. having a mark or marks: as, *marked* cards. 2. singled out to be watched or looked for as an object of suspicion, hostility, etc.: as, a *marked* man. 3. noticeable; obvious; appreciable; distinct; conspicuous: as, a *marked* change in behavior.

mark·ed·ly (mär′kid-li), *adv.* in a marked manner; noticeably; obviously; appreciably.

mark·er (mär′kẽr), *n.* a person or thing that marks; specifically, *a)* a person who keeps score in a game. *b)* a device for keeping score. *c)* a device for marking lines, as on a tennis court. *d)* a bookmark. *e)* a memorial tablet or gravestone. *f)* a milestone or similar sign.

mar·ket (mär′kit), *n.* [ME.; Late AS.; ONorm. Fr. < L. *mercatus,* trade, market place, pp. of *mercari,* to trade < *merx, mercis,* wares, merchandise], 1. *a)* a gathering of people for buying and selling things, especially provisions or livestock. *b)* the people gathered. *c)* the time of such a gathering. 2. an open space or a building where goods are shown for sale, usually with stalls or booths for the various dealers: also **market place.** 3. a store or shop for the sale of provisions: as, a meat *market.* 4. a region in which goods can be bought and sold; place where there is a demand for goods: as, the Latin-American *market.* 5. *a)* buying and selling; trade in goods, stocks, etc.: as, an active *market.* *b)* trade in a specified commodity: as, the wheat *market.* *c)* a place where such trade is carried on. *d)* the group of people associated in such trade. 6. opportunity to sell, or demand (for goods or services): as, industry has a good *market* for its products during boom times. 7. opportunity to buy, or supply (of goods or services): as, industry has a good labor *market* during a depression. 8. market price or market value. Abbreviated **mkt.** *v.t.* 1. to send or take to market. 2. to offer for sale. 3. to sell. *v.i.* 1. to deal in a market; buy or sell. 2. to buy provisions.
at the market, at the price prevailing when the customer's order (for stocks, etc.) is executed.
be in the market for, to be seeking to buy.
be on the market, to be offered for sale.
buyer's market, a state of trade favorable to the buyer (relatively heavy supply and low prices).
put on the market, to offer for sale.
seller's market, a state of trade favorable to the seller (relatively heavy demand and high prices).

mar·ket·a·bil·i·ty (mär′kit-ə-bil′ə-ti), *n.* the quality or condition of being marketable.

mar·ket·a·ble (mär′kit-ə-b'l), *adj.* 1. that can be sold; fit for sale. 2. of buying or selling: as, *marketable* value.

market order, an order to buy or sell goods, stock, etc. at the current market price.

market place, see **market,** *n.,* 2.

market price, the price that a commodity brings when sold in a given market; prevailing price.

market value, the price that a commodity can be expected to bring when sold in a given market: distinguished from *normal value:* abbreviated **m.v.**

Mark·ham, Edwin (mär′kəm), (*Charles Edwin Markham*), 1852–1940: American poet.

Markham, Mount, a mountain in Antarctica: height, 15,100 ft.

mark·ing (mär′kiŋ), *n.* 1. the act of making a mark or marks. 2. a mark or marks. 3. the arrangement of marks; characteristic coloring, as of a plant or animal.

mark·ka (märk′kä), *n.* [*pl.* MARKKAA (-kä)], [Finn. < Sw. *mark;* see MARK (money)], the monetary unit and a nickeled bronze (formerly silver) coin of Finland, worth about 2/5 cent in 1949.

marks·man (märks′mən), *n.* [*pl.* MARKSMEN (-mən)], 1. a person who shoots, especially one who shoots well. 2. in the *United States Army, a)* the lowest of the three ratings of proficiency of a rifleman: see also **sharpshooter, expert.** *b)* a soldier with this rating.

marks·man·ship (märks′mən-ship′), *n.* [see -SHIP], 1. skill in shooting. 2. the condition of being a marksman.

mark·up (märk′up′), *n.* 1. a marking for sale at an increased price. 2. the amount of increase in price. 3. the amount added to the cost to cover overhead and profit in arriving at the selling price.

marl (märl), *n.* [ME. & OFr. *marle;* LL. *margila* (whence G. *mergel*), dim. of L. *marga,* marl; ? < Celt. (so Pliny)], 1. a crumbly soil consisting mainly of clay, sand, and calcium carbonate, used as a fertilizer and in making cement or bricks. 2. any soft, crumbly stratum. 3. [Poetic], earth. *v.t.* to cover or fertilize with marl.

marl (märl), *v.t.* [D. *marlen* < *marren,* to bind], to bind or wind (rope, etc.) with marline, taking a hitch at each turn.

mar·la·ceous (mär-lā′shəs), *adj.* of or like marl; marly.

Marl·bor·ough (märl′bẽr-ō, märl′bẽr-ə; Brit. môl′bẽr-ə, môl′brə), Duke of, (*John Churchill*), 1650–1722; English general and statesman; defeated the French at Blenheim (1704).

mar·lin (mär′lin), *n.* [< *marlinespike:* from the shape], 1. any of several large, slender deep-sea fishes related to the sailfish and spearfish. 2. a spearfish.

mar·line (mär′lin), *n.* [D. *marlijn* < *marren,* to tie + *lijn,* a line; prob. confused with *marling* (< *marren* + *-ing*)], a small cord of two loosely twisted strands, used for winding around the ends of ropes or cables to prevent fraying: also **marling.**

mar·line·spike, mar·lin·spike (mär′lin-spīk′), *n.* a pointed iron instrument for separating the strands of a rope in splicing or marling: also **marlingspike.**

mar·ling (mär′liŋ), *n.* a marline.

mar·ling·spike (mär′liŋ-spīk′), *n.* a marlinespike.

marl·ite (märl′īt), *n.* a variety of marl that resists the action of the air.

Mar·lowe, Christopher (mär′lō), 1564–1593; English dramatist and poet.

Marlowe, Julia, (born *Sarah Frances Frost; Mrs. E. H. Sothern*), 1866–1950; American actress, born in England.

marl·y (mär′li), *adj.* [MARLIER (-li-ẽr), MARLIEST (-li-ist)], 1. of or like marl. 2. containing or full of marl.

mar·ma·lade (mär′mə-lād′), *n.* [OFr. *marmelade;* Port. *marmelada,* orig., confection of quinces < *marmelo,* quince < L. *melimelum* < Gr. *melimēlon,* sweet apple; *meli,* honey + *mēlon,* apple], a jamlike preserve made by boiling the pulp and, usually, the sliced-up rinds of oranges or some other fruits with sugar.

marmalade tree, a tropical American evergreen tree, bearing a plumlike fruit used for preserving: also called *sapodilla, mammee, sapota, mammee colorado.*

Mar·ma·ra, Sea of (mär′mə-rə), a sea between Asiatic and European Turkey, connected with the Black Sea by the Bosporus and with the Mediterranean by the Dardanelles: also **Marmora** : see **Bosporus,** map.

Mar·mo·la·da (mär′mô-lä′dä), *n.* the highest peak of the Dolomites, Italy: height, c. 11,000 ft.

Mar·mo·la·ta (mär′mô-lä′tä), *n.* Marmolada.

Mar·mo·ra, Sea of (mär′mə-rə, mär-môr′ə, mär-mō′rə), the Sea of Marmara.

mar·mo·re·al (mär-môr′i-əl, mär-mō′ri-əl), *adj.* [< L. *marmoreus* < *marmor,* marble; + *-al*], 1. of marble. 2. like marble; cold, white, smooth, hard, etc.

mar·mo·re·an (mär-môr′i-ən, mär-mō′ri-ən), *adj.* marmoreal.

mar·mo·set (mär′mə-zet′), *n.* [Late ME.; OFr. *marmouset,* grotesque figure; prob. ult. < Gr. *mormō, mormous,* bogey for children], one of various very small monkeys of South and Central America, with thick, soft, brightly colored fur; true marmoset or tamarin.

mar·mot (mär′mət), *n.* [Fr. *marmotte* < earlier *marmottaine;* prob. < L. *mus montanus,* mountain mouse], any of a group of small, thick-bodied, gnawing or burrowing rodents with coarse fur and a short, bushy tail, as the ground hog, woodchuck, or prairie dog.

Marne (märn), *n.* a river in northeastern France, flowing into the Seine at Paris: length, 310 mi.: in two battles of the Marne (September, 1914, and July, 1918) the Allies checked German offensives.

Ma·roc (mȧ′rôk′), *n.* Morocco: the French name.

ma·roon (mə-rōōn′), *n. & adj.* [Fr. *marron,* chestnut,

chestnut color < It. *marrone*], dark brownish red.
ma·roon (mə-rōōn′), *n.* [Fr. *marron* < Sp. *cimarrón*, wild, unruly], 1. in the West Indies and Dutch Guiana, *a)* originally, a fugitive Negro slave. *b)* a descendant of such slaves. 2. [Rare], a marooned person. *v.t.* 1. to put (a person) ashore in some desolate place, as a desert island, and leave him there: pirates sometimes marooned people as a punishment. 2. to leave abandoned, isolated, or helpless. *v.i.* 1. in the southern United States, to camp out or picnic for several days. 2. to loiter or loaf.
Ma·ros (mä′rôsh), *n.* Mures: the Hungarian name.
mar·plot (mär′plot′), *n.* a person or, sometimes, a thing that mars or spoils some plan by officious interference.
Marq., 1. Marquess. 2. Marquis.
Mar·quand, J. P. (mär-kwänd′), (*John Phillips Marquand*), 1893–1960; American novelist.
marque (märk), *n.* [Fr., mark, stamp, imprint; Pr. *marca*, seizure, reprisal < *marcar*, to seize as a pledge < *marc*, token of pledge < Gmc.; see MARK (a trace)], reprisal: obsolete except in **letters of marque.**
mar·quee (mär-kē′), *n.* [false sing. < Fr. *marquise*, misunderstood as pl.: so called because regarded as a shelter for a marquise or marchioness], 1. [Brit.]. a large tent with open sides, especially one used for some outdoor entertainment. 2. a rooflike structure or awning projecting over an entrance, as to a theater.
Mar·que·san (mär-kā′sən), *n.* 1. one of the aboriginal people of the Marquesas Islands. 2. their Polynesian language. *adj.* 1. of the Marquesas Islands or their people. 2. of Marquesan.
Mar·que·sas Islands (mär-kā′səs), a group of French islands in the South Pacific: area, 480 sq. mi.; pop., 4,200.
mar·quess (mär′kwis), *n.* a marquis: abbreviated **Marq.**
mar·que·try, mar·que·te·rie (mär′kə-tri), *n.* [Fr. *marqueterie* < *marqueter*, to spot, inlay < *marque*, a mark; cf. MARK (a trace)], decorative inlaid work of wood, ivory, metal, etc., used in furniture and flooring.
Mar·quette, Jacques (zhäk mär-ket′), 1637–1675; French Jesuit missionary and explorer; explored part of the Mississippi River: called *Père Marquette.*
mar·quis (mär′kwis; Fr. mȧr′kē′), *n.* [ME. *markis*; OFr. *marchis* (later *marquis*) < ML. *marchensis*, prefect of a frontier town < *marca*; see MARCH (border)], in some countries of Europe, a nobleman ranking above an earl or count and below a duke: used also in England as a title of courtesy for the eldest son of a duke who is also a marquis: abbreviated **M., m., Marq.**
Mar·quis, Don (mär′kwis), (*Donald Robert Perry Marquis*), 1878–1937; American humorist and journalist.
mar·quis·ate (mär′kwiz-it), *n.* the status, rank, or, sometimes, territory of a marquis or a margrave.
mar·quise (mär-kēz′; Fr. mȧr′kēz′), *n.* [Fr., fem. of *marquis*], 1. *a)* the wife or widow of a marquis. *b)* a lady whose rank in her own right equals that of a marquis. Not used of a British lady of this rank, who is called *marchioness.* 2. a marquee. 3. *a)* a ring with jewels set in the shape of a pointed oval. *b)* a jewel or ring setting of this shape.
mar·qui·sette (mär′ki-zet′, mär′kwi-zet′), *n.* [dim. of Fr. *marquise*, awning, marquise], a thin, lightweight fabric of cotton, silk, rayon, or nylon with square, open meshes, used for curtains, dresses, etc.
Mar·ra·kech, Mar·ra·kesh (mä-rä′kesh), *n.* one of the traditional capitals of Morocco: pop., 220,000: formerly, also called *Morocco.*
Mar·ra·no (mə-rä′nō), *n.* [*pl.* MARRANOS (-nōz)], [Sp., lit., swine (expression of contempt) < Ar. *muḥarram*, forbidden thing; or ? < Heb. *mar'ē*, appearance + Sp. ending], [also m-], in the Spanish Inquisition, a Jew who professed to accept Christianity in order to escape persecution.
mar·riage (mar′ij), *n.* [ME. *mariage*; OFr. < *marier*; see MARRY], 1. the state of being married; relation between husband and wife; married life; wedlock; matrimony. 2. the act of marrying; wedding. 3. the rite or form used in marrying. 4. any close or intimate union. 5. in *pinochle*, etc., the king and queen of a suit.
SYN.—**marriage** refers to the state of, or relation between, a man and woman who have become husband and wife or to the ceremony marking this union; **matrimony**, a formal word, applies specifically to the religious sacrament of marriage and stresses the rights and obligations of the marriage state (the bonds of holy *matrimony*); **wedlock** now applied specifically to marriage as a legal relationship (a child born out of *wedlock*); **wedding** refers specifically to the marriage ceremony and connotes festivities of one sort or another; **nuptials** is a highly formal, sometimes affected, term implying an elaborate ceremony, pomp, etc.
mar·riage·a·bil·i·ty (mar′ij-ə-bil′ə-ti), *n.* the quality or state of being marriageable.
mar·riage·a·ble (mar′ij-ə-b'l), *adj.* 1. old enough to get married. 2. suitable for marriage, as one's age.
marriage portion, a dowry.
mar·ried (mar′id), *adj.* [pp. of *marry*], 1. living together as husband and wife; joined in wedlock. 2. having a husband or wife. 3. of marriage or married people; connubial; conjugal. 4. closely or intimately joined. Abbreviated **M., m., mar.**
mar·ri·er (mar′i-ēr), *n.* a person who marries.
mar·ron (mar′ən; Fr. mȧ′rōn′), *n.* [Fr.; It. *marrone*, chestnut; cf. MAROON (dark red)], 1. a large, sweet European chestnut, often used in confectionery. 2. the color of its shell. 3. a paper shell used to make an explosive noise. 4. *pl.* (mar′ənz; Fr. mȧ′rōn′), chestnuts preserved in vanilla sirup.
‡**mar·rons gla·cés** (mȧ′rōn′glȧ′sā′), [Fr.], marrons in sirup or glazed with sugar; candied chestnuts.
mar·row (mar′ō), *n.* [ME. *maro*, *merowe*, etc.; AS. *mearg*, *mearh*; akin to G. *mark*, marrow; IE. base **mozgho-*, marrow, brains, seen also in Sans. *majján-*, marrow], 1. the soft, vascular, fatty tissue that fills the cavities of most bones: the *spinal marrow* is the spinal cord. 2. the innermost, essential, or choicest part; pith. 3. vitality. 4. [British], vegetable marrow.
mar·row·bone (mar′ō-bōn′), *n.* 1. a bone containing marrow: also **marrow bone.** 2. *pl.* *a)* the knees: humorous usage. *b)* crossbones.
mar·row·fat (mar′ō-fat′), *n.* a variety of large, rich pea: also **marrowfat pea, marrow pea.**
marrow squash, any variety of oblong squash with a hard, smooth rind.
mar·row·y (mar′ə-wi), *adj.* containing or full of marrow.
Mar·ru·e·cos (mär′oo-e′kôs), *n.* Morocco: Spanish name.
mar·ry (mar′i), *v.t.* [MARRIED (-id), MARRYING], [ME. *marien*; OFr. *marier* < L. *maritare* < *maritus*, a husband, married; IE. **merjo*, young man], 1. to join as husband and wife; unite in wedlock. 2. to join (a man) to a woman as her husband, or (a woman) to a man as his wife. 3. to take as husband or wife; take in marriage. 4. to give in marriage (often with *off*): said of a parent or guardian. 5. to join closely or intimately; unite. *v.i.* 1. to get married; take a husband or wife. 2. to enter into a close or intimate relationship; unite.
mar·ry (mar′i), *interj.* [euphemistic respelling of (the Virgin) *Mary*], [Archaic or Dial.], an exclamation of surprise, anger, etc., sometimes a mere intensive.
Mar·ry·at, Frederick (mar′i-ət, mar′i-at′), 1792–1848; British naval captain and novelist.
Mars (märz), *n.* [L.; prob. < IE. base as in *mar*], 1. in *Roman mythology*, the god of war: identified with the Greek Ares. 2. war. 3. a planet of the solar system, fourth in distance from the sun, notable for its red light: diameter, c. 4,230 mi.; diurnal rotation, 24 hrs., 37 min.; year, 686.9 days; symbol, ♂. 4. in *alchemy*, iron.
Mars, Marse (märs), *n.* Master: approximate phonetic spelling of the word as used by Negroes during slavery.
Mar·sa·la (mär-sä′lä), *n.* [< *Marsala*, seaport in western Sicily], a light, sweet white wine originally from Sicily.
Mar·seil·laise (mär′sə-lāz′; Fr. mȧr′se′yez′), *n.* [Fr., lit., of Marseilles: from being first sung by Marseilles volunteers], the national anthem of France, composed by Rouget de Lisle in 1792 during the French Revolution.
Mar·seille (mȧr′se′y′; *for 2,* mär-sāl′), *n.* 1. Marseilles. 2. [m-], marseilles.
Mar·seilles (mär-sālz′), *n.* 1. a seaport in southeastern France, on the Mediterranean: pop., 661,000: French name, *Marseille.* 2. [m-], a thick, strong, figured or striped cotton cloth with a raised weave, somewhat resembling piqué, used for bedspreads, etc.: it was originally made in Marseilles.
marsh (märsh), *n.* [ME. *mersch*, etc.; AS. *mersc*, *merisc*; akin to MLG. *mersch*, *marsch* (whence G. *marsch*); IE. base **mari-*, sea; cf. MARE (sea), MARINE, etc.], a tract of low, wet, soft land; swamp; bog; morass; fen.
Marsh, Reginald (märsh), 1898– ; American painter.
Mar·shal (mär′shəl), [< *marshal*, *n.*], a masculine name.
mar·shal (mär′shəl), *n.* [ME. *marescal*; OFr. *mareschal*, *marescal*; OHG. *marahscalh*, lit., horse servant (whence ML. *marescalcus*, *mariscalus*); *marah*, *marha*, horse (akin to AS. *mearh*, horse) + *scalh*, servant; cf. Fr. *maréchal-ferrant*, farrier], 1. originally, a groom or, later, a master of the horse in a medieval royal household. 2. a high official of a royal household or court, as in medieval times, in charge of military affairs, ceremonies, etc. 3. a military commander; specifically, *a)* a field marshal. *b)* in various foreign armies, a general officer of the highest rank. *c)* in the *British Army*, a commander of a specified branch: as, an air *marshal.* 4. an official in charge of ceremonies, processions, rank and order, etc.: as, the *marshal* of a parade arranges the order of march. 5. in the United States, an officer of various kinds; specifically, *a)* a Federal officer appointed to a judicial district to carry out court orders and perform functions like those of a sheriff. *b)* a minor officer of the law in some cities. *c)* the head of the police or fire department in some cities. Abbreviated **M.** *v.t.* [MARSHALED or MARSHALLED (-shəld), MARSHALING or MARSHALLING], 1. to arrange (troops, things, ideas, etc.) in order; array; dispose: as, he *marshaled* his forces for the battle. 2. *a)* to direct as a marshal; manage. *b)* to lead or guide ceremoniously. 3. in *heraldry*, *a)* to combine (coats of arms) on a single shield. *b)* to associate (accessories) about a shield so as to form a complete escutcheon.
mar·shal·cy (mär′shəl-si), *n.* the position, rank, or authority of a marshal.

Mar·shall (mär′shəl), *n.* the Micronesian language of the natives of the Marshall Islands.
Mar·shall, George Cat·lett (kat′lit mär′shəl), 1880–1959; American general and statesman; chief of staff, United States Army, World War II; secretary of state (1947–1949).
Marshall, John, 1755–1835; American jurist; Chief Justice of the United States (1801–1835).
Marshall Islands, a group of coral atolls in the North Pacific, east of the Caroline Islands: area, 160 sq. mi.; pop., 14,000; chief island, Jaluit: formerly a Japanese mandate, now under United States trusteeship.
Mar·shal·sea (mär′shəl-sē′), *n.* [ME. *marschalcie;* OFr. *mareschancie;* see MARSHAL, *n.*], 1. a court, abolished in 1849, formerly held in London by or for the knight marshal. 2. a prison in Southwark, London, for debtors, etc., abolished in 1842.
mar·shal·ship (mär′shəl-ship′), *n.* [see -SHIP], marshalcy.
marsh elder, 1. any of a group of shrubs of the ragweed family, growing in salt marshes. 2. the guelder-rose.
marsh gas, methane, CH_4, a colorless, odorless, inflammable gas formed from decomposing vegetable matter, as in marshes.
marsh hawk, a large American hawk that lives in marshes and preys on frogs, mice, snakes, etc.
marsh hen, any of several birds; especially, *a*) the American coot. *b*) a kind of rail, found in marshy land along the Atlantic coast of America.
marsh·i·ness (mär′shi-nis), *n.* the quality or state of being marshy.
marsh·mal·low (märsh′mal′ō), *n.* 1. originally, a confection made from the root of the marsh mallow. 2. a soft, spongy candy made of sugar, starch, corn sirup, and gelatin, coated with powdered sugar.
marsh mallow, a plant of the mallow family, with large, pink flowers, growing in marshes: the root is used in medicine and confectionery.
marsh marigold, a plant of the crowfoot family, with bright-yellow flowers, growing in swamps; cowslip.
marsh·y (mär′shi), *adj.* [MARSHIER (-shi-ẽr), MARSHIEST (-shi-ist)], 1. of, consisting of, or containing a marsh or marshes. 2. like a marsh; soft and wet; boggy; swampy. 3. growing in marshes.
Mar·ston, John (mär′stən), 1575?–1634; English dramatist and satirist.
Marston Moor, a place in Yorkshire, northern England: site of a battle (July, 1644) in which the Royalist forces were routed by the Parliamentary army.
mar·su·pi·al (mär-sōō′pi-əl, mär-sū′pi-əl), *adj.* 1. of or like a marsupium, or pouch. 2. of a group of lower mammals that lack a placenta and have an external abdominal pouch containing the teats: the prematurely born offspring is placed within the pouch by the mother immediately after birth to complete its development. *n.* an animal of this kind, as a kangaroo, bandicoot, opossum, wombat, etc.
mar·su·pi·um (mär-sōō′pi-əm, mär-sū′pi-əm), *n.* [*pl.* MARSUPIA (-ə)], [L.; Gr. *marsypion,* dim. of *marsypos,* a pouch, bag], 1. a fold of skin on the abdomen of the female of certain lower mammals (*marsupials*), forming a pouch in which the young are carried and complete their development, feeding from the mammary glands which it encloses. 2. a structure like this, in some crustaceans, fishes, etc.
mart (märt), *n.* [D. *markt*], 1. a market; trading center: as, Chicago is the largest *mart* of the Middle West. 2. [Obs.], *a*) a fair. *b*) buying and selling; trade; bargaining. *c*) a bargain.
Mar·ta·ban, Gulf of (mär′tə-bän′), a part of the Bay of Bengal, on the southern coast of Burma.
Mar·tel, Charles (mär-tel′), 689?–741 A.D.; grandfather of Charlemagne; ruler of the Franks (715–741 A.D.); defeated the Moslems at Tours in 732 A.D., thus checking their invasion of Europe.
Mar·tel·lo tower (mär-tel′ō), [It. *martello,* a hammer (used for *mortella,* a tower < *Mortello,* in Corsica, where such a tower was attacked by the English fleet in 1794)], a circular fort of masonry, formerly built on coasts to protect against invaders: also **martello,** *n.*
mar·ten (mär′t'n), *n.* [*pl.* MARTENS (-t'nz), MARTEN; see PLURAL, II, D, 1], [ME. *martren;* OFr. *martrine, adj.* < *martre,* marten], 1. any of several small, flesh-eating mammals like a weasel but larger, with a long, slender body, short legs, and soft, thick, valuable fur. 2. the fur: also called *sable.*

MARTEN (2 1/2 ft. long)

mar·tens·ite (mär′tenz-īt′), *n.* [after A. *Martens,* G. metallurgist], a very hard, brittle, solid solution of iron and carbon or the carbide of iron, Fe_3C, produced when hot steel is suddenly chilled by cold water.
Mar·tha (mär′thə), [LL.; Gr.; Aram. *Mārthā,* lit., lady], a feminine name: diminutive, *Matty;* equivalents, Fr. *Marthe,* It. & Sp. *Marta.* *n.* 1. in the *Bible,* sister of Lazarus and Mary, and a friend of Jesus: she was rebuked by Jesus for doing housework while he talked with Mary: Luke 10:40; hence, 2. a woman who does the housework and looks after practical affairs.
Martha's Vineyard, an island off the southeastern coast of Massachusetts, south of Cape Cod: summer resort: area, c. 100 sq. mi.; pop., c. 5,800.
Mar·tial (mär′shəl), *n.* (*Marcus Valerius Martialis*), Roman epigrammatist; 1st century A.D.
mar·tial (mär′shəl), *adj.* [Fr.; L. *martialis,* of Mars; see MARS], 1. of or suitable for war: as, *martial* songs. 2. warlike; brave; soldierly. 3. of the army, navy, or military life; military: as, court *martial:* opposed to *civil, civilian.* 4. [Archaic], of or like iron. 5. [M-], in *astrology,* under the dire influence of Mars.
SYN.—**martial** refers to anything connected with or characteristic of war or armies, connoting especially pomp, discipline, etc. (*martial* music, *martial* law); **warlike** stresses the bellicose or aggressive nature or temperament that leads to war or results from preparations for war (a *warlike* nation); **military** applies to anything having to do with armies or soldiers (*military* uniforms, police, etc.).—*ANT.* peacelike, pacifist.
martial law, temporary rule by the military authorities over the civilian population, as in an area of military operations in time of war, or when civil authority has broken down: distinguished from *military law.*
Mar·ti·an (mär′shən), *adj.* [L. *Martius*], of Mars (god or planet). *n.* a hypothetical inhabitant of the planet Mars.
Mar·tin (mär′t'n), [Fr.; L. *Martinus* < *Mars, Martis* (see MARS); hence, lit., warlike], a masculine name.
mar·tin (mär′t'n), *n.* [Fr.; prob. < masc. name *Martin*], 1. any of various birds of the swallow family, as the *purple martin, sand martin, house martin,* etc. 2. a bird like a martin, as a chimney swift.
Martin, Saint, 315?–399? A.D.; bishop of Tours: cf. **Martinmas.**
Mar·tin, Homer Dodge (doj mär′t'n), 1836–1897; American landscape painter.
Mar·ti·neau, Harriet (mär′ti-nō′), 1802–1876; English writer.
Martineau, James, 1805–1900; brother of *Harriet;* English theologian and writer.
Mar·ti·nel·li, Gio·van·ni (jô-vän′nē mär′tē-nel′lē; Eng. mär′t'n-el′i), 1885– ; American tenor, born in Italy.
mar·ti·net (mär′t'n-et′, mär′t'n-et′), *n.* [after *Martinet,* 17th-c. Fr. general & drillmaster], 1. a very strict military disciplinarian. 2. any very strict disciplinarian or stickler for rigid regulations.
mar·tin·gal (mär′t'n-gal′), *n.* a martingale.
mar·tin·gale (mär′t'n-gāl′), *n.* [Fr.; Pr. *martengalo, martegalo,* apparently fem. of *martengo, martego,* inhabitant of Martigues, miserly person; but cf. Sp. *almártaga,* a check, rein < Ar.], 1. the forked strap of a horse's harness passing from the noseband to the girth between the forelegs, to keep the horse from rearing or throwing back its head. 2. *a*) a lower stay for the jib boom or flying jib boom of a sailing vessel, to bear the strain of the head stays. *b*) a short spar extending straight down from the end of the bowsprit: also called *dolphin striker.* 3. any system of trying to make up one's losses in previous bets by doubling or otherwise increasing the amount bet.
mar·ti·ni (mär-tē′ni), *n.* [*pl.* MARTINIS (-niz)], [< *Martini* and Rossi, firm that makes vermouth], [also M-], a cocktail made of gin and dry vermouth, usually served with an olive or a twist of lemon peel.
Mar·ti·nique (mär′t'n-ēk′), *n.* a French island of the Windward group, in the West Indies: area, 385 sq. mi.; pop., 262,000; capital, Fort-de-France.
Mar·tin·mas (mär′t'n-məs), *n.* [see -MAS], Saint Martin's day, a church festival held on November 11.
mart·let (märt′lit), *n.* [Fr. *martelet* < *martinet,* dim. of *martin*], 1. a martin. 2. in *heraldry,* a representation of a bird without feet, used as a crest or bearing.
mar·tyr (mär′tẽr), *n.* [ME. *martir;* AS.; LL.; Gr. *martyr, martys,* a witness], 1. a person who chooses to suffer or die rather than give up his faith or his principles; person tortured or killed because of his beliefs. 2. a person who suffers great pain or misery for a long time. *v.t.* 1. to put to death or torture for adherence to a belief. 2. to torture; make suffer greatly; persecute.
mar·tyr·dom (mär′tẽr-dəm), *n.* 1. the state of being a martyr. 2. the death or sufferings of a martyr. 3. severe, long-continued suffering; torment; torture.
mar·tyr·i·za·tion (mär′tẽr-i-zā′shən, mär′tẽr-ī-zā′shən), *n.* a martyrizing or being martyrized.
mar·tyr·ize (mär′tẽr-īz′), *v.t.* [MARTYRIZED (-īzd′), MARTYRIZING], [LL. *martyrizare*], to make a martyr of. *v.i.* to be or become a martyr.

mar·tyr·ol·o·gy (mär'tẽr-ol'ə-ji), *n.* [*pl.* MARTYROLOGIES (-jiz)], [ML. *martyrologium;* LGr. *martyrologion;* see MARTYR & -LOGY], 1. a list of martyrs. 2. a historical account of religious martyrs, especially Christian martyrs. 3. such accounts collectively. 4. the branch of ecclesiastical history dealing with the lives of martyrs.

mar·tyr·y (mär'tẽr-i), *n.* [*pl.* MARTYRIES (-iz)], [ML. *martyrium;* Gr. *martyrion*], a shrine built in memory of a martyr.

mar·vel (mär'v'l), *n.* [ME. *mervaile;* OFr. *merveille,* a wonder < L. *mirabilia,* wonderful things, neut. pl. of *mirabilis,* wonderful < *mirari,* to wonder at, admire], 1. a wonderful or astonishing thing; prodigy or miracle. 2. [Archaic], astonishment. ***v.i.*** [MARVELED or MARVELLED (-v'ld), MARVELING or MARVELLING], to become full of wonder; be astonished or surprised. ***v.t.*** to wonder at or about (followed by a clause).

Mar·vell, Andrew (mär'v'l), 1621–1678; English poet.

mar·vel-of-Pe·ru (mär'v'l-əv-pə-rōō'), *n.* the four-o'clock (a plant).

mar·vel·ous, mar·vel·lous (mär'v'l-əs), *adj.* [ME. *merveilous;* OFr. *merveillos* < *merveille;* see MARVEL], 1. causing wonder; surprising, astonishing, or extraordinary. 2. so extraordinary as to be improbable, incredible, or miraculous. 3. [Colloq.], fine; splendid: a generalized term of approval.

Mar·vin (mär'v'n), [prob. ult. < Gmc. **mari,* sea + **winiz,* friend; cf. G. *Marwin*], a masculine name.

Mar·war (mär'wär), *n.* Jodhpur, former state of India.

Marx, Karl (märks), 1818–1883; German revolutionary leader and socialist, writer on political economy, philosophy, etc.

Marx·i·an (märk'si-ən), *adj. & n.* Marxist.

Marx·i·an·ism (märk'si-ən-iz'm), *n.* Marxism.

Marx·ism (märk'siz'm), *n.* the system of thought developed by Karl Marx, his co-worker Friedrich Engels, and their followers: see **socialism, communism, dialectical materialism.**

Marx·ist (märk'sist), *adj.* 1. of Karl Marx. 2. of, characteristic of, or in accord with Marxism. ***n.*** a follower of Karl Marx; believer or expert in Marxism.

Mar·y (mâr'i), [ME. *Marie;* AS. *Maria, Marie;* L. *Maria;* Gr. *Maria, Mariam* < Heb. *Miryām* or Aram. *Maryam,* lit., rebellion], a feminine name: diminutives, *Mae, Marietta, May, Molly, Moll, Polly;* variants, *Maria, Marie, Marilyn, Marion, Miriam, Maureen;* equivalents, Fr. *Marie, Marion,* G., It., & Sp. *Maria,* Pol. *Marya.* ***n.*** [*pl.* MARYS, MARIES (-iz)], 1. in the *Bible, a*) the mother of Jesus: Matt. 1:18–25: often referred to as the (*Blessed*) *Virgin Mary, Saint Mary. b*) the sister of Martha and Lazarus: Luke 10:38–42. *c*) Mary Magdalene. 2. in *pidgin English,* a woman. 3. (*Princess Victoria Mary of Teck*), wife of George V; 1867–1953; queen of England (1910–1936). 4. (*Victoria Alexandra Alice Mary*), daughter of George V; 1897– ; Princess Royal of England.

Mary I, (*Mary Tudor*), 1516–1558; daughter of Henry VIII and Catherine of Aragon; queen of England (1553–1558) and wife of Philip II of Spain: called *Bloody Mary.*

Mary II, 1662–1694; daughter of James II; queen of England (1689–1694), ruling jointly with her husband, William III.

Mar·y·land (mâr'i-lənd), *n.* an Eastern State of the United States: area, 10,577 sq. mi.; pop., 3,101,000; capital, Annapolis: abbreviated **Md.**

Mary Magdalene, in the *Bible,* a woman out of whom Jesus cast seven devils: Luke 8:2: usually identified with the repentant woman whom Jesus forgave: Luke 7:37 ff.

Mary, Queen of Scots, (*Mary Stuart*), 1542–1587; queen of Scotland (1542–1567); beheaded.

Mary Tudor, Mary I.

mar·zi·pan (mär'zi-pan'), *n.* marchpane.

-mas (məs), a combining form for *Mass,* meaning *a* (specified) *festival* or *celebration,* as in *Christmas.*

mas., masculine.

Ma·sa·ryk, To·máš Gar·rigue (tô'mash gə-rēg' mȧ'sȧ-rik), 1850–1937; Czechoslovakian statesman; first president of Czechoslovakia (1918–1935).

Mas·ba·te (mäs-bä'te), *n.* one of the Philippine Islands, west of Samar: area, 1,255 sq. mi.; pop., 145,000.

masc., masculine.

Mas·ca·gni, Pie·tro (pye'trô mäs-kä'nyē), 1863–1945; Italian composer of operas.

mas·ca·ra (mas-kar'ə), *n.* [Sp. *máscara,* a mask < Ar. *maskharah,* buffoon], a cosmetic preparation, usually black, dark-blue, or dark-brown, for coloring the eyelashes and eyebrows. ***v.t.*** [MASCARAED (-kar'əd), MASCARAING], to put mascara on.

mas·cle (mas'k'l), *n.* [OFr.; see MACLE], 1. any of many small, diamond-shaped steel plates, linked together to make up a kind of armor used in the 13th century. 2. in *heraldry,* a diamond-shaped figure with a diamond-shaped opening: also called *lozenge voided.*

mas·cot (mas'kot, mas'kət), *n.* [Fr. *mascotte* < Pr. *mascot,* dim. of *masco,* sorcerer, lit., a mask; in pop. use < *La Mascotte* (1880), operetta by the Fr. composer Audran], any person, animal, or thing supposed to bring good luck by being present.

mas·cu·line (mas'kyoo-lin), *adj.* [ME. & OFr. *masculin;* L. *masculinus* < *masculus,* male < *mas,* male], 1. male; of men or boys. 2. having qualities regarded as characteristic of men and boys, as strength, vigor, etc.; manly; virile. 3. suitable for or characteristic of a man. 4. mannish: said of women. 5. in *grammar,* designating or of the gender of words denoting or referring to males or things originally regarded as male: it corresponds to an Indo-European active gender as contrasted with a nonactive gender seen now as feminine and neuter. ***n.*** 1. *a*) that which is male. *b*) a man or boy. 2. *a*) the masculine gender. *b*) a word or form in this gender. Abbreviated **masc., mas., m., M.** —***SYN.*** see **male.**

masculine rhyme, a rhyme of only a single stressed syllable; single rhyme (e.g., *enjoy, destroy*): distinguished from *feminine rhyme.*

mas·cu·lin·i·ty (mas'kyoo-lin'ə-ti), *n.* the quality or state of being masculine.

Mase·field, John (mās'fēld', māz'fēld'), 1878– ; English poet and dramatist; poet laureate (1930–).

ma·ser (mā'zẽr), *n.* [*m*icrowave *a*mplification by *s*timulated *e*mission of *r*adiation], an electronic device that absorbs microwaves, infrared rays, etc., as in a crystal, amplifies them, and emits them in a narrow, very intense beam: see also **laser.**

mash (mash), *n.* [ME. *masche-;* AS. *masc-,* in *mascwyrt,* mashwort, infused malt; akin to G. *meisch, maisch,* crushed grapes, infused malt; IE. base **meiĝh-,* to urinate, seen also in L. *mingere, mictus* (see MICTURATE); basic sense "sprinkled"], 1. crushed or ground malt or meal soaked in hot water for making wort, used in brewing beer. 2. a mixture of bran, meal, etc. in warm water, for feeding horses, cattle, etc. 3. any soft mixture or mass. ***v.t.*** [ME. *maschen* < the ***n.***], 1. to mix (crushed malt, etc.) in hot water for making wort. 2. to change into a soft or uniform mass by beating, crushing, etc. 3. [Earlier Slang], to try to attract the amorous attention of; flirt with or ogle.

Ma·shar·brum (mush'ẽr-broom'), *n.* a peak of the Himalayas, northern Kashmir, India: height, 25,670 ft.

mash·er (mash'ẽr), *n.* a person or thing that mashes; specifically, *a*) a device for mashing vegetables, fruit, etc. *b*) [Slang], a man who annoys women not acquainted with him, by attempting familiarities.

mash·ie, mash·y (mash'i), *n.* [*pl.* MASHIES (-iz)], [? < Fr. *massue,* a club < LL. **mattiuca;* prob. of Celt. origin], an iron-headed golf club of medium loft, for making shots of medium length: now usually called *number 5 iron:* see **golf club,** illus.

Mas·i·nis·sa (mas'ə-nis'ə), *n.* a Numidian king who fought as a Roman ally against Hannibal; lived 238?–149 B.C.: also spelled **Massinissa.**

mas·jid (mus'jid), *n.* [Ar.; see MOSQUE], a mosque; Moslem place of worship: also spelled **musjid.**

mask (mask, mäsk), *n.* [Fr. *masque* < It. *maschera, mascara,* a mask < Ar. *maskharah,* buffoon], 1. a covering for the face or part of the face, to conceal or disguise the identity. 2. anything that conceals or disguises: as, a *mask* of snow on the ground. 3. a party, carnival, etc. where masks are worn; masquerade: often spelled **masque.** 4. a person wearing a mask; masker. 5. a likeness of a person's face, or face and neck; specifically, *a*) a sculptured or molded likeness of the face: as, a death *mask* is a cast of the face made soon after death. *b*) a grotesque or comic representation of a face, worn to amuse or frighten, as at Halloween; false face. *c*) a sculptured head or face, often grotesque, used as an ornament on a building, gargoyle, etc. *d*) a figure of a head worn on the stage by an ancient Greek or Roman actor to identify a character and amplify the voice. 6. a protective covering for the face or head, as a wire screen, metal shield, or respirator (*gas mask*). 7. the face or head of a fox, dog, etc. 8. something serving to conceal artillery, military operations, etc. from observation; piece of camouflage. 9. an opaque border used to cover unwanted parts of a photograph or to alter its shape. 10. a masque (senses 2 & 3). 11. in *zoology,* a masklike formation about the head, as the enlarged lower lip of a dragonfly larva. ***v.t.*** 1. to conceal or cover with or as with a mask. 2. to conceal or disguise. ***v.i.*** to put on a mask; wear a disguise, as for a masquerade.

mas·ka·longe (mas'kə-lonj'), *n.* a muskellunge.

mas·ka·nonge (mas'kə-nonj'), *n.* a muskellunge.

masked (maskt, mäskt), *adj.* 1. wearing a mask. 2. concealed; disguised; camouflaged. 3. in *botany,* masklike; personate. 4. in *zoology,* having masklike markings, as some pupae.

masked ball, a ball at which masks and fancy costumes are worn.

mask·er (mas'kẽr, mäs'kẽr), *n.* a person who wears a mask: also spelled **masquer.**

mask·ing tape (mas'kiŋ, mäs'kiŋ), an adhesive tape for covering and protecting margins, borders, etc. during painting or the like.

mas·ki·nonge (mas'kə-nonj'), *n.* a muskellunge.

mas·och·ism (maz'ə-kiz'm; *now often* mas'ə-kiz'm), *n.* [after Leopold von Sacher-*Masoch* (1835–1895), Austrian writer in whose stories it is described], 1. the getting of sexual pleasure from being dominated, mistreated, or hurt physically or otherwise by one's partner; hence, 2. the getting of pleasure from being dominated, mistreated, or hurt in some way. Cf. **sadism.**

mas·och·ist (maz'ə-kist; *now often* mas'ə-kist), *n.* a person characterized by masochism.

mas·och·is·tic (maz'ə-kis'tik; *now often* mas'ə-kis'tik), *adj.* of or characterized by masochism.

mas·och·is·ti·cal·ly (maz'ə-kis'ti-k'l-i; *now often* mas'ə-kis'tik-li), *adv.* in a masochistic manner.

ma·son (mā's'n), *n.* [ME.; OFr. *masson, maçon;* ML. *matio, macio;* ? < Frank. **mattjo* (akin to Sans. *matya,* club); see MATTOCK], 1. a person whose work is building with stone, brick, etc. 2. a stonecutter. 3. [M-], a Freemason. *v.t.* to build of or reinforce with masonry.

mason bee, a solitary bee that builds its nest of clay, sand, mud, etc.

Mason City, a city in north central Iowa: pop., 31,000.

Ma·son-Dix·on line (mā's'n-dik's'n), the boundary between Pennsylvania and Maryland, surveyed by Charles Mason and Jeremiah Dixon from 1763 to 1767: regarded as the line of demarcation between the North and the South: also **Mason and Dixon's line.**

Ma·son·ic, ma·son·ic (mə-son'ik), *adj.* of Masons (Freemasons) or Masonry (Freemasonry).

ma·son·ite (mā's'n-īt'), *n.* [after W. H. *Mason* (1877–1947?), Am. engineer], a kind of fiberboard made from pressed wood fibers, used as building material, insulation, etc.: a trade-mark (**Masonite**).

Mason jar, a glass jar with a screw top of metal or glass, for home canning or preserving: patented in 1857 by John L. Mason of New York.

ma·son·ry (mā's'n-ri), *n.* [*pl.* MASONRIES (-riz)], [ME. *masonerie;* Fr. *maçonnerie* < *maçon;* see MASON], 1. the trade or art of a mason. 2. something built by a mason or masons, of stone, brick, etc.; brickwork or stonework. 3. [usually M-], Freemasonry; specifically, *a*) the principles of the society of Freemasons. *b*) Freemasons collectively.

Ma·so·ra, Ma·so·rah (mə-sō'rə), *n.* [Mod. Heb. *māsōrāh,* tradition; Heb. *māsōreth*], 1. all the accumulated Jewish tradition concerning the correct Hebrew text of the Old Testament. 2. the marginal notes of Old Testament scripts embodying this tradition, compiled in the 10th century A.D.

Mas·o·rete (mas'ə-rēt'), *n.* [< Heb. *māsōreth*], any of the 10th-century Jewish scribes who compiled the Masora: also **Masorite.**

Mas·o·ret·ic (mas'ə-ret'ik), *adj.* of the Masora or the Masoretes.

Mas·o·ret·i·cal (mas'ə-ret'i-k'l), *adj.* Masoretic.

Mas·o·rite (mas'ə-rīt'), *n.* a Masorete.

Mas·qat (mus-kät'), *n.* Muscat: the Arabian name.

masque (mask, mäsk), *n.* [see MASK], 1. a masquerade; masked ball. 2. a form of dramatic entertainment popular among the aristocracy in England during the 16th and 17th centuries, usually based on a mythical or allegorical theme, and with the dialogue subordinated to lavish costumes, scenery, music, dancing, etc.: originally it contained no dialogue. 3. a dramatic composition written for such an entertainment, usually in verse. Also spelled **mask.**

mas·quer·ade (mas'kə-rād', mäs'kə-rād'), *n.* [altered (after *masque*) < Fr. *mascarade* < Sp. *máscarada* (< *máscara*) or It. *mascherata* (< *maschera*); see MASK, MASCARA], 1. a ball or party at which masks and fancy costumes are worn. 2. a costume for such a ball or party. 3. *a*) a disguise or false show. *b*) a living or acting under false pretenses. *v.i.* [MASQUERADED (-id), MASQUERADING], 1. to take part in a masquerade. 2. to live or act under false pretenses; go about disguised. *v.t.* to cover with a mask or disguise.

Mass, mass (mas, mäs), *n.* [ME. *masse;* AS. *mæsse, messe;* LL. *messa,* dismissal < L. *missa,* pp. of *mittere,* to dismiss < the words *ite, missa est* (go, you are dismissed), addressed to the congregation by the priest toward the end of the service], 1. the celebration or service of the Eucharist, a sacrament of the Roman Catholic Church, consisting of a series of prayers and ceremonies: the term is also used in some High Anglican churches. *High Mass* is celebrated with incense and music, the priest being assisted by a deacon and subdeacon; *Low Mass* is celebrated by one priest, without music and with little ceremony. 2. a musical setting for certain parts of this service. See also **black mass.**

mass (mas), *n.* [ME. & OFr. *masse;* L. *massa,* a lump, mass < Gr. *maza,* barley cake], 1. a quantity of matter forming a body of indefinite shape and size, usually of relatively large size; lump. 2. a large quantity or number: as, a *mass* of bruises. 3. bulk; size; magnitude. 4. the main or larger part; majority. 5. in *mining,* a mineral deposit of irregular shape: distinguished from *bed, vein.* 6. in *pharmacy,* the paste or plastic combination of drugs from which pills are made. 7. in *physics,* the quantity of matter in a body as measured in its relation to inertia: mass is determined for a given body by dividing the weight of the body by the acceleration due to gravity: see **matter,** *n.,* 2. *adj.* 1. of a large number of things; large-scale: as, *mass* production. 2. of, characteristic of, or for the masses: as, *mass* education. *v.t.* & *v.i.* to gather or assemble into a mass. Abbreviated **M., m.** —*SYN.* see **bulk.**
in the mass, collectively; as a whole.
the masses, the common people; the working people; lower classes in the social order: opposed to *the classes.*

Mas·sa·chu·sett (mas'ə-chōō'sit), *n.* [Am. Ind. (Massachusett) *Massa-adchu-es-et,* lit., at the big hill (used as a place name) < *massa,* big + *wadchu,* hill + *-es,* dim. suffix + *-et,* locative suffix], 1. a member of a large tribe of Algonquian Indians ‡who lived around Massachusetts Bay. 2. their language.

Mas·sa·chu·setts (mas'ə-chōō'sits), *n.* 1. a New England State of the United States: area, 8,257 sq. mi.; pop., 5,149,000; capital, Boston: nicknamed *Bay State:* abbreviated **Mass.** 2. Massachusett (sense 2).

Massachusetts Bay, a bay on the eastern coast of Massachusetts: length, 50 mi.; width, 25 mi.

mas·sa·cre (mas'ə-kẽr), *n.* [Fr.; OFr. *maçacre, macecle,* butchery, shambles; origin obscure; ? < *mache-col,* to butcher < *macher,* to smash + *col* (L. *collum*), the neck], 1. the indiscriminate, merciless killing of a number of human beings or, sometimes, animals; wholesale slaughter. 2. [Slang], an overwhelming defeat, as in sports. *v.t.* [MASSACRED (-kẽrd), MASSACRING], 1. to kill (many people or animals) indiscriminately and mercilessly; slaughter wholesale. 2. [Slang], to defeat overwhelmingly. —*SYN.* see **slaughter.**

mas·sage (mə-säzh'), *n.* [Fr. < *masser,* to massage < Port. *amassar,* to knead < *massa,* a lump; L. *massa;* see MASS], a rubbing, kneading, etc. of part of the body, usually with the hands, as to stimulate circulation and make muscles or joints supple. *v.t.* [MASSAGED (-säzhd'), MASSAGING], to give a massage to.

mas·sag·er (mə-säzh'ẽr), *n.* a person who massages.

mas·sag·ist (mə-säzh'ist), *n.* a massager.

mas·sa·sau·ga (mas'ə-sô'gə), *n.* [< *Mississauga,* Ojibway name of river and Indian tribe in Ontario], a variety of small rattlesnake found in dry regions of the southern United States.

Mas·sa·soit (mas'ə-soit'), *n.* American Indian chief of Massachusetts, known as a friend of the Pilgrims; lived 1580?–1661; father of King Philip.

Mas·sa·ua, Mas·sa·wa (mäs-sä'wä), *n.* a seaport in Eritrea, Ethiopia., on the Red Sea: pop., 25,000.

mass defect, in *physics,* the amount by which the mass of the nucleus of an atom is less than the sum of the masses of the particles of which the nucleus is constituted: cf. **packing effect.**

mas·sé (ma-sā'), *n.* [Fr., pp. of *masser,* to make a massé shot < *masse,* billiard cue, lit. mace], a stroke in billiards made by hitting the cue ball on the side with the cue held perpendicularly or almost so, usually so as to make the ball move in a curve around one of the object balls: also **massé shot.**

Mas·sé·na, An·dré (än'drā' ma'sā'na'), Prince d'Essling, 1758–1817; French marshal under Napoleon I.

Mas·se·net, Jules É·mile Fré·dé·ric (zhül ā'mēl' frā'dā'rēk' mas'ne'; Eng. mas'ə-nā'), 1842–1912; French composer.

mas·se·ter (ma-sē'tẽr), *n.* [Mod. L. < Gr. *masētēr,* a chewer < *masasthai,* to chew], either of a pair of large muscles in the angle of the lower jaw, which raise the jaw in chewing, etc.

mas·seur (ma-sũr'; Fr. ma'sẽr'), *n.* [Fr. < *masser;* see MASSAGE], a man whose work is massaging.

mas·seuse (ma-sooz'; Fr. ma'söz'), *n.* [Fr., fem. of *masseur*], a woman whose work is massaging.

mas·si·cot (mas'i-kot'), *n.* [Fr.; It. *marzacotto;* Sp. *mezacote* < Ar. *shabb qubṭi,* Coptic alum; see COPTIC], a yellow oxide of lead, PbO, produced by heating lead in air to just above the melting point, used as a pigment and in the production of red lead.

mas·sif (mas'if; Fr. ma'sēf'), *n.* [Fr., lit., solid; see MASSIVE], in *geology,* 1. the dominant, central mass of a mountain ridge, more or less defined by lengthwise or crosswise valleys. 2. a diastrophic block of the earth's crust that is isolated by boundary faults and has shifted as a whole.

Mas·sil·lon (mas''l-ən), *n.* a city in northeastern Ohio: pop., 31,000.

Mas·sine, Lé·o·nide (lā'ô'nēd' ma'sēn'), 1896– ; Russian ballet dancer, producer, and choreographer.

mass·i·ness (mas'i-nis), *n.* a massy quality or state.

Mas·sin·ger, Philip (mas''n-jẽr), 1584?–1640; English dramatist.

Mas·si·nis·sa (mas'ə-nis'ə), *n.* Masinissa.

mas·sive (mas'iv), *adj.* [Fr. *massif* < *masse;* see MASS (a lump)], 1. forming or consisting of a large mass; large and heavy; big and solid; bulky; ponderous. 2.

solid, not hollow or plated: said of articles made of gold or silver. 3. large and imposing or impressive; of considerable magnitude. 4. in *geology*, *a*) homogeneous in structure, without stratification, foliation, etc.: as, *massive* rock formations. *b*) occurring in thick beds, without minor joints and lamination: said of some stratified rocks. 5. in *mineralogy*, irregular in form, though occasionally crystalline in internal structure. —*SYN.* see **heavy.**

mass meeting, a large public meeting to hear speakers, discuss public affairs, demonstrate public approval or disapproval, etc.

mass number, in *atomic & nuclear physics*, the whole number by which the fundamental unit of mass, 1.6603 $\times 10^{-24}$ gram (almost the mass of a proton, the nucleus of a hydrogen atom), is multiplied to find the approximate mass of the nucleus of an atom: it is equal to the sum of the numbers of protons and neutrons in the nucleus and is always at least twice as great as the atomic number, except in the case of hydrogen and a certain rare isotope of helium.

mas·so·ther·a·py (mas'ō-ther'ə-pi), ***n.*** [< *massage* + *therapy*], the treatment of disease by massage.

mass production, the production or manufacture of goods in large quantities, especially by machinery and division of labor.

mass·y (mas'i), ***adj.*** [MASSIER (-i-ēr), MASSIEST (-i-ist)], [Archaic or Poetic], massive; solid, weighty, bulky, etc.

mast (mast, mäst), ***n.*** [ME. *maste;* AS. *mæst;* akin to G. *mast;* IE. **mazdo-s*, a pole, rod, seen also in L. *malus*, mast (< **madus* with Sabine *l* for *d*), Ir. *maide*, a stick], 1. a tall spar, sometimes in sections, rising vertically from the keel or deck of a vessel and used to support the sails, yards, etc.: modern masts are often hollow structures made of wooden strips, tubular steel, extruded aluminum, etc. 2. a specified section of this: as, the top*mast*. 3. any vertical pole, as in a crane or derrick. 4. the foremast. 5. [M-], in the *United States Navy*, a summary session held by an officer to impose discipline and hear complaints. ***v.t.*** to put a mast or masts on.

before the mast, 1. in the sailors' quarters on a ship, forward of the foremast, as distinguished from the officers' quarters aft; hence, 2. as a common sailor; as an unlicensed seaman.

mast (mast, mäst), ***n.*** [ME. *maste;* AS. *mæst;* akin to G. *mast;* IE. base **mad-*, moist, dripping (with fat, etc.), seen also in Gr. *mazōs*, *mastōs*, a breast (cf. MASTOID) & Eng. *meat*], beechnuts, acorns, chestnuts, etc., especially as food for hogs.

mast-, masto-.

mas·ta·ba, mas·ta·bah (mas'tə-bə), ***n.*** [Ar. *maṣṭabah*], an oblong structure with a flat roof and sloping sides, built over the opening of a mummy chamber or burial pit in ancient Egypt and used as a tomb or mortuary chapel.

MASTABA

mas·tec·to·my (mas-tek'tə-mi), ***n.*** [*mast-* + *-ectomy*], the surgical removal of a breast.

mas·ter (mas'tēr, mäs'tēr), ***n.*** [ME. *maistre* < AS. *mægester*, magister & OFr. *maistre;* both < L. *magister*, a master, chief, leader; orig., double comparative < base of L. *magnus*, great; IE. base **meǵ-*, great, seen also in Gr. *megas*, large (cf. MEGALO-)], 1. a man who rules others or has control, authority, or power over something; specifically, *a*) a man who is head of a household or institution. *b*) an employer. *c*) an owner of an animal or slave. *d*) the captain of a merchant ship. *e*) a victor: as, he proved to be the *master* of the other runners in the race. *f*) [Chiefly British], a male schoolteacher or tutor. *g*) a person whose teachings in religion, philosophy, etc. one follows or professes to follow; hence, *h*) [M-], Jesus Christ (with *our*, *the*, etc.). 2. something regarded as having control, power, etc.: as, love is his *master*. 3. a person very skilled and able in some work, profession, science, etc.; expert; specifically, *a*) a skilled workman or craftsman qualified to follow his trade independently. *b*) an artist regarded as great. 4. a work by such an artist: as, this painting is an old *master*. 5. [M-], a title variously applied to *a*) originally, a man of high rank; hence, *b*) later, any man or youth: now superseded by the variant *Mister*, usually written *Mr*. *c*) a boy regarded as too young to be addressed as *Mr*. *d*) a man who heads some institution, group, activity, or place: as, *Master* of the Foxhounds. *e*) in Scotland, the heir apparent of a viscount or baron. *f*) a person holding a certain degree from a college or university, denoting completion of a prescribed course of graduate study in some field and ranking above that of *Bachelor* and below that of *Doctor*: as, *Master* of Arts. 6. a metal matrix or mold made from the original recording and used to produce phonograph records in quantity. 7. in *law*, any of several court officers appointed to assist the judge by hearing evidence, reporting on certain matters, etc.: as, a *master* in chancery. Abbreviated **M.** ***adj.*** 1. being master. 2. of a master. 3. chief; principal; main; controlling; specifically, designating a mechanism or contrivance that controls others or sets a standard or norm: as, a *master* switch, a *master* test sheet. ***v.t.*** 1. to become master of; subdue, control, conquer, or defeat. 2. to rule or govern as master. 3. to become an expert in (an art, science, etc.).

mas·ter-at-arms (mas'tēr-ət-ärmz', mäs'tēr-ət-ärmz'), ***n.*** [*pl.* MASTERS-AT-ARMS], a naval petty officer responsible for keeping order, maintaining discipline, taking charge of prisoners, etc. on a warship: the rating no longer exists in the United States Navy.

master builder, 1. a person skilled in, or in charge of, building; especially, an architect: often figurative. 2. a building contractor.

mas·ter·dom (mas'tēr-dəm, mäs'tēr-dəm), ***n.*** mastery.

mas·ter·ful (mas'tēr-fəl, mäs'tēr-fəl), ***adj.*** 1. fond of acting the part of a master; arbitrary; imperious. 2. having or showing the ability of a master; expert; skillful.

SYN.—**masterful** implies such strength of personality as enables one to impose his will on others (a *masterful* orchestral conductor); **domineering** implies the arrogant, tyrannical manner of one who openly tries to dominate another (a *domineering* mother); **imperious** suggests the arbitrary ruling of an emperor, but connotes less arrogance than domineering (the *imperious* old dean of the college); **magisterial**, while not suggesting an assumption of arbitrary powers, implies an excessive use or display of such inherent powers as a magistrate might have (he dismissed me with a *magisterial* air).

master hand, 1. an expert. 2. great ability or skill.

master key, a key for opening more than one of a set of locks.

mas·ter·li·ness (mas'tēr-li-nis, mäs'tēr-li-nis), ***n.*** the quality or state of being masterly.

mas·ter·ly (mas'tēr-li, mäs'tēr-li), ***adj.*** showing the ability or skill of a master; expert: as, he did a *masterly* job. ***adv.*** in a masterly manner.

master mason, 1. a skilled mason; expert worker in brick or stone. 2. [often M- M-], a Freemason of the third degree. Abbreviated **M.M.**

master mechanic, a skilled mechanic, especially one serving as foreman: abbreviated **M.M.**

mas·ter·mind (mas'tēr-mīnd', mäs'tēr-mīnd'), ***n.*** [*master* + *mind*], a person of great intelligence, especially one with the ability to plan or direct a group project. ***v.t.*** to be the mastermind of (a project, etc.).

Master of Arts, 1. a degree given by a college or university to a person who has completed a prescribed course of graduate study in the humanities, social sciences, etc.: it ranks above the degree of *Bachelor* and below that of *Doctor*. 2. a person who has this degree. Abbreviated **M.A., A.M.**

master of ceremonies, 1. a person who supervises a ceremony. 2. a person who presides over an entertainment, as on a radio broadcast or in a night club, introducing the speakers or performers, filling in the intervals with jokes, etc. Abbreviated **M.C., m.c.**

Master of Science, 1. a degree given by a college or university to a person who has completed a prescribed course of graduate study in science rather than the humanities: it ranks above the degree of *Bachelor* and below that of *Doctor*. 2. a person who has this degree. Abbreviated **M.S., M.Sc.**

mas·ter·piece (mas'tēr-pēs', mäs'tēr-pēs'), ***n.*** [after G. *meisterstück*], 1. a thing made or done with masterly skill; great work of art or craftsmanship; chef-d'oeuvre. 2. the greatest work made or done by a person or group.

Mas·ters, Edgar Lee (mas'tērz, mäs'tērz), 1869–1950; American poet and novelist.

master sergeant, in the *United States armed forces*, a noncommissioned officer of the highest rank; in the Army, the rank just above sergeant first class; in the Marine Corps and Air Force, the rank just above technical sergeant; since 1948, army personnel with the occupational designation of *first sergeant* hold the rank of *master sergeant*: abbreviated **M.Sgt., M/Sgt** (no period).

mas·ter·ship (mas'tēr-ship', mäs'tēr-ship'), ***n.*** [see -SHIP], 1. the state of being a master; rule; control; dominion. 2. the position, duties, or term of office of a master, especially a schoolmaster. 3. masterly ability; expert skill or knowledge. 4. the status or degree of a master (in a trade, university, etc.).

mas·ter·sing·ers (mas'tēr-siŋ'ērz, mäs'tēr-siŋ'ērz), ***n.pl.*** [transl. of G. *meistersänger*], Meistersinger.

master stroke, a masterly action, move, or achievement.

mas·ter·work (mas'tēr-wūrk', mäs'tēr-wūrk'), ***n.*** a masterpiece.

master workman, 1. an expert workman, craftsman, or artist. 2. in some trades, a foreman or overseer.

mas·ter·y (mas'tēr-i, mäs'tēr-i), ***n.*** [*pl.* MASTERIES (-iz)], [ME. & OFr. *maistrie;* see MASTER], 1. mastership; rule; control. 2. ascendancy or victory in struggle or competition; the upper hand. 3. masterly ability; expert skill or knowledge: as, his *mastery* of chess is famous. 4. the act of mastering (an art, science, etc.).

mast·head (mast'hed', mäst'hed'), *n.* 1. the top part of a ship's mast, especially of the lower mast. 2. a sailor stationed in a crow's-nest near the masthead as a lookout. 3. that part of a newspaper or magazine stating the publishers, owners, and editors, the location of the business, advertising, and editorial offices, etc. *v.t.* 1. to send (a sailor) to the masthead as a punishment. 2. to hoist to or display at the masthead.

mas·tic (mas'tik), *n.* [ME. *mastik;* OFr. *mastic;* LL. *mastichum,* earlier *mastiche;* L. *mastiche;* Gr. *mastichē;* cf. MASTICATE], 1. a yellowish resin obtained from a small Mediterranean evergreen tree, used as an astringent and in making varnish, chewing gum, incense, etc. 2. the tree: often **mastic tree.** 3. a liquor flavored with mastic. 4. any of various quick-drying, pasty cements used for cementing tiles to a wall, etc.

mas·ti·cate (mas'tə-kāt'), *v.t.* [MASTICATED (-id), MASTICATING], [< LL. *masticatus,* pp. of *masticare,* to chew; Gr. *mastichan,* to grind the teeth, gnash < *mastax,* a mouth, morsel; IE. base **menth-*, to chew, mouth, seen also in L. *mandere,* to chew, Eng. *mouth*], 1. to chew up. 2. to grind, cut, or knead (rubber, etc.) to a pulp.

mas·ti·ca·tion (mas'tə-kā'shən), *n.* [LL. *masticatio*], a masticating or being masticated.

mas·ti·ca·tor (mas'tə-kā'tẽr), *n.* a person or thing that masticates; specifically, *a)* a person or animal that chews. *b)* an organ for chewing. *c)* a machine for crushing, grinding, or cutting something into small pieces.

mas·ti·ca·to·ry (mas'ti-kə-tôr'i, mas'ti-kə-tō'ri), *adj.* of or for mastication; specifically, adapted for chewing. *n.* [*pl.* MASTICATORIES (-iz, -riz)], any substance chewed to increase saliva flow.

mas·tiff (mas'tif, mäs'tif), *n.* [ME. *mastif, mestif;* OFr. *mastin* < LL. **mansuetinus* < L. *mansuetus,* tame; confused in OFr. with *mestif,* a mongrel < L. *mixtus,* mixed; see MIX], any of a breed of large, powerful, smooth-coated dog with hanging lips and drooping ears, formerly used for hunting and as watchdogs.

MASTIFF (30 in. high at shoulder)

mas·ti·tis (mas-tī'tis), *n.* [*mast-* + *-itis*], inflammation of the breast, or mammary gland.

mas·to- (mas'tō, mas'tə), [< Gr. *mastos,* the breast], a combining form meaning *of* or *like a breast,* or *mammary gland,* as in *mastodon:* also, before a vowel, **mast-**.

mas·to·don (mas'tə-don'), *n.* [Mod. L. < Gr. *mastos,* a breast + *odous, odontos,* a tooth: so called from the nipplelike processes on the molars], any of various large, extinct animals resembling the elephant but larger, and differing from it and the mammoth mainly in the structure of the molars.

mas·toid (mas'toid), *adj.* [Gr. *mastoeidēs* < *mastos,* a breast + *eidos,* form], 1. shaped like a breast or nipple. 2. designating, of, or near a projection of the temporal bone behind the ear. *n.* 1. the mastoid projection: see **skull,** illus. 2. [Colloq.], mastoiditis.

mas·toid·ec·to·my (mas'toid-ek'tə-mi), *n.* [see -ECTOMY], the surgical removal of part or all of a mastoid.

mas·toid·i·tis (mas'toid-ī'tis), *n.* inflammation of the mastoid.

mas·tur·bate (mas'tẽr-bāt'), *v.i.* [MASTURBATED (-id), MASTURBATING], to engage in masturbation.

mas·tur·ba·tion (mas'tẽr-bā'shən), *n.* [L. *masturbatio* < *masturbatus,* pp. of *masturbari*], genital self-excitation, usually by manipulation; auto-erotism: also called *self-abuse, onanism.*

mas·tur·ba·tor (mas'tẽr-bā'tẽr), *n.* a person who masturbates.

Ma·su·ren (mä-zōō'rən), *n.* Masuria: the German name.

Ma·su·ri·a (mə-zoor'i-ə), *n.* a region in northeastern Poland, formerly in East Prussia.

ma·su·ri·um (mə-soor'i-əm, mə-syoor'i-əm), *n.* [Mod. L. < *Masuria,* where first found], a name given to chemical element 43, supposedly discovered in columbite, gadolinite, etc., in 1925: symbol, Ma: cf. **technetium.**

mat (mat), *n.* [ME. *matte;* AS. *matt, meatt;* LL. *matta* (whence also G. *matte,* etc.)], 1. a flat, coarse fabric made of woven or plaited hemp, straw, rope, rushes, etc., often used as a floor covering. 2. a piece of this, or any more or less similar flat article, often corrugated or roughened, put down near a door, etc., for people to wipe their shoes on; door mat. 3. a flat piece of cloth, woven straw, or other material, put under a vase, dish, etc., or used as an ornament, as on a table. 4. a thickly padded floor covering, especially one used in a gymnasium for tumbling, wrestling, etc. 5. anything densely interwoven or felted, or growing in a thick tangle: as, a *mat* of hair. 6. in *nautical usage, a)* a thick web of rope yarn, used to protect rigging from wear. *b)* a web or pad used as a bumper or to plug large leaks in a hull. *v.t.* [MATTED (-id), MATTING], 1. to cover with or as with a mat or mats. 2. to interweave, felt, or tangle together into a thick mass. *v.i.* to be interwoven, felted, or tangled together into a thick mass.

mat (mat), *adj.* [Fr. < OFr. *mat,* overcome, defeated, exhausted < Ar. *māt;* see CHECKMATE], not glossy or shiny; lusterless; dull: said of a surface, finish, or color. *n.* [Fr.], ‡1. a dull surface or finish, often roughened: also spelled **matte.** 2. a border, as of dull gilt or white cardboard, put around a picture, either as the frame or, usually, between the picture and the frame. 3. in *printing,* a matrix. *v.t.* [MATTED (-id), MATTING], to produce a dull surface or finish on (metal, glass, etc.).

Mat·a·be·le (mat'ə-bē'li), *n.* [*pl.* MATABELE, MATABELES (-liz)], [< Zulu name, lit., vanishing (or hidden) people: from "hiding" behind large oxhide shields in battle], a member of a Zulu tribe driven out of the Transvaal by the Boers in 1837.

Mat·a·be·le·land (mat'ə-bē'li-land'), *n.* a district of Southern Rhodesia, Africa, under British control: the Matabele settled there after 1837.

mat·a·dor (mat'ə-dôr'), *n.* [Sp., lit., killer < *matar,* to kill < *mate,* checkmate; see CHECKMATE], 1. a bullfighter whose specialty is killing the bull with a sword thrust at the end of a bullfight after performing a series of formalized actions with a cape to anger and tire the animal. 2. one of the three principal cards in the games of ombre and quadrille.

Ma·ta·mo·ros (mä'tä-mô'rôs; Eng. mat'ə-môr'əs), *n.* a seaport in northeastern Mexico, on the Rio Grande opposite Brownsville, Texas: pop., 16,000 (1940).

Mat·a·nus·ka (mat'ə-nōōs'kə), *n.* a valley in southern Alaska, under development as an agricultural region since 1935 by homesteaders.

Ma·tan·zas (mə-tan'zəs; Am. Sp. mä-tän'säs), *n.* a seaport in northwestern Cuba: pop., 73,000.

Ma·ta·pan, Cape (mat'ə-pan'), a promontory in the southern Peloponnesus, Greece.

match (mach), *n.* [ME. *macche;* OFr. *mesche* (Fr. *mèche*), wick of a candle, match; prob. < L. *myxa,* wick of a candle; Gr. *myxa,* nozzle of a lamp], 1. originally, a wick or cord prepared to burn at a uniform rate, used for firing guns or explosives. 2. a slender piece of wood, cardboard, waxed cord, etc. tipped with a composition that catches fire by friction, sometimes only on a specially prepared surface. 3. [Obs.], a slip of paper, splinter of wood, etc. dipped in sulfur so that it can be ignited with a spark, for lighting candles, lamps, etc.

match (mach), *n.* [ME. *macche;* AS. *gemæcca,* one suited to another, mate < base of *macian,* to make, form (see MAKE, *v.* & *n.*); sense development: what is put together—what is suitable (for putting together), etc.], 1. any person or thing equal or similar to another in some way; specifically, *a)* a person, group, or thing able to cope with or oppose another as an equal in power, size, etc.; peer. *b)* a counterpart or facsimile. *c)* either of two corresponding things or persons; one of a pair. 2. two or more persons or things that go together in appearance, size, or other quality; pair: as, her purse and shoes were a good *match.* 3. a contest or game involving two or more contestants. 4. *a)* an agreement to marry or mate. *b)* a marriage or mating: as, she made a good *match.* 5. a person regarded as a suitable or possible mate. *v.t.* 1. to join in marriage; get a (suitable) match for; mate. 2. *a)* formerly, to meet as an antagonist; hence, *b)* to compete with successfully. 3. to put in opposition (*with*); pit (*against*). 4. to be equal, similar, suitable, or corresponding to in some way: as, his looks *match* his character. 5. to make, show, produce, or get a competitor, counterpart, or equivalent to: as, I want to *match* this cloth. 6. to suit or fit (one thing) to another. 7. to fit (things) together; make similar or corresponding. 8. to compare. 9. *a)* to flip or reveal (coins) as a form of gambling or to decide something contested, the winner being determined by the combination of faces thus exposed. *b)* to match coins with (another person), usually betting that the same faces will be exposed. *v.i.* 1. to get married; mate. 2. to be equal, similar, suitable, or corresponding in some way.

match·board (mach'bôrd', mach'bōrd'), *n.* any of a number of identical thin boards with a tongue formed along one edge and a groove cut along the other so that the tongue of one can be fitted into the groove of the next, as in making floors or ceilings.

match·box (mach'boks'), *n.* a small box for holding matches.

matched (macht), *adj.* [pp. of *match*], having a tongue formed along one edge and a groove cut along the other, as some boards.

match·less (mach'lis), *adj.* having no equal; peerless.

match·lock (mach′lok′), *n.* 1. an old type of gunlock in which the charge of powder was ignited by a slow match (of wicking or cord). 2. a musket with such a gunlock.

MATCHLOCK MUSKET (1660–1684)

match·mak·er (mach′māk′ẽr), *n.* a person who makes matches (for burning).

match·mak·er (mach′māk′ẽr), *n.* 1. a person who arranges a marriage or marriages for others, or tries to do so by scheming. 2. a person who arranges wrestling matches, prize fights, etc.

match·mak·ing (mach′māk′iŋ), *n.* the work or business of making matches (for burning).

match·mak·ing (mach′māk′iŋ), *n.* 1. the act or practice of arranging or trying to arrange marriages. 2. the arranging of wrestling matches, prize fights, etc.

match·mark (mach′märk′), *n.* a mark put on machine parts to distinguish them as an aid in assembling. *v.t.* to put such a mark on.

match play, 1. play in a match, as in tennis, etc. 2. in *golf,* a form of competitive play in which the score is calculated by counting holes won rather than strokes taken: distinguished from *medal play.*

match point, the final point needed to win the match, as in tennis.

match·wood (mach′wood′), *n.* 1. wood for making matches. 2. very small pieces; splinters.

mate (māt), *n.* [ME.; prob. < MLG. *mate,* a companion, < *gemate* < *ge-,* together + *mat,* meat, food; cf. COMPANION], 1. a companion, comrade, or fellow worker: often used in compounds, as *classmate,* and, among sailors, British workingmen, etc., as a familiar form of address. 2. one of a pair, especially of a matched pair. 3. *a*) a husband or wife; spouse. *b*) the male or female of animals paired for propagation. 4. [Archaic], an equal; fit associate. 5. in *nautical usage, a*) an officer of a merchant ship, ranking below the captain. *b*) an assistant. 6. in the *United States Navy,* any of various petty officers: as, a boatswain's *mate.* *v.t. & v.i.* [MATED (-id), MATING], 1. to join as a pair; couple. 2. to join as mates; couple in marriage or sexual union.

mate (māt), *n., interj., v.t.* [MATED (-id), MATING], checkmate.

ma·té, ma·te (mä′tā, mat′ā), *n.* [Sp. < Peruv. (Quechua) *mati,* calabash: so called in allusion to the gourd or calabash in which it is steeped], 1. a kind of tea made from the dried leaves of a certain South American plant. 2. the plant, a Brazilian holly. 3. the leaves of this plant. Also called *Paraguay tea.*

mat·e·lote (mat′ə-lōt′), *n.* [Fr. < *matelot,* sailor], stewed fish in a sauce of wine, oil, onions, mushrooms, etc.

mat·e·lotte (mat′ə-lot′), *n.* matelote.

Ma·te·os, A·dol·fo Ló·pez (ä-dôl′fô lô′pes mä-te′ôs), 1910– ; president of Mexico, 1958– .

ma·ter (mā′tẽr, mä′tẽr), *n.* [L., mother], 1. [Chiefly British Colloq.], mother: often preceded by *the.* 2. in *anatomy,* either of two membranes (*pia mater* and *dura mater*) forming, with the arachnoid, a covering for the brain and spinal cord.

‡**ma·ter do·lo·ro·sa** (mā′tẽr dō′lə-rō′sə), [L.], sorrowful mother: a name given to the Virgin Mary.

ma·ter·fa·mil·i·as (mā′tẽr-fə-mil′i-əs), *n.* [L.], the mother of a family; woman head of a household.

ma·te·ri·al (mə-têr′i-əl), *adj.* [LL. *materialis* < L. *materia,* matter, stuff, wood], 1. of matter; of substance; relating to or consisting of what occupies space; physical: as, a *material* object, *material* forces. 2. *a*) of the body or bodily needs, satisfactions, etc.; corporeal, sensual, or sensuous: as, *material* pleasures. *b*) of or fond of comfort, pleasure, wealth, etc. rather than spiritual values; worldly: as, *material* success. 3. important, essential, or pertinent (*to* the matter under discussion). 4. in *law,* important enough to affect the outcome of a case, the validity of a legal instrument, etc. 5. in *philosophy,* of the matter of reasoning, as distinguished from the formal element. *n.* 1. what a thing is, or may be, made of; elements, parts, or constituents: as, raw *material.* 2. ideas, notes, observations, sketches, etc. that may be worked up or elaborated; data. 3. cloth or other fabric. 4. *pl.* tools, implements, articles, etc. needed to make or do something: as, writing *materials.*

SYN.—**material** is applied to anything that is formed of matter and has substance (*material* objects, possessions, etc.); **physical** applies either to material things as they are perceivable by the senses or to forces that are scientifically measurable (the *physical* world, the *physical* properties of sound); **corporeal** applies only to such material objects as have bodily form and are tangible (*corporeal* property); **sensible** is specifically applied to anything that can be known through the senses rather than through the intellect (a *sensible* phenomenon). —*ANT.* spiritual, mental, psychical.

ma·te·ri·al·ism (mə-têr′i-əl-iz′m), *n.* 1. in *philosophy, a*) the doctrine that matter is the only reality and that everything in the world, including thought, will, and feeling, can be explained only in terms of matter: opposed to *idealism. b*) the doctrine that comfort, pleasure, and wealth are the only or highest goals or values. 2. the tendency to be more concerned with material than with spiritual goals or values.

ma·te·ri·al·ist (mə-têr′i-əl-ist), *n.* 1. a person who believes in materialism (sense 1). 2. a person characterized by materialism (sense 2). *adj.* of materialism or materialists (esp. in sense 1).

ma·te·ri·al·is·tic (mə-têr′i-ə-lis′tik), *adj.* 1. of materialism or materialists (esp. in sense 2). 2. characterized by materialism; concerned with worldly goals.

ma·te·ri·al·is·ti·cal·ly (mə-têr′i-ə-lis′ti-k'l-i, mə-têr′i-ə-lis′tik-li), *adv.* 1. in a materialist or materialistic manner. 2. from the viewpoint of materialism.

ma·te·ri·al·i·ty (mə-têr′i-al′ə-ti), *n.* 1. the state or quality of being material, or physical. 2. matter; substance. 3. [*pl.* MATERIALITIES (-tiz)], something material; body.

ma·te·ri·al·i·za·tion (mə-têr′i-əl-i-zā′shən, mə-têr′i-əl-i-zā′shən), *n.* a materializing or being materialized.

ma·te·ri·al·ize (mə-têr′i-ə-līz′), *v.t.* [MATERIALIZED (-līzd′), MATERIALIZING], 1. to give material form or characteristics to; represent in material form. 2. to make (a spirit, etc.) appear in bodily form. 3. to make materialistic. *v.i.* 1. to become fact; develop into something real or tangible; be realized: as, this project never *materialized.* 2. to take on, or appear in, bodily form: said of spirits, etc.

ma·te·ri·al·ly (mə-têr′i-əl-i), *adv.* 1. with regard to the matter, substance, or content, and not the form. 2. with regard to material objects, interests, etc.; physically. 3. to a great extent; substantially; considerably.

ma·te·ri·a med·i·ca (mə-têr′i-ə med′i-kə), [ML.; L. *materia,* matter, material + *medica,* fem. of *medicus,* medical], 1. the drugs and other remedial substances used in medicine. 2. the branch of medical science that deals with such substances, their uses, etc.

ma·te·ri·el, ma·té·ri·el (mə-têr′i-el′; Fr. mȧ′tā′ryel′), *n.* [Fr. *matériel;* see MATERIAL], 1. materials and tools necessary to any work, enterprise, etc.; specifically, weapons, equipment, supplies, etc. of armed forces: distinguished from *personnel.* 2. nonexpendable weapons, equipment, etc. of armed forces: distinguished from *supplies.*

ma·ter·nal (mə-tũr′n'l), *adj.* [Fr. *maternel* < L. *maternus* < *mater,* a mother], 1. of, like, or characteristic of a mother or motherhood; motherly. 2. derived, received, or inherited from a mother. 3. on the mother's side of the family: as, *maternal* grandparents.

ma·ter·nal·ize (mə-tũr′nə-līz′), *v.t.* to make maternal.

ma·ter·ni·ty (mə-tũr′nə-ti), *n.* [*pl.* MATERNITIES (-tiz)], [Fr. *maternité;* ML. *maternitas* < L. *maternus;* see MATERNAL], 1. the state of being a mother; motherhood. 2. the character or qualities of a mother; motherliness. *adj.* for prospective mothers; for pregnant women: as, a *maternity* dress.

maternity hospital, a hospital for women giving birth and for the care of newborn babies; lying-in hospital.

mate·y (mā′ti), *adj.* [*mate* (companion) + *-y*], [British Colloq.], friendly; companionable; chummy. *n.* [British Colloq.], a companion; chum.

math (math), *n.* [Colloq.], mathematics.

math·e·mat·ic (math′ə-mat′ik), *adj.* [Rare], mathematical. *n.* [Rare], mathematics.

math·e·mat·i·cal (math′ə-mat′i-k'l), *adj.* [< L. *mathematicus;* Gr. *mathēmatikos,* inclined to learn, mathematical < *mathēma,* what is learned < *manthanein,* to learn; + *-al*], 1. of, having the nature of, or concerned with mathematics; hence, 2. rigorously exact, precise, accurate, etc. Abbreviated **math.**

mathematical logic, a modern type of formal logic using special symbols that can be handled according to exact principles: also called *symbolic logic.*

math·e·mat·i·cal·ly (math′ə-mat′i-k'l-i, math′ə-mat′ik-li), *adv.* 1. by or according to mathematics. 2. in a mathematical manner; with rigorous precision.

math·e·ma·ti·cian (math′ə-mə-tish′ən), *n.* [ME. *mathematicion;* Late OFr. *mathematicien*], an expert or specialist in mathematics: abbreviated **math.**

math·e·mat·ics (math′ə-mat′iks), *n.pl.* [construed as sing.], [see MATHEMATICAL & -ICS], the group of sciences (including arithmetic, geometry, algebra, calculus, etc.) dealing with quantities, magnitudes, and forms, and their relationships, attributes, etc., by the use of numbers and symbols. Abbreviated **math.**

Math·er, Cot·ton (kot′'n math′ẽr), 1663–1728; American clergyman and writer.

Mather, In·crease (in′krēs), 1639–1723; father of *Cotton;* American clergyman and writer.

Ma·til·da, Ma·thil·da (mə-til′də), [ML. *Matilda, Mathildis;* OHG. *Mahthilda* < *maht,* might, power + *hiltia,* battle; hence, lit., powerful (in) battle], a feminine name: diminutives, *Matty, Maud, Tilda, Tilly.*

mat·in (mat′in), *n.* [Early ME. *matyn;* OFr. *matin* < L. *matutinus,* of the morning < *Matuta,* goddess of dawn; cf. MATUTINAL], 1. *pl.* [sometimes M-], *a*) in the *Roman Catholic Church,* the first of the seven canonical hours in the breviary, properly recited at midnight, but often at daybreak, and followed by lauds. *b)* in the *Anglican Church*, the order for, or the service of, public morning prayer: often spelled **mattins** in British usage. 2. [Poetic], a morning song, especially of birds. *adj.* 1. of matins. 2. of morning.

mat·in·al (mat'in-'l), *adj.* 1. of or at matins. 2. of or in the morning.

mat·i·nee, mat·i·née (mat''n-ā', mat''n-ā'), *n.* [Fr. *matinée* < *matin*, morning; see MATIN], a reception or entertainment held in the daytime; especially, a performance, as of a play, held in the afternoon.

matinee idol, an actor whose looks and manner make him popular with women theatergoers.

mat·ing (māt'iŋ), *n.* [see MATE (to join)], a pairing or matching. *adj.* of or for mating: as, the *mating* season.

Ma·tisse, Hen·ri (än'rē' mȧ'tēs'), 1869–1954; French painter.

mat·rass (mat'rəs), *n.* [Fr. *matras* < *matras*, kind of arrow, blunt borer < Gaul. *mataris*, javelin], 1. a glass container with a rounded body and a long neck, formerly used in distilling, etc. 2. a slender, hard glass tube used in blowpipe analysis. Also spelled **mattrass.**

ma·tri- (mā'tri, mat'ri), [< L. *mater, matris*, a mother], a combining form meaning *mother*, as in *matriarch.*

ma·tri·arch (mā'tri-ärk'), *n.* [*matri-* + *-arch* as in *patriarch*], a mother who rules her family or tribe; specifically, in *sociology*, a woman holding a position analogous to that of a patriarch.

ma·tri·ar·chal (mā'tri-är'k'l), *adj.* 1. of, or having the nature of, a matriarch or matriarchy. 2. fit for a matriarch.

ma·tri·arch·ate (mā'tri-är'kit), *n.* 1. a family, tribe, etc. ruled by a matriarch. 2. a matriarchal government or system.

ma·tri·ar·chic (mā'tri-är'kik), *adj.* of, or having the nature of, a matriarchy; matriarchal.

ma·tri·arch·y (mā'tri-är'ki), *n.* [*pl.* MATRIARCHIES (-kiz)], [see MATRIARCH], 1. a form of social organization in which the mother is recognized as the head of the family or tribe, descent and kinship being traced through the mother instead of the father. 2. government by women.

mat·ri·ces (mā'trə-sēz', mat'rə-sēz'), *n.* alternative plural of **matrix.**

ma·tri·cid·al (mā'trə-sīd''l, mat'rə-sīd''l), *adj.* of, like, or having the nature of, matricide or a matricide.

ma·tri·cide (mā'trə-sīd', mat'rə-sīd'), *n.* [L. *matricidium* < *mater*, mother + *caedere*, to kill], 1. the act of killing one's mother; murder of a woman by her child 2. [L. *matricida*], a person who kills his mother.

ma·tric·u·lant (mə-trik'yoo-lənt), *n.* a person matriculating or applying for matriculation.

ma·tric·u·late (mə-trik'yoo-lāt'; *for n.*, mə-trik'yoo-lit), *v.t. & v.i.* [MATRICULATED (-id), MATRICULATING], [< ML., *matriculatus*, pp. of *matriculare*, to register < LL. *matricula*, dim. of *matrix*; see MATRIX], to enroll, especially as a student or candidate for a degree in a college or university. *n.* a person so enrolled.

ma·tric·u·la·tion (mə-trik'yoo-lā'shən), *n.* a matriculating or being matriculated.

ma·tric·u·la·tor (mə-trik'yoo-lā'tẽr), *n.* a matriculant.

ma·tri·lin·e·al (mā'trə-lin'i-əl, mat'rə-lin'i-əl), *adj.* [*matri-* + *lineal*], designating or of descent, kinship, or derivation through the mother instead of the father.

mat·ri·mo·ni·al (mat'rə-mō'ni-əl), *adj.* [Fr.; LL. *matrimonialis*], of matrimony; marital; nuptial; conjugal.

mat·ri·mo·ni·al·ly (mat'rə-mō'ni-əl-i), *adv.* 1. by or as regards matrimony. 2. according to the rules or customs of matrimony.

mat·ri·mo·ny (mat'rə-mō'ni), *n.* [*pl.* MATRIMONIES (-niz)], [ME. & OFr. *matrimoine*; L. *matrimonium* < *mater, matris*, a mother], 1. the act of marrying; rite or sacrament of marriage. 2. the state of being husband and wife. 3. married life. 4. *a)* a card game with any number of players. *b)* a combination of the king and queen of trump, as in this game. —*SYN.* see **marriage.**

matrimony vine, the boxthorn.

ma·trix (mā'triks, mat'riks), *n.* [*pl.* MATRICES (mā'trə-sēz', mat'rə-sēz'), MATRIXES (-iz)], [LL., womb, public register, origin; L., breeding animal < stem of *mater*, a mother], 1. originally, the womb; uterus; hence, 2. that within which, or within and from which, something originates, takes form, or develops; specifically, *a)* the rock in which a gem, mineral, fossil, etc. is enclosed or embedded; also, the impression left in such rock when the embedded object is removed. *b)* a die or mold for casting or shaping. *c)* a metal plate, usually of copper, for molding the face of a type. *d)* a papier-mâché, plaster, or similar impression of type, etc., from which a plate can be made for printing, as in stereotypy: also **mat.** 3. *a)* the substance between the cells of animal or plant tissue. *b)* the formative cells from which a nail, tooth, etc. grows.

ma·tron (mā'trən), *n.* [ME. & OFr. *matrone*; L. *matrona* < *mater*, a mother], 1. a married woman; wife or widow, especially one who has had children or is not very young. 2. a woman superintendent or manager of the domestic arrangements of a hospital, prison, or other institution. 3. a woman attendant or guard in charge of women or children, as in an institution.

ma·tron·age (mā'trən-ij, mat'rən-ij), *n.* [see -AGE], 1. matrons collectively. 2. the state of being a matron. 3. matronly care or supervision.

ma·tron·ize (mā'trən-īz', mat'rən-īz'), *v.t.* [MATRONIZED (-īzd'), MATRONIZING], 1. to make matronly. 2. to chaperon. *v.i.* to become a matron.

ma·tron·li·ness (mā'trən-li-nis), *n.* the quality or state of being matronly.

ma·tron·ly (mā'trən-li), *adj.* of, characteristic of, like, or suitable for a matron; dignified, sedate, staid, etc. *adv.* in a matronly manner.

matron of honor, a married woman acting as chief attendant to the bride at a wedding: cf. **maid of honor.**

mat·ro·nym·ic (mat'rə-nim'ik), *adj.* metronymic.

Ma·tsu·o·ka, Yo·su·ke (yō'soo-ke' mä'tsoo-ō'kä), 1880–1946; Japanese statesman; foreign minister of Japan (1940–1941).

Matt., Matthew.

matte (mat), *n.* [Fr. < dial. *mate*, a lump; prob. ult. < L. *matta*, mat of rushes; see MAT (floor covering)], an impure mixture of sulfides that is produced in smelting the sulfide ores of copper, nickel, lead, etc.

matte (mat), *n.* a mat (dull finish).

mat·ted (mat'id), *adj.* 1. closely tangled together in a dense mass: as, *matted* hair. 2. covered with a dense growth. 3. covered with or enclosed in matting or mats.

mat·ted (mat'id), *adj.* having a mat (dull finish).

mat·ter (mat'ẽr), *n.* [ME. *matere, matiere*; OFr. *matiere, matere* (Fr. *matière*); L. *materia*, material, stuff, wood], 1. what a thing is made of; constituent substance or material. 2. what all (material) things are made of; whatever occupies space and is perceptible to the senses in some way: in modern physics, matter and energy are regarded as equivalents, mutually convertible according to Einstein's formula, $E = mc^2$ (i.e., energy equals mass multiplied by the square of the velocity of light); in dualistic thinking, matter is regarded as the opposite of mind, spirit, etc. 3. any specified sort of substance: as, coloring *matter*. 4. material of thought or expression; what is spoken or written, regarded as distinct from how it is spoken or written; content, as distinguished from manner, style, or form. 5. an amount or quantity, usually indefinite: as, a *matter* of a few days. 6. *a)* something that is the subject of discussion, concern, action, etc.; thing or affair: as, a *matter* of course, a *matter* of fact, business *matters*. *b)* cause, occasion, or grounds: as, no laughing *matter*. 7. *a)* an important affair; thing of some moment or significance. *b)* importance; moment; significance: as, it's of no *matter*. 8. a disagreeable state of affairs; trouble; difficulty (with *the*): as, what's the *matter?* 9. documents, letters, etc. sent, or to be sent, by mail; mail: as, second-class *matter*. 10. pus. 11. in *philosophy*, that which has yet to take on form; undifferentiated substance of reality or experience. 12. in *printing*, *a)* material set up, or to be set up, in type; copy. *b)* type set up. *v.i.* 1. to be of importance or consequence; signify: as, does it really *matter* what I think? 2. to form and discharge pus; suppurate; maturate.

as a matter of fact, in fact; in actuality; really.

for that matter, in regard to that; as far as that is concerned: also **for the matter of that.**

no matter, 1. it is of no importance. 2. regardless of.

Mat·ter·horn (mat'ẽr-hôrn'), *n.* a mountain of the Pennine Alps, between Switzerland and Italy: height, 14,780 ft.: also called *Mont Cervin.*

mat·ter-of-course (mat'ẽr-əv-kôrs', mat'ẽr-əv-kōrs'), *adj.* 1. coming as a natural or logical occurrence in the course of events; to be expected; routine. 2. taking things as a matter of course.

matter of course, a thing to be expected as a natural or logical occurrence in the course of events.

mat·ter-of-fact (mat'ẽr-əv-fakt'), *adj.* sticking strictly to facts; literal, unimaginative, practical, prosaic, etc.

matter of opinion, something about which there can be more than one opinion; debatable question.

Mat·thew (math'ū), [ME. & OFr. *Matheu*; LL. *Matthaeus*; Gr. *Matthaios, Matthias*, contr. < *Mattathias*; Heb. *mattithyāh*, lit., gift of God], a masculine name: diminutive, *Mat(t)*; variant, *Matthias*; equivalents, Fr. *Mathieu*, G. & Sw. *Matthaus*, It. *Matteo*, Sp. *Mateo*. *n.* in the *Bible*, 1. one of the four Evangelists, a customs collector who was a believer in Jesus and was chosen as one of the twelve apostles: also **Saint Matthew.** 2. the first book of the New Testament, telling of Jesus' life: ascribed to Matthew. Abbreviated **Matt.**

Matthew (of) Paris, 1200?–1259; English monk and chronicler.

Mat·thews, (James) Bran·der (bran'dẽr math'ūz), 1852–1929; American scholar and writer.

Mat·thi·as (mə-thī′əs), a masculine name: see **Matthew.** *n.* in the *Bible*, one of the apostles, chosen by lot to replace Judas Iscariot.

mat·ting (mat′iŋ), *n.* **1.** a woven fabric of fiber, as straw or hemp, for mats, floor covering, wrapping, etc. 2. mats collectively. 3. the making of mats.

mat·ting (mat′iŋ), *n.* [see MAT (dull finish)], 1. the production of a dull surface or finish on metal, glass, etc. 2. this surface or finish. 3. a mat, or border.

mat·tins (mat′inz), *n.pl.* matins: Anglican spelling.

mat·tock (mat′ək), *n.* [ME. *mattok;* AS. *mattuc;* IE. base **mat-*, implement for hacking, cutting, etc., seen also in L. *mateola*, mallet, whence Eng. *mace*], a tool for loosening the soil, digging up and cutting roots, etc.: it is like a pickax but has a flat, adz-shaped blade on one or both sides.

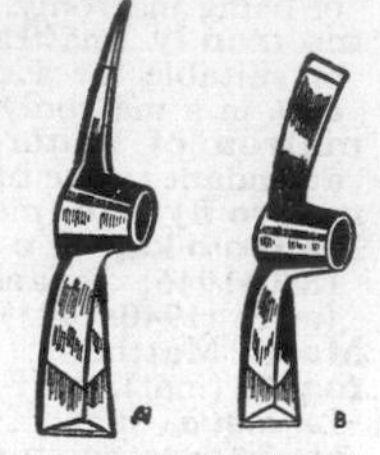
TYPES OF MATTOCK
A, pick mattock; B, cutter mattock

Mat·to Gros·so (mä′too grô′soo), a state of western Brazil, bordering Bolivia and Paraguay: area, 532,210 sq. mi.; pop., 522,000; capital, Cuyabá.

mat·toid (mat′oid), *n.* [It. *mattoide* < *matto*, mad < L. *mattus*, intoxicated < Per. *mat* (via LL.); see CHECKMATE], [Now Rare], a person of unbalanced mind verging on insanity.

mat·trass (mat′rəs), *n.* a matrass.

mat·tress (mat′ris), *n.* [ME. & OFr. *materas;* It. *materasso* < Ar. *maṭraḥ*, place where something is thrown or laid, cushion], 1. a casing of strong cloth or other fabric filled with cotton, hair, foam rubber, etc., often quilted or tufted at intervals, and used on or as a bed: some mattresses (called *innerspring mattresses*) are made with wire springs inside. 2. a mass or mat of interwoven brushwood, poles, etc. used to protect an embankment or dike from erosion, etc.

mat·u·rate (mach′oo-rāt′, mat′yoo-rāt′), *v.i.* [MATURATED (-id), MATURATING], [< L. *maturatus*, pp. of *maturare;* see MATURE], 1. to suppurate; discharge pus. 2. to ripen; mature.

mat·u·ra·tion (mach′oo-rā′shən, mat′yoo-rā′shən), *n.* [Fr.; L. *maturatio* < pp. of *maturare;* see MATURE], 1. the formation or discharge of pus; suppuration. 2. a ripening or maturing. 3. in *biology*, the final stages in the development of gametes in which the normal number of chromosomes is reduced by half: see **meiosis.**

ma·ture (mə-tyoor′, mə-toor′; *now often* mə-choor′), *adj.* [L. *maturus*, seasonable, ripe, mature], 1. full-grown, as plants or animals; ripe, as fruits; fully developed, as a person, a mind, etc. 2. fully or highly developed, perfected, worked out, considered, etc.: as, a *mature* scheme. 3. of a state of full development: as, a person of *mature* age. 4. due; payable: said of a note, bond, etc. 5. in *geology*, having reached maximum development and accentuation of form, or maximum vigor and efficiency of action: said of streams adjusted to their surroundings, topography resulting from erosion, etc. *v.t.* [MATURED (-tyoord′, -toord′, -choord′), MATURING], 1. to bring to full growth or development; cause to ripen. 2. to develop or work out fully. *v.i.* 1. to become fully grown or developed; ripen. 2. to become due: said of a note, etc. —*SYN.* see **ripe.**

ma·tu·ri·ty (mə-tyoor′ə-ti, mə-toor′ə-ti; *now often* mə-choor′ə-ti), *n.* [ME. & OFr. *maturite;* L. *maturitas*], 1. the state or quality of being mature; specifically, *a*) a being full-grown, ripe, or fully developed. *b*) a being perfect, complete, or ready. 2. *a*) a becoming due. *b*) the time at which a note, etc. becomes due. 3. [*pl.* MATURITIES (-tiz)], a mature act, trait, etc.

ma·tu·ti·nal (mə-tū′ti-n'l, mə-to͞o′ti-n'l), *adj.* [L. *matutinalis* < *matutinus*, of morning < *Matuta*, goddess of morning; cf. MATIN], of or in the morning; early.

matz·os (mät′sōs, mät′səs), *n.pl.* matzoth.

matz·oth (mät′sōth, mät′sōs), *n.pl.* [sing. MATSO (-sô, -sə)], [Heb. *matstsōth*, pl. of *matstsāh*, unleavened], flat, thin pieces of unleavened bread, eaten by Jews during the Passover.

Mau·beuge (mō′bözh′), *n.* a city in northeastern France: pop., 21,000.

maud (môd), *n.* [? < the name *Maud*], 1. a gray striped plaid, worn by shepherds in southern Scotland. 2. a shawl, wrap, or rug made of such plaid.

Maud, Maude (môd), a feminine name: see **Matilda.**

maud·lin (môd′lin), *adj.* [< *Maudlin*, Magdalene; ME. *Maudeleyne;* OFr. *Madeleine*: Magdalene was often represented with eyes red from weeping], 1. foolishly and tearfully or weakly sentimental. 2. tearfully sentimental from too much drink. —*SYN.* see **sentimental.**

Maugham, William Som·er·set (sum′ẽr-set′ môm), 1874– ; English writer and dramatist.

mau·gre, mau·ger (mô′gẽr), *prep.* [ME. *maugrie*, etc.; OFr. *maugré, malgré*, lit., with displeasure < *mal*, ill + *gré*, pleasure; see MAL- & AGREE], [Archaic], in spite of.

Mau·i (mou′ē), *n.* one of the Hawaiian Islands, northwest of Hawaii: area, 728 sq. mi.; pop., 36,000.

mau·kin (mô′kin), *n.* [Scot.], a malkin.

maul (môl), *n.* [Early Mod. Eng. phonetic sp. of ME. *malle;* OFr. *maile;* L. *malleus*, a hammer; cf. MALL, MALLET], 1. a very heavy hammer or mallet, often of wood, for driving stakes, wedges, etc. 2. [Archaic], *a*) a mace. *b*) a wooden club. *v.t.* [ME. *mallen;* OFr. *mailler* < the *n.*], 1. to injure by beating or tearing; bruise or lacerate. 2. to handle roughly or clumsily; manhandle; paw. 3. to split (rails, stumps, etc.) with a maul and wedge. Also **mall.** —*SYN.* see **beat.**

maul·er (môl′ẽr), *n.* 1. a person or thing that mauls. 2. [Slang], a boxer or wrestler.

Maul·main (moul-mān′, môl-mān′), *n.* Moulmein.

maul·stick (môl′stik′), *n.* [D. *maalstok* < *malen*, to paint + *stok*, a stick], a long, light stick used by painters as a rest for steadying the brush hand while at work: also **mahlstick.**

Mau Mau (mou′ mou′), [*pl.* MAU MAU, MAU MAUS (mouz′)], a member of a secret society of natives in Kenya, British East Africa, organized c. 1951 to fight against white rule: both the movement and its suppression marked by terrorism and violence.

Mau·mee (mô-mē′, mô′mē′), *n.* a river flowing from northeastern Indiana into Lake Erie: length, 175 mi.

mau·met (mô′mit), *n.* [contr. < *Mahomet*], **1.** [Obs.], an idol: from the notion that Moslems worshiped Mohammed as a god. 2. [British Dial.], *a*) a doll or puppet. *b*) a guy. Also **mammet.**

maun (män, môn), *v.i.* [MScot. *mane* < ON. *man*, pres. t. of *munu*, shall, will, lit. intend], [Scot.], must.

Mau·na Ke·a (mou′nä kā′ä), an extinct volcano on the island of Hawaii: height, 13,825 ft.

Mau·na Lo·a (mou′nä lō′ä), an active volcano in Hawaii National Park, on the island of Hawaii: height, 13,675 ft.: see **Hawaiian Islands**, map.

maund (mônd), *n.* [Hind. & Per. *man;* Sans. *manā;* prob. < Sem.], a unit of weight used in India, Turkey, Iran, etc., varying from somewhat less than 20 to somewhat more than 160 pounds avoirdupois.

maun·der (môn′dẽr), *v.i.* [Early Mod. Eng. *mander, maunder*, to grumble, growl; prob. freq. of obs. *maund*, to beg (slang form < Fr. *quémander;* said to be < OFr. *caimand*, beggar); sense prob. influenced by *meander*], 1. to move or act in a dreamy, vague, aimless way. 2. to talk in an incoherent, rambling way; drivel.

Maun·dy Thursday (môn′di), [ME. *mande;* OFr. *mandé* < L. *mandatum;* see MANDATE: from the use of *mandatum* at the beginning of the prayer for washing the feet, commemorating Jesus' washing of the disciples' feet: John 13:5, 34], the Thursday before Easter.

Mau·pas·sant, Guy de (gē′ də mō′pȧ′sän′; Eng. də mō′pə-sänt′), (*Henri René Albert Guy de Maupassant*), 1850–1893; French writer of short stories and novels.

Mau·reen (mô-rēn′), [Ir. *Mairin*, dim. of *Maire*, Mary; see MARY], a feminine name.

Mau·re·ta·ni·a (môr′ə-tā′ni-ə), *n.* 1. an ancient kingdom, and later a Roman province, in northwestern Africa: see **Roman Empire**, map. 2. Mauritania.

Mau·riac, Fran·çois (fräṅ′swȧ′ mô′ryȧk′), 1885– ; French novelist; received Nobel prize in literature, 1952.

Mau·rice (môr′is, mär′is; Fr. mō′rēs′), [Fr.; LL. *Mauritius* < *Maurus*, a Moor], a masculine name: variant, *Morris;* equivalents, G. *Moritz*, It. *Maurizio*, Sp. *Mauricio.* *n.* elector of Saxony; lived 1521–1553.

Maurice of Nassau, Prince of Orange; 1567–1625; Dutch statesman and military leader.

Mau·ri·ta·ni·a (môr′ə-tā′ni-ə), *n.* 1. a country in western Africa, on the Atlantic: a former French colony, it is now a member of the French Community: area, c. 450,000 sq. mi.; pop., 656,000; capital, Nouakchott. 2. Mauretania.

Mau·ri·ti·us (mô-rish′i-əs, mô-rish′əs), *n.* a British island in the Indian Ocean, east of Madagascar: area, 720 sq. mi.; pop., 501,000; capital, Port Louis.

Mau·rois, An·dré (äṅ′drā′ mô′rwȧ′), (pseudonym of *Émile Salomon Wilhelm Herzog*), 1885– ; French biographer, critic, and novelist.

Mau·ser (mou′zẽr), *n.* [after P. P. *Mauser* (1838–1914), G. inventor], [sometimes m-], a high-powered repeating magazine rifle or pistol: a trade-mark.

mau·so·le·an (mô′sə-lē′ən), *adj.* of or like a mausoleum.

mau·so·le·um (mô′sə-lē′əm), *n.* [*pl.* MAUSOLEUMS (-əmz), MAUSOLEA (-ə)], [L. < Gr. *Mausōleion*], 1. [M-], the tomb of Mausolus, king of Caria, at Halicarnassus: see **Seven Wonders of the World.** 2. a large, imposing tomb: humorously applied to any large building or room regarded as like such a tomb.

mauve (mōv), *n.* [Fr., mallow < L. *malva;* cf. MALLOW: from the resemblance of the color to that of the mallow], 1. a purple dye and pigment obtained from a coal-tar dyestuff produced by oxidizing aniline. 2. any of several shades of delicate purple. *adj.* of such a color.

mav·er·ick (mav′ẽr-ik), *n.* [after Samuel *Maverick*, 19th-c. Texas rancher who did not brand his cattle], 1. an unbranded animal, especially a lost calf, formerly the legitimate property of the first person who branded it; hence, 2. [Colloq.], a person not labeled as belonging to any one party, faction, etc., who acts independently.

ma·vis (mā′vis), *n.* [ME.; OFr. *mauvis;* prob. < OBret. **malhuit* (Bret. *milfid*)], the European song thrush.

ma·vour·neen, ma·vour·nin (mə-voor′nēn, mə-vôr′-nēn), *n.* [Ir. *mo muirnīn*], my darling.
maw (mô), *n.* [ME. *mawe, maugh;* AS. *maga, mage;* akin to G. *magen*, stomach; IE. base **maq-*, prob., skin bag, seen also in W. *megin*, bellows], 1. *a)* originally, the stomach or its cavity. *b)* the stomach of an animal; specifically, the fourth stomach of a cud-chewing animal. 2. the craw or crop of a bird. 3. the air bladder of a fish. 4. the throat, gullet, jaws, or oral cavity (of some voracious animals).
maw (mô), *n.* [Dial.], ma; mamma; mother.
maw·kin (mô′kin), *n.* [Obs.], a malkin.
mawk·ish (môk′ish), *adj.* [lit., maggoty < ME. *mawke* (< ON. *mathkr*), maggot; + *-ish;* cf. MAGGOT], 1. nauseating; sickening; having a sickly, insipid flavor. 2. sentimental in a weak, sickly, insipid way. —*SYN.* see **sentimental.**
Maw·son, Sir **Douglas** (mô′s′n), 1882– ; British geologist and explorer of Antarctica.
Max (maks), a masculine name: see **Maximilian.**
max., maximum.
max·il·la (mak-sil′ə), *n.* [*pl.* MAXILLAE (-ē)], [L., dim.; akin to *mala*, a jaw], 1. in vertebrates, a jaw or jawbone, especially the upper one. 2. in most arthropods, as insects, crabs, etc., either of a pair of accessory jaws or appendages just behind the mandibles.
max·il·lar·y (mak′sə-ler′i, mak-sil′ə-ri), *adj.* [L. *maxillaris*], designating, of, or near the jaw or jawbone, especially the upper one; relating to a maxilla or maxillae. *n.* [*pl.* MAXILLARIES (-iz, -riz)], a maxilla; maxillary bone: see **skull,** illus.
max·il·lo- (mak-sil′ə), a combining form for *maxilla*, meaning *of the maxilla and.*
max·im (mak′sim), *n.* [ME. & Late OFr. *maxime* < L. *maxima* (*propositio*), the greatest (premise); fem. of *maximus*, greatest, superl. of *magnus*, great], a concisely expressed principle or rule of conduct, or a statement of a general truth; precept. —*SYN.* see **saying.**
Max·im, Sir **Hiram Stevens** (mak′sim), 1840–1916; American engineer and inventor of the Maxim gun; became a British subject.
Max·im, Hudson, 1853–1927; brother of *Hiram Stevens;* American engineer and inventor of explosives.
max·i·ma (mak′sə-mə), *n.* alternative plural of **maximum.**
max·i·mal (mak′sə-m′l), *adj.* highest or greatest possible; of or constituting a maximum.
Max·i·mal·ist (mak′sə-m′l-ist), *n.* [*maximal* + *-ist;* cf. BOLSHEVIK], 1. a member of the left wing of the (former) Russian Social Revolutionaries. 2. a Bolshevik (sense 1). Opposed to *Minimalist.*
Maxim gun, a single-barreled, water-cooled machine gun in which the recoil of one shot is used to fire the next one: invented by H. S. Maxim.
Max·i·mil·ian (mak′sə-mil′yən, mak′sə-mil′i-ən), [said (by Camden) to have been devised by Frederick III from names of two Romans he admired, Q. Fabius *Maximus* (cf. MAXIMUM) and Scipio *Aemilianus*], a masculine name: diminutive, *Max.* *n.* (*Ferdinand Maximilian Joseph*), archduke of Austria; emperor of Mexico (1864–1867); lived 1832–1867; executed.
Maximilian I, 1459–1519; emperor of the Holy Roman Empire (1493–1519).
Maximilian II, 1527–1576; emperor of the Holy Roman Empire (1564–1576).
max·im·ite (mak′sə-mīt′), *n.* [after Hudson *Maxim*, the inventor], a high explosive made with picric acid, formerly much used in armor-piercing projectiles.
max·i·mize (mak′sə-mīz′), *v.t.* [MAXIMIZED (-mīzd′), MAXIMIZING], to increase to the maximum; raise to the highest possible degree; enlarge, intensify, etc. as much as possible.
max·i·mum (mak′sə-məm), *n.* [*pl.* MAXIMUMS (-məmz), MAXIMA (-mə)], [L., neut. of *maximus*, superl. of *magnus*, great], 1. the greatest quantity, number, or degree possible or permissible. 2. the highest degree or point (of a varying quantity, as temperature) reached or recorded; upper limit of variation. 3. in *astronomy*, *a)* the moment of greatest brilliance of a variable star. *b)* the star's magnitude at this moment. *adj.* 1. greatest or highest possible, permissible, or reached. 2. of, marking, or setting a maximum or maximums. Opposed to *minimum*. Abbreviated **max.**
Max·ine (mak-sēn′), [fem. of *Max*], a feminine name.
max·well (maks′wel, maks′wəl), *n.* [after James C. *Maxwell* (1831–1879), Scot. physicist], the C.G.S. and international unit of magnetic flux, equal to the flux through one square centimeter normal to a magnetic field with an intensity of one gauss.
May (mā), *n.* [ME. & OFr. *mai* < L. (*mensis*) *Maius*, (month) of May; prob. < *Maia*, goddess of increase < base of *magnus*, great], 1. the fifth month of the year, having 31 days: abbreviated **My.** 2. *a)* springtime. *b)* the springtime of life; youth; prime. 3. [m-], the English hawthorn: also **may bush.** 4. the festivities of May Day. *v.i.* to gather flowers in the spring.
May (mā), [contr. of *Mary, Margaret;* often associated with the name of the month], a feminine name.
may (mā), *v.* [past tense MIGHT (mīt); *archaic* 2d pers. sing. MAYEST (mā′ist) or MAYST (māst); no other forms now in use], [ME. *mai, mei;* akin to G. *mag*, Goth. *magan*, lit., to be physically capable of doing; IE. base **māgh-*, to be able, seen also in *main, might*, Gr. *mēkhos*, means (cf. MECHANIC)], an auxiliary preceding an (expressed or implied) infinitive (without *to*) and expressing: 1. originally, ability or power: now generally replaced by *can.* 2. possibility or likelihood: as, it *may* rain. 3. permission or chance: as, you *may* go: see also **can.** 4. contingency, as in clauses of purpose, result, concession, or condition: as, he is telling us so that we *may* be forewarned. 5. wish, hope, or prayer: used in exclamations and apostrophes, as, *may* he go! —*SYN.* see **can.**
may (mā), *n.* [ME. *may, mey;* prob. merging AS. *mæg*, kinswoman, woman & cognate Anglo-N. form of ON. *mær*, girl, maiden; see MAIDEN], [Archaic], a maiden.
May, Cape, the southernmost point of New Jersey, on Delaware Bay.
Ma·ya (mä′yə), *n.* [< native name], 1. a member of a race of Indians who formerly lived in southeastern Mexico and Central America and are still found in Yucatan, British Honduras, and northern Guatemala: the Mayas had a highly developed civilization when discovered by Europeans early in the 16th century. 2. *a)* their Mayan language. *b)* one of the two branches of the Mayan family of languages. *adj.* of the Mayas or Maya; Mayan.
Ma·ya (mä′yə), *n.* [Sans. *māyā*], 1. the Hindu goddess Devi, or Sakti, consort of Siva. 2. in *Hindu philosophy*, illusion, often personified as a woman.
Ma·ya·güez (mä′yä-gwes′), *n.* a seaport in Puerto Rico: pop., 76,000.
Ma·yan (mä′yən), *adj.* 1. designating or of a Central American Indian linguistic family including the language of the Mayas and consisting of twenty-seven languages divided into two branches, the Maya and the Huastek. 2. Maya. *n.* 1. a Mayan Indian. 2. the Mayan linguistic family.
May apple, 1. a North American plant with shield-shaped leaves and a single large, white, cuplike flower. 2. its edible, yellow, lemon-shaped fruit.
may·be (mā′bi, mā′bē), *adv.* [ME. (for *it may be*)], perhaps; possibly.
May·day (mā′dā′), *n.* [< Fr. *m'aidez*, help me], the international radiotelephonic signal for help, used by ships and aircraft in distress.
May Day, May 1: as a traditional spring festival, often celebrated by dancing, crowning a May queen, etc.; as a more recent international labor holiday (of American origin), observed in many countries by parades, demonstrations, etc.
Ma·yence (mä′yäns′), *n.* Mainz: the French name.
may·est (mā′ist), archaic second person singular of **may:** used with *thou.*
May·fair (mā′fâr′), *n.* [after an annual fair held there (prior to 1708) in May], a fashionable residential district of the West End, London.
May·flow·er (mā′flou′ẽr), *n.* 1. any of various plants that flower in May or early spring; especially, *a)* in the United States, the trailing arbutus, any of several anemones, etc. *b)* in England, the hawthorn, cowslip, marsh marigold, etc. 2. the ship on which the Pilgrims came to America (1620).
May fly, 1. a delicate, slender insect with large forewings and small hind wings: it has a long life in the nymph stage but a very short one in the adult stage. 2. an angler's artificial fly made to resemble this insect. 3. in England, a caddis fly.
may·hap (mā′hap′, mā′hap′), *adv.* [< *it may hap*(*pen*)], [Archaic], perhaps; maybe; perchance.
may·hap·pen (mā′hap′′n), *adv.* [Archaic], mayhap.
may·hem (mā′hem, mā′əm), *n.* [see MAIM], in *law*, the offense of maiming a person; act of intentionally mutilating a person's body or injuring it so as to deprive him of some part or function that he needs to defend or take care of himself: also spelled **maihem.**
May·ing (mā′iŋ), *n.* the celebration of May Day, as by gathering flowers, dancing, etc.
May·nard (mā′nẽrd, mā′närd), [ME.; Anglo-Fr. *Mainard;* OHG. *Maganhard* < *magan*, power, strength + *hart*, strong, hard], a masculine name.
may·n't (mā′nt, mānt), may not.
May·o (mā′ō), *n.* a maritime county of Connaught province, Ireland: pop., 151,000 (est. 1943).
May·o, Charles Horace (mā′ō), 1865–1939; American surgeon.
May·o, William James, 1861–1939; American surgeon: brother of *Charles Horace.*
Ma·yon (mä-yôn′), *n.* an active volcano in Luzon, Philippine Islands: height, 7,900 ft.

may·on·naise (mā'ə-nāz', mā'ə-nāz'), *n.* [Fr., earlier *mahonnaise*, apparently fem. of *mahonais*, of *Mahón*, Minorca; reason for name unknown], 1. a creamy salad dressing or sauce made by beating together egg yolks, olive oil, lemon juice or vinegar, and seasoning. 2. a dish of meat or fish made with this.
may·or (mā'ẽr, mâr), *n.* [ME. & OFr. *maire* < L. *major*, compar. of *magnus*, great], the chief administrative official of a city, town, or other municipality.
may·or·al·ty (mā'ẽr-əl-ti, mâr'əl-ti), *n.* [*pl.* MAYORALTIES (-tiz)], [ME. *mairalte;* OFr. *mairalté*], the office or term of office of a mayor.
Ma·yotte (mȧ'yŏt'), *n.* one of the Comoro Islands: area, 140 sq. mi.; pop., 23,000.
May·pole (mā'pōl'), *n.* a high pole wreathed with flowers, streamers, etc., around which merrymakers dance on May Day.
may·pop (mā'pop'), *n.* [altered < *maracock;* Am. Ind. (Virginian) *maracock*, ult. < Tupi *maracujá*], 1. the small, yellow, edible fruit of a passionflower growing in the southern United States. 2. the plant itself.
May queen, a girl chosen to be queen of the merrymakers on May Day and crowned with flowers.
mayst (māst), archaic second person singular of **may**: used with *thou*.
May·tide (mā'tīd'), *n.* [see TIDE, *n.*], the month of May.
May·time (mā'tīm'), *n.* the month of May.
may tree, [British], the hawthorn.
may·weed (mā'wēd'), *n.* [for *maidweed* < **maythe-weed* < AS. *magothe*, stinking camomile (prob. akin to *mægeth*, maiden); + *weed*], a bad-smelling weed of the composite family, with daisylike flowers of white and yellow: also called *stinking camomile.*
May wine, [after the month of May, when the woodruff blossoms], white wine flavored with woodruff and slices of pineapple and orange.
May·wood (mā'wood'), *n.* a city (officially a village) in northeastern Illinois, near Chicago: pop., 27,000.
maz·ard (maz'ẽrd), *n.* [prob. altered < *mazer*], [Obs.], 1. a mazer. 2. *a*) the head or skull. *b*) the face.
Ma·za·rin, Jules (zhül mȧ'zȧ'ran'; Eng. maz'ə-rin), (*Giulio Mazarini*), Cardinal, 1602–1661; French statesman and prelate, born in Italy.
Maz·da (maz'də), *n.* [after Avestan *mazda;* see ORMAZD: chosen because it suggested the light-giving firmament], [sometimes m-], a trade-mark of electric light bulbs conforming to certain standards.
Maz·da·ism, Maz·de·ism (maz'də-iz'm), *n.* [< Avestan *mazda* (see ORMAZD); + *-ism*], Zoroastrianism.
maze (māz), *v.t.* [MAZED (māzd), MAZING], [ME. *masen*, to confuse, puzzle < AS. **masian* < *amazian* (see AMAZE) & pp. *amasod*, puzzled, confused], [Archaic], 1. to stupefy; daze. 2. to confuse; bewilder. *n.* 1. a confusing, intricate network of winding pathways; labyrinth. 2. a state of confusion or bewilderment.
ma·zer (mā'zẽr), *n.* [ME. *maser;* OFr. *masere*, maple wood < Gmc.; cf. ON. *mösurr*, maple], a large drinking bowl or goblet, originally of a hard wood, probably maple, later of metal: also **mazard.**
ma·zi·ly (mā'z'l-i), *adv.* in a mazy manner.
ma·zi·ness (mā'zi-nis), *n.* a mazy quality or state.
ma·zur·ka, ma·zour·ka (mə-zũr'kə, mə-zoor'kə), *n.* [Pol. *mazurka*, woman from Mazovia (province of Poland)], 1. a lively Polish dance like the polka. 2. music for this, generally in 3/4 or 3/8 time.
ma·zy (mā'zi), *adj.* [MAZIER (-zi-ẽr), MAZIEST (-zi-ist)], like a maze; intricately winding; bewildering.
maz·zard (maz'ẽrd), *n.* [earlier *mazer* (cf. MAZER): apparently from the hardness and knotty appearance of the wood], a small, sweet wild cherry, used as a rootstock for cultivated varieties.
‡**maz·zel·tov** (mä'z'l-tōv'; Yid. mä'z'l-tôf'), *interj.* [Yid. < Heb. *māzal*, luck + *tōv*, good], good luck: an expression of congratulation: also **mazzel tov.**
Maz·zi·ni, Giu·sep·pe (jōō-zep'pe mät-tsē'nē, mäd-dzē'nē), 1805–1872; Italian patriot and revolutionist.
M.B., 1. *Medicinae Baccalaureus*, [L.], Bachelor of Medicine. 2. *Musicae Baccalaureus*, [L.], Bachelor of Music.
M.B.A., Master of Business Administration.
M.B.S., MBS, Mutual Broadcasting System.
M.B.S., M.B.Sc., Master of Business Science.
Mc-, Mc- (mak, mək, mə), Mac-.
M.C., 1. Master Commandant. 2. Master of Ceremonies. 3. Medical Corps. 4. Member of Congress. 5. Member of Council. 6. Military Cross.
Mc·A·doo, William Gibbs (gibz mak'ə-dōō'), 1863–1941; American lawyer and statesman; secretary of the treasury (1913–1918).
Mc·Car·thy·ism (mə-kär'thi-iz'm), *n.* [after J. *McCarthy*, U. S. senator (1946–1957), to whom such practices were attributed], the use of indiscriminate, often unfounded, accusations, sensationalism, inquisitorial investigative methods, etc., ostensibly in the suppression of communism.
Mc·Clel·lan, George Brin·ton (brin't'n mə-klel''n), 1826–1885; Union general in the Civil War.
Mc·Cor·mack, John (mə-kôr'mək), 1884–1945; American tenor, born in Ireland.
Mc·Cor·mick, Cyrus Hall (mə-kôr'mik), 1809–1884; American inventor of the reaping machine.
Mc·Coy, the (real) (mə-koi'), [said to be from advertisements of prize fights stating that a celebrated boxer named *McCoy* would participate, not an inferior boxer of the same name], [Slang], the genuine person or thing; the real thing, not a substitute.
Mc·Dou·gall, William (mək-dōō'g'l), 1871–1938; American psychologist, born in England.
Mc·Dow·ell, Ir·vin (ũr'vin mək-dou'əl), 1818–1885; Union general in the Civil War.
Mc·Guf·fey, William Holmes (mə-guf'i), 1800–1873; American educator: editor of *McGuffey's Readers.*
Mc·In·tosh (mak'in-tosh'), *n.* [after John *McIntosh*, Ontario, who discovered and cultivated it (1796)], a late-maturing variety of red apple: also **McIntosh Red.**
Mc·Kees·port (mə-kēz'pôrt, mə-kēz'pōrt), *n.* a city in southwestern Pennsylvania: pop., 45,000.
Mc·Kin·ley, William (mə-kin'li), 1843–1901; twenty-fifth president of the United States (1897–1901); assassinated in his second term.
McKinley, Mount, a mountain of the Alaska Range, south central Alaska: height, 20,300 ft.: highest peak in North America.
M.C.L., Master of Civil Law.
Mc·Mas·ter, John Bach (bäk mək-mas'tẽr, mək-mäs'tẽr), 1852–1932; American historian.
Mc·Rey·nolds, James Clark (mək-ren''ldz), 1862–1946; associate justice, United States Supreme Court (1914–1941).
M.C.S., Master of Commercial Science.
MD., Middle Dutch.
Md., Maryland.
M/D, m/d, month's date (i.e., months after date).
M.D., 1. Medical Department. 2. *Medicinae Doctor*, [L.], Doctor of Medicine.
M-day (em'dā'), *n.* [*m*obilization *day*], the day on which the War Department orders active mobilization for war.
Mdlle., [*pl.* MDLLES.], Mademoiselle.
Mdm., [*pl.* MDMS.], Madam.
Mdme., [*pl.* MDMES.], Madame.
M.D.S., Master of Dental Surgery.
mdse., merchandise.
me (mē; *unstressed* mi), *pron.* [ME.; AS.; akin to G. *mich*, acc., *mir*, dat.; IE. base **me-*, seen also in L. *me*, acc., *mi*(*hi*), dat.], the objective case of **I**: also used colloquially as a predicate complement with a linking verb (e.g., that's *me*).
Me, methyl.
ME., Middle English.
Me., Maine.
M.E., 1. Mechanical Engineer. 2. Methodist Episcopal. 3. Middle English. 4. Military Engineer. 5. Mining Engineer. 6. Most Excellent.
‡**me·a cul·pa** (mē'ə kul'pə), [L.], (by) my fault; I am to blame.
mead (mēd), *n.* [ME. *mede;* AS. *meodu;* akin to G. *met;* IE. base **medhu-*, honey, seen also in Sans. *mādhu*], 1. an alcoholic liquor made of fermented honey, malt, yeast, spices, and water. 2. formerly, a soft drink made of sarsaparilla sirup and carbonated water.
mead (mēd), *n.* [ME. *mede* < AS. *mæd*, nom. case of base seen in *meadow*], [Poetic], a meadow.
Mead, Lake (mēd), a lake in the Colorado River, formed by Hoover Dam: area, 200 sq. mi.
Mead, Margaret, 1901– ; American anthropologist.
Meade, George Gordon (mēd), 1815–1872; Union general in the Civil War.
mead·ow (med'ō), *n.* [ME. *medwe, medewe* < AS. *mædwe*, oblique case of *mæd* (cf. MEAD, meadow); Gmc. base **mædwa-;* prob. IE. base as in *mow*], 1. a piece of grassland, especially one whose grass is grown for use as hay. 2. low, level grassland near a stream, lake, etc.
meadow bird, a bobolink.
meadow lark, [*pl.* MEADOW LARKS, MEADOW LARK; see PLURAL, II, D, 1], any of a number of related North American songbirds, including the *southern meadow lark*, which is brownish or grayish above with black markings on a yellow breast, and the *eastern meadow lark* and *western meadow lark*, both of which have a yellow breast and are about as large as the robin.
meadow rue, any of a group of plants of the crowfoot family, with leaves like those of rue.
mead·ow·sweet (med'ō-swēt'), *n.* 1. any of a group of plants of the rose family; especially, a shrub with thick clusters of small, fragrant flowers of white or pink. 2. any plant of a related group.
mead·ow·y (med'ō-i, med'ə-wi), *adj.* 1. of or like a meadow. 2. full of meadows.
mea·ger, mea·gre (mē'gẽr), *adj.* [ME. *megre;* OFr. *megre, maigre, magre* < L. *macer*, lean, thin], 1. thin; lean; emaciated. 2. poor; inadequate; not full or rich.
SYN.—**meager** literally implies an emaciated thinness and, hence, connotes a lack of those qualities which give something richness, vigor, strength, etc. (*meager* cultural resources); **scanty** implies an inadequacy in amount, number, quantity, etc. of something essential (a *scanty* income); **scant** is applied to a barely sufficient amount or a stinted quantity (the *scant* attendance at the concert); **spare** implies less than a sufficient

amount but does not necessarily connote great hardship (to live on *spare* rations); **sparse** applies to a scanty quantity that is thinly distributed over a wide area (his *sparse* hair).—*ANT.* ample, abundant, plentiful.

meal (mēl), *n.* [ME. *mele;* AS. *mæl,* a measure, fixed time, meal; akin to G. *mal,* time, *mahl,* meal; IE. base **mē-,* to measure (prob. in extension **mētlom* with sense "time for assembling") seen also in L. *metiri,* to measure, whence *mensa,* dining table, *mensura,* measure (cf. MENSURATION, MEASURE)], 1. any of the times, especially the customary times, for eating; breakfast, lunch, dinner, etc. 2. the food served or eaten at one time.

meal (mēl), *n.* [ME. *mele;* AS. *melu;* akin to G. *mehl;* IE. base **mel-,* to grind, seen also in L. *molere,* to grind (cf. MOLAR), *molina* (cf. MILL)], 1. any edible grain, or the edible part of any grain, coarsely ground and unbolted: as, corn *meal.* 2. any substance similarly ground or powdered.

-meal (mēl), [ME. *-mele;* AS. *-mælum* < *mæl,* measure, time (see MEAL, food) + adv. dat. *-um;* basic sense "measure (taken at a time)"], a suffix used to form adverbs meaning *amount done* or *used at one time:* obsolete except in *piecemeal.*

meal·ies (mēl′iz), *n.pl.* [*sing.* MEALIE, MEALY (-i)], [< S. Afr. D. *milje* < Port. *milho,* millet, in *milho grande,* etc., maize], in South Africa, 1. maize; Indian corn. 2. *sing.* an ear of maize.

meal·i·ness (mēl′i-nis), *n.* a mealy quality or state.

meal ticket, 1. a ticket, card, etc. entitling the owner or bearer to a specified value in meals at the restaurant where it was bought; hence, 2. [Slang], a person, job, etc. depended on as a means of livelihood.

meal·time (mēl′tīm′), *n.* the usual time for serving or eating a meal.

meal worm, the wormlike larva of any of various beetles, which infests granaries and bakeries, destroying flour, meal, etc.

meal·y (mēl′i), *adj.* [MEALIER (-i-ẽr), MEALIEST (-i-ist)], 1. like meal; powdery, dry, soft, etc. 2. of or containing meal. 3. sprinkled or covered with meal. 4. spotty or flecked: said of color, etc. 5. pale; floury in color. 6. mealy-mouthed.

meal·y (mēl′i), *n.* alternative singular of **mealies.**

meal·y-mouthed (mēl′i-mouthd′, mēl′i-moutht′), *adj.* not outspoken or blunt; not willing to state the facts in simple, direct words; euphemistic and insincere.

mean (mēn), *v.t.* [MEANT (ment), MEANING], [ME. *menen;* AS. *mænan;* akin to G. *meinen,* to have in mind, have as opinion; IE. base **main-,* to be of opinion, etc.; prob. < **mēi-na,* estimate, opinion < **mē-,* to measure (cf. MEAL, food)], 1. to have in mind; intend; purpose: as, he *means* to go. 2. to intend to express, signify, or indicate: as, just what do you *mean?* 3. to signify; denote; convey; import: as, the German word "*ja*" *means* "yes." 4. to effect; bring about: as, money *means* happiness. *v.i.* 1. to have a purpose or intention in mind: chiefly in *mean well,* to have good intentions. 2. to have a (specified) degree of importance, effect, or influence: as, money *means* little to me. —*SYN.* see **intend.**

mean well by, to have good intentions or friendly, helpful feelings toward.

mean (mēn), *adj.* [ME. *mene,* common, hence mean; AS. *(ge)mæne;* akin to G. *gemein,* plentiful, common, vulgar; IE. base **mei-,* to change, exchange, barter, seen also in L. *communis* (< OL. *commoin-*), whence Eng. *common, commune, communal,* etc.], 1. low in quality or grade; poor; inferior. 2. low in social status or rank; of humble origin or antecedents. 3. low in dignity; unimposing. 4. of slight value, importance, or consequence; paltry. 5. poor in appearance; shabby: as, a *mean* appearance. 6. ignoble; base; small-minded; petty. 7. stingy; miserly; penurious. 8. bad-tempered; vicious; unmanageable: said of a horse, etc. 9. [Colloq.], *a)* pettily or contemptibly selfish, bad-tempered, disagreeable, malicious, etc. *b)* humiliated or ashamed. *c)* in poor health; not well; ill; indisposed. 10. [Slang], *a)* hard to cope with; difficult: as, he throws a *mean* curve. *b)* skillful; expert. —*SYN.* see **base.**

mean (mēn), *adj.* [ME. *mene;* OFr. *meien* (Fr. *moyen*); L. *medianus* < *medius,* middle], 1. halfway between extremes; in a middle or intermediate position as to place, time, quantity, quality, kind, value, degree, etc. 2. medium; average; middling. *n.* 1. what is between extremes; intermediate state, quality, course, or procedure; hence, 2. moderation; avoidance of extremes or excess. 3. the middle term of a syllogism. 4. in *mathematics, a)* a quantity with a value intermediate between the values of two or more other quantities; especially, the average (also called the *arithmetical mean*), obtained by dividing the sum of two or more quantities by the number of these quantities. *b)* the second or third term of a four-term proportion. *c)* the square root of the product of two given numbers: called the *geometric mean.* See also **means.** —*SYN.* see **average.**

Me·an·der (mi-an′dẽr), *n.* the Menderes River (sense 1): the ancient name: also spelled **Maeander.**

me·an·der (mi-an′dẽr), *n.* [L. *maeander;* Gr. *maiandros* < *Maiandros,* the Meander (noted for its winding course); cf. MAUNDER], 1. *often in pl.* a winding, convolution, or winding course, as of a stream. 2. an ornamental pattern of winding or crisscrossing lines. 3. an aimless wandering; rambling. *v.i.* 1. to take a winding or tortuous course: said of a stream. 2. to wander aimlessly or idly; ramble. *v.t.* to make or traverse by meandering. —*SYN.* see **roam.**

mean distance, the arithmetical mean of the greatest and least distances in the orbit of a planet from the sun, equal to half the major axis of the orbit.

me·an·drous (mi-an′drəs), *adj.* [see MEANDER, *n.*], winding; tortuous.

mean·ing (mēn′iŋ), *n.* 1. what is meant; what is intended to be, or in fact is, signified, indicated, referred to, or understood: signification, purport, import, sense, or significance: as, the *meaning* of a word. 2. [Archaic], intention; purpose. *adj.* 1. that has meaning; significant; expressive. 2. intending; having purpose.

SYN.—**meaning** is the general word for what is intended to be expressed or understood by something (the *meaning* of a sentence); **sense,** in this connection, refers especially to any of the various meanings conveyed by a word or phrase (this word has several slang *senses*); **import** refers to the total implication of something said or done, including the subtle connotations (I didn't get the full *import* of his remark); **purport** refers to the general meaning, or gist, of something (what was the *purport* of her letter?); **signification** is applied especially to the meaning conventionally understood by a sign, symbol, character, etc. (the *signification* of the ace of spades in fortune telling); **significance** refers to the subtle, hidden implications of something as distinguished from its openly expressed meaning (his "no!" had a special *significance* for us).

mean·ing·ful (mēn′iŋ-f′l), *adj.* full of meaning; having significance.

mean·ing·less (mēn′iŋ-lis), *adj.* having no meaning; without significance; senseless.

mean latitude, middle latitude.

mean·ness (mēn′nis), *n.* 1. the quality or state of being mean, low, base, etc. 2. a mean act.

means (mēnz), *n.pl.* [< *mean, n.*], 1. [construed as sing. or pl.], that by which something is done or obtained; agency: as, this is a *means* to an end. 2. resources; property; riches: as, her *means* are adequate.

by all means, 1. without fail. 2. of course; certainly.

by any means, in any way possible; at all; somehow.

by means of, by using; with the aid of; through.

by no (manner of) means, not at all; in no way.

means to an end, a method of getting or accomplishing what one wants.

mean solar time, mean time.

means test, in Great Britain, the test of financial resources that an unemployed person must undergo when his unemployment insurance payments stop, to determine his eligibility for payments from other funds.

mean sun, in *astronomy,* a hypothetical sun thought of as moving uniformly around the celestial equator: a concept used as an aid in calculating time.

meant (ment), past tense and past participle of **mean.**

mean·time (mēn′tīm′), *adv.* 1. in or during the intervening time. 2. at the same time. *n.* the intervening time. Also **meanwhile.**

mean time, time measured by the mean sun and therefore having exactly equal divisions: abbreviated **M.T.:** also **mean solar time.**

mean·while (mēn′hwīl′), *adv.* & *n.* meantime.

Mean·y, George (mēn′i), 1894– ; American labor leader; president of the AFL-CIO (1955–).

meas., measure.

mea·sled (mē′z′ld), *adj.* infected with measles (larval tapeworms).

mea·sles (mē′z′lz), *n.pl.* [construed as sing. in senses 1 & 2*a*], [ME. *maseles,* pl. of *masel,* measle, spot; influenced by *mesel* (< OFr.), leper < L. *misellus,* wretch < *miser,* wretched, miserable], 1. *a)* an acute, infectious, communicable virus disease, characterized by a skin eruption, high fever, nasal catarrh, etc., and occurring most frequently in childhood. *b)* any of various similar but milder diseases; especially, German measles. 2. *a)* a disease of cattle and hogs caused by tapeworm larvae in the flesh. *b)* these larvae.

mea·sly (mēz′li), *adj.* 1. infected with measles (the disease). 2. containing larval tapeworms: said of meat. 3. [Colloq.], contemptibly slight, worthless, or skimpy.

meas·ur·a·bil·i·ty (mezh′ẽr-ə-bil′ə-ti), *n.* the state or quality of being measurable.

meas·ur·a·ble (mezh′ẽr-ə-b'l), *adj.* [ME. & OFr. *mesurable*], that can be measured.

meas·ur·a·bly (mezh′ẽr-ə-bli), *adv.* to a measurable degree or extent; noticeably; perceptibly.

meas·ure (mezh′ẽr), *n.* [ME. & OFr. *mesure;* L. *mensura* < *mensus,* pp. of *metiri,* to measure; cf. MEAL (food)], 1. the extent, dimensions, capacity, etc. of anything, especially as determined by a standard. 2. the act or process of determining extent, dimensions, etc.; measurement. 3. *a)* a standard for determining extent, dimensions, etc.; unit of measurement, as an inch, yard, or bushel. *b)* any standard of valuation, comparison, judgment, etc.; criterion. 4. a system of measurement: as, dry *measure,* board *measure.* 5. an instrument for measuring, or a container of standard capacity: as, a quart *measure.* 6. a definite quantity measured out or thought of as measured. 7. *a)* an extent or degree not to be exceeded: as, remain within *measure. b)* a reasonable limit: as, grieved beyond *measure.* 8. (certain) proportion, quantity, or degree: as, in large *measure.* 9. a procedure; course of action; step: as, take *measures* to stop him. 10. a legislative enactment; statute; law. 11. *a)* rhythm in verse; meter. *b)* a metrical unit; foot of verse. 12. a dance or dance movement, especially if slow or stately. 13. *pl.* in *geology,* related beds or strata, as of coal. 14. in *mathematics,* a divisor that leaves no remainder. 15. in *music, a)* the notes or rests, or both, contained between two vertical lines on the staff, subdividing a part of a composition into equal groups of beats; bar. *b)* musical time or rhythm: see also **mode.** 16. in *printing,* the width of a column or page. *v.t.* [MEASURED (-ẽrd), MEASURING], [ME. *mesuren;* OFr. *mesurer;* LL. *mensurare,* to measure < the L. *n.*], 1. to find out or estimate the extent, dimensions, etc. of, especially by a standard. 2. to get, take, set apart, or mark off by measuring (often with *off* or *out*). 3. to estimate by comparison; judge; appraise: as, he *measured* his foe. 4. to bring into comparison or rivalry (*against*): as, I'll *measure* my talent against his. 5. to be a measure of: as, a clock *measures* time. 6. to adjust or proportion by a standard: as, *measure* your speech by your listeners' reactions. 7. to go over or through; traverse as if measuring. *v.i.* 1. to find out or estimate extent, dimensions, etc.; get or take measurements. 2. to be of a specified dimension, quantity, etc. when measured. 3. to allow of measurement. Abbreviated **meas.**

MEASURE (sense 15*a*)

beyond measure, so much as not to be measurable; exceedingly; extremely.
in a measure, to some extent; somewhat.
made to measure, made to fit one's own measurements; custom-made: said of clothes.
measure one's length, to fall, lie, or be thrown down at full length.
measure out, to give out or allot by measuring.
measure swords, 1. to duel with swords. 2. to duel, fight, or contend.
measure up to, to come up to; meet (expectations, a standard, etc.).
take measures, to take action; do things to accomplish a purpose.
take one's measure, to make an estimate or judgment of one's ability, character, etc.
tread a measure, to dance.

meas·ured (mezh′ẽrd), *adj.* [pp. of *measure*], 1. determined, ascertained, or proportioned by a standard. 2. *a)* regular, steady, or uniform. *b)* steady, slow, and deliberate: as, he walked with *measured* tread. 3. *a)* rhythmical. *b)* metrical. 4. calculated, restrained, and deliberate; careful and guarded: said of speech, etc.

meas·ure·less (mezh′ẽr-lis), *adj.* too large to be measurable; vast; immense; unlimited.

meas·ure·ment (mezh′ẽr-mənt), *n.* 1. a measuring or being measured; mensuration. 2. *a)* extent, quantity, or size as determined by measuring. *b) usually in pl.* a dimension: as, a person's *measurements* are the size of his waist, chest, hips, etc. 3. a system or way of measuring or measures.

meas·ur·er (mezh′ẽr-ẽr), *n.* 1. a person who measures, especially in an official position. 2. a gauge, container, or other device for measuring. 3. a measuring worm.

measuring worm, the caterpillar larva of any geometrid moth: it moves by alternately advancing the front end of its body and bringing the rear end forward to form a loop: also called *looper.*

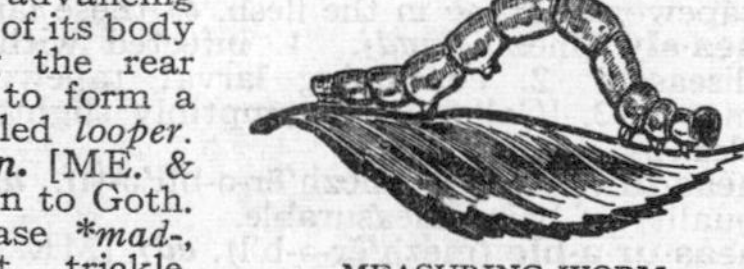
MEASURING WORM

meat (mēt), *n.* [ME. & AS. *mete;* akin to Goth. *mats;* IE. base **mad-,* to be moist, trickle, seen also in *mast* (beechnuts, etc.)], 1. food; especially, solid food, as distinguished from drink: now archaic or dialectal except in *meat and drink.* 2. the flesh of animals used as food; usually, the flesh of mammals, as distinguished from fish and fowl. 3. the edible part: as, the *meat* of a nut. 4. the substance, meaning, or gist: as, the *meat* of a story. 5. a meal; especially, dinner: now obsolete except in *at meat, before meat,* etc. 6. one's quarry. 7. [Slang], something that one especially enjoys or is skillful at: as, golf's my *meat.*

meat·i·ness (mēt′i-nis), *n.* a meaty quality or state.

meat·less (mēt′lis), *adj.* 1. having no meat or food. 2. when no meat is to be eaten: as, a *meatless* day.

meat·man (mēt′man′), *n.* [*pl.* MEATMEN (-men′)], a man who sells meat; butcher.

me·a·tus (mi-ā′təs), *n.* [*pl.* MEATUSES (-iz), MEATUS], [L., a passage, pp. of *meare,* to go, pass], a natural passage or duct in the body, or its opening; foramen.

meat·y (mēt′i), *adj.* [MEATIER (-i-ẽr), MEATIEST (-i-ist)], 1. of, or having the flavor or quality of, meat. 2. like meat. 3. *a)* full of meat. *b)* stout; heavy. 4. full of substance; thought-provoking; pithy.

Mec·ca (mek′ə), *n.* 1. one of the capitals of Saudi Arabia: pop., 220,000 (est. 1948): birthplace of Mohammed and hence a holy city of Islam, to which Moslems make pilgrimages: also spelled **Mekka.** 2. [often m-], *a)* any place visited by many people. *b)* any place that one yearns to go to. *c)* anything that one greatly desires or tries to achieve.

Mec·can (mek′ən), *adj.* of Mecca. *n.* a native or inhabitant of Mecca.

mech., 1. mechanical. 2. mechanics. 3. mechanism.

me·chan·ic (mə-kan′ik), *adj.* [L. *mechanicus;* Gr. *mēchanikos* < *mēchanē,* a machine, contrivance; cf. MAY, *v.*], [Archaic], 1. of or involving manual labor or skill. 2. performing manual labor. 3. mechanical. *n.* 1. a worker skilled in using tools or making, operating, and repairing machines. 2. [Archaic], *a)* an artisan; handicraftsman. *b)* a low, vulgar fellow.

me·chan·i·cal (mə-kan′i-k'l), *adj.* 1. having to do with machinery or tools. 2. produced or operated by machinery or a mechanism. 3. of, in accordance with, or using the principles and terminology of, the science of mechanics. 4. machinelike; automatic, as if from force of habit; lacking spontaneity, expression, intelligence, etc.: as, her acting is *mechanical.* 5. [Archaic], *a)* of manual labor. *b)* of manual laborers; of the artisan class. *c)* base or vulgar. Abbreviated **mech.**

mechanical drawing, a drawing made with the use of T squares, scales, compasses, etc.

me·chan·i·cal·ly (mə-kan′i-k'l-i, mə-kan′ik-li), *adv.* 1. in a mechanical manner. 2. in regard to mechanical features. 3. toward mechanics: as, he is *mechanically* inclined.

mech·a·ni·cian (mek′ə-nish′ən), *n.* a person skilled in the theory, design, operation, or care of machinery.

me·chan·ics (mə-kan′iks), *n.pl.* [construed as sing. in senses 1, 2, and, usually, 3], [see MECHANIC], 1. the branch of physics that deals with motion and the phenomena of the action of forces on bodies: see also **kinetics, kinematics, dynamics, statics.** 2. theoretical and practical knowledge of the design, construction, operation, and care of machinery. 3. the mechanical aspect; technical part: as, the *mechanics* of writing. Abbreviated **mech.**

mech·a·nism (mek′ə-niz'm), *n.* [Mod. L. *mechanismus* < Gr. *mēchanē,* a machine, contrivance], 1. the working parts or arrangement of parts of a machine; works: as, the *mechanism* of a clock. 2. *a)* a system whose parts work together like those of a machine: as, the *mechanism* of the universe. *b)* any system or means for doing something; physical or mental process or processes, whether conscious or unconscious, by which some result is produced; machinery: as, his boasting is a defense *mechanism.* 3. the mechanical aspect; technical part. 4. the theory or doctrine that all the phenomena of the universe, particularly life, can ultimately be explained in terms of physics and chemistry, and that the difference between the organic and the inorganic is only in degree: opposed to *vitalism.* Abbreviated **mech.**

mech·a·nist (mek′ə-nist), *n.* 1. a person who believes in mechanism (sense 4). 2. a mechanician.

mech·a·nis·tic (mek′ə-nis′tik), *adj.* 1. of or characteristic of mechanism (sense 4) or mechanists. 2. of mechanics or mechanical concepts.

mech·a·nis·ti·cal·ly (mek′ə-nis′ti-k'l-i, mek′ə-nis′tik-li), *adv.* in a mechanistic manner.

mech·a·ni·za·tion (mek′ə-ni-zā′shən, mek′ə-nī-zā′shən), *n.* 1. a mechanizing or being mechanized. 2. the degree or extent of this.

mech·a·nize (mek′ə-nīz′), *v.t.* [MECHANIZED (-nīzd′), MECHANIZING], 1. to make mechanical. 2. to do or operate by machinery, not by hand. 3. to bring about the use of machinery in (an industry, etc.). 4. to equip (an army, etc.) with motor vehicles, tanks, self-propelled guns, etc., so as to increase mobility and striking power.

mech·an·o·ther·a·py (mek′ə-nō-ther′ə-pi), *n.* [< Gr. *mēchanē,* a machine; + *therapy*], the treatment of disease by mechanical means, such as massage.

Mech·lin (mek′lin), *n.* 1. Malines: the English name. 2. a fine lace made there, with the design clearly outlined by a thread: also **Mechlin lace, malines.**

Meck·len·burg (mek'lən-boorkh'; Eng. mek'lin-bũrg'), *n.* a former division of northern Germany, earlier a kingdom and duchy.
med., 1. medical. 2. medicine. 3. medieval. 4. medium.
M.Ed., Master of Education.
med·al (med''l), *n.* [Fr. *médaille;* It. *medaglia;* LL. **metallea* < L. *metallum*, metal], a small, flat piece of metal with a design or inscription stamped or inscribed on it, made to commemorate some event, or awarded for some distinguished action, merit, etc. *v.t.* [MEDALED or MEDALLED (-'ld), MEDALING or MEDALLING], to honor or decorate with a medal.
med·al·ist (med''l-ist), *n.* 1. a person who designs or makes medals. 2. a person who has been awarded a medal. 3. in *golf*, the winner at medal play. Abbreviated **med.** Also spelled **medallist.**
me·dal·lic (mə-dal'ik), *adj.* 1. of or like a medal. 2. shown on a medal.
me·dal·lion (mə-dal'yən), *n.* [Fr. *médaillon;* It. *medaglione* < *medaglia;* see MEDAL], 1. a large medal. 2. an oval or circular design, portrait, relief carving, etc. resembling a medal in shape: medallions are sometimes used as a decorative form in carpets, textiles, and lace.
Medal of Honor, the Congressional Medal of Honor.
medal play, in *golf*, a form of competitive play in which the score is calculated by counting the total number of strokes taken to play the designated number of holes: distinguished from *match play.*
Me·dan (me-dän'), *n.* a city on the northeastern coast of Sumatra: pop., 500,000.
med·dle (med''l), *v.i.* [MEDDLED (-'ld), MEDDLING], [ME. *medlen;* OFr. *medler, mesler*, to mix, hence "mix in," meddle; LL. **misculare* < L. *miscere*, to mix], 1. to concern oneself with or take part in other people's affairs without being asked or needed; interfere (*in* or *with*). 2. to tamper (*with*). 3. [Obs.], *a*) to mix; mingle. *b*) to fight; contend.
med·dler (med'lẽr), *n.* a person who meddles; busybody.
med·dle·some (med''l-səm), *adj.* meddling or inclined to meddle; interfering. —*SYN.* see **curious.**
Mede (mēd), *n.* [L. *Medus*, pl. *Medi;* Gr. *Mēdos*, pl. *Mēdoi*], a native or inhabitant of Media.
Me·de·a (mi-dē'ə), *n.* [L.; Gr. *Mēdeia*], in *Greek legend*, a sorceress who helped Jason get the Golden Fleece and, later, when deserted by him, killed her rival and her own children, burned down her palace, and fled to Athens: the subject of several classical tragedies.
Me·del·lín (me'de-yēn', me'*th*e-yēn'), *n.* a city in northwestern Colombia: pop., 579,000.
Med·ford (med'fẽrd), *n.* 1. a city in eastern Massachusetts, near Boston: pop., 65,000. 2. a city in southwestern Oregon: pop., 24,000.
me·di- (mē'di), medio-.
Me·di·a (mē'di-ə), *n.* an ancient country in the part of Asia that is now northwestern Iran.
me·di·a (mē'di-ə), *n.* alternative plural of **medium.**
me·di·a (mē'di-ə), *n.* [*pl.* MEDIAE (-ē')], [Mod. L., fem. < L. *medius*, middle], 1. in *anatomy*, the middle coat of the wall of an artery. 2. in *phonetics*, formerly, a voiced stop.
me·di·a·cy (mē'di-ə-si), *n.* 1. the state or quality of being mediate. 2. mediation.
me·di·ae·val (mē'di-ē'-v'l, med'i-ē'v'l), *adj.* medieval.
me·di·al (mē'di-əl), *adj.* [LL. *medialis* < L. *medius*, middle], 1. of or in the middle; neither beginning nor ending; median. 2. nearer the median plane or axis of a body or part: opposed to *lateral*. 3. *a*) of an average or mean. *b*) average; ordinary. *n.* 1. *a*) a medial letter. *b*) a form (of a letter) used medially. 2. in *phonetics*, any of various voiced stops (*b, d, g*) considered as intermediate in sound between surds (*p, t, k*) and aspirates (Sp. *b*, Ar. *dh*, G. *ch*): term now seldom used.
me·di·al·ly (mē'di-əl-i), *adv.* in a medial position.
Me·di·an (mē'di-ən), *adj.* of Media, its people (the Medes), their Iranian language (Medic), or their culture. *n.* a Mede.
me·di·an (mē'di-ən), *adj.* [L. *medianus* < *medius*, middle], 1. middle; intermediate. 2. *a*) designating the plane that divides a body or part lengthwise into symmetrical halves. *b*) situated in this plane. 3. in *statistics*, *a*) designating the middle number in a series containing an odd number of items (e.g., 7 in the series 1, 4, 7, 16, 43). *b*) designating the number midway between the two middle numbers in a series containing an even number of items (e.g., 10 in the series 3, 4, 8, 12, 46, 72). Distinguished from *average, mean.* *n.* 1. a median number, point, or line. 2. a median artery, vein, nerve, etc. —*SYN.* see **average.**

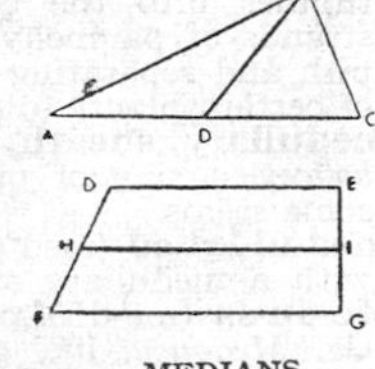

MEDIANS
BD, median of triangle ABC; HI, median of trapezoid DEFG

me·di·ant (mē'di-ənt), *n.* [It. *mediante* < LL. *medians*, ppr. of *mediare;* see MEDIATE], the third tone of a musical scale, halfway between the tonic and the dominant.
me·di·as·ti·num (mē'di-as-tī'nəm), *n.* [*pl.* MEDIASTINA (-nə)], [Mod. L. < ML. *mediastinus*, in the middle < L. *medius*, middle], 1. a membranous partition between two cavities of the body, especially that separating the lungs or the two pleural sacs. 2. the space between the pleural sacs, containing the heart and other chest viscera except the lungs.
me·di·ate (mē'di-āt'; *for adj.*, mē'di-it), *v.i.* [MEDIATED (-id), MEDIATING], [< LL. *mediatus*, pp. of *mediare*, to divide in the middle < L. *medius*, middle], 1. to be in an intermediate position or location. 2. to be an intermediary or conciliator between persons or sides. *v.t.* 1. to settle by mediation; bring about by intervention. 2. to be the medium for bringing about (a result), conveying (an object), communicating (information), etc. *adj.* 1. intermediate or intervening. 2. dependent on, acting by, or connected through some intervening agency; related indirectly: opposed to *immediate*. —*SYN.* see **interpose.**
me·di·a·tion (mē'di-ā'shən), *n.* [Late ME. *mediacioun;* OFr. *mediation;* LL. *mediatio*], 1. a mediating; intercession or friendly intervention, usually by consent or invitation, for settling differences between persons, nations, etc. 2. the state of being mediated.
me·di·a·tive (mē'di-ā'tiv), *adj.* 1. mediating. 2. of mediation.
me·di·a·tize (mē'di-ə-tīz'), *v.t.* [MEDIATIZED (-tīzd'), MEDIATIZING], [< Fr. or G.; Fr. *médiatiser* (< *médiat;* see MEDIATE); or G. *mediatisieren* < Fr.], 1. in Germany under the Holy Roman Empire, to reduce (a prince or state) from the status of an immediate vassal of the Empire to that of a mediate vassal; hence, 2. later, to annex a smaller state to a larger one, leaving the ruler his title and some authority. 3. to make mediate. *v.i.* to mediate.
me·di·a·tor (mē'di-ā'tẽr), *n.* [ME. & OFr. *mediatour;* LL.], a person, nation, etc. that mediates; intercessor.
me·di·a·to·ri·al (mē'di-ə-tôr'i-əl, mē'di-ə-tō'ri-əl), *adj.* mediating; mediatory.
me·di·a·to·ry (mē'di-ə-tôr'i, mē'di-ə-tō'ri), *adj.* of, or having the nature of, a mediator or mediation.
Med·ic (med'ik), *n.* [cf. MEDIC (a plant)], the language of the ancient Medes, regarded by some scholars as identical with Avestan; Median.
med·ic (med'ik), *n.* [Colloq.], 1. a physician or surgeon. 2. a medical student or intern. 3. a member of a military medical corps, especially one who gives first aid in combat.
med·ic (med'ik), *n.* [L. *medica;* Gr. *mēdikē* (*poa*), Median (grass), kind of clover from Media < *Mēdikos*, of Media], any of a number of cloverlike plants with purple or yellow flowers; especially, alfalfa.
med·i·ca·ble (med'i-kə-b'l), *adj.* [L. *medicabilis*], that can be cured, healed, or relieved by medical treatment.
med·i·cal (med'i-k'l), *adj.* [Fr. *médical;* LL. *medicalis* < L. *medicus*, physician; akin to *mederi*, to heal, Avestan *vi-mad-*, healer, physician; prob. IE. base **med-*, to measure, consider, reflect, seen also in L. *meditari* (cf. MEDITATE), AS. *metan*, to measure], 1. of or connected with medicine or the practice or study of medicine. 2. [Rare], medicinal. Abbreviated **med.**
medical examiner, 1. a coroner or similar public officer. 2. a physician who examines applicants for life insurance.
medical jurisprudence, the branch of medicine dealing with the application of medical knowledge to questions of criminal and civil law.
med·i·cal·ly (med'i-k'l-i, med'ik-li), *adv.* 1. by medicine. 2. from the viewpoint of medicine.
me·dic·a·ment (mə-dik'ə-mənt, med'i-kə-mənt), *n.* [L. *medicamentum*], a medicine; substance for curing, healing, or relieving pain.
med·i·cate (med'i-kāt'), *v.t.* [MEDICATED (-id), MEDICATING], [< L. *medicatus*, pp. of *medicari*, to heal], 1. to treat with medicine. 2. to apply a medicinal substance to; tincture or impregnate with medicine.
med·i·ca·tion (med'i-kā'shən), *n.* 1. a medicating or being medicated. 2. a medicament.
med·i·ca·tive (med'i-kā'tiv), *adj.* 1. of, or having the nature of, medication. 2. medicinal; healing.
Med·i·ce·an (med'ə-sē'ən, med'i-chē'ən), *adj.* [< Mod. L. *Mediceus* (< It. *Medici*); + *-an*], of or characteristic of the Medici.
Med·i·ci (med'ə-chē'; It. me'dē-chē'), *n.* name of a rich, powerful family of Florence, Italy, in the 14th, 15th, and 16th centuries, celebrated as bankers, rulers of Tuscany, and patrons of art and literature.
Medici, Catherine de', 1519–1589; queen of Henry II of France (1547–1559); mother of Henry III, Charles IX, and Francis II.
Medici, Cos·i·mo de' (kô'zē-mô' de), 1. 1389–1464;

banker, statesman, and patron of art and literature; head of the Florentine Republic: called *Cosimo the Elder*. 2. (*Cosimo I*), 1519–1574; duke of Florence; first grand duke of Tuscany: called *Cosimo the Great.* Also **Cosmo de' Medici.**

Medici, Giu·lio de' (jōō'lyô de), see **Clement VII.**

Medici, Lo·ren·zo de' (lô-ren'tsô de), 1449–1492; prince of Florence, statesman, poet, scholar, and patron of art and literature: called *Lorenzo the Magnificent.*

Medici, Maria de', see **Marie de Médicis.**

me·dic·i·na·ble (mə-dis''n-ə-b'l), *adj.* [Archaic], medicinal.

me·dic·i·nal (mə-dis''n-'l), *adj.* [ME. *medycinal;* OFr.; L. *medicinalis*], of, or having the properties of, medicine; curing, healing, or relieving.

me·dic·i·nal·ly (mə-dis''n-'l-i), *adv.* as or by medicine.

med·i·cine (med'ə-s'n), *n.* [ME. *medycine;* OFr. *medecine;* L. *medicina* < *medicus;* see MEDICAL], 1. the science and art of diagnosing, treating, curing, and preventing disease, relieving pain, and improving and preserving health. 2. the branch of this science and art that makes use of drugs, diet, etc., as distinguished especially from surgery and obstetrics. 3. *a*) any drug or other substance used in treating disease, healing, or relieving pain. *b*) [Obs.], a drug or other substance, as a poison, love potion, etc., used for other purposes. 4. among North American Indians, *a*) any object, spell, rite, etc. supposed to have natural or supernatural powers as a remedy, preventive, protection, etc. *b*) magical power or rite. 5. [Obs.], a medicine man. *v.t.* [MEDICINED (-s'nd), MEDICINING], to give medicine to; treat medicinally. Abbreviated **M., m., med.**

take one's medicine, to endure punishment, etc.

medicine ball, a large, heavy, leather-covered ball, tossed from one person to another for physical exercise.

Medicine Bow Range, a mountain range in southern Wyoming and northern Colorado.

medicine dance, among North American Indians, etc., a ritual dance to drive out disease or make magic.

medicine man, among North American Indians, etc., a man supposed to have supernatural powers of curing disease and controlling spirits; shaman; magician.

med·i·co (med'i-kō'), *n.* [*pl.* MEDICOS (-kōz')], [It.; L. *medicus;* see MEDICAL], [Colloq.], 1. a physician or surgeon; doctor. 2. a medical student.

med·i·co- (med'i-kō'), a combining form meaning: 1. *medical.* 2. *medical and.*

me·di·e·val (mē'di-ē'v'l, med'i-ē'v'l), *adj.* [< L. *medius,* middle + *aevum,* age], of, like, characteristic of, or suggestive of the Middle Ages: abbreviated **M., med.**: also spelled **mediaeval.**

Medieval Greek, the Greek language as it was used in the Middle Ages, from about 700 A.D. to about 1500: also called *Middle Greek*: abbreviated **MGr.**

me·di·e·val·ism (mē'di-ē'v'l-iz'm, med'i-ē'v'l-iz'm), *n.* 1. the spirit, beliefs, habits of thought, customs, etc. of the Middle Ages. 2. devotion to or acceptance of medieval beliefs, habits, customs, etc. 3. a belief, habit of thought, custom, etc. characteristic of or surviving from the Middle Ages.

me·di·e·val·ist (mē'di-ē'v'l-ist, med'i-ē'v'l-ist), *n.* 1. a student of or specialist in medieval history, literature, art, etc. 2. a person devoted to medieval customs, habits of thought, etc.

Medieval Latin, the Latin language as it was used throughout Europe in the Middle Ages, from about 700 A.D. to about 1500, characterized by many Latinized borrowings from other languages: also called *Middle Latin*: abbreviated **ML., M.L.**

Me·di·na (me-dē'nä, mə-dē'nə), *n.* a city in Hejaz, Saudi Arabia: pop., 40,000 (est. 1948): site of Mohammed's tomb and hence a Moslem holy city.

me·di·o- (mē'di-ō, mē'di-ə), [< L. *medius*], a combining form meaning *middle*: also, before a vowel, **medi-.**

me·di·o·cre (mē'di-ō'kẽr, mē'di-ō'kẽr), *adj.* [Fr. *médiocre;* L. *mediocris* < *medius,* middle + *ocris,* a peak], of middle quality, neither very good nor very bad; ordinary; commonplace; average.

me·di·oc·ri·ty (mē'di-ok'rə-ti), *n.* [*pl.* MEDIOCRITIES (-tiz)], 1. the quality or state of being mediocre. 2. mediocre ability or attainment. 3. a person of mediocre abilities or attainments.

Medit., Mediterranean.

med·i·tate (med'ə-tāt'), *v.t.* [MEDITATED (-id), MEDITATING], [< L. *meditatus,* pp. of *meditari,* to meditate; for base see MEDICAL], 1. [Rare], to think about; contemplate. 2. to plan; intend; purpose. *v.i.* to think deeply and continuously; reflect; ponder; muse. —*SYN.* see **ponder.**

med·i·ta·tion (med'ə-tā'shən), *n.* 1. act of meditating; deep, continued thought; reflection. 2. solemn reflection on sacred matters as a devotional act.

med·i·ta·tive (med'ə-tā'tiv), *adj.* 1. meditating or inclined to meditate. 2. indicating meditation. —*SYN.* see **pensive.**

med·i·ta·tor (med'ə-tā'tẽr), *n.* a person who meditates.

Med·i·ter·ra·ne·an (med'ə-tə-rā'ni-ən), *adj.* [< L. *mediterraneus* < *medius,* middle + *terra,* land], 1. [m-], *a*) far from the coast; inland: said of land. *b*) surrounded, or almost surrounded, by land; landlocked: said of water. 2. of the Mediterranean Sea or near-by regions. 3. of Mediterranean peoples. 4. in *ethnology,* designating or of one of the three main divisions of the Caucasian, or white, race: term used to denote typically long-headed, short, olive-skinned peoples living around the Mediterranean Sea, including ancient Iberian, Ligurian, Pelasgian, and Hamitic peoples and their descendants. *n.* 1. the Mediterranean Sea. 2. a person who lives in a region near this sea. 3. a member of the Mediterranean division of the Caucasian race. Abbreviated **Medit.**

Mediterranean fever, undulant fever.

Mediterranean Sea, a large sea surrounded by Europe, Africa, and Asia: area, 1,145,000 sq. mi.

me·di·um (mē'di-əm), *n.* [*pl.* MEDIUMS (-əmz), MEDIA (-ə)] [L., the middle, neut. of *medius,* middle], 1. *a*) something intermediate. *b*) a middle state or degree; mean. 2. an intervening thing through which a force acts or an effect is produced: as, the ether is a supposed *medium* for radio waves. 3. any means, agency, or instrumentality: as, radio is a *medium* of communication. 4. any surrounding or pervading substance in which bodies exist or move; hence, 5. environment. 6. a sterilized nutritive substance, as agar, for cultivating bacteria, viruses, etc. 7. a person through whom communications are supposedly sent to the living from the spirits of the dead. 8. any material used for expression or delineation in art: as, this sculptor's favorite *medium* is stone. 9. a liquid mixed with pigments to give fluency. 10. a size of writing paper (19 x 24 inches) or printing paper (18 x 23 inches). *adj.* in a middle position; intermediate in quantity, quality, place, size, or degree. Abbreviated **M., m., med.**

me·di·um·is·tic (mē'di-ə-mis'tik), *adj.* of or like a medium (sense 7).

medium of exchange, anything used as money; currency, checks, etc.

me·di·um-sized (mē'di-əm-sīzd'), *adj.* of a medium size; neither large nor small.

med·lar (med'lẽr), *n.* [ME. *medler;* OFr. *medler, meslier* < *mesle, mesple, nesle,* the fruit; L. *mespila, mespilus, mespilum;* Gr. *mespilon, mespilē*], 1. a small tree of the rose family, growing in Europe and Asia. 2. its small, brown, applelike fruit, hard and bitter when ripe and eaten only when partly decayed.

med·ley (med'li), *n.* [*pl.* MEDLEYS (-liz)], [ME. *medle;* OFr. *medlee, meslee,* a mixing, properly fem. of *medle, mesle,* pp. of *medler, mesler;* see MEDDLE], 1. a mixture of things not usually placed together; heterogeneous assortment or collection; hodgepodge. 2. *a*) a musical composition made up of passages, usually incongruous passages, from various other compositions. *b*) a group of dance tunes, etc. arranged for playing as a continuous whole. 3. [Archaic], a melee. *adj.* 1. mixed; made up of heterogeneous parts. 2. [Obs.], motley.

medley race, 1. a relay race in which each contestant must cover a different distance. 2. a swimming race in which a different stroke must be used for each length of the pool.

Mé·doc (me'dôk'), *n.* 1. a grape-growing district of southwestern France. 2. (Eng. mā'dok, mi-dok'), a red wine made there: also **Medoc.**

me·dul·la (mi-dul'ə), *n.* [*pl.* MEDULLAE (-ē)], [L., the marrow], 1. in *anatomy, a*) the marrow of bones. *b*) the medulla oblongata: see **brain,** illus. *c*) the inner substance of an organ, as of the kidney, adrenal gland, etc. 2. in *botany,* the spongy center of the stems of certain plants; pith.

medulla ob·lon·ga·ta (ob'lôŋ-gā'tə), [Mod. L., oblong medulla], the widening continuation of the spinal cord forming the lowest part of the brain and containing vital nerve centers for the control of breathing, circulation, etc.

med·ul·lar·y (med'ə-ler'i, mi-dul'ẽr-i), *adj.* [LL. *medullaris*], of, like, or consisting of the medulla or the medulla oblongata.

medullary ray, 1. in *anatomy,* extensions of the kidney tubules into the cortical substance. 2. in *botany,* strands of parenchymatous tissue extending from the pith and separating the vascular bundles in the stems of certain plants (dicotyledons and gymnosperms).

medullary sheath, 1. in *anatomy,* myelin. 2. in *botany,* a ring of primary xylem around the pith of some stems.

med·ul·lat·ed (med'ə-lā'tid, mi-dul'ā-tid), *adj.* covered with a medullary substance; having myelin sheaths.

Me·du·sa (mə-dōō'sə, mə-dū'zə), *n.* [ME. *Meduse;* L.; Gr. *Medousa,* lit., guardian], 1. in *Greek mythology,* one of the three Gorgons, a monster with snakes for hair and a gaze that turned into stone anyone who looked at her: she was slain by Perseus, who gave her head to Athena. 2. [m-], [*pl.* MEDUSAS (-səz, -zəz), MEDUSAE (-sē, -zē)], in *zoology,* a jellyfish.

me·du·san (mə-dōō's'n, mə-dū'z'n), *adj.* of a medusa, or jellyfish. *n.* a medusa, or jellyfish.

me·du·soid (mə-dōō'soid, mə-dū'zoid), *adj.* like a medusa, or jellyfish. *n.* a medusa-shaped gonophore of a hydrozoan.

meed (mēd), *n.* [ME. *mede;* AS. *med,* a recompense, reward; akin to G. *miete,* pay, rent, etc.; IE. base **mizdhó-,* reward, pay, seen also in Sans. *mīḍhá-,* prize], 1. [Poetic], a merited recompense or reward. 2. [Obs.], *a*) a gift. *b*) a bribe. *c*) merit; worth.
meek (mēk), *adj.* [ME. *meke* (earlier *meoc*) < ON. *miukr,* pliant, gentle; IE. base **meuq-,* **meug-,* slimy, slippery, seen also in L. *mucus,* slime (cf. MUCOUS, MUCILAGE, etc.), Eng. *muck*], 1. patient and mild; not inclined to anger or resentment. 2. *a*) tamely submissive; easily imposed on. *b*) too submissive; spineless; spiritless. 3. [Obs.], gentle or kind. —***SYN.*** see **humble.**
Meer, Jan van der (yän′ vän′ dēr mâr′), 1. 1628–1691; Dutch painter. 2. 1656–1705; his son; Dutch painter.
meer·schaum (mêr′shəm, mêr′shôm′), *n.* [G., lit., sea foam; *meer,* sea + *schaum,* foam; said to be after Per. *kef-i-daryā:* from the foamy appearance; ? after Fr. (*pipe*) *d'écume de mer,* for (*pipe*) *de Kummer,* Kummer's pipe], 1. a soft, white, claylike, heat-resistant mineral, a hydrous magnesium silicate, $H_4Mg_2Si_3O_{10}$, used for tobacco pipes, etc.; sepiolite. 2. a pipe made of this.
Mee·rut (mē′rət), *n.* a city in Uttar Pradesh, in northern India: pop., 284,000.
Meer van Delft, Jan van der, see **Vermeer, Jan.**
meet (mēt), *v.t.* [MET (met), MEETING], [ME. *meten;* AS. *metan* < base of *mot,* a coming together, meeting; see MOOT], 1. to come upon; come across; encounter (a person). 2. to come face to face with or up to (a person or thing moving from a different direction); confront. 3. to be present at the arrival of: as, he *met* the bus. 4. to come into contact, connection, or conjunction with: as, her hand *met* his face in a resounding slap. 5. *a*) to come into the presence or company of. *b*) to be introduced to; get acquainted with. *c*) to keep an appointment or engagement with. 6. *a*) to encounter in or as in battle; fight with. *b*) to face: as, he *met* angry words with a laugh. *c*) to oppose; refute; deal with effectively: as, we can *meet* this objection. 7. to experience: as, their plan will *meet* disaster. 8. to come within the perception of (the eye, ear, etc.). 9. *a*) to comply with; satisfy (a demand, etc.). *b*) to pay (a bill, etc.). *v.i.* 1. to come together, as from different directions. 2. to come into contact, connection, or conjunction. 3. to become acquainted; be introduced. 4. to be opposed in or as in battle; fight; contend. 5. to be united. 6. to assemble. 7. [Archaic], *a*) to agree. *b*) to conflict. *n.* 1. a meeting, gathering, or assembling, as for a sporting event; as, a track *meet.* 2. the people who meet or assemble. 3. the place of meeting.
meet with, 1. to experience. 2. to receive. 3. to come upon or across; encounter.
meet (mēt), *adj.* [ME. *mete* < AS. (*ge*)*mæte,* fitting, made to fit; akin to G. *gemäss,* commensurable; IE. base **mē-,* to measure; see MEAL (food)], suitable; appropriate; proper; fitting: as, it is *meet* that you should go.
meet·ing (mēt′iŋ), *n.* [see MEET, *v.*], 1. a coming together of persons or things. 2. an assembly; gathering of people, especially to discuss or decide on matters. 3. an assembly or place of assembly for purposes of worship, as among the Friends, or Quakers. 4. a point of contact or intersection; junction. 5. a hostile encounter; duel. Abbreviated **mtg.**
meet·ing·house (mēt′iŋ-hous′), *n.* a building used for public worship; church: applied in British usage only to dissenting churches, usually disparagingly except of Friends, or Quakers.
meet·ly (mēt′li), *adv.* [see MEET, *adj.* & -LY], 1. suitably; appropriately; properly. 2. [Obs.], moderately.
meg·a- (meg′ə), [Gr. *mega-* < *megas,* great, mighty], a combining form meaning: 1. *large, great, powerful,* as in *megaphone.* 2. (with reference to metric measurement, electrical units, etc.) *a million times, a million of* (the specified unit), as in *megacycle.* Also, before a vowel, **meg-.**
meg·a·ce·phal·ic (meg′ə-sə-fal′ik), *adj.* [*mega-* + *cephalic*], 1. having a large head. 2. in *craniometry,* having a cranial capacity greater than the average (about 1,500 cubic centimeters). Cf. **macrocephalic.**
meg·a·ceph·a·lous (meg′ə-sef′ə-ləs), *adj.* megacephalic.
meg·a·cy·cle (meg′ə-sī′k'l), *n.* in *physics,* one million cycles.
meg·a·ga·mete (meg′ə-gə-mēt′, meg′ə-gam′ēt), *n.* a macrogamete.
meg·a·lith (meg′ə-lith′), *n.* [*mega-* + *-lith*], a huge stone, especially one used in prehistoric monuments or in the construction work of ancient peoples.
meg·a·lo- (meg′ə-lō, meg′ə-lə), [Gr. *megalo-* < *megas, megalou,* large, great], a combining form meaning: 1. *large, great, powerful,* as in *megalomania.* 2. *abnormal enlargement,* as in *megalocardia.*
meg·a·lo·car·di·a (meg′ə-lō-kär′di-ə), *n.* [Mod. L. < *megalo-* + Gr. *kardia,* heart], abnormal enlargement of the heart.
meg·a·lo·ce·pha·li·a (meg′ə-lō-sə-fā′li-ə), *n.* megalocephaly.
meg·a·lo·ce·phal·ic (meg′ə-lō-sə-fal′ik), *adj.* of or having megalocephaly; megacephalic.
meg·a·lo·ceph·a·lous (meg′ə-lō-sef′ə-ləs), *adj.* megalocephalic.
meg·a·lo·ceph·a·ly (meg′ə-lō-sef′ə-li), *n.* [Mod. L. *megalocephalia* < *megalo-* + Gr. *kephalē,* a head], a condition in which the head is unusually large.
meg·a·lo·ma·ni·a (meg′ə-lə-mā′ni-ə), *n.* [Mod. L.; *megalo-* + *mania*], 1. a mental disorder characterized by delusions of grandeur, wealth, power, etc. 2. a passion for, or for doing, big things; hence, 3. a tendency to exaggerate.
meg·a·lo·ma·ni·ac (meg′ə-lə-mā′ni-ak), *adj.* of or having megalomania. *n.* a person who has megalomania.
meg·a·lop·o·lis (meg′ə-lop′ə-lis), *n.* [Gr. *megalopolis,* great city], an extensive, heavily populated, continuously urban area, including any number of cities.
meg·a·lo·saur (meg′ə-lə-sôr′), *n.* [Mod. L. *megalosaurus; megalo-* + *-saurus*], any of an extinct group of huge, flesh-eating dinosaurs of the Jurassic Period.
meg·a·lo·sau·ri·an (meg′ə-lə-sôr′i-ən), *adj.* of the megalosaurs. *n.* a megalosaur.
meg·a·phone (meg′ə-fōn′), *n.* [*mega-* + *-phone*], a large, funnel-shaped device for increasing the volume of voice sounds or other sounds, or sending them in a desired direction. *v.t.* & *v.i.* [MEGAPHONED (-fōnd′), MEGAPHONING], to magnify or direct (sounds) through or as through a megaphone.
meg·a·pod (meg′ə-pod′), *adj.* [*mega-* + *-pod*], large-footed. *n.* a large-footed, mound-building bird of Australia and the Malay Archipelago.
Meg·a·ra (meg′ə-rə), *n.* the capital of Megaris.
Meg·a·ris (meg′ə-ris), *n.* a district of ancient Greece, on the Isthmus of Corinth.
meg·a·spo·ran·gi·um (meg′ə-spə-ran′ji-əm), *n.* [*pl.* MEGASPORANGIA (-ə)], [Mod. L.; *mega-* + *sporangium*], a sporangium, or spore case, containing only megaspores, as in some ferns; macrosporangium.
meg·a·spore (meg′ə-spôr′, meg′ə-spōr′), *n.* [*mega-* + *spore*], a large asexual spore produced by some seed plants and ferns, which gives rise to a female gametophyte or prothallium, as the embryo sac in a seed plant: also called *macrospore.*
meg·a·spo·ro·phyll (meg′ə-spôr′ə-fil, meg′ə-spō′rə-fil), *n.* a sporophyll producing only megasporangia.
me·gass, me·gasse (mə-gas′, mə-gäs′), *n.* [var. of *bagasse*], bagasse; crushed sugar cane or beet.
meg·a·there (meg′ə-thêr′), *n.* a megatherium.
meg·a·the·ri·um (meg′ə-thêr′i-əm), *n.* [Mod. L. < *mega-* + Gr. *thērion,* beast], any of an extinct group of very large, slothlike, plant-eating animals, whose remains have been found in the Pleistocene of America.
meg·a·ton (meg′ə-tun′), *n.* [*mega-* + *ton*], the explosive force of a million tons of TNT: a unit for measuring the power of thermonuclear weapons.
Me·gid·do (mə-gid′ō), *n.* an ancient city in north Palestine: probably the Biblical Armageddon.
me·gilp (mə-gilp′), *n.* [? < a surname in *Mc-* or *Mac-*], a mixture of linseed oil with mastic varnish or turpentine, etc., used in oil paints: also **magilp, megilph, etc.**
me·gilph (mə-gilf′), *n.* megilp.
meg·ohm (meg′ōm′), *n.* one million ohms.
me·grim (mē′grim), *n.* [Late ME. *migreime;* OFr. *migraine;* see MIGRAINE], 1. a severe headache, usually on only one side, with nausea; migraine. 2. a whim, fancy, or fad. 3. *pl. a*) low spirits; the blues. *b*) vertigo in horses and cattle: also called *blind staggers.*
Me·he·met A·li (me-met′ ä-lē′), 1769–1849; viceroy of Egypt (1805–1848): also **Mohammed Ali.**
Mei·ji (mā′jē′), *n.* [Japan., lit., enlightened peace], the reign name of the emperor Mutsuhito of Japan.
Meil·hac, Hen·ri (än′rē′ me′yák′), 1831–1897; French playwright.
mein·ie, mein·y (mā′ni), *n.* [ME. *meignee, menie,* etc.; OFr. *meisniee, mesnie, maisnie;* see MENIAL], 1. [Obs.], feudal retainers or attendants, collectively; retinue or household. 2. [Scot.], a crowd; throng; multitude.
Mein Kampf (mīn′kämpf′), [G., my battle], a book written by Adolf Hitler while in prison (1924), telling his political beliefs, theories, etc. and outlining a plan for the domination of Europe by Germany.
mei·o·sis (mī-ō′sis), *n.* [Mod. L.; Gr. *meiōsis* < *meioun,* to make smaller < *meiōn,* less], 1. the process of nuclear division in germ cells, in which the number of chromosomes is reduced from the diploid, or double, number found in somatic cells to the haploid, or halved, number found in gametes: also called *maturation, reduction:* distinguished from *mitosis.* 2. litotes.
mei·ot·ic (mī-ot′ik), *adj.* of meiosis.
Meis·sen (mī′sən), *n* a city in eastern Germany, on the Elbe: pop., 50,000: noted for its porcelain.
Meis·so·nier, Jean Louis Er·nest (zhän lwē er′nest′ mā′sô′nyā′), 1815–1891; French painter.
Meis·ter·sing·er (mīs′tēr-siŋ′ēr, mīs′ter-ziŋ′ēr), *n.* [*pl.* MEISTERSINGER], [G., lit., master singer], a member

of one of the guilds, mainly of workingmen, organized in the chief German cities in the 14th, 15th, and 16th centuries for the purpose of cultivating music and poetry: they were successors of the minnesingers.

Mé·ji·co (me'hi-kô'), *n.* Mexico: the Spanish spelling.

Mek·ka (mek'ə), *n.* Mecca.

Mek·nès (mek'nes), *n.* a walled city in French Morocco, one of the traditional capitals of the sultanate: pop., 75,000.

Me·kong (mā'koŋ'), *n.* a river flowing through Tibet and southwestern China into the South China Sea: it forms the boundary between French Indo-China and Thailand: length, 2,600 mi.: Chinese name, *Lantsang.*

mel (mel), *n.* [L.; IE. *melit, seen also in Gr. *meli*, honey, *melissa*, a bee, AS. *meledeaw, mildeaw*, nectar (cf. MILDEW)], honey, especially in the pure, clarified form used in pharmacy.

mel·an-, melano-.

mel·an·cho·li·a (mel'ən-kō'li-ə), *n.* [LL.; see MELANCHOLY], a mental disorder characterized by extreme depression of spirits, brooding, and gloominess.

mel·an·cho·li·ac (mel'ən-kō'li-ak'), *adj.* of or having melancholia. *n.* a person who has melancholia.

mel·an·chol·ic (mel'ən-kol'ik), *adj.* [ME. *melancolike;* OFr. *melancolique;* LL. *melancholicus*], 1. [Now Rare], melancholy. 2. of, like, or having melancholia.

mel·an·chol·i·cal·ly (mel'ən-kol'i-k'l-i, mel'ən-kol'ik-li), *adv.* in a melancholy manner.

mel·an·chol·y (mel'ən-kol'i), *n.* [*pl.* MELANCHOLIES (-iz)], [ME. & OFr. *melancolie;* LL. *melancholia;* Gr. *melancholia* < *melas, melanos*, black + *cholē*, bile, gall], 1. [Obs.], *a)* originally, black bile, one of the four chief humors, or bodily fluids, of obsolete physiology: it was thought to come from the spleen or kidneys and cause gloominess, irritability, or depression. *b)* the condition of having, or the disorder supposed to result from having, too much black bile. *c)* melancholia. 2. *a)* sadness and depression of spirits. *b)* a tendency to be sad, gloomy, or depressed. 3. pensiveness; sad, sober musing. *adj.* 1. sad and depressed; gloomy. 2. *a)* causing sadness, gloom, or depression. *b)* lamentable; deplorable. 3. pensive; sadly or soberly musing. 4. [Obs.], having the disorder of melancholy or melancholia. —*SYN.* see **sad.**

Me·lanch·thon, Philipp (mə-laŋk'thən), (born *Philipp Schwarzert*), 1497–1560; German theologian; a leader of the Lutheran Reformation: also spelled **Melancthon.**

Mel·a·ne·sia (mel'ə-nē'zhə, mel'ə-nē'shə), *n.* [< Gr. *melas*, black + *nesos*, island: prob. from the appearance of the islands from the sea], a group of islands in the South Pacific, extending from the Admiralty to the Fiji Islands.

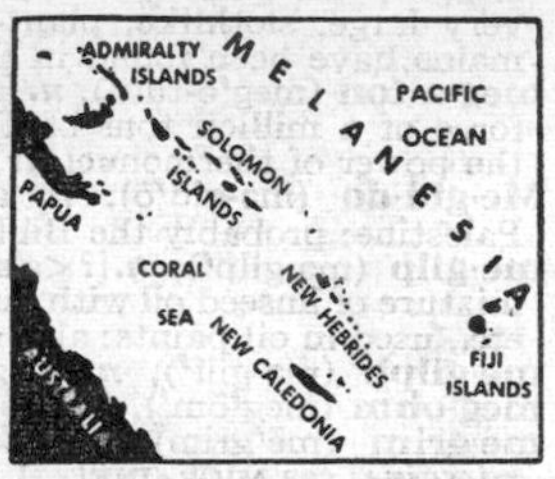

MELANESIA

Mel·a·ne·sian (mel'ə-nē'zhən, mel'ə-nē'shən), *adj.* of Melanesia, its people, or their languages. *n.* 1. a member of the dark-skinned native people of Melanesia. 2. their Austronesian languages and dialects.

‡mé·lange (mā'länzh'), *n.* [Fr. < *mêler*, to mix; see MEDDLE], a mixture; medley; hodgepodge.

me·lan·ic (mə-lan'ik), *adj.* of, characteristic of, or having melanism or melanosis.

mel·a·nin (mel'ə-nin), *n.* [*melan-* + *-in*], a brownish-black pigment found in skin, hair, and other animal tissues.

mel·a·nism (mel'ə-niz'm), *n.* [*melan-* + *-ism*], 1. abnormal development of dark pigmentation in the skin, hair, feathers, etc.: opposed to *albinism.* 2. darkness of skin, hair, eyes, etc., resulting from a high degree of pigmentation.

mel·a·nite (mel'ə-nīt'), *n.* [*melan-* + *-ite*], a black variety of garnet.

mel·a·no- (mel'ə-nō, mel'ə-nə), [< Gr. *melas, melanos*, black], a combining form meaning *black, very dark:* also, before a vowel, **melan-.**

Mel·a·noch·ro·i (mel'ə-nok'rō-ī'), *n.pl.* [Mod. L. < *melano-* + Gr. *ōchros*, pale], members of the Caucasian race having dark hair and a light complexion.

Mel·a·noch·roid (mel'ə-nok'roid), *adj.* of or like the Melanochroi.

mel·a·noid (mel'ə-noid'), *adj.* 1. pigmented black or dark. 2. of or like melanosis.

mel·a·no·ma (mel'ə-nō'mə), *n.* [*pl.* MELANOMATA (-mətə), MELANOMAS (-məz)], [Mod. L. < Gr. *melas, melanos*, black; + *-oma*], a tumor whose cells contain melanin.

mel·a·no·sis (mel'ə-nō'sis), *n.* [Gr. *melanōsis*, a becoming black < *melanousthai*, to become black < *melas, melanos*, black], the abnormal production and deposition of melanin in the body tissues.

mel·a·not·ic (mel'ə-not'ik), *adj.* of, having, or having the nature of, melanosis.

mel·a·nous (mel'ə-nəs), *adj.* [*melan-* + *-ous*], having black or dark skin and hair: opposed to *xanthous.*

mel·an·tha·ceous (mel'ən-thā'shəs), *adj.* [< Mod. L. *Melanthaceae*, name of the family < Gr. *melas, melanos*, black + *anthos*, flower; + *-aceous*], of a family of monocotyledonous plants related to the lily but bulbless.

mel·a·phyre (mel'ə-fīr'), *n.* [Fr. < Gr. *melas*, black + Fr. *porphyre*, porphyry], an igneous porphyritic rock with a dark groundmass.

Mel·ba, Dame **Nellie** (mel'bə), (*Mrs. Helen Mitchell Armstrong*), 1861?–1931; Australian soprano.

Melba toast, [after Dame Nellie *Melba*], slightly stale bread sliced thin and toasted until brown and crisp.

Mel·bourne (mel'bērn), *n.* the capital of Victoria, Australia: pop., 1,227,000 (est. 1947).

Melbourne, second Viscount, (*William Lamb*), 1779–1848; English statesman; prime minister (1834; 1835–1841); adviser to Queen Victoria.

Mel·chior, Lau·ritz (lou'rits mel'kyôr), 1890– ; Danish tenor in America.

Mel·chiz·e·dek, Mel·chis·e·dec (mel-kiz'ə-dek'), *n.* [Heb. *malkī-tsedheq*, lit., king of righteousness], in the *Bible*, the priest and king of Salem who blessed Abraham: Gen. 14:18.

meld (meld), *v.t. & v.i.* [G. *melden*, to announce], in *pinochle*, etc., to declare (a combination of cards in one's hand) for inclusion in one's score. *n.* 1. a melding. 2. a combination of cards melded or to be melded. 3. the score made by melding.

meld (meld), *v.t. & v.i.* [merging of *melt & weld*], to blend; merge; unite.

Mel·e·a·ger (mel'i-ā'jēr), *n.* [L.; Gr. *Meleagros*], in *Greek legend*, one of the Argonauts, the son of Althea, queen of Calydon: he killed the Calydonian boar and, in a quarrel over its head and hide, which he had given to Atalanta, killed his maternal uncles, whereupon his mother caused his death by burning a log that she had removed from the fire at his birth because it was foretold that when it was consumed he would die.

me·lee, mê·lée (mā-lā', mā'lā, mel'ā), *n.* [Fr. *mêlée* < OFr. *meslee;* see MEDLEY], a confused, general hand-to-hand fight between groups or among combatants.

me·li·a·ceous (mē'li-ā'shəs), *adj.* [< Mod. L. *Meliaceae*, the mahogany family < Gr. *melia*, ash tree], of the mahogany family of tropical trees and shrubs.

mel·ic (mel'ik), *adj.* [Gr. *melikos* < *melos*, song], 1. of song or poetry. 2. meant to be sung; lyric. Applied especially to types of Greek poetry written in strophes.

Mel·i·cent (mel'ə-s'nt), a feminine name: see **Millicent.**

mel·i·lot (mel'i-lot'), *n.* [OFr. *mélilot;* L. *melilotos;* Gr. *melilōton, melilōtos*, kind of clover; *meli*, honey + *lōtos*, lotus], any of a group of sweet-smelling, cloverlike plants.

mel·i·nite (mel'i-nīt'), *n.* [Fr. *mélinite* < Gr. *mēlinos*, quince-yellow < *mēlon*, quince, apple: from its color], a powerful explosive like lyddite, made by combining picric acid with guncotton.

mel·io·ra·ble (mēl'yə-rə-b'l), *adj.* that can be meliorated.

mel·io·rate (mēl'yə-rāt'), *v.t. & v.i.* [MELIORATED (-id), MELIORATING], [< LL. *melioratus*, pp. of *meliorare*, to make better < L. *melior*, better], to make or become better; improve; ameliorate.

mel·io·ra·tion (mēl'yə-rā'shən), *n.* 1. a meliorating or being meliorated; improvement. 2. in *linguistics*, a change of meaning for the better. Opposed to *pejoration.*

mel·io·ra·tive (mēl'yə-rā'tiv), *adj.* meliorating or tending to meliorate: applied in linguistics to words whose basic meaning has been changed for the better (e.g., *marshal, knight, steward*). *n.* a meliorative word or form. Opposed to *pejorative.*

mel·io·ra·tor (mēl'yə-rā'tēr), *n.* a person or thing that meliorates.

mel·io·rism (mēl'yə-riz'm), *n.* [L. *melior*, better; + *-ism*], 1. the belief that the world naturally tends to get better and, especially, that it can be made better by human effort. 2. the betterment of society by improving people's health, living conditions, etc.

mel·io·rist (mēl'yə-rist), *n.* a believer in meliorism. *adj.* of meliorism or meliorists.

mel·ior·i·ty (mēl-yôr'ə-ti, mēl-yor'ə-ti), *n.* the quality or condition of being better; superiority.

Me·lis·sa (mə-lis'ə), [Gr. *Melissa*, lit., a bee], a feminine name.

Mel·i·to·pol (mel'i-tô'pôl), *n.* a city in the southern Ukrainian S.S.R., near the Sea of Azov: pop., 76,000.

mell (mel), *v.t. & v.i.* [ME. *mellen;* OFr. *meller*, var. of *mesler;* see MEDDLE], [Obs. or British Dial.], 1. to mingle; mix. 2. to meddle.

mel·lif·er·ous (mə-lif'ēr-əs), *adj.* [L. *mellifer* < *mel*, honey; + *-ous*], producing honey.

mel·lif·lu·ence (mə-lif'lōō-əns), *n.* the quality of being mellifluous.

mel·lif·lu·ent (mə-lif'lōō-ənt), *adj.* [LL. *mellifluens*], mellifluous.

mel·lif·lu·ous (mə-lif'lōō-əs), *adj.* [L. *mellifluus* < *mel, mellis*, honey + *fluere*, to flow], flowing sweetly and smoothly; honeyed: said of words, sounds, etc.

Mel·lon, Andrew William (mel'ən), 1855–1937; American banker; secretary of the treasury (1921–1932).

mel·low (mel'ō), *adj.* [ME. *melwe*, ripe; prob. < AS. *melu* (see MEAL, ground grain) & hence akin to Fl. *meluw*, soft, mellow; influenced in sense by AS. *meru* (ME. *merewe*), soft, tender], 1. soft, sweet, and juicy because ripe: said of fruit. 2. full-flavored; matured; not acid or bitter: said of wine, etc. 3. full, rich, soft, and pure; not harsh: said of sound, light, color, weather, etc. 4. moist and rich; loamy: said of soil. 5. softened and made gentle, understanding, and sympathetic by age and experience. 6. [Colloq.], *a*) genial; jovial. *b*) somewhat drunk; tipsy. 7. [Slang], good; excellent. *v.t.* & *v.i.* to make or become mellow. —***SYN.*** see **ripe.**

me·lo·de·on (mə-lō'di-ən), *n.* [pseudo-Gr. form < *melody*; cf. ACCORDION], 1. a small keyboard organ in which the tones are produced by drawing air through metal reeds by means of a bellows operated by pedals: it is much like a harmonium. 2. a kind of accordion.

me·lo·di·a (mə-lō'di-ə), *n.* [LL.; see MELODY], an 8-foot organ stop with wooden pipes and a flutelike tone; stopped diapason.

me·lod·ic (mə-lod'ik), *adj.* [Fr. *mélodique*; LL. *melodicus*], 1. of, or having the nature of, melody. 2. melodious.

me·lod·i·cal·ly (mə-lod'i-k'l-i, mə-lod'ik-li), *adv.* 1. in a melodic manner. 2. as regards melody. 3. by melody.

me·lod·ics (mə-lod'iks), *n.pl.* [construed as sing.], the branch of musical science dealing with the principles and construction of melody and the pitch of tones.

me·lo·di·ous (mə-lō'di-əs), *adj.* [OFr. *melodieus*], 1. containing or producing melody. 2. pleasing to hear; sounding sweet; tuneful.

mel·o·dist (mel'ə-dist), *n.* a singer or composer of melodies.

mel·o·dize (mel'ə-dīz'), *v.t.* [MELODIZED (-dīzd'), MELODIZING], 1. to make melodious. 2. to set to melody. *v.i.* to make melody; compose melodies.

mel·o·dra·ma (mel'ə-drä'mə, mel'ə-dram'ə), *n.* [Fr. *mélodrame* < Gr. *melos*, a song + *drama*, drama], 1. originally, a sensational or romantic stage play with interspersed songs and an orchestral accompaniment. 2. now, a drama with sensational, romantic, often violent action, extravagant emotions, and, generally, a happy ending. 3. any sensational, extravagantly emotional action, utterance, etc.

mel·o·dra·mat·ic (mel'ə-drə-mat'ik), *adj.* of, characteristic of, like, or fit for melodrama; sensational, violent, and extravagantly emotional.

mel·o·dra·mat·i·cal·ly (mel'ə-drə-mat'i-k'l-i, mel'ə-drə-mat'ik-li), *adv.* in a melodramatic manner.

mel·o·dra·mat·ics (mel'ə-drə-mat'iks), *n.pl.* melodramatic behavior.

mel·o·dy (mel'ə-di), *n.* [*pl.* MELODIES (-diz)], [ME. & OFr. *melodie*; LL. *melodia*; Gr. *melōidia* < *melos*, song + *aeidein*, to sing], 1. *a*) pleasing sounds or arrangement of sounds in sequence. *b*) musical quality, as in the arrangement of words. 2. in *music*, *a*) a sequence of single tones, usually in the same key or mode, to produce a rhythmic whole; often, a tune, air, or song. *b*) the element of form having to do with the arrangement of single tones in sequence: distinguished from *harmony*. *c*) the leading part, or voice, in a harmonic composition; the air. 3. a poem composed to be sung.
SYN.—**melody** refers to the rhythmic arrangement of tones in sequence to express a musical idea; **air**, in strict application, refers to the principal, or leading, melody of a harmonized composition, but it is sometimes used as an equivalent of **tune**, which is the popular term for any easily remembered melody that identifies a song, dance, etc.

mel·oid (mel'oid), *n.* [< Mod. L. *Meloidae*, name of the family < *meloe*, oil beetle], a blister beetle or other insect of the same family. *adj.* of such insects.

mel·o·lon·thine (mel'ə-lon'thin, mel'ə-lon'thin), *adj.* [< Gr. *mēlolonthē*, cockchafer; + *-ine*], of a subfamily of beetles including the cockchafers, June bugs, and rose bugs. *n.* any beetle of this subfamily.

mel·on (mel'ən), *n.* [ME.; OFr.; LL. *melo*, *melonis*, for L. *melopepo*; Gr. *mēlopepōn*, apple-shaped melon; *mēlon*, apple + *pepōn*, melon], 1. any of several large, juicy, many-seeded fruits of certain trailing plants of the gourd family, as the watermelon, muskmelon, cantaloupe, and honeydew melon. 2. any of these plants. 3. [Slang], profits, winnings, political spoils, or the like, for distribution among stockholders, etc.: chiefly in *cut a melon*, to distribute such profits, etc.

Me·los (mē'los), *n.* one of the Cyclades Islands, in the Aegean: area, 57 sq. mi.; pop., 7,000: Italian name, *Milo*.

Mel·pom·e·ne (mel-pom'ə-nē'), *n.* [L.; Gr. *Melpomenē* < *melpein*, to sing], in *Greek mythology*, the Muse of tragedy.

Mel·rose (mel'rōz), *n.* 1. a village in southeastern Scotland: site of ruins of a Cistercian abbey. 2. a city in eastern Massachusetts, near Boston: pop., 30,000.

melt (melt), *v.t.* & *v.i.* [MELTED (-id), MELTING; *archaic* pp. MOLTEN (mōl't'n)], [ME. *melten*; AS. *meltan*, *v.i.*, *mieltan*, *v.t.*; IE. base *mel-d- (< *mel-, to grind; cf. MEAL, ground grain), seen also in L. *mollis*, soft (cf. MOLLIFY)], 1. to change from a solid to a liquid state, generally by heat. 2. to dissolve; disintegrate. 3. to disappear or cause to disappear gradually (often with *away*). 4. to merge gradually; blend: as, the sea seems to *melt* into the sky at the horizon. 5. to soften; make or become gentle and tender: as, her grief *melted* our hearts. *n.* 1. a melting or being melted. 2. something melted. 3. the quantity melted at one operation or during one period. 4. a charge put into a furnace or crucible for melting.
SYN.—**melt** implies the bringing of a substance from its solid to its liquid state, usually by heat (to *melt* butter); **dissolve** refers specifically to the reduction of a solid to a liquid by placing it in another liquid so that its particles are evenly distributed among those of the solvent (to *dissolve* sugar in water); **liquefy** is the general term meaning to change to a liquid state and may be applied to gases as well as solids; **thaw** implies the reducing of a frozen substance to its normal liquid, or to a semiliquid, state by raising its temperature (the ice has *thawed*).—***ANT.*** solidify, freeze.

melt·age (mel'tij), *n.* [see -AGE], 1. the act of melting. 2. the thing or quantity resulting from melting.

melting point, the temperature at which a specified solid becomes liquid: abbreviated **M.P., m.p.**

melting pot, 1. a container in which metals or other substances are melted; crucible. 2. a country, place, etc. in which immigrants of various nationalities and races are assimilated.

mel·ton (mel't'n), *n.* [< *Melton* Mowbray in Leicestershire, England], a heavy woolen cloth with a smooth surface and a short nap, used for overcoats.

Me·lun·geon (mə-lun'jən), *n.* [? < Fr. *mélangé*, mixed; see MÉLANGE], a member of a dark-skinned people of mixed Caucasian, Negro, and Indian stock, inhabiting the Tennessee mountains.

Mel·ville, Herman (mel'vil), 1819–1891; American novelist and poet.

Melville Island, 1. an island in Northwest Territories, Canada, north of Victoria Island: area, 16,164 sq. mi. 2. an island in Northern Territory, Australia: area, 2,400 sq. mi.

Melville Peninsula, a peninsula in Northwest Territories, Canada, opposite Baffin Island: length, 250 mi.

Mel·vin (mel'vin), [ult. prob. < AS. *mæl*, *mæthel*, council + *wine*, friend, protector], a masculine name.

mem (mem), *n.* [Heb. *mēm*, lit., water; see M], the thirteenth letter of the Hebrew alphabet (מ, ם), corresponding to English *M*, *m*: see **alphabet,** table.

mem., 1. member. 2. *memento*, [L.], remember. 3. memoir. 4. memorandum; memoranda. 5. memorial.

mem·ber (mem'bẽr), *n.* [ME. & OFr. *membre*; L. *membrum*], 1. *a*) a leg, arm, or other part or organ of a human or animal body. *b*) a part of a plant considered with regard to structure or position rather than function. 2. *a*) a distinct part or element of a whole, as of a mathematical equation, a sentence, a syllogism, a series, a building, a bridge, etc. *b*) a part or division in a system of classification: as, species are *members* of a genus. 3. a person belonging to some association, society, community, party, etc. 4. [M-], *a*) a Member of Congress, in the House of Representatives. *b*) a Member of Parliament, in the House of Commons. Abbreviated **M., mem.**

mem·ber·ship (mem'bẽr-ship), *n.* [see -SHIP], 1. the state of being, or status as, a member. 2. members collectively, as of an organization. 3. the number of members.

mem·bra·na·ceous (mem'brə-nā'shəs), *adj.* [LL. *membranaceus*], membranous.

mem·brane (mem'brān), *n.* [L. *membrana*, membrane, fine skin, parchment < *membrum*, member; prob. from sense "coating of limb"], a thin, soft, pliable sheet or layer, especially of animal or vegetable tissue, serving as a covering or lining, as for an organ or part.

membrane bone, a bone developed in a connective tissue membrane rather than in cartilage.

mem·bra·nous (mem'brə-nəs, mem-brā'nəs), *adj.* [Fr. *membraneux*], 1. of, having the nature of, or like membrane. 2. characterized by the forming of a membrane: said of some diseases.

Me·mel (mā'məl; Eng. mem'əl), *n.* 1. a territory of Lithuania: now part of the Lithuanian S.S.R. 2. a seaport in the Lithuanian S.S.R.: pop., 89,000. 3. the Niemen River: the German name.

me·men·to (mi-men'tō), *n.* [*pl.* MEMENTOS, MEMENTOES (-tōz)], [L., imperative of *meminisse*, to remember], 1. [M-], in the *Roman Catholic Church*, either of two prayers in the Canon of the Mass, one for the living and one for the dead, beginning "Memento." 2. anything serving as a reminder, warning, or souvenir.

‡me·men·to mo·ri (mi-men'tō mō'rī), [L., remember that you must die], any reminder of death, as a skull.

Mem·ling, Hans (häns mem′liŋ), 1430?–1495; Flemish painter: also **Memlinc** (mem′liŋk).

Mem·non (mem′non), *n.* [L.; Gr. *Memnōn*], 1. in *Greek legend*, an Ethiopian king killed by Achilles in the Trojan War and made immortal by Zeus. 2. a gigantic statue of an Egyptian king at Thebes, Egypt, said to have emitted a musical sound at sunrise.

mem·o (mem′ō), *n.* [*pl.* MEMOS (-ōz)], [Colloq.], a memorandum.

mem·oir (mem′wär), *n.* [Fr. *mémoire*, masc., a memorandum, memoir; fem., memory < L. *memoria*, memory], 1. a biography or biographical notice. 2. a report or record of a scholarly investigation or scientific study; monograph. 3. *pl. a)* a report or record of happenings that is based on the writer's personal observation and knowledge or special information: as, *memoirs* of the French Revolution. *b)* an autobiography or autobiographical record. *c)* a record of the transactions of a learned society. Abbreviated **mem.**

mem·o·ra·bil·i·a (mem′ẽr-ə-bil′i-ə), *n.pl.* [*sing.* MEMORABILE (mem′ə-rab′ə-lē′)], [L., neut. pl. of *memorabilis*, memorable], things worth remembering or recording; noteworthy matters or events.

mem·o·ra·bil·i·ty (mem′ẽr-ə-bil′ə-ti), *n.* the quality or condition of being memorable.

mem·o·ra·ble (mem′ẽr-ə-b'l), *adj.* [L. *memorabilis*], worth remembering; notable; remarkable.

mem·o·ra·bly (mem′ẽr-ə-bli), *adv.* in a memorable manner.

mem·o·ran·dum (mem ə-ran′dəm), *n.* [*pl.* MEMORANDUMS (-dəmz), MEMORANDA (-də)], [L., neut. of *memorandus*, to be remembered, gerundive of *memorare*, to remember], 1. *a)* a short note written to help one remember something or remind one to do something. *b)* a record of events or observations, especially one for future use. 2. an informal written communication, as from one department to another in a business office. 3. in *business*, a statement, made by the consignor, of the goods and terms of a consignment sent with the privilege of return. 4. in *diplomacy*, a summary or outline of a subject under discussion, reasons for or against some action, etc. 5. in *law*, a short written statement of the terms of an agreement, contract, or transaction. Abbreviated **mem.** (*sing. & pl.*).

me·mo·ri·al (mə-môr′i-əl, mə-mō′ri-əl), *adj.* [Late ME.; OFr.; L. *memorialis* < *memoria*; see MEMORY], 1. serving to help people remember some person or event; commemorative. 2. of memory. *n.* 1. anything meant to help people remember some person or event, as a statue, holiday, etc. 2. an informal diplomatic paper. 3. a statement of facts, often with a petition that something be done, sent to a government, official, etc. Abbreviated **mem.**

Memorial Day, a day designated in the United States for honoring dead members of the armed forces; Decoration Day: in most States a legal holiday, falling on May 30; in Southern States, April 26, May 10, or June 3.

me·mo·ri·al·ist (mə-môr′i-əl-ist, mə-mō′ri-əl-ist), *n.* 1. a person who draws up, signs, or presents a memorial. 2. a writer of memoirs.

me·mo·ri·al·ize (mə-môr′i-ə-līz′, mə-mō′ri-ə-līz′), *v.t.* [MEMORIALIZED (-līzd′), MEMORIALIZING], 1. to commemorate. 2. to present a memorial to; petition.

mem·o·ri·za·tion (mem′ẽr-ə-zā′shən, mem′ẽr-ī-zā′shən), *n.* a memorizing or being memorized.

mem·o·rize (mem′ə-rīz′), *v.t.* [MEMORIZED (-rīzd′), MEMORIZING], to commit to memory; learn by heart.

mem·o·ry (mem′ẽr-i), *n.* [*pl.* MEMORIES (-iz)], [ME. & OFr. *memorie*; L. *memoria* < *memor*, mindful, remembering], 1. the power, act, or process of remembering. 2. the total of what one remembers. 3. a person, thing, happening, or act remembered. 4. the length of time over which remembering extends: as, not within the *memory* of living men has this happened. 5. commemoration or remembrance: as, in *memory* of his father. 6. fame after death; posthumous reputation: as, a man of notorious *memory*. 7. [Obs.], a memorial.

SYN.—**memory** refers specifically to the ability or power for retaining or reviving in the mind past thoughts, images, ideas, etc. (I'm losing my *memory*); **remembrance** applies to the act or process of having such events or things come to mind again (the painful *remembrance* of his childhood); **recollection** implies the voluntary and detailed remembering of a half-forgotten event (his *recollection* of the campaign is not too clear); **reminiscence** implies the pensive or wistful recollection of long-past, usually pleasurable, events, or the narration of these (he entertained us with *reminiscences* of his childhood).—*ANT.* forgetfulness, oblivion.

Mem·phi·an (mem′fi-ən), *adj.* 1. of ancient Memphis, Egypt; hence, 2. Egyptian.

Mem·phis (mem′fis), *n.* 1. an ancient city in Egypt, near the mouth of the Nile: former capital of Egypt: see **Egypt**, map. 2. a city in southwestern Tennessee, on the Mississippi: pop., 498,000.

Mem·phre·ma·gog, Lake (mem′fri-mā′gog), a lake in Vermont and Canada: length, 35 mi.; width, 2–5 mi.

mem·sa·hib (mem′sä′ib), *n.* [Anglo-Ind.; *mem* for Eng. *ma'am* + Ar. *sāhib*, a master], in India, lady; mistress: applied to a European woman by servants, etc.

men (men), *n.* plural of **man.**

men·ace (men′is), *n.* [ME. *manasce*, *manace*; OFr. *manace*; L. *minacia* < *minax*, *minacis*, projecting, threatening < *minari*, to threaten], 1. a threat or threatening. 2. anything threatening harm or evil. *v.t. & v.i.* [MENACED (-ist), MENACING], to threaten. —*SYN.* see **threaten.**

me·nad (mē′nad), *n.* a maenad.

mé·nage, me·nage (mə-näzh′, mā-näzh′), *n.* [ME. *maynage*; OFr. *manaige*, etc. (Fr. *ménage*) < LL. **mansionaticum*, domain < L. *mansio*, a house, mansion], 1. a household; domestic establishment. 2. the management of a household; housekeeping.

me·nag·er·ie (mə-naj′ẽr-i, mə-nazh′ẽr-i), *n.* [Fr. *ménagerie* < *ménage*; see MÉNAGE], 1. a collection of wild or strange animals kept in cages or enclosures for exhibition. 2. a place where such animals are kept.

Men·ai Strait (men′ī), a channel off the northwestern coast of Wales, separating Anglesey from the mainland.

Me·nam (me-näm′), *n.* the principal river in Thailand, flowing into the Gulf of Siam: length, 750 mi.

Me·nan·der (mi-nan′dẽr), *n.* Greek comic poet and dramatist; lived 343?–291? B.C.

Men·ci·us (men′shi-əs), *n.* (*Meng-tse*), Chinese philosopher and teacher of Confucianism; 372?–289? B.C.

Men·cken, H. L. (meŋ′k'n), (*Henry Louis Mencken*), 1880–1956; American writer, editor, and critic.

mend (mend), *v.t.* [ME. *menden*; see AMEND], 1. to repair (something broken or worn); remove defects in (something faulty); restore to good condition; make whole. 2. to make better; improve; reform; set right: as, *mend* your manners. 3. to atone for; make amends for: now only in *least said, soonest mended*. *v.i.* to get better; improve, especially in health. *n.* 1. a mending; improvement. 2. a mended place, as on a garment. **on the mend**, improving, especially in health.

SYN.—**mend** is the general word implying a making whole again something that has been broken, torn, etc. (to *mend* a toy, dress, etc.); **repair**, often equivalent to **mend**, is preferred when the object is a relatively complex one that has become damaged or decayed through use, age, exhaustion, etc. (to *repair* an automobile, radio, etc.); **patch** and **darn** imply the mending of a hole, tear, etc., the former by inserting or applying a piece of similar material (to *patch* a coat, a tire tube, etc.), the latter by sewing a network of stitches across the gap (to *darn* a sock).

men·da·cious (men-dā′shəs), *adj.* [< L. *mendax*, *mendacis*; + *-ous*], lying; untruthful; false.

men·dac·i·ty (men-das′ə-ti), *n.* [*pl.* MENDACITIES (-tiz)], [LL. *mendacitas* < L. *mendax*], 1. the quality or state of being mendacious. 2. a lie; falsehood.

Men·del, Gre·gor Jo·hann (grā′gôr yō′hän men′dəl), 1822–1884; Austrian monk and botanist; founder of genetics: see **Mendel's laws.**

Men·de·le·ev, Dmi·tri I·va·no·vich (d′mē′tri i-vä′nô-vich men′dye-lyā′ef; Eng. men′də-lā′ef), 1834–1907; Russian chemist: also spelled **Mendelyeev**, etc.

Mendeleev's law, in *chemistry*, the periodic law.

men·de·le·vi·um (men′də-lē′vi-əm), *n.* a radioactive chemical element produced by bombarding einsteinium with alpha particles having a high energy level: symbol, Mv; at. wt., 256 (?); at. no., 101.

Men·de·li·an (men-dē′li-ən), *adj.* 1. of Gregor Mendel. 2. of, or inherited according to, Mendel's laws.

Men·de·li·an·ism (men-dē′li-ən-iz′m), *n.* Mendelism.

Men·del·ism (men′d'l-iz′m), *n.* the theory of heredity formulated by Gregor Mendel.

Mendel's laws, the three principles of hereditary phenomena discovered and formulated by Gregor Mendel: 1) the law of independent unit characters, which states that characters, or characteristics, as height, color, etc., are inherited separately as units. 2) the law of segregation, which states that body cells and primordial germ cells contain pairs of such unit characters and that when gametes are produced, each gamete receives only one member of each such pair. 3) the law of dominance, which states that in every individual there is a pair of determining factors (see **genes**) for each unit character, one from each parent; if these factors are different (*heterozygous*), one character (the *dominant*) appears in the organism, the other (the *recessive*) being latent; the recessive character can appear in the organism only when the dominant is absent. Hence in all cross-bred generations unit characters are shown in varying combinations, each appearing in a definite proportion of the total number of offspring.

Men·dels·sohn, Fe·lix (fā′liks men′dəls-zōn; Eng. men′d'l-s'n, men′d'l-sōn′), (*Jakob Ludwig Felix Mendelssohn-Bartholdy*), 1809–1847; German composer and conductor; grandson of *Moses*.

Mendelssohn, Mo·ses (mō′zes), 1729–1786; grandfather of *Felix*; German Jewish philosopher.

Men·de·res (men′de-res′), *n.* 1. a river in Asia Minor, flowing into the Aegean: length, 240 mi.: ancient name, *Meander*. 2. a river in Asia Minor, flowing into the Dardanelles: length, 60 mi.: ancient name, *Scamander*.

men·di·can·cy (men′di-kən-si), *n.* [< *mendicant* + *-cy*], the state of being a beggar or the practice of begging.

men·di·cant (men′di-kənt), *adj.* [L. *mendicans*, *mendi-*

cantis, ppr. of *mendicare*, to beg < *mendicus*, needy], 1. begging; asking for alms: as, *mendicant* friars. 2. of or characteristic of a beggar. ***n.*** 1. a beggar; person who begs for alms. 2. a mendicant friar.

men·dic·i·ty (men-dis′ə-ti), ***n.*** [Fr. *mendicité;* L. *mendicitas*], mendicancy.

Men·do·ci·no, Cape (men′də-sē′nō), a cape in northern California: the most westerly point in the State.

Men·do·za (men-dô′sä; Eng. men-dō′zə), ***n.*** a city in western Argentina: pop., 104,000 (est. 1943).

Men·e·la·us (men′ə-lā′əs), ***n.*** [L.; Gr. *Menelaos*], in *Greek legend*, a king of Sparta, son of Atreus, brother of Agamemnon, and husband of Helen.

Men·e·lik II (men′ə-lik′), 1844–1913; emperor of Abyssinia (1889–1910).

‡me·ne, me·ne, tek·el, u·phar·sin (mē′ni mē′ni tek′′l ū-fär′sin), [Aram.], numbered, numbered, weighed, (and) divided: in the *Bible*, the writing on the wall, interpreted by Daniel to mean that God had weighed Belshazzar and his kingdom, found them wanting, and would destroy them: Dan. 5:25.

Me·nén·dez de A·vi·lés, Pe·dro (pe′*th*rô me-nen′deth *the* ä′vē-les′), 1519–1574; Spanish seafarer and explorer; founded St. Augustine, Florida, in 1565.

Me·nes (mē′nēz), ***n.*** founder of 1st dynasty of Egypt; fl. c. 3400 B.C.

men·folk (men′fōk′), ***n.pl.*** [Dial.], men: also **menfolks.**

Meng·tse (meŋ′tsē′; Chin. muŋ′dzu′), ***n.*** Mencius.

Meng·tze (meŋ′tse′; Chin. muŋ′dzu′), ***n.*** a city in Yunnan province, China: pop., 193,000.

men·ha·den (men-hā′d′n), ***n.*** [< Am. Ind. (Narragansett), lit., they fertilize; cf. Algonquian *munnawhat*, fertilizer], a sea fish of the herring family, common along the Atlantic coast from New England southward: it is used for bait or for making oil and fertilizer.

men·hir (men′hir), ***n.*** [Fr.; Bret. *men*, stone + *hir*, long], a tall stone, usually rough, standing upright (either as part of a circle or row, or alone), erected probably as a prehistoric monument; megalith.

me·ni·al (mē′ni-əl, mēn′yəl), ***adj.*** [ME. *meynal, menall;* Anglo-Fr. *meignal, menial* < OFr. *meisniee, maisnie*, household < L. *mansio;* see MANSION], 1. of or fit for servants; hence, 2. servile; low; mean. ***n.*** 1. a domestic servant. 2. a servile, low person. —***SYN.*** see **servile.**

me·nin·ge·al (mə-nin′ji-əl), ***adj.*** of the meninges.

me·nin·ges (mə-nin′jēz), ***n.pl.*** [Mod. L. < Gr. *mēninx, mēningos*, a membrane], the three membranes that envelop the brain and the spinal cord; dura mater, arachnoid, and pia mater.

men·in·git·ic (men′in-jit′ik), ***adj.*** of or having meningitis.

men·in·gi·tis (men′in-jī′tis), ***n.*** [Mod. L.; see MENINGES & -ITIS], inflammation of the meninges, especially as the result of infection by bacteria or viruses: the three principal forms are spinal, cerebral, and cerebrospinal.

me·nin·go·coc·cus (mə-niŋ′gō-kok′əs), ***n.*** [*pl.* MENINGOCOCCI (-kok′sī)], the bacterium causing cerebrospinal meningitis.

me·nis·cus (mi-nis′kəs), ***n.*** [*pl.* MENISCUSES (-iz), MENISCI (-nis′ī)], [Mod. L.; Gr. *meniskos*, dim. of *mēnē*, the moon], 1. a crescent or crescent-shaped thing. 2. a lens convex on one side and concave on the other. 3. in *physics*, the curved upper surface of a column of liquid: as a result of capillarity it is convex when the walls of the container are dry, concave when they are wet.

MENISCUS
A, convex meniscus of mercury; B, concave meniscus of water

men·i·sper·ma·ceous (men′i-spẽr-mā′shəs), ***adj.*** [< Mod. L. *Menispermaceae* < Gr. *mēnē*, the moon + *sperma*, seed; + *-ous*], designating or of the moonseed family of plants, chiefly tropical, climbing, woody plants and herbs with alternate leaves and small flowers, yielding narcotic and toxic substances.

Men·non·ite (men′ən-īt′), ***n.*** [after *Menno* Simons (1492–1559), a leader], a member of an evangelical Protestant Christian sect founded in Friesland in the 16th century and still existing in the United States and Europe: Mennonites oppose the taking of oaths, infant baptism, military service, and the acceptance of public office, and favor plain dress and plain living.

‡me·no (me′nô), ***adv.*** [It. < L. *minus*], in *music*, less.

me·nol·o·gy (mi-nol′ə-ji), ***n.*** [*pl.* MENOLOGIES (-jiz)], [Mod. L. *menologium;* Late Gr. *mēnologion;* Gr. *mēn*, month + *logos*, an account < *legein*, to speak], 1. a calendar of the months, with their events. 2. a register of the saints, with brief biographies, arranged according to months and days, as in the Greek Church.

men·o·pause (men′ə-pôz′), ***n.*** [< Gr. *mēn, mēnos*, month + *pauein*, to cause to cease (see PAUSE)], the permanent cessation of menstruation, normally between the ages of 45 and 50, or the period during which this occurs: female climacteric, or change of life.

Me·nor·ca (me-nôr′kä), ***n.*** Minorca: Spanish spelling.

men·or·rha·gi·a (men′ə-rā′ji-ə), ***n.*** [< Gr. *mēn, mēnos*, month; + *-rrhagia*], excessive menstrual flow.

Me·not·ti, Gian-Car·lo (jän-kär′lō me-nôt′i), 1911– ; American composer and dramatist, born in Italy.

men·sal (men′s′l), ***adj.*** [LL. *mensalis* < L. *mensa*, a table; cf. MEAT], of or used at the table.

men·sal (men′s′l), ***adj.*** [< L. *mensis*, month; + *-al*], monthly.

men·ses (men′sēz), ***n.pl.*** [L., pl. of *mensis*, month], the periodic flow of blood from the uterus, discharged through the genital tract: it normally occurs in women about every four weeks, from puberty to menopause.

Men·she·vik, men·she·vik (men′shə-vik′), ***n.*** [*pl.* MENSHEVIKS (-viks′), MENSHEVIKI (-vē′ki; Russ. men′shə-vi-kē′)], [Russ. (1903) < *menshe*, the smaller, less, minority], 1. *a)* originally, a member of the minority faction (*Mensheviki*) of the Social Democratic Party of Russia, who fought the more radical majority faction (*Bolsheviki*) from 1903 on. *b)* after November, 1917, a member of a political group of similar views, which opposed the policies, actions, and methods of the Soviet government and the Communist (Bolshevik) Party. 2. a person who has Menshevik views and traits: hostile term as applied by Communists. ***adj.*** of or characteristic of the Mensheviks or Menshevism.

Men·she·vism, men·she·vism (men′shə-viz′m), ***n.*** the policies and practices of the Mensheviks.

Men·she·vist, men·she·vist (men′shə-vist), ***n.*** & ***adj.*** Menshevik.

‡mens sa·na in cor·po·re sa·no (menz sā′nə in kôr′pə-ri sā′nō), [L.], a sound mind in a sound body.

men·stru·al (men′strōō-əl), ***adj.*** [ME. *menstruall;* L. *menstrualis* < *menstruus*, monthly < *mensis*, month], 1. of the menses. 2. in *astronomy*, monthly.

men·stru·ate (men′strōō-āt′), ***v.i.*** [MENSTRUATED (-id), MENSTRUATING], [< L. *menstruatus*, pp. of *menstruare*, to menstruate < *menstruus;* see MENSTRUAL], to have a discharge of the menses.

men·stru·a·tion (men′strōō-ā′shən), ***n.*** [see prec.], the discharge of the menses, or the period when this occurs.

men·stru·ous (men′strōō-əs), ***adj.*** [L. *menstruus*, of a month < *mensis*, month], of or having the menses.

men·stru·um (men′strōō-əm), ***n.*** [*pl.* MENSTRUUMS (-əmz), MENSTRUA (-ə)], [neut. of L. *menstruus*, monthly < *mensis*, month: so called from an alchemistic metaphor], a solvent; liquid that dissolves a solid.

men·sur·a·bil·i·ty (men′shẽr-ə-bil′ə-ti), ***n.*** the quality or state of being mensurable.

men·sur·a·ble (men′shẽr-ə-b′l), ***adj.*** [LL. *mensurabilis* < *mensurare;* see MENSURATION], 1. that can be measured; measurable. 2. in *music*, having fixed rhythm and measure.

men·su·ral (men′shẽr-əl), ***adj.*** [ML. *mensuralis*], 1. of measure. 2. in *music*, mensurable.

men·su·ra·tion (men′shə-rā′shən, men′soo-rā′shən), ***n.*** [LL. *mensuratio* < *mensuratus*, pp. of *mensurare*, to measure < L. *mensura*, measure; for base see MEAL (food)], 1. the act, process, or art of measuring. 2. the branch of mathematics dealing with the determination of length, area, or volume.

men·su·ra·tive (men′shə-rā′tiv), ***adj.*** for measuring.

-ment (mənt, mint), [Fr.; L. *-mentum*], a noun-forming suffix added to verbs, verb stems, or, rarely, adjectives, meaning: 1. *a result* or *product of* ______*ing*, as in *improvement, pavement.* 2. *a means, agency*, or *instrument for* ______*ing*, as in *adornment, escapement.* 3. *the act, fact, process*, or *art of* ______*ing*, as in *measurement, movement.* 4. *the state, condition, fact*, or *degree of being* ______*ed*, as in *disappointment.* Final *y* after a consonant becomes *i* before *-ment*, as in *embodiment.*

men·tal (men′t′l), ***adj.*** [ME.; Late OFr.; LL. *mentalis* < L. *mens, mentis*, the mind; for base see MAN], 1. of or for the mind or intellect: as, *mental* powers, *mental* aids. 2. done by, or carried on in, the mind (i.e., without using written symbols): as, *mental* arithmetic. 3. diseased in mind; mentally ill: as, a *mental* patient. 4. for the mentally ill: as, a *mental* hospital.

men·tal (men′t′l), ***adj.*** [< L. *mentum*, the chin; + *-al*], of the chin.

mental age, an individual's degree of mental development measured in terms of the chronological age of the average individual of corresponding mental ability.

mental deficiency, lack of some mental function or functions present in the normal individual; congenital subnormality of intelligence; amentia; feeble-mindedness: it ranges from idiocy to moronity.

mental healing, the treatment of diseases or disorders by mental concentration or hypnotic suggestion.

men·tal·i·ty (men-tal′ə-ti), ***n.*** [*pl.* MENTALITIES (-tiz)], mental capacity, power, or activity; mind.

men·tal·ly (men′t′l-i), ***adv.*** 1. in, with, or by the mind. 2. as regards the mind.

mental reservation, a qualification (of a statement) that one makes to himself but does not express.

men·tha·ceous (men-thā'shəs), *adj.* [< L. *mentha*, mint; + *-aceous*], designating or of a group of plants of the mint family, including spearmint and peppermint.

men·thene (men'thēn), *n.* [< *menthol* + *-ene*], a colorless, oily hydrocarbon, $C_{10}H_{18}$, derived from oil of peppermint or from menthol by dehydration.

men·thol (men'thol, men'thōl, men'thôl), *n.* [G. < L. *mentha*, mint + *-ol*, -ol (sense 1)], a white, waxy, crystalline alcohol, $C_{10}H_{19}OH$, obtained from oil of peppermint and used in medicine and perfumery.

men·tho·lat·ed (men'thə-lā'tid), *adj.* containing menthol; treated or impregnated with menthol.

men·tion (men'shən), *n.* [ME. *mencion; OFr. mention;* L. *mentio* < stem of *mens, mentis*, the mind; for base see MAN], a brief, often incidental, reference (to) or statement (about); a mentioning. *v.t.* to refer to or speak about briefly or incidentally; specify, as by name.
make mention of, to mention.
not to mention, without even mentioning.

Men·ton (män'tōn'), *n.* a resort in southeastern France, on the Mediterranean: pop., 23,000.

Men·to·ne (men-tô'ne), *n.* Menton: the Italian name.

men·tor (men'tẽr), *n.* [Gr. *Mentōr*, lit., adviser], 1. [M-], in *Greek legend*, the loyal friend and wise adviser of Odysseus (Ulysses), and teacher and guardian of Odysseus' son, Telemachus. 2. a wise, loyal adviser.

men·u (men'ū, mā'nū; Fr. mə-nü'), *n.* [*pl.* MENUS (-ūz, -nūz; Fr. -nü')], [Fr., small, detailed < L. *minutus;* see MINUTE, *adj.*], 1. a detailed list of the foods served at a meal; bill of fare. 2. the foods served.

Men·u·hin, Ye·hu·di (yə-hoo'di men'ū-in), 1917– ; American violinist.

me·ow, me·ou (mi-ou', myou), *n.* [echoic], the characteristic vocal sound made by a cat. *v.i.* to make this sound. Also **miaow, mew,** etc.

Me·phis·to (mi-fis'tō), *n.* Mephistopheles.

Me·phis·to·phe·le·an (mef'is-tə-fē'li-ən, mə-fis'tə-fē'li-ən, mef'ə-stof'ə-lē'ən), *adj.* 1. of Mephistopheles. 2. like Mephistopheles; fiendish, diabolical, crafty, malevolent, sardonic, etc. Also **Mephistophelian.**

Meph·i·stoph·e·les (mef'ə-stof'ə-lēz'), *n.* [G.; of obscure origin; earlier written also *Miphostophiles* (as if < Gr. *mē*, not + **phosto*, assumed form of Faust + *philos*, loving), *Mephotophiles* (as if < Gr. *mē* + *phōs, phōtos*, light + *philos*); also said to be < Heb. *mephiz*, destroyer + *tophel*, liar; neither these nor various other derivations have adequate support], 1. in *medieval legend*, a devil to whom Faust, or Faustus, sold his soul for riches and power: a leading character in Goethe's *Faust*, Marlowe's *Dr. Faustus*, Gounod's opera *Faust*, etc. 2. a crafty, powerful, malevolent devil; diabolical person. Also **Mephisto.**

Me·phis·to·phe·li·an (mef'is-tə-fē'li-ən, mə-fis'tə-fē'li-ən), *adj.* Mephistophelean.

me·phit·ic (me-fit'ik), *adj.* 1. of or caused by mephitis. 2. *a)* bad-smelling. *b)* poisonous; noxious.

me·phi·tis (me-fī'tis), *n.* [L.], 1. a harmful, bad-smelling vapor coming out of the earth, as the exhalation from decomposing organic matter or poisonous gas from a mine. 2. a bad smell; stench.

mer., 1. meridian. 2. meridional.

mer·can·tile (mũr'kən-til, mũr'kən-tīl'), *adj.* [Fr.; It. < *mercante*, a merchant; L. *mercans;* see MERCHANT], 1. of or characteristic of merchants or trade; commercial. 2. of mercantilism. Abbreviated **merc.**

mercantile agency, an establishment that gathers and provides for clients information about the credit rating, financial status, etc. of individuals and firms.

mercantile paper, checks, promissory notes, bills of exchange, and other negotiable paper used in business: also called *commercial paper*.

mer·can·til·ism (mũr'kən-til-iz'm, mũr'kən-tīl-iz'm), *n.* 1. *a)* the doctrine or policy that the economic interests of the nation as a whole are more important than those of individuals or parts of the nation, that a balance of exports over imports, with a consequent accumulation of bullion, is desirable, and that industry, agriculture, and commerce should be directed toward this objective: it arose in Europe with the decline of feudalism. *b)* the practice of this policy. Also **mercantile system.** 2. commercialism.

mer·can·til·ist (mũr'kən-til-ist, mũr'kən-tīl-ist), *n.* a person who believes in and advocates mercantilism.

mer·cap·tan (mẽr-kap'tan), *n.* [G. < ML. *mercurium captans*, lit., seizing mercury < L. *mercurius* (see MERCURY) + *captans*, ppr. of *captare*, to seize], any of a class of chemical compounds analogous to the alcohols and characterized by the substitution of sulfur for oxygen in the OH radical: also called *thiol*.

mer·cap·tide (mẽr-kap'tīd), *n.* a metallic salt of a mercaptan, characterized by the substitution of a metal for the hydrogen in the SH radical.

mer·cap·to (mẽr-kap'tō), *n.* [< *mercaptan*], the monovalent radical SH.

Mer·ca·tor, Ger·har·dus (jẽr-här'dəs mẽr-kā'tẽr; Fl. mer-kä'tôr), [Latinized from *Gerhard Kremer:* G. *kremer* & L. *mercator* mean "dealer"], 1512–1594; Flemish mathematician, geographer, and cartographer.

Mercator's projection, a method of making maps in which the earth's surface is shown as a rectangle, with the meridians as parallel straight lines spaced at equal intervals and the parallels of latitude as parallel straight lines intersecting the meridians at right angles but spaced further apart as their distance from the equator increases: areas on such maps become increasingly distorted toward the poles.

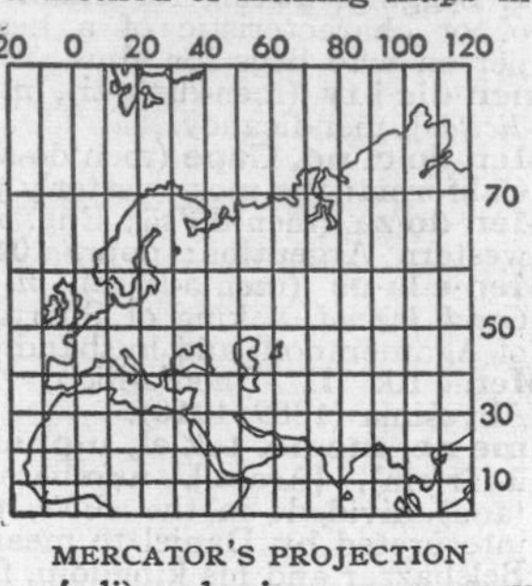

MERCATOR'S PROJECTION

mer·ce·nar·i·ly (mũr'sə-ner'ə-li), *adv.* in a mercenary manner.

mer·ce·nar·i·ness (mũr'sə-ner'i-nis), *n.* the quality or state of being mercenary.

mer·ce·nar·y (mũr'sə-ner'i), *adj.* [L. *mercenarius* < *merces*, pay, wages, reward], 1. working or done for payment only; motivated by a desire for money or other gain; venal; greedy. 2. designating a soldier serving for pay in a foreign army; hired. *n.* [*pl.* MERCENARIES (-iz)], 1. a professional soldier serving in a foreign army for pay. 2. [Archaic], a person paid for his work or services; hireling.

mer·cer (mũr'sẽr), *n.* [ME.; Late OFr. *mercier* < *merz*, goods; L. *merx, mercis*, wares], [British], a dealer in textiles.

mer·cer·ize (mũr'sə-rīz'), *v.t.* [MERCERIZED (-rīzd'), MERCERIZING], [after John *Mercer* (1791–1866), Eng. calico dealer who invented the process], to treat (cotton thread or fabric) with a caustic alkali solution in order to strengthen it, give it a silky luster, and make it more receptive to dyes.

mer·cer·y (mũr'sẽr-i), *n.* [*pl.* MERCERIES (-iz)], [ME. & OFr. *mercerie*], [British], 1. goods sold by a mercer. 2. the business or shop of a mercer.

mer·chan·dise (mũr'chən-dīz'; *for n. also* mũr'chən-dīs'), *n.* [ME. & OFr. *marchandise* < OFr. *marchant;* see MERCHANT], 1. things bought and sold; goods; commodities; wares. 2. [Obs.], buying and selling; trade. *v.t. & v.i.* [MERCHANDISED (-dīzd'), MERCHANDISING], to buy and sell; carry on trade in (some kind of goods). Abbreviated **mdse.** Also spelled **merchandize.**

mer·chant (mũr'chənt), *n.* [ME. *marchant;* OFr. *marchant, marcheant* < LL. **mercatans*, ppr. of **mercatare*, for L. *mercari*, to trade, buy < *merx, mercis*, merchandise, wares], 1. a person whose business is buying and selling goods for profit; trader, especially one in the wholesale trade who deals with foreign countries. 2. a person who sells goods at retail; storekeeper; shopkeeper. *adj.* 1. of or used in trade; mercantile; commercial. 2. of the merchant marine.

mer·chant·a·ble (mũr'chən-tə-b'l), *adj.* marketable.

mer·chant·man (mũr'chənt-mən), *n.* [*pl.* MERCHANTMEN (-mən)], 1. a vessel used in commerce; merchant ship. 2. [Archaic], a merchant.

merchant marine, 1. all the ships of a nation that are used in commerce. 2. their personnel.

Merchant of Venice, The, 1. a comedy (c. 1596) by Shakespeare. 2. Antonio, the merchant of the play.

merchant prince, a rich merchant.

‡**mer·ci** (mâr'sē'), *interj.* [Fr.], thanks; thank you.

Mer·ci·a (mũr'shi-ə, mũr'shə), *n.* a former Anglo-Saxon kingdom of central England.

Mer·ci·an (mũr'shi-ən, mũr'shən), *adj.* of Mercia, its people, or their dialects. *n.* 1. a native or inhabitant of Mercia. 2. the Anglo-Saxon dialects of the Mercians. 3. sometimes, the Middle English dialects descended from these; Midland dialects.

‡**mer·ci beau·coup** (mâr'sē' bō'koo'), [Fr.], thanks very much.

Mer·cier, Dé·si·ré Jo·seph (dā'zē'rā' zhô'zef' mâr'syā'), 1851–1926; Belgian cardinal.

mer·ci·ful (mũr'si-fəl), *adj.* full of mercy; having, feeling, or showing mercy; compassionate; lenient; clement.

mer·ci·less (mũr'si-lis), *adj.* without mercy; having, feeling, or showing no mercy; pitiless; cruel; implacable.

mer·cu·rate (mũr'kyoo-rāt'), *v.t.* [MERCURATED (-id), MERCURATING], to treat or combine with mercury or a compound of mercury.

mer·cu·ri·al (mẽr-kyoor'i-əl), *adj.* [ME.; Late OFr. *mercuriel;* L. *mercurialis*], 1. [M-], of Mercury (the god or planet). 2. of or containing mercury. 3. caused by the action or use of mercury. 4. having qualities attributed to the god Mercury or supposedly influenced by the planet Mercury; eloquent, clever, shrewd, thievish, etc. 5. having qualities suggestive of mercury; quick, quick-witted, volatile, changeable, fickle, etc. *n.* a drug or preparation containing mercury.

mer·cu·ri·al·ism (mẽr-kyoor'i-əl-iz'm), *n.* chronic poisoning caused by mercury or its compounds.

mer·cu·ri·al·ize (mẽr-kyoor′i-ə-līz′), *v.t.* [MERCURIALIZED (-līzd′), MERCURIALIZING], 1. to make mercurial. 2. to treat with mercury or a compound of mercury.

mer·cu·ric (mẽr-kyoor′ik), *adj.* of or containing mercury, especially with a valence of two.

mercuric chloride, a very poisonous, white, crystalline compound, $HgCl_2$, used in engraving and as an antiseptic: also called *corrosive sublimate, bichloride of mercury, mercury chloride.*

mercuric oxide, a poisonous red powder, HgO, used as a chemical reagent and in the manufacture of pigment, cosmetics, and polishing compounds.

mer·cu·ro·chrome (mẽr-kyoor′ə-krōm′), *n.* [see MERCURY & -CHROME], 1. a red, crystalline dye, $C_{20}H_8O_6Br_2Na_2Hg$. 2. an aqueous solution of this, used as an antiseptic. A trade-mark (**Mercurochrome**).

mer·cu·rous (mẽr-kyoor′əs, mũr′kyoo-rəs), *adj.* of or containing mercury, especially with a valence of one.

Mer·cu·ry (mũr′kyoo-ri), *n.* [L. *Mercurius,* Mercury; prob. < base of *merx,* merchandise], 1. in *Roman mythology,* the messenger of the gods, god of commerce, manual skill, eloquence, cleverness, travel, and thievery: identified with the Greek Hermes. 2. the smallest planet in the solar system and the nearest to the sun: diameter, c. 3,000 mi.; diurnal rotation and year, 88 days; symbol, ☿.

MERCURY

mer·cu·ry (mũr′kyoo-ri), *n.* [*pl.* MERCURIES (-riz)], [< *Mercury*], 1. a heavy, silver-white metallic chemical element, liquid at ordinary temperatures, which sometimes occurs in a free state but usually in combination with sulfur; quicksilver: it is used in thermometers, air pumps, dentistry, pharmacy, etc.: symbol, Hg; at. wt., 200.61; at. no., 80. 2. the mercury column in a thermometer or barometer. 3. a messenger or guide. 4. a European plant with edible stems used like asparagus and leaves used like spinach: one variety (*dog's mercury*) is poisonous.

mercury chloride, mercuric chloride.

mer·cu·ry-va·por lamp (mũr′kyoo-ri-vā′pẽr), a glass tube or bulb in which an electric discharge passes through mercury vapor, causing it to give off a bluish-green light rich in ultraviolet and actinic rays.

Mer·cu·ti·o (mẽr-kū′shi-ō′, mẽr-kū′shō), *n.* in Shakespeare's *Romeo and Juliet,* a gay, witty, brave young nobleman, a friend of Romeo.

mer·cy (mũr′si), *n.* [*pl.* MERCIES (-siz)], [ME. *merci;* OFr. *merci;* L. *merces, mercedis,* hire, payment, reward (in LL., mercy, pity, favor); akin to *merx, mercis,* wares], 1. a refraining from harming or punishing offenders, enemies, persons in one's power, etc.; kindness in excess of what may be expected or demanded by fairness; forbearance and compassion. 2. a disposition to forgive, pity, or be kind. 3. the power to forgive or be kind; clemency: as, throw yourself on his *mercy.* 4. kind or compassionate treatment; relief of suffering. 5. a fortunate thing; thing to be grateful for; blessing: as, it's a *mercy* he's still alive. *interj.* a mild exclamation expressing surprise, annoyance, emphasis, etc.

at the mercy of, completely in the power of.

SYN.—**mercy** implies a kindness or forbearance, as in punishing offenders, in excess of what may be demanded by fairness, or it may connote kindness and sympathy to those in distress; **clemency** refers to a tendency toward mercy in one whose duty it is to punish offenders; **lenity** usually implies excessive mercy or mildness toward offenders where greater strictness might be preferable; **charity,** in this connection, implies a kindly understanding and tolerance in judging others.—***ANT.*** severity, cruelty.

mercy killing, euthanasia.

mercy seat, 1. in ancient Jewish ritual, the gold covering on the Ark of the Covenant, which was sprinkled once a year with the blood of sacrificial animals and regarded as the resting place of God: Ex. 25:17; hence, 2. the throne of God or Christ.

mere (mêr), *adj.* [superl. MEREST (-ist)], [< OFr. or L.; OFr. *mier;* L. *merus,* unmixed, pure], 1. nothing more or other than; only (as said to be): as, he's a *mere* boy. 2. [Obs.], unmixed; pure; unqualified; absolute.

mere (mêr), *n.* [ME.; AS.; akin to G. *meer,* sea; IE. base **mari-,* **mori-,* sea, seen also in L. *mare* (cf. MARINE)], [Archaic, Poetic, or British Dial.], 1. *a*) the sea. *b*) an arm of the sea. 2. a lake or pond. 3. a marsh.

mere (mêr), *n.* [ME.; AS. (*ge*)*mære;* base as in *mural, immure*], [Archaic or British Dial.], a boundary.

-mere (mêr), [< Gr. *meros,* a part; cf. MERIT], a combining form meaning *part,* as in *blastomere.*

Mer·e·dith (mer′ə-dith), [W. < *mor,* sea + base of *differaf,* I protect; lit., sea protector], a masculine name.

Mer·e·dith, George (mer′ə-dith), 1828–1909; English novelist and poet.

Meredith, Owen (pseudonym of *Edward Robert Bulwer-Lytton*), 1831–1891; English statesman and poet.

mere·ly (mêr′li), *adv.* [*mere, adj.* + *-ly*], 1. no more than; and nothing else; only. 2. [Obs.], purely; wholly.

mer·e·tri·cious (mer′ə-trish′əs), *adj.* [L. *meretricius* < *meretrix, meretricis,* a prostitute < *mereri,* to serve for hire], 1. originally, of, like, or characteristic of a prostitute; hence, 2. alluring by false, showy charms; speciously attractive; flashy; tawdry.

mer·gan·ser (mẽr-gan′sẽr), *n.* [*pl.* MERGANSERS (-sẽrz), MERGANSER; see PLURAL, II, D, 1], [Mod. L. < L. *mergus,* diver (bird) + *anser,* goose], any of several large, fish-eating, diving ducks with a long, slender, toothed beak hooked at the tip and, usually, a crested head.

merge (mũrj), *v.i. & v.t.* [MERGED (mũrjd), MERGING], [L *mergere,* to dip, plunge, immerse, sink], to lose or cause to lose identity by being absorbed, swallowed up, or combined; unite indistinguishably. —***SYN.*** see **mix.**

mer·gence (mũr′jəns), *n.* a merging or being merged.

merg·er (mũr′jẽr), *n.* 1. a merging; specifically, *a*) the combination of several companies, corporations, etc. in one, as by issuing stock of the controlling corporation to replace the greater part of that of the others. *b*) the absorption of one estate, interest, obligation, contract, etc. in another, or of a lesser offense in a greater. 2. a person or thing that merges.

Mé·ri·da (me′rē-dä′), *n.* the capital of the state of Yucatán, Mexico: pop., 199,000.

Mer·i·den (mer′ə-d′n), *n.* a city in central Connecticut: pop., 52,000.

Me·ri·di·an (mə-rid′i-ən), *n.* a city in eastern Mississippi: pop., 49,000.

me·rid·i·an (mə-rid′i-ən), *adj.* [Late ME.; OFr. *meridien;* L. *meridianus,* of noon, southern < *meridies,* noon, the south < older *medidies* < *medius,* middle + *dies,* day], 1. of or at noon or, especially, of the position or power of the sun at noon. 2. of or passing through the highest point in the daily course of any heavenly body. 3. of or along a meridian. 4. of or at the highest point of prosperity, splendor, power, etc. 5. [Rare], southern. *n.* 1. the highest apparent point reached by a heavenly body in its course. 2. *a*) the highest point of power, prosperity, splendor, etc.; zenith; apex; culmination. *b*) the middle period of one's life, regarded as the highest point of health, vigor, etc.; prime. 3 [Obs.], noon. 4. in *astronomy,* an imaginary great circle of the celestial sphere passing through the poles of the heavens and the zenith and nadir of any given point, and cutting the equator at right angles. 5. in *geography, a*) a great circle of the earth passing through the geographical poles and any given point on the earth's surface. *b*) the half of such a circle between the poles. *c*) any of the lines of longitude running north and south on a globe or map, representing such a circle or half circle. 6. *a*) a place or situation with its own distinctive character. *b*) distinctive character. Abbreviated **M., m., mer.**

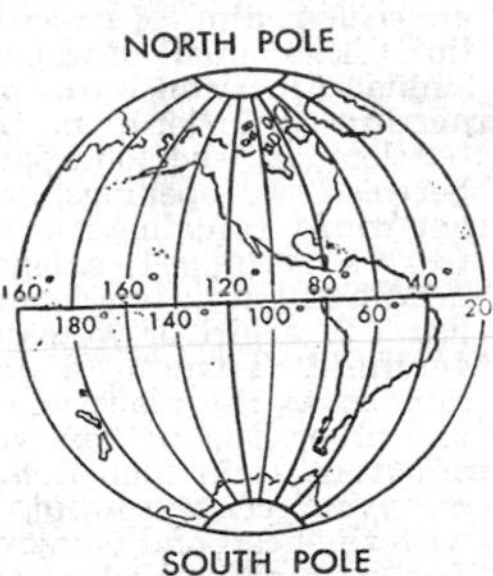

MERIDIANS

me·rid·i·o·nal (mə-rid′i-ə-n′l), *adj.* [Late ME.; OFr.; LL. *meridionalis* < L. *meridianus;* see MERIDIAN], 1. southern; southerly. 2. of or characteristic of the south or people living in the south (of Europe, especially France). 3. of or like a meridian. *n.* [often M-], an inhabitant of the south (of Europe, especially France). Abbreviated **mer.**

me·rid·i·o·nal·ly (mə-rid′i-ə-n′l-i), *adv.* 1. north and south. 2. in the direction of the poles (of a magnet).

Mé·ri·mée, Pros·per (prôs′pâr′ mā′rē′mā′), 1803–1870; French novelist, essayist, and historian.

me·ringue (mə-raŋ′), *n.* [Fr.; G. *meringe,* lit., cake of Mehringen (in Germany)], 1. egg whites beaten stiff and mixed with sugar, often browned in the oven and used as a covering for pies, cakes, etc. 2. a small cake made of this, often filled with fruit, etc.

me·ri·no (mə-rē′nō), *n.* [*pl.* MERINOS (-nōz)], [Sp., roving from pasture to pasture < *merino,* inspector of sheepwalks, shepherd, royal judge < ML. *majorinus,* head of a village, steward < L. *major,* greater], 1. one of a hardy breed of sheep with long, fine, silky wool, originally from Spain. 2. the wool. 3. a fine, soft yarn made from this wool, used to make stockings, underwear, etc. 4. a soft, thin woolen cloth made of this wool or of something like it. *adj.* designating or of this sheep, wool, yarn, or cloth.

Mer·i·on·eth·shire (mer'i-on'ith-shir'), *n.* a county of Wales: pop., 43,000.

mer·i·stem (mer'i-stem'), *n.* [< Gr. *meristos*, divided < *merizein*, to divide < *meros*, a part + *-ēm(a)*, n. suffix; cf. MERIT], undifferentiated plant tissue in the process of formation, consisting of cells actively growing and dividing, as at the tips of roots and stems.

mer·i·ste·mat·ic (mer'i-sti-mat'ik), *adj.* of meristem.

mer·it (mer'it), *n.* [ME.; OFr. *merite;* L. *meritum* < *meritus*, pp. of *merere, mereri*, to deserve, earn; akin to Gr. *meros*, a part, *moira*, lot], 1. *sometimes pl.* the state, fact, or quality of deserving well or, sometimes, ill; desert. 2. worth; value; excellence. 3. something deserving reward, praise, or gratitude. 4. a reward or honor given for praiseworthy qualities or conduct; mark, badge, etc. awarded for excellence. 5. *pl.* actual qualities or facts, good or bad: as, decide the question on its *merits*. *v.t.* to deserve; be worthy of.

mer·it·ed (mer'it-id), *adj.* [pp. of *merit*], deserved.

mer·i·to·ri·ous (mer'ə-tôr'i-əs, mer'ə-tō'ri-əs), *adj.* [ME.; L. *meritorius*, bringing in money < *meritus;* see MERIT], having merit; deserving reward, praise, etc.

merit system, a system of hiring and promoting people to civil service positions on the basis of merit as determined by competitive examinations.

merl, merle (mũrl), *n.* [OFr. *merle;* L. *merula, merulus*], [Archaic or Poetic], the European blackbird.

Merle (mũrl), [Fr.; prob. < *merle*, blackbird; see MERL], a masculine name.

Mer·lin (mũr'lin), [ML. *Merlinus;* W. *Myrrdin, Merddin;* Brythonic **Mori-dūnon* < **mori*, sea + Primitive Celt. **dunom*, hill, fortified hill, fort; hence, lit., sea-hill or sea-fortress], a masculine name. *n.* in *medieval legend*, a magician and seer, helper of King Arthur.

mer·lin (mũr'lin), *n.* [ME. *merlion;* OFr. *emerillon, esmerillon*, dim. of *esmeril*, merlin < OHG. *smirl*, merlin], 1. a small European falcon. 2. a related and similar American bird, the pigeon-hawk.

mer·lon (mũr'lən), *n.* [Fr.; It. *merlone* < *merlo*, a battlement], the solid part of a battlement or parapet, between two openings, or embrasures.

mer·maid (mũr'mād'), *n.* [ME. *mermayde;* see MERE (sea) & MAID], 1. a legendary sea creature with the head and trunk of a beautiful woman and the tail of a fish. 2. a girl or woman who swims well.

Mermaid Tavern, a tavern in London, England, famous as the place where Ben Jonson, Shakespeare, and other Elizabethan writers used to gather.

mer·man (mũr'man'), *n.* [*pl.* MERMEN (-men')], [ME. *mereman;* cf. MERMAID], 1. a legendary sea creature with the head and trunk of a man and the tail of a fish. 2. a man or boy who swims well.

mer·o·blas·tic (mer'ə-blas'tik), *adj.* [< Gr. *meros*, part; + *-blast* + *-ic*], in *embryology*, designating or of ova that undergo only partial segmentation.

Mer·o·ë (mer'ō-ē'), *n.* a ruined city on the Nile: ancient capital of Ethiopa.

-mer·ous (mẽr-əs), [< Gr. *meros*, a part], a suffix that means *having* (a specified number or kind of) *parts*, *partite*, as in *trimerous* (often written *3-merous*).

Mer·o·vin·gi·an (mer'ə-vin'ji-ən, mer'ə-vin'jən), *adj.* [Fr. *Mérovingien* < ML. *Merovingi*, descendants of *Merovaeus*, (Latinized name of) a legendary Frankish king], designating or of the Frankish line of kings who reigned in Gaul (ancient France) from c. 500 to 752 A.D.: the line was founded by Clovis I. *n.* a king of this line.

mer·o·zo·ite (mer'ə-zō'īt), *n.* [< Gr. *meros*, part; + *sporozoa* + *-ite*], any of a form of spore produced in the asexual stage in the reproduction of certain protozoa, as the malaria parasite.

mer·ri·ly (mer'ə-li), *adv.* in a merry manner.

Mer·ri·mac (mer'ə-mak'), *n.* 1. the first armored warship, a United States frigate equipped by the Confederates with iron armor and used to harass Union shipping until engaged in battle (March 9, 1862) at Hampton Roads by the Monitor, a Union ironclad: Confederate name, *Virginia*. 2. the Merrimack.

Mer·ri·mack (mer'ə-mak'), *n.* a river in New Hampshire and Massachusetts, flowing into the Atlantic: length, 110 mi.

mer·ri·ment (mer'i-mənt), *n.* 1. merrymaking; gaiety and fun; mirth; hilarity. 2. [Obs.], something that amuses or entertains. —*SYN.* see **mirth.**

mer·ri·ness (mer'i-nis), *n.* a merry quality or state.

mer·ry (mer'i), *adj.* [MERRIER (-i-ẽr), MERRIEST (-i-ist)], [ME. (South Eastern) *merie;* AS. *myrge;* akin to OHG. *murgi*, short; IE. base **mreĝhu-*, **mr̥ĝhu-*, short, seen also in L. *brevis*, short (cf. BRIEF); basic sense "lasting a short time, seeming brief"], 1. full of fun and laughter; lively and cheerful; gay; mirthful. 2. festive: as, the *merry* month of May. 3. [Archaic], *a)* pleasant. *b)* amusing. *c)* facetious. —*SYN.* see **happy.**

make merry, to be full of laughter and gaiety; be hilarious or festive.

mer·ry-an·drew (mer'i-an'drōō), *n.* [*merry* + *Andrew*, given name: said to be after *Andrew* Boorde, reputed author of jest books in the time of Henry VIII], a buffoon; clown.

mer·ry-go-round (mer'i-gō-round'), *n.* 1. a circular, revolving platform with wooden animals and seats on it, used at carnivals, amusement parks, etc.: it is turned by machinery, usually to music; carrousel. 2. a whirl; swift round, as of social life or business affairs.

mer·ry·mak·er (mer'i-māk'ẽr), *n.* a person taking part in merrymaking.

mer·ry·mak·ing (mer'i-māk'iŋ), *n.* 1. a making merry, laughing, and having fun; conviviality; festivity. 2. a cheerful festival or entertainment. *adj.* taking part in merrymaking; gay and festive.

mer·ry·thought (mer'i-thôt'), *n.* [< the supposed granting of a wish to the person winning the wishbone contest; cf. WISHBONE], the wishbone.

Mer·sey (mũr'zi), *n.* a river in northwest central England, flowing into the Irish Sea: length, 70 mi.: its long estuary forms Liverpool harbor.

mer·thi·o·late (mẽr-thī'ə-lāt'), *n.* [< sodium ethyl-*mer*curi-*thio*salicy*late*], a red or colorless liquid (*sodium ethyl-mercuri-thiosalicylate*), used as an antiseptic and germicide: it contains over 49 per cent of mercury in organic combination: a trade-mark (**Merthiolate**).

Mer·vyn (mũr'vin), [prob. var. of *Marvin*], a masculine name.

Mer·wyn (mũr'win), a masculine name: see **Mervyn.**

mes- (mes), meso-.

me·sa (mā'sə), *n.* [Sp. < L. *mensa*, a table], a small, high plateau or flat tableland with steep sides and, often, a layer of rock covering it.

mé·sal·li·ance (mā-zal'i-əns; Fr. mā'zà'lyäns'), *n.* [Fr.], a marriage with a person of lower social status.

Me·sa Ver·de National Park (mā'sə vâr'dā, mā'sə vũrd'; Am. Sp. me'sä ver'de), a national park in southwestern Colorado, containing prehistoric cliff dwellings: area, 80 sq. mi.

mes·cal (mes-kal'), *n.* [Sp. *mezcal;* Nahuatl *mexcalli*], 1. a colorless alcoholic liquor made from pulque or the fermented juice of an agave. 2. a pulque agave or other plant from which this liquor is made. 3. a small, spineless cactus with rounded stems, whose buttonlike tops (*mescal buttons*) contain a narcotic and are chewed by the Indians for their stimulating effect.

mes·ca·line (mes'kə-lēn', mes'kə-lin), *n.* [*mescal* + *-ine*], a white, crystalline alkaloid, $C_{11}H_{17}O_3N$, obtained from mescal buttons: it has narcotic properties and causes color hallucinations and convulsions: also **mezcaline.**

mes·dames (mā-däm'; Fr. mā'dàm'), *n.pl.* [Fr., lit., my ladies], plural of **madame, madam,** (sense 1), or **Mrs.:** abbreviated **Mmes.**

‡mes·de·moi·selles (mād'mwà'zel'), *n.pl.* [Fr., lit., my young ladies], plural of **mademoiselle:** abbreviated **Mlles.**

me·seems (mē-sēmz'), *impersonal v.* [past tense ME-SEEMED (-sēmd')], [Archaic], it seems to me: also **meseemeth.**

mes·en·ceph·a·lon (mes'en-sef'ə-lon'), *n.* [Mod. L.; *mes-* + *encephalon*], the middle part of the brain; midbrain.

mes·en·chyme (mes'eŋ-kim), *n.* [< *mes-* + Mod. L. *-enchyma*, suffix denoting a type of cell tissue, as in *parenchyma*], in *embryology*, that part of the mesoderm from which the connective tissues, cartilage, bone, blood, heart, and lymphatic vessels are derived.

mes·en·ter·ic (mes''n-ter'ik), *adj.* of the mesentery.

mes·en·ter·i·tis (mes-en'tẽr-ī'tis), *n.* [see -ITIS], inflammation of the mesentery.

mes·en·ter·on (mes-en'tẽr-on'), *n.* [*pl.* MESENTERA (-ə)], [Mod. L.; *mes-* + *enteron*], the middle part of the body cavity of an embryo, from which the alimentary canal, liver, pancreas, etc. develop: it is lined with endoderm.

mes·en·ter·y (mes''n-ter'i), *n.* [*pl.* MESENTERIES (-iz)], [ML. *mesenterium;* Gr. *mesenterion* < *mesos*, middle + *enteron*, intestine], a supporting membrane or membranes enfolding some internal organ and attaching it to either the body wall or another organ; especially, a part of the peritoneum enfolding most of the small intestine and attaching it to the rear wall of the abdominal cavity.

mesh (mesh), *n.* [earlier *meash, meish;* prob. < MD. *maesche;* but the AS. cognate *max* (for **mæsc*), whence dial. *mash*, may have merged with the MD. word; IE. base **mezg-*, to knit, entwine, as also in Lith. *mezgù*, to knit together], 1. any of the open spaces of a net, screen, sieve, etc.: a 50-mesh screen is one with 50 such open spaces per linear inch. 2. *pl.* the threads, cords, etc. forming these openings. 3. a net or network. 4. anything that entangles, snares, or entraps. 5. the engagement of the teeth of gears. *v.t. & v.i.* 1. to entangle or become entangled. 2. to engage or become engaged: said of gears or gear teeth.

in mesh, in gear; interlocked.

Me·shach (mē'shak), *n.* [Heb. *mēshakh*], in the *Bible*, one of the three captives who came out of the blazing furnace miraculously unharmed: Dan. 3.

Mesh·ed (mash-had'; Eng. mə-shed', mesh'hed), *n.* a walled city in northeastern Iran, a Moslem shrine: pop., 176,000 (1942): also spelled **Meshhed.**

mesh knot, a sheet bend: see **knot,** illus.

mesh·work (mesh'wũrk'), *n.* meshes; network.

mesh·y (mesh′i), *adj.* formed, or consisting, of meshes.

me·si·al (mē′zi-əl, mes′i-əl), *adj.* [< Gr. *mesos*, middle; + *-ial*], of, in, toward, or along the middle; middle; median; especially, designating or of a median plane or line.

me·si·al·ly (mē′zi-əl-i, mes′i-əl-i), *adv.* in a mesial position; in or toward the middle.

me·sit·y·lene (mi-sit′ə-lēn′, mes′i-tə-lēn′), *n.* [*mesityl* (< Gr. *mesitēs*, mediator < *mesos*, middle; + *-yl*); + *-ene*], a colorless, aromatic hydrocarbon, $C_6H_3(CH_3)_3$, found in coal tar or made by distillation of a mixture of sulfuric acid and acetone.

mes·mer·ic (mes-mer′ik, mez-mer′ik), *adj.* of or caused by mesmerism; hypnotic.

mes·mer·i·cal·ly (mes-mer′i-k′l-i, mez-mer′ik-li), *adv.* in a mesmeric manner; hypnotically.

mes·mer·ism (mes′mẽr-iz′m, mez′mẽr-iz′m), *n.* [after F. A. *Mesmer* (1734–1815), G. physician], hypnotism.

mes·mer·ist (mes′mẽr-ist, mez′mẽr-ist), *n.* a person who mesmerizes; hypnotist.

mes·mer·ize (mes′mə-rīz′, mez′mə-rīz′), *v.t.* [MESMERIZED (-rīzd′), MESMERIZING], to hypnotize.

mesn·al·ty (mēn′əl-ti), *n.* [Legal Fr. *mesnalte, menalte*], in *law*, the estate or condition of a mesne lord.

mesne (mēn), *adj.* [Legal Fr. form of Anglo-Fr. *meen* < OFr. *meien;* see MEAN (intermediate)], in *law*, middle; intermediate; intervening: *mesne* profits are profits accruing between the illegal ejection of a tenant and his reinstatement in possession of the property.

mesne lord, a feudal lord holding land from a superior.

mes·o- (mes′ō, mes′ə; *occas.* mē′sō, mē′sə), [< Gr. *mesos*, middle], a combining form meaning: 1. *in the middle, intermediate*, as in *mesocarp*. 2. in *anatomy*, *a*) *a mesentery*, as in *mesogastrium*. *b*) *a middle connective part*. Also, before a vowel, **mes-**.

mes·o·blast (mes′ə-blast′), *n.* [*meso-* + *-blast*], the middle germ layer of an embryo; mesoderm.

mes·o·blas·tic (mes′ə-blas′tik), *adj.* of or derived from the mesoblast; mesodermal.

mes·o·carp (mes′ə-kärp′), *n.* [*meso-* + *-carp*], the middle layer of a pericarp.

mes·o·ce·phal·ic (mes′ō-sə-fal′ik), *adj.* [*meso-* + *cephalic*], 1. having a medium cranial capacity. 2. having a head form intermediate between brachycephalic and dolichocephalic; having a cephalic index of from 76 to 81: category used in some systems of cranial measurement. 3. of the mesocephalon.

mes·o·ceph·a·lon (mes′ō-sef′ə-lon′), *n.* [Mod. L.; *meso-* + *cephalon* (< Gr. *kephalē*), a head], the pons Varolii, an organ connecting the cerebrum, cerebellum, and medulla oblongata.

mes·o·crat·ic (mes′ə-krat′ik), *adj.* [< *meso-* + Gr. *kratein*, to rule; + *-ic*], in *geology*, containing light and dark mineral constituents in almost equal proportions, the dark slightly exceeding the light.

mes·o·derm (mes′ə-dũrm′), *n.* [*meso-* + *-derm*], the middle germ layer of an embryo, from which the muscular, vascular, and connective tissues develop; mesoblast.

mes·o·der·mal (mes′ə-dũr′m′l), *adj.* of or derived from the mesoderm.

mes·o·gas·tri·um (mes′ə-gas′tri-əm), *n.* [Mod. L. < *meso-* + Gr. *gastēr*, belly], 1. either mesentery of the stomach of an embryo. 2. the region of the abdomen about the navel.

mes·og·nath·ic (mes′əg-nath′ik), *adj.* mesognathous.

me·sog·na·thous (mi-sog′nə-thəs), *adj.* [*meso-* + *-gnathous*], 1. having medium-sized, slightly projecting jaws. 2. having a gnathic index of from 98 to 103.

mes·o·mor·phic (mes′ə-môr′fik), *adj.* [*meso-* + *-morphic*], 1. of a state intermediate between the liquid and the crystalline. 2. [*meso*derm + *-morphic*], designating or of the muscular or athletic physical type, characterized by predominance of the structures developed from the mesodermal layer of the embryo (i.e., muscle, bone, and connective tissue): distinguished from **ectomorphic, endomorphic.**

mes·on (mes′on, mē′son), *n.* [Mod. L.; Gr. *meson*, middle, neut. of *mesos*], the mesial plane.

mes·on (mes′on, mē′son), *n.* [Gr. *mesōn*, genit. pl. of *mesē*, middle note], in *music*, loosely, a tetrachord.

mes·on (mes′on, mē′son), *n.* [*mesotron*], an unstable particle, first observed in cosmic rays, having a mass between that of the electron and the proton.

mes·o·neph·ros (mes′ə-nef′ros), *n.* [Mod. L.; *meso-* + Gr. *nephros*, kidney], the excretory organ serving as the kidney of a vertebrate embryo: it is a long tube lying between the pronephros and metanephros, and, in the human male, develops into the epididymis and vas deferens: also called *Wolffian body*.

mes·o·phyll (mes′ə-fil′), *n.* [*meso-* + *-phyll*], the soft tissue (*green parenchyma*) inside a leaf, between the lower epidermis and the upper.

mes·o·phyte (mes′ə-fit′), *n.* [*meso-* + *-phyte*], any plant adapted to grow under medium conditions of moisture.

mes·o·phyt·ic (mes′ə-fit′ik), *adj.* of, or having the nature of, a mesophyte.

mes·o·plast (mes′ə-plast′), *n.* [*meso-* + *-plast*], in *biology*, the nucleus of a cell.

Mes·o·po·ta·mi·a (mes′ə-pə-tā′mi-ə), *n.* 1. an ancient country in southwestern Asia, between the Tigris and Euphrates rivers. 2. Iraq: the former name.

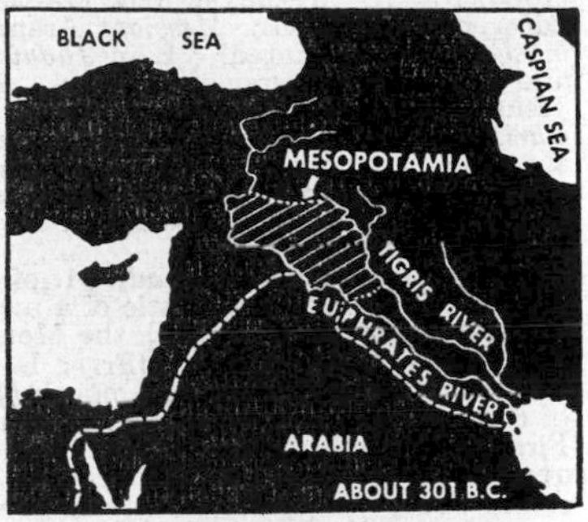

MESOPOTAMIA

Mes·o·po·ta·mi·an (mes′-ə-pə-tā′mi-ən), *adj.* of Mesopotamia, its people, or their culture. *n.* a native of Mesopotamia.

mes·o·the·li·um (mes′ə-thē′li-əm), *n.* [Mod. L.; *meso-* + *epithelium*], 1. epithelium of mesodermal origin. 2. a layer of mesodermal cells lining the serous cavities.

mes·o·tho·rac·ic (mes′ə-thô-ras′ik, mes′ə-thō-ras′ik), *adj.* of the mesothorax.

mes·o·tho·rax (mes′ə-thôr′aks, mes′ə-thō′raks), *n.* the middle one of the three segments of an insect's thorax.

mes·o·tho·ri·um (mes′ə-thôr′i-əm, mez′ə-thō′ri-əm), *n.* [Mod. L.; *meso-* + *thorium*], 1. a radioactive isotope of radium, formed from thorium: also **mesothorium 1.** 2. a radioactive isotope of actinium, formed from this isotope: also **mesothorium 2.** Symbol, Ms-Th, MsTh (no periods).

mes·o·tron (mes′ə-tron′), *n.* [Mod. L.; *meso-* + *electron*], a meson.

Mes·o·zo·ic (mes′ə-zō′ik), *adj.* [*meso-* + *zo-* + *-ic*], designating or of the geological era after the Paleozoic and before the Cenozoic, comprising the Triassic, Jurassic, and Cretaceous periods.

the Mesozoic, the Mesozoic Era or its rocks: see **geology**, chart.

mes·quite, mes·quit (mes-kēt′, mes′kēt), *n.* [Sp. *mezquite* < Nahuatl *mizquitl*], 1. a spiny tree or shrub of the pea family, growing in the southwestern United States and in Mexico and other parts of Latin America: its sugary, beanlike pods are eaten by cattle: also **honey mesquite.** 2. a similar related plant with edible, spiral pods; screwbean: also **screw-pod mesquite.**

mess (mes), *n.* [ME. & OFr. *mes;* L. *missus*, a course (at a meal), orig. pp. of *mittere*, to send, put], 1. a portion or quantity of food for a meal or dish. 2. a portion of soft or semiliquid food, as porridge. 3. unappetizing food; disagreeable concoction. 4. a group of people who regularly have their meals together, as in the army or navy. 5. *a*) the meal eaten by such a group. *b*) the place where it is eaten. 6. a disorderly or confused collection or mass of things; jumble; hodgepodge. 7. a state of embarrassment, trouble, or difficulty; muddle: as, he got himself into a *mess*. 8. a disorderly, untidy, or dirty state of things. *v.t.* 1. to supply meals to. 2. to make a mess of; specifically, *a*) to make dirty, soiled, or untidy. *b*) to bungle; muddle; botch. Often with *up*. 3. [Obs. or Dial.], to serve or divide (food). *v.i.* 1. to eat as one of a mess (sense 4). 2. to make a mess. 3. to putter or meddle.

mess around (or **about**), to be busy in a desultory way, without getting anything done; putter around.

mes·sage (mes′ij), *n.* [ME.; OFr.; ML. *missaticum* < pp. of L. *mittere*, to send], 1. any communication, written or oral, sent between persons. 2. a formal, official communication, written or oral: as, the President's *message* to Congress. 3. the errand or function of a messenger. 4. an inspired or important communication, as of a prophet, poet, or philosopher.

message center, in *military usage*, that agency of a command post by which all messages relating to the post are received for processing and transmission.

Mes·sa·li·na, Valeria (mes′ə-lī′nə), ?–48 A.D.; third wife of the Roman emperor Claudius; notorious for her loose life; executed.

mes·sa·line (mes′ə-lēn′, mes′ə-lēn′), *n.* [Fr.], a thin, soft, lustrous twilled silk cloth.

mes·sei·gneurs (mes′en-yũrz′; Fr. mā′se′nyẽr′), *n.* plural of **monseigneur.**

Mes·se·ne (me-sē′ni), *n.* 1. an ancient city in the southwestern Peloponnesus. 2. Messina: ancient name.

mes·sen·ger (mes′′n-jẽr), *n.* [ME. *messager;* OFr. *messagier* (see MESSAGE); the *-n-* is unhistoric (cf. PASSENGER)], 1. *a*) a person who carries a message or goes on an errand. *b*) a person whose work is delivering telegrams, official dispatches, etc. 2. [Archaic], a harbinger; forerunner.

mess hall, a room or building where a group, as of soldiers or sailors, regularly have their meals.

Mes·si·ah (mə-sī′ə), *n.* [used by the Geneva translators (1560) for LL. *Messias* & ME. *Messie;* both (ME. via OFr. < LL.) < Gr. *Messias;* Aram. *mĕshīḥā*, Heb. *māshīaḥ*, lit., anointed], 1. in *Judaism*, the promised and expected deliverer of the Jews. 2. in *Christianity*, Jesus, regarded as this deliverer, and hence called *the Christ.* 3. [m-], any expected savior or liberator of a people, country, etc. Also **Messias.**

mes·si·ah·ship (mə-sī′ə-ship′), *n.* [see -SHIP], 1. the fact or state of being a messiah. 2. the work or function of a messiah.

Mes·si·an·ic (mes′i-an′ik), *adj.* 1. of the Messiah. 2. [m-], of, like, or characteristic of a messiah.

Mes·si·as (mə-sī′əs), *n.* [LL.], the Messiah.

‡**Mes·si·dor** (me′sē′dôr′), *n.* [Fr. < L. *messis*, a harvest + Gr. *dōron*, gift], the tenth month (June 19–July 18) of the French Revolutionary Calendar, adopted by the First Republic in 1793.

mes·sieurs (mes′ẽrz; Fr. mā′syö′), *n.* plural of **monsieur**: abbreviated **MM.**: see also **Messrs.**

mess·i·ly (mes′ə-li), *adv.* in a messy manner.

Mes·si·na (mə-sē′nə, me-sē′nə), *n.* a seaport in northeastern Sicily: pop., 214,000 (1947): it was destroyed by an earthquake and tidal wave in 1908: ancient name, *Messene.*

Messina, Strait of, the strait between Sicily and Italy: width, 2 1/2–12 mi.

mess·i·ness (mes′i-nis), *n.* messy quality or state.

mess jacket, a man's close-fitting, waist-length jacket, usually white, for semiformal wear in warm weather.

mess kit, the compactly arranged metal plates and eating utensils carried by a soldier or camper for use in the field: also **mess gear.**

mess·mate (mes′māt′), *n.* [*mess* (meal) + *mate* (companion)], a person with whom one regularly has meals, as in the army or navy.

Messrs. (mes′ẽrz), Messieurs: now used chiefly as the plural of **Mr.**

mes·suage (mes′wij), *n.* [Anglo-Fr. *mesuage;* prob. altered < *mesnage;* see MÉNAGE], in *law*, a dwelling house with its outbuildings and adjacent land.

mess·y (mes′i), *adj.* [MESSIER (-i-ẽr), MESSIEST (-i-ist)], in, like, or characterized by a mess; untidy, disordered, dirty, etc.

mes·tee (mes-tē′), *n.* [altered < *mestizo*], a mustee.

mes·ti·za (mes-tē′zə), *n.* a woman or girl mestizo.

mes·ti·zo (mes-tē′zō), *n.* [*pl.* MESTIZOS, MESTIZOES (-zōz)], [Sp. < LL. *misticius, mixticius*, of mixed race < L. *mixtus*, pp. of *miscere*, to mix], a person of mixed parentage; especially, in the western United States and in Latin American countries, the offspring of a Spaniard or Portuguese and an American Indian.

Meš·tro·vić, I·van (ē′vän mesh′trô-vich), 1883– ; Yugoslav sculptor in the United States.

met (met), past tense and past participle of **meet.**

met., 1. metaphor. 2. metaphysical. 3. metropolitan.

met·a- (met′ə), [< Gr. *meta*, along with, after, between, among; akin to G. *mit*, Eng. *mid-* (as in *midwife*)], a prefix meaning: 1. *changed in position* or *form, altered, transposed*, as in *metamorphosis, metathesis:* equivalent to *trans-*. 2. *after*, as in *metaphysics:* sometimes, as in medical terms, equivalent to *post-*. 3. *behind, hinder, at the back*, as in *metathorax:* in anatomical terms, equivalent to *dorso-*. 4. [< supposed analogy to *metaphysics*], *beyond, higher, transcending*, as in *metapsychosis.* 5. in *chemistry, a) a polymer of*, as in *metaldehyde. b) a derivative of*, as in *metaprotein. c) an acid containing less water combined with the anhydride than other acids of the same nonmetallic element*, as in *metaphosphoric. d) characterized by substitutions in the 1, 3 position in the benzene ring:* abbreviated **m-**. Also, before a vowel, **met-.**

met·a·bol·ic (met′ə-bol′ik), *adj.* [Gr. *metabolikos*], 1. of, involving, characterized by, or resulting from metabolism. 2. of or undergoing metamorphosis or transformation.

me·tab·o·lism (mə-tab′ə-liz′m), *n.* [< Gr. *metabolē*, change < *meta*, beyond + *ballein*, to throw; + *-ism*], 1. the chemical and physical processes continuously going on in living organisms and cells, comprising those by which assimilated food is built up (*anabolism*) into protoplasm and those by which protoplasm is used and broken down (*catabolism*) into simpler substances or waste matter, with the release of energy for all vital processes. 2. metamorphosis (of insects).

me·tab·o·lite (mə-tab′ə-līt′), *n.* any substance produced by metabolism.

me·tab·o·lize (mə-tab′ə-līz′), *v.t. & v.i.* [METABOLIZED (-līzd′), METABOLIZING], to change by metabolism.

met·a·car·pal (met′ə-kär′p′l), *adj.* of the metacarpus. *n.* any of the bones of the metacarpus.

met·a·car·pus (met′ə-kär′pəs), *n.* [*pl.* METACARPI (-pī), METACARPUSES (-iz)], [Mod. L. (for *metacarpium*) < Gr. *metakarpion;* see META- & CARPUS], 1. the part of the hand, especially the five bones, between the wrist and the fingers: see **skeleton**, illus. 2. the corresponding part of an animal's forelimb, between the carpus and the phalanges.

met·a·cen·ter, met·a·cen·tre (met′ə-sen′tẽr, met′ə-sen′tẽr), *n.* [Fr. *métacentre;* see META- & CENTER], that point in a floating body at which a vertical line drawn through its center of buoyancy when it is upright meets the vertical line drawn through its center of buoyancy when it is tipped; center of gravity of the unsubmerged part of a floating body: for stability the metacenter must be above the center of gravity.

METACENTER

C, center of gravity; A, center of buoyancy of a floating body; B, center of buoyancy when body is tipped; M, metacenter at point of intersection of verticals MA and MB

met·a·cen·tric (met′ə-sen′trik), *adj.* of or near the metacenter.

met·a·chro·ma·tism (met′ə-krō′mə-tiz′m), *n.* [< *meta-* + Gr. *chrōma, chrōmatos*, color; + *-ism*], a change of color, especially as a result of a change in temperature.

met·a·cy·mene (met′ə-sī′mēn), *n.* one of three isomeric forms of cymene, a hydrocarbon derivative of benzene.

met·a·ga·lac·tic (met′ə-gə-lak′tik), *adj.* of the metagalaxy.

met·a·gal·ax·y (met′ə-gal′ək-si), *n.* in *astronomy*, the entire material universe; system comprising the galaxies, nebulae, etc.

met·age (mēt′ij), *n.* [*mete, v.* + *-age*], 1. official measurement of contents or weight of coal, grain, etc. 2. the charge for this.

met·a·gen·e·sis (met′ə-jen′ə-sis), *n.* [Mod. L.; *meta-* + *-genesis*], in *biology*, reproduction in which there is alternation of generations.

me·tag·na·thous (mi-tag′nə-thəs), *adj.* [*meta-* + *-gnathous*], having the points of the mandibles crossed: said of certain birds.

met·al (met′′l), *n.* [ME.; OFr.; L. *metallum*, metal, mine, quarry; Gr. *metallon*, mine, quarry], 1. *a)* any of a class of chemical elements, as iron, gold, aluminum, etc., generally characterized by ductility, malleability, luster, and conductivity of heat and electricity: these elements form bases with the hydroxyl radical and can replace the hydrogen of an acid to form a salt. *b)* an alloy of such elements, as brass, bronze, etc. 2. any substance consisting of metal. 3. material; substance; stuff. 4. molten cast iron. 5. molten material for making glassware or pottery. 6. [British], broken stone, cinders, etc. used in making roads, ballasting roadbeds, etc. 7. in *heraldry*, either of the tinctures gold (*or*) and silver (*argent*). 8. in the *navy*, the weight of shells that the guns of a warship can shoot at one time. 9. in *printing, a)* type metal. *b)* composed type. *adj.* made of metal. *v.t.* [METALED or METALLED (-′ld), METALING or METALLING], to cover or supply with metal.

metal., 1. metallurgical. 2. metallurgy.

met·al·ist (met′′l-ist), *n.* 1. a person who works in metals. 2. an advocate of the use of metallic instead of paper money. Also spelled **metallist.**

met·al·ize (met′′l-īz′), *v.t.* [METALIZED (-īzd′), METALIZING], 1. to treat, cover, or impregnate with metal or a compound of metal. 2. to change into metal. Also spelled **metallize.**

me·tal·lic (mə-tal′ik), *adj.* [L. *metallicus;* Gr. *metallikos*], 1. of, or having the nature of, metal. 2. containing, yielding, or producing metal. 3. like, characteristic of, or suggestive of metal: as, a *metallic* sound.

me·tal·li·cal·ly (mə-tal′i-k′l-i, mə-tal′ik-li), *adv.* 1. by means of metal or a metal. 2. with reference to the constituent metal: as, *metallically* pure.

metallic soap, a soaplike substance made by combining the salts of lead, aluminum, and some other metals with fatty acids: it is used in making paint, cloth, etc.

met·al·lif·er·ous (met′′l-if′ẽr-əs), *adj.* [L. *metallifer* < *metallum*, metal + *ferre*, to bear; + *-ous*], containing, yielding, or producing metal or ore.

met·al·line (met′′l-in, met′′l-īn′), *adj.* 1. metallic. 2. containing metal or metallic salts.

met·al·list (met′′l-ist), *n.* a metalist.

met·al·lize (met′′l-īz′), *v.t.* [METALLIZED (-īzd′), METALLIZING], to metalize.

met·al·log·ra·phy (met′′l-og′rə-fi), *n.* [< Gr. *metallon*, metal; + *-graphy*], 1. the study of the structure and physical properties of metals and alloys, especially by the use of the microscope and X rays. 2. a method of printing resembling lithography but using metal plates instead of stones.

met·al·loid (met′′l-oid′), *n.* [see -OID], 1. a nonmetal. 2. an element having some of, but not all, the properties of metals, as arsenic or silicon. *adj.* 1. like a metal in appearance. 2. of, or having the nature of, a metalloid.

me·tal·lo·ther·a·py (mə-tal′ō-ther′ə-pi), *n.* [< Gr. *metallon*, metal; + *therapy*], the treatment of disease by the use of metals, or especially of their salts.

met·al·lur·gic (met′′l-ũr′jik), *adj.* metallurgical.

met·al·lur·gi·cal (met′′l-ũr′ji-k′l), *adj.* of metallurgy.

met·al·lur·gist (met′′l-ũr′jist), *n.* an expert in metallurgy.

met·al·lur·gy (met′'l-ũr′ji), *n.* [Mod. L. *metallurgia* < Gr. *metallourgos,* working in metals or mines < *metallon,* metal, mine + *-ergos,* working], the art or science of separating metals from their ores and preparing them for use, by smelting, refining, etc.: abbreviated **metal.**

met·al·work (met′'l-wũrk′), *n.* 1. things made out of metal. 2. the making of such things.

met·al·work·ing (met′'l-wũr′kiŋ), *n.* the act or process of making things out of metal. *adj.* of, for, or engaged in metalworking.

met·a·mer (met′ə-mẽr), *n.* [< *meta-* + Gr. *meros,* a part], any of two or more chemical compounds belonging to the same general class and having identical proportions of the same elements and the same molecular weight, but different chemical properties.

me·tam·er·al (mə-tam′ẽr-əl), *adj.* metameric.

met·a·mere (met′ə-mêr′), *n.* [*meta-* + *-mere*], any of a longitudinal series of similar segments making up the body of a worm, crayfish, etc.; somite.

met·a·mer·ic (met′ə-mer′ik), *adj.* 1. in *chemistry,* being a metamer. 2. in *zoology, a)* of or formed of metameres. *b)* of metamerism.

me·tam·er·ism (mə-tam′ẽr-iz'm), *n.* 1. in *chemistry,* the condition of being metameric. 2. in *zoology,* the condition of being made up of metameres.

met·a·mor·phic (met′ə-môr′fik), *adj.* of, characterized by, causing, or formed by metamorphism or metamorphosis.

met·a·mor·phism (met′ə-môr′fiz'm), *n.* 1. metamorphosis; change of form. 2. change in the structure of rocks under pressure, heat, chemical action, etc., which makes limestone into marble, granite into gneiss, etc.

met·a·mor·phose (met′ə-môr′fōz, met′ə-môr′fōs), *v.t. & v.i.* [METAMORPHOSED (-fōzd, -fōst), METAMORPHOSING], [Fr. *métamorphoser*], to change in form or nature; transform; subject to or undergo metamorphosis. —*SYN.* see **transform.**

met·a·mor·pho·sis (met′ə-môr′fə-sis, met′ə-môr-fō′sis), *n.* [*pl.* METAMORPHOSES (-sēz′, -sēz)], [L.; Gr. *metamorphōsis* < *metamorphoun,* to transform, transfigure < *meta,* over + *morphē,* form, shape], 1. *a)* change of form, shape, structure, or substance; transformation, especially by magic or sorcery. *b)* the form resulting from such change. 2. a marked or complete change of character, appearance, condition, etc. 3. in *biology,* a change in form, structure, or function as a result of development; specifically, *a)* the physical transformation, more or less sudden, undergone by various animals during development after the embryonic state, as of the larva of an insect to the pupa and the pupa to the adult, or the tadpole to the frog. *b)* the development of plant organs, originally similar in morphology, into different forms as a result of adaptation to different functions. *c)* the change of form constantly going on in living cells and tissues. 4. in *medicine,* a morbid change of form of some tissues or parts.

met·a·mor·phous (met′ə-môr′fəs), *adj.* metamorphic.

met·a·neph·ros (met′ə-nef′ros), *n.* [Mod. L.; *meta-* + Gr. *nephros,* kidney], the excretory organ lying behind the mesonephros in an embryo, which in mammals develops into the permanent kidney.

metaph., 1. metaphor. 2. metaphysics.

met·a·phase (met′ə-fāz′), *n.* [*meta-* + *phase*], in *biology,* the stage in mitosis, after the prophase and before the anaphase, during which the split chromosomes are arranged along the equatorial plane of the spindle.

met·a·phor (met′ə-fẽr, met′ə-fôr′), *n.* [Fr. *métaphore;* L. *metaphora;* Gr. *metaphora* < *metapherein,* to carry over; *meta,* over + *pherein,* to carry], a figure of speech in which one thing is likened to another, different thing by being spoken of as if it were that other; implied comparison, in which a word or phrase ordinarily and primarily used of one thing is applied to another (e.g., screaming headlines, "all the world's a stage"): distinguished from *simile:* abbreviated **met., metaph.**

mix metaphors, to use two or more inconsistent metaphors in a single expression (e.g., the storm of protest was nipped in the bud).

met·a·phor·ic (met′ə-fôr′ik, met′ə-for′ik), *adj.* metaphorical.

met·a·phor·i·cal (met′ə-fôr′i-k'l, met′ə-for′i-k'l), *adj.* 1. of or constituting a metaphor. 2. using or containing metaphors; figurative.

met·a·phos·phate (met′ə-fos′fāt), *n.* any salt of metaphosphoric acid.

met·a·phos·phor·ic acid (met′ə-fos-fôr′ik, met′ə-fos-for′ik), glacial phosphoric acid, HPO_3, obtained by heating orthophosphoric acid.

met·a·phrase (met′ə-frāz′), *n.* [Gr. *metaphrasis* < *metaphrazein;* see META- & PHRASE], a translation; especially, a literal, word-for-word translation, as distinguished from a paraphrase. *v.t.* [METAPHRASED (-frāzd′), METAPHRASING], 1. to translate, especially literally. 2. to change the wording of.

met·a·phrast (met′ə-frast′), *n.* [Gr. *metaphrastēs;* see METAPHRASE], a person who puts a piece of writing into another literary form, as prose into verse.

met·a·phras·tic (met′ə-fras′tik), *adj.* having the nature of a metaphrase; literal in translation.

met·a·phys·ic (met′ə-fiz′ik), *n.* 1. metaphysics. 2. [Obs.], a metaphysician. *adj.* [Rare], metaphysical.

met·a·phys·i·cal (met′ə-fiz′i-k'l), *adj.* 1. of, or having the nature of, metaphysics; of the nature of being or essential reality. 2. very abstract, abstruse, or subtle: often used derogatorily of reasoning. 3. based on abstract reasoning. 4. beyond the physical or material; incorporeal, supernatural, or transcendental. 5. fond of or skilled in metaphysics. 6. designating or of the school of early 17th-century English poets, including especially John Donne, George Herbert, Richard Crashaw, and Abraham Cowley, whose verse is characterized by very subtle, highly intellectualized imagery, sometimes deliberately fantastic and far-fetched: term first so used by Samuel Johnson. Abbreviated **met.**

met·a·phys·i·cal·ly (met′ə-fiz′i-k'l-i, met′ə-fiz′ik-li), *adv.* 1. in a metaphysical manner. 2. by, or from the viewpoint of, metaphysics.

met·a·phy·si·cian (met′ə-fə-zish′ən), *n.* [Fr. *métaphysicien*], a person skilled in metaphysics.

met·a·phys·ics (met′ə-fiz′iks), *n.pl.* [construed as sing.], [earlier *metaphysic* < ML. *metaphysica,* neut. pl.; Gr. *meta ta physika,* after the physics (in reference to Aristotle's works following the *Physics,* which dealt with external nature)], 1. the branch of philosophy that deals with first principles and seeks to explain the nature of being or reality (*ontology*) and of the origin and structure of the world (*cosmology*): it is closely associated with a theory of knowledge (*epistemology*). 2. speculative philosophy in general. 3. the theory or principles (of some branch of knowledge). 4. popularly, any very subtle, perplexing, or difficult reasoning. 5. [Archaic], occult lore. Abbreviated **met., metaph.**

met·a·plasm (met′ə-plaz'm), *n.* [L. *metaplasmus;* Gr. *metaplasmos* < *meta,* over, beyond + *plassein,* to form, mold], 1. that part of the contents of a cell which consists of lifeless, nonprotoplasmic matter, as certain inclusions of fatty granules or carbohydrates. 2. a change in a word by adding, leaving out, or transposing letters or syllables.

met·a·plas·mic (met′ə-plaz′mik), *adj.* of or characterized by metaplasm.

met·a·pro·te·in (met′ə-prō′tē-in, met′ə-prō′tēn), *n.* any of a group of substances produced by the action of acids or alkalis on proteins.

met·a·psy·chol·o·gy (met′ə-sī-kol′ə-ji), *n.* speculation about the origin, structure, function, etc. of the mind and about the relation between the mental and the physical, regarded as supplemental to psychology.

me·ta·psy·cho·sis (met′ə-si-kō′sis), *n.* [Mod. L.; see META- & PSYCHOSIS], action or influence between minds that occurs without any known physical medium or agency.

met·a·so·ma·tism (met′ə-sō′mə-tiz'm), *n.* metasomatosis.

met·a·so·ma·to·sis (met′ə-sō′mə-tō′sis), *n.* [Mod. L. < *meta-* + Gr. *sōma, sōmatos,* body], the change of one rock or mineral into another of a different kind.

me·tas·ta·sis (mə-tas′tə-sis), *n.* [*pl.* METASTASES (-sēz′)], [LL., a passing over, transition; Gr. *metastasis* < *methistanai,* to place in another way, change < *meta,* after + *histanai,* to place], 1. [Rare], change of form or matter; transformation. 2. in *biology,* metabolism. 3. in *medicine,* the shifting of disease from one part or organ of the body to another unrelated to it, as by the transfer of pathogenic organisms or of the cells of a malignant tumor. 4. in *rhetoric,* an abrupt transition from one subject to another.

me·tas·ta·size (mə-tas′tə-sīz′), *v.i.* [METASTASIZED (-sīzd′), METASTASIZING], in *medicine,* to spread to some other part or parts of the body by metastasis.

met·a·stat·ic (met′ə-stat′ik), *adj.* of, having the nature of, or caused by metastasis.

met·a·tar·sal (met′ə-tär′s'l), *adj.* of the metatarsus. *n.* any of the bones of the metatarsus.

met·a·tar·sus (met′ə-tär′səs), *n.* [*pl.* METATARSI (-sī)], [Mod. L.; see META- & TARSUS], 1. the part of the foot, especially the five bones, between the ankle and toes: see **skeleton,** illus. 2. *a)* the corresponding part of an animal's hind limb, between the tarsus and phalanges. *b)* the bone between the tibia and the phalanges in a bird's leg.

me·tath·e·sis (mə-tath′ə-sis), *n.* [*pl.* METATHESES (-sēz′)], [LL.; Gr. *metathesis,* transposition, a going over < *metatithenai,* to put over, transpose; *meta,* over + *tithenai,* to place], transposition or interchange; specifically, *a)* the transposition of letters or sounds in a word, or the result of this: as, *clasp* developed from Middle English *clapse* by *metathesis. b)* in *chemistry,* the interchange of elements or radicals between compounds, as when two compounds react with each other to form two new compounds.

met·a·thet·ic (met'ə-thet'ik), ***adj.*** of or by metathesis.

met·a·thet·i·cal (met'ə-thet'i-k'l), ***adj.*** metathetic.

met·a·tho·rac·ic (met'ə-thô-ras'ik, met'ə-thō-ras'ik), ***adj.*** of the metathorax.

met·a·tho·rax (met'ə-thôr'aks, met'ə-thō'raks), ***n.*** [*pl.* METATHORAXES (-iz), METATHORACES (-thôr'ə-sēz', -thō'rə-sēz')], [Mod. L.], the hindmost segment of the thorax of an insect.

Me·tax·as, Jo·an·nes (yô-än'yis me'täk-säs'; Eng. mi-tak'səs), 1871–1941; Greek general and statesman.

met·a·xy·lem (met'ə-zī'lem), ***n.*** [*meta-* + *xylem*], the outer part, and last to be formed, of the primary xylem, or woody tissue of a plant, consisting of thick-walled cells.

Met·a·zo·a (met'ə-zō'ə), ***n.pl.*** [Mod. L. < *meta-* + Gr. *zōion*, animal], the large zoological division made up of all animals whose bodies, originating from a single cell, are composed of many cells: distinguished from *Protozoa*.

met·a·zo·an (met'ə-zō'ən), ***adj.*** of or characteristic of the Metazoa. ***n.*** one of the Metazoa.

met·a·zo·ic (met'ə-zō'ik), ***adj.*** metazoan.

Metch·ni·koff, É·lie (ā'lē' mech'nē'kôf'; Russ. myech'-ni-kôf'), (*Ilya Ilich Mechnikov*), 1845–1916; Russian biologist and physiologist in France; received Nobel prize in physiology, 1908.

mete (mēt), ***v.t.*** [METED (-id), METING], [ME. *meten;* AS. *metan;* akin to G. *messen;* IE. base **med-*, to measure, seen also in L. *meditari* (cf. MEDICAL), *modus* (cf. MODE), Gr. *metron* (cf. METER, rhythm)], 1. to allot; distribute; apportion (usually with *out*). 2. [Archaic or Poetic], to measure. ***n.*** [< the *v.*], [Obs.], measure.

mete (mēt), ***n.*** [ME.; OFr.; L. *meta*, boundary, goal, orig. column; IE. base **mei-t-*, a post, stake, seen also in ON. *meithr*, a tree, MIr. *methos*, boundary mark; cf. MERE (boundary)], 1. a boundary; limit. 2. a boundary mark or line.

met·em·pir·ic (met'em-pir'ik), ***n.*** 1. metempirics. 2. an adherent of metempirics. ***adj.*** metempirical.

met·em·pir·i·cal (met'em-pir'i-k'l), ***adj.*** 1. of metempirics. 2. beyond the knowledge obtained from experience; transcendental.

met·em·pir·ics (met'em-pir'iks), ***n.pl.*** [construed as sing.], [< *met-* + *empiric* + *-ics*], the study or philosophy of things regarded as beyond the knowledge obtained from experience but having some relationship to this; sometimes, transcendental philosophy.

met·em·psy·cho·sis (met'əm-sī-kō'sis, mi-temp'si-kō'-sis), ***n.*** [*pl.* METEMPSYCHOSES (-sēz)], [LL.; Gr. *metempsychosis* < *metempsychoun* < *meta*, over + *empsychoun*, to put a soul into < *en*, in + *psychē*, soul, life], the passing of the soul at death into another body, either human or animal; transmigration of souls.

met·en·ce·phal·ic (met'en-sə-fal'ik), ***adj.*** of the metencephalon.

met·en·ceph·a·lon (met'en-sef'ə-lon'), ***n.*** [*pl.* METENCEPHALA (-lə)], [Mod. L.; *met-* + *encephalon*], 1. that part of the brain of an embryo from which the pons and cerebellum are derived. 2. that part of the brain consisting of the pons and cerebellum. Cf. **hindbrain.**

me·te·or (mē'ti-ēr), ***n.*** [ML. *meteorum;* Gr. *meteōron*, pl. *meteōra*, things in the air < *meteōros*, lifted up, in air < *meta*, beyond + *eōra*, a hovering in the air (akin to *aeirein*, to lift up)], 1. a meteoroid entering the atmosphere of the earth from outer space at very great speed and thus made white-hot and visible by friction with the air; shooting star. 2. any meteoroid or meteorite. 3. in *meteorology*, any atmospheric phenomenon, as hail, a rainbow, etc.

meteor., 1. meteorological. 2. meteorology.

me·te·or·ic (mē'ti-ôr'ik, mē'ti-or'ik), ***adj.*** [ML. *meteoricus;* also < *meteor* + *-ic*], 1. atmospheric or meteorological: as, hail is a *meteoric* phenomenon. 2. of a meteor or meteors. 3. like a meteor; momentarily dazzling or brilliant, flashing, or swift.

me·te·or·i·cal·ly (mē'ti-ôr'i-k'l-i, mē'ti-or'ik-li), ***adv.*** 1. in a meteoric manner. 2. meteorologically.

me·te·or·ite (mē'ti-ēr-īt'), ***n.*** 1. a mass of metal or stone that has fallen upon the earth from outer space; fallen meteor. 2. loosely, a meteor or meteoroid.

me·te·or·it·ic (mē'ti-ə-rit'ik), ***adj.*** of a meteorite or meteorites.

me·te·or·o·graph (mē'ti-ēr-ə-graf', mē'ti-ôr'ə-gräf'), ***n.*** [Fr. *météorographe;* see METEOR & -GRAPH], an apparatus for automatically recording various weather conditions, as moisture, temperature, etc., at the same time.

me·te·or·oid (mē'ti-ēr-oid'), ***n.*** any of the many small, solid bodies traveling through outer space, which become meteors when they enter the earth's atmosphere.

me·te·or·o·log·ic (mē'ti-ēr-ə-loj'ik, mē'ti-ôr'ə-loj'ik), ***adj.*** meteorological.

me·te·or·o·log·i·cal (mē'ti-ēr-ə-loj'i-k'l, mē'ti-ôr'ə-loj'-i-k'l), ***adj.*** 1. of the atmosphere or atmospheric phenomena; of weather or climate. 2. of meteorology. Abbreviated **meteor., meteorol.**

me·te·or·o·log·i·cal·ly (mē'ti-ēr-ə-loj'i-k'l-i, mē'ti-ôr'ə-loj'ik-li), ***adv.*** 1. by or according to meteorology. 2. in meteorological respects.

me·te·or·ol·o·gist (mē'ti-ə-rol'ə-jist), ***n.*** a person trained in meteorology.

me·te·or·ol·o·gy (mē'ti-ə-rol'ə-ji), ***n.*** [Gr. *meteōrologia;* see METEOR & -LOGY], the science of the atmosphere and atmospheric phenomena; study of weather and climate: abbreviated **meteor., meteorol.**

me·ter (mē'tēr), ***n.*** [ME. & OFr. *metre* (Fr. *mètre*); L. *metrum;* Gr. *metron*, measure], 1. *a*) rhythm in verse; measured, patterned arrangement of syllables, primarily according to stress and length: see also **foot** (sense 8). *b*) the specific rhythm as determined by the prevailing foot and the number of feet in the line: as, iambic *meter*. *c*) the specific rhythmic pattern of a stanza as determined by the kind and number of lines. 2. rhythm in music; especially, the division into measures, or bars, having a uniform number of beats; pattern of strong and weak beats in a measure: as, 4/4 *meter* is also called *common time*. 3. [Fr. *mètre*], the basic unit of length in the metric system, equal to 39.37 inches: it was meant to be, and virtually is, one ten-millionth part of the distance along a meridian from the equator to the pole: abbreviated **M., m.** (*sing. & pl.*). Also spelled **metre.**

me·ter (mē'tēr), ***n.*** [< *mete* (to measure)], 1. a person who measures; especially, an official who measures commodities. 2. an instrument or apparatus for measuring; especially, an apparatus for measuring and recording the quantity or rate of flow of gas, electricity, or water passing through it. ***v.t.*** to measure or record with a meter or meters.

-me·ter (mē'tēr, mi-tēr), [Fr. *-mètre* or Mod. L. *-metrum*, both < Gr. *metron*, a measure], a suffix meaning: 1. *a device for measuring* (a specified thing), as in *thermometer, barometer*. 2. *a*) (a specified number of) *meters*, as in *kilometer*. *b*) (a specified fraction of) *a meter*, as in *centimeter*. 3. *having* (a specified number of) *metrical feet*, as in *pentameter*.

me·ter·age (mē'tēr-ij), ***n.*** [*meter* (instrument) + *-age*], 1. measurement. 2. the charge for measurement.

Meth., Methodist.

meth·ac·ry·late (meth-ak'rə-lāt'), ***n.*** a salt or ester of methacrylic acid.

methacrylate resin, any of several plastic substances formed by polymerizing esters of methacrylic acid.

meth·a·cryl·ic acid (meth'ə-kril'ik), [< *methyl* + *acrylic*], a crystalline acid, $C_4H_6O_2$, obtained from camomile or made synthetically.

meth·a·don (meth'ə-don'), ***n.*** [< 6 *dimethylamino-4, 4-diphenyl-3-heptanone* + arbitrary *-on*], a synthetic compound used in medicine as an analgesic more potent than morphine and less rapidly habit-forming: a trade-mark (**Methadon**).

meth·ane (meth'ān), ***n.*** [< *methyl* + *-ane*], a colorless, odorless, inflammable gaseous hydrocarbon, CH_4, present in natural gas and formed by the decomposition of vegetable matter, as in marshes, or produced artificially: it is used as a fuel and for illumination.

methane series, a series of saturated hydrocarbons of the open-chain type, having the general formula C_nH_{2n+2}.

meth·a·nol (meth'ə-nōl', meth'ə-nol'), ***n.*** [< *methane* + *-ol* (alcohol)], a colorless, volatile, inflammable, poisonous liquid, CH_3OH, obtained by the destructive distillation of wood and used in organic synthesis, as a fuel, and in the manufacture of formaldehyde, smokeless powders, paints, etc.: also called *wood alcohol*.

me·theg·lin (mə-theg'lin), ***n.*** [W. *meddyglyn* < *meddyg*, healing (< L. *medicus;* see MEDICAL) + *llyn*, juice, liquor], an alcoholic liquor made of fermented honey.

met·he·mo·glo·bin, met·hae·mo·glo·bin (met-hē'mə-glō'bin, met-hem'ə-glō'bin), ***n.*** [*met-* + *h(a)emoglobin*], a brownish, crystalline substance formed in the blood by the oxidation of hemoglobin, as by the action of certain drugs or in the decomposition of the blood.

me·the·na·min (mə-thē'nə-min), ***n.*** methenamine.

me·the·na·mine (mə-thē'nə-mēn', mə-thē'nə-min), ***n.*** [< *methene* (< *methyl* + *-ene*) + *amine*], hexamethylenetetramine, $(CH_2)_6N_4$, a product of the reaction of ammonia with formaldehyde, used as a diuretic, an internal antiseptic, in vulcanizing rubber, etc.

me·thinks (mi-thiŋks'), ***impersonal v.*** [past tense METHOUGHT (-thôt')], [ME. *me thinketh;* AS. *me thyncth; me*, me, to me + *thyncth*, it seems < *thyncan*, to seem], [Archaic], it seems to me.

me·thi·o·nine (mə-thī'ə-nēn', mə-thī'ə-nin), ***n.*** [< methyl + *thionic* + *-ine*], an amino acid, $C_5H_{11}NO_2S$, obtained from various proteins.

meth·o- (meth'ō, meth'ə), a combining form meaning *methyl:* also, before a vowel, **meth-.**

meth·od (meth'əd), ***n.*** [Fr. *méthode;* L. *methodus;* Gr. *methodos*, a going after, pursuit, investigation, system < *meta*, after + *hodos*, a way], 1. a way of doing anything; mode; procedure; process; especially, a regular, orderly, definite procedure or way of teaching, investigating, etc. 2. regularity and orderliness in action, thought, or expression; system in doing things or handling ideas. 3. regular, orderly arrangement.

SYN.—**method** implies a regular, orderly, logical procedure for doing something (a *method* of vulcanizing rubber); **manner** applies to a distinctive, often personal, procedure or course (her *manner* of speech); **mode** refers to a customary, established, or usual method or manner (their *mode* of dress); **way** is a simple, common, but less explicit synonym for any of the preceding words (a *way* of talking, preparing something, etc.); **fashion,** also a general term, often emphasizes currency of mode (it is the *fashion* to wear bright colors); **system,** in this comparison, implies a carefully developed, relatively complex method (a *system* of government).

me·thod·ic (mə-thod′ik), ***adj.*** methodical.

me·thod·i·cal (mə-thod′i-k'l), ***adj.*** [< LL. *methodicus;* Gr. *methodikos;* + *-al*], characterized by method; orderly; systematic. —***SYN.*** see **orderly.**

me·thod·i·cal·ly (mə-thod′i-k'l-i, mə-thod′ik-li), ***adv.*** in a methodical manner.

Meth·od·ism (meth′əd-iz'm), ***n.*** 1. the doctrines, organization, and way of worship of the Methodists. 2. [m-], excessive adherence to systematic procedure.

Meth·od·ist (meth′əd-ist), ***n.*** 1. a member of any branch of a Protestant Christian denomination that developed from the evangelistic teachings and work of John and Charles Wesley, George Whitefield, and others in the first half of the 18th century: so called from the methodical study and worship practiced by the founders in their "Holy Club" at Oxford University, England (1729). 2. [m-], [Rare], an adherent of method. ***adj.*** of or characteristic of the Methodists or Methodism. Abbreviated **Meth.** Cf. **Wesleyan.**

Meth·od·is·tic (meth′ə-dis′tik), ***adj.*** Methodist.

meth·od·ize (meth′ə-dīz′), ***v.t.*** [METHODIZED (-dīzd′), METHODIZING], to make methodical; systematize.

meth·od·o·log·i·cal (meth′əd-ə-loj′i-k'l), ***adj.*** of methodology.

meth·od·ol·o·gy (meth′ə-dol′ə-ji), ***n.*** [< Gr. *methodos,* method; + *-logy*], 1. the science of method, or orderly arrangement; specifically, the branch of logic concerned with the application of the principles of reasoning to scientific and philosophical inquiry. 2. a system of methods, as in any particular science.

me·thought (mi-thôt′), [Archaic], past tense of **methinks.**

Me·thu·en (mi-thū′in), ***n.*** a city in northeastern Massachusetts: pop., 24,000.

Me·thu·se·lah (mə-thōō′z'l-ə, mə-thū′z'l-ə), ***n.*** [Heb. *methūshelaḥ,* lit., ? man of the dart], 1. in the *Bible,* one of the patriarchs, said to have lived 969 years: Gen. 5:27; hence, 2. a very old man.

meth·yl (meth′əl), ***n.*** [Fr. *méthyle* (or G. *methyl*), back-formation < *méthylène* (or G. *methylen*); see METHYLENE], the monovalent hydrocarbon radical CH_3, found only in combination, as in methyl alcohol: abbreviated **Me** (no period).

methyl acetate, a colorless, volatile, inflammable liquid, $C_3H_6O_2$, that smells like apples: it is a methyl ester of acetic acid and is used as a solvent and in flavoring extracts.

meth·yl·al (meth′ə-lal′, meth′ə-lal′), ***n.*** [Fr. *méthylal* < *méthyle,* methyl + *alcool,* alcohol], a colorless, volatile, inflammable liquid, $CH_2(OCH_3)_2$, that smells like chloroform: it is produced by the incomplete oxidation of methanol and used as a solvent, anesthetic, etc.

methyl alcohol, methanol.

meth·yl·a·mine (meth′əl-ə-mēn′, meth′əl-am′in), ***n.*** [*methyl* + *amine*], a colorless, inflammable gas, CH_3NH_2, that smells like ammonia: it is prepared synthetically or by the distillation of wood, bone, etc.

meth·yl·ate (meth′ə-lāt′), ***n.*** a compound derived from methyl alcohol, in which the hydroxyl hydrogen is replaced by a metal. ***v.t.*** [METHYLATED (-id), METHYLATING], 1. to mix with methyl alcohol, often in order to make the resulting mixture undrinkable. 2. to combine with methyl.

methylated spirit (or **spirits**), ethyl alcohol made unfit to drink by the addition of methanol, or methyl alcohol; denatured alcohol.

methyl benzene, toluene.

methyl chloride, a gas, CH_3Cl, which when compressed becomes a sweet, colorless liquid with an etherlike smell: it is used as a refrigerant and local anesthetic.

meth·yl·ene (meth′ə-lēn′), ***n.*** [Fr. *méthylène* < Gr. *methy,* wine + *hylē,* wood: orig. used to express the idea of "wood spirit," "wood alcohol"], 1. the bivalent hydrocarbon radical CH_2, found only in combination. 2. [Rare], methanol.

methylene blue, a bluish-green aniline dye, $C_{16}H_{18}N_3ClS·3H_2O$, used as a bacteriological stain, an antidote in cyanide poisoning, etc.

me·thyl·ic (me-thil′ik, mə-thil′ik), ***adj.*** of, derived from, or containing methyl.

me·tic·u·los·i·ty (mə-tik′yoo-los′ə-ti), ***n.*** the quality or state of being meticulous.

me·tic·u·lous (mə-tik′yoo-ləs), ***adj.*** [Fr. *méticuleux;* L. *meticulosus,* fearful < *metus,* fear], extremely or excessively careful about details; scrupulous; finical. —***SYN.*** see **careful.**

mé·tier (mā-tyā′), ***n.*** [Fr.; OFr. *mestier;* L. *ministerium;* see MINISTRY], a trade, profession, or occupation; especially, the work that one is particularly suited for.

mé·tif (mā-tēf′), ***n.*** [*pl.* MÉTIFS (-tēfs′), MÉTIS (-tēs′)], [Fr. < L. *misticius* < *miscere,* to mix; cf. MESTIZO], a person of mixed blood; especially, a person one of whose parents was French and the other North American Indian: also spelled **metiff.**

me·tol (mē′tōl, mē′tol), ***n.*** [< *meth*yl-amino-cres*ol*-sulfate], a white, soluble powder, C_7H_9ON, used in its hydrosulfate as a photographic developer: a trademark (**Metol**).

Me·ton·ic cycle (mə-ton′ik), [after *Meton,* Athenian astronomer in the 5th century B.C.], in *astronomy,* a period of about 19 years (almost 235 lunar revolutions) at the end of which the new moon reappears on the same day as at the beginning of the cycle.

met·o·nym (met′ə-nim), ***n.*** a word used in metonymy, as a substitute for another.

met·o·nym·ic (met′ə-nim′ik), ***adj.*** metonymical.

met·o·nym·i·cal (met′ə-nim′i-k'l), ***adj.*** 1. of, or having the nature of, metonymy. 2. using or used in metonymy.

me·ton·y·my (mə-ton′ə-mi), ***n.*** [*pl.* METONYMIES (-miz)], [LL. *metonymia;* Gr. *metōnymia* < *meta,* change + *onoma, onyma,* name], use of the name of one thing for that of another associated with or suggested by it (e.g., "the White House has decided" for "the President has decided"): abbreviated **meton.:** cf. **synecdoche.**

met·o·pe (met′ə-pē′, met′ōp), ***n.*** [L. *metopa;* Gr. *metopē* < *meta,* between + *opē,* an opening, hole in frieze for beam], any of the square areas, whether plain or decorated, between triglyphs in a Doric frieze.

me·top·ic (mi-top′ik), ***adj.*** [< Gr. *metōpon,* forehead; + *-ic*], of the forehead; frontal.

me·tral·gi·a (mi-tral′ji-ə), ***n.*** [Mod. L. < Gr. *mētra,* uterus; + *-algia*], pain in the uterus.

met·ra·zol (met′rə-zōl′, met′rə-zol′), ***n.*** [G. penta*methylenetetrazol*], a drug, $C_6H_{10}N_4$, used to stimulate circulation and respiration and in the treatment of some mental illnesses: a trade-mark (**Metrazol**).

me·tre (mē′tẽr), ***n.*** meter: chiefly British spelling.

met·ric (met′rik), ***adj.*** [L. *metricus;* Gr. *metrikos* < *metron,* measure], 1. of, involving, or used in measurement. 2. [Fr. *métrique*], *a)* of the meter (unit of length). *b)* designating or of the system of measurement based on the meter and the gram: see **metric system.** 3. metrical.

met·ri·cal (met′ri-k'l), ***adj.*** 1. of or composed in meter or verse. 2. of, involving, or used in measurement; metric.

met·ri·cal·ly (met′ri-k'l-i, met′rik-li), ***adv.*** 1. in a metrical manner. 2. in metrical respects.

metric hundredweight, 50 kilograms.

me·tri·cian (me-trish′ən), ***n.*** [ME. (after *physician*); cf. Fr. *métricien*], an expert or specialist in metrics (sense 1); metrist.

met·rics (met′riks), ***n.pl.*** [construed as sing. in senses 1 & 3], 1. the science or art of writing in meter. 2. metrical characteristics and details (of a poem, etc.). 3. in *mathematics,* the theory of measurement.

metric system, a decimal system of weights and measures in which the gram (.0022046 pound), the meter (39.37 inches), and the liter (61.025 cubic inches) are the basic units of weight, length, and capacity, respectively: most names for the various other units are formed by the addition of the following prefixes to these three terms (but see also **are, stere**):

deca- or *deka-* (ten), as, 1 decameter = 10 meters
hecto- (one hundred), as, 1 hectometer = 100 meters
kilo- (one thousand), as, 1 kilometer = 1,000 meters
deci- (one tenth), as, 1 decimeter = 1/10 meter
centi- (one hundredth), as, 1 centimeter = 1/100 meter
milli- (one thousandth), as, 1 millimeter = 1/1000 meter

Other prefixes sometimes used are *myria-* (ten thousand), *mega-* (one million), and *micro-* (one millionth).

metric ton, a measure of weight equal to 1,000 kilograms or 2,204.62 pounds (.984 long ton or 1.1023 short tons): abbreviated **M.T.**

met·ri·fy (met′rə-fī′), ***v.t. & v.i.*** [METRIFIED (-fīd′), METRIFYING], to put into or write in meter; versify.

met·rist (met′rist, mē′trist), ***n.*** [ML. *metrista*], 1. a person who writes in meter; writer of verse. 2. an expert or specialist in metrics (sense 1); metrician.

me·tri·tis (mi-trī′tis), ***n.*** [Mod. L. < Gr. *mētra,* uterus; + *-itis*], inflammation of the uterus.

Met·ro, met·ro (mē′trō), ***n.*** [short for *Metropolitan District Railway,* in London], an underground railway, as in European cities; subway.

met·ro- (mē′trō, met′rə), [< Gr. *metron,* measure], a combining form meaning *measure,* as in *metrology.*

met·ro- (met′rō, met′rə), [< Gr. *mētra,* uterus < *mētēr,* a mother], a combining form meaning *uterus, womb,* as in *metrorrhagia:* also, before a vowel, **metr-.**

met·ro·log·i·cal (met'rə-loj'i-k'l), *adj.* of metrology.
me·trol·o·gy (mi-trol'ə-ji), *n.* [*metro-* (measure) + *-logy*], 1. the science of weights and measures. 2. [*pl.* METROLOGIES (-jiz)], a system of weights and measures.
met·ro·nome (met'rə-nōm'), *n.* [< *metro-* (measure); + Gr. *nomos*, law], 1. a clockwork device with an inverted pendulum that beats time at a rate determined by the position of a sliding weight on the pendulum: it is used especially to help a person maintain regular tempo in practicing on the piano, etc. 2. a similar device for beating time that is operated by a synchronous electric motor.

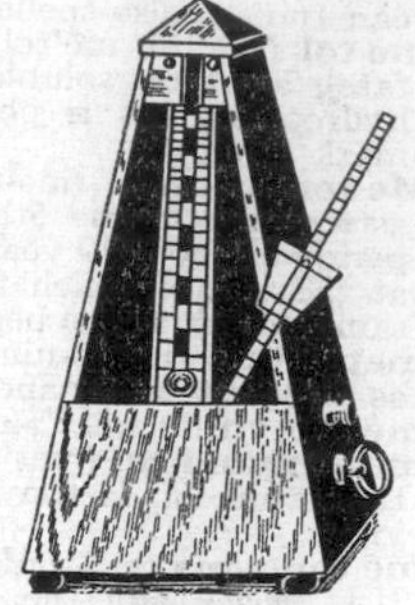
METRONOME

met·ro·nom·ic (met'rə-nom'ik), *adj.* of or like a metronome.
me·tro·nym·ic (mē'trə-nim'ik, met'rə-nim'ik), *adj.* [Gr. *mētrōnymikos* < *mētēr*, a mother + *onoma*, *onyma*, a name], of or derived from the name of the mother or a female ancestor. *n.* a metronymic name. Cf. **patronymic.**
me·trop·o·lis (mə-trop''l-is), *n.* [*pl.* METROPOLISES (-iz)], [L.; Gr. *mētropolis* < *mētēr*, a mother + *polis*, a state, city], 1. the main city, often the capital, of a country, state, or region. 2. any large city or center of population, culture, etc. 3. in ancient Greece, the mother city or state of a colony. 4. the seat, or see, of a metropolitan bishop; main diocese of an ecclesiastical province.
met·ro·pol·i·tan (met'rə-pol'ə-t'n), *adj.* [LL. *metropolitanus*], 1. of or constituting a metropolis (senses 1 & 2). 2. designating or of a metropolitan (sense 2) or metropolis (sense 4). *n.* 1. a person who lives in and knows a metropolis (senses 1 & 2) or one who has the characteristic attitudes and manners of such a person. 2. *a)* an archbishop having authority over the bishops of a church province. *b)* in the *Orthodox Eastern Church*, a bishop ranking just below Patriarch. 3. in ancient Greece, a citizen of a metropolis (sense 3). Abbreviated **met., metrop.**
me·tror·rha·gi·a (mē'trə-rā'ji-ə, met'rə-rā'ji-ə), *n.* [Mod. L. < Gr. *mētra*, uterus; + *-rrhagia*], nonmenstrual bleeding from the uterus.
-metry, [Gr. *-metria* < *metron*, measure; cf. METE (to measure)], a terminal combining form meaning *the process, art,* or *science of measuring*, as in *anthropometry*.
Met·ter·nich, Kle·mens Wen·zel Ne·po·muk Lo·thar, Prince **von** (klā'mens ven'tsəl nā'pō-mook lō'tär fôn met'ēr-niH; Eng. met'ēr-nik), 1773–1859; Austrian statesman; chancellor of state (1809–1848).
met·tle (met''l), *n.* [var. of *metal*, used figuratively], quality of character or temperament; especially, high quality of character; spirit; courage; ardor.
on one's mettle, roused or prepared to do one's best.
met·tled (met''ld), *adj.* mettlesome.
met·tle·some (met''l-səm), *adj.* [see -SOME], full of mettle; spirited; ardent, brave, etc.
Metz (mets), *n.* a fortified city in northeastern France, on the Moselle River: pop., 97,000.
Meuse (möz; Eng. mūz), *n.* a river in northeastern France, Belgium, and the Netherlands, flowing into the North Sea: length, 575 mi.: Dutch name, *Maas*.
Mev, mev (mev), *n.* [*pl.* MEV, MEV], [*m*illion *e*lectron *v*olts], a unit of energy equal to one million electron-volts.
mew (mū), *n.* [ME. & OFr. *mue* < *muer*, to change, molt < L. *mutare*, to change], 1. a cage, as for hawks while molting. 2. a secret place or den. 3. [Obs.], a place of confinement. See also **mews.** *v.t.* 1. [< the *n.*], to confine in or as in a cage; shut up or conceal (often with *up*). 2. [< OFr. *muer*], *a)* [Archaic], to shed or change (feathers); molt. *b)* [Obs.], to cast (horns): said of a stag. *v.i.* [Archaic], to molt.
mew (mū), *n.* [echoic], the characteristic vocal sound made by a cat. *v.i.* to make this sound. Also **meow, miaow,** etc.
mew (mū), *n.* [ME. *mewe;* AS. *mæw;* akin to G. *möwe* (< LG.); echoic of the bird's cry], a sea gull or other gull: also **mew gull.**
mewl (mūl), *v.i.* [freq. of *mew* (to make the sound of a cat)], to cry weakly, like a baby; whimper or whine.
mews (mūz), *n.pl.* [usually construed as sing.], [< *mew* (a cage)], 1. the royal stables in London, built on the site where the royal hawks were mewed; hence, 2. stables grouped around a court or along an alley.
Mex., 1. Mexican. 2. Mexico.
Mex·i·can (mek'si-kən), *adj.* of Mexico, its people, their language, or their culture. *n.* 1. a native or inhabitant of Mexico. 2. Nahuatl. Abbreviated **Mex.**
Mexican bean beetle, a species of spotted ladybug that eats the leaves and pods of bean plants.
Mexican hairless, any of a breed of small dog native to Mexico, hairless except for the end of the tail and a patch on the head.
Mexican War, a war between the United States and Mexico (1846–1848), settled by the Treaty of Guadalupe Hidalgo.
Mex·i·co (mek'si-kō'), *n.* 1. a country in North America, south of the United States: area, 760,290 sq. mi.; pop., 34,626,000; capital, Mexico City. 2. a state of southern Mexico: area, 8,267 sq. mi.; pop., 1,898,000; capital, Toluca: abbreviated **Mex.** 3. Mexico City. Mexican spelling, **México;** Spanish spelling, **Méjico.**
Mexico, Gulf of, a gulf of the Atlantic, east of Mexico and south of the United States: area, c. 716,000 sq. mi.
Mexico City, the capital of the Republic of Mexico and of the Federal District: pop., 3,900,000; officially **México, D.F.**
Mey·er·beer, Gia·co·mo (jä'kô-mô' mī'ēr-bâr'; Eng. mī'ēr-bêr'), (born *Jakob Liebmann Beer*), 1791–1864; German composer.
Mey·er·hof, Otto (mī'ēr-hōf'), 1884–1951; German physiologist; received Nobel prize in physiology, 1922.
Meyn·ell, Alice (men''l, mā'n'l), 1847?–1922; English poet and essayist.
mez·ca·line (mez'kə-lēn', mez'kə-lin), *n.* mescaline.
me·ze·re·on (mi-zē'ri-ən), *n.* [ML.; Ar. & Per. *māzariyūn*], 1. a small European shrub with clusters of fragrant, purplish flowers. 2. mezereum (sense 2).
me·ze·re·um (mi-zē'ri-əm), *n.* [Mod. L.], 1. mezereon. 2. the dried bark of mezereon, used in liniments and in the treatment of some diseases.
me·zu·zah, me·zu·za (mə-zoo'zə, me-zōō'zä), *n.* [*pl.* MEZUZOTH (-zōth)], [Heb. *mĕzūzāh*, doorpost], in *Judaism*, a piece of parchment inscribed on one side with texts from Deuteronomy (6:4–9 & 11:13–21) in 22 lines and on the other side with the name of God (*Shaddai*), rolled and put into a case and attached to the doorpost of the house, as commanded in the Biblical passages.
mez·za·nine (mez'ə-nēn', mez'ə-nin), *n.* [Fr.; It. *mezzanino* < *mezzano*, middle < L. *medianus;* see MEDIAN], 1. a low-ceilinged story between two main stories in a building, usually immediately above the ground floor and sometimes in the form of a balcony projecting only partly over the floor below it: also **mezzanine floor** (or **story**). 2. in some theaters, the first few rows of the balcony, set apart by an aisle.
mez·zo (met'sō, med'zō, mez'ō), *adj.* [It.; L. *medius*, middle, half], in *music*, medium; moderate; half. *adv.* in *music*, moderately; somewhat. Abbreviated **M., m.**
mez·zo-re·lie·vo (met'sō-ri-lē'vō, med'zō-ri-lē'vō, mez'ō-ri-lē'vō), *n.* [*pl.* MEZZO-RELIEVOS (-vōz)], [It. *mezzo rilievo; mezzo* < L. *medius*, middle, half + *rilievo*, relief], sculpture in which the figures project halfway from the background; half relief.
‡**mez·zo-ri·lie·vo** (med'dzô-rē-lye'vô), *n.* [*pl.* MEZZI-RILIEVI (med'dzē-rē-lye'vē)], [It.], mezzo-relievo.
mez·zo-so·pra·no (met'sō-sə-pran'ō, med'sō-sə-prä'nō, mez'ō-sə-pran'ō), *n.* [*pl.* MEZZO-SOPRANOS (-ōz, -nōz), MEZZO-SOPRANI (-i, -ni)], [It.], 1. a voice or part between soprano and contralto. 2. a singer with such a voice. *adj.* designating or of such a voice or singer.
mez·zo·tint (met'sə-tint', med'zə-tint', mez'ə-tint'), *n.* [It. *mezzotinto;* see MEZZO & TINT], 1. a method of engraving on a copper or steel plate by scraping or polishing parts of a roughened surface so that an impression of light and shade can be produced. 2. an engraving or print so produced. *v.t.* to engrave by this method.
MF., Middle French.
mf., 1. in *music*, mezzo forte. 2. microfarad. 3. millifarad.
M.F.A., Master of Fine Arts.
mfd., 1. manufactured. 2. [*pl.* MMFDS.], microfarads.
mfg., manufacturing.
MFr., Middle French.
mfr. [*pl.* MFRS.], 1. manufacture. 2. manufacturer.
Mg, in *chemistry*, magnesium.
mg., milligram; milligrams.
MGael., Middle Gaelic.
MGr., 1. Medieval Greek. 2. Middle Greek.
Mgr., 1. Manager. 2. Monseigneur. 3. Monsignor. 4. Monsignore.
M.H., Medal of Honor.
MHG., M.H.G., Middle High German.
mho (mō), *n.* [*ohm* spelled backward], the unit of electrical conductance, reciprocal of the ohm.
M.H.R., Member of the House of Representatives.
mi (mē), *n.* [It.], in *music*, a syllable representing the third tone of the diatonic scale: see **solfeggio.**
mi., 1. mile; miles. 2. mill; mills. 3. minute. 4. minor.
M.I., 1. Military Intelligence. 2. Mounted Infantry.
Mi·am·i (mī-am'i, mī-am'ə), *n.* [Am. Ind.], 1. [*pl.* MIAMI, MIAMIS (-iz, -əz)], a member of a former tribe of Algonquian Indians who migrated from Wisconsin to Indiana and near-by regions: also **Miami Indian.** 2. a city on the southeastern coast of Florida: winter resort: pop., 292,000. 3. a river in western Ohio, flowing southward into the Ohio: length, 160 mi.: also **Great Miami.**
Miami Beach, a city in southeastern Florida, on an island opposite Miami: winter resort: pop., 63,000.
mi·aow, mi·aou (mi-ou', myou), *n. & v.i.* meow; mew.

mi·as·ma (mī-az′mə, mi-az′mə), *n.* [*pl.* MIASMAS (-məz), MIASMATA (-mə-tə)], [Mod. L.; Gr. *miasma*, pollution < *miainein*, to pollute], poisonous vapor formerly supposed to arise from decomposing animal or vegetable matter, swamps, etc. and infect the air, especially at night: such vapor was once thought to cause malaria.

mi·as·mal (mī-az′m'l, mi-az′m'l), *adj.* of, producing, or caused by miasma; noxious; pestilential.

mi·as·mat·ic (mī′əz-mat′ik), *adj.* miasmal.

mi·as·mic (mī-az′mik, mi-az′mik), *adj.* miasmal.

mi·aul (mi-ôl′, mi-oul′), *n.* & *v.i.* meow; mew.

mib (mib), *n.* [altered < *marble*], [Dial.], 1. a marble. 2. *pl.* the game of marbles.

mi·ca (mī′kə), *n.* [L., a crumb, grain, particle; influenced by *micare*, to shine, glitter], any of a group of minerals (complex silicates) that crystallize in thin, somewhat flexible, easily separated layers, translucent or transparent: mica is resistant to heat and electricity, and when transparent is often called *isinglass*.

mi·ca·ce·ous (mī-kā′shəs), *adj.* [see -ACEOUS], of, containing, characteristic of, or like mica.

Mi·cah (mī′kə), [Heb. *mīkhā(yah)*, lit., who is like (God); cf. MICHAEL], a masculine name. *n.* 1. a Hebrew prophet of the 8th century B.C. 2. a book of the Old Testament. Also, in the Douay Bible, **Micheas.** Abbreviated **Mic.**

Mi·caw·ber, Wilkins (mi-kô′bẽr), a character in Dickens' *David Copperfield* who has very little money but much optimism, and is always sure that "something will turn up."

mice (mīs), *n.* plural of **mouse.**

mi·cel·la (mi-sel′ə, mī-sel′ə), *n.* [*pl.* MICELLAE (-ē)], a micelle.

mi·celle, mi·cell (mi-sel′), *n.* [Mod. L. *micella*, dim. < L. *mica*, a grain, crumb, morsel], 1. a hypothetical structural unit of an organized body. 2. the structural unit of gel-forming colloids, made up of complex molecules: it can change in size without changing chemically and may have crystalline properties.

Mich., 1. Michaelmas. 2. Michigan.

Mi·chael (mī′k'l), [LL.; Gr. *Michaēl*; Heb. *mīkhā'ēl*, lit., who is like God; cf. MICAH], a masculine name: diminutives, *Mike, Micky*; equivalents, Fr. *Michel*, It. *Michele*, Sp. *Miguel*. *n.* 1. son of Carol II; 1921– ; king of Romania (1927–1930; 1940–1947); abdicated. 2. in the *Bible*, the archangel who, with an army of loyal angels, victoriously warred with the rebel angel Lucifer: Rev. 12:7–9.

Mich·ael·mas (mik″'l-məs), *n.* [see -MAS], the feast of the archangel Michael, celebrated September 29: in England, a quarter day: also **Michaelmas Day.**

Michaelmas daisy, any of various asters, wild or cultivated.

miche (mich), *v.i.* [ME. *mychen*; OFr. *muchier* (Fr. *musser*) < Gaul. **mukyare*, to hide; akin to MIr. *muchaim*, I conceal; IE. base **mūg-*, to spy upon, seen also in G. *meuchel-* (in comp.), secret], [Obs. or British Dial.], 1. to pilfer. 2. to skulk. 3. to play truant.

Mi·che·as (mi-kē′əs), *n.* Micah: Douay Bible form.

Mi·chel·an·ge·lo (mī′k'l-an′jə-lō′, mik″'l-an′jə-lō′), *n.* (*Michelangelo Buonarroti*), Italian painter, sculptor, architect, and poet; 1475–1564.

Mi·che·let, Jules (zhül′ mēsh′le′), 1798–1874; French historian.

Mi·chel·son, Albert Abraham (mī′k'l-sən), 1852–1931; American physicist, born in Germany; received Nobel prize in physics, 1907.

Mich·i·gan (mish′ə-gən), *n.* 1. a Middle Western State of the United States: area, 58,216 sq. mi.; pop., 7,823,000; capital, Lansing: abbreviated **Mich.**: nicknamed *Wolverine State*. 2. one of the Great Lakes, between Michigan and Wisconsin: area, 22,400 sq. mi.: usually **Lake Michigan.**

Michigan City, a city in Indiana, on Lake Michigan: pop., 37,000.

Mich·i·gan·der (mish′ə-gan′dẽr), *n.* a native or inhabitant of Michigan.

Mich·i·gan·ite (mish′ə-gən-īt′), *n.* a Michigander.

Mick (mik), *n.* [< *Michael*, taken as typical Irish name], [Slang], an Irishman: hostile or contemptuous term.

mick·ey finn, Mick·ey Finn (mik′i fin′), [Slang], a drink of liquor to which a powerful narcotic or purgative has been added, given to an unsuspecting person: also **mickey, Mickey.**

Mic·kie·wicz, A·dam (ä′däm mits-kye′vich), 1798–1855; Polish poet.

mick·le (mik′'l), *adj., adv., n.* [ME. (Northern) *mikel*; AS. *micel*; influenced by cognate ON. *mykill*; cf. MUCH], [Archaic or Scot.], much: also **muckle.**

Mic·mac (mik′mak), *n.* [*pl.* MICMAC, MICMACS (-maks)], [Am. Ind., lit., allies], a member of a tribe of Algonquian Indians in Newfoundland and the Maritime Provinces of Canada.

mi·cra (mī′krə), *n.* plural of **micron.**

mi·cri·fy (mī′krə-fī′), *v.t.* [MICRIFIED (-fīd′), MICRIFYING], [< *micro-* + *-fy*], to make small or unimportant.

mi·cro- (mī′krō, mī′krə), [Gr. *mikro-* < *mikros*, small], a combining form meaning: 1. *a*) *little, small, minute*. *b*) *exceptionally little, abnormally small*, as in *microcephalic*. 2. *enlarging what is small*, as in *microscope*, *microphone*. 3. *relation to microscopes*, *microscopic*, as in *microchemistry*. 4. in the *metric system*, etc., *one millionth part of* (a specified unit), as in *microgram*, *microfarad*. Also, before a vowel, **micr-.**

mi·cro·a·nal·y·sis (mī′krō-ə-nal′ə-sis), *n.* the chemical analysis and identification of very small quantities.

mi·cro·bar·o·graph (mī′krō-bar′ə-graf′, mī′krō-bar′ə-gräf′), *n.* a barograph for recording very small changes in atmospheric pressure.

mi·crobe (mī′krōb), *n.* [Fr. < Gr. *mikros*, small + *bios*, life], a very minute living thing, whether plant or animal; microorganism; especially, any of the bacteria that cause disease; germ.

mi·cro·bi·al (mī-krō′bi-əl), *adj.* microbic.

mi·cro·bic (mī-krō′bik, mī-krob′ik), *adj.* of or caused by a microbe or microbes.

mi·cro·bi·cide (mī-krō′bə-sīd′), *n.* [< *microbe* + *-cide*], anything that kills microbes.

mi·cro·bi·ol·o·gy (mī′krō-bī-ol′ə-ji), *n.* the branch of biology that deals with microorganisms.

mi·cro·ce·phal·ic (mī′krō-sə-fal′ik), *adj.* microcephalous.

mi·cro·ceph·a·lous (mī′krə-sef′ə-ləs), *adj.* of or having microcephaly.

mic·ro·ceph·a·ly (mī′krə-sef′ə-li), *n.* [*micro-* + *cephal-* + *-y*], a condition in which the head or cranial capacity is abnormally small: opposed to *macrocephaly*.

mi·cro·chem·is·try (mī′krō-kem′is-tri), *n.* the chemistry of microscopic quantities or objects.

mi·cro·cli·ma·tol·o·gy (mī′krō-klī′mə-tol′ə-ji), *n.* the study of climate and its characteristics in a small area.

mi·cro·cline (mī′krə-klīn′), *n.* [< *micro-* + Gr. *klinein*, to incline], a grayish, yellowish, greenish, or reddish mineral of the feldspar family, potassium aluminum silicate, $KAlSi_3O_8$, having a glassy luster and perfect cleavage: it occurs in igneous rocks.

mi·cro·coc·cus (mī′krə-kok′əs), *n.* [*pl.* MICROCOCCI (-kok′sī)], [Mod. L.; *micro-* + *-coccus*], any of a group of spherical or egg-shaped bacteria that occur in irregular masses or plates and feed on dead or living matter.

mi·cro·cosm (mī′krə-koz′m), *n.* a little world; miniature universe; specifically, *a*) man regarded as a miniature or epitome of the world. *b*) a community, village, etc. regarded as a miniature or epitome of the world. Opposed to *macrocosm*.

mi·cro·cos·mic (mī′krə-koz′mik), *adj.* 1. of, being, or like a microcosm. 2. designating a white, crystalline salt, sodium ammonium hydrogen phosphate, $Na(NH_4)HPO_4 \cdot 4H_2O$, used as a reagent in blowpipe analysis, in testing for metallic oxides, etc.: it was originally obtained from human urine.

mi·cro·cos·mi·cal (mī′krə-koz′mi-k'l), *adj.* microcosmic.

mi·cro·crys·tal·line (mī′krō-kris′t'l-in, mī′krō-kris′t'l-īn′), *adj.* having crystalline structure that can be seen only with a microscope.

mi·cro·cyte (mī′krə-sīt′), *n.* [*micro-* + *-cyte*], an abnormally small red blood corpuscle, occurring especially in certain types of anemia.

mi·cro·de·tec·tor (mī′krō-di-tek′tẽr), *n.* [*micro-* + *detector*], an instrument for detecting very small amounts of, or minute changes in, an electric current.

mi·cro·dis·sec·tion (mī′krō-di-sek′shən), *n.* dissection of tissue, etc. under the microscope.

mi·cro·dont (mī′krə-dont′), *adj.* [*micr-* + *-odont*], having very small teeth. *n.* a microdont individual.

mi·cro·far·ad (mī′krə-far′əd), *n.* one millionth of a farad: abbreviated **mf., mfd.**

mi·cro·film (mī′krə-film′), *n.* 1. film on which documents, printed pages, etc. are photographed in a reduced size for convenience in storage and transportation: enlarged prints can be made from such film, or the film can be viewed directly with the help of a special optical apparatus. 2. a reproduction on microfilm. 3. loosely, a microphotograph (sense 3). *v.t.* & *v.i.* to photograph on microfilm.

mi·cro·ga·mete (mī′krō-gə-mēt′, mī′krə-gam′ēt), *n.* the smaller, usually the male, of a pair of conjugating gametes.

mi·cro·gram, mi·cro·gramme (mī′krə-gram′), *n.* one millionth of a gram: symbol, μg (no period).

mi·cro·gram (mī′krə-gram′), *n.* a micrograph (sense 2).

mi·cro·graph (mī′krə-graf′, mī′krə-gräf′), *n.* [*micro-* + *-graph*], 1. an apparatus for doing extremely small writing, drawing, or engraving. 2. a photograph or drawing of an object as seen through a microscope. 3. an apparatus by which, through the movements of a diaphragm, very slight movements can be recorded in magnified visual form and measured.

mi·crog·raph·y (mī-krog′rə-fi), *n.* [*micro-* + *-graphy*],

1. the description or study of microscopic objects. 2. the art or practice of writing in tiny characters.

mi·cro·groove (mī′krə-grōōv′), *n.* 1. a very narrow needle groove, as in a long-playing phonograph record, allowing more matter to be recorded on a record than does the ordinary, wider groove. 2. a record having such narrow grooves. A trade-mark (**Microgroove**).

mi·crol·o·gy (mī-krol′ə-ji), *n.* [Gr. *mikrologia;* see MICRO- & -LOGY], the discussion or study of trivial matters or petty differences.

mi·crom·e·ter (mī-krom′ə-tẽr), *n.* [Fr. *micromètre;* see MICRO- & -METER], 1. an instrument for measuring very small distances, angles, diameters, etc., used on a telescope or microscope. 2. micrometer calipers.

micrometer calipers (or **caliper**), calipers with a micrometer screw, for extremely accurate measurement.

micrometer screw, a finely threaded screw of definite pitch, with a head graduated to show how much the screw has been moved in or out: used in micrometers, etc. to give fine measurements, sometimes to **.0001** of an inch.

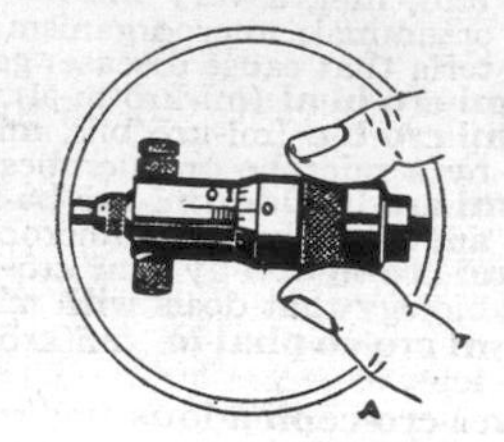

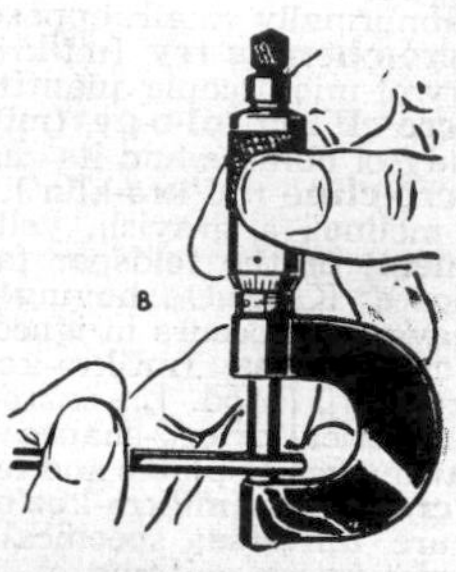

MICROMETER CALIPERS
A, used for measuring inside dimensions; B, used for measuring outside dimensions

mi·crom·e·try (mī-krom′ə-tri), *n.* measurement by means of micrometers.

mi·cro·mil·li·me·ter, mi·cro·mil·li·me·tre (mī′krō-mil′ə-mē′tẽr), *n.* 1. one millionth of a millimeter; one billionth of a meter. 2. a millimicron. 3. in *biology* & *chemistry,* a micron. Symbol, mμ (no period).

mi·cron (mī′kron), *n.* [*pl.* MICRONS (-kronz), MICRA (-krə)], [Mod. L. < Gr. *mikron,* neut. of *mikros,* small, minute], 1. one millionth of a meter; one thousandth of a millimeter: symbol, μ (no period). 2. in *physical chemistry,* a particle having a diameter between .01 and .0001 millimeter. Also spelled **mikron.**

Mi·cro·ne·sia (mī′krə-nē′zhə, mī′krə-nē′shə), *n.* the groups of islands in the Pacific north of the equator and east of the Philippines.

Mi·cro·ne·sian (mī′krə-nē′zhən, mī′krə-nē′shən), *adj.* of Micronesia, its people, their languages, or their culture. *n.* 1. a native of Micronesia, which is inhabited by peoples of mixed Melanesian, Polynesian, and Malayan stock. 2. any of the Austronesian languages spoken in Micronesia.

mi·cro·or·gan·ism, mi·cro·ör·gan·ism, mi·cro-or·gan·ism (mī′krō-ôr′gən-iz′m), *n.* any microscopic or ultramicroscopic animal or vegetable organism; especially, any of the bacteria, protozoa, viruses, etc.

mi·cro·phone (mī′krə-fōn′), *n.* [*micro-* + *-phone*], an instrument for intensifying weak sounds or transmitting sounds by transforming sound waves electromagnetically into variations of an electric current: microphones are used in telephony, radio, etc.

mi·cro·phon·ic (mī′krə-fon′ik), *adj.* of, having the nature of, or like a microphone.

mi·cro·pho·to·graph (mī′krə-fō′tə-graf′, mī′krə-fō′tə-gräf′), *n.* 1. a very small photograph, usually requiring enlargement to bring out the details. 2. a photograph taken through a microscope: usually **photomicrograph.** 3. an enlarged photograph printed from a microfilm.

mi·cro·phyte (mī′krə-fīt′), *n.* [*micro-* + *-phyte*], any microscopically small plant, usually a parasitic one.

mi·cro·phyt·ic (mī′krə-fit′ik), *adj.* of, or having the nature of, a microphyte.

mi·cro·print (mī′krə-print′), *n.* a microphotograph of printed or written matter so greatly reduced that it can be read only through a magnifying device.

mi·cro·py·lar (mī′krə-pī′lẽr), *adj.* of, or having the nature of, a micropyle.

mi·cro·pyle (mī′krə-pīl′), *n.* [Fr. < Gr. *mikros,* small + *pylē,* gate, opening], 1. in *botany, a)* a very small opening in the outer coats of an ovule, through which the pollen tube penetrates. *b)* the corresponding opening in the developed seed. 2. in *zoology,* a very small opening in the vitelline membrane of an ovum, through which spermatozoa can enter.

mi·cro·py·rom·e·ter (mī′krō-pī-rom′ə-tẽr), *n.* [*micro-* + *pyrometer*], an optical instrument for determining temperature, etc. of minute bodies giving off light or heat.

micros., microscopy.

mi·cro·scope (mī′krə-skōp′), *n.* [Mod. L. *microscopium;* see MICRO- & -SCOPE], an instrument consisting essentially of a lens or combination of lenses, for making very small objects, as microorganisms, look larger so that they can be seen and studied: see also **electron microscope.**

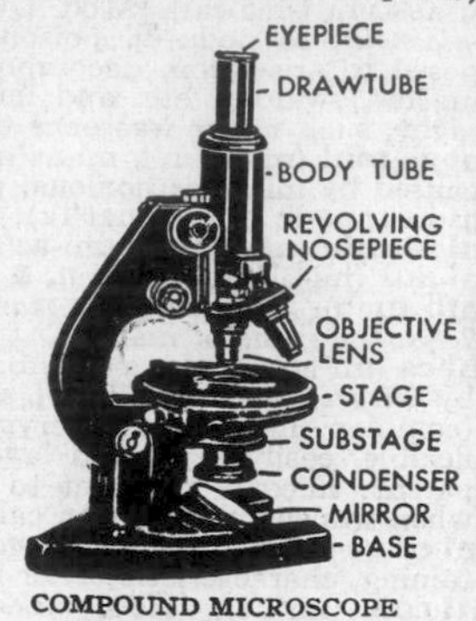

COMPOUND MICROSCOPE

mi·cro·scop·ic (mī′krə-skop′ik), *adj.* 1. so small as to be invisible or obscure except through a microscope; extremely small; minute. 2. of, with, or as with a microscope. 3. like or suggestive of a microscope; searching; minutely observing.

mi·cro·scop·i·cal (mī′krə-skop′i-k′l), *adj.* microscopic.

mi·cro·scop·i·cal·ly (mī′krə-skop′i-k′l-i, mī′krə-skop′ik-li), *adv.* 1. by using a microscope. 2. in careful detail, as if with a microscope; exactly, minutely, and searchingly. 3. so as to be microscopic; extremely: as, *microscopically* small.

mi·cros·co·pist (mī-kros′kə-pist, mī′krə-skō′pist), *n.* a person who uses, or is expert in using, a microscope.

mi·cros·co·py (mī-kros′kə-pi, mī′krə-skō′pi), *n.* the use of a microscope; investigation by means of a microscope. Abbreviated **micros.**

mi·cro·seism (mī′krə-sīz′m, mī′krə-sīs′m), *n.* [< *micro-* + Gr. *seismos,* earthquake], a very slight tremor or quivering of the earth's crust.

mi·cro·some (mī′krə-sōm′), *n.* [*micro-* + *-some* (body)], any of the minute granules in the protoplasm of an active cell.

mi·cro·spo·ran·gi·um (mī′krō-spə-ran′ji-əm), *n.* [*pl.* MICROSPORANGIA (-ə)], a sporangium that contains or produces microspores, as the pollen sac of the anther in seed plants.

mi·cro·spore (mī′krə-spôr′, mī′krə-spōr′), *n.* a small, asexually produced spore from which a male gametophyte develops, as a pollen grain in a seed plant.

mi·cro·spo·ro·phyll (mī′krə-spôr′ə-fil, mī′krə-spō′rə-fil), *n.* a sporophyll that produces microsporangia.

mi·cro·stom·a·tous (mī′krə-stom′ə-təs, mī′krə-stō′mə-təs), *adj.* [*micro-* + *-stomatous*], having a small mouth.

mi·cros·to·mous (mī-kros′tə-məs), *adj.* microstomatous.

mi·cro·tome (mī′krə-tōm′), *n.* [*micro-* + *-tome*], an instrument for cutting thin sections of tissue, etc. for study under the microscope.

mi·cro·tom·ic (mī′krə-tom′ik), *adj.* of microtomy or the microtome.

mi·crot·o·my (mī-krot′ə-mi), *n.* the art of preparing sections for study under the microscope, as by the use of the microtome.

mi·cro·wave (mī′krə-wāv′), *n.* an extremely short electromagnetic wave; wave less than ten meters, or especially less than one meter, in length.

mic·tu·rate (mik′choo-rāt′), *v.i.* [MICTURATED (-id), MICTURATING], [see MICTURITION & -ATE], to urinate.

mic·tu·ri·tion (mik′choo-rish′ən), *n.* [< *micturitus,* pp. of L. *micturire,* to desire to urinate < *mingere,* to urinate; + *-ion*], 1. the act of urinating. 2. formerly, abnormal frequency of urination.

mid (mid), *adj.* [*superl.* MIDMOST], [ME. *myd;* AS. *midd-;* akin to Goth. *midjis;* IE. base **medhjo-,* middle, seen also in L. *medius* (cf. MEDIUM, MEDIA), Gr. *mesos-* (cf. MESO-)], 1. middle. 2. in *phonetics,* pronounced with the tongue in a position approximately midway between high and low: said of certain vowels, as the *a* in *cake* or *o* in *cold.* *n.* [Archaic], the middle.

mid, 'mid (mid), *prep.* [Poetic], amid.

mid- (mid), a combining form meaning *middle* or *middle part of,* as in *midbrain, mid-Atlantic.*

mid., 1. middle. 2. midshipman.

Mi·das (mī′dəs), *n.* [L.; Gr. *Midas*], in *Greek legend,* a king of Phrygia to whom Dionysus granted the power of turning everything that he touched into gold: when even his food and his daughter turned to gold, Midas begged to have the power taken back.

mid-At·lan·tic (mid′ət-lan′tik), *n.* the middle part of the Atlantic Ocean.

mid·brain (mid′brān′), *n.* the mesencephalon.

mid·chan·nel (mid′chan″'l), *n.* the middle part of a channel.

mid·con·ti·nent (mid′kon′tə-nənt), *n.* the middle part of a continent.

mid·day (mid′dā′), *n.* [ME. *middai;* AS. *middæg*], the middle part of the day; noon. *adj.* of midday.

mid·den (mid′'n), *n.* [ME. *midding;* prob. < ON.; cf. Dan. *mögdynge; mög,* muck + *dynge,* a heap], 1. [British Dial.], a dunghill or refuse heap. 2. in *archaeology,* a heap of bones, shells, etc. marking the site of a prehistoric dwelling: usually **kitchen midden.**

mid·dle (mid′'l), *adj.* [ME. & AS. *middel;* akin to G. *mittel;* see MID & -LE], 1. halfway between two given points, times, etc.; equally distant from either end, side, etc.; in the center; mean. 2. intermediate; in between; intervening. 3. in *Greek grammar*, designating or of a voice of the verb, passive in form, in which the subject is represented as acting reflexively. 4. [M-], in *geology*, designating a division of a period or a formation between those called *Upper* and *Lower*. 5. [M-], in *linguistics*, designating a stage in language development intermediate between those called *Old* and *Modern*: as, *Middle* English. 6. in *logic*, designating a term that appears in both premises of a syllogism but not in the conclusion. 7. in *phonetics*, medial. *n.* 1. a point or part halfway between extremes; central point, part, time, etc. 2. something intermediate. 3. the middle part of the body; waist. 4. in *Greek grammar*, the middle voice. 5. in *logic*, a middle term. *v.t. & v.i.* [MIDDLED (-'ld), MIDDLING], 1. to put in the middle. 2. to fold (a rope, etc.) in the middle; double. Abbreviated **M., m., mid.**

SYN.—**middle** refers to the point or part equally distant from either or all sides or extremities and may apply to space, time, etc. (the *middle* of the stage, the day, etc.); **center** more precisely stresses the point equidistant from the bounding lines or surfaces of any plane or solid figure (the *center* of a circle, globe, etc.) and is sometimes used figuratively (the *center* of town, a trade *center*); **midst**, usually used in prepositional phrases, denotes a middle part that is completely surrounded by persons or things or a middle point in some action (in the *midst* of a crowd, one's work, etc.).

middle age, the time of life between youth and old age: now usually applied to the years from about 40 to about 60.

mid·dle-aged (mid′'l-ājd′), *adj.* in, of, characteristic of, or suitable for middle age.

Middle Ages, the period of European history between ancient and modern times, c. 500 A.D.–1450 A.D.

Middle America, the part of Latin America south of the United States and north of South America.

Middle Atlantic States, New York, New Jersey, and Pennsylvania.

mid·dle·break·er (mid′'l-brāk′ẽr), *n.* a kind of plow that throws up the sod equally in both directions from the furrow by means of an added moldboard; lister.

mid·dle·bust·er (mid′'l-bus′tẽr), *n.* a middlebreaker.

middle C, 1. the musical note on the first ledger line below the treble staff and the first above the bass staff. 2. the corresponding tone or key.

mid·dle-class (mid′'l-klas′, mid′'l-kläs′), *adj.* of or characteristic of the middle class: see also **bourgeois.**

middle class, the social class between the aristocracy or very wealthy and the working class, or proletariat: owners of small businesses, professional and white-collar workers, well-to-do farmers, etc. are generally included in the middle class: see also **bourgeoisie.**

Middle Congo, a former French colony in French Equatorial Africa: see **Congo** (sense 3).

middle distance, the space between the foreground and the background in a picture.

middle ear, the tympanum: see **ear.**

Middle East, 1. the area including Iraq, Iran, Afghanistan, and, sometimes, India, Tibet, and Burma. 2. [British], the Near East (sense 1), excluding the Balkans. Cf. **Near East.**

Middle Empire, the Middle Kingdom (sense 1).

Middle English, the English language as written and spoken between about 1150 and about 1475: it is characterized by the loss of Anglo-Saxon inflectional endings, the emergence of a syntax based on word order, a revision of the Anglo-Saxon pronoun system, great diversity of dialectal spellings, extensive vocabulary borrowings from Latin, French, and Low German sources, and the gradual standardization of the South East Midland dialect, used in and around London, as a written language for the whole of England (c. 1375–1475): abbreviated **ME., M.E.**

Middle Greek, Medieval Greek: abbreviated **MGr.**

Middle High German, the language of the highlands of south and central Germany as it was written and spoken between about 1100 and about 1500: in the development of German, it represents a stage analogous to that of Middle English: abbreviated **MHG., M.H.G.**

Middle Irish, the Irish language as it developed in the later Middle Ages: abbreviated **MIr.**

Middle Kingdom, 1. a kingdom of ancient Egypt, c. 2400–1580 B.C., with its capital at Heracleopolis and, later, at Thebes: also **Middle Empire.** 2. [transl. of Chin. *Chung kuo*], *a*) the former Chinese Empire, considered as the center of the world. *b*) China proper.

Middle Latin, Medieval Latin: abbreviated **ML., M.L.**

middle latitude, the latitude midway between two points in the same hemisphere: also **mean latitude.**

Middle Low German, the Germanic language of the northwest European lowlands, chiefly between the Rhine and the Elbe, as written and spoken between about 1100 and about 1450: abbreviated **MLG., M.L.G.**

mid·dle·man (mid′'l-man′), *n.* [*pl.* MIDDLEMEN (-men′)], 1. a trader who buys commodities from the producer and sells them to the retailer or, sometimes, directly to the consumer. 2. a go-between; intermediary. 3. the interlocutor in a minstrel show.

mid·dle·most (mid′'l-mōst′), *adj.* midmost.

middle passage, the passage across the Atlantic from West Africa to the West Indies or America: route of the former slave trade.

Mid·dles·brough (mid′'lz-brə), *n.* a city in northeastern England: pop., 154,000.

Mid·dle·sex (mid′'l-seks′), *n.* 1. a county of England, containing the northwest section of London: pop., 2,269,000. 2. a county in eastern Massachusetts: site of the first battle of the Revolutionary War.

mid·dle-sized (mid′'l-sīzd′), *adj.* of medium size.

Middle States, those eastern States between the New England States and the South; New York, New Jersey, Pennsylvania, Delaware, and Maryland.

Middle Temple, one of two groups of buildings occupied by the Inns of Court in London, England: the other is the Inner Temple.

Mid·dle·ton, Thomas (mid′'l-tən), 1570?–1627; English dramatist.

Mid·dle·town (mid′'l-toun′), *n.* 1. a city in central Connecticut: pop., 33,000. 2. a city in southeastern New York: pop., 23,000. 3. a city in southwestern Ohio: pop., 42,000.

mid·dle·weight (mid′'l-wāt′), *n.* 1. one of average weight. 2. a boxer or wrestler who weighs between 148 and 160 pounds. *adj.* of middleweights.

Middle West, middle west, that part of the United States between the Rocky Mountains and the Allegheny Mountains, north of the Ohio River and the southern borders of Kansas and Missouri: also **Midwest.**

mid·dling (mid′liŋ), *adj.* [< *mid, adj.* + *-ling*], of middle size, quality, grade, state, etc.; medium; ordinary; mediocre. *adv.* [Colloq.], fairly; moderately; somewhat. *n.* [< *mid, n.* + *-ling*], 1. pork or bacon from between the ham and the shoulder. 2. *pl.* products of medium quality, grade, size, or price. 3. *pl.* particles of coarsely ground wheat mixed with bran, valued for their high gluten content.

mid·dy (mid′i), *n.* [*pl.* MIDDIES (-iz)], 1. [Colloq.], a midshipman. 2. a middy blouse.

middy blouse, a loose, hip-length blouse with a sailor collar, worn by women and children.

Mid·gard (mid′gärd′), *n.* [ON. *mithgarthr* < *mithr*, mid + *garthr*, yard, house], in *Norse mythology*, the earth, regarded as midway between heaven and hell and engirdled by a huge serpent: also **Mithgarthr, Midgarth.**

Mid·garth (mid′gärth′), *n.* Midgard.

midge (mij), *n.* [ME. *migge;* AS. *mycg;* akin to G. *mücke;* IE. base **mu-*, a fly, gnat, seen also in L. *musca*, a fly], 1. any very small gnat or gnatlike insect. 2. a very small person; midget.

midg·et (mij′it), *n.* [dim. of *midge*], 1. a very small person. 2. anything very small of its kind. *adj.* very small of its kind; miniature. —*SYN.* see **dwarf.**

mid-gut (mid′gut′), the middle part of the alimentary canal in vertebrate embryos: the ileum and jejunum develop from it.

‡**Mi·di** (mē′dē′), *n.* [Fr., south, lit. midday; *mi-*, half (< L. *medius*, middle) + *di* (L. *dies*), day], southern France.

Mid·i·an·ite (mid′i-ən-īt′), *n.* [< Heb. *midhyān*, name of a son of Abraham (Gen. 25:2); + *-ite*], in the *Bible*, a member of a nomadic tribe of Arabs that fought the Israelites: Ex. 2:15–22, Numb. 31, Judg. 6–8.

mid·i·ron (mid′ī′ẽrn), *n.* [*mid-* + *iron*], in *golf*, a club with a steel or iron head and little loft, used for fairway shots of medium distance: now usually called *number 2 iron*: see **golf club**, illus.

mid·land (mid′lənd), *n.* 1. the middle region of a country; interior. 2. [M-], the dialects of English spoken or formerly spoken in the Midlands: they are divided into eastern and western groups. 3. [M-], a city in west central Texas: pop., 63,000. 4. [M-], a city in central Michigan: pop., 28,000. *adj.* 1. in or of the midland; inland. 2. [M-], of the Midlands.

the Midlands, the middle counties of England.

mid·leg (mid′leg′), *n.* 1. the middle of the leg. 2. one of the middle, or second, pair of legs of an insect. *adv.* to the middle of the leg.

Mid·lo·thi·an (mid-lō′thi-ən), *n.* a county of southeastern Scotland: pop., 575,000; county seat, Edinburgh: formerly called *Edinburgh.*

mid·most (mid′mōst′), *adj.* [ME. *mydmest* (with *-most* for *-mest* < 17th c. onward); AS. *midmest* < **middjumo*, in the middle + suffix *-ist* (see -EST)], exactly in the middle, or nearest the middle; middlemost. *adv.* in the middle or midst. *prep.* in the middle or midst of.

mid·night (mid′nīt′), *n.* 1. the middle of the night: twelve o'clock at night. 2. deep darkness. *adj.* 1. of or at midnight. 2. like or suggestive of midnight; very dark: as, *midnight* blue.
burn the midnight oil, to study or work very late at night.
midnight sun, the sun visible at midnight in the arctic or antarctic regions during the summer.
mid·noon (mid′nōōn′), *n.* [Rare], noon; midday.
Mid·rash (mid′rash, mid′räsh), *n.* [*pl.* MIDRASHIM (mid-rä′shim), MIDRASHOTH (mid-rä′shōth)], [Heb., explanation], any of the Jewish commentaries and explanatory notes on the Scriptures, written between the beginning of the Exile and c. 1200 A.D.: cf. **Haggada.**
mid·rib (mid′rib′), *n.* the central vein, or rib, of a leaf, usually running from the stem to the apex.
mid·riff (mid′rif), *n.* [ME. *mydrif;* AS. *midhrif* < *midd* (see MID) + *hrif,* belly (akin to OHG. *href,* body) < IE. base **qrep-*, body, seen also in L. *corpus* (cf. CORPSE)], 1. the diaphragm; partition of muscles and tendons between the chest cavity and the abdominal cavity. 2. the middle part of the body, between the abdomen and the chest. *adj.* designating or of a garment that bares this part.
mid·ship (mid′ship′), *adj.* of the middle of a ship.
mid·ship·man (mid′ship′mən), *n.* [*pl.* MIDSHIPMEN (-mən)], [for *amidshipmen,* so called from being *amidships* when on duty], 1. a student in training for the rank of ensign in the United States Navy, especially at the Naval Academy at Annapolis. 2. a junior British naval officer ranking between naval cadet and sublieutenant. 3. formerly, one of a class of ship's boys assigned to British naval vessels to be trained as officers. Abbreviated **mid.**
mid·ship·mite (mid′ship′mīt), *n.* a midshipman: a sailors' humorous alteration.
mid·ships (mid′ships′), *adv.* amidships.
midst (midst, mitst), *n.* [ME. *midest;* merging of *middes, mides,* genit. of *mid,* with unhistoric *-t* < *middest,* superl. of *mid*], the middle; central part: now mainly in phrases. —*SYN.* see **middle.**
in our (or **your, their**) **midst,** among, or in the midst of, us (or you, them).
in the midst of, 1. in the middle of; surrounded by. 2. in the course of; during.
midst, 'midst (midst, mitst), *prep.* [Poetic], in the midst of; amidst; amid.
mid·stream (mid′strēm′), *n.* the middle of a stream.
mid·sum·mer (mid′sum′ẽr), *n.* 1. the middle of summer. 2. popularly, the time of the summer solstice, about June 21. *adj.* of, in, or like midsummer.
Midsummer Night's Dream, A, a comedy (c. 1596) by Shakespeare.
mid·term (mid′tũrm′), *adj.* occurring in the middle of the term. *n. often in pl.* [Colloq.], a midterm examination, as in a college course.
mid-Vic·to·ri·an (mid′vik-tôr′i-ən, mid′vik-tō′ri-ən), *adj.* 1. of, like, or characteristic of the middle part of Queen Victoria's reign in Great Britain (c. 1850–1890) or the culture, morals, or art of this period in Britain and the United States; hence, 2. old-fashioned, prudish, morally strict, stuffy, etc. *n.* 1. a person who lived during this period. 2. a person of mid-Victorian ideas, manners, attitudes, etc.
mid·way (mid′wā′; *also, for adj. & adv.,* mid′wā′), *n.* [ME. *midwei;* AS. *midweg*], 1. originally, *a*) the middle of the way or distance. *b*) a middle way or course. 2. that part of a fair or exposition where side shows and other amusements are located. *adj. & adv.* in the middle of the way or distance; halfway.
Midway Islands, a group of islands in the North Pacific, part of the Hawaiian group, about halfway between the United States and the Philippines: area, 28 sq. mi.; pop., 440: an air and naval base.
mid·week (mid′wēk′), *n.* 1. the middle of the week. 2. [M-], Wednesday: so called by the Friends (Quakers). *adj.* in the middle of the week.
mid·week·ly (mid′wēk′li), *adj.* midweek. *adv.* in the middle of the week.
Mid·west (mid′west′), *n.* the Middle West. *adj.* Midwestern.
Mid·west·ern (mid′wes′tẽrn), *adj.* of, in, or characteristic of the Middle West; Middle Western.
Mid·west·ern·er (mid′wes′tẽr-nẽr), *n.* a native or inhabitant of the Middle West; Middle Westerner.
mid·wife (mid′wīf′), *n.* [*pl.* MIDWIVES (-wīvz′)], [ME. *midwyf* < *mid* (AS. *mid;* akin to G. *mit*), with + *wif,* wife (in orig. sense of "woman"); hence basic sense "woman with, woman assisting"], a woman who helps women in childbirth.
mid·wife·ry (mid′wīf′ẽr-i, mid′wif′ri), *n.* the work of a midwife; obstetrics.
mid·win·ter (mid′win′tẽr), *n.* 1. the middle of the winter. 2. popularly, the time of the winter solstice, about December 22. *adj.* of, in, or like midwinter.
mid·year (mid′yêr′), *adj.* occurring in the middle of the (calendar or academic) year. *n. often in pl.* [Colloq.], a midyear examination, as at college.
mien (mēn), *n.* [short for *demean;* associated with Fr. *mine,* look, air, whence also G. *miene*], way of carrying and conducting oneself; manner. —*SYN.* see **bearing.**
miff (mif), *n.* [prob. orig. cry of disgust; cf. G. *muffen,* to sulk], [Colloq.], a trivial quarrel or fit of the sulks; tiff or huff. *v.t. & v.i.* [Colloq.], to offend or take offense; put or be out of humor.
mig·gle (mig′'l), *n.* [dim. of dial. *mig,* a marble], [Dial.], 1. a playing marble. 2. *pl.* the game of marbles.
might (mīt), *v.* [ME. & AS. *mihte*], 1. past tense of **may.** 2. an auxiliary with present or future sense, generally equivalent to *may* in meaning and use, expressing especially a shade of doubt or a smaller degree of possibility (e.g., it *might* rain) or permission (e.g., *might* I go?).
might (mīt), *n.* [ME. *mighte;* AS. *miht, mæht;* akin to G. *macht;* IE. base **māgh-*, **məgh-*, to be able, be capable of; cf. MAY, *v.,* MAIN (strength)], great strength, power, force, or vigor. —*SYN.* see **strength.**
with might and main, with strength and vigor.
might·i·ly (mīt′'l-i), *adv.* 1. in a mighty manner; strongly; powerfully. 2. very much; to a great degree.
might·i·ness (mīt′i-nis), *n.* the quality or state of being mighty.
might·y (mīt′i), *adj.* [MIGHTIER (-i-ẽr), MIGHTIEST (-i-ist)], 1. having might; powerful; strong. 2. great; remarkably large, extensive, etc. *adv.* [Colloq.], very; extremely.
mi·gnon (min′yon; Fr. mē′nyōn′), *adj.* [*fem.* MIGNONNE (min′yən; Fr. mē′nyôn′)], [Fr., for OFr. *mignot,* dainty < Gaul. **mino*, delicate; akin to OIr. *mīn,* gentle, mild], small, delicately formed, and pretty; dainty.
mi·gnon·ette (min′yə-net′), *n.* [Fr. *mignonnette,* dim. of *mignon;* see MIGNON], 1. a plant with wedge-shaped leaves, and spikes of small, fragrant, greenish-white flowers. 2. any of a number of plants related to this.
mi·graine (mī′grān, mi-grān′), *n.* [Fr.; LL. *hemicrania;* Gr. *hēmikrania* < *hēmi-,* half + *kranion,* skull], a type of periodically returning headache, usually limited to one side of the head and often accompanied by vertigo, nausea, etc.
mi·grant (mī′grənt), *adj.* [L. *migrans,* ppr. of *migrare*], migrating; migratory. *n.* a person, bird, or other animal that migrates.
mi·grate (mī′grāt), *v.i.* [MIGRATED (-id), MIGRATING], [< L. *migratus,* pp. of *migrare,* to move from one place to another, change], 1. to move from one place to another; especially, to leave one's country and settle in another. 2. to move from one region to another with the change in seasons, as many birds and some fishes.
SYN.—**migrate** denotes a moving from one region or country to another and may imply, of people, intention to settle in a new land, or, of animals, a periodical movement influenced by climate, food supply, etc.; **emigrate** and **immigrate** are used only of people, **emigrate** specifically denoting the leaving of a country to settle in another, and **immigrate,** the coming into the new country.
mi·gra·tion (mī-grā′shən), *n.* [L. *migratio*], 1. a migrating. 2. a group of people or birds, fishes, etc. migrating together. 3. in *chemistry, a*) the shifting of one or more atoms from one position in the molecule to another. *b*) the movement of ions toward one electrode or the other, under the influence of electromotive force.
mi·gra·tor (mī′grā-tẽr), *n.* a person or animal that migrates; specifically, a migratory bird.
mi·gra·to·ry (mī′grə-tôr′i, mī′grə-tō′ri), *adj.* 1. migrating; characterized by migration. 2. of migration. 3. roving; wandering; nomadic.
mi·ka·do (mi-kä′dō), *n.* [*pl.* MIKADOS (-dōz)], [Japan., lit., exalted gate (i.e., of the Imperial palace); *mi,* exalted + *kado,* gate, door], [often M-], the emperor of Japan: title used by non-Japanese.
mike (mīk), *n.* [Slang], a microphone.
mi·kron (mī′kron), *n.* a micron.
mil (mil), *n.* [L. *mille,* thousand], 1. a unit of length, equal to .001 of an inch (25.4001 microns), used in measuring the diameter of wire. 2. a milliliter; cubic centimeter. 3. a monetary unit or coin of Israel, equal to .001 of the Israeli pound. 4. in *military usage, a*) a unit of angle measurement for artillery fire, equal to 1/6400 of the circumference of a circle: in full, **artillery mil.** *b*) less frequently, a unit equal to 1.018 artillery mils: in full, **infantry mil.**
mil., 1. military. 2. militia.
mi·la·dy, mi·la·di (mi-lā′di), *n.* [Fr. < Eng. *my lady*], an English noblewoman or gentlewoman: Continental term used in speaking to or of such a woman.
mil·age (mīl′ij), *n.* mileage.
Mi·lan (mi-lan′, mil′ən), *n.* a city in northern Italy: pop., 1,264,000 (1947): Italian name, *Milano.*
Mil·a·nese (mil′ə-nēz′), *adj.* of Milan, its people, or their culture. *n.* [*pl.* MILANESE], a native or inhabitant of Milan.
Mi·la·no (mē-lä′nô), *n.* Milan: the Italian name.
Mi·laz·zo (mē-lät′tsô), *n.* a seaport in northeastern Sicily: pop., 20,000.
milch (milch), *adj.* [ME. *milche,* milk-giving; AS. *-milce, -meolc* (akin to G. *melk*); prob. a form of *milk* evolved from use in compounds], giving milk; kept for milking: as, *milch* cows.

mild (mīld), ***adj.*** [ME. & AS. *milde;* akin to G. *mild;* IE. **mel-dh* (cf. L. *mollis,* soft < **moldwis*) < base **mel-,* to rub, grind, triturate, seen also in *melt, malt,* etc. basic sense "softened or weakened by or as by rubbing"], 1. gentle or kind in disposition, action, or effect; not severe, harsh, bitter, etc.; not extreme in any way; moderate; temperate: as, a *mild* nature. 2. having a soft, pleasant taste or flavor; not strong, sour, bitter, biting, or sharp: said of tobacco, cheese, etc. 3. designating steel that is tough but malleable and contains only a small percentage of carbon. —***SYN.*** see **soft.**

mild·en (mīl′d'n), ***v.t. & v.i.*** to make or become mild or milder.

mil·dew (mil′do͞o′, mil′dū′), ***n.*** [ME. *mildewe, meldewe;* AS. *meledeaw, mildeaw;* akin to G. (folk etym.) *mehlthau;* lit. meaning, "honeydew" < Gmc. base **melith,* honey + base of AS. *deaw,* dew], 1. any fungus that attacks various plants or appears on organic matter, paper, leather, etc., especially when exposed to damp, resulting in a thin, furry, whitish coating or discoloration. 2. any such coating or discoloration; mold. 3. any plant disease caused by such a fungus. ***v.t. & v.i.*** to affect or be affected with mildew.

mil·dew·y (mil′do͞o′i, mil′dū′i), ***adj.*** 1. mildewed. 2. like, or having the nature of, mildew.

mild·ly (mīld′li), ***adv.*** 1. in a mild manner. 2. to a mild extent; somewhat.
to put it mildly, to state it with restraint.

Mil·dred (mil′drid), [AS. *Myldthryth* < *milde,* mild + *thryth,* power, strength], a feminine name: diminutives, *Mil, Millie, Milly.*

mile (mīl), ***n.*** [*pl.* MILES (mīlz), *dial.* MILE], [ME.; AS. *mil,* pl. *mila, mile;* L. *milia, millia,* pl. of *mille,* thousand, in *milia passuum,* thousand paces, mile], a unit of linear measure, equal to 1,760 yards (5,280 feet or 1,609.35 meters), used in the United States, Great Britain, etc.: in full, **statute mile:** it is derived from an ancient Roman measure of 1,000 paces (c. 1,620 yards). The *geographical* (or *nautical, sea,* or *air*) *mile* is 1/60 of one degree of the earth's equator, by international agreement (1954), 6,076.10333 feet. Abbreviated **mi., M., m.**

mile·age (mīl′ij), ***n.*** [see -AGE], 1. an allowance for traveling expenses at a specified amount per mile. 2. aggregate distance in miles or total number of miles traveled or covered. 3. expense or charge per mile, as for travel or the use of railroad freight cars. 4. a mileage book. Also spelled **milage.**

mileage book, a book of detachable coupons or tickets (*mileage tickets*), each entitling a person to transportation for a stated number of miles.

mile·post (mīl′pōst′), ***n.*** a signpost showing the distance in miles to or from a specified place.

mil·er (mīl′ẽr), ***n.*** one trained to race a mile.

Miles (mīlz), [OFr. *Miles, Milon* < OHG. *Milo*], a masculine name.

‡**mi·les glo·ri·o·sus** (mī′lēz glō′ri-ō′səs), [L.], a braggart, swashbuckling soldier: the title character in Plautus' comedy.

Mi·le·sian (mə-lē′zhən, mə-lē′shən), ***adj.*** of Miletus. ***n.*** a native or inhabitant of Miletus.

Mi·le·sian (mə-lē′zhən, mə-lē′shən), ***adj.*** [< *Milesius* (Latinized form of Ir. *mileadh,* hero, champion; ult. < L. *miles, militis,* a soldier), legendary Spanish king whose sons reputedly conquered Ireland c. 1300 B.C.; + *-an*], Irish. ***n.*** 1. a legendary ancestor of the Irish. 2. an Irishman.

mile·stone (mīl′stōn′), ***n.*** 1. a stone or pillar set up to show the distance in miles to or from a specified place. 2. a significant or important event in the history or career of a person, the human race, etc.

Mi·le·tus (mī-lē′təs), ***n.*** an ancient Greek city in western Asia Minor, now in ruins.

mil·foil (mil′foil′), ***n.*** [ME.; OFr.; L. *millefolium; mille,* thousand + *folium,* leaf: from the finely divided leaves], the yarrow, a plant of the composite family.

Mil·ford Ha·ven (mil′fẽrd hā′v'n), a seaport in southwestern Wales: pop., 10,000.

Mil·haud, Da·rius (då′ryüs′ mē′yō′), 1892– ; French composer in America.

mil·i·a·ri·a (mil′i-âr′i-ə), ***n.*** [Mod. L.; properly fem. of L. *miliarius;* see MILIARY], an acute skin disease resulting from inflammation of the sweat glands and characterized by small white or red papules or vesicles: also called *prickly heat, heat rash.*

mil·i·ar·y (mil′i-er′i, mil′yə-ri), ***adj.*** [L. *miliarius* < *milium,* millet], 1. like a millet seed or seeds. 2. in *medicine,* characterized or accompanied by papules or vesicles about the size of millet seeds.

miliary tuberculosis, a form of tuberculosis in which the tubercle bacilli spread through the blood stream from a primary focus of infection to other parts of the body, where multiple tubercles are formed.

Mil·i·cent (mil′ə-s'nt), a feminine name: see **Millicent.**

mi·lieu (mēl-yoo′; Fr. mē′lyö′), ***n.*** [Fr., lit., middle; OFr. *mi* (< L. *medius*), middle + *lieu* (< L. *locus*), a place], surroundings; environment.

milit., military.

mil·i·tan·cy (mil′i-tən-si), ***n.*** the state or quality of being militant; fighting spirit, attitude, or policy.

mil·i·tant (mil′i-tənt), ***adj.*** [L. *militans,* ppr. of *militare,* to serve as a soldier < *miles, militis,* a soldier], 1. fighting. 2. ready and willing to fight; warlike; combative. ***n.*** a militant person. —***SYN.*** see **aggressive.**

mil·i·tar·i·ly (mil′ə-ter′ə-li), ***adv.*** 1. in a military manner. 2. from a military standpoint.

mil·i·ta·rism (mil′i-tə-riz′m), ***n.*** [Fr. *militarisme*], 1. military spirit; ideals and attitudes of professional soldiers. 2. the glorification or prevalence of such a spirit, ideals, etc. in a nation, or the predominance of the military caste in government. 3. the policy of maintaining strong armed forces and being ready and willing to use them; aggressive preparedness.

mil·i·ta·rist (mil′i-tə-rist), ***n.*** 1. a person who supports or advocates militarism. 2. an expert or specialist in war and military affairs.

mil·i·ta·ris·tic (mil′i-tə-ris′tik), ***adj.*** of, characteristic of, or characterized by militarism.

mil·i·ta·ris·ti·cal·ly (mil′i-tə-ris′ti-k'l-i, mil′i-tə-ris′tik-li), ***adv.*** in a militaristic manner.

mil·i·ta·ri·za·tion (mil′i-tə-ri-zā′shən, mil′i-tə-rī-zā′shən), ***n.*** a militarizing or being militarized.

mil·i·ta·rize (mil′i-tə-rīz′), ***v.t.*** [MILITARIZED (-rīzd′), MILITARIZING], 1. to make military; equip and prepare for war. 2. to fill with militarism; make warlike.

mil·i·tar·y (mil′ə-ter′i), ***adj.*** [Fr. *militaire;* L. *militaris* < *miles, militis,* a soldier], 1. of, characteristic of, for, fit for, or done by soldiers or the armed forces. 2. of, for, or fit for war. 3. of the army: distinguished from *naval.* ***n.*** soldiers collectively; the army; troops (with *the*): as, the *military* took control of the government. Abbreviated **mil., milit.** —***SYN.*** see **martial.**

military attaché, an army officer attached to his nation's embassy or legation in a foreign country.

military intelligence, 1. any information of military value to a nation. 2. the military department or branch whose work is getting, analyzing, and using such information. Abbreviated **M.I.**

military law, the branch of law concerned with the government and discipline of the armed forces, whether in time of war or in time of peace.

military police, troops assigned to carry on police duties for the army: abbreviated **MP, M.P.**

mil·i·tate (mil′ə-tāt′), ***v.i.*** [MILITATED (-id), MILITATING], [< L. *militatus,* pp. of *militare,* to be a soldier; see MILITANT], 1. originally, to serve as a soldier; fight (*against*); hence, 2. to be directed (*against*); operate or work (*against* or, rarely, *for*): said of facts, evidence, actions, etc., as, his youth *militated* against him.

mi·li·tia (mə-lish′ə), ***n.*** [L., military service, soldiery < *miles, militis,* a soldier], 1. *a*) originally, any military force. *b*) later, any army composed of citizens rather than professional soldiers, called out in time of emergency. 2. in the United States, all able-bodied male citizens between 18 and 45 years old who are not already members of the regular armed forces: members of the National Guard, Organized Reserve Corps (Army and Air), and the Naval and Marine Reserves constitute the *organized militia;* all others, the *unorganized militia.* Abbreviated **mil.**

mi·li·tia·man (mə-lish′ə-mən), ***n.*** [*pl.* MILITIAMEN (-mən)], a member of the militia.

mil·i·um (mil′i-əm), ***n.*** [*pl.* MILIA (-ə)], [L., millet], a small, whitish nodule of the skin, somewhat like a millet seed, resulting from retention of the secretion of a sebaceous gland.

milk (milk), ***n.*** [ME. *milke, melk;* AS. *meolc, milc;* akin to G. *milch;* IE. base **melĝ-,* to stroke, press out, wipe off, hence to milk (an animal), seen also in L. *mulgere,* to milk (cf. EMULSION)], 1. a white or yellowish liquid secreted by the mammary glands of female mammals for suckling their young; especially, cow's milk. 2. any liquid like this, as the juice of various plants, trees, or fruits (e.g., coconut milk), or any of various emulsions. ***v.t.*** 1. *a*) to draw or press milk from the mammary glands of (a cow, etc.). *b*) to draw (milk). 2. to draw (*out*) or drain off; extract as if by milking. 3. to drain off or extract money, ideas, strength, etc. from as if by milking; exploit. 4. to extract juice, sap, venom, etc. from. 5. to draw out (information, etc.), as if by milking. ***v.i.*** 1. to give milk. 2. to draw milk.
cry over spilt milk, to feel sorry in vain about something that has happened and cannot be undone.

milk adder, a milk snake.

milk-and-wa·ter (milk′ən-wô′tẽr, milk′ən-wät′ẽr), ***adj.*** insipid; weak; wishy-washy; namby-pamby.

milk·er (mil′kẽr), ***n.*** 1. a person who milks. 2. a machine for milking cows, etc. 3. a cow or other animal that gives milk (usually preceded by *good, bad,* etc.).

milk fever, 1. a mild fever sometimes occurring with

the first secretion of milk in the breasts after childbirth: it is caused by infection. 2. a somewhat similar condition often occurring in dairy cows shortly after calving, characterized by paralysis, etc.
milk·fish (milk′fish′), *n.* [*pl.* MILKFISH, MILKFISHES (-iz); see FISH], a large, silvery, herringlike sea fish.
milk·i·ness (mil′ki-nis), *n.* a milky quality or state.
milk·ing (mil′kiŋ), *n.* 1. the act of one that milks. 2. the quantity of milk drawn at one time.
milk leg, a condition characterized by painful swelling of the legs, caused by inflammation and clotting of the femoral veins: so called because it occurs most often during lactation after childbirth.
milk-liv·ered (milk′liv′ẽrd), *adj.* timid; cowardly.
milk·maid (milk′mād′), *n.* a girl or woman who milks cows or works in a dairy; dairymaid.
milk·man (milk′man′), *n.* [*pl.* MILKMEN (-men′)], a man who sells or delivers milk.
milk of human kindness, natural feelings of sympathy, generosity, etc.
milk of magnesia, a milky-white fluid, a suspension of magnesium hydroxide, $Mg(OH)_2$, in water, used as a laxative and antacid.
milk shake, a drink made of milk, flavoring, and, usually, ice cream, mixed or shaken until frothy.
milk·shed (milk′shed′), *n.* [*milk* + *-shed* as in *watershed*], all the dairy farm areas supplying milk for a given city.
milk sickness, a rare disease, formerly common in the western United States, caused by drinking the milk or eating the milk products or flesh of cattle that have eaten any of various poisonous weeds.
milk snake, a small, harmless snake, gray with black-rimmed markings, related to the king snake: also called *milk adder, house snake.*
milk·sop (milk′sop′), *n.* an unmanly man or boy; mollycoddle; sissy.
milk sugar, lactose, a sugar obtained from milk.
milk tooth, any of the temporary, first set of teeth in a young child or other mammal: also called *baby tooth.*
milk vetch, a plant that supposedly increases the secretion of milk in goats that eat it.
milk·weed (milk′wēd′), *n.* 1. any of a group of plants with a milky juice, or latex. 2. any of various plants resembling or related to these.
milk-white (milk′hwīt′), *adj.* white as milk.
milk·wort (milk′wũrt′), *n.* any of a group of plants with showy flowers of various colors, including the *orange milkwort* of the southeastern United States: so called from the former notion that they increase the secretion of milk in nursing women.
milk·y (mil′ki), *adj.* [MILKIER (-ki-ẽr), MILKIEST (-ki-ist)], 1. like milk; especially, white as milk. 2. of, containing, or yielding milk. 3. timid, meek, etc.
Milky Way, a broad, faintly luminous band seen across the sky at night, consisting of innumerable stars and nebulae so distant as to be indistinguishable without a telescope; the Galaxy.
mill (mil), *n.* [ME. *myln, mille;* AS. *mylen, myln* < LL. *molina* < *mola,* millstone (whence *molere,* to grind; cf. MOLAR)], 1. a building with machinery for grinding grain into flour or meal. 2. a machine for grinding grain. 3. a machine for grinding or pulverizing any solid material: as, a coffee *mill.* 4. a machine for grinding or crushing fruits or vegetables to press out the juice: as, a cider *mill.* 5. any of various machines for stamping, shaping, polishing, or dressing metal surfaces, coins, etc., or for making something by some action done again and again. 6. a building or group of buildings with machinery for manufacturing something; factory: as, a textile *mill.* 7. a roller of hardened steel with a raised design on it, for making a die or printing plate by pressure. 8. a milling cutter. 9. a raised edge, ridged surface, etc. made by milling. 10. [< the *v.*], [Slang], a fist fight; pugilistic encounter. ***v.t.*** 1. to grind, work, form, polish, etc. by, in, or as in a mill. 2. to raise and ridge the edge of (a coin), as a safeguard against wear and clipping. 3. to beat or whip (chocolate, etc.) to a froth. 4. to put (cattle) into circular motion. 5. [Slang], to beat with or as with the fists; thrash. ***v.i.*** 1. to move slowly in a circle, as cattle or a confused crowd (often with *around*). 2. [Slang], to fight with the fists; box.
through the mill, [Colloq.], through a hard, painful, instructive experience, training, test, etc.
mill (mil), *n.* [for L. *millesimus,* thousandth < *mille,* thousand; cf. CENT], one tenth of a cent; **$.001:** a monetary unit used in calculating but not as a coin: abbreviated **mi., M., m.** (*sing. & pl.*).
Mill, James (mil), 1773–1836; Scottish historian, utilitarian philosopher, and political economist.
Mill, John Stuart, 1806–1873; son of *James;* English philosopher and political economist.
Mil·lais, Sir **John Everett** (mi-lā′), 1829–1896; English painter.
Mil·lay, Edna St. Vincent (mi-lā′), 1892–1950; American poet.
mill·board (mil′bôrd′, mil′bōrd′), *n.* a heavy, flexible pasteboard used in bookbinding, etc.
mill·cake (mil′kāk′), *n.* the residue left after the oil has been pressed from linseed.
mill·dam (mil′dam′), *n.* 1. a dam built across a stream to raise its level enough to provide water power for turning a mill wheel. 2. a millpond.
milled (mild), *adj.* 1. ground, cut, worked, etc. by or in a mill. 2. having the edges raised and ridged or grooved, as a coin.
mil·le·nar·i·an (mil′ə-nâr′i-ən), *adj.* [< LL. *millenarius,* containing a thousand < L. *milleni,* a thousand each < *mille,* thousand; + *-an*], of a thousand years; of the millennium. *n.* a person who believes in the coming of the millennium.
mil·le·nar·y (mil′ə-ner′i), *adj.* [see MILLENARIAN], 1. of or consisting of a thousand, especially a thousand years. 2. of the millennium or millenarians. *n.* [*pl.* MILLENARIES (-iz)], 1. a thousand. 2. a thousand years; millennium. 3. a thousandth anniversary. 4. a millenarian.
mil·len·ni·al (mi-len′i-əl), *adj.* 1. of a thousand years. 2. of, suggestive of, or fit for the millennium.
mil·len·ni·um (mi-len′i-əm), *n.* [*pl.* MILLENNIUMS (-əmz), MILLENNIA (-ə)], [Mod. L. < L. *mille,* thousand + *annus,* year], 1. a period of a thousand years. 2. in *theology,* the period of a thousand years during which Satan will be bound and Christ will reign on earth (with *the*): Rev. 20:1–5; hence, 3. any period of great happiness, peace, prosperity, etc.; imagined golden age.
mil·le·pede (mil′ə-pēd′), *n.* [L. *millepeda* < *mille,* thousand + *pes, pedis,* a foot], a wormlike arthropod (*myriapod*) with two pairs of legs on each of most of its segments: also **millipede, milliped.**
mil·le·pore (mil′ə-pôr′, mil′ə-pōr′), *n.* [Fr. *millépore* < *mille,* thousand + *pore,* a pore], any of a group of hydrozoans that form branching or leaflike masses of coral with many very small openings on the surface.
mill·er (mil′ẽr), *n.* [ME. *mylnere, mulnere*], 1. a person who owns or operates a mill, especially a flour mill. 2. *a*) a milling machine. *b*) a tool to be used in such a machine. 3. any of various moths with wings that look dusty or powdered, suggesting a miller's clothes.
Mil·ler, Arthur (mil′ẽr), 1915– ; American dramatist.
Miller, Joa·quin (wä-kēn′), (pseudonym of *Cincinnatus Heine Miller*), 1841–1913; American poet.
Miller, Joe (jō), 1684–1738; English stage comedian: *Joe Miller's Jest-book* (1739), a book of jokes attributed to him, was published after his death.
Mille·rand, Al·ex·an·dre (à′lek′sän′dr′ mēl′rän′), 1859–1943; French statesman; president (1920–1924).
Mill·er·ite (mil′ẽr-īt′), *n.* a follower of William Miller (1782–1849), an American preacher who prophesied that the end of the world and the second coming of Christ would occur in 1843.
mill·er·ite (mil′ẽr-īt′), *n.* [after W. H. *Miller,* mineralogist at Cambridge University; + *-ite*], native nickel sulfide, NiS, a brassy-yellow, crystalline mineral.
mill·er's-thumb (mil′ẽrz-thum′), *n.* 1. any of several small fresh-water fishes with spiny fins and a broad, flat head. 2. in England, any of various small birds.
mil·les·i·mal (mi-les′i-m′l), *adj.* [L. *millesimus* < *mille,* thousand], 1. thousandth. 2. of or consisting of thousandths. *n.* a thousandth.
mil·let (mil′it), *n.* [see PLURAL, II, D, 3], [Fr., dim. of *mil* < L. *milium,* millet], 1. *a*) a cereal grass whose small grain is used for food in Europe and Asia. *b*) the grain. 2. any of several other similar grasses or their seed, as *Italian millet, pearl millet,* etc. Millet is used for hay in both the United States and Europe.
Mil·let, Jean Fran·çois (zhän′ frän′swå′ mē′le′; Eng. mi-lā′), 1814–1875; French painter.
mil·li- (mil′i, mil′ə), [< L. *mille,* thousand], a combining form meaning: 1. *one thousandth part of* (a specified unit), as in *millimeter.* 2. *one thousand,* as in *millifold.*
mil·li·am·pere (mil′i-am′pêr), *n.* one thousandth of an ampere.
mil·liard (mil′yẽrd, mil′yärd), *n.* [Fr. < Pr. *milhar,* thousand (associated in Fr. with *mille,* thousand) < L. *milliarius,* containing a thousand < *mille,* thousand], [British], one thousand millions; billion.
mil·li·ar·y (mil′i-er′i, mil′i-ẽr-i), *adj.* [L. *milliarius;* see MILLIARD], of the ancient Roman mile, or 1,000 paces. *n.* [*pl.* MILLIARIES (-iz)], an ancient Roman milestone.
mil·li·bar (mil′ə-bär′), *n.* [< *milli-* + Gr. *baros,* weight], a unit of measure of atmospheric pressure, equal to one thousand dynes per square centimeter.
Mil·li·cent (mil′ə-s′nt), [OFr. *Melisent;* OHG. *Amalaswind* < *amal,* work + **swind-,* strong, akin to Goth. *swinths*], a feminine name: also **Melicent, Milicent.**
‡mil·lier (mē′lyā′), *n.* [Fr. < L. *mille,* thousand], a metric ton; 1,000 kilograms.
mil·li·far·ad (mil′ə-far′əd, mil′ə-far′ad), *n.* one thousandth of a farad: abbreviated **mf.**
mil·li·gram, mil·li·gramme (mil′ə-gram′), *n.* [Fr. *milligramme*], one thousandth of a gram (.0154 of a grain): abbreviated **mg.** (*sing. & pl.*).
Mil·li·kan, Robert Andrews (mil′ə-kən), 1868–1953; American physicist; received Nobel prize in physics, 1923.
mil·li·li·ter, mil·li·li·tre (mil′ə-lē′tẽr), *n.* [Fr. *milli-*

litre], one thousandth of a liter (1.000027 cubic centimeters or .06102 cubic inch): abbreviated **ml.**

mil·li·me·ter, mil·li·me·tre (mil'ə-mē'tẽr), *n.* [Fr. *millimètre*], one thousandth of a meter (.03937 inch): abbreviated **mm.** (*sing. & pl.*).

mil·li·mi·cron (mil'ə-mī'kron), *n.* one thousandth of a micron, one millionth of a millimeter, or ten angstroms: a unit of length for measuring waves of light, etc.: symbol, mμ (no period).

mil·line (mil'līn'), *n.* [< *million* + *line*], 1. a unit of measurement equal to a one-column agate line (of an advertisement) in one million copies of some publication. 2. the cost per milline of an advertisement.

mil·li·ner (mil'ə-nẽr), *n.* [< *Milaner*, inhabitant of Milan, importer of silks, ribbons, etc. from Milan], 1. a person who designs, makes, trims, or sells women's hats, headdresses, etc. 2. [Obs.], a dealer in ribbons, lace, gloves, etc., especially those imported from Milan.

mil·li·ner·y (mil'ə-ner'i, mil'ə-nẽr-i), *n.* [< *milliner*], 1. women's hats, headdresses, etc. 2. the work or business of making or selling women's hats, etc.

mill·ing (mil'iŋ), *n.* [< *mill*, *v.*], 1. the process or business of grinding grain into flour or meal. 2. the grinding, cutting, working, or manufacturing of metal, cloth, etc. in a mill. 3. the process of raising and ridging the edge of a coin, etc. 4. the ridging thus produced; milled edge or surface. 5. a slow, circular motion of or as of a herd of cattle. 6. [Slang], a beating; thrashing.

milling machine, a power tool for cutting and grinding metal parts.

mil·lion (mil'yən), *n.* [Late ME.; OFr.; It. *milione* (orig. *millione*) < *mille* (L. *mille*), thousand], 1. a thousand thousands; 1,000,000. 2. a million (unspecified but understood) monetary units, as dollars, pounds, francs, etc.: as, he has made a *million*. 3. an indefinite but very large number; very many. *adj.* 1. one thousand thousand. 2. very many.

the million, the common people; the masses.

mil·lion·aire (mil'yən-âr'), *n.* [Fr. *millionnaire*], 1. a person whose wealth comes to at least a million dollars, pounds, francs, etc. 2. a very wealthy person. Also spelled **millionnaire.**

mil·lion·fold (mil'yən-fōld'), *adj. & adv.* [see -FOLD], a million times as much or as many.

mil·lionth (mil'yənth), *adj.* 1. coming last in a series of a million. 2. designating any of the million equal parts of something. *n.* 1. the millionth one of a series. 2. any of the million equal parts of something.

mil·li·ped (mil'ə-ped'), *n.* a millepede.

mil·li·pede (mil'ə-pēd'), *n.* a millepede.

mil·li·volt (mil'ə-vōlt'), *n.* one thousandth of a volt.

mill·pond (mil'pond'), *n.* a pond formed by a milldam, from which water flows for driving a mill wheel.

mill·race (mil'rās'), *n.* 1. the current of water that drives a mill wheel. 2. the channel in which it runs.

mill·run (mil'run'), *n.* 1. a millrace. 2. a quantity of ore whose quality or mineral content is tested by milling. 3. the mineral obtained by such testing.

mill-run (mil'run'), *adj.* just as it comes out of the mill; ordinary; average: also **run-of-the-mill.**

Mills bomb (or **grenade**) (milz), [after Sir Wm. *Mills* (1856–1932), Brit. inventor], a highly explosive hand grenade weighing about 1 1/2 pounds.

mill·stone (mil'stōn'), *n.* 1. either of a pair of large, flat, round stones used for grinding grain or other substances. 2. stone used for these, usually a hard sandstone or conglomerate. 3. a heavy burden: Matt. 18:6. 4. something that grinds, pulverizes, or crushes.

mill·stream (mil'strēm'), *n.* the water flowing in a millrace.

mill wheel, the wheel, usually a water wheel, that drives the machinery in a mill.

mill·work (mil'wũrk'), *n.* 1. objects made in a mill; especially, doors, windows, etc. made in a planing mill. 2. work done in a mill.

mill·wright (mil'rīt'), *n.* [see WRIGHT, *n.*], 1. a person who designs, builds, or installs mills or their machinery. 2. a worker who installs, attends, or repairs the shafting, belting, and other machinery in a mill.

Milne, A. A. (miln), (*Alan Alexander Milne*), 1882–1956; English playwright, novelist, and writer of children's books.

Mi·lo (mī'lō), a masculine name. *n.* a famous ancient Greek athlete, c. 520 B.C.

Mi·lo (mē'lô), *n.* Melos: the Italian name.

mi·lo (mī'lō), *n.* [< Bantu (Sesuto) *maili*], a sorghum resembling millet, grown as a dry-land forage crop in the United States.

mi·lord (mi-lôrd'), *n.* [Fr. < Eng. *my lord*], an English nobleman or gentleman: Continental term used in speaking to or of such a man.

milque·toast (milk'tōst'), *n.* [< Caspar *Milquetoast*, character of this sort in a comic strip by H. T. Webster (1885–1952), Am. cartoonist; cf. MILKSOP], any timid, shrinking, apologetic person.

mil·reis (mil'rās'), *n.* [*pl.* MILREIS], [Port. *mil reis*, lit., a thousand reis], 1. a former Brazilian monetary unit and silver coin, equivalent to 1,000 reis: superseded in 1942 by the *cruzeiro*. 2. a former Portuguese monetary unit and gold coin: superseded in 1911 by the *escudo*. Also **reis.**

milt (milt), *n.* [ME. *milte;* AS. *milte, multi;* akin to G. *milz;* prob. IE. base **mel-d*, to rub down, grind, weaken; cf. MELT, MILD], 1. the reproductive glands of male fishes, especially when filled with germ cells and the milky fluid containing them. 2. such cells and fluid; fish sperm. *adj.* breeding: said of male fishes. *v.t.* to fertilize (fish roe) with milt.

milt (milt), *n.* [ME. & AS. *milte;* akin to G. *milz;* base as in prec. *milt*: prob. with reference to the supposed digestive function], the spleen.

milt·er (mil'tẽr), *n.* 1. a male fish, especially in breeding time. 2. its milt.

Mil·ti·a·des (mil-tī'ə-dēz'), *n.* Athenian general; fl. c. 500 B.C.; defeated Persia at Marathon in 490 B.C.

Mil·ton (mil't'n), [< surname or place name *Milton*, of two sources: AS. *Middel-tun*, lit., Middletown; or AS. *Mylen-tun*, lit., Mill town], a masculine name: diminutives, *Milt, Miltie*.

Mil·ton, John (mil't'n), 1608–1674; English poet.

Mil·to·ni·an (mil-tō'ni-ən), *adj.* Miltonic.

Mil·ton·ic (mil-ton'ik), *adj.* 1. of John Milton or his writings. 2. like or characteristic of Milton or his writings; solemn, elevated, majestic, etc.

Mil·wau·kee (mil-wô'ki), *n.* a city in southeastern Wisconsin, on Lake Michigan: pop., 741,000.

mim (mim), *adj.* [echoic of pursing lips; cf. MUM], [British Dial.], demure; primly quiet or shy.

mime (mīm), *n.* [L. *mimus;* Gr. *mimos*, imitator, actor], 1. *a*) an ancient Greek or Roman farce, in which people and events were mimicked and burlesqued. *b*) dialogue for this. 2. a modern play of this kind. 3. an actor in such a farce. 4. a clown, jester, buffoon, or mimic. *v.t.* [MIMED (mīmd), MIMING], to imitate, mimic, or act out as a mime. *v.i.* to act as a mime; play a part with gestures and actions, but usually without words.

mim·e·o·graph (mim'i-ə-graf', mim'i-ə-gräf'), *n.* [< Gr. *mimeisthai*, to imitate; + *-graph*], a machine for making copies of written or typewritten matter or drawings by means of a stencil cut on a typewriter or with a stylus: formerly a trade-mark (**Mimeograph**). *v.t.* 1. to make copies of on such a machine. 2. to make (copies) on such a machine.

mi·me·sis (mi-mē'sis, mī-mē'sis), *n.* [Mod. L.; Gr. *mimēsis*, imitation (cf. Aristotle's usage in *Poetics*) < *mimos*, imitator], imitation; specifically, *a*) in *art & literature*, imitation or representation, especially of human speech, behavior, etc. *b*) in *biology*, mimicry.

mi·met·ic (mi-met'ik, mī-met'ik), *adj.* [Gr. *mimētikos* < *mimeisthai*, to imitate], 1. imitative; of or characterized by imitation. 2. make-believe; mimic. 3. of or characterized by mimicry.

mim·ic (mim'ik), *adj.* [L. *mimicus;* Gr. *mimikos* < *mimos*, a mime], 1. imitative; inclined to copy. 2. of, or having the nature of, mimicry or imitation. 3. make-believe; simulated; mock; as, *mimic* battles. *n.* a person or thing that imitates; especially, an actor skilled in mimicry. *v.t.* [MIMICKED (-ikt), MIMICKING], 1. to imitate in speech or action, as in ridicule. 2. to copy closely; imitate accurately. 3. to resemble closely; have or take on the appearance of: as, some animals *mimic* objects in their environment. —*SYN.* see **imitate.**

mim·i·cal (mim'i-k'l), *adj.* [Rare], mimic.

mim·ick·er (mim'ik-ẽr), *n.* a mimic.

mim·ic·ry (mim'ik-ri), *n.* [*pl.* MIMICRIES (-riz)], 1. the practice, art, instance, or way of mimicking. 2. close resemblance of one organism to another or to some object in its environment, as of some insects to the leaves or twigs of plants.

Mi·mir (mē'mir), *n.* [ON. *Mīmir*], in *Norse mythology*, a giant guarding the spring of wisdom at the root of the tree Yggdrasill.

mi·mo·sa (mi-mō'sə, mi-mō'zə), *n.* [Mod. L. < L. *mimus;* see MIME: prob. so called from the apparent mimicry of animal life], any of a large group of trees, shrubs, and herbs of the pea family, growing in warm regions and usually having bipinnate leaves, and heads or spikes of small white, yellow, or pink flowers: the group includes the acacia and the sensitive plant.

mim·o·sa·ceous (mim'ō-sā'shəs, mī'mō-sā'shəs), *adj.* [< *mimosa* + *-aceous*], of the mimosa family of plants.

min., 1. mineralogical. 2. mineralogy. 3. minim; minims. 4. minimum. 5. mining. 6. minister. 7. minor. 8. minute; minutes.

mi·na (mī'nə), *n.* [*pl.* MINAE (-nē), MINAS (-nəz)], [L. < Gr. *mna;* of Sem. origin; cf. MAUND], a varying unit of weight and money used in ancient Greece, Egypt, etc., generally equal to 1/60 talent or 100 drachmas.

mi·na, mi·nah (mī'nə), *n.* a myna.

mi·na·cious (mi-nā′shəs), *adj.* [< L. *minax, minacis;* + *-ous*], menacing; threatening.
mi·nac·i·ty (mi-nas′ə-ti), *n.* the quality of being minacious, or menacing.
min·a·ret (min′ə-ret′, min′ə-ret′), *n.* [Sp. *minarete;* Turk. *manārat* < Ar. *manārah,* lamp, lighthouse, minaret < *minār,* candlestick, lighthouse < base of *nār,* fire], a high, slender tower attached to a Moslem mosque, with one or more projecting balconies, from which a muezzin, or crier, calls the people to prayer.

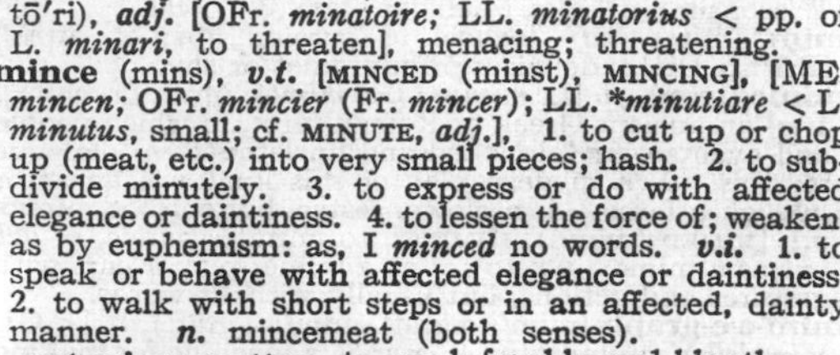

MINARET

Mi·nas Basin (mī′nəs), an eastern arm of the Bay of Fundy, Nova Scotia.
Mi·nas de Ri·o·tin·to (mē′näs de rē′ō-tēn′tō), a city in southwestern Spain, famous for its copper mines: pop., 10,000.
Mi·nas Ge·raes (mē′nə zhi-rīs′), a state of east central Brazil: area, 221,894 sq. mi.; pop., 7,985,000 (est. 1948); capital, Bello Horizonte.
min·a·to·ri·al (min′ə-tôr′i-əl, min′ə-tō′ri-əl), *adj.* minatory.
min·a·to·ry (min′ə-tôr′i, min′ə-tō′ri), *adj.* [OFr. *minatoire;* LL. *minatorius* < pp. of L. *minari,* to threaten], menacing; threatening.
mince (mins), *v.t.* [MINCED (minst), MINCING], [ME. *mincen;* OFr. *mincier* (Fr. *mincer*); LL. **minutiare* < L. *minutus,* small; cf. MINUTE, *adj.*], 1. to cut up or chop up (meat, etc.) into very small pieces; hash. 2. to subdivide minutely. 3. to express or do with affected elegance or daintiness. 4. to lessen the force of; weaken, as by euphemism: as, I *minced* no words. *v.i.* 1. to speak or behave with affected elegance or daintiness. 2. to walk with short steps or in an affected, dainty manner. *n.* mincemeat (both senses).
  not mince matters, to speak frankly and bluntly.
mince·meat (mins′mēt′), *n.* [< *minced meat*], 1. a mixture of chopped apples, spices, suet, raisins, and (now rarely) meat, used as a pie filling. 2. [Obs.], minced meat; meat chopped up into very small pieces.
  make mincemeat of, 1. to chop into small pieces; cut to shreds; hence, 2. to defeat or refute completely.
mince pie, a pie with a filling of mincemeat.
minc·ing (min′siŋ), *adj.* [ppr. of *mince*], 1. affectedly elegant or dainty: of a person or his speech, manner, etc. 2. characterized by short steps or affected daintiness: as, a *mincing* walk.
mind (mīnd), *n.* [ME. *mind, mynd,* etc; AS. *(ge)mynd,* memory; IE. base ***men-**, to think; cf. MAN, MENTAL], 1. memory; recollection or remembrance: as, this brings to *mind* another story. 2. *a)* what one thinks; opinion: as, speak your *mind. b)* what one intends, wishes, or wills; purpose or desire: as, I have a (good) *mind* to go. 3. *a)* that which thinks, perceives, feels, wills, etc.; seat or subject of consciousness. *b)* the thinking and perceiving part of consciousness; intellect or intelligence. *c)* all of an individual's conscious experiences. *d)* the conscious and the unconscious together as a unit; psyche. 4. the intellect in its normal state; reason; sanity: as, he has lost his *mind.* 5. a person having intelligence or regarded as an intellect: as, the great *minds* of the century. 6. way, state, or direction of thinking and feeling: as, the reactionary *mind.* 7. in *philosophy,* consciousness as an element in reality: contrasted with *matter.* 8. in *religion, a)* a Mass in memory of a dead person: a *month's mind* is such a Mass one month after death. *b)* [M-], God: in full, **Divine Mind:** so called in Christian Science. *v.t.* 1. to direct one's mind to; specifically, *a)* to perceive; observe; notice; note. *b)* to pay attention to; heed; hence, *c)* to obey: as, the dog *minds* his master. *d)* to attend to; apply oneself to (a task, etc.). *e)* to tend; take care of; watch over; look after: as, *mind* the baby. *f)* to be careful about; watch out for: as, *mind* those rickety stairs. 2. *a)* to care about; feel concern about. *b)* to object to; dislike: as, I don't *mind* the cold. 3. [Dial.], to remember: sometimes used reflexively. 4. [Dial.], to intend; purpose. 5. [Dial. or Archaic], to remind. *v.i.* 1. to pay attention; give heed. 2. to be obedient. 3. to be careful; watch out. 4. *a)* to care; feel concern. *b)* to object.
  bear in mind, to remember.
  be in one's right mind, to be mentally well; be sane.
  be of one mind, to have the same opinion; agree.
  be of two minds, to be undecided or irresolute.
  be out of one's mind, 1. to be mentally ill; be insane. 2. to be frantic (*with* worry, grief, etc.).
  call to mind, 1. to remember. 2. to be a reminder of.
  change one's mind, 1. to change one's opinion. 2. to change one's intention, purpose, or wish.
  give a person a piece of one's mind, to tell a person plainly one's disapproval of him; rebuke; scold.
  have a (good or **great) mind to,** to feel (strongly) inclined or disposed to.
  have half a mind to, to be somewhat inclined or disposed to.
  have in mind, 1. to remember. 2. to think of. 3. to intend; purpose.
  keep in mind, to remember.
  keep one's mind on, to pay attention to.
  know one's mind, to know one's real thoughts, feelings, desires, or intentions.
  make up one's mind, to form a definite opinion or decision; resolve.
  meeting of minds, an agreement.
  never mind, don't concern yourself; it doesn't matter.
  on one's mind, 1. occupying one's thoughts. 2. worrying one.
  pass out of mind, to be forgotten.
  put in mind, to remind.
  set one's mind on, to be determined on or determinedly desirous of.
  speak one's mind, to say plainly what one thinks.
  take one's mind off, to stop one from thinking about; turn one's attention from.
  to one's mind, in one's opinion.
Min·da·na·o (min′dä-nou′), *n.* the southernmost large island of the Philippine Islands: area, 36,906 sq. mi.; pop., 1,828,000; chief city, Zamboanga: see **Philippine Islands,** map.
mind·ed (mīn′did), *adj.* 1. having a (specified kind of) mind: used in hyphenated compounds, as *high-minded.* 2. having a mind to; inclined; disposed.
mind·ful (mīnd′fəl), *adj.* having in mind; aware, heedful, or careful (*of*): as, I am *mindful* of the danger.
mind·less (mīnd′lis), *adj.* 1. lacking a mind; without intelligence or intellect; senseless. 2. taking no thought; unmindful; heedless or careless (*of*).
Min·do·ro (min-dō′rō), *n.* one of the Philippine Islands, south of Luzon: area, 3,794 sq. mi.; pop., 117,000: see **Philippine Islands,** map.
mind reader, a person who apparently guesses another's thoughts, or professes to be able to perceive them without apparent means of communication.
mind's eye, the imagination.
mine (mīn), *pron.* [ME.; AS. *min,* genit. sing. of *ic,* I; akin to G. *mein;* base as in *me;* cf. MY], that or those belonging to me: the absolute form of *my,* used without a following noun, often after *of,* as, a friend of *mine,* that book is *mine, mine* are better. *possessive pronominal adj.* [Mainly Archaic & Poetic], my: formerly used before a word beginning with a vowel or *h* (e.g. *mine* eyes, *mine* honor), now used after a noun in direct address (e.g., daughter *mine*).
mine (mīn), *n.* [ME.; Late OFr., prob. < the *v.*; many authorities consider the ult. source to be Celtic (cf. Ir. *mein,* vein of metal, metallic ore < IE. **mai-*, to hew, hew off)], 1. a large excavation made in the earth, from which to extract metallic ores, coal, precious stones, salt, or certain other minerals: distinguished from *quarry.* 2. the surface buildings, shafts, elevators, etc. of such an excavation. 3. a deposit of ore, coal, etc. 4. any great source of supply: as, a *mine* of information. 5. a kind of firework that explodes in the air and scatters a number of smaller fireworks. 6. in *military science, a)* a tunnel dug under an enemy's trench, fort, etc., especially one in which an explosive is placed to destroy the enemy or its fortifications. *b)* an explosive charge in a container, buried in the ground for destroying enemy objects on land, or placed in the sea for destroying enemy ships: it can be set off by direct contact, by a time fuse, or by magnetic or chemical action. 7. in *zoology,* the burrow of an insect. *v.i.* [MINED (mīnd), MINING], [ME. *minen;* OFr. *miner*], 1. to dig a mine; specifically, *a)* to dig ores, coal, etc. from the earth. *b)* to tunnel under an enemy installation. 2. to place explosive mines on land or in water. *v.t.* 1. *a)* to dig in (the earth) for ores, coal, etc. *b)* to dig (ores, coal, etc.) from the earth. 2. to dig a tunnel under (an enemy installation). 3. to destroy, or try to destroy, with an explosive mine or mines. 4. to undermine or ruin slowly by secret methods, plotting, etc.

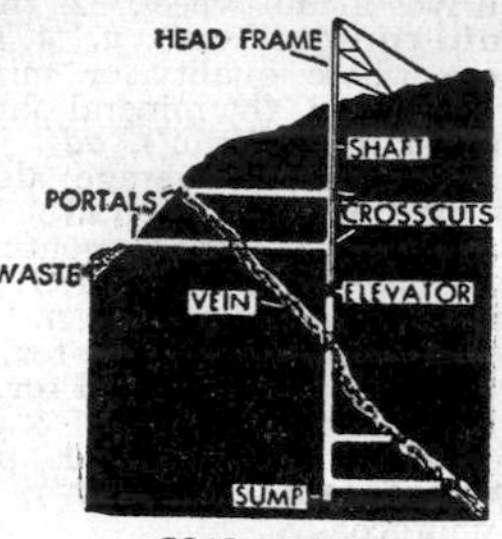

COAL MINE

MINE (contact explosive)

mine detector, an electromagnetic device for locating the position of buried explosive mines.
mine field, an area on land or in water where explosive mines have been set.
mine·lay·er (mīn'lā'ẽr), *n.* a ship especially equipped to lay explosive mines in the water.
min·er (mīn'ẽr), *n.* [ME. & OFr. *minour*], 1. a person whose work is digging coal, ore, etc. in a mine. 2. a soldier who digs or lays military mines.
min·er·al (min'ẽr-əl, min'rəl), *n.* [OFr.; ML. *minerale*, neut. of *mineralis*, mineral < *minera*, a mine < LL. **mina*, a mine; see MINE, *n.*], 1. an inorganic substance occurring naturally in the earth and having a consistent and distinctive set of physical properties (e.g., color, hardness, and crystalline structure) and a composition that can be expressed by a chemical formula: sometimes applied to similar substances of organic origin, as coal. 2. any naturally occurring substance that is neither vegetable nor animal. *adj.* 1. of, having the nature of, consisting of, or containing a mineral or minerals. 2. impregnated with minerals: as, *mineral* water.
mineral., 1. mineralogical. 2. mineralogy.
min·er·al·i·za·tion (min'ẽr-əl-i-zā'shən, min'rəl-ī-zā'shən), *n.* a mineralizing or being mineralized.
min·er·al·ize (min'ẽr-ə-līz', min'rə-līz'), *v.t.* [MINERALIZED (-līzd'), MINERALIZING], 1. to convert (a metal) into an ore: as, exposure to air *mineralizes* iron into iron oxide. 2. to convert (organic matter) into a mineral; petrify. 3. to impregnate (water, etc.) with minerals. *v.i.* to search for or collect minerals for study.
min·er·al·iz·er (min'ẽr-ə-līz'ẽr, min'rə-līz'ẽr), *n.* 1. an element, as arsenic, that combines chemically with a metal to form an ore. 2. a highly volatile substance that helps in the crystallization of minerals.
mineral jelly, petroleum jelly.
min·er·a·log·i·cal (min'ẽr-ə-loj'i-k'l, min'rə-loj'i-k'l), *adj.* of mineralogy: abbreviated **mineral., min.**
min·er·al·o·gist (min'ẽr-al'ə-jist, min'ẽr-äl'ə-jist), *n.* an expert or specialist in mineralogy.
min·er·al·o·gy (min'ẽr-al'ə-ji, min'ẽr-äl'ə-ji), *n.* [< *mineral* + *-logy*], 1. the science of minerals: abbreviated **mineral., min.** 2. [*pl.* MINERALOGIES (-jiz)], a book or article about minerals.
mineral oil, any oil of mineral origin; specifically, *a*) petroleum. *b*) any of various colorless, tasteless oils derived from petroleum and used as a laxative.
mineral pitch, natural asphalt.
mineral spring, any spring of natural mineral water.
mineral tar, a black, semisolid bitumen between petroleum and asphalt in consistency; maltha.
mineral water, water naturally or artificially impregnated with mineral salts or gases; especially, any such water considered to have medicinal values.
mineral wax, ozocerite.
mineral wool, a fibrous material made from melted slag and used as wall insulation in buildings.
Mi·ner·va (mi-nũr'və), [L.; said to be < base of *mens, mentis*, mind (see MAN), but prob. of Etruscan origin], a feminine name. *n.* the ancient Roman goddess of wisdom, technical skill, and invention: identified with the Greek Athena.
mi·ne·stro·ne (min'ə-strō'ni; It. mē'ne-strô'ne), *n.* [It.; < *minestra*, soup < *minestrare*; L. *ministrare*; see MINISTER, *v.*], a thick vegetable soup containing vermicelli, barley, etc. in a meat broth.
mine sweeper, 1. a ship equipped for destroying enemy mines at sea. 2. a heavy roller attached to the front of a military tank for exploding land mines.
mine thrower, any of various trench mortars for throwing high-explosive shells.
min·e·ver (min'ə-vẽr), *n.* miniver.
Ming (miŋ), *n.* [Chin., lit., luminous], a Chinese dynasty that ruled from 1368 to 1644, noted for the artistic works, especially porcelains, produced during its rule. *adj.* of this dynasty: as, a *Ming* vase.
min·gle (miŋ'g'l), *v.t.* [MINGLED (-g'ld), MINGLING], [ME. *mengelen*, freq. of *mengen*; AS. *mengan*, to mix; cf. MONGREL], to mix together; combine; blend; compound. *v.i.* 1. to be or become mixed, blended, etc. 2. to join, unite, or take part with others. —*SYN.* see **mix.**
Mi·nho (mē'nyoo), *n.* a river in Spain and Portugal, flowing into the Atlantic: length, c. 170 mi.: Spanish spelling, **Miño.**
Min·how (min'hō'), *n.* Foochow, a city in China.
min·i·a·ture (min'i-ə-chẽr, min'i-chẽr), *n.* [Fr.; It. *miniatura*; ML. *miniatura* < L. *miniare*, to rubricate, paint red < *minium*, red lead], 1. a small painting or illuminated letter, as in a medieval manuscript. 2. *a*) a small painting, especially a portrait, done on ivory, vellum, etc. *b*) the art of making such paintings. 3. a copy or model on a very small scale. *adj.* done on a very small scale; diminutive; minute. —*SYN.* see **small.**
in miniature, on a small scale; greatly reduced.
miniature camera, a small camera using film of 35 mm. width or less, for taking snapshots; candid camera.
min·i·a·tur·ize (min'i-ə-chẽr-īz', min'i-chẽr-īz'), *v.t.* [MINIATURIZED (-īzd'), MINIATURIZING], to make (industrial and military devices) smaller and more compact, as by using transistors instead of electron tubes.
Min·i·é ball (min'i-ā, min'i; Fr. mē'nyā'), [after C. E. *Minié* (1814–1879), Fr. inventor], a cone-shaped rifle bullet with a cavity in its base, which expanded, when fired, to fit the rifling in the bore: used in 19th century.
min·i·fy (min'ə-fī'), *v.t.* [MINIFIED (-fīd'), MINIFYING], [< L. *minor*, less; + -(*i*)*fy*], to make or make seem smaller or less important: opposed to *magnify*.
min·i·kin (min'i-kin), *n.* [MD. *minneken*, *minnekijn*, dim. of *minne*, love; cf. MINNESINGER, -KIN], 1. [Obs.], a darling. 2. [Rare], anything very small and delicate. *adj.* 1. [Obs.], diminutive. 2. affected or mincing.
min·im (min'im), *n.* [ME. *mynym* (in sense 3); L. *minimus*, least, superl. of *minor*; see MINOR], 1. the smallest liquid measure, equal to 1/60 fluid dram, or about a drop: abbreviated **M., m, min.** (*sing. & pl.*). 2. anything very small; tiny portion. 3. in *music*, a half note (𝅗𝅥). 4. in *penmanship*, a single downstroke, as at the end of the letter *d*. *adj.* smallest; tiniest.
min·i·ma (min'ə-mə), *n.* alternative plural of **minimum.**
min·i·mal (min'ə-m'l), *adj.* smallest or least possible.
Min·i·mal·ist (min'ə-m'l-ist), *n.* [*minimal* + *-ist*; cf. MENSHEVIK], 1. a member of the right wing of the (former) Russian Social Revolutionaries. 2. a Menshevik (sense 1). Opposed to *Maximalist*.
min·i·mi·za·tion (min'ə-mi-zā'shən, min'ə-mī-zā'shən), *n.* a minimizing or being minimized.
min·i·mize (min'ə-mīz'), *v.t.* [MINIMIZED (-mīzd'), MINIMIZING], 1. to reduce to a minimum; decrease to the least possible amount, degree, etc. 2. to estimate or make appear to be of the least possible amount, value, or importance. —*SYN.* see **disparage.**
min·i·miz·er (min'ə-mīz'ẽr), *n.* a person who minimizes; especially, one who tries to make religious or philosophical problems appear easily explained.
min·i·mum (min'ə-məm), *n.* [*pl.* MINIMUMS (-məmz), MINIMA (-mə)], [L., neut. of *minimus*, least], 1. the smallest quantity, number, or degree possible or permissible. 2. the lowest degree or point (of a varying quantity, as temperature) reached or recorded; lower limit of variation. *adj.* 1. smallest possible, permissible, or reached. 2. of, marking, or setting a minimum or minimums. Abbreviated **min.** Opposed to *maximum*.
minimum wage, 1. a wage established by contract or by law as the lowest that may be paid to employees doing a specified type of work. 2. a living wage.
min·ing (mīn'iŋ), *n.* 1. the act, process, or work of removing ores, coal, etc. from a mine. 2. the act or process of laying explosive mines. Abbreviated **min.**
min·ion (min'yən), *n.* [Fr. *mignon*, favorite, darling; cf. MIGNON], 1. a favorite, especially one who is a fawning, servile follower: term of contempt. 2. [Obs.], a mistress; paramour. 3. in *printing*, a size of type, 7 point. The main text of this dictionary is set in minion. *adj.* [Rare], delicate, dainty, etc.
minion of the law, a policeman.
min·ish (min'ish), *v.t. & v.i.* [ME. *minusschen*, *menuschen*; OFr. *menuisier*, to lessen, make small; LL. **minutiare* < L. *minutus*; see MINUTE, *adj.*], [Archaic], to make or become less, smaller, inferior, etc.; diminish.
min·is·ter (min'is-tẽr), *n.* [ME. & OFr. *ministre*; L. *minister*, an attendant, servant (after *magister*, master; cf. MASTER) < base of *minor*, less], 1. a person acting for another as his agent and carrying out his orders or designs; specifically, *a*) a person appointed by the head of a government to take charge of some department of state. *b*) a diplomatic officer sent to a foreign nation to represent his government, and ranking below an ambassador. *c*) anyone authorized to carry out the spiritual functions of a church, conduct worship, administer the sacraments, preach, etc.; clergyman; pastor. 2. any person or thing thought of as serving as the agent of some power, force, etc.: as, a *minister* of evil. *v.t.* [ME. *ministren*; OFr. *ministrer*; L. *ministrare*], 1. [Archaic], to supply; provide. 2. to administer, as a sacrament. *v.i.* 1. to serve; act as an agent. 2. to give help; fill wants; especially, to serve as a nurse.
min·is·te·ri·al (min'is-têr'i-əl), *adj.* [Fr. *ministériel*; LL. *ministerialis*], 1. of ministry, a minister, or ministers collectively. 2. serving as a minister, or agent; subordinate. 3. having the nature of or characteristic of the administrative functions of government; executive. 4. being a cause; instrumental.
min·is·te·ri·al·ist (min'is-têr'i-əl-ist), *n.* a supporter of the government ministry in office.
minister plenipotentiary, [*pl.* MINISTERS PLENIPOTENTIARY], a diplomatic representative with full authority to negotiate.
min·is·trant (min'is-trənt), *adj.* [L. *ministrans*, ppr.; see MINISTER, *v.*], serving as a minister; ministering. *n.* a person who ministers, or serves.

min·is·tra·tion (min′is-trā′shən), *n.* [ME. *ministracion;* L. *ministratio* < pp. of *ministrare;* see MINISTER, *v.*], 1. the act of serving as a minister or clergyman; performance of pastoral duties. 2. service; help.

min·is·tra·tive (min′is-trā′tiv), *adj.* [< L. *ministratus,* pp.; + *-ive*], ministering; giving help or service.

min·is·try (min′is-tri), *n.* [*pl.* MINISTRIES (-triz)], [ME. *mynysterie;* L. *ministerium* < *minister;* see MINISTER], 1. the act of ministering, or serving; ministration. 2. the office, function, or service of a minister of religion. 3. ministers collectively; the clergy. 4. *a)* the department under a minister of government. *b)* the term of office of such a minister. *c)* such ministers collectively. 5. in certain European countries, *a)* a branch of government headed by a minister. *b)* its building or buildings.

min·i·track (min′i-trak′), *n.* a system used to track the path of a satellite in orbit by signals received from miniature transmitters in the satellite.

min·i·um (min′i-əm), *n.* [L.; of Iberian origin; cf. Basque *armineá*], 1. vermilion (the color). 2. red oxide of lead, Pb_3O_4: also called *red lead.*

min·i·ver (min′ə-vẽr), *n.* [ME. *menyuere;* OFr. *menu ver, menu vair,* miniver; *menu* (< L. *minutus*), small + *ver, vair,* kind of fur < L. *varius,* variegated], 1. in medieval times, a kind of white or gray fur used for trimming garments. 2. any fine white fur; especially, the white winter fur of the ermine. Also spelled **minever.**

mink (miŋk), *n.* [*pl.* MINKS (miŋks), MINK; see PLURAL, II, D, 1], [Late ME. *minke* < Scand.; cf. Sw. *menk*], 1. a mammal somewhat like a large weasel, living in water part of the time and found in the cooler latitudes of the Northern Hemisphere. 2. its valuable fur, soft, thick, brown, and lustrous.

MINK (2 ft. long)

Minn., Minnesota.

Min·ne·ap·o·lis (min′i-ap″l-is), *n.* a city in eastern Minnesota, on the Mississippi: pop., 483,000.

Min·ne·ha·ha (min′i-hä′hä), *n.* the Indian girl who becomes the wife of Hiawatha in Longfellow's *The Song of Hiawatha.*

min·ne·sing·er (min′i-siŋ′ẽr), *n.* [G.; *minne,* love, orig. memory (akin to Eng. *mind*) + *singer,* singer; cf. MINIKIN], any of a number of German lyric poets and singers of the 12th to the 14th centuries, corresponding to the minstrels or troubadours.

Min·ne·so·ta (min′i-sō′tə), *n.* a Middle Western State of the United States, adjoining the Canadian border: area, 84,068 sq. mi.; pop., 3,414,000; capital, St. Paul: abbreviated **Minn.**

Min·ne·so·tan (min′i-sō′tən), *adj.* of Minnesota. *n.* a native or inhabitant of Minnesota.

Min·ne·wit, Peter (min′ū-it, min′ə-wit), see **Minuit.**

Min·nie (min′i), [dim. of *Wilhelmina, Mary* or var. of G. *Minne, Minna* < MHG. *minne;* see MINNESINGER], a feminine name.

min·now (min′ō), *n.* [*pl.* MINNOWS (-ōz), MINNOW; see PLURAL, II, D, 1], [ME. *menow,* small fish; prob. merging AS. *myne* (akin to OHG. *munewa*) with OFr. *menu* (< L. *minutus*), small], 1. any of various species of very small fresh-water fish of the carp family, used commonly as bait. 2. any very small fish like these.

min·ny (min′i), *n.* [*pl.* MINNIES (-iz)], [Dial. or Colloq.], a minnow.

Mi·ño (mē′nyô), *n.* the Minho: the Spanish spelling.

Mi·no·an (mi-nō′ən), *adj.* [< *Minos* + *-an*], designating or of an advanced prehistoric culture that flourished in Crete from about 3000 to 1100 B.C.

mi·nor (mī′nẽr), *adj.* [ME. *mynor, menor;* L.], 1. *a)* lesser in size, amount, number, or extent. *b)* lesser in importance or rank: opposed to *major.* 2. under full legal age (usually twenty-one years). 3. constituting the minority: said of a part, etc. 4. in a minor key; sad; melancholy; plaintive. 5. in *education,* designating a field of study in which a student specializes, but to a lesser degree than in his major. 6. in *logic,* narrower; less inclusive: see **minor term, minor premise.** 7. in *music, a)* designating an interval less than the corresponding major interval by a half tone. *b)* designating a tone distant by a minor interval from another tone. *c)* characterized by minor intervals, scales, or tones: as, the *minor* mode. *d)* based on the scale pattern of the minor mode: see **minor scale.** *v.i.* to specialize to a secondary degree in some subject or field of study (with *in*): as, he will *minor* in chemistry. *n.* 1. a person under full legal age, who has not yet acquired all civil rights. 2. in *education,* a minor subject or field of study. 3. in *logic,* a minor term or premise. 4. in *music,* a minor interval, key, mode, etc.

Mi·nor·ca (mi-nôr′kə), *n.* 1. one of the Balearic Islands, east of Majorca: area, 271 sq. mi.: pop., 43,000: Spanish spelling, **Menorca.** 2. any of a breed of large chickens with black, white, or buff feathers.

Mi·nor·ite (mī′nə-rīt′), *n.* [*minor, adj.* + *-ite:* so named because they regarded themselves as of humbler rank than members of other orders], a Franciscan friar.

mi·nor·i·ty (mə-nôr′ə-ti, mī-nor′ə-ti), *n.* [*pl.* MINORITIES (-tiz)], [Fr. *minorité* < *mineur* (L. *minor*), less], 1. the lesser part or smaller number; less than half of a total: opposed to *majority.* 2. a racial, religious, national, or political group smaller than and differing from the larger, controlling group of which it is a part. 3. the period or condition of being under full legal age.

mi·nor-league (mī′nẽr-lēg′), *adj.* of, in, or suitable to a minor league or leagues.

minor league, any of the leagues of professional baseball clubs, etc. other than the major leagues.

minor mode, in *music,* the arrangement of tones in accordance with the intervals of the minor scale, as the basic tonal material of a composition: often associated, in the Occident, with a melancholy mood.

minor premise, the premise (in a syllogism) that contains the minor term.

minor scale, one of the two standard diatonic scales, consisting of eight tones, with half steps instead of whole steps *a)* after the second and seventh tones in ascending and after the sixth and third tones in descending (*melodic minor scale*), or *b)* after the second, fifth, and seventh tones in ascending and after the eighth, sixth, and third tones in descending (*harmonic minor scale*): distinguished from *major scale.*

minor suit, in *bridge,* diamonds or clubs: so called from their lower value in scoring.

minor term, the subject of the conclusion of a syllogism.

Mi·nos (mī′nəs, mī′nos), *n.* [Gr. *Minōs*], in *Greek mythology,* 1. a king of Crete, son of Zeus by Europa, who after he died became one of the three judges of the dead in the lower world, with Aeacus and Rhadamanthus. 2. his grandson, for whom Daedalus built the labyrinth in Crete: see **Minotaur.**

Mi·not (mī′nət), *n.* a city in northern North Dakota: pop., 31,000.

Min·o·taur (min′ə-tôr′), *n.* [ME. *Minotaure;* L. *Minotaurus;* Gr. *Minōtauros;* prob. < *Minōs,* Minos + *tauros,* a bull], in *Greek mythology,* a monster with the body of a man and the head of a bull (in some versions, with the body of a bull and head of a man), confined by Minos in a labyrinth built by Daedalus, and annually fed seven youths and seven maidens from Athens, until killed by Theseus.

MINOTAUR

Minsk (minsk; Russ. mẽnsk), *n.* the capital of the Byelorussian S.S.R.: pop., 509,000.

min·ster (min′stẽr), *n.* [ME. *mynstre, munster, menstre;* AS. *mynster;* LL. *monasterium;* see MONASTERY], 1. the church of a monastery. 2. any of various large churches or cathedrals: *-minster* occurs in some English place names, as *Westminster, Axminster.*

min·strel (min′strəl), *n.* [ME. *menestral;* OFr. *menestrel;* LL. *ministerialis,* servant, jester, singer < L. *minister;* see MINISTER], 1. any of a class of lyric poets and singers of the Middle Ages, who traveled from place to place singing and reciting, usually to the accompaniment of a harp or lute. 2. [Poetic], a poet; singer; musician. 3. a performer in a minstrel show.

minstrel show, [< the Christy *Minstrels,* the first troupe organized (c. 1842, by Edwin P. Christy at Buffalo, New York) to perform such shows in the U.S.], a comic variety show presented by a company of performers in blackface, who sing songs, tell jokes, etc.

min·strel·sy (min′strəl-si), *n.* [*pl.* MINSTRELSIES (-siz)], [ME. & Anglo-Fr. *menestralcie;* OFr. *menestralsie*], 1. the art or occupation of a minstrel. 2. a group of minstrels. 3. a collection of minstrels' ballads or songs.

mint (mint), *n.* [ME. *minte, mynt;* AS. *mynet, mynit,* coin < L. *moneta,* place for coining money < *Moneta,* surname of Juno, in whose temple at Rome money was coined < pp. of *monere,* to warn; cf. MONEY], 1. a place where money is coined by authority of the government. 2. a source of apparently unlimited supply; large amount: as, a *mint* of ideas. 3. a source of manufacture or invention. *adj.* new or in its original condition, as if freshly minted: as, a postage stamp in *mint* condition. *v.t.* 1. to coin or stamp out (money). 2. to invent or create; fabricate.

mint (mint), *n.* [ME. & AS. *minte;* L. *menta, mentha;* Gr. *mintha*], 1. any of various aromatic plants whose leaves are used for flavoring and in medicine: as, spear*mint* and pepper*mint.* 2. a piece of candy or chewing gum flavored with mint.

mint·age (min′tij), *n.* [see -AGE], 1. the act or process of minting money. 2. the act of inventing or making. 3. money produced in a mint. 4. a fee paid to a mint for coining. 5. the stamp impressed on a coin.

mint julep, a frosted drink consisting of whisky or brandy, sugar, and mint leaves in a tall glass packed with chipped ice.

mint sauce, a sauce for meat, especially lamb, consisting of chopped mint leaves, vinegar, sugar, etc.

min·u·end (min′ū-end′), *n.* [L. *minuendus,* to be diminished, gerundive of *minuere;* see MINUTE, *adj.*], in *arithmetic,* the number or quantity from which another (the *subtrahend*) is to be subtracted.

min·u·et (min'ū-et'), *n.* [Fr. *menuet* < *menu* (< L. *minutus*), small: from the small steps taken], 1. a slow, stately dance for groups of couples, introduced in France in the 17th century. 2. the music for this, in 3/4 time: often a movement of certain musical compositions.

Min·u·it, Peter (min'ū-it, min'ə-wit), 1580–1638; first Dutch governor of New Netherland (New York): also spelled **Minnewit.**

mi·nus (mī'nəs), *prep.* [L., neut. sing. of *minor,* less], 1. less; reduced by the subtraction of: as, four *minus* two. 2. [Colloq.], without; lacking: as, *minus* a finger. *adj.* 1. indicating or involving subtraction: as, a *minus* sign. 2. negative: as, a *minus* quantity. 3. somewhat less than: as, a grade of A *minus.* *n.* 1. a minus sign. 2. a negative quantity.

mi·nus·cu·lar (mi-nus'kyoo-lẽr), *adj.* minuscule.

mi·nus·cule (mi-nus'kūl), *n.* [Fr.; L. *minusculus,* rather small, dim. < *minor,* less], 1. a small cursive script developed from the uncial and used in medieval manuscripts: distinguished from *majuscule.* 2. a letter in this script; hence, 3. any small, or lower-case, letter. *adj.* 1. of, in, like, or having the nature of, minuscules; hence, 2. very small; tiny; minute.

minus sign, in *mathematics,* a sign (−), indicating subtraction or negative quantity: opposed to *plus sign* (+).

min·ute (min'it), *n.* [ME. *minut;* via OFr. < ML. *minuta* < L. *minutus;* see MINUTE, *adj.;* cf. MINNOW, MINUET], 1. the sixtieth part of any of certain units; specifically, *a)* 1/60 of an hour; sixty seconds. *b)* 1/60 of a degree of an arc; sixty seconds: indicated by the symbol ('). 2. a very short period of time; moment; instant. 3. a specific point in time. 4. a note or memorandum; specifically, *pl.* an official record of what was said and done at a meeting, convention, etc. Abbreviated **M., m., mi., min.** (*sing. & pl.*). *v.t.* [MINUTED (-id), MINUTING], 1. to time to the minute. 2. to make a minute, or memorandum, of; record.

the minute (that), just as soon as.

up to the minute, in the latest style, fashion, etc.

mi·nute (mī-no͞ot', mi-nūt'), *adj.* [ME.; L. *minutus,* little, small, pp. of *minuere,* to lessen, diminish < *minor,* less], 1. very small; tiny. 2. of little importance or significance; petty; trifling. 3. of, characterized by, or attentive to tiny details; exact; precise. —*SYN.* see **small.**

minute gun, a cannon firing at intervals of a minute, as a distress signal, or as part of a funeral ceremony.

minute hand, the long hand of a clock or watch, which indicates the minutes and moves around the dial once every hour.

min·ute·ly (min'it-li), *adj.* 1. occurring at intervals of a minute. 2. occurring very often or continually. *adv.* 1. every minute. 2. often or continually.

mi·nute·ly (mī-no͞ot'li, mi-nūt'li), *adv.* in a minute manner or in minute detail.

min·ute·man (min'it-man'), *n.* [*pl.* MINUTEMEN (-men')], any of the members of the American citizen army at the time of the Revolution who volunteered to be ready for military service at a minute's notice.

mi·nute·ness (mī-no͞ot'nis, mi-nūt'nis), *n.* [*minute, adj.* + *-ness*], 1. extreme smallness. 2. precise attention to detail; exactness.

min·ute steak (min'it), a small steak, often cubed, that can be cooked quickly.

mi·nu·ti·ae (mi-nū'shi-ē'), *n.pl.* [*sing.* MINUTIA (-ə)], [L., pl. of *minutia,* smallness < *minutus;* see MINUTE, *adj.*], small or relatively unimportant details.

minx (miŋks), *n.* [Early Mod. Eng. < LG.; cf. LG. *minsk,* person, impudent woman; akin to G. *mensch* (OHG. *manisc* < *man,* man)], a pert, saucy girl or young woman.

Mi·o·cene (mī'ə-sēn'), *adj.* [< Gr. *meiōn,* less + *kainos,* recent], designating or of the third epoch of the Tertiary Period in the Cenozoic Era, characterized by the development of large mountain ranges.

the Miocene, the Miocene Epoch or its rocks: see **geology,** chart.

mi·o·sis (mī-ō'sis), *n.* 1. meiosis. 2. myosis.

mi·ot·ic (mī-ot'ik), *adj.* 1. meiotic. 2. myotic. *n.* a myotic.

Mi·que·lon (mik'ə-lon'; Fr. mē'klōn'), *n.* a French island off the southern coast of Newfoundland: area, 83 sq. mi.; pop., 500.

mir (mêr), *n.* [Russ.], in Russia, formerly, a village community of peasant farmers.

MIr., Middle Irish.

Mi·ra·beau, Comte de (də mē'rȧ'bō'; Eng. mir'ə-bō'), (*Honoré Gabriel Victor Riqueti*), 1749–1791; French revolutionist, orator, and statesman.

‡**mi·ra·bi·le dic·tu** (mi-rab'i-li dik'to͞o, dik'tū), [L.], wonderful to tell.

‡**mi·ra·bi·li·a** (mir'ə-bil'i-ə), *n.pl.* [L.], marvels; miracles.

mir·a·cle (mir'ə-k'l), *n.* [ME. *myracle;* OFr.; L. *miraculum* < *mirari,* to wonder at < *mirus,* wonderful; cf. ADMIRE], 1. an event or action that apparently contradicts known scientific laws and is hence thought to be due to supernatural causes, especially to an act of God. 2. a remarkable event or thing; marvel. 3. a wonderful example: as, he is a *miracle* of fortitude. 4. a miracle play.

miracle man, 1. a man who professes, or is believed, to perform miracles. 2. [Colloq.], a man who does something that supposedly could not be done.

miracle play, [after ML. *miraculum*], 1. any of a class of medieval religious dramas based on miracles worked by the saints. 2. in medieval England, a mystery play.

mi·rac·u·lous (mi-rak'yoo-ləs), *adj.* [Fr. *miraculeux;* ML. *miraculosus* < L. *miraculum*], 1. having the nature of a miracle; supernatural. 2. like a miracle; wonderful; marvelous. 3. able to work miracles.

Mi·ra·flo·res (mē'rä-flô'res), *n.pl.* locks near the Pacific end of the Panama Canal.

mi·rage (mi-räzh'), *n.* [Fr. < (*se*) *mirer,* to be reflected; LL. *mirare,* to look at], an optical illusion caused by the reflection of light through layers of air of different temperatures and densities, by which a ship, oasis in the desert, etc. appears to be very near and, often, upside down: often used figuratively of something that falsely appears to be real. —*SYN.* see **delusion.**

Mi·ran·da (mə-ran'də), [L., fem. of *mirandus,* strange, wonderful < *mirari,* to marvel at], a feminine name.

mire (mīr), *n.* [ME.; ON. *myrr, myri;* for base see MOSS], 1. an area of wet, soggy ground; bog. 2. deep mud; wet, soggy earth; slush. *v.t.* [MIRED (mīrd), MIRING], 1. to cause to get stuck in mire. 2. to soil or splatter with mud or dirt. *v.i.* to sink or stick in mud.

Mir·i·am (mir'i-əm), [Heb. *miryām*], a feminine name: see **Mary.** *n.* in the *Bible,* the sister of Moses and Aaron: Ex. 15:20.

mir·i·ness (mīr'i-nis), *n.* a miry quality or condition.

mirk (mũrk), *n.* murk.

mirk·y (mũr'ki), *adj.* [MIRKIER (-ki-ẽr), MIRKIEST (-ki-ist)], murky.

mir·ror (mir'ẽr), *n.* [ME. *mirour;* OFr. *mireor, mirour* < LL. *mirare,* to look at; L. *mirari,* to wonder at; cf. ADMIRE], 1. a smooth surface that reflects the images of objects; especially, a piece of glass coated on the reverse side with silver, etc.; looking glass. 2. anything that gives a true representation or description. 3. something to be imitated or emulated; model. 4. [Archaic], a crystal used by fortunetellers, sorcerers, etc. *v.t.* to reflect, as in a mirror; give or show a likeness of.

mirth (mũrth), *n.* [ME. *myrthe;* AS. *mirigth, mirgth, myrth,* pleasure, joy < base of *mirig, myrig,* pleasant (see MERRY) + *-th*], joyfulness, gaiety, or merriment, especially when characterized by laughter or hilarity.

SYN.—**mirth** implies gaiety, gladness, or great amusement, especially as expressed by laughter; **glee** implies exultant and demonstrative joy or it may suggest malicious delight over another's misfortunes; **jollity** and **merriment** imply exuberant mirth or joy and usually suggest convivial merrymaking; **hilarity** implies boisterous merriment and sometimes suggests an excessively noisy display of high spirits.—*ANT.* sadness, melancholy.

mirth·ful (mũrth'fəl), *adj.* full of, expressing, or causing mirth; merry.

mirth·less (mũrth'lis), *adj.* without mirth; humorless; cheerless; sad; melancholy.

mir·y (mīr'i), *adj.* [MIRIER (-i-ẽr), MIRIEST (-i-ist)], 1. full of, or having the nature of, mire; boggy; swampy. 2. covered or spattered with mire; muddy; dirty.

mir·za (mêr'zä), *n.* [Per. *mīrza,* contr. < *mīrzādah* < *mīr,* prince (< Ar. *amīr,* ruler) + *zād,* born], a Persian title of honor placed after the name of a royal prince or before the name of a high official, scholar, etc.

mis- (mis), [ME. & AS. *mis-;* akin to G. *miss-,* Goth. *missa-;* base as in *miss, v.;* also (in words of French origin) < ME. & OFr. *mes-* < L. *minus,* less], a prefix meaning *wrong, wrongly, bad, badly,* as in *misplace, misconduct, misadventure.*

mis- (mis), miso-.

mis·ad·ven·ture (mis'əd-ven'chẽr), *n.* [ME. & OFr. *mesaventure;* see MIS- & ADVENTURE], an unlucky accident; mishap; bad luck; mischance.

mis·ad·vise (mis'ad-vīz'), *v.t.* to advise wrongly.

mis·al·li·ance (mis'ə-lī'əns), *n.* [after Fr. *mésalliance*], an improper alliance; especially, an unsuitable marriage.

mis·al·ly (mis'ə-lī'), *v.t.* [MISALLIED (-līd'), MISALLYING], to ally unsuitably or inappropriately.

mis·an·thrope (mis'ən-thrōp', miz'ən-thrōp'), *n.* [Gr. *misanthrōpos,* hating mankind < *misein,* to hate + *anthrōpos,* a man], a person who hates or distrusts all people: also **misanthropist.**

mis·an·throp·ic (mis'ən-throp'ik), *adj.* of, having the nature of, or like a misanthrope. —*SYN.* see **cynical.**

mis·an·throp·i·cal (mis'ən-throp'i-k'l), *adj.* misanthropic.

mis·an·thro·pist (mis-an′thrə-pist), *n.* a misanthrope.
mis·an·thro·py (mis-an′thrə-pi), *n.* [Gr. *misanthrōpia*], the feelings or actions of a misanthrope; hatred or distrust of all people.
mis·ap·pli·ca·tion (mis′ap-lə-kā′shən), *n.* a misapplying or being misapplied.
mis·ap·ply (mis′ə-plī′), *v.t.* [MISAPPLIED (-plīd′), MISAPPLYING], 1. to use badly, incorrectly, or uselessly: as, he *misapplies* his energies. 2. to apply dishonestly or illegally: as, he *misapplied* the company's money.
mis·ap·pre·hend (mis′ap-ri-hend′), *v.t.* to fail to apprehend correctly; misunderstand.
mis·ap·pre·hen·sion (mis′ap-ri-hen′shən), *n.* a misapprehending.
mis·ap·pro·pri·ate (mis′ə-prō′pri-āt′), *v.t.* to appropriate to a bad, incorrect, or dishonest use; misapply.
mis·ap·pro·pri·a·tion (mis′ə-prō′pri-ā′shən), *n.* a misappropriating.
mis·ar·range (mis′ə-rānj′), *v.t.* to arrange wrongly or improperly.
mis·be·come (mis′bi-kum′), *v.t.* [MISBECAME (-kām′), MISBECOME, MISBECOMING], to be unbecoming to; be unsuitable or unfit for.
mis·be·got (mis′bi-got′), *adj.* misbegotten.
mis·be·got·ten (mis′bi-got′'n), *adj.* wrongly or unlawfully begotten; specifically, born out of wedlock; illegitimate; bastard: also **misbegot.**
mis·be·have (mis′bi-hāv′), *v.i.* to behave wrongly. *v.t.* to conduct (oneself) improperly.
mis·be·hav·ior (mis′bi-hāv′yẽr), *n.* wrong or improper behavior.
mis·be·lief (mis′bə-lēf′), *n.* wrong, false, or unorthodox belief or opinion, especially in religion.
mis·be·lieve (mis′bə-lēv′), *v.i.* to believe wrongly; hold wrong, false, or unorthodox beliefs or opinions, especially in religion. *v.t.* [Rare], to disbelieve.
mis·be·liev·er (mis′bə-lēv′ẽr), *n.* a person considered to hold a wrong, false, or unorthodox belief, especially in religion.
mis·brand (mis-brand′), *v.t.* to brand or label improperly or falsely.
misc., 1. miscellaneous. 2. miscellany.
mis·cal·cu·late (mis-kal′kyoo-lāt′), *v.t. & v.i.* to calculate incorrectly; miscount or misjudge.
mis·cal·cu·la·tion (mis′kal-kyoo-lā′shən), *n.* a miscalculating; error in figuring or judging.
mis·call (mis-kôl′), *v.t.* 1. to call by a wrong name; misname. 2. [Obs. or British Dial.], to revile; abuse.
mis·car·riage (mis-kar′ij), *n.* 1. failure to reach a proper end; mismanagement. 2. failure of mail, freight, etc. to reach its destination. 3. the premature birth of a fetus, so that it does not live; abortion.
mis·car·ry (mis-kar′i), *v.i.* [MISCARRIED (-id), MISCARRYING], 1. *a)* to go wrong; fail: said of a plan, project, etc. *b)* to go astray; fail to arrive: said of mail, freight, etc. 2. *a)* to give birth prematurely to a fetus, so that it does not live. *b)* [Obs.], to be born prematurely.
mis·cast (mis-kast′, mis-käst′), *v.t.* [MISCAST, MISCASTING], 1. to cast (an actor) for a role not suited to him. 2. to cast (a play) with actors unsuited to their roles.
mis·ce·ge·na·tion (mis′i-jə-nā′shən), *n.* [< L. *miscere*, to mix + *genus*, race; + *-ation*], marriage or interbreeding between members of different races, especially, in the United States, between whites and Negroes.
mis·cel·la·ne·a (mis″l-ā′ni-ə), *n.pl.* [often construed as sing.], [L.; see MISCELLANY], a collection of various kinds, especially of literary works; miscellany.
mis·cel·la·ne·ous (mis″l-ā′ni-əs), *adj.* [L. *miscellaneus* < *miscellus*, mixed < *miscere*, to mix], 1. consisting or formed of various kinds; varied; mixed: as, a box of *miscellaneous* candies. 2. having various qualities, abilities, etc.; many-sided. Abbreviated **misc.**
mis·cel·la·ny (mis″l-ā′ni), *n.* [*pl.* MISCELLANIES (-niz)], [< Fr. or L.; Fr. *miscellanée* < L. *miscellanea*, neut. pl. of *miscellaneus;* see MISCELLANEOUS], 1. a collection of various kinds, especially of literary works. 2. *often pl.* a book made up of such a collection. Abbreviated **misc.**
mis·chance (mis-chans′, mis-chäns′), *n.* [ME. *meschance;* OFr. *meschance, mescheance;* see MIS- & CHANCE], an unlucky accident; bad luck; misadventure.
mis·chief (mis′chif), *n.* [ME. *meschef;* OFr. *meschief, meschef* < *meschever*, to come to grief < *mes-* (see MIS-) + *chief*, end, head (see CHIEF)], 1. harm, damage, or injury, especially that done by a person. 2. a cause or source of harm, damage, or annoyance; specifically, *a)* action or conduct that causes damage or trouble. *b)* a person causing damage or annoyance. 3. a tendency or disposition to annoy or vex with playful tricks. 4. *a)* a troublesome or annoying act; prank; playful, vexing trick. *b)* playful, harmless spirits; gay teasing.
mis·chief-mak·er (mis′chif-māk′ẽr), *n.* a person who causes mischief; especially, one who causes quarrels or hard feelings by gossiping or tale-bearing.
mis·chief-mak·ing (mis′chif-māk′iŋ), *adj.* causing mischief; troublesome; annoying. *n.* the action of a mischief-maker.
mis·chie·vous (mis′chi-vəs), *adj.* [Anglo-Fr. & OFr. *meschevous*], 1. causing mischief; specifically, *a)* injurious; harmful. *b)* prankish; teasing; full of tricks. 2. inclined to annoy or vex with playful tricks; naughty: said especially of a child.
mis·ci·bil·i·ty (mis′ə-bil′ə-ti), *n.* the state or quality of being miscible.
mis·ci·ble (mis′ə-b'l), *adj.* [< L. *miscere*, to mix; + *-ible*], that can be mixed or easily mixed.
mis·col·or (mis-kul′ẽr), *v.t.* 1. to give a wrong color to; hence, 2. to give a false account of; misrepresent.
mis·con·ceive (mis′kən-sēv′), *v.t. & v.i.* to conceive wrongly; interpret incorrectly; misunderstand.
mis·con·cep·tion (mis′kən-sep′shən), *n.* a misconceiving; wrong interpretation; misunderstanding.
mis·con·duct (mis′kən-dukt′; *for n.*, mis-kon′dukt), *v.t.* 1. to manage badly or dishonestly. 2. to conduct (oneself) improperly. *n.* 1. bad or dishonest management; specifically, malfeasance. 2. improper behavior; specifically, adultery or fornication.
mis·con·struc·tion (mis′kən-struk′shən), *n.* a misconstruing; incorrect interpretation; misunderstanding.
mis·con·strue (mis′kən-strōō′, mis-kon′strōō), *v.t.* to construe wrongly; misinterpret; misunderstand.
mis·count (mis-kount′; *also, for n.*, mis′kount′), *v.t. & v.i.* to count incorrectly; miscalculate. *n.* an incorrect count, as of votes in an election.
mis·cre·ance (mis′kri-əns), *n.* [ME.; OFr.; cf. MISCREANT], [Archaic], wrong or false belief or faith.
mis·cre·an·cy (mis′kri-ən-si), *n.* [Archaic], 1. the condition of a miscreant; wickedness. 2. miscreance.
mis·cre·ant (mis′kri-ənt), *adj.* [ME. *miscreaunt, miscreant;* OFr. *mescreant*, unbelieving; *mes-* (see MIS-) + *creant*, ppr. of *creire* (L. *credere*), to believe], 1. villainous; evil. 2. [Archaic], unbelieving; heretical; infidel. *n.* 1. an evil person; criminal; villain. 2. [Archaic], an unbeliever; heretic; infidel.
mis·cre·ate (mis′kri-āt′), *v.t. & v.i.* to create amiss; form badly. *adj.* [Archaic], miscreated.
mis·cre·at·ed (mis′kri-āt′id), *adj.* badly or unnaturally formed; misshapen.
mis·cue (mis-kū′), *n.* 1. in *billiards*, a shot spoiled by the cue's slipping off the ball; hence, 2. [Colloq.], a mistake; error. *v.i.* 1. to make a miscue. 2. in the *theater*, to miss one's cue or to answer the wrong cue.
mis·date (mis-dāt′), *v.t.* to put a wrong date on (a document, letter, etc.) or assign a wrong date to (an event); date incorrectly. *n.* a wrong date.
mis·deal (mis-dēl′), *v.t. & v.i.* [MISDEALT (-delt′), MISDEALING], to deal (playing cards) wrongly. *n.* a wrong deal.
mis·deed (mis-dēd′), *n.* a wrong or wicked act; crime, sin, etc.
mis·de·mean (mis′di-mēn′), *v.t. & v.i.* [*mis-* + *demean*], [Rare], to conduct (oneself) badly; misbehave.
mis·de·mean·ant (mis′di-mēn′ənt), *n.* 1. a person who has misbehaved. 2. in *law*, a person guilty or convicted of a misdemeanor.
mis·de·mean·or (mis′di-mēn′ẽr), *n.* [*mis-* + *demeanor*], 1. [Rare], a misbehaving. 2. in *law*, any minor offense, as the breaking of a municipal ordinance, for which statute provides a lesser punishment than for a felony: the penalty is usually a fine or imprisonment for a short time in a local jail, workhouse, etc. British spelling, **misdemeanour.**
mis·di·rect (mis′də-rekt′, mis′dī-rekt′), *v.t.* to direct wrongly or badly; specifically, *a)* to aim (a blow, etc.) badly. *b)* to address (a letter) incorrectly. *c)* to give incorrect instructions to.
mis·di·rec·tion (mis′də-rek′shən, mis′dī-rek′shən), *n.* a misdirecting.
mis·do (mis-dōō′), *v.t.* [MISDID (-did′), MISDONE (-dun′), MISDOING], [ME. *misdoen;* AS. *misdon*], to do wrongly; bungle. *v.i.* [Obs.], to do evil.
mis·do·ing (mis-dōō′iŋ), *n.* [see MISDO], wrongdoing.
mis·doubt (mis-dout′), *v.t.* [Archaic], 1. to have doubt or suspicion about; distrust. 2. to fear. *v.i.* [Archaic], to have doubts. *n.* [Archaic], suspicion; doubt.
mise (mēz, mīz), *n.* [Anglo-Fr.; OFr., a putting, placing (of expenses, etc.) < *mis*, pp. of *mettre*, to put, lay; L. *mittere*, to send], 1. originally, an agreement or pact. 2. in *law*, the issue in a writ of right.
mis·ease (mis-ēz′), *n.* [ME. *misese;* see MIS- & EASE], [Archaic], 1. discomfort; distress. 2. poverty.
mis·em·ploy (mis′em-ploi′), *v.t.* to employ, or use, wrongly or badly; misuse.
‡**mise en scène** (mē′ zän′ sen′), [Fr.], 1. the staging of a play, including the setting, arrangement of the actors, etc.; hence, 2. general surroundings.
mi·ser (mī′zẽr), *n.* [L., wretched, unhappy, ill, worthless], 1. a greedy, stingy person who hoards money for its own sake, even at the expense of his own comfort. 2. [Obs.], a miserable person; wretch.
mis·er·a·ble (miz′ẽr-ə-b'l, miz′rə-b'l), *adj.* [Fr. *misérable;* L. *miserabilis*, to be pitied, pitiable < *miserari*, to pity], 1. in a condition of misery; wretched; very unhappy. 2. causing misery, discomfort, or suffering: as, *miserable* weather. 3. bad, poor, unpleasant, inadequate, etc.: a generalized term of displeasure or disapproval. 4. pitiable. *n.* [Obs.], a miserable person.
mis·er·a·bly (miz′ẽr-ə-bli, miz′rə-bli), *adv.* 1. in a

miserable manner. 2. [Colloq.], very: a general intensive.

Mis·e·re·re (miz'ə-râr'i, miz'ə-rêr'i), *n.* [ME.; L., have mercy: first word of the psalm in the Vulgate], 1. the 51st Psalm of the Bible (50th in the Douay Version), beginning, "Have mercy upon me, O God." 2. a musical setting for this. 3. [m-], a misericord (sense 1).

mis·er·i·cord, mis·er·i·corde (miz'ẽr-i-kôrd', mi-zer'i-kôrd'), *n.* [ME.; OFr.; L. *misericordia* < base of *misereri*, to pity + *cors, cordis*, heart], 1. formerly, a relaxation of the strict observance of a rule or rules in a monastery; hence, 2. a dining room in a monastery set aside for those who had received such relaxation from fasting. 3. a narrow ledge on the underside of a hinged seat in the choir of a monastic chapel: when turned up, the seat permitted one to relax while standing. 4. a slender dagger used in the Middle Ages for giving the death stroke (*coup de grâce*) to a mortally wounded knight.

mi·ser·li·ness (mī'zẽr-li-nis), *n.* the quality or state of being miserly.

mi·ser·ly (mī'zẽr-li), *adj.* like or characteristic of a miser; greedy and stingy. —*SYN.* see **stingy.**

mis·er·y (miz'ẽr-i), *n.* [*pl.* MISERIES (-iz)], [ME. & OFr. *miserie;* L. *miseria* < *miser*, wretched, etc.; see MISER], 1. a condition of great wretchedness or suffering, because of pain, poverty, etc.; distress. 2. a cause of such suffering; pain, ache, poverty, squalor, etc. 3. [Dial.], a pain (*in* some part of the body).

mis·es·ti·mate (mis-es'tə-māt'; *for n.*, mis-es'tə-mit), *v.t.* to estimate incorrectly. *n.* an incorrect estimate.

mis·fea·sance (mis-fē'z'ns), *n.* [OFr. *mesfaisance* < *mesfaire*, to misdo; see MIS- & FEASANCE], in *law*, wrongdoing; specifically, the doing of a lawful act in an unlawful manner, so that there is an infringement on the rights of another or others: distinguished from *malfeasance, nonfeasance.*

mis·fea·sor (mis-fē'zẽr), *n.* in *law*, a person guilty of misfeasance.

mis·fire (mis-fīr'), *v.i.* [*mis-* + *fire, v.*], 1. to fail to ignite properly or at the right time: said of an internal-combustion engine. 2. to fail to go off, or be discharged: said of a firearm. *n.* a misfiring.

mis·fit (mis-fit'; *for n. 3*, mis'fit'), *v.t. & v.i.* to fail to fit properly; be too large, too small, etc. for (someone or something). *n.* 1. the act or condition of misfitting. 2. anything that misfits, as a badly fitting garment. 3. a person not suited to his position, status, etc.; maladjusted person.

mis·for·tune (mis-fôr'chən), *n.* 1. bad luck; ill fortune; trouble; adversity. 2. an instance of this; unlucky accident; mishap; mischance. —*SYN.* see **affliction.**

mis·give (mis-giv'), *v.t.* [MISGAVE (-gāv'), MISGIVEN (-giv''n), MISGIVING], [*mis-* + *give*], to cause fear, doubt, or suspicion in: said usually of the heart, mind, conscience, etc., as, his heart *misgave* him. *v.i.* to feel fear, doubt, suspicion, etc.

mis·giv·ing (mis-giv'iŋ), *n.* [see prec.], *often in pl.* a disturbed feeling of fear, doubt, apprehension, etc. —*SYN.* see **qualm.**

mis·gov·ern (mis-guv'ẽrn), *v.t.* to govern, administer, or manage badly.

mis·gov·ern·ment (mis-guv'ẽrn-mənt, mis-guv'ẽr-mənt), *n.* a misgoverning.

mis·guid·ance (mis-gīd'əns), *n.* a misguiding.

mis·guide (mis-gīd'), *v.t.* to guide wrongly; lead into error or misconduct; mislead.

mis·guid·ed (mis-gīd'id), *adj.* [pp. of *misguide*], led into or characterized by error or misconduct; misled.

mis·han·dle (mis-han'd'l), *v.t.* to handle badly or roughly; abuse, maltreat, or mismanage.

mis·hap (mis'hap', mis-hap'), *n.* [ME.; prob. after OFr. *mescheance*, mischance], 1. bad luck; adversity; misfortune. 2. an instance of this; unlucky accident.

Mish·a·wa·ka (mish'ə-wô'kə), *n.* a city in northern Indiana: pop., 33,000.

mis·hear (mis-hêr'), *v.t. & v.i.* to hear incorrectly or poorly.

mish·mash (mish'mash'), *n.* [redupl. of *mash*], a hodgepodge; jumble.

Mish·nah, Mish·na (mish'nə), *n.* [*pl.* MISHNAYOTH (mish'nä-yōth')], [Mod. Heb. *mishnāh*, (oral) instruction < Heb. *shānāh*, to repeat, (later) to learn, teach], 1. the first part of the Talmud, containing traditional oral interpretations of scriptural ordinances (*halakoth*), compiled by the rabbis about 200 A.D. 2. any of these interpretations. 3. the teachings of a rabbi.

Mish·na·ic (mish-nā'ik), *adj.* Mishnic.

Mish·nic (mish'nik), *adj.* of the Mishnah.

Mish·ni·cal (mish'ni-k'l), *adj.* Mishnic.

mis·in·form (mis'in-fôrm', mis''n-fôrm'), *v.t.* to supply with false or misleading information. *v.i.* to make false or misleading statements.

mis·in·form·ant (mis'in-fôr'mənt, mis''n-fôr'mənt), *n.* a person who misinforms.

mis·in·for·ma·tion (mis'in-fẽr-mā'shən), *n.* false or misleading information.

mis·in·ter·pret (mis'in-tũr'prit), *v.t.* to interpret wrongly; understand or explain incorrectly.

mis·in·ter·pre·ta·tion (mis'in-tũr'pri-tā'shən), *n.* wrong interpretation; incorrect understanding or explanation.

mis·join·der (mis-join'dẽr), *n.* in *law*, the introduction into a court action of parties or causes not properly belonging to that action.

mis·judge (mis-juj'), *v.t. & v.i.* to judge wrongly or unfairly.

mis·judg·ment, mis·judge·ment (mis-juj'mənt), *n.* wrong or unfair judgment.

mis·lay (mis-lā'), *v.t.* [MISLAID (-lād'), MISLAYING], [see MIS- & LAY, *v.*], 1. to put in a place afterward forgotten or not easily found. 2. to misplace (sense 1).

mis·lead (mis-lēd'), *v.t.* [MISLED (-led), MISLEADING], 1. to lead in a wrong direction; lead astray. 2. to lead into error (of judgment); deceive or delude. 3. to lead into wrongdoing; influence badly. —*SYN.* see **deceive.**

mis·lead·ing (mis-lēd'iŋ), *adj.* that misleads.

mis·like (mis-līk'), *v.t.* [MISLIKED (-līkt'), MISLIKING], 1. to displease. 2. to be displeased at; dislike. *n.* dislike; disapproval.

mis·man·age (mis-man'ij), *v.t. & v.i.* to manage or administer badly or dishonestly.

mis·man·age·ment (mis-man'ij-mənt), *n.* bad management.

mis·match (mis-mach'), *v.t.* to match badly or unsuitably, especially in marriage. *n.* a bad match.

mis·mate (mis-māt'), *v.t. & v.i.* to mate badly or unsuitably.

mis·name (mis-nām'), *v.t.* to call by a wrong name.

mis·no·mer (mis-nō'mẽr), *n.* [ME. *misnoumer;* OFr. *mesnomer, mesnommer*, inf. used as n.; *mes-, mis-* + *nomer, nommer* (L. *nominare*), to name; cf. NOMINATE], 1. *a*) the act of applying a wrong name or epithet to some person or thing. *b*) such a name or epithet. 2. an error in naming a person or place in a legal document.

mis·o- (mis'ō), [Gr. *miso-* < *misein*, to hate], a combining form meaning *hatred* or *hating*, as in *misogyny:* also, before a vowel, **mis-.**

mi·sog·a·mist (mi-sog'ə-mist), *n.* [< *misogamy* + *-ist*], a person who hates marriage.

mi·sog·a·my (mi-sog'ə-mi), *n.* [< *miso-* + Gr. *gamos*, marriage], hatred of marriage.

mi·sog·y·nist (mi-soj'ə-nist), *n.* [see MISOGYNY], a person, especially a man, who hates women.

mi·sog·y·nous (mi-soj'ə-nəs), *adj.* of or characterized by misogyny.

mi·sog·y·ny (mi-soj'ə-ni), *n.* [Gr. *misogynia* < *misein*, to hate + *gynē*, woman], hatred of women.

mi·sol·o·gist (mi-sol'ə-jist), *n.* a person characterized by misology.

mi·sol·o·gy (mi-sol'ə-ji), *n.* [Gr. *misologia;* see MISO- & -LOGY], hatred of argument, debate, or reasoning.

mis·o·ne·ism (mis'ō-nē'iz'm), *n.* [It. *misoneismo* < Gr. *miso-* < *misein*, to hate + *neos*, new + It. *-ismo*, -ism], hatred of innovation or change.

mis·pick·el (mis'pik''l), *n.* [G.; var. of earlier *mispütl*], arsenopyrite.

mis·place (mis-plās'), *v.t.* 1. to put in a wrong place. 2. to bestow (one's trust, affection, etc.) on an unsuitable or undeserving object. 3. [Colloq.], to mislay (sense 1).

mis·place·ment (mis-plās'mənt), *n.* a misplacing or being misplaced.

mis·play (mis-plā'), *v.t. & v.i.* to play wrongly or badly, as in games or sports. *n.* a wrong or bad play.

mis·plead (mis-plēd'), *v.t. & v.i.* [MISPLED (-pled'), MISPLEADING], to plead incorrectly.

mis·plead·ing (mis-plēd'iŋ), *n.* in *law*, an incorrect pleading or error in pleading, as a misstatement of a cause of action.

mis·print (mis-print'; *also, for n.*, mis'print'), *v.t.* to print incorrectly. *n.* an error in printing.

mis·prise (mis-prīz'), *v.t.* [MISPRISED (-prīzd'), MISPRISING], to misprize.

mis·pri·sion (mis-prizh'ən), *n.* [ME.; OFr. *mespresion* < pp. of *mesprendre*, to take wrongly; LL. **minusprehendere;* L. *minus*, less + *prehendere*, to take; see PREHENSILE], 1. misconduct or neglect of duty, especially by a public official. 2. [Archaic], a mistake.

misprision of felony (or **treason**), in *common law*, the offense of concealing knowledge of a felony (or treason) by one who has not participated or assisted in it.

mis·prize (mis-prīz'), *v.t.* [MISPRIZED (-prīzd'), MISPRIZING], [OFr. *mesprisier* < *mes-* (see MIS-) + LL. *pretiare*, to value < L. *pretium*, a price], to despise or undervalue.

mis·pro·nounce (mis'prə-nouns'), *v.t. & v.i.* to pronounce incorrectly; give (a word or words) a pronunciation different from any of the accepted standard pronunciations.

mis·pro·nun·ci·a·tion (mis'prə-nun'si-ā'shən), *n.* 1. a mispronouncing or being mispronounced. 2. a mispronounced word.

mis·quo·ta·tion (mis'kwō-tā'shən), *n.* 1. a misquoting or being misquoted. 2. something misquoted.

mis·quote (mis-kwōt'), *v.t. & v.i.* to quote incorrectly.

mis·read (mis-rēd'), *v.t. & v.i.* [MISREAD (-red'), MISREADING (-rēd'iŋ)], to read wrongly, especially so as to misinterpret or misunderstand.

mis·re·mem·ber (mis'ri-mem'bẽr), *v.t. & v.i.* 1. to make an error in remembering. 2. [Dial.], to forget.

mis·rep·re·sent (mis'rep-ri-zent'), *v.t.* to represent falsely; give an untrue or misleading idea of.

mis·rep·re·sen·ta·tion (mis'rep-ri-zen-tā'shən), *n.* 1. a misrepresenting or being misrepresented. 2. a false or incorrect account, explanation, etc.

mis·rule (mis-rōōl'), *v.t.* to rule badly or unjustly; misgovern. *n.* 1. misgovernment. 2. disorder or riot.

miss (mis), *v.t.* [ME. *missen;* AS. *missan,* to miss, fail to hit, escape the notice of; akin to G. *missen;* IE. base **meit(h)-,* to change, exchange, as also in L. *mutare,* to change (cf. MUTATE, MUTUAL, MIS-)], 1. to fail to hit or land on (something aimed at). 2. to fail to meet, reach, attain, catch, accomplish, see, hear, perceive, etc. 3. to overlook; let (an opportunity, etc.) go by. 4. to escape; avoid: as, he just *missed* being struck. 5. to fail or forget to do, keep, have, be present at, etc.: as, he *missed* class yesterday. 6. to notice the absence or loss of: as, he suddenly *missed* his watch. 7. to feel or regret the absence or loss of; want: as, he *misses* his friends. *v.i.* 1. to fail to hit something aimed at; go wide of the mark. 2. to fail to be successful. 3. [Archaic], to fail to obtain, receive, etc. (with *of* or *in*). *n.* a failure to hit, meet, obtain, see, etc.

a miss is as good as a mile, missing by a narrow margin is as conclusive as missing by a wide one.

miss (mis), *n.* [*pl.* MISSES (-iz)], [contr. of *mistress*], 1. *a)* [M-], a title used in speaking to or of an unmarried woman or girl, placed before the name: as, *Miss* Smith, the *Misses* Smith. *b)* a title used in speaking to an unmarried woman or girl, used without the name. 2. a young unmarried woman or girl: now usually humorous or in trade jargon, as, coats in *misses'* sizes.

Miss., Mississippi.

miss., 1. mission. 2. missionary.

mis·sal (mis''l), *n.* [ME. *missale, messel;* ML. *missale,* neut. of *missalis,* of mass < LL. *missa,* Mass], 1. in the *Roman Catholic Church,* a book containing all the prayers necessary for celebrating Mass throughout the year; hence, 2. any book of prayers or devotions.

mis·say (mis-sā'), *v.t. & v.i.* [MISSAID (-sed'), MISSAYING], [Chiefly Archaic], 1. to say or speak wrongly. 2. to speak evil (of); vilify; abuse; slander.

mis·sel (mis''l), *n.* [< ME. & AS. *mistel,* mistletoe], a variety of large European thrush that eats mistletoe berries: also **missel thrush.**

mis·shape (mis-shāp'), *v.t.* [MISSHAPED (-shāpt'), MISSHAPED or *archaic* MISSHAPEN (-'n), MISSHAPING], to shape badly; deform.

mis·shap·en (mis-shāp''n), *adj.* [ME. *mischapen;* see prec.], badly shaped; deformed.

mis·sile (mis''l), *adj.* [L. *missilis* < *missus,* pp. of *mittere,* to send, throw], 1. that can be, or is, thrown or shot, as from a gun: as, a grenade is a *missile* weapon. 2. [Rare], throwing or shooting missiles. *n.* a weapon or other object, as a spear, bullet, rocket, etc., designed to be thrown, fired, or launched toward a target; often, specifically, a guided missile.

mis·sile·ry (mis''l-ri), *n.* [*missile* + *-ry*], the science of building and launching guided missiles.

miss·ing (mis'iŋ), *adj.* [*miss, v.* + *-ing*], absent; lost; lacking; specifically, absent after combat, but not definitely known to be dead or taken prisoner.

missing link, something necessary for completing a series; specifically, a hypothetical form of animal believed to have existed in the evolutionary process intermediate between man and the anthropoid apes.

mis·sion (mish'ən), *n.* [L. *missio,* a sending, sending away < *missus,* pp. of *mittere,* to send], 1. a sending out or being sent out with authority to perform a special duty; specifically, *a)* the sending out of persons by a religious organization to preach, teach, or proselyte. *b)* the sending out of persons to a foreign government to conduct negotiations. 2. *a)* a group of persons sent by a church to spread its religion, especially in a foreign land. *b)* its organization, headquarters, or place of residence. 3. a group of persons sent to a foreign government to conduct negotiations; diplomatic delegation; embassy. 4. the special duty or function on which someone is sent as a messenger or representative; errand. 5. the special task or purpose for which a person is apparently destined in life; calling: as, he considered it his *mission* to educate the ignorant. 6. any charitable or educational organization for doing welfare work for the needy of a city or district. 7. a series of special religious exercises, sermons, etc. for proselyting. 8. a district without a church of its own, served by the pastor or priest of a near-by parish. 9. *pl.* organized missionary work, especially for spreading Christianity. 10. in *military usage,* a specific combat operation assigned to an individual or unit; especially, a single combat flight by an airplane or group of airplanes. *adj.* of a mission or missions; specifically, of or characteristic of the early Spanish missions in the southwestern United States. *v.t.* 1. to send on a mission. 2. to establish a religious mission in (a district) or among (a people). Abbreviated **miss.**

mis·sion·ar·y (mish'ən-er'i), *adj.* [*mission* + *-ary*], of or characteristic of religious missions or missionaries. *n.* [*pl.* MISSIONARIES (-iz)], a person sent on a mission; specifically, a person sent out by his church to preach, teach, and proselyte in a foreign country, especially in one considered heathen. Abbreviated **miss.**

Missionary Ridge, a ridge in Georgia and Tennessee, near Chattanooga: site of a Civil War battle (1863).

mis·sion·er (mish'ən-ẽr), *n.* a missionary, especially one who conducts the mission of a parish.

mission furniture, a type of heavy, dark furniture with simple, square lines, in imitation of furniture found in the Spanish missions of California.

mis·sis (mis'əz), *n.* [altered < *mistress, Mrs.*], [Colloq. or Dial.], 1. a wife: used with a personal pronoun or *the,* as, the *missis* does all the shopping. 2. the mistress of a household (with *the*). Also spelled **missus.**

Mis·sis·sip·pi (mis'ə-sip'i), *n.* 1. a river in the United States, flowing from northern Minnesota through ten States to the Gulf of Mexico: length, 2,330, mi.: called the *Father of Waters.* 2. a Southern State of the United States, on the Gulf of Mexico: area, 47,716 sq. mi.; pop., 2,178,000; capital, Jackson: abbreviated **Miss.**

Mis·sis·sip·pi·an (mis'ə-sip'i-ən), *adj.* 1. of the Mississippi River. 2. of the State of Mississippi. 3. designating or of the first coal-forming period of the Paleozoic Era in North America, characterized also by the first appearance of reptiles. *n.* a native or inhabitant of Mississippi.

the Mississippian, the Mississippian Period or its rocks: see **geology,** chart.

mis·sive (mis'iv), *adj.* [Fr.; ML. *missivus* < L. *missus,* pp. of *mittere,* to send], [Archaic or Rare], sent or intended to be sent. *n.* a letter or message.

Mis·so·lon·ghi (mis'ə-lôŋ'gi), *n.* a city on the Gulf of Patras, Greece: pop., 12,000.

Mis·sou·la (mi-zōō'lə), *n.* a city in western Montana: pop., 27,000.

Mis·sour·i (mi-zoor'i; *locally, also* mi-zoor'ə), *n.* [< Am. Ind. (Illinois) *Emissourita,* lit., people who dwell on the Big Muddy (the Missouri River), hence Missouri tribe], 1. [*pl.* MISSOURI], a member of a tribe of Siouan Indians that lived in northern Missouri. 2. a Middle Western State of the United States: area, 69,674 sq. mi.; pop., 4,320,000; capital, Jefferson City: abbreviated **Mo.** 3. a river flowing southeastward from Montana to the Mississippi: length, 2,465 mi.: length from its headwaters to the Gulf of Mexico, 3,872 mi.

from Missouri, [Slang], not easily convinced; skeptical until shown definite proof.

Mis·sour·i·an (mi-zoor'i-ən), *adj.* of Missouri. *n.* a native or inhabitant of Missouri.

mis·speak (mis-spēk'), *v.t. & v.i.* [MISSPOKE (-spōk'), MISSPOKEN (-spōk''n), MISSPEAKING], to speak or say incorrectly.

mis·spell (mis-spel'), *v.t. & v.i.* [MISSPELLED (-speld') or MISSPELT (-spelt'), MISSPELLING], to spell incorrectly.

mis·spell·ing (mis-spel'iŋ), *n.* incorrect spelling.

mis·spend (mis-spend'), *v.t.* [MISSPENT (-spent'), MISSPENDING], to spend improperly or wastefully.

mis·state (mis-stāt'), *v.t.* to state incorrectly or falsely.

mis·state·ment (mis-stāt'mənt), *n.* an incorrect or false statement; misrepresentation.

mis·step (mis-step'), *n.* 1. a wrong or awkward step. 2. a mistake in conduct; faux pas.

mis·sus (mis'əz), *n.* [Colloq. or Dial.], missis.

miss·y (mis'i), *n.* [*pl.* MISSIES (-iz)], [Colloq.], miss: diminutive form, used in speaking to or of a young girl.

mist (mist), *n.* [ME.; AS., darkness, mist; common Gmc.; prob. IE. base **meigh-,* to make blink, be dim (via Gmc. **mixstu-*)], 1. a large mass of water vapor at or just above the earth's surface and like a fog, but less dense. 2. a thin film of moisture condensed on a surface in droplets. 3. a cloud of dust, smoke, gas, etc. 4. a cloudiness or film before the eyes, dimming or blurring the vision: as, she smiled in a *mist* of tears. 5. anything that dims or obscures the understanding, memory, etc. *v.t. & v.i.* to be, become, or make misty; dim or obscure with or as with a mist.

SYN.—**mist** applies to a visible atmospheric vapor of rather fine density, that blurs the vision; **haze** suggests a thin dispersion of smoke, dust, etc. that makes objects indistinct; **fog** suggests a greater density of moisture particles than **mist,** sometimes suggesting a thickness impenetrable by the vision; **smog** is applied to a mixture of fog and smoke of a kind that sometimes appears in industrial centers. The first three terms are also used figuratively (lost in the *mists* of the past, a mellow *haze* of intoxication, in a *fog* of doubt).

mis·tak·a·ble (mis-tāk'ə-b'l), *adj.* that can be, or is likely to be, mistaken or misunderstood.

mis·take (mis-tāk'), *v.t.* [MISTOOK (-took'), MISTAKEN (-tāk''n) or *obs.* MISTOOK, MISTAKING], [ME. *mistaken;*

ON. *mistaka*, to take wrongly; see MIS- & TAKE], 1. to understand or perceive wrongly; interpret or estimate incorrectly: as, you *mistake* his real motives. 2. to take (someone or something) to be another; recognize or identify incorrectly: as, he *mistook* me for my brother. *v.i.* to make a mistake. *n.* a fault in understanding, perception, interpretation, etc.; blunder; error; misunderstanding. —*SYN.* see **error.**

and no mistake, [Colloq.], without doubt; certainly.

mis·tak·en (mis-tāk′'n), *adj.* [pp. of *mistake*], 1. wrong; having an incorrect understanding, perception, interpretation, etc.: said of persons. 2. incorrect; misunderstood; erroneous: said of ideas, etc.

mis·ter (mis′tẽr), *n.* [weakened form of *master*], 1. [M-], a title used in speaking to or of a man, placed before the name or title of office and usually written *Mr.*: as, *Mr.* Stein, *Mr.* Secretary. 2. in *military usage*, the official title of address for *a*) a warrant officer in the army. *b*) a cadet in the U. S. Military Academy. *c*) a naval officer below the rank of commander. 3. [Colloq.], sir: as, what time is it, *mister?*

mist·flow·er (mist′flou′ẽr), *n.* any of a group of tall plants with composite flowers of blue or violet.

Mis·ti (mēs′tē), *n.* a volcanic mountain of the Andes, in southern Peru: height, 19,200 ft.

mist·i·ly (mis′tə-li), *adv.* in a misty manner; foggily.

mis·time (mis-tīm′), *v.t.* 1. to time wrongly; do or say at an inappropriate time. 2. to judge incorrectly the time of.

mis·ti·ness (mis′ti-nis), *n.* a misty quality or state.

mis·tle·toe (mis′'l-tō′), *n.* [AS. *misteltan; mistel*, mistletoe + *tan*, a twig; cf. MISSEL], 1. any of various parasitic evergreen plants with small yellowish-green leaves, yellowish flowers, and waxy white berries, growing on the branches of certain trees. 2. a sprig of such a plant, hung as a Christmas decoration: men are by custom privileged to kiss women standing under it.

mis·took (mis-took′), past tense and obsolete past participle of **mistake.**

mis·tral (mis′trəl), *n.* [Fr.; Pr., lit., master-wind < L. *magistralis* < *magister*, a master], a cold, dry, north wind that blows over the Mediterranean coast of France and near-by regions.

Mis·tral, Fré·dé·ric (frā′dā′rēk′ mēs′trȧl′), 1830–1914; French Provençal poet; received Nobel prize in literature, 1904.

mis·trans·late (mis′trans-lāt′, mis-tranz′lāt), *v.t.* to translate incorrectly.

mis·trans·la·tion (mis′trans-lā′shən, mis′tranz-lā′shən), *n.* an incorrect translation.

mis·treat (mis-trēt′), *v.t.* to treat wrongly or badly.

mis·tress (mis′tris), *n.* [ME. & OFr. *maistresse*, fem. of *maistre;* see MASTER], 1. a woman who rules others or has control, authority, or power over something; specifically, *a*) a woman who is head of a household or institution. *b*) a woman owner of an animal or slave. *c*) [Chiefly British], a woman schoolteacher. 2. [sometimes M-], something regarded as feminine that has control, power, etc.: as, England was *Mistress* of the seas. 3. a woman who has sexual intercourse with and, often, is supported by a man for a more or less extended period of time without being married to him; paramour. 4. [Archaic], a sweetheart. 5. [M-], formerly, a title used in speaking to or of a woman, prefixed to the name: now replaced by *Mrs.* or *Miss.*

mis·tri·al (mis-trī′əl), *n.* in *law*, a trial made void because of an error in the proceedings, or because the jury cannot reach a verdict.

mis·trust (mis-trust′), *n.* lack of trust or confidence; suspicion. *v.t. & v.i.* to have no trust or confidence in (someone or something); doubt.

mis·trust·ful (mis-trust′fəl), *adj.* lacking trust or confidence; full of doubt or suspicion.

mist·y (mis′ti), *adj.* [MISTIER (-ti-ẽr), MISTIEST (-ti-ist)], [ME. *misti;* AS. *mistig*], 1. of, or having the nature of, mist. 2. characterized by or covered with mist. 3. blurred or dimmed, as by mist; obscure; vague.

mis·un·der·stand (mis′un-dẽr-stand′, mis-un′dẽr-stand′), *v.t.* [MISUNDERSTOOD (-stood′), MISUNDERSTANDING], to understand incorrectly; miscomprehend or misinterpret.

mis·un·der·stand·ing (mis′un-dẽr-stan′diŋ, mis-un′dẽr-stan′diŋ), *n.* 1. a failure to understand; mistake of meaning or intention. 2. a quarrel; disagreement.

mis·un·der·stood (mis′un-dẽr-stood′, mis-un′dẽr-stood′), *adj.* 1. incorrectly understood. 2. not properly appreciated.

mis·us·age (mis-ūs′ij, mis-ūz′ij), *n.* 1. incorrect usage; misapplication, as of words. 2. bad or harsh treatment.

mis·use (mis-ūz′; *for n.*, mis-ūs′), *v.t.* 1. to use incorrectly or improperly; misapply. 2. to treat badly or harshly; mistreat; abuse. *n.* 1. incorrect or improper use. 2. [Obs. or Rare], bad or harsh treatment; abuse.

mis·us·er (mis-ūz′ẽr), *n.* 1. a person who misuses. 2. in *law*, abuse of some privilege, liberty, benefit, etc.

mis·val·ue (mis-val′ū), *v.t.* to value or esteem wrongly.

mis·word (mis-wũrd′), *v.t.* to word incorrectly.

Mitch·ell, Maria (mich′əl), 1818–1889; American astronomer.

Mitch·ell, Mount (mich′əl), the highest mountain of the Appalachians, in western North Carolina: height, 6,711 ft.

Mitchell, Silas Weir (wêr), 1829–1914; American physician and writer.

Mitchell, William, 1879–1936; American army general; early supporter of a strong air force.

mite (mīt), *n.* [ME. *myte;* AS.; akin to OHG. *mīza*, a gnat; IE. base **mai-*, to cut, cut off, as also in *mad*], any of a large number of tiny arachnids, many of which live as parasites upon animals or plants, or in prepared foods, etc.

mite (mīt), *n.* [ME. < MD.; ult. same as prec. *mite*], 1. *a*) a very small sum of money or contribution. *b*) a coin of very small value; especially, in England, half a farthing: see Mark 12:41–44; hence, 2. a very small creature or object.

mi·ter (mī′tẽr), *n.* [ME. & OFr. *mitre;* L. *mitra;* Gr. *mitra*, a belt, fillet, headband, turban], 1. a headdress; specifically, *a*) a tall, ornamented cap with peaks in front and back, worn by the Pope, bishops, and abbots as a mark of office. *b*) the official headdress of the ancient Jewish high priest. *c*) in ancient Greece, a headband worn by women. 2. the office or rank of a bishop; bishopric. 3. a covering over the top of a chimney that keeps the rain out but permits the smoke to leave. *v.t.* to invest with the office of bishop by placing a miter on. Also spelled **mitre.**

MITER

mi·ter (mī′tẽr), *n.* [? < *miter* (headdress)], in *carpentry*, 1. a kind of joint formed by fitting together two pieces, each of which has been beveled to a specified angle (usually 45°), so that they form a corner (usually a right angle): also **miter joint.** 2. either of the facing surfaces of such a joint. *v.t.* to fit together in a miter. Also spelled **mitre.**

miter box, a device used as a guide in sawing wood at an angle for miter joints.

miter square, a tool with two blades set at a 45° angle or adjustable to any angle, used to mark out angles for miter joints.

MITER JOINTS

mi·ter·wort (mī′tẽr-wũrt′), *n.* any of a group of plants of the saxifrage family, with small, white or greenish flowers and a seed pod shaped like a bishop's miter.

Mit·ford, Mary Russell (mit′fẽrd), 1787–1855; English novelist and playwright.

mith·er (mit*h*′ẽr), *n.* [Scot. & N. Eng. Dial.], mother.

Mith·gar·thr (mit*h*′gär′*th*ẽr), *n.* Midgard.

Mith·ra (mith′rə), *n.* Mithras.

Mith·ra·ic (mith-rā′ik), *adj.* of Mithras or Mithraism.

Mith·ra·i·cism (mith-rā′ə-siz′m), *n.* Mithraism.

Mith·ra·ism (mith′rā-iz′m), *n.* the ancient Persian religion based on worship of Mithras.

Mith·ra·ist (mith′rā-ist), *n.* a believer in Mithraism.

Mith·ra·is·tic (mith′rā-is′tik), *adj.* Mithraic.

Mith·ras (mith′ras), *n.* [L.; Gr. *Mithras;* OPer. *Mithra*], the ancient Persian god of light and truth, opponent of darkness and evil: also **Mithra.**

mith·ri·date (mith′rə-dāt′), *n.* [ML. *mithridatum;* LL. *mithridatium* < *Mithridatius*, of Mithridates VI, said to have become immune to poisons by taking them in gradually increased doses], formerly, a substance supposed to be an antidote against all poisons.

Mith·ri·da·tes VI (mith′rə-dā′tēz), 132?–63 B.C.; king of Pontus (120–63 B.C.): called *the Great.*

mit·i·ga·ble (mit′i-gə-b'l), *adj.* that can be mitigated.

mit·i·gate (mit′ə-gāt′), *v.t. & v.i.* [MITIGATED (-id), MITIGATING], [ME. *myttigaten* < L. *mitigatus*, pp. of *mitigare*, to make mild, soft, or tender < *mitis*, mild, soft + *agere*, to drive, do], to make or become milder, less severe, less rigorous, or less painful; moderate.

mit·i·ga·tion (mit′ə-gā′shən), *n.* 1. a mitigating or being mitigated. 2. anything that mitigates.

mit·i·ga·tive (mit′ə-gā′tiv), *adj.* [LL. *mitigativus*], mitigating or tending to mitigate. *n.* something that mitigates, as a drug that lessens pain.

mit·i·ga·tor (mit′ə-gā′tẽr), *n.* a person or thing that mitigates.

mit·i·ga·to·ry (mit′ə-gə-tôr′i, mit′ə-gə-tō′ri), *adj.* [LL. *mitigatorius*], mitigative.

mi·tis casting (mī′tis, mē′tis), [< L. *mitis*, soft], 1. a method of making malleable iron castings from a

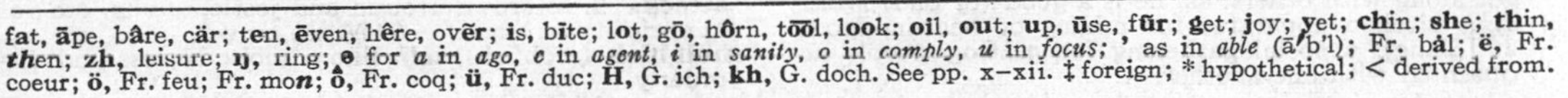
fat, āpe, bâre, cär; ten, ēven, hêre, ovẽr; is, bīte; lot, gō, hôrn, tōōl, look; oil, out; up, ūse, fũr; get; joy; yet; chin; she; thin, *th*en; zh, leisure; ŋ, ring; ə for *a* in *ago*, *e* in *agent*, *i* in *sanity*, *o* in *comply*, *u* in *focus*; ′ as in *able* (ā′b'l); Fr. bȧl; ë, Fr. coeur; ö, Fr. feu; Fr. mon; ô, Fr. coq; ü, Fr. duc; H, G. ich; kh, G. doch. See pp. x–xii. ‡ foreign; * hypothetical; < derived from.

mixture of wrought iron and aluminum. 2. a casting made in this way.
mi·to·sis (mi-tō′sis, mī-tō′sis), *n.* [Mod. L. < Gr. *mitos*, thread; + *-osis*], in *biology*, the indirect, and more common, method of cell division, in which the nuclear chromatin is formed into a long thread which in turn breaks into segments (*chromosomes*) that are split lengthwise: the halves come together in two sets, each set forming the nucleus for a new cell: see also **prophase, metaphase, anaphase, telophase.**
mi·tot·ic (mi-tot′ik, mī-tot′ik), *adj.* of mitosis.
mi·tot·i·cal·ly (mi-tot′i-k'l-i, mī-tot′ik-li), *adv.* by mitosis.
‡**mi·trail·leur** (mē′trȧ′yër′), *n.* [Fr. < *mitrailler*, to fire grapeshot < *mitraille*, grapeshot, small missiles, orig. small coins < OFr. *mitre, mite*, small coin; cf. MITE (small sum)], 1. *a*) a soldier who operated a mitrailleuse. *b*) a machine gunner. 2. a mitrailleuse.
‡**mi·trail·leuse** (mē′trȧ′yöz′), *n.* [Fr.; see MITRAILLEUR], 1. an obsolete, breach-loading machine gun with a cluster of barrels which were fired simultaneously or in rapid succession. 2. any machine gun.
mi·tral (mī′trəl), *adj.* [Fr.; Mod. L. *mitralis*], of or like a miter or the mitral valve.
mitral valve, the valve between the left auricle and left ventricle of the heart.
mi·tre (mī′tēr), *n. & v.t.* [MITRED (-tērd), MITRING], miter.
mits·vah (mits′vä, mits′vô), *n.* [*pl.* MITSVOTH (-vōth)], a mitzvah.
mitt (mit), *n.* [abbrev. of *mitten*], 1. a glove, often of lace or net, covering the forearm, hand, and sometimes part of the fingers. 2. a mitten. 3. [Slang], a hand. 4. in *sports*, *a*) a glove padded on the palm and fingers for protection and worn by baseball players in the field. *b*) *usually in pl.* a padded mitten worn by boxers.
mit·ten (mit′'n), *n.* [ME. *myteyne;* OFr. *mitaine;* extension of *mite* in the same sense; ? < LL. *mi*, pet name for a kitten], 1. a glove with a thumb but no separately divided fingers. 2. a mitt (senses 1 & 4*b*).
get the mitten, [Colloq.], to be rejected as a lover.
give the mitten to, [Colloq.], to reject as a lover.
mit·ti·mus (mit′i-məs), *n.* [L., we send], 1. in *law*, a warrant or writ for putting into prison a person convicted of crime. 2. dismissal, as from office.
mitz·vah (mits′vä, mits′vô), *n.* [*pl.* MITZVOTH (-vōth)], [Heb. *mitswāh*], in *Judaism*, 1. a commandment or precept, as in the Bible or from a rabbi. 2. an act fulfilling such a command or the spirit of such commands: as, an act of charity is a *mitzvah*. Also spelled **mitsvah.**
mix (miks), *v.t.* [MIXED or MIXT (mikst), MIXING], [prob. back-formation < *mixt*, mixed, taken as pp.; Fr. *mixte;* L. *mixtus*, pp. of *miscere*, to mix], 1. to put or blend together in a single mass, collection, or compound. 2. to make by putting ingredients together: as, she's *mixing* a cake. 3. to join; combine: as, we try to *mix* work and play. 4. to cause to join or associate: as, they *mixed* the boys with the girls in our school. 5. to crossbreed. *v.i.* 1. to be mixed or capable of being mixed; be blended; mingle. 2. to associate or get along together. *n.* 1. a mixing or being mixed. 2. a muddle; state of confusion. 3. a prepared blend of various ingredients; mixture. 4. a beverage, usually carbonated, as soda or ginger ale, for mixing with alcoholic liquor.
mix up, 1. to mix thoroughly; mingle together. 2. to confuse; specifically, *a*) to cause confusion in. *b*) to mistake for another (with *with*). 3. to involve or implicate (*in* some matter).
***SYN.*—mix** implies a combining of things so that the resulting substance is uniform in composition, whether or not the separate elements can be distinguished (to *mix* paints); **mingle** usually implies that the separate elements can be distinguished (*mingled* feelings of joy and sorrow); **blend** implies a mixing of different varieties to produce a desired quality (a *blended* tea, whisky, etc.) or the mingling of different elements to form a harmonious whole (a novel *blending* fact and fiction); **merge** stresses the loss of distinction of elements by combination or may suggest the total absorption of one thing in another (the companies *merged* to form a large corporation); **coalesce** implies a union or growing together of things into a single body or mass (the factions *coalesced* into a party of opposition); **fuse** means to unite by melting together and stresses the indissoluble nature of the union.
mixed (mikst), *adj.* [earlier *mixt;* see MIX], 1. joined or mingled in a single mass or compound; blended. 2. made up of different or incongruous parts, elements, classes, races, etc. 3. consisting of or involving both sexes: as, a *mixed* class, *mixed* company. 4. confused; muddled. 5. in *phonetics*, central: said of vowels.
mixed marriage, marriage between persons of different religions or races.
mixed number, a number consisting of a whole number and a fraction, as 3 2/3.
mix·er (mik′sēr), *n.* 1. a person or thing that mixes; specifically, *a*) a person with reference to his ability to get along with others: as, he is a good (or bad) *mixer*. *b*) a kitchen apparatus for mixing or beating foods. 2. [Slang], a social gathering for getting people acquainted with one another.
mixt (mikst), alternative past tense and past participle of **mix.**
mix·ture (miks′chēr), *n.* [Late ME.; OFr.; L. *mixtura* < *mixtus;* see MIX], 1. a mixing or being mixed. 2. something mixed, as a cloth made of differently colored threads. 3. in *chemistry*, a substance containing two or more elements: distinguished from *compound* in that the constituents are not in fixed proportions and do not lose their individual characteristics. Abbreviated **mixt.**
mix-up (miks′up′), *n.* 1. confusion; tangle. 2. [Colloq.], a fight.
miz·zen, miz·en (miz′'n), *adj.* [Late ME. *meseyn;* OFr. *misaine;* It. *mezzana*, fem. of *mezzano*, middle < L. *medianus;* see MEDIAN], of the mizzenmast. *n.* 1. a fore-and-aft sail set on the mizzenmast: see **mainmast,** illus. 2. a mizzenmast.
miz·zen·mast, miz·en·mast (miz′'n-məst, miz′'n-mast′, miz′'n-mäst′), *n.* [see MIZZEN], the mast closest to the stern in a ship with two or three masts: see **mainmast,** illus.
miz·zle (miz′'l), *v.t. & v.i.* [MIZZLED (-'ld), MIZZLING], [Late ME. *miselle;* prob. < a LG. source; cf. D. dial. *miezelen*, LG. *miseln;* for base see MIST], [Obs. or Dial.], to rain in a fine mist; drizzle. *n.* [Obs. or Dial.], a misty rain; drizzle.
mk., [*pl.* MKS.], mark.
mkt., market.
ML., 1. Medieval Latin. 2. Middle Latin.
ml., 1. mail. 2. milliliter; milliliters.
M.L., 1. Medieval Latin. 2. Middle Latin.
M.L.A., Modern Language Association.
MLG., M.L.G., Middle Low German.
Mlle., [*pl.* MLLES.], Mademoiselle.
M.L.S., Master of Library Science.
MM., 1. Their Majesties. 2. Messieurs.
mm., 1. *millia*, [L.], thousands. 2. millimeter; millimeters.
M.M., 1. Master Mason. 2. Master Mechanic.
Mme., [*pl.* MMES.], Madame.
M.M.E., 1. Master of Mechanical Engineering. 2. Master of Mining Engineering.
m.m.f., magnetomotive force.
mmfds., microfarads.
Mn, in *chemistry*, manganese.
M.N.A.S., Member of the National Academy of Sciences.
mne·mon·ic (ni-mon′ik), *adj.* [Gr. *mnēmonikos* < *mnēmōn*, mindful < *mnasthai*, to remember], 1. helping, or meant to help, the memory. 2. of mnemonics or memory.
mne·mon·ics (ni-mon′iks), *n.pl.* [see prec.], 1. [construed as sing.], the science or art of improving the memory, as by the use of certain formulas. 2. formulas or other aids to help in remembering.
Mne·mos·y·ne (ni-mos′ə-nē′, nē-moz′ə-nē′), *n.* [L.; Gr. *mnēmosynē*, memory < *mnasthai*, to remember], in *Greek mythology*, the goddess of memory and mother (by Zeus) of the Muses.
Mngr., 1. Monseigneur. 2. Monsignor.
-mo (mō), [< ending of L. abl. forms of ordinals, after prep. *in*, as *in duodecimo* (< *duodecimus*, twelfth)], a suffix added to numerals or words representing numerals, meaning *having* (a specified number of) *leaves as a result of folding a sheet of paper*, as in *12mo, duodecimo*, or *twelvemo*.
Mo, in *chemistry*, molybdenum.
Mo., 1. Missouri. 2. Monday.
mo., 1. money order. 2. [*pl.* MOS.], month.
M.O., 1. Medical Officer. 2. money order.
mo·a (mō′ə), *n.* [< native (Maori) name], any of an extinct group of very large, flightless birds of New Zealand, related to the ostrich.
Mo·ab (mō′ab), *n.* [Heb. *mō'ābh*], in the *Bible*, 1. a son of Lot: Gen. 19:37. 2. an ancient kingdom east and south of the Dead Sea: see **Judea,** map.
Mo·ab·ite (mō′əb-īt′), *n.* [ME.; L. *Moabita;* ult. < Heb.], in the *Bible*, a native or inhabitant of Moab: Gen. 19:37. *adj.* of Moab or the Moabites.
Mo·ab·it·ish (mō′əb-īt′ish), *adj.* Moabite.
moan (mōn), *n.* [ME. *mone;* prob. < base of AS. *mænen*, to complain], 1. [Rare], a complaint; lamentation. 2. a low, mournful sound of sorrow or pain. 3. any sound like this: as, the *moan* of the wind. *v.i.* 1. to utter a moan or moans. 2. to complain, lament, grieve, etc. *v.t.* 1. to say with a moan. 2. to complain about; bewail: as, he *moaned* his fate. —***SYN.*** see **cry.**
moat (mōt), *n.* [ME. & OFr. *mote;* prob. < Gmc. *motta*, heap of earth], a deep, broad ditch dug around a fortress or castle, and often filled with water, for protection against invasion. *v.t.* to surround with or as with a moat.
mob (mob), *n.* [< L. *mobile* (*vulgus*), movable (crowd)], 1. a disorderly and lawless crowd; rabble. 2. any crowd. 3. the masses; common people collectively: a contemptuous term. 4. [Slang], a gang of criminals. *v.t.* [MOBBED (mobd), MOBBING], 1. to crowd around and attack. 2. to crowd around and jostle, annoy, etc., as in curiosity or anger. —***SYN.*** see **crowd.**
mob·bish (mob′ish), *adj.* like a mob; lawless and disorderly.

mob·cap (mob′kap′), *n.* [< MD. *mop*, woman's cap; + *cap*], formerly, a woman's full, loose cap, often tied under the chin, worn indoors.

Mo·bile (mō-bēl′), *n.* a city in Alabama, on Mobile Bay: pop., 203,000.

mo·bile (mō′b'l; *also, and for adj. 5. and n. usually,* mō′bēl), *adj.* [Fr.; L., neut. of *mobilis*, movable < *movere*, to move], 1. movable. 2. very fluid, as mercury. 3. showing emotional changes by changes in expression: as, *mobile* features. 4. in *military usage*, capable of being moved or transported quickly and with relative ease: as, an armored battalion is a *mobile* unit. 5. designating a form of abstract sculpture which aims to depict movement, i.e., kinetic rather than static rhythms, as by an arrangement of thin forms, rings, rods, etc. suspended in mid-air by fine wires. *n.* a piece of mobile sculpture.

Mo·bile Bay (mō′bēl), a part of the Gulf of Mexico, extending 35 mi. into southwestern Alabama.

mo·bil·i·ty (mō-bil′ə-ti), *n.* [Fr. *mobilité*; L. *mobilitas*], the quality or state of being mobile.

mo·bil·i·za·tion (mō′b'l-i-zā′shən, mō′b'l-ī-zā′shən), *n.* [Fr. *mobilisation*], a mobilizing or being mobilized.

mo·bil·ize (mō′b'l-īz′), *v.t.* [MOBILIZED (-īzd′), MOBILIZING], [Fr. *mobiliser* < *mobile*], 1. *a)* to make mobile, or movable. *b)* to put into motion, circulation, or use. 2. to make (armed forces or a nation) ready for war. 3. to organize and make ready for use. *v.i.* to become organized and ready, as for war.

mob·oc·ra·cy (mob-ok′rə-si), *n.* [*pl.* MOBOCRACIES (-siz)], [< *mob* + *-cracy* (after *democracy*, etc.)], 1. rule or domination by a mob. 2. the mob as ruler.

mob·ster (mob′stẽr), *n.* [Slang], a member of a criminal mob; gangster.

moc·ca·sin (mok′ə-s'n), *n.* [< Am. Ind. (Algonquian); cf. Narragansett *mokussin*, Massachusett *mohkisson*], 1. originally, a heelless slipper of soft, flexible leather, worn by North American Indians. 2. any slipper more or less like this. 3. a poisonous snake of the southeastern United States; especially, the water moccasin.

moccasin flower, a variety of pink or yellow orchid shaped like a slipper.

Mo·cha (mō′kə), *n.* 1. a seaport in Yemen, Arabia, on the Red Sea: pop., 600. 2. [m-], a variety of coffee grown originally in Arabia. 3. [m-], [Colloq.], any coffee. 4. [m-], a soft, velvety leather made from the pelts of certain Arabian goats, and used especially for gloves. *adj.* [m-], flavored with coffee or coffee and chocolate.

mo·chi·la (mō-chē′lə), *n.* [Sp., knapsack], formerly, a leather covering for a saddle.

mock (mok), *v.t.* [ME. *mokken*; OFr. *mocquer, moquer*, to mock], 1. to hold up to scorn or contempt; ridicule. 2. to imitate or mimic, as in fun or derision; burlesque. 3. to lead on and disappoint; deceive: as, the weather *mocked* him. 4. to defy and make futile; defeat: as, the strong fortress *mocked* the invaders. *v.i.* to show or express scorn, ridicule, or contempt; jeer (often with *at*). *n.* 1. an act of mocking; jibe; sneer. 2. a person or thing receiving or deserving ridicule or derision. 3. an imitation; counterfeit. *adj.* sham; false; imitation. —*SYN.* see **imitate, ridicule.**

mock·er·y (mok′ẽr-i), *n.* [*pl.* MOCKERIES (-iz)], 1. a mocking (in various senses). 2. a person or thing receiving or deserving ridicule or derision. 3. a false, derisive, or impertinent imitation; travesty; burlesque. 4. vain effort; disappointment; futility.

mock-he·ro·ic (mok′hi-rō′ik), *adj.* mocking, or burlesquing, heroic manner, action, or character. *n.* a mock-heroic literary work.

mock·ing·bird (mok′iŋ-bũrd′), *n.* a small bird of the thrush family, found in the southern United States and characterized by its practice of imitating the calls of other birds.

mock orange, a shrub with fragrant white flowers resembling those of the orange; syringa.

mock turtle soup, a soup made from calf's head, veal, etc., spiced so as to taste like green turtle soup.

mock-up (mok′up′), *n.* [*mock, v.t.* 2 + *up* (cf. SETUP)], a scale model, usually a full-sized replica in wood, cardboard, canvas, etc., of a structure, apparatus, or weapon, used for instructional purposes, to test the design, or, in military use, as a dummy to draw enemy fire away from a vulnerable point.

mod., 1. moderate. 2. modern. 3. in *music*, moderato. 4. modulus.

mod·al (mō′d'l), *adj.* [ML. *modalis* < L. *modus*, mode, manner], of or indicating a mode or mood; specifically, *a)* in *grammar*, of or expressing a mood: as, a *modal* verb. *b)* in *logic*, expressing or characterized by modality. *c)* in *music*, of or composed in any of the medieval church modes. *d)* in *philosophy*, of mode, or form, as opposed to substance.

modal auxiliary, an auxiliary verb used with another to indicate its mood: *may, might, must, can, would*, and *should* are modal auxiliaries.

mo·dal·i·ty (mō-dal′ə-ti), *n.* [*pl.* MODALITIES (-tiz)], [ML. *modalitas*], the fact, state, or quality of being modal; specifically, in *logic*, the qualification in a proposition affirming or denying possibility, impossibility, necessity, contingency, etc.

mode (mōd), *n.* [ME. *moede* (prob. via OFr.) < L. *modus*; in sense 2, Fr. < L.], 1. a manner or way of acting, doing, or being; method or form. 2. customary usage, or current fashion or style, as in manners or dress. 3. in *grammar*, mood. 4. in *logic*, *a)* modality or the form of a proposition with reference to its modality. *b)* any of the various forms of valid syllogisms, as determined by the quantity and quality of their constituent propositions. 5. in *metaphysics*, the form, or way of being, of something, as apart from its substance. 6. in *music*, *a)* any of the various forms in which the octave was arranged in classical Greek and medieval church music, according to certain fixed intervals between the tones. *b)* either of the two forms of octave arrangement in modern music (*major mode* and *minor mode*). 7. in *petrography*, the actual mineral composition of a rock. 8. in *statistics*, the value, number, etc. that occurs most frequently in a given series. —*SYN.* see **fashion, method.**

mod·el (mod′'l), *n.* [Fr. *modèle*; It. *modello*, dim. of *modo* < L. *modus*; see MODE], 1. *a)* a small copy or imitation of an existing object, as a ship, building, etc., made to scale. *b)* a preliminary representation of something, serving as the plan from which the final, usually larger, object is to be constructed. *c)* a piece of sculpture in wax or clay from which a finished work in bronze, marble, etc. is to be made. 2. a person or thing considered as a standard of excellence to be imitated. 3. a style or design: as, last year's *model* of automobile. 4. *a)* a person who poses for an artist or photographer. *b)* a person, especially a woman, employed to display clothes by wearing them; mannequin. *adj.* serving as a model, pattern, or standard of excellence. *v.t.* [MODELED or MODELLED (-'ld), MODELING or MODELLING], 1. *a)* to make a model of. *b)* to plan, form, or design after a model. *c)* to make conform to a standard of excellence: as, he *modeled* his behavior on that of his father. 2. to display (a dress, etc.) by wearing. *v.i.* 1. to make a model or models: as, she *models* in clay. 2. to serve as a model (sense 4). 3. in *painting, drawing*, etc., to take on a three-dimensional appearance as a result of contrast in lighting and color.

SYN.—**model** refers to a representation made to be copied or, more generally, to any person or thing to be followed or imitated because of his or its excellence, worth, etc.; **example** suggests that which is presented as a sample, or that which sets a precedent for imitation, whether good or bad; a **pattern** is a model, guide, plan, etc. to be strictly followed; **paradigm** is common now only in its grammatical sense of an example of a declension or conjugation, giving all the inflectional forms of a word; **archetype** applies to the original pattern serving as the model for all later things of the same kind; **standard** refers to something established for use as a rule or a basis of comparison in judging quality, etc.

mod·el·er, mod·el·ler (mod′'l-ẽr), *n.* a person who models; especially, one who makes models in clay, etc.

mod·el·ing, mod·el·ling (mod′'l-iŋ, mod′liŋ), *n.* 1. the act or art of making a model, especially of making a pattern in some plastic material to be copied in stone or metal. 2. form; shape: as, the *modeling* of one's features. 3. employment as a model (sense 4). 4. in *painting, drawing*, etc., the indication of three dimensions by means of contrast in lighting and color.

Mo·de·na (mô′de-nä′), *n.* a city in northern Italy: pop., 114,000.

mod·er·ate (mod′ẽr-it; *for v.*, mod′ə-rāt′), *adj.* [ME. *moderat*; L. *moderatus*, pp. of *moderare*, to keep within bounds, restrain < *modus*; see MODE], 1. within reasonable limits; avoiding excesses or extremes; temperate. 2. mild; calm; gentle; not violent: as, *moderate* weather. 3. of medium quality; mediocre: as, *moderate* skills. *n.* a person holding moderate views or opinions in politics or religion. Abbreviated **mod.** *v.t.* [MODERATED (-id), MODERATING], 1. to cause to become moderate; make less extreme, violent, etc.; restrain. 2. to preside over (a meeting, etc.). *v.i.* 1. to become moderate. 2. to serve as a moderator; preside.

SYN.—**moderate** and **temperate** are often interchangeable in denoting a staying within reasonable limits, but in strict discrimination, **moderate** implies merely an absence of excesses or extremes, while **temperate** suggests deliberate self-restraint (*moderate* demands, a *temperate* reply).—*ANT.* excessive, extreme.

mod·er·a·tion (mod′ə-rā′shən), *n.* 1. a moderating, or bringing within bounds. 2. avoidance of excesses or extremes. 3. absence of violence; calmness.

in moderation, to a moderate degree; without excess.

mod·e·ra·to (mod′ə-rä′tō), *adj. & adv.* [It.], in *music*, with moderation in tempo: a direction to the performer: abbreviated **mod.**

mod·er·a·tor (mod′ə-rā′tẽr), *n.* [ME. *moderatour*; L.

moderator], a person or thing that moderates; specifically, *a*) a person who presides at a town meeting, debate, etc. *b*) the presiding officer at a synod or general assembly of the Presbyterian Church. *c*) in *nuclear physics*, a substance, as graphite or heavy water, used to slow down the neutrons in a reactor.

mod·er·a·tor·ship (mod′ə-rā′tẽr-ship′), *n.* [see -SHIP], the position, office, or duties of a moderator.

mod·ern (mod′ẽrn), *adj.* [Fr. *moderne;* LL. *modernus* < L. *modo*, just now, orig. abl. of *modus;* see MODE], 1. of or characteristic of the present or recent times; not ancient: often used to designate certain contemporary tendencies and schools of art, music, literature, etc., as, *modern* architecture and furniture are characterized by functionalism and lack of extraneous ornamentation: see TYPES OF ARCHITECTURE, p. 77. 2. up-to-date; not old-fashioned, antiquated, or obsolete. 3. [often M-], designating a language, or the form of a language, in current use. *n.* 1. a person living in modern times; hence, 2. a person having modern ideas, beliefs, standards, etc. 3. in *printing*, a style of type face characterized by heavy down strokes contrasting with narrow cross strokes. Abbreviated **mod.** —*SYN.* see **new.**

Modern English, the English language since about 1500: cf. **Early Modern English.**

Modern Greek, the Greek language as spoken and written in Greece since about 1500.

Modern Hebrew, Hebrew as spoken and written after Biblical times; especially, Hebrew as the language of modern Israel.

modern history, the history of the world since the fall of Constantinople (1453).

mod·ern·ism (mod′ẽrn-iz′m), *n.* 1. *a*) modern usage, practice, or thought; sympathy with modern ideas. *b*) an instance of this; modern idiom, practice, or usage. 2. [M-], in *Christianity*, any of various movements attempting to redefine Biblical and Christian dogma and teachings in the light of modern science: condemned in the Roman Catholic Church by Pope Pius X in 1907 as a negation of faith.

mod·ern·ist (mod′ẽrn-ist), *n.* 1. a person who follows or is sympathetic to modern ideas and methods. 2. [M-], a follower of Modernism.

mod·ern·is·tic (mod′ẽrn-is′tik), *adj.* 1. of or characteristic of modernism or modernists. 2. modern: used especially to designate certain contemporary tendencies and schools of art, music, etc., often in a somewhat derogatory sense. —*SYN.* see **new.**

mod·ern·is·tic·al·ly (mod′ẽrn-is′ti-k′l-i, mod′ẽrn-is′tikli), *adv.* in a modernistic manner.

mo·der·ni·ty (mo-dũr′nə-ti, mō-dũr′nə-ti), *n.* 1. the state or quality of being modern. 2. [*pl.* MODERNITIES (-tiz)], something modern.

mod·ern·i·za·tion (mod′ẽrn-i-zā′shən, mod′ẽrn-ī-zā′shən), *n.* a modernizing or being modernized.

mod·ern·ize (mod′ẽrn-īz′), *v.t.* [MODERNIZED (-īzd′), MODERNIZING], [Fr. *moderniser*], to make modern; cause to conform to present-day practice, standards, or taste. *v.i.* to adopt modern ways; become modern.

Modern Latin, the Latin that has come into use since the Renaissance, or about 1500, chiefly in scientific literature: it has words formed from Latin and Greek: abbreviated **Mod. L.**: also called *New Latin, Neo-Latin.*

mod·est (mod′ist), *adj.* [Fr. *modeste;* L. *modestus* < *modus;* see MODE], 1. having or showing a moderate or humble opinion of one's own value, abilities, achievements, etc.; unassuming. 2. not forward; shy or reserved: as, *modest* behavior. 3. behaving according to a standard of what is proper or decorous; decent; pure; now, especially, not displaying one's body. 4. showing or caused by moderation; not extreme: as, a *modest* request. 5. quiet and humble in appearance, style, etc.: as, a *modest* home. —*SYN.* see **chaste, humble, shy.**

mod·es·ty (mod′is-ti), *n.* [Fr. *modestie;* L. *modestia*], the quality or state of being modest; specifically, *a*) unassuming or humble behavior. *b*) lack of excesses or pretensions; moderation. *c*) decency; decorum.

Mod. Gr., Modern Greek.

Mod. Heb., Modern Hebrew.

mod·i·cum (mod′i-kəm), *n.* [Late ME.; L., neut. of *modicus*, moderate], a small amount or portion; bit.

mod·i·fi·a·ble (mod′ə-fī′ə-b′l), *adj.* that can be modified.

mod·i·fi·ca·tion (mod′ə-fi-kā′shən), *n.* [< Fr. or L.; Fr. *modification;* L. *modificatio* < pp. of *modificare*], a modifying or being modified; specifically, *a*) a partial or slight change in form. *b*) a product of such a change: as, this automobile is a *modification* of last year's model. *c*) a slight reduction; moderation. *d*) a qualification or limitation of meaning. *e*) in *biology*, a change in an organism caused by its environment and not inheritable. *f*) in *linguistics*, a change in the form of a morpheme within a construction.

mod·i·fi·ca·to·ry (mod′ə-fi-kā′tə-ri), *adj.* [see MODIFICATION & -ORY], modifying or tending to modify.

mod·i·fi·er (mod′ə-fī′ẽr), *n.* a person or thing that modifies; especially, a word, phrase, or clause that limits the meaning of another word or phrase: as, adjectives and adverbs are *modifiers.*

mod·i·fy (mod′ə-fī′), *v.t.* [MODIFIED (-fīd′), MODIFYING], [ME. *modifien;* L. *modificare, modificari*, to limit, regulate < *modus*, measure + *facere*, to make], 1. to change slightly or partially in character, form, etc. 2. to limit or reduce slightly; moderate: as, the judge *modified* her penalty. 3. in *grammar*, to limit or restrict in meaning; qualify: as, "large" *modifies* "house" in *large house.* 4. in *linguistics*, to change (a vowel) by umlaut. *v.i.* to be modified. —*SYN.* see **change.**

Mo·di·glia·ni, A·me·de·o (ä′me-de′ô mô′dē-lyä′nē), 1884–1920; Italian painter in France.

mo·dil·lion (mō-dil′yən), *n.* [It. *modiglione;* LL. **mutilio;* L. *mutulus*, modillion], in *architecture*, an ornamental block or bracket placed under a projecting cornice, especially in the Corinthian order.

mo·di·o·lus (mō-dī′ə-ləs), *n.* [*pl.* MODIOLI (-lī′)], [Mod. L., dim. of L. *modius*, measure for grain], the central bony axis of the cochlea of the ear.

mod·ish (mōd′ish), *adj.* in the current mode; in the latest style; fashionable; stylish.

mo·diste (mō-dēst′), *n.* [Fr. < *mode;* see MODE], a woman who makes or deals in fashionable clothes, hats, etc. for women.

Mo·djes·ka, He·le·na (he-lā′nə mô-jes′kä; Eng. mə-jes′kə), 1840–1909; Polish actress in America.

Mod. L., Modern Latin.

Mod. Pr., Modern Provençal.

Mo·dred (mō′drid), *n.* in *Arthurian legend*, the treacherous nephew of King Arthur: they killed each other in battle: also **Mordred.**

mod·u·lar (moj′oo-lẽr), *adj.* [Mod. L. *modularis*], of a module or modulus.

mod·u·late (moj′oo-lāt′), *v.t.* [MODULATED (-id), MODULATING], [< L. *modulatus*, pp. of *modulari*, to regulate, measure off, arrange < *modulus*, dim. of *modus;* see MODE], 1. to regulate, adjust, or adapt. 2. to vary the pitch, intensity, etc. of (the voice). 3. to sing; intone (a song). 4. in *music*, to cause to shift to another key. 5. in *radio*, to vary the amplitude, frequency, or phase of (a carrier wave) in accordance with another wave. *v.i.* 1. in *music*, to shift from one key to another by the transitional use of a chord common to both. 2. in *radio*, to produce modulation.

mod·u·la·tion (moj′oo-lā′shən), *n.* [ME. *modulacioun;* L. *modulatio*], 1. a modulating or being modulated; specifically, *a*) in *music*, a shifting from one key to another by the transitional use of a chord common to both. *b*) in *radio*, a variation in the amplitude, frequency, or phase of a carrier wave in accordance with another wave. 2. in *linguistics*, the loss of stress and weakening or shortening of the phonetic form of a word when it is used purely as an auxiliary or transitional word. Example: I'*ve* gone vs. I *have* friends.

mod·u·la·tor (moj′oo-lā′tẽr), *n.* [L.], a person or thing that modulates; specifically, in *radio*, a vacuum tube used to produce modulation.

mod·ule (moj′ōōl, moj′ūl), *n.* [< Fr. or L.; Fr. *module;* L. *modulus*, dim. of *modus;* see MODE], 1. a standard or unit of measurement, especially of flowing water. 2. in *architecture*, the length of some part, used as a unit of measurement, as the diameter of the base of a column shaft, used to determine the proportions of a building. 3. in *electronics*, a compact assembly functioning as a component of a larger unit.

mod·u·lus (moj′oo-ləs), *n.* [*pl.* MODULI (-lī′)], [L.; see MODULE], in *physics*, a positive number or quantity expressing the measure of a function, force, or effect, as of elasticity, resistance, etc., especially in relation to a basic unit or to some other factor or factors: symbol, *μ*, M: abbreviated **mod.**

‡mo·dus o·pe·ran·di (mō′dəs op′ə-ran′dī), [L.], manner of working; way of doing or making; procedure.

‡mo·dus vi·ven·di (mō′dəs vi-ven′dī), [L.], 1. manner of living; hence, 2. a temporary agreement in a dispute pending final settlement; compromise.

Moe·si·a (mē′shi-ə), *n.* a Roman province between the Danube River and the Balkan Mountains.

Moe·so-Goth, Moe·so·goth (mē′sō-goth′), *n.* a member of a Gothic tribe that lived in Moesia (c. 300 A.D.).

Moe·so-Goth·ic, Moe·so·goth·ic (mē′sō-goth′ik), *adj.* of the Moeso-Goths or their language. *n.* the language of the Moeso-Goths, as preserved in the translation of the Bible by Bishop Ulfilas (c. 350 A.D.); Gothic.

mo·fette, mof·fette (mō-fet′), *n.* [Fr. < It. *muffare*, to be moldy < G. *muff*, mold], in *geology*, 1. a leakage of carbon dioxide and other gases from a hole or fissure in the earth, marking the last stage in volcanic activity. 2. such a hole or fissure.

Mo·ga·di·scio (mô′gä-dē′shô), *n.* seaport and capital of Somalia: pop., 87,000.

Mo·ga·di·shu (mô′gä-dē′shōō), *n.* Mogadiscio.

Mog·a·dor (mog′ə-dôr′, mog′ə-dōr′; Fr. mô′gà′dôr′), *n.* a seaport in Morocco: pop., 26,000.

Mo·gi·lëv (mô′gi-lyôf′; Eng. mō′gi-lef′), *n.* a city in the Byelorussian S.S.R.: pop., 121,000.

Mo·gul (mō′gul, mō-gul′), *n.* [Per. *Mughul* < Mongol. *Moṅgol*, a Mongol], 1. a Mongol; Mongolian; especially, any of the Mongolian conquerors of India or their descendants. 2. [m-], a powerful or important person, especially one with autocratic power. 3. [m-], a kind of steam locomotive for pulling heavy trains.

mo·hair (mō′hâr′), *n.* [altered (after *hair*) < earlier *moekaire;* It. *moccaiaro* < Ar. *mukhayyar;* cf. MOIRE], 1. the hair of the Angora goat. 2. a fabric made of this; especially, a glossy, tough, napped cloth. 3. a fabric with mohair pile on a cotton or wool backing, used in upholstery. 4. a mohair garment. *adj.* made of or upholstered with mohair.

Mo·ham·med (mō-ham′id), *n.* [Ar. *Muhammed,* lit., praised], Arabian prophet; 570–632 A.D.; founder of the Moslem religion: also **Mahomet, Muhammad.**

Mohammed II, 1430–1481; sultan of Turkey (1451–1481); captured Constantinople (1453).

Mohammed Ali, see **Mehemet Ali.**

Mo·ham·med·an (mō-ham′ə-dən), *adj.* of Mohammed or the Moslem religion. *n.* a follower of Mohammed; believer in the Moslem religion. Abbreviated **Moham.** Also **Muhammadan, Muhammedan.**

Mo·ham·med·an·ism (mō-ham′ə-dən-iz'm), *n.* the Moslem religion, founded by Mohammed; Islam.

Mo·ha·ve (mō-hä′vi), *n.* [< Am. Ind.; cf. Yuman *hamok,* three + *avi,* mountain], a member of a tribe of Yuman Indians that lived around the Colorado River. *adj.* of this people. Also spelled **Mojave.**

Mohave Desert, Mojave Desert.

Mo·hawk (mō′hôk), *n.* [< Am. Ind. (Algonquian); cf. Narragansett *mohowaùuck,* lit., they eat animate things, hence man-eaters: orig. so named by enemy tribes], 1. [*pl.* MOHAWK, MOHAWKS (-hôks)], a member of a tribe of Iroquoian Indians that lived in the Mohawk Valley, New York: see **Five Nations.** 2. a river in central New York, flowing eastward into the Hudson: length, 148 mi. *adj.* of the Mohawk.

Mo·he·gan (mō-hē′gən), *n.* [Am. Ind. (Algonquian), lit., a wolf; cf. MAHICAN], 1. a member of a Mahican tribe of Algonquian Indians that lived in Connecticut, along the Thames River. 2. Mahican. *adj.* of the Mohegans.

Mo·hi·can (mō-hē′kən), *n.* & *adj.* Mahican.

Mo·hock (mō′hok, mō′hôk), *n.* [var. of *Mohawk*], 1. any of a gang of elegant rakes and ruffians who committed outrages at night in the streets of London in the 18th century. 2. [Obs.], Mohawk.

Mohs scale (mōz), [after Friedrich *Mohs* (1773–1839), G. mineralogist who devised it], in *mineralogy,* a scale used to indicate relative hardness, arranged in 10 ascending degrees (1, talc; 2, gypsum; 3, calcite; 4, fluorite; 5, apatite; 6, feldspar; 7, quartz; 8, topaz; 9, sapphire; 10, diamond).

mo·hur (mō′hẽr), *n.* [Hind. *muhur, muhr;* Per. *muhr,* a seal; akin to Sans. *mudrā,* a seal], a former gold coin of India, equal to 15 rupees.

moi·dore (moi′dôr, moi′dōr), *n.* [Port. *moeda d'ouro,* lit., coin of gold < L. *moneta,* money + *aurum,* gold], a former gold coin of Portugal or Brazil.

moi·e·ty (moi′ə-ti), *n.* [*pl.* MOIETIES (-tiz)], [ME. & OFr. *moite* (Fr. *moitié*); L. *medietas* < *medius,* middle], 1. a half. 2. an indefinite share or part. 3. in *anthropology,* either of two primary subdivisions in some tribes.

moil (moil), *v.i.* [ME. *moillen,* to moisten, make wet < OFr. *moillier* < L. *mollis,* soft; hence, basic sense "to work in the wet or wet ground"], to toil; drudge. *n.* 1. drudgery; hard work. 2. confusion; turmoil.

moire (mwär, mwôr, môr, mōr), *n.* [Fr., watered silk < Eng. *mohair*], a fabric, especially silk, having a watered, or wavy, pattern.

‡moi·ré (mwà′rā′; Eng. mwä-rā′, mō′rā′), *adj.* [Fr., pp. of *moirer,* to water < *moire;* see MOIRE], having a watered, or wavy, pattern. *n.* 1. a watered pattern pressed into cloth, etc. with engraved rollers. 2. moire.

moist (moist), *adj.* [ME. & OFr. *moiste* < L. *mucidus,* moldy < *mucus,* mucus], 1. damp; slightly wet. 2. suggestive of the presence of liquid: as, a *moist* sound. —*SYN.* see **wet.**

mois·ten (mois′'n), *v.t.* & *v.i.* to make or become moist.

mois·ture (mois′chẽr), *n.* [ME.; OFr. *moisteur* < *moiste;* see MOIST], water or other liquid causing a slight wetness or dampness.

Mo·ja·ve (mō-hä′vi), *n.* & *adj.* Mohave.

Mojave Desert, a desert in southern California: also spelled **Mohave Desert.**

Mo·ji (mô′jē′), *n.* a city on the northern coast of Kyushu, Japan: pop., 145,000.

moke (mōk), *n.* [prob. < pers. name *Moke,* applied as pet name to the donkey], [Slang], 1. a donkey; hence, 2. a dull, stupid person.

Mo·ki (mō′kē), *n.* a Hopi Indian: also spelled **Moqui.**

mol (mōl), *n.* a mole (a gram molecule).

mol., 1. molecular. 2. molecule.

mo·lal (mō′ləl), *adj.* in *chemistry,* relating to the mole or gram-molecular weight; specifically, designating a solution with a concentration equal to one mole of the solute in 1,000 grams of the solvent.

mo·lar (mō′lẽr), *adj.* [L. *molaris,* a mill < *mola,* millstone; cf. MILL], 1. used for or capable of grinding. 2. designating or of a tooth or teeth adapted for grinding. *n.* a molar tooth: in man there are twelve molars, three on each side of each jaw behind the bicuspids: see **tooth,** illus. Abbreviated **M., m.**

mo·lar (mō′lẽr), *adj.* [< L. *moles,* mass; + *-ar*], 1. in *chemistry,* relating to the mole or gram-molecular weight; specifically, designating a solution containing one mole of solute per liter of solution. 2. in *physics,* of a body (of matter) as a whole: opposed to *molecular, atomic.*

mo·las·ses (mə-las′iz), *n.* [*pl.* MOLASSES], [< Port. *melaço* < LL. *mellaceum,* must < L. *mellaceus,* resembling honey < *mel,* honey], any of various thick, dark-colored sirups, especially that produced during the refining of sugar: cf. **treacle.**

mold (mōld), *n.* [ME. *mold, moolde;* OFr. *molle,* L. *modulus;* see MODULE], 1. a pattern, hollow form, or matrix for giving a certain shape or form to something in a plastic or molten state. 2. a frame, shaped core, etc. on or around which something is modeled. 3. a pattern after which something is formed; model. 4. something formed or shaped in or on, or as if in or on, a mold. 5. *a)* the form or shape given by a mold. *b)* form or shape in general. 6. distinctive character or nature. 7. in *architecture, a)* a molding. *b)* a group of moldings. *v.t.* 1. to make or shape in or on, or as if in or on, a mold. 2. to work into a certain form or shape; shape. 3. to ornament by or with molding. 4. in *founding,* to make a mold of or from in order to make a casting. Also spelled **mould.**

mold (mōld), *n.* [ME. *moul, mowlde,* mold, mildew; sp. prob. influenced by *molde,* earth], 1. a downy or furry growth on the surface of organic matter, caused by fungi, especially in the presence of dampness or decay. 2. any fungus producing such a growth. *v.t.* & *v.i.* [prob. < pp. of ME. *moulen,* to become moldy; IE. base **meuq-,* slimy, as also in L. *mucus* (cf. MUCUS)], to make or become moldy. Also spelled **mould.**

mold (mōld), *n.* [ME. & AS. *molde,* dust, ground, earth; akin to Goth. *mulda;* IE. base **mel-,* to rub away, grind, as also in L. *molere,* to grind (cf. MOLAR) & Eng. *meal*], 1. loose, soft, easily worked soil, especially when rich with decayed animal or vegetable matter and good for growing plants. 2. the material that a thing is made of; matter. 3. [Archaic or Poetic], earth. Also spelled **mould.**

Mol·dau (môl′dou), *n.* a river flowing northward through Czechoslovakia into the Elbe: length, 270 mi.: Czech name, *Vltava.*

Mol·da·vi·a (mol-dā′vi-ə, mol-dāv′yə), *n.* a former principality and district of Romania, now a part of the Moldavian S.S.R.

Mol·da·vi·an Soviet Socialist Republic (mol-dā′vi-ən, mol-dāv′yən), a republic of the U.S.S.R. in southwest European Russia, on the Black Sea: formed (August, 1940) from the former Moldavian A. S. S. R. (in the Ukraine) and Bessarabia: area, 13,680 sq. mi.; pop., 2,880,000; capital, Kishinev.

mold·board (mōld′bôrd′, mōld′bōrd′), *n.* [*mold* (soil) + *board*], a curved plate of iron attached to a plowshare, for turning over the soil: also spelled **mouldboard.**

mold·er (mōl′dẽr), *v.i.* [freq. of obs. *mold, v.,* to molder; see MOLD (soil) & -ER], to crumble into dust; decay; waste away (often with *away*). *v.t.* to cause to molder. Also spelled **moulder.** —*SYN.* see **decay.**

mold·er (mōl′dẽr), *n.* [*mold* (to form) + *-er*], 1. a person or thing that molds or makes molds. 2. in *printing,* one of a set of electrotyped plates used for making duplicate electrotypes. Also spelled **moulder.**

mold·i·ness (mōl′di-nis), *n.* moldy quality or state.

mold·ing (mōl′diŋ), *n.* 1. the act or process of a person or thing that molds; shaping. 2. something molded. 3. *a)* any of various ornamental contours given to cornices, jambs, etc. *b)* a cornice or other shaped member of wood, stone, etc., either sunk or projecting, used for ornament on a surface or angle of a structure. 4. a shaped strip of wood, etc., as around the upper part of the walls of a room, used for ornament or as a support from which to hang pictures. Also spelled **moulding.**

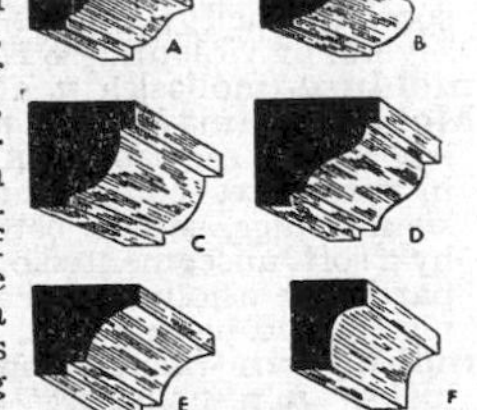

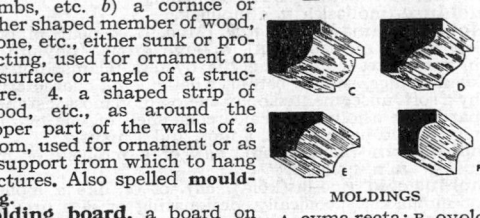

MOLDINGS
A, cyma recta; B, ovolo; C, quarter round; D, cyma reversa; E, cavetto; F, congé

molding board, a board on which dough is kneaded, rolled, cut, etc.

mold·y (mōl′di), *adj.* [MOLDIER (-di-ẽr), MOLDIEST (-di-ist)], [*mold* (furry growth) + *-y*], 1. covered or overgrown with mold. 2. musty or stale, as from age or decay. Also spelled **mouldy.**

mole (mōl), *n.* [ME. & AS. *mal;* akin to Goth. *mail;* IE. base **mei-,* **mai-,* to spot], a small, congenital spot

on the human skin, usually dark-colored and slightly raised, often hairy; especially, a pigmentary nevus.
mole (mōl), *n.* [ME. *molle;* akin to or < MD. *mol;* prob. < same base as *mold* (soil)], any of a number of small, burrowing, insect-eating mammals with very small eyes and ears, broad forefeet, and soft fur: moles live mainly underground.

MOLE (7 in. long)

mole (mōl), *n.* [Fr. *môle* < L. *moles,* a mass, dam, mole], 1. a barrier of stone, etc. built in the water to protect from the force of the waves, as a breakwater. 2. a harbor or anchorage so formed or protected.
mole (mōl), *n.* [G. < *molekül,* molecule], in *chemistry,* a gram molecule; molecular weight (of a substance) in grams: also **mol.**
mole (mōl), *n.* [Fr. *môle;* L. *mola,* false conception, millstone, cake], a fleshy mass or swelling in the uterus, formed by a degenerated or maldeveloped ovum.
Mo·lech (mō′lek), *n.* Moloch (senses 1 & 2).
mo·lec·u·lar (mə-lek′yoo-lẽr), *adj.* [Mod. L. *molecularis*], of, consisting of, produced by, or existing between molecules: abbreviated **mol.**
molecular film, a film or layer (of a substance) one molecule thick: also called *monolayer.*
molecular weight, the relative average weight of a molecule of a substance, expressed by a number in a scale on which the weight of the oxygen atom is represented by 16: abbreviated **mol. wt.**
mol·e·cule (mol′ə-kūl′), *n.* [Fr. *molécule;* Mod. L. *molecula,* dim. < L. *moles,* a mass], 1. the smallest particle of an element or compound that can exist in the free state and still retain the characteristics of the element or compound: the molecules of elements consist of one atom or two or more similar atoms; those of compounds consist of two or more different atoms. 2. a gram molecule. 3. a small particle. Abbreviated **mol.**
mole·hill (mōl′hil′), *n.* a small ridge or mound of earth, formed by a burrowing mole.
make a mountain out of a molehill, to regard a trivial difficulty as a great one.
mole·skin (mōl′skin′), *n.* 1. the soft, dark-gray skin of the mole, used as fur. 2. a strong, twilled cotton fabric with a soft nap, used for work clothes, etc. 3. *pl.* trousers made of this fabric.
mo·lest (mə-lest′), *v.t.* [ME. *molesten;* OFr. *molester;* L. *molestare* < *molestus,* troublesome < *moles,* a burden, etc.], to annoy, interfere with, or meddle with so as to trouble or harm, or with intent to trouble or harm.
mo·les·ta·tion (mō′les-tā′shən, mol′əs-tā′shən), *n.* [ME. *molestacioun*], a molesting or being molested.
Mo·lière (mô′lyâr′; Eng. mō′li-âr′), *n.* (pseudonym of *Jean Baptiste Poquelin*), French writer of comedies; lived 1622–1673.
Mo·line (mō-lēn′), *n.* a city in northern Illinois, on the Mississippi: pop., 43,000.
Moll (mol), a feminine name: see **Mary.** *n.* [usually m-], [Slang], 1. a gangster's mistress. 2. a prostitute.
mol·lah (mol′ə), *n.* a mullah.
mol·les·cence (mə-les′ns), *n.* [< *mollescent*], a softening or tendency to soften.
mol·les·cent (mə-les′nt), *adj.* [L. *mollescens,* ppr. of *mollescere,* to soften < *mollere,* to be soft < *mollis,* soft, flexible], softening or tending to soften.
mol·li·fi·ca·tion (mol′ə-fi-kā′shən), *n.* a mollifying or being mollified.
mol·li·fi·er (mol′ə-fī′ẽr), *n.* a person or thing that mollifies.
mol·li·fy (mol′ə-fī′), *v.t.* [MOLLIFIED (-fīd′), MOLLIFYING], [ME. *molifien;* Late OFr. *mollifier;* LL. *mollificare,* to soften < L. *mollis,* soft + *facere,* to make], 1. to soothe; pacify; appease. 2. to make less intense, severe, or violent. —*SYN.* see **pacify.**
mol·lusc (mol′əsk), *n.* a mollusk.
Mol·lus·ca (mə-lus′kə), *n.pl.* [Mod. L. < neut. pl. of L. *molluscus;* see MOLLUSK], a large group (phylum) of invertebrates comprising the oysters, clams, mussels, snails, slugs, squids, octopi, whelks, etc., characterized by a soft, unsegmented body enclosed, in most instances, partly or wholly in a calcareous shell of one or more pieces, and having gills, a foot, and a mantle.
mol·lus·can (mə-lus′kən), *adj.* of a mollusk or mollusks. *n.* a mollusk.
mol·lus·coid (mə-lus′koid), *adj.* of or like a mollusk or mollusks; specifically, designating or of a group of animals comprising the brachiopods and bryozoans. *n.* a molluscoid animal.
mol·lus·coi·dal (mol′əs-koi′d′l), *adj.* molluscoid.
mol·lus·cous (mə-lus′kəs), *adj.* molluscan.
mol·lusk (mol′əsk), *n.* [Fr. *mollusque* < L. *molluscus,* soft (as a thin-shelled nut) < *mollis,* soft], any of the Mollusca: also spelled **mollusc.**
Mol·ly (mol′i), a feminine name: see **Mary.**
mol·ly (mol′i), *n.* [*pl.* MOLLIES (-iz)], [< Mod. L. *Mollienisia,* genus name < F. N. *Mollien* (1758–1850), Fr. statesman], any of various brightly colored tropical fishes, often kept in aquariums.
mol·ly·cod·dle (mol′i-kod′′l), *n.* [< *Molly,* dim. of *Mary* + *coddle*], a man or boy used to being coddled, or protected, pampered, etc.; milksop. *v.t.* [MOLLYCODDLED (-′ld), MOLLYCODDLING], to pamper; coddle.
Molly Ma·guires (mə-gwīrz′), [so called because members were sometimes disguised as women], 1. a secret society organized in Ireland in 1843 to prevent evictions by terrorizing agents of landlords. 2. a former secret society of Irish-American miners in eastern Pennsylvania (c. 1865–1875), which opposed oppressive industrial and social conditions, sometimes with physical force.
Mol·nár, Fe·renc (fe′rents môl′när), 1878–1952; Hungarian dramatist and novelist.
Mo·loch (mō′lok), *n.* [L. (Vulgate); Gr. (Septuagint) *Moloch;* Heb. *mōlōkh, mōlekh* < *mĕlekh,* a king], 1. in the *Bible,* a god of the ancient Phoenicians and Ammonites, to whom children were sacrificed by burning. 2. anything regarded as demanding terrible sacrifice. Also **Molech.** 3. [m-], a spiny Australian lizard.
Mo·lo·kai (mō′lō-kī′), *n.* one of the Hawaiian Islands, northwest of Maui: area, 259 sq. mi.; pop., 5,000: site of a leper colony: see **Hawaiian Islands,** map.
Mo·lo·tov (mô′lô-tôf), *n.* 1. a region of the R.S.F.S.R. in western Siberia: pop., 2,998,000. 2. its capital, on the Kama River: pop., 628,000. Formerly called *Perm.*
Mo·lo·tov, Vya·che·slav Mi·khai·lo·vich (vyä′chi-släf′ mi-khī′lô-vich mô′lô-tôf), 1890– ; Soviet statesman; minister of foreign affairs (1939–1949; 1953–1956).
Molotov cocktail, [after V. M. *Molotov*], [Slang], a bottle filled with gasoline, etc. and wrapped in a saturated rag, ignited and hurled as an antitank grenade, as by Soviet forces in World War II.
molt (mōlt), *v.i.* [ME. *mouten;* AS. *(be)mutian,* to exchange < L. *mutare,* to change; with unhistoric *l* after words like *fault*], to cast off or shed the hair, outer skin, horns, or feathers at certain intervals, prior to replacement of the castoff parts by a new growth: said of certain animals, as reptiles, birds, etc. *v.t.* to shed and replace by molting. *n.* 1. the act or process of molting. 2. the parts so shed. Also spelled **moult.**
mol·ten (mōl′t′n), archaic past participle of **melt.** *adj.* 1. melted or liquefied by heat. 2. made by being melted and cast in a mold.
Molt·ke, Hel·muth Jo·han·nes Lud·wig von (hel′mōōt yō-hä′nəs lōōt′vikh fôn môlt′kə), Count, 1848–1916; nephew of the following; German general.
Moltke, Helmuth Karl Bern·hard von (kärl bern′härt), Count, 1800–1891; German field marshal.
‡**mol·to** (môl′tô), *adv.* [It. < L. *multum,* much], in *music,* very; much: used in musical directions.
Mo·luc·ca Islands (mō-luk′ə), a group of islands of Indonesia, between Celebes and New Guinea: area, 30,168 sq. mi.; pop., 893,000: also called *Spice Islands.*
Mo·luc·cas (mō-luk′əz), *n.pl.* the Molucca Islands.
mol. wt., molecular weight.
mo·ly (mō′li), *n.* [L.; Gr. *mōly*], 1. a mythical herb of magic powers: in Homer's *Odyssey,* given by Hermes to Odysseus to protect him from Circe's incantation. 2. a European wild garlic.
mol·y (mol′i), *n.* [Colloq.], molybdenum.
mo·lyb·date (mə-lib′dāt), *n.* a salt of molybdic acid.
mo·lyb·de·nite (mə-lib′də-nīt′, mol′ib-dē′nīt), *n.* native molybdenum sulfide, MoS_2, a scaly or foliated, lead-gray mineral, the chief ore of molybdenum.
mo·lyb·de·num (mə-lib′də-nəm, mol′ib-dē′nəm), *n.* [Mod. L.; altered < L. *molybdaena,* lead, galena; Gr. *molybdaina* < *molybdos,* lead], a lustrous, brittle, silver-white metallic chemical element, used in alloys, windings for electrical resistance furnaces, points for spark plugs, etc.: symbol, Mo; at. wt., 95.95; at. no., 42.
mo·lyb·dic (mə-lib′dik), *adj.* designating or of chemical compounds in which molybdenum has a higher valence than in the corresponding molybdous compounds.
mo·lyb·dous (mə-lib′dəs), *adj.* designating or of chemical compounds in which molybdenum has a lower valence than in the corresponding molybdic compounds.
mom (mom), *n.* [Colloq.], mother.
Mom·ba·sa (mom-bas′ə, mom-bä′sä), *n.* a seaport in Kenya, Africa: pop., 146,000.
mo·ment (mō′mənt), *n.* [ME.; L. *momentum,* movement, impulse, brief space of time, importance < *movimentum* < *movere,* to move], 1. an indefinitely brief period of time; instant. 2. a definite point in time or in a series of events. 3. importance; consequence: as, business of great *moment.* 4. in *mechanics, a*) the tendency to cause rotation about a point or axis. *b*) a measure of this tendency. *c*) the product of a (specified) force, mass, volume, etc. and its perpendicular distance from its axis, fulcrum, or plane. 5. in *philosophy,* any of the constituent elements of a complex entity; momentum. —*SYN.* see **importance.**
the moment, the present or the immediate future.
mo·men·tar·i·ly (mō′mən-ter′ə-li, mō′mən-ter′ə-li), *adv.* 1. for a short time. 2. from instant to instant; every moment.
mo·men·tar·i·ness (mō′mən-ter′i-nis), *n.* the quality or condition of being momentary; transitoriness.
mo·men·tar·y (mō′mən-ter′i), *adj.* lasting for only a moment; passing; transitory. —*SYN.* see **transient.**

mo·ment·ly (mō′mənt-li), *adv.* 1. from instant to instant; every moment. 2. instantly. 3. for a single instant.
mo·men·tous (mō-men′təs), *adj.* of great moment; very important: as, a *momentous* decision.
mo·men·tous·ly (mō-men′təs-li), *adv.* with momentous influence or results.
mo·men·tum (mō-men′təm), *n.* [*pl.* MOMENTUMS (-təmz), MOMENTA (-tə)], [L.; see MOMENT], 1. the impetus of a moving object. 2. in *mechanics*, the quantity of motion of a moving object, equal to the product of its mass and its velocity. 3. a moment (sense 5).
Momm·sen, The·o·dor (tā′ô-dôr mōm′zən; Eng. mom′s'n, mom′z'n), 1817–1903; German historian and philologist; received Nobel prize in literature, 1902.
Mo·mus (mō′məs), *n.* [L.; Gr. < *mōmos*, blame, ridicule], 1. in *Greek mythology*, the god of mockery and censure; hence, 2. a faultfinder.
Mon (mōn), *n.* one of the Mon-Khmer languages.
mon- (mon), mono-.
Mon., 1. Monastery. 2. Monday. 3. Monsignor.
mon., 1. monastery. 2. monetary.
Mo·na (mō′nə), [< Ir. *Muadhnait*, dim. of *muadh*, noble], a feminine name.
mon·a·chal (mon′ə-k'l), *adj.* [ML. *monachalis* < LL. *monachus;* see MONK], monastic.
mon·a·chism (mon′ə-kiz'm), *n.* [< L. *monachus* (see MONK); + *-ism*], monasticism.
mon·ac·id (mon-as′id), *adj.* & *n.* monoacid.
Mon·a·co (mon′ə-kō′), *n.* a principality on the Mediterranean, geographically in southeastern France: area, 1/2 sq. mi.; pop., 24,000: Monte Carlo is in Monaco.

MONACO

mon·ad (mon′ad, mō′nad), *n.* [LL. *monas, monadis;* Gr. *monas, monados*, a unit, unity < *monos*, alone], 1. a unit; something simple and indivisible. 2. in *biology*, any simple, single-celled organism; specifically, a type of single-celled, flagellate, ameboid organism. 3. in *chemistry*, an atom, element, or radical with a valence of one. 4. in *philosophy*, an entity or elementary being thought of as a microcosm or ultimate unit. *adj.* of, consisting of, or having the nature of, a monad or monads.
mon·a·del·phous (mon′ə-del′fəs), *adj.* [< *mon-* + Gr. *adelphos*, brother; + *-ous*], in *botany*, 1. having the stamens united by their filaments into one set or bundle, as some plants. 2. united in this way: said of stamens.
mo·nad·ic (mə-nad′ik), *adj.* of or like a monad.
mo·nad·i·cal (mə-nad′i-k'l), *adj.* monadic.
mon·ad·ism (mon′ad-iz'm, mō′nad-iz'm), *n.* in *philosophy*, the theory that the universe consists of monads.
mo·nad·nock (mə-nad′nok), *n.* [after Mt. *Monadnock*, N.H.], in *geology*, a single remnant of a former highland, which rises as an isolated rock mass above a plain.
Mon·a·ghan (mon′ə-gən; Ir. mon′ə-khən), *n.* 1. a county of northeastern Ireland: pop., 58,000. 2. its county seat.
Mo·na Li·sa (mō′nə lē′zə, mon′ə lē′zə), a famous portrait of a faintly smiling woman, by Leonardo da Vinci: also called *La Gioconda*.
mo·nan·drous (mə-nan′drəs), *adj.* [Gr. *monandros*, having one husband; see MON- & -ANDROUS], 1. having only one husband at a time. 2. of or characterized by monandry. 3. in *botany*, *a)* having only one stamen, as some flowers. *b)* having monandrous flowers.
mo·nan·dry (mə-nan′dri), *n.* the state or practice of having only one husband at a time: distinguished from *polyandry*.
mo·nan·thous (mə-nan′thəs), *adj.* [< *mon-* + Gr. *anthos*, a flower; + *-ous*], in *botany*, having only one flower, as some plants.
mon·arch (mon′ẽrk), *n.* [Late ME.; LL. *monarcha;* Gr. *monarchēs* < *monarchos*, ruling alone < *monos*, alone + *archein*, to rule], 1. the single or sole ruler of a state. 2. the hereditary (often constitutional) head of a state; king or emperor. 3. a person or thing that surpasses others of the same kind. 4. a species of large, migrating butterfly of North America, having reddish-brown, black-edged wings: the larvae feed on milkweed.
mo·nar·chal (mə-när′k'l), *adj.* of, like, suitable for, or characteristic of a monarch; royal; regal.
mo·nar·chi·al (mə-när′ki-əl), *adj.* monarchal.
mo·nar·chi·an·ism (mə-när′ki-ən-iz'm), *n.* [see MONARCHY, -AN, & -ISM], the doctrine of several Christian sects in the 2d and 3d centuries that the Three Persons of the Trinity are manifestations of one God, single in person: opposed to *Trinitarianism*.
mo·nar·chic (mə-när′kik), *adj.* [Fr. *monarchique*], monarchical.
mo·nar·chi·cal (mə-när′ki-k'l), *adj.* 1. of, characteristic of, or like a monarch or monarchy. 2. characterized by or favoring a monarchy.
mo·nar·chi·cal·ly (mə-när′ki-k'l-i, mə-när′kik-li), *adv.* in a monarchic manner; royally.
mon·arch·ism (mon′ẽr-kiz'm), *n.* [Fr. *monarchisme*,] monarchical principles or the advocacy of these.
mon·arch·ist (mon′ẽr-kist), *n.* an advocate or supporter of monarchy. *adj.* monarchistic.
mon·arch·is·tic (mon′ẽr-kis′tik), *adj.* of monarchism or monarchists.
mon·arch·y (mon′ẽr-ki), *n.* [*pl.* MONARCHIES (-kiz)], [ME. *monarchie;* L. *monarchia;* Gr. *monarchia* < *monarchos;* see MONARCH], 1. [Rare], rule by only one person. 2. a government or state headed by a king, queen, or emperor: called *absolute* (or *despotic*) when there is no limitation on the monarch's power, *constitutional* (or *limited*) when there is such limitation.
mo·nar·da (mə-när′də), *n.* [Mod. L., after N. *Monardes*, 16th-c. Sp. botanist and physician], any of a group of aromatic plants of the mint family, including the horsemint, Oswego tea, and the wild bergamot, characterized by toothed leaves and large, showy flowers.
mon·as (mon′əs, mō′nəs), *n.* [*pl.* MONADES (mon′ə-dēz′)], [LL.], a monad.
mon·as·te·ri·al (mon′əs-stêr′i-əl), *adj.* [ME.; LL. *monasterialis*], of a monastery or monastic life; monastic.
mon·as·ter·y (mon′əs-ter′i), *n.* [*pl.* MONASTERIES (-iz)], [ME. *monasterie;* LL. *monasterium* < Gr. *monastērion* < *monazein*, to be alone < *monos*, alone, sole, single], 1. a place of residence occupied by a group of people, especially monks, who have retired from the world under religious vows. 2. those living in such a place. Abbreviated **Mon., mon.** —*SYN.* see **cloister.**
mo·nas·tic (mə-nas′tik), *adj.* [Fr. *monastique;* ML. *monasticus;* Gr. *monastikos* < *monazein;* see MONASTERY], 1. of or characteristic of monasteries. 2. of or characteristic of monks or nuns or their way of life: ascetic; self-denying. *n.* a monk.
mo·nas·ti·cal (mə-nas′ti-k'l), *adj.* monastic.
mo·nas·ti·cism (mə-nas′tə-siz'm), *n.* the monastic system, state, or way of life.
Mon·as·tir (mô′nä-stêr′), *n.* Bitolj, Yugoslavia.
mon·a·tom·ic (mon′ə-tom′ik), *adj.* [*mon-* + *atomic*], 1. *a)* consisting of one atom: said of a molecule. *b)* having one atom in the molecule. 2. having one free valence: said of an atom or atomic group. 3. having a valence of one; monad.
mon·au·ral (mon-ô′rəl), *adj.* [*mon-* + *aural*], designating or of sound reproduction in which only one source of sound is used, giving a monophonic effect.
mon·ax·i·al (mon-ak′si-əl), *adj.* 1. having only one axis; uniaxial. 2. developing flowers on the primary axis or along a single axis.
mon·a·zite (mon′ə-zīt′), *n.* [G. *monazit* < Gr. *monazein*, to be alone < *monos*, alone; + G. *-it*, -ite: so named because of its isolated crystals], a brown or brownish-red native phosphate of the cerium metals.
Monck, George (muŋk), see **Monk, George.**
Mon·day (mun′di), *n.* [ME. *Mone(n)dai;* AS. *mon(an)dæg*, moon's day; *monan*, genit. of *mona*, the moon + *dæg*, day; rendering LL. *Lunae dies*], the second day of the week: abbreviated **Mon., Mo.**
‡**monde** (mōnd), *n.* [Fr.], the world; people; society.
‡**mon Dieu** (mōn′dyö′), [Fr.], my God: often used as an interjection.
mo·ne·cious (mə-nē′shəs, mō-nē′shəs), *adj.* monoecious.
Mo·nel metal (mō-nel′), [after Ambrose *Monell* (d. 1921), Am. manufacturer], an alloy of nickel, copper, iron, manganese, silicon, and carbon, very resistant to corrosion: used for screens, cooking ware, acid-resisting equipment, etc.: a trade-mark: also spelled **Monell.**
Mo·net, Claude (klōd mô′ne′; Eng. mō-nā′), 1840–1926; French impressionist painter.
mon·e·tar·i·ly (mon′ə-ter′ə-li, mun′ə-ter′ə-li), *adv.* in regard to monetary matters.
mon·e·tar·y (mon′ə-ter′i, mun′ə-ter′i), *adj.* [L. *monetarius*, of a mint < *moneta*, a mint; see MINT (place for coining money)], 1. of the coinage or currency of a country. 2. of money; pecuniary. Abbreviated **mon.** —*SYN.* see **financial.**
mon·e·ti·za·tion (mon′ə-ti-zā′shən, mun′ə-tī-zā′shən), *n.* a monetizing or being monetized.
mon·e·tize (mon′ə-tīz′, mun′ə-tīz′), *v.t.* [MONETIZED (-tīzd′), MONETIZING], [< L. *moneta*, a mint, money; + *-ize*], 1. to coin into money. 2. to legalize as money.
mon·ey (mun′i), *n.* [*pl.* MONEYS, MONIES (-iz)], [ME. *moneie, moneye;* OFr. *moneie, monnoie* < L. *moneta*, a mint; see MINT (place for coining money)], 1. *a)* standard pieces of gold, silver, copper, nickel, etc., stamped by government authority and used as a medium of exchange and measure of value; coin or coins: also called *hard money*. *b)* any paper note issued by a government or an authorized bank and used in the same way; bank notes; bills: also called *paper money*. 2. any

substance or article used as money, as bank notes, checks, etc. 3. any definite or indefinite sum of money. 4. property; possessions; wealth. 5. any form or denomination of legally current money. 6. a money of account. 7. *pl.* sums of money: now used chiefly in law.

for one's money, [Colloq.], for one's choice; in one's opinion.

in the money, [Slang], 1. among the winners, as in a contest, race, etc. 2. prosperous; wealthy; successful.

make money, to gain profits; become wealthy.

put money into, to invest money in.

put money on, to bet on.

mon·ey·bag (mun'i-bag'), *n.* 1. a bag for holding money. 2. *pl.* [Colloq.], *a*) wealth; riches. *b*) [construed as sing.], a rich person.

mon·ey·chang·er (mun'i-chān'jẽr), *n.* 1. a person whose business is to exchange money, usually of different countries, at a set rate. 2. a machine holding stacked coins for making change quickly.

mon·eyed (mun'id), *adj.* 1. having much money; rich; wealthy. 2. consisting of, derived from, or representing money: as, the *moneyed* interests oppose this bill.

mon·ey·er (mun'i-ẽr), *n.* [ME. *moneyour;* OFr. *monoier;* L. *monetarius*, mint master, orig. of a mint < *moneta*, a mint; see MINT (place for coining money)], [Obs.], 1. a banker or capitalist. 2. a coiner of money.

mon·ey·lend·er (mun'i-len'dẽr), *n.* a person whose business is lending money at interest.

mon·ey-mak·er (mun'i-māk'ẽr), *n.* 1. a person successful at acquiring money. 2. something that produces monetary gain, as a lucrative business.

mon·ey-mak·ing (mun'i-māk'iŋ), *n.* 1. the gaining of money; acquisition of wealth. 2. the coining of money; minting. *adj.* 1. profitable; lucrative. 2. engaged in money-making.

money of account, a monetary denomination used in keeping accounts, etc., especially one not issued as a coin (e.g., the United States mill).

money order, an order for the payment of a specified sum of money, as one issued for a fee at one post office or bank and payable at another: abbreviated **mo., M.O.**

mon·ey·wort (mun'i-wûrt'), *n.* [*money* + *wort*, after the Mod. L. name *Nummularia*], a European creeping plant with yellow flowers and roundish leaves.

mon·ger (muŋ'gẽr), *n.* [ME. *mongere, mangere;* AS. *mangere* < *mangian*, to trade, traffic; cf. ON. *mangari*, L. *mango*, trader], [Chiefly British], a dealer or trader (in a specified commodity): usually in compounds, as *fishmonger*; sometimes used figuratively and derogatorily, as in *scandalmonger.*

Mon·gol (moŋ'gəl, moŋ'gol, moŋ'gōl), *adj.* [Mongol; cf. MOGUL], Mongolian. *n.* 1. a native of Mongolia, Inner Mongolia, or the Buryat Mongol A.S.S.R. 2. a member of the Mongolian race. 3. any of the Mongolian languages.

Mongol., Mongolian.

Mongol Empire, the vast 13th-century empire of Genghis Khan, from the Dnepr to the Pacific.

Mon·go·li·a (moŋ-gō'li-ə, mon-gōl'yə), *n.* a region in central Asia, consisting of the Mongolian People's Republic and Inner Mongolia.

Mon·go·li·an (moŋ-gō'li-ən, mon-gōl'yən), *adj.* 1. of Mongolia, its people, or their culture. 2. designating or of one of the three principal races of mankind, including most of the peoples of Asia, the Eskimos, North American Indians, etc., who are generally characterized by yellowish skins, straight black hair, slanting eyes, etc. 3. designating or of a subfamily of Altaic languages spoken by the Mongols, and probably related to the Turkic and Tungusic languages. Abbreviated **Mongol.** 4. in *medicine*, having Mongolism. *n.* 1. a native of Mongolia. 2. a member of the Mongolian race. 3. any of the Mongolian languages.

Mongolian idiocy, Mongolism.

Mongolian (or **Mongoloid**) **idiot,** a person having Mongolism.

Mongolian People's Republic, a country in central Asia: area, 600,000 sq. mi.; pop., 850,000; capital, Ulan Bator Khoto: formerly called *Outer Mongolia.*

Mon·gol·ic (moŋ-gol'ik, mon-gol'ik), *adj.* Mongolian (senses 1, 2, 3). *n.* any of the Mongolian languages.

Mon·gol·ism (moŋ'gəl-iz'm), *n.* a type of congenital mental deficiency, accompanied with a flattened forehead, slanting eyes set closely together, etc.

Mon·gol·oid (moŋ'gəl-oid'), *adj.* 1. of or characteristic of the natives of Mongolia. 2. of, having the nature of, or resembling the members of the Mongolian race. *n.* a member of the Mongolian race.

mon·goose, mon·goos (moŋ'gōōs, muŋ'gōōs), *n.* [*pl.* MONGOOSES (-iz)], [Marathi *mangūs*], a ferretlike, flesh-eating animal of India, known for its ability to kill rats, poisonous snakes, etc.

mon·grel (mun'grəl, moŋ'grəl), *n.* [ME. *mengrell* < base of AS. *mengan*, to mix + dim. suffix *-rel* as in *cockerel*], 1. an animal or plant produced by the crossing of different breeds or varieties; especially, a dog of this kind. 2. anything produced by the mixture of incongruous things. *adj.* of mixed breed, race, origin, or character. Often used derogatively.

'mongst, mongst (muŋst, muŋkst), *prep.* [Poetic], amongst.

Mon·i·ca (mon'i-kə), [LL.; ? < L. *monere*, to warn], a feminine name.

mon·ick·er (mon'i-kẽr), *n.* a moniker.

Mon·i·er-Wil·liams, Sir **Mon·i·er** (mun'i-ẽr mun'i-ẽr-wil'yəmz), 1819–1899; English Sanskrit scholar.

mon·ies (mun'iz), *n.* alternative plural of **money.**

mon·i·ker (mon'i-kẽr), *n.* [said to be < Shelta via thieves' slang], 1. an initial or other mark of identification used by a tramp. 2. [Slang], a person's name or nickname. Also spelled **monicker.**

mo·nil·i·form (mō-nil'ə-fôrm'), *adj.* [< L. *monile*, necklace; + *-form;* cf. Fr. *moniliforme*], shaped somewhat like a string of beads; specifically, in *botany* & *zoology*, consisting of, or having, a series of alternating swellings and constrictions, as some stems and roots.

mon·ish (mon'ish), *v.t.* [Archaic], to admonish.

mon·ism (mon'iz'm, mō'niz'm), *n.* [Mod. L. *monismus* < Gr. *monos*, single, alone], in *philosophy*, 1. the doctrine that there is only one ultimate substance or principle, whether mind (*idealism*), matter (*materialism*), or some third thing that is the basis of both. 2. the doctrine that reality is an organic whole without independent parts. Cf. **dualism, pluralism.**

mon·ist (mon'ist, mō'nist), *n.* a believer in monism.

mo·nis·tic (mō-nis'tik), *adj.* of monism.

mo·nis·ti·cal (mō-nis'ti-k'l), *adj.* monistic.

mo·ni·tion (mō-nish'ən), *n.* [ME. *monicioun;* OFr.; L. *monitio* < pp. of *monere*, to warn], 1. admonition; warning; caution. 2. an official or legal notice; specifically, a formal notice from a bishop requiring that an ecclesiastical offense be amended. 3. in *law*, a summons to appear and answer in a suit or to contempt charges.

mon·i·tor (mon'ə-tẽr), *n.* [L. < pp. of *monere*, to warn], 1. [Rare], a person who advises, warns, or cautions. 2. in some schools, a student chosen to help keep order, record attendance, etc. 3. something that reminds or warns. 4. any of several species of large, flesh-eating lizards of Africa, southern Asia, and Australia: so called from the notion that they warn of the presence of crocodiles. 5. formerly, an armored warship, or ironclad, with a low freeboard, low flat deck, and heavy guns fitted in one or more revolving turrets; specifically, [M-], the first ship of this kind, the Union ironclad that fought a similar Confederate ship, the Merrimac, March 9, 1862: so named by the designer. 6. a mounting for a nozzle so arranged that a stream of water can be played in any direction desired, as in hydraulic mining or fire fighting. 7. in *radio* & *television*, *a*) a receiver for reproducing transmission without interfering with it, used for checking on the operation of a transmitter with regard to quality, deviation from assigned bands, material transmitted, etc. *b*) a high-fidelity loudspeaker in the control room of a broadcasting studio, used for checking the quality of the transmission. *v.t.* & *v.i.* 1. to watch or check on (a person or thing) as a monitor. 2. in *radio* & *television*, to receive or check on (transmission, a transmitter, etc.) with or as with a monitor.

mon·i·to·ri·al (mon'ə-tôr'i-əl, mon'ə-tō'ri-əl), *adj.* 1. of a monitor or using a monitor or monitors. 2. monitory.

mon·i·tor·ship (mon'ə-tẽr-ship'), *n.* [see -SHIP], the position, function, or period of service, of a monitor (sense 1 or 2).

mon·i·to·ry (mon'ə-tôr'i, mon'ə-tō'ri), *adj.* [Late ME.; L. *monitorius* < *monitor;* see MONITOR], giving or containing monition; admonishing. *n.* [*pl.* MONITORIES (-iz, -riz)], a monitory letter, as from a bishop.

monk (muŋk), *n.* [ME. *munec;* AS. *munuc* < LL. *monachus;* Late Gr. *monachos*, one who lives alone < Gr. *monos*, alone], 1. originally, a man who retired from the world and lived in solitary self-denial for religious reasons. 2. a man who joins a religious order living in retirement according to a rule and under vows of poverty, obedience, and chastity: cf. **friar.**

Monk, George (muŋk), first Duke of Albemarle, 1608–1670; British general; helped Charles II regain the English throne: also spelled **Monck.**

monk·er·y (muŋk'ẽr-i), *n.* [*pl.* MONKERIES (-iz)], 1. *a*) the way of life, condition, behavior, etc. of monks. *b*) *pl.* monastic practices or beliefs. Generally a term of hostility or contempt. 2. a monastery.

mon·key (muŋ'ki), *n.* [*pl.* MONKEYS (-kiz)], [Early Mod. Eng.; prob. < MLG. *Moneke*, name applied in the beast epic *Reynard the Fox* to the son of Martin the Ape; apparently associated with LG. *monnik*, monk (cf. MONK); akin to Sp. & Port. *mono*, ape, with *-ke*, dim. suffix], 1. any of the primates (the highest order of animals) except man and, usually, the lemurs; specifically, any of the smaller, long-tailed members of the primates, excluding the anthropoid apes. 2. the fur of some species of long-haired monkeys. 3. a person regarded as like a monkey in appearance or actions, as a mischievous or imitative child. 4. any of various mechanical devices, as the iron block, or ram, raised and dropped in a pile driver. *v.i.* [Colloq.], to play, fool, trifle, or meddle (often followed by *with* or *around with*). *v.t.* [Rare], to mimic; ape.

monkey bread, 1. the acid, gourd-shaped fruit of the baobab tree, eaten by monkeys. 2. the tree.
monkey business, [Slang], foolish, mischievous, or deceitful tricks or behavior.
monkey flower, any of a group of plants with spotted flowers having a corolla whose appearance suggests a gape or grimace; especially, the scarlet monkey flower.
mon·key·ish (muŋ′ki-ish), ***adj.*** of, like, or characteristic of a monkey; foolish, mischievous, etc.
monkey jacket, [from the resemblance to coats worn by trained monkeys], [Colloq.], a short, tight jacket, as that formerly worn by sailors.
mon·key·pot (muŋ′ki-pot′), ***n.*** 1. the large, woody seed vessel of any of various South American trees: so called from its urnlike shape. 2. any of these trees.
monkey puzzle, a tall South American coniferous tree with stiff pointed leaves, edible nuts, and hard wood.
mon·key·shine (muŋ′ki-shīn′), ***n. usually in pl.*** [Slang], a mischievous or playful trick, joke, or prank.
monkey suit, [see MONKEY JACKET], [Slang], 1. a uniform. 2. a man's dress suit.
monkey wrench, a wrench with a movable jaw, adjusted by a screw to fit various sizes of nuts, etc.: see **wrench,** illus.
Mon-Khmer (mōn′kmer′), ***adj.*** designating or of a group of languages spoken mainly in Indo-China, including Mon and Khmer.
monk·hood (muŋk′hood′), ***n.*** [see -HOOD], 1. the condition or profession of a monk. 2. monks collectively.
monk·ish (muŋk′ish), ***adj.*** of, like, or characteristic of a monk or monks: often used in hostility or contempt.
monk's cloth, 1. originally, a worsted cloth used for monks' garments. 2. now, a heavy cotton cloth with a basket weave, used for drapes, etc.
monks·hood (muŋks′hood′), ***n.*** the aconite plant.
Mon·mouth (mon′məth), ***n.*** 1. Monmouthshire. 2. the county seat of Monmouthshire: pop., 5,000. 3. a county in eastern New Jersey: scene of a battle (1778) of the Revolutionary War.
Monmouth, Duke of, (*James Scott*), 1649–1685; supposed illegitimate son of Charles II; led an insurrection against James II; executed: called the *Protestant Duke.*
Mon·mouth·shire (mon′məth-shir′), ***n.*** a county of England, along the southeast border of Wales: pop., 402,000; county seat, Monmouth.
mon·o- (mon′ō, mon′ə), [Gr. *mono-* < *monos,* single, alone], a prefix meaning: 1. *one, alone, single,* as in *monoclinic.* 2. *containing one atom* or *one group* (of a specified element), as in *monochloride.* 3. [< *mono*-molecular], *having a thickness of one molecule,* as in *monolayer.* Also, before a vowel, **mon-.**
mon·o·ac·id (mon′ō-as′id), ***adj.*** monoacidic. ***n.*** [Rare], an acid having only one replaceable hydrogen atom per molecule.
mon·o·a·cid·ic (mon′ō-ə-sid′ik), ***adj.*** 1. designating a base or alcohol one molecular weight of which can react with only one equivalent weight of an acid, or that has one hydroxyl group capable of replacing one acid hydrogen atom. 2. having only one acid hydrogen atom per molecule.
mon·o·a·tom·ic (mon′ō-ə-tom′ik), ***adj.*** consisting of one atom: said of a molecule.
mon·o·bas·ic (mon′ə-bā′sik), ***adj.*** 1. in *chemistry, a)* designating an acid the molecule of which contains one hydrogen atom replaceable by a metal or positive radical or capable of reacting with the hydroxyl group. *b)* designating a compound in which a metal or positive radical has replaced one acid hydrogen atom. 2. in *biology,* based on only one species; monotypic: said of a genus.
mon·o·carp (mon′ə-kärp′), ***n.*** a monocarpic plant.
mon·o·car·pel·lar·y (mon′ə-kär′pə-ler′i), ***adj.*** consisting of a single carpel.
mon·o·car·pic (mon′ə-kär′pik), ***adj.*** [< *mono-* + Gr. *karpos,* fruit; + *-ic*], bearing fruit only once, and then dying: said of annuals, biennials, and some trees.
mon·o·car·pous (mon′ə-kär′pəs), ***adj.*** 1. having a gynoecium consisting of a single carpel and forming a single ovary. 2. monocarpic.
mon·o·cha·si·al (mon′ə-kā′zhi-əl, mon′ə-kā′zi-əl), ***adj.*** of or characterized by a monochasium or monochasia.
mon·o·cha·si·um (mon′ə-kā′zhi-əm, mon′ə-kā′zi-əm), ***n.*** [*pl.* MONOCHASIA (-ə)], [Mod. L. < *mono-* + Gr. *chasis,* division], a flower cluster in which only a single branch is produced on the main axis.
mon·o·chlo·ride (mon′ə-klôr′īd, mon′ə-klō′rīd), ***n.*** a chloride containing one chlorine atom per molecule.
mon·o·chord (mon′ə-kôrd′), ***n.*** [ME. *monocorde* < ML. *monochordus,* lit., single-stringed; see MONO- & CHORD], 1. an acoustical instrument consisting of a wooden sounding box with a single string and a movable bridge set on a graduated scale: it is used for determining musical intervals mathematically by dividing the string into separate parts whose vibrations can be measured. 2. [Rare], harmony; agreement.
mon·o·chro·ic (mon′ə-krō′ik), ***adj.*** [< Gr. *monochroos;* + *-ic*], of one color; monochromatic.
mon·o·chro·mat·ic (mon′ə-krō-mat′ik), ***adj.*** [< Gr. *monochrōmatos;* see MONOCHROME], 1. of or having one color. 2. of or producing light of one wave length.
mon·o·chrome (mon′ə-krōm′), ***n.*** [Fr.; Gr. *monochrōmos,* of one color < *monos,* single + *chrōma,* color], 1. a painting or drawing in one color or different shades of one color. 2. the art or process of making these.
mon·o·chro·mic (mon′ə-krō′mik), ***adj.*** [< *monochrome* + *-ic*], in one color.
mon·o·chro·mi·cal (mon′ə-krō′mi-k'l), ***adj.*** monochromic.
mon·o·chrom·ist (mon′ə-krōm′ist), ***n.*** a maker of monochromes.
mon·o·cle (mon′ə-k'l), ***n.*** [Fr. < LL. *monoculus,* one-eyed < Gr. *monos,* single + L. *oculus,* eye], an eyeglass for one eye.
mon·o·cled (mon′ə-k'ld), ***adj.*** wearing a monocle.
mon·o·cli·nal (mon′ə-klī′n'l), ***adj.*** in *geology,* 1. dipping in one direction: said of strata, or rock layers. 2. of strata dipping in the same direction. ***n.*** a monocline.
mon·o·cline (mon′ə-klīn′), ***n.*** [< *mono-* + Gr. *klinein,* to incline], in *geology,* a monoclinal rock fold or structure.
mon·o·clin·ic (mon′ə-klin′ik), ***adj.*** [see MONOCLINE], designating or of crystallization characterized by three axes of unequal length, two of which intersect obliquely and are perpendicular to the third.
mon·o·cli·nous (mon′ə-klī′nəs), ***adj.*** [Mod. L. *monoclinus* < *mono-* + Gr. *klinē,* a bed, couch], 1. having the stamens and pistils in the same flower. 2. having both stamens and pistils, as some flowers.
mon·o·cot·y·le·don (mon′ə-kot″l-ē′d'n), ***n.*** in *botany,* a plant with only one cotyledon; specifically, any plant belonging to that one of the two subclasses of seed plants which is characterized by embryos with only one cotyledon, as lilies, orchids, palms, etc.
mon·o·cot·y·le·don·ous (mon′ə-kot″l-ē′d'n-əs, mon′ə-kot″l-ed′n-əs), ***adj.*** having only one cotyledon; belonging to the subclass of monocotyledons.
mo·noc·ra·cy (mə-nok′rə-si), ***n.*** [*pl.* MONOCRACIES (-siz)], [*mono-* + *-cracy*], government by one person; autocracy.
mon·o·crat (mon′ə-krat′), ***n.*** a person who believes in monocracy or monarchy: term applied by Thomas Jefferson c. 1790 to pro-English Federalists in the war between England and France.
mo·noc·u·lar (mə-nok′yoo-lēr), ***adj.*** [< LL. *monoculus* (see MONOCLE); + *-ar*], 1. having only one eye. 2. of, or for use by, only one eye.
mon·o·cul·ture (mon′ə-kul′chēr), ***n.*** [*mono-* + *culture*], the raising of only one crop or product without using the land for other purposes.
mon·o·cyte (mon′ə-sīt′), ***n.*** [*mono-* + *-cyte*], a large, nongranular white blood cell with a relatively small, kidney-shaped nucleus.
mon·o·dac·ty·lous (mon′ə-dak′t'l-əs), ***adj.*** [Gr. *monodaktylos* < *monos,* single + *daktylos,* a finger], having only one finger, toe, or claw: also **monodactyl.**
mo·nod·ic (mə-nod′ik), ***adj.*** [Gr. *monōidikos*], of, or having the nature of, monody.
mo·nod·i·cal (mə-nod′i-k'l), ***adj.*** monodic.
mon·o·dist (mon′ə-dist), ***n.*** a writer or singer of monody.
mon·o·dra·ma (mon′ə-drä′mə, mon′ə-dram′ə), ***n.*** drama acted, or written to be acted, by only one performer.
mon·o·dy (mon′ə-di), ***n.*** [*pl.* MONODIES (-diz)], [LL. *monodia;* Gr. *monōidia* < *monōidos,* singing alone < *monos,* single, alone + *aeidein,* to sing], 1. in ancient Greek literature, an ode sung by a single voice, as in a tragedy; lyric solo, generally a lament or dirge; hence, 2. a poem in which the poet mourns another's death: cf. **elegy, threnody.** 3. a monotonous sound or tone, as of waves. 4. in *music, a)* a style of composition in which one part, or voice, predominates, and the others serve as accompaniment; homophony, as distinguished from polyphony. *b)* a composition in this style.
mo·noe·cious (mə-nē′shəs, mō-nē′shəs), ***adj.*** [< *mon-* + Gr. *oikos,* a house; + *-ious*], 1. in *biology,* having both male and female reproductive organs in the same individual; hermaphroditic. 2. in *botany,* having the stamens and pistils in separate flowers on the same plant, as the oak. Also spelled **monecious.**
mon·o·gam·ic (mon′ə-gam′ik), ***adj.*** monogamous.
mo·nog·a·mist (mə-nog′ə-mist), ***n.*** a person who practices or advocates monogamy.
mo·nog·a·mous (mə-nog′ə-məs), ***adj.*** [LL. *monogamus;* Gr. *monogamos*], 1. practicing or advocating monogamy. 2. of monogamy.
mo·nog·a·my (mə-nog′ə-mi), ***n.*** [Fr. *monogamie;* LL. *monogamia;* Gr. *monogamia* < *monos,* single + *gamos,* marriage], 1. the practice or state of being married to only one person at a time: opposed to *bigamy, polygamy.* 2. [Rare], marriage only once during life: opposed to *digamy, deuterogamy.* 3. in *zoology,* the habit of having only one mate.

mon·o·gen·e·sis (mon'ə-jen'ə-sis), *n.* [Mod. L.; see MONO- & GENESIS], 1. the (hypothetical) descent of all living organisms from a single original organism: opposed to *polygenesis.* 2. monogenism. 3. asexual reproduction, as by budding or spore formation. 4. direct development of an ovum into an organism like the parent, without metamorphosis. Also **monogeny.**

mon·o·ge·net·ic (mon'ə-ji-net'ik), *adj.* 1. of, characterized by, or involving monogenesis. 2. having only one generation in the life cycle, or no intervening asexual generations, as certain worms. 3. in *geology,* produced by one formative process, as a mountain range.

mon·o·gen·ic (mon'ə-jen'ik), *adj.* 1. having a single origin; monogenetic. 2. in *zoology,* reproducing in only one way.

mo·nog·e·nism (mə-noj'ə-niz'm), *n.* [*mono-* + *-gen* + *-ism*], the doctrine that all human beings have descended from a single ancestor or pair of ancestors.

mo·nog·e·ny (mə-noj'ə-ni), *n.* monogenesis.

mon·o·gram (mon'ə-gram'), *n.* [LL. *monogramma;* Late Gr. *monogrammon;* see MONO- & -GRAM], a character or figure made up of two or more letters, often initials of a name, combined in a single design: used on writing paper, ornaments, clothing, etc.

mon·o·gram·mat·ic (mon'ə-grə-mat'ik), *adj.* of or like a monogram.

mon·o·graph (mon'ə-graf', mon'ə-gräf'), *n.* [*mono-* + *-graph*], 1. a book, article, or paper written about a particular subject. 2. originally, a treatise on a single genus, species, etc. of plant or animal.

mo·nog·ra·pher (mə-nog'rə-fẽr), *n.* a writer of a monograph or monographs.

mon·o·graph·ic (mon'ə-graf'ik), *adj.* of, or having the nature of, a monograph.

mo·nog·y·nous (mə-noj'ə-nəs), *adj.* of or characterized by monogyny.

mo·nog·y·ny (mə-noj'ə-ni), *n.* [*mono-* + *-gyny*], the practice or state of being married to only one woman at a time: opposed to *polygyny.*

mon·o·hy·drate (mon'ə-hī'drāt), *n.* a hydrate containing one gram molecular weight of water per gram molecular weight of the combining element or radical.

mon·o·hy·dric (mon'ə-hī'drik), *adj.* [*mono-* + *-hydric*], 1. having one hydroxyl group: as, *monohydric* alcohol. 2. having one atom of replaceable hydrogen.

mo·noi·cous (mə-noi'kəs), *adj.* monoecious.

mo·nol·a·ter (mə-nol'ə-tẽr), *n.* a person who practices monolatry.

mo·nol·a·try (mə-nol'ə-tri), *n.* [< *mono-* + Gr. *latreia,* worship], the worship of only one god, where several are believed to exist: distinguished from *monotheism.*

mon·o·lith (mon'ə-lith'), *n.* [Fr. *monolithe;* L. *monolithus;* Gr. *monolithos,* made of one stone < *monos,* single + *lithos,* stone], 1. a single large block or piece of stone, as in architecture or sculpture. 2. something made of a single block of stone, as an obelisk.

mon·o·lith·ic (mon'ə-lith'ik), *adj.* 1. of, having the nature of, or like a monolith; hence, 2. massively solid, single, and uniform.

mon·o·log·ic (mon'ə-loj'ik), *adj.* of, having the nature of, or like a monologue.

mon·o·log·i·cal (mon'ə-loj'i-k'l), *adj.* monologic.

mon·o·log·ist (mon'ə-lôg'ist, mon'ə-log'ist, mə-nol'ə-jist), *n.* a monologuist.

mon·o·logue (mon'ə-lôg', mon'ə-log'), *n.* [Fr. < Gr. *monologos,* speaking alone < *monos,* single, alone + *legein,* to speak], 1. a long speech by one speaker, sometimes one monopolizing the conversation. 2. a poem or other composition in which one person is represented as speaking alone. 3. a part of a play in which one character speaks alone; soliloquy. 4. a play or playlet for one actor. 5. a type of dramatic entertainment by one speaker only. Also spelled **monolog.**

mon·o·logu·ist (mon'ə-lôg'ist, mon'ə-log'ist), *n.* a person who delivers, or performs in, monologues.

mo·nol·o·gy (mə-nol'ə-ji), *n.* [*pl.* MONOLOGIES (-jiz)], [Gr. *monologia*], 1. the act or habit of soliloquizing. 2. [Obs.], a monologue.

mon·o·ma·ni·a (mon'ə-mā'ni-ə), *n.* [Mod. L.; see MONO- & MANIA], 1. an excessive interest in or enthusiasm for some one thing; craze. 2. a mental disorder characterized by irrationality on one subject.

mon·o·ma·ni·ac (mon'ə-mā'ni-ak'), *n.* a monomaniacal person.

mon·o·ma·ni·a·cal (mon'ō-mə-nī'ə-k'l), *adj.* of, having the nature of, or characterized by monomania.

mo·nom·er·ous (mə-nom'ẽr-əs), *adj.* [< Gr. *monomerēs,* single (< *monos,* alone, only + *meros,* a part); + *-ous*], having one member in each whorl: said of flowers.

mon·o·me·tal·lic (mon'ō-mə-tal'ik), *adj.* 1. of, containing, or using one metal. 2. of or based on monometallism.

mon·o·met·al·lism (mon'ə-met''l-iz'm), *n.* 1. the use of only one metal, usually gold or silver, as the monetary standard. 2. the doctrine or policies supporting this.

mon·o·met·al·list (mon'ə-met''l-ist), *n.* a person who believes in or advocates monometallism.

mo·no·mi·al (mō-nō'mi-əl), *adj.* [< *mono-,* after *binomial*], 1. in *algebra,* consisting of only one term. 2. in *biology,* consisting of only one word: said of a name. *n.* a monomial expression, quantity, or name.

mon·o·mo·lec·u·lar (mon'ō-mə-lek'yoo-lẽr), *adj.* 1. of a single molecule. 2. designating or of a layer one molecule thick.

mon·o·mor·phic (mon'ə-môr'fik), *adj.* [*mono-* + *-morphic*], 1. having only one form. 2. having the same or an essentially similar type of structure.

mon·o·mor·phous (mon'ə-môr'fəs), *adj.* monomorphic.

Mo·non·ga·he·la (mə-noŋ'gə-hē'lə), *n.* a river flowing northward from West Virginia through southwestern Pennsylvania and joining the Allegheny at Pittsburgh to form the Ohio: length, 300 mi.

mon·o·nu·cle·o·sis (mon'ə-nōō'kli-ō'sis, mon'ə-nū'kli-ō'sis), *n.* 1. the presence in the blood of an excessive number of cells having a single nucleus. 2. a disease (*infectious mononucleosis*) resulting from this, characterized by fever and enlargement of the lymph nodes.

mon·o·pet·al·ous (mon'ə-pet''l-əs), *adj.* in *botany,* 1. having only one petal. 2. gamopetalous.

mon·o·pho·bi·a (mon'ə-fō'bi-ə), *n.* [Mod. L.; *mono-* + *-phobia*], an abnormal fear of being alone.

mon·o·phon·ic (mon'ə-fon'ik), *adj.* 1. of, or having the nature of, monophony. 2. designating or of sound reproduction using a single channel to carry and reproduce sounds through one or more loudspeakers: cf. **stereophonic.**

mo·noph·o·ny (mə-nof'ə-ni), *n.* [*mono-* + *-phony*], 1. music having a single melody without accompaniment or harmonizing parts: distinguished from *homophony, polyphony.* 2. monody.

mon·oph·thong (mon'əf-thôŋ', mon'əf-thoŋ'), *n.* [Gr. *monophthongos,* of or with one sound < *monos,* single + *phthongos,* a sound, voice], 1. a single, simple vowel sound. 2. a combination of two letters representing a single vowel sound, as *ea* in *leaf;* vowel digraph.

mon·oph·thon·gal (mon'əf-thôŋ'g'l, mon'əf-thoŋ'g'l), *adj.* of, or having the nature of, a monophthong.

mon·o·phy·let·ic (mon'ə-fī-let'ik), *adj.* [see MONO- & PHYLETIC], 1. of a single stock. 2. developed from a single ancestral type.

mon·o·phyl·lous (mon'ə-fil'əs), *adj.* [Gr. *monophyllos* < *monos,* single + *phyllon,* a leaf], in *botany,* having or consisting of only one leaf.

Mo·noph·y·site (mə-nof'ə-sīt'), *n.* [LGr. *monophysitēs* < Gr. *monos,* single + *physis,* nature], a person who believes that Christ had but one nature, or a composite nature of both the human and the divine, a tenet held by members of the Coptic and some other churches.

Mon·o·phy·sit·ic (mon'ə-fi-sit'ik), *adj.* of, or holding the doctrine of, the Monophysites.

mon·o·plane (mon'ə-plān'), *n.* an airplane with only one main supporting surface, or pair of wings.

mon·o·ple·gi·a (mon'ə-plē'ji-ə), *n.* [Mod. L. < *mono-* + Gr. *plēgē,* a stroke], paralysis of a single limb or part of the body.

mon·o·pleg·ic (mon'ə-plej'ik, mon'ə-plē'jik), *adj.* of or having monoplegia.

MONOPLANE

mon·o·pode (mon'ə-pōd'), *adj.* [LL. *monopodius;* Gr. **monopodios,* for *monopous* < *monos,* single + *pous, podos,* a foot], having only one foot. *n.* 1. a monopode creature; specifically, a member of a fabled race of monopode men. 2. a monopodium.

mon·o·po·di·al (mon'ə-pō'di-əl), *adj.* of, having the nature of, or characterized by a monopodium.

mon·o·po·di·um (mon'ə-pō'di-əm), *n.* [*pl.* MONOPODIA (-ə)], [Mod. L.; see MONO- & -PODIUM], in *botany,* a single main axis that continues to extend at the apex in its original line of growth, giving off lateral branches or axes: also **monopode.**

mo·nop·o·lism (mə-nop'ə-liz'm), *n.* the system or existence of monopolies, or the practice of monopolists.

mo·nop·o·list (mə-nop'ə-list), *n.* 1. a person who has a monopoly. 2. a person who favors or advocates monopoly. *adj.* monopolistic.

mo·nop·o·lis·tic (mə-nop'ə-lis'tik), *adj.* 1. of monopoly, monopolies, or monopolists. 2. monopolizing; having a monopoly.

mo·nop·o·li·za·tion (mə-nop'ə-li-zā'shən, mə-nop'ə-lī-zā'shən), *n.* a monopolizing or being monopolized.

mo·nop·o·lize (mə-nop'ə-līz'), *v.t.* [MONOPOLIZED (-līzd'), MONOPOLIZING], 1. to get, have, or exploit a monopoly of. 2. to get or occupy the whole of; acquire exclusive possession or control of.

mo·nop·o·ly (mə-nop'ə-li), *n.* [*pl.* MONOPOLIES (-liz)], [L. *monopolium;* Gr. *monopōlion,* right of exclusive sale < *monopōlia,* exclusive sale < *monos,* single, alone + *pōlein,* to sell], 1. exclusive control of a commodity or service in a given market, or control that makes possible the fixing of prices and the virtual elimination of free competition. 2. an exclusive privilege of engaging in a particular business or providing a service, granted by a ruler or by the state. 3. exclusive possession or control of something. 4. something that is the subject of a monopoly. 5. a company or combination that has a monopoly. —*SYN.* see next page.

SYN.—**monopoly** applies to the exclusive control of a commodity, etc., as defined above; a **trust** is a combination of corporations, organized for the purpose of gaining a monopoly, in which stock is turned over to trustees who issue stock certificates to the stockholders: trusts are now illegal in the United States; **cartel**, the European term for a trust, now usually implies an international trust; a **syndicate** is now usually a group of bankers, corporations, etc. organized to buy large blocks of securities, afterwards selling them in small parcels to the public at a profit; a **corner** is a temporary speculative monopoly of some stock or commodity for the purpose of raising the price.

mon·o·rail (mon'ə-rāl'), ***n.*** 1. a single rail serving as a track for trucks or cars suspended from it or balanced on it. 2. a railway with such a track.

mon·o·sac·cha·ride (mon'ə-sak'ə-rīd', mon'ə-sak'ə-rid), ***n.*** [*mono-* + *saccharide*], a carbohydrate not decomposable by hydrolysis; simple sugar, as glucose.

mon·o·sep·al·ous (mon'ə-sep''l-əs), ***adj.*** in *botany*, 1. gamosepalous. 2. having only one sepal.

mon·o·so·di·um glu·ta·mate (mon'ə-sō'di-əm glōō'tə-māt'), a white, crystalline powder derived from vegetable protein and used in cooking as a flavor intensifier.

mon·o·sper·mal (mon'ə-spũr'm'l), ***adj.*** monospermous.

mon·o·sper·mous (mon'ə-spũr'məs), ***adj.*** [*mono-* + *-spermous*], in *botany*, having only one seed.

mon·o·stich (mon'ə-stik'), ***n.*** [LL. *monostichum;* Gr. *monostichon* < *monos*, single + *stichos*, a line, verse], 1. a poem or epigram consisting of one metrical line. 2. one line of poetry; a verse.

mon·o·stome (mon'ə-stōm'), ***adj.*** monostomous.

mo·nos·to·mous (mə-nos'tə-məs), ***adj.*** [*mono-* + *-stomous*], having one mouth, stoma, or pore.

mo·nos·tro·phe (mə-nos'trə-fi, mon'ə-strōf'), ***n.*** [< Gr. *monostrophos;* see MONO- & STROPHE], a poem in which all the stanzas have the same metrical form.

mon·o·stroph·ic (mon'ə-strof'ik), ***adj.*** [Gr. *monostrophikos*], of, or having the nature of, a monostrophe.

mon·o·sty·lous (mon'ə-stī'ləs), ***adj.*** in *botany*, having only one style.

mon·o·syl·lab·ic (mon'ə-si-lab'ik), ***adj.*** [ML. *monosyllabicus*], 1. having only one syllable: said of words. 2. consisting of, using, or speaking in, monosyllables.

mon·o·syl·lab·i·cal·ly (mon'ə-si-lab'i-k'l-i, mon'ə-si-lab'ik-li), ***adv.*** in or with monosyllables.

mon·o·syl·la·bism (mon'ə-sil'ə-biz'm), ***n.*** 1. a monosyllabic character. 2. the use of monosyllables.

mon·o·syl·la·ble (mon'ə-sil'ə-b'l), ***n.*** a word of one syllable, as *cat*.

mon·o·the·ism (mon'ə-thē-iz'm), ***n.*** [*mono-* + *theism*], the doctrine or belief that there is only one God.

mon·o·the·ist (mon'ə-thē'ist), ***n.*** a person who believes that there is only one God. ***adj.*** monotheistic.

mon·o·the·is·tic (mon'ə-thē-is'tik), ***adj.*** of or adhering to monotheism.

mon·o·the·is·ti·cal (mon'ə-thē-is'ti-k'l), ***adj.*** monotheistic.

mon·o·tint (mon'ə-tint'), ***n.*** monochrome.

mon·o·tone (mon'ə-tōn'), ***n.*** [Mod. L. *monotonus;* see MONOTONOUS], 1. uninterrupted repetition of the same tone; utterance of successive syllables or words without change of pitch or key. 2. monotony or sameness of tone, style, manner, color, etc. 3. a single, unchanging tone. 4. recitation, chanting, or singing in such a tone. 5. a person who sings in such a tone. ***adj.*** monotonous.

mo·not·o·nous (mə-not'ə-nəs), ***adj.*** [Gr. *monotonos;* see MONO-, TONE, & -OUS], 1. going on in the same tone without variation. 2. having little or no variation or variety. 3. tiresome because unvarying.

mo·not·o·ny (mə-not'ə-ni), ***n.*** [Gr. *monotonia;* see prec.], 1. sameness of tone or pitch, or continuance of the same tone without variation. 2. lack of variation or variety. 3. tiresome sameness; wearisome uniformity.

mon·o·trem·a·tous (mon'ə-trem'ə-təs, mon'ə-trē'mə-təs), ***adj.*** of the monotremes.

mon·o·treme (mon'ə-trēm'), ***n.*** [< Mod. L. *Monotremata* < Gr. *monos*, single + *trēma*, a hole], any of the lowest order of mammals, consisting of the duckbill and the echidnas: it lays eggs and has a single opening for the digestive, urinary, and genital organs.

mo·not·ri·chous (mə-not'ri-kəs), ***adj.*** [< *mono-* + Gr. *thrix*, *trichos*, hair; + *-ic*], having a single flagellum at one end, as some bacteria.

mon·o·type (mon'ə-tīp'), ***n.*** [*mono-* + *-type*], 1. in *biology*, the only type of its group, as a single species constituting a genus. 2. *a*) in *printing*, either of a pair of machines for casting and setting up type in separate characters on individual bodies: one, a casting machine, is controlled by a paper tape perforated on the other, a keyboard machine: a trademark (**Monotype**): cf. **linotype**. *b*) type produced in this way. *c*) a print from a metal plate on which a picture has been made, as with printing ink. *d*) the method of making such prints.

mon·o·typ·ic (mon'ə-tip'ik), ***adj.*** 1. having only one type, as a genus consisting of only one species. 2. having the nature of a monotype.

mon·o·va·lence (mon'ə-vā'ləns), ***n.*** the quality or state of being monovalent.

mon·o·va·len·cy (mon'ə-vā'lən-si), ***n.*** monovalence.

mon·o·va·lent (mon'ə-vā'lənt), ***adj.*** 1. in *bacteriology*, capable of resisting one strain of a given species of disease-producing organism because the right antibodies or antigens are present. 2. in *chemistry*, *a*) having a valence of one. *b*) univalent.

mon·ox·ide (mon-ok'sīd, mə-nok'sīd), ***n.*** an oxide with one atom of oxygen in each molecule.

Mon·roe (mən-rō'), ***n.*** a city in northern Louisiana: pop., 52,000.

Mon·roe, James (mən-rō'), 1758–1831; fifth president of the United States (1817–1825).

Monroe Doctrine, the doctrine, essentially stated by President Monroe in a message to Congress (December, 1823), that the United States would regard as an unfriendly act any attempt by a European nation to interfere in the affairs of the American countries or increase its possessions on the American continents.

Mon·ro·vi·a (mon-rō'vi-ə), ***n.*** seaport and capital of Liberia, Africa: pop., 60,000.

Mons (mōns), ***n.*** a city in southwestern Belgium: pop., 26,000.

mons (monz), ***n.*** [L., mountain, mount, hill], the mons pubis or mons veneris.

Mons., Monsieur.

Mon·sei·gneur, mon·sei·gneur (mon'sen-yũr'; Fr. mōn'se'nyẽr'), ***n.*** [*pl.* MESSEIGNEURS (mes'en-yũrz'; Fr. mā'se'nyẽr')], [Fr., lit., my lord; *mon*, my + *seigneur*, lord < L. *senior*, older], 1. a French title of honor given to persons of high birth or rank, as princes, or to important church officers, as bishops, cardinals, etc. 2. a person with this title. Abbreviated **Mgr., Monsig.**

mon·sieur (mə-syũr'; Fr. mə-syö'), ***n.*** [*pl.* MESSIEURS (mes'ẽrz; Fr. mā'syö')], [Fr., lit., my lord (see SIRE): orig. applied to men of high position], a man; gentleman: French title [M-], equivalent to *Mr.* or *Sir:* abbreviated **M., Mons.**

Mon·si·gnor, mon·si·gnor (mon-sēn'yẽr; It. môn'sē-nyôr'), ***n.*** [*pl.* MONSIGNORS (-yẽrz); It. MONSIGNORI (môn'sē-nyô'rē)], [It., lit., my lord; cf. MONSEIGNEUR], 1. a title given to certain dignitaries of the Roman Catholic Church. 2. a person who has this title. Abbreviated **Mngr., Mon., Monsig., Msgr.**

‡mon·si·gno·re (môn'sē-nyô're), ***n.*** [*pl.* MONSIGNORI (-rē)], [It.], monsignor: abbreviated **Mgr., Msgr.**

mon·soon (mon-sōōn'), ***n.*** [MD. *monssoen;* Port. *monção;* Ar. *mausim*, a time, a season], 1. a seasonal wind of the Indian Ocean and southern Asia, blowing from the southwest from April to October, and from the northeast during the rest of the year. 2. the season during which this wind blows from the southwest, characterized by heavy rains. 3. any wind that reverses its direction seasonally or blows constantly between land and adjacent water.

mons pu·bis (pū'bis), [see MONS & PUBES], the fleshy, rounded elevation, covered with pubic hair, at the lower part of a man's abdomen.

mon·ster (mon'stẽr), ***n.*** [ME. & OFr. *monstre* < L. *monstrum*, divine portent of misfortune, monster < *monere*, to admonish, warn], 1. any plant or animal of abnormal shape or structure, as one greatly malformed or lacking some parts; monstrosity. 2. any imaginary creature part human and part animal in form, as a centaur, or made up of the parts of two or more different animals, as a unicorn. 3. something monstrous. 4. a person so cruel, wicked, depraved, etc. as to horrify others. 5. any huge animal or thing. 6. in *pathology*, a malformed fetus, especially one with an excess or deficiency of limbs or parts; teratism. ***adj.*** huge; enormous; monstrous.

mon·strance (mon'strəns), ***n.*** [ME. *mustraunce*, *munstraunce;* OFr. < ML. *monstrantia* < L. *monstrare*, to show], in the *Roman Catholic Church*, a receptacle in which the consecrated Host is exposed for adoration.

mon·stros·i·ty (mon-stros'ə-ti), ***n.*** [LL. *monstrositas*], 1. the state or quality of being monstrous. 2. [*pl.* MONSTROSITIES (-tiz)], a monstrous thing or creature.

mon·strous (mon'strəs), ***adj.*** [Late ME.; OFr. *monstreux;* L. *monstrosus*, *monstruosus* < *monstrum;* see MONSTER], 1. abnormally or prodigiously large; huge; enormous. 2. very unnatural or abnormal in shape, type, or character. 3. having the character or appearance of a monster. 4. horrible; hideous; shocking. 5. hideously wrong or evil; atrocious. ***adv.*** [Colloq., Now Rare], very; extremely. —***SYN.*** see **outrageous.**

mons ven·er·is (ven'ẽr-is), [L., lit., mount of Venus], the fleshy, rounded elevation, covered with pubic hair, at the lower part of a woman's abdomen.

Mont., Montana.

mon·tage (mon-täzh', mōn-täzh'), ***n.*** [Fr., a mounting, setting together < *monter*, to mount; see MOUNT, *v.*], 1. *a*) the art or process of making a composite picture by bringing together into a single composition a number of different pictures or parts of pictures and arranging these, as by superimposing one on another, so that they form a blended whole while remaining distinct. *b*) a picture so made. 2. in *motion pictures*, *a*) the process of producing a rapid sequence of very short scenes to show a rapid succession of associated ideas or mental images, or a sequence in which images, as of objects, are shown as whirling or flashing rapidly into focus. *b*) a part of a motion picture in which this is used. *c*) the process of cutting and arranging the film. 3. in *radio*, a sequence in which voices or sounds break in on one another or blend to suggest confusion, introspection, etc.

Mon·ta·gu, Lady **Mary Wort·ley** (wûrt′li mon′tə-gū′), (born *Mary Pierrepont*), 1689–1762; English author.

Mon·ta·gue (mon′tə-gū′), *n.* in Shakespeare's *Romeo and Juliet*, Romeo's family name.

Mon·taigne, Mi·chel Ey·quem de (mē′shel′ e′kem′ də mōn′ten′y′; Eng. mon-tān′), 1533–1592; French essayist.

Mon·tan·a (mon-tan′ə), *n.* a Western State of the United States, bordering Canada: area, 147,138 sq. mi.; pop., 675,000; capital, Helena: abbreviated **Mont.**

Mon·tan·an (mon-tan′ən), *adj.* of Montana. *n.* a native or inhabitant of Montana.

mon·tan wax (mon′tan), [< L. *montanus*, of a mountain + *wax*], a brown or whitish hydrocarbon wax extracted from lignite and peat, and used in making candles, polishes, phonograph records, etc.

Mon·tauk Point (mon-tôk′, mon′tôk′), the easternmost point of Long Island, New York.

Mont Blanc (mōn blän′; Eng. mont blaŋk), a mountain in eastern France, on the Italian border: height, 15,781 ft.: highest peak of the Alps: Italian name, *Monte Bianco.*

Mont·calm (mōn′kȧlm′; Eng. mont-käm′), *n.* (*Louis Joseph, Marquis de Montcalm de Saint-Véran*), French field marshal; 1712–1759; defeated by the British led by Wolfe at Quebec (1759).

Mont Cer·vin (mōn′ ser′van′), the Matterhorn.

Mont·clair (mont-klâr′), *n.* a city in northeastern New Jersey: pop., 43,000.

‡**mont-de-pié·té** (mōn′də-pyā′tā′), *n.* [*pl.* MONTS-DE-PIÉTÉ (mōn′-)], [Fr.; It. *monte di pietà*, charitable bank, lit. mount of pity], a public pawnshop, authorized and controlled by the government, for lending money to the poor at a low rate of interest.

mon·te (mon′ti, mōn′tā), *n.* [Sp. *monte*, lit., mountain, hence heap of cards (left after players have their shares); L. *mons, montis*, mountain], a gambling game of Spanish origin, played with a special deck of forty cards, in which the players bet against a banker on the color of cards to be turned up from the deck.

Mon·te Car·lo (mon′ti kär′lō; It. mōn′te kär′lô), a town in Monaco: gambling resort: pop., 11,000.

mon·teith (mon-tēth′), *n.* [said to be named after the inventor], a large bowl for punch, etc., usually of silver, with a brim from which glasses and ladles are hung.

Mon·te·ne·grin (mon′tə-nē′grin), *adj.* of Montenegro or its people. *n.* a native or inhabitant of Montenegro.

Mon·te·ne·gro (mon′tə-nē′grō; It. mōn′te-ne′grô), *n.* a former kingdom north of Albania, now a federated republic of Yugoslavia: area, 5,345 sq. mi.

Mon·te·rey (mon′tə-rā′), *n.* a town on the coast of central California: pop., 23,000: former capital of California (until 1847).

mon·te·ro (mon-târ′ō; Sp. mōn-te′rō), *n.* [*pl.* MONTEROS (-ōz; Sp. -rōs)], [< Sp. *montera* < *monte*, hill], a round cap with a flap, formerly worn by Spanish huntsmen.

Mon·ter·rey (mon′tə-rā′; Mex. mōn′ter-rā′), *n.* the capital of Nuevo Léon, Mexico, in the northeastern part: pop., 564,000.

Mon·tes·pan, Marquise **de** (də mōn′tes′pän′; Eng. mon′təs-pan′), (*Françoise Athénaïs Rochechouart*), 1641–1707; mistress of Louis XIV of France.

Mon·tes·quieu (mōn′tes′kyö′; Eng. mon′təs-kū′, mon′-tes-kū′), *n.* (*Charles Louis de Secondat, Baron de la Brède et de Montesquieu*), French jurist and philosophical writer on history and government; lived 1689–1755.

Mon·tes·so·ri, Maria (mon′tə-sôr′i, mon′tə-sō′ri; It. mōn′tes-sô′rē), 1870–1952; Italian educator.

Montessori method (or **system**), a system of training and teaching young children, devised in 1907 by Maria Montessori, which emphasizes training of the senses and aims at self-education through guiding rather than controlling the child's activity.

Mon·te·ver·di, Clau·di·o (klou′dyô mōn′te-vâr′dē), 1567–1643; Italian composer.

Mon·te·vid·e·o (mon′tə-vi-dā′ō, mon′tə-vid′i-ō′; Sp. mōn′te-vē-*the*′ô), *n.* seaport and capital of Uruguay, on the Plata River: pop., 923,000.

Mon·te·zu·ma II (mon′tə-zōō′mə), 1480?–1520; last Aztec emperor of Mexico (1502–1520); conquered by Cortés.

Mont·fort, Si·mon de (də mont′fērt; Fr. sē′mōn′ də mōn′fôr′), 1. 1160?–1218; French crusader. 2. (*Earl of Leicester*), 1208?–1265; his son; English statesman and soldier.

Mont·gom·er·y (mont-gum′ēr-i, mən-gum′ri), *n.* 1. the capital of Alabama, on the Alabama River: pop., 134,000. 2. Montgomeryshire. 3. the county seat of Montgomeryshire.

Mont·gom·er·y, Sir **Bernard Law** (lô mont-gum′ēr-i, mən-gum′ri), 1887– ; British field marshal; commander of British ground forces, World War II.

Mont·gom·er·y·shire (mont-gum′ēr-i-shir′; mən-gum′-ri-shir′), *n.* a county of Wales: pop., 46,000: county seat, Montgomery.

month (munth), *n.* [ME. *moneth;* AS. *monath* < the base of *mona*, the moon (see MOON & -TH); akin to G. *monat* and parallel in formation to L. *mensis*, month (cf. MENSAL)], 1. any of the main parts (in the Gregorian calendar, twelve) into which the calendar year is divided: also **calendar month.** 2. *a*) the time from any day of one month to the corresponding day of the next. *b*) a period of four weeks or 30 days. 3. the period of a complete revolution of the moon with reference to some fixed point (in full, **lunar month**); especially, the period from one new moon to the next (in full, **synodic month**): equivalent to 29 days, 12 hours, 44 minutes and 2.7 + seconds. 4. one twelfth of the solar year (in full, **solar month**). Abbreviated **M., m., mo.**

month after month, every month.

month by month, each month.

month in, month out, every month.

month·ly (munth′li), *adj.* 1. continuing or lasting for a month. 2. done, happening, appearing, payable, etc. once a month, or every month: as, a *monthly* magazine. 3. of a month, or each month. 4. of the menses. *n.* [*pl.* MONTHLIES (-liz)], 1. a periodical published once a month. 2. *pl.* the menses. *adv.* once a month; every month.

Mon·ti·cel·lo (mon′tə-sel′ō; *occas.* mon′tə-chel′ō), *n.* the home of Thomas Jefferson, three miles from Charlottesville, Virginia.

mon·ti·cule (mon′ti-kūl′), *n.* [Fr.; LL. *monticulus*, dim. of *mons, montis*, mountain], 1. a small mountain or hill. 2. a secondary cone of a volcano.

Mont·mar·tre (mōn′mår′tr′), *n.* a section of the northern part of Paris, famous for its cafés and night life.

Mont·pel·ier (mont-pēl′yēr), *n.* the capital of Vermont: pop., 9,000.

Mont·pel·lier (mōn′pel′yā′), *n.* a city in southern France: pop., 98,000.

Mont·re·al (mont′ri-ôl′, munt′ri-ôl′), *n.* a city in southern Quebec, Canada, on an island in the St. Lawrence: pop., 1,109,000 (with suburbs, 1,621,000).

Mont·rose (mont-rōz′), first Marquis of, (*James Graham*), 1612–1650; Scottish supporter of Charles I; executed.

Mont·ser·rat (mont′sə-rat′), *n.* 1. an island of the Leeward group, in the West Indies Federation: area, 32 sq. mi.; pop., 14,000. 2. a mountain in northeastern Spain: height, 4,058 ft.: site of a monastery.

Mont St. Mi·chel (mōn′ san′ mē′shel′), a small island off the northwestern coast of France, noted for its fortress and abbey: also **Mont-Saint-Michel, Mont Saint Michel.**

mon·u·ment (mon′yoo-mənt), *n.* [ME. *moniment;* OFr.; L. *monumentum* < *monere*, to remind, warn], 1. something set up to keep alive the memory of a person or event, as a tablet, statue, pillar, building, etc. 2. a structure surviving from a former period. 3. a writing or the like serving as a memorial. 4. a work, production, etc. of enduring value or significance: as, *monuments* of learning. 5. a stone shaft or other object set in the earth to mark a boundary. 6. [Obs.], a tomb; sepulcher. 7. [Obs.], a statue; effigy.

mon·u·men·tal (mon′yoo-men′t′l), *adj.* [L. *monumentalis*], 1. of, suitable for, or serving as a monument or monuments. 2. like a monument; massive, enduring, etc. 3. historically notable, important, or of lasting value: as, a *monumental* book. 4. great; colossal: as, *monumental* ineptitude. 5. in *art*, larger than life-size.

mon·u·men·tal·ize (mon′yoo-men′t′l-īz′), *v.t.* [MONUMENTALIZED (-īzd′), MONUMENTALIZING], to make a lasting memorial or record of, as by a monument.

mon·y (mon′i), *adj. & n.* [Scot. & N. Eng. Dial.], many.

-mo·ny (mō′ni), [< Fr. or L.; Fr. *-monie, -moine;* L. *-monia, -monium*], a suffix used to form nouns that mean *a resulting thing, condition,* or *state*, as in *patrimony, sanctimony:* it is sometimes equivalent to *-ment.*

Mon·za (mōn′tsä), *n.* a city in northern Italy: pop., 70,000.

mon·zo·nite (mon′zə-nīt′), *n.* [G. *monzonit* < Mt. *Monzoni* (in Tyrol), where it occurs + *-it*, -ite], an igneous rock containing orthoclase and plagioclase feldspar in nearly equal amounts and, sometimes, biotite in small quantities.

moo (mōō), *n.* [*pl.* MOOS (mōōz)], [echoic], the characteristic vocal sound made by a cow; lowing sound. *v.i.* [MOOED (mōōd), MOOING], to make this sound; low.

mooch (mōōch), *v.i.* [ME. *mowchen*, dial. var. of *mychen*, to pilfer < OFr. *muchier*, to skulk, hide], [Slang], 1. to skulk or sneak. 2. to loiter, loaf, or rove about. *v.t.* [Slang], 1. to steal; pilfer. 2. to get by begging or asking for, without payment, as cigarettes; cadge. Also spelled **mouch.**

mood (mōōd), *n.* [ME. *mode, mood;* AS. *mod,* mind, soul, courage; akin to G. *mut,* mental disposition, spirit, courage; IE. base **mē-,* etc., to strive strongly, be energetic, prob. seen also in L. *mos, moris,* custom, customary behavior (cf. MORAL)], 1. a particular state of mind or feeling; humor, or temper. 2. *pl.* fits of morose, sullen, or uncertain temper. 3. [Obs.], anger. *SYN.*—**mood** is the broadest of these terms referring to a temporary state of mind and emphasizes the constraining or pervading quality of the feeling (she's in a merry *mood*); **humor** emphasizes the variability or capriciousness of the mood (he wept and laughed as his *humor* moved him); **temper,** in this comparison, applies to a mood characterized by a single, strong emotion, especially that of anger (my, he's in a nasty *temper*!); **vein** stresses the transient nature of the mood (if I may speak in a serious *vein* for a moment).

mood (mōōd), *n.* [< *mode,* influenced by prec. *mood*], 1. in *grammar, a*) in many languages, that aspect of verbs which has to do with the speaker's attitude toward the action or state expressed, indicating whether this is regarded as a fact (*indicative mood*), as a matter of supposal, desire, possibility, etc. (*subjunctive mood*), as a command (*imperative mood*), etc.: mood is shown by inflection, as in Latin and Greek, or by auxiliaries, as English *may, might, should,* or by both. *b*) a set of forms expressing this aspect. *c*) any such form. Also **mode.** 2. in *logic,* mode.

mood·i·ly (mōōd'l-i), *adv.* in a moody manner.

mood·i·ness (mōōd'i-nis), *n.* the quality or condition of being moody.

mood·y (mōōd'i), *adj.* [MOODIER (-i-ẽr), MOODIEST (-i-ist)], 1. subject to or characterized by gloomy, sullen moods or changes of mood. 2. resulting from or indicating such a mood. 3. gloomy; sullen; depressed.

Mood·y, Dwight Ly·man (lī'mən mōōd'i), 1837–1899; American evangelist.

Moody, William Vaughan (vôn), 1869–1910; American poet, dramatist, and educator.

moon (mōōn), *n.* [ME. *mone;* AS. *mona* (cf. MONTH); akin to Goth. *mēna;* IE. base **mē-,* to measure; prob. basic sense "that measures (time)"], 1. the heavenly body that revolves around the earth once about every 29 1/2 days and accompanies it in its yearly revolution about the sun, reflecting the sun's light: the moon's diameter is about 2,160 miles, its mean distance from the earth is about 238,857 miles, and its mean density is 0.60. 2. this body as it appears during a particular lunar month or period of time, or at a particular time of the month: the *new moon* (the moon when in conjunction with the sun) becomes visible as a narrow crescent; the *half-moon* (the moon when half of its disk is illuminated) is visible as a half circle; the *full moon* (the moon when its entire disk is illuminated) is visible as a circle; and the *old* (or *waning*) *moon* is the moon at any time after it has been full. 3. a month; especially, a lunar month. 4. moonlight. 5. anything shaped like the moon (i.e., orb or crescent). 6. any planetary satellite. Abbreviated **M., m.** *v.i.* [from the notion of behaving as if moonstruck], to wander or gaze about in an idle, listless, or abstracted manner. *v.t.* to pass (time) in mooning.

moon·beam (mōōn'bēm'), *n.* a ray of moonlight.

moon-blind (mōōn'blind'), *adj.* having moon blindness.

moon blindness, 1. night blindness: formerly attributed to the effects of moonlight. 2. a disease of horses, of undetermined cause, characterized by recurrent inflammation of the eyes and, eventually, blindness.

moon·calf (mōōn'kaf', mōōn'käf'), *n.* [from the notion of being influenced by the moon; cf. LUNATIC], 1. a congenital idiot; born fool. 2. [Obs.], a monstrosity.

mooned (mōōnd), *adj.* 1. shaped like the moon; round or crescent. 2. marked or decorated with moon-shaped signs or devices.

Moo·ney, Tom (mōō'ni), (*Thomas J. Zechariah Mooney*); 1882?–1942; American labor leader; convicted of participation in the bombing of a Preparedness Day parade in San Francisco, 1916; pardoned and freed from prison in 1939.

moon·eye (mōōn'ī'), *n.* 1. an eye of a horse affected with moon blindness. 2. moon blindness.

moon-eyed (mōōn'īd'), *adj.* 1. moon-blind. 2. having the eyes wide open, as from fright or wonder.

moon-faced (mōōn'fāst'), *adj.* having a round face.

moon·fish (mōōn'fish'), *n.* [*pl.* MOONFISH, MOONFISHES (-iz); see FISH], 1. any of a number of sea fishes with a silvery or yellow, deep, sharply compressed body, found in the warmer coastal waters of North and South America. 2. any of various other fishes; especially, *a*) the Mexican top minnow. *b*) the opah.

moon·flow·er (mōōn'flou'ẽr), *n.* 1. a night-blooming plant of the morning-glory family, with large, heart-shaped leaves and white, fragrant, trumpet-shaped flowers. 2. its flower.

moon·ish (mōōn'ish), *adj.* like the moon; changeable; fickle; capricious.

moon·light (mōōn'līt'), *n.* the light of the moon. *adj.* 1. of moonlight. 2. moonlit. 3. done or occurring by moonlight, or at night.

moon·light·ing (mōōn'līt'iŋ), *n.* [from the usual night hours of such second jobs], the practice of holding a second regular job in addition to one's main job.

moon·lit (mōōn'lit), *adj.* lighted by the moon.

moon·rise (mōōn'rīz'), *n.* the rising or time of rising of the moon above the horizon.

moon·seed (mōōn'sēd'), *n.* any of a number of related plants with crescent-shaped seeds, heart-shaped leaves, and greenish-yellow flowers.

moon·set (mōōn'set'), *n.* the setting or time of setting of the moon below the horizon.

moon·shine (mōōn'shīn'), *n.* 1. moonlight; hence, 2. foolish or empty talk, notions, plans, etc.; nonsense. 3. [Colloq.], whisky, etc. unlawfully made or smuggled.

moon·shin·er (mōōn'shīn'ẽr), *n.* [Colloq.], 1. a person who makes alcoholic liquor unlawfully. 2. a person engaged in some unlawful trade at night.

moon·shin·y (mōōn'shīn'i), *adj.* 1. moonlit. 2. like or suggestive of moonlight; hence, 3. unreal, unsubstantial, visionary, foolish, etc.

moon·stone (mōōn'stōn'), *n.* a milky-white, translucent feldspar with a pearly luster, used as a gem.

moon-strick·en (mōōn'strik'ən), *adj.* moonstruck.

moon·struck (mōōn'struk'), *adj.* disordered in mind or otherwise harmfully affected, supposedly by the influence of the moon; crazed; lunatic; dazed.

moon·wort (mōōn'wûrt'), *n.* 1. any of a group of ferns with fleshy leaves and a fruiting spike resembling a bunch of grapes. 2. the honesty, a plant with large, purple flowers and semitransparent pods.

moon·y (mōōn'i), *adj.* [MOONIER (-i-ẽr), MOONIEST (-i-ist)], 1. of or characteristic of the moon. 2. like the moon, especially in shape; round or crescent-shaped. 3. moonlit. 4. like moonlight. 5. mooning; listless.

Moor (moor), *n.* [ME. *More;* OFr. *More, Maure;* L. *Maurus,* a Moor, Mauritanian; Gr. *Mauros*], 1. a member of a Moslem people of mixed Arab and Berber descent living in northwestern Africa. 2. a member of a group of this people that invaded and occupied Spain in the 8th century A.D.

moor (moor), *n.* [ME. *more;* AS. *mor,* wasteland; akin to G. *moor* (< LG.); IE. base **mori-* or **mari-,* sea, as also in L. *mare,* sea, Eng. *marsh,* etc.; basic sense "swampy coast land"], [British], 1. a tract of open wasteland, especially in the British Isles, usually covered with heather and often marshy or peaty; heath. 2. a tract of land with game preserves.

moor (moor), *v.t.* [Early Mod. Eng.; prob. < AS. **marian* (implied in *mærels,* mooring rope); akin to MD. *māren*], 1. to hold (a ship, etc.) in place by cables or chains fastened on shore, or by anchors, etc. 2. to cause to be held in place; secure. *v.i.* 1. to moor a ship, etc. 2. to be secured by cables, chains, etc.

moor·age (moor'ij), *n.* [see -AGE], 1. a mooring or being moored. 2. a place for mooring. 3. a charge for the use of such a place.

moor cock, [British], the male moorfowl, or red grouse.

Moore, George (moor, môr, mōr), 1852–1933; Irish novelist, dramatist, and critic.

Moore, Thomas, 1779–1852; Irish poet.

moor·fowl (moor'foul'), *n.* [British], the red grouse.

moor hen, [British], 1. the female moorfowl, or red grouse. 2. the common European gallinule.

moor·ing (moor'iŋ), *n.* 1. the act of a person or thing that moors. 2. *often in pl.* the lines, cables, etc. by which this is done. 3. *pl.* a place where a ship, etc. is or can be moored; moorage.

mooring mast (or **tower**), a mast (or tower) to which an airship is or can be moored.

Moor·ish (moor'ish), *adj.* 1. of the Moors, their culture, etc. 2. in the style of the Moors: said of architecture, etc.

moor·land (moor'land'), *n.* [British], a moor (sense 1).

moor·wort (moor'wûrt'), *n.* any of a group of low, evergreen shrubs growing in moors or bogs.

moose (mōōs), *n.* [*pl.* MOOSE], [< Am. Ind. (Algonquian); cf. Massachusett *moos,* lit., eats off], 1. the largest animal of the deer family, native to the Northern United States and Canada: the male has huge palmate antlers. 2. the European elk.

Moose·head Lake (mōōs'hed'), a lake in west central Maine: area, 120 sq. mi.

moot (mōōt), *n.* [ME. *mote;* AS. *mot, gemot,* a meeting, assembly; IE. base **mōd-, *măd-,* etc., to encounter; cf. MEET, *v.*], 1. an early English assembly of freemen to administer justice, decide community problems, etc. 2. a discussion or argument, especially of a hypothetical law case, as in a law school. *adj.* subject to or open for discussion or debate; debatable. *v.t.* 1. to debate or discuss. 2. to propose or bring up for discussion or debate. 3. in *law,* to argue or plead (a case, etc.), especially in a mock court.

moot court, a mock court in which hypothetical cases are tried, as to give law students practice.

mop (mop), *n.* [Early Mod. Eng. *mappe;* nautical term, prob. < Walloon *mappe* < L. *mappa,* napkin], 1. a bundle of loose rags, yarns, a sponge, etc. bound to the end of a stick, as for washing floors. 2. anything resembling or suggestive of this, as a thick head of hair. *v.t.* [MOPPED (mopt), MOPPING], to wash, rub, wipe, or remove with or as with a mop (sometimes with *up*).
mop the floor with, [Slang], to defeat decisively.
mop up, 1. [Colloq.], to finish. 2. in *military usage,* to clear out isolated or scattered remnants of beaten enemy forces from (a town, battle area, etc.).

mop (mop), *n. & v.i.* [MOPPED (mopt), MOPPING], [< dial. phr. *mop and mow,* in which both words seem to symbolize the lip puckerings of a grimace], grimace.

mop·board (mop′bôrd′, mop′bōrd′), *n.* a board at the base of the walls of a room; baseboard.

mope (mōp), *v.i.* [MOPED (mōpt), MOPING], [prob. of same origin as *mop* (grimace)], to be gloomy, dull, apathetic, and dispirited. *n.* 1. a person who mopes or is inclined to mope. 2. *pl.* low spirits.

mop·ish (mōp′ish), *adj.* inclined to mope; gloomy.

mop·pet (mop′it), *n.* [dim. of ME. *moppe,* rag doll; prob. < L. *mappa,* a napkin, towel; cf. MOP (cleaning implement)], [Archaic or Humorous], a little child or young girl: a term of affection.

mo·quette (mō-ket′), *n.* [Fr.], a kind of carpet or upholstery fabric with a thick, soft, napped surface.

Mo·qui (mō′kē), *n.* a Moki.

Mor., Morocco.

mo·ra (môr′ə, mō′rə), *n.* [*pl.* MORAE (-ē, -rē), MORAS (-əz, -rəz)], [L. *mora,* delay], in *prosody,* the unit of metrical time, equal to the ordinary short syllable, usually indicated by a breve (˘).

mo·ra·ceous (mô-rā′shəs, mō-rā′shəs), *adj.* [< Mod. L. *Moraceae,* name of the family < L. *morus,* mulberry tree; + *-ous*], in *botany,* of the mulberry family.

Mo·rad·a·bad (mō′rä-dä-bäd′), *n.* a city in the United Provinces, northern India: pop., 111,000.

mo·raine (mə-rān′, mō-rān′), *n.* [Fr. < dial.; cf. Pr. *mourenne* < *mourre,* projecting rock], a mass of rocks, gravel, sand, etc. carried or deposited by a glacier, either along its side (*lateral moraine*) or at its lower end (*terminal moraine*).

mor·al (môr′əl, mor′əl), *adj.* [ME. *morale;* L. *moralis,* of manners or customs < *mos, moris,* pl. *mores,* manners, morals; cf. MOOD], 1. relating to, dealing with, or capable of making the distinction between, right and wrong in conduct. 2. relating to, serving to teach, or in accordance with, the principles of right and wrong. 3. good or right in conduct or character; often, specifically, virtuous in sexual conduct: opposed to *immoral.* 4. based on general observation of people, etc. rather than on what is demonstrable: as, *moral* evidence. 5. designating support, etc. that involves approval and sympathy without action. 6. being virtually such because of its effect on thoughts, attitudes, etc., or because of its general results: as, a *moral* victory. 7. based on strong probability: as, a *moral* certainty. *n.* 1. a moral implication or moral lesson taught by a fable, event, etc. 2. a maxim. 3. *pl.* principles, standards, or habits with respect to right or wrong in conduct; ethics. 4. [Rare], (mə-ral′), morale.
SYN.*—moral** implies conformity with the generally accepted standards of goodness or rightness in conduct or character, sometimes, specifically, in sexual conduct (a *moral* woman); **ethical** implies conformity with an elaborated, ideal code of moral principles, sometimes, specifically, with the code of a particular profession (an *ethical* lawyer); **virtuous** implies a morally excellent character, connoting justice, integrity, and often, specifically, chastity; **righteous** implies a being morally blameless or justifiable (*righteous* anger).—ANT.*** immoral.

mo·rale (mə-ral′, mô-räl′), *n.* [Fr., fem. of *moral;* see MORAL], 1. moral or mental condition with respect to courage, discipline, confidence, enthusiasm, willingness to endure hardship, etc. 2. [Rare], morality.

moral hazard, risk (to an insurance company) arising from the possible dishonesty of the insured.

mor·al·ism (môr′əl-iz′m, mor′əl-iz′m), *n.* 1. moral teaching; moralizing. 2. a moral maxim. 3. belief in or practice of a system of ethics apart from religion.

mor·al·ist (môr′əl-ist, mor′əl-ist), *n.* 1. a teacher of or writer on morals; person who moralizes. 2. a person who lives virtuously, often without reliance on religion.

mor·al·is·tic (môr′ə-lis′tik, mor′ə-lis′tik), *adj.* 1. moralizing. 2. of moralism or moralists.

mo·ral·i·ty (mô-ral′ə-ti, mə-ral′ə-ti), *n.* [*pl.* MORALITIES (-tiz)], [ME. *moralitee;* L. *moralitas* < *moralis*], 1. moral quality or character; rightness or wrongness, as of an action. 2. the character of being in accord with the principles or standards of right conduct; right conduct; often, specifically, virtue in sexual conduct. 3. principles of right and wrong in conduct; ethics. 4. moral instruction or lesson. 5. a morality play.

morality play, any of a class of allegorical dramas of the 15th and 16th centuries, the characters of which were personifications of abstractions, as Everyman, Vice, Virtue, etc.: also **morality.**

mor·al·i·za·tion (môr′əl-i-zā′shən, mor′əl-ī-zā′shən), *n.* a moralizing or being moralized.

mor·al·ize (môr′ə-līz′, mor′ə-līz′), *v.i.* [MORALIZED (-līzd′), MORALIZING], [Fr. *moraliser;* LL. *moralizare* < L. *moralis*], to think, write, or speak about matters of right and wrong. *v.t.* 1. *a*) to interpret or explain in terms of right and wrong. *b*) to point out the moral in or draw a moral from. 2. to improve the morals of.

mor·al·ly (môr′əl-i, mor′əl-i), *adv.* 1. in a moral manner; virtuously. 2. from a moral viewpoint; as regards morals. 3. virtually; practically.

moral philosophy, ethics.

mo·rass (mô-ras′, mə-ras′, mō-ras′), *n.* [D. *moeras,* a marsh, fen; earlier *marasch;* OFr. *maresc* < Frank. *marisk,* a swamp; akin to Eng. *marsh;* cf. MOOR, *n.*], a tract of low, soft, watery ground; bog; marsh; swamp: sometimes used figuratively of a difficult, troublesome, or perplexing state of affairs.

mor·a·to·ri·um (môr′ə-tôr′i-əm, mor′ə-tō′ri-əm), *n.* [*pl.* MORATORIUMS (-əmz), MORATORIA (-ə)], [Mod. L., neut. of LL. *moratorius,* delaying < L. *morari,* to delay < *mora,* a delay], 1. a legal authorization, usually by a law passed in an emergency, to delay payment of money due, as by a bank or debtor nation. 2. the effective period of such an authorization.

mor·a·to·ry (môr′ə-tôr′i, mor′ə-tō′ri), *adj.* [LL. *moratorius;* see MORATORIUM], in *law,* delaying; postponing; especially, designating or of a law authorizing a moratorium.

Mo·ra·va (mô′rä-vä), *n.* 1. a river in Moravia, Czechoslovakia, flowing into the Danube and forming part of the boundary between Czechoslovakia and Austria: length, 180 mi.: German name, *March.* 2. a river in eastern Yugoslavia, flowing into the Danube: length, c. 100 mi. 3. Moravia.

Mo·ra·vi·a (mô-rā′vi-ə, mō-rā′vi-ə), *n.* a former province of Austria: now a part of Czechoslovakia: Czech name, *Morava;* German name, *Mähren.*

Mo·ra·vi·an (mô-rā′vi-ən, mō-rā′vi-ən), *adj.* 1. of Moravia, its people, etc. 2. of the Moravians (religious sect). *n.* 1. a native or inhabitant of Moravia. 2. the Czech dialect of Moravia. 3. a member of a Protestant sect founded in Moravia c. 1722 by disciples of John Huss: also called (***Renewed Church of the***) ***United Brethren, Unity of the Brethren, Moravian Brethren.***

Mo·rav·ská Os·tra·va (mô′räf-skä ôs′trä-vä), *n.* a city in northern Moravia, Czechoslovakia: pop., 125,000: German name, *Mährisch-Ostrau.*

Mor·ay (mŭr′i; Scot. mur′ā), *n.* a county on the coast of northeastern Scotland: pop., 44,000 (est. 1946); county seat, Elgin. Formerly called *Elgin.*

mo·ray (môr′ā, mō-rā′), *n.* [Port. *moreia;* L. *muraena,* kind of fish], any of a number of related eels of warm seas, characterized by brilliant coloring and voracious behavior, found especially among coral reefs: the Mediterranean moray is valued as a food fish.

mor·bid (môr′bid), *adj.* [L. *morbidus,* sickly, diseased < *morbus,* disease], 1. of, having, or caused by disease; unhealthy; diseased. 2. resulting from or as from a diseased state of mind; especially, having or showing an unwholesome tendency to dwell on gruesome or gloomy matters; hence, 3. gruesome; grisly; horrible: as, the *morbid* details of a story. 4. of diseased parts; pathological: as, *morbid* anatomy.

mor·bid·i·ty (môr-bid′ə-ti), *n.* [*pl.* MORBIDITIES (-tiz)], 1. state, quality or instance of being morbid. 2. the rate of disease or proportion of diseased persons in a given locality, nation, etc.

mor·bif·ic (môr-bif′ik), *adj.* [Fr. *morbifique* < LL. *morbificare,* to produce disease < L. *morbus,* disease + *facere,* to make], causing or leading to disease.

mor·bif·i·cal (môr-bif′i-k'l), *adj.* morbific.

mor·bil·li (mor-bil′ī), *n.pl.* [ML., pl. of *morbillus,* dim. of L. *morbus,* disease], measles.

‡mor·ceau (môr′sō′), *n.* [*pl.* MORCEAUX (-sō′)], [Fr.], 1. a morsel; bit; fragment. 2. a short composition, passage, or excerpt, as of poetry or music.

mor·da·cious (môr-dā′shəs), *adj.* [< *mordacity* + *-ous*], biting, sharp, acrid, or caustic.

mor·dac·i·ty (môr-das′ə-ti), *n.* [Fr. *mordacité;* L. *mordacitas* < *mordax,* biting (akin to *mordere,* to bite)], the quality of being biting, sharp, acrid, or caustic.

mor·dan·cy (môr′d'n-si), *n.* the quality of being mordant; mordacity.

mor·dant (môr′d'nt), *adj.* [ME. *mourdant* < OFr. pp. of *mordre* (L. *mordere*), to bite], 1. biting, cutting, caustic, or sarcastic, as speech, wit, etc. 2. corrosive. 3. acting to fix colors in dyeing, etc. *n.* 1. a substance used in dyeing to fix the coloring matter, as a metallic compound that combines with the organic dye to form an insoluble colored compound, or lake, in the fiber of the fabric. 2. an acid or other corrosive substance used in etching to bite lines, etc. into a metal surface. *v.t.* to treat or impregnate with a mordant.

Mor·de·cai (môr′di-kī′, môr′di-kā′ī), [Heb., ult. < Bab. *Marduk,* Marduk], a masculine name: diminutive, *Mordy.* *n.* in the *Bible,* the cousin of Esther (in the Book of Esther), who saved the Jews from the destruction planned by Haman: cf. **Purim.**

mor·dent (môr′d'nt), *n.* [G.; It. *mordente*, ppr. of *mordere* (L. *mordere*), to bite], in *music*, a trill made by a rapid alternation of a principal tone with a supplementary tone a half step below it: in a *single* (or *short*) *mordent* the supplementary tone occurs once, in a *double* (or *long*) *mordent*, more than once; in an *inverted mordent*, or pralltriller, the supplementary tone is a half step above the principal tone.

MORDENTS

Mor·do·vi·an Autonomous Soviet Socialist Republic (môr-dō′vi-ən), a division of the R.S.F.S.R. in east central European Russia: area, 9,843 sq. mi.; pop., 999,000; capital, Saransk.

Mor·dred (môr′drid), *n.* Modred.

more (môr, mōr), *adj.* [superl. MOST (mōst)], [ME.; AS. *mara*, greater, used as compar. of *micel*, big, much (cf. MUCH); akin to Goth. *maiza*; IE. base **mē-*, **mō-*, big], 1. greater in amount, quantity, or degree: used as the comparative of *much*. 2. greater in number: used as the comparative of *many*. 3. additional; further: as, there is *more* tea. *n.* 1. a greater amount, quantity, or degree. 2. [construed as pl.], *a*) a greater number (*of* persons or things): as, *more* of us are going. *b*) a greater number of persons. 3. something additional or further: as, *more* cannot be said. 4. something of greater importance. *adv.* [superl. MOST], [< the above, replacing earlier *mo* (AS. *ma*) < IE. positive **me-ros*, **mō-ro-s* < **mē-*, **mō-*], 1. in or to a greater degree or extent: used with many adjectives and adverbs (regularly with those of three or more syllables) to form the comparative degree: as, *more* satisfying, *more* intensely. 2. in addition; further; again; longer.

more and more, 1. to an increasing degree; increasingly. 2. a constantly increasing amount, quantity, degree, or number (of persons or a specified thing).

more or less, 1. to some extent. 2. approximately.

More, Hannah (môr, mōr), 1745–1833; English writer of religious books and tracts.

More, Paul Elmer, 1864–1937; American essayist, critic, and editor.

More, Sir **Thomas**, 1478–1535; English statesman and author; lord chancellor of England (1529–1532); executed; canonized in 1935: also **Saint Thomas More.**

Mo·re·a (mô-rē′ə, mō-rē′ə), *n.* a peninsula in southern Greece: former name, the *Peloponnesus*.

Mo·reau, Jean Vic·tor (zhän′ vēk′tôr′ mô′rō′), 1763–1813; French general, opposed to Napoleon.

mo·reen (mə-rēn′), *n.* [prob. < *moire* + *-een* as in *velveteen*, etc.], a stout fabric of wool or cotton, or of cotton and wool, silk, or mohair, usually having a watered finish: used for drapes, upholstery, etc.

mo·rel (mə-rel′), *n.* [Fr. *morille*; D. *morilje*; prob. < OHG. *morhila*, dim. of *morha*, *moraha*, carrot; cf. ME. *more*, a root], any of a group of small, edible mushrooms.

mo·rel (mə-rel′), *n.* [ME. & OFr. *morele* (Fr. *morelle*); LL. *maurella*, kind of plant], any of several kinds of nightshade; especially, the black nightshade.

mo·rel·lo (mə-rel′ō), *n.* [Fl. *marelle*, contr. < *amarelle*; It. *amarello*, dim. of *amaro* (< L. *amarus*), bitter], a cultivated cherry with dark-red skin and juice.

MOREL (2 in. high)

more·o·ver (môr-ō′vẽr, mōr-ō′vẽr), *adv.* in addition to what has been said; besides; further; likewise; also.

mo·res (mō′rēz, môr′ēz), *n.pl.* [*sing.* MOS (mōs)], [L., customs], folkways that are considered conducive to the welfare of society and so, through general observance, develop the force of law, often becoming part of the formal legal code.

Mo·resque (mô-resk′, mə-resk′), *adj.* [Fr.; It. *moresco* < *Moro*, a Moor], Moorish: said of decoration, etc. *n.* Moorish style of decoration or architecture, characterized by intricate tracery, bright colors, gilt, etc.

Mor·gain le Fay (môr′gān lə fā′, môr′gən), Morgan le Fay.

Mor·gan (môr′gən), [W., lit., sea dweller], a masculine name. *n.* [after Justin *Morgan* (1747–1798), New Englander who owned the stallion that sired the breed], any of a breed of strong, light trotting horses.

Mor·gan, Daniel (môr′gən), 1736–1802; American general in the Revolutionary War.

Morgan, Sir **Henry**, 1635?–1688; Welsh buccaneer.

Morgan, John Hunt, 1826–1864; Confederate general in the Civil War.

Morgan, John Pier·pont (pêr′pont), 1. 1837–1913; American financier and art collector. 2. 1867–1943; his son; American financier.

Morgan, Thomas Hunt, 1866–1946; American zoologist; received Nobel prize in physiology, 1933.

mor·ga·nat·ic (môr′gə-nat′ik), *adj.* [Mod. L. *morganaticus* < ML. (*matrimonium ad*) *morganaticam* < *morganaticum*; altered < OHG. *morgengeba*, morning gift, gift given on the day after marriage (in lieu of any share in the husband's property)], designating or of a form of marriage in which a man of high rank marries a woman of inferior social status with the stipulation that, although the children, if any, will be legitimate, neither they nor the wife may lay claim to his rank or property.

mor·ga·nat·i·cal·ly (môr′gə-nat′i-k'l-i, môr′gə-nat′ik-li), *adv.* in or by a morganatic marriage.

mor·gan·ic (môr-gan′ik), *adj.* [Rare], morganatic.

mor·gan·ite (môr′gən-īt′), *n.* [after J. P. *Morgan*], a transparent, rose-colored variety of beryl, used as a gem.

Mor·gan le Fay (môr′gən lə fā′), [OFr. *Morgain la fée*, lit., Morgan the fairy; of Celt. origin], in *Arthurian legend*, the fairy half sister of King Arthur, usually shown as doing him harm at every opportunity; in other legends, a fairy who lives in a lake among great treasures: also **Morgain le Fay, (Fata) Morgana.**

Mor·gan·town (môr′gən-toun′), *n.* a town in northern West Virginia: pop., 22,000.

mor·gen (môr′gən), *n.* [*pl.* MORGEN, MORGENS (-gənz)], [< D. & G., lit., morning, hence area plowed in one morning], 1. a land measure formerly used in the Netherlands and its possessions, and still used in South Africa, equal to about 2 acres. 2. a land measure formerly used in Prussia, Denmark, and Norway, equal to about 2/3 acre.

Mor·gen·thau, Henry, Jr. (môr′gən-thô′), 1891– ; American statesman; secretary of the treasury (1934–1945).

morgue (môrg), *n.* [Fr., orig., name of a building in Paris used for this purpose], 1. a place where the bodies of accident victims and unknown persons found dead are kept prior to identification and disposal. 2. in *journalism*, *a*) the reference library of back numbers, photographs, clippings, etc. kept by a newspaper, magazine, etc. *b*) the room in which this is kept.

mor·i·bund (môr′ə-bund′, mor′ə-bənd), *adj.* [L. *moribundus*, dying < *mori*, to die], 1. dying. 2. coming to an end; being terminated.

mo·ri·on (môr′i-on′, mō′ri-on′), *n.* [OFr.; Sp. *morrión* < *morra*, crown of the head], a hatlike, crested helmet without beaver or visor and with a curved brim coming to a peak in front and in back, worn in the 16th and 17th centuries.

mo·ri·on (môr′i-on′, mō′ri-on′), *n.* [misreading of L. *mormorion* (in early editions of Pliny)], a variety of quartz, dark-brown to black in color.

Mo·ris·co (mə-ris′kō), *adj.* [Sp. < *Moro*, Moor], Moorish. *n.* [*pl.* MORISCOS, MORISCOES (-kōz)], a Moor; especially, one of the Moors of Spain.

‡mo·ri·tu·ri te sa·lu·ta·mus (môr′i-tyoor′ī tē sal′yoo-tā′məs), [L.], we (who are) about to die salute you: Roman gladiators' shout to the emperor when they entered the arena.

Mor·ley, Christopher Dar·ling·ton (där′liŋ-t'n môr′li), 1890–1957; American novelist, poet, and essayist.

Morley, John, Viscount Morley of Blackburn, 1838–1923; English statesman and writer.

Mor·mon (môr′mən), *n.* a member of the Church of Jesus Christ of Latter-day Saints (commonly called the *Mormon Church*), founded in the United States in 1830 by Joseph Smith: among its holy books is the Book of Mormon, supposedly an account (by an alleged prophet of the 4th century A.D., named Mormon) of a record of some ancient American peoples, written on plates of gold, and found and translated by Joseph Smith. *adj.* of the Mormons or their religion.

Mor·mon·ism (môr′mən-iz'm), *n.* the religious system of the Mormons.

morn (môrn), *n.* [ME. *morne*, *morwen*; AS. *morne*, dat. of *morgen*, morning], [Poetic], morning.

Mor·nay, Phi·lippe de (fē′lēp′ də môr′nā′), Seigneur du Plessis-Marly, 1549–1623; French Protestant leader, writer, and statesman: also **Duplessis-Mornay.**

morn·ing (môr′niŋ), *n.* [ME. *morweninge* (by analogy with *evening*) < AS. *morgen*, morning; akin to G. *morgen*; IE. base **mer(ə)q-*, glimmer, twinkle], 1. the first or early part of the day, from midnight, or especially dawn, to noon. 2. the first or early part: as, the *morning* of life. 3. *a*) the dawn; daybreak. *b*) [M-], the goddess Aurora or Eos. Abbreviated **M., m.** *adj.* of,

suited to, or occurring, appearing, etc. in the morning.
morn·ing-glo·ry (môr′niŋ-glôr′i, môr′niŋ-glō′ri), ***n.*** [*pl.* MORNING-GLORIES (-iz, -riz)], 1. a twining plant with heart-shaped leaves and trumpet-shaped flowers of lavender, blue, pink, or white. 2. any of a number of plants related or similar to this.
morning sickness, nausea and vomiting occurring in the morning during the first months of pregnancy.
morning star, 1. a planet, especially Venus, visible in the eastern sky before sunrise. 2. a plant with yellow flowers, native to California.
Mo·ro (môr′ō, mō′rō), ***n.*** [*pl.* MOROS (-ōz, -rōz)], [Sp., a Moor], 1. a member of a group of Moslem Malay tribes living in the southern Philippines. 2. their Malay language; Magindanao. ***adj.*** of the Moros or Magindanao.
Mo·roc·can (mə-rok′ən), ***adj.*** of Morocco or its people. ***n.*** a native or inhabitant of Morocco.
Mo·roc·co (mə-rok′ō), ***n.*** 1. a kingdom in northwestern Africa: until 1956, divided into the French zone, the Spanish zone, and Tangier: area, 174,471; pop., 11,598,000; capital, Rabat: French name, *Maroc;* Spanish name, *Marruecos:* abbreviated **Mor.** 2. Marrakech: a former name. 3. [m-], *a*) a fine, soft leather made, originally in Morocco, from goatskins tanned with sumac. *b*) any imitation of this. Also **morocco leather.**
mo·ron (môr′on, mō′ron), ***n.*** [Gr. *mōron*, neut. of *mōros*, foolish], 1. a mentally deficient person with an intelligence quotient ranging from 50 to 75; person mentally equal or inferior to a child between eight and twelve years old: *moron* is the highest classification of mental deficiency, above *imbecile* and *idiot.* 2. loosely, a very foolish or stupid person.
mo·ron·ic (mô-ron′ik, mō-ron′ik), ***adj.*** of, characteristic of, or like a moron.
mo·ron·ism (môr′on-iz'm, mō′ron-iz'm), ***n.*** moronity.
mo·ron·i·ty (mô-ron′ə-ti, mō-ron′ə-ti), ***n.*** the state or quality of being moronic.
mo·rose (mə-rōs′), ***adj.*** [L. *morosus*, peevish, fretful, fastidious < *mos, moris*, manner], gloomy, sullen, surly, etc. —***SYN.*** see **sullen.**
-morph (môrf), [< Gr. *morphē*, form], a combining form meaning *one having a* (specified) *form*, as in *pseudomorph:* used to form nouns generally corresponding to adjectives ending in *-morphic, -morphous.*
mor·pheme (môr′fēm), ***n.*** [< Gr. *morphē*, form; + *-eme* as in *phoneme*], in *linguistics*, any word or part of a word, as an affix or combining form, that conveys meaning, cannot be further divided into smaller elements conveying meaning, and usually occurs in various contexts with relatively stable meaning.
Mor·pheus (môr′fi-əs, môr′fūs), ***n.*** [ME.; L.; Gr. *Morpheus* < *morphē*, form: from the forms seen in dreams], in ***Greek mythology***, the god of dreams, son of the god of sleep.
mor·phi·a (môr′fi-ə), ***n.*** [Mod. L.], morphine.
-mor·phic (môr′fik), [< Gr. *morphē*, form; + *-ic*], a combining form meaning *having a* (specified) *form* or *shape*, as in *anthropomorphic*: also **-morphous.**
mor·phin (môr′fin), ***n.*** morphine.
mor·phine (môr′fēn), ***n.*** [G. *morphin* or Fr. *morphine* < L. *Morpheus;* see MORPHEUS & -INE], a bitter, white, crystalline alkaloid, $C_{17}H_{19}O_3N \cdot H_2O$, derived from opium and used to induce sleep and relieve pain.
mor·phin·ism (môr′fin-iz'm), ***n.*** 1. a diseased condition resulting from the habitual use of morphine. 2. addiction to the use of morphine.
mor·pho·gen·e·sis (môr′fə-jen′ə-sis), ***n.*** [Gr. *morphē*, form; + *-genesis*], the structural changes during the development of an organism.
mor·pho·log·ic (môr′fə-loj′ik), ***adj.*** morphological.
mor·pho·log·i·cal (môr′fə-loj′i-k'l), ***adj.*** of morphology or form; structural.
mor·phol·o·gy (môr-fol′ə-ji), ***n.*** [< Gr. *morphē*, form; + *-logy*], 1. the branch of biology that deals with the form and structure of animals and plants, without regard to function. 2. the branch of linguistics that deals with the internal structure and forms of words: with syntax, it forms a basic division of grammar. 3. any scientific study of form and structure, as in physical geography, etc. 4. *a*) form and structure, as of an organism, regarded as a whole. *b*) morphological features collectively, as of a language. Abbreviated **morph., morphol.**
mor·pho·sis (môr-fō′sis), ***n.*** [*pl.* MORPHOSES (-sēz)], [Mod. L.; Gr. *morphōsis*, form < *morphoun*, to form], the mode of formation or development of an organism or any of its parts.
-mor·phous (môr′fəs), [Gr. *-morphos* < *morphē*, form], a combining form equivalent to *-morphic.*
Mor·ris (môr′is, mor′is), [var. of *Maurice*], a masculine name: diminutives, *Morrie, Morry.*
mor·ris (môr′is, mor′is), ***adj.*** [earlier *morys*, Moorish], designating or of an old folk dance formerly common in England, especially on May Day, in which fancy costumes were worn, often those associated with characters in the Robin Hood legends. ***n.*** this dance.
Mor·ris, Gouv·er·neur (guv′ẽr-nêr′ môr′is, mor′is), **1752–1816; American statesman and lawyer.**
Morris, Robert, 1734–1806; American patriot and financier.
Morris, William, 1834–1896; English poet, artist, craftsman, and socialist.
Morris chair, [after William *Morris*, who popularized it], a large armchair with an adjustable back and removable cushions.
mor·ro (mor′ō; Sp. môr′rô), ***n.*** [*pl.* MORROS (-ōz; Sp. -rôs)], [Sp.], a rounded hill, bluff, or point of land.
mor·row (mor′ō, môr′ō), ***n.*** [ME. *morwe, morwen* < AS. *morgen*, morning; see MORNING], [Archaic or Poetic], 1. morning. 2. the following day; the next day; hence, 3. the time just after some particular event.
Mors (môrz), ***n.*** [L.], in ***Roman mythology***, death regarded as a god: identified with the Greek Thanatos.
Morse (môrs), ***adj.*** [after Samuel F. B. *Morse*, the inventor], 1. designating or of a code, or alphabet, consisting of a system of dots, dashes, and spaces, or sounds corresponding to these, used to represent letters, numerals, etc. in telegraphy, signaling, and the like. 2. loosely, of any similar code. ***n.*** the Morse code.
Morse, Samuel Fin·ley Breese (fin′li brēz môrs), 1791–1872; American inventor of the telegraph.
mor·sel (môr′s'l), ***n.*** [ME.; OFr. *morsel, morcel*, dim. of *mors;* L. *morsum*, a bite, piece < pp. of *mordere*, to bite], 1. a small bite, mouthful, or portion of food; hence, 2. a small piece or amount; bit. 3. a tasty dish. ***v.t.*** to divide into or distribute in small portions.
mort (môrt), ***n.*** [ME.; OFr.; L. *mors, mortis*, death], 1. [Obs.], death. 2. in ***hunting***, a note sounded on a horn to anounce the killing of the quarry.
mort (môrt), ***n.*** [? < *mortal*, used as intens.], [British Dial.], a great quantity or number.
mor·tal (môr′t'l), ***adj.*** [ME.; OFr.; L. *mortalis* < *mors, mortis*, death], 1. that must eventually die: opposed to *immortal.* 2. of man as a being who must eventually die. 3. of this world. 4. of death. 5. causing death; deadly; fatal. 6. causing death of the soul: said of sin: distinguished from *venial.* 7. to the death: as, *mortal* combat. 8. implacable: as, a *mortal* enemy. 9. dire; grievous: as, *mortal* terror. 10. [Colloq.], *a*) extreme; very great. *b*) very long and tedious. *c*) conceivable; possible: as, it's no *mortal* good to anyone. ***n.*** a being who must eventually die; especially, a human being; person. ***adv.*** [Dial.], extremely. —***SYN.*** see **fatal.**
mor·tal·i·ty (môr-tal′ə-ti), ***n.*** [ME. & OFr. *mortalite;* L. *mortalitas* < *mortalis*, mortal], 1. the nature of man, as having eventually to die; mortal nature. 2. death on a large scale, as from disease or war. 3. *a*) the proportion of deaths to the population of a region, nation, etc.; death rate. *b*) the proportion of deaths from a particular disease. 4. human beings collectively; mankind. 5. [Obs.], death.
mortality table, a statistical table, based on a sample group of the population, stating the percentage of people who live to any given age.
mor·tal·ly (môr′t'l-i), ***adv.*** in a mortal manner; especially, *a*) so as to kill; fatally. *b*) grievously. *c*) very.
mor·tar (môr′tẽr), ***n.*** [ME. *mortere* < AS. *mortere* & OFr. *mortier* < L. *mortarium*, vessel or trough in which things are pounded or mixed], 1. a very hard bowl in which softer substances are ground or pounded to a powder with a pestle; hence, 2. any machine in which materials are ground or pounded. 3. [Fr. *mortier*], a short-barreled cannon with a low muzzle velocity, which throws shells in a high trajectory. 4. any of various similar devices, for shooting lifelines, flares, etc. 5. [ME. *morter;* Late OFr. *mortier;* L. *mortarium*, a mixture of sand and lime: so called from the vessel in which it was made], a mixture of cement or lime with sand and water, used between bricks or stones in building, or as plaster. ***v.t.*** to plaster or bind together with mortar.

MORTAR AND PESTLE

mor·tar·board (môr′tẽr-bôrd′, môr′tẽr-bōrd′), ***n.*** 1. a square board with a handle beneath, on which mortar is carried by masons. 2. an academic cap with a square, flat, horizontal top, worn at commencements, etc. in schools and colleges.
mort·gage (môr′gij), ***n.*** [ME.; OFr. *morgage, mort gage*, lit., dead pledge; *mort*, dead + *gage*, a pledge], in *law*, 1. the pledging of property to a creditor as security for the payment of a debt. 2. the deed by which this pledge is made. 3. the claim of the mortgagee on the property. Abbreviated **mtg., mtge.** ***v.t.*** [MORTGAGED (-gijd), MORTGAGING], 1. in *law*, to pledge (property) by a mortgage. 2. to put an advance claim or liability on: as, he *mortgaged* his future happiness.
mort·ga·gee (môr′gi-jē′), ***n.*** a person to whom property is mortgaged.
mort·ga·gor, mort·gag·er (môr′gi-jẽr), ***n.*** a person who mortgages property.
mor·tice (môr′tis), ***n.*** & ***v.t.*** mortise.
mor·ti·cian (môr-tish′ən), ***n.*** [< L. *mors, mortis*, death; + *-ician*], a funeral director; undertaker.

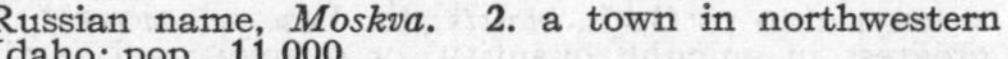

mor·ti·fi·ca·tion (môr′tə-fi-kā′shən), *n.* [ME. *mortificacioun;* LL. *mortificatio* < pp. of *mortificare*], 1. a mortifying or being mortified; specifically, *a)* the control of physical desires and passions by self-denial, fasting, etc. *b)* shame, humiliation, chagrin, etc.; loss of self-respect. *c)* in *medicine*, the death or decay of one part of the body while the rest is alive; gangrene. 2. something causing shame, humiliation, etc.

mor·ti·fi·er (môr′tə-fī′ẽr), *n.* a person or thing that mortifies.

mor·ti·fy (môr′tə-fī′), *v.t.* [MORTIFIED (-fīd′), MORTIFYING], [ME. *mortifien;* OFr. *mortifier;* LL. *mortificare*, to kill, destroy < L. *mors, mortis*, death + *facere*, to make], 1. to punish (one's body) or control (one's physical desires and passions) by self-denial, fasting, etc., as a means of religious or ascetic discipline. 2. to cause to feel shame, humiliation, chagrin, etc.; destroy the self-respect of. 3. in *medicine*, to cause (the tissues or a part of the body) to decay or become gangrenous. *v.i.* 1. to practice mortification (sense 1 *a*). 2. in *medicine*, to decay or become gangrenous.

Mor·ti·mer (môr′tə-mẽr), [< Norm. surname < place name], a masculine name: diminutive, *Mort.*

mor·tise (môr′tis), *n.* [ME. *mortays;* Late OFr. *mortaise*, a mortise; Ar. *murtazza*, joined, fixed in], a notch, hole, or space cut, as in a piece of wood, to receive a projecting part (*tenon*) shaped to fit. *v.t.* [MORTISED (-tist), MORTISING], 1. to join securely; fasten securely, especially with a mortise and tenon. 2. to cut a hole or mortise in. Also spelled **mortice.**

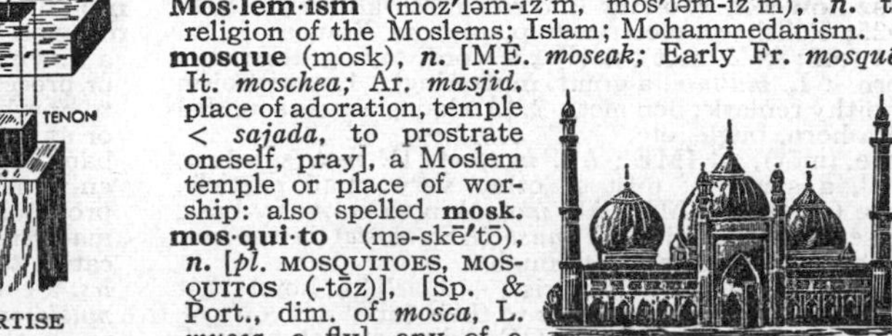

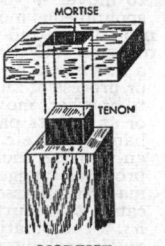

MORTISE

mort·main (môrt′mān), *n.* [Anglo-Fr. *morte mayn;* OFr. *mortemain;* ML. *mortua manus*, lit., dead hand; fem. of L. *mortuus*, pp. of *mori*, to die + *manus*, hand], in *law*, 1. a transfer of lands or houses to a corporate body, such as a school or church, for perpetual ownership. 2. such ownership.

Mor·ton (môr′t'n), [< the surname and place name *Morton* < AS. *Mor-tun; mor*, a swamp, moor + *tun*, a town], a masculine name.

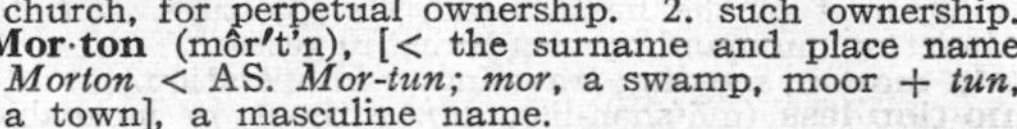

Mor·ton, William Thomas Green (môr′t'n), 1819–1868; American dentist; introduced use of ether for anesthesia.

mor·tu·ar·y (môr′chōō-er′i), *n.* [*pl.* MORTUARIES (-iz)], [ME. *mortuarie* (in sense 2); ML. *mortuarium* < LL. *mortuarius*, of the dead < L. *mortuus*, dead], 1. a place where dead bodies are kept before burial or cremation, as a morgue. 2. formerly, *a)* a gift left by a dying person to his parish priest. *b)* a similar gift left by a priest to his superior. *adj.* 1. of the burial of the dead. 2. of or connected with death.

mor·u·la (mor′yoo-lə, mor′oo-lə), *n.* [*pl.* MORULAE (-lē′)], [Mod. L., dim. of *morum*, mulberry], a solid mass of cells, somewhat like a mulberry in shape, formed by an ovum in the early stages of embryonic development.

mor·u·lar (mor′yoo-lẽr, mor′oo-lẽr), *adj.* of, having the nature of, or characterized by a morula.

mos (mōs), *n.* singular of **mores.**

mos., months.

Mo·sa·ic (mō-zā′ik), *adj.* [Mod. L. *Mosaicus*], of Moses or the writings, laws, etc. attributed to him.

mo·sa·ic (mō-zā′ik), *n.* [ME. *musycke;* OFr. *mosaicq;* It. *mosaico, musaico;* ML. *mosaicus, musaicus* < Gr. *mouseios*, belonging to the Muses, artistic < *Mousa*, a Muse], 1. the process of making pictures or designs by inlaying small bits of colored stone, glass, etc. in mortar. 2. inlaid work made by this process. 3. a picture or design so made. 4. anything resembling this, as, a number of aerial photographs pieced together to show a continuous area. 5. in *botany*, any of the virus diseases that cause wrinkling or mottling of leaves. 6. the photosensitive plate in a television camera. *v.t.* [MOSAICKED (-ikt), MOSAICKING], 1. to make by or as by mosaic. 2. to decorate with mosaics.

mosaic gold, 1. a yellow, crystalline powder, stannic sulfide, SnS_2, used as a pigment. 2. ormolu.

mo·sa·i·cist (mō-zā′ə-sist), *n.* a person who designs, makes, or sells mosaics.

Mosaic law, the ancient law of the Hebrews, ascribed to Moses and contained mainly in the first five books of the Old Testament, the Pentateuch.

mos·chate (mos′kāt, mos′kit), *adj.* [< Mod. L. *moschatus* < ML. *moschus*, musk], having the smell of musk; musky.

mos·cha·tel (mos′kə-tel′, mos′kə-tel′), *n.* [Fr. *moscatelle;* It. *moscatella;* see MUSCATEL], a small plant having greenish-white flowers with a musky smell.

Mos·cow (mos′kou; *for 2, and occas. for 1,* mos′kō), *n.* 1. *a)* a region of the R.S.F.S.R., in central European Russia: pop., 10,938,000. *b)* a city in this region: capital of the R.S.F.S.R. and of the U.S.S.R.: pop., 5,032,000: Russian name, *Moskva.* 2. a town in northwestern Idaho: pop., 11,000.

Mo·sel (mō′zəl), *n.* Moselle (sense 1): the German name.

Mo·selle (mō-zel′; Fr. mô′zel′), *n.* 1. a river flowing through northeastern France and Germany into the Rhine: length, 315 mi.: German name, *Mosel.* 2. a variety of white wine made in the valley of this river.

Mo·ses (mō′ziz, mō′zəs), [L.; Gr. *Mōsēs;* Heb. *mōsheh;* prob. < Egypt. *mes, messu*, child, son], a masculine name: diminutives, *Mo, Mose.* *n.* 1. in the *Bible*, the leader who brought the Israelites out of slavery in Egypt and into the Promised Land, received the Ten Commandments from God, and gave laws to the people; hence, 2. a leader; lawgiver.

Moses, Anna Mary Robertson, (*Grandma Moses*), 1860–1961; American primitive painter.

mo·sey (mō′zi), *v.i.* [< *vamose*], [Slang], 1. to stroll, amble, or shuffle along. 2. to go away; move along.

mosk (mosk), *n.* a mosque.

Mosk·va (môs-kvä′), *n.* Moscow: the Russian name.

Mos·lem (moz′ləm, mos′ləm), *n.* [*pl.* MOSLEMS, MOSLEM], [Ar. *muslim*, true believer < *aslama*, to resign oneself (to God)], an adherent of Islam, or follower of Mohammed. *adj.* of Islam or the Moslems. Also **Muslem, Muslim;** cf. **Mohammedan.**

Mos·lem·ic (moz-lem′ik, mos-lem′ik), *adj.* Moslem.

Mos·lem·ism (moz′ləm-iz′m, mos′ləm-iz′m), *n.* the religion of the Moslems; Islam; Mohammedanism.

mosque (mosk), *n.* [ME. *moseak;* Early Fr. *mosquée;* It. *moschea;* Ar. *masjid*, place of adoration, temple < *sajada*, to prostrate oneself, pray], a Moslem temple or place of worship: also spelled **mosk.**

MOSQUE

mos·qui·to (mə-skē′tō), *n.* [*pl.* MOSQUITOES, MOSQUITOS (-tōz)], [Sp. & Port., dim. of *mosca*, L. *musca*, a fly], any of a large group of two-winged insects, the females of which have skin-piercing mouth parts used to extract blood from animals, including man: some varieties are carriers of certain diseases, as malaria and yellow fever.

mosquito boat, a speedy unarmored motorboat equipped with torpedoes and small guns: now called *PT Boat.*

mosquito hawk, 1. a nighthawk. 2. a dragonfly.

mosquito net, a very fine cloth mesh or curtain for keeping mosquitoes out of a room, bed, etc.

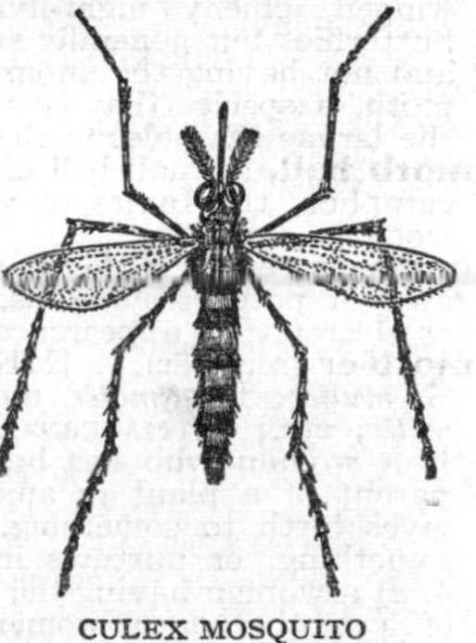
CULEX MOSQUITO (5/16 in. long)

moss (môs, mos), *n.* [ME. *mos*, a bog, moss; AS. *mos*, a swamp; akin to G. *moos*, a bog, moss; IE. *meu-s (as also in L *muscus*, bog & Eng. *mire*) < base *meu-, wet], 1. a very small, green, bryophytic plant that grows in velvety clusters on rocks, trees, moist ground, etc. 2. a growth of these. 3. any of various similar plants, as some lichens. *v.t.* to cover with a growth of moss.

moss agate, a kind of agate with mosslike markings.

moss·back (môs′bak′, mos′bak′), *n.* 1. an old fish, shellfish, turtle, etc. that develops a greenish growth of algae, etc. over the back. 2. [Colloq.], an old-fashioned or very conservative person.

moss·bunk·er (môs′buŋk′ẽr, mos′buŋk′ẽr), *n.* [altered < D. *marsbanker*], the menhaden fish.

moss-grown (môs′grōn′, mos′grōn′), *adj.* 1. overgrown with moss; hence, 2. old-fashioned; antiquated.

moss·i·ness (môs′i-nis, mos′i-nis), *n.* the quality or condition of being mossy.

moss pink, a low, hardy plant with pink, white, or lavender flowers.

moss rose, 1. a variety of rose with a roughened, mossy stem. 2. its flower.

moss·troop·er (môs′trōōp′ẽr, mos′trōōp′ẽr), *n.* [< Scot. *moss*, a swamp], 1. any of the raiders who infested the swampy borderland between England and Scotland in the 17th century. 2. a raider; marauder.

moss·y (môs′i, mos′i), *adj.* [MOSSIER (-i-ẽr), MOSSIEST (-i-ist)], 1. full of or covered with moss or a mosslike growth. 2. as if covered with moss. 3. like moss.

most (mōst), *adj.* [compar. MORE (môr, mōr)], [ME. < AS. *mast, mæst*, used as superl. of *micel*, big (cf.

MUCH); akin to Goth. *maists;* for base see MORE], 1. greatest in amount, quantity, or degree: used as the superlative of *much.* 2. greatest in number: used as the superlative of *many.* 3. in the greatest number of instances: as, *most* fame is fleeting. ***n.*** 1. the greatest amount, quantity, or degree: as, he took *most* of the credit. 2. [construed as pl.], *a)* the greatest number (of persons or things): as, *most* of us are going. *b)* the greatest number of persons. ***adv.*** 1. [compar. MORE], in or to the greatest degree or extent: used with many adjectives and adverbs (regularly with those of three or more syllables) to form the superlative degree: as, *most* horrible, *most* quickly. 2. very (often preceded by *a*): as, a *most* beautiful morning. 3. [for *almost*], [Colloq.], almost; nearly.

at (the) most, at the very limit; not more than.
for the most part, in most instances; mainly.
make the most of, to make the greatest use of; take fullest advantage of.

-most (mōst), [ME., replacing ME. & AS. *-mest,* formed from two older superl. suffixes, *-ma* and *-est*], a suffix used in forming superlatives, as *foremost, hindmost.*

most·ly (mōst′li), ***adv.*** 1. for the most part; in the main. 2. chiefly; principally.

Mo·sul (mō-sōōl′), ***n.*** a city in northern Iraq, near the site of ancient Nineveh: pop., 178,000.

Mosz·kow·ski, Mo·ritz (mō′rits mōsh-kôf′ski), 1854–1925; Polish composer and pianist, in France.

mot (mō; *for 2,* mot), ***n.*** [Fr., a word, saying, tone on a horn < L. *muttum,* a grunt, muttering], 1. a witticism or pithy remark; bon mot. 2. [Archaic], a tone sounded on a horn, bugle, etc.

mote (mōt), ***n.*** [ME.; AS. *mot;* cf. D. *mot,* sawdust, grit], a speck of dust or other very small particle.

mote (mōt), ***v.i.*** [ME.; AS. *mot,* akin to G. *muss;* basic sense "it is permitted"; *must* (AS. *moste*) is the p.t. of this *v.*], [Archaic], may; might.

mo·tel (mō-tel′), ***n.*** [*mo*torist + ho*tel*], a hotel that provides guests ready access to their cars.

mo·tet (mō-tet′), ***n.*** [ME.; OFr., dim. of *mot,* a word, etc.; see MOT], in *music,* a contrapuntal, polyphonic song of a sacred nature, generally unaccompanied.

moth (môth, moth), ***n.*** [*pl.* MOTHS (môthz, moths)], [ME. *motthe;* AS. *moththe;* akin to G. *motte;* the base is prob. that of *midge*], 1. any of a group of four-winged, chiefly night-flying insects related to the butterflies but generally smaller, less brightly colored, and not having the antennae clubbed. 2. the clothes moth, a species that lays eggs in woolens, furs, etc.: the larvae eat holes in the material.

moth ball, a small ball of naphthalene or, sometimes, camphor, the fumes of which repel moths, as from woolens, furs, etc.

moth-eat·en (môth′ē′t'n, moth′ē′t'n), ***adj.*** 1. gnawed away in patches by moths, as cloth; hence, 2. decayed or decrepit in appearance; worn out. 3. out-dated.

moth·er (mu*th*′ēr), ***n.*** [ME. *moder;* AS. *modor;* akin to G. *mutter;* IE. **matēr,* mother (whence L. *mater,* Gr. *mētēr,* etc.; cf. MATERNAL) < child's lip word *ma-*], 1. a woman who has borne a child. 2. the female parent of a plant or animal; hence, 3. that which gives birth to something, is the origin or source of something, or nurtures in the manner of a mother. 4. *a)* a woman having the responsibility and authority of a mother. *b)* a woman who is the head (*mother superior*) of a religious establishment. 5. an elderly woman: used as a title of affectionate respect. 6. the qualities of a mother. ***adj.*** 1. being, or being like, a mother. 2. of or characteristic of a mother: as, *mother* love. 3. derived or learned from one's mother; native: as, *mother* tongue. ***v.t.*** 1. to be the mother of; give birth to: often used figuratively. 2. to look after or care for as a mother does. 3. to acknowledge or admit that one is the mother, author, or originator of.

moth·er (mu*th*′ēr), ***n.*** [prob., by folk etymology, < MD. *moeder;* cf. G. *mutter* in same sense; see also MUD], 1. a stringy, gummy, slimy substance formed by bacteria in vinegar or on the surface of fermenting liquids: also called *mother of vinegar.* 2. [Obs.], dregs.

Mother Car·ey's chicken (kâr′iz), 1. the stormy petrel. 2. any of various other petrels.

mother country, a motherland.

Mother Goose, 1. the imaginary narrator of a collection of tales (c. 1697) by Charles Perrault. 2. the imaginary creator of a collection of nursery rhymes first published in London c. 1760.

moth·er·hood (mu*th*′ēr-hood′), ***n.*** [see -HOOD], 1. the state of being a mother. 2. the qualities or character of a mother. 3. mothers collectively.

Mother Hub·bard (hub′ērd), 1. the subject of an old nursery rhyme. 2. a full, loose gown for women.

moth·er-in-law (mu*th*′ēr-'n-lô′), ***n.*** [*pl.* MOTHERS-IN-LAW], the mother of one's husband or wife.

moth·er·land (mu*th*′ēr-land′), ***n.*** 1. the country of one's birth. 2. the country of one's ancestors.

moth·er·li·ness (mu*th*′ēr-li-nis), ***n.*** a motherly quality.

mother lode, the main lode, or vein of ore, in a mine.

moth·er·ly (mu*th*′ēr-li), ***adj.*** of, like, or befitting a mother; maternal. ***adv.*** in a motherly manner.

Mother of God, the Virgin Mary: title sanctioned by the Council of Ephesus (431 A.D.).

moth·er-of-pearl (mu*th*′ēr-əv-pūrl′), ***n.*** [cf. It. *madreperla,* obs. Fr. *mère perle*], the hard, pearly internal layer of certain marine shells, as of the pearl oyster, abalone, etc., used in the arts and in the manufacture of pearl buttons; nacre. ***adj.*** of mother-of-pearl.

mother of vinegar, mother (stringy substance).

Mother's Day, the second Sunday in May, a day set aside (in the United States) in honor of mothers.

mother superior, the woman head of a convent.

mother tongue, 1. one's native language. 2. a language in its relation to another derived from it.

mother wit, native intelligence; common sense.

moth·er·wort (mu*th*′ēr-wūrt′), ***n.*** [ME. *moderwort;* cf. WORT], an herb of the mint family, with small leaves and prickly, two-lipped flowers of purple, pink, etc.

moth·y (môth′i, moth′i), ***adj.*** [MOTHIER (-i-ēr), MOTHIEST (-i-ist)], 1. infested with moths. 2. moth-eaten.

mo·tif (mō-tēf′), ***n.*** [Fr.; see MOTIVE], a main element, idea, feature, etc.; specifically, in *art, literature,* & *music, a)* a main theme or subject to be elaborated on or developed. *b)* a repeated figure in a design.

mo·tile (mō′t'l, mō′til), ***adj.*** [< L. *motus,* pp. of *movere,* to move; + *-ile*], in *biology,* capable of or exhibiting spontaneous motion.

mo·til·i·ty (mō-til′ə-ti), ***n.*** the quality of being motile.

mo·tion (mō′shən), ***n.*** [ME. *mocioun;* L. *motio, motionis,* a moving < *motus,* pp. of *movere,* to move], 1. the act or process of moving; passage of a body from one place to another; movement. 2. the act of moving the body or any of its parts. 3. a meaningful movement of the hand, eyes, etc.; gesture. 4. the ability to move. 5. an impulse; inclination: as, of one's own *motion.* 6. a proposal; suggestion; especially, a proposal formally made in an assembly or meeting. 7. in *law,* an application to a court for a ruling, order, etc. 8. in *mechanics,* a combination of moving parts; mechanism. 9. in *music,* melodic progression, as a change from one pitch to another in a voice part. ***v.i.*** to make a meaningful movement of the hand, head, etc.; gesture. ***v.t.*** to direct or command by a meaningful gesture.

in motion, moving; traveling or in operation.

mo·tion·less (mō′shən-lis), ***adj.*** without, or incapable of, motion; not moving.

motion picture, 1. a sequence of photographs or drawings projected on a screen in such rapid succession that they create the optical illusion (because of the persistence of vision) of moving persons and objects. 2. a play or story photographed as a motion picture. Also called *moving picture, cinema, movie.*

mo·ti·vate (mō′tə-vāt′), ***v.t.*** [MOTIVATED (-id), MOTIVATING], to provide with, or affect as, a motive or motives; incite; impel.

mo·ti·va·tion (mō′tə-vā′shən), ***n.*** a motivating or being motivated.

mo·ti·va·tion·al research (mō′tə-vā′shən-'l), investigation of the psychological factors that influence the reactions, attitudes, etc. of people; especially, the study of why people buy or do not buy certain products.

mo·tive (mō′tiv), ***n.*** [ME. *motif;* OFr. *motif, adj.* < ML. *motivus,* moving < L. *motus,* pp. of *movere,* to move], 1. some inner drive, impulse, intention, etc. that causes a person to do something or act in a certain way; incentive; goal. 2. in *art, literature,* & *music,* a motif. ***adj.*** [ML. *motivus*], 1. of, causing, or tending to cause motion. 2. [Rare], of, or having the nature of, a motive or motives. ***v.t.*** [MOTIVED (-tivd), MOTIVING], 1. to supply a motive for; motivate. 2. [Rare], to relate (a subject) to the motif of a work of art, literature, etc.

***SYN.*—motive** refers to any impulse, emotion, or desire that moves one to action (greed was his only *motive* for stealing); **incentive** applies to a stimulus, often a reward, that encourages or inspires one to action (he needs no *incentive* other than the desire to be useful); **inducement** always refers to an outer stimulus, rather than an inner urge, that tempts or entices one to do something (the money was an added *inducement*); a **spur** is an impulse or incentive that pricks one on to greatly increased activity or endurance (security for his family was the *spur* that drove him on). See also **cause.**

-mo·tive (mō′tiv), [< *motive, adj.*], a suffix meaning *moving, of motion,* as in *automotive, locomotive.*

motive power, 1. any power, as steam, electricity, etc., used to impart motion; any source of mechanical energy. 2. the locomotives of a railroad, collectively. 3. an impelling force.

mo·tiv·i·ty (mō-tiv′ə-ti), ***n.*** the power of moving or causing motion.

‡mot juste (mō′ zhüst′), [Fr.], the right word; exact, appropriate word or phrase.

mot·ley (mot′li), ***adj.*** [ME. *motteley;* prob. < OFr.; Weekley suggests Anglo-Fr. **moitele* < OFr. *moitie* (cf. MOIETY), on the assumption that the orig. sense was "half and half"], 1. of many colors or patches of color. 2. wearing many-colored garments: as, a *motley* fool. 3. having or composed of many different or clashing elements; heterogeneous: as, a *motley* group. ***n.*** 1. cloth of mixed colors. 2. a garment of various colors, worn by a clown or jester. 3. [Obs.], a fool or jester.

Mot·ley, John Lo·throp (lō'thrəp mot'li), 1814–1877; American historian and diplomat.
mot·mot (mot'mot), *n.* [echoic of its note], any of a group of jaylike birds of tropical and subtropical America, related to the kingfishers and characterized by a long tail, a serrate bill, and plumage of green, blue, tan, and black.
mo·tor (mō'tẽr), *n.* [L., a mover < *motus*, pp. of *movere*, to move], 1. anything that produces or imparts motion. 2. an engine; especially, an internal-combustion engine for propelling a vehicle. 3. a vehicle propelled by an engine; especially, a motorcar; automobile. 4. in *electricity*, a machine for converting electrical energy into mechanical energy. 5. *pl.* in *finance*, securities issued by automobile manufacturers. *adj.* 1. producing or imparting motion. 2. of or powered by a motor or motors: as, a *motor* vehicle. 3. of, by, or for motor vehicles: as, a *motor* trip. 4. in *physiology*, designating or of a nerve carrying impulses from the central nervous system to a muscle producing motion. 5. in *psychology*, of or manifested by muscular movements: as, a tic is a *motor* neurosis. *v.i.* to ride in a motor vehicle; especially, to travel by automobile.
mo·tor·bike (mō'tẽr-bīk'), *n.* [Colloq.], 1. a bicycle propelled by a motor. 2. a motorcycle.
mo·tor·boat (mō'tẽr-bōt'), *n.* a boat propelled by an internal-combustion engine or other kind of motor.
mo·tor·bus (mō'tẽr-bus'), *n.* a passenger bus propelled by a motor, usually an internal-combustion engine.
mo·tor·cade (mō'tẽr-kād'), *n.* [*motor*car + caval*cade*], a procession of automobiles.
mo·tor·car (mō'tẽr-kär'), *n.* an automobile.
mo·tor·cy·cle (mō'tẽr-sī'k'l), *n.* [*motor* + bi*cycle*], a two-wheeled (or, if equipped with a sidecar, three-wheeled) vehicle propelled by an internal-combustion engine and resembling a bicycle, but usually larger and heavier. *v.i.* [MOTORCYCLED (-k'ld), MOTORCYCLING], to ride a motorcycle.
mo·tor·cy·clist (mō'tẽr-sī'klist), *n.* a person who rides a motorcycle.
motor drive, an electric motor and other parts of a mechanical system for operating a machine or machines.
mo·tor·drome (mō'tẽr-drōm'), *n.* [*motor* + *-drome*], a rounded track or course for automobile or motorcycle racing or testing.
mo·tored (mō'tẽrd), *adj.* having a motor or motors; especially, having (a specified number or kind of) motors: generally used in compounds, as *bimotored*.
motor generator, an apparatus consisting of one or more electric motors coupled to one or more generators, for transforming electric currents.
mo·tor·ist (mō'tẽr-ist), *n.* a person who drives an automobile or travels by automobile; especially, one who does so frequently but not as an occupation.
mo·tor·i·za·tion (mō'tẽr-i-zā'shən, mō'tẽr-i-zā'shən), *n.* a motorizing or being motorized.
mo·tor·ize (mō'tẽr-īz'), *v.t.* [MOTORIZED (-īzd'), MOTORIZING], 1. to equip with motor-driven vehicles (in place of horses and horse-drawn vehicles). 2. to equip (vehicles, etc.) with a motor or motors.
mo·tor·man (mō'tẽr-mən), *n.* [*pl.* MOTORMEN (-mən)], 1. a person who drives an electric streetcar or electric locomotive. 2. a person who operates a motor.
motor mimicry, in *psychology*, empathy.
motor scooter, see **scooter**.
motor ship, a ship propelled by Diesels or other internal-combustion engines.
motor truck, a motor-driven truck for hauling loads.
Mott, Lucretia (mot), (born *Lucretia Coffin*), 1793–1880; American social reformer.
motte, mott (mot), *n.* [prob. < Fr. *motte*, a clump, hillock], [Dial.], a small grove of trees on a prairie.
mot·tle (mot''l), *v.t.* [MOTTLED (-'ld), MOTTLING], [back-formation < *mottled*], to mark with blotches, streaks, and spots of different colors or shades. *n.* 1. such a blotch, streak, or spot. 2. a mottled pattern or coloring, as of marble.
mot·tled (mot''ld), *adj.* [< *motley* + *-ed*], marked with blotches or spots of different colors or shades.
mot·to (mot'ō), *n.* [*pl.* MOTTOES, MOTTOS (-ōz)], [It., a word; Fr. *mot;* see MOT], 1. a word, phrase, or sentence inscribed on something, prefixed to a literary work, etc., as expressive of or appropriate to its character. 2. a maxim adopted as a principle of behavior. —*SYN.* see **saying**.
mouch (mōōch), *v.i. & v.t.* to mooch.
‡**mou·choir** (mōō'shwär'), *n.* [Fr. < *moucher*, to wipe the nose < L. *muccare* < *muccus*; see MUCUS], a handkerchief.
‡**moue** (mōō), *n.* [Fr.; see MOW (grimace)], a pouting grimace.
mouf·lon (mōōf'lon), *n.* [*pl.* MOUFLONS (-lonz), MOUFLON; see PLURAL, II, D, 1], [Fr.; It. dial. *muffolo*, for *muffione;* LL. dial. *mufro*], 1. a wild sheep native to the mountainous regions of Corsica and Sardinia: the male has large, curving horns. 2. the wool of this sheep. Also spelled **moufflon**.
mouil·lé (mōō-yā'), *adj.* [Fr., pp. of *mouiller*, to moisten < L. *mollis*, soft], in *phonetics*, palatalized, as Spanish *ñ* in *cañon* or French *ll* in *fille*.
‡**mou·jik** (mōō-zhēk', mōō'zhik), *n.* a muzhik.
Mouk·den (mook'den', mōōk'den'), *n.* Mukden.
mou·lage (mōō-läzh'), *n.* [Fr.], 1. the science or practice of making a mold in some plastic substance, as plaster of Paris, of an object, footprint, etc., as in criminological identification. 2. such a mold.
mould (mōld), *n., v.t. & v.i.* mold (growth).
mould (mōld), *n.* mold (soil).
mould (mōld), *n. & v.t.* mold (form).
mould·board (mōld'bôrd', mōld'bōrd'), *n.* a moldboard.
mould·er (mōl'dẽr), *v.t. & v.i.* to molder (decay).
mould·er (mōl'dẽr), *n.* a molder.
mould·ing (mōl'diŋ), *n.* molding.
mould·y (mōl'di), *adj.* [MOULDIER (-di-ẽr), MOULDIEST (-di-ist)], moldy.
mou·lin (mōō-lan'), *n.* [Fr., lit., a mill; LL. *molinum*], a nearly vertical shaft in a glacier, worn by a stream of surface water falling through a crevice in the ice.
Moul·mein (mool-mān', mōl-mān', mōl-mān'), *n.* a city in Burma, on the Gulf of Martaban: pop., 70,000: also **Maulmain**.
moult (mōlt), *n., v.t. & v.i.* molt.
mound (mound), *n.* [prob. < MD. *mond*, protection; influenced by *mount*, hill], 1. a heap or bank of earth, sand, etc. built over a grave, in a fortification, etc. 2. a natural elevation like this; small hill. 3. any heap or pile. 4. in *baseball*, the slightly raised area in which the pitcher must stand when pitching. *v.t.* 1. to enclose or fortify with a mound. 2. to heap up in a mound.
mound (mound), *n.* [Fr. *monde;* L. *mundus*, the world; ME. had the word in the sense "the earth"], a small, golden ball, often with a cross on top, carried by a monarch as a symbol of his sovereignty; globe.
Mound Builders, the early Indian peoples who built the burial mounds and fortifications found in the Middle West and the Southeast.
mount (mount), *n.* [ME. & AS. *munt* & OFr. *mont*, a mount; both < L. *mons, montis*, hill, mountain], 1. a mountain or hill: now poetic or before a proper name, as *Mount* McKinley: abbreviated **Mt., mt.** 2. [Obs.], a raised fortification. 3. in *palmistry*, any of the fleshy raised parts on the palm of the hand.
mount (mount), *v.i.* [ME. *mounten;* OFr. *munter;* LL. **montare*, lit., to go uphill < L. *mons, montis*, hill, mountain], 1. to climb; ascend (often with *up*). 2. to climb up on something; especially, to get on the back of a horse for riding. 3. to increase in amount: as, his profits are constantly *mounting*. *v.t.* 1. to go up; ascend; climb: as, she *mounted* the stairs. 2. *a)* to get on the back of (a horse) for riding. *b)* to set on a horse. *c)* to climb or get up on (a platform, stool, etc.). 3. to provide with a horse or horses. 4. to climb on for purposes of copulation: said of the male of an animal. 5. to place on something raised (with *on*): as, he *mounted* the statue on a pedestal. 6. to place, fix, or fasten on or in the proper support, backing, etc. for the required purpose; specifically, *a)* to fix (a jewel) in a setting. *b)* to fix (a specimen) on (a slide) for microscopic study. *c)* to arrange (a skeleton, dead animal, etc.) for exhibition. 7. to furnish the necessary costumes, settings, etc. for producing (a play). 8. to put on and display (an article of clothing). 9. in *military & naval usage*, *a)* to raise or adjust (a gun) into proper position for use. *b)* to be armed with (cannon): as, this ship *mounts* six cannon. *c)* to post (a guard) on sentry duty. *d)* to go on (guard) as a sentry. *n.* 1. the act or manner of mounting (a horse, etc.). 2. a horse, bicycle, etc. for mounting and riding. 3. the opportunity for riding a horse, etc., especially in a race. 4. the support, setting, etc. on or in which something is mounted, as the support for a cannon or microscopic slide.
moun·tain (moun't'n), *n.* [ME. *muntaine, monteyne;* OFr. *montaigne;* LL. **montanea, montana;* L. *mons, montis*, hill, mountain], 1. a natural raised part of the earth's surface, usually rising more or less abruptly, and larger than a hill. 2. *pl.* a chain or group of such elevations. 3. a large pile, heap, or mound. *adj.* 1. of a mountain or mountains. 2. situated, living, or used in the mountains. 3. like a mountain; especially, very large. Abbreviated **Mt., mt., mtn., M., m.**
the Mountain, [transl. of Fr. *la Montagne*], the extreme revolutionary party of Danton and Robespierre, which occupied the highest seats in the National Assembly of 1793.
mountain ash, any of various small trees or shrubs with clusters of white flowers and red or orange berries.
mountain avens, a small evergreen plant of the rose family, found on mountains and in arctic regions.
mountain cat, 1. a cougar. 2. a bobcat.

mountain chain, 1. a mountain range. 2. two or more relatively adjacent mountain ranges.
mountain cranberry, a low creeping evergreen with small, dark-green, shining leaves and dark-red berries.
mountain dew, [Colloq.], 1. originally, Scotch whisky. 2. any whisky, especially when illegally distilled, as by mountaineers.
moun·tain·eer (moun'tʼn-êr'), *n.* 1. a person who lives in a mountainous region. 2. a mountain climber. *v.i.* to climb mountains, as for sport.
mountain goat, a long-haired, goatlike mammal found in the mountains of the northwestern United States and western Canada: also **Rocky Mountain goat.**
mountain laurel, an evergreen shrub with pink and white flowers and poisonous, shiny leaves, growing in the eastern United States.
mountain lion, the cougar; puma.
moun·tain·ous (moun'tʼn-əs), *adj.* 1. having or full of mountains. 2. having the nature of or like a mountain; especially, very large.
mountain range, a series of connected mountains considered as a single system because of geographical proximity or common origin.
mountain sheep, any of various wild sheep found in mountain regions; especially, the bighorn of the Rocky Mountains.
mountain sickness, a feeling of weakness, nausea, etc. brought on at high altitudes by the rarefied air.
Mountain Standard Time, one of the four standard times in the United States, corresponding to the mean local time of the 105th meridian west of Greenwich, England: it is seven hours behind Greenwich time and two hours behind Eastern Standard Time: abbreviated **M.S.T.**
Mount·bat·ten, Lord **Louis** (mount-bat'ʼn), (formerly *Prince Louis Francis Battenberg*), 1900– ; British admiral in World War II.
Mount Desert, an island off the coast of Maine: a resort.
moun·te·bank (moun'tə-baŋk'), *n.* [It. *montambanco* < *montare*, to mount + *in*, on + *banco*, a bench], 1. a person who mounts a bench, or platform, in a public place and sells quack medicines, usually attracting an audience by tricks, stories, etc. 2. any charlatan, or quack. *v.i.* to act as a mountebank. —***SYN.*** see **quack.**
mount·ed (moun'tid), *adj.* [pp. of *mount*], 1. seated on horseback, a bicycle, etc. 2. serving on horseback: as, *mounted* police. 3. set up and ready for use: as, a *mounted* gun. 4. fixed on or in the proper backing, support, setting, etc. 5. in *military usage*, regularly equipped with a means of transportation, as with horses, tanks, armored vehicles, etc.
Mount·ie (moun'ti), *n.* [Colloq.], a member of the Royal Canadian Mounted Police.
mount·ing (moun'tiŋ), *n.* 1. the act of a person or thing that mounts. 2. something serving as a backing, support, setting, etc.
Mount McKinley National Park, a national park in Alaska, containing Mount McKinley: area, 3,030 sq. mi.
Mount Rainier National Park, a national park in west central Washington: area, 378 sq. mi.
Mount Robson Park, a national park in eastern British Columbia, in the Rocky Mountains.
Mount Ver·non (vũr'nən), 1. the home and burial place of George Washington, on the Potomac River, in Virginia, near Washington, D.C. 2. a city in New York: suburb of New York City: pop., 76,000.
mourn (môrn, mōrn), *v.i.* [ME. *mournen;* AS. *murnan;* akin to Goth. *maúrnan*, to be anxious; prob. IE. base *(*s*)*mer*-, to remember, think of, seen also in L. *memor*, mindful of (cf. MEMORY, MEMORIAL)], 1. to feel or express sorrow; lament; grieve. 2. to grieve for someone who has died; specifically, to manifest the conventional signs of such grief, as by wearing black clothes. 3. to make the low, continuous sound of a dove. *v.t.* 1. to feel or express sorrow for (something regrettable). 2. to grieve for (someone who has died). 3. to utter in a manner expressing sorrow.
mourn·er (môr'nẽr, mōr'nẽr), *n.* 1. a person who mourns; specifically, one who attends a funeral. 2. in certain revivalist churches, a person who makes a public profession of penitence.
mourners' bench, in certain revivalist churches, a front row of seats reserved for those who are to make professions of penitence.
mourn·ful (môrn'fəl, mōrn'fəl), *adj.* 1. of or characterized by mourning; feeling or expressing grief or sorrow. 2. causing sorrow or depression; melancholy.
mourn·ing (môr'niŋ, mōr'niŋ), *n.* 1. the actions or feelings of one who mourns; specifically, the expression of grief at someone's death. 2. black clothes, drapery, etc., worn or displayed as a conventional sign of grief for the dead. 3. the period during which one mourns the dead. *adj.* of or expressing mourning.
mourning band, a strip of black cloth or crape worn, usually around the arm, to show mourning.
mourning cloak, any of a group of butterflies having purplish-brown wings with a wide yellow border, found throughout Europe and North America.
mourning dove, a small wild dove of the United States: so called because of its cooing, regarded as mournful.
mouse (mous; *for v.*, mouz), *n.* [*pl.* MICE (mīs)], [ME. *mous;* AS. *mus;* akin to G. *maus*, etc.; IE. **mūs*, a mouse, seen also in L. *mus*, mouse & (from the fancied resemblance between the movement of a mouse and that of a muscle) *musculus* (cf. MUSCLE)], 1. any of various large groups of small rodents found throughout the world; especially, the house mouse, which infests human dwellings. 2. *a*) a girl or young woman: a term of endearment. *b*) a timid or spiritless person. 3. [Slang], a dark, swollen bruise under the eye; black eye. 4. in *nautical usage*, *a*) a knot made on a rope to keep a running eye or loop from slipping. *b*) a mousing. *v.i.* [MOUSED (mouzd), MOUSING], 1. to hunt for or catch mice; hence, 2. to seek about or search for something busily and stealthily. *v.t.* 1. [Rare], to tear or rend as a cat does a mouse. 2. to hunt for.
mouse-ear (mous'êr'), *n.* any of various plants with short, hairy leaves resembling the ear of a mouse, as the forget-me-not or the hawkweed.
mous·er (mou'zẽr), *n.* 1. a cat, dog, etc. with reference to its ability to catch mice: as, a good (or poor) *mouser*. 2. a stealthily inquisitive or prying person.
mouse·tail (mous'tāl'), *n.* any of a group of plants of the crowfoot family, with a slender spike resembling the tail of a mouse.
mouse·trap (mous'trap'), *n.* a trap for catching mice.
mous·ey (mou'si, mou'zi), *adj.* mousy.
mous·ing (mou'ziŋ), *n.* 1. the act of hunting or catching mice. 2. in *nautical usage*, a turn of yarn or rope or a metal fastening that holds the point of a hook firm on its shank.
‡mous·que·taire (mōōs'kə-târ'), *n.* [Fr.], a musketeer; especially, [M-], any of the French royal bodyguards of the 17th and 18th centuries. *adj.* designating any of various articles of dress somewhat resembling that of the Mousquetaires.
mousse (mōōs), *n.* [Fr., foam < L. *mulsa*, kind of mead, honey], any of various light frozen desserts, made from whipped cream, white of egg, gelatin, etc., sweetened and flavored.
‡mousse·line (mōōs'lēn'), *n.* [Fr.], 1. muslin. 2. a fine, blown glass with a lacy pattern.
‡mousse·line de laine (mōōs'lēn' də len'), [Fr., lit., muslin of wool], a lightweight woolen cloth, often printed, used for dresses, etc.
‡mousse·line de soie (mōōs'lēn' də swå'), [Fr., lit., muslin of silk], a gauzelike silk or rayon cloth with a plain weave, used for blouses, etc.
Mous·sorg·sky, Mo·dest Pe·tro·vich (mô-dyest' pyi-trô'vich moo-sôrg'ski), 1839–1881; Russian composer: also spelled **Mussorgski.**
mous·tache (məs-tash', mus'tash), *n.* a mustache.
Mous·te·ri·an, Mous·tie·ri·an (mōōs-têr'i-ən), *adj.* [Fr *moustérien:* so named because remains were found at Le *Moustier*, in southern France], in *anthropology*, designating or of a late paleolithic culture, believed to be that of a race of Neanderthal men.
mous·y (mou'si, mou'zi), *adj.* [MOUSIER (-si-ẽr, -zi-ẽr), MOUSIEST (-si-ist, -zi-ist)], 1. of, characteristic of, or like a mouse, in any of various ways; quiet, timid, drab, etc. 2. full of or infested with mice.
mouth (mouth; *for v.*, mouth), *n.* [*pl.* MOUTHS (mouthz)], [ME.; AS. *muth* < **munth*- (cf. SOFT); akin to G. *mund;* IE. base **menth*-, to chew, seen also in L. *mandere*, to chew (cf. MANDIBLE)], 1. the opening through which an animal takes in food; specifically, the cavity, or the entire structure, in the head of any of the higher animals which contains the teeth and tongue and through which sounds are uttered: abbreviated **M., m.** 2. *a*) the mouth regarded as the organ of chewing and tasting. *b*) the mouth regarded as the organ of speech. 3. a person or animal regarded as a being needing food. 4. the lips, or the part of the face surrounding the lips. 5. a wry expression of the face; grimace. 6. any opening regarded as like the mouth; specifically, *a*) the part of a river, stream, etc. where the water empties into another body of water. *b*) the opening of a container, through which it is filled or emptied. *c*) the front opening in the muzzle of a firearm. *d*) the opening between the jaws of a vise. *e*) the opening between the lips of an organ pipe. *f*) the opening in a flute across which the player blows. *v.t.* 1. to say; especially, to say in an affected or oratorical manner with much movement of the mouth; declaim. 2. to take or put into the mouth. 3. to caress or rub with the mouth or lips. 4. to train (a horse) to become accustomed to the bit. *v.i.* 1. to speak in an affected or oratorical manner; declaim. 2. to make a wry face by twisting the mouth; grimace.
down in (or **at**) **the mouth,** [Colloq.], depressed; unhappy; discouraged.
give mouth to, to express in speech; say.
have a big mouth, [Slang], to talk loudly, excessively, or impudently.
mouth·breed·er (mouth'brēd'ẽr), *n.* any of a number of small fishes that carry their young in the mouth.
-mouthed (mouthd), a combining form used in hy-

phenated compounds, meaning *having a* (specified kind of) *mouth* or (specified number of) *mouths.*

mouth·ful (mouth'fool'), *n.* [*pl.* MOUTHFULS (-foolz')], 1. as much as the mouth can hold. 2. as much as is usually taken into the mouth at one time. 3. a small amount. 4. [Colloq.], a long word or group of words hard to pronounce. 5. [Slang], a pertinent, important, or correct remark: usually in *say a mouthful.*

mouth·i·ly (mouth'ʹl-i, mouth'ʹl-i), *adv.* in a mouthy manner.

mouth·i·ness (mouth'i-nis, mouth'i-nis), *n.* the quality or condition of being mouthy; talkativeness; bombast.

mouth organ, 1. a harmonica. 2. a Panpipe.

mouth·piece (mouth'pēs'), *n.* 1. a part placed at, or forming, a mouth: as, the *mouthpiece* of a telephone, of a pipe, of a horse's bit, etc. 2. the part of a musical instrument held in or to the mouth. 3. a person, periodical, etc. serving as a spokesman for another or others. 4. [Slang], a lawyer who defends criminals.

mouth·y (mouth'i, mouth'i), *adj.* [MOUTHIER (-i-ẽr), MOUTHIEST (-i-ist)], very talkative; bombastic.

mou·ton (mōō'ton'), *n.* [Fr., sheep], the fur of any of certain sheep, made water-repellent and dyed to resemble any of various other furs, especially beaver.

mou·ton·née (mōō'tə-nā'), *adj.* [Fr. *moutonnée,* fem. pp. of *moutonner* < *mouton,* sheep; see MUTTON], in *geology,* rounded like the back of a sheep, as by glacial action: said of rock formations.

mov·a·bil·i·ty (mōōv'ə-bil'ə-ti), *n.* the quality or condition of being movable.

mov·a·ble (mōōv'ə-b'l), *adj.* 1. that can be moved from one place to another; transportable; specifically, in *law,* designating personal property (as distinguished from real property). 2. changing in date from one year to the next: as, *movable* holidays. *n.* 1. something movable. 2. *usually pl.* in *law,* personal property, especially furniture. Also spelled **moveable.**

mov·a·bly (mōōv'ə-bli), *adv.* so as to be movable.

move (mōōv), *v.t.* [MOVED (mōōvd), MOVING], [ME. *moven;* Anglo-Fr. *mover;* OFr. *movoir, moveir;* L. *movere*], 1. to change the place or position of; push, carry, or pull from one place or position to another. 2. to set or keep in motion; stir. 3. to cause or persuade (*to act, do, say, speak,* etc.); prompt. 4. to arouse or stir the emotions, passions, or sympathies of; touch the feelings of. 5. to propose or suggest; especially, to propose formally, as in a meeting. 6. to cause (the bowels) to evacuate. 7. in *commerce,* to dispose of (goods) by selling. *v.i.* 1. to change place or position; go (*to* some place). 2. to change one's place of residence. 3. to live or be active; pass one's life: as, we *move* in good society. 4. to make progress; advance. 5. to take action; begin to act. 6. *a*) to be, or be set, in motion. *b*) to operate in a certain fixed motion; turn, revolve, etc.: said of machines. 7. to appeal, make formal application (*for*): as, *move* for a new trial. 8. to be evacuated: said of the bowels. 9. [Colloq.], to start leaving; depart (often with *on*): as, let's be *moving* on. 10. in *chess, checkers,* etc., *a*) to change the position of a piece. *b*) to be put in another position: said of a piece. 11. in *commerce,* to be disposed of by sale: said of goods. *n.* 1. act of moving; movement. 2. one of a series of actions toward some goal. 3. a change of residence. 4. in *chess, checkers,* etc., the act of moving or one's turn to move.

get a move on, [Slang], 1. to start moving. 2. to hurry; go faster.

on the move, [Colloq.], moving about from place to place.

SYN.—**move,** the broadest in scope of these terms, means merely to change from one place or position to another (to *move* a rock, one's foot, a house, etc.); **remove** stresses the departure of the thing moved from its original or usual place or position (to *remove* one's hat, a cause of strife, etc.); **shift** emphasizes the change in position or location and, hence, often connotes instability, unrest, etc. (to *shift* in one's opinions); **transfer** implies a change from one container, vehicle, ownership, etc. to another (we *transferred* to a cross-town bus). See also **affect.**

move·a·ble (mōōv'ə-b'l), *adj. & n.* movable.

move·ment (mōōv'mənt), *n.* [OFr.], 1. a moving; specifically, *a*) an action of a person or group. *b*) an evacuation of the bowels; also, the matter evacuated. *c*) in *military & naval usage,* a change in the location of troops, ships, etc., as part of a maneuver. 2. a particular manner of moving. 3. a series of organized activities by people working concertedly toward some goal: often called *the movement* by those involved in it. 4. a tendency or trend in some particular sphere of activity: as, a *movement* toward formalism in art. 5. the progress of events in a literary work; action. 6. the effect or representation of motion in painting, sculpture, etc. 7. in *commerce,* a change in the price of some stock or commodity. 8. in *mechanics,* the moving parts of a mechanism; especially, a series of connected moving parts: as, the *movement* of a clock. 9. in *music, a*) tempo. *b*) rhythm. *c*) any of the principal divisions of a symphony, sonata, or other extended composition. 10. in *prosody,* rhythmic flow; cadence.

mov·er (mōōv'ẽr), *n.* a person or thing that moves; specifically, a person whose work or business is moving furniture, etc. for those changing residence.

mov·ie (mōōv'i), *n.* [contr. < *moving picture*], [Colloq.], 1. a motion picture. 2. a motion-picture theater.

the movies, [Colloq.], 1. motion pictures collectively. 2. the motion-picture industry. 3. a showing of a motion picture: as, let's go to *the movies* tonight.

mov·ie·go·er (mōōv'i-gō'ẽr), *n.* [Colloq.], a person who goes, especially often, to see motion pictures.

movie house, [Colloq.], a motion-picture theater.

mov·ing (mōōv'iŋ), *adj.* that moves; specifically, *a*) changing, or causing to change, place or position. *b*) causing motion. *c*) causing to act; impelling, instigating, influencing, etc. *d*) arousing or stirring the emotions or feelings; especially, arousing pathos.

SYN.—**moving** implies a general arousing or stirring of the emotions or feelings, sometimes, specifically, of pathos (her *moving* plea for help); **poignant** is applied to that which is sharply painful to the feelings (the *poignant* cry of a lost child); **affecting** applies to that which stirs the emotions, as to tears (the *affecting* scene of their reunion); **touching** is used of that which arouses tender feelings, as of sympathy, gratitude, etc. (her *touching* little gift to me); **pathetic** applies to that which arouses pity or compassion, sometimes pity mingled with contempt (his *pathetic* attempt at wit).

moving picture, a motion picture; photoplay.

moving staircase (or **stairway**), an escalator.

mow (mō), *v.t.* [MOWED (mōd), MOWED or MOWN (mōn), MOWING], [ME. *mowen;* AS. *mawan;* akin to G. *mähen;* IE. base **mē-,* **met-,* to harvest, as also in L. *metere,* to mow], 1. to cut down (standing grass or grain) with a sickle, scythe, lawn mower, etc. 2. to cut grass or grain from (a lawn, field, etc.). 3. to cause to fall like cut grass or grain; kill; destroy (with *down*): as, we *mowed* down the enemy. *v.i.* to cut down standing grass or grain.

mow (mou), *n.* [ME. *mowe;* AS. *muga,* a heap, pile; akin to ON. *mūgi,* a crowd, swath; IE. base **muken-,* a heap, pile], 1. a stack or heap of hay, grain, etc., especially in a barn. 2. the part of a barn where hay or grain is stored: also called *haymow, hayloft.*

mow, mowe (mou, mō), *n. & v.i.* [ME. *mowe;* OFr. *moue;* MD. *mouwe;* cf. MOP (grimace)], [Archaic], grimace.

mow·er (mō'ẽr), *n.* a person or thing that mows; especially, a mowing machine, reaper, or lawn mower.

mow·ing (mō'iŋ), *n.* 1. the act of cutting down grass or grain. 2. the quantity of grass or grain mowed in a single specified period.

mowing machine, a machine with rotating blades for mowing grass, etc.

mown (mōn), alternative past participle of **mow** (to cut down).

mox·a (mok'sə), *n.* [altered < Japan. *mogusa,* a caustic < *moe kusa,* burning herb], 1. a soft, downy material prepared from the leaves of a Chinese plant and burned on the skin as a cauterizing agent or counterirritant. 2. this plant.

‡moy·en âge (mwȧ'ye'näzh'), [Fr., lit., middle age], the Middle Ages.

Mo·zam·bique (mō'zəm-bēk'), *n.* a Portuguese colony in southeastern Africa, on the Mozambique Channel: area, 297,657 sq. mi.; pop., 5,081,000; capital, Lourenço Marques: also called *Portuguese East Africa.*

Mozambique Channel, a part of the Indian Ocean, between eastern Africa and Madagascar.

Moz·ar·ab (mō-zâr'əb), *n.* [Sp. *mozárabe;* Ar. *musta'rib,* would-be Arab], any of a group of Spanish Christians who kept their religion in a modified form during the domination of the Moors.

Mo·zart, Wolf·gang A·ma·de·us (vôlf'gäŋk ä'mä-dā'oos mō'tsärt; *occas. Anglicized to* mō'zärt), 1756–1791; Austrian composer.

moz·zet·ta, mo·zet·ta (mō-zet'ə), *n.* [It. *mozzetta* < *mozza,* shortened], a short cape with a small hood, worn over the rochet by the Pope and other high dignitaries of the Roman Catholic Church.

MP, Military Police: also **M.P.**

mp., *mezzo piano,* [It.], in *music,* moderately soft.

M.P., 1. Member of Parliament. 2. Methodist Protestant. 3. Metropolitan Police. 4. Mounted Police.

M.P., m.p., melting point.

mph, m.p.h., miles per hour.

Mr. (mis'tẽr), [*pl.* MESSRS. (mes'ẽrz)], mister: used before the name or title of a man: see **mister.**

Mrs. (mis'iz), mistress: now used as a title before the name of a married woman.

MS., ms., [*pl.* MSS.], manuscript.

M.S., 1. Master of Science. 2. Master of Surgery. 3. *memoriae sacrum,* [L.], sacred to the memory of.

M/S, 1. in *commerce*, months after sight. 2. motor ship.
M.Sc., Master of Science.
MScand., Middle Scandinavian.
MScot., Middle Scottish.
Msgr., Monsignor.
M. Sgt., M/Sgt, Master Sergeant.
m'sieur (mə-syűr'; Fr. mə-syö'), *n.* monsieur.
m.s.l., mean sea level.
M.S.T., Mountain Standard Time.
Ms-Th, MsTh, in *chemistry*, mesothorium.
Mt., mt., [*pl.* MTS.], 1. mount. 2. mountain.
M.T., 1. Masoretic Text. 2. mean time. 3. metric ton.
mtg., 1. meeting. 2. mortgage.
mtn., mountain.
Mt. Rev., Most Reverend.
mu (mū, mōō), *n.* [Gr. *my*], the twelfth letter of the Greek alphabet (M, μ), corresponding to English *M*, *m*: see **alphabet**, table.
much (much), *adj.* [MORE (môr, mōr), MOST (mōst)], [ME. *muche, miche* < *muchel, michel*, large, much < AS. *mycel*, large in size or quantity; IE. base **meĝ(h)-*, large, as also in L. *magnus, magister, maiestas, Maius* (cf. MAGNUM, MAGISTRATE, MAJESTY, MAY, etc.)], 1. [Obs.], many in number. 2. great in quantity, amount, degree, etc. *adv.* 1. to a great degree or extent: as, he is *much* happier now. 2. just about; almost; nearly: as, he is *much* the same as yesterday. *n.* 1. a great amount or quantity: as, there is *much* to be done. 2. something great, unusual, or important: as, is he *much* of a scholar?
make much of, to treat or consider as of great importance.
Much Ado About Nothing, a comedy (c. 1599) by Shakespeare.
much·ness (much'nis), *n.* greatness, as of quantity, degree, etc.; magnitude.
mu·cic acid (mū'sik), [Fr. *mucique* < L. *mucus* (see MUCUS); + *-ic*], a colorless, crystalline acid, $(CHOH)_4$-$(CO_2H)_2$, formed by oxidizing lactose, gums, etc.
mu·cid (mū'sid), *adj.* [L. *mucidus* < *mucere*, to be moldy; akin to *mucus*, mucus], moldy; musty.
mu·ci·lage (mū's'l-ij), *n.* [ME. *muscilage* (via OFr.) < LL. *mucilago*, musty juice < L. *mucere*, to be musty, be moldy < *mucus*, mucus], 1. any of various thick, sticky substances found in certain plants. 2. any watery solution of gum, glue, etc. used as an adhesive.
mu·ci·lag·i·nous (mū'sə-laj'i-nəs), *adj.* [Fr. *mucilagineux*], 1. of or like mucilage; slimy; sticky. 2. producing or secreting mucilage.
mu·cin (mū'sin), *n.* [Fr. *mucine*; see MUCUS & -IN], in *biochemistry*, any of various nitrogenous substances secreted by the mucous membranes.
muck (muk), *n.* [ME. *muk* < Anglo-N. (ON. *myki*, dung); for IE. base see MEEK], 1. moist manure. 2. black earth containing decaying matter, used as a fertilizer. 3. anything unclean or degrading; dirt; filth. *v.t.* 1. to fertilize with muck. 2. [Colloq.], to dirty with or as with muck. 3. in *mining*, etc., to remove muck from.
muck·er (muk'ẽr), *n.* [prob. < G. *mucker*, low person < *mucken*, to grumble], [British Slang], a coarse or vulgar person, especially, one without honor; cad.
muck·le (muk''l), *adj., adv., n.* [ME. *mikel, mukel, michel*; cf. MUCH], [Archaic or Scot.], much: also **mickle.**
muck·rake (muk'rāk'), *v.i.* [MUCKRAKED (-rākt'), MUCKRAKING], [so used in 1906 by Theodore Roosevelt in allusion to the man with the *muck rake* (in Bunyan's *Pilgrim's Progress*), who was too intent upon raking muck to consider his heavenly crown], to search for and either charge or expose (in newspapers, etc.) corruption by public officials, businessmen, etc.
muck rake, a rake for gathering or spreading muck.
muck·rak·er (muk'rāk'ẽr), *n.* a person, especially a newspaper reporter, who muckrakes.
muck·worm (muk'wűrm'), *n.* 1. a grub, or larva, that lives and develops in muck, or manure. 2. a miser.
muck·y (muk'i), *adj.* [MUCKIER (-i-ẽr), MUCKIEST (-i-ist)], of or like muck; especially, dirty, filthy, etc.
mu·co- (mū'kō, mū'kə), a combining form meaning *mucus* or *mucous membrane*, as in *mucoprotein*: also, before a vowel, **muc-.**
mu·coid (mū'koid), *n.* [*mucin* + *-oid*], in *biochemistry*, any of a group of substances resembling mucin and occurring in connective tissue, etc. *adj.* like mucus.
mu·co·pro·te·in (mū'kō-prō'tē-in, mū'kō-prō'tēn), *n.* in *biochemistry*, any of a class of proteins combined with a carbohydrate complex.
mu·co·sa (mū-kō'sə), *n.* [*pl.* MUCOSAE (-sē)], [Mod. L., fem. of L. *mucosus*; see MUCOUS], a mucous membrane.
mu·cos·i·ty (mū-kos'ə-ti), *n.* the quality or condition of being mucous.
mu·cous (mū'kəs), *adj.* [L. *mucosus*, slimy < *mucus*, mucus], 1. of, containing, or secreting mucus. 2. like mucus or covered with or as with mucus; slimy.
mucous membrane, a mucus-secreting membrane lining body cavities and canals connecting with the external air, as the alimentary canal and respiratory tract.
mu·cro (mū'krō), *n.* [*pl.* MUCRONES (mū-krō'nēz)], [L., sharp point], in *botany & zoology*, a short, sharp point, tip, or process projecting abruptly from certain parts and organs, as at the end of a leaf.
mu·cro·nate (mū'krə-nit, mū'krə-nāt'), *adj.* [L. *mucronatus*], ending in a mucro, or sharp point.
mu·cro·nat·ed (mū'krə-nā'tid), *adj.* mucronate.
mu·cus (mū'kəs), *n.* [L.; IE. base **meuq-*, slimy; cf. MEEK, MUCK], the thick, slimy secretion of the mucous membranes, that moistens and protects them.
mud (mud), *n.* [ME.; prob. < a LG. source; cf. LG. *mudde, mod*; IE. **meut* < base **meu-*, wet, as also in Eng. *mother* (a scum)], 1. wet, soft, sticky earth. 2. defamatory remarks; libel or slander. *v.t.* [MUDDED (-id), MUDDING], to cover or soil with or as with mud.
mud cat, in the Mississippi valley, a full-grown, edible catfish.
mud dauber, any of a variety of wasps that build cells of hard, caked mud for their larvae.
mud·der (mud'ẽr), *n.* in *horse racing*, a horse that runs especially well on a wet, muddy track.
mud·di·ly (mud'ə-li), *adv.* in a muddy manner.
mud·di·ness (mud'i-nis), *n.* the quality or condition of being muddy.
mud·dle (mud''l), *v.t.* [MUDDLED (-'ld), MUDDLING], [< *mud*], 1. to mix up in a confused manner; jumble; bungle. 2. to mix or stir (a drink, etc.). 3. to make (water, etc.) turbid. 4. to confuse mentally; befuddle, as with alcoholic liquor. 5. to confuse (the brain, mind, etc.); befog. *v.i.* to act or think in a confused way. *n.* 1. a confused or disordered condition; mess, jumble, etc. 2. mental confusion. —***SYN.*** see **confusion.**
muddle through, [Chiefly British], to succeed in spite of apparent blunders or confusion.
mud·dle-head·ed (mud''l-hed'id), *adj.* stupid; blundering; confused.
mud·dler (mud'lẽr), *n.* a stick for stirring mixed drinks.
mud·dy (mud'i), *adj.* [MUDDIER (-i-ẽr), MUDDIEST (-i-ist)], 1. full of or spattered with mud. 2. *a*) not clear; containing sediment; cloudy: as, *muddy* coffee. *b*) dull: as, a *muddy* complexion. 3. confused, obscure, vague, etc.: as, *muddy* thinking. *v.t. & v.i.* [MUDDIED (-id), MUDDYING], to make or become muddy.
mud·fish (mud'fish'), *n.* [*pl.* MUDFISH, MUDFISHES (-iz); see FISH], any of various fishes that live in mud or muddy water.
mud flat, low, muddy land that is flooded at high tide and left uncovered at low tide.
mud·guard (mud'gärd'), *n.* a cover or shield over the wheel of a bicycle, automobile, etc., to protect against mud thrown up by the wheel.
mud hen, any of various birds that live in marshes, as the coot, rail, gallinule, etc.; marsh hen.
mud·hole (mud'hōl'), *n.* a hole or low place, as in a field or road, full of mud.
mud puppy, any of various North American salamanders that live in mud under water, especially a large variety with bushy external gills.
mud·sill (mud'sil'), *n.* the lowest timber, or sill, in the foundation of a structure, placed in or on the ground.
mud·sling·er (mud'sliŋ'ẽr), *n.* a person who engages in mudslinging.
mud·sling·ing (mud'sliŋ'iŋ), *n.* the practice of making unscrupulous, malicious attacks against an opponent, as in a political campaign.
mud·stone (mud'stōn'), *n.* a hardened sedimentary rock formed from clay and similar to shale, but not laminated.
mud turtle, any of a large group of small turtles of North and Central America that live in muddy ponds, streams, etc.
mu·ez·zin (mū-ez'in), *n.* [Ar. *mu'adhdhin*, ppr. of *adhdhana*, freq. of *adhana*, to proclaim < *udhn*, an ear], in Moslem countries, a crier in a minaret or other lofty place who calls the people to prayer at the proper hours.
muff (muf), *n.* [D. *mof*; Walloon *moufe*; shortened < Fr. *moufle*, a mitten], 1. a cylindrical covering of fur or other soft material into which the hands are placed from either end for keeping them warm. 2. *a*) in *baseball*, etc., a failure to hold a ball when catching it; hence, *b*) any bungling action. *c*) a bungler. *v.t. & v.i.* to do (something) badly or awkwardly; specifically, in *baseball*, etc., to miss (a catch) or bungle (a play).
muf·fin (muf'in), *n.* [< dial. *mouffin, moufin*; prob. connected with OFr. *moufflet*, soft, as in *pain moufflet*, soft bread], 1. a quick bread made with eggs and baked in a small, cup-shaped mold, usually eaten hot. 2. a similar small bread made from dough leavened with yeast.
muf·fin·eer (muf'in-êr'), *n.* 1. a covered dish for keeping muffins hot. 2. a container with holes in the top for sprinkling sugar, spices, etc. on muffins.
muf·fle (muf''l), *v.t.* [MUFFLED (-'ld), MUFFLING], [prob. contr. < OFr. *enmoufle* < *moufle*, a mitten; cf. MUFF], 1. to wrap up in a shawl, blanket, cloak, etc. so as to hide, keep warm, or protect: often with *up*. 2. to keep (a person) from seeing or speaking by wrapping up the head. 3. to wrap or cover in order to deaden or prevent sound. 4. to deaden (a sound), as by wrapping. *n.* [prob. < Fr. *moufle*], 1. a wrap, covering,

etc. used for muffling. 2. an oven in which pottery, etc. can be fired without being exposed directly to the flame. 3. the fleshy bare part of the upper lip and nose of ruminants and certain other mammals.

muf·fler (muf'lẽr), *n.* 1. a scarf, shawl, etc. worn around the throat, as for warmth. 2. any of various devices for silencing noises, as a baffle in the exhaust pipe of an internal-combustion engine.

muf·ti (muf'ti), *n.* [*pl.* MUFTIS (-tiz)], [Ar., one who gives a decisive response < *āftā*, to judge, give a judicial decision; sense 2 prob. < fancied resemblance to Moslem dress of early 19th-c. dressing gown and tasseled cap, worn by an officer off duty], 1. in Moslem countries, an interpreter or expounder of religious law: cf. **Grand Mufti.** 2. civilian clothes, especially when worn by one who normally wears, or has long worn, a military or other uniform.

mug (mug), *n.* [Early Mod. Eng. *mugg;* akin to Sw. *mug,* D. *mok,* G. *muck, mock,* etc.; prob. < ON. via dial.], 1. a heavy drinking cup of earthenware or metal, usually cylindrical and with a handle, formerly often ornamented with a human face. 2. as much as such a cup will hold. 3. [Slang], *a)* the face. *b)* the mouth. *c)* a grimace. *d)* a rough, uncouth person. ***v.t.*** [MUGGED (mugd), MUGGING], [Slang], 1. to photograph; especially, to photograph (a criminal or suspect) for police records. 2. to assault from behind by strangling with an arm thrown around the neck, especially with intent to rob. ***v.i.*** [Slang], 1. to make a grimace; especially, in the *theater,* to overact by exaggerating the facial expressions. 2. to assault a person from behind by strangling him with an arm thrown around his neck, especially with intent to rob him. Also spelled **mugg** (in sense 2, *v.t.* & *v.i.*).

mug·ger (mug'ẽr), *n.* [Slang], one who mugs; especially, *a)* a robber who assaults his victim from behind. *b)* in the *theater,* an actor who overacts, especially by exaggerating the facial expressions.

mug·ger, mug·gar, mug·gur, (mug'ẽr), *n.* [Hind. *magar;* Sans. *makara,* sea monster], the native crocodile of India and Malaysia, with a broad, wrinkled snout.

mug·gi·ness (mug'i-nis), *n.* the quality or state of being muggy.

mug·gins (mug'inz), *n.* [< personal name *Muggins,* associated with slang *mug,* simpleton, cardsharper's dupe], 1. a variant of the game of dominoes. 2. any of various card games in which players try to match exposed cards. 3. [British], a dupe; fool.

mug·gy (mug'i), *adj.* [MUGGIER (-i-ẽr), MUGGIEST (-i-ist)], [< base of ME. *muggen,* to drizzle < ON.; + *-y*], hot, damp, and close: as, *muggy* weather.

mug·wump (mug'wump'), *n.* [Algonquian *mugquomp,* great man, chief], 1. a Republican who refused to support the party ticket in 1884; hence, 2. any independent, especially in politics.

Mu·ham·mad (moo-ham'əd), *n.* Mohammed.

Mu·ham·mad·an, Mu·ham·med·an (moo-ham'əd-ən), *adj.* & *n.* Mohammedan.

Muhl·bach, Lu·i·se (loo-ē'zə mül'bäkh), (pseudonym of *Klara Müller Mundt*), 1814–1873; German novelist.

Muir, John (myoor), 1838–1914; American naturalist and writer, born in Scotland.

Muir Glacier (myoor), a glacier in southeastern Alaska.

mu·jik (moo-zhēk', moo'zhik), *n.* a muzhik.

Muk·den (mook'den', mook'dən, mook'den'), *n.* the capital of Manchuria: pop., 1,136,000: also called *Feng-Tien:* also spelled **Moukden.**

mu·lat·to (mə-lat'ō, myoo-lat'ō), *n.* [*pl.* MULATTOES (-ōz)], [Sp. & Port. *mulato,* mulatto, of mixed breed, orig. young mule < *mulo,* mule; L. *mulus*], 1. a person one of whose parents is a Negro and the other a Caucasian, or white. 2. popularly, any person with mixed Negro and Caucasian ancestry. ***adj.*** of the light-brown color of a mulatto's skin.

mul·ber·ry (mul'ber'i, mul'bẽr-i), *n.* [*pl.* MULBERRIES (-iz)], [ME. *mulberie,* dissimilated var. of *murberie;* AS. *morberie* < L. *morum,* mulberry + AS. *berie* (see BERRY)], 1. the purplish-red, edible, berrylike fruit of any of a group of trees whose leaves are used as food for silkworms. 2. this tree. 3. purplish-red.

mulch (mulch), *n.* [ME. *molsh,* soft; akin to G. dial. *molsch,* soft; for prob. IE. base see MOLD (earth)], leaves, straw, or other loose material spread on the ground around plants to prevent evaporation of water from soil, freezing of roots, etc. ***v.t.*** to apply mulch to.

mulct (mulkt), *v.t.* [L. *mulctare* < *mulcta, multa,* a fine], 1. to punish (someone) by a fine; penalize by depriving of something. 2. to deprive of something, as by fraud or deceit. ***n.*** a fine or similar penalty.

mule (mūl), *n.* [ME.; OFr.; L. *mulus,* mule], 1. the offspring of a donkey and a horse; especially, the offspring of a jackass and a mare, as distinguished from a *hinny:* mules are usually sterile. 2. a small tractor or electric engine used to tow boats along a canal. 3. a machine for drawing and spinning cotton fibers into yarn and winding the yarn on spindles. 4. [Colloq.], a stubborn person. 5. in *biology,* a hybrid; especially, a sterile hybrid: said especially of the offspring of a canary and some other finch.

mule (mūl), *n.* [Fr.; D. *muil;* L. *mulleus,* red or purple shoe < *mullus,* red mullet, kind of fish], a lounging slipper that does not cover the heel.

mule deer, a long-eared deer of the western United States.

mule skinner, [Colloq.], a mule driver.

mu·le·teer (mū'lə-têr'), *n.* [Fr. *muletier* < *mulet,* dim. of *mule*], a mule driver.

mul·ey (mū'li, mool'i, moo'li), *adj.* & *n.* mulley.

muley saw, [prob. < *mulley,* hornless], a ripsaw, with a long, stiff blade that is not stretched in a frame but is guided by clamps at either end.

Mul·ha·cén (mool'ä-then'), *n.* a mountain in southern Spain: the highest peak in Spain: height, 11,420 ft.

Mül·hau·sen (mül'hou'zən), *n.* Mulhouse.

Mül·heim an der Ruhr (mül'hīm än der roor'), a city in the Rhineland, Germany: pop., 137,000.

Mul·house (mü'looz'), *n.* a city in eastern France, near the Rhine: pop., 88,000 (est. 1946): German name, *Mülhausen.*

mu·li·eb·ri·ty (mū'li-eb'rə-ti), *n.* [LL. *muliebritas* < L. *muliebris,* womanly, womanish < *mulier,* a woman], 1. the condition of being a woman; womanhood. 2. the qualities characteristic of a woman; womanliness; femininity. Opposed to *virility.*

mul·ish (mūl'ish), *adj.* like or characteristic of a mule; specifically, *a)* stubborn; obstinate. *b)* sterile or hybrid.

Mull (mul), *n.* the largest island in the Hebrides.

mull (mul), *v.t.* & *v.i.* [ME. *mullen,* to grind; prob. < *mul,* dust; AS. *myl,* dust; for IE. base see MOLD (earth)], [Colloq.], to cogitate or ponder (usually with *over*).

mull (mul), *v.t.* [prob. < Fr. *mollir,* to soften < *mol,* soft < L. *mollis;* cf. MILL], to heat, sweeten, and flavor with spices, as beer, cider, wine, etc.

mull (mul), *n.* [< Hind. & Per. *malmal*], a thin, soft muslin.

mul·lah, mul·la (mul'ə, mool'ə), *n.* [Turk., Per. & Hind. *mulla;* Ar. *mawla,* a master, sir], a Moslem teacher or interpreter of the religious law: used as a general title of respect for a learned man: also **mollah.**

mul·lein, mul·len (mul'in), *n.* [ME. & OFr. *moleine* < *mol,* soft], any of a group of tall plants of the figwort family, with downy leaves and spikes of variously colored flowers.

mull·er (mul'ẽr), *n.* [< ME. *mullen,* to grind; prob. var. of *millen;* cf. MILL], any of various mechanical or hand devices for grinding; specifically, a flat-bottomed pestle of stone, etc., as for grinding paints or drugs.

Mül·ler, Max (mäks mü'lẽr; Eng. mul'ẽr, mil'ẽr), (*Friedrich Max Müller*), 1823–1900; English philologist and mythologist, born in Germany.

mul·let (mul'it), *n.* [*pl.* MULLETS (-its), MULLET; see PLURAL, II, D, 1], [ME. *molet;* OFr. *mulet,* dim. < L. *mullus,* red mullet; cf. Gr. *myllos,* kind of fish], any of a group of edible fishes found in fresh and salt waters; specifically, *a)* the *gray mullet,* characterized by silvery scales, a small mouth, and feeble teeth. *b)* the *red mullet,* characterized by reddish or golden scales and two long chin barbels; surmullet.

mul·ley (mool'i, moo'li), *adj.* [Scot. *moiley;* prob. < Celt.; orig. meaning "bald"], having had the horns removed; polled: said of cattle. ***n.*** 1. a hornless cow. 2. [British Dial.], any cow. Also **muley.**

mul·li·gan (mul'i-g'n), *n.* [prob. < personal name *Mulligan, Milligan*], [Slang], a stew made of odds and ends of meat and vegetables, especially as prepared by hoboes: also **mulligan stew.**

mul·li·ga·taw·ny (mul'i-gə-tô'ni), *n.* [Tamil *milagutannir,* pepper water], an East Indian soup of meat, etc., flavored with curry.

mul·lion (mul'yən), *n.* [prob. < OFr. *moienel;* L. *medianus,* middle], a slender vertical dividing bar between the lights of windows, screens, etc. ***v.t.*** to furnish with or divide by mullions.

WINDOWS WITH MULLIONS

mul·lock (mul'ək), *n.* [ME. *mulloc* < *mul,* small particles, dust, ashes + *-ock*], in Australia, the refuse earth or rock left over in mining.

Mul·tan (mool-tän'), *n.* a city in West Punjab, Pakistan: pop., 143,000.

mul·ti- (mul'ti, mul'tə), [L. < *multus,* much, many], a combining form meaning: 1. *having, consisting of,* or *affecting many,* as in *multicolored.* 2. *more than two* (or sometimes *one*), as in *multilateral, multicylinder.* 3. *many times more than,* as in *multimillionaire.* Also **mult-.** The meanings of the following words can be determined by combining the meanings of their component elements:

multiangular	**multinucleolar**
multicellular	**multiovular**
multicoil	**multipinnate**
multicolored	**multipolar**
multicostate	**multiradial**
multicuspid	**multiramose**
multicylinder	**multirooted**
multidentate	**multisegmented**
multifoliate	**multiseptate**
multifoliolate	**multispeed**
multilinear	**multispermous**
multilingual	**multispiral**
multilobate	**multistaminate**
multilocular	**multistoried**
multimolecular	**multistriate**
multimotored	**multitubular**
multinominal	**multivalved**
multinuclear	**multivoiced**

mul·ti·far·i·ous (mul'tə-fâr'i-əs), *adj.* [L. *multifarius,* manifold < *multus,* many], having many kinds of parts or elements; of great variety; diverse; manifold. —*SYN.* see **many.**

mul·ti·fid (mul'tə-fid), *adj.* [L. *multifidus* < *multus,* many + base of *findere,* to split], cut into many divisions, or lobes, as a leaf.

mul·ti·flo·rous (mul'tə-flôr'əs, mul'tə-flō'rəs), *adj.* [*multi-* + *-florous*], in *botany,* bearing many flowers.

mul·ti·fold (mul'tə-fōld'), *adj.* [*multi-* + *-fold*], 1. doubled or folded many times. 2. manifold.

mul·ti·form (mul'tə-fôrm'), *adj.* [< Fr. or L.; Fr. *multiforme;* L. *multiformis* < *multus,* many + *forma,* a form], having many forms, shapes, etc.

mul·ti·for·mi·ty (mul'tə-fôr'mə-ti), *n.* the quality or condition of being multiform.

mul·ti·graph (mul'tə-graf', mul'tə-gräf'), *n.* [*multi-* + *-graph*], a type of rotary printing machine used for reproducing typewritten matter: a trade-mark (**Multigraph**). *v.t.* to reproduce with such a machine.

MULTIFID LEAF

mul·ti·lat·er·al (mul'ti-lat'ẽr-əl), *adj.* [*multi-* + *lateral*], 1. many-sided. 2. participated in by more than two nations; multipartite: as, a *multilateral* treaty.

mul·ti·lat·er·al·ly (mul'ti-lat'ẽr-əl-i), *adv.* in a multilateral manner; specifically, by or with multilateral agreement or consent.

mul·ti·mil·lion·aire (mul'ti-mil'yən-âr'), *n.* a person whose wealth amounts to several millions of dollars, francs, pounds, etc.

mul·tip·a·ra (mul-tip'ə-rə), *n.* [*pl.* MULTIPARAE (-rē')], [Mod. L. < *multiparus*], a woman who is bearing her second child or has borne two or more children.

mul·tip·a·rous (mul-tip'ə-rəs), *adj.* [Mod. L. *multiparus;* see MULTI- & -PAROUS], 1. of or being a multipara. 2. in *zoology,* designating an animal that normally bears more than one offspring at a delivery.

mul·ti·par·tite (mul'ti-pär'tīt), *adj.* [L. *multipartitus* < *multus,* many + *pars, partis,* a part], 1. divided into many parts. 2. participated in by more than two nations; multilateral.

mul·ti·ped (mul'ti-ped'), *adj.* [L. *multipes, multipedis* < *multus,* many + *pes, pedis,* a foot], having many feet. *n.* [Rare], a multiped animal or insect.

mul·ti·pede (mul'ti-pēd'), *adj. & n.* multiped.

mul·ti·phase (mul'ti-fāz'), *adj.* having many phases; specifically, in *electricity,* polyphase.

mul·ti·ple (mul'tə-p'l), *adj.* [Fr.; LL. *multiplus,* for L. *multiplex,* manifold < L. *multus,* many + *plicare,* to fold], 1. having or consisting of many parts, elements, etc.; more than one or once; manifold. 2. in *electricity,* designating or of a circuit having two or more conductors connected in parallel. *n.* 1. in *electricity,* a group of terminals so arranged that connection with the circuit can be made at any of a number of points. 2. in *mathematics,* a number which is a product of some specified number and another number: as, 10 is a *multiple* of 5 and 2.

mul·ti·ple-choice test (mul'tə-p'l-chois'), in *education,* an examination in which the person tested must select the correct one of a number of proposed answers for each question.

multiple factors, in *genetics,* a series of two or more independent genes considered to act as a single unit with a cumulative effect in the transmission of certain characteristics, such as size, pigmentation, etc.

multiple fruit, in *botany,* a collective fruit.

multiple neuritis, neuritis affecting several nerves.

multiple sclerosis, a chronic disease in which there is sclerosis in various parts of the nervous system: it is characterized by muscular weakness, tremor, etc.

multiple star, in *astronomy,* three or more stars appearing close together in the sky, often forming a system with a single gravitational center: cf. **binary star.**

multiple voting, the voting of a person at a single election in all districts in which he can meet the legal qualifications, as in Great Britain before 1918.

mul·ti·plex (mul'tə-pleks), *adj.* [L. *multiplex,* manifold < *multus,* many + *-plex,* -fold < base of *plaga,* surface, region; see DUPLEX], 1. multiple; manifold. 2. *a)* designating or of a system of telegraphy or telephony in which two or more messages can be sent simultaneously in either or both directions over the same wire or on the same wave. *b)* in *radio,* designating or of a system in which two or more signals can be transmitted simultaneously on the same wave, as for stereophonic broadcasting. *n.* a multiplex system. *v.t.* to transmit by multiplex.

mul·ti·pli·a·ble (mul'tə-plī'ə-b'l), *adj.* that can be multiplied.

mul·ti·pli·ca·ble (mul'tə-pli-kə-b'l), *adj.* multipliable.

mul·ti·pli·cand (mul'tə-pli-kand'), *n.* [L. *multiplicandus,* to be multiplied, gerundive of *multiplicare,* to multiply], in *mathematics,* the number that is, or is to be, multiplied by another (the *multiplier*).

mul·ti·pli·cate (mul'tə-pli-kāt'), *adj.* [ME.; L. *multiplicatus,* pp. of *multiplicare,* to multiply], multiple.

mul·ti·pli·ca·tion (mul'tə-pli-kā'shən), *n.* [ME. *multiplicacioun;* OFr.; L. *multiplicatio* < *multiplicare,* to multiply], a multiplying or being multiplied; specifically, in *mathematics,* the process of finding the number or quantity (*product*) obtained by repeating a specified number or quantity (*multiplicand*) a specified number of times (*multiplier*), indicated in arithmetic by the symbol ×: opposed to *division.*

multiplication table, a table for memorization showing the results of multiplying each number of a series, usually 1 to 12, by each of the numbers in succession.

mul·ti·pli·ca·tive (mul'tə-pli-kā'tiv), *adj.* [ML. *multiplicativus* < L. *multiplicatus,* pp.; see MULTIPLY], tending to multiply or capable of multiplying.

mul·ti·plic·i·ty (mul'tə-plis'ə-ti), *n.* [LL. *multiplicitas* < L. *multiplex,* manifold], 1. the quality or condition of being manifold or various. 2. a great number.

mul·ti·pli·er (mul'tə-plī'ẽr), *n.* 1. a person or thing that multiplies or increases. 2. in *mathematics,* the number by which another number (the *multiplicand*) is, or is to be, multiplied. 3. in *physics,* any device for multiplying, or intensifying, some effect.

mul·ti·ply (mul'tə-plī'), *v.t.* [MULTIPLIED (-plīd'), MULTIPLYING], [ME. *multiplien;* OFr. *multiplier;* L. *multiplicare* < *multiplex,* manifold], 1. to cause to increase in number, amount, extent, or degree. 2. in *mathematics,* to find the product of by multiplication. *v.i.* 1. to increase in number, amount, extent, or degree; specifically, to increase by procreation. 2. in *mathematics,* to perform multiplication. —*SYN.* see **increase.**

mul·ti·tude (mul'tə-tōōd', mul'tə-tūd'), *n.* [ME.; OFr.; L. *multitudo* < *multus,* many, much], 1. the quality or state of being numerous, or many. 2. a large number of persons or things, especially when gathered together or considered as a unit; host, myriad, etc. 3. the common people (preceded by *the*). —*SYN.* see **crowd.**

mul·ti·tu·di·nous (mul'tə-tōō'd'n-əs, mul'tə-tū'd'n-əs), *adj.* [< L. *multitudo, multitudinis,* multitude; + *-ous*], 1. very numerous; many. 2. consisting of many parts, elements, etc.; manifold. 3. [Rare or Poetic], of or like a multitude; crowded.

mul·ti·va·lence (mul'ti-vā'ləns, mul-tiv'ə-ləns), *n.* the quality or state of being multivalent.

mul·ti·va·lent (mul'ti-vā'lənt, mul-tiv'ə-lənt), *adj.* in *chemistry,* 1. having a valence of more than two. 2. polyvalent.

‡**mul·tum in par·vo** (mul'təm in pär'vō), [L.], much in little.

mul·ture (mul'chẽr), *n.* [ME. *moulture, multure;* OFr. *molture* (Fr. *mouture*) < ML. *molitura* < *molere,* to grind; cf. MILL], formerly, a fee paid to the owner of a mill for the privilege of having one's grain ground there, usually a percentage of the grain or of the ground flour.

mum (mum), *n.* [G. *mumme:* said to be named after Christian *Mumme,* 15th-c. G. brewer], a strong beer.

mum (mum), *v.i.* [MUMMED (mumd), MUMMING], [prob. < MD. *mommen,* to mask, play the mummer; OFr. *momer* < *momon,* a mask; Sp. *momo,* a grimace], to wear a mask or costume in fun; specifically, to act as a mummer at Christmas time: also spelled **mumm.**

mum (mum), *n.* [Colloq.], a chrysanthemum.

mum (mum), *n.* [Colloq.], mother.

mum (mum), *adj.* [ME. *momme;* imitative of a sound made with the lips closed], silent; not speaking. *interj.* be silent! do not speak!

mum's the word, say nothing; remain secretive.

mum·ble (mum'b'l), *v.t. & v.i.* [MUMBLED (-b'ld), MUMBLING], [ME. *momelen;* cf. G. *mummeln,* D. *mommelen;* all directly or ult. of echoic origin], 1. to speak or say indistinctly and in a low voice, as with the mouth partly closed; mutter. 2. [Rare], to chew gently and ineffectively, as with toothless gums. *n.* a mumbled sound or utterance. —*SYN.* see **murmur.**

mum·ble·ty·peg (mum'b'l-ti-peg'), *n.* [altered < *mumble-the-peg* < *mumble,* to bite], a boy's game in which a jackknife must be tossed from a number of positions so that it always lands upright with the blade stuck in the ground, the loser originally having to draw a peg from the ground with his teeth.

mum·bo jum·bo (mum'bō jum'bō), [orig. *mama dyambo,* in a Mandingo dialect], 1. [M- J-], among certain African tribes of western Sudan, a medicine man who is supposed to protect his people from evil and terrorize the women into subjection. 2. an idol or fetish; hence, 3. any object of fear or dread. 4. meaningless ritual, unintelligible expression, gibberish, etc.

mum·mer (mum'ẽr), *n.* [MFr. *momeur* < OFr. *momer;* see MUM, *v.*], 1. a person who wears a mask or disguise for fun; specifically, in England, any of the masked and costumed persons who travel from house to house, as at Christmas time, acting out short pantomimes; hence, 2. humorously, any actor.

mum·mer·y (mum'ẽr-i), *n.* [*pl.* MUMMERIES (-iz)], [MFr. *mommerie* < OFr. *momer;* see MUM, *v.*], 1. performance by mummers. 2. any show or ceremony regarded as pretentious or hypocritical.

mum·mi·fi·ca·tion (mum'ə-fi-kā'shən), *n.* a mummifying or being mummified.

mum·mi·fy (mum'ə-fī'), *v.t.* [MUMMIFIED (-fīd'), MUMMIFYING], [Fr. *momifier;* see MUMMY & -FY], to make into or like a mummy. *v.i.* to shrivel up; dry.

mum·my (mum'i), *n.* [*pl.* MUMMIES (-iz)], [Fr. *mumie, momie;* ML. *mumia;* Ar. *mūmiyā,* embalmed body, mummy < *mum,* wax], 1. a dead body preserved by embalming, as by the ancient Egyptians. 2. any dead body that has been naturally well preserved. 3. any thin, withered person regarded as looking like a mummy. *v.t.* [MUMMIED (-id), MUMMYING], to mummify.

mump (mump), *v.t.* & *v.i.* [cf. D. *mompelen,* var. of *mommelen,* to mumble], 1. [Dial.], to mumble; mutter. 2. [cf. D. *mompen,* to cheat; prob. akin to *mompelen*], [Old Slang], *a)* to beg. *b)* to cheat.

mumps (mumps), *n.pl.* [construed as sing.], [pl. of obs. *mump,* a grimace: prob. from patient's appearance], an acute communicable disease, usually of childhood, caused by a virus and characterized by swelling of the salivary glands, especially the parotid, or, occasionally in adults, by inflammation of the testes, breasts, etc.

mun., municipal.

munch (munch), *v.t.* & *v.i.* [ME. *munchen;* echoic, prob. after *maungen* (OFr. *manger*), to eat & *crunch*], to chew vigorously, and often with a crunching sound.

Mun·chau·sen, Baron (mun-chô'zən, mun'chou-zən), (*Karl Friedrich Hieronymus von Münchhausen*), 1720–1797; German adventurer and soldier; known for his exaggerated tales of his exploits, as collected by Rudolph Eric Raspe.

Mün·chen (mün'Hən), *n.* Munich.

Mun·cie (mun'si), *n.* a city in eastern Indiana: pop., 69,000.

mun·dane (mun'dān), *adj.* [Fr. *mondain;* L. *mundanus* < *mundus,* world], of the world; especially, worldly, as distinguished from heavenly, spiritual, etc. —*SYN.* see **earthly.**

mun·dun·go (mun-duŋ'gō), *n.* mundungus.

mun·dun·gus (mun-duŋ'gəs), *n.* [orig. facetious use of Sp. *mondongo,* tripe], [Archaic], a dark tobacco with a disagreeable smell.

mun·go (muŋ'gō), *n.* [< Yorkshire dial.; prob. after personal name *Mungo*], the waste of milled wool used with cotton, etc. to make a cheap cloth: cf. **shoddy.**

Mu·nich (mū'nik), *n.* the capital of Bavaria, Germany: pop., 1,034,000: German name, *München.*

Munich Pact (or **Agreement**), a pact signed September 29, 1938, at Munich by Great Britain, France, Italy, and Germany, which provided that Germany was to get the Sudetenland.

mu·nic·i·pal (mū-nis'ə-p'l), *adj.* [L. *municipalis* < *municipium,* a town subject to Rome but governed by its own laws < *municeps,* inhabitant of a free town, free citizen < *munia,* official duties, functions + *capere,* to take], 1. *a)* of or characteristic of a city, town, etc. or its local government. *b)* having self-government locally. 2. of the internal, as distinguished from the international, affairs of a state or nation. Abbreviated **mun.**

mu·nic·i·pal·ism (mū-nis'ə-p'l-iz'm), *n.* 1. self-government by a municipality. 2. the theory that such government should be fostered.

mu·nic·i·pal·ist (mū-nis'ə-p'l-ist), *n.* a supporter of municipalism.

mu·nic·i·pal·i·ty (mū-nis'ə-pal'ə-ti), *n.* [*pl.* MUNICIPALITIES (-tiz)], [Fr. *municipalité* < *municipal;* L. *municipalis;* see MUNICIPAL], 1. a city, town, etc. having its own incorporated government. 2. the officials governing such a community.

mu·nic·i·pal·i·za·tion (mū-nis'ə-p'l-i-zā'shən, mū-nis'ə-p'l-ī-zā'shən), *n.* a municipalizing or being municipalized.

mu·nic·i·pal·ize (mū-nis'ə-p'l-īz'), *v.t.* [MUNICIPALIZED (-īzd'), MUNICIPALIZING], 1. to bring under the control or ownership of a municipality. 2. to make a municipality of.

mu·nif·i·cence (mū-nif'ə-s'ns), *n.* [Fr.; L. *munificentia*], quality, state, or instance of being munificent.

mu·nif·i·cent (mū-nif'ə-s'nt), *adj.* [L. *munificens* < *munificus,* bountiful < *munus,* a gift + *facere,* to make], 1. very generous in giving; lavish. 2. characterized by great generosity: as, a *munificent* reward.

mu·ni·ment (mū'ni-mənt), *n.* [ME. *munimente;* OFr.; L. *munimentum,* a fortification, defense, protection < *munire,* to furnish with walls, fortify], 1. a means of protection or defense. 2. *pl.* in *law,* a document or documents serving as evidence of title to property, etc.

mu·ni·tion (mū-nish'ən), *v.t.* [< *munitions*], to provide with munitions.

mu·ni·tions (mū-nish'ənz), *n.pl.* [Fr. *munition;* L. *munitio,* a fortifying, defending < *munire,* to fortify], military supplies; especially, weapons and ammunition.

Mun·ká·csy, Mi·haly von (mi'häl'y' fôn moon'kä-chi), (born *Michael Lieb*), 1844–1900; Hungarian painter.

mun·nion (mun'yən), *n.* a mullion.

Mun·ro, Hector Hugh (mən-rō'), see **Saki.**

Mun·ster (mun'stẽr), *n.* a province of southwestern Ireland: area, 9,316 sq. mi.; pop., 877,000.

Mün·ster (mün'stẽr; Eng. min'stẽr), *n.* a city in western Germany: pop., 151,000.

munt·jac, munt·jak (munt'jak), *n.* [< Jav. & Malay *mĕnjangan*], any of various small, horned deer of southeastern Asia and the East Indies.

mu·ral (myoor'əl), *adj.* [Fr.; L. *muralis,* of a wall < *murus,* a wall], 1. of, on, in, or for a wall. 2. like a wall. *n.* a picture, especially a large one, painted directly on a wall (or, by extension, on a ceiling).

mu·ral·ist (myoor'əl-ist), *n.* a painter of murals.

Mu·ra·sa·ki, Baroness (mōō'rä-sä'kē), (*Murasaki Shikibu*), 11th-century Japanese writer.

Mu·rat, Jo·a·chim (zhô'à'kēm' mü'rà'; *occas. Anglicized to* mū-rat'), 1767?–1815; marshal of France (1804–1805); king of Naples (1808–1815).

Mur·ci·a (mũr'shi-ə, mũr'shə; Sp. mōōr'thyä), *n.* a city in southeastern Spain: pop., 211,000.

mur·der (mũr'dẽr), *n.* [ME. & AS. *morthor;* akin to Goth. *maurthr;* base as in L. *mors, mortis,* death (cf. MORTAL)], the unlawful and malicious or premeditated killing of one human being by another; also, any killing done while committing some other felony, as rape or robbery: see also **homicide, manslaughter.** *v.t.* 1. to kill (a person) unlawfully and with malice. 2. to kill inhumanly or barbarously, as in warfare. 3. to spoil, mar, etc., as by giving a poor performance: as, she *murdered* that song. *v.i.* to commit murder. —*SYN.* **kill.**

get away with murder, [Slang], to escape detection of or punishment for a blameworthy act.

murder will out, 1. a murder or murderer will always be revealed; hence, 2. any secret or wrongdoing will be revealed sooner or later.

mur·der·er (mũr'dẽr-ẽr), *n.* a person guilty of murder.

mur·der·ess (mũr'dẽr-is), *n.* a woman guilty of murder.

mur·der·ous (mũr'dẽr-əs), *adj.* 1. of, having the nature of, or characteristic of murder; brutal: as, a *murderous* act. 2. capable or guilty of, or intending, murder.

Mu·reş (moo'resh), *n.* a river flowing from the Carpathian Mountains to the Tisza River, through Romania and Hungary: length, 400 mi.: Hungarian name, *Maros.*

mu·rex (myoor'eks), *n.* [*pl.* MURICES (-ə-sēz'), MUREXES (-iz)], [L., the purple fish; akin to Gr. *myax,* sea mussel], any of a group of whelks with rough shells, living in tropical seas: some species secrete a purple dye.

Mur·frees·bor·o (mũr'friz-bũr'ō), *n.* a city in Tennessee: pop., 19,000: site of a battle (1863) in the Civil War.

mu·ri·ate (myoor'i-āt', myoor'i-it), *n.* [Fr. < *muriatique* < L. *muriaticus;* see MURIATIC], [Now Rare], a salt of hydrochloric acid; chloride; especially, potassium chloride, used as a fertilizer.

mu·ri·at·ed (myoor'i-ā'tid), *adj.* [< *muriate* + *-ed*], [Now Rare], containing or treated with hydrochloric acid or a chloride.

mu·ri·at·ic acid (myoor'i-at'ik), [L. *muriaticus,* pickled < *muria,* brine], hydrochloric acid: now only a commercial term.

Mu·ri·el (myoor'i-əl), [prob. < Celt.; cf. Ir. *Muirgheal* < *muir,* the sea + *geal,* bright], a feminine name.

Mu·ril·lo, Bar·to·lo·mé Es·te·ban (bär'tô-lô-me' este'bän mōō-rē'lyô; Eng. myoo-ril'ō), 1617–1682; Spanish painter.

mu·rine (myoor'in, myoor'in), *adj.* [L. *murinus* < *mus, muris,* a mouse; akin to Eng. *mouse*], of the family of rodents including the rats and mice. *n.* a murine rodent.

murk (mũrk), *n.* [ME. *mirke* (chiefly N.) < ON. *myrkr,* dark; akin to AS. *mirce,* dark], darkness; gloom. *adj.* dark or dim. Also spelled **mirk.**

murk·i·ly (mũr'kə-li), *adv.* in a murky manner; darkly.

murk·i·ness (mũr′ki-nis), *n.* murky quality or state.
murk·y (mũr′ki), *adj.* [MURKIER (-ki-ẽr), MURKIEST (-ki-ist)], [ME. (N. dial.) *mirky*], 1. dark or gloomy. 2. heavy and obscure with smoke, mist, etc.: as, the *murky* air. Also spelled **mirky**. —*SYN.* see **dark**.
Mur·man Coast (moor-män′), the coast of the Kola Peninsula, U.S.S.R., on the Arctic Ocean.
Mur·mansk (moor-mänsk′), *n.* 1. a region in the R.S.F.S.R., on the Kola Peninsula: pop., 291,000. 2. its capital, an Arctic seaport: pop., 117,000.
mur·mur (mũr′mẽr), *n.* [OFr.; L., a murmur, roaring sound, muttering; echoic word], 1. a low, indistinct, continuous sound, as of a stream, far-off voices, etc. 2. a mumbled or muttered complaint. 3. in *medicine*, any abnormal sound heard by auscultation of various parts of the body; especially, such a sound in the region of the heart, resulting from lesions of the heart valves. ***v.i.*** 1. to make a murmur. 2. to mumble or mutter a complaint. ***v.t.*** to say in a murmur.
SYN.—**murmur** implies a continuous flow of words or sounds in a low, indistinct voice and may apply to utterances of satisfaction or dissatisfaction (he *murmured* words of love in her ear); **mutter** usually suggests angry or discontented words or sounds of this kind (to *mutter* curses); to **mumble** is to utter almost inaudible or inarticulate sounds in low tones, with the mouth nearly closed (an old woman *mumbling* to herself).
mur·mur·ous (mũr′mẽr-əs), *adj.* characterized by or making a murmur or murmurs.
mur·phy (mũr′fi), *n.* [*pl.* MURPHIES (-fiz)], [< the Irish surname], [Slang], a potato.
Mur·phy, Frank (mũr′fi), 1890–1949; American jurist; associate justice, United States Supreme Court (1940–1949).
mur·rain (mũr′in), *n.* [ME. *moreine;* OFr. *morine* < L. *mori*, to die], 1. any of various infectious diseases of cattle. 2. [Archaic], a pestilence; plague.
Mur·ray (mũr′i), [< the surname *Murray*; ? < Celt.; cf. W. *mor*, the sea], a masculine name.
Mur·ray (mũr′i), *n.* a river in southeastern Australia, flowing into the Indian Ocean: length, 2,310 mi.
Mur·ray, Gilbert (mũr′i), 1866–1957; English classical scholar and statesman.
Murray, Sir **James Augustus Henry,** 1837–1915; English linguist and lexicographer, born in Scotland.
Murray, Lind·ley (lind′li), 1745–1826; English grammarian, born in America.
Murray, Philip, 1886–1952; American labor leader, born in Scotland; president of the C.I.O. (1940–1952).
murre (mũr), *n.* [*pl.* MURRES (mũrz), MURRE; see PLURAL, II, D, 1], [var. of dial. *marrot, morrot, marrock;* prob. of Celt. origin], 1. any bird of the guillemot family. 2. a kind of auk.
murre·let (mũr′lit), *n.* [*murre* + *-let*], any of various small sea birds found chiefly on North Pacific islands.
mur·rey (mũr′i), *n.* [ME. *morreye;* OFr. *moree*, a dark-red color < L. *morum*, a mulberry], a purplish-red color; mulberry. *adj.* of this color.
mur·rhine (mũr′in, mũr′in), *adj.* [L. *murr(h)inus* < *murr(h)a*], of an ancient Roman semiprecious stone, variously believed to be jade, fluorite, etc., used for making vases and drinking cups.
murrhine glass, 1. glassware believed to resemble ancient Roman murrhine cups. 2. a delicate glassware having embedded pieces of colored metal, glass, etc.
Mur·rum·bidg·ee (mũr′um-bij′i), *n.* a river in New South Wales, Australia, flowing westward into the Murray River: length, 1,350 mi.
mur·ther (mũr′*th*ẽr), *n., v.t. & v.i.* [Obs. or Dial.], murder.
mus., 1. museum. 2. music. 3. musical. 4. musician.
mu·sa·ceous (mū-zā′shəs), *adj.* [< Mod. L. *Musaceae*, name of the family < *Musa*, type genus < Ar. *mawzah*, banana; + *-ous*], of the banana family of plants.
Mus. B., Mus. Bac., *Musicae Baccalaureus*, [L.], Bachelor of Music.
Mus·ca (mus′kə), *n.* [L., a fly], a southern constellation, supposedly outlining a fly: see **constellation**, chart.
mus·ca·del (mus′kə-del′), *n.* muscatel.
mus·ca·dine (mus′kə-din, mus′kə-dīn′), *n.* [Eng. formation based on Pr. *muscade*, fem. of *muscat;* see MUSCAT], 1. a variety of grape grown in the southern United States. 2. [Obs.], muscatel (wine).
‡**mus·cae vo·li·tan·tes** (mus′sē vol′i-tan′tēz), [L., flying flies], specks that appear to float before the eyes, caused by defects or impurities in the vitreous humor.
mus·ca·rin (mus′kə-rin), *n.* muscarine.
mus·ca·rine (mus′kə-rin, mus′kə-rēn′), *n.* [< Mod. L. (*Amanita*) *muscaria*, fly (agaric) < L. *muscarius*, of flies < *musca*, a fly], an extremely poisonous alkaloid, $C_8H_{19}O_3N$, found in certain mushrooms, rotten fish, etc.
Mus·cat (mus-kat′), *n.* seaport and capital of Oman, Arabia: pop., 4,200: Arabian name, *Masqat*.
mus·cat (mus′kət, mus′kat), *n.* [Fr.; Pr.; It. *moscato*, musk, wine, lit., having the smell or flavor of musk < LL. *muscus*, musk], 1. a variety of sweet European grape from which muscatel is made. 2. muscatel (wine).
Muscat and Oman, see **Oman**.
mus·ca·tel (mus′kə-tel′), *n.* [ME. *muscadelle;* OFr., dim. of *muscal;* see MUSCAT], 1. a rich, sweet wine made from the muscat. 2. the muscat. Also **muscadel**.
mus·cid (mus′id), *adj.* [< Mod. L. *Muscidae*, name of the family < L. *musca*, a fly], of the family of two-winged insects that includes the common housefly. ***n.*** a muscid insect.
mus·cle (mus′'l), *n.* [Fr.; L. *musculus*, a muscle, lit., little mouse, dim. of *mus*, a mouse], 1. any of the body organs consisting of bundles of fibers that can be contracted and expanded to produce bodily movements. 2. the tissue making up such an organ. 3. muscular strength; brawn. ***v.i.*** [MUSCLED (-'ld), MUSCLING], [Colloq.], to make one's way by sheer strength or force (usually with *in*).
mus·cle-bound (mus′'l-bound′), *adj.* having some of the muscles enlarged and less elastic, as from too much exercise.
muscle sense, that sense by which muscular movement is perceived through stimuli transmitted by nerves whose ends lie in the muscles, tendons, skin, etc.
Muscle Shoals, former rapids in the Tennessee River, northwestern Alabama: now a lake created by Wilson Dam.
mus·co·va·do (mus′kə-vā′dō), *n.* [Sp. *mascabado* or Port. *mascavado*, unrefined, of inferior quality < Sp. *mascabar*, to depreciate, for *menoscabar* < *menos* (L. *minus*) less + *cabo* (L. *caput*), a head], the dark raw sugar that remains after the molasses has been extracted from the juice of the sugar cane.
Mus·co·vite (mus′kə-vīt′), *n.* a native or inhabitant of Muscovy; Russian. *adj.* of Muscovy; Russian.
mus·co·vite (mus′kə-vīt′), *n.* [formerly called Muscovy glass; see -ITE], the common, light-colored mica, $KH_2Al_3(SiO_4)_3$, used as an electrical insulator.
Mus·co·vy (mus′kə-vi), *n.* Russia: the ancient name.
Muscovy duck, [altered < *musk duck*], any of a group of ducks commonly domesticated in tropical America, characterized by a large crest, red wattles and by the fact that it does not quack.
mus·cu·lar (mus′kyoo-lẽr), *adj.* [< L. *musculus* (see MUSCLE); + *-ar*], 1. of, consisting of, or accomplished by a muscle or muscles. 2. having well-developed or prominent muscles; strong; brawny.
muscular dystrophy, a chronic, noncontagious disease characterized by a progressive wasting of the muscles.
mus·cu·lar·i·ty (mus′kyoo-lar′ə-ti), *n.* the quality or condition of being muscular.
mus·cu·la·ture (mus′kyoo-lə-chẽr), *n.* [Fr. < L. *musculus*], the arrangement of the muscles of a body or of some part of the body; muscular system.
mus·cu·lo- (mus′kyoo-lō, mus′kyoo-lə), [< L. *musculus*, muscle], a combining form meaning *muscle* or *the muscles:* also **muscul-**.
Mus. D., Mus. Doc., Mus. Dr., *Musicae Doctor*, [L.], Doctor of Music.
Muse (mūz), *n.* [Fr.; L. *musa;* Gr. *mousa*, a Muse, music, eloquence < IE. base **monthī;* akin to OHG. *mendi*, excitement, joy, OS. *mendian*, to rejoice], 1. in *Greek mythology*, any of the nine goddesses who presided over literature and the arts and sciences; Calliope, Clio, Euterpe, Melpomene, Terpsichore, Erato, Polyhymnia (or Polymnia), Urania, or Thalia; hence, 2. [m-], the spirit regarded as inspiring a poet or other artist; source of genius or inspiration.
muse (mūz), *v.t. & v.i.* [MUSED (mūzd), MUSING], [ME. *musen;* OFr. *muser*, to ponder, loiter, trifle; cf. AMUSE], to think or consider deeply and at length; meditate. ***n.*** a musing; deep meditation. —*SYN.* see **ponder**.
muse·ful (mūz′fəl), *adj.* [*muse* + *-ful*], meditative.
mu·sette (mū-zet′), *n.* [ME.; OFr. < *muser*, to play music; prob. < ML. *musus*, a mouth], 1. formerly, a variety of small French bagpipe. 2. a soft pastoral melody, in imitation of the tunes played on this.
musette bag, in *military usage*, a small bag of canvas or leather for toilet articles, etc., worn suspended from a shoulder strap or strapped to the back.
mu·se·um (mū-zē′əm), *n.* [L.; Gr. *mouseion*, place for the Muses or for study, library < *mousa*, a Muse], a building, room, etc. for preserving and exhibiting artistic, historical, or scientific objects: abbreviated **mus.**
mush (mush), *n.* [var. of *mash* (mixture)], 1. a thick porridge made by boiling meal, especially cornmeal, in water or milk. 2. any thick, soft, yielding mass. 3. [Colloq.], maudlin sentimentality.
mush (mush), ***interj.*** [? altered < Fr. *marche*, imperative of *marcher*, to go, move forward], in Canada and Alaska, a shout commanding sled dogs to start or to go faster. ***v.i.*** to travel on foot over snow, usually with a dog sled. ***n.*** a journey by mushing.
mush·room (mush′room, mush′room), *n.* [ME. *muscheron;* OFr. *mouscheron, mouseron*, mushroom < *mousse*, moss], 1. any of various rapid-growing, fleshy fungi, having a stalk capped with an umbrellalike top; especially, in popular use, any edible variety, as distinguished from the poisonous ones (*toadstools*). 2. anything like a mushroom in shape or rapid growth. ***adj.*** 1. of or made with mushrooms. 2. like a mushroom in shape or rapid, ephemeral growth. ***v.i.*** 1. to grow or spread rapidly. 2. to flatten out at the end so as to resemble a mushroom.

mush·y (mush'i), *adj.* [MUSHIER (-i-ẽr), MUSHIEST (-i-ist)], 1. like mush; thick, soft, and yielding. 2. [Colloq.], sentimental in a maudlin fashion.
mu·sic (mū'zik), *n.* [ME. *musike, musyk;* OFr. *musique;* L. *musica;* Gr. *mousikē* (*technē*), musical (art), orig. an art of the Muses < *mousa*, a Muse], 1. the art and science of combining vocal or instrumental sounds or tones in varying melody, harmony, rhythm, and timbre, especially so as to form structurally complete and emotionally expressive compositions. 2. the sounds or tones so arranged, or the arrangement of these. 3. any rhythmic sequence of pleasing sounds, as of birds, water, etc. 4. *a*) a musical composition; especially, the written or printed score of this. *b*) such compositions collectively: as, the *music* of Brahms. 5. ability to respond to or take pleasure in music: as, he has no *music* in his soul. 6. [Rare or Obs.], a group of musical performers. Abbreviated **mus.**
face the music, [orig. with reference to a performer's overcoming stage fright], [Colloq.], to accept the consequences, however unpleasant.
set to music, to compose music for (a poem, etc.).
mu·si·cal (mū'zi-k'l), *adj.* [ME. *musycal;* ML. *musicalis* < L. *musica*], 1. of or for the creation, production, or performance of music. 2. having the nature of music; melodious or harmonious. 3. fond of, sensitive to, or skilled in music. 4. set to music; accompanied by music: as, a *musical* comedy. *n.* 1. a musical comedy. 2. [Colloq.], a musicale. Abbreviated **mus.**
musical comedy, a theatrical production consisting of musical numbers, dances, and humorous or satirical skits, centered upon some slight plot and usually having elaborate costuming and staging.
mu·si·cale (mū'zi-kal'), *n.* [Fr.], a party or social affair featuring a musical program.
music box, a mechanical musical instrument consisting of a case containing a bar with tuned steel teeth that are struck by pins so arranged on a revolving cylinder as to produce a certain tune or tunes.
music hall, 1. an auditorium for musical or theatrical productions. 2. [British], a vaudeville theater.
mu·si·cian (mū-zish'ən), *n.* [ME. & Late OFr. *musicien*], a person skilled in music; especially, a professional performer of music: abbreviated **mus.**
music of the spheres, an ethereal music supposed by Pythagoras and other early mathematicians to be produced by the movements of the heavenly bodies.
mu·si·col·o·gist (mū'zi-kol'ə-jist), *n.* an expert in musicology.
mu·si·col·o·gy (mū'zi-kol'ə-ji), *n.* the systematized study of the science, history, forms, and methods of music.
music stand, a rack to hold sheets of music for a performer.
mus·ing (mūz'iŋ), *adj.* that muses; meditative; reflective. *n.* meditation; reflection; contemplation.
mus·jid (mus'jid), *n.* a masjid.
musk (musk), *n.* [ME.; OFr. *musc;* LL. *muscus;* Gr. *moschos;* Ar. *mushk, musk*, musk; Sans. *mushka*, testicle, dim. of *mus*, a mouse], 1. a substance with a strong, penetrating odor, obtained from a small sac (*musk bag*) under the skin of the abdomen in the male musk deer: used as the basis of numerous perfumes. 2. a similar substance secreted by certain other animals. 3. the odor of any of these substances, now often created synthetically. 4. the musk deer.
mus·kal·longe (mus'kə-lonj'), *n.* [*pl.* MUSKALLONGE], a muskellunge.
mus·kal·lunge (mus'kə-lunj'), *n.* [*pl.* MUSKALLUNGE], a muskellunge.
musk deer, any of a group of small, hornless deer of central Asia: the male secretes musk.
musk duck, 1. any of a group of Australian ducks with an inflatable leathery pouch beneath the lower jaw, spikelike tail feathers, and a musklike odor during the breeding season. 2. the Muscovy duck.
mus·keg (mus'keg), *n.* [< Am. Ind. (Ojibway) native name], a kind of bog or marsh formed by the deposit of thick layers of decaying vegetable matter, mosses, etc. in a depression or hollow in the earth's surface.
Mus·ke·gon (mus-kē'gən), *n.* a city in Michigan, on Lake Michigan: pop., 46,000.
mus·kel·lunge (mus'kə-lunj'), *n.* [*pl.* MUSKELLUNGE], [Algonquian *maskinonge; mas*, great + *kinonge*, a pike (fish)], any of a group of very large pike of the Great Lakes and Mississippi Valley, valued as a game and food fish: also **maskalonge, maskanonge,** etc.
mus·ket (mus'kit), *n.* [Fr. *mousquet* < OFr. *mousket, moschet;* It. *moschetto*, musket, orig. sparrow hawk (cf. FALCONET) < L. *musca*, a fly], a smooth-bore, long-barreled hand firearm, used especially by infantry soldiers before the invention of the rifle.
mus·ket·eer (mus'kə-têr'), *n.* [Fr. *mousquetaire*], formerly, a soldier armed with a musket; cf. **mousquetaire.**
mus·ket·ry (mus'kit-ri), *n.* [Fr. *mousqueterie*], 1. the art or practice of firing muskets or other small arms. 2. *a*) muskets collectively. *b*) musketeers collectively.
Mus·kho·ge·an (mus-kō'gi-ən, mus'kō-gē'ən), *adj.* designating or of a linguistic stock of North American Indians of the southeastern United States, including the Creek, Chickasaw, Choctaw, and Seminole tribes.
musk·mel·on (musk'mel'ən), *n.* [*musk* + *melon*], 1. any of several round or oblong fruits of the melon family, as the cantaloupe, with a thick rind and sweet, juicy flesh. 2. the trailing plant on which it grows.
Mus·ko·gee (mus-kō'gi), *n.* a city in eastern Oklahoma: pop., 38,000.
musk ox, any of a group of hardy oxen of arctic America and Greenland, with a long, coarse, hairy coat, large, curved horns, and a musklike odor.
musk·rat (musk'rat'), *n.* [*pl.* MUSKRATS (-rats'), MUSKRAT; see PLURAL, II, D, 1], 1. a North American rodent living in water and having a glossy brown fur, a long tail, and a musklike odor. 2. its fur.
musk rose, a Mediterranean rose with fragrant flowers, usually white.

MUSKRAT (20 in. long)

musk·y (mus'ki), *adj.* [MUSKIER (-ki-ẽr), MUSKIEST (-ki-ist)], of, like, or smelling of musk.
Mus·lem, Mus·lim (muz'ləm), *n.* & *adj.* Moslem.
mus·lin (muz'lin), *n.* [Fr. *mousseline;* It. *mussolino* < *mussolo*, muslin < *Mussolo* (< Ar. *Mosul*), Mosul, city in Iraq, where it was made], any of various fine cotton cloths of plain weave, often dyed or printed; especially, a heavy variety used for sheets, pillowcases, etc.
muslin delaine, delaine.
Mus. M., *Musicae Magister*, [L.], Master of Music.
mus·quash (mus'kwäsh), *n.* [*pl.* MUSQUASHES (-iz), MUSQUASH; see PLURAL, II, D, 1], [< Am. Ind. (Algonquian); cf. Abnaki *muskwessu*, it is red], a muskrat.
muss (mus), *n.* [prob. var. of *mess*], [Colloq. or Dial.], 1. a mess; disorder. 2. a squabble; row; commotion. *v.t.* [Colloq. or Dial.], to make messy (often with *up*).
mus·sel (mus''l), *n.* [ME. *muscle;* AS. *mus(c)le;* LL. *muscula* < L. *musculus*, mussel, muscle, orig. dim. of *mus*, a mouse], any of various bivalve mollusks; specifically, *a*) a salt-water variety used as food. *b*) a fresh-water variety whose shell is made into buttons, etc.
Mus·set, Al·fred de (ål'fred' də mü'se'), (*Louis Charles Alfred de Musset*), 1810–1857; French poet, dramatist, and novelist.
Mus·so·li·ni, Be·ni·to (be-nē'tô mōōs'sô-lē'nē; Eng. mōōs'ə-lē'ni, mus'ə-lē'ni), 1883–1945; Italian dictator; Fascist prime minister of Italy (1922–1943); executed.
Mussorgski, Modest Petrovich, see **Moussorgsky.**
Mus·sul·man (mus''l-mən), *n.* [*pl.* MUSSULMANS (-mənz)], [Turk. & Per. *musulmān*, a Moslem < Ar. *muslim, moslim*, Moslem], a Moslem.
muss·y (mus'i), *adj.* [MUSSIER (-i-ẽr), MUSSIEST (-i-ist)], [Colloq.], messy; disordered, untidy, rumpled, etc.
must (must), *v.aux.* [*p.t.* MUST], [ME. *moste*, p.t., had to; AS. *moste*, p.t. of *motan*, may], an auxiliary used with the infinitive of various verbs (without *to*) to express: 1. *compulsion, obligation, requirement*, or *necessity:* as, I *must* pay her. 2. *probability:* as, then you *must* be my cousin. 3. *certainty* or *inevitability:* as, it *must* have rained while we were in. *Must* is sometimes used elliptically, the verb being understood: as, I *must* forth, shoot if you *must*. *n.* something that must be done, had, read, seen, etc.: as, this book is a *must*. *adj.* that must be done, etc.; necessary; essential.
must (must), *n.* [Hind. *mast*, intoxicated < Per. *mast*], 1. a state of frenzy in animals, especially in the male elephant, usually associated with sexual heat. 2. an elephant in this state. *adj.* in must. Also spelled **musth.**
must (must), *n.* [ME.; AS.; L. *mustum*, new wine, neut. of *mustus*, new, fresh], the juice pressed from grapes or other fruit before it has fermented; new wine.
must (must), *n.* [back-formation < *musty*], mustiness.
mus·tache (məs-tash', mus'tash), *n.* [Fr. *moustache;* It. *mostacchio, mustacchio*, mustache; Gr. *mystax*, upper lip, mustache < *mastax*, a mouth, jaws], 1. the hair on the upper lip of men: sometimes used in the plural in reference to the two halves of the upper lip. 2. the hair or bristles growing about the mouth in some animals. Also spelled **moustache.**
mus·ta·chio (məs-tä'shō), *n.* [*pl.* MUSTACHIOS (-shōz)], [< Sp. *mostacho* or It. *mostaccio*], a mustache.
Mustafa Kemal, see **Kemal Ataturk.**
Mus·tagh (mōōs-täkh'), *n.* Karakoram, a mountain range in India.
mus·tang (mus'taŋ), *n.* [Sp. *mesteño*, earlier *mestengo*, belonging to the graziers, wild < *mesta*, company of graziers, orig. a group < L. *mixtus*, a mingling, orig. pp. of *miscere*, to mix], a small wild or half-wild horse of the southwestern plains of the United States.

mus·tard (mus′tẽrd), *n.* [ME. *mustarde;* OFr. *moustarde;* Pr. & It. *mostarda,* mustard < L. *mustum,* must: because orig. made with a little must mixed in it], 1. any of several plants with yellow flowers and slender pods containing round seeds. 2. the ground or powdered seeds of this plant, often prepared as a paste, used as a pungent seasoning for foods or as a counterirritant in medicine. 3. the color of ground mustard, a dark yellow.

mustard gas, [from its odor, like that of ground mustard], an oily, volatile liquid, $(CH_2ClCH_2)_2S$, used in warfare as a poison gas because of its extremely irritating, blistering, and disabling effects.

mustard oil, an oil extracted from mustard seed, used in making soap.

mustard plaster, a paste made with powdered mustard, spread on a cloth and applied to the skin as a counterirritant and rubefacient.

mus·tee (mus-tē′, mus′tē), *n.* [altered < *mestizo*], 1. the offspring of a white and a quadroon; octoroon. 2. any person of mixed ancestry.

mus·te·line (mus′tə-līn′, mus′tə-lin), *adj.* [L. *mustelinus* < *mustela,* a weasel; akin to *mus,* a mouse], designating or of a large group of fur-bearing mammals, including the weasel, marten, polecat, mink, wolverine, etc.

mus·ter (mus′tẽr), *v.t.* [ME. *mousteren;* OFr. *moustrer, mostrer, monstrer,* to exhibit, show; L. *monstrare,* to show < *monere,* to warn, admonish], 1. to assemble or summon (troops, etc.), as for inspection, roll call, or service. 2. to gather together and display; collect; summon (often with *up*): as, he *mustered* up strength. *v.i.* to come together or gather; specifically, to assemble as for inspection or roll call: said of troops, etc. *n.* 1. a gathering together or assembling, especially of troops for inspection, roll call, service, etc. 2. the persons or things assembled; assemblage. 3. the sum or total of persons or things assembled. 4. the roll, or list, of men in a military or naval unit: also **muster roll.** —*SYN.* see **gather.**

muster in (or **out**), to enlist in (or discharge from) military service.

pass muster, to measure up to the required standard.

musth (must), *n. & adj.* must (frenzy).

mus·ti·ly (mus′t'l-i), *adv.* in a musty manner.

mus·ti·ness (mus′ti-nis), *n.* a musty quality or state.

must·n't (mus′'nt), must not.

mus·ty (mus′ti), *adj.* [MUSTIER (-ti-ẽr), MUSTIEST (-ti-ist)], [prob. < earlier *moisty* < *moist*], 1. having a stale, moldy smell or taste, as an unused room, food kept in a damp place, etc.; hence, 2. stale or trite; antiquated: as, *musty* scholarship. 3. dull; apathetic. —*SYN.* see **stinking.**

mut., 1. mutilated. 2. mutual.

mu·ta·bil·i·ty (mū′tə-bil′ə-ti), *n.* [L. *mutabilitas*], the quality or state of being mutable.

mu·ta·ble (mū′tə-b'l), *adj.* [ME.; L. *mutabilis,* changeable < *mutare,* to change], 1. that can be changed. 2. tending to frequent change; inconstant; fickle.

mu·ta·bly (mū′tə-bli), *adv.* in a mutable manner.

mu·tant (mū′tənt), *adj.* [< L. *mutans,* ppr. of *mutare,* to mutate], undergoing mutation, or changing. *n.* an animal or plant with inheritable characteristics that differ from those of the parents; sport.

mu·tate (mū′tāt), *v.i. & v.t.* [MUTATED (-id), MUTATING], [< L. *mutatus,* pp. of *mutare,* to change], to change; specifically, to undergo or cause to undergo mutation.

mu·ta·tion (mū-tā′shən), *n.* [ME. *mutacioun;* L. *mutatio* < *mutare,* to change], 1. a changing or being changed. 2. a change, as in form, nature, qualities, etc. 3. in *biology, a*) a sudden variation in some inheritable characteristic of an individual animal or plant, as distinguished from a variation resulting from generations of gradual change. *b*) an individual resulting from such variation; mutant. 4. in *linguistics,* umlaut.

‡**mu·ta·tis mu·tan·dis** (mū-tā′tis mū-tan′dis), [L.], the necessary changes having been made.

mu·ta·tive (mū′tə-tiv), *adj.* [ML. *mutativus;* cf. OFr. *mutatif*], of, tending to, or characterized by mutation.

mutch·kin (much′kin), *n.* [< obs. D. *mudseken,* a measure of capacity], [Scot.], a measure of liquid volume, equal to a little less than a pint.

mute (mūt), *adj.* [ME. *muet* (via OFr.) < LL. **mutettus,* dim. of L. *mutus,* dumb, silent; sp. Latinized in 16th c.], 1. not speaking; voluntarily silent: often used figuratively. 2. unable to speak; dumb. 3. in *law,* refusing to plead when arraigned: used especially in *stand mute,* to refuse to plead guilty or not guilty. 4. in *linguistics, a*) not pronounced; silent, as the *e* in *mouse. b*) pronounced with a complete temporary stoppage of the breath, as the sounds of *p* or *k:* in this sense now generally replaced by *stopped. n.* 1. a person who does not speak; specifically, one who cannot speak because deaf; deaf-mute. 2. [Obs.], a hired mourner at a funeral. 3. in *law,* a defendant who refuses to plead when arraigned. 4. in *linguistics, a*) a silent letter. *b*) a consonant, as *p* or *k,* formed by a complete temporary stoppage of the breath; stop. 5. in *music,* any of various devices used to soften or muffle the tone of an instrument, as a pear-shaped block placed within the bell of a brass instrument. *v.t.* [MUTED (-id), MUTING], to soften or muffle the sound of (a musical instrument, etc.), as with a mute. —*SYN.* see **voiceless.**

mu·ti·late (mū′t'l-āt′), *v.t.* [MUTILATED (-id), MUTILATING], [< L. *mutilatus,* pp. of *mutilare,* to maim, mutilate < *mutilus,* maimed], 1. to cut off or damage a limb or other important part of (a person or animal). 2. to damage, injure, or otherwise make imperfect, especially by removing an essential part or parts: as, the censors *mutilated* his speech. —*SYN.* see **maim.**

mu·ti·la·tion (mū′t'l-ā′shən), *n.* 1. a mutilating or being mutilated. 2. the injury resulting from this.

mu·ti·la·tive (mū′t'l-ā′tiv), *adj.* that mutilates or tends to mutilate.

mu·ti·la·tor (mū′t'l-ā′tẽr), *n.* a person or thing that mutilates.

mu·ti·neer (mū′t'n-êr′), *n.* [Fr. *mutinier* < *mutin;* see MUTINY], a person guilty of mutiny.

mu·ti·nous (mū′t'n-əs), *adj.* 1. of, engaged in, or inclined to mutiny. 2. like or characteristic of mutiny.

mu·ti·ny (mū′t'n-i), *n.* [*pl.* MUTINIES (-iz)], [< earlier *mutine* < Fr. *mutiner,* to rebel < OFr. *mutin, meutin,* mutinous, riotous < *meute,* a revolt < LL. **movita,* movement < L. *movere, motus,* to move], revolt against and, often, forcible resistance to constituted authority; especially, rebellion of soldiers or sailors against their officers. *v.i.* [MUTINIED (-id), MUTINYING], to participate in a mutiny; revolt against constituted authority. —*SYN.* see **rebellion.**

mut·ism (mūt′iz'm), *n.* [Fr. *mutisme*], the condition of being mute, especially, in *psychiatry,* as the result of psychic, rather than organic, disorders.

Mu·tsu·hi·to (mōō′tsōō-hē′tô), *n.* emperor of Japan (1867–1912); lived 1852–1912.

mutt (mut), *n.* [? contr. of *mutton-head*], [Slang], 1. a stupid person; blockhead. 2. a mongrel dog; cur.

mut·ter (mut′ẽr), *v.i.* [ME. *materen;* of freq. echoic formation; akin to G. *muttern*], 1. to speak in low, indistinct tones without much movement of the lips, as in complaining or in speaking to oneself; hence, 2. to complain or grumble. 3. to make a low, rumbling, threatening sound, as thunder. *v.t.* to say in low, indistinct, often angry or discontented, tones. *n.* 1. a muttering. 2. something muttered; especially, a complaint or grumble. —*SYN.* see **murmur.**

mut·ton (mut′'n), *n.* [ME. *moton, mouton;* OFr. *molton, moton* (Fr. *mouton*), a ram; ML. *multo,* sheep; prob. of Celt. origin; cf. W. *mollt,* Ir. *molt*], 1. the flesh of sheep used as food; especially, the flesh of grown sheep, as distinguished from lamb. 2. [Rare], a sheep.

mutton chop, 1. a piece cut from the rib of a sheep for broiling or frying. 2. *pl.* side whiskers shaped like mutton chops (i.e., narrow at the top, and broad and rounded at the bottom), with a clean-shaven chin separating the two whiskers; burnsides.

mut·ton-head (mut′'n-hed′), *n.* [Slang], a stupid person; blockhead.

mut·ton·y (mut′'n-i), *adj.* like mutton in taste, smell, etc.

Mut·tra (mut′rə), *n.* a city in western Uttar Pradesh, India: pop., 117,000: it is said to be the birthplace of Krishna.

mu·tu·al (mū′chōō-əl), *adj.* [Fr. *mutuel;* LL. *mutualis* < L. *mutuus,* mutual, reciprocal < *mutare,* to change, exchange], 1. *a*) done, felt, etc. by each of two or more for or toward the other or others; reciprocal: as, *mutual* hate. *b*) of, or having the same relationship toward, each other or one another: as, *mutual* enemies. 2. shared in common; joint: as, our *mutual* friend. 3. designating or of a type of insurance in which the policyholders elect their own directors, share in the profits, and agree to indemnify one another against loss. Abbreviated **mut.**

SYN.—**mutual** may be used of an interchange of feeling between two persons (John and Joe are *mutual* enemies) or may imply a sharing jointly with others (the *mutual* efforts of a group); **reciprocal** implies a return in kind or degree by each of two sides of what is given or demonstrated by the other (a *reciprocal* trade agreement), or it may refer to any inversely corresponding relationship (the *reciprocal* functions of two machine parts); **common** simply implies a being shared by others or by all the members of a group (our *common* interests).

mutual fund, an investment fund that issues on a continuous basis shares that can be redeemed at any time at their underlying asset value: also called *open-end investment fund.*

mu·tu·al·ism (mū′chōō-əl-iz'm), *n.* in *biology,* symbiosis with mutual advantage to both or all organisms involved.

mu·tu·al·i·ty (mū′chōō-al′ə-ti), *n.* [*pl.* MUTUALITIES (-tiz)], the quality or condition of being mutual.

mu·tu·al·ize (mū′chōō-əl-īz′), *v.t. & v.i.* [MUTUALIZED (-īzd′), MUTUALIZING], 1. to make or become mutual. 2. to organize or reorganize (a corporation) so that a majority of shares are held by the employees or customers.

mutual savings bank, a savings bank that has no capital, its depositors sharing in the profits.

mu·tule (mū′chōōl), *n.* [Fr.; L. *mutulus*], in *architecture,* a flat block projecting beneath, and supporting, the corona of a Doric cornice.

‡**mu·zhik, muz·jik** (mōō-zhēk′, mōō′zhik), *n.* [Russ.], in czarist Russia, a peasant: also spelled **moujik, mujik.**

muz·zle (muz′'l), *n.* [ME. *mosel;* OFr. *musel, museau,* muzzle, snout; ML. *musellum,* dim. of *musus*], 1. the projecting part of the head of a dog, horse, etc., including the mouth, nose, and jaws; snout. 2. a device, as of wire or straps, fastened over the mouth of an animal to prevent its biting or eating. 3. the front end of the barrel of a firearm. *v.t.* [MUZZLED (-'ld), MUZZLING], 1. to put a muzzle on (an animal). 2. to prevent from talking or expressing an opinion; gag.

muz·zle-load·er (muz′'l-lōd′ẽr), *n.* any firearm loaded through the muzzle.

muzzle velocity, the velocity of a projectile as it leaves the muzzle of a firearm: expressed in feet per second, with reference to the firearm.

muz·zy (muz′i), *adj.* [MUZZIER (-i-ẽr), MUZZIEST (-i-ist)], [prob. formed after *muse, bemuse,* etc.], [Colloq.], confused; befuddled.

Mv, in *chemistry,* mendelevium.

m.v., 1. market value. 2. mean variation.

MVD, M.V.D., [first letters of Russ. *Ministerstvo Vnutrennikh Del,* ministry of internal affairs], the state security police, or secret service, of the Soviet Union: a renaming in 1946 of the NKVD, which had succeeded the Gay-Pay-Oo in 1934.

Mwe·ru (mwā′rōō), *n.* a lake between Northern Rhodesia and the Belgian Congo: length, 68 mi.

my (mī), *pron.* [ME. *mi,* shortened form of *min* used before consonants; AS. *min,* of me, my, mine; cf. MINE, ME], possessive form of **I.** ***possessive pronominal adj.*** of, belonging to, or done by me: also used before some formal titles of address: as, *my* lord, *my* dear Mr. Brown. ***interj.*** an exclamation of surprise, dismay, etc. (often preceded by *oh*).

my- (mī), myo-.

my·al·gi·a (mī-al′ji-ə), *n.* [*my-* + *-algia*], pain in a muscle or muscles.

my·as·the·ni·a (mī′as-thē′ni-ə), *n.* [*my-* + *asthenia*], an abnormal condition characterized chiefly by muscular weakness or fatigue.

my·ce·li·al (mī-sē′li-əl), *adj.* of, or having the nature of, mycelium.

my·ce·li·an (mī-sē′li-ən), *adj.* mycelial.

my·ce·li·oid (mī-sē′li-oid′), *adj.* mycelial.

my·ce·li·um (mī-sē′li-əm), *n.* [Mod. L. (after *epithelium*) < Gr. *mykēs,* a mushroom], the thallus, or vegetative part, of a fungus, made of threadlike tubes.

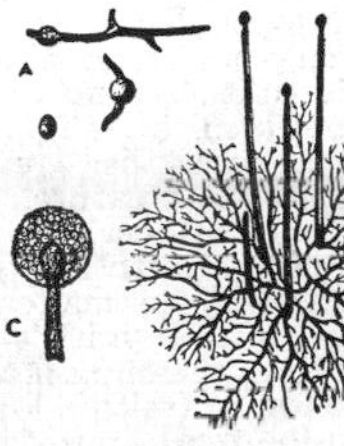

my·ce·loid (mī′sə-loid′), *adj.* mycelial.

My·ce·nae (mī-sē′nē), *n.* an ancient Greek city in the northeastern Peloponnesus.

My·ce·nae·an (mī′si-nē′ən), *adj.* 1. of Mycenae. 2. designating or of the civilization which existed in Greece, Crete, Asia Minor, etc. from 1500 to 1100 B.C.

MYCELIUM

A, germination of a spore; B, mycelium; C, cross section of a spore

-my·cete (mī-sēt′), [< *-my-cetes*], a combining form meaning *one of a* (specified) *group of fungi,* as *schizomycete.*

-my·ce·tes (mī-sē′tēz), [Mod. L. < Gr. *mykētes,* pl. of *mykēs,* a mushroom], a combining form used in forming the names of large groups of fungi.

my·ce·to·zo·an (mī-sē′tə-zō′ən), *adj.* myxomycetous.

my·co- (mī′kō, mī′kə), [< Gr. *mykēs,* fungus], a combining form meaning *fungus,* as in *mycology:* also, before a vowel, **myc-.**

my·co·bac·te·ri·um (mī′kō-bak-têr′i-əm), *n.* [*pl.* MYCOBACTERIA (-ə)], [Mod. L.; see MYCO- & BACTERIA], any of a group of rod-shaped, Gram-positive bacteria, including those causing tuberculosis and leprosy.

my·co·log·i·cal (mī′kə-loj′i-k'l), *adj.* of mycology.

my·col·o·gy (mī-kol′ə-ji), *n.* [*myco-* + *-logy*], 1. the branch of botany dealing with fungi. 2. all the fungi native to a specific region.

my·co·sis (mī-kō′sis), *n.* [*pl.* MYCOSES (-sēz)], [*myc-* + *-osis*], 1. the growth of parasitic fungi in any part of the body. 2. a disease caused by such fungi.

my·cot·ic (mī-kot′ik), *adj.* of or caused by a mycosis.

my·dri·a·sis (mi-drī′ə-sis, mī-drī′ə-sis), *n.* [L.; Gr.], prolonged or excessive dilatation of the pupil of the eye, as the result of disease or the administration of a drug.

myd·ri·at·ic (mid′ri-at′ik), *adj.* of or causing mydriasis. *n.* any drug causing mydriasis.

myel-, myelo-.

my·e·len·ceph·a·lon (mī′ə-len-sef′ə-lon′), *n.* [*myel-* + *encephalon*], the posterior part of the hindbrain; afterbrain.

my·e·lin (mī′ə-lin), *n.* [G. < Gr. *myelos,* marrow], the white, fatty substance forming a sheath about certain nerve fibers.

my·e·line (mī′ə-lēn′, mī′ə-lin), *n.* myelin.

my·e·li·tis (mī′ə-lī′tis), *n.* [*myel-* + *-itis*], inflammation of the spinal cord or the bone marrow.

my·e·lo- (mī′ə-lō), [< Gr. *myelos,* marrow], a combining form meaning *the marrow* or *the spinal cord:* also, before a vowel, **myel-.**

my·e·loid (mī′ə-loid′), *adj.* [*myel-* + *-oid*], 1. of the spinal cord. 2. of, like, or derived from bone marrow.

my·na, my·nah (mī′nə), *n.* [Hind. *mainā*], any of a group of tropical birds of southeastern Asia related to the starling; especially, such a bird of India that has the ability to mimic human speech and is often kept as a pet: also spelled **mina.**

Myn·heer (mīn-hâr′, mīn-hêr′), *n.* [D. *mijn heer,* lit., my lord], 1. Sir; Mr.: a Dutch title of address; hence, 2. [m-], [Colloq.], a Dutchman.

my·o- (mī′ō, mī′ə), [< Gr. *mys, myos,* a muscle], a combining form meaning *muscle,* as in *myograph:* also, before a vowel, **my-.**

my·o·car·di·o·graph (mī′ō-kär′di-ə-graf′, mī′ō-kär′di-ə-gräf′), *n.* [*myo-* + *cardiograph*], an instrument for recording the movements of the heart muscle.

my·o·car·di·tis (mī′ō-kär-dī′tis), *n.* [Mod. L.; see -ITIS], inflammation of the myocardium.

my·o·car·di·um (mī′ō-kär′di-əm), *n.* [Mod. L.; see MYO- & CARDIO-], the muscular substance of the heart.

my·o·ge·net·ic (mī′ō-jə-net′ik), *adj.* [*myo-* + *genetic*], originating in or produced by a muscle or muscle tissue.

my·o·graph (mī′ə-graf′, mī′ə-gräf′), *n.* [*myo-* + *-graph*], an instrument for recording muscular contractions.

my·ol·o·gy (mī-ol′ə-ji), *n.* [Mod. L. *myologia;* see MYO- & -LOGY], the branch of anatomy dealing with the muscles.

my·o·ma (mī-ō′mə), *n.* [*pl.* MYOMATA (-mə-tə), MYOMAS (-məz)], [Mod. L.; see MY- & -OMA], any tumor consisting of muscular tissue.

my·om·a·tous (mī-om′ə-təs), *adj.* of, or having the nature of, a myoma.

my·op·ath·y (mī-op′ə-thi), *n.* [*myo-* + *-pathy*], any disease of a muscle.

my·ope (mī′ōp), *n.* [Fr.; LL. *myops,* Gr. *myōps,* short-sighted, blinking < *myein,* to close + *ōps,* an eye], a person having myopia; nearsighted person.

my·o·pi·a (mī-ō′pi-ə), *n.* [Mod. L. < LL. *myops;* see MYOPE], an abnormal eye condition in which light rays from distant objects are focused in front of the retina instead of on it, so that the objects are not seen distinctly; nearsightedness.

my·op·ic (mī-op′ik), *adj.* of or having myopia; nearsighted.

my·o·py (mī′ə-pi), *n.* [Fr. *myopie*], myopia.

my·o·sin (mī′ə-sin), *n.* [< Gr. *mys, myos,* a muscle; + *-in*], a soluble protein resembling globulin, present in the tissue of the contractile muscles: its coagulation into an insoluble fibrin is believed to be the cause of rigor mortis.

my·o·sis (mī-ō′sis), *n.* [< Gr. *myein,* to close; + *-osis*], prolonged or excessive contraction of the pupil of the eye, resulting from disease or the use of a drug.

my·o·sote (mī′ə-sōt′), *n.* a myosotis.

my·o·so·tis (mī′ə-sō′tis), *n.* [Mod. L. *Myosotis,* name of the genus; Gr. *myosōtis,* lit., mouse ear < *mys, myos,* a mouse + *ōtos,* genit. of *ous,* an ear], any of a large group of plants, including the forget-me-not, with light-green leaves and white, blue, or pink flowers.

my·ot·ic (mī-ot′ik), *adj.* of, causing, or having myosis. *n.* any drug causing myosis.

My·ra (mī′rə), [? < Ir. *Moira, Moyra*], a feminine name.

My·ra (mī′rə) *n.* a city in ancient Lycia, Asia Minor.

myr·i·a- (mir′i-ə), [< Gr. *myrias;* cf. MYRIAD], a combining form meaning: 1. *many, numerous,* as in *myriapod.* 2. in the *metric system, ten thousand,* as in *myriameter.*

myr·i·ad (mir′i-əd), *n.* [< Gr. *myrias, myriados,* the number ten thousand < *myrios,* countless], 1. ten thousand; hence, 2. any indefinitely large number. 3. a large number of persons or things. *adj.* of an indefinitely large number; countless.

myr·i·a·pod (mir′i-ə-pod′), *adj.* [Mod. L.; see MYRIA- & -POD], having many legs; specifically, of or belonging to a large group of arthropods having long bodies consisting of many segments, each of which bears one or more pairs of jointed legs, as the millipedes and centipedes. *n.* any animal of this group.

myr·i·ap·o·dan (mir′i-ap′ə-dən), *adj.* & *n.* myriapod.

myr·i·ap·o·dous (mir′i-ap′ə-dəs), *adj.* myriapod.

myr·me·co- (mũr′mi-kō, mũr′mi-kə), a combining form meaning *ant,* as in *myrmecology.*

myr·me·co·log·i·cal (mũr′mi-kə-loj′i-k'l), *adj.* of myrmecology.

myr·me·col·o·gy (mũr′mi-kol′ə-ji), *n.* [*myrmeco-* + *-logy*], the branch of entomology dealing with ants.

myr·me·coph·a·gous (mũr'mi-kof'ə-gəs), *adj.* [< Gr. *myrmēx, myrmēkos*, ant (akin to Eng. *-mire*, in *pismire*); + *-phagous*], feeding on ants.

Myr·mi·don (mũr'mi-don', mũr'mi-dən), *n.* [*pl.* MYRMIDONS (-donz', -dənz), MYRMIDONES (mẽr-mid'ə-nēz')], [ME. *mirmidones* < L. *Myrmidones*, pl.; Gr. *Myrmidones*, the Myrmidons], 1. any of a tribe of Thessalian warriors who, according to Greek legend, fought under Achilles, their king, in the Trojan War. 2. [m-], an unquestioning follower or subordinate.

my·rob·a·lan (mī-rob'ə-lən, mi-rob'ə-lən), *n.* [Fr.; L. *myrobalanum;* Gr. *myrobalanon* < *myron*, plant juice (for base cf. SMEAR) + *balanos*, a nut], any of the dried, astringent, prunelike fruits of various tropical trees, containing tannin and used for dyeing and tanning.

My·ron (mī'rən), [? < Gr. *myron*, an ointment, perfume], a masculine name. *n.* Greek sculptor; 5th century B.C.

myrrh (mũr), *n.* [ME. *mirre;* AS. *myrre* & OFr. *mirre;* both < L. *myrrha, murrha, murra;* Gr. *myrrha;* Ar. *murr*, myrrh, bitter; cf. Heb. *mōr*, myrrh], 1. a fragrant, bitter-tasting gum resin exuded from any of several shrubs of Arabia and eastern Africa, used in making incense, perfume, etc. 2. any of these shrubs.

myr·ta·ceous (mũr-tā'shəs), *adj.* [< Mod. L. *Myrtaceae*, name of the family < L. *myrtus* (Gr. *myrtos*); + *-ous*], designating, of, or like a group of trees and shrubs, the myrtle family, including the myrtle, eucalyptus, and various spice-bearing trees, as the clove and allspice.

Myr·tle (mũr't'l), [< *myrtle*, shrub], a feminine name.

myr·tle (mũr't'l), *n.* [ME. & OFr. *myrtille;* ML. *myrtillus*, dim. < L. *myrtus;* Gr. *myrtos*, myrtle], 1. any of a group of shrubs with evergreen leaves, white or pinkish flowers, and dark, fragrant berries: in ancient times, it was held sacred to Venus. 2. any of various other plants; especially, the periwinkle.

my·self (mī-self', mə-self'), *pron.* [ME. *meself, miself;* AS. *me sylf;* see ME & SELF], a form of the first person singular pronoun, used: *a*) as an intensive: as, I went *myself*. *b*) as a reflexive: as, I hurt *myself*. *c*) as a quasi-noun meaning "my real, true, or actual self" (e.g., I am not *myself* when I rage like that): in this construction *my* may be considered a possessive pronominal adjective and *self* a noun, and they may be separated: as, *my* own sweet *self*.

My·si·a (mish'i-ə), *n.* an ancient country in northwestern Asia Minor.

My·sore (mī-sôr', mī-sōr'), *n.* a state of southern India: area, 74,210 sq. mi.; pop., 23,586,000; capital, Bangalore.

mys·ta·gog·ic (mis'tə-goj'ik), *adj.* of a mystagogue or mystagogy.

mys·ta·gogue (mis'tə-gôg', mis'tə-gog'), *n.* [Fr.; L. *mystagogus* < Gr. *mystagōgos* < *mystēs*, one initiated in mysteries + *agōgos*, leader], a person who interprets religious mysteries or initiates others into them.

mys·ta·go·gy (mis'tə-gō'ji), *n.* the teachings or doctrines of a mystagogue.

mys·te·ri·ous (mis-têr'i-əs), *adj.* [< L. *mysterium*], of, containing, implying, or characterized by mystery. *SYN.*—**mysterious** is applied to that which excites curiosity, wonder, etc. but is impossible or difficult to explain or solve (a *mysterious* murder); that is **inscrutable** which is completely mysterious and is altogether incapable of being searched out, interpreted, or understood (the *inscrutable* ways of God); **mystical** applies to that which is occult or esoteric in connection with religious rites or spiritual experience.

mys·ter·y (mis'tẽr-i, mis'tri), *n.* [*pl.* MYSTERIES (-iz, -triz)], [ME. *mysterye;* L. *mysterium;* Gr. *mystērion*, secret worship of a deity, secret thing < *mystēs*, one initiated into the mysteries < *myein*, to initiate into the mysteries < *myein*, to shut the eyes], 1. something unexplained, unknown, or kept secret: as, the *mystery* of life. 2. *a*) any thing or event that remains so secret or obscure as to excite curiosity: as, a murder *mystery*. *b*) a novel, story, or play involving such an event. 3. the quality of being inexplicable; obscurity or secrecy: as, an air of *mystery* surrounds this affair. 4. *pl.* secret rites or doctrines known only to a small, esoteric group; specifically, in ancient Greece, religious ceremonies or doctrines revealed only to the initiated. 5. *pl.* any of the ancient cults characterized by such ceremonies: as, the Eleusinian *mysteries*. 6. [? influenced by *mystery*, a craft], a mystery play. 7. in *Christianity*, *a*) the Mass. *b*) a sacrament; especially, the Eucharist. *c*) any of fifteen events in the lives of Jesus and Mary serving as a subject for meditation during the saying of the rosary. 8. in *theology*, any assumed truth that cannot be comprehended by the human mind but must be accepted on faith.
SYN.—**mystery** is applied to something beyond human knowledge or understanding, or it merely refers to any unexplained or seemingly inexplicable matter; **enigma** specifically applies to that whose meaning is hidden by cryptic or ambiguous allusions, and generally, to anything very difficult to explain; a **riddle** is an enigma (usually in the form of a question in guessing games) that involves paradoxes; a **puzzle** is a situation, problem, or, often, a contrivance, that requires some ingenuity to solve or explain; **conundrum** is specifically applied to a riddle whose answer is a pun, and generally, to any puzzling question or problem.

mys·ter·y (mis'tẽr-i), *n.* [*pl.* MYSTERIES (-iz)], [ME. *misterie, mysterie*, a trade, craft; ML. *misterium* < L. *ministerium*, office, occupation, by confusion with *mysterium* (cf. prec. entry)], [Archaic], a craft or trade.

mystery play, any of a class of medieval dramatic representations of Biblical events, especially of the life and death of Jesus: they originated in the church liturgy but were later presented by craft guilds on improvised platforms or wagons in market places, etc.: cf. **miracle play, morality play.**

mys·tic (mis'tik), *adj.* [ME. *mistik;* L. *mysticus;* Gr. *mystikos*, belonging to secret rites < *mystēs*, one initiated], 1. of mysteries, or esoteric rites or doctrines. 2. of mystics or mysticism. 3. of obscure or occult character or meaning: as, *mystic* powers. 4. beyond human comprehension; mysterious or enigmatic. 5. [Rare], mystical (sense 1). *n.* 1. a person initiated into esoteric mysteries. 2. a believer in mysticism; specifically, one who professes to undergo mystical experiences by which he intuitively comprehends truths beyond human understanding.

mys·tic·al (mis'ti-k'l), *adj.* 1. spiritually significant or symbolic; allegorical: as, the *mystical* rose, a symbol of the Virgin Mary. 2. mystic (senses 2 & 3). 3. [Rare], mysterious; enigmatic. —*SYN.* see **mysterious.**

mys·ti·cism (mis'tə-siz'm), *n.* [*mystic* + *-ism*], 1. the doctrines or beliefs of mystics; specifically, the doctrine that it is possible to achieve communion with God through contemplation and love without the medium of human reason. 2. any doctrine that asserts the possibility of attaining knowledge of spiritual truths through intuition acquired by fixed meditation. 3. vague or obscure thinking or belief.

mys·ti·fi·ca·tion (mis'tə-fi-kā'shən), *n.* [Fr.], a mystifying or being mystified.

mys·ti·fy (mis'tə-fī'), *v.t.* [MYSTIFIED (-fīd'), MYSTIFYING], [Fr. *mystifier* < *mystique*, mystic], 1. to puzzle or perplex; especially, to bewilder deliberately; play on the credulity of; hoax. 2. to involve in mystery, or obscurity; make obscure or hard to understand.

mys·tique (mis-tēk'), *n.* [Fr., mystic], a complex of quasi-mystical attitudes and feelings surrounding some person, institution, activity, etc.

myth (mith), *n.* [LL. *mythos;* Gr. *mythos*, a word, speech, story, legend], 1. a traditional story of unknown authorship, ostensibly with a historical basis, but serving usually to explain some phenomenon of nature, the origin of man, or the customs, institutions, religious rites, etc. of a people: myths usually involve the exploits of gods and heroes: cf. **legend.** 2. such stories collectively; mythology. 3. any fictitious story. 4. any imaginary person or thing spoken of as though existing.

myth·ic (mith'ik), *adj.* mythical.

myth·i·cal (mith'i-k'l), *adj.* 1. of, or having the nature of, a myth or myths. 2. existing only in a myth or myths: as, a *mythical* creature. 3. imaginary or fictitious. —*SYN.* see **fictitious.**

myth·i·cize (mith'i-sīz'), *v.i.* [MYTHICIZED (-sīzd'), MYTHICIZING], to make into, or explain as, a myth.

myth·o- (mith'ō, mith'ə), [< Gr. *mythos*, myth], a combining form meaning *myth*, as in *mythology*.

myth·o·log·ic (mith'ə-loj'ik), *adj.* mythological.

myth·o·log·i·cal (mith'ə-loj'i-k'l), *adj.* of mythology: abbreviated **myth., mythol.**

my·thol·o·gist (mi-thol'ə-jist), *n.* 1. an expert in mythology. 2. a writer or compiler of myths.

my·thol·o·gize (mi-thol'ə-jīz'), *v.i.* [MYTHOLOGIZED (-jīzd'), MYTHOLOGIZING], [Fr. *mythologiser*], to relate, explain, classify, or write about myths. *v.t.* to mythicize.

my·thol·o·gy (mi-thol'ə-ji), *n.* [*pl.* MYTHOLOGIES (-jiz)], [ME. *methologie;* LL. *mythologia;* Gr. *mythologia*, a telling of tales or legends < *mythos*, myth + *-logia* < *legein*, to speak], 1. the science or study of myths. 2. a book of or about myths. 3. myths collectively; especially, all the myths of a specific people or about a specific being. Abbreviated **myth., mythol.**

myth·o·ma·ni·a (mith'ə-mā'ni-ə), *n.* [Mod. L. < *mytho-* + *-mania*], in *psychiatry*, an abnormal tendency to lie or exaggerate.

myth·o·poe·ic, myth·o·pe·ic (mith'ə-pē'ik), *adj.* [< Gr. *mythopoios* (< *mythos*, myth + *poiein*, to make); + *-ic*], of, or engaged in, the making of myths.

Myt·i·le·ne, Myt·i·le·ni (mit'ə-lē'nē), *n.* a Greek island in the Aegean, off the coast of Asia Minor: area, 675 sq. mi.; pop., 140,000; ancient name, *Lesbos*.

myx·e·de·ma, myx·oe·de·ma (mik'si-dē'mə), *n.* [Mod. L.; see MYXO- & EDEMA], a disease caused by a decreased functioning of the thyroid gland and characterized by a drying and thickening of the skin and a slowing down of physical and mental activity.

myx·o- (mik'sō, mik'sə), [< Gr. *myxa*, mucus], a combining form meaning *slime* or *mucus*, as in *myxomycete:* also, before a vowel, **myx-.**

myx·o·my·cete (mik'sō-mī-sēt'), *n.* [*myxo-* + *-mycete*], any of a class of primitive organisms, the slime molds, consisting of masses of naked protoplasm and having some characteristics of both plants and animals, but generally classified as plants (fungi).

myx·o·my·ce·tous (mik'sō-mī-sē'təs), *adj.* [*myxo-* + *-mycetous*], designating or of the class of myxomycetes.

N

N, n (en), *n.* [*pl.* N's, n's, Ns, ns (enz)], 1. the fourteenth letter of the English alphabet: from the Greek *nu*, a borrowing from the Phoenician: see **alphabet,** table. 2. the sound of N or n: normally, in English, it is a voiced tongue-apex nasal continuant. 3. a type or impression for N or n. 4. *a symbol for* the fourteenth (or the thirteenth if J is omitted) in a sequence or group. 5. in *printing*, an en (half an em). *adj.* 1. of N or n. 2. fourteenth (or thirteenth if J is omitted) in a sequence or group.
N (en), *n.* 1. an object shaped like N. 2. a Roman numeral for 90: with a superior bar ($\overline{N}$), 90,000. 3. in *chemistry, the symbol for* nitrogen. *adj.* shaped like N.
n (en), *n.* 1. in *mathematics, the symbol for* an indefinite number: see **nth.** 2. in *physics, the symbol for* neutron.
N., 1. National. 2. Nationalist. 3. Norse. 4. November.
N., n., 1. nail. 2. name. 3. *natus,* [L.], born. 4. navy. 5. neuter. 6. new. 7. nominative. 8. noon. 9. northern. 10. noun. 11. in *chemistry*, normal.
N, N., n, n., North.
n., 1. nephew. 2. net. 3. note. 4. number.
na (nä, nə), *adv.* [cf. AS. *ne,* not & *a,* ever], [Chiefly Scot.], 1. no. 2. not: usually with auxiliary verbs, as, *wouldna.* Also **nae. conj.** [Chiefly Scot.], nor.
Na, *natrium,* [L.], in *chemistry,* sodium.
n/a, in *banking,* no account.
N.A., 1. National Academician. 2. National Academy. 3. National Army. 4. North America.
N.A.A.C.P., NAACP, National Association for the Advancement of Colored People.
nab (nab), *v.t.* [NABBED (nabd), NABBING], [< thieves' slang (16th-17th c.); prob. var. of dial. *nap,* to snatch < ON.; cf. earlier Dan. *nappe,* Sw. *nappa,* to snatch], [Colloq.], 1. to snatch or seize suddenly. 2. to arrest or catch (a felon or wrongdoer) —*SYN.* see **catch.**
na·bob (nā′bob), *n.* [Hind. *navvāb, navāb;* Ar. *nuwwāb,* pl. of *nā'ib,* deputy, viceroy], 1. a native provincial deputy or governor of the old Mogul Empire in India; native district ruler in India. 2. a European who has become rich in India; hence, 3. a very rich man.
na·bob·ish (nā′bob-ish), *adj.* of or like a nabob.
Na·both (nā′both, nā′bōth), *n.* [Heb. *nābhōth*], in the *Bible,* the owner of a vineyard: Jezebel had him killed so that Ahab could seize the vineyard: I Kings 21.
NACA, N.A.C.A., National Advisory Committee for Aeronautics.
na·celle (nə-sel′), *n.* [Fr.; LL. *navicella,* dim. of *navis,* a ship], 1. an enclosed part in an airplane, dirigible, or other aircraft, for housing the engine, cargo, etc. or sheltering passengers. 2. the basket or car suspended from a balloon.
na·cre (nā′kẽr), *n.* [Fr.; It. *nacchera;* Ar. *naqqārah,* small kettledrum], 1. a shellfish yielding mother-of-pearl. 2. mother-of-pearl.
na·cred (nā′kẽrd), *adj.* 1. covered or lined with nacre. 2. nacreous.
na·cre·ous (nā′kri-əs), *adj.* 1. of or like nacre. 2. yielding nacre. 3. iridescent; lustrous.
Na-Dene (nə-dēn′), *n.* a family of American Indian languages, including Athapascan, Tlingit, and Haida.
Na·dine (nə-dēn′, nā-dēn′), [Fr. < Russ. *nadezhda,* hope], a feminine name.
na·dir (nā′dẽr, nā′dêr), *n.* [ME.; OFr.; Ar. *naẓīr,* in *naẓīr as-samt,* lit., opposite to the zenith; *naẓīr,* opposite + *as-samt,* zenith], 1. that point of the celestial sphere directly opposite to the zenith; point directly beneath the observer. 2. the lowest point; time of greatest depression or dejection: as, the *nadir* of human progress.
nae (nā), *adj. & adv.* [Scot.], 1. no. 2. not. Also **na.**
nae·thing (nā′thiŋ), *n. & adv.* [Scot.], nothing.
nae·void (nē′void), *adj.* nevoid.
nae·vus (nē′vəs), *n.* [*pl.* NAEVI (-vī)], a nevus.
nag (nag), *v.t.* [NAGGED (nagd), NAGGING], [of Scand. origin; cf. Sw. *nagga,* Dan. *nage* (earlier *nagge*), to nibble, gnaw, fret, etc.; prob. akin to AS. *gnagan* (cf. GNAW); for sense development cf. FRET, *v.*], to annoy by continual scolding, faultfinding, complaining, urging, etc. *v.i.* to urge, scold, find fault, etc. constantly. *n.* 1. the act of nagging. 2. [Colloq.], a person who nags, particularly a woman.
nag (nag), *n.* [ME. *nagge, nagghe;* akin to obs. D. *negghe* (D. *negge, neg*); ? < *nag, v.,* with reference to gnawing the bridle; or ? akin to *neigh*], 1. a small saddle horse; pony; sometimes, any horse. 2. a mediocre or poor horse.
na·ga·na (nə-gä′nə), *n.* [< Zulu *u(lu)-nakane*], an infectious disease affecting horses and cattle in South Africa: it is caused by the bite of infected tsetse flies.
Na·ga·sa·ki (nä′gä-sä′kē), *n.* a seaport on the western coast of Kyushu, Japan: pop., 253,000 (1940), c. 175,000 (1946): on August 9, 1945 it was largely destroyed by an atomic bomb dropped by American airmen: cf. **Hiroshima.**
nag·ger (nag′ẽr), *n.* a person who nags.
nag·gy (nag′i), *adj.* [NAGGIER (-i-ẽr), NAGGIEST (-i-ist)], nagging.
Na·go·ya (nä′gô-yä′), *n.* a city in southern Honshu, Japan: pop., 1,328,000 (1940); 700,000 (est. 1946).
Nag·pur (näg′poor), *n.* the capital of Central Provinces, India: pop., 302,000.
Na·gy·vá·rad (näd′y′-vä′räd), *n.* Oradea, a city in Romania: the Hungarian name.
Na·hua (nä′wä), *n.* a member of the various North and Central American Indian tribes of the Nahuatl linguistic group, including the Aztecs, Toltecs, etc.
Na·hua·tl (nä′wä-t'l), *n.* a group of Uto-Aztecan languages, spoken by various tribes of North and Central American Indians. *adj.* Nahuatlan.
Na·hua·tlan (nä-wät′län), *adj.* of the Nahuatl group of languages. *n.* Nahuatl.
Na·hum (nā′əm, nā′hum), *n.* [Heb. *naḥūm,* lit., comfort], in the *Bible,* 1. a Hebrew prophet of the 7th century B.C. 2. a book of the Old Testament containing his prophecies. Abbreviated **Nah.**
nai·ad (nā′ad, nī′ad), *n.* [*pl.* NAIADS (-adz), NAIADES (-ə-dēz′)], [Fr. *naiade;* L. *Naias, Naiadis;* Gr. *Naïas* (pl. *Naïades*) < *naein,* to flow], 1. in *Greek & Roman mythology,* any of the nymphs who lived in and gave life to springs, fountains, rivers, and lakes. 2. a girl or woman swimmer.
na·if, na·ïf (nä-ēf′), *adj.* [Fr.; see NAIVE], naive.
nail (nāl), *n.* [ME. *naile, neil;* AS. *nægl;* akin to G. *nagel;* IE. base **onogh* (**ongh-, *nogh-,* etc.), nail, seen also in L. *unguis,* fingernail, *ungula,* claw, hoof (cf. UNGULATE), etc.], 1. the thin, horny plate at the ends of the fingers and toes of man, monkeys, etc.; claw of a bird or animal. 2. a tapered piece of metal or wood, commonly pointed and having a flattened head, driven with a hammer, and used for holding pieces of wood together, as a peg, or for decoration. 3. an old cloth measure, equal to 2 1/4 inches. Abbreviated **N., n.** 4. [Slang], a cigarette: short for *coffin nail.* *v.t.* 1. to attach or fasten together or onto something else with nails; hence, 2. to fasten as if with nails: as, he *nailed* a tent flap to the ground with a bayonet. 3. to secure, hold, or fasten shut with nails; hence, 4. to secure; make sure: as, he *nailed* the bargain. 5. to fix (the eyes, attention, etc.) steadily on an object. 6. to discover or expose, as a lie. 7. [Colloq.], to catch, capture, or seize. 8. [Colloq.], to intercept and detain: as, *nail* him before he leaves.
hit the nail on the head, to do or say whatever is exactly right.
nail up, 1. to fasten to a wall or at some height. 2. to fasten tightly with nails, as a door no longer used.
on the nail, [Colloq.], 1. immediately. 2. at the exact spot or time.
nail·brush (nāl′brush′), *n.* a small, stiff brush for cleaning the fingernails.
nail file, a small file for trimming the fingernails.
nail·set (nāl′set′), *n.* a tool for sinking the head of a nail so that it is level with, or below, the surface of the wood: also **nail set.**

nain·sook (nān′sook, nan′sook), *n.* [Hind. *nainsukh; nain,* the eye + *sukh,* pleasure], a thin, plain-woven, lightweight cotton, sometimes striped.

Nairn (nârn), *n.* 1. Nairnshire. 2. its county seat: pop., 4,700.

Nairn·shire (nârn′shir), *n.* a county of northern Scotland: pop., 8,300; county seat, Nairn.

Nai·ro·bi (nī-rō′bi), *n.* the capital of Kenya, Africa: pop., 289,000.

na·ïve, na·ive (nä-ēv′), *adj.* [Fr., fem. of *naïf* < L. *nativus,* natural, native], unaffectedly or, sometimes, foolishly simple; childlike; artless; unsophisticated.

SYN.—**naive** implies a genuine, innocent simplicity or lack of artificiality but sometimes connotes an almost foolish lack of worldly wisdom (his *naive* belief in the kindness of others); **ingenuous** implies a frankness or straightforwardness that suggests the simplicity of a child (her *ingenuous* smile at my discomfiture); **artless** suggests a lack of artificiality or guile that derives from indifference to the effect one has upon others (her *artless* beauty); **unsophisticated,** like **naive,** implies a lack of worldly wisdom but connotes that this is the result merely of a lack of experience (an *unsophisticated* freshman).—*ANT.* sophisticated, artful.

na·ïve·té, na·ive·te (nä-ēv′tā′, nä-ēv′tā), *n.* [Fr.], 1. the quality or state of being naive; simplicity; artlessness. 2. a naive action or remark.

na·ive·ty (nä-ēv′ti), *n.* [*pl.* NAIVETIES (-tiz)], naïveté.

na·ked (nā′kid), *adj.* [ME.; AS. *nacod, næcad,* etc.; akin to G. *nackt* (OHG. *nakot*); IE. base **nogw-,* naked, seen also in L. *nudus* (< **nogwodhos* or **nogwedhos*); cf. NUDE], 1. *a*) completely unclothed; bare; nude. *b*) uncovered; exposed: said of parts of the body. 2. lacking clothing, means of support, etc.; destitute. 3. without protection or defense. 4. without conventional or usual covering; specifically, *a*) out of its sheath: as, a *naked* sword. *b*) without leaves, grass, vegetation, etc. *c*) without furnishing, decoration, etc.: as, a *naked* wall. 5. without additions, ornaments, disguises, or embellishments; plain; stark: as, the *naked* truth. 6. in *law,* without objective support; lacking a necessary condition; invalid: as, a *naked* contract. 7. in *zoology,* without hair, scales, feathers, shell, etc. —*SYN.* see **bare.**

naked eye, the unaided eye; eye without the help of any optical device.

Na·khi·che·van Autonomous Soviet Socialist Republic (nä-khē′che-vän′), a division of the Azerbaijan S.S.R., in the Transcaucasus: area, 2,277 sq. mi.; pop., 142,000; capital, Nakhichevan.

Nam (näm), *n.* the Menam, a river in Thailand.

N.A.M., NAM, National Association of Manufacturers.

Na·ma (nä′mä), *n.* [< the native name], 1. the chief tribe of the Hottentots. 2. a Hottentot. 3. the language of the Hottentots: it belongs to the Hottentot-Bushman family and is characterized by the use of initial click sounds and three speech tones.

nam·a·ble (nām′ə-b'l), *adj.* 1. that can be named. 2. worthy of being mentioned; notable. Also spelled **nameable.**

Na·ma Land (nä′mä), Namaqua Land.

Na·man·gan (nä-män-gän′), *n.* a city in the northwestern Uzbek S.S.R.: pop., 122,000.

Na·ma·qua Land (nä-mä′kwə), a region in South West Africa, occupied by Hottentots: also **Nama Land, Great Namaqua Land.**

nam·ay·cush (nam′i-kush′, nam′ā-kush′), *n.* [Algonquian (Cree) *namekus,* trout; dim. of *namew,* a fish], a large, light-spotted lake trout, found from Maine to Vancouver and north to Alaska: also called *Mackinaw trout, Great Lakes trout, lake trout.*

nam·by-pam·by (nam′bi-pam′bi), *adj.* [< nickname of *Ambrose Philips,* 18th-c. Eng. poet: so called in ridicule of his sentimental pastorals], weakly sentimental; wishy-washy; without vigor; insipidly pretty or nice. *n.* [*pl.* NAMBY-PAMBIES (-biz)], 1. namby-pamby talk or writing. 2. a namby-pamby person.

name (nām), *n.* [ME. *name, naam;* AS. *nama;* akin to G. *name;* IE. base **enomen-, *nōmen-,* name, seen also in L. *nomen* (cf. NOMINAL, NOMENCLATURE), Gr. *onoma* (cf. ONOMATOPOEIA)], 1. a word or phrase by which a person, thing, or class of things is known, called, or spoken to or of; appellation; title: abbreviated N., n. 2. a word or words expressing some quality considered characteristic or descriptive of a person or thing; epithet: as, they called him *names.* 3. *a*) fame, reputation, or character: as, a good *name.* *b*) good reputation. 4. a family or clan: as, the last of my *name.* 5. reputation or appearance only, not reality; semblance: as, chief in *name* only. 6. a distinguished or noted person: as, the greatest *name* in science. 7. in *logic,* a designation for a concept; term. *adj.* having a good reputation; well-known. *v.t.* [NAMED (nāmd), NAMING], 1. to give a name or title to (anything); entitle; style. 2. to designate, mention, or refer to (a person or object) by name. 3. to identify by the right name: as, he *named* the States of the Union. 4. to nominate or appoint (a person) to a post, situation, or office. 5. to set or fix; specify (a date, price, etc.). 6. to speak about; mention.

call names, to mention in an abusive manner; swear at.

in the name of, 1. in appeal or reference to. 2. by the authority of; as the representative of.

know only by name, to be familiar with the name of but not know personally.

to one's name, belonging to one; owned by one.

name·a·ble (nām′ə-b'l), *adj.* namable.

name day, 1. the feast day of the saint after whom a person is named. 2. day of baptism.

name-drop·per (nām′drop′ẽr), *n.* a person who seeks to impress others by frequently mentioning famous or important persons in a familiar way.

name·less (nām′lis), *adj.* 1. not having a name. 2. left unnamed; anonymous: as, a rogue who shall be *nameless.* 3. not publicly known; obscure. 4. lacking a legal name; illegitimate. 5. that cannot be named; indescribable: as, *nameless* dread. 6. unfit for mention: as, *nameless* practices.

name·ly (nām′li), *adv.* [ME. *nameliche, nameli;* see NAME & -LY], that is to say; specifically; to wit.

name·sake (nām′sāk′), *n.* [earlier *name's sake*], a person with the same name as another; especially, a person named after another.

Na·mur (nȧ′mür′; Eng. nä-moor′, nā′moor), *n.* 1. a province of southern Belgium. 2. its capital, on the Meuse River: pop., 33,000.

Nan·chang (nän′chäŋ′), *n.* the capital of Kiangsi province, China: pop., 267,000.

Nan·cy (nän′sē′; Eng. nan′si), *n.* a city in northeastern France: pop., 125,000.

Nan·cy (nan′si), [prob. by faulty division of *mine + Ancy,* dim. form of ME. *Annis,* Agnes, confused with *Anne;* cf. ANNA], a feminine name.

Nan·da De·vi, Mount (nun′dä dā′vē), a mountain of the Himalayas, in Uttar Pradesh, India: height, 25,645 ft.

Nan·ga Par·bat, Mount (nuŋ′gä pũr′but), a mountain of the Himalayas, in northern India: height, 26,620 ft.

nan·keen, nan·kin (nan-kēn′), *n.* [< *Nankin(g),* China, where first made], 1. a buff-colored, durable cotton cloth, originally from China. 2. buff (color). 3. *pl.* trousers made of this cloth.

Nan·kin (nan′kin′), *n.* Nanking.

Nan·king (nan′kiŋ′; Chin. nän′kiŋ′), *n.* a city in southeastern China, on the Yangtze River: former capital: pop., 1,092,000.

Nan Ling (nän′liŋ′), Nan Shan.

Nan·nette (nan-et′), a feminine name: see **Anna.**

Nan·ning (nän′niŋ′; Eng. nan′niŋ′), *n.* the capital of Kwangsi province, China: pop., 203,000.

nan·ny (nan′i), *n.* [*pl.* NANNIES (-iz)], [< *Nan,* dim. of *Ann(a)*], [British], a child's nurse.

nanny goat, [see prec.], [Colloq.], a female goat.

Nan·sen, Fridt·jof (frit′yof nän′sən; Eng. nan′s'n), 1861–1930; Norwegian arctic explorer, naturalist, writer, and statesman.

Nan Shan (nän′ shän′), a mountain range in northern Chinghai and southern Kansu provinces, China.

Nantes (nänt; Eng. nants), *n.* a city in western France, on the Loire: pop., 223,000.

Nantes, Edict of, a decree issued in 1598 by Henry IV of France, giving political equality to the Huguenots: it was revoked in 1685.

Nan·tuck·et (nan-tuk′it), *n.* an island and summer resort off Massachusetts: area, 51 sq. mi.

Na·o·mi (nā-ō′mi, na-ō′mi, nā′ə-mī′), [Heb. *nā'omī,* lit., my delight], a feminine name. *n.* in the *Bible,* the mother-in-law of Ruth: Ruth 1.

na·os (nā′os), *n.* [Mod. L.; Gr. *naos*], 1. a temple. 2. the inner part of a temple; cella.

nap (nap), *v.i.* [NAPPED (napt), NAPPING], [ME. *nappen;* AS. *hnappian, hnæppian;* akin to OHG. *hnaffezan,* to sleep; IE. base **qenebh-* < **qen-,* to rub, scratch, pinch (cf. NAB, NAP, *n.*); prob. basic sense "to close the eyes"], 1. to doze or sleep lightly for a short time; hence, 2. to be off one's guard: as, he was caught *napping.* *n.* a brief, light sleep; doze.

nap (nap), *n.* [ME. *noppe;* AS. *-cnoppa;* cf. MD. & MLG. *noppe* (G. *noppe*), Dan. *nappe;* IE. base as in prec.], 1. the downy or hairy surface of cloth formed by short hairs or fibers, especially when artificially raised by brushing, etc.; pile of velvet, etc. 2. the downy surface of some plants. 3. the short, downy fibers on a new wool rug which come off in early sweepings, as contrasted with the pile, which does not brush off. *v.t.* [NAPPED (napt), NAPPING], 1. to place or raise nap on (fabric) by brushing, etc. 2. to smooth or trim (cloth) by shearing the nap or pile.

nap (nap), *n.* napoleon (senses 1 & 2).

na·palm (nā′päm), *n.* [< *na*phthenic and *palm*itic acids, whose aluminum salts are used in its manufacture], jellied gasoline used in flame throwers and bombs.

nape (nāp, nap), *n.* [ME. *naape, nape;* prob. specialized sense < AS. *cnæp,* summit, fibula (with reference to the spinal projection) or *hnæpp,* a bowl (with reference to the hollow)], the back of the neck.

na·per·y (nā′pẽr-i), *n.* [ME. *naprye;* OFr. *naperie* < *nappe;* see NAPKIN], household linen; especially, table linen; napkins, doilies, etc.

Naph·ta·li (naf′tə-lī′), *n.* [Heb. < *hipotēl,* to wrestle:

see Gen. 30:7], in the *Bible*, 1. a son of Jacob: Gen. 30:7, 8. 2. that one of the twelve tribes of Israel which was named after him: Numb. 1:15, 43.

naph·tha (naf′thə, nap′thə), *n.* [L.; Gr. *naphtha*, naphtha, bitumen < Per. *naft;* cf. Aram. *napṭā* < Assyr. *napṭu*, petroleum], 1. an inflammable, volatile, oily liquid produced by the fractional distillation of petroleum: it is the fraction that boils at 80°–110° C. and is used as a fuel, solvent, and illuminant. 2. petroleum. 3. any of several inflammable, volatile liquids produced by the distillation of coal tar, wood, coal, and other carbonaceous materials.

naph·tha·lene (naf′thə-lēn′, nap′thə-lēn′), *n.* [*naphtha* + *al*cohol + *-ene*], a white, crystalline, aromatic hydrocarbon, $C_{10}H_8$, produced in the fractional distillation of coal tar: it is used in moth repellents and in the manufacture of certain dyes and other organic compounds: also **naphthalin, naphthaline.**

naph·thal·ic (naf-thal′ik, nap-thal′ik), *adj.* of or derived from naphthalene.

naph·tha·lin (naf′thə-lin, nap′thə-lin), *n.* naphthalene.

naph·tha·line (naf′thə-lēn′, nap′thə-lēn′), *n.* naphthalene.

naph·thol (naf′thōl, naf′thol, nap′thôl), *n.* [*naphth*alene + *-ol* (-ole)], either of two white, crystalline isomeric compounds, $C_{10}H_7OH$, derived from naphthalene and used as antiseptics and in the manufacture of dyes.

naph·thous (naf′thəs, nap′thəs), *adj.* of or like naphtha.

naph·tol (naf′tōl, nap′tol), *n.* naphthol.

Na·pi·er, Sir **Charles James** (nā′pi-ẽr, nə-pêr′), 1782–1853; British general.

Napier, John, 1550–1617; Scottish mathematician; inventor of logarithms.

na·pi·form (nā′pi-fôrm′), *adj.* [< L. *napus*, turnip; + *-form*], large and round at the top, tapering sharply below; turnip-shaped: said of roots.

nap·kin (nap′kin), *n.* [ME. *nap(p)ekyn(n)*, dim. (via MD.) < OFr. *nap(p)e*, cloth, tablecloth < L. *mappa*, cloth, napkin; cf. MAP], 1. a small piece of cloth or paper, usually square, used at table for protecting the clothes and wiping the fingers or lips; serviette. 2. a small towel. 3. [Chiefly British], a baby's diaper. 4. see **sanitary napkin.** 5. [Obs. exc. Scot.], a pocket handkerchief.

Na·ples (nā′p'lz), *n.* a city in Italy, on the Bay of Naples: pop., 970,000 (est. 1947): Italian name, *Napoli.*

Naples, Bay of, an inlet of the Tyrrhenian Sea, on the southwestern coast of Italy.

na·po·le·on (nə-pō′li-ən, nə-pōl′yən), *n.* [after *Napoleon*], 1. a former gold coin of France, equivalent to 20 francs, with a portrait of Napoleon I (or III) on it. 2. *a)* a card game. *b)* a bid in this game by which a player agrees to take all five tricks. Often shortened to **nap.** 3. a French pastry with a cream filling.

Na·po·le·on I (nə-pō′li-ən, nə-pōl′yən), (*Napoléon Bonaparte*), 1769–1821; emperor of the French (1804–1815); extended French Empire by military victories; defeated at Waterloo (1815): called the *Little Corporal.*

Napoleon II, (*François Charles Joseph Bonaparte, duc de Reichstadt*), 1811–1832; son of Napoleon I; titular emperor of France.

Napoleon III, see **Louis Napoleon.**

Na·po·le·on·ic (nə-pō′li-on′ik), *adj.* of, characteristic of, or like Napoleon I, his campaigns, period, etc.

Na·po·li (nä′pô-lē′), *n.* Naples: the Italian name.

nap·per (nap′ẽr), *n.* a person who naps or is in the habit of taking naps.

nap·per (nap′ẽr), *n.* an instrument or machine for putting a nap on cloth.

nap·py, nap·pie (nap′i), *n.* [*pl.* NAPPIES (-iz)], [prob. dim. of ME. *hnap, nap*, a bowl; AS. *hnæp(p); cf.* NAPE], a shallow, flat-bottomed, rounded dish with sloping sides, used for serving or cooking food.

nap·py (nap′i), *adj.* having or covered with nap; hairy or downy.

nap·py (nap′i), *adj.* [prob. < *nappy* (hairy, downy)], 1. foaming; heady; strong: said of ale. 2. slightly intoxicated. *n.* [Scot.], ale.

na·pra·path (nap′rə-path′), *n.* a person who practices naprapathy.

na·prap·a·thy (nə-prap′ə-thi), *n.* [< Czech *naprava*, correction; + *-pathy*], a system of treatment based on the theory that disease symptoms are due to strained or contracted ligaments and disorders of the connective tissue and can be cured by massage.

Nar·bad·a (nur-bud′ä), *n.* a river in central India, flowing westward into the Arabian Sea: length, 800 mi.: also **Nerbudda.**

nar·ce·in (när′si-in), *n.* narceine.

nar·ce·ine (när′si-ēn′, när′si-in), *n.* [Fr. *narcéine* < Gr. *narkē*, numbness, stupor; + *-ine*], a bitter, white, crystalline alkaloid, $C_{22}H_{27}O_8N$, obtained from opium: it is a narcotic.

nar·cism (när′siz'm), *n.* narcissism.

nar·cis·sism (när-sis′iz'm), *n.* [G. *Narzissismus;* see NARCISSUS & -ISM], 1. self-love; excessive interest in one's own appearance, comfort, importance, abilities, etc. 2. in *psychoanalysis*, arrest at or regression to the first stage of sexual development, in which the self is an object of sexual pleasure.

nar·cis·sist (när-sis′ist), *n.* a person characterized by narcissism.

nar·cis·sis·tic (när′sə-sis′tik), *adj.* of or characterized by narcissism.

Nar·cis·sus (när-sis′əs), *n.* [L.; Gr. *Narkissos*], 1. in *Greek mythology*, a beautiful youth for unrequited love of whom Echo died: Nemesis in punishment caused him to pine away for love of his own reflection in a spring and changed him into the narcissus. 2. [n-], [*pl.* NARCISSUSES (-iz), NARCISSI (-ī)], [L.; Gr. *narkissos* < *narkē*, stupor: in reference to the sedative effect], any of a number of related bulb plants with smooth leaves and clusters of white, yellow, or orange flowers.

nar·cist (när′sist), *n.* a narcissist.

nar·co·lep·sy (när′kə-lep′si), *n.* [< Gr. *narkē* (see NARCOTIC); + *-lepsy*], a condition of frequent and uncontrollable desire for sleep; paroxysmal sleep.

nar·co·lep·tic (när′kə-lep′tik), *adj.* of or having narcolepsy.

nar·co·ma·ni·a (när′kə-mā′ni-ə), *n.* [Mod. L. < Gr. *narkē* (see NARCOTIC); + *-mania*], 1. an abnormal craving to gain relief from pain through the use of drugs. 2. mental derangement resulting from the excessive use of alcohol.

nar·co·sis (när-kō′sis), *n.* [Mod. L.; Gr. *narkōsis*], a condition of deep unconsciousness caused by a narcotic.

nar·co·syn·the·sis (när′kō-sin′thə-sis), *n.* [< Gr. *narkē* (see NARCOTIC); + *synthesis*], a method of treating a neurosis by working with a patient while he is under the influence of a narcotic, as pentothal sodium.

nar·cot·ic (när-kot′ik), *adj.* [ME. *narcotike;* OFr. *narcotique;* Gr. *narkōtikos* < *narkoun*, to benumb < *narkē*, numbness, stupor; IE. base *(*s*)*narq-*, to turn, twist < *(*s*)*ner-*, to turn, wind, seen also in *snare, narrow*], 1. of, like, or capable of producing narcosis. 2. for treating narcotism. *n.* 1. any drug that induces profound sleep, lethargy, and relief of pain: it is usually an opiate. 2. a person addicted to narcotics. 3. anything that causes drowsiness, lethargy, etc.

nar·co·tism (när′kə-tiz'm), *n.* 1. the condition induced by a narcotic; narcosis. 2. a method or influence producing narcosis. 3. addiction to narcotics.

nar·co·ti·za·tion (när′kə-ti-zā′shən, när′kə-tī-zā′shən), *n.* a narcotizing or being narcotized.

nar·co·tize (när′kə-tīz′), *v.t.* [NARCOTIZED (-tīzd′), NARCOTIZING], to subject to a narcotic; stupefy; produce narcotism in.

nard (närd), *n.* [ME. & OFr. *narde;* L. *nardus;* Gr. *nardos;* Heb. *nērd;* Per. *nārdēn;* Sans. *naladā*, lit., perfume-giving; *nala*, fragrance + *dā*, giving], 1. any of several plants with heart-shaped leaves, small greenish-white flowers, and reddish berries; spikenard. 2. an ointment made from the roots of these plants.

na·res (nâr′ēz), *n.pl.* [*sing.* NARIS (-is)], [L.], the nasal passages; especially, the nostrils.

Na·rev (nä′ref), *n.* Narew: the Russian spelling.

Na·rew (nä′ref), *n.* a river in northeastern Poland, flowing into the Bug River: length, 290 mi.

nar·ghi·le (när′gə-li, när′gə-lā′), *n.* [Turk. & Per. *nārgīleh* < Per. *nargīl*, coconut tree; prob. < Sans. *nārikera*, coconut: so called because orig. made of coconut shell], an Oriental pipe with a long, flexible tube so arranged that it draws the smoke through water in a vase or bowl and cools it; hookah: also spelled **nargile, nargileh.**

nar·i·al (nâr′i-əl), *adj.* of the nares.

nar·ine (nâr′in, nâr′in), *adj.* narial.

nark (närk), *n.* [< Gypsy *nāk*, a nose], [British Slang], an informer; stool pigeon. *v.i.* to act as a nark.

Nar·ra·gan·sett (nar′ə-gan′sit), *n.* [*pl.* NARRAGANSETT, NARRAGANSETTS (-sits)], [Algonquian, lit., on a small cape], a member of an extinct tribe of Algonquian Indians who lived around Narragansett Bay. *adj.* of this tribe.

Narragansett Bay, an inlet of the Atlantic, extending into Rhode Island: length, c. 28 mi.

nar·rate (na-rāt′, nar′āt), *v.t. & v.i.* [NARRATED (-id), NARRATING], [< L. *narratus*, pp. of *narrare*, to tell], 1. to tell (a story) in writing or speech. 2. to give an account of (happenings, etc.). —***SYN.*** see **tell.**

nar·ra·tion (na-rā′shən), *n.* [ME. *narracion;* Late OFr.; L. *narratio*], 1. the act or process of narrating; telling a story or giving an account of happenings, etc., in writing or speech. 2. a story or account; narrative. 3. writing or speaking that narrates, as history, biography, and fiction: conventionally distinguished from *argumentation, description, exposition.*

nar·ra·tive (nar′ə-tiv), *adj.* [L. *narrativus*], 1. of, or having the nature of, narration; in story form. 2.

occupied or concerned with narration: as, a *narrative* poet. ***n.*** 1. a story; account; tale. 2. the art or practice of relating stories or accounts; narration. — ***SYN.*** see **story.**

nar·ra·tor, nar·rat·er (na-rā′tēr; *now often* nar′ā-tēr), ***n.*** [L. < *narratus;* see NARRATE], 1. a person who relates a story or account. 2. a person who reads descriptive or narrative passages between the speeches or scenes of a play, radio show, etc.

nar·row (nar′ō), ***adj.*** [ME. *narwe;* AS. *nearu;* akin to MD. *nare,* OS. *naru;* IE. base *(*s*)*ner-*, to turn, wind, seen also in Gr. *narkē*, stupor (cf. NARCOTIC); basic sense "twisted up"], 1. small in width as compared to length; especially, less wide than is customary or expected; not wide. 2. limited in meaning, size, amount, extent: as, a *narrow* majority. 3. limited in outlook; without breadth of view or generosity; not liberal; prejudiced. 4. close; careful; minute; thorough: as, a *narrow* inspection. 5. with limited margin; with barely enough space, time, etc.; barely successful: as, a *narrow* escape. 6. limited in means; with hardly enough to live on: as, *narrow* circumstances. 7. in *phonetics*, tense: said of the tongue. ***v.i.*** to decrease in width; contract: as, the river *narrows.* ***v.t.*** to decrease or limit (something) in width, extent, or scope; restrict: as, he *narrowed* the argument. ***n.*** 1. a narrow part or place; especially, a narrow part of a valley, mountain pass, road, etc. 2. *usually pl.* a narrow passage, as between two bodies of water; strait.

The Narrows, 1. the strait between Staten Island and Long Island, New York: least width, 1 1/4 mi. 2. the narrowest part of the Dardanelles, c. 3/4 mi.

nar·row-gauge (nar′ō-gāj′), ***adj.*** 1. for or having a narrow gauge. 2. [Colloq.], narrow-minded.

narrow gauge, 1. a width (between the rails) of less than 56 1/2 inches (standard gauge). 2. a railroad having such a gauge. 3. a locomotive or car for such a railroad.

nar·row-mind·ed (nar′ō-mīn′did), ***adj.*** limited in outlook; not liberal; bigoted; prejudiced.

nar·thex (när′theks), ***n.*** [L.; Gr. *narthex*, giant fennel (in LGr. also narthex): from a supposed resemblance of the architectural part to the hollow, reedlike stem], 1. *a*) in ancient Christian churches, a porch at the west end for penitents and others not admitted to the church itself. *b*) later, a vestibule within the church, for the same purpose. 2. any church vestibule leading to the nave.

Nar·vá·ez, Pán·fi·lo de (päm′fē-lô *th*e när-vä′eth), 1480?–1528; Spanish soldier and conqueror in America.

nar·wal (när′wəl), ***n.*** a narwhal.

nar·whal (när′wəl, när′hwəl), ***n.*** [prob. < D. *narwal* or Dan. & Sw. *narhval;* modified after *whale;* apparently < ON. *nāhvalr*, said to be < *nār*, corpse + *hvalr*, a whale (with reference to the whitish underside)], an arctic cetacean valued for its oil and ivory; sea unicorn: the male has a long, spiral tusk extending from the upper jaw.

NARWHAL (15–20 ft. long)

nar·whale (när′hwāl), ***n.*** a narwhal.

nar·y (nâr′i), ***adj.*** [altered < *ne'er a*, never a], [Dial. & Colloq.], not any; no (with *a* or *an*): as, *nary* a doubt.

NASA, National Aeronautics and Space Administration.

na·sal (nā′z'l), ***adj.*** [Mod. L. *nasalis* < L. *nasus*, a nose; see NOSE], 1. of the nose. 2. produced by stopping all or part of the breath in the mouth and permitting it to pass through the nose, as the sounds of *m, n, ng* (ŋ), and the French nasalized vowels. 3. characterized by such production of sounds: as, a *nasal* voice. ***n.*** 1. a nasal sound or a letter representing such a sound. 2. in *anatomy*, a bone or plate of the nose. 3. [ME.; OFr. *nasal, nasel* < L. *nasus*], the protective nosepiece of a helmet.

nasal index, 1. in *cephalometry*, the ratio of the greatest breadth of the nose to its greatest height. 2. in *craniometry*, the ratio of the greatest breadth of the nasal aperture (of the skull) to its greatest height.

na·sal·i·ty (nā-zal′ə-ti), ***n.*** the quality of being nasal.

na·sal·i·za·tion (nā′z'l-i-zā′shən, nā′z'l-ī-zā′shən), ***n.*** 1. a nasalizing or being nasalized. 2. the result of nasalizing.

na·sal·ize (nā′z'l-īz′), ***v.i.*** [NASALIZED (-īzd′), NASALIZING], to permit all or part of the breath to pass through the nose in pronouncing certain sounds, especially sounds not nasals; talk through the nose. ***v.t.*** to pronounce with a nasal sound.

Nas·by, Pe·tro·le·um V. (pi-trō′li-əm naz′bi), see **Locke, David Ross.**

nas·cence (nas′'ns, nā′s'ns), ***n.*** nascency.

nas·cen·cy (nas′'n-si, nā′s'n-si), ***n.*** [L. *nascentia* < *nascens;* see NASCENT], the process of being brought into being, formed, or started; birth.

nas·cent (nas′'nt, nā′s'nt), ***adj.*** [L. *nascens*, ppr. of *nasci*, to be born], 1. coming into being; being born; hence, 2. beginning to form, start, grow, or develop: said of ideas, cultures, etc. 3. in *chemistry*, designating or of the state of an element just released from a compound and having unusual chemical activity because atoms of the element have not combined to form molecules: as, *nascent* chlorine.

nascent state (or **condition**), 1. the earliest state of development. 2. in *chemistry*, the earliest state of an element at liberation from a compound.

nase·ber·ry (nāz′ber′i, nāz′bēr-i), ***n.*** [*pl.* NASEBERRIES (-iz)], [Sp. *níspero*, medlar tree, *néspero*, medlar; L. *mespilus;* see MEDLAR], 1. a variety of West Indian tree. 2. its edible fruit: also called *sapodilla* (*plum*).

Nase·by (nāz′bi), ***n.*** a parish in Northamptonshire, England: site of a Royalist defeat (1645).

Nashe, Thomas (nash), 1567–1601; English satirist, dramatist, and novelist: also spelled **Nash.**

Nash·u·a (nash′ōō-ə), ***n.*** a city in southern New Hampshire, on the Merrimack River: pop., 39,000.

Nash·ville (nash′vil), ***n.*** the capital of Tennessee, on the Cumberland River: pop., 171,000.

na·si·al (nā′zi-əl), ***adj.*** of the nasion.

na·si·on (nā′zi-on′), ***n.*** [Mod. L. < *nasus*, nose], in *craniometry*, the point in the skull at which the suture between the two nasal bones meets the suture between these and the frontal bone.

na·so- (nā′zō), [< L. *nasus;* see NOSE], a combining form meaning: 1. *nose, nasal.* 2. *nasal and*, as in *nasofrontal.*

na·so·fron·tal (nā′zō-frun′t'l), ***adj.*** of the nose and the frontal bone.

na·so·phar·ynx (nā′zō-far′iŋks), ***n.*** the part of the pharynx lying directly behind the nasal passages and above the soft palate.

Nas·sau (nas′ô), ***n.*** 1. the capital of the Bahama Islands, on New Providence Island: pop., 50,000. 2. a former duchy in western Germany: now in Hesse. 3. the ruling family of the Netherlands since 1815.

Nassau Mountains, a mountain range in Netherlands New Guinea: highest peak, Mt. Carstensz, 16,404 ft.

Nas·ser, Ga·mal Ab·del (gä-mäl′ äb′dəl nä′sēr), 1918– ; Egyptian president of the United Arab Republic (1958–).

Nast, Thomas (nast), 1840–1902; American caricaturist and illustrator, born in Germany.

nas·tic (nas′tik), ***adj.*** [< Gr. *nastos*, pressed close; + *-ic*], designating, of, or exhibiting a characteristic reaction of plants by which an inequality of cellular growth or pressure on one side of the axis results in a change in the form or position of the axis.

-nas·tic (nas′tik), a combining form meaning *nastic by some* (specified) *means* or *in some* (specified) *direction.*

nas·ti·ly (nas′t'l-i), ***adv.*** in a nasty manner.

nas·ti·ness (nas′ti-nis), ***n.*** 1. the quality or condition of being nasty. 2. a nasty act, word, expression, etc.

na·stur·tium (nə-stũr′shəm), ***n.*** [L., kind of cress < **nasitortium*, lit., nose-twist < *nasus*, nose + pp. of *torquere*, to turn, twist: from the pungent odor of the plant], 1. any of a number of related plants with shield-shaped leaves and funnel-shaped red, orange, or yellow flowers. 2. the flower of this plant.

nas·ty (nas′ti), ***adj.*** [NASTIER (-ti-ēr), NASTIEST (-ti-ist)], [ME. *nasty, nasky, naxty;* ? < or akin to D. *nestig*, dirty; or ? < ON.; cf. Sw. dial. *naskug*, foul], 1. filthy; foul. 2. offensive in taste or smell; nauseating. 3. morally offensive; obscene. 4. very unpleasant; objectionable: as, *nasty* weather. 5. mean; malicious; ill-humored: as, a *nasty* temper. 6. very harmful or troublesome; dangerous: as, a *nasty* bruise.

-nas·ty (nas′ti), a combining form used to form nouns corresponding to adjectives ending in *-nastic.*

nat., 1. national. 2. native. 3. natural. 4. naturalist. 5. *natus*, [L.], born.

Na·tal (nə-tal′, nə-täl′), ***n.*** a province of the Union of South Africa, on the Indian Ocean: area, 33,578 sq. mi.; pop., 2,415,000; capital, Pietermaritzburg.

na·tal (nā′t'l), ***adj.*** [L. *natalis* < *natus*, pp. of *nasci*, to be born; IE. base *ĝen-, to bring forth; cf. GENUS], 1. of or connected with one's birth. 2. [Poetic], native.

Nat·a·lie (nat′'l-i), [Fr.; LL. *Natalia* < L. *natalis* (*dies*), natal (day), name given to children born on Christmas Day], a feminine name.

na·tal·i·ty (nā-tal′ə-ti), ***n.*** [Fr. *natalité* < L. *natalis;* see NATAL, *adj.*], 1. [Rare], birth. 2. birth rate.

na·tant (nā′t'nt), ***adj.*** [L. *natans*, ppr. of *natare*, to swim], swimming or floating; especially, floating on water: as, the *natant* leaves of water lilies.

na·ta·tion (nā-tā′shən), ***n.*** [L. *natatio* < pp. of *natare*, to swim], the act or art of swimming.

na·ta·to·ri·al (nā′tə-tôr′i-əl, nā′tə-tō′ri-əl), ***adj.*** natatory.

na·ta·to·ri·um (nā′tə-tôr′i-əm, nā′tə-tō′ri-əm), ***n.*** [*pl.* NATATORIUMS (-əmz), NATATORIA (-ə)], [LL. < *natatorius*], a swimming pool, especially one indoors.

na·ta·to·ry (nā′tə-tôr′i, nā′tə-tō′ri), ***adj.*** [LL. *natatorius* < L. *natator*, swimmer; cf. NATATION], of, characterized by, or adapted for swimming.

Natch·ez (nach′iz), ***n.*** 1. [*pl.* NATCHEZ], a member of an extinct tribe of Muskhogean Indians who lived in southwestern Mississippi. 2. a city in southwestern Mississippi: pop., 24,000.

na·tes (nā′tēz), ***n.pl.*** [L., pl. of *natis;* akin to Gr. *nōton*, the back], the buttocks.

Na·than (nā′thən), [Heb. *nāthān*, lit., gift], a masculine name: diminutives, *Nat, Nate.* ***n.*** in the *Bible,* a prophet who rebuked David for the death of Uriah: II Sam. 12:1-14.
Na·than, George Jean (nā′thən), 1882–1958; American dramatic critic, writer, and editor.
Na·than·a·el (nə-than′yəl, nə-than′i-əl), [LL.; Gr. *Nathanaēl;* Heb. *nĕthan'ēl,* lit., gift of God], a masculine name: diminutive, *Nat*: also spelled **Nathaniel.** ***n.*** in the *Bible,* one of the disciples of Jesus: John 1:45-51.
nathe·less (nāth′lis, nath′lis), ***adv.*** [ME. *natheles;* AS. *nathelæs,* etc.; *na,* never + *the* (for *thy,* instrumental case of def. art.) + *læs,* less], [Archaic], nevertheless. ***prep.*** [Archaic], notwithstanding.
nath·less (nath′lis), ***adv. & prep.*** [Archaic], natheless.
na·tion (nā′shən), ***n.*** [ME. & OFr. *nacion* < L. *natio* < *natus,* pp. of *nasci,* to be born], 1. a stable, historically developed community of people with a territory, economic life, distinctive culture, and language in common. 2. the people of a territory united under a single government; country; state. 3. *a)* a people or tribe. *b)* a tribe of North American Indians belonging to a confederation: as, the Six *Nations. c)* the territory of such a tribe.
the nations, 1. in the *Bible,* the non-Jewish nations; the Gentiles. 2. [Poetic], all the peoples of the earth.
Na·tion, Carry (nā′shən), (born *Carry Amelia Moore*), 1846–1911; American agitator for temperance: first name often wrongly spelled **Carrie.**
na·tion·al (nash′ən-'l), ***adj.*** [Fr.], 1. of a nation or the nation; affecting the nation as a whole. 2. strongly devoted to one's nation or its interests; patriotic. ***n.*** 1. a person who belongs to a certain nation by birth or naturalization. 2. loosely, a fellow citizen. Abbreviated **natl., nat., N.**—***SYN.*** see **citizen.**
national bank, 1. a bank that manages and controls the finances of a nation. 2. in the United States, a bank chartered by the Federal government and under certain controls by the Federal Reserve System, of which it is a member: national banks formerly issued bank notes secured by government bonds.
National Guard, in the United States, that part of the militia consisting of the properly organized, equipped, and trained forces of the individual States, supported in part by the Federal government: it becomes a definite component of the Army of the United States when called into active Federal service.
National Guard of the United States, those members and units of the National Guard who have been accorded Federal recognition as a component part of the Army of the United States.
national income, the total income of a nation, including all profits, rents, interest, wages, salaries, etc., during a specified period, usually a year.
na·tion·al·ism (nash′ən-'l-iz'm), ***n.*** 1. *a)* devotion to one's nation; patriotism. *b)* excessive, narrow, or jingoist patriotism; chauvinism. 2. the doctrine that national interests, security, etc. are more important than international considerations: opposed to *internationalism.* 3. national quality or character; nationality. 4. a national idiom, trait, or custom. 5. the desire for or advocacy of national independence. 6. the policy of nationalizing all industry.
na·tion·al·ist (nash′ən-'l-ist), ***n.*** a person who believes in or advocates nationalism. ***adj.*** of nationalism or nationalists. Abbreviated **Nat., N.**
na·tion·al·is·tic (nash′ən-'l-is′tik), ***adj.*** nationalist.
na·tion·al·is·ti·cal·ly (nash′ən-'l-is′ti-k'l-i, nash′ən-'l-is′tik-li), ***adv.*** in a nationalistic manner.
na·tion·al·i·ty (nash′ə-nal′ə-ti), ***n.*** [*pl.* NATIONALITIES (-tiz)], 1. national quality or character. 2. the condition or fact of belonging to a nation by birth or naturalization. 3. the condition or fact of being a nation. 4. a nation or national group.
na·tion·al·i·za·tion (nash′ən-'l-i-zā′shən, nash′ən-'l-ī-zā′shən), ***n.*** a nationalizing or being nationalized.
na·tion·al·ize (nash′ən-'l-īz′), ***v.t.*** [NATIONALIZED (-īzd′), NATIONALIZING], 1. to make national in character. 2. to transfer ownership or control of land, resources, industries, etc. to the nation. 3. to make into a nation.
na·tion·al·ly (nash′ən-'l-i), ***adv.*** 1. so as to affect the whole nation; throughout the nation. 2. as a nation.
national monument, a natural geographic feature or historic site, as a mountain, canyon, fort, etc., maintained and preserved by the national government for public enjoyment.
national park, an area of scenic beauty, historical importance, etc. maintained and preserved by the national government for the enjoyment of the public.
National Socialism, National Socialist German Workers' Party, see **Nazi.**
na·tion-wide (nā′shən-wīd′), ***adj.*** by or through the whole nation; national.
na·tive (nā′tiv), ***adj.*** [replacing ME. *natyf* (OFr. *natif*) < L. *nativus* < *natus,* pp. of *nasci,* to be born], 1. inborn; innate; not acquired. 2. belonging to a locality or country by birth, production, or growth; indigenous: as, a *native* Bostonian, *native* industry, *native* plants. 3. *a)* related to one as the place of one's birth: as, one's *native* land. *b)* belonging to one because of the place of one's birth: as, one's *native* language. 4. as found in nature; natural; not refined, adorned, or altered by man. 5. occurring in a pure state in nature: as, *native* gold. 6. of or characteristic of the inhabitants of any given region. 7. of, characteristic of, or belonging to primitive or uncivilized peoples, particularly nonwhites, living in their place of origin: as, *native* customs in Borneo. ***n.*** 1. a person born or thing produced in the place or country indicated. 2. *a)* an original or indigenous inhabitant of a region, as distinguished from an invader, explorer, colonist, etc. *b)* an indigenous plant or animal. 3. a permanent resident, as distinguished from a temporary resident or visitor. 4. in *astrology,* a person born under a certain sign. Abbreviated **nat.**
go native, to adopt a primitive mode of life.
SYN.—**native** applies to a person or thing born or originating in a certain place or country (a *native* Italian, *native* fruits); **indigenous,** which also suggests natural origin in a particular region, is applied to races or species rather than to individuals (the potato is *indigenous* to South America); **aboriginal** applies to the earliest known inhabitants (or, rarely, animals or plants) of a region (the Indians are the *aboriginal* Americans); **endemic,** applied especially to plants and diseases, implies prevalence in or restriction to a particular region (typhus is *endemic* in various countries.) See also **citizen.**—***ANT.*** alien, foreign.
na·tive-born (nā′tiv-bôrn′), ***adj.*** born in a specified place or country.
na·tiv·ism (nā′tiv-iz'm), ***n.*** 1. the practice or policy of favoring native-born citizens as against immigrants. 2. in *philosophy,* the doctrine of innate ideas.
na·tiv·i·ty (nə-tiv′ə-ti, nā-tiv′ə-ti), ***n.*** [*pl.* NATIVITIES (-tiz)], [ME. *natiuite;* OFr. *nativite;* LL. *nativitas* < L. *nativus;* see NATIVE], 1. birth. 2. the conditions accompanying birth. 3. the horoscope for one's birth.
the Nativity, 1. the birth of Jesus. 2. a representation of this. 3. Christmas Day.
natl., national.
NATO (nā′tō), North Atlantic Treaty Organization.
na·tri·um (nā′tri-əm), ***n.*** [Mod. L. < Fr.; see NATRON], sodium: symbol, Na (no period).
nat·ro·lite (nat′rə-līt′, nā′trə-līt′), ***n.*** [< *natron* + *-lite*], a hydrous silicate of sodium and aluminum, $Na_2O \cdot Al_2O_3 \cdot 3SiO_2 \cdot 2H_2O$.
na·tron (nā′tron), ***n.*** [Fr.; Sp. *natrón;* Ar. *natrūn;* Gr. *nitron;* see NITRE], hydrated sodium carbonate, $Na_2CO_3 \cdot 10H_2O$, a mineral occurring in salt lakes or, mixed with other substances, in deposits.
nat·ti·ly (nat′'l-i), ***adv.*** in a natty manner.
nat·ti·ness (nat′i-nis), ***n.*** natty quality or condition.
nat·ty (nat′i), ***adj.*** [NATTIER (-i-ẽr), NATTIEST (-i-ist)], [? < *neat, adj.*], trim and smart in appearance or dress.
nat·u·ral (nach′ẽr-əl), ***adj.*** [ME. *naturel;* OFr.; L. *naturalis,* by birth, according to nature], 1. of, forming a part of, or arising from nature; in accordance with what is found or expected in nature. 2. produced or existing in nature; real; not artificial or manufactured. 3. dealing with nature: as, a *natural* science. 4. *a)* in a state provided by nature, without man-made changes; wild; uncultivated. *b)* unenlightened; primitive. 5. of the physical world as distinguished from the spiritual world. 6. *a)* present by virtue of nature; innate; not acquired: as, *natural* abilities. *b)* having certain qualities, abilities, etc. innately: as, a *natural* comedian. 7. innately felt to be right; based on instinctive moral feeling: as, *natural* rights. 8. true to nature; realistic in appearance; lifelike: as, a *natural* likeness. 9. normal for a given person or thing; in the ordinary course of events: as, a *natural* outcome. 10. customarily expected or uncritically accepted: as, a *natural* courtesy. 11. free from affectation or restraint; at ease. 12. illegitimate: as, a *natural* child. 13. in *mathematics, a)* designating or of an integer or any number referred to 1 as the base. *b)* designating or of an actual number as distinguished from a logarithm: as, a *natural* sine, cosine, etc. 14. in *music, a)* without flats or sharps, as the key of C major. *b)* modified in pitch by the sign (♮). *c)* neither sharped nor flatted. ***n.*** 1. a person without normal intelligence; fool; idiot. 2. [Colloq.], a person who is or seems to be naturally expert. 3. [Colloq.], a thing that is, or promises to be, immediately and remarkably successful. 4. in *music, a)* the sign (♮), used to remove the effect of a preceding sharp or flat within the measure in which it occurs: in full, **natural sign.** *b)* the note so changed. *c)* a white key on a piano. Abbreviated **nat.** —***SYN.*** see **normal.**
Natural Bridge, a natural bridge over Cedar Creek in west central Virginia: height, 215 ft.; span, 90 ft.
Natural Bridges, three natural bridges in south-

eastern Utah, the largest having a span of 261 ft.

natural gas, a mixture of gaseous hydrocarbons, chiefly methane, occurring naturally in the earth in certain places, from which it is piped to cities, etc., to be used as a fuel.

natural history, 1. formerly, zoology, botany, mineralogy, geology, and other subjects dealing with the animal, vegetable, and mineral world. 2. the study of these subjects, especially of animal and plant life, in a popular, nontechnical manner.

nat·u·ral·ism (nach′ẽr-əl-iz'm), ***n.*** 1. action or thought based on natural desires or instincts. 2. in *literature, painting,* etc., *a*) faithful adherence to nature; realism; specifically, the variety of realism based on the principles and methods of a group of 19th-century writers, including Émile Zola, Gustave Flaubert, and Guy de Maupassant, who believed that the writer or artist should apply scientific objectivity and precision in his observation and treatment of life, without idealizing, imposing value judgments, or avoiding what is regarded as repulsive. *b*) the quality resulting from the use of such realism. 3. in *philosophy,* the belief that the natural world is the whole of reality and that there is no supernatural or spiritual creation, value, control, or significance: it holds that scientific laws can explain all phenomena. 4. in *religion,* the doctrine that religion does not depend on supernatural experience, divine revelation, etc., and that all religious truth may be derived from the natural world.

nat·u·ral·ist (nach′ẽr-əl-ist), ***n.*** [Fr. *naturaliste*], 1. a person who studies nature, especially by direct observation of animals and plants. 2. a person who believes in or practices naturalism in art, literature, philosophy, or religion. Abbreviated **nat.**

nat·u·ral·is·tic (nach′ẽr-ə-lis′tik), ***adj.*** 1. of natural history or naturalists. 2. of or characterized by naturalism in art, literature, philosophy, or religion. 3. in accordance with, or in imitation of, nature.

nat·u·ral·i·za·tion (nach′ẽr-əl-i-zā′shən, nach′ẽr-əl-ī-zā′shən), ***n.*** a naturalizing or being naturalized.

nat·u·ral·ize (nach′ẽr-ə-līz′), ***v.t.*** [NATURALIZED (-līzd′), NATURALIZING], [Fr. *naturaliser* < *naturel; see* NATURAL], 1. to confer the rights of citizenship upon (an alien). 2. to adopt and make common (a custom, word, etc.) from another locality. 3. to adapt (a plant or animal) to an environment not native; acclimate. 4. to explain (occurrences) by natural law, rejecting supernatural influence. 5. to make natural or less artificial; free from conventionality. ***v.i.*** 1. to become naturalized, or as if native. 2. to study nature.

natural law, 1. rules of conduct supposedly inherent in the relations between human beings and discoverable by reason; law based upon man's innate moral sense: contrasted with *statute law, common law.* 2. a law of nature: see **law** (sense 10). 3. the laws of nature, collectively.

nat·u·ral·ly (nach′ẽr-əl-i), ***adv.*** 1. in a natural manner. 2. by nature; innately. 3. as one might expect; of course.

natural philosophy, 1. the study of nature generally, or of the entire physical universe. 2. physics.

natural resources, those actual and potential forms of wealth supplied by nature, as coal, oil, waterpower, arable land, etc.

natural science, 1. the systematized knowledge of nature and the physical world, including zoology, botany, chemistry, physics, geology, etc. 2. any of these branches of knowledge. Also **science.**

natural selection, in evolution, the process by which those individuals (of a species) with characteristics that help them to become adapted to their specific environment tend to survive (*survival of the fittest*) and transmit their characteristics, while those less able to become adapted tend to die out, so that in the course of generations there is a progressive tendency in the species to a greater degree of adaptation: see also **Darwinian theory.**

na·ture (nā′chẽr), ***n.*** [ME.; OFr.; L. *natura* < *natus,* born, produced, pp. of *nasci,* to be born; cf. NATAL, *adj.*], 1. the essential character of a thing; quality or qualities that make something what it is; essence. 2. inborn character; innate disposition; inherent tendencies of a person. 3. the vital functions, forces, and activities of the organs: often euphemistic. 4. kind; sort; type: as, things of that *nature.* 5. any or all of the instincts, desires, appetites, drives, etc. of a person. 6. the sum total of all things in time and space; the entire physical universe. 7. [sometimes N-], the power, force, principle, etc. that seems to regulate this: often personified. 8. the primitive state of man. 9. natural scenery, including the plants and animals that are part of it. 10. in *religion,* the state of man unredeemed by grace. —***SYN.*** see **type.**

by nature, naturally; inherently.

in a state of nature, 1. completely naked. 2. not cultivated or tamed; wild. 3. uncivilized.

of (or **in**) **the nature of,** having the essential character of; like.

-na·tured (nā′chẽrd), a combining form used to form hyphenated compounds meaning *having* or *showing a* (specified kind of) *nature, disposition,* or *temperament,* as *good-natured.*

nature study, the study of plant and animal life by direct observation, especially in a popular, nontechnical manner.

nature worship, 1. worship of natural forces as gods. 2. poetic love for nature.

na·tur·op·a·thy (nā′chẽr-op′ə-thi), ***n.*** [< L. *natura,* nature; + *-pathy*], a system of treating diseases, largely employing natural agencies, such as air, sunshine, etc., and rejecting the use of drugs and medicines.

Nau·cra·tis (nô′krə-tis), ***n.*** an ancient Greek city in the Nile delta, Egypt.

naught (nôt), ***n.*** [ME. *nauht;* AS. *nawiht; na* (see NA, NO) + *wiht* (see WIGHT, WIT)], 1. nothing. 2. in *arithmetic,* the figure zero (0). See also **nought.** ***adj.*** [Archaic or Obs.], 1. worthless; useless. 2. wicked; evil. ***adv.*** [Obs.], in no degree; not in the least.

set at naught, to defy; scorn.

naught·i·ly (nô′t'l-i), ***adv.*** in a naughty manner.

naugh·ti·ness (nô′ti-nis), ***n.*** quality, state, or instance of being naughty.

naugh·ty (nô′ti), ***adj.*** [NAUGHTIER (-ti-ẽr), NAUGHTIEST (-ti-ist)], [ME. *naugti;* see NAUGHT, *adj.* & -Y], 1. [Obs.], wicked; bad; evil. 2. not behaving properly; mischievous; disobedient: usually of children or their behavior. 3. showing lack of decorum; improper; indelicate; obscene. —***SYN.*** see **bad.**

nau·ma·chi·a (nô-mā′ki-ə), ***n.*** [*pl.* NAUMACHIAS (-əz), NAUMACHIAE (-ē′)], [L.; Gr. *naumachia* < *naus,* ship + *machē,* battle], 1. in ancient Rome, a mock sea fight. 2. a place constructed for this.

nau·ma·chy (nô′mə-ki), ***n.*** [*pl.* NAUMACHIES (-kiz)], a naumachia.

nau·pli·us (nô′pli-əs), ***n.*** [*pl.* NAUPLII (-ī′)], [L., kind of shellfish; Gr. *nauplios,* kind of shellfish said to sail in its shell as in a ship < *naus,* ship + *pleiein,* to sail], the first, or larval, stage in the development of certain crustaceans.

Na·u·ru (nä-ōō′rōō), ***n.*** a British island in Micronesia, in the Pacific: area, 8 sq. mi.; pop., 3,400: former name, *Pleasant Island.*

nau·se·a (nô′shə, nô′shi-ə, nô′zi-ə, nô′zhə, nô′si-ə), ***n.*** [L.; Gr. *nausia, nautia,* seasickness < *naus,* a ship], 1. a feeling of sickness at the stomach, with an impulse to vomit. 2. any stomach disorder causing this feeling, as seasickness. 3. disgust; loathing.

nau·se·ate (nô′shi-āt′, nô′zi-āt′, nô′zhi-āt′, nô′si-āt′), ***v.t.*** [NAUSEATED (-id), NAUSEATING], [< L. *nauseatus,* pp. of *nauseare,* to be seasick; see NAUSEA], 1. to cause to feel nausea; make sick. 2. [Rare], to feel nausea at; loathe. ***v.i.*** to feel nausea; become sick.

nau·seous (nô′shəs, nô′shi-əs, nô′zi-əs, nô′zhəs, nô′si-əs), ***adj.*** [L. *nauseosus*], causing nausea; specifically, *a*) sickening. *b*) disgusting.

Nau·sic·a·ä (nô-sik′ā-ə, nou-sik′i-ə), ***n.*** in Homer's *Odyssey,* King Alcinoüs's daughter, who discovered the shipwrecked Ulysses and brought him to her father, from whom he received safe passage to Ithaca.

nautch (nôch), ***n.*** [Hind. *nāc;* Prakrit *nacca;* Sans. *nṛtya,* dancing < *nṛt,* to dance], in India, a performance by professional dancing girls (***nautch girls***).

nau·ti·cal (nô′ti-k'l), ***adj.*** [Fr. *nautique;* L. *nauticus;* Gr. *nautikos* < *nautēs,* sailor, seaman < *naus,* a ship], of sailors, ships, or navigation: abbreviated **naut.**

nautical mile, a unit of linear measure for ships and aircraft, equal to 1/60 of a degree, or about 6,076 ft.

nau·ti·lus (nô′t'l-əs), ***n.*** [*pl.* NAUTILUSES (-iz), NAUTILI (-ī′)], [L.; Gr. *nautilos,* sailor, nautilus < *naus,* a ship], 1. any of a group of tropical mollusks with a many-chambered, spiral shell, having a pearly interior: also **pearly nautilus.** 2. the paper nautilus.

PEARLY NAUTILUS (8 in. long)

nav., 1. naval. 2. navigable. 3. navigation. 4. navy.

Nav·a·ho, Nav·a·jo (nav′ə-hō′), ***n.*** [*pl.* NAVAHOS, NAVAJOS (-hōz′); NAVAHOES, NAVAJOES (-hōz′)], [< Sp. Apaches de *Navajó* < Am. Ind. (Tewa) *Navahú,* lit., great fields, name of the Tewa pueblo near which the Spaniards first met Navahos], a member of a tribe of Athapascan Indians now living on a reservation in Arizona, New Mexico, and Utah.

na·val (nā′v'l), ***adj.*** [< Fr. or L.; Fr. *naval;* L. *navalis* < *navis,* a ship], 1. [Obs.], of ships or shipping. 2. of, having, characteristic of, or for a navy, its ships, personnel, etc. Abbreviated **nav.**

naval academy, a college for training naval officers.

Na·var·ra (nä-vär′rä), ***n.*** Navarre: the Spanish name.

Na·varre (nə-vär′), ***n.*** a former kingdom of northern Spain and southwestern France.

nave (nāv), *n.* [OFr. < L. *navis*, a ship], that part of a church which is between the side aisles and extends from the chancel to the principal entrance, forming the main part of the building.

nave (nāv), *n.* [ME.; AS. *nafu;* akin to G. *nabe;* for base see NAVEL], the hub of a wheel.

na·vel (nā'v'l), *n.* [ME.; AS. *nafela;* akin to G. *nabel;* IE. base ***enebh-**, ***ombh-**, ***nōbh-**, etc., navel, seen also in L. *umbilicus*, Eng. *nave* (hub)], 1. the small scar, usually a depression in the middle of the abdomen, marking the place where the umbilical cord was attached to the fetus; umbilicus. 2. a similar point or depression centrally located on something or in some place.

navel orange, a seedless orange having at its apex a depression like a navel, containing a small, undeveloped secondary fruit.

nav·i·cert (nav'i-sûrt'), *n.* [*navi*gation *cert*ificate], a document issued by a nation at war, declaring that a ship of a friendly or neutral nation carries no contraband and authorizing it to move through the belligerent's blockade.

na·vic·u·lar (nə-vik'yoo-lẽr), *adj.* [LL. *navicularis* < L. *navicula*, dim. of *navis*, a ship], shaped like a boat: said especially of certain bones. *n.* any of various boat-shaped bones; especially, *a)* the outer bone of the first row of carpal bones in the wrist. *b)* a bone on the inner side of the human foot, in front of the ankle-bone.

na·vic·u·la·re (nə-vik'yoo-lâr'i), *n.* a navicular.

nav·i·ga·bil·i·ty (nav'i-gə-bil'ə-ti), *n.* the quality or state of being navigable.

nav·i·ga·ble (nav'i-gə-b'l), *adj.* [L. *navigabilis* < *navigare;* see NAVIGATE], 1. wide or deep enough, or free enough from obstructions, to be traveled on by ships: as, a *navigable* river. 2. that can be steered, or directed: as, a *navigable* balloon. Abbreviated **nav.**

nav·i·gate (nav'ə-gāt'), *v.i.* [NAVIGATED (-id), NAVIGATING], [< L. *navigatus*, pp. of *navigare*, to sail < *navis*, a ship + *agere*, to lead, go], 1. to travel by ship. 2. to steer, or direct, a ship or aircraft. *v.t.* 1. to travel through, on, or over (land, air, sea, etc.) in a boat or aircraft. 2. to steer, or direct (a ship or aircraft). 3. to plot the course for (a ship or aircraft).

nav·i·ga·tion (nav'ə-gā'shən), *n.* [L. *navigatio*], the act or practice of navigating; especially, the science of locating the position and plotting the course of ships and aircraft: abbreviated **nav., navig.**

nav·i·ga·tor (nav'ə-gā'tẽr), *n.* [L.], 1. a person who navigates; especially, one skilled or employed in navigation, either of a ship or an aircraft: abbreviated **navig.** 2. [British], a navvy.

Navigators Islands, Samoa: the former name.

nav·vy (nav'i), *n.* [*pl.* NAVVIES (-iz)], [abbrev. of *navigator*], [British], an unskilled laborer, as on canals, roads, etc.

na·vy (nā'vi), *n.* [*pl.* NAVIES (-viz)], [ME. & OFr. *navie;* LL. *navia* (for L. *navis*, a ship)], 1. [Archaic or Poetic], a fleet of ships. 2. all the warships of a nation. 3. [often N-], *a)* the entire sea force of a nation, including vessels, officers, men, stores, yards, etc. *b)* the governmental department in charge of this. 4. navy blue. Abbreviated **N., n., nav.**

navy bean, [from common use in the U.S. Navy], a small, white bean related to the kidney bean, dried for use as a food.

navy blue, [from the color of the Brit. naval uniform], very dark blue.

Navy Cross, a decoration awarded by the United States Navy for conspicuous heroism or service in war.

navy yard, a dockyard for building and repairing naval ships, storing naval supplies, etc.

na·wab (nə-wôb'), *n.* [Hind. *navāb;* see NABOB], in India, 1. a native ruler under the Mogul government. 2. [N-], a title of courtesy, especially for a Moslem prince. 3. a rich Anglo-Indian who has retired; nabob.

Nax·os (nak'sos; Gr. näk'sôs), *n.* the largest of the Cyclades Islands, in the Aegean: area, 171 sq. mi.; pop., 17,000.

nay (nā), *adv.* [ME. *nai, nei;* ON. *nei* < *ne*, not + *ei*, ever (see AYE)], 1. [Archaic], no. 2. not that only, but also: used to deny a statement mildly or to introduce an argument, as, I will permit, *nay*, encourage it. *n.* 1. a refusal or denial. 2. a negative vote or voter. 3. a negative answer.

say (someone) nay, to refuse or forbid (someone).

Naz·a·rene (naz'ə-rēn', naz'ə-rēn'), *adj.* [ME. *Nazaren;* LL. *Nazarenus;* Gr. *Nazarēnos*], of Nazareth or the Nazarenes. *n.* 1. a native or inhabitant of Nazareth; especially, Jesus (*the Nazarene*). 2. any member of an early sect of Jewish Christians who kept the Mosaic ritual. 3. [Obs.], a Christian: term formerly used by Moslems, Jews, etc.

Naz·a·reth (naz'ə-rəth, naz'rith), *n.* an ancient town in northern Palestine, where Jesus lived as a child.

Naz·a·rite (naz'ə-rīt'), *n.* [LL. *Nazaraeus;* Gr. *Nazēraios*, for Heb. *nāzīr* < *nāzar*, to separate, consecrate], 1. among the ancient Hebrews, a person who voluntarily assumed certain strict religious vows, such as abstaining from wine, not cutting his hair, etc.: as, Samson was a *Nazarite.* 2. [Rare], a Nazarene. Also spelled **Nazirite.**

Na·zi (nä'tsi, na'tsi, na'zi), *adj.* [G., contr. of party name, *Na*tionalso*zi*alistische Deutsche Arbeiterpartei], designating, of, or characteristic of the German fascist political party (*National Socialist German Workers' Party*, abbrev. **NSDAP**), founded in 1919 and abolished in 1945: under Hitler this party seized control of Germany in 1933, systematically eliminated opposition, and put into effect its program of nationalism, racism, rearmament, aggression, etc. *n.* 1. a member of this party. 2. [often n-], a supporter or follower of this party; fascist.

Na·zi·fy (nä'tsi-fī', na'tsi-fī'), *v.t.* [NAZIFIED (-fīd'), NAZIFYING], to place under Nazi control or influence; cause to be Nazi or like the Nazis: also **nazify.**

Na·zi·ism (nä'tsi-iz'm, na'tsi-iz'm), *n.* Nazism.

Na·zim·o·va, Al·la (äl'ə nə-zim'ə-və), 1879–1945; Russian actress in America.

na·zir (nä'zir), *n.* [Ar. *nazir*, overseer], in India, etc., any of various officials.

Naz·i·rite (naz'ə-rīt'), *n.* a Nazarite.

Na·zism (nä'tsiz'm, na'tsiz'm), *n.* the philosophy, aims, or characteristics of the Nazi Party; German fascism.

Nb, in *chemistry*, niobium.

N.B., 1. New Brunswick. 2. North Britain.

N.B., n.b., *nota bene*, [L.], note well.

N.B.C., NBC, National Broadcasting Company.

NbE, north by east.

NbW, north by west.

N.C., 1. New Caledonia. 2. North Carolina.

N.C.O., noncommissioned officer.

Nd, in *chemistry*, neodymium.

N.D., n.d., no date.

N.D., N. Dak., North Dakota.

ne- (nē), neo-.

Ne, in *chemistry*, neon.

NE, N.E., n.e., northeast.

N.E., 1. Naval Engineer. 2. New England. 3. Northeastern (postal district).

N.E.A., National Education Association.

Neal (nēl), [ME. *Nel, Neel, Nele;* prob. < Ir. *Niul* (Gael. *Niall*) < *niadh*, a champion], a masculine name: also spelled **Neil.**

Ne·an·der·thal (ni-an'dẽr-täl'; *now often* **ni-an'dẽr-thôl'**; G. nä-än'dẽr-täl'), *adj.* [G., lit., Neander valley (G. *thal, tal*, valley; akin to Eng. *dale*): named in honor of Joachim *Neander* (1650–1680), G. hymn writer], 1. designating, of, or from a valley in the Rhine Province, Germany. 2. designating or of a race of early man of the paleolithic period, whose skeletal remains were first found in this valley.

NEANDERTHAL HEAD (reconstructed)

neap (nēp), *adj.* [ME. *neep;* AS. *nep-* in *nepflod*, neap tide; prob. Gmc. base ***nōpi-**, scarcely touching, seen also in Norw. dial. *næpen*, scarcely touching, *nöpen*, hardly enough, *nōpa, næpa*, hardly to disturb], designating the tide occurring just after the first and third quarters of the lunar month: at these times the difference between high and low tides is smallest. *n.* neap tide.

neap (nēp), *n.* [prob. < ON.; cf. Norw. dial. *neip*, forked pole], [Dial.], the tongue of a wagon drawn by two animals.

Ne·a·pol·i·tan (nē'ə-pol'ə-t'n), *adj.* [L. *Neapolitanus* < *Neapolis*, Naples; Gr. *Neapolis*, lit., new town], of Naples. *n.* a native or inhabitant of Naples.

Neapolitan ice cream, brick ice cream containing several flavors in layers, usually chocolate, strawberry, and vanilla.

near (nêr), *adv.* [ME. *nere, neer;* AS. *near*, compar. of *neah, adv.*, nigh (see NIGH); akin to G. *näher*], 1. at a relatively short distance in space or time: as, summer is drawing *near.* 2. relatively close in degree; almost: as, you are *near* right: now usually *nearly.* 3. closely; intimately. 4. in a stingy manner; thriftily. *adj.* 1. close in distance or time; not far. 2. close in relationship; akin. 3. close in feelings, desires, etc.; close in friendship; intimate. 4. close in degree; narrow: as, a *near* escape. 5. on the left side: said of animals, vehicles, etc., as, the *near* horse. 6. short or quick; direct: as, he took the *near* way. 7. stingy; niggardly. 8. somewhat resembling; approximating: as, *near* beer.

prep. at a relatively short distance from in space, time, degree, etc.; close to. *v.t. & v.i.* to come or draw near (to); approach. Abbreviated **nr.**

near at hand, very close in time or space.

near-by, near·by (nêr′bī′), *adj. & adv.* near; close at hand.

near by, near; close at hand; close to: used adverbially or prepositionally.

Ne·arc·tic (nē-ärk′tik), *adj.* [*ne-* + *arctic*], designating the arctic and north temperate parts of North America: used in classifying some plants and animals according to geographical distribution.

Near East, 1. variously, the countries near or east of the eastern Mediterranean, including southwestern Asia (Turkey, Syria, Lebanon, Israel, Jordan, Saudi Arabia, etc.) and, sometimes, the Balkans and Egypt. 2. [British], the Balkans; especially, the lower Balkans. Cf. **Middle East.**

Nearer Tibet, formerly, the eastern part of Tibet: now part of Chinghai and Szechwan provinces, China.

near-hand (nêr′hand′), *adj.* [Scot. & British Dial.], close at hand; near-by. *adv.* [Scot. & British Dial.], 1. near-by. 2. nearly; almost.

near·ly (nêr′li), *adv.* [*near* + *-ly*], 1. almost; not quite; all but: as, I'm *nearly* finished. 2. closely; intimately: as, they are *nearly* related. 3. parsimoniously.

near miss, in *military usage,* a shell, aerial bomb, etc. that does not score a direct hit on the target but comes close enough to inflict some damage.

near·sight·ed (nêr′sīt′id), *adj.* seeing only near objects distinctly; myopic.

neat (nēt), *adj.* [Fr. *net* < L. *nitidus,* shining, elegant, smart, trim < *nitere,* to shine], 1. unmixed with anything; pure; undiluted: said especially of liquor drunk without a mixer or chaser. 2. [Rare], free of deductions; net. 3. *a)* trim; tidy; clean. *b)* characterized by tidiness; skillful and precise: as, a *neat* worker. 4. well proportioned; shapely. 5. cleverly or smartly phrased or done; adroit.

SYN.—**neat** suggests cleanness and orderliness and, hence, connotes a lack of superfluous or confusing details (a *neat* house, design, etc.); **tidy** emphasizes painstaking, orderly arrangement rather than cleanliness (a *tidy* closet); **trim** adds to the sense of **neat** connotations of smartness, dapperness, good proportion, etc. (a *trim* figure, ship, etc.).—*ANT.* slovenly, sloppy.

neat (nēt), *n.* [*pl.* NEAT], [ME. *nete, neet;* AS. *neat* (akin to ON. *naut,* D. *noot*) < base of *neotan,* to enjoy, possess; basic sense "what is possessed"], [Obs.], an animal of the ox family; cow, steer, etc.

'neath, neath (nēth, nēth), *prep.* [Poetic], beneath.

neat·herd (nēt′hūrd′), *n.* [ME. *netherd;* see NEAT (animal) & HERD (herdsman)], a cowherd.

neat's-foot oil (nēts′foot′), a light-yellow oil obtained by boiling the feet and shinbones of cattle, used mainly as a dressing for leather.

neb (neb), *n.* [ME. *nebbe;* AS. *nebb;* akin to MD. *nebbe,* ON. *nef,* etc.; Gmc. base **nefj-*], 1. *a)* the bill, or beak, of a bird. *b)* the snout of an animal; hence, 2. the nose or mouth of a person. 3. the projecting end or point of anything; nib; **tip.**

Neb., Nebraska.

NEbE, northeast by east.

Ne·bi·im (neb′i-ēm′; Heb. nə-vē′im), *n.pl.* [Heb. *nebī'īm,* pl. of *nābī,* prophet], in the *Old Testament,* the books of the Prophets.

NEbN, northeast by north.

Ne·bo, Mount (nē′bō), in the *Bible,* the mountain (summit of Mount Pisgah) from which Moses saw the Promised Land: Deut. 34:1-4.

Ne·bras·ka (nə-bras′kə), *n.* a Middle Western State of the United States: area, 77,237 sq. mi.; pop. 1,411,000; capital, Lincoln: abbreviated **Neb., Nebr.**

Ne·bras·kan (nə-bras′kən), *adj.* of Nebraska. *n.* a native or inhabitant of Nebraska.

Neb·u·chad·nez·zar (neb′yoo-kəd-nez′ẽr, neb′ə-kəd-nez′ẽr), *n.* [Assyr.-Bab. *nabū-kudurri-utsur,* lit., Nebo, defend the boundary], fl. 6th century B.C.; Chaldean king of Babylon (604?–562? B.C.) who conquered Jerusalem and destroyed the Temple: Dan. 1-4, II Kings 24.

Neb·u·chad·rez·zar (neb′yoo-kəd-rez′ẽr, neb′ə-kəd-rez′ẽr), *n.* [Heb. *nebhūkhadhre'tstsar*], Nebuchadnezzar.

neb·u·la (neb′yoo-lə), *n.* [*pl.* NEBULAE (-lē′), NEBULAS (-ləz)], [L.; IE. base **nebh-,* moist, vapor, cloud, seen also in Gr. *nephelē,* cloud, AS. *nifol,* mist, darkness (cf. NIBELUNG & G. *nebel,* mist), Avestan *nabah-,* air, sky], 1. any of several light, misty, cloudlike patches seen in the night sky, consisting of groups of stars too far away to be seen singly, or of masses of gaseous matter. 2. in *medicine, a)* a small, cloudy opacity on the cornea. *b)* a cloudiness in the urine. *c)* an oily preparation used as a spray.

neb·u·lar (neb′yoo-lẽr), *adj.* of a nebula or nebulae.

nebular hypothesis, the theory that the solar system was once a nebula which condensed to form the sun and planets.

neb·u·li·za·tion (neb′yoo-lə-zā′shən, neb′yoo-lī-zā′shən), *n.* a nebulizing or being nebulized.

neb·u·lize (neb′yoo-līz′), *v.t.* [NEBULIZED (-līzd′), NEBULIZING], [< L. *nebula,* mist (see NEBULA); + *-ize*], 1. to reduce (a liquid) to a fine spray. 2. to spray (a diseased or injured surface) with a medicated liquid.

neb·u·lose (neb′yoo-lōs′), *adj.* nebulous.

neb·u·los·i·ty (neb′yoo-los′ə-ti), *n.* [Fr. *nébulosité;* LL. *nebulositas*], 1. the quality or condition of being nebulous. 2. [*pl.* NEBULOSITIES (-tiz)], a nebula.

neb·u·lous (neb′yoo-ləs), *adj.* [ME. *nebulus;* L. *nebulosus*], 1. of or like a nebula or nebulae. 2. cloudy; misty; indistinct; hence, 3. unclear; vague; indefinite.

nec·es·sar·i·an (nes′ə-sâr′i-ən), *n. & adj.* necessitarian.

nec·es·sar·i·ly (nes′ə-ser′ə-li, nes′ə-sâr′ə-li), *adv.* 1. because of necessity; by or of necessity: as, that is not *necessarily* so. 2. as a necessary result.

nec·es·sar·y (nes′ə-ser′i), *adj.* [ME.; L. *necessarius* < *necesse,* unavoidable, necessary < *ne-,* not + *cedere,* to give way], 1. that cannot be dispensed with; essential; indispensable: as, water is *necessary* to life. 2. resulting from necessity; inevitable. 3. that must be done; mandatory; not voluntary; required. 4. inherent in the situation; undeniable; unavoidable from the premises. 5. [Archaic], rendering some essential and intimate service. *n.* [*pl.* NECESSARIES (-iz)], 1. *often in pl.* a necessary thing; thing essential to life, some purpose, etc. 2. [Dial.], a privy or water closet; toilet. 3. *pl.* in *law,* those things essential to maintaining an incompetent or dependent in comfort and well-being. —*SYN.* see **essential.**

ne·ces·si·tar·i·an (nə-ses′ə-târ′i-ən), *n.* a person who believes in necessitarianism. *adj.* of or like necessitarianism. Also **necessarian.**

ne·ces·si·tar·i·an·ism (nə-ses′ə-târ′i-ən-iz′m), *n.* the theory that every event is determined by causal necessity and that the action of the human will is not free, but is caused by previous actions and experiences.

ne·ces·si·tate (nə-ses′ə-tāt′), *v.t.* [NECESSITATED (-id), NECESSITATING], [< ML. *necessitatus,* pp. of *necessitare* < L. *necessitas,* necessity], 1. to make (something) necessary or unavoidable; involve or imply as a logical outcome. 2. to compel; require; force: usually in passive, as, I am *necessitated* to act alone.

ne·ces·si·tous (nə-ses′ə-təs), *adj.* [Fr. *nécessiteux;* see NECESSITY & -OUS], in great need; destitute; needy.

ne·ces·si·ty (nə-ses′ə-ti), *n.* [*pl.* NECESSITIES (-tiz)], [ME. *necessite* (cf. Fr. *nécessité*); L. *necessitas* < *necesse;* see NECESSARY], 1. the power of natural law that cannot be other than it is; natural causation; physical compulsion placed on man by nature; fate. 2. anything that is inevitable, unavoidable, etc. as a result of natural law; that which is necessary in natural sequence: as, death is a *necessity* to life. 3. the compulsion or constraint of man-made circumstances, habit, custom, law, etc.; logical or moral conditions making certain actions inevitable or obligatory. 4. what is required by this social or legal compulsion; that which is necessary in logical or moral sequence: as, a passport is a *necessity.* 5. great or imperative need: as, call me in case of *necessity.* 6. *often in pl.* something that cannot be done without; necessary. 7. the state or quality of being necessary. 8. **want;** poverty; neediness. —*SYN.* see **need.**

of necessity, necessarily; inevitably.

neck (nek), *n.* [ME. *nekke;* AS. *hnecca;* akin to G. *nacken;* Gmc. **hanak-;* IE. base **keng-,* peg, hook (cf. HANG); for *v.t.* 2 & *v.i.,* cf. AS. *healsgebedda,* beloved bedfellow, *healsmægeth,* beloved maid < *heals* (G. *hals*), the neck], 1. that part of man or animal joining the head to the body, including the part of the backbone between the skull and the shoulders; hence, 2. a narrow part between the head or end and the body or base of any object: as, the *neck* of a violin, *neck* of a goblet. 3. that part of a garment which covers, encircles, or is nearest the neck. 4. the narrowest part of any object, considered to be like a neck; specifically, *a)* a narrow strip of land. *b)* the narrowest part of an organ: as, the *neck* of the femur, *neck* of a tooth. *c)* the narrowest or tapering part of a bottle, vase, etc. *d)* a strait or channel. 5. in *geology,* a column of molten rock that has hardened in the passage connecting a volcanic crater with the underground source of the lava and has been exposed later by weathering. *v.t.* 1. to kill (a fowl) by breaking its neck. 2. [Slang], to kiss and caress in making love: cf. **pet.** *v.i.* [Slang], to engage in such love-making. —*SYN.* see **caress.**

get it in the neck, [Slang], to be severely reprimanded or punished.

neck and crop, completely; entirely.

neck and neck, side by side; in a contest or election, so close together that the winner is not determined until the very end.

neck or nothing, with determination to succeed completely or fail; at the risk of everything.

risk one's neck, to put one's life in danger; do something very dangerous.

win by a neck, 1. in *horse racing,* to win by the length of a horse's head and neck. 2. to win any contest by a narrow margin.

neck·band (nek′band′), *n.* 1. a band worn around the neck. 2. the part of a garment that encircles the neck; especially, the part to which the collar is fastened.
neck·cloth (nek′klôth′), *n.* a scarf for the neck; neckerchief; cravat.
Neck·er, Jacques (zhäk ne′kâr′; Eng. nek′ẽr), 1732–1804; father of Madame de Staël; French statesman; minister of finance (1776–1781; 1788–1790).
neck·er·chief (nek′ẽr-chif), *n.* [*neck* + *kerchief*], a handkerchief or scarf worn around the neck.
neck·ing (nek′iŋ), *n.* [see NECK, *v.*], 1. in *architecture*, any small molding around the top of a column below the capital. 2. [Slang], the act of kissing and caressing in making love.
neck·lace (nek′lis), *n.* [*neck* + *lace* (string)], a string or chain of gold, silver, jewels, wood, shells, etc., worn around the neck as an ornament.
neck·let (nek′lit), *n.* 1. a closely fitting band of fur or cloth worn around the neck. 2. a necklace.
neck·piece (nek′pēs′), *n.* 1. a decorative scarf, often of fur, worn around the neck. 2. the part of a garment closest to the neck. 3. a piece of armor for the neck.
neck·tie (nek′tī′), *n.* 1. a band, usually narrowest in the middle and widening at one or both ends, to be worn around the neck, usually under a collar and tied in a bow, knotted, or looped in front; cravat: often **tie.** 2. a bow fastened in front of the neck.
necktie party, [Slang], a hanging, especially in lynching.
neck·wear (nek′wâr′), *n.* articles worn about the neck; especially, neckties, scarfs, and collars.
nec·ro- (nek′rō, nek′rə), [< Gr. *nekros*, dead body], a combining form meaning *death, corpse, dead tissue*, as in *necrology*: also, before a vowel, **necr-**.
nec·ro·bi·o·sis (nek′rə-bī′ə-sis), *n.* [Mod. L.; *necro-* + *-biosis*], the process of decay and death of body cells.
ne·crol·a·try (ne-krol′ə-tri), *n.* [< *necro-* + *-latry*], worship of, or excessive reverence for, the dead.
nec·ro·log·i·cal (nek′rə-loj′i-k'l), *adj.* of or like a necrology.
ne·crol·o·gist (ne-krol′ə-jist), *n.* a writer of necrologies.
ne·crol·o·gy (ne-krol′ə-ji), *n.* [*pl.* NECROLOGIES (-jiz)], [*necro-* + *-logy*], 1. a list or register of people who have died in a certain time or place, as that in a newspaper. 2. a death notice; obituary.
nec·ro·man·cer (nek′rə-man′sẽr), *n.* [ME. *nigromanciere;* OFr. *nigromanceur* < *nigromance;* see NECROMANCY], 1. a person who claims to foretell the future through alleged communication with the dead. 2. a conjurer; wizard; sorcerer.
nec·ro·man·cy (nek′rə-man′si), *n.* [ME. *nigromancie;* OFr. *nigromance;* ML. *nigromantia* (altered by association with L. *niger*, black) < L. *necromantia;* Gr. *nekromanteia* < *nekros*, corpse + *manteia*, divination], 1. the art claiming to foretell the future by alleged communication with the dead. 2. black magic.
nec·ro·man·tic (nek′rə-man′tik), *adj.* [LL. *necromanticus*], of, like, used in, or done by necromancy.
nec·ro·phil·i·a (nek′rə-fil′i-ə), *n.* [Mod. L.], necrophilism.
ne·croph·i·lism (ne-krof′ə-liz'm), *n.* [< *necro-* + Gr. *philos*, loving; + *-ism*], an abnormal attraction, especially an erotic attraction, to corpses; necrophilia.
nec·ro·pho·bi·a (nek′rə-fō′bi-ə), *n.* [*necro-* + *-phobia*], an abnormal fear of death or of dead bodies.
ne·crop·o·lis (ne-krop′ə-lis), *n.* [*pl.* NECROPOLISES (-iz), NECROPOLEIS (-lis′)], [Gr. *nekropolis* < *nekros*, dead body + *polis*, city], a cemetery, especially one belonging to an ancient city.
nec·rop·sy (nek′rop-si), *n.* [*pl.* NECROPSIES (-siz)], [< *necr-* + Gr. *opsis*, sight; + *-y*], an autopsy; examination of a dead body.
ne·cros·co·py (ne-kros′kə-pi), *n.* a necropsy.
ne·crose (ne-krōs′, nek′rōs), *v.t.* [NECROSED (-krōst′, -rōst), NECROSING], to make necrotic. *v.i.* to be or become necrotic.
ne·cro·sis (ne-krō′sis), *n.* [*pl.* NECROSES (-sēz)], [Mod. L.; Gr. *nekrōsis* < *nekroun*, to make dead, mortify < *nekros*, dead body], 1. the death or decay of tissue in a part of the body, as a bone: it is the result of loss of blood supply, burning, and other severe injuries. 2. in *botany*, gradual decay of trees or plants.
ne·crot·ic (ne-krot′ik), *adj.* of or undergoing necrosis.
ne·crot·o·my (ne-krot′ə-mi), *n.* [*pl.* NECROTOMIES (-miz)], [*necro-* + *-tomy*], 1. the dissection of corpses. 2. the surgical removal of dead bone.
nec·tar (nek′tẽr), *n.* [L.; Gr. *nektar* < base of *necros*, dead, dead body + *-tar*, who overcomes (akin to Sans. *tarati*, he overcomes); hence, death-overcoming: so named because the drink was held to confer immortality], 1. in *Greek mythology*, the drink of the gods; hence, 2. any very delicious beverage. 3. in *botany*, the sweetish liquid in many flowers, used by bees for the making of honey.
nec·tar·e·an (nek-târ′i-ən), *adj.* like nectar.
nec·tar·e·ous (nek-târ′i-əs), *adj.* [L. *nectareus;* Gr. *nektareos*], 1. producing nectar. 2. like nectar; sweet; delicious.
nec·tar·i·al (nek-târ′i-əl), *adj.* of, or having the nature of, a nectary.
nec·tar·ine (nek′tə-rēn′, nek′tə-rēn′), *n.* [< *nectar*], a kind of peach that has a smooth skin without down.
nec·ta·ry (nek′tə-ri), *n.* [*pl.* NECTARIES (-riz)], [Mod. L. *nectarium*], 1. an organ or part (of a flower) that secretes nectar. 2. either of a pair of abdominal tubes in aphids, for sucking nectar from flowers.
Ned (ned), [by faulty division of *mine Ed*], a masculine name: see **Edgar, Edmund, Edward.**
N.E.D., NED, New English Dictionary (Oxford English Dictionary).
nee, née (nā), *adj.* [Fr., fem. of *né*, pp. of *naître* < L. *nasci*, to be born], born: used to introduce the maiden name of a married woman, as, Mrs. Helen Jones, *nee* Smith.
need (nēd), *n.* [ME. *nede;* AS. *nead, neod, nied, ned;* akin to G. *not* (Goth. *nauths*); IE. **nəu-ti* < base **nəu-*, to collapse with weariness, seen also in Goth. *naus*, corpse], 1. necessity; compulsion; obligation: as, there is no *need* to worry now. 2. a lack of something useful, required, or desired; call or demand for the presence, possession, etc. of something: as, I feel the *need* of a long rest. 3. something useful, required, or desired that is lacking; want; requirement: as, what are his daily *needs?* 4. *a)* a condition in which there is a deficiency of something; time or situation of difficulty; condition requiring relief or supply: as, a friend in *need.* *b)* a condition of poverty; state of extreme want. *v.t.* to have need of; want. *Need* is often used as an auxiliary, either uninflected and followed by an infinitive without *to*, or inflected and followed by an infinitive with *to*, meaning "to be obliged, must": as, he *need* not come, he *needs* to be careful. *v.i.* 1. [Archaic], to be necessary: chiefly in impersonal constructions, as, it *needs* not. 2. to be in need. See also **needs.**
have need to, to be compelled or required to; must.
if need be, if it is required; if the occasion demands.
SYN.—**need** refers to an urgent requirement of something essential or desirable that is lacking; **necessity,** a more formal word, suggests an imperative need for something indispensable but lacks the emotional connotations of **need** (they are in *need* of food, food is a *necessity* for all living things); **exigency** refers to a necessity created by some emergency, crisis, or compelling circumstances (the *exigencies* created by the flood); **requisite** applies to something that is indispensable to a particular end or goal (a sense of rhythm is a *requisite* in a dancer). See also **lack.**
need·ful (nēd′fəl), *adj.* 1. necessary; needed; required. 2. [Archaic], characterized by great need or distress; needy.
need·i·ness (nēd′i-nis), *n.* the quality or state of being needy; poverty; indigence; want.
nee·dle (nē′d'l), *n.* [ME. *nedle, nedel;* AS. *nædl;* akin to G. *nadel;* IE. base *(*s*)*nē-*, *(*s*)*nēi-*, to sew, spin, seen also in L. *nere*, to spin & Eng. *snood*], 1. *a)* a small, slender piece of steel with a sharp point at one end and a hole for thread at the other, used for sewing by hand. *b)* a similar implement with a hole for thread near the pointed end, used especially on sewing machines. 2. *a)* a slender rod of steel, bone, wood, etc. with a hook at one end, used for crocheting. *b)* a similar rod, usually larger and without a hook, used in knitting. 3. the short, pointed piece of metal, often tipped as with diamond, that moves in the grooves of a phonograph record and transmits vibrations. 4. *a)* the magnetized pointer of a compass. *b)* the indicator or pointer of a speedometer or other gauge. 5. the thin, short, pointed leaf of such trees as the pine, spruce, etc. 6. the thin rod which, when moved, opens or closes a passage in a valve and permits close adjustment. 7. the sharp, very slender metal tube at the end of a hypodermic syringe. 8. an electric needle. 9. any object roughly resembling a needle or its point in shape, as the sharp point of some crystals, a narrow, jutting, pointed rock, an obelisk, etc. *v.t.* [NEEDLED (-d'ld), NEEDLING], 1. to sew, puncture, etc. with a needle. 2. [Colloq.], *a)* to provoke into doing something; goad; prod. *b)* to tease or heckle. 3. [Slang], to strengthen by adding alcohol: as, they *needled* the beer. *v.i.* 1. to work with a needle. 2. to form needles in crystallization.
nee·dle·fish (nē′d'l-fish′), *n.* [*pl.* NEEDLEFISH, NEEDLEFISHES (-iz); see FISH], 1. any of a group of long, pipelike, voracious marine fishes with a pointed snout and many sharp teeth, somewhat resembling the garfish. 2. a pipefish.
nee·dle·ful (nē′d'l-fool′), *n.* [*pl.* NEEDLEFULS (-foolz′)], the length of thread conveniently used in a needle at one time.
nee·dle-point (nē′d'l-point′), *adj.* designating lace made on a pattern with a needle instead of a bobbin.
needle point, 1. an embroidery of woolen threads upon canvas, used as a covering in upholstery. 2. needle-point lace.

needle shower, a shower bath in which the water is sprayed out in fine jets.
need·less (nēd′lis), *adj.* not needed; unnecessary.
needle valve, a type of valve in which a long, cone-shaped plug instead of a disk controls the flow of fluid: used especially on high-pressure gas cylinders.
nee·dle·wom·an (nē′d'l-woom′ən), *n.* [*pl.* NEEDLEWOMEN (-wim′in)], a woman who does needlework; especially, a seamstress.
nee·dle·work (nē′d'l-wũrk′), *n.* work done with a needle; embroidery; sewing.
need·n't (nēd′'nt), need not.
needs (nēdz), *adv.* [ME. *nedes;* AS. *nedes, nydes* < *nied* (see NEED) + *-s*, genit. & adv. suffix], of necessity; necessarily (with *must*): as, he must *needs* obey.
need·y (nēd′i), *adj.* [NEEDIER (-i-ẽr), NEEDIEST (-i-ist)], in, or characterized by, need; not having enough to live on; very poor; destitute; indigent.
neep (nēp), *n.* [ME.; AS. *næp* < L. *napus*], [Scot. & British Dial.], a turnip.
ne'er (nâr), *adv.* [Poetic], never.
ne'er-do-well (nâr′doo-wel′), *n.* a person who never does anything of value; person who cannot make a living, get along, etc. *adj.* worthless; good-for-nothing.
ne·far·i·ous (ni-fâr′i-əs), *adj.* [L. *nefarius* < *nefas*, crime, wrong; *ne-*, not + *fas*, lawful], very wicked; villainous; iniquitous. —*SYN.* see **vicious.**
Ne·fud Desert (ne-fo͞od′), a desert in north central Saudi Arabia: also called *Red Desert.*
ne·gate (ni-gāt′, nē′gāt), *v.t.* [NEGATED (-id), NEGATING], [< L. *negatus;* see NEGATION], 1. to deny the existence or truth of. 2. to make ineffective. —*SYN.* see **nullify.**
ne·ga·tion (ni-gā′shən), *n.* [< Fr. or L.; Fr. *négation;* L. *negatio* < *negatus*, pp. of *negare*, to deny < *ne-*, *neg-, not + *aio*, I say], 1. act or instance of denying; negative answer; denial. 2. the lack or opposite of some positive character or quality, as annihilation, destruction, etc. 3. something negative; nonentity.
neg·a·tive (neg′ə-tiv), *adj.* [< Fr. or L.; Fr. *négatif;* L. *negativus* < *negatus;* see NEGATION], 1. containing, expressing, or implying a denial or refusal; saying "no": opposed to *affirmative.* 2. opposite to something considered as positive; specifically, *a*) lacking in positive character or quality; lacking evidence, affirmation, etc.; having the effect of diminishing, depriving, or denying: as, a *negative* personality. *b*) not demonstrating or proving the presence or existence of symptoms, bacteria, etc. 3. in *logic*, denying the subject or predicate of a proposition. 4. in *mathematics*, designating a quantity less than zero, or one to be subtracted; minus. 5. in *photography*, reversing the relation of light and shade of the original subject. 6. in *physics*, of negative electricity. *n.* 1. a word, term, or phrase that denies, rejects, or refuses (e.g., *no, not, by no means*). 2. a statement of denial, refusal, or rejection. 3. the point of view that denies or attacks the positive or affirmative: as, the *negative* won the debate. 4. the right of veto. 5. the plate in a voltaic battery where the lower potential is; negative plate or pole. 6. in *mathematics*, a quantity less than zero, or one to be subtracted; minus quantity. 7. in *photography*, an exposed and developed photographic film or plate on which light and shadow are the reverse of what they are in the positive printed from this. Abbreviated **neg.** *v.t.* [NEGATIVED (-tivd), NEGATIVING], 1. to refuse; reject; veto (a candidate, motion, or bill). 2. to deny; contradict. 3. to prove false; disprove. 4. to counteract; neutralize.
in the negative, 1. in refusal or denial of a plan, suggestion, etc. 2. with a denial or negative answer.
negative electricity, 1. electricity made by friction on resin or wax, as distinct from that made on glass. 2. electricity appearing at the pole of the plate having the lower potential in a voltaic cell.
negative sign, in *mathematics*, the sign (−), used to indicate a negative quantity.
neg·a·tiv·ism (neg′ə-tiv-iz'm), *n.* 1. in *philosophy*, any system of thought opposed to positivism; doctrine characterized not by approval and acceptance, but by doubt and question, as agnosticism or skepticism. 2. in *psychology*, an attitude characterized by ignoring or opposing suggestions or orders from others, most often manifested in children.
neg·a·tiv·ist (neg′ə-tiv-ist), *n.* a believer in negativism. *adj.* of negativism or negativists.
neg·a·tiv·is·tic (neg′ə-ti-vis′tik), *adj.* negativist.
neg·a·tiv·i·ty (neg′ə-tiv′ə-ti), *n.* the quality or condition of being negative.
neg·a·to·ry (neg′ə-tôr′i, neg′ə-tō′ri), *adj.* [LL. *negatorius*], negative; constituting or expressing negation.
neg·a·tron (neg′ə-tron′), *n.* [*negative* + *electron*], [Rare], in *chemistry & physics*, an electron.
Ne·geb (neg′eb), *n.* Negev.
Ne·gev (neg′ev), *n.* a region in southern Israel, of partially reclaimed desert.
neg·lect (ni-glekt′), *v.t.* [< L. *neglectus*, pp. of *negligere, neglegere*, not to heed, be regardless of < *neg-, not + *egere*, to gather], 1. to ignore or disregard (something): as, we *neglect* modern art. 2. not to care for or attend to (something) sufficiently or properly; slight; treat as unimportant: as, he *neglected* his clothes. 3. to fail to carry out (an expected or required action) through carelessness or by intention; leave undone. *n.* 1. a neglecting. 2. lack of sufficient or proper care; negligence; disregard. 3. the state of being neglected.
SYN.—**neglect** implies a failure to carry out some expected or required action, either through carelessness or by intention (I *neglected* to wind the clock); **omit,** in this connection, implies a neglecting through oversight, absorption, etc. (she should not *omit* to visit the Louvre); **overlook** suggests a failure to see or to take action, either inadvertently or indulgently (I'll *overlook* your errors this time); **disregard** implies inattention or neglect, usually intentional (she always *disregards* his wishes); **ignore** suggests a deliberate disregarding, sometimes through stubborn refusal to face the facts (but you *ignore* the necessity for action); **slight** implies a disregarding or neglecting in an indifferent or disdainful way (he seems to *slight* the newer writers); **forget,** in this connection, implies an intentional disregarding or omitting (after his election he *forgot* the wishes of the voters).
neg·lect·er, neg·lect·or (ni-glek′tẽr), *n.* a person who neglects.
neg·lect·ful (ni-glekt′fəl), *adj.* characterized by neglect; heedless; negligent (often with *of*). —*SYN.* see **remiss.**
‡né·gli·gé (nā′glē′zhā′; Eng. neg′li-zhā′) *n.* & *adj.* [Fr.], negligee.
neg·li·gee (neg′li-zhā′, neg′li-zhā′), *n.* [Fr. *négligée*, fem. of *négligé*, pp. of *négliger*, to neglect; L. *negligere;* see NEGLECT], 1. a woman's loosely fitting dressing gown, usually decorative and of a soft, flowing material. 2. any informal, careless, or incomplete attire. *adj.* carelessly or incompletely dressed.
neg·li·gence (neg′li-jəns), *n.* [ME. *neglygence, necligens;* OFr.; L. *negligentia*], 1. the quality or condition of being negligent; specifically, *a*) habitual failure to do the required thing. *b*) carelessness in manner or appearance; indifference. 2. an instance of such failure, carelessness, or indifference. 3. in *law*, failure to use a reasonable amount of care when such failure results in injury to another.
neg·li·gent (neg′li-jənt), *adj.* [ME. *necligent*, etc. < OFr. or L.; OFr. *negligent;* L. *negligens*, ppr. of *negligere;* see NEGLECT], 1. habitually failing to do the required thing; neglectful. 2. careless, lax, inattentive, or indifferent. —*SYN.* see **remiss.**
neg·li·gi·bil·i·ty (neg′li-jə-bil′ə-ti), *n.* the quality or state of being negligible.
neg·li·gi·ble (neg′li-jə-b'l), *adj.* [< L. *negligere* (see NEGLECT); + *-ible*], that can be neglected or disregarded because small, unimportant, etc.; trifling.
neg·li·gi·bly (neg′li-jə-bli), *adv.* in a negligible manner; so as to be negligible.
ne·go·ti·a·bil·i·ty (ni-gō′shi-ə-bil′ə-ti, ni-gō′shə-bil′ə-ti), *n.* the state or quality of being negotiable.
ne·go·ti·a·ble (ni-gō′shi-ə-b'l, ni-gō′shə-b'l), *adj.* that can be negotiated; specifically, *a*) transferable to a third person: said of promissory notes, checks, etc. *b*) that can be passed, crossed, surmounted, etc.
ne·go·ti·ate (ni-gō′shi-āt′), *v.i.* [NEGOTIATED (-id), NEGOTIATING], [< L. *negotiatus*, pp. of *negotiari*, to carry on business < *negotium*, business < *nec-*, not + *otium*, ease], to confer, bargain, or discuss with a view to reaching agreement. *v.t.* 1. to make arrangements for, settle, or conclude (a business transaction, treaty, etc.). 2. to transfer, assign, or sell (negotiable paper). 3. [Colloq.], to succeed in crossing, surmounting, accomplishing, etc.
ne·go·ti·a·tion (ni-gō′shi-ā′shən), *n.* [L. *negotiatio*], a negotiating; specifically, *often in pl.*, a conferring, discussing, or bargaining to reach agreement, as in business transactions or state matters.
ne·go·ti·a·tor (ni-gō′shi-ā′tẽr), *n.* [L.], a person who negotiates.
Ne·gress (nē′gris), *n.* [Fr. *négresse*, fem. of *négro*, a Negro], [sometimes n-], a Negro woman or girl: often a patronizing or contemptuous term.
Ne·gril·lo (ni-gril′ō), *n.* [*pl.* NEGRILLOS (-ōz)], [Sp., dim. of *negro*, black; see NEGRO], an African Pygmy or Bushman.
Ne·gri Sem·bi·lan (nā′grē sem′bē-län′), a native state of the Federation of Malaya: area, 2,580 sq. mi.; pop., 286,000; capital, Seremban.
Ne·grit·ic (ni-grit′ik), *adj.* [sometimes n-], of or like Negroes or Negritos.
Ne·gri·to (ni-grē′tō), *n.* [*pl.* NEGRITOS, NEGRITOES (-tōz)], [Sp., dim. of *negro*, black; see NEGRO], a member of any of various groups of dwarfish Negroid peoples living in the East Indies, the Philippines, and Africa.
Ne·gro (nē′grō), *n.* [*pl.* NEGROES (-grōz)], [Sp. & Port. *negro*, black, black person < L. *niger*, black], 1. *a*) a member of the dominant black race of Africa, living chiefly in the Congo and Sudan regions. *b*) a member of any of the other black races of Africa, as a Bantu, Hottentot, etc. 2. any person with some Negro ancestors. *adj.* of, for, or being a Negro or Negroes. Less often **negro.**
Ne·gro, Rí·o (rē′ō nā′grō; Sp. rē′ô ne′grô), 1. a river in northern Brazil, flowing into the Amazon: length, 1,400 mi. 2. a river in central Argentina, flowing into the Atlantic: length, 630 mi.

Ne·groid (nē'groid), *adj.* [sometimes n-], of, like, or characteristic of the Negro or Negroes. *n.* [sometimes n-], a member of any dominantly Negro people.
Ne·gro·phil (nē'grə-fil), *n.* [sometimes n-], a Negrophile.
Ne·gro·phile (nē'grə-fil', nē'grə-fil), *n.* [*Negro* + *-phile*], [sometimes n-], a person who admires, likes, or champions Negroes, their culture, etc.: often used contemptuously by Negrophobes.
Ne·gro·phobe (nē'grə-fōb'), *n.* [*Negro* + *-phobe*], [sometimes n-], a person who hates or fears Negroes.
Ne·gro·pho·bi·a (nē'grə-fō'bi-ə), *n.* [*Negro* + *-phobia*], [sometimes n-], hatred or fear of Negroes.
Neg·ro·pon·te (neg'rô-pôn'te), *n.* Evvoia, a Greek island in the Aegean: the Italian name.
Ne·gros (nā'grōs; Sp. ne'grôs), *n.* one of the Philippine Islands, between Panay and Cebu: area, 4,903 sq. mi.; pop., 1,219,000.
Ne·gus (nē'gəs), *n.* [Amharic *nĕgūš*, king], the title of the ruler of Ethiopia.
ne·gus (nē'gəs), *n.* [after Col. Francis *Negus* (d. 1732), who first made it], a beverage of hot water, wine, and lemon juice, sweetened and spiced.
Ne·he·mi·ah (nē'ə-mī'ə), *n.* [Heb. *neḥemyāh*, lit., comfort of Jah (God)], in the *Bible*, 1. a Hebrew leader of about the 5th century B.C. 2. a book of the Old Testament about his work. Abbreviated **Neh.**
Ne·he·mi·as (nē'ə-mī'əs), *n.* Nehemiah: form used in the Douay Bible.
Neh·ru, Ja·wa·har·lal (jə-wä'hẽr-läl' nā'rōō), 1889– ; Hindu leader of the National Congress Party in India; prime minister of India (1947–).
neigh (nā), *v.i.* [ME. *neyen, nayen;* AS. *hnægan;* akin to MD. *neyen;* echoic], to utter the loud, characteristic cry of a horse; whinny. *n.* this cry; a whinny.
neigh·bor (nā'bẽr), *n.* [ME. *neighbour, nyebour*, etc.; AS. *neahgebur* < *neah, nigh* (see NIGH) + **gebur*, freeholder, peasant, farmer (cf. BOOR, BOER); akin to G. *nachbar* (MHG. *nachbūr*), etc.], 1. a person who lives near another. 2. a person or thing situated near another. 3. a fellow man: as, love thy *neighbor*. 4. any person: used as a term of direct address. *adj.* near-by; adjacent. *v.t.* 1. to live or be situated near (someone or something). 2. [Rare], to bring near or into close association with. *v.i.* 1. to live or be situated near-by. 2. to have friendly relations; associate on friendly terms (often followed by *with*). British spelling, **neighbour.**
neigh·bor·hood (nā'bẽr-hood'), *n.* [see -HOOD], 1. [Rare], friendly relations, as of neighbors; neighborliness. 2. the state or quality of being neighbors. 3. a community, region, area, or territory, especially with regard to some characteristic: as, they live in an attractive *neighborhood*. 4. the people living near one another; community.
in the neighborhood of, [Colloq.], 1. near; close to (a place). 2. about; approximately; roughly.
neigh·bor·ing (nā'bẽr-iŋ), *adj.* [ppr. of *neighbor*], near-by; adjacent; close together; in the same region. —*SYN.* see **adjacent.**
neigh·bor·li·ness (nā'bẽr-li-nis), *n.* the quality or condition of being neighborly.
neigh·bor·ly (nā'bẽr-li), *adj.* like, characteristic of, or appropriate to neighbors; kind, friendly, sociable, etc.
Neil (nēl), a masculine name: see **Neal.**
Neil·son, William Allan (nēl'sən), 1869–1946; American educator, writer, and editor, born in Scotland; president of Smith College (1917–1939).
nei·ther (nē'*th*ẽr, nī'*th*ẽr), *adj.* [ME. *naither, neyther*, etc.; altered (after *eyther, either;* see EITHER) < *nauther, nother*, etc. < AS. *na-hwæther*, lit., not whether (cf. NA, NO, WHETHER), not either of two], not one or the other of two; not either: as, use *neither* hand. *pron.* not one or the other (of two); not either: as, *neither* of the reasons is adequate. *conj.* 1. not either: the first element of the pair of correlatives *neither. . .nor*, implying negation of both parts of the statement: as, I can *neither* go nor stay. 2. nor yet; and. . .not: as, he doesn't smoke, *neither* does he drink. *adv.* [Dial. or Colloq.], any more than the other; also (following negative expressions): as, if she won't go, I won't *neither*.
Nejd (nezhd), *n.* an inland state of Saudi Arabia: area, c. 170,000 sq. mi.; pop., 3,000,000; capital, Riyadh.
nek·ton (nek'ton), *n.* [Mod. L.; Gr. *nektōn*, neut. of *nektos*, swimming], all the minute organisms swimming in large numbers on or near the surface of the sea.
Nell (nel), a feminine name: see **Helen, Eleanor.**
Nel·lie, Nel·ly (nel'i), a feminine name: see **Helen, Eleanor.**
Nel·son (nel's'n), [< the surname *Nelson;* ME. *Nel* (see NEAL); + *son*], a masculine name. *n.* a river in Manitoba, flowing into Hudson Bay: length, 390 mi.
nel·son (nel's'n), *n.* [< personal name *Nelson*], a hold in wrestling: see **full nelson, half nelson.**
Nelson, Horatio, Viscount Nelson, 1758–1805; English admiral; victor over Napoleon at Trafalgar (1805).
ne·lum·bo (ni-lum'bō), *n.* [Mod. L. < Singhalese *nelumbu*], any of a group of water lilies with blue-green leaves and flowers of white to dark red.
Ne·man (nye'mān), *n.* the Niemen: the Russian name.
nem·a·tel·minth (nem'ə-tel'minth), *n.* a nemathelminth.
nem·a·thel·minth (nem'ə-thel'minth), *n.* [*nemat-* + *helminth*], any of a large group of round, unsegmented worms, as the nematodes.
nem·a·to- (nem'ə-tō), [< Gr. *nēma, nēmatos*, what is spun, thread], a combining form meaning *thread, threadlike*, as in *nematocyst:* also, before a vowel, **nemat-.**
nem·a·to·cyst (nem'ə-tō-sist'), *n.* [*nemato-* + *-cyst*], any of the stinging cells of certain hydrozoans, as the jellyfish, containing a threadlike sting.
nem·a·to·cys·tic (nem'ə-tō-sis'tik), *adj.* of, like, or forming a nematocyst.
nem·a·tode (nem'ə-tōd'), *adj.* [< Mod. L. *Nematoda*, name of the group < *Nematoidea* < *nemato-* + *-ode*], designating or of a group of worms with long, cylindrical, unsegmented bodies, as the hookworm, pinworm, etc. *n.* a worm of this group.
Nem·bu·tal (nem'byoo-tôl', nem'byoo-tal'), *n.* [*Na* (sodium) + *e*thyl + *m*ethyl + *bu*tyl + barbi*tal*], pentobarbital sodium, used in medicine as a sedative, hypnotic, and analgesic: a trade-mark.
Ne·me·a (nē'mi-ə), *n.* a valley in ancient Argolis, in southeastern Greece.
Ne·me·an (ni-mē'ən, nē'mi-ən), *adj.* of Nemea.
Nemean games, an ancient Greek festival held every other year at Nemea, consisting chiefly of athletic and musical contests.
Nemean lion, in *Greek mythology*, a fierce lion killed by Hercules in the course of his twelve labors.
ne·mer·te·an, ne·mer·ti·an (ni-mûr'ti-ən), *adj.* [< Mod. L. *Nemertea*, name of the group < Gr. *Nēmertēs*, name of a sea nymph < *nēmertēs*, unerring], belonging to a group of brightly colored marine worms living in coastal mud or sand. *n.* a worm of this group.
nem·er·tin·e·an (nem'ẽr-tin'i-ən), *adj. & n.* nemertean.
Nem·e·sis (nem'ə-sis), *n.* [L.; Gr. *Nemesis* < *nemein*, to distribute, deal out], 1. in *Greek mythology*, the goddess of retributive justice, or vengeance. 2. [usually n-], [*pl.* NEMESES (-sēz')], *a)* just punishment; retribution. *b)* one who imposes retribution.
‡**ne·mi·ne con·tra·di·cen·te** (nem'ə-nē' kon'trə-di-sen'ti), [L.], (with) no one contradicting; hence, unanimously: abbreviated **nem. con.**
‡**ne·mi·ne dis·sen·ti·en·te** (nem'ə-nē' di-sen'shi-en'ti), [L.], (with) no one dissenting; hence, unanimously: abbreviated **nem. diss.**
Ne·mu·nas (nye'moo-näs'), *n.* the Niemen: the Lithuanian name.
N.Eng., 1. New England. 2. North England.
ne·o- (nē'ō, nē'ə), [< Gr. *neos*, new, recent, young], a combining form meaning: 1. [sometimes N-], *new, recent, latest*, as in *Neo-Catholic, neoclassic*. 2. [N-], in *geology, the chronologically last subdivision of a period*, as in *Neocene*. Also **ne-.**
ne·o·ars·phen·am·in (nē'ō-ärs'fen-am'in), *n.* neoarsphenamine.
ne·o·ars·phen·a·mine (nē'ō-ärs'fen-ə-mēn', nē'ō-ärs'-fen-am'in), *n.* a sodium compound of arsphenamine, used instead of arsphenamine because it is less toxic and more soluble: also called *Neosalvarsan*.
Ne·o-Cath·o·lic (nē'ō-kath'ə-lik, nē'ō-kath'lik), *adj.* 1. designating or of a group in the Anglican Church that tends toward Roman Catholic doctrine and practice. 2. in France, designating or of a group of liberal Catholics opposed to the religious supremacy of the Pope. *n.* a member of either of these groups.
Ne·o·cene (nē'ə-sēn'), *adj.* [< *neo-* + Gr. *kainos*, new], designating or of the latter epoch of the Tertiary, including the Miocene and the Pliocene, when mammals underwent their greatest development and manlike types appeared.
the Neocene, the Neocene Epoch or its rocks.
ne·o·clas·sic (nē'ō-klas'ik), *adj.* designating or of a revival of classic style and form in art, literature, etc., as in England from c. 1660 to c. 1740.
ne·o·clas·si·cal (nē'ō-klas'i-k'l), *adj.* neoclassic.
Ne·o-Dar·win·ism (nē'ō-där'win-iz'm), *n.* a biological theory which maintains that natural selection is the main factor in the evolution of animals and plants, and denies the inheritance of acquired characteristics.
ne·o·dym·i·um (nē'ə-dim'i-əm), *n.* [Mod. L. < *neo-* + *didymium*], a metallic chemical element of the rare-earth group: symbol, Nd; at. wt., 144.27; at. no., 60.
Ne·o·gae·a (nē'ə-jē'ə), *n.* [Mod. L. < *neo-* + Gr. *gaia*, earth], the Neotropical area of the earth, considered as one of the primary realms.
Ne·o-He·bra·ic (nē'ō-hē-brā'ik), *n. & adj.* Modern Hebrew.
ne·o·im·pres·sion·ism (nē'ō-im-presh'ən-iz'm), *n.* a

late 19th-century theory and practice of painting, based on a strict scientific application of impressionist techniques, especially pointillism.

Ne·o-La·marck·ism (nē'ō-lə-märk'iz'm), *n.* a theory of inheritance based on a modification and extension of Lamarckism, essentially maintaining the principle that acquired characters can be inherited, but admitting the importance of natural selection.

Ne·o-Lat·in (nē'ō-lat''n), *n.* Modern Latin.

ne·o·lith (nē'ə-lith'), *n.* a neolithic tool.

ne·o·lith·ic (nē'ə-lith'ik), *adj.* [*neo-* + *-lith* + *-ic*], designating or of the later part of the Stone Age (in the Old World), during which man developed polished stone tools and weapons, raised cattle, etc.

ne·o·log·i·cal (nē'ə-loj'i-k'l), *adj.* of or characterized by neology or (a) neologism.

ne·ol·o·gism (nē-ol'ə-jiz'm), *n.* [Fr. *néologisme;* see NEO-, -LOGY & -ISM], 1. a new word or a new meaning for an established word. 2. the use of new words or of new meanings for established words.

ne·ol·o·gist (nē-ol'ə-jist), *n.* [Fr. *néologiste*], a person who invents, or makes a practice of using, neologisms.

ne·ol·o·gis·tic (nē-ol'ə-jis'tik), *adj.* of or characterized by neologism.

ne·ol·o·gis·ti·cal (nē-ol'ə-jis'ti-k'l), *adj.* neologistic.

ne·ol·o·gize (nē-ol'ə-jīz'), *v.i.* [NEOLOGIZED (-jīzd'), NEOLOGIZING], [Fr. *néologiser;* see NEO-, -LOGY & -IZE], to invent, or make a practice of using, new words or new meanings for established words.

ne·ol·o·gy (nē-ol'ə-ji), *n.* [*pl.* NEOLOGIES (-jiz)], [Fr. *néologie*], neologism.

ne·o·my·cin (nē'ə-mī'sin), *n.* [< *neo-* + Gr. *mykēs*, fungus; + *-in*], an antibiotic drug similar to streptomycin, used in the treatment of various skin and eye infections and certain systemic infections.

ne·on (nē'on), *n.* [Mod. L. < Gr. *neon*, neut. of *neos*, new], a rare, colorless, and inert gaseous chemical element, found in the earth's atmosphere: symbol, Ne; at. wt., 20.183; at. no., 10.

neon lamp, a glass tube filled with neon, which ionizes and glows when an electric current is sent through it.

ne·o·phyte (nē'ə-fīt'), *n.* [LL. *neophytus;* Gr. *neophytos*, newly planted < *neos*, new + *phytos* < *phyein*, to produce, grow], 1. a new convert; especially, a newly baptized member of the early Christian Church. 2. a newly ordained priest or new member of a convent. 3. any beginner; novice. —***SYN.*** see **amateur.**

ne·o·plasm (nē'ə-plaz'm), *n.* [*neo-* + *-plasm*], any abnormal growth of tissue; tumor, etc.

ne·o·plas·tic (nē'ə-plas'tik), *adj.* of a neoplasm.

ne·o·plas·ti·cism (nē'ō-plas'tə-siz'm), *n.* [*neo-* + *plastic* + *-ism*], an early 20th-century school of abstract painting, characterized by nonsymmetrical geometric figures.

ne·o·plas·ty (nē'ə-plas'ti), *n.* [*neo-* + *-plasty*], the use of plastic surgery to restore a destroyed or mutilated part of the body.

Ne·o·pla·to·nism, Ne·o-Pla·to·nism (nē'ō-plā't'n-iz'm), *n.* a school of philosophy, founded at Alexandria in the 3d century A.D., that tried to combine the doctrines of Plato and some other Greek philosophers with the ethical concepts common to Judaism and Christianity, and with the mysticism of the Near East.

ne·o·prene (nē'ə-prēn'), *n.* [*neo-* + chloro*prene*], a synthetic rubber produced by the polymerization of a chlorine derivative of acetylene: it is highly resistant to oil, heat, light, and oxidation.

Ne·o·sal·var·san (nē'ō-sal'vẽr-san), *n.* [*neo-* + *salvarsan*], neoarsphenamine: a trade-mark.

Ne·o-Scho·las·ti·cism (nē'ō-skə-las'tə-siz'm), *n.* a philosophical system based on scholasticism but incorporating new elements, particularly emphasis on research, to make it applicable to contemporary life.

ne·o·style (nē'ə-stīl'), *n.* [*neo-* + *style*], a type of cyclostyle for multiple reproduction of a writing, drawing, etc. *v.t.* [NEOSTYLED (-stīld'), NEOSTYLING], to reproduce by means of a neostyle.

ne·o·ter·ic (nē'ə-ter'ik), *adj.* [LL. *neotericus;* Gr. *neōterikos* < *neōteros*, compar. of *neos*, young], recent; new; newly invented. *n.* a modern person; one accepting new ideas and practices.

Ne·o·trop·ic (nē'ə-trop'ik), *adj.* Neotropical.

Ne·o·trop·i·cal (nē'ə-trop'i-k'l), *adj.* [*neo-* + *tropical*], designating or of that region of the New World extending southward from the Tropic of Cancer.

Ne·o·zo·ic (nē'ə-zō'ik), *adj.* [< *neo-* + Gr. *zōē*, life; + *-ic*], in *geology*, 1. designating or of the period including the Mesozoic and the Cenozoic. 2. Cenozoic: former name.

NEP, Nep, nep, (nep), *n.* New Economic Policy.

Ne·pal (ni-pôl'), *n.* a country in the Himalaya Mountains, between India and Tibet; area, 54,000 sq. mi.; pop., 9,180,000; capital, Katmandu.

Nep·a·lese (nep'ə-lēz'), *adj.* of Nepal, its people, or their culture. *n.* [*pl.* NEPALESE], a native of Nepal.

ne·pen·the (ni-pen'thi), *n.* [L. < Gr. *nepenthēs*, removing sorrow < *ne-*, not + *penthos*, sorrow, grief], 1. a drug supposed by the ancient Greeks to cause forgetfulness of sorrow. 2. anything causing this state.

ne·pen·the·an (ni-pen'thi-ən), *adj.* of, or having the nature of, nepenthe; causing forgetfulness.

ne·pen·thes (ni-pen'thēz), *n.* nepenthe.

neph·e·line (nef'ə-lin), *n.* [Fr. *néphéline*], nephelite.

neph·e·lin·ite (nef'ə-lin-īt'), *n.* [< *nepheline* + *-ite*], a dark, granular volcanic rock composed of nephelite and pyroxene.

neph·e·lite (nef'ə-līt'), *n.* [< Gr. *nephelē*, a cloud (see NEBULA); + *-ite*], a silicate of aluminum, sodium, and potassium, found in many igneous rocks: also **nepheline.**

neph·e·lom·e·ter (nef'ə-lom'ə-tẽr), *n.* [< Gr. *nephelē*, a cloud; + *-meter*], an apparatus for measuring the concentration of a suspension, as of bacteria or some chemical substance in solution, by comparing the brightness of light passed through it with that passed through a set of standard solutions of barium chloride.

neph·ew (nef'ū; *esp.* Brit., nev'ū), *n.* [ME. *neve, neveu;* OFr. *neveu* < L. *nepos*], 1. *a*) the son of one's brother or sister. *b*) the son of one's brother-in-law or sister-in-law. 2. an illegitimate son, as of a medieval prelate: a euphemism. 3. [Obs.], a grandson.

neph·o- (nef'ō, nef'ə), [< Gr. *nephos*, cloud], a combining form meaning *cloud, clouds*, as in *nephology.*

neph·o·gram (nef'ə-gram'), *n.* [*nepho-* + *-gram*], a photograph of a cloud.

ne·phol·o·gy (ni-fol'ə-ji), *n.* [*nepho-* + *-logy*], the branch of meteorology dealing with clouds.

neph·o·scope (nef'ə-skōp'), *n.* [*nepho-* + *-scope*], an instrument for determining the altitude of a cloud and the direction and velocity of its drift.

nephr-, nephro-.

ne·phral·gi·a (ne-fral'ji-ə), *n.* [*nephr-* + *-algia*], pain in the kidneys.

ne·phrec·to·my (ne-frek'tə-mi), *n.* [*pl.* NEPHRECTOMIES (-miz)], [*nephr-* + *-ectomy*], surgical removal of a kidney.

neph·ric (nef'rik), *adj.* of or near the kidneys.

ne·phrid·i·al (ne-frid'i-əl), *adj.* of a nephridium.

ne·phrid·i·um (ne-frid'i-əm), *n.* [*pl.* NEPHRIDIA (-ə)], [Mod. L.; Gr. *nephridion*, dim. of *nephros*, kidney], 1. the waste-discharging organ of some invertebrates, as worms, mollusks, etc. 2. the waste-discharging organ of vertebrate embryos; embryonic tube from which the kidney is developed.

neph·rism (nef'riz'm), *n.* [*nephr-* + *-ism*], the abnormal condition caused by chronic kidney disease.

neph·rite (nef'rīt), *n.* [G. *nephrit;* Gr. *nephritēs*, of the kidneys < *nephros*, kidney], the less valuable of the two varieties of jade, compact in structure and varying in color from white to dark green: it was formerly worn as a supposed remedy for kidney ailments.

ne·phrit·ic (ne-frit'ik), *adj.* [LL. *nephriticus;* Gr. *nephritikos* < *nephros*, kidney], 1. of a kidney or the kidneys; renal. 2. of or having nephritis.

ne·phri·tis (ne-frī'tis), *n.* [LL.; Gr. *nephritis;* see NEPHRO- & -ITIS], an acute or chronic disease of the kidneys, characterized by inflammation, degeneration, fibrosis, etc.: certain types are called *Bright's disease.*

neph·ro- (nef'rō, nef'rə), [< Gr. *nephros*, kidney], a combining form meaning *kidney* or *nephric and*, as in *nephrotomy:* also, before a vowel, **nephr-.**

ne·phro·sis (ne-frō'sis), *n.* [*nephr-* + *-osis*], a disease of the kidneys in which there is degeneration of the renal tubules, but no inflammation.

ne·phrot·o·my (ne-frot'ə-mi), *n.* [*pl.* NEPHROTOMIES (-miz)], [*nephro-* + *-tomy*], surgical incision into the kidney, as for removing a renal calculus.

‡ne plus ul·tra (nē plus ul'trə), [L., lit., no more beyond], 1. the furthest limit or highest point of perfection. 2. (go) no further.

Ne·pos, Cornelius (nē'pos, nep'os), 1st century B.C.; Roman historian.

nep·o·tism (nep'ə-tiz'm), *n.* [Fr. *népotisme;* It. *nepotismo* < L. *nepos, nepotis*, grandson, nephew + *-ism:* from favoritism shown to "nephews" by medieval prelates], favoritism shown to relatives, especially in appointment to desirable positions.

nep·o·tist (nep'ə-tist), *n.* one who practices nepotism.

Nep·tune (nep'tōōn, nep'chōōn), *n.* [ME.; L. *Neptunus*], 1. in *Roman mythology*, the god of the sea: identified with the Greek Poseidon. 2. the sea personified. 3. the third largest planet in the solar system and the eighth in distance from the sun: diameter, 33,000 mi.; period of revolution, 164.79 yrs.; symbol, ♆. Abbreviated **Nep.**

Nep·tu·ni·an (nep-tōō'ni-ən, nep-chōō'ni-ən), *adj.* 1. of the sea god Neptune. 2. of the planet Neptune. 3. [often n-], in *geology*, formerly, designating or of water-formed strata.

nep·tu·ni·um (nep-tōō'ni-əm, nep-chōō'ni-əm), *n.* a chemical element produced by irradiating uranium atoms with neutrons: it does not occur naturally on earth: symbol, Np; at. wt., 239; at. no., 93.

Ner·bud·da (nẽr-bud'ə), *n.* Narbada.

Ne·re·id (nêr'i-id), *n.* [L. *Nereis, Nereidis;* Gr. *Nērēis, Nērēidos* < *Nēreus*, Nereus], in *Greek mythology*, a sea nymph, one of the fifty daughters of Nereus.

Ne·reus (nêr'ōōs, nêr'yōōs), *n.* [L.; Gr. *Nereus*], in *Greek mythology*, a sea god, father of the fifty Nereids.

Nernst, Wal·ther Her·mann (väl′ter her′män nernst), 1864–1941; German physicist and chemist.

Ne·ro (nêr′ō), (*Nero Claudius Caesar Drusus Germanicus*), *n.* emperor of Rome (54–68 A.D.); lived 37 A.D.–68 A.D.; notoriously cruel and depraved.

ner·o·li (nâr′ə-li), *n.* [Fr. *néroli;* It. *neroli, nerolo;* said to be from name of the discoverer, an Italian princess], an oil distilled from orange flowers and used in perfumery: also **neroli oil.**

Ne·ro·ni·an (ni-rō′ni-ən), *adj.* [L. *Neronianus*], 1. of or connected with Nero or his reign. 2. like or characteristic of Nero; cruel, depraved, despotic, etc.

nerv·ate (nũr′vāt), *adj.* in *botany,* having nerves, or veins.

ner·va·tion (nũr-vā′shən), *n.* [< *nerve* + *-ation*], the arrangement of nerves, or veins, in a leaf or insect's wing; venation; neuration.

nerve (nũrv), *n.* [ME. *nerfe;* OFr. *nerf;* L. *nervus*], 1. originally, a sinew or tendon: now poetic except in *strain every nerve.* 2. any of the cordlike fibers or bundles of fibers connecting the body organs with the central nervous system (the brain and the spinal cord) and parts of the nervous system with each other, and carrying impulses to and from the brain or a nerve center. 3. emotional control; coolness in danger; courage: as, a man of *nerve.* 4. strength; energy; vigor. 5. [Colloq.], impudent boldness; audacity; brazenness. 6. in *botany* & *zoology,* a rib or vein in a leaf or insect's wing; nervure. *v.t.* [NERVED (nũrvd), NERVING], to give strength or courage to. —*SYN.* see **temerity.**

get on one's nerves, [Colloq.], to make one irritable or exasperated.

nerve oneself, to collect one's energies or courage for an effort.

nerves, 1. the nervous system regarded as indicating health, courage, endurance, etc. 2. *a*) nervousness. *b*) an attack of this; hysteria.

strain every nerve, to try as hard as possible.

nerve block, a method of anesthesia by stopping the passage of impulses through a particular nerve.

nerve cell, a cell which with its processes forms the structural and functional unit of the nervous system; especially, a cell of the gray matter of the brain or of a ganglion; neuron.

nerve center, any group of nerve cells that function together in controlling some specific sense or bodily activity, as breathing.

nerve fiber, any of the threadlike elements making up a nerve: it is the main process of a nerve cell and conducts the impulses.

MOTOR NEURON
SPINAL CORD
SENSORY NEURON
END ORGAN
CELL BODY OF NEURON

NERVE CELL

nerve·less (nũrv′lis), *adj.* 1. without strength, vigor, force, or courage; weak; inert; unnerved. 2. in *anatomy, botany* & *zoology,* having no nerve or nerves.

nerve-rack·ing, nerve-wrack·ing (nũrv′rak′iŋ), *adj.* very trying to one's patience or equanimity; causing irritation or exasperation.

nerv·ine (nũr′vēn, nũr′vin), *adj.* [Mod. L. *nervinus* < L. *nervus*], 1. of the nerves. 2. affecting, especially soothing or calming, the nerves. *n.* a medicine supposed to soothe or calm the nerves; nerve tonic.

nerv·ing (nũr′viŋ), *n.* in *veterinary medicine,* the removal of part of a nerve trunk, as when it is chronically inflamed.

ner·vos·i·ty (nũr-vos′ə-ti), *n.* [L. *nervositas,* strength], the state of being, or a tendency to be, abnormally nervous.

nerv·ous (nũr′vəs), *adj.* [ME. *neruous;* L. *nervosus*], 1. originally, strong; sinewy. 2. vigorous in expression; animated. 3. of the nerves. 4. made up of or containing nerves. 5. characterized by or having a disordered state of the nerves. 6. characterized by or showing emotional tension, restlessness, agitation, etc. 7. fearful; apprehensive.

nervous prostration, neurasthenia.

nervous system, all the nerve cells and nervous tissues in an organism, including, in the vertebrates, the brain, spinal cord, ganglia, nerves, and nerve centers: it co-ordinates and controls responses to stimuli and conditions behavior and consciousness.

ner·vure (nũr′vyoor), *n.* [Fr.; see NERVE & -URE], a vein or rib in a leaf or insect's wing.

nerv·y (nũr′vi), *adj.* [NERVIER (-vi-ẽr), NERVIEST (-vi-ist)], 1. [Rare], strong; vigorous; sinewy. 2. [British], nervous; excitable; jittery. 3. full of courage; bold. 4. [Slang], rudely bold; brazen; impudent.

nes·ci·ence (nesh′əns, nesh′i-əns), *n.* [LL. *nescientia* < L. *nesciens;* see NESCIENT], 1. ignorance. 2. agnosticism.

nes·ci·ent (nesh′ənt, nesh′i-ənt), *adj.* [L. *nesciens,* ppr. of *nescire,* to be ignorant of; *ne-,* not + *scire,* to know], 1. ignorant. 2. agnostic.

ness (nes), *n.* [ME. *nesse, nasse* < AS. *næs* & ON. *nes;* akin to AS. *nosu,* nose (cf. NOSE, NASAL)], a promontory; headland: now chiefly in place names, as *Inverness.*

-ness (nis, nəs), [ME. *-nesse, -nisse;* AS. *-nes(s), -nis(s);* akin to G. *-niss,* Goth. *-nassus* (for *-assus,* with *n-* < end of the base of weak verbs ending in *-atjan*)], a noun-forming suffix meaning: 1. *condition, quality* or *state of being,* as in *greatness, sadness, togetherness.* 2. *a single instance of such a condition, quality,* or *state.*

Nes·sel·rode (nes′′l-rōd′), *n.* [after Count K. R. *Nesselrode*], a mixture of preserved fruits, chopped nuts, etc., used in ice cream, pudding, or the like.

Nes·sel·rode, Count **Karl Robert** (nes′′l-rōd′; Russ. nyes′sil-rô′dye), 1780–1862; Russian statesman of German descent; imperial chancellor (1844).

Nes·sus (nes′əs), *n.* [L.; Gr. *Nessos*], in *Greek legend,* a centaur killed with a poisoned arrow by Hercules for trying to carry off his wife Deianira: a shirt that she steeped in Nessus' blood as a love charm caused the death of Hercules.

nest (nest), *n.* [ME.; AS.; akin to G. *nest;* IE. **nizdos* < base **ni-,* down + **sed-,* to sit, as also in L. *nidus* (cf. NIDUS)], 1. the structure made or the place chosen by birds for laying their eggs and sheltering their young. 2. the place used by turtles, hornets, fish, etc. for spawning or breeding. 3. a cozy or snug place to live or rest; retreat. 4. *a*) a resort, haunt, or den: especially in an unfavorable sense. *b*) the people who frequent such a place: as, a *nest* of criminals. 5. a brood, swarm, or colony of birds, insects, etc. 6. a set or series of similar things, each fitting within the one next larger. *v.i.* 1. to build or live in a nest. 2. to hunt for birds' nests: usually in the present participle. *v.t.* 1. to make a nest for. 2. to place or settle in or as in a nest.

‡n'est-ce pas? (nes′pä′), [Fr., lit., is it not?], isn't that so?

nest egg, 1. an artificial or real egg left in a nest to induce a hen to lay more eggs; hence, 2. money, etc. put aside as a reserve or to establish a fund.

nes·tle (nes′′l), *v.i.* [NESTLED (-′ld), NESTLING], [ME. *nestlen, nestlien;* AS. *nestlian;* see NEST & -LE], 1. [Rare], to nest. 2. to settle down comfortably and snugly. 3. to draw or press close for comfort or in affection. 4. to lie sheltered or partly hidden, as a house among trees. *v.t.* 1. to rest or press (a baby, one's head, etc.) in a snug, affectionate manner. 2. to settle or house as in a nest; shelter.

nes·tler (nes′′l-ẽr, nes′lẽr), *n.* 1. a person or thing that nestles. 2. a nestling.

nest·ling (nest′liŋ, nes′liŋ), *n.* [ME. (akin to G. *nestling, nistling*); see NEST & -LING], 1. a young bird not yet ready to leave the nest. 2. a baby.

Nes·tor (nes′tẽr), [L.; Gr. *Nestōr*], a masculine name. *n.* 1. in *Greek legend,* a wise old counselor who fought with the Greeks at Troy; hence, 2. a wise old man.

Nes·to·ri·an (nes-tôr′i-ən; nes-tō′ri-ən), *n.* [< LL.], a follower of Nestorius; believer in Nestorianism. *adj.* of or accepting the teachings of Nestorius.

Nes·to·ri·an·ism (nes-tôr′i-ən-iz′m, nes-tō′ri-ən-iz′m), *n.* the doctrine of Nestorius (declared heretical in 431 A.D.) that divinity and humanity existed as two distinct natures in Jesus and were not unified into a single personality.

Nes·to·ri·us (nes-tôr′i-əs, nes-tō′ri-əs), *n.* Syrian prelate; ?–c. 451 A.D.; patriarch of Constantinople (428–431 A.D.); banished for heresy.

net (net), *n.* [ME.; AS. *nett;* akin to G. *netz* (Goth. *nati*); IE. base **ned-,* to twist together, seen also in L. *nodus,* a knot (cf. NODE, NODULE)], 1. a fabric made from string, cord, etc., loosely knotted or woven in an openwork pattern and used to trap or snare birds, fish, etc. 2. anything that catches or entraps; trap; snare. 3. any of various meshed fabrics used to hold, protect, or mark off something: as, a hair *net,* tennis *net.* 4. a fine, meshed, lacelike cloth of cotton or silk. 5. a network. 6. in *tennis,* etc., a ball hit into the net. *v.t.* [NETTED (-id), NETTING], 1. to make into net or a net. 2. to make with net. 3. to trap or snare with or as with a net. 4. to protect, shelter, or enclose with or as with a net. 5. in *tennis,* to drive (the ball) into the net. *v.i.* to make nets or network. *adj.* 1. of or like net. 2. caught in a net; netted.

net (net), *adj.* [Fr., clean, clear, pure; see NEAT, *adj.*], left over after certain deductions or allowances have been made, as for expenses, weight of containers or waste materials, nonessential considerations, etc. *n.* a net amount, profit, weight, price, result, etc. Abbreviated **n.** *v.t.* [NETTED (-id), NETTING], to get or bring in as a net; gain.

neth·er (neth′ẽr), *adj.* [ME. *nethere;* AS. *neothera, nithera,* etc.; akin to G. *nieder;* IE. base **ni-,* down (as also in L. *nidus*, nest; cf. NEST) + compar. suffix; cf. Sans. *nitarām*], 1. lying, or thought of as lying, below the earth's surface: as, the *nether* world. 2. lower or under: as, *nether* garments.

Neth·er·land·er (neth′ẽr-lan′dẽr, neth′ẽr-lən-dẽr), *n.* a native or inhabitant of the Netherlands.

Neth·er·lands (neth′ẽr-ləndz), *n.* 1. a country in western Europe, on the North Sea: area, 12,868 sq. mi.; pop., 11,861,000; commercial capital, Amsterdam; political capital, The Hague: abbreviated **Neth.**: also called *Holland.* 2. a kingdom consisting of the independent states of the Netherlands, Surinam, and Netherlands Antilles.

Netherlands Antilles, a group of islands in the West Indies constituting part of the Netherlands (sense 2), and comprising two of the Windward Islands and part of another and three of the Leeward Islands: total area, 394 sq. mi.; pop., 194,000; capital, Willemstad.

Netherlands Guiana, Surinam.

Netherlands Indies, formerly, islands in the East Indies belonging to the Netherlands: also called *Dutch East Indies:* see **Indonesia.**

Netherlands New Guinea, a former territory of the Netherlands, comprising the western part of New Guinea: see **West Irian.**

neth·er·most (neth′ẽr-mōst′, neth′ẽr-məst), *adj.* [ME. *nethermest;* see NETHER & -MOST], lowest; farthest down.

neth·er·ward (neth′ẽr-wẽrd), *adv.* in a downward course, or direction.

nether world, the world of the dead or of punishment after death; hell.

Né·thou, Pic de (pĕk′ də nā′to͞o′), Pico de Aneto, highest mountain in the Pyrenees: the French name.

Net·tie, Net·ty (net′i), a feminine name: see **Antoinette, Henrietta, Jeannette.**

net·ting (net′iŋ), *n.* 1. the act or process of making nets or fishing with them. 2. netted material.

netting knot, a sheet bend: see **knot,** illus.

net·tle (net′'l), *n.* [ME. *netle, netel;* AS. *netele;* akin to G. *nessel;* IE. base **ned-*, to twist together, seen also in *net*: from the use of such plants as a source of spinning fiber], any of a number of related weeds with stinging hairs. *v.t.* [NETTLED (-'ld), NETTLING], 1. to sting with or as with nettles; hence, 2. to irritate; annoy; vex. —*SYN.* see **irritate.**

nettle rash, an allergic skin condition characterized by itching, burning, stinging, and the formation of smooth, usually red patches, or wheals; hives; urticaria.

net ton, a short ton.

net·work (net′wûrk′), *n.* [*net* (knotted fabric) + *work*], 1. any arrangement or fabric of parallel wires, threads, etc. crossed at regular intervals by others fastened to them so as to leave open spaces; netting; mesh. 2. a thing resembling this in some way; specifically, *a*) a system of crossed roads, canals, etc. *b*) in *radio* & *television*, a chain of transmitting stations controlled and operated as a unit. 3. the making of nets or netted fabric. *adj.* broadcast simultaneously over all or most of the stations of a network.

Neu·châ·tel, Lake of (nö′shȧ′tel′), a lake in western Switzerland: area, 85 sq. mi.

Neuf·châ·tel (no͞o′shə-tel′, nū′shə-tel′; Fr. nö′shȧ′tel′), *n.* [after *Neufchâtel*, town in northern France], a soft, white cheese prepared from sweet milk with or without cream: also **Neufchâtel cheese.**

Neuil·ly (nö′yē′), *n.* a city in France, near Paris: pop., 66,000.

neuk (nūk), *n.* [Scot.], a nook; corner.

neume, neum (no͞om, nūm), *n.* [Fr. *neume;* ML. *neuma* < Gr. *pneuma*, breath: so named from being orig. a group of notes sung to a final syllable for the duration of the breath], in *music*, 1. any of a set of signs used in the Middle Ages in written church music to indicate melody, manner of performance, etc. 2. the tone or group of tones indicated by these.

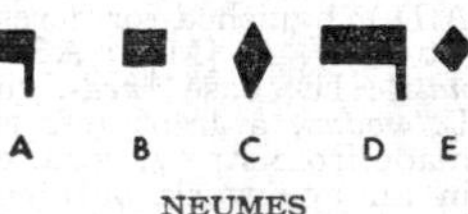

NEUMES
A, long; B, breve; C, semibreve; D, double long; E, minim

neur-, neuro-.

neu·ral (noor′əl, nyoor′əl), *adj.* [*neur-* + *-al*], of a nerve, nerves, or the nervous system.

neu·ral·gia (noo-ral′jə, nyoo-ral′jə), *n.* [Mod. L.; *neur-* + *-algia*], 1. a pain in a nerve or nerves; severe pain along the course of a nerve or in its area of distribution. 2. the condition characterized by such pain.

neu·ral·gic (noo-ral′jik, nyoo-ral′jik), *adj.* of or having neuralgia.

neu·ras·the·ni·a (noor′əs-thē′ni-ə, nyoor′əs-thē′ni-ə), *n.* [Mod. L. < *neur-* + Gr. *astheneia*, weakness], 1. formerly, weakness or exhaustion of the nervous system, as from excessive expenditure of energy; nervous prostration. 2. a type of neurosis, usually the result of emotional conflicts, characterized by fatigue, depression, worry, and, often, localized pains without apparent objective causes.

neu·ras·then·ic (noor′əs-then′ik, nyoor′əs-then′ik), *adj.* of or having neurasthenia. *n.* a neurasthenic person.

neu·ra·tion (noo-rā′shən, nyoo-rā′shən), *n.* [*neur-* + *-ation*], nervation.

neu·rec·to·my (noo-rek′tə-mi, nyoo-rek′tə-mi), *n.* [*pl.* NEURECTOMIES (-miz)], [*neur-* + *-ectomy*], surgical removal of a nerve or part of a nerve.

neu·ri·lem·ma (noor′i-lem′ə, nyoor′i-lem′ə), *n.* [Mod. L.; altered (after Gr. *lemma*, skin, peel) < *neurilema* < Gr. *neuron*, nerve + *eilēma*, a covering], the thin outer sheath covering a nerve fiber.

neu·rit·ic (noo-rit′ik, nyoo-rit′ik), *adj.* of or having neuritis.

neu·ri·tis (noo-rī′tis, nyoo-rī′tis), *n.* [Mod. L.; *neur-* + *-itis*], inflammation of a nerve or nerves, characterized by pain and muscle tenderness and accompanied by changes in sensory and motor activity in the region of the affected nerve.

neu·ro- (noor′ō, nyoor′ə), [< Gr. *neuron*, sinew], a combining form meaning *of a nerve, nerves,* or *the nervous system*, as in *neuropath:* also, before a vowel, **neur-.**

neu·ro·blast (noor′ə-blast′, nyoor′ə-blast′), *n.* [*neuro-* + *-blast*], any of the embryonic cells from which the nerve cells develop.

neu·ro·coele (noor′ə-sēl′, nyoor′ə-sēl′), *n.* [*neuro-* + *-coele*], the cavity of the cerebrospinal system, consisting of the ventricles of the brain and the central canal of the spinal cord, regarded as a unit.

neu·rog·li·a (noo-rog′li-ə, nyoo-rog′li-ə), *n.* [Mod. L.; *neuro-* + *-glia* (< Gr. *glia*, glue), suffix denoting gluelike or fine fibrillar tissue], the connective tissue, consisting of a special type of branched cells, that binds together and supports the nerve tissue of the central nervous system.

neu·ro·log·i·cal (noor′ə-loj′i-k'l, nyoor′ə-loj′i-k'l), *adj.* of or in neurology.

neu·rol·o·gist (noo-rol′ə-jist, nyoo-rol′ə-jist), *n.* an expert or specialist in neurology.

neu·rol·o·gy (noo-rol′ə-ji, nyoo-rol′ə-ji), *n.* [*neuro-* + *-logy*], the branch of medicine dealing with the nervous system, its structure, and its diseases.

neu·rol·y·sis (noo-rol′ə-sis, nyoo-rol′ə-sis), *n.* [Mod. L.; cf. NEURO- & -LYSIS], destruction of nerve tissue.

neu·ro·ma (noo-rō′mə, nyoo-rō′mə), *n.* [*pl.* NEUROMAS (-məz), NEUROMATA (-mə-tə)], [Mod. L.; *neur-* + *-oma*], a tumor derived from nervous tissue, consisting of nerve cells and fibers.

neu·ron (noor′on, nyoor′on), *n.* [Mod. L.; Gr. *neuron*, nerve], the structural and functional unit of the nervous system, consisting of the nerve cell body and all its processes, as the dendrites and axon: see **nerve cell,** illus.

neu·rone (noor′ōn, nyoor′ōn), *n.* a neuron.

neu·ron·ic (noo-ron′ik, nyoo-ron′ik), *adj.* of neurons.

neu·ro·path (noor′ə-path′, nyoor′ə-path′), *n.* [< *neuropathic* (person)], [Rare], 1. a person having a tendency to neurosis. 2. a neuropathist.

neu·ro·path·ic (noor′ə-path′ik, nyoor′ə-path′ik), *adj.* of or having neuropathy. *n.* a neuropathic person.

neu·rop·a·thist (noo-rop′ə-thist, nyoo-rop′ə-thist), *n.* [< *neuropathy* + *-ist*], a doctor who specializes in nervous diseases; neurologist.

neu·ro·pa·thol·o·gy (noor′ō-pə-thol′ə-ji, nyoor′ō-pə-thol′ə-ji), *n.* the pathology of the nervous system and its parts; branch of medicine dealing with diseases of the nervous system.

neu·rop·a·thy (noo-rop′ə-thi, nyoo-rop′ə-thi), *n.* [*neuro-* + *-pathy*], any disease of the nervous system.

neu·ro·phys·i·ol·o·gy (noor′ō-fiz′i-ol′ə-ji, nyoor′ō-fiz′i-ol′ə-ji), *n.* the physiology of the nervous system.

neu·ro·psy·chi·a·try (noor′ō-sī-kī′ə-tri, nyoor′ō-sī-kī′ə-tri), *n.* the branch of medicine dealing with disorders of both the psyche, or mind, and the nervous system.

neu·ro·psy·cho·sis (noor′ō-sī-kō′sis, nyoor′ō-sī-kō′sis), *n.* [*pl.* NEUROPSYCHOSES (-sēz)], a psychosis: distinguished from *psychoneurosis.*

neu·rop·ter·an (noo-rop′tẽr-ən, nyoo-rop′tẽr-ən), *adj.* [< Mod. L. *Neuroptera*, name of the order (< *neuro-* + Gr. *pteron*, a feather, wing); + *-an*], of the neuropterous insects. *n.* a neuropterous insect; neuropteron.

neu·rop·ter·oid (noo-rop′tẽr-oid′, nyoo-rop′tẽr-oid′), *adj.* like a neuropterous insect.

neu·rop·ter·on (noo-rop′tẽr-on′, nyoo-rop′tẽr-on′), *n.* a neuropterous insect; neuropteran.

neu·rop·ter·ous (noo-rop′tẽr-əs, nyoo-rop′tẽr-əs), *adj.* [< Mod. L. *Neuroptera* (see NEUROPTERAN); + *-ous*], of a group of insects with four membranous wings, transparent except for a lacelike framework of ribs, as the ant lion.

neu·ro·sis (noo-rō′sis, nyoo-rō′sis), *n.* [*pl.* NEUROSES (-sēz)], [Mod. L. < Gr. *neuron*, nerve], 1. formerly, a functional disorder of the nervous system. 2. any of various psychic, or mental, disorders characterized by special combinations of anxieties, compulsions, obsessions, phobias, and motor or sensory manifestations, such as tics, without apparent organic or structural change: it results in partial disorganization of the personality and is less serious both in form and prognosis than a psychosis: also **psychoneurosis.**

neu·ro·sur·ger·y (noor′ō-sũr′jẽr-i, nyoor′ō-sũr′jẽr-i), *n.*

surgery involving some part of the nervous system, including the brain and the spinal cord.

neu·rot·ic (noo-rot′ik, nyoo-rot′ik), *adj.* 1. of, characteristic of, or having a neurosis. 2. neural. *n.* 1. a neurotic person. 2. [Obs.], a drug that acts on the nervous system.

neu·rot·o·my (noo-rot′ə-mi, nyoo-rot′ə-mi), *n.* [*pl.* NEUROTOMIES (-miz)], [*neuro-* + *-tomy*], surgical cutting, or severing, of a nerve, as for relieving pain.

Neu·satz (noi′zäts′), *n.* Novi Sad: the German name.

Neu·stri·a (nōō′stri-ə, nū′stri-ə), *n.* the western part of the empire of the Franks, now included in northern and northwestern France.

neut., neuter.

neu·ter (nōō′tẽr, nū′tẽr), *adj.* [Late ME. < Fr. or L.; Fr. *neutre;* L. *neuter*, neither; *ne-*, not + *uter*, either; cf. NEITHER], 1. [Archaic], neutral. 2. in *biology*, *a)* having no sexual organs; asexual. *b)* having undeveloped or imperfect sexual organs in the adult, as the worker bee. 3. in *grammar*, *a)* designating or of one of the three genders of many highly inflected languages: most words of this gender designate or refer to things that are neither male nor female. *b)* neither active nor passive; intransitive: said of verbs. *n.* 1. a castrated animal. 2. [Archaic], a neutral person or group. 3. in *biology*, a plant or animal lacking, or having undeveloped, sexual organs. 4. in *grammar*, *a)* the neuter gender. *b)* a neuter word.

neu·tral (nōō′trəl, nū′trel), *adj.* [L. *neutralis* < *neuter*; see NEUTER], 1. *a)* not taking part in either side of a quarrel. *b)* not taking part in a war; giving no active aid to any belligerent. 2. of, belonging to, or characteristic of a nation not taking part in a war. 3. belonging to neither of two classes; in a middle position between extremes; not one thing or the other; indifferent. 4. *a)* having little or no decided color; not vivid. *b)* free from mixture of other colors. 5. in *botany*, without stamens or pistils. 6. in *chemistry*, giving neither acid nor alkaline reaction. 7. in *electricity*, neither negative nor positive; uncharged. 8. in *phonetics*, reduced in quality, especially through lack of stress, so as to become (ə) or (i): said of vowels, as, *a* in *about*. 9. in *zoology*, neuter. *n.* 1. a nation not taking part in a war; neutral power. 2. a neutral person or a citizen of a neutral country. 3. a neutral color. 4. in *mechanics*, a disengaged position of gears; the position of gears when they do not transmit power from the engine to the operating parts.

neu·tral·i·ty (nōō-tral′ə-ti, nū-tral′ə-ti), *n.* 1. the quality, state, or character of being neutral. 2. the status, policy, or attitude of a nation not participating directly or indirectly in a war between other nations. 3. neutral status, as of a seaport in wartime.

neu·tral·i·za·tion (nōō′trəl-i-zā′shən, nū′trəl-ī-zā′shən), *n.* a neutralizing or being neutralized.

neu·tral·ize (nōō′trə-līz′, nū′trə-līz′), *v.t.* [NEUTRALIZED (-līzd′), NEUTRALIZING], [Fr. *neutraliser*], 1. to declare (a territory, nation, etc.) neutral; declare open to all nations and inviolable from attack; exempt from war or military operations. 2. to make ineffective; paralyze, destroy, or counteract the effectiveness, force, disposition, etc. of. 3. in *chemistry*, to destroy the distinctive or active properties of: as, an alkali *neutralizes* an acid. 4. in *electricity*, to make electrically neutral.

neu·tret·to (nōō-tret′ō, nū-tret′ō), *n.* [*pl.* NEUTRETTOS (-ōz)], [< *neutron* + It. dim. suffix *-etto* (cf. -ET)], a neutral meson transformed from a positive meson that has collided with a neutron, or from a negative meson that has collided with a proton.

neu·tri·no (nōō-trē′nō, nū-trē′nō), *n.* [*pl.* NEUTRINOS (-nōz)], [< L. *neuter* (cf. NEUTRON) + It. dim. suffix *-ino*], in *physics*, a neutral particle smaller than a neutron, having a mass approaching zero.

neu·tro·dyne (nōō′trə-dīn′, nū′trə-dīn′), *adj.* [*neutro-* (< *neutral*) + *dyne*], in *radio*, designating or of a high-frequency amplifying circuit that has a small condenser to neutralize the instability between the input and output circuits. *n.* such a circuit.

neu·tron (nōō′tron, nū′tron), *n.* [< *neutral* + *-on* as in *electron*], one of the fundamental particles of an atom: neutrons are uncharged and have approximately the same mass as protons: symbol, n (no period).

Ne·va (nē′və; Russ. nye-vä′), *n.* a river in European Russia, flowing from Lake Ladoga through Leningrad into the Gulf of Finland: length, 46 mi.

Ne·vad·a (nə-vad′ə, nə-vä′də), *n.* a Western State of the United States: area, 110,540 sq. mi.; pop., 285,000; capital, Carson City: abbreviated **Nev.**

Ne·vad·an (nə-vad′′n, nə-vä′d′n), *adj.* of Nevada. *n.* a native or inhabitant of Nevada.

né·vé (nā′vā′), *n.* [Fr. (via Swiss dial. of Fr.), glacier; ult. < L. *nix*, *nivis*, snow; for base see SNOW], the granular, crystallized snow that accumulates in snowfields of glaciers and is later solidified into ice.

nev·er (nev′ẽr), *adv.* [ME. *naefre;* AS. *næfre; ne*, not + *æfre*, ever; see EVER], 1. not ever; at no time. 2. not at all; by no chance; in no case; under no conditions.

nev·er·more (nev′ẽr-môr′, nev′ẽr-mōr′), *adv.* never again; at no future time.

nev·er·the·less (nev′ẽr-*thə*-les′), *adv.* none the less; in spite of that; however.

Nev·il, Nev·ile, Nev·ill, Nev·ille (nev′′l, nev′il), [< Norman surname *Nevil*, *Néville* < *Neuville*, town in Normandy (lit., new city)], a masculine name.

Nev·in, Ethelbert Wood·bridge (wood′brij′ nev′in), 1862-1901; American composer.

Nev·is (nev′is, nē′vis), *n.* an island of the Leeward group, West Indies Federation: area, 50 sq. mi.: see **St. Kitts.**

ne·void (nē′void), *adj.* of or like a nevus: also spelled **naevoid.**

ne·vus (nē′vəs), *n.* [*pl.* NEVI (-vī)], [L. *naevus* < base **gna-*, seen also in *genus*, *gnatus* (cf. GENUS)], a colored spot on the skin, usually congenital; birthmark or mole: also spelled **naevus.**

new (nōō, nū), *adj.* [ME. *newe;* AS. *niwe;* akin to G. *neu;* IE. **newos*, **newios*, new, seen also in L. *novus*, new, etc. (cf. NOVEL, NOVICE), Gr. *nēos* (cf. NEO-)], 1. never existing before; appearing, thought of, developed, made, produced, etc. for the first time. 2. *a)* existing before, but known or discovered for the first time: as, a *new* planet. *b)* recently observed, experienced, manifested, etc.; different: as, this is a *new* aspect of your personality. *c)* strange; unfamiliar; foreign. 3. not yet familiar or accustomed; inexperienced: as, he is *new* to the work. 4. *a)* designating the more or most recent of two or more things of the same class, though both may be old: as, *New* York. *b)* taking the place of what has existed; recently appointed, acquired, etc.: as, a *new* teacher. 5. recently grown; fresh: as, *new* potatoes. 6. not worn out; not used up; not previously used. 7. modern; recent; fashionable; recently current. 8. more; additional. 9. beginning again; starting as a repetition of a cycle, series, etc.; making another start: as, the *new* moon. 10. having just come; having just reached a position, rank, place, etc.: as, a *new* arrival. 11. refreshed in spirits, health, etc.: as, a *new* man. 12. [N-], modern; in use since the Middle Ages: said of languages. Abbreviated **N., n.** *n.* something new. *adv.* 1. again. 2. newly; recently.

SYN.—**new** is applied to that which has never existed before or which has only just come into being, possession, use, etc. (a *new* coat, teacher, etc.); **fresh** implies such newness that the original appearance, quality, vigor, etc. have not been affected by time or use (*fresh* eggs, a *fresh* start); **novel** implies a newness that is strikingly unusual or strange (a *novel* idea, combination, etc.); **modern** and **modernistic** apply to that which is of the present time, as distinguished from earlier periods, and connotes up-to-dateness, the latter word, sometimes, with derogatory implications; **original** is used of that which is not only new but is also the first of its kind (an *original* plan, melody, etc.).—*ANT.* old.

New Albany, a city in southern Indiana, on the Ohio: pop., 38,000.

New Amsterdam, a Dutch colonial town on Manhattan Island: it later became New York City.

New·ark (nōō′ẽrk, nū′ẽrk), *n.* 1. a city in northeastern New Jersey: pop., 405,000. 2. a city in central Ohio: pop., 42,000.

New Bedford, a seaport in southeastern Massachusetts: pop., 102,000.

New·bolt, Sir **Henry John** (nōō′bōlt′, nū′bōlt′), 1862–1938; English poet and naval historian.

new·born (nōō′bôrn′, nū′bôrn′), *adj.* [ME.; akin to MD. *nieboren*], 1. recently born; just born. 2. reborn.

New Britain, 1. an island in the Bismarck Archipelago: area, 14,500 sq. mi.; pop., 102,000; chief city, Rabaul. 2. a city in central Connecticut: pop., 82,000.

New Brunswick, 1. a province of Canada, on the southeastern coast: area, 27,985 sq. mi.; pop., 598,000; capital, Fredericton: abbreviated **N.B.** 2. a city in central New Jersey: pop., 40,000.

New·burg (nōō′bẽrg, nū′bẽrg), *adj.* served in a specially prepared sauce: see **à la Newburg.**

New·burgh (nōō′bẽrg, nū′bẽrg), *n.* a city in southeastern New York, on the Hudson: pop., 31,000.

New Caledonia, 1. a French island in Melanesia, in the Coral Sea: area, 6,296 sq. mi.; pop., 72,000; capital, Nouméa. 2. a French territory including New Caledonia and adjacent islands. Abbreviated **N.C.**

New Castile, a former province of central Spain: Spanish name, *Castilla la Nueva.*

New·cas·tle (nōō′kas′′l, nū′käs′′l), *n.* the county seat of Northumberland, England: pop., 269,000.

carry coals to Newcastle, 1. to take things to a place where they are plentiful or are not needed: Newcastle was a center for coal. 2. to waste time or effort.

New Castle, a city in western Pennsylvania: pop., 45,000.

New·cas·tle-u·pon-Tyne (nōō'kas''l-ə-pon'tin', nū'-käs''l-ə-pon'tin'), *n.* Newcastle.

New Church, New Jerusalem Church: abbreviated **N.C.**

New·chwang (nōō'chwäŋ', nū'chwäŋ'), *n.* Yingkow: a former name.

new·com·er (nōō'kum'ẽr, nū'kum'ẽr), *n.* a person who has come recently; recent arrival.

New Deal, 1. the economic and political principles and policies adopted by President Franklin D. Roosevelt and his associates to advance the economic and social welfare of the American people. 2. the Roosevelt administration.

New Dealer, a supporter or advocate of the New Deal.

New Delhi, the capital of India, adjacent to Delhi: pop., 276,000.

New Economic Policy, the policy of restoring certain features of capitalist economy, such as private trade in commodities and private manufacture of certain goods, instituted as a temporary expedient by the Soviet government under Lenin in 1921 and gradually liquidated with the advance of socialization: also **NEP, Nep, nep.**

New Egyptian, the Hamitic language of the Copts; Coptic.

new·el (nōō'əl, nū'əl), *n.* [OFr. *nuel, nouel* < LL. *nucalis*, like a nut < L. *nux, nucis*, nut], 1. the central upright pillar around which the steps of a winding staircase turn. 2. the post at the top or bottom of a flight of stairs, supporting the handrail: also **newel post.**

New England, [the name occurs on Italian maps antedating Captain John Smith, its reputed originator], the six northeastern States of the United States; Maine, Vermont, New Hampshire, Massachusetts, Rhode Island, and Connecticut: abbreviated **N.Eng.**

New England aster, a variety of aster that grows in the eastern part of North America, having a purplish flower.

New England boiled dinner, a dish consisting of meat, usually beef, and whole potatoes, onions, carrots, etc., cooked together.

New Englander, a native or inhabitant of New England.

New English, [term popularized by Henry Sweet after G. *neuhochdeutsch*, New High German, etc.], Modern English, as distinguished from Early Modern English, Middle English, and Old English (Anglo-Saxon).

new·fan·gled (nōō'faŋ'g'ld, nū'faŋ'g'ld), *adj.* [ME. *newefangel; newe*, new + *-fangel* < base of AS. *fon*, to take; cf. FANG], 1. new; novel; newly done, made, etc. 2. tending toward the recent, different, or novel; fond of new theories, etc. A contemptuous term.

new-fash·ioned (nōō'fash'ənd, nū'fash'ənd), *adj.* 1. recently come into fashion. 2. made in a new and different form or style.

New Forest, a forest district and national park in Hampshire, England: area, 145 sq. mi.

New·found·land (nōō'fənd-land', nū'fənd-lənd; *officially* nū-found'land'), *n.* 1. an island off the eastern coast of Canada: area, 42,734 sq. mi. 2. a province of Canada comprising Newfoundland and Labrador: area, 156,185 sq. mi.; pop., 415,000; capital, St. John's. Abbreviated **Nfld., Nfd., Newf., N.F.**

New·found·land dog (nōō-found'lənd, nū-found'lənd), any of a North American breed of large, usually black, shaggy-haired dogs of above average intelligence.

New·found·land·er (nōō-found'lən-dẽr, nū-found'lən-dẽr), *n.* a native or inhabitant of Newfoundland.

New France, a French territory (1609–1763) in North America, including Canada and the Mississippi Valley.

New·gate (nōō'gāt', nū'gāt'), *n.* a former prison in London, England: it was destroyed in 1902.

New Georgia, one of the British Solomon Islands.

New Granada, 1. Panama and Colombia when owned by Spain. 2. the former Spanish possessions in northwestern South America and Central America, including New Granada, Ecuador, and Venezuela.

New Guinea, a large island in the East Indies, north of Australia: divided between Netherlands New Guinea, in the western half, and two territories (*Territories of Papua* and *New Guinea*) jointly administered by Australia, in the eastern half: abbreviated **N.G.**: also called *Papua.*

New Guinea, Territory of, an Australian trust territory including northeastern New Guinea, the Bismarck Archipelago, Bougainville, Buka, and smaller adjacent islands of the Solomons: area, 93,000 sq. mi.; pop., 1,341,000; capital, Rabaul.

New Hampshire, a New England State of the United States: area, 9,304 sq. mi.; pop., 607,000; capital, Concord: abbreviated **N.H.**

New Haven, a city in southern Connecticut, on Long Island Sound: pop., 152,000.

New Hebrides, a group of Melanesian islands in the South Pacific, under the joint control of Britain and France: area, 5,700 sq. mi.; pop., 56,000; capital, Vila: abbreviated **N.Heb.**

New High German, see **German, High German.**

New Ireland, an island in the Bismarck Archipelago: area, 3,800 sq. mi.; pop., 38,000.

new·ish (nōō'ish, nū'ish), *adj.* somewhat new.

New Jersey, an Eastern State of the United States: area, 7,836 sq. mi.; pop., 6,067,000; capital, Trenton: abbreviated **N.J.**

New Jer·sey·ite (jũr'zi-īt'), a native or inhabitant of New Jersey.

New Jerusalem, 1. in the *Bible*, the Holy City of Heaven: Rev. 21:2. 2. heaven.

New Jerusalem Church, the church that holds to the doctrines taught by Emanuel Swedenborg: the members are usually called *Swedenborgians.*

New Kensington, a city in western Pennsylvania: pop., 23,000.

New Latin, Modern Latin: abbreviated **NL., N.L.**

New London, a city in southeastern Connecticut: pop. 34,000: site of the United States Coast Guard Academy.

new·ly (nōō'li, nū'li), *adv.* 1. recently; lately. 2. anew; afresh.

new·ly·wed (nōō'li-wed', nū'li-wed'), *n.* a recently married person.

New·man, John Henry (nōō'mən, nū'mən), Cardinal Newman, 1801–1890; English theologian and writer.

New·mar·ket (nōō'mär'kit, nū'mär'kit), *n.* a city in Cambridgeshire, southeastern England: pop., 10,000: many horse races are held near by.

new·mar·ket (nōō'mär'kit, nū'mär'kit), *n.* [< *Newmarket*, where orig. worn], 1. a long, close-fitting coat: also **Newmarket coat.** 2. a kind of card game.

New Mexican, 1. of New Mexico. 2. a native or inhabitant of New Mexico.

New Mexico, a Southwestern State of the United States, on the Mexican border: area, 121,666 sq. mi.; pop., 951,000; capital, Santa Fe: abbreviated **N. Mex., N. M., New M.**

new moon, 1. that phase of the moon when it is between the earth and the sun, with the dark side of its disk toward the earth: it appears as a thin crescent curving toward the right. 2. the time of the new moon.

new-mown (nōō'mōn', nū'mōn'), *adj.* freshly mown; just cut: said of hay or grass.

New Netherland, a former Dutch colony (1613–1664) in North America, later comprising the British colonies of New York, New Jersey, and Delaware.

New Order, the fascist political and economic system that the Nazis set up in Germany and tried to establish throughout Europe.

New Or·le·ans (ôr'li-ənz; *esp. formerly*, ôr-lēnz'; *esp. Southern*, ôr'lənz), a city in southeastern Louisiana, on the Mississippi: pop., 628,000: site of an unsuccessful attack (1815) by the British after the War of 1812.

New·port (nōō'pôrt', nū'pôrt'), *n.* 1. a resort town in southern Rhode Island, on Narragansett Bay: pop., 47,000. 2. a city in Kentucky, on the Ohio, opposite Cincinnati: pop., 30,000. 3. a city in southeastern Wales: pop., 104,000.

Newport News, a city and naval base in Virginia, at the mouth of the James River: pop., 114,000.

New Ro·chelle (rə-shel'), a city in New York, north of New York City: pop., 77,000.

news (nōōz, nūz), *n.pl.* [construed as sing.], [ME. *newes*, novelties (pl. of *newe, adj.*); after OFr. *noveles* (Fr. *nouvelles*) or ML. *nova*, pl. of *novum*, what is new; see NEW], 1. new information about anything; information previously unknown: as, that's *news* to me. 2. recent happenings, especially those broadcast over the radio, printed in a newspaper, etc. 3. reports of such events, collectively. 4. a newspaper.

news·boy (nōōz'boi', nūz'boi'), *n.* a boy who sells or delivers newspapers.

news·cast (nōōz'kast', nūz'käst'), *n.* [*news* + *broadcast*], a radio or television broadcast of news reports. *v.t. & v.i.* to broadcast (news).

news·cast·er (nōōz'kas'tẽr, nūz'käs'tẽr), *n.* a person who broadcasts news reports on radio or television.

news·deal·er (nōōz'dēl'ẽr, nūz'dēl'ẽr), *n.* a person who sells newspapers, magazines, etc.

New Siberian Islands, a group of islands in the U.S.S.R., in the Arctic Ocean, north of eastern Siberia.

news·let·ter (nōōz'let'ẽr, nūz'let'ẽr), *n.* 1. a bulletin issued at regular intervals to subscribers, containing recent news, particularly political and economic, and often including interpretations and predictions. 2. any similar report issued by a firm, governmental agency, etc. to keep employees or the public informed of pertinent matters.

news·man (nōōz'man', nūz'mən), *n.* [*pl.* NEWSMEN (-men', -mən)], 1. a person who sells or delivers newspapers. 2. a newspaper reporter.

news·mon·ger (nōōz'muŋ'gẽr, nūz'muŋ'gẽr), *n.* a person who spreads news; especially, a gossip; tattler.

New South Wales, a state of southeastern Australia: area, 309,433 sq. mi.; pop., 3,756,000; capital, Sydney: abbreviated **N.S.W.**

New Spain, the former Spanish possessions in Mexico, the southwestern United States, Central America (excluding Panama), the West Indies, and the Philippine Islands.

news·pa·per (nōōz'pā'pẽr, nūz'pā'pẽr), *n.* 1. a publication regularly printed and distributed, usually daily or weekly, containing news, opinions, advertisements, and other items of general interest. 2. newsprint.

news·print (nōōz'print', nūz'print'), *n.* a cheap, thin paper made mainly from wood pulp and used for newspapers, etc.

news·reel (nōōz'rēl', nūz'rēl'), *n.* a motion picture showing events of current interest.

news room, 1. a room in a newspaper office containing the desks of reporters, copy editors, etc., where the news is written and edited: sometimes called *city room.* 2. a similar room for preparing news in a radio or television station.

news·stand (nōōz'stand', nūz'stand'), *n.* a stand at which newspapers, magazines, etc. are sold: also [British], **news stall.**

New Style, the method of reckoning time in accordance with the Gregorian calendar: abbreviated **N.S.**

news·wor·thy (nōōz'wūr'*th*i, nūz'wūr'*th*i), *adj.* having the qualities of news; timely, important, and interesting.

news·y (nōōz'i, nūz'i), *adj.* [NEWSIER (-i-ēr), NEWSIEST (-i-ist)], [Colloq.], containing much news. *n.* [*pl.* NEWSIES (-iz)], [Colloq.], a newsboy.

newt (nōōt, nūt), *n.* [ME. *neute,* for *eute,* by syllabic merging < *an eute;* AS. *efete;* see EFT, *n.*], any of various small salamanders that can live both on land and in water: also called *eft, triton.*

SMOOTH NEWT (3–6 in. long)

New Testament, 1. in *Christian theology,* the promises of God to man that are embodied in the life and teachings of Jesus. 2. the part of the Bible that contains the life and teachings of Jesus and his followers, including the four Gospels, the Acts of the Apostles, the Epistles, and the Revelation of Saint John. Abbreviated **NT., N.T.**

New Thought, a modern religious philosophy emphasizing the power of the mind over the body and its ills: also called *Higher Thought, Practical Christianity.*

New·ton (nōō't'n, nū't'n), [< surname *Newton* < common Eng. place name *Newton* < AS. *neowa tun,* new town], a masculine name. *n.* a city in Massachusetts, near Boston: pop., 92,000.

New·ton, Sir **Isaac** (nōō't'n, nū't'n), 1642–1727; English mathematician and philosopher; formulated the binomial theorem, the laws of gravity and motion, and the elements of differential calculus.

New·to·ni·an (nōō-tō'ni-ən, nū-tō'ni-ən), *adj.* of or agreeing with Sir Isaac Newton or his discoveries and theories. *n.* an advocate of Newton's theories.

new-world (nōō'wūrld', nū'wūrld'), *adj.* of or from the New World.

New World, the Western Hemisphere.

new year, 1. the year just about to begin or just begun (usually with *the*). 2. the first day or days of the new year (with *the* or *a*): as, a fine *new year*: also **New Year's.**

New Year's Day, January 1, the first day of a calendar year, usually celebrated as a legal holiday: also **New Year's.**

New Year's Eve, the evening before New Year's Day.

New York, 1. an Eastern State of the United States: area, 49,576 sq. mi.; pop., 16,782,000; capital, Albany. 2. the largest city in the United States, in southeastern New York State, at the mouth of the Hudson: area, 309 sq. mi.; pop., 7,782,000: divided into five boroughs (the Bronx, Brooklyn, Manhattan, Queens, Richmond): often **New York City** (abbreviated **N.Y.C.**): also called *Greater New York,* as distinguished from the metropolitan area of New York, which includes all the region within a 40-mile radius of City Hall (area, 2,514 sq. mi.; pop., 10,695,000). Abbreviated **N.Y.**

New York Bay, an inlet of the Atlantic, south of Manhattan Island.

New York·er (yôr'kēr), a native or inhabitant of New York (State or, especially, City).

New York State Barge Canal, 1. the New York State canal system: total length, 525 mi. 2. the canal from Buffalo, on Lake Erie, to Troy, on the Hudson: length, 363 mi.: originally called *Erie Canal.*

New Zea·land (zē'lənd), a British dominion made up of two large and several small islands in the Pacific, southeast of Australia: total area, 103,934 sq. mi.; pop., 2,174,000; capital, Wellington: abbreviated **N.Z., N.Zeal.**

New Zea·land·er (zē'lən-dēr), a native or inhabitant of New Zealand.

Nex·ö, Mar·tin An·der·sen (mär'tēn ån'ēr-s'n nik'sö), 1869–1954; Danish novelist.

next (nekst), *adj.* [older superlative of *nigh*], [ME. *nexte;* AS. *neahst, niehst,* superl. of *neah,* nigh (see NIGH); akin to G. *nächst* (OHG. *nāhist-*)], nearest; just before or after in time, space, degree, or rank; immediately preceding or following. *adv.* 1. in the time, place, degree, or rank nearest, or immediately preceding or following. 2. on the first subsequent occasion: as, when *next* we meet. *prep.* beside; nearest to: as, sit *next* the tree. *n.* the one immediately following.

get next to, [Slang], to ingratiate oneself with; become friendly or intimate with.

next door (to), in or at the next house, building, etc. (adjacent to).

next-door (neks'dôr', neks'dōr'), *adj.* in or at the next house, building, etc.

next friend, in *law,* a person who, though not legally a guardian, acts for another legally unable to act for himself.

next of kin, 1. a person's nearest relative or relatives. 2. in *law, a)* the blood relatives who may be entitled to share in the estate of a person who dies without a will. *b)* sometimes, the nearest relative by blood as defined in the law of the various States.

nex·us (nek'səs), *n.* [*pl.* NEXUSES (-iz), NEXUS], [L. < pp. of *nectere,* to bind; cf. ANNEX], 1. a connection, tie, or link between individuals of a group, members of a series, etc. 2. the group or series connected.

Ney, Mi·chel (mē'shel' nā), Duc d'Elchingen, Prince de La Moskova, 1769–1815; French soldier; marshal of France during Napoleon's reign; executed.

Nez Per·cé (nā' pâr'sā'; Eng. nez' pūrs'), *n.* [*pl.* NEZ PERCÉS (pâr'sā'; Eng. pūr'siz)], [Fr., lit., pierced nose: from the practice of several western tribes (but not of this tribe) of piercing the nose for insertion of a shell ornament], a member of a tribe of North American Indians who lived in Idaho, Washington, and Oregon.

N.F., 1. Newfoundland. 2. Norman French.

N.F., n/f, in *banking,* no funds.

Nfd., Nfld., Newfoundland.

N.G., 1. National Guard. 2. New Guinea.

N.G., n.g., [Slang], no good.

Ngan·hui (n'gän'hwi'), *n.* Anhwei, a province of China.

NGr., N.Gr., New Greek.

N.H., New Hampshire.

N.Heb., New Hebrides.

NHG., N.H.G., New High German.

Ni, in *chemistry,* nickel.

N.I., Northern Ireland.

ni·a·cin (nī'ə-s'n), *n.* [*ni*cotinic *ac*id + *-in*], nicotinic acid.

Ni·ag·a·ra (nī-ag'rə, nī-ag'ə-rə), *n.* a river between New York and Ontario, Canada, flowing from Lake Erie into Lake Ontario: length, 36 mi.

Niagara Falls, 1. the waterfall of the Niagara River, between New York and Ontario, Canada: it is divided into two great falls, Horseshoe, or Canadian, Falls (height, 158 ft.) and American Falls (height, 167 ft.). 2. a city in New York, near Niagara Falls: pop., 102,000. 3. a city in Ontario, Canada, near Niagara Falls: pop., 23,000.

nib (nib), *n.* [var. of *neb*], 1. the bill or beak of a bird. 2. *a)* originally, the split and sharpened end of a quill pen; hence, *b)* the point of a pen, or the entire pen, meant to be inserted in a holder. 3. the projecting end of anything; point; sharp prong. 4. the short grip handles on the shaft of a scythe. 5. *pl.* crushed coffee or cocoa beans. *v.t.* [NIBBED (nibd), NIBBING], 1. originally, to sharpen and split the end of (a quill) to make a pen. 2. to mend (a pen point). 3. to put a point on (a pen).

nib·ble (nib''l), *v.t.* [NIBBLED (-'ld), NIBBLING], [prob. < Late MD. or MLG. *nibbelen* or base of *nip, v.* + freq. suffix *-le*], 1. to eat (food) with quick bites, taking only a small amount at a time, as a mouse does. 2. to continue to bite (food) with small bites, gently and intermittently: as, a fish *nibbles* the bait. *v.i.* 1. to take only small bites; bite cautiously or gently (usually with *at*). 2. to show little interest in food by taking only small bites intermittently (usually with *at*). *n.* 1. a small bite, morsel, or quantity. 2. act or instance of nibbling.

Ni·be·lung (nē'bə-looŋ'; *sometimes Anglicized to* nib''l-ooŋ'), *n.* [G.], in *Norse mythology,* 1. any of a race of dwarfs, the children of the mist, who owned a magic ring and a hoard of gold, taken from them by Siegfried. 2. any of Siegfried's followers. 3. any of the Burgundian kings in the Nibelungenlied.

Ni·be·lung·en·lied (nē'bə-looŋ'ən-lēt'; *sometimes Anglicized to* nib''l-ooŋ'ən-lēd'), *n.* [G., song of the Nibelungs], a Middle High German epic poem by an unknown author, written in the first decade of the 13th century and based on two main legends of the Burgundain kings, which were in turn ultimately based on various compilations of legends: Wagner's cycle of operas, *The Ring of the Nibelung,* is based chiefly on Norse variants of these legends.

nib·lick (nib'lik), *n.* [? < D. *kneppelig* < *kneppel,* *knuppel*, a club (akin to G. *knebel*): golf shows D. influences], a heavy, iron-headed golf club with much loft, used in sand and for short shots in which the ball must be stopped quickly: now usually called *number 8 iron*: see **golf club**, illus.

nibs (nibz), *n.* [earlier also *his nabs;* ? var. of Brit. slang *nob* (wealthy, highly placed person)], [Colloq.], a person of importance or authority (with *his*): said especially of self-important persons.

Ni·cae·a (nī-sē′ə), *n.* 1. an ancient city in Bithynia, near the Sea of Marmara: at an important church council held here in 325 A.D. the Nicene Creed was formulated: English name, *Nice.* 2. Nice (city in France): the ancient name.

Ni·cae·an (nī-sē′ən), *adj.* Nicene.

Nic·a·ra·gua (nik′ə-rä′gwə), *n.* a country in Central America, on the Caribbean and Pacific: area, 57,143 sq. mi.; pop., 1,471,000; capital, Managua: abbreviated **Nicar.**

Nicaragua, Lake, a lake in southwestern Nicaragua: area, 3,089 sq. mi.

Nic·a·ra·guan (nik′ə-rä′gwən), *adj.* of Nicaragua, its people, or their culture. *n.* a native or inhabitant of Nicaragua.

nic·co·lite (nik′ə-līt′), *n.* [< Mod. L. *niccolum* (see NICKEL); + *-ite*], a pale-red native arsenide of nickel, NiAs: also called *copper nickel.*

Nice (nēs), *n.* 1. a seaport and resort in southeastern France, on the Mediterranean: pop., 244,000: ancient name, *Nicaea.* 2. (nīs), Nicaea: the English name.

nice (nīs), *adj.* [NICER (-ēr), NICEST (-ist)], [ME., foolish; OFr. *nice, niche, nisce,* stupid, foolish < L. *nescius,* ignorant, not knowing < *nescire,* to be ignorant; *ne-,* not + *scire,* to know], 1. difficult to please; very careful; fastidious; refined. 2. delicate; precise; minute; discriminative; subtle: as, a *nice* distinction. 3. calling for delicacy, accuracy, or precision in handling, discrimination, or adjustment; calling for great care, tact, etc.: as, a *nice* problem. 4. *a)* able to make fine or delicate distinctions; delicately skillful; finely discriminating. *b)* minutely accurate, as an instrument. 5. having high standards of conduct; scrupulous. 6. *a)* agreeable; pleasant; delightful. *b)* attractive; pretty. *c)* kind; thoughtful; considerate. *d)* modest; well-mannered; reserved. *e)* in good taste. *f)* good; excellent. A generalized term of approval, having very wide application. 7. [Obs.], *a)* ignorant; foolish. *b)* wanton. *c)* coy; shy. —*SYN.* see **dainty.**

nice·ly (nīs′li), *adv.* 1. in an attractive or pleasing manner. 2. exactly; precisely. 3. satisfactorily.

Ni·cene (nī-sēn′, nī′sēn′), *adj.* of Nicaea.

Nicene Council, 1. the church council that met at Nicaea in 325 A.D. to condemn Arianism and adopt the Nicene Creed. 2. the church council that met in 787 A.D. to restore images, pass disciplinary measures, etc.

Nicene Creed, a confession of faith for Christians, originally adopted at the first Nicene Council (325 A.D.): it was later expanded at the Council of Constantinople (381 A.D.) and in this form is accepted by the Orthodox Eastern Church; the Roman Catholic Church uses a form containing one extra clause, and various Protestant denominations have accepted modifications of this.

Ni·ce·tas (nī-sē′təs), see **Ignatius,** Saint (sense 2).

ni·ce·ty (nī′sə-ti), *n.* [*pl.* NICETIES (-tiz)], [ME. *nicete, nycete;* OFr. *nicete,* folly < *nice;* see NICE], 1. the quality or state of being nice; specifically, *a)* [Obs.], foolishness. *b)* coyness; modesty. *c)* excessive elegance. *d)* scrupulosity. *e)* precision; accuracy; minuteness; exactness, as of discrimination or perception. *f)* fastidiousness; refinement; delicacy of taste. 2. the quality of calling for delicacy, accuracy, or precision in handling, discrimination, or adjustment. 3. anything involving or calling for delicacy, accuracy, or precision; subtle or minute detail, distinction, etc. 4. something choice, dainty, or elegant.

to a nicety, to a precise degree; exactly.

niche (nich), *n.* [Fr. < OFr. *nichier,* to nest; LL. **nidicare* < L. *nidus,* a nest; see NEST], 1. a recess or hollow in a wall, usually intended for a statue, bust, or vase. 2. a place or position particularly suitable for the person or thing in it. *v.t.* [NICHED (nicht), NICHING], to place in or as in a niche.

NICHE

Nich·o·las (nik′'l-əs), [ME.; OFr. *Nicolas;* L. *Nicolaus;* Gr. *Nikolaos* < *nikē,* victory + *laos,* the people], a masculine name: diminutive, *Nick;* equivalents, L. *Nicolaus,* Fr. & Sp. *Nicolas,* G. *Nikolaus,* It. *Niccolo:* also spelled **Nicolas.**

Nicholas I, (*Nikolai Pavlovich*), 1796–1855; czar of Russia (1825–1855).

Nicholas I, Saint, 800?–867 A.D.; Pope (858–867 A.D.); excommunicated Photius, patriarch of Constantinople, causing a schism between the Roman and Byzantine churches: his day is November 13.

Nicholas II, (*Nikolai Aleksandrovich*), 1868–1918; czar of Russia (1894–1917); forced to abdicate; executed.

Nicholas V, 1397?–1455; Pope (1447–1455).

Nicholas, Saint, ?–342 A.D.; bishop of Myra; patron saint of Russia and of young people, sailors, etc.: his day is December 6: cf. **Santa Claus.**

‡**nicht wahr?** (niHt vär′), [G., lit., not true?], isn't that so?

Nic·i·as (nish′i-əs), *n.* Athenian statesman and general; ?–413 B.C.; defeated at Syracuse; executed.

Nick (nik), a masculine name: see **Nicholas.** *n.* the Devil; Satan: usually **Old Nick.**

nick (nik), *v.t.* [prob. < MLG. *knicken* (akin to ON. *kneikja,* to squeeze, pinch); IE. base **gneig-* < **gen-,* to squeeze together (cf. KNIGHT, KNOT, KNIT, etc.)], 1. to make a nick or nicks in. 2. to score or tally by means of notches. 3. to cut through or into. 4. to strike or catch at the exact or proper time; hit, guess, grasp, etc. exactly. 5. [Slang], *a)* to catch off guard. *b)* to trick; cheat; defraud. 6. [British Slang], to arrest; nab. *n.* [< the *v.*], 1. a small notch or slit; especially, a small cut, indention, or chip on the edge or surface of wood, metal, china, etc. 2. any of certain winning throws or casts in a game of dice. 3. a channel cut in the bottom of a printing type. 4. a tally or record kept by notching something.

in the nick of time, at the critical moment.

nick·el (nik′'l), *n.* [Sw.; contr. < *kopparnickel* < G. *kupfernickel,* copper nickel; *kupfer,* copper + *nickel,* demon (assumed to be contr. of *Nikolaus,* Nick, but prob. akin to G. *nix;* see NICK, devil): so called because in spite of its copperlike appearance the ore contained no copper], 1. a hard, silver-white, malleable metallic chemical element, used extensively in alloys and for plating because of its resistance to oxidation: symbol, Ni; at. wt., 58.69; at. no., 28. 2. a United States or Canadian coin made of an alloy of nickel and copper and equal to five cents. *v.t.* to plate with nickel.

nick·el·ic (nik′'l-ik), *adj.* of or containing nickel, especially trivalent nickel.

nick·el·if·er·ous (nik′'l-if′ēr-əs), *adj.* [< *nickel* + *-ferous*], containing nickel: said of ore, etc.

nick·el·o·de·on (nik′'l-ō′di-ən), *n.* [*nickel* + *odeon* (< Fr. *odéon*), odeum], 1. formerly, a motion-picture theater, variety show, etc. where admission was five cents. 2. a player piano or phonograph which can be operated by the insertion of a nickel in a slot.

nick·el·ous (nik′'l-əs), *adj.* containing nickel, especially bivalent nickel.

nick·el-plate (nik′'l-plāt′), *v.t.* to plate with nickel by electrolysis, etc.

nickel plate, a thin layer of nickel placed by electrolysis on objects made of other metal, to improve the finish and prevent rust.

nickel silver, a hard, tough, ductile, malleable, silver-white alloy composed essentially of nickel, copper, and zinc: used in the manufacture of tableware, electric-resistance wire, etc.: also called *German silver.*

nickel steel, a steel alloy made harder than ordinary steel by the addition of small amounts of nickel.

nick·er (nik′ēr), *n.* [*nick, v.* + *-er*], a person or thing that nicks (esp. in sense 4); specifically, any of a group of 18th-century English rowdies who broke windows by throwing copper coins.

nick·er (nik′ēr), *n.* & *v.i.* [prob. var. of *nicher, neigher,* freq. of *neigh;* cf. LG. *gnickern*], [Chiefly British Dial.], 1. neigh. 2. laugh; snicker.

nick·nack (nik′nak′), *n.* a knickknack.

nick·name (nik′nām′), *n.* [by syllabic merging < *an ekename;* ME. *ekename,* surname; see EKE & NAME; cf. NEWT], 1. an additional or substitute name given to a person, place, or thing: usually descriptive and given in fun, affection, or derision, as "Doc," "Shorty," etc. 2. a familiar form of a proper name, as "Freddy" for "Frederick," "Davey" for "David," etc. *v.t.* 1. to give a nickname to; call by a specified nickname. 2. to call by a wrong name.

Nic·o·bar Islands (nik′ə-bär′), a group of islands in the Bay of Bengal, southwest of Burma: with the Andaman Islands, constituting a state of India (*Andaman and Nicobar Islands*): area (of the state), 3,215 sq. mi.; pop. (of the state), 31,000.

Nic·o·las (nik′'l-əs), a masculine name: see **Nicholas.**

nic·o·tin (nik′ə-tin), *n.* nicotine.

nic·o·tin·am·ide (nik′ə-tin-am′īd, nik′ə-tin′ə-mīd′), *n.* a white crystalline powder, $C_5H_4N{\cdot}CONH_2$, the amide of nicotinic acid, used in treating pellagra.

nic·o·tine (nik′ə-tēn′, nik′ə-tin), *n.* [Fr. < Jacques *Nicot,* Fr. ambassador at Lisbon, who first introduced tobacco into France (1560)], a poisonous alkaloid, $C_{10}H_{14}N_2$, found in tobacco leaves, from which it is extracted as a colorless, oily, acrid, transparent liquid and used, ordinarily in an aqueous solution of its sulfate, as an insecticide.

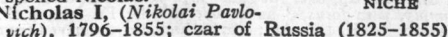

nic·o·tin·ic acid (nik'ə-tin'ik), a white, odorless, crystalline substance, $C_6H_5O_2N$, found in protein foods like lean meat, eggs, whole-grain cereals, etc. and prepared synthetically by the oxidation of nicotine: it is a member of the vitamin B complex and is used in the treatment of pellagra: also called *niacin.*

nic·o·tin·ism (nik'ə-tēn'iz'm, nik'ə-tin-iz'm), *n.* a diseased condition caused by the ingestion of nicotine, as from tobacco; nicotine poisoning.

nic·tate (nik'tāt), *v.i.* [NICTATED (-id), NICTATING], to nictitate.

nictating membrane, a nictitating membrane.

nic·ta·tion (nik-tā'shən), *n.* nictitation.

Nic·the·roy (nik'te-roi'), *n.* a city in Brazil, near Rio de Janeiro: pop., 171,000: also **Niteroi.**

nic·ti·tate (nik'tə-tāt'), *v.i.* [NICTITATED (-id), NICTITATING], [< ML. *nictitatus*, pp. of *nictitare*, freq. < L. *nictare*, to wink, blink < *nicere*, to beckon], to wink or blink rapidly, as birds and animals with a nictitating membrane: also **nictate.**

nictitating membrane, a transparent third eyelid hinged at the inner side or lower lid of the eye of various animals, serving to keep the eye clean and moist: also **nictating membrane.**

nic·ti·ta·tion (nik'tə-tā'shən), *n.* a nictitating.

Ni·da·ros (nē'dä-rōs'), *n.* Trondheim: the former name.

nid·der·ing, nid·er·ing (nid'ẽr-iŋ), *n.* [popularized by Scott (*Ivanhoe*, XLIII) < error in printed text (1596) of William of Malmesbury, for ME. *nithing* (< ON. *nithingr*), mean person, coward], [Archaic], coward; wretch. *adj.* [Archaic], base; cowardly.

nide (nīd), *n.* [< L. *nidus*, a nest], a nest or brood of pheasants. *v.i.* [NIDED (-id), NIDING], [Rare], to nest.

nid·i·fi·cate (nid'ə-fi-kāt'), *v.i.* [NIDIFICATED (-id), NIDIFICATING], [< L. *nidificatus*, pp. of *nidificare;* see NIDIFY], to build a nest; nidify.

nid·i·fi·ca·tion (nid'ə-fi-kā'shən), *n.* [see prec.], the act of building a nest; nesting.

nid·i·fy (nid'ə-fī'), *v.i.* [NIDIFIED (-fīd'), NIDIFYING], [L. *nidificare* < *nidus*, a nest + *facere*, to make; cf. NEST], to build a nest; nidificate.

ni·dus (nī'dəs), *n.* [*pl.* NIDI (-dī), NIDUSES (-iz)], [L. < **nizdos;* see NEST], 1. a nest, especially one in which insects or spiders deposit their eggs. 2. a breeding place; specifically, *a)* a place where spores or seeds are developed. *b)* a source of infection or disease.

Nie·buhr, Bar·thold Ge·org (bär'tôlt gā-ôrkh' nē'-boor), 1776–1831; German statesman and historian.

niece (nēs), *n.* [ME. *nece;* OFr. *niece, niepce;* LL. *neptia* < L. *neptis*, granddaughter, niece; akin to *nepos*, nephew; cf. NEPOTISM], 1. the daughter of one's brother or sister. 2. the daughter of one's brother-in-law or sister-in-law. 3. an illegitimate daughter, as of a medieval prelate: a euphemism.

ni·el·list (ni-el'ist), *n.* a person who works with niello.

ni·el·lo (ni-el'ō), *n.* [*pl.* NIELLI (-i), NIELLOS (-ōz)], [It.; ult. < L. *nigellus*, somewhat black, dark < *niger*, black], 1. any of a number of alloys of sulfur with silver, lead, copper, etc., characterized by a deep-black color and used to decorate objects of other metals by means of inlay. 2. the process of decorating with niello. 3. something decorated in this way. *v.t.* to decorate with niello.

Nie·men (nē'mən; Pol. nye'men), *n.* a river in Byelorussia and Lithuania, flowing into the Baltic Sea: length, 500 mi.: Lithuanian name, *Nemunas;* Russian name, *Neman, Nyeman;* German name, *Memel.*

Nier·stein·er (nêr'stīn-ẽr; G. nêr'shtīn-ẽr), *n.* [G. < *Nierstein*, place in Germany, where it was made], a variety of white Rhine wine.

Nie·tzsche, Frie·drich Wil·helm (frē'driH vil'helm nē'chə), 1844–1900; German philosopher.

Nie·tzsche·an (nē'chi-ən), *adj.* of Nietzsche or his philosophy: see **superman.** *n.* a follower of Nietzsche.

nieve (nēv), *n.* [ME. *neve;* ON. *hnefi*], [Archaic or Scot. & British Dial.], a fist or hand.

nif·fer (nif'ẽr), *v.* & *n.* [freq. formation < ME. *neve;* see NIEVE], [Scot.], exchange; barter; trade.

Ni·fl·heim, Ni·fel·heim (niv''l-hām'), *n.* [ON. *Niflheimr;* cf. NIBELUNG], in *Norse mythology*, the regions of darkness and cold, or realm of the dead; hell.

Ni·fl·heimr (niv''l-hām'ẽr), *n.* Niflheim.

nif·ty (nif'ti), *adj.* [NIFTIER (-ti-ẽr), NIFTIEST (-ti-ist)], [orig. theatrical slang; prob. < *magnificent*], [Slang], attractive, smart, stylish, enjoyable, etc.: a generalized term of approval. *n.* [Slang], a clever remark.

Ni·ger (nī'jẽr, nī'gẽr), *n.* 1. a river in west central Africa, flowing through Nigeria into the Gulf of Guinea: length, 2,600 mi. 2. a country in central Africa: a former French colony, it is now a member of the French Community: area, 459,000 sq. mi.; pop., 2,850,000; capital, Niamey.

Ni·ger·i·a (nī-jêr'i-ə), *n.* a country in west central Africa, on the Gulf of Guinea: a former British colony and protectorate, it is now a member of the British Commonwealth of Nations: the northern section of the Cameroons joined Nigeria by plebescite in 1961: area, 356,670 sq. mi.; pop., 30,500,000; capital, Lagos.

Ni·ge·ri·an (nī-jêr'i-ən), *adj.* of Nigeria, its people, or their culture. *n.* a native or inhabitant of Nigeria.

nig·gard (nig'ẽrd), *n.* [ME. *negarde;* prob. < Norm. Fr.; the base, prob. < ON., seems to be akin to Norw. dial. *knika, gnikka*, to rub, pinch, be mean or niggardly (cf. NIGGLE); for prob. IE. base see NICK (cut)], a stingy person; miser. *adj.* stingy; miserly.

nig·gard·li·ness (nig'ẽrd-li-nis), *n.* the quality or state of being niggardly.

nig·gard·ly (nig'ẽrd-li), *adj.* 1. like or characteristic of a niggard; stingy; miserly. 2. small, few, or scanty, as if given by a niggard: as, a *niggardly* sum. *adv.* in the manner of a niggard; stingily. —*SYN.* see **stingy.**

nig·ger (nig'ẽr), *n.* [earlier *neger;* Fr. *nègre;* Sp. *negro;* see NEGRO], 1. a Negro. 2. a member of any dark-skinned people. A vulgar, offensive term of hostility and contempt, as used by Negrophobes.

nig·gle (nig''l), *v.i.* [NIGGLED (-'ld), NIGGLING], [North Brit. dial.; prob. < ON.; as if < base of *niggard* + *-le*, freq. suffix; cf. Norw. *nigla* in same sense], to work fussily; pay too much attention to details; putter.

nigh (nī), *adv.* [ME. *neih, nyh*, etc.; AS. *neh, neah;* akin to G. *nahe;* prob. < IE. prefix **an-*, **anō-*, **no-*, up to, toward + base **oqw-*, to see (cf. EYE, OCULIST); basic sense "turned toward, looking toward"; cf. NEAR, NEXT], [Chiefly Archaic or Dial.], 1. near in time, place, etc. 2. nearly; almost. *adj.* [NIGHER (-ẽr), NIGHEST (-ist) or, *older*, NEXT (nekst)], [Chiefly Archaic or Dial.], 1. near; close. 2. direct or short. 3. on the left: said of animals, vehicles, etc. 4. parsimonious. *prep.* [Chiefly Archaic or Dial.], near; near to. *v.i.* & *v.t.* [Archaic], to draw near; approach.

night (nīt), *n.* [ME. *nyht;* AS. *niht, neaht;* akin to G. *nacht;* IE. base **noqt-*, night, seen also in L. *nox, noctis* (cf. NOCTURNAL)], 1. *a)* the period from sunset to sunrise. *b)* the period of actual darkness after sunset and before sunrise. 2. the darkness of this period; hence, 3. any period or condition of darkness or gloom; specifically, *a)* a period of intellectual or moral degeneration. *b)* a time of grief. *c)* death. *adj.* of or for the night.

make a night of it, to celebrate all or most of night.

night and day, continuously or continually.

night blindness, imperfect vision in the dark or in dim light; nyctalopia: a sign of vitamin A deficiency.

night-bloom·ing cereus (nīt'bloom'iŋ), any of various kinds of cactus, especially one with large, white flowers that open at night.

night·cap (nīt'kap'), *n.* 1. a cap worn in bed to protect the head from cold. 2. [Colloq.], an alcoholic drink taken just before going to bed.

night clothes, clothes to be worn in bed, as pajamas.

night club, a place of entertainment open at night for eating, drinking, etc., often having a floor show.

night crawler, a large earthworm that comes out of the earth at night; nightwalker.

night·dress (nīt'dres'), *n.* 1. a nightgown. 2. night clothes.

night·fall (nīt'fôl'), *n.* the close of the day; dusk.

night·gown (nīt'goun'), *n.* 1. a loose gown, usually long, worn in bed by women or children. 2. a nightshirt. 3. [Obs.], a dressing gown.

night·hawk (nīt'hôk'), *n.* 1. any of a group of night birds related to the whippoorwill, with brown, mottled feathers and a broad, deeply cleft bill; goatsucker. 2. the European nightjar. 3. a night owl (sense 2).

night heron, any of various herons most active at night or twilight.

night·in·gale (nīt''n-gāl', nīt'iŋ-gāl'), *n.* [ME. *nihtyngale*, for earlier *nihtegale;* AS. *nehtgale, nihtegale*, etc. (akin to G. *nachtigall*) < *niht*, night + base of *galan*, to sing], any of various small European thrushes with a russet back and buff to white underparts: it is characterized by the varied, melodious singing of the male, especially at night during the breeding season.

Night·in·gale, Florence (nīt''n-gāl', nīt'iŋ-gāl'), 1820–1910; English nurse in the Crimean War; regarded as the founder of modern nursing.

night·jar (nīt'jär'), *n.* [*night* + *jar, v.:* so called from the whirring noise made by the male], the European goatsucker; nighthawk.

night latch, a kind of door latch opened on the outside by a key, and on the inside by a knob.

night letter, a telegram with a minimum charge for fifty words or fewer, sent at night to be delivered the next morning, and cheaper than a regular telegram: distinguished from *day letter.*

night light, a small, dim light kept burning all night, as in the halls of rooming houses, etc.

night·long (nīt'lôŋ'), *adj.* lasting the entire night. *adv.* during the entire night.

night·ly (nīt'li), *adj.* 1. of, like, or characteristic of

the night. 2. done or occurring every night. *adv.* 1. at night. 2. every night.
night·mare (nīt′mâr′), *n.* [ME. *nihtmare; niht,* night + *mare,* demon (< AS. *mara*); akin to G. dial. *mahr,* incubus], 1. formerly, an evil spirit that was believed to haunt and suffocate sleeping people. 2. a frightening dream, often accompanied by a sensation of oppression and helplessness. 3. any experience like a nightmare in its frightening or oppressing aspects.
night·mar·ish (nīt′mâr′ish), *adj.* like a nightmare.
night owl, 1. an owl that is active almost exclusively at night. 2. a person who works at night or otherwise stays up late.
night raven, [Poetic], any of various birds, especially the night heron, that are most active at night.
night·rid·er (nīt′rī′dẽr), *n.* in the southern United States, any of a band of masked mounted men who perform lawless acts of violence and terror at night, generally to intimidate, punish, etc.
night robe, a nightgown.
nights (nīts), *adv.* [Colloq. or Dial.], at or by night.
night school, a school held in the evening for people, usually adults, unable to attend by day.
night·shade (nīt′shād′), *n.* [ME.; AS. *nihtscada,* lit., shade, or shadow, of night: with reference to narcotic qualities], any of a group of flowering plants related to the potato and tomato; especially, any of various poisonous varieties, including the belladonna (*deadly nightshade*) and the henbane.
night·shirt (nīt′shũrt′), *n.* a loose, shirtlike garment reaching to the knees, worn in bed by men or boys.
night soil, [from being collected at night], excrement removed from a cesspool or privy and used as fertilizer.
night·spot (nīt′spot′), *n.* [Colloq.], a night club.
night stick, a long, heavy club carried by a policeman, especially at night.
night·tide (nīt′tīd′), *n.* [Poetic], nighttime.
night·time (nīt′tīm′), *n.* the period of darkness from sunset to sunrise.
night·walk·er (nīt′wôk′ẽr), *n.* 1. a large earthworm that comes out of the earth at night; night crawler. 2. [Rare], a person who goes about at night, as a thief, prostitute, etc.
night watch, 1. a watching or guarding during the night. 2. the person or persons doing such guarding. 3. the time of their guarding. 4. *usually in pl.* any of the periods into which the night was formerly divided for such guarding.
night watchman, a watchman hired for duty at night.
night·wear (nīt′wâr′), *n.* night clothes.
night·y (nīt′i), *n.* [*pl.* NIGHTIES (-iz)], a nightgown or nightshirt: a diminutive.
ni·gres·cence (nī-gres′'ns), *n.* [< *nigrescent*], 1. the process of becoming black. 2. blackness, especially of the skin, hair, or eyes.
ni·gres·cent (nī-gres′'nt), *adj.* [L. *nigrescens,* ppr. of *nigrescere,* to grow black < *niger,* black], becoming or tending to become black.
nig·ri·fy (nig′rə-fī′), *v.t.* [NIGRIFIED (-fīd′), NIGRIFYING], [L. *nigrificare* < *niger,* black + *facere,* to make], to make black.
nig·ri·tude (nig′rə-tōōd′, nig′rə-tūd′), *n.* [L. *nigritudo* < *niger,* black], 1. blackness. 2. something black.
‡**ni·hil** (nī′hil), *n.* [L., contr. < *nihilum* < **nehilum; ne-,* not + *hilum,* little thing, trifle], 1. nothing. 2. a thing of slight value or importance; a mere nothing.
ni·hil·ism (nī′ə-liz′m), *n.* [< L. *nihil* (see NIHIL); + *-ism*], 1. in *philosophy, a)* the denial of the existence of any basis for knowledge or truth. *b)* the general rejection of customary beliefs in morality, religion, etc.: also **ethical nihilism.** 2. in *politics, a)* the doctrine that all social, political, and economic institutions must be completely destroyed in order to make way for new institutions; specifically, *b)* [N-], a movement in Russia (c. 1860–1917) which advocated such revolutionary reform and attempted to carry it out through the use of some terrorism and assassination; hence, 3. loosely, any violent revolutionary movement involving some use of terrorism.
ni·hil·ist (nī′ə-list), *n.* 1. an advocate of any form of philosophical or political nihilism. 2. [N-], formerly, any adherent of Nihilism.
ni·hil·is·tic (nī′ə-lis′tik), *adj.* of or characteristic of nihilism or nihilists.
ni·hil·i·ty (nī-hil′ə-ti), *n.* [ML. *nihilitas*], nothingness.
Ni·hon (nē′hon′), *n.* Japan: original Japanese name.
Ni·i·ga·ta (nē′ē-gä′tä), *n.* a city on the western coast of Honshu, Japan: pop., 151,000.
Ni·i·ha·u (nē′ē-hä′ōō), *n.* one of the Hawaiian Islands, west of Kauai: area, 72 sq. mi.; pop., 180.
Ni·jin·sky, Vas·lav (väs-läf′ ni-zhēn′ski; Eng. nə-jin′ski), 1890–1950; Russian ballet dancer.
Nij·me·gen (nī′mā-gən; D. nī′mā-khən), *n.* a city in the eastern Netherlands: pop., 107,000 (1947): also called *Nymwegen.*
Ni·ke (nī′kē), *n.* [Gr. *Nikē*], in *Greek mythology,* 1. the winged goddess of victory: identified by the Romans with Victoria. 2. the goddess Athena as giver of victory. 3. a United States Army guided missile launched from the ground, capable of automatically steering a course to strike attacking enemy aircraft.
Ni·ko·la·ev (nē′kô-lä′yef), *n.* a city in the Ukrainian S.S.R., on the Bug River: pop., 167,000: formerly called *Vernoleninsk.*
nil (nil), *n.* [L., contr. of *nihil;* see NIHIL], nothing.
‡**nil de·spe·ran·dum** (nil des′pə-ran′dəm), [L.], nothing should be despaired of; never despair.
Nile (nīl), *n.* a river in eastern Africa, flowing through Egypt into the Mediterranean: length, 4,000 mi.
Nile-green (nīl′grēn′), *adj.* of Nile green.
Nile green, yellowish green.
nil·gai, nil·ghai (nil′gī), *n.* [*pl.* NILGAIS, NILGHAIS (-gīz), NILGAI, NILGHAI; see PLURAL, II, D, 1], [Hind. & Per. *nīlgāw,* lit., blue cow < Per. *nīl,* blue + *gāw,* cow], any of a group of large, slate-blue antelopes of India: also **nylghai, nylghau.**
nil·gau, nil·ghau (nil′gô), *n.* [*pl.* NILGAUS, NILGHAUS (-gôz), NILGAU, NILGHAU; see PLURAL, II, D, 1], a nilgai.
nill (nil), *v.t. & v.i.* [ME. *nille;* AS. *nylle, nelle* (1st pers. sing., pres. indic.) < *ne,* not + *wille,* to will], [Archaic], not to will (something); refuse: as, will I *nill* I: see also **willy-nilly.**
‡**nil ni·si bo·num** (nil nī′sī bō′nəm), [L.], nothing but good: see **de mortuis nil nisi bonum.**
Ni·lom·e·ter (nī-lom′ə-tẽr), *n.* [Gr. *Neilometrion* < *Neilos,* the Nile + *metron,* measure], an instrument for measuring the rise of the Nile during flood time: it consists of a graduated pillar with a water chamber.
Ni·lot·ic (nī-lot′ik), *adj.* [L. *Niloticus;* Gr. *Neilōtikos* < *Neilos,* the Nile], 1. of the Nile or the Nile Valley. 2. designating or of the Sudanese Negroes who live in the valley of the White Nile.
Ni·lus (nī′ləs), *n.* the Nile: the Roman name.
nim (nim), *v.t.* [NAM (näm, nam) or NIMMED (nimd), NOMEN (nō′mən) or NOME (nōm), NIMMING], [ME. *nimen;* AS. *niman;* akin to G. *nehmen,* to take], [Obs.], 1. to take. 2. to steal; filch.
nim·ble (nim′b'l), *adj.* [NIMBLER (-blẽr), NIMBLEST (-blist)], [with intrusive *-b-* (cf. THIMBLE) < ME. *nimmel;* AS. *numol* < *niman,* to take, seize (cf. NIM); basic sense "capable of taking," etc.], 1. mentally quick; quick-witted; alert: as, a *nimble* mind. 2. showing mental quickness: as, a *nimble* reply. 3. moving or acting quickly and lightly. —***SYN.*** see **agile.**
nim·bly (nim′bli), *adv.* in a nimble manner; agilely.
nim·bo-stra·tus (nim′bō-strā′təs), *n.* [*nimbo-* (< L. *nimbus,* black rain cloud; see NIMBUS) + *stratus*], a low, gray cloud layer that covers the sky and brings rain or snow.
nim·bus (nim′bəs), *n.* [*pl.* NIMBUSES (-iz), NIMBI (-bī)], [L., violent rain, black rain cloud, nimbus; IE. base **enebh-,* **nebh-,* **embh-,* moist, water, vapor, seen also in L. *nebula* (cf. NEBULA)], 1. a bright cloud supposedly surrounding gods or goddesses when they appeared on earth; hence, 2. an aura of splendor about any person or thing. 3. a halo or bright disk surrounding the heads of divinities, saints, and sovereigns on pictures, medals, etc. 4. a nimbo-stratus.
Nîmes (nēm), *n.* a city in southern France: pop., 104,000 (1946).
ni·mi·e·ty (ni-mī′ə-ti), *n.* [L. *nimietas* < *nimius, adj., nimis, adv.,* too much], excess; redundancy.
nim·i·ny-pim·i·ny (nim′ə-ni-pim′ə-ni), *adj.* [imitative of mincing speech], fussily dainty or refined; mincing.
Nim·itz, Chester William (nim′its), 1885– ; American admiral in command of United States Pacific fleet, World War II.
‡**n'im·porte** (nan′pôrt′), [Fr.], it doesn't matter.
Nim·rod (nim′rod), *n.* [Heb. *nimrōdh*], 1. in the *Bible,* the son of Cush, referred to as a mighty hunter: Gen. 10:8-9; hence, 2. a hunter.
nin·com·poop (nin′kəm-pōōp′, niŋ′kəm-pōōp′), *n.* [earlier also *nicompoop;* early forms disprove deriv. < *non compos mentis;* ? < *Nick* + D. *poep,* a fool (so Weekley)], a stupid, silly person; fool; simpleton.
nine (nīn), *adj.* [ME. *nyen,* etc.; AS. *nigon;* indirectly akin to G. *neun;* IE. **enewen,* etc., nine, seen also in L. *novem,* nine (cf. NOVEMBER), *nonus,* ninth (cf. NOON); IE. form < extension of base **newo-,* new (cf. NEW), indicating a new division of the numeral system commencing with 9], totaling one more than eight. *n.* 1. the cardinal number between eight and ten; 9; IX. 2. any group of nine persons or things; especially, a baseball team. 3. a playing card marked with the number 9 and nine spots of its suit.
the Nine, the nine Muses.
nine days' wonder, anything that arouses great excitement and interest for a short time.
nine·fold (nīn′fōld′), *adj.* [see -FOLD], 1. having nine parts. 2. having nine times as much or as many. *adv.* nine times as much or as many.
nine·pence (nīn′pəns), *n.* 1. the sum of nine British pennies, equal to approximately eighteen American cents. 2. a British coin of this value.
nine·pins (nīn′pinz′), *n.pl.* 1. [construed as sing.], a game like tenpins, in which nine wooden pins are set up at one end of an alley and bowled at. 2. the pins used in this game.

nine·teen (nīn′tēn′), *adj.* [AS. *nigontyne;* see NINE & -TEEN], nine more than ten. *n.* the cardinal number between eighteen and twenty; 19; XIX.
nine·teenth (nīn′tēnth′), *adj.* [ME. *nyntenthe;* AS. *nigonteotha;* see NINE & TENTH], 1. preceded by eighteen others in a series; 19th. 2. designating any of the nineteen equal parts of something. *n.* 1. the one following the eighteenth. 2. any of the nineteen equal parts of something; 1/19.
nineteenth hole, [Colloq.], any place, such as the locker room or bar of a clubhouse, where golfers meet for drinks and conviviality after playing a round of golf.
nine·ti·eth (nīn′ti-ith), *adj.* [ME. *nyntithe;* see NINETY & -TH], 1. preceded by eighty-nine others in a series; 90th. 2. designating any of the ninety equal parts of something. *n.* 1. the one following the eighty-ninth. 2. any of the ninety equal parts of something; 1/90.
nine·ty (nīn′ti), *adj.* [ME. *nigenty;* AS. *nigontig;* see NINE & -TY (tens)], nine times ten. *n.* [*pl.* NINETIES (-tiz)], the cardinal number between eighty-nine and ninety-one; 90; XC (or LXXXX).
the nineties, the years from ninety through ninety-nine (of a century or a person's age).
Nin·e·veh (nin′ə-və), *n.* a city in ancient Assyria, on the Tigris, near modern Mosul: Latin name, *Ninus.*
Ning·po (niŋ′pō′), *n.* a city in Chekiang province, China: pop., 219,000.
Ning·sia (niŋ′syä′), *n.* 1. a province of Inner Mongolia: area, 112,831 sq. mi.; pop., 1,023,000. 2. its capital: pop., 20,000.
nin·ny (nin′i), *n.* [*pl.* NINNIES (-iz)], [prob. by syllabic merging and contr. of *an innocent*], a fool; dolt.
ninth (nīnth), *adj.* [ME. *ninthe;* AS. *nigonthe;* see NINE & -TH], 1. preceded by eight others in a series; 9th. 2. designating any of the nine equal parts of something. *n.* 1. the one following the eighth. 2. any of the nine equal parts of something; 1/9. 3. in *music, a*) an interval in pitch of an octave and a second. *b*) the tone at the upper limit of such an interval. *c*) the combination of this tone and of the tone at the lower limit of such an interval, written or sounded together.
ninth chord, in *music,* a chord consisting of the third, fifth, seventh, and ninth above the root.
ninth·ly (nīnth′li), *adv.* in the ninth place.
Ni·nus (nī′nəs), *n.* Nineveh: the Latin name.
Ni·o·be (nī′ə-bi), *n.* [L. *Nioba, Niobe;* Gr. *Niobē*], in *Greek mythology,* a mother whose children were slain by Artemis and Apollo when she boastfully compared herself to their mother, Leto: the weeping Niobe was changed by Zeus into a stone from which tears continued to flow.
Ni·o·be·an (nī′ə-bē′ən), *adj.* of or like Niobe.
ni·o·bi·um (nī-ō′bi-əm), *n.* [Mod. L. < L. *Niobe,* Niobe, daughter of Tantalus: from association with tantalum; see TANTALUM], a rare metallic chemical element with properties like those of tantalum: symbol, Nb; at. wt., 92.91; at. no., 41: formerly also called *columbium.*
Ni·o·brar·a (nī′ə-brâr′ə), *n.* a river in eastern Wyoming and northern Nebraska, flowing eastward into the Missouri: length, 450 mi.
Nip (nip), *n.* & *adj.* [Slang], Nipponese; Japanese: usually contemptuous.
nip (nip), *v.t.* [NIPPED (nipt), NIPPING], [ME. *nippen;* prob. < MLG. *nippen* or ON. *hnippa;* akin to *nib-* in *nibble;* IE. base **qneib-* < **qen-,* to scratch, rub], 1. to catch, pinch, or squeeze between two surfaces, points, or edges; pinch; bite. 2. to sever (shoots, etc.) by pinching or clipping with a tool. 3. to check the growth or development of. 4. to have a painful or injurious effect on: said of cold, as, frost *nipped* the plants. 5. [Slang], *a*) to snatch. *b*) to steal. *v.i.* 1. to give a nip or nips. 2. [British Colloq.], to move quickly or nimbly (with *off, away, along,* etc.). *n.* 1. the act of nipping; pinch; bite. 2. a piece nipped off; small bit. 3. a stinging quality, as in cold or frosty air. 4. stinging cold; frost. 5. a stinging remark. 6. a tang in cheese.
nip and tuck, so close, even, or critical as to leave the outcome in doubt; neck and neck.
nip in the bud, to check (something) at the start.
nip (nip), *n.* [prob. contr. < *nipperkin* < D. *nippertje,* small measure for liquors < base of *nippen,* to sip, nip], a small drink of liquor; dram; sip. *v.t.* & *v.i.* [NIPPED (nipt), NIPPING], to drink (liquor) in nips.
ni·pa (nē′pə, nī′pə), *n.* [Sp.; Malay *nipah*], 1. an Asiatic palm with feathery leaves and large bunches of fruit. 2. the liquor made from its sap.
Nip·i·gon, Lake (nip′ə-gon′), a lake in Ontario, Canada, above Lake Superior: area, 1,730 sq. mi.
Nip·is·sing, Lake (nip′ə-siŋ′), a lake in southeastern Ontario, Canada, northeast of Georgian Bay: area, 332 sq. mi.
nip·per (nip′ẽr), *n.* 1. anything that nips, or pinches. 2. *pl.* any of various tools for grasping or severing wire, etc., as pliers, pincers, or forceps. 3. any of certain organs of animals, used in biting, grasping, holding, etc.; specifically, *a*) an incisor tooth of a horse. *b*) the pincerlike claw of a crab. 4. [British Colloq.], a small boy. 5. *pl.* [Slang], *a*) handcuffs. *b*) leg irons.
nip·ping (nip′iŋ), *adj.* 1. that nips, or pinches. 2. sharp; biting; nippy. 3. sarcastic.
nip·ple (nip′'l), *n.* [earlier *neble;* prob. dim. of *neb*], 1. the small protuberance on a breast or udder, through which the milk passes in suckling the young; teat; pap: it is rudimentary in the male. 2. a rubber cap with a teatlike part, for a baby's feeding bottle. 3. any projection, part, or thing resembling a nipple in shape or function; specifically, *a*) a threaded piece of pipe at the end of a water line, to which is fastened a nozzle, faucet, etc. *b*) a short piece of pipe with both ends threaded. *c*) a small projection on glass or metal.
Nip·pon (nip′on, ni-pon′), *n.* Japan: Japanese name.
Nip·pon·ese (nip′ə-nēz′), *adj.* & *n.* [*pl.* NIPPONESE], [< *Nippon*], Japanese.
Nip·pur (ni-poor′), *n.* a city in ancient Mesopotamia.
nip·py (nip′i), *adj.* [NIPPIER (-i-ẽr), NIPPIEST (-i-ist)], 1. nipping or tending to nip, or pinch; sharp; biting. 2. [British Colloq.], quick; active; nimble.
NIRA, N.I.R.A., National Industrial Recovery Act.
nir·va·na (nẽr-van′ə, nir-vä′nə), *n.* [Sans. *nirvāṇa* < *nirwā,* to blow], 1. in *Hinduism,* a blowing out, or extinction, of the flame of life; reunion with Brahma. 2. in *Buddhism,* the state of perfect blessedness achieved by the extinction of individual existence and by the absorption of the soul into the supreme spirit, or by the extinction of all desires and passions.
Ni·san (nī′san, nis′ən; Heb. ni-sän′), *n.* [Heb. *nīsān*], the seventh month of the Jewish year: see **Jewish calendar.**
ni·sei (nē′sā′), *n.* [*pl.* NISEI, NISEIS (-sāz′)], [Japan., lit., second generation], [also N-], a native American citizen born of immigrant Japanese parents and educated in the United States: distinguished from *issei, kibei.*
Ni·sha·pur (nē′shä-poor′, nē′shä-boor′), *n.* a town in northeastern Iran: birthplace of Omar Khayyam.
ni·si (nī′sī), *conj.* [L.], unless: used in law after *decree, order,* etc. to indicate that it shall take permanent effect at a specified time unless cause is shown why it should not, or unless it is changed by further proceedings.
nisi pri·us (prī′əs), [L., unless before: used orig. in a writ directing a sheriff to summon a jury to Westminster on a certain date "unless before" that date the trial had been held in his own county], in *law,* a civil action tried in a court of record before a judge and jury: abbreviated **N.P., n.p.**
Nis·sen hut (nis′'n), [after P. N. *Nissen* (1871–), engineer in the Canadian Army], a prefabricated shelter of corrugated metal shaped like a cylinder cut vertically in two and resting on its flat surface: it was first used by the British Army in World War II: see also **Quonset hut.**
Nis·tru (nē′stroo), *n.* the Dnestr: the Romanian name.
ni·sus (nī′səs), *n.* [*pl.* NISUS], [L. < *nisus,* pp. of *niti,* to strive], effort; endeavor; impulse; striving.
nit (nit), *n.* [ME. *nitte, nete;* AS. *hnitu;* akin to G. *nisse, niss;* IE. base **qonid-, *qnid-,* etc., louse, nit; prob. < **qen-,* to scratch], 1. the egg of a louse or similar insect. 2. the young insect.
ni·ter (nī′tẽr), *n.* [Fr. *nitre;* L. *nitrum;* Gr. *nitron,* native soda, natron; Heb. *nether;* prob. < Egypt. *ntr(j)*], 1. potassium nitrate, a crystalline salt found in nature and used as a preservative, in making gunpowder, etc.; saltpeter. 2. sodium nitrate, a crystalline salt, used as a fertilizer, etc.; Chile saltpeter. Also spelled **nitre.**
Ni·te·roi (nē′te-roi′), *n.* Nictheroy.
ni·ton (nī′ton), *n.* [Mod. L. < L. *nitere,* to shine; + *-on* as in *argon*], radon, a radioactive chemical element: symbol, Nt: former name.
nitr-, nitro-.
ni·trate (nī′trāt, nī′trit), *n.* [< *nitre* + *-ate;* cf. Fr. *nitrate*], 1. a salt or ester of nitric acid. 2. potassium nitrate or sodium nitrate, used as a fertilizer. *v.t.* [NITRATED (-id), NITRATING], to treat or combine with nitric acid or a nitrate; make into a nitrate.
ni·tra·tion (nī-trā′shən), *n.* the process of nitrating; especially, the introduction of the NO_2 group into an organic compound.
ni·tre (nī′tẽr), *n.* niter.
ni·tric (nī′trik), *adj.* [Fr. *nitrique;* see NITRO- & -IC], 1. of or containing nitrogen. 2. designating or of compounds in which nitrogen has a higher valence than in the corresponding nitrous compounds.
nitric acid, a colorless, fuming acid, HNO_3, that is highly corrosive: it is prepared by the action of sul-

furic acid on nitrates and by the oxidation of ammonia: also called *aqua fortis*.

nitric bacteria, see **nitrobacteria**.

nitric oxide, a colorless gas, NO, prepared by the action of nitric acid on copper, etc.

ni·trid (nī′trid), *n.* a nitride.

ni·tride (nī′trīd, nī′trid), *n.* [*nitr-* + *-ide*], a compound of nitrogen with a more positive element, as phosphorus, boron, or a metal.

ni·tri·fi·ca·tion (nī′trə-fi-kā′shən), *n.* a nitrifying.

ni·tri·fi·er (nī′trə-fī′ẽr), *n.* anything that nitrifies; especially, soil bacteria that oxidize ammonium salts into nitrites and nitrates.

ni·tri·fy (nī′trə-fī′), *v.t.* [NITRIFIED (-fīd′), NITRIFYING], [Fr. *nitrifier;* see NITER & -FY], 1. to combine with nitrogen or nitrogen compounds. 2. to impregnate (soil, etc.) with nitrates. 3. to cause the oxidation of (ammonium salts, etc.) to nitrites and nitrates, as by the action of soil bacteria, etc.

ni·tril (nī′tril), *n.* a nitrile.

ni·trile (nī′tril, nī′trēl, nī′trīl), *n.* [< *nitrogen* + *-ile*, n. suffix used in chem.], an organic cyanide of an alkyl group, yielding the corresponding acid and ammonia on hydrolysis.

ni·trite (nī′trīt), *n.* [*nitr-* + *-ite;* cf. Fr. *nitrite*], a salt or ester of nitrous acid.

ni·tro (nī′trō), *adj.* [see NITRO-], 1. designating certain compounds containing nitrogen and produced by the action of nitric or nitrous acid. 2. designating the NO_2 radical or compounds in which one or more NO_2 radicals have replaced atoms of hydrogen.

ni·tro- (nī′trō, nī′trə), [< L. *nitrum;* Gr. *nitron;* see NITER], a combining form used to indicate: 1. *the presence of nitrogen compounds made by the action of nitric* or *nitrous acid and other substances*, as in *nitrocellulose*. 2. *the presence of the NO_2 radical*, as in *nitrobenzene*. 3. *niter*, as in *nitrobacteria*. Also, before a vowel, **nitr-**.

ni·tro·bac·te·ri·a (nī′trō-bak-têr′i-ə), *n.pl.* [Mod. L.; *nitro-* + *bacteria*], bacteria in the soil that oxidize ammonia compounds into nitrites (*nitrous bacteria*), or nitrites into nitrates (*nitric bacteria*).

ni·tro·ben·zene (nī′trə-ben′zēn), *n.* a poisonous yellow liquid, $C_6H_5NO_2$, prepared by treating benzene with nitric acid, used in making dyes, perfumes, etc.

ni·tro·cel·lu·lose, ni·tro·cel·lu·lose (nī′trə-sel′yoo-lōs′), *n.* an amorphous yellow substance obtained by treating cellulose in the form of cotton or wood fiber with nitric acid, used in making explosives, photographic films, lacquers, etc.; cellulose nitrate.

ni·tro·chlo·ro·form (nī′trə-klôr′ə-fôrm′, nī′trə-klō′rə-fôrm′), *n.* chloropicrin.

ni·tro·gen (nī′trə-jən), *n.* [Fr. *nitrogène;* see NITRO- & -GEN], a colorless, tasteless, odorless gaseous chemical element forming nearly four fifths of the atmosphere: it is a component of all living things: symbol, N; at. wt., 14.008; at. no., 7.

nitrogen cycle, the cycle of processes by which atmospheric nitrogen is converted by natural agencies into compounds used by plants and animals in the formation of proteins, and is eventually returned to its original state.

nitrogen fixation, 1. the conversion of atmospheric nitrogen into nitrates by soil bacteria (*nitrogen fixers*), found in the nodules of certain legumes. 2. the conversion of free nitrogen into nitrogenous compounds of commercial value by any of various processes.

ni·tro·gen-fix·ing (nī′trə-jən-fik′siŋ), *adj.* capable of nitrogen fixation: said of nitrobacteria, etc.

ni·trog·e·nize (nī-troj′ə-nīz′, nī′trə-jən-īz′), *v.t.* [NITROGENIZED (-nīzd′, -īzd′), NITROGENIZING], to combine or impregnate with nitrogen or its compounds.

ni·trog·e·nous (nī-troj′ə-nəs), *adj.* of or containing nitrogen or nitrogen compounds.

ni·tro·glyc·er·in, ni·tro·glyc·er·ine (nī′trə-glis′ẽr-in), *n.* a thick, pale-yellow, explosive oil, $C_3H_5(NO_3)_3$, prepared by treating glycerin with a mixture of nitric and sulfuric acids; glyceryl trinitrate: it is used in medicine and as an ingredient of dynamite.

ni·tro·hy·dro·chlor·ic acid (nī′trə-hī′drə-klôr′ik, nī′-trə-hī′drə-klō′rik), a mixture of one part of concentrated nitric acid with three parts of concentrated hydrochloric acid, used as a solvent for gold and platinum: also called *aqua regia*.

ni·trol·ic (nī-trol′ik), *adj.* [< *nitro-* + *-ol* + *-ic*], designating or of any of a series of acids formed by the action of nitrous acid on nitroparaffin and containing the CH_2-NO_2 group.

ni·trom·e·ter (nī-trom′ə-tẽr), *n.* [*nitro-* + *-meter*], an apparatus for measuring the amount of nitrogen, or certain of its compounds, in a substance.

ni·tro·par·af·fin (nī′trə-par′ə-fin), *n.* a nitrogen compound derived from any member of the methane, or paraffin, series of hydrocarbons and containing an NO_2 group in place of one of the hydrogen atoms normally present in the hydrocarbon.

ni·tros·am·in (nī′trōs-am′in), *n.* a nitrosamine.

ni·tros·a·mine (nī′trōs-ə-mēn′, nī′trōs-am′in), *n.* [< *nitroso-* + *amine*], any of a series of organic compounds derived from amines and containing the divalent =N·NO radical.

ni·tro·so (nī-trō′sō), *adj.* [see NITROSO-], designating or containing the NO radical, or group.

ni·tro·so- (nī-trō′sō, nī-trō′sə), [< L. *nitrosus*, full of natron < *nitrum;* see NITER], a combining form used to indicate the presence of *the NO radical*.

ni·tro·syl (nī-trō′sil, nī′trə-sēl′, nī′trə-sil′), *n.* [< *nitroso-* + *-yl*], the nitroso radical, or group.

ni·trous (nī′trəs), *adj.* [L. *nitrosus;* see NITRO- & -OUS], 1. of, like, or containing niter. 2. designating or of compounds in which nitrogen has a lower valence than in the corresponding nitric compounds.

nitrous acid, an acid, HNO_2, known only in solution: it forms salts called *nitrites*.

nitrous bacteria, see **nitrobacteria**.

nitrous oxide, a colorless gas, N_2O, used as an anesthetic: also called *laughing gas*.

nit·ty (nit′i), *adj.* full of nits.

nit·wit (nit′wit′), *n.* [*nit* (< G. dial. for G. *nicht*, not) or *nit* (louse) + *wit*], a stupid person.

Ni·u·e (nē-ōō′ā), *n.* an island in the South Pacific, east of Tonga, belonging to New Zealand: area, 100 sq. mi.: also called *Savage Island*.

ni·val (nī′v'l), *adj.* [L. *nivalis* < *nix, nivis*, snow], of, or growing under, snow.

niv·e·ous (niv′i-əs), *adj.* [L. *niveus*, snowy < *nix, nivis*, snow], snowy; snowlike.

Ni·ver·nais (nē′vâr′ne′), *n.* a former province of central France.

‡Ni·vôse (nē′vōz′), *n.* [Fr. < L. *nivosus*, snowy < *nix, nivis*, snow; cf. NÉVÉ], the fourth month (December 21–January 19) of the French Revolutionary Calendar.

nix (niks), *n.* [*pl.* NIXES (-iz); G. NIXE (nik′sə)], [G. *nix*, masc., *nixe*, fem.; OHG. *nihhus*, sea beast, *nicchussa*, water sprite, goblin; akin to AS. *nicor*, water sprite, ON. *nykr*, fabulous water-being < Gmc. **nik-*, **nikwus-*, water spirit; IE. base **neigw-*, to wash], in *Germanic mythology*, a water sprite or water fairy, usually small and of human or partly human form.

nix (niks), *adv.* [G. *nichts*], [Slang], 1. nothing. 2. no. 3. not at all. *interj.* an exclamation meaning: 1. stop! 2. I forbid, refuse, disagree, etc.

nix·ie (nik′si), *n.* [G. *nixe*], a female nix.

Nix·on, Richard M. (nik′s'n), 1913– ; vice-president of the United States (1953–1961).

Ni·zam (ni-zäm′, nī-zam′), *n.* [Hind. & Per. *niẓām;* Ar. *niẓām*, to order, arrange < *naẓama*, to govern], 1. the title of the native ruler in Hyderabad, India. 2. [n-], [*pl.* NIZAM], a soldier in the Turkish regular army.

Nizh·ni Nov·go·rod (nēzh′ni nôv′gô-rôt), Gorki, a city in the central European U.S.S.R.: the former name.

N.J., New Jersey.

Njord (nyôrd), *n.* Njorth.

Njorth (nyôrth), *n.* [ON. *Njörthr*], in *Norse mythology*, a Vanir, the father of Frey and Freya.

NKVD, N.K.V.D., [first letters of Russ. *Narodnii Kommissariat Vnutrennikh Del*, people's commissariat of internal affairs], the MVD (from 1934 to 1946).

NL., N.L., New Latin (Modern Latin).

n.l., 1. in *printing*, new line. 2. *non licet*, [L.], it is not lawful. 3. *non liquet*, [L.], it is not clear.

N. Lat., N. lat., north latitude.

NLRB, N.L.R.B., National Labor Relations Board.

N.M., New Mexico: also **N. Mex.**

N.M.U., NMU, National Maritime Union.

NNE, N.N.E., n.n.e., north-northeast.

NNW, N.N.W., n.n.w., north-northwest.

no (nō), *adv.* [ME.; AS. *na* < *ne a*, lit., not ever (see AYE, ever)], 1. [Scot. or Rare], not: as, whether or *no*. 2. not in any degree; not at all: as, he is *no* worse. 3. nay; not so: the opposite of *yes*, used to deny, refuse, or disagree. *adj.* [ME., form of *non, none* (cf. NONE) used only before a consonant; AS. *nan* < *ne an*, lit., not one (cf. ONE)], not any; not a; not one: as, he is *no* fool. *n.* [*pl.* NOES (nōz)], 1. an utterance of *no;* refusal or denial. 2. a negative vote or a person voting in the negative.

no (nō), *n.* [*pl.* NO], [Japan. *nō*], a type of Japanese play with a highly stylized plot, almost no stage accessories, elaborate costuming, and much singing and dancing: also **no-gaku, noh.**

No, in *chemistry*, nobelium.

No., 1. Noah. 2. north. 3. northern.

No., no., 1. number. 2. *numero*, [L.], by number.

No·a·chi·an (nō-ā′ki-ən), *adj.* 1. of Noah or his time; hence, 2. ancient; antique.

No·ach·ic (nō-ak′ik), *adj.* Noachian.

No·ach·i·cal (nō-ak′i-k'l), *adj.* Noachian.

No·ah (nō′ə), [Heb. *nōaḥ*, lit., rest, comfort], a masculine name. *n.* in the *Bible*, the patriarch commanded by God to build the ark on which he, his family, and two of every kind of creature survived the Flood: Gen. 5:28-10. Abbreviated **No.**

nob (nob), *n.* [later form of *knob*], 1. a knob. 2. [Slang], the head. 3. in *cribbage*, the jack of the same suit as the card turned over by the dealer: it counts one point for the player holding it in his hand or playing it from the crib.

nob (nob), *n.* [? contr. < *nabob;* cf. NIBS], [Slang], a person of wealth and high social status.

no-ball (nō′bôl′), *n.* in *cricket,* a ball that has not been bowled in the manner specified by the rules.

nob·ble (nob′'l), *v.t.* [NOBBLED (-'ld), NOBBLING], [? freq. of *nab*], [British Slang], 1. to disable or harm (a horse) to keep it from winning a race, as by drugging, etc. 2. *a)* to win (a race or other contest) by bribery or other underhand methods. *b)* to win over by bribery. 3. to cheat; steal; swindle; bribe.

nob·by (nob′i), *adj.* [NOBBIER (-i-ẽr), NOBBIEST (-i-ist)], [< *nob* (wealthy person)], [Slang], 1. of or for nobs; stylish; fashionable. 2. excellent; first-rate.

No·bel, Al·fred Bern·hard (ál′fred bâr′nárd nō-bel′), 1833–1896; Swedish industrialist, philanthropist, and inventor of dynamite; established Nobel prizes.

no·bel·i·um (nō-bel′i-əm), *n.* [after *Nobel* Institute in Stockholm, where discovered], a radioactive chemical element produced by the nuclear bombardment of curium: symbol, No; at. wt., 255(?); at. no., 102.

Nobel prizes, the five annual prizes amounting to nearly $40,000 each, given by the Nobel Foundation for distinction in physics, chemistry, medicine, and literature, and for the promotion of peace.

no·bil·i·ar·y (nō-bil′i-er′i, nō-bil′yẽr-i), *adj.* [Fr. *nobiliarie;* see NOBLE & -ARY], of nobles or nobility.

no·bil·i·ty (nō-bil′ə-ti), *n.* [*pl.* NOBILITIES (-tiz)], [ME. *nobylyte;* OFr. *noblete, nobilité;* L. *nobilitas*], 1. the quality or state of being noble. 2. high station or rank in society, especially when accompanied by a title. 3. the class of people of noble rank; in Great Britain, the peerage (usually with *the*).

no·ble (nō′b'l), *adj.* [ME.; OFr.; L. *nobilis,* lit., well-known < base of *(g)noscere,* to know; see KNOW], 1. famous, illustrious, or renowned; having eminence, dignity, fame, etc. 2. having or showing high moral qualities or ideals; characterized by or characteristic of greatness of character; lofty. 3. having excellent qualities. 4. grand; stately; splendid; magnificent: as, a *noble* view. 5. of high rank, title, or birth; of ancient lineage; aristocratic. 6. not corroding or deteriorating rapidly; precious; pure: said of metals, especially gold, silver, etc.: distinguished from *base.* *n.* 1. a person having hereditary rank or title; nobleman; peer. 2. a former gold coin of England, equal (until 1461) to 6 shillings, 8 pence. 3. [Slang], a leader of men hired to break a strike.

noble fir, a variety of very large fir that grows in the western United States.

no·ble·man (nō′b'l-mən), *n.* [*pl.* NOBLEMEN (-mən)], a member of the nobility; peer; titled person.

no·blesse (nō-bles′), *n.* [ME. *noblesse, noblesce;* OFr. *noblesce, noblece;* ML. *nobilitia*], 1. noble birth or status. 2. the nobility; aristocrats collectively.

‡no·blesse o·blige (nô′bles′ ô′blēzh′; Eng. nō-bles′ ō-blēzh′), [Fr., lit., nobility obliges], people of high birth or social position should behave nobly toward others: said sometimes of the rich in regard to charity.

no·ble·wom·an (nō′b'l-woom′ən), *n.* [*pl.* NOBLEWOMEN (-wim′in)], a woman member of the nobility; peeress.

no·bly (nō′bli), *adv.* 1. with noble courage or spirit; gallantly. 2. *a)* idealistically; loftily. *b)* excellently; splendidly. 3. of titled birth; of the peerage.

no·bod·y (nō′bəd-i, nō′bod′i), *pron.* not any person; not anybody; no one. *n.* [*pl.* NOBODIES (-iz)], a person of no influence, authority, or importance.

no·cent (nō′s'nt), *adj.* [Late ME. < L. *nocens,* ppr. of *nocere,* to harm], [Obs. or Rare], 1. causing harm or injury; hurtful. 2. guilty.

no·ci·as·so·ci·a·tion (nō′si-ə-sō′si-ā′shən, nō′si-ə-sō′-shi-ā′shən), *n.* [< L. *nocere,* to hurt; + *association*], a discharge of nervous energy as the result of trauma or pain, manifested as shock or profound exhaustion.

nock (nok), *n.* [ME. *nocke;* prob. < ON.; cf. Sw. dial. *nokke,* notch], 1. a notch for holding the string at either end of a bow. 2. a similar notch in the end of an arrow, for the insertion of the bowstring. *v.t.* 1. to make a notch in (a bow or arrow). 2. to set (an arrow) into the bowstring.

noc·tam·bu·la·tion (nok-tam′byoo-lā′shən), *n.* noctambulism.

noc·tam·bu·lism (nok-tam′byoo-liz'm), *n.* [< L. *nox, noctis,* night + *ambulare,* to walk; + *-ism*], walking in one's sleep; somnambulism.

noc·tam·bu·list (nok-tam′byoo-list), *n.* a person suffering from noctambulism; somnambulist; sleepwalker.

noc·ti- (nok′ti), [< L. *nox, noctis,* night], a combining form meaning *night:* also, before a vowel, **noct-.**

noc·ti·lu·ca (nok′ti-lōō′kə, nok′ti-lū′kə), *n.* [L., something that shines at night < *nox, noctis,* night + *lucere,* to shine < *lux,* a light], any of a group of very small phosphorescent marine organisms that occur in vast numbers in the sea, causing parts of it to appear luminous at night.

noc·tu·id (nok′choo-id), *n.* [< Mod. L. *Noctuidae,* name of the family < L. *noctua,* night owl < *nox, noctis,* night], any of a large group of moths which fly at night, including most of those flying into lighted houses, as the cutworm moth, dagger moth, etc.: their larvae are very destructive. *adj.* of this group.

noc·tule (nok′chōōl), *n.* [Fr., after It. *nottola,* a bat < L. *nox, noctis,* night], a variety of large brown bat of Europe and the British Isles.

noc·turn (nok′tẽrn), *n.* [ME. & OFr. *nocturne;* ML. *nocturna* < L. *nocturnus;* see NOCTURNAL], 1. in the *Orthodox Eastern & Roman Catholic churches,* any of the three divisions of the office of Matins; early morning service between midnight and daybreak. 2. in *music,* a nocturne.

noc·tur·nal (nok-tũr′n'l), *adj.* [LL. *nocturnalis* < L. *nocturnus* < *nox, noctis,* night; cf. NIGHT], 1. of the night. 2. functioning at night; active during the night. 3. having blossoms that open at night, as the moonflower. 4. done or happening in the night.

noc·turne (nok′tẽrn, nok-tũrn′), *n.* [Fr. < L. *nocturnus;* see NOCTURNAL], 1. in *art,* a painting of a night scene. 2. in *music,* a composition of a romantic or dreamy character thought appropriate to night.

noc·u·ous (nok′ū-əs), *adj.* [L. *nocuus* < *nocere,* to do hurt to], harmful; poisonous; noxious.

nod (nod), *v.i.* [NODDED (-id), NODDING], [ME. *nodden,* prob. in basic sense "to shake the head"; akin to G. *notten,* to move about, OHG. *hnotōn,* to shake (also AS. *hnossian,* to knock); IE. *qeneudh < base *qen-, to scratch, rub, etc. (cf. NAP, NIP)], 1. to bend the head forward slightly and raise it again quickly, as a sign of agreement, greeting, command, acknowledgment, or invitation. 2. to say "yes" by doing this. 3. to allow the head to fall forward involuntarily because of drowsiness; be very sleepy; hence, 4. to be inattentive; be careless; make a slip: as, even Homer *nods.* 5. to sway back and forth or up and down, as the tops of trees, flowers, plumes, etc. *v.t.* 1. to bend (the head) forward slightly and raise it again quickly. 2. to signify (assent, approval, agreement, etc.) by doing this. *n.* 1. a nodding, as of the head, treetops, etc. 2. a sign of affirmation, assent, etc.: as, he gave my plans the *nod.* 3. [N-], the imaginary realm of sleep and dreams: usually **land of Nod.**

nod·al (nō′d'l), *adj.* of or like a node or nodes.

nod·der (nod′ẽr), *n.* a person or thing that nods.

nod·ding acquaintance (nod′iŋ), 1. a slight, not intimate, acquaintance with a person or thing. 2. a person whom one knows slightly.

nod·dle (nod″l), *n.* [ME. *nodle;* prob. extension of earlier *nolle,* influenced by *nodden,* to nod], [Colloq.], the head; pate: a humorous term.

nod·dy (nod′i), *n.* [*pl.* NODDIES (-iz)], [? < *nod*], 1. a fool; simpleton. 2. any of several kinds of tame tropical sea birds, easily caught and so considered stupid.

node (nōd), *n.* [L. *nodus;* cf. KNOT], 1. a dilemma or complication, as of a story or play. 2. a knot; knob; swelling. 3. a point of concentration; central point. 4. in *anatomy,* a protuberance; knotty, localized swelling. 5. in *astronomy, a)* either point at which the orbit of a planet intersects the apparent path of the sun. *b)* either point at which the orbit of a satellite intersects the plane of the orbit of its planet. 6. in *botany,* that part of a stem from which a leaf starts to grow; joint of a stem. 7. in *geometry,* the point where a continuous curve crosses or meets itself. 8. in *physics,* the point, line, or surface of a vibrating object, as a string, where there is comparatively no vibration.

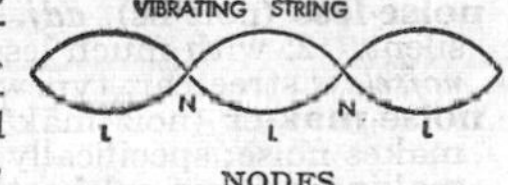

NODES

N, nodes formed when vibrating string is stopped at intervals along its length; L, loops between nodes

nod·i·cal (nod′i-k'l, nō′di-k'l), *adj.* in *astronomy,* of the nodes.

no·dose (nō′dōs, nō-dōs′), *adj.* [L. *nodosus*], having nodes; knotty: said of roots, etc.

no·dos·i·ty (nō-dos′ə-ti), *n.* [L. *nodositas*], 1. the state or quality of being full of nodes; knottiness or knobbiness. 2. [*pl.* NODOSITIES (-tiz)], a knot; knob.

no·dous (nō′dəs), *adj.* [< *node* + *-ous,* after L. *nodosus,* full of knots], full of knots; knotty.

nod·u·lar (noj′oo-lẽr, nod′yoo-lẽr), *adj.* of, having, or in the form of, a nodule or nodules.

nod·ule (noj′ōōl, nod′ūl), *n.* [L. *nodulus,* dim. of *nodus,* a knot], 1. a small knot or irregular, rounded lump. 2. in *anatomy,* a small node. 3. in *botany,* a small knot or joint on a stem or root.

nod·u·lose (noj′oo-lōs′, nod′yoo-lōs′), *adj.* having nodules.

nod·u·lous (noj′oo-ləs, nod′yoo-ləs), *adj.* nodulose.

no·dus (nō′dəs), *n.* [ME.; L., a knot], complication; difficulty; knotty situation, as in a play or story.

No·el (nō′əl), [OFr. *Nouel, Noel,* lit., natal; see NATALIE], a masculine or feminine name.

no·el, no·ël (nō-el′, nō′el), *n.* [< Fr. *noël,* replacing ME. *nowel;* OFr. *nowel, nouel* < L. *natalis,* pertaining to birth, a birthday < *natus,* born], 1. an expression of joy used in Christmas carols. 2. a Christmas carol. 3. [N-], Christmas.

no·e·sis (nō-ē′sis), *n.* [Gr. *noēsis* < *noein,* to perceive < *nous,* the mind], 1. comprehension by operation of the intellect alone. 2. cognition.

no·et·ic (nō-et′ik), *adj.* [Gr. *noētikos* < *noēsis;* see NOESIS], 1. of, or existing or originating in, the intellect. 2. interested in intellectual activity. *n.* an intellectual person.

nog (nog), *n.* [prob. Early Mod. Eng. form of ME. *knagge* in the same sense; ? < base of *knock*], 1. a wooden pin or block set in a wall, for nails, etc. 2. a log of wood supporting a mine roof. *v.t.* [NOGGED (nogd), NOGGING], 1. to build brickwork within a frame of wood. 2. to hold or fasten with wooden pegs, or nogs.

nog, nogg (nog), *n.* [< East Anglian dial.], 1. [British], a kind of strong ale. 2. eggnog.

no·ga·ku (nōn′gä′koo), *n.* no (Japanese drama).

nog·gin (nog′in), *n.* [prob. < *nog* (ale)], 1. a small cup or mug. 2. one fourth of a pint: a measure for ale or liquor. 3. [Colloq.], the head.

nog·ging (nog′iŋ), *n.* [< *nog, v.*], [British], brick masonry used to fill up the spaces of a wooden frame.

No·gu·chi, Hi·de·yo (hi′de-yō′ nō-gōō′chi), 1876–1928; Japanese bacteriologist in America.

noh (nō), *n.* no (Japanese drama).

no·how (nō′hou′), *adv.* in no manner; not at all: generally regarded as substandard.

noil (noil), *n.* [< SW. Yorkshire dial.; ? < Walloon Fr.], 1. a short piece or knot of wool combed from the long staple. 2. shreds of wool, hair, or silk.

noise (noiz), *n.* [ME.; OFr.; prob. < L. *nausea* (see NAUSEA)], 1. *a*) loud shouting; clamor; din. *b*) any loud, discordant, or disagreeable sound or sounds. 2. *a*) sound: as, the *noise* of the rain. *b*) an unexpected or unusual sound: as, do you hear that *noise?* 3. [Obs.], bad report; rumor; scandal. 4. in *radio, acoustics,* etc., any sound that interferes with the sound impulse being communicated. *v.t.* [NOISED (noizd), NOISING], to spread about (a report, rumor, etc.). *v.i.* 1. to talk much or loudly. 2. to make noise or a noise.
***SYN.*—noise** is the general word for any loud, unmusical, or disagreeable sound; **din** refers to a loud, prolonged, deafening sound, painful to the ears (the *din* of the steeple bells); **uproar** applies to a loud, confused sound, as of shouting, laughing, etc., and connotes commotion or disturbance (his remarks threw the audience into an *uproar*); **clamor** suggests loud, continued, excited shouting, as in protest or demand (the *clamor* of an aroused people); **hubbub** implies the confused mingling of many voices (the *hubbub* of a subway station); **racket** refers to a loud, clattering combination of noises regarded as annoyingly excessive (he couldn't work for the *racket* next door). See also **sound.**—*ANT.* quiet.

noise·less (noiz′lis), *adj.* 1. without noise; very quiet; silent. 2. with much less noise than is expected: as, a *noiseless* streetcar, typewriter, etc. —*SYN.* see **still.**

noise·mak·er (noiz′māk′ẽr), *n.* a person or thing that makes noise; specifically, a horn, cowbell, etc. used for making noise in celebration, as on New Year's Eve.

nois·i·ly (noiz′ə-li), *adv.* in a noisy manner.

nois·i·ness (noiz′i-nis), *n.* the quality of being noisy.

noi·some (noi′səm), *adj.* [ME. *noyesum;* see ANNOY & -SOME], 1. injurious to health; noxious; harmful. 2. foul-smelling; offensive. —*SYN.* see **stinking.**

nois·y (noiz′i), *adj.* [NOISIER (-i-ẽr), NOISIEST (-i-ist)], 1. making, or accompanied by, noise. 2. making more sound than is expected or customary. 3. full of noise; clamorous; turbulent: as, the *noisy* city.

‡**no·lens vo·lens** (nō′lenz vō′lenz), [L.], unwilling (or) willing; whether or not one wishes to; willy-nilly.

‡**no·li me tan·ge·re** (nō′lī mē tan′jə-ri), [L., lit., touch me not], 1. a warning against meddling. 2. a painting showing Jesus appearing to Mary Magdalene after his resurrection: from the Latin form of his caution to her: John 20:17. 3. any of several plants whose ripe seed cases burst when touched. 4. any of several skin diseases characterized by ulcers.

‡**nol·le pros·e·qui** (nol′i pros′i-kwī′), [L., to be unwilling to prosecute], in *law,* 1. formal notice by the prosecutor that prosecution in a criminal case will be partly or entirely ended. 2. similar formal notice by the plaintiff in a civil suit. Abbreviated **nol. pros.**

‡**no·lo con·ten·de·re** (nō′lō kən-ten′də-ri), [L., I do not wish to contest (it)], in *law,* a plea by the defendant in a criminal case declaring that he will not make a defense, but not admitting guilt: also **nolo.**

nol-pros (nol′pros′), *v.t.* [NOL-PROSSED (-prost′), NOL-PROSSING], [< abbrev. of *nolle prosequi*], to abandon (all or part of a suit) by entering a *nolle prosequi* on the court records.

nom., nominative.

no·ma (nō′mə), *n.* [Mod. L. < Gr. *nomē,* lit., a feeding], a severe ulcerous condition of the mouth, occurring especially in young children, as after debilitating disease, and usually resulting in gangrene.

no·mad (nō′mad, nom′ad), *n.* [L. *nomas;* Gr. *nomas, nomados,* living on pasturage < *nemein,* to distribute, feed, pasture], 1. a member of a tribe, nation, or race having no permanent home, but moving about constantly in search of food, pasture, etc. 2. any person who changes his residence frequently; wanderer. *adj.* nomadic; wandering.

no·mad·ic (nō-mad′ik), *adj.* of, characteristic of, or like nomads or their way of life. —*SYN.* see **itinerant.**

no·mad·i·cal·ly (nō-mad′i-k′l-i, nō-mad′ik-li), *adv.* in a nomadic manner.

no·mad·ism (nō′mad-iz′m, nom′ad-iz′m), *n.* the state of being nomadic.

no man's land, 1. a piece of land, usually wasteland, to which no one has a recognized title. 2. the area on a battlefield separating the combatants.

nom·arch (nom′ärk), *n.* [Gr. *nomarchēs* < *nomos,* province + *archein,* to rule], the governor of a nome or nomarchy.

nom·arch·y (nom′är-ki), *n.* [*pl.* NOMARCHIES (-kiz)], [Gr. *nomarchia*], a province of modern Greece; nome.

nom·bles (num′b'lz), *n.pl.* [Archaic], numbles.

nom·bril (nom′bril), *n.* [Fr., the navel, for OFr. *lombril* < LL. **umbiliculus,* dim. < L. *umbilicus,* navel], the point on an escutcheon just below the true center and above the center of the base; navel point.

‡**nom de guerre** (nōn′ də gâr′), [Fr., lit., a war name], a pseudonym.

nom de plume (nom′ də plōōm′; Fr. nōn′ də plüm′), [Eng. expression formed < Fr.], a pen name; pseudonym. —*SYN.* see **pseudonym.**

Nome (nōm), *n.* a mining town near Cape Nome, Alaska: pop., 2,300.

nome (nōm), *n.* [Gr. *nomos* < *nemein,* to divide], 1. a province of ancient Egypt. 2. a nomarchy.

Nome, Cape, a cape on Seward Peninsula, western Alaska.

no·men·cla·tor (nō′mən-klā′tẽr), *n.* [L. < *nomen* (see NOMINAL) + *calator,* caller, crier < pp. of *calare,* to call], 1. in ancient Rome, a person who announced the names of guests or assigned them places at dinner. 2. an announcer of names, as at a reception. 3. a person who invents names for, or assigns them to, things, as in scientific classification.

no·men·cla·ture (nō′mən-klā′chẽr), *n.* [L. *nomenclatura;* see NOMENCLATOR], the system of names used in a branch of learning or activity, for the parts of a mechanism or device, or by some person or group.

nom·i·nal (nom′ə-n'l), *adj.* [ME. *nominalle;* L. *nominalis,* of a name < *nomen,* name; for IE. base see NAME], 1. of, consisting of, having the nature of, or giving a name or names. 2. of or having to do with a noun or nouns. 3. in name only, not in fact: as, the *nominal* leader. 4. very small compared to expectations; slight: as, a *nominal* fee. *n.* in *linguistics,* a nounlike word: nouns, adjectives, and pronouns are called *nominals:* distinguished from *verbal.*

nom·i·nal·ism (nom′ə-n'l-iz′m), *n.* [Fr. *nominalisme;* see NOMINAL & -ISM], a doctrine of the late Middle Ages that all universal or abstract terms are mere necessities of thought or conveniences of language and therefore exist as names only and have no realities corresponding to them: opposed to (medieval) *realism.*

nom·i·nal·ist (nom′ə-n'l-ist), *n.* a person who believes in nominalism. *adj.* nominalistic.

nom·i·nal·is·tic (nom′ə-n'l-is′tik), *adj.* of nominalism or the nominalists.

nom·i·nal·ly (nom′ə-n'l-i), *adv.* 1. in a nominal way; in name. 2. by name.

nominal value, stated or par value, as for a stock certificate: distinguished from *actual* or *market value.*

nominal wages, wages stated in terms of money paid, not in terms of purchasing power: distinguished from *real wages.*

nom·i·nate (nom′ə-nāt′), *v.t.* [NOMINATED (-id), NOMINATING], [< L. *nominatus,* pp. of *nominare,* to name < *nomen;* see NOMINAL], 1. originally, to name, call, or designate. 2. to name or appoint (a person) to an office or position. 3. to name (a person) as a candidate for election or appointment; propose for office.

nom·i·na·tion (nom′ə-nā′shən), *n.* [ME., a naming or calling by name; L. *nominatio* < pp. of *nominare;* see NOMINATE], 1. the naming or appointing of a person to an office. 2. the naming of a person as a candidate for election or appointment to an office. 3. the state of being chosen or named for office, or as a candidate.

nom·i·na·tive (nom′i-nə-tiv; *for adj. 1 & 2, usually* nom′ə-nā′tiv), *adj.* [ME. *nomenatyf;* Late OFr. *nominatif;* L. *nominativus,* belonging to a name < pp. of *nominare;* see NOMINATE], 1. named or appointed to a position or office: distinguished from *elected.* 2. having the name of a person on it: as, a *nominative* will. 3. in *grammar,* designating or of the case of the subject of a finite verb and the words (appositives, predicate nouns or adjectives, and nouns of direct address) that agree with it; active or actor case. *n.* [L. *nominativus* (*casus*)], 1. the nominative case. 2. a word in this case. Abbreviated **nom., nomin., N., n.**

nom·i·na·tor (nom′ə-nā′tẽr), *n.* one who nominates.

nom·i·nee (nom′ə-nē′), *n.* [< *nominate* + *-ee*], a person who is nominated, especially a candidate for election.

no·mism (nō′miz′m), *n.* [< Gr. *nomos*, law; + *-ism*], legalism in religion; basing of conduct upon adherence to a law or holy scripture.

no·mis·tic (nō-mis′tik), *adj.* of or based on nomism.

no·mog·ra·phy (nō-mog′rə-fi), *n.* [Gr. *nomographia* < *nomos*, law + *graphein*, to write], 1. the art of drafting laws. 2. a treatise on law or on the drafting of laws.

no·mol·o·gy (nō-mol′ə-ji), *n.* [< Gr. *nomos*, law; + *-logy*], 1. the science of law and lawmaking. 2. the branch of a science, as of psychology, that investigates and formulates the principles governing its phenomena.

nom·o·thet·ic (nom′ə-thet′ik), *adj.* [Gr. *nomothetikos* < *nomothetēs*, lawgiver < *nomos*, law + *tithenai*, to make, assign], 1. giving or enacting laws. 2. based on law. 3. of a science of general or universal laws.

nom·o·thet·i·cal (nom′ə-thet′i-k′l), *adj.* nomothetic.

No·mu·ra, Ki·chi·sa·bu·ro (kē′chē-sä′boo-rô′ nô′moo-rä′), 1877– ; Japanese admiral; ambassador to the United States (1940–1941).

-nomy, [Gr. *-nomia* < *nomos*, law], a combining form meaning *the systematized knowledge of*, as in *astronomy*.

non- (non), [< L. *non*, not], a prefix meaning *not*, used to give a negative force, especially to nouns, adjectives, and adverbs, as in *nonresident: non-* is less emphatic than *in-* and *un-*, which often give a word an opposite meaning (e.g., *non-American, un-American*); a hyphen may be used after *non-* and is generally used when the base word begins with a capital letter. The list below includes the more common compounds formed with *non-* that do not have special meanings; they will be understood if *not* is used before the meaning of the base word.

non·age (non′ij, nō′nij), *n.* [ME. & Anglo-Fr. *nounage;* OFr. *nonage;* see NON- & AGE], 1. in *law*, the state of being under the lawful age for doing certain things, as making contracts, marrying, etc.; usually, the state of being under twenty-one. 2. the period of immaturity; early stage.

non·a·ge·nar·i·an (non′ə-ji-nâr′i-ən, nō′nə-ji-nâr′i-ən), *adj.* [L. *nonagenarius* < *nonageni*, ninety each < *nonaginta*, ninety], ninety years old, or between the ages of ninety and one hundred. *n.* a person of this age.

non·ag·gres·sion pact (non′ə-gresh′ən), an agreement between two nations in which each guarantees not to aggress against the other, usually for a specified period of years.

non·a·gon (non′ə-gon′), *n.* [< L. *nonus*, ninth + Gr. *gōnia*, an angle], a plane figure having nine angles and nine sides.

nonce (nons), *n.* [ME. (*for the*) *nones*, formed by syllabic merging < (*for then*) *ones*, lit., the once, in which *then* (earlier *than*, etc.) is the dat. sing. of the def. art.; cf. NICKNAME], the present use, occasion, or time; time being: chiefly in *for the nonce*.

nonce word, a word coined and used for a single occasion.

non·cha·lance (non′shə-ləns, non′shə-läns′), *n.* [Fr.], the state or quality of being nonchalant. —*SYN.* see **equanimity.**

non·cha·lant (non′shə-lənt, non′shə-länt′), *adj.* [Fr. < *non* (L. *non*), not + *chaloir*, to care for < L. *calere*, to be warm or ardent], 1. without warmth or enthusiasm; not showing interest. 2. showing cool lack of concern; casually indifferent. —*SYN.* see **cool.**

non·com (non′kom′), *n.* [Colloq.], a noncommissioned officer.

non·com·bat·ant (non-kom′bə-tənt, non-kum′bə-tənt), *n.* 1. a civilian in wartime. 2. a member of the armed forces whose activities do not include actual combat, as a chaplain. *adj.* 1. not involving combat. 2. of noncombatants.

non·com·mis·sioned officer (non′kə-mish′ənd), an enlisted person in the armed forces appointed by a proper authority to any of the ranks above private first class and below warrant officer: abbreviated **N.C.O.:** distinguished from *commissioned officer*.

non·com·mit·tal (non′kə-mit′′l), *adj.* not committing one to any point of view or course of action; not revealing one's position or purpose.

non·com·pli·ance (non′kəm-plī′əns), *n.* failure to comply; refusal to yield, agree, etc.; obstinance.

‡non com·pos men·tis (non kom′pəs men′tis), [L.], in *law*, not of sound mind; mentally incapable of handling one's own affairs: often **non compos.**

non·con·duc·tor (non′kən-duk′tẽr), *n.* a substance that does not readily transmit certain forms of energy, as sound, heat, and, especially, electricity.

non·con·form·ist (non′kən-fôr′mist), *n.* a person who does not act in harmony with the practices and doctrines of an established church; especially, [N-], a Protestant in England who is not a member of the Anglican Church; Dissenter.

non·con·form·i·ty (non′kən-fôr′mə-ti), *n.* 1. failure or refusal to act in conformity with generally accepted beliefs and practices; especially, [N-], refusal to accept the doctrines or follow the practices of the Anglican Church. 2. the doctrines and rites of Nonconformists.

nonabsorbent
nonabstainer
nonaccent
nonacceptance
nonacid
nonactinic
nonactive
nonadhesive
nonadjacent
nonadjectival
nonadministrative
nonadmission
nonadvantageous
nonadverbial
nonaesthetic
non-African
nonaggression
nonaggressive
nonagreement
nonagricultural
nonalcoholic
nonalgebraic
nonallegorical
nonalliterative
nonalphabetic
nonamendable
non-American
non-Anglican
nonantagonistic
nonapologetic
nonapostolic
nonappearance
nonappearing
nonapprehension
nonaquatic
non-Arab
non-Arabic
nonaristocratic
nonarithmetical
non-Aryan
non-Asiatic
nonassertive
nonassessable
nonassignable
nonassimilable
nonassimilation
nonassociable
nonathletic
nonatmospheric
nonattendance
nonattributive
nonauricular
nonauthoritative
nonautomatic
nonautomotive
nonbacterial
nonbasic
nonbeliever
nonbelieving
nonbelligerent
nonbenevolent
non-Biblical
nonblooming
non-Bolshevist
nonbreakable
non-British
non-Buddhist
nonbudding
nonbureaucratic
nonburnable
nonbusiness
noncaking
noncalcareous
non-Calvinist
noncanonical
noncapitalistic
noncapsizable
noncarnivorous
noncategorical
non-Catholic
non-Caucasian
noncelestial
noncellular
non-Celtic
noncensored
noncentral
noncereal
noncertified
nonchargeable
nonchemical
non-Chinese
non-Christian
nonchurch
nonciliate
noncivilized
nonclassifiable
nonclerical
nonclinical
noncoagulating
noncoalescing
noncoercive
noncognitive
noncoherent
noncohesive
noncollaborative
noncollapsible
noncollectable
noncollegiate
noncolloid
noncombat
noncombining
noncombustible
noncommercial
noncommissioned
noncommunicant
noncommunicating
non-Communist
noncompensating
noncompetency
noncompeting
noncompetitive
noncomplaisant
noncompletion
noncomplying
noncompressible
noncompression
noncompulsion
nonconcealment
nonconcentration
nonconciliating
nonconcordant
nonconcurrence
noncondensing
nonconducive
nonconducting
nonconferrable
nonconfidential
nonconfiscable
nonconflicting
nonconforming
noncongealing
noncongenital
noncongestion
non-Congressional
nonconnective
nonconnivance
nonconsecutive
nonconsent
nonconservative
nonconspiring
nonconstitutional
nonconstructive
nonconsultative
noncontagious
noncontemplative
noncontemporary
noncontentious
noncontiguous
noncontinental
noncontinuance
noncontinuous
noncontraband
noncontradiction
noncontradictory
noncontributory
noncontrolled
noncontroversial
nonconventional
nonconvergent
nonconversant
nonconvertible
nonconviction

non·co·op·er·a·tion (non'kō-op'ə-rā'shən), ***n.*** 1. failure to work together or act jointly; refusal to work in unison with a person, group, or organization. 2. refusal to perform civic duties, pay taxes, etc.: often used to protest against a government, as by Gandhi formerly against the British government in India.

non·de·script (non'di-script'), ***adj.*** [< L. *non*, not + *descriptus*, described], so lacking in recognizable character or qualities as to belong to no definite class or type; hard to classify or describe. ***n.*** a nondescript person or thing.

non·dis·junc·tion (non'dis-juŋk'shən), ***n.*** in *biology*, the failure of paired chromosomes to pass to separate cells in mitosis.

none (nun), ***pron.*** [ME. *none, non;* AS. *nan* < *ne*, not + *an*, one; see NO & ONE], 1. no one; not anyone: as, *none* but Jack can do it. 2. no persons or things; not any: usually used with a plural verb, as, there are *none* on the table. ***n.*** not any (of); no part; nothing: as, I want *none* of it. ***adv.*** in no way; not at all: as, he is *none* the stronger for it. ***adj.*** [Obs.], not any: used before a vowel, as, of *none* effect.

none the less, nevertheless; notwithstanding.

non·e·go (non-ē'gō, non-eg'ō), ***n.*** [*pl.* NONEGOS (-gōz, -ōz)], 1. anything or everything that is not the self; hence, 2. the external world.

non·en·ti·ty (non-en'tə-ti), ***n.*** [*pl.* NONENTITIES (-tiz)], 1. the state of not existing. 2. something without existence. 3. a person considered of little importance; person having little influence or individuality.

nones (nōnz), ***n.pl.*** [ME. < L. *nonae* < *nonus*, ninth < *novem*, nine; cf. NINE], 1. in the ancient Roman calendar, the ninth day before the ides of a month; the seventh of March, May, July, and October, and the fifth of the other months. 2. [< *none, sing.;* AS. *non;* see NOON], in the early Christian Church, the fifth of the seven canonical hours, coming at the ninth hour of the day, or about 3:00 P.M. 3. the service of this hour, now usually recited somewhat earlier than 3:00 P.M.

non·es·sen·tial (non'i-sen'shəl), ***adj.*** not essential; of relatively no importance; unnecessary. ***n.*** a nonessential person or thing.

none·such (nun'such'), ***n.*** 1. a person or thing unrivaled or unequaled; something or someone unique; paragon. 2. a variety of apple. Also spelled **nonsuch.**

non·ex·ist·ence (non'ig-zis'təns), ***n.*** 1. the condition of not existing. 2. something that does not exist.

non·fea·sance (non-fē'z'ns), ***n.*** in *law*, failure to do what duty requires to be done: distinguished from *malfeasance, misfeasance.*

no·nil·lion (nō-nil'yən), ***n.*** [Fr. < L. *nonus*, ninth + Fr. *million*], 1. in the United States and France, the number represented by 1 followed by 30 zeros. 2. in Great Britain and Germany, the number represented by 1 followed by 54 zeros. ***adj.*** amounting to one nonillion in number.

non·in·duc·tive (non'in-duk'tiv), ***adj.*** in *electricity*, not inductive: as, a *noninductive* resistance.

non·in·ter·ven·tion (non'in-tẽr-ven'shən), ***n.*** refusal or failure to intervene; a refraining from interference; especially, a refraining by one nation from interference in the affairs of another.

non·join·der (non-join'dẽr), ***n.*** in *law*, the failure of

non-co-operative
non-co-ordinating
noncorrective
noncorresponding
noncorroborative
noncorroding
noncorrosive
noncosmic
noncreative
noncredible
noncreditor
noncriminal
noncritical
noncrucial
noncrystalline
nonculpable
noncultivation
noncumulative
non-Czech
nondamageable
non-Darwinian
nondecaying
nondeceptive
nondeciduous
nondefamatory
nondefensive
nondeferential
nondefilement
nondefining
nondegeneration
nondehiscent
nondelineation
nondelirious
nondelivery
nondemand
nondemocratic
nondepartmental
nondeparture
nondependence
nondepletion
nondepositor
nondepreciating
nonderivative
nonderogatory
nondespotic
nondestructive
nondetachable
nondetonating
nondevelopment
nondevotional
nondialectal
nondictatorial
nondidactic
nondifferentiation
nondiffractive
nondiffusing
nondilatable
nondiplomatic
nondirectional
nondirigible
nondisappearing
nondischarging
nondisciplinary
nondiscountable
nondiscrimination
nondisfranchised
nondisparaging
nondispersion
nondisposal
nondistinctive
nondistributive
nondivergent
nondivisible
nondoctrinal
nondocumentary
nondogmatic
nondomesticated
nondramatic
nondrying
nondutiable
nondynastic
nonearning
nonecclesiastical
noneclectic
noneconomic
nonedible
noneditorial
noneducable
noneducational
noneffective
noneffervescent
nonefficacious
nonefficient
nonelastic
nonelective
nonelectric
nonelementary
nonemotional
nonemphatic
nonempirical
nonencyclopedic
nonendemic
non-English
nonentailed
nonephemeral
nonepiscopal
nonequal
nonequivalent
nonequivocating
nonerotic
noneternal
nonethical
nonethnological
non-Euclidean
noneugenic
non-European
nonevangelical
nonevasion
noneviction
nonevolutionary
nonexchangeable
nonexclusive
nonexcusable
nonexecution
nonexecutive
nonexempt
nonexistent
nonexisting
nonexotic
nonexpansive
nonexperienced
nonexperimental
nonexploitation
nonexplosive
nonexportable
nonextended
nonextension
nonexternal
nonextraditable
nonextraneous
nonfactual
nonfading
nonfanatical
nonfanciful
non-Fascist
nonfastidious
nonfatal
nonfatalistic
nonfederal
nonfederated
nonfermentable
nonfermented
nonfertile
nonfestive
nonfeudal
nonfiction
nonfictional
nonfiduciary
nonfigurative
nonfinancial
nonfireproof
nonfiscal
nonflowering
nonflowing
nonfluctuating
nonflying
nonfocal
nonforfeiting
nonforfeiture
nonformal
nonfortuitous
nonfraudulent
nonfreezing
non-French
nonfricative
nonfulfillment
nonfunctional
nonfundamental
nongaseous
nongelatinous
nongenerative
nongenetic
non-Gentile
non-German
non-Germanic
nongovernmental
nongranular
non-Greek
nongregarious)
nonhabitable
nonhabitual
nonharmonious
nonhazardous
nonheathen
nonhedonistic
non-Hellenic
nonhereditary
nonheritable
non-Hibernian
nonhistoric
nonhomogeneous
nonhostile
nonhuman
nonhumorous
nonidentical
nonidentity
nonidiomatic
nonidolatrous
nonignitible
nonimaginary
nonimitative
nonimmune
nonimmunized
nonimperative
nonimperial
nonimportation
nonimpregnated
nonincandescent
noninclusive
nonindependent
non-Indian
nonindictable
nonindividualistic
non-Indo-European
nonindustrial
noninfallible
noninfected
noninfectious
noninfinite
noninflammable
noninflammatory
noninflectional
noninformative
noninheritable
noninjurious
noninstructional
noninstrumental
nonintellectual
nonintelligent
noninterchangeable
nonintercourse
noninterference
nonintermittent
noninternational
noninterrupted
nonintersecting
nonintoxicant
nonintoxicating
nonintuitive
noninverted
noniodized
nonionized
non-Irish
nonirradiated
nonirrigated
nonirritant
nonirritating
non-Islamic
non-Israelite
non-Italian
non-Japanese
non-Jew
non-Jewish
nonjudicial

a plaintiff to include in his suit some person or cause of action that should have been included.

non·ju·ror (non-joor′ēr), *n.* a person who refuses to take an oath of allegiance to his ruler or government; specifically, [N-], any of the clergymen of the Church of England who refused to take such an oath at the accession of William and Mary in 1689.

non·met·al (non-met′'l, non′met′'l), *n.* any of those elements lacking the characteristics of a metal; specifically, any of the electronegative elements (e.g., oxygen, carbon, nitrogen, fluorine) whose oxides are not basic.

non·mor·al (non-môr′əl, non-mor′əl), *adj.* not connected in any way with morality or ethical concepts; not moral and not immoral; amoral.

non·ni·trog·e·nous (non′nī-troj′i-nəs), *adj.* having no nitrogen.

non·ob·jec·tive (non′ob-jek′tiv), *adj.* nonrepresentational.

‡non ob·stan·te (non ob-stan′ti), [L. < *non*, not + *obstans*, *obstantis*, ppr. of *obstare;* see OBSTACLE: from use in medieval legal clauses permitting (to the king) certain actions notwithstanding statutes to the contrary], notwithstanding; despite (a law, decision, etc.).

non·pa·reil (non′pə-rel′), *adj.* [Fr.; *non*, not + *pareil*, equal < LL. *pariculus*, dim. of *par*, equal], unequaled; unrivaled; peerless. *n.* 1. someone or something unequaled or unrivaled. 2. the painted bunting. 3. [Fr. *nonpareille*], in *printing*, a size of type between agate and minion; 6 point. This line is in nonpareil.

non·par·ous (non-par′əs), *adj.* [*non-* + *-parous*], having borne no children.

non·par·tic·i·pat·ing (non′pēr-tis′ə-pāt′iŋ, non′pär-tis′ə-pāt′iŋ), *adj.* not participating; especially, in *insurance*, not giving the right to participate in the dividends from the profits or surplus of the company.

non·par·ti·san, non·par·ti·zan (non-pär′tə-z'n), *adj.* not partisan; especially, not controlled or influenced by, or supporting, any single political party.

non·plus (non-plus′, non′plus), *n.* [L. *non*, not + *plus*, more, further], a condition of perplexity in which one is unable to go, speak, or act further. *v.t.* [NONPLUSED or NONPLUSSED (-plust′, -plust), NONPLUSING or NONPLUSSING], to cause to be in a nonplus. —*SYN.* see **puzzle.**

‡non pos·su·mus (non pos′ū-məs), [L.], we cannot: used to signify the impossibility of doing something specified.

non·pro·duc·tive (non′prə-duk′tiv), *adj.* not productive; specifically, *a)* not resulting in the production of the goods sought or the realization of the effects expected: as, a *nonproductive* plan. *b)* not directly related to the production of goods; as, clerks, salesmen, etc. are *nonproductive* personnel.

non·prof·it (non-prof′it), *adj.* not intending or intended to earn a profit: as, a *nonprofit* organization.

non-pros (non′pros′), *v.t.* [NON-PROSSED (-prost′), NON-PROSSING], to enter a judgment of *non prosequitur* against (a plaintiff or his suit).

‡non pro·se·qui·tur (non prō-sek′wi-tēr), [L., he does not prosecute], in *law*, a judgment entered against a plaintiff who fails to appear at the court proceedings of his suit: abbreviated **non pros.**

non·rep·re·sen·ta·tion·al (non′rep-ri-zen-tā′shən-'l), *adj.* not representational; specifically, designating or of art that does not attempt to represent in recognizable form any object in nature; abstract; nonobjective.

non·res·i·dence (non-rez′ə-dəns), *n.* the fact or condition of being nonresident.

non·res·i·dent (non-rez′ə-dənt), *adj.* not residing in a specified place; especially, having one's home in some locality other than where one works, attends school, etc. *n.* 1. a person whose permanent home is not where he is staying. 2. a person who lives away from the locality of his business, school, etc.

non·re·sist·ance (non′ri-zis′təns), *n.* the fact of not resisting; especially, the policy or practice of submitting to force or arbitrary authority without opposition or retaliation.

non·re·sist·ant (non′ri-zis′tənt), *adj.* not resistant; submitting to force or arbitrary authority. *n.* 1. a person who believes that force and violence should not be used to oppose arbitrary authority, however unjust. 2. a person who refuses to use force even to defend himself.

non·re·straint (non′ri-strānt′), *n.* the absence of restraint; especially, in *psychiatry*, the management of psychotic persons without the use of a strait jacket or other physical restraint.

non·re·stric·tive (non′ri-strik′tiv), *adj.* in *grammar*, designating a clause, phrase, or word felt as not essential to the sense, or purely descriptive, and hence

non-Latin
nonlegal
nonlicensed
nonlimiting
nonliquefying
nonliquidating
nonliterary
nonliturgical
nonlocal
nonluminous
nonlustrous
non-Lutheran
nonmagnetic
non-Magyar
nonmaintenance
non-Malay
nonmalignant
nonmalleable
nonmarital
nonmaritime
nonmarriageable
nonmarrying
nonmartial
nonmaterial
nonmaterialistic
nonmaternal
nonmathematical
nonmatrimonial
nonmechanical
nonmechanistic
nonmedicinal
nonmelodious
nonmember
nonmercantile
nonmetallic
nonmetaphysical
nonmetropolitan
nonmigratory
nonmilitant
nonmilitary
nonmimetic
nonmineral
nonministerial
nonmiraculous
nonmischievous
nonmobile
non-Mohammedan
non-Mongolian
non-Mormon
nonmortal
non-Moslem
nonmotile
nonmunicipal
nonmuscular
nonmystical
nonmythical
nonnational
nonnative
nonnatural
nonnautical
nonnaval
nonnavigable
nonnecessity
nonnegotiable
non-Negro
nonneutral
non-Norse
nonnitrogenous
nonnucleated
nonnutritious
nonnutritive
nonobedience
nonobligatory
nonobservance
nonobservant
nonobstructive
nonoccupational
nonoccurrence
nonodorous
nonofficial
nonoperative
nonoptional
nonoriental
non-Oriental
nonorthodox
nonoxidizing
nonoxygenated
nonpacific
nonpagan
nonpalatal
nonpalatalization
nonpapal
nonpapist
nonparallel
nonparasitic
nonparental
nonparishioner
nonparliamentary
nonparochial
nonparticipation
nonpartisanship
nonpaying
nonpayment
nonpensionable
nonperceptual
nonperforated
nonperformance
nonperforming
nonperiodical
nonperishing
nonpermanent
nonpermeable
nonpermissible
nonperpendicular
nonpersecution
nonpersistent
nonphilosophical
nonphysical
nonphysiological
nonplastic
nonplausible
nonpoetic
nonpoisonous
nonpolarizable
non-Polish
nonpolitical
nonporous
non-Portuguese
nonpredatory
nonpredictable
nonpreferential
nonprejudicial
nonprepositional
non-Presbyterian
nonprescriptive
nonpreservative
nonpresidential
nonprevalent
nonpriestly
nonproducer
nonprofessional
nonprofessorial
nonproficient
nonprofiteering
nonprogressive
nonprohibitive
nonprolific
nonprophetic
nonproportional
nonproprietary
nonproscriptive
nonprotective
non-Protestant
non-Prussian
nonpsychic
nonpuncturable
nonpunishable
nonpurulent
nonracial
nonradiating
nonradical
nonratable
nonrational
nonreactive
nonreality
nonreceiving
nonreciprocal
nonreciprocating
nonrecognition
nonrecoverable
nonrecurring
nonrefillable
nonrefueling
nonregenerating
nonregimented
nonregistered
nonregistrable
nonreigning
nonrelative
nonreligious
nonremission
nonremunerative
nonrenewable
nonrepayable
nonrepentance
nonreprehensible
nonrepresentative
nonreproductive
nonresidential
nonresidual
nonresonant
nonrestricted

usually set off by commas (e.g., John, *who is six feet tall*, is younger than Bill): opposed to *restrictive*.

non·sec·tar·i·an (non'sek-târ'i-ən), *adj.* not sectarian; not confined to or affiliated with any specific religion.

non·sense (non'sens, non'səns), *n.* [*non-* + *sense*], 1. words or actions that convey an absurd meaning or no meaning at all. 2. things of relatively no importance or value; trivialities. 3. impudent, foolish, or evasive behavior. **interj.** how foolish! how absurd!: an exclamation of impatience, contradiction, contempt, etc.

non·sen·si·cal (non-sen'si-k'l), *adj.* unintelligible, foolish, silly, absurd, etc.

‡**non se·qui·tur** (non sek'wi-tẽr), [L., lit., it does not follow], in *logic*, a conclusion or inference which does not follow from the premises or evidence upon which it is based: abbreviated **non seq.**

non·skid (non'skid'), *adj.* having the tread so constructed as to reduce skidding: said of a tire, etc.

non·stop (non'stop'), *adj.* & *adv.* without a stop.

non·stri·at·ed (non'strī'ā-tid), *adj.* not striated; without stripes, as certain muscle tissues.

non·such (nun'such'), *n.* nonesuch.

non·suit (non'sōōt', non'sūt'), *n.* [ME. *noun suyt;* Anglo-Fr. *nonsute;* see NON- & SUIT], in *law*, 1. originally, the ending of a lawsuit by the voluntary withdrawal of the plaintiff. 2. a judgment against a plaintiff because of his failure to establish that he has a valid case or to produce adequate evidence. *v.t.* to bring a nonsuit against (a plaintiff or his case).

non·sup·port (non'sə-pôrt', non'sə-pōrt'), *n.* failure to provide for a legal dependent.

‡**non trop·po** (nôn trôp'pô), [It.], in *music*, not too much; moderately: a direction to the performer, as in *allegro non troppo*, fast, but not too fast.

non·un·ion (non-ūn'yən), *n.* failure to mend or unite: said of a broken bone. *adj.* 1. not belonging to a labor union. 2. not made or serviced by union workers or under conditions required by a labor union. 3. refusing to recognize, or sign a contract with, a labor union.

non·un·ion·ism (non-ūn'yən-iz'm), *n.* theories and practices of those who oppose or refuse to accept labor unions.

non·un·ion·ist (non-ūn'yən-ist), *n.* 1. a believer in nonunionism. 2. a person who is not a member of a labor union.

non·vot·er (non-vōt'ẽr), *n.* a person who does not vote or is not permitted to vote.

noo·dle (nōō'd'l), *n.* [? < *noddy, noddle*, etc. (with *oo* < *fool*)], 1. a simpleton; fool. 2. [Slang], the head.

noo·dle (nōō'd'l), *n.* [G. *nudel*, macaroni], a flat, narrow strip of dry dough, usually containing egg and served in soup, etc.

nook (nook), *n.* [ME. (chiefly Northern) *nok;* akin to Norw. *nakke, nokke*, a hook, ON. *hnekkja*, to hem in, drive back, AS. *hnecca*, the neck (see NECK); despite Scand. parallels, the prob. etymon is AS. *hnoc*, orig. < same base; prob. IE. base *qneg- < *qen-, to squeeze together, pinch, nip (cf. NUT)], 1. a corner, especially of a room. 2. a small recess or secluded spot; retreat.

noon (nōōn), *n.* [AS. *non*, orig., the ninth hour (by the Roman method, reckoning from sunrise; hence about 3:00 P.M.); L. *nona* (*hora*), ninth (hour); see NONES, etym. & senses 2, 3], 1. twelve o'clock in the daytime; midday: abbreviated **N., n.** 2. the highest point or culmination; time of greatest power, etc.: as, in the *noon* of his life. 3. [Rare or Poetic], *a)* midnight: now only in *noon of night*. *b)* the position of the moon at this time. *adj.* of or occurring at noon (midday).

noon·day (nōōn'dā'), *n.* & *adj.* noon (midday).

no-one (nō'wun', nō'ən), *pron.* no one.

no one, no person; not anybody; nobody.

noon·ing (nōōn'iŋ), *n.* [Archaic or Dial.], 1. noon. 2. a stop at midday for rest or food. 3. a meal or refreshment at noon.

noon·tide (nōōn'tīd'), *n.* noon (midday).

noon·time (nōōn'tīm'), *n.* & *adj.* noon (midday).

noose (nōōs), *n.* [Pr. *nous* < L. *nodus;* cf. KNOT], 1. a loop formed in a rope, cord, etc. by means of a slip knot so that the loop tightens as the rope is pulled: often used figuratively with reference to death by hanging. 2. anything that restricts one's freedom; tie, bond, snare, trap, etc. *v.t.* [NOOSED (nōōst), NOOSING], 1. to catch or hold in or as in a noose; trap, ensnare, etc. 2. to form a noose in or of (a rope, cord, etc.). 3. [Rare], to execute by hanging.

no·pal (nō'pəl), *n.* [Sp.; Nahuatl *nopalli*], 1. any of a group of cactuses, formerly raised as a plant on which to breed cochineal insects. 2. the prickly pear.

no-par (nō'pär'), *adj.* having no stated par value: as, a *no-par* certificate of stock.

nope (nōp), *adv.* [Slang], no: a negative reply.

nor (nôr; *unstressed* nẽr), *conj.* [ME., contr. of *nother;* akin to OFris. *noer;* see NEITHER], and not; and not either: usually as the second of the correlatives *neither . . .nor*, implying negation of both parts of the statement, as, I can neither go *nor* stay; occasionally used in poetry or rhetoric: *a)* without the preceding *neither*: as, he doesn't smoke, *nor* does he drink. *b)* substituting for *neither* as the first in a pair of negative correlatives: as, *nor* flood *nor* fire.

nor (nôr), *conj.* [Northern ME.], [Dial.], than.

nor', nor, north: used especially in compounds, as in *nor'western*.

Nor., 1. Norman. 2. North. 3. Norway. 4. Norwegian.

No·ra (nôr'ə, nō'rə), [Ir., contr. of *Honora, Eleanor, Leonora*], a feminine name: see **Eleanor, Leonora.**

Nor·dau, Max Simon (nôr'dou), (*Max Simon Südfeld*), 1849–1923; German physician, miscellaneous writer, and Zionist leader, born in Hungary.

Nor·den·skjöld Sea (nōōr'dən-shüld'), an arm of the Arctic Ocean, between the Taimyr Peninsula and the New Siberian Islands: also called *Laptev Sea*.

Nord·hau·sen (nôrt'hou'zən), *n.* 1. a city in south central Prussia, Germany: pop., 38,000. 2. a Nazi

nonretentive
nonretiring
nonretraceable
nonretractile
nonretroactive
nonreturnable
nonrevealing
nonreversible
nonrevertible
nonreviewable
nonrevolting
nonrevolving
nonrhetorical
nonrhyming
nonrhythmic
nonrigid
nonritualistic
nonrival
non-Roman
nonromantic
nonrotating
nonroyal
nonruminant
nonrural
non-Russian
nonrustable
nonsacred
nonsacrificial
nonsalable
nonsalaried
nonsalutary
nonsaturated
non-Scandinavian
nonscholastic
nonscientific
nonscoring
nonseasonal
nonsecret
nonsecretory
nonsectional

nonsecular
nonsedentary
nonseditious
nonselective
non-Semitic
nonsensitive
nonsensitized
nonservile
non-Shakespearean
nonsharing
nonshattering
nonshrinkable
nonsilver
nonsinkable
nonslaveholding
non-Slavic
nonsmoker
nonsocial
nonsocialist
nonsolid
nonsolvent
nonsovereign
non-Spanish
nonsparing
nonspecializing
nonspectral
nonspeculative
nonspherical
nonspiritual
nonspirituous
nonspottable
nonstaining
nonstandardized
nonstarting
nonstatic
nonstationary
nonstatistical
nonstatutory
nonstrategic
nonstretchable

nonstriker
nonstriking
nonstructural
nonsubmissive
nonsubscriber
nonsuccessive
nonsupporting
nonsuppurative
nonsustaining
non-Swedish
non-Swiss
nonsymbolic
nonsymmetrical
nonsympathizer
nonsymphonic
nonsymptomatic
nonsynchronous
nonsyntactic
nonsynthesized
nonsystematic
nontarnishable
nontaxable
nonteachable
nontechnical
nonterrestrial
nonterritorial
nontestamentary
nontheatrical
nontheological
nontherapeutic
nonthinking
nontitular
nontoxic
nontragic
nontransferable
nontransitional
nontransparent
nontreasonable
nontributary
nontropical

nontuberculous
non-Turkish
nontypical
nontyrannical
nonulcerous
nonunderstandable
non-Unitarian
nonuniversal
nonuniversity
nonuser
nonuterine
nonutilitarian
nonutilized
nonvascular
nonvegetative
nonvenereal
nonvenomous
nonvenous
nonverminous
nonvernacular
nonvertical
nonvesicular
nonviable
nonvibratory
nonvicarious
nonviolation
nonvirulent
nonviscous
nonvisiting
nonvisual
nonvitreous
nonvocal
nonvocational
nonvolatile
nonvolcanic
nonvoluntary
nonvoting
nonvulcanizable
nonworker
nonyielding

concentration camp in this city: notorious as an extermination center.

Nor·dic (nôr′dik), *adj.* [ML. *Nordicus* < G. or Fr. *nord*, north; see NORTH], in *ethnology*, designating or of one of the three main divisions of the Caucasian, or white, race: term used to denote typically long-headed, tall, blond peoples of northern Europe, as the Scandinavians. *n.* a member of the Nordic division of the Caucasian race.

Nord·kyn, Cape (nôr′kün′), a cape in northern Norway: it is the northernmost part of the mainland of Europe.

Nor·folk (nôr′fək), *n.* 1. a seaport in southeastern Virginia, on Hampton Roads: pop., 305,000. 2. a county on the eastern coast of England: pop., 548,000; county seat, Norwich.

Norfolk Island, an Australian island, 930 mi. northeast of Sydney: area, 13 1/2 sq. mi.; pop., 1,000.

Norfolk jacket, a loose-fitting, single-breasted, belted jacket with a pocket on each side and box pleats in front and back: also **Norfolk coat**.

Nor·ge (nôr′gə), *n.* Norway: the Norwegian name.

no·ri·a (nō′ri-ə), *n.* [Sp. < Ar. *nā'ūrah*], a water wheel with buckets at its circumference, used in Spain and the Orient to raise and discharge water.

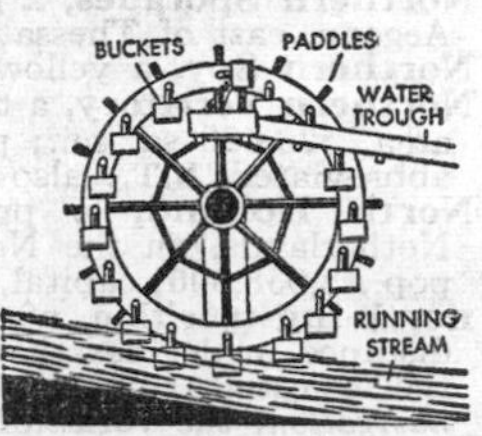

NORIA

Nor·i·cum (nor′i-kəm), *n.* a Roman province south of the Danube, in the region of modern Austria.

norm (nôrm), *n.* [L. *norma*, carpenter's square, rule, for **gnorima*; ult. < IE. base **ĝenē-*, **ĝenō-*, to recognize, know, seen also in Eng. *know*], a standard, model, or pattern for a group; especially, such a standard of achievement as represented by the median or average achievement of a large group. —*SYN.* see **average**.

Norm., Norman.

Nor·ma (nôr′mə), [< L. *norma;* see NORM], a feminine name. *n.* a southern constellation: see **constellation**, chart.

nor·mal (nôr′m'l), *adj.* [L. *normalis* < *norma*, a rule, etc.; see NORM], 1. conforming with or constituting an accepted standard, model, or pattern; especially, corresponding to the median or average of a large group in type, appearance, achievement, function, development, etc.; natural; standard; regular. 2. in *biology*, *a)* not immunized or otherwise exposed to an infectious agent: as, a *normal* animal. *b)* happening naturally. 3. in *chemistry*, *a)* designating or of a salt formed by replacing all the replaceable hydrogen of an acid with a metal or metals. *b)* designating or of a solution which contains an amount of the dissolved substance chemically equivalent to one gram-atomic weight of hydrogen per liter of solution. *c)* designating or of a fatty hydrocarbon, the chain of which is continuous rather than branched, in which no carbon atom is united directly to more than two others. Abbreviated **N., n.** 4. in *economics*, designating a price for a commodity approximately equal to the highest cost of production. 5. in *mathematics*, perpendicular; at right angles. 6. in *psychology*, average in intelligence or emotional stability. *n.* 1. anything normal. 2. the usual state, amount, degree, etc.; especially, the median or average. 3. in *mathematics*, a perpendicular; especially, a perpendicular to a line tangent to a curve, at its point of tangency.

SYN.—**normal** implies conformity with the established norm or standard for its kind (*normal* intelligence); **regular** implies conformity with the prescribed rule or accepted pattern for its kind (the *regular* working day); **typical** applies to that which has the representative characteristics of its type or class (a *typical* southern town); **natural** implies behavior, operation, etc. that conforms with the nature or innate character of the person or thing (a *natural* comedian); **usual** applies to that which conforms to the common or ordinary use or occurrence (the *usual* price); **average**, in this connection, implies conformity with what is regarded as normal or ordinary (the *average* man).—*ANT.* abnormal, unusual.

nor·mal·cy (nôr′m'l-si), *n.* the fact or condition of being normal; normality.

nor·mal·i·ty (nôr-mal′ə-ti), *n.* normalcy.

nor·mal·ize (nôr′m'l-īz′), *v.t.* [NORMALIZED (-īzd′), NORMALIZING], to make normal; bring into conformity with a standard, pattern, model, etc.

nor·mal·ly (nôr′m'l-i), *adv.* 1. in a normal manner. 2. under normal circumstances; ordinarily.

normal school, [after Fr. *école normale*], a school for training high-school graduates to become teachers.

normal value, the average price of a commodity in a given market over a long period of time: distinguished from *market value*.

Nor·man (nôr′mən), [< AS. *Northman*, OHG. *Nordemann*, lit., Northman], a masculine name: diminutive, *Norm.* *n.* [ME.; OFr. *Normant* (Fr. *Normand*), pl. *Normans, Normanz* < early ON.; cf. Dan. *Normand*, ON. *Northmathr*, Northman], 1. any of the Northmen who occupied Normandy in the 10th century A.D. 2. a descendant of the Normans and French who conquered England in 1066. 3. Norman French. 4. a native or inhabitant of Normandy. 5. the modern French dialect of Normandy. *adj.* 1. of Normandy, the Normans, their language, or culture. 2. designating or of the Romanesque style of architecture as it flourished in Normandy and, after the Norman Conquest, as developed in England: characterized by massive construction, round arches over recessed doors and windows, and carving. Abbreviated **Norm., Nor.**

Norman Conquest, the conquest of England by the Normans under William the Conqueror in 1066.

Nor·man·dy (nôr′mən-di), *n.* 1. a former province of France, on the English Channel: capital, Rouen. 2. a district on the northern coast of France, between Dieppe and Mont St. Michel.

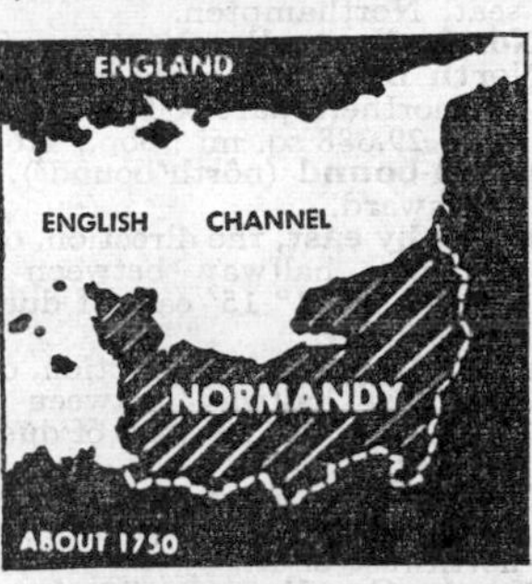

NORMANDY

Nor·man·esque (nôr′mən-esk′), *adj.* in the style of the Normans.

Nor·man-French (nôr′mən-french′), *adj.* 1. of or using Norman French. 2. of the Norman-French people. *n.* Norman French.

Norman French, 1. the French of the Normans or Normandy, as spoken in England by the Norman conquerors; Anglo-French: it was not imposed on the English as an official language at the Conquest, but gained legal and administrative currency after the accession of Eleanor of Aquitaine as queen (1152). 2. the later form of this language used as the legal jargon of England until the late 17th century; Law French.

Nor·man·ize (nôr′mən-īz′), *v.i. & v.t.* [NORMANIZED (-īzd′), NORMANIZING], to make or become Norman in style, character, language, customs, law, etc.

nor·ma·tive (nôr′mə-tiv), *adj.* 1. of or establishing a norm, or standard. 2. having to do with usage norms: as, *normative* grammar.

Norn (nôrn), *n.* [ON. *norn;* IE. base **(s)ner-*, **(s)nur-*, to snarl, mutter, seen also in Eng. *sneer*, Norw. dial. *norna*, to warn, give secret tidings], in *Norse mythology*, any of the three goddesses, Urth (the Past), Verthandi (the Present), and Skuld (the Future), who determined the destiny of gods and men.

Nor·ris, Frank (nôr′is, nor′is), (*Benjamin Franklin Norris*), 1870–1902; American novelist and journalist.

Norris, George William, 1861–1944; American statesman; United States senator from Nebraska (1913–1943).

Norris, Kathleen, 1880– ; American novelist.

Nor·ris·town (nôr′is-toun′, nor′is-toun′), *n.* a city in Pennsylvania, near Philadelphia: pop., 39,000.

Norr·kö·ping (nôr′chö′piŋ), *n.* a city in southeastern Sweden: pop., 90,000.

Norse (nôrs), *adj.* [prob. < D. *Noorsch*, a Norwegian, var. of *Noordsch; noord*, north + *-sch*, -ish], 1. Scandinavian. 2. West Scandinavian (Norwegian, Icelandic, and Faroese). *n.* 1. the Scandinavian group of languages. 2. the West Scandinavian group of languages. Abbreviated **N.**

the Norse, 1. the Scandinavians. 2. the West Scandinavians.

Norse·man (nôrs′mən), *n.* [*pl.* NORSEMEN (-mən)], a member of the ancient Scandinavian people; Northman.

north (nôrth), *n.* [ME.; AS.; akin to D. *noord*, G. *nord;* IE. base **ner-*, beneath, below: said to be so called from being to the left of worshipers praying to the East], 1. the direction to the right of a person facing the sunset; direction of the North Pole from any other point on the earth's surface: the needle of a compass points to the *magnetic north pole* rather than to the geographic pole. 2. the point on a compass at 0° or 360°, directly opposite south. 3. a region or district in or toward this direction. 4. [often N-], the northern part of the earth, especially the arctic regions. 5. [Poetic], the north wind. *adj.* 1. in, of, to, toward, or facing the north. 2. from the north: as, a *north* wind. 3. [N-], designating the northern part of a continent, country, etc.: as, *North* America, *North* India. *adv.* in or toward the north; in a northerly direction. Abbreviated **N, N., n, n., Nor., No.**

the North, that part of the United States which is

bounded on the south by Maryland, the Ohio River, and Missouri; States opposed to the Confederacy in the Civil War.

North, Frederick, 1732–1792, second Earl of Guilford, eighth Baron North; English statesman; prime minister of England (1770–1782).

North Adams, a city in northwestern Massachusetts: pop., 20,000.

North America, the northern continent in the Western Hemisphere: area, 8,500,000 sq. mi.; pop., 241,000,000: abbreviated **N.A.**

North American, 1. of North America or its people. 2. a native or inhabitant of North America.

North·amp·ton (nôr-thamp′tən), *n.* 1. Northamptonshire. 2. the county seat of Northamptonshire, England: pop., 100,000. 3. a city in western Massachusetts: pop., 30,000.

North·amp·ton·shire (nôr-thamp′tən-shir′), *n.* a county of central England: pop., 360,000; county seat, Northampton.

North Australia, Northern Territory, Australia.

North Borneo, a territory in British Borneo, including the northern part of Borneo and the island of Labuan: area, 29,388 sq. mi.; pop., 416,000.

north·bound (nôrth′bound′), *adj.* bound north; going northward.

north by east, the direction, or the point on a mariner's compass, halfway between due north and north-northeast; 11° 15′ east of due north: abbreviated **NbE** (no period).

north by west, the direction, or the point on a mariner's compass, halfway between due north and north-northwest; 11° 15′ west of due north: abbreviated **NbW** (no period).

North Cape, a cape on an island in Norway: it is the northernmost part of Europe, except for an island northwest of it.

North Carolina, a Southern State of the United States: area, 52,712 sq. mi.; pop., 4,556,000; capital, Raleigh: abbreviated **N.C.**

North Carolinian, 1. of North Carolina. 2. a native or inhabitant of North Carolina.

North Channel, the narrow channel between Northern Ireland and Scotland.

North·cliffe, Viscount (nôrth′klif), (*Alfred Charles William Harmsworth*), 1865–1922; English newspaper publisher, born in Ireland.

North Dakota, a Middle Western State of the United States: area, 70,665 sq. mi.; pop., 632,000; capital, Bismarck: abbreviated **N. Dak., N.D.**

North Da·ko·tan (də-kō′tən), 1. of North Dakota. 2. a native or inhabitant of North Dakota.

north·east (nôrth′ēst′; *in nautical usage,* nôr-ēst′), *n.* 1. the direction, or the point on a mariner's compass, halfway between north and east; 45° east of due north. 2. a region or district in or toward this direction. *adj.* 1. in, of, to, toward, or facing the northeast. 2. from the northeast, as a wind. *adv.* in, toward, or from the northeast. Abbreviated **NE, N.E., n.e.**
the Northeast, the northeastern part of the United States, especially New England, but sometimes including New York City and its environs.

northeast by east, the direction, or the point on a mariner's compass, halfway between northeast and east-northeast; 11° 15′ east of northeast: abbreviated **NEbE** (no period).

northeast by north, the direction, or the point on a mariner's compass, halfway between northeast and north-northeast; 11° 15′ north of northeast: abbreviated **NEbN** (no period).

north·east·er (nôrth′ēs′tẽr; *in nautical usage,* nôr-ēs′tẽr), *n.* a storm or strong wind from the northeast.

north·east·er·ly (nôrth′ēs′tẽr-li; *in nautical usage,* nôr-ēs′tẽr-li), *adj. & adv.* 1. in or toward the northeast. 2. from the northeast: as, a *northeasterly* wind.

north·east·ern (nôrth′ēs′tẽrn; *in nautical usage,* nôr-ēs′tẽrn), *adj.* 1. in, of, or toward the northeast. 2. from the northeast: as, a *northeastern* wind. 3. [N-], of or characteristic of the Northeast or New England.

Northeast Passage, a water route from the Atlantic to the Pacific through the seas north of Europe and Asia.

north·east·ward (nôrth′ēst′wẽrd; *in nautical usage,* nôr-ēst′wẽrd), *adv. & adj.* toward the northeast. *n.* a northeastward direction, point, or region.

north·east·ward·ly (nôrth′ēst′wẽrd-li; *in nautical usage,* nôr-ēst′wẽrd-li), *adj. & adv.* 1. toward the northeast. 2. from the northeast, as a wind.

north·east·wards (nôrth′ēst′wẽrdz; *in nautical usage,* nôr-ēst′wẽrdz), *adv.* northeastward.

north·er (nôr′*th*ẽr), *n.* a storm or strong wind from the north; especially, such a wind in the area about the Gulf of Mexico.

north·er·ly (nôr′*th*ẽr-li), *adj.* 1. in, of, or toward the north. 2. from the north: as, a *northerly* wind. *adv.* 1. toward the north. 2. from the north.

north·ern (nôr′*th*ẽrn), *adj.* [ME. *northren;* AS. *northern*], 1. in, of, toward, or facing the north. 2. from the north: as, a *northern* wind. 3. [N-], of or characteristic of the North. *n.* a northerner. Abbreviated **N., n., No., north.**

Northern Cross, the northern constellation Cygnus, the brighter stars of which form a cross.

Northern Crown, the constellation Corona Borealis.

Northern Dvina, a river in northern European Russia, flowing into the White Sea: length, 1,100 mi.

north·ern·er (nôr′*th*ẽr-nẽr; nôr′*th*ən-ẽr), *n.* 1. a native or inhabitant of the north. 2. [N-], a native or inhabitant of the northern part of the United States.

Northern Hemisphere, that half of the earth north of the equator.

Northern Ireland, a division of the United Kingdom, in northeastern Ireland: it consists of the major part of the former province of Ulster: area, 5,241 sq. mi.; pop., 1,371,000; capital, Belfast: abbreviated **N.I.**

northern lights, the aurora borealis.

north·ern·most (nôr′*th*ẽrn-mōst′), *adj.* farthest north.

Northern Rhodesia, a British protectorate in southern Africa: part of the Federation of Rhodesia and Nyasaland: area, 288,130 sq. mi.; pop., 2,430,000; capital, Lusaka.

Northern Sporades, a group of Greek islands in the Aegean, east of Thessaly, Greece.

Northern Spy, a yellowish-red winter apple.

Northern Territory, a territory of northern Australia: area, 523,620 sq. mi.; pop., 36,000; capital, Darwin: abbreviated **N.T.:** also called *North Australia.*

North Holland, a province of the northwestern Netherlands, on the North Sea: area, 1,058 sq. mi.; pop., 2,038,000; capital, Haarlem.

north·ing (nôr′thiŋ, nôr′*th*iŋ), *n.* 1. in *astronomy,* the distance in degrees that a heavenly body is north of the celestial equator; northern declination. 2. in *navigation,* the variation in latitude toward the north from the last reckoning of position.

North Island, the northern of the two chief islands of New Zealand: area, 44,281 sq. mi.

north·land (nôrth′lənd, nôrth′land′), *n.* 1. the northern region of a country; land in the north. 2. [N-], [Poetic], *a*) the northern part of the earth. *b*) the Scandinavian Peninsula.

north·land·er (nôrth′lənd-ẽr, nôrth′land′ẽr), *n.* a native or inhabitant of the northland.

North Little Rock, a city in central Arkansas, on the Arkansas River: pop., 58,000.

North·man (nôrth′mən), *n.* [*pl.* NORTHMEN (-mən)], 1. a Norseman. 2. a native or inhabitant of northern Europe.

North Miami, a city on the southeastern coast of Florida: suburb of Miami: pop., 29,000.

north-north·east (nôrth′nôrth′ēst′; *in nautical usage,* nôr′nôr-ēst′), *n.* the direction, or the point on a mariner's compass, halfway between due north and northeast; 22° 30′ east of due north. *adj. & adv.* 1. in or toward this direction. 2. from this direction, as a wind. Abbreviated **NNE, N.N.E., n.n.e.**

north-north·west (nôrth′nôrth′west′; *in nautical usage,* nôr′nôr-west′), *n.* the direction, or the point on a mariner's compass, halfway between due north and northwest; 22° 30′ west of due north. *adj. & adv.* 1. in or toward this direction. 2. from this direction, as a wind. Abbreviated **NNW, N.N.W., n.n.w.**

North Ossetian Autonomous Soviet Socialist Republic, a division of the R.S.F.S.R., in the Caucasus: area, 2,393 sq. mi.; pop., 449,000; capital, Ordzhonikidze.

North Platte, a river in Colorado, Wyoming, and Nebraska, joining the South Platte to form the Platte: length, 618 mi.

North Pole, the northern end of the earth's axis: its zenith (called the *north pole of the heavens*) is slightly more than 1° from Polaris, the North Star.

North Riding, a division of Yorkshire, England: pop., 525,000.

North River, an estuary of the Hudson, between New York City and New Jersey.

North Sea, an arm of the Atlantic, between Great Britain on the west and Norway and Denmark on the east: length, c. 600 mi.: also called *German Ocean.*

North Star, Polaris, the bright star almost directly above the northern end of the earth's axis; polestar.

North Ton·a·wan·da (ton′ə-wän′də), a city in western New York: pop., 35,000.

North·um·ber·land (nôr-thum′bẽr-lənd), *n.* the northernmost county of England: pop., 798,000; county seat, Newcastle: abbreviated **Northum., Northumb.**

North·um·bri·a (nôr-thum′bri-ə), *n.* a former Anglo-Saxon kingdom of northeastern England, north of the River Humber.

North·um·bri·an (nôr-thum′bri-ən), *adj.* 1. of Northumbria, its people, or their dialect. 2. of Northumberland, its people, or their dialect. *n.* 1. a native or inhabitant of Northumbria. 2. the Anglo-Saxon dialect of Northumbria. 3. a native or inhabitant of Northumberland. 4. the dialect of Northumberland.

north·ward (nôrth′wẽrd; *in nautical usage,* nôr′*th*ẽrd), *adv. & adj.* [see -WARD], toward the north. *n.* a northward direction, point, or region.

north·ward·ly (nôrth′wẽrd-li; *in nautical usage,* nôr′*th*ẽrd-li), *adj. & adv.* 1. toward the north. 2. from the north: as, a *northwardly* wind.
north·wards (nôrth′wẽrdz), *adv.* northward.
north·west (nôrth′west′; *in nautical usage,* nôr-west′), *n.* 1. the direction, or the point on a mariner's compass, halfway between north and west; 45° west of due north. 2. a district or region in or toward this direction. *adj.* 1. in, of, toward, or facing the northwest. 2. from the northwest: as, a *northwest* wind. *adv.* in, toward, or from the northwest. Abbreviated NW, N.W., n.w.
the Northwest, 1. the northwestern part of the United States when its western boundary was the Mississippi. 2. the northwestern part of the United States, especially Washington, Oregon, and Idaho. 3. the northwestern part of Canada.
northwest by north, the direction, or the point on a mariner's compass, halfway between northwest and north-northwest; 11° 15′ north of northwest: abbreviated NWbN (no period).
northwest by west, the direction, or the point on a mariner's compass, halfway between northwest and west-northwest; 11° 15′ west of northwest: abbreviated NWbW (no period).
north·west·er (nôrth′wes′tẽr; *in nautical usage,* nôr-wes′tẽr), *n.* a storm or strong wind from the northwest.
north·west·er·ly (nôrth′wes′tẽr-li; *in nautical usage,* nôr-wes′tẽr-li), *adj. & adv.* 1. in or toward the northwest. 2. from the northwest: as, a *northwesterly* wind.
north·west·ern (nôrth′wes′tẽrn; *in nautical usage,* nôr-wes′tẽrn), *adj.* 1. in, of, or toward the northwest. 2. from the northwest: as, a *northwestern* wind. 3. [N-], of or characteristic of the Northwest. Abbreviated NW, N.W., n.w.
North-West Frontier Agencies and Tribal Areas, a group of native agencies and tribal areas of British India: since 1947, part of West Pakistan.
North-West Frontier Province, a former province of northwestern Pakistan: now part of West Pakistan.
Northwest Passage, a water route from the Atlantic to the Pacific through the northern coastal waters of North America.
Northwest Territories, a division of northern Canada, subdivided into the Districts of Mackenzie, Keewatin, and Franklin: area, 1,304,903 sq. mi.; pop., 19,000: abbreviated N.W.T.
Northwest Territory, a region north of the Ohio, between Pennsylvania and the Mississippi, ceded (1783) by England to the United States: it now forms Ohio, Indiana, Illinois, Michigan, Wisconsin, and part of Minnesota.
north·west·ward (nôrth′west′wẽrd; *in nautical usage,* nôr-west′wẽrd), *adv. & adj.* toward the northwest. *n.* a northwestward direction, point, or region.
north·west·ward·ly (nôrth′west′wẽrd-li; *in nautical usage,* nôr-west′wẽrd-li), *adj. & adv.* 1. toward the northwest. 2. from the northwest, as a wind.
north·west·wards (nôrth′west′wẽrdz; *in nautical usage,* nôr-west′wẽrdz), *adv.* northwestward.
Nor·ton, Thomas (nôr′t′n), 1532–1584; English poet and playwright.
Norw., 1. Norway. 2. Norwegian.
Nor·walk (nôr′wôk), *n.* 1. a city in southwestern Connecticut: pop., 68,000. 2. a city in southwestern California: suburb of Los Angeles: pop., 89,000.
Nor·way (nôr′wā), *n.* a country in northern Europe, in the western part of the Scandinavian Peninsula: area, 124,556 sq. mi.; pop., 3,572,000; capital, Oslo: abbreviated **Norw., Nor.:** Norwegian name, *Norge.*
Norway rat, the common brown rat, which is larger than the black English rat.
Nor·we·gian (nôr-wē′jən), *adj.* [ML. *Norwegia, Norvegia,* Norway (< ON. *Norvegr* < *northr,* north + *vegr,* way); + *-an*], of Norway, its people, their language, or culture. *n.* 1. a native or inhabitant of Norway. 2. the Scandinavian language of the Norwegians, in any of its forms: as a literary language the older form of Norwegian was succeeded in Norway by a form of Danish (*Riksmaal*) during the late Middle Ages, but this Danish is now being replaced by a standard form of the language (*Landsmaal*) based on Norwegian dialects. Abbreviated **Norw., Nor., Ng.**
Norwegian Sea, the part of the Atlantic between Iceland and Norway.
Nor·wich (nôr′ij, nor′ich), *n.* 1. the county seat of Norfolk, England: famous for its cathedral: pop., 118,000. 2. (nôr′wich), a city in eastern Connecticut: pop., 39,000.
Nor·wood (nôr′wood′), *n.* a city in southwestern Ohio: suburb of Cincinnati: pop., 35,000.
nose (nōz), *n.* [ME.; AS. *nosu* (akin to OFris. *nosi*), orig. a dual, meaning "the two nostrils" (cf. AS. *doru,* door, orig. pair of doors); IE. base **nas-,* nostril, seen also in Sans. *nāsā,* the nose, lit., pair of nostrils, L. *nasus,* etc.; cf. NASAL], 1. the part of the face between the mouth and the eyes, having two openings for breathing and smelling. 2. the part that corresponds to this in animals; snout; muzzle. 3. the sense of smell; hence, 4. *a*) scent. *b*) power of tracking or perceiving by or as if by scent. 5. anything resembling a nose in shape or position; projecting or foremost part, as a nozzle, spout, prow of a ship, front of an airplane, etc. 6. [British Slang], a spy; informer. *v.t.* [NOSED (nōzd), NOSING], 1. to discover or perceive by or as if by the sense of smell; scent. 2. to touch or rub with the nose. 3. to make or push (a way, etc.) with the front forward: as, the ship *nosed* its way into the harbor. 4. to defeat by a very small margin (with *out*). *v.i.* 1. to smell; sniff. 2. to pry inquisitively. 3. to advance; move forward. 4. [British Slang], to act as a spy or informer.
by a nose, 1. in *horse racing,* etc., by the length of the animal's nose; hence, 2. by a very small margin.
count noses, to count the number of people present, voting, etc.
cut off one's nose to spite one's face, to injure one's own interests in a fit of anger, resentment, etc.
follow one's nose, to go straight forward.
lead by the nose, to dominate completely.
look down one's nose at, [Colloq.], to be disdainful of.
nose over, to turn over on its nose: said of an airplane on the ground.
on the nose, [Slang], 1. in *racing,* that (a specified horse, etc.) will finish first. 2. precisely; exactly.
pay through the nose, to pay an unreasonable price.
poke one's nose into, to interfere with; pry into.
put one's nose out of joint, 1. to replace one in another's affection, regard, etc. 2. to ruin one's plans, hopes, etc.
turn up one's nose at, to sneer at; scorn.
under one's (very) nose, in plain view.
nose bag, a canvas bag for holding feed for a horse, etc., hung over the animal's head.
nose·band (nōz′band′), *n.* that part of a bridle or halter which passes over the animal's nose.
nose·bleed (nōz′blēd′), *n.* a bleeding from the nose; nasal hemorrhage; epistaxis.
nose-dive (nōz′dīv′), *v.i.* [NOSE-DIVED (-dīvd′), NOSE-DIVING], to make a nose dive.
nose dive, 1. a swift, steep downward plunge of an airplane, with the nose toward the earth; hence, 2. any sudden, sharp drop.
nose·gay (nōz′gā′), *n.* [*nose* + *gay* (in obs. sense of "gay object, bright flower")], a bunch of flowers; small bouquet.
nose·piece (nōz′pēs′), *n.* 1. that part of a helmet which covers and protects the nose. 2. a noseband. 3. anything like a nose in form or position, as the nozzle of a hose or lower end of a microscope. 4. loosely, the bridge of a pair of glasses.
nose ring, 1. a metal ring passed through the nose of an animal for leading it about. 2. a ring of bone or metal worn in the nose as an ornament.
nos·ey (nōz′i), *adj.* [NOSIER (-i-ẽr), NOSIEST (-i-ist)], nosy.
nos·ing (nōz′iŋ), *n.* [< *nose, n.* + *-ing*], 1. the projecting edge of a step; that part of the tread which extends beyond the riser. 2. a strip, as of metal, for protecting this edge from wear. 3. any projection like a stair nosing.
nos·o- (nō′sō, nos′ə), [< Gr. *nosos,* disease], a combining form meaning *disease,* as in *nosology:* also, before a vowel, **nos-.**
no·sog·ra·phy (nō-sog′rə-fi), *n.* [*noso-* + *-graphy*], the systematic description of diseases.
nos·o·log·i·cal (nos′ə-loj′i-k′l), *adj.* of or in nosology.
no·sol·o·gy (nō-sol′ə-ji), *n.* [Mod. L. *nosologia;* see NOSO- & -LOGY], 1. the classification of diseases. 2. the branch of medicine dealing with this.
nos·tal·gi·a (nos-tal′jə, nos-tal′ji-ə), *n.* [Mod. L. < Gr. *nostos,* a return; + *-algia*], 1. homesickness; a longing to go back to one's home, home town, or homeland; hence, 2. a longing for something far away or long ago.
nos·tal·gic (nos-tal′jik), *adj.* of, having, or causing nostalgia.
nos·toc (nos′tok), *n.* [Mod. L.; coined by Paracelsus], any of a group of algae having blue-green cells surrounded by a stiff, jellylike substance.
nos·to·log·ic (nos′tə-loj′ik), *adj.* of nostology.
nos·tol·o·gy (nos-tol′ə-ji), *n.* [< Gr. *nostos,* a return; + *-logy*], the scientific study of old age in man and animals; geriatrics.
nos·to·ma·ni·a (nos′tō-mā′ni-ə), *n.* [< *nost*algia + *-mania*], in *psychiatry,* excessive or abnormal nostalgia.
Nos·tra·da·mus (nos′trə-dā′məs), *n.* (*Michel de Notredame*), French astrologer; lived 1503–1566.
nos·tril (nos′trəl), *n.* [ME. *nostril, nosethirl;* AS. *nos-*

thyrl < *nos*, for *nosu*, the nose + *thyrel*, a hole < *thurh*, through; see NOSE & THROUGH], either of the external openings of the nose.

nos·trum (nos′trəm), *n.* [*pl.* NOSTRUMS (-trəmz)], [L., neut. of *noster*, ours: so called from the seller's calling it "our" remedy], 1. *a)* a medicine prepared by the person selling or recommending it. *b)* a quack medicine. *c)* a patent medicine. 2. a favorite remedy, as a pet plan or scheme for solving some social or political problem; panacea.

nos·y (nōz′i), *adj.* [NOSIER (-i-ẽr), NOSIEST (-i-ist)], [< *nose* + *-y*], [Colloq.], given to prying; inquisitive: also spelled **nosey**.

not (not), *adv.* [ME. *not*, unstressed form of *noht*, *nought*, *naught;* see NOUGHT], in no manner, to no degree, etc.: a particle of negation, or word expressing the idea of *no*, often implying refusal, affirmation of the opposite, etc.; sometimes used elliptically (e.g., whether you like it or *not*).

not- (nōt), noto-.

‡no·ta be·ne (nō′tə bē′ni), [L.], note well; take particular notice: abbreviated **N.B., n.b.**

no·ta·bil·i·ty (nō′tə-bil′ə-ti), *n.* 1. [*pl.* NOTABILITIES (-tiz)], a person who is notable or prominent. 2. the quality of being notable.

no·ta·ble (nō′tə-b'l; *for adj. 2, also* not′ə-b'l), *adj.* [ME.; OFr.; L. *notabilis* < *notare*, to mark, note < *nota*, a mark], 1. worthy of notice; remarkable; striking; distinguished; eminent. 2. [Dial.], industrious, capable, or efficient in housekeeping: said of women. *n.* 1. a person of distinction; famous or well-known person. 2. [N-], formerly, in France, any of the persons of authority, rank, etc. summoned by the king as a deliberative assembly in emergencies.

no·ta·bly (nō′tə-bli), *adv.* 1. in a notable manner. 2. to a notable degree.

no·tar·i·al (nō-târ′i-əl), *adj.* 1. of or characteristic of a notary. 2. drawn up or executed by a notary.

no·ta·rize (nō′tə-rīz′), *v.t.* [NOTARIZED (-rīzd′), NOTARIZING], to certify or attest (a document) as a notary.

no·ta·ry (nō′tẽr-i), *n.* [*pl.* NOTARIES (-iz)], [ME. *notarye;* OFr. *notaire;* L. *notarius* < *notare*, to note], an official authorized to certify or attest documents, take depositions and affidavits, etc.

notary public, [*pl.* NOTARIES PUBLIC], a notary: abbreviated **N.P., n.p.**

no·ta·tion (nō-tā′shən), *n.* [L. *notatio* < *notare*, to note], 1. the use of a system of signs or symbols to represent words, phrases, numbers, quantities, etc. 2. any such system of signs or symbols, as in arithmetic, algebra, music, etc. 3. a noting. 4. a note; annotation.

no·ta·tion·al (nō-tā′shən-'l), *adj.* of notation.

notch (noch), *n.* [prob. by syllabic merging of ME. *an oche;* OFr. *oche, osche*, a notch < *oschier*, to notch], 1. a V-shaped cut in an edge or across a surface. 2. a narrow pass with steep sides; defile; gap. 3. [Colloq.], a step; grade; degree; peg: as, his average dropped a *notch*. *v.t.* 1. to cut a notch or notches in. 2. to record or tally, as by means of notches.

note (nōt), *n.* [ME.; OFr.; L. *nota*, a mark, sign, character, letter < *notus*, pp. of *noscere*, to know < *gnoscere;* for IE. base see KNOW], 1. a mark of some quality, condition, or fact; distinguishing or characteristic feature: as, *a note* of sadness. 2. importance, distinction, or eminence: as, a person of *note*. 3. any sign or character, other than a letter, used in writing or printing (e.g., ? ! *). 4. *a)* a brief statement of a fact, experience, etc. written down for review, as an aid to memory, or to inform someone else; memorandum. *b)* *pl.* a record of experiences, etc.: as, the *notes* of a journey. 5. a comment, explanation, or elucidation, as at the foot of a page; annotation. 6. notice; heed; observation: as, please take *note* of this. 7. any of certain types of correspondence, as a short informal letter or a formal diplomatic or other official communication. 8. any of certain commercial papers, some of which are negotiable, relating to the owing of debts or payment of money: as, a promissory *note*, a bank *note*. 9. a cry; call; sound. 10. the cry or call of a bird. 11. a signal or intimation: as, a *note* of admonition. 12. [Archaic or Poetic], a melody, tune, or song. 13. in *music*, *a)* a tone of definite pitch, as made by a voice or musical instrument. *b)* a symbol for a tone, indicating the duration by its form and the pitch by its position on the staff. *c)* a key of a piano or similar musical instrument. Abbreviated **n.** *v.t.* [NOTED (-id), NOTING], 1. to pay close attention to; heed; notice; observe. 2. to set down in writing; make a note of. 3. to mention particularly. 4. to denote, signify, or indicate. 5. to annotate. 6. to write down in or supply with musical notes.

MUSICAL NOTES
A, whole note; B, half notes; C, quarter notes; D, eighth notes; E, sixteenth notes; F, thirty-second notes; G, sixty-fourth notes; H, double notes

compare notes, to exchange views; discuss.

strike the right note, to say, write, or do what is specially suitable.

take notes, to put facts, events, conversations, etc. in writing for later reference.

note·book (nōt′book′), *n.* 1. a book in which notes, or memorandums, are kept. 2. a record book for registering promissory notes.

not·ed (nōt′id), *adj.* [pp. of *note*], distinguished; well-known; renowned; eminent. —***SYN.*** see **famous.**

note·less (nōt′lis), *adj.* 1. not noted; unnoticed; undistinguished. 2. unmusical; voiceless.

note of hand, a promissory note.

note paper, paper for writing notes (letters).

note·wor·thi·ly (nōt′wũr′*th*ə-li), *adv.* in a noteworthy manner; so as to be noteworthy.

note·wor·thi·ness (nōt′wũr′*th*i-nis), *n.* the quality or condition of being noteworthy.

note·wor·thy (nōt′wũr′*th*i), *adj.* worthy of note; deserving notice; outstanding; remarkable; notable.

noth·ing (nuth′iŋ), *n.* [ME.; AS. *na thing, nan thing*], 1. no thing; not anything; nought: opposed to *anything, something*. 2. *a)* lack of existence; nonexistence; nothingness. *b)* insignificance; unimportance. 3. a thing that does not exist. 4. *a)* something of little or no value, seriousness, importance, etc.; triviality. *b)* a person considered of no value or importance. 5. in *mathematics*, lack of any quantity either plus or minus; zero. *adv.* not at all; in no manner or degree.

for nothing, 1. free; at no cost. 2. in vain; uselessly. 3. without reason.

make nothing of, 1. to treat as of little importance. 2. to fail to understand. 3. to fail to use or do.

nothing but, only; nothing other than.

nothing doing, [Colloq.], 1. no: used as a refusal of a request to do something. 2. no result, accomplishment, etc.: an exclamation of disappointment.

nothing less than, no less than; just the same as: also **nothing short of.**

think nothing of, to regard as unimportant, easy, etc.

noth·ing·ness (nuth′iŋ-nis), *n.* 1. the quality or condition of being nothing; lack of existence; extinction. 2. lack of value or worth; uselessness; insignificance. 3. unconsciousness. 4. anything that is nonexistent, worthless, insignificant, etc.

no·tice (nō′tis), *n.* [Fr.; L. *notitia* < *notus;* see NOTE], 1. information, announcement, or warning; especially, formal announcement or warning, as in a newspaper: as, a legal *notice*. 2. a short article about a work of art, book, play, etc. 3. a written or printed sign giving some public information, warning, or rule. 4. *a)* the act of observing; attention; regard; heed; cognizance. *b)* courteous attention; civility. 5. a formal announcement or warning of intention to end an agreement, relation, or contract at a certain time: as, the tenant gave *notice*. *v.t.* [NOTICED (-tist), NOTICING], 1. *a)* to mention; refer to; comment on. *b)* to review briefly. 2. *a)* to regard; observe; pay attention to. *b)* to be courteous, civil, or responsive to. 3. [Rare], to serve with a notice; give formal warning to. —***SYN.*** see **discern.**

serve notice, to give formal warning or information, as of intentions; announce.

take notice, to take cognizance; become aware; pay attention; observe.

no·tice·a·ble (nō′tis-ə-b'l), *adj.* 1. easily seen; conspicuous. 2. worth noticing; significant.

***SYN.*—noticeable** is applied to that which must inevitably be noticed (a *noticeable* coolness in his manner); **remarkable** applies to that which is noticeable because it is unusual or exceptional (*remarkable* beauty); **prominent** refers to that which literally or figuratively stands out from its background (a *prominent* nose, a *prominent* author); an **outstanding** person or thing is remarkable as compared with others of its kind (an *outstanding* sculptor); **conspicuous** applies to that which is so obvious or manifest as to be immediately perceptible (*conspicuous* gallantry); **striking** is used of something so out of the ordinary that it leaves a sharp impression on the mind (a *striking* epigram).

no·tice·a·bly (nō′tis-ə-bli), *adv.* 1. in a noticeable manner. 2. to a noticeable degree.

no·ti·fi·ca·tion (nō′tə-fi-kā′shən), *n.* [< *notify*], 1. a notifying or being notified. 2. the notice given or received. 3. the letter, form, etc. used to convey such a notice.

no·ti·fi·er (nō′tə-fī′ẽr), *n.* a person or thing that notifies.

no·ti·fy (nō′tə-fī′), *v.t.* [NOTIFIED (-fīd′), NOTIFYING], [ME. *notifien;* OFr. *notifier;* L. *notificare* < *notus* (see NOTE) + *facere*, to make], 1. to give notice to; inform; announce to. 2. [Chiefly British], to give notice of; announce; make known.

***SYN.*—notify** implies a sending of a formal notice imparting required or pertinent information (*notify* me when you are ready); **inform** implies a making aware of something by giving knowledge of it (he *informed* me of your decision to join us); **acquaint** suggests a making familiar with something hitherto unknown to one (she *acquainted* me with her problems); **apprise** implies a notifying someone of something that has particular interest for him (I have *apprised* him of your arrival).

no·tion (nō′shən), *n.* [OFr.; L. *notio* < *notus*, pp. of *noscere;* see NOTE], 1. *a)* a mental image; general idea. *b)* a vague thought. 2. a belief; opinion; view. 3. a desire; inclination; whim. 4. an intention: as, I have no *notion* of going yet. 5. *pl.* small, useful articles, as needles, thread, etc., sold in a store. —*SYN.* see **idea.**

no·tion·al (nō′shən-'l), *adj.* 1. of, expressing, or consisting of notions, or concepts. 2. imaginary; not actual: as, a *notional* value of one's own skills. 3. having visionary ideas; given to whims; fanciful. 4. in *grammar, a)* having full lexical, as distinguished from relational, meaning. *b)* of the meaning expressed by a linguistic form. 5. in *semantics*, presentive.

no·to- (nō′tō, nō′tə), [< Gr. *nōton*, the back], a combining form meaning *the back, dorsum*, as in *notochord:* also, before a vowel, **not-.**

no·to·chord (nō′tə-kôrd′), *n.* [*noto-* + *chord*], 1. a rod-shaped, elastic structure of cells forming the primitive supporting axis of the body in the lowest vertebrates. 2. a similar structure in the embryonic stages of higher vertebrates, which later develops into the backbone.

No·to·gae·a (nō′tə-jē′ə), *n.* [Mod. L. < Gr. *notos*, the south + *gaia*, earth, land], a primary zoological region of the earth's land area, including Australia, New Zealand, and the Neotropical regions.

No·to·gae·an, No·to·ge·an (nō′tə-jē′ən), *adj.* of or from Notogaea.

no·to·ri·e·ty (nō′tə-rī′ə-ti), *n.* [*pl.* NOTORIETIES (-tiz)], [Fr. *notorieté;* ML. *notorietas* < *notorius*], 1. the quality or state of being notorious. 2. a prominent or well-known person.

no·to·ri·ous (nō-tôr′i-əs, nō-tō′ri-əs), *adj.* [ML. *notorius* < L. *notus*, pp. of *noscere;* see NOTE], 1. [Rare], well-known; publicly discussed. 2. widely but unfavorably known or talked about. —*SYN.* see **famous.**

no·tor·nis (nō-tôr′nis), *n.* [Mod. L. < Gr. *notos*, the south + *ornis*, bird], any of a rare or extinct group of nonflying birds related to the coot and rail, formerly found in New Zealand.

No·tre Dame (nō′trə däm′; Fr. nô′tr′ dȧm′), [Fr.], 1. Our Lady (Mary, mother of Jesus). 2. a famous early Gothic cathedral in Paris: in full, **Notre Dame de Paris.**

no-trump (nō′trump′), *adj.* 1. without trumps. 2. in *bridge*, designating or of a bid to play with no suit being trumps. *n.* 1. a bid in bridge to play with no suit being trumps. 2. the hand so played.

Not·ting·ham (not′iŋ-əm), *n.* 1. Nottinghamshire. 2. the county seat of Nottinghamshire: pop., 278,000.

Not·ting·ham·shire (not′iŋ-əm-shir′), *n.* a county of central England: pop., 749,000; county seat, Nottingham.

no·tun·gu·late (nō-tuŋ′gyoo-lāt′), *adj.* [< Mod. L. *Notungulata*, name of the order; see NOTO- & UNGULATE], of an extinct order of plant-eating mammals.

not·with·stand·ing (not′with-stan′diŋ, not′*with*-stan′diŋ), *prep.* in spite of: as, they traveled on, *notwithstanding* the storm. *adv.* all the same; nevertheless: as, they will do it, *notwithstanding*. *conj.* in spite of the fact that; although.

nou·gat (no͞o′gət, no͞o′gä), *n.* [Fr.; Pr. *nogat* < *noga, nuga*, nut < L. *nux*, nut], a confection of sugar paste with almonds or other nuts.

nought (nôt), *n.* [ME. *nouht*, etc.; AS. *nowiht, nowuht* < *ne*, not + *owiht, awiht*, aught (cf. AUGHT); akin to OHG. *neowiht* (G. *nicht*, not); cf. NOT], 1. nothing. 2. a person or thing considered of no value. 3. in *arithmetic*, the figure zero (0). *adj.* worthless; useless. *adv.* [Archaic], in no way; not at all.

Nou·mé·a (no͞o′mā-ä′), *n.* the capital of New Caledonia: pop., 11,100.

nou·me·nal (no͞o′mi-n'l, nou′mi-n'l), *adj.* in *philosophy*, of noumena or the noumenon.

nou·me·nal·ism (no͞o′mi-n'l-iz'm, nou′mi-n'l-iz'm), *n.* the doctrine maintaining the existence of noumena.

nou·me·non (no͞o′mi-non′, nou′mi-non′), *n.* [*pl.* NOUMENA (-nə)], [Gr. *nooumenon*, neut. of *nooumenos*, ppr. pass. of *noein*, to perceive < *noos*, the mind], in *Kantian philosophy*, an object understood by intellectual intuition, without the aid of the senses: opposed to *phenomenon.*

noun (noun), *n.* [ME. *nowne;* OFr. *noun, nun, non, nom* < L. *nomen*, a name], in *grammar*, 1. any of a class of words naming or denoting a person, thing, action, quality, etc.: as, *boy, water*, and *truth* are *nouns.* 2. any word, phrase, or clause similarly used; substantive. Abbreviated **n., N.**

noun·al (noun′'l), *adj.* of or like a noun. *n.* a nominal.

nour·ish (nũr′ish), *v.t.* [ME. *norischen, norisen* < OFr. *nurir, nurrir, norrir* < L. *nutrire;* see NURSE], 1. to feed or sustain (any plant or animal) with substances necessary to life and growth. 2. to stimulate; foster; develop; support (a feeling, attitude, habit, etc.).

nour·ish·ing (nũr′ish-iŋ), *adj.* [ppr. of *nourish*], nutritious; contributing to health or growth.

nour·ish·ment (nũr′ish-mənt), *n.* [OFr. *norissement, nourissement*], 1. a nourishing or being nourished. 2. something that nourishes; food; nutriment.

nous (no͞os, nous), *n.* [Gr. *nous, noos*], in *philosophy*, mind; understanding; reason; intellect.

‡nou·veau riche (no͞o′vō′ rēsh′), [*pl.* NOUVEAUX RICHES (no͞o′vō′ rēsh′)], [Fr., newly rich], a person who has only recently become rich: often implying tasteless ostentation, lack of culture, etc.

‡nou·veau·té (no͞o′vō′tā′), *n.* [Fr.], a novelty.

‡nou·velles (no͞o′vel′), *n.pl.* [Fr.], news.

Nov., November.

nov., novelist.

no·va (nō′və), *n.* [*pl.* NOVAS (-vəz), NOVAE (-vē)], [L., *nova* (*stella*), new (star) < *novus*, new], in *astronomy*, a star that suddenly increases greatly in brilliance and then gradually grows fainter.

no·vac·u·lite (nō-vak′yoo-līt′), *n.* [< L. *novacula*, razor; + *-ite*], a hard, extremely fine-grained siliceous rock, supposedly sedimentary in origin: it is used for whetstones.

No·va·ra (nô-vä′rä), *n.* a city in northwestern Italy: pop., 71,000 (est. 1947).

No·va Sco·tia (nō′və skō′shə), a peninsular maritime province of southeastern Canada: area, 21,068 sq. mi.; pop., 643,000; capital, Halifax: abbreviated **N.S.:** formerly called *Acadia.*

Nova Sco·tian (skō′shən), 1. of Nova Scotia, its people, or their culture. 2. a native or inhabitant of Nova Scotia.

no·va·tion (nō-vā′shən), *n.* [L. *novatio* < *novare*, to make new < *novus*, new], in *law*, the substitution of a new obligation for an old one: any obligation may be legally terminated by novation.

No·va·ya Zem·lya (nô′vä-yä zem′lyä), two large islands in the European U.S.S.R., in the Arctic Ocean: area, 36,000 sq. mi.

nov·el (nov′'l), *adj.* [OFr. *novel, nouvel* < L. *novellus*, dim. of *novus*, new; akin to Gr. *neos*, new; cf. NEW], new; recent; strange; unusual. *n.* [Fr. *nouvelle*, short story, or It. *novella;* both < L. *novella*, neut. pl. of *novellus* (see the *adj.*); hence, orig., new things, news], 1. *usually in pl.* a novella. 2. a relatively long fictional prose narrative with a more or less complex plot or pattern of events, about human beings, their feelings, thoughts, actions, etc.: cf. **romance, novelette, short story.** 3. the type or form of literature represented by such narratives (with *the*). 4. *usually in pl.* in *Roman law*, a new law or decree, specifically one made by Justinian supplementary to the Justinian Code. —*SYN.* see **new.**

nov·el·ette (nov′ə-let′), *n.* a short novel (usually c. 30,000–50,000 words).

nov·el·ist (nov′'l-ist), *n.* a person who writes novels.

nov·el·is·tic (nov″'l-is′tik), *adj.* of, characteristic of, or like novels.

nov·el·i·za·tion (nov″'l-i-zā′shən, nov″'l-ī-zā′shən), *n.* a novelizing or being novelized.

nov·el·ize (nov″'l-īz′), *v.t.* [NOVELIZED (-īzd′), NOVELIZING], to give the form or characteristics of a novel to; make into or like a novel.

‡no·vel·la (nô-vel′lä), *n.* [*pl.* NOVELLE (nô-vel′le)], [It.; see NOVEL, *n.*], a short prose narrative, usually with a moral and often satiric, as any of the tales in Boccaccio's *Decameron.*

nov·el·ty (nov′'l-ti), *n.* [*pl.* NOVELTIES (-tiz)], [ME. *novelte;* OFr. *noveleté;* L. *novellitas*], 1. the quality of being novel; newness; freshness. 2. something new, fresh, or unusual; change; innovation. 3. *usually in pl.* a small, often cheap, cleverly made article, usually for play or adornment.

No·vem·ber (nō-vem′bẽr), *n.* [L. *November* or *Novembris* (*mensis*), ninth (month) of the ancient Roman year < *novem*, nine], the eleventh month of the year, having 30 days: abbreviated **Nov., N.**

no·ve·na (nō-vē′nə), *n.* [*pl.* NOVENAS (-əz), NOVENAE (-nē)], [ML., neut. pl. of L. *novenus*, nine each < *novem*, nine], in the *Roman Catholic Church*, the recitation of prayers and the practicing of devotions during a nine-day period, usually for some special religious purpose.

no·ver·cal (nō-vũr′k'l), *adj.* [L. *novercalis* < *noverca*, a stepmother], of, like, or befitting a stepmother.

Nov·go·rod (nov′gə-rod′; Russ. nôv′gô-rôt′), *n.* a city in the northwestern R.S.F.S.R.: pop., 31,000: an important political and commercial center during the Middle Ages; former capital of Russia.

nov·ice (nov′is), *n.* [ME. *novis;* OFr. *novice;* L. *novicius,* new, fresh < *novus,* new], 1. a person on probation in a religious group or order before taking the final vows; neophyte. 2. a recent convert; specifically, a recent convert to Christianity. 3. a person new to a particular occupation, activity, etc.; apprentice; beginner; tyro. —*SYN.* see **amateur.**

No·vi Sad (nô′vi säd′), a city in northeastern Yugoslavia, on the Danube: pop., 64,000: German name, *Neusatz.*

no·vi·ti·ate, no·vi·ci·ate (nō-vish′i-it, nō-vish′i-āt′), *n.* [Fr. *noviciat;* ML. *novitiatus*], 1. the period of probation of a novice in a religious order. 2. the state or period of being a novice. 3. a novice. 4. the housing and training quarters of religious novices.

no·vo·cain, no·vo·caine (nō′və-kān′), *n.* [*novo-* (< L. *novus,* new) + *cocaine*], an alkaloid compound resembling cocaine but less toxic and irritant, used as a local anesthetic; procaine: a trade-mark (**Novocain**).

No·vo·ros·siisk (nô′vô-rô-sēsk′), a city in the southeastern R.S.F.S.R., on the Black Sea: pop., 95,000.

No·vo·si·birsk (nô′vô-si-bērsk′), *n.* 1. a territory of the U.S.S.R., in western Siberia: pop., 4,023,000. 2. its capital, on the Ob River: pop., 406,000.

now (nou), *adv.* [ME. *nou, nu;* AS. *nu* (form in all Gmc. languages); IE. base ***nū-*,** as also in L. *nunc* (< **numce*), *num,* etc.], 1. *a*) at the present time; at this moment. *b*) at once. 2. at the time referred to; then; next: usually in narrative, as, *now* a series of catastrophes occurred. 3. at a time very close to the present; specifically, *a*) very recently; not long ago (with *just*): as, he left just *now.* *b*) very soon (often with *just*): as, they are leaving just *now.* 4. given the situation; with things as they are: as, *now* we'll never know what happened. *Now* is often used without any definite meaning, especially to introduce or emphasize: as, come *now,* don't be absurd. ***conj.*** since; seeing that: as, *now* (that) the rain has come, we won't starve. ***n.*** the present time. ***interj.*** an exclamation expressing warning, reproach, etc.

now and then, occasionally: also **now and again.**

now·a·days (nou′ə-dāz′), *adv.* [ME. *nou adaies, now on dayes* < *now* + *on* + *day* + *-s* adv. suffix], in these days; at the present time. ***n.*** the present time.

no·way (nō′wā′), *adv.* in no manner; by no means; not at all; nowise.

no·ways (nō′wāz′), *adv.* noway.

now·el (nō-el′, nō′el), *n.* [Archaic], noel.

no·where (nō′hwâr′), *adv.* [ME. *nowher;* AS. *nahwær*], not in, at, or to any place; not anywhere.

be (or **get**) **nowhere,** to have no success; fail.

nowhere near, not nearly; not by a wide margin.

no·wheres (nō′hwârz′), *adv.* [Dial.], nowhere.

no·whith·er (nō′hwith′ẽr), *adv.* [ME. *nowhider;* AS. *nahwider*], in, at, or to no place; nowhere.

no·wise (nō′wīz′), *adv.* in no manner; noway.

nowt (nout), *n.pl.* [sing. NOWT], [ME.; ON. *naut,* cattle; akin to AS. *neat;* cf. NEAT (cattle)], [Scot. & British Dial.], cattle; oxen.

Nox (noks), *n.* [L.], in *Roman mythology,* the goddess of night: identified with the Greek Nyx.

nox·ious (nok′shəs), *adj.* [L. *noxius* < *noxa,* injury, hurt < *nocere,* to hurt, injure], harmful to health or morals; unwholesome. —*SYN.* see **pernicious.**

no·yade (nwä-yäd′), *n.* [Fr. < *noyer,* to drown < L. *necare,* to kill (in LL., to drown)], a mass execution of persons by drowning, as practiced at Nantes, France, during the Reign of Terror (1794).

Noyes, Alfred (noiz), 1880–1958; English poet.

noz·zle (noz′'l), *n.* [dim. of *nose*], 1. the small mouthpiece or spout of a hose, pipe, teakettle, pair of bellows, etc. 2. [Slang], the nose; snout.

NP, neuropsychiatric.

Np, in *chemistry,* neptunium.

N.P., n.p., 1. new paragraph. 2. nisi prius. 3. no protest. 4. Notary Public.

nr., near.

NRA, N.R.A., National Recovery Administration.

N.S., 1. National Society. 2. New Series. 3. New Style. 4. Nova Scotia. 5. Numismatic Society.

N/S, n/s, in *banking,* not sufficient funds: also **N.S.F.**

N.S.P.C.A., National Society for the Prevention of Cruelty to Animals.

N.S.P.C.C., National Society for the Prevention of Cruelty to Children.

N.S.W., New South Wales.

-n't, a contracted and enclitic form of *not,* as in *aren't.*

Nt, in *chemistry,* niton.

NT., N.T., New Testament.

N.T., Northern Territory.

nth (enth), *adj.* 1. expressing the ordinal equivalent to *n;* hence, 2. of the indefinitely large or small quantity represented by *n.*

to the nth degree (or **power**), 1. to an indefinite degree or power. 2. to an extreme.

nt. wt., net weight.

nu (nōō, nū), *n.* [Gr. *ny*], the thirteenth letter of the Greek alphabet (Ν, ν), corresponding to English *N, n:* see **alphabet,** table.

nu·ance (nōō-äns′, nū′äns), *n.* [Fr. < *nuer,* to shade < *nue;* L. *nubes,* a cloud], a slight or delicate variation in tone, color, meaning, etc.; shade of difference.

nub (nub), *n.* [var. of *knub,* for *knob*], 1. a knob; lump. 2. [Colloq.], the point of a story, etc.; gist.

Nu·ba (nōō′bä), *n.* [*pl.,* for 1 & 2, NUBA], 1. a Nubian. 2. a member of a Negro tribe in the Anglo-Egyptian Sudan, related to the Nubians. 3. the language of the Nuba.

nub·bin (nub′in), *n.* [dim. of *nub*], 1. a small lump. 2. a small or imperfect ear of Indian corn. 3. an undeveloped fruit.

nub·ble (nub′'l), *n.* [dim. of *nub*], a small knob or lump.

nub·bly (nub′li), *adj.* [NUBBLIER (-li-ẽr), NUBBLIEST (-li-ist)], full of, or in the form of, nubbles; knobby.

nub·by (nub′i), *adj.* covered with small nubs; nubbly: said especially of a fabric with a rough, knotted weave.

Nu·bi·a (nōō′bi-ə, nū′bi-ə), *n.* a former kingdom of northeastern Africa, between the Red Sea and the Sahara Desert: now part of Egypt and the Anglo-Egyptian Sudan.

nu·bi·a (nōō′bi-ə, nū′bi-ə), *n.* [< L. *nubes,* a cloud], a woman's light, fleecy wrap, worn over the head and shoulders.

Nu·bi·an (nōō′bi-ən, nū′bi-ən), *adj.* of Nubia, its people, or their language. ***n.*** 1. a member of a Negroid people of Nubia. 2. the language of the Nubians.

Nubian Desert, a desert in the northeastern Anglo-Egyptian Sudan.

nu·bile (nōō′b'l, nū′bil), *adj.* [< Fr. or L.; Fr. *nubile;* L. *nubilis* < *nubere,* to veil oneself, marry], marriageable: said of women, with reference to their age or physical development.

nu·bil·i·ty (nōō-bil′ə-ti, nū-bil′ə-ti), *n.* the state of being nubile.

nu·bi·lous (nōō′b'l-əs, nū′bil-əs), *adj.* [LL. *nubilosus,* cloudy, for L. *nubilus* < *nubes,* a cloud], 1. cloudy; misty; foggy. 2. obscure; indefinite.

nu·cel·lar (nyoo-sel′ẽr), *adj.* of a nucellus or nucelli.

nu·cel·lus (nyoo-sel′əs), *n.* [*pl.* NUCELLI (-ī)], [Mod. L. < L. *nucella,* dim. of *nux, nucis,* nut], the central part of an ovule, containing the embryo sac.

nu·cha (nū′kə), *n.* [*pl.* NUCHAE (-kē)], [ME.; ML.; Ar. *nukhā‘,* spinal marrow], the nape of the neck.

nu·chal (nū′k'l), *adj.* of or connected with the nucha.

nu·ci- (nū′si), [< L. *nux, nucis,* nut], a combining form meaning *nut,* as in *nuciferous.*

nu·cif·er·ous (nyoo-sif′ẽr-əs), *adj.* [*nuci-* + *-ferous*], bearing nuts.

nu·cle·ar (nōō′kli-ẽr, nū′kli-ẽr), *adj.* of, like, or forming a nucleus.

nuclear fission, the splitting of the nuclei of atoms, accompanied by conversion of part of the mass into energy: the principle of the atomic bomb.

nuclear fusion, the fusion of atomic nuclei, as of heavy hydrogen or tritium, into a nucleus of heavier mass, as of helium, with a resultant loss in the combined mass, which is converted into energy: the principle of the hydrogen bomb.

nuclear physics, the branch of physics dealing with the structure of atomic nuclei and the energies involved in nuclear changes.

nu·cle·ate (nōō′kli-it, nū′kli-āt′), *adj.* [L. *nucleatus,* having a kernel], having a nucleus. ***v.t.*** (nōō′kli-āt′, nū′kli-āt′), [NUCLEATED (-id), NUCLEATING], [< L. *nucleatus,* pp. of *nucleare,* to become like a kernel < *nucleus;* see NUCLEUS], to form into or around a nucleus. ***v.i.*** to form a nucleus.

nu·cle·a·tion (nōō′kli-ā′shən, nū′kli-ā′shən), *n.* a nucleating or being nucleated.

nu·cle·i (nōō′kli-ī′, nū′kli-ī′), *n.* plural of **nucleus.**

nu·cle·ic acid (nōō-klē′ik, nū-klē′ik), any of a group of acids occurring in organic nuclear material and consisting of a combination of phosphoric acid with a carbohydrate and a base.

nu·cle·in (nōō′kli-in, nū′kli-in), *n.* [< *nucleus* + *-in*], any of a group of colorless, amorphous protein substances found in all cell nuclei and consisting of nucleic acids combined with a base.

nu·cle·o·lar (nōō-klē′ə-lẽr, nū-klē′ə-lẽr), *adj.* of, or having the nature of, a nucleolus.

nu·cle·o·late (nōō-klē′ə-lit, nū-klē′ə-lāt′), *adj.* nucleolated.

nu·cle·o·lat·ed (nōō-klē′ə-lā′tid, nū-klē′ə-lā′tid), *adj.* having a nucleolus or nucleoli.

nu·cle·ole (nōō′klē-ōl′, nū′klē-ōl′), *n.* a nucleolus.

nu·cle·o·lus (nōō-klē′ə-ləs, nū-klē′ə-ləs), *n.* [*pl.* NUCLEOLI (-lī′)], [LL., dim. of *nucleus*], a conspicuous body, usually spherical, found in the nucleus of most cells.

nu·cle·on (nōō′kli-on, nū′kli-on), *n.* a proton or neutron in the nucleus of an atom.

nu·cle·on·ics (nōō′kli-on′iks, nū′kli-on′iks), *n.pl.* [construed as sing.], [*nuclear* + *electronics*], the branch of physics dealing with nucleons or with nuclear action.

nu·cle·o·plasm (nōō′kli-ə-plaz′m, nū′kli-ə-plaz′m), *n.* [< *nucleus* + *-plasm*], the protoplasm that composes the nucleus of a cell.

nu·cle·o·plas·mic (nōō′kli-ə-plaz′mik, nū′kli-ə-plaz′-

mik), ***adj.*** of, constituting, or like nucleoplasm.

nu·cle·o·pro·te·in (nōō′kli-ō-prō′tē-in, nū′kli-ō-prō′tēn), ***n.*** [< *nucleus* + *protein*], any of a class of compound proteins found in the nuclei of plant and animal cells, consisting of a simple protein combined with a nuclein and either a pentose or a hexose.

nu·cle·us (nōō′kli-əs, nū′kli-əs), ***n.*** [*pl.* NUCLEI (-ī′), NUCLEUSES (-iz)], [L., a nut, kernel, fruit stone, for **nuculeus*, dim. < *nux, nucis*, nut], 1. a thing or part forming the center, around which other parts or things are grouped or collected. 2. anything serving as a center of growth or development: as, the *nucleus* of an art collection. 3. in *anatomy*, a group of nerve cells in the brain or spinal column. 4. in *astronomy*, the bright central part of the head of a comet. 5. in *biology*, the central, spherical or egg-shaped mass of protoplasm present in most plant and animal cells and necessary to such functions as growth, reproduction, etc. 6. in *botany*, *a)* a nucellus. *b)* the kernel of a nut or seed. *c)* the central point in a starch grain. 7. in *chemistry & physics*, the central part of an atom, the fundamental particles of which are the proton and neutron: it carries a positive charge and constitutes almost all of the mass of the atom. 8. in *organic chemistry*, a fundamental, stable arrangement of atoms (e.g., the benzene ring) that may occur in many compounds by atomic substitution without structural change.

nude (nōōd, nūd), ***adj.*** [L. *nudus*, naked < **nogwodos* < IE. base **nogwo-dho-*; cf. NAKED], 1. naked; bare; unclothed; uncovered. 2. in *law*, without consideration: said of contracts, etc. ***n.*** [obs. Fr. *nud* < L. *nudus*, naked], a nude figure, especially as represented in painting, sculpture, etc. —*SYN.* see **bare.**

the nude, 1. the nude human figure. 2. the representation of this in art. 3. a nude condition.

nudge (nuj), ***v.t.*** [NUDGED (nujd), NUDGING], [Eng. dial. *nidge* (to strike sharp blows, shake, etc.) suggests that this and *nudge* are both < an AS. **nycgan* (transmitted via dial.); akin to MLG. *nucken*, to shake the head, *nuck, nucke*, sudden shove; IE. base **neu-*, to give a push, shove, seen also in L. *nuere*, to nod, *nutare*, to rock, shake, etc., & prob. in Norw. dial. *nugga, nyggja*, to push, jostle], to push gently, especially with the elbow, in order to get attention, hint slyly, etc. ***n.*** a gentle push with the elbow, etc.; jog.

nu·di- (nōō′di, nū′di), [< L. *nudus*], a combining form meaning *nude, bare*, as in *nudibranchiate*.

nu·di·bran·chi·ate (nōō′di-braŋ′ki-it, nū′di-braŋ′ki-āt′), ***n.*** [< Mod. L. *Nudibranchiata*, name of the suborder; see NUDI- & BRANCHIATE], any of a variety of mollusks lacking both a shell and true gills.

nu·di·caul (nōō′di-kôl′, nū′di-kôl′), ***adj.*** in *botany*, having stems without leaves.

nu·di·cau·lous (nōō′di-kô′ləs, nū′di-kô′ləs), ***adj.*** nudicaul.

nud·ism (nōōd′iz′m, nūd′iz′m), ***n.*** the practice or cult of going nude for hygienic reasons.

nud·ist (nōōd′ist, nūd′ist), ***n.*** a person who believes in or practices nudism. ***adj.*** of nudism or nudists.

nu·di·ty (nōōd′ə-ti, nūd′ə-ti), ***n.*** [< Fr. or L.; Fr. *nudité*; L. *nuditas*], 1. the state, quality, or fact of being nude; nakedness. 2. [*pl.* NUDITIES (-tiz)], anything nude.

Nu·e·ces (nōō-ā′sās), ***n.*** a river in southern Texas, flowing into the Gulf of Mexico: length, c. 310 mi.

Nue·vo Le·on (nwe′vô le-ôn′), a state of northeastern Mexico: area, 25,134 sq. mi.; pop., 525,000; capital, Monterrey.

nu·ga·to·ry (nōō′gə-tôr′i, nū′gə-tō′ri), ***adj.*** [L. *nugatorius* < *nugari*, to trifle], 1. trifling; worthless. 2. not operative; ineffectual; invalid.

nug·get (nug′it), ***n.*** [prob. dim. of Eng. dial. *nug*, a lump], a lump; especially, a lump of native gold.

nui·sance (nōō′s'ns, nū′s'ns), ***n.*** [ME. *nusance;* OFr. < *nuisir, noisir* < L. *nocere*, to annoy], an act, condition, thing, or person causing trouble, annoyance, or inconvenience.

nuisance tax, a tax considered a nuisance because it is paid in very small amounts by the consumer.

null (nul), ***adj.*** [< Fr. or L.; Fr. *nul;* L. *nullus*, not any, none < *ne-*, not + *ullus*, any, dim. of *unus*, one], 1. without legal force; not binding; void; invalid. 2. amounting to nought; nil. 3. of no value, effect, or consequence; insignificant.

null and void, without legal force; invalid.

nul·lah (nul′ə), ***n.*** [Hind. *nālā*, brook, ravine], in India, etc., 1. a gully; ravine. 2. a watercourse.

nul·li·fi·ca·tion (nul′ə-fi-kā′shən), ***n.*** [LL. *nullificatio*], 1. a nullifying or being nullified. 2. in United States history, the refusal of a State to recognize or enforce within its territory any act of Congress held to be an infringement on its sovereignty.

nul·li·fid·i·an (nul′ə-fid′i-ən), ***n.*** [< L. *nullus*, none + *fides*, faith], a person having no religious faith.

nul·li·fi·er (nul′ə-fī′ẽr), ***n.*** a person or thing that nullifies.

nul·li·fy (nul′ə-fī′), ***v.t.*** [NULLIFIED (-fīd′), NULLIFYING], [LL. *nullificare* < L. *nullus*, none + *facere*, to make], 1. to make legally null; make void; annul. 2. to make valueless or useless; bring to nothing.

SYN.—to **nullify** is literally to bring to nought, as by depriving of effectiveness, validity, etc. (the bad weather *nullified* whatever advantage we'd had); **invalidate** and **void** specifically imply a depriving of legal force or authority (to *invalidate*, or *void*, a contract); **negate** implies a bringing to a state of nonexistence, as by destroying or denying (good *negates* evil).

nul·lip·a·ra (nə-lip′ẽr-ə), ***n.*** [*pl.* NULLIPARAE (-ē′)], [Mod. L. < L. *nullus*, none (see NULL) + *parere*, to bring forth, bear], in *obstetrics*, a woman who has never given birth to a child.

nul·lip·a·rous (nə-lip′ẽr-əs), ***adj.*** of, or having the nature of, a nullipara; barren.

nul·li·pore (nul′i-pôr′, nul′i-pōr′), ***n.*** [< L. *nullus*, none (see NULL) + *porus*, a pore], a red-spored, lime-secreting seaweed.

nul·li·ty (nul′ə-ti), ***n.*** [Fr. *nullité;* ML. *nullitas*], 1. the state, quality, or fact of being null. 2. [*pl.* NULLITIES (-tiz)], anything that is null.

Num., Numbers, the fourth book of the Old Testament.

num., 1. number. 2. numeral; numerals.

Nu·man·ti·a (nōō-man′shi-ə, nū-man′shi-ə), ***n.*** an ancient city in northern Spain: beseiged and captured by Scipio the Younger (134 B.C.).

numb (num), ***adj.*** [< ME. *nome, nomen, numen*, pp. of *nimen*, to take; with unhistoric *-b* (cf. THUMB)], 1. weakened in or deprived of the power of feeling or moving; benumbed; deadened; insensible: as, *numb* with cold, *numb* with grief. 2. having the nature of numbness, as a feeling. ***v.t.*** to make numb.

num·ber (num′bẽr), ***n.*** [ME. & OFr. *nombre* < L. *numerus;* IE. base **nem-*, to distribute, seen also in Gr. *nemein*, to divide, distribute], 1. a symbol or word, or a group of either of these, showing how many or what place in a sequence: 1, 2, 3, 13, 23, 123 (one, two, three, thirteen, twenty-three, one hundred and twenty-three) are called *cardinal numbers;* 1st, 2d, 3d, 4th, 24th, 100th, 124th (first, second, third, fourth, twenty-fourth, one hundredth, one hundred and twenty-fourth) are called *ordinal numbers*. The symbol (#) is often used with a definite numeral, as in designating grade, size, rank, position, etc. See also **Arabic numerals, Roman numerals, integer, fraction, decimal, mixed number.** 2. *pl.* arithmetic. 3. the sum of any collection of persons or things; amount of units; total; aggregate. 4. a collection of persons or things; company; assemblage. 5. *a)* *also pl.* a certain, usually a considerable, company or collection; many. *b)* *pl.* numerical superiority. 6. quantity, as consisting of units. 7. one of a series or group that is numbered or thought of as numbered; specifically, *a)* a single issue of a periodical: as, the June *number* of a magazine. *b)* a single or distinct part of a program of entertainment; any of a sequence of songs, skits, etc. 8. [Colloq.], a person or thing singled out: as, this hat is a smart *number;* see also **opposite number.** 9. in *grammar*, *a)* a difference of word form to show whether one or more than one person or thing is meant. *b)* the form itself. See **dual, plural, singular.** 10. in *music*, *a)* *pl.* measures. *b)* rhythm. 11. in *poetry*, *a)* *pl.* metrical feet, verses, or verse. *b)* metrical rhythm. Abbreviated **No., no., num., n.** ***v.t.*** 1. to total the number of persons or things in; count; enumerate. 2. to give a number to; designate by number. 3. to include as one of a group, class, collection, etc. 4. to fix or limit the number or the duration of: as, his days are *numbered*. 5. to have or comprise in number. 6. to add up to; total; equal. 7. [Obs.], to allot or appoint. ***v.i.*** 1. to total; count; enumerate. 2. to be numbered; be included.

a number of, an unspecified number of; several or many.

beyond number, too numerous to be counted.

get one's number, [Slang], to discover one's true character or motives.

have one's number on it, [Slang], to be assumed to have been marked by fate for the person whom it kills: said of a bullet, etc.

one's number is up, [Slang], one's time to die, suffer, etc. has arrived.

the numbers, numbers pool.

without number, too numerous to be counted.

num·ber·less (num′bẽr-lis), ***adj.*** 1. without number; countless. 2. without a number or numbers.

number one, [Colloq.], 1. oneself. 2. the first, usually the very best, quality or grade.

Num·bers (num′bẽrz), ***n.pl.*** [construed as sing.], [transl. of Gr. *Arithmoi* (cf. ARITHMETIC): so named from containing the census of the Hebrews after the Exodus], the fourth book of the Old Testament: abbreviated **Numb., Num.**

numbers pool (or **game, racket**), an illegal lottery in which people place small bets on the order of certain numbers, usually the last three, in some tabulation of game scores, financial reports, etc. published in the daily newspapers: also called *policy game.*

numb·fish (num'fish'), *n.* [*pl.* NUMBFISH, NUMBFISHES (-iz); see FISH], a fish that can give numbing shocks by means of its electric organs; electric ray.

num·bles (num'b'lz), *n.pl.* [ME. *noumbles;* OFr. *numbles, nombles;* by dissimilation < L. *lumbulus,* dim. of *lumbus,* loin], [Archaic], the heart, lungs, liver, etc. of a deer, etc., used for food: also spelled **nombles:** cf. **humble pie.**

nu·men (nū'men), *n.* [*pl.* NUMINA (-mi-nə)], [L., akin to *-nuere,* to nod; cf. NUDGE], in *Roman mythology,* a presiding spirit; divinity.

nu·mer·a·ble (nōō'mẽr-ə-b'l, nū'mẽr-ə-b'l), *adj.* [L. *numerabilis*], that can be numbered or counted.

nu·mer·al (nōō'mẽr-əl, nū'mẽr-əl), *adj.* [LL. *numeralis* < L. *numerus;* see NUMBER], of, expressing, or denoting number or numbers. *n.* 1. a figure, letter, or word, or a group of any of these, expressing a number: see **Arabic numerals, Roman numerals.** 2. *pl.* the numerals of the year of graduation of one's class in college, etc., awarded and worn for participation in sports, etc. Abbreviated **num.** (*sing. & pl.*).

nu·mer·ar·y (nōō'mẽr-er'i, nū'mẽr-er'i), *adj.* [ML. *numerarius*], of a number or numbers.

nu·mer·ate (nōō'mə-rāt', nū'mə-rāt'), *v.t.* [NUMERATED (-id), NUMERATING], [< L. *numeratus,* pp. of *numerare;* see NUMBER], 1. to count; enumerate. 2. to read (a number or numbers expressed in figures).

nu·mer·a·tion (nōō'mə-rā'shən, nū'mə-rā'shən), *n.* [ME. *numeracioun;* L. *numeratio* < *numerare;* see NUMBER], 1. a numbering or counting; calculation. 2. a system of numbering or of reading numbers expressed in figures: see **billion, trillion, quadrillion,** etc. for differences in these as between the French system of numeration (used also in the United States) and the English system (used also in Germany).

nu·mer·a·tor (nōō'mə-rā'tẽr, nū'mə-rā'tẽr), *n.* [LL. < *numerare;* see NUMBER], 1. that term of a fraction which shows how many of the specified parts of a unit are taken: in common fractions, it is written above the line; in decimal fractions, it is written to the right of the decimal point. 2. a person or thing that numbers.

nu·mer·ic (nōō-mer'ik, nū-mer'ik), *adj.* [Fr. *numérique* < L. *numerus,* a number], numerical.

nu·mer·i·cal (nōō-mer'i-k'l, nū-mer'i-k'l), *adj.* 1. of, or having the nature of, number. 2. in or by numbers. 3. denoting (a) number. 4. expressed by a number or numbers, not by a letter or letters. 5. in *mathematics,* designating or of value or magnitude regardless of sign: as, the *numerical* value of −3 is smaller than that of −7.

nu·mer·i·cal·ly (nōō-mer'i-k'l-i, nū-mer'ik-li), *adv.* in a numerical manner; by or with respect to numbers.

nu·mer·ol·o·gy (nōō'mə-rol'ə-ji, nū'mə-rol'ə-ji), *n.* [< L. *numerus,* a number; + *-logy*], a system of occultism built around numbers, especially those giving birth dates, those which are the sum of the letters in one's name, etc.; divination by numbers.

nu·mer·ous (nōō'mẽr-əs, nū'mẽr-əs), *adj.* [L. *numerosus* < *numerus,* a number], 1. consisting of many persons or things. 2. very many. —***SYN.*** see **many.**

Nu·mid·i·a (nōō-mid'i-ə, nū-mid'i-ə), *n.* an ancient kingdom, and later a Roman province, on the northern coast of Africa.

Nu·mid·i·an (nōō-mid'i-ən, nū-mid'i-ən), *adj.* of Numidia, its people, or their language. *n.* 1. a native or inhabitant of Numidia. 2. the Hamitic language of the Numidians.

Numidian crane, the demoiselle, a variety of crane.

numis., numism., 1. numismatic. 2. numismatics.

nu·mis·mat·ic (nōō'miz-mat'ik, nū'mis-mat'ik), *adj.* [Fr. *numismatique* < L. *numisma,* a coin < Gr. *nomisma,* a coin, lit. what is sanctioned by law < *nomizein,* to sanction < *nomos,* law, custom], 1. of coins or medals or both. 2. of numismatics or numismatists.

nu·mis·mat·i·cal (nōō'miz-mat'i-k'l, nū'mis-mat'i-k'l), *adj.* numismatic.

nu·mis·mat·ics (nōō'miz-mat'iks, nū'mis-mat'iks), *n.pl.* [construed as sing.], [< *numismatic*], the study or collection of coins and medals.

nu·mis·ma·tist (nōō-miz'mə-tist, nū-mis'mə-tist), *n.* [Fr. *numismatiste;* see NUMISMATIC], a specialist in or collector of coins and medals.

nu·mis·ma·tol·o·gy (nōō-miz'mə-tol'ə-ji, nū-mis'mə-tol'ə-ji), *n.* numismatics.

num·mu·lar (num'yoo-lẽr), *adj.* [L. *nummularius* < *nummulus,* dim. of *nummus,* a coin], in *medicine,* 1. coin-shaped. 2. piled up like a roll of coins: said of agglutinating red blood cells.

num·mu·lite (num'yoo-lit'), *n.* [< L. *nummus,* a coin; + *-lite*], any of a group of nearly extinct one-celled animals with a somewhat coin-shaped shell.

num·mu·lit·ic (num'yoo-lit'ik), *adj.* containing or consisting of nummulites.

num·skull (num'skul'), *n.* [< *numb* + *skull*], a stupid person; dolt; blockhead; dunce.

Nun (nōōn), *n.* the chief mouth of the Niger River.

nun (nun), *n.* [ME. *nunne, nonne;* AS. *nunne* < LL. *nonna,* nun, child's nurse, old lady; like Gr. *nanna,* aunt, Sans. *nanā,* mother, ult. < baby talk; cf. MAMMA, PAPA], 1. a woman devoted to a religious life; especially, a member of a convent under vows, as of chastity, obedience, and poverty. 2. any of various birds, as the pigeon.

nun (nōōn, noon), *n.* [Heb. *nūn,* lit., fish], the fourteenth letter of the Hebrew alphabet (נ,ן), corresponding to English *N, n:* see **alphabet,** table.

Nunc Di·mit·tis (nuŋk di-mit'is), [L., now thou lettest depart: first words of the L. version], the song of Simeon, sung as a hymn or canticle in various liturgies: Luke 2:29-32. 2. [n- d-], *a*) departure or farewell, especially from life. *b*) permission to depart; dismissal.

nun·ci·a·ture (nun'shi-ə-chẽr), *n.* [It. *nunziatura*], the office or term of office of a nuncio.

nun·ci·o (nun'shi-ō'), *n.* [*pl.* NUNCIOS (-ōz')], [It. *nuncio, nunzio* < L. *nuncius, nuntius,* messenger; ? contr. < ***noventius** < *novus,* new + *venire,* to come], the permanent official representative of the Pope to a foreign government; papal ambassador.

nun·cle (nuŋ'k'l), *n.* [by syllabic merging of *mine* (or *an*) *uncle*], [Dial.], uncle.

nun·cu·pa·tive (nuŋ'kyoo-pā'tiv, nuŋ-kū'pə-tiv), *adj.* [LL. *nuncupativus,* so-called, nominal < L. *nuncupare,* to call by name, name before witnesses as one's heir < *nomen,* a name + *capere,* to take], oral, not written: said especially of wills.

nun·na·tion (nun-ā'shən), *n.* [Mod. L. *nunnatio* < Ar. *nun,* the letter *n;* cf. NUN (Heb. letter)], the addition of final *n* to words in which it does not historically occur, as in the declension of certain Arabic nouns.

nun·ner·y (nun'ẽr-i), *n.* [*pl.* NUNNERIES (-iz)], [ME. & OFr. *nounerie*], a community of nuns and the building or buildings in which they live; convent. —***SYN.*** see **cloister.**

nun's veiling, a soft, loosely woven, untwilled woolen material, used for veils, light dresses, etc.

nup·tial (nup'shəl, nup'chəl), *adj.* [< Fr. or L.; Fr. *nuptial;* L. *nuptialis* < *nuptiae,* marriage < *nuptus,* pp. of *nubere,* to marry], of marriage or a wedding. *n. pl.* a wedding; marriage ceremony.

Nu·rem·berg (nyoor'əm-bũrg', noor'əm-bũrg'), *n.* a city in Bavaria, Germany: pop., 431,000: site of trials (1945–1946) of Nazis accused of war crimes.

Nürn·berg (nür'n-berkh'), *n.* Nuremberg: German name.

nurse (nũrs), *n.* [ME. *norice, nurice;* OFr. *norice, nurrice;* LL. *nutricia,* a nurse, governess < L. *nutricius,* that suckles or nourishes < *nutrix, nutricis,* wet nurse, nurse < *nutrire,* to nourish, feed; IE. base ***sneu-, *snāu-,*** to trickle, seen also in Sans. *snauti,* she drips, gives milk, Gr. *naein,* to flow], 1. a woman who suckles a child not her own: now usually *wet nurse.* 2. a woman hired to take full care of another's young child or children. 3. a person trained to take care of the sick, injured, or aged, assist surgeons, etc. 4. a person or thing that nourishes, fosters, protects, or develops someone or something. 5. in *zoology,* a sexually incomplete worker bee or ant that cares for the young. *v.t.* [NURSED (nũrst), NURSING], 1. to suckle (an infant); be wet nurse for. 2. to take care of (a child or children). 3. to tend (the sick, injured, or aged). 4. to take special care of; nourish, foster, develop, or cherish: as, she's *nursing* her anger. 5. to treat; try to cure: as, he is *nursing* a cold. 6. *a*) to use, operate, or handle cautiously or carefully, so as to avoid injury, pain, exhaustion, etc.: as, he's *nursing* his injured leg. *b*) to drink slowly, so as to conserve: as, she *nursed* her highball. 7. to clasp; hold carefully; fondle. 8. in *billiards,* to keep (the balls) close together for a series of caroms. *v.i.* 1. to be suckled; feed at the breast. 2. to suckle a child. 3. to serve as a nurse.

nurse·ling (nũrs'liŋ), *n.* a nursling.

nurse·maid (nũrs'mād'), *n.* a girl or woman hired to take care of a child or children.

nurs·er·y (nũr'sẽr-i, nũrs'ri), *n.* [*pl.* NURSERIES (-iz, -riz)], [ME. *norcery;* see NURSE], 1. *a*) an infant's bedroom. *b*) a room or apartment in a home, set aside for the children as a playroom, study, dining room, etc. *c*) specially equipped quarters, as in a theater or store, where parents may temporarily leave children with trained attendants while they shop, etc. *d*) a nursery school. 2. a place where young trees or other plants are raised for experimental purposes, for transplanting, or for sale. 3. anything that nourishes, protects, develops, or fosters.

nurs·er·y·maid (nũr'sẽr-i-mād', nũrs'ri-mād'), *n.* a nursemaid.

nurs·er·y·man (nũr'sẽr-i-mən, nũrs'ri-mən), *n.* [*pl.* NURSERYMEN (-mən)], a person who owns, operates, or works in a nursery for growing trees, plants, etc.

nursery rhyme, a short, rhymed poem for children.

nursery school, a prekindergarten school for young children between the ages of 3 and 5.

nurs·ing bottle (nŭr′siŋ), a bottle with a detachable rubber nipple, for feeding liquids to babies.

nursing home, [Chiefly British], a small private hospital, especially one for **convalescents.**

nurs·ling (nŭrs′liŋ), *n.* 1. a young baby still being nursed. 2. anything that is being carefully tended or cared for. Also spelled **nurseling.**

nur·ture (nŭr′chẽr), *n.* [ME. *nuriture;* OFr. *norreture, nourture;* LL. *nutritura* < L. *nutrire*, to nourish; see NURSE], 1. anything that nourishes; food; nutriment. 2. the act or process of raising or promoting the development of; training; rearing; upbringing. 3. in *sociology*, all the environmental factors, collectively, to which the individual is subjected from conception onward, as distinguished from his nature, or heredity. *v.t.* [NURTURED (-chẽrd), NURTURING], 1. to feed or nourish; maintain; foster. 2. to raise or promote the development of; train; educate; rear.

nut (nut), *n.* [ME. *nutte, note;* AS. *hnutu;* akin to G. *nuss;* IE. base **qneu-*, little lumpish object (< **qen-*, to squeeze together), seen also in L. *nux, nucis*, nut (cf. NUX VOMICA)], 1. the dry, one-seeded fruit of any of various trees or bushes, consisting of a kernel, often edible, in a hard and woody or tough and leathery shell, more or less separable from the seed itself: walnuts, pecans, chestnuts, acorns, etc. are all *nuts*. 2. the kernel, or meat, of such a fruit. 3. loosely, any hard-shelled fruit that will keep more or less indefinitely: peanuts, almonds, and cashews are often called *nuts*. 4. a person, problem, or thing difficult to understand or handle. 5. a small block, usually of metal, with a threaded hole through the center, for screwing onto a bolt, etc. 6. [Slang], *a)* the head. *b) usually in pl.* a testicle. 7. [Slang], a queer, foolish, or demented person; eccentric. 8. *a)* a ridge of wood, ebony, etc. at the top of the fingerboard of a stringed instrument, over which the strings pass. *b)* the small knob at the end of a violin bow, for tightening or loosening the hairs. See also **nuts.** *v.i.* [NUTTED (-id), NUTTING], to hunt for or gather nuts.
 hard (or **tough**) **nut to crack,** 1. any problem, task, etc. that is difficult to solve or do. 2. a person who cannot be persuaded or convinced easily.
 off one's nut, [Slang], insane; crazy.

nu·tant (nōō′t'nt, nū′t'nt), *adj.* [L. *nutans*, ppr. of *nutare*, to nod], with the top bent downward; drooping; nodding: said of plants.

nu·ta·tion (nōō-tā′shən, nū-tā′shən), *n.* [L. *nutatio* < *nutare*, to nod], 1. the act or an instance of nodding the head. 2. in *astronomy*, a slight vibratory movement of the earth's axis. 3. in *botany*, a slight rotatory movement in the stem of a growing plant, due to the varying rates of growth in the parts of the stem.

nut-brown (nut′broun′), *adj.* dark-brown, like some ripe nuts.

nut·crack·er (nut′krak′ẽr), *n.* 1. *sometimes pl.* an instrument for cracking the shells of nuts, usually consisting of two hinged metal levers, between which the nut is squeezed. 2. *a)* a white-spotted, dark-brown European bird of the crow family, that feeds on nuts. *b)* a similar bird of western North America, with grayish plumage. *c)* a nuthatch.

nut·gall (nut′gôl′), *n.* a small, nut-shaped gall on the oak and other trees.

nut·hatch (nut′hach′), *n.* [ME. *notehach, nuttehache*, etc.; the 2d element is akin to *hack*], any of various small, nut-eating birds related to the creepers and titmice, having a sharp beak and a short tail.

nut·let (nut′lit), *n.* 1. a small nut or nutlike fruit. 2. the pit, or stone, of a cherry, peach, plum, etc.

Nut·ley (nut′li), *n.* a city in northeastern New Jersey: pop., 30,000.

nut·meat (nut′mēt′), *n.* the kernel of a nut, especially when edible.

nut·meg (nut′meg), *n.* [ME. *notemuge, nutmuge* (partial transl. of OFr. *nois mugue*) < *nut*, nut + OFr. *mugue*, musk < L. *muscus*, musk], 1. the hard, aromatic kernel of the seed of an East Indian tree: it is grated and used as a spice. 2. the tree itself.

NUTMEG
A, seed; B, ripe fruit

nut·pick (nut′pik′), *n.* a small, sharp instrument for digging out the kernels of cracked nuts.

nu·tri·a (nōō′tri-ə, nū′tri-ə), *n.* [Sp. *nutria, lutria* < L. *lutra*, otter], 1. a beaver-like South American water-dwelling rodent; coypu. 2. its short-haired, soft, brown fur, often dyed to look like beaver.

nu·tri·ent (nōō′tri-ənt, nū′tri-ənt), *adj.* [L. *nutriens*, ppr. of *nutrire*, to nourish], nutritious; nourishing. *n.* anything nutritious.

nu·tri·ment (nōō′trə-mənt, nū′trə-mənt), *n.* [L. *nutrimentum* < *nutrire*, to nourish], 1. anything that nourishes; food. 2. anything that promotes growth or development.

nu·tri·men·tal (nōō′trə-men′t'l, nū′trə-men′t'l), *adj.* having or providing nutriment; nutritious.

nu·tri·tion (nōō-trish′ən, nū-trish′ən), *n.* [< L. *nutrire*, to nourish; see NURSE], 1. a nourishing or being nourished; especially, the series of processes by which an organism takes in and assimilates food for promoting growth and replacing worn or injured tissues. 2. anything that nourishes; nourishment; food.

nu·tri·tion·al (nōō-trish′ən-'l, nū-trish′ən-'l), *adj.* of nutrition.

nu·tri·tion·ist (nōō-trish′ən-ist, nū-trish′ən-ist), *n.* a specialist in the problems of nutrition.

nu·tri·tious (nōō-trish′əs, nū-trish′əs), *adj.* [L. *nutricius;* see NURSE], nourishing; promoting growth and repairing tissues of the body.

nu·tri·tive (nōō′trə-tiv, nū′trə-tiv), *adj.* [ME. *nutritiff;* OFr. *nutritif;* ML. *nutritivus*], 1. having to do with nutrition. 2. promoting nutrition; nutritious.

nuts (nuts), *adj.* [see NUT, 6, 7], [Slang], crazy; foolish. *interj.* [Slang], an exclamation of disgust, scorn, disappointment, disapproval, refusal, etc.
 be nuts about, [Slang], 1. to be greatly in love with. 2. to like very much; be very enthusiastic about.
 nuts to (someone or **something)!,** [Slang], an exclamation indicating anger or disappointment at, disapproval or refusal of, etc. (someone or something).

nut·shell (nut′shel′), *n.* the shell enclosing the kernel of a nut.
 in a nutshell, in brief or concise form; in a few words.

nut·ter (nut′ẽr), *n.* a person who gathers nuts.

nut·ti·ness (nut′i-nis), *n.* 1. the quality or state of being nutty. 2. a nutty flavor or consistency.

nut·ting (nut′iŋ), *n.* the act or process of gathering or hunting for nuts.

nut·ty (nut′i), *adj.* [NUTTIER (-i-ẽr), NUTTIEST (-i-ist)], 1. containing or producing many nuts. 2. having a nutlike flavor. 3. [Slang], *a)* enthusiastic, often to excess. *b)* queer, foolish, demented, etc.

nux vom·i·ca (nuks′ vom′i-kə), [ML. < L. *nux*, nut (cf. NUT) + *vomere*, to vomit], 1. the poisonous, disk-like seed of an Asiatic tree, containing strychnine. 2. the tree itself. 3. a medicine made from the seed, used as a heart stimulant.

nuz·zle (nuz′'l), *v.t.* [NUZZLED (-'ld), NUZZLING], [ME. *noselen;* see NOSE, -LE, -EN], 1. to push against or rub with the nose, snout, muzzle, etc. 2. to root up with the nose or snout: said of a pig, etc. *v.i.* 1. to push or rub with the nose, etc. against or into something. 2. to lie close; nestle; snuggle.

NW, N.W., n.w., 1. northwest. 2. northwestern.

NWbN, northwest by north.

NWbW, northwest by west.

N.W.T., Northwest Territories (Canada).

N.Y., New York.

NYA, N.Y.A., National Youth Administration.

Nya·sa (nyä′sä, ni-as′ə), *n.* a lake in southeastern Africa, bordering on Nyasaland: length, 350 mi.; width, 45 mi.; area, 14,000 sq. mi.: also spelled **Nyassa.**

Nya·sa·land (nyä′sä-land′, ni-as′ə-land′), *n.* a British protectorate in southeastern Africa: part of the Federation of Rhodesia and Nyasaland: area, 47,949 sq. mi.; pop., 2,830,000; capital, Zomba.

N.Y.C., 1. New York Central. 2. New York City.

nyc·ta·gi·na·ceous (nik′tə-ji-nā′shəs), *adj.* [< Mod. L. *Nyctago*, old name of the genus (< Gr. *nyx, nyktos*, night); + *-aceous*], belonging to the four-o'clock family of plants.

nyc·ta·lo·pi·a (nik′tə-lō′pi-ə), *n.* [LL. < Gr. *nyktalōps* < *nyx, nyktos*, night + *alaos*, blind + *ōps*, the eye], night blindness.

nyc·ti- (nik′ti), [< Gr. *nyx, nyktos*, night], a combining form meaning *of* or *at night*, as in *nyctitropic*: also **nycto-** and, before a vowel, **nyct-.**

nyc·ti·trop·ic (nik′ti-trop′ik), *adj.* [*nycti-* + *-tropic*], changing position at night: said of the leaves of certain plants.

nyc·tit·ro·pism (nik-tit′rə-piz′m), *n.* the tendency of the leaves of certain plants to be nyctitropic.

nyc·to- (nik′tō, nik′tə), nycti-.

nyc·to·pho·bi·a (nik′tə-fō′bi-ə), *n.* [*nycto-* + *-phobia*], an unnatural or excessive fear of darkness or night.

Nye, Edgar Wilson (nī), (called *Bill Nye*); 1850–1896; American humorist.

Nye·man (nye′män), *n.* Niemen: the Russian name.

nyl·ghai (nil′gī), *n.* [*pl.* NYLGHAIS (-gīz), NYLGHAI; see PLURAL, II, D, 1], a nilgai.

nyl·ghau (nil′gô), *n.* [*pl.* NYLGHAUS (-gôz), NYLGHAU; see PLURAL, II, D, 1], a nilgai.

ny·lon (nī′lon), *n.* [arbitrary formation; cf. RAYON],

1. a highly elastic, very strong, synthetic material derived from coal, water, and air, and made into thread, bristles, sheets, etc. 2. *pl.* stockings made of this.

nymph (nimf), *n.* [ME. *nimphe;* OFr. *nymphe, nimphe;* L. *nympha;* Gr. *nymphē*], 1. in *Greek & Roman mythology,* any of a group of minor nature goddesses, represented as beautiful maidens living in rivers, mountains, trees, etc. 2. *a)* a lovely young woman. *b)* a young woman; maiden: literary or playful usage. 3. in *entomology, a)* the young of an insect without complete metamorphosis. *b)* a pupa.

nym·pha (nim′fə), *n.* [*pl.* NYMPHAE (-fē)], [L.], 1. a nymph (sense 3*a*). 2. *pl.* the labia minora.

nym·phae·a·ceous (nim′fi-ā′shəs), *adj.* [< L. *nymphaea,* water lily; Gr. *nymphaia* < *nymphaios,* of nymphs; + *-aceous*], belonging to the water-lily family of plants.

nymph·al (nim′f'l), *adj.* [L. *nymphalis*], of or like a nymph or nymphs.

nym·pha·lid (nim′fə-lid), *n.* [< Mod. L. *Nymphalidae,* name of the family < *Nymphalis,* name of the type genus < Gr. *nymphē,* nymph], any of a group of butterflies with very short forelegs. *adj.* of this group.

nym·phe·an (nim-fē′ən), *adj.* nymphal.

nym·pho·lep·si·a (nim′fə-lep′si-ə), *n.* nympholepsy.

nym·pho·lep·sy (nim′fə-lep′si), *n.* [< Gr. *nymphē,* nymph; + *-lepsy*], 1. in ancient times, a state of frenzy that was believed to seize any man who looked at a nymph. 2. a violent emotional state, especially that believed to result from desire for some unattainable ideal.

nym·pho·lept (nim′fə-lept′), *n.* a person who has nympholepsy.

nym·pho·lep·tic (nim′fə-lep′tik), *adj.* of or having nympholepsy.

nym·pho·ma·ni·a (nim′fə-mā′ni-ə), *n.* [Mod. L. < Gr. *nymphē,* bride; + *-mania*], excessive and uncontrollable sexual desire in a woman: cf. **satyriasis.**

nym·pho·ma·ni·ac (nim′fə-mā′ni-ak′), *adj.* of, characteristic of, or having nymphomania. *n.* a woman having nymphomania.

Nym·we·gen (nim′vā-gən), *n.* Nijmegen.

nys·tag·mic (nis-tag′mik), *adj.* of, like, or characterized by nystagmus.

nys·tag·mus (nis-tag′məs), *n.* [Mod. L.; Gr. *nystagmos,* drowsiness < *nystazein,* to be sleepy], an involuntary rapid movement of the eyeball, usually from side to side.

Nyx (niks), *n.* [Gr.], in *Greek mythology,* the goddess of night.

N.Z., N. Zeal., New Zealand.

O, o (ō), *n.* [*pl.* O's, o's, Os, os, oes (ōz)], 1. the fifteenth letter of the English alphabet: from the Greek *omega* (long *o*) and *omicron* (short *o*), both borrowed from the Phoenician: see **alphabet,** table. 2. a sound of O or o: in English, the mid back vowel, IPA [o] of cold, or its equivalent diphthong [ou]; the low central or low back vowel, IPA [a] or [ɑ] of hot; and the low back vowel, IPA [ɔ] of wrong. 3. a type or impression for O or o. 4. the numeral zero; a cipher. 5. an object shaped like O or o. 6. *a symbol for* the fifteenth (or the fourteenth if J is omitted) in a sequence or group. 7. in *physics, the symbol for* ohm. *adj.* 1. of O or o. 2. circular or oval in shape. 3. fifteenth (or fourteenth if J is omitted) in a sequence or group.

O (ō), *interj.* an exclamation variously used: 1. in direct address: as, *O* God, save us! 2. to express surprise, fear, wonder, pain, etc.: now usually *oh.* 3. at the end of a line in some ballads and songs. *n.* [*pl.* O's (ōz)], any instance of this exclamation. *O* and *oh* are now sometimes used interchangeably.

o' (ō; *unstressed* ə), *prep.* an abbreviated form of: 1. *of,* as in *o'clock.* 2. [Archaic or Dial.], *on.*

O' (ō), [Ir. *ō,* descendant], a prefix of some Irish surnames, meaning *a descendant of,* as in *O'Reilly.*

o-, in *chemistry,* ortho-.

O, 1. in *chemistry,* oxygen. 2. in *linguistics,* Old, as in *OFr.* 3. in *mathematics,* a medieval Roman numeral for 11: with a superior bar ($\bar{O}$), 11,000.

O., 1. Ocean. 2. October. 3. Ohio. 4. Ontario. 5. Oregon.

O., o., 1. *octarius,* [L.], in *pharmacy,* a pint. 2. octavo. 3. old.

o., 1. off. 2. only. 3. order. 4. in *baseball,* outs, or put-outs.

oaf (ōf), *n.* [*pl.* OAFS (ōfs), OAVES (ōvz)], [earlier *auf, ouphe* < ON. *alfr,* elf; cf. ELF], 1. originally, a changeling; child supposedly substituted by elves for a normal child; hence, 2. a misshapen or idiotic child. 3. a stupid, clumsy fellow; lout.

oaf·ish (ōf′ish), *adj.* like or characteristic of an oaf.

O·a·hu (ō-ä′hōō), *n.* the chief island of the Hawaiian Islands: area, 595 sq. mi.; pop., 500,000; chief city, Honolulu: see **Hawaiian Islands,** map.

oak (ōk), *n.* [see PLURAL, II, D, 3], [ME. *oke;* AS. *ac;* akin to G. *eiche;* IE. base **aig-,* oak, prob. seen also in L. *aesculus* (< **aig-selos*), mountain oak], 1. any of a number of large hardwood trees and bushes bearing nuts called *acorns.* 2. the wood. 3. any of various plants resembling these trees: as, poison *oak.* 4. a wreath of oak leaves. 5. woodwork, furniture, etc. made of oak. 6. [British University Slang], a door, usually of oak. *adj.* of oak; oaken.

sport one's oak, [British University Slang], to shut one's door as a sign that one does not want visitors.

oak apple (or **gall**), an applelike gall on oak trees.

oak·en (ōk′ən), *adj.* made of the wood of the oak.

Oak·land (ōk′lənd), *n.* a city in western California, on San Francisco Bay: pop., 368,000.

Oak Leaf Cluster, a bronze decoration consisting of a small cluster of oak leaves and acorns, awarded to the holder of a United States military decoration for any further award of the same medal.

Oakley, Annie, see **Annie Oakley.**

Oak Park, a city (legally, a village) in northeastern Illinois: suburb of Chicago: pop., 61,000.

Oak Ridge, a city in eastern Tennessee, near Knoxville: a center of atomic research: pop., 27,000.

oa·kum (ō′kəm), *n.* [ME. *okonie;* AS. *acumba, æcemba,* tow, oakum < *a-,* away, out + *camb,* a comb < base of *cemban,* to comb (cf. COMB, UNKEMPT); lit., what is combed out], loose, stringy, hemp fiber got by taking apart old ropes: used in packing the seams of boats.

oar (ôr, ōr), *n.* [ME. *ore;* AS. *ar;* akin to ON. *ār;* prob. IE. **ojes,* shaft, seen also in Czech *oje,* rod], 1. a long wooden pole with a broad, thin blade at one end, used in rowing or, sometimes, in steering a boat. 2. a person who uses an oar; rower. *v.t. & v.i.* to row.

put one's oar in, to be meddlesome; interfere.

rest on one's oars, to stop one's efforts in order to rest.

OAr., Old Arabic.

oared (ôrd, ōrd), *adj.* equipped with oars: often used in hyphenated compounds, meaning *equipped with* (a specified number of) *oars,* as *two-oared.*

oar·fish (ôr′fish′, ōr′fish′), *n.* [*pl.* OARFISH, OARFISHES (-iz); see FISH], any of a group of large, long deep-sea fishes, having long fins with flattened ends.

oar·less (ôr′lis, ōr′lis), *adj.* 1. having no oars: said of a boat. 2. not stirred or rippled by oars.

oar·lock (ôr′lok′, ōr′lok′), *n.* a device, often U-shaped, for holding the oar in place in rowing or steering; rowlock.

oars·man (ôrz′mən, ōrz′mən), *n.* [*pl.* OARSMEN (-mən)], a man who rows; especially, an expert at rowing.

oars·man·ship (ôrz′mən-ship′, ōrz′mən-ship′), *n.* [*oarsman* + *-ship*], the art of, or skill at, rowing.

oar·y (ôr′i, ōr′i), *adj.* like an oar in shape or function.

OAS, O.A.S., Organization of American States: see **Pan American Union.**

o·a·sis (ō-ā′sis, ō′ə-sis), *n.* [*pl.* OASES (-sēz, -sēz′)], [L.; Gr. *oasis,* fertile spot; orig. Coptic], a fertile place in a desert, due to the presence of water.

oast (ōst), *n.* [ME. *ost;* AS. *ast;* Gmc. **aist-;* IE. base **aidh-,* to burn, seen also in L. *aestus,* a heat, glow, *aestas,* summer (cf. ESTIVAL)], a kiln for drying hops, malt, or tobacco.

oat (ōt), *n.* [ME. *ote;* AS. *ate;* not found in other Gmc. languages; IE. base **oid-,* to swell, seen also in Russ. *yadritsa,* groats, Gr. *oidos,* a swelling], 1. *usually in pl. a)* a hardy cereal grass. *b)* the edible grain of this grass. 2. any of various related grasses; especially, the wild oat. 3. [Obs. or Poetic], a simple musical pipe made of an oat stalk.

feel one's oats, [Slang], 1. to be in high spirits; be frisky. 2. to feel and act important.

oat·cake (ōt′kāk′), *n.* a thin, flat, hard cake made of oatmeal.

oat·en (ōt′'n), *adj.* of or made of oats, oatmeal, or oat straw.

Oates, Titus (ōts), 1649–1705; English conspirator who fabricated the Popish Plot, a supposed Roman Catholic plot (1678) to massacre Protestants, burn London, and kill the king; convicted of perjury but later pardoned.

oat grass, any of various oatlike grasses; especially, any wild oat.

oath (ōth), *n.* [*pl.* OATHS (ōthz, ōths)], [ME. *oth;* AS. *ath;* akin to G. *eid;* IE. base **ei-*, to go; basic sense "a going to fulfill a promise"; cf. L. *ire*, to go, *iter*, a journey (cf. ITINERARY), *initium*, a beginning (cf. INITIAL), etc. < the same base], 1. *a)* a ritualistic declaration, based on an appeal to God or to some revered person or object, that one will speak the truth, keep a promise, remain faithful, etc. *b)* the pattern of words or ritual form used in making such a declaration. *c)* the thing promised or declared in this way. 2. the irreverent or profane use of the name of God or of a sacred thing to express anger or emphasize a statement. 3. a swearword; curse.

take oath, to promise or declare by making an oath; swear solemnly.

oat·meal (ōt′mēl′), *n.* 1. oats crushed into meal or flakes; rolled or ground oats. 2. a porridge made from such oats.

Oa·xa·ca (wä-hä′kä), *n.* 1. a state of southern Mexico, on the Pacific: area, 36,371 sq. mi.; pop., 1,193,000. 2. its capital: pop., 34,000.

Ob (ōb), *n.* a river in western Siberia, flowing into the Gulf of Ob: length, 3,200 mi.

Ob, Gulf of, an arm of the Arctic Ocean, in northwestern Siberia: length, c. 600 mi.

ob- (ob, əb, ōb), [< L. *ob*, prep.], a prefix meaning: 1. *to, toward, before,* as in *object.* 2. *opposed to, against,* as in *obnoxious.* 3. *upon, over,* as in *obfuscate.* 4. *completely, totally,* as in *obsolete.* 5. *inversely, oppositely,* as in *objurgate.* In words of Latin origin, *ob-* assimilates to *oc-* before *c*, as in *occur; of-* before *f*, as in *offer;* and *op-* before *p*, as in *oppress;* it becomes *o-* before *m*, as in *omit.*

ob., 1. [L.], *obiit.* 2. *obiter,* [L.], in passing. 3. oboe.

O.B., 1. Benedictine Order. 2. obstetrics.

O·ba·di·ah (ō′bə-dī′ə), [LL.; Heb. *'ōbadhyah*, lit., servant of the Lord], a masculine name. *n.* in the *Bible,* 1. one of the minor Hebrew prophets. 2. a book of the Old Testament containing his prophecies. Abbreviated **Ob., Obad.**

ob·bli·ga·to (ob′li-gä′tō), *adj.* [It., lit., obliged; L. *obligatus*, pp. of *obligare;* see OBLIGE], in *music,* not to be left out; indispensable: said of an accompaniment that has its own character and importance and is necessary to the proper performance of a piece: abbreviated **obb.** *n.* [*pl.* OBBLIGATOS (-tōz), OBBLIGATI (-tī)], a musical accompaniment, especially one of this kind. Also spelled **obligato.**

ob·cor·date (ob-kôr′dāt), *adj.* [*ob-* + *cordate*], in *botany,* heart-shaped and joined to the stem at the apex: said of certain leaves.

obdt., obedient.

ob·du·ra·cy (ob′doo-rə-si, ob′dyoo-rə-si), *n.* the quality or state of being obdurate.

ob·du·rate (ob′doo-rit, ob′dyoo-rit), *adj.* [ME.; L. *obduratus*, pp. of *obdurare*, to harden; *ob-*, intens. + *durare*, to harden < *durus*, hard], 1. not easily moved to pity or sympathy; hardhearted. 2. hardened and unrepenting; impenitent. 3. not giving in readily; stubborn; obstinate; inflexible. —*SYN.* see **inflexible.**

o·be·ah (ō′bi-ə), *n.* [of W. Afr. origin], 1. [often O-], a form of witchcraft or magic practiced by some Negroes in Africa, and formerly also in the West Indies. 2. a talisman or fetish used in such witchcraft. Also **obi.**

o·be·di·ence (ō-bē′di-əns, ə-bē′di-əns), *n.* [ME.; OFr.; L. *obedientia* < *obediens*], 1. the state or fact of being obedient; doing what is ordered; submission. 2. in the *Roman Catholic Church, a)* the Church's jurisdiction. *b)* all those who submit to this jurisdiction.

o·be·di·ent (ō-bē′di-ənt, ə-bē′di-ənt), *adj.* [ME.; L. *obediens*, ppr. of *obedire;* see OBEY], obeying or willing to obey; docile; tractable: abbreviated **obdt.**

SYN.—**obedient** suggests a giving in to the orders or instructions of one in authority or control (an *obedient* child); **docile** implies a temperament that submits easily to control or that fails to resist domination (a *docile* wife); **tractable** implies ease of management or control but does not connote the submissiveness of **docile** and applies to things as well as people (silver is a *tractable*, i.e., malleable, metal); **compliant** suggests a weakness of character that allows one to yield meekly to another's request or demand (army life had made him *compliant*); **amenable** suggests such amiability or desire to be agreeable as would lead one to submit readily (he is *amenable* to discipline). —*ANT.* disobedient, refractory.

o·bei·sance (ō-bā′s'ns, ō-bē′s'ns), *n.* [ME. *obeisaunce;* OFr. *obeissance* < *obeissant*, ppr. of *obeir*, to obey; cf. OBEY], 1. a gesture of respect or reverence, such as a bow, curtsy, etc. 2. the attitude shown by this; homage; deference: as, they did *obeisance* to him.

o·bei·sant (ō-bā′s'nt, ō-bē′s'nt), *adj.* showing or doing obeisance; respectful.

ob·e·lisk (ob′'l-isk′), *n.* [L. *obeliscus;* Gr. *obeliskos*, dim. of *obelos;* see OBELUS], 1. a tall, four-sided stone pillar tapering toward its pyramidal top: it often has hieroglyphics on it. 2. an obelus.

ob·e·lize (ob′'l-īz′), *v.t.* [OBELIZED (-īzd′), OBELIZING], [Gr. *obelizein*], to mark with an obelus.

ob·e·lus (ob′'l-əs), *n.* [*pl.* OBELI (-ī′)], [ME.; LL.; Gr. *obelos*, a needle, spit], 1. a mark (– or ÷) used in ancient manuscripts to indicate questionable passages or readings. 2. in *typography,* a reference mark (†), used to indicate footnotes, etc.; dagger; obelisk.

O·ber·am·mer·gau (ō′bẽr-äm′ẽr-gou′, ō′bẽr-am′ẽr-gou′), *n.* a town in southern Bavaria, Germany, where the Passion play is normally presented every ten years: pop., 2,000.

O·ber·hau·sen (ō′bẽr-hou′z'n), *n.* a city in the Rhine Province, Germany: pop., 174,000 (est. 1946).

O·ber·land (ō′bẽr-länt′), *n.* a mountainous district in central Switzerland.

O·ber·on (ō′bə-ron′, ō′bẽr-ən), *n.* [Fr.; OFr. *Auberon* < Gmc. base of *elf, oaf*], in early folklore, the king of fairyland and husband of Titania.

o·bese (ō-bēs′), *adj.* [L. *obesus*, pp. of *obedere*, to devour; *ob-* (see OB-) + *edere*, to eat], very fat; stout; corpulent.

o·bes·i·ty (ō-bēs′ə-ti, ō-bes′ə-ti), *n.* [Fr. *obésité;* L. *obesitas*], the quality or state of being obese.

o·bey (ō-bā′, ə-bā′), *v.t.* [ME. *obeien;* OFr. *obeir;* L. *obedire*, to obey; OL. *oboedire* < *ob-* (see OB-) + *audire*, to hear], 1. to carry out the instructions or orders of. 2. to carry out (an instruction, order, etc.). 3. to be guided by; submit to the control of: as, *obey* your common sense. *v.i.* to be obedient.

ob·fus·cate (ob-fus′kāt, ob′fəs-kāt′), *v.t.* [OBFUSCATED (-id), OBFUSCATING], [< L. *obfuscatus*, pp. of *obfuscare*, *offuscare*, to darken < *ob-* (see OB-) + *fuscare*, to obscure < *fuscus*, dark], 1. to darken; obscure; hence, 2. to confuse; stupefy; bewilder.

ob·fus·ca·tion (ob′fus-kā′shən), *n.* 1. an obfuscating or being obfuscated. 2. something that obfuscates.

o·bi (ō′bi), *n.* obeah.

o·bi (ō′bi), *n.* [Japan.], a broad sash with a bow in the back, worn by Japanese women and children.

‡ob·i·it (ob′i-it, ō′bi-it), [L.], he (or she) died: abbreviated **ob.**

o·bit (ō′bit, ob′it), *n.* [ME. *obite;* OFr.; L. *obitus*, death < pp. of *obire*, to go down, fall, die; *ob-* (see OB-) + *ire*, to go; cf. OATH], an obituary.

ob·i·ter dic·tum (ob′i-tẽr dik′təm), [*pl.* OBITER DICTA (-tə)], [L.], 1. an incidental opinion expressed by a judge, having no bearing upon the case in question, hence not binding. 2. any incidental remark.

o·bit·u·ar·y (ō-bich′ōō-er′i, ə-bich′ōō-er′i), *n.* [*pl.* OBITUARIES (-iz)], [ML. *obituarius* < L. *obitus;* see OBIT], a notice of someone's death, as in a newspaper, usually with a short biography of the deceased. *adj.* of or recording a death or deaths.

obj., 1. object. 2. objection. 3. objective.

ob·ject (ob′jikt; *for v.*, əb-jekt′, ob-jekt′), *n.* [ME.; ML. *objectum*, something thrown in the way; L. *objectus*, a casting before, that which appears, orig. pp. of *objicere* < *ob-* (see OB-) + *jacere*, to throw], 1. a thing that can be seen or touched; material thing. 2. *a)* a person or thing to which action, thought, or feeling is directed. *b)* [Colloq.], a person or thing that excites pity or ridicule. 3. what is aimed at; purpose; end; goal. 4. in *grammar,* a noun or substantive that directly or indirectly receives the action of a verb, or one that is governed by a preposition. In "Give me the book," *book* is the *direct object* and *me* is the *indirect object.* Abbreviated **obj.** 5. in *philosophy,* anything that can be known or perceived by the mind. *v.t.* 1. formerly, *a)* to oppose. *b)* to thrust in; interpose. *c)* to expose. *d)* to bring forward as a reason, instance, etc.; adduce. 2. to put forward in opposition; state by way of objection: as, it was *objected* that the new tax law was unfair to property owners. *v.i.* 1. to put forward an objection or objections; enter a protest; be opposed. 2. to feel or express disapproval or dislike.

SYN.—**object** implies opposition to something because of strong dislike or disapproval (I *object* to her meddling); **protest** implies the making of strong, formal, often written objection to something (they *protested* the new tax increases); **remonstrate** implies protest and argument in demonstrating to another that he is wrong or blameworthy (he *remonstrated* against her hostile attitude); **expostulate** suggests strong, earnest pleading or argument to change another's views or actions (I *expostulated* with him about his self-sacrifice); **demur** implies the raising of objections or the taking of exception so as to delay action (I *demurred* at her proposal to dine out). See also **intention.**—*ANT.* agree, consent, acquiesce.

object., objective.

object ball, in *billiards & pool*, the ball that the player aims to hit with the cue ball, or any ball that may be hit by the cue ball.

object glass, an objective (sense 4).

ob·jec·ti·fy (əb-jek′tə-fī′, ob-jek′tə-fī′), *v.t.* [OBJECTIFIED (-fīd′), OBJECTIFYING], [< *object* + *-fy*], to give objective form to; make objective; materialize.

ob·jec·tion (əb-jek′shən, ob-jek′shən), *n.* [ME. *objeccioun;* LL. *objectio* < pp. of *objicere;* see OBJECT], 1. a feeling or expression of opposition, disapproval, or dislike. 2. a cause for objecting; reason for opposing, disapproving, or disliking. Abbreviated **obj.**

ob·jec·tion·a·ble (əb-jek′shən-ə-b'l, ob-jek′shən-ə-b'l), *adj.* 1. open to objection. 2. disagreeable; offensive.

ob·jec·tion·a·bly (əb-jek′shən-əb-li, ob-jek′shən-əb-li), *adv.* in an objectionable manner; so as to be objectionable.

ob·jec·tive (əb-jek′tiv, ob-jek′tiv), *adj.* [ML. *objectivus*], 1. of or having to do with a known or perceived object as distinguished from something existing only in the mind of the subject, or person thinking; hence, 2. being, or regarded as being, independent of the mind; real; actual. 3. determined by and emphasizing the features and characteristics of the object, or thing dealt with, rather than the thoughts, feelings, etc. of the artist, writer, or speaker: as, an *objective* description, painting, etc.; hence, 4. without bias or prejudice; detached; impersonal. 5. being the aim or goal: as, an *objective* point. 6. in *grammar*, designating or of the case of an object of a preposition or transitive verb. 7. in *medicine*, designating or of a symptom or condition perceptible to others besides the patient. *n.* 1. anything external to or independent of the mind; something objective; reality. 2. something aimed at or striven for. 3. in *grammar*, *a)* the objective case. *b)* a word in this case. 4. in *optics*, the lens or lenses nearest to the object observed, in a microscope, telescope, etc.: see **microscope,** illus. Abbreviated **obj., object.** —*SYN.* see **fair, intention.**

ob·jec·tiv·ism (əb-jek′tiv-iz'm, ob-jek′tiv-iz'm), *n.* 1. any of various philosophical doctrines that stress the objective reality of all that is known or perceived. 2. the use of objective methods in art or literature.

ob·jec·tiv·i·ty (ob′jek-tiv′ə-ti), *n.* 1. the state or quality of being objective. 2. objective reality.

ob·ject·less (ob′jikt-lis), *adj.* 1. having no object, or purpose; aimless. 2. having no visible or concrete object: as, an *objectless* stretch of land.

object lesson, an actual or practical demonstration or exemplification of some principle.

ob·jec·tor (əb-jek′tẽr, ob-jek′tẽr), *n.* a person who objects.

‡ob·jet d'art (ôb′zhe′dȧr′), [*pl.* OBJETS D'ART (ôb′-zhe′ dȧr′)], [Fr., lit., object of art], a relatively small object of artistic value, as a figurine, vase, etc.

ob·jur·gate (ob′jẽr-gāt′, əb-jũr′gāt), *v.t.* [OBJURGATED (-id), OBJURGATING], [< L. *objurgatus*, pp. of *objurgare; ob-* (see OB-) + *jurgare*, to chide], to chide vehemently; upbraid sharply; rebuke; berate.

ob·jur·ga·tion (ob′jẽr-gā′shən), *n.* an objurgating.

ob·jur·ga·to·ry (əb-jũr′gə-tôr′i, ob-jũr′gə-tō′ri), *adj.* [L. *objurgatorius*], objurgating or tending to objurgate.

obl., 1. oblique. 2. oblong.

ob·lan·ce·o·late (ob-lan′si-ə-lit, ob-lan′si-ə-lāt′), *adj.* [*ob-* + *lanceolate*], lance-shaped, with the broad end at the top: said of a leaf.

ob·late (ob′lāt, ob-lāt′), *adj.* [ML. *oblatus*, offered, thrust forward (in L., pp. of *offerre;* see OFFER)]. 1. dedicated to a religious or monastic life. 2. [Mod. L. *oblatus; ob-* (see OB-) + *-latus* as in *prolatus* (see PROLATE): from being thrust forward at the equator], in *geometry*, flattened at the poles: as, an *oblate* spheroid. *n.* a person dedicated to a religious or monastic life.

ob·la·tion (ob-lā′shən, əb-lā′shən), *n.* [ME. *oblacioun;* OFr.; L. *oblatio*, an offering < *oblatus;* see OBLATE], 1. an offering of a sacrifice, thanksgiving, etc. to God or a god. 2. the thing or things offered; especially, the bread and wine of the Eucharist.

ob·la·to·ry (ob′lə-tôr′i, ob′lə-tō′ri), *adj.* of an oblation.

ob·li·gate (ob′lə-gāt′; *for adj.*, ob′lə-gət), *v.t.* [OBLIGATED (-id), OBLIGATING], [< L. *obligatus*, pp. of *obligare;* see OBLIGE], to bind by a contract, promise, sense of duty, etc.; put under obligation. *adj.* [ME. < L. *obligatus*], 1. bound; obliged. 2. in *biology*, limited to a certain condition of life, as a parasite.

ob·li·ga·tion (ob′lə-gā′shən), *n.* [ME. *obligacioun;* OFr.; L. *obligatio*], 1. an obligating or being obligated. 2. the contract, promise, moral responsibility, etc. binding one. 3. a duty imposed legally or socially; thing that one is bound to do as a result of a contract, promise, moral responsibility, etc. 4. the binding power of a contract, promise, moral responsibility, etc. 5. *a)* the condition or fact of being indebted to another for a favor or service received. *b)* a favor or service. 6. in *law*, *a)* an agreement by which the *obligor* is bound under penalty of law to make payment or perform services for the benefit of the *obligee*. *b)* the bond, contract, or other written document setting forth the terms of this agreement. —*SYN.* see **duty.**

ob·li·ga·to (ob′li-gä′tō), *adj.* & *n.* [*pl.* OBLIGATOS (-tōz), OBLIGATI (-ti)], obbligato.

ob·lig·a·tor·i·ly (ə-blig′ə-tôr′ə-li, ob′lig-ə-tō′rə-li), *adv.* in an obligatory manner.

ob·lig·a·tor·y (ə-blig′ə-tôr′i, ob′li-gə-tō′ri), *adj.* [Late ME.; LL. *obligatorius*], 1. legally or morally binding; constituting, or having the nature of, an obligation required. 2. in *biology*, obligate.

o·blige (ə-blīj′, ō-blīj′), *v.t.* [OBLIGED (-blījd′), OBLIGING], [ME. *obligen;* OFr. *obligier;* L. *obligare*, to bind, oblige; *ob-* (see OB-) + *ligare*, to bind], 1. to compel by moral, legal, or physical force; constrain. 2. to make indebted for a favor or kindness done; do a favor for.

ob·li·gee (ob′li-jē′), *n.* [< *oblige* + *-ee*], 1. a person obliged to do something for another: opposed to *obliger*. 2. in *law*, a person to whom another is bound by contract: opposed to *obligor*.

o·blig·er (ə-blīj′ẽr, ō-blīj′ẽr), *n.* a person who obliges.

o·blig·ing (ə-blīj′iŋ, ō-blīj′iŋ), *adj.* [ppr. of *oblige*], 1. [Rare], obligatory. 2. ready to do favors; helpful; courteous; accommodating. —*SYN.* see **amiable.**

ob·li·gor (ob′li-gôr′, ob′li-gôr′), *n.* [< *oblige* + *-or*], in *law*, a person who binds himself to another by contract: opposed to *obligee*.

ob·lique (ə-blēk′; *esp. in military use,* ō-blīk′), *adj.* [L. *obliquus* < *ob-* (see OB-) + *liquis*, awry], 1. having a slanting position or direction; neither perpendicular nor horizontal; not level or upright; inclined. 2. not straight to the point; not straightforward; indirect; hence, 3. evasive, disingenuous, underhand, etc. 4. indirectly aimed at or attained, as results, etc. 5. in *anatomy*, designating or of any of certain muscles obliquely placed and attached. 6. in *botany*, having the sides unequal, as some leaves. 7. in *grammar*, designating or of any case except the nominative and the vocative (and sometimes the accusative). 8. in *rhetoric*, indirect: said of discourse. *v.i.* [OBLIQUED (-blēkt′, -blīkt′), OBLIQUING], 1. to veer from the perpendicular; slant. 2. in *military usage*, to change the original direction of march by approximately 45 degrees. Abbreviated **obl.**

oblique angle, any angle other than a right angle; acute or obtuse angle.

oblique sailing, a ship's movement in sailing on a course that forms an oblique angle with the meridian.

ob·liq·ui·tous (ə-blik′wə-təs), *adj.* characterized by or having obliquity.

ob·liq·ui·ty (ə-blik′wə-ti), *n.* [*pl.* OBLIQUITIES (-tiz)], [ME. *obliquitee;* L. *obliquitas*], 1. the state or quality of being oblique. 2. a turning aside from moral conduct or sound thinking. 3. in *astronomy*, the angle between the planes of the earth's equator and orbit. 4. in *mathematics*, *a)* deviation of a line or plane from the perpendicular or parallel. *b)* the degree of this.

OBLIQUE ANGLES (ABC, DBA, DBC, DBE, EBN, NBC, ABT, etc.)

ob·lit·er·ate (ə-blit′ə-rāt′), *v.t.* [OBLITERATED (-id), OBLITERATING], [< L. *obliteratus*, pp. of *obliterare*, to blot out < *ob-* (see OB-) + *litera*, a letter], 1. to blot out, leaving no traces; erase; efface. 2. to do away with as if by effacing; destroy. —*SYN.* see **erase.**

ob·lit·er·a·tion (ə-blit′ə-rā′shən), *n.* [L. *obliteratio*], an obliterating or being obliterated.

ob·lit·er·a·tive (ə-blit′ə-rā′tiv), *adj.* obliterating or tending to obliterate.

ob·lit·er·a·tor (ə-blit′ə-rā′tẽr), *n.* [LL.], a person or thing that obliterates.

ob·liv·i·on (ə-bliv′i-ən), *n.* [ME.; OFr.; L. *oblivio* < *oblivisci*, to forget], 1. a forgetting or having forgotten; forgetfulness. 2. the condition or fact of being forgotten. 3. official overlooking of offenses; pardon.

ob·liv·i·ous (ə-bliv′i-əs), *adj.* [ME. *obliuyous;* L. *obliviosus* < *oblivio;* see OBLIVION], 1. forgetful; unmindful (with *of* or *to*). 2. causing forgetfulness.

ob·long (ob′lôŋ), *adj.* [ME. *oblonge;* L. *oblongus*, rather long; *ob-* (see OB-) + *longus*, long], longer than broad; elongated; specifically, *a)* rectangular and longer in one direction than in the other. *b)* elliptical. *n.* an oblong figure; anything oblong in form. Abbreviated **obl.**

ob·lo·quy (ob′lə-kwi), *n.* [*pl.* OBLOQUIES (-kwiz)], [LL. *obloquium* < *obloqui*, to speak against; *ob-* (see OB-) + *loqui*, to speak], 1. verbal abuse of a person or thing; censure or vituperation, especially when widespread or general. 2. ill repute, disgrace, or infamy resulting from this.

ob·nox·ious (əb-nok′shəs, ob-nok′shəs), *adj.* [L. *obnoxiosus* < *obnoxius*, subject, liable, or exposed to danger < *ob-* (see OB-) + *noxa,* a harm, hurt < base of *nocere,* to hurt], 1. very unpleasant; objectionable; offensive. 2. [Archaic], *a)* exposed or liable to injury, evil, or harm. *b)* liable to punishment; censurable. 3. in *law,* answerable; responsible. —*SYN.* see **hateful.**

o·boe (ō′bō, ō′boi), *n.* [It.; Fr. *hautbois;* see HAUTBOY], 1. a double-reed wood-wind instrument having a range of nearly three octaves and a high, penetrating, melancholy tone. 2. an organ stop producing an oboelike sound. Abbreviated **ob.**

OBOE

o·bo·ist (ō′bō-ist), *n.* a person who plays an oboe.

ob·ol (ob′'l), *n.* an obolus.

ob·o·lus (ob′'l-əs), *n.* [*pl.* OBOLI (-ī′)], [L.; Gr. *obolos*], 1. in ancient Greece, *a)* a coin valued at 1/6 drachma. *b)* a weight equal to 11 1/4 grains. 2. any of several small coins formerly current in Europe.

ob·o·vate (ob-ō′vāt), *adj.* inversely ovate; having the shape of the longitudinal section of an egg, with the broad end at the top, as some leaves: see **leaf,** illus.

ob·o·void (ob-ō′void), *adj.* [*ob-* + *ovoid*], egg-shaped, with the broad end at the top: said of some fruits, etc.

O·bre·gón, Ál·va·ro (äl′vä-rô′ ô′bre-gôn′), 1880–1928; Mexican soldier; president of Mexico (1920–1924).

Obs., obs., 1. obsolete. 2. observatory.

ob·scene (ob-sēn′, əb-sēn′), *adj.* [Fr. *obscène;* L. *obscenus, obscaenus* < *obs-,* var. of *ob-* (see OB-) + *caenum,* filth], 1. offensive to modesty or decency; lewd. 2. disgusting; filthy; repulsive. —*SYN.* see **coarse.**

ob·scen·i·ty (ob-sen′ə-ti, əb-sē′nə-ti), *n.* [Fr. *obscénité;* L. *obscenitas*], 1. the state or quality of being obscene. 2. [*pl.* OBSCENITIES (-tiz)], something obscene, as language, conduct, a remark, an expression, an act, etc.

ob·scur·ant (əb-skyoor′ənt, ob-skyoor′ənt), *n.* [< L. *obscurans*], a person or thing that obscures, especially one that tends to prevent human progress and enlightenment. *adj.* of or constituting an obscurant.

ob·scur·ant·ism (əb-skyoor′ən-tiz′m, ob-skyoor′ən-tiz′m) *n.* the principles or practice of an obscurant; opposition to human progress and enlightenment.

ob·scur·ant·ist (əb-skyoor′ən-tist, ob-skyoor′ən-tist), *n.* a person who advocates obscurantism. *adj.* of or like obscurantism or an obscurantist.

ob·scu·ra·tion (ob′skyoo-rā′shən), *n.* [L. *obscuratio*], an obscuring or being obscured.

ob·scure (əb-skyoor′, ob-skyoor′), *adj.* [ME.; OFr. *obscur;* L. *obscurus,* lit., covered over < base seen in Eng. *shower, sky,* etc.], 1. dim; dark; murky; gloomy: as, an *obscure* corner of the room. 2. not easily perceived; specifically, *a)* not clear or distinct; faint or undefined: as, an *obscure* figure or sound. *b)* not easily understood; vague; cryptic; ambiguous: as, an *obscure* explanation. *c)* in an inconspicuous position; hidden; hence, 3. not well known; not famous: as, an *obscure* scientist. *v.t.* [OBSCURED (-skyoord′), OBSCURING], [L. *obscurare* < the *adj.*], 1. to make obscure; specifically, *a)* to darken; make dim. *b)* to conceal from view; hide. *c)* to make less conspicuous; overshadow: as, his success *obscured* his failures. *d)* to make less intelligible; confuse: as, his testimony *obscured* the issue. 2. in *phonetics,* to decrease the quality of (a vowel) to a more or less neutral sound, as that of (ə) or (i). *n.* [Rare], obscurity.

SYN.—**obscure** applies to that which is perceived with difficulty either because it is concealed or veiled or because of obtuseness in the perceiver (his reasons remain *obscure*); **vague** implies such a lack of preciseness or exactness as to be indistinct or unclear (a *vague* idea); **enigmatic** and **cryptic** are used of that which baffles or perplexes, the latter word implying deliberate intention to puzzle (his *enigmatic* behavior, a *cryptic* warning); **ambiguous** applies to that which puzzles because it allows of more than one interpretation (an *ambiguous* title); **equivocal** is used of something ambiguous that is deliberately used to mislead or confuse (an *equivocal* answer). —*ANT.* clear, distinct, obvious.

ob·scu·ri·ty (əb-skyoor′ə-ti, ob-skyoor′ə-ti), *n.* 1. the quality or condition of being obscure. 2. [*pl.* OBSCURITIES (-tiz)], an obscure person or thing.

ob·se·crate (ob′si-krāt′), *v.t.* [OBSECRATED (-id), OBSECRATING], [< L. *obsecratus,* pp. of *obsecrare,* to beseech (on religious grounds) < *ob-* (see OB-) + *sacrare,* to make sacred < *sacer,* holy], [Rare], to beg for (something) or supplicate (someone); entreat.

ob·se·cra·tion (ob′si-krā′shən), *n.* [ME. *obsecracioun;* L. *obsecratio* < pp. of *obsecrare;* see OBSECRATE], 1. a supplication or entreaty. 2. any prayer or petition in the Litany beginning with the word *by* (L. *per*).

ob·se·qui·ous (əb-sē′kwi-əs, ob-sē′kwi-əs), *adj.* [Fr. *obséquieux;* L. *obsequiosus* < *obsequium,* complaisance < *obsequi,* to comply with], 1. excessively willing to serve or obey; overly submissive; fawning. 2. [Now Rare], compliant; devoted; dutiful. —*SYN.* see **servile.**

ob·se·quy (ob′si-kwi), *n.* [*pl.* OBSEQUIES (-kwiz)], [ME.; OFr. *obseques;* ML. *obsequiae,* by confusion with *exsequiae,* funeral < L. *obsequium,* complaisance], *usually in pl.* a funeral rite or ceremony.

ob·serv·a·ble (əb-zũr′və-b'l, ob-zũr′və-b'l), *adj.* [L. *observabilis*], 1. that can be observed; specifically, *a)* visible; discernible; noticeable. *b)* that can be kept or celebrated: as, Lincoln's birthday is an *observable* holiday. 2. that should or must be observed; specifically, *a)* deserving of attention; noteworthy. *b)* that must be kept or celebrated.

ob·serv·a·bly (əb-zũr′və-bli), *adv.* so as to be observable.

ob·serv·ance (əb-zũr′vəns, ob-zũr′vəns), *n.* [ME. *observaunce;* OFr. *observance;* L. *observantia*], 1. the act or practice of observing, or keeping a law, duty, custom, rule, etc. 2. a customary act, rite, ceremony, etc. 3. observation. 4. [Archaic], respectful attention; deference. 5. in the *Roman Catholic Church, a)* the rule or constitution to be observed by a religious order. *b)* an order observing such a rule.

ob·serv·ant (əb-zũr′vənt, ob-zũr′vənt), *adj.* [Fr., ppr. of *observer;* see OBSERVE], 1. strict in observing, or keeping, a law, custom, duty, rule, etc. (often with *of*): as, *observant* of the rules of etiquette. 2. paying careful attention; keenly watchful. 3. perceptive or alert. *n.* [O-], in the *Roman Catholic Church,* any member of a Franciscan order strictly observing the original rules, especially that of poverty.

ob·ser·va·tion (ob′zẽr-vā′shən), *n.* [ME. *observacioun;* L. *observatio*], 1. originally, observance, as of laws, customs, etc. 2. *a)* the act, practice, or power of noticing. *b)* something noticed. 3. the fact of being seen or noticed: as, let's try to avoid *observation.* 4. *a)* the act or practice of noting and recording facts and events, as for some scientific study. *b)* the data so noted and recorded. 5. a comment or remark based on something observed. 6. in *navigation, a)* the act of determining the altitude of the sun, a star, etc., in order to find the ship's position at sea. *b)* the result obtained. *adj.* for observing. —*SYN.* see **remark.**

ob·ser·va·tion·al (ob′zẽr-vā′shən-'l), *adj.* of or based on observation rather than experimentation.

observation car, a railway car at the end of a train with extra-large windows or, formerly, an open platform at the rear, for viewing the scenery along the route.

observation post, an advanced military position from which movements of the enemy can be observed, artillery fire directed, etc.: abbreviated **OP, O.P.**

ob·serv·a·to·ry (əb-zũr′və-tôr′i, ob-zũr′və-tō′ri), *n.* [*pl.* OBSERVATORIES (-iz, -riz)], [Fr. *observatoire*], 1. a building equipped for scientific observation, especially for astronomical or meteorological research. 2. any building or place providing an extensive view of the surrounding terrain. Abbreviated **Obs., obs.**

ob·serve (əb-zũrv′, ob-zũrv′), *v.t.* [OBSERVED (-zũrvd′), OBSERVING], [ME. *observen;* OFr. *observer;* L. *observare,* to watch, note; *ob-* (see OB-) + *servare,* to keep or hold], 1. to adhere to, follow, keep, or abide by (a law, custom, duty, rule, etc.). 2. to celebrate or keep (a holiday, etc.) according to custom. 3. *a)* to notice or perceive (something). *b)* to pay special attention to. 4. to say or mention casually; remark. 5. to examine scientifically. *v.i.* 1. to take notice. 2. to comment or remark (*on* or *upon*). 3. to act as an observer. —*SYN.* see **celebrate, discern.**

ob·serv·er (əb-zũr′vẽr, ob-zũr′vẽr), *n.* a person who observes something; specifically, *a)* a member of an aircraft crew whose job is to keep a lookout for the enemy and, often, to operate a machine gun. *b)* a soldier manning an observation post. *c)* an unofficial delegate to an assembly, convention, etc., sent only to observe and report the proceedings.

ob·sess (əb-ses′, ob-ses′), *v.t.* [< L. *obsessus,* pp. of *obsidere,* to besiege < *ob-* (see OB-) + *sedere,* to sit], to haunt or trouble in mind; beset; harass; preoccupy: usually in the passive voice, followed by *with* or *by.*

ob·ses·sion (əb-sesh′ən, ob-sesh′ən), *n.* [L. *obsessio*], 1. originally, the act of an evil spirit in possessing or ruling a person. 2. *a)* the fact or state of being obsessed with an idea, desire, emotion, etc. *b)* such an idea, desire, emotion, etc.

ob·ses·sive (əb-ses′iv, ob-ses′iv), *adj.* of, having the nature of, or causing an obsession or obsessions.

ob·sid·i·an (əb-sid′i-ən, ob-sid′i-ən), *n.* [L. *obsidianus,* a faulty reading of *obsianus* in Pliny, who claimed it was discovered by a person named *Obsius*], a dark, hard, glassy volcanic rock, usually having the same composition as volcanic granite.

ob·so·les·cence (ob′sə-les′'ns), *n.* [< *obsolescent*], the process or state of becoming obsolete.

ob·so·les·cent (ob′sə-les′'nt), *adj.* [L. *obsolescens*], becoming obsolete; passing out of general use, etc.

ob·so·lete (ob′sə-lēt′), *adj.* [L. *obsoletus,* pp. of *obso-*

lescere, to go out of use < *ob-* (see OB-) + *solere*, to become accustomed], 1. no longer in use or practice; discarded: distinguished from *archaic*. 2. no longer in fashion; out of date; passé: as, *obsolete* guns. 3. in *biology*, rudimentary or poorly developed as compared with its counterpart in other individuals of a related species, the opposite sex, etc.: said of an organ or the like. Abbreviated **Obs., obs.** —*SYN.* see **old.**

ob·sta·cle (ob′sti-k'l), *n.* [ME.; OFr.; L. *obstaculum*, obstacle < *obstare*, to withstand; *ob-* (see OB-) + *stare*, to stand], anything that gets in the way or hinders; impediment; obstruction; hindrance.
SYN.—**obstacle** is used of anything which literally or figuratively stands in the way of one's progress (her father's opposition remained their only *obstacle*); **impediment** applies to anything that delays or retards progress by interfering with the normal action (a speech *impediment*); **obstruction** refers to anything that blocks progress or some activity as if by stopping up a passage (your interference is an *obstruction* of justice); **hindrance** applies to anything that thwarts progress by holding back or delaying (lack of supplies is the greatest *hindrance* to my experiment); **barrier** applies to any apparently insurmountable obstacle that prevents progress or keeps separate and apart (language differences are often a *barrier* to understanding).

obstacle race, a race in which the runners must surmount obstacles, such as fences, ditches, etc.

ob·stet·ric (ob-stet′rik, əb-stet′rik), *adj.* [Mod. L. *obstetricus*, for L. *obstetricius*, belonging to a midwife < *obstetrix*, midwife, lit. she who stands before < *ob-* (see OB-) + *stare*, to stand], of childbirth or obstetrics.

ob·stet·ri·cal (ob-stet′ri-k'l, əb-stet′ri-k'l), *adj.* obstetric: abbreviated **obstet.**

ob·ste·tri·cian (ob′ste-trish′ən), *n.* a doctor who specializes in obstetrics: abbreviated **obstet.**

ob·stet·rics (ob-stet′riks, əb-stet′riks), *n.pl.* [construed as sing.], [< *obstetric*], the branch of medicine concerned with the care and treatment of women during pregnancy, childbirth, and the period immediately following: abbreviated **O.B., obstet.**

ob·sti·na·cy (ob′sti-nə-si), *n.* [ME. *obstinacie*; LL. *obstinatio*], 1. the state or quality of being obstinate; specifically, *a*) stubbornness. *b*) resistance to treatment; persistence, as of a disease. 2. [*pl.* OBSTINACIES (-siz)], an obstinate act, attitude, etc.

ob·sti·nate (ob′sti-nit), *adj.* [ME.; L. *obstinatus*, pp. of *obstinare*, to set one's mind firmly on, resolve on < *obstare*, to stand against, oppose; *ob-* (see OB-) + *stare*, to stand], 1. unreasonably determined to have one's own way; not yielding to reason or plea; stubborn; dogged; mulish. 2. resisting remedy or treatment: as, an *obstinate* fever. 3. not easily subdued, ended, etc. —*SYN.* see **stubborn.**

ob·sti·pant (ob′sti-pənt), *n.* in *medicine*, any substance that causes obstipation.

ob·sti·pa·tion (ob′sti-pā′shən), *n.* [L. *obstipatio*], in *medicine*, severe constipation.

ob·strep·er·ous (əb-strep′ẽr-əs, ob-strep′ẽr-əs), *adj.* [L. *obstreperus* < *obstrepere*, to roar at; *ob-* (see OB-) + *strepere*, to roar], noisy, boisterous, or unruly, especially in resisting or opposing. —*SYN.* see **vociferous.**

ob·struct (əb-strukt′, ob-strukt′), *v.t.* [< L. *obstructus*, pp. of *obstruere*, to block up, build against; *ob-* (see OB-) + *struere*, to pile up], 1. to block or stop up (a passage) with obstacles or impediments; dam; bar. 2. to hinder (progress, an activity, etc.); impede; check. 3. *a*) to get in the way of; cut off (an object) from view. *b*) to block (the view). —*SYN.* see **hinder.**

ob·struc·tion (əb-struk′shən, ob-struk′shən), *n.* 1. an obstructing or being obstructed. 2. anything that obstructs; hindrance. —*SYN.* see **obstacle.**

ob·struc·tion·ism (əb-struk′shən-iz'm, ob-struk′shən-iz'm), *n.* the action or policy of an obstructionist.

ob·struc·tion·ist (əb-struk′shən-ist, ob-struk′shən-ist), *n.* anyone who obstructs progress; especially, a member of a legislative group who hinders the passage of legislation by various technical maneuvers. *adj.* of obstructionists or obstructionism.

ob·struc·tive (əb-struk′tiv, ob-struk′tiv), *adj.* obstructing or tending to obstruct.

ob·stru·ent (ob′stroo͞-ənt), *adj.* [L. *obstruens*, ppr. of *obstruere*, to block up], obstructing; especially, blocking up a natural passage of the body. *n.* something, as a kidney stone, that blocks a passage of the body.

ob·tain (əb-tān′, ob-tān′), *v.t.* [ME. *obtenen*, *obteinen*; OFr. *obtenir*; L. *obtinere*, to obtain, acquire, prevail, maintain < *ob-* (see OB-) + *tenere*, to hold], 1. to get possession of, especially by trying; procure. 2. [Archaic], to arrive at; reach; achieve. *v.i.* 1. to be in force or in general usage; be established; prevail: as, peace will *obtain*. 2. [Archaic], to succeed. —*SYN.* see **get.**

ob·tain·a·ble (əb-tān′ə-b'l, ob-tān′ə-b'l), *adj.* capable of being obtained.

ob·tain·ment (əb-tān′mənt, ob-tān′mənt), *n.* [Rare], an obtaining.

ob·tect·ed (ob-tek′tid), *adj.* [< L. *obtectus*, pp. of *obtegere*, to cover over; *ob-* (see OB-) + *tegere*, to cover], enclosed in or covered with a hard outer shell: said of the pupae of certain insects.

ob·test (ob-test′, əb-test′), *v.t.* [L. *obtestari*; *ob-* (see OB-) + *testari*, to witness < *testis*, a witness], 1. to beg for; beseech; supplicate. 2. to call to witness.

ob·tes·ta·tion (ob′tes-tā′shən), *n.* an obtesting.

ob·trude (əb-tro͞od′, ob-tro͞od′), *v.t.* [OBTRUDED (-id), OBTRUDING], [L. *obtrudere*; *ob-* (see OB-) + *trudere*, to thrust], 1. to thrust forward; push out; eject. 2. to offer or force (oneself, one's opinions, etc.) upon others without being asked or wanted. *v.i.* to obtrude oneself (*on* or *upon*). —*SYN.* see **intrude.**

ob·tru·sion (əb-tro͞o′zhən, ob-tro͞o′zhən), *n.* [LL. *obtrusio*], 1. an obtruding. 2. something obtruded.

ob·tru·sive (əb-tro͞o′siv, ob-tro͞o′siv), *adj.* [L. *obtrusus*], 1. inclined to obtrude. 2. obtruding itself.

ob·tund (ob-tund′, əb-tund′), *v.t.* [ME. *obtunden*; L. *obtundere*, to strike at or upon, blunt; *ob-* (see OB-) + *tundere*, to strike], to make blunt or dull; take the edge off; make less acute; deaden.

ob·tu·rate (ob′tyoo-rāt′), *v.t.* [OBTURATED (-id), OBTURATING], [< L. *obturatus*, pp. of *obturare*, to stop up], 1. to close (an opening); stop up; obstruct. 2. to close (a gun breech) so as to keep gas from escaping when the gun is fired.

ob·tu·ra·tion (ob′tyoo-rā′shən), *n.* an obturating or being obturated.

ob·tu·ra·tor (ob′tyoo-rā′tẽr), *n.* [Mod. L. < L. *obturare*; see OBTURATE], a thing that stops or closes an opening or passage; specifically, *a*) a device on a gun breech to prevent the escape of gas on firing. *b*) in *surgery*, a plate for closing a cleft palate or other abnormal opening.

ob·tuse (əb-to͞os′, ob-tūs′), *adj.* [L. *obtusus*, blunted, dull, pp. of *obtundere*; see OBTUND], 1. not sharp or pointed; blunt. 2. greater than 90 degrees: said of an angle. 3. slow to understand or perceive; insensitive. 4. not producing a sharp impression; not acute; dull, as pain, etc. —*SYN.* see **dull.**

OBTUSE ANGLES (ABE, DBE, CBE)

ob·tu·si- (əb-to͞o′si, ob-tū′si), a combining form meaning *obtuse*, as in *obtusipennate*.

ob·tu·si·pen·nate (əb-to͞o′si-pen′āt, ob-tū′si-pen′āt), *adj.* [*obtusi-* + *pennate*], having obtuse wings.

ob·verse (əb-vũrs′; *also, & for n. always*, ob′vẽrs), *adj.* [L. *obversus*, pp. of *obvertere*, to turn toward; *ob-* (see OB-) + *vertere*, to turn], 1. turned toward the observer: opposed to *reverse*. 2. narrower at the base than at the top: as, an *obverse* leaf. 3. forming a counterpart. *n.* 1. the side, as of a coin or medal, bearing the main design: opposed to *reverse*. 2. the front or main surface of anything. 3. a counterpart. 4. in *logic*, the negative counterpart of an affirmative proposition, or the affirmative counterpart of a negative: as, "no one is infallible" is the *obverse* of "everyone is fallible."

ob·ver·sion (əb-vũr′shən, ob-vũr′zhən), *n.* [LL. *obversio* < L. *obversus*; see OBVERSE], 1. an obverting. 2. in *logic*, inference of the obverse.

ob·vert (əb-vũrt′, ob-vũrt′), *v.t.* [L. *obvertere*; see OBVERSE], 1. to turn the main surface or a different surface of (a thing) toward. 2. in *logic*, to state the obverse of (a proposition).

ob·vi·ate (ob′vi-āt′), *v.t.* [OBVIATED (-id), OBVIATING], [< L. *obviatus*, pp. of *obviare*, to prevent < *obvius*; see OBVIOUS], to do away with or prevent by effective measures; make unnecessary. —*SYN.* see **prevent.**

ob·vi·a·tion (ob′vi-ā′shən), *n.* an obviating.

ob·vi·ous (ob′vi-əs), *adj.* [L. *obvius*, in the way, meeting; see OB- & VIA], 1. easy to see or understand; plain; evident. 2. [Obs.], standing or lying in the way. —*SYN.* see **evident.**

ob·vo·lute (ob′və-lo͞ot′, ob′və-lūt′), *adj.* [L. *obvolutus*, pp. of *obvolvere*, to wrap around; *ob-* (see OB-) + *volvere*, to roll], having overlapping margins: said of leaves or petals.

ob·vo·lu·tion (ob′və-lo͞o′shən, ob′və-lū′shən), *n.* the condition of being obvolute.

ob·vo·lu·tive (ob′və-lo͞o′tiv, ob′və-lū′tiv), *adj.* obvolute.

oc- (ok, ək, ōk), ob-: used before *c*, as in *occur*.

Oc., oc., ocean.

o.c., *opere citato*, [L.], in the work cited.

oc·a·ri·na (ok′ə-rē′nə), *n.* [It., dim. of *oca*, a goose; L. *auca*, a goose: so called from its shape], a small, simple wind instrument shaped like a sweet potato and usually made of terra cotta, with finger holes and a mouthpiece: it produces soft, hollow tones.

OCARINA

O'Ca·sey, Sean (shôn ō-kā′si), 1884- ; Irish dramatist.

Occam, William of, see **Ockham, William of.**

occas., 1. occasion. 2. occasional. 3. occasionally.

oc·ca·sion (ə-kā′zhən), *n.* [ME. *occasioun*; OFr.; L. *occasio*, accidental opportunity, fit time < *occasus*, pp. of *occidere*, to fall < *ob-* (see OB-) + *cadere*, to fall], 1. a favorable time or juncture; opportunity. 2. a fact, event, or state of affairs that is the immediate cause of something: as, a mere chance meeting was the *occasion* of the renewal of their friendship. 3. *a*) a happening; occurrence. *b*) the time at which something happens; particular time: as, on the *occasion* of our last meeting. 4. a special time or event. 5. need arising from circumstances. 6. *pl.* *a*) [Obs.], needs; requirements. *b*) [Archaic], affairs; business. ***v.t.*** to be the occasion of; give occasion to; cause.

on occasion, once in a while; sometimes; occasionally.

rise to the occasion, to do whatever suddenly becomes necessary; meet an emergency.

take occasion, to use an opportunity (to do something); choose a favorable time.

oc·ca·sion·al (ə-kā′zhən-'l), ***adj.*** 1. occurring on a particular occasion. 2. of or for a special occasion. 3. acting only on special occasions. 4. of irregular occurrence; happening now and then; infrequent. 5. designating chairs, tables, etc. intended for occasional or auxiliary use. Abbreviated **occas.**

oc·ca·sion·al·ism (ə-kā′zhən-'l-iz'm), ***n.*** in *Cartesian philosophy,* the doctrine that the interaction of mind and body is occasioned by God through His producing activities in one corresponding to those in the other.

oc·ca·sion·al·ly (ə-kā′zhən-'l-i), ***adv.*** now and then; sometimes; on occasion: abbreviated **occas.**

oc·ci·dent (ok′sə-dənt), ***n.*** [ME. < L. *occidens,* direction of the setting sun < *occidere,* to fall, set; cf. ORIENT], 1. [Poetic], the west. 2. [O-], the countries west of Asia; specifically, *a*) formerly, Europe. *b*) now, also, the Western Hemisphere. Opposed to *orient, Orient.*

oc·ci·den·tal (ok′sə-den′t'l), ***adj.*** [ME. *occidentale*], 1. western. 2. [O-], of the Occident, its people, or their culture; Western. ***n.*** [usually O-], a native of the Occident, or a member of a people native to that region. Opposed to *oriental, Oriental.*

Oc·ci·den·tal·ism (ok′sə-den′t'l-iz'm), ***n.*** the spirit, character, culture, customs, etc. of the Occident.

Oc·ci·den·tal·ize (ok′sə-den′t'l-iz′), ***v.t.*** [OCCIDENTALIZED (-īzd′), OCCIDENTALIZING], to make Occidental in spirit, character, culture, customs, etc.

oc·cip·i·tal (ok-sip′ə-t'l), ***adj.*** [ML. *occipitalis*], of the occiput or the occipital bone. ***n.*** the occipital bone.

occipital bone, the bone that forms the back part of the skull: see **skull,** illus.

oc·cip·i·to- (ok-sip′ə-tō, ok-sip′ə-tə), a combining form meaning *occipital and.*

oc·ci·put (ok′si-put′), ***n.*** [*pl.* OCCIPITA (ok-sip′ə-tə)], [L. < *ob-* (see OB-) + *caput,* head], the back part of the skull or head.

oc·clude (ə-klōōd′, o-klōōd′), ***v.t.*** [OCCLUDED (-id), OCCLUDING], [L. *occludere* < *ob-* (see OB-) + *claudere,* to shut], 1. to close, shut, or block (a passage). 2. to prevent the passage of (something) by closing; shut in or out. 3. in *chemistry,* to absorb (a gas or liquid): as, palladium *occludes* hydrogen. ***v.i.*** in *dentistry,* to meet with the cusps fitting close together: said of the upper and lower teeth.

oc·clu·sion (ə-klōō′zhən, o-klōō′zhən), ***n.*** [< L. *occlusus*], an occluding or being occluded.

oc·clu·sive (ə-klōō′siv, o-klōō′siv), ***adj.*** occluding or tending to occlude.

oc·cult (ə-kult′, ok′ult), ***adj.*** [L. *occultus,* concealed, pp. of *occulere,* to cover over], 1. hidden; concealed. 2. secret; esoteric. 3. beyond human understanding; mysterious. 4. designating or of certain mystic arts or studies, such as magic, alchemy, astrology, etc. ***v.t. & v.i.*** to hide or become hidden from view; specifically, in *astronomy,* to hide by occultation.

the occult, the occult arts or studies.

oc·cul·ta·tion (ok′ul-tā′shən), ***n.*** [ME. *occultacioun;* L. *occultatio,* a hiding < *occultus;* see OCCULT], 1. concealment; disappearance. 2. in *astronomy,* the disappearance of one heavenly body behind another.

oc·cult·ism (ə-kul′tiz'm, ok′əl-tiz'm), ***n.*** 1. belief in occult forces and powers. 2. the study or practice of occult arts. Abbreviated **occult.**

oc·cu·pan·cy (ok′yoo-pən-si), ***n.*** [*pl.* OCCUPANCIES (-siz)], [< *occupant*], 1. *a*) an occupying; a taking or keeping in possession. *b*) the period during which a house, etc. is occupied. 2. in *law,* the taking possession of a previously unowned object, thus establishing ownership.

oc·cu·pant (ok′yoo-pənt), ***n.*** [< Fr. or L.; Fr. *occupant;* L. *occupans*], 1. a person who occupies. 2. a person who acquires a title to anything by occupancy.

oc·cu·pa·tion (ok′yoo-pā′shən), ***n.*** [ME. *occupacion;* OFr.; L. *occupatio*], 1. an occupying or being occupied. 2. what occupies, or engages, one's time; business; employment; vocation.

oc·cu·pa·tion·al (ok′yoo-pā′shən-'l), ***adj.*** of occupation or an occupation.

occupational disease, a disease commonly acquired by people in a particular occupation: as, silicosis is an *occupational disease* of miners.

occupational therapy, the treatment of mental and physical ailments by work designed to divert the mind or to correct a particular physical defect.

oc·cu·pi·er (ok′yoo-pī′ēr), ***n.*** a person who occupies.

oc·cu·py (ok′yoo-pī′), ***v.t.*** [OCCUPIED (-pīd′), OCCUPYING], [ME. *occupien;* OFr. *occuper;* L. *occupare,* to take possession of, possess < *ob-* (see OB-) + *capere,* to seize], 1. to take possession of by settlement or seizure. 2. to hold possession of by tenure; specifically, *a*) to dwell in. *b*) to hold (a position or office). 3. to take up or fill up (space, time, etc.). 4. to employ, busy, or engage (oneself, one's attention, mind, etc.).

oc·cur (ə-kũr′), ***v.i.*** [OCCURRED (-kũrd′), OCCURRING], [L. *occurrere,* to run, come up to, meet < *ob-* (see OB-) + *currere,* to run], 1. to be or be met with; exist: as, fish *occur* in most waters. 2. to present itself; come to mind: as, it never *occurred* to him to call. 3. to take place; happen. —***SYN.*** see **happen.**

oc·cur·rence (ə-kũr′əns), ***n.*** 1. the act or fact of occurring. 2. something that occurs; event; incident.

SYN.—**occurrence** is the general word for anything that happens or takes place (an unforeseen *occurrence*); an **event** is an occurrence of relative significance, especially one growing out of earlier happenings or conditions (the *events* that followed the surrender); an **incident** is an occurrence of relatively minor significance, often one connected with a more important event (the award was just another *incident* in his career); an **episode** is a distinct event that is complete in itself but forms part of a larger event or is one of a series of events (an *episode* of his childhood); a **circumstance** is an event that is either incidental to, or a determining factor of, another event (the *circumstances* surrounding my decision).

oc·cur·rent (ə-kũr′ənt), ***adj.*** [Fr.; L. *occurrens,* ppr.], [Rare], occurring. ***n.*** [Obs.], something that occurs.

o·cean (ō′shən), ***n.*** [ME. *occean;* L. *oceanus,* outer sea (in contrast with the Mediterranean); Gr. *ōkeanos*], 1. the great body of salt water that covers more than two thirds of the surface of the earth. 2. any of its five principal geographical divisions: the Atlantic, Pacific, Indian, Arctic, and Antarctic oceans. 3. any great expanse or quantity. Abbreviated **O., Oc., oc.**

O·ce·an·i·a (ō′shi-an′i-ə), ***n.*** the islands in the Pacific, including Melanesia, Micronesia, and Polynesia, and sometimes New Zealand, Australia, and the Malay Archipelago: also **Oceanica.**

O·ce·an·i·an (ō′shi-an′i-ən), ***adj.*** of Oceania or its peoples. ***n.*** a native of Oceania.

o·ce·an·ic (ō′shi-an′ik), ***adj.*** 1. of, living in, or produced by the ocean. 2. like the ocean; vast.

O·ce·an·i·ca (ō′shi-an′i-kə), ***n.*** Oceania.

O·ce·an·id (ō-sē′ə-nid), ***n.*** [Gr. *Ōkeanis, Ōkeanidos*], in *Greek mythology,* one of the three thousand ocean nymphs, daughters of Oceanus and Tethys.

o·ce·a·nog·ra·pher (ō′shi-ə-nog′rə-fẽr, ō′shən-og′rə-fẽr), ***n.*** a student of or specialist in oceanography.

o·ce·a·no·graph·ic (ō′shi-ən-ə-graf′ik, ō′shən-ə-graf′ik), ***adj.*** of or connected with oceanography.

o·ce·a·nog·ra·phy (ō′shi-ə-nog′rə-fi, ō′shən-og′rə-fi), ***n.*** [< *ocean* + *-graphy*], the branch of geography dealing with the ocean: abbreviated **oceanog.**

O·ce·an·us (ō-sē′ən-əs), ***n.*** [L.; Gr. *Ōkeanos;* cf. OCEAN], in *Greek mythology,* 1. a Titan who was god of the sea before Poseidon and father of the Oceanids. 2. the great outer stream supposedly encircling the earth.

o·cel·lar (ō-sel′ẽr), ***adj.*** of an ocellus or ocelli.

oc·el·late (os′ə-lāt′, ō-sel′it), ***adj.*** ocellated.

oc·el·lat·ed (os′ə-lā′tid, ō-sel′ə-tid), ***adj.*** [L. *ocellatus* < *ocellus,* little eye], 1. like an ocellus. 2. having an ocellus or ocelli. 3. spotted.

oc·el·la·tion (os′ə-lā′shən), ***n.*** 1. the condition of being ocellated. 2. an eyelike spot.

o·cel·lus (ō-sel′əs), ***n.*** [*pl.* OCELLI (-ī)], [L., dim. of *oculus,* an eye], 1. a small eye; especially, the simple, or rudimentary, eye of certain invertebrates, as distinguished from the compound eye of an insect. 2. an eyelike spot, as on a peacock's feathers.

o·ce·lot (ō′sə-lot′, os′ə-lət), ***n.*** [*pl.* OCELOTS (-lots′, -ləts), OCELOT; see PLURAL, II, D, 1], [Fr.; contr. by Buffon < Mex. *tlalocelotl* < *tlalli,* a field + *ocelotl,* jaguar], a large cat of North and South America, with a yellow or gray hide marked with black spots.

OCelt., Old Celtic.

o·cher (ō′kẽr), ***n.*** [ME. *ocra* < L. *ochra;* Gr. *ōchra* < *ōchros,* pale, pale-yellow; mod. form via. Fr. *ocre*], 1. an earthy clay containing iron ore, usually yellow or reddish brown in color: used as a pigment in paints. 2. the color of ocher; especially, dark yellow. ***v.t.*** to color or mark with ocher. Also spelled **ochre.**

o·cher·ous (ō′kẽr-əs), ***adj.*** like or containing ocher.

och·loc·ra·cy (ok-lok′rə-si), ***n.*** [Fr. *ochlocratie;* Gr. *ochlokratia* < *ochlos,* a mob, populace + *kratos,* strength, rule], government by the mob; mob rule.

och·lo·crat (ok′lə-krat′), ***n.*** [see OCHLOCRACY], a member of or believer in an ochlocracy.

och·lo·crat·ic (ok′lə-krat′ik), ***adj.*** of, like, or advocating ochlocracy.

och·one (ə-khōn′), ***interj.*** [Scot. & Irish], alas!
o·chre (ō′kẽr), ***n. & v.t.*** [OCHRED (-kẽrd), OCHRING], ocher.
o·chre·ous (ō′kẽr-əs, ō′kri-əs), ***adj.*** ocherous.
o·chroid (ō′kroid), ***adj.*** [Gr. *ōchroeidēs*, pale, like ocher < *ōchros*, pale, pale-yellow + *eidos*, a form], resembling ocher; of a dark-yellow color.
Ochs, Adolph Simon (oks), 1858–1935; American newspaper publisher.
-ock (ək), [ME. *-ok;* AS. *-oc, -uc,* dim.], a suffix used originally to form the diminutive, as in ***hillock:*** it has lost its meaning in such words as ***buttock, tussock.***
Ock·ham, William of (ok′əm), 1300?–1349?; English scholastic philosopher: also spelled **Occam.**
o'clock (ə-klok′, ō-klok′), of or according to the clock.
O'Con·nell, Daniel (ō-kon′'l), 1775–1847; Irish nationalist.
O'Con·nor, Thomas Pow·er (pou′ẽr ō-kon′ẽr), 1848–1929; Irish journalist and nationalist politician.
o·co·til·lo (ō′kə-tēl′yō; Sp. ô′kô-tē′yô), ***n.*** [*pl.* OCOTILLOS (-yōz; Sp. -yôs)], [Sp., dim. of *ocote*, Mexican pine < Nahuatl *ocotl*], a spiny desert plant with scarlet flowers.
oc·re·a (ok′ri-ə, ō′kri-ə), ***n.*** [*pl.* OCREAE (-ē′)], [L., a legging, greave], 1. in *botany*, a tubelike covering around some stems. 2. in *zoology*, a sheath.
oc·re·ate (ok′ri-it, ō′kri-āt′), ***adj.*** having an ocrea or ocreae; sheathed.
oct-, 1. octa-. 2. octo-.
Oct., October.
oct., octavo.
oc·ta- (ok′tə), [Gr. *okta-* < *oktō;* cf. EIGHT], a combining form meaning *eight*, as in *octagon*: also **octo-, oct-.**
oc·ta·chord (ok′tə-kôrd′), ***n.*** [LL. *octachordus;* Gr. *oktachordos*, eight-stringed < *oktō*, eight + *chordē*, a string], in *music*, 1. a series of eight tones; especially, an octave of the diatonic scale. 2. a musical instrument with eight strings.
oc·tad (ok′tad), ***n.*** [Gr. *oktas, oktados* < *oktō*, eight], 1. a series or group of eight. 2. in *chemistry*, an element, atom, or radical with a valence of eight.
oc·ta·gon (ok′tə-gon′, ok′tə-gən), ***n.*** [L. *octagonos;* Gr. *oktagōnos*, eight-cornered < *okta-*, eight + *gōnia*, an angle], a plane figure with eight angles and eight sides.
oc·tag·o·nal (ok-tag′ə-n'l), ***adj.*** of, or having the form of, an octagon.
oc·tag·o·nal·ly (ok-tag′ə-n'l-i), ***adv.*** in the form of an octagon.
oc·ta·he·dral (ok′tə-hē′drəl), ***adj.*** of, or having the form of, an octahedron.
oc·ta·he·drite (ok′tə-hē′drīt), ***n.*** [< LL. *octaedros* (< Gr. *oktaedros;* see OCTAHEDRON); + *-ite*], titanium dioxide, TiO_2, occurring in octahedral crystals.
oc·ta·he·dron (ok′tə-hē′drən), ***n.*** [*pl.* OCTAHEDRONS (-drənz), OCTAHEDRA (-drə)], [Gr. *oktaedron;* see OCTA- & -HEDRON], a solid figure with eight plane surfaces.

OCTAHEDRON

oc·tam·er·ism (ok-tam′ẽr-iz'm), ***n.*** the state of being octamerous.
oc·tam·er·ous (ok′tam′ẽr-əs), ***adj.*** [*octa-* + *-merous*], having eight parts in each whorl: said of flowers: also written **8-merous.**
oc·tam·e·ter (ok-tam′ə-tẽr), ***n.*** [LL., having eight feet; Gr. *oktametros;* see OCTA- & -METER], a line of verse with eight metrical feet. ***adj.*** containing eight metrical feet.
oc·tan (ok′tən), ***adj.*** [< L. *octo*, eight; + *-an*], occurring every eighth day (counting both days of occurrence). ***n.*** an octan fever, etc.
oc·tane (ok′tān), ***n.*** [*oct-* + *-ane*], an oily hydrocarbon, C_8H_{18}, occurring in petroleum, or any of a group of isomers of this substance.
octane number (or **rating**), a number representing the antiknock properties of a gasoline, etc., determined by the percentage of 2·2·4-trimethylpentane that must be mixed with *n*-heptane to produce the knocking quality of the fuel being tested: the higher the number, the greater the antiknock properties.
oc·tan·gle (ok′taŋ-g'l), ***n.*** [*oct-* + *angle*], an octagon.
oc·tan·gu·lar (ok-taŋ′gyoo-lẽr), ***adj.*** having eight angles.
Oc·tans (ok′tanz), ***n.*** [Mod. L.; see OCTANT], a southern constellation: see **constellation**, chart.
oc·tant (ok′tənt), ***n.*** [LL. *octans*, eighth part < *octo*, eight], 1. an eighth of a circle; 45° angle or arc. 2. an instrument like the sextant, for measuring angles. 3. in *astronomy*, the position of one heavenly body when it is 45° distant from another. 4. in *mathematics*, any of the eight parts into which a space is divided by three planes intersecting at a single point and at right angles to one another.
oc·tarch·y (ok′tär-ki), ***n.*** [*pl.* OCTARCHIES (-kiz)], [*oct-* + *-archy*], 1. government by eight rulers. 2. a group of eight governments or kingdoms: sometimes applied to the Heptarchy of Anglo-Saxon England: see **heptarchy.**
oc·ta·val (ok-tā′v'l, ok′ti-v'l), ***adj.*** of or in an octave or octaves.
oc·tave (ok′tāv; *also, and in music usually,* ok′tiv), ***n.*** [ME.; L. *octavus*, eighth < *octo*, eight], 1. *a*) the eighth day following a church festival, counting the festival day as the first. *b*) the entire period between the festival and this day. 2. a group of eight lines of verse; especially, the first eight lines of the Italian sonnet: also called *octet.* 3. any group of eight. 4. in *fencing*, a position of thrust or parry in which the hand is rotated with the palm up. 5. in *music*, *a*) the eighth full tone above a given tone, having twice as many vibrations per second, or below a given tone, having half as many vibrations per second. *b*) the interval of eight diatonic degrees between a tone and either of its octaves. *c*) the series of tones contained within this interval, or the keys of an instrument producing such a series. *d*) a tone and either of its octaves sounded together. *e*) an organ stop producing tones an octave above those ordinarily produced by the keys struck. ***adj.*** 1. consisting of eight, or an octave. 2. in *music*, producing tones an octave higher: as, an *octave* key.
Oc·ta·vi·a (ok-tā′vi-ə), [L., fem. of *Octavius*], a feminine name. ***n.*** the wife of Mark Antony; ?–11 B.C.
Oc·ta·vi·an (ok-tā′vi-ən), ***n.*** see **Augustus.**
Oc·ta·vi·us (ok-tā′vi-əs), [L. < *octavus*, eighth], a masculine name: feminine, *Octavia.*
oc·ta·vo (ok-tā′vō, ok-tä′vō), ***n.*** [*pl.* OCTAVOS (-vōz)], [< L. *in octavo*, in eight; *in*, in + *octavo*, abl. of *octavus*, eighth], 1. the page size of a book made up of printer's sheets folded into eight leaves, each leaf being from 5 by 8 inches to 6 by 9 1/2 inches. 2. a book consisting of pages of this size: also called *eightvo*, and written *8vo* or *8°*. ***adj.*** consisting of pages of this size. Abbreviated **O., o., oct.**
oc·ten·ni·al (ok-ten′i-əl), ***adj.*** [< LL. *octennium*, period of eight years (< L. *octo*, eight + *annus*, year); + *-al*], 1. happening every eight years. 2. lasting for eight years.
oc·ten·ni·al·ly (ok-ten′i-əl-i), ***adv.*** every eight years.
oc·tet, oc·tette (ok-tet′), ***n.*** [< L. *octo*, eight; + *duet*], 1. any group of eight; especially, an octave (sense 2). 2. in *music*, *a*) a composition for eight voices or eight instruments. *b*) the eight performers of this.
oc·til·lion (ok-til′yən), ***n.*** [Fr. < L. *octo*, eight + Fr. *million*], 1. in the United States and France, the number represented by 1 followed by 27 zeros. 2. in Great Britain and Germany, the number represented by 1 followed by 48 zeros. ***adj.*** amounting to one octillion in number.
oc·to- (ok′tō, ok-tō′, ok′tə), [Gr. *oktō-* < *oktō;* cf. EIGHT], a combining form meaning *eight*, as in *octopod:* also **octa-** and, before a vowel, **oct-.**
Oc·to·ber (ok-tō′bẽr), ***n.*** [ME.; AS.; L. < *octo*, eight: it was the eighth month of the early Roman calendar], 1. the tenth month of the year, having 31 days: abbreviated **Oct., O.** 2. [British], ale brewed in October.
October Revolution, the Russian revolution of November, 1917 (October, Old Style), in which the Kerensky government was overthrown by workers, peasants, soldiers, and sailors led by the Bolsheviks, or Communists, under Lenin, and the Soviet government was set up: see also **Russian Revolution.**
oc·to·dec·i·mo (ok′tō-des′ə-mō′), ***n.*** [*pl.* OCTODECIMOS (-mōz′)], [< L. *in octodecimo*, in eighteen; *in*, in + *octodecimo*, abl. of *octodecimus*, eighteenth], 1. the page size of a book made up of printer's sheets folded into eighteen leaves, each leaf being approximately 4 by 6 1/3 inches. 2. a book consisting of pages of this size: also called *eighteenmo*, and written ***18mo*** or ***18°***. ***adj.*** consisting of pages of this size.
oc·to·ge·nar·i·an (ok′tə-ji-nâr′i-ən), ***adj.*** [L. *octogenarius* < *octogeni*, eighty each < *octoginta*, eighty], eighty years old, or between the ages of eighty and ninety. ***n.*** a person of this age.
oc·tog·e·nar·y (ok-toj′ə-ner′i), ***adj. & n.*** [*pl.* OCTOGENARIES (-iz)], [Rare], octogenarian.
oc·to·nar·y (ok′tə-ner′i), ***adj.*** [L. *octonarius*, of eight], of or consisting of eight or groups of eight. ***n.*** [*pl.* OCTONARIES (-iz)], 1. a group of eight; ogdoad. 2. in *prosody*, a stanza of eight lines; octave.
oc·to·pod (ok′tə-pod′), ***n.*** [*octo-* + *-pod*], any animal with eight limbs; specifically, the octopus.
oc·to·pus (ok′tə-pəs), ***n.*** [*pl.* OCTOPUSES (-iz), OCTOPODES (ok-top′ə-dēz′), OCTOPI (-pī′)], [Mod. L.; Gr. *oktōpous*, eight-footed; *oktō*, eight + *pous, podos*, a foot], 1. any of a group of mollusks having a soft, saclike body, a large head with a mouth on the undersurface, and eight arms covered with suckers. 2. anything supposedly like an octopus; especially, an organization with branches that reach out in a powerful and influential manner.

OCTOPUS (4-8 ft. across)

oc·to·roon (ok'tə-rōōn'), *n.* [*octo-* + quad*roon*], a person with one Negro and seven white great-grandparents; offspring of a white and a quadroon.
oc·to·syl·lab·ic (ok'tə-si-lab'ik), *adj.* 1. containing eight syllables, as a line of verse. 2. containing lines of eight syllables. *n.* an octosyllabic line or verse.
oc·to·syl·la·ble (ok'tə-sil'ə-b'l), *n.* a line or word of eight syllables. *adj.* octosyllabic.
oc·troi (ok'troi; Fr. ôk'trwä'), *n.* [*pl.* OCTROIS (-troiz; Fr. -trwä')], [Fr. < *octroyer*, for earlier *ottroyer*, *otreier*, to grant; LL. *auctorizare* < *auctor;* see AUTHOR], 1. a tax on certain goods entering a town. 2. the place where this tax is collected. 3. the official or officials collecting this tax.
oc·tu·ple (ok'too-p'l, ok'tyoo-p'l), *adj.* [L. *octuplus* < *octo*, eight + *plicare*, to fold], 1. eightfold. 2. consisting of eight parts. *n.* something eight times as great as something else. *v.t.* [OCTUPLED (-p'ld), OCTUPLING], to multiply by eight.
oc·u·lar (ok'yoo-lẽr), *adj.* [L. *ocularis* < *oculus*, the eye], 1. of, for, or like the eye. 2. by eyesight: as, an *ocular* demonstration. *n.* the lens or lenses constituting the eyepiece of an optical instrument.
oc·u·list (ok'yoo-list), *n.* [Fr. *oculiste* < L. *oculus*, the eye], a physician specializing in the treatment of abnormalities and diseases of the eye; ophthalmologist.
oc·u·lo- (ok'yoo-lō, ok'yoo-lə), [< L. *oculus*, the eye], a combining form meaning *the eye*: also, before a vowel, **ocul-**.
oc·u·lo·mo·tor (ok'yoo-lō-mō'tẽr), *adj.* [*oculo-* + *motor*], moving the eyeball; specifically, designating the third pair of cranial nerves, arising in the midbrain and supplying four of the six muscles that move each eyeball.
OCym., Old Cymric.
Od, 'Od (od), *interj.* [often o-], [Archaic], a euphemism for *God*, used in oaths, etc.: also spelled **Odd.**
od (od), *n.* [*pl.* OD], [G.; arbitrary formation], a theoretical force formerly supposed by some to exist in nature and manifest itself in such phenomena as hypnotism, magnetism, light, etc.: also **odyl, odyle.**
O.D., 1. Doctor of Optometry. 2. Old Dutch: also **OD.** 3. overdraft. 4. overdrawn. 5. Officer of the Day.
O.D., o.d., 1. olive drab. 2. outside diameter.
o·da·lisque, o·da·lisk (ō'də-lisk'), *n.* [Fr. *odalisque* < Turk. *ōdaliq*, chambermaid < *ōdah*, chamber + *-liq*, suffix expressing function], a female slave or concubine in an Oriental harem.
ODan., Old Danish.
Odd (od), *interj.* [often o-], Od.
odd (od), *adj.* [ME. *odde;* ON. *odda-*, combining form < *oddi*, point of land, triangle, hence (from the third angle) odd number; akin to AS. *ord*, a point], 1. being one of a pair of which the other is missing: as, an *odd* glove. 2. having a remainder of one when divided by two; not even: said of numbers; hence, 3. characterized by an odd number: as, an *odd* month. 4. additional to a whole mentioned in round numbers; left over after taking a round number: as, a library of 5,000 and *odd* books, *odd* change. 5. with a relatively small amount or number over that specified: as, thirty *odd* years ago. 6. additional to what is usual, regular, habitual, accounted for, etc.; extra; occasional; incidental: as, *odd* jobs. 7. being one or more of a set, series, or group separated from the others: as, a few *odd* volumes of Dickens. 8. *a)* not usual or ordinary; singular; peculiar. *b)* queer; eccentric. *n.* an odd, or additional, thing; specifically, in *golf*, *a)* a stroke more than one's opponent has played. *b)* [British], a stroke taken from a player's total score for a hole, to give him odds. —*SYN.* see **strange.**
Odd Fellow, a member of the Independent Order of Odd Fellows, a fraternal and benevolent secret society, originated in England in the 18th century.
odd·ish (od'ish), *adj.* somewhat odd; rather queer.
odd·i·ty (od'ə-ti), *n.* 1. the state or quality of being odd; queerness; peculiarity; strangeness. 2. [*pl.* ODDITIES (-tiz)], an odd person or thing.
odd·ment (od'mənt), *n.* [*odd* + *-ment*], 1. something left over; scrap; remnant. 2. *pl.* in *printing*, parts of a book, as the title page, etc., not included in the text.
odd-pin·nate (od'pin'āt), *adj.* in *botany*, pinnate with an odd, or single, terminal leaflet: see **leaf**, illus.
odds (odz), *n.pl.* [sometimes construed as sing.], [< *odd*], 1. unequal things; inequalities. 2. [Rare], difference or amount of difference. 3. difference in favor of one side and against the other; advantage. 4. advantage given by a bettor or competitor in proportion to the assumed chances in his favor.
at odds, in disagreement; quarreling; antagonistic.
by (all) odds, by far.
the odds are, the likelihood is; the chances are.
odds and ends, scraps; remnants; oddments.
ode (ōd), *n.* [Fr.; LL. *ode, oda;* Gr. *ōidē*, song; contr. < *aoidē* < *aeidein*, to sing], 1. originally, a poem written to be sung. 2. in modern use, a lyric poem, rhymed or unrhymed, usually addressed to some person or thing and characterized by lofty feeling, elaborate form, and dignified style, but sometimes simple in form and style: see also **Pindaric.**
-ode (ōd), [< Gr. *hodos*, path, way], a suffix meaning *way, path*, as in *anode, cathode.*
-ode (ōd), [Gr. *-ōdēs, -odes* < *-o-*, ending of base or thematic vowel + *-eidēs*, like, having the same form], a suffix meaning *like* or *something like*, as in *phyllode.*
O·den·se (ō'thən-sā'), *n.* a seaport on Fyn Island, Denmark: pop., 106,000.
O·der (ō'dẽr), *n.* a river in Czechoslovakia and Poland, forming part of the boundary between Poland and Germany, flowing into the Baltic Sea: length, c. 550 mi.
O·des·sa (ō-des'ə, ə-des'ə), *n.* 1. a city in the Ukrainian S.S.R., on the Black Sea: pop., 667,000. 2. a city in west central Texas: pop., 80,000.
o·de·um (ō-dē'əm), *n.* [*pl.* ODEUMS (-əmz), ODEA (-ə)], [L.; Gr. *ōideion* < *ōidē;* see ODE], 1. in ancient Greece and Rome, a roofed building for musical performances; hence, 2. a modern concert hall.
od·ic (ōd'ik), *adj.* of or forming an ode.
od·ic (od'ik, ōd'ik), *adj.* of or connected with od.
O·din (ō'din), *n.* [Dan.; ON. *Odinn;* cf. EDDA, WEDNESDAY], in *Norse mythology*, the supreme deity, god of art, culture, war, and the dead: identified with the Teutonic Woden: also **Othin.**
o·di·ous (ō'di-əs), *adj.* [ME.; OFr. *odieus;* L. *odiosus* < *odium*, hatred], hateful; disgusting; offensive. —*SYN.* see **hateful.**
o·di·um (ō'di-əm), *n.* [L. *odium*, hatred, ill will < *odi*, I hate], 1. *a)* hatred. *b)* the state, quality, or fact of being hated. 2. the disgrace or infamy brought on by hateful action; opprobrium. —*SYN.* see **disgrace.**
O·do·a·cer (ō'dō-ā'sẽr), *n.* first barbarian ruler of Italy (476–493 A.D.); lived 434?–493 A.D.: also **Odovacar.**
o·do·graph (ō'də-graf', ō'də-gräf'), *n.* [< Gr. *hodos*, way; + *-graph*], 1. a device that records the distance traveled by a vehicle or a pedestrian. 2. a device that records the number, length, and rapidity of steps taken by a person walking.
o·dom·e·ter (ō-dom'ə-tẽr), *n.* [Gr. *hodometros* < *hodos*, way + *metron*, a measure], an instrument for measuring the distance traveled by a vehicle.
-odont (ə-dont'), [< Gr. *odōn, odontos*, a tooth], a combining form meaning *tooth*, as in *macrodont.*
o·don·tal·gi·a (ō'don-tal'ji-ə, od'on-tal'ji-ə), *n.* [Gr. *odontalgia;* see ODONTO- & -ALGIA], toothache.
o·dont·o- (ō-don'tō, ō-don'tə), [< Gr. *odōn, odontos*, a tooth], a combining form meaning *tooth* or *teeth*, as in *odontoblast, odontology:* also, before a vowel, **odont-.**
o·don·to·blast (ō-don'tə-blast'), *n.* [*odonto-* + *-blast*], one of the layers of connective tissue cells forming the outer surface of the pulp of a tooth: these cells secrete a substance which develops into dentine.
o·don·to·blas·tic (ō-don'tə-blas'tik), *adj.* of an odontoblast.
o·don·to·glos·sum (ō-don'tə-glos'əm), *n.* [Mod. L. < *odonto-* + Gr. *glōssa*, a tongue], any of a group of tropical American orchids with large flowers.
o·don·to·graph (ō-don'tə-graf', ō-don'tə-gräf'), *n.* [*odonto-* + *-graph*], 1. an instrument for laying out or marking gear teeth. 2. an instrument for recording irregularities of surface of tooth enamel.
o·don·toid (ō-don'toid), *adj.* [Gr. *odontoeidēs;* see ODONTO- & -OID], 1. toothlike. 2. designating or of a toothlike process, called the *odontoid peg* or *process*, projecting from the second vertebra of the neck, on which the top vertebra moves and rotates.
o·don·to·log·i·cal (ō-don'tə-loj'i-k'l), *adj.* of or connected with odontology.
o·don·tol·o·gy (ō'don-tol'ə-ji, od'on-tol'ə-ji), *n.* [*odonto-* + *-logy*], the science dealing with the structure, growth, and diseases of the teeth; dentistry.
o·don·toph·o·ral (ō'don-tof'ẽr-əl), *adj.* of an odontophore.
o·don·to·phore (ō-don'tə-fôr', ō-don'tə-fōr'), *n.* [*odonto-* + *-phore*], 1. the ribbonlike tongue of certain mollusks having minute teeth; radula. 2. a structure, usually protrusible, supporting the radula.
o·don·toph·o·rine (ō'don-tof'ə-rīn', ō'don-tof'ẽr-in), *adj.* of or like an odontophore.
o·don·toph·o·rous (ō'don-tof'ẽr-əs), *adj.* having an odontophore.
o·dor (ō'dẽr), *n.* [ME. via OFr. < L.], 1. that characteristic of a substance which makes it perceptible to the sense of smell; any smell, pleasant or unpleasant; fragrance; aroma. 2. a perfume. —*SYN.* see **smell.**
be in bad (or **ill**) **odor**, to have a poor reputation; be in ill repute.
o·dor·if·er·ous (ō'də-rif'ẽr-əs), *adj.* [ME. *odoryferous;* L. *odorifer* < *odor*, odor + *ferre*, to bear], giving off an odor, especially a fragrant odor.
o·dor·less (ō'dẽr-lis), *adj.* having no odor.

o·dor·ous (ō′dẽr-əs), *adj.* having an odor; especially, sweet-smelling; fragrant.
o·dour (ō′dẽr), *n.* odor: British spelling.
O·do·va·car (ō′dō-vā′kẽr), *n.* Odoacer.
-o·dus (ə-dəs), [Mod. L.; Gr. *-odous* < *odōn, odontos,* tooth], a combining form meaning *having teeth, toothed.*
od·yl, od·yle (od′il, ōd′il), *n.* [< *od* + Gr. *hylē*, matter], od.
-o·dyn·i·a (ə-din′i-ə, ə-dī′ni-ə), [Gr. *-odynia* < *odynē*, a pain], a combining form meaning *pain in* (a specified organ or part), as in *osteodynia.*
Od·ys·se·an (od′i-sē′ən), *adj.* of or like the (or an) Odyssey.
O·dys·seus (ō-dis′ūs, ō-dis′i-əs), *n.* [Gr. *Odysseus*], the hero of the *Odyssey,* a king of Ithaca and one of the Greek leaders in the Trojan War; Ulysses.
Od·ys·sey (od′ə-si), *n.* [L. *Odyssea;* Gr. *Odysseia*], 1. an ancient Greek epic poem describing the wanderings of Odysseus during the ten years after the fall of Troy: it is generally attributed to Homer. 2. [sometimes o-], [*pl.* ODYSSEYS (-sēz′)], any extended wandering or journey.
oe- (ē), e-: most words beginning with *oe-* are now more commonly written with *e-.*
OE., O.E., Old English (Anglo-Saxon).
O.E., o.e., omissions excepted.
oec·u·men·i·cal (ek′yoo-men′i-k′l, ē′kyoo-men′i-k′l), *adj.* ecumenical.
O.E.D., OED, Oxford English Dictionary.
oe·de·ma (ē-dē′mə), *n.* [*pl.* OEDEMATA (-mə-tə)], edema.
Oed·i·pus (ed′ə-pəs, ē′də-pəs), *n.* [L.; Gr. *Oidipous*], in *Greek legend,* the son of Laius and Jocasta, king and queen of Thebes, who, abandoned by his parents at birth because of the prophecy of an oracle, was raised by the king of Corinth, eventually returned to Thebes, and unwittingly killed his father and married his mother: subject of a tragedy by Sophocles.
Oedipus complex, in *psychoanalysis,* the unconscious tendency of a child to be attached to the parent of the opposite sex and hostile toward the other parent: its persistence in adult life results in neurotic disorders: sometimes restricted to a son's attachment, the term *Electra complex* being used for a daughter's.
‡oeil-de-boeuf (ö′y′-də-böf′), *n.* [*pl.* OEILS-DE-BOEUF (ö′y′-də-böf′)], [Fr., lit., eye of an ox, bull's-eye], a round or oval window.
‡oeil·lade (ö′yȧd′), *n.* [Fr. < *oeil*, an eye < L. *oculus*], an amorous or flirting glance; ogle.
oe·no·log·i·cal (ē′nə-loj′i-k′l), *adj.* of or by oenology.
oe·nol·o·gy (ē-nol′ə-ji), *n.* [< Gr. *oinos,* wine; + *-logy*], the knowledge or study of wines.
oe·no·mel (ē′nə-mel′), *n.* [LL. *oenomeli* (later also *oenomelum*); Gr. *oinomeli* < *oinos,* wine + *meli,* honey], 1. a beverage of wine and honey, drunk by the ancient Greeks. 2. [Poetic], strong, sweet speech, etc.
Oe·no·ne (ē-nō′ni), *n.* [L.; Gr. *Oinōnē*], in *Greek mythology,* a nymph who became the wife of Paris and was deserted by him for Helen of Troy.
o'er (ôr, ōr), *prep. & adv.* [Poetic], over.
oer·sted (ũr′sted), *n.* [after Hans Christian *Oersted* (1777–1851), Dan. physicist], 1. formerly, the C.G.S. unit of magnetic reluctance. 2. the C.G.S. unit of magnetic intensity.
Oe·sel (ü′zəl), *n.* an Estonian island in the Gulf of Riga: area, 1,010 sq. mi.
oe·soph·a·gus (i-sof′ə-gəs), *n.* esophagus.
oes·trin (es′trin, ēs′trin), *n.* estrin.
oes·trous (es′trəs, ēs′trəs), *adj.* estrous.
oes·trum (es′trəm, ēs′trəm), *n.* estrum.
oes·trus (es′trəs, ēs′trəs), *n.* estrus.
‡oeu·vres (ö′vr′), *n.pl.* [Fr.], works, as of literature.
of (uv, ov; *unstressed* əv), *prep.* [ME.; AS., unstressed var. of *af, æf,* away (from); akin to G. *ab;* IE. base *apo-, from, away from, as also in L. *ab* (cf. AB-), Gr. *apo-*, etc.], 1. from; specifically, *a)* derived or coming from: as, *of* good family, men *of* Ohio. *b)* resulting from; caused by; through: as, he died *of* starvation. *c)* at a distance from; apart from: as, a mile east *of* the river. *d)* proceeding as a product from; by: as, the stories *of* Poe. *e)* deprived, relieved, or separated from: as, cured *of* his disease, robbed *of* his money. *f)* from the whole, or total number, constituting: as, he gave *of* his time, one *of* his brothers. *g)* made from; using (a specified substance) as the material: as, a house *of* wood, made *of* plastic. 2. belonging to: as, the leaves *of* the book, the square root *of* a number. 3. *a)* having; possessing: as, a man *of* property. *b)* containing: as, a bag *of* peanuts. 4. that is; having the designation; specified as: as, the State *of* Utah, a height *of* six feet. 5. with (something specified) as object, goal, etc.: as, a reader *of* books. 6. having as a distinguishing quality or attribute; characterized by: as, a man *of* honor, a period *of* plenty. 7. having to do with; relating to; pertaining to; with reference to; concerning; about: as, don't think harshly *of* me. 8. set aside for; dedicated to: as, a week *of* festivities. 9. *a)* during: as, *of* recent years. *b)* on (a specified time): as, he came *of* a Saturday. 10. before: used in telling time, as, twenty *of* twelve. *Of* is also used in various idiomatic expressions (e.g., *of* course), many of which are entered in this dictionary under the key words.
of- (ôf, of, əf), ob-: used before *f,* as in *offer.*
OF., O.F., Old French.
off (ôf), *adv.* [a Late ME. variant spelling of *of,* later generalized for all occurrences of *of* in stressed positions; *off* is thus merely *of* stressed], 1. so as to be away, at a distance, to a side, etc.: as, he moved *off* toward the door. 2. so as to be no longer on, attached, united, in contact, etc.: as, he took *off* his coat, he tore a sheet *off.* 3. (a specified distance) away: *a)* in space: as, the road is 200 yards *off. b)* in time: as, my vacation is only two weeks *off.* 4. *a)* so as to be no longer in operation, function, continuance, etc.: as, he turned the motor *off. b)* to the point of completion or exhaustion: as, drink it *off.* 5. so as to be less, smaller, fewer, etc.: as, the number of customers dropped *off.* 6. away from one's work or usual activity: as, let's take the week *off. prep.* 1. (so as to be) no longer (or not) on, attached, united, etc.: as, it rolled *off* the table, the car is *off* the road. 2. from the substance of; on: as, he lived *off* the fat of the land. 3. coming or branching out from: as, an alley *off* Main Street. 4. free or relieved from: as, *off* duty. 5. not up to the usual level, standard, etc. of: as, badly *off* one's game. 6. [Colloq.], no longer using, engaging in, supporting, etc.; abstaining from: as, he's *off* liquor for life. 7. in *nautical usage,* away from (shore): as, a mile *off* shore. *adj.* 1. not on, attached, united, etc.: as, his hat is *off.* 2. not in operation, function, continuance, etc.: as, the motor is *off.* 3. gone away; on the way: as, the children are *off* to school. 4. less, smaller, fewer, etc.: as, profits are *off* this year. 5. away from work, etc.; absent: as, the office force is *off* today. 6. not up to the usual level, standard, etc.: as, an *off* season. 7. more remote; further: as, on the *off* chance, *off* side. 8. on the right: said of a horse in double harness, etc. 9. in (specified) circumstances: as, they are well *off.* 10. wrong; in error: as, you are *off* in your calculations. 11. in *cricket,* designating the side of the field facing the batsman. 12. in *nautical usage,* toward the sea; seaward. *n.* 1. the fact or condition of being off: as, I've had my *offs* and ons. 2. in *cricket,* the off side. *interj.* go away! stay away! *Off* is also used in various idiomatic expressions, many of which are entered in this dictionary under the key words. Abbreviated **o.**
be (or **take**) **off,** to go away; depart.
off and on, now and then; intermittently.
off with, put off! take off! remove!
off with you! go away! depart!
off., 1. office. 2. officer. 3. official. 4. officinal.
of·fal (ôf′'l, of′'l), *n.* [ME. *ofall,* lit., off-fall], 1. [construed as sing. or pl.], waste parts; especially, the entrails, etc. of a butchered animal. 2. refuse; garbage.
off·beat (ôf′bēt′), *n.* in *music,* any of the beats of a measure that have weak, or secondary, accents. *adj.* 1. in *jazz,* having the strong, or primary, accent on the second and fourth beats in 4/4 time: as, *offbeat* rhythm. 2. [Colloq.], not conforming to the usual pattern or trend; unconventional, unusual, strange, etc.
off·cast, off-cast (ôf′kast′, ôf′käst′), *adj. & n.* castoff.
off-chance (ôf′chans′, ôf′chäns′), *n.* a very slight chance; remote possibility.
off-col·or (ôf′kul′ẽr), *adj.* 1. varying from the usual, standard, or required color. 2. not quite proper; in rather poor taste; risqué: as, an *off-color* joke.
Of·fen·bach (ôf′ən-bäkh′), *n.* a city in Hesse, Germany: pop., 81,000.
Of·fen·bach, Jacques (zhȧk ôf′en′bäk′; G. ôf′ən-bäkh′), 1819–1880; French composer of operettas, born in Germany.
of·fend (ə-fend′), *v.i.* [ME. *offenden;* OFr. *offendre;* L. *offendere,* to strike against < *ob-* (see OB-) + OL. *fendere,* to hit, thrust], 1. to break moral laws or religious commandments; commit an offense. 2. to create resentment, anger, or displeasure; give offense. *v.t.* 1. to hurt the feelings of; cause to feel resentful, angry, or displeased; insult. 2. to be displeasing to (the taste, sense, etc.). 3. [Obs.], *a)* to transgress; violate. *b)* to cause to sin.
SYN.—**offend** implies a causing displeasure or resentment in another, intentionally or unintentionally, by wounding his feelings or by a breach of his sense of propriety (he will be *offended* if he is not invited); **affront** implies open and deliberate disrespect or offense (to *affront* one's modesty); **insult** implies an affront so insolent or contemptuously rude as to cause deep humiliation and resentment (he *insulted* me by insinuating that I had lied); **outrage** implies an extreme offense against one's sense of right, justice, propriety, etc. (he was *outraged* by the offer of a bribe).
of·fense (ə-fens′), *n.* [ME.; OFr.; L. *offensa*], 1. an offending; specifically, *a)* the act of breaking the law; sin; crime; transgression. *b)* the act of creating resentment, hurt feelings, displeasure, etc. 2. the condition of being offended, especially of feeling hurt, resentful, or angry; umbrage. 3. something that causes sinning or wrongdoing. 4. something that causes resentment, anger, etc. 5. the act of attacking

or assaulting; aggression. 6. the person, team, army, etc. that is attacking. Also spelled **offence.**

give offense, to offend; anger, insult, displease, etc.

take offense, to become offended; feel hurt, resentful, angry, etc.

SYN.—**offense** implies displeased or hurt feelings as the result of a slight, insult, etc. (don't take *offense* at my criticism); **resentment** adds implications of indignation, a brooding over an injury, and ill will toward the offender (a *resentment* cherished for days); **umbrage** implies offense or resentment at being slighted or having one's pride hurt (he took *umbrage* at the tone of her letter); **pique** suggests a passing feeling of ruffled pride, usually over a petty matter; **displeasure** may describe a feeling varying from dissatisfaction or disapproval to anger and indignation.

of·fense·less (ə-fens'lis), *adj.* 1. not offending. 2. lacking or incapable of offense.

of·fen·sive (ə-fen'siv), *adj.* [ML. *offensivus* < L. *offensa;* see OFFENSE], 1. attacking. 2. of or for attack. 3. unpleasant, as to the senses; disgusting; revolting; repugnant: as, an *offensive* odor. 4. causing resentment, anger, etc.; insulting. *n.* attitude, position, or operation of attack (often with *the*).

of·fer (ôf'ẽr, of'ẽr), *v.t.* [ME. *offrien;* AS. *offrian;* L. *offerre* < *ob-* (see OB-) + *ferre,* to bring], 1. to present to God or a god in an act of worship (often with *up*): as, he will *offer* prayers, they are *offering* up sacrifices. 2. to present for approval or acceptance; proffer; tender: as, I *offered* my services. 3. to present for consideration; suggest; propose: as, she *offered* a plan. 4. to indicate intention of; threaten or attempt: as, he *offered* to strike me, they *offered* resistance. 5. to bid (a price, etc.). *v.i.* 1. to make a presentation or sacrifice in worship. 2. to occur; present itself: as, opportunity *offered.* *n.* 1. the act of offering. 2. something offered; presentation, proposal, suggestion, bid, etc. 3. in *law,* a proposal the acceptance of which constitutes a contract.

SYN.—**offer** is the general term meaning to hold out before one for acceptance or refusal (to *offer* money, help, etc.); **proffer,** a literary term, is usually used of something intangible (she accepted the *proffered* assistance); **tender** is a formal or polite synonym (to *tender* one's thanks, resignation, etc.) and is specifically applied to something offered in payment of an obligation; **present** often adds to **offer** the idea of outward show, formality, or ceremony (to *present* a petition to Congress, to *present* a new play).

of·fer·ing (ôf'ẽr-iŋ, of'ẽr-iŋ), *n.* 1. the act of making an offer. 2. something offered; specifically, *a)* a gift or contribution. *b)* presentation in worship; oblation.

of·fer·to·ry (ôf'ẽr-tôr'i, of'ẽr-tō'ri), *n.* [*pl.* OFFERTORIES (-iz, -riz)], [ME. *offertorie;* OFr. *offertoire;* LL. *offertorium,* place for offerings], 1. that part of the Mass or Holy Communion during which the unconsecrated bread and wine of the Eucharist are offered to God: in the Anglican Church, alms are collected at this time. 2. the prayers recited or hymn sung at this time. 3. the alms collected at this time; hence, 4. any money collected at a church service.

off·hand (ôf'hand'), *adv.* without prior preparation or study; at once; extemporaneously. *adj.* 1. said or done offhand; extemporary; unpremeditated; hence, 2. casual, curt, informal, brusque, etc.

off·hand·ed (ôf'han'did), *adj.* offhand.

of·fice (ôf'is, of'is), *n.* [ME. *offiz,* etc.; OFr.; L. *officium;* prob. < *opus,* a work + *facere,* to make], 1. something performed or intended to be performed for another; (specified kind of) service: as, this was done through his good (or ill) *offices.* 2. a function or duty assigned to someone, especially as an essential part of his work or position. 3. a position of authority or trust, especially in a government, corporation, etc.: as, the *office* of president. 4. any of the branches of the United States Government ranking next below the departments: as, the Printing *Office.* 5. *a)* the building, room, or series of rooms in which the affairs of a business, professional person, branch of government, etc. are carried on. *b)* all the people working in such a place; staff. *c)* all the administrative officers or executives of a business, etc. 6. *pl.* the rooms or buildings of a house or estate in which the servants carry out their duties. 7. a religious or social ceremony or rite; specifically, *a)* the daily service of the Roman Catholic breviary: also called *Divine Office.* *b)* the Morning and Evening Prayer of the Anglican Church. *c)* the service of Holy Communion. *d)* prayers or rites for any special purpose: as, the *Office* of the Dead. Abbreviated **off.** —*SYN.* see **function, position.**

office boy, a boy hired to do the small tasks in an office.

of·fice·hold·er (ôf'is-hōl'dẽr, of'is-hōl'dẽr), *n.* a person holding an office; especially, a government official holding office through political patronage.

office hours, the time of day during which an office is normally open for business.

of·fi·cer (ôf'ə-sẽr, of'ə-sẽr), *n.* [ME.; Anglo-Fr. & OFr. *officier;* ML. *officiarius* < L. *officium,* office], 1. anyone elected or appointed to an office or position of authority in a government, business, institution, social club, etc. 2. a policeman or constable. 3. a person appointed to a position of authority in the armed forces of a country, especially one holding a commission or rank; commissioned officer. 4. the captain or any of the mates of a ship. 5. in certain honorary societies, a member holding one of the higher grades. Abbreviated **off.** *v.t.* 1. to provide with officers. 2. to command; direct; manage.

officer of the day, in *military usage,* the officer in over-all charge of the interior guard and security of his garrison for any given day: abbreviated **O.D.**

officer of the guard, in *military usage,* an officer detailed under the officer of the day to be in immediate command of the interior guard of a garrison: abbreviated **O.G.**

office seeker, a person who tries to get himself appointed to public office.

of·fi·cial (ə-fish'əl), *adj.* [ME.; OFr.; LL. *officialis*], 1. of or holding an office, or position of authority. 2. coming from the proper authority; authorized: as, an *official* reprimand. 3. befitting a person of authority in his capacity as an officer; formal; ceremonious. 4. in *pharmacy,* contained in the current pharmacopoeia; authorized for use in medicine. *n.* a person holding office, especially public office. Abbreviated **off.**

of·fi·cial·dom (ə-fish'əl-dəm), *n.* 1. officials collectively. 2. excessive adherence to official routine; officialism. 3. the domain or position of officials.

official family, the cabinet of the President of the United States: a journalistic term.

of·fi·cial·ism (ə-fish'əl-iz'm), *n.* 1. the characteristic practices and behavior of officials; especially, excessive adherence to official routine and regulations; red tape. 2. officials collectively; officialdom.

of·fi·cial·ly (ə-fish'əl-i), *adv.* in an official manner or capacity.

of·fi·ci·ant (ə-fish'i-ənt), *n.* [< ML. *officians*], an officiating priest, minister, etc.

of·fi·ci·ar·y (ə-fish'i-er'i), *n.* [*pl.* OFFICIARIES (-iz)], [ML. *officiarius*], a group of officials. *adj.* connected with or resulting from the holding of an office.

of·fi·ci·ate (ə-fish'i-āt'), *v.i.* [OFFICIATED (-id), OFFICIATING], [ML. *officiare*], 1. to perform the duties of an office; act as an officer. 2. to perform the functions of a priest, minister, etc.; conduct a religious service.

of·fi·ci·a·tion (ə-fish'i-ā'shən), *n.* the act of officiating.

of·fi·ci·a·tor (ə-fish'i-ā'tẽr), *n.* a person who officiates.

of·fic·i·nal (ə-fis'i-n'l), *adj.* [ML. *officinalis* < L. *officina,* workshop, contr. of *opificina* < *opifex,* worker < *opus,* a work + *facere,* to do], authorized and kept in stock in a pharmacy: said of drugs, etc. *n.* an officinal drug or preparation. Abbreviated **off.**

of·fi·cious (ə-fish'əs), *adj.* [< Fr. or L.; Fr. *officieux;* L. *officiosus* < *officium,* office], 1. [Obs.], ready to serve; obliging. 2. offering unnecessary and unwanted advice or services; meddlesome. 3. in *diplomacy,* unofficial; informal: as, an *officious* statement.

off·ing (ôf'iŋ), *n.* [< *off*], 1. the distant part of the sea visible from the shore. 2. distance, or position at a distance, from the shore.

in the offing, 1. barely visible from shore. 2. far but in sight. 3. at some vague future time.

off·ish (ôf'ish), *adj.* [Colloq.], inclined to remain aloof.

off·print (ôf'print'), *n.* a separate reprint of an article etc. that first appeared in a magazine or other larger publication. *v.t.* to reprint (an excerpt, etc.) separately.

off·scour·ing (ôf'skour'iŋ), *n.* *usually pl.* something scoured off; garbage; rubbish; refuse; filth.

off·set (ôf'set'; *for v.,* ôf-set'), *n.* 1. something that is set off, or has sprung or developed, from something else; offshoot; extension; branch; spur. 2. anything that balances, counteracts, or compensates for something else; compensation. 3. in *architecture,* a ledge or recess formed in a wall by a reduction in its thickness above. 4. in *botany,* a side shoot that takes root and starts a new plant. 5. in *electricity,* a branch off a main power line. 6. in *mechanics,* a curve or bend in a metal bar, pipe, etc. to permit it to pass an obstruction. 7. in *printing,* *a)* offset printing. *b)* an impression made by this process. *c)* an ink smudge transferred from a freshly printed sheet to the one next to it. 8. in *surveying,* a short distance measured at right angles from the main line to help in computing the area of an irregular plot of ground. *v.t.* [OFFSET, OFFSETTING], 1. to balance, complement, counteract, compensate for, etc. 2. to make an offset in. 3. in *printing,* *a)* to make (an impression) by offset printing. *b)* to smudge with an offset. *v.i.* 1. to come out or develop as an offset. 2. in *printing,* to make an offset.

offset printing, a printing process in which the inked impression is first made on a rubber-covered roller, then transferred to paper.

off·shoot (ôf′sho͞ot′), *n.* anything that branches off, or derives from, a main source; specifically, a shoot or stem growing laterally from the main stem of a plant.

off·shore (ôf′shôr′, ôf′shōr′), *adj.* 1. moving off or away from the shore. 2. situated or in operation at some distance from shore. *adv.* away or far from the shore; seaward.

off·side (ôf′sīd′), *adj.* in certain sports, not in the proper position for play; specifically, in *football*, over the line of scrimmage or otherwise ahead of the ball before the play has properly begun, and hence subject to penalty: said of a player, team, or play. *n.* an offside play. Also **off side.**

off·spring (ôf′spriŋ′), *n.* [sometimes construed as pl.], [ME. & AS. *ofspring;* see OFF & SPRING], 1. a child or children; descendant or descendants; progeny; issue: as, John is my only *offspring*, she has six *offspring*. 2. a product, outcome, or result.

off-stage (ôf′stāj′), *n.* that part of a stage not visible to the audience. *adj.* in or from the off-stage: as, an *off-stage* whisper. *adv.* to the off-stage: as, he went *off-stage*.

off-white (ôf′hwīt′), *adj.* of an off shade of white; especially, grayish-white.

O'Fla·her·ty, Li·am (lē′əm ō-fla′hẽr-ti), 1896– ; Irish novelist and short-story writer.

OFr., Old French.

OFris., Old Frisian.

oft (ôft), *adv.* [ME.; AS.; akin to G. *oft*, Dan. *ofte*, Sw. *ofta*, Goth. *ufta*, etc.], [Rare or Poetic], often.

of·ten (ôf′′n; *frequently* ôf′t′n), *adv.* [ME. var. of *oft(e)*, with adj. suffix used before vowels; see OFT], many times; repeatedly; frequently. *adj.* [Archaic], frequent.

oft·en·times (ôf′′n-tīmz′, ôf′t′n-tīmz′), *adv.* often.

oft·times (ôf′tīmz′, ôft′tīmz′), *adv.* [Archaic or Poetic], often.

OG., Old German.

O.G., 1. Officer of the Guard. 2. in *philately*, original gum.

O·ga·sa·wa·ra Ji·ma (ô-gä′sä-wä′rä jē′mä), the Bonin Islands in the Pacific: the Japanese name.

Og·den (og′dən, ôg′dən), *n.* a city in northern Utah: pop., 70,000.

og·do·ad (og′dō-ad′), *n.* [< Gr. *ogdoas* < *oktō*, eight (via L.)], 1. the number eight. 2. any group or series of eight.

o·gee (ō-jē′, ō′jē), *n.* [ME. (pl.) *oggez;* OFr. *ogive, augive;* cf. OGIVE], 1. a molding having an S-shaped curve in profile. 2. any S-shaped curve or line. 3. an ogee arch.

ogee arch, a pointed arch formed with the curve of an ogee on each side.

O·gil·vie, John (ō′g′l-vi), 1797–1867; Scottish lexicographer.

o·gi·val (ō-jī′v′l), *adj.* 1. of, or having the form of, an ogive. 2. characterized by ogives.

o·give (ō′jīv, ō-jīv′), *n.* [Fr.], 1. the diagonal rib or groin of a Gothic vault. 2. a pointed, or Gothic, arch.

OGEE ARCH

o·gle (ō′g′l), *v.i. & v.t.* [OGLED (-g′ld), OGLING], [prob. < LG. *oegeln* < *oog*, the eye], to keep looking (at) with fondness or desire; make eyes (at). *n.* an ogling look.

O·gle·thorpe, James Edward (ō′g′l-thôrp′), 1696–1785; English general; founder of the colony of Georgia.

Og·pu (og′po͞o), *n.* [Russ. < *O*tdelenie *G*osudarstvenni *P*oliticheskoi *U*pravi, Special Government Political Administration], formerly, the state security police, or secret service, of the Soviet Union, succeeding the Cheka in 1922, and now abolished: also called *Gay-Pay-Oo, G.P.U.*: see **MVD.**

o·gre (ō′gẽr), *n.* [Fr.; first used in Perrault's fairy tales & prob. coined by him], 1. in fairy tales and folklore, a man-eating monster or giant. 2. a hideous, coarse, or cruel man.

o·gre·ish (ō′gẽr-ish), *adj.* like or characteristic of an ogre.

o·gress (ō′gris), *n.* a female ogre.

o·grish (ō′grish), *adj.* ogreish.

O·gyg·i·a (ō-jij′i-ə), *n.* [L.; Gr. *Ōgygia*], in Homer's *Odyssey*, the island of the sea nymph Calypso.

oh (ō), *interj.* an exclamation expressing surprise, fear, wonder, pain, etc. *n.* [*pl.* OH'S, OHS (ōz)], any instance of this exclamation. See also **O.**

O. Henry, see **Henry, O.**

OHG., O.H.G., Old High German.

O·hi·o (ō-hī′ō), *n.* 1. a Middle Western State of the United States: area, 41,222 sq. mi.; pop., 9,706,000; capital, Columbus: abbreviated **O.**: nicknamed *Buckeye State*. 2. a river formed by the junction of the Monongahela and the Allegheny at Pittsburgh, flowing southwestward into the Mississippi: length, 981 mi.

O·hi·o·an (ō-hī′ə-wən), *adj.* of Ohio. *n.* a native or inhabitant of Ohio.

ohm (ōm), *n.* [after Georg S. *Ohm*], the unit of electrical resistance, equal to the resistance of a circuit in which an electromotive force of one volt maintains a current of one ampere: symbol, Ω (no period).

Ohm, Ge·org Si·mon (gā-ôrkh′ zē′môn ōm), 1787–1854; German physicist.

ohm·age (ōm′ij), *n.* [*ohm* + *-age*], the electrical resistance of a conductor, expressed in ohms.

ohm·ic (ōm′ik), *adj.* 1. of the ohm. 2. measured in ohms.

ohm·me·ter (ōm′mē′tẽr), *n.* [*ohm* + *-meter*], an instrument for measuring electrical resistance in ohms.

O.H.M.S., On His (or Her) Majesty's Service.

Ohm's law, a law, formulated by Ohm, which states that the intensity of a constant electrical current in a circuit is directly proportional to the electromotive force and inversely proportional to the resistance.

o·ho (ō-hō′), *interj.* [ME. phr. *o ho!;* cf. O, OH], an exclamation expressing surprise, taunting, etc.

Oh·ře (ôr′zhe), *n.* a river in northern Bohemia, Czechoslovakia, flowing into the Elbe: length, 190 mi.: German name, *Eger*.

-oid (oid), [Gr. *-o-eidēs; -o-*, termination of prec. element + *-eidēs*, -oid < *eidos*, a form, shape], a suffix meaning *like, resembling*, as in *anthropoid, celluloid*.

-oi·de·a (oi′di-ə), [Mod. L.; see -OID], a combining form used in zoology to form the names of classes or superfamilies.

oil (oil), *n.* [ME. *oile* (also, earlier *oli*); OFr. *oile, oille;* L. *oleum*, oil], 1. any of various kinds of greasy, combustible substances obtained from animal, vegetable, and mineral matter: oils are liquid at ordinary temperatures and soluble in certain organic solvents, as ether, but not in water. 2. petroleum. 3. any of various substances having the consistency of oil. 4. an oil color. 5. an oil painting. 6. [Colloq.], flattery. *v.t.* 1. to smear, lubricate, or supply with oil. 2. to bribe. *v.i.* to turn into oil by melting. *adj.* of, from, like, or yielding oil, or having to do with the production or use of oil.

pour oil on troubled waters, to settle quarrels, differences, etc. by calm, soothing methods.

strike oil, 1. to discover oil under the ground by drilling a shaft for it. 2. to become suddenly wealthy.

oil·bird (oil′bũrd′), *n.* the guacharo, a bird of South America, from which an oily fat is extracted.

oil cake, a cake or mass of crushed linseed, rapeseed, cottonseed, etc. from which the oil has been extracted: it is used as feed for cattle and as a fertilizer.

oil·can (oil′kan′), *n.* a can for holding oil, especially one with a spout, used for lubricating machinery, etc.

Oil City, a city in northwestern Pennsylvania: pop., 18,000.

oil·cloth (oil′klôth′), *n.* cloth made waterproof by being coated with paint or treated with oil, used for covering tables, shelves, etc.

oil color, a color or paint made by grinding a pigment in oil, often linseed oil.

oil·cup (oil′kup′), *n.* a cylindrical container (in a machine) for holding oil and releasing it gradually as lubrication for the moving parts.

oil·er (oil′ẽr), *n.* 1. a person or thing that oils machinery, engines, etc. 2. an oilcan. 3. a ship for transporting oil; tanker. 4. [Colloq.], an oilskin coat.

oil field, a place where oil deposits of value are found.

oil·i·ly (oil′ə-li), *adv.* in an oily manner.

oil·i·ness (oil′i-nis), *n.* an oily quality or condition.

oil of turpentine, a colorless, volatile oil distilled from the oleoresin of any of several trees, as the terebinth, pine, fir, etc., used in paints, varnishes, and disinfectants, in pharmacy, etc.: also **turpentine, spirits of turpentine.**

oil of vitriol, [so called because green vitriol was its source], sulfuric acid.

oil painting, 1. a picture painted in oil colors. 2. the art of painting in oil colors.

oil·pa·per (oil′pā′pẽr), *n.* paper made transparent and waterproof by treatment with oil.

Oil Rivers, 1. the rivers of the Niger Delta. 2. the region surrounding these rivers, formerly a British protectorate, now a part of Nigeria.

oil·skin (oil′skin′), *n.* 1. cloth made waterproof by treatment with oil. 2. *often in pl.* a garment made of this.

oil·stone (oil′stōn′), *n.* a whetstone treated with oil.

oil well, a well bored through layers of rock, etc. to a supply of petroleum.

oil·y (oil′i), *adj.* [OILIER (-i-ẽr), OILIEST (-i-ist)], 1. of, like, consisting of, or containing oil. 2. covered with oil; fat; greasy. 3. too smooth; slippery; unctuous.

oint·ment (oint′mənt), *n.* [ME. & OFr. *oignement;* LL. **unguimentum*, for L. *unguentum* (see UNGUENT): the *-t-* in Eng. results from association with obs. v. *oint*, to anoint], a fatty substance applied to the skin for healing or cosmetic purposes; salve; **unguent.**

OIr., Old Irish.

Oir·each·tas (er′əkh-təs), *n.* [Ir.], the legislature of Ireland, consisting of the Dail Eireann (lower house) and the Seanad Eireann (upper house).

Oi·rot Autonomous Region (oi-rot′), a division of

the R.S.F.S.R., in south central Siberia: area, 35,936 sq. mi.; pop., 159,000; capital, Oirot-Tura.

Oise (wȧz), *n.* a river in Belgium and France, flowing into the Seine: length, 186 mi.

OIt., Old Italian.

O·jib·wa (ō-jib′wā), *adj. & n.* [*pl.* OJIBWA, OJIBWAS (-wāz)], Ojibway.

O·jib·way (ō-jib′wā), *n.* [*pl.* OJIBWAY, OJIBWAYS (-wāz)], [Am. Ind. dial. *ojibway*, to roast till puckered (< *ojib*, to pucker + *ub-way*, to roast): from the puckered seam on their moccasins], 1. a Chippewa, member of a tribe of Algonquian Indians. 2. their language. *adj.* of this tribe.

O.K., OK (ō′kā′; *for the v.*, ō′kā′), *adj., adv., interj.* [orig. U.S. colloq.; first used in name of Democratic *O.K.* Club (earliest recorded meeting March 24, 1840), in which *O.K.* is abbrev. of *Old Kinderhook*, name of the native village of Martin Van Buren, whom the Club supported for a 2d term (cf. *Saturday Review of Literature*, July 19, 1941, pp. 3-10; also H. L. Mencken, *Am. Lang., Suppl. I*, pp. 269-279)], all right; correct. *n.* approval; endorsement. *v.t.* [O.K.'D, OK'D (-kād′), O.K.'ING, OK'ING], to put an O.K. on; approve; endorse. Also spelled **okay**.

O·ka (ô-kä′), *n.* a river in the central European U.S.S.R., flowing northeastward into the Volga: length, 950 mi.

o·ka (ō′kə), *n.* [It. *oc(c)a*; Turk. *ōqah*; Ar. *ūqīyah*; Gr. *oungia* (L. *uncia*); see OUNCE (unit of weight)], in Turkey, Egypt, Bulgaria, etc., a unit of weight, equal to 2 3/4 pounds, or of liquid measure, equal to 1 1/3 quarts: also **oke**.

o·ka·pi (ō-kä′pi), *n.* [*pl.* OKAPIS (-piz), OKAPI; see PLURAL, II, D, 1], [native Afr. name], an African animal related to the giraffe, but having a short neck.

O·ka·van·go River (ō′kä-väŋ′gō), the Kabango River.

o·kay (ō′kā′; *for the v.*, ō′kā′), *adj., adv., interj., n., v.t.* [Colloq.], O.K.

O·ka·ya·ma (ô′kȧ-yä′mȧ), *n.* a city on the southwest coast of Honshu, Japan: pop., 236,000.

oke (ōk), *n.* an oka.

O·kee·cho·bee, Lake (ō′ki-chō′bi), a lake in south central Florida: length, 40 mi.; width, 25 mi.: see **Everglades**, map.

O'Keeffe, Georgia (ō-kēf′), 1887– ; American painter.

O'Kel·ley, Sean Thomas (shôn ō-kel′i), 1883– ; Irish political leader; president of Ireland (1945–1959).

O·khotsk, Sea of (ō-kotsk′; Russ. ô-khôtsk′), an arm of the Pacific, east of Siberia: area, 590,000 sq. mi.; average depth, c. 10,500 ft.

O·kie (ō′ki), *n.* [< *Oklahoma*], a migratory agricultural worker, especially one forced to migrate from Oklahoma or other parts of the dust bowl through drought, farm foreclosure, etc., in the late 1930's.

O·ki·na·wa (ō′ki-nä′wä), *n.* one of the Ryukyu Islands, in the North Pacific, between Taiwan and Kyushu: captured by American forces (1945) in World War II.

O·kla·ho·ma (ō′klə-hō′mə), *n.* a Southern State of the United States: area, 69,919 sq. mi.; pop., 2,328,000; capital, Oklahoma City: abbreviated **Okla.**

Oklahoma City, the capital of Oklahoma: pop., 324,000.

O·kla·ho·man (ō′klə-hō′mən), *adj.* of Oklahoma. *n.* a native or inhabitant of Oklahoma.

o·kra (ō′krə), *n.* [< W. Afr. (Tshi) name, *nkruman*], 1. a tall plant with sticky green pods, used in soups, stews, etc. 2. the pod or pods of this plant. 3. a soup, stew, etc. made from these pods. Also called *gumbo*.

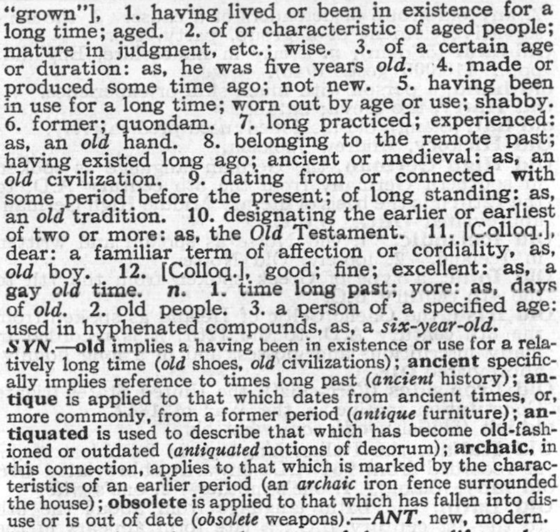

OKRA (with pods)

-ol (ōl, ol), [in sense 1 < *alcohol*; in sense 2 < L. *oleum*, oil], a suffix used in chemistry to mean: 1. *an alcohol* or *phenol*, as in *menthol, thymol*. 2. -ole.

OL., O.L., Old Latin.

O·laf I (ō′ləf, ō′läf), (*Olaf Tryggvesson*), 969–1000; king of Norway (995–1000); subject of many legends.

Olaf II, Saint, (*Olaf Haraldsson*), 995?–1030; king of Norway (1016–1028): Latin form, *Olaus*.

Olaf V, 1903– ; king of Norway (1957–).

Ö·land (ö′länd′), *n.* a Swedish island in the Baltic Sea: area, 519 sq. mi.; pop., 27,000.

O·la·us (ō-lā′əs), see **Olaf II.**

Ol·cott, Chauncey (ol′kət), (*Chancellor John Olcott*), 1860–1932; American actor and tenor.

old (ōld), *adj.* [OLDER (-ẽr) or ELDER (el′dẽr), OLDEST (-ist) or ELDEST (el′dist)], [ME.; AS. (Anglian) *ald*; W.S. *eald*; akin to G. *alt*; IE. base **al-*, to grow, as also in L. *alere*, to nourish; cf. ADULT; basic sense "grown"], 1. having lived or been in existence for a long time; aged. 2. of or characteristic of aged people; mature in judgment, etc.; wise. 3. of a certain age or duration: as, he was five years *old*. 4. made or produced some time ago; not new. 5. having been in use for a long time; worn out by age or use; shabby. 6. former; quondam. 7. long practiced; experienced: as, an *old* hand. 8. belonging to the remote past; having existed long ago; ancient or medieval: as, an *old* civilization. 9. dating from or connected with some period before the present; of long standing: as, an *old* tradition. 10. designating the earlier or earliest of two or more: as, the *Old* Testament. 11. [Colloq.], dear: a familiar term of affection or cordiality, as, *old* boy. 12. [Colloq.], good; fine; excellent: as, a gay *old* time. *n.* 1. time long past; yore: as, days of *old*. 2. old people. 3. a person of a specified age: used in hyphenated compounds, as, a *six-year-old*.

SYN.—**old** implies a having been in existence or use for a relatively long time (*old* shoes, *old* civilizations); **ancient** specifically implies reference to times long past (*ancient* history); **antique** is applied to that which dates from ancient times, or, more commonly, from a former period (*antique* furniture); **antiquated** is used to describe that which has become old-fashioned or outdated (*antiquated* notions of decorum); **archaic**, in this connection, applies to that which is marked by the characteristics of an earlier period (an *archaic* iron fence surrounded the house); **obsolete** is applied to that which has fallen into disuse or is out of date (*obsolete* weapons).—*ANT.* new, modern.

old age, the advanced years of human life, when strength and vigor decline: cf. **middle age.**

Old Arabic, Arabic in its oldest stage, chiefly as recorded in Northern Arabian inscriptions from the 1st century A.D. to the 6th, and in inscriptions of Mecca from 328 A.D. on: abbreviated **OAr.**

Old Bai·ley (bā′li), formerly, the criminal court of London.

Old Castile, a former province of central Spain: Spanish name, *Castilla la Vieja*.

Old Catholic, a member of a religious sect organized by Roman Catholics who, in 1870, refused to accept the doctrine of papal infallibility: abbreviated **O.C.**

Old Celtic, all the branches of the Celtic language as supposedly spoken at the close of the 4th century A.D.: abbreviated **OCelt.**

Old Church Slavic, see **Old Slavic.**

old country, the country from which an immigrant came: said especially of a country in Europe.

Old Cymric, Cymric in its oldest stage: abbreviated **OCym.**

Old Danish, the Danish language in its oldest recorded stage, as found in literary remains from the 13th century A.D., as conjectured from loan words in Middle English, and as preserved in certain Norman place names: abbreviated **ODan.**

Old Delhi, capital of Delhi state, India: see **Delhi.**

Old Dominion, Virginia.

Old Dutch, the Dutch language in its oldest stage: it is actually recorded only on fragmentary relics, but may be reconstructed from Middle Dutch and from loan words in neighboring languages: cf. **Old Low Frankish**: abbreviated **OD., O.D.**

old·en (ōl′d'n), *adj.* [ME., inflected form of *old*], [Poetic], old; ancient; of old, or of former times.

Ol·den·burg (ōl′d'n-bũrg′; G. ōl′dən-boorkh′), *n.* 1. a former division of northwestern Germany: earlier, a duchy. 2. a city in northwestern Germany: pop., 121,000.

Old English, 1. the West Germanic, Low German language of the Anglo-Saxons; language spoken in England from the 5th century A.D. until shortly after the Norman Conquest (1066); Anglo-Saxon: abbreviated **OE., O.E.** 2. a style of black letter.

old-fash·ioned (ōld′fash′ənd), *adj.* styled or done in accordance with, or favoring, the methods, manners, or ideas of past times; **out-of-date**; antiquated; outmoded. *n.* [also O- F-], an iced cocktail containing whisky, a dash of soda, bitters, sweetening, and fruit.

old-fo·gy, old-fo·gey (ōld′fō′gi), *adj.* old-fogyish.

old fogy, old fogey, a person who is old-fashioned or overly conservative in ideas and actions.

old-fo·gy·ish, old-fo·gey·ish (ōld′fō′gi-ish), *adj.* of, like, characteristic of, or suitable for an old fogy.

Old French, the French language as spoken from the 9th century A.D. until Modern French developed in the 16th century: abbreviated **OFr., OF., O.F.**

Old Frisian, a West Germanic language spoken from the 11th century A.D. to the 16th, closely related to Anglo-Saxon and Old Saxon: the oldest documents date from the 13th century: abbreviated **OFris.**

Old Glory, the flag of the United States.

old gold, a soft, yellowish, metallic color.

Old Guard, [transl. of Fr. *Vieille Garde*: so named in contrast to the Young Guard, formed in 1810], 1. the imperial guard, organized by Napoleon I in 1804.

2. any old group of defenders of a cause. 3. the conservative element of a group, party, etc.
Old·ham (ōl'dəm), *n.* a city in Lancashire, England: pop., 118,000 (est. 1946).
old hand, a person with much skill or experience.
Old Harry, the Devil; Satan.
old hat, [Slang], old-fashioned: used predicatively.
Old Hickory, Andrew Jackson.
Old High German, the German language as spoken in southern Germany from the 8th century A.D. to the 12th: it is the basis of literary Middle High German: abbreviated **OHG., O.H.G.**
Old Icelandic, 1. Old Norse as spoken and written in Iceland. 2. loosely, Old Norse.
Old Ionic, a type of Greek spoken from the 7th to the 4th century B.C.
Old Irish, the Gaelic Celtic of Ireland as spoken from the 8th century A.D. to the 12th: it is recorded in many inscriptions and glosses, and in a long homily: abbreviated **OIr.**
Old I·ron·sides (ī'ẽrn-sīdz'), the United States frigate Constitution, active in the War of 1812.
old·ish (ōld'ish), *adj.* somewhat old.
Old Italian, the Italian language in its oldest stage, as recorded from 964 A.D. onward: abbreviated **OIt.**
old lady, [Slang], 1. one's mother. 2. one's wife.
Old Latin, the Latin language from about the 6th to the 1st century B.C.: a late form appears in the comedies of Plautus: abbreviated **OL., O.L.**
old-line (ōld'līn'), *adj.* 1. with an old, well-established history. 2. following tradition in action, thought, etc.; conservative.
Old Low Frankish, the language of the Franks of the lower Rhine, the ancestor of Dutch, Flemish, etc.: cf. **Old Dutch.**
Old Low German, the language of northern Germany and the Netherlands from the 8th century A.D. to the 12th, the ancestor of Modern Low German: abbreviated **OLG., O.L.G.**
old maid, 1. a woman who is unmarried and seems likely to remain so. 2. a prim, prudish, fussy person. 3. a simple card game in which the players draw cards from one another's hands to match pairs.
old-maid·ish (ōld'mād'ish), *adj.* characteristic of or suitable for an old maid; prim, prudish, fussy, etc.
old man, [Slang], 1. one's father. 2. one's husband. 3. any man in a position of authority, as the head of a business concern, captain of a vessel, military commander, etc. 4. old Mr.——: used with reference to an elderly man, or to distinguish the father from the son. Also used as a term of address, as to a friend.
Old Man of the Sea, 1. in the *Arabian Nights,* an old man who clung to the back of Sinbad for many days and nights; hence, 2. any person or thing hard to shake off or get rid of.
old master, 1. any of the great European painters before the 18th century. 2. a painting by any of these.
old moon, the phase of the moon in which it appears as a crescent curving toward the left; last quarter.
Old Nick, [usually assumed to be contr. < *Nicholas,* but prob. < Gmc. **niq-,* water sprite, goblin; see NIX, *n.,* NICKEL], the Devil; Satan: see **Nick.**
Old Norman French, Norman French; Anglo-French: abbreviated **ONorm.Fr.**
Old Norse, the language spoken in Norway, Denmark, and Iceland from the 8th century A.D. to the 14th, recorded in the sagas, in the *Elder Edda,* and in the skaldic poetry: abbreviated **ON., O.N.:** also called *Old Icelandic.*
Old North French, the dialectal forms of Old French spoken in northern France: abbreviated **ONFr.**
Old Northwest, the Northwest Territory.
Old Orchard Beach, a seaside resort town in southern Maine: pop., 5,000.
Old Persian, the oldest form of Persian, preserved in stone inscriptions dating from the 7th to the 4th century B.C.: abbreviated **OPer.**
Old Prussian, a Baltic language spoken from the 15th century A.D. to the early 18th.
old-rose (ōld'rōz'), *adj.* of old rose.
old rose, a grayish or purplish red.
Old Saxon, a Low Germanic dialect once common in part of northern Germany, known chiefly from manuscripts of the 9th and 10th centuries A.D.: its chief literary monument is the *Heliand* ("savior"), a poem composed about 830 A.D.: abbreviated **OS., O.S.**
old school, a group of people who cling to traditional or conservative ideas, methods, etc.: abbreviated **O.S.**
Old Serbian, an old Bulgarian dialect that developed about the 10th century A.D., the ancestor of modern Serbian: abbreviated **OSerb.**
Old Slavic, Slavic in its oldest stage, as represented by Bible translations and other church documents recorded in the Bulgarian dialect of Salonika in the second half of the 9th century A.D.: as *Old Church Slavic,* it is still used in the Orthodox liturgies in Slavic-speaking countries: abbreviated **OSlav.**
old sledge, the card game seven-up.
Old South, the South before the Civil War.
Old Spanish, the Spanish language as spoken from the 12th century A.D. to the 16th, first recorded in a document dated 1145: abbreviated **OSp.**
old squaw, a sea duck common to northern regions.
old·ster (ōld'stẽr), *n.* [Colloq.], a person who is no longer a youngster; old or elderly person.
old-style (ōld'stīl'), *adj.* in or according to old style.
old style, 1. in *typography,* an old style of type, modern varieties of which are in popular use: abbreviated **O.S., O/S, o/s.** 2. [O- S-], the old method of reckoning time according to the Julian calendar, which was off one day every 128 years.
Old Testament, [see TESTAMENT, 2], the first of the two general divisions of the Bible, containing the history of the Hebrews, the Mosaic law, the writings of the prophets, the Psalms, etc.: abbreviated **O.T., OT., OT** (no period).
Old Teutonic, Germanic: the former name: abbreviated **O Teut.**
old-time (ōld'tīm'), *adj.* of, like, or characteristic of past times.
old-tim·er (ōld'tīm'ẽr), *n.* [Colloq.], 1. a person who has been a resident, employee, member, etc. for a long time. 2. a person who is old-fashioned.
old·wife (ōld'wīf'), *n.* [*pl.* OLDWIVES (-wīvz')], 1. an old woman. 2. an old squaw. 3. *a)* any of several related fishes of the herring family, including the alewife and menhaden. *b)* any of several species of triggerfishes found near the West Indies.
old wives' tale, a silly story or superstitious belief such as might be passed around by gossipy old women.
old-wom·an·ish (ōld'woom'ən-ish), *adj.* like, characteristic of, or suitable for an old woman; fussy.
old-world (ōld'wũrld'), *adj.* 1. of or belonging to the ancient world. 2. characteristic of or belonging to former times. 3. of the Old World.
Old World, the Eastern Hemisphere; the world of Europe, Asia, and Africa: opposed to *New World.*
-ole (ōl), [< L. *oleum,* oil], a suffix used in chemistry: 1. to indicate a closed-chain compound with five members, as in *pyrrole.* 2. to form the names of certain aldehydes and ethers, as in *anethole.* Also **-ol.**
o·le·a·ceous (ō'li-ā'shəs), *adj.* [< Mod. L. *oleaceae,* olive trees < L. *olea,* olive tree], designating or belonging to the olive family of trees and shrubs, which includes the ash, lilac, forsythia, etc.
o·le·ag·i·nous (ō'li-aj'i-nəs), *adj.* [Fr. *oléagineux;* L. *oleaginus* < *olea,* the olive], oily; greasy; unctuous.
O·le·an (ō'li-an'), *n.* a city in southwestern New York: pop., 23,000.
o·le·an·der (ō'li-an'dẽr), *n.* [ML.; earlier also *lorandrum;* ? altered < L. *rhododendron*], a poisonous evergreen shrub with fragrant flowers of white, pink, or red.
o·le·as·ter (ō'li-as'tẽr), *n.* [ME. *oliaster;* L. < *olea,* olive tree], a southern European shrub resembling the wild olive, having fragrant, yellow flowers and olive-like fruit.
o·le·ate (ō'li-āt'), *n.* a salt or ester of oleic acid.
o·lec·ra·non (ō-lek'rə-non', ō'li-krā'nən), *n.* [Mod. L.; Gr. *ōlekranon* (for *ōlenokronon*) < *ōlenē,* the elbow + *kranion,* the head], the part of the ulna projecting behind the elbow joint.
o·le·fin (ō'lə-fin), *n.* [< Fr. *oléfiant* < L. *oleum,* an oil + *-ficare* (< *facere*), to make], any of a series of unsaturated open-chain hydrocarbons containing one double bond and corresponding in composition to the general formula C_nH_{2n}: similar compounds containing more than one double bond are called *diolefins, triolefins,* etc.
o·le·fine (ō'lə-fin, ō'lə-fēn'), *n.* olefin.
o·le·ic (ō-lē'ik, ō'li-ik), *adj.* [< L. *oleum,* an oil; + *-ic*], of or obtained from oil.
oleic acid, an oily acid, $C_{17}H_{33}COOH$, present in the form of the glyceryl ester in most animal and vegetable fats and oils, used in making soap, ointments, etc.
o·le·in (ō'li-in), *n.* [Fr. *oléine* < L. *oleum,* an oil], 1. a liquid glyceride of oleic acid, present in olive oil and certain other oils and fats. 2. the liquid part of any fat, as distinguished from the solid part.
o·le·o (ō'li-ō'), *n.* oleomargarine.
o·le·o- (ō'li-ə, ō'li-ō), [L. < *oleum,* an oil], a combining form meaning *oil, olein,* or *oleic,* as in *oleomargarine.*
o·le·o·graph (ō'li-ō-graf', ō'li-ə-gräf'), *n.* [*oleo-* + *-graph*], 1. a chromolithograph made in imitation of an oil painting. 2. the outline, or form, assumed by a drop of oil placed on the surface of water.
o·le·o·graph·ic (ō'li-ə-graf'ik), *adj.* of or like an oleograph or oleography.
o·le·og·ra·phy (ō'li-og'rə-fi), *n.* 1. the art or process of making oleographs. 2. the process of identifying an oil by its oleograph.
o·le·o·mar·ga·rin (ō'li-ō-mär'jə-rin; *occas.* ō'li-ō-mär'gə-rin), *n.* oleomargarine.
o·le·o·mar·ga·rine (ō'li-ō-mär'jə-rin, ō'li-ō-mär'jə-rēn'; *occas.* ō'li-ō-mär'gə-rēn'), *n.* [*oleo-* + *margarine*], margarine.
oleo oil, a butterlike oil obtained from animal fat.
o·le·o·res·in (ō'li-ō-rez''n), *n.* 1. a solution of a resin in an essential oil, as turpentine, occurring naturally

in various plants. 2. a prepared mixture of an essential oil containing resin in solution.

oleo strut, a shock-absorbing strut on airplanes, consisting of a telescopic cylinder containing oil.

ol·fac·tion (ol-fak′shən; *now often* ōl-fak′shən), *n.* [< L. *olfacere;* see OLFACTORY], 1. the sense of smell. 2. the act of smelling.

ol·fac·to·ry (ol-fak′tẽr-i, ōl-fak′tẽr-i), *adj.* [< L. *olfactus*, pp. of *olfacere*, to smell < *olere*, to have a smell + *facere*, to make], of the sense of smell. *n.* [*pl.* OLFACTORIES (-iz)], *usually in pl.* 1. an organ of smell. 2. the sense of smell.

OLG., O.L.G., Old Low German.

Ol·ga (ol′gə, ôl′gə), [Russ.; ? < *Oleg*, holy, or < N. *Helga*, holy], a feminine name.

o·lib·a·num (ō-lib′ə-nəm), *n.* [ME.; ML. < L. *libanum* < Gr. *libanos*, frankincense], a gum resin used as an incense and medicine; frankincense.

ol·i·garch (ol′i-gärk′), *n.* [Gr. *oligarchēs*], any of the rulers of an oligarchy.

ol·i·gar·chic (ol′i-gär′kik), *adj.* [Gr. *oligarchikos*], of, constituting, or advocating an oligarchy.

ol·i·gar·chi·cal (ol′i-gär′ki-k′l), *adj.* oligarchic.

ol·i·garch·y (ol′i-gär′ki), *n.* [*pl.* OLIGARCHIES (-kiz)], [Gr. *oligarchia;* see OLIGO- & -ARCHY], 1. a form of government in which the ruling power belongs to a few persons. 2. a state governed in this way. 3. the persons ruling such a state.

ol·i·go- (ol′i-gō), [Gr. *oligo-* < *oligos*, small], a combining form meaning *few, scant, small, a deficiency of*, as in *oligocythemia:* also, before a vowel, **olig-**.

Ol·i·go·cene (ol′ig-ə-sēn′), *adj.* [< *oligo-* + Gr. *kainos*, new, recent], designating or of the second epoch of the Tertiary Period in the Cenozoic Era, characterized by the development of the higher mammals.
the Oligocene, the Oligocene Epoch or its rocks: see **geology**, chart.

ol·i·go·chae·tous (ol′i-gō-kē′təs), *adj.* [< *oligo-* + Gr. *chaitē*, hair; + *-ous*], designating or of any member of a group of hermaphroditic worms, as the earthworm, having a segmented body and no distinct head.

ol·i·go·clase (ol′i-gō-klās′), *n.* [< *oligo-* + Gr. *klasis*, a fracture < *klan*, to break], a crystalline variety of feldspar, containing both sodium and calcium.

ol·i·go·cy·the·mi·a (ol′i-gō-sī-thē′mi-ə), *n.* [Mod. L. < *oligo-* + Gr. *kytos*, a hollow + *haima*, blood], a form of anemia characterized by a deficiency of red corpuscles in the blood: also spelled **oligocythaemia**.

ol·i·gu·re·sis (ol′i-gyoo-rē′sis), *n.* oliguria.

ol·i·gu·ri·a (ol′i-gyoor′i-ə), *n.* [Mod. L.; see OLIGO- & -URIA], a condition characterized by an abnormally small amount of urine secretion and a greatly decreased frequency of urination.

o·li·o (ō′li-ō′), *n.* [*pl.* OLIOS (-ōz′)], [< Sp. *olla;* see OLLA], 1. a highly spiced stew of meat and vegetables; olla. 2. a medley; sundry assortment; miscellany.

ol·i·va·ceous (ol′i-vā′shəs), *adj.* [Mod. L. *olivaceus*], of or like the olive, especially in color; olive-green.

ol·i·var·y (ol′ə-ver′i), *adj.* [L. *olivarius*], in *anatomy*, 1. shaped like an olive. 2. designating or of either of two oval bodies protruding from the sides of the medulla oblongata.

Ol·ive (ol′iv), [OFr.; It. *Olivia* < L. *oliva*, an olive], a feminine name: variant, *Olivia*.

ol·ive (ol′iv), *n.* [ME.; OFr.; L. *oliva*, an olive], 1. an evergreen tree of southern Europe and the Near East, with leathery leaves, yellow flowers, and an edible fruit. 2. the small, oval fruit of this tree, eaten green or ripe as a relish, or pressed to extract olive oil. 3. the wood of this tree. 4. an olive branch or wreath. 5. the dull, yellowish-green color of the unripe olive fruit. *adj.* 1. of the olive. 2. *a)* olive-colored. *b)* having a dark complexion tinged with this color.

olive branch, 1. the branch of the olive tree, traditionally a symbol of peace; hence, 2. any peace offering.

ol·ive-drab (ol′iv-drab′), *adj.* of olive drab.

olive drab, 1. any of various shades of greenish brown, much used as a camouflage color in the armed forces. 2. woolen cloth dyed this color and used for uniforms by the United States Army: distinguished from *khaki*. 3. *pl.* a uniform of this cloth. Abbreviated **O.D., o.d.**

olive green, the color of the unripe olive.

o·liv·en·ite (ō-liv′ən-īt′, ol′i-vən-īt′), *n.* [G. *olivenerz*, olive ore; + *-ite*], a native copper arsenate, $CuO \cdot As_2O_3 \cdot H_2O$, usually of olive green.

olive oil, a light-yellow oil pressed from ripe olives, used in cooking, salad dressings, liniments, soap, etc.

Ol·i·ver (ol′ə-vẽr), [Fr. *Olivier;* form assimilated to OFr. *olivier*, olive tree < L. *olivarius*, but prob. < MLG. *alfihar*, lit., elf-army < *alf*, elf + *hari*, a host, army], a masculine name. *n.* one of Charlemagne's twelve peers, a friend of Roland: see **Roland**.

Olives, Mount of, a hilly ridge east of Jerusalem.

Ol·i·vet, Mount (ol′ə-vet′), the Mount of Olives.

O·liv·i·a (ō-liv′i-ə, ə-liv′yə), a feminine name: see **Olive**.

ol·i·vine (ol′ə-vēn′, ol′ə-vēn′), *n.* [< *olive* + *-ine*], a silicate of magnesium and iron, $(MgFe)_2SiO_4$, existing usually as green crystals in many rocks and used as a semiprecious stone; green garnet; chrysolite.

ol·la (ol′ə; Sp. ôl′yä), *n.* [Sp.; L.], 1. a large-mouthed pot or jar used in Spain and Latin America. 2. a highly spiced stew of meat and vegetables.

ol·la-po·dri·da (ol′ə-pə-drē′də; Sp. ôl′yä-pô-*th*rē′*th*ä), *n.* [Sp., lit., rotten pot; *olla* (L. *olla*), pot + *podrida* (L. *putridus*), rotten], 1. an olla (stew). 2. any assortment, medley, or miscellany; olio.

Ol·mütz (ôl′müts), *n.* Olomouc: the German name.

ol·o·gy (ol′ə-ji), *n.* [*pl.* OLOGIES (-jiz)], [properly a suffix < Gr. *logos*, description, with *-o-* of prec. element], a branch of learning; science: a humorous usage.

Ol·o·mouc (ô′lô-mōts′), *n.* a city in Moravia, Czechoslovakia: pop., 74,000.

O·lym·pi·a (ō-lim′pi-ə, ə-lim′pi-ə), [L.; Gr. *Olympia*, fem. of *Olympios*, lit., of Olympus], a feminine name. *n.* 1. a plain in ancient Elis, Greece: site of the Olympic games: see **Greece**, map. 2. the capital of Washington, on Puget Sound: pop., 18,000.

O·lym·pi·ad (ō-lim′pi-ad′, ə-lim′pi-ad′), *n.* [Fr. *olympiade* < Gr. *Olympias, Olympiados* < *Olympia*, district in ancient Elis where the Olympic games were held < *Olympos*, Mt. Olympus; in ME. *olympias*], 1. in ancient Greece, any of the four-year periods between Olympic games: used by the Greeks in computing time. 2. a celebration of the modern Olympic games.

O·lym·pi·an (ō-lim′pi-ən, ə-lim′pi-ən), *n.* [LL.; Gr. *Olympios*], 1. in *Greek mythology*, any of the twelve major gods who were supposed to live on the slopes of Mount Olympus. 2. a native of Olympia. 3. any participant in the ancient or modern Olympic games. *adj.* 1. of Olympia or Mount Olympus. 2. like an Olympian god; exalted; celestial; godlike; majestic. 3. designating or of the Olympic games of ancient Greece.

O·lym·pic (ō-lim′pik, ə-lim′pik), *adj.* [L. *Olympicus;* Gr. *Olympikos*], Olympian. *n.* 1. an Olympic game. 2. *pl.* the Olympic games (preceded by *the*).

Olympic games, 1. in ancient Greece, a festival consisting of various contests in athletics, poetry, and music, held every four years at Olympia in honor of Zeus: also called *Olympian games*. 2. an international athletic competition of modern times, patterned after this festival and generally held every four years at some city chosen for this event: the competition, first held at Athens in 1896, includes track and field events, swimming, fencing, team games, etc.

Olympic Mountains, a part of the Coast Range, in western Washington: highest peak, Mount Olympus.

Olympic National Park, a national park in western Washington, around Mount Olympus: area, 1,305 sq. mi.

O·lym·pus (ō-lim′pəs, ə-lim′pəs), *n.* 1. a mountain in northern Greece: height, 9,793 ft.: in *Greek mythology*, the home of the gods. 2. heaven; the sky.

Olympus, Mount, 1. Olympus. 2. the highest peak of the Olympic Mountains, in northwestern Washington: height, 8,150 ft.

O·lyn·thus (ō-lin′thəs), *n.* a city in ancient Greece, on the Chalcidice Peninsula.

Om., Ostmark.

O.M., Order of Merit (British).

-o·ma (ō′mə), [Gr. *-ōma*], a suffix meaning *morbid growth, tumor*, as in *lymphoma, sarcoma*.

O·ma·ha (ō′mə-hô′, ō′mə-hä′), *n.* 1. a city in eastern Nebraska, on the Missouri: pop., 302,000. 2. a member of a tribe of Siouan Indians who migrated from the Ohio River Valley to northeastern Nebraska.

O·man (ō-män′), *n.* a country in southeastern Arabia, on the Arabian Sea and the Gulf of Oman: area, 82,000 sq. mi.; pop., 550,000; capital, Muscat: also called *Muscat and Oman*.

Oman, Gulf of, an arm of the Arabian Sea, between Iran and Arabia.

O·mar Khay·yám (ō′mär kī-yäm′, ō′mẽr kī-yam′), ?–1123; Persian poet; author of the *Rubáiyát* translated into English by Edward FitzGerald.

o·ma·sum (ō-mā′səm), *n.* [*pl.* OMASA (-sə)], [L., paunch], the third division in the stomach of a cud-chewing animal, as the cow: also called *psalterium, manyplies:* see **ruminant**, illus.

O·may·yad (ō-mī′ad), *n.* an Ommiad.

om·ber, om·bre (om′bẽr), *n.* [Fr. *ombre;* Sp. *hombre;* L. *homo*, a man], 1. a card game of Spanish origin, played with forty cards by three players: popular in England in the 17th and 18th centuries. 2. the player attempting to win the pool in this game.

Om·dur·man (om′door-män′), *n.* a city on the Nile, opposite Khartoum, in Sudan: pop., 114,000.

o·me·ga (ō-meg′ə, ō-mē′gə, ō′mi-gə), *n.* [Gr. *o* + *mega*, great; lit., great, long *o*], 1. the twenty-fourth and final letter of the Greek alphabet (Ω, ω), corresponding to English long *O, o:* see **alphabet**, table. 2. the last (of any series); end.

om·e·let, om·e·lette (om′lit, om′ə-let), *n.* [Fr. *omelette*, earlier *amelette;* by metathesis < *alemette* < *alemelle* < L. *lamella*, small plate; see LAMELLA], a dish consisting of eggs beaten up, often with milk or water, and cooked in a frying pan.

o·men (ō′mən), *n.* [L., earlier *osmen;* ? akin to Gr. *oiomai*, I have a foreboding], a thing or happening supposed to foretell a future (good or evil) event; sign; portent; augury. *v.t.* to be an omen of; presage; augur.

o·men·tal (ō-men′t'l), *adj.* of the omentum.

o·men·tum (ō-men′təm), *n.* [*pl.* OMENTA (-tə)], [L.], a free fold of peritoneum connecting the stomach to the other visceral organs and supporting blood vessels, nerves, and lymphatics.

o·mer (ō′mẽr), *n.* [Heb. *'ōmer*], an ancient Hebrew dry measure equal to about 3.7 quarts.

om·i·cron, om·i·kron (om′i-kron′, ō′mi-kron′), *n.* [Gr. *o mikron*, lit., small *o;* cf. MICRO-], the fifteenth letter of the Greek alphabet (O, o), corresponding to English short *O, o:* see **alphabet**, table.

om·i·nous (om′ə-nəs), *adj.* [L. *ominosus*], of or serving as an omen; especially, having the character of an evil omen; threatening; sinister; menacing.

SYN.—**ominous** implies a threatening character but does not necessarily connote a disastrous outcome (his request was met by an *ominous* silence); **portentous** literally implies a foreshadowing, especially of evil, but is now more often used of that which arouses awe or amazement because of its prodigious or marvelous character (a *portentous* event); **fateful** may imply a fatal character or control by fate, but is now usually applied to that which is of momentous or decisive significance (a *fateful* truce conference); **foreboding** implies a portent or presentiment of something evil or harmful (a *foreboding* anxiety).

o·mis·si·ble (ō-mis′ə-b'l), *adj.* that can be omitted.

o·mis·sion (ō-mish′ən), *n.* [ME. *omissioun;* LL. *omissio*], 1. an omitting or being omitted. 2. anything omitted.

o·mis·sive (ō-mis′iv), *adj.* [< L. *omissus*, pp. of *omittere;* + *-ive*], failing to do or include; omitting.

o·mit (ō-mit′), *v.t.* [OMITTED (-id), OMITTING], [ME. *omitten;* L. *omittere* < *ob-* (see OB-) + *mittere*, to send], 1. to fail to include; leave out. 2. to fail to do; neglect. —*SYN.* see **neglect.**

om·ma·tid·i·al (om′ə-tid′i-əl), *adj.* of an ommatidium.

om·ma·tid·i·um (om′ə-tid′i-əm), *n.* [*pl.* OMMATIDIA (-ə)], [Mod. L., dim. < Gr. *omma, ommatos*, the eye], one of the elements forming the compound eye of an insect, etc., each element corresponding to a simple eye, or ocellus.

om·mat·o·phore (ə-mat′ə-fôr′, ə-mat′ə-fōr′), *n.* [< Gr. *omma, ommatos*, the eye; + *-phore*], a movable stalk to which the eye is attached, as in the mud puppy, snail, lobster, etc.

om·ma·toph·o·rous (om′ə-tof′ẽr-əs), *adj.* having an ommatophore.

Om·mi·ad (ō-mī′ad), *n.* [*pl.* OMMIADS (-adz), OMMIADES (-ə-dēz′)], [< *Omayya*, great-grandfather of the first caliph in the dynasty], any of a dynasty of Moslem caliphs who ruled in Damascus from 661 to 750 A.D., or of a closely related branch ruling in Spain from 756 to 1031 A.D.

om·ni- (om′ni, om′nə), [L. < *omnis*, all], a combining form meaning *all, everywhere*, as in *omniscient.*

‡om·ni·a vin·cit a·mor (om′ni-ə vin′sit ā′môr), [L.], love overcomes all (things): a quotation from Virgil.

om·ni·bus (om′ni-bus′, om′nə-bəs), *n.* [*pl.* OMNIBUSES (-iz)], [Fr.; L., for all, dat. pl. of *omnis*, all], 1. a large motor coach that can carry many passengers, generally following a regular route; bus. 2. a book containing a collection of stories, essays, poems, etc., all written by the same author or bearing on the same subject. *adj.* providing for many things at once; having many purposes or uses.

omnibus bill, a legislative bill containing many miscellaneous provisions, appropriations, etc.

om·ni·far·i·ous (om′ni-fâr′i-əs), *adj.* [L. *omnifarius*, of all sorts < *omnis*, all + *-farius* < *fari*, to speak], of all kinds, varieties, or forms.

om·nif·er·ous (om-nif′ẽr-əs), *adj.* [< L. *omnifer* < *omnis*, all + *ferre*, to bear; + *-ous*], producing all kinds or varieties.

om·nif·ic (om-nif′ik), *adj.* [ML. *omnificus* < L. *omnis*, all + *facere*, to make], all-creating.

om·nip·o·tence (om-nip′ə-təns), *n.* [Fr.; LL. *omnipotentia*], 1. the state or quality of being omnipotent. 2. [O-], God.

om·nip·o·tent (om-nip′ə-tənt), *adj.* [ME.; OFr.; L. *omnipotens* < *omnis*, all + *potens*, able, powerful], having unlimited power or authority; all-powerful.

the Omnipotent, God.

om·ni·pres·ence (om′ni-prez′'ns), *n.* [ML. *omnipraesentia*], the state or quality of being omnipresent.

om·ni·pres·ent (om′ni-prez′'nt), *adj.* [ML. *omnipraesens* < L. *omnis*, all + *praesens*, present], present in all places at the same time.

SYN.—**omnipresent**, strictly applicable only to the Deity in its implication of presence in all places at the same time, is loosely used of anything that is always present within a given sphere (the *omnipresent* spirit of competition in business); **ubiquitous** implies a being present, or seeming to be present, everywhere but not always at the same time or place (the trillium is a *ubiquitous* spring wildflower).

om·nis·cience (om-nish′əns), *n.* 1. the state or quality of being omniscient. 2. [O-], God.

om·nis·cient (om-nish′ənt), *adj.* [Mod. L. *omnisciens* < L. *omnis*, all + *sciens*, ppr. of *scire*, to know], having infinite knowledge; knowing all things.

the Omniscient, God.

om·ni·um-gath·er·um (om′ni-əm-gath′ẽr-əm), *n.* [L. *omnium*, all + Latinized form of Eng. *gather*], a miscellaneous collection of persons or things.

om·niv·o·rous (om-niv′ẽr-əs), *adj.* [L. *omnivorus* < *omnis*, all + *vorare*, to devour], 1. eating any sort of food, especially both animal and vegetable food. 2. taking in everything indiscriminately, as with the intellect: as, an *omnivorous* reader.

o·mo·pha·gi·a (ō′mə-fā′ji-ə), *n.* [Gr. *ōmophagia* < *ōmos*, raw + *phagein*, to eat], the eating of raw flesh.

o·mo·phag·ic (ō′mə-faj′ik), *adj.* omophagous.

o·moph·a·gist (ō-mof′ə-jist), *n.* [see OMOPHAGOUS & -IST], an eater of raw flesh.

o·moph·a·gous (ō-mof′ə-gəs), *adj.* [Gr. *ōmophagos* < *ōmos*, raw + *phagein*, to eat], eating raw flesh.

omphal-, omphalo-.

Om·pha·le (om′fə-lē′), *n.* [L.; Gr. *Omphalē*], in *Greek mythology*, a queen of Lydia in whose service Hercules, dressed as a woman, spun wool and performed other womanly tasks for three years to appease the gods.

om·pha·lo- (om′fə-lō, om′fə-lə), [< Gr. *omphalos*, the navel], a combining form meaning *the navel, umbilicus:* also, before a vowel, **omphal-.**

Omsk (ômsk), *n.* 1. a region of the U.S.S.R., in northwestern Siberia: pop., 2,367,000. 2. its capital, on the Irtish River: pop., 281,000.

On (on), *n.* Heliopolis, in Egypt: the Biblical name.

on (on, ôn), *prep.* [ME.; AS. *on, an;* akin to G. *an;* basic Gmc. senses "in contact with, in motion toward"; IE. **an, *anō*, prob. meaning "obliquely toward, slanting toward," as also in Gr. *ana* (cf. ANA-)], 1. upon; in a position above, but in contact with and supported by. 2. in contact with (any surface regardless of position). 3. near to; by: as, a cottage *on* the lake, seated *on* my right. 4. at the time of: as, *on* entering, *on* the first of the month. 5. indicating the ground or basis of: as, *on* authority, *on* purpose. 6. connected with; engaged in: as, *on* the faculty board, *on* a trip. 7. in a condition or state of: as, *on* parole. 8. as a result of: as, he made a profit *on* the sale. 9. toward; in the direction of: as, the light shone *on* us. 10. through the use of: as, to live *on* bread and water. 11. concerning or about: as, an essay *on* war. 12. [Colloq.], chargeable to; at the expense of: as, a drink *on* the house. *adv.* 1. in or into a situation or position of contacting, being supported by, or covering: as, put your shoes *on.* 2. in a direction to or toward: as, he looked *on.* 3. in advance; forward; ahead: as, move *on.* 4. lastingly; continuously: as, she sang *on.* 5. into operation, performance, or action: as, switch *on* the light. *adj.* 1. in action, operation, or occurrence: as, the play is *on*, the light is *on.* 2. near or nearer. 3. in *cricket*, designating that side of the field, or of the wicket, where the batsman stands. *n.* 1. the fact or state of being on. 2. in *cricket*, the on side.

and so on, and more like the preceding; and so forth.

have something on one, [Colloq.], to be in possession of unfavorable evidence against one.

on and off, not continuously; intermittently.

on and on, continuously; at great length.

on to, [Slang], aware of; cognizant of.

ON., O.N., Old Norse.

on·a·ger (on′ə-jẽr), *n.* [*pl.* ONAGRI (-grī′), ONAGERS (-jẽrz)], [ME.; L. < Gr. *onagros*, wild ass < *onos*, ass + *agrios*, wild], 1. the wild ass of Central Asia. 2. a catapult for throwing stones, used in ancient and medieval warfare.

on·a·gra·ceous (on′ə-grā′shəs), *adj.* [< Mod. L. *Onograceae*, name of the family (< L. *onagra*, fem. of *onager;* see ONAGER); + *-ous*], of or belonging to the evening-primrose family of plants.

o·nan·ism (ō′nan-iz′m), *n.* [< *Onan* (Gen. 38:9)], 1. withdrawal in coition before ejaculation. 2. masturbation.

once (wuns), *adv.* [ME. *ones;* AS. *anes*, genit. of *an*, one; see ONE], 1. one time; one time only: as, the rent is due *once* a month. 2. at any time; at all; ever. 3. at some time in the past; formerly: as, a *once* celebrated actress. *conj.* as soon as; if ever; whenever: as, *once* he is tired he will quit. *adj.* former; quondam. *n.* one time: as, let him go this *once.*

all at once, 1. all at the same time. 2. suddenly.

at once, 1. immediately. 2. at the same time.

for once, for at least one time.

once and again, time after time; repeatedly.

once (and) for all, finally; decisively; conclusively.

once in a while, now and then; occasionally.
once or twice, not often; a few times.
once upon a time, a long time ago.

once-o·ver (wuns'ō'vẽr), *n.* [Slang], a quick, comprehensive look or examination; swiftly appraising glance.

on·col·o·gy (oŋ-kol'ə-ji), *n.* [< Gr. *onkos*, a mass, bulk; + *-logy*], the study of tumors.

on·com·ing (on'kum'iŋ), *adj.* coming nearer in position or time; approaching. *n.* an approach.

on·ding (on'diŋ), *n.* [*on, adv.* + dial. *ding*, to drive], [Scot.], a heavy fall of snow or rain.

‡**on dit** (ōn'dē'), [Fr.], 1. they say; it is said; hence, 2. a bit of gossip; common report: often **on-dit.**

on·do·gram (on'də-gram'), *n.* the record made on an ondograph.

on·do·graph (on'də-graf', on'də-gräf'), *n.* [< Fr. *onde* (< L. *unda*), a wave; + *-graph*], in *electricity*, an instrument that records wave forms, as in alternating currents.

on·dom·e·ter (on-dom'ə-tẽr), *n.* [see ONDOGRAPH & -METER], an instrument for measuring the frequency of an alternating current or radio carrier wave.

one (wun), *adj.* [ME. *oon, one;* AS. *an;* akin to G. *ein* (Goth. *ain-s*); IE. **oi-nos* (as also in L. *unus;* cf. UNIT) < a prefixed pronominal stem meaning "the, this, this one"], 1. being a single thing or unit; not two or more. 2. characterized by unity; forming a whole; united; undivided: as, with *one* accord. 3. designating a person or thing as contrasted with or opposed to another: as, from *one* end of town to the other. 4. designating a single person or thing that is not clearly defined; some or any; a certain: as, *one* day last week. 5. single in kind; the same. *n.* 1. the number expressing unity or designating a single unit: it is the lowest cardinal number and the first used in counting a series, etc.; 1; I. 2. a single person or thing. *pron.* 1. a certain person or thing; some person or thing. 2. any person or thing; anybody or anything. 3. the same person or thing.
all one, 1. united or agreed. 2. of no importance.
at one, of the same opinion; in accord.
make one, 1. to be a member of a group, part, etc.; join or take part in something. 2. to unite (a couple) in marriage.
one and all, everybody.
one another, each person or thing the other: said of an action, relation, etc. reciprocally involving more than two individuals.
one by one, individually in succession.

-one (ōn), [Gr. *-ōnē*, used to signify a female descendant of], a suffix used in chemistry, meaning *a ketone*, as in *acetone, butanone.*

one-bag·ger (wun'bag'ẽr), *n.* [Slang], a one-base hit.

one-base hit (wun'bās'), in *baseball*, a hit by which the batter can reach first base without benefit of an error: also called *single.*

O·ne·ga (ō-nē'gə; Russ. ô-nye'gä), *n.* 1. a river in the northwestern U.S.S.R., flowing into Onega Bay. 2. a lake located chiefly in the Karelo-Finnish S.S.R.: area, 3,764 sq. mi.

Onega Bay, an arm of the White Sea, extending into the northwestern U.S.S.R.

one-horse (wun'hôrs'), *adj.* 1. drawn by or using a single horse. 2. [Colloq.], having little importance; limited in resources, scope, etc.; petty; inferior.

O·nei·da (ō-nī'də), *n.* [*pl.* ONEIDA, ONEIDAS (-dəz)], [< Am. Ind. (Iroquois) *Oněñiute*], a member of a tribe of Iroquoian Indians who lived near Oneida Lake.

Oneida Lake, a lake near Syracuse, New York: length, 22 mi.; width, 6 mi.

O'Neill, Eugene (ō-nēl'), (*Eugene Gladstone O'Neill*), 1888–1953; American dramatist.

o·nei·ro·crit·ic (ō-nī'rə-krit'ik), *n.* [< Gr. *oneirokritikos*, concerning the interpretation of dreams < *oneiros*, a dream + *kritikos*, critical; see CRITIC], a person who interprets dreams.

o·nei·ro·crit·i·cal (ō-nī'rə-krit'i-k'l), *adj.* of, or having the power of, an oneirocritic.

o·nei·ro·man·cy (ō-nī'rə-man'si), *n.* [< Gr. *oneiros*, a dream; + *-mancy*], the art claiming to foretell the future by the interpretation of dreams.

one·ness (wun'nis), *n.* 1. the quality or state of being one; singleness; unity. 2. unity of mind, feeling, or purpose. 3. sameness; identity.

one-night stand (wun'nīt'), a single night performance of a show, lecture, etc. at a given town.

on·er·ous (on'ẽr-əs), *adj.* [ME. (*h*)*onerous;* OFr. (*h*)*onereus;* L. *onerosus* < *onus*, a load], 1. burdensome; laborious. 2. in *law*, involving a legal obligation.
SYN.—**onerous** applies to that which is laborious or troublesome, often because of its annoying or tedious character (the *onerous* duties of a janitor); **burdensome** applies to that which is wearisome or oppressive to the mind or spirit as well as to the body (*burdensome* responsibilities); **oppressive** stresses the overbearing cruelty of the person or thing that inflicts hardship, or emphasizes the severity of the hardship itself (*oppressive* weather, an *oppressive* king); **exacting** suggests the making of great demands on the attention, skill, care, etc. (an *exacting* supervisor, *exacting* work).

one·self (wun'self', wunz'self'), *pron.* a person's own self; himself or herself: also **one's self.**
be oneself, 1. to function physically and mentally as one normally does. 2. to be natural or sincere.
by oneself, alone; unaccompanied; withdrawn.
come to oneself, 1. to recover one's senses. 2. to recover one's capacity for sound judgment.

one-sid·ed (wun'sīd'id), *adj.* 1. on, having, or involving only one side. 2. larger or more developed on one side; leaning to one side. 3. favoring one side; uneven or unfair; partial; prejudiced.

one-step (wun'step'), *n.* 1. a ballroom dance characterized by quick walking steps in 2/4 time. 2. music for this dance. *v.i.* to dance the one-step.

one-time (wun'tīm'), *adj.* at some past time; former.

one-track (wun'trak'), *adj.* 1. having a single track. 2. [Colloq.], able to deal with only one thing at a time; limited in scope: as, a *one-track* mind.

one-way (wun'wā'), *adj.* moving, or providing for movement, in one direction only: as, a *one-way* street.

ONFr., Old North French.

on·ion (un'yən), *n.* [ME.; OFr. *oignon;* L. *unio, unionis*, unity, hence single onion, pearl < *unus*, one], 1. a plant of the lily family, having an edible bulb with a strong, sharp smell and taste. 2. the bulb of this plant, formed of close, concentric layers of tissue.

on·ion·skin (un'yən-skin'), *n.* 1. the thin, translucent outer coating of an onion; hence, 2. a tough, thin, translucent paper with a glossy surface.

on·look·er (on'look'ẽr), *n.* a person who looks on; spectator.

on·look·ing (on'look'iŋ), *adj.* watching but not taking part; looking on. *n.* the act of looking on.

on·ly (ōn'li), *adj.* [ME. *onli, onlich;* AS. *anlic; an*, one + *-lic*, -ly], 1. alone of its or their kind; by itself or by themselves; sole. 2. alone in its or their superiority; best; finest. *adv.* and no other; and no (or nothing) more; singly; solely; merely; exclusively. *conj.* [Colloq.], were it not that; except that; but: as, I should have gone, *only* it rained. Abbreviated **o.**
only too, very; exceedingly.

on·o·mat·o·poe·ia (on'ə-mat'ə-pē'ə, ō-nom'ə-tə-pē'ə), *n.* [LL.; Gr. *onomatopoiia* < *onoma, onomatos*, a name + *poiein*, to make], 1. the formation of a word by imitating the natural sound associated with the object or action involved (e.g., *tinkle, buzz, chickadee*, etc.). 2. a word formed in this way. 3. the use of such words, as in poetry or rhetoric.

on·o·mat·o·poe·ic (on'ə-mat'ə-pē'ik), *adj.* of, having the nature of, or like onomatopoeia: see also **echoic.**

on·o·mat·o·po·et·ic (on'ə-mat'ə-pō-et'ik), *adj.* onomatopoeic.

on·o·mat·o·poi·et·ic (on'ə-mat'ə-poi-et'ik), *adj.* onomatopoetic.

On·on·da·ga (on'ən-dô'gə, on'ən-dä'gə), *n.* [*pl.* ONONDAGA, ONONDAGAS (-gəz)], [< Am. Ind. (Iroquois) *Ononta'ge'*, lit., on top of the hill (name of the chief Onondaga village)], a member of a tribe of Iroquoian Indians who lived near Onondaga Lake.

Onondaga Lake, a salt lake near Syracuse, New York: length, 5 mi.; width, 1 mi.

ONorm.Fr., Old Norman French.

on·rush (on'rush'), *n.* a headlong dash forward; strong onward flow.

on·set (on'set'), *n.* 1. an attack; assault. 2. a setting out; beginning; start.

on·shore (on'shôr', on'shōr'), *adj.* 1. moving onto or toward the shore. 2. situated or operating on land: as, an *onshore* patrol. *adv.* toward the shore; landward.

on·side (on'sīd'), *adj. & adv.* in *football, hockey*, etc., in the proper position for play, according to the rules.

on·slaught (on'slôt'), *n.* [prob. < D. *aanslag* < *slagen*, to strike; modified after words like *draught, slaughter*, etc.; early forms *anslacht, anslaight* exist], a violent, intense attack.

On·tar·i·an (on-târ'i-ən), *adj.* of Ontario. *n.* a native or inhabitant of Ontario.

On·tar·i·o (on-târ'i-ō'), *n.* 1. the smallest of the Great Lakes, between New York and Ontario, Canada: area, 7,540 sq. mi. 2. a province of south central Canada, on the Great Lakes: area, 412,582 sq. mi.; pop., 4,598,000; capital, Toronto. Abbreviated **Ont., O.**

on·to (on'tōō, on'tə), *prep.* 1. to and upon; to a position on. 2. [Slang], aware of; cognizant of: as, father is *onto* you and your excuses. Also **on to.**

on·to- (on'tō, on'tə), [Gr. *ōn, ontos*, ppr. of *einai*, to be], a combining form meaning *being, existence*, as in *ontology, ontogenesis.*

on·to·gen·e·sis (on'tō-jen'ə-sis), *n.* [*onto-* + Gr. *genesis*, generation], ontogeny.

on·to·ge·net·ic (on'tō-jə-net'ik), *adj.* of ontogeny.

on·tog·e·ny (on-toj′ə-ni), *n.* [*onto-* + *-geny*], the life cycle of a single organism; biological development of the individual: distinguished from *phylogeny*.

on·to·log·i·cal (on′tə-loj′i-k'l), *adj.* of ontology.

ontological argument, in *metaphysics*, an a priori argument for the existence of God, based upon the widespread existence of the idea of God.

on·tol·o·gism (on-tol′ə-jiz'm), *n.* [see ONTOLOGY & -ISM], the philosophical doctrine that the knowledge of God is immediate and intuitive, and that all other knowledge is dependent upon this.

on·tol·o·gy (on-tol′ə-ji), *n.* [Mod. L. *ontologia;* see ONTO- & -LOGY], the branch of metaphysics dealing with the nature of being or reality: cf. **phenomenology.**

o·nus (ō′nəs), *n.* [L., a load, burden; IE. base **enos-* or **onos-*, seen also in Sans. *ánas*, freight cart], anything burdensome; task; responsibility.

‡**o·nus pro·ban·di** (ō′nəs prō-ban′dī), [L., lit., burden of proving], the burden of proof.

on·ward (on′wērd), *adv.* [ME.; see ON & -WARD], toward or at a position or point ahead in space or time; forward. *adj.* moving or directed onward or ahead; advancing: as, an *onward* trend.

on·wards (on′wērdz), *adv.* onward.

on·yx (on′iks, ō′niks), *n.* [ME. & OFr. *oniche;* L.; Gr. *onyx*, the nail: the color of the gem resembles that of the nail], a variety of agate with alternate layers of color, used as a semiprecious stone, especially in making cameos.

o·ö- (ō′ə), [< Gr. *ōion*, an egg], a combining form meaning *egg* or *ovum*, as in *oögenesis*, *oölogy*.

o·ö·cyte (ō′ə-sīt′), *n.* [*oö-* + *-cyte*], in *embryology*, 1. an egg that has not yet undergone maturation. 2. in certain protozoans, an immature female gamete.

oo·dles (ōō′d'lz), *n.pl.* [said to be dial. form of *huddle*], [Slang], a great amount; very many.

o·ög·a·mous (ō-og′ə-məs), *adj.* [*oö-* + *-gamous*], in *biology*, having reproductive cells that are sexually differentiated; heterogamous.

o·ö·gen·e·sis (ō′ə-jen′ə-sis), *n.* [*oö-* + *-genesis*], in *biology*, the process by which the ovum is formed in preparation for its fertilization and development.

o·ö·go·ni·um (ō′ə-gō′ni-əm), *n.* [*pl.* OÖGONIA (-ə), OÖGONIUMS (-əmz)], [Mod. L., dim. < *oö-* + Gr. *gonos*, offspring], 1. the female reproductive organ in thallophytic plants, consisting of a large cell in which the eggs (*oöspheres*) are developed. 2. in *embryology*, any of the cells from which the oöcytes derive.

o·ö·lite (ō′ə-līt′), *n.* [Fr. *oölithe;* see OÖ- & -LITE], a limestone composed of many small grains of carbonate of lime cemented together like fish eggs in a layer of sedimentary rock.

o·ö·lit·ic (ō′ə-lit′ik), *adj.* of oölite.

o·ö·log·i·cal (ō′ə-loj′i-k'l), *adj.* of oölogy.

o·öl·o·gy (ō-ol′ə-ji), *n.* [*oö-* + *-logy*], that branch of ornithology concerned with the study of birds' eggs.

oo·long (ōō′lôŋ, ōō′loŋ), *n.* [Chin. dial. form of *wu-lung*, lit., black dragon], a Chinese variety of black tea that is partly fermented before being dried.

oo·mi·ac, oo·mi·ak (ōō′mi-ak′), *n.* an umiak.

Oom Paul (ōom pō′ool), see **Kruger, Paul.**

oomph (oomf), *n.* [echoic of involuntary expression of approval], [Slang], 1. sex appeal. 2. vigor; energy.

o·ö·phore (ō′ə-fôr′, ō′ə-fōr′), *n.* [*oö-* + *-phore*], an oöphyte.

o·ö·pho·rec·to·my (ō′ə-fə-rek′tə-mi), *n.* [*oöphor-* + *-ectomy*], the surgical removal of one or both ovaries.

o·ö·pho·ri·tis (ō′ə-fə-rī′tis), *n.* [Mod. L. < *oöphor-* + *-itis*], inflammation of an ovary or the ovaries.

o·öph·o·ro- (ō-of′ə-rə), [< Mod. L. *oöphoron*, ovary < Gr. *ōion*, an egg + *-phoros*, bearing], a combining form meaning *ovary* or *ovaries:* also, before a vowel, **oöphor-.**

o·ö·phyte (ō′ə-fīt′), *n.* [*oö-* + *-phyte*], in plants undergoing alternation of generations, as ferns, mosses, etc., that generation in which the reproductive organs are developed.

o·ö·sperm (ō′ə-spûrm′), *n.* [*oö-* + Gr. *sperma*, a seed], 1. in *botany*, an oöspore. 2. in *zoology*, a zygote.

o·ö·sphere (ō′ə-sfēr′), *n.* [*oö-* + *sphere*], any of the unfertilized eggs that develop in the female reproductive organ of a thallophytic plant.

o·ö·spore (ō′ə-spôr′), *n.* [*oö-* + *spore*], an oösphere after it has been fertilized.

o·ö·the·ca (ō′ə-thē′kə), *n.* [*pl.* OÖTHECAE (-sē)], [Mod. L. < *oö-* + Gr. *thēkē*, a case], the egg case of certain mollusks and insects.

ooze (ōōz), *n.* [ME. *wose, wos;* AS. *wos*, sap, juice; akin to MLG. *wose*, scum; IE. base **wes-*, wet; meaning influenced by AS. *wase*, mire, dirt], 1. an infusion of oak bark, sumac, etc., used in tanning leather. 2. [< the *v.*], *a*) an oozing; gentle flow. *b*) something that oozes. *v.i.* [OOZED (ōōzd), OOZING], 1. to flow or leak out slowly, as through very small holes. 2. to give forth moisture, as through pores. 3. to escape or disappear imperceptibly: as, his desire to go *oozed* away. *v.t.* to give forth, or exude (a fluid).

ooze (ōōz), *n.* [ME. *wose, wase;* AS. *wase;* IE. base **weis-*, to flow away], 1. soft mud or slime; especially, the deep layers of sediment at the bottom of a lake, ocean, etc. 2. an area of muddy ground; bog; marsh.

oo·zi·ly (ōō′z'l-i), *adv.* in an oozy manner.

oo·zi·ness (ōō′zi-nis), *n.* an oozy quality or state.

oo·zy (ōō′zi), *adj.* [OOZIER (-zi-ēr), OOZIEST (-zi-ist)], oozing; giving forth moisture.

oo·zy (ōō′zi), *adj.* [OOZIER (-zi-ēr), OOZIEST (-zi-ist)], full of or like ooze; slimy.

op- (op, əp), ob-: used before *p*, as in *oppose.*

OP, O.P., observation post.

op., 1. opera. 2. operation. 3. opposite. 4. opus.

O.P., o.p., 1. out of print. 2. overproof. 3. in *philately*, overprint.

OPA, O.P.A., Office of Price Administration.

o·pac·i·ty (ō-pas′ə-ti), *n.* [Fr. *opacité;* L. *opacitas* < *opacus*, shady], 1. the state or quality of being opaque. 2. [*pl.* OPACITIES (-tiz)], something opaque.

o·pah (ō′pə), *n.* [W. Afr. *úbà*], a very large, brightly spotted, silvery fish of the Atlantic Ocean.

o·pal (ō′p'l), *n.* [L. *opalus*, opal; Gr. *opalios, opallios;* Sans. *upala*, precious stone], any of a large group of glassy, translucent silicas of various colors, capable of refracting light and then reflecting it in a play of colors: some varieties, used as semiprecious stones, include the *common opal*, with a generally milky appearance, the *black opal*, with a very dark-green background, and the *fire opal*, with flamelike colors.

o·pal·esce (ō′pə-les′), *v.i.* [OPALESCED (-lest′), OPALESCING], [*opal* + *-esce*], to show a play of colors like that of the opal.

o·pal·es·cence (ō′pə-les′'ns), *n.* the quality of being opalescent.

o·pal·es·cent (ō′pə-les′'nt), *adj.* [*opal* + *-escent*], showing a play of colors like that of the opal; iridescent.

o·pal·ine (ō′p'l-in, ō′p'l-īn′), *adj.* [*opal* + *-ine*], of or like opal. *n.* a translucent, milky variety of glass.

o·paque (ō-pāk′, ə-pāk′), *adj.* [ME. *opake;* L. *opacus*, shady], 1. not letting light pass through; not transparent. 2. not reflecting light; not shining or lustrous; dull or dark. 3. not allowing electricity, heat, etc. to pass through. 4. hard to understand; obscure. 5. slow in understanding; obtuse. *n.* 1. anything opaque. 2. in *photography*, an opaque liquid used in blocking out parts of a negative.

op. cit., *opere citato*, [L.], in the work cited.

ope (ōp), *adj., v.t. & v.i.* [OPED (ōpt), OPING], [Late ME. < *open(en)*], [Poetic], open.

o·pen (ō′p'n), *adj.* [ME.; AS.; akin to G. *offen;* for IE. base see UP (of which *open* is a semantic extension)], 1. in a state which permits entrance or exit; not closed, covered, clogged, or shut: as, *open* eyes, *open* doors. 2. in a state which permits freedom of view or passage; not enclosed, fenced in, sheltered, screened, etc.; unobstructed; clear: as, an *open* field. 3. unsealed; unwrapped. 4. *a*) not covered over; without covering, top, etc.: as, an *open* boat. *b*) liable to attack, etc.; unprotected. 5. spread out; unfolded; unclosed; expanded: as, an *open* book. 6. having spaces between; having gaps, holes, interstices, etc.: as, *open* ranks. 7. free from ice: as, the lake is *open* in May. 8. free from frost: as, an *open* winter. 9. free to be entered, used, competed in, shared, visited, etc. by all: as, an *open* meeting or tournament. 10. free to be argued or contested; not settled or decided: as, an *open* question. 11. *a*) free from prejudice or bigotry; not closed to new ideas, etc.: as, an *open* mind. *b*) liberal; generous. 12. *a*) free from restrictions: as, an *open* season. *b*) free from effective regulation with respect to drinking, gambling, etc.: as, the city is wide *open*. 13. in force or operation: as, an *open* account. 14. *a*) not already taken, occupied, or engaged; not filled: as, the job is still *open*. *b*) free to be accepted or rejected. 15. not closed against access; accessible; available. 16. not hidden or secret; generally known; public: as, an *open* quarrel. 17. frank; candid; direct; honest: as, an *open* manner. 18. in *music*, *a*) not stopped by the finger: said of a string. *b*) not closed at the top: said of an organ pipe. *c*) produced by an open string or pipe, or, in wind instruments, brasses, etc., without a slide or key: said of a tone. 19. in *nautical usage*, not hazy or foggy; clear. 20. in *phonetics*, *a*) pronounced with the tongue as low as possible; low: said of a vowel. *b*) pronounced with the organs of speech not in close contact; fricative: said of a consonant. *c*) ending in a vowel or diphthong: said of a syllable. 21. in *printing*, designating or of a style of type the letters of which are cast in outline. *v.t.* 1. to make or cause to be open (senses 1, 2, 3); unclose; unfasten: as, *open* the door. 2. to make an opening or openings in: as, the doctor *opened* the abscess. 3. to make spaces between; make less compact; spread out; expand: as, the soldiers *opened* their ranks. 4. to unclose; unfold; unroll: as, he *opened* the book. 5. to make available for use, competition, or participation, without restriction, taxation, fee, etc. 6. to free from prejudice and bigotry; make liberal and generous. 7. to make known, public, etc.; reveal; disclose. 8. to begin; enter upon; start; commence: as, he *opened* the session with a greeting. 9. to cause to start operating, going, etc.: as, he *opened* a new night club. 10. to undo, recall, set aside (a judgment, settlement, etc.), so as to leave the matter open to further action. *v.i.* 1. to become open. 2. to spread out; expand; unroll; unfold. 3. to become free from prejudice, etc.; become liberal and generous. 4. to become revealed, disclosed, etc.; come into view. 5. to be or act as an opening; give access. 6. to begin; start. 7. to start operating, going, etc. —*SYN.* see **frank.**

open out, 1. to make or become extended or larger. 2. to develop. 3. to disclose to view; reveal.

open to, 1. glad or willing to receive, discuss, etc. 2. liable to; subject to. 3. available to or for.

open up, 1. to make or become open. 2. to spread out; unfold. 3. to start; begin. 4. [Colloq.], to speak freely or with great feeling.

the open, 1. any open, unobstructed space on land or water. 2. an unenclosed area; the outdoors. 3. public knowledge. 4. in golf, *a)* any tournament open to both professionals and amateurs. *b)* [O-], an open tournament played annually in the United States to decide the national championship: properly called the *National Open.*

o·pen-air (ō′p'n-âr′), *adj.* outdoor.

open air, out of doors.

o·pen-and-shut (ō′p'n-'n-shut′), *adj.* that can be clearly and easily determined or decided; simple; obvious: as, an *open-and-shut* case.

open chain, a molecular formation in which the chain of elements does not form a ring.

open city, a city which is a military objective but is completely demilitarized and left open to enemy occupation in order to gain immunity, under international law, from bombardment and attack.

o·pen-door (ō′p'n-dôr′, ō′p'n-dōr′), *adj.* designating or of the policy or principle of the open door.

open door, 1. unrestricted admission. 2. free and equal opportunity for all nations to trade with a given nation, without any restrictive terms.

o·pen·er (ō′p'n-ẽr), *n.* 1. a person or thing that opens. 2. any of several devices for opening bottles, cans, etc. 3. the first game in a series.

o·pen-eyed (ō′p'n-īd′), *adj.* 1. having the eyes open or wide-open; awake, aware, watchful, discerning, amazed, etc. 2. done with the eyes open.

o·pen-faced (ō′p'n-fāst′), *adj.* 1. with the face uncovered. 2. having a frank, honest face.

o·pen·hand·ed (ō′p'n-han′did), *adj.* generous.

open hand knot, a loop knot: see **knot,** illus.

o·pen·heart·ed (ō′p'n-här′tid), *adj.* 1. not reserved; frank; candid. 2. kindly; generous.

o·pen-hearth (ō′p'n-härth′), *adj.* 1. designating a furnace with a wide, saucer-shaped hearth and a low roof, used in making steel. 2. using a furnace of this kind: as, the *open-hearth* process.

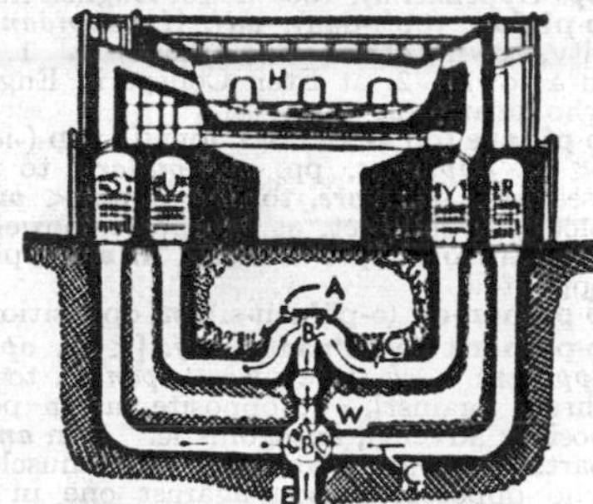

OPEN-HEARTH FURNACE
A, air valve; B, B, reversing valves; W, chimney; C, C, ports to chimney; E, gas main valve; H, hearth; R, S, U, V, regenerators

open house, 1. a house that extends hospitality to all who wish to come. 2. an occasion when a school, institution, etc. is open to visitors for inspection and observation of activities.

keep open house, to be ready to entertain guests at all times.

o·pen·ing (ō′p'n-iŋ), *n.* [ME. *openyng*], 1. a becoming open or causing to be open. 2. an open place or part; hole; gap; aperture. 3. a clearing in the midst of a wooded area. 4. *a)* a beginning; first part; commencement. *b)* start of operations; formal beginning. 5. a favorable chance or occasion; opportunity. 6. an unfilled position, or office for which a person is wanted. 7. in *chess, checkers,* etc., the series of moves at the beginning of a game.

open letter, a letter written as to a specific person, usually in attack, criticism, etc., but published for everyone to read.

o·pen-mind·ed (ō′p'n-mīn′did), *adj.* having a mind open to new ideas; free from prejudice or bigotry.

o·pen-mouthed (ō′p'n-mou*th*d′, ō′p'n-moutht′), *adj.* 1. having the mouth open. 2. gaping, as in astonishment. 3. greedy; ravenous. 4. clamorous; vociferous.

o·pen·ness (ō′p'n-nis), *n.* the quality or condition of being open; specifically, *a)* absence of secrecy. *b)* frankness; forthrightness. *c)* absence of prejudice or bigotry.

open season, any of various annual periods during which it is legal to kill or capture certain specified game, wild fowl, or fish.

open secret, something supposed to be secret but known to almost everyone.

open sesame, 1. magic words spoken to open the door of the robbers' den in the story of Ali Baba in the *Arabian Nights;* hence, 2. any unfailing means of gaining admission, etc., as a password.

open shop, 1. a factory, business, etc. operating under the system of employing workers without regard to whether or not they are members of a union, or, especially, not knowingly employing any union members, and following an antiunion policy. 2. this system. Distinguished from *closed shop, union shop,* etc.

open stock, merchandise sold in sets, the individual pieces of which are kept in stock in quantity so that replacements or additions are always available.

o·pen·work (ō′p'n-wũrk′), *n.* ornamental work, as in cloth, metal, etc., with openings in the material.

OPer., Old Persian.

op·er·a (op′ẽr-ə), *n.* [It. < L. *opera,* a work, labor], 1. a play having all or most of its text set to music, with arias, recitatives, choruses, duets, trios, etc. sung to orchestral accompaniment, usually characterized by elaborate costuming, scenery, and choreography: see **grand opera, comic opera, light opera.** 2. the branch of art represented by such plays. 3. the score, libretto, or performance of such a play. 4. a theater in which operas are given. Abbreviated **op.**

op·er·a (op′ẽr-ə), *n.* plural of **opus.**

op·er·a·ble (op′ẽr-ə-b'l), *adj.* [< L. *operari,* to work; + *-able*], 1. practicable. 2. that can be treated by a surgical operation.

‡o·pé·ra bouffe (ô′pā′rȧ′ bōōf′; Eng. op′ẽr-ə bōōf′), [Fr.], comic opera, especially if farcical.

‡o·pé·ra co·mique (ô′pā′rȧ′ kô′mēk′), [Fr., lit., comic opera], French opera with spoken dialogue: it may or may not be comic.

opera glasses, a small binocular telescope used at the opera, in theaters, etc.

opera hat, a man's tall, collapsible silk hat.

opera house, a theater chiefly for the performance of operas.

op·er·ant (op′ẽr-ənt), *adj.* [< L. *operans,* ppr. of *operari;* see OPERATE], operating, or producing an effect or effects. *n.* a person or thing that operates.

op·er·ate (op′ə-rāt′), *v.i.* [OPERATED (-id), OPERATING], [< L. *operatus,* pp. of *operari,* to work < *opus, operis,* a work], 1. to be in action so as to produce an effect; act; work. 2. to bring about a desired or appropriate effect; have a certain influence. 3. to carry on strategic military movements (usually with *against*). 4. to perform a surgical operation. *v.t.* 1. to bring about as an effect. 2. to put or keep in action; conduct.

op·er·at·ic (op′ə-rat′ik), *adj.* [< *opera,* after *dramatic*], of or like the opera.

op·er·at·i·cal·ly (op′ə-rat′i-k'l-i, op′ə-rat′ik-li), *adv.* in an operatic manner.

op·er·a·tion (op′ə-rā′shən), *n.* [ME. *operacion;* OFr.; L. *operatio*], 1. the act, process, or method of operating. 2. the condition of being in action or at work. 3. the power to act; force; influence. 4. a process or action that is part of a series in some work. 5. *a)* any movement or series of movements made in carrying out strategic military plans; hence, *b)* any specific plan or project: as, the atomic bomb test at Bikini was called *Operation* Crossroads. 6. any surgical procedure performed with or without the aid of instruments, usually to remedy a physical ailment or defect. 7. in *mathematics,* any process involving a change or transformation in a quantity: as, the *operations* of addition, subtraction, etc. Abbreviated **op.**

in operation, 1. in the act or process of making, working, etc. 2. having an influence or effect; in force.

op·er·a·tive (op′ə-rā′tiv, op′ẽr-ə-tiv), *adj.* [Fr. *opératif;* LL. *operativus*], 1. capable of, characterized by, or in operation. 2. accomplishing what is desired; effective; efficient. 3. connected with physical work or mechanical action. 4. in *surgery,* of or resulting from a surgical operation. *n.* 1. a worker, especially one employed or skilled in some sort of industrial work. 2. a detective.

op·er·a·tor (op′ə-rā′tẽr), *n.* [LL.], a person who operates; specifically, *a)* a person who effects something; agent. *b)* a person who works some machine: as, a telephone *operator. c)* a person who performs surgical operations. *d)* a person engaged in financial, commercial, or industrial operations; owner or manager of a mine, railroad, factory, etc.

o·per·cu·lar (ō-pũr′kyoo-lẽr), *adj.* of, or having the nature of, an operculum.

o·per·cu·late (ō-pũr′kyoo-lit, ō-pũr′kyoo-lāt′), ***adj.*** [L. *operculatus*], having an operculum.

o·per·cu·lat·ed (ō-pũr′kyoo-lā′tid), ***adj.*** operculate.

o·per·cu·lum (ō-pũr′kyoo-ləm), ***n.*** [*pl.* OPERCULA (-lə), OPERCULUMS (-ləmz)], [L. < *operire*, to close, shut], any of various covering flaps or lidlike structures in plants and animals; specifically, *a*) the bony covering protecting the gills of fishes. *b*) in many gastropods, the horny plate serving to close the shell when the animal is retracted. *c*) the lid of the spore cases in mosses. *d*) the lid of a pitcher-shaped leaf.

‡o·pe·re ci·ta·to (op′ə-ri sī-tā′tō), [L.], in the work cited, or quoted: abbreviated **op. cit., o.c.**

op·er·et·ta (op′ə-ret′ə), ***n.*** [It., dim. of *opera*], a short, amusing musical play.

op·er·ose (op′ə-rōs′), ***adj.*** [L. *operosus* < *opera*, a service, pains, work], 1. done with or requiring much toil. 2. very busy; industrious.

O·phe·lia (ō-fēl′yə, ə-fēl′yə), [prob. < Gr. *ōphelia*, a help, succor], a feminine name. ***n.*** in Shakespeare's *Hamlet*, Polonius's daughter, in love with Hamlet.

oph·i·cleide (of′i-klīd′), ***n.*** [Fr. *ophicléide* < Gr. *ophis*, serpent + *kleis*, a key], an early brass-wind instrument consisting of a long tube doubled back on itself, with keys for fingering.

o·phid·i·an (ō-fid′i-ən), ***n.*** [< Mod. L. *Ophidia*, name of the order (< Gr. *ophis*, a snake); + *-an*], any of a large group of reptiles that includes all the snakes, or serpents. ***adj.*** of or like a snake, or serpent.

oph·i·ol·a·try (of′i-ol′ə-tri), ***n.*** [< Gr. *ophis*, a snake; + *-latry*], the worship of serpents.

oph·i·ol·o·gy (of′i-ol′ə-ji), ***n.*** [< Gr. *ophis*, a snake; + *-logy*], the branch of zoology dealing with snakes.

O·phir (ō′fẽr), ***n.*** [Heb. *ōphīr*], in the *Bible*, a land rich in gold: I Kings 9:28, 10:11, 22:48.

oph·ite (of′īt, ō′fīt), ***n.*** [L. *ophites;* Gr. *ophitēs* (*lithos*), snake (stone) < *ophis*, a snake], a green, mottled rock.

o·phit·ic (ō-fit′ik), ***adj.*** of or like ophite: consisting of feldspar crystals in a matrix of augite.

Oph·i·u·chus (of′i-ū′kəs, ō′fi-ū′kəs), ***n.*** [L.; Gr. *ophiouchos*, lit., holding a serpent], a northern constellation: see **constellation**, chart.

ophth., ophthalm., ophthalmology.

oph·thal·mi·a (of-thal′mi-ə), ***n.*** [ME. *obtalmia;* LL.; Gr. *ophthalmia* < *ophthalmos*, the eye], a severe inflammation involving the eyeball or the conjunctiva.

oph·thal·mic (of-thal′mik), ***adj.*** [L. *ophthalmicus;* Gr. *ophthalmikos* < *ophthalmos*, the eye], 1. of or connected with the eyes. 2. having ophthalmia.

oph·thal·mi·tis (of′thal-mī′tis), ***n.*** ophthalmia.

oph·thal·mo- (of-thal′mō, of-thal′mə), [< Gr. *ophthalmos*, the eye], a combining form meaning *the eye* or *eyes*, as in *ophthalmoscope:* also, before a vowel, **ophthalm-**.

oph·thal·mo·log·i·cal (of-thal′mə-loj′i-k'l), ***adj.*** of ophthalmology.

oph·thal·mol·o·gist (of′thal-mol′ə-jist), ***n.*** a specialist in ophthalmology.

oph·thal·mol·o·gy (of′thal-mol′ə-ji), ***n.*** [*ophthalmo-* + *-logy*], the branch of medicine dealing with the structure, functions, and diseases of the eye.

oph·thal·mo·scope (of-thal′mə-skōp′), ***n.*** [*ophthalmo-* + *-scope*], an instrument used to examine the interior of the eye: it consists of a perforated mirror arranged to reflect light from a small bulb into the eye.

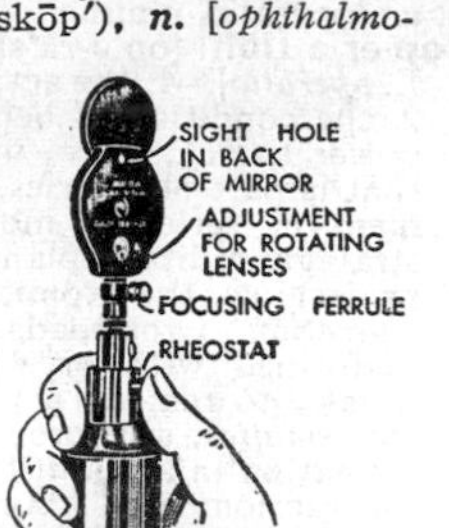

OPHTHALMOSCOPE

oph·thal·mo·scop·ic (of-thal′mə-skop′ik), ***adj.*** of the ophthalmoscope or ophthalmoscopy.

oph·thal·mos·co·py (of′thal-mos′kə-pi), ***n.*** the examination of the interior of the eye with the ophthalmoscope.

-o·pi·a (ō′pi-ə), [Gr. *-ōpia* < *ōps*, *ōpos*, an eye], a combining form meaning *a* (specified kind of) *eye defect*, as in *diplopia:* also **-opy**.

o·pi·ate (ō′pi-it, ō′pi-āt′), ***n.*** [ML. *opiatus;* see OPIUM], 1. any medicine containing opium or any of its derivatives, and acting as a sedative and narcotic. 2. anything tending to quiet or soothe. ***adj.*** 1. containing opium. 2. bringing sleep, quiet, or ease; narcotic. ***v.t.*** (ō′pi-āt′), [OPIATED (-id), OPIATING], [Rare], 1. to treat with an opiate. 2. to dull; deaden.

o·pine (ō-pīn′), ***v.t. & v.i.*** [OPINED (-pīnd′), OPINING], [Fr. *opiner;* L. *opinari*, to think], to hold or express (an opinion); think; suppose: now usually humorous.

o·pin·ion (ə-pin′yən), ***n.*** [ME. *opinioun;* OFr.; L. *opinio* < *opinari*, to think], 1. a belief not based on absolute certainty or positive knowledge but on what seems true, valid, or probable to one's own mind; what one thinks; judgment. 2. an evaluation, impression, or estimation of the quality or worth of a person or thing. 3. the formal judgment of an expert on a matter in which his advice is sought. 4. in *law*, 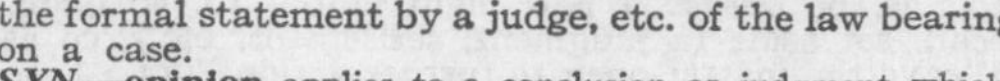 the formal statement by a judge, etc. of the law bearing on a case.

SYN.—**opinion** applies to a conclusion or judgment which, while it remains open to dispute, seems true or probable to one's own mind (it's my *opinion* that he'll agree); **belief** refers to the mental acceptance of an idea or conclusion, often a doctrine or dogma proposed to one for acceptance (*religious* beliefs); a **view** is an opinion affected by one's personal manner of looking at things (she gave us her *views* on life); a **conviction** is a strong belief about whose truth one has no doubts (I have a *conviction* of his innocence); **sentiment** refers to an opinion that is the result of deliberation but is colored with emotion; **persuasion** refers to a strong belief that is unshakeable because one wishes to believe in its truth.

o·pin·ion·at·ed (ə-pin′yən-ā′tid), ***adj.*** holding unreasonably or obstinately to one's own opinions.

o·pin·ion·a·tive (ə-pin′yən-ā′tiv), ***adj.*** 1. of opinion; consisting in opinion. 2. opinionated.

op·is·thog·na·thous (op′is-thog′nə-thəs), ***adj.*** [< Gr. *opisthen*, behind; + *-gnathous*], having receding jaws: opposed to *prognathous*.

o·pi·um (ō′pi-əm), ***n.*** [L.; Gr. *opion* < *opos*, vegetable juice], a narcotic drug prepared from the juice of the unripe seed capsules of the opium poppy: it contains such alkaloids as morphine, codeine, and papaverine, and is used as an intoxicant and medicinally to relieve pain and produce sleep.

o·pi·um·ism (ō′pi-əm-iz'm), ***n.*** 1. opium addiction. 2. the condition resulting from this.

opium poppy, a plant with grayish-green leaves and large white or purple flowers, the source of opium.

op·o·del·doc (op′ō-del′dok), ***n.*** [said to have been coined by Paracelsus; prob. < Gr. *opos*, a juice], a soap liniment, especially one containing camphor.

O·por·to (ō-pôr′tō), ***n.*** a seaport in northern Portugal: pop., 262,000: Portuguese name, *Porto*.

o·pos·sum (ə-pos′əm), ***n.*** [*pl.* OPOSSUMS (-əmz), OPOSSUM; see PLURAL, II, D, 1], [N. Am. Ind., lit., white beast], a small, tree-dwelling mammal, the female of which carries its young in a pouch: it is active at night and pretends to be dead when trapped: also **possum**.

opossum shrimp, a shrimplike crustacean, the female of which carries her eggs in a pouch between the legs.

OPOSSUM (15 in. long)

opp., 1. opposed. 2. opposite.

Op·pen·heim, E. Phillips (op′'n-hīm′), (*Edward Phillips Oppenheim*), 1866–1946; English novelist.

op·pi·dan (op′i-dən), ***adj.*** [L. *oppidanus* < *oppidum*, city, town], of a town; urban. ***n.*** 1. a person living in a town. 2. at Eton College in England, a student who boards in town.

op·pi·late (op′ə-lāt′), ***v.t.*** [OPPILATED (-id), OPPILATING], [< L. *oppilatus*, pp. of *oppilare*, to stop up < *ob-* (see OB-) + *pilare*, to ram down < *pilum*, pestle], to block or obstruct, as the pores, bowels, etc.

op·pi·la·tion (op′ə-lā′shən), ***n.*** an oppilating or being oppilated.

op·po·nen·cy (ə-pō′nən-si), ***n.*** opposition; resistance.

op·po·nent (ə-pō′nənt), ***adj.*** [< L. *opponens*, ppr. of *opponere* < *ob-* (see OB-) + *ponere*, to set, put, place, thrust against], 1. opposite, as in position. 2. opposing; adverse; antagonistic. 3. in *anatomy*, bringing parts into opposition: said of a muscle. ***n.*** a person who opposes; person against one in a fight, game, debate, argument, etc.; adversary.

SYN.—**opponent**, an unemotional word, refers to anyone who is opposed to one, as in a fight, game, debate, etc.; **antagonist** implies more active opposition, especially in a struggle for control or power; **adversary** usually suggests actual hostility in the conflict; **enemy** may imply actual hatred in the opponent and a desire to injure, or it may simply refer to any member of the opposing group, nation, etc., whether or not there is personal animosity or hostility involved; **foe**, now a somewhat literary synonym for **enemy**, connotes more active hostility.—***ANT.*** ally, confederate.

op·por·tune (op′ẽr-tōōn′, op′ẽr-tūn′), ***adj.*** [ME.; L. *opportunus*, lit., at or before the port < *ob-* (see OB-) + *portus*, a port, harbor, haven], 1. right for the purpose; fitting in regard to circumstances: said of time. 2. happening or done at the right time; seasonable; well-timed; timely. —***SYN.*** see **timely**.

op·por·tun·ism (op′ẽr-tōōn′iz'm, op′ẽr-tūn′iz'm), ***n.*** [< *opportune*, after Fr. *opportunisme*], the policy or habit of adapting one's actions, thoughts, and utterances to circumstances, as in politics, in order to further one's immediate interests, without regard for basic principles or eventual consequences.

op·por·tun·ist (op′ẽr-tōōn′ist, op′ẽr-tūn′ist), ***n.*** a person who practices opportunism. ***adj.*** opportunistic.

op·por·tun·is·tic (op′ẽr-tōō-nis′tik, op′ẽr-tū-nis′tik), ***adj.*** of an opportunist or opportunism.

op·por·tu·ni·ty (op′ẽr-tōō′nə-ti, op′ẽr-tū′nə-ti), ***n.*** [*pl.* OPPORTUNITIES (-tiz)], [ME. *opportunite;* OFr. *opportunité;* L. *opportunitas* < *opportunus;* see OPPORTUNE], a combination of circumstances favorable for the purpose; fit time; good chance or occasion.

op·pos·a·bil·i·ty (ə-pōz'ə-bil'ə-ti), *n.* the quality or condition of being opposable.

op·pos·a·ble (ə-pōz'ə-b'l), *adj.* 1. that can be opposed. 2. that can be placed opposite something else.

op·pose (ə-pōz'), *v.t.* [OPPOSED (-pōzd'), OPPOSING], [ME. *opposen;* OFr. *opposer* < *poser;* see POSE, *v.*], 1. to set against; place opposite, in balance or contrast. 2. to resist; withstand; contend with in speech or action. *v.i.* to bring opposition: as, I choose to *oppose*.
SYN.—**oppose** implies offensive action taken against something that threatens or interferes with one; **resist** implies defensive action taken against something that is already in active opposition to one (one *opposes* legislative action under consideration, one *resists* a measure already passed by refusing to comply with it); **withstand** usually implies resistance that successfully thwarts or frustrates the attack (can they *withstand* the new onslaught?).—*ANT.* submit, succumb, comply.

op·po·site (op'ə-zit), *adj.* [ME.; OFr.; L. *oppositus*, pp. of *opponere;* see OPPONENT], 1. opposed to. 2. set against; in a contrary position or direction (often with *to*). 3. characterized by hostility or resistance. 4. extremely different; exactly contrary; antithetical. 5. in *botany*, *a*) growing in pairs, but separated by a stem. *b*) having one part before another, as a stamen in front of a petal. *n.* anything opposed. *adv.* on opposing sides; in opposite positions; specifically, in the *theater*, in a complementary role (of the opposite sex) to: as, he played *opposite* her. *prep.* fronting; across from. Abbreviated **opp., op.**
SYN.—**opposite** is applied to things that are symmetrically opposed in position, direction, etc. (they sat at *opposite* ends of the table); **contrary** adds to this connotations of conflict or antagonism (they hold *contrary* views); **antithetic(al)** implies diametrical opposition so that the contrasted things are as far apart or as different as is possible (our interests are completely *antithetical*); **reverse** applies to that which moves or faces in the opposite direction (the *reverse* side of a fabric); **antonymous** is used specifically of words that are so opposed in meaning that each contradicts, reverses, or negates the other (good and bad are *antonymous* terms).—*ANT.* same, identical, like.

opposite number, a person having a position, rank, etc. comparable with that of another in a different place, organization, or situation.

op·po·si·tion (op'ə-zish'ən), *n.* [ME. *opposicioun;* OFr. < L. *oppositio* < *oppositus*, pp. of *opponere;* see OPPOSITE], 1. an opposing or being opposed. 2. resistance; contradiction; contrast; hostility. 3. anything that opposes. 4. [sometimes O-], a minority political party serving as a check on the party in power. 5. in *astrology* & *astronomy*, the position of two heavenly bodies when their longitudes differ by 180°; especially, such position of a planet with respect to the sun. 6. in *law*, the refusal of a creditor to assent to a debtor's release under the bankruptcy law. 7. in *logic*, the relation of exclusion or inclusion which exists between propositions having the same subject and predicate but differing in quality, quantity, or both.

op·press (ə-pres'), *v.t.* [ME. *oppressen;* OFr. *oppresser;* ML. *oppressare* < L. *oppressus*, pp. of *opprimere*, to press against < *ob-* (see OB-) + *primere*, to press], 1. to weigh heavily on the mind, spirits, or senses of; lie heavily on; burden. 2. to keep down by the cruel or unjust use of power or authority; burden with harsh, rigorous impositions; tyrannize over. 3. [Obs.], *a*) to crush; trample down. *b*) to overpower; subdue. —*SYN.* see **wrong.**

op·pres·sion (ə-presh'ən), *n.* 1. an oppressing or being oppressed. 2. a thing that oppresses. 3. a feeling of being weighed down; physical or mental distress.

op·pres·sive (ə-pres'iv), *adj.* [ML. *oppressivus* < L. *oppressus;* see OPPRESS], 1. hard to put up with; burdensome. 2. cruelly overbearing; tyrannical. 3. weighing heavily on the mind, spirits, or senses; causing physical or mental distress. —*SYN.* see **onerous.**

op·pres·sor (ə-pres'ẽr), *n.* [ME. *oppressour* < Anglo-Fr.], a person who oppresses.

op·pro·bri·ous (ə-prō'bri-əs), *adj.* [ME.; LL. *opprobriosus*], 1. expressing opprobrium; abusive; disrespectful. 2. deserving opprobrium; disgraceful; infamous.

op·pro·bri·um (ə-prō'bri-əm), *n.* [L. < *opprobrare*, to reproach < *ob-* (see OB-) + *probrum*, a disgrace], 1. the disgrace attached to shameful conduct or status; scorn; reproach; infamy. 2. anything bringing shame or disgrace.

op·pugn (ə-pūn'), *v.t.* [ME. *oppugnen;* L. *oppugnare* < *ob-* (see OB-) + *pugnare* < *pugna*, a fight], to oppose with argument; reason against; criticize adversely; call in question; controvert.

op·pug·nan·cy (ə-pug'nən-si), *n.* the quality or state of being oppugnant.

op·pug·nant (ə-pug'nənt), *adj.* [L. *oppugnans*, ppr.; see OPPUGN], hostile; antagonistic; opposing.

OPr., Old Provençal.

Ops (ops), *n.* [L., lit., strength, riches], in *Roman mythology*, the wife of Saturn and goddess of the harvest: identified with the Greek Rhea.

OPS, O.P.S., Office of Price Stabilization.

-op·sis (op'sis), [Gr. *-opsis* < *opsis*, a sight, appearance], a combining form meaning *sight* or *view*, as in *synopsis*.

op·son·ic (op-son'ik), *adj.* of, or having the effect of, opsonin.

opsonic index, the ratio of the number of bacteria destroyed by phagocytes in an individual's blood serum to the number destroyed in a normal blood serum.

op·son·i·fi·ca·tion (op-son'ə-fi-kā'shən), *n.* the act, process, or result of opsonifying.

op·son·i·fy (op-son'ə-fī'), *v.t.* [OPSONIFIED (-fīd'), OPSONIFYING], to make bacteria more liable to destruction by phagocytes: said of opsonins.

op·so·nin (op'sō-nin), *n.* [< Gr. *opsōnein*, to buy food, cater < *opson*, meat, fish, food eaten with bread; *o-*, together with + **pson*, food, bread; akin to *psōmos*, mouthful], a substance in the blood which acts on bacteria, making them more liable to destruction by phagocytes.

op·so·nize (op'sə-nīz'), *v.t.* [OPSONIZED (-nīzd'), OPSONIZING], to form opsonins in.

opt (opt), *v.i.* [Fr. *opter;* L. *optare*], to make a choice.

opt., 1. optative. 2. optician. 3. optics. 4. optional.

op·ta·tive (op'tə-tiv), *adj.* [Fr. *optatif;* LL. *optativus* < *optare*, to desire], 1. expressing wish or desire. 2. designating or of the grammatical mood in Greek, etc. which expresses wish or desire. *n.* 1. the optative mood. 2. a verb in this mood. Abbreviated **opt.**

op·tic (op'tik), *adj.* [Fr. *optique;* ML. *opticus;* Gr. *optikos* < base *op*, seen in *opsomai*, I shall see], of the eye or sense of sight. *n.* [Colloq.], an eye.

op·ti·cal (op'ti-k'l), *adj.* 1. of or connected with the sense of sight; visual; ocular. 2. of the relation between light and vision. 3. having to do with optics. 4. made to give help in seeing: as, *optical* instruments.

optical activity, the ability of certain substances to rotate the plane of polarization when transmitting polarized light.

optic axis, in a crystal not having the same properties in all directions with regard to light, the direction or directions along which there is no double refraction.

op·ti·cian (op-tish'ən), *n.* [Fr. *opticien*], a person who makes or sells eyeglasses and other optical instruments.

optic nerves, the second pair of cranial nerves; the nerves of sight, connecting the retina of the eye with the brain: see **eye,** illus.

op·tics (op'tiks), *n.pl.* [construed as sing.], [< *optic*], the branch of physics dealing with the nature and properties of light and vision: abbreviated **opt.**

optic thalamus, a mass of gray matter located at the base of the brain on either side, functioning as a visual center.

op·ti·mism (op'tə-miz'm), *n.* [Fr. *optimisme* < L. *optimus*, best], 1. in *philosophy*, *a*) the doctrine of Leibnitz that the existing world is the best possible. *b*) the doctrine or belief that good ultimately prevails over evil. 2. the tendency to take the most hopeful view of matters or to expect the best outcome in any circumstances; practice of looking on the bright side of things: opposed to *pessimism*.

op·ti·mist (op'tə-mist), *n.* a person who believes in or is given to optimism.

op·ti·mis·tic (op'tə-mis'tik), *adj.* of or characterized by optimism; hopeful; sanguine.

op·ti·mis·ti·cal·ly (op'tə-mis'ti-k'l-i, op'tə-mis'tik-li), *adv.* in an optimistic manner.

op·ti·mize (op'tə-mīz'), *v.i.* [OPTIMIZED (-mīzd'), OPTIMIZING], to be given to optimism. *v.t.* to consider with optimism.

op·ti·mum (op'tə-məm), *n.* [*pl.* OPTIMUMS (-məmz), OPTIMA (-mə)], [L., neut. of *optimus*, best], 1. the best or most favorable degree, condition, amount, etc. 2. in *biology*, the amount of heat, light, moisture, food, etc. most favorable for growth and reproduction. *adj.* best; most favorable.

op·tion (op'shən), *n.* [Fr.; L. *optio* < *optare*, to wish, desire], 1. a choosing; choice. 2. the power, right, or liberty of choosing. 3. something that is or can be chosen. 4. the right, acquired for a consideration, to buy or sell something at a fixed price within a specified time. —*SYN.* see **choice.**

op·tion·al (op'shən-'l), *adj.* left to one's option; open to choice; not compulsory; elective: abbreviated **opt.**

op·tion·al·ly (op'shən-'l-i), *adv.* by option, or choice.

op·tom·e·ter (op-tom'ə-tẽr), *n.* [see OPTIC & -METER], an instrument for measuring the range and power of vision and determining the focal lengths of lenses necessary to correct nearsightedness or farsightedness.

op·tom·e·trist (op-tom'ə-trist), *n.* a specialist in optometry: see also **ophthalmologist, oculist, optician.**

op·tom·e·try (op-tom'ə-tri), *n.* [see OPTIC & -METRY], 1. measurement of the range and power of vision.

2. examination of the eyes (without the use of drugs or medicine) for nearsightedness, farsightedness, etc., and the fitting of glasses to correct these defects; work of an optometrist.

op·u·lence (op′yoo-ləns), *n.* [L. *opulentia* < *opulens;* see OPULENT], 1. wealth; riches. 2. abundance.

op·u·len·cy (op′yoo-lən-si), *n.* opulence.

op·u·lent (op′yoo-lənt), *adj.* [L. *opulentus* or *opulens* < *ops, opis,* might, wealth], 1. wealthy; rich. 2. abundant; profuse; luxuriant. —*SYN.* see **rich.**

o·pun·ti·a (ō-pun′shi-ə), *n.* [Mod. L. < *Opus,* city in Locris, Greece, where such plants were plentiful], any of a large group of cactus plants with red, purple, or yellow flowers and fleshy or dry berries; prickly pear.

o·pus (ō′pəs), *n.* [*pl.* OPERA (op′ẽr-ə); *now also* OPUSES (-iz)], [L., a work], a work; composition: the term when applied to a musical composition is followed by a number showing its place in order of composition or publication among the works of the composer: abbreviated **op.**

o·pus·cule (ō-pus′kūl), *n.* [Fr.; L. *opusculum,* dim. of *opus,* a work], a small or trivial work or composition.

-o·py (ō′pi), -opia.

o·quas·sa (ō-kwas′ə), *n.* [< *Oquassa* Lake, in Maine], a small lake trout of Maine, with a red-spotted, dark-blue body.

or (ôr; *unstressed* ẽr), *conj.* [ME., in form a contr. of *other, auther,* either, but actually < AS. *oththe* (in *āther. . .oththe,* either. . .or)], a co-ordinating conjunction introducing an alternative; specifically, *a*) introducing the second of two choices: as, I'll offer him beer *or* wine. *b*) introducing any of the choices in a series, but usually used only before the last: as, apples, (*or*) pears, (*or*) peaches, *or* plums. *c*) introducing a synonymous word or phrase: as, botany, *or* the science of plants. *d*) introducing the second of two choices when the first is introduced by *either* or *whether:* as, either go *or* stay, whether to go *or* stay. *e*) in *poetry,* sometimes substituted for *either* as the first correlative: as, "*or* in the heart *or* in the head."

or (ôr), *conj. & prep.* [ME.; AS. *ār,* var. of *ǣr,* ere; cf. ERE], [Archaic or Dial.], before; ere.

or (ôr), *n.* [Fr.; L. *aurum,* gold], in *heraldry,* gold or yellow, represented in engraving by small dots powdered over a plain field.

-or (ẽr; *rarely* ôr), a suffix of varied origins: 1. [ME. *-our;* OFr. *-our, -or, -eur;* L. *-or, -ator*], a noun-forming suffix meaning *a person* or *thing that,* as in *inventor, juror, tractor.* 2. [ME. & OFr. *-our;* L. *-or*], a noun-forming suffix meaning *quality* or *condition,* as in *horror, error, favor:* in British usage, often *-our.*

Or., 1. Oregon. 2. Oriental.

o.r., owner's risk.

‡o·ra (ō′rə), *n.* plural of **os** (a mouth).

or·ach, or·ache (ôr′əch, or′əch), *n.* [ME. *orage;* Anglo-Fr. *orache;* OFr. *arroche;* altered < L. *atriplex,* orach], a garden plant with red or green leaves, sometimes used as a vegetable.

or·a·cle (ôr′ə-k'l, or′i-k'l), *n.* [ME.; OFr.; L. *oraculum,* divine announcement, oracle, prophecy < *orare,* to speak, pray, beseech, entreat < *os, oris,* the mouth], 1. among the ancient Greeks and Romans, the place where or medium by which deities were consulted. 2. the revelation or response of a medium or priest. 3. *a*) any person or agency believed to be in communication with a deity; hence, *b*) any person of great knowledge. *c*) opinion or statements of such a person. 4. the holy of holies of the ancient Jewish Temple: I Kings 6:16, 19–23. 5. *pl.* the Scriptures.

o·rac·u·lar (ō-rak′yoo-lẽr, ō-rak′yoo-lẽr), *adj.* 1. of, or having the nature of, an oracle. 2. very wise; prophetic; mysterious.

O·ra·de·a (ô-räd′yä), *n.* a city in northwestern Romania: pop., 104,000: German name, *Grosswardein;* Hungarian name, *Nagyvárad.*

o·ral (ôr′əl, ō′rəl), *adj.* [< L. *os, oris,* the mouth], 1. uttered by the mouth; spoken. 2. of speech; using speech. 3. of, at, or near the mouth. 4. in *phonetics,* having mouth resonance only: distinguished from *nasal.* 5. in *zoology,* on or of the same side as the mouth. *n.* an oral examination, as in a university.

SYN.—**oral** refers to that which is spoken, as distinguished from that which is written or otherwise communicated (an *oral* promise, request, etc.); **verbal,** though sometimes synonymous with **oral,** in strict discrimination refers to anything using words, either written or oral, to communicate an idea or feeling (a *verbal* image, caricature, etc.).

o·ral·ly (ôr′ə-li, ō′rə-li), *adv.* [*oral* + *-ly*], 1. by speech, or spoken words. 2. by the mouth.

O·ran (ō-ran′; Fr. ô′rän′), *n.* a city in northwestern Algeria, on the Mediterranean: pop., 299,000.

o·rang (ō-raŋ′), *n.* an orangutan.

Or·ange (ôr′ənj, or′inj; *also for 3 & 4,* Fr. ô′ränzh′), *n.* 1. a city in New Jersey, near Newark: pop., 36,000. 2. a river in the Union of South Africa, flowing westward into the Atlantic: length, 1,300 mi. 3. a former principality of western Europe: now a part of southeastern France. 4. a town in southeastern France: site of Roman ruins.

or·ange (ôr′ənj, or′inj), *n.* [ME. & OFr. *orenge;* Pr. *auranja* (with sp. influenced by L. *aurum,* gold & loss of initial *n* through faulty separation of art. *une*) < Sp. *naranja;* Ar. *naranj;* Per. *narang*], 1. a reddish-yellow, round fruit of the citrus family, with a sweet, juicy pulp. 2. the evergreen tree producing this fruit, having white, fragrant blossoms. 3. any of several shrubs resembling this tree. 4. reddish yellow. *adj.* 1. of an orange or oranges. 2. reddish-yellow.

or·ange·ade (ôr′ənj-ād′, or′inj-ād′), *n.* [Fr.; see ORANGE & -ADE], a drink made of orange juice mixed with water and sugar, usually iced.

Orange Free State, a province of the Union of South Africa: area, 49,647 sq. mi.; pop., 1,017,000; capital, Bloemfontein: formerly a Boer republic (1854–1900) and then a British colony (*Orange River Colony,* 1900–1910): abbreviated **O.F.S.**

Or·ange·ism (ôr′ənj-iz'm, or′inj-iz'm), *n.* the principles and practices of the Orangemen.

Or·ange·man (ôr′ənj-mən, or′inj-mən), *n.* [*pl.* ORANGEMEN (-mən)], [named after William III of England, Prince of *Orange*], a member of a secret society organized in northern Ireland in 1795 to support Protestantism.

Orange Mountains, a mountain range in central New Guinea; highest peak, Mt. Wilhelmina, 15,580 ft.

orange pekoe, a black tea grown in Ceylon and India: see **pekoe.**

or·ange·ry (ôr′ənj-ri, or′inj-ri), *n.* [*pl.* ORANGERIES (-riz)], [Fr. *orangerie* < *oranger,* orange tree < *orange*], a place where orange trees are grown: usually with reference to a hothouse or other sheltered place used for this purpose in cooler climates.

orange stick, a pointed stick of orangewood, used in manicuring.

or·ange·wood (ôr′ənj-wood′, or′inj-wood′), *n.* the wood of the orange tree, used in woodwork, etc. *adj.* of orangewood.

o·rang·ou·tang (ō-raŋ′oo-taŋ′), *n.* an orangutan.

o·rang·u·tan (ō-raŋ′oo-tan′), *n.* [Malay *orañ utan,* wild man, lit., man of the forest; *orañ,* man + *utan,* forest: first applied to the ape by Europeans], a manlike ape with shaggy, reddish-brown hair, very long arms, small ears, and a hairless face: it is smaller than the gorilla and is found only in the jungles of Borneo and Sumatra: often **orang.**

ORANGUTAN (4-5 ft. high)

‡o·ra pro no·bis (ō′rə prō nō′bis), [L.], pray for us: in the Roman Catholic liturgy, a plea to the Virgin Mary.

o·rate (ôr′āt, ō-rāt′), *v.i. & v.t.* [ORATED (-id), ORATING], [< *oration*], to make (an oration); say (something) in a pompous or bombastic manner: a humorously derogatory term.

o·ra·tion (ô-rā′shən, ō-rā′shən), *n.* [ME. (Scot.) *oracione;* L. *oratio* < *orare,* to speak], a formal public speech, especially one given in connection with a ceremony, anniversary, etc. —*SYN.* see **speech.**

or·a·tor (ôr′ə-tẽr, or′ə-tẽr), *n.* [ME. *oratour;* OFr. *orateur;* L. *orator*], 1. a person who delivers an oration. 2. a skilled, eloquent public speaker. 3. in *law,* a petitioner; plaintiff.

or·a·tor·i·cal (ôr′ə-tôr′i-k'l, or′ə-tō′ri-k'l), *adj.* 1. of or characteristic of orators or oratory; in the manner of an orator or oratory. 2. given to oratory.

or·a·to·ri·o (ôr′ə-tôr′i-ō′, or′ə-tō′ri-ō′), *n.* [*pl.* ORATORIOS (-ōz′)], [It., lit., small chapel (< LL. *oratorium;* see ORATORY, 2): music so called from the performance of such compositions at the oratory of Saint Philip Neri in Rome], a long, dramatic musical composition, usually on a religious theme, consisting of arias, recitatives, duets, trios, choruses, etc. sung to orchestral accompaniment: it is presented without stage action, scenery, or costumes.

or·a·to·ry (ôr′ə-tôr′i, or′ə-tō′ri), *n.* [*pl.* ORATORIES (-iz, -riz)], [ME. *oratorie;* L. *oratoria*], 1. the art of an orator; skill or eloquence in public speaking. 2. [ME. *oratorie;* LL. *oratorium* < L. *oratorius,* of praying < *orator*], a small chapel, especially one for private prayer. 3. [O-], in the *Roman Catholic Church,* a religious society of secular priests, founded by Saint Philip Neri in 1564: also called *Fathers of the Oratory, Oratorians.*

orb (ôrb), *n.* [< Fr. or L.; Fr. *orbe;* L. *orbis,* a circle], 1. a sphere; globe. 2. *a*) any of the heavenly spheres, as the sun, moon, etc. *b*) [Obs.], the earth. *c*) [Obs.], the orbit of a planet, etc. 3. [Poetic], the eye or eyeball. 4. a sphere surmounted by a cross, as a symbol of royal power. 5. [Archaic], *a*) a sphere of activity; province. *b*) rank; status. 6. a collective body; organized whole. 7. [Rare], anything circular in form;

circle. 8. in *astrology*, the sphere of influence of a planet, star, or house. ***v.t.*** 1. to form into a sphere or circle. 2. [Poetic], to enclose or encircle. ***v.i.*** 1. to move in an orbit. 2. [Poetic], to take on the shape of an orb.

or·bic·u·lar (ôr-bik′yoo-lẽr), ***adj.*** [ME. *orbiculer;* LL. *orbicularis* < L. *orbiculus*, dim. of *orbis*, a circle], 1. in the form of an orb; spherical or circular. 2. in *botany*, round and flat, as a leaf: see **leaf**, illus.

or·bic·u·late (ôr-bik′yoo-lit, ôr-bik′yoo-lāt′), ***adj.*** [L. *orbiculatus*], orbicular.

or·bic·u·lat·ed (ôr-bik′yoo-lā′tid), ***adj.*** orbiculate.

or·bit (ôr′bit), ***n.*** [< Fr. or L.; Fr. *orbite;* L. *orbita*, path, track < *orbis*, a circle, wheel], 1. the bony cavity containing the eye; eye socket. 2. the path taken by a heavenly body during its periodic revolution around another body. 3. the range of one's experience or activity; ordinary course of life. 4. in *zoology*, the skin around the eye of a bird. ***v.t. & v.i.*** to put or go in an orbit (sense 2), as an artificial satellite.

or·bit·al (ôr′bit-'l), ***adj.*** of or in an orbit.

orbital index, the ratio between the length and the greatest height of the orbit of the eye.

orb·y (ôr′bi), ***adj.*** 1. of, or having the form of, an orb. 2. revolving as an orb.

orc (ôrk), ***n.*** [Fr. *orque;* L. *orca*, kind of whale], 1. the grampus, or killer whale. 2. any dolphin whale resembling the grampus.

O.R.C., 1. Officers' Reserve Corps. 2. Order of the Red Cross.

or·ce·in (ôr′si-in), ***n.*** [< *orcin*], a brownish-red, crystalline coloring matter, $C_{28}H_{24}O_7N_2$, obtained by treating orcinol with ammonia and oxygen.

orch., orchestra.

or·chal (ôr′kəl), ***n.*** orchil.

or·chard (ôr′chẽrd), ***n.*** [ME.; AS. *orceard, ortgeard; ort* (? < ML. *ortus*, for L. *hortus*), a garden + *geard* (see YARD, enclosure)], 1. an area of land, generally enclosed, devoted to the cultivation of fruit trees, nut trees, etc. 2. such trees, collectively.

or·chard·ist (ôr′chẽrd-ist), ***n.*** a person skilled or engaged in the cultivation of orchards.

or·ches·tra (ôr′kis-trə), ***n.*** [L.; Gr. *orchēstra* < *orcheisthai*, to dance; IE. base **ergh-*, extension of **er-*, swift movement, rise abruptly, seen also in Sans. *ṛghāyati*, he trembles or is agitated, L. *oriri*, to rise], 1. in ancient Greek theaters, the semicircular space in front of the stage, used by the chorus. 2. in modern theaters, the narrow space in front of and below the stage, where the musicians sit: also called *orchestra pit.* 3. *a)* the section of seats near the pit on the main floor of a theater. *b)* the main floor of a theater. 4. *a)* a group of musicians playing together; especially, a symphony orchestra. *b)* the instruments of such a group. Abbreviated **orch.**

or·ches·tral (ôr-kes′trəl), ***adj.*** of, for, or by an orchestra.

or·ches·trate (ôr′kis-trāt′), ***v.t. & v.i.*** [ORCHESTRATED (-id), ORCHESTRATING], to compose or arrange (music) for an orchestra.

or·ches·tra·tion (ôr′kis-trā′shən), ***n.*** arrangement of music for an orchestra; instrumentation.

or·ches·tri·na (ôr′kis-trē′nə), ***n.*** an orchestrion.

or·ches·tri·on (ôr-kes′tri-ən), ***n.*** a large, mechanical music box, somewhat like a barrel organ, that produces an effect imitative of that of an orchestra.

or·chi- (ôr′ki), orchido-.

or·chid (ôr′kid), ***n.*** [< L. **orchid-*, falsely assumed stem of *orchis;* see ORCHIS], 1. any of a number of related plants having flowers with three petals, two regularly shaped and the third (the lip) enlarged and irregular in form. 2. the flower of such a plant; especially, any of the brightly colored tropical varieties cultivated for wear by women and regarded as a symbol of luxury. 3. a light bluish red. ***adj.*** light bluish-red.

or·chi·da·ceous (ôr′ki-dā′shəs), ***adj.*** [< Mod. L. *Orchidaceae* (see ORCHID); + *-ous*], 1. of the orchid family. 2. like an orchid in showiness, beauty, etc.

or·chi·do- (ôr′ki-dō, ôr′ki-də), [< Gr. **orchidos*, falsely assumed genit. of *orchis*, testicle], a combining form meaning: 1. *testicle*, as in *orchidotomy*. 2. *orchid*, as in *orchidology*. Also **orchi-** and, before a vowel, **orchid-**.

or·chid·ol·o·gy (ôr′ki-dol′ə-ji), ***n.*** [*orchido-* + *-logy*], the branch of horticulture dealing with orchids.

or·chi·dot·o·my (ôr′ki-dot′ə-mi), ***n.*** [*orchido-* + *-tomy*], surgery on the testicles.

or·chil (ôr′kil, ôr′chil), ***n.*** [OFr. *orcheil, orchel;* see ARCHIL], archil, a purple dye or the lichen from which it is obtained: also **orchal.**

or·chis (ôr′kis), ***n.*** [L.; Gr. *orchis*, testicle: from the shape of the roots], an orchid; specifically, a variety with small purplish or white flowers growing in spikes.

or·cin (ôr′sin), ***n.*** orcinol.

or·cin·ol (ôr′si-nōl′, ôr′si-nol′), ***n.*** [< It. *orcello*, archil (see ARCHIL); + *-in* + *-ol*], a colorless, crystalline compound, $C_6H_3 \cdot CH_3(OH)_2$, obtained from aloes, some lichens, etc., used as a medicine or in making dyes.

Or·cus (ôr′kəs), ***n.*** [L.], in *Roman mythology*, 1. the lower world; Hades. 2. Pluto; Dis.

ord., 1. ordained. 2. order. 3. ordinal. 4. ordinance. 5. ordinary. 6. ordnance.

or·dain (ôr-dān′), ***v.t.*** [ME. *ordeinen;* OFr. *ordener;* L. *ordinare*, to order < *ordo, ordinis*, an order], 1. originally, to put in order; arrange; prepare. 2. to appoint; decree; order; establish; enact. 3. to appoint or admit to the Christian ministry. 4. to qualify (a man) as a rabbi.

or·deal (ôr-dēl′, ôr-dē′əl, ôr′dēl), ***n.*** [ME. *ordal;* AS. *ordal, ordel* (akin to G. *urteil*, judgment) < *or-*, out + *dæl* (see DEAL), what is dealt: the prevailing sense seems to be due to adoption of the L. *ordela*, itself a borrowing of the Gmc. word], 1. an ancient method of trial in which the accused was exposed to physical dangers, which were supposed to be harmless to him if he was innocent. 2. any difficult, painful, or trying experience; severe trial.

or·der (ôr′dẽr), ***n.*** [ME. & OFr. *ordre;* L. *ordo, ordinis*, straight row, regular series], 1. social position; rank in the community. 2. a state of peace and serenity; observance of the law; orderly conduct. 3. the sequence or arrangement of things or events; series; succession. 4. a fixed or definite plan; system; law of arrangement. 5. a group or class set off from others by some trait or quality. 6. *a)* a group of men constituting a military or monastic brotherhood: as, the *Order* of Knights Templars, the Franciscan *Order.* *b)* an organized group of persons united by common interests or for social purposes, often in the form of a secret organization or lodge: as, the *Order* of the Eastern Star. 7. *a)* a group of persons distinguished by having received a certain award or citation, as for outstanding service to a state: as, the *Order* of the Purple Heart. *b)* the insignia or badge of such a group. 8. a state or condition in which everything is in its right place and functioning properly. 9. condition or state in general: as, the motor was in very poor *order.* 10. a command, direction, or instruction, usually backed by authority. 11. a class; kind; sort; group determined by distinction or uniqueness: as, sentiments of a high *order.* 12. an established method or system, as of conduct or action in meetings, worship, court, etc. 13. *a)* a request or commission to make or supply something: as, have you received my *order* for books? *b)* the goods so made or supplied: as, I delivered her grocery *order.* *c)* a single portion of some food, as served in a public eating place: as, I'll have an *order* of cole slaw. 14. in *architecture*, *a)* any of several classical styles of structure, determined chiefly by the type of column: see **Doric, Ionic,** etc. *b)* a style of building. 15. in *finance*, written instructions to pay money or surrender property. 16. in *law*, a decision of a court or judge, usually not a final judgment. 17. in *mathematics*, the degree or stage of complexity of a sum or figure. 18. in *military science*, *a) pl.* commands or announcements issued by the War Department or by military commanders. *b)* the position of a rifle following the command *order arms.* 19. in *scientific classification*, a group in botany or zoology next larger than the family and smaller than the class. 20. in *theology*, *a)* one of the nine classifications or grades of angels. *b)* any rank or grade in the Christian clergy. *c) pl.* the position of ordained minister: as, he took holy *orders.* *d)* the ceremony of ordaining a minister. Abbreviated **O., ord.** ***v.t.*** 1. to put or keep in order; organize; arrange. 2. to instruct (another) to do something; command. 3. to request (something to be supplied): as, *order* the groceries. 4. in *theology*, to ordain. ***v.i.*** 1. to give a command. 2. to request that something be supplied. —***SYN.*** see **command.**

by order, in observance of an order given by someone.

call to order, 1. to request to be quiet and busy at work. 2. to start (a meeting).

in order, 1. in proper sequence or position. 2. in good condition. 3. in accordance with the rules, as of a meeting. 4. appropriate to the occasion; suitable.

in order that, so that; to the end that.

in order to, for the purpose of; as a means to; to.

in short order, in a short time; without delay; quickly.

on order, ordered, or requested, but not yet supplied.

on the order of, somewhat resembling; similar to.

out of order, 1. out of proper sequence or position. 2. not in operation; in poor condition. 3. not in accordance with the rules, as of a meeting. 4. not appropriate to the occasion; not suitable.

to order, in accordance with the specifications made by the purchaser.

order arms, in *military usage*, 1. to bring the rifle to an upright position with its butt on the ground beside the right foot, and remain at attention. 2. a command to do this.

or·der·li·ness (ôr′dẽr-li-nis), *n.* the quality or condition of being orderly.

or·der·ly (ôr′dẽr-li), *adj.* 1. neat; tidy; well-arranged. 2. well-behaved; law-abiding; peaceable. 3. having to do with the transmission of military orders. *n.* [*pl.* ORDERLIES (-liz)], 1. a soldier assigned to an officer for carrying messages, performing personal services, etc. 2. a male hospital attendant.

SYN.—**orderly** implies freedom from disorder or confusion as by observing a proper arrangement, a set rule, etc. (an *orderly* desk, crowd, meeting, etc.); **methodical** implies a following closely and regularly a definite procedure that is carefully planned in detail (a *methodical* investigation, worker, etc.); **systematic** often adds the implications of thoroughness and elaborateness and stresses the over-all purpose, design, pattern, etc. (a *systematic* suppression of the opposition, etc.)—*ANT.* disorderly, haphazard, chaotic.

Order of the Garter, the highest order of British knighthood, instituted about 1344 by Edward III.

Order of the Purple Heart, a United States military order of soldiers wounded in action: instituted by George Washington as a medal of merit and revived in its present form in 1932.

or·di·nal (ôr′d'n-əl, ôr′di-n'l), *adj.* [ME. *ordynal,* conforming to order; LL. *ordinalis* < L. *ordo, ordinis,* an order], 1. expressing order or succession, specifically of a number in a series: the ordinal numbers are *first, second, third,* etc., or *1st, 2d, 3d,* etc.: distinguished from *cardinal.* 2. of an order of animals or plants. *n.* 1. an ordinal number. 2. [often O-], a book of prescribed forms used in church services or certain church ceremonies. Abbreviated **ord.**

or·di·nance (ôr′di-nəns), *n.* [ME. *ordenaunce;* OFr. *ordenance* < *ordener;* see ORDAIN], 1. a direction or command of an authoritative nature. 2. a custom or practice established by usage or authority. 3. an established religious rite; specifically, the Communion. 4. in *law,* a statute enacted by the legislative department of a city government. Abbreviated **ord.** —*SYN.* see **law.**

or·di·nar·i·ly (ôr′d'n-er′ə-li, ôr′də-nâr′ə-li), *adv.* usually; generally; as a rule.

or·di·nar·i·ness (ôr′d'n-er′i-nis), *n.* the quality or condition of being ordinary.

or·di·nar·y (ôr′d'n-er′i), *n.* [*pl.* ORDINARIES (-iz)], [ME. *ordinarie;* L. *ordinarius* < *ordo,* an order], 1. an official of church or court whose power or jurisdiction is original and not that of a deputy. 2. a book containing the form or order for divine service. 3. a set meal served from day to day at the same price. 4. a tavern. 5. a prison chaplain. 6. an early type of bicycle having wheels of different size. 7. in *heraldry,* any one of the major devices used as heraldic distinctions. *adj.* 1. customary; usual; regular; normal. 2. familiar; unexceptional; common Abbreviated **ord.** —*SYN.* see **common.**

in ordinary, in regular, permanent service.

out of the ordinary, unusual; extraordinary.

ordinary seaman, 1. a sailor of less experience than, and ranking below, an able-bodied seaman. 2. formerly, in the United States Navy, a seaman second class.

or·di·nate (ôr′d'n-āt′, ôr′d'n-it), *n.* [ME. *ordynat;* L. *ordinatus,* well-ordered, ordained, pp. of *ordinare,* to order, arrange < *ordo, ordinis,* an order], in *mathematics,* one of two lines used in fixing a point on a geometric graph.

or·di·na·tion (ôr′də-nā′shən), *n.* [ME. *ordinacioun;* L. *ordinatio* < *ordinare;* see ORDINATE], 1. an ordaining or being ordained. 2. admission to the Christian ministry.

ORDINATE
ME or YO, ordinate of point M; OE or YM, abscissa of M; NN, axis of ordinates; DD, axis of abscissas

ord·nance (ôrd′nəns), *n.* [contr. < *ordinance,* in restricted meaning], 1. artillery. 2. *a*) all weapons and ammunition used in warfare. *b*) any equipment or supplies used in servicing weapons. Abbreviated **ord., ordn.**

‡**or·do** (ôr′dō), *n.* [*pl.* ORDINES (-di-nēz′)], [L., order], 1. order; arrangement. 2. [O-], in the *Roman Catholic Church,* an annual calendar that gives directions for each day's Mass and Office.

or·don·nance (ôr′də-nəns; Fr. ôr′dô′näns′), *n.* [Fr.; cf. ORDINANCE], 1. the proper or orderly arrangement of parts, as in a painting, literary composition, etc. 2. in France and other European countries, an ordinance, law, or decree.

Or·do·vi·cian (ôr′də-vish′ən), *adj.* [< L. *Ordovices,* Roman name for ancient Celtic tribe in Wales], designating or of the period of the Paleozoic Era immediately following the Cambrian and preceding the Silurian, characterized by an abundance of invertebrate life and, in rock strata, by deposits of limestone, lead, and zinc.

the Ordovician, the Ordovician Period or its rocks: see **geology,** chart.

or·dure (ôr′jẽr, ôr′dyoor), *n.* [ME.; OFr. < *ord,* filthy; L. *horridus,* horrid], dung; filth; manure; excrement.

Or·dzho·ni·kid·ze (ôr′jô-ni-kēd′ze), *n.* 1. the capital of the North Ossetian A.S.S.R., in the Caucasus: pop., 164,000: formerly called *Vladikavkaz.* 2. a city in the eastern Ukrainian S.S.R.: pop., 92,000.

ore (ôr, ōr), *n.* [ME. *or;* AS. *ar,* brass, copper, identified with *ora,* unwrought metal; hence, the form is from the former, the meaning from the latter], 1. any natural combination of minerals, especially one from which a metal or metals can be profitably extracted. 2. a natural substance from which a nonmetallic material, such as sulfur, can be extracted.

o·re·ad (ôr′i-ad′, ō′ri-ad′), *n.* [Gr. *oreias, oreiados* < *oros,* mountain], in *Greek mythology,* a mountain nymph.

o·rec·tic (ō-rek′tik), *adj.* [Gr. *orektikos* < *orektos,* stretched out < *oregein,* to stretch out for, reach, desire], in *philosophy,* of or characterized by appetite or desire.

o·re·ga·no (ō-re′gə-nō′), *n.* [Sp. *orégano*], any of a number of plants of the mint family, the fragrant leaves of which are used for seasoning.

Or·e·gon (ôr′i-gon′, or′i-gən), *n.* a Northwestern State of the United States: area, 96,981 sq. mi.; pop., 1,769,000; capital, Salem: abbreviated **Oreg., Ore., Or., O.**: nicknamed *Beaver State.*

Oregon fir, the Douglas fir: also **Oregon pine.**

Oregon grape, 1. a North American evergreen shrub having clusters of small, blue berries: it is the state flower of Oregon. 2. its berry.

Or·e·go·ni·an (ôr′i-gō′ni-ən, or′i-gō′ni-ən), *adj.* of Oregon. *n.* 1. a native or inhabitant of Oregon. 2. a member of a linguistic family of American Indians who lived in the northwestern United States.

Oregon Trail, a former route extending northwest about 2,000 miles, from the Mississippi to the Columbia River in Oregon: it was used by pioneers (c. 1804–1850).

Or·el (ō-rel′; Russ. or-yôl′), *n.* 1. a region of the R.S.F.S.R., in central European Russia: pop., 3,482,000. 2. its capital: pop., 152,000.

Or·en·burg (or′en-boorkh′), *n.* Chkalov, a city in European Russia: the former name.

O·res·tes (ô-res′tēz, ō-res′tēz), *n.* [L.; Gr. *Orestēs* < *oros,* mountain], in *Greek legend,* son of Agamemnon and Clytemnestra, who, with the aid of his sister Electra, avenged the murder of his father by killing his mother and her lover Aegisthus.

Ö·re·sund (ö′rə-soon′), *n.* The Sound: Danish and Swedish name.

org., 1. organic. 2. organization. 3. organized.

or·gan (ôr′gən), *n.* [ME. *organe;* both OFr. *organe* & AS. *organa* < L. *organum* < Gr. *organon,* an instrument, implement, engine], 1. a large wind instrument consisting of various sets of pipes which, as they are opened by their corresponding keys on the keyboard, allow passage to a column of compressed air that causes sound by vibration. 2. any of several other musical instruments resembling this instrument. 3. in animals and plants, a part composed of several tissues and adapted to the performance of a specific function or functions. 4. a means or instrument for the performance of some action. 5. a means of communicating ideas or opinions, as a periodical.

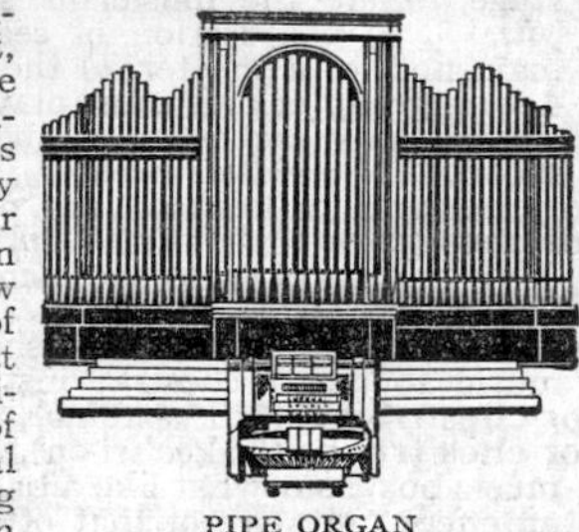
PIPE ORGAN

or·gan·dy, or·gan·die (ôr′gən-di), *n.* [*pl.* ORGANDIES (-diz)], [Fr. *organdi;* prob. < altered name of a Chinese town or locality], a very sheer, stiff, lightweight cotton material, used for blouses, etc. *adj.* made of organdy.

organ grinder, a person who makes a living by playing a barrel organ in the street.

or·gan·ic (ôr-gan′ik), *adj.* [L. *organicus;* Gr. *organikos*], 1. of or having to do with an organ. 2. inherent; inborn; constitutional. 3. organized; systematically arranged. 4. *a*) designating or of any chemical compound containing carbon: some of the simple compounds of carbon, as carbon dioxide, are frequently classified as inorganic compounds. *b*) designating or of the branch of chemistry dealing with carbon compounds. 5. of, having the characteristics of, or derived from living organisms. 6. in *law,* fundamental: as, the *organic* law of the United States is the Constitution. 7. in *medicine,* producing or involving alteration in the structure of an organ: opposed to *functional.* 8. in *philosophy,* having a complex but necessary interrelationship of parts, similar to that in living things. Abbreviated **org.**

or·gan·i·cal·ly (ôr-gan′i-k'l-i, ôr-gan′ik-li), *adv.* 1. in an organic manner. 2. as regards organic structure.

organic disease, a disease caused or accompanied by visible structural changes in the tissues or organs.

or·gan·i·cism (ôr-gan′ə-siz'm), *n.* 1. in *medicine, a*) the theory that each bodily organ has its own constitution. *b*) the theory that all disease is caused by organic lesions. *c*) the theory that the bodily organs determine all symptoms. 2. in *philosophy*, the theory of biology that an organism's own dynamic system constitutes life: opposed to *mechanism*, *vitalism*.

or·gan·ism (ôr′gən-iz'm), *n.* 1. any living thing. 2. anything resembling a living thing in its complexity of structure or functions.

or·gan·ist (ôr′gən-ist), *n.* [< *organ*, after Fr. *organiste*], one who plays, or is skilled at playing, the organ.

or·gan·iz·a·ble (ôr′gən-īz′ə-b'l), *adj.* that can be organized.

or·gan·i·za·tion (ôr′gən-i-zā′shən, ôr′gən-ī-zā′shən), *n.* [ME. *organizacion;* ML. *organizatio*], 1. an organizing or being organized. 2. organic structure; manner of being organized. 3. an organism. 4. any unified, consolidated group of elements; systematized whole; especially, a body of persons organized for some specific purpose, as a club, union, or society. 5. the administrative personnel or executive structure of a business. 6. all the functionaries, committees, etc. of a political party. Abbreviated **org.**

or·gan·ize (ôr′gən-īz′), *v.t.* [ORGANIZED (-īzd′), ORGANIZING], [ME. *organyzen;* ML. *organizare* < L. *organum*], 1. to provide with an organic structure; systematize. 2. to arrange; establish; institute; bring into being. 3. *a*) to enlist in, or cause to form, a labor union. *b*) to enlist the employees of (an industry, store, etc.) in a labor union. *v.i.* 1. to become organic or organized. 2. to form or join a labor union.

or·gan·iz·er (ôr′gən-īz′ẽr), *n.* a person who organizes; specifically, a labor-union official whose work is enlisting and orienting members.

organ loft, the gallery, as in a church, for the organ.

or·ga·no- (ôr′gə-nō), [< Gr. *organon*, organ], a combining form meaning *organ* or *organic*, as in *organography*.

or·ga·no·gen·e·sis (ôr′gə-nō-jen′ə-sis), *n.* [Mod. L.; see ORGANO- & -GENESIS], in *biology*, the origin and development of organs.

or·ga·nog·ra·phy (ôr′gə-nog′rə-fi), *n.* [*organo-* + *-graphy*], a scientific description of plant or animal organs.

or·ga·nol·o·gy (ôr′gə-nol′ə-ji), *n.* [*organo-* + *-logy*], that branch of science dealing with the form, structure, development, and functions of animal organs.

or·ga·non (ôr′gə-non′), *n.* [*pl.* ORGANA (-nə), ORGANONS (-nonz′)], [Gr.], 1. a method, means, or agency for communicating knowledge. 2. in *philosophy*, a system used in investigation.

or·ga·no·ther·a·peu·tics (ôr′gə-nō-ther′ə-pū′tiks), *n.pl.* [construed as sing.], organotherapy.

or·ga·no·ther·a·py (ôr′gə-nō-ther′ə-pi), *n.* [*organo-* + *therapy*], the treatment of disease with extracts of animal organs, as of the glands of internal secretion.

organ pipe, 1. one of the pipes in a pipe organ. 2. something resembling this.

or·ga·num (ôr′gə-nəm), *n.* [*pl.* ORGANUMS (-nəmz), ORGANA (-nə)], [L.; Gr. *organon*, a tool], 1. an organon. 2. in *music*, an early type of two-part harmony in which the voices are separated by an interval of a fourth or fifth.

or·gasm (ôr′gaz'm), *n.* [Fr. *orgasme;* Gr. *orgasmos* < *organ*, to swell with moisture, lust; akin to Sans. *ūrjā*, violence, vigor, sap], a frenzy; great excitement; especially, the climax or culmination of a sexual act.

or·geat (ôr′zhat; Fr. ôr′zhä′), *n.* [Fr.; Pr. *orjat* < *ordi*, *orge*, barley < L. *hordeum*], a sirup or beverage made of barley water flavored with almonds or orange flowers.

or·gi·as·tic (ôr′ji-as′tik), *adj.* [Gr. *orgiastikos* < *orgiastēs* < *orgiazein*, to celebrate orgies; see ORGY], having to do with or resembling an orgy.

or·gy (ôr′ji), *n.* [*pl.* ORGIES (-jiz)], [earlier chiefly in pl.; Fr. *orgies;* L. *orgia*, *pl.*; Gr. *orgia*, *pl.*, secret rites, secret worship; akin to *ergon*, a work; for IE. base see WORK], 1. *usually in pl.* in ancient Greece and Rome, feasting and wild celebration in worship of certain gods. 2. any wild, riotous merrymaking. 3. an overindulgence in any activity: as, an *orgy* of work.

or·i·bi (ôr′ə-bi), *n.* [S.Afr.D. < Nama *arab*], any of several species of African pygmy antelopes distinguished by a long tuft of hair growing from each knee.

o·ri·el (ôr′i-əl, ō′ri-əl), *n.* [ME.; OFr. *oriol;* ML. *oriolum*, porch, gallery], a large window built out from a wall and resting on a bracket or a corbel; large bay window.

or·i·ent (ôr′i-ənt, ō′ri-ənt; *for n. also, and for v. usually*, ôr′i-ent′, ō′ri-ent′), *n.* [ME.; OFr. < L. *oriens;* see the *adj.*], 1. [Poetic], the east. 2. [O-], *a*) the East; Asia. *b*) the Far East; eastern Asia. Opposed to *occident*, *Occident*. 3. *a*) the quality that determines a pearl's value; luster. *b*) a pearl of high quality. *adj.* [L. *oriens*, direction of the rising sun, ppr. of *oriri*, to arise; cf. OCCIDENT], 1. [Poetic], oriental; belonging to the east. 2. brilliant; shining; precious: originally of pearls, now more general. 3. [Chiefly Poetic], rising, as the sun. *v.t.* [Fr. *orienter* < the *adj.*], 1. to cause to turn to or face the east. 2. *a*) to set, as a map, in agreement with the points of the compass; hence, *b*) figuratively, to adjust or adapt to a particular situation (often used reflexively). 3. to show or establish relationship with others by placing or arranging in a certain manner. *v.i.* 1. to turn to or face the east. 2. to become adjusted to a situation.

or·i·en·tal (ôr′i-en′t'l, ō′ri-en′t'l), *adj.* [ME. *orientale*], 1. eastern. 2. [O-], of the Orient, its people, or their culture; Eastern. *n.* [usually O-], a native of the Orient or a member of a people native to that region. Opposed to *occidental*, *Occidental*. Abbreviated **Or.**

O·ri·en·tal·ism (ôr′i-en′t'l-iz'm, ō′ri-en′t'l-iz'm), *n.* [*oriental* + *-ism*], [sometimes o-], 1. any trait, quality, mannerism, etc. usually associated with people of the East. 2. study of Eastern culture.

O·ri·en·tal·ist (ôr′i-en′t'l-ist, ō′ri-en′t'l-ist), *n.* [*oriental* + *-ist*], [sometimes o-], a student of Eastern culture.

O·ri·en·tal·ize (ôr′i-en′t'l-īz′, ō′ri-en′t'l-īz′), *v.t. & v.i.* [ORIENTALIZED (-īzd′), ORIENTALIZING], [sometimes o-], to make or become Oriental in character.

Oriental rug, any of various kinds of handmade rugs made in the Orient: also **Oriental carpet.**

o·ri·en·tate (ôr′i-en-tāt′, ō′ri-en′tāt), *v.t.* [ORIENTATED (-id), ORIENTATING], [*orient* + *-ate*, after Fr. *orienter*], to orient. *v.i.* 1. to face east, or in any specified direction. 2. to adjust to a situation.

o·ri·en·ta·tion (ôr′i-en-tā′shən, ō′ri-en-tā′shən), *n.* 1. an orienting or being oriented. 2. *a*) position with relation to the points of the compass. *b*) the planning of church architecture so that the altar is in the east end. 3. familiarization with and adaptation to a situation or environment; specifically, in *psychology*, interpretation of the environment as to time, space, objects, and persons. 4. in *zoology*, the homing faculty or instinct of certain animals.

O·rien·te (ô-ryen′te), *n.* a province of eastern Cuba: area, 14,211 sq. mi.; pop., 1,143,000; capital, Santiago de Cuba: former name, *Santiago de Cuba*.

or·i·fice (ôr′ə-fis, or′ə-fis), *n.* [Fr.; LL. *orificium* < L. *os*, *oris*, a mouth + *facere*, to make], an opening; mouth or outlet of a tube, cavity, etc.; vent.

or·i·flamme (ôr′ə-flam′, or′ə-flam′), *n.* [Fr.; OFr. *orieflambe* < L. *aurea flamma* < *aurum*, gold + *flamma*, a flame], 1. the ancient royal standard of France, a red silk banner split at one end to form flame-shaped streamers, used as the early French kings' military ensign. 2. any battle standard.

orig., 1. origin. 2. original. 3. originally.

or·i·gan (ôr′i-gən, or′i-gən), *n.* [ME. *origane;* Late OFr.; L. *origanum;* Gr. *origanon*, lit., mountain brightness], marjoram; especially, wild marjoram.

Or·i·gen (ôr′i-jən, or′ə-jen′), *n.* (*Origenes Adamantius*), Christian theologian, teacher, and writer, born in Alexandria; lived 185?–254? A.D.

or·i·gin (ôr′ə-jin, or′ə-jin), *n.* [Fr. *origine;* L. *origo*, *originis* < *oriri*, to rise], 1. a coming into existence or use; beginning. 2. parentage; birth; lineage. 3. that in which something has its beginning; source; root; cause. 4. in *anatomy*, the less movable of the two points of attachment of a muscle, usually the end attached to the more rigid part of the skeleton: opposed to *insertion*. Abbreviated **orig.**

SYN.—**origin** is applied to that from which a person or thing has its very beginning (the *origin* of a word); **source** is applied to the point or place from which something arises, comes, or develops (the sun is our *source* of energy); **beginning** is the basic general term for a starting point or place (the *beginning* of a quarrel); **inception** is specifically applied to the beginning of an undertaking, organization, etc. (Smith headed the business from its *inception*); **root** suggests an origin so deep and basic as to be the ultimate cause from which something stems (to go to the *root* of the matter).

o·rig·i·nal (ə-rij′ə-n'l), *adj.* [ME.; OFr.; L. *originalis* < *origo;* see ORIGIN], 1. having to do with an origin; initial; first; earliest. 2. never having occurred or existed before; not copied; fresh; new; novel. 3. capable of or given to inventing or creating something new, or thinking or acting in an independent, individual, fresh way. 4. coming from someone as the originator, maker, author, etc. 5. being that or those from which reproductions, copies, etc. have been made. *n.* [Fr. < the *adj.*], 1. a pristine form or primary type that has given rise to varieties. 2. an original work, as of art or literature, in contradistinction to any reproduction, copy, etc. 3. the person or thing represented in a painting or the like. 4. a person of original mind, character, or behavior. 5. an eccentric person. 6. [Archaic], an originator. Abbreviated **orig.** —*SYN.* see **new.**

o·rig·i·nal·i·ty (ə-rij′ə-nal′ə-ti), *n.* [Fr. *originalité*], 1. the quality or condition of being original. 2. [*pl.* ORIGINALITIES (-tiz)], anything original.

o·rig·i·nal·ly (ə-rij′ə-n'l-i), *adv.* 1. with reference to origin, or beginning. 2. at or from the beginning; initially. 3. in the first place; chiefly. 4. in an original, independent, or novel manner. Abbreviated **orig.**

original sin, a tendency to sin and depravity which, in Christian theology, is held to be inherent in mankind as a direct result of Adam's sin of rebellion and which, in Roman Catholicism, is held to have resulted in the loss of sanctifying grace.

o·rig·i·nate (ə-rij′ə-nāt′), *v.t.* [ORIGINATED (-id), ORIGINATING], [*origin* + *-ate*], to bring into being; especially, to create (something original); invent. *v.i.* to come into being; begin; start. —*SYN.* see **rise.**

o·rig·i·na·tion (ə-rij′ə-nā′shən), *n.* [LL. *originatio*], 1. an originating or being originated. 2. origin.

o·rig·i·na·tive (ə-rij′ə-nā′tiv), *adj.* able to originate; inventive; creative.

o·rig·i·na·tor (ə-rij′ə-nā′tẽr), *n.* a person or thing that originates something.

o·ri·na·sal (ôr′i-nā′z'l, ō′ri-nā′z'l), *adj.* [< L. *os, oris,* a mouth; + *nasal*], in *phonetics,* pronounced with the nasal passage open to the breath. *n.* an orinasal sound, as a French nasalized vowel.

O·ri·no·co (ôr′ə-nō′kō, ō′ri-nō′kō), *n.* a river in Venezuela, flowing into the Atlantic: length, 1,600 mi.

o·ri·ole (ôr′i-ōl′, ō′ri-ōl′), *n.* [OFr. *oriol;* ML. *oriolus;* L. *aureolus,* dim. of *aureus,* golden < *aurum,* gold], 1. any of a group of chiefly yellow and black birds, including the golden oriole, found from Europe to Australia. 2. any of a group of American birds, including the Baltimore oriole, related to the starlings and characterized by bright-orange (or yellow) and black plumage and hanging nests.

O·ri·on (ō-rī′ən), *n.* [ME.; L.; Gr. *Ōriōn,* mythological hunter, handsomest of his race], 1. in *Greek & Roman mythology,* a hunter whom Diana loved but accidentally killed: he was placed in the heavens by her as a constellation. 2. in *astronomy,* an equatorial constellation near Taurus, containing the first-magnitude stars Rigel and Betelgeuse: see **constellation,** chart.

O·ris·ka·ny (ō-ris′kə-ni), *n.* a village in central New York, on the Mohawk River: site of a battle (1777) of the Revolutionary War.

or·i·son (ôr′i-z'n, or′i-z'n), *n.* [ME. *oreisun;* OFr. *oreison;* L. *oratio* < *orare,* to pray], *usually in pl.* a prayer.

O·ris·sa (ō-ris′ə), *n.* a state of eastern India, on the Bay of Bengal: area, 60,136 sq. mi.; pop., 14,646,000; capital, Bhubaneshwar.

O·ri·za·ba (ō′rē-sä′bä), *n.* 1. a volcanic mountain in southeastern Mexico: height, 18,701 ft.: also called *Citlaltepetl.* 2. a city near this mountain: pop., 56,000.

Ork·ney Islands (ôrk′ni), a group of islands north of Scotland, forming Orkney County of Scotland: area, 376 sq. mi.; pop., 20,000; county seat, Kirkwall.

ORKNEY ISLANDS

Or·lan·do (ôr-lan′dō), [It.], a masculine name: see **Roland.** *n.* a city in central Florida: pop., 88,000.

Or·lan·do, Vit·to·rio E·ma·nue·le (vēt-tô′ryô e′mä-nwe′le ôr-län′dô; Eng. ôr-lan′dō), 1860–1952; Italian statesman and jurist; premier of Italy (1917–1919).

orle (ôrl), *n.* [Fr.; OFr. *ourle, urle,* dim. < L. *ora,* margin, border], in *heraldry,* the inner border on an escutcheon, following the outline of the edge of the shield.

Or·lé·a·nais (ôr′lā′á′ne′), *n.* a former province of north central France.

Or·le·an·ist (ôr′li-ən-ist), *n.* a supporter of the house of Orleans' claim to the French throne through the Duke of Orleans, a younger brother of Louis XIV.

Or·lé·ans (ôr′lā′än′; Eng. ôr′li-ənz), *n.* a city in north central France, on the Loire River: pop., 76,000: site of a battle (1429) of the Hundred Years' War, in which Joan of Arc saved the city, besieged by the English, and secured French independence.

Orléans, Louis Phi·lippe Jo·seph d' (lwē′ fē′lēp′ zhô′zef′ də), Duc d'Orléans, 1747–1793; French political leader.

or·lon (ôr′lon), *n.* a synthetic acrylic fiber somewhat similar to nylon, or a fabric made from this fiber: a trade-mark (**Orlon**).

or·lop (ôr′lop), *n.* [D. *overloop* < *over,* over + *loopen,* to run: so called because it covers the hold], the lowest deck of a ship, especially of a warship.

Or·mazd (ôr′məzd), *n.* [Per. *Ormazd;* OPer. *Auramazda;* Zend *Ahuro-Mazdao,* wise lord], the supreme deity and creator of the world, in the Zoroastrian, or ancient Persian, religion: also spelled **Ormuzd**: cf. **Ahriman.**

or·mer (ôr′mẽr), *n.* [Fr. dial. (Channel Islands) < Fr. *ormier;* altered < *oreille de mer,* ear of the sea: so named from the shape], an abalone shell; ear shell.

or·mo·lu (ôr′mə-lōō′), *n.* [Fr. *or moulu; or,* gold + *moulu,* pp. of *moudre* < L. *molere,* to grind], 1. an imitation gold consisting of an alloy of copper and tin, used in making ornaments, moldings, inexpensive jewelry, etc. 2. imitation gold leaf.

Or·muz, Strait of (ôr′muz), the Strait of Hormuz, connecting the Persian Gulf and the Gulf of Oman.

or·na·ment (ôr′nə-mənt; *for v.,* ôr′nə-ment′), *n.* [ME. *ournement;* OFr. *ornement;* L. *ornamentum* < *ornare,* to adorn], 1. anything serving to adorn; decoration; embellishment; hence, 2. a person whose character or talent adds luster to his surroundings, society, etc. 3. an adorning or being adorned; ornamentation. 4. mere external display. 5. in *ecclesiastical usage,* an adjunct, accessory, or article of equipment. 6. in *music,* a tone or tones used to embellish a principal melodic tone. *v.t.* to decorate; beautify; furnish with ornaments or be an ornament to. —*SYN.* see **adorn.**

or·na·men·tal (ôr′nə-men′t'l), *adj.* serving as an ornament; decorative. *n.* something ornamental; specifically, a plant or shrub grown for its decorative effect.

or·na·men·ta·tion (ôr′nə-men-tā′shən), *n.* 1. an ornamented condition or appearance. 2. an ornamenting or being ornamented. 3. ornaments collectively; decoration.

or·nate (ôr-nāt′), *adj.* [ME.; L. *ornatus,* pp. of *ornare,* to adorn], 1. heavily ornamented; overadorned. 2. flowery; showy; unnatural: said of literary style.

or·ner·y (ôr′nẽr-i), *adj.* [altered < *ordinary*], [Chiefly Dial.], 1. having an ugly or mean disposition. 2. obstinate. 3. base; low. 4. ordinary.

or·nis (ôr′nis), *n.* [Gr. *ornis,* bird], all the birds of a certain region; avifauna.

ornith., 1. ornithological. 2. ornithology.

or·nith·ic (ôr-nith′ik), *adj.* [Gr. *ornithikos* < *ornis, ornithos,* bird], of or characteristic of birds.

or·ni·thin (ôr′nə-thin), *n.* ornithine.

or·ni·thine (ôr′nə-thēn′, ôr′nə-thin), *n.* [< Gr. *ornis, ornithos,* bird; + *-ine*], an amino acid, $C_5H_{12}O_2N_2$, found in the urine and excrement of birds.

or·ni·tho- (ôr′ni-thō, ôr′ni-thə), [< Gr. *ornis, ornithos,* bird], a combining form meaning *a bird* or *birds,* as in *ornithology:* also, before a vowel, **ornith-.**

or·ni·thoid (ôr′nə-thoid′), *adj.* [*ornith-* + *-oid*], like a bird in appearance or structure.

or·ni·tho·log·i·cal (ôr′ni-thə-loj′i-k'l), *adj.* having to do with ornithology: abbreviated **ornith., ornithol.**

or·ni·thol·o·gy (ôr′ni-thol′ə-ji), *n.* [Mod. L. *ornithologia* < Gr. *ornithologos;* see ORNITHO- & -LOGY], the branch of zoology dealing with birds: abbreviated **ornith., ornithol.**

or·ni·tho·pod (ôr′ni-thə-pod′, ôr-ni′thə-pod′), *adj.* [*ornitho-* + *-pod*], of a group of dinosaurs that walked upright on digitigrade hind feet. *n.* such a dinosaur.

or·ni·thop·ter (ôr′ni-thop′tẽr), *n.* an orthopter.

or·ni·tho·rhyn·chus (ôr′ni-thō-riŋ′kəs), *n.* [< *ornitho-* + Gr. *rhynchos,* bill, snout], a duckbill, or platypus.

o·ro- (ôr′ō, or′ə), [< Gr. *oros,* mountain], a combining form meaning *mountain,* as in *orography.*

or·o·ban·cha·ceous (ôr′ə-baŋ-kā′shəs), *adj.* [< Mod. L. *Orobanchaceae,* name of the family (< L. *orobanche,* broomrape); + *-ous*], of the broomrape family of leafless parasitic plants.

or·o·gen·e·sis (ôr′ə-jen′ə-sis), *n.* orogeny.

o·rog·e·ny (ô-roj′ə-ni), *n.* [*oro-* + *-geny*], the formation of mountains, especially through a disturbance in the earth's crust.

or·o·graph·ic (ôr′ə-graf′ik), *adj.* of orography.

or·o·graph·i·cal (ôr′ə-graf′i-k'l), *adj.* orographic.

o·rog·ra·phy (ô-rog′rə-fi), *n.* [*oro-* + *-graphy*], the branch of physical geography dealing with mountains.

o·ro·ide (ō′rō-id′, ō′rō-id), *n.* [Fr. *or* (L. *aurum*), gold + Gr. *eidos,* a form], an alloy, mainly of copper, tin, and zinc, resembling gold, used in inexpensive jewelry.

or·o·log·i·cal (ôr′ə-loj′i-k'l), *adj.* of orology.

o·rol·o·gy (ô-rol′ə-ji), *n.* [*oro-* + *-logy*], the study of mountains.

o·rom·et·er (ô-rom′ə-tẽr), *n.* [*oro-* + *-meter*], a barometric instrument indicating distances above sea level, for measuring the altitudes of mountains.

or·o·met·ric (ôr′ə-met′rik), *adj.* 1. of or for the measurement of the altitudes of mountains. 2. of an orometer.

O·ron·tes (ō-ron′tēz), *n.* a river in northwestern Syria, flowing from the Lebanon Valley into the Mediterranean: length, c. 250 mi.

O·ro·si·us, Pau·lus (pô′ləs ô-rō′zhi-əs), fl. 5th century A.D.; Spanish theologian and historian.

o·ro·tund (ôr′ə-tund′, ō′rə-tund′), *adj.* [< L. *ore rotundo,* lit., with a round mouth < *os, oris,* a mouth + *rotundus,* round, smooth], 1. full; mellow; resonant; clear; strong: said of the voice. 2. showy; bombastic; pompous: said of a style of speaking or writing.

O·roz·co, Jo·sé Cle·men·te (hô-se′ kle-men′te ô-rôs′kô), 1883–1949; Mexican painter.

Or·pen, Sir **William New·en·ham Montague** (nū′ən-əm ôr′pən), 1878–1931; British painter.

or·phan (ôr′fən), *n.* [LL. *orphanus;* Gr. *orphanos*], a child whose father and mother are dead: sometimes applied to a child who has lost only one parent by death. *adj.* 1. being an orphan. 2. of or for orphans: as, an *orphan* home. *v.t.* to cause to become an orphan; bereave of parents or a parent.

or·phan·age (ôr′fən-ij), *n.* [see -AGE], 1. the condition of being an orphan. 2. an institution for orphans. 3. orphans collectively.

or·phan·hood (ôr′fən-hood′), *n.* [see -HOOD], the state of being an orphan.

Or·phe·an (ôr-fē′ən), *adj.* of or like Orpheus or his music; melodious; charming; bewitching.

Or·pheus (ôr′fi-əs, ôr′fūs), *n.* [L.; Gr. *Orpheus*], in *Greek mythology*, a musician whose magic ability on the lyre affected beasts and even rocks and trees: when his wife Eurydice died, he obtained her release from the underworld on the condition that he would not look at her until they had reached the upper world, but he failed of his purpose at the last moment: the subject of operas by Monteverde, Gluck, etc.

Or·phic (ôr′fik), *adj.* [L. *Orphicus;* Gr. *Orphikos*], 1. of or characteristic of Orpheus or the mystic doctrines and rites in worship of Dionysus ascribed to him. 2. like the music attributed to Orpheus; entrancing. 3. [also o-], mystic; occult; oracular.

Or·phism (ôr′fiz'm), *n.* the rites and religion ascribed to Orpheus as founder.

or·phrey (ôr′fri), *n.* [ME. *orferey*, falsely assumed as sing. of OFr. *orfreis* < L. *aurum*, gold + *Phrygius*, Phrygian], a richly embroidered decorative band on the front of some ecclesiastical robes.

or·pi·ment (ôr′pi-mənt), *n.* [ME. *orpemente;* OFr.; L. *auripigmentum*, pigment of gold], native arsenic trisulfide, As_2S_3, having a lemon-yellow color and a resinous luster: it is used as a pigment.

or·pine, or·pin (ôr′pin), *n.* [Fr. *orpin;* shortened < *orpiment* (see ORPIMENT): orig. used of a yellow-flowered plant], any of a number of related plants with fleshy leaves and stems, and white or purple flowers.

Or·ping·ton (ôr′piŋ-tən), *n.* [after *Orpington*, village in Kent, England], any of a breed of heavy, full-bodied chickens having black, white, buff, or blue plumage, single combs, and featherless legs.

or·ra (ôr′ə), *adj.* [Scot. dial.; prob. < Gael.], [Scot.], odd (occasional, extra).

or·rer·y (ôr′ẽr-i, or′ẽr-i), *n.* [*pl.* ORRERIES (-iz)], [so called after Charles Boyle, Earl of *Orrery*, for whom one was made], a mechanical apparatus which illustrates with balls of various sizes the relative motions and positions of the bodies in the solar system: also called *planetarium*.

or·ris, or·rice (ôr′is, or′is), *n.* [prob. altered < MIt. *ireos* < L. *iris*, iris], a plant of the iris family, having fragrant roots used in perfumes and medicines.

or·ris·root (ôr′is-rōōt′, or′is-root′), *n.* the rootstock of the orris: used, when pulverized, in perfumery or as a powder to whiten the hair in stage make-up.

Or·son (ôr′s'n), [< Fr. *ourson*, dim. of *ours*, a bear (< L. *ursus*); Eng. sp. after It. *orso*, a bear], a masculine name.

ort (ôrt), *n.* [prob. < Early Mod. D. *oor-aete*, remains of food, lit., out-eat], *usually in pl.* [Dial. or Obs.], a scrap or fragment of food left from a meal.

Or·te·gal, Cape (ôr′te-gäl′), a headland in northwestern Spain.

Or·te·ga y Gas·set, Jo·sé (hô-se′ ôr-te′gä ē gäs′set), 1883–1955; Spanish author and philosopher.

Or·thi·con (ôr′thi-kon′), *n.* [*orth(o)-* + *Iconoscope*], an improved television pickup tube, developed from the Iconoscope: a trade-mark.

or·tho- (ôr′thō, ôr′thə), [< Gr. *orthos*, straight], a combining form meaning: 1. *straight, regular, upright*, as in *orthodontia, orthognathous*. 2. *right angle*, as in *orthorhombic*. 3. *proper, correct, standard*, as in *orthography*. 4. in *chemistry*, *a) that acid (of a group containing the same nonmetallic element) which has the largest number of OH groups per atom of the nonmetal*, as in *orthophosphoric*. *b) characterized by substitutions in the 1, 2 position in the benzene ring.* Abbreviated o- (no period). 5. in *medicine, correction of deformities*, as in *orthopedics*. Also, before a vowel, **orth-**.

or·tho·ce·phal·ic (ôr′thō-sə-fal′ik), *adj.* [*ortho-* + *-cephalic*], 1. having a skull whose height is 70 to 75 per cent of its length. 2. having a skull midway between brachycephalic and dolichocephalic; mesocephalic.

or·tho·ceph·a·lous (ôr′thō-sef′ə-ləs), *adj.* orthocephalic.

or·tho·ceph·a·ly (ôr′thō-sef′ə-li), *n.* the condition of being orthocephalic.

or·tho·chro·mat·ic (ôr′thō-krō-mat′ik), *adj.* [*ortho-* + *chromatic*], of, producing, or having tone values corresponding to natural colors, as a photographic film.

or·tho·clase (ôr′thə-klās′, ôr′thə-klāz′), *n.* [< *ortho-* + Gr. *klasis*, a breaking < *klan*, to break, cleave], a mineral of the feldspar family, having a vitreous luster and perfect cleavage: it occurs in igneous rocks.

or·tho·clas·tic (ôr′thə-klas′tik), *adj.* [< *ortho-* + Gr. *klastos*, broken < *klan*, to break; + *-ic*], having cleavages at right angles, as orthoclase.

or·tho·cy·mene (ôr′thə-sī′mēn), *n.* one of the three isomeric forms of cymene.

or·tho·don·ti·a (ôr′thə-don′shə, ôr′thə-don′shi-ə), *n.* [Mod. L.; see ORTH-, -ODONT & -IA], the branch of dentistry concerned with correcting and preventing irregularities of the teeth so as to bring about proper occlusion.

or·tho·don·tic (ôr′thə-don′tik), *adj.* of or for orthodontia.

or·tho·don·tist (ôr′thə-don′tist), *n.* a dentist specializing in orthodontia.

or·tho·dox (ôr′thə-doks′), *adj.* [< Fr. or LL.; Fr. *orthodoxe;* LL. *orthodoxus;* Gr. *orthodoxos* < *orthos*, correct + *doxa*, opinion < *dokein*, to think], 1. conforming to the usual beliefs or established doctrines, especially in religion; proper, correct, or conventional: as, *orthodox* ideas: opposed to *heterodox*. 2. conforming to the Christian faith as formulated in the early ecumenical creeds and confessions. 3. [O-], designating or of any of the churches comprised in the Orthodox Eastern Church.

Orthodox Eastern Church, the dominant Christian church in eastern Europe, western Asia, and northern Africa: originally it consisted of the four patriarchates of the Eastern Roman Empire that broke with the Roman See in 1054; now it includes the churches that recognize the primacy of the patriarchs of Constantinople, Alexandria, Antioch, and Jerusalem, as well as the autonomous churches of the Soviet Union, Greece, Romania, Bulgaria, Yugoslavia, etc., all of which agree in matters of dogma, ritual, and liturgy, and deny the supreme authority of the Pope: also called *Eastern Church, Orthodox Church*, and less properly, *Greek (Orthodox) Church*.

or·tho·dox·y (ôr′thə-dok′si), *n.* [*pl.* ORTHODOXIES (-siz)], [Gr. *orthodoxia*], quality, practice, or instance of being orthodox; orthodox belief, character, etc.

or·tho·ëp·ic (ôr′thō-ep′ik), *adj.* of orthoëpy.

or·tho·ë·pist (ôr-thō′i-pist, ôr′thō-i-pist), *n.* a student of or expert in orthoëpy.

or·tho·ë·py (ôr-thō′i-pi, ôr′thō-i-pi), *n.* [Gr. *orthoepeia* < *orthos*, right + *epos*, a word], 1. the branch of grammar dealing with pronunciation; phonology. 2. the customary pronunciation of educated people; standard pronunciation.

or·thog·a·mous (ôr-thog′ə-məs), *adj.* of or reproducing by orthogamy.

or·thog·a·my (ôr′thog′ə-mi), *n.* [*ortho-* + *-gamy*], self-fertilization, as in some plants or animals.

or·tho·gen·e·sis (ôr′thə-jen′ə-sis), *n.* [Mod. L.; see ORTHO- & -GENESIS], 1. in *biology*, progressive evolution in a certain direction, seen in successive generations and leading toward a definitely new form; determinate evolution. 2. in *sociology*, the theory that every culture or society follows the same fixed course of evolution, uninfluenced by differing environmental factors.

or·tho·ge·net·ic (ôr′thō-jə-net′ik), *adj.* of or by orthogenesis.

or·thog·nath·ic (ôr′thog-nath′ik), *adj.* orthognathous.

or·thog·na·thism (ôr-thog′nə-thiz'm), *n.* the condition of being orthognathous.

or·thog·na·thous (ôr-thog′nə-thəs), *adj.* [*ortho-* + *-gnathous*], 1. having the jaws straight or in line, with the lower jaw neither projecting nor receding. 2. designating a skull with the forehead and lower jaw in line.

or·thog·o·nal (ôr-thog′ə-n'l), *adj.* [< Fr. *orthogone* (LL. *orthogonium*, neut. of *orthogonius* < Gr. *orthogōnios*, rectangular < *orthos*, right + *gōnia*, an angle); + *-al*], having to do with right angles; rectangular.

or·thog·ra·pher (ôr-thog′rə-fẽr), *n.* a person skilled in orthography; expert speller.

or·tho·graph·ic (ôr′thə-graf′ik), *adj.* 1. of orthography. 2. characterized by correct spelling. 3. in *geometry*, of right angles and perpendicular lines.

or·tho·graph·i·cal (ôr′thə-graf′i-k'l), *adj.* orthographic.

orthographic projection, in *geometry & architecture*, a projection in which the projecting lines are perpendicular to the plane of projection.

or·thog·ra·phy (ôr-thog′rə-fi), *n.* [*pl.* ORTHOGRAPHIES (-fiz)], [OFr. *ortographie;* L. *orthographia;* Gr. *orthographia;* see ORTHO- & -GRAPHY], 1. correct spelling. 2. any style or way of spelling. 3. spelling as a subject or science. 4. orthographic projection.

or·tho·pe·dic, or·tho·pae·dic (ôr′thə-pē′dik), *adj.* [< *ortho-* + Gr. *paideia*, training of children < *pais*, *paidos*, child; + *-ic*], of orthopedics.

or·tho·pe·dics, or·tho·pae·dics (ôr′thə-pē′diks), *n.pl.* [construed as sing.], [< *orthopedic*], the branch of surgery dealing with the treatment of deformities, diseases, and injuries of the bones and joints.

or·tho·pe·dist, or·tho·pae·dist (ôr'thə-pē'dist), *n.* an expert or specialist in orthopedics.

or·tho·pe·dy (ôr'thə-pē'di), *n.* [Fr. *orthopédie;* see ORTHOPEDIC], orthopedics.

or·tho·phos·phor·ic acid (ôr'thō-fos-fôr'ik, ôr'thō-fos-for'ik), [*ortho-* + *phosphoric*], a clear, colorless, sirupy liquid or a colorless crystalline acid, H_3PO_4, produced from phosphorus or phosphate rock and used in the manufacture of fertilizers, textiles, etc.

or·tho·psy·chi·a·try (ôr'thō-sī-kī'ə-tri), *n.* [*ortho-* + *psychiatry*], the study and treatment of disorders of behavior and personality, with emphasis on prevention.

or·thop·ter (ôr-thop'tẽr), *n.* [Fr. *orthoptère* < Gr. *orthos,* straight + *pteron,* a wing], a type of aircraft designed to be propelled by wing flapping, never proved practical: also **ornithopter.**

or·thop·ter·an (ôr-thop'tẽr-ən), *adj.* orthopterous. *n.* an orthopteron.

or·thop·ter·on (ôr-thop'tẽr-on'), *n.* [*pl.* ORTHOPTERA (-ə)], [Mod. L. < *ortho-* + Gr. *pteron,* feather, wing], any of an order of insects, including cockroaches, crickets, grasshoppers, etc., having biting mouth parts and narrow, hard forewings that cover longitudinally folded, membranous hind wings.

or·thop·ter·ous (ôr-thop'tẽr-əs), *adj.* of an orthopteron or the orthoptera.

or·thop·tic (ôr-thop'tik), *adj.* [*orth-* + *optic*], correcting any deviations of the visual axis of the eye.

orthoptic exercises, the exercising of weakened eye muscles by the use of prisms to strengthen them and overcome any deviation.

or·tho·rhom·bic (ôr'thə-rom'bik), *adj.* [*ortho-* + *rhombic*], with the three axes unequal and at right angles to one another: said of a type of crystallization.

or·tho·scope (ôr'thə-skōp'), *n.* [*ortho-* + *-scope*], an instrument containing a layer of water which is held in contact with the eye, allowing an examination of the interior of the eye without the distortion due to corneal refraction.

or·tho·scop·ic (ôr'thə-skop'ik), *adj.* [< *ortho-* + Gr. *skopein,* to view; + *-ic*], giving a true flat image without distortion.

or·thos·ti·chous (ôr-thos'ti-kəs), *adj.* characterized by or arranged in orthostichies.

or·thos·ti·chy (ôr-thos'ti-ki), *n.* [*pl.* ORTHOSTICHIES (-kiz)], [< *ortho-* + Gr. *stichos,* a row; + *-y*], a vertical arrangement of leaves or flowers on a stem.

or·tho·trop·ic (ôr'thə-trop'ik), *adj.* in *botany,* designating, of, or showing vertical growth.

or·thot·ro·pism (ôr-thot'rə-piz'm), *n.* [*ortho-* + *-tropism*], in *botany,* growth, or a tendency to grow, in a vertical direction or position.

or·thot·ro·pous (ôr-thot'rə-pəs), *adj.* [*ortho-* + *-tropous*], in *botany,* growing straight: said of a nucellus.

Ort·ler Range (ôrt'lẽr), a range of the Eastern Alps, in northern Italy: highest peak (Ortler), 12,800 ft.

or·to·lan (ôr'tə-lən), *n.* [Fr.; Pr.; It. *ortolana,* gardener, ortolan; L. *hortulanus,* dim. of *hortus,* a garden: so named from its frequenting gardens], 1. an Old World bunting, prized as a table delicacy. 2. the bobolink. 3. the sora.

O·ru·ro (ô-rōō'rô), *n.* a city in western Bolivia: pop., 75,000: a former capital.

Or·ville (ôr'vil), [Fr. < identical place name], a masculine name.

-o·ry (ôr'i; *for 2, also* ẽr-i), 1. [ME. *-orie;* OFr. *-oire;* L. *-orius, -oria, -orium*], an adjective-forming suffix meaning *of, having the nature of,* as in *hortatory, commendatory.* 2. [ME. *-orie;* OFr. *-oire, -orie;* L. *-orium*], a noun-forming suffix meaning *a place* or *thing for,* as in *refectory, directory.*

o·ryx (ôr'iks, ō'riks, or'iks), *n.* [*pl.* ORYXES (-iz), ORYX; see PLURAL, II, D, 1], [ME. *orix;* ML.; L., gazelle; Gr. *oryx* < *oryssein,* to dig: so called from its pointed horns], any of a group of large African antelopes with long, straight horns projecting backward; gemsbok.

‡**os** (os), *n.* [*pl.* OSSA (os'ə)], [L.], a bone.

‡**os** (os), *n.* [*pl.* ORA (ō'rə)], [L.], a mouth; opening.

os (ōs), *n.* [*pl.* OSAR (ō'sär)], [Sw. *ås,* ridge, pl. *åsar*], a gravel mound or ridge formed by a glacier; esker.

Os, in *chemistry,* osmium.

O/S, o/s, Old Style.

OS., O.S., Old Saxon.

O.S., 1. Old School. 2. Old Series. 3. Old Style. 4. ordinary seaman.

o.s., out of stock.

O·sage (ō-sāj', ō'sāj), *n.* [Am. Ind. (Osage) *Wazhazhe,* war people], 1. a member of a tribe of Siouan Indians who migrated from the Ohio River Valley to the Osage River in Missouri. 2. their Siouan language, closely allied to Omaha. 3. a river in Kansas and Missouri, flowing into the Missouri: length, 500 mi.

O·sage orange (ō'sāj'), 1. a spiny tree with orange-colored wood, used for hedges, etc. 2. its greenish-yellow, orangelike, inedible fruit.

O·sa·ka (ō'sä-kä; Eng. ō-sä'kə), *n.* a city on the southern coast of Honshu, Japan: pop., 2,547,000.

Os·born, Henry Fair·field (fâr'fēld oz'bẽrn), 1857–1935; American paleontologist.

Os·borne, Thomas Mott (mot oz'bẽrn), 1859–1926; American prison reformer.

Os·can (os'kən), *n.* [L. *Oscus,* pl. *Osci;* + *-an*], 1. a member of an ancient people who lived in Campania, Italy. 2. the Italic language of the Oscans. *adj.* of the Oscans or their language.

Os·car (os'kẽr), [AS. *Osgar* < *os,* a god + *gar,* a spear], a masculine name. *n.* [Slang], any of the statuettes awarded annually in the United States for outstanding contributions to the motion-picture industry.

Os·ce·o·la (os'i-ō'lə), *n.* American Indian chief, leader of the Seminoles; lived 1804?–1838.

os·cil·late (os'ə-lāt'), *v.i.* [OSCILLATED (-id), OSCILLATING], [< L. *oscillatus,* pp. of *oscillare,* to swing < *oscillum,* a swing, lit. a little face or mask hung to a tree and swaying with the wind, dim. of *os,* a mouth, face], 1. to swing to and fro. 2. to be indecisive in purpose or opinion; vacillate. 3. in *physics,* to vary between maximum and minimum values, as an electric current. *v.t.* to cause to oscillate. —***SYN.*** see **swing.**

os·cil·la·tion (os'ə-lā'shən), *n.* [L. *oscillatio*], 1. an oscillating. 2. fluctuation; instability; variation. 3. in *electricity,* variation between maximum and minimum values, as of current or voltage. 4. in *physics,* a single swing of an oscillating object between the two extremes of its arc.

os·cil·la·tor (os'ə-lā'tẽr), *n.* 1. a person or thing that oscillates. 2. in *electricity,* an apparatus producing oscillations, as a radio-frequency generator.

os·cil·la·to·ry (os'ə-lə-tôr'i, os'ə-lə-tō'ri), *adj.* oscillating.

os·cil·lo·graph (ə-sil'ə-graf', os'i-lə-gräf'), *n.* [< L. *oscillare,* to swing; + *-graph*], an instrument which registers oscillations of an electric current and photographically records the variation.

os·cil·lo·scope (ə-sil'ə-skōp'), *n.* [< L. *oscillare,* to swing (cf. OSCILLATE); + *-scope*], a type of oscillograph that visually records an electrical wave on a fluorescent screen, as of a cathode ray tube.

os·cine (os'in, os'īn), *adj.* [< Mod. L. *Oscines,* name of the group < L. *oscen, oscinis,* singing bird], designating a special group of perching birds, as the finches, shrikes, larks, buntings, etc., with highly developed vocal organs and certain other structures in common: some do not sing. *n.* a bird of this group.

os·ci·tan·cy (os'i-tən-si), *n.* [< L. *oscitans,* ppr. of *oscitare,* to yawn; *os,* a mouth + *citare,* to move], drowsiness; apathy; stupor; dullness.

Os·co-Um·bri·an (os'kō-um'bri-ən), *adj.* designating or of the group of Italic languages comprising Oscan and Umbrian.

os·cu·lant (os'kyoo-lənt), *adj.* [L. *osculans,* ppr. of *osculari;* see OSCULATE], 1. kissing; hence, 2. touching; connecting. 3. in *biology,* intermediate; linking; shared: said of a characteristic common to two or more groups.

os·cu·lar (os'kyoo-lẽr), *adj.* [L. *osculum* (see OSCULATE); + *-ar*], 1. of the mouth or kissing. 2. in *biology,* of an osculum.

os·cu·late (os'kyoo-lāt'), *v.t. & v.i.* [OSCULATED (-id), OSCULATING], [L. *osculari,* to kiss < *osculum,* little mouth, kiss, dim. of *os,* a mouth], 1. to kiss. 2. to touch closely. 3. in *biology,* to have (characteristics) in common. 4. in *mathematics,* to touch, as two curves, at three or more points.

os·cu·la·tion (os'kyoo-lā'shən), *n.* [L. *osculatio*], 1. a kissing or being kissed. 2. a kiss. 3. a close contact. 4. in *mathematics,* a contact between osculating curves, etc.

os·cu·la·to·ry (os'kyoo-lə-tôr'i, os'kyoo-lə-tō'ri), *adj.* osculating.

os·cu·lum (os'kyoo-ləm), *n.* [*pl.* OSCULA (-lə)], [L., dim. of *os,* a mouth], 1. any of the openings for outflowing currents of water in sponges. 2. any of the suckers on the head of a tapeworm.

-ose (ōs), [Fr. < *glucose;* see GLUCOSE], a suffix meaning: 1. *a carbohydrate,* as in *cellulose, sucrose.* 2. *the product of a protein hydrolysis,* as in *proteose.*

-ose (ōs), [Fr.; L. *-osus*], a suffix meaning *full of, having the qualities of, like,* as in *bellicose, morose.*

OSerb., Old Serbian.

O.S.F., Order of Saint Francis.

Osh·kosh (osh'kosh), *n.* a city in eastern Wisconsin, on Lake Winnebago: pop., 45,000.

o·sier (ō'zhẽr), *n.* [ME. *osiere;* OFr.; ML. *ausaria,* bed of willows], any of a number of related willows whose wood is used for baskets and furniture.

O·si·ris (ō-sī'ris), *n.* [L.; Gr. *Osiris* < Egypt. *Ås-år* or *Us-år*], the ancient Egyptian god of the lower world and judge of the dead, husband and brother of Isis.

-o·sis (ō'sis), [L.; Gr. *-osis*], a suffix meaning: 1. *state, condition, action,* as in *osmosis.* 2. *an abnormal* or *diseased condition,* as in *neurosis.*

-os·i·ty (os'ə-ti), [< Fr. or L.; Fr. *-osité;* L. *-ositas;* cf. -OSE, -ITY], a suffix used to form nouns corresponding to adjectives ending in *-ose* or *-ous.*

OSlav., Old Slavic.

Os·ler, Sir **William** (ōs'lẽr), 1849–1919; Canadian physician and writer.

Os·lo (os′lō, oz′lō; Norw. oos′loo), *n.* the capital of Norway, on Oslo Fjord: pop., 462,000: formerly called *Christiania.*
Oslo Fjord, an arm of the Skagerrak: length, 80 mi.
Os·man (oz′män, os′mən; Turk. os-män′), *n.* founder of the Ottoman empire; lived 1259–1326: called *the Conqueror:* Arabic name, *Othman.*
Os·man·li (oz-man′li, os-man′li), *n.* [Turk. < *Osman;* Ar. *Uthman,* Osman (Eng. Ottoman)], 1. [*pl.* OSMANLIS (-liz)], an Ottoman Turk. 2. the language of the Ottoman Turks. *adj.* Ottoman.
os·mic (oz′mik, os′mik), *adj.* designating or of chemical compounds in which osmium has a higher valence than in the corresponding osmious compounds.
os·mi·ous (oz′mi-əs, os′mi-əs), *adj.* designating or of chemical compounds in which osmium has a lower valence than in the corresponding osmic compounds.
os·mir·i·di·um (oz′mə-rid′i-əm, os′mə-rid′i-əm), *n.* [*osmium* + *iridium*], a very hard native alloy of iridium and osmium with a small amount of various other metals of the platinum group, used especially in pen points: also called *iridosmine, iridosmium.*
os·mi·um (oz′mi-əm, os′mi-əm), *n.* [Mod. L. < Gr. *osmē,* odor: so called from the odor of one of its oxides], a bluish-white, amorphous, metallic chemical element of the platinum group: it occurs in the form of an alloy with platinum and iridium: symbol, Os; at. wt., 190.2; at. no., 76.
os·mose (oz′mōs, os′mōs), *v.i.* [OSMOSED (-mōst), OSMOSING], [< *osmosis*], to undergo osmosis.
os·mo·sis (oz-mō′sis, os-mō′sis), *n.* [Mod. L.; ult. < Gr. *ōsmos,* impulse < *ōthein,* to push], 1. the tendency of a fluid to pass through a semipermeable membrane, as the wall of a living cell, into a solution of higher concentration, so as to equalize concentrations on both sides of the membrane. 2. the diffusion of fluids through a membrane or porous partition.
os·mot·ic (oz-mot′ik, os-mot′ik), *adj.* of osmosis.
os·mot·i·cal·ly (oz-mot′i-k'l-i, os-mot′ik-li), *adv.* by or according to osmosis.
os·mund (os′mənd, oz′mənd), *n.* [ME. *osmunde;* via Anglo-Fr. < ML. *osmunda*], any of a number of related flowering ferns.
Os·na·brück (ôs′nä-brük′; Eng. oz′nə-brook′), *n.* a city in western Germany: pop., 133,000.
os·na·burg (oz′nə-bũrg′), *n.* [after *Osnaburg* (*Osnabrück*), Germany], a type of coarse, heavy cloth, originally of linen and now of cotton, used in making sacks, work clothes, etc.
OSp., Old Spanish.
os·prey (os′pri), *n.* [*pl.* OSPREYS (-priz)], [Late ME. *ospray* < L. *osifraga,* osprey, lit., the bone-breaker < *os,* a bone + *frangere,* to break: the name was apparently first applied to another bird of prey], a large bird of prey of the hawk family, which feeds solely on fish and is an excellent diver: the plumage is glossy-brown on top, and the underparts are white with a brown band across the breast: also called *fish hawk, ossifrage.*
O.S.S., OSS, Office of Strategic Services.
Os·sa (os′ə), *n.* [L.; Gr. *Ossa*], a mountain in northeastern Greece: height, c. 6,400 ft.: in *Greek mythology,* the Titans, in their futile attempt to reach and attack the gods in heaven, piled Ossa on Pelion and both on Olympus.
‡os·sa (os′ə), *n.* plural of **os** (bone).
os·se·in (os′i-in), *n.* [< L. *osseus,* bony < *os,* a bone; + *-in*], in *biochemistry,* the organic basis of bone, the part left after the mineral matter is dissolved in dilute acids.
os·se·ous (os′i-əs), *adj.* [L. *osseus* < *os,* a bone], composed of, containing, or like bone; bony.
Os·set (os′et), *n.* one of a people who live in the Caucasus, U.S.S.R.
Os·se·tia (o-sē′shə; Russ. o-set′i-ə), *n.* a region in the Caucasus, U.S.S.R.: see **North Ossetian A.S.S.R., South Ossetian Autonomous Region.**
Os·se·tian (o-sē′shən, o-set′i-ən), *adj.* 1. of the Ossets. 2. of Ossetia. *n.* an Osset.
Os·set·ic (o-set′ik), *adj.* Ossetian. *n.* the Iranian language of the Ossets.
Os·sian (osh′ən, os′i-ən), *n.* [Gael. *Oisin,* dim. of *os,* a fawn], in *Gaelic folklore,* a bard and hero of the 3d century A.D.: James Macpherson published pieces of rhythmic prose (1761–1765) which he claimed were his translations of Ossian's poetry from old Gaelic manuscripts.
Os·si·an·ic (os′i-an′ik, osh′i-an′ik), *adj.* of or like the supposed translations of Ossian by James Macpherson; pompous; flowery; bombastic.
os·si·cle (os′i-k'l), *n.* [< L. *ossiculum,* dim. of *os,* a bone], a small bone or bonelike structure; especially, any of the three small bones in the tympanic cavity of the ear.
Os·si·etz·ky, Carl von (kärl fôn ôs′i-et′ski), 1889–1938; German pacifist and writer; awarded Nobel peace prize, 1935.
os·sif·er·ous (o-sif′ẽr-əs), *adj.* [< L. *os, ossis,* a bone; + *-ferous*], containing bones, as a geological deposit.
os·si·fi·ca·tion (os′ə-fi-kā′shən), *n.* 1. an ossifying or being ossified. 2. any bone structure. 3. the pathological or abnormal conversion of soft tissue into bone.
os·si·frage (os′ə-frij), *n.* [L. *ossifraga, ossifragus,* sea eagle, osprey < *ossifragus,* bone-breaking < *os, ossis,* a bone + *frangere,* to break], either of two hawks, the European lammergeier or the osprey.
os·si·fy (os′ə-fī′), *v.t. & v.i.* [OSSIFIED (-fīd′), OSSIFYING], [< L. *os, ossis,* a bone; + *-fy*], 1. in *physiology,* to change or develop into bone; hence, 2. to settle or fix rigidly in a practice, custom, etc.
Os·si·ning (os′ə-niŋ), *n.* a town in southeastern New York, on the Hudson: pop., 19,000: site of Sing Sing, State prison.
os·su·ar·y (os′ū-er′i, osh′ū-er′i), *n.* [*pl.* OSSUARIES (-iz)], [LL. *ossuarium* < *ossuarius,* of or for bones < L. *os, ossis,* a bone], a container, as an urn, vault, etc., for the bones of the dead.
os·te·al (os′ti-əl), *adj.* [< Gr. *osteon,* a bone; + *-al*], osseous; bony.
os·te·i·tis (os′ti-ī′tis), *n.* [< Gr. *osteon,* a bone; + *-itis*], an inflammation of the bone or bony tissue.
Ost·end (os-tend′), *n.* a seaport and summer resort in northwestern Belgium: pop., 55,000.
os·ten·si·bil·i·ty (os-ten′sə-bil′ə-ti), *n.* the state or quality of being ostensible.
os·ten·si·ble (os-ten′sə-b'l), *adj.* [Fr.; ML. *ostensibilis* < L. *ostendere,* to show < *ob(s)-,* against + *tendere,* to stretch], apparent; seeming; professed.
os·ten·si·bly (os-ten′sə-bli), *adv.* in an ostensible manner; apparently.
os·ten·sive (os-ten′siv), *adj.* [ML. *ostensivus*], 1. ostensible; exhibiting; revealing. 2. in *logic,* characterized by proof through broad principle.
os·ten·ta·tion (os′tən-tā′shən), *n.* [ME. *ostentacioun;* L. *ostentatio* < *ostentare* < *ostendere;* see OSTENSIBLE], outright display; showiness; boastful exhibition.
os·ten·ta·tious (os′tən-tā′shəs), *adj.* characterized by or given to ostentation; showy; pretentious.
os·te·o- (os′ti-ō, os′ti-ə), [< Gr. *osteon,* a bone], a combining form meaning *a bone* or *bones,* as in *osteopath:* also, before a vowel, **oste-.**
os·te·o·blast (os′ti-ə-blast′), *n.* [*osteo-* + *-blast*], any cell which develops into bone or secretes substances producing bony tissue.
os·te·oc·la·sis (os′ti-ok′lə-sis), *n.* [Mod. L. < *osteo-* + Gr. *klasis,* a breaking < *klan,* to break], 1. the breaking of a bone to correct a deformity; especially, such breaking of a bone badly healed after a previous fracture. 2. the breaking down and absorption of bony tissue.
os·te·o·clast (os′ti-ə-klast′), *n.* [< *osteo-* + Gr. *klastos,* broken < *klan,* to break], 1. any of the large multinuclear cells in developing bone which absorb bony tissue, thus forming certain hollow parts in the bone, as canals and marrow cavities. 2. an instrument used to perform osteoclasis.
os·te·oid (os′ti-oid′), *adj.* [*oste-* + *-oid*], like bone.
os·te·o·log·i·cal (os′ti-ə-loj′i-k'l), *adj.* of osteology.
os·te·ol·o·gy (os′ti-ol′ə-ji), *n.* [Mod. L.; see OSTEO- & -LOGY], the study of the bones of vertebrates.
os·te·o·ma (os′ti-ō′mə), *n.* [*pl.* OSTEOMAS (-məz), OSTEOMATA (-mə-tə)], [Mod. L.; see OSTEO- & -OMA], a tumor composed of bony tissue.
os·te·o·my·e·li·tis (os′ti-ō-mī′ə-lī′tis), *n.* [*osteo-* + *myelitis*], inflammation of the bone marrow.
os·te·o·path (os′ti-ə-path′), *n.* a person who practices osteopathy.
os·te·o·path·ic (os′ti-ə-path′ik), *adj.* of or based on osteopathy.
os·te·op·a·thist (os′ti-op′ə-thist), *n.* 1. an osteopath. 2. a believer in osteopathy.
os·te·op·a·thy (os′ti-op′ə-thi), *n.* [*osteo-* + *-pathy*], a theory and system of treating ailments based on the belief that they generally result from the pressure of displaced bones on nerves, etc. and are curable by manipulation.
os·te·o·phyte (os′ti-ə-fīt′), *n.* [*osteo-* + *-phyte*], in *medicine,* a small bony outgrowth.
os·te·o·phyt·ic (os′ti-ə-fit′ik), *adj.* of, or having the nature of, an osteophyte.
os·te·o·plas·tic (os′ti-ə-plas′tik), *adj.* [< *osteoplasty* + *-ic*], in *surgery,* of or based on the replacement of bone.
os·te·o·plas·ty (os′ti-ə-plas′ti), *n.* [*osteo-* + *-plasty*], in *surgery,* bone grafting.
os·te·o·tome (os′ti-ə-tōm′), *n.* [*osteo-* + *-tome*], a surgical instrument for cutting or dividing bone.
os·te·ot·o·my (os′ti-ot′ə-mi), *n.* [*pl.* OSTEOTOMIES (-miz)], [*osteo-* + *-tomy*], surgical operation of dividing a bone or cutting out a piece of bone.

Ös·ter·reich (ös′tẽr-rīH′), *n.* Austria: German name.
Os·tia (os′ti-ə; It. ôs′tyä), *n.* a city at the mouth of the Tiber, Italy: the ancient port of Rome.
Os·ti·ak (os′ti-ak′), *n.* Ostyak.
os·ti·ar·y (os′ti-er′i), *n.* [*pl.* OSTIARIES (-iz)], [L. *ostiarius* < *ostium*, door, entrance], 1. a person who guards an entrance, usually of a church. 2. in the *Roman Catholic Church*, *a)* the lowest of the minor orders. *b)* a member of this order.
‡**os·ti·na·to** (ôs′tē-nä′tô), *n.* [*pl.* OSTINATOS (-tôs)], [It., lit., obstinate], in *music*, a short melodic phrase constantly repeated by the same voice or instrument and in the same pitch.
os·ti·o·lar (os′ti-ə-lẽr, os-tī′ə-lẽr), *adj.* of an ostiole.
os·ti·ole (os′ti-ōl′), *n.* [L. *ostiolum*, dim. of *ostium*, door], a small opening or orifice, as a pore.
ost·ler (os′lẽr), *n.* [ME. *osterlere*, var. of *hostelere*, with phonetic omission of mute *h*], a hostler; stableman.
Ost·mark (ôst′märk′), *n.* [*pl.* OSTMARK; Eng. OSTMARKS (-märks′)], the monetary unit of the Soviet zone of occupation in Germany, valued at 7.5 cents in 1948: abbreviated **Om.**
os·to·sis (os-tō′sis), *n.* [Mod. L.; see OSTEO- & -OSIS], the formation of bone.
Ost·preus·sen (ôst′proi′sən), *n.* East Prussia, Germany: the German name.
os·tra·cism (os′trə-siz′m), *n.* [Mod. L. *ostracismus*; Gr. *ostrakismos* < *ostrakizein*; see OSTRACIZE], 1. in ancient Greece, the temporary banishment of a citizen by popular vote: ballots were cast on shells or potsherds. 2. a rejection or exclusion by general consent, as from society.
os·tra·cize (os′trə-sīz′), *v.t.* [OSTRACIZED (-sīzd′), OSTRACIZING], [Gr. *ostrakizein* < *ostrakon*, a shell, potsherd], to banish, bar, shut out, etc. by ostracism. —*SYN.* see **banish.**
os·trich (ôs′trich, os′trich), *n.* [*pl.* OSTRICHES (-iz), OSTRICH; see PLURAL, II, D, 1], [ME. *ostrice*; OFr. *ostrusce*, *ostruche*; LL. *avistruthius* < L. *avis*, bird + *struthio* (Gr. *strouthiōn*), ostrich], 1. a large, swift-running bird of Africa and the Near East, belonging to the largest and most powerful species of birds: it has a long neck, very long legs with two toes on each foot, and small, useless wings; the white tail and wing feathers of the male are used in millinery and as trimming. 2. a smaller South American bird related to this species and having three toes; rhea.
Os·tro·goth (os′trə-goth′), *n.* [LL. *Ostrogothus* < *ostro-* (prob. < OHG. *ostar*), east + *Gothus*; see GOTH], an East Goth; especially, a member of the tribe which conquered Italy in the 5th century A.D.
Os·tro·goth·ic (os′trə-goth′ik), *adj.* of the Ostrogoths.
Ost·wald, Wil·helm (vil′helm ōst′vält), 1853–1932; German chemist; received Nobel prize in chemistry, 1909.
Os·ty·ak (os′ti-ak′), *n.* 1. a member of a Finno-Ugric people living in western Siberia. 2. the Ugric language of the Ostyaks. Also spelled **Ostiak.**
Os·wald, Os·wold (oz′wəld, oz′wôld), [AS. *Osweald* < *os*, a god + *weald*, power], a masculine name.
Os·we·go (os-wē′gō), *n.* a city in New York, on Lake Ontario: pop., 22,000.
Oswego tea, 1. a plant of the mint family, with red flowers and lance-shaped, saw-edged leaves. 2. the tea brewed from its leaves.
Oś·wię·cim (ôsh-vyan′tsim), *n.* Auschwitz: city and Nazi concentration camp in Poland: the Polish name.
ot-, oto-.
O.T., OT, OT., Old Testament.
O·ta·hei·te (ō′tə-hē′ti), *n.* Tahiti: the former name.
o·tal·gi·a (ō-tal′ji-ə), *n.* [Mod. L.; Gr. *ōtalgia*; see OTO- & -ALGIA], an earache; pain in the ear.
O·ta·ru (ô′tȧ-rōō′), *n.* a city on the western coast of Hokkaido, Japan: pop., 188,000.
‡**O tem·po·ra! O mo·res!** (ō tem′pẽr-ə ō mō′rēz), [L.], O the times! O the customs!: a quotation from Cicero.
OTeut., Old Teutonic.
O·thel·lo (ə-thel′ō, ō-thel′ō), *n.* [It.], a tragedy (1604?) by Shakespeare in which the title character, a noble Moor, made madly jealous by the villainous Iago, kills his faithful and loving wife, Desdemona: subject of operas by Rossini (1816) and Verdi (1887).
oth·er (uth′ẽr), *adj.* [ME.; AS. < **anthor*; akin to G. *ander*, Goth. *anthar*; IE. base **ono-* < **no-*, that one], 1. *a)* being the remaining one of two or more: as, the *other* foot. *b)* being the remaining ones of several: used before a plural noun, as, his *other* books are better than this. 2. different or distinct from that or those referred to or implied: as, any *other* girl. 3. different in nature or kind: as, I wouldn't want it *other* than it is. 4. further or additional: as, he has no *other* coat. 5. former: as, *other* times had their own customs. *pron.* 1. the other one: as, each loved the *other*. 2. another or some other person or thing: as, how many *others* are there? *adv.* otherwise; differently: as, he can't do *other* than go.
every other, every second; every alternate.
of all others, above all others.
the other day (or **night**, etc.), not long ago; recently.
oth·er·guess (uth′ẽr-ges′), *adj.* [var. of dial. *othergates*, otherwise], [Obs.], of another kind; different. *adv.* [Obs.], in another way; differently; otherwise.
oth·er·where (uth′ẽr-hwâr′), *adv.* [Archaic or Dial.], in or to another place; elsewhere.
oth·er·while (uth′ẽr-hwīl′), *adv.* [Archaic or Dial.], at some other time or times.
oth·er·whiles (uth′ẽr-hwīlz′), *adv.* [Archaic or Dial.], otherwhile.
oth·er·wise (uth′ẽr-wīz′), *adv.* [ME. *othre wise*; AS. *on othre wisan*], 1. in another manner; differently: as, she believed *otherwise*. 2. in all other points or respects: as, he is *otherwise* intelligent. 3. in other circumstances. *adj.* in another condition; different: as, his answer could not be *otherwise*.
other world, the world of the dead, or the supposed world after death.
oth·er·world·li·ness (uth′ẽr-wũrld′li-nis), *n.* the quality or state of being otherworldly.
oth·er·world·ly (uth′ẽr-wũrld′li), *adj.* being apart from material or earthly interests; spiritual or concerned with life in a future world.
O·thin (ō′thin), *n.* Odin.
Oth·man (oth′män, oth′mən), *n.* 1. [*pl.* OTHMANS (-mänz, -mənz)], an Ottoman. 2. (Ar. ooth-män′), Osman.
O·tho I (ō′thō), Otto I.
o·tic (ō′tik, ot′ik), *adj.* [Gr. *ōtikos* < *ous*, *ōtos*, ear], of or connected with the ear.
-ot·ic (ot′ik), [Gr. *-ōtikos*], a suffix used to form adjectives corresponding to nouns ending in *-osis*, meaning: 1. *of* or *affected with*, as in *sclerotic*. 2. *producing*, as in *narcotic*.
o·ti·ose (ō′shi-ōs′, ō′ti-ōs′), *adj.* [L. *otiosus* < *otium*, leisure], 1. at leisure; idle; indolent. 2. ineffective; futile; sterile. 3. useless; superfluous. —*SYN.* see **vain.**
o·ti·os·i·ty (ō′shi-os′ə-ti, ō′ti-os′ə-ti), *n.* [L. *otiositas*], the state or condition of being otiose.
o·ti·tis (ō-tī′tis), *n.* [Mod. L.; see OTO- & -ITIS], inflammation of the ear.
otitis media, inflammation of the middle ear.
o·to- (ō′tō, ō′tə), [< Gr. *ous*, *ōtos*, the ear], a combining form meaning *the ear*, as in *otology*, *otoscope*: also, before a vowel, **ot-**.
o·to·cyst (ō′tə-sist′), *n.* [*oto-* + *-cyst*], a small cavity containing fluid and otoliths, believed to serve as a balancing or hearing organ in invertebrates.
o·to·lar·yn·gol·o·gy (ō′tə-lâr′iŋ-gol′ə-ji), *n.* the branch or practice of medicine combining the fields of laryngology and otology.
o·to·lith (ō′tə-lith′), *n.* [*oto-* + *-lith*], a tiny bonelike particle or stony platelike structure in the internal ear of vertebrates and in the otocyst of invertebrates.
o·to·log·i·cal (ō′tə-loj′i-k′l), *adj.* of or having to do with otology.
o·tol·o·gist (ō-tol′ə-jist), *n.* a specialist in otology.
o·tol·o·gy (ō-tol′ə-ji), *n.* [*oto-* + *-logy*], the branch of medicine dealing with the ear and its diseases.
o·to·scope (ō′tə-skōp′), *n.* [*oto-* + *-scope*], 1. an instrument for examining the tympanic membrane and external canal of the ear. 2. a type of stethoscope for auscultating the middle ear.
O·tran·to, Strait of (ō-trän′tō; It. ô-trän′tô), the strait between Albania and Italy: width, 44 mi.
ot·ta·va ri·ma (ə-tä′və rē′mə; It. ôt-tä′vä rē′mä), [It.; see OCTAVE & RHYME], a stanza of eight lines with the rhyme scheme *abababcc*: the Italian form has eleven syllables in a line, the English, ten or eleven.
Ot·ta·wa (ot′ə-wə, ot′ə-wä′), *n.* [Canad. Fr. *Otaua* < Am. Ind. (Algonquian); cf. Cree *atâweu*, trader], 1. a member of a tribe of Algonquian Indians that lived near the Ottawa River: formerly called *Algonquin*. 2. a river in Canada, between Ontario and Quebec, flowing into the St. Lawrence River: length, 685 mi. 3. the capital of Canada, in eastern Ontario: pop., 234,000 (with suburbs, 285,000).
ot·ter (ot′ẽr), *n.* [*pl.* OTTERS (-ẽrz), OTTER; see PLURAL, II, D, 1], [ME. *oter*; AS. *otor*, *oter*; akin to ON. *otr*; IE. base **wed-*, to make wet, be wet, as also in *water*, *wet*, *winter*], 1. any of a group of furry, flesh-eating mammals related to the weasel and mink, with webbed feet used in swimming and a long, slightly flattened tail. 2. the short, thick, lustrous fur of this animal.
Ot·to (ot′ō), [OHG. *Otho*, *Odo* < *auda*, rich; also contr. for compounds containing *Od-*, *Ot-* (of same origin) as first element], a masculine name.
Otto I, 912–973 A.D.; king of Germany (936–973 A.D.) and emperor of the Holy Roman Empire (962–973 A.D.): called *the Great*: also **Otho I.**
Ot·to·man (ot′ə-mən), *adj.* [Fr.; It. *Ottomano*; ML. *Ottomanus*; Ar. *'Uthmānī*, of *'Uthmān* (Osman)], Turkish; Osmanli. *n.* [*pl.* OTTOMANS (-mənz)], 1. a Turk, especially one belonging to the tribe or family of Osman; Othman. 2. [Fr. *ottomane*], [o-], *a)* a low, cushioned seat without a back or arms. *b)* a kind of couch or divan, with or without a back. *c)* a low, cushioned footstool. *d)* a corded fabric of silk, rayon, etc., used for trimming.

Ottoman Empire, the empire (c. 1300–1919) of the Turks in southeastern Europe, southwestern Asia, and northeastern Africa: capital, Constantinople: also called *Turkish Empire.*

OTTOMAN EMPIRE

Ot·tum·wa (o-tum′wə), *n.* a city in southern Iowa, on the Des Moines River: pop., 34,000.
Ot·way, Thomas (ot′wā), 1652–1685; English dramatist.
Ouach·i·ta (wäsh′i-tô′, wôsh′i-tô′), *n.* a river in Arkansas, flowing into the Red River in Louisiana: length, 545 mi.: also spelled **Washita.**
oua·na·niche (wä′nə-nēsh′), *n.* [*pl.* OUANANICHE], [Canad. Fr. < Am. Ind. (Algonquian) *wananish*], a fresh-water salmon, related to the Atlantic salmon, found from New York to Labrador.
Ou·ban·gui (ōō′bän′gē′), *n.* the Ubangi, a river in Africa: the French spelling.
Ou·ban·gui-Cha·ri (ōō′bän′gē′shȧ′rē′), *n.* Ubangi-Shari, a French colony in Africa: the French spelling.
ou·bli·ette (ōō′bli-et′), *n.* [Fr. < *oublier,* to forget], a concealed dungeon having a trap door in the ceiling as its only opening.
ouch (ouch), *interj.* [cf. G. *autsch*], an exclamation expressing sudden pain.
ouch (ouch), *n.* [ME. *anouche, a nouche;* OFr. *nousche,* collar, necklace < Gmc.], [Archaic], a clasp or buckle; specifically, an ornamental brooch, especially when set with precious stones. *v.t.* [Archaic], to ornament with or as with ouches.
Oudh (oud), *n.* a part of Uttar Pradesh, in northern India.
ought (ôt), *v. aux.* [orig., p.t. of *owe;* ME. *aughte;* AS. *ahte,* pp. of *agan,* to owe, possess], an auxiliary used with the infinitives of various verbs to express: 1. *obligation* or *duty*: as, he *ought* to pay his debts. 2. *desirability*: as, you *ought* to eat more slowly. 3. *expectancy* or *probability:* as, I *ought* to be through by Monday. Past time is expressed by combining *ought* with the perfect infinitive of the verb being used: as, I *ought* to have told you.
ought (ôt), *n.* anything whatever; aught. *adv.* to any degree; in any way; at all; aught.
ought (ôt), *n.* a nought; cipher; zero.
‡**oui** (wē), *adv.* [Fr.], yes.
Oui·da (wē′də), *n.* (pseudonym of *Marie Louise de la Ramée*), English novelist and writer of children's stories; 1839–1908.
oui·ja (wē′jə), *n.* [Fr. *oui,* yes + G. *ja,* yes], a device consisting of a planchette and a board bearing the alphabet and various other symbols, used in spiritualistic séances, etc., supposedly to convey and record messages from the spirits: a trade-mark (**Ouija**).

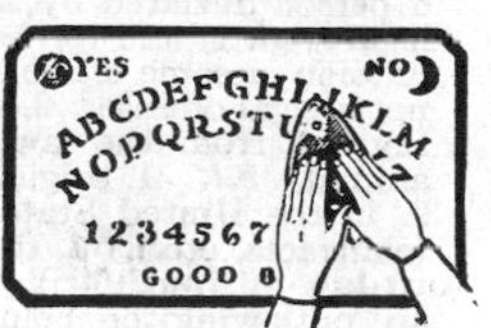

OUIJA BOARD

ounce (ouns), *n.* [ME. *unce, ounce;* OFr. *once;* L. *uncia,* a twelfth, twelfth part of a foot or pound, orig., unit; akin to L. *unus,* one], 1. a unit of weight equal to 1/16 pound avoirdupois, or 1/12 pound troy. 2. any small amount: as, an *ounce* of care. 3. a fluid ounce. Abbreviated **oz.** (*sing. & pl.*).
ounce (ouns), *n.* [ME. *once, unce;* OFr. *l'once, lonce;* LL. **luncea* < L. *lynx;* see LYNX], the rarely seen snow leopard of the mountains of Central Asia and Siberia: it has woolly, gray-white fur marked with black.
ouphe (ouf, ōōf), *n.* [var. of *oaf*], an elf; goblin.
our (our; *often* är), *pron.* [ME. *ure;* AS. *ure,* earlier *user,* genit. of *us* (see US); akin to G. *unser*], possessive form of **we.** *possessive pronominal adj.* of, belonging to, or done by us.
ou·ra·ri (ōō-rä′rē), *n.* [Braz. native name], curare.
Our Lady, the Virgin Mary.
ours (ourz; *often* ärz), *pron.* [ME. *ures; ure* (cf. OUR) + genit. *-s;* hence, in form, a double possessive], that or those belonging to us: the absolute form of *our,* used without a following noun, often after *of,* as, a friend of *ours,* that book is *ours, ours* are better.
our·self (our-self′), *pron.* a form corresponding to *ourselves,* used, as in royal proclamations, of one person: cf. **we** (for *I*).
our·selves (our-selvz′; *often* är-selvz′), *pron.* [Late ME. *ure selves,* for Midland *ure selven,* replacing *us selven,* lit., us selves], a form of the first person plural pronoun, used: *a*) as an intensive: as, we went *ourselves. b*) as a reflexive: as, we hurt *ourselves. c*) as a quasi-noun meaning "our real, true, or actual selves" (e.g., we are not *ourselves* when we rage like that): in this construction *our* may be considered a possessive pronominal adjective and *selves* a noun, and they may be separated: as, *our* own sweet *selves.*
-ous (əs), [ME.; OFr. *-ous, -os;* L. *-osus*], an adjective-forming suffix meaning: 1. *having, full of, characterized by,* as in *pious.* 2. in *chemistry, having a lower valence than is indicated by the suffix -ic,* as in *nitrous.*
Ouse (ōōz), *n.* 1. a river in northern England, flowing into the River Humber: length, c. 60 mi. 2. a river in east central England, flowing into the North Sea: length, c. 160 mi.: also **Great Ouse.** 3. a river in southeastern England, flowing into the English Channel: length, 30 mi.
ou·sel (ōō′z'l), *n.* the ouzel.
oust (oust), *v.t.* [Anglo-Fr. *ouster;* OFr. *ouster, oster* (Fr. *ôter*); said to be < L. *ostare,* to obstruct < *ob-,* against + *stare,* to stand], to force out; expel; drive out; dispossess; eject. —***SYN.*** see **eject.**
oust·er (ous′tẽr), *n.* [Anglo-Fr., inf. used as n.; see OUST], 1. a person or thing that ousts. 2. in *law,* an ousting or being ousted, especially from real property, usually by illegal means.
out (out), *adv.* [ME. *out, ut;* AS. *ut;* akin to G. *aus;* IE. base **ud-,* up, up away, etc., seen also in L. *usque*], 1. *a*) away from, forth from, or removed from a place, position, or situation: as, *out* of the house. *b*) away from home. *c*) on strike. 2. into or in the open air: as, come *out* and play. 3. into or in existence or activity: as, disease broke *out.* 4. *a*) to a conclusion or result: as, argue it *out. b*) completely, fully, or to the point of exhaustion: as, tired *out,* dry *out.* 5. into sight or notice: as, the moon came *out;* hence, 6. *a*) into or in circulation: as, the firm put *out* a new line of shoes. *b*) into or in society: as, this girl has just come *out.* 7. from existence, operation, or activity: as, fade *out,* burn *out,* die *out.* 8. forcefully; aloud: as, sing *out,* speak *out.* 9. beyond a regular or normal surface, condition, or position: as, stand *out,* eke *out,* lengthen *out.* 10. away from the interior, center, or midst: as, spread *out,* reach *out,* branch *out:* sometimes implying sharing or dividing, as, deal *out,* sort *out.* 11. from one state, as of composure, harmony, or agreement, into another, as of annoyance, discord, or disagreement: as, I felt put *out* about it, friends may fall *out.* 12. into or in disuse, retirement, or discard: as, new cars went *out* for the duration. 13. from a number, group, or stock: as, pick *out.* 14. [Colloq.], out on or along: as, *out* our way. 15. [Slang], into or in unconsciousness: as, he passed *out.* 16. in *baseball,* etc., in a manner producing an out: as, he struck *out.* *adj.* 1. external: usually in combination, as in *outpost, outfield, outlying.* 2. irregular: said of sizes of clothes, etc. 3. beyond regular limits. 4. outlying. 5. away from work, class, etc.: as, *out* because of sickness. 6. bared because of torn clothing, etc.: as, *out* at the elbow. 7. deviating from what is accurate or right: as, *out* in my estimates. 8. having suffered a financial loss: as, *out* five dollars. 9. not in effective use, operation, etc. 10. lacking enough practice: as, his hand is *out.* 11. in disagreement; at variance. 12. in *baseball, a*) not at bat; fielding. *b*) failing to get on a base. *prep.* 1. forth from: usually after *from.* 2. on the outside of: as, *out* this window. *n.* 1. something that is out. 2. [Slang], a way out; means of avoiding; excuse. 3. in *baseball, a*) a failure to get on a base; retirement of a batter or of a player who has reached base. *b*) *pl.* the players on the team not batting. 4. *pl.* in *politics,* the party not in office. 5. in *printing, a*) the omission of a word or words. *b*) the word or words omitted. 6. in *tennis,* a return that lands outside the court. *v.i.* to go out; come out. *v.t.* to put out. *interj.* get out! begone!
all out, [Colloq.], completely; wholeheartedly.
at (or **on**) **the outs,** [Colloq.], on unfriendly terms.
out and away, by far; without comparison.
out and out, completely; thoroughly.
out for, making a determined effort to get or do.
out from under, [Colloq.], away from difficulty or danger.
out of, 1. from inside of. 2. from the number of. 3. past the boundaries or scope of; beyond. 4. from (material, etc.): as, buildings made *out of* stone. 5. because of: as, *out of* spite. 6. given birth by: said of animals. 7. not in possession of: as, *out of* money. 8. so as to deprive or be deprived of: as, cheat *out of* money.
out to, making a determined effort to.
out- (out), [< *out*], a combining form meaning: 1.

situated at or *coming from a point away, outside, external*, as in *outbuilding, outpatient*. 2. *going away* or *forth, outward*, as in *outbound, outcast*. 3. *better, greater*, or *more than*, as in *outrun, outdo, outsell*.

out·age (out′ij), *n.* [*out-* + *-age*], an interruption; accidental suspension of operation: as, the power company reported an *outage* lasting two hours.

out-and-out (out′′n-out′), *adj.* complete; thorough.

out·bal·ance (out-bal′əns), *v.t.* to be greater than in weight, value, etc.

out·bid (out-bid′), *v.t.* [for prin. pts. see BID], to bid more than (someone else).

out·board (out′bôrd′, out′bōrd′), *adj.* situated near or located on the outer surface of a water craft. *adv.* in a direction away from the center of a craft.

outboard motor, a portable gasoline engine, attached to a small craft for the purpose of propelling it.

out·bound (out′bound′), *adj.* outward bound.

out·brave (out-brāv′), *v.t.* [OUTBRAVED (-brāvd′), OUTBRAVING], 1. to overcome through bravery. 2. to defy.

out·break (out′brāk′), *n.* a breaking out; sudden occurrence, as of disease, looting, anger, etc.

out·breed (out-brēd′), *v.t.* & *v.i.* [OUTBRED (-bred′), OUTBREEDING], to practice, or subject to, outbreeding.

out·breed·ing (out′brēd′iŋ), *n.* 1. the breeding of unrelated stocks or individuals. 2. in *sociology*, a marrying out of the family or tribe because of a taboo against marriage of persons related by blood.

out·build·ing (out′bil′diŋ), *n.* a structure, as a garage or barn, separate from the house or main building.

out·burst (out′bũrst′), *n.* an outbreak; outpouring.

out·cast (out′kast′, out′käst′), *adj.* [Rare], driven out; rejected. *n.* 1. a person or thing cast out or rejected; hence, 2. a worthless or degraded person.

out·caste (out′kast′, out′käst′), *n.* in India, a person expelled from his caste.

out·class (out-klas′, out-kläs′), *v.t.* to surpass by a wide margin.

out·come (out′kum′), *n.* [Early ME. *utcome*], result; consequence; aftermath. —*SYN.* see **effect.**

out·crop (out′krop′; *for v.*, out-crop′), *n.* the emergence of a mineral from the earth so as to be exposed on the surface of the ground. *v.i.* [OUTCROPPED (-kropt′), OUTCROPPING], to emerge from the earth in this way.

out·cry (out′krī′), *n.* [*pl.* OUTCRIES (-krīz′)], 1. a crying out; hence, 2. a strong protest or objection.

out·curve (out′kũrv′), *n.* in *baseball*, a pitch curving away or out from the batter.

out·dat·ed (out-dāt′id), *adj.* 1. old-fashioned. 2. no longer popular.

out·dis·tance (out-dis′təns), *v.t.* [OUTDISTANCED (-tənst), OUTDISTANCING], 1. to leave behind in a race; hence, 2. to get ahead of in any competition; outstrip.

out·do (out-dōō′), *v.t.* [OUTDID (-did′), OUTDONE (-dun′), OUTDOING], to exceed; surpass. —*SYN.* see **excel.**

outdo oneself, 1. to do something better than one ever did before, or believed himself capable of doing. 2. to make a supreme effort.

out·door (out′dôr′, out′dōr′), *adj.* 1. being outside of a building or shelter; open-air. 2. having to do with those activities of an institution, as a hospital, which are carried on outside its premises.

out·doors (out′dôrz′, out′dōrz′; *for n.*, out-dôrz′, out-dōrz′), *adv.* in or into the open; outside a building or shelter. *n.* 1. any area or place outside a building or shelter. 2. the outdoor world.

out·er (out′ẽr), *adj.* [ME. *outter*; new form < *out* + *-er*, replacing *uttere* < AS. *uterra* (cf. UTTER)], 1. located farther from a certain point or place than something else; external; nearer the outside. 2. relatively far out or far removed: as, the *outer* regions: opposed to *inner*. *n.* 1. that part of a target outside the rings. 2. a shot hitting this part.

Outer Mongolia, the Mongolian People's Republic: the former name.

out·er·most (out′ẽr-mōst′, out′ẽr-məst), *adj.* & *adv.* in a position farthest from the inside or center.

out·face (out-fās′), *v.t.* [OUTFACED (-fāst′), OUTFACING], 1. to stare down (another person); overcome or subdue with a look or stare; hence, 2. to defy or resist.

out·fall (out′fôl′), *n.* the outlet of a river, sewer, etc.

out·field (out′fēld′), *n.* 1. distant or outlying farmland. 2. in *baseball*, *a*) the playing area beyond the four lines connecting the bases. *b*) the outfielders collectively. 3. in *cricket*, the part of the field farthest from the batsman. Distinguished from *infield*.

out·field·er (out′fēl′dẽr), *n.* in *baseball* & *cricket*, a player whose position is in the outfield: distinguished from *infielder*.

out·fit (out′fit′), *n.* 1. *a*) a set of articles for fitting out, or equipping. *b*) the equipment used in any craft or activity; paraphernalia: as, a carpenter's *outfit*, camping *outfit*. 2. a group of people associated in some undertaking or activity; especially, a military unit. 3. a fitting out; equipping. *v.t.* [OUTFITTED (-id), OUTFITTING], to fit out; equip. —*SYN.* see **furnish.**

out·fit·ter (out′fit′ẽr), *n.* a person who furnishes, sells, or makes outfits.

out·flank (out-flaŋk′), *v.t.* 1. to maneuver into a position on the flank, or side, of (a body of enemy troops); go beyond or turn the flank of; hence, 2. to thwart; outwit.

out·flow (out′flō′), *n.* 1. the act of flowing out. 2. *a*) that which flows out. *b*) the amount flowing out.

out·foot (out-foot′), *v.t.* 1. to walk, run, etc. faster or farther than. 2. to sail faster than (another): said of a ship.

out·gen·er·al (out-jen′ẽr-əl), *v.t.* [OUTGENERALED or OUTGENERALLED (-əld), OUTGENERALING or OUTGENERALLING], to surpass in leadership or management.

out·go (out-gō′; *for n.*, out′gō′), *v.t.* [OUTWENT (-went′), OUTGONE (-gôn′), OUTGOING], to exceed in progress; go beyond; surpass. *n.* [*pl.* OUTGOES (-gōz′)], 1. a going out. 2. that which goes or is paid out; outflow or expenditure: opposed to *income*.

out·go·ing (out′gō′iŋ), *adj.* 1. going out; leaving. 2. expansive; sociable; gregarious: as, an *outgoing* personality. *n.* 1. the act of going out. 2. something that goes out; especially, *usually in pl.*, an outlay.

out-group (out′grōōp′), *n.* all the people not belonging to a specific in-group.

out·grow (out-grō′), *v.t.* [OUTGREW (-grōō′), OUTGROWN (-grōn′), OUTGROWING], 1. to exceed in growing. 2. to lose or get rid of by becoming mature: as, he *outgrew* his credulity. 3. to grow too large for.

out·growth (out′grōth′), *n.* 1. a growing out. 2. a result; consequence; development. 3. an offshoot.

out·guess (out-ges′), *v.t.* to outwit.

out·haul (out′hôl′), *n.* in *nautical usage*, a rope used to haul the corners of a sail out to the end of a boom.

out-Her·od (out-her′əd), *v.t.* 1. to be more violent or cruel than (Herod): Hamlet's reference to the usual characterization of Herod in the old mystery plays; hence, 2. to surpass, as in excess.

out·house (out′hous′), *n.* a building separate from but located near any main building or dwelling; specifically, an outdoor latrine; privy.

out·ing (out′iŋ), *n.* [*out* + *-ing*], 1. a pleasure trip or holiday spent outdoors or away from home. 2. an airing; walk in the open air. *adj.* used on or suitable for such a trip: as, *outing* equipment.

outing flannel, a warm cotton fabric in a plain or twill weave with a nap on both sides.

out·land (out′land′), *n.* [ME.; AS. *utlond*], 1. the outlying part of an estate. 2. [Archaic or Poetic], a foreign land. *adj.* (*also* out′lənd), 1. outlying. 2. [Archaic or Poetic], foreign.

out·land·er (out′lan′dẽr), *n.* [*out* + *land* + *-er*, after D. *uitlander*, foreigner], a foreigner; alien; stranger.

out·land·ish (out-lan′dish), *adj.* [ME. *utlandisch*; AS. *utlandisc*; see OUT, LAND, -ISH], 1. strange; alien. 2. peculiar; fantastic; bizarre; barbarous. 3. remote; out-of-the-way. —*SYN.* see **strange.**

out·last (out-last′, out-läst′), *v.t.* 1. to endure longer than. 2. to outlive. —*SYN.* see **outlive.**

out·law (out′lô′), *n.* [ME. *utlage*; AS. *utlaga*; ON. *utlagi*, lit., outlawed; see OUT & LAW], 1. originally, a person declared by a court of law to be deprived of legal rights and protection, generally for the commission of some crime: the killing of such a person was not a legal offense. 2. a habitual or notorious criminal; fugitive from the law. 3. a fierce or uncontrollable animal. *v.t.* 1. originally, to declare to be an outlaw. 2. in the United States, to remove the legal force of (contracts, etc.). 3. to declare unlawful or illegal.

out·law·ry (out′lô′ri), *n.* [*pl.* OUTLAWRIES (-riz)], 1. an outlawing or being outlawed. 2. the state or condition of being an outlaw; hence, 3. disregard or defiance of the law.

out·lay (out′lā′; *for the v.*, out-lā′), *n.* 1. a spending (of money). 2. money, or amount of money, spent. *v.t.* [OUTLAID (-lād′), OUTLAYING], to spend (money).

out·let (out′let′), *n.* 1. a passage or vent for letting something out; hence, 2. a means of expression: as, an *outlet* for the emotions. 3. in *commerce*, *a*) a market for goods. *b*) a store, agency, etc. that sells the goods of a specific manufacturer or wholesaler. 4. in *electricity*, any point in a wiring system at which current may be taken for consumption.

out·li·er (out′lī′ẽr), *n.* any person or thing that lies, dwells, exists, etc. away from the main body or expected place; specifically, *a*) a person who resides away from his place of work or business. *b*) a person who is excluded, or excludes himself, from some group; outsider. *c*) in *geology*, a mass of rock at some distance from the main formation as the result of the wearing away of the intermediate rock.

out·line (out′līn′), *n.* 1. a profile line; line bounding the limits of an object. 2. a sketch showing only the contours of an object, without use of shading. 3. an undetailed general plan. 4. a summary of a subject, consisting of a systematic listing of its most important points. *v.t.* [OUTLINED (-līnd′), OUTLINING], 1. to draw a profile of; draw in outline. 2. to give or write an outline of; list or present the main points of.

SYN.—**outline** is used of the line bounding the limits of an object (the sketch shows only the *outline* of the skyscrapers);

contour, specifically applied to the configuration of a land mass, in extension stresses the shape of an object or mass as determined by its outline (the soft *contour* of her waist); **profile** is used of the outline or contour of the face in a side view or of the outline of any object as it is seen against a background (the *profile* of the trees against the sky); **silhouette** applies to a profile portrait, especially of the head and usually in solid black, or it may be used of any dark shape seen against a light background (the *silhouette* of a house against the moonlight). See also **form.**

out·live (out-liv′), ***v.t.*** to live or endure longer than; survive or outlast.

SYN.—**outlive, outlast,** and **survive** all imply a continuing to exist longer than others or after a specified occasion, **outlive** stressing one's power to endure, as in competition with others or in overcoming a difficulty (to *outlive* one's enemies, a disgrace, etc.), **outlast,** a remaining existent for a longer time (to *outlast* one's usefulness), and **survive,** a remaining alive after another's death (two sons *survive* the deceased) or after a perilous incident (they *survived* the tornado).

out·look (out′look′), ***n.*** 1. a place for watching or looking out. 2. the view from such a place. 3. the act of looking out. 4. viewpoint; mental view. 5. expectation; prospect; probable result.

out·ly·ing (out′lī′iŋ), ***adj.*** relatively far out from a certain point or center; out of the midst; remote.

out·man (out-man′), ***v.t.*** [OUTMANNED (-mand′), OUTMANNING], 1. to surpass in number of men; outnumber. 2. to outdo in manliness.

out·ma·neu·ver, out·ma·noeu·vre (out′mə-nōō′vẽr), ***v.t.*** to maneuver with better effect than; outwit.

out·match (out-mach′), ***v.t.*** to be superior to; outdo.

out·mod·ed (out-mōd′id), ***adj.*** no longer in fashion or accepted; obsolete.

out·most (out′mōst′), ***adj.*** [ME.; altered form of *utmost,* refashioned on *out*], most remote; outermost.

out·num·ber (out-num′bẽr), ***v.t.*** to be more numerous than.

out-of-date (out′əv-dāt′, out′ə-dāt′), ***adj.*** not current; obsolete; old-fashioned.

out-of-door (out′əv-dôr′, out′ə-dōr′), ***adj.*** open-air; outdoor.

out-of-doors (out′əv-dôrz′, out′ə-dōrz′), ***adj.*** out-of-door. ***n. & adv.*** outdoors.

out-of-the-way (out′əv-*th*ə-wā′, out′ə-*th*ə-wā′), ***adj.*** 1. not near a frequented road or populous place; secluded. 2. unusual. 3. not conventional or proper.

out·pa·tient (out′pā′shənt), ***n.*** a patient who receives treatment at a hospital without being an inmate.

out·play (out-plā′), ***v.t.*** to play better than.

out·point (out-point′), ***v.t.*** 1. to score more points than. 2. in ***nautical usage,*** to get into a position closer to the wind than (another vessel).

out·post (out′pōst′), ***n.*** 1. in ***military science,*** *a)* a small group stationed at a distance from the main force in order to prevent an enemy surprise attack. *b)* the place or station occupied by such a group. 2. a settlement on the border of a country or frontier.

out·pour (out′pôr′, out′pōr′; *for the v.,* out-pôr′, out-pōr′), ***n.*** a pouring out. ***v.t. & v.i.*** to pour out.

out·put (out′poot′), ***n.*** 1. the total quantity of any product manufactured or produced, especially over a given period of time. 2. in ***mechanics,*** the amount of power or energy produced by a machine, etc.

out·rage (out′rāj′), ***n.*** [ME.; OFr. *oultrage;* LL. ****ultragium*** < L. ***ultra,*** beyond], 1. an extremely vicious or violent act. 2. a deep insult or offense. 3. any serious breach of legal or moral codes. ***v.t.*** [OUTRAGED (-rājd′), OUTRAGING], 1. to commit an outrage upon or subject to outrage. 2. to rape. —***SYN.*** see **offend.**

out·ra·geous (out-rā′jəs), ***adj.*** [ME.; OFr. *outrageus* < *outrage, oultrage;* see OUTRAGE], 1. having the nature of, involving, or doing great injury or wrong. 2. exceeding all bounds of decency or reasonableness; very offensive or shocking. 3. violent in action or disposition.

SYN.—**outrageous** applies to that which so exceeds all bounds of right, morality, decency, etc. as to be intolerable (an *outrageous* insult); **flagrant** implies a glaringly bad or openly evil character in persons or their acts (a *flagrant* sinner, a *flagrant* violation); **monstrous** and **atrocious** are applied to that which is extremely or shockingly wrong, bad, evil, cruel, etc. (a *monstrous* vice, lie, etc., *atrocious* cruelty, manners, etc.); **heinous** implies such extreme wickedness as to arouse the strongest hatred and revulsion (a *heinous* crime).

‡ou·trance (ōō′träns′), ***n.*** [Fr.; cf. ME. & OFr. *ou(l)trance* (< OFr. *ou(l)trer,* to pass beyond), OUTRÉ, OUTRAGE], the extreme limit; utmost extremity.

out·range (out-rānj′), ***v.t.*** to have a greater range than, or to range beyond.

out·rank (out-raŋk′), ***v.t.*** to exceed in rank.

‡ou·tré (ōō′trā′; Eng. *also* ōō′trā), ***adj.*** [Fr.], 1. exaggerated. 2. eccentric; bizarre.

out·reach (out-rēch′), ***v.t. & v.i.*** 1. to reach farther (than); exceed; surpass. 2. to reach out; extend.

ou·tre·mer (ōō′trə-mâr′), ***n.*** [Fr.; *outre,* beyond (< L. *ultra*) + *mer* (< L. *mare*), sea], the lands beyond the sea; foreign countries. ***adv.*** beyond the sea.

out·ride (out-rīd′), ***v.t.*** [OUTRODE (-rōd′), OUTRIDDEN (-rid′′n), OUTRIDING], to surpass or outstrip in riding.

out·rid·er (out′rīd′ẽr), ***n.*** 1. an attendant on horseback who rides out ahead of or beside a carriage on the highway. 2. a person who rides out or forth.

out·rig·ger (out′rig′ẽr), ***n.*** 1. any temporary support extending out from the main structure. 2. in *nautical usage, a)* any of a variety of frameworks extended beyond the rail of a ship for various purposes. *b)* a brace holding an oarlock out from the side of a boat, to give the rower more leverage. *c)* a timber rigged out from the side of native canoes to prevent tipping. *d)* a canoe of this type. 3. a projection for supporting the lesser airfoils of an airplane.

OUTRIGGER

out·right (out′rīt′; *for adv.,* out′rīt′), ***adj.*** 1. without reservation; downright. 2. straightforward. 3. complete; total; whole. ***adv.*** 1. entirely; wholly. 2. without reservation; openly. 3. at once. 4. [Obs.], straight ahead.

out·root (out-rōōt′, out-root′), ***v.t.*** 1. to uproot. 2. to wipe out; destroy; eradicate.

out·run (out-run′), ***v.t.*** [for prin. pts. see RUN], 1. to run faster, longer, or better than. 2. to exceed. 3. to escape (a pursuer) by or as by running.

out·run·ner (out′run′ẽr), ***n.*** 1. a person or thing that runs out. 2. an attendant running alongside or in front of a carriage. 3. the leader of a team of dogs.

out·sell (out-sel′), ***v.t.*** [OUTSOLD (-sōld′), OUTSELLING], 1. to sell more easily or readily than. 2. to sell in greater volume than. 3. to have a higher price than.

out·set (out′set′), ***n.*** 1. a setting out. 2. a beginning.

out·shine (out-shīn′), ***v.t.*** [OUTSHONE (-shōn′), OUTSHINING], 1. to shine brighter or longer than (another). 2. to surpass; excel. ***v.i.*** to shine forth.

out·shoot (out-shōōt′; *for n.,* out′shōōt′), ***v.t.*** [OUTSHOT (-shot′), OUTSHOOTING], 1. to shoot more effectively than. 2. to shoot out. ***v.i.*** to shoot out; protrude. ***n.*** 1. a shooting or being shot out. 2. that which shoots out, or protrudes. 3. in ***baseball,*** a pitch curving away or out from the batter.

out·side (out′sīd′; *for prep., usually* out-sīd′), ***n.*** 1. the exterior; outer side or surface. 2. the unenclosed portion of anything partly enclosed. 3. *a)* that part of an object which can be seen; hence, *b)* that which is obvious or superficial. 4. the most; absolute limit (with *the*). ***adj.*** 1. outer; having to do with, or located on, the outside. 2. originating, coming from, or situated beyond the limits of a given boundary or classification: as, the club would accept no *outside* help. 3. extreme: as, an *outside* estimate. 4. mere; slight: as, an *outside* chance. ***adv.*** 1. externally; on the exterior. 2. to or toward the exterior. 3. beyond certain limits. 4. in or into the open air. ***prep.*** 1. on or to the outer side of. 2. outside the limits of. 3. [Colloq.], except.

at the outside, at the most; at the absolute limit.

outside of, 1. outside. 2. [Colloq.], other than; with the exception of.

out·sid·er (out-sīd′ẽr), ***n.*** 1. one who is outside, or not included; especially, one not a member of or in sympathy with a given group; alien. 2. a horse which has little chance of winning a given race.

out sister, a nun who manages the affairs of her order outside the convent.

out·sit (out-sit′), ***v.t.*** [for prin. pts. see SIT], 1. to sit longer than (another). 2. to sit beyond the time of.

out·size (out′sīz′), ***n.*** 1. a size varying from the usual standard; odd size; especially, an unusually large size. 2. a garment of such a size.

out·skirt (out′skũrt′), ***n.*** ***usually in pl.*** a part or district remote from the center or midst, as of a city.

out·smart (out-smärt′), ***v.t.*** [Colloq.], to overcome by cunning or cleverness; outwit.

out·soar (out-sôr′, out-sōr′), ***v.t.*** to soar beyond or higher than.

out·span (out-span′), ***v.t. & v.i.*** [OUTSPANNED (-spand′), OUTSPANNING], [S.Afr.D. *uitspannen;* D. *uit,* out, away from + *spannen,* to drag, stretch], in South Africa, to unyoke or unharness (animals). ***n.*** the act or place of outspanning.

out·speak (out-spēk′), ***v.t.*** [OUTSPOKE (-spōk′), OUTSPOKEN (-spō′k'n), OUTSPEAKING], 1. to speak better, more loudly, or more forcibly than. 2. to say boldly or candidly. ***v.i.*** to speak out boldly or candidly.

out·spo·ken (out′spō′kən), ***adj.*** 1. unrestrained in speech; frank; candid. 2. spoken boldly or candidly. —*SYN.* see **frank.**

out·spread (out-spred′; *also for adj., and for n. usually,* out′spred′), *v.t. & v.i.* [OUTSPREAD (-spred′), OUTSPREADING], to spread out; extend; expand. *n.* a spreading out; extension; expansion. *adj.* 1. extended; expanded. 2. diffused.

out·stand (out-stand′), *v.i.* [OUTSTOOD (-stood′), OUTSTANDING], 1. to project; stand out plainly. 2. in *nautical usage,* to leave port; sail out to sea. *v.t.* 1. to withstand. 2. to endure or stay beyond.

out·stand·ing (out′stan′diŋ), *adj.* 1. projecting. 2. prominent; distinguished; conspicuous. 3. unfulfilled; unpaid; unsettled. 4. resisting. —*SYN.* see **noticeable.**

out·stare (out-stâr′), *v.t.* 1. to outdo in staring; stare down. 2. to gaze at steadily without blinking.

out·stay (out-stā′), *v.t.* to stay longer than or beyond.

out·stretch (out-strech′), *v.t.* 1. to stretch out; extend; expand. 2. to stretch beyond.

out·strip (out-strip′), *v.t.* [OUTSTRIPPED (-stript′), OUTSTRIPPING], 1. to go at a faster pace than; pass or leave behind; get ahead of. 2. to excel; surpass.

out·stroke (out′strōk′), *n.* a stroke outward, as when an engine's piston goes out toward the crankshaft.

out·talk (out-tôk′), *v.t.* to talk more skillfully, loudly, or forcibly than; surpass in talking.

out·turn (out′tũrn′), *n.* the total quantity turned out, or produced, over a given period of time; output.

out·vote (out-vōt′), *v.t.* [OUTVOTED (-id), OUTVOTING], to defeat or surpass in voting.

out·ward (out′wẽrd), *adj.* [ME. *outeward;* AS. *uteweard* < *ut,* out + *-weard,* -ward], 1. having to do with the outside or exterior; outer; hence, 2. obvious; observable; visible. 3. away from the interior; to or toward the outside. 4. having to do with the physical or the body as opposed to the mind or spirit. 5. concerning the surface only; superficial. *adv.* 1. externally; on the outside. 2. away from the interior or from port; toward the outside. 3. visibly; openly; publicly. *n.* 1. the outward part; exterior. 2. the material or external world. 3. outward form or appearance.

out·ward·ly (out′wẽrd-li), *adv.* 1. toward or on the outside. 2. in regard to external appearance or action.

out·wards (out′wẽrdz), *adv.* [*outward* + adv. genit. *-(e)s*], outward.

out·wear (out-wâr′), *v.t.* [OUTWORE (-wôr′, -wōr′), OUTWORN (-wôrn′, -wōrn′), OUTWEARING], 1. to wear out; use up. 2. to be more lasting than; outlast. 3. to outgrow or outlive. 4. to exhaust, as in strength.

out·weigh (out-wā′), *v.t.* 1. to weigh more than. 2. to be more important, valuable, etc. than.

out·wit (out-wit′), *v.t.* [OUTWITTED (-id), OUTWITTING], 1. to overcome, or get the better of, by cunning or cleverness. 2. [Archaic], to be more intelligent than.

out·work (out′wũrk′; *for v.,* out-wũrk′), *n.* in *military usage,* a lesser trench or fortification built out beyond the main defenses. *v.t.* 1. to work better, faster, or harder than. 2. to work out to completion.

ou·zel (ōō′z′l), *n.* [ME. & AS. *osle* < **amsla;* akin to OHG. *amsala* (G. *amsel*); IE. base **ames-,* aphetisized in L. *merula*], 1. the European blackbird. 2. any of several thrushes or related birds. Also spelled **ousel.**

o·va (ō′və), *n.* plural of **ovum.**

o·val (ō′v′l), *adj.* [Fr. *oval, ovale* < L. *ovum,* an egg], 1. egg-shaped. 2. resembling an egg in shape; ellipsoidal. *n.* anything shaped like an egg or an ellipse.

o·var·i·an (ō-vâr′i-ən), *adj.* of an ovary.

o·var·i·ot·o·my (ō-vâr′i-ot′ə-mi), *n.* [OVARIOTOMIES (-miz)], [see -TOMY], 1. a surgical operation on an ovary. 2. the surgical removal of an ovary.

o·va·ri·tis (ō′və-rī′tis), *n.* [see -ITIS], inflammation of an ovary.

o·va·ry (ō′vẽr-i), *n.* [*pl.* OVARIES (-iz)], [Mod. L. *ovarium* < L. *ovum,* an egg], 1. in *anatomy & zoology,* the female reproductive gland, in which the ova are formed. 2. in *botany,* the enlarged hollow part of the pistil in angiosperms, containing ovules.

o·vate (ō′vāt), *adj.* [L. *ovatus* < *ovum,* an egg], 1. egg-shaped. 2. in *botany,* a) having the shape of the longitudinal section of an egg. b) having such a shape with the broader end at the base, as some leaves: see **leaf,** illus.

o·va·tion (ō-vā′shən), *n.* [L. *ovatio* < *ovare,* to celebrate a triumph], 1. in ancient Rome, a lesser ceremonial tribute to a hero whose deeds were not great enough to justify a full triumph. 2. an enthusiastic outburst of applause or an enthusiastic public welcome.

ov·en (uv′ən), *n.* [ME.; AS. *ofen;* akin to G. *ofen;* IE. base **augʷ-,* cooking vessel, seen also in L. *aulla, olla* (cf. OLLA PODRIDA)], a compartment or receptacle for heating, baking, or drying by means of heat.

ov·en·bird (uv′ən-bũrd′), *n.* 1. any of a group of South American passerine birds that build a two-chambered, dome-shaped, ovenlike nest from clay. 2. a North American warbler that builds a domelike nest on the ground.

o·ver (ō′vẽr), *prep.* [ME. & AS. *ofer,* over, above, upon, beside, beyond; akin to G. *über, ober;* IE. **upere,* over, above, an old compar. (seen also in L. *super*) on the base of **upo,* up], 1. in, at, or to a position up from; higher than; above: as, the branch hung *over* the house. 2. so as to cover or close: as, they boarded *over* the window. 3. while occupied or engaged in: as, we'll discuss it *over* our dinner. 4. upon; upon the surface of: as, she spread the frosting *over* the cake. 5. upon, as an effect or influence: as, he cast a spell *over* the group. 6. above in authority, position, power, etc.: as, he will preside *over* the meeting. 7. in a course leading along or across, or above and to the other side of: as, fly *over* the lake; hence, 8. on the other side of: as, a city *over* the border. 9. here and there in, or through all parts of: as, *over* the whole state. 10. during; through: as, the dictionary was in production *over* a period of several years. 11. more than, or above in degree, amount, number, etc.: as, it cost *over* five dollars. 12. up to and including; until after: as, stay *over* Easter. 13. in preference to. 14. concerning; about; regarding. *adv.* 1. a) above, across, or to the other side. b) across the brim or edge. 2. more; in excess; beyond: as, they were gone three hours or *over.* 3. completely; covering the entire area: as, the wound healed *over.* 4. through; from start to finish: as, he took out his money and counted it *over.* 5. a) from an upright position: as, the tree fell *over.* b) upside down; into an inverted position: as, they turned the plank *over.* 6. again; another time: as, go back and do it *over.* 7. at or on the other side, as of an intervening space, or at an unspecified distance but in a specified direction or place: as, *over* in England, *over* by the park. 8. from one side, belief, viewpoint, etc. to another: as, the party's new policy won him *over.* 9. from one person, etc. to another: as, make your property *over* to her. *adj.* 1. upper, outer, superior, excessive, or extra: often in combination, as in *overcoat, overseer, oversupply.* 2. finished; done with; past: as, the game is *over.* 3. having reached the other side; having got across. 4. [Colloq.], having a surplus: as, he is three hours *over* for the week. *n.* 1. something in addition; excess; surplus. 2. in *cricket,* a) the set number of balls bowled during a single turn at one end of the wicket. b) the period of time during which this takes place. 3. in *military usage,* a shot that hits or explodes beyond the target. *v.t. & v.i.* [Poetic], to pass above and across.

all over, 1. on or in every part (of). 2. throughout. 3. finished; ended: also **all over with.**

over again, again; another time; anew.

over against, opposite to or in contrast with.

over all, over the whole extent; from end to end.

over and above, in addition to; more than; besides.

over and over (again), repeatedly; time after time.

over there, [Colloq.], in Europe: World War I expression.

o·ver- (ō′vẽr), a combining form meaning: 1. *above in position, upper, superior, eminent,* as in *overhead, overbearing, overlord.* 2. *excessive, too much, beyond the normal,* as in *overrate, oversell, oversleep.* 3. *passing across* or *beyond,* as in *overshoot, overpass, overrun.* 4. *causing a change from the original position to one lower,* as in *overset, overweigh, overwhelm.* The list below includes the more common compounds formed with *over-* that do not have special meanings; they will be understood if *too much* or *excessively* is used with the meaning of the base word.

overactive
overambitious
overanxious
overattentive
overbusy
overcareful
overcareless
overcaution
overcautious
overconscientious
overconservative
overconsiderate
overcook
overcritical
overeager
overemotional
overemphasize
overenthusiastic
overexercise
overexert
overexpansion
overexposure
overfond
overgenerous
overgreedy
overhasty
overindulge
overmeasure
overnegligent
overobedient
overpopulate
overprecise
overreligious
oversensitive
oversentimental
overspecialize
overstimulate
overstretch
overstrict
oversufficient
oversuspicious
overtire
overvehement
overzealous

o·ver·a·bun·dance (ō′vẽr-ə-bun′dəns), *n.* more than an abundance; superfluous plenty.

o·ver·act (ō′vẽr-akt′), *v.t. & v.i.* to act with exaggeration.

o·ver·age (ō′vẽr-āj′), *adj.* over the age fixed as a standard.

o·ver·age (ō′vẽr-ij), *n.* [*over-* + *-age*], a surplus or excess, as of goods.

o·ver-all, o·ver·all (ō′vẽr-ôl′), *adj.* 1. from end to end. 2. comprehensive; total; including everything.

o·ver·alls (ō′vẽr-ôlz′), *n.pl.* 1. loose-fitting trousers,

often with the front extending up over the breast, and usually of some strong cotton cloth, worn over other clothing as a protection against dirt and wear. 2. *sing.* [British], a smock or loose-fitting housedress.
o·ver·arch (ō'vẽr-ärch'), ***v.t. & v.i.*** to form an arch over (something).
o·ver·awe (ō'vẽr-ô'), ***v.t.*** [OVERAWED (-ôd'), OVERAWING], to overcome or subdue by inspiring awe.
o·ver·bal·ance (ō'vẽr-bal'əns), ***v.t.*** [OVERBALANCED (-ənst), OVERBALANCING], 1. to weigh more than. 2. to throw off balance. ***n.*** something that outweighs or overbalances.
o·ver·bear (ō'vẽr-bâr'), ***v.t.*** [for prin. pts. see BEAR], 1. to press or bear down by weight or physical power. 2. to dominate, domineer over, overrule, or subdue. ***v.i.*** to be too fruitful; bear to excess.
o·ver·bear·ing (ō'vẽr-bâr'iŋ), ***adj.*** disregarding the wishes of others; arrogant; domineering. —***SYN.*** see **proud.**
o·ver·bid (ō'vẽr-bid'), ***v.t. & v.i.*** [for prin. pts. see BID], 1. to outbid (another person). 2. to bid more than the worth of (a thing). ***n.*** (ō'vẽr-bid'), a higher or excessive bid.
o·ver·bite (ō'vẽr-bīt'), ***n.*** faulty occlusion of the teeth in which the upper incisors and canines project over the lower to an abnormal extent.
o·ver·blow (ō'vẽr-blō'), ***v.t.*** [for prin. pts. see BLOW], 1. to blow across, away, or down. 2. to cover with something blown, as sand.
o·ver·blown (ō'vẽr-blōn'), ***adj.*** 1. past the stage of full bloom. 2. blown down or over.
o·ver·board (ō'vẽr-bôrd', ō'vẽr-bōrd'), ***adv.*** [ME. *over borde;* AS. *ofer bord;* cf. OVER & BOARD], 1. over a ship's side. 2. from a ship into the water.
o·ver·bold (ō'vẽr-bōld'), ***adj.*** too bold; rash.
o·ver·build (ō'vẽr-bild'), ***v.t.*** [for prin. pts. see BUILD], 1. to build over or on top of. 2. to build too elaborately. 3. to erect too many buildings in or on (an area).
o·ver·bur·den (ō'vẽr-bũr'd'n; *for n.*, ō'vẽr-bũr'd'n), ***v.t.*** to burden oppressively; weigh down. ***n.*** something that overburdens.
o·ver·buy (ō'vẽr-bī'), ***v.t. & v.i.*** [OVERBOUGHT (-bôt'), OVERBUYING], to buy more than is needed or justified by ability to pay.
o·ver·cap·i·tal·ize (ō'vẽr-kap'ə-t'l-īz'), ***v.t.*** 1. to capitalize beyond what is warranted by the state of the business, etc.; furnish too much capital for or overestimate the capital value of. 2. to set the nominal value of the capital of (a corporation) higher than is lawful or justifiable.
o·ver·cast (ō'vẽr-kast', ō'vẽr-käst'; *for v. 1 & 2,* ō'vẽr-kast', ō'vẽr-käst'), ***n.*** 1. a covering, especially of clouds. 2. an arch in a mine, supporting an overhead passage. 3. in *fishing,* a cast made to a point beyond the one intended. ***adj.*** 1. covered over; coated. 2. cloudy; dark: said of the sky or weather. 3. in *sewing,* made with overcasting. ***v.t.*** [OVERCAST, OVERCASTING], 1. *a*) to overspread. *b*) to overcloud; darken. 2. in *fishing,* to cast beyond the point intended. 3. in *sewing,* to sew over (an edge) with long, loose stitches so as to prevent raveling.
o·ver·charge (ō'vẽr-chärj'; *for n.*, ō'ver-chärj'), ***v.t.*** 1. to charge too high a price for; charge too much for. 2. to overload or fill too full. 3. to exaggerate. ***n.*** 1. an excessive charge. 2. a load that is too full or heavy. Abbreviated **o/c** (no period).
o·ver·check (ō'vẽr-chek'), ***n.*** a checkrein that is passed over the head and between the ears of a horse.
o·ver·clothes (ō'vẽr-klōz', ō'vẽr-klō*th*z'), ***n.pl.*** outer garments worn over the usual clothing.
o·ver·cloud (ō'vẽr-kloud'), ***v.t.*** 1. to darken or cover over with clouds; obscure; dim. 2. to make gloomy, angry, etc. in appearance: as, despair *overclouded* his face. ***v.i.*** to become cloudy, gloomy, etc.
o·ver·coat (ō'vẽr-kōt'), ***n.*** a coat worn over the usual clothing for warmth; topcoat or greatcoat.
o·ver·come (ō'vẽr-kum'), ***v.t.*** [OVERCAME (-kām'), OVERCOME, OVERCOMING], [ME. *overcomen;* AS. *ofercuman*], 1. to get the better of in competition, struggle, etc.; conquer. 2. to master, suppress, prevail over, surmount, or overwhelm: as, *overcome* obstacles, be *overcome* by grief. 3. [Archaic], to spread over or overrun. ***v.i.*** to be victorious; win. —***SYN.*** see **conquer.**
o·ver·com·pen·sa·tion (ō'vẽr-kom'pən-sā'shən), ***n.*** in *psychoanalysis,* an intensified and exaggerated striving to compensate for a strong feeling, as of inferiority.
o·ver·con·fi·dent (ō'vẽr-kon'fə-dənt), ***adj.*** confident without good reason; too confident.
o·ver·crop (ō'vẽr-krop'), ***v.t.*** [OVERCROPPED or *occas.* OVERCROPT (-kropt'), OVERCROPPING], to deplete the fertility of (land) by overproduction of crops.
o·ver·crowd (ō'vẽr-kroud'), ***v.t.*** to crowd too many people in or on.
o·ver·de·vel·op (ō'vẽr-di-vel'əp), ***v.t.*** 1. to develop too much. 2. in *photography,* to develop (a film, plate, etc.) too long or with too strong a developer.
o·ver·do (ō'vẽr-dōō'), ***v.t.*** [OVERDID (-did'), OVERDONE (-dun'), OVERDOING], 1. to do too much, or to excess. 2. to spoil the effect of by exaggeration: as, she *overdid* her apology. 3. to cook too long; overcook. 4. to overwork; exhaust; tire. ***v.i.*** to do too much.
o·ver·dose (ō'vẽr-dōs'; *for v.*, ō'vẽr-dōs'), ***n.*** too large a dose. ***v.t.*** to dose to excess.
o·ver·draft, o·ver·draught (ō'vẽr-draft', ō'vẽr-dräft'), ***n.*** 1. a withdrawal of money from a bank in excess of the amount credited to the drawer. 2. the amount withdrawn in excess. Abbreviated **O.D.** 3. a draft, or current of air, passed over a fire, as in a furnace, or passing down through a kiln.
o·ver·draw (ō'vẽr-drô'), ***v.t.*** [OVERDREW (-drōō'), OVERDRAWN (-drôn'), OVERDRAWING], 1. to spoil the effect of by exaggeration; overdo. 2. to draw on in excess of the amount credited to the drawer. 3. to draw (a bow, etc.) too far or too much.
o·ver·dress (ō'vẽr-dres'), ***v.t. & v.i.*** to dress extravagantly or beyond the call of good taste or the occasion.
o·ver·drive (ō'vẽr-drīv'), ***n.*** a gear that at a certain speed automatically reduces an engine's power output without reducing its driving speed: used to lessen fuel consumption and engine wear.
o·ver·due (ō'vẽr-dōō', ō'vẽr-dū'), ***adj.*** 1. past the time for payment. 2. delayed beyond the time set for arrival or occurrence. —***SYN.*** see **tardy.**
o·ver·dye (ō'vẽr-dī'), ***v.t.*** 1. to subject too long to the dyeing process; make too dark a color. 2. to dye over (a color previously dyed).
o·ver·eat (ō'vẽr-ēt'), ***v.i.*** [for prin. pts. see EAT], to eat too much.
o·ver·es·ti·mate (ō'vẽr-es'tə-māt'; *for n., usually* ō'vẽr-es'tə-mit), ***v.t.*** to set too high an estimate on or for. ***n.*** an estimate that is too high.
o·ver·ex·ert (ō'vẽr-ig-zũrt'), ***v.t. & v.i.*** to exert too much or too long (often used reflexively).
o·ver·ex·pose (ō'vẽr-ik-spōz'), ***v.t.*** to expose too much or too long.
o·ver·flow (ō'vẽr-flō'; *for n.*, ō'vẽr-flō'), ***v.t.*** 1. to flow or spread over or across; flood. 2. to flow over the brim or edge of. 3. to cause to overflow; fill beyond capacity. ***v.i.*** 1. to flow or spread beyond the limits; run over. 2. to be more than full or complete; be superabundant. ***n.*** 1. an overflowing or being overflowed. 2. the amount that overflows; quantity or number in excess; superabundance. 3. an outlet; vent for overflowing liquids.
o·ver·gar·ment (ō'vẽr-gär'mənt), ***n.*** an outer garment.
o·ver·glaze (ō'vẽr-glāz'; *for v.*, ō'vẽr-glāz'), ***n.*** in *ceramics,* 1. a second glaze applied over the first. 2. a decoration applied over a glaze. ***v.t.*** to cover with a glaze or overglaze; glaze over.
o·ver·grow (ō'vẽr-grō'), ***v.t.*** [OVERGREW (-grōō'), OVERGROWN (-grōn'), OVERGROWING], 1. to overspread with growth or foliage; grow over so as to cover. 2. to grow too large for; outgrow. ***v.i.*** 1. to grow too large or too fast. 2. to grow beyond normal size.
o·ver·grown (ō'vẽr-grōn'), ***adj.*** 1. overspread with foliage. 2. grown excessively or beyond normal size.
o·ver·hand (ō'vẽr-hand'; *for adv., also* ō'vẽr-hand'), ***adj.*** 1. descending; down from above: as, an *overhand* gesture. 2. performed with the hand raised above the elbow or the arm above the shoulder: as, an *overhand* pitch. 3. designating or of a style of sewing, or a seam, in which the stitches are passed over two edges to sew them together. ***adv.*** in an overhand manner. ***v.t.*** to sew overhand. ***n.*** in *sports,* skill or style in performing or delivering overhand strokes.
overhand knot, a kind of knot: see **knot,** illus.
o·ver·hang (ō'vẽr-haŋ'; *for n.*, ō'vẽr-haŋ'), ***v.t.*** [OVERHUNG (-huŋ'), OVERHANGING], 1. to hang over or above; project beyond; hence, 2. to impend; threaten. 3. to decorate with hangings. ***v.i.*** to hang over; project or jut out over something. ***n.*** 1. the projection of one thing over or beyond another. 2. the amount of such projection. 3. in *architecture,* a projection of one part of a structure over another. 4. in *aeronautics,* one half the difference in span of two main airfoils.
o·ver·haul (ō'vẽr-hôl'; *for n.*, ō'vẽr-hôl'), ***v.t.*** 1. to haul over, as for examination; hence, 2. *a*) to examine thoroughly and check for needed repairs. *b*) to make the repairs, adjustments, etc. needed to restore (a motor, etc.) to good working order. 3. to gain on, catch up with, or overtake. ***n.*** an overhauling; thorough examination or restoration to good working order.
o·ver·head (ō'vẽr-hed'; *for adv.*, ō'vẽr-hed'), ***adj.*** 1. located or operating above the level of the head. 2. in the sky. 3. on a higher level, with reference to related objects: as, the machine had an *overhead* drive. 4. having to do with the overhead of a business. ***n.*** the general, continuing costs involved in running a business, as of fuel, maintenance, breakage, rent, etc. ***adv.*** aloft; above the level of the head.
o·ver·hear (ō'vẽr-hēr'), ***v.t.*** [OVERHEARD (-hũrd'), OVER-

HEARING], to hear (something spoken or a speaker) without the speaker's knowledge or intention.

o·ver·heat (ō'vẽr-hēt'), *v.t.* to make too hot.

o·ver·in·dul·gence (ō'vẽr-in-dul'jəns), *n.* excessive indulgence.

o·ver·is·sue (ō'vẽr-ish'ōō, ō'vẽr-ish'ū), *n.* an issue, as of bonds or stocks, that exceeds authorization, credit limits, etc.

o·ver·joy (ō'vẽr-joi'), *v.t.* to give great joy to; delight.

o·ver·lad·en (ō'vẽr-lād''n), *adj.* having too heavy a load; overloaded; overburdened.

o·ver·land (ō'vẽr-land'), *adv. & adj.* by, on, or across land.

o·ver·lap (ō'vẽr-lap'; *for n.*, ō'vẽr-lap'), *v.t. & v.i.* 1. to lap over; lie upon and extend beyond (something or each other). 2. to extend over part of (a period of time, sphere of activity, etc.); coincide in part (with). *n.* 1. an overlapping. 2. a part that overlaps. 3. the amount or extent of overlapping. 4. the place of overlapping.

o·ver·lay (ō'vẽr-lā'; *for n.*, ō'vẽr-lā'), *v.t.* [OVERLAID (-lād'), OVERLAYING], 1. to lay or spread over. 2. to cover or overspread, as with a decorative layer of something. 3. to put too much upon; weigh down; burden; oppress. 4. in *printing*, to place an overlay upon. *n.* 1. anything laid over another thing; covering. 2. a decorative layer or the like, applied in overlaying. 3. in *printing*, a sheet of paper fastened on the printing surface of a press to make a heavier impression. 4. [Scot.], a cravat.

o·ver·leap (ō'vẽr-lēp'), *v.t.* 1. to leap over or across. 2. to omit; pass over; ignore. 3. to leap farther than. 4. to overreach (oneself) by leaping too far.

o·ver·lie (ō'vẽr-lī'), *v.t.* [for prin. pts. see LIE], 1. to lie on or over. 2. to stifle or smother by lying on.

o·ver·live (ō'vẽr-liv'), *v.t.* to live longer than; outlive. *v.i.* to continue living or existing; endure; survive.

o·ver·load (ō'vẽr-lōd'; *for n.*, ō'vẽr-lōd'), *v.t.* to put too great a load upon. *n.* too great a load.

o·ver·long (ō'vẽr-lôŋ'), *adj. & adv.* too long.

o·ver·look (ō'vẽr-look'; *for n.*, ō'vẽr-look'), *v.t.* 1. to look at from above. 2. to give a view of from above. 3. to rise above; overtop. 4. *a)* to look over or beyond and not see. *b)* to ignore; neglect; hence, 5. to pass over indulgently; excuse. 6. to inspect; look over. 7. to oversee; supervise; manage. 8. to bewitch by looking at. *n.* 1. a height from which to survey surroundings. 2. the view from such a height. 3. a viewing or surveying. —*SYN.* see **neglect.**

o·ver·lord (ō'vẽr-lôrd'), *n.* a lord ranking over other lords, especially in the feudal system.

o·ver·ly (ō'vẽr-li), *adv.* [ME. *ouerly*, *ouerliche;* cf. ON. *ofrligr*], too or too much; excessively.

o·ver·man (ō'vẽr-mən; *for n. 3*, ō'vẽr-man'; *for v.*, ō'vẽr-man'), *n.* [*pl.* OVERMEN (-mən; *for 3*, -men')], 1. a man above others in power or authority; leader; foreman. 2. an arbitrator; referee. 3. [transl. of G.; cf. ÜBERMENSCH], a superman. *v.t.* [OVERMANNED (-mand'), OVERMANNING], to supply with more men than necessary.

o·ver·mas·ter (ō'vẽr-mas'tẽr, ō'vẽr-mäs'tẽr), *v.t.* [ME. *overmaistren*], to overcome; conquer; subdue.

o·ver·match (ō'vẽr-mach'), *v.t.* to more than match; exceed; surpass.

o·ver·much (ō'vẽr-much'), *adj. & adv.* too much. *n.* too great a quantity; excessive amount.

o·ver·nice (ō'vẽr-nīs'), *adj.* too nice; too fastidious, precise, etc.

o·ver·night (ō'vẽr-nīt'), *adv.* 1. during or through the night. 2. on or during the previous evening. *adj.* 1. done, happening, or lasting during the night. 2. of the previous evening. 3. of or for only one night: as, an *overnight* guest. 4. of or for a short journey or visit: as, an *overnight* bag. *n.* (ō'vẽr-nīt'), the previous evening.

o·ver·pass (ō'vẽr-pas', ō'vẽr-päs'; *for v.*, ō'vẽr-pas', ō'vẽr-päs'), *n.* a bridge or other passageway over or across a road, railway, etc. *v.t.* 1. to pass over, across, or through. 2. to surpass; exceed; outdo. 3. to overlook; ignore. 4. to transgress.

o·ver·pay (ō'vẽr-pā'), *v.t. & v.i.* 1. to pay too much, or more than (the due or proper amount). 2. to pay too much to (someone).

o·ver·peo·pled (ō'vẽr-pē'pəld), *adj.* filled with too many people.

o·ver·per·suade (ō'vẽr-pẽr-swād'), *v.t.* to win over by persuading; especially, to persuade (someone) against his natural inclinations.

o·ver·play (ō'vẽr-plā'), *v.t.* 1. to overact or overdo. 2. in *card games*, to overestimate the strength of (one's hand) and be defeated as a result. 3. in *golf*, to hit (the ball) beyond the flag or green.

o·ver·plus (ō'vẽr-plus'), *n.* [ME. *ouer*, over + *pluse* (< L. *plus*), more; prob. after Late OFr. *surplus;* cf. SURPLUS], 1. an amount left over; surplus. 2. too great an amount; excess.

o·ver·pow·er (ō'vẽr-pou'ẽr), *v.t.* 1. to make helpless; subdue; overwhelm. 2. to furnish with too much power: as, the motorboat was *overpowered.*

o·ver·pow·er·ing (ō'vẽr-pou'ẽr-iŋ), *adj.* that overpowers; overwhelming.

o·ver·print (ō'vẽr-print'; *for n.*, ō'vẽr-print'), *v.t.* to print over or on top of (a previously printed surface). *n.* 1. anything overprinted. 2. *a)* anything officially printed over the original design on a stamp. *b)* a stamp so overprinted: abbreviated **O.P., o.p.**

o·ver·pro·duce (ō'vẽr-prə-dōōs', ō'vẽr-prə-dūs'), *v.t. & v.i.* to produce in a quantity that is too great or that exceeds demand.

o·ver·pro·duc·tion (ō'vẽr-prə-duk'shən), *n.* 1. the production of more than is necessary. 2. the production of more goods than the public will or can buy at the market price.

o·ver·proof (ō'vẽr-prōōf'), *adj.* containing more alcohol than proof spirit does: abbreviated **O.P., o.p.**

o·ver·rate (ō'vẽr-rāt'), *v.t.* to rate, assess, or estimate too highly.

o·ver·reach (ō'vẽr-rēch'), *v.t.* 1. to reach or stretch beyond or above; extend beyond. 2. figuratively, to extend beyond in time. 3. to spread over and cover. 4. to reach too far for and miss. 5. to cheat; outdo by cunning. *v.i.* 1. to reach too far. 2. to cheat. 3. to reach or stretch beyond or above something. 4. to strike the forefoot with the hind foot: said of hoofed animals.

overreach oneself, 1. to fail because of trying to do more than one can. 2. to fail because of being too crafty or eager.

o·ver·re·fined (ō'vẽr-ri-fīnd'), *adj.* too refined.

o·ver·ride (ō'vẽr-rīd'), *v.t.* [OVERRODE (-rōd'), OVERRIDDEN (-rid''n), OVERRIDING], 1. to ride over. 2. to trample down. 3. to suppress, oppress, or domineer over. 4. to disregard; nullify: as, he *overrode* their pleas. 5. to fatigue (a horse, etc.) by riding too long. 6. to pass or extend over. 7. in *surgery*, to overlap.

o·ver·ripe (ō'vẽr-rīp'), *adj.* too ripe.

o·ver·rule (ō'vẽr-rōōl'), *v.t.* 1. to set aside or decide against by virtue of higher authority; rule out; annul: as, the major *overruled* the captain's order. 2. to have influence over or prevail over.

o·ver·run (ō'vẽr-run'; *for n.*, ō'vẽr-run'), *v.t.* [OVERRAN (-ran'), OVERRUN, OVERRUNNING], 1. to run or spread out over so as to cover: as, the flooded river *overran* the valley. 2. to spread over with a harmful result; infest or swarm over, as vermin, or rove over and ravage, as an invading army. 3. to spread swiftly throughout, as ideas, a fad, etc. 4. to run or extend beyond (certain limits): as, the program *overran* its schedule. 5. [Archaic], to outrun. 6. in *printing*, to rearrange (lines of type, columns, or pages) by shifting words or letters from one line to another. *v.i.* 1. to overflow. 2. to run over or beyond certain limits. *n.* 1. an overrunning. 2. the amount that overruns, or by which something overruns.

o·ver·score (ō'vẽr-skôr', ō'vẽr-skōr'; *for n.*, ō'vẽr-skôr', ō'vẽr-skōr'), *v.t.* [OVERSCORED (-skôrd', -skōrd'), OVERSCORING], 1. to put a line above (a word, sentence, etc.). 2. to mark lines through. *n.* a line over or through a word, sentence, etc.

o·ver·sea (ō'vẽr-sē'), *adj. & adv.* overseas.

o·ver·seas (ō'vẽr-sēz'), *adv.* abroad; over or beyond the sea. *adj.* 1. foreign; having to do with foreign countries. 2. from beyond the sea. 3. over or across the sea.

overseas cap, a small, soft cap without a visor or brim, worn by U. S. forces since World War I.

o·ver·see (ō'vẽr-sē'), *v.t.* [OVERSAW (-sô'), OVERSEEN (-sēn'), OVERSEEING], [ME. *oversene;* AS. *oferseon*], 1. to watch over and manage; supervise; superintend. 2. to survey; watch. 3. [Obs.], to examine; inspect.

o·ver·se·er (ō'vẽr-sē'ẽr), *n.* 1. one who watches over and directs the work of others; supervisor. 2. in England, a parish official: in full, **overseer of the poor.**

o·ver·sell (ō'vẽr-sel'), *v.t.* [OVERSOLD (-sōld'), OVERSELLING], 1. to sell more than can be supplied. 2. to sell to an excessive degree.

o·ver·set (ō'vẽr-set'; *for n.*, ō'vẽr-set'), *v.t.* [OVERSET, OVERSETTING], 1. to overcome or upset. 2. to overturn or overthrow. 3. to set too great an amount of (type or copy), or too much type for (a given space). *v.i.* to overturn; tip over. *n.* an overturning.

o·ver·sew (ō'vẽr-sō', ō'vẽr-sō'), *v.t.* [for prin. pts. see SEW], to sew together (two pieces of material) by passing small, close stitches over their coinciding edges; overhand.

o·ver·shade (ō'vẽr-shād'), *v.t.* [OVERSHADED (-id), OVERSHADING], to overshadow.

o·ver·shad·ow (ō'vẽr-shad'ō), *v.t.* 1. to cast a shadow over; hence, 2. to darken; obscure; dim. 3. to loom over, dominate, or be more significant or important than by comparison.

o·ver·shine (ō'vẽr-shīn'), *v.t.* [OVERSHONE (-shōn'), OVERSHINING], 1. to shine over or upon. 2. to outshine.

o·ver·shoe (ō'vẽr-shōō'), *n.* a kind of shoe or boot of rubber or fabric, worn over the regular shoe as a protection from cold or dampness; galosh; rubber.

o·ver·shoot (ō'vẽr-shōōt'), *v.t.* [OVERSHOT (-shot'), OVERSHOOTING], 1. to shoot or pass over or beyond.

2. to go farther than (an intended or normal limit); exceed. 3. to cause (a thing) to go beyond a proper limit. *v.i.* to shoot or go too far.

o·ver·shot (ō′vẽr-shot′), ***adj.*** 1. with the upper part or half extending past the lower: as, an *overshot* jaw. 2. driven by water flowing onto the upper part: as, an *overshot* water wheel.

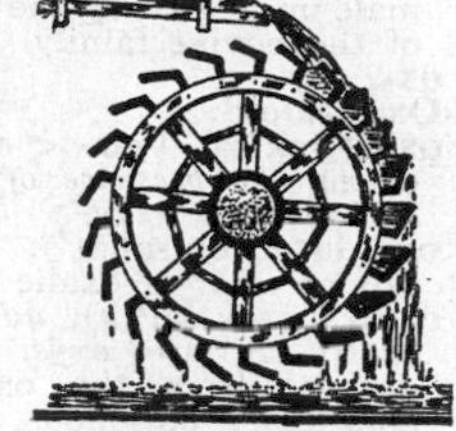
OVERSHOT WATER WHEEL

o·ver·side (ō′vẽr-sīd′), ***adv.*** over the side, as of a ship. ***adj.*** (ō′vẽr-sīd′), discharging or working over the side, as a dredge.

o·ver·sight (ō′vẽr-sīt′), ***n.*** 1. a superintendence; supervision. 2. an overlooking; failure to see or notice; hence, 3. an unintentional, careless mistake or omission.

o·ver·size (ō′vẽr-sīz′; *for n.*, ō′vẽr-sīz′), ***adj.*** 1. too large. 2. outsize; larger than the normal or usual. ***n.*** an outsize; size larger than regular sizes.

o·ver·skirt (ō′vẽr-skũrt′), ***n.*** an outer skirt.

o·ver·sleep (ō′vẽr-slēp′), ***v.t.*** [OVERSLEPT (-slept′), OVERSLEEPING], to sleep longer than (the intended time). ***v.i.*** to sleep too long.

o·ver·soul (ō′vẽr-sōl′), ***n.*** the spirit which inspires and motivates all living things: a concept in the transcendentalist philosophy of Emerson and others.

o·ver·spend (ō′vẽr-spend′), ***v.t.*** [OVERSPENT (-spent′), OVERSPENDING], 1. [Rare], to use till worn out; exhaust. 2. to spend more than. ***v.i.*** to spend more than one can afford.

o·ver·spread (ō′vẽr-spred′), ***v.t. & v.i.*** [OVERSPREAD, OVERSPREADING], to spread over or cover over.

o·ver·state (ō′vẽr-stāt′), ***v.t.*** [OVERSTATED (-id), OVERSTATING], to give an extravagant or magnified account of (facts, truth, etc.); exaggerate.

o·ver·state·ment (ō′vẽr-stāt′mənt), ***n.*** an extravagant statement; exaggeration.

o·ver·stay (ō′vẽr-stā′), ***v.t.*** to stay beyond the time, duration, or limits of.

o·ver·step (ō′vẽr-step′), ***v.t.*** [for prin. pts. see STEP], to go beyond: usually in a figurative application.

o·ver·stock (ō′vẽr-stok′; *for n.*, ō′vẽr-stok′), ***v.t.*** to stock more of than can be readily used. ***n.*** too large a stock.

o·ver·strain (ō′vẽr-strān′), ***v.t.*** to put under very great strain; overwork. ***v.i.*** to exert great effort.

o·ver·stride (ō′vẽr-strīd′), ***v.t.*** [for prin. pts. see STRIDE], 1. to stride across or over; go beyond. 2. to outdo; surpass. 3. to bestride.

o·ver·strung (ō′vẽr-struŋ′), ***adj.*** too highly strung; tense; jittery.

o·ver·stud·y (ō′vẽr-stud′i), ***v.t. & v.i.*** to study too hard or too much. ***n.*** too much study.

o·ver·stuff (ō′vẽr-stuf′), ***v.t.*** 1. to stuff with too much of something. 2. to upholster (furniture) with deep stuffing.

o·ver·sub·scribe (ō′vẽr-səb-skrīb′), ***v.t. & v.i.*** to subscribe for more (of) than is available or asked.

o·ver·sup·ply (ō′vẽr-sə-plī′), ***v.t.*** to supply in excess. ***n.*** too great a supply.

o·vert (ō′vẽrt, ō-vũrt′), ***adj.*** [ME. *overte;* OFr. *overt,* pp. of *ovrir,* to open; L. *aperire,* to open], 1. open; public; observable. 2. in *law,* done outwardly, without attempt at concealment and with evident intent.

o·ver·take (ō′vẽr-tāk′), ***v.t.*** [OVERTOOK (-took′), OVERTAKEN (-tāk′'n), OVERTAKING], 1. to catch up with. 2. to come upon unexpectedly or suddenly.

o·ver·task (ō′vẽr-task′, ō′vẽr-täsk′), ***v.t.*** to impose too great or heavy a task or tasks upon.

o·ver·tax (ō′vẽr-taks′), ***v.t.*** 1. to tax too heavily. 2. to make excessive demands on.

o·ver-the-count·er (ō′vẽr-*thə*-koun′tẽr), ***adj.*** 1. sold directly to buyers rather than through an exchange, as stocks and bonds. 2. sold or carried on in retail stores rather than by mail: as, *over-the-counter* sales.

o·ver·throw (ō′vẽr-thrō′; *for n.*, ō′vẽr-thrō′), ***v.t.*** [OVERTHREW (-thrōō′), OVERTHROWN (-thrōn′), OVERTHROWING], 1. to throw or turn over; upset. 2. to overcome; conquer; end. ***n.*** 1. an overthrowing or being overthrown. 2. destruction; ruin; end. —***SYN.*** see **conquer.**

o·ver·time (ō′vẽr-tīm′; *for v.*, ō′vẽr-tīm′), ***n.*** 1. time beyond the established limit, especially beyond the regular number of working hours. 2. pay for such time. 3. in *sports,* an extra time period added to the game to decide a tie. ***adj. & adv.*** of, for, or during a period of overtime. Abbreviated **o.t.** ***v.t.*** [OVERTIMED (-tīmd′), OVERTIMING], to exceed the proper limit in timing (a photographic exposure, etc.).

o·ver·tone (ō′vẽr-tōn′), ***n.*** [transl. of G. *oberton,* contr. < *oberpartialton,* upper partial tone], 1. any of the higher tones which faintly accompany the fundamental tone produced by a musical instrument, created by the vibration of small sections of the string or air column; upper partial; harmonic. 2. *pl.* implications; associations; suggestions: as, a reply full of *overtones.*

o·ver·top (ō′vẽr-top′), ***v.t.*** [OVERTOPPED (-topt′), OVERTOPPING], 1. to rise beyond or above. 2. to exceed in height; tower over. 3. to excel; surpass.

o·ver·trade (ō′vẽr-trād′), ***v.i.*** to trade beyond one's means of paying for or selling goods bought.

o·ver·train (ō′vẽr-trān′), ***v.t. & v.i.*** to train too long or too hard.

o·ver·trick (ō′vẽr-trik′), ***n.*** in *card games,* a trick taken in excess of the number bid or needed to win the game.

o·ver·trump (ō′vẽr-trump′), ***v.t. & v.i.*** in *card games,* to trump with a higher card than has been played.

o·ver·ture (ō′vẽr-chẽr), ***n.*** [ME., an opening; OFr. < *ovrir;* see OVERT], 1. an introductory proposal or offer; indication of willingness to negotiate. 2. *a)* a musical introduction to an opera or other large musical work. *b)* an independent orchestral composition of varying form. 3. in Presbyterian churches, *a)* the submitting of a proposal or a question, as of doctrine, by the highest church court to the presbyteries for consideration preceding formal decision. *b)* the proposal or question submitted. 4. an introductory section, as of a poem.

o·ver·turn (ō′vẽr-tũrn′; *for n.*, ō′vẽr-tũrn′), ***v.t.*** 1. to turn or throw over; upset. 2. to conquer; defeat; ruin. ***v.i.*** to turn or tip over; capsize. ***n.*** an overturning or being overturned. —***SYN.*** see **upset.**

o·ver·use (ō′vẽr-ūs′), ***n.*** too much use. ***v.t.*** (ō′vẽr-ūz′), to use too much, too long, etc.

o·ver·val·ue (ō′vẽr-val′ū), ***v.t.*** to value too highly.

o·ver·watch (ō′vẽr-wäch′, ō′vẽr-wôch′), ***v.t.*** 1. to watch over. 2. to watch to the point of weariness.

o·ver·wear (ō′vẽr-wâr′), ***v.t.*** [for prin. pts. see WEAR], 1. to wear until no longer fit for use. 2. to outgrow.

o·ver·wea·ry (ō′vẽr-wêr′i), ***adj.*** too weary; exhausted. ***v.t.*** [OVERWEARIED (-id), OVERWEARYING], to make overweary; tire out.

o·ver·ween·ing (ō′vẽr-wēn′iŋ), ***adj.*** [ME. *oferweninge,* ppr. of *oferwenen;* AS. *oferwenan; ofer,* over + *wenan,* to hope], arrogant; excessively proud; conceited.

o·ver·weigh (ō′vẽr-wā′), ***v.t.*** 1. to outweigh. 2. to burden; oppress; weigh down.

o·ver·weight (ō′vẽr-wāt′; *for adj. & v.*, ō′vẽr-wāt′), ***n.*** 1. more weight than is needed or allowed; extra or surplus weight. 2. a greater amount of importance or weight; preponderance. ***adj.*** above normal or legal weight: opposed to *underweight.* ***v.t.*** to overweigh.

o·ver·whelm (ō′vẽr-hwelm′), ***v.t.*** [ME. *oferwhelmen; ofer,* over + *whelmen,* to turn], 1. to pour down upon and cover over or bury beneath. 2. to make helpless; overcome; crush; overpower. 3. [Obs.], to overthrow.

o·ver·whelm·ing (ō′vẽr-hwel′miŋ), ***adj.*** that overwhelms.

o·ver·wind (ō′vẽr-wīnd′), ***v.t.*** to wind too far or too tightly, as a winch.

o·ver·work (ō′vẽr-wũrk′; *for n. 2,* ō′vẽr-wũrk′), ***v.t.*** to work or use to excess: as, he *overworked* the horse, she *overworks* that excuse. ***v.i.*** to work too hard or too long. ***n.*** 1. work that is severe or burdensome. 2. work beyond the amount agreed upon; extra work.

o·ver·write (ō′vẽr-rīt′), ***v.t. & v.i.*** [OVERWROTE (-rōt′), OVERWRITTEN (-rit′'n), OVERWRITING], 1. *a)* to write (something) over other writing. *b)* to write over (other writing). 2. to write too much, or in too flowery or labored a style, about (some subject).

o·ver·wrought (ō′vẽr-rôt′), ***adj.*** 1. overworked; fatigued; hence, 2. nervous; strained; excited. 3. with the surface adorned. 4. too elaborate; ornate.

o·vi- (ō′vi), [< L. *ovum,* an egg], a combining form meaning *egg* or *ovum,* as in *oviduct, oviform.*

Ov·id (ov′id), ***n.*** (*Publius Ovidius Naso*), Roman poet; lived 43 B.C.–17? A.D.

o·vi·duct (ō′vi-dukt′), ***n.*** [Mod. L. *oviductus;* see OVI- & DUCT], a duct or tube through which the ova pass from the ovary to the uterus or to the outside.

O·vie·do (ô-vye′*th*ô), ***n.*** a city in northwestern Spain: pop., 78,000.

o·vif·er·ous (ō-vif′ẽr-əs), ***adj.*** [*ovi-* + *-ferous*], in *anatomy & zoology,* bearing, producing, or carrying ova.

o·vi·form (ō′vi-fôrm′), ***adj.*** [*ovi-* + *-form*], egg-shaped.

o·vine (ō′vīn, ō′vin), ***adj.*** [LL. *ovinus* < L. *ovis,* sheep; akin to Gr. *ois;* for IE. base see EWE], of, like, or having the nature of, sheep.

o·vip·a·ra (ō-vip′ẽr-ə), ***n.pl.*** [Mod. L. < L. *oviparus;* see OVIPAROUS], the egg-laying animals.

o·vi·par·i·ty (ō′vi-par′ə-ti), ***n.*** the quality or condition of being oviparous.

o·vip·a·rous (ō-vip′ẽr-əs), ***adj.*** [L. *oviparus* < *ovum,* an egg + *parere,* to produce], 1. producing eggs which hatch after leaving the body of the female. 2. designating or of this type of reproduction. Opposed to *viviparous.*

o·vi·pos·it (ō′vi-poz′it), *v.i.* [< *ovi-* + L. *positus,* pp. of *ponere,* to place], to deposit or lay eggs: usually said of insects having an ovipositor.
o·vi·po·si·tion (ō′vi-pə-zish′ən), *n.* the act of depositing eggs, as with an ovipositor.
o·vi·pos·i·tor (ō′vi-poz′i-tẽr), *n.* [*ovi-* + L. *positor,* one who places < *ponere,* to place], 1. a special organ of insects for depositing eggs in a suitable place, usually situated at the end of the abdomen. 2. an extension of the genital orifice of a fish.
o·vi·sac (ō′vi-sak′), *n.* [*ovi-* + *sac*], 1. an egg capsule or case; oötheca. 2. an egg receptacle. 3. a Graafian follicle.
o·void (ō′void), *adj.* [*ovi-* + *-oid*], egg-shaped; oviform. *n.* anything of ovoid form.
o·vo·lo (ō′və-lō′), *n.* [*pl.* OVOLI (-lē′)], [obs. It. (now *uovolo*), dim. of *ovo* < L. *ovum,* an egg], a convex molding, usually a quarter section of a circle; quarter round: see **molding,** illus.
o·vo·vi·vip·a·rous (ō′vō-vi-vip′ẽr-əs), *adj.* [< L. *ovum,* an egg + *viviparous*], designating various animals which produce hard-shelled eggs that are hatched within the female's body, as some reptiles and fishes.
o·vu·lar (ō′vyoo-lẽr), *adj.* [Mod. L. *ovularis* < *ovulum;* see OVULE], like or having to do with an ovule or ovum.
o·vu·lar·y (ō′vyoo-ler′i), *adj.* ovular.
o·vu·late (ō′vyoo-lāt′; *for adj.,* ō′vyoo-lit), *v.i.* [OVULATED (-id), OVULATING], [< *ovule* + *-ate*], to discharge ova from the ovary; produce ova. *adj.* having an ovule or ovules.
o·vu·la·tion (ō′vyoo-lā′shən), *n.* [< *ovule* + *-ation*], the physiological process by which a mature ovum escapes from a ruptured Graafian follicle.
o·vule (ō′vūl), *n.* [Fr.; Mod. L. *ovulum,* dim. < L. *ovum*], 1. in *zoology,* the immature ovum while still in the Graafian follicle; any small egg. 2. in *botany,* that part of a plant which develops into a seed.
o·vum (ō′vəm), *n.* [*pl.* OVA (ō′və)], [L., an egg], in *biology,* an egg; female germ cell which, generally only after fertilization, develops into a new member of the same species.
OW., Old Welsh.
owe (ō), *v.t.* [OWED (ōd), *obs.* OUGHT (ôt); OWING], [ME. *owen, aghen;* AS. *agan,* to own, possess, have; akin to Goth. *aigan* (OHG. *eigan;* cf. G. *eigen,* own); IE. base **ēik-,* to have as one's own, be able; cf. OUGHT], 1. to have an obligation to pay; be indebted to the amount of. 2. to be morally obligated to: as, I *owe* him my thanks. 3. to have or cherish (a certain feeling) toward another; bear: as, he *owed* ill will. 4. to be indebted to for the existence of. 5. [Obs.], to own; have. *v.i.* to be in debt.
Ow·en (ō′in, ō′wən), [W. < *Owein,* earlier *Ewein* < Celt. **Esu-ganyos;* akin to Gr. *Eugenios;* see EUGENE], a masculine name.
Ow·en, Robert (ō′in, ō′wən), 1771–1858; British industrialist and socialist.
Owen, Wilfred, 1893–1918; English poet.
O·wens·bor·o (ō′inz-būr′ō), *n.* a city in northwestern Kentucky, on the Ohio: pop., 42,000.
Ow·en-Stan·ley (ō′in-stan′li), *n.* a mountain range in northeastern New Guinea: highest peak, Mount Victoria, 13,121 ft.
OWI, Office of War Information.
ow·ing (ō′iŋ), *adj.* [ME. *owynge*], 1. that owes. 2. due; unpaid: as, there are three dollars *owing.*
  owing to, resulting from; caused by; on account of.
owl (oul), *n.* [ME. & AS. *ule;* akin to G. *eule* < echoic base seen also in L. *ulula,* owl, *ululare,* to howl; cf. HOWL], any of a group of night birds of prey found throughout the world, distinguished by a large head, eyes surrounded by stiff-feathered disks, a short hooked beak, feathered legs with sharp talons, and soft plumage which permits noiseless flight: applied figuratively to a person of nocturnal habits, solemn appearance, etc.
owl·et (oul′it), *n.* 1. any young or small owl. 2. a certain small European owl.
owl·ish (oul′ish), *adj.* like or characteristic of an owl.
owl's-clo·ver (oulz′klō′vẽr), *n.* a plant of the figwort family, with spikes of red or purple tubelike flowers.
own (ōn), *adj.* [ME. *owen, agen;* AS. *agen,* pp. of *agan,* to possess; cf. OWE], belonging, relating, or peculiar to oneself or itself: used to strengthen a preceding possessive, as, he wants his *own* book, he prefers his *own* doctor. *n.* that which belongs to oneself: as, that is his *own,* he came into his *own,* I'm on my *own.* *v.t.* 1. to possess; hold as personal property; have. 2. to admit; recognize; acknowledge. *v.i.* to confess (with *to*). —*SYN.* see **acknowledge, have.**
  come into one's own, to receive what properly belongs to one, especially acclaim or recognition.
  hold one's own, to maintain one's place or condition in spite of attack, criticism, illness, etc.
  of one's own, belonging strictly to oneself.
  on one's own, [Colloq.], by one's own efforts; on one's own resources, responsibility, etc.
own·er (ōn′ẽr), *n.* a person who owns; proprietor.
own·er·ship (ōn′ẽr-ship′), *n.* [see -SHIP], 1. the state or fact of being an owner. 2. legal right of possession; lawful title (to something); proprietorship.
ox (oks), *n.* [*pl.* OXEN (ok′s'n), *rarely* OX; see PLURAL, II, D, 1], [ME.; AS. *oxa;* akin to G. *ochse;* IE. base **wegw-, ūgw-,* wet, to make wet (with sense of the male impregnating the female)], 1. loosely, any animal of the bovine family. 2. a castrated bull.
ox-, oxy-.
Ox., Oxford.
ox·a- (ok′sə), [var. < *oxy-*], in *chemistry,* a prefix indicating *the presence of oxygen, especially as replacing carbon in a ring.*
ox·a·late (ok′sə-lāt′), *n.* [Fr.; see OXALIC & -ATE], a salt or ester of oxalic acid.
ox·al·ic (ok-sal′ik), *adj.* [Fr. *oxalique;* L. *oxalis;* Gr. *oxalis,* sorrel < *oxys,* acid], 1. having to do with or derived from the oxalis. 2. designating or of a colorless, poisonous, crystalline acid, $(COOH)_2$, found in oxalis and other plants or prepared synthetically: used in dyeing, bleaching, etc.
ox·a·lis (ok′sə-lis), *n.* [L., garden sorrel; Gr. *oxalis* < *oxys,* acid, sour], any of a number of related plants with cloverlike leaves and flowers of white, red, etc.
ox·a·zin (ok′sə-zin), *n.* oxazine.
ox·a·zine (ok′sə-zēn′, ok′sə-zin), *n.* [*oxygen* + *azine*], any of six compounds having a composition corresponding to the formula C_4H_5NO and composed of molecules which contain four atoms of carbon and one atom each of oxygen and nitrogen united in a ring structure.
ox·blood (oks′blud′), *n.* a deep red color.
ox·bow (oks′bō′), *n.* [ME. *oxboue*], 1. the U-shaped part of an ox yoke which passes under and around the neck of the animal. 2. a crescent-shaped bend in a river; hence, 3. the land within such a bend.

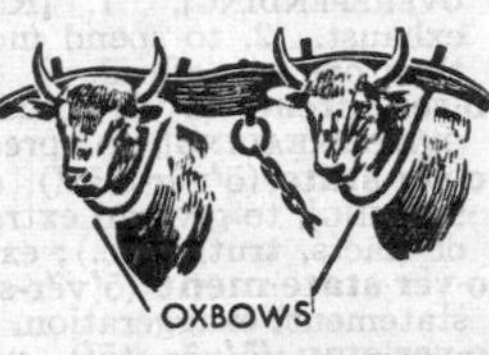

YOKE WITH OXBOWS

ox·en (ok′s'n), *n.* plural of **ox.**
ox·eye (oks′ī′), *n.* [ME. *oxie*], any of a number of related daisylike plants.
ox-eyed (oks′īd′), *adj.* with eyes large and full like those of an ox.
oxeye daisy, a daisylike plant with flowers of yellow rays around a brown disk; black-eyed Susan.
Ox·ford (oks′fẽrd), *n.* 1. Oxfordshire. 2. the county seat of Oxfordshire: pop., 104,000: home of Oxford University. Abbreviated **Ox., Oxf.**
ox·ford (oks′fẽrd), *n.* [after *Oxford*], [sometimes O-], 1. a type of low shoe laced over the instep: also **oxford shoe.** 2. a type of cotton cloth with a basketlike weave, used for men's shirts, etc.: also **oxford cloth.**
Oxford gray, a very dark gray, approaching black.
Oxford group movement, a religious movement started about 1921 by the Reverend Frank Buchman and based on early, or primitive, Christianity, emphasizing the fellowship of man and God, and the importance of confession: also called *Buchmanism.*
Oxford movement, a movement begun at Oxford University in 1833 by certain Anglican clergymen to bring Catholic doctrine and ritual into the Anglican Church in opposition to the liberal movement in religion: see **Tractarianism.**
Ox·ford·shire (oks′fẽrd-shir′), *n.* a county of south central England: pop., 276,000; county seat, Oxford: also called *Oxford, Oxon.*
ox·heart (oks′härt′), *n.* 1. a large cherry shaped like a heart. 2. a kind of cabbage.
ox·id (ok′sid), *n.* oxide.
ox·i·dase (ok′sə-dās′, ok′sə-dāz′), *n.* [*oxidize* + *-ase*], any of a group of enzymes which act as oxidizing agents.
ox·i·da·tion (ok′sə-dā′shən), *n.* [Fr. < *oxide;* see OXIDE], 1. the union of a substance with oxygen. 2. the process of increasing the positive valence or of decreasing the negative valence of an element or ion. 3. the process by which electrons are removed from atoms or ions. Cf. **reduction.**
ox·i·da·tive (ok′sə-dā′tiv), *adj.* of or characterized by oxidation; able to oxidize.
ox·ide (ok′sīd, ok′sid), *n.* [Fr. < Gr. *oxys,* acid, sour + Fr. *acide,* acid], a binary compound of oxygen with some other element or with a radical: also **oxid.**
ox·i·diz·a·ble (ok′sə-dīz′ə-b'l), *adj.* that can be oxidized.
ox·i·dize (ok′sə-dīz′), *v.t.* [OXIDIZED (-dīzd′), OXIDIZING], [< *oxide* + *-ize*], 1. to unite with oxygen. 2. to increase the positive valence or decrease the negative valence of (an element or ion). 3. to remove electrons from (an atom or ion). *v.i.* to become oxidized.
ox·i·diz·er (ok′sə-dīz′ẽr), *n.* any substance that oxidizes or causes another to oxidize; oxidizing agent.
ox·im (ok′sim), *n.* oxime.
ox·ime (ok′sēm, ok′sim), *n.* [< *oxygen* + *imide*], any of a series of compounds formed by the action of hydroxylamine on an aldehyde or ketone, in which the oxygen atom of the CHO group of the aldehyde, or of the CO group of the ketone, is replaced by the :NOH group.

ox·lip (oks′lip′), **n.** [AS. *oxanslyppe; oxan*, genit. of *oxa* (see OX) + *slyppe*, dropping; cf. COWSLIP], a plant of the primrose family, having yellow flowers.
Ox·on (ok′son), **n.** Oxfordshire.
Oxon., 1. *Oxonia*, [L.], Oxford. 2. *Oxoniensis*, [L.], of Oxford.
Ox·o·ni·an (ok-sō′ni-ən), **adj.** [< ML. *Oxonia*, Oxford], of Oxford (England) or Oxford University. **n.** 1. a student or alumnus of Oxford University. 2. a native or inhabitant of Oxford, England.
ox·peck·er (oks′pek′ẽr), **n.** any of a group of African starlings that feed on the parasitic larvae found on the hide of oxen.
ox·tail (oks′tāl′), **n.** the tail of an ox, especially when skinned and used to make a soup.
ox·ter (ok′stẽr), **n.** [Late ME. *oxtere;* AS. *ohsta;* akin to G. *achsel*, shoulder; IE. base **aǵes-*, as also in L. *axis* (cf. AXIS), *axilla*, shoulder; cf. AXLE, AISLE], [Scot. & British Dial.], the armpit.
ox·tongue (oks′tuŋ′), **n.** any of a number of related plants with rough, tongue-shaped leaves.
Ox·us (ok′səs), **n.** the Amu Darya, a river in western Asia: the ancient name, still used.
ox·y- (ok′si), [< *oxygen*], a combining form meaning *a) containing oxygen:* also, before a vowel, **ox-**. *b) containing the hydroxyl radical:* in this sense *hydroxy-* is preferred.
ox·y- (ok′si, ok′sə), [< Gr. *oxys*, sharp, acid], a combining form meaning *sharp, pointed, acute*, or *acid*, as in *oxycephalic, oxymoron, oxygen.*
ox·y·a·cet·y·lene (ok′si-ə-set′'l-ēn′), **adj.** [*oxy-* (oxygen) + *acetylene*], of or using a mixture of oxygen and acetylene.
oxyacetylene torch, a blowpipe in which the oxyacetylene flame produced is much hotter than an oxyhydrogen flame, used for cutting and welding steel: also **oxyacetylene blowpipe.**
ox·y·ac·id (ok′si-as′id), **n.** an acid containing oxygen.
ox·y·cal·ci·um light (ok′si-kal′si-əm), [*oxy-* (oxygen) + *calcium*], a light produced by white-hot lime.
ox·y·ce·phal·ic (ok′si-sə-fal′ik), **adj.** [*oxy-* (sharp) + *cephalic*], designating or having a skull coming to a more or less cone-shaped point on top.
ox·y·gen (ok′si-jən), **n.** [Fr. *oxygène;* see OXY- (acid) & -GEN], a colorless, odorless, tasteless, gaseous chemical element, the most abundant of all elements: it occurs free in the atmosphere, forming one fifth of its volume, and in combination in water, sandstone, limestone, etc.; it is very active, being able to combine with nearly all other elements, and is essential to life processes and to combustion: symbol, O; at. wt., 16.000; at. no., 8.
oxygen acid, an acid that contains oxygen; oxyacid.
ox·y·gen·ate (ok′si-jə-nāt′), **v.t.** [OXYGENATED (-id), OXYGENATING], [< Fr. *oxygèner*], to mix, treat, or combine with oxygen; oxidize.
ox·y·gen·a·tion (ok′si-jə-nā′shən), **n.** a mixing or being mixed with oxygen; oxidation.
ox·y·gen·ize (ok′si-jə-nīz′), **v.t.** [OXYGENIZED (-nīzd′), OXYGENIZING], to oxygenate; oxidize.
oxygen tent, a boxlike enclosure supplied with oxygen, in which a patient is kept to facilitate his breathing: used chiefly in cases of pneumonia and cardiac disease.

OXYGEN TENT

ox·y·hem·o·glo·bin (ok′si-hē′mə-glō′bin), **n.** [*oxy-* (oxygen) + *hemoglobin*], a substance found in the arterial blood, formed in the lungs by the loose union of hemoglobin with oxygen, which is thus carried to the body tissues.
ox·y·hy·dro·gen (ok′si-hī′drə-jən), **adj.** [*oxy-* (oxygen) + *hydrogen*], of or using a mixture of oxygen and hydrogen. **n.** oxyhydrogen gas.
oxyhydrogen torch (or **blowpipe**), a blowpipe which burns a mixture of oxygen and hydrogen at a very high temperature, used for cutting and welding steel.
ox·y·mo·ron (ok′si-môr′on, ok′si-mō′ron), **n.** [*pl.* OXYMORA (-ə)], [Mod. L.; Gr. *oxymōron* < *oxys*, sharp + *mōros*, foolish, dull], a figure of speech in which opposite or contradictory ideas or terms are combined (e.g., thunderous silence, sweet sorrow).
ox·y·salt (ok′si-sôlt′), **n.** any salt of an oxyacid.
ox·y·sul·fide (ok′si-sul′fīd, ok′si-sul′fid), **n.** a compound formed of an element or positive radical with oxygen and sulfur, in which oxygen may be thought of as replacing a part of the sulfur.
ox·y·to·cic (ok′si-tō′sik, ok′si-tos′ik), **adj.** [< Gr. *oxytokion*, medicine for speeding childbirth; + *-ic*], in *medicine*, promoting or hastening the process of childbirth by stimulating the contractions of the involuntary muscles of the uterus. **n.** an oxytocic medicine.
ox·y·to·cin (ok′si-tō′sin, ok′si-tos′in), **n.** [< Gr. *oxys*, quick, sharp + *tokos*, birth; + *-in*], one of the hormones of the posterior pituitary gland, serving to increase the contractions of the uterus during childbirth and to prevent or stop bleeding afterward.
ox·y·tone (ok′si-tōn′), **adj.** [Gr. *oxytonos* < *oxys*, sharp + *tonos*, a tone], with an acute accent on the last syllable. **n.** an oxytone word.
o·yer (ō′yẽr, oi′ẽr), **n.** [ME.; Anglo-Fr., inf. used as n.; L. *audire*, to hear], a copy of a bond or other instrument that is the subject of a suit, given to the opposite party instead of being read aloud, as formerly.
oyer and ter·mi·ner (tũr′mi-nẽr), [Archaic], a hearing and determining: used in the United States to designate the higher criminal courts.
o·yez, o·yes (ō′yes, ō′yez), **interj.** [ME.; Anglo-Fr., hear ye < *oyer;* see OYER], hear ye! attention!: usually cried out three times by officials to command silence before a proclamation is made. **n.** a cry of *oyez.*
oys·ter (ois′tẽr), **n.** [ME. & OFr. *oistre;* L. *ostrea, ostreum;* Gr. *ostreon*, oyster; akin to *osteon*, a bone, *ostrakon*, hard shell of a shellfish], 1. any of a group of marine mollusks with an irregularly shaped hinged shell, found especially on the bottom of the sea and widely used as food. 2. any of numerous similar bivalve mollusks, as the scallop, pearl oyster, etc. 3. the oyster-shaped bit of meat contained in a depression on each side of the pelvic bone of a fowl. Applied figuratively to a taciturn person or to a thing from which profit or advantage can be extracted.
oyster bed, a place on the ocean floor naturally suited to, or artificially prepared for, the breeding and cultivation of oysters.
oyster catcher, any of several species of wading birds of the plover family, with a strong, wedge-shaped beak and stout legs.
oyster crab, any of a group of crabs that live as commensals in the gill cavities of oysters.
oyster cracker, a small, round soda cracker eaten with oyster stews, etc.
oyster farm, a place where oyster beds are maintained.
oys·ter·man (ois′tẽr-mən), **n.** [*pl.* OYSTERMEN (-mən)], 1. a person who gathers, sells, or raises oysters. 2. a vessel used in gathering oysters.
oyster plant, 1. salsify. 2. the sea lungwort.
oyster rake, a rake with a long handle and curved teeth for gathering in oysters from shallow waters.
oys·ter·root (ois′tẽr-rōōt′, ois′tẽr-root′), **n.** salsify.
oyster stew, a dish consisting of whole oysters in a soup of heated milk or cream, butter, and seasoning.
oyster white, a very light gray, with a creamy or yellowish cast.
oz., [*pl.* oz., ozs.], ounce.
O·zark Mountains (ō′zärk), a low mountain range in southwestern Missouri, northwestern Arkansas, and northeastern Oklahoma: also **Ozarks.**
o·zo·ce·rite (ə-zō′kə-rīt′, ə-zō′sə-rīt′), **n.** [G. *ozokerit* < Gr. *ozein*, to smell + *kēros*, wax], a mineral wax used in making candles, electrical insulation, etc.
o·zone (ō′zōn, ō-zōn′), **n.** [Fr. < Gr. *ozein*, to smell], 1. a blue gas, O_3, with a penetrating odor: it is an allotropic form of oxygen, formed usually by a silent electrical discharge in air, and is used as an oxidizing, deodorizing, and bleaching agent and in the purification of water. 2. [Slang], pure air.
o·zon·ic (ō-zon′ik, ō-zō′nik), **adj.** containing or having to do with ozone.
ozonic ether, a solution of ethylic ether, hydrogen peroxide, and alcohol, used as an antiseptic.
o·zo·nid (ō′zō-nid), **n.** an ozonide.
o·zo·nide (ō′zō-nīd′), **n.** any of a series of compounds of ozone.
o·zo·nif·er·ous (ō′zə-nif′ẽr-əs), **adj.** [< *ozone* + *-ferous*], having or containing ether.
o·zo·nize (ō′zə-nīz′), **v.t.** [OZONIZED (-nīzd′), OZONIZING], 1. to change (oxygen) into ozone. 2. to treat or impregnate with ozone.
o·zo·nous (ō′zə-nəs), **adj.** ozonic.
ozs., ounces.

P

P, p (pē), *n.* [*pl.* **P's, p's, Ps, ps** (pēz)], 1. the sixteenth letter of the English alphabet: from the Greek *pi*, a borrowing from the Phoenician: see **alphabet**, table. 2. the sound of P or p: normally in English, a voiceless lip stop consonant: *p* is silent before *n* in words of Greek origin. 3. a type or impression for P or p. 4. *a symbol for* the sixteenth in a sequence or group (or the fifteenth if J is omitted). *adj.* 1. of P or p. 2. sixteenth (or fifteenth if J is omitted) in a sequence or group.

mind one's p's and q's, to be careful of one's words and actions.

P (pē), *n.* 1. an object shaped like P. 2. a Roman numeral for 400: with a superior bar (P̄), 400,000. 3. in *genetics, the symbol for* parental generation. 4. in *chemistry, the symbol for* phosphorus. 5. in *mechanics, the symbol for*: *a*) power. *b*) pressure.

P, in *chess*, pawn.

P-, pursuit: followed by a number to designate a specific model of United States Air Force fighter airplane.

p-, in *chemistry*, para-.

P., p., 1. pastor. 2. post. 3. power. 4. president. 5. pressure. 6. priest. 7. prince.

p., 1. [*pl.* PP.], page. 2. part. 3. participle. 4. past. 5. penny. 6. per. 7. pint. 8. pipe. 9. pitcher. 10. pole. 11. population. 12. pro. 13. in *music*, piano.

Pa, in *chemistry*, protactinium.

pa (pä; *dial., often* pô), *n.* [Colloq.], father; papa.

Pa., Pennsylvania.

P.A., 1. Passenger Agent. 2. Post Adjutant. 3. Purchasing Agent. 4. [Slang], *a*) press agent. *b*) prosecuting attorney. *c*) public address (system).

p.a., 1. participial adjective. 2. per annum.

pab·u·lum (pab′yoo-ləm), *n.* [L.], food; sustenance.

Pac., Pacific.

pa·ca (pä′kə, pak′ə), *n.* [Port. & Sp. < Tupi *páca*], any of a number of related short-tailed or tailless rodents of South and Central America, with spotted brown fur and hooflike toes.

pace (pās), *n.* [ME.; OFr. *pas*; L. *passus*, a step, lit., a stretching out of the leg in walking < pp. of *pandere*, to stretch out], 1. a step in walking, running, etc.; stride. 2. a conventional measure of length, approximately the distance covered in a step or stride: it is generally estimated at 2 1/2 feet, or sometimes in measuring, 3 feet or 3.3 feet (1/5 of a rod). The regulation pace of the United States Army is 30 inches, or 36 inches for double time. The *Roman pace*, measured from the heel of one foot to the heel of the same foot in the next stride, was 5 Roman feet, or 58.1 inches: it is now known as a *geometric pace*, about 5 feet. 3. the rate of speed in walking, running, etc.; hence, 4. *a*) rate of movement, progress, development, etc. *b*) an equal rate or speed: as, try to keep *pace* with me. 5. a particular way of walking, running, etc. (of a person or animal); gait; walk. 6. a gait of a horse in which both legs on the same side are raised together. *v.t.* [PACED (pāst), PACING], 1. to walk or stride back and forth across. 2. to measure by paces. 3. to train, develop, or guide the pace of (a horse). 4. to set the pace for (a runner, horse, etc.). *v.i.* 1. to walk with slow or regular steps. 2. to raise both legs on the same side at the same time in moving: said of a horse.

put one through his paces, to test one's abilities, accomplishments, capabilities, etc.

set the pace, 1. to go at a speed that others try to equal, as in a race; hence, 2. to do or be something for others to emulate.

paced (pāst), *adj.* 1. having a specified pace: used in hyphenated compounds, as *fast-paced*. 2. measured by paces or pacing. 3. in *horse racing*, having its pace set by a pacemaker.

pace·mak·er (pās′mā′kēr), *n.* a runner, horse, automobile, etc. that sets the pace for others, as in a race.

pace·mak·ing (pās′mā′kiŋ), *n.* a setting of a pace, as by a runner, horse, etc.

pac·er (pā′sēr), *n.* 1. a horse whose normal gait is a pace. 2. a pacemaker.

pa·cha (pə-shä′, pash′ə, pä′shə), *n.* a pasha.

pa·cha·lic (pə-shä′lik), *n.* a pashalik.

pa·chi·si (pə-chē′zi, pä-chē′zi), *n.* [Hind. *pacīsī* < *pacīs*, twenty-five: so named from the highest throw], 1. in India, a game for four players in which the moves of the pieces around a board are determined by the throwing of cowrie shells. 2. in England and the United States, a similar game in which dice replace the shells: also **parcheesi, parchesi, parchisi.**

Pach·mann, Vlad·i·mir de (vlá-dē′mir dye pákh′mán), 1848–1933; Russian pianist.

pach·ou·li (pach′oo-li, pə-chōō′li), *n.* patchouli.

Pa·chu·ca (pä-chōō′kä), *n.* a city in east central Mexico: pop., 53,000.

pach·y·derm (pak′ə-dũrm′), *n.* [Fr. *pachyderme*; Gr. *pachydermos*, thick-skinned < *pachys*, thick + *derma*, a skin], 1. any of certain large, thick-skinned, hoofed animals, as the elephant, rhinoceros, and hippopotamus, formerly classified together; hence, 2. a thick-skinned, insensitive, stolid person.

pach·y·der·ma·tous (pak′ə-dũr′mə-təs), *adj.* 1. of, or having the nature of, a pachyderm. 2. thick-skinned; insensitive to criticism, insult, etc.

pach·y·der·mous (pak′ə-dũr′məs), *adj.* pachydermatous.

pach·y·san·dra (pak′i-san′drə), *n.* [Mod. L. < Gr. *pachys*, thick; + *-androus*], any of various dense-growing plants, mainly evergreen, used as a ground cover.

pac·i·fi·a·ble (pas′ə-fī′ə-b'l), *adj.* that can be pacified.

Pa·cif·ic (pə-sif′ik), *n.* [see next entry; so called by Magellan because of its tranquil appearance], the largest of the earth's oceans, between Asia and the American continents; area, 63,750,000 sq. mi. *adj.* 1. designating, of, in, on, or near this ocean. 2. on, along, or near the Pacific Coast of the United States. Abbreviated **Pac., Pacif.**

pa·cif·ic (pə-sif′ik), *adj.* [Fr. *pacifique*; L. *pacificus* < *pacificare*; see PACIFY], 1. making or tending to make peace; appeasing; conciliatory. 2. of a peaceful nature or disposition; not warlike; mild; tranquil; calm.

pa·cif·i·cal (pə-sif′i-k'l), *adj.* pacific.

pa·cif·i·cate (pə-sif′i-kāt′), *v.t.* [PACIFICATED (-id), PACIFICATING], [< L. *pacificatus*], to pacify.

pac·i·fi·ca·tion (pas′ə-fi-kā′shən), *n.* [Fr.; L. *pacificatio*], a pacifying or being pacified.

pa·cif·i·ca·tor (pə-sif′i-kā′tēr, pas′ə-fi-kā′tēr), *n.* a person who pacifies; peacemaker.

pa·cif·i·ca·to·ry (pə-sif′i-kə-tôr′i, pə-sif′i-kə-tō′ri), *adj.* tending to pacify, or make peace; conciliatory.

pa·cif·i·cism (pə-sif′ə-siz′m), *n.* pacifism.

‡**pa·ci·fi·co** (pä-sē′fē-kô′), *n.* [*pl.* PACIFICOS (-kôs′)], [Sp.], a peaceful person; nonresister; specifically, a Cuban or Filipino who submitted to Spanish rule.

Pacific Standard Time, one of the four standard times in the United States, corresponding to the mean local time of the 120th meridian west of Greenwich, England: it is eight hours behind Greenwich time and three behind Eastern Standard Time: abbreviated **P.S.T.**

pac·i·fi·er (pas′ə-fī′ēr), *n.* 1. a person or thing that pacifies. 2. a nipple or teething ring for babies.

pac·i·fism (pas′ə-fiz′m), *n.* [< *pacific* + *-ism*], opposition to all war and armed hostility; belief that national or international disputes should be settled by peaceful means rather than by force or war.

pac·i·fist (pas′ə-fist), *n.* a person who advocates pacifism; one opposed to war or the use of force.

pac·i·fis·tic (pas′ə-fis′tik), *adj.* of pacifism or pacifists.

pac·i·fy (pas′ə-fī′), *v.t.* [PACIFIED (-fīd′), PACIFYING], [Fr. *pacifier*; L. *pacificare* < *pax*, *pacis*, peace + *facere*, to make], 1. to make peaceful or calm; appease; tranquilize. 2. to establish or secure peace in (a nation, etc.).

SYN.—**pacify** implies a making quiet and peaceful that which has become noisy or disorderly (to *pacify* a crying child); **appease** suggests a pacifying by gratifying or giving in to the demands of (to *appease* one's hunger); **mollify** suggests a soothing of wounded feelings or an allaying of indignation (his compliments failed to *mollify* her); **placate** implies the changing of a hostile or angry attitude to a friendly or favorable one (to *placate* an offended colleague); **propitiate** implies an allaying or forestalling of hostile feeling by winning the good will of (to *propitiate* a deity); **conciliate** implies the use of arbitration, concession, persuasion, etc. in an attempt to win over.—*ANT.* anger, enrage.

pack (pak), *n.* [ME. *pakke* < a LG. source; cf. MD., MLG. *pak*, MFl. *pac*: the word was carried throughout Europe via the Low Countries' wool trade (cf. It.

pacco, Ir. *pac*, ML. *paccus*, etc.)], 1. a large bundle of things wrapped or tied up for carrying, as on the back of an animal; load; burden; bale. 2. a number of similar or related persons or things; specifically, *a*) a number; group; collection: as, a *pack* of lies. *b*) a package of a standard number: as, a *pack* of cigarettes. *c*) a set of playing cards, usually 52; deck. *d*) a set of hunting hounds. *e*) a number of wild animals living together: as, a *pack* of wolves. *f*) a united group; gang. 3. a mass of floating pieces of ice driven together. 4. *a*) treatment by wrapping a patient in blankets or sheets that are wet or dry and hot or cold. *b*) the blankets or sheets used. *c*) a folded towel or cloth filled with crushed ice: also **ice pack**. 5. any of various cosmetic pastes applied to the skin and left to dry. 6. the amount of food put in cans, etc. in a season or year. ***v.t.*** 1. to make a pack, or bundle, of. 2. *a*) to put together compactly in a box, trunk, etc. for carrying or storing. *b*) to fill (a box, trunk, etc.) for carrying or storing: as, he *packed* his bags. 3. *a*) to put (food) in cans, boxes, etc. for preservation or sale. *b*) to put food in (cans, boxes, etc.) for preservation or sale. 4. *a*) to crowd; fill closely; cram: as, the audience *packed* the hall. *b*) to crowd (people) together; press together. 5. to fill in or surround tightly for protection, prevention of leaks, etc.: as, *pack* a joint. 6. to press together firmly: as, *packed* earth. 7. to load (an animal) with a pack; hence, 8. to carry (goods, equipment, etc.) in or as in a pack: said of an animal. 9. to carry or wear as part of one's regular clothing, equipment, etc.: as, he *packs* a gun. 10. to wrap in a pack (sense 4*b*). 11. to send (*off*): as, they *packed* him off to school. 12. [Slang], to deliver or be able to deliver (a blow, punch, etc.) with force. ***v.i.*** 1. to make up packs. 2. to put one's clothes, belongings, etc. into luggage for a trip: as, are you going to *pack* tonight? 3. to press, crowd, or throng together in a small space. 4. to admit of being folded compactly, put in a container, etc.: as, this suit *packs* well. 5. to settle into a compact or solid mass. 6. to go away in haste (sometimes with *off*). ***adj.*** 1. *a*) used in packing. *b*) suitable for packing. 2. formed in a pack or packs. 3. used for carrying packs, loads, etc. —***SYN.*** see **bundle, group.**

send packing, to dismiss (a person) without delay.

pack (pak), ***v.t.*** [< prec. *pack*, *v.t.*], to choose or arrange (a jury, committee, etc.) in such a way as to get desired decisions, results, etc.

pack·age (pak′ij), ***n.*** [see -AGE], 1. the act or process of packing. 2. a wrapped or boxed thing or group of things; parcel. 3. a box, case, etc. in which things are packed. ***v.t.*** [PACKAGED (-ijd), PACKAGING], to wrap or box, as for selling, carrying, etc. —***SYN.*** see **bundle.**

package store, a retail store where alcoholic beverages are sold by the bottle to be drunk off the premises.

pack animal, an animal used for carrying packs or loads.

pack·er (pak′ẽr), ***n.*** a person or thing that packs; specifically, *a*) a person who packs goods for preservation, transportation, or sale. *b*) a person who owns or manages a packing house.

pack·et (pak′it), ***n.*** [Anglo-Fr. *pacquet*, dim. of ME. *pakke*; see PACK], 1. a small package or parcel. 2. a packet boat. Abbreviated **pkt.** ***v.t.*** to make up into or wrap in a packet.

packet boat, [so called from orig. carrying mail; cf. Fr. *paquebot*], a boat that travels a regular route between ports, as along a coast or on a river, carrying passengers, freight, and mail.

pack horse, 1. a horse used to carry packs, luggage, etc.; hence, 2. a drudge.

pack·ing (pak′iŋ), ***n.*** 1. the act or process of a person or thing that packs; specifically, *a*) the canning of meats, fruits, or vegetables. *b*) in *medicine*, the filling of a wound or cavity with gauze, etc. to permit drainage and prevent closure. 2. any material used in packing, as a fibrous substance placed around valves to make them watertight, etc.

packing box (or **case**), a large wooden box for storing or shipping goods; crate.

packing effect, in *physics*, the loss of mass in the nucleus of an atom attributed to the loss of energy resulting in the building up of the nucleus from its component parts.

packing house, a place where meats, and sometimes fruits, vegetables, etc., are prepared for future sale, by processing, canning, packaging, etc.

pack·man (pak′mən), ***n.*** [*pl.* PACKMEN (-mən)], a man who carries a pack of goods for sale; peddler.

pack rat, a kind of North American rat that carries and hides small articles that it finds.

pack·sack (pak′sak′), ***n.*** a traveling sack of canvas or leather, usually carried strapped on the shoulders.

pack·sad·dle (pak′sad′′l), ***n.*** a saddle designed to support the load carried by a pack animal.

pack·thread (pak′thred′), ***n.*** strong, thick thread or twine for tying bundles, packages, etc.

pack train, a train, or procession, of pack animals.

pact (pakt), ***n.*** [ME.; OFr. *pacte*; L. *pactum*, neut. of *pactus*, pp. of *paciscere*, to agree < *pax, pacis*, peace], a compact, covenant, or agreement.

pad (pad), ***n.*** [chiefly echoic, but influenced by *pad* (to travel)], the dull sound made by a footstep or staff on the ground.

pad (pad), ***n.*** [prob. var. of *pod*, and, like that word < a LG. source; prob. IE. base **bu-*, **bhu-*, to blow out (as the cheeks), seen also in *bud*, obs. *pad*, a toad, etc.], 1. a soft, stuffed saddle. 2. anything made of or stuffed with soft material and used to fill hollow spaces or to protect from friction, jarring, blows, etc.; cushion or something like a cushion: as, a shoulder *pad*. 3. the foot or footprint of certain animals, as the wolf, fox, etc. 4. the cushionlike part of the foot of some animals, birds, and insects. 5. the floating leaf of a water plant, as the water lily. 6. a number of sheets of paper for writing or drawing, fastened along one edge; tablet. 7. an absorbent cushion soaked with ink for inking a rubber stamp. 8. the leather cushion that lines the valves of certain wind instruments. ***v.t.*** [PADDED (-id), PADDING], 1. to stuff, cover, or line with soft material. 2. to lengthen (a speech or piece of writing) by inserting unnecessary or irrelevant material. 3. to fill (an expense account, etc.) with fraudulent or invented entries.

pad (pad), ***v.i.*** [PADDED (-id), PADDING], [< *pad* (path); cf. LG. *padden*], 1. to travel on foot; walk; tramp. 2. to walk or run with a soft, almost soundless, step.

pad (pad), ***n.*** [D. *pad*, path], 1. a horse with an easy, slow pace. 2. [Rare], a highwayman; footpad. 3. [British Slang or Dial.] a path; road; way.

Pa·dang (pä-däŋ′), ***n.*** a city on the western coast of Sumatra, Netherlands Indies: pop., 52,000.

padded cell, a cell, or room, lined with heavy, soft material for the confinement of violently deranged patients or prisoners.

pad·ding (pad′iŋ), ***n.*** 1. the action of a person who pads. 2. any soft material used to pad, as cotton, felt, etc. 3. material, often unnecessary or irrelevant, inserted in a speech, writing, etc. to make it longer.

Pad·ding·ton (pad′iŋ-tən), ***n.*** a borough of London: pop., 145,000.

pad·dle (pad′′l), ***n.*** [ME. *padell*, small spade; prob. var. of *patel*, shallow pan (< L. *patella*), with medial voicing; the form *pattel* actually exists], 1. a relatively short oar with a wide blade at one end or both ends, used, without an oarlock, to propel a canoe. 2. any of various implements shaped like this; specifically, *a*) a metal tool for stirring iron in a furnace. *b*) a small, flat, wooden instrument for working butter, stirring clay, etc. *c*) a wooden device used in washing clothes by hand. *d*) a flat, wooden stick for administering punishment by beating. 3. any of the propelling boards in a water wheel or paddle wheel. ***v.i.*** [PADDLED (-′ld), PADDLING], 1. to propel a canoe, etc. by means of a paddle. 2. to row slowly and gently. ***v.t.*** 1. to propel (a canoe, etc.) by means of a paddle or paddles. 2. to punish by beating with or as with a paddle; spank. 3. to stir, work, etc. with a paddle.

paddle one's own canoe, to depend entirely on oneself; be self-reliant.

pad·dle (pad′′l), ***v.i.*** [PADDLED (-′ld), PADDLING], [prob. freq. < *pad*, *v.i.*], 1. to walk or move the feet in shallow water; wade; dabble. 2. to toy or play idly, as with the fingers (with *in, on, with,* or *about*). 3. to walk like a small child; toddle.

paddle box, a case often enclosing the upper part of a paddle wheel on a boat.

pad·dle·fish (pad′′l-fish′), ***n.*** [*pl.* PADDLEFISH, PADDLEFISHES (-iz); see FISH], a large fish of the Mississippi, with a snout that looks somewhat like a paddle.

pad·dler (pad′lẽr), ***n.*** a person or thing that paddles.

paddle wheel, a wheel with boards, or paddles, around its circumference for propelling a steamboat.

PADDLE WHEEL

pad·dock (pad′ək), ***n.*** [ME. *paddoke* < *padde* (AS. *pad*, frog, toad) + *-ock*; cf. PAD (cushion)], 1. [Obs. or Scot.], a frog. 2. [Obs.], a toad.

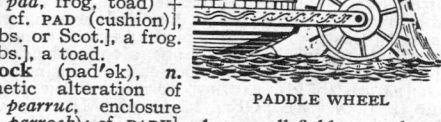

pad·dock (pad′ək), ***n.*** [phonetic alteration of AS. *pearruc*, enclosure (dial. *parrock*); cf. PARK], 1. a small field or enclosure near a stable, in which horses are exercised. 2. an enclosure near a race track, where horses are assembled before a race. 3. in Australia, an enclosed piece of land. ***v.t.*** to shut in a paddock.

Pad·dy (pad′i), ***n.*** [*pl.* PADDIES (-iz)], [< *Pādraig*, Ir. form of *Patrick*, after Saint *Patrick*], [Slang], an Irishman: a nickname.

pad·dy (pad′i), ***n.*** [*pl.* PADDIES (-iz)], [Malay *padi*], 1.

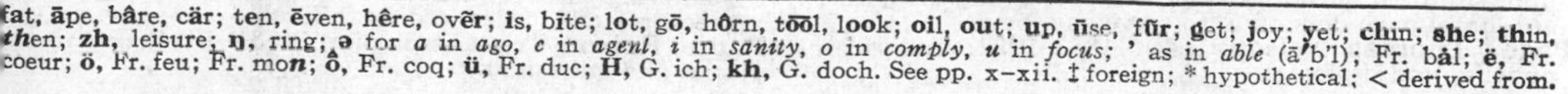

rice in the husk, growing or gathered. 2. rice in general. 3. loosely, a rice field.

paddy wagon, [prob. < *Paddy* (an Irishman); cf. PADDYWHACK], [Slang], a patrol wagon.

pad·dy·whack (pad′i-hwak′), *n.* [< *Paddy* + *whack*; orig., Irishman; cf. "get one's Irish up"], 1. [British Dial.], a rage; temper. 2. [Colloq.], a beating.

Pa·de·rew·ski, I·gnace Jan (ē′nyås′ yän pä′de-ref′ski; Eng. pad′ə-ref′ski), 1860–1941; Polish pianist, composer, and statesman; prime minister of Poland (1919).

pa·di·shah (pä′di-shä′), *n.* [Per. *pādshāh* < *pati*, master + *shāh*, shah], 1. a great king; emperor. 2. [often P-], *a*) the shah of Iran. *b*) formerly, the sultan of Turkey. *c*) formerly, the British sovereign as emperor of India.

pad·lock (pad′lok′), *n.* [ME. *padlocke*; ? < *padde*, toad, frog, because of the shape], a removable lock with a hinged or pivoted link to be passed through a staple, chain, or eye. *v.t.* 1. to fasten with or as with a padlock. 2. to close (a building) against entrance.

pad·nag (pad′nag′), *n.* [< *pad*, to pace + *-nag*], an easygoing, ambling nag.

Pa·do·va (pä′dô-vä), *n.* Padua: the Italian name.

pa·dre (pä′dri; It. pä′dre; Sp. pä′*thre*), *n.* [*pl.* PADRES (-riz; Sp. -*thres*); It. PADRI (-drē)], [Sp.; It.; Port. < L. *pater*, a father], 1. father: the title of a priest in Italy, Spain, Portugal, and Latin America. 2. [Military Slang], a chaplain.

pa·dro·ne (pə-drō′ni; It. pä-drô′ne), *n.* [*pl.* PADRONI (-nē)], [It.; L. *patronus*, patron], 1. patron; master; boss. 2. in Italy, *a*) a master of a Mediterranean trading ship. *b*) a person who employs street musicians, child beggars, etc. *c*) an innkeeper. 3. a contractor for Italian laborers in America.

Pad·u·a (paj′oo-ə, pad′ū-ə), *n.* a city in northeastern Italy: pop., 173,000: Italian name, *Padova*.

pad·u·a·soy (paj′oo-ə-soi′), *n.* [altered (after *Padua*, Italy) < Fr. *pou-de-soie*, earlier *poudesoy*], 1. a corded silk cloth used extensively in the 18th century. 2. a garment made of this. *adj.* made of paduasoy.

Pa·du·cah (pə-dōō′kə, pə-dū′kə), *n.* a city in western Kentucky, on the Ohio: pop., 34,000.

Pa·dus (pā′dəs), *n.* the Po River: the ancient name.

pae·an (pē′ən), *n.* [L.; Gr. *paian*, hymn < *Paian*, Apollo], 1. in ancient Greece, a hymn of thanksgiving to the gods, especially to Apollo; hence, 2. a song of joy, triumph, etc. Also spelled **pean**.

pae·do- (pē′də, ped′ə), pedo-.

pae·on (pē′ən), *n.* [L.; Gr. (Attic) *paiōn*; see PAEAN], in *Greek & Latin prosody*, a foot of three short syllables and one long syllable occurring in any order.

Paes·tum (pes′təm), *n.* an ancient Greek city in southern Italy: modern name, *Pesto*.

pa·gan (pā′gən), *n.* [ME.; L. *paganus* (in LL., a pagan), a peasant or civilian, hence (among early Christians) the opposite of the Christian "soldier" (i.e., a heathen) < *pagus*, country], 1. *a*) formerly, a person who was not a Christian. *b*) now, a person who is not a Christian, Moslem, or Jew; heathen. 2. a person who has no religion. *adj.* 1. of pagans or paganism; not Christian, Moslem, or Jewish. 2. not religious; heathen.

SYN.—**pagan** and **heathen** are both applied to one who is neither Jewish, Christian, nor Moslem by one who is, but **pagan** specifically refers to one of the ancient polytheistic peoples, such as the Greeks and Romans, and **heathen** is applied to any of the peoples regarded as uncivilized idolaters; **gentile** (often **Gentile**) is applied to one who is not a Jew, or among Mormons, to one who is not a Mormon.

pa·gan·dom (pā′gən-dəm), *n.* 1. all pagans. 2. a place or all the places inhabited by pagans.

Pa·ga·ni·ni, Ni·co·lò (nē′kô-lô′ pä′gä-nē′nē; Eng. pag′ə-nē′ni), 1782–1840; Italian violinist and composer.

pa·gan·ish (pā′gən-ish), *adj.* of or like a pagan.

pa·gan·ism (pā′gən-iz′m), *n.* 1. the state of being pagan. 2. pagan beliefs, customs, and attitudes.

pa·gan·ize (pā′gən-īz′), *v.t. & v.i.* [PAGANIZED (-īzd′), PAGANIZING], [Fr. *paganiser*], to make or become pagan.

page (pāj), *n.* [Fr.; L. *pagina*, a page < base of *pangere*, to fasten], 1. *a*) one side of a leaf of a book, newspaper, letter, etc. *b*) the printing or writing on such a leaf. Often loosely applied (in sense *a*) to the entire leaf. Abbreviated **p.** 2. *often pl.* a record; writing: as, the *pages* of history. 3. an episode; event or series of events that might fill a page: as, a colorful *page* in his life. 4. in *printing*, the type set for printing a page. *v.t.* [PAGED (pājd), PAGING], to number the pages of.

page (pāj), *n.* [ME.; OFr.; It. *paggio*; ML. *pagius*; ? < Gr. *paidion*, dim. of *pais, paidos*, child], 1. formerly, a boy training for knighthood, who acted as an attendant on a knight. 2. *a*) a boy attendant or servant, especially one serving a person of high rank, as in court; hence, *b*) a title of various officers of a royal household. 3. a boy, often in uniform, who runs errands, carries messages, etc., as in a hotel or office building. 4. an attendant in Congress or a legislature. *v.t.* [PAGED (pājd), PAGING], 1. to attend as a page. 2. to try to find, summon, or notify (a person) by calling his name, as a hotel page does. *v.i.* to serve as a page.

Page, Thomas Nelson (pāj), 1853–1922; American novelist and diplomat.

Page, Walter Hines (hīnz), 1855–1918; American diplomat, writer, and editor.

pag·eant (paj′ənt), *n.* [ME. *pagine, pagend, pagent*, scaffold for scenic exhibitions, also the exhibitions themselves; Anglo-L. *pagina*; prob. < base of L. *pangere*, to fix], 1. *a*) originally, an individual scene in a medieval mystery play. *b*) [Anglo-L. *paganus*], any of a series of movable outdoor platforms on which a mystery play was performed. 2. a spectacular exhibition, elaborate parade, etc., as a procession with floats. 3. an outdoor drama celebrating a historical event or presenting, with local actors, the history of a community. 4. empty pomp or display; mere show.

pag·eant·ry (paj′ən-tri), *n.* [*pl.* PAGEANTRIES (-triz)], 1. pageants collectively. 2. grand spectacle; gorgeous display. 3. empty show or display.

pag·i·nal (paj′ə-n'l), *adj.* [LL. *paginalis*], 1. of a page or pages; consisting of pages. 2. page for page.

pag·i·nate (paj′ə-nāt′), *v.t.* [PAGINATED (-id), PAGINATING], to number the pages of (a book, etc.); page.

pag·i·na·tion (paj′ə-nā′shən), *n.* 1. the act of numbering the pages of a book, etc. 2. the marks, figures, etc. with which pages are numbered. 3. the arrangement and number of pages, as noted in a catalogue.

pag·od (pag′əd, pə-god′), *n.* [Archaic], a pagoda.

pa·go·da (pə-gō′də), *n.* [Port. *pagode*; prob. < Per. *bulkadah*, house of idols; *but*, idol + *kadah*, house, dwelling; ? influenced by Tamil *pagavadi*, temple < Sans. *bhagavati*, divine, deity], in India, China, Japan, and the Far East, a temple in the form of a pyramidal tower of several stories, commonly built over a sacred relic or as a work of devotion.

PAGODA

Pa·go Pa·go (päŋ′ō päŋ′ō, pä′gō pä′gō), the main seaport of American Samoa, on Tutuila Island: also called *Pango Pango*.

pa·gu·ri·an (pə-gyoor′i-ən), *adj.* [< L. *pagurus*, kind of crab; Gr. *pagouros* < base of *pagos*, hard object + *oura*, tail; + *-ian*], in *zoology*, of a family of crustaceans including the hermit crab. *n.* a member of this family.

pa·gu·rid (pə-gyoor′id, pag′yoo-rid), *n.* a pagurian.

pah (pä, pa, pə), *interj.* an exclamation of disgust, contempt, or disbelief.

Pa·hang (pä-häŋ′), *n.* a state of the Federation of Malaya: area, 13,820 sq. mi.; pop., 313,000.

Pah·la·vi (pä′lə-vē′), *n.* [Per. < OPer. *Parthava*, Parthia], an Iranian language spoken and written in Persia from about the 3d to the 10th century A.D.; Middle Persian: the name is often restricted to the literary language of the Zoroastrian books, written c. 224–651 A.D., one form of which (Huzvarišn) writes Semitic words with Iranian inflections: also **Pehlevi**.

pah·la·vi (pä′lə-vē′), *n.* [*pl.* PAHLAVI], [Pers., belonging to Riza Khan *Pahlavi*, Shah of Persia], a gold coin of Iran, equivalent to 20 rials.

paid (pād), past tense and past participle of **pay**. *adj.* 1. receiving pay; hired: as, a *paid* advisor. 2. *a*) given in payment, as money (also with *out*). *b*) discharged; settled, as a debt (also with *up*). Abbreviated **pd.**

pail (pāl), *n.* [ME. *paile* < AS. *pægel*, small measure, wine vessel & OFr. *paile, paele*; L. *patella*, a pan], 1. a container made of wood, metal, etc., cylindrical or almost cylindrical in shape, usually with a handle, for holding liquids, etc.; bucket. 2. a pailful.

pail·ful (pāl′fool′), *n.* [*pl.* PAILFULS (-foolz′)], as much as a pail will hold.

pail·lasse (pal-yas′, pal′yas), *n.* [Fr.; It. *pagliaccio*; LL. *paleaceum* < L. *palea*, straw, chaff], a mattress filled with straw, sawdust, etc.: also spelled **palliasse**.

pail·lette (pal-yet′), *n.* [Fr., dim. of *paille*, straw < L. *palea*], 1. a piece of metal or foil used in enamel painting. 2. a small disk of shiny metal used in decorating women's dresses, etc.; spangle.

pain (pān), *n.* [ME. *peine*; OFr. *peine, poine*; L. *poena*, penalty, punishment; Gr. *poinē*, penalty], 1. originally, penalty. 2. the sensations one feels when hurt, mentally or physically, especially distress, suffering, great anxiety, anguish, grief, etc.: opposed to *pleasure*. 3. a sensation of hurting, or strong discomfort, in some part of the body, caused by an injury, disease, or functional disorder, and transmitted through the nervous system. 4. *pl.* the labor of childbirth. 5. *pl.* great care or effort: as, he took *pains* with his work. *v.t.* to cause pain to; cause to suffer; hurt; distress.

on (or **upon, under**) **pain of**, with the probability of suffering (death, punishment, etc.) unless a specified requirement, order, etc. is fulfilled.

Paine, Robert Treat (trēt pān), 1731–1814; American jurist and statesman.

Paine, Thomas, 1737–1809; American Revolutionary patriot, writer, and political thinker, born in England.

pained (pānd), *adj.* [pp. of *pain*], 1. hurt or distressed; having the feelings hurt; offended. 2. showing hurt feelings or resentment: as, a *pained* expression.

pain·ful (pān′fəl), *adj.* 1. causing pain; hurting; distressing. 2. full of or suffering with pain; aching: as, a *painful* finger. 3. requiring trouble and care; exacting and difficult; irksome. 4. [Archaic], painstaking.

pain·kill·er (pān′kil′ẽr), *n.* [Colloq.], a medicine that relieves pain; especially, any patented tonic medicine.

pain·less (pān′lis), *adj.* 1. free from or without pain. 2. not causing or involving pain: as, *painless* childbirth.

pains·tak·ing (pānz′tāk′iŋ), *n.* the act of taking pains; great care or diligence. *adj.* 1. taking pains; very careful; diligent. 2. characterized by great care.

paint (pānt), *v.t.* [ME. *peinten* < OFr. *peint,* pp. of *peindre;* L. *pingere,* to paint], 1. *a*) to make (a picture, design, etc.) in colors by means of pigments, brushes, etc. *b*) to depict or portray with paints; represent in colors: as, he *painted* a landscape. 2. to describe colorfully or vividly; picture in words for the mind. 3. to cover or decorate with paint; color: as, he *painted* the walls; hence, 4. to decorate with or as with colors, cosmetics, etc.; adorn; beautify. 5. *a*) to apply (a medicine, etc.) like paint. *b*) to treat in this way, as a wound. *v.i.* 1. to practice the art of painting pictures. 2. to use cosmetics. *n.* 1. *a*) a mixture of colored pigment with oil, water, etc., in liquid or paste form, applied as with a brush, roller, or spray gun, and used for protective covering or coloring of a surface or for making pictures on canvas, paper, etc. *b*) dry or solid pigment; hence, 2. a dried coat of paint: as, this *paint* chips off. 3. coloring matter, such as lipstick, rouge, etc., used to ornament or beautify the face or body. 4. in the *theater,* grease paint.

paint out, to cover up with or as with a coat of paint.

paint·brush (pānt′brush′), *n.* 1. a brush used for applying paint. 2. the painted cup, a plant.

paint·ed (pān′tid), *adj.* [pp. of *paint*], 1. represented in colors as a picture, likeness, etc. 2. coated with paint. 3. pretended; feigned. 4. highly colored.

painted bunting, a brightly colored variety of finch found in the southern United States.

painted cup, any of several American plants of the figwort family, having brilliantly colored bracts and inconspicuous flowers.

Painted Desert, a desert plateau in north central Arizona, east of the Little Colorado River.

paint·er (pān′tẽr), *n.* 1. an artist who paints pictures. 2. a person whose work is covering surfaces, as walls, with paint.

paint·er (pān′tẽr), *n.* [Early Mod. Eng. *peyntour;* OFr. *pentour;* ult. < L. *pendere,* to hang], a rope attached to the bow of a boat for tying it to a wharf, mooring, etc.

paint·er (pān′tẽr), *n.* [var. of *panther;* via Fr. *panthère*], [Dial.], the American panther; mountain lion; cougar.

painter's colic, a form of lead poisoning characterized by intense abdominal pains: also called *lead colic.*

paint·ing (pān′tiŋ), *n.* 1. the act or occupation of covering surfaces with paint. 2. *a*) the act, art, or occupation of picturing scenes, objects, persons, etc. in paint. *b*) a picture in paint, as an oil, water color, etc.

paint·y (pān′ti), *adj.* [PAINTIER (-ti-ẽr), PAINTIEST (-ti-ist)], 1. of, smeared, or covered with paint. 2. having more paint than necessary: said of a picture.

pair (pâr), *n.* [*pl.* PAIRS (pârz); *sometimes, after a number,* PAIR], [ME. *paire, peir;* OFr. *paire;* L. *paria,* neut. pl. of *par,* equal], 1. two similar or corresponding things joined, associated, or used together: as, a *pair* of gloves. 2. a single thing made up of two corresponding parts that must be used together: as, a *pair* of pants. 3. two persons or animals; specifically, *a*) a married or engaged couple. *b*) two mated animals. *c*) any two people considered as having something in common: as, a *pair* of rascals. *d*) a brace; span: as, a *pair* of horses. *e*) two members of opposing parties in a legislative body who agree to withhold their vote on a given question; also, this agreement. 4. two playing cards of the same denomination. 5. [Rare or Dial.], a set or flight: used only in *a pair of stairs, a pair of steps.* Abbreviated **pr.** *v.t.* 1. to make a pair of (two persons or things) by matching, joining, grouping, mating, etc. 2. to arrange in pairs (sometimes with *together*). 3. to provide with a partner (followed by *with*). *v.i.* 1. to form a pair or couple; match. 2. to join in marriage; mate.

pair off, 1. to join or arrange (two people or things) in a pair. 2. to go apart or separate into pairs.

***SYN.*—pair** is used of two similar things that are associated together or are necessary in twos for proper use (a *pair* of socks) or of a single thing made up of two corresponding parts (a *pair* of scissors); **couple** applies to any two similar things that are somehow associated (a *couple* of dollars) or it is used colloquially to mean several or a few (I must buy a *couple* of things); a **brace** is a couple, especially of certain birds or animals (a *brace* of pheasants, hounds, etc.); **yoke** applies to a pair of animals harnessed together for pulling (a *yoke* of oxen); **span** is used especially of a pair of horses harnessed together.

pair-oar (pâr′ôr′, pâr′ōr′), *n.* a boat to be rowed by two persons who sit one behind the other, each using one oar. *adj.* of such a boat.

Pais·ley (pāz′li), *n.* a city in Scotland, near Glasgow: pop., 97,000.

pais·ley (pāz′li), *adj.* [after *Paisley,* Scotland], 1. [also P-], designating a shawl of soft wool, having an elaborate, colorful pattern, originally made in Paisley, Scotland. 2. designating cloth having the characteristic pattern of such a shawl. 3. made of such cloth or having the characteristic pattern of such cloth. *n.* 1. paisley cloth. 2. a paisley shawl.

Pai·ute (pī-ūt′), *n.* [orig. used of Corn Creek tribe in Utah], a member of a tribe of Uto-Aztecan Indians that lived in Nevada, Utah, Arizona, and California.

pa·ja·mas (pə-jam′əz, pə-jä′məz), *n.pl.* [Hind. *pājāmā, paijāmā* < Per. *pāi,* a leg + *jāmah,* garment], 1. in the Orient, a pair of loose silk or cotton trousers. 2. a loosely fitting sleeping or lounging suit consisting of jacket (or blouse) and trousers of silk, cotton, etc. Also spelled **pyjamas.**

Pa·ki·stan (pä′ki-stän′, pak′i-stan′), *n.* a country on the peninsula of India, consisting of two provinces, one in the northwestern part (*West Pakistan*) and the other in the northeastern part (*East Pakistan*): a member of the British Commonwealth of Nations: area, 364,737 sq. mi.; pop., 86,823,000; capital, Rawalpindi. See also **Kashmir.**

Pa·ki·stan·i (pä′ki-stän′i, pak′i-stan′i), *adj.* of Pakistan or its people. *n.* a native or inhabitant of Pakistan.

pal (pal), *n.* [Eng. Gypsy, brother, mate (for *prāl,* in dial. on European continent) < Sans. *bhrātṛ.,* brother; see BROTHER], [Colloq.], an intimate friend; comrade; chum. *v.i.* [PALLED (pald), PALLING], [Colloq.], 1. to associate as pals. 2. to be or become a pal with another.

pal., 1. paleography. 2. paleontology.

pal·ace (pal′is), *n.* [ME. & OFr. *palais;* L. *palatium* < *Palatium,* one of the seven hills of Rome, where Augustus lived], 1. the official residence of a king, emperor, bishop, etc. 2. any large, magnificent house or building. 3. a large, ornate place of entertainment.

pal·a·din (pal′ə-din), *n.* [Fr.; It. *paladino;* L. *palatinus,* officer of a palace < *palatium;* see PALACE], 1. any of the twelve peers, or douzepers, of Charlemagne's court; hence, 2. a knight; heroic champion.

pa·lae·o- (pā′li-ō; *occas.* pal′i-ō), paleo-.

pa·laes·tra (pə-les′trə), *n.* [*pl.* PALAESTRAE (-trē), PALAESTRAS (-trəz)], [L.; Gr. *palaistra* < *palaiein,* to wrestle], 1. in ancient Greece, a public place for exercise in wrestling and athletics. 2. *a*) a wrestling school. *b*) a gymnasium. Also spelled **palestra.**

pal·an·quin, pal·an·keen (pal′ən-kēn′), *n.* [Port. *palanquim;* Jav. *pĕlangki;* Sans. *palyaṅka, paryaṅka*], in the Orient, a covered litter, usually for one person, carried by poles on the shoulders of two or more men.

pal·at·a·bil·i·ty (pal′i-tə-bil′ə-ti), *n.* a palatable quality.

pal·at·a·ble (pal′i-tə-b'l), *adj.* [< *palate* + *-able*], 1. pleasant to the taste; savory; tasty; hence, 2. pleasing to the mind; agreeable.

pal·at·a·bly (pal′i-tə-bli), *adv.* so as to be palatable.

pal·a·tal (pal′i-t'l), *adj.* [Fr. < L. *palatum,* palate], 1. of the palate. 2. in *phonetics,* pronounced with the front of the tongue raised against or near the hard palate: said of consonants, as *ch* in German *ich* or *y* in English *young*: the term is now often extended to include consonants produced by raising the main body of the tongue toward the palate (e.g., *ch* in *chill*) and also front vowels. *n.* a palatal sound.

pal·a·tal·i·za·tion (pal′i-t'l-i-zā′shən, pal′i-t'l-ī-zā′shən), *n.* a palatalizing or being palatalized.

pal·a·tal·ize (pal′i-t'l-īz′), *v.t.* [PALATALIZED (-īzd′), PALATALIZING], in *phonetics,* to pronounce as a palatal sound; specifically, to change (a nonpalatal sound) into a palatal sound: as, the *t* in *nature* is now invariably *palatalized* to *ch.*

pal·ate (pal′it), *n.* [ME. & OFr. *palat;* L. *palatum*], 1. the roof of the mouth, consisting of a hard bony forward part (the *hard palate*) and a soft fleshy back part (the *soft palate,* or *velum*). 2. taste or sense of taste: the palate was incorrectly thought to be the organ of taste; hence, 3. intellectual taste; liking.

pa·la·tial (pə-lā′shəl), *adj.* [< L. *palatium,* palace], 1. of, suitable for, or like a palace; hence, 2. large and ornate; magnificent; stately.

pa·lat·i·nate (pə-lat′'n-āt′, pə-lat′'n-it), *n.* 1. the territory ruled by a palatine. 2. the office of a palatine. 3. [P-], a native or inhabitant of the Palatinate.

the (Rhine) Palatinate, a district west of the Rhine, formerly a state of the German empire: in 1945, it was incorporated into a state of West Germany (**Rhineland-Palatinate**): German name, *Pfalz.*

pal·a·tine (pal′ə-tīn′, pal′ə-tin), *adj.* [ME.; L. *palatinus* < *palatium*, palace], 1. of a palace. 2. having royal privileges: as, a count *palatine*. 3. of or belonging to a count, earl, or county palatine. 4. [P-], of the Palatinate. *n.* 1. an officer of an imperial palace; hence, 2. a medieval vassal lord having the rights of royalty in his own territory, or palatinate. 3. a fur piece covering the shoulders. 4. [P-], one of the seven hills on which Rome was built. 5. [P-], a native or inhabitant of the Palatinate.

pal·a·tine (pal′ə-tīn′, pal′ə-tin), *adj.* [Fr. *palatin;* see PALATE & -INE], in *anatomy*, having to do with the palate. *n.* in *anatomy*, either of the two bones forming the hard palate.

Pa·la·u Islands (pä-lou′), a group of islands in the Pacific, between Mindanao and the Caroline Islands: area, 175 sq. mi.; pop., 8,000: also called *Pelew*.

pa·lav·er (pə-lav′ẽr), *n.* [Port. *palavra*, a word; L. *parabola*, a speech, comparison; cf. PARABOLA], 1. a conference, especially among or with African tribes. 2. talk; especially, idle chatter. 3. flattery; cajolery. *v.i.* to talk glibly or flatteringly. *v.t.* to flatter; wheedle.

Pa·la·wan (pä-lä′wän), *n.* one of the Philippine Islands, near Mindoro: area, 4,500 sq. mi.; pop., 44,000.

pale (pāl), *adj.* [ME.; OFr.; L. *pallidus*, pale < *pallere*, to be pale], 1. of a whitish or colorless complexion; pallid; wan. 2. faint; dim; lacking intensity or brilliance: said of color, light, etc.; hence, 3. feeble; weak; faint: as, a *pale* imitation. *v.i.* [PALED (pāld), PALING], 1. to turn or become pale; lose color; hence, 2. to dim; lessen in importance, significance, etc.: as, my work *paled* beside his. *v.t.* to make pale.

SYN.—**pale**, in this comparison the least connotative of these words, implies merely an unnatural whiteness or colorlessness, often temporary, of the complexion; **pallid** suggests a paleness resulting from exhaustion, faintness, emotional strain, etc.; **wan** suggests the paleness resulting from an emaciating illness; **ashen** implies the grayish paleness of the skin as in death; **livid** refers to a grayish-blue complexion, as of one in great rage or fear.—*ANT.* ruddy, rosy.

pale (pāl), *n.* [ME. & OFr. *pal;* L. *palus;* a stake], 1. a pointed stake; narrow, upright, pointed piece of wood used in fences; picket. 2. a fence; enclosure; limit; boundary; restriction: now chiefly figurative, as, outside the *pale* of the law. 3. a territory or district enclosed within bounds. 4. in *heraldry*, a vertical third of the field; an ordinary.

the (English) Pale, a district in eastern Ireland, around Dublin, included in the Angevin Empire of Henry II, and later regarded as English.

pa·le- (pā′li; *occas.* pal′i), paleo-: words beginning with *pale-* are also spelled **palae-**.

pa·le·a (pā′li-ə), *n.* [*pl.* PALEAE (-ē′)], [L., chaff], in *botany*, 1. a chaffy bract or scale; especially, a bract at the base of a floret of a composite flower. 2. the upper, or inner, bract enclosing the flower in grasses.

pa·le·a·ceous (pā′li-ā′shəs), *adj.* in *botany*, having, consisting of, or resembling paleae.

pa·le·eth·no·log·ic (pā′li-eth′nə-loj′ik), *adj.* paleethnological.

pa·le·eth·no·log·i·cal (pā′li-eth′nə-loj′i-k'l), *adj.* of paleethnology.

pa·le·eth·nol·o·gy (pā′li-eth-nol′ə-ji), *n.* [*pale-* + *ethnology*], the study of prehistoric races of man.

pale·face (pāl′fās′), *n.* a white person: a term alleged to have been first used by North American Indians.

Pa·lem·bang (pä′lem-bäŋ′), *n.* a city in southeastern Sumatra: pop., 108,000.

Pa·len·que (pä-leŋ′kā), *n.* a village in northern Chiapas state, Mexico: site of notable ancient ruins.

pa·le·o- (pā′li-ō; *occas.* pal′i-ō), [< Gr. *palaios*, ancient], a combining form meaning: 1. *ancient*, *historically early*, or *prehistoric*, as in *Paleozoic*. 2. *primitive*, as in *paleolithic*. 3. *paleontological*, as in *paleozoology*. Also, before vowels, **pale-**. Words beginning with *paleo-* are also spelled **palaeo-**.

pa·le·o·bo·tan·ic (pā′li-ō-bə-tan′ik), *adj.* of paleobotany.

pa·le·o·bo·tan·i·cal (pā′li-ō-bə-tan′i-k'l), *adj.* paleobotanic.

pa·le·o·bot·a·ny (pā′li-ō-bot′ə-ni), *n.* [*paleo-* + *botany*], the study of fossil plants: abbreviated **paleob., paleobot.**

Pa·le·o·cene (pā′li-ə-sēn′), *adj.* [< *paleo-* + Gr. *kainos*, recent], in some geological classifications, designating or of an epoch preceding the Eocene in the Tertiary Period.

the Paleocene, the Paleocene Epoch or its rocks.

pa·le·og·ra·pher (pā′li-og′rə-fẽr), *n.* a student of or specialist in paleography.

pa·le·o·graph·ic (pā′li-ə-graf′ik), *adj.* of paleography.

pa·le·o·graph·i·cal (pā′li-ə-graf′i-k'l), *adj.* paleographic.

pa·le·og·ra·phy (pā′li-og′rə-fi), *n.* [*paleo-* + *-graphy*], 1. ancient writing or forms of writing, collectively. 2. the study of describing or deciphering ancient writings, manuscripts, etc. Abbreviated **pal., paleog.**

pa·le·o·lith (pā′li-ə-lith′), *n.* [*paleo-* + *-lith*], a primitive stone tool.

pa·le·o·lith·ic (pā′li-ə-lith′ik), *adj.* [*paleo-* + *-lithic*], designating or of the period of the Stone Age between the eolithic and the neolithic, or its culture, characterized by the use of stone tools.

paleolithic man, in *anthropology*, any of the types of man of the paleolithic period, including Cro-Magnon, Heidelberg, and Neanderthal man.

pa·le·on·to·graph·ic (pā′li-on′tə-graf′ik), *adj.* paleontographical.

pa·le·on·to·graph·i·cal (pā′li-on′tə-graf′i-k'l), *adj.* of paleontography.

pa·le·on·tog·ra·phy (pā′li-on-tog′rə-fi), *n.* [< *paleo-* + Gr. *ōn*, *ontos*, a being; + *-graphy*], the description of fossils.

pa·le·on·to·log·ic (pā′li-on′tə-loj′ik), *adj.* paleontological.

pa·le·on·to·log·i·cal (pā′li-on′tə-loj′i-k'l), *adj.* of paleontology.

pa·le·on·tol·o·gy (pā′li-ən-tol′ə-ji), *n.* [< *paleo-* + Gr. *ōn*, *ontos*, a being; + *-logy*], 1. the branch of geology that deals with prehistoric forms of life through the study of plant and animal fossils. 2. a treatise on this subject. Abbreviated **pal., paleon., paleont., paleontol.**

Pa·le·o·zo·ic (pā′li-ə-zō′ik), *adj.* [*paleo-* + *zo-* + *-ic*], 1. designating or of the era between the Proterozoic and the Mesozoic, characterized by the development of fish and sea plants, the first amphibians, land plants, and reptiles, and later by temperature extremes which destroyed many of these: coal, oil, and many fossils were produced at this time. 2. of the rocks of this era.

the Paleozoic, the Paleozoic Era or its rocks: see **geology**, chart.

pa·le·o·zo·o·log·i·cal (pā′li-ō-zō′ə-loj′i-k'l), *adj.* of paleozoology.

pa·le·o·zo·ol·o·gy (pā′li-ō-zō-ol′ə-ji), *n.* [*paleo-* + *zoology*], the branch of paleontology that deals with fossil animals.

Pa·ler·mo (pə-lûr′mō; It. pä-ler′mô), *n.* a seaport in northern Sicily: pop., 454,000 (est. 1947).

Pal·es·tine (pal′əs-tīn′), *n.* 1. a territory on the eastern coast of the Mediterranean, the country of the Jews in Biblical times. 2. part of this territory, exclusive of Trans-Jordan and parts in Syria, under a British mandate after World War I: area, 10,157 sq. mi.; pop., 1,900,000; capital, Jerusalem: divided into separate independent Arab and Jewish states by action of the United Nations in 1947: cf. **Israel**: Biblical name, *Canaan;* also called *Holy Land.* Abbreviated **Pal.**

Pal·es·tin·i·an (pal′əs-tin′i-ən, pal′əs-tin′yən), *adj.* of Palestine or its people. *n.* a native or inhabitant of Palestine.

pa·les·tra (pə-les′trə), *n.* [*pl.* PALESTRAE (-trē), PALESTRAS (-trəz)], a palaestra.

Pal·es·tri·na, Gio·van·ni (jô-vän′nē pä′les-trē′nä; Eng. pal′ə-strē′nə), 1526?–1594; Italian composer of religious music.

pal·e·tot (pal′ə-tō′, pal′tō), *n.* [Fr.; OFr. *palletoc* (whence ME. *paltok*)], 1. an overcoat; greatcoat. 2. a loose jacket worn by women and children.

pal·ette (pal′it), *n.* [Fr., dim. of *pale*, a shovel; L. *pala*, a spade, shovel], 1. a thin, oval or oblong board with a hole at one end for the thumb, on which an artist arranges and mixes his paints: also **pallet**; hence, 2. the colors used by a particular artist or for a particular painting.

PALETTE

palette knife, a thin, flexible, steel blade with a blunt edge and a wooden handle, used by artists to mix oil colors and clean the palette.

pal·frey (pôl′fri), *n.* [*pl.* PALFREYS (-friz)], [ME. & OFr. *palefrei;* LL. *palafredus*, *parafredus* < *paraveredus*, extra post horse < Gr. *para*, beside + L. *veredus*, post horse < Gaul. **vorēdos;* akin to W. *gorwydd*, horse], [Archaic], a saddle horse, especially one for a woman.

Pal·grave, Francis Turner (pôl′grāv, pal′grāv), 1824–1897; English poet, critic, and anthologist.

Pa·li (pä′lē), *n.* [Sans. *pāli*, lit., a row, line, canon; short for *pāli bhāsā*, canon language], the Old Indic Prakrit, or dialect, of the Buddhist scriptures, which has become the religious language of Buddhism.

pal·i·kar (pal′i-kär′), *n.* [Mod. Gr. *palikari*, young man; Gr. *pallēx*, a youth], a soldier in the Greek or Albanian militia; especially, one in the Greek war of independence against Turkey (1821–1828).

pal·imp·sest (pal′imp-sest′), *n.* [L. *palimpsestus;* Gr. *palimpsēstos*, lit., rubbed again (*palimpsēston*, a palimpsest) < *palin*, again + *psēn*, to rub smooth], a parchment, tablet, etc. that has been written upon or inscribed two or three times, the previous text or texts having been imperfectly erased and remaining, therefore, still visible. *adj.* of or in the form of a palimpsest; written upon or engraved more than once.

pal·in·drome (pal′in-drōm′), *n.* [Gr. *palindromos*, running back < *palin*, again + *dramein*, to run], a word, verse, or sentence which reads the same backward or forward (e.g., "madam"; "able was I ere I saw Elba.").

pal·ing (pā'liŋ), *n.* 1. the action of making a fence of pales; fencing. 2. a fence made of pales. 3. pales collectively; material for fencing. 4. a strip of wood used in making a fence; pale.

pal·in·gen·e·sis (pal'in-jen'ə-sis), *n.* [Mod. L. < Gr. *palin*, again + *genesis*, generation, birth], 1. birth over again; regeneration. 2. the doctrine of successive rebirths; metempsychosis. 3. that phase in the development of an individual plant or animal which repeats the evolutionary history of the group to which it belongs: opposed to *cenogenesis*. 4. the change in form and structure of an insect during its development; metamorphosis. 5. [Obs.], spontaneous generation.

pal·i·node (pal'ə-nōd'), *n.* [MFr. *palinod;* LL. *palinodia;* Gr. *palinōidia* < *palin*, again + *ōidē*, song; see ODE], 1. an ode or poem written to retract something said in a previous poem; hence, 2. a retraction.

pal·i·sade (pal'ə-sād'), *n.* [Fr. *palissade;* Pr. *palisada* < *palisa*, a pale; L. *palus*, a stake], 1. any one of a row of large pointed stakes set in the ground to form a fence used for fortification or defense. 2. a fence of such stakes. 3. *pl.* a line of very steep cliffs, usually along a river. *v.t.* to fortify or defend with a palisade.

the Palisades, the line of steep cliffs in New Jersey on the west shore of the Hudson: length, c. 20 mi.

pal·ish (pāl'ish), *adj.* somewhat pale.

pall (pôl), *v.t.* [PALLED (pôld), PALLING], [ME. *pallen*, for *appallen*, to appall], to satiate; weary; disgust. *v.i.* 1. to become cloying, insipid, boring, wearisome, etc. 2. to become cloyed or satiated.

pall (pôl), *n.* [ME. *pal;* AS. *pæll;* L. *pallium*, a cover (akin to *palla*, a robe, mantle)], 1. a black, purple, or white piece of velvet, etc. used to cover a coffin, hearse, or tomb. 2. a dark or gloomy covering: as, a *pall* of smoke. 3. [Obs.], a rich cloth or coverlet. 4. [Obs.], a cloak or mantle. 5. in *Christian churches*, *a)* a piece of cloth, or cardboard covered with cloth, used to cover the chalice. *b)* an altar cloth. *v.t.* [PALLED (pôld), PALLING], to cover with or as with a pall.

Pal·la·di·an (pə-lā'di-ən), *adj.* [< L. *Palladius* (< *Pallas*); + *-an*], 1. of Pallas Athena, Greek goddess of wisdom; hence, 2. of wisdom or learning.

Pal·la·di·an (pə-lā'di-ən), *adj.* of or in the classical Roman style of Andrea Palladio.

pal·lad·ic (pə-lad'ik, pə-lā'dik), *adj.* designating or of chemical compounds containing palladium with a valence of four.

Pal·la·dio, An·dre·a (än-dre'ä päl-lä'dyô), 1518–1580; Italian architect.

Pal·la·di·um (pə-lā'di-əm), *n.* [*pl.* PALLADIA (-ə)], [L.; Gr. *palladion*, sacred statue or image < *Pallas*], 1. in ancient Greece and Rome, any statue of the Greek goddess Pallas Athena; specifically, the statue in Troy on the preservation of which the safety of the city was supposed to depend; hence, 2. [p-], any safeguard, as of a city or institution. 3. [p-], an object or principle upon which the safety of something is dependent.

pal·la·di·um (pə-lā'di-əm), *n.* [Mod. L. < *Pallas*, the asteroid < Gr. *Pallas*, the goddess], a rare, silvery-white, ductile, malleable, metallic chemical element of the platinum group: it is used as a catalyst, or in alloys with gold, silver, and other metals: symbol, Pd; at. wt., 106.7; at. no., 46.

pal·la·dous (pə-lā'dəs, pal'ə-dəs), *adj.* designating or of chemical compounds containing palladium with a valence of two.

Pal·las (pal'əs), *n.* [L.; Gr. *Pallas*], 1. in *Greek mythology*, a name for Athena, the goddess of wisdom: also **Pallas Athena.** 2. one of the asteroids, or small planets, between Jupiter and Mars.

pall·bear·er (pôl'bâr'ẽr), *n.* [*pall* (cloth) + *bearer:* formerly, one who held the edges of the pall], one of the persons who attend or bear the coffin at a funeral.

pal·let (pal'it), *n.* [Fr. *palette;* see PALETTE], 1. a wooden tool consisting of a flat blade with a handle; especially, such a tool used by potters for smoothing and rounding. 2. a painter's palette. 3. a low, portable platform, usually double-faced, on which materials are stacked for storage or transportation, as in a warehouse. 4. in *bookbinding*, a tool for printing letters on the binding of a book. 5. in *mechanics*, a part of a machine that changes back-and-forth motion to circular motion, or vice versa, by engaging the teeth of a ratchet wheel; pawl; click; especially, any of the clicks or pawls in the escapement of a clock or watch, which regulate the speed by releasing one tooth of a ratchet wheel at each swing of the pendulum or turn of the balance wheel.

pal·let (pal'it), *n.* [ME. & OFr. *paillet* < *paille*, straw; L. *palea*, chaff], a straw bed or mattress: often connoting a poor or inferior bed.

pal·let (pal'it), *n.* [dim. of *pale*, *n.* 4], in *heraldry*, a vertical stripe on an escutcheon, half as wide as a pale.

pal·lette (pal'it), *n.* [Fr. *palette;* see PALETTE], a plate in the armpit of a suit of armor.

pal·liasse (pal-yas', pal'yas), *n.* a paillasse.

pal·li·ate (pal'i-āt'), *v.t.* [PALLIATED (-id), PALLIATING], [< L. *palliatus*, cloaked < *pallium*, a cloak], 1. to lessen the pain or severity of without curing; alleviate; ease. 2. to make (a crime, offense, etc.) appear less serious than it is; excuse; extenuate.

pal·li·a·tion (pal'i-ā'shən), *n.* [Fr.; ML. *palliatio*, a cloaking], 1. a palliating. 2. a thing that palliates.

pal·li·a·tive (pal'i-ā'tiv, pal'i-ə-tiv), *adj.* serving or tending to palliate; specifically, *a)* alleviating. *b)* excusing; extenuating. *n.* a thing that palliates.

pal·li·a·tor (pal'i-ā'tẽr), *n.* a person who palliates.

pal·lid (pal'id), *adj.* [L. *pallidus* < *pallere*, to become pale], faint in color; pale; wan. —*SYN.* see **pale.**

pal·li·um (pal'i-əm), *n.* [*pl.* PALLIUMS (-əmz), PALLIA (-ə)], [L., a cloak, mantle], 1. in ancient Greece, a large, oblong mantle worn by men: also called *himation.* 2. in *anatomy*, the cortex of the cerebrum. 3. in the *Roman Catholic Church*, a circular white wool band with pendants, worn over the shoulders at certain times by archbishops. 4. in *zoology*, the soft layer of tissue next to the shell in mollusks and brachiopods; mantle.

pall-mall (pel'mel'), *n.* [obs. Fr. *palemail;* It. *pallamaglio; palla*, var. of *balla*, ball + *maglio* (L. *maleus*), a mallet], 1. an old game in which a boxwood ball was struck by a mallet through an iron ring hung at the end of an alley. 2. the alley in which it was played.

Pall Mall (pel mel, pal mal), a London street, noted for its clubs, built on the site of an old pall-mall alley.

pal·lor (pal'ẽr), *n.* [L. < base of *pallere*, to be pale; for IE. base see FALLOW (yellow)], lack of color; unnatural paleness, as of the face.

palm (päm), *n.* [ME. *palme;* AS. *palm;* L. *palma:* so named because the fronded leaf somewhat resembles the palm of the hand], 1. any of several kinds of tropical or subtropical trees having a tall branchless trunk with a bunch of huge leaves at the top. 2. a leaf of this tree carried or worn as a symbol of victory, triumph, joy, etc.; hence, 3. victory; triumph. 4. a representation of a palm leaf or frond given in lieu of a second award of the same military decoration, as of the croix de guerre.

bear (or **carry off**) **the palm**, to be the winner; take the prize; be supreme.

yield the palm to, to acknowledge the superiority of; admit to defeat by.

PALM (60 80 ft. high)

palm (päm), *n.* [ME. & OFr. *paume;* L. *palma*, palm of the hand: the mod. spelling is Latinized], 1. the inner part or surface of the hand between the fingers and wrist. 2. the part of a glove, etc. that covers the palm. 3. the broad, flat part of an antler, as of a moose, deer, etc. 4. a unit of measure equal to either the width of the hand (3 to 4 inches) or its length (7 to 9 inches). 5. any broad, flat part at the end of an arm, handle, etc., as the blade of an oar. 6. a metal disk used by sailmakers over the palm of the hand to push a needle through canvas. *v.t.* 1. to hide (something) in the palm or about the hand, as a coin in a sleight-of-hand trick. 2. to touch with the palm.

grease the palm of, to bribe.

have an itching palm, [Colloq.], to desire money greedily.

palm off, to pass off by fraud or deceit.

Pal·ma (päl'mä), *n.* 1. a city on Majorca, capital of the Balearic Islands, Spain: pop., 148,000: also called *Palma de Mallorca.* 2. one of the Canary Islands: area, 280 sq. mi.; capital, Santa Cruz de la Palma.

pal·ma·ceous (pal-mā'shəs), *adj.* [< Mod. L. *Palmaceae*, palms], of or like a palm tree.

Pal·ma de Mal·lor·ca (päl'mä de mä-lyôr'kä), Palma.

pal·mar (pal'mẽr), *adj.* [L. *palmaris*], of, in, or corresponding to the palm of the hand.

pal·ma·ry (pal'mə-ri), *adj.* [L. *palmarius*], bearing or worthy to bear the palm; pre-eminent; victorious.

pal·mate (pal'māt, pal'mit), *adj.* [L. *palmatus* < *palma*, the palm], shaped like a hand with the fingers spread; specifically, *a)* in *botany*, having veins or lobes radiating from a common center: said of some leaves: see **leaf**, illus. *b)* in *zoology*, web-footed, as many water birds.

pal·mat·ed (pal'mā-tid), *adj.* palmate.

pal·ma·tion (pal-mā'shən), *n.* 1. the state or quality of being palmate; palmate formation or structure. 2. a part or division of a palmate formation.

Palm Beach, a town in southeastern Florida: a winter ocean resort: pop., 6,000.

Palm Beach cloth, a lightweight cotton and mohair fabric used for men's summer suits: a trade-mark.

palm·er (päm′ẽr), *n.* [ME. *palmere;* Anglo-Fr. *palmer, paumer;* OFr. *paumier, palmier;* ML. *palmarius* < L. *palma,* the palm], 1. a pilgrim who carried a palm leaf as a sign that he had been to the Holy Land; hence, 2. any pilgrim. 3. a palmer worm.

Palm·er, George Herbert (päm′ẽr), 1842–1933; American educator and author.

Palmer Peninsula, a peninsula of Antarctica, south of South America.

Palm·er·ston (päm′ẽr-stən), third Viscount, (*Henry John Temple*), 1784–1865; English statesman; prime minister (1855–1858; 1859–1865).

palmer worm, 1. any of a number of wandering caterpillars harmful to plants. 2. the larva of a small North American moth, destructive to apple leaves.

pal·met·to (pal-met′ō), *n.* [*pl.* PALMETTOS, PALMETTOES (-ōz)], [Sp. *palmito,* dim. < L. *palma,* the palm], any of several small palm trees with fan-shaped leaves, as the dwarf fan palm of southern Europe and North Africa or the cabbage palm of the southeastern United States.

palm·ist (päm′ist), *n.* [back-formation < *palmistry*], a person who practices palmistry.

palm·is·try (päm′is-tri), *n.* [ME. *paumestrie;* prob. contr. < *paume,* the palm + *maistrie,* mastery], the pretended art of telling a person's character or fortune by the lines and marks of the palm of his hand.

pal·mi·tate (pal′mə-tāt′), *n.* a salt or ester of palmitic acid.

pal·mit·ic (pal-mit′ik), *adj.* [Fr. *palmitique* < L. *palma,* the palm], designating or of a colorless, crystalline fatty acid, $CH_3(CH_2)_{14}CO_2H$, found uncombined in palm oil and as the glyceryl ester in other vegetable and animal fats and oils.

pal·mi·tin (pal′mə-tin), *n.* [G.; contr. < *palmitinsaure,* transl. of Fr. *acide palmitique;* see PALMITIC], a colorless crystalline compound, $C_3H_5(C_{15}H_{31}COO)_3$, found in palm oil and many other fats: it is the glyceryl ester of palmitic acid.

palm leaf, the leaf of a palm tree, especially of one of the palmettos, used to make fans, hats, etc.

palm oil, a yellow or reddish fat obtained from the fruit of several kinds of palms, especially the West African oil palm, used in making soap, candles, etc.

palm sugar, sugar from the sap of certain palm trees.

Palm Sunday, the Sunday before Easter, commemorating in Christian churches Jesus' entry into Jerusalem, when palm branches were strewn before him.

palm·y (päm′i), *adj.* [PALMIER (-i-ẽr), PALMIEST (-i-ist)], 1. abounding in or shaded by palm trees. 2. of or like a palm or palms. 3. bearing or worthy to bear the palm; triumphant; hence, 4. flourishing; prosperous; successful: as, *palmy* days.

Pal·my·ra (pal-mī′rə), *n.* an ancient city in Syria.

pal·my·ra (pal-mī′rə), *n.* [Port. *palmeira* < L. *palma,* the palm: sp. affected by false association with *Palmyra,* city in Syria], a kind of palm tree, grown in India and Ceylon, having large rounded leaves that are shaped like a fan and are used to make matting, hats, etc.: also **palmyra palm, palmyra tree.**

Palmyra Island, an atoll in the central Pacific, belonging to the United States: used as an air base.

Pal·o Al·to (pal′ō al′tō), a city in California, near San Francisco: pop., 52,000.

pal·o·mi·no (pal′ə-mē′nō), *n.* [Am. Sp. (for Sp. *palomillo*), dim. of *paloma,* pigeon, dove; LL. *palumbus,* for L. *palumbes,* ringdove; hence, orig. applied to horses of a dovelike color], a brownish-gray or golden horse that has a silvery-white or ivory mane and tail.

pa·loo·ka (pə-lōō′kə), *n.* [coined by Jack Conway (died 1928), one-time baseball player, and later writer for *Variety*], [Slang], in *sports,* an incompetent or easily defeated player.

Pa·los (pä′lôs), *n.* a town in southwestern Spain: port where Columbus embarked on his first western voyage.

palp (palp), *n.* a palpus.

pal·pa·bil·i·ty (pal′pə-bil′ə-ti), *n.* a palpable quality.

pal·pa·ble (pal′pə-b'l), *adj.* [ME.; LL. *palpabilis* < L. *palpare,* to touch], 1. that can be touched, felt, or handled; tangible. 2. easily perceived by the senses; audible, recognizable, perceptible, noticeable, etc.; hence, 3. clear to the mind; obvious; evident; plain. —*SYN.* see **evident, perceptible.**

pal·pa·bly (pal′pə-bli), *adv.* in a palpable manner; specifically, *a*) obviously. *b*) to the touch.

pal·pate (pal′pāt), *v.t.* [PALPATED (-id), PALPATING], [< L. *palpatus,* pp. of *palpare,* to touch], to examine by touching, as for medical diagnosis.

pal·pate (pal′pāt), *adj.* [< *palpus* + *-ate*], having a palpus or palpi.

pal·pa·tion (pal-pā′shən), *n.* [L. *palpatio*], a palpating or being palpated; medical examination by touching.

pal·pe·bral (pal′pə-brəl), *adj.* [LL. *palpebralis* < *palpebra,* eyelid], of the eyelids.

pal·pi (pal′pī), *n.* plural of **palpus.**

pal·pi·tant (pal′pə-tənt), *adj.* [Fr.; L. *palpitans*], throbbing; trembling; palpitating; quivering.

pal·pi·tate (pal′pə-tāt′), *v.i.* [PALPITATED (-id), PALPITATING], [< L. *palpitatus,* pp. of *palpitare,* freq. of *palpare,* to feel, stroke], 1. to beat rapidly or flutter, as the heart. 2. to throb; quiver; tremble.

pal·pi·ta·tion (pal′pə-tā′shən), *n.* [L. *palpitatio*], 1. a rapid, often irregular, beating of the heart from functional disorder, emotion, etc. 2. a trembling; palpitating; quivering; throbbing.

pal·pus (pal′pəs), *n.* [*pl.* PALPI (-pī)], [Mod. L. < L. *palpus,* the soft palm of the hand], in *zoology,* a jointed organ or feeler for touching or tasting, attached to the mouth of insects, lobsters, some worms, etc.

pals·grave (pôlz′grāv′, palz′grāv′), *n.* [D. *paltsgrave* < *palts* (< L. *palatium*), palace + *graaf,* count; akin to G. *pfalzgraf*], formerly, in Germany, a count palatine.

pals·gra·vine (pôlz′grə-vēn′, palz′grə-vēn′), *n.* the wife or widow of a palsgrave.

pal·sied (pôl′zid), *adj.* [pp. of *palsy*], 1. having palsy; paralyzed. 2. shaking; tottering; trembling.

pal·sy (pôl′zi), *n.* [*pl.* PALSIES (-ziz)], [ME. *palesie, parlesie;* OFr. *paralisie;* L. *paralysis;* see PARALYSIS], paralysis in any part of the body, sometimes accompanied with involuntary tremors. *v.t.* [PALSIED (-zid), PALSYING], 1. to afflict with palsy; paralyze; hence, 2. to make powerless or helpless, as with fear.

pal·ter (pôl′tẽr), *v.i.* [freq. formation < dial. *palt,* rag, piece of cloth (< a LG. source); the word prob. arose with reference to haggling over cloth prices], 1. to talk or act insincerely; deal crookedly; prevaricate. 2. to trifle; treat facts, decisions, etc. lightly or carelessly. 3. to quibble, as in bargaining.

pal·tri·ly (pôl′trə-li), *adv.* in a paltry manner.

pal·tri·ness (pôl′tri-nis), *n.* the quality of being paltry.

pal·try (pôl′tri), *adj.* [PALTRIER (-tri-ẽr), PALTRIEST (-tri-ist)], [prob. < LG. *paltrig, palterig,* ragged < *palte,* a rag; cf. PALTER], trifling; insignificant; practically worthless; contemptible; petty. —*SYN.* see **petty.**

pa·lu·dal (pə-lōō′d'l, pal′yoo-d'l), *adj.* [< L. *palus, paludis,* marsh], 1. of a marsh or marshes; marshy. 2. in *medicine,* caused by a marsh; malarial, as fever.

pal·u·dism (pal′yoo-diz'm), *n.* [< L. *palus, paludis,* marsh; + *-ism*], in *medicine,* malaria.

pal·y (pāl′i), *adj.* [Poetic], palish.

pal·y (pā′li), *adj.* [Fr. *palé* < *pal,* a stake; see PALE (stake)], in *heraldry,* divided into four or more vertical stripes, or pales, of equal width, in alternating colors: said of the field of an escutcheon.

pam (pam), *n.* [< Fr. *pamphile* < Gr. *Pamphilos* (proper name), lit., beloved of all < *pan,* all + *philos,* beloved], in *card playing,* 1. the jack of clubs, as in the game of loo. 2. a game like napoleon in which the jack of clubs is the highest trump.

pam., pamphlet.

Pam·e·la (pam′ə-lə), [apparently coined by Sir Philip Sidney for a character in his *Arcadia* (1590)], a feminine name.

Pa·mir (pä-mêr′), *n.* Galcha, the Iranian language of the Pamiri.

Pa·mir·i (pä-mêr′i), *n.* [*pl.* PAMIRI], a Galcha, one of a people living in the Pamirs.

Pa·mirs (pä-mêrz′), *n.pl.* a mountain system and high tableland in the Tadzhik S.S.R.: highest known peak, Muztagh Ata, across the border of Sinkiang, 24,388 ft.

Pam·li·co Sound (pam′li-kō′), a channel between the coast and islands off North Carolina: length, 80 mi.

pam·pas (pam′pəz; *for adj.,* pam′pəs; Sp. päm′päs), *n.pl.* [Sp., pl. of *pampa* < Quechua *pampa,* plain, field], the extensive treeless plains of Argentina and some other parts of South America. *adj.* of the pampas.

pampas grass, a very tall, bluish-green South American grass with long, silky, silvery-white panicles, or plumes.

pam·pe·an (pam′pi-ən, pam-pē′ən), *adj.* of the pampas or their Indian natives. *n.* an Indian who lives in the pampas.

Pam·pe·lu·na (päm′pe-lōō′nä), *n.* Pamplona: the former name.

pam·per (pam′pẽr), *v.t.* [ME. *pampren;* prob. < a LG. source; cf. W.Fl. *pampren* in the same sense; *pampen,* to cram, also occurs in ME.], 1. originally, to feed too much; gratify to excess; glut. 2. to be overindulgent with; give too many privileges to; coddle: as, he *pampers* the child. —*SYN.* see **indulge.**

pam·pe·ro (päm-pâr′ō; Sp. päm-pe′rô), *n.* [*pl.* PAMPEROS (-rōz; Sp. -rôs)], [Sp. < *pampa,* steppe, plain], a strong cold wind that blows from the Andes across the South American pampas.

pam·phlet (pam′flit), *n.* [ME. *paunflet, pamfilet, pamflet;* OFr. *Pamphilet,* familiar name of a popular ML. poem *Pamphilus, seu de Amore*], 1. a small, thin, unbound book made up of sheets of paper stapled or stitched together and usually having a paper cover. 2. a treatise published in this form, usually as an argument on some topic of current interest. Abbreviated **pam., pamph., pph.**

pam·phlet·eer (pam′fli-têr′), *n.* a writer or publisher of pamphlets. *v.i.* to write or publish pamphlets.

Pam·phyl·i·a (pam-fil′i-ə), *n.* an ancient land in southern Asia Minor.

Pam·plo·na (päm-plô′nä), *n.* a city in northern Spain: pop., 86,000: former name, *Pampeluna.*

Pan (pan), *n.* [L.; Gr. *Pan*], in *Greek mythology,* a god of fields, forests, wild animals, flocks, and shepherds, represented with the legs (and sometimes horns and ears) of a goat: identified by the Romans with Faunas.

PAN

pan (pan), *n.* [ME. & AS. *panne;* akin to G. *pfanne;* said to be early loan word < LL. *panna* < L. *patina,* a pan; cf. PATINA, PATELLA], 1. any of many kinds of dishes, usually broad, shallow, without a cover, and made of metal, and used for domestic purposes: often in combination, as, a frying *pan, saucepan, dishpan,* etc. 2. any object or part of an apparatus shaped like a pan; specifically, *a*) an open container for washing out gold, tin, etc. from gravel or the like, in mining. *b*) either receptacle in a pair of scales. *c*) a container for heating, evaporating, etc. 3. the amount a pan will hold; panful. 4. a hollow, natural depression in the ground. 5. a layer of hard soil, impervious to water; hardpan. 6. a small ice floe. 7. the part of the flintlock that held the firing powder in old guns and pistols. 8. [Slang], a face. *v.t.* [PANNED (pand), PANNING], 1. to cook in a pan. 2. [Colloq.], to give an unfavorable criticism of: as, the critic *panned* the play. 3. in *mining, a*) to wash (gravel, etc.) in a pan, as for separating gold. *b*) to separate (gold, etc.) from gravel by washing in a pan. *v.i.* in *mining,* 1. to wash gravel in a pan, searching for gold. 2. to yield gold in this process.
pan out, 1. in *mining,* to yield gold, as gravel, a mine, etc. 2. [Colloq.], to turn out (in some way); transpire. 3. [Colloq.], to turn out well; succeed.

pan (pän), *n.* [Hind. *pān;* Sans. *parṇa,* a leaf, feather], 1. a leaf of the betel palm. 2. a substance made of this leaf, chewed to increase the flow of saliva.

pan (pan), *v.t. & v.i.* [PANNED (pand), PANNING], [abbrev. < *panorama*], to move (a motion-picture or television camera) in order to get a panoramic effect or to follow a moving object.

pan- (pan), [< Gr. *pan,* neut. of *pas,* all, every, universal], a combining form meaning: 1. *all,* as in *panchromatic, pantheism.* 2. [P-], *a*) *of, comprising, embracing, or common to all or every,* as in *Pan-American. b*) *(belief in) the co-operation, unity, or union of all members of* (a specified nationality, race, church, etc.), as in *Pan-Americanism.* In sense 2, usually followed by a hyphen, as in the following words:

Pan-Asiatic	**Pan-Islam**
Pan-European	**Pan-Slavic**
Pan-Germanic	**Pan-Slavism**

Pan., Panama.

pan·a·ce·a (pan'ə-sē'ə), *n.* [L.; Gr. *panakeia* < *pan,* all + *akeisthai,* to cure], a supposed remedy, cure, or medicine for all diseases or ills; cure-all.

pa·nache (pə-nash', pə-näsh'), *n.* [Fr.; It. *pennachio;* L. *penna,* a feather], a plume of feathers; especially, such a plume on a helmet.

pa·na·da (pə-nä'də, pə-nā'də), *n.* [Sp. < L. *panis,* bread], a dish made of bread or crackers boiled to a pulp and flavored.

Pan·a·ma (pan'ə-mä', pan'ə-mô'), *n.* 1. a republic of Central America, on the Isthmus of Panama: area, 32,001 sq. mi.; pop., 1,053,000. 2. its capital: seaport on the Gulf of Panama: pop., 200,000: also **Panama City.**

Panama, Gulf (or **Bay**) **of,** an arm of the Pacific, on the southern coast of Panama.

Panama, Isthmus of, a strip of land connecting North and South America: 31 mi. across its narrowest point: former name, *Isthmus of Darien.*

Panama Canal, a ship canal across the Isthmus of Panama, connecting the Atlantic and Pacific Oceans: length, 50.7 mi.: see **Central America,** map.

Panama Canal Zone, see **Canal Zone.**

Panama hat, [after *Panama* (city), once a main distributing center], 1. a fine, hand-plaited hat made from select leaves of a Central and South American palm tree. 2. any similar straw hat.

Pan·a·ma·ni·an (pan'ə-mā'ni-ən, pan'ə-män'yən), *adj.* of Panama. *n.* a native or inhabitant of Panama.

Pan-A·mer·i·can (pan'ə-mer'ə-kən), *adj.* of North America, South America, and Central America, collectively, or their peoples.

Pan-A·mer·i·can·ism (pan'ə-mer'ə-kən-iz'm), *n.* belief in, or any theory or policy of, political and economic co-operation, mutual social and cultural understanding, international alliance, etc. among the nations of North, Central, and South America.

Pan American Union, the official agency of the Organization of American States (OAS) through which the twenty-one member American republics work to develop closer co-operation among themselves.

Pan·a·mint Mountains (pan'ə-mint'), a mountain range in eastern California, forming the western rim of Death Valley.

Pa·nay (pä-nī'; Eng. pə-nī'), *n.* one of the Philippine Islands, between Mindoro and Negros: area, 4,448 sq. mi.; pop., 1,424,000; chief city, Iloilo: see **Philippine Islands,** map.

pan·cake (pan'kāk', paŋ'kāk'), *n.* 1. a thin, flat cake of batter fried on a griddle or in a pan; griddlecake: also called *flapjack.* 2. a landing in which the airplane in a horizontal position drops almost vertically to the ground, after leveling off higher than for a normal landing. *v.i. & v.t.* [PANCAKED (-kākt'), PANCAKING], to make or cause (an airplane) to make such a landing.

pan·chro·mat·ic (pan'krō-mat'ik), *adj.* [*pan-* + *chromatic*], sensitive to light of all colors: as, *panchromatic* film.

pan·chro·ma·tism (pan-krō'mə-tiz'm), *n.* the condition of being panchromatic.

pan·crat·ic (pan-krat'ik), *adj.* of the pancratium or pancratia.

pan·cra·ti·um (pan-krā'shi-əm), *n.* [*pl.* PANCRATIA (-shi-ə)], [L.; Gr. *pankration* < *pan,* all + *kratos,* strength], in ancient Greece and Rome, an athletic contest combining boxing and wrestling.

pan·cre·as (pan'kri-əs, paŋ'kri-əs), *n.* [Mod. L. < Gr. *pankreas; pan,* all + *kreas,* flesh], a large, elongated gland situated behind the stomach and secreting a digestive juice (*pancreatic juice*) into the small intestine: groups of differentiated cells (*islands of Langerhans*) in the gland produce the hormone insulin: the pancreas of animals, used as food, is also called *sweetbread.*

ESOPHAGUS
PYLORUS
BILIARY DUCT
STOMACH
PANCREATIC DUCT
PANCREAS
DUODENUM

PANCREAS

pan·cre·at·ic (pan'kri-at'ik, paŋ'kri-at'ik), *adj.* of or secreted from the pancreas.

pancreatic juice, the clear, alkaline juice secreted by the pancreas into the small intestine, where its constituent enzymes act on food passed down from the stomach.

pan·cre·a·tin (pan'kri-ə-tin, paŋ'kri-ə-tin), *n.* 1. any of the pancreatic enzymes or a mixture of these. 2. a commercial preparation of pancreas extract from cattle or hogs, used as an aid to digestion.

pan·cre·a·to- (pan'kri-ə-tō, paŋ'kri-ə-tō), a combining form meaning *of the pancreas,* as in *pancreatotomy:* also, before a vowel, **pancreat-**.

pan·cre·a·tot·o·my (pan'kri-ə-tot'ə-mi, paŋ'kri-ə-tot'ə-mi), *n.* [*pl.* PANCREATOTOMIES (-miz)], surgical incision of the pancreas.

pan·da (pan'də), *n.* [< the native (? Nepal) name], 1. a small, reddish-brown animal, resembling the raccoon, native to the Himalayas. 2. a white-and-black, bearlike animal of Asia: also called *giant panda.*

GIANT PANDA (6 ft. long)

pan·da·nus (pan-dā'nəs), *n.* [Mod. L.; Malay *pandan*], a variety of Asiatic shrublike tree of the screw pine group.

Pan·da·rus (pan'də-rəs), *n.* [L.; Gr. *Pandaros*], one of the leaders of the Lycians in the Trojan War; in medieval romances and in Boccaccio, Chaucer, and Shakespeare, he acts as the go-between who arranges the meeting of Troilus and Cressida, and is often represented as Cressida's uncle: see also **Cressida, Troilus.**

Pan·de·an (pan-dē'ən), *adj.* [< *Pan*], of Pan.

Pandean pipes, a Panpipe.

pan·dect (pan'dekt), *n.* [Fr. *pandecte;* L. *pandectae, pandectes;* Gr. *pandektēs,* lit., all-receiving < *pan,* all + *dechesthai,* to contain, receive], 1. [P-], *pl.* a digest of Roman civil law in fifty books, compiled for the emperor Justinian in the 6th century A.D.: also called *the Digest.* 2. *often pl.* any complete body of laws; legal code. 3. any complete or comprehensive digest.

pan·dem·ic (pan-dem'ik), *adj.* [< LL. *pandemus;* Gr. *pandēmos; pan,* all + *dēmos,* the people], of all the people; prevalent over a whole area, country, etc.; universal; general; specifically, epidemic over a large region: said of a disease.

Pan·de·mo·ni·um (pan'di-mō'ni-əm), ***n.*** [Mod. L. < *pan-* + Gr. *daimōn*, demon], 1. the abode of all demons: in ***Paradise Lost*** it is the palace built under Satan's orders as the capital of Hell; hence, 2. hell. 3. [p-], any place or scene of wild disorder, noise, or confusion. 4. [p-], wild disorder, noise, or confusion.

pan·der (pan'dēr), ***n.*** [< *Pandarus* (ME. *Pandare*)], 1. a go-between in a sexual intrigue; procurer; pimp. 2. a person who provides the means of helping to satisfy the ambitions, vices, etc. of another. ***v.t.*** [Archaic], to be a pander for. ***v.i.*** to act as a pander (with *to*).

pan·dit (pun'dit; pan'dit *is a sp. pronun.*), ***n.*** [var. of *pundit*], in India, a learned man; scholar: used [P-] as a title of respect.

P. and L., P. & L., profit and loss.

Pan·do·ra (pan-dôr'ə, pan-dō'rə), ***n.*** [L.; Gr. *Pandōra* < *pan*, all + *dōron*, a gift], in ***Greek mythology***, the first mortal woman, sent by Zeus as a punishment to mankind for the theft of fire by Prometheus: Zeus gave her a box which she opened, letting out all human ills into the world (or, in a later version, letting all human blessings escape and be lost, leaving only hope).

pan·do·ra (pan-dôr'ə, pan-dō'rə), ***n.*** [It.; see BANDORE], a bandore, ancient stringed instrument.

pan·dore (pan-dôr', pan'dōr), ***n.*** a bandore.

pan·dour (pan'door), ***n.*** [Fr.; G. & Croatian *pandur*, constable; ML. *banderius*, one who follows a banner; see BANNER], 1. a member of a force of Croatian soldiers organized in 1741 to quell frontier brigands and used in the Austrian army to fight the Turks: noted for their brutality. 2. any brutal soldier.

pan·dow·dy (pan-dou'di), ***n.*** [*pl.* PANDOWDIES (-diz)], [< *pan:* 2d element is said to be equivalent to *-doulde* in obs. Somersetshire dial. word, *pandoulde*], deep-dish apple pie or pudding, having a top crust only.

pan·du·rate (pan'doo-rāt', pan'dyoo-rit), ***adj.*** [< L. *pandura*, stringed instrument; + *-ate*], panduriform.

pan·du·ri·form (pan-door'ə-fôrm', pan-dyoor'ə-fôrm'), ***adj.*** [< LL. *pandura* (see BANDORE); + *-form*], in ***botany***, shaped somewhat like a violin, as some leaves.

pan·dy (pan'di), ***n.*** [*pl.* PANDIES (-diz)], [L. *pande*, open (your hand), imperative of *pandere*, to extend, open, stretch out], [Scot.], a stroke on the palm of the hand with a strap or cane, as a punishment. ***v.t.*** [PANDIED (-did), PANDYING], [Scot.], to punish in this way.

pane (pān), ***n.*** [ME.; OFr. *pane*, *panne;* L. *pannus*, piece of cloth], 1. a piece or division, especially if flat and rectangular. 2. a flat side, or face, of something that has several sides, as of a nut, bolthead, cut diamond, etc. 3. *a*) a single division of a window, etc., consisting of a sheet of glass in a frame. *b*) the sheet of glass or a substitute. 4. a panel, as of a door, wall, etc.

pan·e·gyr·ic (pan'ə-jir'ik), ***n.*** [Fr. *panégyrique;* L. *panegyricus;* Gr. *panēgyris*, public meeting < *pan*, all + *ageirein*, to bring together], 1. a formal speech or writing praising a person or event; hence, 2. superlative praise; eulogy; laudation. —***SYN.*** see **tribute.**

pan·e·gyr·i·cal (pan'ə-jir'i-k'l), ***adj.*** of, or having the nature of, panegyric or a panegyric; praising; eulogistic.

pan·e·gyr·ist (pan'ə-jir'ist, pan'ə-jir'ist), ***n.*** a person who writes or speaks panegyrics; eulogist; encomiast.

pan·e·gy·rize (pan'ə-ji-rīz'), ***v.t. & v.i.*** [PANEGYRIZED (-rīzd'), PANEGYRIZING], [Gr. *panēgyrizein* < *panēgyris*, to write or speak a panegyric (on); eulogize.

pan·el (pan''l), ***n.*** [ME.; OFr.; ML. *pannellus*, dim. < L. *pannus*, piece of cloth], 1. *a*) a piece of cloth placed under a saddle; saddle lining. *b*) a soft saddle. 2. a section or division of a wall, ceiling, or other surface; specifically, *a*) a section of a fence or railing between two posts. *b*) a flat piece of material, as wood or metal, usually rectangular, forming a part of the surface of a wall, door, cabinet, etc., and usually set off from the surrounding surface by being raised, recessed, framed, etc. *c*) a compartment or pane of a window. *d*) an insulated board, or flat surface, for instruments or controls, as of an electric circuit, airplane, etc. 3. *a*) a thin board used for oil painting. *b*) a painting on such a board. *c*) any picture very much longer than it is wide. 4. a list or group of persons selected for a specific purpose, as judging, discussing, etc. 5. in ***aeronautics***, *a*) one complete section of a wing. *b*) in dirigibles, the quadrilateral area bounded by two adjacent longerons and transverses. 6. in ***dressmaking***, a lengthwise strip, as of contrasting material, in a skirt or dress. 7. in ***law***, *a*) originally, a piece of parchment on which were recorded the list of persons summoned for jury duty. *b*) later, the list itself. *c*) the jurors as a whole. 8. in ***mining***, a compartment of a mine. ***v.t.*** [PANELED or PANELLED (-'ld), PANELING or PANELLING], 1. to cover, provide, fit, or decorate with panels. 2. in ***law***, to impanel (a jury). 3. in ***Scottish law***, to indict.

panel discussion, a discussion carried on by a selected group of speakers before an audience.

pan·el·ing, pan·el·ling (pan''l-iŋ), ***n.*** 1. the action of a person who panels. 2. panels collectively; series of panels in a wall, etc.

pan·el·ist (pan''l-ist), ***n.*** 1. a participant in a panel discussion. 2. in ***radio & television***, a person who serves on a panel, as on a quiz program.

pan·e·tel·a, pan·e·tel·la (pan'ə-tel'ə), ***n.*** [Sp.], a long, slender cigar.

pan fish, any small fish that can be fried whole in a pan.

pan-fry (pan'frī'), ***v.t.*** to fry in a shallow skillet or frying pan, with fat.

pang (paŋ), ***n.*** [altered < ME. *prong*, *prang*, itself prob. special use of *prong*, a point], a sudden, sharp, and brief pain, physical or emotional; spasm of distress.

pan·gen·e·sis (pan-jen'ə-sis), ***n.*** [Mod. L.; *pan-* + *-genesis*], an abandoned theory advanced by Darwin that each unit or cell of the body throws off very minute particles (*gemmules*) into the blood which circulate freely and undergo division and are collected in the reproductive cells; thus each part of the body is represented in the germ cell through these gemmules, which are regarded as the units of hereditary transmission.

pan·ge·net·ic (pan'jə-net'ik), ***adj.*** of pangenesis.

Pan-Ger·man (pan'jūr'mən), ***adj.*** of or having to do with all Germans as a group or Pan-Germanism. ***n.*** an advocate of Pan-Germanism.

Pan-Ger·man·ism (pan'jūr'mən-iz'm), ***n.*** the theory of, or a movement toward, the political unification of all German peoples, especially by annexing to the German state all near-by territories inhabited by German-speaking peoples.

pan·go·lin (paŋ-gō'lin), ***n.*** [Malay *pĕngulin*, roller < *gulin*, to roll], any of a number of related, toothless, scaly mammals of Asia and Africa, able to roll into a ball when attacked: also called *scaly anteater*.

Pang·o Pang·o (päŋ'ō päŋ'ō), Pago Pago.

pan·han·dle (pan'han'd'l), ***n.*** 1. the handle of a pan; hence, 2. [often P-], a strip of land resembling the handle of a pan, as the northern extension of the state of Texas between Oklahoma and New Mexico.

pan·han·dle (pan'han'd'l), ***v.t. & v.i.*** [PANHANDLED (-d'ld), PANHANDLING], [prob. < *panhandler*], [Slang], to beg, especially on the streets.

pan·han·dler (pan'han'dlēr), ***n.*** [*pan* (dish) + *handler*], [Slang], a beggar.

Panhandle State, West Virginia.

Pan·hel·len·ic (pan'hə-len'ik), ***adj.*** 1. of all the Greek peoples. 2. of Panhellenism. 3. of all Greek-letter fraternities and sororities.

Pan·hel·len·ism (pan-hel''n-iz'm), ***n.*** [see PAN-, HELLENE, -ISM], formerly, the theory of, or a movement toward, the political unification of all the Greek peoples.

pan·ic (pan'ik), ***n.*** [ME. *panyk;* L. *panicum*, kind of millet], any of several related grasses, as millet, used as fodder: also **panic grass.**

pan·ic (pan'ik), ***adj.*** [Fr. *panique;* Gr. *panikos*, of Pan < *Pan*, Pan], 1. literally, of Pan; hence, 2. of sudden fear, as supposedly inspired by him. 3. having the nature of, or showing or resulting from, panic. ***n.*** 1. a sudden, unreasoning, hysterical fear, often spreading quickly. 2. a widespread fear of the collapse of the financial system, resulting in unreasoned attempts to turn property into cash, withdraw money, etc. 3. [Slang], a person or thing considered extremely humorous or entertaining. ***v.t.*** [PANICKED (-ikt), PANICKING], 1. to affect with panic. 2. [Slang], to delight; win laughter and applause from.—***SYN.*** see **fear.**

pan·ick·y (pan'ik-i), ***adj.*** 1. having the nature of, or showing or resulting from, panic. 2. liable or susceptible to panic; liable to be in a panic.

pan·i·cle (pan'i-k'l), ***n.*** [L. *panicula*, tuft on plants, panicle, dim. of *panus*, a swelling, ear of millet; Gr. *pēnos*, thread wound on the bobbin in a shuttle], a loose, irregularly branched flower cluster; compound raceme.

PANICLE (of oat)

pan·ic-strick·en (pan'ik-strik''n), ***adj.*** stricken with panic; badly frightened; hysterical and out of control from fear.

pan·ic-struck (pan'ik-struk'), ***adj.*** panic-stricken.

pa·nic·u·late (pə-nik'yoo-lāt', pə-nik'yoo-lit), ***adj.*** [Mod. L. *paniculatus*], growing or arranged in panicles.

pa·nic·u·lat·ed (pə-nik'yoo-lā'tid), ***adj.*** paniculate.

pa·nic·u·late·ly (pə-nik'yoo-lāt'li, pə-nik'yoo-lit-li), ***adv.*** in or with panicles.

Pan-Is·lam·ism (pan'is'ləm-iz'm), ***n.*** a theory of, or movement toward, the political unification of all Islamic peoples.

Pan·ja·bi (pun-jä'bi), ***n.*** [Hind. *panjābī* < *Panjāb;* see PUNJAB], 1. the Indic language spoken in the Punjab, India: also spelled **Punjabi.** 2. a native of the Punjab: usually **Punjabi.**

pan·jan·drum (pan-jan'drəm), ***n.*** [arbitrary formation from a nonsense story by Samuel Foote (1755)], a self-important, pompous official: a satirical title.

Pank·hurst, Emmeline Goul·den (gōōl'dən paŋk'hūrst'), 1858–1928; English suffragist.

panne (pan), ***n.*** [Fr.], a soft cloth resembling velvet, but having a longer nap and a lustrous finish.

pan·nier (pan′yẽr, pan′i-ẽr), *n.* [ME. & OFr. *panier;* L. *panarium,* breadbasket < *panis,* bread], 1. a large basket; specifically, *a)* a wicker basket for carrying loads on the back. *b)* either one of a pair of baskets hung across the back of a mule, horse, etc. for carrying market produce. 2. *a)* a framework, as of whalebone, wire, etc., used to puff out a skirt at the hips. *b)* a skirt extended or puffed at the hips to give the effect of a pannier.

PANNIERS

pan·ni·kin (pan′ə-kin), *n.* [dim. of *pan* (dish)], 1. a small pan. 2. a metal cup.

Pan·no·ni·a (pə-nō′ni-ə), *n.* an ancient Roman province, between the Danube and Sava Rivers.

pa·no·cha (pə-nō′chə), *n.* [Sp. < L. *panucula, panicula;* see PANICLE], 1. a coarse sugar made in Mexico. 2. a candy, resembling fudge, made of brown sugar, milk, butter, and, sometimes, nuts. Also **penuche, penuchi.**

pa·no·che (pə-nō′chi), *n.* panocha.

pan·o·plied (pan′ə-plid), *adj.* equipped with a complete suit of armor; completely or elaborately arrayed.

pan·o·ply (pan′ə-pli), *n.* [*pl.* PANOPLIES (-pliz)], [Gr. *panoplia* < *pan,* all + *hopla,* arms], 1. a complete suit of armor; hence, 2. any complete or magnificent covering or array.

pan·op·tic (pan-op′tik), *adj.* [*pan-* + *optic*], including in one view everything within sight.

pan·o·ra·ma (pan′ə-ram′ə, pan′ə-rä′mə), *n.* [< *pan-* + Gr. *horama,* a view < *horān,* to see], 1. *a)* a picture or series of pictures of a landscape, historical event, etc. presented on a continuous surface encircling the spectator; cyclorama. *b)* a picture unrolled before the spectator in such a way as to give the impression of a continuous view. 2. an unlimited view in all directions. 3. a comprehensive survey of a subject. 4. a continuous series of scenes or events; constantly changing scene.

pan·o·ram·ic (pan′ə-ram′ik), *adj.* of, or having the nature of, a panorama; specifically, *a)* presenting an unlimited view in all directions. *b)* passing before the eyes in a continuous picture or series of pictures.

pan·o·ram·i·cal·ly (pan′ə-ram′i-k′l-i, pan′ə-ram′ik-li), *adv.* in a panoramic manner; as a panorama.

panoramic sight, a kind of periscopic gun sight that provides a greatly enlarged field of view.

pa·nou·chi (pə-nōō′chi), *n.* panocha.

Pan·pipe (pan′pīp′), *n.* a primitive musical instrument made of a row of reeds or tubes of graduated lengths bound together lengthwise and played by blowing across the top, open ends: also called *Pandean pipes, Panpipes, Pan's pipes, syrinx.*

Pan-Slav·ism (pan′släv′iz′m), *n.* a theory of, or movement toward, the political unification of all Slavic peoples.

pan·soph·ic (pan-sof′ik), *adj.* of pansophy.

pan·soph·i·cal (pan-sof′i-k′l), *adj.* pansophic.

pan·so·phism (pan′sə-fiz′m), *n.* [< Gr. *pansophos,* all-wise (< *pan,* all + *sophia,* wisdom); + *-ism*], pretension to universal wisdom or knowledge.

pan·so·phy (pan′sə-fi), *n.* [< Gr. *pansophos,* all-wise < *pan,* all + *sophia,* wisdom], 1. universal knowledge or wisdom. 2. a system or work embracing all knowledge.

Pan's pipes, a Panpipe.

pan·sy (pan′zi), *n.* [*pl.* PANSIES (-ziz)], [Fr. *pensée,* a thought < *penser,* to think], 1. a small plant of the violet family, with flat, broad, velvety petals in many colors: also called *heartsease.* 2. [Slang], an effeminate man or male homosexual: contemptuous term.

pant (pant), *v.i.* [ME. *pantyn;* prob. shortened < OFr. *pantaisier* < LL. **phantasiare,* to suffer from a nightmare < L. *phantasia,* nightmare, fantasy], 1. to breathe rapidly and heavily; gasp for breath, as from running fast. 2. to throb; pulsate; beat rapidly, as the heart. 3. to gasp with desire; yearn eagerly (with *for* or *after*). 4. to give off steam, smoke, etc. in loud puffs, as an engine. *v.t.* to utter hurriedly and breathlessly; gasp out (often with *out* or *forth*). *n.* 1. any of a series of rapid, heavy breaths, as from exertion; gasp. 2. a throb or pulsation, as of the heart. 3. a puff of an engine.

Pan·tag·ru·el (pan-tag′rōō-el; Fr. pän′tȧ′grü′el′), *n.* [Fr., coined by Rabelais < Gr. *panta,* all + "Hagarene" (i.e., Arabic) *gruel,* athirst, hence, lit., all-thirsty], the boisterous, young giant son of Gargantua in Rabelais' *Gargantua and Pantagruel:* he is a jovial drunkard characterized by rough, extravagant humor.

Pan·ta·gru·el·i·an (pan′tə-grōō-el′i-ən), *adj.* of or like Pantagruel or Pantagruelism.

Pan·ta·gru·el·ism (pan′tə-grōō′əl-iz′m, pan-tag′rōō-el-iz′m), *n.* [Fr. *pantagruélisme*], rough, extravagant humor with a satirical intent, like that of Pantagruel.

pan·ta·lets, pan·ta·lettes (pan′tə-lets′), *n.pl.* [dim. of *pantaloon*], 1. long, loose drawers frilled at the ankle and showing beneath the skirt, worn by women during the middle of the 19th century. 2. detachable ruffles for the legs of drawers.

pan·ta·loon (pan′tə-lōōn′), *n.* [Fr. *pantalon;* It. *pantalone,* name of a character in an Italian comedy, from the Venetian patron saint *Pantolone* or *Pantaleon:* said also of the garment worn by this character], 1. [P-], *a)* a stock character in an old Italian comedy, usually a slender, foolish old man wearing tight trousers which extended to the feet; hence, *b)* a similar figure in modern pantomime, the butt of the clown's jokes. 2. *pl. a)* formerly, tight trousers fastened below the calf or strapped under the boots; trousers and hose in one garment. *b)* later, any trousers: see **pants.**

pan·tech·ni·con (pan-tek′ni-kon′, pan-tek′ni-kən), *n.* [< *pan-* + Gr. *technikon, neut. adj.,* of the arts < *technē,* art], [British], 1. originally, a bazaar where all kinds of things were sold. 2. a storage warehouse. 3. a furniture van: also **pantechnicon van.**

Pan·tel·le·ri·a (pän-tel′le-rē′ä), *n.* an Italian island between Sicily and Tunisia: area, 32 sq. mi.; pop., 9,800: ancient name, *Cosyra.*

Pan-Teu·ton·ism (pan′tōō′t′n-iz′m, pan′tū′t′n-iz′m), *n.* Pan-Germanism.

pan·the·ism (pan′thē-iz′m), *n.* [*pan-* + *theism*], 1. the doctrine or belief that God is not a personality, but that all laws, forces, manifestations, etc. of the self-existing universe are God; belief that God is everything and everything is God. 2. the worship of all gods.

pan·the·ist (pan′thē-ist), *n.* a believer in pantheism.

pan·the·is·tic (pan′thē-is′tik), *adj.* of, or having the nature of, pantheism or pantheists.

pan·the·is·ti·cal (pan′thē-is′ti-k′l), *adj.* pantheistic.

pan·the·on (pan′thē-on′, pan′thi-ən, pan-thē′ən), *n.* [ME. *Panteon;* L.; Gr. *pantheion* < *pan,* all + *theos,* a god], 1. a temple for all the gods; especially, [P-], a temple built by Agrippa in Rome in 27 B.C., and rebuilt in the 2d century A.D. by Hadrian: used since 609 A.D. as a Christian church (*Santa Maria Rotunda*). 2. all the gods of a people. 3. [often P-], a building in which the famous dead persons of a nation are entombed or commemorated, as Westminster Abbey in England or the church of Sainte-Geneviève in Paris.

pan·ther (pan′thẽr), *n.* [*pl.* PANTHERS (-thẽrz), PANTHER; see PLURAL, II, D, 1], [ME. *pantere;* L. *panthera;* Gr. *panthēr*], 1. a puma; cougar; mountain lion. 2. a leopard, especially one of dark color. 3. a jaguar.

pan·ther·ess (pan′thẽr-is), *n.* a female panther.

pan·ties (pan′tiz), *n.pl.* women's or children's short underpants.

pan·tile (pan′tīl′), *n.* [*pan* (dish) + *tile*], a roofing tile having an S curve, laid with the large curve of one tile overlapping the small curve of the next.

LAID TILE

SINGLE TILE

PANTILE

pan·to- (pan′tō, pan′tə), [< Gr. *pantos,* genit. of *pan;* see PAN-], a combining form meaning *all* or *every,* as in *pantograph, pantoscope:* also, before a vowel, **pant-.**

pan·to·fle, pan·tof·fle (pan′tə-f′l, pan-tof′′l, pan-tōō′f′l), *n.* [Fr. *pantoufle;* It. *pantofola;* MGr. *pantophellos,* whole cork < Gr. *pantos* (see PANTO-) + *phellos,* a cork], a slipper.

pan·to·graph (pan′tə-graf′, pan′tə-gräf′), *n.* [*panto-* + *-graph*], 1. a mechanical device for reproducing a map, drawing, etc. on the same or a different scale, consisting of a framework of jointed rods in a roughly parallelogram form. 2. any similar framework, as an extendible arm for a telephone, a trolley on an electric locomotive, etc.

pan·to·mime (pan′tə-mīm′), *n.* [Fr.; L. *pantomimus;* Gr. *pantomimos* < *pas, pantos,* all + *mimos,* a mimic], 1. in ancient Rome, *a)* an actor who played his part by gestures and action without words. *b)* a drama played in action and gestures to the accompaniment of words sung by the chorus or music. 2. any drama played without words, using action and gestures only. 3. action or gestures without words as a means of expression. 4. in England, a type of entertainment presented at Christmas time. *adj.* pantomimic. *v.t. & v.i.* [PANTOMIMED (-mīmd′), PANTOMIMING], to express or act in pantomime.

pan·to·mim·ic (pan′tə-mim′ik), *adj.* [L. *pantomimicus*], of, or having the nature of, pantomime.

pan·to·mim·ist (pan′tə-mīm′ist), *n.* an actor in a pantomime.

pan·to·scope (pan′tə-skōp′), *n.* [*panto-* + *-scope*], a form of photographic lens having a very wide angle.

pan·to·scop·ic (pan'tə-skop'ik), ***adj.*** [< *panto-* + *-scope* + *-ic*], having a wide range of view.

pan·to·then·ic acid (pan'tə-then'ik), a B-complex vitamin, $C_9H_{17}O_5N$, widely distributed in animal and plant tissues and prepared synthetically: thought to be essential for cell growth and helpful in preventing gray hair.

pan·toum (pan-tōōm'), ***n.*** [Fr.; Malay *pantun*], a verse form made up of quatrains rhyming *abab, bcbc, cdcd,* etc.: a European imitation of the Malayan pantun.

pan·try (pan'tri), ***n.*** [*pl.* PANTRIES (-triz)], [ME. & OFr. *paneterie;* ML. *panetaria* < L. *panis,* bread], 1. a small room or closet off the kitchen, where cooking ingredients and utensils, china, etc. are kept. 2. a small room between the kitchen and dining room for serving meals and storing tableware: also called *butler's pantry.*

pants (pants), ***n.pl.*** [abbrev. of *pantaloons*], 1. an outer garment extending from the waist to the knees or ankles and divided into separate coverings for the legs: more formally called *trousers.* 2. drawers or panties.

pan·tun (pan-tōōn'), ***n.*** [Malay], a Malayan verse form, consisting of rhymed quatrains: see also **pantoum.**

pan·ty·waist (pan'ti-wāst'), ***n.*** 1. originally, a child's two-piece undergarment that buttoned together at the waist; hence, 2. [Slang], a person considered as like a child in strength, courage, etc.; weakling; sissy.

Pan·urge (pan-ũrj'; Fr. pȧ'nürzh'), ***n.*** [Fr. < Gr. *panourgos,* ready to do anything; *pan* (see PAN-) + *-ourgos,* worker], the gay, cowardly companion of Pantagruel in Rabelais' *Gargantua and Pantagruel.*

Panza, Sancho, see **Sancho Panza.**

pan·zer (pan'zẽr; G. pän'tsẽr), ***adj.*** [G., armor; MHG. *panzier;* OFr. *pancier* < It. *pancia,* belly; L. *pantex;* cf. PAUNCH], armored: as, a *panzer* division.

Pao·ting (bou'tiŋ'), ***n.*** a city in Hopeh province, northeastern China: pop., 100,000.

pap (pap), ***n.*** [ME. *pappe* < ON.; cf. Sw. *papp, pappe*], 1. [Archaic], a nipple or teat. 2. something shaped like a nipple.

pap (pap), ***n.*** [? < L. *pappa, papa,* infant's cry for food], 1. any soft or semiliquid food for babies or invalids. 2. any mash, paste, or pulp. 3. political patronage; money or favors from public office.

pa·pa (pä'pə; *now less freq.,* pə-pä'), ***n.*** [like Fr. & L. *papa,* Gr. *pappas* < baby talk; cf. MAMMA], father: a child's word, corresponding to *mamma* for *mother:* also **pa, paw, pop,** etc.

pa·pa·cy (pā'pə-si), ***n.*** [*pl.* PAPACIES (-siz)], [ME. *papacie;* ML. *papatia,* papacy < *papa,* pope, bishop], 1. the position, authority, or rank of the Pope. 2. the period of time during which a pope rules. 3. the succession of popes; popes collectively. 4. [also P-], the government of the Roman Catholic Church, headed by the Pope.

pa·pa·in (pə-pā'in, pā'pə-in), ***n.*** [*papaya* + *-in*], a protein-splitting enzyme obtained from the juice of unripe papaya and used as an aid to digestion.

pa·pal (pā'p'l), ***adj.*** [ME.; OFr. < ML. *papa,* pope], 1. of the Pope. 2. of the papacy. 3. of the Roman Catholic Church.

Papal States, the lands in central and north central Italy that were ruled by the Pope until 1870: also called *States of the Church.*

pa·pav·er·a·ceous (pə-pav'ə-rā'shəs), ***adj.*** [< Mod. L. *Papaveraceae,* name of the family (< L. *papaver,* poppy); + *-ous*], in *botany,* of the poppy family.

pa·pav·er·in (pə-pav'ẽr-in, pə-pä'vẽr-in), ***n.*** papaverine.

pa·pav·er·ine (pə-pav'ə-rēn', pə-pä'vẽr-in), ***n.*** [L. *papaver,* poppy; + *-ine*], a white, crystalline alkaloid, $C_{20}H_{21}NO_4$, derived from opium and used in medicine to relax muscles in spasms and as a local anesthetic.

pa·paw (pô'pô, pə-pô'), ***n.*** [Sp. *papaya* (fruit), *papayo* (tree) < Carib name], 1. a papaya. 2. *a*) a tree of the custard apple family, growing in the central and southern United States and having an oblong, yellowish, edible fruit with many seeds. *b*) its fruit. Also **pawpaw.**

pa·pa·ya (pə-pä'yə), ***n.*** [Sp., fruit of the papaw], 1. a tropical tree of America, Hawaii, and the Philippines, resembling a palm, having a bunch of large leaves at the top, and bearing a large, oblong, yellowish-orange fruit like a melon. 2. its fruit, eaten raw or cooked, and also valued for its juice.

PAPAYA
A, tree (15–20 ft. high); B, cross section of fruit

Pa·pe·e·te (pä'pi-ā'tā), ***n.*** a seaport on Tahiti: capital of the Society Islands and French Oceania: pop., 8,500.

pa·per (pā'pẽr), ***n.*** [ME. *papire;* OFr. *papier;* L. *papyrus;* Gr. *papyros,* Egyptian reed, from the inner bark of which a kind of writing paper was made in ancient Egypt], 1. a thin flexible material in sheets or leaves, made from rags, wood pulp, or other fibrous material, and used to write or print on, wrap, decorate, etc. 2. a single piece, sheet, or leaf of paper. 3. a printed or written sheet or piece of paper; writing; specifically, *a*) an official document. *b*) an essay, monograph, or dissertation, as read before a learned society, published in a scholarly journal, etc. *c*) a written examination, report, theme, etc. 4. *a*) checks, promissory notes, bills of exchange, and other negotiable papers used in business: also **commercial paper.** *b*) paper money. 5. a newspaper. 6. a small wrapper or card of paper, usually including its contents: as, a *paper* of pins. 7. wallpaper. 8. any material like paper, as papyrus. 9. *a*) a free pass or passes to a theater, etc. *b*) the people admitted by free passes. 10. *pl. a*) documents proving the identity of a person; credentials. *b*) a collection of documents, letters, writings, etc., especially of one person: as, the Lincoln *papers.* Abbreviated **pap.** ***adj.*** 1. of paper; made of paper. 2. like paper; thin. 3. existing only in written or printed form; theoretical; spurious: as, *paper* profits. ***v.t.*** 1. to cover with paper, especially wallpaper. 2. to write down on paper; describe in writing. 3. to wrap or enclose in paper. 4. [Slang], to help to fill (a theater, etc.) by issuing free passes.
on paper, 1. in written or printed form. 2. in theory.

pa·per·back (pā'pẽr-bak'), ***n.*** a book bound in paper, instead of leather, cardboard, etc.

paper birch, the North American birch with white or ash-colored, paperlike bark: also called *white birch.*

pa·per·boy (pā'pẽr-boi'), ***n.*** a boy or man who sells or delivers newspapers.

paper cutter, 1. a paper knife. 2. a machine used to cut and trim paper to required dimensions.

paper hanger, a person whose work is to cover walls with wallpaper.

paper hangings, wallpaper.

paper knife, a dull, narrow knife of metal, wood, ivory, etc., used to cut folded paper, as sealed envelopes or the uncut pages of books: also called *paper cutter.*

paper money, noninterest-bearing notes issued by a government or its banks, circulating as a substitute for metallic money: as, a dollar bill is *paper money.*

paper nautilus, an eight-armed mollusk related to the octopus: the female has a thin paperlike shell in which the young develop.

pa·per·weight (pā'pẽr-wāt'), ***n.*** any small, heavy object to be placed on papers to keep them from being blown away or otherwise scattered.

paper work, the keeping of records, filing of reports, etc. that is incidental to some work or task: as, a teacher must spend several hours a day on *paper work.*

pa·per·y (pā'pẽr-i), ***adj.*** like paper, as in consistency.

pap·e·terie (pap'ə-tri; Fr. pȧp'trē'), ***n.*** [Fr. < *papetier,* paper-maker, stationer < *papier;* see PAPER], a box for paper and other writing materials.

Pa·phi·an (pā'fi-ən), ***adj.*** 1. of Paphos. 2. erotic.

Paph·la·go·ni·a (paf'lə-gō'ni-ə), ***n.*** an ancient country and Roman province in Asia Minor, on the Black Sea.

Pa·phos (pā'fos), ***n.*** an ancient city in Cyprus.

‡**pa·pier col·lé** (pȧ'pyā' kô'lā'), [*pl.* PAPIERS COLLÉS (-pyā' -lā')], [Fr., lit., pasted paper; see COLLAGE], a kind of collage in which the pasted objects are grouped for pattern rather than for symbolism.

pa·pier-mâ·ché (pā'pẽr-mə-shā'; Fr. pȧ'pyā'mȧ'shā'), ***n.*** [Fr. *papier,* paper + *mâché,* pp. of *mâcher* (L. *masticare*), to chew], a material made of paper pulp mixed with rosin, oil, etc., that can be molded into various objects when moist. ***adj.*** made of papier-mâché.

pa·pil·i·o·na·ceous (pə-pil'i-ə-nā'shəs), ***adj.*** [< L. *papilio,* butterfly (akin to AS. *fifealde*); + *-aceous*], in *botany,* shaped like a butterfly, as certain flowers.

pa·pil·la (pə-pil'ə), ***n.*** [*pl.* PAPILLAE (-ē)], [L., dim. of *papula,* pimple], 1. *a*) any small nipplelike projection or process of connective tissue, as the small elevations at the root of a developing tooth, hair, feather, etc. or the many and variously shaped elevations on the surface of the tongue. *b*) the nipple. 2. in *botany,* a tiny, protruding cell.

pap·il·lar·y (pap'ə-ler'i, pə-pil'ẽr-i), ***adj.*** 1. of, or having the nature of, a papilla. 2. provided with, consisting of, or affecting papillae.

pap·il·lo·ma (pap'ə-lō'mə), ***n.*** [*pl.* PAPILLOMATA (-mə-tə), PAPILLOMAS (-məz)], [Mod.L. < *papilla* + *-oma*], a tumor of the skin or mucous membrane, consisting of a thickened and enlarged papilla or group of papillae, as a corn or wart.

pa·pil·lon (pap'ə-lon'; Fr. pȧ'pē'yōn'), ***n.*** [Fr., a butterfly: from the shape of the ears], any of a breed of toy spaniel: one type has erect, fringed ears.

pap·il·lose (pap'ə-lōs'), ***adj.*** covered with or having many papillae.

pap·il·los·i·ty (pap'ə-los'ə-ti), ***n.*** the quality of being papillose.

pap·il·lote (pap'ə-lōt'), ***n.*** [Fr. < *papilloter,* to strew with tinsel (prob. influenced also by association with *papier,* paper) < MFr. *papillot,* butterfly, dim. of *papillon* < L. *papilio*], 1. a paper for curling the hair; curlpaper. 2. a paper frill placed on the end of the bone of a chop, cutlet, etc. before serving.

pa·pist (pā′pist), *n.* [Fr. *papiste;* ML. *papista* < L. *papa;* see POPE], 1. a person who believes in papal supremacy. 2. a Roman Catholic. *adj.* Roman Catholic. A hostile term.
pa·pis·tic (pā-pis′tik, pə-pis′tik), *adj.* papist.
pa·pis·ti·cal (pā-pis′ti-k'l, pə-pis′ti-k'l), *adj.* papistic.
pa·pist·ry (pā′pis-tri), *n.* [see PAPIST & -(E)RY], the beliefs and practices of the Roman Catholic Church: hostile term.
pa·poose (pa-po͞os′), *n.* [< Am. Ind. (Algonquian) *papoos*], a North American Indian baby.
pap·pose (pap′ōs), *adj.* in *botany*, provided or covered with pappus, or downy chaff.
pap·pous (pap′əs), *adj.* pappose.
pap·pus (pap′əs), *n.* [*pl.* PAPPI (-ī)], [Mod. L.; Gr. *pappos*, old man, grandfather, hence substance resembling gray hairs], in *botany*, a downy or feathery tuft of chaff or bristles on certain fruits, especially of the composite family, as on the seeds of the dandelion.
pap·py (pap′i), *n.* [Dial. or Colloq.], papa; father.
pap·py (pap′i), *adj.* [< *pap* (soft food) + *-y*], like pap; soft; mushy.
pap·ri·ka, pap·ri·ca (pa-prē′kə, pap′ri-kə), *n.* [G.; Hung.; Gr. *peperi*, a pepper], 1. the fruit of the capsicum or various other pepper plants. 2. a mild, red condiment ground from it.
Pap·u·a (pä′po͞o-ə; Eng. pap′ū-ə), *n.* 1. New Guinea, an island in the East Indies. 2. the Territory of Papua.
Papua, Territory of, an Australian territory including the southeastern part of New Guinea and near-by islands: area, 90,540 sq. mi.; pop., 300,000 (est. 1947); capital, Port Moresby: also called *British New Guinea*.
Pap·u·an (pap′ū-ən), *adj.* [Malay, lit., frizzled, from the characteristic hair], of Papua, its people, or their languages. *n.* 1. a member of a Negroid people living in New Guinea and near-by islands. 2. a member of any of the dark-skinned peoples of Oceania. 3. any of a number of languages spoken in New Guinea, New Caledonia, and elsewhere in the Southwest Pacific. 4. the Papuan family of languages.
pap·u·lar (pap′yoo-lẽr), *adj.* of, or having the nature of, a papule.
pap·ule (pap′ūl), *n.* [L., akin to *papilla*, nipple < IE. base seen also in Lettish *pampt*, to swell, Sans. *pippalī*, berry; cf. PEPPER], a small, usually inflammatory, elevation of the skin; pimple.
pap·y·ra·ceous (pap′ə-rā′shəs), *adj.* [< L. *papyrus* (see PAPER); + *-aceous*], like paper; papery.
pa·py·rus (pə-pī′rəs), *n.* [*pl.* PAPYRI (-rī), PAPYRUSES (-iz)], [ME. *papirus;* L.; see PAPER], 1. a variety of tall water plant of the sedge family, formerly abundant in the Nile region of Egypt. 2. a writing material made from this plant by the ancient Egyptians, Greeks, and Romans, by soaking, pressing, and drying thin slices of its pith laid crosswise. 3. any ancient document or manuscript on papyrus.

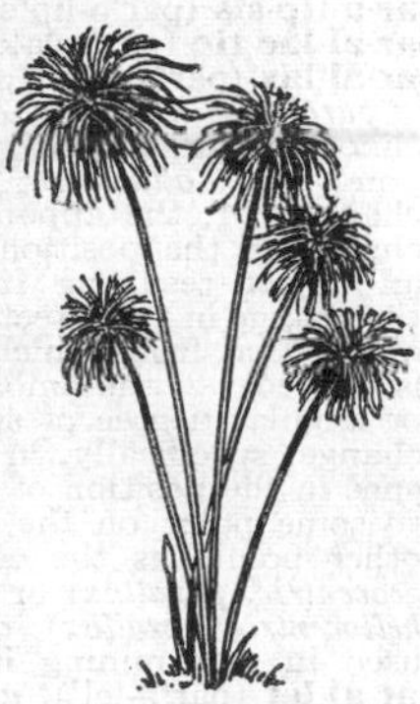

PAPYRUS
(3–12 ft. high)

par (pär), *n.* [L., an equal], 1. the established or recognized value of the money of one country in terms of the money of another country, based on the same metal as standard of value. 2. an equal or common status, standing, footing, level, etc. (with *on* or *upon*): as, he is on a *par* with his associates in ability. 3. the average or normal state, condition, degree, etc.: as, his work is above *par*. 4. in *commerce*, the nominal, or face, value of stocks, bonds, etc.: as, a stock is at *par* when it can be sold for its face value. 5. in *golf*, the number of strokes established as an expert score for any given hole or for a whole course. *adj.* 1. of or at par. 2. average; normal.
par-, para- (beside, etc.).
par., 1. [*pl.* PARS.], paragraph. 2. parallel. 3. [*pl.* PARENS.], parenthesis. 4. parish.
Pa·rá (pä-rä′), *n.* 1. the southern estuary of the Amazon, also forming the estuary of the Tocantins River: length, 200 mi. 2. a state of northern Brazil: area, 443,789 sq. mi.; pop., 1,094,000 (est. 1948). 3. Belém, its capital. 4. Pará rubber.
pa·ra (pä-rä′, pä′rä), *n.* [Turk. & Per. *pārah*, a piece], 1. a Turkish copper coin equal to 1/40 piaster. 2. a small Yugoslavian coin equal to 1/100 dinar.
par·a- (par′ə), [Gr. *para-* < *para*, at the side of, alongside, etc.], a prefix meaning: 1. *by the side of, beside, alongside of, by, past, beyond, to one side, aside from,* or *amiss*, as in *parallel*. 2. in *chemistry*, *an isomer, modification, polymer, derivative, etc. of* (a specified substance): used especially to designate a derivative of benzene in which two atoms or radicals are substituted in positions directly opposite each other in the ring, as in *paradichlorobenzene:* abbreviated **p-** (no period). 3. in *medicine*, *a) in a secondary or accessory capacity. b) functionally disordered, abnormal*, as in *parafunctional*. *c) like* or *resembling*, as in *paracholera*. Also **par-**.
par·a- (par′ə), [Fr. < It. *para*, imperative of *parare*, to ward off; L. *parare*, to prepare], a combining form meaning: 1. *a thing that protects from*, as in *parachute, parapet*. 2. *using a parachute*, as in *paratroop*.
Para., Paraguay.
par·a·a·mi·no·ben·zo·ic acid (par′ə-ə-mē′nō-ben-zō′ik, par′ə-am′i-nō-ben-zō′ik), [*para-* + *amino-* + *benzoic*], a yellowish crystalline compound, $C_7H_7NO_2$, considered a member of the vitamin B complex, present in yeast and commercially prepared: a deficiency of this factor causes prematurely gray hair.
par·a·blast (par′ə-blast′), *n.* [*para-* (beside, etc.) + *-blast*], in *embryology*, the nutritive yolk of a meroblastic ovum: distinguished from *archiblast*.
par·a·blas·tic (par′ə-blas′tik), *adj.* of a parablast.
par·a·ble (par′ə-b'l), *n.* [OFr. *parabole;* L. *parabola;* Gr. *parabolē* < *paraballein*, to throw beside, compare; *para-*, beside + *ballein*, to throw; cf. PARABOLA], 1. a short, simple story from which a moral lesson may be drawn: it is usually an allegory. 2. [Archaic], an obscure or enigmatic saying.
pa·rab·o·la (pə-rab′ə-lə), *n.* [*pl.* PARABOLAS (-ləz)], [Mod.L.; Gr. *parabolē* < *para-*, beside + *ballein*, to throw: so called from its axis being parallel to the side of the cone], in *geometry*, a plane curve, the path, or locus, of a moving point that remains equally distant from a fixed point (*focus*) and from a fixed straight line (*directrix*); curve formed by the intersection of a cone with a plane parallel to its side.

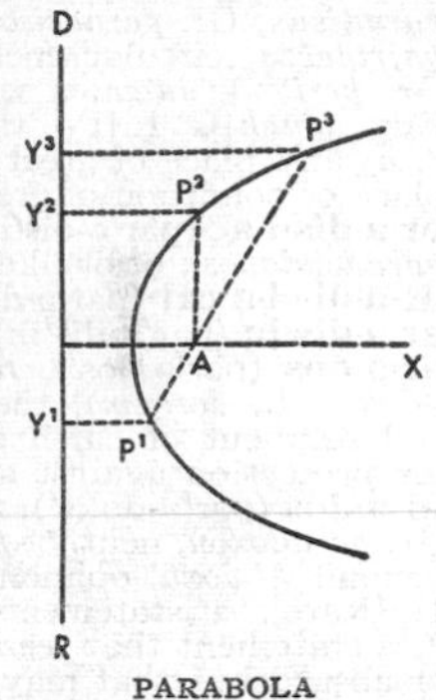

PARABOLA
A, focus; AX, axis; DR, directrix; P^1, P^2, P^3, points on the parabola; $P^3Y^3 = P^3A$, $P^2Y^2 = P^2A$, $P^1Y^1 = P^1A$

par·a·bol·ic (par′ə-bol′ik), *adj.* [LL. *parabolicus*], of, in the form of, or expressed by a parable; allegorical.
par·a·bol·ic (par′ə-bol′ik), *adj.* of or like a parabola.
par·a·bol·i·cal (par′ə-bol′i-k'l), *adj.* parabolic; allegorical.
par·a·bol·i·cal·ly (par′ə-bol′i-k'l-i, par′ə-bol′ik-li), *adv.* 1. in parables. 2. by means of parabolas.
pa·rab·o·lize (pə-rab′ə-liz′), *v.t.* [PARABOLIZED (-līzd′), PARABOLIZING], 1. to tell in a parable or parables. 2. to make parabolic in shape.
pa·rab·o·loid (pə-rab′ə-loid′), *n.* the surface or solid formed by a parabola revolving around its axis.
pa·rab·o·loi·dal (pə-rab′ə-loi′d'l), *adj.* of, or in the form of, a paraboloid.
Par·a·cel·sus, Phil·ip·pus Au·re·o·lus (fi-lip′əs ô-rē′ə-ləs par′ə-sel′səs), (born *Theophrastus Bombastus von Hohenheim*), 1493?–1541; German physician and alchemist, born in Switzerland.
par·a·chute (par′ə-sho͞ot′), *n.* [Fr.; *para-* (see PARA-, protecting) + *chute*, a fall], 1. a large cloth contrivance shaped like an umbrella when expanded, and used to retard the falling speed of a person or thing dropping from an airplane, etc.: it is generally carried folded in a pack, from which it is released by a rip cord or other device. 2. something shaped like or having the effect of a parachute. 3. in *zoology*, a fold of skin between the fore and hind limbs of flying squirrels, flying lizards, etc., enabling them to glide through the air; patagium. *v.t.* [PARACHUTED (-id), PARACHUTING], to drop by a parachute. *v.i.* to descend by means of a parachute.
par·a·chut·ist (par′ə-sho͞ot′ist), *n.* a person who descends by parachute.
par·a·clete (par′ə-klēt′), *n.* [OFr. *paraclet;* LL. *paracletus;* Gr. *paraklētos* < *parakalein; para-*, to + *kalein*, to call], 1. an advocate; intercessor; pleader. 2. [P-], in *Christianity*, the Holy Spirit, considered as comforter, intercessor, or advocate.
par·a·cy·mene (par′ə-sī′mēn), *n.* [*para-* (beside, etc.) + *cymene*], a colorless liquid, $C_{10}H_{14}$, insoluble in water: made from oils of eucalyptus, cumin, thyme, etc., and used as a solvent: see **cymene**.
pa·rade (pə-rād′), *n.* [Fr., show, display, military parade, etc.; Sp. *parada*, a parade, place for the exercise of troops < L. *parare*, to set or place in order, to prepare], 1. ostentatious or pompous display. 2. *a*) a military display or assembly; review of troops. *b*) a place where troops assemble regularly for parade; parade ground.

3. any organized procession or march, as for display. 4. *a*) a public walk or promenade. *b*) persons promenading; strollers. *v.t.* [PARADED (-id), PARADING], 1. to bring together (troops, etc.) for inspection or display. 2. to march or walk through, as for display: as, the band *paraded* the streets. 3. to make a display of; show off: as, he always *parades* his knowledge. *v.i.* 1. to march in a parade or procession. 2. to walk about ostentatiously; show off. 3. to assemble in military formation for review or display.

on parade, on display.

parade rest, in *military usage,* 1. a formal position of rest, distinguished by its prescribed stance from the informal position of *at ease.* 2. the command to assume this position.

par·a·di·chlo·ro·ben·zene (par'ə-dī-klôr'ə-ben'zēn, par'ə-dī-klō'rə-ben-zēn'), *n.* [*para-* (beside, etc.) + *di-* + *chloro-* + *benzene*], a white crystalline compound, $C_6H_4Cl_2$, used as an insecticide, deodorant, etc.

par·a·digm (par'ə-dim, par'ə-dīm'), *n.* [Fr. *paradigme;* LL. *paradigma;* Gr. *paradeigma; para-,* beside + *deigma,* example < *deiknynai,* to show], 1. a pattern, example, or model. 2. in *grammar,* an example of a declension or conjugation, giving all the inflectional forms of a word. —***SYN.*** see **model.**

par·a·dig·mat·ic (par'ə-dig-mat'ik), *adj.* of, or having the nature of, a paradigm; exemplary.

par·a·di·sa·ic (par'ə-di-sā'ik), *adj.* paradisiac.

par·a·di·sa·i·cal (par'ə-di-sā'i-k'l), *adj.* paradisiacal.

par·a·dise (par'ə-dīs'), *n.* [ME. & OFr. *paradis;* L. *paradisus;* Gr. *paradeisos,* a garden < Per.; cf. Avestan *pairidaēza,* circular enclosure; *pairi,* around (akin to Gr. *peri*) + *daēza,* a wall (akin to Gr. *teichos,* wall, Eng. *dough*)], 1. [P-], the garden of Eden. 2. heaven. 3. *a*) any place of great beauty and perfection. *b*) any place or condition of great happiness.

par·a·dis·i·ac (par'ə-dis'i-ak'), *adj.* [L. *paradisiacus;* Gr. *paradeisiakos*], of or like paradise or a paradise.

par·a·di·si·a·cal (par'ə-di-sī'ə-k'l), *adj.* paradisiac.

par·a·dis·ic (par'ə-dis'ik), *adj.* paradisiac.

par·a·dos (par'ə-dos'), *n.* [Fr. < *para-* (that protects) + *dos* (L. *dorsum*), the back], in *military usage,* an embankment of earth at the back edge of a trench for protection against gunfire from the rear.

par·a·dox (par'ə-doks'), *n.* [Fr. *paradoxe;* L. *paradoxum;* Gr. *paradoxon,* neut. of *paradoxos,* paradoxical < *para-,* beyond + *doxa,* opinion < *dokein,* to think, suppose], 1. [Rare], a statement contrary to common belief. 2. a statement that seems contradictory, unbelievable, or absurd but that may actually be true in fact. 3. a statement that is self-contradictory in fact and, hence, false. 4. *a*) something inconsistent with common experience or having contradictory qualities. *b*) a person who is inconsistent or contradictory in character or behavior.

par·a·dox·i·cal (par'ə-dok'si-k'l), *adj.* 1. of, having the nature of, or expressing a paradox or paradoxes. 2. fond of using paradoxes.

par·aes·the·si·a (par'es-thē'zhə, par'es-thē'zhi-ə), *n.* paresthesia.

par·af·fin (par'ə-fin), *n.* [G. < L. *parum,* too little + *affinis,* akin: from its resistance to chemical reagents], 1. a white, waxy solid substance consisting of a mixture of hydrocarbons: it is obtained chiefly from the distillation of petroleum and is used for making candles, sealing preserving jars, waterproofing paper, etc. 2. in *chemistry,* any member of the methane series, the group of hydrocarbons having the general formula C_nH_{2n+2}. *v.t.* to coat or impregnate with paraffin.

par·af·fine (par'ə-fin, par'ə-fēn'), *n.* & *v.t.* [PARAFFINED (-find, -fēnd'), PARAFFINING], paraffin.

paraffin series, in *chemistry,* the methane series of hydrocarbons: see **methane series.**

paraffin wax, solid paraffin.

par·a·ge·ne·si·a (par'ə-jə-nē'si-ə), *n.* paragenesis.

par·a·gen·e·sis (par'ə-jen'ə-sis), *n.* [Mod. L.; *para-* (beside, etc.) + *-genesis*], the formation of minerals in close contact, with a resulting interlocking of their crystals, as in granite, marble, etc.

par·a·ge·net·ic (par'ə-jə-net'ik), *adj.* of or resulting from paragenesis.

par·a·go·ge (par'ə-gō'ji), *n.* [L.; Gr. *paragōge,* drawing out < *paragein,* to draw out < *para-,* beyond + *agein,* to lead], in *grammar,* the adding of a letter or syllable to the end of a word, either functionally, as in *drowned,* or unnecessarily, as in substandard *drowneded.*

par·a·gog·ic (par'ə-goj'ik), *adj.* of, having the nature of, or forming a paragoge.

par·a·gon (par'ə-gon', par'ə-gən), *n.* [OFr.; It. *paragone,* touchstone < Gr. *parakonaein,* to test with a whetstone < *para-,* against + *akonē,* whetstone], 1. a model or pattern of perfection or excellence. 2. a perfect diamond weighing a hundred carats or more. 3. in *printing,* a size of type, 20-point. *v.t.* 1. [Poetic], to put side by side; compare. 2. [Poetic], to be equal to; match. 3. [Obs.], to surpass. 4. [Obs.], to set forth as a paragon.

pa·rag·o·nite (pə-rag'ə-nīt'), *n.* [< Gr. *paragōn,* ppr. of *paragein,* to mislead < *para-,* beside + *agein,* to lead; + *-ite*], a kind of mica distinguished from common mica by containing sodium instead of potassium.

par·a·graph (par'ə-graf', par'ə-gräf'), *n.* [Fr. *paragraphe;* ML. *paragraphus;* Gr. *paragraphē,* marginal note < *para-,* beyond, beside + *graphein,* to write], 1. a distinct section or subdivision of a chapter, letter, etc., usually dealing with a particular point: it is always begun on a new line and is often indented: abbreviated **para., par.** 2. a mark (¶ or ⁋) used chiefly by proofreaders to indicate the beginning of a separate passage or paragraph, or a sign marking material referred to elsewhere. 3. a brief article, item, or note in a newspaper or magazine. *v.t.* 1. to treat in a paragraph or paragraphs. 2. to separate or arrange in paragraphs. *v.i.* to write paragraphs, especially for a newspaper.

par·a·graph·er (par'ə-graf'ẽr, par'ə-gräf'ẽr), *n.* a writer of paragraphs, as for newspaper editorials.

par·a·graph·i·a (par'ə-graf'i-ə), *n.* [Mod. L. < *para-* (beside, etc.) + Gr. *graphein,* to write], a mental disorder, generally due to cerebral injury, characterized by the unintentional omission, transposition, or insertion of letters or words in writing.

par·a·graph·ic (par'ə-graf'ik), *adj.* of or forming a paragraph or paragraphs.

par·a·graph·i·cal (par'ə-graf'i-k'l), *adj.* paragraphic.

Par·a·guay (par'ə-gwā', par'ə-gwī'; Sp. pä-rä-gwī'), *n.* 1. a country in central South America: area, 157,047 sq. mi.; pop., 1,768,000; capital, Asunción. 2. a river in southern Brazil and Paraguay flowing into the Paraná River: length, 1,500 mi. Abbreviated **Para.**

Par·a·guay·an (par'ə-gwā'ən, par'ə-gwī'ən), *adj.* of Paraguay, its people, or culture. *n.* a native or inhabitant of Paraguay.

Paraguay tea, 1. a beverage made from the leaves of a South American plant. 2. this plant. Also called *maté.*

par·a·keet (par'ə-kēt'), *n.* [OFr. *paroquet* (prob. < *perrot*); see PARROT], any of certain small, slender parrots with long, tapering tails: also **parrakeet, parroket, paroquet, parroquet.**

par·al·de·hyde (pə-ral'də-hīd'), *n.* [*par-* + *aldehyde*], a colorless liquid, $(CH_3CHO)_3$, produced by the polymerization of acetaldehyde, having a strong, nauseating smell and used in medicine as a hypnotic and sedative.

par·a·leip·sis (par'ə-līp'sis), *n.* [Gr. *paraleipsis,* omission < *para-,* beyond + *leipein,* to leave], in *rhetoric,* a device in which a point is stressed by suggesting that it is too obvious or well-known to mention, as in the phrase, "not to mention the expense involved."

par·a·lep·sis (par'ə-lep'sis), *n.* paraleipsis.

par·a·lip·sis (par'ə-lip'sis), *n.* paraleipsis.

par·al·lac·tic (par'ə-lak'tik), *adj.* of a parallax.

par·al·lax (par'ə-laks'), *n.* [Fr. *parallaxe;* Gr. *parallaxis* < *parallassein,* to vary, decline, wander < *para-,* beyond + *allassein,* to change], 1. the apparent change in the position of an object resulting from the change in the direction or position from which it is viewed. 2. the amount or angular degree of such change; specifically, in *astronomy,* the apparent difference in the position of a heavenly body with reference to some point on the surface of the earth and some other point, as the center of the earth (*diurnal,* or *geocentric, parallax*) or a point on the sun (*annual,* or *heliocentric, parallax*): the parallax of an object may be used in determining its distance from the observer.

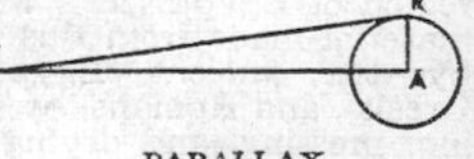

PARALLAX

P, star; R, point on earth's surface; A, center of the earth; angle RPA, parallax

par·al·lel (par'ə-lel'), *adj.* [Fr. *parallèle;* L. *parallelus;* Gr. *parallēlos* < *para-,* side by side + *allēlos,* one another < *allos,* other], 1. extending in the same direction and at the same distance apart at every point, so as never to meet, as lines, planes, etc.: in modern non-Euclidian geometry, such lines and planes are considered to meet at infinity. 2. having parallel parts or movements, as some machines, tools, etc. 3. closely similar or corresponding, as in purpose, tendency, time, or essential parts. 4. in *music,* having consistently equal intervals in pitch, as two parts of harmony, a series of chords, etc. *n.* 1. something parallel to something else, as a line or surface. 2. any person or thing essentially the same as, or closely similar or corresponding to, something else; counterpart. 3. the condition of being parallel; conformity in essential points. 4. any comparison showing the existence of similarity or likeness. 5. any of the imaginary lines parallel to the equator and representing degrees of latitude on the earth's surface; hence, 6. such a line drawn on a map or globe. 7. in *electricity,* a hookup of lights, cells, etc. in which all positive poles or terminals are connected in one conductor and all negatives in another: also called *multiple circuit.* 8. in *military science,* a trench, usually one of a series, running parallel to and opposing a position. 9. *pl.* in *printing,* a sign (‖) marking material referred to in a note. Abbreviated **par.** *v.t.* [PARALLELED or PARALLELLED (-leld'), PARALLELING or PARALLELLING], 1. *a*) to make (one thing) parallel to another.

b) to make parallel to each other. 2. to be parallel with; extend parallel to: as, the highway *parallels* the river. 3. to compare (things, ideas, etc.) in order to show similarity or likeness. 4. to find a counterpart for; match. 5. to be a counterpart for; match; equal.

parallel bars, two bars parallel to each other and set horizontally on adjustable upright posts: used in gymnastics.

PARALLEL BARS

par·al·lel·e·pi·ped (par'ə-lel'ə-pi'pid, par'ə-lel'ə-pip'id), *n.* [< Gr. *parallēlos,* parallel + *epipedos,* on the ground, on a level with it, plane, superficial < *epi,* upon + *pedon,* the ground], a solid with six faces, each of which is a parallelogram.

par·al·lel·e·pip·e·don (par'ə-lel'ə-pip'ə-don'), *n.* a parallelepiped.

par·al·lel·ism (par'ə-lel-iz'm), *n.* [Gr. *parallēlismos*], 1. the state of being parallel. 2. close resemblance; similarity. 3. in *philosophy,* the theory that mind and matter, though independent, function together in a parallel, but without an interactive causal relationship.

parallel of latitude, parallel (senses 5 & 6).

par·al·lel·o·gram (par'ə-lel'ə-gram'), *n.* [Fr. *parallélogramme;* L. *parallelogrammum;* Gr. *parallēlogrammon* < *parallēlos,* parallel + *grammē,* stroke in writing < *graphein,* to write], a plane figure with four sides, having the opposite sides parallel and equal.

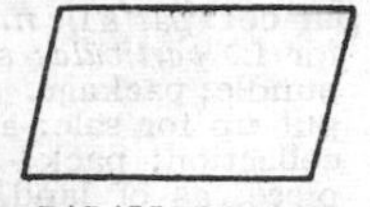

PARALLELOGRAM

pa·ral·o·gism (pə-ral'ə-jiz'm), *n.* [Fr. *paralogisme;* LL. *paralogismus;* Gr. *paralogismos* < *paralogizesthai,* to reason illogically; *para-,* beyond + *logizesthai,* to reason < *logos,* a discourse, reason], reasoning contrary to the rules of logic; faulty reasoning.

pa·ral·o·gis·tic (pə-ral'ə-jis'tik), *adj.* of or by a paralogism; faulty in logic.

pa·ral·o·gize (pə-ral'ə-jīz'), *v.i.* [PARALOGIZED (-jīzd'), PARALOGIZING], [Gr. *paralogizesthai;* see PARALOGISM], to reason falsely or illogically.

pa·ral·y·sis (pə-ral'ə-sis), *n.* [*pl.* PARALYSES (-sēz')], [L.; Gr. *paralysis* < *paralyein,* to loosen, dissolve, or weaken at the side; *para-,* beside + *lyein,* to loose], 1. (partial or complete) loss of the power of motion or sensation, especially voluntary motion, in some part or all of the body, as the result of injury to the nervous system or to some muscular mechanism. 2. a condition of helpless inactivity; crippling of activities.

par·a·lyt·ic (par'ə-lit'ik), *adj.* [OFr. *paralytique;* L. *paralyticus;* Gr. *paralytikos*], 1. of, or having the nature of, paralysis. 2. having or subject to paralysis. *n.* a person having paralysis.

par·a·lyze (par'ə-līz'), *v.t.* [PARALYZED (-līzd'), PARALYZING], [Fr. *paralyser*], 1. to cause paralysis in; make paralytic. 2. to bring into a condition of helpless inactivity; make ineffective or powerless. —*SYN.* see **shock.**

par·a·mag·net (par'ə-mag'nit), *n.* any paramagnetic substance or thing.

par·a·mag·net·ic (par'ə-mag-net'ik), *adj.* having a magnetic permeability greater than unity; having a capacity for magnetization greater than that of a vacuum.

par·a·mag·net·ism (par'ə-mag'nə-tiz'm), *n.* the quality or condition of being paramagnetic.

Par·a·mar·i·bo (par'ə-mar'i-bō'), *n.* seaport and capital of Surinam: pop., 61,000 (1944).

par·a·mat·ta (par'ə-mat'ə), *n.* [after *Parramatta,* Australia], a soft, lightweight dress fabric of wool and cotton or, formerly, wool and silk: also spelled **parramatta.**

par·a·me·ci·um (par'ə-mē'shi-əm, par'ə-mē'si-əm), *n.* [*pl.* PARAMECIA (-ə)], [Mod. L.; Gr. *paramēkēs,* oval], any of a number of related one-celled, elongated animals having a large mouth in a fold at the side and moving by means of cilia.

pa·ram·e·ter (pə-ram'ə-tēr), *n.* [Mod. L. *parametrum* < Gr. *para-,* beside + *metron,* a measure], in *mathematics,* a quantity or constant whose value varies with the circumstances of its application, as the radius line of a group of concentric circles, which varies with the circle under consideration.

pa·ra·mo (par'ə-mō'; Sp. pä'rä-mô'), *n.* [*pl.* PARAMOS (-mōz'; Sp. -môs')], [Sp. *páramo;* prob. < the native name], any high, barren plain in the South American tropics.

par·a·mor·phic (par'ə-môr'fik), *adj.* of or by paramorphism.

par·a·mor·phism (par'ə-môr'fiz'm), *n.* [< *para-* (beside, etc.) + Gr. *morphē,* a form; + *-ism*], the process by which some minerals undergo a change in physical character without change of their chemical composition.

par·a·mount (par'ə-mount'), *adj.* [OFr. *paramont; par* (L. *per*), by + *amont, à mont* (< L. *ad montem,* to the hill), uphill], ranking higher than any other, as in power or importance; chief; supreme. *n.* a person having supreme power. —*SYN.* see **dominant.**

par·a·mount·cy (par'ə-mount'si), *n.* the quality or condition of being paramount.

par·a·mour (par'ə-moor'), *n.* [< ME. & OFr. phr. *par amour,* with love; *par* (L. *per*), by + *amour* (L. *amor*), love; orig. in *love par amour,* sexual love as distinct from other kinds of love], 1. a man's mistress or a woman's lover. 2. [Archaic or Poetic], a sweetheart.

Pa·ra·ná (par'ə-nä'; Sp. pä'rä-nä'), *n.* a river in Brazil and Argentina, flowing into the Plata River: it forms the southeastern boundary of Paraguay: length, 2,450 mi.

par·a·neph·ric (par'ə-nef'rik), *adj.* 1. located near the kidney. 2. of a paranephros.

par·a·neph·ros (par'ə-nef'ros), *n.* [Mod. L.; *para-* (beside, etc.) + Gr. *nephros,* kidney], an adrenal gland.

pa·rang (pä-räŋ'), *n.* [Malay], a heavy sheath knife used by the Malays as a tool and weapon.

par·a·noe·a (par'ə-nē'ə), *n.* paranoia.

par·a·noi·a (par'ə-noi'ə), *n.* [Mod. L.; Gr. *paranoia* < *para-,* beside + *nous,* the mind], in *psychiatry,* a mental disorder characterized by systematized delusions, as of grandeur or, especially, persecution.

par·a·noi·ac (par'ə-noi'ak), *n.* a person having paranoia. *adj.* of, like, or having paranoia.

par·a·noid (par'ə-noid'), *adj.* of or like paranoia.

par·a·nymph (par'ə-nimf), *n.* [LL. *paranymphus;* Gr. *paranymphos* < *para-,* beside + *nymphē,* bride], 1. in ancient Greece, *a*) a friend of the bridegroom who escorted him when he went to take his bride home. *b*) a bridesmaid who escorted the bride to the bridegroom. 2. a best man or bridesmaid at a wedding.

par·a·pet (par'ə-pit, par'ə-pet'), *n.* [Fr.; It. *parapetto* < *parare,* to guard + *petto,* breast < L. *pectus*], 1. a wall or bank used to screen troops from frontal enemy fire, sometimes placed along the top of a rampart. 2. a wall or railing to protect people from falling, as on a balcony or bridge.

par·a·pet·ed (par'ə-pit-id, par'ə-pet'id), *adj.* having a parapet or parapets.

par·aph (par'əf), *n.* [ME. *parafe;* OFr. *paraphe;* ML. *paraphus,* contr. < LL. *paragraphus;* see PARAGRAPH], a flourish made after a signature, originally as a safeguard against forgery.

par·a·pher·na·li·a (par'ə-fēr-nā'li-ə, par'ə-fə-nāl'yə), *n.pl.* [ML., short for *paraphernalia bona,* wife's own goods < LL. *parapherna* < Gr. *parapherna,* what a bride has over and above her dower < *para-,* beyond + *phernē,* a dowry, portion < *pherein,* to bear, bring], 1. personal belongings. 2. any collection of articles, usually things used in some activity; equipment; apparatus; trappings; gear. 3. in *law,* formerly, property or possessions (other than dower) given over to the control, but not complete possession, of a wife.

par·a·phrase (par'ə-frāz'), *n.* [Fr.; L. *paraphrasis;* Gr. *paraphrasis* < *paraphrazein,* to say in other words; *para-,* beyond + *phrazein,* to tell], 1. a rewording of the thought or meaning expressed in something that has been said or written before. 2. the use or process of paraphrase as an educational or literary method. *v.t. & v.i.* [PARAPHRASED (-frāzd'), PARAPHRASING], to express in a paraphrase. —*SYN.* see **translation.**

par·a·phrast (par'ə-frast'), *n.* a person who paraphrases.

par·a·phras·tic (par'ə-fras'tik), *adj.* [ML. *paraphrasticus;* Gr. *paraphrastikos*], 1. of, having the nature of, or forming a paraphrase. 2. using paraphrase.

par·a·phras·ti·cal·ly (par'ə-fras'ti-k'l-i, par'ə-fras'tik-li), *adv.* in a paraphrastic manner; so as to paraphrase.

pa·raph·y·sis (pə-raf'ə-sis), *n.* [*pl.* PARAPHYSES (-sēz')], [Mod. L.; *para-* (beside, etc.) + Gr. *physis,* a growth], a sterile, threadlike part found with the spore-bearing organs of some ferns and mosses.

par·a·ple·gi·a (par'ə-plē'ji-ə), *n.* [Mod. L.; Gr. *paraplēgia,* a stroke at one side < *paraplēssein,* to strike at the side; *para-,* beside + *plēssein,* to strike], motor and sensory paralysis of the entire lower half of the body.

par·a·pleg·ic (par'ə-plej'ik, par'ə-plē'jik), *adj.* of or having paraplegia. *n.* a person having paraplegia.

par·a·psy·chol·o·gy (par'ə-sī-kol'ə-ji), *n.* [*para-* (beside, etc.) + *psychology*], the study that investigates the psychological aspect of apparently supernatural phenomena as telepathy, clairvoyance, apparitions, etc.

par·a·quet (par'ə-ket'), *n.* a parakeet.

Pará rubber, crude rubber obtained from several South American trees.

par·a·sang (par'ə-saŋ'), *n.* [L. *parasanga;* Gr. *parasangēs* < OPer.; cf. Per. *farsang*], an ancient Persian measure of length, equal to about 3 1/2 miles.

par·a·se·le·ne (par'ə-si-lē'ni), *n.* [*pl.* PARASELENAE

(-nē)], [Mod. L. < *para-* (beside, etc.) + Gr. *selēnē*, the moon], a bright moonlike spot on a lunar halo.

par·a·shah (pär′ə-shä′, pär′shô), *n.* [*pl.* PARASHOTH (-shōth′)], [Heb. *pārāshāh*], a lesson read from the five books of the Mosaic law, or Pentateuch, as part of the Jewish synagogue service on the Sabbath and holidays.

par·a·site (par′ə-sīt′), *n.* [Fr.; L. *parasitus;* Gr. *parasitos*, one who eats beside or at the table of another, parasite, toady; *para-*, beside + *sitos*, food], 1. in ancient Greece, *a)* a person who flattered and amused his host in return for free meals. *b)* a priest's helper who feasted with the priests after sacrificial rites. 2. a person who lives at the expense of another or others without making any useful contribution or return; hanger-on. 3. in *biology*, a plant or animal that lives on or within another organism, from which it derives sustenance or protection without making compensation.

SYN.—**parasite** refers to one who derives advantage or sustenance from another and gives nothing in return; a **sycophant** is one who seeks advantage or favor from the wealthy or powerful by flattery, fawning, etc.; **toady** suggests the servility and snobbery of one who seeks familiarity with those whom he regards as his superiors; **hanger-on** is applied to anyone regarded contemptuously for his close adherence to and dependence on another; **leech** is applied to a parasite who clings closely to another and extracts whatever he can for his own advantage; **sponge** is a colloquial term for a parasite and stresses his total dependence, disinclination to work, etc.

par·a·sit·ic (par′ə-sit′ik), *adj.* [L. *parasiticus;* Gr. *parasitikos*], 1. of or like a parasite; living at the expense of others. 2. caused by parasites, as a disease.

par·a·sit·i·cal (par′ə-sit′i-k'l), *adj.* parasitic.

par·a·sit·i·cal·ly (par′ə-sit′i-k'l-i, par′ə-sit′ik-li), *adv.* in the manner of a parasite.

par·a·sit·i·cide (par′ə-sit′ə-sīd′), *adj.* [< *parasite* + *-cide*], that destroys parasites. *n.* anything used to destroy parasites.

par·a·sit·ism (par′ə-sīt-iz'm), *n.* 1. the state or condition of being a parasite. 2. the habits of a parasite. 3. in *medicine*, *a)* the condition of being infested with parasites. *b)* any of various diseases, as of the skin, caused by parasites.

par·a·sol (par′ə-sôl′, par′ə-sol′), *n.* [Fr.; It. *parasole* < *parare*, to ward off + *sole* (L. *sol*), the sun], a light umbrella carried by women as a sunshade.

pa·ras·ti·chy (pə-ras′tə-ki), *n.* [*pl.* PARASTICHIES (-kiz)], [< *para-* (beside, etc.) + Gr. *stichos*, a row], a secondary spiral in leaf or scale arrangement on an axis, stem, etc., as on a pine cone.

par·a·sym·pa·thet·ic (par′ə-sim′pə-thet′ik), *adj.* [*para-* (beside, etc.) + *sympathetic*], in *anatomy & physiology*, designating or of that part of the autonomic nervous system whose nerves originate in the midbrain, the hindbrain, and the sacral region of the spinal cord and whose functions include the constriction of the pupils of the eyes, the slowing of the heartbeat, and the stimulation of certain digestive glands: cf. **sympathetic**.

par·a·syn·ap·sis (par′ə-si-nap′sis), *n.* [Mod. L.; *para-* (beside, etc.) + *synapsis*], the conjunction of chromosomes side by side.

par·a·syn·the·sis (par′ə-sin′thə-sis), *n.* [Mod. L.; Gr. *parasynthesis;* see PARA- (beside, etc.) & SYNTHESIS], in *linguistics*, the process of forming words by both derivation and composition (e.g., *big-hearted* < *big heart* + *-ed*, not < *big* + *hearted*).

par·a·syn·thet·ic (par′ə-sin-thet′ik), *adj.* of or formed by parasynthesis.

par·a·tac·tic (par′ə-tak′tik), *adj.* of or constituting parataxis.

par·a·tac·ti·cal (par′ə-tak′ti-k'l), *adj.* paratactic.

par·a·tax·is (par′ə-tak′sis), *n.* [Mod. L.; Gr. *parataxis*, a placing beside < *para-*, beside + *tassein*, to place], the placing of related clauses, etc. in a series without the use of connecting words (e.g., "I came, I saw, I conquered."): opposed to *hypotaxis*.

par·a·thy·roid (par′ə-thī′roid), *adj.* [*para-* (beside, etc.) + *thyroid*], 1. situated alongside or near the thyroid gland. 2. designating or of any of four small, oval glands located on or embedded in the thyroid gland: they secrete a hormone that increases the calcium content of the blood. *n.* a parathyroid gland.

par·a·troop·er (par′ə-trōōp′ẽr), *n.* a soldier in the paratroops.

par·a·troops (par′ə-trōōps′), *n.pl.* a unit of infantry soldiers trained and equipped to land behind enemy lines from airplanes by means of parachutes.

par·a·ty·phoid (par′ə-tī′foid), *adj.* [*para-* + *typhoid*], designating, of, or causing an infectious disease closely resembling typhoid fever but usually milder and caused by a different bacillus. *n.* paratyphoid fever.

par·a·vane (par′ə-vān′), *n.* [*para-* (beside, etc.) + *vane*], 1. one of a pair of large, torpedo-shaped devices towed under water on either side of a ship and equipped with sharp teeth for cutting the moorings of submerged mines, allowing them to float and be destroyed. 2. a similar device loaded with explosives for attacking submerged submarines.

‡**par a·vi·on** (pȧr′ ȧ′vyōn′), [Fr., lit., by airplane], by air mail.

par·boil (pär′boil′), *v.t.* [ME. *parboilen;* OFr. *parboullir; par* (L. *per*), through, thoroughly + *boullir* (L. *bullire*), to boil: Mod. Eng. meaning influenced by association of *par-* with *part*], 1. to boil until partly cooked: usually in preparation for roasting, etc. 2. to make uncomfortably hot; overheat.

par·buck·le (pär′buk″'l), *n.* [Early Mod. Eng. *parbunkel*, altered after *buckle*], 1. a sling for a log, barrel, etc., made by passing a doubled rope around the object and pulling the rope ends through the loop. 2. a device consisting of a doubled rope, the middle of which is attached at a given height and the ends passed around either side of a cylindrical object which may then be raised or lowered by hauling in or paying out the rope ends. *v.t.* [PARBUCKLED (-'ld), PARBUCKLING], to raise or lower by using a parbuckle.

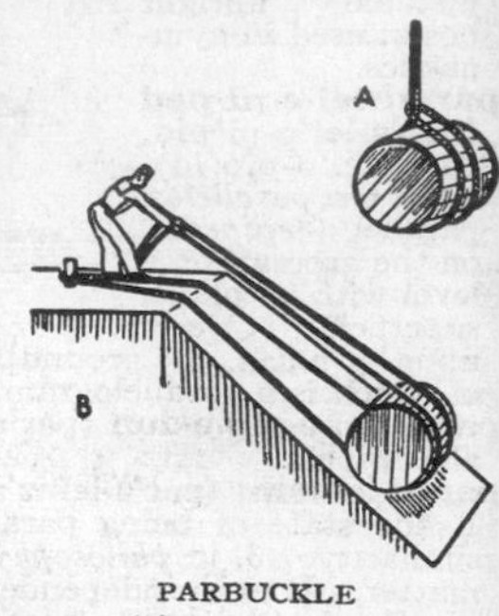

PARBUCKLE
A, for lifting; B, for rolling

Par·cae (pär′sē), *n.pl.* [ME.; L., pl. of *Parca*, one of the Fates < *parere*, to produce], in *Roman mythology*, the three Fates.

par·cel (pär′s'l), *n.* [ME. & OFr. *parcelle;* LL. *particella* for L. *particula;* see PARTICLE], 1. a small, wrapped bundle; package. 2. a quantity or a collection of items put up for sale: as, a *parcel* of books. 3. a group or collection; pack; bunch: as, a *parcel* of fools. 4. a piece, as of land, usually a specific part of a large acreage or estate. 5. a portion or part; especially, an inseparable or essential part: now only in *part and parcel*. *v.t.* [PARCELED or PARCELLED (-s'ld), PARCELING or PARCELLING], 1. to separate into parts and distribute; apportion (with *out*). 2. to make up in or as a parcel. 3. in *nautical usage*, to wrap in canvas strips. *adj. & adv.* part; partly. —***SYN.*** see **bundle**.

par·cel·ing, par·cel·ling (pär′s'l-iŋ), *n.* 1. a separating into parts and distributing. 2. in *nautical usage*, canvas strips, usually covered with tar, wrapped around a rope to protect it.

parcel post, that branch of the post office which carries and delivers parcels: abbreviated **P.P., p.p.**

par·ce·nar·y (pär′sə-ner′i), *n.* [Anglo-Fr. *parcenerie;* OFr. *parçonerie* < *parçonier;* see PARCENER], inheritance by two or more persons; partnership in inheritance.

par·ce·ner (pär′sə-nẽr), *n.* [ME.; Anglo-Fr. *parcenier;* OFr. *parçonnier;* ML. *partionarius*, contr. of *partitionarius* < L. *partitio;* see PARTITION], one of two or more persons sharing an inheritance; joint heir.

parch (pärch), *v.t.* [ME. *perchen, parchen*, contr. of *perischen* (see PERISH)], 1. to expose to great heat so as to dry or roast slightly, as corn, peas, etc. 2. to dry up with heat; make hot and dry; hence, 3. to make very thirsty. 4. to dry up and shrivel with cold. *v.i.* to become very dry and, usually, hot.

par·chee·si, par·che·si, par·chi·si (pär-chē′zi), *n.* pachisi.

parch·ment (pärch′mənt), *n.* [ME. *perchemin;* OFr. *parchemin;* ML. **particaminum* (altered through association with OFr. *parche*, parchment < LL. *parthica pellis*, lit., Parthian leather) < LL. (*charta*) *Pergamenum*, (paper) of Pergamum (now Bergama), city in Asia Minor, where it was used as a substitute for papyrus], 1. the skin of an animal, usually a sheep or goat, prepared as a surface for writing or painting. 2. a sheet of parchment used in this way; document or manuscript on parchment. 3. an imitation of this material used for lampshades, etc. 4. a fine paper having a texture resembling parchment.

pard (pärd), *n.* [ME. *parde;* OFr.; L. *pardus;* Gr. *pardos*], [Archaic or Poetic], a leopard, or panther.

pard (pärd), *n.* [contr. of *pardner*, altered < *partner*], [Slang], a partner; companion.

par·die, par·di (pär-dē′), *adv. & interj.* [ME. *parde;* OFr. *par dé* (Fr. *pardieu*), by God!], [Archaic], verily; indeed: also spelled **pardy**.

par·don (pär′d'n), *v.t.* [OFr. *perdoner, pardoner;* LL. *perdonare;* L. *per-*, through, quite + *donare*, to give], 1. to release (a person) from punishment; not punish for crimes or offenses. 2. to cancel or not exact penalty for (an offense); forgive. 3. *a)* to excuse or forgive (a person) for some minor fault, discourtesy, etc. *b)* to overlook (a discourtesy, etc.). *n.* 1. a pardoning or being pardoned; forgiveness. 2. an official document granting a legal or ecclesiastical pardon. 3. in the *Roman Catholic Church*, a release from temporal or purgatorial punishment; indulgence. —***SYN.*** see **absolve**.

par·don·a·ble (pär′d'n-ə-b'l), *adj.* [Fr. *pardonnable*], that can be pardoned, overlooked, or forgiven.

par·don·a·bly (pär′d'n-ə-bli), *adv.* in a pardonable manner; so as to be pardonable.

par·don·er (pär′d'n-ẽr), *n.* [ME. *pardonere;* OFr. *par* donaire], 1. historically, a person authorized by the Roman Catholic Church to grant or sell ecclesiastical pardons, or indulgences. 2. a person who pardons.

par·dy (pär-dē′), *adv. & interj.* pardie.

pare (pâr), *v.t.* [PARED (pârd), PARING], [ME. *pairen;* Late OFr. *parer*, to prepare, trim, pare; L. *parare*, to prepare], 1. to cut or trim away the rind, skin, covering, rough surface, etc. of; shave; peel. 2. to cut or trim away (rind, skin, covering, rough surface, etc.) of anything. 3. to reduce gradually; make less, as savings.

Pa·ré, Am·broise (än′brwȧz′ pȧ′rā′), 1517?–1590; French surgeon.

pa·re·cious (pə-rē′shəs), *adj.* paroecious.

par·e·gor·ic (par′ə-gôr′ik, par′ə-gor′ik), *adj.* [LL. *paregoricus;* Gr. *parēgorikos* < *parēgoros*, exhorting, mitigating < *para-*, beside + *agora*, assembly], soothing or lessening pain. *n.* a medicine that soothes or lessens pain; specifically, a camphorated tincture of opium, used in cough mixtures and to relieve diarrhea.

pa·rei·ra bra·va (pə-râr′ə brä′və, brā′və), [Port. *parreira brava*, wild vine; *parreira*, vine + *brava*, wild], the root of a South American plant, used as a diuretic and tonic: also **pareira.**

paren., parenthesis.

pa·ren·chy·ma (pə-reŋ′ki-mə), *n.* [Mod. L.; Gr. *parenchyma*, anything poured in beside < *para-*, beside + *enchyma*, infusion < *enchein*, to pour in; *en-*, in + *chein*, to pour], 1. in *anatomy*, the essential or functional tissue of an organ, as distinguished from its connective tissue, etc. 2. in *botany*, a soft tissue of roundish, thin-walled cells in a plant stem or the pulp of fruits. 3. in *zoology*, the endoplasm of a protozoan.

par·en·chym·a·tous (par′eŋ-kim′ə-təs), *adj.* of, or having the nature of, parenchyma.

par·ent (pâr′ənt), *n.* [ME.; OFr.; L. *parens*, parent (orig. ppr. of *parere*, to beget)], 1. a father or mother. 2. any animal, organism, or plant in relation to another which it has produced. 3. any cause or source.

par·ent·age (pâr′ənt-ij), *n.* [see -AGE], 1. descent or derivation from parents or ancestors; family; birth; origin. 2. parenthood.

pa·ren·tal (pə-ren′t'l), *adj.* [L. *parentalis*], 1. of or characteristic of a parent or parents. 2. constituting the source or origin of something. 3. in *biology*, of or designating the generation in which fertilization produces hybrids: symbol, P (no period).

par·en·ter·al (par-en′tēr-əl), *adj.* [< *par-* + Gr. *enteron*, intestine; + *-al*], not intestinal; by some way other than through the digestive tract, as intravenous or intramuscular.

pa·ren·the·sis (pə-ren′thə-sis), *n.* [*pl.* PARENTHESES (-sēz′)], [ML.; Gr. *parenthesis* < *parentithenai*, to put beside < *para-*, beside + *entithenai*, to insert], 1. an additional word, clause, etc. placed as an explanation or comment within an already complete sentence: in writing or printing it is usually marked off by curved lines, dashes, or commas. 2. *usually in pl.* either or both of the curved lines ( ) used to mark off parenthetic words, etc. or to enclose mathematical quantities that are to be treated as a single quantity. 3. an episode or incident, often an irrelevant one; interlude. Abbreviated **par., paren.**

pa·ren·the·size (pə-ren′thə-sīz′), *v.t.* [PARENTHESIZED (-sīzd′), PARENTHESIZING], 1. *a)* to insert (a word, phrase, etc.) as a parenthesis. *b)* to put into parentheses (sense 2). 2. to place a parenthesis within: as, he *parenthesized* the rule with his own comment.

par·en·thet·ic (par′ən-thet′ik), *adj.* parenthetical.

par·en·thet·i·cal (par′ən-thet′i-k'l), *adj.* [ML. *parentheticus*], 1. *a)* of, or having the nature of, a parenthesis. *b)* marked off or placed within parentheses; hence, 2. giving qualifying information or explanation. 3. using or containing parentheses.

par·en·thet·i·cal·ly (par′ən-thet′i-k'l-i, par′ən-thet′ik-li), *adv.* in a parenthetical manner; as a parenthesis.

par·ent·hood (pâr′ənt-hood′), *n.* [see -HOOD], the fact or state of being a parent; relation or authority of a parent.

pa·re·sis (pə-rē′sis, par′ə-sis), *n.* [Mod. L.; Gr. *paresis* < *parienai*, to relax], 1. partial paralysis. 2. a disease of the brain caused by syphilis of the central nervous system and characterized by inflammation of the meninges, mental and emotional instability, paralytic attacks, etc.: usually **general paresis**: also called *general paralysis*: abbreviated **G.P., g.p.**

par·es·the·si·a (par′es-thē′zhə, par′es-thē′zhi-ə), *n.* [Mod. L. < Gr. *para-*, beside + *aisthēsis*, sensation], in *medicine*, abnormal sensation, as of burning, prickling, etc. on the skin: also spelled **paraesthesia.**

par·es·thet·ic (par′es-thet′ik), *adj.* of or having paresthesia.

pa·ret·ic (pə-ret′ik, pə-rē′tik), *adj.* of, resulting from, or having paresis. *n.* a person having paresis.

Pa·re·to, Vil·fre·do (vēl-frā′dô pä-rā′tô), 1848–1923; Italian economist and sociologist in Switzerland.

par ex·cel·lence (pär ek′sə-läns′; Fr. pȧr′ ek′se′läns′), [Fr., lit., by way of excellence], in the greatest degree of excellence; beyond comparison; pre-eminently.

‡**par ex·em·ple** (pȧr′ eg′zän′pl′), [Fr.], 1. for example; for instance. 2. really! well!: exclamation of surprise.

par·fait (pär-fā′), *n.* [Fr., perfect], 1. a dessert made of rich cream, eggs, sirup, etc. frozen together and served in a tall, narrow glass. 2. a dessert of ice cream with crushed fruit or sirup, served in a similar glass.

par·fleche (pär′flesh, pär-flesh′), *n.* [Canad. Fr.], 1. a rawhide with the hair removed by soaking it in water and lye. 2. something made of this, as a case or shield.

par·get (pär′jit), *v.t.* [PARGETED or PARGETTED (-id), PARGETING or PARGETTING], [ME. *pargeten;* OFr. *pargeter, parjeter; par*, all over + *jeter*, to throw], to put plaster on, especially in a decorative way. *n.* 1. plaster or any similar wall coating. 2. ornamental plasterwork on walls or ceilings. 3. a kind of plaster used for lining chimneys.

par·get·ing, par·get·ting (pär′jit-iŋ), *n.* [ME.], 1. ornamental plasterwork on walls or ceilings. 2. plasterwork on the inside of chimneys.

par·he·li·a·cal (pär′hi-lī′ə-k'l), *adj.* parhelic.

par·he·lic (pär-hē′lik, pär-hel′ik), *adj.* of or like a parhelion or parhelia.

parhelic circle, a bright circular band or halo that appears to intersect the sun in a plane parallel to the horizon: also **parhelic ring.**

par·he·li·on (pär-hē′li-ən, pär-hēl′yən), *n.* [*pl.* PARHELIA (-ə, -yə)], [L. *parelion;* Gr. *parēlion* < *para-*, beside + *hēlios*, the sun], a bright spot of light sometimes seen on the ring of a solar halo; mock sun; sun dog.

par·i- (par′i), [< L. *par, paris*], a combining form used in botany and zoology to mean *equal*, as in *paripinnate.*

pa·ri·ah (pə-rī′ə, par′i-ə, pä′ri-ə), *n.* [Tamil *paraiyan*, drummer < *parai*, a drum: the pariah was a hereditary drumbeater], 1. a member of one of the oppressed social castes in the former caste system of India. 2. any outcast; someone despised or rejected by others.

Par·i·an (pâr′i-ən), *adj.* 1. of Paros. 2. *a)* designating a fine, white marble found in Paros. *b)* like this marble. *n.* 1. a native or inhabitant of Paros. 2. a fine, white porcelain that resembles Parian marble.

Pa·ri·cu·tín (pä-rē-ko͞o-tēn′), *n.* a volcanic mountain in west central Mexico: height, 8,200 ft.: the youngest mountain on earth, it first erupted on Feb. 20, 1943.

pa·ri·es (pâr′i-ēz′), *n.* [*pl.* PARIETES (pə-rī′ə-tēz′)], [L., a wall], *usually in pl.* in *biology*, a wall, as of a hollow organ, cavity, cell, etc.

pa·ri·e·tal (pə-rī′ə-t'l), *adj.* [Fr. *pariétal;* LL. *parietalis* < *paries, parietis*, a wall], 1. [Rare], living within, or having to do with life within, a college. 2. in *anatomy*, of the parietes, or walls, of a hollow organ, cavity, cell, etc.; especially, designating either of the two bones between the frontal and occipital bones, forming part of the top and sides of the skull: see **skull**, illus. 3. in *botany*, attached to the wall of the ovary, as the placenta in some plants.

parietal lobe, the part of each hemisphere of the brain between the frontal and the occipital lobes.

pa·ri·e·to- (pə-rī′ə-tō, pə-rī′ə-tə), a combining form meaning *parietal and*, as in *parietomastoid.*

par·i-mu·tu·el (par′i-mū′cho͞o-əl), *n.* [Fr., lit., mutual stakes or bets], 1. a system of betting on races in which those backing the winners divide, in proportion to their wagers, the total amount bet, after a percentage has been taken by the agency conducting the betting. 2. a machine used in registering such bets.

par·ing (pâr′iŋ), *n.* 1. a cutting away or trimming off of a rind, skin, covering, rough surface, etc. 2. a thin piece or strip pared off, as of the skin of a potato.

‡**pa·ri pas·su** (par′i pas′ū, pâr′i pas′o͞o), [L.], 1. with equal pace; with equal speed. 2. in equal proportion. 3. at the same time.

par·i·pin·nate (par′ə-pin′āt), *adj.* [*pari-* + *pinnate*], in *botany*, having an equal number of leaves on either side of the stem.

Par·is (par′is), *n.* [L.; Gr. *Paris*], in *Greek legend*, a son of Priam, king of Troy: his kidnaping of Helen, wife of Menelaus, caused the Trojan War.

Par·is (par′is; Fr. pȧ′rē′), *n.* capital of France, on the Seine: pop., 2,725,000 (1946): ancient name, *Lutetia.*

Paris, Matthew, see **Matthew Paris.**

Paris Commune, see **commune.**

Paris green, [after *Paris*, France, where once manufactured], a poisonous, bright-green powder made from arsenic trioxide and cupric acetate and used as an insecticide and pigment.

par·ish (par′ish), *n.* [ME. *parissche, parosche;* OFr. *parosse, parroche, paroiche;* LL. *parochia*, for *paroecia;* Gr. *paroikia*, neighborhood, diocese < *para-*, beside + *oikos*, dwelling], 1. originally, a British church district with its own church, under the charge of one clergyman; hence, 2. a district of British local civil government, often identical with the original church parish. 3. *a)* an administrative district of various churches, especially a part of a diocese, under the charge of a priest or minister. *b*) the members of the congregation of any church, without regard to the territory in which they live; congregation. *c*) the territory in which the members of a congregation live. 4. a civil division in Louisiana, corresponding to a county. 5. the people of a parish (senses 1, 2, 3*a*, 4). Abbreviated **par.**

pa·rish·ion·er (pə-rish′ən-ẽr), *n.* [ME. *parishion* < OFr. *paroissien* < *paroiche;* + *-er*], a member of a parish.

parish register, a book for recording every baptism, marriage, and death of the members of a parish.

Pa·ri·sian (pə-rizh′ən), *adj.* of or like Paris, its people, or culture. *n.* a native or inhabitant of Paris.

par·i·ty (par′ə-ti), *n.* [Fr. *parité;* L. *paritas* < *par,* equal], 1. the state or condition of being the same in power, value, rank, etc.; equality. 2. resemblance; similarity. 3. the equivalent in value of a sum of money expressed in terms of another country's currency. 4. equality of value at a given ratio between different kinds of money, commodities, etc.

par·i·ty (par′ə-ti), *n.* [< L. *parere,* to bear; + *-ity*], in *medicine,* the state or fact of having borne offspring.

park (pärk), *n.* [ME. & OFr. *parc;* ML. *parricus* < a Gmc. equivalent of AS. *pearroc* (dial. *parrock*); cf. PADDOCK], 1. in *English law,* an enclosed area of land, held by authority of the king or by prescription, stocked and preserved for hunting; hence, 2. an area of land containing pasture, woods, lakes, etc., surrounding a large country house or private estate. 3. an area of public land; specifically, *a*) an area in or near a city, usually laid out with walks, drives, playgrounds, etc., for public recreation. *b*) an open square in a city, with benches, trees, etc. *c*) a large area known for its natural scenery and preserved for public recreation by a state or national government. 4. a stadium or other enclosed area for baseball games: in full, **(base)ball park.** 5. a level, open area surrounded by mountains or forest. 6. a space set aside for leaving vehicles temporarily. 7. in *military usage, a*) an area set aside for vehicles, supplies, and other equipment. *b*) things kept in such an area: as, a *park* of tanks. Abbreviated **pk.** *v.t.* 1. to enclose in or as in a park. 2. to place or arrange (military equipment) in a park. 3. to leave (a vehicle) in a certain place temporarily. 4. to maneuver (a vehicle) into a space where it can be left temporarily; hence, 5. [Slang], to put or leave in a particular place; deposit. *v.i.* to park a vehicle.

Park, Mun·go (muŋ′gō pärk), 1771–1806; Scottish explorer in Africa.

par·ka (pär′kə), *n.* [Aleutian], a fur jacket or heavy, long, woolen shirt, often lined with pile or fleece, with an attached hood for protecting the head from the cold.

Park Avenue, a wealthy residential street in New York City: a symbol of high society, fashion, etc.

Par·ker, Sir **Gilbert** (pär′kẽr), (*Horatio Gilbert Parker*), 1862–1932; Canadian novelist.

Parker, Theodore, 1810–1860; American clergyman and antislavery reformer.

Par·kers·burg (pär′kẽrz-bũrg′), *n.* a city in West Virginia, on the Ohio River: pop., 45,000.

parking meter, a coin-operated timing device installed near a parking space for indicating the length of time that a parked vehicle has occupied that space.

parking ticket, a police summons given for violating regulations concerning the parking of vehicles.

Par·kin·son's disease (pär′kin-s′nz), [after James *Parkinson* (1755–1824), English physician who first described it], shaking palsy.

Park·man, Francis (pärk′mən), 1823–1893; American historian.

Park Range, a mountain range of the Rocky Mountain system, in northern Colorado.

park·way (pärk′wā′), *n.* a broad roadway bordered or divided with plantings of trees, bushes, and grass.

Parl., 1. Parliament. 2. Parliamentary.

parl·ance (pär′ləns), *n.* [OFr. < *parler,* to speak], 1. conversation; speech; especially, parley or debate. 2. a style or manner of speaking or writing; language; idiom; phraseology: as, military or newspaper *parlance.*

par·lay (pär′li, pär-lā′), *v.t.* & *v.i.* [Fr. & It. *paroli* < *paro,* an equal], 1. to bet (an original wager plus its winnings) on another race, contest, etc. 2. to exploit (an asset) successfully: as, he *parlayed* his voice into fame. *n.* a bet or series of bets made by parlaying.

par·ley (pär′li), *v.i.* [< Fr. *parlée,* pp., or *parlez,* imperative, of *parler,* to speak; LL. *parabolare,* to speak < L. *parabola;* see PARABLE], to have a conference or discussion, especially with an enemy; confer. *n.* [*pl.* PARLEYS (-liz)], a talk or conference for the purpose of discussing a specific matter or of settling a dispute, as a military conference with an enemy, under a temporary truce, for discussing terms.

par·lia·ment (pär′lə-mənt), *n.* [ME. & OFr. *parlement* < *parler,* to speak], 1. an official or formal conference or council, usually concerned with government or public affairs. 2. [P-], the national legislative body of Great Britain: it is composed of the House of Commons (elected) and the House of Lords (mostly hereditary). 3. [P-], any of several similar bodies in countries of the British Empire and in other countries. 4. any of several high courts of justice in France before 1789.

par·lia·men·tar·i·an (pär′lə-men-târ′i-ən), *n.* 1. [P-], a supporter of the Long Parliament in opposition to Charles I of England; Roundhead. 2. a person skilled in parliamentary rules, practice, or debate.

par·lia·men·ta·ry (par′lə-men′tə-ri), *adj.* 1. of or like a parliament. 2. decreed or established by a parliament. 3. conforming to the customs and rules of a parliament or other public assembly. 4. having or governed by a parliament. Abbreviated **Parl.**

par·lor (pär′lẽr), *n.* [ME. *parlour;* OFr. *parleor;* ML. *parlatorium* < *parlare,* to speak], 1. *a*) originally, a room set aside for the entertainment of guests; formal sitting room. *b*) now, any living room. 2. a small, semiprivate sitting room separate from the main lounges in a hotel, inn, etc. 3. *a*) originally, a business establishment elegantly furnished to resemble a private sitting room: as, an ice-cream *parlor. b*) now, a shop or business establishment, often with some special equipment or furnishings for personal services: as, a beauty *parlor.* British spelling, **parlour.**

parlor car, a railroad car for daytime travel, having comfortable individual chairs.

par·lor·maid (pär′lẽr-mād′), *n.* a maid who serves at table, answers the door, etc.

par·lous (pär′ləs), *adj.* [ME. *perlous, parlous;* contr. of *perilous*], [Chiefly Archaic], 1. perilous; dangerous; risky. 2. dangerously clever; cunning, mischievous, shrewd, etc. *adv.* [Chiefly Archaic], extremely; very.

Par·ma (pär′mä, pär′mə), *n.* 1. a city in northern Italy: pop., 124,000. 2. a former duchy of Italy. 3. (pär′mə), a city in northeastern Ohio: suburb of Cleveland: pop., 83,000.

Par·men·i·des (pär-men′ə-dēz′), *n.* Greek Eleatic philosopher; fl. 5th century B.C.

Par·me·san (pär′mə-zan′), *adj.* [Fr. *parmesan;* It. *parmegiano* < *Parma,* city in Italy], of or from Parma, Italy. *n.* Parmesan cheese.

Parmesan cheese, a dry, hard, yellow Italian cheese made from skim milk and usually grated for use as a flavoring, as with spaghetti.

Par·na·hy·ba, Par·na·hi·ba (pär′nä-ē′bə), *n.* a river in northeastern Brazil, flowing into the Atlantic: length, 850 mi.

Par·nas·si·an (pär-nas′i-ən), *adj.* [L. *Parnasius, Parnassius* < *Parnasus, Parnassus;* Gr. *Parnasos*], 1. of Mount Parnassus or the Parnassians. 2. of the art of poetry. *n.* [Fr. *parnassien*], a member of a school of late 19th-century French poets: their first collection (1866) was titled *Le Parnasse contemporain.*

Par·nas·sus (pär-nas′əs), *n.* [L.; Gr. *Parnasos,* later *Parnassos*], 1. a mountain in southern Greece: height, 8,070 ft.: in ancient times it was sacred to Apollo and the Muses; hence, 2. *a*) poetry or poets collectively. *b*) any center of poetic or artistic activity. 3. formerly, a common title for collections of poetry.

Par·nell, Charles Stewart (pär′n'l, pär-nel′), 1846–1891; Irish statesman and nationalist leader.

pa·ro·chi·al (pə-rō′ki-əl), *adj.* [ME. *perochiele;* OFr.; ML. *parochialis* < *parochia;* see PARISH], 1. of or in a parish or parishes. 2. restricted to a small area or scope; narrow; limited; provincial.

pa·ro·chi·al·ism (pə-rō′ki-əl-iz′m), *n.* the quality or condition of being parochial; narrowness of thought, interest, or activity; provincialism.

parochial school, a school supported and controlled by a church.

par·o·dist (par′ə-dist), *n.* a writer of parodies.

par·o·dy (par′ə-di), *n.* [*pl.* PARODIES (-diz)], [Fr. *parodie;* L. *parodia;* Gr. *parōidia,* counter song < *para-,* beside + *ōidē,* song], 1. literary or musical composition imitating the characteristic style of some other work or of a writer or composer, but treating a serious subject in a nonsensical manner, as in ridicule. 2. a poor or weak imitation. *v.t.* [PARODIED (-did), PARODYING], to make a parody of. —*SYN.* see **caricature.**

pa·roe·cious (pə-rē′shəs), *adj.* [< *para-* (beside, etc.) + Gr. *oikia,* a house; + *-ous*], in *botany,* having the male and female organs in the same flower cluster: also **parecious, paroicous.**

pa·roi·cous (pə-roi′kəs), *adj.* paroecious.

pa·role (pə-rōl′), *n.* [Fr., a word; It. *parola;* LL. *parabola,* a parable, speech, word], 1. word of honor; promise; especially, the promise of a military prisoner that, if released from captivity or given certain privileges, he will meet requirements made by his captors: usually a promise to take no further part in the fighting. 2. the condition of being on parole. 3. a release from prison, given to a prisoner before his sentence has expired, on condition of future good behavior: the sentence is not set aside and he remains under the supervision of a parole board. 4. the conditional freedom granted by such release, or the period of such freedom. 5. in *military usage,* a special password used as a check on the countersign for more complete identification. *v.t.* [PAROLED (-rōld′), PAROLING], to release on parole. **on parole,** at liberty under conditions of parole.

pa·rol·ee (pə-rō′lē′), *n.* [< *parole* + *-ee*], a person who has been released from prison on parole.

par·o·no·ma·si·a (par′ə-nō-mā′zhə, par′ə-nō-mā′zhi-ə), *n.* [L.; Gr. *paranomasia; para-*, beside + *onomasia*, naming < *onomazein*, to name < *onoma*, a name], 1. a pun. 2. the act or practice of punning.

par·o·no·mas·tic (par′ə-nō-mas′tik), *adj.* of or by paronomasia.

par·o·nym (par′ə-nim), *n.* [< Gr. *para-*, beside + *onoma*, a name], a paronymous word.

pa·ron·y·mous (pə-ron′ə-məs), *adj.* [Gr. *parōnymos* < *para-*, beside + *onyma*, a name; + *-ous*], 1. derived from the same root; cognate: said of words (e.g., *differ* and *defer*). 2. differing in spelling, origin, and meaning, but pronounced alike (e.g., *pair, pare,* and *pear*).

par·o·quet (par′ə-ket′), *n.* a parakeet.

Par·os (pâr′os; Gr. pä′rôs), *n.* an island of Greece in the Aegean Sea, known for its fine, white marble: area, 80 sq. mi.; pop., 7,700.

pa·rot·ic (pə-rot′ik, pə-rō′tik), *adj.* [Mod. L. *paroticus* < Gr. *para-*, beside + *ous, ōtos*, ear], situated near the ear.

pa·rot·id (pə-rot′id), *adj.* [< Fr. or L.; Fr. *parotide;* L. *parotis;* Gr. *parōtis*, a tumor near the ear < *para-*, beside + *ous, ōtos*, ear], situated near or beside the ear; especially, designating or of either of the salivary glands situated below and in front of each ear. *n.* a parotid gland.

par·o·tit·ic (par′ə-tit′ik), *adj.* of or having parotitis, or the mumps.

par·o·ti·tis (par′ə-tī′tis), *n.* [see -ITIS], inflammation of the parotid gland; especially, the mumps.

pa·ro·toid (pə-rō′toid), *adj.* [*paro*tid + *oid*], in *zoology*, designating or of skin glands forming warty growths near the ear in some frogs, toads, and related animals. *n.* a parotoid gland.

-par·ous (pẽr′əs), [L. *-parus* < *parere*, to bring forth, bear], a combining form meaning *bringing forth, producing, bearing,* as in *viviparous.*

par·ox·ysm (par′ək-siz′m), *n.* [Fr. *paroxysme;* ML. *paroxysmus;* Gr. *paroxysmos* < *paroxynein*, to excite, sharpen < *para-*, beyond, in excess + *oxynein*, to sharpen < *oxys*, sharp], 1. a sudden attack, or intensification of the symptoms, of a disease, usually recurring periodically. 2. a sudden convulsion or outburst, as of laughter, rage, sneezing, etc.; fit; spasm.

par·ox·ys·mal (par′ək-siz′m′l), *adj.* of, like, having, or characterized by a paroxysm or paroxysms.

par·ox·y·tone (par-ok′sə-tōn′), *n.* [Mod.L. *paroxytonus;* Gr. *paroxytonos; para-*, beside + *oxytonos*, having the acute accent < *oxys*, sharp + *tonos*, a tone, sound], in *Greek grammar*, a word having an acute accent on the next to the last syllable. *adj.* accented in this way.

par·quet (pär-kā′, pär-ket′), *n.* [Fr., dim. of *parc*, a park], 1. the main floor of a theater, especially that part from the orchestra to the parquet circle: usually called *orchestra.* 2. a flooring of parquetry. *v.t.* [PARQUETED (-kād′, -ket′id), PARQUETING], 1. to use parquetry to make (a floor, etc.). 2. to decorate the floor of (a room) with parquetry.

parquet circle, the part of a theater beneath the balcony and behind the parquet on the main floor: also called *orchestra circle.*

par·quet·ry (pär′kit-ri), *n.* [Fr. *parqueterie;* see PARQUET], inlaid woodwork in geometric forms, usually in different colors: used especially in flooring.

parr (pär), *n.* [*pl.* PARRS (pärz), PARR; see PLURAL, II, D, 1], [? a Scot. dial. word], 1. a young salmon before it enters salt water. 2. the young of certain other fish.

Parr, Catherine (pär), 1512–1548; sixth wife of Henry VIII.

par·ra·keet (par′ə-kēt′), *n.* a parakeet.

par·ra·mat·ta (par′ə-mat′ə), *n.* paramatta.

Par·ran, Thomas (par′ən), 1892– ; American physician; surgeon general of the United States Public Health Service (1936–1948).

par·rel, par·ral (par′əl), *n.* [ME. *perell;* var. of *parail* < *aparail*, equipment; cf. OFr. *parail* in the same sense], in *nautical usage*, a loop of rope, chain, etc. or a metal collar used to fasten a yard to a mast.

par·ri·cid·al (par′ə-sīd′'l), *adj.* [L. *parricidalis*], of or guilty of parricide.

par·ri·cide (par′ə-sīd′), *n.* [Fr.; L. *parricida* < *parri-* (? < *pater*), father + *caedere*, to kill; cf. PATRICIDE], 1. a person who murders either or both of his parents or someone else who stands to him in a somewhat similar relationship. 2. the act of a parricide.

Par·ring·ton, Vernon Louis (par′iŋ-tən), 1871–1929; American educator and literary critic.

Par·rish, Max·field (maks′fēld par′ish), 1870– ; American painter and illustrator.

par·ro·ket, par·ro·quet (par′ə-ket′), *n.* a parakeet.

par·rot (par′ət), *n.* [Fr. *perrot;* prob. < *Perrot*, dim. of *Pierre*, Peter], 1. any of a number of related birds with hooked bills, brightly colored feathers, and feet having two toes pointing forward and two backward: some parrots can imitate sounds and learn to repeat words. 2. a person who mechanically repeats the words or acts of others without fully understanding what he does or says. *v.t.* to repeat or imitate without understanding.

parrot fever, psittacosis.

parrot fish, any of a number of related brightly colored fishes found in warm seas, with parrotlike jaws and a spoon-shaped body.

par·ry (par′i), *v.t.* [PARRIED (-id), PARRYING], [< a form of Fr. *parer;* It. *parare*, to ward off; L. *parare*, to prepare, keep off], 1. to ward off; deflect, as a blow. 2. to evade; avoid answering, as a question, etc. *v.i.* to make a parry or evasion. *n.* [*pl.* PARRIES (-iz)], 1. a warding off or a turning aside of an attack, blow, etc., as in fencing. 2. an evasion; evasive reply.

Par·ry, Sir William Edward (par′i), 1790–1855; English arctic explorer.

parse (pärs), *v.t.* [PARSED (pärst), PARSING], [< L. *pars*, a part, in *Quae pars orationis?* What part of speech?], 1. to break (a sentence) down into parts, explaining the grammatical form, function, and interrelation of each part. 2. to describe the form, part of speech, and function of (a word) in a sentence.

par·sec (pär′sek′), *n.* [*par*allax + *sec*ond], a unit of measure of astronomical distance, equal to 3.26 light years, or 19,200,000,000,000 miles: also called *secpar.*

Par·see, Par·si (pär′sē, pär-sē′), *n.* [Per. *Parsi*, a Persian < *Pars*, Persia], a member of a Zoroastrian religious sect in India descended from a group of Persian refugees who fled from the Moslem persecutions of the 7th and 8th centuries.

Par·see·ism, Par·si·ism (pär′sē-iz′m, pär-sē′iz′m), *n.* the Zoroastrian religion of the Parsees.

Par·si·fal (pär′si-fäl′, pär′sə-f′l), *n.* [G.; MHG. *Parzival;* OFr. *Perceval;* cf. PERCIVAL], the title character in Wagner's music drama (1882) of the knights of the Holy Grail: he gets from Klingsor a magic spear with which he heals the wound of Amfortas.

par·si·mo·ni·ous (pär′sə-mō′ni-əs), *adj.* characterized by parsimony; miserly; close. —***SYN.*** see **stingy.**

par·si·mo·ny (pär′sə-mō′ni), *n.* [ME. *parcimony;* L. *parsimonia, parcimonia* < *parcere*, to spare], a tendency to be overcareful in spending; unreasonable economy; stinginess; extreme frugality.

pars·ley (pärs′li), *n.* [ME. *perseli, persil* < AS. *petersilie* & OFr. *persil*, both < LL. *petrosilium;* L. *petroselinum;* Gr. *petroselinon*, rock parsley < *petros*, a rock + *selinon*, parsley], a plant with greenish-yellow flowers and curled leaves used to flavor or garnish some foods.

pars·nip (pärs′nip), *n.* [ME. *pasnepe*, altered by association with *nepe*, turnip; OFr. *pasnaie;* L. *pastinaca* < *pastinare*, to dig up < *pastinum*, two-forked dibble], 1. a plant with yellow flowers and a long, thick, sweet, white root used as a vegetable. 2. the root.

par·son (pär′s'n), *n.* [ME. *persone;* see PERSON], 1. a clergyman or minister in charge of a parish. 2. [Colloq.], any clergyman or minister.

par·son·age (pär′s'n-ij), *n.* [ME. *personage;* OFr. *personage;* see PERSON & -AGE], 1. the dwelling provided by a church for the use of its parson, or minister. 2. in *English ecclesiastical law*, the land or income provided by a parish for its parson.

part (pärt), *n.* [ME. *part, parte;* L. *pars, partis;* IE. base **per-*, to sell, hand over in sale, as also in L. *parere* (cf. PARE), *comparare* (cf. COMPARE), etc.], 1. a portion or division of a whole; specifically, *a)* any of several equal portions, quantities, numbers, pieces, etc. of which something is composed or into which it can be divided: as, an hour is the twenty-fourth *part* of a day. *b)* an essential element or constituent; integral portion which can be separated: as, an automobile *part.* *c)* a portion detached or cut from a whole; fragment; piece. *d)* a certain amount but not all: as, he lost *part* of his fortune. *e)* a certain amount or section regarded as a separate division: as, which *part* of the book did you like best? *f)* a segment or organ of the body of men and animals. *g)* a division of a literary work. *h)* in *mathematics*, an aliquot part. 2. a portion assigned or given; share; specifically, *a)* something a person must do; business; duty: as, we do our *part.* *b)* interest; concern: as, it was no *part* of his to interfere. *c) usually pl.* talent; ability: as, a man of *parts.* *d)* a character in a drama; theatrical role. *e)* the words, actions, etc. of a character in a play. *f)* in *music*, the score for a particular voice or instrument in a concerted piece; also, any of the voices or instruments in a musical ensemble. 3. a region; area; especially, *usually pl.* a portion of a country; district; quarter: as, he left these *parts.* 4. one of the different sides or parties in a transaction, dispute, conflict, etc. 5. the dividing line formed by combing the hair in opposite directions. *v.t.* [ME. *parten;* OFr. *partir;* L. *partire*, to divide, separate < the *n.*], 1. to break or divide into separate parts. 2.

to comb (the hair) in opposite directions so as to leave a dividing line. 3. to break up (a connection or relationship) by separating the people or parties involved; hence, 4. to separate (two or more persons or things); break or hold apart; put asunder. 5. to separate in the mind; distinguish, as two theories. 6. to separate (substances) as by a chemical process. 7. [Archaic], to distribute; share; apportion. 8. in *nautical usage*, to break or incur the breaking of (a hawser, chain, etc.). ***v.i.*** 1. to break or divide into two or more pieces; shift apart. 2. to separate and go different ways, as branches of a river. 3. to separate; go away from each other; cease associating. 4. to go away; leave; depart. 5. to die. ***adj.*** less than a whole; as, *part* interest. ***adv.*** partly; in part. Abbreviated **p.**

for one's part, so far as one is concerned.

for the most part, in the greatest part or to the greatest extent; mostly; generally.

in good part, good-naturedly; without offense.

in part, to a certain extent or degree; partly.

on the part of one, 1. as far as one is concerned. 2. by or coming from one. Also **on one's part.**

part and parcel, an essential or necessary part: used emphatically.

part from, to depart or separate from; leave.

part with, to give up; let go; relinquish.

play a part, 1. to behave unnaturally in an attempt to deceive. 2. to participate or share: also **take part.**

take one's part, to support one in a struggle or disagreement; side with one.

SYN.—**part** is the general word for any of the components of a whole (a *part* of one's life); a **portion** is specifically a part allotted to someone or something (his *portion* of the work); a **piece** is either a part separated from the whole (a *piece* of pie) or a single standardized unit of a collection (a *piece* of statuary); a **division** is a part formed by cutting, partitioning, classifying, etc. (the fine arts *division* of a library); **section** is equivalent to **division** but usually connotes a smaller part (a *section* of a bookcase); **segment** implies a part separated along natural lines of division (a *segment* of a tangerine); a **fraction** is strictly a part contained by the whole an integral number of times, but generally it connotes an insignificant part (he received only a *fraction* of the benefits); a **fragment** is a relatively small part separated by or as by breaking (a *fragment* of rock). See also **separate.**—***ANT.*** whole.

part., 1. participial. 2. participle. 3. particular.

part. adj., participial adjective.

par·take (pär-tāk′), ***v.i.*** [PARTOOK (-took′), PARTAKEN (-tāk′′n), PARTAKING], [back-formation < *partaker*, contr. of *part taker*, used to translate L. *particeps* < *pars, partis*, a part + *capere*, to take], 1. to take part in an activity; participate. 2. to take a portion; eat or drink something, especially in company with others. ***v.t.*** [Rare], to take or have a part or share in, as a meal, responsibility, etc. —***SYN.*** see **share.**

partake of, 1. *a*) to take or have a share in, as a meal. *b*) to take; take of; take some of. 2. to have or show a trace or suggestion of; have some of the qualities or nature of.

par·tan (pär′tən), ***n.*** [Scot. & British Dial.], a crab.

part·ed (pär′tid), ***adj.*** 1. divided; separated; split. 2. [Archaic], dead. 3. in *botany*, divided almost to the base, as some leaves.

par·terre (pär-târ′), ***n.*** [Fr.; *par*, on + *terre* (L. *terra*), earth], 1. an ornamental garden area in which the flower beds and paths form a pattern. 2. the part of a theater beneath the balcony and behind the parquet; parquet circle: also called *orchestra circle*.

par·the·no·gen·e·sis (pär′thə-nō-jen′ə-sis), ***n.*** [Mod.L. < Gr. *parthenos*, maiden, virgin + *genesis*, origin], reproduction by the development of an unfertilized ovum, seed, or spore, as in certain polyzoans, insects, algae, etc.: *artificial parthenogenesis* is the development of an ovum stimulated by chemical or mechanical means.

par·the·no·ge·net·ic (pär′thə-nō-jə-net′ik), ***adj.*** of, reproducing by, or produced by parthenogenesis.

Par·the·non (pär′thə-non′, pär′thə-nən), ***n.*** [L.; Gr. *Parthenōn* < *parthenos*, a virgin (i.e., Athena)], the Doric temple of Athena built (5th century B.C.) on the Acropolis in Athens: sculpture is attributed to Phidias.

Par·then·o·pe (pär-then′ə-pē′), ***n.*** [L.; Gr. *Parthenopē*], in *Greek mythology*, the siren who threw herself into the sea after her songs failed to lure Ulysses into a shipwreck.

Par·the·nos (pär′thə-nos′), ***n.*** [< Gr. *parthenos*, a virgin], a virgin: an epithet of several Greek goddesses, especially of Athena.

Par·thi·a (pär′thi-ə), ***n.*** an ancient kingdom southeast of the Caspian Sea.

Par·thi·an (pär′thi-ən), ***adj.*** of Parthia, its people, or culture. ***n.*** a native or inhabitant of Parthia.

Parthian shot, any hostile gesture or remark made in leaving; parting shot: Parthian cavalrymen usually shot at the enemy while retreating or pretending to retreat.

par·tial (pär′shəl), ***adj.*** [ME. *parcial;* LL. *partialis* < L. *pars, partis*, a part], 1. favoring one person, faction, etc. more than another; biased; prejudiced. 2. of, being, or affecting only a part; not complete or total.

partial to, fond of; having a liking for.

partial fractions, the fractions into which a given fraction may be separated and whose sum equals the given fraction: as, $\frac{a}{2xy}$ and $\frac{a}{xy}$ are the *partial fractions* of $\frac{3a}{2xy}$.

par·ti·al·i·ty (pär′shi-al′ə-ti, pär-shal′ə-ti), ***n.*** [ME. *parcialitee;* OFr. *partialité*], 1. the state or quality of being partial; bias; tendency to favor unfairly. 2. particular fondness; strong liking. —***SYN.*** see **prejudice.**

par·tial·ly (pär′shəl-i), ***adv.*** 1. with partiality or bias; in a manner showing prejudice. 2. not completely or totally; in part; partly.

partial tone, in *acoustics* & *music*, any of the pure, or harmonic, tones forming a complex tone.

par·ti·ble (pär′tə-b'l), ***adj.*** [LL. *partibilis* < *partiri*, to divide < *pars, partis*, a part], that can be divided, separated, or parted; divisible.

‡par·ti·ceps cri·mi·nis (pär′ti-seps′ krim′i-nis), [L.], a partner in crime; accomplice.

par·tic·i·pance (pär-tis′ə-pəns, pẽr-tis′ə-pəns), ***n.*** participation.

par·tic·i·pan·cy (pär-tis′ə-pən-si, pẽr-tis′ə-pən-si), ***n.*** participance.

par·tic·i·pant (pär-tis′ə-pənt, pẽr-tis′ə-pənt), ***adj.*** [L. *participans*, ppr. of *participare*], participating. ***n.*** a person who participates or shares in something.

par·tic·i·pate (pär-tis′ə-pāt′, pẽr-tis′ə-pāt′), ***v.i.*** [PARTICIPATED (-id), PARTICIPATING], [< L. *participatus*, pp. of *participare* < *pars, partis*, a part + *capere*, to take], to have or take a part or share with others (*in* some activity, enterprise, etc.); partake. ***v.t.*** [Rare], to have or take a part or share in. —***SYN.*** see **share.**

par·tic·i·pa·tion (pär-tis′ə-pā′shən, pẽr-tis′ə-pā′shən), ***n.*** a participating; act or fact of sharing or partaking.

par·tic·i·pa·tor (pär-tis′ə-pā′tẽr, pẽr-tis′ə-pā′tẽr), ***n.*** a person who participates.

par·ti·cip·i·al (pär′tə-sip′i-əl, pär′tə-sip′yəl), ***adj.*** [L. *participialis*], of, based on, or having the nature and use of a participle. ***n.*** a verbal derivative (as a gerund or infinitive) used as a noun or adjective. Abbreviated **part.**

par·ti·cip·i·al·ly (pär′tə-sip′i-əl-i, pär′tə-sip′yəl-i), ***adv.*** as a participle; with participial function.

par·ti·ci·ple (pär′tə-si-p'l), ***n.*** [ME.; OFr. *participe, participle;* L. *participium* < *particeps*, participating, partaking < *pars, partis*, a part + *capere*, to take: so named from participating in the nature of both verb & adjective], a word derived from a verb and having the qualities of both verb and adjective: a participle may be active (e.g., I am *asking*) or passive (e.g., I am *asked*) and is referred to as having tense (e.g., present, *asking;* past, *asked;* perfect, *having asked*) but does not indicate time except in relation to its context. Participles are used: *a*) in various verb forms. *b*) as adjectives (e.g., a club *used* in golf; a car *rushing* downhill). *c*) in absolute constructions, modifying a whole sentence (e.g., generally *speaking*, these principles can be accepted). In any of these functions a participle may take an object or be modified by an adverb. The present participle is sometimes used with adverbial force (e.g., *raving* mad). Abbreviated **p., part.**

par·ti·cle (pär′ti-k'l), ***n.*** [ME. *partycle;* OFr. *particul(e);* L. *particula*, dim. of *pars, partis*, a part], 1. an extremely small piece; tiny fragment; slightest trace; speck: as, a dust *particle*, not a *particle* of truth. 2. a small, individual section of written matter; clause; article in a document. 3. in *grammar*, *a*) a short and indeclinable part of speech, as an article, preposition, conjunction, or interjection. *b*) a prefix or suffix. 4. in *physics*, a piece of matter so small as to be considered without magnitude though having inertia and the force of attraction. 5. in the *Roman Catholic Church*, a small piece of the consecrated Host or any of the small Hosts given in a lay communion.

par·ti-col·ored (pär′ti-kul′ẽrd), ***adj.*** [*parti-* < Fr. *parti;* see PARTY], 1. having different colors in different parts. 2. showing variations or differences in form, quality, etc.; diversified; variegated. Also spelled **party-colored.**

par·tic·u·lar (pẽr-tik′yoo-lẽr, pär-tik′yoo-lẽr), ***adj.*** [ME. *particuler;* Fr. *particulier;* LL. *particularis* < L. *particula;* see PARTICLE], 1. of or belonging to a single, definite person, part, group, or thing; not general; distinct; peculiar to one. 2. apart from any other; regarded separately; specific: as, why did she choose that *particular* hat? 3. out of the ordinary; unusual; noteworthy; special: as, no *particular* reason for going. 4. dealing with particulars; itemized; detailed. 5. not satisfied with anything considered inferior; exacting; extremely careful; fastidious; hard to please. 6. in *logic*, designating a proposition which affirms or denies its predicate to a part of, but not to the whole of, a subject; limited in application to part of a class: as, "some people have red hair" is a *particular* proposition: opposed to *universal*. ***n.*** 1. a separate and distinct individual, fact, item, or instance which may be classified or included under a generalization; single case. 2. a detail; item of information; point. 3. in *logic*,

a particular proposition. Abbreviated **part.** —*SYN.* see **dainty, item, single, special.**
in particular, particularly; especially.

par·tic·u·lar·ism (pẽr-tik′yoo-lẽr-iz'm, pär-tik′yoo-lẽr-iz'm), *n.* 1. the theological doctrine that redemption is possible only for certain individuals. 2. undivided adherence or devotion to one particular party, system, interest, etc. 3. the policy of allowing each member or state in a federation to function independently without regard for the whole.

par·tic·u·lar·i·ty (pẽr-tik′yoo-lar′ə-ti, pär-tik′yoo-lar′ə-ti), *n.* [*pl.* PARTICULARITIES (-tiz)], [Fr. *particularité;* LL. *particularitas*], 1. the state, quality, or fact of being particular; specifically, *a)* individuality; characteristic quality: opposed to *generality, universality. b)* the quality of being detailed or minute, as a description. *c)* attention to detail; minute exactness; painstaking care. *d)* the quality of being fastidious or hard to please. 2. something particular; specifically, *a)* an individual trait or characteristic; peculiarity, as of circumstance or detail. *b)* a minute detail.

par·tic·u·lar·i·za·tion (pẽr-tik′yoo-lẽr-i-zā′shən, pär-tik′yoo-lẽr-i-zā′shən), *n.* a particularizing or being particularized.

par·tic·u·lar·ize (pẽr-tik′yoo-lẽr-īz′, pär-tik′yoo-lẽr-īz′), *v.t.* [PARTICULARIZED (-īzd′), PARTICULARIZING], [Fr. *particulariser*], to state or name individually or in detail; itemize. *v.i.* to give particulars or details.

par·tic·u·lar·ly (pẽr-tik′yoo-lẽr-li, pär-tik′yoo-lẽr-li), *adv.* 1. so as to be particular; in detail. 2. especially; unusually; extraordinarily. Abbreviated **part.**

part·ing (pär′tiŋ), *adj.* [ppr. of *part*], 1. dividing; separating. 2. departing; hence, 3. dying. 4. given, spoken, done, etc. at parting. *n.* 1. a breaking, dividing, or separating. 2. a place of division or separation; dividing point or line. 3. something that separates or divides. 4. a separation of two or more persons; leavetaking. 5. a departure; hence, 6. death.

parting strip, a thin strip of wood, metal, etc. for separating adjoining parts of a structure.

‡par·ti pris (pȧr′tē′ prē′), [Fr.], preconceived opinion.

par·ti·san (pär′tə-z'n), *n.* [Fr.; It. *partigiano* < *parte* < L. *pars, partis;* see PART], 1. a person who takes the part of or strongly supports a side, a party, or another person: often said of an unreasoning, emotional adherent. 2. a member of a group of irregular troops engaged in guerrilla fighting, often behind enemy lines. *adj.* 1. of, like, or characteristic of a partisan; hence, 2. blindly or unreasonably devoted. 3. of or having to do with partisans or their type of fighting. Also spelled **partizan.** —*SYN.* see **follower.**

par·ti·san (pär′tə-z'n), *n.* [OFr. *partizane, partisane;* It. *partesana, partigiana;* prob. < *pertugiare,* to pierce (or ? n. use of fem. of *partigiano;* see prec.)], a variety of pike or halberd used by infantry in the 16th and 17th centuries.

par·ti·san·ship (pär′tə-z'n-ship′), *n.* [*partisan* + *-ship*], 1. the strong supporting or endorsement of a side, party, etc. 2. a strong, often unreasoning, attachment; blind loyalty.

par·tite (pär′tīt), *adj.* [L. *partitus,* pp. of *partire,* to part], parted; having divisions; divided into parts: often in compounds, as *tripartite.*

par·ti·tion (pär-tish′ən, pẽr-tish′ən), *n.* [ME. *particioune;* L. *partitio*], 1. a parting or being parted; division into parts; separation; apportionment. 2. something that separates or divides, as an interior wall dividing one room from another. 3. a part or section; portion; compartment. 4. in *law,* the process of dividing property and giving separate title to those who previously had joint title. 5. in *logic,* the separation of a class into its elements or parts: a method of analysis. 6. in *mathematics,* division. *v.t.* 1. to divide into parts or shares; apportion. 2. to set off or divide by a partition.

par·ti·tive (pär′tə-tiv), *adj.* [Fr. *partitif;* L. *partitus;* see PARTITE], 1. used in setting off or separating; making a division. 2. in *grammar,* restricting to or involving only a part of a whole. *n.* a partitive word or form (e.g., *few, some, any*).

par·ti·zan (pär′tə-z'n), *n. & adj.* partisan (adherent).

part·let (pärt′lit), *n.* [earlier *patlet, patelet;* OFr. *patelette,* band of stuff, orig., dim. of *pate,* a paw], a covering for the neck and upper chest, often ruffled or embroidered: popular in the 16th century.

part·ly (pärt′li), *adv.* in some measure or degree; in part; not fully or completely.

part·ner (pärt′nẽr), *n.* [ME. *partener;* prob. < *parcener* (see PARCENER), influenced by *part*], 1. a person who takes part or engages in some activity in common with another or others; sharer; associate; specifically, *a)* one of two or more persons engaged in the same business enterprise and sharing its profits and risks: as, each *partner* is an agent for the other or others and is liable for the debts of the firm. *b)* a husband or wife. *c)* either of two persons dancing together. *d)* either or any one of the players on the same side or team, especially one of two playing on the same side against two others, as in bridge. 2. in *nautical usage,* one of the reinforcing timbers used to support a mast or other upright and to strengthen the deck at the point where the mast, etc. enters. *v.t.* 1. to join (others) together as partners. 2. to join with (another) as a partner; be or provide a partner for.

part·ner·ship (pärt′nẽr-ship′), *n.* [see -SHIP], 1. the state of being a partner; participation. 2. the relationship of partners; joint interest; association. 3. *a)* an association of two or more people who contribute money or property to carry on a joint business and who share profits or losses in certain proportion. *b)* a contract by which such an association is created. *c)* the people so associated.

part of speech, in *grammar,* 1. any of the traditional form classes comprising the words of a language, to which a word is assigned according to its function (e.g., in Latin grammar, noun, verb, pronoun, adjective, adverb, preposition, conjunction, and interjection). 2. any word considered as belonging to one of these classes.

par·took (pär-took′), past tense of **partake.**

par·tridge (pär′trij), *n.* [*pl.* PARTRIDGES (-iz), PARTRIDGE; see PLURAL, II, D, 1], [ME. *partriche, pertriche;* OFr. *pertris, perdriz,* earlier *perdiz;* L. *perdix;* Gr. *perdix*], any of a number of game birds resembling domestic fowls, as the ruffed grouse, pheasant, quail, etc.

par·tridge·ber·ry (pär′trij-ber′i), *n.* [*pl.* PARTRIDGEBERRIES (-iz)], 1. a trailing evergreen with rounded leaves, pinkish flowers, and red berries. 2. its berry. 3. the wintergreen.

part song, a homophonic song for several voices, usually three or more, singing in harmony, generally without accompaniment.

part-time (pärt′tīm′), *adj.* for, during, or by part time: as, *part-time* work.

part time, a part of the normal or customary time.

par·tu·ri·ent (pär-tyoor′i-ənt, pär-toor′i-ənt), *adj.* [L. *parturiens,* ppr. of *parturire,* to be in labor < *parere,* to bring forth], 1. giving birth or about to give birth to young. 2. of childbirth, or parturition. 3. on the point of coming forth with a discovery, idea, etc.

par·tu·ri·en·cy (pär-tyoor′i-ən-si, pär-toor′i-ən-si), *n.* the quality or condition of being parturient.

par·tu·ri·fa·cient (pär-tyoor′i-fā′shənt, pär-toor′i-fā′shənt), *adj.* [< L. *parturire* (see PARTURIENT); + *-facient*], inducing or easing labor in childbirth. *n.* a parturifacient medicine.

par·tu·ri·tion (pär′choo-rish′ən, pär′tyoo-rish′ən), *n.* [L. *parturitio* < *parturire;* see PARTURIENT], the act of giving birth; act of bringing forth young; childbirth.

par·ty (pär′ti), *n.* [*pl.* PARTIES (-tiz)], [ME. & OFr. *parti, partie* < *partir,* to divide; L. *partiri* < *pars, partis,* a part], 1. a group of people working together to establish, promote, or gain acceptance for, some kind of government, cause, or theory which they hold in common; especially, an organized political group which tries to elect its candidates to office. 2. the political practice of forming and supporting such groups. 3. a group of persons acting together; specifically, *a)* a group sent out on a task or mission: as, a surveying *party. b)* a group meeting together socially to accomplish a task: as, a quilting *party. c)* a group assembled for amusement or recreation: as, the fishing *party* arrived early. 4. a gathering for social entertainment or the entertainment itself, often of a specific nature: as, a card *party,* cocktail *party.* 5. a person who participates or is concerned in an action, proceeding, plan, etc. (often with *to*): as, I'll not be a *party* to the affair. 6. either of the persons or sides concerned in a legal matter. 7. [Colloq.], a person: often used facetiously.

par·ty-col·ored (pär′ti-kul′ẽrd), *adj.* parti-colored.

party line, 1. a line marking the boundary between adjoining properties owned by two parties (sense 6). 2. a single circuit connecting two or more telephone users with the exchange. 3. *usually in pl.* a political tenet regarded as a line, or boundary, beyond which a political party or its members are not supposed to go: as, *party lines* are strictly drawn on this issue. 4. the line of policy followed by a political party, especially a Communist party.

party man, a faithful supporter of a political party.

party politics, political acts and principles directed toward the interests of one political party or its members without reference to the common good.

party wall, a wall separating and common to two buildings or properties: each owner has a partial right in its use.

pa·rure (pə-roor′; Fr. pȧ′rür′), *n.* [ME. *parure, paroure* < OFr. < L. *paratura:* the Mod. word is reborrowed < Fr.], a number of pieces of jewelry, as earrings, bracelet, and necklace, intended to be worn as a set.

par value, the value of a stock, bond, etc. fixed at the time of its issue; face value: abbreviated **p.v.**

par·ve·nu (pär′və-no͞o′, pär′və-nū′), ***n.*** [Fr., pp. of *parvenir;* L. *parvenire,* to arrive], a person who has suddenly acquired wealth or power, especially one who fails to conform to the established forms, customs, and habits of the class into which he has risen; person considered an upstart. ***adj.*** 1. being a parvenu. 2. like or characteristic of a parvenu.

par·vis (pär′vis), ***n.*** [ME.; OFr. *parevis;* L. *paradisum,* lit., Paradise, name of the court before St. Peter's in Rome], 1. an enclosed court or yard in front of a building, especially a church. 2. a portico or single line of columns in front of a church.

par·vo·lin (pär′və-lin), ***n.*** parvoline.

par·vo·line (pär′və-lēn′, pär′və-lin), ***n.*** [< L. *parvus,* small, after Eng. *quinoline:* so named because of its low volatility], any of the isomeric, liquid, basic compounds, $C_9H_{13}N$, derived from pyridine and found in decaying fish or meat.

‡pas (pä), ***n.*** [Fr.; L. *passus,* a step], 1. the right to precede; precedence. 2. a step or series of steps in dancing. 3. a dance, as in *pas de deux.*

Pas·a·de·na (pas′ə-dē′nə), ***n.*** 1. a city in California, near Los Angeles: pop., 116,000. 2. a city in southeastern Texas: suburb of Houston: pop., 59,000.

Pas·cal, Blaise (blez pȧs′kȧl′; Eng. pas′k′l), 1623–1662; French mathematician and philosopher.

Pasch (pask), ***n.*** [ME. *paske, pasche;* OFr. *pasque, pasche;* LL. *pascha;* LGr. *pascha* < Heb. *pesaḥ,* usually interpreted "passage," as if < *pāṣah,* to pass over, but prob. < base akin to Assyr. *pašāḫu,* to propitiate], [Chiefly Archaic], 1. the Passover. 2. Easter.

pas·chal (pas′k′l), ***adj.*** [ME. *pascall;* Late OFr. *pascal;* LL. *paschalis* < L. *pascha;* see PASCH], 1. of or connected with the Passover. 2. of or connected with Easter.

paschal flower, a pasqueflower.

paschal lamb, 1. in ancient times, the lamb slain and eaten at the Passover. 2. [P- L-], in the *Christian Church, a)* Jesus. *b)* any of several symbolic representations of Jesus, as Agnus Dei.

Pas de Cal·ais (pä′ də kȧ′le′), the Strait of Dover: the French name.

‡pas de deux (pä′ də dö′), [Fr.], in *ballet,* a dance or figure for two performers.

pash (pash), ***v.t. & v.i.*** [ME. *passchen,* prob. echoic after *smash, dash, bash,* etc.; but cf. Sw. *paska;* see DASH], [Obs. or Dial.], to hurl or be hurled violently so as to break or smash; dash. ***n.*** [Obs. or Dial.], a smashing blow.

pash (päsh), ***n.*** [prob. < *pash, v.,* with reference to blows on the head], [Obs. or British Dial.], the head.

pa·sha (pə-shä′, pash′ə, pä′shə), ***n.*** [Turk. *pāshā, bāshā;* prob. < *bāsh,* a head], in Turkey, 1. a title of rank or honor placed after the name. 2. a high civil or military official. Also spelled **pacha.**

pa·sha·lik, pa·sha·lic (pə-shä′lik), ***n.*** [Turk. *pāshālik; pāshā* + *-lik,* suffix of condition], the jurisdiction of or area governed by a pasha: also spelled **pachalic.**

Pash·to (push′tō), ***n.*** Pushtu, language of Afghanistan.

Pa·siph·a·ë (pə-sif′ə-ē′), ***n.*** [L.; Gr. *Pasiphaē*], in *Greek mythology,* the wife of Minos and mother of the Minotaur by a white bull belonging to Minos.

pasque·flow·er (pask′flou′ẽr), ***n.*** [earlier *passeflower;* Fr. *passefleur* < *passer,* to surpass + *fleur,* a flower, altered after Fr. *pasque;* see PASCH], any of a number of related plants with hairy leaves and blue or purplish flowers shaped like cups: also **paschal flower.**

pas·quil (pas′kwil), ***n.*** a pasquinade.

pas·quin·ade (pas′kwi-nād′), ***n.*** [Fr.; It. *pasquinata* < *Pasquino,* statue in Rome to which it was the custom to attach satirical verses], a satire or sarcastic squib posted in a public place; lampoon. ***v.t.*** [PASQUINADED (-id), PASQUINADING], to criticize or ridicule with such satire; lampoon.

pass (pas, päs), ***n.*** [ME. *pas;* see PACE], a narrow passage or opening especially between mountains; gap; defile.

pass (pas, päs), ***v.i.*** [PASSED (past, päst), PASSED or, *rare,* PAST (past, päst), PASSING], [ME. *passen;* OFr. *passer;* LL. **passare* < L. *passus,* a step], 1. to go; move; move forward; proceed. 2. to extend; lead: as, the road *passes* around the hill. 3. to go from person to person; circulate; be handed on from one to another. 4. to go, shift, or be conveyed from one place, form, condition, circumstance, possession, etc. to another. 5. to be spoken or exchanged between persons, as greetings. 6. *a)* to cease; come to an end: as, the fever *passed. b)* to go away; depart; hence, 7. to die. 8. to go by; move by or past; hence, 9. to slip by or elapse: as, the hour *passed* quickly. 10. to get or make a way (with *through* or *by*). 11. to go, take place, or be accepted without question, dispute, or challenge; hence, 12. to go through the necessary stages and be sanctioned, ratified, or approved by some authority, as a legislative body. 13. to go through a trial, test, or examination successfully; satisfy given requirements or standards. 14. to happen; take place; occur: as, what *passed* in my absence? 15. *a)* to sit in inquest or judgment. *b)* to give a judgment, opinion, or sentence; decide: as, the jury *passed* upon the case. 16. to be rendered or pronounced: as, the judgment *passed* against us. 17. in *card games,* to decline a chance to bid, play a round, etc.; skip a bid or round of play. 18. in *sports,* to make a pass. ***v.t.*** 1. to go by, beyond, past, over, or through; specifically, *a)* to leave behind: as, we have *passed* her house. *b)* [Archaic], to cross; traverse. *c)* to undergo. *d)* to go by without noticing; disregard; hence, *e)* to omit the payment of (a regular dividend). *f)* to go through (a trial, test, course, examination, etc.) successfully; satisfy the requirements or standards of. *g)* to go beyond or above the powers or limits of; surpass; excel. 2. to cause or allow to go, move, or proceed; specifically, *a)* to send; dispatch. *b)* to cause to move in a certain way; direct the movement of: as, he *passed* his hand through his hair. *c)* to guide into position: as, he *passed* the rope around the stake. *d)* to cause to go through, or penetrate. *e)* to cause to move past: as, the troops were *passed* in review. *f)* to cause or allow (a person or thing) to get by an obstacle, obstruction, etc. *g)* to cause or allow to progress by stages; ratify; sanction; enact; approve. *h)* to cause or allow to go through an examination, test, etc. successfully. *i)* to allow to go by, or elapse; spend: as, we *passed* a pleasant hour. *j)* to discharge or expel from the bowels, bladder, etc.; excrete; void. *k)* in *baseball,* to walk (a batter). 3. to cause to move from place to place or person to person; transport; transmit; hand on; specifically, *a)* to hand to another: as, please *pass* the salt. *b)* to cause (money, etc.) to circulate: as, he tried to *pass* a bad check. *c)* to hand, throw, or hit (a ball, etc.) from one player to another. *d)* to hit a tennis ball past (an opponent) so as to score a point. 4. [Rare], to pledge. 5. to pronounce, give, or utter, as an opinion or judgment. 6. to manipulate (cards, etc.) or trick (a person), as by sleight of hand. ***n.*** [Fr. *passe* < *passer* (see the *v.*); influenced by the Eng. *v.*], 1. an act of passing; passage. 2. the successful completion of a scholastic course or examination, often without securing honors. 3. a mark, etc. indicating this. 4. condition; situation: as, a strange *pass.* 5. *a)* a ticket, certificate, etc. giving permission or authorization to come or go freely or without charge. *b)* a written leave of absence for a brief period, given to a soldier. 6. a motion of the hands that is meant to deceive, as in card tricks or magic; sleight of hand. 7. a motion or stroke of the hand, as in mesmerism or hypnotism. 8. [Slang], an attempt to embrace, caress, or kiss, often an improper or overfamiliar one. 9. in *card games,* a declining or refusal of a chance to bid or play a round, etc. 10. in *sports, a)* an intentional transfer of the ball, puck, etc. to another player during play. *b)* a lunge or thrust made in fencing. *c)* a walk in baseball.

a pretty pass, [Colloq.], a difficult, unfortunate, or critical situation; extremity.

bring to pass, to cause tc come about or happen.

come to pass, to come about or happen.

make a pass at, 1. to attempt to strike. 2. [Slang], to make an attempt to caress, embrace, or kiss, often an improper or overfamiliar attempt.

pass away, 1. to come to an end; cease; hence, 2. to die. 3. to spend (time, etc.).

pass current, 1. to have a certain accepted value, as money. 2. to be common; circulate, as a rumor.

pass for, to be accepted or looked upon as: usually said of an imitation or counterfeit.

pass off, 1. to come to an end; cease. 2. to take place; go through, as a transaction. 3. to be accepted or cause to be accepted as genuine, true, etc., especially by using deceit.

pass one's lips, 1. to be eaten or drunk by one. 2. to be said by one.

pass out, [Slang], to become unconscious; faint.

pass over, to disregard; ignore; omit.

pass through, to experience or undergo, as the different phases of an illness.

pass up, [Slang], to reject, refuse, or let go, as an opportunity.

pass., 1. passenger. 2. passive. 3. passim.

pass·a·ble (pas′ə-b'l, päs′ə-b'l), ***adj.*** [ME.; OFr. < *passer*], 1. that can be passed, traveled over, or crossed. 2. that can be circulated; genuine, as coin. 3. good enough for the purpose; moderate; adequate; fair. 4. that can be enacted, as a proposed law.

pass·a·bly (pas′ə-bli, päs′ə-bli), ***adv.*** so as to be passable; fairly; moderately.

pass·a·cagl·ia (pas′ə-käl′yə; It. päs′sä-käl′yä), ***n.*** [pseudo-It. < Sp. *pasacalle* < *pasar,* to pass + *calle,* street: so named from often being performed in the streets], 1. formerly, a slow, stately Italian dance similar to the chaconne. 2. the music for this dance. 3. a musical form based on this dance, characterized by 3/4 meter and a continuous ground bass.

pas·sade (pə-sād′), ***n.*** [Fr.; Pr. *passada* (It. *passata*); see PASS & -ADE], in *horsemanship,* the movement of a horse backward and forward over the same course.

pas·sa·do (pə-sä′dō), ***n.*** [*pl.* PASSADOS, PASSADOES (-dōz)], [altered < Fr. *passade* < It. *passata* or Pr. *passada,* both < pp. of LL. *passare*, to pass], in *fencing*, a thrust or lunge with one foot advanced.

pas·sage (pas′ij), *n.* [ME.; OFr. < *passer*], 1. the act of passing; specifically, *a)* movement from one place to another; migration: as, birds of *passage*. *b)* change or progress from one process or condition to another; transition. *c)* the enactment of a law by a legislative body. 2. permission, right, or a chance to pass. 3. a journey by water; voyage; crossing. 4. *a)* passenger accommodations on a ship. *b)* the charge for this. 5. a way or means of passing; specifically, *a)* a road; path; opening. *b)* a hall or corridor that is an entrance or exit or onto which several rooms open; passageway. 6. that which happens or takes place between persons; interchange, as of blows or vows. 7. a portion of something spoken or written: as, a *passage* from *The Tempest*. 8. in *medicine*, a bowel movement. 9. in *music*, *a)* a run consisting of the tones of a scale or chord. *b)* a short section of a composition. *v.i.* [PASSAGED (-ijd), PASSAGING], 1. to make a passage, or voyage; journey. 2. to take part in a fight or quarrel.

pas·sage·way (pas′ij-wā′), *n.* a narrow way for passage, as a hall, corridor, or alley; passage.

Pas·sa·ic (pə-sā′ik, pa-sā′ik), *n.* 1. a river in northeastern New Jersey, flowing into Newark Bay: length, 100 mi. 2. a city on this river: pop., 54,000.

Pas·sa·ma·quod·dy Bay (pas′ə-mə-kwod′i), an arm of the Atlantic between Maine and New Brunswick, Canada.

pas·sant (pas′ənt), *adj.* [ME. (only in sense "excelling, passing") < OFr. *passant* < *passer*, to pass], in *heraldry*, walking toward the (viewer's) left side of the shield with the right forepaw raised: said of an animal.

pass·book (pas′book′, päs′book′), *n.* 1. a bankbook. 2. a customer's record in which a merchant or dealer records items bought on credit.

pass degree, [Chiefly British], a scholastic degree indicating that the receiver has satisfied graduation requirements, but without any special distinction.

pas·sé (pa-sā′, pas′ā; Fr. pȧ′sā′), *adj.* [Fr.], past; out of date; old-fashioned.

passed (past, päst), *adj.* [see PASS, *v.*], 1. having satisfied some requirement, as for promotion; qualified. 2. left unpaid, as a dividend.

passed ball, in *baseball*, a pitch that gets by the catcher when he could be expected to catch it, and allows a man on base to advance to another base.

passe·men·terie (pas-men′tri; Fr. päs′män′trē′), *n.* [Fr. < *passement*, lace], trimming made of gimp, cord, beads, braid, etc.

pas·sen·ger (pas′'n-jẽr), *n.* [ME. & OFr. *passager* < *passage* (see PASSAGE); the *n* is intrusive, as in *messenger*], 1. [Rare], a person passing by or through, usually on foot. 2. a person traveling in a train, bus, boat, etc., especially a person having no part in the operation of the conveyance. Abbreviated **pass.**

passenger pigeon, an extinct variety of North American pigeon with a narrow tail longer than its wings.

passe par·tout (pas pär-to͞o′; Fr. päs′ pȧr′to͞o′), [Fr., pass everywhere], 1. originally, that which passes or allows passage everywhere. 2. a passkey or master key. 3. a mat used in mounting pictures. 4. a picture mounting in which glass, picture, backing, and often a mat are bound together, as by strips of gummed paper along the edges. 5. such gummed paper.

‡passe·pied (pȧs′pyā′), *n.* [Fr. < *passer*, to pass, pace + *pied*, a foot], 1. a lively, 17th-century French dance, similar to the minuet but faster in tempo: now sometimes a movement in ballet. 2. the music for this.

pass·er-by (pas′ẽr-bī′, päs′ẽr-bī′), *n.* [*pl.* PASSERS-BY (-ẽrz-bī′)], a person who passes by.

pas·ser·ine (pas′ẽr-in, pas′ẽr-īn′), *adj.* [L. *passerinus* < *passer*, a sparrow], of a group of small or medium-sized, perching songbirds having grasping feet with the first toe directed backward: more than half of all birds belong to this group. *n.* a bird of this group.

‡pas seul (pä′ söl′), [Fr., lit., solo dance], a (ballet) dance performed by one person.

pas·si·bil·i·ty (pas′ə-bil′ə-ti), *n.* a passible quality.

pas·si·ble (pas′ə-b'l), *adj.* [ME.], that can feel or suffer; sensible.

pas·si·flo·ra·ceous (pas′i-flō-rā′shəs), *adj.* [< Mod. L. *Passifloraceae*, name of the family (< L. *passio*, passion + *flos*, *floris*, a flower); + *-ous*], of the passionflower family.

‡passim (pas′im) *adv.* [L.], throughout; in various parts (of a book, etc.): abbreviated **pass.**

pass·ing (pas′iŋ, päs′iŋ), *adj.* [ME.], 1. going by, beyond, past, over, or through. 2. lasting only a short time; short-lived; fleeting; momentary. 3. casual; cursory; incidental: as, a *passing* remark. 4. permitting one to go through a test, examination, course, etc. successfully: as, a *passing* grade. 5. that is happening; current. 6. [Chiefly Archaic], surpassing; extreme; very. *adv.* [Chiefly Archaic], exceedingly; unusually; very. *n.* 1. the act of a person or thing that passes. 2. a means or place of passing. 3. [Poetic], death.
in passing, casually; incidentally.

passing bell, a bell tolled to indicate a death.

passing note, in *music*, a note that is not part of the harmonic scheme, but is introduced for ornamentation or to make the movement from one tone or chord to another smoother.

pas·sion (pash′ən), *n.* [ME.; OFr.; LL. *passio* < L. *passus*, pp. of *pati*, to endure, suffer], 1. originally, suffering or agony, as of a martyr. 2. [P-], *a)* the agony and sufferings of Jesus during the Crucifixion or during the period following the Last Supper. *b)* any of the gospel descriptions of this. *c)* an artistic representation of this. 3. the state or power of receiving or being affected by outside influences; condition of being acted upon: opposed to *action*. 4. *a)* any one of the emotions, as hate, grief, love, fear, joy, etc. *b)* *pl.* all of these emotions. 5. extreme, compelling emotion; intense emotional drive or excitement; specifically, *a)* great anger; rage; fury. *b)* enthusiasm or fondness, as for music. *c)* strong love or affection. *d)* sexual drive or desire; lust. 6. the object of any strong desire or fondness.
***SYN.*—passion** usually implies a strong emotion that has an overpowering or compelling effect (his *passions* overcame his reason); **fervor** and **ardor** both imply emotion of burning intensity, **fervor** suggesting a constant glow of feeling (religious *fervor*), and **ardor**, a restless, flamelike emotion (the *ardors* of youth); **enthusiasm** implies strongly favorable feelings for an object or cause and usually suggests eagerness in the pursuit of something (his *enthusiasm* for golf); **zeal** implies intense enthusiasm for an object or cause, usually as displayed in vigorous and untiring activity in its support (inflamed with a *zeal* for reform). See also **feeling.**

pas·sion·al (pash′ən-'l), *adj.* of, characterized by, or due to passion. *n.* a book describing the sufferings of saints and martyrs: usually read during their festivals.

pas·sion·ate (pash′ən-it), *adj.* [ML. *passionatus*], 1. having or showing strong feelings; capable of or susceptible to passion. 2. easily angered; hot-tempered. 3. resulting from, expressing, or tending to arouse strong feeling; ardent; intense; impassioned: as, a *passionate* speech. 4. lustful; amorous. 5. strong; vehement: said of an emotion.
***SYN.*—passionate** implies strong or violent emotion, often of an impetuous kind (a *passionate* rage); **impassioned** suggests an expression of emotion that is deeply and sincerely felt (an *impassioned* plea for tolerance); **ardent** and **fervent** suggest a fiery or glowing feeling of eagerness, enthusiasm, devotion, etc. (an *ardent* pursuit of knowledge, a *fervent* prayer); **fervid** differs from **fervent** in often suggesting an outburst of intense feeling that is at a fever pitch (a vengeful, *fervid* hatred).

pas·sion·flow·er (pash′ən-flou′ẽr), *n.* any of a number of related plants with white, red, purple, or orange flowers and yellow, egglike fruit: so called because parts of the flower are supposed to resemble Jesus' wounds, crown of thorns, etc.

passion fruit, the pale-yellow, usually small, edible fruit of the passionflower.

pas·sion·less (pash′ən-lis), *adj.* free from passion or emotion; impassive; calm.

Passion play, a religious play representing the Passion of Jesus, as the one given every ten years at Oberammergau, Bavaria.

Passion Sunday, [cf. PASSION, 2*a*], the fifth Sunday in Lent, two weeks before Easter Sunday.

Passion Week, 1. the week begining on Passion Sunday. 2. formerly, the week before Easter; Holy Week.

pas·sive (pas′iv), *adj.* [L. *passivus* < *passus*, pp. of *pati*, to suffer], 1. influenced or acted upon without exerting influence or acting in return; inactive, but acted upon. 2. offering no opposition or resistance; submissive; yielding; patient. 3. taking no part; inactive; inert. 4. in *chemistry*, inert. 5. in *grammar*, indicating that the subject is the receiver (object) of the action the verb denotes (e.g., in "the tree was struck by lightning," *was struck* is said to be in the passive voice). 6. in *law & finance*, noninterest-bearing, as certain bonds, shares, etc. 7. in *medicine*, designating certain abnormal conditions in which there is lowered activity and reaction. *n.* 1. *usually pl.* a passive thing, quality, trait, etc. 2. in *grammar*, *a)* the passive voice. *b)* a verb in this voice. Abbreviated **pass.** —***SYN.*** see **inactive.**

passive immunity, immunity to a disease acquired by injecting into the blood stream serum from an individual who has acquired active immunity by recovering from the disease.

passive resistance, opposition offered to a law, tax, or government by refusal to comply or obey or by such nonviolent acts as voluntary fasting.

pas·siv·ism (pas′iv-iz'm), *n.* 1. a passive quality or character. 2. the principle of or belief in being passive.

pas·siv·i·ty (pa-siv′ə-ti), *n.* the state or quality of being passive; inaction; submissiveness.

pass·key (pas′kē′, päs′kē′), *n.* 1. a key that will open every one of a group of locks, as those of a certain building; master key. 2. any private key.

Pass·o·ver (pas'ō'vẽr, päs'ō'vẽr), *n.* [*pass* + *over*, used to transl. Heb. *pesaḥ;* see PASCH], 1. a Jewish holiday (*Pesach*) commemorating the deliverance of the ancient Hebrews from slavery in Egypt: Ex. 12: see **Jewish holidays.** 2. [p-], formerly, the paschal lamb.

pass·port (pas'pôrt', päs'pōrt'), *n.* [Fr. *passeport*, safe-conduct, orig., permission to leave a port or sail into it < *passer* (see PASS) + *port*, a port], 1. a government document granting permission to a citizen to travel in certain specified foreign countries and certifying his identity and citizenship: it entitles the bearer to the protection of his own country and that of the countries visited. 2. a safe-conduct. 3. a government document permitting a vessel to leave port and requesting permission for it to enter and leave certain foreign ports. 4. anything that enables a person to be accepted, admitted, or successful.

pas·sus (pas'əs), *n.* [*pl.* PASSUS, PASSUSES (-iz)], [L., a step; see PACE], a part or section of a poem or story.

pass·word (pas'wũrd', päs'wũrd'), *n.* a secret word or phrase used by the members of a military unit, etc. to identify themselves, as in passing a guard.

Pas·sy, Paul É·dou·ard (pōl ā'dwȧr' pȧ'sē'), 1859–1940; French phonetician; principal originator of the International Phonetic Alphabet.

past (past, päst), past participle of **pass.** *adj.* 1. gone by; ended; over: as, his worries were *past.* 2. of a former time; bygone. 3. immediately preceding; just gone by: as, the *past* week. 4. having served formerly: as, a *past* chairman. 5. in *grammar*, indicating a time or condition gone by or an action completed or in progress at a former time. *n.* 1. the history, former life, or experiences of a person, group, or institution: often used, with the indefinite article, to indicate a hidden or questionable past, as the actress was found to have a *past.* 2. in *grammar*, *a*) the past tense. *b*) a verb form in this tense. *prep.* 1. beyond in time; later than. 2. beyond in space; farther on than. 3. beyond in amount or degree. 4. beyond the extent, power, limits, scope, etc. of: as, it's *past* belief. *adv.* to and beyond a point in time or space; by; so as to pass. Abbreviated **p.**
the past, something that has gone before; past time, state, or happenings.

paste (pāst), *n.* [ME.; OFr.; LL. *pasta;* Gr. *pastē*, mess of barley porridge < *passein*, to sprinkle], 1. dough used in making rich pastry. 2. any of various soft, moist, smooth-textured substances: as, tooth *paste*, shoe *paste.* 3. a foodstuff, pounded or ground until fine and made creamy, soft, etc.: as, almond *paste.* 4. a jellylike candy. 5. a mixture of flour or starch, water, and occasionally alum, resin, etc., used as an adhesive for light materials, as paper or gold leaf. 6. the moistened clay used in manufacturing pottery and porcelain. 7. *a*) a hard, brilliant glass containing oxide of lead: used in making artificial gems. *b*) such a gem or gems. 8. [Slang], a blow, or punch, as with the fist. *v.t.* [PASTED (-id), PASTING], 1. to fasten or make adhere, with or as with paste. 2. to cover with pasted material: as, he *pasted* the window with paper. 3. [Slang], to hit; beat; punch.

paste·board (pāst'bôrd', pāst'bōrd'), *n.* 1. a stiff material made of layers of paper pasted together or of pressed and dried paper pulp. 2. [Slang], something made of pasteboard, as a playing card, ticket, etc. *adj.* 1. of or like pasteboard; hence, 2. flimsy; sham.

pas·tel (pas'tel), *n.* [Fr.; Pr.; LL. **pastellum;* see the next entry], 1. a plant whose leaves yield a blue dye. 2. this dye. Also called *woad.*

pas·tel (pas-tel', pas'tel), *n.* [Fr.; It. *pastello;* LL. **pastellum*, dim. of *pasta*, a paste], 1. *a*) ground coloring matter mixed with gum and formed into a crayon. *b*) a crayon so made. 2. a picture drawn with such crayons. 3. drawing with pastels as an art form or medium. 4. a light, brief prose work. 5. a soft, pale shade of some color. *adj.* 1. soft and pale: said of colors. 2. of pastel.

pas·tel·ist, pas·tel·list (pas'tel-ist, pas-tel'ist), *n.* an artist who draws with pastels.

past·er (pās'tẽr), *n.* 1. a person or thing that pastes. 2. a slip of gummed paper used to paste on or over something.

pas·tern (pas'tẽrn), *n.* [ME. *pastron;* OFr. *pasturon* < *pasture*, tether for cattle; LL. *pastoria*, a tether < L. *pastorius*, pastoral < *pastor;* see PASTOR], the part of a horse's foot between the fetlock and the hoof.

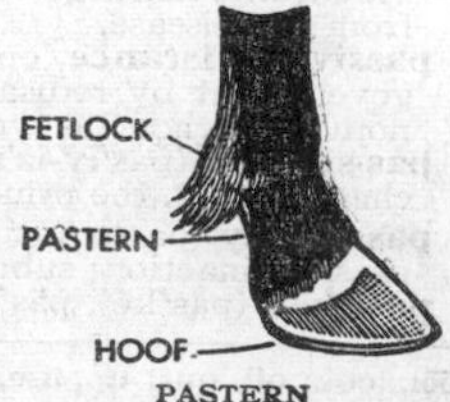

PASTERN

Pas·teur, Lou·is (lwē päs'tẽr'; Eng. pas-tũr'), 1822–1895; French chemist and bacteriologist.

pas·teur·ism (pas'tẽr-iz'm), *n.* the theories or methods of Louis Pasteur; specifically, *a*) pasteurization. *b*) the Pasteur treatment for rabies.

pas·teur·i·za·tion (pas'tẽr-i-zā'shən, pas'chẽr-ī-zā'shən), *n.* [< *pasteurize* (*Pasteur* + *-ize*) + *-ation*], a method of destroying disease-producing bacteria, and checking the activity of fermentative bacteria, in milk, beer, etc. by exposing the liquid to a temperature of 142°–145° F. for thirty minutes.

pas·teur·ize (pas'tẽr-īz', pas'chẽr-īz'), *v.t.* [PASTEURIZED (-īzd'), PASTEURIZING], 1. to subject (milk, beer, etc.) to pasteurization. 2. to give the Pasteur treatment to.

Pasteur treatment, a method of preventing certain diseases, especially rabies, by successive inoculations with the specific virus in increasing strength: first used by Louis Pasteur.

‡pas·tic·cio (päs-tēt'chô), *n.* [*pl.* PASTICCI (-chē)], [It.; ML. *pasticius;* LL. **pasticius*, composed of paste < *pasta*, a paste], a literary, artistic, or musical composition made up of bits from various sources; potpourri; medley.

pas·tiche (pas-tēsh', päs-tēsh'), *n.* [Fr.; It. *pasticcio*], a pasticcio, especially one done in imitation or ridicule of the style of another artist.

pas·til (pas'til), *n.* pastille.

pas·tille (pas-tēl'), *n.* [Fr.; L. *pastillus*, little roll, lozenge < *pascere*, to feed], 1. a small tablet or lozenge containing medicine, flavoring, etc. 2. a pellet of aromatic paste, burned for fumigating or deodorizing. 3. pastel for crayons. 4. a crayon of pastel.

pas·time (pas'tīm', päs'tīm'), *n.* [< *pass* + *time*, transl. of Fr. *passe-temps*], a way of spending spare time; anything done for amusement, recreation, or diversion.

past·i·ness (pās'ti-nis), *n.* a pasty state or quality.

past master, 1. a person who formerly held the position of master, as in a lodge or club. 2. a person who has had long experience in some occupation, art, etc.; expert. Abbreviated **P.M.**

Pas·to (päs'tô), *n.* 1. a city in southwestern Colombia: pop., 60,000 (1945). 2. a volcano near this city: height, 13,990 ft.

pas·tor (pas'tẽr, päs'tẽr), *n.* [ME. *pastour;* OFr.; L. < *pascere*, to feed], 1. originally, a shepherd; hence, 2. a clergyman or priest in charge of a church or congregation. Abbreviated **P., p.**

pas·to·ral (pas'tẽr-əl, päs'tẽr-əl), *adj.* [ME. *pastoralle;* L. *pastoralis* < *pastor*, a shepherd], 1. of shepherds or their work, way of life, etc. 2. of or portraying rural life, especially a conventionalized form of rustic life among shepherds, dairymaids, etc. 3. of pastoral literature or a pastoral. 4. characteristic of pleasant rural life; peaceful, simple, and natural. 5. of a pastor or his duties. *n.* 1. a piece of literature dealing with life in the country; especially, a poem, play, etc. treating the rustic lives and loves of shepherds in a conventionalized, artificial manner. 2. such writing as a literary form. 3. a pastoral picture or scene. 4. a book treating of the functions of a pastor. 5. a letter from a pastor to his congregation or from a bishop to his clergy. 6. a crosier. 7. in *music*, a pastorale. —*SYN.* see **rural.**

pas·to·ra·le (pas'tə-rä'li; It. päs'tô-rä'le), *n.* [*pl.* PASTORALES (-liz), PASTORALI (-lē)], [It.], in *music*, 1. a composition in simple and idyllic style suggesting rural scenes. 2. a composition, as an opera or cantata, with a rural theme or subject.

pas·to·ral·ism (pas'tẽr-əl-iz'm, päs'tẽr-əl-iz'm), *n.* pastoral character or style.

pas·to·ral·ist (pas'tẽr-əl-ist, päs'tẽr-əl-ist), *n.* a writer of pastorals.

pastoral staff, a crosier.

pas·tor·ate (pas'tẽr-it, päs'tẽr-it), *n.* 1. the position, rank, or duties of a pastor. 2. a pastor's term of office with one church or parish. 3. *a*) a group of pastors serving one locality. *b*) pastors collectively.

pas·to·ri·um (pas-tôr'i-əm, pas-tō'ri-əm), *n.* [Mod. L. < L. *pastorius*, of a shepherd < *pastor*, a shepherd], in the southern United States, a parsonage.

pas·tor·ship (pas'tẽr-ship', päs'tẽr-ship'), *n.* [see -SHIP], a pastorate.

past participle, a participle used usually with an auxiliary to indicate a time or state gone by or an action completed in the past (e.g., in "the garden has grown well because it has been properly tended," *grown* and *tended* are past participles): abbreviated **pp., past. part., P.P., p.p.**

past perfect, in *grammar*, 1. expressing action completed before a given or implied time; pluperfect (e.g., in "he had locked the door before he left," *had locked* is past perfect). 2. a past perfect tense or form.

pas·tra·mi (pə-strä'mi), *n.* [Yid.; Hung.], rolled beef, especially a shoulder cut, highly spiced and smoked.

pas·try (pās'tri), *n.* [*pl.* PASTRIES (-triz)], [< *paste;* cf. OFr. *pastaierie* (< *pastaier*, pastry cook)], 1. flour dough or paste made with shortening and used for the crust of pies, tarts, etc. 2. articles of food made with this, as pies, tarts, etc. 3. in a broad sense, all fancy baked goods, including cakes, pies, tarts, etc.

pas·tur·a·ble (pas'chẽr-ə-b'l, päs'chẽr-ə-b'l), *adj.* that can be used for pasture.

pas·tur·age (pas'chẽr-ij, päs'chẽr-ij), *n.* [OFr. < *pasturer;* see -AGE], 1. pasture. 2. *a*) the pasturing of cattle. *b*) the right or business of doing this.

pas·ture (pas'chẽr, päs'chẽr), ***n.*** [ME.; OFr.; LL. *pastura* < L. *pascere*, to feed], 1. grass or other growing plants used as food by grazing animals. 2. ground suitable for grazing, or a field, plot, etc. set aside for this. ***v.t.*** [PASTURED (-chẽrd), PASTURING], 1. to put (cattle, etc.) out to graze in a pasture. 2. to graze or feed on (grass, etc.). 3. to provide with pasture: said of land. ***v.i.*** to feed on growing grass or herbage.

pas·tur·er (pas'chẽr-ẽr, päs'chẽr-ẽr), ***n.*** a person who pastures cattle, etc.

past·y (pās'ti), ***adj.*** [PASTIER (-ti-ẽr), PASTIEST (-ti-ist)], of or like paste in color or texture.

pas·ty (pas'ti, päs'ti; pās'ti *is a sp. pronun.*), ***n.*** [*pl.* PASTIES (-tiz)], [ME. *pastee;* OFr. *pastée* < LL. *pasta*, a paste], [Chiefly British], a pie, especially a meat pie.

pat (pat), ***adj.*** [prob. < *pat, v.*], 1. apt; timely; opportune. 2. exactly suitable: as, a *pat* hand in poker. ***adv.*** aptly; perfectly; suitably.
 have (or **know**) **pat,** [Colloq.], to know thoroughly.
 stand pat, [Colloq.], 1. to refuse to turn aside from an opinion, course of action, etc. 2. in *poker*, to draw no further cards, but play the hand as dealt.

pat (pat), ***n.*** [ME. *patte;* prob. echoic], 1. a quick, gentle tap, touch, or stroke with the hand or other flat surface. 2. a sound made by this. 3. a small lump or mass, as of butter. ***v.t.*** [PATTED (-id), PATTING], 1. *a*) to tap, touch, or stroke quickly or gently, especially with the hand as in affection, sympathy, or encouragement. *b*) to tap or stroke lightly with a flat surface. 2. to give a certain shape to, as mud, by patting. ***v.i.*** to make a patting sound, as in running.

pat., 1. patent. 2. patented. 3. pattern.

pat-a-cake (pat'ə-kāk'), ***n.*** 1. the opening words of a nursery rhyme. 2. a game played by clapping the hands in rhythm to this rhyme. Also **patty-cake.**

pa·ta·gi·um (pə-tā'ji-əm), ***n.*** [*pl.* PATAGIA (-ə)], [Mod. L.; L., gold edging of a tunic, border; Gr. *patageion*], 1. a fold of skin between the fore and hind limbs of flying squirrels, flying lizards, etc., enabling them to glide through the air. 2. a fold of skin between the shoulder and fore part of a bird's wing.

Pat·a·go·ni·a (pat'ə-gō'ni-ə, pat'ə-gōn'yə), ***n.*** a region in southern Argentina and Chile.

PATAGONIA

Pat·a·go·ni·an (pat'ə-gō'ni-ən, pat'ə-gōn'yən), ***adj.*** of Patagonia, its people, or their culture. ***n.*** a member of a tribe of very tall South American Indians that live in Patagonia.

patch (pach), ***n.*** [ME. *pacche;* prob. var. of *peche*, a piece < OFr. *pieche* (Fr. *pièce;* cf. PIECE); for form, cf. MATCH], 1. a piece of material applied to cover or mend a hole or tear or to strengthen a weak spot. 2. a dressing applied to a wound or sore. 3. a pad or shield worn over an injured eye. 4. a little piece of black paper, cloth, etc., put on a woman's face, back, etc. to emphasize the beauty or whiteness of her skin; beauty spot. 5. a surface area differing from its surroundings in nature or appearance: as, *patches* of blue sky. 6. a small plot of ground: as, a potato *patch*. 7. a small piece of any material; scrap; bit; remnant. ***v.t.*** 1. to put a patch or patches on. 2. to serve as a patch for. 3. to form or make by the use of patches, as a quilt. 4. to produce or bring together roughly, crudely, or hurriedly; piece together (often with *up* or *together*). —***SYN.*** see **mend.**
 patch up, to bring to an end; make right; settle, as differences or a quarrel.

Patch, Alexander Mc·Car·rell (mə-kar'əl pach), 1889–1945; American general in World War II.

patch·i·ly (pach'ə-li), ***adv.*** so as to be patchy; in patches.

patch·i·ness (pach'i-nis), ***n.*** the state or quality of being patchy.

patch·ou·li, patch·ou·ly (pach'oo-li, pə-chōō'li), ***n.*** [Fr. < Tamil *paccilai*, lit., green leaf < *paccu*, green + *ilai*, a leaf], 1. an East Indian plant of the mint family. 2. a perfume made from its fragrant oil.

patch pocket, a pocket made by sewing a patch of shaped material to the outside of a garment.

patch test, in *medicine*, a test for determining allergy to a specific substance, made by placing on the skin small pieces of cloth or blotting paper soaked in this substance and observing the reaction of the skin.

patch·work (pach'wũrk'), ***n.*** 1. anything formed of irregular, incongruous, odd, or miscellaneous parts; jumble. 2. needlework, as a quilt, made of odd patches of cloth, etc. sewn together at the edges. 3. any design or surface like this.

patch·y (pach'i), ***adj.*** [PATCHIER (-i-ẽr), PATCHIEST (-i-ist)], 1. *a*) made up of or characterized by patches. *b*) forming or like patches. 2. giving the effect of patches; not consistent or uniform in quality; irregular.

patd., patented.

pate (pāt), ***n.*** [ME.; prob. orig. euphemistic (like Fr. *tête*, G. *kopf*, etc.); ? < or associated with L. *patina* (cf. PATEN)], 1. the head. 2. the top of the head. 3. intelligence. A humorous or derogatory term.

‡pâte (pät), ***n.*** [Fr.], paste; especially, the clay paste used in making pottery or porcelain.

‡pâ·té (pä'tā'), ***n.*** [Fr.], 1. a pie or pasty. 2. a meat paste.

-pat·ed (pāt'id), a combining form meaning *having a* (specified kind of) *pate*, or *head*, as in *bald-pated*.

‡pâ·té de foie gras (pä'tā' də fwä' grä'), [Fr.], a paste made of the livers of fattened geese.

pa·tel·la (pə-tel'ə), ***n.*** [*pl.* PATELLAS (-əz), PATELLAE (-ē)], [L., dim. of *patina*, a pan < *patere*, to be open], 1. a small, shallow pan. 2. in *anatomy*, the kneecap: see **skeleton,** illus. 3. in *botany* & *zoology*, any panlike formation.

pa·tel·lar (pə-tel'ẽr), ***adj.*** in *anatomy*, of the patella.

patellar reflex, in *medicine*, a reflex kick with extension of the leg at the knee, produced by sharply tapping the tendon below the patella: it is a normal reaction in health: also called *knee jerk*.

pa·tel·late (pə-tel'it, pə-tel'āt), ***adj.*** having or like a patella.

pa·tel·li·form (pə-tel'ə-fôrm'), ***adj.*** [< *patella* + *-form*], 1. having the form of a flattened cone. 2. having the shape of a limpet shell.

pat·en (pat''n), ***n.*** [ME. & OFr. *patene;* L. *patina*, a pan < *patere*, to be open], 1. a metal plate or dish; especially, the plate holding the bread in the Eucharist. 2. a thin, flat piece of metal; disk. Also **patin, patina, patine.**

pa·ten·cy (pā't'n-si), ***n.*** 1. the state or quality of being patent, or obvious. 2. in *medicine*, the state of being open or unobstructed.

pat·ent (pat''nt; *also, esp. Brit.*, pā't'nt; *for adj. 2, 3, & 4, usually* pā't'nt), ***adj.*** [ME.; partly < OFr., partly < L. *patens* < *patere*, to be open], 1. that can be examined by the public: said of a document granting some right, as, formerly, a commission to hold public office. 2. open to all; generally accessible or available. 3. obvious; plain; evident. 4. unobstructed. 5. *a*) protected by a document (letters patent) granting exclusive right to the production, use, sale, and profit of an invention, process, etc. *b*) having received such a document, as an inventor. 6. new, unusual, practical, individual, etc.: as, a *patent* method of lighting a fire. 7. of high quality: said of flour. 8. in *botany* & *zoology*, spreading out or open; patulous. ***n.*** 1. a document open to public examination and granting a certain right or privilege; letters patent; especially, a document granting the monopoly right to produce, use, sell, or get profit from an invention, process, etc. for a certain number of years. 2. *a*) the right so granted. *b*) the thing protected by such a right; patented article or process. 3. land or title to land granted by letters patent. 4. any exclusive right, title, or license: as, she had no *patent* on charm. ***v.t.*** 1. [Rare], to grant a patent to or for. 2. to secure exclusive right to produce, use, and sell (an invention or process) by a patent; get a patent for. Abbreviated **pat.**

pat·ent·ee (pat''n-tē'), ***n.*** a person who has been granted a patent.

patent leather, leather having a hard, glossy, usually black finish: made by a process formerly patented.

pa·tent·ly (pā't'nt-li, pat''nt-li), ***adv.*** in a patent manner; clearly, obviously, evidently, openly, etc.

patent medicine, a trade-marked medical preparation usually containing secret ingredients or made by secret formula.

Patent Office, an office in the Department of Commerce which administers the patent and trade-mark laws: abbreviated **Pat. Off.**

pat·en·tor (pat''n-tẽr), ***n.*** a person or agent who grants a patent.

patent right, an exclusive right established by letters patent, especially the right to an invention.

pa·ter (pā'tẽr), ***n.*** [L.; for cognates & IE. base see FATHER], [Chiefly British Colloq.], father.

Pa·ter, Walter Horatio (pā'tẽr), 1839–1894; English essayist, critic, and novelist.

pa·ter·fa·mil·i·as (pā'tẽr-fə-mil'i-əs), ***n.*** [*pl.* PATRESFAMILIAS (pā'trēz-)], [L.], the father of a family; male head of a household.

pa·ter·nal (pə-tũr'n'l), ***adj.*** [ML. *paternalis* < L. *paternus* < *pater*, father], 1. of, like, or characteristic of a father or fatherhood; fatherly. 2. derived, received, or inherited from a father. 3. on the father's side of the family: as, *paternal* grandparents.

pa·ter·nal·ism (pə-tũr'n'l-iz'm), ***n.*** [*paternal* + *-ism*], the principle or system of governing or controlling a country, group of employees, etc. in a manner suggesting a father's relationship with his children.

pa·ter·nal·is·tic (pə-tũr'n'l-is'tik), *adj.* of or characterized by paternalism.

pa·ter·nal·is·ti·cal·ly (pə-tũr'n'l-is'ti-k'l-i, pə-tũr'n'l-is'tik-li), *adv.* in a paternalistic manner; by paternalism.

pa·ter·ni·ty (pə-tũr'nə-ti), *n.* [Fr. *paternité;* LL. *paternitas* < L. *paternus,* paternal], 1. the state of being a father; fatherhood. 2. male parentage; paternal origin. 3. origin or authorship in general.

pa·ter·nos·ter (pā'tẽr-nos'tẽr, pat'ẽr-nos'tẽr), *n.* [ME.; L., our father], 1. the Lord's Prayer, especially in Latin: often **Pater Noster.** 2. every eleventh bead of a rosary on which this prayer is said. 3. a rosary. 4. any muttered prayer or incantation.

Pat·er·son (pat'ẽr-s'n), *n.* a city in northeastern New Jersey: pop., 144,000.

path (path, päth), *n.* [ME.; AS. *pæth;* akin to G. *pfad;* thought to be orig. an Iranic loan word < IE. base **penth-,* to step, go (as also in L. *pons,* bridge, etc.); cf. Avestan *path-*], 1. a track or way worn by footsteps; trail. 2. a walk or way for the use of people on foot, as in a park or garden. 3. a line of movement; course taken: as, the *path* of the meteor. 4. a course or manner of conduct or procedure.

path., 1. pathological. 2. pathology.

Pa·than (pə-tän', pət-hän'), *n.* [Hind. *Paṭhān* < Afghan *Pĕṣtāna,* pl. of *Pĕṣtūn,* an Afghan], a member of a Moslem, Indo-Iranian people of Afghanistan.

pa·thet·ic (pə-thet'ik), *adj.* [LL. *patheticus;* Gr. *pathētikos* < *pathos,* suffering], 1. expressing, arousing, or intended to arouse pity, sorrow, sympathy, or compassion; pitiful. 2. of the feelings or emotions. —*SYN.* see **moving.**

pa·thet·i·cal (pə-thet'i-k'l), *adj.* [Rare], pathetic.

pa·thet·i·cal·ly (pə-thet'i-k'l-i, pə-thet'ik-li), *adv.* in a pathetic manner.

pathetic fallacy, the literary device of portraying inanimate nature as having human feelings and character. Examples: "the angry sea," "a stubborn door."

path·find·er (path'fīn'dẽr, päth'fīn'dẽr), *n.* one who makes a path or way where none had existed, as in an unknown region, wilderness, etc.

-path·i·a (path'i-ə), -pathy.

-path·ic (path'ik), [see -PATHY & -IC], a combining form used to form adjectives corresponding to nouns ending in *-pathy,* as in *osteopathic, psychopathic.*

path·less (path'lis, päth'lis), *adj.* without a path or track; untrodden.

path·o- (path'ō, path'ə), [< Gr. *pathos* < *pathein,* to suffer], a combining form meaning *suffering, disease, feeling,* as in *pathology:* also, before a vowel, **path-.**

path·o·gen (path'ə-jen), *n.* [*patho-* + *-gen*], any microorganism or virus that can cause disease.

path·o·gene (path'ə-jēn'), *n.* a pathogen.

path·o·gen·e·sis (path'ə-jen'ə-sis), *n.* [Mod. L.; see PATHO- & -GENESIS], the production or development of a disease.

path·o·ge·net·ic (path'ō-jə-net'ik), *adj.* of or causing pathogenesis; pathogenic.

path·o·gen·ic (path'ə-jen'ik), *adj.* pathogenetic.

pa·thog·e·ny (pə-thoj'ə-ni), *n.* pathogenesis.

path·o·log·ic (path'ə-loj'ik), *adj.* pathological.

path·o·log·i·cal (path'ə-loj'i-k'l), *adj.* 1. of pathology; of or concerned with diseases. 2. due to or involving disease. Abbreviated **path., pathol.**

path·o·log·i·cal·ly (path'ə-loj'i-k'l-i, path'ə-loj'ik-li), *adv.* of or with reference to pathology.

pa·thol·o·gist (pə-thol'ə-jist), *n.* a specialist in pathology.

pa·thol·o·gy (pə-thol'ə-ji), *n.* [Fr. *pathologie;* Mod.L. *pathologia;* see PATHO- & -LOGY], 1. the branch of medicine that deals with the nature of disease, especially with the structural and functional changes caused by disease. 2. [*pl.* PATHOLOGIES (-jiz)], all the conditions, processes, or results of a particular disease. Abbreviated **path., pathol.**

pa·thos (pā'thos), *n.* [Gr. *pathos,* suffering, disease, feeling < base of *pathein, paschein,* to suffer, feel], 1. [Rare], suffering. 2. the quality in something experienced or observed which arouses feelings of pity, sorrow, sympathy, or compassion. 3. the personal or emotional element in art: opposed to *ethos.*

SYN.—**pathos** names that quality, in a real situation or in a literary or artistic work, which evokes sympathy and a sense of sorrow or pity; **bathos** applies to a false or overdone pathos that is absurd in its effect; **poignancy** implies an emotional quality that is keenly felt, often to the point of being sharply painful.

path·way (path'wā', päth'wā'), *n.* a path.

-pa·thy (pə-thi), [< Gr. *pathos,* suffering], a combining form meaning *feeling, suffering, disease, treatment of disease,* as in *antipathy, osteopathy:* also **-pathia.**

Pat·i·a·la (put'i-ä'lə), *n.* a city in northern India, in the state of Punjab: pop., 70,000.

Patiala and East Punjab, a former state of northwestern India: now part of the state of Punjab.

pa·tience (pā'shəns), *n.* [ME. & OFr. *pacience;* L. *patientia* < *pati,* to suffer], 1. the state, quality, ability, or fact of being patient; specifically, *a)* the will or ability to wait or endure without complaint. *b)* steadiness, endurance, or perseverance in performing a task. 2. [Chiefly British], any of a number of card games, usually for one player; solitaire.

SYN.—**patience** implies the bearing of suffering, provocation, delay, tediousness, etc. with calmness and self-control (her *patience* with children); **endurance** stresses the capacity to bear suffering or hardship (Job's *endurance* of his afflictions); **fortitude** suggests the resolute endurance that results from firm, sustained courage (the *fortitude* of the pioneers); **forbearance** implies restraint under provocation or a refraining from retaliation for a wrong (he acted with *forbearance* toward the hecklers); **stoicism** suggests such endurance of suffering without flinching as to indicate an almost austere indifference to pain or pleasure. —*ANT.* impatience.

pa·tient (pā'shənt), *adj.* [ME. & OFr. *pacient;* L. *patiens,* patient, ppr. of *pati,* to suffer], 1. bearing or enduring pain, trouble, etc. without complaining, losing self-control, making a disturbance, etc. 2. refusing to be provoked or angered, as by an insult; forbearing; tolerant. 3. calmly tolerating delay, confusion, inefficiency, etc.; able to wait calmly. 4. showing or characterized by patience: as, a *patient* face. 5. steady; diligent; persevering, as a worker. 6. [Rare], receiving action; passive. *n.* 1. a person receiving care or treatment; especially, a person under the care of a doctor. 2. a person who receives action or is affected.

patient of, 1. capable of bearing (fatigue, thirst, etc.). 2. admitting of or having (a particular meaning).

pat·in (pat''n), *n.* a paten.

pat·i·na (pat'i-nə), *n.* [*pl.* PATINAE (-nē')], [L.], a paten.

pat·i·na (pat''n-ə), *n.* [< It. (? via Fr. *patine*); orig., tarnish (on a metal plate); cf. PATEN], 1. a fine crust or film on bronze or copper: it is usually green or greenish-blue and is formed by natural oxidation: it is valued as being ornamental. 2. any thin coating or color change resulting from age, as on old wood.

pat·ine (pat''n), *n.* a paten.

pa·ti·o (pä'ti-ō', pat'i-ō'; Sp. pä'tyô), *n.* [*pl.* PATIOS (-ōz'; Sp. -tyôs)], [Sp.; prob. < L. *patere,* to lie open], 1. a courtyard or inner area open to the sky: common in Spanish and Spanish-American architecture. 2. a terrace (sense 4).

Pat·more, Cov·en·try (kuv'ən-tri pat'môr, pat'mōr), (*Coventry Kersey Dighton Patmore*), 1823–1896; English poet.

Pat·mos (pät'môs; Eng. pat'məs), *n.* a Greek island in the Aegean: area, 22 sq. mi.; pop., 3,000: cf. Rev. 1:9.

Pat·na (put'nə, pat'nə), *n.* the capital of Bihar province, India, on the Ganges: pop., 283,000.

Pat. Off., Patent Office.

pat·ois (pat'wä; Fr. på'twå'), *n.* [*pl.* PATOIS (pat'wäz; Fr. på'twå')], [Fr.], 1. a form of a language differing generally from the accepted standard, as a provincial or local dialect. 2. in *linguistics,* the blend of a provincial dialect with a standard form of a language.

pat. pend., patent pending.

Pa·tras (pä-träs'), *n.* a seaport in Greece, on the northwestern Peloponnesus: pop., 79,000.

Patras, Gulf of, an arm of the Ionian Sea, between the western Peloponnesus and the mainland of Greece, connecting with the Gulf of Corinth.

pat·ri- (pat'rə, pat'ri), [L.; Gr. *patri-* < *patēr,* father], a combining form meaning *father,* as in *patrimony.*

pa·tri·arch (pā'tri-ärk'), *n.* [ME. & OFr. *patriarche;* LL. *patriarcha* < Gr. *patriarchēs* < *patria,* family < *patēr,* father + *archein,* to rule], 1. the father and ruler of a family or tribe, as one of the founders of the ancient Hebrew families: in the Bible, Abraham, Isaac, Jacob and Jacob's twelve sons were patriarchs. 2. a person regarded as the founder or father of a colony, religion, business, etc. 3. *a)* a bishop in the early Christian Church, especially a bishop of Rome, Constantinople, Alexandria, Antioch, or Jerusalem. *b)* in the *Roman Catholic Church,* a bishop who holds the highest rank, after the Pope, in the hierarchy of the jurisdiction: patriarchs with jurisdiction are the Pope as Patriarch of the West; those of Constantinople, Alexandria, Antioch, and Jerusalem; those of the Melkite, Syrian, Maronite, Armenian, Chaldean Churches, etc. *c)* in the *Orthodox Eastern Church,* the highest ranking bishop at Constantinople, Alexandria, Antioch, Jerusalem, Moscow, Bucharest, etc. *d)* the jurisdictional head of any of certain other churches, as the Coptic, Nestorian, Armenian, etc. 4. a man of great age and dignity. 5. the oldest individual of a class or group.

pa·tri·ar·chal (pā'tri-är'k'l), *adj.* [ML. *patriarchalis*], 1. of, ruled by, suitable to, or characteristic of a patriarch; hence, 2. venerable. 3. having the position or jurisdiction of a patriarch.

pa·tri·arch·ate (pā'tri-är'kit), *n.* [ML. *patriarchatus*], 1. the position, rank, jurisdiction, territory, etc. of a patriarch. 2. a patriarchal government or system.

pa·tri·arch·y (pā'tri-är'ki), *n.* [*pl.* PATRIARCHIES (-kiz)], [Gr. *patriarchia;* see PATRIARCH], 1. a form of social organization in which the father or the eldest male is recognized as the head of the family or tribe, descent and kinship being traced through the male line. 2. government by men. Opposed to *matriarchy.*

Pa·tri·cia (pə-trish′ə), [L., fem. of *patricius;* see PATRICK], a feminine name: diminutive, *Pat.*

pa·tri·cian (pə-trish′ən), *adj.* [ME. *patricion;* OFr. *patricien;* L. *patricius,* of the rank of the patricians < *patres,* pl. of *pater,* father], 1. of or characteristic of patricians. 2. noble; aristocratic. *n.* [L. *patricius* < the *adj.*], 1. in ancient Rome, *a)* originally, a member of any of the ancient Roman citizen families. *b)* later, a member of the nobility: opposed to *plebeian. c)* a member of a class of honorary nobility of the later Empire. *d)* a chief administrator in the Roman provinces in Africa and Italy. 2. a person of high rank in some medieval Italian republics and in certain Free Cities of the German Empire. 3. any person of high social rank; aristocrat.

pa·tri·ci·ate (pə-trish′i-it, pə-trish′i-āt′), *n.* [ML. *patriciatus* < L. *patricius*], 1. the rank or position of a patrician. 2. the patrician class; aristocracy.

pat·ri·ci·dal (pat′rə-sī′d′l), *adj.* of, like, or having the nature of, patricide or a patricide.

pat·ri·cide (pat′rə-sīd′), *n.* [< L. *pater,* father; + *-cide* (killing)], 1. the act of killing one's own father; murder of a man by his child. 2. [< L. *pater,* father; + *-cide* (killer)], a person who kills his own father.

Pat·rick (pat′rik), [L. *patricius,* a patrician], a masculine name: diminutives, *Paddy, Pat;* feminine, *Patricia.*

Patrick, Saint, 389?–461? A.D.; British bishop who converted the Irish to Christianity; patron saint of Ireland: his day is March 17.

pa·tri·lin·e·al (pā′trə-lin′i-əl, pat′rə-lin′i-əl), *adj.* [*patri-* + *lineal*], designating or of descent, kinship, or derivation through the father instead of the mother.

pat·ri·mo·ni·al (pat′rə-mō′ni-əl), *adj.* [LL. *patrimonialis*], of a patrimony; hereditary.

pat·ri·mo·ny (pat′rə-mō′ni), *n.* [*pl.* PATRIMONIES (-niz)], [ME. *patrimoigne;* OFr. *patrimoine;* L. *patrimonium* < *pater,* father], 1. property inherited from one's father or ancestors. 2. property endowed to an institution, as a church. 3. anything inherited, as a trait or character. —*SYN.* see **heritage.**

pa·tri·ot (pā′tri-ət, pā′tri-ot′; *esp. Brit.* pat′ri-ət), *n.* [Fr. *patriote;* LL. *patriota,* fellow countryman; Gr. *patriōtēs* < *patris,* fatherland], a person who loves and loyally or zealously supports his own country.

pa·tri·ot·ic (pā′tri-ot′ik; *esp. Brit.* pat′ri-ot′ik), *adj.* [Fr. *patriotique;* LL. *patrioticus*], 1. having or showing the qualities and feelings of a patriot. 2. characteristic of or suitable to a patriot; inspired by patriotism.

pa·tri·ot·i·cal·ly (pā′tri-ot′i-k′l-i; *esp. Brit.* pat′ri-ot′ik-li), *adv.* in a patriotic manner.

pa·tri·ot·ism (pā′tri-ət-iz′m; *esp. Brit.* pat′ri-ət-iz′m), *n.* [*patriot* + *-ism*], love and loyal or zealous support of one's own country, especially in all matters involving other countries; nationalism.

Patriots' Day, April 19, a legal holiday in Maine and Massachusetts commemorating the battles of Lexington and Concord (1775).

pa·tris·tic (pə-tris′tik), *adj.* [< L. *patres,* pl. of *pater,* father; + *-istic*], of the early leaders, or fathers, of the Christian Church or the writings and doctrines attributed to them.

pa·tris·ti·cal (pə-tris′ti-k′l), *adj.* patristic.

Pa·tro·clus (pə-trō′kləs), *n.* [L.; Gr. *Patroklos*], in *Greek legend,* a Greek warrior and friend of Achilles in the Trojan War: while wearing Achilles' armor he was mistaken for him and slain by Hector.

pa·trol (pə-trōl′), *v.t. & v.i.* [PATROLLED (-trōld′), PATROLLING], [Fr. *patrouiller,* altered < *patouiller,* to paddle, puddle, patrol (prob. < *patte,* a paw, foot)], to make a regular and repeated circuit of (an area, town, camp, etc.) in guarding or inspecting: as, an armed guard is *patrolling* the area. *n.* [Fr. *patrouille* < the *v.*], 1. a patrolling. 2. a person or persons patrolling. 3. a group of ships, airplanes, etc. used in guarding or gathering information about the enemy. 4. a group of eight boy scouts, constituting a subdivision of a troop.

pa·trol·ler (pə-trōl′ẽr), *n.* a person who patrols.

pa·trol·man (pə-trōl′mən), *n.* [*pl.* PATROLMEN (-mən)], a man who patrols; especially, a policeman assigned to make a circuit of a certain area.

patrol wagon, a small, enclosed truck used by the police in transporting prisoners.

pa·tron (pā′trən), *n.* [ME. *patron, patroun;* OFr. *patron, patrun;* L. *patronus* < *pater,* father], 1. a person corresponding in some respects to a father; protector; benefactor. 2. a person empowered with the granting of an English church benefice. 3. a patron saint. 4. *a)* a person, usually a wealthy and influential one, who sponsors and supports some person, activity, etc.: as, the book was dedicated to the author's *patron. b)* a champion; advocate; supporter. 5. a regular customer, as of a store. 6. in ancient Rome, a person who had freed his slave but still retained a certain paternal control over him. —*SYN.* see **sponsor.**

pa·tron·age (pā′trən-ij, pat′rən-ij), *n.* [ME. < ML. *patronagium*], 1. *a)* the function or status of a patron. *b)* support, favor, encouragement, sponsorship, etc. given by a patron. 2. the power to grant an English church benefice. 3. good will, favor, courtesy, etc. shown to people considered inferior; condescension. 4. *a)* patrons collectively; clientele. *b)* business; trade; custom. 5. the power to appoint to office or grant other favors, especially political ones. 6. offices or other favors distributed through this power.

pa·tron·al (pā′trən-′l, pat′rən-′l), *adj.* [Fr.; LL. *patronalis*], of or characteristic of a patron or patron saint; protective; guardian.

pa·tron·ess (pā′trən-is, pat′rən-is), *n.* [ME. *patronesse;* ML. *patronissa*], a woman patron, especially one who sponsors or supports some activity, as the opera.

pa·tron·ize (pā′trə-nīz′, pat′rə-nīz′), *v.t.* [PATRONIZED (-nīzd′), PATRONIZING], 1. to act as a patron toward; sponsor; support; protect. 2. to show favor or kindness to in a condescending manner. 3. to be a regular customer of (a store, etc.); give one's trade to.

patron saint, a saint looked upon as the special guardian of a person, place, or institution.

pat·ro·nym·ic (pat′rə-nim′ik), *adj.* [LL. *patronymicus;* Gr. *patrōnymikos* < *patēr,* father + *onoma, onyma,* a name], 1. derived from the name of a father or ancestor. 2. showing such descent: as, a *patronymic* suffix. *n.* 1. a name showing descent from a given person as by the addition of a prefix or suffix (e.g., *Stevenson,* son of Steven, *O'Brien,* descendant of Brien). 2. a family name; surname.

pa·troon (pə-trōōn′), *n.* [D., protector < Fr. *patron;* see PATRON], 1. a person who held a large estate with manorial rights in return for founding a colony under the old Dutch governments of New York and New Jersey. 2. [Fr. *patron*], [Obs.], a patron.

pat·ten (pat′′n), *n.* [ME. *paten;* OFr. *patin,* a clog, patten < *patte,* a paw, foot], 1. a thick wooden sandal mounted on an iron support and worn in wet weather. 2. a wooden shoe or overshoe.

pat·ter (pat′ẽr), *v.i.* [freq. of *pat,* to tap gently], 1. to make a patter. 2. to move so as to make a patter. *v.t.* to cause to patter. *n.* a series of light, rapid taps: as, the *patter* of rain on dry leaves.

pat·ter (pat′ẽr), *v.t. & v.i.* [ME. *patteren* < *pater,* in *paternoster,* as pronounced in rapid and mechanical recitation], to speak or mumble rapidly or glibly; recite mechanically or thoughtlessly, as prayers. *n.* 1. language peculiar to a group, class, etc., and not generally understood by outsiders; cant; jargon. 2. the glib, rapid speech of salesmen, circus barkers, magicians, etc. 3. [Colloq.], idle, meaningless chatter.

pat·ter (pat′ẽr), *n.* a person or thing that pats.

pat·tern (pat′ẽrn), *n.* [ME. & OFr. *patron,* patron, hence something to be imitated, pattern; see PATRON], 1. a person or thing so ideal as to be worthy of imitation or copying. 2. a model, guide, plan, etc. used in making things. 3. the full-scale model used in making a sand mold for casting metal. 4. something representing a class or type; example; sample. 5. an arrangement of form; disposition of parts or elements; design or decoration: as, wallpaper *patterns,* the *pattern* of a novel. 6. definite direction, tendency, or characteristics: as, behavior *patterns.* 7. *a)* grouping or distribution, as of a number of bullets fired at a mark. *b)* a diagram showing such distribution. 8. sufficient material for making a garment. *v.t.* 1. to make or do (something) in imitation of a model or pattern (with *on, upon,* or *after*). 2. to supply with a pattern or design; put a pattern on. Abbreviated **pat.** —*SYN.* see **model.**

pat·tern·mak·er (pat′ẽrn-māk′ẽr), *n.* a person who makes patterns, especially patterns for molds: also **pattern maker.**

patter song, a musical comedy song with a simple tune and comic lyrics sung with great rapidity.

Pat·ti, A·de·li·na (ä′de-lē′nä pät′tē; Eng. pat′i), (*Baroness Cederström*), 1843–1919; Italian operatic soprano, born in Spain.

Pat·ton, Jr., George Smith (pat′′n), 1885–1945; American general in World War II.

pat·ty (pat′i), *n.* [*pl.* PATTIES (-iz)], [Fr. *pâté;* see PÂTÉ], 1. a small pie. 2. a small, flat cake of ground meat, fish, etc., usually fried. 3. any disk-shaped piece of food.

pat·ty-cake (pat′i-kāk′), *n.* pat-a-cake.

patty pan, a pan used for baking patties (sense 1).

pat·u·lous (pach′oo-ləs), *adj.* [L. *patulus* < *patere,* to be open], in *botany,* standing open, or spreading.

Pau (pō), *n.* a city in southwestern France: pop., 46,000 (1946).

‡pau·cis ver·bis (pô′sis vũr′bis), [L.], in a few words.

pau·ci·ty (pô′sə-ti), *n.* [< Fr. or L.; Fr. *paucité;* L. *paucitas* < *paucus,* few], 1. fewness; small number. 2. scarcity; dearth; insufficiency.

Paul (pôl), [L. *Paulus* (or Gr. *Paulos*), a Roman surname of the Aemilian gens, prob. < or akin to *paulus,* small], a masculine name: feminine, *Paula, Pauline;* equivalents, L. *Paulus,* It. *Paolo,* Sp. *Pablo.*

Paul, Saint, ?–67? A.D.; a Jew of Tarsus, apostle of Christianity to the Gentiles; author of the Pauline Epistles: his day is January 25: originally called *Saul.*

Paul I, (*Pavel Petrovich*), 1754–1801; son of *Catherine the Great* and *Peter III;* emperor of Russia (1796–1801).

Paul III, (*Alessandro Farnese*), 1468–1549; Italian church official; Pope (1534–1549).

Pau·la (pô′lə), [G. or LL., fem. of L. *Paulus,* Paul], a feminine name.

Paul-Bon·cour, Jo·seph (zhô′zef′ pôl′bōn′kōōr′), 1873– ; French statesman; premier (1932–1933).

Paul Bun·yan (bun′yən), in *American legend,* a giant lumberjack who, with the help of his blue ox, Babe, performed various superhuman feats.

paul·dron (pôl′drən), *n.* [OFr. *espauleron* < *espaule,* the shoulder (Fr. *épaule*); see EPAULET], a piece of plate armor to protect the shoulder: see **armor,** illus.

Pau·line (pô-lēn′), [L. < *Paulinus,* belonging to a *Paulus;* see PAUL], a feminine name.

Paul·ine (pôl′in, pôl′ēn), *adj.* of or characteristic of the Apostle Paul, his writings, or doctrines.

Paul·ist (pôl′ist), *n.* 1. in India, a Jesuit. 2. a Roman Catholic priest belonging to the Missionary Society of St. Paul the Apostle, founded in New York in 1858.

pau·low·ni·a (pô-lō′ni-ə), *n.* [after Anna *Pavlovna,* Russ. princess], any of various Asiatic trees with large, heart-shaped leaves and large clusters of violet flowers.

Pa·u·mo·to Archipelago (pä′oo-mō′tōō), Tuamotu Archipelago, a group of islands in the South Pacific.

paunch (pônch), *n.* [ME. *paunche, panche;* OFr. *panche;* L. *pantex, panticis,* belly], 1. the abdomen, or belly; especially, a large, protruding belly; potbelly. 2. the first and largest stomach of a cud-chewing animal.

paunch·i·ness (pôn′chi-nis), *n.* the state or quality of being paunchy.

paunch·y (pôn′chi), *adj.* having a large, protruding belly.

pau·per (pô′pẽr), *n.* [L., poor person], 1. a person who lives on charity, especially on tax-supported charity. 2. any person who is extremely poor.

pau·per·ism (pô′pẽr-iz′m), *n.* 1. the condition of being a pauper. 2. paupers collectively.

pau·per·i·za·tion (pô′pẽr-i-zā′shən, pô′pẽr-ī-zā′shən), *n.* a pauperizing or being pauperized.

pau·per·ize (pô′pẽr-iz′), *v.t.* [PAUPERIZED (-īzd′), PAUPERIZING], to make a pauper of.

Pau·sa·ni·us (pô-sā′ni-əs), *n.* Greek traveler, geographer, and chronicler; 2d century A.D.

pause (pôz), *n.* [Fr.; L. *pausa;* Gr. *pausis,* a stopping < *pauein,* to bring to an end, stop], 1. a short period of inaction; temporary stop, break, or rest, as in speaking or reading. 2. hesitation; interruption; delay: as, pursuit without *pause.* 3. *a*) a stop or break in speaking or reading to clarify meaning. *b*) any mark of punctuation indicating this. 4. in *music,* a sign (𝄐 or 𝄑) placed above or below a note or rest that is to be prolonged. 5. in *prosody,* a rhythm break or caesura. *v.i.* [PAUSED (pôzd), PAUSING], 1. to make a pause; be temporarily inactive; stop; hesitate. 2. to dwell or linger (with *on* or *upon*): as, to *pause* on a point.
 give one pause, to make one hesitant or uncertain.

pav·an (pav′ən), *n.* [Fr. *pavane;* Sp. *pavana* < *pavo,* peacock; L. *pavus*], 1. a slow, stately court dance of Spanish or Italian origin, performed by couples. 2. the music for this. Also **pavane, pavin.**

pav·ane (pav′ən; Fr. pȧ′vȧn′), *n.* a pavan.

pave (pāv), *v.t.* [PAVED (pāvd), PAVING], [ME. *paven;* OFr. *paver;* LL. **pavare,* for L. *pavire,* to ram, beat; akin to Lith. *piauti,* to cut, L. *putare,* to cut], 1. to cover over the surface of (a road, etc.), as with concrete, asphalt, brick, etc.. 2. to be the top surface or covering of. 3. to cover closely or thickly; stud; overlay.
 pave the way (for), to prepare the way (for); facilitate the introduction (of).

‡pa·vé (pȧ′vā′), *n.* [Fr., orig. pp. of *paver;* see PAVE], 1. pavement. 2. a setting of jewelry in which the gems are placed close together so that no metal shows.

pave·ment (pāv′mənt), *n.* [ME.; OFr.; L. *pavimentum* < *pavire,* to beat down], 1. a paved surface or covering, as of concrete, brick, etc. 2. a paved street or road. 3. the material used in paving.

pav·er (pāv′ẽr), *n.* 1. a person or thing that paves. 2. a paving stone, etc.

Pa·vi·a (pä-vē′ä), *n.* a city in northern Italy: pop., 64,000 (est. 1947): ancient Lombard capital.

pav·id (pav′id), *adj.* [L. *pavidus* < *pavere,* to be afraid], fearful; afraid; timid.

pa·vil·ion (pə-vil′yən), *n.* [ME. *pavilon;* OFr. *pavillon;* L. *papilio,* butterfly, also tent (from its shape)], 1. a large tent, usually with a peaked top. 2. *a*) a building or part of a building used for entertainment, exhibits, etc., as at a fair or park: often open-air and highly ornamented. *b*) a decorative shelter or summerhouse. 3. part of a building jutting out from the main part and often ornamented. 4. any of the separate or connected parts of a group of related buildings, as of a hospital or sanitarium. 5. the auricle of the ear. 6. the part of a brilliant-cut gem between the girdle and the culet. *v.t.* to furnish with or shelter in or as in a pavilion.

pav·in (pav′′n), *n.* a pavan.

pav·ing (pāv′iŋ), *n.* 1. a pavement. 2. material for a pavement.

pav·ior, pav·iour (pāv′yẽr), *n.* [altered < ME. *pavier* (cf. LAWYER)], a paver.

pav·is (pav′is), *n.* [OFr. *pavais* (Fr. *pavois*); It. *pavese* < *Pavia,* Italy, where first made], in medieval times, a large shield for protecting the entire body.

Pav·lov, I·van Pe·tro·vich (i-vän′ pye-trô′vich päv′lôf), 1849–1936; Russian physiologist; received Nobel prize in physiology, 1904.

Pav·lo·va, An·na (än′ä päv′lô-vä; *sometimes Anglicized to* päv-lō′və), 1885–1931; Russian ballet dancer.

Pa·vo (pā′vō), *n.* [L., peacock], a constellation near the southern pole: see **constellation,** chart.

pav·o·nine (pav′ə-nīn′, pav′ə-nin), *adj.* [L. *pavoninus* < *pavo,* peacock], 1. of or resembling a peacock. 2. rainbowlike in color, as a peacock's tail; iridescent.

paw (pô), *n.* [ME. *pawe;* OFr. *poue, poe;* prob. < Gmc. **pauta,* a paw; cf. G. *pfote*], 1. the foot of a four-footed animal having claws. 2. [Colloq.], a hand. *v.t. & v.i.* 1. to touch, dig, strike, etc. with the paws or feet: as, the wild horse *pawed* the air. 2. to handle clumsily, roughly, or overintimately; maul.

paw (pô), *n.* [Dial.], pa; papa; father.

pawk·y (pô′ki), *adj.* [PAWKIER (-ki-ẽr), PAWKIEST (-ki-ist)], [Scot. & British Dial.], cunning; shrewd; crafty.

pawl (pôl), *n.* [? < Fr. *épaule,* a shoulder; or ? < D. *pal,* pawl, stake, pole], a mechanical device allowing rotation in only one direction: one type consists of a hinged tongue, the tip of which engages the notches of a cogwheel, preventing backward motion.

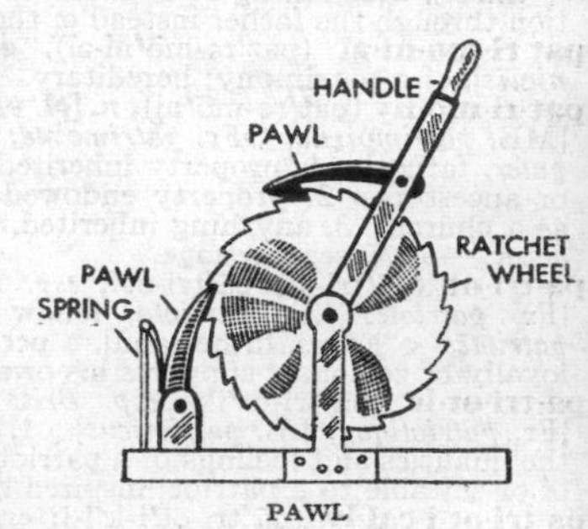

pawn (pôn), *n.* [OFr. *pan, pant;* akin to D. *pand,* G. *pfand;* thought by some to be borrowed < the Gmc. word & akin to *penny,* by others to be < L. *pannus,* piece of cloth (OFr. *pan*) with specialized sense < D. or G.], 1. anything given as security, as for a debt, performance of an action, etc.; pledge; guaranty. 2. a hostage. 3. the state of being pledged: as, his ring was in *pawn.* 4. the act of pawning. *v.t.* 1. to give as security; put in pawn. 2. to stake, wager, or risk: as, he *pawned* his honor. —*SYN.* see **pledge.**

pawn (pôn), *n.* [ME. *poun;* OFr. *peon;* LL. *pedo,* foot soldier < L. *pes, pedis,* a foot], 1. a chessman of the lowest value: it can be moved only forward and but one square at a time (or two squares on the first move), but it captures with a diagonal move: symbol, P. 2. a person subject to the will of another; tool.

pawn·age (pôn′ij), *n.* [see -AGE], a pawning or being pawned.

pawn·bro·ker (pôn′brō′kẽr), *n.* [*pawn* (pledged property) + *broker*], a person licensed to loan money at a legally specified rate of interest on personal property left with him as security.

pawn·bro·king (pôn′brō′kiŋ), *n.* the business of a pawnbroker.

Paw·nee (pô-nē′), *n.* [said to be < Pawnee *pariki,* horn, with reference to the custom of dressing the forelock to resemble a horn], 1. [*pl.* PAWNEE, PAWNEES (-nēz′)], a member of a confederacy of North American Plains Indians of Caddoan linguistic stock, formerly living in the valley of the Platte River, Nebraska, and now in northern Oklahoma. 2. their language. *adj.* of this tribe or their language.

pawn·er (pôn′ẽr), *n.* a person who pawns something.

pawn·or (pôn′ẽr), *n.* a pawner.

pawn·shop (pôn′shop′), *n.* a pawnbroker's shop.

pawn ticket, a receipt for goods in pawn.

paw·paw (pô′pô′), *n.* the papaw.

Paw·tuck·et (pô-tuk′it), *n.* a city in Rhode Island: pop., 81,000.

pax (paks), *n.* [ME.; L., peace], 1. [P-], the Roman goddess of peace. 2. a small tablet representing the Crucifixion, the Virgin, a saint, etc.: formerly kissed during the Roman Catholic Eucharistic service.

‡pax in bel·lo (paks in bel′ō), [L.], peace in war.

Pax Ro·man·a (paks rō-mā′nə), [L., Roman peace], 1. the terms of peace imposed by Rome on any of its dominions; hence, 2. a peace dictated to a subjugated people by a conquering nation.

‡pax vo·bis·cum (paks vō-bis′kəm), [L.], peace (be) with you.

pax·wax (paks′waks′), *n.* [ME., earlier *faxwax, fexwex* < AS. *feax,* hair + *weaxan,* to grow; cf. G. *haarwachs*], a strong, elastic ligament in the back of the neck in many mammals, serving to support the head.

pay (pā), *v.t.* [PAID or *obs.* (except in phrase *pay out,* sense 2) PAYED (pād), PAYING], [ME. *paien, payen,* to pay, satisfy; OFr. *paier, paer;* L. *pacare,* to pacify < *pax, pacis,* peace], 1. to give to (a person) what is due, as for goods received, services rendered, etc.; remunerate; recompense. 2. to make return or recompense for; repay: as, she *paid* kindness with evil. 3. to give (what is due or owed) in return, as for goods or services. 4. to discharge or settle (a debt, obligation, etc.) by giving something in return. 5. *a)* to give or offer (a compliment, respects, attention, etc.). *b)* to make (a visit, call, etc.). 6. to yield as a recompense or return: as, this job *pays* fifty dollars a week. 7. to give satisfaction or be profitable to: as, it will *pay* you to read the book. *v.i.* 1. to give due or adequate compensation; make payment. 2. to be profitable. *n.* 1. a paying or being paid: said of wages, hire, etc. 2. compensation, especially money, for goods, services, etc.; wages or salary. 3. anything, good or evil, given or done in return. 4. a person regarded from the standpoint of his financial credit or willingness to pay. *adj.* 1. rich enough in minerals, etc. to make mining profitable: as, *pay* gravel. 2. operated by depositing a coin or coins, as a telephone or public toilet.

in the pay of, employed and paid by.

pay as you go, to pay expenses as they arise.

pay back, to repay.

pay down, 1. to pay in cash. 2. to pay (part of the purchase price of an article) at the time of purchase: used in installment buying.

pay for, 1. to suffer or undergo punishment because of. 2. to atone or make amends for.

pay off, 1. to pay all that is owed on (a debt, etc.) or to (a person, as in discharging from employment). 2. to take revenge on (a wrongdoer) or for (a wrong done). 3. to yield full recompense or return, for either good or evil. 4. in *nautical usage,* to cause or allow the bow of (a vessel) to veer to leeward.

pay one's way, to pay one's share of the expenses.

pay out, 1. to give out (money, etc.); expend. 2. to let out (a rope, cable, etc.).

pay up, to pay in full or on time.

SYN.—**pay** is the simple, direct word meaning to give money, etc. due for services rendered, goods received, etc.; **compensate** implies a return, whether monetary or not, thought of as equivalent to the service given, the effort expended, or the loss sustained (he could never be *compensated* for the loss of his son); **remunerate** stresses the idea of payment for a service rendered, but it often also carries an implication of reward (a bumper crop *remunerated* the farmer for his labors); to **reimburse** is to pay back what has been expended (the salesman was *reimbursed* for his traveling expenses); to **indemnify** is to pay for what has been lost or damaged (they were *indemnified* for the war destruction); **repay** implies a paying back of money given to one or it may refer to a doing or giving of anything in requital (how can I *repay* you for your kindness?); **recompense** stresses the idea of compensation or requital. See also **wage.**

pay (pā), *v.t.* [PAYED (pād), PAYING], [ONorm.Fr. *peier* < L. *picare,* to cover with pitch < *pix, picis,* pitch], to coat with tar, etc. in order to make waterproof.

pay·a·ble (pā'ə-b'l), *adj.* 1. that can be paid. 2. that is to be paid (on a specified date); due. 3. that is or can be profitable, as a mine or business venture.

pay·day (pā'dā'), *n.* the day on which wages are paid.

pay dirt, soil, gravel, ore, etc. rich enough in minerals to make mining profitable.

pay·ee (pā-ē'), *n.* the person to whom a check, note, money, etc. is payable.

pay·er (pā'ẽr), *n.* the person who pays or is to pay.

pay·load (pā'lōd'), *n.* 1. a cargo, or the part of a cargo, producing income: also **pay load** 2. *a)* the war head of a ballistic missile, the instruments of an artificial satellite, etc., along with the compartment or final stage carrying these. *b)* the weight of such a load or of the load and its container.

pay·mas·ter (pā'mas'tẽr, pā'mäs'tẽr), *n.* the official in charge of paying wages to employees.

pay·ment (pā'mənt), *n.* 1. a paying or being paid. 2. something that is paid. 3. penalty or reward.

Payne, John Howard (pān), 1791–1852; American actor and playwright; wrote "Home, Sweet Home."

pay·nim (pā'nim), *n.* [ME. *painim;* OFr. *paienime,* heathendom; LL. *paganismus,* paganism], [Archaic], 1. a pagan; heathen. 2. a non-Christian; especially, a Moslem. 3. the pagan world. *adj.* [Archaic], 1. pagan. 2. non-Christian.

pay-off (pā'ôf'), *n.* [Colloq.], 1. originally, the act or time of payment; hence, 2. settlement or reckoning. 3. something that is unexpected or almost incredible, especially when coming as a climax or culmination.

pay·o·la (pā-ō'lə), *n.* [*pay* + ? *-ola* as in *Pianola,* trade-mark for a player piano], [Slang], 1. the practice of paying bribes for commercial advantage, as to a disk jockey for promoting a song unfairly. 2. such a bribe.

pay roll, 1. a list of employees to be paid, with the amount due to each. 2. the total amount needed for this for a given period.

payt., pay't, payment.

Pb, *plumbum,* [L.], in *chemistry,* lead.

P.B., 1. *Pharmacopoeia Britannica,* [L.], British Pharmacopoeia. 2. Prayer Book.

PBX, P.B.X., [*p*rivate *b*ranch e*x*change], a telephone system operating within one building, company, etc., usually having outside telephone lines.

pc., 1. piece. 2. prices.

P/C, p/c, 1. petty cash. 2. prices current.

P.C., 1. Past Commander. 2. Police Constable. 3. Post Commander. 4. Privy Council (or Councilor).

p.c., 1. per cent. 2. postal card. 3. post card.

pct., per cent.

Pd, in *chemistry,* palladium.

pd., paid.

P.D., 1. Police Department. 2. postal district. 3. potential difference. 4. per diem: also **p.d.**

Pd.B., Bachelor of Pedagogy.

Pd.D., Doctor of Pedagogy.

Pd.M., Master of Pedagogy.

P.D.Q. (pē'dē'kū'), [*p*retty *d*amn *q*uick], [Slang], quickly or immediately.

pe (pā), *n.* peh.

P.E., 1. Presiding Elder. 2. probable error. 3. Protestant Episcopal.

pea (pē), *n.* [*pl.* PEAS, or *archaic* or *Brit. dial.* PEASE (pēz)], [back-formation < ME. *pese, pees,* a pea, taken as sing.; AS. *pise;* LL. *pisa* < L. *pisa,* pl. of *pisum,* a pea; Gr. *pison,* a pea], 1. a climbing plant with white or pinkish flowers and green seed pods. 2. its small, round seed, used as a vegetable. 3. any of a number of related plants.

as like as two peas, exactly alike.

pea bean, a small, nearly round variety of white bean.

Pea·bod·y (pē'bod'i, pē'bəd-i), *n.* a city in northeastern Massachusetts: pop., 32,000.

Pea·bod·y, George (pē'bod'i, pē'bəd-i), 1795–1869; American merchant and banker in England.

pea·bod·y bird (pē'bod'i), [echoic of its note], the white-throated sparrow.

peace (pēs), *n.* [ME. *pees, pais;* OFr. *pais;* L. *pax, pacis* < base of *pangere,* to fix (cf. PACT); the native word was *frith*], 1. freedom from war or civil strife. 2. a treaty or agreement to end war. 3. freedom from public disturbance or disorder; public security; law and order. 4. freedom from disagreement or quarrels; harmony; concord. 5. an undisturbed state of mind; absence of mental conflict; serenity. 6. calm; quiet; tranquillity. *v.i.* [PEACED (pēst), PEACING], [Obs. except in imperative], to be or become silent or quiet.

at peace, 1. free from war. 2. quiet; in repose.

hold (or **keep**) **one's peace,** to be silent; keep quiet.

keep the peace, to avoid or prevent violation of law and good order.

make one's peace with, to effect a reconciliation with.

make peace, to end hostilities, settle arguments, etc.

peace·a·ble (pēs'ə-b'l), *adj.* [ME. *peisible;* OFr. *paisible*], 1. fond of, inclined toward, or promoting peace; not quarrelsome. 2. at peace; peaceful.

peace·a·bly (pēs'ə-bli), *adv.* in a peaceable manner.

peace conference, a conference for the purpose of ending a war or for seeking ways to establish lasting peace.

peace·ful (pēs'fəl), *adj.* 1. not quarrelsome; peaceable. 2. characterized by peace; free from disturbance or disorder; calm; quiet; tranquil. 3. of or characteristic of a time of peace. —***SYN.*** see **calm.**

peace·mak·er (pēs'māk'ẽr), *n.* one who makes peace, as by settling the disagreements or quarrels of others.

peace·mak·ing (pēs'māk'iŋ), *n.* the action of making peace. *adj.* that makes peace.

peace offering, 1. an offering or sacrifice in thanksgiving to God. 2. an offering made to maintain or bring about peace.

peace officer, an officer entrusted with maintaining law and order, as a sheriff, constable, or policeman.

peace pipe, a ceremonial pipe smoked by American Indians as part of a peace conference; calumet.

Peace River, a river in British Columbia and Alberta, flowing into the Slave River: length, 1,050 mi.

peace·time (pēs'tīm'), *n.* a time of peace. *adj.* of or characteristic of such a time.

peach (pēch), *n.* [ME. *peche;* OFr. *pesche;* LL. *persica* < L. *Persicum* (*malum*), Persian (apple)], 1. a small tree with lance-shaped leaves, pink flowers, and round, juicy, orange-yellow fruit, with a fuzzy skin and a single, rough pit. 2. its fruit. 3. the orange-yellow color of this fruit. 4. [Slang], any person or thing well liked. *adj.* 1. of the peach. 2. orange-yellow.

peach (pēch), *v.t.* [ME. *apechen;* via Anglo-Fr. < OFr. *empechier, empeechier;* see IMPEACH], [Obs.], to name in an indictment; impeach. *v.i.* [Slang], to give evidence against another; turn informer.

peach·blow (pēch′blō′), *n.* [*peach* + *blow* (blossom)], 1. a delicate, purplish-pink color. 2. a porcelain glaze of this color.
peach brandy, brandy distilled from fermented peach juice.
peach·i·ness (pē′chi-nis), *n.* the quality of being peachy.
peach·y (pē′chi), *adj.* [PEACHIER (-chi-ẽr), PEACHIEST (-chi-ist)], 1. peachlike, as in color or texture. 2. [Slang], fine, excellent, beautiful, etc.
pea·cock (pē′kok′), *n.* [*pl.* PEACOCKS (-koks′), PEACOCK; see PLURAL, II, D, 1], [ME. *pacok; pa,* peacock (< AS. *pawa, pea;* L. *pavo*) + *cok,* a cock], 1. any of a number of large related birds, especially the male with a crest and a long tail which has rainbow-colored, eyelike spots and can spread out like a fan: conventionally regarded as a symbol of vanity. 2. a vain person. *v.i.* to be vain; strut.

PEACOCK (body, 20 in. tall)

Pea·cock, Thomas Love (pē′kok′), 1785–1866; English poet and novelist.
pea·cock-blue (pē′kok-blōō′), *adj.* greenish-blue.
peacock blue, a greenish blue.
pea·cock·ish (pē′kok′ish), *adj.* like or characteristic of a peacock; vain; inclined to strut.
peacock ore, bornite, a copper ore.
pea·cock·y (pē′kok′i), *adj.* 1. colored like a peacock. 2. peacockish.
pea·fowl (pē′foul′), *n.* [*pl.* PEAFOWLS (-foulz′), PEAFOWL; see PLURAL, II, D, 1], a peacock or peahen.
peag, peage (pēg), *n.* [< Am. Ind. (Algonquian) (*wampum*)*peage,* (white) string], wampum.
pea-green (pē′grēn′), *adj.* light yellowish-green.
pea green, a light yellowish green.
pea·hen (pē′hen′), *n.* the female of the peacock.
pea jacket, [1st element prob. < D. *pij,* coarse, thick cloth, warm jacket], a short coat of heavy woolen cloth, worn by sailors.
peak (pēk), *v.i.* [prob. < *peak, n.,* with idea of emaciated appearance], to become sickly; fade or waste away; droop.
peak (pēk), *n.* [var. of *pike* (peak, summit)], 1. a tapering part that projects; pointed end or top, as of a cap, roof, etc. 2. part of the hairline coming to a point on a person's forehead; widow's peak. 3. [Rare], a promontory. 4. the crest or summit of a hill or mountain ending in a point. 5. a mountain with such a pointed summit. 6. the highest or utmost point of anything; height; maximum: as, the *peak* of production. 7. in *electricity,* the maximum value of a varying quantity during a specified period. 8. in *nautical usage, a)* the top rear corner of a fore-and-aft (gaff) sail. *b)* the narrowed part of the hull, front or rear. Abbreviated **pk.** *v.t. & v.i.* to bring or come to a vertical position; tilt up, as a sail yard or spar. —*SYN.* see **summit.**
peaked (pēkt, pēk′id), *adj.* having or ending in a peak; pointed.
peak·ed (pēk′id), *adj.* [< *peak* (to shrink), or *peak, n.*], having sharp features; thin and drawn, as from illness.
peal (pēl), *n.* [ME. *pele,* shortened < *apele,* appeal; see APPEAL], 1. the loud ringing of a bell or set of bells. 2. the ringing of changes on a set of bells. 3. a set of matched bells; chime; carillon. 4. any loud, prolonged sound, as of gunfire, thunder, laughter, etc. *v.i. & v.t.* to sound in a peal; resound; ring.
Peale, Charles Will·son (wil′sən pēl), 1741–1827; American portrait painter, especially of George Washington.
pe·an (pē′ən), *n.* a paean.
pea·nut (pē′nut′), *n.* 1. a vine of the pea family, with yellow flowers and brittle pods ripening underground and containing edible seeds. 2. the pod or its seed.
peanut butter, a paste or spread made by grinding roasted peanuts.
pear (pâr), *n.* [ME. *pere;* AS. *pere, peru;* LL. *pera, pira* < L. *pira,* pl. of *pirum,* pear], 1. a tree with glossy leaves, white flowers, and greenish-yellow fruit. 2. the soft, juicy fruit, round at the base and narrowing toward the stem.

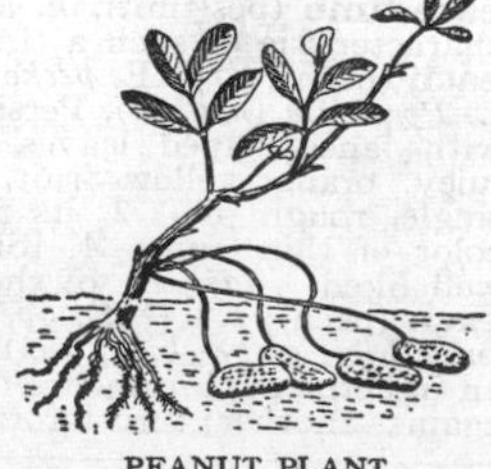
PEANUT PLANT (1–2 ft. high)

Pearl (pũrl), [< *pearl*], a feminine name.
pearl (pũrl), *n.* [ME. & OFr. *perle;* ML. *perla, perula* < L. *perua,* kind of shellfish, lit., a ham: so called from the shape], 1. a smooth, hard, usually white or bluish-gray, abnormal growth of various, usually roundish, shapes, formed around a parasitic worm or other foreign body within the shell of some oysters and certain other mollusks: it is used as a gem. 2. mother-of-pearl. 3. anything pearllike in size, shape, color, beauty, value, etc. 4. the color of pearl, a bluish-gray. 5. in *printing,* a size of type, 5 point. *v.t.* 1. to adorn or cover with pearls or pearllike drops. 2. to make like a pearl in shape or color. *v.i.* to fish for pearl-bearing mollusks, especially oysters. *adj.* 1. of, like, or having pearls. 2. like a pearl in shape or color.
cast pearls before swine, to present something of great interest or value to someone incapable of appreciating it.
pearl (pũrl), *v.t. & v.i., n.* purl.
pearl·ash (pũrl′ash′), *n.* a refined potash, potassium carbonate.
pearl barley, barley seed rubbed to a rounded granular shape.
pearl diver (or **fisher**), a person who dives for pearl-bearing mollusks.
pearl gray, a pale bluish gray.
Pearl Harbor, an inlet on the southern coast of Oahu, Hawaii, near Honolulu: site of the United States naval base attacked by Japan, December 7, 1941: see **Hawaiian Islands,** map.
pearl·i·ness (pũr′li-nis), *n.* a pearly quality or state.
pearl·ite (pũrl′īt), *n.* 1. perlite. 2. an alloy of carbon and iron used in making steel and cast iron.
pearl millet, a tall cereal and forage grass having pearly white seeds.
Pearl River, 1. a river in central Mississippi, flowing into the Gulf of Mexico: length, 490 mi. 2. a river forming a gulf between Canton, China, and the South China Sea: Chinese name, *Chu-Kiang.*
pearl·y (pũr′li), *adj.* [PEARLIER (-li-ẽr), PEARLIEST (-li-ist)], 1. of or like a pearl, as in color or luster. 2. adorned or covered with pearls or mother-of-pearl.
pearly nautilus, a sea mollusk having a spiral chambered shell with a pearly lining.
pear·main (pâr′mān), *n.* [ME. *parmayn;* OFr. *parmain,* lit., Parman < *Parma,* Italy], a variety of apple.
Pear·son, Lester B. (pêr′s′n), 1879– ; prime minister of Canada (1963–); received Nobel peace prize, 1957.
peart (pêrt, pũrt), *adj.* [Dial.], 1. pert; lively. 2. clever.
Pear·y, Robert Edwin (pêr′i), 1856–1920; American arctic explorer; discovered the North Pole (1909).
peas·ant (pez′'nt), *n.* [Anglo-Fr. *paisant;* OFr. *paisent, paisenc* < *pais, pays,* country; LL. *pagensis* < *pagus,* district, province; cf. PAGAN], 1. in Europe, a worker who farms the land; agricultural worker; farmer; rustic. 2. [Obs.], a person considered inferior.
peas·ant·ry (pez′'n-tri), *n.* 1. peasants collectively. 2. a peasant's rank or condition.
peas·cod (pēz′kod′), *n.* a peasecod.
pease (pēz), *n.* [see PEA], 1. [*pl.* PEASES (-iz), PEASEN (-'n)], [Obs.], a pea. 2. archaic or British dialectal plural of **pea.**
pease·cod (pēz′kod′), *n.* [ME. *pesecod;* cf. PEASE & COD], the pod of the pea plant.
pea·shoot·er (pē′shōōt′ẽr), *n.* a toy consisting of a tube through which dried peas, etc. are blown.
pea soup, 1. a heavy soup made from dried peas. 2. [Slang], a dense, yellowish fog.
peat (pēt), *n.* [ME. *pete;* ML. *peta,* piece of turf; prob. specialized var. of *petia,* a piece (cf. PIECE) < Celt.], 1. partly decayed, moisture-absorbing plant matter found in ancient bogs and swamps, used as a plant covering or fuel. 2. a dried block of this used as fuel.
peat moss, 1. a certain moss found especially in the peat of northern Europe. 2. a peat bog.
peat·y (pēt′i), *adj.* [PEATIER (-i-ẽr), PEATIEST (-i-ist)], of, like, or having the odor of peat.
peau de soie (pō′də swä′), [Fr., lit., silk skin], a soft, rich, silk or rayon cloth with a dull satiny finish.
pea·vey (pē′vi), *n.* [*pl.* PEAVEYS (-viz)], [after Joseph *Peavey,* its inventor], a heavy wooden lever with a pointed metal tip and a hinged hook near the end: used by lumbermen in handling logs.
pea·vy (pē′vi), *n.* [*pl.* PEAVIES (-viz)], a peavey.
peb·ble (peb′'l), *n.* [ME. *pobble, pubel,* etc.; AS. *papol-*(*stan*), *popol-*(*stan*), pebble (stone); ? orig. of echoic origin], 1. a small stone worn smooth and round, as by the action of water. 2. clear, transparent quartz or a lens made from it. 3. a surface grain of pebbly appearance, artificially produced on leather, paper, etc. *v.t.* [PEBBLED (-'ld), PEBBLING], to stamp (leather) so as to produce a pebbly appearance.
peb·bly (peb′li), *adj.* [PEBBLIER (-li-ẽr), PEBBLIEST (-li-ist)], 1. having many pebbles. 2. having an uneven surface or grain, somewhat resembling pebbles.
pe·can (pi-kan′, pi-kän′, pē′kan), *n.* [earlier *paccan* < Am. Ind. (Algonquian) name; cf. Ojibway *pagân,* hard-shelled nut], 1. an olive-shaped nut with a thin, smooth shell. 2. the tree it grows on, related to the hickory.
pec·ca·bil·i·ty (pek′ə-bil′ə-ti), *n.* a peccable state.

pec·ca·ble (pek'ə-b'l), *adj.* [OFr.; ML. *peccabilis* < L. *peccare*, to sin], liable to or capable of sin.
pec·ca·dil·lo (pek'ə-dil'ō), *n.* [*pl.* PECCADILLOES, PECCADILLOS (-ōz)], [Sp., dim. < *pecado;* L. *peccatum*, a sin < *peccare*, to sin], a minor or petty sin; slight fault.
pec·can·cy (pek'ən-si), *n.* [LL. *peccantia* < L. *peccare*, to sin], 1. sinfulness. 2. [*pl.* PECCANCIES (-siz)], a sin.
pec·cant (pek'ənt), *adj.* [L. *peccans*, ppr. of *peccare*, to sin], 1. sinful; sinning. 2. breaking or disregarding a rule or practice; faulty. 3. [OFr.], causing disease.
pec·ca·ry (pek'ə-ri), *n.* [*pl.* PECCARIES (-riz), PECCARY; see PLURAL, II, D, 1], [Sp. *pecari* < Carib (dial.) *pakira*], any of a number of related grayish, piglike animals of tropical America, with sharp tusks and porklike flesh.
‡**pec·ca·vi** (pe-kā'vi, pe-kä'vē), [L.], I have sinned. *n.* [*pl.* PECCAVIS (-vīz, -vēz)], a confession of sin or of guilt.
Pe·cho·ra (pe-chôr'ə; Russ. pye-chô'rä), *n.* a river in the northeastern European U.S.S.R., flowing into the Barents Sea: length, 975 mi.
peck (pek), *v.t.* [ME. *pecken*, var. of *pikken*, to pick (cf. PICK) in specialized senses], 1. to strike with a pointed object, as with a beak. 2. to make by doing this: as, the bird *pecked* a hole in the bread. 3. to pick up with the beak; get by pecking. *v.i.* to make strokes with a pointed object, as a beak. *n.* 1. a stroke so made, as with the beak. 2. a mark made by pecking. 3. [Colloq.], a quick, casual kiss.
peck at, 1. to make a pecking motion at. 2. [Colloq.], to eat very little of; eat carefully or sparingly. 3. [Colloq.], to criticize or find fault with constantly.
peck (pek), *n.* [ME. *pekke;* Anglo-Fr. *pek*, chiefly of oats for horses; prob. akin to *pic-* in Fr. *picotin*, a peck; thought by some to be < *pick*, *v.t.*], 1. a unit of dry measure equal to 1/4 bushel or eight quarts. 2. any container with a capacity of one peck. Abbreviated **pk.** 3. [Colloq.], a large amount, as of trouble.
peck·er (pek'ēr), *n.* 1. a person or thing that pecks; specifically, a woodpecker. 2. a pointed object used in pecking; pick. 3. [British Slang], courage; pluck.
peck·ing order (pek'iŋ), [transl. < G., a hierarchy among birds, as hens, in which the most aggressive pecks, and the least aggressive is pecked by, all the others], social organization in which status is determined by aggressive awareness of rank, income, etc.
Peck·sniff·i·an (pek-snif'i-ən), *adj.* [after *Pecksniff*, unctuous hypocrite in Dickens' *Martin Chuzzlewit*], hypocritical; insincere; falsely moralistic.
Pe·cos (pā'kōs, pā'kəs), *n.* a river in New Mexico and Texas, flowing into the Rio Grande: length, 735 mi.
Pe·cos Bill (pā'kōs bil'), in *American legend*, the original cowboy, who performed such superhuman feats as digging the Rio Grande.
Pécs (pāch), *n.* a city in southwestern Hungary: pop., 70,000: German name, *Fünfkirchen*.
pec·tase (pek'tās), *n.* [< *pectin* + *-ase*], an enzyme in fruits that converts pectin into pectic acid.
pec·tate (pek'tāt), *n.* a salt or ester of pectic acid.
pec·ten (pek'tən), *n.* [*pl.* PECTINES (-tə-nēz')], [L. *pecten*, a comb, kind of shellfish < *pectere*, to comb], in *zoology*, a comblike tissue around the transparent, jellylike part of the eye in many birds and reptiles.
pec·tic (pek'tik), *adj.* [Gr. *pēktikos*, congealing < *pēktos*, congealed < *pēgnynai*, to fix], of, containing, or derived from pectin.
pectic acid, an acid of the methyl ester groups of pectins, $C_{17}H_{24}O_{16}$, insoluble in water.
pec·tin (pek'tin), *n.* [< Gr. *pēktos* (see PECTIC); + *-in*], a water soluble carbohydrate, a mixed polysaccharide obtained from certain ripe fruits, which yields a gel that is the basis of fruit jellies.
pec·ti·nate (pek'tə-nāt'), *adj.* [L. *pectinatus*, pp. of *pectinare*, to comb < *pecten*, a comb], having toothlike projections like those on a comb.
pec·ti·nat·ed (pek'tə-nā'tid), *adj.* pectinate.
pec·ti·na·tion (pek'tə-nā'shən), *n.* [see PECTINATE & -ION], 1. an interlocking or being fitted together, as the teeth of two combs. 2. a comblike part.
pec·to·ral (pek'tə-rəl), *adj.* [< Fr. or L.; Fr. *pectoral;* L. *pectoralis* < *pectus*, *pectoris*, breast], 1. of or located in or on the breast or chest. 2. of or used in treating diseases of the chest or lungs. 3. worn on the chest or breast. 4. influenced by or resulting from personal feelings; subjective. *n.* [OFr.; L. *pectorale*], 1. something worn on the breast, as an ornamental plate. 2. a pectoral medicine. 3. a pectoral fin or muscle.
pectoral arch (or **girdle**), in *anatomy & zoology*, the bony or cartilaginous structure to which the forelimbs (or arms) of a vertebrate are attached.
pectoral fin, either of a pair of fins just behind the head of a fish, corresponding to the forelimbs of a vertebrate.
pectoral sandpiper, a variety of sandpiper with a heavily streaked breast, found in the Arctic.
pec·tose (pek'tōs), *n.* [< Gr. *pēktos;* see PECTIC], a substance found with cellulose in the pulpy tissue of unripe fruits: the ripening process converts it into pectin.
pec·u·late (pek'yoo-lāt'), *v.t. & v.i.* [PECULATED (-id), PECULATING], [< L. *peculatus*, pp. of *peculari*, to embezzle < *peculium*, private property < *pecus*, cattle], to steal or misuse (money or property entrusted to one's care, especially public funds); embezzle.
pec·u·la·tion (pek'yoo-lā'shən), *n.* the act of peculating; embezzlement.
pec·u·la·tor (pek'yoo-lā'tēr), *n.* [L.], a person who peculates; embezzler.
pe·cul·iar (pi-kūl'yēr), *adj.* [obs. Fr. *peculier;* L. *peculiaris* < *peculium;* see PECULATE], 1. of only one person, thing, group, country, etc.; distinctive; exclusive. 2. particular; unique; special: as, a *peculiar* talent for distorting the truth. 3. out of the ordinary; queer; odd; strange. *n.* 1. something belonging to one only, as a privilege. 2. a church or parish under a jurisdiction other than that of the diocese in which it is located. —*SYN.* see **strange.**
pe·cu·li·ar·i·ty (pi-kū'li-ar'ə-ti, pi-kūl'yar'ə-ti), *n.* 1. the quality or condition of being peculiar. 2. [*pl.* PECULIARITIES (-tiz)], something that is peculiar, as a trait or habit.
peculiar people, 1. in the *Bible*, the Jews, considered as Jehovah's own people: Deut. 26:18. 2. the followers of any of several Christian creeds.
pe·cu·li·um (pi-kū'li-əm), *n.* [L.], 1. in *Roman law*, property given to a slave, wife, or child to hold as his own; hence, 2. a private property or possession.
pe·cu·ni·ar·i·ly (pi-kū'ni-er'ə-li), *adv.* in a pecuniary manner; with respect or regard to money.
pe·cu·ni·ar·y (pi-kū'ni-er'i), *adj.* [L. *pecuniarius* < *pecunia*, money < *pecus*, cattle; cf. PECULATE], 1. of or involving money. 2. involving a money penalty, or fine: as, a *pecuniary* offense. —*SYN.* see **financial.**
ped- (ped), 1. pedo-. 2. pedi-.
-ped (ped), -pede.
ped., 1. pedal. 2. pedestal.
ped·a·gog (ped'ə-gog', ped'ə-gôg'), *n.* a pedagogue.
ped·a·gog·ic (ped'ə-goj'ik), *adj.* [Gr. *paidagōgikos* < *paidagōgos;* see PEDAGOGUE], of or characteristic of teachers or of teaching.
ped·a·gog·i·cal (ped'ə-goj'i-k'l), *adj.* pedagogic.
ped·a·gog·i·cal·ly (ped'ə-goj'i-k'l-i, ped'ə-goj'ik-li), *adv.* 1. in a pedagogic manner. 2. by means of or according to pedagogy.
ped·a·gog·ics (ped'ə-goj'iks), *n.pl.* [construed as sing.], pedagogy.
ped·a·gog·ism (ped'ə-gog-iz'm, ped'ə-gôg-iz'm), *n.* 1. the characteristics, practices, beliefs, etc. of a pedagogue, especially of a pedantic one. 2. the state of being a pedagogue.
ped·a·gogue (ped'ə-gog', ped'ə-gôg'), *n.* [ME. *pedagoge;* OFr.; L. *paedagogus;* Gr. *paidagōgos* < *pais*, *paidos*, child + *agein*, to lead], a teacher; especially, a pedantic, dogmatic teacher.
ped·a·gogu·ism (ped'ə-gog-iz'm, ped'ə-gôg-iz'm), *n.* pedagogism.
ped·a·go·gy (ped'ə-gō'ji, ped'ə-goj'i), *n.* [Fr. *pédagogie;* Gr. *paidagōgia;* see PEDAGOGUE], 1. the profession or function of a teacher; teaching. 2. the art or science of teaching; especially, instruction in teaching methods.
ped·al (ped''l; *also, for adj. 1*, pē'd'l), *adj.* [L. *pedalis* < *pes*, *pedis*, a foot], 1. of the foot or feet. 2. of or operated by a pedal or pedals. *n.* [Fr. *pédale;* It. *pedale;* L. *pedalis;* see the *adj.*], a lever operated by the foot, used in transmitting motion, as in a bicycle or sewing machine, or in changing the tone or volume of a musical instrument, as an organ or harp: abbreviated **ped.** *v.t. & v.i.* [PEDALED or PEDALLED (-'ld), PEDALING or PEDALLING], to move or operate by a pedal or pedals; use the pedals (of).
pe·dal·fer (pi-dal'fēr), *n.* [Gr. *ped*on, ground + L. *al*umen (see ALUMINUM) + *fer*rum, iron (metal)], soil containing alumina and iron oxide and lacking a layer of calcium and magnesium carbonates: usually found in areas having an annual rainfall of 25 inches or more.
pedal point, in *music*, a single continuous tone, usually in the bass, held against the changing figures or harmonies of the other parts.
pedal pushers, knee-length trousers for women or girls, used originally for bicycle riding.
ped·ant (ped''nt), *n.* [Fr. *pédant*, pedant, schoolmaster; It. *pedante*, prob. contr. < *pedagogante* < L. *paedagogans*, ppr. of *paedagogare*, to educate; see PEDAGOGUE], 1. a person who lays unnecessary stress on minor or trivial points of learning, displaying a scholarship lacking in judgment or sense of proportion. 2. a narrow-minded teacher who insists on exact adherence to a set of arbitrary rules. 3. [Obs.], a schoolmaster.
pe·dan·tic (pi-dan'tik), *adj.* of, like, or characteristic of a pedant or pedantry.
pe·dan·ti·cal·ly (pi-dan'ti-k'l-i, pi-dan'tik-li), *adv.* in a pedantic manner.

ped·ant·ry (ped'n-tri), *n.* [Fr. *pédanterie;* It. *pedanteria* < *pedante;* see PEDANT], 1. the qualities, characteristics, practices, beliefs, etc. of a pedant; display of narrow-minded and trivial scholarship or arbitrary adherence to rules and forms. 2. [*pl.* PEDANTRIES (-triz)], a pedantic act or expression.

ped·ate (ped'āt), *adj.* [L. *pedatus* < *pes, pedis,* a foot], 1. having feet. 2. footlike. 3. in *botany,* in a fanlike arrangement with subdivided leaves.

pe·da·ti- (pi-dat'i, pi-dā'ti), a combining form meaning *pedately,* as in *pedatifid.*

pe·dat·i·fid (pi-dat'ə-fid, pi-dā'tə-fid), *adj.* [*pedati-* + *-fid*], in *botany,* cleft pedately.

ped·dle (ped''l), *v.i.* [PEDDLED (-'ld), PEDDLING], [back-formation < *peddler*], 1. to go from place to place selling small articles. 2. [var. of *piddle*], to spend time on trifles; piddle; dally. *v.t.* 1. to carry from place to place and offer for sale. 2. to deal in or dispense, especially in small amounts, as, narcotics, gossip, etc.

ped·dler (ped'lēr), *n.* [ME. *pedlare, pedlere,* prob. < *peddare,* peddler < *ped, pedde,* a basket, via. dim. *pedle*], a person who peddles: also spelled **pedlar.**

ped·dler·y (ped'lēr-i), *n.* 1. the business or trade of a peddler. 2. the goods or wares sold by a peddler. Also spelled **pedlary.**

ped·dling (ped'liŋ), *adj.* [< *peddle* + *-ing;* associated in meaning with *piddling*], busy with trifles; trifling; petty.

-pede (pēd), [< L. *pes, pedis,* a foot], a combining form meaning *foot* or *feet,* as in *centipede:* also **-ped.**

ped·er·ast (ped'ə-rast', pē'də-rast'), *n.* a man who practices pederasty.

ped·er·as·ty (ped'ə-ras'ti, pē'də-ras'ti), *n.* [Mod.L. *paederastia;* Gr. *paiderastia* < *paiderastēs,* lover of boys < *pais, paidos,* boy + *eran,* to love], a form of sodomy between men, especially as practiced by a man with a boy: also spelled **paederasty.**

ped·es·tal (ped'is-t'l), *n.* [Fr. *piédestal;* It. *piedestallo, piedistallo* < *piè* (L. *pes, pedis*), a foot + *di,* of + *stal* (OHG. *stal*), a rest, place], 1. the foot or bottom support of a column, pillar, vase, lamp, statue, etc. 2. any foundation, base, support, etc. Abbreviated **ped.** *v.t.* [PEDESTALED or PEDESTALLED (-t'ld), PEDESTALING or PEDESTALLING], to place on or furnish with a pedestal.

put (or **set**) **on a pedestal,** to regard with great or excessive admiration; idolize.

pe·des·tri·an (pə-des'tri-ən), *adj.* [< L. *pedester* < *pes, pedis,* a foot], 1. going or done on foot; walking. 2. lacking interest or imagination; prosaic; dull, as a literary style, etc. *n.* one who goes on foot; walker.

pe·des·tri·an·ism (pə-des'tri-ən-iz'm), *n.* 1. the practice of walking, as for exercise. 2. a pedestrian quality, literary style, etc.

ped·i- (ped'i), [< L. *pes, pedis,* a foot], a combining form meaning *foot* or *feet,* as in *pedicure:* also, before a vowel, **ped-.**

pe·di·at·ric (pē'di-at'rik, ped'i-at'rik), *adj.* [see PEDO- & -IATRIC], of pediatrics.

pe·di·a·tri·cian (pē'di-ə-trish'ən, ped'i-ə-trish'ən), *n.* a specialist in pediatrics.

pe·di·at·rics (pē'di-at'riks, ped'i-at'riks), *n.pl.* [construed as sing.], [< *pediatric*], the branch of medicine dealing with the development and care of infants and children, and with the treatment of their diseases.

pe·di·at·rist (pē'di-at'rist, ped'i-at'rist), *n.* a pediatrician.

ped·i·cel (ped'i-s'l), *n.* [< Mod.L. *pedicellus,* dim. of L. *pediculus,* dim. of *pes, pedis,* a foot], in *botany* & *zoology,* a small, stalklike structure; peduncle.

ped·i·cel·lar (ped'i-sel'ēr), *adj.* of or like a pedicel.

ped·i·cel·late (ped'i-s'l-it, ped'i-s'l-āt'), *adj.* having or supported by a pedicel.

ped·i·cle (ped'i-k'l), *n.* [L. *pediculus*], a pedicel.

pe·dic·u·lar (pi-dik'yoo-lēr), *adj.* [L. *pedicularis* < *pediculus,* dim. of *pedis,* a louse], 1. of lice. 2. infested with lice; lousy.

pe·dic·u·late (pi-dik'yoo-lit, pi-dik'yoo-lāt'), *adj.* [< L. *pediculus* (see PEDICEL); + *-ate*], belonging to a group of fishes having pectoral fins attached to an armlike base. *n.* a fish of this group.

pe·dic·u·lo·sis (pi-dik'yoo-lō'sis), *n.* [< L. *pediculus* (see PEDICULAR); + *-osis*], infestation with lice.

pe·dic·u·lous (pi-dik'yoo-ləs), *adj.* [L. *pediculosus;* see PEDICULAR], infested with lice; lousy.

ped·i·cure (ped'i-kyoor'), *n.* [Fr. *pédicure* < L. *pes, pedis,* a foot + *cura,* care], 1. a chiropodist. 2. chiropody. 3. [by analogy with *manicure*], popularly, a cleaning, trimming, and polishing of the toenails.

ped·i·form (ped'i-fôrm'), *adj.* [*pedi-* + *-form*], foot-shaped.

ped·i·gree (ped'ə-grē'), *n.* [ME. *pedegru, pe de gre,* etc.; OFr. *pié de grue,* lit., crane's foot < L. *pes,* foot & *grus,* a crane: so called from the lines in the genealogical tree], 1. a list of ancestors; record of ancestry; family tree. 2. descent; lineage; ancestry. 3. a recorded or known line of descent, especially of a pure-bred animal.

ped·i·greed (ped'ə-grēd'), *adj.* having a known or recorded pedigree: as, a *pedigreed* dog.

ped·i·ment (ped'ə-mənt), *n.* [altered < earlier *periment* (alteration of *pyramid*) by association with L. *pes, pedis,* a foot], 1. a low-pitched gable on the front of some buildings in the Grecian style of architecture. 2. any similar triangular piece used in decorating, as over a doorway, fireplace, etc.

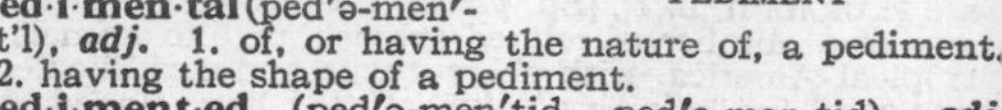

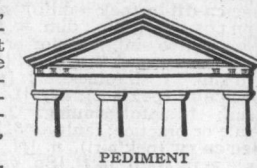

PEDIMENT

ped·i·men·tal (ped'ə-men't'l), *adj.* 1. of, or having the nature of, a pediment. 2. having the shape of a pediment.

ped·i·ment·ed (ped'ə-men'tid, ped'ə-mən-tid), *adj.* having a pediment.

ped·lar (ped'lēr), *n.* a peddler.

pe·do- (pē'dō, pē'də), [< Gr. *pais, paidos,* a child], a combining form meaning *child, children, offspring,* as in *pedobaptism:* also spelled **paedo-:** also, before a vowel, **ped-.**

pe·do·bap·tism (pē'dō-bap'tiz'm), *n.* [*pedo-* + *baptism*] baptism of children.

pe·do·don·ti·a (pē'də-don'shə), *n.* [*ped-* + *-odont* + *-ia*], the branch of dentistry concerned with the care of children's teeth.

ped·o·graph (ped'ə-graf', ped'ə-gräf'), *n.* [< Gr. *pedon* the ground; + *-graph*], an instrument which records the topography of the ground covered by a person carrying it while walking.

pe·dol·o·gy (pi-dol'ə-ji), *n.* [*pedo-* + *-logy*], the systematic study of the behavior and development of children.

pe·dom·e·ter (pi-dom'ə-tēr), *n.* [Fr. *pédomètre* < L. *pes pedis,* a foot + Gr. *metron,* a measure], an instrument which measures approximately distance covered in walking by recording the number of steps taken.

pe·dro (pē'drō), *n.* [Sp. *Pedro,* Peter; LL. *Petrus;* see PETER], in *card games,* 1. a variety of seven-up in which the five of trumps counts five. 2. the five of trumps in this game.

pe·dun·cle (pi-duŋ'k'l), *n.* [Mod.L. *pedunculus,* dim of L. *pes, pedis,* a foot], 1. a flower stalk. 2. in *anatomy* a stalklike bundle of nerve fibers connecting various parts of the brain. 3. in *zoology,* a slender, stalklike part, as between the abdomen and middle section of an insect; pedicel.

pe·dun·cu·lar (pi-duŋ'kyoo-lēr), *adj.* of or like a peduncle.

pe·dun·cu·late (pi-duŋ'kyoo-lit, pi-duŋ'kyoo-lāt'), *adj* growing on or having a peduncle.

pe·dun·cu·lat·ed (pi-duŋ'kyoo-lā'tid), *adj.* pedunculate.

Pee·bles (pē'b'lz), *n.* 1. a county of southern Scotland pop., 14,500 (est. 1946): also **Peeblesshire, Tweeddale** 2. its county seat: pop., 6,000.

Pee·bles·shire (pē'b'lz-shir'), *n.* Peebles.

Pee Dee (pē' dē'), a river flowing through North and South Carolina: length, 415 mi.: also called *Yadkin* (in North Carolina).

peek (pēk), *v.i.* [Early Mod. Eng. phonetic sp. < ME *piken,* prob. var. of *kiken,* to peer, influenced by *peep* etc.], to glance or peer quickly and furtively, especially through an opening or from behind something. *n.* a glance or look; peep. —*SYN.* see **look.**

peek·a·boo (pēk'ə-bōō'), *n.* a child's game in which someone hides his face, as behind his hands, and then suddenly reveals it, calling "peekaboo!"

peel (pēl), *v.t.* [ME. *pelen;* OFr. *peler,* to strip, pare L. *pilare,* to make bald < *pilus,* a hair], 1. to cut or trim away the rind, skin, covering, surface, etc. of pare. 2. to cut or trim away (rind, skin, covering surface, etc.) of anything. *v.i.* 1. to shed skin or the outer surface; become bare. 2. to come off: as, sunburned skin often *peels.* 3. [Slang], to undress. *n.* the rind or skin of fruit. —*SYN.* see **skin.**

keep one's eyes peeled, [Colloq.], to keep alert or on the watch.

peel off, in *aviation,* to veer away from a flight formation in order to make a dive at a target or to land.

peel (pēl), *n.* [ME. & OFr. *pele;* L. *pala,* a spade], a long shovellike tool used by bakers for moving bread into and out of the ovens.

peel (pēl), *n.* [ME. & OFr. *pel,* a fort, stake; L. *palus;* see PALE (a stake)], a fortified house or tower of a type built on the Scottish border during the 16th century.

Peel, Sir Robert (pēl), 1788–1850; English statesman prime minister of England (1834–1835; 1841–1846).

Peele, George (pēl), 1558?–1597?; English dramatist.

peel·er (pēl'ēr), *n.* [after Sir Robert *Peel,* who first organized Irish constabulary], [Obs. Irish & British Slang], a policeman.

peel·ing (pēl'iŋ), *n.* anything peeled off, as an apple skin.

peen (pēn), *n.* [prob. via dial. < ON.; cf. Norw. *pænn,* sharpened end of a hammer, Sw. *pæna,* to beat out, etc.], the part of the head of a hammer opposite to the flat striking surface: it is often hemispherical or wedge-shaped. *v.t.* to hammer, bend, etc. with a peen.

peep (pēp), *n.* [prob. suggested by rhyme with *jeep* (see JEEP) and by dim. quality of sound made by small birds and chicks], [Military Slang], a jeep (sense 1): the more common name in some military units.
peep (pēp), *v.i.* [ME. *pepen;* prob. echoic formation], 1. to make the short, high-pitched cry of a young bird or chick; chirp; cheep. 2. to speak in a small, weak voice, as from fear. *n.* a short, high-pitched sound like that made by a young bird; chirp; cheep.
peep (pēp), *v.i.* [ME. *pepen;* prob. symbolistic formation after earlier *keken* (*kiken*), to peep; cf. PEEK], 1. to look through a small opening or from a place of hiding; hence, 2. to peer slyly or secretly; take a hasty, furtive look. 3. to come into view; show or appear gradually or partially, as though from hiding: as, stars *peeped* through clouds. *v.t.* to cause to appear or protrude. *n.* 1. a brief, hasty look or restricted view; secret or furtive glimpse or glance. 2. the first appearance; crack, as of dawn. 3. an opening to peep through.
peep·er (pēp′ẽr), *n.* 1. a person who peeps or pries. 2. [Slang], an eye.
peep·er (pēp′ẽr), *n.* 1. a person or thing that peeps, cheeps, chirps, etc. 2. any of several species of frogs.
peep·hole (pēp′hōl′), *n.* a hole to peep through.
Peeping Tom, 1. in *English legend*, the Coventry tailor who was struck blind after peeping at Lady Godiva. 2. [p- T-], a person who gets pleasure, especially sexual pleasure, from watching others from a place of concealment.
peep show, a device containing a pictured scene or group of objects and a small opening, often with a magnifying lens, through which they may be viewed.
peep sight, a rear sight for a firearm, usually consisting of an adjustable disk with a small opening in the center through which the front sight and target are lined up.
peer (pêr), *n.* [ME. *peir, peer;* OFr. *per, pair;* L. *par*, an equal], 1. a person or thing of the same rank, value, quality, ability, etc.; equal; specifically, an equal before the law. 2. a noble; especially, a British duke, marquis, earl, viscount, or baron. *v.t.* 1. to match or equal. 2. to make a nobleman of.
peer of the realm, any of the class of British peers entitled to a seat in the House of Lords.
peer (pêr), *v.i.* [prob. contr. < *appear*], 1. to look closely and searchingly, as in trying to see more clearly. 2. [Poetic], to appear. 3. to come out or show slightly; come partly into sight. —*SYN.* see **look.**
peer·age (pêr′ij), *n.* [see -AGE], 1. all the peers of a particular country. 2. the rank or dignity of a peer. 3. a book or list of peers with their lineage.
peer·ess (pêr′is), *n.* 1. the wife of a peer. 2. a woman having the rank of peer in her own right.
peer·less (pêr′lis), *adj.* without equal; unrivaled.
peet·weet (pēt′wēt′), *n.* [echoic], the spotted sandpiper.
peeve (pēv), *v.t. & v.i.* [PEEVED (pēvd), PEEVING], [back-formation < *peevish*], [Colloq.], to make or become peevish or bad-tempered. *n.* [Colloq.], an object of dislike; annoyance. —*SYN.* see **irritate.**
peeved (pēvd), *adj.* [pp. of *peeve*], irritated; annoyed.
pee·vish (pēv′ish), *adj.* [ME. *pevische* < ?], 1. irritable; fretful; cross; hard to please. 2. showing ill humor or impatience, as a glance or remark.
pee·wee (pē′wē′), *n.* [said to be < Am.Ind. (Massachusett) *pewe*, little], [Colloq.], a person or thing that is unusually small.
peg (peg), *n.* [ME. *pegge;* prob. < LG. source; cf. D. *peg*, wooden plug; IE. base **bak-*, staff, as also in L. *baculum*, stick (cf. BACILLUS)], 1. a short, usually tapering or pointed piece used to hold parts together or to close an opening, as in a barrel. 2. a projecting pin or bolt used to hang things on, fasten ropes to, mark degrees of measurement or the score in a game, etc. 3. any of the pins which hold, and are used in regulating the tension of, the strings of a violin or other stringed instrument: see **violin,** illus. 4. the distance between pegs; hence, 5. a step or degree. 6. a point or prong for tearing, hooking, etc. 7. [Colloq.], the foot or leg: as, he was knocked off his *pegs*. 8. [Colloq.], a tooth. 9. [British], an alcoholic drink, usually brandy and soda. *v.t.* [PEGGED (pegd), PEGGING], 1. to put a peg or pegs into so as to fasten, secure, mark, etc. 2. to mark, as a score or distance, with pegs. 3. to strike with a peg so as to pierce or hook. 4. to maintain the price of, as a stock, by regulations or by buying and selling freely. 5. [Colloq.], to throw: as, he *pegged* the ball to first base. *v.i.* 1. to work, progress, etc. steadily and persistently: as, *peg* away at your studies. 2. to keep score with pegs, as in cribbage. 3. to hit a croquet peg, as in ending a game.
round peg in a square hole, a person in a position, situation, etc. for which he is unfitted or unqualified: also **square peg in a round hole.**
take down a peg, to lower the pride or conceit of; make rather humble or dispirited.
Peg·a·sus (peg′ə-səs), *n.* [ME. *Pegasee;* via OFr. < L.; Gr. *Pēgasos*], 1. in *Greek mythology*, a winged horse which sprang from the body of Medusa at her death: a stamp of his hoof caused Hippocrene, the fountain of the Muses, to issue from Mount Helicon; hence, 2. poetic inspiration. 3. a northern constellation near the vernal equinox: see **constellation,** chart.
peg·board, peg-board (peg′bôrd′, peg′bōrd′), *n.* a board with holes for inserting pegs; specifically, *a*) a small board used for scoring in cribbage. *b*) boardlike material, or a piece of this, perforated with rows of holes, for arranging pegs or hooks to hold displays, tools, etc.: a trade-mark (**Peg-Board**).
Peg·gy (peg′i), a feminine name: see **Margaret.**
peg leg, [Colloq.], 1. a wooden leg. 2. a person with a wooden leg.
peg·ma·tite (peg′mə-tīt′), *n.* [< Gr. *pēgma*, framework; + *-ite:* so called from closeness of texture], 1. a very coarse igneous rock, usually granitic, containing large crystals of quartz, feldspar, and mica, usually found in fissures and cracks of other rocks. 2. graphic granite.
peg-top (peg′top′), *adj.* pear-shaped like a peg top; especially, designating trousers that are full at the hips and narrow at the cuffs.
peg top, 1. a child's spinning toy having a pear-shaped body with a metal tip; top. 2. *pl.* peg-top trousers.
peh (pā), *n.* [Heb. *peh*, lit., mouth], the seventeenth letter of the Hebrew alphabet (פּ, פ), corresponding to English *P, p:* see **alphabet,** table: also spelled **pe.**
Peh·le·vi (pā′lə-vē′), *n.* Pahlavi.
P.E.I., Prince Edward Island.
peign·oir (pān-wär′, pān′wär), *n.* [Fr. < *peigner*, to comb < *peigne;* L. *pecten*, a comb], a negligee.
Pei·ping (pā′piŋ′; Chin. bā′piŋ′), *n.* Peking.
Peip·si (pāp′si), *n.* Peipus: the Estonian name.
Pei·pus (pī′poos), *n.* a lake between the Estonian S.S.R. and the Leningrad region, U.S.S.R.: area, 1,350 sq. mi.: Estonian name, *Peipsi;* Russian name, *Chudskoe.*
Pei·rae·us (pī-rē′əs), *n.* Piraeus.
Pei·rai·evs (pē′re-efs′), *n.* Piraeus: the Greek name.
Peirce, Charles San·ders (san′dẽrz pûrs), 1839–1914; American mathematician, philosopher, and logician.
pe·jo·ra·tion (pē′jə-rā′shən, pej′ə-rā′shən), *n.* [see PEJORATIVE], 1. a worsening. 2. in *linguistics*, a change of meaning for the worse. Opposed to *melioration.*
pe·jo·ra·tive (pē′jə-rā′tiv, pej′ə-rā′tiv, pi-jôr′ə-tiv), *adj.* [< L. *pejoratus*, pp. of *pejorare*, to make worse < *pejor*, worse], making or becoming worse; disparaging: applied in linguistics to words whose basic meaning has been changed for the worse (e.g., *silly, cretin*). *n.* a pejorative word or form. Opposed to *meliorative.*
pek·an (pek′ən), *n.* [Canad.Fr. < Am.Ind. (Algonquian) name; cf. Abnaki *pĕkanê*], 1. a North American animal of the weasel family, with blackish fur above and brown or gray below. 2. its fur.
Pe·kin (pē′kin′), *n.* 1. Peking: a former variant. 2. (pē′kin), a city in central Illinois: pop., 28,000.
pe·kin (pē′kin′), *n.* [Fr. *pékin* < *Pékin*, Peking], a patterned silk or satin material, originally from China.
Pe·kin·ese (pē′kə-nēz′), *adj. & n.* Pekingese.
Pe·king (pē′kiŋ′; Chin. bā′jiŋ′), *n.* the capital of the Chinese People's Republic, in northeastern China: the former capital of Hopeh province: pop., 5,420,000: former name (1928–1949), *Peiping:* see **China.**
Peking duck, a large, white domesticated duck of a breed originating in China: also **Peking.**
Pe·king·ese (pē′kiŋ-ēz′), *adj.* of Peking or its people. *n.* [*pl.* PEKINGESE], 1. a native or inhabitant of Peking, China: abbreviated **Pek.** 2. the Chinese dialect of Peking. 3. a small dog with long, silky hair, protruding eyes, short legs, and a pug nose: originally bred in China. Also **Pekinese.**

PEKINGESE (8 in. high at shoulder)

Peking man, a type of primitive man of about 475,000 B.C. whose fossil remains were found near Peking, China in 1929.
pe·koe (pē′kō; Brit. pek′ō), *n.* [< Chin. dial. *pek-ho*, lit., white down: so called from being picked while leaves still have the down on them], a black tea grown in Ceylon and India, made from the small leaves at the tips of the stem.
pel·age (pel′ij), *n.* [Fr. < OFr. *pel*, hair; L. *pilus*, hair], the coat, or covering, of a mammal, as hair, fur, etc.
Pe·la·gi·an (pə-lā′ji-ən), *n.* [LL. *Pelagianus*], a follower of Pelagius, a 4th-century British monk who denied the doctrine of original sin and maintained that man has freedom of will. *adj.* of Pelagius or his followers.
Pe·la·gi·an·ism (pə-lā′ji-ən-iz′m), *n.* the doctrines of Pelagius.

pe·lag·ic (pə-laj′ik), *adj.* [L. *pelagicus;* Gr. *pelagikos* < *pelagos,* the sea], of the ocean surface or the open sea, especially as distinguished from coastal waters.
pel·ar·gon·ic (pel′är-gon′ik, pel′är-gō′nik), *adj.* 1. of or obtained from a pelargonium. 2. designating or of a monobasic organic acid, $CH_3(CH_2)_7CO_2H$, extracted from the leaves of a pelargonium.
pel·ar·go·ni·um (pel′är-gō′ni-əm), *n.* [Mod.L. < Gr. *pelargos,* stork], any of a number of related plants with deeply cut leaves and variously colored flowers; geranium.
Pe·las·gi (pi-laz′jī), *n.pl.* a prehistoric people believed to have lived in Greece, Asia Minor, and the Aegean Islands.
Pe·las·gi·an (pi-laz′ji-ən), *adj.* of the Pelasgi. *n.* one of the Pelasgi.
Pe·las·gic (pi-laz′jik), *adj.* Pelasgian.
Pe·lee, Mount (pə-lā′), a volcanic mountain on Martinique Island, in the West Indies: height, 4,430 ft.
pel·er·ine (pel′ə-rēn′), *n.* [Fr. *pèlerine* < *pèlerin,* a pilgrim; L. *peregrinus;* see PILGRIM], a woman's cape, usually of fur, tapering to long points in the front.
Pe·leus (pēl′yoos, pē′li-əs), *n.* in *Greek legend,* a king of the Myrmidons, father of Achilles.
Pe·lew Islands (pē-lōō′), Palau Islands.
pelf (pelf), *n.* [ME.; Anglo-Fr. *pelfe, adduced < ONorm.Fr. *peuffe* < base seen in OFr. *pelfre,* a plunder; cf. PILFER], 1. [Rare], ill-gotten gains; booty. 2. mere money or wealth: a term of contempt.
Pe·li·as (pē′li-əs, pel′i-əs), *n.* in *Greek mythology,* a king of Thessaly: he was the uncle and guardian of Jason, whom he sent in search of the Golden Fleece.
pel·i·can (pel′i-kən), *n.* [ME. & AS. *pellicane;* LL. *pelicanus;* Gr. *pelekan,* a pelican, apparently < *pelekys,* an ax (in reference to the shape of the bill)], any of a number of large, related water birds with completely webbed feet and a distensible pouch which hangs from the lower bill and serves to scoop up fish.

PELICAN (5 ft. long)

Pe·li·des (pi-lī′dēz), *n.* [L.; Gr. *Pēleidēs*], 1. any male descendant of Peleus; specifically, 2. Achilles.
Pe·li·on (pē′li-ən), *n.* a mountain in eastern Thessaly, Greece: height, 5,300 ft.: see **Ossa.**
pe·lisse (pə-lēs′), *n.* [Fr.; ML. *pellicia* (*vestis*) < L. *pellicius,* made of skins < *pellis,* a skin], a long cloak or outer coat, especially one made or lined with fur.
pe·lite (pē′līt), *n.* [< Gr. *pelos,* earth, clay; + *-ite*], any sedimentary rock, as shale, composed of minute particles of clay, mud, etc.
pel·la·gra (pə-lā′grə, pə-lag′rə), *n.* [It. < *pelle* (L. *pellis*), the skin + *agra,* hard, or *-agra* < Gr. *agra,* seizure], a chronic disease caused by a deficiency of nicotinic acid in the diet and characterized by gastrointestinal disturbances, skin eruptions, and nervous disorders: it is endemic in some parts of the world.
pel·la·grin (pə-lā′grin, pə-lag′rin), *n.* a person who has pellagra.
pel·la·grous (pə-lā′grəs, pə-lag′rəs), *adj.* of or having pellagra.
pel·let (pel′it), *n.* [ME. & OFr. *pelote;* ML. *pilota, pelota,* dim. of L. *pila,* a ball; cf. PELOTA], 1. a little ball or rounded mass, as of clay, paper, medicine, etc. 2. a crude projectile of stone, etc., as used in a catapult or early cannon. 3. a bullet. 4. a small lead shot. *v.t.* 1. to make pellets of. 2. to shoot or hit with pellets.
pel·li·cle (pel′i-k'l), *n.* [L. *pellicula,* dim. of *pellis,* skin], a thin, skinlike substance, as a membrane, or the scum on a liquid.
pel·lic·u·lar (pə-lik′yoo-lẽr), *adj.* of, or in the form of, a pellicle.
pel·li·to·ry (pel′ə-tôr′i, pel′ə-tō′ri), *n.* [*pl.* PELLITORIES (-iz, -riz)], [ME. *peletre,* altered < OFr. *paritoire, paritaire;* L. *parietaria* < *parietarius,* of walls < *paries, parietis,* a wall], 1. any of a number of related climbing plants of the nettle family. 2. a plant of the composite family whose root is used in medicine as a sedative, etc.: in full, **pellitory of Spain.**
pell-mell, pell·mell (pel′mel′), *adv.* [Fr. *pêle-mêle;* OFr. *pesle mesle,* redupl. < *mesler,* to mix], 1. in a jumbled, confused mass or manner; without order or method. 2. in wild, disorderly haste; with reckless speed; headlong. *adj.* 1. jumbled; confused; disorderly. 2. headlong. *n.* a jumble; confusion; disorder.
pel·lu·cid (pə-lōō′sid), *adj.* [L. *pellucidus; pel* for *per,* intens. + *lucidus,* bright], 1. transparent or translucent; clear; hence, 2. easy to understand; clear and simple in style: as, a *pellucid* explanation. —*SYN.* see **clear.**
pel·lu·cid·i·ty (pel′oo-sid′ə-ti), *n.* the quality or condition of being pellucid.
Pe·lop·i·das (pi-lop′ə-dəs), *n.* a general of Thebes; died 364 B.C.
Pel·o·pon·ne·sian (pel′ə-pə-nē′shən, pel′ə-pə-nē′zhən), *adj.* of the Peloponnesus or its people. *n.* a native or inhabitant of the Peloponnesus.
Peloponnesian War, a war between Athens and Sparta (431–404 B.C.) ending with the victory of Sparta.
Pel·o·pon·ne·sus, Pel·o·pon·ne·sos (pel′ə-pə-nē′səs), *n.* the peninsula of southern Greece: seat of early Mycenaean civilization and of Sparta: see **Greece,** map.
Pe·lops (pē′lops), *n.* [L.; Gr. *Pelops* < *pelos,* dark + *ops,* an eye], in *Greek mythology,* the son of Tantalus: served up to the gods as food by his father and later restored to life by them.
pe·lo·ri·a (pi-lôr′i-ə, pi-lō′ri-ə), *n.* [Mod.L. < Gr. *pelōros,* monstrous < *pelōr,* monster], an abnormal regularity of form in a flower that is normally irregular.
pe·lor·ic (pi-lôr′ik, pi-lō′rik), *adj.* of or constituting peloria.
pe·lo·ta (pe-lō′tə; Sp. pe-lô′tä), *n.* [Sp., lit., a ball; see PELLET], a Spanish game somewhat like handball, played in a walled court with a hard ball and a long, curved wicker basket strapped to the arm: in Spanish America, called *jai-alai.*
pelt (pelt), *v.t.* [ME. *pelten;* prob. var. of *pulten, pilten, pelten,* to thrust, hasten < L. *pultare,* freq. of *pillare,* to drive; cf. *n.* 2], 1. to throw things at; strike with or as with missiles. 2. to beat or pound heavily and repeatedly. 3. to throw or cast (missiles). *v.i.* 1. to beat or strike heavily or steadily, as hard rain. 2. to rush or hurry. *n.* 1. the act of pelting; blow. 2. speed; tilt: as, running at full *pelt.*
pelt (pelt), *n.* [ME.; prob. back-formation < OFr. *peleterie;* see PELTRY], 1. the skin of a fur-bearing animal, especially when prepared for tanning. 2. an animal skin used as a garment. 3. the human skin: a humorous usage. —*SYN.* see **skin.**
pel·tast (pel′tast), *n.* [L. *peltasta;* Gr. *peltastēs* < *peltē,* light shield], in ancient Greece, a soldier carrying a light shield.
pel·tate (pel′tāt), *adj.* [< L. *pelta* (< Gr. *peltē*), light shield; + *-ate*], having a stalk attached to the center of the lower surface: said of a leaf: see **leaf,** illus.
pelt·ing (pel′tiŋ), *adj.* [prob. < obs. *pelt,* to haggle; cf. PALTRY], [Archaic], mean; miserly; paltry.
pelt·ry (pel′tri), *n.* [*pl.* PELTRIES (-triz)], [ME.; OFr. *peleterie* < *peletier,* furrier < *pel* (L. *pellis*), a skin], 1. pelts, or fur-bearing skins, collectively. 2. a pelt.
pel·vic (pel′vik), *adj.* of or situated near the pelvis.
pel·vis (pel′vis), *n.* [*pl.* PELVES (-vēz)], [L., a basin], in *anatomy* & *zoology,* any basinlike or funnel-shaped structure; specifically, *a*) the basinlike cavity formed by the ring of bone in the posterior part of the trunk in many vertebrates: in man, it is formed by the ilium, ischium, pubis, and sacrum, supporting the spinal column and resting upon the legs. *b*) these bones collectively: also **pelvic arch** (or **girdle**). *c*) the funnel-shaped part of the kidney leading into the ureter.
Pem·ba (pem′bə), *n.* an island off Tanganyika Territory, Africa: it is attached to the British protectorate of Zanzibar: area, 380 sq. mi.; pop., 98,000.
Pem·broke (pem′brook, pem′brōk), *n.* 1. Pembrokeshire. 2. its county seat: pop., 12,000.
Pem·broke·shire (pem′brook-shir′, pem′brōk-shir′), *n.* a county of southwestern Wales: pop., 87,000; county seat, Pembroke.
pem·mi·can, pem·i·can (pem′i-kən), *n.* [< Am.Ind. (Cree) *pemikkân,* fat meat < *pimiy,* fat], 1. dried lean meat, pounded into a paste with fat and preserved in the form of pressed cakes. 2. dried beef, raisins, suet, and sugar prepared as a concentrated food, as for explorers.
pem·phi·gus (pem′fi-gəs, pem-fi′gəs), *n.* [Mod.L. < Gr. *pemphix, pemphigos,* bubble], a disease characterized by the formation of watery blisters on the skin.
pen (pen), *n.* [ME.; AS. *penn;* for IE. base see PIN], 1. a small yard or enclosure for domestic animals. 2. the animals so confined. 3. any small enclosure: as, a play *pen* for babies. *v.t.* [PENNED (pend) or PENT (pent), PENNING], to confine or enclose in or as in a pen.
pen (pen), *n.* [ME. *penne;* OFr. *penne, pene,* a pen, feather < L. *penna,* a feather < **petna;* IE. base **pet-,* to fly, go, seen also in Gr. *petomai,* I fly, Eng. *feather*], 1. originally, a heavy quill or feather trimmed to a split point, used for writing with ink. 2. now, any of various devices used in writing or drawing with ink, usually with a half-tubular metal point split into two nibs: see also **ball point pen.** 3. the metal point for such a device. 4. *a*) the pen regarded as an instrument of writing; hence, *b*) literary style or expression. *c*) writing as a profession. *d*) a writer. 5. [Archaic], a feather or quill; especially, a heavy wing feather. 6. in *zoology,* the long, pen-shaped, internal shell of a squid. *v.t.* [PENNED (pend), PENNING], to write with or as with a pen.
pen (pen), *n.* [Slang], a penitentiary.
Pen., pen., peninsula.

P.E.N., International Association of Poets, Playwrights, Editors, Essayists, and Novelists.

pe·nal (pē'n'l), *adj.* [ME.; L. *poenalis* < *poena*, punishment], 1. of, for, or constituting punishment, especially legal punishment. 2. specifying or prescribing punishment: as, a *penal* code. 3. making a person liable to punishment, as an offense.

penal code, a body of law dealing with various crimes or offenses and their legal penalties.

pe·nal·i·za·tion (pē'n'l-i-zā'shən, pen''l-i-zā'shən), *n.* a penalizing or being penalized.

pe·nal·ize (pē'n'l-īz', pen''l-īz'), *v.t.* [PENALIZED (-īzd'), PENALIZING], 1. to make punishable; set a penalty for, as an offense. 2. to impose a penalty on; specifically, to subject to a handicap, as in a contest, as penalty for the infraction of a rule.

penal servitude, imprisonment, usually at hard labor: the legal punishment for conviction of certain crimes.

pen·al·ty (pen''l-ti), *n.* [*pl.* PENALTIES (-tiz)], [ML. *poenalitas* < L. *poenalis*], 1. a punishment fixed by law, as for a crime or breach of contract. 2. the disadvantage, suffering, handicap, etc. imposed upon an offender, as a fine or forfeit. 3. any unfortunate consequence or result of an act or condition.

pen·ance (pen'əns), *n.* [ME.; OFr. *penance, peneance;* L. *paenitentia, poenitentia* < *paenitens;* see PENITENT], 1. *a*) a sacrament of the Roman Catholic Church involving the confession of sin, repentance, and submission to penalties imposed, followed by absolution by a priest. *b*) the penalty or penalties so imposed. 2. any voluntary suffering or punishment to show repentance for a sin or wrongdoing. *v.t.* [PENANCED (-ənst), PENANCING], to impose a penance on.

Pe·nang (pi-naŋ'), *n.* 1. an island northwest of the Malay Peninsula: area, 110 sq. mi.; pop., 240,000. 2. Georgetown, a seaport on this island. 3. a state of the Federation of Malaya, including this island and part of the Malay Peninsula: area, 290 sq. mi.; pop., 399,000.

pe·na·tes (pi-nā'tēz), *n.pl.* [L.; prob. akin to *penus*, inner part of temple of Vesta < base **pen-*, seen also in *penes*, near, *penetrare*, to enter], the household gods of the ancient Romans: see **lares**.

pence (pens), *n.* [ME. *pens*, contr. of *penies*, pl. of *peny, pening;* see PENNY], [British], plural of **penny**: used also in compounds, as *twopence:* abbreviated **d.**

pen·cel (pen's'l), *n.* [ME.; Anglo-Fr., contr. < OFr. *penoncel*, dim. of *penon*, a pennon], [Archaic], a small pennon, or narrow flag.

pen·chant (pen'chənt; Fr. pän'shän'), *n.* [Fr. < *pencher*, to incline; LL. **pendicare* < L. *pendere*, to hang], a strong liking or fondness; inclination; taste.

pen·cil (pen's'l), *n.* [ME. *pencel;* OFr. *pincel;* L. *penicillus*, a brush < *peniculus*, dim. of *penis*, a tail: mod. sense & form of *pencil* have been influenced by *pen* (writing instrument)], 1. originally, an artist's brush, especially a small, fine one. 2. the style or ability of a given artist. 3. a pointed, rod-shaped instrument of wood, metal, etc. with a center or core of graphite or crayon, used for marking, writing, and drawing. 4. something shaped or used like a pencil; specifically, *a*) a small cosmetic stick for touching up the eyebrows. *b*) a stick of some medicated substance: as, a styptic *pencil*. 5. a series of lines or rays coming to or spreading out from a point. *v.t.* [PENCILED or PENCILLED (-s'ld), PENCILING or PENCILLING], 1. to mark, write, or draw with or as with a pencil. 2. to use a pencil on.

pen·cil·er, pen·cil·ler (pen's'l-ẽr), *n.* a person who pencils.

pend (pend), *v.i.* [Fr. *pendre;* L. *pendere*, to hang], 1. to await judgment or decision. 2. [Dial.], to depend.

pend·ant (pen'dənt), *n.* [ME.; OFr., ppr. of *pendre* < L. *pendere*, to hang], 1. a hanging object, as an earring, used as an ornament or decoration. 2. the stem and ring of a pocket watch. 3. one of a pair; match or parallel. 4. anything hanging, as the pull chain on a lamp. 5. in *architecture*, a decorative piece suspended from a ceiling or roof: used especially in Gothic architecture. Also spelled **pendent**. *adj.* pendent.

pend·en·cy (pen'dən-si), *n.* the state or condition of being pendent or pending.

pend·ent (pen'dənt), *adj.* [ME. *pendant, pendent;* L. *pendens*, ppr. of *pendere*, to hang], 1. hanging; suspended. 2. overhanging. 3. undecided; pending. Also spelled **pendant**. *n.* pendant.

‡**pen·den·te li·te** (pen-den'ti lī'ti), [L.], while a lawsuit or action is pending.

pen·den·tive (pen-den'tiv), *n.* [Fr. *pendentif* < L. *pendens*, ppr. of *pendere*, to hang], in *architecture*, one of the triangular pieces of vaulting springing from the corners of a rectangular area, serving to support a rounded or polygonal dome: usually supported by a single pier.

pend·ing (pen'diŋ), *adj.* [ppr. of *pend*, after Fr. *pendant*, L. *pendens*], 1. not decided, determined, or established: as, a *pending* patent. 2. impending. *prep.* 1. throughout the course or process of; during. 2. while awaiting; until: as, *pending* his arrival.

pen·drag·on (pen-drag'ən), *n.* [W. *pen*, head + *dragon*, dragon symbol, war standard, hence leader], supreme chief or leader: a title used in ancient Britain.

pen·du·lous (pen'joo-ləs), *adj.* [L. *pendulus* < *pendere*, to hang], 1. hanging freely or loosely without a rigid attachment; hence, 2. swinging.

pen·du·lum (pen'joo-ləm, pen'd'l-əm), *n.* [*pl.* PENDULUMS (-ləmz, -əmz)], [Mod. L. < L. *pendulus;* see PENDULOUS], a body hung from a fixed point in such a way that it can swing freely to and fro under the combined forces of gravity and momentum: often used in regulating the movement of clocks.

Pē·nei·os (pē'nē-ôs'; Eng. pi-nē'əs), *n.* Salambria, a river in Greece: the Modern Greek name.

Pe·nel·o·pe (pə-nel'ə-pi), [L.; Gr. *Pēnelopē, Pēnelopeia*], a feminine name. *n.* the faithful wife of Ulysses: during his absence she was courted by many suitors, who were asked to wait until she had woven a certain garment: she was able to delay its completion, since each night she secretly unraveled that day's work.

pe·ne·plain, pe·ne·plane (pē'nə-plān'), *n.* [L. *pene, paene*, almost; + *plain, n.*], land worn down by erosion almost to a level plain.

pen·e·tra·bil·i·ty (pen'i-trə-bil'ə-ti), *n.* the quality or condition of being penetrable.

pen·e·tra·ble (pen'i-trə-b'l), *adj.* [ME.; L. *penetrabilis*], that can be penetrated.

pen·e·tra·bly (pen'i-trə-bli), *adv.* so as to be penetrable.

pen·e·tra·li·a (pen'ə-trā'li-ə), *n.pl.* [L., neut. pl. of *penetralis*, penetrating, inward], 1. the innermost parts, as of a temple. 2. things kept private or secret.

pen·e·trant (pen'ə-trənt), *adj.* [Fr. *pénétrant;* L. *penetrans*, ppr. of *penetrare*], sharp; acute; penetrating.

pen·e·trate (pen'ə-trāt'), *v.t.* [PENETRATED (-id), PENETRATING], [< L. *penetratus*, pp. of *penetrare*, to pierce into, penetrate < base of *penitus*, inward + **trare*, in *intrare*, to go into], 1. to find or force a way into or through; enter by piercing. 2. to have an effect throughout; spread through; permeate. 3. to affect or move deeply; imbue. 4. to grasp mentally; understand. *v.i.* 1. to make a way into and through something; pierce. 2. to have a marked effect on the mind.

pen·e·trat·ing (pen'ə-trāt'iŋ), *adj.* 1. that can penetrate; sharp; piercing: as, a *penetrating* sound or smell. 2. that has entered deeply: as, a *penetrating* wound. 3. showing keenness of mind; acute; discerning.

pen·e·tra·tion (pen'ə-trā'shən), *n.* [LL. *penetratio*], 1. a penetrating. 2. the depth to which a projectile sinks into a target. 3. the extension of the influence of a country over a weaker one by means of commercial investments, loans, strong diplomatic posts, etc. 4. keenness of mind; discernment; insight.

pen·e·tra·tive (pen'ə-trā'tiv), *adj.* penetrating.

pen·e·tron (pen'ə-tron'), *n.* [Mod.L. < *penetrate* + *electron*], a meson.

Pe·ne·us (pi-nē'əs), *n.* Salambria: the ancient name.

pen·gö (pen'gö'), *n.* [*pl.* PENGO, PENGOS (-göz')], [Hung.], the former monetary unit of Hungary, discontinued August 1, 1946 and replaced by the forint.

pen·guin (peŋ'gwin, pen'gwin), *n.* [in early accounts attributed to "Welsh fishermen," but prob. applied by Bret. fishermen in the Newfoundland seas; cf. W. *pen*, head, + *gwyn*, white, Bret. *pen gouin*, white head: the great auk has white spots near its eyes], 1. [Obs.], the great auk. 2. any of a number of related flightless birds found in the Southern Hemisphere, having webbed feet and paddlelike flippers for swimming and diving.

KING PENGUIN (36 in. tall)

pen·hold·er (pen'hōl'dẽr), *n.* 1. the handle or holder into which a pen point fits. 2. a container or rack for a pen or pens.

pen·i·cil (pen'ə-sil), *n.* [< L. *penicillus*, paintbrush; cf. PENCIL], in *botany* & *zoology*, a small tuft of hairs resembling a painter's brush.

pen·i·cil·late (pen'ə-sil'it, pen'ə-sil'āt), *adj.* [< L. *penicillus* (see PENCIL); + *-ate*], having a penicil or penicils.

pen·i·cil·lin (pen'ə-sil'in), *n.* a powerful antibiotic substance obtained from certain penicilliums and used in the treatment and prevention of some infections due to its ability to inhibit growth of certain bacteria.

pen·i·cil·li·um (pen'ə-sil'i-əm), *n.* [*pl.* PENICILLIUMS (-əmz), PENICILLIA (-ə)], [Mod.L. < L. *penicillus* (see PENCIL): so named because of the tuftlike ends of the conidiophores], any of a group of fungi growing as green mold on stale bread, ripening cheese, decaying fruit, etc.: penicillin is derived from some species.

pen·in·su·la (pə-nin′sə-lə, pə-nin′syoo-lə), *n.* [L. *paeninsula* < *paene,* almost + *insula,* an isle], 1. a land area almost entirely surrounded by water and connected with the mainland by an isthmus. 2. any land area projecting out into the water. Abbreviated **Pen., pen.**

pen·in·su·lar (pə-nin′sə-lẽr, pə-nin′syoo-lẽr), *adj.* 1. of or forming a peninsula. 2. like a peninsula.

pe·nis (pē′nis), *n.* [*pl.* PENES (-nēz), PENISES (-iz)], [L., orig., a tail], the male organ of sexual intercourse: in mammals it is also the organ through which urine is ejected.

pen·i·tence (pen′ə-təns), *n.* [ME.; OFr.; L. *penitentia, poenitentia*], the state of being penitent; repentance. *SYN.*—**penitence** implies sorrow over having sinned or done wrong; **repentance** implies full realization of one's sins or wrongs and a will to change one's ways; **contrition** implies a deep, crushing sorrow for one's sins (theologically, as motivated by a love of God and a sense of his mercy) with a true purpose of amendment; **compunction** implies a pricking of the conscience and therefore suggests a sharp but passing feeling of uneasiness about wrongdoing; **remorse** implies a deep and torturing sense of guilt; **regret** may refer to sorrow over any unfortunate occurrence as well as over a fault or act of one's own.

pen·i·tent (pen′ə-tənt), *adj.* [ME. *penitaunt;* OFr.; L. *paenitens, poenitens,* ppr. of *paenitere, poenitere,* to repent], sorry or ashamed for having done wrong and willing to atone; repentant. *n.* 1. a penitent person. 2. in the *Roman Catholic Church,* a person undergoing the sacrament of penance.

pen·i·ten·tial (pen′ə-ten′shəl), *adj.* [ML. *penitentialis*], of, constituting, or expressing penitence or penance. *n.* 1. a penitent. 2. a list or book of rules governing religious penance.

pen·i·ten·tia·ry (pen′ə-ten′shə-ri), *adj.* [ML. *penitentiarius* < L. *paenitentia;* see PENANCE], 1. of or for penance. 2. used in punishing, disciplining, and reforming: as, a *penitentiary* device. 3. that makes one liable to imprisonment in a penitentiary. *n.* [*pl.* PENITENTIARIES (-riz)], 1. [ML. *penitentiaria* < the *adj.*], a prison; especially, a State or Federal prison for persons convicted of serious crimes. 2. [ML. *penitentiarius* < the *adj.*], in the *Roman Catholic Church, a*) an office or tribunal headed by a cardinal (the *grand penitentiary*) and dealing with matters of penance, confession, dispensation, absolution, etc. *b*) an officer empowered to give absolution in cases normally reserved to a bishop.

pen·knife (pen′nīf′), *n.* [*pl.* PENKNIVES (-nīvz′)], a small pocketknife: originally used in making quill pens.

pen·man (pen′mən), *n.* [*pl.* PENMEN (-mən)], 1. a person employed to write or copy; scribe. 2. a person skilled in penmanship. 3. an author.

pen·man·ship (pen′mən-ship′), *n.* [*penman* + *-ship*], 1. handwriting considered as an art or skill. 2. a style of handwriting.

Penn, William (pen), 1644–1718; English Quaker; founder of Pennsylvania.

Penn., Penna., Pennsylvania.

pen·na (pen′ə), *n.* [*pl.* PENNAE (-ē)], [L.; see PEN (quill)], any of the feathers forming the general outer covering, or contour, of a bird.

pen name, a name used by an author in place of his true name; nom de plume. —*SYN.* see **pseudonym.**

pen·nant (pen′ənt), *n.* [< *pennon;* influenced by *pendant*], 1. any long, narrow, usually triangular flag, as used for naval signaling, a school banner, etc. 2. any such flag symbolizing a championship, as in baseball.

pen·nate (pen′āt), *adj.* [L. *pennatus,* winged < *penna,* quill, wing], in *botany,* pinnate.

pen·nat·ed (pen′ā-tid), *adj.* pennate.

Pen·nell, Joseph (pen″l), 1857–1926; American etcher and book illustrator.

pen·ni (pen′i), *n.* [*pl.* PENNIA (-ə)], [Finn. < G. *pfennig;* see PENNY], a Finnish coin equal to 1/100 markka.

pen·ni- (pen′i), [< L. *penna* (see PEN, quill)], a combining form meaning *feather, featherlike,* as in *penniform.*

pen·ni·form (pen′i-fôrm′), *adj.* [< Mod. L.; see PENNI- & -FORM], like a feather, as in appearance or structure.

pen·ni·less (pen′i-lis), *adj.* without even a penny; extremely poor.

Pen·nine Alps (pen′īn, pen′in), a range of the Alps between Switzerland and northwestern Italy: highest point, Monte Rosa, 15,196 ft.

Pennine Chain, a range of English hills and mountains extending from the Peak of Derbyshire in the south to the Cheviot Hills of the Scottish Border in the north.

pen·non (pen′ən), *n.* [ME. & OFr. *penon;* L. *penna,* a feather], 1. a long, narrow, triangular or swallow-tailed flag used as an ensign by a knight or regiment of lancers. 2. any flag or pennant. 3. a pinion; wing.

Penn·syl·va·ni·a (pen′s'l-vān′yə, pen′s'l-vā′ni-ə), *n.* an Eastern State of the United States: area, 45,333 sq. mi.; pop., 11,319,000; capital, Harrisburg: nicknamed *Keystone State:* abbreviated **Pa., Penn., Penna.**

Penn·syl·va·ni·a-Dutch (pen′s'l-vān′yə-duch′), *adj.* 1. of the Pennsylvania Dutch or their language. 2. designating or of a style of furniture, etc. characterized by carved or painted decorations of flowers, fruits, etc.

Pennsylvania Dutch, 1. the descendants of early German immigrants to Pennsylvania. 2. their German dialect. Also called *Pennsylvania German.*

Penn·syl·va·ni·an (pen′s'l-vān′yən, pen′s'l-vā′ni-ən), *adj.* 1. of Pennsylvania. 2. designating or of the second coal-forming period of the Paleozoic Era in North America. *n.* a native or inhabitant of Pennsylvania.

the Pennsylvanian, the Pennsylvanian Period or its rocks: see **geology,** chart.

pen·ny (pen′i), *n.* [*pl.* PENNIES (-iz); for 1 (esp. collective), PENCE (pens)], [ME. *peny, pening;* AS. *penig, pening;* akin to G. *pfennig;* Gmc. forms suggest base form **panding* < **pand-,* base of *pawn* + *-ing,* as in *farthing, shilling,* etc.], 1. a British bronze coin equal to one twelfth of a shilling: abbreviated **d.** 2. a cent (U.S. or Canadian). 3. a sum of money: as, a pretty *penny.* Abbreviated **p.**

a pretty penny, [Colloq.], a large sum of money.

turn an honest penny, to earn money fairly and honestly.

-pen·ny (pen′i; *esp. Brit.,* pə-ni), a combining form meaning *costing* (a specified number of) *pennies,* as in *sixpenny:* formerly applied to nails to indicate the cost per hundred, but now simply a measure of their length.

pen·ny-a-line (pen′i-ə-līn′), *adj.* 1. receiving a penny per line of writing; i.e., having a low rate of pay; hence, 2. of inferior quality; cheap: said of writing.

pen·ny-a-lin·er (pen′i-ə-līn′ẽr), *n.* a writer paid at a low rate, especially a hack writer.

penny ante, a game of poker in which the ante is limited to one cent.

penny dreadful, [British Colloq.], a cheap book or magazine containing stories of crime, terror, the supernatural, etc.; dime novel.

pen·ny·roy·al (pen′i-roi′əl), *n.* [altered < earlier *pulyol ryal;* Anglo-Fr. *puliol real;* OFr. *poliol, pouliol* (< L. *pulegium,* fleabane) + *real, roial,* royal], 1. a hairy plant of the mint family. 2. the oil it yields.

pen·ny·weight (pen′i-wāt′), *n.* a unit of weight, equal to 24 grains or 1/20 ounce troy weight: abbreviated **dwt., pwt.**

pen·ny-wise (pen′i-wīz′), *adj.* careful or thrifty in regard to small matters.

penny-wise and pound-foolish, careful or thrifty in small matters but careless or wasteful in major ones.

pen·ny·wort (pen′i-wũrt′), *n.* [ME. *penywort;* see PENNY & WORT], any of various plants with small round leaves, growing in crevices of rocks and walls or in marshy places.

pen·ny·worth (pen′i-wũrth′), *n.* 1. the amount that can be bought for one penny. 2. the value of something bought, with regard to the price paid: as, a good *pennyworth.* 3. a small amount.

Pe·nob·scot (pi-nob′skot), *n.* [< Am.Ind. (Algonquian); cf. *penaubsket,* it flows on stones, *penabskat,* plenty stones], 1. a river in central Maine, flowing southward to the Atlantic: length, 300 mi. 2. a member of a tribe of Algonquian Indians living around this river and its bay. *adj.* of the Penobscots.

Penobscot Bay, an inlet at the mouth of the Penobscot River: length, 30 mi.

pe·no·log·i·cal (pē′nə-loj′ə-k'l), *adj.* of penology.

pe·nol·o·gy (pē-nol′ə-ji), *n.* [Gr. *poinē* (L. *poena,* punishment); + *-logy*], the study of the reformation and rehabilitation of criminals and of the management of prisons: abbreviated **penol.:** also spelled **poenology.**

Pen·sa·co·la (pen′sə-kō′lə), *n.* a seaport in northwestern Florida: pop., 57,000.

Pensacola Bay, an arm of the Gulf of Mexico, in northwestern Florida.

pen·sile (pen′sil), *adj.* [L. *pensilis* < *pendere,* to hang] 1. hanging. 2. having or building a hanging nest, as the Baltimore oriole.

pen·sion (pen′shən; *for n. 3* pon′si-on′, Fr. pän′syōn′), *n.* [ME. *pensioun;* OFr.; L. *pensio,* a paying < *pendere,* to weigh, pay], 1. a payment, not wages, made regularly to a person (or to his family) who has fulfilled certain conditions of service, reached a certain age, etc.: as, a soldier's *pension,* old-age *pension.* 2. a regular payment, not a fee, given to artists, etc. by their patrons or benefactors; subsidy. 3. in France and other Continental countries, a boarding school or boardinghouse. *v.t.* to grant a pension to.

pension off, to dismiss from service with a pension.

pen·sion·a·ble (pen′shən-ə-b'l), *adj.* having or giving a right to a pension: as, sixty-five is a *pensionable* age.

pen·sion·ar·y (pen′shən-er′i), *adj.* [ML. *pensionarius*], 1. of or constituting a pension. 2. receiving a pension; hence, 3. dependent; hireling. *n.* [*pl.* PENSIONARIES (-iz)], 1. a pensioner. 2. a hireling; tool; puppet.

pen·sion·er (pen′shən-ẽr), *n.* [ME. *pensyonere,* in sense 2; OFr. *pensionnier*], 1. a person who receives a pension; pensionary. 2. an undergraduate who pays his own expenses at Cambridge University, England. 3. [Obs.], a gentleman-at-arms.

pen·sive (pen′siv), *adj.* [ME. & OFr. *pensif* < *penser,* to think, reflect; L. *pensare,* to weigh, consider, freq. of *pendere,* to weigh], 1. thinking deeply or seriously, often of sad or melancholy things. 2. expressing deep thoughtfulness, often with some sadness.

SYN.—**pensive** suggests a dreamy, often somewhat sad or melancholy concentration of thought (the *pensive* look in her eye); **contemplative** implies intent concentration of thought as on some abstract matter, often connoting this as a habitual practice (a *contemplative* scholar); **reflective** suggests an orderly, often analytical turning over in the mind with the aim of reaching some definite understanding (after a *reflective* pause he answered); **meditative,** on the other hand, implies a quiet and sustained musing, but with no definite intention of understanding or reaching a conclusion (a *meditative* walk in the cloister).

pen·stock (pen'stok'), *n.* [*pen* (enclosure) + *stock*], 1. a gate or sluice used in controlling the flow of water. 2. a tube or trough for carrying water to a water wheel.

pent (pent), alternative past tense and past participle of **pen** (to shut in). *adj.* held or kept in; confined; penned (often with *up*).

pen·ta- (pen'tə), [Gr. *penta-* < *pente*, five (see FIVE)], a combining form meaning *five*, as in *pentamerous:* also, before a vowel, **pent-**.

pen·ta·cle (pen'tə-k'l), *n.* [MFr.; ML. *pentaculum* < Gr. *penta-*, five + L. *-culum*, dim. suffix], a symbol, usually a five-pointed star, formerly used in magic.

pen·tad (pen'tad), *n.* [Gr. *pentas, pentados* < *pente*, five], 1. the number five. 2. a series or group of five. 3. a five-year period. 4. in *chemistry*, an element or radical with a valence of five.

pen·ta·dac·tyl (pen'tə-dak'til), *adj.* [< *penta-* + Gr. *daktylos*, a finger], having five fingers or toes on each hand or foot.

pen·ta·gon (pen'tə-gon'), *n.* [LL. *pentagonium;* Gr. *pentagōnon* < *penta-*, five + *gōnia*, an angle], a plane figure with five angles and five sides.

the Pentagon, the pentagonal building in Arlington, Virginia, in which the offices of the National Military Establishment are located.

pen·tag·o·nal (pen-tag'ə-n'l), *adj.* of, or having the form of, a pentagon.

pen·ta·gram (pen'tə-gram'), *n.* [Gr. *pentagrammon*, neut. of *pentagrammos*, having five lines; see PENTA- & -GRAM], 1. a pentacle. 2. any figure of five lines.

pen·ta·he·dral (pen'tə-hē'drəl), *adj.* of, or having the form of, a pentahedron.

pen·ta·he·dron (pen'tə-hē'drən), *n.* [*pl.* PENTAHEDRONS (-drənz), PENTAHEDRA (-drə)], [Mod. L.; see PENTA- & -HEDRON], a solid figure with five plane surfaces.

pen·tam·er·ism (pen-tam'ẽr-iz'm), *n.* the condition of being pentamerous.

pen·tam·er·ous (pen-tam'ẽr-əs), *adj.* [*penta-* + *-merous*], in *botany* & *zoology*, made up of five parts or divisions: also written **5-merous.**

pen·tam·e·ter (pen-tam'ə-tẽr), *n.* [L.; Gr. *pentametros;* see PENTA- & METER (rhythm)], 1. a line of verse containing five metrical feet or measures; especially, English iambic pentameter. Example: "Yŏu blócks, | yŏu stónes, | yŏu wórse | thăn sénse | lĕss thíngs." 2. verse consisting of pentameters; heroic verse. *adj.* having five metrical feet or measures.

pen·tane (pen'tān), *n.* [*pent-* + *-ane*], any of three known isomeric, colorless hydrocarbons, C_5H_{12}, of the methane series, occurring in petroleum, etc.

pen·tan·gu·lar (pen-taŋ'gyoo-lẽr), *adj.* [*pent-* + *angular*], having five angles.

pen·tarch·y (pen'tär-ki), *n.* [*pl.* PENTARCHIES (-kiz)], [Gr. *pentarchia;* see PENTA- & -ARCHY], 1. a federation of five states, each under an individual leader or ruler. 2. government by five rulers.

pen·ta·stich (pen'tə-stik'), *n.* [Gr. *pentastichos; penta-*, five + *stichos*, a verse], a poem or stanza of five lines.

Pen·ta·teuch (pen'tə-tōōk', pen'tə-tūk'), *n.* [LL. *Pentateuchus;* Gr. *pentateuchos*, composed of five books; *penta-*, five + *teuchos*, an implement, book], the first five books of the Old Testament.

pen·tath·lon (pen-tath'lən, pen-tath'lon), *n.* [Gr. < *penta-*, five + *athlon*, a contest], 1. an athletic contest in which each contestant takes part in five events (broad jump, javelin throw, 200-meter dash, discus throw, and 1500-meter run). 2. in the Olympic games, a contest consisting of five events (5000-meter cross-country horseback ride, 4000-meter cross-country run, 300-meter swim, foil fencing, and pistol shooting): in full, **modern pentathlon.**

pen·ta·ton·ic (pen'tə-ton'ik), *adj.* [see PENTA- & TONIC], designating or of a musical scale having only five tones.

pen·ta·va·lent (pen'tə-vā'lənt, pen-tav'ə-lənt), *adj.* 1. having a valence of five. 2. having five valences. Also, esp. for 2, **quinquevalent.**

Pen·te·cost (pen'ti-kôst', pen'ti-kost'), *n.* [ME.; L. *pentecoste;* Gr. *pentēkostē* (*hēmera*), the fiftieth (day) < *pentēkonta*, fifty < *pente*, five], 1. Shabuoth, the Jewish holiday. 2. a Christian festival on the seventh Sunday after Easter, celebrating the descent of the Holy Spirit upon the Apostles; Whitsunday. Abbreviated **Pent.**

Pen·te·cos·tal (pen'ti-kôs't'l, pen'ti-kos't'l), *adj.* [LL. *pentecostalis*], of or taking place during Pentecost.

Pen·tel·i·cus (pen-tel'i-kəs), *n.* a mountain near Athens, Greece, known for its fine marble: height, 3,640 ft.

pent·house (pent'hous'), *n.* [altered < *pentice;* ME. *pentis*, penthouse; OFr. *apentis;* ML. *appenditium* < LL. *appendicium*, lit., an appendage < L. *appendere;* see APPEND], 1. a small structure, especially one with a sloping roof, attached to a larger building. 2. a sloping roof extending out from a wall or building. 3. a house or apartment built on the roof of a building. 4. a structure built on the roof of a building, to house machinery, etc. 5. anything like a penthouse, as a canopy.

pen·to·bar·bi·tal sodium (pen'tə-bär'bi-tôl', pen'tə-bär'bi-tal'), *n.* [*pento-* for *penta-* (because of methylbutyl five-carbon group) + *barbital*], the soluble sodium salt of ethyl (1-methylbutyl) barbituric acid, used in medicine as a sedative, hypnotic, and analgesic.

pen·to·san (pen'tə-san'), *n.* [< *pentose* + *-an*], any of a group of plant carbohydrates which form pentoses upon undergoing hydrolysis.

pen·to·sane (pen'tə-sān'), *n.* pentosan.

pen·tose (pen'tōs), *n.* [*pent-* + *-ose*], any of a group of monosaccharides having a composition corresponding to the formula $C_5H_{10}O_5$.

pen·to·thal sodium (pen'tə-thal'), [*pento-* for *penta-* (because of methylbutyl five-carbon group) + *th*iobarbiturate + *-al* (as in *veronal, barbital*)], a drug, sodium ethyl-(1-methylbutyl)-thiobarbiturate, injected intravenously as an anesthetic and hypnotic: a trade-mark (**Pentothal Sodium**).

pent·ste·mon (pent-stē'mən), *n.* [Mod. L. < Gr. *penta-*, five + *stēmōn*, warp; see STAMEN], any of a number of related plants with clusters of white, red, blue, or purple flowers; beardtongue.

pent-up (pent'up'), *adj.* held in check; curbed; confined: as, *pent-up* emotion.

pe·nu·che, pe·nu·chi (pə-nōō'chi), *n.* panocha.

pe·nuch·le, pe·nuck·le (pē'nuk''l), *n.* pinochle.

pe·nult (pē'nult, pi-nult'), *n.* [L. *paenultima* < *paene*, almost + *ultima*, fem. of *ultimus*, last], the one next to the last; specifically, the second last syllable in a word.

pe·nul·ti·mate (pi-nul'tə-mit), *adj.* [< L. *paenultimus*, after *ultimate*], 1. next to the last. 2. of the penult. *n.* the penult.

pe·num·bra (pi-num'brə), *n.* [*pl.* PENUMBRAE (-brē), PENUMBRAS (-brəz)], [Mod.L. < L. *paene*, almost + *umbra*, shade], 1. the partly lighted area surrounding the complete shadow of a body, as the moon, in full eclipse. 2. a partly lighted area around any area of full shadow, as of a sunspot.

PENUMBRA

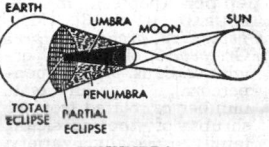

pe·num·bral (pi-num'brəl), *adj.* of or like a penumbra.

pe·nu·ri·ous (pə-nyoor'i-əs, pə-noor'i-əs), *adj.* [ML. *penuriosus* < L. *penuria*, penury], 1. unwilling to part with money or possessions; mean; miserly; stingy. 2. poorly supplied; scanty; barren —*SYN.* see **stingy.**

pen·u·ry (pen'yoo-ri), *n.* [ME. *pennury;* L. *penuria*, want, scarcity], lack of money or property; extreme poverty; destitution. —*SYN.* see **poverty.**

Pe·nu·ti·an (pə-nōō'ti-ən, pə-nōō'shən), *n.* a family of western North American Indian languages.

Pen·za (pen'zä), *n.* 1. a region of the R.S.F.S.R., in central European Russia: pop., 1,510,000. 2. its capital: pop., 286,000.

Pen·zance (pen-zans'), *n.* a seaport in Cornwall, England: pop., 19,000.

pe·on (pē'ən), *n.* [< Sp. *peón* or (in sense 2) Port. *peão*, both < ML. *pedo, pedonis*, foot soldier < L. *pes, pedis*, a foot; see PAWN], 1. in Latin America, *a*) a member of the laboring class. *b*) formerly, a person forced to work off a debt or to perform penal servitude. 2. in the southwestern U.S., a person forced into servitude to work off a debt. 3. in India, *a*) a foot soldier. *b*) a native policeman. *c*) an attendant or footman.

pe·on·age (pē'ən-ij), *n.* [see -AGE], 1. the condition of a peon. 2. the system by which debtors or legal prisoners are held in servitude to labor for their creditors or for persons who lease their services from the state.

pe·o·ny (pē'ə-ni), *n.* [*pl.* PEONIES (-niz)], [ME. *pione* < AS. *peonie* & OFr. *peoine*, both < L. *poeonia;* Gr. *paiōnia* < *Paiōn*, epithet of Apollo, physician of the gods; so called from its former medicinal use], 1. any of a number of related plants with large pink, white, red, or yellow, showy flowers. 2. the flower.

peo·ple (pē'p'l), *n.* [*pl.* PEOPLE], [ME. *peple, people;* Anglo-Fr. *poeple, people;* OFr. *pople;* L. *populus*, nation, crowd < base seen also in *plebs*, the common people], 1. [*pl.* PEOPLES (-p'lz)], *a*) all the persons of a racial, cultural, religious, or linguistic group; nation, race, etc. *b*) specifically, all the members of a group having in common traditional, historical, or cultural ties, as distinct from racial or political unity: as, the Jewish *people*. 2. the persons belonging to a certain place, community, or class: as, the *people* of Cleveland, *people* of wealth. 3. the members of a group under the leadership, influence, or control of a particular person or body, as a number of servants, royal subjects, etc. 4. the members of a person's class, set, race, tribe, etc. as, the miner spoke for his *people*. 5. one's family; relatives; ancestry. 6. persons without wealth, influence, privilege, or distinction; populace. 7. the citizens or electorate of a state. 8. persons considered indefinitely: as, I don't care what *people* say. 9. [*pl.* PEOPLES (-p'lz)], a tribe or kind, as of animals; group of creatures: as, the ant *people*, fairies are the little *people*. 10. human beings, as distinct from other animals. *v.t.* [PEOPLED (-p'ld), PEOPLING], [Fr. *peupler* < the *n.*], to fill with or as with people; populate; stock.

people's front, popular front.

People's party, an American political party (1891–1904) advocating free coinage of gold and silver, public ownership of utilities, an income tax, and support of labor and agriculture: its members were called *Populists*.

Pe·or·i·a (pi-ôr'i-ə, pi-ō'ri-ə), *n.* a city in central Illinois, on the Illinois River: pop., 103,000.

pep (pep), *n.* [< *pepper*], [Slang], energy; briskness; vigor; spirit. *v.t.* [PEPPED (pept), PEPPING], [Slang], to fill with pep; invigorate; encourage (with *up*).

Pep·in the Short (pep'in), 714?–768 A.D.; father of *Charlemagne;* king of the Franks (751–768 A.D.).

pep·los (pep'ləs), *n.* [Gr. *peplos*], a large shawl or scarf worn draped about the body by women in ancient Greece: also spelled **peplus**.

pep·lum (pep'ləm), *n.* [*pl.* PEPLUMS (-ləmz), PEPLA (-lə)], [L. < Gr. *peplos;* see PEPLOS], 1. a peplos. 2. a flounce or short, flared skirt attached at the waist of a dress, blouse, coat, etc., and extending around the hips.

PEPLUM

pe·po (pē'pō), *n.* [L., large species of melon], any fleshy gourd fruit with a hard rind and many seeds, as the melon, squash, etc.

pep·per (pep'ẽr), *n.* [see PLURAL, II, D, 3], [ME. *peper;* AS. *pipor;* L. *piper;* Gr. *peperi;* of Oriental origin; cf. Sans. *pippali*, peppercorn], 1. *a)* any of a number of related tropical shrubs of the capsicum family, especially a variety with a many-seeded, red or green, sweet or hot fruit. *b)* the fruit. 2. *a)* a pungent condiment prepared from any of a group of plants: *black pepper* is ground from the dried berries; *white pepper* consists of the dried seeds with the coatings removed. *b)* any of these plants. 3. cayenne; red pepper. *v.t.* 1. to sprinkle or flavor with ground pepper. 2. to sprinkle freely or thickly. 3. to shower or pelt with many small objects: as, the lawn was *peppered* with hailstones. 4. to beat or thrash.

pep·per-and-salt (pep'ẽr-'n-sôlt'), *adj.* consisting of a fine weave or mixture of black with white, so as to appear grayish: said of cloth.

pep·per·box (pep'ẽr-boks'), *n.* a small container with holes in the top, used in sprinkling pepper on food.

pep·per·corn (pep'ẽr-kôrn'), *n.* [ME. *pepercorn;* AS. *piporcorn*], 1. the dried berry of the black pepper: formerly used in a nominal payment of rent; hence, 2. something insignificant or trifling.

pep·per·grass (pep'ẽr-gras', pep'ẽr-gräs'), *n.* a plant with white or greenish flowers formed like a cross; garden cress: the leaves are used in salads.

pep·per·idge (pep'ẽr-ij), *n.* [var. of Brit. dial. *pipperidge*, the barberry], the black gum tree; tupelo.

pep·per·i·ness (pep'ẽr-i-nis), *n.* a peppery quality.

pep·per·mint (pep'ẽr-mint'), *n.* 1. a plant of the mint family, with lance-shaped leaves and pink flowers. 2. the pungent oil it yields, used for flavoring. 3. a candy or lozenge flavored with this oil.

pepper pot, 1. a pepperbox. 2. a West Indian stew of vegetables and meat or fish, flavored with cassava juice, red pepper, etc. 3. a thick, hotly seasoned stew of vegetables, dumplings, tripe, and other meat. 4. a soup of meat and vegetables flavored with hot spices.

pepper tree (or **shrub**), a tree with loose-hanging branches, clusters of yellow flowers, and reddish berries.

pep·per·wort (pep'ẽr-wũrt'), *n.* peppergrass.

pep·per·y (pep'ẽr-i), *adj.* 1. of, like, or highly seasoned with pepper. 2. sharp; fiery; hot, as speech or writing. 3. hot-tempered; easily angered; irritable.

pep·py (pep'i), *adj.* [PEPPIER (-i-ẽr), PEPPIEST (-i-ist)], [Slang], full of pep, or energy; brisk; vigorous; spirited.

pep·sin (pep'sin), *n.* [G. < Gr. *pepsis*, digestion < *peptein*, to digest], 1. an enzyme secreted in the stomach, aiding in the digestion of proteins by splitting them into the less complex proteoses and peptones. 2. an extract of pepsin from the stomachs of calves, sheep, etc., used as a medicine in aiding digestion.

pep·sin·ate (pep'sin-āt'), *v.t.* [PEPSINATED (-id), PEPSINATING], to treat, mix, or infuse with pepsin, as milk.

pep·sine (pep'sin), *n.* pepsin.

pep·sin·o·gen (pep-sin'ə-jən), *n.* [< *pepsin* + *-gen*], a substance in the cells of the gastric glands of the stomach, from which pepsin is produced by the action of hydrochloric acid.

pep·tic (pep'tik), *adj.* [Gr. *peptikos* < *peptein*, to digest], 1. of or aiding digestion. 2. that can digest. 3. of, like, or caused by pepsin or other digestive secretions: as, a *peptic* ulcer. *n.* anything that aids digestion.

pep·tid (pep'tid), *n.* peptide.

pep·tide (pep'tīd, pep'tid), *n.* [*pept*one + *-ide*], a combination of amino acids formed by the linkage of the amino groups of some of the acids with the carboxyl groups of others.

pep·tize (pep'tīz), *v.t.* & *v.i.* [PEPTIZED (-tīzd), PEPTIZING], [*pept*one + *-ize*], to change into a colloid, usually through the action of an added chemical; especially, to change (a sol) into a gel.

pep·tone (pep'tōn), *n.* [G. *pepton;* Gr. *pepton*, neut. of *peptos*, digested], any of a group of soluble and diffusible simple proteins formed by the action of pepsin on albuminous substances, as in the process of digestion.

pep·ton·ic (pep-ton'ik), *adj.* of, like, or constituting a peptone.

pep·to·ni·za·tion (pep'tə-ni-zā'shən, pep'tə-nī-zā'shən), *n.* a peptonizing or being peptonized.

pep·to·nize (pep'tə-nīz'), *v.t.* [PEPTONIZED (-nīzd'), PEPTONIZING], 1. to change (proteins) into peptones. 2. to subject to the action of pepsin or other protein-converting agents.

Pepys, Samuel (pēps; *occas.* peps, pep'is), 1633–1703; English diarist and government official.

Pe·quot (pē'kwot), *n.* [< Am. Ind. (Algonquian) *Paquatauog*, destroyers], a member of a tribe of Algonquian Indians that settled in Connecticut. *adj.* of this tribe.

per (pũr; *unstressed* pẽr), *prep.* [L.], 1. through; by; by means of. 2. for each; for every: as, fifty cents *per* yard, the fare *per* mile. Abbreviated **p.**

per- (pũr; *unstressed* pẽr), [< L. *per*, through], a prefix meaning: 1. *through, throughout, away*, as in *perceive, percolate*. 2. *thoroughly, completely, very*, as in *persuade*. 3. in *chemistry, containing* (a specified element or radical) *in its maximum, or a relatively high, valence*, as in *perchlorate*.

Per., 1. Persia. 2. Persian.

per., 1. period. 2. person.

Per·a (pâr'ä), *n.* the modern section of Istanbul, Turkey: also called *Beyoglu*.

per·ac·id (pũr'as'id), *n.* an acid containing a larger proportion of oxygen than other acids containing the same elements, as perboric acid, perchloric acid, etc.

per·ad·ven·ture (pũr'əd-ven'chẽr), *adv.* [ME. *perauenture;* OFr. *par aventure; par* (L. *per*), by + *aventure*, a chance, adventure], [Archaic], 1. perhaps; possibly; maybe: as, *peradventure* it will rain. 2. by chance: as, if, *peradventure*, he comes. *n.* [Archaic], chance; question; doubt: as, we shall win without *peradventure*.

Per·ae·a (pə-rē'ə), *n.* an ancient division of Palestine, beyond the Jordan.

Pe·rak (pā'rak'; Malay pä'rä), *n.* a state of the Federation of Malaya: area, 7,980 sq. mi.; pop., 1,221,000.

per·am·bu·late (pẽr-am'byoo-lāt'), *v.t.* [PERAMBULATED (-id), PERAMBULATING], [< L. *perambulatus*, pp. of *perambulare; per*, through + *ambulare*, to walk], 1. to walk through, over, around, etc., especially in examining or inspecting. 2. to walk round in order to fix the boundary of (a forest, etc.). *v.i.* to walk or move about; stroll.

per·am·bu·la·tion (pẽr-am'byoo-lā'shən), *n.* a perambulating or that which is perambulated.

per·am·bu·la·tor (pẽr-am'byoo-lā'tẽr), *n.* 1. a person who perambulates. 2. a wheeled instrument that measures the distance over which it is rolled: used by surveyors. 3. [Chiefly British], a baby carriage, or buggy.

per·am·bu·la·to·ry (pẽr-am'byoo-lə-tôr'i, pẽr-am'byoo-lə-tō'ri), *adj.* of perambulation.

per an·num (pẽr an'əm), [L.], by the year; annually: abbreviated **per an., per ann., p.a.**

per·bo·rate (pẽr-bôr'āt, pẽr-bō'rāt), *n.* a salt of perboric acid.

per·bor·ic acid (pẽr-bôr'ik, pẽr-bō'rik), [*per-* + *boric*], the hypothetical acid, HBO_3, whose salts, the perborates, are formed by the action of hydrogen peroxide on borates.

per·cale (pẽr-kāl', pẽr-kal'), *n.* [Fr. < Per. *pargāl*], fine, closely woven cotton cloth, used for sheets, etc.

per·ca·line (pũr'kə-lēn'), *n.* [Fr. < *percale*], a fine cotton cloth, usually with a glazed or watered finish and used for linings.

per ca·pi·ta (pẽr kap′ə-tə), [L., lit., by heads], for each person.

per·ceiv·a·ble (pẽr-sē′və-b'l), ***adj.*** that can be perceived.

per·ceiv·a·bly (pẽr-sē′və-bli), ***adv.*** in a perceivable manner.

per·ceive (pẽr-sēv′), ***v.t. & v.i.*** [PERCEIVED (-sēvd′), PERCEIVING], [ME. *perceyven* < (via OFr.) L. *percipere*, to take hold of, feel, comprehend < *per*, through + *capere*, to take], 1. to grasp mentally; take note (of); recognize; observe. 2. to become aware (of) through sight, hearing, touch, taste, or smell. —***SYN.*** see **discern.**

per·cent (pẽr-sent′), ***n.*** per cent.

per cent, [L. *per centum*], per hundred; by the hundred; in, to, or for every hundred: as, a 20 *per cent* casualty rate means that 20 in every 100 were casualties: symbol, %. ***n.*** 1. [Colloq.], percentage. 2. *pl.* bonds, government securities, etc. bearing regular interest of a (stated) per cent: as, the three *per cents*. Abbreviated **p.c., pct., per ct.**

per cent., per centum.

per·cent·age (pẽr-sen′tij), ***n.*** [see -AGE], 1. a given rate or proportion in every hundred; hence, 2. any number or amount, as of interest, tax, etc., stated in per cent. 3. part; portion; share: as, only a small *percentage* of the people came. 4. [Colloq.], use; advantage; profit: as, there's no *percentage* in worry.

per·cen·tile (pẽr-sen′til, pẽr-sen′tīl), ***n.*** [*per cent* + *-ile*], in *statistics*, 1. any of the values in a series dividing the distribution of the individuals in the series into one hundred groups of equal frequency. 2. any of these groups. ***adj.*** of a percentile or division into percentiles.

per cen·tum (pẽr sen′təm), [L.], by the hundred: abbreviated **per cent.**: symbol, %.

per·cept (pũr′sept), ***n.*** [< L. *perceptum* < *percipere*, to perceive], a recognizable sensation or impression received by the mind through the senses; something perceived.

per·cep·ti·bil·i·ty (pẽr-sep′tə-bil′ə-ti), ***n.*** the state or quality of being perceptible.

per·cep·ti·ble (pẽr-sep′tə-b'l), ***adj.*** [LL. *perceptibilis* < pp. of L. *percipere*], that can be perceived.

SYN.—**perceptible** is applied to anything that can be apprehended by the senses but often connotes that the thing is just barely visible, audible, etc. (a *perceptible* smell of coffee); **sensible** applies to that which can clearly be perceived (a *sensible* difference in their size); **palpable** refers to anything that can be perceived by or as by the sense of touch (a *palpable* fog); **tangible** applies to that which can be grasped, either with the hand or the mind (*tangible* property, ideas, etc.); **appreciable** is used of that which is sufficiently perceptible to be measured, estimated, etc. or to have significance (an *appreciable* amount). —***ANT.*** imperceptible.

per·cep·ti·bly (pẽr-sep′tə-bli), ***adv.*** in a perceptible manner; so as to be perceptible.

per·cep·tion (pẽr-sep′shən), ***n.*** [< OFr. & L.; OFr. *perception*; L. *perceptio* < pp. of *percipere*; see PERCEIVE], 1. consciousness; awareness. 2. the awareness of objects or other data through the medium of the senses. 3. the process or faculty of perceiving. 4. the result of this; knowledge, etc. gained by perceiving. 5. insight or intuition, as of an abstract quality.

per·cep·tion·al (pẽr-sep′shən-'l), ***adj.*** of or constituting perception.

per·cep·tive (pẽr-sep′tiv), ***adj.*** [< L. *perceptus*; + *-ive*], 1. of perception. 2. capable of perceiving; especially, perceiving readily.

per·cep·tiv·i·ty (pũr′sep-tiv′ə-ti), ***n.*** the state of being perceptive.

per·cep·tu·al (pẽr-sep′chōō-əl), ***adj.*** of or involving perception.

Per·ce·val (pũr′sə-v'l), a masculine name: see **Percival.** ***n.*** Percivale.

perch (pũrch), ***n.*** [*pl.* PERCH, PERCHES (-iz); see PLURAL, II, D, 2], [ME. & OFr. *perche*; L. *perca*; Gr. *perkē* < *perknos*, dark-colored], 1. any of a number of related small, spiny-finned, fresh-water food fishes. 2. any of a number of similar, often marine, fishes.

perch (pũrch), ***n.*** [ME. & OFr. *perche*; L. *pertica*, a pole, staff], 1. a horizontal pole provided as a roost for birds. 2. anything, as a branch or wire, upon which a bird rests; hence, 3. any resting place or position, especially a high or insecure one. 4. a measure of length, equal to 5 1/2 yards; rod. 5. a measure of area, equal to 30 1/4 square yards. 6. a cubic measure for stone, usually equal to 24 3/4 cubic feet. 7. a pole connecting the front and hind gear of a spring carriage. ***v.i.*** [Fr. *percher*], to alight and rest on or as on a perch. ***v.t.*** to place or set on or as on a perch.

per·chance (pẽr-chans′, pẽr-chäns′), ***adv.*** [ME. *par chance*; OFr. *par* (L. *per*), by + *chance*, chance], [Archaic or Poetic], 1. by chance. 2. perhaps; possibly.

Perche (persh), ***n.*** a former division in northern France.

perch·er (pũr′chẽr), ***n.*** a person or thing that perches; specifically, a bird having feet adapted for perching.

Per·che·ron (pũr′chə-ron′, pũr′shə-ron′), ***n.*** [Fr. < Le *Perche*, district of France], any of a breed of large, fast-trotting draft horses: also **Percheron Norman.**

per·chlo·rate (pẽr-klôr′āt, pẽr-klō′rāt), ***n.*** a salt of perchloric acid.

per·chlo·ric acid (pẽr-klôr′ik, pẽr-klō′rik), [*per-* + *chloric*], a colorless, liquid acid, $HClO_4$, with a higher oxygen content for the same weight of chlorine than chloric acid.

per·chlo·rid (pẽr-klôr′id, pẽr-klō′rid), ***n.*** perchloride.

per·chlo·ride (pẽr-klôr′id, pẽr-klō′rid), ***n.*** a chloride in which the proportion of chlorine is relatively high as compared with other chlorides of the same element.

per·cip·i·ence (pẽr-sip′i-əns), ***n.*** [< *percipient*], the act or power of perceiving; perception.

per·cip·i·en·cy (pẽr-sip′i-ən-si), ***n.*** percipience.

per·cip·i·ent (pẽr-sip′i-ənt), ***adj.*** [L. *percipiens*, ppr. of *percipere*; see PERCEIVE], perceiving, especially keenly or readily. ***n.*** a person who perceives.

Per·ci·val (pũr′sə-v'l), [OFr. *Perceval*; prob. < *perce val*, pierce valley; apparently coined by Chrétien de Troyes (12th c.)], a masculine name: diminutive, ***Percy.*** ***n.*** Percivale. Also spelled **Perceval.**

Per·ci·vale (pũr′sə-v'l), ***n.*** [see prec. entry], a knight of King Arthur's Round Table: he was one of the few to glimpse the Holy Grail.

per·coid (pũr′koid), ***adj.*** [< L. *perca*, a perch; + *-oid*], belonging to a group including the perches and related fishes. ***n.*** a fish of this group.

per·coi·de·an (pẽr-koi′di-ən), ***adj.*** percoid.

per·co·late (pũr′kə-lāt′), ***v.t.*** [PERCOLATED (-id), PERCOLATING], [< L. *percolatus*, pp. of *percolare*, to strain; *per*, through + *colare*, to strain], 1. to pass (a liquid) gradually through small spaces or a porous substance; filter. 2. to drain or ooze through (a porous substance); permeate. 3. to brew (coffee) in a percolator. ***v.i.*** to pass or ooze through a porous substance. ***n.*** a liquid product of percolation.

per·co·la·tion (pũr′kə-lā′shən), ***n.*** act of percolating.

per·co·la·tor (pũr′kə-lā′tẽr), ***n.*** 1. a thing that percolates. 2. a kind of coffeepot in which the boiling water repeatedly bubbles up through a tube and filters back to the bottom through the coffee grounds, which are held in a perforated container.

per con·tra (pẽr kon′trə), [L.], on the contrary.

per·cuss (pẽr-kus′), ***v.t.*** [< L. *percussus*, pp. of *percutere*, to strike], to rap gently and firmly, as in medical diagnosis.

per·cus·sion (pẽr-kush′ən), ***n.*** [L. *percussio* < *percussus*; see PERCUSS], 1. the hitting or impact of one body against another, as the hammer of a firearm against a powder cap. 2. the shock, vibration, etc. resulting from this. 3. the impact of sound waves on the ear. 4. in *medicine*, the striking or tapping of the chest, back, etc., with the fingertips so as to determine from the sound produced the condition of any of the internal organs. 5. percussion instruments collectively.

percussion cap, a small metal cap containing gunpowder that explodes when struck: formerly used in firearms to set off the main charge.

percussion instrument, a musical instrument in which the tone is produced when some part is struck, as the drums, cymbals, tambourine, triangle, bells, xylophone, etc., and, broadly, the piano.

per·cus·sive (pẽr-kus′iv), ***adj.*** of or characterized by percussion.

Per·cy, Sir Henry (pũr′si), 1364–1403; English soldier: called *Hotspur.*

Percy, Thomas, 1729–1811; English bishop, poet, and collector of early English ballads.

Per·di·do, Mon·te (môn′te per-dē′thô), a mountain in the central Pyrenees, Spain: height, 10,997 ft.: French name, *Mont Perdu.*

per·die (pẽr-dē′), ***adv. & interj.*** [Archaic], pardie.

per diem (pẽr dī′əm), [L.], by the day; daily.

per·di·tion (pẽr-dish′ən), ***n.*** [ME. & OFr. *perdicium*; L. *perditio* < *perditus*, pp. of *perdere*, to lose, ruin], 1. complete and irreparable loss; ruin. 2. in ***theology,*** *a)* the loss of the soul or of hope for salvation; damnation. *b)* the place or condition of damnation; hell.

per·du, per·due (pẽr-dōō′, pẽr-dū′), ***adj.*** [Fr. *perdu*, masc., *perdue*, fem., pp. of *perdre*, to lose; L. *perdere*], out of sight; in hiding; concealed, as in a military ambush. ***n.*** [< the *adj.*; also contr. of Fr. *sentinelle perdue*, advanced (lit., lost) sentry, or *enfants perdus*, forlorn hope], [Obs.], a soldier or group of soldiers on an especially dangerous assignment.

Per·du, Mont (mōn′ per′dü′), Monte Perdido.

per·dur·a·ble (pẽr-door′ə-b'l, pẽr-dyoor′ə-b'l), ***adj.*** [ME.; OFr.; LL. *perdurabilis* < L. *perdurare*, to harden; *per-*, intens. + *durare* < *durus*, hard], extremely durable or lasting; everlasting; permanent.

per·dur·a·bly (pẽr-door′ə-bli, pẽr-dyoor′ə-bli), ***adv.*** in a perdurable manner.

‡père (pâr), ***n.*** [Fr.], 1. father: often used after the

surname, like English *Senior*, as, Dumas *père*. 2. [P-], the title of certain priests.
per·e·grin (per'ə-grin), *adj.* peregrine.
per·e·gri·nate (per'ə-gri-nāt'), *v.t.* [PEREGRINATED (-id), PEREGRINATING], [< L. *peregrinatus*, pp. of *peregrinari* < *peregrinus;* see PILGRIM], to follow (a route, etc.); travel along. *v.i.* to journey or travel.
per·e·gri·na·tion (per'ə-gri-nā'shən), *n.* [< Fr. or L.; Fr. *pérégrination;* L. *peregrinatio*], a journeying or traveling.
per·e·gri·na·tor (per'ə-gri-nā'tẽr), *n.* a person who peregrinates.
per·e·grine (per'ə-grin, per'ə-grīn'), *adj.* [ME. *peregryne;* L. *peregrinus;* see PILGRIM], foreign; traveling or migratory. *n.* a large, swift falcon: also **peregrine falcon.**
pe·rei·ra bark (pə-rā'rə), [< Mod.L. *Pereira,* former genus name, after J. *Pereira* (1804–1853), Eng. medical professor], the medicinal bark of a Brazilian tree, used as a tonic and in reducing fever: also **pereira.**
pe·rei·rine (pə-rā'rēn, pə-rā'rin), *n.* an alkaloid, $C_{19}H_{24}N_2O$, prepared as a powder from pereira bark and used in medicine as a tonic and to reduce fevers.
per·emp·to·ri·ly (pẽr-emp'tẽr-ə-li), *adv.* in a peremptory manner.
per·emp·to·ri·ness (pẽr-emp'tẽr-i-nis), *n.* the state or quality of being peremptory.
per·emp·to·ry (pẽr-emp'tẽr-i; *occas.* per'əmp-tôr'i, per'əmp-tō'ri), *adj.* [Fr. *peremptoire;* L. *peremptorius* < *peremptus,* pp. of *perimere,* to destroy < *per-,* intens. + *emere,* to take, buy], 1. in *law,* barring further action, debate, question, etc.; final; absolute; decisive. 2. that cannot be denied, changed, delayed, opposed, etc., as a command. 3. intolerantly positive; dictatorial; dogmatic; imperious: as, a *peremptory* manner.
per·en·ni·al (pə-ren'i-əl), *adj.* [< L. *perennis,* lasting through the year < *per,* through + *annus,* a year], 1. lasting or active throughout the whole year. 2. lasting or continuing for a long time: as, a *perennial* youth. 3. returning or becoming active again and again; perpetual. 4. having a life cycle of more than two years: said of plants. *n.* a perennial plant.
per·en·ni·al·ly (pə-ren'i-ə-li), *adv.* in a perennial manner; every year; perpetually.
perf., 1. perfect. 2. perforated.
per·fect (pũr'fikt; *for v., usually* pẽr-fekt'), *adj.* [ME. *perfit;* OFr. *parfit;* L. *perfectus,* pp. of *perficere,* to finish < *per,* through + *facere,* to make, do: mod. sp. is Latinized], 1. complete in all respects; without defect or omission; sound; flawless; hence, 2. in a condition of complete excellence, as in skill or quality; faultless; most excellent: sometimes used comparatively, as, to create a more *perfect* union. 3. completely correct or accurate; exact; precise: as, a *perfect* copy. 4. without reserve or qualification; pure; utter; sheer; complete: as, a *perfect* fool, *perfect* stranger. 5. in *botany,* having stamens and pistils in the same flower; monoclinous. 6. in *grammar,* expressing or showing a state or action completed at the time of speaking or at the time indicated: verbs have three perfect tenses; simple (or present) perfect, past perfect (or pluperfect), and future perfect. 7. in *music, a)* designating an interval (i.e., the fourth, fifth, or octave) whose character is not altered by inversion. *b)* designating a cadence that satisfactorily ends a composition according to the standards of classical harmony. *v.t.* 1. to bring to completion. 2. to make perfect or more nearly perfect according to a given standard, as by training or improvement. *n.* 1. the perfect tense. 2. a verb form in this tense. Abbreviated **perf., pf.**
perfect cadence, in *music,* a cadence in which the dominant passes into the harmony of the tonic.
per·fect·i·bil·i·ty (pẽr-fek'tə-bil'ə-ti), *n.* the quality or condition of being perfectible.
per·fect·i·ble (pẽr-fek'tə-b'l), *adj.* that can become, or be made, perfect.
per·fec·tion (pẽr-fek'shən), *n.* [ME. *perfeccioun;* OFr.; L. *perfectio*], 1. the act or process of perfecting: as, the *perfection* of the machine took many months. 2. the quality or condition of being perfect; extreme degree of excellence according to a given standard. 3. a person or thing that is the perfect embodiment of some quality. **to perfection,** completely; perfectly.
per·fec·tion·ism (pẽr-fek'shən-iz'm), *n.* any doctrine that holds that moral, religious, or social perfection can and should be attained in this life.
per·fec·tion·ist (pẽr-fek'shən-ist), *n.* 1. a person who believes in a doctrine of perfectionism. 2. a person who strives for perfection.
per·fec·tive (pẽr-fek'tiv), *adj.* 1. tending to bring to perfection. 2. in *grammar,* designating an aspect of verbs, as in Russian, expressing completion of the action or state. *n.* 1. the perfective aspect. 2. a verb in this aspect.
per·fect·ly (pũr'fikt-li), *adv.* 1. so as to be perfect; to a perfect degree. 2. completely; fully.
per·fec·to (pẽr-fek'tō), *n.* [*pl.* PERFECTOS (-tōz)], [Sp., perfect], a cigar of a standard shape, thick in the center and tapering to a point at either end.
perfect participle, the past participle: abbreviated **perf. part.**
perfect rhyme, a rhyme of two words or syllables spelled or pronounced alike but differing in meaning, as *dear* and *deer:* also called *rich rhyme.*
per·fer·vid (pẽr-fũr'vid), *adj.* [*per-,* intens. + *fervid*], extremely fervid; ardent.
per·fid·i·ous (pẽr-fid'i-əs), *adj.* [L. *perfidiosus*], characterized by perfidy; treacherous. —***SYN.*** see **faithless.**
per·fi·dy (pũr'fə-di), *n.* [*pl.* PERFIDIES (-diz)], [Fr. *perfidie;* L. *perfidia* < *per,* through + *fides,* faith], the deliberate breaking of faith; betrayal of trust; treachery.
per·fo·li·ate (pẽr-fō'li-it, pẽr-fō'li-āt'), *adj.* [*per-,* through + L. *folium,* a leaf; + *-ate*], having a stem that seems to pass through it: said of a leaf.

PERFOLIATE LEAVES
A, perfoliate (of bellwort); B, connate perfoliate (of wild honeysuckle)

per·fo·rate (pũr'fə-rāt'; *for adj., usually* pũr'fə-rit), *v.t. & v.i.* [PERFORATED (-id), PERFORATING], [< L. *perforatus,* pp. of *perforare; per,* through + *forare,* to bore], 1. to make a hole or holes through, as by punching or boring; pierce; penetrate. 2. to pierce with holes in a row, as a pattern, sheet of stamps, etc. *adj.* pierced with holes, especially with a row of holes, as to facilitate tearing.
per·fo·rat·ed (pũr'fə-rāt'id), *adj.* perforate: abbreviated **perf.**
per·fo·ra·tion (pũr'fə-rā'shən), *n.* 1. a perforating or being perforated. 2. a hole or any of a series of holes punched or drilled, as between postage stamps on a sheet.
per·fo·ra·tive (pũr'fə-rā'tiv), *adj.* [Fr. *perforatif*], that perforates readily.
per·fo·ra·tor (pũr'fə-rā'tẽr), *n.* a person or instrument that perforates.
per·force (pẽr-fôrs', pẽr-fōrs'), *adv.* [ME. & OFr. *par force;* see PER & FORCE], of or through necessity; necessarily. *n.* [Rare], necessity; compulsion.
per·form (pẽr-fôrm'), *v.t.* [ME. *parfournen* < OFr. *parfournir,* to perform, consummate < *par* (< L. *per-,* intens.) + *fornir,* to accomplish, furnish], 1. to act on so as to accomplish or bring to completion; execute; do, as a task, process, etc. 2. to carry out; meet the requirements of; fulfill, as a promise or command. 3. to give a performance of; render or enact, as a piece of music or a dramatic role. *v.i.* to carry out or execute an action or process; especially, to give a public exhibition of skill, as in music, drama, magic, etc.
SYN.—**perform,** often a mere formal equivalent for **do,** is usually used of a more or less involved process rather than a single act (to *perform* an experiment); **execute** implies a putting into effect or completing that which has been planned or ordered (to *execute* a law); **accomplish** suggests effort and perseverance in carrying out a plan or purpose (to *accomplish* a mission); **achieve** implies the overcoming of obstacles in accomplishing something of worth or importance (to *achieve* a lasting peace); **effect** also suggests the conquering of difficulties but emphasizes what has been done to bring about the result (his cure was *effected* by the use of certain drugs); **fulfill,** in strict discrimination, implies the full realization of what is expected or demanded (to *fulfill* a promise).
per·form·ance (pẽr-fôr'məns), *n.* 1. the act of performing; execution; accomplishment. 2. operation or functioning, usually with regard to effectiveness, as of an airplane. 3. something done or performed; deed or feat. 4. a formal exhibition of skill or talent, as a play, musical program, etc.; show.
per·form·er (pẽr-fôr'mẽr), *n.* a person who performs; specifically, a person who takes part in a public entertainment or exhibition.
perf. part., perfect participle.
per·fume (pẽr-fūm'; *for n., usually* pũr'fūm), *v.t.* [PERFUMED (-fūmd'), PERFUMING], [Fr. *parfumer;* It. *perfumare;* L. *per-,* intens. + *fumare,* to smoke < *fumus,* smoke], to fill with a fragrant or pleasing odor; scent with perfume. *n.* [Fr. *parfum* < the *v.*], 1. a pleasing smell or odor; sweet scent, as of flowers; fragrance. 2. a substance producing a pleasing odor; especially, a liquid extract of the scent of flowers or a substance like this prepared synthetically. —***SYN.*** see **scent.**
per·fum·er (pẽr-fūm'ẽr), *n.* 1. a person who makes or sells perfumes. 2. a person or thing that perfumes.
per·fum·er·y (pẽr-fūm'ẽr-i), *n.* [*pl.* PERFUMERIES (-iz)], [< *perfume* + *-ery;* cf. Fr. *parfumerie*], 1. the trade of a perfumer. 2. a perfume, or perfumes collectively. 3. a place where perfume is made or sold.
per·func·to·ri·ly (pẽr-fuŋk'tẽr-ə-li), *adv.* in a perfunctory manner.
per·func·to·ri·ness (pẽr-fuŋk'tẽr-i-nis), *n.* the quality of being perfunctory.
per·func·to·ry (pẽr-fuŋk'tẽr-i), *adj.* [LL. *perfunctorius* < L. *perfunctus,* pp. of *perfungi,* to get rid of, discharge; *per-,* intens. + *fungi,* to perform], 1. done without care or interest or merely as a form or routine; superficial: as, a *perfunctory* examination. 2. without concern or solicitude; indifferent: as, a *perfunctory* lecturer.
per·fuse (pẽr-fūz'), *v.t.* [PERFUSED (-fūzd'), PERFUSING],

[< L. *perfusus*, pp. of *perfundere; per*, through + *fundere*, to pour], 1. to sprinkle, cover over, or permeate with or as with a liquid; suffuse. 2. to pour or spread (a liquid, etc.), through or over something.
per·fu·sion (pẽr-fū′zhən), *n.* [L. *perfusio*], a perfusing or being perfused.
per·fu·sive (pẽr-fū′siv), *adj.* that perfuses readily.
Per·ga·mum (pũr′gə-məm), *n.* an ancient Greek city in Mysia, on the site of modern Bergama, Turkey.
Per·ga·mus (pũr′gə-məs), *n.* Pergamum.
per·go·la (pũr′gə-lə), *n.* [It., arbor; L. *pergula*, arbor < *pergere*, to proceed], a tunnel-shaped structure of latticework, upon which climbing plants are grown.
Per·go·le·si, Gio·van·ni Bat·tis·ta (jô-vän′nē bät-tēs′tä pâr′gô-le′si), 1710–1736; Italian composer.
per·haps (pẽr-haps′, pẽr-aps′), *adv.* [*per-* + *haps*, pl. of *hap*, chance], 1. possibly; probably; maybe: as, *perhaps* we'd better go. 2. by chance; perchance: as, if, *perhaps*, he shouldn't come. Abbreviated **perh.**
pe·ri (pêr′i), *n.* [Per. *parī*], 1. in *Persian mythology*, a fairy or elf descended from evil angels and barred from paradise until penance has been done. 2. any fairylike or elfin being.
per·i- (per′i, per′ə), [Gr. *peri-* < *peri*, around], a prefix meaning: 1. *around, about, encircling, surrounding*, as in *periscope*. 2. *near*, as in *perigee*.
per·i·anth (per′i-anth′), *n.* [Fr. *périanthe;* Mod. L. *perianthium* < Gr. *peri-*, around + *anthos*, a flower], the envelope of a flower, especially one in which the calyx and corolla are indistinguishable.
per·i·apt (per′i-apt′), *n.* [Fr. *périapte;* Gr. *periapton* < *periaptein*, to fit about, tie about], an amulet.
per·i·blem (per′ə-blem′), *n.* [via G. < Gr. *periblēma*, something that surrounds], in *botany*, the undifferentiated embryonic tissue in the growing points of plant stems and roots which develops into the cortex.
per·i·car·di·ac (per′ə-kär′di-ak′), *adj.* pericardial.
per·i·car·di·al (per′ə-kär′di-əl), *adj.* of the pericardium.
per·i·car·di·tis (per′i-kär-dī′tis), *n.* [see -ITIS], inflammation of the pericardium.
per·i·car·di·um (per′ə-kär′di-əm), *n.* [*pl.* PERICARDIA (-ə)], [Mod. L.; Gr. *perikardion* < *perikardios*, around the heart < *peri-*, around + *kardia*, heart], the thin, membranous sac enclosing the heart.
per·i·carp (per′ə-kärp′), *n.* [Fr. *péricarpe;* Mod. L. *pericarpium;* Gr. *perikarpion* < *peri-*, around + *karpos*, a fruit], in *botany*, the wall of a ripened ovary, sometimes consisting of three distinct layers, the endocarp, mesocarp, and epicarp.
per·i·car·pi·al (per′ə-kär′pi-əl), *adj.* of the pericarp.
per·i·chon·dri·al (per′ə-kon′dri-əl), *adj.* of or characterized by perichondrium.
per·i·chon·dri·um (per′ə-kon′dri-əm), *n.* [*pl.* PERICHONDRIA (-ə)], [< *peri-* + Gr. *chondros*, cartilage; + *-ium*], the membrane of white, fibrous connective tissue covering cartilage, except at the joints.
Per·i·cle·an (per′ə-klē′ən), *adj.* 1. of Pericles. 2. of the period of great intellectual achievement in Athens (c. 495–429 B.C.), in the lifetime of Pericles.
Per·i·cles (per′ə-klēz′), *n.* Athenian statesman and general; ? –429 B.C.
per·i·cline (per′ə-klīn′), *n.* [< Gr. *periklinēs*, sloping on all sides < *peri-*, around + *klinein*, to slope, incline], a kind of albite found in white, crystalline form.
per·i·cra·ni·al (per′ə-krā′ni-əl), *adj.* of the pericranium.
per·i·cra·ni·um (per′ə-krā′ni-əm), *n.* [*pl.* PERICRANIA (-ə)], [Mod. L. < Gr. *perikranion*, orig. neut. adj., around the skull; *peri-*, around + *kranion*, skull], the periosteum of the external surface of the skull.
per·i·cy·cle (per′ə-sī′k'l), *n.* [< Gr. *perikyklos*, spherical; *peri-*, around + *kyklos*, a ring, circle], the outer layer of the stele in the root and stem of most plants.
per·i·derm (per′ə-dũrm′), *n.* [*peri-* + *-derm*], the outer bark and the layer of soft, growing tissue between the bark and the wood in plants.
pe·rid·i·al (pi-rid′i-əl), *adj.* of or forming the peridium.
pe·rid·i·um (pi-rid′i-əm), *n.* [*pl.* PERIDIA (-ə)], [Mod. L. < Gr. *pēridion*, dim. of *pēra*, leather sack, wallet], the outer coat of the spore-bearing organ in certain fungi.
per·i·dot (per′ə-dot′), *n.* [ME. *peridod;* OFr. *peritot;* reintroduced < Fr. *péridot* in 17th c.], a kind of yellowish-green chrysolite, used as a gem: also called *olivine*.
per·i·dot·ic (per′ə-dot′ik), *adj.* of or like peridot.
per·i·do·tite (per′ə-dō′tīt), *n.* [Fr. *péridotite* < *péridot*, peridot], a rare, dark, heavy rock of the igneous type, consisting of ferromagnesian minerals and olivine.
per·i·ge·al (per′ə-jē′əl), *adj.* perigean.
per·i·ge·an (per′ə-jē′ən), *adj.* of, or at the time of, the perigee.
per·i·gee (per′ə-jē′), *n.* [Fr. *périgée;* Mod. L. *perigium;* LGr. *perigeion* < Gr. *perigeios*, around the earth < *peri-*, around + *gē*, the earth], 1. the point nearest to the earth in the orbit of the moon or of a man-made satellite: abbrev. **peri., perig.:** see **apogee,** illus. 2. the lowest or nearest point.
pe·rig·y·nous (pi-rij′ə-nəs), *adj.* [Mod. L. *perigynus;* see PERI- & -GYNOUS], in *botany*, 1. growing in a ring around the pistil, as the stamens. 2. having stamens, etc. growing in this way: said of a flower.

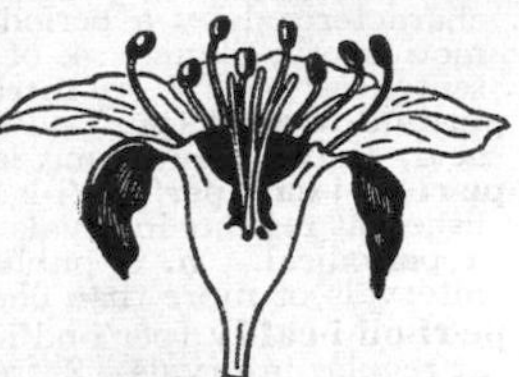
PERIGYNOUS FLOWER (of pear)

pe·rig·y·ny (pi-rij′ə-ni), *n.* the condition of being perigynous.
per·i·he·li·on (per′ə-hē′li-ən), *n.* [*pl.* PERIHELIA (-ə)], [Mod. L. < Gr. *peri-*, around + *hēlios*, the sun], that point in the orbit of a planet or comet nearest the sun: opposed to *aphelion:* see **aphelion,** illus.
per·il (per′əl), *n.* [ME.; OFr.; L. *periculum, periclum*, a danger < base seen in *experiri*, to try, attempt], exposure to harm or injury; risk; jeopardy. *v.t.* [PERILED or PERILLED (-əld), PERILING or PERILLING], to expose to danger; risk; imperil. —*SYN.* see **danger.**
per·il·ous (per′ə-ləs), *adj.* [ME.; Anglo-Fr. *perillous;* L. *periculosus*], involving peril or risk; dangerous.
pe·rim·e·ter (pə-rim′ə-tẽr), *n.* [L. *perimetros;* Gr. *perimetros* < *peri-*, around + *metron*, a measure], 1. the outer boundary of a figure or area: as, a fence marked the *perimeter* of the field. 2. the total length of this. 3. an optical instrument for testing the scope of vision and the visual powers of various parts of the retina. —*SYN.* see **circumference.**
per·i·met·ric (per′ə-met′rik), *adj.* 1. of a perimeter, or boundary. 2. of or by a perimeter or perimetry.
per·i·met·ri·cal (per′ə-met′ri-k'l), *adj.* perimetric.
pe·rim·e·try (pə-rim′ə-tri), *n.* the testing of the scope of vision by means of the perimeter.
per·i·morph (per′ə-môrf′), *n.* [*peri-* + *-morph*], a mineral of one kind enclosing one of another kind.
per·i·ne·al (per′ə-nē′əl), *adj.* of the perineum.
per·i·neph·ri·um (per′ə-nef′ri-əm), *n.* [Mod. L. < *peri-* + Gr. *nephros*, kidney], the envelope of connective and fatty tissue surrounding the kidney.
per·i·ne·um (per′ə-nē′əm), *n.* [*pl.* PERINEA (-ə)], [Mod. L.; LL. *perinaeon;* Gr. *perineon* < *peri-*, around + *inaō*, I discharge, I evacuate], the region of the body between the thighs, at the outlet of the pelvis; specifically, the small triangular region including the anus and the vulva or the base of the penis.
per·i·neu·ri·tis (per′i-nyoo-rī′tis), *n.* [see -ITIS], inflammation of the perineurium.
per·i·neu·ri·um (per′ə-nyoor′i-əm), *n.* [*pl.* PERINEURIA (-ə)], [Mod. L. < *peri-* + Gr. *neuron*, a nerve; + *-ium*], the sheath of dense connective tissue that envelops a bundle of nerve fibers composing a peripheral nerve.
pe·ri·od (pêr′i-əd), *n.* [Fr. *période;* L. *periodus;* Gr. *periodos*, a going around, cycle < *peri-*, around + *hodos*, way], 1. the interval between the successive occurrences of an astronomical event: as, the portion of time between two full moons is a *period*. 2. the interval between certain happenings: as, a ten-year *period* of peace. 3. a portion of time, often indefinite, distinguished by the existence of certain processes, characteristics, or conditions; stage: as, a *period* of change, the present *period*. 4. any of the portions of time into which an event of fixed duration, as a game or school day, is divided. 5. the full course or one of the stages of a disease. 6. the time of menstruation; menses. 7. an end, completion, or conclusion or a point of time marking this: as, death put a *period* to his plans. 8. in *geology*, a subdivision of a geological era, in which rock strata and fossils form a definite sequence. 9. in *grammar & rhetoric*, *a*) a complete sentence. *b*) the natural pause, in speaking, or a mark of punctuation (.), in writing, used to indicate the end of a sentence. *c*) the dot (.) following most abbreviations. 10. in *music*, a group of measures, usually eight or sixteen, arranged in two phrases and forming a complete statement ending with a cadence. 11. in *physics*, the interval of time necessary for a regularly recurring motion to make a complete cycle. 12. in *prosody*, a rhythm group of two or more cola in the Greek system. *adj.* of or like that of a certain period or age: as, *period* furniture or painting. Abbreviated **per.**
SYN.—**period** is the general term for any portion of time; **epoch** and **era** are often used interchangeably, but in strict discrimination, **epoch** applies to the beginning of a new period marked by radical changes, new developments, etc. and **era**, to the entire period (the steam engine marked an *epoch* in transportation, an *era* of revolution); **age** is applied to a period identified with some dominant personality or distinctive characteristic (the Stone *Age*); **eon** (or **aeon**) refers to an indefinitely long period (it all happened *eons* ago).
per·i·o·date (pẽr-ī′ə-dāt′), *n.* a salt of periodic acid.
pe·ri·od·ic (pêr′i-od′ik), *adj.* [Fr. *périodique;* L. *periodicus;* Gr. *periodikos*], 1. occurring, appearing, or

recurring at regular intervals: as, a *periodic* fever. 2. occurring from time to time; intermittent. 3. of or characterized by a period or periods: as, the *periodic* motion of a planet. 4. of or characterized by periodic sentences. —*SYN.* see **intermittent.**

per·i·od·ic acid (pũr'ī-od'ik), [*per-* + *iodic*], an oxygen acid, H_5IO_6, containing iodine in its highest valence.

pe·ri·od·i·cal (pêr'i-od'i-k'l), *adj.* 1. periodic. 2. published at regular intervals of more than one day. 3. of a periodical. *n.* a publication appearing at regular intervals of more than one day, as a weekly magazine.

pe·ri·od·i·cal·ly (pêr'i-od'i-k'l-i, pêr'i-od'ik-li), *adv.* 1. at regular intervals. 2. from time to time; recurrently.

pe·ri·o·dic·i·ty (pêr'i-ə-dis'ə-ti), *n.* [*pl.* PERIODICITIES (-tiz)], [Fr. *périodicité* < *période*], 1. a tendency to recur at regular intervals, as of some fevers; periodic character. 2. in *chemistry*, the occurrence of similar properties in elements occupying similar positions in the periodic table. 3. in *electricity*, frequency.

periodic law, the principle that the physical and chemical properties of the chemical elements recur periodically when the elements are arranged in increasing order of their atomic numbers.

periodic sentence, a sentence in which the grammatical form and essential meaning are not completed until the end is reached: distinguished from *loose sentence.*

periodic system, the system governing the classification of the elements: see **periodic law.**

periodic table, an arrangement of the chemical elements according to their atomic numbers, to exhibit the periodic law: the vertical columns (*groups*) include elements having related properties; the aligned subgroups (*families*) in these columns include elements having more closely related properties; the horizontal columns (*periods*) show the periodic shift in the properties of the elements: see chart on facing page.

per·i·o·dide (pẽr-ī'ə-dīd'), *n.* an iodide in which the proportion of iodine is relatively high as compared with other iodides of the same element.

per·i·o·don·tal (per'i-ə-don't'l), *adj.* [< *peri-* + Gr. *odōn, odontos*, tooth; + *-al*], in *anatomy*, situated or occurring around a tooth.

per·i·os·te·al (per'i-os'ti-əl), *adj.* of the periosteum.

per·i·os·te·um (per'i-os'ti-əm), *n.* [*pl.* PERIOSTEA (-ə)], [Mod. L.; L. *periosteon;* Gr. *periosteon; peri-*, around + *osteon*, a bone], the membrane of tough, fibrous connective tissue covering all bones except at the joints.

per·i·os·ti·tis (per'i-os-tī'tis), *n.* [see -ITIS], inflammation of the periosteum.

per·i·o·tic (per'i-ō'tik, per'i-ot'ik), *adj.* [< *peri-* + Gr. *otikos* < *ous, ōtos*, an ear], in *anatomy* & *zoology*, surrounding the inner ear; specifically, of the bony structure (*periotic bone*) forming a capsule enclosing the labyrinth.

per·i·pa·tet·ic (per'i-pə-tet'ik), *adj.* [ME. *parypatetik, n.;* L. *peripateticus;* Gr. *peripatētikos* < *peripatein*, to walk about; *peri-*, around + *patein*, to walk], 1. [P-], of the philosophy or the followers of Aristotle, who walked about in the Lyceum while he was teaching. 2. moving from place to place; walking about; itinerant. *n.* 1. [P-], a follower of Aristotle. 2. a person who walks from place to place. —*SYN.* see **itinerant.**

pe·riph·er·al (pə-rif'ẽr-əl), *adj.* 1. of or forming a periphery. 2. in *anatomy*, outer; external; distal.

pe·riph·er·al·ly (pə-rif'ẽr-əl-i), *adv.* so as to be peripheral.

pe·riph·er·y (pə-rif'ẽr-i), *n.* [*pl.* PERIPHERIES (-iz)], [Fr. *périphérie;* LL. *peripheria;* Gr. *periphereia* < *peripherēs*, moving around < *peri-*, around + *pherein*, to bear], 1. a boundary line, especially that of a rounded figure; perimeter. 2. an outside surface, especially that of a rounded object or body. 3. surrounding space or area; environs. 4. in *anatomy*, the area surrounding a nerve ending. —*SYN.* see **circumference.**

per·i·phrase (per'ə-frāz'), *n.* periphrasis.

pe·riph·ra·sis (pə-rif'rə-sis), *n.* [*pl.* PERIPHRASES (-sēz')], [L.; Gr. *periphrasis* < *peri-*, around + *phrazein*, to speak], 1. the use of many words where one or a few would do; roundabout way of speaking; circumlocution. 2. a periphrastic expression.

per·i·phras·tic (per'ə-fras'tik), *adj.* [Gr. *periphrastikos*], 1. of, like, or expressed in periphrasis. 2. in *grammar*, formed with a particle or auxiliary verb instead of by inflection (e.g., "she did sing" for "she sang" is a *periphrastic* construction).

per·i·phras·ti·cal·ly (per'ə-fras'ti-k'l-i, per'ə-fras'tik-li), *adv.* in a periphrastic manner.

per·ip·ter·y (pə-rip'tẽr-i), *n.* [*pl.* PERIPTERIES (-iz)], [< L. *peripteros;* Gr. *peripteros*, flying about < *peri-*, around + *pteron*, a feather], that area around a moving body within which air currents are set up by the motion.

pe·rique (pə-rēk'), *n.* [Fr., supposedly after *Pierre* Chenet, who introduced tobacco-growing to French colonists in Louisiana, but actually < Fr. pronun. of *prick*, vulgar for penis, so called from the shape of the dried, compacted plug], a strong, black tobacco grown in Louisiana: used in blending.

per·i·sarc (per'ə-särk'), *n.* [< *peri-* + Gr. *sarx, sarkos*, flesh], the tough outer layer of a hydrozoan animal.

per·i·scope (per'ə-skōp'), *n.* [*peri-* + *-scope*], 1. a periscopic lens. 2. an optical instrument consisting of a tube holding a system of lenses with a mirror at either end arranged so that a person looking through the eyepiece at one end can see objects reflected by the mirror at the other end: used on submerged submarines, etc.

MIRROR REFLECTING VIEW
PERISCOPE
MIRROR

PERISCOPE

per·i·scop·ic (per'ə-skop'ik), *adj.* 1. providing clear lateral or oblique range of view, as certain lenses. 2. of or by a periscope.

per·ish (per'ish), *v.i.* [ME. *perischen, perissen* < ppr. stem of OFr. *perir;* L. *perire*, to go through, perish; *per-*, intens. + *ire*, to go], to be utterly destroyed or ruined; end; specifically, to die a violent or untimely death. —*SYN.* see **die.**

perish the thought! do not even consider such a possibility!

per·ish·a·ble (per'ish-ə-b'l), *adj.* that may perish; liable to spoil or deteriorate, as some foods. *n.* something liable to spoil or deteriorate, especially such a food.

pe·ris·so·dac·tyl, pe·ris·so·dac·tyle (pə-ris'ə-dak'til), *adj.* [Mod. L. *perissodactylus* < Gr. *perissos*, uneven (< *peri-*, over) + *daktylos*, finger], having an uneven number of toes on each foot as a horse, rhinoceros, etc. *n.* a hoofed animal with an uneven number of toes.

per·i·stal·sis (per'ə-stal'sis), *n.* [*pl.* PERISTALSES (-sēz)], [Mod. L.; see PERISTALTIC], the rhythmic, wavelike motion of the walls of the alimentary canal and certain other hollow organs, consisting of alternate muscular contractions and dilations that move the contents of the tube onward.

per·i·stal·tic (per'ə-stal'tik), *adj.* [Gr. *peristaltikos* < *peristellein*, to surround, involve; *peri-*, around + *stellein*, to place], of or characterized by peristalsis.

per·i·stome (per'ə-stōm'), *n.* [Mod. L. *peristoma* < *peri-* + Gr. *stoma*, a mouth], 1. in *botany*, the fringe around the opening of the spore case in mosses. 2. in *zoology*, the area or parts surrounding the mouth or a mouthlike part of an organism.

per·i·sty·lar (per'ə-stī'lẽr), *adj.* of or like a peristyle.

per·i·style (per'ə-stīl'), *n.* [Fr. *péristyle;* L. *peristylum;* Gr. *peristylon* < *peri-*, around + *stylos*, a column], 1. a row of columns forming an enclosure or supporting a roof. 2. any space or enclosure, as a court, so formed.

per·i·the·ci·um (per'ə-thē'shi-əm, per'ə-thē'si-əm), *n.* [*pl.* PERITHECIA (-ə)], [Mod. L. < *peri-* + Gr. *thēkē*, a case, box], in certain fungi, a flasklike case containing the spore sacs.

per·i·to·ne·al, per·i·to·nae·al (per'i-tə-nē'əl), *adj.* of the peritoneum.

per·i·to·ne·um, per·i·to·nae·um (per'i-tə-nē'əm), *n.* [*pl.* PERITONEA (-ə)], [LL.; Gr. *peritonaion* < *peri-*, around + *teinein*, to stretch], the transparent serous membrane lining the abdominal cavity and reflected inward at various places to cover the visceral organs.

per·i·to·ni·tis (per'i-tə-nī'tis), *n.* [see -ITIS], inflammation of the peritoneum.

per·i·wig (per'ə-wig'), *n.* [earlier *perwyke, perruck;* altered < Fr. *perruque;* see PERUKE], a wig.

per·i·win·kle (per'ə-wiŋ'k'l), *n.* [ME. *pervenke;* AS. *pervince;* L. *pervinca*, periwinkle], a creeping plant with evergreen leaves and white or blue flowers; myrtle.

per·i·win·kle (per'ə-wiŋ'k'l), *n.* [AS. *perwynke;* prob. confusion of earlier *pinewincle* with the prec. word], 1. any of a number of small, related salt-water snails having a thick, brown or yellowish, cone-shaped shell with dark spiral bands. 2. such a shell.

per·jure (pũr'jẽr), *v.t.* [PERJURED (-jẽrd), PERJURING], [ME. *parjuren;* OFr. *parjurer;* L. *perjurare; per*, through + *jurare*, to swear], 1. to make (oneself) guilty of perjury by speaking falsely under oath. 2. to prove guilty of perjury: in the passive.

per·jured (pũr'jẽrd), *adj.* guilty of perjury; having lied under oath: as, a *perjured* witness.

per·jur·er (pũr'jẽr-ẽr), *n.* a person guilty of perjury.

per·ju·ry (pũr'jẽr-i), *n.* [*pl.* PERJURIES (-iz)], [ME. *perjurie, parjurie;* OFr. *parjurie;* L. *perjurium* < *perjurus*, false, breaking oath < *per*, through + *jus, juris*, a right, justice], 1. in *law*, the willful telling of a lie while under oath to tell the truth in a matter material to the point of inquiry. 2. the breaking of any oath or formal promise.

perk (pũrk), *v.t.* [ME. *perken;* prob. < ONorm.Fr. *perquer*, to perch], 1. to raise, as the head, briskly or spiritedly (often with *up*). 2. to make (oneself) smart or jaunty in appearance (often with *up* or *out*). *v.i.* 1. to lift one's head or straighten one's posture, as in

PERIODIC TABLE OF THE ELEMENTS

	GROUP 0	GROUP I		GROUP II		GROUP III		GROUP IV		GROUP V		GROUP VI		GROUP VII		GROUP VIII		
Type of Hydride		RH		RH_2		RH_3		RH_4		RH_3		RH_2		RH				
Type of Oxide		R_2O		RO		R_2O_3		RO_2		R_2O_5		RO_3		R_2O_7		RO_4		
SUBGROUP		A	B	A	B	A	B	A	B	A	B	A	B	A	B			
PERIOD 0		1 H 1.0080																
1	2 He 4.003	3 Li 6.940		4 Be 9.02		5 B 10.82		6 C 12.01		7 N 14.008		8 O 16.0000		9 F 19.00				
2	10 Ne 20.183	11 Na 22.997		12 Mg 24.32		13 Al 26.97		14 Si 28.06		15 P 30.98		16 S 32.06		17 Cl 35.457				
3	18 A 39.944	19 K 39.096		20 Ca 40.08		21 Sc 45.10		22 Ti 47.90		23 V 50.95		24 Cr 52.01		25 Mn 54.93		26 Fe 55.85	27 Co 58.94	28 Ni 58.69
			29 Cu 63.54		30 Zn 65.38		31 Ga 69.72		32 Ge 72.60		33 As 74.91		34 Se 78.96		35 Br 79.916			
4	36 Kr 83.7	37 Rb 85.48		38 Sr 87.63		39 Y 88.92		40 Zr 91.22		41 Nb 92.91		42 Mo 95.95		43 Tc 99(?)		44 Ru 101.7	45 Rh 102.91	46 Pd 106.7
			47 Ag 107.880		48 Cd 112.41		49 In 114.76		50 Sn 118.70		51 Sb 121.76		52 Te 127.61		53 I 126.92			
5	54 Xe 131.3	55 Cs 132.91		56 Ba 137.36		57–71* RARE-EARTH METALS		72 Hf 178.6		73 Ta 180.88		74 W 183.92		75 Re 186.31		76 Os 190.2	77 Ir 193.1	78 Pt 195.23
			79 Au 197.2		80 Hg 200.61		81 Tl 204.39		82 Pb 207.21		83 Bi 209.00		84 Po 210.0		85 At 211(?)			
6	86 Rn 222	87 Fr 223(?)		88 Ra 226.05		89–103** ACTINIDE SERIES												

*RARE-EARTH METALS 57–71 (LANTHANIDE SERIES)	57 La 138.92	58 Ce 140.13	59 Pr 140.92	60 Nd 144.27	61 Pm 146.7(?)	62 Sm 150.43	63 Eu 152.0	64 Gd 156.9	65 Tb 159.2	66 Dy 162.46	67 Ho 164.94	68 Er 167.2	69 Tm 169.4	70 Yb 173.04	71 Lu 174.99
**ACTINIDE SERIES	89 Ac 227(?)	90 Th 232.12	91 Pa 231	92 U 238.07	93 Np 239	94 Fu 239	95 Am 241(?)	96 Cm 242(?)	97 Bk 243(?)	98 Cf 244(?)	99 E 247(?)	100 Fm 254(?)	101 Mv 256(?)	102 No 255(?)	103 Lw 257(?)

acting jaunty. 2. to become lively or animated; recover one's spirits (with *up*).

perk (pũrk), *v.t. & v.i.* [Colloq.], to percolate.

Per·kin, Sir **William Henry** (pũr'kin), 1838–1907; English chemist.

Per·kins, Frances (pũr'kinz), 1882– ; American sociologist; secretary of labor (1933–1945).

perk·y (pũr'ki), *adj.* [PERKIER (-ki-ẽr), PERKIEST (-ki-ist)], 1. spirited; aggressive. 2. brisk; gay; saucy; jaunty.

per·lite (pũr'līt), *n.* [Fr. < *perle,* pearl], a glassy volcanic rock with a pearly luster: it is a form of obsidian appearing as an aggregation of small, rounded masses.

per·lit·ic (pẽr-lit'ik), *adj.* of or like perlite.

Perm (perm), *n.* Molotov, Siberia: the former name.

perm·al·loy (pũrm'al'oi), *n.* [*perm*eable + *alloy*], any of various alloys of iron and nickel having a high magnetic permeability: a trade-mark (**Permalloy**).

per·ma·nence (pũr'mə-nəns), *n.* [ME.; ML. *permanentia*], the state or quality of being permanent.

per·ma·nen·cy (pũr'mə-nən-si), *n.* 1. permanence. 2. [*pl.* PERMANCIES (-siz)], something permanent.

per·ma·nent (pũr'mə-nənt), *adj.* [ME.; OFr.; L. *permanens,* ppr. of *permanere; per,* through + *manere,* to remain], 1. lasting or intended to last indefinitely without change: opposed to *temporary.* 2. lasting a relatively long time. *n.* [Colloq.], a permanent wave.

permanent wave, a hair wave produced by use of chemicals or heat and lasting for months.

per·man·ga·nate (pẽr-maŋ'gə-nāt'), *n.* a salt of permanganic acid, generally dark purple.

per·man·gan·ic acid (pũr'man-gan'ik), [*per-* + *manganic*], an unstable acid, $HMnO_4$, that is a strong oxidizing agent in aqueous solution.

per·me·a·bil·i·ty (pũr'mi-ə-bil'ə-ti), *n.* 1. the state or quality of being permeable. 2. the power of conducting lines of magnetic force.

per·me·a·ble (pũr'mi-ə-b'l), *adj.* [ME.; L. *permeabilis*], that can be permeated; open to passage or penetration, especially by fluids.

per·me·ance (pũr'mi-əns), *n.* 1. a permeating or being permeated. 2. the quality of being permeable.

per·me·ant (pũr'mi-ənt), *adj.* permeating or tending to permeate.

per·me·ate (pũr'mi-āt'), *v.t.* [PERMEATED (-id), PERMEATING], [< L. *permeatus,* pp. of *permeare; per,* through + *meare,* to glide, flow, pass], to pass into and affect every part of; penetrate and spread through: as, water will *permeate* blotting paper. *v.i.* to spread or diffuse; penetrate (with *through* or *among*).

per·me·a·tion (pũr'mi-ā'shən), *n.* a permeating or being permeated.

per·me·a·tive (pũr'mi-ā'tiv), *adj.* permeating; penetrative; diffusive.

‡per men·sem (pẽr men'səm), [L.], by the month.

Per·mi·an (pũr'mi-ən), *adj.* [after *Perm,* former province of Russia], designating or of the geological period following the Pennsylvanian in the Paleozoic Era and preceding the Triassic in the Mesozoic: it was characterized by increased reptile life, major mountain building of the Appalachian ranges, and much glaciation, especially in the Southern Hemisphere.

the Permian, the Permian Period or its rocks: see **geology,** chart.

per·mis·si·bil·i·ty (pẽr-mis'ə-bil'ə-ti), *n.* the state or quality of being permissible.

per·mis·si·ble (pẽr-mis'ə-b'l), *adj.* [ME. *permyssyble;* OFr.; ML. *permissibilis* < L. *permissus,* pp. of *permittere*], that can be permitted; allowable.

per·mis·si·bly (pẽr-mis'ə-bli), *adv.* so as to be permissible.

per·mis·sion (pẽr-mish'ən), *n.* [ME.; L. *permissio* < pp. of *permittere*], the act of permitting; formal consent; leave; license: as, you have my *permission* to go.

per·mis·sive (pẽr-mis'iv), *adj.* [ME. *permyssyue;* OFr.; *permissif* < pp. of L. *permittere*], 1. giving permission; that permits; allowing. 2. permitted; allowable, at one's option; not forbidden.

per·mit (pẽr-mit'; *for n., usually* pũr'mit), *v.t.* [PERMITTED (-id), PERMITTING], [L. *permittere* (pp. *permissus*); *per,* through + *mittere,* to send], 1. to allow; consent to; tolerate: as, smoking is not *permitted.* 2. to give permission to; authorize: as, he is *permitted* to leave. 3. to give opportunity for: as, an intermission that *permits* conversation. *v.i.* to give opportunity or possibility: as, I'll come if time and weather *permit.* *n.* 1. permission. 2. a document granting permission to do something; license; warrant. —*SYN.* see **let.**

per·mit·ter (pẽr-mit'ẽr), *n.* a person who permits.

per·mut·a·ble (pẽr-mū'tə-b'l), *adj.* that can be permuted.

per·mu·ta·tion (pũr'myoo-tā'shən), *n.* [ME. *permutacioun;* OFr. *permutacion;* L. *permutatio* < *permutare;* see PERMUTE], 1. a change; alteration; rearrangement. 2. any one of the combinations or changes in position possible within a group: as, the *permutations* of *1, 2,* and *3* are *123, 132, 213, 231, 312, 321.*

per·mute (pẽr-mūt'), *v.t.* [PERMUTED (-id), PERMUTING], [ME. *permuten;* L. *permutare,* to change thoroughly; *per-,* intens. + *mutare,* to change], 1. to make different; alter. 2. to rearrange the order or sequence of.

Per·nam·bu·co (pũr'nəm-boo'kō; Port. per'năm-boo'koo), *n.* Recife, a city of Brazil.

per·ni·cious (pẽr-nish'əs), *adj.* [Fr. *pernicieux;* L. *perniciosus* < *pernicies,* destruction < *pernecare,* to kill; *per,* thoroughly + *necare,* to kill < *nex, necis,* death], 1. causing injury, destruction, or ruin; fatal; deadly. 2. [Rare], wicked; evil.

SYN.—**pernicious** applies to that which does great harm by insidiously undermining or weakening (*pernicious* anemia, a *pernicious* dogma); **baneful** implies a harming by or as by poisoning (a *baneful* superstition); **noxious** refers to anything that is injurious to physical or mental health (*noxious* fumes); **deleterious** implies slower, less irreparable injury to the health (the *deleterious* effects of an unbalanced diet); **detrimental** implies a causing of damage, loss, or disadvantage to something specified (his interference was *detrimental* to our cause).—*ANT.* harmless, innocuous.

pernicious anemia, a severe form of anemia characterized by a gradual reduction in the number of the red blood cells, general weakness, gastrointestinal and nervous disturbances, etc.: it can be successfully treated by the administration of liver or liver extracts.

per·nick·et·y (pẽr-nik'ə-ti), *adj.* [< Scot. dial.; prob. echoic expansion of *pernicky* in same sense; ? altered < *pertickie,* child's word for *particular*], [Colloq.], 1. too particular or precise; fastidious; fussy. 2. showing or requiring extremely careful treatment. Also **persnickety.**

Pe·rón, Juan Do·min·go (hwän dô-mēŋ'gô pe-rôn'), 1896?– ; president of Argentina, 1946–1955; deposed.

per·o·ne·al (per'ə-nē'əl), *adj.* [Gr. *peronē,* a pin, fibula; + *-al*], of or near the fibula.

per·o·rate (per'ə-rāt'), *v.i.* [PERORATED (-id), PERORATING], [< L. *peroratus;* see PERORATION], 1. to make a speech; especially, to speak at some length; harangue. 2. to sum up or conclude a speech.

per·o·ra·tion (per'ə-rā'shən), *n.* [L. *peroratio* < *perorare* (pp. *peroratus*); *per,* through + *orare,* to pray, speak], the concluding part of a speech, in which there is a summing up and emphatic recapitulation.

per·ox·id (pẽr-ok'sid), *n.* peroxide.

per·ox·ide (pẽr-ok'sīd), *n.* [*per-* + *oxide*], any oxide containing the O_2 group in which the two atoms of oxygen are linked by a single bond; specifically, hydrogen peroxide. *v.t.* [PEROXIDED (-id), PEROXIDING], to bleach with hydrogen peroxide. *adj.* bleached with hydrogen peroxide: as, *peroxide* hair.

per·pend (pũr'pənd), *n.* [Fr. *parpaing, parpain* < LL. **perpannius* < base seen also in Fr. *pan* (*de mur*), side (of a wall)], a large stone extending through a wall from one side to the other, used as a binder.

per·pend (pẽr-pend'), *v.t. & v.i.* [L. *perpendere; per-,* intens. + *pendere,* to weigh], [Archaic], to ponder.

per·pen·dic·u·lar (pũr'pən-dik'yoo-lẽr), *adj.* [ME.; OFr. *perpendiculer;* L. *perpendicularis* < *perpendiculum,* plumb line < *per-,* intens. + *pendere,* to hang], 1. at right angles to a given plane or line. 2. exactly upright; vertical; straight up or down. 3. [P-], of or designating the third and latest style of English Gothic architecture of the 14th, 15th, and 16th centuries, characterized by vertical lines in its tracery. *n.* 1. a device used in finding or marking the vertical line from any point. 2. a line at right angles to the plane of the horizon. 3. a straight line at right angles to another line or plane. 4. a perpendicular or upright position. —*SYN.* see **vertical.**

PERPENDICULAR PD, perpendicular to HR

per·pen·dic·u·lar·i·ty (pũr'pən-dik'yoo-lar'ə-ti), *n.* the state or quality of being perpendicular.

per·pent (pũr'pənt), *n.* a perpend.

per·pe·trate (pũr'pə-trāt'), *v.t.* [PERPETRATED (-id), PERPETRATING], [< L. *perpetratus,* pp. of *perpetrare* < *per,* thoroughly + *patrare,* to effect], to do or perform (something evil, criminal, or offensive); be guilty of; commit (a blunder), impose (a hoax), etc.

per·pe·tra·tion (pũr'pə-trā'shən), *n.* 1. the act of perpetrating. 2. something perpetrated, as an offense.

per·pe·tra·tor (pũr'pə-trā'tẽr), *n.* a person who perpetrates.

per·pet·u·al (pẽr-pech'ōō-əl), *adj.* [ME. & OFr. *perpetuel;* L. *perpetualis* < *perpetuus,* constant], 1. lasting or enduring forever or for an indefinitely long time; eternal; permanent. 2. continuing indefinitely without interruption; unceasing; constant: as, a *perpetual* nuisance. 3. in *gardening,* blooming continuously throughout the growing season. *n.* a perpetual plant; especially, a variety of perpetual hybrid rose. —*SYN.* see **continual.**

perpetual calendar, a calendar that is mathematically so arranged that the correct day of the week can be determined for any given date over a wide range of years.

per·pet·u·al·ly (pẽr-pech'ōō-əl-i), *adv.* 1. forever; eternally. 2. constantly; incessantly.

perpetual motion, the motion of a hypothetical device which, once set in motion, would operate indefinitely by creating its own energy.

per·pet·u·ate (pẽr-pech′ōō-āt′), *v.t.* [PERPETUATED (-id), PERPETUATING], [< L. *perpetuatus*, pp. of *perpetuare*], to make perpetual; cause to continue or be remembered; preserve from oblivion.

per·pet·u·a·tion (pẽr-pech′ōō-ā′shən), *n.* [ML. *perpetuatio*], a perpetuating or being perpetuated.

per·pet·u·a·tor (pẽr-pech′ōō-ā′tẽr), *n.* a person who perpetuates.

per·pe·tu·i·ty (pũr′pə-tōō′ə-ti, pũr′pə-tū′ə-ti), *n.* [*pl.* PERPETUITIES (-tiz)], [ME. *perpetuite;* L. *perpetuitas*], 1. the state or quality of being perpetual. 2. something perpetual, as an annuity or pension to be paid indefinitely. 3. unlimited time; eternity. 4. in *law, a)* a limitation upon the transference of an estate: it is valid only for a legally specified period. *b)* an estate so limited.

in perpetuity, forever.

Per·pi·gnan (per′pē′nyän′), *n.* a city in southern France: pop., 75,000 (1946).

per·plex (pẽr-pleks′), *v.t.* [Late ME., involved; OFr. *perplexe;* L. *perplexus*, entangled, confused, involved; *per*, through + *plexus*, pp. of *plectere*, to twist, plait], 1. to make (a person) uncertain, doubtful, or hesitant; confuse; puzzle. 2. to make intricate or complicated; make confusing or hard to understand: as, don't *perplex* the problem. —*SYN.* see **puzzle.**

per·plexed (pẽr-plekst′), *adj.* [pp. of *perplex*], 1. full of doubt or uncertainty; puzzled. 2. hard to understand; confusing.

per·plex·ing (pẽr-plek′siŋ), *adj.* that perplexes.

per·plex·i·ty (pẽr-plek′sə-ti), *n.* [ME. *perplexite;* OFr. *perplexité;* LL. *perplexitas*], 1. the condition of being perplexed; bewilderment; confusion. 2. [*pl.* PERPLEXITIES (-tiz)], something that perplexes or is perplexed, as a complication or intricacy.

per pro., *per procurationem*, [L.], by proxy.

per·qui·site (pũr′kwə-zit), *n.* [ML. *perquisitum* < L. *perquisitus*, pp. of *perquirere*, to search diligently for < *per-*, intens. + *quaerere*, to seek], 1. something additional to regular profit or pay, resulting from one's position or employment, especially something customary or expected, as a tip or gratuity. 2. something to which a person, institution, etc. is entitled by virtue of status, position, or character; prerogative; right: as, the frank is a *perquisite* of congressmen.

Per·rault, Charles (shärl′ pe′rō′), 1628–1703; French writer and compiler of fairy tales.

Per·rin, Jean Bap·tiste (zhän′ bȧ′tēst′ pe′ran′), 1870–1942; French physicist; received Nobel prize in physics, 1926.

per·ron (per′ən; Fr. pe-rōn′), *n.* [ME. *peroun;* OFr. *perron* < *pierre;* L. *petra*, a stone], an outside staircase, usually extending up the slope of a terrace, as to the front entrance of a building.

per·ry (per′i), *n.* [ME. *pereye;* OFr. *peré;* LL. *pera* < L. *pirum*, pear], a fermented drink made from pear juice.

Per·ry, Matthew Cal·braith (kal′breth per′i), 1794–1858; brother of *Oliver Hazard;* American commodore; negotiated first treaty between the United States and Japan.

Perry, Oliver Haz·ard (haz′ẽrd), 1785–1819; American naval officer; defeated the British at the Battle of Lake Erie (1813).

Perry, Ralph Barton (bär′t'n), 1876–1957; American educator and philosopher.

Pers., 1. Persia. 2. Persian.

pers., 1. person. 2. personal. 3. personally.

per·salt (pũr′sôlt′), *n.* a salt of a peracid.

perse (pũrs), *adj.* [ME.; OFr. *pers;* LL. *persus*], grayish-blue. *n.* grayish blue.

per se (pũr′ sē′), [L.], by (or in) itself; inherently.

per·se·cute (pũr′sə-kūt′), *v.t.* [PERSECUTED (-id), PERSECUTING], [Fr. *persécuter;* back-formation < *persécuteur*, L. *persecutor* < L. *persequi*, to pursue; *per*, through + *sequi*, to follow], 1. to afflict or harass constantly so as to injure or distress; oppress cruelly, especially for reasons of religion, politics, or race. 2. to trouble or annoy constantly: as, *persecuted* by mosquitoes. —*SYN.* see **wrong.**

per·se·cu·tion (pũr′sə-kū′shən), *n.* [ME. & OFr. *persecucio(u)n;* L. *persecutio*], a persecuting or being persecuted.

per·se·cu·tive (pũr′sə-kū′tiv), *adj.* of, like, or constituting persecution.

per·se·cu·tor (pũr′sə-kū′tẽr), *n.* [Anglo-Fr. *persecutour;* L.], a person who persecutes.

Per·se·id (pũr′si-id), *n.* [< Mod. L. *Perseis* (pl. *Perseides*), daughter of Perseus: so named because apparently radiating from Perseus], any of a group of meteors that appear annually about August 11.

Per·seph·o·ne (pẽr-sef′ə-ni), *n.* [L.; Gr. *Persephonē*], in *Greek mythology*, the daughter of Zeus and Demeter, abducted by Hades (Pluto) and made his wife: identified by the Romans with Proserpina.

Per·sep·o·lis (pẽr-sep′ə-lis), *n.* a ruined city in southern Iran: ancient capital of Persia.

Per·seus (pũr′sūs, pũr′si-əs), *n.* [L.; Gr. *Perseus*], 1. in *Greek mythology*, the son of Zeus and Danaë and slayer of Medusa: he married Andromeda after rescuing her from a sea monster. 2. a northern constellation between Taurus and Cassiopeia: see **constellation,** chart.

per·se·ver·ance (pũr′sə-vêr′əns), *n.* [ME.; OFr.; L. *perseverantia* < *perseverans*, ppr. of *perseverare*], 1. the act of persevering. 2. the quality of one who perseveres; persistence. 3. in *Calvinist theology*, the continuance in grace of people elected to eternal salvation.

SYN.—**perseverance** implies a continuing to do something in spite of difficulties, obstacles, etc.; **persistence,** in a favorable sense, implies steadfast perseverance, in an unfavorable sense, annoyingly stubborn continuance; **tenacity** and **pertinacity** imply firm adherence to some purpose, action, belief, etc., the former word in a favorable sense, and the latter, with the unfavorable connotation of annoying obstinacy.

per·se·vere (pũr′sə-vêr′), *v.i.* [PERSEVERED (-vêrd′), PERSEVERING], [ME. *perseveren;* OFr. *perseverer;* L. *perseverare* < *perseverus*, very severe, strict; *per-*, intens. + *severus*, severe, serious, grave, strict], to continue doing something in spite of difficulty, opposition, etc.; be steadfast in purpose; persist.

per·se·ver·ing (pũr′sə-vêr′iŋ), *adj.* refusing to give up; showing perseverance; unrelenting; persistent.

Per·shing, John Joseph (pũr′shiŋ), 1860–1948; American general; commander in chief of American Expeditionary Forces, World War I.

Per·sia (pũr′zhə, pũr′shə), *n.* 1. the Persian Empire. 2. Iran, a country in western Asia: the former name: abbreviated **Per., Pers.**

Per·sian (pũr′zhən, pũr′shən), *adj.* of Persia, ancient or modern, its people, their language, or culture; Iranian. *n.* 1. a native or inhabitant of Persia. 2. the Iranian language of the Persians: its historical forms are Old Persian, Avestan, and Pahlavi; the current form is Modern Persian. Abbreviated **Per., Pers.**

Persian blinds, persiennes.

Persian cat, a variety of domestic cat with long, silky hair.

Persian Empire, an empire of southwestern Asia, from the Indus River to the Mediterranean: it was founded by Cyrus the Great (6th century B.C.) and destroyed by Alexander the Great (331 B.C.).

Persian Gulf, an arm of the Arabian Sea, between Arabia and Iran: length, 420 mi.

Persian lamb, 1. the lamb of certain Asiatic sheep. 2. its black, gray, or brown curly fleece, used for fur coats, etc.

Persian rug (or **carpet**), an Oriental rug made in Persia, having rich, soft colors in an intricate pattern.

per·si·car·y (pũr′si-ker′i), *n.* [*pl.* PERSICARIES (-iz)], [ML. *persicarius*, peach tree < L. *persicum*, peach], any of a group of plants of the knotweed family, characterized by jointed stems.

per·si·ennes (pũr′zi-enz′; Fr. per′syen′), *n.pl.* [Fr., fem. pl. of *persien*, Persian], outside shutters for windows, having adjustable, horizontal slats like those on Venetian blinds: also **Persian blinds.**

per·si·flage (pũr′si-fläzh′), *n.* [Fr. < *persifler*, to banter < L. *per* + Fr. *siffler*, to whistle, hiss; L. *sifilare, sibilare;* cf. SIBILANT], 1. a light, frivolous or flippant style of writing or speaking. 2. talk or writing of this kind; banter; raillery.

per·sim·mon (pẽr-sim′ən), *n.* [< Am. Ind. (Algonquian); cf. Cree *pasiminan*, dried fruit], 1. any of a number of related trees with white, cup-shaped flowers, hard wood, and yellow or orange-red, plumlike fruit. 2. the fruit, sour and astringent when green, but sweet and edible when thoroughly ripe.

per·sist (pẽr-sist′, pẽr-zist′), *v.i.* [Fr. *persister;* L. *persistere; per*, through + *sistere*, to cause to stand], 1. to refuse to give up, especially when faced with opposition or difficulty; continue firmly or steadily. 2. to continue insistently, as in repeating a question. 3. to continue to exist or prevail; endure; remain. —*SYN.* see **continue.**

per·sist·ence (pẽr-sis′təns, pẽr-zis′təns), *n.* [Fr. *persistance*], 1. the act of persisting; stubborn or enduring continuance, as in a chosen course or purpose. 2. a persistent or lasting quality; resoluteness; tenacity. 3. continuous existence; endurance, as of a headache. 4. the continuance of an effect after the removal of its cause: as, *persistence* of vision causes visual impressions to continue upon the retina for some time. —*SYN.* see **perseverance.**

per·sist·en·cy (pẽr-sis′tən-si, pẽr-zis′tən-si), *n.* persistence.

per·sist·ent (pẽr-sis′tənt, pẽr-zis′tənt), *adj.* [L. *persistens*, ppr. of *persistere;* see PERSIST], 1. refusing to relent; continuing, especially in the face of opposition, etc.; stubborn; persevering. 2. continuing to exist or endure; lasting without change. 3. constantly repeated; continued. 4. in *botany*, remaining attached for a long time, as some withered leaves. 5. in *zoology*, remaining for life: said of such parts which in other animals disappear or wither at an early stage.

per·snick·e·ty (pẽr-snik'ə-ti), *adj.* [Colloq.], pernickety.

per·son (pũr's'n), *n.* [ME. & OFr. *persone;* L. *persona*, lit., face mask used by actors, hence a character, person; cf. IMPERSONATE, PARSON], 1. a human being, especially as distinguished from a thing or lower animal; individual man, woman, or child: as, he is a kind *person*, three *persons* are missing. 2. a common individual: used in slight or contempt. 3. *a*) a living human body. *b*) bodily form or appearance: as, she was neat and clean about her *person*. 4. personality; self; being: as, his very *person* is offensive. 5. in *grammar*, *a*) division into three classes of pronouns and, in most languages, corresponding verb forms, the use of which indicates and is determined by the identity of the subject, thus: the *first person* (*I* or *we*) is used when the subject is the speaker; the *second person* (*you*) when the subject is spoken to; the *third person* (*he, she, it*, or *they*) when the subject is spoken of. *b*) any of these three classes. 6. in *law*, any individual or incorporated group having certain legal rights and responsibilities. 7. in *theology*, one of the three modes of being (Father, Son, and Holy Ghost) in the Trinity. 8. [Archaic], a role in a play; character. Abbreviated **pers., per.**

in person, in the flesh; in bodily presence.

per·so·na (pẽr-sō'nə), *n.* [*pl.* PERSONAE (-nē)], [L.], 1. person. 2. *pl.* the characters of a drama, novel, etc.

per·son·a·ble (pũr's'n-ə-b'l), *adj.* having an attractive personal appearance; good-looking; handsome; comely.

per·son·age (pũr's'n-ij), *n.* [OFr.; see -AGE], 1. a person of importance or distinction; notable. 2. a person. 3. a character in history, a play, novel, etc. 4. [Archaic], physical appearance.

‡**per·so·na gra·ta** (pẽr-sō'nə grā'tə, grä'tə), [L.], a person who is acceptable; one who is always welcome.

per·son·al (pũr's'n-əl), *adj.* [ME. *personele;* OFr. *personel;* L. *personalis*], 1. of or peculiar to a certain person; private; individual. 2. done in person or by oneself without the use of another person or outside agency: as, a *personal* interview. 3. of the person, body, or physical appearance: as, *personal* hygiene. 4. having to do with the character, personality, intimate affairs, conduct, etc. of a certain person: as, a *personal* remark. 5. tending to make remarks, or be inquisitive, about the private affairs of others. 6. of, like, or having the nature of a person, or rational, self-conscious being: as, a *personal* God. 7. in *grammar*, indicating grammatical person, as the inflectional endings of verbs in Latin and Greek: see also **personal pronoun.** 8. in *law*, of or constituting personal property. *n.* 1. a local news item about a person or persons. 2. a brief newspaper advertisement concerning a personal matter. Abbreviated **pers.**

personal effects, personal property; intimate belongings.

personal equation, see **equation** (sense 2).

per·son·al·i·ty (pũr'sə-nal'ə-ti), *n.* [*pl.* PERSONALITIES (-tiz)], [ME. *personalite;* OFr. *personalité;* ML. *personalitas* < L. *personalis*, personal], 1. the quality or fact of being a person. 2. the quality or fact of being a particular person; personal identity; individuality. 3. habitual patterns and qualities of behavior of any individual as expressed by physical and mental activities and attitudes; distinctive individual qualities of a person, considered collectively. 4. the sum of such qualities as impressing or likely to impress others: as, she has *personality*. 5. a person; especially a notable person; personage. 6. *usually pl.* any remark, usually an offensive or disparaging one, aimed at or referring to a person. —*SYN.* see **disposition.**

per·son·al·ize (pũr's'n-əl-īz'), *v.t.* [PERSONALIZED (-īzd'), PERSONALIZING], 1. to make personal; apply to a specific person, especially to oneself: as, she *personalized* his general criticism of her group. 2. to personify; endow with personality. 3. to have printed with one's name: as, *personalized* checks.

per·son·al·ly (pũr's'n-əl-i), *adv.* 1. without the use of another person or an agent; in person: as, he attended to it *personally*. 2. as a person: as, though I dislike him *personally*, I admire his taste. 3. in one's own opinion; as far as oneself is concerned: as, *personally*, I'd rather not go. 4. as though directed at one's person: as, she took his remarks *personally*.

personal pronoun, any of a group of pronouns referring to the speaker(s), the person(s) spoken to, or any other person(s) or thing(s). The English personal pronouns, nominative case form, are:

	sing.	*pl.*
1st pers.	I	we
2d pers.	you (*archaic* thou)	you (*archaic* ye)
3d pers.	he, she, it	they

personal property, any property that is movable or not attached to the land: opposed to *real property*.

per·son·al·ty (pũr's'n-əl-ti), *n.* [*pl.* PERSONALTIES (-tiz)], [Anglo-Fr. *personaltie* for OFr. *personalité;* see PERSONALITY], personal property: opposed to *realty*.

‡**per·so·na non gra·ta** (pẽr-sō'nə non grā'tə, grä'tə), [L.], a person who is not acceptable; an unwelcome person.

per·son·ate (pũr's'n-āt'; *for adj., usually* pũr's'n-it), *v.t.* [PERSONATED (-id), PERSONATING], [< L. *personatus*, masked < *persona;* see PERSON], 1. to act or play the part of, as in a drama or masquerade; portray. 2. to personify, as in poetry. 3. in *law*, to assume the character or identity of with intent to defraud; impersonate. *adj.* having a single-petaled flower with two lips and a projection in its throat.

per·son·a·tion (pũr's'n-ā'shən), *n.* a personating or being personated; impersonation.

per·son·a·tive (pũr's'n-ā'tiv), *adj.* personating; especially, representing dramatically.

per·son·a·tor (pũr's'n-ā'tẽr), *n.* one who personates.

per·son·i·fi·ca·tion (pẽr-son'ə-fi-kā'shən), *n.* 1. a personifying or being personified. 2. a person or thing thought of as representing some quality, thing, or idea; embodiment; type; perfect example: as, the old man was the very *personification* of evil, Cupid is the *personification* of love. 3. a figure of speech in which a thing, quality, or idea is represented as a person.

per·son·i·fi·er (pẽr-son'ə-fī'ẽr), *n.* a person or thing that personifies.

per·son·i·fy (pẽr-son'ə-fī'), *v.t.* [PERSONIFIED (-fīd'), PERSONIFYING], [Fr. *personnifier* < L. *persona*, person + *facere*, to make], 1. to think or speak of (a thing) as having life or personality; represent as a person: as, we *personify* a ship by referring to it as "she." 2. to symbolize (an abstract idea) by a human figure, as in art. 3. to be a perfect example of (some quality, thing, or idea); typify; embody. 4. [Rare], to personate.

per·son·nel (pũr'sə-nel'), *n.* [Fr.; see PERSONAL], persons employed in any work, enterprise, service, establishment, etc.: distinguished in military usage from *matériel*. *adj.* of or in charge of personnel.

per·spec·tive (pẽr-spek'tiv), *adj.* [ME. *perspectif;* LL. *perspectivus* < L. *perspicere*, to look through < *per*, through + *specere*, to look], 1. of perspective. 2. drawn in perspective. *n.* [ML. *perspectiva* < LL. *perspectivus;* see the *adj.*], 1. the art of picturing objects or a scene in such a way as to show them as they appear to the eye with reference to relative distance or depth. 2. *a*) the appearance of objects or scenes as determined by their relative distance and positions. *b*) the effect of relative distance and position. 3. the relationship or proportion of the parts of a whole, regarded from a particular standpoint or point in time. 4. a proper evaluation with proportional importance given to the component parts. 5. a picture in perspective. 6. a distant view; vista. 7. [Obs.], an optical instrument.

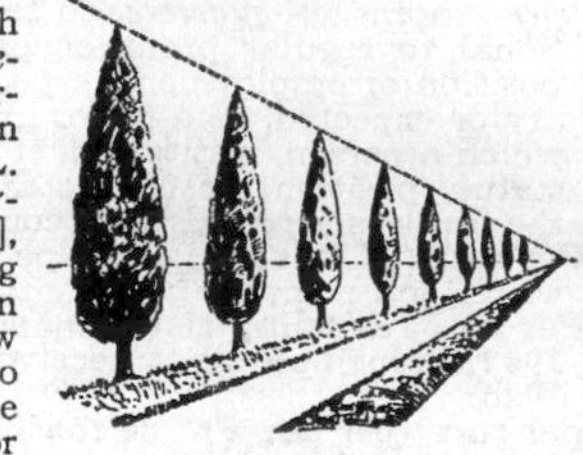
PERSPECTIVE

per·spi·ca·cious (pũr'spi-kā'shəs), *adj.* [< L. *perspicax, perspicacis* < *perspicere*, to see through], 1. having keen judgment or understanding; acutely perceptive. 2. [Archaic], having keen vision. — *SYN.* see **shrewd.**

per·spi·cac·i·ty (pũr'spi-kas'ə-ti), *n.* [L. *perspicacitas*], 1. keenness of judgment or understanding. 2. [Archaic], keenness of sight.

per·spi·cu·i·ty (pũr'spi-kū'ə-ti), *n.* [Fr. *perspicuité;* L. *perspicuitas*], quality of being perspicuous; lucidity.

per·spic·u·ous (pẽr-spik'ū-əs), *adj.* [L. *perspicuus*, transparent < *perspicere*, to see through], clear in statement or expression; easily understood; lucid.

per·spi·ra·tion (pũr'spə-rā'shən), *n.* [Fr.], 1. the act of perspiring; sweating. 2. moisture given off in perspiring; sweat.

per·spir·a·to·ry (pẽr-spīr'ə-tôr'i, pẽr-spīr'ə-tō'ri), *adj.* of or causing perspiration.

per·spire (pẽr-spīr'), *v.t. & v.i.* [PERSPIRED (-spīrd'), PERSPIRING], [Fr. *perspirer;* L. *perspirare*, to breathe everywhere; *per*, through + *spirare*, to breathe], to give forth (a characteristic salty moisture) through the pores of the skin; sweat.

per·suad·a·ble (pẽr-swād'ə-b'l), *adj.* that can be persuaded.

per·suade (pẽr-swād'), *v.t.* [PERSUADED (-id), PERSUADING], [Fr. *persuader;* L. *persuadere; per-*, intens. + *suadere*, to urge], 1. to cause (someone) to do something, especially by reasoning, urging, or inducement; prevail upon. 2. to induce (someone) to believe something; convince.

SYN.—**persuade** implies an influencing of a person to an action, belief, etc. by an overt appeal to his reason or emotions (after some coaxing, pleading, and arguing, we *persuaded* him to go); **induce** suggests a subtler leading of a person to a course of action so that the decision seems finally to come from him (he was *induced* to accept the position); **prevail on,** interchangeable with either of the preceding, often suggests stronger resistance overcome only after considerable argument, etc. (he could not be *prevailed on* to change his mind).

per·sua·si·bil·i·ty (pēr-swā'sə-bil'ə-ti), *n.* the state or quality of being persuasible.
per·sua·si·ble (pēr-swā'sə-b'l), *adj.* [ME.; L. *persuasibilis* < *persuasus*, pp. of *persuadere*], that can be persuaded.
per·sua·sion (pēr-swā'zhən), *n.* [ME. *persuacioun;* L. *persuasio* < pp. of *persuadere*], 1. a persuading or being persuaded. 2. power of persuading. 3. a strong belief; conviction. 4. a particular religious belief or system or the persons adhering to this; religion. 5. a particular party, sect, group, etc. 6. [Colloq.], kind, sort, sex, etc.: used humorously. —*SYN.* see **opinion.**
per·sua·sive (pēr-swā'siv), *adj.* [Fr. *persuasif;* ML. *persuasivus* < L. *persuasus*, pp. of *persuadere*], having the power, or tending, to persuade. *n.* [Rare], something that persuades; inducement.
per·sul·fate (pũr-sul'fāt), *n.* [*per-* + *sulfate*], a salt containing the S_2O_8 radical, produced by the electrolysis of a sulfate solution.
pert (pũrt), *adj.* [contr. < ME. & OFr. *apert;* L. *apertus*, open], 1. bold or impudent in speech or behavior; saucy; forward. 2. [Dial.], in good spirits; lively; brisk. 3. [Obs.], *a*) expert; skilled. *b*) clever.
pert., pertaining.
per·tain (pēr-tān'), *v.i.* [ME. *partenen;* OFr. *partenir;* L. *pertinere*, to stretch out, reach < *per-*, intens. + *tenere*, to hold], 1. to belong; be connected or associated; be a part or accessory. 2. to be appropriate or suitable: as, the conduct that *pertains* to a gentleman. 3. to have reference or relevance: as, his remark did not *pertain* to the question.
pertaining to, having to do with; belonging to; of.
Perth (pũrth), *n.* 1. a county of central Scotland: pop., 127,000: also **Perthshire.** 2. its county seat: pop., 41,000. 3. seaport and capital of Western Australia: pop., 389,000.
Perth Am·boy (am'boi), a city in eastern New Jersey, on Raritan Bay: pop., 38,000.
Perth·shire (pũrth'shir), *n.* Perth.
per·ti·na·cious (pũr'tə-nā'shəs), *adj.* [< L. *pertinax*, firm < *per-*, intens. + *tenax, tenacis*, holding fast], 1. holding firmly to some purpose, belief, or action, often stubbornly or obstinately. 2. hard to get rid of; unyielding; persistent, as an illness. —*SYN.* see **stubborn.**
per·ti·nac·i·ty (pũr'tə-nas'ə-ti), *n.* [Fr. *pertinacité*], the quality or condition of being pertinacious; stubborn persistence; obstinacy. —*SYN.* see **perseverance.**
per·ti·nence (pũr't'n-əns), *n.* the quality of being pertinent or appropriate; relevance.
per·ti·nen·cy (pũr't'n-ən-si), *n.* pertinence.
per·ti·nent (pũr't'n-ənt), *adj.* [ME. *pertynent;* L. *pertinens*, ppr. of *pertinere;* see PERTAIN], of or connected with the matter in hand; relevant; to the point. —*SYN.* see **relevant.**
per·turb (pēr-tũrb'), *v.t.* [ME. *perturben;* OFr. *perturber;* L. *perturbare; per-*, intens. + *turbare*, to disturb < *turba*, turmoil], to cause to be alarmed, agitated, or upset; disturb or trouble greatly. —*SYN.* see **disturb.**
per·tur·ba·tion (pũr'tēr-bā'shən), *n.* [ME. *perturbacioun;* OFr. *perturbacion;* L. *perturbatio*], 1. a perturbing or being perturbed. 2. something that perturbs; disturbance. 3. in *astronomy*, an irregularity in the motion or orbit of a heavenly body caused by some force other than that which determines its usual path.
per·tur·ba·tive (pũr'tēr-bā'tiv), *adj.* [LL. *perturbativus*], tending to perturb or disturb.
per·tus·sal (pēr-tus''l), *adj.* of or having pertussis, or whooping cough.
per·tus·sis (pēr-tus'is), *n.* [Mod. L.; L. *per-*, intens. + *tussis*, a cough], whooping cough.
Pe·ru (pə-rōō'), *n.* a country in South America, on the Pacific: area, 482,133 sq. mi.; pop., 10,857,000; capital, Lima.
Pe·ru·gia (pe-rōō'jä), *n.* a city in central Italy: pop., 95,000.
Per·u·gi·no, Il (ēl pe'rōō-jē'nô), (born *Pietro Vannucci*), 1446–1523?; Italian painter.
pe·ruke (pə-rōōk'), *n.* [Fr. *perruque;* It. *perruca, parruca;* cf. PERIWIG], a wig.
pe·rus·a·ble (pə-rōō'zə-b'l), *adj.* that can be perused.
pe·rus·al (pə-rōō'z'l), *n.* a perusing; a careful or thorough reading.
pe·ruse (pə-rōōz'), *v.t.* [PERUSED (-rōōzd'), PERUSING], [prob. L. *per-*, intens.; + *use, v.*], 1. [Rare], to examine in detail; scrutinize. 2. to read carefully or thoroughly; study. 3. to read.
Pe·ru·vi·an (pə-rōō'vi-ən), *adj.* of Peru, its people, or culture. *n.* a native or inhabitant of Peru. Abbreviated **Peruv.**
Peruvian bark, cinchona.
per·vade (pēr-vād'), *v.t.* [PERVADED (-id), PERVADING], [L. *pervadere; per*, through + *vadere*, to go], 1. to pass through; spread or be diffused throughout. 2. to be abundant or prevalent throughout.
per·va·sion (pēr-vā'zhən), *n.* [LL. *pervasio* < L.; see PERVADE], a pervading or being pervaded; diffusion.
per·va·sive (pēr-vā'siv), *adj.* tending to pervade or spread throughout.
per·verse (pēr-vũrs'), *adj.* [ME. *peruers;* OFr. *pervers;* L. *perversus*, pp. of *pervertere;* see PERVERT], 1. deviating from what is considered right or acceptable; perverted; hence, 2. wicked. 3. persisting in error or fault; stubbornly contrary. 4. obstinately disobedient or difficult; intractable. —*SYN.* see **contrary.**
per·ver·sion (pēr-vũr'zhən, pēr-vũr'shən), *n.* [ME. *peruersion;* L. *perversio* < pp. of *pervertere*], 1. a perverting or being perverted. 2. something perverted; abnormal form. 3. any of various sexual acts or practices deviating from what is considered normal.
per·ver·si·ty (pēr-vũr'sə-ti), *n.* [Fr. *perversité;* L. *perversitas* < *perversus*], 1. the quality or condition of being perverse. 2. an instance of this.
per·ver·sive (pēr-vũr'siv), *adj.* [< L. *perversus;* + *-ive*], tending to pervert.
per·vert (pēr-vũrt'; *for n.*, pũr'vērt), *v.t.* [ME. *peruerten;* L. *pervertere*, to overturn, corrupt; *per-*, intens. + *vertere*, to turn], 1. to cause to turn from what is considered right, natural, or true; misdirect; lead astray; corrupt. 2. to turn to an improper use; misuse. 3. to change or misapply the meaning of; misinterpret; distort; twist. 4. to bring into a worse condition; debase. *n.* a perverted person; especially, a person who practices sexual perversions. —*SYN.* see **debase.**
per·vert·ed (pēr-vũr'tid), *adj.* [pp. of *pervert*], 1. deviating from what is considered right, natural, or true; characterized by perversion; misdirected. 2. of or practicing sexual perversions. 3. misinterpreted; distorted; twisted.
per·vert·i·ble (pēr-vũr'tə-b'l), *adj.* that can be perverted.
per·vi·ous (pũr'vi-əs), *adj.* [L. *pervius* < *per*, through + *via*, way], 1. allowing passage through; that can be penetrated or permeated. 2. having a mind open to influence, argument, or suggestion.
Pe·sach (pā'säkh), *n.* [Heb. *pēsaḥ*, a passing over], a Jewish holiday, the Passover: see **Jewish holidays.**
pe·sade (pə-säd', pə-zäd'), *n.* [Fr., earlier *posade;* It. *posata*, a halt; cf. POSE], in *horsemanship*, the action of a horse in rearing, or bringing the forelegs up into the air without moving the hind legs.
Pes·ca·do·res (pes'kä-dô'res), *n.* a group of islands in Formosa Strait, belonging to Taiwan: area, 50 sq. mi.; pop., 84,000: Japanese name, *Hoko Gunto.*
pe·se·ta (pə-sā'tə; Sp. pe-se'tä), *n.* [Sp., dim. of *pesa*, a weight], a monetary unit and silver coin of Spain, equal to 100 centimos and valued at about 9 cents in 1950.
Pe·sha·war (pe-shä'wēr), *n.* a city in northwestern Pakistan: pop., 152,000.
Pe·shi·to (pe-shē'tō), *n.* [Syr. *peshīttō*, lit., plain, simple], the standard translation of the Old and New Testaments in ancient Syriac.
Pe·shit·ta (pe-shēt'tä), *n.* Peshito.
pes·ky (pes'ki), *adj.* [PESKIER (-ki-ēr), PESKIEST (-ki-ist)], [prob. var. of *pesty*], [Colloq.], annoying; disagreeable; troublesome.
pe·so (pā'sō; Sp. pe'sô), *n.* [*pl.* PESOS (-sōz; Sp. -sôs)], [Sp., lit., a weight; L. *pensum*, something weighed], 1. any of the monetary units and silver coins of certain Latin American countries, as the peso of Mexico, valued at 10 1/2 cents in 1950, or that of Cuba, valued at one dollar in 1950. 2. a monetary unit and silver coin of the Philippines, valued at 50 cents in 1947.
pes·sa·ry (pes'ə-ri), *n.* [*pl.* PESSARIES (-riz)], [ML. *pessarium;* L. *pessum;* Gr. *pessos*, oval pebble], 1. *a*) a device worn in the vagina as a support for a displaced or weak uterus. *b*) a somewhat similar contraceptive device. 2. a vaginal suppository.
pes·si·mism (pes'ə-miz'm), *n.* [L. *pessimus*, worst, superl. of *pejor*, worse; + *-ism*], 1. *a*) the doctrine or belief that the existing world is the worst possible. *b*) the doctrine or belief that the evil in life outweighs the good. 2. the tendency to expect misfortune or the worst outcome in any circumstances; practice of looking on the dark side of things: opposed to *optimism.*
pes·si·mist (pes'ə-mist), *n.* a person who believes in or is given to pessimism.
pes·si·mis·tic (pes'ə-mis'tik), *adj.* of or characterized by pessimism; expecting the worst. —*SYN.* see **cynical.**
pes·si·mis·ti·cal·ly (pes'ə-mis'ti-k'l-i, pes'ə-mis'tik-li), *adv.* in a pessimistic manner.
pest (pest), *n.* [Fr. *peste;* L. *pestis*, a plague], 1. a person or thing that causes trouble, annoyance, discomfort, etc.; nuisance; specifically, any destructive insect or other small animal; vermin. 2. [Now Rare], a fatal epidemic disease; especially, the plague.
Pes·ta·loz·zi, Jo·hann Hein·rich (yô-hän' hin'riH pes'tä-lô'tsi), 1746–1827; Swiss educational reformer.
pes·ter (pes'tēr), *v.t.* [< obs. *impester* < OFr. *empestrer*, orig., to shackle the feet of a horse at pasture, entangle,

embarrass < *em-* (L. *in*, in) + LL. *pastorium*, foot shackles < L. *pascere*, *pastus*, to feed: meaning has been influenced by *pest*, a plague], 1. to annoy constantly or repeatedly with petty irritations; bother; vex. 2. [Obs.], to block (a space) by overcrowding.

pest·hole (pest'hōl'), *n.* [*pest* + *hole*], a place infested or likely to be infested with an epidemic disease.

pest·house (pest'hous'), *n.* [*pest* + *house*], [Archaic], a hospital for the isolation of people with contagious or epidemic diseases.

pes·tif·er·ous (pes-tif'ẽr-əs), *adj.* [L. *pestiferus* < *pestis*, a plague + *ferre*, to bear], 1. *a*) bringing or carrying disease. *b*) infected with an epidemic disease. 2. dangerous to morals or to the welfare of society; noxious; evil. 3. [Colloq.], annoying; mischievous; bothersome.

pes·ti·lence (pes'tə-ləns), *n.* [ME.; OFr.; L. *pestilentia* < *pestilens*; see PESTILENT], 1. any virulent or fatal contagious disease. 2. an epidemic of such a disease; especially, the bubonic plague; hence, 3. anything, as a doctrine, regarded as harmful or dangerous.

pes·ti·lent (pes'tə-lənt), *adj.* [ME.; L. *pestilens* < *pestis*, plague], 1. likely to cause death; deadly. 2. [Rare], *a*) contagious; pestilential. *b*) likely to produce a contagious disease. 3. dangerous to morals or to the welfare of society; pernicious. 4. annoying; troublesome.

pes·ti·len·tial (pes'tə-len'shəl), *adj.* [ME. *pestilencial*; ML. *pestilentialis*], 1. of, causing, or likely to cause pestilence or infection. 2. like or constituting a pestilence; widespread and deadly. 3. pernicious; dangerous; harmful, as to morals.

pes·tle (pes''l, pes't'l), *n.* [ME. & OFr. *pestel*; L. *pistillum* < *pinsere*, *pistus*, to pound, beat], 1. a tool used to pound or grind substances, as in a mortar: see **mortar**, illus. 2. a heavy bar moved vertically in pounding or stamping, as in a mill. *v.t.* & *v.i.* [PESTLED (-'ld, -t'ld), PESTLING], to pound, grind, crush, or mix with or as with a pestle.

Pes·to (pe'stô), *n.* Paestum: the modern name.

pet (pet), *n.* [orig. Scot. dial.; ? connected with obs. Fr. *peton*, lit., little foot, or with Fr. *petit*, small]], 1. an animal that is tamed or domesticated and kept as a favorite or treated with affection. 2. a person who is treated with particular affection or indulgence; favorite; darling. *adj.* 1. kept or treated as a pet: as, a *pet* duck. 2. especially liked; favorite. 3. greatest; especial; particular: used humorously, as, my *pet* peeve. *v.t.* [PETTED (-id), PETTING], 1. [Rare], to treat as a pet. 2. to stroke or pat gently; fondle; caress: as, most dogs like to be *petted*. *v.i.* [Colloq.], to make love; kiss, embrace, fondle, etc. —*SYN.* see **caress**.

pet (pet), *n.* [< obs. phr. *to take the pet*], a state of sulky peevishness or ill-humor. *v.i.* [PETTED (-id), PETTING], to be in a pet; sulk.

Pet., Peter.

Pé·tain, Hen·ri Phi·lippe (än'rē' fē'lēp' pā'taṅ'), 1856–1951; French general; marshal of France (1918); premier of French government at Vichy (1940–1944); convicted of treason (1945).

pet·al (pet''l), *n.* [Mod. L. *petalum* (L., metal plate); Gr. *petalon*, a leaf < *petalos*, outspread], any of the component parts, or leaves, of a corolla.

-petal, [< Mod. L. *-petus* (< L. *petere*, to seek); + *-al*], a combining form meaning *moving toward*, *seeking*, as in *centripetal*.

pet·aled, pet·alled (pet''ld), *adj.* having petals.

pet·al·if·er·ous (pet'ə-lif'ẽr-əs), *adj.* [< *petal* + *-ferous*], having petals.

pet·al·ine (pet''l-in, pet''l-īn'), *adj.* of petals.

pet·a·lod·ic (pet'ə-lod'ik), *adj.* of, like, or characterized by petalody.

pet·a·lo·dy (pet'ə-lō'di), *n.* [< Gr. *petalōdēs*, leaflike < *petalon*, a leaf + *eidos*, a form], in *botany*, a change of stamens or other organs into petals.

pet·al·oid (pet''l-oid'), *adj.* [Mod. L. *petaloideus*; see PETAL & -OID], resembling a petal.

pet·al·ous (pet''l-əs), *adj.* with petals.

pe·tard (pi-tärd'), *n.* [Fr. *pétard* < *péter*, to break wind, bounce < *pet*; L. *peditum* < *peditus*, pp. of *pedere*, to break wind], 1. a metal cone filled with explosives: in ancient warfare it was fastened to walls and gates and exploded to force an opening. 2. a kind of firecracker.

hoist with one's own petard, destroyed by the very devices with which one meant to destroy others; caught in one's own trap: *Hamlet*, III, iv.

pet·a·sos, pet·a·sus (pet'ə-səs), *n.* [Gr. *petasos* < *petannynai*, to spread out], 1. a flat, wide-brimmed hat worn in ancient Greece. 2. the winged hat of Hermes.

pet·cock (pet'kok'), *n.* [? < obs. *pett*, *pet*, breaking of wind + *cock* (valve)], a small faucet or valve used in draining unwanted or excess water or air from pipes, radiators, steam boilers, etc.: also **pet cock**.

Pe·ter (pē'tẽr), [ME.; LL. *Petrus*; Gr. *Petros* (< *petros*, a stone, *petra*, a rock), used as transl. of Aram. *kēphā*, a rock], a masculine name: diminutive, *Pete*; equivalents, L. *Petrus*, Fr. *Pierre*, It. *Pietro*, Sp. *Pedro*. *n.* 1. in the *Bible*, one of the twelve Apostles, a fisherman on the Sea of Galilee; ?–67 A.D.; reputed author of two books of the New Testament that bear his name; considered first pope and founder of the Christian church: also called *Simon Peter*, *Saint Peter*. 2. either of the two Epistles of Peter. Abbreviated **Pet.**

pe·ter (pē'tẽr), *v.i.* [? < name *Peter*, with sexual allusion], [Colloq.], to become gradually smaller, weaker, etc. and then cease or disappear (with *out*).

Peter I, 1. (*Peter Karageorgevich*), 1844–1921; king of Serbia (1903–1921). 2. (*Pëtr Alekseyevich*; called *Peter the Great*), 1672–1725; czar of Russia (1682–1725); responsible for westernization of Russia.

Peter II, 1923– ; son of *Alexander I*; king of Yugoslavia (1934–1941).

Peter III, (*Pëtr Feodorovich*), 1728–1762; czar of Russia (1762); assassinated, and succeeded by his wife, Catherine II.

Pe·ter·bor·ough (pē'tẽr-bũr'ō, pē'tẽr-bũr'ə), *n.* 1. a city in the Soke of Peterborough: pop., 53,000. 2. a city in Ontario, Canada, near Toronto: pop., 61,000.

Peterborough, Soke of (sōk), a division of Northampton county, England: pop., 64,000.

Peter Pan, the title character of J. M. Barrie's play (1904), a little boy who ran away to "Never-Never Land" and never grew up.

Pe·ters·burg (pē'tẽrz-bũrg'), *n.* a city in southeastern Virginia: pop., 37,000: scene of Civil War battles.

Pe·ter·sham (pē'tẽr-shəm), *n.* [after Lord *Petersham*, who set the fashion (c. 1812)], 1. a rough, heavy, woolen cloth. 2. formerly, an overcoat made of this.

Peter's pence (or **penny**), 1. an annual tax, originally of one penny, paid to the papal see by certain English property owners before the Reformation. 2. an annual voluntary donation made by Catholics to the papal treasury. Also **Peter pence**, **Peter penny**.

pet·i·o·lar (pet'i-ə-lẽr), *adj.* of or attached to the petiole.

pet·i·o·late (pet'i-ə-lāt'), *adj.* [< *petiole* + *-ate*], in *botany* & *zoology*, having a stalk or stalklike part.

pet·i·o·lat·ed (pet'i-ə-lā'tid), *adj.* petiolate.

pet·i·ole (pet'i-ōl'), *n.* [Mod. L. *petiolus*; L., a little foot, little leg, stalk, dim. < *pes*, *pedis*, a foot], 1. in *botany*, the stalk to which a leaf is attached. 2. in *zoology*, a slender, stalklike part, as between the abdomen and middle section of an insect; peduncle.

pet·it (pet'i; Fr. pə-tē'), *adj.* [ME.; OFr.; var. of *petty*], of small importance; petty: now used only in law.

pe·tite (pə-tēt'), *adj.* [Fr., fem. of *petit*], small and trim in figure: said of a woman. —*SYN.* see **small**.

pe·ti·tion (pə-tish'ən), *n.* [ME. *peticioun*; L. *petitio*, *petitionis* < *petere*, to seek, ask, make for, attack], 1. a solemn, earnest supplication or request to a superior or to a person or group in authority; prayer; entreaty. 2. a formal writing or document embodying such a request, addressed to a specific person or group and often signed by a number of petitioners. 3. something that is asked or entreated: as, the king was forced to grant their *petition*. 4. in *law*, a written request or plea in which specific court action is asked for: as, a *petition* for rehearing. *v.t.* 1. to address a petition to; ask formally or earnestly. 2. to ask for; solicit. *v.i.* to make a petition or entreaty: as, he *petitioned* for stay of execution. —*SYN.* see **appeal**.

pe·ti·tion·ar·y (pə-tish'ən-er'i), *adj.* 1. of, like, or constituting a petition. 2. [Archaic], begging; suppliant.

pe·ti·tion·er (pə-tish'ən-ẽr), *n.* a person who petitions.

‡**pe·ti·ti·o prin·ci·pi·i** (pi-tish'i-ō' prin-sip'i-ī'), [L., lit., a begging of the question], in *logic*, the fallacy of assuming in the premise of an argument the conclusion which is to be proved.

petit jury, a group of twelve citizens picked to weigh the evidence in and decide the issues of a trial in court: distinguished from *grand jury*.

petit larceny, petty larceny.

‡**petit mal** (pə-tē' mȧl'), [Fr., lit., small ailment], a relatively mild form of epilepsy in which there are short attacks of unconsciousness without convulsions: distinguished from *grand mal*.

pet·it point (pet'i), 1. any of various small stitches, as tent stitch, used in embroidering designs, pictures, etc. on canvas. 2. embroidery done in small stitches.

pe·tits fours (pet'i fôrz', pet'i fōrz'; Fr. pə-tē' fōōr'), [Fr., small cakes < *petits*, pl. of *petit*, small + *fours*, pl. of *four*, lit., oven < L. *furnus*; see FURNACE], cupcakes made of spongecake, etc., usually frosted.

‡**pe·tits pois** (pə-tē' pwȧ'), [Fr., little peas], green peas, especially small ones.

pet name, a term of address used to express affection.

Pe·tö·fi, Sán·dor (shän'dôr pe'tö-fi), (born *Sandor Petrovics*), 1823–1849; Hungarian national poet.

Pe·tra (pē'trə), *n.* an ancient city in modern Jordan.

Pe·trarch (pē'trärk), *n.* (*Francesco Petrarca*), Italian poet, rhetorician, and humanist; 1304–1374.

Pe·trar·chan sonnet (pē-trär'kən), a sonnet composed of a group of eight lines (*octave*) with two rhymes *abba*, *abba*, and a group of six lines (*sestet*) with two or three rhymes variously arranged, typically *cdc dcd* or *cde cde*: the thought or theme is stated and developed in the octave, and expanded, contradicted, etc. in the sestet: also called *Italian sonnet*.

pet·rel (pet'rəl), *n.* [earlier *pitteral*; said to be a dim. of

Peter, in allusion to St. Peter's walking on the sea; cf. Fr. *pétrel, pétérel*], any of various related small, dark, sea birds with long wings; especially, the stormy petrel.

Pe·trie, Sir Flin·ders (flin′dẽrz pē′tri), (*William Matthew Flinders Petrie*), 1853–1942; English archaeologist, Egyptologist, and historical theorist.

pet·ri·fac·tion (pet′rə-fak′shən), ***n.*** [< *petrify*], 1. a petrifying or being petrified. 2. something petrified.

pet·ri·fac·tive (pet′rə-fak′tiv), ***adj.*** [< *petrify*], tending to cause petrifaction.

pet·ri·fi·ca·tion (pet′rə-fi-kā′shən), ***n.*** petrifaction.

Petrified Forest, a national monument in east central Arizona, containing three forests of petrified pines and cedars.

pet·ri·fy (pet′rə-fī′), ***v.t.*** [PETRIFIED (-fīd′), PETRIFYING], [Fr. *pétrifier* < L. *petra*, a stone, rock (< Gr. *petra*) + *facere*, to make], 1. to replace the normal cells of (organic matter) with silica or other mineral deposits; change into a stony substance. 2. to make stiff or inflexible; deaden; harden. 3. to make rigid or numb; stupefy; stun, as with fear. ***v.i.*** to change into stone or a stony substance.

Pe·trine (pē′trīn, pē′trin), ***adj.*** [< *Peter* + *-ine*], of or characteristic of the Apostle Peter or his teachings.

pet·ro- (pet′rə), [< Gr. *petra*, a rock, or *petros*, a stone], a combining form meaning *rock* or *stone*, as in *petrography*: also, before a vowel, **petr-**.

pet·ro·glyph (pet′rə-glif′), ***n.*** [Fr. *pétroglyphe* < Gr. *petra*, a rock + *glyphē*, carving], a rock carving, especially a prehistoric one.

pe·trog·ly·phy (pi-trog′lə-fi), ***n.*** [< *petroglyph*], the art or practice of carving petroglyphs.

Pet·ro·grad (pet′rə-grad; Russ. pyet′rô-grät′), ***n.*** Leningrad: the name from 1914 to 1924.

pe·trog·ra·pher (pi-trog′rə-fẽr), ***n.*** an expert in petrography.

pet·ro·graph·ic (pet′rə-graf′ik), ***adj.*** of petrography.

pet·ro·graph·i·cal (pet′rə-graf′i-k′l), ***adj.*** petrographic.

pe·trog·ra·phy (pi-trog′rə-fi), ***n.*** [*petro-* + *-graphy*], the science dealing with the description or classification of rocks: abbreviated **petrog.**

pet·rol (pet′rəl), ***n.*** [Fr. *pétrole; ML. petroleum;* see PETROLEUM], [British], 1. gasoline. 2. [Obs.], petroleum.

pet·ro·la·tum (pet′rə-lā′təm), ***n.*** [Mod. L. < *petroleum*], a greasy, jellylike substance consisting of a mixture of semisolid hydrocarbons obtained from petroleum: it is used as a base for ointments, in leather dressing, etc.

pe·tro·le·um (pə-trō′li-əm), ***n.*** [ML. < L. *petra*, a rock + *oleum*, oil], an oily, liquid solution of hydrocarbons, yellowish-green to black in color, occurring naturally in the rock strata of certain geological formations: when fractionally distilled it yields paraffin, kerosene, benzene, naphtha, fuel oil, gasoline, etc.

petroleum ether, an inflammable, volatile, liquid hydrocarbon produced by the fractional distillation of petroleum: it is the fraction that boils at 40°–60° C. and is used as a solvent.

petroleum jelly, petrolatum.

pe·trol·ic (pə-trol′ik), ***adj.*** of or produced from petroleum.

pet·ro·log·ic (pet′rə-loj′ik), ***adj.*** of petrology.

pet·ro·log·i·cal (pet′rə-loj′i-k′l), ***adj.*** petrologic.

pet·ro·log·i·cal·ly (pet′rə-loj′i-k′l-i, pet′rə-loj′ik-li), ***adv.*** in accordance with the science of petrology.

pe·trol·o·gy (pi-trol′ə-ji), ***n.*** [*petro-* + *-logy*], the study of the composition, structure, and origin of rocks: abbreviated **petrol.**

pet·ro·nel (pet′rə-nəl), ***n.*** [Fr. *petrinal* < OFr. *peitrine* (Fr. *poitrine*), breast, chest < L. *pectus*, chest: said to be so named from being rested against the chest in firing], a carbinelike firearm of heavy caliber, used in the 15th to 17th centuries.

Pe·tro·ni·us, Gai·us (gā′əs or gī′əs pi-trō′ni-əs), 1st century A.D.; Roman satirist: called *Arbiter Elegantiae* (*Judge of Elegance*).

pe·tro·sal (pi-trō′s′l), ***adj.*** [< L. *petrosus*, rocky < *petra*, a rock], 1. very hard or stony; petrous. 2. in *anatomy & zoology*, of or located near the stonelike part of the temporal bone of the ear. ***n.*** a petrosal bone.

pet·rous (pet′rəs, pē′trəs), ***adj.*** [L. *petrosus*, rocky < *petra*, a rock], 1. of or like rock; hard; stony. 2. of or designating that part of the temporal bone which surrounds and protects the internal ear.

Pet·sa·mo (pet′sä-mô′), ***n.*** a seaport in the U.S.S.R., on the Arctic Ocean.

pet·ti·coat (pet′i-kōt′), ***n.*** [< *petty* + *coat*], 1. a skirt, now especially an underskirt, worn by women and young children. 2. something suggestive of a petticoat, as any of the flanges of a petticoat insulator. 3. [Colloq.], a woman or girl. ***adj.*** 1. feminine; womanly. 2. of or by women: as, *petticoat* government.

petticoat insulator, a tumbler-shaped electric insulator with a flared base or ringed flanges around the center.

pet·ti·fog (pet′i-fog′, pet′i-fôg′), ***v.i.*** [PETTIFOGGED (-fogd′, -fôgd′), PETTIFOGGING], [back-formation < *pettifogger*], to act as a pettifogger.

pet·ti·fog·ger (pet′i-fog′ẽr, pet′i-fôg′ẽr), ***n.*** [< *petty* + *fogger*; ? < obs. D. *focker*, cheater], a lawyer who handles petty cases, especially one who uses unethical methods in conducting trumped-up cases.

pet·ti·fog·ger·y (pet′i-fog′ẽr-i, pet′i-fôg′ẽr-i), ***n.*** pettifogging.

pet·ti·fog·ging (pet′i-fog′iŋ, pet′i-fôg′iŋ), ***adj.*** tricky or dishonest, especially in petty matters. ***n.*** petty dishonesty; trickery.

pet·ti·ly (pet′ə-li), ***adv.*** in a petty manner.

pet·ti·ness (pet′i-nis), ***n.*** the quality of being petty.

pet·tish (pet′ish), ***adj.*** [< *pet* (a fit)], peevish; ill-humored; petulant; cross.

pet·ti·toes (pet′i-tōz′), ***n.pl.*** [orig., giblets & said to be < Fr. *petite oie*, little goose, goose giblets, understood as *petty toe*], 1. pigs' feet, as an article of food. 2. feet or toes, especially a child's.

‡**pet·to** (pet′tô), ***n.*** [*pl.* PETTI (-tē)], [It.; L. *pectus*], the breast.

in petto, in one's breast; in secret; not disclosed.

pet·ty (pet′i), ***adj.*** [PETTIER (-i-ẽr), PETTIEST (-i-ist)], [ME. *peti, petit;* OFr. *petit;* cf. PETIT], 1. relatively worthless or unimportant; trivial; insignificant. 2. small-scale; minor. 3. tending to make much of small matters; narrow-minded; mean. 4. relatively low in rank; subordinate.

SYN.—**petty** is applied to that which is comparatively small, minor, unimportant, etc. of its kind, or it is often used to imply small-mindedness (*petty* larceny, a *petty* grudge); **trivial**, in strict usage, applies to that which, because it is both petty and commonplace, is quite insignificant (a *trivial* remark); **trifling** applies to something so small and unimportant as to be negligible or of very little account (a *trifling* matter); **paltry** is applied to something contemptibly small or worthless (a *paltry* wage); **picayune** is used of a person or thing considered small, mean, or insignificant (a *picayune* objection). —***ANT.*** important, significant.

petty cash, a cash fund from which small incidental expenses are paid: abbreviated **P/C, p/c** (no period).

petty jury, a petit jury.

petty larceny, theft involving a sum smaller than that which constitutes grand larceny: see **grand larceny**.

petty officer, a naval enlisted man whose rank corresponds to that of a noncommissioned officer in the army: abbreviated **P.O., p.o.**

pet·u·lance (pech′oo-ləns), ***n.*** the state or quality of being petulant; peevishness; ill-humor.

pet·u·lan·cy (pech′oo-lən-si), ***n.*** petulance.

pet·u·lant (pech′oo-lənt), ***adj.*** [Fr. *pétulant;* L. *petulans, petulantis*, forward, petulant < base of *petere*, to make for, aim at, attack], 1. [Obs.], *a*) forward; immodest. *b*) pert; insolent. 2. impatient or irritable, especially over a petty annoyance; peevish; bad-tempered.

pe·tu·ni·a (pə-tōōn′yə, pə-tū′ni-ə), ***n.*** [Mod. L. < Fr. *petun* < Braz. *petun*, tobacco], 1. any of a number of related plants of the nightshade family, with funnel-shaped flowers of various colors. 2. the flower.

pe·tun·se (pe-toon′se), ***n.*** petuntse.

pe·tun·tse, pe·tun·tze (pe-toon′tse; Chin. bi′dun′dzu′), ***n.*** [< Chin. *pai-tun-tze*, lit., white stone], a kind of white clay made of powdered granite and used in making Chinese porcelain.

‡**peu à peu** (pö ′à pö′), [Fr.], little by little.

‡**peu de chose** (pöd′ shōz′), [Fr.], a trifle; thing of slight importance.

pew (pū), ***n.*** [ME. *pue;* OFr. *puie*, balcony, balustrade; L. *podia*, pl. of *podium*, balcony; Gr. *podion* < *pous, podos*, a foot], 1. any of the rows of fixed benches with a back, in the auditorium of a church. 2. especially formerly, any of several boxlike enclosures with seats, in a church, for the use of a particular family, etc.

pe·wee (pē′wē), ***n.*** [echoic of its call], 1. the phoebe. 2. any of several other small flycatchers; especially, the wood pewee.

pe·wit (pē′wit, pū′it), ***n.*** [echoic of its call], 1. the lapwing. 2. the phoebe; pewee. 3. the European black-headed gull.

pew·ter (pū′tẽr), ***n.*** [ME. *peutre;* OFr. *peutre, peautre, piautre;* prob. for earlier **peltre;* cf. It. *peltro*], 1. an alloy of tin with lead, brass, or copper: it takes on a grayish, silvery luster when polished. 2. articles made of pewter collectively. ***adj.*** made of pewter.

pe·yo·te (pā-ō′ti; Sp. pe-yô′te), ***n.*** [Sp. < Nahuatl *peyotl*, caterpillar, with reference to the down in the center], any of various mescal cactuses of Mexico and the southwestern United States having buttonlike tops yielding an intoxicating drug.

pf., 1. perfect. 2. pfennig. 3. pianoforte. 4. preferred.

p.f., *più forte*, [It.], a little louder.

Pfalz (pfälts), ***n.*** the Palatinate: the German name.

Pfc., Private First Class.

pfd., preferred.

pfen·nig (fen′ig; G. pfen′iH), *n.* [*pl.* PFENNIGS (-igz); G. PFENNIGE (-i-gə)], [G.; see PENNY], a minor bronze coin of Germany, equal to 1/100 mark: abbreviated **pfg., pf.**

Pforz·heim (pfôrts′hīm), *n.* a city in Baden, southwestern Germany: pop., 80,000.

Pg., 1. Portugal. 2. Portuguese.

P.G., 1. Past Grand. 2. Postgraduate.

Ph, phenyl.

***p*H** (pē′āch′), [*p*otential of *H*ydrogen], *the symbol for* the logarithm of the reciprocal of the hydrogen ion concentration, expressed in gram atoms per liter of a solution, and used to indicate acidity or alkalinity: *p*H 7 (.0000001 gram atom of hydrogen ion per liter), the value for pure water, is regarded as neutral; *p*H values from 0 to 7 indicate acidity and *p*H values from 7 to 14 indicate alkalinity.

Phae·dra (fē′drə), *n.* [L.; Gr. *Phaidra*], in *Greek legend,* the daughter of Minos and wife of Theseus: she killed herself and, through a suicide note, was responsible for the death of her stepson, Hippolytus, who had rejected her advances.

Phae·drus (fē′drəs), *n.* Roman writer of fables of the 1st century A.D.

Pha·ë·thon (fā′ə-thən, fā′ə-t'n), *n.* [L. *Phaethon;* Gr. *Phaethōn,* lit., shining (< *phaethein,* to shine)], in *Greek & Roman mythology,* son of Helios, the sun god: he borrowed his father's sun chariot and, through careless driving, would have set the world on fire had not Zeus struck him down with a thunderbolt.

pha·e·ton, pha·ë·ton (fā′ə-t'n), *n.* [Fr. *phaéton* < L. *Phaethon;* see PHAËTHON], 1. a light, four-wheeled carriage, drawn by either one or two horses, with front and back seats and, usually, a folding top. 2. an open automobile with front and back seats and a folding top, usually furnished with side curtains; touring car.

PHAETON

-phage (fāj), [< Gr. *phagein,* to eat], a combining form meaning *eating* or *destroying,* as in *xylophage.*

phag·e·de·na, phag·e·dae·na (faj′ə-dē′nə), *n.* [L. *phagedaenos;* Gr. *phagedaina* < *phagein,* to eat], 1. a rapidly spreading ulcer accompanied by sloughing, or the separation of dead tissue. 2. gangrene.

-pha·gi·a (fā′ji-ə), -phagy.

phag·o- (fag′ō, fag′ə), [< Gr. *phagein,* to eat], a combining form meaning: 1. *eating* or *destroying,* as in *phagocyte.* 2. *phagocyte.* Also, before a vowel, **phag-.**

phag·o·cyte (fag′ə-sīt′), *n.* [*phago-* + *-cyte*], any leucocyte that ingests and destroys other cells, microorganisms, or other foreign matter in the blood and tissues.

phag·o·cyt·ic (fag′ə-sit′ik), *adj.* of phagocytes or phagocytosis.

phagocytic index, the average number of bacteria ingested by a single leucocyte in an incubated mixture of normal or immune serum, bacteria, and normal leucocytes.

phag·o·cy·to·sis (fag′ə-sī-tō′sis), *n.* [< *phagocyte* + *-osis*], the ingestion and destruction by phagocytes of cells, microorganisms, and other foreign matter in the blood or tissues.

-pha·gous (fə-gəs), [< Gr. *phagein,* to eat], a combining form used to form adjectives corresponding to nouns ending in *-phage,* as in *xylophagous.*

-pha·gy (fə-ji), [Mod. L. *-phagia* < Gr. *phagein,* to eat], a combining form meaning *the practice of eating* (something specified), as in *anthropophagy*: also **-phagia.**

pha·lan·gal (fə-laŋ′g'l), *adj.* phalangeal.

phal·ange (fal′ənj, fə-lanj′), *n.* [Fr. < *phalanges,* pl. of *phalanx*], in *anatomy,* a phalanx.

pha·lan·ge·al (fə-lan′ji-əl), *adj.* [< Mod. L. *phalangeus;* + *-al*], of a phalanx or the phalanges.

pha·lan·ger (fə-lan′jẽr), *n.* [Mod. L. < Gr. *phalanx,* bone between two joints (of the fingers or toes): so named because of the structure of the 2d and 3d phalanges of the hind feet], any of a number of related small, pouched Australian animals with a long tail.

pha·lan·ges (fə-lan′jēz), *n.* alternative plural of **phalanx.**

phal·an·ste·ri·an (fal′ən-stêr′i-ən), *adj.* of or relating to a phalanstery. *n.* a member of a phalanstery.

phal·an·ster·y (fal′ən-ster′i), *n.* [*pl.* PHALANSTERIES (-iz)], [Fr. *phalanstère* < *phalange* (lit., phalange, term used by Fourier to designate a socialistic community) + mona*stère,* monastery], 1. a socialistic community of the type planned by F. M. C. Fourier. 2. any communal association. 3. the buildings housing one of these communities.

pha·lanx (fā′laŋks, fal′aŋks), *n.* [*pl.* PHALANXES (-iz), PHALANGES (fə-lan′jēz)], [L.; Gr. *phalanx,* line or order of battle, battle array], 1. an ancient military formation of infantry in close and deep ranks with shields joined together and spears overlapping. 2. a massed group of individuals; compact body. 3. a group of individuals united for a common purpose. 4. the people forming a phalanstery. 5. [*pl.* PHALANGES], in *anatomy,* any of the bones forming the fingers or toes: see **skeleton,** illus.

phal·a·rope (fal′ə-rōp′), *n.* [Fr.; Mod. L. *phalaropus,* name of the type genus < Gr. *phalaris,* coot + *pous,* a foot], any of a number of related small swimming and wading birds that resemble the sandpiper: the male is less brightly colored than the female.

phal·lic (fal′ik), *adj.* [Gr. *phallikos*], 1. of the phallus. 2. of phallicism.

phal·li·cism (fal′ə-siz'm), *n.* worship of the phallus as a symbol of the male generative power.

phal·li·cist (fal′ə-sist), *n.* a person practicing phallicism.

phal·lism (fal′iz'm), *n.* phallicism.

phal·list (fal′ist), *n.* a phallicist.

phal·lus (fal′əs), *n.* [*pl.* PHALLI (-ī)], [L.; Gr. *phallos*], 1. a representation or image of the penis as the reproductive organ, worshiped as a symbol of generative power, as in the Dionysiac festivals of ancient Greece. 2. the penis or clitoris. 3. in *psychoanalysis,* the penis during the period of infantile sexuality.

-phane (fān), [< Gr. *phainein,* to appear], a combining form meaning *resembling, appearing like,* as in *allophane.*

phan·er·o·gam (fan′ẽr-ə-gam′), *n.* [Fr. *phanérogame* < Gr. *phaneros,* visible + *gamos,* marriage], a flowering plant with distinctly developed pistils and stamens: opposed to *cryptogam.*

phan·er·o·gam·ic (fan′ẽr-ə-gam′ik), *adj.* of a phanerogam.

phan·er·og·a·mous (fan′ẽr-og′ə-məs), *adj.* [*phanerogam* + *-ous*], having stamens and pistils; flowering.

phan·tasm (fan′taz'm), *n.* [ME. & OFr. *fantasme;* L. *phantasma;* Gr. *phantasma* < *phantazein,* to show < stem of *phainein,* to show], 1. a perception of something that has no physical reality; figment of the mind; especially, a specter, or ghost. 2. a deceptive likeness (*of* something). 3. in *philosophy,* a mental image of a real person or thing. Also spelled **fantasm.**

phan·tas·ma (fan-taz′mə), *n.* [*pl.* PHANTASMATA (-mə-tə)], [L.; see PHANTASM], a phantasm (sense 1).

phan·tas·ma·go·ri·a (fan-taz′mə-gôr′i-ə, fan′taz-mə-gō′ri-ə), *n.* [Mod. L. < Gr. *phantasma,* phantasm + (prob.) *agora,* assembly], 1. a magic-lantern show consisting of various optical illusions in which objects rapidly change size, blend into one another, etc. 2. a rapidly changing series of things seen or imagined, as the figures or events of a dream.

phan·tas·ma·go·ri·al (fan-taz′mə-gôr′i-əl, fan′taz-mə-gō′ri-əl), *adj.* of, like, or constituting a phantasmagoria.

phan·tas·ma·gor·ic (fan-taz′mə-gôr′ik, fan′taz-mə-gor′ik), *adj.* phantasmagorial.

phan·tas·ma·go·ry (fan-taz′mə-gôr′i, fan-taz′mə-gō′ri), *n.* [*pl.* PHANTASMAGORIES (-iz, -riz)], a phantasmagoria.

phan·tas·mal (fan-taz′m'l), *adj.* of, like, or constituting a phantasm; illusory; unreal; spectral.

phan·tas·mic (fan-taz′mik), *adj.* phantasmal.

phan·ta·sy (fan′tə-si, fan′tə-zi), *n.* [*pl.* PHANTASIES (-siz, -ziz)], a fantasy.

phan·tom (fan′təm), *n.* [ME. *fantome, fantosme;* OFr. *fantosme;* L. *phantasma;* see PHANTASM], 1. something that seems to appear to the sight but has no physical existence; apparition; vision; specter. 2. something that exists only in the mind; illusion. 3. a person or thing that is something in appearance but not in fact: as, a *phantom* of a leader. 4. any mental image or representation: as, the *phantoms* of things past. *adj.* of, like, or constituting a phantom; unreal; phantasmal. Also spelled **fantom.**

-phan·y (fə-ni), [< Gr. *phainein,* to appear], a terminal combining form meaning *appearance, manifestation,* as in *epiphany.*

Phar., 1. pharmaceutical. 2. pharmacopoeia. 3. pharmacy.

Phar·aoh (fâr′ō; *occas.* fâr′ā-ō′), *n.* [ME. & AS. *Pharaon* < L. acc.; LL. *Pharao;* Gr. *Pharaō;* Heb. *par'ōh;* Egypt. *pr-'o,* great house], the title of the rulers of ancient Egypt: sometimes used as a proper name in the Bible.

Phar·a·on·ic (fâr′ā-on′ik), *adj.* of or like a Pharaoh.

Phar·a·on·i·cal (fâr′ā-on′i-k'l), *adj.* Pharaonic.

Phar. B., *Pharmaciae Baccalaureus,* [L.], Bachelor of Pharmacy.

Phar. D., Doctor of Pharmacy.

Phar·i·sa·ic (far′ə-sā′ik), *adj.* [LL. *Pharisaicus;* Gr. *pharisaïkos* < *pharisaios;* see PHARISEE], 1. of the Pharisees. 2. [p-], emphasizing or observing the letter but not the spirit of religious law; self-righteous; sanctimonious. 3. [p-], pretending to be highly moral or virtuous without actually being so; hypocritical.

phar·i·sa·i·cal (far′ə-sā′i-k'l), *adj.* pharisaic.

phar·i·sa·i·cal·ly (far′ə-sā′i-k'l-i, far′ə-sā′ik-li), *adv.* in a pharisaic manner.

Phar·i·sa·ism (far′ə-sā-iz'm), *n.* [Mod. L. *Pharisaïsmus* < Gr. *pharisaios* (see PHARISEE); + *-ism*], 1. the beliefs and practices of the Pharisees. 2. [p-], pharisaic behavior, character, principles, etc.; hypocrisy.

Phar·i·see (far'ə-sē'), ***n.*** [ME. *pharise;* AS. *fariseus;* OFr. *pharisé;* LL. *Pharisaeus;* Gr. *pharisaios;* Aram. *pĕrīshaiyā,* pl. of *pĕrīsh;* Heb. *pārūsh,* separated < *parash,* to cleave, divide, separate], 1. a member of an ancient Jewish sect that rigidly observed the written law, but also insisted on the validity of the oral, or traditional, law, that had grown out of popular usage: opposed to *Sadducee.* 2. [p-], a pharisaic person.

Pharm., 1. pharmaceutical. 2. pharmacopoeia. 3. pharmacy.

phar·ma·ceu·tic (fär'mə-sōō'tik, fär'mə-sū'tik), ***adj.*** pharmaceutical.

phar·ma·ceu·ti·cal (fär'mə-sōō'ti-k'l, fär'mə-sū'ti-k'l), ***adj.*** [LL. *pharmaceuticus;* Gr. *pharmakeutikos* < *pharmakeuein,* to practice witchcraft, use medicine < *pharmakon,* a poison, medicine], 1. of pharmacy or pharmacists. 2. of or by drugs: as, *pharmaceutical* cure. Abbreviated **Phar., Pharm.**

phar·ma·ceu·tics (fär'mə-sōō'tiks, fär'mə-sū'tiks), ***n.pl.*** [construed as sing.], [< LL], pharmacy (sense 1).

phar·ma·ceu·tist (fär'mə-sōō'tist, fär'mə-sū'tist), ***n.*** a pharmacist.

phar·ma·cist (fär'mə-sist), ***n.*** a person licensed to practice pharmacy; druggist.

phar·ma·co·log·i·cal (fär'mə-kə-loj'i-k'l), ***adj.*** of or by pharmacology.

phar·ma·col·o·gist (fär'mə-kol'ə-jist), ***n.*** a specialist in pharmacology.

phar·ma·col·o·gy (fär'mə-kol'ə-ji), ***n.*** [Mod. L. *pharmacologia* < Gr. *pharmakon,* a drug; + *-logy*], the study of the preparation, qualities, uses, and effects of drugs.

phar·ma·co·poe·ia (fär'mə-kə-pē'ə), ***n.*** [Mod. L.; Gr. *pharmakopoiia* < *pharmakon,* a drug + *poiein,* to make], 1. an official book issued by the proper authorities with a list of drugs and medicines and a description of their properties, preparation, and use. 2. a stock of drugs. Abbreviated **Phar., Pharm.**

phar·ma·co·poe·ial (fär'mə-kə-pē'əl), ***adj.*** of a pharmacopoeia.

phar·ma·cy (fär'mə-si), ***n.*** [*pl.* PHARMACIES (-siz)], [ME. *fermacie;* OFr. *farmacie;* ML. *pharmacia;* Gr. *pharmakeia* < *pharmakon,* a drug], 1. the art or profession of preparing and dispensing drugs and medicines. 2. a place where pharmacy is practiced; drugstore. Abbreviated **Phar., Pharm.**

Pharm. D., Doctor of Pharmacy.

Pharm. M., Master of Pharmacy.

Pha·ros (fâr'os), ***n.*** 1. a small peninsula at Alexandria, in northern Egypt: in ancient times it was an island with a large lighthouse on it. 2. this lighthouse, one of the Seven Wonders of the World. 3. [p-], any lighthouse or marine beacon.

Phar·sa·li·a (fär-sā'li-ə), ***n.*** an ancient Greek district of Thessaly, surrounding the city of Pharsalus.

Phar·sa·lus (fär-sā'ləs), ***n.*** an ancient city in Thessaly, Greece: scene of a battle (48 B.C.) of the Roman Civil War, in which Caesar defeated Pompey.

pha·ryn·gal (fə-riŋ'g'l), ***adj.*** pharyngeal.

pha·ryn·ge·al (fə-rin'ji-əl, far'in-jē'əl), ***adj.*** [< Mod. L. *pharyngeus*], of, or in the region of, the pharynx.

phar·yn·gi·tis (far'in-jī'tis), ***n.*** [Mod. L.; see -ITIS], inflammation of the mucous membrane of the pharynx; sore throat.

pha·ryn·go- (fə-riŋ'gō, fə-riŋ'gə), [< Gr. *pharynx, pharyngos*], a combining form meaning *the pharynx* or *the pharynx and,* as in *pharyngology:* also, before a vowel, **pharyng-.**

phar·yn·gol·o·gy (far'iŋ-gol'ə-ji), ***n.*** [*pharyngo-* + *-logy*], the branch of medicine dealing with the pharynx and its diseases.

pha·ryn·go·scope (fə-riŋ'gə-skōp'), ***n.*** [*pharyngo-* + *-scope*], an instrument for examining the pharynx.

phar·yn·gos·co·py (far'iŋ-gos'kə-pi), ***n.*** examination of the pharynx, especially with a pharyngoscope.

phar·yn·got·o·my (far'iŋ-got'ə-mi), ***n.*** [*pharyngo-* + *-tomy*], surgical incision of the pharynx.

phar·ynx (far'iŋks), ***n.*** [*pl.* PHARYNXES (-iz), PHARYNGES (fə-rin'jēz)], [Mod. L.; Gr. *pharynx, pharyngos,* the throat], the muscular and membranous cavity of the alimentary canal leading from the mouth and nasal passages to the larynx and esophagus.

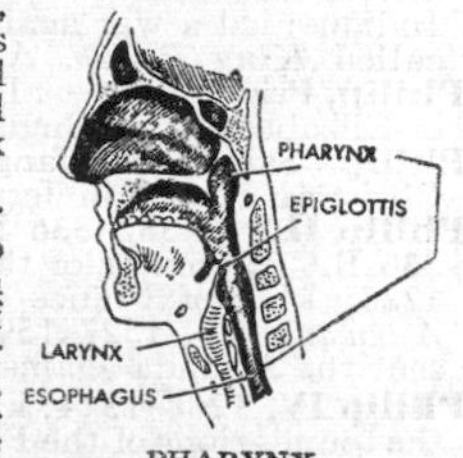

PHARYNX

phase (fāz), ***n.*** [Mod. L. *phasis;* Gr. *phasis* < *phainesthai,* to appear; cf. Fr. *phase*], 1. in *astronomy,* any of the stages of variation in the illumination or appearance of the moon or a planet. 2. any of the stages or forms in any series or cycle of changes, as in development. 3. any of the ways in which something may be observed, considered, or presented; aspect; side; part: as, this is but one *phase* of the subject. 4. in *physical chemistry,* a solid, liquid, or gaseous homogeneous form existing as a distinct part in a heterogeneous system: as, ice is a *phase* of H_2O. 5. the stage or progress of any cyclic movement, as of sound or light waves, alternating electric current, etc., with reference to a standard position or assumed starting point. 6. in *zoology,* any of the characteristic variations in color of the fur or plumage of an animal, according to season, age, etc.

SYN.—**phase** applies to any of the ways in which something may be observed, considered, or presented, and often refers to a stage in development, in a cycle of changes, etc. (the *phases* of the moon); **aspect** emphasizes the appearance of a thing as seen or considered from a particular point of view (to consider a problem from all *aspects*); **facet** literally or figuratively applies to any of the faces of a many-sided object (the *facets* of a diamond, a personality, etc.); **angle** suggests a specific aspect seen from a point of view sharply limited in scope, or, sometimes, an aspect seen only by a sharply acute observer (he knows all the *angles*).

-pha·si·a (fā'zhə, fā'zhi-ə), [Mod. L. < Gr. *phanai,* to speak], a combining form meaning *a* (specified) *speech disorder,* as in *aphasia.*

pha·sis (fā'sis), ***n.*** [*pl.* PHASES (-sēz)], [Mod. L.], a phase; aspect; way; stage.

-pha·sy (fə-si), -phasia.

Ph.B., *Philosophiae Baccalaureus,* [L.], Bachelor of Philosophy.

Ph. C., Pharmaceutical Chemist.

Ph.D., *Philosophiae Doctor,* [L.], Doctor of Philosophy.

pheas·ant (fez''nt), ***n.*** [*pl.* PHEASANTS (-'nts), PHEASANT; see PLURAL, II, D, 1], [ME. & Anglo-Fr. *fesant;* OFr. *faisan, faisant;* L. *phasianus;* Gr. *phasianos* < *Phasis,* river of Asia: the birds are said to have been numerous near its mouth], 1. any of a number of related chickenlike game birds with a long, sweeping tail and brilliant feathers. 2. any of a number of birds resembling the pheasant, as the ruffed grouse.

Phe·be (fē'bi), a feminine name: see **Phoebe.**

Phei·dip·pi·des (fī-dip'ə-dēz'), ***n.*** the Athenian courier who ran to Sparta to seek aid against the Persians before the battle of Marathon; lived in the 5th century B.C.: also spelled **Phidippides.**

phel·lo·derm (fel'ə-dũrm'), ***n.*** [< Gr. *phellos,* a cork; + *-derm*], in *botany,* the layer of soft, green tissue developed on the inner side of the cork from the phellogen.

phel·lo·der·mal (fel'ə-dũr'm'l), ***adj.*** of or like phelloderm.

phel·lo·gen (fel'ə-jən), ***n.*** [< Gr. *phellos,* a cork; + *-gen*], in *botany,* the layer of embryonic tissue from which the cork and phelloderm are developed.

phel·lo·ge·net·ic (fel'ə-jə-net'ik), ***adj.*** phellogenic.

phel·lo·gen·ic (fel'ə-jen'ik), ***adj.*** of or like phellogen.

Phelps, William Lyon (felps), 1865–1943; American literary critic, author, and educator.

phen-, [Fr. *phén-* < Gr. *phainein,* to show, shine: term first used by Laurent, 19th-c. Fr. chemist, to indicate derivation from coal tar, a by-product in manufacturing illuminating gas], a combining form meaning *of* or *derived from benzene,* as in *phenazine:* also **pheno-.**

phe·na·caine (fē'nə-kān', fen'ə-kān'), ***n.*** [*phene*tidyl*acet*phenetid*ine* + co*caine*], a colorless, odorless, crystalline compound, $C_{18}H_{22}N_2O_2{\cdot}HCl$, used as a local anesthetic, especially for the eyes: also called *holocaine hydrochloride.*

phe·nac·e·tin, phe·nac·e·tine (fi-nas'ə-tin), ***n.*** [*phen-* + *acetin*], a coal-tar preparation of white crystals or powder, $C_{10}H_{13}O_2N$, used in medicine to reduce fever.

phen·a·cite (fen'ə-sīt'), ***n.*** [< Gr. *phenax, phenakos,* cheat; + *-ite:* so named because mistaken for quartz], a silicate of glucinum: it is colorless or red, yellow, or brown with white streaks: used as a gem.

phe·nan·threne (fi-nan'thrēn), ***n.*** [*phen-* + *anthracene*], a colorless, crystalline hydrocarbon, $C_{14}H_{10}$, an isomer of anthracene present in coal tar, used in making dyes and other products.

phen·a·zin (fen'ə-zin), ***n.*** phenazine.

phen·a·zine (fen'ə-zēn', fen'ə-zin), ***n.*** [*phen-* + *az-* + *-ine*], a yellow crystalline base, $C_6H_4{:}N_2{:}C_6H_4$, from which many dyes are derived.

phe·net·i·din (fi-net'ə-din), ***n.*** phenetidine.

phe·net·i·dine (fi-net'ə-dēn', fi-net'ə-din), ***n.*** [*phen*ol + *-et-* + amido + *-ine*], any of three isomeric compounds, $C_8H_{11}ON$, especially the para form, used in the manufacture of phenacetin.

phen·e·tol (fen'ə-tol), ***n.*** phenetole.

phen·e·tole (fen'ə-tōl', fen'ə-tol), ***n.*** [*phen*ol + *-et-* + *-ole*], a colorless liquid, $C_6H_5OC_2H_5$, the ethyl ether of phenol.

Phe·ni·cia (fə-nish'ə, fə-nish'i-ə), ***n.*** Phoenicia.

phe·nix (fē'niks), ***n.*** phoenix.

phe·no- (fē'nō, fen'ə), phen-.

phe·no·bar·bi·tal (fē'nə-bär'bi-tal', fen'ə-bär'bi-tôl'), *n.* [*pheno-* + *barbital*], an odorless, white crystalline powder, $C_{12}O_3N_2H_{12}$, used as a sedative and soporific: also called *luminal.*

phe·no·cryst (fē′nə-krist, fen′ə-krist), *n.* [Fr. *phénocryste* < Gr. *phainein*, to show + *krystallos*, crystal], an isolated or conspicuous crystal embedded in porphyritic rock.

phe·nol (fē′nôl, fē′nol, fē′nōl), *n.* [*phen-* + *-ol*], 1. a white crystalline compound, C_6H_5OH, produced from coal tar, and used in making explosives, etc.: it is a strong, corrosive poison, and its dilute aqueous solution, commonly called carbolic acid, is used as an antiseptic. 2. any of a group of aromatic hydroxyl derivatives, similar in structure and composition to phenol.

phe·no·late (fē′nə-lāt′), *n.* a salt of carbolic acid (phenol in a dilute aqueous solution); carbolate.

phe·no·lic (fi-nol′ik, fi-nō′lik), *adj.* of, derived from, or containing phenol.

phe·no·log·i·cal (fē′nə-loj′i-k'l), *adj.* of phenology.

phe·nol·o·gy (fi-nol′ə-ji), *n.* [contr. of *phenomenology*], the study of natural phenomena that recur periodically, as migration, blossoming, etc., and of their relation to climate and changes in season.

phe·nol·phthal·ein, phe·nol-phthal·ein (fē′nôl-thal′ēn, fē′nōl-fthal′i-in), *n.* [*phenol* + *phthalein*], a white to pale-yellow, crystalline powder, $C_{20}H_{14}O_4$, used as a laxative, in making dyes, and as an acid-base indicator in chemical analysis: it is red in a solution containing a base and colorless in a solution containing an acid.

phe·nom·e·na (fi-nom′ə-nə), *n.* plural of **phenomenon.**

phe·nom·e·nal (fi-nom′ə-n'l), *adj.* 1. of or constituting a phenomenon or phenomena. 2. extremely unusual; extraordinary; highly remarkable. 3. in *philosophy*, apparent to or perceptible by the senses.

phe·nom·e·nal·ism (fi-nom′ə-n'l-iz'm), *n.* the philosophic theory that knowledge is limited to phenomena, either because there is no reality beyond phenomena or because such reality is unknowable.

phe·nom·e·nal·is·tic (fi-nom′ə-n'l-is′tik), *adj.* of or constituting phenomenalism.

phe·nom·e·nol·o·gy (fi-nom′ə-nol′ə-ji), *n.* [< *phenomenon* + *-logy*], 1. the science dealing with phenomena as distinct from the science of being (*ontology*). 2. the branch of a science that classifies and describes its phenomena without any attempt at explanation.

phe·nom·e·non (fi-nom′ə-non′), *n.* [*pl.* PHENOMENA (-nə); also, esp. for 3 & 4, PHENOMENONS (-nonz′)], [LL. *phaenomenon;* Gr. *phainomenon*, neut. ppr. of *phainesthai*, to appear], 1. any fact, circumstance, or experience that is apparent to the senses and that can be scientifically described or appraised: as, an eclipse is a *phenomenon* of astronomy. 2. the appearance or observed features of something experienced as distinguished from reality or the thing in itself. 3. anything that is extremely unusual; extraordinary occurrence. 4. [Colloq.], a person with some extraordinary quality, aptitude, etc.; prodigy.

phe·no·type (fē′nə-tīp′), *n.* [*pheno-* (as in *phenomenon*) + *-type*], in *biology*, 1. a type distinguished by visible characters rather than by hereditary or genetic traits. 2. all the individuals belonging to such a type. Opposed to *genotype.*

phe·no·typ·ic (fē′nə-tip′ik), *adj.* of or characteristic of a phenotype.

phe·nox·ide (fi-nok′sīd), *n.* phenolate.

phen·yl (fen′il, fē′nil), *n.* [*phen-* + *-yl*], a monovalent radical, C_6H_5, forming the basis of phenol, benzene, aniline, and various other aromatic compounds.

phen·yl·am·ine (fen′il-ə-mēn′, fē′nil-am′in), *n.* [*phenyl* + *amine*], aniline.

phen·yl·ene (fen′ə-lēn′, fē′nə-lēn′), *n.* [*phenyl* + *-ene*], a divalent radical, C_6H_4, derived from benzene by replacement of two hydrogen atoms.

phew (fū, fyoo: *conventionalized pronun.*), *interj.* an exclamation expressing disgust, surprise, relief, etc.

phi (fī, fē), *n.* [Gr.], the twenty-first letter of the Greek alphabet (Φ, φ), generally equivalent to English *ph* (*f*): see **alphabet**, table.

phi·al (fī′əl), *n.* [ME. *fiole;* OFr. *fiole, phiole;* Pr. *fiola;* LL. *fiola;* L. *phiala;* Gr. *phialē*, broad, shallow drinking vessel], a small glass bottle; vial.

Phi Be·ta Kap·pa (fī bā′tə kap′ə, bē′tə), [< the initial letters of the Gr. words *philosophia biou kybernētēs*, philosophy the guide of life], an honorary society composed of American college students of high scholastic rank: founded 1776.

Phid·i·an (fid′i-ən), *adj.* of or characteristic of Phidias.

Phid·i·as (fid′i-əs), *n.* Greek sculptor of 5th century B.C.

Phi·dip·pi·des (fi-dip′ə-dēz′), *n.* Pheidippides.

phil- (fil), philo-.

-phil (fil), -phile.

Phil., 1. Philippians. 2. Philippine.

phil., philosophy.

Phil·a·del·phi·a (fil′ə-del′fi-ə, fil′ə-del′fyə), *n.* 1. a city in southeastern Pennsylvania, on the Delaware River: pop., 2,003,000 (metropolitan area, 4,343,000). 2. an ancient city in Asia Minor.

Philadelphia lawyer, [Slang], a clever or shrewd lawyer, especially one skilled in the subtleties of legal technicalities: a somewhat opprobrious term connoting unscrupulous behavior.

phi·lan·der (fi-lan′dẽr), *n.* [< Gr. *philandros*, fond of men < *philos*, loving + *anēr, andros*, a man: used in fiction as a name for a lover], [Rare], a man who philanders; philanderer. *v.i.* to engage lightly in passing love affairs; make love insincerely: said of a man.

phi·lan·der·er (fi-lan′dẽr-ẽr), *n.* a man who philanders.

phil·an·throp·ic (fil′ən-throp′ik), *adj.* [Fr. *philanthropique*], of, showing, or constituting philanthropy; charitable; benevolent; generous; humane.

SYN.—**philanthropic** implies interest in the general human welfare, especially as shown in large-scale gifts to charities, the endowment of institutions for human advancement, etc.; **humanitarian** implies more direct concern with promoting the welfare of humanity, especially through reducing pain and suffering; **charitable** implies the giving of money or other help to those in need; **altruistic** implies a putting the welfare of others before one's own interests and therefore stresses freedom from selfishness.

phil·an·throp·i·cal (fil′ən-throp′i-k'l), *adj.* philanthropic.

phi·lan·thro·pist (fi-lan′thrə-pist), *n.* a person who practices philanthropy.

phi·lan·thro·pize (fi-lan′thrə-pīz′), *v.t.* [PHILANTHROPIZED (-pīzd′), PHILANTHROPIZING], to deal with philanthropically. *v.i.* to practice philanthropy.

phi·lan·thro·py (fi-lan′thrə-pi), *n.* [LL. *philanthropia;* Gr. *philanthrōpia* < *philein*, to love + *anthrōpos*, man], 1. a desire to help mankind as indicated by acts of charity, etc.; love of mankind. 2. [*pl.* PHILANTHROPIES (-piz)], something that helps mankind; philanthropic service, act, gift, institution, etc.

phil·a·tel·ic (fil′ə-tel′ik), *adj.* of philately.

phi·lat·e·list (fi-lat′'l-ist), *n.* a person who practices philately; stamp collector.

phi·lat·e·ly (fi-lat′'l-i), *n.* [Fr. *philatélie* < Gr. *philos*, loving + *ateleia*, exemption from (further) tax (i.e., with postage prepaid), taken as equivalent of Fr. *franco*, Eng. *frank;* see FRANK (to send free)], the collection and study of postage stamps, postmarks, stamped envelopes, etc., usually as a hobby.

-phile (fil, fīl), [< Gr. *philos*, loving], a combining form meaning *loving, liking, favorably disposed to,* as in *Anglophile:* also **-phil.**

Phi·le·mon (fi-lē′mən, fī-lē′mən), [L.; Gr. *Philēmōn*, lit., affectionate], a masculine name. *n.* 1. the Epistle to Philemon, a book in the New Testament which was a message from the Apostle Paul to his convert Philemon: abbreviated **Philem.** 2. in *Greek mythology*, an old man who, with his wife, Baucis, shared what little he had with the disguised Zeus and Hermes.

phil·har·mon·ic (fil′här-mon′ik, fil′ẽr-mon′ik), *adj.* [Fr. *philharmonique*, after It. *filharmonico* < Gr. *philos*, loving + *harmonia*, harmony], 1. loving or devoted to music. 2. of or by a philharmonic group or society. *n.* 1. [P-], a society formed to sponsor a symphony orchestra. 2. [P-], [Colloq.], an orchestra or concert sponsored by such a society.

philharmonic pitch, in *music*, the standard pitch, in which middle A has a frequency of 440 vibrations per second: cf. **concert pitch.**

phil·hel·lene (fil-hel′ēn), *n.* [see PHILO- & HELLENE], a friend or supporter of the Greeks.

phil·hel·len·ic (fil′he-len′ik, fil′he-lē′nik), *adj.* friendly toward or supporting the Greeks.

phil·hel·len·ism (fil-hel′ən-iz'm), *n.* friendliness toward or support of the Greeks.

phil·hel·len·ist (fil-hel′ən-ist, fil′he-lē′nist), *n.* a philhellene.

Phil. I., Philippine Islands.

-phil·i·a (fil′i-ə), [< Gr. *philos*, loving], a combining form meaning: 1. *tendency toward*, as in *hemophilia.* 2. *abnormal attraction to*, as in *coprophilia.*

Phil·ip (fil′əp), [L. *Philippus;* Gr. *Philippos*, lit., fond of horses < *philos*, loving + *hippos*, a horse], a masculine name: diminutive, *Phil;* feminine, *Philippa;* equivalents, L. *Philippus*, Fr. *Philippe*, G. *Philipp*, It. *Filippo*, Sp. *Felipe*: also spelled **Phillip.** *n.* 1. one of the twelve Apostles. 2. (Indian name, *Metacomet*), son of Massasoit; ?–1676; chief of the Wampanoag Indians; led a war against the New England colonists: called *King Philip*. Abbreviated **Phil.**

Philip, Prince, 1921– ; Duke of Edinburgh and husband of Elizabeth II of England.

Philip, Saint, an evangelist and deacon of the early Christian church in Jerusalem: his day is June 6.

Philip II, 1. 382–336 B.C.; king of Macedonia (359–336 B.C.); creator of the Macedonian army. 2. 1165–1223; king of France (1180–1223): also called *Philip Augustus.* 3. 1527–1598; king of Spain (1556–1598); sent the Armada against England.

Philip IV, 1268–1314; king of France (1285–1314); laid the foundations of the French monarchy: called *the Fair.*

Philip V, 1683–1746; king of Spain (1700–1746); founder of the House of Bourbon.

Philip Augustus, see **Philip II.**

Phi·lip·pa (fi-lip′ə), [fem. of *Philip*], a feminine name.

Phi·lip·pi (fi-lip′ī), *n.* an ancient city in Macedonia:

scene of two battles (42 B.C.), in which Mark Antony and Octavius defeated Brutus and Cassius.

Phi·lip·pi·an (fi-lip'i-ən), *adj.* of Philippi or its people. *n.* a native or inhabitant of Philippi.

Phi·lip·pi·ans (fi-lip'i-ənz), *n.pl.* [construed as sing.], an Epistle to the Philippians, a book of the New Testament which was a message from the Apostle Paul to the Christians of Philippi: abbreviated **Phil.**

Phi·lip·pic (fi-lip'ik), *n.* [L. *Philippicus;* Gr. *Philippikos,* belonging to Philip < *Philippos,* Philip], 1. any of the orations of Demosthenes against Philip, king of Macedon. 2. [p-], any bitter verbal attack.

Phil·ip·pine (fil'ə-pēn'), *adj.* of the Philippine Islands or their people: abbreviated **Phil.**

Philippine Islands, a group of 7,083 islands in the Pacific, northeast of Borneo, comprising a republic (*Republic of the Philippines*): under the jurisdiction of the United States until 1946, and called the Commonwealth of the Philippines from 1935 to 1946: area, 114,830 sq. mi.; pop., 27,456,000; capital, Quezon City: abbreviated **P.I., Phil. I.**

PHILIPPINE ISLANDS

Phil·ip·pines (fil'ə-pēnz'), *n.* the Philippine Islands.

Phil·ip·pop·o·lis (fil'ə-pop'ə-lis), *n.* Plovdiv: the Greek name.

Phi·lis·ti·a (fə-lis'ti-ə), *n.* an ancient country on the southern coast of Palestine.

Phi·lis·tine (fə-lis'tin, fil'əs-tēn', fil'əs-tīn'), *n.* [ME., also *Palestine;* LL. *Philistinus,* usually in pl. *Philistini;* Gr. *philistinoi, palaistinoi;* Heb. *p'lishtīm;* akin to Eng. *Palestine*], 1. a member of a non-Semitic people who lived in southwestern Palestine from c. 1200 B.C. on: they repeatedly warred with the Israelites for control of the country. 2. [adapted by Matthew Arnold < G. *Philister*], a person regarded as smugly narrow and conventional in his views and tastes, lacking in and indifferent to cultural and aesthetic values, etc. *adj.* 1. of the ancient Philistines. 2. smugly conventional, lacking in culture, etc.

Phi·lis·tin·ism (fə-lis'tin-iz'm, fil'əs-tin-iz'm), *n.* attitudes, views, etc. characteristic of a Philistine (sense 2).

Phil·lip (fil'əp), a masculine name: see **Philip.**

Phil·lips, Stephen (fil'əps), 1868–1915; English poetic dramatist.

Phillips, Wendell, 1811–1884; American abolitionist and orator.

Phil·lis (fil'is), a feminine name: see **Phyllis.**

phil·o- (fil'ō, fil'ə), [< Gr. *philos,* loving], a combining form meaning *loving, liking, having a predilection for,* as in *philology:* also, **phil-.**

Phil·oc·te·tes (fil'ok-tē'tēz), *n.* in *Greek legend,* the Greek warrior who killed Paris in the Trojan war with one of the poisoned arrows given him by Hercules.

phil·o·den·dron (fil'ə-den'drən), *n.* [Mod. L. < Gr. *philodendros,* loving trees < *philos,* loving + *dendron,* a tree], any of a number of tropical American plants of the arum family, usually climbing, with tough, leathery leaves.

phi·log·y·nist (fi-loj'ə-nist), *n.* [< *philogyny* + *-ist*], a person who loves or is fond of women.

phi·log·y·nous (fi-loj'ə-nəs), *adj.* of or like a philogynist; fond of women.

phi·log·y·ny (fi-loj'ə-ni), *n.* [Gr. *philogynia* < *philein,* to love + *gynē,* woman], love of or fondness for women: opposed to *misogyny.*

Phi·lo Ju·dae·us (fī'lō jōō-dē'əs), ? B.C.– c.50 A.D.; Jewish Platonist philosopher.

phi·lol·o·ger (fi-lol'ə-jẽr), *n.* a philologist.

phil·o·lo·gi·an (fil'ə-lō'ji-ən, fil'ə-lō'jən), *n.* philologist.

phil·o·log·ic (fil'ə-loj'ik), *adj.* philological.

phil·o·log·i·cal (fil'ə-loj'i-k'l), *adj.* of philology.

phi·lol·o·gist (fi-lol'ə-jist), *n.* a person skilled in philology: now generally replaced by *linguist.*

phi·lol·o·gy (fi-lol'ə-ji), *n.* [Fr. *philologie;* L. *philologia,* love of learning; Gr. *philologia,* love of literature < *philein,* to love + *logos,* a word], 1. originally, the love of learning and literature; study; scholarship. 2. the study of written records, especially literary texts, in order to determine their authenticity, meaning, etc. 3. linguistics: a former term. Abbreviated **philol.**

phil·o·mel (fil'ə-mel'), *n.* [ME. *Philomene;* OFr. *philomèle;* L. *Philomela*], [Poetic], the nightingale.

Phil·o·me·la (fil'ə-mē'lə), *n.* [L.; Gr. *Philomēla* < *philein,* to love + *melos,* song], 1. in *Greek mythology,* the daughter of a king of Athens: her sister Procne's husband, Tereus, raped her and tore out her tongue; when, in revenge, the sisters killed his son and fled, the gods changed Philomela into a nightingale, Procne into a swallow, and Tereus into a hawk. 2. [Poetic], a nightingale; philomel.

phil·o·pe·na (fil'ə-pē'nə), *n.* [altered < Fr. *philippine* < G. *Philippchen,* little Philip < *vielliebchen,* lit., sweetheart, pop. name for the joined kernels of nuts, hence the game played with such kernels; dim. < *viel,* much + *lieb,* dear; influenced in Eng. by association with Gr. *philos,* loving & L. *poena,* a penalty, because of the forfeit paid to one of the "friends" playing the game], 1. a nut with two kernels. 2. a game in which the two kernels of a nut are shared by two people, one of whom, if failing to fulfill a given condition, must pay a forfeit to the other. 3. the forfeit, usually a gift.

phil·o·pro·gen·i·tive (fil'ə-prō-jen'ə-tiv), *adj.* [*philo-* + *progenitive*], 1. productive of offspring; prolific. 2. loving offspring, especially one's own. 3. of such love.

philos., philosophy.

phi·los·o·pher (fi-los'ə-fẽr), *n.* [ME. *philosophre, filosophe;* OFr. *philosophe;* L. *philosophus;* Gr. *philosophos* < *philos,* loving + *sophos,* wise], 1. a person who studies or is learned in philosophy. 2. a person who lives and thinks according to a system of philosophy. 3. a person who meets all events, whether favorable or unfavorable, with calmness and composure. 4. [Obs.], an alchemist, magician, etc.

philosophers' (or **philosopher's**) **stone,** an imaginary substance sought for by alchemists in the belief that it would change base metals into gold or silver.

phil·o·soph·ic (fil'ə-sof'ik), *adj.* [L. *philosophicus;* Gr. *philosophikos*], 1. of or according to a philosophy or a philosopher. 2. devoted to or learned in philosophy. 3. like or suited for a philosopher; hence, 4. rational; sensibly composed; calm, as in a difficult situation.

phil·o·soph·i·cal (fil'ə-sof'i-k'l), *adj.* philosophic.

phil·o·soph·i·co- (fil'ə-sof'i-kō, fil'ə-sof'i-kə), a combining form meaning *philosophical and.*

phil·o·soph·i·co-re·li·gious (fil'ə-sof'i-kō-rə-lij'əs), *adj.* philosophical and religious.

phi·los·o·phism (fi-los'ə-fiz'm), *n.* [Fr. *philosophisme* < *philosophe*], 1. false or faulty philosophy; sophistry. 2. a philosophic proposition intended to deceive.

phi·los·o·phize (fi-los'ə-fīz'), *v.i.* [PHILOSOPHIZED (-fīzd'), PHILOSOPHIZING], to deal philosophically with abstract matter; think or reason like a philosopher.

phi·los·o·phy (fi-los'ə-fi), *n.* [*pl.* PHILOSOPHIES (-fiz)], [ME. & OFr. *philosophie;* L. *philosophia;* Gr. *philosophia* < *philosophos;* see PHILOSOPHER], 1. originally, love of wisdom or knowledge. 2. a study of the processes governing thought and conduct; theory or investigation of the principles or laws that regulate the universe and underlie all knowledge and reality: included in the study are aesthetics, ethics, logic, metaphysics, etc. 3. the general principles or laws of a field of knowledge, activity, etc.: as, the *philosophy* of economics. 4. *a)* a particular system of principles for the conduct of life. *b)* a treatise covering such a system. 5. a study of human morals, character, and behavior; hence, 6. the mental balance believed to result from this; calmness; composure. Abbreviated **phil., philos.**

-phi·lous (fi-ləs), [< Gr. *philos,* loving; + *-ous*], a combining form meaning *loving, liking,* as in *photophilous.*

Phil. Sp., Philippine Spanish.

phil·ter (fil'tẽr), *n.* [Fr. *philtre;* L. *philtrum;* Gr. *philtron* < *philein,* to love], 1. a potion or charm thought to cause a person to fall in love. 2. any magic potion. *v.t.* to charm or bewitch with a philter.

phil·tre (fil'tẽr), *n.* & *v.t.* [PHILTRED (-tẽrd), PHILTRING], philter.

phi·mo·sis (fī-mō'sis), *n.* [Mod. L.; Gr. *phimōsis,* a muzzling < *phimos,* a muzzle], 1. an abnormal condition in which the foreskin of the penis is so tight as to prevent its being drawn back over the glans. 2. a similar condition of the clitoris.

Phin·e·as (fin'i-əs), [LL. *Phinees;* Gr. *Phinees;* Heb. *pīnĕhās;* prob. < Egypt. *pe-neḥase*], a masculine name.

phiz (fiz), *n.* [contr. < *physiognomy*], [Slang], a face or facial expression.

phle·bit·ic (fli-bit'ik), *adj.* of or having phlebitis.

phle·bi·tis (fli-bī'tis), *n.* [*phleb-* + *-itis*], inflammation of a vein or veins.

phleb·o- (fleb'ō, fleb'ə), [< Gr. *phleps, phlebos,* a vein], a combining form meaning *vein,* as in *phlebotomy:* also, before a vowel, **phleb-.**

phleb·o·scle·ro·sis (fleb'ō-skli-rō'sis), *n.* [*phlebo-* + *sclerosis*], hardening of the walls of a vein or veins.

phle·bot·o·mist (fli-bot'ə-mist), *n.* a practitioner of or believer in phlebotomy.

phle·bot·o·mize (fli-bot'ə-mīz'), *v.t.* & *v.i.* [PHLEBOTOMIZED (-mīzd'), PHLEBOTOMIZING], to practice phlebotomy (on).

phle·bot·o·my (fli-bot'ə-mi), *n.* [ME. *flebotomie;* OFr. *flebothomie;* LL. *phlebotomia;* Gr. *phlebotomia* < *phleps, phlebos,* a vein + *temnein,* to cut], the formerly common act or practice of bloodletting as a therapeutic measure.

Phleg·e·thon (fleg′ə-thon, flej′ə-thon), *n.* [L.; Gr. *Phlegethōn*, orig. ppr. of *phlegethein*, to flame, blaze], in *Greek mythology*, a river of fire in Hades.

phlegm (flem), *n.* [ME. & OFr. *fleume;* LL. *phlegma*, clammy humor of the body; Gr. *phlegma*, inflammation, hence, humors caused by inflammation < *phlegein*, to burn], 1. the thick, stringy mucus secreted by the mucous glands of the respiratory tract and discharged from the throat, as during a cold. 2. in *early physiology*, that one of the four humors of the body which was believed to cause sluggishness or dullness; hence, 3. *a)* sluggishness; apathy. *b)* calmness; equanimity.

phleg·mat·ic (fleg-mat′ik), *adj.* [ME. & OFr. *fleumatike;* LL. *phlegmaticus;* Gr. *phlegmatikos* < *phlegma;* see PHLEGM], 1. hard to rouse to action; specifically, *a)* sluggish; dull; apathetic. *b)* calm; cool; imperturbable. 2. [Obs.], of, like, or producing the humor phlegm. — *SYN.* see **impassive.**

phleg·mat·i·cal (fleg-mat′i-k'l), *adj.* phlegmatic.

phlegm·y (flem′i), *adj.* 1. of, like, containing, or characterized by phlegm. 2. [Rare], phlegmatic.

phlo·em, phlo·ëm (flō′em), *n.* [G. < Gr. *phloos*, the bark], the cell tissue serving as a path for the distribution of food material in a plant; bast.

phlo·gis·tic (flō-jis′tik), *adj.* [< Gr. *phlogistos*, inflammable], 1. of phlogiston. 2. [Obs.], fiery; flaming. 3. in *medicine*, inflammatory; of inflammation.

phlo·gis·ton (flō-jis′ton, flō-jis′tən), *n.* [Mod. L. < Gr. *phlogistos* < *phlogizein*, to burn, inflame < *phlegein*, to burn], an imaginary element formerly believed to cause combustion and to be given off by anything burning; matter or principle of fire.

phlog·o·pite (flog′ə-pīt′), *n.* [< Gr. *phlogōpos*, fiery (< *phlox*, a flame + *ōps*, a face); + *-ite*], a kind of magnesium mica, usually light brown in color.

phlo·go·sis (flə-gō′sis), *n.* [Mod. L.; Gr. *phlogōsis*, burning heat < *phlox*, *phlogos*, a flame], [Now Rare], inflammation, especially of the skin; erysipelas.

phlo·got·ic (flə-got′ik), *adj.* [Now Rare], of or having phlogosis.

phlo·rhi·zin (flə-rē′zin), *n.* phlorizin.

phlo·rid·zin (flə-rid′zin), *n.* phlorizin.

phlor·i·zin (flôr′ə-zin, flə-rī′zin), *n.* [< Gr. *phloios*, *phloos*, a bark + *rhiza*, a root; + *-in*], a bitter, white, crystalline substance, $C_{21}H_{24}O_{10}$, found in the root bark of the apple, pear, plum, and cherry trees: used in medicine as a tonic and to combat periodic fevers, as in malaria.

phlox (floks), *n.* [L., a flower, flame; Gr. *phlox*, a flame < *phlegein*, to burn: from the appearance of the flowers], any of a number of related plants with small leaves and clusters of red, pink, violet, blue, or white flowers.

phlyc·tae·na (flik-tē′nə), *n.* [*pl.* PHLYCTAENAE (-nē)], a phlyctena.

phlyc·te·na (flik-tē′nə), *n.* [*pl.* PHLYCTENAE (-nē)], [Mod. L.; Gr. *phlyktaina*, a blister < *phlyein*, to swell], a small blister or pustule.

-phobe (fōb), [Fr.; L. *-phobus;* Gr. *-phobos* < *phobos*, a fear], a combining form, used in forming adjectives and nouns, meaning *fearing* or *hating*, as in *Francophobe.*

pho·bi·a (fō′bi-ə), *n.* [Mod. L. < Gr. *phobos*, a fear], an irrational, excessive, and persistent fear of some particular thing or situation.

-pho·bi·a (fō′bi-ə), [Gr. *-phobia* < *phobos*, a fear, flight], a combining form meaning *fear, dread, hatred*, as in *claustrophobia, Anglophobia.*

pho·bic (fō′bik, fob′ik), *adj.* of, like, or constituting a phobia.

Pho·cae·a (fō-sē′ə), *n.* an ancient Ionian city in Asia Minor.

pho·cine (fō′sīn, fō′sin), *adj.* [< L. *phoca*, a seal; + *-ine*], in *zoology*, of or relating to the seals.

Pho·ci·on (fō′shi-on′, fō′shi-ən), *n.* Athenian statesman and general; lived 402?–317 B.C.

Pho·cis (fō′sis), *n.* an ancient region in central Greece, on the Gulf of Corinth.

Phoe·be (fē′bi), [L.; Gr. *Phoibē*, fem. of *Phoibos;* see PHOEBUS], a feminine name: also spelled **Phebe.** *n.* 1. in *Greek mythology*, Artemis, goddess of the moon: identified by the Romans with Diana. 2. [Poetic], the moon.

phoe·be (fē′bi), *n.* [echoic; sp. influenced by *Phoebe*], a small bird, one of the flycatchers, with a greenish-brown back, light-yellow breast, and a short crest: also called *pewit, pewee.*

Phoe·bus (fē′bəs), *n.* [ME. *Phebus;* L.; Gr. *Phoibos*, bright one < *phoibos*, bright], 1. in *Greek mythology*, Apollo, god of the sun. 2. [Poetic], the sun.

Phoe·ni·ci·a (fə-nish′ə, fə-nish′i-ə, fə-nē′shə), *n.* an ancient kingdom on the Mediterranean in the region of modern Syria and Palestine: also spelled **Phenicia:** see **Israel,** map.

Phoe·ni·cian (fi-nish′ən, fə-nē′shən), *adj.* of Phoenicia, its people, their language, or culture. *n.* 1. a native of Phoenicia: the Phoenicians were famous as navigators and traders. 2. the extinct Northwest Semitic language of the Phoenicians, closely related to Moabite and Hebrew. Abbreviated **Phoen.**

Phoe·nix (fē′niks), *n.* the capital of Arizona, on the Salt River: pop., 439,000.

phoe·nix (fē′niks), *n.* [altered (after L.) < AS. & OFr. *fenix;* ML. *phenix;* L. *phoenix;* Gr. *phoinix*], 1. in *Egyptian mythology*, a beautiful, lone bird which lived in the Arabian desert for 500 or 600 years and then consumed itself in fire, rising renewed from the ashes to start another long life: it is used as a symbol of immortality. 2. [P-], in *astronomy*, a southern constellation: see **constellation,** chart. Also spelled **phenix.**

phon- (fōn), phono-.

phon., phonetics.

pho·nate (fō′nāt), *v.i.* [PHONATED (-id), PHONATING], [Gr. *phōnē*, a voice; + *-ate*], to utter a voiced sound; vocalize.

pho·na·tion (fō-nā′shən), *n.* the act of phonating.

phon·au·to·graph (fōn-ô′tə-graf′, fōn-ô′tə-gräf′), *n.* [*phon-* + *auto-* + *-graph*], 1. an instrument which makes a graphic record of the vibrations set up by a sound. 2. a record or graph so made.

phone (fōn), *n.* [Gr. *phōnē*, a sound, voice], any single speech sound: a phoneme is composed of various *phones.*

phone (fōn), *n., v.t. & v.i.* [PHONED (fōnd), PHONING], [abbrev. of *telephone*], [Colloq.], telephone.

-phone (fōn), [< Gr. *phōnē*, a sound, voice], a combining form meaning *producing*, or *connected with, sound*, as in *saxophone, megaphone.*

pho·neme (fō′nēm), *n.* [Fr. *phonème;* Gr. *phōnēma*, a sound < *phōnē*, a voice], in *linguistics*, a class, or family, of closely related speech sounds (*phones*) regarded as a single sound and represented in phonetic transcription by the same symbol, as the sounds of *r* in *bring, red,* and *round:* the discernible phonetic differences between such sounds are due to the modifying influence of the adjacent sounds.

pho·ne·mic (fō-nē′mik), *adj.* 1. of or based on phonemes: as, a *phonemic* analysis of the sounds of a language. 2. of phonemics.

pho·ne·mi·cist (fō-nē′mə-sist), *n.* an expert in phonemics.

pho·ne·mics (fō-nē′miks), *n.pl.* [construed as sing.], the branch of language study dealing with the phonemic system of a particular language.

pho·net·ic (fə-net′ik, fō-net′ik), *adj.* [Mod. L. *phoneticus;* Gr. *phōnētikos* < *phōnētos*, to be spoken < *phōnein*, to speak < *phōnē*, a sound], 1. of speech sounds or the production or recording of these. 2. of phonetics. 3. conforming to pronunciation: as, *phonetic* spelling.

pho·net·i·cal·ly (fə-net′i-k'l-i, fō-net′ik-li), *adv.* in accordance with the principles of phonetics; so as to represent the sounds of speech.

pho·ne·ti·cian (fō′nə-tish′ən), *n.* an expert in phonetics.

pho·net·i·cist (fə-net′ə-sist, fō-net′ə-sist), *n.* a phonetist.

pho·net·ics (fə-net′iks, fō-net′iks), *n.pl.* [construed as sing.], [see PHONETIC], 1. the branch of language study dealing with speech sounds, their production and combination, and their representation by written symbols. 2. the phonetic system of a particular language. Abbreviated **phon., phonet.**

pho·ne·tist (fō′nə-tist), *n.* [< Gr. *phōnētos*, to be spoken < *phōnē*, a voice; + *-ist*], 1. a phonetician. 2. a person who advocates or uses a system of phonetic spelling.

pho·ney (fō′ni), *adj. & n.* [Slang], phony.

-pho·ni·a (fō′ni-ə), -phony.

phon·ic (fon′ik, fō′nik), *adj.* [< Gr. *phōnē*, a voice; + *-ic*], 1. of, or having the nature of, sound; especially, of speech sounds. 2. [Rare], voiced; sonant.

phon·ics (fon′iks, fō′niks), *n.pl.* [construed as sing.], [< *phonic*], 1. the science of sound; acoustics. 2. [Rare], phonetics. 3. the use of elementary phonetics in teaching beginners to read or enunciate.

pho·no- (fō′nō, fō′nə), [< Gr. *phōnē*, a sound, voice], a combining form meaning *sound, tone, speech*, as in *phonology:* also, before a vowel, **phon-.**

pho·no·gram (fō′nə-gram′), *n.* [*phono-* + *-gram*], 1. a sign or symbol representing a word, syllable, or sound, as in shorthand. 2. [Now Rare], a phonograph record.

pho·no·gram·ic, pho·no·gram·mic (fō′nə-gram′ik), *adj.* of or by a phonogram or phonograms.

pho·no·graph (fō′nə-graf′, fō′nə-gräf′), *n.* [*phono-* + *-graph*], an instrument that records or, especially, reproduces sound from tracings made on a flat disk or, formerly, a cylinder: cf. **record.**

pho·no·graph·ic (fō′nə-graf′ik), *adj.* 1. of a phonograph or the sounds made by one. 2. of phonography.

pho·no·graph·i·cal·ly (fō′nə-graf′i-k'l-i, fō′nə-graf′ik-li), *adv.* 1. in a phonographic manner. 2. by means of a phonograph.

pho·nog·ra·phy (fō-nog′rə-fi), *n.* [*phono-* + *-graphy*], 1. a written or printed representation of the sounds of speech; phonetic spelling or transcription. 2. any system of shorthand based on a phonetic transcription of speech; especially, the system invented by Isaac Pitman (1813–1897). 3. the use of a phonograph in recording or reproducing sound. Abbreviated **phonog.**

pho·no·lite (fō′nə-līt′), *n.* [*phono-* + *-lite*], a fine-grained igneous rock consisting chiefly of alkali feldspar and nephelite: it rings when struck: also called *clinkstone.*

pho·no·lit·ic (fō′nə-lit′ik), *adj.* of or like phonolite.

pho·no·log·ic (fō′nə-loj′ik), *adj.* phonological.

pho·no·log·i·cal (fō'nə-loj'i-k'l), *adj.* of phonology; in accordance with the principles of phonology.
pho·nol·o·gist (fō-nol'ə-jist), *n.* an expert in phonology; phonemicist or phonetician.
pho·nol·o·gy (fō-nol'ə-ji), *n.* [*phono-* + *-logy*], 1. *a*) phonetics. *b*) phonemics. *c*) phonetics and phonemics. 2. the study of the evolution of speech sounds, especially from one status to another within a particular language.
pho·nom·e·ter (fō-nom'ə-tẽr), *n.* [*phono-* + *-meter*], an instrument used to measure the intensity and vibration frequency of sound.
pho·no·scope (fō'nə-skōp'), *n.* [*phono-* + *-scope*], an instrument used to observe or exhibit the properties of a sounding body; especially, such an instrument for testing the quality of strings for musical instruments.
pho·no·type (fō'nə-tip'), *n.* [*phono-* + *-type*], a phonetic symbol or character, as used in printing.
pho·no·typ·y (fō'nə-tī'pi), *n.* [< *phonotype*], a system of phonetic writing, as some systems of shorthand.
pho·ny (fō'ni), *adj.* [PHONIER (-ni-ẽr), PHONIEST (-ni-ist)], [said to be altered < *Forney*, cheap jewelry < *Forney rings*, brass rings made by a manufacturer named *Forney* for sale by street peddlers], [Slang], not genuine; false; counterfeit; spurious; fake; sham. *n.* [*pl.* PHONIES (-niz)], [Slang], 1. something not genuine; sham; fake. 2. a person who pretends to be what he is not; charlatan; impostor. Also spelled **phoney.**
-pho·ny (fō'ni, fə-ni), [< Gr. *phōnē*, a sound, voice], a combining form meaning *a* (specified kind of) *sound*, as in *cacophony:* also **-phonia.**
-phore (fôr, fōr), [Mod. L. *-phorus, -phorum;* Gr. *-phoros, -phoron* < *pherein*, to bear], a combining form meaning *bearer, producer*, as in *carpophore.*
-phor·ous (fôr'əs, fō'rəs), [Mod. L. *-phorus;* Gr. *-phoros* < *pherein*, to bear], a combining form meaning *bearing, producing.*
phos·gene (fos'jēn), *n.* [< Gr. *phōs*, a light; + *-gene* (for *-gen*)], carbonyl chloride, $COCl_2$, a colorless gas formed by the reaction of carbon monoxide and chlorine in the sunlight: used in making dyes and other organic compounds, and as a lung irritant in warfare.
phos·ge·nite (fos'jə-nīt'), *n.* [< *phosgene* + *-ite*], a grayish mineral, $Pb_2Cl_2CO_3$, composed of carbonate and chloride of lead, and occurring in tetragonal crystals.
phosph-, phospho-.
phos·pha·tase (fos'fə-tās'), *n.* [< *phosphate* + *-ase*], any of various enzymes found in body tissues and fluids that split the phosphate-carbohydrate compounds.
phos·phate (fos'fāt), *n.* [Fr.; see PHOSPHORUS & -ATE], 1. a salt or ester of phosphoric acid. 2. any substance containing phosphates, used as a fertilizer. 3. a soft drink made with soda water, sirup, and a few drops of phosphoric acid.
phos·phat·ic (fos-fat'ik), *adj.* of or containing phosphoric acid or phosphates.
phos·pha·tize (fos'fə-tīz'), *v.t.* [PHOSPHATIZED (-tīzd'), PHOSPHATIZING], to change into, or treat with, a phosphate or phosphates.
phos·pha·tu·ri·a (fos'fə-tyoor'i-ə), *n.* [Mod. L.; see PHOSPHATE & -URIA], an excess of phosphates in the urine.
phos·pha·tu·ric (fos'fə-tyoor'ik), *adj.* of or characterized by phosphaturia.
phos·phene (fos'fēn), *n.* [< Gr. *phōs*, a light + *phainein*, to show], a bright visual image produced by mechanical stimulation of the retina, as by pressure on the eyeball through the closed eyelids.
phos·phid (fos'fid), *n.* phosphide.
phos·phide (fos'fīd, fos'fid), *n.* a compound consisting of trivalent phosphorus with another element or a radical.
phos·phin (fos'fin), *n.* phosphine.
phos·phine (fos'fēn, fos'fin), *n.* [*phosph-* + *-ine*], 1. hydrogen phosphide, PH_3, a colorless, poisonous gas with a garliclike odor. 2. a synthetic yellow dye.
phos·phite (fos'fīt), *n.* [Fr.; see PHOSPH- & -ITE], a salt or ester of phosphorous acid.
phos·pho- (fos'fō, fos'fə), [< *phosphorus*], a combining form meaning *phosphorus*, as in *phosphoprotein:* also, before a vowel, **phosph-.**
phos·pho·ni·um (fos-fō'ni-əm), *n.* [Mod. L.; *phosph-* + *ammonium*], the monovalent radical PH_4, which is related to PH_3 as the ammonium radical NH_4 is related to NH_3.
phos·pho·pro·te·in (fos'fō-prō'tē-in), *n.* any of a group of proteins in which the protein molecule is combined with some phosphorous compound other than lecithin or a nucleic acid, as casein of milk.
phos·phor (fos'fẽr), *n.* [L. *Phosphorus;* see PHOSPHORUS], 1. [P-], [Poetic], the morning star, especially Venus. 2. [Archaic & Poetic], phosphorus or any other phosphorescent substance. 3. in *physics*, any substance that gives off light when subjected to radiation. *adj.* [Rare], phosphorescent.
phos·pho·rate (fos'fə-rāt'), *v.t.* [PHOSPHORATED (-id), PHOSPHORATING], [< *phosphorus* + *-ate*], to combine or impregnate with phosphorus.
phos·phore (fos'fôr, fos'fōr), *n.* phosphor.
phos·pho·resce (fos'fə-res'), *v.i.* [PHOSPHORESCED (-rest'), PHOSPHORESCING], [< *phosphorus* + *-esce*], to give off light without noticeable heat or combustion; gleam or shine, as phosphorus in the dark.
phos·pho·res·cence (fos'fə-res''ns), *n.* [< *phosphorus* + *-escence*], 1. the condition or property of giving off light without noticeable heat or combustion, as shown by phosphorus, decayed wood, etc. 2. such a light.
phos·pho·res·cent (fos'fə-res''nt), *adj.* showing phosphorescence.
phos·pho·ret·ed, phos·pho·ret·ted (fos'fə-ret'id), *adj.* combined or impregnated with phosphorus: also **phosphureted, phosphuretted.**
phos·phor·ic (fos-fôr'ik, fos-for'ik, fos-fō'rik), *adj.* [Fr. *phosphorique*], 1. of, like, or containing phosphorus, especially with a valence of five. 2. designating any of three oxygen acids of phosphorus, especially orthophosphoric acid, H_3PO_4, a colorless crystalline acid, soluble in water and used as a reagent.
phos·pho·rism (fos'fə-riz'm), *n.* chronic phosphorus poisoning.
phos·pho·rite (fos'fə-rīt'), *n.* 1. a fibrous variety of apatite. 2. any mineral phosphate used as fertilizer.
phos·pho·ro- (fos'fẽr-ō, fos'fẽr-ə), a combining form meaning *phosphorus* or *phosphorescence*, as in *phosphoroscope:* also, before a vowel, **phosphor-.**
phos·phor·o·scope (fos-fôr'ə-skōp', fos-for'ə-skōp'), *n.* [*phosphoro-* + *-scope*], a device used in observing and measuring the persistence of phosphorescence after the source of light has been removed.
phos·pho·rous (fos'fẽr-əs, fos-fôr'əs, fos-fō'rəs), *adj.* [< *phosphorus* + *-ous*], 1. [Rare], phosphorescent. 2. [Fr. *phosphoreux*], of, like, or containing phosphorus, especially with a valence of three. 3. designating a white or yellowish, crystalline acid, H_3PO_3, that absorbs oxygen readily: used as a chemical reducing agent.
phos·pho·rus (fos'fẽr-əs), *n.* [*pl.* PHOSPHORI (-fə-rī')], [Mod. L.; L. *Phosphorus*, morning star; Gr. *phōsphoros*, bringer of light < *phōs*, a light + *pherein*, to bear], 1. any phosphorescent substance or object. 2. a nonmetallic chemical element, normally a white, phosphorescent, waxy solid, becoming yellow when exposed to light: it is poisonous and unites easily with oxygen so that it ignites spontaneously at room temperature: when heated in sealed tubes it is converted into a red form which is nonpoisonous, and less inflammable than the white: when heated under a pressure of 15,000 atmospheres it is converted into a black powder: symbol, P; at. wt., 30.98; at. no., 15.
phos·phu·ret·ed, phos·phu·ret·ted (fos'fyoo-ret'id), *adj.* phosphoreted.
phot (fot, fōt), *n.* [< Gr. *phōs, phōtos*, a light], the C.G.S. unit of illumination, equal to one lumen per square centimeter, or the direct illumination produced by a uniform point source of one international foot-candle upon a surface one centimeter distant.
phot., 1. photograph. 2. photographer. 3. photographic. 4. photography.
pho·tic (fō'tik), *adj.* [< Gr. *phōs, phōtos*, a light; + *-ic*], 1. of light. 2. in *biology*, having to do with the effect of light upon, or the production of light by, organisms.
pho·tics (fō'tiks), *n.pl.* [construed as sing.], [see PHOTIC], the science of light.
pho·to (fō'tō), *n.* [*pl.* PHOTOS (-tōz)], [contr. of *photograph*], [Colloq.], a photograph.
pho·to- (fō'tō, fō'tə), [< Gr. *phōs, phōtos*, a light], a combining form meaning: 1. *of or produced by light*, as in *photograph, photosynthesis.* 2. *of a photograph or photography*, as in *photoplay, photomontage.*
pho·to·ac·tin·ic (fō'tō-ak-tin'ik), *adj.* [*photo-* + *actinic*], that can produce actinic effect, as ultraviolet rays.
pho·to·bi·ot·ic (fō'tō-bī-ot'ik), *adj.* [< *photo-* + Gr. *bios*, life], in *biology*, dependent upon light for existence.
pho·to·cell (fō'tə-sel'), *n.* a photoelectric cell.
pho·to·chem·i·cal (fō'tə-kem'ə-k'l), *adj.* [*photo-* + *chemical*], of or resulting from the chemical action of light.
pho·to·chem·is·try (fō'tō-kem'is-tri), *n.* [*photo-* + *chemistry*], the branch of chemistry having to do with the effect of light or other radiant energy in producing chemical action, as in photography.
pho·to·chro·my (fō'tə-krō'mi), *n.* [< *photo* + Gr. *chrōma*, a color], color photography.
pho·to·chron·o·graph (fō'tə-kron'ə-graf', fō'tə-kron'ə-gräf'), *n.* [*photo-* + *chrono-* + *-graph*], 1. an instrument that records motion, as of a bird, in a series of photographs taken at regular, extremely brief, intervals. 2. a photograph so taken. 3. in *physics*, an instrument for recording the exact time of an event by exposing a moving photographic plate to the tracing of a thin beam of light synchronized with the event.

pho·to·dis·in·te·gra·tion (fō'tō-dis-in'tə-grā'shən), *n.* [*photo-* + *disintegration*], in *physics*, the breaking down of the nucleus of an atom by the action of radiant energy.

pho·to·dra·ma (fō'tə-drä'mə, fō'tə-dram'ə), *n.* a photoplay.

pho·to·dy·nam·ics (fō'tō-dī-nam'iks), *n.pl.* [construed as sing.], [*photo-* + *dynamics*], 1. the effect of light on living organisms, as in causing phototropism. 2. the science dealing with this.

pho·to·e·lec·tric (fō'tō-i-lek'trik), *adj.* [*photo-* + *electric*], of or having to do with the electric effects produced by light, especially as in the emission of electrons by certain substances when subjected to light or radiation of suitable wave length.

photoelectric cell, any device in which light controls the electron emission from a cathode, the electrical resistance of an element, or the electromotive force produced by a cell: it is usually incorporated in an electric circuit and used in controlling mechanical devices, as for opening doors: also called *electric eye.*

pho·to·e·lec·tro·type (fō'tō-i-lek'trə-tīp'), *n.* an electrotype plate made by a photographic process.

photoeng., photoengraving.

pho·to·en·grave (fō'tō-in-grāv'), *v.t.* [PHOTOENGRAVED (-grāvd'), PHOTOENGRAVING], to reproduce by the process of photoengraving.

pho·to·en·grav·ing (fō'tō-in-grāv'iŋ), *n.* [*photo-* + *engraving*], 1. a process by which photographs are reproduced on printing plates, especially one in which the reproduction is in relief: opposed to *photogravure.* 2. a plate so made. 3. a print from such a plate.

photo finish, 1. a race finish so close that the winner can be determined only from a photograph of the contestants as they cross the finish lines; hence, 2. any close finish of a game, competition, etc.

pho·to·flash (fō'tə-flash'), *adj.* 1. designating an electric bulb containing oxygen and fine aluminum foil which when lighted gives off a single bright flash of white light: used in photography. 2. *a)* of or for such a bulb. *b)* made with the aid of such a bulb. *n.* a photoflash bulb or photograph.

pho·to·flood (fō'tə-flud'), *adj.* 1. designating an electric bulb of low voltage which when connected to a circuit of standard voltage burns with a sustained intense light: used in photography. 2. *a)* of or for such a bulb. *b)* made with the aid of such a bulb. *n.* a photoflood bulb or photograph.

photog., 1. photograph. 2. photographer. 3. photographic. 4. photography.

pho·to·gel·a·tin (fō'tə-jel'ə-t'n), *adj.* of, designating, or produced by a photographic process in which prints are made from a film of hardened gelatin.

pho·to·gen (fō'tə-jen), *n.* [*photo-* + *-gen*], a light solvent or illuminating oil prepared by the distillation of bituminous shale, coal, etc.

pho·to·gene (fō'tə-jēn'), *n.* photogen.

pho·to·gene (fō'tə-jēn'), *n.* [see PHOTO- & -GEN], an afterimage.

pho·to·gen·ic (fō'tə-jen'ik), *adj.* [*photo-* + *-genic*], 1. [Rare], due to or produced by light. 2. artistically suitable for being photographed, as a person. 3. in *biology*, producing or giving off light; phosphorescent.

pho·to·gen·i·cal·ly (fō'tə-jen'i-k'l-i, fō'tə-jen'ik-li), *adv.* in a photogenic manner.

pho·to·gram·me·try (fō'tə-gram'ə-tri), *n.* [*photogram* (var. of *photograph*, after *telegram*, etc.) + *-metry*], the art or process of surveying or mapping with the help of photographs.

pho·to·graph (fō'tə-graf', fō'tə-gräf'), *n.* [*photo-* + *-graph*], an image or picture made by means of photography: abbreviated **phot., photog.** *v.t.* to take a photograph of. *v.i.* 1. to practice photography. 2. to undergo being photographed, with reference to photogenic qualities: as, she *photographs* well.

pho·tog·ra·pher (fə-tog'rə-fẽr), *n.* a person who takes photographs; especially, one whose occupation is photography: abbreviated **phot., photog.**

pho·to·graph·ic (fō'tə-graf'ik), *adj.* 1. of or like a photograph or photography: as, his *photographic* writing. 2. used in or made by photography, as equipment, records, etc. Abbreviated **phot., photog.**

pho·to·graph·i·cal (fō'tə-graf'i-k'l), *adj.* photographic.

pho·to·graph·i·cal·ly (fō'tə-graf'i-k'l-i, fō'tə-graf'ik-li), *adv.* 1. in a photographic manner. 2. by a photograph or photographs.

pho·tog·ra·phy (fə-tog'rə-fi), *n.* [*photo-* + *-graphy*], the art or process of producing images of objects upon a photosensitive surface by the chemical action of light or other radiant energy: abbreviated **phot., photog.**

pho·to·gra·vure (fō'tō-grə-vyoor', fō'tə-grā'vyoor), *n.* [Fr.; *photo-* + *gravure*, engraving], 1. a photoengraving process by which photographs are reproduced on intaglio printing plates or rolls from which they may be transferred to paper. 2. a print so made, usually with a velvety, satinlike finish.

pho·to·he·li·o·graph (fō'tə-hē'li-ə-graf', fō'tə-hē'li-ə-gräf'), *n.* [*photo-* + *heliograph*], a telescopic camera made especially for photographing the sun.

pho·to·ki·ne·sis (fō'tō-ki-nē'sis, fō'tō-kī-nē'sis), *n.* [Mod. L.; *photo-* + *kinesis*, motion < Gr. *kinēsis* < *kinein*, to move], in *physiology*, movement in response to light.

pho·to·ki·net·ic (fō'tō-ki-net'ik), *adj.* of photokinesis.

pho·to·lith·o·graph (fō'tə-lith'ə-graf', fō'tə-lith'ə-gräf'), *n.* a lithograph produced by photoengraving.

pho·to·lith·o·graph·ic (fō'tə-lith'ə-graf'ik), *adj.* of, like, or produced by photolithography.

pho·to·li·thog·ra·phy (fō'tō-li-thog'rə-fi), *n.* the art or process of making photolithographs.

pho·tol·y·sis (fō-tol'ə-sis), *n.* [Mod. L.; see PHOTO- & -LYSIS], chemical decomposition due to the action of light.

pho·to·lyt·ic (fō'tə-lit'ik), *adj.* of photolysis.

photom., photometry.

pho·to·map (fō'tə-map'), *n.* a map made by piecing together aerial photographs.

pho·to·me·chan·i·cal (fō'tō-mə-kan'i-k'l), *adj.* [*photo-* + *mechanical*], designating or of any process by which prints are made from photographic plates.

pho·tom·e·ter (fō-tom'ə-tẽr), *n.* [*photo-* + *-meter*], an instrument used in measuring the intensity of light, especially in determining the relative intensity of different lights; light meter.

pho·to·met·ric (fō'tə-met'rik), *adj.* of or by photometry or a photometer.

pho·to·met·ri·cal (fō'tə-met'ri-k'l), *adj.* photometric.

pho·tom·e·try (fō-tom'ə-tri), *n.* [Mod. L. *photometria;* see PHOTO- & -METRY], 1. the measurement of the intensity of light. 2. the branch of optics dealing with this. Abbreviated **photom.**

pho·to·mi·cro·graph (fō'tə-mī'krə-graf', fō'tə-mī'krə-gräf'), *n.* [*photo-* + *micro-* + *-graph*], 1. a photograph taken through a microscope. 2. a very small photograph, usually requiring enlargement to bring out the details: usually **microphotograph.**

pho·to·mi·crog·ra·phy (fō'tō-mī-krog'rə-fi), *n.* the process of making photomicrographs.

pho·to·mon·tage (fō'tō-mon-täzh', fō'tō-mōn-täzh'), *n.* montage done in photographs.

pho·to·mu·ral (fō'tə-myoor'əl), *n.* a large photograph used as a mural.

pho·ton (fō'ton), *n.* [< *photo-* + *-on*, as in *electron*], a quantum of light energy, analogous to the electron.

pho·to·neu·tron (fō'tə-nōō'tron, fō'tə-nū'tron), *n.* a neutron given off in the photodisintegration of an atomic nucleus.

pho·to-off·set (fō'tō-ôf'set'), *n.* a method of offset printing in which the pictures or text are photographically transferred to a metal plate from which inked impressions are made on the rubber roller.

pho·toph·i·lous (fō-tof'ə-ləs), *adj.* [*photo-* + *-philous*], in *biology*, thriving in light.

pho·to·pho·bi·a (fō'tə-fō'bi-ə), *n.* [Mod. L.; see PHOTO- & -PHOBIA], 1. an abnormal fear of light. 2. in *medicine*, an abnormal sensitivity to light, especially of the eyes as in measles and certain eye conditions.

pho·to·play (fō'tə-plā'), *n.* [*photo-* + *play*], a play presented in motion pictures; screen play.

pho·to·sen·si·tive (fō'tə-sen'sə-tiv), *adj.* reacting or sensitive to radiant energy, especially to light.

pho·to·spec·tro·scope (fō'tə-spek'trə-skōp'), *n.* an instrument used in making a photographic record of spectra.

pho·to·sphere (fō'tə-sfêr'), *n.* [*photo-* + *sphere*], the white-hot envelope of gas surrounding the sun.

pho·to·stat (fō'tə-stat'), *n.* [*photo-* + *-stat*], 1. a device used in making inexpensive photographic reproductions of printed matter, maps, drawings, etc.: the image is made directly as a positive upon special paper: a trademark (**Photostat**). 2. a reproduction or copy so made. *v.t.* [PHOTOSTATED or PHOTOSTATTED (-id), PHOTOSTATING or PHOTOSTATTING], to make a photostatic copy of.

pho·to·stat·ic (fō'tə-stat'ik), *adj.* of, like, or by a photostat.

pho·to·syn·the·sis (fō'tə-sin'thə-sis), *n.* [Mod. L.; see PHOTO- & SYNTHESIS], the formation of carbohydrates in living plants from water and carbon dioxide, by the action of sunlight on the chlorophyll.

pho·to·syn·thet·ic (fō'tō-sin-thet'ik), *adj.* of or by photosynthesis.

pho·to·tax·is (fō'tə-tak'sis), *n.* [Mod. L.; see PHOTO- & -TAXIS], the movement of an organism in response to stimulus from light.

pho·to·tax·y (fō'tə-tak'si), *n.* phototaxis.

pho·to·tel·e·graph (fō'tə-tel'ə-graf', fō'tə-tel'ə-gräf'), *v.t.* & *v.i.* to send by phototelegraphy. *n.* something sent by phototelegraphy.

pho·to·te·leg·ra·phy (fō'tō-tə-leg'rə-fi), *n.* 1. communication by means of light, as by flashing reflections of the sun's rays. 2. the sending of photograph facsimiles by telegraphy.

pho·to·tel·e·scope (fō'tə-tel'ə-skōp'), *n.* a telescope equipped with a camera and used for photographing the heavenly bodies.

pho·to·ther·a·peu·tic (fō'tə-ther'ə-pū'tik), *adj.* of or by phototherapy.

pho·to·ther·a·peu·tics (fō′tə-ther′ə-pū′tiks), ***n.pl.*** [construed as sing.], phototherapy.
pho·to·ther·a·py (fō′tə-ther′ə-pi), ***n.*** [*photo-* + *therapy*], the treatment of disease, especially of certain skin diseases, by the use of light rays.
pho·to·ther·mic (fō′tə-thũr′mik), ***adj.*** [*photo-* + *thermic*], of both light and heat.
pho·to·ton·ic (fō′tə-ton′ik), ***adj.*** of or by phototonus: as, *phototonic* movement of plants.
pho·tot·o·nus (fō-tot′ə-nəs), ***n.*** [Mod. L.; see PHOTO- & TONE], in *biology*, the state of being responsive to or irritated by exposure to light.
pho·to·trop·ic (fō′tə-trop′ik), ***adj.*** of or by phototropism.
pho·to·trop·i·cal·ly (fō′tə-trop′i-k'l-i, fō′tə-trop′ik-li), ***adv.*** in a phototropic manner.
pho·tot·ro·pism (fō-tot′rə-piz'm), ***n.*** [*photo-* + *tropism*], in *biology*, tropism toward or away from light.
pho·to·tube (fō′tə-tōōb′, fō′tə-tūb′), ***n.*** a photoelectric cell.
pho·to·type (fō′tə-tīp′), ***n.*** [*photo-* + *-type*], 1. a printing block or plate upon which a photograph is reproduced. 2. the process used in producing such a block. 3. a print from such a block.
pho·to·typ·ic (fō′tə-tip′ik), ***adj.*** 1. of or like a phototype. 2. by phototype.
pho·to·ty·pog·ra·phy (fō′tō-tī-pog′rə-fi), ***n.*** any mechanical printing process in which photographs are reproduced in relief for use with type.
pho·to·typ·y (fō′tə-tīp′i, fō-tot′ə-pi), ***n.*** the art or process of making phototypes.
pho·to·vol·ta·ic (fō′tō-vol-tā′ik), ***adj.*** [*photo-* + *voltaic*], photoelectric.
pho·to·zin·cog·ra·phy (fō′tō-ziŋ-kog′rə-fi), ***n.*** [*photo-* + *zincography*], the use of a zinc plate in photoengraving.
phr., phrase.
phras·al (frāz′'l), ***adj.*** of or forming a phrase or phrases.
phrase (frāz), ***n.*** [Fr.; L. *phrasis*, diction; Gr. *phrasis* < *phrazein*, to speak], 1. a manner or style of speech; expression; phraseology. 2. a short, colorful, or forceful expression. 3. a connected series of movements in a formal dance. 4. in *grammar*, a sequence of a few words conveying a single thought or forming a separate part of a sentence but not containing a subject and predicate (cf. **clause**); specifically, in *linguistics*, a group of two or more words that can function as a grammatical structure (e.g., *of mine*, *giving parties*, *fresh milk*). 5. in *music*, a short, distinct part or passage, usually of two, four, or eight measures. ***v.t. & v.i.*** [PHRASED (frāzd), PHRASING], 1. to express in words or in a phrase. 2. in *music*, to mark off or divide (notes) into phrases. Abbreviated **phr.**
phra·se·o·gram (frā′zi-ə-gram′), ***n.*** [< *phrase* + *-gram*], a mark or symbol representing a phrase, as in shorthand.
phra·se·o·graph (frā′zi-ə-graf′, frā′zi-ə-gräf′), ***n.*** a phrase for which there is a phraseogram.
phra·se·o·log·i·cal (frā′zi-ə-loj′i-k'l), ***adj.*** 1. expressing or expressed in phrases. 2. of phraseology.
phra·se·ol·o·gist (frā′zi-ol′ə-jist), ***n.*** 1. a person who deals with, or pays much attention to, phraseology. 2. a person skilled at coining phrases, catchwords, etc.
phra·se·ol·o·gy (frā′zi-ol′ə-ji), ***n.*** [*pl.* PHRASEOLOGIES (-jiz)], [Mod. L. *phraseologia;* see PHRASE & -LOGY], choice or pattern of words; way of speaking or writing; diction.
phras·ing (frāz′iŋ), ***n.*** 1. the act or manner of making phrases; phraseology. 2. a style of making melodic phrases.
phra·try (frā′tri), ***n.*** [*pl.* PHRATRIES (-triz)], [Gr. *phratria* < *phratēr*, brother, akin to L. *frater*, Eng. *brother*], 1. a subdivision of an ancient Greek phyle, or tribe. 2. any of the similar units, as clans, of a primitive tribe.
phren., 1. phrenological. 2. phrenologist. 3. phrenology.
phre·net·ic (fri-net′ik), ***adj.*** [ME. *frenetik;* OFr. *frenetique;* L. *phreneticus;* Gr. *phrenētikos*, mad, suffering with inflammation of the brain], 1. wild; delirious; insane; frenetic. 2. excessively excited; fanatic. ***n.*** a phrenetic person.
phre·net·i·cal (fri-net′i-k'l), ***adj.*** phrenetic.
phren·ic (fren′ik), ***adj.*** [see PHRENO- & -IC], 1. of the diaphragm. 2. of the mind; mental.
phre·nit·ic (fri-nit′ik), ***adj.*** of or having phrenitis.
phre·ni·tis (fri-nī′tis), ***n.*** [L.; Gr. *phrenitis;* see PHRENO- & -ITIS], 1. formerly, inflammation of the brain, with fever and delirium. 2. inflammation of the diaphragm.
phren·o- (fren′ō, fren′ə), [< Gr. *phrēn*, *phrenos*, midriff, also mind, mental capacity (thought by the ancients to reside in the diaphragm)], a combining form meaning *the diaphragm* or *the diaphragm and:* also, before a vowel, **phren-**.
phren·o·log·ic (fren′ə-loj′ik), ***adj.*** phrenological.
phren·o·log·i·cal (fren′ə-loj′i-k'l), ***adj.*** of phrenology: abbreviated **phren., phrenol.**
phre·nol·o·gist (fre-nol′ə-jist, fri-nol′ə-jist), ***n.*** a person who practices phrenology: abbreviated **phren., phrenol.**
phre·nol·o·gy (fre-nol′ə-ji, fri-nol′ə-ji), ***n.*** [*phreno-* (in ancient sense of "mind") + *-logy*], a system by which an analysis of character and of the development of the faculties can allegedly be made by studying the shape and protuberances of the skull: abbreviated **phren., phrenol.**
phren·sy (fren′zi), ***n.*** [*pl.* PHRENSIES (-ziz)], & ***v.t.*** [PHRENSIED (-zid), PHRENSYING], frenzy.
Phryg·i·a (frij′i-ə), ***n.*** an ancient country in central Asia Minor.
Phryg·i·an (frij′i-ən), ***adj.*** of Phrygia, its people, their language, etc. ***n.*** 1. a native or inhabitant of Phrygia. 2. the Indo-Hittite language of the ancient Phrygians, preserved only in fragmentary inscriptions: also **Thraco-Phrygian.**
PHS, P.H.S., Public Health Service.
phthal·ein (thal′ēn, fthal′ē-in), ***n.*** [< *phthalic*], any of a group of synthetic dyes manufactured from phenols and phthalic anhydride.
phthal·ic acid (thal′ik, fthal′ik), [na*phthal*ene + *-ic*], any of three isomeric acids, $C_6H_4(CO_2H)_2$; specifically, orthophthalic acid which is produced by the oxidation of naphthalene and is used in the manufacture of dyes, medicines, phenolphthalein, synthetic perfumes, etc.
phthalic anhydride, a white solid substance, $C_6H_4(CO)_2O$, produced by the oxidation of naphthalene and used to make the phthalein dyes, certain synthetic resins, and other products.
phthal·in (thal′in, fthal′in), ***n.*** [*phthal*ic + *-in*], any of a series of compounds produced by the reduction of the phthaleins.
phthal·o·cy·a·nine (thal′ō-sī′ə-nēn′, fthal′ō-sī′ə-nin), ***n.*** [< *phthalic* + *cyan-* + *-ine*], any of a group of synthetic organic dyes of blue or green.
phthi·o·col (thī′ə-kōl′, thī′ə-kol′), ***n.*** [< *phthisic* + *-ol*, with *-oc-* interpolated], a yellow crystalline pigment, $C_{11}H_8O_3$, extracted from tubercle bacilli found in the body and used to prevent or stop hemorrhage.
phthis·ic (tiz′ik), ***n.*** [ME. *tisik;* OFr. *tisique;* L. *phthisica*, fem. of *phthisicus;* Gr. *phthisikos* < *phthisis;* see PHTHISIS], phthisis. ***adj.*** phthisical.
phthis·i·cal (tiz′i-k'l), ***adj.*** of or having phthisis.
phthis·ick·y (tiz′i-ki), ***adj.*** phthisical.
phthi·sis (thī′sis, fthī′sis), ***n.*** [L.; Gr. *phthisis*, a decay < *phthiein*, to waste away], a wasting away of the body or any of its parts; especially, tuberculosis of the lungs; consumption.
-phy·ce·ae (fī′si-ē′, fis′i-ē′), [Mod. L. < Gr. *phykos*, seaweed], a combining form meaning *seaweed*, used in forming the botanical names of algae.
-phy·ceous (fish′əs), a combining form used to form adjectives derived from nouns ending in *phyceae*.
phy·col·o·gy (fī-kol′ə-ji), ***n.*** [< Gr. *phykos*, seaweed; + *-logy*], the branch of botany dealing with algae; algology.
phy·co·my·ce·tous (fī′kō-mī-sē′təs), ***adj.*** [< Gr. *phykos*, seaweed + *mykēs*, *mykētos*, mushroom, fungus; + *-ous*], of a group of fungi closely resembling the algae.
Phyfe, Duncan (fīf), 1768-1854; American cabinetmaker and furniture designer, born in Scotland.
phy·la (fī′lə), ***n.*** plural of **phylon.**
phy·la (fī′lə), ***n.*** plural of **phylum.**
phy·lac·ter·y (fi-lak′tẽr-i, fə-lak′tri), ***n.*** [*pl.* PHYLACTERIES (-iz, -triz)], [ME. *filaterie;* ML. *philaterium;* LL. *phylacterium;* Gr. *phylaktērion*, a fort < *phylassein*, to defend, guard], 1. a small, leather case holding slips inscribed with scripture passages: one is fastened with leather thongs to the forehead and one to the left arm by men of orthodox Jewish faith during morning prayer: cf. Deut. 11:18. 2. a reminder. 3. something worn as a charm or safeguard.
phy·lax·is (fi-lak′sis), ***n.*** [Mod. L.; Gr. *phylaxis*, a watching, guarding < *phylassein*, to watch, keep guard], in *medicine*, any of the body's natural defenses against infection, as immunity, phagocytosis, etc.

PHYLACTERIES

phy·le (fī′lē), ***n.*** [*pl.* PHYLAE (-lē)], [Mod. L. < Gr. *phylē*, tribe], the largest political subdivision in the ancient Athenian state.
phy·let·ic (fī-let′ik), ***adj.*** [Gr. *phyletikos* < *phyletēs*, tribesman < *phylon*, tribe], in *biology*, of a phylum or subkingdom; racial.
-phyll (fil), [< Gr. *phyllon*, a leaf], a combining form meaning *leaf*, as in *sporophyll*.
Phyl·lis (fil′is), [L.; Gr. *Phyllis*, lit., green leaf, green

bough], a feminine name. *n.* 1. a country maiden in Virgil's *Eclogues;* hence, 2. [Poetic], *a)* any pretty country girl. *b)* a sweetheart. Also spelled **Phillis.**

phyl·lo- (fil'ō, fil'ə), [Gr. *phyllon*, a leaf], a combining form meaning *leaf*, as in *phyllophagous:* also **phyll-.**

phyl·lo·clad (fil'ə-klad'), *n.* phylloclade.

phyl·lo·clade (fil'ə-klād'), *n.* [Mod. L. *phyllocladium* < Gr. *phyllon*, a leaf + *klados*, a branch], a flattened branch or stem functioning as a leaf.

phyl·lode (fil'ōd), *n.* [Fr.; Mod. L. *phyllodium* < Gr. *phyllōdēs*, leaflike < *phyllon*, a leaf + *eidos*, a form], a flat leafstalk that functions as a leaf.

phyl·loid (fil'oid), *adj.* [Mod. L. *phylloides;* see PHYLL- & -OID], leaflike.

phyl·lome (fil'ōm), *n.* [Mod. L. *phylloma;* Gr. *phyllōma*, foliage < *phylloun*, to cover with leaves < *phyllon*, a leaf], in *botany*, a leaf or analogous member.

phyl·lom·ic (fi-lom'ik, fi-lō'mik), *adj.* of a phyllome.

phyl·lo·pod (fil'ə-pod'), *n.* [Mod. L. *Phyllopoda*, name of the group < Gr. *phyllon*, a leaf + *pous, podos*, a foot], any of a number of related crustaceans with leaflike, swimming feet. *adj.* of the phyllopods.

phyl·lop·o·dan (fi-lop'ə-dən), *adj.* & *n.* phyllopod.

phyl·lo·tax·is (fil'ə-tak'sis), *n.* phyllotaxy.

phyl·lo·tax·y (fil'ə-tak'si), *n.* [*phyllo-* + *-taxy*], 1. the arrangement of leaves on a stem. 2. the principles of such arrangement.

-phyl·lous (fil'əs), [see PHYLLO- & -OUS], a combining form meaning *having* (a specified number or kind of) *leaves, leaflets*, etc., as in *heterophyllous.*

phyl·lox·er·a (fil'ək-sêr'ə, fi-lok'sẽr-ə), *n.* [Mod. L. < Gr. *phyllon*, a leaf + *xēros*, dry], any of a number of related plant lice that attack the leaves and roots of certain grapevines, chiefly the European variety.

phy·lo- (fi'lō, fi'lə), [< Gr. *phylon, phylē*, tribe], a combining form meaning *tribe, race, phylum*, etc., as in *phylogeny:* also, before a vowel, **phyl-.**

phy·lo·gen·e·sis (fi'lə-jen'ə-sis), *n.* phylogeny.

phy·lo·ge·net·ic (fi'lō-jə-net'ik), *adj.* of phylogeny.

phy·lo·gen·ic (fi'lə-jen'ik), *adj.* of phylogeny.

phy·log·e·ny (fi-loj'ə-ni), *n.* [*pl.* PHYLOGENIES (-niz)], [G. *phylogenie;* see PHYLO- & -GENY], the racial history or evolutionary development of any plant or animal species.

phy·lon (fi'lon), *n.* [*pl.* PHYLA (-lə)], [Mod. L.; Gr. *phylon*, tribe], in *biology*, a phylum.

phy·lum (fi'ləm), *n.* [*pl.* PHYLA (-lə)], [Mod. L. < Gr. *phylon*, tribe], 1. any of the broad, basic divisions of the plant or animal kingdom. 2. any of the broad, basic divisions of the linguistic families.

-phyre (fir), [Fr. < *porphyre;* see PORPHYRY], a combining form meaning *a porphyritic rock.*

phys., 1. physical. 2. physician. 3. physics. 4. physiological. 5. physiology.

phys. ed., physical education.

phys·ic (fiz'ik), *n.* [ME. *fisike;* OFr. *phisique, phisike;* L. *physica*, natural science; Gr. *physikē* < *physis*, nature < *phyein*, to produce], 1. [Rare], the science of physics. 2. [Archaic], the art or science of healing; medical science. 3. a medicine or remedy, especially a laxative or cathartic. *v.t.* [PHYSICKED (-ikt), PHYSICKING], 1. to dose with medicine, especially with a cathartic; hence, 2. to cause to have a bowel movement. 3. to have a curative effect on; heal; relieve. *SYN.*—**physic** is the general word for anything taken to relieve constipation or to effect a bowel movement; **laxative** and **aperient** are usually used of milder physics of a kind that are ordinarily taken to promote discharge from the bowels, such as mineral oil, agar-agar, certain fruit juices, etc.; **purgative** and **cathartic** apply to stronger physics, such as castor oil, Epsom salts, calomel, etc., that are more drastic in their action.

phys·i·cal (fiz'i-k'l), *adj.* [ME. *phisical*, having to do with medicine; ML. *physicalis* < L. *physica;* see PHYSIC], 1. of nature and all matter; natural; material: opposed to *spiritual, moral, mental.* 2. of natural science or natural philosophy. 3. of or according to the laws of nature: as, the force of gravity is a *physical* fact. 4. of, or produced by the forces of, physics. 5. of the body as opposed to the mind: as, *physical* exercise. Abbreviated **phys.** —*SYN.* see **bodily, material.**

physical chemistry, the branch of chemistry dealing with the physical properties of substances as they relate to the chemical properties and changes.

physical education, instruction in the exercise, care, and hygiene of the human body; especially, a course in gymnastics, athletics, etc., as in a school or college.

physical geography, the study of the features and nature of the earth's surface, atmosphere and climate, distribution of plant and animal life, etc.

phys·i·cal·ly (fiz'i-k'l-i, fiz'ik-li), *adv.* 1. with reference to the laws of nature; materially. 2. with regard to the body; corporeally.

physical science, any of the sciences that deal with inanimate matter or energy, as physics, chemistry, geology, etc.

physical therapy, the treatment of disease, injury, etc. by physical means rather than with drugs, as by massage, infrared or ultraviolet light, electrotherapy, hydrotherapy, heat, or exercise: also called *physiotherapy.*

phy·si·cian (fə-zish'ən), *n.* [ME. & OFr. *fisicien* < L. *physica;* see PHYSIC], 1. a person licensed to practice medicine; doctor of medicine. 2. a general medical practitioner, as distinguished from a surgeon. 3. any person or thing that heals, relieves, or comforts. Abbreviated **phys.**

phys·i·cist (fiz'ə-sist), *n.* an expert in physics.

phys·ics (fiz'iks), *n.pl.* [construed as sing. in senses 1 & 2], [< *physic*], 1. originally, natural science or natural philosophy. 2. the science dealing with the properties, changes, interaction, etc. of matter and energy: physics is subdivided into mechanics, thermodynamics, optics, acoustics, etc. 3. a book or treatise on this. 4. physical properties or processes: as, the *physics* of flight. Abbreviated **phys.**

phys·i·o- (fiz'i-ō, fiz'i-ə), [< Gr. *physis*, nature], a combining form meaning *nature, natural*, as in *physiography:* also, before a vowel, **physi-.**

phys·i·o·crat (fiz'i-ə-krat'), *n.* [Fr. *physiocrate;* see PHYSIO- & -CRAT], a believer in the economic theory that land and its products are the only true wealth and hence the only logical sources of revenue and that freedom of opportunity and trade and security of person and property are essential to prosperity.

phys·i·og·nom·ic (fiz'i-og-nom'ik, fiz'i-ə-nom'ik), *adj.* [ML. *physiognomonicus;* Gr. *physiognōmonikos*], of physiognomy.

phys·i·og·nom·i·cal (fiz'i-og-nom'i-k'l, fiz'i-ə-nom'i-k'l), *adj.* physiognomic.

phys·i·og·no·mist (fiz'i-og'nə-mist, fiz'i-on'ə-mist), *n.* [Fr. *physionomiste* < *physionomie;* see PHYSIOGNOMY], a person who tries to judge character and mental qualities by observing the facial features.

phys·i·og·no·my (fiz'i-og'nə-mi, fiz'i-on'ə-mi), *n.* [ME. *fisonomie;* OFr. *phisonomie;* ML. *physonomia, phisionomia* < Gr. *physiognōmonia* < *physis*, nature + *gnōmōn*, one who knows < base of *gignōskein*, to know], 1. the practice of trying to judge character and mental qualities by observation of bodily, especially facial, features. 2. the face; facial features and expression, especially as supposedly indicative of character. 3. apparent characteristics; outward features or appearance. —*SYN.* see **face.**

phys·i·og·ra·pher (fiz'i-og'rə-fẽr), *n.* a specialist in physiography.

phys·i·o·graph·ic (fiz'i-ə-graf'ik), *adj.* of physiography.

phys·i·o·graph·i·cal (fiz'i-ə-graf'i-k'l), *adj.* physiographic.

phys·i·og·ra·phy (fiz'i-og'rə-fi), *n.* [*physio-* + *-graphy*], 1. a description of the features and phenomena of nature. 2. physical geography. Abbreviated **physiog.**

phys·i·o·log·ic (fiz'i-ə-loj'ik), *adj.* physiological.

phys·i·o·log·i·cal (fiz'i-ə-loj'i-k'l), *adj.* 1. of physiology. 2. characteristic of or promoting normal, or healthy, functioning. Abbreviated **phys., physiol.**

phys·i·o·log·i·cal·ly (fiz'i-ə-loj'i-k'l-i, fiz'i-ə-loj'ik-li), *adv.* 1. according to the principles of physiology. 2. so as to be physiological.

phys·i·ol·o·gist (fiz'i-ol'ə-jist), *n.* a specialist in physiology.

phys·i·ol·o·gy (fiz'-i-ol'ə-ji), *n.* [Fr. *physiologie;* L. *physiologia;* Gr. *physiologia* < *physis*, nature + *logos*, a discourse], 1. the branch of biology dealing with the functions and vital processes of living organisms or their parts and organs. 2. a book or treatise on this subject. 3. the functions and vital processes, collectively (*of* an organism). Distinguished from *anatomy, morphology.* Abbreviated **phys., physiol.**

phys·i·o·ther·a·py (fiz'i-ō-ther'ə-pi), *n.* physical therapy.

phy·sique (fi-zēk'), *n.* [Fr.; see PHYSIC], the structure, constitution, strength, form, or appearance of the body.

phy·so·stig·min (fi'sō-stig'min), *n.* physostigmine.

phy·so·stig·mine (fi'sō-stig'mēn, fi'sō-stig'min), *n.* [< Mod. L. *Physostigma*, name of the genus including the Calabar bean (< Gr. *physan*, to inflate + *stigma*, a prick, spot); + *-ine*], a colorless or pinkish crystalline alkaloid, $C_{15}H_{21}O_2N_3$, extracted from the Calabar bean, used in medicine for stimulating intestinal muscles and for contracting the pupils of the eyes.

phy·sos·to·mous (fi-sos'tə-məs), *adj.* [< Gr. *physa*, bellows; + *-stomous*], in *zoology*, 1. having a tube connecting the air bladder with the digestive tract. 2. of a group of fishes with such an arrangement.

-phyte (fit), [< Gr. *phyton*, a plant; akin to *phyein*, to grow], a combining form meaning *a plant growing in a* (specified) *way or place*, as in *microphyte.*

phy·tin (fi'tin), *n.* [< Gr. *phyton*, a plant; + *-in*], a calcium-magnesium salt derived from the seeds of hemp, sunflowers, peas, beans, etc.

phy·to- (fi'tō, fi'tə), [< Gr. *phyton*, a plant], a combining form meaning *a plant, flora, vegetation*, as in *phytogeography:* also **phyt-.**

phy·to·gen·e·sis (fi'tō-jen'ə-sis), *n.* [*phyto-* + *-genesis*], the history of the development of plants.

phy·to·ge·net·ic (fi'tō-jə-net'ik), *adj.* of or according to phytogenesis.

phy·to·ge·net·i·cal (fi'tō-jə-net'i-k'l), *adj.* phytogenetic.

phy·to·gen·ic (fī'tō-jen'ik), *adj.* 1. of, or largely of, plant origin, as peat or coal. 2. phytogenetic.
phy·tog·e·nous (fī-toj'ə-nəs), *adj.* phytogenic.
phy·tog·e·ny (fī-toj'ə-ni), *n.* phytogenesis.
phy·to·ge·og·ra·phy (fī'tō-ji-og'rə-fi), *n.* [*phyto-* + *geography*], the geography of the distribution of plant life.
phy·tog·ra·phy (fī-tog'rə-fi), *n.* [Mod. L. *phytographia;* see PHYTO- & -GRAPHY], the branch of botany dealing with the description of plants.
phy·to·log·ic (fī'tə-loj'ik), *adj.* of or according to phytology.
phy·to·log·i·cal (fī'tə-loj'i-k'l), *adj.* phytologic.
phy·tol·o·gy (fī-tol'ə-ji), *n.* [Mod. L. *phytologia;* see PHYTO- & -LOGY], [Rare], the study of plants; botany.
phy·toph·a·gous (fī-tof'ə-gəs), *adj.* [*phyto-* + *-phagous*], in *zoology*, eating plants; herbivorous.
pi (pī), *n.* [see PIE, var. sp.], 1. a mixed, disordered collection of printing type; hence, 2. any jumble or mixture. *v.t.* [PIED (pīd), PIEING], to make jumbled or disordered; mix up, as type. Also spelled **pie**.
pi (pī, pē), *n.* [Gr.], 1. the sixteenth letter of the Greek alphabet (Π, π), corresponding to English *P, p:* see **alphabet**, table. 2. the symbol (π) designating the ratio of the circumference of a circle to its diameter: π equals 3.14159265+.
P.I., Philippine Islands.
Pia·cen·za (pyä-chen'tsä), *n.* a city in northern Italy, on the Po River: pop., 79,000 (est. 1947): ancient name, *Placentia*.
pi·ac·u·lar (pī-ak'yoo-lẽr), *adj.* [L. *piacularis* < *piaculum*, expiatory sacrifice < *piare*, to appease, expiate], 1. expiatory; atoning. 2. calling for expiation or atonement; sinful; wicked.
piaffe (pyaf), *v.i.* [PIAFFED (pyaft), PIAFFING], to perform the piaffer.
piaf·fer (pyaf'ẽr), *n.* [substantive use of Fr. *piaffer*, to paw the ground < Pr. *piafá*, to prance; of Gmc. origin], a slow movement in horsemanship in which the animal simultaneously raises one forefoot and the opposite hind foot while standing in place.
pi·a ma·ter (pī'ə mā'tẽr), [ML. < L., lit., pious or gentle mother], the vascular membrane immediately enveloping the brain and spinal chord and surrounded by the arachnoid and dura mater.
pi·a·nis·si·mo (pē'ə-nis'ə-mō'; It. pyä-nēs'sē-mô'), *adj.* & *adv.* [It., superl. of *piano;* see PIANO, *adj.* & *adv.*], in *music*, very soft: a direction to the performer; opposed to *fortissimo*: abbreviated **pp, pp.** *n.* [*pl.* PIANISSIMOS (-mōz'); It. PIANISSIMI (-mē')], a passage to be performed pianissimo.
pi·an·ist (pi-an'ist, pyan'ist, pē'ə-nist), *n.* [Fr. *pianiste;* It. *pianista*], a person who plays the piano.
pi·an·o (pi-an'ō, pyan'ō), *n.* [*pl.* PIANOS (-ōz)], [It., contr. < *pianoforte*], a large, stringed, percussion instrument played from a keyboard, each key of which operates a small, felt-covered hammer that strikes and vibrates a corresponding steel wire: the wires produce tones ranging over seven octaves and are mounted on a harp-shaped frame in a wooden case of various forms: cf. **grand piano, upright piano.**
pi·an·o (pi-ä'nō, pyä'nō), *adj.* & *adv.* [It., soft, smooth < L. *planus*, plain, smooth], in *music*, soft: a direction to the performer: abbreviated **p.** *n.* [*pl.* PIANOS (-nōz)], a passage to be performed piano.
pi·an·o·for·te (pi-an'ə-fôrt', pyan'ə-fōr'ti), *n.* [It. < *piano* (soft) + *forte* (loud)], a piano: abbreviated **pf.**
pi·as·sa·ba, pi·a·sa·ba (pē'ə-sä'bə), *n.* piassava.
pi·as·sa·va, pi·a·sa·va (pē'ə-sä'və), *n.* [Port. *piassaba* < Tupi *piaçâba*], 1. either of two Brazilian palms whose leafstalks yield a stiff, coarse fiber. 2. the fiber.
pi·as·ter, pi·as·tre (pi-as'tẽr), *n.* [Fr. *piastre;* It. & Sp. *piastra*, thin plate of metal, dollar; ult. < L. *emplastrum;* see PLASTER], 1. [Rare], the Spanish dollar. 2. a monetary unit and coin of Turkey and Egypt.
Pia·ve (pyä've), *n.* a small river in northeastern Italy.
pi·az·za (pi-az'ə; It. pyät'tsä), *n.* [It.; L. *platea;* see PLACE], 1. in Italy, an open, public square, especially one surrounded by buildings. 2. a covered gallery or arcade. 3. a large, covered porch; veranda.
pi·broch (pē'brok; Scot. pē'brokh), *n.* [Gael. *piobaireachd*, pipe music < *piobair*, piper < *piob*, a pipe, bagpipe], a piece of music for the bagpipe, consisting of a theme with variations, usually martial in character but sometimes dirgelike.
pi·ca (pī'kə), *n.* [ML., directory, hence prob. applied to the type used in printing it], 1. a size of type, 12 point. This line is in pica. 2. the height of this type, about 1/6 inch: used as a measure.
pi·ca (pī'kə), *n.* [L., magpie], an abnormal craving for certain unnatural foods, as clay or chalk, sometimes occurring in pregnancy, hysteria, and chlorosis.
pic·a·dor (pik'ə-dôr'), *n.* [Sp. < *picar*, to prick < *pica*, a pike], any of the horsemen who irritate the bull by pricking him with a lance at the start of a bullfight.
Pic·ar·dy (pik'ẽr-di), *n.* a former province of northern France, once a part of Flanders.

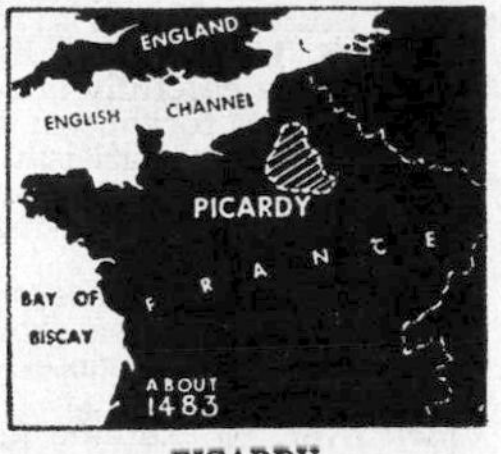

PICARDY

pic·a·resque (pik'ə-resk'), *adj.* [Sp. *picaresco* < *picaro*, a rascal, orig., a Picard], 1. of or dealing with sharp-witted vagabonds and their roguish adventures. 2. designating a style of fiction originating in Spain and having a roguish hero.
pic·a·roon (pik'ə-rōōn'), *n.* [Sp. *picaron* < *picaro*, a rogue], 1. a rogue, adventurer, or thief. 2. a pirate. 3. a pirate ship. *v.i.* to act as a pirate.
Pi·cas·so, Pa·blo (pä'blô pē-kä'sô; Eng. pi-kä'sō), 1881– ; Spanish painter and sculptor in France.
pic·a·yune (pik'i-ūn'), *n.* [Fr. *picaillon*, farthing; Pr. *picaioun, picalhoun*, dim. of *picalho*, money], 1. any coin of small value. 2. anything trivial or worthless. *adj.* trivial; cheap; contemptible.—***SYN.*** see **petty.**
pic·a·yun·ish (pik'i-ūn'ish), *adj.* picayune.
Pic·ca·dil·ly (pik'ə-dil'i), *n.* a fashionable street in London, between Haymarket and Hyde Park Corner.
pic·ca·lil·li (pik'ə-lil'i), *n.* [prob. < *pickle;* formerly also *piccalillo*, etc.], a relish, originally East Indian, of chopped vegetables, mustard, vinegar, and hot spices.
Pic·card, Au·guste (ô'güst' pē'kar'; Eng. pi-kärd'), 1884– ; Swiss physicist; known for balloon ascents into the stratosphere and descents in a bathyscaphe.
Piccard, Jean Fé·lix (zhän fā'lēks'), 1884– ; American chemist and aeronautical engineer, born in Switzerland; twin brother of *Auguste*: he also made balloon ascents.
pic·co·lo (pik'ə-lō'), *n.* [*pl.* PICCOLOS (-lōz')], [It., small], a small instrument of the flute family pitched an octave above the ordinary flute.
pic·co·lo·ist (pik'ə-lō'ist), *n.* a player on the piccolo.
pice (pīs), *n.* [Hind. *paisā*], a small coin of India, equal to 1/4 of an anna.
pic·e·ous (pis'i-əs, pī'si-əs), *adj.* [L. *piceus* < *pix*, pitch], of or like pitch; specifically, *a)* inflammable. *b)* in *zoology*, black as pitch.
pich·i·ci·a·go (pich'i-si-ä'gō, pich'ə-si-ā'gō), *n.* [Sp. *pichiciego* < Guarani *pichey*, little armadillo + Sp. *ciego* (L. *caecus*), blind], a burrowing South American animal, related to the armadillo but smaller.
pick (pik), *v.t.* [var. of *pitch* (to throw)], in *weaving*, to throw (a shuttle); cast. *n.* 1. one passage of, or the blow that drives, the shuttle of a loom. 2. one of the weft threads, or filling yarns.
pick (pik), *n.* [var. of *pike* (weapon)], 1. a heavy, two-headed metal tool used in breaking up soil, rock, etc.: it is long, narrow, and slightly curved, and pointed at one or both ends, with a wooden handle fitted into its center. 2. any of several pointed tools or instruments for picking: usually in combination, as, *icepick*. 3. a small, thin piece of metal, bone, etc., used in plucking the strings of a guitar, banjo, etc.; plectrum.
pick (pik), *v.t.* [ME. *picken* < AS. **pician, pican;* inferred < *picung*, a pricking; akin to & ? influenced by ON. *pikka;* also influenced by OFr. *piquer*, to pierce; cf. PECK], 1. to break up, pierce, or dig up (soil, rock, etc.) with something sharply pointed; use a pick on. 2. to make or form, as a hole, with something pointed. 3. *a)* to dig, probe, or scratch at with the fingers or with something pointed in an attempt to remove, as a scab. *b)* to clear something from (the teeth, etc.) in this way. 4. to remove by pulling with or as with the fingers; specifically, to pluck or gather (flowers, berries, etc.). 5. to clear (something) in this way; specifically, *a)* to prepare (a fowl) by removing the feathers. *b)* to remove the fruit from (a tree). 6. to take up (food, etc.) in small pieces, as a bird with its bill; peck; hence, 7. to eat sparingly or daintily. 8. to pull apart, as fibers, rags, etc. 9. to choose; select; cull. 10. to look for and find excuse or occasion for (a quarrel or fight). 11. to look for purposefully and find: as, *pick* flaws. 12. *a)* to pluck (the strings on a guitar, etc.). *b)* to play (a guitar, etc.) in this way. 13. to open (a lock) with a wire, etc. instead of a key, especially in a stealthy manner. 14. to steal from (one's pocket, purse, etc.). *v.i.* 1. to eat sparingly or in a fussy manner. 2. to thieve or pilfer. 3. to use a pick. 4. to gather berries, flowers, etc. from the plants upon which they grow. 5. to be picked: as, grapes *pick* easily. 6. to select or choose, especially in a careful or fussy manner. *n.* 1. the act of picking; stroke or blow with something pointed. 2. the act of choosing or a thing chosen; choice. 3. the most desirable; best. 4. the amount of a crop picked at one time.—***SYN.*** see **choose.**
pick and choose, to choose or select carefully.
pick apart (or **to pieces**), 1. to separate or tear into many parts. 2. to find flaws in by examining critically.

pick at, 1. to eat small portions of, especially in a dainty or fussy manner. 2. [Colloq.], to nag at; find fault with. 3. to toy or meddle with; finger.
pick off, 1. to remove by picking or plucking. 2. to hit with a carefully aimed shot.
pick on, 1. to choose; select. 2. [Colloq.], to single out for abuse, criticism, etc.; annoy; tease.
pick one's way, to progress slowly, choosing each move with care, as in crossing muddy ground or in painstaking study.
pick out, 1. to choose; select. 2. to single out from or recognize among a group; distinguish. 3. to make out (meaning or sense). 4. to play (a tune) note by note, as on a piano.
pick over, to examine (a number of things) item by item; sort out.
pick up, 1. to break up (soil, etc.) with a pick. 2. to grasp and raise or lift; take up. 3. to get; gain; find; learn, especially by chance or in a casual manner. 4. to stop for and take or bring along. 5. to accelerate; gain speed. 6. to regain (health, power, efficiency, etc.); improve. 7. to bring into range of sight, hearing, radio reception, etc. 8. to make a room, etc. tidy. 9. [Colloq.], to become acquainted with casually or informally, usually for purposes of love-making.

pick·a·back (pik′ə-bak′), ***adv.*** [var. of *pickapack, pickpack,* redupl. of *pack*], on the shoulders or back: as, he carried the child *pickaback.* ***adj.*** designating an airplane which is carried on the take-off by a larger airplane and later released in mid-air. Also **piggyback.**

pick·a·nin·ny (pik′ə-nin′i), ***n.*** [*pl.* PICKANINNIES (-iz)], [dim. < Sp. *pequeño,* little], a Negro baby or child: a patronizing or contemptuous term.

pick·ax (pik′aks′), ***n.*** [altered (after *ax*) < ME. *pikois* OFr. *picquois,* pickax; prob. < *pic,* a pike], a pick with a point at one end of the head and a chisel-like edge at the other; mattock. ***v.t. & v.i.*** to use a pickax (on).

PICKAX

pick·axe (pik′aks′), ***n., v.t. & v.i.*** [PICKAXED (-akst′), PICKAXING], pickax.

picked (pikt), ***adj.*** [< *pick,* to pierce], 1. selected or chosen, especially with care: as, *picked* men. 2. gathered from plants rather than from the ground, as berries, apples, etc. 3. worked over with a pick or mattock.

Pick·ens, Andrew (pik′inz), 1739–1817; American general in the Revolutionary War.

pick·er (pik′ẽr), ***n.*** a person or thing that picks; especially, a machine for picking fibers.

pick·er (pik′ẽr), ***n.*** [< *pick,* to throw], in *weaving,* a device that throws the shuttle through the warp.

pick·er·el (pik′ẽr-əl, pik′rəl), ***n.*** [*pl.* PICKEREL, PICKERELS (-əlz, -rəlz); see **PLURAL,** II, D, 2], [ME. < *pike* (fish) + *-rel,* dim. suffix], any of a number of related, fierce fresh-water fishes of the pike family, especially a small variety with a narrow, pointed snout, projecting lower jaw, and sharp teeth.

pick·er·el·weed (pik′ẽr-əl-wēd′, pik′rəl-wēd′), ***n.*** any of a number of related water plants with large, arrow-shaped leaves and spikes of blue-violet flowers.

Pick·er·ing, Edward Charles (pik′ẽr-iŋ, pik′riŋ), 1846–1919; American physicist and astronomer.

Pickering, William Henry, 1858–1938; brother of *Edward Charles;* American astronomer.

pick·et (pik′it), ***n.*** [Fr. *piquet,* dim. of *pic,* a pike], 1. a stake or slat, usually pointed, used as an upright in a fence, a hitching post for animals, a marker, etc. 2. a group of soldiers or a single soldier used to guard a body of troops from surprise attack: a picket is usually stationed at an outpost. 3. a person, as a member of a labor union on strike, stationed outside a factory, store, public building, etc., often carrying a sign, to demonstrate protest, keep strikebreakers from entering, dissuade people from buying, etc. ***v.t.*** 1. to enclose, shut in, or protect with a picket fence or palisade. 2. to hitch (an animal) to a picket. 3. *a*) to post as a military picket. *b*) to guard (a body of troops) with a picket. 4. to place pickets, or serve as a picket, at (a factory, etc.). ***v.i.*** to serve as a picket (sense 3).

picket fence, a fence made of upright pales or stakes.

picket line, a line or cordon of people serving as pickets.

Pick·ett, George Edward (pik′it), 1825–1875; American Confederate general.

Pick·ford, Mary (pik′fẽrd), (born *Gladys Smith*), 1893– ; American motion-picture actress born in Canada.

pick·ing (pik′iŋ), ***n.*** 1. the act of a person who picks. 2. *usually pl.* something that is or may be picked, or the amount of this; specifically, *a*) small scraps or refuse that may be gleaned. *b*) something got by dishonest or unethical means; spoils; pilferings.

pick·le (pik′'l), ***n.*** [ME. *pikil;* MD. *pekel;* prob. < *pikken,* to prick, prob. in sense "that which pricks, or is piquant"], 1. any brine, vinegar, or spicy solution used to preserve or flavor food. 2. a vegetable, specifically cucumber, preserved in such a solution. 3. a chemical bath used to clear metal of scale, preserve wood, etc. 4. [Colloq.], an awkward or difficult situation; plight. ***v.t.*** [PICKLED (-'ld), PICKLING], to treat with or preserve in a pickle solution. —***SYN.*** see **predicament.**

pick·led (pik′'ld), ***adj.*** [Slang], intoxicated; drunk.

pick·lock (pik′lok′), ***n.*** 1. a person, especially a thief, who picks locks. 2. an instrument for picking locks.

pick-me-up (pik′mi-up′), ***n.*** [Colloq.], an alcoholic drink taken for quick stimulation.

pick·pock·et (pik′pok′it), ***n.*** a person who steals from pockets.

pick·up (pik′up′), ***n.*** 1. the act of picking up, as in fielding a rapidly rolling baseball. 2. the process or power of increasing in speed; acceleration. 3. a small, often open, truck used in collecting and delivering parcels, etc. 4. [Colloq.], a casual or informal acquaintance, as one formed for purposes of love-making. 5. [Colloq.], improvement; recovery, as in trade. 6. [Colloq.], *a*) a stimulant; bracer. *b*) stimulation. 7. *a*) in an electric phonograph, a device that produces audio-frequency currents from the vibrations of the needle moving over the record. *b*) the pivoted arm holding the needle and this device. 8. in *radio & television, a*) the reception of sound or light for conversion into electrical energy in the transmitter. *b*) the apparatus used for this. *c*) any place outside a studio where a broadcast originates. *d*) the electrical system connecting the program from this place to the broadcasting station.

Pick·wick, Mr. (Samuel) (pik′wik), the naive, benevolent president of the Pickwick Club in Dickens' *Pickwick Papers* (1836).

Pick·wick·i·an (pik-wik′i-ən), ***adj.*** 1. of or characteristic of Mr. Pickwick or the Pickwick Club. 2. used with a special or esoteric sense: said of a word or phrase.

pic·nic (pik′nik), ***n.*** [Fr. *piquenique;* prob. redupl. < *piquer,* to pick], 1. a pleasure outing at which a meal is eaten outdoors. 2. [Slang], any pleasant experience. ***v.i.*** [PICNICKED (-nikt), PICNICKING], to hold or attend a picnic.

pic·nick·er (pik′nik-ẽr), ***n.*** a person taking part in a picnic.

Pi·co del·la Mi·ran·do·la, Gio·van·ni (jô-vän′nē pē′kô del′lä mē-rän′dô-lä), Count, 1463–1494; Italian humanist scholar.

pic·o·lin (pik′ə-lin), ***n.*** picoline.

pic·o·line (pik′ə-lēn′, pik′ə-lin), ***n.*** [< L. *pix, picis,* pitch; + *-ol* + *-ine*], any of three isomeric, colorless, strong-smelling, liquid bases, C_6H_7N, found in the oil produced by the distillation of bones and coal, and used in medicine as a nerve sedative.

pi·cot (pē′kō), ***n.*** [*pl.* PICOTS (-kōz)], [Fr., dim. of *pic,* a point, pike], any of a number of small, threadlike loops forming an ornamental edging on lace, ribbon, etc. ***v.t. & v.i.*** [PICOTED (-kōd), PICOTING], to trim or edge with such loops.

pic·o·tee (pik′ə-tē′), ***n.*** [Fr. *picoté, picotée,* pp. of *picoter,* to mark with dots or pricks < *picot;* see **PICOT**], a variety of carnation whose light-colored petals are bordered with another, usually darker, color.

pic·rate (pik′rāt), ***n.*** a salt or ester of picric acid, usually highly explosive.

pic·ric acid (pik′rik), [< Gr. *pikros,* bitter; + *-ic*], a yellow, crystalline, bitter acid, $C_6H_2(NO_2)_3OH$, used in making dyes and explosives.

pic·rite (pik′rīt), ***n.*** [*picr-* + *-ite:* so named from its content of magnesia], a dark, heavy, igneous rock consisting mostly of augite and olivine and resembling peridotite.

pic·ro- (pik′rō, pik′rə), [< Gr. *pikros,* bitter], a combining form meaning ***bitter:*** also, before a vowel, **picr-.**

pic·rol (pik′rōl, pik′rol), ***n.*** [*picr-* + *-ol*], a colorless, bitter, crystalline compound, soluble in water, used in medicine as an antiseptic.

pic·ro·tox·in (pik′rō-tok′sin), ***n.*** [*picro-* + *toxin*], a bitter, poisonous, crystalline compound, $C_{30}H_{34}O_{13}$, resembling strychnine in properties and used in medicine.

Pict (pikt), ***n.*** [Late ME.; LL. *Picti,* pl., said to be < L. *pictus,* pp. of *pingere,* to paint (hence, lit., painted people); cf. AS. *Peohtas*], one of an ancient people of Great Britain, driven into Scotland by the Britons and Romans.

Pict·ish (pik′tish), ***adj.*** of the Picts, their language, or their culture. ***n.*** the language of the Picts: its relationship is not established.

pic·to·graph (pik′tə-graf′, pik′tə-gräf′), ***n.*** [< L. *pictus* (see **PICTURE**); + *-graph*], 1. a picture representing an idea, as in primitive writing; hieroglyph. 2. writing of this kind.

pic·to·graph·ic (pik′tə-graf′ik), ***adj.*** of pictographs.

pic·tog·ra·phy (pik-tog′rə-fi), ***n.*** writing by the use of pictographs.

Pic·tor (pik′tẽr), ***n.*** [L., painter], a southern constellation: see **constellation,** chart.

pic·to·ri·al (pik-tôr′i-əl, pik-tō′ri-əl), ***adj.*** [L. *pictorius* < *pictor,* painter < pp. of *pingere,* to paint], 1. [Rare], of a painter or painting. 2. of, containing, or expressed in pictures. 3. invoking or suggesting a mental image or picture; vivid; graphic, as a description. *n.* a periodical featuring many pictures. —*SYN.* see **graphic.**

pic·ture (pik'chẽr), *n.* [ME. *pycture, pictour;* L. *pictura* < *pictus,* pp. of *pingere,* to paint], 1. an image or likeness of an object, person, or scene produced on a flat surface, especially by painting, drawing, or photography. 2. a printed reproduction of any of these. 3. anything closely resembling or strikingly typifying something else; perfect likeness; image: as, she's the *picture* of her mother, that cat is the *picture* of laziness. 4. anything admired for beauty: as, the garden was a *picture.* 5. a mental image or impression; idea. 6. a description: as, this is a poor *picture* of the times. 7. all the pertinent facts or conditions of an event. 8. a tableau. 9. a motion picture. *v.t.* [PICTURED (-chẽrd), PICTURING], 1. to make a picture of by painting, drawing, photographing, etc. 2. to make visible; show clearly; reflect. 3. to describe or explain. 4. to form a mental picture or impression of; imagine.

picture gallery, a place for exhibiting pictures.

picture hat, a woman's wide-brimmed hat with plumes, flowers, etc., like those seen in some famous paintings.

picture show, a motion picture or motion-picture theater.

pic·tur·esque (pik'chẽr-esk'), *adj.* [Fr. *pittoresque;* It. *pittoresco* < *pittore,* painter; L. *pictor,* painter], 1. like or suggesting a picture; specifically, *a)* having a wild or natural beauty, as mountain scenery. *b)* pleasantly unfamiliar or strange; quaint; informal: as, a *picturesque* Indian village. 2. suggesting or calling up a mental picture; striking; vivid. —*SYN.* see **graphic.**

picture window, a large window, especially in a living room, that seems to frame the outside view.

picture writing, 1. writing consisting of pictures or figures representing ideas. 2. the pictures or figures so used; pictographs; hieroglyphs.

EGYPTIAN PICTURE WRITING

pic·tur·i·za·tion (pik'chẽr-i-zā'shən, pik'-chẽr-i-zā'shən), *n.* 1. a picturizing or being picturized. 2. something that is picturized.

pic·tur·ize (pik'chẽr-īz'), *v.t.* [PICTURIZED (-īzd'), PICTURIZING], to make into a picture, especially a motion picture.

pic·ul (pik'ul), *n.* [*pl.* PICUL, PICULS (-ulz)], [Jav. & Malay *pikul,* a man's load < *pikul,* to carry on one's back], a measure of weight used in the Orient, equal to 100 catties: it varies between 132 and 140 pounds.

pid·dle (pid''l), *v.i. & v.t.* [PIDDLED (-'ld), PIDDLING], [euphemistic dim. < base of *piss*], 1. to dawdle or trifle (sometimes with *away*): as, he *piddles* the time away. 2. to urinate: child's term.

pid·dling (pid'liŋ), *adj.* useless; insignificant; trifling.

pid·dock (pid'ək), *n.* [< Brit. dial.; prob. < same base as *piddle;* cf. AS. *puduc,* a wart], any of a number of related burrowing mollusks with a two-valved shell.

pidg·in (pij'in), *n.* [Chin. pronun. of *business*], a mixed language, or jargon, originally developed for purposes of trade, incorporating the vocabulary of one or more languages with a very simplified form of the grammatical system of one of these; pidgin English, Beach-la-Mar, or any similar jargon: also spelled **pigeon.**

pidgin English, [see prec.], a simplified form of English used by Orientals and South Pacific natives in dealing with foreigners: there are two forms, Chinese pidgin and Melanesian pidgin, the former based on the syntax of Chinese, the latter on the syntax of certain aboriginal languages of Melanesia and Northern Australia.

pie (pī), *n.* [ME.; prob. same word as *pie* (magpie), with reference to the magpie's habit of collecting oddments and to the miscellaneous character of the dish; several early quotations support this view], 1. a baked dish consisting of fruit, meat, etc., with either an under crust, an upper crust, or both. 2. a layer cake filled with custard, cream, jelly, etc. 3. [Slang], *a)* something extremely good or easy. *b)* political graft.

pie (pī), *n.* [prob. < same source as *pie* (baked dish), from similar notion], 1. a mixed, disordered collection of printing type; hence, 2. any jumble or mixture. *v.t.* [PIED (pīd), PIEING], to make jumbled or disordered; mix up, as type. Usually spelled **pi.**

pie (pī), *n.* [ME.; OFr.; L. *pica,* magpie], a magpie.

pie (pī), *n.* [transl. of L. *pica* in the same sense; hence same word as prec.], in England, a form or table of rules used before the Reformation in selecting the correct church service or office for the day: also spelled **pye.**

pie (pī), *n.* [Hind. *pā'ī*], a small bronze coin of India, equal to 1/12 of an anna.

pie·bald (pī'bôld'), *adj.* [*pie* (magpie) + *bald*], covered with patches or spots of two colors, especially with white and black. *n.* a piebald horse or other animal.

piece (pēs), *n.* [ME. & OFr. *pece;* LL. **pettia,* **pecia;* prob. of Celt. origin (cf. W. *peth,* little); see PATCH], 1. a part or fragment broken or separated from the whole. 2. a section, division, or quantity regarded as complete in itself and distinct from the whole of which it is a part. 3. any single thing, amount, specimen, example, etc.; specifically, *a)* an artistic work or composition, as of music, literature, painting, drama, etc. *b)* an action or its result: as, a *piece* of nonsense, business, etc. *c)* a firearm; specifically, a rifle. *d)* a coin: as, a fifty-cent *piece.* *e)* one of a set, as of silver or china. *f)* a counter or man, as used in various games; specifically, in *chess,* any man other than a pawn. 4. the quantity or size, as of cloth or wallpaper, that is manufactured as a unit. 5. an amount of work constituting a single job. 6. [Archaic or Dial.], an amount of time or space, especially a small amount; bit. 7. [Archaic or Dial.], a person; individual. *v.t.* [PIECED (pēst), PIECING], 1. to add a piece or pieces to, as in repairing or enlarging. 2. to join or put (*together*) the pieces of, as in mending; hence, 3. to join or unite. *v.i.* [Colloq.], to eat between meals. Abbreviated **pc.** —*SYN.* see **part.**

a piece of one's mind, [Colloq.], a severe reprimand or frankly expressed, unfavorable opinion.

go to pieces, 1. to break into pieces; fall apart. 2. to lose all self-control, morally or emotionally.

of a (or **one**) **piece,** of the same sort; consistent (*with*).

speak one's piece, to vent one's views or opinions.

‡**pièce de ré·sis·tance** (pyes' də rā'zēs'täns'), [Fr., piece of resistance], 1. the principal dish of a meal; hence, 2. the main item or event in a series.

piece-dyed (pēs'dīd'), *adj.* dyed after being woven or knitted: said of cloth.

piece goods, textiles made and sold in standard sizes.

piece·meal (pēs'mēl'), *adv.* [ME. *pecemel* < *pece* (see PIECE) + *-mele* (AS. *-mæl*), a part: the word is a ME. modernization of AS. *styccemæl*], 1. piece by piece; in small amounts or degrees. 2. into pieces or parts. *adj.* made or done in pieces or one piece at a time.

piece of eight, the obsolete Spanish and Spanish-American silver dollar, equal to eight reals.

piec·er (pēs'ẽr), *n.* a person whose work is to piece or patch, as by sewing together pieces, joining threads in spinning, etc.

piece·work (pēs'wũrk'), *n.* work paid for at a fixed rate (**piece rate**) per piece of work done.

piece·work·er (pēs'wũr'kẽr), *n.* a person who does piecework.

pied (pīd), *adj.* [ME. *pyed,* orig., black and white like a magpie < *pie* (magpie)], 1. covered with patches or spots of two or more colors; piebald; variegated. 2. wearing a garment of this description.

‡**pied-à-terre** (pye'dȧ'târ'), *n.* [Fr., lit., foot on the ground], a lodging, especially for a short time.

Pied·mont (pēd'mont), *n.* 1. a plateau between the Atlantic coast and the Appalachians, covering parts of Alabama, Georgia, the Carolinas, and Virginia. 2. a former principality, and now a department, of northwestern Italy: chief city, Turin: Italian name, *Piemonte.*

pied·mont (pēd'mont), *adj.* [< *Piedmont,* Italy; L. *Pedimontium* < *pes, pedis,* a foot + *mons, montis,* mountain], at the base of a mountain or mountains: as, a *piedmont* stream. *n.* a piedmont area, plain, etc.

Pied·mon·tese (pēd'mon-tēz'), *adj.* of Piedmont, Italy, its people, or culture. *n.* [*pl.* PIEDMONTESE], a native or inhabitant of Piedmont, Italy.

Pied Piper (of Hamelin), in *German legend,* a musician who rid Hamelin of its rats by leading them with his piping to the river, where they drowned: in revenge for not receiving his reward, he later led the children of the village to a mountain, where they disappeared: the subject of a poem by Robert Browning.

Pie·mon·te (pye-môn'te), *n.* Piedmont, Italy.

pie·plant (pī'plant'), *n.* [*pie* (dish) + *plant*], the rhubarb: so called from its use in pies.

pier (pêr), *n.* [ME. & OFr. *pere;* ML. *pera;* ? connected with OFr. (Walloon) *pire,* breakwater; Weekley suggests connection with OHG. *pero,* boar, a word sometimes found in the sense "breakwater" in its LG. cognates], 1. a heavy structure supporting the spans of a bridge, especially, as distinguished from an abutment, one supporting the adjacent ends of two center spans of a long bridge. 2. a structure built out over the water and supported by pillars or piles: used as a landing place, pleasure pavilion, etc. 3. in *architecture,* *a)* a heavy column, usually square, used to support weight, as at the end of an arch. *b)* the part of a wall between windows or other openings. *c)* a reinforcing part built out from the surface of a wall; buttress.

pierce (pêrs), *v.t.* [PIERCED (pêrst), PIERCING], [ME. *percen;* OFr. *percer;* cf. PERISH, with which early forms often coincide], 1. to pass into or through as a pointed instrument does; penetrate; stab. 2. to affect sharply the senses or feelings of. 3. to make a hole in or through; perforate; bore. 4. to make (a hole), as by boring or stabbing. 5. to force a way into or through; break through. 6. to sound sharply through: as, a shriek *pierced* the air. 7. to penetrate with the sight or mind. ***v.i.*** to penetrate.

Pierce, Franklin (pêrs), 1804-1869; fourteenth president of the United States (1853-1857).

pierc·ing (pêr′siŋ), ***adj.*** penetrating; sharp.

pier glass, a tall mirror such as was formerly set in the pier, or wall section, between windows.

Pi·er·i·a (pī-êr′i-ə), ***n.*** a region in ancient Macedonia.

Pi·er·i·an (pī-êr′i-ən), ***adj.*** 1. of Pieria, where the Muses were worshiped. 2. of the Muses or the arts.

pi·er·i·dine (pī-er′ə-dīn′, pī-er′ə-din), ***adj.*** [< Mod. L. *Pieridinae,* name of a subfamily < *Pieris,* type genus < Gr. *Pieris,* one of the Muses], of a family of small or medium-sized butterflies, usually white or yellow with dark markings.

Pierre (pi-er′; Fr. pyâr), [Fr.; see PETER], a masculine name.

Pierre (pêr), ***n.*** the capital of South Dakota, on the Missouri: pop., 10,000.

Pi·er·rot (pē′ẽr-ō′, pē′ə-rō′; Fr. pye′rō′), ***n.*** [Fr., dim. of *Pierre* < L. *Petrus,* Peter], a comedy character having a whitened face and wearing loose white pantaloons and a jacket with large buttons: originally a stock figure in French pantomime.

pier table, a low table set in the pier, or wall section, between windows, often below a pier glass.

pi·et (pī′ət), ***n.*** [ME. *piot* < *pie,* magpie + *-ot,* dim. suffix], 1. the magpie. 2. the water ouzel.

‡Pie·tà (pyā-tä′), ***n.*** [It.; L. *pietas,* piety], a representation in painting, sculpture, etc. of Mary, the mother, grieving over the body of Jesus after the Crucifixion.

Pie·ter·mar·itz·burg (pē′tẽr-mâr′its-bũrg′), ***n.*** the capital of Natal province, Union of South Africa: pop., 74,000.

pi·e·tism (pī′ə-tiz′m), ***n.*** [G. *pietismus*], 1. a system which stresses the devotional ideal in religion. 2. [P-], the principles and practices of the Pietists. 3. exaggerated pious feeling or attitude.

Pi·e·tist (pī′ə-tist), ***n.*** [G. < L. *pietas,* piety; orig. used as a nickname for the followers of P. J. Spener (1635-1705), G. mystic], 1. a member of a group of Germans who advocated a revival of the devotional ideal in the Lutheran Church. 2. [p-], a pious person.

pi·e·tis·tic (pī′ə-tis′tik), ***adj.*** of or characterized by pietism.

pi·e·tis·ti·cal (pī′ə-tis′ti-k'l), ***adj.*** pietistic.

pi·e·ty (pī′ə-ti), ***n.*** [*pl.* PIETIES (-tiz)], [ME. *piete;* OFr. *pieté;* L. *pietas* < *pius,* pious], 1. devotion to religious duties and practices. 2. loyalty and devotion to parents, family, etc. 3. a pious act, statement, etc. 4. [Obs.], pity.

pi·e·zo·e·lec·tric (pī-ē′zō-i-lek′trik), ***adj.*** of or exhibiting piezoelectricity.

pi·e·zo·e·lec·tri·cal·ly (pī-ē′zō-i-lek′tri-k'l-i, pī-ē′zō-i-lek′trik-li), ***adv.*** in a piezoelectric manner.

pi·e·zo·e·lec·tric·i·ty (pī-ē′zō-i-lek′tris′ə-ti), ***n.*** [< Gr. *piezein,* to press; + *electricity*], charges of electricity induced in crystalline substances by pressure.

pi·e·zom·e·ter (pī′ə-zom′ə-tẽr), ***n.*** [< Gr. *piezein,* to press; + *-meter*], any of various instruments used in measuring pressure, compressibility, etc.

pi·e·zo·met·ric (pī-ē′zə-met′rik), ***adj.*** 1. of piezometry. 2. determined by piezometry.

pi·e·zo·met·ri·cal (pī-ē′zə-met′ri-k'l), ***adj.*** piezometric.

pi·e·zom·e·try (pī′ə-zom′ə-tri), ***n.*** [see PIEZOMETER], the measurement of the compressibility of fluids.

pif·fle (pif″l), ***n.*** [< Brit. dial.; cf. PIDDLE], [Colloq.], anything regarded as insignificant or nonsensical. ***v.i.*** [PIFFLED (-'ld), PIFFLING], [Colloq.], to talk nonsense.

pig (pig), ***n.*** [*pl.* PIGS (pigz), PIG; see PLURAL, II, D, 1], [ME. *pigge,* orig., young pig, replacing AS. *swin* (cf. SWINE); akin to D. *big* (MD. *vigghe*) & LG. *bigge,* young pig; the AS. etymon is *picg-,* as in *picg-bred,* mast (food for hogs)], 1. a domesticated animal with a long, broad snout and a thick, fat body covered with coarse bristles; swine; hog. 2. a young hog. 3. meat from a pig; pork. 4. [Colloq.], a person regarded as acting or looking like a pig; greedy or filthy person. 5. *a)* an oblong casting of iron or other metal poured from the smelting furnace. *b)* any of the molds in which these are cast. *c)* pig iron collectively. ***v.i.*** [PIGGED (pigd), PIGGING], 1. to bear pigs. 2. to live like pigs (usually with *it*).

buy a pig in a poke, to buy, get, or agree to something without sight or knowledge of it in advance.

pig bed, the sand bed into which molten iron is poured in molding pigs.

pig·boat (pig′bōt′), ***n.*** [so named from resembling suckling pigs when nosed against a tender], [Navy Slang], a submarine.

pi·geon (pij′ən), ***n.*** [*pl.* PIGEONS (-ənz), PIGEON; see PLURAL, II, D, 1], [ME. *pyjon, pijon;* OFr. *pijon;* LL. *pipio, pipionis,* chirping bird, squab < *pipire,* to peep, chirp], 1. any of a number of related birds with a small head, plump body, long, pointed wings, and short legs; dove. 2. [Slang], a person easily deceived; dupe.

pi·geon (pij′in), ***n.*** pidgin.

pigeon breast, a deformity of the human chest occurring in rickets, etc. and characterized by a sharply projecting sternum like that of a pigeon.

pi·geon-breast·ed (pij′ən-bres′tid), ***adj.*** having a pigeon breast.

pigeon hawk, a small variety of hawk; merlin.

pi·geon-heart·ed (pij′ən-här′tid), ***adj.*** cowardly; timid.

pi·geon·hole (pij′ən-hōl′), ***n.*** 1. a small recess or hole for pigeons to nest in, usually in a compartmented box. 2. a small open compartment, as in a desk, for filing papers, etc. ***v.t.*** [PIGEONHOLED (-hōld′), PIGEONHOLING], 1. to put in the pigeonhole of a desk, etc.; hence, 2. to put aside indefinitely, with the intention of ignoring; shelve. 3. to arrange systematically.

pi·geon-toed (pij′ən-tōd′), ***adj.*** having the toes or feet turned in.

pi·geon·wing (pij′ən-wiŋ′), ***n.*** 1. a fancy dance step performed by jumping and striking the feet together. 2. a figure in skating, outlining a pigeon wing.

pig·fish (pig′fish′), ***n.*** [*pl.* PIGFISH, PIGFISHES (-iz); see FISH], any of a number of fishes that make a grunting noise when taken out of water, as the grunt.

pig·ger·y (pig′ẽr-i), ***n.*** [*pl.* PIGGERIES (-iz)], a place where pigs are raised; pigpen; pigsty.

pig·gin (pig′in), ***n.*** [Early Mod. Eng. < Brit. dial.; dim. of *pig* in dial. & obs. sense "a pail"], a small wooden pail with one long stave that serves as a handle.

pig·gish (pig′ish), ***adj.*** like a pig; gluttonous; filthy.

pig·gy (pig′i), ***n.*** [*pl.* PIGGIES (-iz)], a little pig: also spelled **piggie.** ***adj.*** piggish.

pig·gy·back (pig′i-bak′), ***adv. & adj.*** 1. pickaback. 2. designating or by means of a transportation system in which loaded truck trailers are carried on railroad flatcars: in this sense, usually **piggy-back.**

piggy bank, any small savings bank, especially one shaped like a pig, with a slot for receiving coins.

pig·head·ed (pig′hed′id), ***adj.*** stubborn; obstinate.

pig iron, [from being cast in molds, or pigs], crude iron, as it comes from the blast furnace.

pig Latin, a playful code in speaking, in which each word is begun with its first vowel and any preceding consonants are moved to the end to form a new syllable with the vowel sound (ā), as "oybay" for *boy.*

pig·let (pig′lit), ***n.*** a little pig.

pig·ment (pig′mənt), ***n.*** [ME.; L. *pigmentum* < base of *pingere,* to paint], 1. coloring matter, usually in the form of an insoluble powder, mixed with oil, water, etc. to make paints. 2. any coloring matter in the cells and tissues of plants or animals.

pig·men·tar·y (pig′mən-ter′i), ***adj.*** of or containing pigment.

pig·men·ta·tion (pig′mən-tā′shən), ***n.*** [*pigment* + *-ation*], coloration in plants or animals due to the presence of pigment in the tissue.

pig·men·ted (pig′mən-tid), ***adj.*** having pigmentation.

Pig·my (pig′mi), ***adj. & n.*** [*pl.* PIGMIES (-miz)], Pygmy.

pig·nus (pig′nəs), ***n.*** [*pl.* PIGNORA (-nə-rə)], [L.], in *law,* a pledge; pawn.

pig·nut (pig′nut′), ***n.*** 1. the thin-shelled nut of a kind of hickory. 2. the tree it grows on. 3. the tuber of a variety of European earthnut.

pig·pen (pig′pen′), ***n.*** a pen where pigs are confined.

pig·skin (pig′skin′), ***n.*** 1. the skin of a pig. 2. leather made from this. 3. [Colloq.], a football. 4. [Colloq.], a saddle.

pig·stick·ing (pig′stik′iŋ), ***n.*** the hunting of wild boars with spears.

pig·sty (pig′stī′), ***n.*** [*pl.* PIGSTIES (-stīz′)], a pigpen.

pig·tail (pig′tāl′), ***n.*** 1. tobacco in a twisted roll. 2. a long braid of hair hanging at the back of the head.

pig·weed (pig′wēd′), ***n.*** any of a number of related coarse plants with tassellike heads of reddish flowers.

pi·ka (pī′kə), ***n.*** [< E. Siberian (Tungusic) name, *peeka*], any of a number of related animals resembling the guinea pig, found in North America and Asia; cony.

pike (pīk), ***n.*** [short for *turnpike*], 1. a gate or place on a road where a toll is paid. 2. the toll paid there. 3. a toll road. ***v.i.*** [PIKED (pīkt), PIKING], [Slang], to move quickly (usually with *along*).

pike (pīk), ***n.*** [Fr. *pique* < *piquer,* to pierce, prick < *pic,* a pike, pickax], a weapon, formerly used by foot soldiers, consisting of a metal spearhead on a long wooden shaft. ***v.t.*** [PIKED (pīkt), PIKING], to pierce or kill with or as with a pike.

pike (pīk), ***n.*** [*pl.* PIKE, PIKES (pīks); see PLURAL, II, D, 2], [ME. *pik* for *pikefish:* from the pointed head; see PIKE (pointed weapon); cf. PICKEREL], any of various slender, fierce fresh-water fishes with a narrow, pointed snout, projecting lower jaw, and sharp teeth.

pike (pīk), ***n.*** [ME. *pike;* AS. *piic,* a pickax; prob. < OFr. *pic,* a pick, pickax; cf. ON. *pik*], a spike; point, as the pointed tip of a spear.

pike (pīk), ***n.*** [ME.; prob. < ON. *pik;* akin to AS. *piic* (cf. PIKE, a point)], [British Dial.], 1. a peaked summit. 2. a mountain or hill with a peaked summit.

Pike, Zeb·u·lon Montgomery (zeb′yoo-lən), 1779-1813; American general and explorer.

pike·man (pīk′mən), ***n.*** [*pl.* PIKEMEN (-mən)], a soldier armed with a pike.
pike perch, a fish of the perch family resembling the pike, as the walleyed pike.
pik·er (pī′kẽr), ***n.*** [< dial. *pike*, var. of *pick*, in sense "petty pilferer"], [Slang], a person who does things in a petty or niggardly way; especially, one who gambles or speculates in an overly cautious way.
Pikes Peak (pīks), ***n.*** a mountain of the Front Range, in central Colorado: height, 14,110 ft.: also **Pike's Peak.**
pike·staff (pīk′staf′, pīk′stäf′), ***n.*** [*pl.* PIKESTAVES (-stāvz′)], 1. the shaft of a pike. 2. a traveler's staff with a sharp iron or steel point.
pi·laf, pi·laff (pi-läf′), ***n.*** pilau.
pi·las·ter (pi-las′tẽr), ***n.*** [Fr. *pilastre;* It. *pilastro;* L. *pila*, a pile, column; cf. PILLAR], a rectangular support or pier treated architecturally as a column, with a base, shaft, and capital.

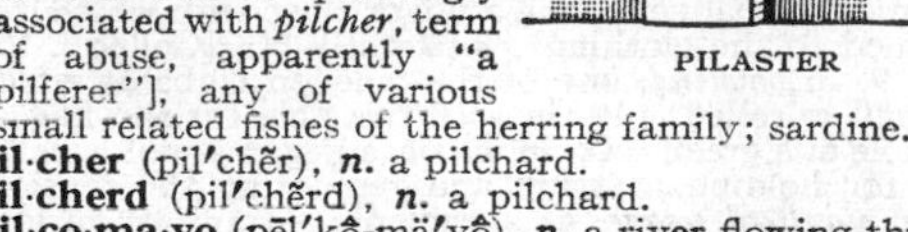
PILASTER

Pi·late, Pon·tius (pon′shəs, pon′chəs, or pon′ti-əs pī′lət), the Roman governor of Judea (26–36? A.D.) when Jesus was crucified.
pi·lau, pi·law (pi-lô′), ***n.*** [Per. & Turk. *pilāw*], an Oriental dish of rice boiled with meat or fish and spiced.
pil·chard (pil′chẽrd), ***n.*** [earlier *pilcher;* ? < ME. *pilken, pilchen*, to pluck, pick (later, to pilfer); in Early Mod. Eng., the name of the fish is punningly associated with *pilcher*, term of abuse, apparently "a pilferer"], any of various small related fishes of the herring family; sardine.
pil·cher (pil′chẽr), ***n.*** a pilchard.
pil·cherd (pil′chẽrd), ***n.*** a pilchard.
Pil·co·ma·yo (pēl′kô-mä′yô), ***n.*** a river flowing through southeastern Bolivia and Paraguay into the Paraguay River: length, 1,000 mi.: see **Chaco**, map.
pile (pīl), ***n.*** [ME.; OFr.; L. *pila*, a pillar], 1. a mass of things heaped together; heap. 2. a heap of wood or other combustible material on which a corpse or sacrifice is burned. 3. a large building or group of buildings. 4. [Colloq.], a large amount or number. 5. [Slang], a lot of money; fortune. 6. in *electricity, a*) originally, a series of alternate plates of dissimilar metals with acid-saturated cloth or paper between them, for making an electric current. *b*) any similar arrangement that produces an electric current; battery. 7. in *physics*, a device for controlling the nuclear chain reaction in the production of atomic energy, consisting primarily of a latticework arrangement of uranium and some moderating material, as graphite. ***v.t.*** [PILED (pīld), PILING], 1. to put or set in a pile; heap up. 2. to accumulate (with *up*). 3. to cover with a pile; load. ***v.i.*** 1. to form a pile or heap. 2. to move confusedly in a mass; crowd (with *in, out, on, off*, etc.). 3. to accumulate (with *up*). —***SYN.*** see **building.**
pile (pīl), ***n.*** [ME. *pile*, bird's down; L. *pilus*, a hair], 1. a raised surface on material, produced by making yarn loops on the body of the cloth and, often, shearing them to produce a soft, velvety surface. 2. any of these loops. 3. soft, fine hair; down, wool, fur, etc.
pile (pīl), ***n.*** [ME. & AS. *pil*, a stake; L. *pilum*, a javelin], 1. a long, heavy timber or beam driven into the ground, sometimes under water, to support a bridge, dock, etc. 2. any similar supporting member, as of concrete. 3. in *heraldry*, a wedge-shaped charge with the point downward. ***v.t.*** [PILED (pīld), PILING], 1. to drive piles into. 2. to support or strengthen with piles.
pi·le·ate (pī′li-it, pil′i-āt′), ***adj.*** [L. *pileatus* < *pileus*], 1. having a pileus. 2. having a crest extending from the bill to the nape, as some birds.
pi·le·at·ed (pī′li-ā′tid, pil′i-ā′tid), ***adj.*** pileate.
pileated woodpecker, a North American woodpecker with a black and white body and a red crest.
piled (pīld), ***adj.*** having a pile, as certain textiles.
pile driver (or **engine**), a machine with a drop hammer for driving piles.
pi·le·ous (pī′li-əs), ***adj.*** [L. *pilosus* < *pilus*, a hair], hairy.
piles (pīlz), ***n.pl.*** [LL. *pilae*, pl. of L. *pila*, a ball], hemorrhoids.
pi·le·um (pī′li-əm, pil′i-əm), ***n.*** [*pl.* PILEA (-ə)], [Mod. L. < L. *pilleum*, felt cap], the top of a bird's head from the bill to the nape.
pi·le·us (pī′li-əs, pil′i-əs), ***n.*** [*pl.* PILEI (-ī′)], [< L. *pilleus* (or *pilleum*), felt cap], 1. in ancient Rome, a cap without a brim. 2. in *botany*, the cap of a mushroom. 3. in *zoology, a*) the umbrella-shaped disk of a jellyfish. *b*) the pileum.
pile·wort (pīl′wũrt′), ***n.*** a plant of the crowfoot family, with yellow flowers and a grainlike, underground stem.
pil·fer (pil′fẽr), ***v.t. & v.i.*** [OFr. *pelfrer*, to plunder < *pelfre*, goods, booty; ? < Eng.; cf. PELF], to steal (especially small sums or petty objects); filch. —***SYN.*** see **steal.**
pil·fer·age (pil′fẽr-ij), ***n.*** [see -AGE], 1. a pilfering. 2. something pilfered.
pil·gar·lic (pil-gär′lik), ***n.*** [altered < *pilled* (peeled) *garlic*], 1. a bald-headed man. 2. a person regarded with contempt or pretended pity.
pil·grim (pil′grim), ***n.*** [ME. *pelegrim;* OFr. **pelegrin* (later *pèlerin*, Pr. *pelegrin*); L. *peregrinus*, foreigner < *pereger*, one on a journey < *per*, through + *ager*, country; cf. PEREGRINE], 1. a wanderer; sojourner. 2. a person who travels to a shrine or holy place. 3. [P-], a member of the band of English Puritans who founded Plymouth Colony in 1620.
pil·grim·age (pil′grə-mij), ***n.*** [ME. *pilegrimage, pelrimage;* OFr. *pelerinage* < *peleriner*, to go on a journey < *pelerin*, a pilgrim; see PILGRIM], 1. a journey made by a pilgrim, especially to a shrine or holy place. 2. any long journey.
Pilgrim Fathers, the Pilgrims.
Pilgrim's Progress, a religious allegory by John Bunyan (1678).
pi·li (pē-lē′), ***n.*** [Tag.], 1. the edible nut, somewhat like an almond, of a tropical tree of the Philippines. 2. the tree itself.
pil·i- (pil′i, pī′li), [< L. *pilus*, a hair], a combining form meaning *hair*, as in ***piliform.***
pi·lif·er·ous (pī-lif′ẽr-əs), ***adj.*** [*pili-* + *-ferous*], having hair or hairs.
pil·i·form (pil′ə-fôrm′), ***adj.*** [Mod. L. *piliformis;* see PILI- & -FORM], in the form of a hair; hairlike.
pil·ing (pīl′iŋ), ***n.*** 1. a supplying with piles. 2. piles collectively. 3. a structure of piles.
pill (pil), ***n.*** [prob. MD. *pille* < L. *pilula*, dim. of *pila*, a ball], 1. a small ball or pellet of medicine to be swallowed whole. 2. anything unpleasant but unavoidable. 3. [Slang], a baseball, golf ball, etc. 4. [Slang], an unpleasant or boring person. ***v.t.*** 1. to dose with pills. 2. to form into pills. 3. [Slang], to blackball.
pill (pil), ***v.t. & v.i.*** [ME. *pilien, pillen;* Late AS. *pylian;* prob. < L. *pilare*, to make bare of hair, hence, fig., to peel, plunder, etc.; doublet of PEEL, *v.*], 1. [Archaic], to pillage; plunder. 2. [Archaic or Dial.], to peel, skin, etc. 3. [Obs.], to become or cause to become bald.
pil·lage (pil′ij), ***n.*** [ME. *pilage;* Late OFr. < *piller*, to rob < same source as *pill, v.*], 1. a plundering. 2. that which is plundered; booty; loot. ***v.t.*** [PILLAGED (-ijd), PILLAGING], 1. to deprive of money or property by violence; loot. 2. to take as booty or loot. ***v.i.*** to engage in plunder; take loot. —***SYN.*** see **ravage, spoil.**
pil·lar (pil′ẽr), ***n.*** [ME. & OFr. *piler;* LL. *pilare* < L. *pila*, a column], 1. a long, slender, vertical structure used to support a superstructure; column. 2. such a column standing alone as a monument. 3. anything resembling a pillar in form or function. 4. a person who is a main support of an institution, movement, etc. ***v.t.*** to support or brace with or as with pillars.
from pillar to post, from one predicament, place of appeal, etc. to another, usually under harassment.
pillar box, [British], a mail collection box.
Pillars of Hercules, the two points of land, Gibraltar and Jebel Musa, on either side of the Strait of Gibraltar.
pill·box (pil′boks′), ***n.*** 1. a small, shallow box, often cylindrical, for holding pills. 2. an enclosed gun emplacement of concrete and steel. 3. a woman's short, cylindrical hat with a flat top.

PILLBOX (fort)

pill bug, any of a number of related land crustaceans with a flat body, capable of rolling up into a ball.
pil·lion (pil′yən), ***n.*** [Gael. *pillean* < *peall*, a hide, skin; L. *pellis*], 1. a cushion attached behind a saddle for an extra rider, especially a woman. 2. an extra seat behind the driver's saddle on a motorcycle.
pil·lo·ry (pil′ə-ri), ***n.*** [*pl.* PILLORIES (-riz)], [ME. & OFr. *pilori;* Pr. *espilori*], 1. a device with holes for the head and hands, in which petty offenders were formerly locked and exposed to public scorn. 2. any exposure to public scorn, etc. ***v.t.*** [PILLORIED (-rid), PILLORYING], 1. to punish by placing in a pillory. 2. to lay open to public ridicule, scorn, or abuse.
pil·low (pil′ō), ***n.*** [ME. *pylwe;* AS. *pyle;* akin to G. *pfühl;* W. Gmc. borrowing of L. *pulvinus*, a cushion],

1. a cloth case filled with feathers, down, air, etc., used as a support for the head, as in sleeping. 2. any object used as a headrest. 3. anything like a pillow or cushion, as a pad on which certain laces are made. 4. anything that supports like a pillow, as the block supporting the inner end of a bowsprit. *v.t.* 1. to rest on or as on a pillow. 2. to be a pillow for. *v.i.* to rest the head on or as on a pillow.

pillow block, a block that supports the journal of a shaft, spindle, etc.

pil·low·case (pil'ō-kās'), *n.* a removable cotton or linen covering for a pillow.

pillow lace, lace made by drawing and interlacing thread from bobbins around pins set into a pillow; bobbin lace.

pillow sham, a decorative cover to be laid over a bed pillow.

pil·low·slip (pil'ō-slip'), *n.* a pillowcase.

pil·low·y (pil'ō-i, pil'ə-wi), *adj.* like a pillow; soft; yielding.

pi·lo·car·pin (pī'lō-kär'pin, pil'ō-kär'pin), *n.* pilocarpine.

pi·lo·car·pine (pī'lō-kär'pēn, pil'ō-kär'pin), *n.* [< Mod. L. *Pilocarpus*, type genus (< Gr. *pilos*, felt + *karpos*, a fruit); + *-ine*], an alkaloid, $C_{11}H_{16}N_2O_2$, extracted from the leaves of the jaborandi plant and used in medicine to stimulate sweating.

pi·lose (pī'lōs), *adj.* [L. *pilosus* < *pilus*, a hair], covered with hair, especially fine, soft hair.

pi·los·i·ty (pī-los'ə-ti), *n.* [< *pilose* + *-ity*], hairiness.

pi·lot (pī'lət), *n.* [Fr. *pilote;* It. *pilota;* MGr. **pēdōlēs* < Gr. *pēdon*, an oar (in pl., rudder)], 1. a steersman; specifically, a person licensed to steer ships into or out of a harbor or through difficult waters. 2. a person who flies an airplane, airship, or balloon. 3. a guide; leader. 4. a device that guides the action of a machine or machine part. 5. a pilot light. *v.t.* 1. to act as a pilot of, on, in, or over. 2. to guide; conduct; lead. *adj.* 1. that serves as a guide or guiding device. 2. that serves as a device to start operation of a larger device: as, a *pilot* light. 3. that serves as a trial unit on a small scale for experimentation or testing. —*SYN.* see **guide.**

pi·lot·age (pī'lət-ij), *n.* [Fr.; see -AGE], 1. a piloting. 2. the fee paid to a pilot.

pilot balloon, a small balloon sent up to determine the direction and velocity of the wind.

pilot biscuit (or **bread**), hard, unleavened biscuit used on ships; hardtack.

pilot engine, a locomotive sent on in front to clear the line.

pilot fish, a narrow, spiny-finned fish with a widely forked tail, often seen swimming near sharks.

pi·lot·house (pī'lət-hous'), *n.* an enclosed place on the upper deck of a ship, where the helmsman works the steering gear.

pilot lamp, 1. an electric lamp which indicates the location of a switch or circuit breaker. 2. an electric lamp placed in an electric circuit to indicate when the current is on.

pilot light, 1. a small gas burner which is kept lighted to rekindle a principal burner when needed: also **pilot burner.** 2. a pilot lamp.

pilot plant, a small factory or manufacturing unit for making experimental tests of new methods and techniques of production.

pi·lous (pī'ləs), *adj.* pilose.

Pil·sen (pil'z'n), *n.* a city in western Bohemia, Czechoslovakia: pop., 118,000 (est. 1947): Czech name, *Plzeň.*

Pil·sud·ski, Jó·zef (yoo'zef pil-soot'ski; Eng. pil-sud'ski), 1867–1935; Polish statesman and general; president of Poland (1918–1922); premier (1926–1928; 1930).

Pilt·down man (pilt'doun'), a species of prehistoric man whose existence was presumed on the basis of bone fragments found in Piltdown (Sussex, England) in 1911. These were exposed as a hoax in 1953.

pil·u·lar (pil'yoo-lẽr), *adj.* of or like a pill.

pil·ule (pil'ūl), *n.* [Fr.; L. *pilula;* cf. PILL, *n.*], a small pill.

Pi·ma (pē'mə), *n.* [*pl.* PIMA, PIMAS (-məz)], a member of a tribe of Nahuatl Indians that live in the Gila and Salt River Valleys, Arizona. *adj.* of this tribe.

Pima cotton, [< *Pima* County, Ariz.], a tough, strong, smooth cotton grown in the southwestern United States, and used in tire fabrics, clothes, etc.

Pi·man (pē'mən), *n.* 1. one of the three branches of the Uto-Aztecan family of languages. 2. [*pl.* PIMANS (-mənz), PIMAN], a Pima Indian. *adj.* 1. of Piman. 2. of the Pimans.

pi·men·to (pi-men'tō), *n.* [*pl.* PIMENTOS (-tōz)], [Sp. *pimienta;* ML. *pigmentum*, a spice, spiced drink; L. *pigmentum*, coloring matter, pigment], 1. the pimiento. 2. a tropical tree, its berry, or the spice made from it; allspice.

pimento cheese, a processed cheese containing pimientos.

pi·mien·to (pi-myen'tō), *n.* [*pl.* PIMIENTOS (-tōz)], [Sp.; see PIMENTO], a variety of garden pepper or its sweet, red fruit, used as a relish, for stuffing olives, etc.; Spanish paprika.

pim·o·la (pi-mō'lə), *n.* [< *pimiento*], an olive stuffed with pimiento.

pimp (pimp), *n.* [prob. < or connected with OFr. *pimper*, to allure, entice (esp. by dressing smartly)], a go-between in illicit sexual affairs; especially, a prostitute's agent; pander. *v.i.* to act as a pimp.

pim·per·nel (pim'pẽr-nel', pim'pẽr-nəl), *n.* [ME. *pympernelle;* OFr. *piprenelle* (Fr. *pimprenelle*); ML. *pipinella;* LL. **piperinella;* L. *piperinus*, as if composed of peppercorns < *piper*, pepper; the fruit of the pimpernel resembles small peppercorns], a plant of the primrose family, with red, white, or blue, starlike flowers which close in bad weather.

pimp·ing (pim'piŋ), *adj.* [< dial.; prob. akin to D. *pimpel*, weak man, G. *pimpelig*, womanish], [Colloq.], 1. petty; mean. 2. sickly; puny.

pim·ple (pim'p'l), *n.* [ME. (pl.) *pinplis*, prob. a repatterning of the base of AS. *piplian*, to be pimpled (inferred < *pipligende*, affected with herpes), after *dimple*, etc.], any small, usually inflamed, swelling of the skin; papule or pustule.

pim·pled (pim'p'ld), *adj.* having pimples.

pim·ply (pim'pli), *adj.* [PIMPLIER (-pli-ẽr), PIMPLIEST (-pli-ist)], pimpled.

pin (pin), *n.* [ME. *pinne;* AS. *pinn;* akin to G. *pinne*, pin; IE. base **bend-*, erect point, as also in Eng. *pintle*, MIr. *benn*, a peak, etc.; cf. PEN (enclosure)], 1. a peg of wood, metal, etc., used for fastening or holding things together, as a support for hanging things, etc. 2. a little piece of stiff wire with a pointed end and flattened or rounded head, for fastening things together; hence, 3. something worthless or insignificant; trifle. 4. a pointed instrument for holding the hair, a hat, etc. in place. 5. a clothespin, hairpin, cotter pin, rolling pin, etc. 6. anything like a pin in form, use, etc. 7. an ornament or badge having a pin or clasp with which it is fastened to the clothing. 8. *usually pl.* [Colloq.], the leg. 9. in *bowling*, one of the wooden clubs at which the ball is rolled. 10. in *golf*, the pole for the flag at the hole of a green. 11. in *music*, a peg in a violin, cello, etc., for holding a string and regulating the tension. 12. in *nautical usage*, *a*) a tholepin. *b*) any of various pegs or bolts used in fastening the rigging. *v.t.* [PINNED (pind), PINNING], 1. to fasten with or as with a pin. 2. to pierce with a pin. 3. to hold firmly in one place or position. 4. [College Slang], to give one's fraternity pin to, as an informal token of betrothal.

on pins and needles, filled with anxiety; in a state of suspense or nervous anticipation.

pin one down, to get a person to commit himself as to his opinion, a course of action, etc.

pin (something) on one, [Colloq.], to lay the blame of (something) on one.

pi·ña (pē'nyä), *n.* [Sp., pineapple, orig., pine cone; L. *pinea;* see PINE], 1. the pineapple. 2. piña cloth.

pi·na·ceous (pī-nā'shəs), *adj.* [< *pine* (a tree) + *-aceous*], of the pine family of trees, including the pine, cedar, fir, etc.

piña cloth, [see PIÑA], a fabric made of the fibers of pineapple leaves.

pin·a·fore (pin'ə-fôr', pin'ə-fōr'), *n.* [*pin* + *afore*], a sleeveless, apronlike garment worn especially by girls.

pi·nas·ter (pi-nas'tẽr, pi-nas'tẽr), *n.* [Fr.; L., wild pine < *pinus*, a pine], a Mediterranean pine.

pin·ball (pin'bôl'), *n.* a game of chance played on an inclined board, typically containing a number of holes surrounded by numerous pins, springs, etc. and marked with scores credited to the player if he causes a number of spring-driven balls to strike the pins or roll into the holes.

pin boy, in *bowling*, a boy or man who sets up the pins after each frame and returns the balls to the bowlers.

pince-nez (pans'nā', pins'nā'; Fr. pans'nā'), *n.* [*pl.* PINCE-NEZ], [Fr., nose-pincher], eyeglasses kept in place by a spring gripping the bridge of the nose.

pin·cers (pin'sẽrz), *n.pl.* [occas. construed as sing.], [ME. *pinsours*, *pynsours* < OFr. *pincier*, to pinch], 1. a tool with two parts pivoted together to form two handles and two jaws, used in gripping or nipping things. 2. in *zoology*, a grasping claw, as of a crab or lobster; chela. Also **pinchers.**

PINCERS

pincers movement, a military maneuver in which simultaneous flank movements are used to converge upon an enemy force or stronghold and cut it off from support and supplies.

pinch (pinch), *v.t.* [ME. *pinchen;* ONorm.Fr. *pincher;* prob. < Gmc.], 1. to squeeze between a finger and the thumb or between two surfaces, edges, etc. 2. to press painfully upon (some part of the body). 3. to cause distress or discomfort to. 4. to cause to become thin, cramped, etc., as by hunger, pain, cold, etc. 5. to restrict closely; straiten; stint (often in the passive). 6. [Slang], to steal. 7. [Slang], to arrest or make a police raid on. 8. in *nautical usage*, to sail close-hauled. *v.i.* 1. to squeeze painfully. 2. to be stingy or niggardly. 3. in *mining*, to become narrower; hence, to give (*out*): said of a vein of ore. ***n.*** 1. a pinching; squeeze or nip. 2. the quantity that may be grasped between the finger and thumb; small amount. 3. distress; hardship; difficulty. 4. an emergency; urgent situation or time. 5. [Slang], a theft. 6. [Slang], an arrest or raid. —***SYN.*** see **steal.**

pinch bar, a kind of crowbar with a pointed, projecting end, used to roll heavy wheels, etc.

pinch·beck (pinch′bek), ***n.*** [after Christopher *Pinchbeck*, Eng. jeweler who invented it c. 1725], 1. an alloy of copper and zinc used to imitate gold in cheap jewelry. 2. anything cheap or imitation. ***adj.*** 1. made of pinchbeck. 2. cheap; imitation; spurious.

pinch·cock (pinch′kok′), ***n.*** [*pinch* + *cock* (valve)], any of various clamps for compressing a tube of rubber, etc. so as to control the flow of a fluid.

pinch·ers (pin′chẽrz), ***n.pl.*** pincers.

pinch-hit (pinch′hit′), ***v.i.*** [PINCH-HIT, PINCH-HITTING], 1. in *baseball*, to bat in place of the regular player when a hit is especially needed; hence, 2. to act as a substitute in an emergency (*for*).

pinch hitter, a person who pinch-hits.

Pinck·ney, Charles Cotes·worth (kōts′wẽrth piŋk′ni), 1746–1825; American statesman and general.

pin·cush·ion (pin′koosh′ən), ***n.*** a small cushion in which pins and needles are stuck to keep them handy for use.

Pin·dar (pin′dẽr), ***n.*** Greek lyric poet; 522?–443 B.C.

Pin·dar·ic (pin-dar′ik), ***adj.*** [L. *Pindaricus;* Gr. *Pindarikos*], 1. of, characteristic of, or in the style of, Pindar. 2. elaborate or regular in metrical structure. 3. designating an ode in which the strophe and antistrophe have the same form, in contrast to the epode, which has a different form. ***n.*** a Pindaric ode.

pin·dling (pin′dliŋ), ***adj.*** [euphemized var. of *piddling*], [Dial.], puny; weak and undersized.

Pin·dus (pin′dəs), ***n.*** a mountain range in northwestern Greece.

pine (pīn), ***n.*** [see PLURAL, II, D, 3], [ME.; AS. *pin;* L. *pinus*, pine tree], 1. any of various evergreen trees having cones and clusters of needle-shaped leaves: many pines are valuable for their wood and their resin, from which turpentine, tar, etc. are obtained. 2. the wood of such a tree. 3. [Colloq.], a pineapple.

pine (pīn), ***v.i.*** [PINED (pīnd), PINING], [ME. *pinen, pinien;* AS. *pinian*, to torment < *pin* (L. *poena*), a pain], 1. to waste (*away*) through grief, pain, hunger, etc. 2. to have an intense longing or desire; yearn: (with *for, after*, or an infinitive). ***v.t.*** [Archaic], to mourn for. ***n.*** [Archaic], torment; suffering; want.

pin·e·al (pin′i-əl), ***adj.*** [Fr. *pinéal* < L. *pinea*, a pine cone < *pinus*, a pine], 1. shaped like a pine cone. 2. designating or of a small, cone-shaped body or gland in the brain of all vertebrates having a cranium. It has no known function, but is believed to be a vestigial sensory organ.

pine·ap·ple (pīn′ap′'l), ***n.*** [ME. *pinappel*, pine cone; mod. sense from shape of the fruit], 1. a juicy, edible tropical fruit somewhat resembling a pine cone: it consists of the fleshy inflorescence of a collective fruit developed from a spike of flowers. 2. the plant it grows on, having a short stem and spiny-edged recurved leaves. 3. [Slang], a small dynamite bomb or hand grenade.

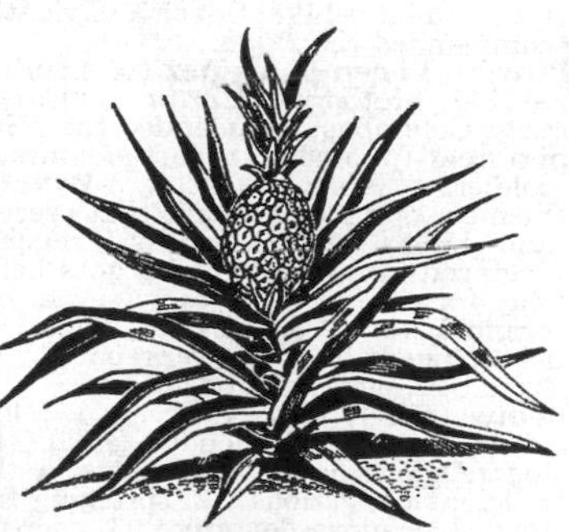

PINEAPPLE

pine cone, the cone (sense 3) of a pine tree.

pine·drops (pīn′drops′), ***n.*** [*pl.* PINEDROPS], a purplish-red, leafless plant with white flowers, parasitic on the roots of pines.

pi·nene (pī′nēn), ***n.*** [*pine* (a tree) + *-ene*], either of two isomeric terpenes, $C_{10}H_{16}$, occurring in oil of turpentine and other essential oils.

pine needle, the needlelike leaf of a pine tree.

Pi·ner·o, Sir **Arthur Wing** (wiŋ pi-ner′ō, pi-nêr′ō), 1855–1934; English dramatist.

pin·er·y (pīn′ẽr-i), ***n.*** [*pl.* PINERIES (-iz)], [< *pine* (a tree) + *-ery*], 1. a forest of pine trees. 2. a pineapple plantation or hothouse.

Pines, Isle of, a Cuban island, south of western Cuba: area, 1,180 sq. mi.; pop., 9,000.

pine·sap (pīn′sap′), ***n.*** any of a number of related whitish or reddish plants living on dead vegetable material or as a parasite on roots.

pine siskin, a small, streaked, brown finch with yellow markings on the wings and tail: also **pine finch.**

pine tar, a viscid, blackish-brown liquid prepared by the destructive distillation of pine wood and used in the preparation of expectorants, disinfectants, tar paints, roofing materials, etc.

pi·ne·tum (pī-nē′təm), ***n.*** [*pl.* PINETA (-tə)], [L., pine wood], an arboretum of pine trees, etc.

pine warbler, a variety of small warbler living in the pine forests of the eastern United States.

pin·ey (pīn′i), ***adj.*** piny.

pin·feath·er (pin′feth′ẽr), ***n.*** an undeveloped feather that is just emerging through the skin.

pin·fish (pin′fish′), ***n.*** [*pl.* PINFISH, PINFISHES (-iz); see FISH], any of various small fish of the porgy family, having a sharp dorsal spine and found in the South Atlantic along the southern coast of the United States.

pin·fold (pin′fōld′), ***n.*** [ME. *pynfold, ponfolde;* AS. *pundfald; pund*, a pound (cf. POUND, enclosure) + *fald* (see FOLD, pen)], a place where stray animals are confined; animal pound. ***v.t.*** to confine in a pinfold.

ping (piŋ), ***n.*** [echoic], 1. the sound made by a bullet striking something sharply. 2. the sound made by a bullet cutting through the air. ***v.i. & v.t.*** to travel or strike with a ping.

ping-pong (piŋ′poŋ′, piŋ′pôŋ′), ***n.*** [echoic], a game somewhat like tennis in miniature, played on a large, rectangular table, usually indoors, with a small, hollow celluloid ball and small, racket-shaped paddles; table tennis: a trade-mark (**Ping-pong**).

pin·guid (piŋ′gwid), ***adj.*** [L. *pinguis*, fat], 1. fat; oily; greasy. 2. rich; fertile: said of soil.

pin·guid·i·ty (piŋ-gwid′ə-ti), ***n.*** the quality or condition of being pinguid.

pin·head (pin′hed′), ***n.*** 1. the head of a pin. 2. anything very small or trifling. 3. a stupid or silly person.

pin·hole (pin′hōl′), ***n.*** 1. a tiny hole made by or as by a pin. 2. a hole into which a pin or peg goes.

pin·ion (pin′yən), ***n.*** [Fr. *pignon* (in OFr., a battlement); ult. < L. *pinna*, a pinnacle], a small cogwheel the teeth of which fit into those of a larger gear wheel or those of a rack.

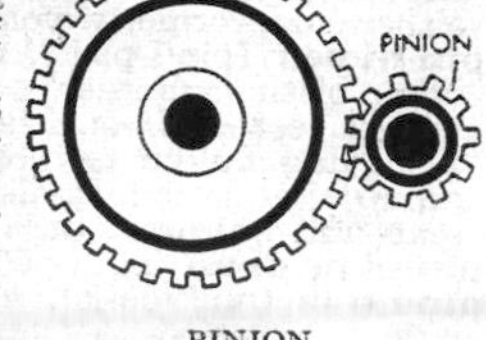

PINION

pin·ion (pin′yən), ***n.*** [ME.; OFr. *pignon;* L. *pinna, penna*, a feather], 1. the end joint of a bird's wing. 2. a wing. 3. any wing feather. 4. the anterior border of an insect's wing. ***v.t.*** 1. to cut off or bind the pinions of (a bird) to keep it from flying. 2. to bind (the wings). 3. to disable or impede by binding the arms of. 4. to confine or shackle.

pin·ite (pin′īt, pī′nīt), ***n.*** [G. *pinit* < *Pini*, mine in Saxony], a hydrous silicate of aluminum and potassium, occurring as an amorphous mineral.

pi·ni·tol (pī′ni-tōl′, pin′i-tol), ***n.*** [Fr. *pinite, pinitol* < L. *pinus*, pine (tree); + *-ol*], a sweet crystalline compound, $C_6H_6(OH)_5OCH_3$, occurring in the resin of the sugar pine.

pink (piŋk), ***n.*** [? < *pinkeye*, lit., little eye (cf. *pinkie*, little finger), a transl. of Fr. *oeillet*, the pink (lit., little eye)], 1. any of a number of related plants with five-petaled, pale-red flowers and sticky stems. 2. the flower. 3. its pale-red color. 4. the highest or finest condition, example, degree, etc. 5. [British], the scarlet worn by a fox hunter; hence, 6. [British], a fox hunter. 7. [sometimes P-], a person whose political views are somewhat radical: a derogatory term. ***adj.*** 1. pale-red. 2. mildly radical.

pink (piŋk), ***v.t.*** [ME. *pynken;* ? nasalized form of *pick, v.;* ? < AS. *pyngan*, to prick], 1. to ornament (cloth, leather, paper, etc.) by making perforations in a pattern. 2. to cut a saw-toothed edge on (cloth, etc.) so as to prevent unraveling or for decorative purposes. 3. to prick; stab. 4. to adorn; embellish.

pink (piŋk), ***n.*** [MD. *pinke;* M.Scot. has *pink botes*], a ship with a narrow stern: also **pinkie, pinky.**

Pink·er·ton, Allan (piŋ′kẽr-t'n), 1819–1884; American private detective, born in Scotland.

pink·eye (piŋk′ī′), ***n.*** an acute, contagious form of conjunctivitis in which the eyeball and the mucous membrane lining the eyelid become red and inflamed: also **pink eye.**

pink·ie (piŋk′i), ***n.*** the fifth, or smallest, finger: also spelled **pinky.**

pink·ie (piŋk′i), ***n.*** a pink (ship).

pink·ing shears (piŋk′iŋ), shears with notched blades, used for pinking the edges of cloth, etc.

pink·ish (piŋk′ish), ***adj.*** somewhat pink.

pink·root (piŋk′rōōt′, piŋk′root′), ***n.*** 1. a plant with tufted stems, stemless leaves, and red flowers with yellow throats. 2. its root, used as a vermifuge.

Pink·ster (piŋk'stẽr), *n.* [D. < (? via Goth. *paintēkustē*) Gr. *pentēkostē;* see PENTECOST], [Dial.], Whitsuntide.

pinkster flower, a variety of azalea with pink, sweet-smelling flowers, purplish-red at the base.

pink tea, [Colloq.], any frivolous social gathering, especially one attended largely by women.

pink·y (piŋk'i), *n.* [*pl.* PINKIES (-iz)], a pinkie.

pink·y (piŋk'i), *n.* [*pl.* PINKIES (-iz)], a pink (ship).

pin money, 1. an allowance of money given to a wife for her personal use. 2. any small sum of money, as for incidental minor expenses.

pin·na (pin'ə), *n.* [*pl.* PINNAE (-ē), PINNAS (-əz)], [L., a feather, projection], 1. in *anatomy*, the external ear; auricle. 2. in *botany*, one leaflet of a group arranged in feather fashion on a stem. 3. in *zoology*, a feather, wing, fin, or similar structure.

pin·nace (pin'is), *n.* [Fr. *pinasse;* It. *pinaccia;* LL. **pinacea* < L. *pinus*, a pine], 1. a small sailing ship formerly used as a tender, scout, etc. 2. a ship's boat.

pin·na·cle (pin'ə-k'l), *n.* [ME. & OFr. *pinacle;* LL. *pinnaculum*, dim. < L. *pinna*, a wing, pinnacle], 1. a small turret or spire on a buttress or an angle pier. 2. a slender, pointed formation, as at the top of some mountains; peak. 3. the highest point; culmination; acme. *v.t.* [PINNACLED (-k'ld), PINNACLING], 1. to set on a pinnacle. 2. to furnish or ornament with pinnacles. 3. to form the pinnacle of. —***SYN.*** see **summit**.

pin·nal (pin'əl), *adj.* of or like a pinna.

pin·nate (pin'āt, pin'it), *adj.* [L. *pinnatus* < *pinna*, a feather, fin], 1. resembling a feather. 2. in *botany*, with leaflets on each side of a common stem in a featherlike arrangement: see **leaf**, illus.

pin·nat·ed (pin'ā-tid), *adj.* pinnate.

pin·nat·i- (pi-nat'i), [< L. *pinnatus*, pinnate], a combining form meaning *pinnately*, as in *pinnatifid*.

pin·nat·i·fid (pi-nat'i-fid), *adj.* [*pinnati-* + *-fid*], having leaves in a featherlike arrangement, with narrow lobes whose clefts extend more than halfway to the stem.

pin·na·tion (pi-nā'shən), *n.* the condition or fact of being pinnate.

pin·ner (pin'ẽr), *n.* 1. a person or thing that pins. 2. a caplike headdress with a long, hanging flap pinned on either side, formerly worn by women.

pin·ni·ped (pin'i-ped'), *adj.* [< Mod. L. *Pinnipedia*, name of the suborder < L. *pinnapes*, *pinnipes*, having winged feet < *pinna*, a feather, fin + *pes*, *pedis*, a foot], 1. having finlike feet or flippers. 2. belonging to a group of aquatic animals having flippers, including the seals and walruses. *n.* a pinniped animal.

pin·ni·pe·di·an (pin'i-pē'di-ən), *adj. & n.* pinniped.

pin·nu·la (pin'yoo-lə), *n.* [*pl.* PINNULAE (-lē')], a pinnule.

pin·nu·lar (pin'yoo-lẽr), *adj.* of or like a pinnule.

pin·nu·late (pin'yoo-lāt'), *adj.* having pinnules.

pin·nu·lat·ed (pin'yoo-lā'tid), *adj.* pinnulate.

pin·nule (pin'ūl), *n.* [L. *pinnula*, dim. of *pinna*, a wing, feather], 1. any of the leaflets of a pinnate leaf. 2. a small fin or finlike part in animals; specifically, any of the lateral branches of the arm of a crinoid.

pi·noch·le, pi·noc·le (pē'nuk''l), *n.* [earlier also *penuchle*, *binochle:* the form of the word and the relation of the game to bezique suggest Fr. origin], 1. a game of cards for two, three, or four persons, played with a special deck of 48 cards, consisting of a double deck of all cards above the eight (including the ace). 2. the combination of the queen of spades and the jack of diamonds in this game. Also **penuchle, penuckle.**

pi·no·le (pi-nō'lā; Sp. pē-nô'le), *n.* [Sp. < Nahuatl *pinolli*], flour made of ground corn, mesquite beans, etc. in the southwestern United States and Mexico.

pi·ñon (pin'yən, pēn'yōn; Sp. pē-nyôn'), *n.* [Sp., pine nut < L. *pinea*, pine cone < *pinus*, a pine (tree)], 1. any of a number of related pine trees with large, edible seeds. 2. the seed.

pin·point (pin'point'), *v.t.* 1. to show the location of by sticking a pin into, as on a map; hence, 2. to show the precise location of. *n.* 1. the point of a pin. 2. something trifling or insignificant.

pinpoint bombing, bombing directed precisely at a particular objective.

pin·prick (pin'prik'), *n.* 1. any tiny puncture made by or as by a pin. 2. a minor irritation or annoyance.

pins and needles, paresthesia characterized by a tingling and prickling feeling in some parts of the body, as in the fingers and toes.

Pinsk (pēnsk; Eng. pinsk), *n.* a town in Byelorussian S.S.R.: pop., 32,000.

pin stripe, a slender, light-colored stripe, about the width of a pin, as in the fabric of some suits.

pint (pīnt), *n.* [ME. *pynte;* OFr. *pinte* < MD.], a measure of capacity (liquid or dry) equal to 1/2 quart: abbreviated **pt., p.**

pin·ta (pin'tə; Sp. pēn'tä), *n.* [Sp., a spot < *pintado*, pp. of *pintar*, to paint; see PINTO & PAINT], a contagious skin disease of tropical America, characterized by patches of various colors.

pin·ta·do (pin-tä'dō), *n.* [*pl.* PINTADOS, PINTADOES (-dōz)], [Port., painted, pp. of *pintar*, to paint; LL. **pinctare* < **pinctus*, for L. *pictus*, pp. of *pingere*, to paint], a long, silvery food and game fish with brown spots and a widely forked tail: it is common in the waters surrounding Florida and Cuba.

pin·tail (pin'tāl'), *n.* [*pl.* PINTAILS (-tālz'), PINTAIL; see PLURAL, II, D, 1], 1. a variety of duck with a long neck, white belly, and long, pointed, middle tail feathers. 2. a variety of grouse with a long, pointed tail.

pin·ta·no (pin-tä'nō), *n.* [*pl.* PINTANOS (-nōz)], a brightly colored fish found chiefly among coral reefs: also called *cow pilot*.

pin·tle (pin't'l), *n.* [ME. *pintil*, penis; AS. *pintel;* for IE. base see PIN; cf. PEN], a pin or bolt upon which some other part pivots or turns.

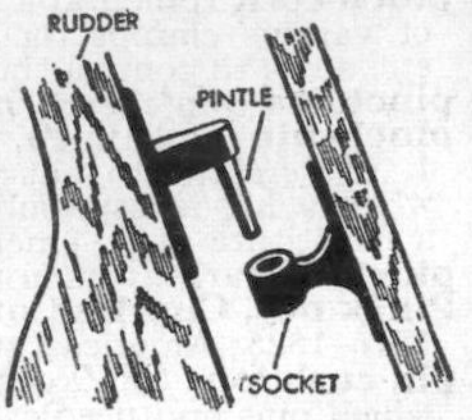

RUDDER
PINTLE
SOCKET

PINTLE

pin·to (pin'tō), *adj.* [Sp. < LL. **pinctus;* see PINTADO], marked with spots of two or more colors; mottled; piebald. *n.* [*pl.* PINTOS (-tōz)], 1. a pinto horse or pony. 2. the pinto bean.

pinto bean, a kind of mottled kidney bean found in the southwestern United States.

Pintsch gas (pinch), [after Richard *Pintsch* (1840–1919), G. inventor of the process], a gas obtained by the destructive distillation of petroleum, used for lighting.

pin-up (pin'up'), *adj.* 1. that is or can be pinned up or otherwise fastened to a wall: as, a *pin-up* lamp. 2. [Slang], designating a girl whose sexual attractiveness makes her a suitable subject for a picture to be displayed on a wall, as of a barracks. *n.* [Slang], a pin-up girl, picture, etc.

pin·weed (pin'wēd'), *n.* any of a number of related plants with thin stems and leaves, and small, purplish or greenish flowers.

pin·wheel (pin'hwēl'), *n.* 1. a small wheel with variously colored vanes of paper, etc. pinned to a stick so as to revolve in the wind. 2. a firework that revolves and throws off colored lights when set off. Also **pin wheel.**

pin·worm (pin'wũrm'), *n.* a small, threadlike worm with an unsegmented body, sometimes found as a parasite in the human rectum.

pin wrench, a type of wrench with a projecting polygonal pin that fits into a corresponding hole in a nut, etc. so as to secure a firm hold.

‡pinx·it (piŋk'sit), [L.], he (or she) painted (it): often placed after the artist's name on a painting: abbreviated **pnx., pxt.**

pinx·ter flower (piŋk'stẽr), a pinkster flower.

pin·y (pīn'i), *adj.* [PINIER (i-ẽr), PINIEST (-i-ist)], 1. abounding in pines. 2. of or like pines. Also spelled **piney.**

Pin·zón, Mar·tín A·lon·so (mär-tēn' ä-lôn'sô pēn-thôn'), 1440?–1493; Spanish navigator with Columbus; commanded the *Pinta*.

Pinzón, Vi·cen·te Yá·ñez (vē-then'te yä'nyeth), 1460?–1524?; brother of *Martín Alonso;* Spanish navigator with Columbus; commanded the *Nina*.

pi·o·neer (pī'ə-nêr'), *n.* [Fr. *pionnier;* OFr. *peonier*, foot soldier < *peon;* see PEON, PAWN (chessman)], 1. a member of a military unit that precedes the main body and builds bridges, roads, trenches, etc.; military engineer. 2. a person who goes before, preparing the way for others, as, an early settler or a scientist doing original work. 3. [Obs.], a digger; miner. *v.i.* to act as a pioneer. *v.t.* 1. to prepare or open (a way, etc.). 2. to be a pioneer in or of.

pi·ous (pī'əs), *adj.* [< Fr. or L.; Fr. *pieux;* L. *pius*, pious, devout, affectionate, good], 1. having or showing religious devotion; zealous in the performance of religious obligations. 2. springing from actual or pretended religious devotion. 3. sacred, as distinguished from secular or profane. 4. [Archaic], having or showing a sense of duty and loyalty to parents, family, friends, etc. —***SYN.*** see **devout.**

pip (pip), *n.* [abbrev. of *pippin*], 1. a small seed, as of an apple, pear, orange, etc. 2. [slang], a person or thing much admired.

pip (pip), *n.* [earlier *peep* < ?], 1. any of the figures or spots on playing cards, dominoes, dice, etc. 2. any of the diamond-shaped divisions of the skin of a pineapple. 3. a single rootstock or flower of the lily of the valley, peony, etc.

pip (pip), *v.i.* [PIPPED (pipt), PIPPING], [prob. var. of *peep* (to cry)], to peep or chirp, as a young bird. *v.t.* to break through (the shell): said of a hatching bird.

pip (pip), *n.* [ME. & MD. *pippe;* LL. *pipita* for L. *pituita*, phlegm, slime, pip], 1. a contagious disease of fowl, characterized by the secretion of mucus in the throat and the formation of a scab on the tongue. 2. any minor human ailment: a humorous usage.

pip·age (pīp'ij), *n.* [see -AGE], 1. transportation, as of water, gas, oil, etc., by pipes. 2. the charge for this transportation. 3. a system of such pipes.

pi·pal (pē′pəl), *n.* [Hind. *pīpal;* Sans. *pippala*], a fig tree of India; bo tree: also **pipal tree.**
pipe (pīp), *n.* [ME.; AS.; LL. **pipa* < L. *pipare*, to cheep, chirp, peep; echoic word], 1. a cylindrical tube, as of reed, straw, wood, or metal, for making musical sounds by the vibration of an air column; specifically, *pl. a)* the Panpipe. *b)* the bagpipe. 2. any of the wooden or metal tubes in an organ, that produce the tones. 3. *a)* a boatswain's whistle. *b)* the sounding of such a whistle to signal a ship's crew. 4. the voice in singing. 5. *often pl.* the singing voice. 6. the call, song, or note of a bird. 7. a long tube of clay, concrete, metal, wood, etc., for conveying water, gas, oil, or other fluids. 8. a tubular organ or canal of the body; especially, *pl.* the respiratory organs. 9. anything tubular in form. 10. *a)* a tube with a small bowl at one end, in which tobacco, etc. is smoked. *b)* enough tobacco to fill such a bowl. 11. a large cask for wine, oil, etc., having a capacity of about two hogsheads, or 126 gallons. 12. this volume as a unit of measure. 13. [Slang], something regarded as easy to accomplish. *v.i.* [PIPED (pīpt), PIPING], 1. to play on a pipe. 2. to utter shrill, reedy sounds or tones. 3. in *metallurgy*, to develop longitudinal cavities, as steel sometimes does in ingots and castings during solidification. 4. in *nautical usage*, to signal a ship's crew by sounding the boatswain's pipe. *v.t.* 1. to play (a tune, etc.) on a pipe. 2. to utter in a shrill, reedy voice or tone. 3. to affect or bring to some condition by or as by piping: as, he *piped* the children of Hamelin to their destruction. 4. to convey (water, gas, oil, etc.) by means of pipes. 5. to provide with pipes. 6. to trim with piping, as a dress. 7. in *nautical usage*, to order or call together by sounding the boatswain's pipe.
  pipe down, [Slang], to become quiet or quieter; stop shouting, talking, etc.
  pipe up, 1. to begin to play or sing (music). 2. to speak up or say in a piping voice.
pipe-clay (pīp′klā′), *v.t.* to whiten with pipe clay.
pipe clay, a white, plastic clay used for whitening, making clay pipes, etc.
pipe dream, [Colloq.], a fantastic idea, vain hope, or impossible plan such as might be produced in the mind of an opium smoker.
pipe·fish (pīp′fish′), *n.* [*pl.* PIPEFISH, PIPEFISHES (-iz); see FISH], any of a number of related long, narrow, bony-scaled fishes with a tubelike snout.
pipe·ful (pīp′fool′), *n.* [*pl.* PIPEFULS (-foolz′)], the amount (of tobacco, etc.) put in a pipe at one time.
pipe-line (pīp′lin′), *v.t.* 1. to convey by a pipe line. 2. to supply with a pipe line.
pipe line, 1. a line of pipes for conveying water, gas, oil, etc. 2. any channel or means whereby something is conveyed: as, a *pipe line* of information.
pipe of peace, a peace pipe; calumet.
pipe organ, a musical instrument with a keyboard that controls the flow of compressed air through one or more sets of pipes of varying length: cf. **organ, reed organ.**
pip·er (pīp′ẽr), *n.* [ME. & AS. *pipere*], a person who plays on a pipe; especially, a bagpiper.
  pay the piper, to pay for one's pleasures or undertakings; bear the consequences.
pip·er·a·ceous (pip′ə-rā′shəs, pī′pə-rā′shəs), *adj.* [L. *piper*, a pepper; + *-aceous*], of the pepper family.
pi·per·a·zin (pi-per′ə-zin, pip′ẽr-ə-zin), *n.* piperazine.
pi·per·a·zine (pi-per′ə-zēn′, pip′ẽr-ə-zin), *n.* [*piperine* + *azote* + *-ine*], a crystalline compound, $(C_2H_4NH)_2$, used in the treatment of gout.
pi·per·i·dine (pi-per′ə-dēn′, pip′ẽr-ə-din), *n.* [Fr. < *piperine;* cf. -IDE & -INE], a colorless, liquid hydrocarbon, $C_5H_{11}N$, found in many alkaloids and obtained by treating piperine with alkalis.
pip·er·in (pip′ẽr-in), *n.* piperine.
pip·er·ine (pip′ə-rēn′, pip′ẽr-in), *n.* [L. *piper*, a pepper; + *-ine*], a colorless, crystalline alkaloid, $C_{17}H_{19}O_3N$, found in black pepper and used in medicine to reduce fever.
pip·er·o·nal (pip′ẽr-ə-nal′), *n.* [G. < *piperin*, piperine + *-on*, -one + *al*dehyd, aldehyde], an aldehyde, $C_8H_6O_3$, obtained from piperine and having a strong smell like that of heliotrope: used in making perfume.
pipe·stem (pīp′stem′), *n.* 1. the long, slender stem of a tobacco pipe through which the smoke is drawn. 2. anything like this in form, as a very thin leg.
pipe·stone (pīp′stōn′), *n.* a reddish, claylike stone used by the American Indians to make tobacco pipes.
pi·pette, pi·pet (pi-pet′, pi-pet′), *n.* [Fr., dim. of *pipe*], a slender pipe or tube, usually of glass, for removing, transferring, or measuring small amounts of liquids.
pip·ing (pīp′iŋ), *n.* 1. the act of a person who pipes. 2. the music made by pipes. 3. a shrill voice or sound. 4. a system of pipes. 5. material that resembles or can be used for pipes. 6. in *cookery*, ornamental pipelike lines of icing. 7. in *dressmaking*, etc., a pipelike fold of material with which edges or seams are trimmed. *adj.* 1. playing on a pipe. 2. characterized by the music of the "peaceful" pipe rather than of the "warlike" drums, trumpets, etc.; hence, 3. peaceful; tranquil. 4. sounding high and shrill. *adv.* so as to hiss or sizzle: as, *piping* hot.
pip·it (pip′it), *n.* [echoic of its cry], any of a number of small related birds with a slender bill, streaked breast, and constantly wagging tail.
pip·kin (pip′kin), *n.* [dim. of *pipe;* cf. -KIN], 1. a small earthenware pot. 2. a piggin.
pip·pin (pip′in), *n.* [ME. *pipyn;* OFr. *pepin*, seed, pip], 1. any of a number of varieties of apple. 2. in *botany*, a seed. 3. [Slang], a person or thing much admired.
pip·sis·se·wa (pip-sis′ə-wə), *n.* [< Am. Ind. (Algonquian); cf. Cree *pipisisikweu*, lit., breaks it (i.e., gallstone) into fragments], any of a number of related plants with pink or white flowers and jagged, leathery leaves, used in medicine as a diuretic and tonic.
pip-squeak (pip′skwēk′), *n.* [first applied to a small high-velocity shell used by the Germans in World War I: apparently echoic in origin], anything or anyone regarded as small or insignificant.
pip·y (pīp′i), *adj.* [PIPIER (-i-ẽr), PIPIEST (-i-ist)], 1. pipelike; tubular. 2. sounding like a pipe; shrill.
pi·quan·cy (pē′kən-si), *n.* piquant quality, flavor, etc.
pi·quant (pē′kənt), *adj.* [Fr., ppr. of *piquer*, to prick, sting], 1. agreeably pungent or stimulating to the taste; pleasantly sharp or biting. 2. exciting interest or curiosity; stimulating; provocative. 3. [Archaic], piercing or stinging; bitter. —*SYN.* see **pungent.**
pique (pēk), *n.* [Fr. < *piquer*, to prick, sting], 1. resentment at being slighted or disdained; ruffled pride. 2. a fit of displeasure. *v.t.* [PIQUED (pēkt), PIQUING], [Fr. *piquer*], 1. to arouse resentment in, as by slighting; offend; ruffle the pride of. 2. to excite; arouse; provoke. 3. to pride (oneself). —*SYN.* see **offense, provoke.**
  pique oneself on (or **upon**), to be proud of.
pi·qué (pi-kā′), *n.* [Fr., pp. of *piquer*, to prick, sting], a firmly woven cotton fabric with vertical cords.
pi·quet (pi-ket′), *n.* [Fr., spade at cards; prob. dim. < *pique*, a pike], a game of cards for two persons, played with 32 cards.
pi·ra·cy (pī′rə-si), *n.* [*pl.* PIRACIES (-siz)], [ML. *piratia;* Gr. *peirateia* < *peiratēs*, a pirate], 1. robbery of ships on the high seas. 2. the unauthorized publication or use of a copyrighted or patented work.
Pi·rae·us (pī-rē′əs), *n.* a city in Greece: seaport of Athens: pop., 251,000: also spelled **Peiraeus:** Greek name, *Peiraievs.*
pi·ra·gua (pi-rä′gwə, pi-rag′wə), *n.* [Sp.; see PIROGUE], 1. a canoe made by hollowing out a large log: also **pirogue.** 2. a flat-bottomed, two-masted sailing boat.
Pi·ran·del·lo, Lu·i·gi (lōō-ē′jē pē′rän-del′lô; Eng. pir′ən-del′ō), 1867–1936; Italian dramatist and novelist; received Nobel prize in literature, 1934.
pi·ra·nha (pi-rän′yə), *n.* [Braz. Port. < Tupi *piranha*, toothed fish < *piro*, a fish + *sainha*, a tooth], any of a group of small but voracious South American fish that attack large mammals in the water, including man.
pi·rate (pī′rit), *n.* [ME.; L. *pirata;* Gr. *peiratēs* < *peirān*, attack], 1. a person who practices piracy; especially, a robber of ships on the high seas. 2. a ship used by pirates in attacking other vessels. *v.i. & v.t.* [PIRATED (-id), PIRATING], 1. to practice piracy (upon). 2. to publish or use (a literary work, etc.) in violation of a copyright or patent.
pi·rat·ic (pī-rat′ik), *adj.* piratical.
pi·rat·i·cal (pī-rat′i-kl), *adj.* [< L. *piraticus;* + *-al*], 1. of or like a pirate. 2. engaged in piracy.
Pi·rith·o·üs (pī-rith′ō-əs), *n.* in *Greek mythology*, a king of the Lapithae who, with his friend Theseus, attempted to abduct Persephone from Hades: he was apprehended by Pluto and bound there to a rock.
pirn (pũrn), *n.* [ME. *pyrne;* ? by metathesis < dial. *prin, preen*, a pin, pointed twig; cf. SPOOL, of which orig. sense was reed, quill], 1. the bobbin or spool of a weaver's shuttle. 2. [Scot.], a fishing reel.
pi·rogue (pi-rōg′), *n.* [Fr.; Sp. *piragua* < the W.Ind. (Carib) name], 1. a canoe made by hollowing out a large log: also **piragua.** 2. any canoe-shaped boat.
pir·ou·ette (pir′ōō-et′), *n.* [Fr., spinning top; prob. < dial. *piroue*, a top; source may be LL. **piro*, a plug, peg, whence notion "peg-top"], in *dancing*, a whirling on the toes. *v.i.* [PIROUETTED (-id), PIROUETTING], [Fr. *pirouetter* < the *n.*], to do a pirouette.
Pi·sa (pē′zə; It. pē′sä), *n.* a city in northwestern Italy, on the Arno River: famous for its Leaning Tower: pop., 82,000 (est. 1947).
‡pis al·ler (pē′zà′lā′), [Fr., lit., to go worse], last resort; last expedient.
Pi·sa·no, Ni·co·la (nē-kô′lä pē-sä′nô; Eng. pi-sä′nō), 1225?–1278?; Italian sculptor and architect.
pis·ca·ry (pis′kə-ri), *n.* [*pl.* PISCARIES (-riz)], [ML. *piscaria* < L. *piscarius*, of fish, of fishing < *piscis*, a fish], 1. in *law*, the right of fishing in waters owned

by another: now only in *common of piscary.* 2. a place for fishing.

pis·ca·tol·o·gy (pis′kə-tol′ə-ji), *n.* [< L. *piscatus*, pp. of *piscari*, to fish; + *-logy*], the art or science of fishing.

pis·ca·to·ri·al (pis′kə-tôr′i-əl, pis′kə-tō′ri-əl), *adj.* [L. *piscatorius* < *piscator*, fisherman], of fishes, fishermen, or fishing.

pis·ca·to·ry (pis′kə-tôr′i, pis′kə-tō′ri), *adj.* piscatorial.

Pis·ces (pis′ēz), *n.* [ME.; L., pl. of *piscis*, a fish], 1. a constellation south of Andromeda, supposedly resembling a fish in shape: see **constellation**, chart. 2. the twelfth sign of the zodiac (♓), entered by the sun about February 21: see **zodiac**, illus. 3. the class of vertebrates including the fishes.

pis·ci- (pis′i), [< L. *piscis*, a fish], a combining form meaning *fish*, as in *piscivorous*.

pis·ci·cul·ture (pis′i-kul′chẽr), *n.* [*pisci-* + *culture*], the breeding and rearing of fish as an art or industry.

pis·ci·na (pi-sī′nə, pi-sē′nə), *n.* [L., a tank, cistern, orig., fishpond < *piscis*, a fish], a basin with a drain, near the altar of a church, for the disposal of water used for sacred purposes.

pis·cine (pis′īn, pis′in), *adj.* [< L. *piscis*, a fish; + *-ine*], of or resembling fish.

Pis·cis Aus·tri·nus (or **Aus·tra·lis**), (pis′is ôs-trī′nəs, ôs-trā′lis), a southern constellation: see **constellation**, chart.

pis·civ·o·rous (pi-siv′ẽr-əs), *adj.* [*pisci-* + *-vorous*], fish-eating.

Pis·gah, Mount (piz′gə), [Heb. *pisgāh*, lit., prob., cleft], the mountain ridge east of Jordan from which Moses saw the Promised Land.

pish (pish, psh; *conventionalized pronun.*), *interj. & n.* an exclamation of disgust or impatience. *v.i. & v.t.* to make this exclamation (at).

Pi·sid·i·a (pi-sid′i-ə), *n.* an ancient country in southern Asia Minor: it later became a Roman province.

pi·si·form (pī′sə-fôrm′), *adj.* [< L. *pisum*, pea; + *-form*], 1. resembling a pea in shape and size. 2. designating a small round bone of the wrist.

Pi·sis·tra·tus (pī-sis′trə-təs, pi-sis′trə-təs), *n.* ruler and tyrant of Athens; lived 605–527 B.C.

pis·mire (pis′mīr′), *n.* [ME. *pissemire; pisse*, urine + *mire*, ant: so named because it discharges an irritant fluid popularly regarded as urine], an ant.

pi·so·lite (pī′sə-līt′, piz′ə-līt′), *n.* [< Gr. *pison*, a pea; + *-lite*], a limestone composed of pea-shaped pebbles.

pi·so·lit·ic (pī′sə-lit′ik, piz′ə-lit′ik), *adj.* of or like pisolite.

piss (pis), *v.i.* [ME. *pissen;* OFr. *pissier;* prob. of echoic origin], to urinate. *v.t.* to discharge as or with the urine. *n.* urine. Now vulgar.

Pis·sar·ro, Ca·mille (kȧ′mē′y′ pē′sȧ′rō′), 1831–1903; French impressionist painter.

pis·ta·chi·o (pis-tä′shi-ō′, pis-tash′i-ō′), *n.* [*pl.* PISTACHIOS (-ōz′)], [It. *pistacchio;* L. *pistacium;* Gr. *pistakion* < *pistakē*, pistachio tree], 1. a small tree of the cashew family. 2. its edible, greenish seed (*pistachio nut*). 3. the flavor of this nut. 4. a light yellow-green color.

PISTACHIO (branch bearing fruit)

pis·ta·reen (pis′tə-rēn′), *n.* [dim. of *peseta*, dim. of *peso;* see PESO], a former Spanish silver coin of the American colonies and the West Indies. *adj.* concerned with petty affairs; trifling.

pis·til (pis′til, pis′t'l), *n.* [Fr.; L. *pistillum*, a pestle], the seed-bearing organ of a flower consisting of the ovary, stigma, and style.

pis·til·late (pis′tə-lit, pis′tə-lāt′), *adj.* in *botany*, having a pistil or pistils; especially, having pistils but no stamens.

Pis·to·ia (pē-stô′yä), *n.* a city in central Italy: pop., 74,000 (est. 1947).

pis·tol (pis′t'l), *n.* [Fr. & G. *pistole;* Czech *píšťal*, a pipe, pistol < *pisk*, echoic word for a whistling sound], a small firearm made to be held and fired with one hand: most pistols are now either revolvers or magazine-fed automatics. *v.t.* [PISTOLED or PISTOLLED (-t'ld), PISTOLING or PISTOLLING], to shoot with a pistol.

pis·tole (pis-tōl′), *n.* [Fr., lit., pistol (see PISTOL): so named in Fr., after a debasement of the coin, in punning allusion to a double use of the original name of the coin, *écu*, which also meant "shield"], 1. a former Spanish gold coin, valued at about $4.00. 2. any of various similar obsolete gold coins of Europe.

pis·to·leer, pis·to·lier (pis′tə-lêr′), *n.* [Fr. *pistolier*], formerly, a soldier armed with a pistol.

pis·ton (pis′t'n), *n.* [Fr. *piston;* It. *pistone*, piston < *pestone*, a pestle < *pistare*, *pestare*, to beat, pound; LL. *pistare* < L. *pisere*, *pinsere*, to pound, beat], 1. a disk or short cylinder closely fitted in a hollow cylinder and moved back and forth by the pressure of a fluid so as to transmit reciprocating motion to the piston rod attached to it, or moved by the rod so as to exert pressure on the fluid. 2. in *music*, a sliding valve moved in the cylinder of a brass-wind instrument to change the pitch.

PISTON ROD
CYLINDER WALL
PISTON

PISTON

piston ring, a split metal ring placed around a piston to make it fit the cylinder closely.

piston rod, a rod which moves, or is moved by, the piston to which it is attached.

pit (pit), *n.* [D. *pit, pitte*, kernel, pith; akin to Eng. *pith*], the hard stone, as of the plum, peach, cherry, etc., which contains the seed. *v.t.* [PITTED (-id), PITTING], to remove the pit from.

pit (pit), *n.* [ME.; AS. *pytt;* ON. *pyttr;* L. *puteus*, a well], 1. a hole or cavity in the ground. 2. an abyss. 3. hell. 4. a covered hole used to trap wild animals; pitfall. 5. any concealed danger; trap; snare. 6. an enclosed area in which animals are kept or made to fight: as, a bear *pit*. 7. *a*) the shaft of a coal mine. *b*) the coal mine itself. 8. an indentation or depression on a part of the human body: as, an arm*pit*. 9. a small hollow in a surface; specifically, a depressed scar on the skin as that resulting from smallpox. 10. [British], *a*) the ground floor of a theater, especially the part at the rear. *b*) the spectators in that section. 11. the small, often depressed, section in front of the stage where the orchestra sits. 12. the part of the floor of an exchange where a special branch of business is transacted: as, the wheat *pit*. *v.t.* [PITTED (-id), PITTING], 1. to put, cast, or store in a pit. 2. to make pits in. 3. to mark with small scars: as, *pitted* by smallpox. 4. to set (cocks, etc.) in a pit to fight; hence, 5. to set in competition (*against*). *v.i.* to become marked with pits.

pi·ta (pē′tə), *n.* [Sp. < Quechua *pita*, fine thread], any of a number of related agave plants yielding a fiber used in paper and cord. 2. the fiber.

pit·a·pat (pit′ə-pat′), *adv.* [redupl. of *pat*], with rapid and strong beating; palpitatingly. *n.* a rapid succession of beats or taps. *v.i.* [PITAPATTED (-id), PITAPATTING], to go pitapat; palpitate.

Pit·cairn Island (pit′kârn), a British island in Polynesia in the South Pacific, settled by mutineers of the British ship *Bounty* in 1790: area, 2 sq. mi.; pop., 210.

pitch (pich), *n.* [ME. *pich;* AS. *pic;* L. *pix, picis*, pitch], 1. a black, sticky substance formed in the distillation of coal tar, wood tar, petroleum, etc. and used for waterproofing, roofing, pavements, etc. 2. any of certain bitumens, as mineral pitch or asphaltum. 3. a resin found in certain evergreen trees. *v.t.* to cover or smear with or as with pitch.

pitch (pich), *v.t.* [ME. *picchen;* prob. form of *pick*, to strike], 1. to set up; erect: as, *pitch* a tent. 2. to throw; cast; fling; hurl; toss. 3. to set in order for battle: obsolete except in *pitched battle*. 4. to fix or set at a particular point, level, degree, etc. 5. in *baseball*, to throw (the ball) to the batter. 6. in *card games*, *a*) to lead (a card of a certain suit), thus establishing trump. *b*) to establish (trump) thus. 7. in *music*, to determine or set the key of (a tune, an instrument, or the voice). *v.i.* 1. to encamp. 2. to take up one's position; settle. 3. to pitch anything, as hay, a ball, etc. 4. to fall or plunge headlong. 5. to incline downward; dip. 6. to plunge or toss with the bow and stern rising and falling: said of a ship; hence, 7. to plunge forward; lurch, as a person or animal does when off balance. *n.* 1. act or manner of pitching. 2. a throw; fling; toss. 3. a plunging forward; especially, the rising and falling of the bow and stern of a ship in a rough sea. 4. anything pitched. 5. the amount pitched. 6. a place where a street hawker or carnival hawker sets up his stand. 7. a point or degree: as, excitement was at a high *pitch*. 8. the degree of slope or inclination. 9. [Slang], a line of talk, such as a hawker uses. 10. in *aeronautics*, the distance advanced by a propeller in one revolution. 11. in *architecture*, the slope of the sides of a roof, expressed by the ratio of its height to its span. 12. in *geology & mining*, the dip of a stratum or vein. 13. in *machinery*, *a*) the distance between corresponding points on two adjacent gear teeth. *b*) the distance between corresponding points on two adjacent threads of a screw, measured along the axis. 14. in *music, speech*, etc., *a*) that quality of a tone or sound determined by the frequency of vibration of the sound waves reaching the ear: the greater the frequency, the higher the pitch. *b*) a standard of pitch for tuning instruments: see **concert pitch, philharmonic pitch.** —*SYN.* see **throw.**

pitch in, [Colloq.], to set to work energetically.

pitch into, [Colloq.], to attack physically or verbally.

pitch on (or **upon**), to select; decide on.

pitch-black (pich′blak′), ***adj.*** very black.

pitch·blende (pich′blend′), ***n.*** [G. *pechblende; pech,* pitch + *blende;* see BLENDE], a brown to black lustrous mineral containing uranium, radium, etc.

pitch circle, a circle touching the teeth of a gear wheel at points where they mesh with the teeth of another gear wheel.

pitch-dark (pich′därk′), ***adj.*** very dark.

pitched battle (picht), a battle in which placement of troops and the line of combat are prearranged.

pitch·er (pich′ẽr), ***n.*** [ME. *picher;* OFr. *pichier* or ML. *picher;* ult. < LL. *bicarium,* a jug; Gr. *bikos,* wine jar], 1. a container, usually with a handle and lip, for holding and pouring liquids. 2. as much as a pitcher will hold. 3. in *botany,* a leaf, shaped somewhat like a pitcher, which attracts insects; ascidium. Abbreviated **p.**

pitch·er (pich′ẽr), ***n.*** [*pitch, v.* + *-er*], 1. a person who pitches; especially, in *baseball,* the player who pitches the ball to the batter. 2. in *golf,* an iron club with the face slanted sharply backward.

pitcher plant, any of a number of related plants with pitcherlike leaves which attract and trap insects.

pitch·fork (pich′fôrk′), ***n.*** a large, long-handled fork used for lifting and tossing hay, straw, etc. ***v.t.*** to lift and toss with or as with a pitchfork.

pitch·i·ness (pich′i-nis), ***n.*** the quality of being pitchy.

pitch·man (pich′mən), ***n.*** [*pl.* PITCHMEN (-mən)], [Slang], a person who makes his living by setting up small stands at carnivals or on city streets and hawking novelties, jewelry, etc.

pitch·out (pich′out′), ***n.*** in *baseball,* a ball pitched deliberately away from the plate, as in an attempt to trap a base runner stealing a base.

PITCHER PLANT
(2 ft. high)

pitch pine, any of several resinous pines from which pitch or turpentine is obtained.

pitch pipe, a small metal pipe which produces a fixed tone used as a standard in tuning an instrument or establishing the pitch for a singer.

pitch·stone (pich′stōn′), ***n.*** [*pitch* (black substance) + *stone,* after G. *pechstein*], a glassy, lustrous volcanic rock with a pitchy appearance.

pitch·y (pich′i), ***adj.*** [PITCHIER (-i-ẽr), PITCHIEST (-i-ist)], 1. full of pitch; smeared with pitch. 2. resembling pitch in consistency or stickiness. 3. black; very dark.

pit·e·ous (pit′i-əs), ***adj.*** [ME. & OFr. *pitous;* LL. **pietosus* < L. *pietas,* piety, (later) pity], 1. arousing pity or compassion; deserving pity. 2. [Archaic], having or showing pity. —*SYN.* see **pitiful.**

pit·fall (pit′fôl′), ***n.*** [ME. *putfal, pitfalle,* etc.; 2d element < AS. *fealle,* a trap], 1. a lightly covered pit used as a trap for animals. 2. any concealed danger or trap for an unsuspecting person. —*SYN.* see **trap.**

pith (pith), ***n.*** [ME. *pithe;* AS. *pitha;* akin to MD. *pitte,* pit of a fruit, kernel, pith of a tree, etc.; only W.Gmc.], 1. the soft, spongy tissue in the center of certain plant stems. 2. the soft core of various other things, as of a bone, feather, etc. 3. the essential part; substance; gist. 4. strength; vigor; force. ***v.t.*** 1. to remove the pith from (a plant stem). 2. to pierce or sever the spinal cord of (an animal) in order to kill it or make it insensible for experimental purposes.

pith·e·can·thrope (pith′ə-kan′thrōp), ***n.*** a member of the genus *Pithecanthropus.*

Pith·e·can·thro·pus e·rec·tus (pith′ə-kan′thrə-pəs, pith′ə-kan-thrō′pəs i-rek′təs), [Mod. L. < Gr. *pithēkos,* ape + *anthrōpos,* man; see ERECT], an extinct early species of man, an apelike creature of the Pleistocene Epoch, remains of which were found in Java; Java man.

pith·i·ly (pith′ə-li), ***adv.*** in a pithy manner.

pith·i·ness (pith′i-nis), ***n.*** the quality of being pithy.

pith·y (pith′i), ***adj.*** [PITHIER (-i-ẽr), PITHIEST (-i-ist)], 1. of, like, or full of pith. 2. full of substance, meaning, or force: as, a *pithy* style. —*SYN.* see **concise.**

pit·i·a·ble (pit′i-ə-b′l), ***adj.*** [ME. & OFr. *piteable* < *pitier;* see PITY], 1. arousing or deserving pity. 2. deserving contempt; despicable; mean. —*SYN.* see **pitiful.**

pit·i·a·bly (pit′i-ə-bli), ***adv.*** in a pitiable manner.

pit·i·er (pit′i-ẽr), ***n.*** a person who pities.

pit·i·ful (pit′i-fəl), ***adj.*** 1. full of pity or compassion. 2. exciting or deserving pity. 3. deserving contempt; despicable; mean.

SYN.—**pitiful** applies to that which arouses or deserves pity because it is sad, pathetic, etc. (the suffering of the starving natives was *pitiful*); **pitiable** is the preferred term when a greater or lesser degree of contempt is mingled with commiseration (the opposition shrunk to a *pitiable* minority); **piteous** stresses the nature of the thing calling for pity rather than its influence on the observer (*piteous* groans).

pit·i·less (pit′i-lis), ***adj.*** without pity. —*SYN.* see **cruel.**

pit·man (pit′mən), ***n.*** [*pl.* PITMEN (-mən)], 1. a person who works in a pit; especially, a coal miner. 2. [*pl.* PITMANS (-mənz)], in *machinery,* a connecting rod.

Pi·tot tube (pē-tō′), [after Henri *Pitot* (1695–1771), Fr. physicist, who invented the original instrument], an instrument for measuring the velocity of flow of a fluid by differential pressure between openings at the tip and side: it is used on airplanes to measure air speed.

pit saw, a large saw worked by two men, one standing on the log, the other in a pit below it: also **pitsaw,** ***n.***

Pitt, William (pit), 1. first Earl of Chatham, 1708–1778; English statesman and orator: called *The Great Commoner.* 2. 1759–1806; son of the above; English statesman; prime minister (1783–1801; 1804–1806).

pit·tance (pit′əns), ***n.*** [ME. *pitaunce;* OFr. *pitance,* portion of food allowed a monk; ML. *pietantia* < L. *pietas,* piety], 1. a small or barely sufficient allowance of money. 2. a small amount or share, as of income.

pit·ted (pit′id), ***adj.*** 1. marked with pits or hollows. 2. pockmarked.

pit·ter-pat·ter (pit′ẽr-pat′ẽr), ***n.*** [ME. *pyter-pater;* echoic], a rapid succession of light beating or tapping sounds. ***adv.*** with a pitter-patter.

Pitts·burgh (pits′bẽrg), ***n.*** a city in western Pennsylvania, at the juncture of the Allegheny and Monongahela rivers: pop., 604,000 (metropolitan area, 2,405,000).

Pitts·field (pits′fēld), ***n.*** a city in western Massachusetts: pop., 58,000.

pi·tu·i·tar·y (pi-tōō′ə-ter′i, pi-tū′ə-ter′i), ***adj.*** [L. *pituitarius* < *pituita,* phlegm, rheum < IE. base **pī-,* a juice, sap, seen also in Gr. *pitys,* a juice, drink, L. *pinus,* pine], 1. of or secreting mucus. 2. of the pituitary gland. 3. designating a type of body structure characterized by large bones and abnormally long arms and legs, believed to be caused by excessive secretion by the pituitary gland. ***n.*** 1. the pituitary gland. 2. any of various preparations made from extracts of either of the lobes of the pituitary gland.

pituitary gland (or **body**), a small, oval endocrine gland attached by a stalk to the base of the brain and consisting of an anterior and a posterior lobe: it secretes hormones influencing body growth, metabolism, etc.

pi·tu·i·tous (pi-tōō′ə-təs, pi-tū′ə-təs), ***adj.*** [L. *pituitosus* < *pituita,* phlegm], of, like, or discharging mucus.

pit·y (pit′i), ***n.*** [*pl.* PITIES (-tiz)], [ME. *pite;* OFr. *pite, pitet;* L. *pietas,* piety < *pius,* pious], 1. sorrow felt for another's suffering or misfortune; compassion; sympathy. 2. a cause for sorrow or regret. ***v.t.* & *v.i.*** [PITIED (-id), PITYING], to feel pity (for).

have (or **take**) **pity on,** to show pity or compassion for.

SYN.—**pity** implies sorrow felt for another's suffering or misfortune, sometimes connoting slight contempt because the object is regarded as weak or inferior (he felt *pity* for a man so ignorant); **compassion** implies pity accompanied by an urge to help or spare (moved by *compassion,* I did not press for payment); **commiseration** implies deeply felt and openly expressed feelings of pity (she wept with her friend in *commiseration*); **sympathy,** in this connection, implies such kinship of feeling as enables one to really understand or even to share the sorrow, etc. of another (he always turned to his wife for *sympathy*); **condolence** now usually implies a formal expression of sympathy with another in sorrow (a letter of *condolence*).

pit·y·ri·a·sis (pit′ə-ri′ə-sis), ***n.*** [Mod. L.; Gr. *pityriasis* < *pityrion,* bran, scale], 1. any of various skin diseases characterized by the shedding of scaly flakes of epidermis. 2. a skin disease of domestic animals, characterized by the formation of dry scales.

‡**più** (pū), ***adv.*** [It.], more: a direction in music, as in *più allegro,* more quickly.

Pi·us VII (pī′əs), 1742–1823; Pope (1800–1823).

Pius IX, 1792–1878; Pope (1846–1878).

Pius X, Saint, 1835–1914; Pope (1903–1914).

Pius XI, 1857–1939; Pope (1922–1939).

Pius XII, 1876–1958; Pope (1939–1958).

piv·ot (piv′ət), ***n.*** [Fr.; cf. It. *pivolo,* peg], 1. a point, shaft, pin, etc. on which something turns. 2. a person or thing on or around which something turns, depends, etc.; central point. 3. a pivoting movement. ***adj.*** pivotal. ***v.t.*** to provide with, attach by, or mount on a pivot or pivots. ***v.i.*** to turn on or as on a pivot.

piv·ot·al (piv′ət-'l), ***adj.*** 1. of or acting as a pivot. 2. on which something turns or depends; cardinal.

pix (piks), ***n.*** a pyx.

pix·i·lat·ed (pik′sə-lā′tid), ***adj.*** [< *pixy* + *titillated*], 1. slightly unbalanced mentally. 2. [Slang], drunk.

pix·y (pik′si), ***n.*** [*pl.* PIXIES (-siz)], [< S.W. Brit. dial. *pixey, pisky*], a fairy; sprite: also spelled **pixie.**

Pi·zar·ro, Fran·cis·co (frän-thēs′kō pē-thär′rō; Eng.

pi-zä'rō), 1470?–1541; Spanish conqueror of Peru.
piz·za (pēt'sə), ***n.*** [It.], an Italian dish consisting of a breadlike crust covered with a spiced preparation of tomatoes and cheese and baked.
piz·ze·ri·a (pēt'sə-rē'ə), ***n.*** [It.], a place where pizzas are prepared and sold.
piz·zi·ca·to (pit'sə-kä'tō; It. pēt'tsē-kä'tô), ***adj.*** [It., pp. of *pizzicare*, to pluck, pinch], in *music*, plucked: a direction to performers on stringed instruments to pluck the strings with the fingers instead of running the bow across them. ***adv.*** in a pizzicato manner. Abbreviated **pizz.** ***n.*** 1. the act or art of plucking the strings on a violin, etc. 2. [*pl.* PIZZICATI (-tē)], a note or passage played in this way.
pk., [*pl.* PKS.], 1. pack. 2. park. 3. peak. 4. peck.
pkg., package; packages.
pl., 1. place. 2. plate. 3. plural.
pla·ca·bil·i·ty (plā'kə-bil'ə-ti, plak'ə-bil'ə-ti), ***n.*** [L. *placabilitas*], the quality of being placable.
pla·ca·ble (plā'kə-b'l, plak'ə-b'l), ***adj.*** [ME.; OFr.; L. *placabilis* < *placare*, to quiet, soothe, appease, pacify], capable of being placated; readily pacified; forgiving.
pla·ca·bly (plā'kə-bli, plak'ə-bli), ***adv.*** in a placable manner.
plac·ard (plak'ärd; *for v., usually* plə-kärd'), ***n.*** [OFr. *placart, plackart;* Pr. **placat* < *placa*, plaque; see PLAQUE], a notice for display in a public place; poster. ***v.t.*** 1. to place placards on or in. 2. to advertise or give notice of by means of placards. 3. to display as a placard. ***v.i.*** to set up placards.
pla·cate (plā'kāt, plak'āt), ***v.t.*** [PLACATED (-id), PLACATING], [< L. *placatus*, pp. of *placare*, to appease], to quiet the anger of; appease; pacify. —***SYN.*** see **pacify.**
pla·ca·tion (plā-kā'shən), ***n.*** a placating; appeasement.
pla·ca·tive (plā'kə-tiv, plak'ə-tiv), ***adj.*** tending to placate.
pla·ca·to·ry (plā'kə-tôr'i, plak'ə-tō'ri), ***adj.*** [LL. *placatorius*], serving or intended to placate.
place (plās), ***n.*** [ME.; OFr.; L. *platea;* Gr. *plateia*, a street < *platys*, broad], 1. a square or court in a city. 2. a short, usually narrow, street. 3. space; room. 4. a particular area or locality; region. 5. *a*) the part of space occupied by a person or thing. *b*) situation. 6. a city, town, or village. 7. a residence; dwelling; house and grounds. 8. a building or space devoted to a special purpose: as, a *place* of amusement. 9. a particular spot on or part of the body or a surface: as, a sore *place* in the back. 10. a particular passage or page in a book, magazine, etc. 11. position or standing as determined by others: as, his *place* in history is assured. 12. a step or point in a sequence: as, in the first *place.* 13. the customary, proper, or natural position, time, or character. 14. a space used, reserved, or customarily occupied by a person, as a seat in a theater, at a table, etc. 15. the space or position customarily or formerly occupied by another: as, a regent ruled in *place* of the boy king. 16. (another's) situation or state: as, you would have acted quite the same if you were in my *place.* 17. an office; employment; position. 18. official position. 19. the duties of any position. 20. the duty or business (of a person). 21. in *arithmetic*, the position of an integer, as in noting decimals: as, the third decimal *place.* 22. in *racing*, *a*) a position among the leaders, usually first, second, or third, at the finish. *b*) the second position at the finish. Abbreviated **pl.** ***v.t.*** [PLACED (plāst), PLACING], [Fr. *placer*], 1. to put in a particular place, condition, or relation. 2. to find employment or a position for; appoint to an office. 3. to arrange for a desired handling, treatment, or allocation of: as, he *placed* the whole shipment, the child was *placed* for adoption. 4. to repose (confidence, trust, hope, etc.) *in* a person or thing. 5. to identify by connecting with some place, time, circumstance, class, etc. 6. to pitch (the voice) in singing or speaking. ***v.i.*** in *sports*, to finish among the first three in a contest; specifically, to finish second in a horse or dog race.
give place, 1. to make room. 2. to yield.
go places, [Slang], to achieve success.
in place, 1. in the customary, proper, or assigned place. 2. fitting; proper; timely.
know one's place, to be conscious of one's (inferior) position or rank in life and act accordingly.
out of place, 1. not in the customary, proper, or assigned place. 2. not fitting, proper, or timely.
put one in one's place, to humble a person who is overstepping bounds.
take place, to come into being; happen; occur.
take the place of, to be a substitute for.
pla·ce·bo (plə-sē'bō), ***n.*** [*pl.* PLACEBOS, PLACEBOES (-bōz)], [ME.; L., I shall please], 1. in the *Roman Catholic Church*, the first antiphon of the Vespers for the dead, beginning with the word *placebo.* 2. a medicine given merely to humor the patient; especially, a preparation containing no medicine but given for its psychological effect. 3. something said or done to win the favor of another.
place card, a small card bearing the name of a guest and placed at the seat that he is to occupy at a table.
place-kick (plās'kik'), ***v.i.*** to make a place kick.
place kick, in *football*, a kick performed while the ball is held in place on the ground, used in kicking off or, sometimes, in attempting to make a field goal or a point after a touchdown.
place·man (plās'mən), ***n.*** [*pl.* PLACEMEN (-mən)], [Chiefly British], a person who holds a government position or the like: usually contemptuous.
place mat, a small mat of cloth, paper, etc. serving as an individual table cover for each person at a meal.
place·ment (plās'mənt), ***n.*** 1. a placing or being placed. 2. the finding of employment for a person. 3. location or arrangement. 4. in *football*, the setting of the ball on the ground in position for a place kick.
pla·cen·ta (plə-sen'tə), ***n.*** [*pl.* PLACENTAE (-tē), PLACENTAS (-təz)], [L., lit., a cake < Gr. *plakounta*, acc. of *plakous*, a flat cake < *plax*, *plakos*, a flat object], 1. in *anatomy* & *zoology*, a vascular organ within the uterus, connected to the fetus by the umbilical cord: it serves as the structure through which the fetus receives nourishment from, and eliminates waste matter into, the circulatory system of the mother. 2. in *botany*, that part of the lining of the ovary which bears the ovules; tissue that bears sporangia.
pla·cen·tal (plə-sen't'l), ***adj.*** of or having a placenta.
pla·cen·tate (plə-sen'tāt), ***adj.*** having a placenta.
plac·en·ta·tion (plas''n-tā'shən), ***n.*** 1. in *anatomy* & *zoology*, *a*) the formation or structure of a placenta. *b*) the manner in which the placenta is attached to the uterus. 2. in *botany*, the manner in which the placenta is arranged in the ovary.
Pla·cen·tia (plə-sen'shə), ***n.*** Piacenza: the ancient name.
plac·er (plās'ēr), ***n.*** a person who places.
plac·er (plas'ēr), ***n.*** [Sp. < *plaza*, a place], a waterborne or glacial deposit of gravel or sand containing heavy ore minerals, as gold, platinum, etc., which have been eroded from their original bedrock and concentrated as small particles that can be washed out.
plac·er mining (plas'ēr), mining of placers (deposits) by washing, dredging, or other hydraulic methods.
pla·cet (plā'sit), ***n.*** [L., it pleases], a vote of assent expressed by saying *placet.*
plac·id (plas'id), ***adj.*** [L. *placidus* < *placere*, to please], undisturbed; tranquil; calm; quiet. —***SYN.*** see **calm.**
pla·cid·i·ty (plə-sid'ə-ti), ***n.*** [L. *placiditas*], the state or quality of being placid.
plack·et (plak'it), ***n.*** [var. of *placard*, in obs. sense "breastplate, top of skirt," etc.; the word *placard* is recorded in this sense], 1. a slit at the top of a skirt to make it easy to put on and take off: also **placket hole.** 2. a pocket, especially in a woman's skirt. 3. [Archaic], a petticoat.
plac·oid (plak'oid), ***adj.*** [< Gr. *plax*, *plakos*, flat plate, tablet; + *-oid*], in *zoology*, of or having horny scales consisting of a bony base and an enamel-covered, toothlike spine. ***n.*** a fish with such scales.
‡pla·fond (plà'fōn'), ***n.*** [Fr., earlier *platfond; plat*, flat + *fond*, background, bottom], 1. a decorated ceiling. 2. a painted or carved design on a ceiling.
pla·gal (plā'g'l), ***adj.*** [ML. *plagalis* < *plaga*, plagal mode; MGr. *plagios*, plagal (in Gr., oblique, slanting) < Gr. *plagos*, a side], in *music*, 1. with its keynote in the middle of the compass, as a mode. 2. designating a cadence with the subdominant chord immediately preceding the tonic chord.
pla·gi·a·rism (plā'jə-riz'm, plā'ji-ə-riz'm), ***n.*** [< L. *plagiarius*, kidnaper; + *-ism*], 1. the act of plagiarizing. 2. an idea, passage, plot, etc. that has been plagiarized.
pla·gi·a·rist (plā'jə-rist, plā'ji-ə-rist), ***n.*** [see PLAGIARISM], a person who plagiarizes.
pla·gi·a·ris·tic (plā'jə-ris'tik, plā'ji-ə-ris'tik), ***adj.*** of or characterized by plagiarism.
pla·gi·a·rize (plā'jə-rīz', plā'ji-ə-rīz'), ***v.t.*** [PLAGIARIZED (-rīzd'), PLAGIARIZING], [see PLAGIARISM], 1. to take and pass off as one's own (the ideas, writings, etc. of another). 2. to take ideas, writings, etc. from and pass them off as one's own.
pla·gi·a·ry (plā'jə-ri, plā'ji-ə-ri), ***n.*** [*pl.* PLAGIARIES (-riz)], [L. *plagiarius*, kidnaper, plunderer, literary thief < *plagium*, a kidnaping < Gr. *plagios*, oblique, crooked], 1. a plagiarist. 2. plagiarism.
pla·gi·o- (plā'ji-ō, plā'ji-ə), [< Gr. *plagios*, oblique, crooked], a combining form meaning *oblique, slanting*, as in *plagiotropic:* also **plagi-.**
pla·gi·o·clase (plā'ji-ə-klās'), ***n.*** [G. *plagioklas* < Gr. *plagios*, oblique + *klasis*, a cleaving, fracture], any of a group of minerals of the feldspar family, containing calcium and sodium and having oblique cleavage.
pla·gi·o·clas·tic (plā'ji-ə-klas'tik), ***adj.*** 1. of plagioclase. 2. having oblique cleavage.
pla·gi·o·trop·ic (plā'ji-ə-trop'ik), ***adj.*** [*plagio-* + *-tropic*], in *botany*, having the longer axes of roots or branches slanting from the vertical line.
pla·gi·ot·ro·pism (plā'ji-ot'rə-piz'm), ***n.*** the state or fact of being plagiotropic.
plague (plāg; *chiefly dial.*, pleg), ***n.*** [ME. & OFr. *plage;* L. *plaga;* Gr. *plēgē*, a blow, misfortune], 1. anything that afflicts or troubles; calamity; scourge. 2. divine punishment. 3. any contagious epidemic disease that is deadly; specifically, the bubonic plague. 4. [Colloq.],

a nuisance; annoyance. ***v.t.*** [PLAGUED (plāgd; *chiefly dial.*, plegd), PLAGUING], 1. to afflict with a plague. 2. to vex; harass; trouble; torment. —***SYN.*** see **annoy.**

pla·gui·ly (plā′gə-li; *chiefly dial.*, pleg′ə-li), ***adv.*** [Colloq.], in a plaguy manner.

pla·guy (plā′gi; *chiefly dial.*, pleg′i), ***adj.*** [Colloq.], annoying; vexatious; disagreeable. ***adv.*** [Colloq.], plaguily. Also spelled **plaguey.**

plaice (plās), ***n.*** [*pl.* PLAICE, PLAICES (-iz); see PLURAL, II, D, 2], [ME. *plais, plaice;* OFr. *plais, plaïz;* LL. *platessa*, flatfish; prob. < Gr. *platys*, broad], any of a number of related American and European fishes having a flat, olive-brown body with white spots.

plaid (plad), ***n.*** [Gael. *plaide*, a blanket, plaid; said to be contr. < *peallaid*, sheepskin], 1. a long piece of twilled woolen cloth with a checkered or crossbarred pattern, worn over the shoulder by Scottish Highlanders. 2. cloth with a checkered or crossbarred pattern. 3. any pattern of this kind.

plaid·ed (plad′id), ***adj.*** 1. wearing a plaid. 2. made of plaid. 3. with a plaid pattern.

plain (plān), ***adj.*** [ME.; OFr.; L. *planus*, flat, level], 1. flat; level; plane. 2. free from obstructions; open; clear: as, in *plain* view. 3. clearly understood; evident; obvious: as, a *plain* prose style. 4. outspoken; downright; straightforward: as, *plain* talk. 5. not luxurious; unembellished: as, a *plain* meal. 6. not complicated; simple: as, *plain* sewing. 7. not good-looking; homely: as, a *plain* face. 8. unfigured, undyed, or untwilled: as, *plain* cloth. 9. not of high rank or position; such as characterizes the common people; ordinary: as, a *plain* man. ***n.*** an extent of level country. ***adv.*** in a plain manner; clearly. —***SYN.*** see **evident.**

the Plain, the less radical party in the French legislature during the Revolution.

the Great Plains, the broad expanse of level land stretching westward from the Mississippi Valley.

plain (plān), ***v.i.*** [OFr. *plaindre;* L. *plangere*, to beat the breast, lament], [Archaic & Dial.], to complain.

plain chant, [Fr.], plain song.

plain-clothes man (plān′klōz′, plān′klōthz′), a detective or policeman who wears civilian clothes on duty.

plain dealing, straightforward dealing with others.

Plain·field (plān′fēld′), ***n.*** a city in central New Jersey: pop., 45,000.

plain-laid (plān′lād′), ***adj.*** made of three strands laid together with a right-handed twist: said of a rope.

plain sailing, 1. sailing on a smooth, clear course. 2. a smooth, clear course of action.

Plains Indian, a member of any of the American Indian tribes formerly inhabiting the prairie region of the United States: they were of various linguistic stocks but shared certain culture traits in common, and were characterized especially by the nomadic following of bison herds.

plains·man (plānz′mən), ***n.*** [*pl.* PLAINSMEN (-mən)], a person who lives on the plains.

Plains of Abraham, Battle of the, a battle of the French and Indian War, fought near Quebec in 1759, in which the British under Wolfe defeated the French under Montcalm.

plain song, [transl. of ML. *cantus planus*], early Christian church music, still used in Roman Catholic and Anglican services, in free rhythm and the limited Gregorian scale, sung in unison without accompaniment: also **plain chant.**

plain-spo·ken (plān′spō′k′n), ***adj.*** speaking or spoken plainly or frankly.

plaint (plānt), ***n.*** [ME. *plainte;* OFr. *plaint, plainte;* LL. *plancta;* L. *planctus* < *plangere*, to beat the breast in token of grief, lament; akin to Gr. *plēssein*, to strike], 1. [Poetic], lamentation; lament. 2. a complaint.

plain·tiff (plān′tif), ***n.*** [ME. & OFr. *plaintif*, mournful, making complaint < *plaindre;* see PLAIN, *v.*], a person who brings a suit into a court of law; complainant.

plain·tive (plān′tiv), ***adj.*** [ME. *pleintif;* OFr. *plaintif;* see PLAINTIFF], expressing sorrow or melancholy; mournful; sad.

plais·ter (plās′tẽr), ***n.*** [Obs.], a plaster.

plait (plāt; *occas., but less properly*, plēt; *for n. 2 and v. 2 & 3, sometimes* plat), ***n.*** [ME. *playt;* OFr. *ploit, pleit;* L. *plicitum*, neut. pp. of *plicare*, to fold], 1. a flattened fold, as of cloth doubled back on itself; pleat. 2. a braid of hair, ribbon, etc. ***v.t.*** 1. to pleat. 2. to braid. 3. to make by braiding.

plan (plan), ***n.*** [Fr. *plan*, earlier also *plant;* It. *pianta* (< L. *planta*, sole of the foot) or *piano* (< L. *planus*, plane, level)], 1. an outline; draft; map. 2. a drawing or diagram showing the arrangement in horizontal section of a structure, piece of ground, etc. 3. a scheme for making, doing, or arranging something; project; program; schedule. 4. in perspective, one of several planes thought of as perpendicular to the line of sight and between the eye and the object. ***v.t.*** [PLANNED (pland), PLANNING], 1. to make a plan of (a structure, piece of ground, etc.). 2. to devise a scheme for doing, making, or arranging. 3. to have in mind as a project or purpose. ***v.i.*** to make plans.

SYN.—**plan** refers to any detailed method, formulated beforehand, for doing or making something (vacation *plans*); **design** stresses the final outcome of a plan and implies the use of skill or craft, sometimes in an unfavorable sense, in executing or arranging this (it was his *design* to separate us); **project** implies the use of enterprise or imagination in formulating an ambitious or extensive plan (they've begun work on the housing *project*); **scheme**, a less definite term than the preceding, often connotes either an impractical, visionary plan or an underhand intrigue (a *scheme* to embezzle the funds).

plan- (plan), plano- (wandering).

pla·nar·i·an (plə-nâr′i-ən), ***n.*** [LL. *planarius*, flat; L. *planus*, plane, flat], any of a number of related small, flat-bodied worms moving by means of cilia.

planch, planche (planch, plänch), ***n.*** [ME. *plaunche;* OFr. *planche;* see PLANK], [Obs. or British Dial.], 1. a plank; board. 2. a floor.

planch·et (plan′chit), ***n.*** [Fr. *planchette*, dim. of *planche*, a plank], a disk of metal to be stamped as a coin.

plan·chette (plan-chet′, plan-shet′), ***n.*** [Fr.; see prec.], a three-cornered board, often having as one of its supports a pencil, that is supposed to spell out a message as it moves with the fingers resting lightly on it.

Planck, Max (mäks plāŋk), 1858–1947; German physicist; formulated the quantum theory; received Nobel prize in physics, 1918.

plane (plān), ***n.*** [ME. *playn;* OFr. *plasne;* L. *platanus;* Gr. *platanos* < *platys*, broad: so called from its broad leaves], any of a number of related trees with large leaves and streaky bark that sheds, as the sycamore.

plane (plān), ***adj.*** [L. *planus*], 1. flat; level; even. 2. in *mathematics*, *a*) lying on a surface that is a plane. *b*) of such surfaces. ***n.*** 1. a surface that wholly contains every straight line joining any two points lying in it. 2. a flat, level, or even surface. 3. a level of development, achievement, existence, etc.: as, a low *plane* of culture. 4. an airplane. 5. any airfoil; especially, a wing of an airplane. —***SYN.*** see **level.**

plane (plān), ***n.*** [Fr.; LL. *plana* < *planare*, to plane, make level < L. *planus*, level, flat], 1. a kind of trowel used for smoothing the surface of sand, clay, etc. 2. a carpenter's tool for leveling, smoothing, or removing wood. ***v.t.*** [PLANED (plānd), PLANING], 1. to make smooth or level with or as with a plane. 2. to remove with or as with a plane (with *off* or *away*). ***v.i.*** 1. to work with a plane. 2. to do the work of a plane.

PLANE

plane (plān), ***v.i.*** [Fr. *planer* < *plan*, a plane: from the position of a bird's wings while soaring], 1. to soar or glide. 2. to rise partly out of the water while in motion at a high speed, as a hydroplane does.

plane angle, an angle made by two straight lines that lie in the same plane.

plane geometry, the branch of geometry dealing with plane figures.

plan·er (plān′ẽr), ***n.*** 1. a person or thing that planes. 2. a machine that smooths or finishes the surface of wood or metal by planing. 3. in *printing*, a block of wood used to level type or in taking proofs.

planer tree, a small tree resembling an elm, with egg-shaped leaves and a nutlike fruit.

plan·et (plan′it), ***n.*** [ME. & OFr. *planete;* LL. *planeta;* Gr. *planētēs*, wanderer < *planan*, to lead astray, wander], 1. originally, any of the heavenly bodies with apparent motion (as distinguished from the fixed stars), including the sun, moon, Mercury, Venus, Mars, Jupiter, and Saturn. 2. now, any heavenly body that shines by reflected sunlight and revolves about the sun: the major planets, in their order from the sun, are Mercury, Venus, Earth, Mars, Jupiter, Saturn, Uranus, Neptune, and Pluto; the minor planets are the asteroids, or planetoids, which move in orbits between Mars and Jupiter. 3. in *astrology*, any heavenly body supposed to influence a person's life.

plane table, a surveying device for plotting maps in the field; it consists of a drawing board mounted on a tripod with an alidade pivoted over its center.

plan·e·tar·i·um (plan′ə-târ′i-əm), ***n.*** [*pl.* PLANETARIUMS (-əmz), PLANETARIA (-ə)], [Mod. L. < LL. *planeta;* see PLANET], 1. a model of the solar system in which, by means of clockwork, the relative motion of the planets around the sun can be demonstrated; orrery. 2. an arrangement for projecting the images of the sun, moon, planets, and stars on the inside of a large hemispherical dome by means of a large, complex optical instrument which is revolved to show the principal celestial motions. 3. the room or building in which this is contained.

plan·e·tar·y (plan'ə-ter'i), ***adj.*** [LL. *planetarius*], 1. of a planet or the planets. 2. terrestrial; worldly. 3. wandering; erratic. 4. in *astrology*, under the influence of a planet. 5. in *machinery*, designating or of an epicyclic train of gears in an automobile transmission. 6. in *physics*, moving in an orbit, like a planet.

plan·e·tes·i·mal (plan'ə-tes'i-m'l), ***adj.*** [< *planet* + *infinitesimal*], of very small bodies in space that move in planetary orbits. ***n.*** any of these small bodies.

planetesimal hypothesis, a hypothesis that the planets were formed by the uniting of planetesimals created by the tidal eruptions caused on the sun by the passage of a star close to it.

plan·et·oid (plan'ə-toid'), ***n.*** [*planet* + *-oid*], 1. any of a group of minor planets with orbits between those of Mars and Jupiter; asteroid. 2. a man-made satellite.

plane tree, a plane (tree).

plan·et-strick·en (plan'it-strik''n), ***adj.*** 1. stricken by the supposed influence of the planets; blasted; hence, 2. panic-stricken.

plan·et-struck (plan'it-struk'), ***adj.*** planet-stricken.

planet wheel, a gearwheel that meshes with and revolves around another wheel in an epicyclic train.

plan·gen·cy (plan'jən-si), ***n.*** [< L. *plangens*], the quality of being plangent.

plan·gent (plan'jənt), ***adj.*** [L. *plangens*, ppr. of *plangere*, to beat], beating with a loud or deep sound, as breaking waves, etc.

pla·ni- (plā'ni, plan'i), [< L. *planus*, flat, level], a combining form meaning *plane, level, flat*, as in *planimeter*.

pla·nim·e·ter (plə-nim'ə-tẽr), ***n.*** [Fr. *planimètre;* see PLANI- & -METER], an instrument for measuring the area of a regular or irregular plane figure by tracing the perimeter of the figure.

plan·i·met·ric (plan'ə-met'rik), ***adj.*** of or by planimetry or a planimeter.

pla·nim·e·try (plə-nim'ə-tri), ***n.*** [*plani-* + *-metry*], the measurement of plane surfaces; plane geometry.

plan·ish (plan'ish), ***v.t.*** [< OFr. *planir*, to flatten < L. *planus*, smooth], to toughen, smooth, or polish (metal) by hammering or rolling.

plan·i·sphere (plan'ə-sfêr'), ***n.*** [OFr. *planisphère;* ML. *planisphaerium;* see PLANI- & SPHERE], 1. a map or chart that is the projection of all or part of a sphere on a plane. 2. a projection of the celestial sphere on a plane with the zenith of the North Pole or of the South Pole as the center.

plank (plaŋk), ***n.*** [ME. & ONorm. Fr. *planke;* OFr. *planche;* LL. *planca*, a board, plank], 1. a long, broad, thick board. 2. timber cut into planks; planking. 3. something that supports or forms a foundation. 4. any of the articles or principles in a platform, as of a political party. ***v.t.*** 1. to cover, lay, or furnish with planks. 2. to broil and serve on a board, as fish or steak. 3. [Colloq.], to lay or set down with force or emphasis; hence, 4. [Colloq.], to pay (usually with *down* or *out*).
walk the plank, to walk blindfold off a plank projecting over the water from the side of a ship, as the victims of pirates were forced to do.

plank·ing (plaŋk'iŋ), ***n.*** 1. the act of laying planks. 2. planks in quantity. 3. the planks of a structure.

plank-sheer (plaŋk'shêr'), ***n.*** in *shipbuilding*, a timber extending around the hull of a ship at the line of junction with the deck.

plank·ton (plaŋk'tən), ***n.*** [G. < Gr. *planktos*, wandering < *plazesthai*, to wander], the microscopic animal and plant life found floating or drifting in the ocean or in bodies of fresh water, used as food by fish.

plan·ner (plan'ẽr), ***n.*** a person who plans.

plan·o- (plan'ō, plan'ə), [< Gr. *planos*, wandering], a combining form meaning *wandering*, as in *planoblast:* also, before a vowel, **plan-.**

pla·no- (plā'nō), [< L. *planus*, level, flat], a combining form meaning *plane, flat*, or *having one side plane and* (the other as specified), as in *plano-concave*.

plan·o·blast (plan'ə-blast'), ***n.*** [*plano-* (wandering) + *-blast*], a tiny, free-swimming jellyfish; medusa form of a hydroid.

pla·no-con·cave (plā'nō-kon'kāv), ***adj.*** having one side plane and the other concave: see **concave,** illus.

pla·no-con·vex (plā'nō-kon'veks), ***adj.*** having one side plane and the other convex: see **convex,** illus.

pla·nom·e·ter (plə-nom'ə-tẽr), ***n.*** [*plano-* + *-meter*], a device, as a flat plate of iron, for gauging the accuracy of a plane surface.

plant (plant, plänt), ***n.*** [ME. & AS. *plante;* L. *planta*, a plant; prob. ult. < base of *planus*, level, flat (via *plantare*, to level ground for sowing); senses 4, 5, 6, 7 < the *v.*], 1. a young tree, shrub, or herb, ready to put into other soil for growth to maturity; a slip, cutting, or set. 2. any living thing that cannot move voluntarily, has no sense organs, and generally makes its own food by photosynthesis; vegetable organism, as distinguished from an animal organism; any tree, shrub, herb, etc. 3. a soft-stemmed organism of this kind, as distinguished from a tree or shrub. 4. the tools, machinery, fixtures, buildings, grounds, etc. of a factory or business. 5. the equipment, buildings, etc. used by any institution, as a hospital, school, etc. 6. the apparatus or equipment for a certain mechanical operation or process: as, the power *plant* of a ship. 7. [Slang], a swindling scheme; trick; trap. 8. [Slang], a person placed or thing planned to trick, mislead, or trap. ***v.t.*** [ME. *planten* < AS. & OFr. (AS. *plantian*, OFr. *planter*); both < L. *plantare* < the *n.*], 1. to put into the ground to grow. 2. to set firmly; fix in position. 3. to fix in the mind; implant, as an idea. 4. to establish in a specified place, as a religion. 5. to settle; found, as a colony. 6. to furnish; stock, as a piece of land with plants or a body of water with fish. 7. to put a stock of (oysters, young fish, etc.) in a body of water. 8. [Slang], to deliver (a punch, blow, etc.) on the spot aimed at. 9. [Slang], to place (a person or thing) in such a way as to trick, mislead, or trap. 10. [Slang], to hide (stolen articles, etc.).

Plan·tag·e·net (plan-taj'ə-nit), ***n.*** the ruling family of England (1154–1399) or any member of this family.

plan·tain (plan'tin), ***n.*** [ME.; OFr.; L. *plantago* < *planta*, sole of the foot: from the shape of the leaves], 1. any of a number of related plants with leaves toward the bottom of the stem and spikes of tiny, greenish flowers. 2. a weed with broad, ribbed leaves.

plan·tain (plan'tin), ***n.*** [earlier *platan, plantan;* Sp. *plátano, plántano* < W.Ind. native name; form influenced in Sp. by *plátano, plántano*, plane tree, and in Eng. by *plantain* (a weed)], 1. a tropical plant yielding a kind of banana. 2. its fruit.

plan·tar (plan'tẽr), ***adj.*** [L. *plantaris* < *planta*, sole of the foot], of the sole of the foot.

plan·ta·tion (plan-tā'shən), ***n.*** [L. *plantatio* < *plantare*, to plant], 1. formerly, a colony or new settlement. 2. an area growing cultivated crops. 3. an estate, as in a tropical or semitropical region, cultivated by workers living on it: as, a sugar *plantation*. 4. a large, cultivated planting of trees: as, a rubber *plantation*.

plant·er (plan'tẽr, plän'tẽr), ***n.*** 1. the owner of a plantation. 2. a person or machine that plants. 3. a container, usually decorative, for potted or unpotted house plants. 4. a colonist; pioneer.

Planter's Punch, [prob. so called because served by *planters* (plantation owners)], an alcoholic drink made by shaking Jamaica rum, lemon or lime juice, and sugar together with fine ice, served unstrained.

plan·ti·grade (plan'tə-grād'), ***adj.*** [Fr. < L. *planta*, sole + *gradi*, to walk], walking on the whole sole of the foot, as a bear, man, etc. ***n.*** a plantigrade animal.

plant louse, any of a number of related small, usually green, sucking insects harmful to plants; aphid.

plan·u·la (plan'yoo-lə), ***n.*** [*pl.* PLANULAE (-lē')], [Mod. L.; LL., little plane, dim. < L. *planus*, flat, plane], the young, free-swimming larva of a coelenterate.

plan·u·lar (plan'yoo-lẽr), ***adj.*** of or like a planula.

plan·u·late (plan'yoo-lit, plan'yoo-lāt'), ***adj.*** planular.

plaque (plak), ***n.*** [Fr.; D. *plak*, a disk, plate], 1. any thin, flat piece of metal, wood, porcelain, terra-cotta, etc., used for ornamentation, as on a wall. 2. a platelike brooch or pin worn as a badge or ornament.

plash (plash), ***n.*** [ME. *plasche;* AS. *plæsc;* akin to MD. & MFl. *plasch*, pool; prob. echoic], a pool or puddle.

plash (plash), ***v.t. & v.i.*** [origin echoic; cf. PLASH, *n.*, SPLASH], to splash. ***n.*** a splash.

plash (plash), ***v.t.*** [OFr. *plaissier;* LL. **plectiare* < L. *plectere*, to weave], 1. to bend and intertwine (branches, stems, etc.) so as to form a hedge. 2. to make or trim (a hedge) in this way.

-pla·si·a (plā'zhə, plā'zhi-ə), [Mod. L. < Gr. *plasis*, a molding < *plassein*, to mold], a combining form signifying *change, development*, as in *cataplasia:* also **-plasis, -plasy.**

plasm (plaz'm), ***n.*** plasma (senses 1, 2, 3).

-plasm (plaz'm), [< Gr. *plasma;* see PLASMA], a terminal combining form meaning: 1. *the fluid substances of an animal* or *vegetable cell*. 2. *protoplasm*, as in *ectoplasm*.

plas·ma (plaz'mə), ***n.*** [LL., something shaped or molded; Gr. *plasma* < *plassein*, to form, mold], 1. a green, somewhat translucent variety of quartz. 2. the fluid part of blood, lymph, milk, or intramuscular liquid; especially, the fluid part of blood, as distinguished from the corpuscles. 3. protoplasm. 4. a hot ionized gas composed of nearly equal numbers of electrons and positive ions: it can be confined and compressed by a magnetic field, as for controlled nuclear fusion.

plas·mat·ic (plaz-mat'ik), ***adj.*** of plasma.

plas·mic (plaz'mik), ***adj.*** plasmatic.

-plas·mic (plaz'mik), a combining form used in forming adjectives derived from nouns ending in *-plasm*.

plas·mo- (plaz'mō, plaz'mə), a combining form meaning *plasma*, as in *plasmolysis:* also **plasm-.**

plas·mo·chin (plaz'mə-kin), ***n.*** [see PLASMA, CHINA BARK, QUININE], an antimalarial drug, $C_{19}H_{29}N_3O$, prepared synthetically from quinoline: a trade-mark (**Plasmochin**): also **plasmoquine, plasmoquin.**

plas·mo·di·um (plaz-mō'di-əm), ***n.*** [*pl.* PLASMODIA (-ə)], [Mod. L.; see PLASMA & -ODE], 1. a mass of protoplasm with many nuclei, formed by the fusion of a number of one-celled organisms. 2. any of various unicellular parasites found in red blood corpuscles: one variety causes malaria.

plas·mol·y·sis (plaz-mol'ə-sis), *n.* [Mod. L.; see PLASMO- & -LYSIS], a shrinking of the protoplasm of a cell due to loss of water by osmosis.

plas·mo·lyze (plaz'mə-līz'), *v.t. & v.i.* [PLASMOLYZED (-līzd'), PLASMOLYZING], to subject to or undergo plasmolysis.

plas·mo·quin (plaz'mə-kwin), *n.* plasmochin.

plas·mo·quine (plaz'mə-kwīn'), *n.* plasmochin.

Plas·sey (plä'si), *n.* a village in Bengal, India: scene of a battle (1757), in which the British under Clive defeated the French.

-plast (plast), [< Gr. *plastos,* formed < *plassein,* to form, mold], a combining form meaning *a unit of protoplasm,* as in *chromoplast.*

plas·ter (plas'tẽr, pläs'tẽr), *n.* [ME.; AS. *plaster* (in sense 3) & OFr. *plastre* (in senses 1 & 2); both < LL. *plastrum,* for L. *emplastrum;* Gr. *emplastron,* plaster < *emplassein,* to daub over < *en,* on, in + *plassein,* to form, mold], 1. a pasty mixture of lime, sand, and water, hard when dry, for coating walls, ceilings, and partitions. 2. plaster of Paris. 3. a pasty preparation spread on cloth and applied to the body, used medicinally as a curative or irritant. *v.t.* 1. to cover, smear, overlay, etc. with or as with plaster. 2. to apply or affix like a plaster: as, we *plastered* posters on the walls.

plas·ter·board (plas'tẽr-bôrd', pläs'tẽr-bōrd'), *n.* a thin board formed of layers of plaster and paper, used in building walls, partitions, etc.

plaster cast, 1. a copy or mold of a statue or other object, cast in plaster of Paris. 2. in *surgery,* a rigid cast to hold a fractured bone in place and prevent movement, made by wrapping the limb or part with a bandage of gauze soaked in wet plaster of Paris.

plas·tered (plas'tẽrd, pläs'tẽrd), *adj.* [pp. of *plaster;* orig. military slang], [Slang], intoxicated; drunk.

plas·ter·ing (plas'tẽr-iŋ, pläs'tẽr-iŋ), *n.* 1. the act or process of applying plaster. 2. a coating of plaster on a wall, ceiling, etc.

plaster of Paris, [so called from use of gypsum from Montmartre in Paris, France, in its manufacture], a heavy white powder, calcined gypsum, which, when mixed with water, forms a thick paste that sets quickly: used for casts, moldings, statuary, etc.

plas·ter·y (plas'tẽr-i, pläs'tẽr-i), *adj.* like plaster.

plas·tic (plas'tik), *adj.* [L. *plasticus;* Gr. *plastikos* < *plassein,* to form], 1. molding or shaping matter; formative. 2. that can be molded or shaped; hence, 3. impressionable; easily influenced; flexible. 4. dealing with molding or modeling. 5. in *biology,* capable of undergoing metabolic changes. 6. in *medicine, a)* of or helpful in the renewal of destroyed or injured tissue. *b)* that can be so renewed. 7. in *physics,* capable of continuous and permanent change of shape in any direction without breaking apart. *n.* 1. any of various nonmetallic compounds, synthetically produced (usually from organic compounds by polymerization), which can be molded into various forms and hardened for commercial use: among the various trade-mark names for plastics are *Lucite, Vinylite, Bakelite,* etc. 2. any article made of plastic. —*SYN.* see **pliable.**

-plas·tic (plas'tik), [< Gr. *plastikos;* see PLASTIC], a combining form meaning: 1. *forming, developing,* as in *cytoplastic.* 2. *of* ——*plasty* or *a* ——*plast,* as in *neuroplastic.*

plas·ti·cal·ly (plas'ti-k'l-i, plas'tik-li), *adv.* in a plastic manner.

plastic arts, any of the arts concerned with molding or modeling, as sculpture, ceramics, etc.

plas·tic·i·ty (plas-tis'ə-ti), *n.* the quality or state of being plastic.

plas·ti·cize (plas'tə-sīz'), *v.t. & v.i.* [PLASTICIZED (-sīzd'), PLASTICIZING], to make or become plastic.

plas·ti·ciz·er (plas'tə-sīz'ẽr), *n.* any of various substances added to a plastic material to keep it soft and viscous.

plastic memory, the tendency of certain plastics to resume their original form when heated.

plastic surgery, surgery dealing with the repair or restoration of injured, deformed, or destroyed parts of the body, especially by transferring tissue, as skin or bone, from other parts or from another individual.

plastic wood, a synthetic product which dries and hardens to the consistency of wood when exposed to the air: used in repairing wooden articles or as a filler in cracks, etc.

plas·tid (plas'tid), *n.* [G. *plastiden* (pl.); Gr. *plastides,* pl. of *plastis,* fem. of *plastēs,* molder < *plassein,* to form], 1. a unit of protoplasm; cell. 2. a granule of specialized protoplasm occurring in the cytoplasm of some cells.

plas·tral (plas'trəl), *adj.* of a plastron.

plas·tron (plas'trən), *n.* [Fr.; It. *piastrone* < *piastra;* see PIASTER], 1. a metal breastplate worn under a coat of mail. 2. a leather breastplate worn over the chest by fencers. 3. an ornamental, detachable trimming tapering from the shoulders to the waist on the front of a woman's dress. 4. a starched shirt front. 5. the under shell of a turtle or tortoise.

-plas·ty (plas'ti), [Gr. *-plastia* < *plastos,* formed < *plassein,* to form], a terminal combining form meaning: 1. *the act* or *means of forming, growth, development,* as in *genioplasty, dermatoplasty.* 2. in *surgery, a) plastic surgery in which a* (specified) *part of the body is involved,* as in *thoracoplasty. b) plastic surgery in which tissue from a* (specified) *source is used,* as in *autoplasty. c) plastic surgery for a* (specified) *purpose,* as in *kineplasty.*

-pla·sy (plā'si), -plasia.

plat (plat), *v.t.* [PLATTED (-id), PLATTING], [ME. *platten;* var. of *playten;* see PLAIT], to interweave; braid; plait. *n.* [Dial.], a braid; plait.

plat (plat), *n.* [var. of *plot;* influenced by ME. *plat,* flat < OFr.; ult. < Gr. *platys,* broad], 1. a small piece of ground. 2. a map; plan. *v.t.* [PLATTED (-id), PLATTING], to make a map or plan of.

plat- (plat), platy-.

plat., 1. plateau. 2. platoon.

Pla·ta, Ri·o de la (rē'ô de lä plä'tä), the estuary of the Paraná and Uruguay Rivers, between Argentina and Uruguay: length, 200 mi.: English name, *River Plate.*

Pla·tae·a (plə-tē'ə), *n.* an ancient city in Boeotia, Greece: scene of a battle (479 B.C.), in which the Greeks defeated the Persians.

plat·an (plat'ən), *n.* a plane tree.

plate (plāt), *n.* [ME.; OFr.; ML. *platta;* ult. < Gr. *platys,* broad], 1. a smooth, flat, relatively thin piece of any material, as metal. 2. sheet metal made by beating, rolling, or casting. 3. one of the thin pieces or sheets of metal used in armor. 4. armor made of these. 5. a thin flat piece of metal on which an engraving is, or is to be, cut. 6. an impression taken from the engraved metal. 7. loosely, a print of a woodcut, lithograph, etc., especially when used in a book. 8. a full-page book illustration of any kind, printed on paper of a stock different from that which carries the text. 9. dishes, utensils, and similar household articles of silver or gold. 10. metal dishes, utensils, etc. that are plated, or coated with gold or silver. 11. a shallow dish, usually circular, from which food is eaten. 12. a plateful. 13. the food in a dish; course: as, a fruit *plate.* 14. food and service for an individual at a meal: as, dinner at three dollars a *plate.* 15. a dishlike object passed in churches, etc. for donations of money. 16. a thin cut of beef from the forequarter, just below the short ribs: see **beef,** illus. 17. in *anatomy* & *zoology,* a thin layer, plate, or scale, as of bone, horny tissue, etc.; lamina; scute. 18. in *architecture,* a horizontal wooden girder that supports the trusses or rafters of a roof. 19. in *baseball,* the home base (usually a small five-sided piece of rubber, etc., set into the ground), beside which the batter stands and which a player must touch after a circuit of the bases in order to score a run. 20. in *dentistry, a)* that part of a set of false teeth which fits to the mouth and holds the teeth. *b)* loosely, a set of false teeth. 21. in *electricity,* the anode, or positive element, of an electron tube, a flat plate or cylinder toward which the stream of electrons flows. 22. in *photography,* a sheet of glass, metal, etc. coated with a film sensitive to light, upon which the image is formed. 23. in *printing,* a cast, to be printed from, made from a mold of set type by the electrotype or stereotype process. 24. in *sports, a)* a prize, originally a gold or silver cup, given to the winner of a race or contest. *b)* loosely, a contest, especially a horse race, in which the prize is a plate: also called *plate race.* *v.t.* [PLATED (-id), PLATING], 1. to overlay or coat with gold, silver, tin, etc. 2. to cover with metal plates for protection. 3. in *printing,* to make a streotype or electrotype plate of. Abbreviated **pl.**

Plate, River (plāt), Rio de la Plata.

pla·teau (pla-tō'), *n.* [*pl.* PLATEAUS, PLATEAUX (-tōz)], [Fr.; OFr. *platel,* dim. < *plat;* see PLAT], an elevated tract of more or less level land; tableland: abbreviated **plat.**: applied figuratively to a period in the evolution of something, as of an individual's learning, characterized by a relative absence of progress, as represented by a flat extent in a graph, etc.

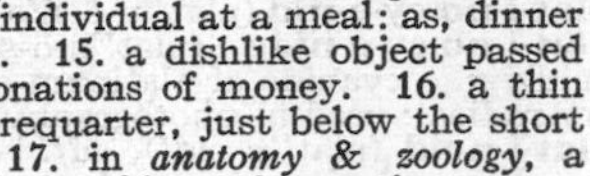

SEA LEVEL COASTAL PLAIN PLATEAU MOUNTAIN PLATEAU

PLATEAUS

plat·ed (plāt'id), *adj.* 1. covered or protected with plates, as of armor. 2. knitted of two kinds of yarn, one forming the face and the other the back. 3. overlaid or coated with a metal, especially a precious one: sometimes used in hyphenated compounds, meaning *coated with* (a specified metal), as in *silver-plated.*

plate·ful (plāt'fool'), *n.* [*pl.* PLATEFULS (-foolz')], as much as a plate will hold.

plate glass, polished, clear glass in thick sheets, used for shop windows, mirrors, etc.
plate·let (plāt′lit), *n.* [*plate* + *-let*], any of certain round or oval disks, one-third to one-half the size of a red blood cell but containing no hemoglobin, found in the blood of mammals and associated with the process of blood clotting; thrombocyte: in full, **blood platelet.**
plat·en (plat′'n), *n.* [ME. *plateyne;* OFr. *platine,* flat plate, metal plate < *plat,* flat], 1. in a printing press, a flat metal plate or rotating cylinder that presses the paper against the inked type. 2. in a typewriter, the roller against which the keys strike.
plat·er (plāt′ẽr), *n.* 1. a person or thing that plates. 2. [cf. PLATE, *n.* 24 *b*], an inferior race horse.
plate rail, a shelflike molding along a wall to hold ornamental plates, etc.
plat·form (plat′fôrm′), *n.* [Fr. *plateforme,* lit., flat form], 1. a raised horizontal surface of wood, stone, or metal; specifically, *a*) a raised stage or flooring beside railroad tracks, streetcar tracks, etc. *b*) a vestibule at the end of a railway car, streetcar, etc. *c*) a raised flooring or stage for performers, speakers, etc. 2. the statement of principles and policies of a political party or other organization. *adj.* 1. designating a shoe sole, from 1/2 to 3 inches thick, usually made of cork or wood. 2. designating a shoe with such a sole.
platform car, a railroad freight car without a roof or raised sides; flatcar.
plat·i·na (plat′'n-ə, plə-tē′nə), *n.* [Mod. L.; Sp., dim. < *plata,* silver, orig. thin plate of metal], [Obs. or Rare], platinum.
plat·ing (plāt′iŋ), *n.* 1. the act or process of a person or thing that plates. 2. an external layer of metal plates. 3. a thin coating of gold, silver, tin, etc.
pla·tin·ic (plə-tin′ik), *adj.* of, like, or containing platinum, especially with a valence of four.
plat·i·nif·er·ous (plat′ə-nif′ẽr-əs), *adj.* [< *platinum* + *-ferous*], yielding platinum.
plat·in·i·rid·i·um (plat′'n-i-rid′i-əm, plat′'n-ī-rid′i-əm), *n.* [Mod. L.], a native alloy of platinum and iridium, often containing other related metals.
plat·i·nize (plat′'n-īz′), *v.t.* [PLATINIZED (-īzd′), PLATINIZING], to coat or combine with platinum.
plat·i·no·cy·an·ic (plat′ə-nō-sī-an′ik), *adj.* designating or of an acid containing platinum and the cyanogen radical.
plat·i·no·cy·a·nid (plat′'n-ō-sī′ə-nid), *n.* platinocyanide.
plat·i·no·cy·a·nide (plat′'n-ō-sī′ə-nīd′, plat′'n-ō-sī′ə-nid), *n.* a cyanide of platinum and some other element or radical: used in photography, etc.
plat·i·noid (plat′'n-oid′), *adj.* [< *platinum* + *-oid*], resembling platinum. *n.* 1. an alloy of copper, nickel, zinc, and tungsten, used in electrical resistance coils, etc. 2. any of the metals of the platinum group.
plat·i·no·type (plat′'n-ō-tīp′), *n.* 1. a process of printing photographs in platinum black by using a platinum salt in the sensitizing solution or developer. 2. a print produced by this process.
plat·i·nous (plat′'n-əs), *adj.* of, like, or containing platinum, especially with a valence of two.
plat·i·num (plat′'n-əm), *n.* [Mod. L. < Sp. *platina* < *plata,* silver], a steel-gray, malleable, ductile metallic chemical element, highly resistant to corrosion and electricity: used as a chemical catalyst, for acid-proof containers, ignition fuses, jewelry, dental equipment, etc.: symbol, Pt; at. wt., 195.23; at. no., 78.
platinum black, a black powder of finely divided metallic platinum, made by reduction of platinum salts and used as a catalyst, as in organic synthesis.
platinum blonde, a girl or woman who has very light pale-yellow hair.
plat·i·tude (plat′ə-tōōd′, plat′ə-tūd′), *n.* [Fr. < *plat,* flat, after *latitude, rectitude*], 1. commonplaceness; flatness; dullness. 2. a commonplace or trite remark, especially one uttered as if it were fresh or original.
SYN.—a **platitude** is a trite remark or idea, especially one uttered as if it were novel or momentous; a **commonplace** is any obvious or conventional remark or idea; a **truism** is a statement whose truth is widely known and whose utterance, therefore, seems superfluous; a **cliché** is an expression or idea which, though it was once fresh and forceful, has become hackneyed and weak through frequent repetition; **bromide** is an informal term for a platitude that is especially dull, tiresome, or annoying.
plat·i·tu·di·nize (plat′ə-tōō′d'n-īz′, plat′ə-tū′d'n-īz′), *v.i.* [PLATITUDINIZED (-īzd′), PLATITUDINIZING], to write or speak platitudes.
plat·i·tu·di·nous (plat′ə-tōō′d'n-əs, plat′ə-tū′d'n-əs), *adj.* of or like a platitude; characterized by, full of, or using platitudes; trite; commonplace.
Pla·to (plā′tō), *n.* Greek philosopher; lived 427–347 B.C.
Pla·ton·ic (plə-ton′ik, plā-ton′ik), *adj.* [L. *Platonicus;* Gr. *Platōnikos* < *Platōn,* Plato], 1. of or characteristic of Plato or his philosophy. 2. idealistic, visionary, or impractical. 3. [also p-], not amorous or sensual but purely spiritual: as, *Platonic* love.
Pla·ton·i·cal·ly (plə-ton′i-k'l-i, plā-ton′ik-li), *adv.* in a Platonic manner.
Pla·ton·ism (plā′t'n-iz'm), *n.* [Mod. L. *platonismus*], 1. the philosophy of Plato or his school: see **idealism.** 2. a doctrine or saying typical of Platonic philosophy. 3. [also p-], the theory or practice of Platonic love.
Pla·to·nist (plā′t'n-ist), *adj.* of Plato, his ideas, or his school. *n.* [ML. *platonista*], a follower of Plato, or a student of his philosophy.
Pla·to·nize (plā′t'n-īz′), *v.i.* [PLATONIZED (-īzd′), PLATONIZING], to follow the philosophy of Plato; philosophize in a Platonic manner. *v.t.* to make Platonic.
pla·toon (plə-tōōn′), *n.* [Fr. *peloton,* a ball, group, platoon < *pelote,* a ball], 1. a military unit composed of two or more squads or sections, normally under the command of a lieutenant: it is a subdivision of a company, troop, etc. 2. a group or unit like this: as, a *platoon* of police. 3. in professional football, either of the two squads (offensive and defensive) constituting a single team. Abbreviated **plat.**
Platt·deutsch (plät′doich′), *n.* [G.; *platt,* lit., flat, low + *deutsch,* German; orig. < D. *plat,* lit., flat, plain (as in *ic segg't uw plat,* I say it plainly, clearly), hence "in the vernacular"], the Low German vernacular language of northern Germany.
Platte (plat), *n.* a river in Nebraska, flowing eastward into the Missouri: length, 310 mi.
Platte National Park (plat), a national park in southern Oklahoma, containing sulfur springs.
Plat·ten·see (plät′ən-zā′), *n.* Balaton: the German name.
plat·ter (plat′ẽr), *n.* [ME. *plater* < OFr. *plat,* flat], 1. a large, shallow dish, usually oval, for serving food. 2. [Slang], in *baseball,* the home base: also called *plate.* 3. [Slang], a phonograph record.
Platts·burg (plats′bẽrg), *n.* a town in northeastern New York, on Lake Champlain: pop., 20,000: scene of a naval battle (1814) in the War of 1812, in which the Americans defeated the British.
plat·y- (plat′i), [< Gr. *platys,* broad, flat], a combining form meaning *broad* or *flat,* as in *platypus:* also **plat-.**
plat·y·hel·minth (plat′i-hel′minth), *n.* [< *platy-* + Gr. *helmins, helminthos,* a worm], any of a number of related worms with a soft, flattish body, as a tapeworm, fluke, etc.; flatworm.
plat·y·pus (plat′ə-pəs), *n.* [*pl.* PLATYPUSES (-iz), PLATYPI (-pī′)], [Mod. L. < *platy-* + Gr. *pous,* a foot], a duckbill: also called *duckbilled platypus.*
plat·yr·rhin·i·an (plat′ə-rin′i-ən), *adj.* [Mod. L. *platyrrhinus* < *platy-* + Gr. *rhis, rhinos,* a nose], having a broad, flat nose with the nostrils wide apart. *n.* a platyrrhinian person, monkey, or skull.
plau·dit (plô′dit), *n.* [L. *plaudite,* imperative of *plaudere,* to applaud], *usually in pl.* 1. an applauding or round of applause. 2. any expression of approval or praise.
Plau·en (plou′ən), *n.* a city in east central Germany: pop., 85,000.
plau·si·bil·i·ty (plô′zə-bil′ə-ti), *n.* a plausible quality.
plau·si·ble (plô′zə-b'l), *adj.* [L. *plausibilis* < *plaudere,* to applaud, clap hands], 1. seemingly true, acceptable, etc.: often implying disbelief; hence, 2. specious. 3. seemingly honest, trustworthy, etc.: often implying distrust, as, a *plausible* rogue.
SYN.—**plausible** applies to that which at first glance appears to be true, reasonable, valid, etc. but which may or may not be so, although there is no connotation of deliberate deception (a *plausible* argument); **credible** is used of that which is believable because it is supported by evidence, sound logic, etc.; (a *credible* account); **specious** applies to that which is superficially reasonable, valid, etc. but is actually not so, and it connotes intention to deceive (a *specious* excuse).—***ANT.*** genuine, actual.
plau·si·bly (plô′zə-bli), *adv.* in a plausible manner.
plau·sive (plô′siv), *adj.* 1. applauding or showing praise. 2. [Obs.], plausible.
Plau·tus (plô′təs), *n.* (*Titus Maccius Plautus*), Roman writer of comedies; lived 254?–184 B.C.
play (plā), *v.i.* [ME. *pleien;* AS. *plegan, plegian,* to play, be active; akin to G. *pflegen,* to take care of, be used to; basic sense "to bestir oneself, be busy"; IE. base **dhlgh-,* prob., to take up one's promise, responsibility, etc.], 1. to move lightly, rapidly, or erratically; frisk; flutter: as, sunlight *plays* on the waves, a smile *played* on his lips. 2. to have fun; amuse oneself; take part in a game or sport; engage in recreation. 3. to take part in a game for money; gamble. 4. to make love playfully. 5. to handle anything carelessly or treat anyone lightly; trifle (*with* a thing or person). 6. to perform on a musical instrument. 7. to give out musical sounds: said of an instrument. 8. to act in a specified way: as, *play* fast and loose. 9. to act in or as in a drama; perform on the stage. 10. to lend itself to performance: as, the new piano *plays* well, that drama will *play.* 11. to be performed in a theater, on the radio, etc.: as, a new movie is *playing* tonight. 12. to move freely within limits, as parts of a machine. 13. to be ejected, discharged, or directed repeatedly or continuously, as a fountain, a gun, a spotlight, etc. (with *on, over,* or *along*). *v.t.* 1. to take part in (a game or sport). 2. to engage in a game or contest against. 3. to enter or use (a player, etc.) in a game or contest: as, the coach *played* Jones at center. 4. to do (something), often in fun or to deceive: as, *play*

tricks. 5. *a*) to bet. *b*) to bet on: as, *play* the horses. 6. to cause to move, act, operate, etc.; put into or keep in action; wield; ply. 7. to cause; effect: as, *play* hob, *play* havoc. 8. to perform (music). 9. to perform on (an instrument); cause to give out musical sounds. 10. to accompany or lead (a person or persons) with music (with *in, off, down,* etc.). 11. to perform (a drama or dramatic passage). 12. to act the part of: as, *play* Iago, *play* the fool. 13. to pretend or imitate for amusement: as, *play* soldier. 14. to give performances in: as, they *played* New York for a month. 15. to eject, discharge, or direct repeatedly or continuously, as a fountain, etc. (with *on, over,* or *along*). 16. to let (a fish) tire itself while hooked by tugging at the line. ***n.*** 1. action, motion, or activity, especially when free, rapid, or light: as, the *play* of muscles. 2. freedom or scope for motion or action. 3. action or exercise for amusement; recreation; sport. 4. fun; joking: as, do a thing in *play*: opposed to *earnest*. 5. the playing of a game. 6. the way of playing a game. 7. a maneuver, move, or act in a game. 8. gambling. 9. a dramatic composition or performance; drama.

in (or **out of**) **play,** in *sports,* in (or not in) such a condition or position that play may legitimately be continued: said of a ball, etc.

make a play for, [Colloq.], 1. to employ one's arts and wiles in order to fascinate. 2. to use all one's skill in order to obtain.

play at, 1. to participate in. 2. to pretend to be engaged in. 3. to perform or work at halfheartedly.

play both ends against the middle, 1. to take chances on alternatives in order to win something no matter what the outcome. 2. to play off opposing factions, etc. against one another to one's own profit.

play down, to attach little importance to; give little publicity to; minimize.

played out, 1. finished. 2. worn out; exhausted. 3. out of date.

play fair, 1. to play according to the rules. 2. to behave honorably.

play for time, to maneuver so as to delay an outcome, gain a respite, etc.

play into (someone's) hands, to act in such a way as to give the advantage to (someone).

play off, 1. to pit (a person or thing) against another. 2. to palm off. 3. in *games,* to break (a tie) by playing once more.

play on (or **upon**), to make adroit or unscrupulous use of (a person's feelings or susceptibilities) for one's own purposes.

play one's cards well, to use one's resources in the most effective manner.

play out, 1. to play to the finish; end. 2. to pay out (a rope, etc.).

play second fiddle, to take a subordinate position.

play up, [Colloq.], to give prominence to; advertise.

play up to, [Colloq.], to try to please by flattery, etc.

***SYN.*—play,** the general term, implies activity, physical or mental, whose sole aim is diversion or amusement; **sport,** in this connection now somewhat literary, implies active physical play out-of-doors (children *sporting* in the woods); **frolic** implies lighthearted, carefree gaiety in playing (*frolicking* at a New Year's Eve party); **romp** suggests active, boisterous play that involves running about and jumping (I see them *romping* on the beach); **gambol** suggests the skipping about of lambs or young children in play (let them *gambol* on the lawn).

pla·ya (plä'yə), ***n.*** [*pl.* PLAYAS (-yəz)], [Sp.; Pr.; LL. *plagia,* for L. *plaga,* an area], a dried-up lake basin.

play·a·ble (plā'ə-b'l), ***adj.*** 1. that can be played. 2. that can be played on; in suitable condition for playing.

play·back (plā'bak'), ***n.*** 1. a playing back. 2. the part of an electric recorder that serves as a phonograph to play back transcriptions, etc.

play·bill (plā'bil'), ***n.*** 1. a poster or circular advertising a play. 2. a program of a play.

play·boy (plā'boi'), ***n.*** [Colloq.], a man who is carefree, gay, and fond of playing; specifically, a well-to-do man who spends much time and energy in pleasure-seeking and dissipation.

play-by-play (plā'bī-plā'), ***adj.*** of each play as it occurs: as, a *play-by-play* description of a game.

play·day (plā'dā'), ***n.*** a day for playing; holiday.

play·er (plā'ẽr), ***n.*** 1. a person who plays a game: as, a football *player*. 2. a performer in a drama; actor. 3. a person who plays a musical instrument. 4. a gambler. 5. an apparatus for playing a musical instrument mechanically.

player piano, a piano that plays automatically.

play·fel·low (plā'fel'ō), ***n.*** a playmate.

play·ful (plā'fəl), ***adj.*** 1. fond of play or fun; sportive; frisky; frolicsome. 2. humorous; joking; merry.

play·go·er (plā'gō'ẽr), ***n.*** a person who goes to the theater frequently or regularly.

play·ground (plā'ground'), ***n.*** a place, often near a schoolhouse, for outdoor games and recreation.

play hook·y (hook'i), [*hooky* prob. < *hook it,* to run away], to stay away from school without permission; be a truant.

play·house (plā'hous'), ***n.*** [AS. *pleghus* < *plega,* a play + *hus,* a house], 1. a theater. 2. a small house for children to play in. 3. a building used for recreation. 4. a child's toy house or doll house.

playing cards, cards used in playing various games, arranged in decks of four suits (spades, clubs, diamonds, and hearts).

play·let (plā'lit), ***n.*** a short drama.

play·mate (plā'māt'), ***n.*** a companion in games and recreation; playfellow.

play-off (plā'ôf'), ***n.*** in *games,* a match played to break a tie.

play on words, a pun or punning.

play·room (plā'ro͞om', plā'room'), ***n.*** a room for playing or recreation.

play·thing (plā'thiŋ'), ***n.*** a thing to play with; a toy.

play·time (plā'tīm'), ***n.*** time for play or recreation.

play·wright (plā'rīt'), ***n.*** [see WRIGHT], a person who writes plays; dramatist.

pla·za (plaz-ə, plä'zə), ***n.*** [Sp.; L. *platea;* see PLACE], a public square or market place in a city or town.

plea (plē), ***n.*** [ME. *plee, plead, pleid;* OFr. *plai, plaid, plait,* a suit, plea; L. *placitum,* an opinion, determination, that which is pleasing, orig. neut. pp. of *placere,* to please], 1. a statement in defense or justification; excuse. 2. an appeal; request; entreaty. 3. in *law, a*) a pleading or allegation. *b*) a statement made by, or on behalf of, a defendant, either answering the charges or showing why he should not be required to answer.

pleach (plēch), ***v.t.*** [ME. *plechen;* ONorm.Fr. *plechier,* for OFr. *plessier, plaissier,* to weave, plait; see PLASH (to bend)], to bend and interlace (branches); plait.

plead (plēd), ***v.i.*** [PLEADED (-id), PLEADING; *colloq.* or *dial.* p.t. & pp. PLEAD, PLED (pled)], [ME. *plaiden;* OFr. *plaidier* < *plaid;* see PLEA], 1. to present a plea in a law court; argue the case of either party; hence, 2. to make an earnest appeal; supplicate; beg: as, *plead* for mercy. ***v.t.*** 1. to discuss or defend (a law case) by argument. 2. to declare oneself to be (guilty or not guilty) in answer to a charge. 3. to offer as an excuse or defense: as, *plead* ignorance. **—*SYN.*** see **appeal.**

plead·er (plēd'ẽr), ***n.*** 1. a person who pleads in a law court; advocate. 2. a person who entreats or intercedes.

plead·ings (plēd'iŋz), ***n.pl.*** the statements setting forth to the court the claims or allegations of the plaintiff and the answer of the defendant.

pleas·ance (plez''ns), ***n.*** [ME. *plesaunce;* OFr. *plaisance* < *plaisir,* to please], 1. [Archaic], pleasure or pleasantry. 2. a pleasure ground or garden, usually part of an estate.

pleas·ant (plez''nt), ***adj.*** [ME. *plesaunte;* OFr. *plaisant,* ppr. of *plaisir,* to please], 1. agreeable to the mind or senses; pleasing; delightful. 2. having an agreeable manner, appearance, etc.; amiable. 3. *a*) gay; merry. *b*) jesting; jocular; playful.

SYN.*—pleasant** and **pleasing** both imply the producing of an agreeable effect upon the mind or senses, but the former word stresses the effect produced (a *pleasant* smile) and the latter, the ability to produce such an effect (her *pleasing* ways); **agreeable** is used of that which is in accord with one's personal likes, mood, etc. (*agreeable* music); **enjoyable** implies the ability to give enjoyment or pleasure (an *enjoyable* picnic); **gratifying** implies the ability to give satisfaction or pleasure by indulging the wishes, hopes, etc. (a *gratifying* experience).**—*ANT. unpleasant, disagreeable.

Pleasant Island, Nauru Island: the former name.

pleas·ant·ry (plez''n-tri), ***n.*** [*pl.* PLEASANTRIES (-triz)], [Fr. *plaisanterie*], 1. the quality or state of being pleasant, or playful, in conversation; jocularity. 2. a humorous remark or action; joke. 3. [Archaic], pleasure.

please (plēz), ***v.t.*** [PLEASED (plēzd), PLEASING], [ME. *plesen, plaisen;* OFr. *plaisir;* L. *placere,* to please < base seen also in *placidus,* gentle, mild, *placare,* to calm, soothe; orig. idea, to make smooth, level], 1. to be agreeable to; give pleasure to; satisfy. 2. to be the will or wish of: as, it *pleased* him to remain. ***v.i.*** 1. to be agreeable; give pleasure; satisfy: as, we aim to *please.* 2. to have the will or wish; like: as, I'll do as I *please:* also used passively, as, you are *pleased* to scoff. *Please* is also used, followed by an infinitive, for politeness in requests or commands to mean "be obliging enough": as, *please* (to) do this for me.

if you please, if you wish or like; if you permit: sometimes used in ironic exclamation.

please God, if it pleases God; if it is God's will.

please oneself, to do as one wishes.

pleas·ing (plēz'iŋ), ***adj.*** giving pleasure; pleasant; agreeable; gratifying. **—*SYN.*** see **pleasant.**

pleas·ur·a·ble (plezh'ẽr-ə-b'l), ***adj.*** [< *pleasure,* after *comfortable*], pleasant; enjoyable; agreeable.

pleas·ur·a·bly (plezh'ẽr-ə-bli), ***adv.*** in a pleasurable manner.

pleas·ure (plezh′ẽr), *n.* [ME. *plesir;* OFr. *plesir, plaisir,* pleasure; orig. inf.; see PLEASE], 1. a pleased feeling; enjoyment; delight; satisfaction. 2. one's wish, will, or choice: as, what is his *pleasure* in the matter? 3. a thing that gives delight or satisfaction. 4. gratification of the senses; sensual satisfaction. *v.t.* [PLEASURED (-ẽrd), PLEASURING], [Archaic], to give pleasure to; please. *v.i.* [Archaic], to take pleasure; delight.

SYN.—**pleasure** is the general term for an agreeable feeling of satisfaction, ranging from a quiet sense of gratification to a positive sense of happiness; **delight** implies a high degree of obvious pleasure, openly and enthusiastically expressed (a child's *delight* with a new toy); **joy** describes a keenly felt, exuberant, often demonstrative happiness (their *joy* at his safe return); **enjoyment** suggests a somewhat more quiet feeling of satisfaction with that which pleases (our *enjoyment* of the recital).—*ANT.* displeasure, sorrow, vexation.

pleasure principle, in *psychoanalysis,* the automatic adjustment of the mental activity to secure pleasure, or gratification, and avoid pain, or unpleasantness.

pleat (plēt), *n.* [ME. *pleten,* var. of *playten;* cf. PLAIT, PLAT], a flat double fold in cloth or other material, of uniform width and pressed or stitched in place. *v.t.* to lay and press (cloth) in a pleat or series of pleats.

pleat·er (plēt′ẽr), *n.* a person or thing that pleats; specifically, an attachment on a sewing machine for making pleats.

pleb (pleb), *n.* 1. a plebeian. 2. a plebe (sense 3).

plebe (plēb), *n.* [Fr. *plèbe;* L. *plebs*], 1. [Obs.], the Roman plebs; hence, 2. the common people of a nation. 3. [short for *plebeian*], a member of the lowest, or freshman, class at the United States Military Academy at West Point or the Naval Academy at Annapolis.

ple·be·ian (pli-bē′ən), *n.* [< L. *plebeius* < *plebs, plebis,* common people], 1. a member of the ancient Roman lower class; hence, 2. one of the common people. 3. a vulgar, coarse person. *adj.* 1. of or characteristic of the Roman lower class or the common people; hence, 2. of low rank. 3. vulgar, coarse, or common.

ple·be·ian·ism (pli-bē′ən-iz'm), *n.* 1. a plebeian characteristic, act, or remark. 2. plebeian quality or manners; vulgarity.

pleb·i·scite (pleb′ə-sīt′, pleb′ə-sit), *n.* [Fr. *plébiscite;* L. *plebiscitum* < *plebs,* common people + *scitum,* decree, neut. pp. of *scire,* to know], an expression of the people's will by direct ballot of all eligible voters on a political issue, as on choice of national sovereignty.

plebs (plebz), *n.* [*pl.* PLEBES (plē′bēz)], [L.], 1. the lower class in ancient Roman society: distinguished from *patricians.* 2. the common people; the masses.

plec·tog·nath (plek′tog-nath′), *adj.* [< Mod. L. *Plectognathi,* name of the order < Gr. *plektos,* twisted + *gnathos,* a jaw], in *zoology,* of an order of fishes found in warm seas, having a small mouth with powerful jaws and bony or spiny scales. *n.* a fish of this order.

plec·tron (plek′tron), *n.* a plectrum.

plec·trum (plek′trəm), *n.* [*pl.* PLECTRUMS (-trəmz), PLECTRA (-trə)], [L.; Gr. *plēktron,* an instrument for striking (the lyre) < *plēssein,* to strike], a small, thin piece of metal, bone, plastic, etc., used for plucking the strings of a guitar, mandolin, etc.

pled (pled), colloquial or dialectal past tense and past participle of **plead.**

pledge (plej), *n.* [ME. *plege;* OFr. *pleige;* ML. *plegium, plivium* < Gmc. base of AS. *plegian,* to play; cf. PLAY], 1. the condition of being given or held as security for a contract, payment, etc.: as, a thing held in *pledge.* 2. a person or thing given or held as security for the performance of a contract, as guarantee of faith, etc.; something pawned; hostage. 3. a token or earnest. 4. a drinking of one's health to express good will or allegiance; toast. 5. a promise or agreement. 6. a person who has promised to become a member of a fraternity and who goes through a trial period before being initiated. *v.t.* [PLEDGED (plejd), PLEDGING], 1. to present as security or guarantee, especially for the repayment of a loan; pawn. 2. to drink a health to; toast. 3. to bind by a promise or agreement. 4. to promise to join (a fraternity); hence, 5. to accept (someone) as a candidate for membership in a fraternity.

take the pledge, to take a vow to stop drinking, or never to drink, alcoholic liquor.

SYN.—**pledge** applies to anything given as security for the performance of an act or contract or for the payment of a debt (she gave her a ring as a *pledge*); **earnest,** in current usage, applies to anything given or done as an indication, promise, or assurance of more to follow (his early triumphs are an *earnest* of his success); **token** is used of anything serving or given as evidence of authority, genuineness, good faith, etc. (this watch is a *token* of our gratitude); **pawn** now usually refers to an article left as security for the money loaned on it by a pawnbroker; **hostage** is applied to a person handed over as a pledge for the fulfillment of certain terms or one seized and kept to force others to comply with demands.

pledg·ee (plej′ē′), *n.* a person with whom a pledge is deposited.

pledge·or (plej′ôr′), *n.* a pledgor.

pledg·er (plej′ẽr), *n.* a person who pledges.

pledg·et (plej′it), *n.* [< ?], a small wad of wool, cotton, or linen, used as a dressing for a wound or sore.

pledg·or (plej′ôr′), *n.* in *law,* a person who deposits something as security: distinguished from *pledgee.*

-ple·gi·a (plē′ji-ə), [Gr. *-plēgia* < *plēgē,* a stroke; akin to *plēssein,* to strike], in *medicine,* a combining form meaning *paralysis,* as in *paraplegia.*

-ple·gy (plē′ji), -plegia.

Ple·ia·des (plē′ə-dēz′, plī′ə-dēz′), *n.pl.* [*sing.* PLEIAD (plē′əd, plī′ad)], [ME. *Pliades;* L.], 1. in *Greek mythology,* the seven daughters of Atlas and Pleione, who were placed by Zeus among the stars; hence, 2. in *astronomy,* a large group of stars in the constellation Taurus, six of which are visible and represent the daughters of Atlas, the seventh being "lost" (the *Lost Pleiad*).

plein-air (plān′âr′), *adj.* [Fr., lit., open air], designating or of certain schools of French impressionist painting engaged mainly in representing effects of outdoor light and atmosphere.

Plei·o·cene (plī′ə-sēn′), *adj.* Pliocene.

Pleis·to·cene (plīs′tə-sēn′), *adj.* [< Gr. *pleistos,* most + *kainos,* new], designating or of the first epoch of the Quaternary Period in the Cenozoic Era, characterized by the rise and recession of continental ice sheets and by the appearance of man.

the Pleistocene, the Pleistocene Epoch or its rocks: see **geology,** chart.

ple·na·ri·ly (plē′nə-rə-li, plen′ə-rə-li), *adv.* in a plenary manner.

ple·na·ry (plē′nə-ri, plen′ə-ri), *adj.* [LL. *plenarius;* L. *plenus,* full], 1. full; complete; absolute. 2. attended by all members: said of an assembly.

plenary indulgence, in the *Roman Catholic Church,* an indulgence remitting in full the temporal punishment incurred by a sinner.

plen·i·po·ten·ti·ar·y (plen′i-pə-ten′shi-er′i, plen′i-pə-ten′shə-ri), *adj.* [ML. *plenipotentiarius* < LL. *plenipotens* < L. *plenus,* full + *potens,* powerful], 1. having or conferring full power or authority. 2. full; plenary: said of power, etc. *n.* [*pl.* PLENIPOTENTIARIES (-iz, -riz)], a person given full authority to act as representative of a government; ambassador.

plen·ish (plen′ish), *v.t.* [< OFr. *pleniss-,* ppr. stem of *plenir,* to fill < L. *plenus,* full], [Scot. & Dial.], to fill up; furnish; stock.

plen·i·tude (plen′ə-tōōd′, plen′ə-tūd′), *n.* [OFr.; L. *plenitudo* < *plenus,* full], 1. fullness; completeness. 2. abundance; plenty.

plen·te·ous (plen′ti-əs), *adj.* [ME. *plenteus, plentevous;* OFr. *plentieus, plentevous*], 1. abundant; plentiful; copious. 2. producing abundantly; fruitful.

plen·ti·ful (plen′ti-fəl), *adj.* 1. having or yielding plenty. 2. sufficient; abundant.

SYN.—**plentiful** implies a large or full supply (a *plentiful* supply of food); **abundant** implies a very plentiful or very large supply (a forest *abundant* in wild game); **copious,** now used chiefly with reference to quantity produced, used, etc., implies a rich abundance (a *copious* harvest, vocabulary, etc.); **profuse** implies a giving or pouring forth abundantly or lavishly, often to excess (*profuse* in his thanks); **ample** applies to that which is large enough to meet all demands (his savings are *ample* to see him through this crisis).—*ANT.* scarce, scant.

plen·ty (plen′ti), *n.* [*pl.* PLENTIES (-tiz)], [ME. *plente, plenteth;* OFr. *plentet, plente;* L. *plenitas* < *plenus,* full], 1. prosperity; opulence. 2. a sufficient supply; enough. *adj.* plentiful; enough; ample: generally used in the predicate. *adv.* [Colloq.], fully; very: as, *plenty* good.

ple·num (plē′nəm), *n.* [*pl.* PLENUMS (-nəmz), PLENA (-nə)], [L., neut. of *plenus,* full], 1. space filled with matter: opposed to *vacuum.* 2. fullness. 3. a full assembly, as of all members of a legislative body. 4. an enclosed volume of gas under greater pressure than that surrounding the container.

ple·o·nasm (plē′ə-naz'm), *n.* [LL. *pleonasmus;* Gr. *pleonasmos* < *pleonazein,* to be in excess < *pleon,* neut. of *pleōn, pleiōn,* more, compar. of *polys,* much], 1. the use of more words than are necessary for the expression of an idea; redundancy. 2. an instance of this. 3. the redundant word or expression.

ple·o·nas·tic (plē′ə-nas′tik), *adj.* characterized by pleonasm; redundant.

ple·o·nas·ti·cal·ly (plē′ə-nas′ti-k'l-i, plē′ə-nas′tik-li), *adv.* in a pleonastic manner.

ple·o·pod (plē′ə-pod′), *n.* [< Gr. *pleōn,* ppr. of *plein,* to swim; + *-pod*], in *zoology,* one of the limbs attached to the abdomen of a crustacean.

ple·si·o·saur (plē′si-ə-sôr′), *n.* [Mod. L. *plesiosaurus* < Gr. *plēsios,* close, near + *sauros,* lizard], any of an extinct group of large water reptiles of the Mesozoic Era, characterized by a small head, long neck, short tail, and four paddlelike limbs: also **plesiosaurus.**

ple·si·o·sau·rus (plē′si-ə-sôr′əs), *n.* a plesiosaur.

ples·sor (ples′ẽr), *n.* [< Gr. *plēssein,* to strike], in *medicine,* a small hammer with a soft head, as of rubber, used in percussion: also **plexor.**

pleth·o·ra (pleth′ə-rə), *n.* [ML.; Gr. *plēthōrē* < *plēthein,* to become full < *plēthos,* fullness], 1. the state of being too full; overabundance; excess. 2. an abnormal condition characterized by an excess of blood in the circulatory system or in some part of it.

ple·thor·ic (ple-thôr′ik, ple-thor′ik, pleth′ə-rik), *adj.*

[ML. *plethoricus;* Gr. *plēthōrikos*], 1. too full; swollen; hence, 2. bombastic. 3. of or characterized by plethora; having an excess of blood.

ple·thor·i·cal·ly (ple-thôr'i-k'l-i, ple-thor'ik-li), *adv.* in a manner characterized by plethora.

pleu·ra (ploor'ə), *n.* [*pl.* PLEURAE (-ē)], [ML. < Gr. *pleura,* a rib, side], a thin serous membrane lining each half of the chest cavity and enveloping the lungs.

pleu·ral (ploor'əl), *adj.* of the pleura.

pleu·ri·sy (ploor'ə-si), *n.* [OFr. *pleurisie;* LL. *pleurisis;* L. *pleuritis;* Gr. *pleuritis* < *pleura,* a rib, side], inflammation of the pleura, characterized by difficult, painful breathing, fever, and a dry cough, and often accompanied by the exudation of liquid into the chest cavity.

pleurisy root, 1. a plant with orange flowers; butterfly weed. 2. its root, formerly used as a cure for pleurisy.

pleu·rit·ic (ploo-rit'ik), *adj.* [L. *pleuriticus;* Gr. *pleuritikos*], of, indicating, or having pleurisy.

pleu·ro- (ploor'ō, ploor'ə), [< Gr. *pleura,* a rib, side], a combining form meaning: 1. *on* or *near the side,* as in *pleurodont.* 2. *of* or *near the pleura,* as in *pleurotomy.* 3. *pleural and,* as in *pleuropneumonia.* Also, before a vowel, **pleur-.**

pleu·ro·dont (ploor'ə-dont'), *adj.* [*pleur-* + *-odont*], in *zoology,* having teeth growing from the side of the jawbone instead of from separate sockets, as some lizards.

pleu·ron (ploor'on), *n.* [*pl.* PLEURA (-ə)], [Gr. *pleuron,* a rib], either of the lateral plates on the thorax of an insect.

pleu·ro·pneu·mo·ni·a (ploo'rō-nōō-mō'ni-ə, ploo'rō-nū-mō'ni-ə), *n.* [*pleuro-* + *pneumonia*], pneumonia complicated by pleurisy.

pleu·rot·o·my (ploo-rot'ə-mi), *n.* [*pl.* PLEUROTOMIES (-miz)], [*pleuro-* + *-tomy*], surgical incision of the pleura to permit drainage of exuded liquids.

plex·i·form (plek'sə-fôrm'), *adj.* [< *plexus* + *-form*], 1. like a network. 2. complicated.

plex·i·glass (plek'si-glas', plek'si-gläs'), *n.* [< L. *plexus,* a twining; + *glass*], a lightweight, transparent thermoplastic substance, used as a cockpit cover for aircraft, etc.: a trade-mark (**Plexiglas**).

plex·im·e·ter (plek-sim'ə-tẽr), *n.* in *medicine,* a small, thin plate, as of ivory, placed against some part of the body and struck with a plessor in percussion.

plex·or (plek'sẽr), *n.* a plessor.

plex·us (plek'səs), *n.* [*pl.* PLEXUSES (-iz), PLEXUS], [L., a twining, braid < *plexus,* pp. of *plectere,* to twine, braid; akin to *plicare;* see PLY], an interwoven arrangement of parts; network; specifically, in *anatomy,* a network of blood vessels, lymphatic vessels, nerves, etc.: as, the solar *plexus* (of nerves) in the abdomen.

pli·a·bil·i·ty (plī'ə-bil'ə-ti), *n.* a pliable quality.

pli·a·ble (plī'ə-b'l), *adj.* [Fr. < *plier,* to bend, fold < L. *plicare,* to fold, bend], 1. easily bent or molded; flexible. 2. easily influenced or persuaded; adaptable; tractable.

SYN.—**pliable** and **pliant** both imply capability of being easily bent, physically suggesting the suppleness of a wooden switch and figuratively, a yielding nature or adaptability; **plastic** is used of substances, such as plaster or clay, that can be molded into various forms which are retained upon hardening, and figuratively suggests an impressionable quality; **ductile** literally and figuratively suggests that which can be finely drawn or stretched out (copper is a *ductile* metal); **malleable** literally or figuratively suggests that which can be hammered, beaten, or pressed into various shapes (copper is *malleable* as well as ductile).—*ANT.* inflexible, rigid, brittle.

pli·a·bly (plī'ə-bli), *adv.* in a pliable manner.

pli·an·cy (plī'ən-si), *n.* the quality of being pliant.

pli·ant (plī'ənt), *adj.* [ME. *plyande,* etc.; OFr., ppr. of *plier;* see PLIABLE], 1. easily bent; pliable. 2. adaptable; compliant. —*SYN.* see **pliable.**

pli·ca (plī'kə), *n.* [*pl.* PLICAE (-sē)], [ML., a fold < L. *plicare,* to fold], 1. in *anatomy,* a fold or folding, especially of the skin or mucous membrane. 2. in *medicine,* a matted, diseased condition of the hair, in which it becomes covered with crusts and vermin.

plica po·lon·i·ca (pə-lon'i-kə), plica (sense 2).

pli·cate (plī'kāt), *adj.* [L. *plicatus,* pp. of *plicare,* to fold], folded; plaited; arranged in pleats, as a fan.

pli·cat·ed (plī'kā-tid), *adj.* plicate.

pli·ca·tion (plī-kā'shən, pli-kā'shən), *n.* [ME. *plicacioun;* OFr. < L. *plicare,* to fold], 1. a folding or being folded. 2. a fold. 3. in *geology,* a stratum fold.

plic·a·ture (plik'ə-chẽr), *n.* plication.

pli·er (plī'ẽr), *n.* a person or thing that plies.

pli·ers (plī'ẽrz), *n.pl.* [< *ply* (to bend)], small pincers for handling small objects, cutting wire, etc.

plight (plīt), *n.* [ME. *plit,* a state, condition; Anglo-Fr. *plit,* for OFr. *ploit,* a fold, way of folding, condition (see PLAIT, *n.*); in mod. sense prob. influenced by AS. *pliht,* a pledge, danger (see PLIGHT, *v.*)], a condition, state of affairs, or situation; especially, now, a dangerous or awkward situation. —*SYN.* see **predicament.**

plight (plīt), *v.t.* [ME. *plihten;* AS.‡*plihtan,* to pledge, expose to danger < *pliht,* a pledge, danger; akin to *pleon,* to risk, G. *pflicht,* duty, *pflegen,* to take care of, nourish], 1. to pledge or engage: as, *plight* one's troth. 2. to bind (oneself) by a promise; engage; betroth.

plight one's troth, 1. to pledge one's truth; give one's word. 2. to make a promise of marriage.

Plim·soll mark (or **line**), (plim'səl, plim'sol), [after Samuel *Plimsoll* (1824–1898), Brit. statesman who was instrumental in having legislation passed against overloading vessels], a line on the outside of British merchant ships, showing the lawful submergence level: also **Plimsoll's mark** (or **line**).

plinth (plinth), *n.* [L. *plinthus;* Gr. *plinthos,* a brick, tile], 1. the square block at the base of a column, pedestal, etc. 2. the rectangular or circular base on which a statue is placed.

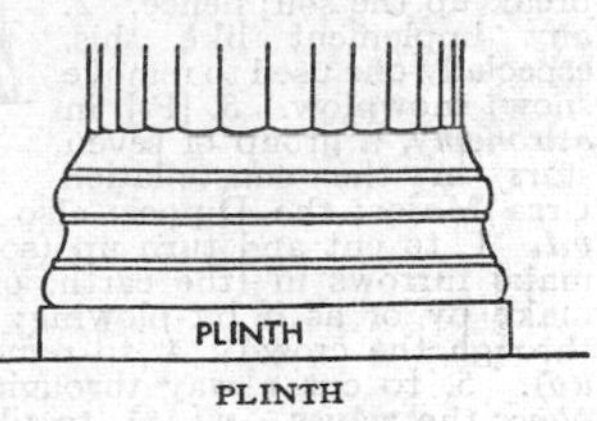

PLINTH

Plin·y (plin'i), *n.* 1. (*Gaius Plinius Secundus*), Roman naturalist and writer; lived 23–79 A.D.: called *the Elder.* 2. (*Gaius Plinius Caecilius Secundus*), nephew of the above; lived 62–113 A.D.; Roman statesman and writer: called *the Younger.*

Pli·o·cene (plī'ə-sēn'), *adj.* [< Gr. *pleiōn, pleōn,* more (see PLEONASM) + *kainos,* recent, new], designating or of the last epoch of the Tertiary Period in the Cenozoic Era, during which modern plants and animals developed: also spelled **Pleiocene.**

the Pliocene, the Pliocene Epoch or its rocks: see **geology,** chart.

pli·o·film (plī'ə-film'), *n.* [< *pliable* + *film*], a type of waterproof, transparent rubber sheeting used for raincoats, wrapping material, etc.: a trade-mark (**Pliofilm**).

plod (plod), *v.i.* [PLODDED (-id), PLODDING], [origin prob. echoic], 1. to walk or move heavily and laboriously; trudge. 2. to work steadily and monotonously; drudge. *n.* 1. a plodding. 2. a heavy step. 3. the sound of this.

plod·der (plod'ẽr), *n.* 1. a person who plods. 2. a dull or stolid person.

Plo·eș·ti (plô-yesht'), *n.* a city in Romania, north of Bucharest: pop., 105,000 (est. 1945).

-ploid (ploid), [< Gr. *-ploos,* -fold; + *-oid*], a combining form meaning *of a* (specified) *multiple of chromosomes,* as in *diploid.*

plop (plop), *v.t. & v.i.* [PLOPPED (plopt), PLOPPING], [echoic], to drop with a sound like that of something flat falling into water without splashing. *n.* 1. such a sound. 2. a plopping. *adv.* with a plop.

plo·sion (plō'zhən), *n.* [< *explosion*], 1. the articulation of a plosive sound. 2. loosely, the final stage, or sudden release of breath, in the articulation of a plosive.

plo·sive (plō'siv), *adj.* [< *explosive*], designating or of a speech sound produced by the complete stoppage and sudden release of the breath, as the consonants *k, p,* and *t* when used initially. *n.* a plosive sound.

plot (plot), *n.* [ME. (& once in Late AS.), an area of ground; ? < OFr. *pelote,* clod; meaning later influenced, prob. by *complot*], 1. an area marked on a surface, usually of ground; patch; plat. 2. a chart, diagram, or map, as of a building, estate, etc. 3. a secret, usually evil, project or scheme; conspiracy. 4. the plan of action of a play, novel, poem, short story, etc. *v.t.* [PLOTTED (-id), PLOTTING], 1. to draw a plan, chart, or map of (a building, ship's course, etc.). 2. to make secret plans for: as, to *plot* someone's destruction. 3. to plan the action of (a story, etc.). 4. in *mathematics, a)* to represent (an equation) by locating points on a graph and joining them to form a curve. *b)* to draw (the curve). *v.i.* to plan; scheme; conspire.

SYN.—**plot** is used of a secret, usually evil, project or scheme the details of which have been carefully worked out (the *plot* to deprive him of his inheritance failed); **intrigue,** implying more intricate scheming, suggests furtive, underhand maneuvering often of an illicit nature (the *intrigues* at the royal court); **machination** stresses deceit and cunning in devising plots or schemes intended to harm someone (the *machinations* of the villain); **conspiracy** suggests a plot in which a number of people plan and act together secretly for an unlawful or harmful purpose (a *conspiracy* to seize the throne); **cabal** suggests a small group of persons involved in a political intrigue.

Plo·ti·nus (plō-tī'nəs), *n.* Roman philosopher born in Egypt; lived 205?–270 A.D.; Neoplatonist.

plot·tage (plot'ij), *n.* the area of a plot of land.

plot·ter (plot'ẽr), *n.* a person who plots; conspirator.

plotting paper, paper ruled into uniform small squares, for plotting graphs, etc.

plough (plou), *n., v.t. & v.i.* plow.

Plov·div (plôv'dif), *n.* a city in south central Bulgaria: pop., 100,000: Greek name, *Philippopolis.*

plov·er (pluv'ẽr, plō'vẽr), *n.* [*pl.* PLOVERS (-ẽrz, -vẽrz),

PLOVER; see PLURAL, II, D, 1], [ME.; OFr. *plovier*, lit., rain bird; LL. **pluviarius* < L. *pluvia*, rain; reason for name obscure], 1. any of a number of related shore birds of North America, having a short tail, long, pointed wings, and, usually, brown or gray feathers mixed with white. 2. any of a number of similar birds.

plow (plou), *n.* [ME. *plou, plogh;* Late AS. *ploh;* akin to G. *pflug;* appears late in Gmc. languages & is prob. borrowed < non-Indo-European], 1. a farm implement used to cut, turn up, and break up the soil; hence, 2. any implement like this, especially one used to remove snow; snowplow. 3. [P-], in *astronomy*, a group of seven stars in the constellation Ursa Major; the Dipper: also called *Charles's Wain. v.t.* 1. to cut and turn up (soil) with a plow. 2. to make furrows in (the earth, one's face, etc.). 3. to make by or as if by plowing: as, he *plowed* his way through the crowd. 4. to remove with a plow (with *up*). 5. to cut a way through (water): as, the ship *plows* the waves. *v.i.* 1. to till the soil with a plow; use a plow. 2. to take plowing; be in a specified condition for plowing: as, the field *plows* well. 3. to cut a way (*through* water, snow, etc.), as a plow does. 4. to advance laboriously; plod. Also spelled **plough.**

PLOW

plow into, to begin work vigorously on (a job, etc.).

plow·boy (plou'boi'), *n.* 1. a boy who leads the horse or horses drawing a plow. 2. a country boy.

plow·land (plou'land'), *n.* 1. in medieval England, an assessment unit of land, approximately the area that could be plowed by a team of eight oxen in a year. 2. land being cultivated or suitable for cultivation.

plow·man (plou'mən), *n.* [*pl.* PLOWMEN (-mən)], 1. a person who plows. 2. a farm worker; rustic.

plow·share (plou'shâr'), *n.* the share, or cutting blade, of a moldboard plow.

ploy (ploi), *n.* [? < em*ploy*], an action or maneuver intended to outwit or disconcert another person.

pluck (pluk), *v.t.* [ME. *plukken;* AS. *pluccian;* akin to G. *pflücken;* thought by some to be < LL. **piluccare* (cf. It. *piluccare*, to pluck) < L. *pilus*, hair], 1. to pull off or out; pick. 2. to drag or snatch. 3. to pull out the feathers of (a fowl). 4. to pull at and release quickly with little jerking movements of the fingers, as the strings of a musical instrument. 5. [Slang], to rob or swindle. 6. [British Slang], to reject (a candidate) in an examination. *v.i.* to pull; tug; snatch (with *at*). *n.* 1. a pulling; tug. 2. an animal's heart, liver, and lungs, used for food. 3. courage; spirit; fortitude. —*SYN.* see **fortitude.**

pluck up, to rouse one's (courage); take heart.

pluck·i·ly (pluk''l-i), *adv.* in a plucky manner.

pluck·y (pluk'i), *adj.* [PLUCKIER (-i-ẽr), PLUCKIEST (-i-ist)], [< *pluck, n.* 3 + *-y*], brave; spirited; resolute. —*SYN.* see **brave.**

plug (plug), *n.* [MD. *plugge*, a bung, plug, block; akin to G. *pflock*], 1. an object used to stop up a hole, gap, outlet, etc. 2. *a*) a cake of pressed tobacco. *b*) a piece of chewing tobacco. 3. an electrical device, as with projecting prongs, to be fitted into an outlet, etc., thus making contact or closing the circuit. 4. a spark plug. 5. a fireplug. 6. [Slang], a plug hat. 7. [Slang], an inferior or worthless animal or thing; especially, an old, worn-out horse. 8. [Slang], an advertisement, especially one interpolated in a radio program; hence, 9. [Slang], a recommendation, or boost, for someone or something. 10. in *geology*, an extrusive rock which has filled in the vent of a volcano and hardened: it is often exposed by erosion. *v.t.* [PLUGGED (plugd), PLUGGING], 1. to stop up or fill (a hole, gap, etc.) by inserting a plug (usually with *up*). 2. to insert as a plug. 3. to cut and remove a small wedge from (a melon) to test its ripeness. 4. [Slang], to shoot a bullet into. 5. [Slang], to hit with the fist. 6. [Slang], to advertise or recommend insistently; hence, 7. [Slang], to advertise or publicize (a song, etc.) by singing or playing frequently. *v.i.* 1. [Colloq.], to work doggedly and laboriously; plod. 2. [Slang], to shoot or hit (at).

plug in, to connect (an electrical device) with an outlet, etc. by inserting a plug in a socket.

plug·ger (plug'ẽr), *n.* a person or thing that plugs; specifically, *a*) [Colloq.], one who keeps steadily and doggedly at work. *b*) [Slang], one who advertises or publicizes: as, a song *plugger*.

plug hat [Slang], a man's high silk hat.

plug-ug·ly (plug'ug'li), *n.* [*pl.* PLUG-UGLIES (-liz)], [cf. PLUG, *v.t.* 5], [Slang], a city ruffian or gangster; rowdy.

plum (plum), *n.* [ME. & AS. *plume;* LL. *pruna;* L. *prunum;* Gr. *prounon* < *proumnon*, plum], 1. any of a number of related trees having smooth-skinned fruit with a smooth pit. 2. the fruit. 3. a raisin, when used in pudding or cake. 4. the dark bluish-red color of some plums. 5. a choice or desirable object.

plum·age (plōōm'ij), *n.* [ME.; OFr. < *plume*, a feather], a bird's feathers.

plu·mate (plōō'māt, plōō'mit), *adj.* [L. *plumatus*], in *zoology*, resembling plumage or a feather.

plumb (plum), *n.* [ME.; OFr. *plom* (Fr. *plomb*); L. *plumbum*, lead (metal)], a lead weight hung at the end of a line, used to determine how deep water is or whether a wall, etc. is vertical: also called *plumb bob. adj.* vertical; exactly perpendicular. *adv.* 1. in a vertical direction; straight down; directly. 2. [Colloq.], entirely; wholly; absolutely: as, he's *plumb* exhausted. *v.i.* [ME. *plumben*], 1. to fall or sink straight down; plump. 2. to hang vertically. 3. to work with lead, as a plumber. *v.t.* 1. to test or sound with a plumb; hence, 2. to discover the facts or contents of; fathom; solve; understand. 3. to make vertical. 4. to weight or seal with lead. 5. to work on (pipes, etc.) as a plumber. —*SYN.* see **vertical.**

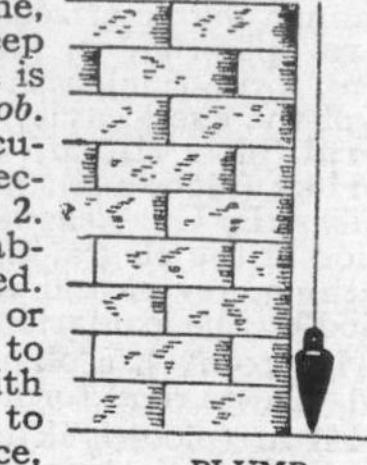
PLUMB

out of plumb, not vertical: also **off plumb.**

plum·bag·i·nous (plum-baj'i-nəs), *adj.* of, like, or containing plumbago.

plum·ba·go (plum-bā'gō), *n.* [*pl.* PLUMBAGOS (-gōz)], [L. *plumbago* < *plumbum*, lead (metal)], 1. graphite. 2. a drawing made with a lead-pointed instrument.

plumb bob, the weight at the end of a plumb line.

plum·be·ous (plum'bi-əs), *adj.* [L. *plumbeus* < *plumbum*, lead (metal)], of, like, or containing lead; leaden.

plumb·er (plum'ẽr), *n.* [ME. *plomere, plummer;* OFr. *plommier;* L. *plumbarius*, lead-worker < *plumbum*, lead (metal)], a skilled worker who fits and repairs the pipes, fixtures, etc. of gas and water systems.

plumb·er·y (plum'ẽr-i), *n.* [*pl.* PLUMBERIES (-iz)], 1. a plumber's workshop. 2. a plumber's work.

plum·bic (plum'bik), *adj.* [< L. *plumbum*, lead (metal)], 1. of or containing lead, especially with a valence of four. 2. in *medicine*, caused by the presence of lead.

plum·bif·er·ous (plum-bif'ẽr-əs), *adj.* [< *plumbum* + *-ferous*], that contains or produces lead.

plumb·ing (plum'iŋ), *n.* [< *plumber*], 1. the using of a plumb. 2. the work or trade of a plumber. 3. the pipes and fixtures with which a plumber works.

plum·bism (plum'biz'm), *n.* [< L. *plumbum*, lead (metal); + *-ism*], lead poisoning.

plumb line, a cord suspending a lead weight, or plumb, used in sounding and in determining vertical direction.

plum·bous (plum'bəs), *adj.* [L. *plumbosus* < *plumbum*, lead (metal)], of or containing lead, especially with a valence of two.

plumb rule, a narrow board equipped with a plumb line and bob, used by carpenters, etc.

plum·bum (plum'bəm), *n.* [L.], lead (the metal).

plume (plōōm), *n.* [ME.; OFr. < L. *pluma*, downy part of a feather, small soft feather], 1. *a*) a feather, especially a large and wavy one. *b*) a group of such feathers. 2. an ornament made of a large feather or feathers, or of a feathery tuft of hair, especially when worn on a helmet, etc. as a mark of rank or distinction; hence, 3. any token of worth or achievement; prize. 4. plumage or down. 5. something like a plume in shape or lightness: as, a *plume* of smoke. 6. in *botany* & *zoology*, a featherlike formation or part. *v.t.* [PLUMED (plōōmd), PLUMING], 1. to provide, cover, or adorn with plumes. 2. to smooth its feathers: used reflexively, of a bird. 3. to pride (oneself). 4. to preen.

plume·let (plōōm'lit), *n.* a small plume.

plum·met (plum'it), *n.* [ME. *plomet;* OFr. *plommet*, dim. of *plom;* see PLUMB], 1. a weight attached to a plumb line; plumb bob. 2. the line and bob together. 3. a thing that weighs heavily. *v.i.* to fall straight downward.

plum·my (plum'i), *adj.* 1. full of plums. 2. like a plum. 3. [Colloq.], good; desirable.

plu·mose (plōō'mōs), *adj.* [L. *plumosus* < *pluma*, a feather], 1. feathered. 2. like a feather.

plu·mos·i·ty (plōō-mos'ə-ti), *n.* the quality or state of being plumose.

plump (plump), *adj.* [Late ME.; MD. *plomp*, unwieldy, bulky, dull; prob. < same echoic base as *plump, v.*], full and rounded in form; chubby. *v.t.* & *v.i.* to fatten or fill out (sometimes with *up* or *out*).

plump (plump), *v.i.* [ME. *plumpen;* MD. *plompen;* origin echoic], 1. to fall suddenly or with full impact. 2. to come in contact abruptly or heavily (*against* something). 3. to go or come in a rush (with *in* or *out*). *v.t.* to drop or throw; put down heavily or all at once. *n.* 1. a falling, plunging, or colliding suddenly or heavily. 2. the sound of this. *adv.* 1. with a plump; suddenly; heavily. 2. straight down. 3. in plain words; bluntly. *adj.* blunt; downright; straightforward.

plump for, 1. to vote for. 2. to support strongly.

plump (plump), *n.* [cf. PLUMP, *v.* & CLUMP], [Archaic or British Dial.], a compact group; cluster.

plump·er (plump'ẽr), *n.* a person or thing that plumps, or fattens; specifically, something carried in the mouth to plump out hollow cheeks.

plump·er (plump'ẽr), *n.* 1. a plumping (dropping heavily). 2. a vote or votes for only one of several candidates running for the same office, when two or more may be voted for. 3. [Slang], a downright lie.

plum pudding, [orig. made with *plums*], 1. a rich pudding made of suet, raisins, currants, etc., boiled or steamed, as in a linen bag. 2. [British], a baked pudding containing similar ingredients in a crust.

plu·mule (plōō'mūl), *n.* [L. *plumula*, dim. of *pluma*, a feather], 1. in *botany*, a little seed bud. 2. a small or downy feather.

plum·y (plōō'mi), *adj.* 1. made of or adorned with plumes or down; feathered. 2. like a plume; feathery.

plun·der (plun'dẽr), *v.t.* [G. *plündern* < *plunder*, trash, baggage], 1. to rob or despoil (a person or place) by force, especially in warfare. 2. to take (property) by force or fraud. *v.i.* to steal. *n.* 1. the act of plundering; pillage; robbery. 2. goods taken by force or fraud; loot; booty. —*SYN.* see **ravage, spoil.**

plun·der·age (plun'dẽr-ij), *n.* [see -AGE], 1. robbery. 2. an embezzling of property on shipboard. 3. the property embezzled.

plunge (plunj), *v.t.* [PLUNGED (plunjd), PLUNGING], [ME. *plungen;* OFr. *plongier;* LL. **plumbicare* < L. *plumbum*, lead (metal)], to thrust, throw, or force suddenly (*into* a liquid, hole, condition, etc.): as, he *plunged* his head into the water, they will *plunge* us into debt. *v.i.* 1. to throw oneself, dive, or rush, as into water, a fight, etc. 2. to move violently and rapidly downward or forward. 3. to pitch, as a ship. 4. to slope steeply, as a road. 5. [Colloq.], to spend or gamble heavily or rashly. *n.* 1. a place for plunging; swimming pool. 2. *a)* a dive or downward leap. *b)* a swim. 3. any sudden, violent plunging motion. 4. [Colloq.], a heavy, rash investment or speculation.

take the plunge, to start on some new and seemingly uncertain enterprise.

plung·er (plun'jẽr), *n.* 1. a person who plunges, or dives. 2. [Colloq.], a person who acts hastily or recklessly; especially, a rash gambler or speculator. 3. in *mechanics*, any cylindrical part that operates with a plunging motion, as a piston, dasher, firing pin, etc.

plunk (pluŋk), *v.t.* [echoic], 1. to pluck or strum (a banjo, etc.). 2. to throw or put down heavily; plump. *v.i.* 1. to give out a twanging sound: said of a banjo, guitar, etc. 2. to fall or sink heavily. *n.* 1. a plunking. 2. the sound made by plunking. 3. [Colloq.], a hard blow. 4. [Slang], a dollar. *adv.* with a twang or thud.

plu·per·fect (plōō-pũr'fikt, plōō'pũr'fikt), *adj.* [abbrev. of L. *plus quam perfectum*, lit., more than perfect], in *grammar*, expressing action completed before a given or implied past time; past perfect. *n.* a pluperfect tense or form. Abbreviated **plup., plupf.**

plu·ral (ploor'əl), *adj.* [ME. & OFr. *plurel;* L. *pluralis* < *plus, pluris*, more], 1. of or including more than one. 2. of, involving, or being one of, a plurality of persons or things: as, *plural* marriage, a *plural* mate. 3. in *grammar*, *a)* designating or of more than one (of what is referred to). *b)* in languages having dual number, designating or of more than two (of what is referred to). *n.* in *grammar*, 1. the plural number. 2. a plural form of a word. 3. a word in plural form. Distinguished from *singular*. Abbreviated **pl., plur.**

NOUN PLURALS IN ENGLISH.— The principle of plural formation is this: 1. according to *sound*, the regular plural suffix is (-iz) after the sound of *s* or any *s*-like sound, (-z) after all other voiced sounds, and (-s) after all other voiceless sounds. 2. according to *spelling*, the regular plural suffix is -*(e)s*. Even Latin, Greek, or other foreign words often have alternative plurals in this form, in addition to their original plurals. Words with alternative plurals in the regular -*(e)s* form are marked (*).

I. Regular English Plurals.

A. By *sound:*

1. Add (-iz) after *s* and *s*-like sounds (sh, z, zh, ch, j): *glasses, flashes, roses, rouges, matches, bridges.*

2. Add (-z) after all other voiced sounds: *heads, legs, pills, trees.*

3. Add (-s) after all other voiceless sounds: *lips, bats, rocks.*

B. By *spelling:*

1. Add -*s* in all cases except as noted below.

2. Add -*es* after final -*ss*, -*sh*, -*ch*, -*s*, -*x*, and -*zz: glass-es, ash-es, witch-es, gas-es, box-es, buzz-es.*

3. Add -*es* after -*y* preceded by a consonant or by -*qu*-, and change the -*y* to -*i: fly, fli-es; army, armi-es; soliloquy, soliloqui-es*, etc. (Add -*s* after -*y* preceded by a vowel: *day, day-s; monkey, monkey-s*, etc.)

4. Add -*es* to some words ending in -*o* preceded by a consonant: **buffalo-es*, **domino-es*, *echo-es, hero-es, potato-es*, etc. (Add -*s* to most words ending in -*o* preceded by a consonant, and to all words ending in -*o* preceded by a vowel: *piano-s, radio-s, studio-s*, etc.)

II. Minor English Plurals.

A. Regular plural with change in preceding consonant:

1. Change *f* to *v* in many words, and add -*(e)s* (-z): *half, self, life, leaf*, **scarf*, **wharf*, etc.

2. Change (th) to (*th*) in many words, and add -*s* (-z): *path, mouth, sheath, wreath*, **truth*, **youth*, etc.

3. Change (s) to (z) and add -*s* (-iz) for *house.*

B. Regular plural replaced:

1. By -*en* (-'n): *ox-en.*

2. By -*ren* (-rən, -rin), with vowel change: *child-ren* (chil'drən, chil'drin), etc.

3. By vowel change: *man, men; foot, feet; mouse, mice*, etc.

C. Plural the same as the singular: *alms, barracks, Chinese, deer* (occas. *deers*), *forceps, gallows, gross, Iroquois, Japanese, means, moose, salmon, sheep, Swiss*, etc.

D. Plural either different from or the same as the singular:

1. Plural usually different, but sometimes the same, especially in the usage of hunters and fishermen:

albacore	**guanaco**	**porgy**
albatross	**gull**	**porpoise**
anchovy	**gurnard**	**pronghorn**
antelope	**gurnet**	**ptarmigan**
argali	**hare**	**puma**
badger	**hart**	**quail**
bear	**hartebeest**	**rabbit**
beaver	**heron**	**raccoon**
bighorn	**herring**	**rail**
bittern	**hind**	**rhinoceros**
blackcock	**hippopotamus**	**robalo**
blenny	**hog**	**roebuck**
boar	**horse**	**sable**
bobcat	**ibex**	**sambar**
bobwhite	**ibis**	**sambur**
bonito	**jack**	**sandpiper**
brant	**jackal**	**sardine**
buck	**jacksnipe**	**scaup**
buffalo	**jaguar**	**scoter**
canvasback	**kangaroo**	**seal**
carabao	**killdee**	**sheldrake**
caribou	**killdeer**	**shiner**
cat	**kittiwake**	**shrimp**
char	**klipspringer**	**skate**
charr	**kudu**	**skipjack**
chub	**lemming**	**skunk**
clam	**leopard**	**smelt**
cock	**lion**	**snapper**
codling	**llama**	**snipe**
coot	**lobster**	**squid**
cougar	**lynx**	**squirrel**
coyote	**mallard**	**stag**
coypu	**marten**	**stilt**
crake	**meadow lark**	**stint**
crane	**merganser**	**stoat**
crappie	**mink**	**stork**
croppie	**minnow**	**sturgeon**
curlew	**mouflon, mouffion**	**surmullet**
dhole		**swan**
doe	**mullet**	**tapir**
dog	**murre**	**tarpon**
dotterel	**muskrat**	**teal**
dowitcher	**musquash**	**tench**
duck	**nilgai, nilghai**	**tiger**
duiker	**nilgau, nilghau**	**tortoise**
dunlin	**nylghai, nylghau**	**tunny**
eel	**ocelot**	**turkey**
egret	**okapi**	**turtle**
eider	**opossum**	**vicuña**
elephant	**oryx**	**wallaby**
ermine	**ostrich**	**walrus**
fisher	**otter**	**wapiti**
flounder	**ox**	**waterfowl**
fowl	**panther**	**weasel**
fox	**parr**	**whale**
gadwall	**partridge**	**whippoorwill**
gannet	**peacock**	**whiting**
gazelle	**peafowl**	**widgeon**
giraffe	**peccary**	**wigeon**
gnu	**pheasant**	**wildcat**
goat	**pig**	**wildebeest**
goby	**pigeon**	**willet**
goldeneye	**pintail**	**wolverine**
goose	**plover**	**woodcock**
goral	**pochard**	**yak**
grebe	**polecat**	**yellowtail**
grouper	**porcupine**	**zebra**
		zebu

2. Plural usually the same, but different if referring to different kinds, species, varieties, etc.: as, the *fishes* of the South Pacific:

barracuda	**dace**	**pollock**
barramunda	**duikerbok**	**pout**
barramundi	**duikerbuck**	**quagga**
bass	**eelpout**	**reedbuck**
beluga	**eland**	**roach**
blaubok	**elk**	**roe**
bleak	**fish** (and its compounds, as, *bluefish*)	**salmon**
blesbok		**scad**
blesbuck		**scup**
bontebok	**gar**	**shad**
boschbok	**gemsbok**	**sheepshead**
boshbok	**grayling**	**springbok**
bream	**grilse**	**springbuck**
brill	**haddock**	**steelhead**
burbot	**hake**	**steenbok**
bushbuck	**halibut**	**steinbock**
capelin	**holibut**	**steinbok**
carp	**ling**	**torsk**
cavalla	**mackerel**	**trout**
cavally	**perch**	**tuna**
cero	**pickerel**	**turbot**
cod	**pike**	**vendace**
codling	**plaice**	**waterbuck**
cusk	**pollack**	

3. Plural usually lacking, but given in -(*e*)*s* form when different kinds are referred to: as, the many *steels* produced.

barley	**iron**	**rye**
brass	**linen**	**silk**
coffee	**millet**	**steel**
copper	**oak**	**tea**
corn	**pepper**	**wheat**
fruit	**pine**	**wool**

4. Plural and collective singular interchangeable: *cannons, cannon,* etc.

III. Forms Singular or Plural Only.
A. Singular only (or when a generalized abstraction): *chess, clearness, fishing, information, knowledge, luck, music, nonsense, truth,* etc.
B. Plural only (even when singular in meaning). This includes certain senses of nouns otherwise singular: *Balkans, blues* (depression), *bowels, glasses, lodgings, overalls, pliers, remains* (corpse), *scissors, tongs, trousers,* etc.
C. Plural in form but construed as singular: *cards* (game), *checkers* (game), *measles, news,* etc.
D. Nouns ending in *-ics* are singular when they denote scientific subjects, as *mathematics, physics,* etc., and plural when they denote activities or qualities, as *acrobatics, acoustics,* etc.

IV. Latin and Greek Plurals.
A. With suffix *-a* and loss of singular ending:
1. Latin nouns in *-um: agendum, agend-a; datum, dat-a; *medium, medi-a,* etc.
2. Greek nouns in *-on: criterion, criteri-a; phenomenon, phenomen-a,* etc.
B. With Latin suffix *-i* and loss of singular ending *-us: alumnus, alumn-i; *focus, foc-i; *radius, radi-i,* etc.
C. With Latin suffix *-ae* and loss of singular ending *-a: alumna, alumn-ae; *formula, formul-ae,* etc.
D. With suffix *-es* (ēz):
1. Latin nouns in *-ex* or *-ix* change the ending to *-ic* and add *-es* (-ə-sēz, -i-sēz): **appendix, append-ices; *index, ind-ices,* etc.
2. Latin or Greek nouns in *-is* change *-is* to *-es: analysis, analys-es; axis, ax-es,* etc.
E. Miscellaneous Latin plurals: **phalanx, phalang-es; *stigma, stigma-ta,* etc.

V. Foreign Plurals.
A. Hebrew: **cherub, cherub-im; *seraph, seraph-im,* etc.
B. Italian: **bandit, bandit-ti; *prima donna, prim-e donn-e; *dilettante, dilettant-i; *virtuoso, virtuos-i,* etc.
C. French: *bijou, bijou-x; *château, château-x; *portmanteau, portmanteau-x,* etc.

VI. Plurals of Numbers, Letters, Signs, Words (when thought of as things), etc. add *-'s*: *8's, B's, &'s, whereas's.*

plu·ral·ism (ploor'əl-iz'm), *n.* 1. the quality or condition of existing in more than one part or form. 2. the holding by one person of more than one office or church benefice at the same time. 3. in *philosophy*, the theory that reality is composed of a multiplicity of ultimate beings, principles, or substances: it opposes the position of monism that reality is ultimately one, but agrees in denying the dualism of mind and body.

plu·ral·ist (ploor'əl-ist), *n.* 1. a person who holds two or more offices or church benefices at once. 2. a person who believes in pluralism.

plu·ral·is·tic (ploor'əl-is'tik), *adj.* of pluralists or pluralism.

plu·ral·i·ty (ploo-ral'ə-ti), *n.* [*pl.* PLURALITIES (-tiz)], [ME. *pluralite;* OFr. *pluralité;* LL. *pluralitas*], 1. the condition of being plural or numerous; hence, 2. a great number; multitude. 3. the holding of two or more church benefices at the same time. 4. any of the benefices so held. 5. a majority. 6. the number of votes in an election that the leading candidate obtains over his nearest rival. Abbreviated **plur.**

plu·ral·ize (ploor'əl-iz'), *v.t.* [PLURALIZED (-īzd'), PLURALIZING], [Fr. *pluraliser*], to make plural; put into plural form. *v.i.* to hold two or more offices or church benefices at the same time.

plu·ral·ly (ploor'əl-i), *adv.* in a plural sense; so as to express a plural.

plu·ri- (ploor'ə), [L. < *plus, pluris,* several], a combining form meaning *several* or *many.*

plus (plus), *prep.* [L., more], 1. added to: as, two *plus* two equals four (2 + 2 = 4): opposed to *minus.* 2. increased by; and in addition: as, the salary *plus* bonuses came to $3,000. *adj.* 1. indicating or involving addition: as, a *plus* sign. 2. positive: as, a *plus* quantity. 3. somewhat higher than: as, a grade of B *plus.* 4. [Colloq.], having something added, gained, etc.: as, I'm *plus* a dollar. 5. [Colloq.], and more: as, she has personality *plus.* 6. in *bookkeeping*, credit: as, the *plus* column of an account. 7. in *botany*, designating or of a differentiation in physiology, found in fungi and some other plants, which is like maleness. 8. in *electricity*, positive: opposed to *negative.* 9. in *golf*, *a)* already counted: as, a handicap of *plus* one. *b)* having a handicap of (a specified number of strokes). *n.* 1. a plus sign. 2. an added or extra quantity or thing. 3. a plus quantity. *adv.* in *electricity*, positively.

plus fours, [orig. a tailoring term indicating added length of material for overlap below the knee], loose knickerbockers worn for active sports.

plush (plush), *n.* [Fr. *pluche* < *peluche;* It. *peluzzo;* LL. **piluceus* < L. *pilus,* hair], a fabric having a soft pile over one eighth of an inch long. *adj.* 1. of or made of plush. 2. [Slang], luxurious, as in furnishings.

plush·y (plush'i), *adj.* [PLUSHIER (-i-ēr), PLUSHIEST (-i-ist)], of or like plush.

plus sign, in *mathematics*, the sign (+), indicating addition or positive quantity: opposed to *minus sign* (−).

Plu·tarch (ploo'tärk), *n.* Greek biographer and moralist; lived 46?–120? A.D.

Plu·to (ploo'tō), *n.* [L.; Gr. *Ploutōn*], 1. in *Greek & Roman mythology*, the god ruling over the lower world: also called *Hades* by the Greeks and *Dis* by the Romans. 2. the outermost planet of the solar system, discovered in 1930, ninth in distance from the sun: diameter, 7,600 mi.; period of revolution, 248.42 yrs.; symbol, ♇.

plu·toc·ra·cy (ploo-tok'rə-si), *n.* [*pl.* PLUTOCRACIES (-siz)], [Gr. *ploutokratia* < *ploutos,* wealth + *kratein,* to rule], 1. government by the wealthy. 2. a government or state in which the wealthy rule. 3. a group of wealthy people who control or influence a government.

plu·to·crat (ploo'tə-krat'), *n.* [< Gr. *ploutos,* wealth; + *-crat*], 1. a member of a wealthy ruling class; hence, 2. a person whose wealth gives him control or great influence. 3. [Colloq.], any wealthy person.

plu·to·crat·ic (ploo'tə-krat'ik), *adj.* of, like, or characterized by plutocracy or plutocrats.

plu·to·crat·i·cal (ploo'tə-krat'i-k'l), *adj.* plutocratic.

Plu·to·ni·an (ploo-tō'ni-ən), *adj.* [L. *Plutonius;* Gr. *Ploutōnios*], of or like Pluto or the infernal regions.

Plu·ton·ic (ploo-ton'ik), *adj.* [< L. *Pluto, Plutonis;* + *-ic*], 1. Plutonian. 2. [sometimes p-], in *geology*, formed far below the earth's crust by the action of intense heat, and then crystallized; igneous: as, *Plutonic* rock.

plu·to·ni·um (ploo-tō'ni-əm), *n.* [after *Pluto* (planet); cf. NEPTUNIUM, URANIUM], a radioactive chemical element formed by the transformation of neptunium: symbol, Pu; at. wt., 239; at. no., 94.

Plu·tus (ploo'təs), *n.* [L.; Gr. *Ploutos* < *ploutos,* wealth], in *Greek mythology*, the blind god of wealth.

plu·vi·al (ploo'vi-əl), *adj.* [L. *pluvialis* < *pluvia,* rain], 1. of or having to do with rain; having much rain. 2. in *geology*, formed by rain.

plu·vi·om·e·ter (ploo'vi-om'ə-tēr), *n.* [< L. *pluvia,* rain; + *-meter*], a gauge for measuring the depth of a rainfall.

plu·vi·o·met·ric (ploo'vi-ə-met'rik), *adj.* having to do with a pluviometer or pluviometry.

plu·vi·o·met·ri·cal (ploo'vi-ə-met'ri-k'l), *adj.* pluviometric.

plu·vi·om·e·try (ploo'vi-om'ə-tri), *n.* [< L. *pluvia,* rain; + *-metry*], the science of measuring rainfall.

‡Plu·viôse (plü'vyōz'; Eng. ploo'vi-ōs'), *n.* [Fr. < L. *pluviosus,* rainy < *pluvia,* rain], the fifth month (January 20–February 18) of the French Revolutionary Calendar, adopted by the First Republic in 1793.

plu·vi·ous (ploo'vi-əs), *adj.* [L. *pluviosus* < *pluvia,* rain], of or characterized by rain; rainy.

ply (plī), *v.t.* [PLIED (plīd), PLYING], [ME. *plien;* OFr. *plier, ploier;* L. *plicare,* to fold], to bend, twist, fold, or mold. *v.i.* [Obs.], 1. to bend or be bent. 2. to be pliable or adaptable; yield or consent (*to* a person or thing). *n.* [*pl.* PLIES (plīz)], [OFr. *pli* < the *v.*], 1. a single thickness, fold, or layer, as of doubled cloth, plywood, etc. 2. one of the twisted strands in rope, yarn, etc. 3. the state of being bent or twisted; hence,

4. bent, bias, or inclination. *adj.* having (a specified number of) layers, thicknesses, or strands: usually in hyphenated compounds, as, *three-ply*.

ply (plī), *v.t.* [PLIED (plīd), PLYING], [contr. < *apply*], 1. to use; do work with; wield (a tool, faculty, etc.). 2. to work at (a trade); keep working on (*with* a tool, process, etc.). 3. to address (someone) urgently and constantly (*with* questions, etc.). 4. to keep supplying (*with* presents, food, etc.). 5. to sail back and forth across: as, boats *ply* the channel. *v.i.* 1. to keep busy; work (*at* something); apply oneself (*to* something). 2. to sail or travel regularly back and forth (*between* places): said of ships, buses, etc. 3. [Poetic], to steer a course. 4. in *navigation*, to sail in a zigzag course into the wind; tack. —*SYN.* see **handle.**

Plym·outh (plim′əth), *n.* 1. a city in Devonshire, England, on the English Channel: pop., 216,000. 2. a town on the coast of Massachusetts: pop., 6,000: settled by the Pilgrims (1620).

Plymouth Brethren, a small Christian sect, founded in 1830 at Plymouth, England: it has no formal creed or organization, and makes the Bible its only guide.

Plymouth Colony, the colony founded by the Pilgrims in 1620 on the shores of Massachusetts Bay.

Plymouth Rock, 1. the rock at Plymouth, Massachusetts, where the Pilgrims who sailed on the *Mayflower* are said to have landed in 1620. 2. one of a breed of American chickens: the most common variety has gray and bluish-black striped feathers.

ply·wood (plī′wood′), *n.* [*ply* (*n.*) + *wood*], a construction material made of thin layers of wood glued and pressed together, usually with their grains at right angles to one another.

Plzeň (pul′zen-y′), *n.* Pilsen: the Czech name.

Pm, in *chemistry*, promethium.

pm., premium.

P.M., 1. Past Master. 2. Paymaster. 3. Police Magistrate. 4. Postmaster. 5. Provost Marshal.

P.M., p.m., *post meridiem*, [L.], after noon.

p.m., *post-mortem*, [L.], after death.

P.M.G., 1. Paymaster General. 2. Postmaster General.

P/N, p.n., promissory note.

pneum., 1. pneumatic. 2. pneumatics.

pneu·ma (nōō′mə, nū′mə), *n.* [Gr. *pneuma* < *pnein*, to breathe], 1. the breath of life; soul or spirit. 2. in *Christian theology*, the Holy Spirit.

pneu·mat·ic (nōō-mat′ik, nū-mat′ik), *adj.* [L. *pneumaticus;* Gr. *pneumatikos* < *pneuma*, breath < *pnein*, to breathe], 1. of or containing wind, air, or gases. 2. worked by or filled with compressed air. 3. equipped with pneumatic tires. 4. in *theology*, having to do with the spirit or soul; spiritual. 5. in *zoology*, having hollows filled with air, as the bones of certain birds. *n.* 1. a pneumatic tire. 2. a vehicle with pneumatic tires.

pneu·mat·i·cal·ly (nōō-mat′i-k′l-i, nū-mat′ik-li), *adv.* in a pneumatic manner; especially, by air pressure.

pneu·mat·ics (nōō-mat′iks, nū-mat′iks), *n.pl.* [construed as sing.], [< *pneumatic*], the branch of physics that deals with the properties, such as pressure, density, etc., of air and other gases: abbreviated **pneum.**

pneumatic tire, a rubber tire inflated with compressed air.

pneu·ma·to- (nōō′mə-tō, nū′mə-tə), [< Gr. *pneuma*, *pneumatos*, air, spirit, breath < *pnein*, to breathe], a combining form meaning: 1. *air, vapor*, as in *pneumatolysis, pneumatophore*. 2. *breathing*, as in *pneumatometer*. 3. *spirits*, as in *pneumatology*.

pneu·ma·tol·o·gy (nōō′mə-tol′ə-ji, nū′mə-tol′ə-ji), *n.* [*pneumato-* + *-logy*], 1. in *theology*, the study or doctrine of spirits or spiritual phenomena; hence, 2. in *Christian theology*, the doctrine of the Holy Ghost. 3. [Obs.], psychology. 4. pneumatics.

pneu·ma·tol·y·sis (nōō′mə-tol′ə-sis, nū′mə-tol′ə-sis), *n.* [Mod. L.; see PNEUMATO- & -LYSIS], the natural process that forms pneumatolytic ores and minerals.

pneu·ma·to·lyt·ic (nōō′mə-tō-lit′ik, nū′mə-tō-lit′ik), *adj.* [*pneumato-* + *-lytic*], in *geology*, formed by steam pressure: said of ores and minerals found near igneous or volcanic formations: also spelled **pneumatolitic.**

pneu·ma·tom·e·ter (nōō′mə-tom′ə-tẽr, nū′mə-tom′ə-tẽr), *n.* [*pneumato-* + *-meter*], in *physiology*, an instrument for measuring the amount of air breathed in or out at a single time, thus determining the force of the lungs in respiration.

pneu·ma·to·phore (nōō′mə-tō-fôr′, nū-mat′ə-fôr′), *n.* [*pneumato-* + *-phore*], 1. in *botany*, a porous structure, used as a breathing organ, on the roots of certain tropical plants. 2. in *zoology*, a cavity that contains air.

pneu·ma·to·ther·a·py (nōō′mə-tō-ther′ə-pi, nū′mə-tō-ther′ə-pi), *n.* [*pneumato-* + *therapy*], the treatment of disease by the use of rarefied or condensed air.

pneu·mec·to·my (nōō-mek′tə-mi, nū-mek′tə-mi), *n.* [< *pneumo-* + *-ectomy*], the surgical removal of part of a lung.

pneu·mo- (nōō′mō, nū′mə), pneumono-.

pneu·mo·ba·cil·lus (nōō′mō-bə-sil′əs, nū′mō-bə-sil′əs), *n.* [*pl.* PNEUMOBACILLI (-ī)], [Mod. L.; *pneumo-* + *bacillus*], a bacillus found in some respiratory infections, but not regarded as the causative agent of pneumonia.

pneu·mo·coc·cal (nōō′mə-kok′əl, nū′mə-kok′əl), *adj.* of or caused by pneumococci.

pneu·mo·coc·cic (nōō′mə-kok′sik, nū′mə-kok′sik), *adj.* pneumococcal.

pneu·mo·coc·cus (nōō′mə-kok′əs, nū′mə-kok′əs), *n.* [*pl.* PNEUMOCOCCI (-sī)], [Mod. L.; *pneumo-* + *coccus*], a bacterium, occurring in a large number of strains, that is the causative agent of lobar pneumonia and certain other diseases.

pneu·mo·co·ni·o·sis (nōō′mə-kon′i-ō′sis, nū mə-kon′i-ō′sis), *n.* [< *pneumo-* + Gr. *konia*, dust; + *-osis*], any of various diseased conditions of the lungs characterized by fibrous hardening as a result of chronic inhalation of irritating dust particles, as by miners, etc.

pneu·mo·dy·nam·ics (nōō′mō-dī-nam′iks, nū′mō-dī-nam′iks), *n.* [*pneumo-* + *dynamics*], pneumatics.

pneu·mo·gas·tric (nōō′mə-gas′trik, nū′mə-gas′trik), *adj.* [*pneumo-* + *gastric*], of the lungs and stomach; especially, designating or of the vagus nerve. *n.* the vagus nerve.

pneu·mo·nec·to·my (nōō′mə-nek′tə-mi, nū′mə-nek′tə-mi), *n.* [see PNEUMONO- & -ECTOMY], the surgical removal of an entire lung.

pneu·mo·ni·a (nōō-mō′nyə, nū-mō′ni-ə), *n.* [Mod. L.; Gr. *pneumonia* < *pneumōn*, a lung < *pnein*, to breathe], a disease of the lungs in which the tissue becomes inflamed, hardened, and watery: there are several types of pneumonia, as lobar and bronchial.

pneu·mon·ic (nōō-mon′ik, nū-mon′ik), *adj.* [Mod. L. *pneumonicus;* Gr. *pneumonikos*], 1. [Rare], of or affecting the lungs; pulmonary. 2. of, like, or having pneumonia.

pneu·mo·no- (nōō′mə-nō, nū′mə-nə), [< Gr. *pneumōn*, a lung], a combining form meaning *lung* or *lungs*, as in *pneumonophorous:* also **pneumo-, pneumon-.**

pneu·mo·no·pho·rous (nōō′mə-nō-fôr′əs, nū′mə-nō-fō′rəs), *adj.* [*pneumono-* + *-phorous*], having lungs.

pneu·mo·tho·rax (nōō′mō-thôr′aks, nū′mō-thō′raks), *n.* [*pneumo-* + *thorax*], the presence of air or gas in the pleural cavity, sometimes artificially induced for collapsing and immobilizing the lung in the treatment of tuberculosis.

Pnom-Penh (pnoom′pen′y′; Eng. nom′pen′), *n.* the capital of Cambodia, on the Mekong River: pop., 500,000.

pnxt., *pinxit*, [L.], he (or she) painted it.

Po (pō), *n.* a river in northern Italy, flowing into the Adriatic: length, 415 mi.: ancient name, *Padus*.

Po, in *chemistry*, polonium.

P.O., p.o., 1. petty officer. 2. postal order. 3. post office.

po·a·ceous (pō-ā′shəs), *adj.* [< Gr. *poa*, grass; + *-aceous*], in *botany*, of the grass family.

poach (pōch), *v.t.* [OFr. *pochier*, to pocket < *poche*, a pouch, pocket: used because the yolk is "pocketed" in the white], to place the unbroken contents of (an egg) in boiling water, or in a small receptacle put over boiling water, and cook until the white of the egg coagulates.

poach (pōch), *v.t.* [Fr. *pocher;* OFr. *pochier*, to tread upon, poach into < MHG. *bochen, puchen*, to strike upon, plunder < same Gmc. base as Eng. *poke* (to thrust)], 1. to soften, tear up, or make holes in (ground) by stamping; trample. 2. to mix with water until smooth. 3. to trespass on (private property), especially for hunting or fishing; hence, 4. to hunt or catch (game or fish) illegally. 5. to take (anything) by unfair or illegal methods; steal. *v.i.* 1. to sink into soft or wet earth when walking. 2. to become soggy or full of holes when trampled; turn into mud. 3. to hunt or fish on another's property; trespass.

poach·y (pōch′i), *adj.* [POACHIER (-i-ẽr), POACHIEST (-i-ist)], [*poach* (to trample) + *-y*], soggy or swampy; sodden: said of land.

P.O.B., POB, Post Office Box.

Po·ca·hon·tas (pō′kə-hon′təs), *n.* daughter of *Powhatan;* lived 1595?–1617; American Indian princess; reputed to have saved Captain John Smith from execution.

po·chard (pō′chẽrd, pō′kẽrd), *n.* [*pl.* POCHARDS (-chẽrdz, -kẽrdz), POCHARD; see PLURAL, II, D, 1], [prob. < Fr. *pocher*, to poach, thrust], a European diving duck with a brownish-red head: it is related to the American widgeon and redhead.

pock (pok), *n.* [ME. *pocke;* AS. *pocc;* akin to D. *pok;* IE. base as in *pod* (seedcase)], 1. a pimple or pustule caused by smallpox and some other diseases. 2. a scar or pit in the skin left by such a pustule. See **pox.**

pock·et (pok′it), *n.* [ME. *poket;* Anglo-Fr. *pokete*, for ONorm.Fr. *poquette*, dim. of *poque, poche;* see POKE (a bag)], 1. [British], a sack, especially when used to measure something. 2. a little bag or pouch, now usually when sewed into clothing, for carrying money and small articles. 3. any cavity or enclosure which holds or can hold something. 4. the condition of being surrounded and hemmed in, as in a race. 5. an atmospheric current or condition that causes an airplane to drop suddenly: also called *air pocket*. 6. an open pouch at the side or corner of a billiard or pool table. 7. in *mining*, *a)* a cavity filled with ore. *b)* a small deposit of ore. 8. in *zoology*, a sac or cavity in an animal's body. ***adj.*** 1. that is or can be carried in a pocket; hence, 2. small. ***v.t.*** 1. to put into a pocket; hence, 2. to envelop; enclose. 3. to take dishonestly; appropriate, as money, profits, etc. 4. to submit to or put up with (an insult, gibe, etc.) without answering or showing anger. 5. to hide or suppress: as, *pocket* one's pride. 6. in *politics*, to prevent passage of (a bill) by the pocket veto.

in one's pocket, completely under one's influence.

line one's pockets, to get or make much money.

pocket battleship, a type of small battleship of 10,000 tons displacement, carrying heavier guns than a cruiser.

pock·et·book (pok'it-book'), ***n.*** 1. a case or folder, usually of leather, for carrying money and papers in one's pocket; billfold. 2. a woman's purse or handbag.

pocket book, a book small enough to be carried in one's pocket.

pocket borough, in Great Britain, a borough whose parliamentary representation, before 1832, was controlled by one family or person.

pock·et·ful (pok'it-fool'), ***n.*** [*pl.* POCKETFULS (-foolz')], as much as a pocket will hold.

pock·et·knife (pok'it-nīf'), ***n.*** [*pl.* POCKETKNIVES (-nīvz')], a small knife with a blade or blades folding into the handle.

pocket money, cash for small expenses; small change.

pocket veto, the method whereby the President of the United States can veto a bill passed by Congress and presented to him within ten days of its adjournment by failing to sign and return the bill by the time of adjournment.

pock·mark (pok'märk'), ***n.*** a scar or pit in the skin left by a pustule, as in smallpox.

pock-marked (pok'märkt'), ***adj.*** having, or marked with, pockmarks.

pock·y (pok'i), ***adj.*** 1. covered with pocks or pockmarks. 2. of or like a pock. 3. of or having the pox.

‡**po·co** (pô'kô; Eng. pō'kō), ***adv.*** [It.], in *music*, somewhat: a direction to the performer. ***n.*** a little.

‡**po·co a po·co** (pô'kô ä pô'kô; Eng. pō'kō ä pō'kō), [It.], little by little; by degrees; gradually.

po·co·cu·ran·te (pō'kō-koo-ran'ti; It. pô'kô-kōō-rän'te), ***adj.*** [It. *poco curante* < *poco* (L. *paucus*), little + *curante*, ppr. of *curare* (L. *curare*), to care], caring little; indifferent; apathetic. ***n.*** a pococurante person; trifler.

po·co·cu·ran·te·ism (pō'kō-koo-ran'ti-iz'm), ***n.*** the attitude or behavior of a pococurante.

po·co·cu·ran·tism (pō'kō-koo-ran'tiz'm), ***n.*** pococuranteism.

pod (pod), ***n.*** [Early Mod. Eng., replacing earlier *cod;* prob. < a LG. source; IE. base **bu-*, **bhu-*, to blow out or up, swell, inflate; hence akin to *bud, pock, poke,* etc.], 1. the seedcase of peas, beans, etc.; hence, 2. a podlike container, as a cocoon, etc. ***v.i.*** [PODDED (-id), PODDING], 1. to bear pods. 2. to swell out into a pod. ***v.t.*** to take (peas, etc.) out of pods; shell.

pod (pod), ***n.*** [prob. a special application of prec. *pod*], a flock or school, as of birds, whales, etc. ***v.t.*** [PODDED (-id), PODDING], to herd (animals) together.

pod (pod), ***n.*** [prob. var. of *pad*, in same sense], in *mechanics*, 1. the sharp groove in certain boring tools, as the pod auger. 2. the socket for the bit in a brace.

-pod (pod), [< Gr. *pous, podos*, a foot], a combining form used to form nouns and adjectives, meaning: 1. *foot*, as in *pleopod*. 2. (*one*) *having* (a specified number or kind of) *feet*, as in *tripod*. Also **-pode.**

P.O.D., 1. pay on delivery. 2. Post Office Department.

-pod·a (pə-də), in *zoology*, plural of **-pod.**

po·dag·ra (pə-dag'rə, pod'ə-grə), ***n.*** [L.; Gr. < *pous, podos*, a foot + *agra*, a seizure], gout, especially in a foot.

po·dag·ric (pə-dag'rik), ***adj.*** of or having podagra.

-pode (pōd), -pod.

po·des·ta (pō-des'tə; It. pô'de-stä'), ***n.*** [It. *podestà;* L. *potestas*, power < *potis*, able], 1. a governor or chief magistrate of a medieval Italian town. 2. a judge or minor official in an Italian town. 3. under Fascism, a chief executive, or mayor, of a commune.

podg·i·ness (poj'i-nis), ***n.*** the condition or quality of being podgy.

podg·y (poj'i), ***adj.*** [PODGIER (-i-ẽr), PODGIEST (-i-ist)], [var. of *pudgy*], short and thick; squat; pudgy.

po·di·a·trist (pō-dī'ə-trist), ***n.*** a specialist in podiatry.

po·di·a·try (pō-dī'ə-tri), ***n.*** [< Gr. *pous, podos*, foot; + *-iatry*], the branch of medicine having to do with the care of the feet and, especially, the treatment of foot disorders.

po·di·um (pō'di-əm), ***n.*** [*pl.* PODIA (-ə)], [L. < Gr. *podion*, dim. of *pous, podos*, a foot], 1. a low wall serving as a pedestal or foundation. 2. a wall separating the seats from the arena in an amphitheater. 3. a continuous bench projecting from the walls of a room. 4. a raised platform for the conductor of an orchestra; dais. 5. in *zoology*, a structure or part serving as a foot.

-po·di·um (pō'di-əm), [Mod. L. < Gr. *pous, podos*, a foot], a combining form meaning *footstalk, supporting part*, as in *monopodium*.

pod·o·phyl·lin (pod'ə-fil'in), ***n.*** [< Mod. L. *Podophyllum*, name of the genus (< Gr. *pous, podos*, a foot + *phyllon*, a leaf); + *-in*], a yellow cathartic resin with a bitter taste, taken from the rootstock of the mandrake.

-pod·ous (pə-dəs), [Gr. *-podos* < *pous, podos*, a foot], a combining form signifying *having* (a specified number or kind of) *feet:* used to form adjectives corresponding to nouns that end in *-pod* or *-poda*.

Po·dunk (pō'duŋk'), ***n.*** [after *Podunk*, Massachusetts; of Am. Ind. origin], [Colloq.], an imaginary typical small town in the United States: humorous usage.

pod·zol (pod'zol), ***n.*** [Russ., lit., ashlike], a type of relatively infertile soil found typically in forests and consisting of a thin, ash-colored layer overlaying a brown, acidic humus.

Poe, Edgar Allan (pō), 1809–1849; American poet, critic, and fiction writer.

po·em (pō'im), ***n.*** [Fr. *poème;* L. *poema;* Gr. *poiēma*, anything made, poem < *poiein*, to make], 1. an arrangement of words in verse; especially, a rhythmical composition, sometimes rhymed, expressing facts, ideas, or emotions in a style more concentrated, imaginative, and powerful than that of ordinary speech: some poems are in meter, some in free verse. 2. a composition, whether in verse or prose, having beauty of thought or language. 3. anything beautiful in a way suggesting a poem.

poe·nol·o·gy (pē-nol'ə-ji), ***n.*** penology.

po·e·sy (pō'i-si, pō'i-zi), ***n.*** [*pl.* POESIES (-siz, -ziz)], [ME. & OFr. *poesie;* L. *poesis;* Gr. *poiēsis* < *poiein*, to make], 1. [Archaic], poetry; poems generally, or the art of writing poems. 2. [Obs.], a poem. 3. [Obs.], a motto. 4. [Obs.], a nosegay. See **posy.**

po·et (pō'it), ***n.*** [ME. & OFr. *poete;* L. *poeta;* Gr. *poiētēs*, one who makes, poet < *poiein*, to make], 1. a person who writes poems or verses. 2. a person who writes or expresses himself with imaginative power and beauty of thought, language, etc.

SYN.—**poet,** the general term for a writer of poems or verses, is sometimes used specifically to designate a writer of verse, or, in extended use, of elevated prose, who has great powers of imagination, intuition, and expression; **rhymer, rhymester,** and **versifier** do not in themselves carry the special favorable connotations of **poet** and, when used in contrast to it, specifically suggest a lack of true poetic powers; **poetaster** is always a term of contempt for a writer of inferior or trashy verse.

poet., 1. poetic. 2. poetry.

po·et·as·ter (pō'it-as'tẽr), ***n.*** [Mod. L.; see POET & -ASTER], a writer of mediocre verse; rhymester; would-be poet.—***SYN.*** see **poet.**

po·et·ess (pō'it-is), ***n.*** a woman poet.

po·et·ic (pō-et'ik), ***adj.*** [Fr. *poétique;* L. *poeticus;* Gr. *poiētikos*], 1. of, characteristic of, like, or fit for a poet or poetry. 2. skilled in or fond of poetry. 3. written in verse. 4. having the beauty, imagination, etc. of good poetry. 5. imaginative. ***n.*** poetics.

po·et·i·cal (pō-et'i-k'l), ***adj.*** poetic: now used chiefly in reference to form, whereas *poetic* refers to the basic qualities of poetry.

poetic justice, justice, as in some plays, stories, etc., in which good is properly rewarded and evil punished; justice as one might wish it to be.

poetic license, a poet's or artist's right to deviate, for artistic effect, from literal fact and strict rules of form, grammar, etc.

po·et·ics (pō-et'iks), ***n.pl.*** [construed as sing.], 1. the part of literary criticism that has to do with poetry; theory of poetry. 2. a treatise on poetry. 3. [P-], a famous treatise on poetic drama by Aristotle.

po·et·ize (pō'it-īz'), ***v.i.*** [POETIZED (-īzd'), POETIZING], [Fr. *poétiser*], to write poetry. ***v.t.*** 1. to make poetic. 2. to express, or deal with, in poetry.

poet laureate, [*pl.* POETS LAUREATE, POET LAUREATES], 1. the court poet of England, appointed by the monarch to write poems celebrating official occasions, national events, etc. 2. any official poet of a State, nation, etc.

po·et·ry (pō'it-ri), ***n.*** [ME. & OFr. *poetrie;* ML. *poetria* < L. *poeta*, a poet], 1. the writing of poems; art of writing poems. 2. poems; poetical works. 3. something like poetry in quality or emotional effect: as, that acting is pure *poetry*. 4. poetic quality or spirit: as, the *poetry* of motion. Abbreviated **poet.** Cf. **verse.**

po·go·ni·a (pə-gō'ni-ə, pə-gōn'yə), ***n.*** [Mod. L. < Gr. *pōgōn*, a beard], 1. a small orchid with a single white or pinkish flower having a lip tufted with yellow-brown hairs. 2. the flower.

pog·o·nip (pog'ə-nip), ***n.*** [< Shoshonean], a heavy winter fog containing ice particles, occurring in the Sierra Nevada Mountains of the western United States.

po·go stick (pō'gō), [arbitrary coinage], a stiltlike toy consisting of a strong stick with a metal spring at one end to which are fastened two pedals: by holding the stick in the hands and pushing down on the pedals with the feet, one can propel himself in a series of short jumps.

po·grom (pō′grəm, pō-grom′), ***n.*** [Russ., devastation], 1. an organized massacre of or attack on the Jews, as in Czarist Russia. 2. any similar persecution of a minority group. —***SYN.*** see **slaughter.**

po·gy (pō′gi, pog′i), ***n.*** [*pl.* POGIES (-giz, -iz)], [contr. < Am. Ind. (Algonquian) native name *pauhaugen*], the menhaden, a kind of fish.

Po·hai (pō′hī′; Chin. bō′hī′), ***n.*** a gulf of the Yellow Sea, off northeastern China: former name, *Gulf of Chihli.*

po·i (poi, pō′i), ***n.*** [Haw.], a Hawaiian food made of taro root pounded to a paste and then fermented.

-poi·et·ic (poi-et′ik), [< Gr. *poiētikos* < *poiēsis*, a creating, making], a combining form meaning *making, producing, forming,* as in *onomatopoietic.*

poign·an·cy (poin′ən-si, poin′yən-si), ***n.*** the condition or quality of being poignant. —***SYN.*** see **pathos.**

poign·ant (poin′ənt, poin′yənt), ***adj.*** [ME. *poynant, poinaunt;* OFr. *poignant*, ppr. of *poindre* < L. *pungere*, to prick], 1. sharp or biting to the smell or taste; tart; piquant. 2. sharply painful to the feelings; piercing. 3. keen; pointed: as, *poignant* wit. —***SYN.*** see **moving.**

poi·kil·o·therm·al (poi′kə-lō-thũr′m′l), ***adj.*** [< Gr. *poikilos*, variegated (akin to L. *pingere*, to paint; cf. PAINT); + *thermal*], having a body temperature that varies with the environmental temperature, as fish.

poi·lu (pwä′loo; Fr. pwȧ′lü′), ***n.*** [Fr., hairy, virile, bold < *poil*, hair], [Slang], in World War I, a soldier in the French army.

Poin·ca·ré, Jules Hen·ri (zhül′ än′rē′ pwan′kȧ′rā′), 1854–1912; French mathematician.

Poincaré, Ray·mond (rā′mōn′), 1860–1934; cousin of *Jules Henri;* prime minister of France (1912–1913; 1922–1924; 1926–1929); president (1913–1920).

poin·ci·a·na (poin′si-ā′nə, poin′si-an′ə), ***n.*** [Mod. L., after M. de *Poinci*, early governor of the French West Indies], any of a number of related small tropical trees with showy red, orange, or yellow flowers.

poind (poind; Scot. pünd), ***v.t.*** [MScot. *poynd*, var. of ME. *pinden* < AS. *pyndan*, to enclose, impound], [Scot.], 1. *a)* to seize and sell (the property of a debtor) under a warrant. *b)* to distrain the goods of (a debtor). 2. to impound. ***n.*** the act or an instance of poinding; distraint.

poin·set·ti·a (poin-set′i-ə, poin-set′ə), ***n.*** [Mod. L.; after Joel R. *Poinsett* (d. 1851), Am. ambassador to Mexico], a Mexican and South American shrub with yellow flowers surrounded by tapering red leaves resembling petals.

point (point), ***n.*** [ME.; OFr. *point*, a dot, prick < L. *punctum*, a dot, neut. of *punctus*, pp. of *pungere*, to prick; also < OFr. *pointe*, sharp end; ML. *puncta* < L. *punctus*], 1. a prick, speck, or dot. 2. a dot in print or writing, as a period, decimal point, vowel point, etc. 3. something thought of as having definite position in space, but no size or shape; location: as, a straight line is the shortest distance between two *points.* 4. the position of a certain player in cricket and other games; hence, 5. the player. 6. [British], a policeman's fixed station for duty, as distinguished from a beat. 7. a particular time; exact moment: as, at this *point* she left the room, the *point* of death. 8. a stage or condition reached: as, boiling *point.* 9. a part of something; item; detail: as, he explained the problem *point* by *point.* 10. *a)* a distinguishing feature; characteristic. *b)* a physical characteristic or quality of an animal, used as a standard in judging breeding. 11. a unit, as of measurement, value, game scores, etc. 12. a sharp or projecting end of something; hence, 13. something with a sharp end. 14. needle-point lace. 15. a projecting or tapering piece of land; promontory; cape; peak. 16. a small party before an advance guard or behind a rear guard in a military maneuver. 17. *pl.* a horse's extremities. 18. a branch of a deer's antler: as, a ten-*point* buck. 19. the exact or essential fact or idea under consideration (preceded by *the*). 20. a purpose; object; use: as, what's the *point* of acting like a child? 21. the important or main idea, as of a joke, speech, dispute, etc.; hence, 22. an impressive or telling argument, fact, or idea: as, you have a *point* there! 23. the posture of a hunting dog to show the presence and position of game. 24. [Archaic], a cord with metal tags, formerly used to lace up articles of clothing. 25. in *commerce*, a standard unit of value, as $1 or 1¢, used in quoting current prices of stocks, commodities, etc. 26. in *craps*, the number that the thrower must make in order to win. 27. in *education*, a unit for grading school work: as, a grade of A is worth four *points.* 28. in *electricity*, *a)* either of the two contacts, tipped with tungsten or platinum, that make or break the circuit in a distributor. *b)* [British], an outlet or socket. 29. in *hunting*, *a)* a spot or landmark serving as the goal for a straight run. *b)* a cross-country run. 30. in *music*, a short tune, sometimes sounded on an instrument as a military signal: as, *point* of war. 31. in *navigation*, *a)* one of the thirty-two marks showing direction on the circumference of a compass card. *b)* the corresponding position on the horizon. *c)* the angle between two successive compass points. 32. in *printing*, a unit measure for type bodies, equal to about 1/72 of an inch. 33. *usually in pl.* [British], in *railroading*, a tapering rail in a switch. ***v.t.*** 1. to put punctuation marks or pauses in: as, *point* a sentence or a speech. 2. to mark off (parts of a sentence, sum, etc.) with points, as especially a decimal fraction from a whole number (with *off*). 3. to sharpen to a point, as a pencil. 4. to give (a story, remark, anecdote, action, etc.) force, purpose, or point (sometimes with *up*). 5. to show or call attention to (usually with *out*): as, *point* the way, he likes to *point* out the shortcomings of others. 6. to aim or direct (a gun, finger, etc.). 7. to show the presence and location of (game) by standing still and facing toward it: said of hunting dogs. 8. in *linguistics*, to put vowel points in (Hebrew writing). 9. in *masonry*, to fill the joints of (brickwork) with mortar. ***v.i.*** 1. to direct one's finger (*at* or *to* something). 2. to call attention (*to* something); hint (*at* something). 3. to aim or be directed (*to* or *toward* something); extend in a specified direction; face. 4. to stand rigid and look in the direction of game: said of pointers and setters. 5. [British], to come to a head, as an abscess. 6. in *navigation*, to sail close to the wind. Abbreviated **pt.**

at the point of, very close to.

beside the point, not pertinent; irrelevant.

in point, appropriate; pertinent; apt.

in point of, in the matter of; as concerns.

make a point of, to make (something) one's strict rule, habit, or purpose; insist on.

on the point of, almost in the act of; on the verge of.

point up, to give more point to; make more emphatic, as by a lengthier treatment, reiteration, etc.

stretch (or **strain**) **a point,** to make an exception or concession.

to the point, pertinent; apt.

point-blank (point′blaŋk′), ***adj.*** [*point* + *blank* (white center of the target) < Fr. *blanc*], 1. in *gunnery*, *a)* aimed horizontally, straight at a mark, without allowing for rise and fall in the projectile's flight. *b)* of or suitable for this type of fire: as, *point-blank* range or distance. 2. straightforward; plain; blunt: as, a *point-blank* answer. ***adv.*** 1. straight: as, he fired the gun *point-blank* at the burglar. 2. without hesitation or quibbling; directly; bluntly: as, she refused *point-blank.*

‡point d'ap·pui (pwan′ dȧ′pwē′), [Fr.], point of support, as for a battle line; basis; fulcrum.

point-de·vice, point-de·vise (point′di-vīs′), ***adj.*** [ME. *at point devis; at*, at + *point*, a point + *devis*, exact (see DEVICE); prob. for OFr. *à point devis*, to the point arranged, to perfection], [Archaic], completely correct; precise. ***adv.*** [Archaic], to perfection; completely.

point·ed (poin′tid), ***adj.*** 1. having a sharp end; tapering. 2. sharp; incisive; to the point, as an epigram. 3. clearly aimed at, or referring to, someone, as a remark. 4. very evident; emphasized; conspicuous.

pointed fox, red fox fur dyed black, with white hairs inserted, to simulate silver fox fur.

point·er (poin′tẽr), ***n.*** 1. a person or thing that points. 2. a long, tapered rod used by teachers and lecturers for calling attention to things on a map, blackboard, etc. 3. an indicator on a clock, meter, scales, etc. 4. a large, lean hunting dog with a smooth coat, usually white with brown spots: it smells out game and then points until the hunter is ready to fire. 5. [Colloq.], a hint; clue; tip. 6. [P-], *pl.* in *astronomy*, the two stars in the Big Dipper that are almost in a direct line with the North Star.

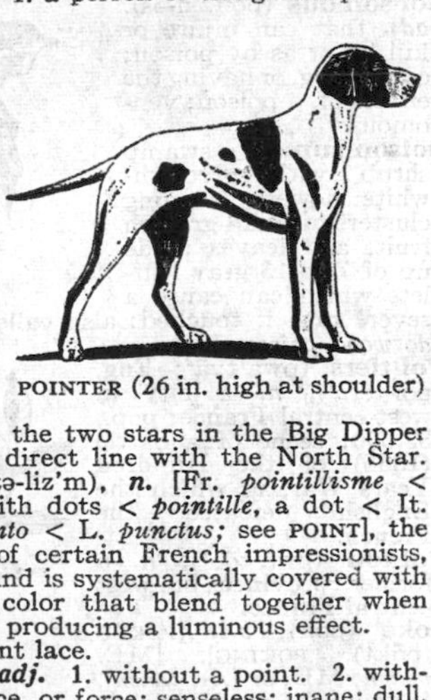

POINTER (26 in. high at shoulder)

poin·til·lism (pwan′tə-liz′m), ***n.*** [Fr. *pointillisme* < *pointiller*, to mark with dots < *pointille*, a dot < It. *puntiglio*, dim. of *punto* < L. *punctus;* see POINT], the method of painting of certain French impressionists, in which a white ground is systematically covered with tiny points of pure color that blend together when seen from a distance, producing a luminous effect.

point lace, needle-point lace.

point·less (point′lis), ***adj.*** 1. without a point. 2. without meaning, relevance, or force; senseless; inane; dull.

point of honor, a matter affecting a person's honor.

point of order, a question as to whether the rules of parliamentary procedure are being observed.

point of view, 1. the place from which, or way in which, something is viewed or considered; standpoint. 2. a mental attitude or opinion.

point rationing, a system of rationing food, clothing, etc., in which each item or a specified amount of a commodity is assigned a number of points, and each purchaser is permitted a fixed number of points for a given period of time.

points of the compass, 1. the thirty-two directional lines on the face of a compass. 2. the imagined points around the horizon corresponding to these.

point system, 1. in *education,* a system of averaging a student's grades by giving them equivalent numerical value in points: the average attained is called the *grade-point average.* 2. in *typography,* a system of graduating the sizes of type on a uniform scale of which the unit, called a *point,* is about 1/72 inch: each type body is a multiple of the point unit and is designated by its number of points, as in *eight-point* type. 3. any system of writing or printing for the blind in which raised points or dots in certain combinations are used to represent the alphabet: Braille is a variety of this.

poise (poiz), *n.* [ME. *pois,* weight; OFr. *pois, peis;* LL. *pesum* < L. *pensum,* something weighed < *pendere,* to weigh], 1. balance; stability. 2. ease and dignity of manner. 3. carriage; bearing, as of the body or head. 4. a suspension of activity in a condition of balance. 5. suspense; irresolution; indecision. *v.t.* [POISED (poizd), POISING], [ME. *poisen;* OFr. *poiser* < *peise, poise,* inflected form of *peser,* to weigh; LL. *pesare;* L. *pensare,* to weigh out < *pensus,* pp. of *pendere,* to weigh], 1. [Rare], to weigh mentally; ponder. 2. [Rare], to make (one thing) balance (*with* or *against* another); equalize (two things). 3. to balance; keep steady. 4. to suspend (usually passive or reflexive): as, the earth is *poised* in space. *v.i.* 1. to be suspended or balanced. 2. to hover. —*SYN.* see **tact.**

poi·son (poi′z'n), *n.* [ME. *poisoun, puison;* OFr. *poison, puison;* L. *potio,* potion; see POTION], 1. a substance, usually a drug, causing illness or death when eaten, drunk, or absorbed in relatively small quantities. 2. anything harmful or destructive to happiness or welfare, such as an idea, emotion, etc. *v.t.* 1. to give poison to; harm or destroy by means of poison. 2. to put poison on or into. 3. to influence wrongfully; corrupt: as, they *poisoned* his mind. *adj.* poisonous.

poison dogwood, poison sumac.

poison gas, any of several toxic chemical agents, in the form of gases, liquids, or solids, used in chemical warfare to kill or harass through inhalation or contact.

poison hemlock, a bad-smelling plant with finely cut leaves, small white flowers, and a very poisonous root.

poison ivy, any of several American sumacs with grayish berries and pointed leaves that grow in groups of three and can cause a skin rash if touched: also called *poison oak.*

POISON IVY

poison oak, 1. a shrubby western variety of poison ivy. 2. poison sumac.

poi·son·ous (poi′z'n-əs), *adj.* that can injure or kill by or as by poison; containing, or having the effects of, a poison; venomous.

poison sumac, a swamp shrub with greenish-white flowers, hanging clusters of small grayish fruit, and leaves made up of 7 to 13 gray leaflets which can cause a severe rash if touched: also called *poison oak, poison dogwood, poison elder.*

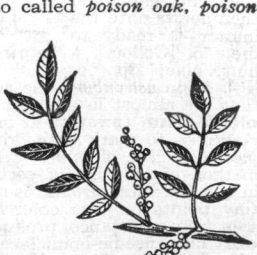

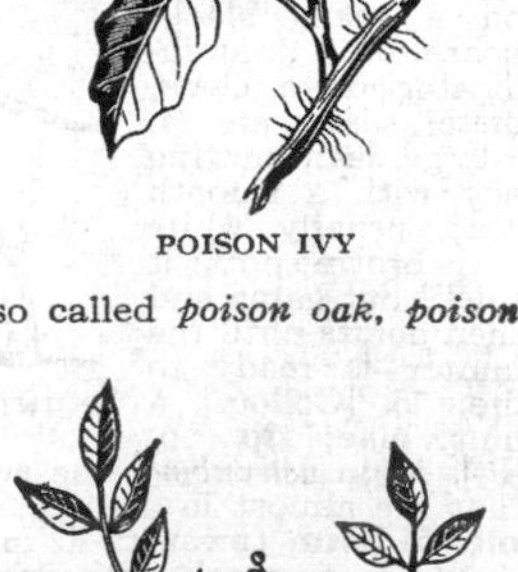

POISON SUMAC

Poi·tiers (pwȧ′tyā′; Eng. poi-têrz′), *n.* a city in west central France: pop., 53,000: scene of a battle (1356) of the Hundred Years War, in which the English defeated the French.

Poi·tou (pwȧ′to͞o′), *n.* a former province of west central France.

poke (pōk), *v.t.* [POKED (pōkt), POKING], [ME. *poken;* MD. or LG. *poken*], 1. to push; prod; jab, as with a stick, an elbow, etc.: as, *poke* him in the ribs. 2. [Slang], to hit with the fist. 3. to make by poking: as, she *poked* a hole in the wallpaper. 4. to stir up (a fire) by jabbing the coals with a poker (sometimes with *up*). 5. to thrust; put forward; intrude: as, *poke* the stake into the ground, don't *poke* your nose into my affairs. *v.i.* 1. to make jabs with a stick, poker, etc. (*at* something). 2. to intrude; meddle. 3. to pry or search (sometimes with *about* or *around*). 4. to live or move slowly or lazily; loiter; putter; dawdle (often with *along*). *n.* 1. a poking; jab; thrust; nudge. 2. [Slang], a blow with the fist. 3. a lazy or slow-moving person; dawdler; slowpoke. 4. a poke bonnet. 5. the projecting brim at the front of a poke bonnet.

poke fun (at); to ridicule or deride, especially satirically or slyly.

poke (pōk), *n.* [ME.; OFr. *poke, poque* < Gmc. base **pokka;* for IE. base cf. POD, BUD], [Archaic & Dial.], 1. a sack; bag. 2. a pocket. 3. a baglike growth on the neck, especially of sheep.

poke (pōk), *n.* [earlier *pocan* < Am. Ind. (Virginian) *pakon,* weed used for staining < *pak,* blood], pokeweed.

poke·ber·ry (pōk′ber′i, pōk′bẽr-i), *n.* [*pl.* POKEBERRIES (-iz)], [*poke* (pokeweed) + *berry*], 1. the reddish-purple berry of the pokeweed, containing poisonous seeds. 2. the pokeweed.

poke bonnet, a bonnet with a projecting front brim.

pok·er (pō′kẽr), *n.* [corresponds to G. *pochspiel* < *pochen,* to brag: variety of older game *brag*], a card game in which the players bet on the value of their hands, the bets forming a pool to be taken by the winner: there are several varieties (see **draw poker, stud poker**).

pok·er (pō′kẽr), *n.* 1. a person or thing that pokes. 2. a bar, usually of iron, for stirring a fire.

poker face, [Colloq.], an expressionless face, as of a poker player trying to conceal the nature of his hand.

poke·root (pōk′ro͞ot′, pōk′root′), *n.* a pokeweed.

poke·weed (pōk′wēd′), *n.* [see POKE (weed)], any of several North American weeds with clusters of purplish-white flowers, reddish-purple berries, and smooth leaves and stems: the roots and berry seeds are poisonous.

pok·y, pok·ey (pō′ki), *adj.* [POKIER (-ki-ẽr), POKIEST (-ki-ist)], [< *poke* (to push)], 1. slow; dull; trifling. 2. small and uncomfortable; stuffy, as a place. 3. shabbily dressed; dowdy. *n.* [< ?], [Slang], a jail.

Pol., 1. Poland. 2. Polish.

pol., 1. political. 2. politics.

Po·la (pô′lä), *n.* Pulj, Yugoslavia: the Italian name.

Po·lack (pō′läk, pō′lak), *n.* [< Pol. *Polak*], 1. [Obs.], a Pole. 2. [Slang], a person of Polish descent: vulgar term of prejudice and contempt. *adj.* [Slang], Polish.

Po·land (pō′lənd), *n.* a country in central Europe, on the Baltic Sea: area, 150,470 sq. mi.; pop., 29,480,000; capital, Warsaw: Polish name, *Polska.*

Poland China, an American breed of large hogs, usually black and white.

po·lar (pō′lẽr), *adj.* [ML. *polaris* < L. *polus;* see POLE], 1. of, connected with, or near the North or South Pole. 2. of a pole or poles. 3. having polarity. 4. having two opposite natures, directions, etc. 5. central and guiding, like the earth's pole or the polestar.

polar bear, a large white bear of the arctic regions.

polar body, one of the two cells cast off from a dividing ovum during maturation: also **polar cell** (or **globule**).

polar circle, 1. Arctic Circle. 2. Antarctic Circle.

polar distance, in *astronomy* & *navigation,* the complement of the declination; codeclination.

polar front, in *meteorology,* the region, or belt, serving as the boundary or transition between the cold air of a polar region and the warmer air of the middle or tropical regions.

po·lar·im·e·ter (pō′lə-rim′ə-tẽr), *n.* [< ML. *polaris* (see POLAR); + *-meter*], an instrument for measuring the degree of polarization in light, the amount of polarized light in a ray, or the amount of rotation of the plane of polarization.

Po·la·ris (pō-lâr′is), *n.* [Mod. L., short for ML. *stella polaris,* polar star], the North Star; polestar; star of the second magnitude, standing alone and forming the end of the tail of the constellation Ursa Minor: it marks very nearly the position of the north celestial pole: see **constellation,** chart.

po·lar·i·scope (pō-lar′ə-skōp′), *n.* [< ML. *polaris* (see POLAR); + *-scope*], an instrument for demonstrating the polarization of light, or for looking at things in polarized light.

po·lar·i·ty (pō-lar′ə-ti), *n.* 1. the property possessed by bodies having magnetic poles (one positive and attracting, one negative and repelling) of placing themselves so that their two extremities point to the two poles of the earth. 2. any tendency to turn, grow, think, feel, etc. in a certain way, as if because of magnetic attraction or repulsion. 3. the having or showing of two contrary qualities, powers, tendencies, etc. 4. in *electricity,* the condition of being positive or negative in relation to a magnetic pole.

po·lar·iz·a·ble (pō′lẽr-iz′ə-b'l), *adj.* that can be polarized.

po·lar·i·za·tion (pō′lẽr-i-zā′shən, pō′lẽr-ī-zā′shən), *n.* [< *polarize* + *-ation*], 1. the producing of polarity in something, or the acquiring of polarity. 2. in *electricity,* the production of a reverse electromotive force at the electrodes of a cell, by the depositing on them of gases produced during electrolysis. 3. [Fr. *polarisation*], in *optics, a)* a condition of light or radiant heat, in which the transverse vibrations of the rays assume different forms in different planes. *b)* the production of this condition.

po·lar·ize (pō′lẽr-īz′), ***v.t.*** [POLARIZED (-īzd′), POLARIZING], [Fr. *polariser* < *polaire*, polar], to give polarity to; produce polarization in. ***v.i.*** to acquire polarity.

polar lights, 1. the aurora borealis: also called *northern lights.* 2. the aurora australis.

po·lar·oid (pō′lẽr-oid′), ***n.*** [*polar* + *-oid*], a thin, transparent, filmlike material capable of polarizing light, used in optics, photography, etc.: a trade-mark (**Polaroid**).

pol·der (pōl′dẽr), ***n.*** [D.; prob. akin to Eng. *pool*], an area of low-lying land reclaimed from a sea, lake, or river by the protection of dikes.

Pole (pōl), ***n.*** a native or inhabitant of Poland.

pole (pōl), ***n.*** [ME.; AS. *pol, pal;* L. *palus*, a stake; cf. PALE (a stake)], 1. a long, slender piece of wood, usually rounded; long rod of any material: as, a tent *pole*, telephone *pole*. 2. a tapering wooden shaft attached to the front axle of a wagon or carriage and to the collars of the horses. 3. a unit of measure, equal to one rod in linear measure or one square rod in square measure. Abbreviated **p.** ***v.t. & v.i.*** [POLED (pōld), POLING], to propel (a boat or raft) with a pole.

under bare poles, 1. with all sails furled because of the force of a gale; hence, 2. naked; stripped.

pole (pōl), ***n.*** [ME.; OFr.; L. *polus*, pole of the heavens, heavens; Gr. *polos*, axis of the sphere, firmament < *pelein*, to be in motion], 1. either end of any axis, as of the earth, of the celestial sphere, or of a cell nucleus. 2. a region contiguous to either end of the earth's axis, as the North and South Poles. 3. either of two opposed or differentiated forces, parts, or principles, such as the ends of a magnet, the terminals of a battery, cell, motor, or dynamo, or two extremes of opinion, etc. 4. a point of reference, as for a system of points or lines in mathematics, or for a series of arguments in logic. Abbreviated **p.**

poles apart, widely separated; having opposite natures, opinions, etc.; at opposite extremes.

Pole, Reginald (pōl), 1500–1558; English cardinal and Roman Catholic archbishop of Canterbury.

pole·ax, pole·axe (pōl′aks′), ***n.*** [ME. *pollax* < *pol*, poll, head + *ax*], 1. a long-handled battle-ax. 2. any ax with a spike, hook, or hammer opposite the blade. ***v.t.*** to attack or fell with or as with a poleax.

POLEAX

pole·cat (pōl′kat′), ***n.*** [*pl.* POLECATS (-kats′), POLECAT; see PLURAL, II, D, 1], [ME. *polcat;* prob. < OFr. *pole, poule*, a hen; + *cat*], 1. a small, bad-smelling, weasellike carnivore of Europe. 2. a skunk.

pole horse, a horse harnessed to the pole of a wagon, tandem, etc., and nearest the wheels.

po·lem·ic (pō-lem′ik), ***adj.*** [Gr. *polemikos* < *polemos*, a war], 1. of or involving dispute; controversial. 2. argumentative. ***n.*** 1. an argument or controversial discussion. 2. a person inclined to argument.

po·lem·i·cal (pō-lem′i-k′l), ***adj.*** polemic.

po·lem·i·cist (pō-lem′ə-sist), ***n.*** a skilled debater or writer of polemic discussions.

po·lem·ics (pō-lem′iks), ***n.pl.*** [construed as sing.], [see POLEMIC & -ICS], 1. the art or practice of disputation or controversy. 2. a dispute.

pol·e·mist (pol′ə-mist), ***n.*** an argumentative person.

pol·e·mo·ni·a·ceous (pol′ə-mō′ni-ā′shəs), ***adj.*** [< Mod. L. *Polemoniaceae*, name of the family (< Gr. *polemōnion*, kind of plant); + *-ous*], of the phlox family of plants.

po·len·ta (pō-len′tə), ***n.*** [It.; L., peeled or pearl barley], a porridge made of barley, chestnut meal, or corn meal, eaten especially in Italy.

pol·er (pōl′ẽr), ***n.*** 1. a pole horse. 2. a person who poles a boat.

pole·star (pōl′stär′), ***n.*** Polaris: also called *North Star.*

pole-vault (pōl′vôlt′), ***v.i.*** to perform the pole vault.

pole vault, in *track & field*, 1. an event in which the contestant leaps for height, vaulting over a bar with the aid of a long pole. 2. a leap so performed.

po·lice (pə-lēs′), ***n.*** [Fr.; LL. *politia*, administration of the commonwealth (in L., the state); Gr. *politeia*, the state, citizenship < *politēs*, citizen < *polis*, city], 1. the regulation of morals, safety, sanitation, etc.; public order; law enforcement. 2. the governmental department (of a city, state, etc.) organized for keeping order and for preventing, detecting, and punishing crimes. 3. an official force, or body of persons, established and maintained for keeping order, etc. 4. [construed as pl.], the members of such a force or governmental department. 5. in the *United States Army*, *a)* the act or duty of maintaining order or cleanliness in a camp, etc. *b)* the soldiers charged with maintaining order. *c)* any nonmilitary duty or detail: as, kitchen *police.* ***v.t.*** [POLICED (-lēst′), POLICING], 1. to control, protect, or keep orderly with or as police or the like: as, *police* the street. 2. to make or keep (a military camp, etc.) clean or orderly (sometimes with *up*).

police court, an inferior court having jurisdiction over minor offenses and misdemeanors, and the power to hold for trial those charged with more serious crimes.

police dog, a dog specially trained to assist police, etc.; especially, in popular use, a German shepherd (or German police).

POLICE DOG (German shepherd)

po·lice·man (pə-lēs′mən), ***n.*** [*pl.* POLICEMEN (-mən)], a member of a police force.

police state, a government that seeks to intimidate and suppress political opposition by means of a secret police force.

police station, the headquarters of a local or district police force, where arrested persons are first charged.

po·lice·wom·an (pə-lēs′woom′ən), ***n.*** [*pl.* POLICEWOMEN (-wim′in)], a woman member of a police force.

pol·i·clin·ic (pol′i-klin′ik), ***n.*** [G. *poliklinik* < Gr. *polis*, city + G. *klinik*, clinic], the department of a hospital where outpatients are treated: cf. **polyclinic.**

pol·i·cy (pol′ə-si), ***n.*** [*pl.* POLICIES (-siz)], [ME. & OFr. *policie;* L. *politia;* Gr. *politeia;* see POLICE], 1. political wisdom or cunning; diplomacy; prudence; artfulness. 2. wise, expedient, or crafty conduct or management. 3. any governing principle, plan, or course of action.

pol·i·cy (pol′ə-si), ***n.*** [*pl.* POLICIES (-siz)], [Fr. *police;* It. *polizza;* ML. *apodixa;* Gr. *apodeixis*, proof < *apodeiknynai*, to display, make known], 1. a written contract in which one party guarantees to insure another against a specified loss or misfortune, in consideration of periodic payments called premiums: in full, **insurance policy.** 2. a gambling on lottery numbers: see **policy racket.**

pol·i·cy·hold·er (pol′ə-si-hōl′dẽr), ***n.*** a person to whom an insurance policy is issued.

policy racket, a lottery based on the appearance of a specific number in some daily statistical table: see **numbers pool.**

pol·i·o (pō′li-ō′; pol′i-ō′ *is preferred by the National Foundation for Infantile Paralysis*), ***n.*** [Colloq.], poliomyelitis.

pol·i·o·my·e·li·tis (pol′i-ō-mī′ə-lī′tis), ***n.*** [Mod. L. < Gr. *polios*, gray; + *myelitis*], inflammation of the gray matter of the spinal cord; especially, infantile paralysis.

Pol·ish (pō′lish), ***adj.*** of Poland, its people, their language, or culture. ***n.*** the West Slavic language of the Poles. Abbreviated **Pol.**

pol·ish (pol′ish), ***v.t.*** [ME. *polischen* < inflected form of OFr. *polir;* L. *polire*, to polish], 1. to smooth and brighten, as by rubbing. 2. to remove crudity or vulgarity from; make elegant or polite; refine (manners, style, appearance, literary work, etc.). 3. to complete or embellish; finish; perfect. ***v.i.*** to take a polish; become glossy, elegant, or refined. ***n.*** 1. surface gloss. 2. elegance; refinement; finish. 3. a substance used to polish. 4. a polishing or being polished.

polish off, [Colloq.], 1. to finish (a meal, job, etc.) completely and quickly. 2. to overcome or get rid of (a competitor, enemy, etc.).

polish up, [Colloq.], to improve.

***SYN.*—polish** implies a rubbing, as with a cloth or tool and, often, an abrasive, paste, etc., to produce a smooth or glossy surface (to *polish* silver, glass, furniture, etc.); **burnish** specifically suggests a rubbing of metals to make them bright and lustrous (*burnished* steel); **buff** implies polishing with a stick or tool covered with specially treated leather (originally buffalo hide) or other material (to *buff* the fingernails); **shine** implies a making bright and clean by polishing (to *shine* shoes).

Polish Corridor, the narrow strip of Poland between Germany and East Prussia, extending to the Baltic Sea (1919–1945).

pol·ished (pol′isht), ***adj.*** 1. *a)* made smooth and shiny, as by rubbing. *b)* having a naturally smooth and shiny surface. 2. elegant; refined; polite. 3. without error or flaw: as, a *polished* performance.

polit., 1. political. 2. politics.

Po·lit·bu·ro (pə-lit′byoor′ō), ***n.*** [< Russ. *Polit*icheskoe *Buro*, political bureau], a former committee of the Communist Party of the Soviet Union, having the responsibility of analyzing events, determining policy, etc. between sessions of the larger Central Committee: replaced by a presidium in 1952.

po·lite (pə-līt′), *adj.* [L. *politus*, pp. of *polire*, to polish], 1. polished; cultured; refined; correct: as, *polite* society, *polite* letters. 2. having good manners; courteous.

pol·i·tesse (pol′ə-tes′; Fr. pô′lē′tes′), *n.* [Fr.; It. *politezza, pulitezza*, cleanliness, courtliness], politeness.

pol·i·tic (pol′ə-tik), *adj.* [ME. *polytyk;* L. *politicus;* Gr. *politikos*, of a citizen < *politēs;* see POLICE], 1. having practical wisdom; prudent; shrewd; diplomatic; hence, 2. crafty; unscrupulous. 3. prudently or artfully contrived; expedient, as a plan, action, remark, etc. 4. [Rare], political: see **body politic.** *v.i.* [POLITICKED] (-tikt), POLITICKING], to engage in political campaigning, vote-getting, etc. —*SYN.* see **suave.**

po·lit·i·cal (pə-lit′i-k′l), *adj.* [< L. *politicus*], 1. of or concerned with government, the state, or politics. 2. having a definite governmental organization. 3. engaged in or taking sides in politics: as, *political* parties. 4. of or characteristic of political parties or politicians: as, *political* pressure. Abbreviated **pol., polit.**

political economy, economics.

political liberty, the right to participate in determining the form, choosing the officials, making the laws, and carrying on the functions of one's government.

po·lit·i·cal·ly (pə-lit′i-k′l-i, pə-lit′ik-li), *adv.* 1. in a political manner. 2. with reference to government or politics.

political science, the science of political institutions, or of the principles, organization, and methods of government.

pol·i·ti·cian (pol′ə-tish′ən), *n.* [see POLITIC & -IAN; cf. Fr. *politicien*], 1. a person actively engaged in politics, especially party politics, professionally or otherwise; often, a person holding or seeking political office: frequently used in a derogatory sense, with implications of seeking personal or partisan gain, scheming, opportunism, etc., as distinguished from *statesman*, which suggests able, far-seeing, principled conduct of public affairs. 2. [Now Rare], a person skilled or experienced in practical politics or political science.

po·lit·i·cize (pə-lit′ə-sīz′), *v.i.* [POLITICIZED (-sīzd′), POLITICIZING], 1. to talk politics. 2. to take part in politics. *v.t.* 1. to make political. 2. to discuss politically.

pol·i·tic·ly (pol′ə-tik-li), *adv.* in a politic manner.

po·lit·i·co (pə-lit′i-kō′), *n.* [Sp. *político* or It. *politico*], a politician.

po·lit·i·co- (pə-lit′i-kō), a combining form meaning *political and.*

pol·i·tics (pol′ə-tiks), *n.pl.* [construed as sing. except in sense 6], [< *politic*], 1. the science and art of political government; political science. 2. [P-], a treatise on political science by Aristotle (384–322 B.C.). 3. political affairs. 4. the conducting of or participation in political affairs, often as a profession. 5. political methods, tactics, etc. 6. political opinions, principles, or party connections. 7. factional scheming within a group: as, office *politics.* Abbreviated **polit., pol.**

pol·i·ty (pol′ə-ti), *n.* [*pl.* POLITIES (-tiz)], [OFr. *politie;* L. *politia;* see POLICY (wisdom)], 1. the governmental organization or constitution of a state, church, etc. 2. a society or institution with an organized government; state; body politic.

Polk, James Knox (pōk), 1795–1849; eleventh president of the United States (1845–1849).

pol·ka (pōl′kə), *n.* [Fr. & G.; prob. < Czech *pulka*, half step], 1. a fast dance for couples, developed in Bohemia in the early 19th century. 2. the basic step of this dance, a hop followed by three small steps. 3. music for this dance, in fast duple time. *v.i.* to dance the polka.

pol·ka dot (pō′kə), [from the popularity of the *polka* dance in the late 19th c.; *polka gauze, polka hats*, etc. were formerly popular], 1. one of the small round dots regularly spaced to form a pattern on cloth. 2. a pattern or cloth with such dots.

poll (pōl), *n.* [ME. *pol, polle;* MD. *polle, pol*, top of the head, head], 1. the head; especially, the crown, back, or hair of the head. 2. an individual person, especially one among several, as one of twelve jurors. 3. a counting, listing, or register of persons, especially of voters. 4. a voting or expression of opinion by individuals. 5. the amount of voting; number of votes recorded. 6. *usually in pl.* a place where votes are cast and recorded. 7. a poll tax. 8. a canvassing of a selected sample group of people in an attempt to discover public opinion on some question. 9. the blunt end of a hammer head. *v.t.* [ME. *pollen*], 1. to cut off or cut short. 2. to cut off or trim the wool, hair, horns, or branches of. 3. to take or register the votes of: as, *poll* a county. 4. to receive (a certain number or proportion of votes); receive the votes of (certain voters): said of a candidate. 5. to cast (a vote). 6. to canvass in a poll (sense 8). *v.i.* to vote in an election.

pol·lack (pol′ək), *n.* [*pl.* POLLACK, POLLACKS (-əks); see PLURAL, II, D, 2], [for early Scot. *podlok*, prob. under influence of Scot. Gael. *pollag*, fresh-water fish; for base, see POD; cf. COD], any of several related food fishes of the Atlantic coast, having tiny scales and a projecting lower jaw: also spelled **pollock.**

pol·lard (pol′ẽrd), *n.* [< *poll* (to cut off)], 1. a hornless animal, as a goat, deer, ox, etc. 2. a tree with its top branches cut back to the trunk, so as to cause a dense growth of new shoots. *v.t.* to change into a pollard.

poll·book (pōl′book′), *n.* a book or list of registered voters in a precinct, county, etc.

polled (pōld), *adj.* 1. [Archaic], with the wool, hair, horns, or branches cut off or trimmed. 2. hornless.

poll·ee (pōl′ē′), *n.* a person questioned in a poll.

pol·len (pol′ən), *n.* [L., fine flour, dust], the yellow, powderlike male sex cells on the stamens of a flower.

pollen count, the number of grains of a specified variety of pollen, usually ragweed, present in a given volume of air, usually a cubic yard, at a specified time and place.

pol·lex (pol′eks), *n.* [*pl.* POLLICES (-ə-sēz′)], [L.], the thumb; innermost digit of a forelimb.

pol·li·nate (pol′ə-nāt′), *v.t.* [POLLINATED (-id), POLLINATING], to place pollen on the upper tip of the pistil of.

pol·li·na·tion (pol′ə-nā′shən), *n.* the transfer of pollen from the stamen to the pistil.

pol·li·nif·er·ous (pol′ə-nif′ẽr-əs), *adj.* [< L. *pollen, pollinis;* + *-ferous*], bearing, yielding, or carrying pollen.

pol·lin·i·um (pə-lin′i-əm), *n.* [Mod. L. < L. *pollen;* see POLLEN], a mass of pollen grains.

pol·li·no·sis (pol′ə-nō′sis), *n.* [Mod. L. < L. *pollen, pollinis*, pollen; + *-osis*], hay fever.

pol·li·wog (pol′i-wog′), *n.* [ME. *polwygle;* cf. POLL (the head) & WIGGLE], a tadpole: also spelled **pollywog.**

pol·lock (pol′ək), *n.* [*pl.* POLLOCK, POLLOCKS (-əks); see PLURAL, II, D, 2], a pollack.

Pol·lock, Sir Frederick (pol′ək), 1845–1937; English jurist and writer.

poll·ster (pōl′stẽr), *n.* a person who conducts polls (sense 8).

poll-tax (pōl′taks′), *adj.* of, having, or advocating a poll tax, especially as a means of limiting the electorate.

poll tax, a tax per head: in some States payment of a poll tax is a prerequisite for voting.

pol·lute (pə-lōōt′), *v.t.* [POLLUTED (-id), POLLUTING], [ME. *poluten* < L. *pollutus*, pp. of *polluere*, to pollute], to make unclean, impure, or corrupt; desecrate; defile; contaminate; dirty. —*SYN.* see **contaminate.**

pol·lu·tion (pə-lōō′shən), *n.* [ME. *poluccion;* LL. *pollutio*], a polluting or being polluted.

Pol·lux (pol′əks), *n.* [L., earlier *Polluces;* Gr. *Polydeukēs*], 1. in *Greek & Roman mythology*, one of the twin sons of Zeus: see **Dioscuri.** 2. in *astronomy*, the brighter of the two first-magnitude stars in the constellation Gemini: the other star is Castor.

Pol·ly (pol′i), a feminine name: see **Mary.**

Pol·ly·an·na (pol′i-an′ə), *n.* [name of the young heroine of a novel by Eleanor H. Porter (1868–1920), Am. writer], an excessively or persistently optimistic person.

pol·ly·wog (pol′i-wog′), *n.* a polliwog.

po·lo (pō′lō), *n.* [prob. < Tibet. dial. *polo*, var. of *pulu*, properly, the name of the ball], 1. a game played on horseback by two teams of four players each, who attempt to drive a small wooden ball through the opponents' goal with long-handled mallets. 2. water polo.

Po·lo, Mar·co (mär′kō pō′lō), 1254?–1324?; Venetian traveler in Asia.

polo coat, a type of loose, tailored overcoat made of camel's hair or a similar fabric.

po·lo·ist (pō′lō-ist), *n.* a person who plays polo.

po·lo·naise (pol′ə-nāz′, pō′lə-nāz′), *n.* [Fr., fem. of *polonais*, Polish], 1. a dress with the skirt divided in front and worn looped back over an elaborate underskirt: originally worn by Polish women. 2. a stately Polish dance in triple time, almost processional in character. 3. music for, or in the rhythm of, this dance.

POLONAISE

po·lo·ni·um (pə-lō′ni-əm), *n.* [Mod. L.; so named by its co-discoverer, Marie Curie, after her native land, Poland (ML. *Polonia*)], a radioactive chemical element formed by the disintegration of radium: symbol, Po; at. wt., approximately 210; at. no., 84: also called *radium F.*

Po·lo·ni·us (pə-lō′ni-əs), *n.* in Shakespeare's *Hamlet*, a voluble, sententious old courtier, lord chamberlain to the king and father of Ophelia and Laertes.

polo shirt, a short-sleeved, usually knitted, pull-over sport shirt for men and boys, somewhat like a T-shirt, but generally with a buttoned collar.

Pol·ska (pôl′skä), *n.* Poland: the Polish name.

Pol·ta·va (pôl-tä′vä), *n.* a city in the Ukrainian S.S.R.: pop., 130,000: scene of a battle (1709) in which Russia defeated Sweden.

pol·ter·geist (pōl′tẽr-gīst′), *n.* [G.; *polter*, uproar + *geist*, a spirit], a ghost supposed to be responsible for table rappings and other mysterious noisy disturbances.

pol·troon (pol-trōōn′), *n.* [Fr. *poltron;* It. *poltrone,* coward < OHG. *polstar,* a bed; prob. ult. < *bolstar,* a pillow; cf. BOLSTER, *n.*], a thorough coward; craven.

pol·troon·er·y (pol-trōōn′ẽr-i), *n.* cowardice.

pol·y- (pol′i), [Gr. *poly-* < *polys,* much, many], a combining form meaning: 1. *much, many, more than one,* as in *polychromatic, polyandry.* 2. *more than usual, excessive,* as in *polyphagia.* 3. *in* or *of many kinds* or *parts,* as in *polymorphous.*

pol·y·an·drist (pol′i-an′drist), *n.* a person who practices polyandry.

pol·y·an·drous (pol′i-an′drəs), *adj.* 1. practicing polyandry. 2. of or characterized by polyandry. 3. in *botany,* having many stamens.

pol·y·an·dry (pol′i-an′dri, pol′i-an′dri), *n.* [Gr. *polyandria* < *poly-,* many + *anēr, andros,* a man], 1. the state or practice of having two or more husbands at the same time. 2. in *botany,* the presence of twenty or more stamens in one flower. 3. in *zoology,* the mating of one female animal with more than one male.

pol·y·an·thus (pol′i-an′thəs), *n.* [Mod. L.; Gr. *polyanthos; poly-,* many + *anthos,* a flower], 1. a kind of primrose with many flowers; oxlip. 2. a kind of narcissus with many star-shaped flowers.

pol·y·bas·ic (pol′i-bās′ik), *adj.* [*poly-* + *basic*], 1. designating an acid having more than one hydrogen atom (per molecule) replaceable by basic atoms or radicals. 2. designating a salt having more than one atom (per molecule) of a monovalent metal.

pol·y·bas·ite (pol′i-bās′it, pə-lib′ə-sit′), *n.* [G.; see POLY-, BASE, -ITE], an iron-black ore with a metallic luster, Ag_9SbS_6, a sulfide of silver and antimony.

Po·lyb·i·us (pə-lib′i-əs), *n.* Greek historian; lived 205?–125? B.C.

Pol·y·carp, Saint (pol′i-kärp′), 69?–155? A.D.; Christian prelate and martyr in Smyrna: his day is January 26.

pol·y·chae·tous (pol′i-kē′təs), *adj.* [< Mod. L. *Polychaeta,* name of the order < *poly-* + Gr. *chaitē,* hair], belonging to a group of segmented worms having short, fleshy limbs with bristles.

pol·y·cha·si·um (pol′i-kā′zi-əm, pol′i-kā′zhi-əm), *n.* [*pl.* POLYCHASIA (-ə)], [Mod. L. < *poly-* + Gr. *chasis,* division], a broad cluster of flowers in which each main stem sends forth more than two branches.

pol·y·chro·mat·ic (pol′i-krō-mat′ik), *adj.* [*poly-* + *chromatic*], having various or changing colors.

pol·y·chrome (pol′i-krōm′), *adj.* [Fr.; Gr. *polychrōmos* < *poly-,* many + *chrōma,* a color], 1. polychromatic. 2. done in several colors: as, *polychrome* printing.

pol·y·chro·mic (pol′i-krō′mik), *adj.* polychromatic.

pol·y·chro·my (pol′i-krō′mi), *n.* [Fr. *polychromie;* see POLYCHROME], the art of tastefully combining many different colors, especially in painting statues, decorating buildings, etc.

pol·y·clin·ic (pol′i-klin′ik), *n.* [*poly-* + *clinic*], a clinic or hospital for the treatment of various kinds of diseases: cf. **policlinic.**

Pol·y·cli·tus, Pol·y·clei·tus (pol′i-klī′təs), *n.* Greek sculptor; lived 5th century B.C.

pol·y·con·ic projection (pol′i-kon′ik), a type of map projection in which the parallels are arcs of nonconcentric circles and the meridians are curves equally spaced from the central, straight meridian.

Po·lyc·ra·tes (pə-lik′rə-tēz′), *n.* Greek tyrant and pirate of Samos; crucified by Persians (c. 522 B.C.).

pol·y·dac·tyl, pol·y·dac·tyle (pol′i-dak′til), *adj.* [*poly-* + *dactyl*], having more than the normal number of fingers or toes. *n.* a polydactyl person or animal.

pol·y·dac·tyl·ism (pol′i-dak′til-iz′m), *n.* the condition of being polydactyl.

Pol·y·dor·us (pol′i-dôr′əs, pol′i-dō′rəs), *n.* Greek sculptor; lived 1st century B.C.

pol·y·em·bry·o·ny (pol′i-em′bri-ə-ni), *n.* [< *poly-* + *embryo*], the production of two or more embryos or individuals from a single fertilized ovum.

pol·y·es·ter (pol′i-es′tẽr), *n.* [*poly*mer + *ester*], any of several polymeric resins with ester groups in the main chain: used in making plastics, fibers, etc.

pol·y·eth·yl·ene (pol′i-eth′ə-lēn′), *n.* [*poly*mer + *ethylene*], any of several thermoplastic resins, $(C_2H_4)_n$, made by the polymerization of ethylene: used in making plastics, films, containers, insulation, etc.

po·lyg·a·la (pə-lig′ə-lə), *n.* [L., milkwort; Gr. *polygalon* < *poly-,* much + *gala,* milk], any of a number of related plants with yellow or rosy-purple, irregular flowers and small, two-seeded pods.

po·lyg·a·mist (pə-lig′ə-mist), *n.* a person who practices or favors polygamy.

po·lyg·a·mous (pə-lig′ə-məs), *adj.* [Gr. *polygamos*], 1. of, engaging in, or characterized by polygamy. 2. in *botany,* having two-sexed flowers and one-sexed flowers on the same plant or on different plants.

po·lyg·a·my (pə-lig′ə-mi), *n.* [Fr. *polygamie;* Gr. *polygamia* < *poly-,* many + *gamos,* marriage], the state or practice of having two or more wives, husbands, or mates at the same time; plural marriage or mating.

pol·y·gen·e·sis (pol′i-jen′ə-sis), *n.* [Mod. L.; see POLY- & GENESIS], in *biology,* 1. derivation from more than one kind of germ cell. 2. the theory that different species are descended from different ultimate ancestors.

pol·y·ge·net·ic (pol′i-jə-net′ik), *adj.* [*poly-* + *genetic*], 1. having more than one source or origin. 2. in *biology,* of or characterized by polygenesis.

pol·y·glot (pol′i-glot′), *adj.* [Gr. *polyglōttos* < *poly-,* many + *glōtta,* the tongue], 1. speaking or writing several languages. 2. containing, composed of, or written in several languages. *n.* 1. a person who speaks or writes several languages. 2. a book written in several languages. 3. a mixture or confusion of languages.

Pol·yg·no·tus (pol′ig-nō′təs), *n.* Greek painter; lived 5th century B.C.

pol·y·gon (pol′i-gon′), *n.* [LL. *polygonum;* Gr. *polygōnon,* neut. of *polygōnos;* see POLY- & -GON], a plane figure with several angles and sides, usually over four.

po·lyg·o·nal (pə-lig′ə-n′l), *adj.* of, or having the form of, a polygon.

po·lyg·o·num (pə-lig′ə-nəm), *n.* [Mod. L.; L. *polygonos, polygonon;* Gr. *polygonon,* kind of plant, knotgrass < *poly-,* many + *gony,* a knee, joint: so named because of the many joints], any of a number of related plants with large leaves and small white, greenish-white, or pink flowers in spikes or clusters.

pol·y·graph (pol′i-graf′, pol′i-gräf′), *n.* [Gr. *polygraphos;* see POLY- & -GRAPH], 1. a device for reproducing writings or drawings; especially, a gelatin copying pad. 2. an instrument for recording simultaneously changes in blood pressure, respiration, pulse rate, etc. 3. an author of many works or many kinds of works.

pol·y·graph·ic (pol′i-graf′ik), *adj.* of or reproduced by a polygraph.

po·lyg·y·nous (pə-lij′ə-nəs), *adj.* [Mod. L. *polygynus;* see POLYGYNY], of, or characterized by polygyny.

po·lyg·y·ny (pə-lij′ə-ni), *n.* [< *poly-* + Gr. *gynē,* a female], 1. the state or practice of having two or more wives or concubines at the same time. 2. the mating of a male animal with several females. 3. in *botany,* the fact of having many styles or pistils.

pol·y·he·dral (pol′i-hē′drəl), *adj.* of, or having the form of, a polyhedron.

pol·y·he·dron (pol′i-hē′drən), *n.* [*pl.* POLYHEDRONS (-drənz), POLYHEDRA (-drə)], [Mod. L.; Gr. *polyhedron,* neut. of *polyhedros;* see POLY- & -HEDRON], a solid figure with several plane surfaces, usually more than six.

Pol·y·hym·ni·a (pol′i-him′ni-ə), *n.* [L.; Gr. *Polymnia* < *poly-,* many + *hymnos,* a hymn], in *Greek mythology,* the Muse of sacred poetry: also **Polymnia.**

pol·y·mer (pol′i-mẽr), *n.* [< Gr. *poly-,* many + *meros,* a part], any of two or more polymeric compounds, especially one with a higher molecular weight.

pol·y·mer·ic (pol′i-mer′ik), *adj.* [< *poly-* + Gr. *meros,* a part; + *-ic*], composed of the same chemical elements in the same proportions by weight, but differing in molecular weight.

po·lym·er·ism (pə-lim′ẽr-iz′m, pol′i-mẽr-iz′m), *n.* the condition of being polymeric or polymerous.

pol·y·mer·i·za·tion (pol′i-mẽr-i-zā′shən, pə-lim′ẽr-ī-zā′shən), *n.* 1. the process of joining two or more like molecules to form a more complex molecule whose molecular weight is a multiple of the original and whose physical properties are different. 2. the changing of a compound into a polymeric form by this process.

pol·y·mer·ize (pol′i-mẽr-īz′, pə-lim′ẽr-īz′), *v.t. & v.i.* [POLYMERIZED (-īzd′), POLYMERIZING], to subject to or undergo polymerization.

po·lym·er·ous (pə-lim′ẽr-əs), *adj.* [*poly-* + *-merous*], in *botany,* consisting of many parts or having many members in each whorl.

Po·lym·ni·a (pə-lim′ni-ə), *n.* Polyhymnia.

pol·y·morph (pol′i-môrf′), *n.* [< Gr. *polymorphos* < *poly-,* many + *morphē,* a form], 1. in *biology,* a polymorphous organism or one of its forms. 2. in *chemistry & mineralogy, a)* a substance that can crystallize in two or more different forms. *b)* one of these forms.

pol·y·mor·phic (pol′i-môr′fik), *adj.* polymorphous.

pol·y·mor·phism (pol′i-môr′fiz′m), *n.* the condition or quality of being polymorphous.

pol·y·mor·phous (pol′i-môr′fəs), *adj.* [Gr. *polymorphos* < *poly-,* many + *morphē,* a form], having, occurring in, or passing through several or various forms.

Pol·y·ne·sia (pol′ə-nē′zhə, pol′ə-nē′shə), *n.* a scattered group of islands in the Pacific, east of Micronesia and Melanesia.

Pol·y·ne·sian (pol′ə-nē′zhən, pol′ə-nē′shən), *adj.* of Polynesia, its people, their language, or culture. *n.* 1. a member of the brown people of Polynesia, including the Hawaiians, Tahitians, Samoans, and Maoris. 2. the group of Austronesian languages of Polynesia.

Pol·y·ni·ces (pol′i-nī′sēz), *n.* [L. *Polynices;* Gr. *Polyneikēs*], in *Greek legend*, a son of Oedipus and the brother of Eteocles: see **Seven against Thebes.**

pol·y·no·mi·al (pol′i-nō′mi-əl), *n.* [*poly-* + bi*nomial*], 1. in *algebra*, an expression consisting of two or more terms: as, $x^2 - 2xy + y^2$ is a *polynomial.* 2. in *biology*, a species name consisting of more than two terms. *adj.* consisting of or characterized by polynomials.

pol·y·nu·cle·ar (pol′i-nōō′kli-ẽr, pol′i-nū′kli-ẽr), *adj.* [*poly-* + *nuclear*], having many nuclei.

pol·yp (pol′ip), *n.* [Fr. *polype;* L. *polypus;* Gr. *polypous; poly-*, many + *pous*, a foot], 1. any of a number of small, flowerlike water animals having a mouth fringed with many small, slender tentacles at the top of a tubelike body, as the sea anemone, hydra, etc. 2. a smooth projecting growth of hypertrophied mucous membrane in the nasal passages, bladder, rectum, etc.

pol·y·par·y (pol′i-per′i), *n.* [*pl.* POLYPARIES (-iz)], [Mod. L. *polyparium* < L. *polypus;* see POLYP], in *zoology*, the base or the connecting tissue to which each member of a colony of polyps is attached; polypidom.

pol·y·pet·al·ous (pol′i-pet′′l-əs), *adj.* [*poly-* + *petalous*], having separate petals.

pol·y·pha·gi·a (pol′i-fā′ji-ə), *n.* [Mod. L.; Gr. *polyphagia* < *poly-*, many + *phagein*, to eat], 1. an abnormal or excessive desire for food. 2. the practice of subsisting on many kinds of food.

po·lyph·a·gous (pə-lif′ə-gəs), *adj.* [*poly-* + *-phagous*], in *zoology*, living on various kinds of food.

pol·y·phase (pol′i-fāz′), *adj.* in *electricity*, having or generating two or more phases: as, a *polyphase* current.

Pol·y·phe·mus (pol′i-fē′məs), *n.* [L.; Gr. *Polyphēmos*], in *Greek legend*, the Cyclops who confined Odysseus and his companions in a cave and ate two of them daily, until Odysseus blinded him with a stake as he slept and escaped along with those still alive.

Polyphemus moth, a large, yellowish-brown American silkworm moth with an eyelike spot on each hind wing.

pol·y·phone (pol′i-fōn′), *n.* in *phonetics*, a polyphonic letter or other symbol.

pol·y·phon·ic (pol′i-fon′ik), *adj.* [Gr. *polyphōnos*, having many tones < *poly-*, many + *phōnē*, a voice, sound], 1. having or making many sounds. 2. in *music*, *a*) of, having, or in polyphony; having two or more harmonized melodies; contrapuntal. *b*) that can produce more than one tone at a time, as a piano. 3. in *phonetics*, representing more than one sound, as *c* in *cat* and *cereal.*

po·lyph·o·nous (pə-lif′ə-nəs), *adj.* polyphonic.

po·lyph·o·ny (pə-lif′ə-ni, pol′i-fō′ni), *n.* [Gr. *polyphōnia;* see POLYPHONIC], 1. multiplicity of sounds, as in an echo. 2. in *music*, a combining of a number of individual but harmonizing melodies, as in a fugue, canon, etc.; counterpoint: opposed to *monody, homophony.* 3. in *phonetics*, the representation of two or more sounds by the same letter or symbol, as *c* in *ace* and *act.*

pol·y·phy·let·ic (pol′i-fī-let′ik), *adj.* [< *poly-* + Gr. *phylētēs*, of the same clan < *phylēs*, a clan], in *biology*, derived from more than one ancestral type.

po·lyp·i·dom (pə-lip′i-dəm), *n.* [< *polypus* + L. *domus* (Gr. *domos*), a house], a polypary.

pol·y·ploid (pol′i-ploid′), *adj.* [*poly-* + *-ploid*], having the number of chromosomes in the somatic cells more than twice the haploid number. *n.* a polyploid cell or organism.

pol·y·po·dy (pol′i-pō′di), *n.* [*pl.* POLYPODIES (-diz)], [ME. *polipodye;* L. *polypodium;* see POLY- & -POD], any of a number of related ferns with rather coarse and leathery leaves.

pol·y·pous (pol′i-pəs), *adj.* of or like a polyp.

pol·yp·tych (pol′ip-tik), *n.* [Gr. *polyptychos*, having many folds < *polys*, many + *ptyx*, a fold; cf. TRIPTYCH], any arrangement, as an altarpiece, having more than three leaves or panels hinged or folded together.

pol·y·pus (pol′i-pəs), *n.* [*pl.* POLYPI (-pī′)], [L.], a polyp.

pol·y·sac·cha·ride (pol′i-sak′ə-rīd′, pol′i-sak′ə-rid), *n.* [*poly-* + *saccharide*], any of a group of carbohydrates that decompose by hydrolysis into more than three molecules of monosaccharides.

pol·y·sty·rene (pol′i-stī′rēn, pol′i-stir′ēn), *n.* a clear, colorless plastic material, a polymer of styrene (C_8H_8).

pol·y·sul·fide (pol′i-sul′fīd), *n.* [*poly-* + *sulfide*], a binary compound of sulfur containing more atoms of sulfur than the valence of the combining element requires.

pol·y·syl·lab·ic (pol′i-si-lab′ik), *adj.* [ML. *polysyllabus;* Gr. *polysyllabos* < *poly-*, many + *syllabē*, a syllable], 1. having many, or more than three, syllables. 2. characterized by polysyllables.

pol·y·syl·lab·i·cal (pol′i-si-lab′i-k′l), *adj.* polysyllabic.

pol·y·syl·la·ble (pol′i-sil′ə-b′l), *n.* [ML. *polysyllaba* < *polysyllabus*], a word of more than three syllables.

pol·y·syn·de·ton (pol′i-sin′də-ton′), *n.* [Mod. L. < *poly-* + Gr. *syndetos*, bound together < *syndein*, to bind together], in *rhetoric*, the use or repetition of conjunctions in close succession: opposed to *asyndeton.*

pol·y·tech·nic (pol′i-tek′nik), *adj.* [Fr. *polytechnique;* Gr. *polytechnos* < *poly-*, many + *technē*, an art], of or providing instruction in many scientific and technical subjects (and, formerly, arts). *n.* a polytechnic institution, usually one offering instruction in engineering.

pol·y·the·ism (pol′i-thē-iz′m), *n.* [Fr. *polythéisme;* Gr. *polytheos*, of many gods; *poly-*, many + *theos*, god], belief in or worship of many gods, or more than one god: opposed to *monotheism.*

pol·y·the·ist (pol′i-thē′ist), *n.* a person who believes in or practices polytheism.

pol·y·the·is·tic (pol′i-thē-is′tik), *adj.* of or characterized by polytheism.

pol·y·to·nal·i·ty (pol′i-tō-nal′ə-ti), *n.* [*poly-* + *tonality*], in *music*, the simultaneous use of several, or especially of two, keys in the various voices, or parts, of a composition: cf. **atonality.**

pol·y·troph·ic (pol′i-trof′ik), *adj.* [Gr. *polytrophos*, nutritious; *poly-*, many + *trophos*, feeder < *trophein*, to nourish], in *bacteriology*, obtaining nourishment from more than one kind of organic material, as many pathogenic bacteria.

pol·y·typ·ic (pol′i-tip′ik), *adj.* [< *poly-* + *-type* + *-ic*], having or involving several different types.

pol·y·u·ri·a (pol′i-yoor′i-ə), *n.* [Mod. L. < Gr. *poly-*, many + *ouron*, urine], excessive urination, as in certain diseases.

pol·y·u·ric (pol′i-yoor′ik), *adj.* of or characterized by polyuria.

pol·y·va·lence (pol′i-vā′ləns, pə-liv′ə-ləns), *n.* the quality or state of being polyvalent.

pol·y·va·lent (pol′i-vā′lənt, pə-liv′ə-lənt), *adj.* 1. in *bacteriology*, designating a vaccine containing two or more strains of the same species of bacteria. 2. in *chemistry*, having more than one valence.

pol·y·vi·nyl (pol′i-vī′nil, pol′i-vin′il), *adj.* designating or of any of a group of polymerized vinyl compounds.

Po·lyx·e·na (pə-lik′sə-nə), *n.* in *Greek legend*, a daughter of Priam and betrothed of Achilles.

pol·y·zo·an (pol′i-zō′ən), *adj.* [< *poly-* + *-zoa* + *-an*], of or belonging to a group of tiny, mollusklike water animals that live together, forming branching colonies resembling brownish moss or seaweed. *n.* any member of this group; bryozoan.

pol·y·zo·ar·i·um (pol′i-zō-âr′i-əm), *n.* [*pl.* POLYZOARIA (-ə)], [Mod. L.; see POLYZOAN & -ARY], in *zoology*, 1. a polyzoan colony. 2. its supporting skeleton.

pol·y·zo·ic (pol′i-zō′ik), *adj.* 1. of the polyzoans. 2. consisting of many zooids. 3. designating or of a spore that produces many sporozoites.

pom·ace (pum′is), *n.* [ML. *pomacium*, cider < L. *pomum*, apple, fruit], 1. the crushed pulp of apples or other fruit pressed for juice. 2. the crushed matter of anything pressed, as seeds for oil.

po·ma·ceous (pō-mā′shəs), *adj.* [Mod. L. *pomaceus* < L. *pomum*, apple, fruit], 1. [Poetic], having to do with apples. 2. in *botany*, of or like the pomes.

po·made (pō-mād′, pə-mäd′), *n.* [Fr. *pommade;* It. *pomata* < *pomo* (L. *pomum*), apple, fruit], a perfumed ointment, now usually one for the hair: so called because it is said to have been made originally with apples. *v.t.* [POMADED (-id), POMADING], to apply pomade to.

po·man·der (pə-man′dẽr, pō′man-dẽr), *n.* [earlier *pomamber;* OFr. *pome ambre, pomme d'ambre* < *pome* (see POME) + *ambre*, amber], 1. a ball made of a mixture of perfumes, formerly carried as a supposed safeguard against infection or bad luck. 2. a case for carrying this, as a perforated box, bag, or hollow ball.

po·ma·tum (pō-mā′təm, pō-mä′təm), *n.* [Mod. L. < L. *pomum*, apple, fruit], pomade.

pome (pōm), *n.* [ME.; OFr. (Fr. *pomme*) < L. *pomum*, apple, fruit], any fleshy fruit containing a core and seeds, as an apple, quince, pear, etc.

pome·gran·ate (pom′gran′it, pum′gran′it, pum-gran′it), *n.* [ME. *pomegarnet, pomgarnade;* OFr. *pome granade* < *pome* (L. *pomum*), apple, fruit + *granade, grenate* < L. *granatum*, pomegranate, lit. having seeds, grained, neut. of *granatus* < *granum*, grain, seed], 1. a round, red, juicy, pulpy fruit with a hard rind and many seeds. 2. the bush or small tree that bears it.

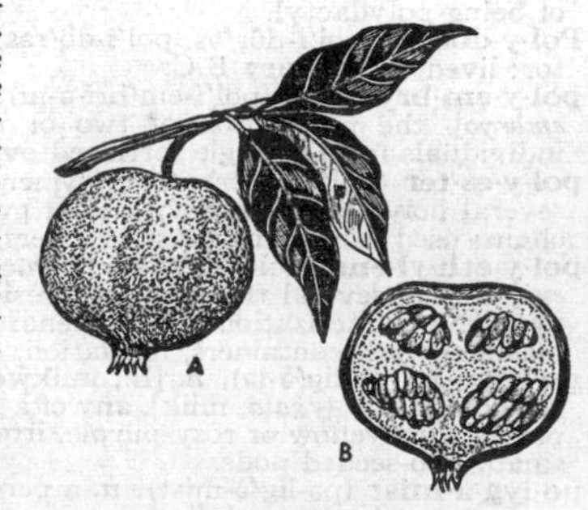

POMEGRANATE
A, leaves and fruit; B, cross section of fruit

pom·e·lo (pom′ə-lō′), *n.* [*pl.* POMELOS (-lōz′)], [prob. trade name based on *pome* and suggested by D. *pompelmoes*, the E. Ind. shaddock], 1. the shaddock. 2. the grapefruit.

Pom·er·a·ni·a (pom′ə-rā′ni-ə), *n.* a former province of Prussia, on the Baltic Sea: pop., 2,405,000; capital, Stettin: divided between Germany and Poland (1945): German name, *Pommern.*

Pom·er·a·ni·an (pom'ə-rā'ni-ən), *adj.* of Pomerania or its people. *n.* 1. a native or inhabitant of Pomerania. 2. a dog of a small breed with long, silky hair, pointed ears and muzzle, and a bushy tail turned over the back.

POMERANIAN (14 in. high at shoulder)

po·mi·cul·ture (pō'mi-kul'chẽr), *n.* [< L. *pomum*, apple, fruit; + *culture*], cultivation of fruit.

po·mif·er·ous (pō-mif'ẽr-əs), *adj.* [< L. *pomum*, fruit; + *-ferous*], bearing fruit, especially pomes.

pom·mel (pum''l; *also, for n.,* pom''l), *n.* [ME. & OFr. *pomel*, dim. of *pome* < L. *pomum*, apple, fruit], 1. a round knob on the end of the hilt of a sword, etc. 2. the rounded, upward-projecting front part of a saddle. *v.t.* [POMMELED or POMMELLED (-'ld), POMMELING or POMMELLING], to beat (formerly, with a sword pommel; now, usually, with the fists). —*SYN.* see **beat.**

Pom·mern (pôm'ẽrn), *n.* Pomerania: the German name.

po·mo·log·i·cal (pō'mə-loj'i-k'l), *adj.* of pomology.

po·mol·o·gy (pō-mol'ə-ji), *n.* [Mod. L. *pomologia;* see POME & -LOGY], the science of fruit cultivation.

Po·mo·na (pə-mō'nə), *n.* [L. < *pomum*, apple, fruit], 1. in *Roman mythology*, the goddess of fruits and fruit trees. 2. a city in southern California: pop., 67,000. 3. the largest of the Orkney Islands: area, 190 sq. mi.; pop., 14,000: also called *Mainland.*

pomp (pomp), *n.* [ME. & OFr. *pompe;* L. *pompa* < Gr. *pompē*, solemn procession < *pempein*, to send], 1. stately or brilliant display; splendor; magnificence. 2. ostentatious or vain show. 3. [Obs.], a pageant.

pom·pa·dour (pom'pə-dôr', pom'pə-door', pom'pə-dōr'), *n.* [after the Marquise de *Pompadour*], 1. a woman's hairdo in which the hair is swept up high from the forehead, usually over a roll. 2. a man's hairdo in which the hair is brushed up straight from the forehead.

Pom·pa·dour, Marquise **de,** (də pom'pə-dôr', pom'pə-door', pom'pə-dōr'; Fr. pōn'pà'do͞or'), (*Jeanne Antoinette Poisson*), 1721–1764; mistress of Louis XV.

pom·pa·no (pom'pə-nō'), *n.* [*pl.* POMPANOS (-nōz')], [Sp. *pámpano*], any of a number of related North American and West Indian food fishes with spiny fins and a widely forked tail.

Pom·pei·an (pom-pā'ən, pom-pē'ən), *adj.* of Pompeii, its people, or culture. *n.* an inhabitant of Pompeii.

Pom·pe·ii (pom-pā'ē, pom-pā'), *n.* an ancient city on the Bay of Naples: destroyed by the eruption of Mount Vesuvius (79 A.D.).

Pom·pey the Great (pom'pi), (*Gnaeus Pompeius Magnus*), 106–48 B.C.; Roman general and statesman; member of the first triumvirate.

pom-pom (pom'pom'), *n.* [echoic], 1. in World War I, a type of large machine gun firing one-pound shells. 2. in World War II, a rapid-firing, automatic anti-aircraft gun firing explosive shells.

pom·pon (pom'pon; Fr. pōn'pōn'), *n.* [Fr. < MFr. *pomper*, to exhibit pomp < OFr. *pompe;* see POMP], 1. an ornamental ball or tuft of silk, wool, feathers, etc., sometimes worn on women's or children's hats, or on the front of a soldier's shako. 2. *a)* a kind of chrysanthemum with small, round flowers. *b)* its flower.

pom·pos·i·ty (pom-pos'ə-ti), *n.* [*pl.* POMPOSITIES (-tiz)], [ME. *pomposite;* ML. *pompositas* < LL. *pomposus*], quality or instance of being pompous; pompous behavior, speech, etc.; ostentation; self-importance.

pom·pous (pom'pəs), *adj.* [ME.; OFr. *pompeus;* LL. *pomposus* < L. *pompa*], 1. full of pomp; stately; magnificent. 2. characterized by exaggerated stateliness; pretentious, as in speech or manner; self-important.

Pon·ca (poŋ'kə), *n.* [*pl.* PONCA, PONCAS (-kəz)], a member of a tribe of Siouan Indians on reservations in Nebraska and Oklahoma. *adj.* of this tribe.

Pon·ce (pôn'se), *n.* a city on the southern coast of Puerto Rico: pop., 114,000.

Pon·ce de Le·ón, Juan (hwän pôn'the *th*e le-ôn'; Eng. pons' də lē'ən), 1460?–1521; Spanish explorer; discovered Florida while seeking the Fountain of Youth.

pon·cho (pon'chō), *n.* [*pl.* PONCHOS (-chōz)], [Sp. < Araucan *poncho, pontho*], 1. a cloak like a blanket with a hole in the middle for the head, worn in Spanish America. 2. any similar garment, especially one of rubber, etc., worn as a raincoat.

pond (pond), *n.* [ME. *ponde*, artificially enclosed body of water; form of *pound*, enclosure], a body of standing water smaller than a lake, often artificially formed.

pon·der (pon'dẽr), *v.t.* [ME. *ponderen;* OFr. *ponderer;* L. *ponderare*, to weigh < *pondus, ponderis*, a weight], to weigh mentally; think deeply about; consider carefully. *v.i.* to think deeply; deliberate; meditate.

SYN.—**ponder** implies a weighing mentally and suggests careful consideration of a matter from all sides (to *ponder* over a problem); **meditate,** in intransitive use, suggests quiet, deep contemplation (he *meditated* on the state of the world) and, transitively, deliberate consideration of some plan (to *meditate* revenge); **muse** implies such contemplation or reflection as seems to absorb one completely (to *muse* over the past); **ruminate** suggests turning a matter over and over in the mind.

pon·der·a·bil·i·ty (pon'dẽr-ə-bil'ə-ti), *n.* the state or quality of being ponderable.

pon·der·a·ble (pon'dẽr-ə-b'l), *adj.* [LL. *ponderabilis* < L. *ponderare;* see PONDER], 1. that can be weighed. 2. that can be mentally weighed; appreciable.

pon·der·os·i·ty (pon'dẽr-os'ə-ti), *n.* [LL. *ponderositas* < L. *ponderosus*], the state or quality of being ponderous.

pon·der·ous (pon'dẽr-əs), *adj.* [ME.; L. *ponderosus* < *pondus*, a weight], 1. very heavy; hence, 2. unwieldy because of weight. 3. that seems heavy; bulky; massive. 4. labored; dull: as, *ponderous* words. —*SYN.* see **heavy.**

Pon·di·cher·ry (pon'di-cher'i), *n.* Pondichéry.

Pon·di·ché·ry (pōn'dē'she'rē'), *n.* 1. a former French dependency in India, on the Coromandel Coast: since 1954, part of India: area, 196 sq. mi.; pop., 317,000. 2. its chief city: pop., 60,000. English name, *Pondicherry.*

pond lily, the water lily.

pond scum, a mass of one-celled plants floating on the surface of ponds, etc., forming a green scum.

pond·weed (pond'wēd'), *n.* any of a number of related plants with straplike or long, grasslike leaves.

pone (pōn), *n.* [< Am. Ind. (Algonquian); cf. Virginian *äpân*, bread], in the southern United States, 1. bread made of corn meal. 2. a loaf or cake of this.

pone (pōn), *n.* [< L. *pone*, imperative of *ponere*, to place], in certain card games, the player to the right of the dealer.

pon·gee (pon-jē'), *n.* [< Chin. dial. *pen-chi*, domestic loom], 1. a soft, thin cloth of Chinese or Indian silk, usually left in its natural light-brown color. 2. a cloth, as of rayon, like this. *adj.* made of pongee.

pon·iard (pon'yẽrd), *n.* [Fr. *poignard* < *poing;* L. *pugnus*, fist], a dagger. *v.t.* to stab with a poniard.

pons (ponz), *n.* [*pl.* PONTES (pon'tēz)], [L., a bridge], in *anatomy & zoology*, 1. a narrow piece of tissue connecting two parts of an organ. 2. the pons Varolii.

Pons, Lily (pons; Fr. pōns), 1904– ; French operatic soprano in America.

pons as·i·no·rum (as'i-nō'rəm, as'i-nôr'əm), [L., bridge of asses], 1. in *geometry*, the fifth proposition of the first book of Euclid (that the base angles of an isosceles triangle are equal); hence, 2. any problem that is hard for beginners.

pons Va·ro·li·i (və-rō'li-ī'), [Mod. L., bridge of Varoli: after Costanzo *Varoli* (1542–1575), It. anatomist], a broad band of nerve fibers that arch across the upper part of the medulla oblongata and connect the cerebrum, cerebellum, and medulla oblongata.

Pon·ta Del·ga·da (pôn'tà *th*el-gä'*th*à; Eng. pon'tə del-gä'də), seaport and capital of São Miguel Island, in the Azores: pop., 23,000.

Pont·char·train, Lake (pon'chẽr-trān'), a lake in southeastern Louisiana: area, 600 sq. mi.

Pon·ti·ac (pon'ti-ak'), *n.* 1. chief of the Ottawa Indians; lived ?–1769. 2. a city in southeastern Michigan: pop., 82,000.

Pon·tic (pon'tik), *adj.* [L. *Ponticus;* Gr. *Pontikos* < *pontos*, sea, esp. the Black Sea], 1. of Pontus. 2. of the Black Sea.

pon·ti·fex (pon'tə-feks'), *n.* [*pl.* PONTIFICES (pon-tif'ə-sēz')], [L.; see PONTIFF], in ancient Rome, a member of the supreme college of priests, the Pontifical College.

pon·tiff (pon'tif), *n.* [Fr. *pontife;* L. *pontifex, pontificis*, high priest; prob. < Osco-Umbrian *puntis*, sacrificial offering + L. *facere*, to make], 1. a pontifex. 2. a bishop. 3. the Pope. 4. a high priest.

pon·tif·i·cal (pon-tif'i-k'l), *adj.* [ME. *pontificall;* L. *pontificalis* < *pontifex;* see PONTIFF], 1. having to do with a pontifex, a high priest, or a bishop; episcopal. 2. having to do with the Pope; papal. 3. having the pomp, dignity, or dogmatism of a pontiff: often used to imply arrogance or haughtiness. *n.* 1. *pl.* a pontiff's vestments and insignia. 2. a book of offices for a bishop.

pon·tif·i·cate (pon-tif'i-kit; *also, and for v.i. always,* pon-tif'i-kāt'), *n.* [L. *pontificatus* < *pontifex;* see PONTIFF], the office, or term of office, of a pontiff. *v.i.* [PONTIFICATED (-id), PONTIFICATING], [< ML. *pontificatus*, pp. of *pontificare*], 1. to officiate as a pontiff. 2. to behave in the manner of a pontiff; be dogmatic.

pon·tif·i·ces (pon-tif'ə-sēz'), *n.* plural of **pontifex.**

pon·til (pon'til), *n.* [Fr.; It. *pontello, puntello*, dim. of *punto*, a point], a punty.

Pon·tine (pon'tin, pon'tīn), *adj.* having to do with the Pontine Marshes.

Pontine Marshes, a region in Italy, between Rome and Naples, formerly swampy, now largely reclaimed.

Pontius, see **Pilate, Pontius.**

pont·lev·is (pont-lev′is; Fr. pōn′le′vē′), *n.* [Fr. < *pont* (L. *pons*), a bridge + *levis*, movable in a vertical plane; OFr. *leveïs;* ult. < L. *levare*, to raise], a drawbridge.

pon·ton (pon′t'n), *n.* [Fr.], in the *United States Army*, a pontoon.

pon·to·nier (pon′tə-nêr′), *n.* [Fr. *pontonnier*], a military engineer or other member of the armed forces who builds, or is in charge of building, a pontoon bridge.

pon·toon (pon-to͞on′), *n.* [Fr. *ponton;* L. *ponto* < *pons, pontis*, a bridge], 1. a flat-bottomed boat. 2. any of a number of these, or of some other floating objects, as hollow cylinders, used as supports for a temporary bridge. 3. either of two boatlike floats used on the landing gear of small airplanes to allow them to land on water: see **amphibian**, illus. Cf. **ponton.**

pontoon bridge, a temporary bridge supported on pontoons: in military usage, usually **ponton bridge.**

PONTOON BRIDGE

Pon·top·pi·dan, Hen·rik (hen′rēk pon-top′i-dän′), 1857–1943; Danish novelist; received Nobel prize in literature, 1917.

Pon·tus (pon′təs), *n.* an ancient kingdom in Asia Minor, on the Black Sea.

po·ny (pō′ni), *n.* [*pl.* PONIES (-niz)], [Scot. *powny;* prob. < OFr. *poulenet*, dim. of *poulain*, a colt, foal; LL. *pullanus* < L. *pullus*, young animal, foal; akin to Eng. *foal*], 1. a horse of any of a number of small breeds, usually not over 14 hands high. 2. something small of its kind. 3. [Colloq.], *a*) a small liqueur glass. *b*) the amount of liqueur, brandy, etc. this will hold. 4. [Colloq.], a literal translation of a literary work in a foreign language, used in doing schoolwork, often dishonestly; a crib. 5. [British Racing Slang], the sum of twenty-five pounds. ***v.t. & v.i.*** [Slang], to pay (money), as to settle an account (with *up*).

pony express, a system of carrying and delivering mail by riders on swift ponies; specifically, such a system in operation from 1860 to 1861 between St. Joseph, Missouri, and Sacramento, California.

pooch (po͞och), *n.* [coincides with dial. & obs. form of *pouch;* ? with reference to appetite], [Slang], a dog, especially a mongrel.

pood (po͞od), *n.* [Russ. *pud;* LG. *pund;* see POUND], a Russian weight, equal to 36.113 pounds avoirdupois.

poo·dle (po͞o′d'l), *n.* [G. *pudel;* LG. *pudel, pudel-hund* < *pudeln*, to splash], any of a breed of curly-haired dogs having a solid-colored coat.

POODLE (15 in. high at shoulder)

pooh (po͞o, poo, pə), *interj.* [? imitative of blowing away], an exclamation of contempt, disbelief, or impatience.

pooh (po͞o), *v.t.* [Slang], to tire; exhaust.

pooh-pooh (po͞o′po͞o′), *v.t.* [redupl. of *pooh*, *interj.*], to express contempt for; make light of; disregard. *n.* a pooh-poohing.

pool (po͞ol), *n.* [ME. & AS. *pol;* akin to D. *poel* & G. *pfuhl;* prob. IE. base **bhel-*, to shine, glimmer], 1. a small pond, as in a garden. 2. a puddle. 3. a swimming pool. 4. a deep, still spot in a river.

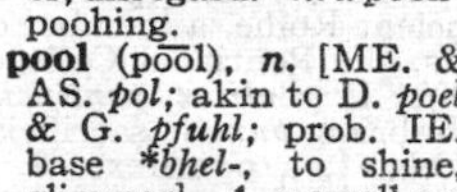

pool (po͞ol), *n.* [Fr. *poule*, pool, stakes, orig. hen < LL. *pulla*, hen; associated in Eng. with *pool* (of water)], 1. the total amount of the players' stakes, played for in a card game, etc. 2. a container for this. 3. *a*) any of several related games of billiards played with object balls numbered from 1 to 15 and a cue ball, on a table with six pockets. *b*) [British], a game of billiards for a pool (sense 1). 4. a combination of resources, funds, etc. for some common purpose or benefit; specifically, *a*) the combined wagers of betters on a horse race, etc., the gains or losses from which are to be divided proportionately. *b*) the combined investments of a group of persons or corporations undertaking, and sharing responsibility for, a joint enterprise. *c*) a common fund of stockholders, for speculation, manipulation of prices, etc. 5. the persons or parties forming such a combination. 6. a combination of business firms for elimination of competition in, and for control of, a common market; trust; monopoly. 7. in *fencing*, a contest in which each member of a team successively competes with each member of the opposing team. ***v.t. & v.i.*** to contribute to a pool, or common fund; make a common interest or form a pool (of).

pool·room (po͞ol′ro͞om′, po͞ol′room′), *n.* 1. a room or establishment where pool is played. 2. a room or place where bets are made on sporting events.

pool table, a billiard table with a pocket at each corner and at the middle of both sides, for playing pool.

poon (po͞on), *n.* [Singh. *pūna*], 1. any of a number of related East Indian trees whose seeds yield a bitter oil. 2. the wood of any of these trees. Also **poon tree.**

Poo·na (po͞o′nə), *n.* a city in Bombay province, India: pop., 250,000.

poop (po͞op), *n.* [OFr. *pupe* (Fr. *poupe*); Pr. *popa* or It. *poppa;* L. *puppis*, stern of a ship], 1. originally, the stern section of a ship. 2. on sailing ships, a raised deck at the stern, sometimes forming the roof of a cabin: also **poop deck.** *v.t.* 1. to break over the poop or stern of: said of waves. 2. to receive (a wave) over the poop or stern.

POOP

poop (po͞op), *v.t.* [via dial. < ME. *puopen*, to make an abrupt sound, blow, gulp; echoic origin], [Slang], to cause to become exhausted, out of breath, etc.: usually in the passive voice: also **pooh.**

Po·o·pó (pô′ô-pô′), *n.* a lake in west central Bolivia: length, 75 mi.; altitude, 12,120 ft.

poor (poor), *adj.* [ME. *pore, povre;* OFr. *poure, povre* (Fr. *pauvre*); L. *pauper*, poor], 1. lacking material possessions; having little or no means to support oneself; needy; impoverished. 2. indicating or characterized by poverty. 3. lacking in some quality. 4. lacking abundance; scanty; inadequate: as, *poor* crops. 5. lacking productivity; barren; sterile: as, *poor* soil. 6. lacking nourishment; feeble; emaciated: as, a *poor* body. 7. lacking excellence; paltry; mean; insignificant; inferior. 8. lacking good moral or mental qualities; mean-spirited; contemptible: as, he is a *poor* creature. 9. lacking pleasure, comfort, or satisfaction: as, we had a *poor* time. 10. worthy of pity; unfortunate.

the poor, poor, or needy, people collectively.

SYN.—**poor** is the simple, direct term for one who lacks the resources for reasonably comfortable living; **impoverished** is applied to one who having once had plenty is now reduced to poverty (an *impoverished* aristocrat); **destitute** implies such great poverty that the means for mere subsistence, such as food and shelter, are lacking (left *destitute* by the war); **impecunious** applies to one in a habitual state of poverty and suggests that this results from his own practices (an *impecunious* gambler); **indigent** implies such relative poverty as results in a lack of luxuries and the endurance of hardships (books for *indigent* children).—***ANT.*** rich, wealthy.

poor farm, a farm for paupers, supported by a county or other local government.

poor·house (poor′hous′), *n.* a house or institution for paupers, supported from public funds.

poor laws, laws that provide for public relief and support of the poor.

poor·ly (poor′li), *adv.* 1. in a poor manner; scantily; badly; defectively. 2. with a low opinion; disparagingly: as, I think *poorly* of it. *adj.* [Colloq.], in poor health.

poor-spir·it·ed (poor′spir′it-id), *adj.* having or showing a poor spirit; cowardly; timorous; abject.

poor white, in the southern United States, a white person who lives in great poverty and ignorance, often as a tenant farmer: also, collectively, **poor white trash:** contemptuous term.

pop (pop), *n.* [ME. *poppe;* echoic], 1. a sudden, short, light, explosive sound. 2. a shot with a revolver, rifle, etc. 3. any carbonated, nonalcoholic beverage: so called from the sound produced when the cork, now generally replaced by a bottle cap, was removed from a bottle. *v.i.* [POPPED (popt), POPPING], 1. to make a pop. 2. to burst with a pop. 3. to move, go, come, etc. suddenly and quickly, and usually unexpectedly: as, he *popped* into the room. 4. to open wide suddenly, or protrude, as with amazement: said of the eyes. 5. to shoot a pistol, etc. 6. in *baseball*, to be put out by hitting the ball high in the air so that it is easily caught: usually with *out* or *up*. *v.t.* [ME. *poppen*], 1. to cause to pop, as corn by roasting, etc. 2. to fire (a pistol, etc.). 3. to shoot. 4. to put suddenly, quickly, or unexpectedly: as, he *popped* his head in the door, they *popped* a question at him. 5. in *baseball*, to hit (the ball) high in the air, but in or near the infield, so that it is easily caught. *adv.* with or like a pop.

pop the question, [Colloq.], to propose marriage.

pop (pop), *n.* [contr. < *poppa*, var. of *papa*], [Slang], father: often a familiar or humorous term of address applied to any elderly man.

pop., 1. popular. 2. popularly. 3. population.

pop concert, a popular concert, chiefly of semiclassical and light classical music.

pop·corn (pop′kôrn′), *n.* 1. a variety of Indian corn with small ears and hard grains which pop open into a white, puffy mass when heated. 2. the popped grains, eaten as a confection.

pope (pōp), *n.* [ME. *pape, pope;* AS. *papa;* LL. *papa;* LGr. *papas*, father, bishop; Gr. *pappas*, father], 1. [usually P-], in the *Roman Catholic Church*, the bishop of Rome and head of the Church. 2. a person who assumes, or is thought to have, popelike authority.

3. in the *Orthodox Eastern Church*, a parish priest.

Pope, Alexander (pōp), 1688–1744; English poet.

Pope, John, 1822–1892; Union general in the Civil War.

pope·dom (pōp′dəm), *n.* [ME.; AS. *papdom;* see POPE & -DOM], the office, tenure, or jurisdiction of a pope.

Pope Joan (jōn), [after a fictitious female pope Joan, but prob. < Fr. *jaune*, yellow, in *nain jaune*, lit., yellow dwarf, Fr. name of this game], a card game played by any number of players with a deck from which the eight of diamonds has been removed.

pop·er·y (pōp′ẽr-i), *n.* [< *pope* + *-ery*], the doctrines, beliefs, and rituals of the Roman Catholic Church: a hostile term.

pop·eyed (pop′īd′), *adj.* having wide, protruding eyes.

pop·gun (pop′gun′), *n.* a toy gun that shoots harmless pellets or corks by air compression, with a pop.

pop·in·jay (pop′in-jā′), *n.* [ME. *papejai, papegai;* OFr. *papagai;* altered by association with *gai* (see JAY) < Ar. *babaghā*], 1. originally, a parrot. 2. formerly, a target consisting of a wooden parrot on a pole. 3. a talkative, vain person; fop. 4. the green woodpecker.

pop·ish (pōp′ish), *adj.* having to do with popery; characteristic of the Roman Catholic Church: a hostile term.

pop·lar (pop′lẽr), *n.* [ME. *popler;* OFr. *poplier;* L. *populus*], 1. any of a number of related tall, fast-growing trees with small leaves. 2. the wood of any of these.

pop·lin (pop′lin), *n.* [Fr. *popeline, papeline;* It. *papalino*, lit., papal: so called because made in Avignon, a papal town], a silk, rayon, cotton, or woolen cloth with a ribbed surface, used for dresses, etc.

pop·lit·e·al (pop-lit′i-əl, pop′lə-tē′əl), *adj.* [< L. *poples, poplitis*, the ham; + *-al*], of or near the ham, or that part of the leg behind the knee.

Po·po·ca·te·petl (pô-pô′kä-te′pet′l; Eng. pō′pə-kat′ə-pet″l), *n.* a volcanic mountain in western Puebla state, Mexico: height, 17,888 ft.

pop·o·ver (pop′ō′vẽr), *n.* a very light, puffy, hollow muffin: so called because it rises over the baking tin.

Pop·pae·a Sa·bi·na (po-pē′ə sə-bī′nə), ?–65? A.D.; mistress and later wife of the emperor Nero.

pop·per (pop′ẽr), *n.* 1. a person or thing that pops. 2. a covered wire basket or pan for popping corn.

pop·pet (pop′it), *n.* [form of *puppet*], 1. a poppethead. 2. a valve that moves up out of and down into its port, often used for regularly interrupted flow, as in a gasoline engine: also **poppet valve.** 3. a piece of wood on the gunwale of a boat, for supporting an oarlock. 4. *a)* [Obs.], a doll. *b)* [British Dial.], a little person: term of endearment, as for a child.

pop·pet·head (pop′it-hed′), *n.* the tailstock or headstock of a lathe.

pop·pied (pop′id), *adj.* 1. covered with poppies. 2. drugging or drugged, as by opium.

pop·ping crease (pop′iŋ), in *cricket*, a line marking the batsman's position.

pop·ple (pop″l), *v.i.* [POPPLED (-′ld), POPPLING], [ME. *poplen;* prob. of echoic origin], to heave, toss, bubble, or ripple, as water in a choppy sea. *n.* a poppling.

pop·py (pop′i), *n.* [*pl.* POPPIES (-iz)], [ME. *popi;* AS. *popæg;* altered < LL. **papau* < L. *papaver*], 1. any of a number of related plants with deeply cut leaves, a milky or colored juice, and pink, red, white, orange, or yellow flowers. 2. the flower of any of these plants. 3. a pharmaceutical extract made from poppy juice. 4. opium. 5. poppy red.

pop·py·cock (pop′i-kok′), *n.* [prob. < obs. *pop*, darling, dear], [Colloq.], nonsense; foolish talk.

pop·py·head (pop′i-hed′), *n.* an ornament in the form of a small head, cluster of foliage, fleur-de-lis, finial, etc., carved at the top of pew ends or stall ends in Gothic churches.

poppy red, a yellowish red, the color of some poppies.

poppy seed, the small, dark seed of the poppy, used in cooking, especially as a flavoring or topping for bread, rolls, and the like.

pop·u·lace (pop′yoo-lis), *n.* [Fr.; It. *popolaccio* < *popolo;* L. *populus*], the common people; the masses.

pop·u·lar (pop′yoo-lẽr), *adj.* [L. *popularis* < *populus*, the people], 1. of or carried on by the common people or all the people: as, *popular* opinion. 2. suitable or intended for the people at large: as, *popular* music. 3. within the means of the ordinary person: as, *popular* prices. 4. accepted among the people; common; prevalent: as, a *popular* misconception. 5. liked by the people or by most people: as, a *popular* magazine. 6. very well liked by one's friends and acquaintances. Abbreviated **pop.** —***SYN.*** see **common.**

popular etymology, folk etymology.

popular front, a coalition of leftist and centrist political parties and other groups, as in France (1936–1939), to combat fascism and promote social reforms: also **people's front.**

pop·u·lar·i·ty (pop′yoo-lar′ə-ti), *n.* [Fr. *popularité;* L. *popularitas*], the state or quality of being popular.

pop·u·lar·i·za·tion (pop′yoo-lẽr-i-zā′shən, pop′yoo-lẽr-i-zā′shən), *n.* a popularizing or being popularized.

pop·u·lar·ize (pop′yoo-lə-rīz′), *v.t.* [POPULARIZED (-rīzd′), POPULARIZING], to make popular.

pop·u·lar·ly (pop′yoo-lẽr-li), *adv.* 1. in a popular manner; so as to be popular. 2. by the people; generally. Abbreviated **pop.**

pop·u·late (pop′yoo-lāt′), *v.t.* [POPULATED (-id), POPULATING], [< ML. *populatus*, pp. of *populare*, to populate < L. *populus*, the people], 1. to be or become the inhabitants of; inhabit. 2. to supply with inhabitants; people.

pop·u·la·tion (pop′yoo-lā′shən), *n.* [LL. *populatio*], 1. all the people in a country, region, etc. 2. the number of these. 3. a (specified) part of the people in a given area: as, the Japanese *population* of Hawaii. 4. a populating or being populated. 5. in *biology*, all the organisms living in a given area. 6. in *statistics*, a group of items or individuals. Abbreviated **pop., p.**

Pop·u·lism (pop′yoo-liz′m), *n.* [< L. *populus*, the people; + *-ism*], 1. the theory and policies of Populists. 2. the Populistic movement.

Pop·u·list (pop′yoo-list), *n.* [see POPULISM], a member of the People's party: see **People's party.** *adj.* Populistic.

Pop·u·lis·tic (pop′yoo-lis′tik), *adj.* 1. of Populists or their views. 2. having to do with the People's party.

pop·u·lous (pop′yoo-ləs), *adj.* [L. *populosus*], full of people; thickly populated.

por·bea·gle (pôr′bē′g'l), *n.* [< Corn. dial.; form suggests Fr. *porc bégueule*, lit., pig with gaping mouth (cf. BEAGLE, PORCUPINE, PORPOISE)], any of a number of related large, fierce sharks of northern seas, which bring forth living young rather than eggs.

por·ce·lain (pôr′s'l-in, pōrs′lin), *n.* [Fr. *porcelaine;* It. *porcellana* < *porcella*, little pig: so called from its resemblance to the Venus shell, the upper surface of the shell resembling the curve of a pig's back], 1. a fine, white, translucent, hard earthenware with a transparent glaze; china. 2. porcelain dishes or ornaments, collectively. *adj.* made of porcelain.

por·ce·la·ne·ous, por·cel·la·ne·ous (pôr′sə-lā′ni-əs, pōr′sə-lā′ni-əs), *adj.* of or resembling porcelain.

porch (pôrch, pōrch), *n.* [ME. & OFr. *porche;* L. *porticus* < *porta*, a gate, entrance, passage], 1. a covered entrance to a building, usually projecting from the wall and having a separate roof. 2. an open or enclosed gallery or room on the outside of a building; veranda. 3. a portico.

the Porch, a portico in Athens where the Stoic philosopher Zeno taught his disciples.

por·cine (pôr′sīn, pôr′sin), *adj.* [Fr. *porcin, porcine;* L. *porcinus* < *porcus*, a hog], of or like pigs or hogs.

por·cu·pine (pôr′kyoo-pīn′), *n.* [*pl.* PORCUPINES (-pīnz′), PORCUPINE; see PLURAL, II, D, 1], [ME. *porkepyn, pork despyne;* OFr. *porc espin*, spinous hog, spine hog < L. *porcus*, a pig + *spina*, a spine, thorn], any of a number of related gnawing animals having coarse hair mixed with long, stiff, sharp spines.

PORCUPINE (3 ft. long)

porcupine anteater, an echidna, an anteating mammal resembling a porcupine.

pore (pôr, pōr), *v.i.* [PORED (pôrd, pōrd), PORING], [ME. *poren, pouren;* the form suggests AS. **purian;* ? doublet of **pyrian* (cf. PEER, *v.*)], 1. to gaze intently or steadily. 2. to look searchingly; read carefully; study minutely (with *over*): as, he *pored* over the book. 3. to think deeply and thoroughly; ponder; meditate (with *on, upon*, or *over*): as, he *pored* on the wonders of science.

pore (pôr, pōr), *n.* [ME. *pore, poor;* L. *porus;* Gr. *poros*], 1. originally, a passage; channel. 2. a tiny opening, usually microscopic, as in plant leaves, skin, etc., through which fluids may be absorbed or discharged. 3. a similar opening in rock or other substances.

por·gy (pôr′gi, pôr′ji), *n.* [*pl.* PORGIES (-giz, -jiz), PORGY; see PLURAL, II, D, 1], [prob. var. of *pogy*, with intrusive *-r* common in the Coastal New England dial.], any of a number of related salt-water food fishes having spiny fins and a wide body covered with large scales.

po·rif·er·an (pō-rif′ẽr-ən), *n.* [< L. *porus*, pore + *ferre*, to bear; + *-an*], in *zoology*, any of the family of sponges.

po·rif·er·ous (pō-rif′ẽr-əs), *adj.* [< *poriferan* + *-ous*], 1. having pores. 2. in *zoology*, of the sponges.

po·rism (pôr′iz'm, pō′riz'm), *n.* [ME. *porysme;* ML. *porisma;* Gr. *porisma*, lit., a thing brought < *porizein*, to bring; see PORE], in *ancient mathematics*, a geometrical proposition variously defined; specifically, *a)* a proposition deduced from some other demonstrated proposition; corollary. *b)* a proposition that uncovers the possibility of finding such conditions as to make a specific problem capable of innumerable solutions.

pork (pôrk, pōrk), *n.* [ME. & OFr. *porc;* L. *porcus,* a pig], 1. originally, a pig or hog. 2. the flesh of a pig or hog, used, fresh or cured, as food. 3. [Slang], money, position, etc. received from the government through political patronage.

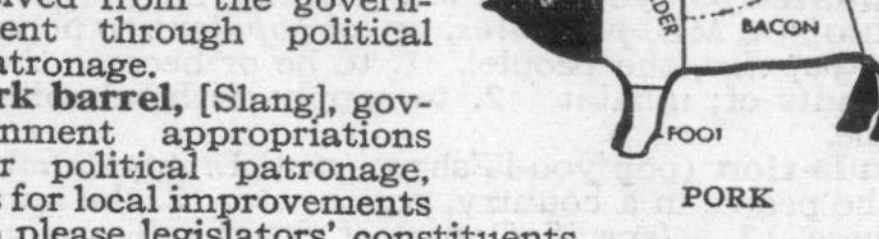

PORK

pork barrel, [Slang], government appropriations for political patronage, as for local improvements to please legislators' constituents.

pork·er (pôr′kẽr, pōr′kẽr), *n.* a hog, especially a young one, fattened for use as food.

pork pie, 1. a meat pie made of chopped pork, usually eaten cold. 2. a soft hat with a round, flat crown, worn by men: now often **pork·pie** (pôrk′pī′, pōrk′-pī′), *n.*

PORK PIE (hat)

pork·y (pôr′ki, pōr′ki), *adj.* [PORKIER (-ki-ẽr), PORKIEST (-ki-ist)], 1. of or like pork. 2. fat, as though overfed.

por·no·graph·ic (pôr′nə-graf′ik), *adj.* of, or having the nature of, pornography; obscene.

por·nog·ra·phy (pôr-nog′rə-fi), *n.* [< Gr. *pornē,* a prostitute; + *-graphy*], 1. originally, a description of prostitutes and their trade; hence, 2. writings, pictures, etc. intended to arouse sexual desire.

po·ros·i·ty (pô-ros′ə-ti, pō-ros′ə-ti), *n.* [*pl.* POROSITIES (-tiz)], [ME. *porositee;* ML. *porositas* < *porosus* < L. *porus,* a pore], 1. the quality or state of being porous. 2. the ratio of the volume of a material's pores to that of its solid content. 3. anything porous. 4. a pore.

po·rous (pôr′əs, pō′rəs), *adj.* full of pores, or tiny holes through which fluids, air, or light may pass.

por·phy·rin (pôr′fə-rin), *n.* [< *hematoporphyrin* < *hemato-* + Gr. *porphyra,* purple, purple product of hemoglobin decomposition], any of a group of pyrrole derivatives of hemoglobin and chlorophyll, containing no iron or magnesium.

por·phy·rit·ic (pôr′fə-rit′ik), *adj.* [ME. *porphiritike;* ML. *porphyriticus* < L. *porphyrites*], 1. of porphyry. 2. like porphyry; having distinct crystals embedded in a fine-grained mass.

por·phy·roid (pôr′fə-roid′), *n.* a rock that resembles, or has the structure of, porphyry.

por·phy·ry (pôr′fə-ri), *n.* [*pl.* PORPHYRIES (-riz)], [ME. *purfire, porfirie;* OFr. *porfire;* ML. *porphyreus* < Gr. *porphyros,* purple], 1. originally, a hard Egyptian rock having red and white feldspar crystals embedded in a fine-grained, dark-red or purplish groundmass. 2. any igneous rock of similar texture.

por·poise (pôr′pəs), *n.* [*pl.* PORPOISES (-iz), PORPOISE; see PLURAL, II, D, 1], [ME. *porpoys, porpeys;* OFr. *porpeis, porpois,* lit., swine fish < L. *porcus,* a pig, swine + *piscis,* a fish], 1. any of a number of small related cetaceans, dark above and white below, with a triangle-shaped fin on the back, a blunt snout, and many teeth. 2. a dolphin or any of several other small cetaceans.

por·ridge (pôr′ij, por′ij), *n.* [altered < *pottage* by confusion with ME. *porrey;* OFr. *poree;* LL. *porrata,* leek broth < L. *porrum,* leek], 1. originally, pottage. 2. [Chiefly British], a soft food made of cereal or meal boiled in water or milk until thick.

por·rin·ger (pôr′in-jẽr, por′in-jẽr), *n.* [earlier *pottanger, pottager* < Fr. *potager,* soup dish; altered by association with *porridge*], a bowl for porridge; small, shallow bowl of pewter, etc., used for cereal, children's food, etc.

Por·se·na, Lars (lärz pôr′si-nə), an Etruscan king of the 6th century B.C. who, according to legend, attacked Rome in an unsuccessful effort to restore Tarquin to the throne.

Por·sen·na, Lars (pôr-sen′ə), Lars Porsena.

port (pôrt, pōrt), *n.* [ME. < OFr. & AS. *port;* both < L. *portus,* a haven], 1. a harbor. 2. a city or town with a harbor where ships arrive and depart, and load or unload cargoes. 3. a port of entry. Abbreviated **Pt.**

port (pôrt, pōrt), *n.* [< *Oporto,* city in Portugal], a sweet, fortified, usually dark-red wine.

port (pôrt, pōrt), *v.t.* [ME. *porten;* OFr. *porter;* L. *portare,* to carry], 1. originally, to carry. 2. to carry, hold, or place (a rifle or sword) diagonally in front of one, crossing the left shoulder, as for inspection. *n.* [ME. *porte;* OFr. < the *v.*], 1. the manner in which one carries oneself; carriage; deportment; demeanor. 2. the position of porting a weapon. 3. purport; meaning.

port (pôrt, pōrt), *n.* [< *port* (harbor), with reference to the side opposite the steering oar; cf. LARBOARD], the left-hand side of a ship or airplane as one faces forward, toward the bow; larboard: opposed to *starboard.* ***adj.*** of or on the port. ***v.t. & v.i.*** to move or turn (the helm) to the left.

port (pôrt, pōrt), *n.* [ME. *porte, port;* OFr. *porte;* L. *porta,* a door], 1. [Obs. except Scot.], a portal; gateway; hence, 2. *a*) a porthole. *b*) the covering for this. 3. an opening, as in a cylinder face or valve face, for the passage of steam, gas, water, etc.

Port., 1. Portugal. 2. Portuguese.

port·a·bil·i·ty (pôr′tə-bil′ə-ti, pōr′tə-bil′ə-ti), *n.* the condition or quality of being portable.

port·a·ble (pôr′tə-b'l, pōr′tə-b'l), *adj.* [ME.; LL. *portabilis* < L. *portare,* to carry], 1. that can be carried. 2. easily carried. 3. [Obs.], bearable; endurable.

por·tage (pôr′tij, pōr′tij), *n.* [ME.; OFr.; ML. *portaticum* < L. *portare,* to carry], 1. the act of carrying or transporting. 2. its cost. 3. a carrying or transporting of boats and supplies overland between navigable rivers, lakes, etc., as during a canoe trip. 4. any place or route over which this is done. ***v.t. & v.i.*** [PORTAGED (-tijd), PORTAGING], to carry or transport (boats, etc.) over a portage.

por·tal (pôr′t'l, pōr′t'l), *n.* [ME.; OFr.; ML. *portale,* orig. neut. of *portalis,* of a door < L. *porta,* a gate], 1. a doorway, gate, or entrance, especially a large and imposing one. 2. [Poetic], any entrance: often figurative, as, the *portal* of wisdom. 3. the portal vein. ***adj.*** [ML. *portalis*], designating, of, or like the vein carrying blood from the intestines, stomach, etc. to the liver.

por·tal-to-por·tal pay (pôr′t'l-tə-pôr′t'l, pōr′t'l-tə-pōr′t'l), wages for workers based on the total time spent from the moment of entering the mine, factory, etc. until the moment of leaving it.

por·ta·men·to (pôr′tə-men′tō; It. pôr′tä-men′tô), *n.* [*pl.* PORTAMENTI (-tē)], [It. < *portare,* to carry; L. *portare*], in *music,* a continuous gliding from one note to another, sounding all intervening tones; glide.

port·ance (pôr′t'ns, pōr′t'ns), *n.* [Early Mod. Eng. < Fr. *portance* < *porter,* to bear, carry; cf. -ANCE], [Archaic], conduct; bearing; carriage; demeanor.

Port Arthur, 1. a seaport in northeastern China: Japanese name, *Ryojun:* for pop. see **Dairen.** 2. a city in eastern Texas, on Sabine Lake: pop., 67,000.

por·ta·tive (pôr′tə-tiv, pōr′tə-tiv), *adj.* [ME. & OFr. *portatif,* lit., that is carried < L. *portatus,* pp. of *portare,* to carry + OFr. *-if* (cf. -IVE)], 1. of or having the power of carrying a load, charge, etc. 2. that can be carried; portable.

Port-au-Prince (pôrt′ō-prins′, pōrt′ō-prins′; Fr. pôrt′-ō′prans′), *n.* seaport and capital of Haiti: pop., 200,000.

port authority, a governmental commission in charge of the traffic, regulations, etc. of a port.

Port Chester, a city in southeastern New York, on Long Island Sound: pop., 25,000.

port·cul·lis (pôrt-kul′is, pōrt-kul′is), *n.* [ME. *portcoles;* OFr. *porte coleïce; porte,* a gate + *coleïce,* fem. of *coleis,* gliding, sliding < L. *colare,* to strain, filter], a large, heavy iron grating suspended by chains and lowered between grooves to bar the gateway of a castle or fortified town.

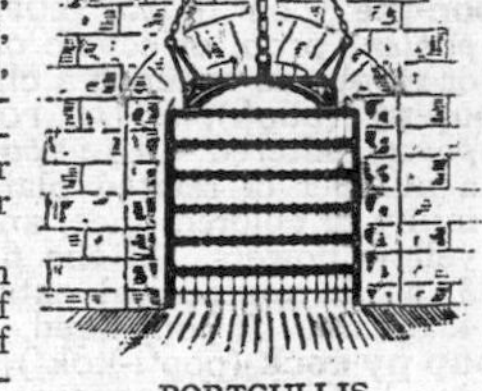
PORTCULLIS

Porte (pôrt, pōrt), *n.* [Fr., in *la Sublime Porte,* transl. of Turk. *Babi Ali,* the chief office of the Ottoman Empire, lit. the High Gate: from the gate (*bāb*) of the palace at which justice was administered], the Ottoman Turkish government.

porte-co·chere (pôrt′kō-shâr′; Fr. pôrt′kô′shâr′), *n.* [Fr. *porte,* a gate + *cochère,* coach, fem. adj. < *coche;* see COACH], 1. a large entrance gateway into a courtyard. 2. a kind of porch roof projecting over a driveway at an entrance, as of a house. Also **porte-cochère.**

Port Elizabeth, a seaport in southern Cape province, Union of South Africa: pop., 189,000.

‡porte·mon·naie (pôrt′mô′nā′; Eng. pôrt′mun′i, pōrt′-mun′i), *n.* [Fr., carry-money], a purse or pocketbook.

por·tend (pôr-tend′, pōr-tend′), *v.t.* [ME. *portenden;* L. *portendere,* old form of *protendere; pro-,* forth + *tendere,* to stretch; cf. PORTENT], to be an omen or warning of; foreshadow; presage.

por·tent (pôr′tent, pōr′tent), *n.* [L. *portentum* < *portendere;* see PORTEND], 1. something that portends an event about to occur, especially an unfortunate or evil event; an omen. 2. a portending; significance: as, a howl of dire *portent;* hence, 3. something regarded as portentous; marvel; prodigy.

por·ten·tous (pôr-ten′təs, pōr-ten′təs), *adj.* [L. *portentosus* < *portentum,* portent], 1. that portends; portending evil; ominous. 2. arousing awe or amazement; marvelous; prodigious. —***SYN.*** see **ominous.**

por·ter (pôr′tẽr, pōr′tẽr), *n.* [ME.; OFr. *portier;* LL. *portarius* < L. *porta,* a gate], a doorman; gatekeeper.

por·ter (pôr′tẽr, pōr′tẽr), *n.* [ME. *portour, portere;* OFr. *porteour;* LL. *portator* < L. *portare,* to carry], 1. a person who carries things; especially, a man who carries luggage, etc. for hire or as an attendant at a railroad station, hotel, etc. 2. a man who sweeps, cleans, does errands, etc. in a bank, store, restaurant, etc. 3. a railroad employee who waits on passengers in a parlor car or sleeper. 4. [abbrev. of *porter's ale*], a dark-brown beer resembling light stout, made from charred or browned malt.

Por·ter, Cole (kōl pôr'tẽr, pōr'tẽr), 1893– ; American composer of popular songs.

Porter, David, 1780–1843; American naval officer and diplomat; father of *David Dixon.*

Porter, David Dix·on (dik's'n), 1813–1891; American admiral.

Porter, Noah, 1811–1892; American clergyman, educator, and editor.

Porter, William Sydney, see **Henry, O.**

por·ter·age (pôr'tẽr-ij, pōr'tẽr-ij), *n.* [see -AGE], 1. a porter's work. 2. the charge for this.

por·ter·house (pôr'tẽr-hous', pōr'tẽr-hous'), *n.* 1. formerly, a place where beer, porter, etc. (and sometimes steaks and chops) were served. 2. a porterhouse steak.

porterhouse steak, [said to be so named as a specialty at a former New York porterhouse], a choice cut of beef from between the tenderloin and the sirloin.

port·fo·li·o (pôrt-fō'li-ō', pōrt-fōl'yō), *n.* [*pl.* PORTFOLIOS (-ōz', -yōz)], [earlier *porto folio* < It. *portafoglio* < *portare* (L. *portare*), to carry + *foglio* (L. *folium*), a leaf], 1. a flat, portable case, usually of leather, for carrying loose sheets of paper, manuscripts, drawings, etc.; brief case. 2. such a case for state documents; hence, 3. the office of a minister of state: as, a minister without *portfolio*. 4. a list of the stocks, bonds, and commercial paper owned by a bank, an investor, etc.

port·hole (pôrt'hōl', pōrt'hōl'), *n.* 1. an opening in a ship's side to admit light and air, load cargo, or fire a gun through. 2. an opening to shoot through, in the wall of a fort, etc.; embrasure. 3. an opening shaped somewhat like this, as in a furnace door.

Port Huron, a port in southeastern Michigan, on the St. Clair River and Lake Huron: pop., 36,000.

Por·ti·a (pôr'shə, pōr'shi-ə), [L. *Porcia*, fem. of *Porcius*, name of a Roman gens; prob. < *porcus*, a hog], a feminine name. *n.* the heroine of Shakespeare's *Merchant of Venice.*

por·ti·co (pôr'ti-kō', pōr'ti-kō'), *n.* [*pl.* PORTICOES, PORTICOS (-kōz')], [It.; L. *porticus;* see PORCH], a porch or covered walk, consisting of a roof supported by columns; colonnade.

PORTICO

por·tiere, por·tière (pôr-tyâr', pōr'ti-âr'), *n.* [Fr. *portière* < *porte*, a door], a heavy curtain hung in a doorway.

por·tion (pôr'shən, pōr'shən), *n.* [ME. *porcioun;* OFr. *porcion;* L. *portio, portionis*, a portion; akin to *pars, partis*, a part < *partiri*, to divide], 1. a part or limited quantity of anything, especially that allotted to a person; share. 2. the part of an estate received by an heir. 3. the part of a man's money or property contributed by his bride; a marriage portion; dowry. 4. the part of experience supposedly allotted to a person by fate; one's lot; destiny. 5. the part of a meal or quantity of food served to a person; serving; helping. *v.t.* [OFr. *portionner*, to divide, separate], 1. to divide into portions. 2. to give as a portion to; apportion. 3. to give a portion to; endow; dower. —*SYN.* see **fate, part.**

Port·land (pōrt'lənd), *n.* 1. a city on the coast of southern Maine: pop., 73,000. 2. a city in northwestern Oregon: pop., 373,000.

portland cement, [so called from resemblance of the concrete made from it to stone quarried on the Isle of *Portland*, England], [sometimes P-], a kind of cement that hardens under water, made by burning a mixture of limestone and clay or similar materials.

port·li·ness (pôrt'li-nis, pōrt'li-nis), *n.* the quality or state of being portly; corpulence.

Port Louis, seaport and capital of Mauritius, in the Indian Ocean: pop., 104,000.

port·ly (pôrt'li, pōrt'li), *adj.* [PORTLIER (-li-ẽr), PORTLIEST (-li-ist)], 1. originally, having a dignified and stately port or demeanor; hence, 2. stout; obese.

port·man·teau (pôrt-man'tō, pōrt-man'tō), *n.* [*pl.* PORTMANTEAUS, PORTMANTEAUX (-tōz)], [Fr. *portemanteau* < *porter*, to carry + *manteau*, a cloak], 1. originally, a case or bag for carrying clothes on a trip. 2. a stiff leather suitcase that opens like a book into two compartments.

portmanteau word, a word that is a combination of two other words in form and meaning (e.g., *smog*, from *smoke* and *fog*).

Port Mores·by (môrz'bi, mōrz'bi), a seaport in southeastern New Guinea; capital of joint administration of Territories of Papua and New Guinea: pop., 15,000.

Por·to (pôr'too), *n.* Oporto: the Portuguese name.

Porto A·le·gre (ä-le'gri), a seaport in southeastern Brazil: pop., 375,000.

port of entry, any place where customs officials are stationed to check the entry of foreign goods into a country.

Port of Spain, seaport and capital of Trinidad and of the West Indies Federation: pop., 99,000.

Por·to No·vo (pôr'tō, pōr'tō nō'vō), seaport and capital of Dahomey, on the Gulf of Guinea: pop., 32,000.

Por·to Ri·can (pôr'tə, pōr'tə rē'kən), Puerto Rican.

Por·to Ri·co (pôr'tə, pōr'tə rē'kō), Puerto Rico.

Port Phillip Bay, a bay off Melbourne, Australia.

por·trait (pôr'trāt, pōr'trit), *n.* [Fr., pp. of *portraire;* see PORTRAY], 1. originally, a drawn, painted, or carved picture of something. 2. a picture of a person, especially of his face, drawn, painted, photographed, etc. from life. 3. a description, dramatic portrayal, etc. of a person.

por·trait·ist (pôr'trāt-ist, pōr'trāt-ist), *n.* a person who makes portraits.

por·trai·ture (pôr'tri-chẽr, pōr'tri-chẽr), *n.* [ME. *purtreiture*, etc.; OFr.], 1. the process, practice, or art of portraying. 2. a portrait. 3. portraits collectively.

por·tray (pôr-trā', pōr-trā'), *v.t.* [ME. *purtreien;* OFr. *pourtraire, portraire;* L. *protrahere*, to draw forth; *pro-*, forth + *trahere*, to draw], 1. to make a picture or portrait of; depict; delineate. 2. to make a word picture of; describe graphically. 3. to picture on the stage.

por·tray·al (pôr-trā'əl, pōr-trā'əl), *n.* 1. the act of portraying. 2. a portrait; description; representation.

por·tress (pôr'tris, pōr'tris), *n.* a woman porter (doorkeeper).

Port Royal, 1. a town in South Carolina, on Port Royal Island: colony established by the French in 1562. 2. a town in southeastern Jamaica.

Port Sa·id (pôrt sä-ēd', pōrt sä'id), a seaport in Egypt, at the Mediterranean end of the Suez Canal: pop., 227,000.

Ports·mouth (pôrts'məth, pōrts'məth), *n.* 1. a seaport in Southampton, England: pop., 220,000. 2. a seaport in southeastern Virginia, near Norfolk: pop., 115,000. 3. a city in south central Ohio, on the Ohio River: pop., 34,000. 4. a seaport in southeastern New Hampshire: pop., 26,000: treaty signed here in 1905 between Russia and Japan.

Por·tu·gal (pôr'chə-g'l, pōr'choo-gəl; Port. pôr'too-gäl'), *n.* a country in southwestern Europe, on the Atlantic: area, 35,490 sq. mi.; pop., 9,149,000; capital, Lisbon: ancient name, *Lusitania:* abbreviated **Port., Pg.**

Por·tu·guese (pôr'chə-gēz', pōr'choo-gēz'), *adj.* of Portugal, its people, their language, or culture. *n.* 1. [*pl.* PORTUGUESE], a native or inhabitant of Portugal. 2. the Romance language spoken in Portugal and Brazil. Abbreviated **Port., Pg.**

Portuguese East Africa, Mozambique, a Portuguese overseas territory in southeastern Africa.

Portuguese Guinea, a Portuguese overseas territory on the coast of western Africa: area, 13,948 sq. mi.; pop., 511,000; capital, Bissau.

Portuguese India, a Portuguese overseas territory consisting of Goa, Damao, and Diu, on the west coast of India: capital, Nova Goa.

Portuguese man-of-war, any of several large, tubelike, warm-sea animals having a large, bladderlike sac, with a saillike structure on top, which enables them to float on the water.

Portuguese Timor, the Portuguese overseas territory on eastern Timor Island, in the East Indies: area, 7,330 sq. mi.; pop., 442,000; capital, Dili.

Portuguese West Africa, Angola, a Portuguese overseas territory in southwestern Africa.

por·tu·lac·a (pôr'choo-lak'ə, pōr'choo-lak'ə), *n.* [L., purslane], any of a number of related fleshy plants with yellow, pink, or purple flowers.

por·tu·la·ca·ceous (pôr'choo-lə-kā'shəs, pōr'choo-lə-kā'shəs), *adj.* [< Mod. L. *Portulacaceae*, name of the family; see PORTULACA], of the purslane family of plants.

pos., 1. positive. 2. possessive.

pose (pōz), *v.t.* [POSED (pōzd), POSING], [ME.; OFr. *poser*, to put in position; L. *pausare* (see PAUSE), confused in meaning by association in LL. with *positus*, pp. of *ponere*, to place, put], 1. to put forth; lay down; assert, as a claim, argument, etc. 2. to put forward or propose, as a question, problem, etc. 3. to put (an artist's model, etc.) in a certain attitude. *v.i.* 1. to assume or hold a certain attitude, as in having one's portrait made. 2. to strike attitudes; attitudinize: as, look at her *posing*. 3. to assume or maintain a mental attitude; set oneself up: as, he *poses* as a scholar. *n.* [OFr. < the *v.*], 1. a bodily attitude, especially one held for or pictured by an artist, photographer, etc. 2. a mental attitude assumed for effect; pretense.

SYN.—**pose** refers to an attitude or manner that is assumed for the effect that it will have on others (her generosity is a mere *pose*); **affectation** is used of a specific instance of artificial behavior intended obviously to impress others (an *affectation* of speech); a **mannerism** is a peculiarity in behavior, speech, etc. (often originally an affectation) that has become habitual and unconscious (his *mannerism* of raising one eyebrow in surprise); **airs** is used of an affected pretense of superior manners and graces (she's always putting on *airs*). See also **posture**.

pose (pōz), *v.t.* [POSED (pōzd), POSING], [abbrev. < *oppose* or *appose*], 1. [Obs.], to question. 2. to puzzle or disconcert, as by an almost unanswerable question; baffle; nonplus.

Po·sei·don (pō-sī'd'n), *n.* [L.; Gr. *Poseidōn*], in *Greek mythology*, god of the sea and of horses: identified by the Romans with Neptune.

Po·sen (pō'zən), *n.* Poznán: the German name.

pos·er (pōz'ẽr), *n.* a person who poses; affected person.

pos·er (pōz'ẽr), *n.* a baffling question or problem.

po·seur (pō-zūr'; Fr. pô'zër'), *n.* [Fr.], a poser (person who poses).

pos·it (poz'it), *v.t.* [< L. *positus*, pp. of *ponere*, to place], 1. to set in place or position; situate. 2. to set down as fact; assume; postulate.

po·si·tion (pə-zish'ən), *n.* [Fr.; L. *positio* < *positus*, pp. of *ponere*, to place; ME. (Chaucer) has *possession* rendering the L. word], 1. a positing; placing. 2. a positing of a proposition; affirmation. 3. the manner in which a person or thing is placed or arranged; attitude; posture; disposition. 4. a person's mental attitude toward or opinion on a subject; stand: as, the senator's *position* on international affairs. 5. the place where a person or thing is, especially in relation to other persons or things; location; situation; site: as, the ship's *position*. 6. the usual or proper place of a person or thing; station: as, the players were in *position*. 7. a location or condition in which one has the advantage: as, jockey for *position;* hence, 8. a strategic military site. 9. a person's relative place, as in society; rank; status. 10. a place high in society, business, etc.: as, a man of *position*. 11. a post of employment; office; job: as, he's got a good *position*. 12. in *arithmetic*, a method of finding an unknown quantity by assuming various trial values for it until the true value is arrived at: also called *rule of trial and error*. 13. in *music*, *a)* the arrangement of the notes of a chord with respect to their relative closeness or distance apart: as, open *position*. *b)* the location of the left hand on the finger board of a violin: as, second *position*. *c)* a corresponding location on a trombone slide. *v.t.* 1. to put in a particular position; place. 2. [Rare], to locate.

SYN.—**position** applies to any specific employment for salary or wages, but often connotes white-collar or professional employment; **situation** now usually refers to a position that is open or to one that is desired (*situation* wanted as instructor); **office** refers to a position of authority or trust, especially in government, a corporation, etc.; a **post** is a position or office that carries heavy responsibilities, especially one to which a person is appointed; **job** is now the common, comprehensive equivalent for any of the preceding terms.

po·si·tion·al (pə-zish'ən-'l), *adj.* of position.

pos·i·tive (poz'ə-tiv), *adj.* [ME. & OFr. *positif;* L. *positivus* < *positus*, pp. of *ponere*, to place], 1. formally or arbitrarily set; conventional; artificial: opposed to *natural*. 2. definitely set; explicitly laid down; admitting of no question or modification; express; precise; specific: as, *positive* instructions. 3. having the mind set or settled; confident; assured: as, a *positive* person; hence, 4. overconfident; dogmatic; opinionated. 5. showing resolution or agreement; affirmative; certain: as, a *positive* answer. 6. tending in the direction regarded as that of increase, progress, etc.: as, clockwise motion is *positive*. 7. making a definite contribution; constructive: as, *positive* criticism. 8. unrelated to anything else; independent of circumstances; absolute; unqualified: distinguished from *relative, comparative*. 9. that has, or is considered as having, real existence; characterized by the presence of certain attributes, not their absence: as, a *positive* evil. 10. based, or asserted as based, on reality or facts: as, *positive* proof. 11. concerned only with real things and experience; empirical; practical: distinguished from *speculative, theoretical*. 12. [Colloq.], complete; downright; out-and-out: as, a *positive* devil. 13. in *bacteriology*, showing the presence of a specific disease, condition, etc. 14. in *biology*, directed toward the source of a stimulus: as, *positive* tropism. 15. in *electricity*, *a)* designating or of the kind of electricity generated on a glass rod when it is rubbed with a piece of silk; hence, *b)* of, generating, or charged with positive electricity. Opposed to *negative*. 16. in *grammar*, *a)* of an adjective or adverb in its simple, uncompared form or degree. *b)* of this degree. Distinguished from *comparative, superlative*. 17. in *mathematics*, greater than zero; plus. 18. in *photography*, with the lights and shades corresponding to those of the subject: opposed to *negative*. *n.* something positive, as a degree, quality, quantity, battery terminal, photographic print, etc. Abbreviated **pos.** —*SYN.* see **sure**.

pos·i·tiv·ism (poz'ə-tiv-iz'm), *n.* [Fr. *positivisme* < *positif*], 1. the quality or state of being positive; certainty; assurance. 2. dogmatism. 3. a system of philosophy that is based solely on the positive data of sense experience; empiricism; especially, [also P-], a system of philosophy, originated by Auguste Comte, which is based solely on positive, observable, scientific facts and their relations to each other and to natural law: it rejects speculation on or search for ultimate origins.

pos·i·tiv·ist (poz'ə-tiv-ist), *n.* [Fr. *positiviste*], a believer in positivism. *adj.* positivistic.

pos·i·tiv·is·tic (poz'ə-tiv-is'tik), *adj.* of or characteristic of positivism or positivists.

pos·i·tron (poz'ə-tron'), *n.* [*positive* + *electron*], the positive counterpart of an electron, having approximately the same mass and magnitude of charge.

poss., 1. possession. 2. possessive. 3. possibly.

pos·se (pos'i), *n.* [ML., power, armed force; L. inf., to be able], 1. *a)* the body of men liable to be summoned by a sheriff to assist him in keeping the peace, etc. *b)* a band of men, usually armed, so summoned: in full, **posse comitatus**. 2. any body of men armed with legal authority.

in posse, potentially.

‡**pos·se co·mi·ta·tus** (pos'i kom'ə-tā'təs), [ML. *posse*, power (< L. *posse*, to be able) + *comitatus*, county < *comes*, a count], a posse (sense 1).

pos·sess (pə-zes'), *v.t.* [OFr. *possessier* < L. *possessus*, pp. of *possidere*, to possess < *pos-* (of obscure origin; ? akin to *post*, after) + *sedere*, to sit], 1. to have as belonging to one; own. 2. to have as an attribute, quality, faculty, etc.: as, he *possesses* wisdom. 3. to have knowledge or mastery of (a language, etc.). 4. to gain strong influence or control over; dominate: as, the idea *possessed* him. 5. to keep control over; maintain: as, *possess* your mind in peace. 6. to have sexual intercourse with. 7. to put in possession of; cause to have. 8. [Archaic], to seize; win; gain. 9. [Archaic], to cause to be possessed, as by a passion. —*SYN.* see **have**.

pos·sessed (pə-zest'), *adj.* [pp. of *possess*], 1. owned. 2. controlled by an evil spirit; crazed; mad.

possessed of, in possession of.

pos·ses·sion (pə-zesh'ən), *n.* [ME.; OFr.; L. *possessio*], 1. a possessing or being possessed; ownership, occupancy, hold, etc. 2. anything possessed. 3. *pl.* property; wealth. 4. any territory belonging to an outside country. 5. self-possession. Abbreviated **poss.**

pos·ses·sive (pə-zes'iv), *adj.* [L. *possessivus*], 1. of possession, or ownership. 2. showing, or characterized by a desire for, possession: as, a *possessive* person, *possessive* gestures. 3. in *grammar*, designating or of a case, form, or construction expressing possession or some like relationship: in English, this is expressed (*a*) by a final *s* (of nouns and some pronouns) preceded or followed by an apostrophe, or sometimes by an apostrophe only, following a final *s* sound (e.g., *John's* book, *men's* lives, *boys'* games, *conscience'* sake); (*b*) by change of form of pronouns (e.g., *my, mine, your, yours, his, her, hers, its, our, ours, their, theirs, whose*); (*c*) by *of* preceding a form in the objective case (e.g., the lives *of men*) or preceding a form in the possessive case (e.g., a play *of Shakespeare's*, a friend *of mine* — called a *double possessive*): cf. **genitive.** *n.* in *grammar*, 1. the possessive case. 2. a possessive form or construction. Abbreviated **poss., pos.**

pos·ses·sor (pə-zes'ẽr), *n.* [ME. & OFr. *possessour;* L.], a person who possesses; owner.

pos·ses·so·ry (pə-zes'ẽr-i), *adj.* 1. of, being, or characterizing a possessor. 2. of or based upon possession.

pos·set (pos'it), *n.* [ME. *poshote, poshoote, possot;* the early forms suggest ME. *hote, hoot*, hot, as the 2d element; the 1st may be ME. *pott* or AS. *pos*, head cold], a hot drink made of milk curdled with ale, wine, etc., usually spiced.

pos·si·bil·i·ty (pos'ə-bil'ə-ti), *n.* 1. the quality or condition of being possible. 2. [*pl.* POSSIBILITIES (-tiz)], something that is possible.

pos·si·ble (pos'ə-b'l), *adj.* [ME.; OFr.; L. *possibilis* < *posse*, to be able < *potis*, able + *esse*, to be], 1. that can be; capable of existing. 2. that can be in the future; that may or may not happen: distinguished from *probable*. 3. that can be done, known, acquired, etc. by a person or thing expressed or implied. 4. that can be used, selected, done, etc., depending on circumstances; potential: as, a *possible* location. 5. that may be done, known, etc. if allowed; permissible. 6. [Colloq.], that can be put up with; tolerable.

SYN.—**possible** is used of anything that may exist, occur, be done, etc., depending on circumstances (a *possible* solution to a problem); **practicable** applies to that which can readily be effected under the prevailing conditions or by the means available (a *practicable* plan); **feasible** is used of that which can easily be carried through to a successful conclusion and, hence, connotes the desirability of doing so (a *feasible* enterprise). See also **probable.**

pos·si·bly (pos'ə-bli), *adv.* 1. by any possible means; in any case: as, it can't *possibly* work. 2. by some possibility; perhaps; maybe: as, it may *possibly* be so. Abbreviated **poss.**

pos·sum (pos'əm), *n.* [Colloq.], an opossum.

play possum, to pretend or feign ignorance, illness, etc.: opossums feign death when attacked.

post (pōst), *n.* [ME.; AS.; L. *postis*, a post, doorpost], 1. a piece of wood, metal, etc., usually long and square or cylindrical, set upright to support a building, sign, gate, etc.; pillar; pole. 2. anything resembling this in shape or purpose. 3. any place originally marked by or associated with a post, as the starting point of a horse race. Abbreviated **P., p.** *v.t.* 1. to put up (a poster, notice, etc.) on a wall, post, or other conspicuous place (also with *up*). 2. to announce, publicize, or advertise by posting notices, etc.: as, *post* a reward. 3. to put posters, etc. on; placard. 4. to warn persons against trespassing on (grounds, etc.) by posted notices. 5. to put (a person's name) on a posted or published list. 6. to denounce by a public notice. 7. to publish the name of (a ship) as lost or missing.

post (pōst), *n.* [Fr. *poste;* It. *posto;* LL. *postum;* contr. < L. *positum*, neut. pp. of *ponere*, to place], 1. the place where a soldier is stationed. 2. a place where a body of troops is stationed or is in occupation. 3. the troops at such a place; garrison. 4. a local unit of a veterans' organization. 5. in the British Army, either of two bugle calls (*first post* and *last post*) sounded at tattoo. 6. a place where a person is stationed, as at a machine. 7. a position or job, especially one to which a person is appointed. 8. a trading post. Abbreviated **P., p.** *v.t.* 1. to station at or assign to a post. 2. to appoint to a military post or command. —***SYN.*** see **position.**

post (pōst), *n.* [Fr. *poste;* It. *posta*, orig., a station; LL. *posta*, for L. *posita*, fem. pp. of *ponere*, to place], 1. originally, one of a number of riders or runners posted at intervals to carry letters and packages in relays or stages along a route or, later, to provide fresh horses for a courier; hence, 2. formerly, *a*) a postrider or courier. *b*) a stage of a post route. *c*) a post horse or a station for one. *d*) a packet (ship). 3. [Chiefly British], *a*) (the) mail. *b*) a post office. *c*) a mail box. *d*) [Dial.], a postman. 4. a size of paper, approximately 16 by 20 inches: so called because the original watermark was a postman's horn. Abbreviated **P., p.** *v.i.* 1. formerly, to travel in posts or stages; hence, 2. to travel fast; hasten. *v.t.* 1. originally, *a*) to send by or as by post. *b*) to hasten. 2. [Chiefly British], to mail; put in a mailbox, etc. 3. to inform, as of events (usually in the passive): as, he is kept well *posted.* 4. in *bookkeeping, a*) to transfer (an item) from a daybook, etc. to the ledger. *b*) to enter in the correct form and place. *c*) to enter all necessary items in (a ledger, etc.).

post- (pōst), [L. < *post*, behind, after], a prefix meaning: 1. *after in time, later, following*, as in *postgraduate, postglacial.* 2. *after in space, behind*, as in *postaxial.*

post·age (pōs'tij), *n.* [*post* (mail) + *-age*], the amount charged for mailing a letter or package.

postage stamp, a government stamp to be put on a letter or package as a sign that the postage has been prepaid: it is either a small printed gummed label or a design imprinted on an envelope, postal card, etc.

post·al (pōs't'l), *adj.* [Fr. < *poste*], having to do with mail or post offices. *n.* [Colloq.], a postal card.

postal card, 1. a card with a printed postage stamp, issued by a government for sending messages at a rate lower than that for letters. 2. loosely, a post card. Abbreviated **p.c.**

post·ax·i·al (pōst'ak'si-əl), *adj.* in *anatomy & zoology*, situated behind the axis of the body, as the posterior part of a limb.

post-bel·lum (pōst'bel'əm), *adj.* occurring after the war, specifically after the American Civil War.

‡post bel·lum (pōst bel'əm), [L.], after the war.

post·box (pōst'boks'), *n.* a mailbox.

post·boy (pōst'boi'), *n.* 1. formerly, a man or boy who rode with the post. 2. a letter carrier. 3. a postilion.

post card, 1. a postal card. 2. an unofficial card, often a picture card, that can be sent through the mail when a postage stamp is affixed. Abbreviated **p.c.**

post chaise, a closed, four-wheeled coach or carriage drawn by fast horses, which were changed at each post, formerly used to carry mail and passengers.

post·date (pōst'dāt'), *v.t.* [POSTDATED (-id), POSTDATING], 1. to assign a later date to than the actual date. 2. to write such a date on. 3. to be subsequent to.

post·di·lu·vi·an (pōst'di-lōō'vi-ən), *adj.* [*post-* + *diluvian*], living or happening after the Flood. *n.* a postdiluvian person.

post·er (pōs'tẽr), *n.* 1. a person who posts notices, bills, etc. 2. a relatively large printed card or sheet of paper, often illustrated, posted to advertise or publicize something; placard.

post·er (pōs'tẽr), *n.* 1. originally, a person who traveled by post, or rapidly. 2. a post horse.

poste res·tante (pōst' res-tänt'), [Fr., remaining post], 1. a notation on a letter asking that it be held at the post office until called for; hence, 2. [Chiefly British], a post-office department for letters of this kind.

pos·te·ri·or (pos-têr'i-ẽr), *adj.* [L., compar. of *posterus*, following < *post*, after], 1. later; following after; subsequent: opposed to *prior.* 2. coming after in order; succeeding. 3. located behind; hinder; rear: opposed to *anterior.* 4. in *anatomy*, at or toward the hind part of the body; dorsal. 5. in *botany*, on the side next to the main stem. *n. sometimes pl.* the buttocks.

pos·te·ri·or·i·ty (pos-têr'i-ôr'ə-ti), *n.* [ME. *posteriorite;* ML. *posterioritas*], 1. the condition or quality of being posterior. 2. posterior position in space or time.

pos·ter·i·ty (pos-ter'ə-ti), *n.* [ME. *posterite;* MFr. *postérité;* L. *posteritas* < *posterus;* see POSTERIOR], 1. all of a person's descendants: opposed to *ancestry.* 2. all succeeding generations; the future.

pos·tern (pōs'tẽrn, pos'tẽrn), *n.* [ME.; OFr. *posterne, posterle;* LL. *posterula*, a small back door, postern, dim. < *posterus;* see POSTERIOR], 1. formerly, a back door or gate; private entrance. 2. a hidden, often underground, entrance or exit to a castle; hence, 3. a way of escape, refuge, dishonorable entrance, etc. *adj.* 1. of or resembling a postern. 2. rear; posterior; hence, 3. lesser; inferior. 4. private; undercover.

Post Exchange, a nonprofit general store at an army post or camp, for the sale of small articles for personal use, refreshments, etc.: abbreviated **PX** (no period).

post·ex·il·i·an (pōst'eg-zil'i-ən, pōst'ek-sil'i-ən), *adj.* of that period of Jewish history following the Babylonian exile (6th century B.C.).

post·ex·il·ic (pōst'eg-zil'ik, pōst'ek-sil'ik), *adj.* postexilian.

post·fix (pōst'fiks), *n.* [*post-* + af*fix*], a suffix. *v.t.* (pōst'fiks'), to suffix.

post·free (pōst'frē'), *adj.* 1. that can be mailed free of charge. 2. [British], postpaid.

post·gla·cial (pōst'glā'shəl), *adj.* existing or happening after the glacial, or Pleistocene, Epoch.

post·grad·u·ate (pōst'graj'ōō-it, pōst'graj'ōō-āt'), *adj.* of or taking a course of study after graduation. *n.* a student taking such courses. Abbreviated **P.G.**

post·haste (pōst'hāst'), *n.* [Archaic], great haste, as of a postrider. *adv.* with great haste.

‡post hoc, er·go prop·ter hoc (pōst' hok ũr'gō prop'tẽr hok'), [L.], after this, therefore because of this: in *logic*, the fallacy of thinking that a happening which follows another must be its result.

post horse, formerly, a horse kept at a post house, or inn, for couriers and post chaises or for hire to travelers.

post house, formerly, an inn or other place where post horses were kept.

post·hu·mous (pos'choo-məs), *adj.* [LL., for L. *postumus*, last, superl. of *posterus* (see POSTERIOR); altered in LL. after *humus*, ground, or *humare*, to bury (as if meaning "born after the father is buried")], 1. born after the father's death. 2. published after the author's death. 3. arising or continuing after one's death.

post·hu·mous·ly (pos'choo-məs-li), *adv.* after death.

‡pos·tiche (pôs'tēsh'), *adj.* [Fr.; It. *posticcio;* LL. *appositicius* < L. *appositus;* see APPOSITE], 1. counterfeit; artificial. 2. superfluously or inappropriately decorative. *n.* 1. a substitute; counterfeit. 2. pretense.

pos·ti·cous (pos-tī'kəs), *adj.* [L. *posticus* < *post*, after, behind], in *botany*, posterior.

pos·til·ion, pos·til·lion (pō-til'yən, pos-til'yən), *n.* [Fr. *postillon;* It. *postiglione* < *posta*, a post], 1. a person who rides the left-hand horse of the leaders of a four-horse carriage. 2. one who rides the left-hand horse of a two-horse carriage when there is no driver.

post·im·pres·sion·ism (pōst'im-presh'ən-iz'm), *n.* the theory, practice, or methods of a group of late 19th-century painters who revolted against the objectivity and scientific naturalism of impressionism, and placed emphasis upon the subjective viewpoint of the artist rather than upon literal representation.

post·im·pres·sion·ist (pōst'im-presh'ən-ist), *adj.* of or characteristic of postimpressionism. *n.* an artist of the period or school of postimpressionism, as Cézanne, Van Gogh, or Gauguin.

post·im·pres·sion·is·tic (pōst'im-presh'ən-is'tik), *adj.* postimpressionist.

post·li·min·i·um (pōst'li-min'i-əm), *n.* [L. < *post*, behind + *limen, liminis*, threshold], in *international law*, the rule by which persons or things captured in war by an enemy regain their former rights when restored to the jurisdiction of their own country.

post·lim·i·ny (pōst'lim'ə-ni), *n.* postliminium.

post·lude (pōst'lōōd', pōst'lūd'), *n.* [*post-* + pre*lude*], 1. an organ voluntary played at the end of a church service. 2. a phrase or movement played at the end of a musical composition.

post·man (pōst'mən), *n.* [*pl.* POSTMEN (-mən)], a person who collects and delivers mail; letter carrier.

post·mark (pōst'märk'), *n.* a post-office mark stamped on a piece of mail, canceling the postage stamp and recording the date, time, and place of sending or receiving: abbreviated **pmk.** *v.t.* to stamp with a postmark.

post·mas·ter (pōst'mas'tẽr, pōst'mäs'tẽr), *n.* 1. originally, a person in charge of a station for post horses. 2. a person in charge of a post office: abbreviated **P.M.**

postmaster general, [*pl.* POSTMASTERS GENERAL, POSTMASTER GENERALS], the head of a government's postal system: abbreviated **P.M.G.**

post·mas·ter·ship (pōst′mas′tẽr-ship′, pōst′mäs′tẽr-ship′), *n.* [see -SHIP], the office or term of a postmaster.

post·me·rid·i·an (pōst′mə-rid′i-ən), *adj.* [L. *postmeridianus;* see POST- & MERIDIAN], of or occurring in the time after the sun has passed the meridian; of or happening after noon.

‡**post me·ri·di·em** (pōst mə-rid′i-em′), [L.], after noon: abbreviated **P.M., p.m.**

post·mil·len·ni·al (pōst′mə-len′i-əl), *adj.* existing or happening after the millennium.

post·mil·len·ni·al·ism (pōst′mə-len′i-əl-iz′m), *n.* the religious doctrine that the second coming of Christ will occur after, not at, the millennium.

post·mis·tress (pōst′mis′tris), *n.* a woman postmaster (sense 2).

post-mor·tem (pōst′môr′təm), *adj.* [L., after death], 1. happening, done, or made after death. 2. having to do with a post-mortem examination. *n.* a post-mortem examination. Abbreviated **p.m.**

post-mortem examination, the examination of a human body after death; autopsy.

post·na·tal (pōst′nā′t'l), *adj.* [*post-* + *natal*], after birth.

post·nup·tial (pōst′nup′shəl), *adj.* [*post-* + *nuptial*], after marriage.

post-o·bit (pōst′ō′bit, pōst′ob′it), *adj.* [contr. < L. *post obitum,* after death < *post,* after + *obitus,* death; see OBIT], being, or to be, in effect after a person's death. *n.* a bond given by a borrower pledging to pay his debt upon the death of a specified person from whom he expects to inherit money.

post-of·fice (pōst′ôf′is), *adj.* of a post office.

post office, 1. the governmental department in charge of the mails. 2. an office or building where mail is sorted for distribution, postage stamps are sold, etc.

post·op·er·a·tive (pōst′op′ə-rā′tiv, pōst′op′ẽr-ə-tiv), *adj.* of or occurring in the period after a surgical operation.

post·or·bit·al (pōst-ôr′bi-t'l), *adj.* in *anatomy* & *zoology,* situated behind the orbit, or eye socket. *n.* a post-orbital bone or scale, as in certain reptiles.

post·paid (pōst′pād′), *adj.* with the postage prepaid: abbreviated **P.P., p.p.**

post·par·tum (pōst′pär′təm), *adj.* [L.; *post,* after + *partum,* acc. of *partus,* a bringing forth < *parere,* to bear], after childbirth.

post·pon·a·ble (pōst-pōn′ə-b'l), *adj.* that can be postponed.

post·pone (pōst-pōn′), *v.t.* [POSTPONED (-pōnd′), POSTPONING], [L. *postponere; post,* after + *ponere,* to put], 1. to put off until later; defer; delay. 2. [Rare], to consider less important; subordinate. *v.i.* in *medicine,* to delay in coming on or recurring. —*SYN.* see **adjourn.**

post·pone·ment (pōst-pōn′mənt), *n.* a postponing or being postponed.

post·po·si·tion (pōst′pə-zish′ən), *n.* [< L. *postpositus,* pp. of *postponere;* see POSTPONE], 1. a placing after or being placed after. 2. [*post-* + pre*position*], a word placed after another word; especially, a word that has the function of a preposition but follows its object.

post·pos·i·tive (pōst′poz′ə-tiv), *adj.* [< L. *postpositus*], placed after or added to another word; enclitic; suffixed. *n.* a postpositive word; postposition.

post·pran·di·al (pōst′pran′di-əl), *adj.* [< *post-* + L. *prandium,* noonday meal; + *-al*], after-dinner.

post·rid·er (pōst′rid′ẽr), *n.* a person who carries the post, or mail, on horseback; post.

post road, 1. formerly, a road provided with post houses. 2. a road over which the post, or mail, is or formerly was carried.

post·script (pōst′skript′, pōs′skript′), *n.* [L. *postscriptum,* neut. pp. of *postscribere; post-,* after + *scribere,* to write], a note, paragraph, etc. added below the signature line of a letter, or added to a book or article, as an afterthought or to give supplementary information: abbreviated **P.S., p.s., PS.**

pos·tu·lant (pos′choo-lənt), *n.* [Fr. < L. *postulans,* ppr. of *postulare;* see POSTULATE], a petitioner or candidate, especially one for admission into a religious order.

pos·tu·late (pos′choo-lāt′; *for n., usually* pos′choo-lit), *v.t.* [POSTULATED (-id), POSTULATING], [< L. *postulatus,* pp. of *postulare,* to demand; prob. < base of *poscere,* to demand], 1. to claim; demand; require. 2. to assume without proof to be true, real, or necessary, especially as a basis for argument. 3. to assume; take as self-evident or axiomatic. *n.* [L. *postulatum,* prop. neut. pp.], 1. something postulated (in senses 2 & 3). 2. a prerequisite. 3. a basic principle. —*SYN.* see **presume.**

pos·tu·la·tion (pos′choo-lā′shən), *n.* 1. a postulating or being postulated. 2. something postulated.

pos·tu·la·tor (pos′choo-lā′tẽr), *n.* one who postulates.

pos·tur·al (pos′chẽr-əl), *adj.* having to do with posture.

pos·ture (pos′chẽr), *n.* [Fr. < L. *positura,* a position < *ponere,* to place], 1. the position of the body or of parts of the body; carriage; bearing. 2. such a position assumed as in posing, etc.; hence, 3. the way things stand; condition with respect to circumstances: as, the delicate *posture* of foreign affairs. 4. an attitude of mind; frame of mind. *v.t.* [POSTURED (-chẽrd), POSTURING], to place in a posture; pose. *v.i.* to assume a bodily or mental posture, as for effect; pose; attitudinize.

SYN.—**posture** refers to the habitual or assumed disposition of the parts of the body in standing, sitting, etc. (erect *posture*); **attitude** refers to a posture assumed either unconsciously, as in manifesting a mood or emotion, or intentionally for carrying out a particular purpose (an *attitude* of watchfulness); **pose** suggests a posture assumed, usually deliberately, as for artistic effect (the photographer wants you to hold that *pose*); **stance** refers to a particular way of standing, especially with reference to the position of the feet, as in certain sports (the *stance* of a golfer).

pos·tur·ize (pos′chẽr-īz′), *v.t.* [POSTURIZED (-īzd′), POSTURIZING], to posture.

post·war (pōst′wôr′), *adj.* after the (or a) war.

po·sy (pō′zi), *n.* [*pl.* POSIES (-ziz)], [contr. < *poesy*], 1. originally, a verse or motto inscribed inside a ring, etc. 2. a flower or bouquet: so called probably from the use of flower imagery in posies (sense 1).

pot (pot), *n.* [ME.; AS. *pott;* akin to D. *pot;* for prob. IE. base see POD; prob. named from the shape], 1. a round vessel of any size, made of metal, earthenware, or glass, used for holding liquids, cooking or preserving food, etc. 2. a pot with its contents; hence, 3. a potful. 4. a pot of liquor; drink; potation. 5. something resembling a pot in shape or use: as, a chimney *pot,* lobster *pot.* 6. [Colloq.], *a)* all the money bet at a single time; pool; kitty. *b)* a large amount of money. 7. [Colloq.], a pot shot. *v.t.* [POTTED (-id), POTTING], 1. to put into a pot. 2. to preserve in a pot or jar. 3. to cook in a pot. 4. to shoot (game) for food instead of for sport. 5. to hit or secure by or as by a pot shot. 6. [Colloq.], to secure, win, or capture; bag. *v.i.* [Colloq.], to take a pot shot; shoot.

go to pot, to go to ruin; deteriorate.

pot., potential.

po·ta·ble (pō′tə-b'l), *adj.* [Fr.; LL. *potabilis* < L. *potare,* to drink], drinkable. *n. usually in pl.* something drinkable; beverage.

‡**po·tage** (pô′tȧzh′), *n.* [Fr.], soup; broth.

pot·ash (pot′ash′), *n.* [earlier in pl., *potashes;* D. *potasschen* < *pot,* pot + *asch,* ash: so called from being prepared for commercial purposes by evaporating the lixivium of wood ashes in iron pots], 1. an oxide, K_2O, derived from natural brines, distillery waste from alcohol manufacture, flue dusts of blast furnaces, wood ashes, etc., used in fertilizer, soaps, etc. 2. caustic potash (potassium hydroxide). 3. potassium carbonate.

po·tas·sic (pə-tas′ik), *adj.* of or containing potassium.

po·tas·si·um (pə-tas′i-əm), *n.* [Mod. L. < *potassa;* D. *potasch;* see POTASH], a soft, silver-white, waxlike metallic chemical element that oxidizes rapidly when exposed to air: it occurs abundantly in nature in the form of its salts, which are used in fertilizers, glass, etc.: symbol, K; at. wt., 39.096; at. no., 19.

potassium bromide, a white, crystalline compound, KBr, used in photography, medicine, etc.

potassium carbonate, a strongly alkaline, white, crystalline compound, K_2CO_3, used in the manufacture of soap and glass, in medicine, etc.

potassium chlorate, a colorless, crystalline salt, $KClO_3$, a strong oxidizing agent used in the manufacture of explosives, matches, tooth pastes, etc.

potassium chloride, a colorless, crystalline salt, KCl, used in fertilizers, explosives, etc.; sylvite.

potassium cyanide, an extremely poisonous, white, crystalline compound, KCN, used in metallurgy for extracting gold, in electroplating, as an insecticide, etc.

potassium dichromate, a yellowish-red, crystalline compound, $K_2Cr_2O_7$, used as an oxidizing agent and in photography, dyeing, etc.

potassium hydroxide, a white, crystalline salt or deliquescent solid, KOH, used in the manufacture of soap, glass, etc.: it is a very strong alkali and absorbs carbon dioxide from the air: also called *caustic potash.*

potassium my·ron·ate (mī′rə-nāt′), [< *myronic* (*acid*); Fr. *myronique* < Gr. *myron,* fragrant ointment; + *-ate*], a colorless, crystalline, glucoside salt, $KC_{10}H_{18}O_{10}NS_2$, extracted from the seeds of black mustard: it yields glucose by hydrolysis: also called *sinigrin.*

potassium nitrate, a colorless, crystalline compound, KNO_3, used in fertilizers, gunpowder, preservatives, etc., in medicine, and as a reagent and oxidizing agent in chemistry: also called *niter, saltpeter.*

potassium permanganate, a dark-purple, crystalline compound, $KMnO_4$, used as an oxidizing agent, disinfectant, antiseptic, etc.

po·ta·tion (pō-tā′shən), *n.* [ME. *potacioun;* OFr. *potacion, potation;* L. *potatio* < *potare,* to drink], 1. the act of drinking. 2. a drink or draft. 3. excessive drinking. 4. a liquor.

po·ta·to (pə-tā′tō), *n.* [*pl.* POTATOES (-tōz)], [Sp. *patata,* var. of *batata,* sweet potato < a Haitian word], 1. originally, a sweet potato. 2. the starchy, brown-skinned or red-skinned tuber of a widely cultivated plant of the nightshade family, used as a vegetable: also **Irish potato.** 3. this plant.

potato beetle (or **bug**), a black-striped, yellow beetle that eats the leaves of potatoes.

potato chip, a very thin slice of potato fried crisp and then salted.

‡**pot-au-feu** (pô'tō'fö'), *n.* [Fr., lit., pot on the fire], beef stew with vegetables.

pot·bel·lied (pot'bel'id), *adj.* having a potbelly.

pot·bel·ly (pot'bel'i), *n.* [*pl.* POTBELLIES (-iz)], 1. a protruding belly. 2. a potbellied person.

pot·boil·er (pot'boil'ẽr), *n.* a work of art or literature, often inferior, produced only to make money.

pot·boy (pot'boi'), *n.* [Chiefly British], 1. a boy who carries pots of ale, etc. in a public house or inn. 2. a person who serves customers, cleans up, etc. in a tavern.

pot cheese, cottage cheese.

po·teen (pō-tēn'), *n.* [Ir. *poitin*, dim. of *poite*, a pot], in Ireland, illicitly distilled whisky: also **potheen.**

Po·tëm·kin, Gri·go·ri A·le·ksan·dro·vich (gri-gô'ri ä'-lyek-sän'drô-vich po-tyôm'kin; Eng. pō-tem'kin), Prince, 1739–1791; Russian statesman and field marshal; favorite of Catherine the Great.

po·tence (pō't'ns), *n.* potency.

po·ten·cy (pō't'n-si), *n.* [*pl.* POTENCIES (-siz)], [L. *potentia*], 1. the state or quality of being potent, or the degree of this; power; strength. 2. capacity for development; potentiality. 3. something or someone influential or powerful. —*SYN.* see **strength.**

po·tent (pō't'nt), *adj.* [L. *potens, potentis*, ppr. of *posse*, to be able < *potis*, able + *esse*, to be], 1. able to control or influence; having authority or power; mighty: as, a *potent* monarch. 2. convincing; cogent; influential: as, a *potent* argument. 3. effective or powerful in action, as a drug or drink. 4. able to perform sexual intercourse: said of a male.

po·ten·tate (pō't'n-tāt'), *n.* [ME. *potentat;* LL. *potentatus* < L. *potentatus*, power, rule < *potens*, powerful], a potent, or powerful, person; ruler; monarch.

po·ten·tial (pə-ten'shəl), *adj.* [ME. *potenciall;* LL. *potentialis* < L. *potentia;* see POTENT], 1. originally, that has power; potent. 2. that can, but has not yet, come into being; possible; latent; unrealized; undeveloped: opposed to *actual*. 3. in *grammar*, expressing possibility, capability, or the like: as, the *potential* mood. *n.* 1. something potential; a potentiality. 2. in *electricity*, the relative voltage, amount of electric charge, or degree of electrification at a point in an electric circuit or field, as referred to some other point in the same circuit or field. 3. in *grammar*, *a*) the potential mood or aspect. *b*) a potential construction or form. 4. in *physics*, any scalar quantity in which energy is involved as a function of position or condition. Abbreviated **pot.** —*SYN.* see **latent.**

potential energy, energy that is the result of relative position instead of motion, as in a coiled spring.

po·ten·ti·al·i·ty (pə-ten'shi-al'ə-ti), *n.* [ML. *potentialitas*], 1. the state or quality of being potential; possibility or capability of becoming; latency. 2. [*pl.* POTENTIALITIES (-tiz)], something potential; a possibility of developing, coming to fruition, etc.

po·ten·tial·ly (pə-ten'shəl-i), *adv.* possibly or hypothetically, but not yet actually.

po·ten·til·la (pō'ten-til'ə), *n.* [Mod. L., dim. < L. *potens;* see POTENT], any of a number of related plants of the rose family, with flowers of various colors and saw-edged leaves, generally five, growing along the stem; cinquefoil; five-finger.

po·ten·ti·om·e·ter (pə-ten'shi-om'ə-tẽr), *n.* [< L. *potentia*, power; + *-meter*], an instrument for measuring or controlling electric potential.

poth·e·car·y (poth'ə-ker'i), *n.* [*pl.* POTHECARIES (-iz)], [ME. *potecarie*], [Obs. or Dial.], an apothecary.

po·theen (pō-thēn', pō-tēn'), *n.* poteen.

poth·er (poth'ẽr), *n.* [earlier *pudder, puther;* vowel after *bother*, etc.; Early Mod. Eng.; prob. < Continental military slang; ? < or akin to G. *poltern* (cf. POLTERGEIST)], 1. a choking cloud of smoke, dust, etc. 2. an uproar; commotion; fuss. *v.t. & v.i.* to bother; worry.

pot·herb (pot'ũrb', pot'hũrb'), *n.* any herb whose fleshy leaves and stems are boiled and eaten, or used to flavor food.

pot·hold·er (pot'hōl'dẽr), *n.* a small pad, or piece of thick cloth, for holding and handling hot pots, etc.

pot·hole (pot'hōl'), *n.* a deep hole or pit; especially, a deep, round hole formed in the rock of a river bed by gravel whirling in water.

pot·hook (pot'hook'), *n.* 1. an S-shaped hook for hanging a pot or kettle over a fire. 2. a hooked rod for lifting hot pots, etc. 3. an S-shaped mark, as one made by children learning to write.

pot·house (pot'hous'), *n.* [British], an alehouse or tavern, especially a disreputable one.

pot·hunt·er (pot'hun'tẽr), *n.* 1. a hunter who kills game indiscriminately, disregarding the rules of sport. 2. a person who enters contests merely to win prizes.

‡**po·tiche** (pô'tēsh'), *n.* [*pl.* POTICHES (-tēsh')], [Fr. < *pot*, a pot], a vase or jar of porcelain, etc., with a rounded or polygonal body narrowing toward the top.

po·tion (pō'shən), *n.* [ME. *pocion;* L. *potio* < *potare*, to drink], a drink, especially of medicine or poison; dose.

pot·latch (pot'lach'), *n.* [< Am. Ind. (Chinook) *patshatl*, a gift], 1. among some American Indians of the northern Pacific coast, *a*) [often P-], a winter festival. *b*) a distribution of gifts, as during such a festival. 2. a ceremonial feast at which gifts are exchanged in a rivalry to display wealth.

pot·luck (pot'luk'), *n.* whatever the family meal happens to be: as, will you take *potluck* with us?

pot·man (pot'mən), *n.* [*pl.* POTMEN (-mən)], [British], a serving man, or waiter, as in a public house.

pot marigold, any of various plants of the daisy family, with showy yellow or orange flowers; calendula.

pot metal, 1. originally, an alloy of lead and copper used to make pots. 2. a kind of iron suitable for making pots. 3. stained glass that is colored throughout while still molten.

Po·to·mac (pə-tō'mək), *n.* a river forming the boundaries of West Virginia, Virginia, and Maryland, flowing into Chesapeake Bay: length, 287 mi.

Po·to·sí (pô'tô-sē'), *n.* 1. a mountain of the Andes, in southwestern Bolivia: height, 15,925 ft. 2. a city on its slopes: pop., 51,000.

pot·pie (pot'pī'), *n.* 1. a meat pie made in a pot or deep dish. 2. a stew with dumplings.

pot·pour·ri (pō'poo-rē', pot-poor'i), *n.* [Fr.; *pot*, a pot + *pourri*, pp. of *pourrir*, to rot; transl. of Sp. *olla podrida;* see OLLA-PODRIDA], 1. originally, a stew. 2. a mixture, as of dried flower petals with spices, kept in a jar for its fragrance. 3. a medley, miscellany, or anthology.

pot roast, meat, usually beef, cooked by braising.

Pots·dam (pots'dam'; G. pôts'däm), *n.* a city in eastern Germany, near Berlin: pop., 114,000: scene of a conference (July-August, 1945) of Truman, Churchill (later replaced by Attlee), and Stalin.

pot·sherd (pot'shũrd'), *n.* [ME. *potschoord, potszherd;* see POT & SHARD], a piece of broken pottery.

pot shot, 1. originally, a pothunter's shot; hence, 2. an easy shot, as one at close range. 3. a random shot. 4. a haphazard try at something.

pot·stone (pot'stōn'), *n.* a kind of soapstone of which cooking vessels were made in prehistoric times.

pot·tage (pot'ij), *n.* [ME. & OFr. *potage* < *pot*, a pot], a kind of stew made of vegetables, or meat and vegetables; thick soup.

pot·ted (pot'id), *adj.* 1. put into a pot or pots. 2. cooked or preserved in a pot or can. 3. [Slang], intoxicated; drunk.

pot·ter (pot'ẽr), *n.* [ME. *pottare* < *pot*, a pot], a person who makes earthenware pots, dishes, etc.

pot·ter (pot'ẽr), *v.i. & v.t.*, *n.* [freq. formation < obs. *pote;* AS. *potian*, to push], [Chiefly British], putter.

Pot·ter, Paul (pot'ẽr), 1625–1654; Dutch painter.

potter's field, [after an old burial place for strangers in Jerusalem, said to have been orig. a potter's field (Matt. 27:7)], a burial ground for poverty-stricken, friendless, or unknown persons.

potter's wheel, a rotating horizontal disk, usually operated by a treadle or motor, upon which clay is molded into bowls, etc.

pot·ter·y (pot'ẽr-i), *n.* [*pl.* POTTERIES (-iz)], [Fr. *poterie* < *potier*, a potter < *pot*, a pot], 1. a place where earthenware is made; potter's workshop or factory. 2. the art or occupation of a potter; ceramics. 3. pots, bowls, dishes, etc. made of clay hardened by heat; earthenware.

POTTER'S WHEEL

pot·tle (pot''l), *n.* [ME. & OFr. *potel*, dim. of *pot*, a pot], 1. formerly, a liquid measure, equal to a half gallon. 2. a pot or tankard having this capacity. 3. the contents of such a pot; hence, 4. alcoholic liquor.

Pott's disease (pots), [after Percival *Pott* (1714–1788), Eng. surgeon], tuberculous caries of the vertebrae, resulting in curvature of the spine.

Potts·town (pots'toun), *n.* a city in southeastern Pennsylvania: pop., 26,000.

Potts·ville (pots'vil), *n.* a city in east central Pennsylvania: pop., 22,000.

pot·ty (pot'i), *adj.* [POTTIER (-i-ẽr), POTTIEST (-i-ist)], [from phr. *go to pot* or from notion of drunkenness], [British Colloq.], 1. trivial; petty. 2. slightly crazy.

pot-val·iant (pot'val'yənt), *adj.* valiant and bold from drunkenness.

pot·wal·lop·er (pot′wäl′əp-ẽr), *n.* [altered (after *wallop*, to boil) < *potwaller*, lit., a pot boiler < *pot* + obs. *wall*, to boil; ME. *wallen;* AS. *weallan*], in *English history*, a person considered a householder by virtue of owning a hearth, and therefore qualified to vote.

pouch (pouch), *n.* [ME. *pouche;* OFr. *pouche, poche*, forms of *poque;* see POKE (sack)], 1. a smallish bag or sack. 2. a small bag for carrying ammunition. 3. a small bag of leather, rubberized cloth, plastic, etc., for carrying pipe tobacco in one's pocket. 4. a mailbag. 5. anything shaped like a pouch. 6. [Scot.], a pocket (in clothing). 7. [Archaic], a purse. 8. in *anatomy*, any pouchlike cavity or part. 9. in *botany*, a pod that looks almost square, with an upper and lower lid. 10. in *zoology*, *a*) a saclike structure on the abdomen of some animals, as the kangaroo and the opossum, used to carry young. *b*) a baglike part, as of a pelican's bill or a gopher's cheeks, used to carry food. *v.t.* 1. to put in a pouch. 2. to make into a pouch; make pouchy. 3. to swallow. *v.i.* to form a pouch or pouchlike cavity.

pouched (poucht), *adj.* 1. having a pouch or pouches. 2. pouchy.

pouch·y (pouch′i), *adj.* [POUCHIER (-i-ẽr), POUCHIEST (-i-ist)], resembling a pouch; baggy.

pouf (po͞of), *n.* [Fr., a puff; see PUFF], 1. an elaborate headdress worn by women, especially in the 18th century, and characterized by high rolls or puffs of hair. 2. any part of a dress, etc. gathered into a puff, or projection. 3. a kind of ottoman (sense 2*a*).

Pough·keep·sie (pə-kip′si), *n.* a city in southeastern New York, on the Hudson: pop., 38,000.

pou·lard (po͞o-lärd′), *n.* [Fr. *poularde* < *poule*, hen], 1. a young hen spayed for fattening. 2. a fat young hen.

poult (pōlt), *n.* [ME. *pulte;* contr. of *pulete;* see PULLET], a young turkey, chicken, pheasant, or similar fowl.

poul·ter·er (pōl′tẽr-ẽr), *n.* [ME. *pulter;* OFr. *pouletier* < *poulet* (see PULLET); + *-er*], [Chiefly British], a person who deals in poultry: also, [Archaic], **poulter.**

poul·tice (pōl′tis), *n.* [earlier *pultes;* ML. *pultes*, thick pap, orig. pl. of L. *puls, pultis*, pap], a hot, soft, moist mass, as of flour, mustard, etc., applied to a sore or inflamed part of the body. *v.t.* [POULTICED (-tist), POULTICING], to apply a poultice to.

poul·try (pōl′tri), *n.* [ME. *pulitrie;* OFr. *pouleterie* < *poulet;* see PULLET], domestic fowls; chickens, turkeys, ducks, geese, etc., collectively.

pounce (pouns), *n.* [prob. < ME. & OFr. *pounson;* see PUNCHEON], 1. a claw or talon of a bird of prey. 2. a swoop, as by a bird of prey; act of pouncing. *v.i.* [POUNCED (pounst), POUNCING], to swoop down, spring, or leap (*on, upon*, or *at* a person or thing) and, or as if to, attack or seize.

pounce (pouns), *n.* [Fr. *ponce;* L. *pumex*, pumice], 1. a fine powder, as pulverized cuttlefish bone, formerly used to prevent ink from blotting or to prepare the writing surface of parchment. 2. powdered charcoal, etc. sprinkled over a stencil to make a design, as on cloth. *v.t.* [POUNCED (pounst), POUNCING], 1. to sprinkle, rub, finish, or prepare with pounce. 2. to stencil with pounce.

poun·cet box (poun′sit), [cf. Fr. *poncette*, box for sprinkling pounce (powder)], [Archaic], a small box with a perforated lid, for perfumes: also **pouncet,** *n.*

pound (pound), *n.* [*pl.* POUNDS (poundz), collectively POUND], [ME.; AS. *pund;* L. *pondo*, a pound, orig. abl. of *pondus*, a weight (in *libra pondo*, a pound in weight)], 1. a unit of weight, equal to 16 ounces (7,000 grains) avoirdupois or 12 ounces (5,760 grains) troy: abbreviated **lb.** 2. the monetary unit of Great Britain, equal to 20 shillings or 240 pence and, from 1940 to 1949, having a par exchange value in United States money of $4.035; devalued in 1949 to a par exchange value of $2.80: symbol, £ (no period). 3. the monetary unit of various other countries, including Australia, Egypt, Ireland, Lebanon, New Zealand, Israel, Syria, and the Union of South Africa. 4. in the New Testament, a mina. 5. a former Scottish monetary unit (*pound Scots*), originally equal to the British pound.

pound (pound), *v.t.* [ME. *pownen* (AS. *punian*); with unhistoric *-d* (cf. SOUND, COMPOUND); akin to D. *puin*, rubbish], 1. to beat to a pulp, powder, etc.; pulverize. 2. to strike or drive with repeated, heavy blows. *v.i.* 1. to deliver repeated, heavy blows (*at* or *on* a door, etc.). 2. to move with heavy steps or come down heavily while moving. 3. to beat heavily; throb. *n.* 1. a pounding. 2. a hard blow. 3. the sound of this; thud; thump. —*SYN.* see **beat.**

pound out, 1. to flatten, smooth, etc. by pounding. 2. to play with a very heavy touch, as on a piano.

pound (pound), *n.* [ME. *poonde;* AS. *pund-* (in compounds); akin to AS. *pyndan*, to shut up (cf. PINDER); IE. base prob. as in *pin, pen* (to enclose)], 1. an enclosure, maintained by a town, etc., for confining stray animals until claimed. 2. an enclosure for keeping or sheltering animals. 3. an enclosure for trapping animals. 4. a place of confinement, as for arrested persons. 5. an enclosed area for catching or keeping fish. *v.t.* to confine in a pound; impound.

Pound, Ezra Loo·mis (lo͞o′mis pound), 1885– ; American poet; in Italy (1924–1945; 1958–); institutionalized as mentally unsound after indictment for treason (1945–1958).

Pound, Louise, 1872–1958; American linguist.

Pound, Roscoe, 1870– ; brother of *Louise;* American educator and legal scholar.

pound·age (poun′dij), *n.* [see -AGE], a tax, rate, or commission, etc. per pound (sterling or weight).

pound·age (poun′dij), *n.* [see -AGE], 1. confinement in or as in a pound, or enclosure. 2. the fee required to free animals from a pound.

pound·al (poun′d'l), *n.* [< *pound* (weight)], a unit of force that, acting on it for one second, will give to a one-pound mass a velocity of one foot per second.

pound·cake (pound′kāk′), *n.* 1. a rich cake made with a pound each of its principal ingredients, as flour, butter, sugar, etc. 2. a cake resembling this.

pound·er (poun′dẽr), *n.* a person or thing that pounds.

pound·er (poun′dẽr), *n.* something weighing or worth a pound: often used in hyphenated compounds meaning *weighing, worth*, or *having to do with* (a specified number of) *pounds*, as *eight-pounder.*

pound-fool·ish (pound′fo͞ol′ish), *adj.* foolish in handling large sums of money: cf. **penny-wise.**

pound net, a fish trap consisting of nets arranged so as to form an enclosure with a narrow opening.

pound sterling, a pound (the British monetary unit).

pour (pôr, pōr), *v.t.* [ME. *pouren;* prob. a dial. word; the mod. vowel is phonetically puzzling; ? < ONorm. Fr. *purer* (L. *purare*), to purify, in the sense "to pour off impurities"], 1. to cause to flow in a continuous stream. 2. to emit, discharge, utter, etc. profusely or steadily. *v.i.* 1. to flow freely, continuously, or copiously. 2. to rain heavily. 3. to rush in a crowd; swarm. 4. to serve as a hostess at a reception or the like, by pouring tea, coffee, etc. for the guests. *n.* 1. a pouring. 2. a heavy rain; downpour.

‡**pour·boire** (po͞or′bwår′), *n.* [Fr.; *pour*, for + *boire*, to drink], a tip, or gratuity.

‡**pour·par·ler** (po͞or′pår′lā′), *n.* [Fr.; *pour*, for + *parler*, to speak], a preliminary, informal discussion.

pour·point (poor′point′), *n.* [ME. *purpoynt, purpont;* OFr. *porpoint;* prob. < *pourpoindre*, to perforate], a quilted doublet worn in the late Middle Ages.

pousse-ca·fé (po͞os′ka-fā′; Fr. po͞os′kå′fā′), *n.* [Fr. < *pousser*, to push + *café*, coffee], 1. a liqueur drunk with after-dinner coffee. 2. a drink made of several liqueurs, each forming its own layer in the glass.

pous·sette (po͞o-set′), *n.* [Fr., dim. of *pousse*, a push], a dance figure in which a couple or several couples dance round and round with hands joined. *v.i.* [POUSSETTED (-id), POUSSETTING], to perform a poussette.

Pous·sin, Ni·co·las (nē′kô′lä′ po͞o′san′), 1594–1665; French painter.

‡**pou sto** (po͞o′ stō′, pou′ stō′), [Gr. *pou stō*, where I may stand: from a saying of Archimedes, *dos moi pou stō, kai kinō tēn gēn*, give me (a place) where I may stand, and I will move the earth], 1. literally, a place to stand on; hence, 2. a basis of operations.

pout (pout), *v.i.* [ME. *pouten;* prob. < ON. **puta*, to swell; cf. Sw. *puta*, to be swollen; for IE. base see BUD], 1. to thrust out the lips, as in sullenness or displeasure; hence, 2. to sulk. 3. to protrude, as the lips. *v.t.* 1. to thrust out (the lips or mouth). 2. to utter with a pout. *n.* 1. a pouting. 2. *pl.* a fit of sulking.

pout (pout), *n.* [*pl.* POUT, POUTS (pouts); see PLURAL, II, D, 2], [AS. *pute* (found only in compounds, as in *ælpute*, eelpout); IE. base as in *bud, pod*], any of several fishes, as the horned pout, eelpout, or whiting pout.

pout·er (pout′ẽr), *n.* 1. a person who pouts. 2. a breed of long-legged pigeon that can distend its crop to produce a large, puffed-up breast.

pov·er·ty (pov′ẽr-ti), *n.* [ME. *poverte;* OFr. *poverté, povreté;* L. *paupertas* < *pauper*, poor], 1. the condition or quality of being poor; indigence; need. 2. deficiency in necessary properties or desirable qualities, or in a specific quality, etc.; inferiority; inadequacy. 3. unproductiveness, as of soil. 4. smallness in amount; scarcity; paucity; dearth; scantiness.

SYN.—**poverty,** the broadest of these terms, implies a lack of the resources for reasonably comfortable living; **destitution** and **want** imply such great poverty that the means for mere subsistence, such as food and shelter, are lacking; **indigence,** a somewhat euphemistic term, implies a lack of luxuries to which one was formerly accustomed; **penury** suggests such severe poverty as to cause abjectness, or a loss of self-respect.—*ANT.* wealth, affluence, plenty.

pov·er·ty-strick·en (pov′ẽr-ti-strik′'n), *adj.* 1. stricken with poverty; very poor. 2. characteristic of, or giving the appearance of, poverty.

pow (pō, pou), *n.* [Chiefly Scot.], the poll (head).

POW (pē′ō′dub′'l-ū′), prisoner of war: also **P.O.W.**

pow·der (pou′dẽr), *n.* [ME. *poudre;* OFr. *poudre, pouldre;* L. *pulvis, pulveris*, dust, powder], 1. any dry substance in the form of very fine, dustlike particles, produced by crushing, grinding, etc. 2. a specific kind of powder: as, bath *powder*. 3. *a*) a drug in the form of powder. *b*) a dose of this. 4. gunpowder. *v.t.* 1. to sprinkle or cover with or as with powder. 2. to ornament thus.

3. to make into powder; pulverize. ***v.i.*** 1. to be made into powder. 2. to use powder as a cosmetic.

powder blue, pale-blue.

powder burn, a skin burn caused by exploding gunpowder.

pow·dered sugar (pou′dẽrd), granulated sugar ground into a powder: cf. **confectioners' sugar.**

powder flask, a small, flat container for gunpowder.

powder horn, 1. a container for carrying gunpowder, made of an animal's horn. 2. loosely, a powder flask.

powder magazine, a fireproof vault or compartment for storing gunpowder and explosives.

powder metallurgy, the science or process of working metals and alloys by reducing them to powder and shaping this into solids under great heat and pressure.

powder monkey, formerly, a boy who carried powder from the magazine to the guns aboard a man-of-war.

powder puff, a soft pad for applying cosmetic powder.

powder room, a toilet or lavatory, especially one for women, as in a public building.

pow·der·y (pou′dẽr-i), ***adj.*** 1. of, like, or in the form of, powder. 2. easily crumbled into powder; friable. 3. covered with or as with powder; dusty.

pow·er (pou′ẽr), ***n.*** [ME. *pouer, poer;* OFr. *poeir,* earlier *poter,* orig. inf. < LL. *potere,* to be able, for L. *posse,* to be able; see POTENT], 1. ability to do; capacity to act; capability of performing or producing. 2. a specific ability or faculty: as, the *power* of hearing, beyond one's *powers.* 3. great ability to do, act, or affect strongly; vigor; force; strength. 4. *a)* the ability to control others; authority; sway; influence. *b)* legal ability or authority. *c)* a document giving it. 5. physical force or energy: as, electric *power.* 6. the capacity to exert physical force or energy, usually in terms of the rate or results of its use: as, 60-watt *power:* symbol, P (no period). 7. a person or thing having great influence, force, or authority. 8. a nation, especially one possessed of influence over other nations: as, the big *powers.* 9. national might or political strength. 10. a spirit or divinity. 11. [Archaic], an armed force; army; navy. 12. [Colloq.], a large number or quantity (of something specified). 13. in *mathematics,* the product of the multiplication of a quantity by itself: as, 4 is the second *power* of 2 (2^2), 32 is the fifth *power* of 2 (2^5). 14. in *optics,* the degree of magnification of a lens, microscope, telescope, etc., expressed as a ratio of the diameters of image and object. 15. *pl.* in *theology,* one of the nine orders of angels. Abbreviated **P., p., pr.** ***v.t.*** 1. to supply with a source of power. 2. [Colloq.], to make (one's way) with force. ***adj.*** 1. operated by electricity, etc.: as, *power* tools. 2. served by an auxiliary, engine-powered system that reduces the effort of the operation: as, *power* steering in an automobile.

in power, 1. in authority or control. 2. in office.

the powers that be, the persons in control.

SYN.—**power** denotes the inherent ability or the admitted right to rule, govern, determine, etc. (the limited *power* of a president); **authority** refers to the power, because of rank or office, to give commands, enforce obedience, make decisions, etc. (the *authority* of a teacher); **jurisdiction** refers to the power to rule or decide within certain defined limits (the *jurisdiction* of the courts); **dominion** implies sovereign or supreme authority (*dominion* over a dependent state); **sway** stresses the predominance or sweeping scope of power (the Romans held *sway* over the ancient world); **control,** in this connection, implies authority to regulate, restrain, or curb (under the *control* of a guardian); **command** implies such authority that enforces obedience to one's orders (in *command* of a regiment). See also **strength.**

pow·er·boat (pou′ẽr-bōt′), ***n.*** a fast motorboat.

power dive, in *aviation,* a dive speeded by engine power.

power drill, 1. a portable drill operated by an electric motor. 2. a large drilling machine in which a vertical power-driven drill is lowered onto material by a lever.

pow·er·ful (pou′ẽr-fəl), ***adj.*** full of power; having power; strong; mighty; influential. ***adv.*** [Dial.], very.

pow·er·house (pou′ẽr-hous′), ***n.*** 1. a building where power, especially electric power, is generated. 2. [Slang], a person with a great deal of energy, etc.

pow·er·less (pou′ẽr-lis), ***adj.*** without power; weak, feeble, impotent, unable, not empowered, etc.

power of appointment, the authority granted by one person to another to dispose of his property.

power of attorney, a written statement legally authorizing a person to act for one: abbreviated **P/A, P.A.**

power plant, 1. the entire apparatus serving as the source of power for some particular operation: as, the *power plant* of an automobile. 2. a factory for generating power, especially electric power.

power politics, international political relations in which each nation attempts to increase its own power and interests by using military force or the threat of it.

Pow·ha·tan (pou′ə-tan′), ***n.*** father of *Pocahontas;* lived 1550?–1618; Algonquian Indian chief in Virginia.

pow·wow (pou′wou′), ***n.*** [< Am. Ind. (Algonquian); cf. Massachusett *pauwaw,* he dreams, hence medicine man], 1. a North American Indian medicine man or priest. 2. among North American Indians, a ceremony to conjure the cure of disease, success in war, etc., marked by feasting, dancing, etc. 3. a conference of or with North American Indians. 4. [Colloq.], any conference. ***v.i.*** 1. to hold a powwow. 2. [Colloq.], to confer.

Pow·ys, John Cowper (pō′is), 1872–1963; English novelist, poet, and critic.

Powys, Llewellyn, 1884–1939; brother of *John Cowper;* English writer.

Powys, Theodore Francis, 1875–1953; brother of *John Cowper;* English novelist.

pox (poks), ***n.*** [for *pocks,* ME. *pokkes,* pl. of *pokke;* see POCK], 1. any of various diseases characterized by skin eruptions, as smallpox or chicken pox. 2. syphilis.

Po·yang (pô′yäŋ′), ***n.*** a lake in Kiangsi province, eastern China: length, 90 mi.; width, 20 mi.

Poz·nań (pôz′nän′y′), ***n.*** a city in western Poland: pop., 408,000: German name, *Posen.*

Po·zsony (pô′zhôn′y′), ***n.*** Bratislava, a city in Czechoslovakia: the Hungarian name.

poz·zo·la·na (pot′sə-lä′nə), ***n.*** pozzuolana.

poz·zuo·la·na (pot′swə-lä′nə), ***n.*** [It. < *Pozzuoli,* a city in Italy, where the rock was quarried], a volcanic rock, powdered and used in making a hydraulic cement.

Poz·zuo·li (pôt-tswô′lē), ***n.*** a seaport in Italy, near Naples: pop., 37,000.

pp, pp., in *music,* pianissimo.

pp., 1. pages. 2. past participle. 3. privately printed.

P.P., p.p., 1. parcel post. 2. parish priest. 3. past participle. 4. postpaid.

ppd., prepaid.

ppr., p. pr., present participle.

P.P.S., p.p.s., *post postscriptum,* [L.], an additional postscript.

P.Q., 1. previous question. 2. Province of Quebec.

Pr, in *chemistry,* praseodymium.

Pr., 1. Priest. 2. Prince. 3. Provençal.

pr., 1. [*pl.* PRS.], pair. 2. power. 3. preferred (stock). 4. present. 5. [*pl.* PC.], price. 6. pronoun.

P.R., 1. Puerto Rico. 2. proportional representation. 3. public relations.

prac·tic (prak′tik), ***n.*** [Archaic], practice. ***adj.*** [Obs.], practical.

prac·ti·ca·bil·i·ty (prak′ti-kə-bil′ə-ti), ***n.*** the quality or condition of being practicable.

prac·ti·ca·ble (prak′ti-kə-b'l), ***adj.*** [Fr. *praticable* < *pratiquer;* see PRACTICE], 1. that can be done or put into practice; feasible: as, a *practicable* plan. 2. that can be used; usable; useful: as, a *practicable* tool. —***SYN.*** see **possible, practical.**

prac·ti·ca·bly (prak′ti-kə-bli), ***adv.*** in a practicable manner.

prac·ti·cal (prak′ti-k'l), ***adj.*** [obs. *practic* < obs. Fr. *practique, pratique* < LL. *practicus* (see PRACTICE); + *-al*], 1. of, exhibited in, or obtained through practice or action: as, *practical* knowledge: opposed to *theoretical, speculative, ideal.* 2. that can be used; workable; useful: as, *practical* proposals. 3. designed for use; utilitarian: as, a *practical* dress. 4. concerned with the application of knowledge to useful ends, as distinguished from speculation, etc.: as, *practical* science, a *practical* mind. 5. given to or experienced from actual practice: as, a *practical* farmer. 6. of, concerned with, or dealing efficiently with everyday activities, work, etc. 7. that is so in practice, whether or not in theory, intention, law, etc.; virtual. 8. matter-of-fact.

SYN.—**practical** stresses effectiveness as tested by actual experience or as measured by a completely realistic approach to life or the particular circumstances involved; **practicable** is used of something that appears to be capable of being put into effect, but has not yet been developed or tried (before the era of electronics, television did not seem *practicable;* today it is but one of the *practical* applications of the science).—***ANT.*** impractical, impracticable.

prac·ti·cal·i·ty (prak′ti-kal′ə-ti), ***n.*** 1. the quality of being practical. 2. [*pl.* PRACTICALITIES (-tiz)], something practical.

practical joke, a trick played on someone, meant in fun.

prac·ti·cal·ly (prak′tik-li, prak′ti-k'l-i), ***adv.*** 1. in a practical manner. 2. from a practical viewpoint. 3. for all practical purposes; in effect; virtually: as, he is *practically* the boss. 4. [Colloq.] almost; nearly

practical nurse, an experienced nurse who is neither a graduate of a nursing school nor a registered nurse.

prac·tice (prak′tis), ***v.t.*** [PRACTICED (-tist), PRACTICING], [ME. *practisen;* OFr. *practiser* < *practiquer, pratiquer;* ML. *practicare* < LL. *practicus;* Gr. *praktikos,* concerning action, practical < *prassein,* to do], 1. to do, exercise, or perform frequently or usually; make a habit or custom of. 2. to do repeatedly in order to learn or become proficient; exercise oneself in: as, he *practices* batting every day. 3. to put into practice; use one's knowledge of; work at, especially as a profession: as, she *practices* medicine. 4. to teach or train through practice; exercise. *v.i.* 1. to do something repeatedly in order to learn or acquire proficiency; exercise oneself, as in music, etc. 2. to put knowledge into practice; work at or follow a profession, as medicine, law, etc. 3. [Archaic or Rare], to scheme; intrigue. Also spelled **practise.** *n.* 1. a practicing; specifically, *a)* a frequent or usual action; habit; usage: as, he makes a *practice* of coming early. *b)* a usual method; custom; convention: as, tipping is the *practice* in most restaurants: also used in the plural in a disapproving sense, as, the *practices* of a shyster. 2. repeated mental or physical action for the purpose of learning or acquiring proficiency: as, *practice* makes perfect. 3. proficiency or skill acquired through this: as, he's out of *practice.* 4. the doing of something, often as an application of knowledge: as, theory is useless without *practice.* 5. the exercise of a profession or occupation: as, the *practice* of law. 6. a business based on this, often regarded as a legal property: as, he bought their law *practice.* 7. a scheming, intriguing, or trickery. 8. *a)* a scheme; intrigue. *b)* a stratagem; maneuver. 9. in *arithmetic,* an abridged method of multiplying quantities of different denominations by the use of aliquot parts. 10. in *law,* an established method of court procedure. Abbreviated **prac.**

***SYN.*—practice** implies repeated performance for the purpose of learning or acquiring proficiency (he *practiced* on the violin every day, *practice* makes perfect); **exercise** implies a putting to or keeping at work (to *exercise* one's rights) or refers to activity, often of a systematic formal kind, that trains or develops the body or mind (gymnastic *exercises*); **drill** suggests disciplined group training in which something is taught by constant repetition (to *drill* a squad, an arithmetic *drill*). See also **habit.**

prac·ticed (prak'tist), *adj.* 1. proficient through practice; experienced; skilled. 2. learned or perfected by practice. Also spelled **practised.**

prac·tise (prak'tis), *v.t. & v.i.* [PRACTISED (-tist), PRACTISING], to practice.

prac·ti·tion·er (prak-tish'ən-ẽr), *n.* [formerly *practicioner* < *practician* (*practic* + *-ian*) + *-er*], 1. a person who practices a profession, art, etc.: as, a medical *practitioner.* 2. a Christian Science healer.

prae- (prē), [L. < *prae,* before], pre-: the preferred form in certain words, as *praenomen, praetor,* etc.

prae·di·al (prē'di-əl), *adj.* [ML. *praedialis* < L. *praedium,* a farm, estate], of land or stationary property: also spelled **predial.**

prae·fect (prē'fekt), *n.* a prefect.

prae·mu·ni·re (prē'myoo-nī'rē), *n.* [short for ML. *praemunire* (*facias*), (see to it) that you warn, used for L. *praemonere,* to forewarn; *prae-,* before + *monere,* to advise, warn], in *English law,* 1. the offense of obeying other authority than that of the Crown. 2. a writ charging this offense. 3. the penalty for this offense, as imprisonment, forfeiture, etc.

prae·no·men (prē-nō'men), *n.* [*pl.* PRAENOMINA (-nom'i-nə)], [L.; *prae-,* before + *nomen,* a name], in ancient Rome, a person's first, or personal, name, preceding the nomen and cognomen (e.g., *Marcus* Tullius Cicero).

prae·nom·i·nal (prē-nom'i-n'l), *adj.* of a praenomen.

prae·pos·tor (prē-pos'tẽr), *n.* a prepositor.

prae·tor (prē'tẽr, prē'tôr), *n.* [ME. (northern) *pretour;* L. < *praeire,* to precede, go before; *prae-,* before + *ire,* to go], a magistrate of ancient Rome, next below a consul in rank: also spelled **pretor.**

prae·to·ri·al (pri-tôr'i-əl, pri-tō'ri-əl), *adj.* of a praetor or the rank of a praetor: also spelled **pretorial.**

prae·to·ri·an (pri-tôr'i-ən, pri-tō'ri-ən), *adj.* 1. praetorial. 2. [often P-], designating or of the bodyguard (*Praetorian Guard*) of a Roman commander or emperor. *n.* 1. a man with the rank of a praetor or ex-praetor. 2. [often P-], a member of the Praetorian Guard. Also spelled **pretorian.**

Prag (präkh), *n.* Prague: the German name.

prag·mat·ic (prag-mat'ik), *adj.* [Fr. *pragmatique;* L. *pragmaticus,* skilled in business or law; Gr. *pragmatikos* < *pragma,* business, orig. a thing done < *prassein,* to do], 1. *a)* busy; active. *b)* practical. 2. pragmatical; meddlesome, officious, conceited, etc. 3. having to do with the affairs of a state or community. 4. dealing with historical facts in their interrelations. 5. of or belonging to philosophical pragmatism. *n.* 1. a pragmatic sanction. 2. a pragmatical person.

prag·mat·i·cal (prag-mat'i-k'l), *adj.* 1. officious; meddlesome. 2. dogmatic; opinionated; conceited. 3. in *philosophy,* pragmatic.

pragmatic sanction, any of various royal decrees that had the force of fundamental law.

prag·ma·tism (prag'mə-tiz'm), *n.* 1. the quality or condition of being pragmatic. 2. an instance of this. 3. a system of or tendency in philosophy which tests the validity of all concepts by their practical results.

prag·ma·tist (prag'mə-tist), *n.* 1. a pragmatic person. 2. an adherent of pragmatism.

Prague (präg, prāg), *n.* the capital of Czechoslovakia, on the Moldau River: pop., 921,000 (est. 1947): Czech name, *Praha;* German name, *Prag.*

Pra·ha (prä'hä), *n.* Prague.

‡Prai·ri·al (pre'rē'äl'), *n.* [Fr. < *prairie;* see PRAIRIE], the ninth month (May 20—June 18) of the French Revolutionary Calendar, adopted by the First Republic in 1793.

prai·rie (prâr'i), *n.* [Fr., meadowland < ML. *prataria* < L. *pratum,* meadow], a large area of level or slightly rolling grassland, especially one in the Mississippi Valley.

prairie chicken, a large, brown and white, henlike grouse with a short, rounded tail, found on the North American prairies: also **prairie hen.**

prairie dog, any of a number of related small, squirrel-like animals of North America, having a barking cry.

prairie schooner, a large covered wagon used by pioneers to cross the American prairies.

prairie wolf, any of a number of related wolflike animals of the western plains of North America; coyote.

PRAIRIE DOG (1 ft. long)

praise (prāz), *v.t.* [PRAISED (prāzd), PRAISING], [ME. *preisen;* OFr. *preiser, preisier;* LL. *pretiare* < L. *pretium,* worth, price], 1. originally, to set a price on; appraise; hence, 2. to commend the worth of; express approval or admiration of. 3. to laud the glory of (God, etc.), as in song; glorify; extol. *n.* 1. a praising or being praised; commendation; approbation; glorification. 2. [Archaic], a reason or basis for praise. 3. [Obs.], an object of praise.

PRAIRIE SCHOONER

sing one's praise (or **praises**), to praise one highly.

***SYN.*—praise** is the simple, basic word implying an expression of approval, esteem, or commendation (to *praise* one's performance); **laud** implies great, sometimes extravagant praise (the critics *lauded* the actor to the skies); **acclaim** suggests an outward show of strong approval, as by loud applause, cheering, etc. (he was *acclaimed* the victor); **extol** implies exalting or lofty praise (the scientist was *extolled* for his work); **eulogize** suggests formal praise in speech or writing, as on a special occasion (the minister *eulogized* the exemplary life of the deceased).

praise·wor·thi·ly (prāz'wũr'thə-li), *adv.* in a praiseworthy manner.

praise·wor·thi·ness (prāz'wũr'thi-nis), *n.* the quality of being praiseworthy.

praise·wor·thy (prāz'wũr'thi), *adj.* worthy of praise; laudable.

Pra·ja·dhi·pok (prə-chä'ti-pok'), *n.* 1893–1941; king of Siam (1925–1935); abdicated.

Pra·krit (prä'krit), *n.* [Sans. *prakṛta,* natural, simple, vulgar < *pra-* (akin to Eng. *for*), before + *kr,* to do, make; cf. SANSKRIT], any of several vernacular Indic languages used in India, chiefly in the period B.C.

pra·line (prä'lēn, prā'lēn), *n.* [Fr. < the name of Marshal Duplessis-*Praslin* (1598–1675), whose cook invented it], a crisp candy made of pecans, almonds, or other nuts browned in boiling sugar.

prall·tril·ler (präl'tril'ẽr), *n.* [G.; *prall,* elastic, springy + *triller,* a trill], in *music,* a figure in which a principal note is played, then the note above, and then the principal note again, all in very rapid succession: symbol, 𝆗, placed over the principal note: also called *inverted mordent.*

pram (pram), *n.* [British Colloq.], a perambulator.

prance (prans, präns), *v.i.* [PRANCED (pranst, pränst), PRANCING], [ME. *prauncen;* prob. < OFr. (Norm. dial.); ? < ON. (cf. Dan. dial. *pranse*) or < OFr. **paravancier,* intens. < *avancier,* to advance], 1. to rise up on the hind legs; especially, to move along in this way: said of a horse. 2. to ride on a prancing horse. 3. to move about in a way suggestive of a prancing horse; caper. 4. to move or go gaily or arrogantly; swagger; strut. 5. to ride gaily or arrogantly. *v.t.* to cause (a horse) to prance. *n.* a prancing or prancing movement.

pran·di·al (pran'di-əl), *adj.* [< L. *prandium,* early dinner; + *-al*], of a meal, especially dinner.

prank (praŋk), *n.* [? < *prank, v.t. & v.i.*], 1. a mischievous trick; practical joke. 2. a frolicsome movement of an animal.

prank (praŋk), *v.t.* [Early Mod. Eng.; prob. < a LG. source; cf. D. *pronken,* to make a show], to dress showily; dress up; adorn (also with *out* or *up*). *v.i.* to dress up; make a show.

prank·ish (praŋk'ish), *adj.* 1. full of pranks; mischievous; frolicsome. 2. like a prank.

Pra·sad, Ra·jen·dra (rä-jān'drə prə-säd'), 1884– ; Indian nationalist leader and statesman; president of the Republic of India (1950–).

prase (prāz), *n.* [Fr.; L. *prasius;* Gr. *prasios,* leek-green < *prason,* leek], a translucent, leek-green quartz.

pra·se·o·dym·i·um (prā′zi-ə-dim′i-əm, prā′si-ə-dim′i-əm), *n.* [Mod. L. < Gr. *prasios*, green; + *didymium*], a metallic chemical element of the rare-earth group, whose salts are generally green in color: symbol, Pr; at. wt., 140.92; at. no., 59.

prat (prat), *n.* [< thieves' slang; ? a euphemistic alteration < *prate*, *v.*], *sometimes pl.* [Slang], the buttocks.

prate (prāt), *v.i.* [PRATED (-id), PRATING], [ME. *praten* < MD. *praten*; prob. of echoic origin], to talk much and foolishly; chatter. *v.t.* to tell or repeat idly; blab. *n.* foolish or idle talk; chatter.

prat·fall (prat′fôl′), *n.* [Slang], a fall on the buttocks.

prat·in·cole (prat′iŋ-kōl′), *n.* [Mod. L. *pratincola* < L. *pratum*, meadow + *incola*, inhabitant], any of a number of related swallowlike or ploverlike shore birds with long, pointed wings and a forked tail.

pra·tique (pra-tēk′, prat′ik), *n.* [Fr. < *pratiquer*; see PRACTICE], permission to carry on business with a port, granted to a ship that has complied with quarantine or health regulations.

prat·tle (prat′′l), *v.i.* & *v.t.* [PRATTLED (-′ld), PRATTLING], [MLG. *pratelen*; see PRATE], 1. to prate. 2. to speak in a childish manner; babble. *n.* 1. prate. 2. babble.

prawn (prôn), *n.* [ME. *prayne*, *prane*; prob. < East Anglian dial.; no cognates outside Eng.], any of a number of related edible, shrimplike animals having a thin, leathery shell with many reddish-brown dots. *v.i.* to catch, or fish for, prawns.

prax·is (prak′sis), *n.* [Mod. L.; Gr. *praxis* < *prassein*, to do], 1. practice (sense 4): distinguished from *theory*. 2. established practice; custom. 3. a set of examples or exercises, as in grammar.

Prax·it·e·les (prak-sit′ə-lēz′), *n.* Athenian sculptor of the 4th century B.C.

pray (prā), *v.t.* [ME. *preien*; OFr. *preier*; LL. *precare*, for L. *precari* < *prex*, *precis*, prayer], 1. originally, to implore; beseech; entreat: now seldom used except as the elliptical form of *I pray you*, as, *pray* tell me. 2. to ask for by prayer or supplication; beg for imploringly. 3. to bring about, get, etc. by praying. *v.i.* to ask very earnestly; make supplication; say prayers, as to God. —*SYN.* see **appeal.**

prayer (prâr), *n.* [ME. & OFr. *preiere*; ML. *precaria* < L. *precarius*, obtained by begging < *precari*, to entreat], 1. the act or practice of praying. 2. an earnest request; entreaty; supplication. 3. *a*) humble entreaty addressed to God, to a god, etc. *b*) a request made to God, etc.: as, her *prayer* for his safe return. *c*) any set formula for praying, as to God. 4. *often pl.* in some religions, a devotional service consisting chiefly of prayers. 5. any spiritual communion with God, etc. 6. something prayed for or requested, as in a petition.

pray·er (prā′ẽr), *n.* a person who prays.

prayer book, 1. a book of formal religious prayers. 2. [P- B-], the Book of Common Prayer.

prayer·ful (prâr′fəl), *adj.* 1. given to frequent praying; devout. 2. like or expressive of prayer.

prayer shawl, a tallith.

prayer wheel, a revolving drum containing written prayers, used by Buddhists of Tibet.

praying mantis, any of a number of related long, slender insects with grasping, spiny forelegs often held together as if in prayer.

pre- (prē; *unstressed* pri, prə), [< Fr. or L.; Fr. *pré-*; L. *prae-* < *prae*, before, in front of], a prefix meaning: 1. *before in time, earlier* (*than*), *prior* (*to*), as in *presuppose*, *prewar*. 2. *before in place, in front* (*of*), *anterior* (*to*), as in *preaxial*. 3. *before in rank, superior, surpassing*, as in *pre-eminent*. 4. *preliminary to, in preparation for*, as in *preschool*. Cf. **prae-**. Words formed with *pre-* are generally written without a hyphen unless the element following *pre-* begins with *e* or a capital letter.

preach (prēch), *v.i.* [ME. *prechen*; OFr. *precher*, *prechier* (Fr. *prêcher*); L. *praedicare*, to proclaim, declare in public; *prae-*, before + *dicare*, to proclaim, akin to *dicere*, to say], 1. to speak in public on religious matters; give a sermon, as from the Gospel. 2. to give moral or religious advice, especially in a tiresome manner. *v.t.* 1. to expound or proclaim by preaching. 2. to advocate by or as by preaching; urge strongly or persistently. 3. to deliver (a sermon).

preach·er (prē′chẽr), *n.* [ME. *prechur*; OFr. *prechor*; L. *praedicator* < pp. of *praedicare*; see PREACH], a person who preaches; especially, a clergyman.

preach·i·fy (prē′chə-fī′), *v.i.* [PREACHIFIED (-fīd′), PREACHIFYING], [Colloq.], to preach or moralize in a tiresome manner.

preach·ing (prē′chiŋ), *n.* 1. the act or art of one who preaches. 2. an instance of this. 3. a sermon.

preach·ment (prēch′mənt), *n.* [ME. & OFr. *prechement*; L. *praedicamentum*; cf. PREDICAMENT], a preaching or sermon, especially a long, tiresome one.

preach·y (prē′chi), *adj.* [PREACHIER (-chi-ẽr), PREACHIEST (-chi-ist)], [Colloq.], given to or resembling preaching.

pre·ad·am·ite (prē-ad′əm-īt′), *adj.* [cf. Fr. *préadamite*, Mod. L. *praeadamita*], 1. that existed before Adam. 2. of the preadamites. *n.* 1. a preadamite person. 2. one who believes that people existed before Adam.

pre·am·ble (prē′am′b′l, prē-am′b′l), *n.* [Fr. *préambule*; ML. *praeambulum*, neut. of LL. *praeambulus*, going before < L. *praeambulare*, to precede; *prae-*, before + *ambulare*, to go], 1. an introduction, especially one to a constitution, statute, etc., stating its reason and purpose. 2. an introductory fact, event, etc.; preliminary. —*SYN.* see **introduction.**

pre·ar·range (prē′ə-rānj′), *v.t.* to arrange beforehand.

pre·ar·range·ment (prē′ə-rānj′mənt), *n.* arrangement made beforehand.

Pre-AS., Pre-Anglo-Saxon.

pre·ax·i·al (prē-ak′si-əl), *adj.* in *anatomy*, situated in front of the axis of the body; especially, of the radial side of the arm or the tibial side of the leg.

preb·end (preb′ənd), *n.* [ME.; OFr. *prebende*; ML. *praebenda*, things to be furnished or supplied < L. *praebere*, to give, grant < *prae-*, before + *habere*, to have], 1. the part of the revenues of a cathedral or collegiate church paid as a clergyman's salary. 2. the property or tax yielding such revenue. 3. a prebendary or his benefice.

pre·ben·dal (pri-ben′d′l), *adj.* [ML. *praebendalis*], of a prebend or prebendary.

preb·en·dar·y (preb′ən-der′i), *n.* [*pl.* PREBENDARIES (-iz)], [ME. *prebendarie*; ML. *praebendarius*], 1. a person receiving a prebend. 2. in the *Church of England*, an honorary canon with only the title of a prebend.

prec., 1. preceding. 2. preceded.

Pre-Cam·bri·an (prē′kam′bri-ən), *adj.* designating or of all the geologic time before the Cambrian Era: it is now divided into the Archeozoic and Proterozoic Eras. **the Pre-Cambrian**, the Pre-Cambrian Era or its rocks: see **geology**, chart.

pre·can·cel (prē-kan′s′l), *v.t.* [PRECANCELED or PRECANCELLED (-s′ld), PRECANCELING or PRECANCELLING], to cancel (a postage stamp) before use in mailing: chiefly in the past participle. *n.* a precanceled stamp.

pre·car·i·ous (pri-kâr′i-əs), *adj.* [L. *precarius*; see PRAYER], 1. dependent upon the will or favor of another person: as, a *precarious* allowance. 2. dependent upon circumstances; uncertain; insecure: as, a *precarious* living. 3. dependent upon chance; risky; dangerous: as, a *precarious* foothold. 4. dependent upon mere assumption; unwarranted: as, a *precarious* assertion.

prec·a·tive (prek′ə-tiv), *adj.* precatory.

prec·a·to·ry (prek′ə-tôr′i, prek′ə-tō′ri), *adj.* [LL. *precatorius* < L. *precari*, to pray, entreat], of, having the nature of, or expressing entreaty.

pre·cau·tion (pri-kô′shən), *n.* [Fr. *précaution*; LL. *praecautio* < L. *praecautus*, pp. of *praecavere*; *prae-*, before + *cavere*, to take care], 1. care taken beforehand; caution used in advance. 2. a measure taken beforehand against possible danger, failure, etc.

pre·cau·tion·ar·y (pri-kô′shən-er′i), *adj.* of, advising, or using precaution.

pre·cau·tious (pri-kô′shəs), *adj.* using, or giving evidence of, precaution.

pre·cede (pri-sēd′, prē-sēd′), *v.t.* [PRECEDED (-id), PRECEDING], [ME. *preseden*; L. *praecedere*; *prae-*, before + *cedere*, to move], 1. to be, come, or go before in time, place, order, rank, or importance. 2. to introduce with prefatory remarks, etc. *v.i.* to be, come, or go before.

pre·ced·ence (pri-sē′d′ns, pres′ə-dəns), *n.* [< *precedent*], 1. the act, right, privilege, or fact of preceding in time, place, order, or importance. 2. superiority in rank.

pre·ced·en·cy (pri-sē′d′n-si, pres′ə-dən-si), *n.* [*pl.* PRECEDENCIES (-siz)], [Rare], precedence.

pre·ced·ent (pri-sē′d′nt; *for n.*, pres′ə-dənt), *adj.* [ME.; Early Fr. *précédent* < L. *praecedens*, ppr. of *praecedere*; *prae-*, before + *cedere*, to go], preceding. *n.* an act, statement, legal decision, case, etc. that may serve as an example, reason, or justification for a later one.

prec·e·den·tial (pres′ə-den′shəl), *adj.* 1. of, or having the nature of, a precedent; serving as an example for future cases. 2. having precedence; preliminary.

pre·ced·ing (pri-sēd′iŋ, prē-sēd′iŋ), *adj.* that precedes: abbreviated **prec.** —*SYN.* see **previous.**

pre·cen·tor (pri-sen′tẽr), *n.* [LL. *praecentor* < L. *praecinere*, to sing or play before < *prae-*, before + *canere*, to sing], a person who directs a church choir or congregation in singing.

pre·cen·tor·ship (pri-sen′tẽr-ship′), *n.* [see -SHIP], the office of a precentor.

pre·cept (prē′sept), *n.* [ME. *precep*; OFr. *precep*, *precept*; L. *praeceptum* < *praecipere*, to admonish, teach < *prae-*, before + *capere*, to take], 1. a commandment or direction meant as a rule of action or conduct. 2. a rule of moral conduct; maxim. 3. a rule or direction, as for doing something technical. 4. in *law*, a written order; warrant; writ. —*SYN.* see **doctrine.**

pre·cep·tive (pri-sep′tiv), *adj.* [LL. *praeceptivus*], 1. of, having the nature of, or expressing a precept. 2. giving precepts; instructive; didactic.

pre·cep·tor (pri-sep'tẽr), *n.* [L. *praeceptor* < *praecipere;* see PRECEPT], 1. a teacher. 2. the head of a preceptory.

pre·cep·to·ri·al (prē'sep-tôr'i-əl, prē'sep-tō'ri-əl), *adj.* 1. of a preceptor. 2. employing preceptors.

pre·cep·to·ry (pri-sep'tə-ri), *adj.* preceptive.

pre·cep·to·ry (pri-sep'tə-ri), *n.* [*pl.* PRECEPTORIES (-riz)], [ML. *praeceptoria,* estate of a preceptor < L. *praeceptor;* see PRECEPT], 1. a provincial community or religious house of the medieval Knights Templars, subordinate to the London Temple. 2. its estates.

pre·cep·tress (pri-sep'tris), *n.* 1. a woman preceptor. 2. a governess.

pre·ces·sion (pri-sesh'ən, prē-sesh'ən), *n.* [ME.; LL. *precessio* < L. *praecedere,* to go before], 1. a preceding; precedence. 2. the precession of the equinoxes.

pre·ces·sion·al (pri-sesh'ən-'l, prē-sesh'ən-'l), *adj.* of or resulting from the precession of the equinoxes.

precession of the equinoxes, in *astronomy,* 1. the occurrence of the equinoxes earlier in each successive sidereal year, caused by the gradual westward movement of the equinoctial points along the ecliptic as the result of the change in direction of the earth's axis as it turns around the axis of the ecliptic so as to describe a complete cone approximately every 26,000 years. 2. the westward movement of the equinoctial points. Precession is the result of the action of the sun and the moon upon protuberances about the earth's equator.

pre·cinct (prē'siŋkt), *n.* [ME. *precincte;* ML. *praecinctum* < L. *praecinctus,* pp. of *praecingere,* to encompass; *prae-,* before + *cingere,* to surround, gird], 1. an enclosure between buildings, walls, etc.; specifically, the grounds immediately surrounding a religious house or church. 2. *usually pl.* environs; a neighborhood. 3. a subdivision of a city, ward, etc.: as, police *precincts.* 4. any limited area, as of thought. 5. a boundary.

pre·ci·os·i·ty (presh'i-os'ə-ti), *n.* [*pl.* PRECIOSITIES (-tiz)], [ME. *preciousite;* OFr. *preciosité;* L. *pretiositas* < *pretiosus;* see PRECIOUS], great fastidiousness, overrefinement, or affectation, especially in language.

pre·cious (presh'əs), *adj.* [ME.; OFr. *precios, precieus;* L. *pretiosus* < *pretium,* a price, value], 1. of great price or value; costly. 2. of great desirability; held in high esteem: as, freedom is *precious.* 3. beloved; dear. 4. very fastidious, overrefined, or affected, as in behavior, language, etc. 5. egregious; arrant. 6. [Colloq.], very great: as, a *precious* liar. *adv.* [Colloq.], very.

precious stone, a rare and costly gem.

prec·i·pice (pres'ə-pis), *n.* [Fr. *précipice;* L. *praecipitium* < *praeceps,* headlong < *prae-,* before + *caput,* a head], 1. a vertical, almost vertical, or overhanging rock face; steep cliff; crag; hence, 2. a hazardous situation.

pre·cip·i·tance (pri-sip'ə-təns), *n.* quality, fact, or instance of being precipitant; great haste; rashness.

pre·cip·i·tan·cy (pri-sip'ə-tən-si), *n.* [*pl.* PRECIPITANCIES (-siz)], precipitance.

pre·cip·i·tant (pri-sip'ə-tənt), *adj.* [< Fr. or L.; Fr. *précipitant;* L. *praecipitans,* ppr. of *praecipitare;* see PRECIPICE], 1. falling steeply or rushing headlong. 2. acting very hastily or rashly; precipitate. 3. very abrupt, sudden, or unexpected. *n.* a substance which, when added to a solution, causes the formation of a precipitate.

pre·cip·i·tate (pri-sip'ə-tāt'; *also, for adj. & n.,* prisip'ə-tit), *v.t.* [PRECIPITATED (-id), PRECIPITATING], [< L. *praecipitatus,* pp. of *praecipitare* < *praeceps;* see PRECIPICE], 1. to throw headlong; hurl downward. 2. to cause to happen before expected, warranted, needed, or desired; bring on; hasten: as, he *precipitated* the crisis. 3. in *chemistry,* to cause (a slightly soluble substance) to become insoluble and separate out from a solution. 4. in *meteorology,* to condense (vapor, etc.) and cause to fall as rain, snow, sleet, etc. *v.i.* 1. in *chemistry,* to be precipitated. 2. in *meteorology,* to condense and fall as rain, snow, sleet, etc. *adj.* [L. *praecipitatus;* see the *v.*], 1. falling steeply, rushing headlong, flowing swiftly, etc. 2. acting, happening, or done very hastily or rashly; impetuous; headstrong. 3. very sudden, unexpected, or abrupt. *n.* a substance that is separated out from a solution as a solid by the action of chemical reagents, temperature, etc. —*SYN.* see **sudden.**

pre·cip·i·ta·tion (pri-sip'ə-tā'shən), *n.* [Fr. *précipitation;* L. *praecipitatio*], 1. a precipitating or being precipitated; specifically, a headlong fall or rush. 2. precipitance; rash haste; impetuosity. 3. a bringing on suddenly; acceleration. 4. in *chemistry, a)* a precipitating or being precipitated from a solution. *b)* a precipitate. 5. in *meteorology, a)* a depositing of rain, snow, sleet, etc. *b)* rain, snow, sleet, etc. *c)* the amount of this. 6. in *spiritualism,* materialization.

pre·cip·i·ta·tor (pri-sip'ə-tā'tẽr), *n.* a person or thing that precipitates.

pre·cip·i·tin (pri-sip'ə-tin), *n.* [*precipitate* + *-in*], an antibody produced in the blood of an animal injected with an antigen: when the antigen is added to the blood serum of such an animal, a precipitate is formed.

pre·cip·i·tous (pri-sip'ə-təs), *adj.* [obs. Fr. *precipiteux;* LL. **precipitosus* < L. *praeceps;* see PRECIPICE], 1. steep like a precipice; sheer. 2. having precipices. 3. [Rare], rash; precipitate. —*SYN.* see **steep.**

pré·cis (prā-sē', prā'sē), *n.* [*pl.* PRÉCIS (-sēz', -sēz)], [Fr.; see PRECISE], a concise abridgment; summary; abstract. *v.t.* to make a précis of.

pre·cise (pri-sīs'), *adj.* [Fr. *précis;* L. *praecisus* < *praecidere,* to cut off, be brief < *prae-,* before + *caedere,* to cut], 1. strictly defined; accurately stated; definite. 2. speaking definitely or distinctly. 3. with no variation; minutely exact: as, the *precise* amount. 4. *a)* that strictly conforms to usage, etc.; scrupulous; fastidious. *b)* overnice or finicky. —*SYN.* see **correct, explicit.**

pre·cise·ly (pri-sīs'li), *adv.* in a precise manner; exactly: also used as an affirmative reply, equivalent to "I agree," "quite true."

pre·ci·sian (pri-sizh'ən), *n.* a person who is punctilious and precise in observing customs, especially of religion; specifically, a 16th- or 17th-century English Puritan.

pre·ci·sion (pri-sizh'ən), *n.* [Fr.; L. *praecisio*], the quality of being precise; exactness; accuracy; definiteness.

precision bombing, the dropping of bombs on narrowly defined targets with maximum accuracy obtained through the use of bombsights.

pre·ci·sion·ist (pri-sizh'ən-ist), *n.* a person who considers precision very important.

pre·clin·i·cal (prē-klin'i-k'l), *adj.* [*pre-* + *clinical*], in *medicine,* of or in the period of a disease before any of the symptoms appear.

pre·clude (pri-klōōd'), *v.t.* [PRECLUDED (-id), PRECLUDING], [L. *praecludere,* to shut off < *prae-,* before + *claudere,* to shut], to shut out; hinder; prevent; make impossible, especially in advance. —*SYN.* see **prevent.**

pre·clu·sion (pri-klōō'zhən), *n.* [L. *praeclusio* < pp. of *praecludere*], a precluding or being precluded.

pre·clu·sive (pri-klōō'siv), *adj.* [< L. *praeclusus,* pp. of *praecludere* (see PRECLUDE); + *-ive*], precluding or tending to preclude; preventive.

pre·co·cial (pri-kō'shəl), *adj.* [see PRECOCIOUS & -AL], designating or of birds whose newly hatched young are covered with down and are able to run about.

pre·co·cious (pri-kō'shəs), *adj.* [L. *praecox* < *praecoquere,* to boil beforehand; *prae-,* before + *coquere,* to cook, mature], 1. developed or matured earlier than usual, as a child or a child's mentality. 2. of or showing premature development.

pre·coc·i·ty (pri-kos'ə-ti), *n.* [*pl.* PRECOCITIES (-tiz)], [Fr. *précocité*], the condition or quality of being precocious; premature development.

pre·con·ceive (prē'kən-sēv'), *v.t.* to form a conception or opinion of beforehand; conceive in advance.

pre·con·cep·tion (prē'kən-sep'shən), *n.* 1. a preconceiving. 2. a preconceived idea or opinion. 3. prejudice.

pre·con·cert (prē'kən-sũrt'), *v.t.* [*pre-* + *concert, v.*], to arrange or settle beforehand, as by agreement.

pre·co·nize (prē'kə-nīz'), *v.t.* [PRECONIZED (-nīzd'), PRECONIZING], [ME. *preconisen;* ML. *praeconizare* < L. *praeco, praeconis,* public crier], 1. to proclaim or extol in public. 2. to approve and announce the name of (a new bishop) publicly: said of the Pope.

pre·con·tract (prē-kon'trakt; *for v., usually* prē'kəntrakt'), *n.* a previous contract, as, formerly, of marriage. *v.t.* 1. formerly, to betroth beforehand. 2. to agree to by advance contract. *v.i.* to contract beforehand.

pre·cool (prē-kōōl'), *v.t.* to cool artificially before packing or shipment.

pre·crit·i·cal (prē-krit'i-k'l), *adj.* [*pre-* + *critical*], in *medicine,* coming before the crisis (of a disease).

pre·cur·sor (pri-kũr'sẽr), *n.* [L. *praecursor* < *praecurrere,* to run ahead; *prae-,* before + *currere,* to run], 1. a person or thing that goes before; forerunner; harbinger. 2. a predecessor, as in office. —*SYN.* see **forerunner.**

pre·cur·so·ry (pri-kũr'sə-ri), *adj.* [L. *praecursorius*], 1. serving as a precursor, or harbinger; indicating something to follow. 2. introductory; preliminary.

pred., predicate.

pre·da·ceous, pre·da·cious (pri-dā'shəs), *adj.* [< L. *praeda,* a prey], preying on other animals; predatory.

pre·dac·i·ty (pri-das'ə-ti), *n.* the condition or quality of being predaceous.

pre·date (prē-dāt'), *v.t.* 1. to date before the actual date. 2. to come before in date; antedate.

pred·a·tor (pred'ə-tẽr), *n.* a predatory person or animal.

pred·a·to·ri·ly (pred'ə-tôr'ə-li, pred'ə-tō'rə-li), *adv.* in a predatory manner.

pred·a·to·ri·ness (pred'ə-tôr'i-nis, pred'ə-tō'ri-nis), *n.* the condition or quality of being predatory.

pre·da·to·ry (pred'ə-tôr'i, pred'ə-tō'ri), *adj.* [L. *praedatorius* < *praeda,* a prey], 1. of, living by, or characterized by plundering or robbing: as, a *predatory* class of people. 2. predaceous.

pre·de·cease (prē'di-sēs'), *v.t.* [PREDECEASED (-sēst'), PREDECEASING], [*pre-* + *decease*], to die before (someone else or some event).

pred·e·ces·sor (pred'ə-ses'ẽr, pred'ə-ses'ẽr), *n.* [ME. *predecessour;* OFr. *predecesseur;* LL. *praedecessor;* L. *prae-,* before + *decessor,* retiring officer < *decessus,* pp. of *decedere,* to go away, depart; *de-,* from + *cedere,* to go], 1. a person who precedes or preceded another, as in office. 2. a thing replaced by another thing, as in use. 3. an ancestor; forefather.

pre·des·ig·nate (prē-dez′ig-nāt′, prē-des′ig-nāt′), *v.t.* 1. to designate beforehand. 2. in *logic*, to prefix a sign of quantity, as *all, no, few*, etc., to.

pre·des·ti·nar·i·an (pri-des′tə-nâr′i-ən), *adj.* [*predestinate* + *-arian*], of or believing in predestination. *n.* a person who believes in predestination.

pre·des·ti·nar·i·an·ism (pri-des′tə-nâr′i-ən-iz′m), *n.* the doctrine of predestinarians; belief in predestination.

pre·des·ti·nate (pri-des′tə-nit; *for v.*, pri-des′tə-nāt′), *adj.* [ME. *predestynat(e)*; L. *praedestinatus*, pp. of *praedestinare*, to predestine, foretell; *prae-*, before + *destinare*, to determine], predestinated *v.t.* [PREDESTINATED (-id), PREDESTINATING], 1. in *theology*, to foreordain by divine decree or intent. 2. to predestine.

pre·des·ti·na·tion (pri-des′tə-nā′shən), *n.* [ME. *predestinacioun*; LL. *praedestinatio*], 1. in *theology*, *a)* the act by which God supposedly foreordained everything that would happen. *b)* God's predestinating of certain souls to damnation and others to salvation. 2. a predestinating or being predestinated; destiny; fate.

pre·des·tine (pri-des′tin), *v.t.* to destine or decree beforehand; foreordain.

pre·de·ter·mi·nate (prē′di-tũr′mə-nit), *adj.* predetermined.

pre·de·ter·mi·na·tion (prē′di-tũr′mə-nā′shən), *n.* a predetermining or being predetermined.

pre·de·ter·mine (prē′di-tũr′min), *v.t.* [LL. *praedeterminare*; L. *prae-*, before + *determinare*; see DETERMINE], 1. to determine, decide, or decree beforehand. 2. to give a tendency to or impel beforehand; prejudice.

pre·di·al (prē′di-əl), *adj.* praedial.

pred·i·ca·bil·i·ty (pred′i-kə-bil′ə-ti), *n.* the state or quality of being predicable.

pred·i·ca·ble (pred′i-kə-b′l), *adj.* [Fr. *prédicable*; L. *praedicabilis* < *praedicare*; see PREACH], that can be predicated. *n.* 1. something predicable. 2. in *logic*, any of the several sorts of predicate that can be used of a subject, as, in Aristotelian logic, genus, species, difference, property, and accident.

pred·i·ca·bly (pred′i-kə-bli), *adv.* in a predicable manner.

pre·dic·a·ment (pri-dik′ə-mənt), *n.* [ME.; LL. *praedicamentum* < L. *praedicare*; see PREACH, PREACHMENT], 1. a condition or situation, especially one that is dangerous, unpleasant, embarrassing, or, sometimes, comical. 2. in *Aristotelian logic*, a category.

SYN.—**predicament** implies a complicated, perplexing situation from which it is difficult to disentangle oneself; **dilemma** implies a predicament necessitating a choice between equally disagreeable alternatives; **quandary** emphasizes a state of great perplexity and uncertainty; **plight** emphasizes a distressing or unfortunate situation; **fix** and **pickle** are both colloquial terms loosely interchangeable with any of the preceding, although more precisely **fix** is equivalent to **predicament** and **pickle**, to **plight**.

pre·dic·a·men·tal (pri-dik′ə-men′t′l), *adj.* of, or having the nature of, a predicament.

pred·i·cant (pred′i-kənt), *adj.* [L. *praedicans*, ppr. of *praedicare*; see PREACH], preaching. *n.* a preacher.

pred·i·cate (pred′i-kāt′; *for n. and adj.*, pred′i-kit), *v.t.* [PREDICATED (-id), PREDICATING], [ML. *praedicatum*, that which is declared of the subject < L. *praedicatus*, pp. of *praedicare*; see PREACH], 1. [Rare], to proclaim; preach; declare; affirm. 2. to affirm as a quality, attribute, or property of a person or thing: as, let us *predicate* greenness of grass. 3. to involve as a connotation; imply: as, grass *predicates* greenness. 4. to affirm or base upon facts, arguments, conditions, etc. *v.i.* to make an affirmation or statement. *n.* [L. *praedicatum*, neut. of *praedicatus*; see the *v.*], 1. in *grammar*, the word or words that make a statement about the subject of a clause or sentence: a predicate may be: *a)* a verb of complete meaning, as, the wind *blows*. *b)* a verb and its adverbial modifier, as, the wind *blows from the east*. *c)* a transitive verb and its object, as, John *threw the ball*. *d)* a linking verb and its complement, as, the grass *is green*, grass *is a plant*. 2. in *logic*, something that is affirmed or denied about the subject of a proposition (e.g., *green* in "grass is green," *red* in "grass is not red"). Abbreviated **pred.** *adj.* 1. predicated. 2. in *grammar*, of, having the nature of, or involved in a predicate: as, a *predicate* noun or adjective.

pred·i·ca·tion (pred′i-kā′shən), *n.* 1. a predicating or being predicated. 2. a predicate.

pred·i·ca·tive (pred′i-kā′tiv), *adj.* [L. *praedicativus* < *praedicare*; see PREACH], 1. predicating or expressing predication. 2. serving as or in a predicate.

pred·i·ca·to·ry (pred′i-kə-tôr′i, pred′i-kə-tō′ri), *adj.* [LL. *praedicatorius*, praising, laudatory < L. *praedicare*; see PREACH], 1. preaching. 2. having to do with preaching. 3. preached.

pre·dict (pri-dikt′), *v.t.* [< L. *praedictus*, pp. of *praedicere*; *prae-*, before + *dicere*, to tell], to state that there will be; make known beforehand; foretell. *v.i.* to make a prediction or predictions. —*SYN.* see **prophesy.**

pre·dic·tion (pri-dik′shən), *n.* 1. a predicting or being predicted. 2. a prophecy.

pre·dic·tive (pri-dik′tiv), *adj.* predicting; prophetic.

pre·dic·tor (pri-dik′tẽr), *n.* 1. a person who predicts. 2. an antiaircraft aiming device that calculates flying speeds, courses, and altitudes of approaching planes.

pre·di·gest (prē′di-jest′, prē′dī-jest′), *v.t.* to digest beforehand; specifically, to make (food) more digestible by an artificial process before it is eaten.

pre·di·ges·tion (prē′di-jes′chən, prē′dī-jes′chən), *n.* a predigesting or being predigested.

pre·di·lec·tion (prē′də-lek′shən, pred″l-ek′shən), *n.* [Fr. *prédilection* < ML. *praediligere*, to prefer; L. *prae-*, before + *diligere*, to prefer], a preconceived liking; partiality; preference. —*SYN.* see **prejudice.**

pre·dis·pose (prē′dis-pōz′), *v.t.* 1. to dispose, or make receptive, beforehand; make susceptible: as, fatigue *predisposes* one to colds. 2. to dispose of beforehand.

pre·dis·po·si·tion (prē′dis-pə-zish′ən), *n.* 1. a predisposing. 2. the condition of being predisposed; previous inclination; tendency; predilection; susceptibility.

pre·dom·i·nance (pri-dom′ə-nəns), *n.* the quality or condition of being predominant.

pre·dom·i·nan·cy (pri-dom′ə-nən-si), *n.* predominance.

pre·dom·i·nant (pri-dom′ə-nənt), *adj.* [Fr. *prédominant* < ML. *predominans*, ppr. of *predominari*; see PRE- & DOMINANT], 1. having ascendancy, influence, or authority over others; superior; dominating. 2. most frequent, noticeable, etc.; prevailing; preponderant. —*SYN.* see **dominant.**

pre·dom·i·nate (pri-dom′ə-nāt′), *v.i.* [< ML. *predominatus*, pp. of *predominari*; see PRE- & DOMINATE], 1. to have ascendancy, influence, or authority (*over* others); be superior; hold sway. 2. to be dominant over all others; prevail; preponderate.

pre·dom·i·na·tion (pri-dom′ə-nā′shən), *n.* a predominating.

pre·e·lec·tion, pre·ë·lec·tion (prē′i-lek′shən), *adj.* occurring before an election. *n.* a previous choice.

pre·em·i·nence, pre·ëm·i·nence (prē-em′ə-nəns), *n.* the quality or condition of being pre-eminent.

pre·em·i·nent, pre·ëm·i·nent (prē-em′ə-nənt), *adj.* [ME.; L. *praeeminens*, ppr. of *praeeminere*, to project forward; *prae-*, before + *eminere*, to project], eminent above others; excelling others, especially in a particular quality; prominent; surpassing. —*SYN.* see **dominant.**

pre-empt, pre·ëmpt (prē-empt′), *v.t.* [back-formation < *pre-emption*], 1. to acquire by pre-emption; settle on (public land) to establish pre-emption. 2. to seize before anyone else can, excluding others; appropriate.

pre-emp·tion, pre·ëmp·tion (prē-emp′shən), *n.* [< ML. *preemptus*, pp. of *preemere*, to buy beforehand < L. *prae-*, before + *emere*, to buy], the act or right of buying land, etc. before, or in preference to, others.

pre-emp·tive, pre·ëmp·tive (prē-emp′tiv), *adj.* of, or having the nature of, pre-emption.

pre-emp·tor, pre·ëmp·tor (prē-emp′tẽr), *n.* a person who pre-empts.

pre-emp·to·ry, pre·ëmp·to·ry (prē-emp′tə-ri), *adj.* pre-emptive.

preen (prēn), *v.t.* [var. of *prune* (to trim); influenced by ME. *preonen*, to prick with a pin < *preon*; AS. *preon*, a pin], 1. to clean and trim (the feathers) with the beak: said of birds. 2. to make (oneself) trim; dress up or adorn (oneself); hence, 3. to show satisfaction with or vanity in (oneself). *v.i.* to prink; primp.

pre-Eng·lish (prē′iŋ′lish), *n.* the Continental Low Germanic language from which Anglo-Saxon (Old English) developed; Anglo-Frisian. *adj.* 1. of this language. 2. of the peoples and languages of England before the Anglo-Saxon conquest.

pre-es·tab·lish, pre·ës·tab·lish (prē′ə-stab′lish), *v.t.* to establish in advance.

pre-ex·il·i·an, pre·ëx·il·i·an (prē′ig-zil′i-ən, prē′ik-sil′i-ən), *adj.* [< *pre-* + *exile* (or L. *exilium*, exile) + *-an*], of or in that period of Jewish history preceding the Babylonian exile (6th century B.C.).

pre-ex·il·ic, pre·ëx·il·ic (prē′ig-zil′ik, prē′ik-sil′ik), *adj.* pre-exilian.

pre-ex·ist, pre·ëx·ist (prē′ig-zist′), *v.i. & v.t.* to exist previously or before (another person or thing).

pre-ex·ist·ence, pre·ëx·ist·ence (prē′ig-zis′təns), *n.* previous existence, as supposedly of the soul.

pre-ex·ist·ent, pre·ëx·ist·ent (prē′ig-zis′tənt), *adj.* existing previously or before another person or thing.

pref., 1. preface. 2. prefaced. 3. prefatory. 4. preference. 5. preferred. 6. prefix.

pre·fab·ri·cate (prē-fab′rə-kāt′), *v.t.* [PREFABRICATED (-id), PREFABRICATING], 1. to fabricate beforehand. 2. to make or build in standardized sections for shipment and quick assembly, as a house.

pref·ace (pref′is), *n.* [ME. *prefas*; OFr.; L. *praefatio* < *prae-*, before + *fari*, *fatus*, to speak], 1. [usually P-], in Christian liturgy, the introduction to the Canon of the Mass. 2. a statement preliminary or introductory to an article, book, or speech, telling its subject, purpose, plan, etc. 3. something preliminary or introductory; prelude. *v.t.* [PREFACED (-ist), PREFACING], 1. to furnish or introduce with a preface. 2. to be or serve as a preface to; begin. —*SYN.* see **introduction.**

pref·a·to·ri·al (pref'ə-tôr'i-əl, pref'ə-tō'ri-əl), *adj.* prefatory.

pref·a·to·ri·ly (pref'ə-tôr'ə-li, pref'ə-tō'rə-li), *adv.* in a prefatory manner; as a preface.

pref·a·to·ry (pref'ə-tôr'i, pref'ə-tō'ri), *adj.* [< L. *praefatio* (see PREFACE); + *-ory*], of, like, serving as, or given as a preface; introductory: abbreviated **pref.**

pre·fect (prē'fekt), *n.* [ME. *prefecte;* OFr.; L. *praefectus,* pp. of *praeficere,* to set over < *prae-,* before + *facere,* to make], 1. in ancient Rome, any of various high-ranking officials or chief magistrates in charge of governmental or military departments. 2. in modern times, any of various administrative officials; specifically, *a*) the head of a department of France. *b*) the chief of the Paris police. *c*) an ecclesiastical dean. Also spelled **praefect.**

pre·fec·tur·al (pri-fek'chẽr-əl), *adj.* of a prefecture.

pre·fec·ture (prē'fek-chẽr), *n.* [L. *praefectura*], the office, authority, territory, or residence of a prefect.

pre·fer (pri-fũr'), *v.t.* [PREFERRED (-fũrd'), PREFERRING], [ME. *preferren;* L. *praeferre,* to place before; *prae-,* before + *ferre,* to bear, carry], 1. to put before a magistrate, administrator, court, etc. for consideration, sanction, or redress: as, he *preferred* charges against his assaulter. 2. to put before someone else in rank, office, etc.; promote; advance. 3. to put before something else in one's liking, opinion, etc.; like better. —*SYN.* see **choose.**

pref·er·a·bil·i·ty (pref'ẽr-ə-bil'ə-ti), *n.* the quality or condition of being preferable.

pref·er·a·ble (pref'ẽr-ə-b'l, pref'rə-b'l), *adj.* to be preferred; more desirable (than something else).

pref·er·a·bly (pref'ẽr-ə-bli, pref'rə-bli), *adv.* by preference; by choice.

pref·er·ence (pref'ẽr-əns, pref'rəns), *n.* [Fr. *préférence;* ML. *praeferentia* < L. *praeferens,* ppr. of *praeferre;* see PREFER], 1. a preferring or being preferred; greater liking. 2. the right, power, or opportunity of prior choice or claim: as, you have your *preference* of seats. 3. something preferred; one's first choice. 4. a giving of priority or advantage to one person, country, etc. over others, as in payment of debts or granting of credit. Abbreviated **pref.** —*SYN.* see **choice.**

pref·er·en·tial (pref'ə-ren'shəl), *adj.* [ML. *praeferentia* (see PREFERENCE); + *-al*], 1. of, having, giving, or receiving preference. 2. offering a preference; showing one's preference: as, a *preferential* ballot.

pref·er·en·tial·ism (pref'ə-ren'shəl-iz'm), *n.* the practice of giving preferences, as to certain countries in establishing tariffs.

preferential shop, a union shop in which the management by contract or agreement gives preference to union members, as in hiring, layoffs, promotion, etc.

preferential voting, a system of voting in which the voter indicates an order of preference for several candidates.

pre·fer·ment (pri-fũr'mənt), *n.* 1. a preferring, or advancement in rank or office; promotion. 2. an office, rank, or honor to which a person is advanced.

preferred stock, stock on which dividends must be paid before those of common stock: it also has preference in the distribution of assets: abbreviated **PR., Pr., pr.**

pre·fer·rer (pri-fũr'ẽr), *n.* a person who prefers.

pre·fig·u·ra·tion (prē'fig-yoo-rā'shən, prē-fig'yoo-rā'shən), *n.* 1. a prefiguring. 2. something in which something else is prefigured; prototype.

pre·fig·ur·a·tive (prē-fig'yẽr-ə-tiv), *adj.* [ML. *praefiguratívus* < LL. *praefiguratus,* pp.], prefiguring.

pre·fig·ure (prē-fig'yẽr), *v.t.* [LL. *praefigurare;* L. *prae-,* before + *figurare,* to fashion], 1. to suggest or represent beforehand; be an antecedent figure or type of; foreshadow. 2. to figure to oneself, or imagine, beforehand.

pre·fix (prē-fiks'; *for n.,* prē'fiks), *v.t.* [ME. *prefyxen;* OFr. *prefixer* < L. *praefixus,* pp. of *praefigere; prae-,* before + *figere,* to fix], 1. [Rare], to fix beforehand. 2. to fix to the beginning of a word, etc.; place before; add as a prefix. *n.* [Mod. L. < L. *praefixus;* see the *v.*], a syllable, group of syllables, or word united with or joined to the beginning of another word to alter its meaning or create a new word: as, *pre-* is a *prefix* added to *cool* to form *precool.* Abbreviated **pref.**

pre·fix·al (prē'fik-s'l, prē-fik's'l), *adj.* of or as a prefix.

pre·fix·ion (prē-fik'shən), *n.* a prefixing or being prefixed.

pre·for·ma·tion (prē'fôr-mā'shən), *n.* 1. previous formation. 2. in *biology,* a former theory that every germ cell contains every part of the future organism in miniature, development being merely growth in size.

preg·na·bil·i·ty (preg'nə-bil'ə-ti), *n.* the condition or quality of being pregnable.

preg·na·ble (preg'nə-b'l), *adj.* [ME. *prenable* < Late OFr. *prenable* < *prendre* (L. *prehendere*), to take], 1. that can be captured, as a fortress. 2. that can attacked or injured; assailable or vulnerable.

preg·nan·cy (preg'nən-si), *n.* [*pl.* PREGNANCIES (-siz the condition, quality, or period of being pregnar

preg·nant (preg'nənt), *adj.* [ME. *preignant;* L. *pregnar pregnantis,* heavy with young < *prae-,* before + base OL. *gnasci,* to be born], 1. having a fetus or fetus growing in the uterus; that has conceived; with you or with child. 2. mentally fertile; prolific of ideas; i ventive. 3. productive of results; fruitful: as, a *pre nant* cause. 4. full of or rich in meaning, significanc etc. 5. filled (*with*) or rich (*in*); abounding.

pre·heat (prē-hēt'), *v.t.* to heat beforehand.

pre·hen·sile (pri-hen'sil, pri-hen's'l), *adj.* [Fr. *préhe sile* < L. *prehensus,* pp. of *prehendere,* to take], adapt for seizing or grasping, especially by wrapping folding around something, as the tail of a monke

pre·hen·sil·i·ty (prē'hen-sil'ə-ti), *n.* the state or quali of being prehensile.

pre·hen·sion (pri-hen'shən), *n.* [L. *prehensio*], 1. seizing or grasping. 2. mental apprehension.

pre·his·tor·ic (prē'his-tôr'ik, prē'his-tor'ik), *adj.* of t period before recorded history.

pre·his·tor·i·cal (prē'his-tôr'i-k'l, prē'his-tor'i-k'l), *a* prehistoric.

pre·his·tor·i·cal·ly (prē'his-tôr'i-k'l-i, prē'his-tor'ik-l *adv.* before recorded history.

pre·his·to·ry (prē-his'tə-ri), *n.* history before record history, as learned from archaeology, etc.

pre·ig·ni·tion (prē'ig-nish'ən), *n.* in an internal-co bustion engine, ignition occurring before the inta valve is closed or before compression is at a maximu

pre·judge (prē-juj'), *v.t.* [Fr. *préjuger;* L. *praejudicar prae-,* before + *judicare,* to judge], to judge beforehan prematurely, or without all the evidence.

pre·judg·ment, pre·judge·ment (prē-juj'mənt), [Fr. *préjugement*], a prejudging or being prejudged.

prej·u·dice (prej'oo-dis), *n.* [ME.; OFr. *prejudice* (F *préjudice*); L. *praejudicium; prae-,* before + *judiciu* judgment < *judex, judicis,* a judge], 1. a judgment opinion formed before the facts are known; preco ceived idea, favorable or, more usually, unfavorab 2. a judgment or opinion held in disregard of fac that contradict it; unreasonable bias: as, a *prejudi* against Northerners. 3. the holding of such judgmen or opinions. 4. suspicion, intolerance, or hatred other races, creeds, regions, occupations, etc. 5. inju or harm resulting as from some judgment or action another or others. *v.t.* [PREJUDICED (-dist), PREJUDI ING], 1. to injure or harm, as by some judgment action: as, his mistake *prejudiced* the outcome. 2. cause to have prejudice; cause to be prejudiced; bias

without prejudice to, in *law,* without dismissal of detriment to a legal right, claim, or the like.

SYN.—**prejudice** implies a preconceived and unreasona judgment or opinion, usually an unfavorable one marked suspicion, fear, intolerance, or hatred (the lynch mob was cited by race *prejudice*); **bias** implies a mental leaning in fav of or against someone or something (few of us are without *b* of any kind); **partiality** implies an inclination to favor a pers or thing because of strong fondness or attachment (the c ductor has a *partiality* for the works of Brahms); **predilecti** implies a preconceived liking, formed as a result of one's bac ground, temperament, etc., that inclines one to a particu preference (he has a *predilection* for murder mysteries).

prej·u·di·cial (prej'oo-dish'əl), *adj.* causing prejudic or harm; injurious; detrimental.

prel·a·cy (prel'ə-si), *n.* [*pl.* PRELACIES (-siz)], [M *prelacie;* ML. *praelatia*], 1. the office or rank of prelate. 2. prelates collectively. 3. church gover ment by prelates: often a hostile term.

prel·ate (prel'it), *n.* [ME. & OFr. *prelat;* ML. *praelatu* ruler < L. *praelatus,* pp. of *praeferre; prae-,* before *ferre,* to bear], a high-ranking ecclesiastic, as a bisho

prel·ate·ship (prel'it-ship'), *n.* [see -SHIP], the office tenure of a prelate.

pre·lat·ic (pri-lat'ik), *adj.* of a prelate or prelacy.

prel·a·tism (prel'it-iz'm), *n.* prelacy (sense 3).

prel·a·ture (prel'ə-chẽr), *n.* [Fr. *prélature;* ML. *pra latura*], prelacy (senses 1 & 2).

pre·lect (pri-lekt'), *v.i.* [< L. *praelectus,* pp. of *praeleger* to read before, lecture; *prae-,* before + *legere,* to rea choose], to lecture; give lectures.

pre·lec·tion (pri-lek'shən), *n.* [L. *praelectio* < *praeleger* see PRELECT], a lecture, especially at a university.

pre·lec·tor (pri-lek'tẽr), *n.* [L. *praelector;* see PRELE TION], [Chiefly British], a college or university lecture

pre·li·ba·tion (prē'li-bā'shən), *n.* [LL. *praelibatio* < *praelibare; prae-,* before + *libare,* to taste], [Rare], foretaste.

pre·lim·i·nar·i·ly (pri-lim'ə-ner'ə-li), *adv.* in a prelin inary manner; as a preliminary.

pre·lim·i·nar·y (pri-lim'ə-ner'i), *adj.* [< *pre-* + L. *li inaris,* of a threshold < *limen,* threshold, limit], comi before or leading up to the main action, discussio business, etc.; introductory; prefatory; preparator *n.* [*pl.* PRELIMINARIES (-iz)], *often in pl.* 1. a prelin inary step, procedure, arrangement, etc. 2. a prelin inary examination. Abbreviated **prelim.**

pre·lit·er·ate (prē-lit'ẽr-it), *adj.* [*pre-* + *literate*], designating or of a culture developed before the invention of writing and, hence, leaving no written records.

prel·ude (prel'ūd, prē'lōōd), *n.* [Fr. *prélude;* ML. *praeludium* < L. *praeludere*, to play beforehand; *prae-*, before + *ludere*, to play], 1. a thing serving as the introduction to a principal event, action, performance, etc.; preliminary part; preface; opening. 2. in *music, a)* an introductory section or movement of a suite, fugue, etc. *b)* since the 19th century, any short romantic composition. *v.t.* [PRELUDED (-id), PRELUDING], [L. *praeludere;* see the *n.*], 1. to serve as or be a prelude to. 2. to introduce by or as by a prelude. *v.i.* 1. to serve as or be a prelude. 2. to play or provide a prelude.

pre·lu·sion (pri-lōō'zhən), *n.* [L. *praelusio* < *praelusus*, pp. of *praeludere;* see PRELUDE], a prelude.

pre·lu·sive (pri-lōō'siv), *adj.* [< L. *praelusus*, pp. of *praeludere* (see PRELUDE); + *-ive*], introductory.

pre·lu·so·ry (pri-lōō'sə-ri), *adj.* prelusive.

prem., premium.

pre·ma·ture (prē'mə-tyoor', prē'mə-toor', prē'mə-choor'), *adj.* [L. *praematurus; prae-*, before + *maturus*, ripe], happening, done, arriving, or existing before the proper or usual time; unexpectedly early; too early.

pre·ma·ture·ly (prē'mə-tyoor'li, prē'mə-toor'li, prē'mə-choor'li), *adv.* before the proper time; too soon.

pre·max·il·la (prē'mak-sil'ə), *n.* [*pl.* PREMAXILLAE (-ē)], [Mod. L.; *pre-* + *maxilla*], in *anatomy & zoology*, either of two bones in the upper jaw of vertebrates, situated between and in front of the maxillae, and fusing with them in the adult human being.

pre·max·il·lar·y (prē-mak'sə-ler'i), *adj.* having to do with the premaxillae.

pre·med·i·cal (prē-med'i-k'l), *adj.* designating or of the studies preparatory to the study of medicine.

pre·med·i·tate (prē-med'ə-tāt'), *v.t.* [PREMEDITATED (-id), PREMEDITATING], [< L. *praemeditatus*, pp. of *praemeditari*, to think over, premeditate; *prae-*, before + *meditari;* see MEDITATE], to think out, plan, or scheme beforehand. *v.i.* to think or meditate beforehand.

pre·med·i·ta·tion (prē'med-ə-tā'shən), *n.* a premeditating; specifically, in *law*, a degree of planning and forethought sufficient to show intent to commit an act.

pre·med·i·ta·tive (prē-med'ə-tā'tiv), *adj.* that results from or shows premeditation.

pre·mi·er (prē'mi-ẽr, prem'yẽr; *for n., usually* pri-mêr'), *adj.* [Fr.; L. *primarius* < *primus*, first], 1. first in importance or rank; chief; foremost. 2. first in time; earliest. *n.* a chief official; specifically, a prime minister.

pre·mière (pri-mêr'; Fr. prə-myâr'), *n.* [Fr., fem. of *premier*], 1. a first performance of a play, etc. 2. the leading lady (in the cast of a play, etc.).

pre·mier·ship (pri-mêr'ship, prē'mi-ẽr-ship'), *n.* [see -SHIP], the office or term of a premier.

pre·mil·le·nar·i·an (prē'mil-ə-nâr'i-ən), *adj.* 1. occurring or living before the millennium. 2. designating or of the doctrine that the second coming of Christ will precede the millennium. *n.* a person who believes in this doctrine.

pre·mil·len·ni·al (prē'mə-len'i-əl), *adj.* of or happening in the period before the millennium.

pre·mil·len·ni·al·ism (prē'mə-len'i-əl-iz'm), *n.* the doctrine that the second coming of Christ will occur before the millennium.

prem·ise (prem'is; *for v., usually* pri-mīz'), *n.* [ME. *premisse;* ML. *praemissa* < L. *praemissus*, pp. of *praemittere*, to send before; *prae-*, before + *mittere*, to send], 1. a previous statement or assertion that serves as the basis for an argument. 2. *pl. a)* the part of a deed or lease that states its reason, the parties involved, and the property in conveyance. *b)* the property so mentioned; hence, 3. *pl.* a piece of real estate; house or building and its land: as, keep off the *premises*. 4. in *logic*, either of the two propositions of a syllogism from which the conclusion is drawn: see **syllogism.** *v.t.* [PREMISED (-mīzd', -ist), PREMISING], 1. to state beforehand; give as a premise. 2. to introduce or preface (a discourse, etc.), as with explanatory remarks. *v.i.* to make a premise. —*SYN.* see **presume.**

prem·iss (prem'is), *n.* a premise.

pre·mi·um (prē'mi-əm), *n.* [*pl.* PREMIUMS (-əmz)], [L. *praemium*, a reward, recompense < *prae-*, before + *emere*, to take], 1. a reward or prize, especially one offered as an added inducement to win, buy, etc.; bonus. 2. an additional amount paid or charged; specifically, *a)* an amount paid for a loan in addition to interest. *b)* an amount paid, as for stock, above the nominal or par value. 3. a payment; specifically, *a)* the amount payable or paid, in one sum or periodically, for an insurance policy. *b)* a fee paid for instruction in a trade, etc. *c)* a fee paid by a borrower of stock to the lender. 4. very high value: as, he put a *premium* on punctuality. 5. in *economics*, the amount by which one form of money exceeds another (of the same nominal value) in exchange value, or buying power. Abbreviated **pm., prem.** —*SYN.* see **bonus, reward.**

at a premium, 1. at a value or price higher than normal. 2. very valuable, usually because hard to get.

pre·mo·lar (prē-mō'lẽr), *adj.* designating or of any of the (bicuspid) teeth situated in front of the molars. *n.* a premolar tooth. See **tooth,** illus.

pre·mon·ish (pri-mon'ish), *v.t. & v.i.* [< L. *praemonere*, to forewarn, formed after *admonish*], [Rare], to advise or caution beforehand; forewarn.

pre·mo·ni·tion (prē'mə-nish'ən), *n.* [OFr. *premonicion;* LL. *praemonitio* < L. *praemonere; prae-*, before + *monere*, to warn], 1. a forewarning. 2. a foreboding; presentiment.

pre·mon·i·to·ry (pri-mon'ə-tôr'i, pri-mon'ə-tō'ri), *adj.* [LL. *praemonitorius*], that gives warning in advance; serving as a premonition.

pre·morse (pri-môrs'), *adj.* [L. *praemorsus*, pp. of *praemordere*, to bite off, orig. to bite in front or at the end; *prae-*, before + *mordere*, to bite], ending abruptly, as if bitten off: said of a leaf or root.

pre·mun·dane (prē-mun'dān), *adj.* antemundane.

pre·na·tal (prē-nā't'l), *adj.* [*pre-* + *natal*], existing or happening before birth.

pre·na·tal·ly (prē-nā't'l-i), *adv.* before birth.

pre·nom·i·nate (prē-nom'ə-nāt'; *also, for adj.,* prē-nom'ə-nit), *v.t.* [*pre-* + *nominate*, after L. *praenominare*], [Obs.], to name, or mention, beforehand. *adj.* [Obs.], previously mentioned; forenamed.

pre·no·tion (prē-nō'shən), *n.* [*pre-* + *notion*], [Rare], a preconception.

pren·tice, 'pren·tice (pren'tis), *n.* [ME. *prentis;* aphetic for *apprentice*], [Archaic or Dial.], an apprentice. *adj.* [Archaic or Dial.], characteristic of an apprentice.

pre·oc·cu·pan·cy (prē-ok'yoo-pən-si), *n.* [*pl.* PREOCCUPANCIES (-siz)], prior occupancy; preoccupation.

pre·oc·cu·pa·tion (prē-ok'yoo-pā'shən, prē'ok-yoo-pā'shən), *n.* [L. *praeoccupatio*], a preoccupying or being preoccupied.

pre·oc·cu·pied (prē-ok'yoo-pīd'), *adj.* 1. previously or already occupied. 2. occupied with or absorbed in one's thoughts; engrossed. 3. in *biology*, designating or of a name already used and hence no longer available. —*SYN.* see **absent-minded.**

pre·oc·cu·py (prē-ok'yoo-pī'), *v.t.* [PREOCCUPIED (-pīd'), PREOCCUPYING], [L. *praeoccupare; prae-*, before + *occupare*, to seize], 1. to occupy the thoughts of; engross; absorb. 2. to occupy or take possession of before someone else or beforehand.

pre·o·ral (prē-ôr'əl, prē-ō'rəl), *adj.* [*pre-* + *oral*], in *zoology*, located in front of, or anterior to, the mouth.

pre·or·dain (prē'ôr-dān'), *v.t.* to ordain or decree beforehand; foreordain.

pre·or·di·na·tion (prē'ôr-d'n-ā'shən), *n.* a preordaining or being preordained.

prep (prep), *adj.* [Colloq.], preparatory: as, a *prep* school. *n.* [Colloq.], a preparatory school.

prep., 1. preparation. 2. preparatory. 3. preposition.

pre·paid (prē-pād'), past tense and past participle of **prepay:** abbreviated **ppd.**

prep·a·ra·tion (prep'ə-rā'shən), *n.* [ME. *preparacion;* L. *praeparatio*], 1. a preparing. 2. a being prepared; readiness. 3. something done to prepare; preparatory measure. 4. something prepared for a special purpose, as a medicine, cosmetic, condiment, etc. 5. in *music, a)* the preparing for a dissonant chord by using the dissonant tone as a consonant tone in the immediately preceding chord. *b)* a tone so used. Abbreviated **prep.**

pre·par·a·tive (pri-par'ə-tiv), *adj.* [Fr. *preparatif;* ML. *praeparativus*], that tends or serves to prepare; preparatory. *n.* 1. something preparative. 2. a preparation.

pre·par·a·to·ry (pri-par'ə-tôr'i, pri-par'ə-tō'ri), *adj.* [ME. *preparatorye;* ML. *praeparatorius*], 1. that prepares or serves to prepare; preliminary; introductory. 2. undergoing preparation, or preliminary instruction, especially for college entrance: as, a *preparatory* student.

preparatory school, a private school for preparing students to enter college.

pre·pare (pri-pâr'), *v.t.* [PREPARED (-pârd'), PREPARING], [Fr. *préparer;* L. *praeparare; prae-*, before + *parare*, to set or place in order, get ready], 1. to make ready, usually for a specific purpose; make suitable; fit; adapt; train. 2. to make receptive; dispose; accustom: as, he *prepared* them for the bad news. 3. to equip or furnish with necessary provisions, accessories, etc.; fit out: as, they *prepared* an expedition. 4. to put together or make out of materials, ingredients, parts, etc., or according to a plan or formula; construct; compound: as, they *prepared* dinner, he *prepared* the medicine. 5. in *music*, to use (a dissonant tone) in preparation (sense 5). *v.i.* 1. to make things ready. 2. to make oneself ready.

pre·par·ed·ly (pri-pâr'id-li), *adv.* 1. in a manner showing preparation. 2. in such a way as to be prepared.

pre·par·ed·ness (pri-pâr'id-nis, pri-pârd'nis), *n.* the state of being prepared; specifically, possession of sufficient armed forces, matériel, etc. for waging war.

pre·pay (prē-pā′), *v.t.* [PREPAID (-pād′), PREPAYING], to pay or pay for in advance.

pre·pay·ment (prē-pā′mənt), *n.* payment in advance.

pre·pense (pri-pens′), *adj.* [earlier *prepensed, purpensed;* OFr. *purpense,* pp. of *purpenser,* to meditate < *pur-,* pro- + *penser* (L. *pensare*), to think], planned beforehand; premeditated.

pre·pon·der·ance (pri-pon′dẽr-əns), *n.* the condition of being preponderant; superiority in amount, weight, power, influence, importance, etc.

pre·pon·der·an·cy (pri-pon′dẽr-ən-si), *n.* preponderance.

pre·pon·der·ant (pri-pon′dẽr-ənt), *adj.* that preponderates; greater in amount, weight, power, influence, importance, etc.; predominant. —*SYN.* see **dominant.**

pre·pon·der·ate (pri-pon′də-rāt′), *v.i.* [PREPONDERATED (-id), PREPONDERATING], [< L. *praeponderatus,* pp. of *praeponderare; prae-,* before + *ponderare,* to weigh < *pondus, ponderis,* a weight], 1. to weigh more than something else. 2. to sink or incline downward, as a scale of a balance. 3. to surpass in amount, number, power, influence, importance, etc.; predominate.

pre·pon·der·a·tion (pri-pon′də-rā′shən), *n.* a preponderating; preponderance.

prep·o·si·tion (prep′ə-zish′ən), *n.* [ME. *preposicioun;* L. *praepositio* < *praepositus,* pp. of *praeponere; prae-,* before + *ponere,* to place], 1. in some languages, a relation word, as English *in, by, for, with, to,* etc., that connects a noun, pronoun, or noun phrase to another element of the sentence, as to a verb (e.g., he went *to* the store), to a noun (e.g., the sound *of* tramping feet), or to an adjective (e.g., old *in* years). 2. any construction of similar function (e.g., *in back of,* equivalent to *behind*). The noun or pronoun usually following the preposition (as *store, feet,* and *years* in the preceding examples) is called its *object.* Abbreviated **prep.**

prep·o·si·tion·al (prep′ə-zish′ən-′l), *adj.* of, functioning as, or formed with a preposition.

prep·o·si·tion·al·ly (prep′ə-zish′ən-′l-i), *adv.* 1. as a preposition. 2. by means of a preposition.

prepositional phrase, a preposition and its object.

pre·pos·i·tive (prē-poz′ə-tiv), *adj.* [LL. *praepositivus* < L. *praeponere;* see PREPOSITION], in *grammar,* put before; prefixed. *n.* a prepositive word.

pre·pos·i·tor (prē-poz′ə-tẽr), *n.* [altered < L. *praepositus;* see PROVOST], in some English public schools, a senior student with authority to discipline: also **praepostor, prepostor.**

pre·pos·sess (prē′pə-zes′), *v.t.* 1. [Rare], to take possession of or occupy beforehand or before another. 2. to possess or preoccupy beforehand to the exclusion of later thoughts, feelings, etc.; hence, 3. to prejudice; bias. 4. to impress favorably beforehand or at once.

pre·pos·sess·ing (prē′pə-zes′iŋ), *adj.* that prepossesses, or impresses favorably; pleasing; attractive.

pre·pos·ses·sion (prē′pə-zesh′ən), *n.* a prepossessing or being prepossessed; bias; predilection.

pre·pos·ter·ous (pri-pos′tẽr-əs), *adj.* [L. *praeposterus; prae-,* before + *posterus,* coming after], 1. originally, with the first last and the last first; inverted; hence, 2. contrary to nature, reason, or common sense; senseless; absurd; ridiculous. —*SYN.* see **absurd.**

pre·pos·tor (pri-pos′tẽr), *n.* a prepositor.

pre·po·ten·cy (pri-pō′t′n-si), *n.* [*pl.* PREPOTENCIES (-siz)], [L. *praepotentia; prae-,* before + *potentia,* power], 1. the condition or quality of being prepotent. 2. in *biology,* the greater capacity of one parent to transmit certain characteristics to offspring.

pre·po·tent (pri-pō′t′nt), *adj.* [L. *praepotens; prae-,* before + *potens;* see POTENT], 1. superior in power, force, or influence. 2. in *biology,* of or having prepotency.

pre·puce (prē′pūs), *n.* [Fr. *prépuce;* L. *praeputium* < *prae-,* before + base akin to Lith. *pusti,* to swell, Byelorussian *potka,* penis], the foreskin; fold of skin covering the end (glans) of the penis or clitoris.

pre·pu·tial (pri-pū′shəl), *adj.* of the prepuce.

Pre-Raph·a·el·ite (prē-raf′i-ə-līt′, prē-raf′ə-līt′, prē-rā′fi-ə-līt′), *n.* 1. a member of the Pre-Raphaelite Brotherhood, a society of artists led by Dante Gabriel Rossetti, Holman-Hunt, and J. E. Millais, formed in England in 1848 to encourage painting with the fidelity to nature and delicacy of treatment characteristic of Italian art before the time of Raphael. 2. any modern artist with similar aims. 3. any Italian painter before Raphael. *adj.* 1. of or characteristic of the Pre-Raphaelites or their followers. 2. designating or of Italian painters or painting before Raphael.

pre·req·ui·site (prē-rek′wə-zit), *adj.* required beforehand, especially as a necessary condition for something following. *n.* something prerequisite.

pre·rog·a·tive (pri-rog′ə-tiv), *n.* [ME. *prerogatif;* OFr.; L. *praerogativa,* called upon to vote first < *praerogare,* to ask before; *prae-,* before + *rogare,* to ask], 1. a prior or exclusive right or privilege, especially one peculiar to a rank, class, etc. 2. priority or precedence, as that derived from such a right or privilege. 3. a superior advantage. *adj.* of or having a prerogative.

prerogative court, 1. formerly, any of certain courts in England and Ireland with jurisdiction over testamentary matters. 2. the New Jersey probate cou

Pres., 1. Presbyterian. 2. President.

pres., 1. present. 2. presidency.

‡**pre·sa** (pre′sä), *n.* [*pl.* PRESE (-se)], [It., lit., a taki up, seizure < pp. of *prendere* (L. *prehendere*), to tak in *music,* a sign (:S:, +, ※) showing where each su cessive voice enters in a canon.

pres·age (pres′ij; *for v.,* pri-sāj′), *n.* [ME. < L. *pra sagium,* a foreboding < *prae-,* before + *sagire,* to pe ceive], 1. a sign or warning of a future event; ome portent; augury. 2. a foreboding; presentime 3. [Rare], a prediction. 4. meaning; import: as, ominous *presage.* *v.t.* [PRESAGED (-sājd′), PRESAGIN [Fr. *présager* < the *n.*], 1. to give a presage, or warnin of; portend. 2. to have a foreboding or presentime of. 3. to predict. *v.i.* 1. to have a presentiment. to make a prediction. —*SYN.* see **foretell.**

pres·by·o·pi·a (prez′bi-ō′pi-ə, pres′bi-ō′pi-ə), *n.* [Mo L. < Gr. *presbys,* old + *ōps,* an eye], a form of fa sightedness occurring after middle age, caused by diminished elasticity of the crystalline lens.

pres·by·op·ic (prez′bi-op′ik, pres′bi-op′ik), *adj.* of having presbyopia.

pres·by·ter (prez′bi-tẽr, pres′bi-tẽr), *n.* [LL., an eld see PRIEST], 1. in the early Christian church and the Presbyterian Church, an elder. 2. in the Episcop Church, a priest or minister.

pres·byt·er·al (prez-bit′ẽr-əl, pres-bit′ẽr-əl), *adj.* [I *presbytéral;* ML. *presbyteralis*], presbyterial.

pres·byt·er·ate (prez-bit′ẽr-it, pres-bit′ə-rāt′), *n.* [M *presbyteratus*], 1. the office of a presbyter. 2. a pre bytery.

pres·by·te·ri·al (prez′bə-têr′i-əl, pres′bə-têr′i-əl), *a* having to do with presbyters or a presbytery.

Pres·by·te·ri·an (prez′bə-têr′i-ən, pres′bə-têr′i-ən), *a* [< LL. *presbyterium,* presbytery; + *-an*], 1. [p-], havi to do with church government by presbyters. 2. de ignating or of a church of a Calvinistic Protesta denomination governed by presbyters, or elders. *n.* believer in Presbyterianism or a member of a Pre byterian church. Abbreviated **Pres., Presb., Presby**

Pres·by·te·ri·an·ism (prez′bə-têr′i-ən-iz′m, pres′bə-têr i-ən-iz′m), *n.* 1. church government by presbyters, elders of equal rank, over whom there is no high authority. 2. the doctrines and beliefs of the Presb terian churches.

pres·by·ter·y (prez′bi-ter′i, pres′bi-ter′i), *n.* [*pl.* PRE BYTERIES (-iz)], [ME. *presbetory;* OFr. *presbiterie;* L *presbyterium,* council of elders < *presbyter;* see PRIES 1. a body of presbyters; specifically, in Presbyteri churches, an ecclesiastical court made up of all t ministers and one or two presbyters from each pari in a given district. 2. the district of such a cour 3. the part of a church reserved for the officiating clerg 4. in the *Roman Catholic Church,* a priest's house.

pre·school (prē′skōōl′), *adj.* designating, of, or for child between infancy and school age, or in the a group 2–4, 2–5, or 2–6.

pre·sci·ence (prē′shi-əns, presh′i-əns), *n.* [ME.; OF L. *praescientia* < *praescire; prae-,* before + *scire,* know], knowledge of things before they happen come into being; foreknowledge; foresight.

pre·sci·ent (prē′shi-ənt, presh′i-ənt), *adj.* [Fr.; L. *pra sciens,* ppr.], having prescience.

pre·scind (pri-sind′), *v.t.* [L. *praescindere,* to cut off front; *prae-,* before + *scindere,* to cut], to detac abstract, or isolate (a meaning, one's mind, etc.).

Pres·cott, William Hick·ling (hik′liŋ pres′kət), 179 1859; American historian.

pre·scribe (pri-skrīb′), *v.t.* [PRESCRIBED (-skrībd′), PR SCRIBING], [L. *praescribere; prae-,* before + *scribere,* write], 1. originally, to write beforehand; hence, 2. set down as a rule or direction; order; ordain; direc 3. to order or advise as a medicine or treatment: sa of physicians, etc. 4. in *law,* to invalidate or outla by negative prescription. *v.i.* 1. to set down or gi rules, directions, etc. 2. to give medical advice prescriptions. 3. in *law, a)* to claim a right or tit through long use or possession (often with *to* or *for b)* to become invalidated or outlawed by negati prescription.

pre·script (pri-skript′; *also, and for n. always,* prē skript), *adj.* [L. *praescriptus,* pp. of *praescribere;* s PRESCRIBE], prescribed. *n.* [L. *praescriptum* < *pra scriptus*], something prescribed; order; direction; ru

pre·scrip·ti·ble (pri-skrip′tə-b′l), *adj.* 1. that can effectively prescribed for: as, a *prescriptible* illnes 2. acquired or acquirable by prescription (sense 5).

pre·scrip·tion (pri-skrip′shən), *n.* [ME. *prescripcio* L. *praescriptio*], 1. a prescribing. 2. something pr scribed; order; direction; prescript. 3. a doctor's writte direction for the preparation and use of a medicin 4. a medicine so prescribed. 5. in *law, a)* the acqui ment of the title or right to something through continued use or possession from time immemorial over a long period. *b)* a right or title so acquired.

pre·scrip·tive (pri-skrip′tiv), *adj.* [LL. *praescriptivus* 1. that prescribes. 2. based on legal prescription. prescribed by custom or long use.

pres·ence (prez'ns), *n.* [ME.; OFr.; L. *praesentia* < *praeesse;* see PRESENT, *adj.*], 1. the fact, condition, or quality of being present. 2. immediate surroundings; vicinity within close view: as, I was admitted to his *presence.* 3. attendance; company. 4. a person who is present, especially a royal person. 5. a person's bearing, personality, or appearance: as, he has a poor *presence.* 6. pleasing deportment; dignity: as, he has no *presence.* 7. an influence or supernatural spirit felt to be present; ghost. 8. [Archaic], people present; an assemblage. 9. [Obs.], a presence chamber.

saving your presence, though I apologize for saying or doing this in your presence.

presence chamber, the room in which a king or other person of rank or distinction formally receives guests.

presence of mind, ability to think clearly and act quickly and intelligently in an emergency.

pres·ent (prez''nt; *for v.,* pri-zent'), *adj.* [ME.; OFr.; L. *praesens,* ppr. of *praeesse,* to be present; *prae-,* before + *esse,* to be], 1. being at the specified or understood place; at hand; in attendance: opposed to *absent.* 2. existing or happening now; in process: contrasted with *past, future.* 3. now being discussed, considered, written, read, etc.: as, the *present* writer. 4. [Archaic], self-possessed; collected; ready. 5. [Obs.], prompt to act, understand, or assist; efficacious. 6. in *grammar,* designating or of a tense or verb form expressing action as now taking place or state as now existing (e.g., he *goes*), action that is habitual (e.g., he *speaks* with an accent), or action that is always true (e.g., two and two *is* four). *n.* 1. the present time. 2. the present occasion. 3. in *grammar, a)* the present tense. *b)* a verb in it. 4. [OFr., in phr. *mettre en present à,* to put before (someone), present, offer, hence a gift], something presented; gift. Abbreviated **pr., pres.** (in sense 3). *v.t.* [ME. *presenten;* OFr. *presenter;* L. *praesentare,* to place before, present, hold out, lit., to make present < *praesens;* see the *adj.*], 1. to bring (a person) into the presence of another or others; introduce, especially to a superior. 2. to offer to view or notice; exhibit; display; show. 3. to offer for consideration. 4. to offer for acceptance; make a gift of; bestow. 5. to make a gift or donation to: as, he *presented* the college with a library. 6. to represent (a character) on the stage; act; perform. 7. to point, level, or aim, as a weapon. 8. to nominate to an ecclesiastical benefice. 9. in *law, a)* to lay before a legislature, court, etc. for consideration. *b)* to bring a charge or indictment against.

by these presents, in *law,* by this document.

present arms, in *military usage,* 1. to hold a rifle vertically in line with the middle of the body, with the muzzle up, at eye level, and the trigger away from the body: a position of salute. 2. *a)* this position. *b)* the command to assume it.

***SYN.*—present** and **gift** both refer to something given as an expression of friendship, affection, esteem, etc., but **gift,** in current use, more often suggests formal bestowal (Christmas *presents,* the painting was a *gift* to the museum); **donation** applies to a gift of money, etc. for a philanthropic, charitable, or religious purpose, especially as solicited in a public drive for funds (a *donation* to the Community Chest); **gratuity** applies to a gift of money, etc. for services rendered, such as a tip to a waiter. See also **give, offer.**

pre·sent·a·bil·i·ty (pri-zen'tə-bil'ə-ti), *n.* the condition or quality of being presentable.

pre·sent·a·ble (pri-zen'tə-b'l), *adj.* 1. capable of being presented; suitable for presentation. 2. fit to be seen; suitable, as in appearance, for introduction into society.

pre·sent·a·bly (pri-zen'tə-bli), *adv.* in a presentable manner; so as to be presentable.

pres·en·ta·tion (prez''n-tā'shən, prē'zen-tā'shən), *n.* [ME.; OFr. *presentacion;* L. *praesentatio* < *praesentare;* see PRESENT, *v.*], 1. a presenting or being presented. 2. something that is presented; specifically, *a)* a performance, as of a play. *b)* a gift. 3. in *commerce,* a presentment. 4. in *ecclesiastical usage, a)* the naming of a clergyman to a benefice. *b)* a request to the bishop to institute the clergyman named. 5. in *obstetrics,* the position of the fetus in the uterus at the time of delivery, with reference to the part presenting itself at the mouth of the uterus: as, an arm or breech *presentation.* 6. in *philosophy & psychology,* anything present in the consciousness at a single moment as an actual sensation or a mental image; perception.

pres·en·ta·tion·al (prez''n-tā'shən-'l, prē'zen-tā'shən-'l), *adj.* 1. of (a) presentation. 2. presentive.

pres·en·ta·tion·ism (prez''n-tā'shən-iz'm, prē'zen-tā'shən-iz'm), *n.* in *philosophy,* the theory that in perception the mind is directly aware of an external object without any intervening medium: opposed to *representationism.*

pre·sent·a·tive (pri-zen'tə-tiv), *adj.* 1. serving to present; presenting. 2. in *ecclesiastical usage,* designating a benefice to or for which a patron has the right of presentation. 3. in *philosophy & psychology,* capable of being known directly without the use of reason.

pres·ent-day (prez''nt-dā'), *adj.* of the present time.

pres·en·tee (prez''n-tē'), *n.* [< Anglo-Fr.], 1. a person presented, especially for institution to a benefice. 2. a person to whom something is presented.

pre·sen·ti·ment (pri-zen'tə-mənt), *n.* [obs. Fr. < L. *praesentire;* see PRE- & SENTIMENT], a feeling that something, especially of an unfortunate or evil nature, is about to take place; premonition; foreboding.

pre·sen·tive (pri-zen'tiv), *adj.* presenting an object or idea directly to the mind: as, a *presentive* word: opposed to *representative, symbolic.*

pres·ent·ly (prez''nt-li), *adv.* 1. in a little while; soon; shortly. 2. at present; at this time; now. 3. [Archaic or Dial.], at once; instantly.

pre·sent·ment (pri-zent'mənt), *n.* [ME.; OFr. *presentement* < *presenter;* see PRESENT, *v.*], 1. presentation. 2. an exhibition; thing presented to view. 3. in *commerce,* the producing of a note, bill of exchange, etc. for acceptance or payment at the proper time and place. 4. in *law,* the notice taken or report made by a grand jury of an offense on the basis of the jury's knowledge and without a bill of indictment. 5. in *philosophy,* a presentation.

present participle, in *grammar,* a participle of present meaning (e.g., *running* in "running water"): abbreviated **ppr., p.pr., pres. part.**

present perfect, in *grammar,* 1. expressing action or state as completed at the time of speaking but not at any definite time in the past. 2. the present perfect tense: it is formed in English by using the present tense of *have* with a past participle (e.g., he *has* gone). 3. a verb in this tense.

pre·serv·a·ble (pri-zũr'və-b'l), *adj.* that can be preserved.

pres·er·va·tion (prez'ẽr-vā'shən), *n.* [Fr. *préservation;* ML. *praeservatio*], a preserving or being preserved.

pre·serv·a·tive (pri-zũr'və-tiv), *adj.* [ME. *preseruatyve;* ML. *praeservativus*], having the quality of preserving. *n.* anything that preserves; especially, a substance added to a food to keep it from spoiling or rotting.

pre·serve (pri-zũrv'), *v.t.* [PRESERVED (-zũrvd'), PRESERVING], [ME. *preserven;* LL. *praeservare;* L. *prae-,* before + *servare,* to keep], 1. to keep from harm, damage, danger, evil, etc.; protect; save. 2. to keep from spoiling or rotting. 3. to prepare (food), as by canning, pickling, salting, etc., for future use. 4. to keep up; carry on; maintain. 5. to maintain and protect (game, fish, etc.) for private use in hunting or fishing. *v.i.* 1. to preserve fruit, etc. 2. to maintain a game preserve. *n.* 1. *usually pl.* fruit preserved whole by cooking with sugar. 2. a place where game, fish, etc. are preserved. 3. something that preserves or is preserved. —***SYN.*** see **defend.**

pre-shrunk (prē'shruŋk'), *adj.* shrunk by a special process in manufacture so that there is little or no shrinkage in laundering or dry cleaning.

pre·side (pri-zīd'), *v.i.* [PRESIDED (-id), PRESIDING], [Fr. *présider;* L. *praesidere* < *prae-,* before + *sedere,* to sit], 1. to be in the position of authority; take charge of a meeting; act as chairman. 2. to have control or authority. 3. to be in the leading place, as a featured instrumentalist, etc.

pres·i·den·cy (prez'i-dən-si), *n.* [*pl.* PRESIDENCIES (-siz)], [ML. *praesidentia* < L. *praesidens;* see PRESIDENT], 1. the office or function of president. 2. the term during which a president is in office. 3. [often P-], the office of President of the United States. 4. [P-], formerly, any of the three original provinces of British India (Bengal, Bombay, and Madras), originally governed by presidents of the East India Company's holdings. 5. in the *Mormon Church, a)* a council of three with local jurisdiction. *b)* a council of three (*First Presidency*) that is the highest administrative body. Abbreviated **pres.**

pres·i·dent (prez'i-dənt), *n.* [ME. < L. *praesidens,* ppr. of *praesidere;* see PRESIDE], 1. the highest officer of a company, society, university, club, etc. 2. [often P-], the chief executive of a republic. 3. the formal head of a republic, with little or no executive power, usually the presiding member of the legislative assembly or council. Abbreviated **Pres., P., p.**

pres·i·dent-e·lect (prez'i-dənt-i-lekt'), *n.* an elected president who has not yet taken office.

pres·i·den·tial (prez'i-den'shəl), *adj.* [ML. *praesidentialis*], of or having to do with a president or presidency.

pres·i·dent·ship (prez'i-dənt-ship'), *n.* [see -SHIP], [British], the office or term of a president.

pre·sid·i·al (pri-sid'i-əl), *adj.* [Fr. *présidial;* LL. *praesidialis*], of or having a presidio, or garrison.

pre·sid·i·ar·y (pri-sid'i-er'i), *adj.* [L. *praesidiarius*], presidial.

pre·sid·i·o (pri-sid'i-ō'), *n.* [*pl.* PRESIDIOS (-ōz')], [Sp.; L. *praesidium,* a garrison, orig. a presiding over, hence defense, protection], 1. a fortified place; military post; fort; garrison. 2. a (Spanish) penal settlement.

pre·sid·i·um (pri-sid'i-əm), *n.* [L. *praesidium,* a presiding over, protection], in the Soviet Union, *a*) any of a number of permanent administrative committees meeting regularly and empowered to act for a larger body between its sessions. *b*) [P-], the permanent administrative committee of the Supreme Soviet.

pre·sig·ni·fy (prē-sig'nə-fī'), *v.t.* [PRESIGNIFIED (-fīd'), PRESIGNIFYING], to signify, or give an indication of, beforehand; foreshadow.

pres. part., present participle.

press (pres), *v.t.* [ME. *pressen;* OFr. *presser;* L. *pressare,* freq. of *premere,* to press], 1. to act on with steady force or weight; push steadily against; squeeze. 2. *a*) to extract juice, etc. from by squeezing. *b*) to squeeze (juice, etc.) out; express. 3. *a*) to squeeze for the purpose of making smooth, compact, etc.; compress. *b*) to iron, as clothes. 4. to embrace closely. 5. to force; compel; constrain. 6. to urge or solicit earnestly or persistently; entreat; importune. 7. to impose by persistent entreaty; try to force: as, she *pressed* the gift on her friend. 8. to lay stress on; be insistent about; emphasize. 9. to distress; embarrass; straiten: as, they were *pressed* with want. 10. to urge on; drive on. 11. Archaic], to crowd; throng. 12. [Obs.], to oppress. *v.i.* to exert pressure; specifically, *a*) to weigh down; bear heavily. *b*) to go forward with energetic or determined effort. *c*) to force one's way. *d*) to crowd; throng. *e*) to be urgent or insistent. *n.* 1. a pressing or being pressed; pressure, urgency, etc. 2. a crowd; throng. 3. an instrument or machine by which something is crushed, stamped, smoothed, etc. by pressure. 4. *a*) any of various machines for printing; printing press. *b*) a printing establishment. *c*) the art, business, or practice of printing. *d*) newspapers, magazines, etc. in general, or the persons who write for them; journalism or journalists. *e*) publicity, criticism, etc. in newspapers, magazines, etc. 5. an upright closet in which clothes or other articles are kept. —*SYN.* see **urge.**

go to press, to start to be printed.

press (pres), *v.t.* [altered (by association with prec. *press*) < obs. *prest,* to engage for military service by advance payment on wages; OFr. *prester;* L. *praestare,* to vouch for, warrant; *prae-,* before + *stare,* to stand], 1. to force into military or naval service. 2. to force or urge into any kind of service. 3. to use in a way different from the ordinary. *n.* 1. an impressment, or forcing into service, usually naval or military. 2. an order for impressing recruits.

press agent, a person whose business is to advance the interests of a person, organization, etc., usually by getting publicity; publicity agent: abbreviated **P.A.**

press·board (pres'bôrd', pres'bōrd'), *n.* 1. a heavy glazed paper used to cover the cylinder or platen of printing presses. 2. a smooth board of stiff, heavy paper or wood, used in presses for finishing paper, books, etc.

press box, a place reserved for reporters at sports events, etc.

Press·burg (pres'boorkh), *n.* Bratislava, a city in Czechoslovakia: the German name.

press conference, a collective interview granted to journalists, as by a celebrity or personage.

press·er (pres'ẽr), *n.* a person or thing that presses; specifically, a person whose work is pressing newly made or freshly cleaned clothes.

press gallery, a section set apart for journalists in a chamber where an official body meets.

press·gang (pres'gaŋ'), *n.* a press gang.

press gang, [for *prest gang;* see PRESS (to force into service)], a group of men who round up other men and force them into naval or military service.

press·ing (pres'iŋ), *adj.* [ppr. of *press* (to push against)], 1. calling for immediate attention; urgent. 2. persistent in request or demand; importunate.

press·man (pres'mən), *n.* [*pl.* PRESSMEN (-mən)], an operator of a printing press.

press·mark (pres'märk'), *n.* a letter, number, etc. stamped on a book to show its place on a library shelf.

press of sail (or **canvas**), in *nautical usage,* the maximum amount of sail that a ship can safely carry under any particular wind pressure.

pres·sor (pres'ẽr), *adj.* [< *pressure,* after *motor, adj.*], 1. increasing the pressure. 2. designating a nerve which, when stimulated, causes a rise in blood pressure and increased activity of some motor center.

press proof, the last proof examined before the matter is printed or the electrotype or stereotype is made.

press·room (pres'rōōm', pres'room'), *n.* the room where the printing presses are located, as in a newspaper building or printing establishment.

pres·sure (presh'ẽr), *n.* [ME.; OFr.; L. *pressura* < *pressus,* pp. of *premere,* to press], 1. a pressing or being pressed; compression; squeezing. 2. a condition of distress; oppression; affliction. 3. a compelling influence; constraining force: as, we all react to social *pressure.* 4. demands requiring immediate attention; urgency. 5. [Obs.], an impression; mark made by pressing. 6. in *electricity,* electromotive force. 7. in *physics,* force exerted against an opposing body; the thrust distributed over a surface: expressed in weight per unit of area: symbol, P (no period). Abbreviate **P., p., press.** *v.t.* [PRESSURED (-ẽrd), PRESSURING [Colloq.], to exert pressure, or compelling influence, o

pressure cooker, an airtight metal container for quic cooking by means of steam under pressure.

pressure gauge, 1. a gauge for measuring the pressu of steam, water, gas, etc. 2. a mechanism for measurin explosive pressure, as in the barrel of a gun.

pressure group, any group that exerts pressure upc legislators and the public through lobbies, propagand etc. in order to affect legislation or policies.

pressure point, any of a number of points on the bod where an artery passes close to the surface and front of a bony structure so that pressure applie there will check bleeding from a distal injured par

pres·sur·ize (presh'ẽr-īz'), *v.t.* [PRESSURIZED (-īzd' PRESSURIZING], to keep nearly normal atmospher pressure inside of (an airplane, etc.), as at high altitud or in rising or descending.

pressurized suit, a garment with pneumatic pads f protecting an aviator from the effects of changes pressure and the force of gravity in high-altitude fligh test dives, etc.

press·work (pres'wũrk'), *n.* 1. the operation or ma agement of a printing press. 2. work done by a prin ing press.

prest (prest), *n.* [ME. *preste;* OFr. (Fr. *prêt*) < *prest* (Fr. *prêter*), to lend, afford < L. *praestare;* see PRE (to force into service)], 1. originally, a loan; advan of money. 2. an advance of money to men enlistin in the British army or navy: also **prest money.** *ad* [Obs.], ready; prepared.

pres·ter (pres'tẽr), *n.* [OFr. *prestre;* LL. *presbyter*], priest; presbyter.

Pres·ter John (pres'tẽr), [ME. *Prestre Johan;* OF *prestre Jehan;* ML. *presbyter Iohannes*], a legenda medieval Christian king and priest thought to ha ruled either in the Far East or in Ethiopia.

pres·ti·dig·i·ta·tion (pres'tə-dij'i-tā'shən), *n.* [Fr.; s PRESTIDIGITATOR], the performance of tricks by quic skillful use of the hands; sleight of hand; legerdema

pres·ti·dig·i·ta·tor (pres'tə-dij'i-tā'tẽr), *n.* [Fr. *pres digitateur* (after L. *prestigiator,* juggler, deceiver) < *presto* (see PRESTO) + L. *digitus,* a finger (cf. DIGIT an expert at prestidigitation.

pres·tige (pres-tēzh', pres'tij), *n.* [Fr.; L. *praestigiu* delusion, illusion, juggler's trick < *praestinguere* *praestingere,* to bind tight, blindfold], 1. the pow to command admiration or esteem. 2. reputation distinction based on brilliance of achievement, cha acter, etc.; renown. —*SYN.* see **influence.**

pres·tis·si·mo (pres-tis'ə-mō'; It. pres-tēs'sē-mô'), *ad & adj.* [It., superl. of *presto;* see PRESTO], in *music,* ve fast; as fast as possible: a direction to the perform *n.* a prestissimo musical passage or movement.

pres·to (pres'tō), *adv. & adj.* [It., quick, nimble; L *praestus,* at hand, ready], 1. fast. 2. in *music,* in fa tempo: a direction to the performer. *n.* a music passage or movement performed in fast tempo.

Pres·ton (pres'tən), *n.* a seaport in Lancashire, Englan near Liverpool: pop., 116,000 (est. 1946).

Pres·ton·pans (pres't'n-panz'), *n.* a resort in sout eastern Scotland: site of a battle (1745).

pre·sum·a·ble (pri-zōōm'ə-b'l, pri-zūm'ə-b'l), *adj.* th may be presumed, or taken for granted; probable.

pre·sum·a·bly (pri-zōōm'ə-bli, pri-zūm'ə-bli), *adv.* may be presumed, or taken for granted; probably.

pre·sume (pri-zōōm', pri-zūm'), *v.t.* [PRESUM (-zōōmd', -zūmd'), PRESUMING], [ME. *presumen;* OF *presumer;* L. *praesumere; prae-,* before + *sumere,* take], 1. to take upon oneself without permission authority; dare (to say or do something); venture. 2. take for granted; accept as true until proof to t contrary is furnished; suppose; presuppose. 3. to co stitute reasonable evidence for supposing: as, a sign invoice *presumes* receipt of the shipment. *v.i.* 1. to a presumptuously; take liberties. 2. to rely too mu (*on* or *upon*), as in taking liberties. 3. to take som thing for granted; make suppositions.

SYN.—**presume** implies a taking something for granted accepting it as true, usually on the basis of probable evidence its favor and the absence of proof to the contrary (the man *presumed* to be of sound mind); **presuppose** is the broade term here, sometimes suggesting a taking something for grant unwarrantedly (this writer *presupposes* a too extensive vocab lary in children) and, in another sense, implying that somethi is required as a preceding condition (brilliant technique in pia playing *presupposes* years of practice); **assume** implies the su position of something as the basis for argument or action (let *assume* his motives were good); **postulate** implies the assum tion of something as an underlying factor, often one that incapable of proof (his argument *postulates* the inherent goo ness of man); **premise** implies the setting forth of a propositi on which a conclusion can be based.

pre·sum·ed·ly (pri-zōōm'id-li, pri-zūm'id-li), *adv.* as or may be presumed; supposedly.

pre·sump·tion (pri-zump'shən), *n.* [ME.; OFr. *pr somption;* L. *praesumptio,* a taking beforehand < *pra sumptus,* pp. of *praesumere;* see PRESUME], 1. the a of presuming; specifically, *a*) an overstepping of prop bounds; forwardness; effrontery. *b*) the taking of something for granted. 2. the thing presumed; supposition. 3. a ground or reason for presuming; evidence that points to the probability of something. 4. in *law*, the inference that a fact exists, based on the proved existence of other facts.

re·sump·tive (pri-zump′tiv), *adj.* [Fr. *présomptif;* LL. *praesumptivus* < L. *praesumptus;* see PRESUMPTION], 1. giving reasonable ground for belief: as, *presumptive* evidence. 2. based on probability; presumed: as, an heir *presumptive.*

re·sump·tu·ous (pri-zump′choo-əs), *adj.* [ME.; OFr. *presuntuex;* LL. *praesumptuosus* < L. *praesumptus;* see PRESUMPTION], 1. too bold or forward; taking too much for granted; showing overconfidence, arrogance, or effrontery; taking liberties. 2. [Obs.], presumptive.

re·sup·pose (prē′sə-pōz′), *v.t.* 1. to suppose or assume beforehand; take for granted. 2. to require or imply as a preceding condition: as, a healthy body *presupposes* healthful living. —*SYN.* see **presume.**

re·sup·po·si·tion (prē′sup-ə-zish′ən), *n.* [ML. *praesuppositio*], 1. a presupposing. 2. the thing, fact, idea, etc. presupposed.

re·sur·mise (prē′sũr-mīz′), *v.t.* to surmise beforehand. *n.* a surmise made in advance; presentiment.

ret., preterit.

re·tence (pri-tens′, prē′tens), *n.* pretense: British spelling.

re·tend (pri-tend′), *v.t.* [ME. *pretenden,* to intend; OFr. *pretendre;* L. *praetendere; prae-,* before + *tendere,* to reach, stretch], 1. to claim; profess; allege: as, he *pretended* ignorance of the law. 2. to claim or profess falsely; feign; simulate: as, he *pretended* that he was ill. 3. to suppose in play; make believe: as, she *pretended* that she was a princess. *v.i.* 1. to lay claim (with *to*). 2. to make believe in play or in an attempt to deceive; feign. —*SYN.* see **assume.**

re·tend·ed (pri-ten′did), *adj.* [pp. of *pretend*], 1. not genuine; feigned. 2. reputed or alleged.

re·tend·er (pri-ten′dẽr), *n.* 1. a person who pretends. 2. a claimant to a throne; specifically, [P-], in English history, the son (James Edward, called *Old Pretender*) or the grandson (Charles Edward, called *Young Pretender*) of James II. 3. an aspirant.

re·tense (pri-tens′, prē′tens), *n.* [ME.; Anglo-Fr. *pretensse;* ML. *pretensa* < *praetensus,* alleged < L. *praetentus,* pp. of *praetendere;* see PRETEND], 1. a claim, as to some distinction or accomplishment; pretension: as, he made no *pretense* to being infallible. 2. a false claim or profession: as, under the *pretense* of friendship. 3. a false show of something. 4. something said or done for show. 5. a pretending, as at play; make-believe. 6. a false reason or plea; pretext. 7. [Rare], aim; intention. 8. pretentiousness.

re·ten·sion (pri-ten′shən), *n.* [ML. *praetensio* < *praetensus;* see PRETENSE], 1. a pretext or allegation. 2. a claim, as to a right, title, distinction, dignity, etc. 3. assertion of a claim. 4. pretentiousness.

re·ten·tious (pri-ten′shəs), *adj.* [Fr. *prétentieux* < L. *praetentus,* pp. of *praetendere;* see PRETEND], 1. making claims, explicit or implicit, to some distinction, importance, dignity, or excellence. 2. showy; ostentatious.

re·ter- (prē′tẽr), [L. *praeter-* < *praeter,* beyond, past, compar. of *prae,* before, ahead], a prefix meaning *past, beyond, outside the bounds of,* as in *preternatural.*

re·ter·hu·man (prē′tẽr-hū′mən), *adj.* beyond that which is human; especially, superhuman.

ret·er·it, pret·er·ite (pret′ẽr-it), *adj.* [ME. & OFr. *preterit;* L. *praeteritus,* gone by, pp. of *praeterire; praeter-,* beyond + *ire,* to go], 1. in *grammar,* expressing past action or state. 2. [Rare], past; bygone; former. *n.* 1. the past tense. 2. a verb in it. Abbreviated **pret.**

ret·er·i·tion (pret′ẽr-ish′ən), *n.* [LL. *praeteritio* < L. *praeteritus;* see PRETERIT], 1. a passing over; omission. 2. in *law,* an omitting of one or more legal heirs from a will. 3. in *theology,* the passing over by God of those not elect: a doctrine of Calvinism.

re·ter·mis·sion (prē′tẽr-mish′ən), *n.* [L. *praetermissio*], a pretermitting or being pretermitted.

re·ter·mit (prē′tẽr-mit′), *v.t.* [PRETERMITTED (-id), PRETERMITTING], [L. *praetermittere,* to let go by; *praeter-,* beyond + *mittere,* to send], 1. to leave out or undone; neglect or omit. 2. to let pass unnoticed; overlook.

re·ter·nat·u·ral (prē′tẽr-nach′ẽr-əl), *adj.* [ML. *praeternaturalis*], 1. differing from or beyond what is natural; out of the ordinary. 2. supernatural.

re·ter·nat·u·ral·ism (prē′tẽr-nach′ẽr-əl-iz′m), *n.* 1. the quality or condition of being preternatural. 2. a preternatural occurrence. 3. a preternatural doctrine or system.

re·text (prē′tekst), *n.* [Fr. *pretexte;* L. *praetextum,* neut. of *praetextus,* pp. of *praetexere,* to weave before, pretend, disguise; *prae-,* before + *texere,* to weave], a false reason or motive put forth to hide the real one; excuse.

re·tor (prē′tẽr, prē′tôr), *n.* a praetor.

Pre·to·ri·a (pri-tôr′i-ə, pri-tō′ri-ə), *n.* the capital of Transvaal and seat of government of the Union of South Africa, in southern Transvaal: pop., 129,000.

pre·to·ri·an (pri-tôr′i-ən, pri-tō′ri-ən), *adj. & n.* praetorian.

pret·ti·fy (prit′i-fī′), *v.t.* [PRETTIFIED (-fīd′), PRETTIFYING], to make pretty, especially in a finical way.

pret·ti·ly (prit′′l-i), *adv.* in a pretty manner.

pret·ti·ness (prit′i-nis), *n.* a pretty quality or state.

pret·ty (prit′i; *by metathesis, esp. unstressed,* pũr′ti), *adj.* [PRETTIER (-i-ẽr), PRETTIEST (-i-ist)], [ME. *prati;* AS. *prættig,* crafty < *prætt,* a craft, trick], 1. pleasing; attractive: implying daintiness, delicacy, or gracefulness rather than striking beauty, elegance, grandeur, or stateliness. 2. fine; good; nice: often used ironically. 3. foppish. 4. [Archaic], elegant. 5. [Archaic or Scot.], brave; bold; gallant. 6. [Colloq.], considerable; rather large in amount or extent. *adv.* somewhat; to some extent or degree. *n.* [*pl.* PRETTIES (-iz)], a pretty person or thing. —*SYN.* see **beautiful.**

sitting pretty, [Slang], in a favorable position.

pret·ty·ish (prit′i-ish), *adj.* somewhat pretty.

pre·typ·i·fy (prē-tip′ə-fī′), *v.t.* to typify beforehand; prefigure; foreshadow.

pret·zel (pret′s′l), *n.* [G. *brezel;* OHG. *brezitella;* prob. ult. < L. *brachium,* an arm; basic sense "armlet, bracelet"], a hard, brittle biscuit made from slender rolls of dough heavily sprinkled with salt and usually baked in the form of a loose knot.

Preus·sen (proi′sən), *n.* Prussia: the German name.

pre·vail (pri-vāl′), *v.i.* [ME. *prevaylen;* L. *praevalere; prae-,* before + *valere,* to be strong, be well], 1. to gain the advantage or mastery; be victorious; triumph (often with *over* or *against*). 2. to be effective; produce or achieve the desired effect; succeed. 3. to be or become stronger or more widespread; predominate; hence, 4. to exist widely; be in general use; be prevalent.

prevail on (or **upon, with**), to persuade; induce.

pre·vail·ing (pri-vāl′iŋ), *adj.* [ppr. of *prevail*], 1. being superior in strength or influence. 2. predominant. 3. widely existing; prevalent. 4. efficacious.

SYN.—**prevailing** applies to that which leads all others in acceptance, usage, belief, etc. at a given time and in a given place (a *prevailing* practice); **current** refers to that which is commonly known or accepted or in general usage at the time specified or, if unspecified, at the present time (that pronunciation was *current* in the 18th century); **prevalent** implies widespread occurrence or acceptance but does not now connote the predominance of **prevailing** (a *prevalent* belief); **rife** implies rapidly increasing prevalence and often connotes excitement or commotion (rumors about the plague were *rife*).

prev·a·lence (prev′ə-ləns), *n.* [Fr. *prévalence;* ML. *praevalentia* < L. *praevalere;* see PREVAIL], 1. [Rare], predominance. 2. widespread existence, general practice, occurrence, or acceptance.

prev·a·lent (prev′ə-lənt), *adj.* [L. *praevalens,* ppr. of *praevalere;* see PREVAIL], 1. [Rare], predominant. 2. widely existing; generally practiced, occurring, or accepted. —*SYN.* see **prevailing.**

pre·var·i·cate (pri-var′ə-kāt′), *v.i.* [PREVARICATED (-id), PREVARICATING], [< L. *praevaricatus,* pp. of *praevaricari,* to prevaricate, lit., to walk crookedly < *prae-,* before + *varicare,* to straddle < *varicus,* straddling < *varus,* bent]. 1. to turn aside from or evade the truth; equivocate. 2. loosely, to lie. —*SYN.* see **lie.**

pre·var·i·ca·tion (pri-var′ə-kā′shən), *n.* a prevaricating.

pre·var·i·ca·tor (pri-var′ə-kā′tẽr), *n.* [L. *praevaricator*], a person who prevaricates.

pre·ven·ience (prē-vēn′yəns), *n.* the condition or fact of being prevenient.

pre·ven·ient (prē-vēn′yənt), *adj.* [L. *praeveniens,* ppr. of *praevenire;* see PREVENT], 1. going before; preceding; hence, 2. anticipating; expectant. 3. antecedent to human action: as, *prevenient* grace.

pre·vent (pri-vent′), *v.t.* [ME. *preventen* < L. *praeventus,* pp. of *praevenire,* to anticipate; *prae-,* before + *venire,* to come], 1. formerly, *a*) to act in anticipation of (an event or a fixed time). *b*) to anticipate (a desire, want, objection, etc.). *c*) to anticipate in action. *d*) to precede. *e*) to forestall; balk; frustrate. 2. to stop or keep from doing something. 3. to keep from happening; make impossible by prior action; hinder.

SYN.—**prevent** implies a stopping or keeping from happening, as by some prior action or by interposing an obstacle or impediment (to *prevent* disease); **forestall** suggests advance action to stop something in its course and thereby make it ineffective (try to *forestall* their questions); **preclude** implies a making impossible by shutting off every possibility of occurrence (guards at all the doors *precluded* his escape); **obviate** suggests the preventing of some unfavorable outcome by taking the necessary anticipatory measures (his forthright statement *obviated* any possible objections); **avert** suggests a warding off of imminent danger or misfortune (the use of diplomacy to *avert* war).—*ANT.* permit, allow.

pre·vent·a·ble (pri-ven′tə-b′l), *adj.* capable of being prevented: also spelled **preventible.**

pre·vent·a·tive (pri-ven′tə-tiv), *adj.* & *n.* preventive.
pre·ven·tion (pri-ven′shən), *n.* 1. a preventing. 2. a means of preventing; hindrance.
pre·ven·tive (pri-ven′tiv), *adj.* preventing or serving to prevent; specifically, in *medicine*, preventing disease. *n.* anything that prevents; specifically, in *medicine*, anything that prevents disease; prophylactic. Also **preventative.**
pre·view (prē-vū′; *also, and for n. always,* prē′vū′), *v.t.* to view or show beforehand. *n.* 1. a previous view or survey. 2. *a*) a private showing of a motion picture, fashion show, etc. before exhibition to the public. *b*) a showing of scenes from a motion picture in order to advertise its coming appearance: also spelled **prevue.**
pre·vi·ous (prē′vi-əs, prēv′yəs), *adj.* [L. *praevius* < *prae-*, before + *via*, a way], 1. occurring before in time or order; going before; prior. 2. [Colloq.], premature.
previous to, before.
SYN.—**previous** implies rather generally a coming before in time or order (during a *previous* encounter); **prior** adds to this a connotation of greater importance or claim as a result of being first (a *prior* commitment); **preceding,** especially when used with the definite article, implies a coming immediately before (the *preceding* night); **antecedent** adds to the meaning of **previous** a connotation of direct causal relationship with what follows the events *antecedent* to the war); **foregoing** applies specifically to something previously said or written (the *foregoing* examples); **former** always connotes comparison, stated or implied, with what follows (termed *latter*).—*ANT.* following.
pre·vi·ous·ly (prē′vi-əs-li), *adv.* at a previous time.
previous question, the question whether a matter under consideration by a parliamentary body should be voted on immediately: in the United States, generally, a negative vote does not postpone further consideration of the matter as it does in England.
pre·vise (prē-vīz′), *v.t.* [PREVISED (-vīzd′), PREVISING], [< L. *praevisus*, pp. of *praevidere*, to foresee; *prae-*, before + *videre*, to see], [Rare], 1. to foresee; forecast. 2. to warn; inform beforehand.
pre·vi·sion (prē-vizh′ən), *n.* [Fr. *prévision;* ML. *praevisio* < L. *praevisus;* see PREVISE], 1. foresight; knowledge of the future. 2. a prophetic or anticipatory vision or prognostication.
pre·vi·sion·al (prē-vizh′ən-′l), *adj.* of prevision.
pre·vo·ca·tion·al (prē′vō-kā′shən-′l), *adj.* designating or of training or instruction given as a prerequisite for admission to a vocational school.
Pré·vost, Mar·cel (mȧr′sel′ prā′vō′), 1862–1941; French novelist.
Pré·vost d'Ex·iles, An·toine Fran·çois (än′twän′ frän′swȧ′ prā′vō′ deg′zēl′), 1697–1763; French novelist: called *Abbé Prévost.*
pre·vue (prē′vū′), *n.* a preview (sense 2*b*).
pre·war (prē′wôr′), *adj.* before the war.
prex·y (prek′si), *n.* [*pl.* PREXIES (-siz)], [contr. of *president*], [Slang], the president, especially of a college or university.
prey (prā), *n.* [ME. *preie, preye;* OFr. *preie, praie;* L. *praeda;* prob. < base of *prehendere*, to seize], 1. originally, plunder; booty. 2. an animal hunted or killed for food by another animal. 3. a person or thing that falls victim to someone or something. 4. the act or habit of seizing other animals for food: as, a bird of *prey.* *v.i.* 1. to plunder; pillage; rob. 2. to hunt or kill other animals for food. 3. to make profit from a victim by swindling, etc. 4. to have a wearing or destructive influence; weigh heavily. Generally used with *on* or *upon.*
Pri·am (prī′əm), *n.* [L. *Priamus;* Gr. *Priamos*], in *Greek legend*, the last king of Troy, who reigned during the Trojan War, father of Hector and Paris.
pri·a·pism (prī′ə-piz′m), *n.* [LL. *priapismus;* Gr. *priapismos* < *priapizein*, to act the part of Priapus], a pathological condition characterized by persistent erection of the penis.
Pri·a·pus (prī-ā′pəs), *n.* [L.; Gr. *Priapos*], 1. in *Greek & Roman mythology*, a god personifying the male procreative power, conceived as the son of Dionysus and Aphrodite. 2. [p-], a phallus.
Pri·bi·lof Islands (prē′bi-lôf′; Eng. prib′ə-lof′), a group of Alaskan islands in the Bering Sea, north of the Aleutian Islands: noted as a breeding place of seals.
price (prīs), *n.* [ME. & OFr. *pris;* L. *pretium*, a price], 1. the amount of money, etc. asked or given for something; cost; charge. 2. value; worth. 3. a reward for the capture or death of a person. 4. money or other consideration as a bribe: as, some people think that every man has his *price.* 5. the cost, as in life, labor, sacrifice, etc., of obtaining some benefit or advantage. Abbreviated **pr.** *v.t.* [PRICED (prīst), PRICING], 1. to put a price on; fix the price of. 2. [Colloq.], to ask or find out the price of.
at any price, no matter what the cost.
beyond (or **without**) **price,** priceless; invaluable.
price control, the establishment of ceiling prices on basic commodities by a government to prevent or combat inflation.
price·less (prīs′lis), *adj.* 1. of too great worth to be measured by price; invaluable. 2. [Colloq.], very amusing or absurd.

prick (prik), *n.* [ME. *prike;* AS. *prica*, a point, do akin to D. *prik;* ? < IE. base **bhrei-*, to cut, seen als in L. *friare*, to rub away (cf. FRIABLE), *frivolus*, lit breakable (cf. FRIVOLOUS)], 1. a very small punctu or, formerly, dot, made by a sharp point. 2. [Archaic any of various pointed objects, as a thorn, goad, et 3. a pricking. 4. a sharp pain caused by or as by being pricked. *v.t.* 1. to make a very small ope ing in with a sharp point. 2. to make (a hole) with sharp point. 3. to pain sharply or sting: as, remor *pricked* his conscience. 4. to mark or trace by dots points. 5. to pierce (a horse's foot) to the quick shoeing, causing lameness. 6. [Archaic], to spur urge on; goad; incite. *v.i.* 1. to give or feel a sligl piercing or sharp pain. 2. to have a prickly or stingir sensation; tingle. 3. [Archaic], to spur a horse o ride fast. 4. in *horticulture*, to transfer seedlings fro seed pans to shallow boxes (with *off* or *out*). *ad* carried stiffly erect: said of a dog's ears.
prick up, to rise erect; point or stick up.
prick up one's (or **its**) **ears,** 1. to raise the ears wi the points upward. 2. to listen closely.
prick·et (prik′it), *n.* [ME. *pryket*], 1. a small spike which to stick a candle. 2. a candlestick having su a spike. 3. a male deer in his second year, with straigh unbranched antlers.
prick·ing (prik′iŋ), *n.* 1. the act or process of one th pricks. 2. a prickly feeling.
prick·le (prik′′l), *n.* [ME. *prykel;* AS. *pricel*, earli *pricels* < base of *prica* (see PRICK) + *-els*, instrument suffix], 1. a small, sharply pointed growth; spin thorn. 2. a prickly sensation; stinging or tingling. 3. *botany*, a small, sharply pointed process growing fro the tissue under the outer layer of a plant. *v* [PRICKLED (-′ld), PRICKLING], 1. to prick as with spine or thorn. 2. to cause to feel a tingling sensatio *v.i.* to tingle.
prick·li·ness (prik′li-nis), *n.* the quality or state being prickly.
prick·ly (prik′li), *adj.* [PRICKLIER (-li-ẽr), PRICKLIE (-li-ist)], 1. full of prickles, or sharp points. 2. stingin smarting; tingling.
prickly ash, a shrub or small tree with prickles a yellowish flowers.
prickly heat, a noncontagious, itching and prickli skin eruption caused by inflammation of the swe glands, as in hot weather.
prickly pear, 1. the pear-shaped fruit of any of a nu ber of related flat-stemmed cactuses. 2. any of the cactuses.
prickly poppy, any of a number of related plants wi prickles, yellow juice, and large flowers of various colo
prick song, 1. [Obs.], music written down in pricks, dots; written music. 2. counterpoint; descant.
pride (prīd), *n.* [ME. *pride, prude, prute;* AS. *pryte prut*, proud; cf. PROUD], 1. an overhigh opinion oneself; exaggerated self-esteem; conceit. 2. the sho ing of this in behavior; haughtiness; arrogance. 3. sense of one's own dignity or worth; self-respect. delight or satisfaction in one's achievements, posse sions, children, etc. 5. a person or thing in whi pride is taken: as, his daughters are his *pride.* 6. t best of a class, group, society, etc.; pick; flower: the *pride* of the Yankees. 7. the best part or tim prime; flowering: as, in the *pride* of manhood. mettle (in a horse). 9. [Archaic], *a*) magnificen splendor. *b*) ornament. 10. [Obs.], sexual desire. *v* [PRIDED (-id), PRIDING], [Rare], to make proud.
pride oneself on, to be proud of.
SYN.—**pride** refers either to a justified or excessive belief one's own worth, merit, superiority, etc. (he takes *pride* in accuracy); **conceit** always implies an exaggerated opinion oneself, one's achievements, etc. (blinded by his overweeni *conceit*); **vanity** suggests an excessive desire to be admired others for one's achievements, appearance, etc. (his *vanity* wounded by criticism); **vainglory** implies extreme conceit manifested by boasting, swaggering, arrogance, etc. (the *va glory* of a conquering general); **self-esteem** implies a high op ion of oneself, sometimes a higher opinion than is held by othe —*ANT.* humility.
Pride, Thomas (prīd), ?–1658; English general a antiroyalist; signed death warrant of Charles I.
pride·ful (prīd′fool), *adj.* full of pride; proud; haught
pride of India, a tropical tree with purple or wh flowers: also called *pride of China.*
Pride's Purge (prīdz), the expulsion in 1648 of over 1 Royalist and Presbyterian members from the Engli House of Commons: conducted by Thomas Pride.
‡prie-dieu (prē′dyö′), *n.* [Fr. *prier*, to pray + *di* God], a small, low reading desk with a ledge kneeling at prayer.
pri·er (prī′ẽr), *n.* a person who pries: also spelled **pry**
priest (prēst), *n.* [ME. *prest, preost;* AS. *preost* < L *presbyter*, an elder; Gr. *presbyteros*, elder, compar. *presbys*, old, an old man; IE. base **pres-*, ahead **gweu-*, ox; cf. Sans. *purugava*, a guide, leader (ori of a herd of oxen)], 1. originally, in the early Christi church, a presbyter, or elder. 2. in hierarchical Chr tian churches, a clergyman ranking next below a bish

and authorized to administer the sacraments and pronounce absolution. 3. any clergyman: distinguished from *layman*. 4. a minister of any religion. 5. a person whose function is to make sacrificial offerings and perform other religious rites. 6. a person whose duties, attitude, etc. are like a priest's. Abbreviated **P., p., Pr.**

priest·craft (prēst′kraft′, prēst′kräft′), ***n.*** the craft, policies, methods, etc. of priests.

priest·ess (prēs′tis), ***n.*** a girl or woman priest, as of a pagan religion.

priest·hood (prēst′hood), ***n.*** [ME. *preosthood;* AS. *preosthad*], 1. the office, rank, or characteristics of a priest. 2. priests collectively.

Priest·ley, J. B. (prēst′li), (*John Boynton Priestley*), 1894– ; English critic, novelist, and playwright.

Priestley, Joseph, 1733–1804; English theologian and chemist; discoverer of oxygen.

priest·li·ness (prēst′li-nis), ***n.*** priestly state or quality.

priest·ly (prēst′li), ***adj.*** [PRIESTLIER (-li-ẽr), PRIESTLIEST (-li-ist)], of, like, or suitable for a priest or priests.

priest-rid·den (prēst′rid″n), ***adj.*** dominated or tyrannized by priests.

prig (prig), ***n.*** [< 16th-c. cant, but prob. a merging of several words; cf. next *prig*], 1. originally, any person regarded with dislike. 2. a person who affects great preciseness or propriety in matters of learning or morals, to the annoyance of others; smug, pedantic person.

prig (prig), ***v.t.*** [PRIGGED (prigd), PRIGGING], [cf. prec. *prig*], [British Slang], to steal. ***v.i.*** [Scot. or Dial.], to haggle. ***n.*** [British Slang], a thief or pickpocket.

prig·ger·y (prig′ẽr-i), ***n.*** the character or behavior of a prig; priggishness.

prig·gish (prig′ish), ***adj.*** like or characteristic of a prig; smug; overprecise.

prig·gism (prig′iz′m), ***n.*** priggery; priggishness.

prim (prim), ***adj.*** [PRIMMER (-ẽr), PRIMMEST (-ist)], [prob. < OFr. *prim*, prime, first; also, sharp, thin, slender, hence neat < L. *primus*, first], stiffly formal, precise, or correct; proper; demure. ***v.t.*** [PRIMMED (primd), PRIMMING], to produce a prim expression on (one's face or mouth). ***v.i.*** to assume a prim manner.

prim., 1. primary. 2. primitive.

pri·ma·cy (prī′mə-si), ***n.*** [*pl.* PRIMACIES (-siz)], [ME. *primacie;* OFr. *primacie, primatie;* ML. *primatia* < LL. *primas;* see PRIMATE], 1. the state of being first in time, order, rank, etc.; supremacy. 2. the rank, duties, or authority of a primate. 3. in the *Roman Catholic Church*, the supreme authority of the Pope.

pri·ma don·na (prē′mə don′ə), [*pl.* PRIMA DONNAS], [It., lit., first lady], 1. the principal woman singer in an opera or concert. 2. [Colloq.], a temperamental, conceited, or vain person; especially, such a woman.

pri·ma-fa·ci·e (prī′mə-fā′shi-ē′, prī′mə-fā′shi), ***adj.*** [see next entry], in *law*, adequate to establish a fact or raise a presumption of fact unless refuted: said of evidence.

pri·ma fa·ci·e (prī′mə fā′shi-ē′, fā′shi), [L.], at first sight; on first view, before further examination.

pri·mage (prī′mij), ***n.*** [ML. *primagium;* ? < It. *primo* (*legno*), keel], 1. formerly, a small fee paid by a shipper to a ship's master and crew for loading and taking care of his freight. 2. now, a small percentage added to freight charge and paid to the ship's owner.

pri·mal (prī′m'l), ***adj.*** [ML. *primalis* < L. *primus*, first], 1. first in time; original; primitive; primeval. 2. first in importance; chief; primary.

pri·ma·quine (prī′mə-kwēn′), ***n.*** a synthetic chemical compound, an aminoquinoline, used as a cure for malaria.

pri·ma·ri·ly (prī′mer′ə-li, prī′mẽr-ə-li; *esp. when emphatic* prī-mâr′ə-li), ***adv.*** 1. at first; in the first instance; originally. 2. in the first place; principally.

pri·ma·ry (prī′mer′i, prī′mẽr-i), ***adj.*** [L. *primarius* < *primus*, first], 1. first in time or order of development; primitive; original; earliest: as, a *primary* instinct. 2. *a*) from which others are derived; fundamental; elemental. *b*) designating the colors regarded as basic, or as those from which all others may be derived: the classification of colors as primary differs according to the point of view; thus, in color photography, red, green, and blue are considered primary, but in painting the term is applied to red, yellow, and blue: cf. **color.** 3. of or in the first stage of a succession; elementary; preparatory: as, *primary* studies: distinguished from *secondary, tertiary*, etc. 4. first in importance; chief; principal: as, a *primary* policy. 5. in *chemistry*, *a*) characterized by or resulting from the replacement of one atom or radical. *b*) designating or characterized by one carbon atom united to not more than one other carbon atom in a molecule. 6. in *electricity*, designating or of an inducing current, circuit, or coil in an induction coil, etc. 7. in *geology*, designating or of the earliest periods, up through the Paleozoic Era. 8. in *linguistics*, *a*) having as its fundamental form a base or other element that cannot be broken down: said of derivation. *b*) referring to present or future time: said of Latin, Greek, and Sanskrit tenses. 9. in *zoology*, of the large, stiff feathers on the end joint of a bird's wing. ***n.*** [*pl.* PRIMARIES (-iz)], 1. something first in order, quality, importance, etc. 2. in the United States, a local meeting of voters of a given political party to prepare for choosing candidates for public office, by selecting delegates to a nominating convention, etc. 3. *often in pl.* a direct primary election. 4. one of the primary colors. 5. in *astronomy*, a planet, etc. in relation to one or more smaller bodies (satellites) revolving around it. 6. in *electricity*, a primary coil. 7. in *zoology*, a primary feather. Abbreviated **prim.**

primary accent, 1. the heaviest accent, or stress, in pronouncing a word. 2. the mark for this, in this dictionary (′), as in *prim′rōz′* (primrose).

primary cell, in *electricity*, a battery cell whose energy is derived from an irreversible electrochemical reaction and which is hence incapable of being recharged by an electric current.

primary election, see **direct primary election.**

primary school, a school providing elementary instruction; specifically, a school providing instruction for the first few years of the public-school course, as in the United States.

pri·mate (prī′mit, prī′māt), ***n.*** [ME. & OFr. *primat* < LL. *primas, primatis*, of the first, chief < L. *primus*, first], 1. [Rare], a person with primacy. 2. an archbishop, or the highest-ranking bishop in a province, etc. 3. any member of the most highly developed order of animals, composed of man, the apes, monkeys, lemurs, etc.

pri·mate·ship (prī′mit-ship′, prī′māt-ship′), ***n.*** [see -SHIP], the rank or duties of a primate; a primacy.

pri·ma·tial (prī-mā′shəl), ***adj.*** [Fr. < ML. *primatia*, primacy], having to do with a primate.

prime (prīm), ***adj.*** [OFr.; L. *primus*, first, compar. of OL. *pri*, before], 1. first in time; original; primitive; primary. 2. first in rank or authority; chief: as, *prime* minister. 3. first in importance or value; principal; main: as, a *prime* advantage. 4. first in quality; of the highest excellence; first-rate: as, *prime* beef. 5. from which others are derived; fundamental; elemental: as, the *prime* reason. 6. in *mathematics*, *a*) that can be divided by no other whole number than itself or 1, as 3, 5, or 7. *b*) that cannot be divided by the same whole number except 1: as, 9 and 16 are *prime* to one another. ***n.*** [AS. *prim* < L. *prima* (*hora*), first (hour); see the *adj.*], 1. the first daylight canonical hour or office, usually beginning at 6 A.M. or sunrise. 2. the first hour of the day, usually corresponding to this; dawn. 3. the earliest part; beginning; hence, 4. springtime. 5. the springtime of life; youth; hence, 6. the best, most vigorous, or most fully mature period or stage of a person or thing: as, the soprano was in her *prime*. 7. the best part of anything. 8. the best of several or many; pick; cream. 9. any of a number of equal parts, usually sixty, into which a unit of measure, as a degree, is divided, and which usually may in turn be subdivided in the same proportion. 10. the mark indicating this (′): it is also used to distinguish a letter, etc. from another of the same kind, as *A′*. 11. in *arithmetic*, a prime number. 12. in *music*, unison. ***v.t.*** [PRIMED (prīmd), PRIMING], 1. to make ready; prepare. 2. to prepare (a gun) for firing by providing, formerly, with a charge of gunpowder, now, with a primer. 3. to get (a pump) into operation by pouring in water until the suction is established. 4. to undercoat, size, or otherwise prepare (a surface) for painting. 5. to provide (a person) beforehand with information, answers, etc. ***v.i.*** 1. to prime a gun, pump, surface, person, etc. 2. to let water in the form of spray mix with the steam forced into the cylinder: said of steam engines.

prime cost, the direct cost of labor and material in producing an article, exclusive of capital, overhead, etc.

prime·ly (prīm′li), ***adv.*** [Colloq.], extremely well: excellently.

prime meridian, the meridian from which longitude is measured both east and west; 0°: it passes through Greenwich, England.

prime minister, in some countries, the chief executive of the government and, usually, head of the cabinet.

prime mover, 1. the original force in a series of transmissions of force. 2. any natural force applied by man to produce power, as muscular energy, flowing water, etc. 3. a machine, as a turbine, that converts a natural force into productive power. 4. in *Aristotelian philosophy*, the first cause of all movement.

prim·er (prim′ẽr), ***n.*** [ME.; ML. *primarius* < L. *primus*, first], 1. originally, a prayer book. 2. a book for teaching children how to spell or read. 3. a textbook that gives the first principles of any subject. 4. in *printing*, either of two sizes of type: *a*) **great primer,** or 18 point. *b*) **long primer,** or 10 point.

prim·er (prīm′ẽr), ***n.*** 1. a person or thing that primes.

2. a small cap, tube, etc. containing explosive, used to fire the main charge of a big gun.
prime ribs, a choice cut of beef consisting of the seven ribs immediately before the loin.
pri·me·ro (pri-mâr′ō), *n.* [Sp. *primera*, fem. of *primero*, first; see PRIMARY], a card game popular in the 16th and 17th centuries.
pri·me·val (prī-mē′v'l), *adj.* [< L. *primaevus* < *primus*, first + *aevum*, an age; + *-al*], of the first age or ages; primitive: as, *primeval* forests.
pri·mi·ge·ni·al (prī′mi-jē′ni-əl), *adj.* [< L. *primigenius*; see PRIMOGENITURE], 1. [Obs.], earliest produced or generated; original; primitive. 2. in *zoology*, designating or of a species of a primitive type.
pri·mine (prī′min), *n.* [< L. *primus*, first; + *-ine*; cf. Fr. *primine*], in *botany*, the outer covering of the ovule.
prim·ing (prīm′iŋ), *n.* 1. the act of a person or thing that primes. 2. the gunpowder or other explosive used to fire a charge in a gun or in blasting. 3. an undercoat or first coat of paint, sizing, etc.
pri·mip·a·ra (prī-mip′ə-rə), *n.* [*pl.* PRIMIPARAE (-rē′)], [L. < *primus*, first + *parere*, to bear], a woman who is pregnant for the first time or who has borne just one child.
pri·mi·par·i·ty (prī′mi-par′ə-ti), *n.* the fact or condition of being a primipara.
pri·mip·a·rous (prī-mip′ə-rəs), *adj.* of or being a primipara or primiparae.
prim·i·tive (prim′ə-tiv), *adj.* [ME. *primitif* < L. *primitivus* < *primus*, first], 1. of or existing in the beginning or the earliest time or ages; ancient; original. 2. characteristic or imitative of the earliest ages; crude; simple; rough; uncivilized. 3. underived; primary; basic. 4. in *biology*, *a)* primordial. *b)* designating species, etc. very little evolved from early ancestral types. *n.* 1. a primitive person or thing. 2. an artist or a work of art that belongs to or is suggestive of an early period. 3. in *algebra & geometry*, a form from which another is derived. 4. in *grammar*, the form from which a certain word or other form has been derived; root; base: distinguished from *derivative*. Abbreviated **prim.**
prim·i·tiv·ism (prim′ə-tiv-iz'm), *n.* belief in or practice of primitive ways, living, etc.
Pri·mo de Ri·ve·ra, Mi·guel (mē-gel′ prē′mô *the* rē-ve′-rä), Marquis of Estella, 1870–1930; Spanish general; military and civil head of Spain (1923–1930).
pri·mo·gen·i·tor (prī′mə-jen′i-tẽr), *n.* [ML. < L. *primus*, first + *genitor*, a father], 1. an ancestor; forefather. 2. the earliest ancestor of a family, race, etc.
pri·mo·gen·i·ture (prī′mə-jen′i-chẽr), *n.* [ML. *primogenitura* < L. *primus*, first + *genitura*, a begetting < *gignere*, to beget], 1. the condition or fact of being the first-born of the same parents. 2. in *law*, the right of the eldest son to inherit his father's estate.
pri·mor·di·al (prī-môr′di-əl), *adj.* [ME.; LL. *primordialis* < L. *primordium*, the beginning < *primus*, first + *ordiri*, to begin], 1. first in time; existing at or from the beginning; primitive; primeval. 2. underived; fundamental; original. 3. in *biology*, earliest formed in the development of an organism or organ; primitive.
pri·mor·di·um (prī-môr′di-əm), *n.* [*pl.* PRIMORDIA (-ə)], [L., earliest beginning; cf. PRIMORDIAL], in *embryology*, the first recognizable aggregation of cells that will form a distinct organ or part of the embryo.
primp (primp), *v.t. & v.i.* [dial. extension of *prim*], to dress overcarefully or showily; prink.
prim·rose (prim′rōz′), *n.* [altered (by association with *rose*) < ME. & OFr. *primerole*, primrose; ML. *primula*, a flower, daisy, primrose < L. *primus*, first], 1. any of a number of related plants having variously colored, tubelike flowers with five lobes. 2. the flower of any of these plants. 3. the light yellow of some primroses. *adj.* 1. of the primrose. 2. light-yellow.
primrose path, [popularized after Shakespeare, *Hamlet*, I, iii], the path of pleasure.
prim·u·la (prim′yoo-lə), *n.* [ML.], the primrose.
prim·u·la·ceous (prim′yoo-lā′shəs), *adj.* [< Mod. L. *Primulaceae*, name of the family < ML. *primula*; see PRIMROSE], of the primrose family of plants.
‡pri·mum mo·bi·le (prī′məm mob′ə-lē′), [L., first moving thing; see PRIME, *adj.* & MOBILE], in *Ptolemaic astronomy*, the tenth and outermost concentric sphere, revolving from east to west about the earth as a center and causing all heavenly bodies to revolve with it.
prin., 1. principal. 2. principally. 3. principle.
prince (prins), *n.* [ME.; OFr.; L. *princeps*, first, chief, prince < *primus*, first + *capere*, to take], 1. a monarch; especially, a king. 2. a ruler whose rank is below that of king; head of a principality. 3. a nonreigning male member of a royal family. 4. in Great Britain, a son of the sovereign or of a son of the sovereign. 5. the English equivalent of any of various titles of nobility in other languages. 6. a pre-eminent person in any class or group: as, a merchant *prince*. Abbreviated **Pr., P., p.**
Prince Albert, [after *Prince Albert*, consort of Victoria of England], a long, double-breasted frock coat.
Prince Albert National Park, a Canadian national park in central Saskatchewan: area, 1,869 sq. mi.
prince consort, the husband of a queen or empress wh reigns in her own right.
prince·dom (prins′dəm), *n.* 1. the territory over whic a prince rules; a principality. 2. the rank or digni of a prince.
Prince Edward Island, an island province of Canad in the Gulf of St. Lawrence: area, 2,184 sq. mi.; pop 98,000; capital, Charlottetown: abbreviated **P.E.I.**
prince·kin (prins′kin), *n.* [*prince* + *-kin*], a princelin
prince·let (prins′lit), *n.* a princeling.
prince·li·ness (prins′li-nis), *n.* the condition or quali of being a prince.
prince·ling (prins′liŋ), *n.* a young, small, or subordina prince.
prince·ly (prins′li), *adj.* [PRINCELIER (-li-ẽr), PRINC LIEST (-li-ist)], 1. of a prince; royal; regal; noble. that is a prince. 3. characteristic of a prince; libera generous. 4. worthy of a prince; magnificent; lavis
Prince of Darkness, the Devil; Satan.
Prince of Peace, Jesus Christ.
Prince of Wales, the oldest son and heir apparent of British king or queen.
Prince of Wales, Cape, a promontory of the Sewa Peninsula, Alaska, on the Bering Strait: the wester most point of North America.
Prince of Wales Island, 1. an island of the Alexand Archipelago, southeastern Alaska. 2. an island b tween Victoria Island and Somerset Island, Northwe Territories, Canada: area, 14,004 sq. mi.
prince royal, the oldest son of a king or queen.
Prince Rupert, a seaport in western British Columbi Canada: pop., 7,000.
prince's-feath·er (prin′siz-feth′ẽr), *n.* a graceful pla with a few large leaves and dense spikes of red flowe
prin·cess (prin′sis, prin′ses), *n.* [ME.; OFr.; see PRINC & -ESS], 1. originally, a woman sovereign. 2. a no reigning female member of a royal family. 3. in Gre Britain, a daughter of the sovereign or of a son of t sovereign. 4. the wife of a prince. 5. any wom regarded as having the characteristics, position, et of a princess.
prin·cesse, prin·cess (prin-ses′, prin′sis), *adj.* [Fr., princess], of or designating a woman's one-piece, clos fitting garment, gored and unbroken at the waistlin
princess royal, the oldest daughter of a king or quee
Prince·ton (prins′tən), *n.* a town in central New Jerse pop., 12,000: scene of a battle (1777) of the Revolutio ary War, in which Washington defeated the British.
prin·ci·pal (prin′sə-p'l), *adj.* [ME.; OFr.; L. *principa* < *princeps*; see PRINCE], first in rank, authority, i portance, degree, etc. *n.* 1. a principal person thing; specifically, *a)* a chief; head. *b)* a governing presiding officer, as of a school. *c)* a main actor performer. *d)* a combatant in a duel: distinguish from *second*. 2. one of the main end rafters of a ro supporting the purlins, which in turn support the or nary rafters. 3. in *finance*, *a)* the amount of a debt, vestment, etc. minus the interest, or on which intere is computed. *b)* the face value of a stock or bond. *c)* t main body of an estate, etc., as distinguished fro income. 4. in *law*, *a)* a person who employs anoth to act as his agent. *b)* the person primarily responsib for an obligation: distinguished from *surety*. *c)* a pers who commits a crime or is present as an abettor to distinguished from *accessory*. 5. in *music*, *a)* in Germ organs, the open diapason in 4-foot, 8-foot, 16-foot, a 32-foot stops. *b)* in American and British organs, 4-foot open diapason, or an 8-foot open diapason on t pedal. *c)* the soloist in a concert. *d)* the first player any division of orchestral instruments except the fi violins. *e)* the subject of a fugue: opposed to *answ* Abbreviated **prin.** —***SYN.*** see **chief.**
prin·ci·pal·i·ty (prin′sə-pal′ə-ti), *n.* [*pl.* PRINCIPALITI (-tiz)], 1. [Rare], the state or quality of being princip or a principal. 2. the rank, dignity, or jurisdiction of prince. 3. the territory ruled by a prince. 4. a count with which a prince's title is identified. 5. *pl.* in *the ogy*, one of the nine orders of angels.
prin·ci·pal·ly (prin′sə-p'l-i, prin′sip-li), *adv.* chiefl mainly; for the most part: abbreviated **prin.**
principal parts, the principal inflected forms of a ver from which the other forms may be derived: in Englis the principal parts are the present infinitive, the pa tense, and the past participle (e.g., *drink, drank, drun go, went, gone; add, added, added*).
prin·ci·pal·ship (prin′sə-p'l-ship), *n.* [see -SHIP], t position, duties, or term of a principal.
prin·cip·i·um (prin-sip′i-əm), *n.* [*pl.* PRINCIPIA (-ə) [L. < *princeps*; see PRINCE], 1. a principle. 2. first principles; fundamentals.
prin·ci·ple (prin′sə-p'l), *n.* [< L. *principium*, aft *manciple, participle*, etc.; see PRINCIPIUM], 1. the ult mate source, origin, or cause of something. 2. a natur or original tendency, faculty, or endowment. 3. fundamental truth, law, doctrine, or motivating forc upon which others are based. 4. a rule of conduc especially of right conduct: as, the *principle* of raci equality. 5. *a)* such rules collectively. *b)* adheren to them; integrity; uprightness: as, a person of *pri*

ciple. 6. an essential element, constituent, or quality, especially one that produces a specific effect: as, the active *principle* of a medicine. 7. the law of nature by which a thing operates: as, capillary attraction is the *principle* of a blotter. 8. the method of a thing's operation: as, the *principle* of a gasoline engine is internal combustion. Abbreviated **prin.**

in principle, as far as the principle is concerned; theoretically or in essence.

on principle, because of or according to a principle.

prin·ci·pled (prin′sə-p'ld), *adj.* having principles, as of conduct: often in hyphenated compounds, as *high-principled.*

prin·cox (prin′koks), *n.* [earlier also *princocks, princock;* the 1st element is prob. < *preen, v.,* the 2d < *cox-, cocks-,* as in *coxcomb*], [Obs. or Dial.], a coxcomb; fop.

prink (priŋk), *v.t.* [prob. related to *prank,* with association of *preen, v.*], to dress (oneself) up. *v.i.* 1. to dress up; preen. 2. to fuss over one's appearance; primp.

print (print), *n.* [ME. *prente, preinte;* OFr. *priente, preinte* < *prient,* pp. of *preindre* < L. *premere,* to press], 1. a mark made in or on a surface by pressing or hitting with an object; impression; imprint: as, the *print* of a heel. 2. an object for making such a mark, as a stamp, die, seal, mold, etc. 3. an object or mass that has received such a mark: as, a *print* of butter. 4. a cloth printed with a design, or a dress made of this. 5. the condition of being printed. 6. printed letters, words, etc.; the impression made by inked type; typography: as, uneven *print.* 7. a picture or design printed from a plate, block, roll, etc., as an etching, woodcut, lithograph, etc. 8. printed material: as, news*print.* 9. a publication. 10. an edition or printing, as of a book. 11. a photograph made by exposing sensitized paper to light passed through a negative. *v.t.* [ME. *prenten, printen* < the *n.*], 1. to mark by pressing or stamping; make a print on or in. 2. to press or stamp (a mark, letter, etc.) on or in a surface; hence, 3. to draw, trace, carve, or otherwise make (a mark, letter, etc.) on a surface. 4. to produce on the surface of (paper, etc.) the impression of inked type, plates, etc. by means of a printing press; hence, 5. to perform or cause to be performed all processes connected with the printing of (a book, etc.), as typesetting, presswork, binding, etc. 6. to publish (a manuscript, one's ideas, etc.) in print. 7. to write in letters resembling printed ones: as, *print* the name. 8. to produce (a photograph) by exposing sensitized paper to light passed through a negative. 9. to impress upon the mind, memory, etc. *v.i.* 1. to practice the art or trade of a printer. 2. to produce an impression, print, photograph, etc.: as, this negative *prints* well. 3. to draw letters resembling printed ones.

in print, 1. in printed form; published. 2. still purchasable from the publisher: said of books, etc.

out of print, no longer procurable for purchase from the publisher: said of books, etc.

print·a·ble (prin′tə-b'l), *adj.* 1. that can be printed or printed from. 2. fit to print.

printed circuit, an electrical circuit formed by applying conductive material in fine lines or other shapes to an insulating sheet, as by printing with electrically conductive ink, by electroplating, etc.

print·er (prin′tẽr), *n.* a person or thing that prints; especially, a person whose work or business is printing.

print·er·y (prin′tẽr-i), *n.* [*pl.* PRINTERIES (-iz)], 1. a printing shop. 2. a factory where cloth is printed.

print·ing (prin′tiŋ), *n.* 1. the act of a person or thing that prints. 2. the production of printed matter. 3. this as an art; typography. 4. something printed; the printed part. 5. all the copies of a book, etc. printed at one time. 6. letters made like printed ones; lettering.

printing press, a machine for printing from inked type, plates, or rolls.

print·less (print′lis), *adj.* having, making, or leaving no print or mark.

print shop, 1. a shop where printing is done. 2. a shop where prints, etchings, etc. are sold.

pri·or (prī′ẽr), *adj.* [L., former, superior, compar. of OL. *pri,* before; akin to L. *prae,* before, *primus,* first], 1. preceding in time; earlier; previous; former. 2. preceding in order or importance; preferred: as, a *prior* choice. *n.* [ME. < AS. *prior* & OFr. *prior, priur;* both < ML. *prior,* a prior < L. *prior;* see the *adj.*], 1. the head of a priory or other religious house. 2. in an abbey, the person in charge next below the abbot. —*SYN.* see **previous.**

prior to, before: as, it happened *prior to* my arrival.

Pri·or, Matthew (prī′ẽr), 1664–1721; English poet.

pri·or·ate (prī′ẽr-it), *n.* [ME.; ML. *prioratus*], 1. the rank, office, or term of a prior. 2. a priory.

pri·or·ess (prī′ẽr-is), *n.* [see PRIOR & -ESS], 1. the woman head of a priory of nuns, etc. 2. in an abbey of nuns, the woman in charge next below the abbess.

pri·or·i·ty (prī-ôr′ə-ti, prī-or′ə-ti), *n.* [*pl.* PRIORITIES (-tiz)], [ME. *priorite;* ML. *prioritas*], 1. the quality or condition of being prior; precedence in time, order, importance, etc. 2. *a*) a right to precedence in obtaining travel reservations, purchasing certain commodities, etc. *b*) an order granting this.

pri·or·ship (prī′ẽr-ship′), *n.* [see -SHIP], the rank, office, or term of a prior; priorate.

pri·o·ry (prī′ẽr-i), *n.* [*pl.* PRIORIES (-iz)], [ME. < Anglo-Fr. *priorie;* ML. *prioria*], a monastery governed by a prior, or a nunnery governed by a prioress, sometimes as a subordinate branch of an abbey. —*SYN.* see **cloister.**

Pri·pet (prē′pet), *n.* a river in Poland and the Byelorussian S.S.R., flowing into the Dnepr: length, c. 500 mi.: also **Pripyat.**

Pripet Marshes, a marshy region in eastern Poland and the Byelorussian S.S.R.: area, c. 20,000 sq. mi.

Pri·pyat (prē′pyät′y'), *n.* Pripet.

Pris·cian (prish′ən, prish′i-ən), *n.* Latin grammarian of the 5th century A.D.

Pris·cil·la (pri-sil′ə), [L. (Gr. *Priskilla*), dim. of *Prisca,* fem. of *Priscus,* a Roman surname < *priscus,* ancient, primitive], a feminine name.

prise (prīz), *n.* & *v.t.* [PRISED (prīzd), PRISING], prize (lever, etc.).

prism (priz'm), *n.* [LL. *prisma;* Gr. *prisma,* lit., something sawed < *prizein,* to saw], 1. in *geometry,* a solid figure whose ends are polygonal, equal in size and shape, and parallel, and whose sides are parallelograms. 2. a crystalline body having parallel faces. 3. anything that refracts light, as a drop of water. 4. in *optics, a*) a transparent body, as of glass, whose ends are equal and parallel triangles, and whose three sides are parallelograms: used for refracting or dispersing light, as into the spectrum. *b*) any similar body of three or more sides.

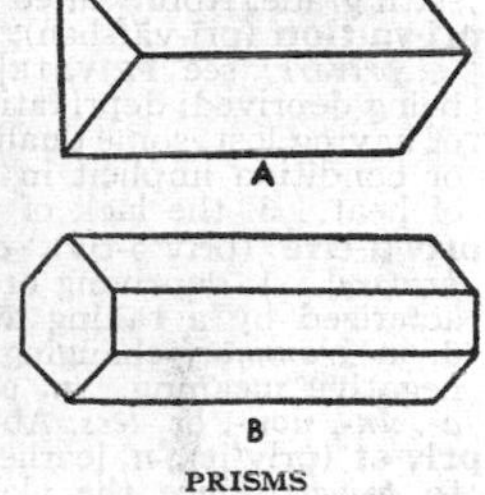

PRISMS
A, triangular prism; B, hexagonal prism

pris·mat·ic (priz-mat′ik), *adj.* [< Gr. *prisma, prismatos* (see PRISM); + *-ic*], 1. of or resembling a prism. 2. that refracts light as a prism. 3. that forms or resembles prismatic colors; hence, 4. many-colored; brilliant; dazzling. 5. in *mineralogy,* orthorhombic.

pris·mat·i·cal (priz-mat′i-k'l), *adj.* prismatic.

pris·mat·i·cal·ly (priz-mat′i-k'l-i, priz-mat′ik-li), *adv.* 1. through, or as if through, a prism. 2. with prismatic colors.

prismatic colors, the colors of the visible spectrum produced by passing white light through a prism; red, orange, yellow, green, blue, indigo, and violet.

pris·moid (priz′moid), *n.* [see PRISM & -OID; cf. Fr. *prismoïde*], a prismlike solid figure whose ends are parallel but unequal polygons, and whose sides are consequently trapezoids instead of parallelograms.

pris·moi·dal (priz-moi′d'l), *adj.* of or like a prismoid.

pris·on (priz′'n), *n.* [ME.; OFr.; L. *prehensio, prensio,* a taking < *prehendere, prendere,* to take; cf. PREHENSILE], 1. a place where persons are confined. 2. a building, usually with cells, where convicted criminals are confined or accused persons are held awaiting trial; jail. 3. in the United States, a State prison: distinguished from *reformatory.* 4. imprisonment.

pris·on·er (priz′'n-ẽr, priz′nẽr), *n.* [ME.; OFr. *prisonier*], 1. a person confined in prison, as for some crime. 2. a person held in custody. 3. a person who is captured or held captive: as, a *prisoner* of war. 4. a person who is detained or confined in any way: as, a *prisoner* of love.

prisoner's base, a children's game in which each side has a base to which captured opponents are brought.

pris·sy (pris′i), *adj.* [PRISSIER (-i-ẽr), PRISSIEST (-i-ist)], [< *precise* or *prim* + *sissy*], [Colloq.], 1. very prim or precise; fussy. 2. overrefined; prudish.

pris·tine (pris′tēn, pris′tin), *adj.* [L. *pristinus,* former < OL. *pri,* before; cf. PRIOR], 1. characteristic of the earliest, or an earlier, period or condition; original. 2. still pure or untouched; uncorrupted; unspoiled.

prith·ee (prith′i), *interj.* [altered < *pray thee*], [Archaic], I pray thee; please: also spelled **prythee.**

priv., 1. private. 2. privative.

pri·va·cy (prī′və-si), *n.* [*pl.* PRIVACIES (-siz)], [< *private*], 1. the quality or condition of being private; withdrawal from public view or company; seclusion. 2. secrecy.

‡**Pri·vat·do·cent** (pri-vät′dō-tsent′), *n.* [*pl.* PRIVATDOCENTEN (-ən)], [G. < *privat,* private + *docent, dozent,* teacher; see DOCENT], in European, especially German, universities, a lecturer paid only by his students' fees.

pri·vate (prī′vit), *adj.* [ME. *pryvat;* L. *privatus,* belonging to oneself, not public or of the state < *privare,* to separate, deprive < *privus,* separate, peculiar], 1. of, belonging to, or concerning a particular person or group of persons; not common or general: as, *private* property, a *private* joke. 2. not open to, intended for, or controlled by the public: as, a *private* school. 3. not holding public office: as, a *private* citizen. 4. away from public view; secluded: as, a *private* dining room. 5. not known to the public; secret; confidential: as, one's *private* opinion. *n.* 1. *pl.* genitals. 2. in the *United States armed forces,* the lowest rank of enlisted man: in the Army, there are two ranks of private, comprising the sixth and seventh grades of enlisted man (see **recruit**); in the Marine Corps and Air Force, it is the seventh, or lowest grade: abbreviated **Pvt.** (as a title), **priv.**

in private, privately or secretly; not publicly.

pri·va·teer (prī'və-têr'), *n.* [< *private,* after *buccaneer*], 1. a privately owned and manned armed ship commissioned by a belligerent government to attack and capture enemy ships, especially merchant ships. 2. a commander or crew member of a privateer. *v.i.* to sail on or as a privateer.

pri·va·teers·man (prī'və-têrz'mən), *n.* a privateer (sense 2).

private first class, in the *United States armed forces,* a rank of enlisted man, just below a corporal: in the Army, it is the fifth grade of enlisted man (formerly *corporal*); in the Marine Corps and Air Force, it is the sixth grade. Abbreviated **Pfc, PFC** (no period).

pri·va·tion (prī-vā'shən), *n.* [ME. *privacion;* L. *privatio* < *privare;* see PRIVATE], 1. [Rare], a depriving or being deprived; deprivation. 2. the absence of, or state of having lost, some quality or condition, or the quality or condition implicit in this: as, cold is the *privation* of heat. 3. the lack of usual necessities or comforts.

priv·a·tive (priv'ə-tiv), *adj.* [L. *privativus* < pp. of *privare*], 1. depriving or tending to deprive. 2. characterized by a taking away or loss of some quality. 3. in *grammar,* changing a positive term to give it a negative meaning. *n.* a privative prefix or suffix, as *a-, un-, non-,* or *-less.* Abbreviated **priv.**

priv·et (priv'it), *n.* [earlier *primprint, primet;* form due to *private,* since the plant is chiefly used to screen], any of a number of related shrubs of the olive family, with bluish-black berries and spikes of white flowers.

priv·i·lege (priv''l-ij), *n.* [ME.; OFr.; L. *privilegium,* an exceptional law made in favor of or against any individual < *privus,* separate, peculiar + *lex, legis,* a law], 1. a right, advantage, favor, or immunity granted to some person, group of persons, or class, not enjoyed by others and sometimes detrimental to them. 2. a basic civil right, guaranteed by a government: as, the *privilege* of equality for all. *v.t.* [PRIVILEGED (-ijd), PRIVILEGING], to grant a privilege or privileges to.

priv·i·leged (priv''l-ijd), *adj.* enjoying a privilege or privileges.

privileged communication, in *law,* 1. a communication that one cannot legally be compelled to divulge, as that to a lawyer from his client. 2. a communication made under such circumstances, as in a legislative proceeding, that it is not actionable as slander or libel.

priv·i·ly (priv''l-i), *adv.* in a privy manner.

priv·i·ty (priv'ə-ti), *n.* [*pl.* PRIVITIES (-tiz)], [ME. *privete;* OFr. *priveté* < L. *privus,* private], 1. *a)* private or secret knowledge, as shared between persons. *b)* participation in this. 2. in *law,* a successive relationship to or mutual interest in the same property, etc., established by law or legalized by contract, as between a testator and legatee, lessor and lessee, etc. 3. [Obs.], privacy.

priv·y (priv'i), *adj.* [ME. & OFr. *prive;* L. *privatus;* see PRIVATE], 1. originally, private; not public; confidential: now used only in such phrases as *privy council.* 2. [Archaic], hidden, secret, clandestine, surreptitious, or furtive. *n.* [*pl.* PRIVIES (-iz)], 1. a toilet; especially, a small shelter outside of a house, etc., containing a toilet. 2. in *law,* one of the parties to a privity.

privy to, secretly or privately informed about.

privy council, a group of confidential counselors appointed by a ruler to advise him: abbreviated **P.C.**

privy seal, in Great Britain, the seal placed on documents which are later to receive the great seal or which are not important enough to receive the great seal: abbreviated **P.S.**

‡prix fixe (prē' fēks'), [Fr., fixed price], 1. a meal for which a fixed price is charged; table d'hôte: distinguished from *à la carte.* 2. its price.

prize (prīz), *v.t.* [PRIZED (prīzd), PRIZING], [ME. *pris;* var. of *price;* see PRICE], 1. to set a value upon; appraise; price. 2. to value highly; esteem. *n.* 1. something offered or given to a person winning a contest. 2. something won in a game of chance, lottery, etc. 3. anything worth striving for; any enviable or highly valued possession. *adj.* 1. that has received a prize: as, a *prize* novel. 2. that could win a prize; first-rate: as, a *prize* answer: sometimes used ironically. 3. given as a prize. —*SYN.* see **appreciate, reward.**

prize (prīz), *n.* [ME. *prise,* a taking hold, lever; OFr. *prise,* a taking < *prise,* fem. pp. of *prendre,* to take; L. *prehendere;* see PREHENSILE], 1. originally, the act of capturing; seizure. 2. something taken by force, as in war; especially, a captured enemy warship or its cargo. 3. [Dial.], *a)* an instrument for prying; lever. *b)* leverag also spelled **prise.** *v.t.* [PRIZED (prīzd), PRIZING], 1. t seize as a prize of war. 2. to pry, as with a lever: als spelled **prise.** —*SYN.* see **spoil.**

prize court, in *law,* a military court having authorit over the disposition of prizes, or property captured a sea in wartime.

prize fight, [use of *prize* prob. merging archaic sens of "contest" with sense of "reward, payment"], professional boxing match.

prize fighter, a professional boxer.

prize fighting, professional boxing.

prize money, part of the money from the sale of ship and cargo captured in battle, usually divided pr portionately according to rank among the officers an crew who made the capture.

priz·er (prī'zẽr), *n.* [Archaic], a person competing fo a prize, as in a contest.

prize ring, 1. a square platform or similar space, en closed by ropes, where prize fights are held. 2. priz fighting.

pro (prō), *adv.* [L., for], on the affirmative side; favo ably. *adj.* favorable. *n.* [*pl.* PROS (prōz)], 1. a perso who favors the affirmative side of some debatab question. 2. an argument in favor of something: a the *pros* and cons of the matter. 3. a vote for th affirmative. Abbreviated **p.**

pro (prō), *adj.* & *n.* [*pl.* PROS (prōz)], [contr. < *pro fessional*], [Colloq.], professional.

pro- (prō), [Gr. *pro-* < *pro,* before; akin to Eng. *for* a prefix meaning: 1. *before in place* or *position,* as i *prostrate.* 2. *before in time,* as in *prophet.*

pro- (prō), [L. < *pro,* before, forward, for], a prefi meaning: 1. *moving forward* or *ahead of,* as in *progres* 2. *substituting for, acting for,* as in *pronoun.* 3. *defendin acting in behalf of,* as in *prolocutor.* 4. *favoring,* as i *prolabor, pro-German.*

pro·a (prō'ə), *n.* [Malay *prau, prao*], a swift Malaya canoe having a lateen sail and an outrigger.

PROA

prob., 1. probable. 2. probably. 3. problem.

prob·a·bil·ism (prob'ə-b'l-iz'm), *n.* 1. in the *Roman Catholic Church,* the doctrine that in matters concerning which there are two opinions, both probable but neither decisive, it is lawful to follow the one preferred: opposed to *rigorism.* 2. in *philosophy,* the doctrine that certainty in knowledge is impossible and that probability is a sufficient basis for action and belief.

prob·a·bil·i·ty (prob'ə-bil'ə-ti), *n.* [*pl.* PROBABILITII (-tiz)], [Fr. *probabilité;* L. *probabilitas*], 1. likelihoo chance stronger than possibility but falling short certainty; quality or state of being probable. 2. som thing probable.

in all probability, very likely; quite probably.

prob·a·ble (prob'ə-b'l), *adj.* [ME.; L. *probabilis* *probare,* to prove], 1. likely to occur or to be so; th can reasonably be expected or believed on the bas of the available evidence, though not proved or certai 2. such as to establish a probability: said of evidenc

SYN.—**probable** applies to that which appears reasonable the basis of evidence or logic but is neither certain nor prove **possible** applies to that which, although not probable, can co ceivably exist, occur, be done, etc.; **likely** suggests great probability than **possible,** but less credibility than **probab** (there are a number of *possible* explanations; the first three a all *likely,* but the second seems the *probable* one).—*ANT.* i probable, unlikely.

probable cause, in *law,* reasonable grounds for pr suming guilt in someone charged with a crime.

prob·a·bly (prob'ə-bli), *adv.* with probability; mo likely: abbreviated **prob.**

pro·bang (prō'baŋ), *n.* [earlier *provang* < obs. *prov* probe + *fang;* altered by association with *probe,* v a flexible, slender rod tipped with a ball, sponge, tuft, used to remove obstructions from, or to tre diseases of, the esophagus or larynx.

pro·bate (prō'bāt), *n.* [ME. *probat;* L. *probatus,* pp. *probare,* to prove; see PROBE], the official establishi of the genuineness or validity of a will left, or presur ably left, by some person deceased. *adj.* having to with such action: as, a *probate* judge. *v.t.* [PROBATI (-id), PROBATING], 1. to establish officially the genuin ness or validity of (a will). 2. to put on probatio 3. to certify in a probate court as mentally unsoun

probate court, a court for probating wills and, wh necessary, administering estates.

pro·ba·tion (prō-bā'shən), *n.* [ME. & OFr. *probacio* L. *probatio* < *probare,* to prove; see PROBE], 1. a testi or trial, as of a person's character, his ability to me certain requirements, or his fitness for a position. the conditional suspension of sentence of a person co victed but not yet imprisoned: after promising good behavior he is placed under the supervision of a probation officer. 3. the status of a person being tested or on trial: as, he is on *probation* because of low grades. 4. the period of testing or trial. 5. [Rare], proof.

pro·ba·tion·al (pro-bā'shən-'l), *adj.* probationary.

pro·ba·tion·ar·y (prō-bā'shən-er'i), *adj.* of, serving for, or undergoing probation.

pro·ba·tion·er (prō-bā'shən-ẽr), *n.* a person on probation.

probation officer, an officer appointed by a magistrate to watch and report on a person placed on probation.

pro·ba·tive (prō'bə-tiv, prob'ə-tiv), *adj.* [L. *probativus* < *probatus,* pp.; see PROBE], 1. serving to test or try. 2. providing proof or evidence.

pro·ba·to·ry (prō'bə-tôr'i, prō'bə-tō'ri), *adj.* [ML. *probatorius* < L. *probatus,* pp.; see PROBE], of or serving as proof; probative.

probe (prōb), *n.* [LL. *proba,* proof < L. *probare,* to test, prove < *probus,* good, proper], 1. a slender, blunt surgical instrument for exploring a wound or the like. 2. the act of probing; hence, 3. a searching investigation, as by a committee appointed for the purpose, of alleged corrupt practices, illegal transactions, and the like. *v.t.* [PROBED (prōbd), PROBING], 1. to explore (a wound or the like) with a probe, as in searching for a bullet embedded in the flesh. 2. to investigate with great thoroughness. *v.i.* to search (with *into*). —*SYN.* see **investigation.**

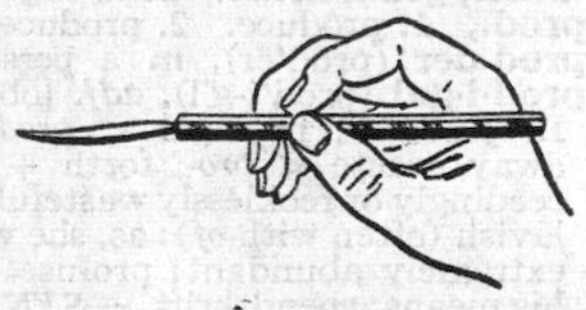

PROBE

prob·i·ty (prō'bə-ti, prob'ə-ti), *n.* [Fr. *probité;* L. *probitas* < *probus,* good, proper], integrity; uprightness in one's dealings; complete honesty. —*SYN.* see **honesty.**

prob·lem (prob'ləm), *n.* [ME. *probleme;* prob. via OFr. < L. *problema;* Gr. *problēma* < *proballein,* to throw forward; *pro-,* forward + *ballein,* to throw, drive], 1. a question proposed for solution or consideration. 2. a question, matter, situation, or person that is perplexing or difficult. 3. in *mathematics,* anything required to be done, or requiring the doing of something. Abbreviated **prob.** *adj.* 1. presenting a problem of human conduct or social relationships: as, a *problem* novel. 2. very difficult to train or discipline: as, a *problem* child.

prob·lem·at·ic (prob'lə-mat'ik), *adj.* [Fr. *problématique*], problematical.

prob·lem·at·i·cal (prob'lə-mat'i-k'l), *adj.* [< Fr. *problématique;* L. *problematicus;* Gr. *problematikos* < *problēma* (see PROBLEM); + *-al*], 1. having the nature of a problem; hence, 2. uncertain. —*SYN.* see **doubtful.**

pro bo·no pu·bli·co (prō bō'nō pub'li-kō'), [L.], for the public good; for the commonweal.

pro·bos·cid·i·an (prō'bə-sid'i-ən), *adj.* [see PROBOSCIS & -AN], in *zoology,* of a group of animals having tusks and a long, flexible, tubelike snout, as the elephant or the extinct mastodon. *n.* any member of this group. Also spelled **proboscidean.**

pro·bos·cis (prō-bos'is), *n.* [*pl.* PROBOSCISES (-iz), PROBOSCIDES (-ə-dēz')], [L. < Gr. *proboskis* < *pro-,* before + *boskein,* to feed, graze], 1. an elephant's trunk, or a long, flexible snout, as of a tapir. 2. a tubular sucking organ, as of some insects, worms, and mollusks. 3. a person's nose: humorously so called.

proc., 1. proceedings. 2. process. 3. proctor.

pro·caine (prō-kān', prō'kān), *n.* [*pro-* + *cocaine*], a synthetic crystalline compound, $C_{13}H_{20}O_2N_2 \cdot HCl$, resembling, but less toxic than, cocaine, used as a local anesthetic in medicine and dentistry.

pro·cam·bi·al (prō-kam'bi-əl), *adj.* of the procambium.

pro·cam·bi·um (prō-kam'bi-əm), *n.* [Mod. L.; see PRO- & CAMBIUM], the growing layer of plant tissue from which wood cells and cells conducting food and water are formed.

pro·carp (prō'kärp), *n.* [*pro-* + *-carp*], in *botany,* a female reproductive organ in certain algae.

pro·ca·the·dral (prō'kə-thē'drəl), *n.* a church used as a temporary substitute for a cathedral.

pro·ce·dur·al (prə-sē'jẽr-əl, prō-sē'jẽr-əl), *adj.* of or according to procedure.

pro·ce·dure (prə-sē'jẽr, prō-sē'jẽr), *n.* [Fr. *procédure* < *procéder;* see PROCEED], 1. the act, method, or manner of proceeding in some process or course of action. 2. a particular course of action or way of doing something. 3. the established way of carrying on the business of a legislature, law court, etc.

pro·ceed (prə-sēd', prō-sēd'), *v.i.* [ME. *proceden;* L. *proceder; pro-,* forward + *cedere,* to go], 1. to advance or go on, especially after stopping: as, we then *proceeded* to the next town. 2. to go on speaking, especially after an interruption. 3. to undertake and carry on some action or process: as, he *proceeded* to eat his dinner. 4. to take legal action (often with *against*). 5. to issue; come forth. See also **proceeds.**

pro·ceed·ing (prə-sēd'iŋ, prō-sēd'iŋ), *n.* 1. an advancing or going on with what one has been doing. 2. action or course of action. 3. a particular course of action. 4. *pl.* transactions. 5. *pl.* a record of the business transacted by a learned society or other organized group. 6. *a*) *pl.* legal action. *b*) the taking of legal action.

pro·ceeds (prō'sēdz), *n.pl.* that which proceeds or results, as from a transaction; especially, the sum derived from a sale, venture, etc.

proc·e·leus·mat·ic (pros'i-lōōs-mat'ik), *adj.* [LL. *proceleusmaticus;* Gr. *prokeleusmatikos* < *prokeleusma,* incitement < *prokeleuein; pro-,* before + *keleuein,* to incite], 1. animating; stirring: said of a song. 2. in *prosody, a*) designating a metrical foot of four short syllables. *b*) of such feet. *n.* in *prosody,* a proceleusmatic foot.

pro·ce·phal·ic (prō'sə-fal'ik), *adj.* [*pro-* + *cephalic*], of the fore part of the head.

proc·ess (pros'es; *mainly Brit.* prō'ses), *n.* [ME. & OFr. *proces;* L. *processus,* pp. of *procedere;* see PROCEED], 1. the course of being done: chiefly in *in process.* 2. course, as of time. 3. a continuing development involving many changes: as, the *process* of digestion. 4. a particular method of doing something, generally involving a number of steps or operations. 5. in *anatomy,* a projection or outgrowth from a larger structure, usually a bone: as, the alveolar *process* of the jaw. 6. in *botany & zoology,* an appendage or projecting part of an organism. 7. in *law, a*) an action or suit. *b*) a writ or summons directing a defendant to appear in court. *c*) the total of such writs in any action or proceeding. 8. in *printing,* photomechanical or photoengraving methods collectively. *v.t.* 1. to prepare by or subject to a special treatment or process. 2. in *law, a*) to prosecute. *b*) to serve a process on. *adj.* 1. prepared by a special treatment or process. 2. of, made by, used in, or using photomechanical or photoengraving methods. Abbreviated **proc.**

in (the) process of, in or during the course of.

proc·ess·ing tax (pros'es-iŋ; *mainly Brit.* prō'ses-iŋ), a tax levied on the processing of certain agricultural products.

pro·ces·sion (prə-sesh'ən, prō-sesh'ən), *n.* [ME.; AS.; OFr.; L. *processio* < *procedere;* see PROCEED], 1. the act of proceeding, especially in an orderly manner. 2. a number of persons or things moving forward, ordinarily in a long line, in orderly fashion toward some set destination. *v.i.* to form or take part in a procession.

pro·ces·sion·al (prə-sesh'ən-'l, prō-sesh'ən-'l), *adj.* [ME.; ML. *processionalis*], of, or used in connection with, a procession or processions. *n.* 1. a book setting forth the ritual to be observed in processions of the church. 2. a hymn sung at the beginning of a church service during the entrance of the clergy. 3. any musical composition intended for performance in connection with a procession, as at a university convocation.

process printing, a method of printing colored reproductions of paintings, etc. by use of plates made from half tones.

process server, in *law,* a policeman, sheriff, or deputy who delivers an official order, or process, to a person, commanding him to be in court at a time and place named in the order.

‡pro·cès-ver·bal (prô'se' vâr'bȧl'), *n.* [*pl.* PROCÈS-VERBAUX (-bō')], [Fr., a verbal process], an authenticated official report of proceedings or facts; authorized statement; minutes (of a meeting).

‡pro·chain (prô'shan'), *adj.* [Fr.], prochein.

pro·chein (prō'shen), *adj.* [Fr. < LL. **propeanus* < L. *prope,* near], in *law,* next; closest.

pro·claim (prō-klām'), *v.t.* [ME. *proclame(n);* OFr. *proclamer;* L. *proclamare; pro-,* before + *clamare,* to cry out], 1. to announce officially; announce to be: as, they *proclaimed* her queen. 2. to outlaw, ban, or otherwise restrict by a proclamation. 3. to show to be: as, her every act *proclaimed* her a snob. —*SYN.* see **declare.**

proc·la·ma·tion (prok'lə-mā'shən), *n.* [ME. *proclamasion;* OFr. *proclamacion;* L. *proclamatio* < *proclamare*], 1. a proclaiming or being proclaimed. 2. something that is proclaimed, or announced officially.

pro·clit·ic (prō-klit'ik), *adj.* [Mod. L. *procliticus* < Gr. *proklinein,* to lean forward; *pro-,* forward + *klinein,* to lean, incline], pronounced, in ordinary speech, with the word that follows it, and so having no accent of its own: said of such words as *to* in a phrase like *to be or not to be:* distinguished from *enclitic.* *n.* a proclitic word.

pro·cliv·i·ty (prō-kliv'ə-ti), *n.* [*pl.* PROCLIVITIES (-tiz)], [Fr. *proclivité;* L. *proclivitas* < *proclivus,* downward; *pro-,* before + *clivus,* a slope], a natural tendency in human nature; inclination, especially toward something discreditable: as, a *proclivity* to vice. —*SYN.* see **inclination.**

Proc·ne (prok′ni), *n.* [L.; Gr. *Proknē*], in *Greek & Roman mythology*, Pandion's daughter, transformed into a swallow by the gods: see **Philomela.**

pro·con·sul (prō-kon′s'l), *n.* [ME.; L.; *pro*, for + *consul*, a consul], 1. a Roman official invested with consular authority who commanded an army in one or more of the provinces and often acted as a provincial governor. 2. a governing official in a modern British colony.

pro·con·su·lar (prō-kon′s'l-ẽr, prō-kon′syoo-lẽr), *adj.* [L. *proconsularis*], of or governed by a proconsul.

pro·con·su·late (prō-kon′s'l-it, prō-kon′syoo-lit), *n.* [L. *proconsulatus*], the office or term of office of a proconsul.

pro·con·sul·ship (prō-kon′s'l-ship′), *n.* [see -SHIP], proconsulate.

Pro·co·pi·us (prō-kō′pi-əs), *n.* Byzantine historian of the 6th century A.D.

pro·cras·ti·nate (prō-kras′tə-nāt′), *v.i.* [PROCRASTINATED (-id), PROCRASTINATING], [< L. *procrastinatus*, pp. of *procrastinare* < *pro-*, forward + *crastinus*, belonging to the morrow < *cras*, tomorrow], to put off doing something until a future time; postpone or defer taking action. *v.t.* to defer; postpone.

pro·cras·ti·na·tion (prō-kras′tə-nā′shən), *n.* [L. *procrastinatio*], the act or habit of procrastinating.

pro·cras·ti·na·tor (prō-kras′tə-nā′tẽr), *n.* a person who procrastinates, especially habitually.

pro·cre·ant (prō′kri-ənt), *adj.* [L. *procreans*, ppr. of *procreare;* see PROCREATE], 1. producing young; fruitful. 2. of procreation.

pro·cre·ate (prō′kri-āt′), *v.t. & v.i.* [PROCREATED (-id), PROCREATING], [< L. *procreatus*, pp. of *procreare*, to procreate; *pro-*, before + *creare*, to create], 1. to produce (young); beget (offspring); hence, 2. to produce or bring into existence.

pro·cre·a·tion (prō′kri-ā′shən), *n.* a procreating or being procreated.

pro·cre·a·tive (prō′kri-ā′tiv), *adj.* 1. of procreation, or the producing of young. 2. productive.

pro·cre·a·tor (prō′kri-ā′tẽr), *n.* [L.], one who procreates.

Pro·crus·te·an (prō-krus′ti-ən), *adj.* 1. of Procrustes or his famous bedstead. 2. designed to secure conformity at any cost; drastic, as methods.

Pro·crus·tes (prō-krus′tēz), *n.* [L.; Gr. *Prokroustēs* < *prokrouein*, to beat out], in *Greek mythology*, a giant of Attica who seized travelers and tied them to an iron bedstead, after which he either cut off their legs or stretched his victims till they fitted it.

proct-, procto-.

proc·to- (prok′tō, prok′tə), [< Gr. *prōktos*, anus], a combining form meaning *rectum*, as in *proctology*.

proc·tol·o·gy (prok-tol′ə-ji), *n.* [*procto-* + *-logy*], the branch of medicine dealing with the rectum and its diseases.

proc·tor (prok′tẽr), *n.* [ME. *proketour;* contr. < *procuratour;* see PROCURATOR], 1. a person employed to manage the affairs of another; agent. 2. a college or university official who maintains order, supervises examinations, etc.: abbreviated **proc.** *v.t.* to supervise (an academic examination).

proc·to·ri·al (prok-tôr′i-əl, prok-tō′ri-əl), *adj.* of or employing a proctor or proctors.

proc·tor·ship (prok′tẽr-ship′), *n.* [see -SHIP], the office or term of office of a proctor.

proc·to·scope (prok′tə-skōp′), *n.* [*procto-* + *-scope*], an instrument used for the direct examination of the interior of the rectum.

pro·cum·bent (prō-kum′bənt), *adj.* [L. *procumbens*, ppr. of *procumbere*, to lean forward; *pro-*, forward + *-cumbere* < *cubare*, to lie down], 1. lying face down. 2. in *botany*, trailing along the ground.

pro·cur·a·ble (prō-kyoor′ə-b'l), *adj.* that can be procured, or obtained.

proc·u·ra·cy (prok′yoor-ə-si), *n.* [*pl.* PROCURACIES (-siz)], the act or office of a procurator.

pro·cur·ance (prō-kyoor′əns), *n.* the act of procuring, obtaining, or bringing about; agency.

proc·u·ra·tion (prok′yoo-rā′shən), *n.* [ME. *procuracioun;* OFr.; L. *procuratio*], 1. management of the affairs of another. 2. power of attorney. 3. a procuring.

proc·u·ra·tor (prok′yoo-rā′tẽr), *n.* [ME. & OFr. *procuratour;* L. *procurator* < *procurare;* see PROCURE], 1. in the Roman Empire, an official who managed the financial affairs of a province or acted as governor of a territory, such as Judaea, not having the status of a province. 2. a person employed to manage the affairs of another.

proc·u·ra·to·ri·al (prok′yoo-rə-tôr′i-əl, prok′yoo-rə-tō′ri-əl), *adj.* of a procurator or proctor.

proc·u·ra·to·ry (prok′yoo-rə-tôr′i, prō-kyoor′ə-tō′ri), *adj.* [LL. *procuratorius*, belonging to a procurator], [Rare], of a procurator or procuration. *n.* [ML. *procuratorium*], an authorization to act as a procurator.

pro·cure (prō-kyoor′), *v.t.* [PROCURED (-kyoord′), PROCURING], [ME. *procuren;* OFr. *procurer*, to procure < L. *procurare*, to take care of, attend to; *pro*, for + *curare*, to attend to < *cura*, a care], 1. to obtain or secure: as, he *procured* work. 2. [Rare], to cause. 3. to obtain (girls) for the purpose of prostitution. *v.i.* to obtain girls for the purpose of prostitution. —***SYN.*** see **get.**

pro·cure·ment (prō-kyoor′mənt), *n.* a procuring, o obtaining.

pro·cur·er (prō-kyoor′ẽr), *n.* [ME. & Anglo-Fr. *pro curour* (OFr. *procureor*); L. *procurator;* see PROCURATOR] 1. a person who procures, or obtains. 2. a man who ob tains girls for the purpose of prostitution; pimp.

pro·cur·ess (prō-kyoor′is), *n.* [OFr. *procureresse*, fem of *procureor;* see PROCURER], a woman who obtains girl for the purpose of prostitution.

Pro·cy·on (prō′si-on′, prō′si-ən), *n.* [L.; Gr. *Prokyōn* < *pro-*, before + *kyōn*, dog: so named because it rise before the Dog Star], a star of the first magnitude i the constellation Canis Minor.

prod (prod), *n.* [prob. merging of *prog* & *brod*, both o which mean "to stab"], 1. a thrust or dig with some thing pointed; a prodding. 2. something that serves t goad or urge on: as, many stockyards use an electri *prod* to keep the cattle moving. *v.t.* [PRODDED (-id) PRODDING], 1. to jab or poke with or as with a pointe stick; goad; hence, 2. to urge or rouse.

prod., 1. produce. 2. produced. 3. product.

prod·der (prod′ẽr), *n.* a person or thing that prods

prod·i·gal (prod′i-g'l), *adj.* [obs. Fr.; ML. *prodigalis* < L. *prodigus*, prodigal < *prodigere*, to drive forth c away, waste < *pro-*, forth + *agere*, to drive], 1. ex ceedingly or recklessly wasteful. 2. extremely generous lavish (often with *of*): as, she was *prodigal* of praise. 3 extremely abundant; profuse. *n.* a person who waste his means; spendthrift. —***SYN.*** see **profuse.**

prod·i·gal·i·ty (prod′i-gal′ə-ti), *n.* [*pl.* PRODIGALITIE (-tiz)], [ME. *prodigalite;* OFr. *prodigalité;* LL. *prodi galitas*], 1. reckless wastefulness. 2. abundant gener osity or liberality; lavishness. 3. extreme abundance.

pro·di·gious (prə-dij′əs), *adj.* [L. *prodigiosus*, marvelou < *prodigium;* see PRODIGY], 1. wonderful; amazing 2. enormous; huge. 3. monstrous. 4. [Obs.], portentous

prod·i·gy (prod′ə-ji), *n.* [*pl.* PRODIGIES (-jiz)], [L. *pro digium* < *pro-*, before + OL. **agiom*, a thing said < *aio*, I say], 1. [Rare], an extraordinary happening thought to foretell good or evil fortune. 2. a marve person, thing, or act so extraordinary as to inspir wonder: as, a child *prodigy*. 3. something monstrous

prod·ro·mal (prod′rə-məl), *adj.* in *medicine*, of or bein a prodrome; premonitory.

pro·drome (prō′drōm), *n.* [Fr.; L. *prodromus;* Gr *prodromos*, forerunner; *pro-*, before + *dromos*, a run ning], in *medicine*, a warning symptom indicating th onset of a disease.

pro·duce (prə-dōōs′, prə-dūs′; *for n.*, prod′ōōs, prō′dūs) *v.t.* [PRODUCED (-dōōst′, -dūst′), PRODUCING], [L. *pro ducere; pro-*, forward + *ducere*, to lead, draw], 1. t bring to view; offer for inspection: as, at the officer' request he *produced* his driver's license. 2. to bear bring forth; create; yield: as, biennial plants *produc* seed every other year, a well that *produces* oil. 3. t make or manufacture. 4. to cause; give rise to: a anything out of the ordinary *produces* a flood of rumor 5. to get ready and present (a play, motion picture etc.) on the stage or screen. 6. in *economics*, to creat (anything having exchange value). 7. in *geometry* t extend (a line or plane). *v.i.* to bear, yield, manu facture, etc. the customary product or product *n.* something that is produced; yield; especially, far products collectively. Abbreviated **prod.**

pro·duc·er (prə-dōōs′ẽr, prə-dūs′ẽr), *n.* 1. a perso who produces; specifically, in *economics*, one who pro duces goods and services: opposed to *consumer*. 2. special type of furnace for making producer gas. 3. person who is in charge of the production of a pla motion picture, etc.

producer gas, a gas prepared by burning low-grad coal with a limited supply of air so that a combustib mixture of nitrogen and carbon monoxide is obtaine

producers' goods, goods, such as raw materials an machines, that are used in producing consumers' good

pro·duc·i·ble (prə-dōōs′ə-b'l, prə-dūs′ə-b'l), *adj.* capab of being produced.

prod·uct (prod′əkt), *n.* [ME.; L. *productus*, pp. of *pro ducere;* see PRODUCE], 1. something that is produce by nature or made by industry or art. 2. result; ou growth: as, war is a *product* of greed. 3. in *chemistr* any substance resulting from a chemical change. 4 in *mathematics*, the number obtained by multiplyin two or more numbers together. Abbreviated **prod.**

pro·duc·tion (prə-duk′shən), *n.* [ME. *produccioun;* I *productio*], 1. the act or process of producing. 2. th rate of producing. 3. *a*) something produced; produc *b*) a work of art, literature, the theater, etc. 4. i *economics*, the creation of economic value; producin of goods and services: opposed to *consumption*.

pro·duc·tive (prə-duk′tiv), *adj.* [ML. *productivus* < I *productus*, pp. of *producere;* see PRODUCE], 1. producin abundantly; fertile. 2. marked by abundant pro duction: as, a *productive* time. 3. bringing as a resu (with *of*): as, waste is *productive* of many evils. 4. i *economics*, of or engaged in the creating of econom value, or the producing of goods and services.

pro·duc·tiv·i·ty (prō′duk-tiv′ə-ti), *n.* the quality c state of being productive.

ro·em (prō′em), *n.* [ME. & OFr. *proeme;* L. *prooemium;* Gr. *prooimion* < *pro-*, before + *oimē*, song], a brief introduction or preface.

ro·e·mi·al (prō-ē′mi-əl), *adj.* of a proem; prefatory.

rof (prof), *n.* [contr. < *professor*], [Colloq.], a professor.

'rof., Professor.

rof·a·na·tion (prof′ə-nā′shən), *n.* [Fr.; LL. *profanatio*], a profaning or being profaned; desecration or defilement. —*SYN.* see **sacrilege.**

ro·fan·a·to·ry (prə-fan′ə-tôr′i, prō-fan′ə-tō′ri), *adj.* involving profanation; profaning.

ro·fane (prə-fān′, prō-fān′), *adj.* [Fr.; L. *profanus* < *pro-*, before + *fanum*, a temple; lit., before the temple, hence not sacred, common, profane], 1. not concerned with religion or religious matters; secular: as, *profane* art. 2. not initiated into the inner mysteries of something: as, the *profane* herd. 3. not hallowed or consecrated. 4. showing disregard or contempt for sacred things; irreverent. *v.t.* [PROFANED (-fānd′), PROFANING], 1. to treat (sacred things) with irreverence or contempt; desecrate. 2. to put to a base or improper use; debase; defile.

ro·fan·i·ty (prə-fan′ə-ti, prō-fan′ə-ti), *n.* [LL. *profanitas*], 1. the state or quality of being profane. 2. [*pl.* PROFANITIES (-tiz)], something that is profane, especially profane language. —*SYN.* see **blasphemy.**

ro·fert (prō′fẽrt), *n.* [L., he brings forward (< *proferre;* cf. PROFFER); in phr. *profert in curia*, he brings forward in court], in *law*, a formal offer in a pleading to produce in court the documentary evidence on which the pleader's action is based.

ro·fess (prə-fes′), *v.t.* [< ME. *professed*, pp.; OFr. *profes, professe*, bound by vows; L. *professus*, pp. of *profiteri*, to avow publicly < *pro-*, before + *fateri*, to avow], 1. to make an open declaration of; affirm: as, he *professed* his admiration of our ideals. 2. to lay claim to (some feeling) insincerely: as, she *professed* a gratitude she did not feel. 3. to practice as one's profession. 4. to declare one's belief in: as, to *profess* Christ. 5. to accept into a religious order. *v.i.* 1. to make profession. 2. to make one's profession (sense 5).

ro·fessed (prə-fest′), *adj.* [ME. *professed, profest*], 1. openly declared; avowed: as, a *professed* opponent of free trade. 2. insincerely avowed; pretended: as, their *professed* neutrality. 3. having made one's profession (sense 5).

ro·fess·ed·ly (prə-fes′id-li), *adv.* avowedly, allegedly, or ostensibly.

ro·fes·sion (prə-fesh′ən), *n.* [ME.; OFr.; L. *professio*], 1. a professing, or declaring; avowal, whether true or pretended: as, a *profession* of faith. 2. *a*) the avowal of belief in a religion. *b*) a faith or religion professed. 3. a vocation or occupation requiring advanced training in some liberal art or science, and usually involving mental rather than manual work, as teaching, engineering, writing, etc.; especially, medicine, law, or theology (formerly called *the learned professions*). 4. the body of persons in a particular calling or occupation. 5. the avowal made on formally entering a religious order.

ro·fes·sion·al (prə-fesh′ən-'l), *adj.* 1. of, engaged in, or worthy of the high standards of, a profession. 2. making some activity not usually followed for gain, such as a sport, the source of one's livelihood. 3. engaged in by professionals (sense 2): as, *professional* hockey. 4. engaged in a specified occupation for pay or as a means of livelihood: as, a *professional* writer. 5. having much experience and great skill in a specified role: as, a *professional* rabble-rouser. *n.* 1. a person belonging to one of the professions. 2. a person who makes some activity not usually followed for gain, such as a sport, the source of his livelihood.

ro·fes·sion·al·ism (prə-fesh′ən-'l-iz'm), *n.* 1. professional quality, status, etc. 2. the practice or fact of using professional players in organized sports.

ro·fes·sor (prə-fes′ẽr), *n.* [ME. *professoure;* L., a teacher < *professus;* see PROFESS], 1. a person who professes something; especially, one who openly declares his sentiments, religious beliefs, etc. 2. a teacher; specifically, a college teacher of the highest rank, usually in a specific field. 3. any person claiming or assumed to be especially skilled or experienced in some art, sport, etc.: a popular or humorous usage. Abbreviated **Prof.**

ro·fes·sor·ate (prə-fes′ẽr-it), *n.* the office or term of office of a professor.

ro·fes·so·ri·al (prō′fə-sôr′i-əl, prof′ə-sō′ri-əl), *adj.* [L. *professorius*], of or characteristic of a professor.

ro·fes·so·ri·ate (prō′fə-sôr′i-it, prof′ə-sō′ri-it), *n.* 1. the professors of a school collectively. 2. a professorship.

ro·fes·sor·ship (prə-fes′ẽr-ship′), *n.* [see -SHIP], the position of a professor (sense 2).

rof·fer (prof′ẽr), *v.t.* [ME. *profren;* Anglo-Fr. & OFr. *proffrir* < *poroffrir; por-*, pro- + *offrir* < LL. **offerire*, for L. *offerre*, to offer, proffer], to offer (usually something intangible): as, to *proffer* friendship. *n.* [ME. & Anglo-Fr. *profre* < the *v.*], an offer. —*SYN.* see **offer.**

pro·fi·cien·cy (prə-fish′ən-si), *n.* [*pl.* PROFICIENCIES (-siz)], the state, quality, or fact of being proficient.

pro·fi·cient (prə-fish′ənt), *adj.* [L. *proficiens*, ppr. of *proficere*, to advance < *pro-*, forward + *facere*, to make], highly competent; skilled. *n.* an expert.

pro·file (prō′fīl), *n.* [It. *profilo* < *profilare*, to outline < *pro-* (L. *pro-*), before + *filo*, a thread < L. *filum*, a thread, line, outline], 1. a side view of the face. 2. a drawing of such a view. 3. outline: as, the *profile* of a distant hill. 4. a short, vivid biography, briefly outlining the most outstanding characteristics of the subject. 5. in *architecture*, a side or sectional elevation of a building or the like. *v.t.* [PROFILED (-fīld), PROFILING], 1. to sketch a profile of. 2. to form as to profile. 3. to write a profile of. —*SYN.* see **outline.**

prof·it (prof′it), *n.* [ME.; OFr.; L. *profectus*, pp. of *proficere*, to profit, lit. to move forward, advance < *pro-*, toward + *facere*, to make], 1. advantage; gain; benefit. 2. *often pl. a*) financial or monetary gain obtained from the use of capital in a transaction or series of transactions. *b*) the ratio of this to the amount of capital invested. *c*) proceeds from property or the like. 3. *often pl.* in *economics*, the net income, as of a business, or the difference between the income and the costs, direct and indirect. *v.i.* 1. to be of advantage or benefit. 2. to benefit; reap an advantage, financial or otherwise. *v.t.* to be of advantage to.

prof·it·a·ble (prof′it-ə-b'l), *adj.* yielding profit, gain, or benefit.

prof·it·a·bly (prof′it-ə-bli), *adv.* with profit, gain, or benefit.

prof·it-and-loss (prof′it-ən-lôs′), *adj.* of or showing profit and loss.

profit and loss, the gain and loss from business transactions, etc.: applied especially to a bookkeeping account at the close of a fiscal period: abbreviated **P. & L., P. and L.**

prof·it·eer (prof′ə-têr′), *n.* [*profit* + *-eer*], a person who makes excessive profits by taking advantage of a shortage of supply to charge unreasonably high prices. *v.i.* to be a profiteer.

prof·it-shar·ing (prof′it-shâr′iŋ), *adj.* of profit sharing.

profit sharing, the practice of giving employees a share in the profits of a business, in addition to paying them stipulated wages.

prof·li·ga·cy (prof′lə-gə-si), *n.* the state or quality of being profligate.

prof·li·gate (prof′lə-git), *adj.* [L. *profligatus*, pp. of *profligare*, to strike to the ground, rout, ruin < *pro-*, forward + *fligere*, to drive, dash], 1. abandoned to vice; dissolute. 2. extremely wasteful; recklessly extravagant. *n.* a profligate person.

prof·lu·ent (prof′lōō-ənt), *adj.* [ME.; L. *profluens*, ppr. of *profluere; pro-*, forth + *fluere*, to flow], flowing smoothly and copiously.

‡pro for·ma (prō fôr′mə), [L.], for (the sake of) form; as a matter of form.

pro·found (prə-found′), *adj.* [ME.; OFr. *profund, profond;* L. *profundus; pro-*, forward + *fundus*, bottom], 1. very deep or low: mainly poetic when used of the physical features of the earth's surface. 2. marked by intellectual depth: as, a *profound* discussion of good and evil. 3. deeply or intensely felt: as, *profound* grief. 4. thoroughgoing: as, *profound* changes in our mode of living. 5. unbroken: as, a *profound* silence. *n.* [Poetic], 1. an abyss or deep, as of the ocean or of space. 2. that which is profound.

pro·fun·di·ty (prə-fun′də-ti), *n.* [*pl.* PROFUNDITIES (-tiz)], [ME. *profundite;* OFr. *profondite;* LL. *profunditas*], 1. depth, especially great depth. 2. something profound, as a thought. 3. a very deep place; abyss.

pro·fuse (prə-fūs′), *adj.* [ME.; L. *profusus*, pp. of *profundere*, to pour out; *pro-*, forth + *fundere*, to pour], 1. giving or pouring forth freely; generous, often to the point of excess (usually with *in*): as, she was *profuse* in her apologies for being late. 2. given, poured forth, or produced freely and abundantly.

SYN.—**profuse** implies a pouring or giving forth freely, often to the point of excess (*profuse* apologies); **lavish** implies an unstinted, generous, sometimes unreasonably liberal, giving (*lavish* attentions); **extravagant** always suggests unreasonably excessive, wasteful spending or giving (*extravagant* living); **prodigal** implies such reckless extravagance as to suggest eventual impoverishment (the *prodigal* heirs to a fortune); **luxuriant** suggests production in great and rich abundance (*luxuriant* foliage); **lush** implies such great luxuriance as to seem excessive (a *lush* jungle). See also **plentiful.**—*ANT.* limited, scant, spare.

pro·fu·sion (prə-fū′zhən), *n.* [Fr.; L. *profusio* < *profusus;* see PROFUSE], 1. a pouring forth or expending with great liberality or wastefulness. 2. great liberality or wastefulness. 3. abundant supply; abundance.

prog (prog), *v.i.* [PROGGED (progd), PROGGING], [via dial. < ME. *prokken*, to beg (prob. < LG.); cf. D.

prachen (whence G. *prachern*, Dan. *prakke*, etc.) in the same sense], [Obs. or British Dial.], to prowl about, as in search of food or plunder; forage. *n.* [Obs. or British Dial.], food obtained as by progging.

Prog., progressive.

pro·gen·i·tive (prō-jen′ə-tiv), *adj.* [see PROGENITOR], capable of begetting offspring; reproductive.

pro·gen·i·tor (prō-jen′ə-tẽr), *n.* [ME. *progenitour;* Fr. *progeniteur;* L. < *progignere*, to beget; *pro-*, forth + *gignere*, to beget], a forefather; ancestor in direct line.

prog·e·ny (proj′ə-ni), *n.* [*pl.* PROGENIES (-niz)], [ME. & OFr. *progenie;* L. *progenies*, descent, lineage, race, family < *progignere;* see PROGENITOR], children, descendants, or offspring collectively; issue.

pro·ges·ter·one (prō-jes′tə-rōn′), *n.* [*pro-* + *ges*tation + *ster*ol + *-one*], a crystalline hormone, $C_{21}H_{30}O_2$, secreted by the corpus luteum or prepared synthetically, serving to prepare the uterus for the reception and development of the fertilized ovum.

pro·ges·tin (prō-jes′tin), *n.* [*pro-* + *gestation* + *-in*], 1. progesterone: the earlier name. 2. any substance whose action is like that of progesterone.

pro·glot·tic (prō-glot′ik), *adj.* of or forming a proglottid.

pro·glot·tid (prō-glot′id), *n.* [< Mod. L. *proglottis, proglottidis* < Gr. *pro-*, forward + *glōtta*, the tongue], any of the segments of a tapeworm's body: each segment has both male and female reproductive organs and can become an independent organism.

pro·glot·tis (prō-glot′is), *n.* [*pl.* PROGLOTTIDES (-ə-dēz′)], a proglottid.

prog·nath·ic (prog-nath′ik), *adj.* prognathous.

prog·na·thism (prog′nə-thiz′m), *n.* the condition of being prognathous, or a tendency toward this condition.

prog·na·thous (prog′nə-thəs, prog-nā′thəs), *adj.* [*pro-* + Gr. *gnathos*, a jaw], 1. having either or both jaws projecting abnormally. 2. projecting abnormally: said of a jaw.

prog·na·thy (prog′nə-thi), *n.* prognathism.

prog·no·sis (prog-nō′sis), *n.* [*pl.* PROGNOSES (-sēz)], [LL.; Gr. *prognōsis* < *progignōskein; pro-*, before + *gignōskein*, to know], a forecast or forecasting; especially, in *medicine*, a prediction of the probable course of a disease and the chances of recovery.

prog·nos·tic (prog-nos′tik), *n.* [ME. *pronostike;* OFr. *pronostique;* L. *prognosticum;* Gr. *prognōstikon* < *progignōskein;* see PROGNOSIS], 1. a sign or indication of things to come; omen. 2. a forecast; prediction. 3. in *medicine*, a symptom indicating the probable course of a disease. *adj.* 1. foretelling; predictive. 2. in *medicine*, of, or serving as a basis for, prognosis.

prog·nos·ti·cate (prog-nos′tə-kāt′), *v.t.* [PROGNOSTICATED (-id), PROGNOSTICATING], [< ML. *prognosticatus*, pp. of *prognosticare* < *prognosticus;* see PROGNOSTIC], 1. to foretell; predict. 2. to indicate beforehand. —*SYN.* see **foretell.**

prog·nos·ti·ca·tion (prog-nos′tə-kā′shən), *n.* 1. the act of prognosticating. 2. a prophecy or prediction.

prog·nos·ti·ca·tive (prog-nos′tə-kā′tiv), *adj.* characterized by or tending to prognostication.

prog·nos·ti·ca·tor (prog-nos′tə-kā′tẽr), *n.* a person who prognosticates; predictor.

pro·gram, pro·gramme (prō′gram, prō′grəm), *n.* [< LL. & Fr.; Fr. *programme;* LL. *programma;* Gr. *programma*, an edict < *prographein*, to write in public; *pro-*, before + *graphein*, to write], 1. originally, *a*) a proclamation. *b*) a prospectus or syllabus. 2. *a*) a list of the events, pieces, performers, speakers, etc. of an entertainment, ceremony, or the like. *b*) the events or pieces collectively. 3. a plan of procedure. *v.t.* (prō′gram), [PROGRAMED or PROGRAMMED (-gramd), PROGRAMING or PROGRAMMING (-gram-iŋ)], to enter or schedule in a program.

pro·gram·mat·ic (prō′grə-mat′ik), *adj.* of, or having the nature of, a program or program music.

program music, instrumental music that depicts or suggests a particular scene, story, etc.

prog·ress (prog′res, prō′gres; *for v.*, prə-gres′), *n.* [ME. *progresse;* OFr. *progres;* L. *progressus*, pp. of *progredi* < *pro-*, before + *gradi*, to step, go], 1. [Archaic], an official journey, as of a sovereign. 2. a moving forward or onward. 3. forward course; development. 4. improvement; advance toward perfection or to a higher state. *v.i.* 1. to move forward or onward. 2. to continue toward completion; come along. 3. to improve; advance toward perfection or to a higher state.

pro·gres·sion (prə-gresh′ən), *n.* [ME.; L. *progressio*], 1. a moving forward or onward; progress. 2. a sequence or succession, as of acts, happenings, etc. 3. in *astronomy*, direct planetary motion (as contrasted to retrograde). 4. in *mathematics*, a series of numbers increasing or decreasing by proportional differences: see **arithmetic progression, geometric progression.** 5. in *music*, *a*) the movement forward from one tone or chord to another. *b*) a succession of tones or chords.

pro·gres·sion·al (prə-gresh′ən-'l), *adj.* of or involving progression.

pro·gres·sion·ist (prə-gresh′ən-ist), *n.* a person who believes in progress, particularly in the progress of human society toward desirable ends through natura processes or human effort.

pro·gres·sive (prə-gres′iv), *adj.* [Fr. *progressif* < *progrès* see PROGRESS], 1. moving forward or onward. 2. con tinuing by successive steps: as, the *progressive* declin of Macbeth's fortunes. 3. marked by progress, reform or a continuing improvement: as, a *progressive* peopl *progressive* education. 4. favoring progress throug political or other reform. 5. in *bridge*, involving certai regular changes of partners and tables after each gam 6. in *grammar*, indicating continuing action: said c certain verb forms, such as *am working* (as compare with the simple form *work.*) 7. in *medicine*, becomin more severe or spreading to other parts: said of disease. 8. [P-], in *politics*, of a Progressive Party *n.* 1. a person who is progressive, especially one wh favors political progress or reform. 2. [P-], a membe of a Progressive Party. —*SYN.* see **liberal.**

Progressive Party, 1. an American political part organized in 1912 by followers of Theodore Roosevel with a program of direct primaries, extension of th franchise to women, the initiative, referendum, an recall, etc.: in full, **National Progressive Party.** 2. a American political party formed in 1924 under the lea ership of Robert M. LaFollette. 3. an American politica party formed in 1948, originally under the leadershi of Henry A. Wallace.

pro·gres·siv·ism (prə-gres′iv-iz′m), *n.* the doctrine principles, and practices of progressives.

pro·hib·it (prō-hib′it, prə-hib′it), *v.t.* [ME. *prohibeten* L. *prohibitus*, pp. of *prohibere*, to prohibit < *pro-*, be fore + *habere*, to have], 1. to refuse to permit; forbi as by law. 2. to prevent; hinder. —*SYN.* see **forbid.**

pro·hi·bi·tion (prō′ə-bish′ən), *n.* [ME. *prohibicion;* I *prohibitio*], 1. a prohibiting or being prohibited. 2. a order or law forbidding something to be done. 3. th forbidding by law of the manufacture, transportatio and sale of alcoholic liquors for beverage purpose specifically [P-], in the United States, the perio (1920–1933) of prohibition by federal law.

pro·hi·bi·tion·ist (prō′ə-bish′ən-ist), *n.* 1. one in fav of prohibiting by law the manufacture and sale of alc holic drinks. 2. [P-], a member of the Prohibition Part

Prohibition Party, an American political party, esta lished in 1869, advocating the prohibition by law of th manufacture and sale of alcoholic drinks.

pro·hib·i·tive (prō-hib′ə-tiv, prə-hib′ə-tiv), *adj.* 1. pr hibiting or tending to prohibit something. 2. such a to prevent purchase, use, etc.: as, *prohibitive* prices.

pro·hib·i·to·ry (prō-hib′ə-tôr′i, prə-hib′ə-tō′ri), *n.* [*prohibitorius*], prohibitive.

proj·ect (proj′ekt, proj′ikt; *for v.*, prə-jekt′), *n.* [M *projecte;* L. *projectum*, neut. of *projectus*, pp. of *pr iicere* < *pro-*, before, forward + *jacere*, to throw], 1. proposal of something to be done; scheme. 2. an unde taking: as, all drainage *projects* have been complete *v.t.* 1. to propose (an act or plan of action). 2. throw or hurl forward. 3. to send forth in one thoughts or imagination: as, *project* yourselves into th world of tomorrow. 4. to cause to stick out. 5. cause (a shadow, image, etc.) to fall or appear upon surface. 6. in *geometry*, to represent (a solid, etc.) c a plane surface by means of lines of correspondenc 7. in *psychology*, to externalize (a thought or feeling) that it appears to have objective reality. *v.i.* to stic out; protrude. —*SYN.* see **plan.**

pro·jec·tile (prə-jek′t'l), *n.* [Fr. < L. *projectus;* s PROJECT], 1. an object, as a bullet, shell, rocket, etc designed to be hurled or shot forward, as from a gu 2. anything thrown or hurled forward. *adj.* 1. d signed to be hurled forward: as, a javelin is a *projecti* weapon. 2. hurling forward: as, *projectile* energy. in *zoology*, that can be thrust out, as a tentacle.

pro·jec·tion (prə-jek′shən), *n.* [< Fr. or L.; Fr. *pr jection;* L. *projectio*], 1. a projecting or being projecte 2. something that projects, or sticks out. 3. somethir that is projected; specifically, in *map making*, the repr sentation on a plane of the earth's surface (or t celestial sphere) or of a part thereof. 4. in *psychiatr* the unconscious act or process of ascribing to othe one's own ideas or impulses, especially when suc ideas or impulses are considered undesirable. 5. *photography*, *a*) the process of causing an image appear upon a screen, etc.: as, the *projection* of motic pictures. *b*) the representation thus produced.

SYN.—**projection** implies a jutting out abruptly beyond t rest of the surface (the *projection* of the eaves beyond the sid of a house); **protrusion** suggests a thrusting or pushing out an abnormal or disfiguring nature (*protrusion* of the eyeball **protuberance** suggests a swelling out, usually in rounded for (the tumor on his arm formed a *protuberance*); **bulge** sugges an outward swelling of a kind that may result from intern pressure (the *bulge* in the can resulted from the fermentation its contents).

projection booth, the small chamber at the rear of motion-picture theater from which the pictures a projected onto a screen at the front.

pro·jec·tion·ist (prə-jek′shən-ist), *n.* the operator of motion-picture projector.

ro·jec·tive (prə-jek′tiv), *adj.* of or made by projection.
rojective geometry, the branch of geometry dealing with those properties of a figure (*projective properties*) that do not vary when the figure is projected.
ro·jec·tor (prə-jek′tẽr), *n.* a person or thing that projects; specifically, a machine for throwing an image on a screen: as, a motion-picture *projector*.
ro·kof·iev, Ser·ge·i (syer-gyā′ prô-kôf′yef), 1891–1953; Russian composer.
ro·ko·pi·evsk (prô-kô′pyefsk′), *n.* a city in the southern Siberian U.S.S.R., near Stalinsk: pop., 107,000.
ro·lac·tin (prō-lak′tin), *n.* [*pro-* + *lact-* + *-in*], a pituitary hormone stimulating milk secretion in mammals and gland secretion in birds.
ro·lan (prō′lan), *n.* [< L. *proles*, offspring; + *-an* as in *pentosan;* cf. -ANE], a hormone found in the urine during pregnancy, hence serving to diagnose pregnancy in the early stages.
ro·lapse (prō-laps′), *n.* [L. *prolapsus*, pp. of *prolabi*, to fall forward; *pro-*, forward + *labi*, to fall], in *medicine*, the falling or slipping out of place of an internal organ, as the uterus or rectum. *v.i.* [PROLAPSED (-lapst′), PROLAPSING], in *medicine*, to fall or slip out of place.
ro·lap·sus (prō-lap′səs), *n.* prolapse.
ro·late (prō′lāt, prō-lāt′), *adj.* [L. *prolatus*, pp. of *proferre*, to bring forward], extended or elongated at the poles: as, a *prolate* spheroid: opposed to *oblate*.

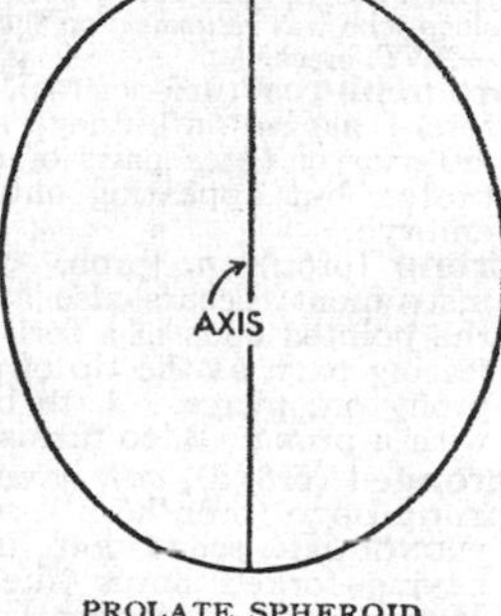

PROLATE SPHEROID

ro·leg (prō′leg′), *n.* [*pro-* (for) + *leg*], in *zoology*, any of the stubby, fleshy limbs attached to the abdomen of certain insect larvae.
ro·le·gom·e·non (prō′li-gom′ə-non), *n.* [*pl.* PROLEGOMENA (-nə)], [Gr. *prolegomenon* < *prolegein*, to say beforehand; *pro-*, before + *legein*, to speak], *usually in pl.* a preliminary remark; foreword.
ro·le·gom·e·nous (prō′li-gom′ə-nəs), *adj.* [see PROLEGOMENON & -OUS], 1. preliminary; prefatory. 2. having or giving too lengthy prefatory matter.
ro·lep·sis (prō-lep′sis), *n.* [*pl.* PROLEPSES (-sēz)], [L.; Gr. *prolēpsis*, an anticipating < *prolambanein*, to take before; *pro-*, before + *lambanein*, to take], an anticipating; especially, the describing of an event as taking place before it could have done so, the treating of a future event as if it had already happened, or the anticipating and answering of an argument before one's opponent has a chance to advance it.
ro·lep·tic (prō-lep′tik), *adj.* of prolepsis; anticipatory.
ro·le·tar·i·an (prō′lə-târ′i-ən), *adj.* [< L. *proletarius*, citizen of the lowest class; see PROLETARY], of the proletariat. *n.* a member of the proletariat; worker.
ro·le·tar·i·at (prō′lə-târ′i-ət), *n.* [Fr. *prolétariat* < L. *proletarius;* see PROLETARY], 1. the class of lowest status in ancient Roman society; hence, 2. [Rare], the class of lowest status in any society or community. 3. the working class; especially, the industrial working class: the current sense, as in Marxism.
ro·le·tar·y (prō′lə-ter′i), *n.* [*pl.* PROLETARIES (-iz)], L. *proletarius*, a citizen of the lowest class, who served the state only by having children, since he had no property < *proles*, offspring], in ancient Rome, a member of the lowest class of citizens, who had no property.
ro·li·cide (prō′lə-sīd′), *n.* [< L. *proles*, offspring + *caedere*, to slay], the crime of killing one's own child or children before or after birth.
ro·lif·er·ate (prō-lif′ə-rāt′), *v.t.* [PROLIFERATED (-id), PROLIFERATING], [*proliferous* + *-ate*], to reproduce (new parts) in quick succession. *v.i.* to grow by multiplying new parts, as by budding, in quick succession.
ro·lif·er·a·tion (prō-lif′ə-rā′shən), *n.* a proliferating or being proliferated.
ro·lif·er·ous (prō-lif′ẽr-əs), *adj.* [< ML. *prolifer* (< L. *proles, prolis*, offspring + *ferre*, to bear); + *-ous*], 1. in *botany*, *a*) multiplying freely by means of buds, side branches, etc. *b*) having leafy shoots growing from a flower or fruit. 2. in *zoology*, reproducing by budding, as coral.
ro·lif·ic (prə-lif′ik), *adj.* [Fr. *prolifique;* ML. *prolificus* < L. *proles, prolis*, offspring + *facere*, to make], 1. producing many young or much fruit. 2. turning out many products of the mind: as, a *prolific* scholar or poet. 3. fruitful; abounding (often with *in* or *of*). —*SYN.* see **fertile.**
o·lif·i·ca·cy (prə-lif′i-kə-si), *n.* the quality or state of being prolific.
pro·lif·i·cal·ly (prə-lif′i-k′l-i, prə-lif′ik-li), *adv.* in a prolific manner; abundantly.
pro·lin (prō′lin), *n.* proline.
pro·line (prō′lēn, prō′lin), *n.* [< *pyrrole* + *-ine*], an amino acid, $C_5H_9O_2N$, formed by the decomposition of proteins.
pro·lix (prō-liks′, prō′liks), *adj.* [ME. *prolixe;* L. *prolixus*, extended, prolix < *pro-*, forth + base of *liquere*, to flow], so wordy as to be tiresome; verbose or long-winded. —*SYN.* see **wordy.**
pro·lix·i·ty (prō-lik′sə-ti), *n.* [*pl.* PROLIXITIES (-tiz)], the state or quality of being prolix.
pro·loc·u·tor (prō-lok′yoo-tẽr), *n.* [L. < *prolocutus*, pp. of *proloqui*, to declare; *pro*, for + *loqui*, to speak], 1. a person who speaks for another person or for a group; spokesman. 2. a chairman.
pro·logue (prō′lôg, prō′log), *n.* [ME. *prolog;* OFr.; L. *prologus;* Gr. *prologos; pro-*, before + *logos*, a discourse], 1. an introduction to a poem, play, etc.; especially, introductory lines or verses spoken, ordinarily by one of the principal members of the cast, before a dramatic performance. 2. the person who speaks such lines or verses. 3. a preliminary act or course of action foreshadowing greater events. Also spelled **prolog.** —*SYN.* see **introduction.**
pro·logu·ize (prō′lô-gīz′), *v.i.* [PROLOGUIZED (-gīzd′), PROLOGUIZING], to compose or deliver a prologue: also spelled **prologize.**
pro·long (prə-lôŋ′), *v.t.* [ME. *prolongen;* OFr. *prolonguer;* LL. *prolongare* < L. *pro-*, forth + *longus*, long], to lengthen or extend in time or space. —*SYN.* see **extend.**
pro·lon·gate (prə-lôŋ′gāt), *v.t.* [PROLONGATED (-id), PROLONGATING], [< LL. *prolongatus*, pp.], to prolong.
pro·lon·ga·tion (prō′lôŋ-gā′shən), *n.* [Fr.; ML. *prolongatio*], 1. a prolonging or being prolonged. 2. the part added in lengthening something.
pro·longe (prō-lonj′; Fr. prô′lōnzh′), *n.* [Fr. < *prolonger;* see PROLONG], in *military science*, a heavy rope having a hook and toggle, used to drag a gun carriage, etc.
prolonge knot, a kind of knot: see **knot,** illus.
pro·lu·sion (prō-lōō′zhən, prō-lū′zhən), *n.* [L. *prolusio*, a prelude < *prolusus*, pp. of *proludere*, to play beforehand; *pro-*, before + *ludere*, to play], a preliminary piece, performance, essay, etc.
pro·lu·so·ry (prō-lōō′sə-ri, prō-lū′sə-ri), *adj.* [ML. *prolusorius*], of, having the nature of, or serving as a prolusion; preliminary.
prom (prom), *n.* [contr. < *promenade*], [Colloq.], a ball or dance, usually given by a particular group or class of students at a college, high school, etc.
prom·e·nade (prom′ə-nād′, prom′ə-näd′), *n.* [Fr. < *se promener*, to go for a walk, *promener*, to take for a walk < LL. *prominare*, to drive (animals) onward; L. *pro-*, forth + *minare*, to drive (animals) < *minari*, to threaten], 1. a leisurely walk taken for pleasure, to display one's finery, etc. 2. a public place for walking, as an avenue, the deck of a ship, or the hall of a building. 3. in *dancing*, *a*) a ball. *b*) a march, ordinarily participated in by all the guests, beginning a formal ball. *c*) a march introduced between the figures of a square dance. *v.i.* [PROMENADED (-id), PROMENADING], to take a promenade; walk about for pleasure, display, etc. *v.t.* 1. to take a promenade along or through. 2. to take or show on or as on a promenade; parade.
Pro·me·the·an (prə-mē′thi-ən), *adj.* 1. of, like, or suggestive of Prometheus. 2. life-bringing, creative, or courageously original. *n.* a person who is Promethean in spirit or deeds.
Pro·me·theus (prə-mē′thūs, prə-mē′thi-əs), *n.* [L.; Gr. *Promētheus;* prob. < *promēthes*, forethinking < *pro-*, before + *mathein*, to learn], in *Greek mythology*, a Titan who taught mankind the use of fire, which he had stolen from heaven for their benefit: he was punished by Zeus by being chained to a rock where a vulture came each day to eat away his liver, which was made whole again each night.
pro·me·thi·um (prō-mē′thi-əm), *n.* [< *Prometheus*], a metallic chemical element of the rare-earth group: symbol, Pm: at. wt., 147(?); at. no., 61: formerly designated as *illinium*.
prom·i·nence (prom′ə-nəns), *n.* [obs. Fr.; L. *prominentia* < *prominens;* see PROMINENT], 1. the state or quality of being prominent. 2. something prominent.
prom·i·nen·cy (prom′ə-nən-si), *n.* prominence.
prom·i·nent (prom′ə-nənt), *adj.* [L. *prominens*, ppr. of *prominere*, to project], 1. sticking out; projecting: as, a *prominent* chin. 2. noticeable at once; conspicuous. 3. widely and favorably known. —*SYN.* see **noticeable.**
prom·is·cu·i·ty (prom′is-kū′ə-ti, prō′mis-kū′ə-ti), *n.* [*pl.* PROMISCUITIES (-tiz)], 1. state, quality, or instance of being promiscuous, especially in sexual relations. 2. an indiscriminate mixture; jumble.
pro·mis·cu·ous (prə-mis′kū-əs), *adj.* [L. *promiscuus* < *pro-*, forth + *miscere*, to mix], 1. consisting of different elements mixed together or mingled without sorting

or discrimination. 2. characterized by a lack of discrimination; specifically, engaging in sexual intercourse indiscriminately or with many persons. 3. [Colloq.], without plan or purpose; casual.

prom·ise (prom′is), *n.* [ME. *promis;* L. *promissum* < *promittere,* to send before or forward; *pro-,* forth + *mittere,* to send], 1. an oral or written agreement to do or not to do something; vow. 2. indication, as of a successful prospect or future; basis for expectation. 3. anything promised. *v.i.* [PROMISED (-ist), PROMISING], 1. to make a promise. 2. to give a basis for expectation (often with *well* or *fair*). *v.t.* 1. to make a promise of (something) to somebody. 2. to engage or pledge (followed by an infinitive or a clause): as, *promise* to go. 3. to give a basis for expecting. 4. to pledge to give in marriage.

Promised Land, Land of Promise.

prom·is·ee (prom′is-ē′), *n.* a person to whom a promise is made.

prom·is·er (prom′is-ẽr), *n.* a person who promises.

prom·is·ing (prom′is-iŋ), *adj.* likely to be successful, excellent, etc.; showing promise.

prom·i·sor (prom′is-ôr′, prom′is-ôr′), *n.* in *law,* a person who makes a promise.

prom·is·so·ry (prom′ə-sôr′i, prom′ə-sō′ri), *adj.* [ML. *promissorius* < L. *promissor,* one who promises], 1. containing a promise. 2. having the nature of a promise: as, a *promissory* representation in selling insurance.

promissory note, a written promise to pay a certain sum of money to a certain person or bearer on demand or on a specified date.

prom·on·to·ry (prom′ən-tôr′i, prom′ən-tō′ri), *n.* [*pl.* PROMONTORIES (-iz, -riz)], [LL. *promontorium;* L. *promunturium;* prob. < *prominere;* see PROMINENT], 1. a peak of high land that juts out over an expanse of water; headland. 2. in *anatomy,* a prominent part.

pro·mote (prə-mōt′), *v.t.* [PROMOTED (-id), PROMOTING], [ME. *promoten* < L. *promotus,* pp. of *promovere,* to move forward; *pro-,* forward + *movere,* to move], 1. to raise or move (a person) forward to a higher or better position: as, *promoted* to a foremanship. 2. to further the growth or establishment of (something). 3. to work actively and stir up interest for the accomplishment of (something): as, *promote* a new law. 4. in *education,* to move forward a grade in school. ***—SYN.*** see **advance.**

pro·mot·er (prə-mōt′ẽr), *n.* [Anglo-Fr. *promotour;* ML. *promotor*], 1. a person or thing that promotes. 2. a person who begins and furthers the organization of a new business undertaking, the selling of its stock, etc.

pro·mo·tion (prə-mō′shən), *n.* 1. a promoting; furtherance. 2. the result of promoting; advancement. 3. the stirring up of interest in an enterprise.

pro·mo·tion·al (prə-mō′shən-'l), *adj.* of or for a promotion.

pro·mo·tive (prə-mō′tiv), *adj.* tending to promote.

prompt (prompt), *adj.* [ME. *prompte;* Late OFr.; L. *promptus,* brought out, hence at hand, ready, quick < *promptus,* pp. of *promere,* to bring forth < *pro-,* forth + *emere,* to take], 1. ready; quick; immediately or instantly at hand. 2. done, spoken, etc. at once or without delay. *n.* 1. in *commerce, a)* the time limit specified for the payment of an account. *b)* the contract in which the due date is specified. 2. any reminder or notice of payment due. *v.t.* 1. to urge into action. 2. to remind (a person) of something he has forgotten; help with a cue. 3. to move or inspire by suggestion. ***—SYN.*** see **quick.**

prompt·book (prompt′book′), *n.* in the *theater,* a fully annotated copy of the script of a play, for the use of the director or prompter, containing full directions for action, settings, properties, etc.

prompt·er (promp′tẽr), *n.* 1. a person who prompts. 2. the person in an operatic or theatrical company whose task is to cue the actors or singers when they forget their words, entrances, etc.: abbreviated **P., p.**

promp·ti·tude (promp′tə-to͞od′, promp′tə-tūd′), *n.* [Fr.; LL. *promptitudo*], the quality of being prompt.

pro·mul·gate (prō-mul′gāt, prom′əl-gāt′), *v.t.* [PROMULGATED (-id), PROMULGATING], [< L. *promulgatus,* pp. of *promulgare,* to publish; prob. altered < *provulgare,* to publish < *pro-,* forth, before + *vulgus,* the people], 1. to publish or make known officially (a decree, church dogma, etc.); hence, 2. *a)* to make known the terms of (a new or proposed law or statute). *b)* to put (a law) into effect by publishing its terms. 3. to make widespread: as, *promulgate* learning and culture.

pro·mul·ga·tion (prō′mul-gā′shən, prom′əl-gā′shən), *n.* [Fr.; L. *promulgatio*], a promulgating.

pro·mul·ga·tor (prō-mul′gā-tẽr, prom′əl-gā′tẽr), *n.* [L.], a person who promulgates.

pro·mulge (prō-mulj′), *v.t.* [PROMULGED (-muljd′), PROMULGING], [Archaic], to promulgate.

pro·my·ce·li·um (prō′mi-sē′li-əm), *n.* [*pl.* PROMYCELIA (-ə)], [*pro-* + *mycelium*], in *botany,* a short filament bearing sporidia, developed in spore germination.

pron., 1. pronominal. 2. pronoun. 3. pronounced. 4. pronunciation.

pro·nate (prō′nāt), *v.t.* [PRONATED (-id), PRONATING], [< LL. *pronatus,* pp. of *pronare,* to bend forward < L. *pronus;* see PRONE], 1. to bend or turn face downward; make prone. 2. to turn (the hand or forelimb) with the palm down or toward the body. *v.i.* to bow or bend forward; assume a prone position.

pro·na·tion (prō-nā′shən), *n.* [ML. *pronatio* < LL. *pronatus*], 1. a pronating; especially, in *physiology,* a turning of the hand so that the palm faces downward or a similar turning of the forelimb of an animal. 2. the position resulting from this. Opposed to *supination.*

pro·na·tor (prō-nā′tẽr), *n.* the muscle in the forearm or forelimb by which pronation is effected.

prone (prōn), *adj.* [ME. *proone;* L. *pronus* < *pro* before], 1. lying or leaning face downward; pronated; hence, 2. lying flat or prostrate; in a horizontal position: as, he fell *prone* on the floor. 3. having a natural bent toward; disposed or inclined (with *to*): as, *prone* to error. 4. groveling: as, *prone* before tyranny. 5. [Poetic], leaning forward or sloping downward.

SYN.*—prone,** in strict use, implies a position in which the front part of the body lies upon or faces the ground (he fell *prone* upon the ground and drank from the brook); **supine** implies a position in which one lies on his back (he snores when he sleeps in a *supine* position); **prostrate** implies the position of one thrown or lying flat in a prone or supine position, as in great humility or complete submission, or because laid low (the victim lay *prostrate* at the murderer's feet); **recumbent** suggests a lying down or back in any position one might assume for rest or sleep (she was *recumbent* on the chaise longue). See also **likely.** ***—ANT. erect.

pro·neph·ros (prō-nef′rəs), *n.* [Mod. L.; Gr. *pro-,* before + *nephros,* a kidney], a primitive kidney, the most anterior of three pairs of renal organs in lower vertebrates, but appearing only transiently in the human embryo.

prong (prôŋ), *n.* [prob. < MLG. *prange,* a pinching instrument; occurs also as *prang, sprong*], 1. one of the pointed ends of a fork; tine. 2. any pointed projecting part, as the tip of an antler. *v.t.* 1. to use a prong on; pierce. 2. to break up (clods) with or as with a prong. 3. to furnish with prongs or tines.

pronged (prôŋd), *adj.* having prongs.

prong·horn (prôŋ′hôrn′), *n.* [*pl.* PRONGHORNS (-hôrns′), PRONGHORN; see PLURAL, II, D, 1], an antelopelike deer having forked horns like those of cattle, found in Mexico and the western United States.

pro·nom·i·nal (prō-nom′ə-n'l), *adj.* [LL. *pronominalis* < L. *pronomen*], in *grammar,* of, or having the function of, a pronoun: abbreviated **pron., pronom.**

pro·nom·i·nal·ly (prō-nom′ə-n'l-i), *adv.* as a pronoun.

pro·noun (prō′noun), *n.* [Fr. *pronom;* L. *pronomen* < *pro,* for + *nomen,* noun], in *grammar,* a word used in the place of or as a substitute for a noun: *I, you, he, she, it, we, they,* etc. are *pronouns*: abbreviated **pron., pr.**

pro·nounce (prə-nouns′), *v.t.* [PRONOUNCED (-nounst′), PRONOUNCING], [ME. *pronouncen;* OFr. *pronuncier, prononcier;* L. *pronuntiare; pro-,* before + *nuntiare,* to announce < *nuntius,* messenger], 1. to say officially, solemnly, or with ceremony: as, the judge *pronounced* the sentence. 2. to announce or declare (someone or something) to be as specified: as, the coroner *pronounced* him dead. 3. *a)* to utter or articulate (a sound or word): as, I *pronounce* it differently. *b)* to utter or articulate (a word or sound) in the required or standard manner: as, he couldn't *pronounce* my name. *c)* to indicate the pronunciation of (a word) with phonetic symbols. *v.i.* 1. to state or pass a judgment; make a pronouncement (with *on*). 2. to pronounce words, etc.

pro·nounced (prə-nounst′), *adj.* [pp. of *pronounce*], 1. spoken or uttered. 2. clearly marked; unmistakable: as, a *pronounced* accent. 3. decided: as, *pronounced* opinions. Abbreviated **pron., pron'd.**

pro·nounce·ment (prə-nouns′mənt), *n.* [Fr. *prononcement*], 1. a pronouncing. 2. a formal statement of fact, opinion, or judgment.

pron·to (pron′tō), *adv.* [Sp. < L. *promptus;* see PROMPT], [Slang], at once; quickly; immediately.

pro·nu·cle·us (prō-no͞o′kli-əs, prō-nū′kli-əs), *n.* [*pl.* PRONUCLEI (-ī′)], [*pro-* + *nucleus*], in *zoology,* the nucleus of either the male gamete (spermatozoon) or the female gamete (ovum) which unite in fertilization to form the double nucleus of the fertilized ovum.

pro·nun·ci·a·men·to (prə-nun′si-ə-men′tō, prō-nun′shi-ə-men′tō), *n.* [*pl.* PRONUNCIAMENTOS (-tōz)], [Sp. < L. *pronuntiare;* see PRONOUNCE], 1. a public declaration or pronouncement; proclamation. 2. a manifesto.

pro·nun·ci·a·tion (prə-nun′si-ā′shən, prə-nun′shi-ā′shən), *n.* [ME. *pronunciacion;* L. *pronuntiatio*], 1. the act or manner of pronouncing words with reference to the production of sounds, the placing of stress, intonation, etc. 2. the transcription in phonetic symbols of the accepted or standard pronunciation or pronunciations of a word: as, variant *pronunciations* of many words are recorded here. Abbreviated **pronun., pron.**

proof (pro͞of), *n.* [*pl.* PROOFS (pro͞ofs)], [ME. *profe, preove, preve;* OFr. *prueve, preve;* LL. *proba;* see PROBE], 1. the act or process of proving; testing or trying of something. 2. anything serving or tending to establish the truth of something, or to convince one of its truth conclusive evidence. 3. the establishment of the truth of something: as, he is completing the *proof* of his theory. 4. a test or trial of the truth, worth, quality, etc. of something: as, the *proof* of the pudding is in the eating. 5. the quality or condition of having been tested or proved. 6. tested or proved strength, as of armor. 7. the relative strength of an alcoholic liquor with reference to the arbitrary standard for proof spirit, taken as 100 proof. 8. in *engraving*, a trial impression taken from a plate before its completion. 9. in *law*, all the facts, admissions, etc. which together operate to determine a verdict or judgment. 10. in *mathematics*, a process for checking the correctness of a computation, as by adding the result to the subtrahend to get the minuend. 11. in *photography*, a trial print of a negative. 12. in *printing*, a trial impression of composed type for checking against the original manuscript to find and correct errors or make changes. *adj.* [contr. < *of proof*], 1. of tested and proved strength; impervious to (with *against*): as, *proof* against criticism. 2. used in proving or testing: as, a printer's *proof* sheet. 3. of standard strength: said of alcoholic liquors.

SYN.—**proof**, as compared here, applies to facts, documents, etc. that are so certain or convincing as to demonstrate the validity of a conclusion beyond reasonable doubt; **evidence** applies to something presented before a court, as a witness's statement, an object, etc. which bears on or establishes a fact; **testimony** applies to verbal evidence given by a witness under oath; **exhibit** applies to a document or object produced as evidence in a court.

-proof (proof), [< *proof, adj.*], a suffix used in forming adjectives (and verbs) meaning: 1. *impervious to*, as in *waterproof*. 2. *protected from* or *against*, as in *foolproof*, *weatherproof*. 3. *as strong as*, as in *armorproof*. 4. *resistive to, unaffected by*, as in *pityproof*, *womanproof*.

roof·ing (proof'iŋ), *n.* 1. the act or process of making (something) proof, especially waterproof. 2. the chemical, etc. used in this process.

roof·read (proof'rēd'), *v.t. & v.i.* to read (printers' proofs, etc.) in order to make corrections.

roof sheet, a printer's proof.

roof spirit, an alcoholic liquor, or a mixture of alcohol and water, containing 50 per cent of its volume of alcohol having a specific gravity of .7939 at 60° F.

rop (prop), *n.* [ME. *proppe;* MD. *proppe*, a prop; akin to G. *propfe*, a peg], 1. a rigid support, as a beam, stake, or pole, placed under or against a structure or part; hence, 2. a person who is one of the main supports of an enterprise, institution, etc. *v.t.* [PROPPED (propt), PROPPING], 1. to support, hold up, or hold in place with or as with a prop (often with *up*). 2. to lean (something) *against* a support. 3. to sustain or bolster.

rop (prop), *n.* a property (sense 7).

rop., 1. proper(ly). 2. property. 3. proposition.

ro·pae·deu·tic (prō'pi-dū'tik), *adj.* [< Gr. *propaideuein*, to teach beforehand; *pro-*, before + *paideuein*, to instruct < *pais, paidos*, a child], of, or having the nature of, elementary or introductory instruction. *n.* an elementary or introductory subject or study.

ro·pae·deu·ti·cal (prō'pi-dū'ti-k'l), *adj.* propaedeutic.

ro·pae·deu·tics (prō'pi-dū'tiks), *n.pl.* [construed as sing.], [see PROPAEDEUTIC], the basic principles and rules preliminary to the study of some art or science.

rop·a·ga·ble (prop'ə-gə-b'l), *adj.* [< L. *propagare* (see PROPAGATE); + *-able*], capable of being propagated.

rop·a·gan·da (prop'ə-gan'də), *n.* [contr. < L. *congregatio de propaganda fide*, the congregation for propagating the faith; see PROPAGATE], 1. [P-], in the Roman Catholic Church, a committee of cardinals, the Congregation for the Propagation of the Faith, in charge of the foreign missions; hence, 2. any organization or movement working for the propagation of particular ideas, doctrines, practices, etc. 3. the ideas, doctrines, practices, etc. spread in this way. 4. any systematic, widespread, deliberate indoctrination or plan for such indoctrination: now often used in a derogatory sense, connoting deception or distortion.

rop·a·gan·dism (prop'ə-gan'diz'm), *n.* the art, system, or use of propaganda.

rop·a·gan·dist (prop'ə-gan'dist), *n.* one who propagandizes. *adj.* of, or having the nature of, propaganda.

rop·a·gan·dize (prop'ə-gan'dīz), *v.t.* [PROPAGANDIZED (-dīzd), PROPAGANDIZING], 1. to spread (a doctrine or theory) by propaganda. 2. to subject (someone) to propaganda. *v.i.* to organize or conduct propaganda.

op·a·gate (prop'ə-gāt'), *v.t.* [PROPAGATED (-id), PROPAGATING], [< L. *propagatus*, pp. of *propagare*, to peg down, set < *propago*, slip for transplanting < *pro-*, before + *pag*, base of *pangere*, to fasten], 1. to cause a plant or animal) to reproduce itself; raise or breed. to reproduce (itself); multiply: said of a plant or animal. 3. to transmit (hereditary characteristics) by reproduction. 4. to spread (ideas, customs, etc.) from person to person or generation to generation. 5. to extend or transmit through space: as, *propagate* light. 6. [Obs. or Rare], to cause to increase or multiply. *v.i.* to reproduce or multiply, as plants or animals.

prop·a·ga·tion (prop'ə-gā'shən), *n.* [Fr.; L. *propagatio*], a propagating or being propagated.

prop·a·ga·tive (prop'ə-gā'tiv), *adj.* capable of propagating or tending to propagate.

prop·a·ga·tor (prop'ə-gā'tẽr), *n.* [L.], a person or thing that propagates.

pro·pane (prō'pān), *n.* [*propyl* + meth*ane*], a gaseous hydrocarbon of the methane series, C_3H_8, occurring naturally in petroleum.

pro·par·ox·y·tone (prō'par-ok'sə-tōn'), *adj.* [Gr. *proparoxytonos;* see PRO-, PARA- (beside), OXYTONE], in *Greek grammar*, having an acute accent on the antepenult. *n.* a proparoxytone word.

‡pro pa·tri·a (prō pā'tri-ə), [L.], for (one's) country.

pro·pel (prə-pel'), *v.t.* [PROPELLED (-peld'), PROPELLING], [L. *propellere; pro-*, forward + *pellere*, to drive], to push, drive, or impel onward, forward, or ahead. —*SYN.* see **push**.

pro·pel·lant (prə-pel'ənt), *n.* a person or thing that propels; specifically, the explosive charge that propels a shell from a gun.

pro·pel·lent (prə-pel'ənt), *adj.* [L. *propellens*, ppr.], propelling or tending to propel. *n.* a propellant.

pro·pel·ler (prə-pel'ẽr), *n.* a person or thing that propels; specifically, any of various propellent devices on a ship or aircraft, consisting typically of a series of blades mounted at an angle in a revolving hub and serving to propel the craft forward by a driving action on the water or air: see **airplane**, illus.

pro·pend (prō-pend'), *v.i.* [L. *propendere*, to hang forward; *pro-*, before + *pendere*, to hang], [Obs.], to incline, or be disposed (*to* or *toward* something).

pro·pene (prō'pēn), *n.* [*propyl* + *-ene*], propylene.

pro·pen·si·ty (prə-pen'sə-ti), *n.* [*pl.* PROPENSITIES (-tiz)], [< L. *propensus*, pp. of *propendere*, to hang forward; + *-ity*], 1. a natural inclination or tendency; bent. 2. [Rare], favorable inclination; bias (with *for*). —*SYN.* see **inclination.**

prop·er (prop'ẽr), *adj.* [ME. & OFr. *propre;* L. *proprius*, one's own], 1. specially adapted or suitable to a specific purpose or specific conditions; appropriate: as, the *proper* tool for this job. 2. naturally belonging or peculiar (*to* a specified person or thing): as, this weather is *proper* to Florida. 3. conforming to an accepted standard or to good usage; correct. 4. fitting; seemly; right: as, it was *proper* for him to strike back. 5. decent; decorous; chaste; modest: often connoting exaggerated respectability. 6. understood in its most restricted sense; strictly so called: usually following the noun modified, as, the population of Cleveland *proper* (i.e., apart from its suburbs). 7. [Archaic or Dial.], *a)* fine; good; excellent. *b)* becoming in appearance; handsome. 8. [British Colloq.], complete; thorough: as, a *proper* scoundrel. 9. [Obs.], one's own; belonging to oneself or itself. 10. in *ecclesiastical usage*, reserved for a particular day or festival: said of prayers, rites, etc. 11. in *grammar*, used to designate a specific individual, place, etc.: *Donald, Rover, Boston*, etc. are *proper* nouns, written with an initial capital letter. 12. in *heraldry*, represented in its natural colors. *n.* in *ecclesiastical usage*, the special office or prayers for a particular day or festival. Abbreviated **prop.** —*SYN.* see **fit.**

proper fraction, in *mathematics*, a fraction in which the numerator is less, or of lower degree, than the denominator, as 2/5 or x/x^2.

prop·er·ly (prop'ẽr-li), *adv.* in a proper manner (in various senses): abbreviated **prop.**

prop·er·tied (prop'ẽr-tid), *adj.* owning property.

Pro·per·tius, Sex·tus (seks'təs prō-pũr'shəs), fl. c. 30–15 B.C.; Roman poet.

prop·er·ty (prop'ẽr-ti), *n.* [*pl.* PROPERTIES (-tiz)], [ME. *proprete, properte;* OFr. *proprieté;* L. *proprietas* < *proprius*, one's own], 1. the right to possess, use, and dispose of something; ownership: as, *property* in land. 2. a thing or things owned; holdings or possessions collectively; especially, land or real estate owned. 3. a specific piece of land or real estate. 4. any trait or attribute proper to a thing or, formerly, to a person; characteristic quality; peculiarity; specifically, any of the principal characteristics of a substance, especially as determined by the senses: as, the *properties* of a chemical compound. 5. something regarded as being possessed by, or at the disposal of, a person or group of persons: as, that joke is common *property*. 6. in *logic*, an essential quality common to all members of a species or class. 7. in the *theater & motion pictures*, any of the movable articles used as part of the setting or in a piece of stage business, except the costumes, backdrops, etc. Abbreviated **prop.** —*SYN.* see **quality.**

pro·phase (prō'fāz'), *n.* [*pro-* (before) + *phase*], in *biology*, the first stage in mitosis, during which the chromatin is formed into chromosomes.

proph·e·cy (prof'ə-si), *n.* [*pl.* PROPHECIES (-siz)], [ME. *prophecie;* OFr. *prophecie, prophetie;* LL. *prophetia;* Gr. *prophēteia* < *prophētēs*], 1. prediction of the future under the influence of divine guidance; act or practice of a prophet. 2. any prediction. 3. something prophesied or predicted; specifically, the utterance or utterances of a prophet. 4. a book of prophecies.

proph·e·si·er (prof'ə-sī'ẽr), *n.* a person who prophesies.

proph·e·sy (prof'ə-sī'), *v.t.* [PROPHESIED (-sīd'), PROPHESYING], [ME. *prophecien;* OFr. *prophecier* < *prophecie;* see PROPHECY], 1. to declare or predict (something) by or as by the influence of divine guidance; hence, 2. to predict (a future event) in any way. 3. [Rare], to foreshadow. *v.i.* 1. to speak as a prophet; utter or make prophecies. 2. to teach religious matters; preach. —*SYN.* see **foretell.**

proph·et (prof'it), *n.* [ME. & OFr. *prophete;* LL. *propheta* < Gr. *prophētēs* < *pro-*, before + *phanai*, to speak], 1. a person who speaks for God or a god, or as though under divine guidance. 2. a religious teacher or leader regarded as, or claiming to be, divinely inspired. 3. a spokesman for some cause, group, movement, etc. 4. a person who predicts future events in any way.

the Prophet, 1. in *Moslemism*, Mohammed. 2. in *Mormonism*, Joseph Smith.

the Prophets, 1. the writers of the prophetic books of the Old Testament. 2. these books, forming a division distinct from the Law and the Hagiographa.

proph·et·ess (prof'it-is), *n.* a woman prophet.

proph·et·hood (prof'it-hood'), *n.* [see -HOOD], the office, condition, powers, etc. of a prophet.

pro·phet·ic (prə-fet'ik), *adj.* [Fr. *prophétique;* LL. *propheticus;* Gr. *prophētikos*], 1. of, or having the powers of, a prophet. 2. of, or having the nature of, prophecy or a prophecy. 3. containing a prophecy: as, a *prophetic* utterance. 4. that prophesies, predicts, or foreshadows.

pro·phet·i·cal (prə-fet'i-k'l), *adj.* prophetic.

pro·phy·lac·tic (prō'fə-lak'tik, prof'ə-lak'tik), *adj.* [Gr. *prophylaktikos* < *prophylassein*, to be on guard; *pro-*, before + *phylassein*, to guard], preventive or protective; especially, preventing or guarding against disease. *n.* a prophylactic medicine, device, treatment, etc.

pro·phy·lax·is (prō'fə-lak'sis, prof'ə-lak'sis), *n.* [*pl.* PROPHYLAXES (-sēz)], [Mod. L.], the prevention of or protection from disease; prophylactic treatment.

pro·pin·qui·ty (prō-piŋ'kwə-ti), *n.* [ME. & OFr. *propinquite;* L. *propinquitas* < *propinquus*, near], 1. nearness in time or place. 2. nearness of relationship; kinship. 3. likeness or affinity of nature.

pro·pi·on·ic (prō'pi-on'ik, prō'pi-ō'nik), *adj.* [*proto-* + Gr. *piōn*, fat; + *-ic*], designating a colorless, sweet-smelling, liquid fatty acid, $C_2H_5CO_2H$, found in chyme and sweat, and produced in the distillation of wood.

pro·pi·ti·a·ble (prə-pish'i-ə-b'l), *adj.* that can be propitiated.

pro·pi·ti·ate (prə-pish'i-āt'), *v.t.* [PROPITIATED (-id), PROPITIATING], [< L. *propitiatus*, pp. of *propitiare*, to propitiate < *propitius;* see PROPITIOUS], to cause to become favorably inclined; win or regain the good will of; appease or conciliate. —*SYN.* see **pacify.**

pro·pi·ti·a·tion (prə-pish'i-ā'shən), *n.* [ME. *propiciacioun;* LL. *propitiatio*], 1. a propitiating or being propitiated. 2. something that propitiates.

pro·pi·ti·a·tive (prə-pish'i-ā'tiv, prə-pish'i-ə-tiv), *adj.* that propitiates or tends to propitiate.

pro·pi·ti·a·tor (prə-pish'i-ā'tẽr), *n* [LL.], a person who propitiates.

pro·pi·ti·a·to·ry (prə-pish'i-ə-tôr'i, prə-pish'i-ə-tō'ri), *adj.* that propitiates or is intended to propitiate; conciliatory. *n.* in ancient Jewish ritual, the mercy seat.

pro·pi·tious (prə-pish'əs), *adj.* [OFr. *propicius;* L. *propitius*, favorable; generally supposed to be formed < *pro-*, before, forward + *petere*, to seek, orig. to fly], 1. favorably inclined or disposed; gracious: as, the gods were *propitious*. 2. favorable; boding well; auspicious: as, a *propitious* omen. 3. that favors or furthers; advantageous: as, *propitious* winds. —*SYN.* see **favorable.**

prop·o·lis (prop'ə-lis), *n.* [L.; Gr. *propolis*, suburb, also bee glue; *pro-*, before + *polis*, city], a brownish, waxy substance collected from the buds of certain trees by bees and used by them to cement or caulk their hives.

pro·pone (prə-pōn'), *v.t.* [PROPONED (-pōnd'), PROPONING], [MScot. < L.; see PROPONENT], [Scot.], to bring forward as a plan, excuse, etc.; propose.

pro·po·nent (prə-pō'nənt), *n.* [< L. *proponens*, ppr. of *proponere*, to set forth; *pro-*, forth + *ponere*, to place], 1. a person who makes a proposal or proposition. 2. a person who supports a cause, etc. 3. in *law*, one who propounds something, especially a will for probate.

pro·por·tion (prə-pôr'shən, prə-pōr'shən), *n.* [ME. *proporcioun;* OFr. *proporcion;* L. *proportio; pro-*, before + *portio*, a part, share], 1. a part, share, or portion, especially in its relation to the whole; quota. 2. the comparative relation between parts or things with respect to size, amount, quantity, etc.; ratio. 3. a harmonious relationship between parts or things; balance or symmetry. 4. size, degree, or extent relative to a standard. 5. *pl.* dimensions: as, a building of large *proportions*. 6. [Rare], relation, other than of quantity, between things; comparison; analogy. 7. in *mathematics*, *a*) an equality between ratios; relationship between four quantities in which the quotient of the first divided by the second is equal to that of the third divided by the fourth (e.g., 2 is to 6 as 3 is to 9): also **geometrical proportion.** *b*) a method for finding the fourth quantity in such a relationship when three are given; rule of three. *v.t.* 1. to cause (something) to be in proper relation, harmony, or symmetry with something else: as, *proportion* the penalty to the nature of the crime. 2. to arrange the parts of (a whole) so as to be harmonious or symmetrical. —*SYN.* see **symmetry.**

pro·por·tion·a·ble (prə-pôr'shən-ə-b'l, prə-pōr'shən-ə-b'l), *adj.* [ME. *proporcionable* < OFr.], in proper proportion; having due correspondence; proportional.

pro·por·tion·al (prə-pôr'shən-'l, prə-pōr'shən-'l), *adj.* [ME.; L. *proportionalis*], 1. of or determined by proportion; relative: as, the *proportional* meanings of life and death. 2. having, or being in, proportion: as, his pay is *proportional* to his work. 3. in *mathematics*, having the same or a constant ratio. *n.* a quantity in a mathematical proportion. —*SYN.* see **proportionate.**

pro·por·tion·al·i·ty (prə-pôr'shə-nal'ə-ti, prə-pōr'shə-nal'ə-ti), *n.* [ML. *proportionalitas*], the quality or condition of being proportional, or in proportion.

proportional representation, a system of voting that gives minority parties representation in a legislature in proportion to their popular vote: abbreviated **P.R.**

pro·por·tion·ate (prə-pôr'shən-it, prə-pōr'shən-it; *for v.*, prə-pôr'shə-nāt', prə-pōr'shə-nāt'), *adj.* in proper proportion; proportional. *v.t.* [PROPORTIONATED (-id), PROPORTIONATING], to make proportionate.

SYN.—**proportionate** and **proportional** both imply a being in due proportion, the former usually being preferred with reference to two things that have a reciprocal relationship to each other (the output was *proportionate* to the energy expended) and the latter, with reference to a number of similar or related things (*proportional* representation); **commensurable** applies to things measurable by the same standard or to things properly proportioned; **commensurate**, in addition, implies equality in measure or size of things that are alike or somehow related to each other (a reward *commensurate* with his heroism).—*ANT.* disproportionate.

pro·por·tioned (prə-pôr'shənd, prə-pōr'shənd), *adj.* 1. in proportion. 2. having specified proportions.

pro·por·tion·ment (prə-pôr'shən-mənt, prə-pōr'shən-mənt), *n.* a proportioning or being proportioned.

pro·pos·al (prə-pō'z'l), *n.* 1. a proposing. 2. a plan, scheme, etc. proposed. 3. an offer of marriage.

SYN.—**proposal** refers to a plan, offer, etc. presented for acceptance or rejection (his *proposal* for a decrease in taxes was approved); **proposition**, commonly used in place of **proposal** with reference to business dealings and the like, in a strict sense applies to a statement, theorem, etc. set forth for argument, demonstration, proof, etc. (the *proposition* that all men are created equal).

pro·pose (prə-pōz'), *v.t.* [PROPOSED (-pōzd'), PROPOSING], [Late ME.; Early Fr. *proposer; pro-* (L. *pro-*), forth + *poser* < L. *positus*, pp. of *ponere*, to place], 1. to put forth for consideration or acceptance. 2. to purpose, plan; intend. 3. to present as a toast in drinking. 4. to nominate (someone) for membership, office, etc. *v.i.* 1. to make a proposal; form or declare a purpose or design. 2. to offer marriage. —*SYN.* see **intend.**

prop·o·si·tion (prop'ə-zish'ən), *n.* [ME. *proposicioun;* L. *propositio* < *proponere;* see PROPONENT], 1. a proposing. 2. *a*) something proposed; proposal; plan. *b*) [Colloq.], an indecent or immoral proposal. 3. [Archaic], a setting forth; offering. 4. [Colloq.], a project; business undertaking. 5. [Colloq.], a person, problem, undertaking, etc. to be dealt with. 6. in *logic*, an expression in which the predicate affirms or denies something about the subject. 7. in *mathematics*, a theorem to be demonstrated or a problem to be solved. 8. in *rhetoric*, a subject to be discussed or a statement to be upheld. Abbreviated **prop.** *v.t.* [Colloq.], to make an indecent or immoral proposal to. —*SYN.* see **proposal.**

prop·o·si·tion·al (prop'ə-zish'ən-'l), *adj.* 1. of a proposition. 2. having the character of a proposition.

pro·pound (prə-pound'), *v.t.* [earlier *propone;* L. *proponere;* see PROPONENT], to put forward for consideration; set forth; propose.

pro·prae·tor, pro·pre·tor (prō-prē'tẽr), *n.* [L. *propraetor*, orig. *pro praetore* < *pro*, for + *praetor*, praetor], in ancient Rome, a magistrate who was sent to govern a province after having served as praetor in Rome.

pro·pri·e·tar·y (prə-prī'ə-ter'i), *n.* [*pl.* PROPRIETARIES (-iz)], [LL. *proprietarius* < L. *proprietas;* see PROPERTY], 1. a proprietor; owner. 2. a group of proprietors. 3. proprietorship. 4. in *American history*, the owner of a proprietary colony. 5. a proprietary medicine. *adj.* 1. belonging to a proprietor. 2. holding property. 3. of property or proprietorship. 4. held under patent, trade-mark, or copyright by a private person or company: as, a *proprietary* medicine.

proprietary colony, in *American history*, any of certain North American colonies that were granted by the British Crown to an individual or group of individuals in whom all governing rights were vested.

pro·pri·e·tor (prə-prī'ə-tẽr), *n.* [irregular formation *proprietary* + *-or*], 1. a person who has a legal title or exclusive right to some property; owner. 2. the owner of a proprietary colony. Abbreviated **propr.**

ro·pri·e·tor·ship (prə-prī′ə-tẽr-ship′), *n.* ownership.

ro·pri·e·tress (prə-prī′ə-tris), *n.* a woman proprietor.

ro·pri·e·ty (prə-prī′ə-ti), *n.* [*pl.* PROPRIETIES (-tiz)], [Fr. *propriété;* OFr. *proprieté;* see PROPERTY], 1. the quality of being proper, fitting, or suitable; fitness. 2. conformity with what is proper or fitting. 3. conformity with accepted standards of manners or behavior. 4. [Obs.], *a*) peculiar or proper nature or state. *b*) a peculiarity. 5. [Obs.], private property. —*SYN.* see **decorum.**

the proprieties, accepted standards of behavior in polite society.

ro·pri·o·cep·tive (prō′pri-ə-sep′tiv), *adj.* [< L. *proprius,* one's own; + *-ceptive* as in *inceptive*], designating or of stimuli produced in body tissues, as the muscles or tendons, and received there by the proprioceptors.

ro·pri·o·cep·tor (prō′pri-ə-sep′tẽr), *n.* any of the sensory end organs in the muscles, tendons, etc. that are sensitive to the stimuli originating in these tissues by the movement of the body or its parts.

rop root, any root that helps support the plant stem, as on the mangrove or banyan tree.

rop·to·sis (prop-tō′sis), *n.* [Mod. L.; Gr. *proptōsis* < *propiptein,* to fall forward; *pro-,* before + *piptein,* to fall], a displacement or tipping forward; protrusion, especially of the eyeball.

ro·pul·sion (prə-pul′shən), *n.* [Fr. < L. *propulsus,* pp. of *propellere;* see PROPEL], 1. a propelling or being propelled. 2. something that propels; propelling force.

ro·pul·sive (prə-pul′siv), *adj.* [< L. *propulsus,* pp. of *propellere;* + *-ive*], propelling, tending to propel, or having the power to propel.

ro·pyl (prō′pil), *n.* [*prop*ionic + *-yl*], the monovalent radical C_3H_7, derived from propane.

rop·y·lae·um (prop′i-lē′əm), *n.* [*pl.* PROPYLAEA (-ə)], L.; Gr. *propylaion,* orig. neut. of *propylaios,* before the gate < *pro-,* before + *pylē,* gate], in *Greek & Roman architecture,* an entrance, vestibule, or portico before a building or group of buildings; especially, *pl.* the architectural structure forming the entrance to the Acropolis.

ro·pyl·ene (prō′pə-lēn′), *n.* [*propyl* + *-ene*], an unsaturated hydrocarbon, C_3H_6, a colorless gas obtained in the refining of petroleum: also called *propene.*

rop·y·lite (prop′ə-lit′), *n.* [< Gr. *propylon,* gateway (< *pro-,* before + *pylē,* gate); + *-ite*], a type of volcanic rock found in silver-mining regions, a form of andesite.

ro ra·ta (prō rā′tə; *occas.,* rä′tə), [L., *pro rata* (*parte*), according to the calculated (share)], in proportion; proportionately.

ro·rat·a·ble (prō-rāt′ə-b'l), *adj.* capable of being prorated.

ro·rate (prō′rāt′, prō′rāt′), *v.t.* & *v.i.* [PRORATED (-id), PRORATING], [< *pro rata*], to divide, assess, or distribute proportionally.

ro·ro·ga·tion (prō′rō-gā′shən), *n.* [ME. & OFr. *prorogacion;* L. *prorogatio,* extension, deferring < pp. of *prorogare*], a proroguing, as of a legislative assembly.

ro·rogue (prō-rōg′), *v.t.* [PROROGUED (-rōgd′), PROROGUING], [ME. *prorogen;* 14th-c. Fr. *proroguer;* L. *prorogare,* to defer, prolong; *pro-,* for + *rogare,* to ask], 1. to discontinue or end a session of (a legislative assembly, as the British Parliament). 2. [Rare], to defer; delay; postpone. —*SYN.* see **adjourn.**

ros., prosody.

ro·sa·ic (prō-zā′ik), *adj.* [ML. *prosaicus* < L. *prosa,* prose], 1. of or like prose; unpoetic. 2. matter-of-fact; commonplace; dull.

ro·sa·i·cal·ly (prō-zā′i-k'l-i, prō-zā′ik-li), *adv.* in a prosaic manner.

ro·sa·ism (prō′zā-iz'm), *n.* [Fr. *prosaïsme*], 1. prosaic quality or style. 2. a prosaic expression.

ros. Atty., prosecuting attorney.

ro·sce·ni·um (prō-sē′ni-əm), *n.* [*pl.* PROSCENIA (-ə)], L. < Gr. *proskēnion* < *pro-,* before + *skēnē,* a tent, stage], 1. the stage of the ancient Greek and Roman theater. 2. *a*) the front area of the stage that is still visible to the audience when the curtain is lowered.) the curtain and the arch or framework that holds it.

o·scribe (prō-skrīb′), *v.t.* [PROSCRIBED (-skrībd′), PROSCRIBING], [L. *proscribere; pro-,* before + *scribere,* to write], 1. in ancient Rome, to publish the name of (a person) condemned to death, banishment, etc. 2. to deprive of the protection of the law; outlaw. 3. to banish; exile. 4. to denounce; forbid; interdict.

o·scrip·tion (prō-skrip′shən), *n.* [ME. *proscripcioun;* .. *proscriptio* < *proscriptus,* pp.], 1. a proscribing or being proscribed. 2. interdiction; prohibition.

ro·scrip·tive (prō-skrip′tiv), *adj.* of proscription; proscribing or tending to proscribe.

ose (prōz), *n.* [ME.; OFr.; L. *prosa,* for *prorsa* (*oratio*), direct (speech) < *prorsus,* forward, straight on < *pro-,* forward + *versus,* pp. of *vertere,* to turn], 1. the ordinary form of written or spoken language, without rhyme or meter: opposed to *verse, poetry.* 2. dull, commonplace talk or expression. 3. in the *Roman Catholic Church,* a hymn sung after the gradual: also called *sequence.* *adj.* 1. of prose. 2. in prose. 3. dull; unimaginative; commonplace; prosaic. *v.t.* & *v.i.* [PROSED (prōzd), PROSING], to speak, write, or express (one's thoughts, etc.) in prose.

pro·sec·tor (prō-sek′tẽr), *n.* [LL., anatomist < L. *prosectus,* pp. of *prosecare,* to cut up; *pro-,* before + *secare,* to cut], a person skilled in dissection who prepares subjects for anatomical demonstration.

pros·e·cute (pros′i-kūt′), *v.t.* [PROSECUTED (-id), PROSECUTING], [ME. *prosecuten* < L. *prosecutus,* pp. of *prosequi; pro-,* before + *sequi,* to follow], 1. to follow up or pursue (something) so as to complete it: as, *prosecute* a war with great vigor. 2. to carry on; practice; engage in: as, *prosecute* your studies. 3. to institute legal proceedings against, or conduct criminal proceedings in court against. 4. to try to get, enforce, etc. by legal process. *v.i.* 1. to institute and carry on a legal suit. 2. to act as prosecutor.

prosecuting attorney, a public official who conducts criminal prosecutions on behalf of the State or people: abbreviated **Pros. Atty., P.A.**

pros·e·cu·tion (pros′i-kū′shən), *n.* [< OFr. or LL.; OFr. *prosecution;* LL. *prosecutio*], 1. a prosecuting, or following up. 2. the conducting of a lawsuit. 3. the party who institutes and carries on criminal proceedings in court.

pros·e·cu·tor (pros′i-kū′tẽr), *n.* [ML. (in LL., a companion, attendant)], 1. a person who prosecutes. 2. in *law, a*) a person who institutes a prosecution in court. *b*) a prosecuting attorney.

pros·e·lyte (pros′'l-īt′), *n.* [ME. *proselite;* ML. *proselytus;* Gr. *prosēlytos* < *pros,* toward + an aorist stem of *proserchesthai,* to come], a person who has been converted from one religion, opinion, or party to another. *v.t.* & *v.i.* [PROSELYTED (-id), PROSELYTING], 1. to proselytize. 2. to persuade (an athlete), usually by an attractive offer, to attend and play for a certain school.

pros·e·lyt·ism (pros′'l-i-tiz'm, pros′'l-īt-iz'm), *n.* 1. the fact of becoming or being a proselyte. 2. the act or practice of proselytizing.

pros·e·lyt·ize (pros′'l-i-tīz′, pros′'l-īt-īz′), *v.i.* [PROSELYTIZED (-tīzd′, -īzd′), PROSELYTIZING], to make proselytes, or converts. *v.t.* to make a convert of.

pros·en·ce·phal·ic (pros′en-sə-fal′ik), *adj.* of the prosencephalon.

pros·en·ceph·a·lon (pros′en-sef′ə-lon′), *n.* [Mod. L.; Gr. *pros,* in front; + *encephalon*], the forebrain.

pros·en·chy·ma (pros-eŋ′ki-mə), *n.* [Mod. L. (after *parenchyma*); Gr. *pros,* to, toward, near + *enchyma,* infusion], in *botany,* a tissue of thick-walled, elongated cells without much protoplasm, found in some plants.

pros·en·chym·a·tous (pros′eŋ-kim′ə-təs), *adj.* of, or having the nature of, prosenchyma.

pros·er (prō′zẽr), *n.* a person who proses; especially, one who talks or writes in a prosaic manner.

Pro·ser·pi·na (prō-sūr′pi-nə), *n.* [L.], in *Roman mythology,* the daughter of Ceres and wife of Pluto: identified with the Greek Persephone.

Pro·ser·pi·ne (prō-sūr′pi-nē′, pros′ẽr-pīn′), *n.* Proserpina.

pros·i·ly (prō′zə-li), *adv.* in a prosy manner.

pros·i·ness (prō′zi-nis), *n.* the quality of being prosy.

‡pro·sit (prō′sit; G. prō′zit), *interj.* [L., 3d pers. sing., subj., of *prodesse,* to do good < *pro,* for + *esse,* to be], to your health: a toast, especially among Germans.

pro·slav·er·y (prō-slāv′ẽr-i), *adj.* in favor of slavery; especially, in *United States history,* in favor of preserving the institution of Negro slavery. *n.* support or advocacy of slavery.

pros·o·di·a·cal (pros′ə-dī′ə-k'l), *adj.* prosodic.

pro·sod·ic (prə-sod′ik), *adj.* of, or according to the principles of, prosody.

pro·sod·i·cal·ly (prə-sod′i-k'l-i, prə-sod′ik-li), *adv.* 1. in a prosodic manner. 2. as regards prosody.

pros·o·dist (pros′ə-dist), *n.* a person skilled in prosody.

pros·o·dy (pros′ə-di), *n.* [*pl.* PROSODIES (-diz)], [L. *prosodia;* Gr. *prosōidia,* tone, accent, voice modulation, song sung to music < *pros,* to + *ōdē,* song], 1. the science or art of versification, including the study of metrical structure, rhyme, stanza forms, etc. 2. a particular system of versification and metrical structure: as, Dryden's *prosody.* Abbreviated **pros.**

pro·so·po·poe·ia (prə-sō′pō-pē′ə), *n.* [L.; Gr. *prosōpopoiia* < *prosōpon,* person + *poiein,* to make], in *rhetoric,* 1. a figure in which an absent, dead, or imaginary person is represented as speaking. 2. personification.

pros·pect (pros′pekt), *n.* [ME. *prospecte;* L. *prospectus,* lookout < *prospicere,* to look forward < *pro-,* forward + *specere,* to look], 1. a broad view; scene. 2. the view obtained from any particular point; outlook. 3. a looking forward; anticipation. 4. *a*) something hoped for or expected; probable outcome. *b*) *usually in pl.* apparent chance for success, gain, etc. 5. a likely customer, candidate, etc. 6. in *mining, a*) a place where a mineral deposit is sought or found. *b*) a sample of gravel, earth, etc. tested for a particular mineral, or the resulting yield of mineral. ***v.t. & v.i.*** to explore or search (*for*): as, *prospect* for gold. —***SYN.*** see **view.**

in prospect, expected.

pro·spec·tive (prə-spek′tiv), ***adj.*** [obs. Fr. *prospectif;* L. *prospectivus* < *prospectus;* see PROSPECT], 1. looking forward into the future. 2. expected; likely; future.

pros·pec·tor (pros′pek-tẽr), ***n.*** [LL.], a person who prospects, or searches, for precious minerals, oil, etc.

pro·spec·tus (prə-spek′təs, pros-pek′təs), ***n.*** [L.; see PROSPECT], a statement outlining the main features of a new work or business enterprise, or the attractions of an established institution such as a college, hotel, etc.

pros·per (pros′pẽr), ***v.i.*** [Fr. *prospérer;* L. *prosperare,* to cause to prosper < *prosperus,* favorable, fortunate], to succeed; be prosperous; thrive; flourish. ***v.t.*** to cause to succeed or flourish. —***SYN.*** see **succeed.**

pros·per·i·ty (pros-per′ə-ti), ***n.*** [*pl.* PROSPERITIES (-tiz)], [ME. & OFr. *prosperite;* L. *prosperitas* < *prosperus*], prosperous condition; good fortune; wealth; success.

Pros·per·o (pros′pẽr-ō′), ***n.*** [It.], in Shakespeare's *The Tempest,* the deposed Duke of Milan, who by magic raises a tempest off the island which he inhabits with his daughter Miranda, and then acts as host to the shipwrecked malefactors.

pros·per·ous (pros′pẽr-əs), ***adj.*** [ME.; L. *prosperus*], 1. prospering; successful; flourishing. 2. well-to-do; well-off. 3. conducive to success; favorable; propitious.

prostat-, prostato-.

pros·tate (pros′tāt), ***adj.*** [ML. *prostata* < Gr. *prostatēs,* one standing before < *proistanai,* to set before < *pro-,* before + *histanai,* to set], designating or of a partly muscular gland surrounding the urethra at the base of the bladder in the male: it secretes an alkaline fluid that is discharged with the sperm. ***n.*** the prostate gland.

pros·ta·tec·to·my (pros′tə-tek′tə-mi), ***n.*** [see PROSTATO- & -ECTOMY], the surgical removal of all or part of the prostate gland.

pro·stat·ic (prō-stat′ik), ***adj.*** of the prostate gland.

pros·ta·ti·tis (pros′tə-tī′tis), ***n.*** [see -ITIS], inflammation of the prostate gland.

pros·ta·to- (pros′tə-tō), a combining form meaning *of the prostate:* also, before a vowel, **prostat-.**

pros·the·sis (pros′thə-sis), ***n.*** [LL.; Gr. *prosthesis* < *prostithenai; pros,* to + *tithenai,* to place], 1. in *grammar,* prothesis. 2. in *medicine, a*) the replacement of a missing part of the body, as a limb, eye, or tooth, by an artificial substitute. *b*) such a substitute.

pros·thet·ic (pros-thet′ik), ***adj.*** [Gr. *prosthetikos*], of prosthesis.

prosthetic dentistry, prosthodontia.

pros·thet·ics (pros-thet′iks), ***n.pl.*** [construed as sing.], [< *prosthetic*], the branch of surgery dealing with the replacement of missing parts, especially limbs, by artificial substitutes.

pros·tho·don·ti·a (pros′thə-don′shə, pros′thə-don′shi-ə), ***n.*** [Mod. L.; see PROSTHETIC & -ODONT], the branch of dentistry dealing with the replacement of missing teeth, as by bridges or artificial dentures.

pros·tho·don·tist (pros′thə-don′tist), ***n.*** a specialist in prosthodontia.

pros·ti·tute (pros′tə-tōōt′, pros′tə-tūt′), ***v.t.*** [PROSTITUTED (-id), PROSTITUTING], [< L. *prostitutus,* pp. of *prostituere* < *pro-,* before + *statuere,* to cause to stand], 1. to sell the services of (oneself or another) for purposes of sexual intercourse. 2. to sell (oneself, one's artistic or moral integrity, etc.) for low or unworthy purposes. ***adj.*** given over to base purposes; debased; corrupt. ***n.*** 1. a woman who engages in promiscuous sexual intercourse for pay; whore; harlot; hence, 2. a person, as a writer, artist, etc., who sells his services for low or unworthy purposes.

pros·ti·tu·tion (pros′tə-tōō′shən, pros′tə-tū′shən), ***n.*** the act or practice of prostituting, or the fact of being prostituted; especially, the trade of a prostitute.

pros·ti·tu·tor (pros′tə-tōō′tẽr, pros′tə-tū′tẽr), ***n.*** [LL.], a person or thing that prostitutes.

pros·trate (pros′trāt), ***adj.*** [ME. *prostrat;* L. *prostratus,* pp. of *prosternere,* to lay flat; *pro-,* before + *sternere,* to stretch out], 1. lying with the face downward in demonstration of great humility or abject submission. 2. lying flat, prone, or supine. 3. thrown or fallen to the ground. 4. laid low; completely subjugated; overcome; submissive. 5. in *botany,* growing on the ground; trailing. ***v.t.*** [PROSTRATED (-id), PROSTRATING], 1. to throw prostrate; lay flat on the ground. 2. to lay low; overcome; exhaust or subjugate. —***SYN.*** see **prone.**

pros·tra·tion (pros-trā′shən), ***n.*** 1. a prostrating or being prostrated. 2. utter exhaustion or dejection.

pro·style (prō′stīl), ***adj.*** [L. *prostylus;* Gr. *prostylos; pro-,* before + *stylos,* pillar], in *architecture,* having a portico whose columns, usually four in number, extend in a line across the front only, as in a Greek temple. ***n.*** 1. such a portico. 2. a prostyle building.

pros·y (prō′zi), ***adj.*** [PROSIER (-zi-ẽr), PROSIEST (-zi-ist)], 1. like, or having the nature of, prose. 2. prosaic; commonplace, unimaginative, dull, or tedious.

Prot., Protestant.

pro·tac·tin·i·um (prō′tak-tin′i-əm), ***n.*** [Mod. L. < *proto-* + *actinium*], a rare radioactive chemical element: symbol, Pa; at. wt., 231; at. no., 91: formerly called *protoactinium.*

pro·tag·o·nist (prō-tag′ə-nist), ***n.*** [Gr. *prōtagōnistēs* < *prōtos,* first + *agōnistēs,* actor], 1. the main character in a drama, novel, or story, about whom the action centers. 2. a person who plays a leading or active part.

Pro·tag·o·ras (prō-tag′ẽr-əs), ***n.*** Greek philosopher; lived 481–411 B.C.; first of the Sophists.

pro·ta·min (prō′tə-min), ***n.*** protamine.

pro·ta·mine (prō′tə-mēn′, prō-tə-min), ***n.*** [see PROTO- & AMINE], any of a class of simple proteins that are soluble in ammonia, do not coagulate by heat, and yield relatively few amino acids upon hydrolysis.

prot·a·sis (prot′ə-sis), ***n.*** [LL.; Gr. *protasis* < *proteinein,* to stretch before, present; *pro-,* before + *teinein,* to stretch], 1. in *classical drama,* the opening of the play in which the characters are introduced. 2. in *grammar* the clause that expresses the condition in a conditional sentence: cf. **apodosis.**

pro·te·an (prō′ti-ən, prō-tē′ən), ***adj.*** 1. [P-], of or like Proteus. 2. very changeable; readily taking on different shapes and forms.

pro·te·ase (prō′ti-ās′), ***n.*** [*prote*in + dias*tase*], an enzyme that digests proteins.

pro·tect (prə-tekt′), ***v.t.*** [< L. *protectus,* pp. of *protegere* to protect; *pro-,* before + *tegere,* to cover], 1. to shield from injury, danger, or loss; guard; defend. 2. in *commerce,* to set aside funds toward the payment of (a note, draft, etc.) at maturity. 3. in *economics,* to guard (domestic industry) by tariffs on imported products. —***SYN.*** see **defend.**

pro·tec·tion (prə-tek′shən), ***n.*** [ME. *proteccioun;* OFr. LL. *protectio*], 1. a protecting or being protected. 2. an instance of this. 3. a person or thing that protects. 4. a writing, pass, etc. that makes it possible for one to travel with safety; passport. 5. [Colloq.], *a*) money extorted by racketeers as insurance against threatened violence. *b*) extortion of this kind. 6. in *economics,* the system of protecting domestic products by taxing imported goods: opposed to *free trade.*

pro·tec·tion·ism (prə-tek′shən-iz′m), ***n.*** in *economics* the system, theory, or policy of protection.

pro·tec·tion·ist (prə-tek′shən-ist), ***n.*** a person advocating protectionism and opposed to free trade. ***adj.*** of protectionists or protectionism.

pro·tec·tive (prə-tek′tiv), ***adj.*** protecting, or serving, intended, or alleged to protect: as, a *protective* gesture, *protective* custody; specifically, in *political economy* serving or intended to protect domestic products, industries, etc. in competition with foreign products, industries, etc.: as, a *protective* tariff.

protective coloration (or **coloring**), the natural coloration of any of certain organisms by means of which it is blended in with its normal environment and thus protected from detection by its enemies.

protective tariff, a tax or duty imposed on imported goods to protect domestic industry.

pro·tec·tor (prə-tek′tẽr), ***n.*** [ME.; OFr. *protectour;* LL. 1. a person or thing that protects; guardian; defender. 2. in *English history, a*) a person who rules a kingdom during the minority, absence, or incapacity of the sovereign. *b*) [P], the title (in full, *Lord Protector*) held by Oliver Cromwell (1653–1658) and his son Richard (1658–1659), during the British Commonwealth.

pro·tec·tor·al (prə-tek′tẽr-əl), ***adj.*** of a protector.

pro·tec·tor·ate (prə-tek′tẽr-it), ***n.*** 1. government by a protector. 2. the office or term of office of a protector. 3. [P-], the government of England under Oliver Cromwell and his son Richard (1653–1659). 4. the relation of a strong state to a weaker state under its control and protection. 5. a state or territory so controlled and protected. 6. the authority exercised by the controlling state. Abbreviated **protec.**

pro·tec·tor·ship (prə-tek′tẽr-ship′), ***n.*** [see -SHIP], the office or government of a protector.

pro·tec·to·ry (prə-tek′tẽr-i), ***n.*** [*pl.* PROTECTORIES (-iz)], an institution for the protection of destitute children.

pro·tec·tress (prə-tek′tris), ***n.*** a woman who protects.

pro·té·gé (prō′tə-zhā′; Fr. prô′tā′zhā′), ***n.*** [Fr., pp. *protéger* < L. *protegere;* see PROTECT], a person under the patronage, protection, or care of another.

pro·té·gée (prō′tə-zhā′; Fr. prô′tā′zhā′), ***n.*** feminine of **protégé.**

pro·te·id (prō′ti-id), ***n.*** & ***adj.*** proteide.

pro·te·ide (prō′ti-īd′, prō′ti-id), ***n.*** [*protein* + *-id*] protein. ***adj.*** containing proteins.

pro·te·in (prō′tē-in, prō′tēn), ***n.*** [G. < Gr. *prōtei*[os], prime, chief < *prōtos,* first: so called because of being the chief constituent of plant and animal bodies], any of a class of nitrogenous substances consisting of a complex union of amino acids and containing carbon, hydrogen, nitrogen, oxygen, and frequently sulfur: proteins occur in all animal and vegetable matter and are essential to the diet of animals.

pro·te·in·ase (prō′tē-in-ās′), *n.* any enzyme that promotes proteolysis.
pro tem·po·re (prō tem′pə-rē′), [L.], for the time (being); temporary; temporarily: shortened to **pro tem.**
pro·te·ol·y·sis (prō′ti-ol′ə-sis), *n.* [Mod. L.: see PROTEIDE & -LYSIS], in *biochemistry*, a breaking down of proteins, as by gastric juices, to form simpler, soluble substances.
pro·te·o·lyt·ic (prō′ti-ə-lit′ik), *adj.* of proteolysis.
pro·te·ose (prō′ti-ōs′), *n.* [*protein* + *-ose*], any of a class of water-soluble products formed in the hydrolysis of proteins, as albumose.
prot·er·o- (prot′ẽr-ō, prot′ẽr-ə), [< Gr. *proteros*, former], a combining form meaning *former, earlier*, as in *Proterozoic*.
Prot·er·o·zo·ic (prot′ẽr-ə-zō′ik), *adj.* [*protero-* + *zo-* + *-ic*], designating or of the geological era following the Archeozoic and preceding the Paleozoic, characterized by the appearance of the simplest types of algae, widespread glaciation and mountain formation, and the laying down of iron and copper deposits: sometimes called *Cryptozoic*.
the Proterozoic, the Proterozoic Era or its rocks: see **geology**, chart.
pro·test (prə-test′; *for n.*, prō′test), *v.t.* [ME. *protesten;* L. *protestari; pro-*, forth + *testari*, to affirm < *testis*, a witness], 1. to state positively; affirm solemnly; assert. 2. to make objection to; speak strongly against. 3. to make a written declaration of the nonpayment of (a bill of exchange or a promissory note). *v.i.* 1. to make solemn affirmation. 2. to express disapproval; object; dissent. *n.* 1. an objection; remonstrance. 2. a document formally objecting to something. 3. in *law*, *a*) a declaration by a notary to the holder of a bill or note, showing that it has not been honored by the drawer. *b*) a declaration made by the master of a ship before an authorized officer, attesting to the causes of damages or losses sustained by the ship, as from a disaster, and protesting the freedom from liability of the officers and crew. *c*) a declaration by a payer that he does not concede the legality of a claim he has paid. —*SYN.* see **object**.
under protest, having first expressed one's objections.
Prot·es·tant (prot′is-tənt; *also, for n. 3 & adj. 2*, prə-tes′tənt), *n.* [Fr. < L. *protestans*, ppr. of *protestari;* see PROTEST], 1. [P-], originally, any of the German princes and free cities that formally protested to the Diet of Spires (1529) its decision to uphold the edict of the Diet of Worms against the Reformation. 2. [P-], any Christian not belonging to the Roman Catholic or Orthodox Eastern Church: in the 17th century the term was restricted to Lutherans and Anglicans. 3. a person who protests. *adj.* 1. [P-], of Protestants or Protestantism. 2. protesting. Abbreviated **Prot.**
Protestant Episcopal Church, the Protestant church in the United States that conforms to the practices and principles of the Church of England.
Prot·es·tant·ism (prot′is-tənt-iz′m), *n.* 1. the religion of Protestants. 2. the condition of being a Protestant. 3. Protestants or Protestant churches, collectively.
prot·es·ta·tion (prot′əs-tā′shən), *n.* [ME. *protestacioun;* OFr.; LL. *protestatio*], 1. a protesting; strong declaration or affirmation. 2. a protest; objection.
Pro·teus (prō′tūs, prō′ti-əs), *n.* [ME. *protheus;* L.; Gr. *Prōteus*], 1. in *Greek mythology*, a sea god who attended Poseidon and had the power of changing his own form or appearance at will; hence, 2. a person who changes his appearance or principles with ease.
pro·tha·la·mi·on (prō′thə-lā′mi-on), *n.* [*pl.* PROTHALAMIA (-ə)], [Mod. L.; coined by Spenser (after *epithalamion*) < Gr. *pro-*, before + *thalamos*, bridechamber], a nuptial song.
pro·tha·la·mi·um (prō′thə-lā′mi-əm), *n.* [*pl.* PROTHALAMIA (-ə)], prothalamion.
pro·thal·li·al (prō-thal′i-əl), *adj.* of a prothallium.
pro·thal·line (prō-thal′īn, prō-thal′in), *adj.* having the nature of a prothallium.
pro·thal·li·um (prō-thal′i-əm), *n.* [*pl.* PROTHALLIA (-ə)], [Mod. L. < Gr. *pro-*, before + *thallos*, a shoot], that part of a fern which bears the sex organs.
pro·thal·lus (prō-thal′əs), *n.* the prothallium.
proth·e·sis (proth′ə-sis), *n.* [LL.; Gr. *prothesis*, a placing before or in public < *protithenai*, to set before; *pro-*, before + *tithenai*, to place], 1. in *grammar*, the addition of a letter, syllable, or phoneme to the beginning of a word, as of *be-* in *beloved*, *a-* in *ahead*: also **prosthesis**. 2. in the *Orthodox Eastern Church*, *a*) the preparation and preliminary oblation of the elements of the Eucharist. *b*) the table on which this is done. *c*) the place where this table stands.
pro·thet·ic (prō-thet′ik), *adj.* of prothesis.
pro·thon·o·tar·i·al (prō-thon′ə-târ′i-əl), *adj.* of or belonging to a prothonotary.
pro·thon·o·tar·y (prō-thon′ə-ter′i, prō′thə-nō′tẽr-i), *n.* [*pl.* PROTHONOTARIES (-iz)], [ML. *protonotarius;* LGr. *prōtonotarios* < Gr. *prōtos*, first + L. *notarius;* see NOTARY], 1. a chief notary or clerk. 2. in the *Roman Catholic Church*, one of the seven members of the College of Prothonotaries Apostolic, who record important pontifical events: sometimes held as an honorary title by other ecclesiastics. Also **protonotary.**
pro·tho·rac·ic (prō′thô-ras′ik), *adj.* of or connected with the prothorax.
pro·tho·rax (prō-thôr′aks, prō-thō′raks), *n.* [Mod. L.; *pro-*, before, in front + *thorax*], in *zoology*, that division of an insect's body nearest the head.
pro·throm·bin (prō-throm′bin), *n.* [Mod. L. < Gr. *pro-*, before + *thrombos*, a clot, curd], a factor in the blood plasma that takes part in the blood-clotting process: believed to be a precursor of thrombin.
pro·tist (prō′tist), *n.* [< Gr. *prōtistos*, first < *prōtos*, first], any one-celled plant or animal.
pro·tis·tan (prō-tis′tən), *adj.* of or belonging to the protists. *n.* a protist.
pro·tis·tic (prō-tis′tik), *adj.* of the protists.
pro·ti·um (prō′ti-əm, prō′shi-əm), *n.* [Mod. L. < *proto-* + *-ium*, n. suffix], the most common isotope of hydrogen, H^1, having a mass number of 1.
pro·to- (prō′tō, prō′tə), [Gr. *prōto-* < *prōtos*, first], a combining form meaning: 1. *first in time, original, primitive*, as in *protocol, protoplast*. 2. *first in importance, principal, chief*, as in *protagonist*. 3. (of people, their language, etc.) *primitive, original*, as in *proto-Arabic*. 4. in *chemistry*, *a*) *being that member of a series of compounds having the lowest proportion of* (the specified element or radical). *b*) *being the parent form of* (a specified substance), as in *protoactinium*. Also **prot-**.
pro·to·ac·tin·i·um (prō′tō-ak-tin′i-əm), *n.* protactinium.
pro·to·col (prō′tə-kol′), *n.* [Early Mod. Eng. *prothocoll;* OFr. *prothocole;* ML. *protocollum;* Late Gr. *prōtokollon*, first leaf glued to a manuscript (containing an account of the contents) < Gr. *prōtos*, first + *kolla*, glue], 1. an original draft or record of a document, negotiation, etc. 2. [Fr. *protocole*], in *diplomacy*, *a*) a signed document containing a record of the points on which agreement has been reached by negotiating parties preliminary to a final treaty or compact. *b*) the ceremonial forms and courtesies that are established as proper and correct in official intercourse between heads of states and their ministers. *v.i.* to draw up a protocol.
Protocols of the Elders of Zion, a set of forged writings created by Russian reactionaries in 1903 and circulated by anti-Semitic propagandists, purporting to be a record of a series of meetings in Basle in 1897 for plotting the overthrow of Christian civilization by Jews and Freemasons.
pro·to·gine (prō′tə-jin, prō′tə-jēn′), *n.* [Fr. < Gr. *prōtos*, first + base of *gignesthai*, to be born], a kind of granite with a foliated structure, found mainly in the Alps.
pro·to·lith·ic (prō′tə-lith′ik), *adj.* [*proto-* + *-lithic*], designating or of the earliest Stone Age; eolithic.
pro·to·mar·tyr (prō′tō-mär′tẽr), *n.* [ML.; see PROTO- & MARTYR], the first martyr (of some cause); especially, Saint Stephen, the first Christian martyr.
pro·to·morph (prō′tə-môrf′), *n.* [*proto-* + *-morph*], in *biology*, a primitive form.
pro·to·mor·phic (prō′tə-môr′fik), *adj.* [*proto-* + *-morphic*], in *biology*, primitive in form or character.
pro·ton (prō′ton), *n.* [Mod. L. < Gr. *prōton*, neut. of *prōtos*, first], the nucleus of an atom of the protium isotope of hydrogen, having a mass number of 1: it is considered to be one of the fundamental particles of the nuclei of all atoms and carries a unit positive charge of electricity: see also **neutron.**
pro·to·ne·ma (prō′tə-nē′mə), *n.* [*pl.* PROTONEMATA (-tə)], [Mod. L. < Gr. *prōto-*, first + *nēma, nēmatos*, a thread], a threadlike growth in mosses, developing small buds that grow into leafy moss plants.
pro·ton·o·tar·y (prō-ton′ə-ter′i, prō′tə-nō′tẽr-i), *n.* [*pl.* PROTONOTARIES (-iz)], a prothonotary.
pro·to·path·ic (prō′tə-path′ik), *adj.* [*proto-* + *-pathic*], in *physiology*, designating or of primary, or primitive, sensibility, which can perceive and localize only strong, gross stimuli, as pain.
pro·to·plasm (prō′tə-plaz′m), *n.* [G. *protoplasma* < Gr. *prōtos*, first + *plasma*, anything formed or molded < *plassein*, to mold], 1. a semifluid, viscous, translucent colloid, the essential matter of all animal and plant cells: it consists largely of water, proteins, lipoids, carbohydrates, and inorganic salts. 2. formerly, cytoplasm.
pro·to·plas·mic (prō′tə-plaz′mik), *adj.* of protoplasm.
pro·to·plast (prō′tə-plast′), *n.* [Fr. *protoplaste;* LL. *protoplastus;* Gr. *prōtoplastos*, formed first < *prōtos*, first + *plastos*, formed < *plassein*, to form], 1. a thing or being that is the first of its kind. 2. in *biology*, a unit of protoplasm, such as makes up a single cell; plastid.
pro·to·plas·tic (prō′tə-plas′tik), *adj.* of a protoplast.
pro·to·ste·le (prō′tə-stē′li, prō′tə-stēl′), *n.* [*proto-* + *stele*], a simple central cylinder in the stems and roots of plants, through which food and liquids pass.

pro·to·ste·lic (prō'tə-stē'lik), *adj.* of or characterized by a protostele.

pro·to·troph·ic (prō'tə-trof'ik), *adj.* [*proto-* + *trophic*], nourished by uncombined elements, as the nitrogen-fixing bacteria.

pro·to·typ·al (prō'tə-tīp''l), *adj.* 1. having the nature of a prototype. 2. of a prototype.

pro·to·type (prō'tə-tīp'), *n.* [Fr.; Mod. L. *prototypon;* Gr. *prōtotypon* < *prōtotypos*, original; *prōtos*, first + *typos*, a type, form, model], the first thing or being of its kind; original; model; pattern; archetype.

pro·to·typ·ic (prō'tə-tip'ik), *adj.* prototypal.

pro·tox·ide (prō-tok'sīd, prō-tok'sid), *n.* that one of any series of oxides that contains the lowest proportion of oxygen.

Pro·to·zo·a (prō'tə-zō'ə), *n.pl.* [Mod. L., pl. of *protozoon* < Gr. *prōtos*, first + *zōion*, an animal], the phylum of protozoans.

pro·to·zo·an (prō'tə-zō'ən), *n.* [< *Protozoa* + *-an*], any of a number of one-celled animals, usually microscopic, belonging to the lowest division of the animal kingdom. *adj.* of or belonging to the one-celled animals.

pro·to·zo·ic (prō'tə-zō'ik), *adj.* 1. in *geology*, designating strata containing the earliest traces of organic life. 2. in *zoology*, protozoan.

pro·to·zo·ol·o·gy (prō'tə-zō-ol'ə-ji), *n.* that branch of zoology devoted to the study of the protozoans.

pro·to·zo·on (prō'tə-zō'on), *n.* [*pl.* PROTOZOA (-ə)], [Mod. L.], a protozoan.

pro·tract (prō-trakt'), *v.t.* [< L. *protractus*, pp. of *protrahere; pro-*, forward + *trahere*, to draw], 1. to draw out; lengthen in duration; prolong. 2. to draw to scale, using a protractor and scale. 3. in *zoology*, to extend; thrust out: opposed to *retract*. —*SYN.* see **extend.**

pro·trac·tile (prō-trak't'l, prō-trak'til), *adj.* that can be protracted or thrust out; extensible.

pro·trac·tion (prō-trak'shən), *n.* 1. a protracting; extension. 2. a drawing to scale of any figure, plan, etc.

pro·trac·tive (prō-trak'tiv), *adj.* protracting or tending to protract.

pro·trac·tor (prō-trak'tẽr), *n.* [ML.], 1. a person who protracts. 2. an instrument in the form of a graduated semicircle, used for drawing and measuring angles. 3. in *anatomy*, a muscle that protracts, or extends, a limb.

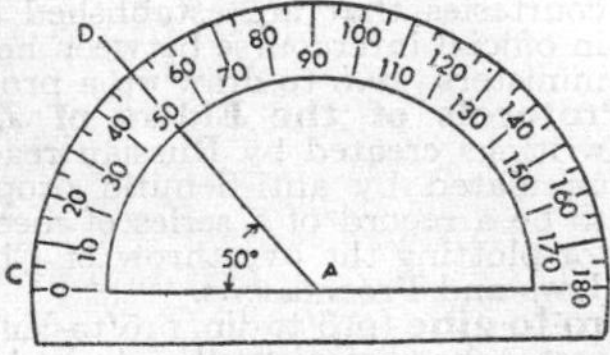

PROTRACTOR
DAC, angle measured

pro·trude (prō-trōōd'), *v.t.* & *v.i.* [PROTRUDED (-id), PROTRUDING], L. *protrudere; pro-*, forth + *trudere* to thrust], to thrust or jut out; project.

pro·trud·ent (prō-trōō'd'nt), *adj.* protruding.

pro·tru·si·ble (prō-trōō'sə-b'l), *adj.* protrusile.

pro·tru·sile (prō-trōō's'l, prō-trōō'sil), *adj.* [< L. *protrusus*, pp. of *protrudere* (see PROTRUDE); + *-ile*], that can be protruded, or thrust out, as a tentacle, an elephant's trunk, etc.

pro·tru·sion (prō-trōō'zhən), *n.* [Fr. < L. *protrusus*, pp. of *protrudere*], 1. a protruding or being protruded. 2. a protruding part or thing. —*SYN.* see **projection.**

pro·tru·sive (prō-trōō'siv), *adj.* [< L. *protrusus*, pp. of *protrudere* (see PROTRUDE); + *-ive*], 1. protruding; jutting or bulging out. 2. obtrusive.

pro·tu·ber·ance (prō-tōō'bẽr-əns, prō-tū'bẽr-əns), *n.* 1. the condition or fact of being protuberant. 2. a part or thing that protrudes; projection; bulge; swelling. —*SYN.* see **projection.**

pro·tu·ber·an·cy (prō-tōō'bẽr-ən-si, prō-tū'bẽr-ən-si), *n.* [*pl.* PROTUBERANCIES (-siz)], protuberance.

pro·tu·ber·ant (prō-tōō'bẽr-ənt, prō-tū'bẽr-ənt), *adj.* [LL. *protuberans*, ppr. of *protuberare*, to bulge out < L. *pro-*, forth + *tuber*, a bump, bulge], bulging or swelling out; protruding; prominent.

pro·tu·ber·ate (prō-tōō'bə-rāt', prō-tū'bə-rāt'), *v.i.* [PROTUBERATED (-id), PROTUBERATING], [< LL. *protuberatus*, pp. of *protuberare;* see PROTUBERANT], to bulge or swell out.

pro·tyle (prō'tīl, prō'til), *n.* [< *prot-* + Gr. *hylē*, substance, stuff], the hypothetical primordial substance from which all elements are supposed to be derived.

proud (proud), *adj.* [ME.; AS. *prud, prut;* prob. < OFr. *prud* (cf. Fr. *preux*) < LL. **prodis*, supposedly a back-formation < *prod-esse*, to be of value; cf. PRIDE], 1. having or showing a proper pride in oneself, one's position, etc. 2. having or showing an overweening opinion of oneself, one's position, etc.; arrogant; haughty. 3. feeling or showing great pride or joy. 4. that is an occasion or cause of pride; highly gratifying. 5. arising from or caused by pride; presumptuous. 6. stately; splendid: as, a *proud* fleet. 7. spirited; of high mettle: as, a *proud* stallion. 8. [Obs.], valiant.

do oneself proud, [Colloq.], to do extremely well.

proud of, highly pleased with or exulting in.

SYN.—**proud** is the broadest term in this comparison, ranging in implication from proper self-esteem or pride to an overweening opinion of one's importance (too *proud* to beg, *proud* as a peacock); **arrogant** implies an aggressive, unwarranted assertion of superior importance or privileges (the *arrogant* colonel); **haughty** implies such consciousness of high station, rank, etc. as is displayed in scorn of those one considers beneath one (a *haughty* dowager); **insolent**, in this connection, implies both haughtiness and great contempt, especially as manifested in behavior or speech that insults or affronts others (she has an *insolent* disregard for her servant's feelings); **overbearing** implies extreme, domineering insolence (an *overbearing* supervisor); **supercilious** stresses an aloof, scornful manner towards others (a *supercilious* intellectual snob); **disdainful** implies even stronger and more overt feelings of scorn for that which is regarded as beneath one.—*ANT.* humble.

proud flesh, [so called from the notion of swelling up], an abnormal growth of flesh around a healing wound, caused by excessive granulation.

Prou·dhon, Pierre Jo·seph (pyâr' zhō'zef' prōō'dōn'), 1809–1865; French socialist and author.

Proust, Mar·cel (mȧr'sel' prōōst'), 1871–1922; French novelist.

Prov., 1. Provençal. 2. Proverbs. 3. Province.

prov., 1. provincial. 2. provisional. 3. provost.

prov·a·ble (prōōv'ə-b'l), *adj.* that can be proved.

prov·a·bly (prōōv'ə-bli), *adv.* in a provable manner.

prove (prōōv), *v.t.* [PROVED (prōōvd), PROVED or PROVEN (prōōv''n), PROVING], [ME. *proven;* Late AS. *profian;* OFr. *prover;* L. *probare;* see PROBE], 1. to test by experiment, standard, etc.; subject to a testing process; try out. 2. to establish (something) as true; demonstrate to be a fact. 3. to establish the validity or authenticity of (a will, etc.); demonstrate to be as is claimed. 4. [Archaic], to experience; learn or know by experience. 5. in *mathematics*, to test or verify the correctness of (a calculation, etc.). 6. in *printing*, to take a proof of (type, etc.). *v.i.* 1. to be found or shown by experience or trial; turn out to be: as, the operation *proved* fatal. 2. [Archaic], to make trial.

the exception proves the rule, the exception puts the rule to the test.

prov·e·nance (prov'ə-nəns), *n.* [Fr. < *provenir;* L. *provenire*, to come forth; *pro-*, forth + *venire*, to come], origin; derivation.

Pro·ven·çal (prō'vən-säl', prov'ən-säl'; Fr. prô'vän'säl'), *adj.* [Fr.], of Provence, its people, their language, etc. *n.* 1. the vernacular of southern France, a distinct Romance language comprising several dialects. 2. the medieval language of southern France: as cultivated by the troubadours, it was one of the great literary languages of Europe. 3. a native or inhabitant of Provence. Abbreviated **Prov., Pr.**

Pro·vence (prov'ens; Fr. prô'väns'), *n.* a former province of southeastern France, on the Mediterranean.

prov·en·der (prov'ən-dẽr), *n.* [ME. & OFr. *provendre* var. of *provende;* L. *praebenda;* see PREBEND], 1. dry food for livestock, as hay, corn, oats, etc.; fodder. 2. [Colloq.], food: used humorously.

Prov. Eng., Provincial English.

pro·ve·ni·ence (prō-vē'ni-əns, prō-vēn'yəns), *n.* [< L. *proveniens*, ppr. of *provenire*], provenance; origin.

prov·erb (prov'ẽrb), *n.* [ME. & OFr. *proverbe;* L. *proverbium* < *pro-*, before + *verbum*, a word], 1. a short saying in common use that strikingly expresses some obvious truth or familiar experience; adage; maxim. 2. a person or thing that has become commonly recognized as a type of specified characteristics; byword. 3. in the *Bible*, an enigmatical saying in which a profound truth is cloaked; parable; allegory. *v.t.* [ME. *prouerben*], 1. to make a proverb or byword of. 2. to describe in a proverb. —*SYN.* see **saying.**

pro·ver·bi·al (prə-vũr'bi-əl), *adj.* [ME.; LL. *proverbialis*], 1. of, or having the nature of, a proverb. 2. expressed in a proverb. 3. that has become an object of common reference, as in a proverb.

pro·ver·bi·al·ly (prə-vũr'bi-əl-i), *adv.* 1. by means of or as expressed in, a proverb. 2. to the point or degree of becoming a proverb; notoriously.

Prov·erbs (prov'ẽrbz), *n.pl.* [construed as sing.], a book of the Old Testament, containing various maxims ascribed to Solomon and others: abbreviated **Prov.**

pro·vide (prə-vīd'), *v.t.* [PROVIDED (-id), PROVIDING], [ME. *providen;* L. *providere; pro-*, before + *videre*, to see], 1. to get ready beforehand; obtain in advance. 2. to make available; supply; afford. 3. to furnish (*with*). *v.i.* 1. to prepare (*for* or *against*) some probable or possible situation, occurrence, condition, etc. 2. to make a condition; stipulate. 3. to furnish the means of support (usually with *for*).

pro·vid·ed (prə-vīd'id), *conj.* [pp. of *provide*], on the condition or understanding; if (often with *that*).

Prov·i·dence (prov'ə-dəns), *n.* seaport and capital of Rhode Island, on Narragansett Bay: pop., 207,000.

prov·i·dence (prov'ə-dəns), *n.* [ME.; L. *providentia*], foresight < *providere;* see PROVIDE], 1. a looking to, or preparation for, the future; provision; hence, 2. skill or wisdom in management; prudence. 3. the care or benevolent guidance of God or nature. 4. an instance of this. 5. [P-], God.

prov·i·dent (prov'ə-dənt), *adj.* [ME.; L. *providens*, ppr.

1. providing for future needs or events; exercising or characterized by foresight. 2. prudent; economical. —*SYN.* see **thrifty.**

rov·i·den·tial (prov'ə-den'shəl), *adj.* [< L. *providentia*], 1. of providence. 2. decreed by Providence. 3. fortunate; lucky. —*SYN.* see **lucky.**

ro·vid·ing (prə-vīd'iŋ), *conj.* [ppr. of *provide*], on the condition or understanding (that); provided.

rov·ince (prov'ins), *n.* [ME.; OFr.; L. *provincia*, province; prob. < IE. **pro-wo-s*, inclined forward], 1. a territory, outside Italy, governed by ancient Rome. 2. an administrative division of a country. 3. any of the British colonies in North America now administrative divisions of Canada. 4. any of certain British colonies now a part of the United States. 5. *a*) a region; district; territory. *b*) *pl.* the parts of a country removed from the capital and the populated, cultural centers. 6. proper duties or functions; sphere. 7. a department; division; branch of learning. 8. in *ecclesiastical usage*, a division of a country under the jurisdiction of an archbishop or metropolitan. 9. a division of the world according to the plants or animals found there: it is smaller in size than a region. Abbreviated **Prov.**

rov·ince·town (prov'ins-toun'), *n.* a resort town in Massachusetts, at the tip of Cape Cod: pop., 3,000.

ro·vin·cial (prə-vin'shəl), *adj.* [ME. *prouyncial;* L. *provincialis*], 1. of or belonging to the provinces. 2. having the ways, speech, attitudes, etc. of people in a province. 3. countrified; rustic; local. 4. narrow; limited: as, a *provincial* outlook. *n.* 1. a native of a province. 2. *pl.* troops raised in a province. 3. a provincial person. Abbreviated **prov.**

ro·vin·cial·ism (prə-vin'shəl-iz'm), *n.* 1. the condition or fact of being provincial. 2. narrowness of outlook. 3. a provincial custom, characteristic, etc. 4. a word, phrase, or pronunciation peculiar to a province.

ro·vin·ci·al·i·ty (prə-vin'shi-al'ə-ti), *n.* [*pl.* PROVINCIALITIES (-tiz)], provincialism.

rov·ing ground (prōōv'iŋ), a place for testing new equipment, theories, etc.

ro·vi·sion (prə-vizh'ən), *n.* [ME. *provysion;* L. *provisio*, a foreseeing < *provisus*, pp. of *providere;* see PROVIDE], 1. a providing, preparing, or supplying of something. 2. something provided, prepared, or supplied for the future; specifically, *pl.* a stock of food and other supplies assembled for future needs. 3. preparatory arrangements or measures taken in advance for meeting some future needs. 4. a clause, as in a legal document, agreement, etc., stipulating or requiring some specific thing; condition. 5. in *ecclesiastical usage*, appointment to an office; especially, advance appointment by the Pope to a see or benefice that is not yet vacant. *v.t.* to supply with provisions, especially with a stock of food. —*SYN.* see **food.**

o·vi·sion·al (prə-vizh'ən-'l), *adj.* having the nature of a temporary provision; having a conditional or temporary character; arranged or established for the time being, pending permanent arrangement or establishment: abbreviated **prov.** —*SYN.* see **temporary.**

o·vi·sion·ar·y (prə-vizh'ən-er'i), *adj.* provisional.

o·vi·sion·er (prə-vizh'ən-ēr), *n.* a person who supplies provisions.

o·vi·so (prə-vī'zō), *n.* [*pl.* PROVISOS, PROVISOES (-zōz)], L., it being provided, abl. of *provisus*, pp. of *providere;* see PROVIDE], 1. a clause, as in a document or statute, making some condition or stipulation; hence, 2. a condition; stipulation.

o·vi·so·ry (prə-vī'zēr-i), *adj.* [ML. *provisorius* < L. *provisus*, pp. of *providere;* see PROVIDE; cf. Fr. *provisoire*], conditional. 2. provisional.

o·vi·ta·min (prō-vī'tə-min), *n.* any substance in the body believed to be the precursor or source of a vitamin.

ov·o·ca·tion (prov'ə-kā'shən), *n.* [ME. *provocacion;* L. *provocatio*], 1. a provoking. 2. something that provokes; cause of resentment or irritation; incitement.

o·voc·a·tive (prə-vok'ə-tiv), *adj.* [ME. *prouocatyue*, aphrodisiac; LL. *provocativus* < L. *provocare;* see PROVOKE], provoking or tending to provoke, as to action, thought, anger, etc. *n.* something that provokes.

o·voke (prə-vōk'), *v.t.* [PROVOKED (-vōkt'), PROVOKING], [ME. *provokin;* OFr. *provoquer;* L. *provocare*, to call forth; *pro-*, forth + *vocare*, to call], 1. to excite to some action or feeling. 2. to anger; irritate. 3. to stir up (action or feeling). 4. to call forth; evoke.

SYN.—**provoke**, in this connection, implies rather generally an arousing to some action or feeling (thought-*provoking*); **excite** suggests a more powerful or profound stirring or moving of the thoughts or emotions (it *excites* my imagination); **stimulate** implies an arousing as if by goading or pricking and, hence, often connotes a bringing out of a state of inactivity or indifference (to *stimulate* one's enthusiasm); **pique** suggests a stimulating as if by irritating (to *pique* one's curiosity). See also **irritate.**

o·vok·ing (prə-vōk'iŋ), *adj.* [ppr. of *provoke*], that provokes; especially, annoying; vexing.

prov·ost (prov'əst; *esp. in military usage*, prō'vō), *n.* [ME. < AS. & OFr.; AS. *profost, prafost;* OFr. (& Anglo-Fr.) *provost;* LL. *propositus*, for L. *praepositus*, chief, director, prefect, orig. pp. of *praeponere*, to set before, place first; *prae-*, before + *ponere*, to put, place], 1. a superintendent; official in charge. 2. the chief magistrate in a Scottish burgh. 3. [Obs.], a jailer. 4. in *ecclesiastical usage*, the head of a cathedral chapter or principal church. 5. in *education*, *a*) the head of any of certain colleges in England and Ireland. *b*) in certain American universities, an administrator concerned with educational matters. Abbreviated **prov.**

pro·vost court (prō'vō), a military court for trying soldiers or civilians charged with minor offenses in occupied territory.

pro·vost guard (prō'vō), a detail of military police headed by a provost marshal.

pro·vost marshal (prō'vō), 1. in the *army*, an officer in charge of military police. 2. in the *navy*, an officer charged with the custody of prisoners on trial by court-martial. Abbreviated **P.M.**

pro·vost sergeant (prō'vō), a sergeant who heads a detachment of military police.

prov·ost·ship (prov'əst-ship'), *n.* [see -SHIP], the office, rank, or authority of a provost.

Prov. Scot., Provincial Scotch.

prow (prou), *n.* [Fr. *proue;* Pr. *proa;* L. *prora;* Gr. *prōira*, a prow], 1. the forward part of a ship. 2. a part resembling this, as the front end of an airship.

prow (prou), *adj.* [ME.; OFr. *prou, prouz, preu*, brave (also, as *n.*, benefit); LL. *prode*, brave; back-formation < L. *prodesse*, to be of use < *pro-, prod-*, for, on behalf of + *esse*, to be], [Archaic], valiant; brave.

prow·ess (prou'is), *n.* [ME. *prowess, proues;* OFr. *prouesse, proece* < *prou*, brave; see PROW, *adj.*], 1. bravery; valor; gallantry. 2. a valorous act. 3. superior ability, skill, ingenuity, or technique.

prowl (proul), *v.i.* & *v.t.* [ME. *prollen, prolen;* the mod. vowel is based on an Early Mod. Eng. var. sp.; ? < OFr. **parrouler*, intens. of *rouler*, to roll; see ROLL], to roam about furtively in search of prey. *n.* a prowling. —*SYN.* see **lurk.**

on the prowl, prowling about.

prowl car, a squad car.

prox·i·mal (prok'sə-m'l), *adj.* 1. proximate; next or nearest. 2. in *anatomy*, situated nearest the center of the body or the point of attachment of a limb, etc.

prox·i·mate (prok'sə-mit), *adj.* [LL. *proximatus*, pp. of *proximare*, to come near < L. *proximus*, nearest, superl. of *prope*, near], 1. next or nearest in space, order, time, etc. 2. approximate.

prox·im·i·ty (prok-sim'ə-ti), *n.* [Fr. *proximité;* L. *proximitas* < *proximus;* see PROXIMATE], the state or quality of being near; nearness in space, time, etc.

prox·i·mo (prok'sə-mō'), *adv.* [L. *proximo (mense)*, in the next (month), abl. of *proximus;* see PROXIMATE], in or of the next month: as, on the 9th *proximo*: abbreviated **prox.**

prox·y (prok'si), *n.* [*pl.* PROXIES (-siz)], [ME. *prokecie*, contr. < *procuracie;* see PROCURACY], 1. the agency or function of a deputy. 2. the authority to act for another. 3. a document empowering a person to act for another, as in voting. 4. a person empowered to act for another. —*SYN.* see **agent.**

prude (prōōd), *n.* [Fr.; prob. a back-formation < *prudefemme*, excellent woman < OFr. *prou* (see PROW, *adj.*) + *de*, of + *feme*, woman], a person who is overly modest or proper in behavior, dress, or speech.

Pru·dence (prōō'd'ns), [LL., fem. of *Prudentius* < L. *prudentia*, prudence, discretion], a feminine name: diminutive, *Prue.*

pru·dence (prōō'd'ns), *n.* [ME.; OFr.; L. *prudentia*], 1. the quality or fact of being prudent. 2. an instance of this. 3. careful management; economy.

pru·dent (prōō'd'nt), *adj.* [ME.; OFr.; L. *prudens*, for *providens;* see PROVIDENT], 1. capable of exercising sound judgment in practical matters. 2. cautious or discreet in conduct; circumspect; sensible; not rash. —*SYN.* see **careful, wise.**

pru·den·tial (prōō-den'shəl), *adj.* 1. characterized by or resulting from prudence. 2. exercising prudence, or sound judgment. 3. discretionary or advisory.

prud·er·y (prōōd'ēr-i), *n.* [Fr. *pruderie*], 1. the quality or condition of being prudish; exaggerated modesty in behavior, etc. 2. [*pl.* PRUDERIES (-iz)], an instance of this.

prud·ish (prōōd'ish), *adj.* like or characteristic of a prude; overly modest or proper.

pru·i·nose (prōō'i-nōs'), *adj.* [L. *pruinosus*, frosty < *pruina*, hoarfrost, for earlier **pruswina;* IE. base **preus-*, to freeze; cf. AS. *freosan*, to freeze], in *botany*, covered with a white, powdery substance or bloom.

prune (prōōn), *n.* [ME.; OFr.; ML. *pruna* < L. *prunum;* Gr. *prounon*, plum], 1. a dried plum. 2. any kind of plum that can be easily dried without spoiling. 3.

[Slang], a person regarded as stupid, silly, or unpleasant.

prune (prōōn), *v.t.* [PRUNED (prōōnd), PRUNING], [ME. *proinen, prunen*, to trim; OFr. *proignier, prooignier;* prob. < *provaignier*, to cut < *provain* (< L. *propago*), a slip; influenced by *rooignier*, to cut off; LL. **rotundiare* < L. *rotundus*, round], 1. to remove dead or living parts from (a plant) so as to increase fruit or flower production or improve the form. 2. to cut out or get rid of, as unnecessary parts. *v.i.* to cut away or remove unnecessary branches or parts.

prune (prōōn), *v.t. & v.i.* [PRUNED (prōōnd), PRUNING], [ME. *proinen;* OFr. *poroindre; por-* (for *pro-*) + *oindre* (< L. *ungere*), to anoint], [Archaic], to preen or dress up.

pru·nel·la (prōō-nel′ə), *n.* [Fr., lit., sloe-colored, dim. < *prune* (see PRUNE, *n.*); prob. so named because of orig. color of the material], a strong textile, usually a worsted twill, used for clerical, academic, and legal gowns, shoe uppers, etc.

pru·nelle (prōō-nel′), *n.* [Fr., dim. of *prune;* see PRUNE, *n.*], a small, yellow prune with the skin removed.

pruning hook, a pair of shears with one hooked blade, used for pruning branches, vines, etc.

pru·ri·ence (proor′i-əns), *n.* the condition or fact of being prurient.

pru·ri·en·cy (proor′i-ən-si), *n.* prurience.

pru·ri·ent (proor′i-ənt), *adj.* [L. *pruriens* < *prurire*, to itch or long for a thing, be lecherous], 1. having lustful ideas or desires. 2. lustful; lascivious; lewd: as, *prurient* longings. 3. [Rare], itching.

pru·rig·i·nous (proo-rij′ə-nəs), *adj.* [Fr. *prurigineux;* LL. *pruriginosus* < L. *prurigo* < *prurire*, to itch], of, having the nature of, causing, or having prurigo.

pru·ri·go (proo-rī′gō), *n.* [L.; see PRURIGINOUS], a chronic, inflammatory skin disease characterized by pale-red papules and intense itching.

pru·rit·ic (proo-rit′ik), *adj.* of or having pruritus.

pru·ri·tus (proo-rī′təs), *n.* [< L. *prurire*, to itch], intense itching of the skin without eruption.

Prus., 1. Prussia. 2. Prussian.

Prus·sia (prush′ə), *n.* a former state of Germany, in the northern part: previously a kingdom: German name, *Preussen.*

Prus·sian (prush′ən), *adj.* 1. of Prussia, its people, their language, etc. 2. like or characteristic of the Junkers and military caste of Prussia, regarded as harsh in discipline, militaristic, arrogant, etc. *n.* 1. originally, a member of a Lettic people formerly living in the coastal regions of the southeastern Baltic. 2. a native or inhabitant of Prussia. 3. any of the German dialects of East or West Prussia. 4. Old Prussian.

Prussian blue, [so called from being discovered in Berlin, by Diesbach, in 1704], any of a group of dark-blue powders, ferrocyanides of iron, used as dyes or pigments; especially, ferric ferrocyanide, $Fe_4[Fe(CN)_6]_3$.

Prus·sian·ism (prush′ən-iz′m), *n.* the principles, practices, and doctrines of the Prussians; specifically, the despotic militarism and harsh discipline of the Prussian ruling classes.

prus·si·ate (prus′i-āt′, prush′i-āt′), *n.* [Fr.], 1. a salt of prussic acid; cyanide. 2. a ferrocyanide or ferricyanide.

prus·sic acid (prus′ik), [Fr. *prussique* < Mod. L. *prussia*, Prussian blue: so named from its chemical relationship to Prussian blue], a colorless, volatile, highly poisonous gaseous acid, HCN, soluble in water and having the odor of bitter almonds: it is used in mining and metallurgy, as an insecticide, etc.: also called *hydrocyanic acid.*

Prut, Pruth (prōōt), *n.* a river in south central Europe, joining the Danube near the Black Sea: length, 500 mi.

pry (prī), *n.* [*pl.* PRIES (prīz)], [back-formation < *prize* (a lever)], 1. a lever, crowbar, etc.; tool for raising or moving something by leverage. 2. leverage. *v.t.* [PRIED (prīd), PRYING], 1. to raise, move, or force with a lever, crowbar, etc. 2. to draw forth with difficulty.

pry (prī), *v.i.* [PRIED (prīd), PRYING], [ME. *prien*, to peer; the semantic development suggests metathetic connection with *peer*], to look closely or inquisitively; peer. *n.* [*pl.* PRIES (prīz)], 1. a prying. 2. a person who is improperly curious or inquisitive.

pry·er (prī′ẽr), *n.* a prier.

pry·ing (prī′iŋ), *adj.* [ppr. of *pry* (to peer)], improperly curious; inquisitive; peering. —*SYN.* see **curious.**

pryth·ee (prith′i), *interj.* prithee.

Prze·myśl (pshe′mish-′l), *n.* a city in southern Poland: pop., 37,000 (est. 1946).

ps., 1. pieces. 2. pseudonym.

P.S., 1. passenger steamer. 2. permanent secretary. 3. Privy Seal. 4. Public School.

PS., P.S., p.s., [*pl.* P.SS.], postscript.

Ps., Psa., Psalm; Psalms.

psalm (säm), *n.* [ME. *psalme, salm, saume* < AS. & OFr.; AS. *sealm, psalm;* OFr. *salme, psaume;* both < LL. *psalmus;* Gr. *psalmos*, song sung to the harp, lit. a pulling or twanging with the fingers < *psallein*, to twitch], 1. a sacred song or poem; hymn. 2. any of the sacred songs or hymns composing the Book of Psalms in the Old Testament. *v.t.* to sing or glorify in psalms; hymn.

psalm·book (säm′book′), *n.* a collection of psalms for use in religious worship.

psalm·ist (säm′ist), *n.* a composer of psalms.
the Psalmist, King David, to whom all or certain of the Psalms are variously attributed.

psal·mo·dic (säm′ə-dik, sal′mə-dik), *adj.* of psalmody

psal·mo·dist (säm′ə-dist, sal′mə-dist), *n.* a person skilled in psalmody; singer of psalms.

psal·mo·dy (säm′ə-di, sal′mə-di), *n.* [ME. *psalmodye*, LL. *psalmodia;* Gr. *psalmōdia* < *psalmos* (see PSALM) + *ōdē*, a song], 1. the act, practice, or art of singing psalms. 2. psalms collectively. 3. the arrangement of psalms for singing.

Psalms (sämz), *n.pl.* [construed as sing.], a book of the Old Testament, consisting of 150 psalms; Book of Psalms: abbreviated **Ps., Psa.**

Psal·ter (sôl′tẽr), *n.* [AS. *psaltere, saltere* < L. *psalterium* Gr. *psaltērion*, stringed instrument < *psallein*, to pull twitch; replacing ME. *psauter, sauter* < Anglo-Fr *sauter* (OFr. *psaltier*) < L.], 1. the Book of Psalms 2. [also p-], a version of the Psalms for use in religious services.

psal·te·ri·um (sôl-têr′i-əm), *n.* [*pl.* PSALTERIA (-ə)], [L. see PSALTER: so called from the appearance of the many folds it contains], the omasum, or third stomach of cud-chewing animals; manyplies.

psal·ter·y (sôl′tẽr-i, sôl′tri), *n.* [*pl.* PSALTERIES (-iz -triz)], [ME. *psauterie;* OFr. *sautere, psalterie;* L. *psalterium;* see PSALTER], 1. an ancient stringed instrument with a shallow sound box, played by plucking the strings with the fingers or a plectrum. 2. [P-], the Psalter.

PSALTERY

psam·mite (sam′īt), *n.* [Fr. < Gr. *psammos*, sand], sandstone.

psam·mit·ic (sa-mit′ik), *adj.* [< *psammite* + *-ic*], of or consisting of sandstone.

pse·phite (sē′fīt), *n.* [< Gr. *psēphos*, a pebble; + *-ite*], conglomerate or fragmental rock.

pseud-, pseudo-.

pseud., pseudonym.

pseu·dax·is (sōō-dak′sis), *n.* [*pseud-* + *axis*], in *botany*, a sympodium.

pseu·de·pig·ra·pha (sōō′də-pig′rə-fə, sū′də-pig′rə-fə) *n.pl.* [Mod. L.; Gr. *pseudepigrapha*, neut. pl. of *pseudepigraphos*, having a false title < *pseudēs*, false + *epigraphein*, to inscribe; *epi*, upon + *graphein*, to write], writings falsely ascribed to Biblical characters

pseu·de·pig·ra·phous (sōō′də-pig′rə-fəs, sū′də-pig′rə-fəs), *adj.* [Gr. *pseudepigraphos*], of, or having the nature of, pseudepigrapha; spurious.

pseu·do (sōō′dō, sū′dō), *adj.* [ME.; see PSEUDO-], sham false; spurious; pretended; counterfeit.

pseu·do- (sōō′də, sū′dō), [Gr. *pseudo-* < *pseudēs*, false < *pseudein*, to deceive], a combining form meaning: *fictitious, pretended, sham*, as in *pseudonym*. 2. *counterfeit, spurious*, as in *pseudepigrapha*. 3. *closely* or *deceptively similar to* (a specified thing), as in *pseudomorph* 4. *not corresponding to the reality, illusory*. 5. in *chemistry, an isomer* or *related form of* (the specified compound). Also, before a vowel, **pseud-.**

pseu·do·a·quat·ic (sōō′dō-ə-kwat′ik, sū′dō-ə-kwät′ik *adj.* having a moist or wet habitat, but not truly aquatic

pseu·do·carp (sōō′də-kärp′, sū′də-kärp′), *n.* [< *pseud-* + Gr. *karpos*, a fruit], a fruit made up of more than the ripened seedcase and its contents, as the strawberry.

pseu·do·car·pous (sōō′də-kär′pəs, sū′də-kär′pəs), *adj.* of or like a pseudocarp.

pseu·do·clas·sic (sōō′dō-klas′ik, sū′dō-klas′ik), *adj.* pretending, or falsely seeming, to be classic.

pseu·do·morph (sōō′də-môrf′, sū′də-môrf′), *n.* [< Gr. *pseudomorphos*, having a false form < *pseudēs*, false *morphē*, a form], 1. a false or irregular form. 2. mineral possessing the external form characteristic of another.

pseu·do·mor·phic (sōō′də-môr′fik, sū′də-môr′fik), *adj.* pseudomorphous.

pseu·do·mor·phism (sōō′də-môr′fiz′m, sū′də-môr′fiz′m), *n.* 1. the condition or quality of being pseudomorphous. 2. the formation or occurrence of pseudomorphs.

pseu·do·mor·phous (sōō′də-môr′fəs, sū′də-môr′fəs), *adj.* possessing the qualities of a pseudomorph.

pseu·do·nym (sōō′də-nim′, sū′də-nim′), *n.* [Fr. *pseudonyme* < Gr. *pseudōnymos;* see PSEUDONYMOUS], fictitious name, as assumed by an author; pen name abbreviated **pseud., ps.**

SYN.—a **pseudonym** is a fictitious name assumed, especially by a writer, as for anonymity, for effect, etc.; **pen name** and **nom de plume** are applied specifically to the pseudonym of a writer; **alias** also refers to an assumed name and, in popular use is specifically applied to one taken by a criminal to disguise identity; **incognito** is usually applied to a fictitious name temporarily assumed by a famous person, as in traveling, to avoid being recognized.

pseu·do·nym·i·ty (sōō′də-nim′ə-ti, sū′də-nim′ə-ti),

1. the practice or fact of using a pseudonym. 2. pseudonymous character.

seu·don·y·mous (sōō-don′ə-məs, sū-don′ə-məs), ***adj.*** [Mod. L. *pseudonymus;* Gr. *pseudōnymos,* having a false name < *pseudēs,* false + *onyma,* a name], 1. bearing a pseudonym. 2. written under a pseudonym.

seu·do·pod (sōō′də-pod′, sū′də-pod′), ***n.*** a pseudopodium.

seu·do·po·di·um (sōō′də-pō′di-əm, sū′də-pō′di-əm), ***n.*** [*pl.* PSEUDOPODIA (-ə)], [Mod. L.; *pseudo-* + *-podium* < Gr. *pōdion,* dim. of *pous,* a foot], in *zoology,* a temporary projection of the protoplasm of certain one-celled organisms, serving as a means of moving about or for taking in food: see **amoeba,** illus.

shaw (shô), ***interj. & n.*** an exclamation of impatience, disgust, contempt, etc. ***v.i. & v.t.*** to express impatience, contempt, etc. at, for, or to (someone or something) by saying "pshaw."

si (sī; Gr. psē), ***n.*** [Gr.], the twenty-third letter of the Greek alphabet (Ψ, ψ), corresponding to English *ps,* as in *lips* (usually pronounced in English derivatives simply as *s,* as in *psychology*): see **alphabet,** table.

si·lan·thro·pism (sī-lan′thrə-piz′m), ***n.*** psilanthropy.

si·lan·thro·pist (sī-lan′thrə-pist), ***n.*** [< Gr. *psilanthropos,* merely human < *psilos,* bare, mere + *anthrōpos,* a man], a believer in psilanthropy.

si·lan·thro·py (sī-lan′thrə-pi), ***n.*** [see PSILANTHROPIST], the doctrine that Jesus was merely a human being.

si·lom·e·lane (sī-lom′ə-lān′), ***n.*** [< Gr. *psilos,* bare, mere + *melan,* neut. of *melas,* black], a mineral, essentially manganese oxide, occurring in rounded, grapelike, black masses.

si·lo·ri·ti, Mount (psē′lô-rē′tē), a mountain on Crete: height, 8,960 ft.: ancient name, *Mount Ida.*

si·lo·sis (sī-lō′sis), ***n.*** [Mod. L.; Gr. *psilōsis* < *psiloun,* to strip bare < *psilos,* bare, mere], 1. a falling out of hair. 2. sprue.

sit·ta·co·sis (sit′ə-kō′sis), ***n.*** [Mod. L. < Gr. *psittakos,* a parrot; + *-osis*], an acute infectious virus disease affecting birds of the parrot family, often transmitted to man, in whom it is characterized by high fever and pulmonary disorders resembling pneumonia: also called *parrot fever.*

skov (pskôf), ***n.*** 1. a city in the western part of the U.S.S.R.: pop., 60,000. 2. a lake near this city, connecting with Lake Peipus.

so·as (sō′əs), ***n.*** [Mod. L.; acc. pl. of Gr. *psoa,* muscle of the loins], either of two muscles of the loin that connect the spinal column and the thighbone.

so·ra (sō′rə), ***n.*** [L.; Gr. *psōra,* an itch], any itching disease of the skin, especially psoriasis or scabies.

so·ra·le·a (sə-rā′li-ə), ***n.*** [Mod. L. < Gr. *psōraleos,* scaly], any of a number of related plants with pink, purple, or white flower clusters and short pods with single seeds.

so·ri·a·sis (sō-rī′ə-sis, sə-rī′ə-sis), ***n.*** [Mod. L.; Gr. *psōriasis* < *psōra,* an itch], a chronic skin disease characterized by scaly, reddish patches.

so·ri·at·ic (sôr′i-at′ik, sō′ri-at′ik), ***adj.*** of or having psoriasis.

so·ro·sis (sə-rō′sis), ***n.*** [Mod. L. < Gr. *psōra,* an itch; + *-osis*], a plant disease affecting citrus fruit trees: also called *scaly bark.*

SS., postscripts.

S.T., Pacific Standard Time.

sych., 1. psychological. 2. psychology.

y·chas·the·ni·a (sī′kas-thē′ni ə, sī′kas-thi-nī′ə), ***n.*** [Mod. L.; see PSYCHO- & ASTHENIA], a type of neurosis characterized by obsessions, morbid anxieties, etc.

sy·che (sī′ki), ***n.*** [L.; Gr. *Psychē* < *psychē,* the soul], in *Greek & Roman mythology,* a maiden who, after undergoing many hardships due to Venus' jealousy of her beauty, is reunited with Cupid and made immortal by Jupiter: she personifies the soul.

y·che (sī′ki), ***n.*** [Gr. *psychē*], 1. the human soul. 2. the mind; especially, in psychiatry, the mind considered as an organic system reaching all parts of the body and serving to adjust the total organism to the needs or demands of the environment.

yche knot, a woman's coiffure in which a knot or coil of hair projects from the back of the head.

y·chi·a·ter (sī-kī′ə-tẽr), ***n.*** a psychiatrist.

y·chi·at·ric (sī′ki-at′rik), ***adj.*** 1. of psychiatry: as, *psychiatric* clinic. 2. employing psychiatry: as, *psychiatric* treatment.

y·chi·at·ri·cal (sī′ki-at′ri-k′l), ***adj.*** psychiatric.

y·chi·a·trist (sī-kī′ə-trist), ***n.*** a specialist in psychiatry.

y·chi·a·try (sī-kī′ə-tri), ***n.*** [Mod. L. *psychiatria* < Gr. *psychē,* the soul + *iatreia,* healing], the branch of medicine concerned with the study and treatment of disorders of the mind, including psychoses and neuroses.

y·chic (sī′kik), ***adj.*** [< Gr. *psychikos,* of the soul, spiritual < *psychē,* the soul, spirit], 1. of the psyche, or mind. 2. beyond natural or known physical processes. 3. apparently sensitive to forces beyond the physical world. ***n.*** 1. a person who is supposedly sensitive to forces beyond the physical world. 2. a spiritualistic medium.

psy·chi·cal (sī′ki-k′l), ***adj.*** psychic.

psychic trauma, an emotional hurt or shock which makes a permanent impression on the mind, particularly in the unconscious.

psy·cho (sī′kō), ***adj. & n.*** [Colloq.], psychoneurotic.

psy·cho- (sī′kō, sī′kə), [< Gr. *psychē,* breath, spirit, soul], a combining form meaning *the mind* or *mental processes,* as in *psychology, psychoanalysis, psychosis:* also **psych-,** as in *psychiatry.*

psy·cho·a·nal·y·sis (sī′kō-ə-nal′ə-sis), ***n.*** [Mod. L.; *psycho-* + *analysis*], 1. a method, developed by Freud and others, of treating neuroses and some other disorders of the mind: it is based on the assumption that such disorders are the result of the rejection by the conscious mind of factors that then persist in the unconscious as dynamic repressions, causing conflicts which may be resolved by discovering and analyzing the repressions through the use of such techniques as free association, dream analysis, etc. 2. the theory or practice of this. Often shortened to **analysis.**

psy·cho·an·a·lyst (sī′kō-an′əl-ist), ***n.*** a specialist in psychoanalysis: often shortened to **analyst.**

psy·cho·an·a·lyt·ic (sī′kō-an′ə-lit′ik), ***adj.*** of or connected with psychoanalysis.

psy·cho·an·a·lyt·i·cal (sī′kō-an′ə-lit′i-k′l), ***adj.*** psychoanalytic.

psy·cho·an·a·lyt·i·cal·ly (sī′kō-an′ə-lit′i-k′l-i, sī′kō-an′ə-lit′ik-li), ***adv.*** 1. in a psychoanalytic manner. 2. from a psychoanalytic standpoint.

psy·cho·an·a·lyze (sī′kō-an′ə-līz′), ***v.t.*** [PSYCHOANALYZED (-līzd′), PSYCHOANALYZING], to treat or investigate by means of psychoanalysis.

psy·cho·bi·ol·o·gy (sī′kō-bi-ol′ə-ji), ***n.*** [*psycho-* + *biology*], 1. that branch of biology dealing with the interrelationship of the mental processes and the anatomy and physiology of the individual. 2. psychology as investigated by biological methods.

psy·cho·dra·ma (sī′kə-drä′mə, sī′kə-dram′ə), ***n.*** in *psychiatry,* a form of cathartic therapy in which a patient acts out by spontaneous improvisation situations related to his problem, often with the aid of others who represent persons near his problem.

psy·cho·gen·e·sis (sī′kə-jen′ə-sis), ***n.*** [Mod. L.; see PSYCHO- & -GENESIS], 1. origination and development within the psyche, or mind. 2. the origin and development of the psyche, or mind.

psy·cho·ge·net·ic (sī′kə-jə-net′ik), ***adj.*** psychogenic.

psy·cho·gen·ic (sī′kə-jen′ik), ***adj.*** [< *psychogenesis*], of psychic origin; caused by mental conflicts.

psy·chog·no·sis (sī-kog′nə-sis, sī′kog-nō′sis), ***n.*** [*psycho-* + *-gnosis*], [Rare], any investigation or diagnosis of the psyche.

psy·cho·graph (sī′kə-graf′, sī′kə-gräf′), ***n.*** [*psycho-* + *-graph*], in *psychology,* a graphic chart outlining the relative strength of the fundamental personality traits in an individual.

psy·cho·log·ic (sī′kə-loj′ik), ***adj.*** psychological.

psy·cho·log·i·cal (sī′kə-loj′i-k′l), ***adj.*** 1. of psychology. 2. of the mind; mental. Abbreviated **psych., psychol.**

psy·cho·log·i·cal·ly (sī′kə-loj′i-k′l-i, sī′kə-loj′ik-li), ***adv.*** 1. in a psychological manner. 2. from a psychological standpoint.

psychological moment, 1. the moment when the mind is most willing to accept a fact, suggestion, etc.; most propitious time to act. 2. the critical moment.

psy·chol·o·gist (sī-kol′ə-jist), ***n.*** a student of or specialist in psychology: abbreviated **psych., psychol.**

psy·chol·o·gize (sī-kol′ə-jīz′), ***v.i.*** [PSYCHOLOGIZED (-jīzd′), PSYCHOLOGIZING], 1. to study psychology. 2. to reason psychologically. ***v.t.*** to analyze psychologically.

psy·chol·o·gy (sī-kol′ə-ji), ***n.*** [*pl.* PSYCHOLOGIES (-jiz)], [Mod. L. *psychologia;* see PSYCHO- & -LOGY], 1. *a*) the science dealing with the mind and mental processes, feelings, desires, etc. *b*) the science of human and animal behavior. 2. the sum of a person's actions, traits, attitudes, thoughts, etc.: as, the *psychology* of the adolescent. 3. a treatise on psychology. 4. a system of psychology. Abbreviated **psych., psychol.**

psy·cho·met·ric (sī′kə-met′rik), ***adj.*** of psychometry.

psy·cho·met·ri·cal (sī′kə-met′ri-k′l), ***adj.*** psychometric.

psy·chom·e·try (sī-kom′ə-tri), ***n.*** [*psycho-* + *-metry*], 1. the supposed faculty of divining knowledge about an object, or about a person connected with it, through contact with the object. 2. the measurement of the duration, force, precision, etc. of mental processes.

psy·cho·mo·tor (sī′kō-mō′tẽr), ***adj.*** of the motor effects of mental processes.

psy·cho·neu·ro·sis (sī′kō-nyoo-rō′sis, sī′kō-noo-rō′sis), ***n.*** [*pl.* PSYCHONEUROSES (-sēz)], [Mod. L.; see PSYCHO- & NEUROSIS], a neurosis.

psy·cho·neu·rot·ic (sī'kō-nyoo-rot'ik, sī'kō-noo-rot'ik), *adj.* & *n.* [see prec.], neurotic.
psy·cho·path (sī'kə-path'), *n.* a person affected with psychopathy; specifically, a psychopathic personality.
psy·cho·path·ic (sī'kə-path'ik), *adj.* of or characterized by psychopathy.
psychopathic personality, 1. a person characterized by emotional instability, lack of sound judgment, perverse and impulsive (often criminal) behavior, inability to learn from experience, amoral and asocial feelings, and other serious personality defects: he may or may not have psychotic attacks or symptoms. 2. the personality of such a person.
psy·chop·a·thist (sī-kop'ə-thist), *n.* [Obs.], a psychiatrist.
psy·cho·pa·thol·o·gy (sī'kō-pə-thol'ə-ji), *n.* [*psycho-* + *pathology*], the science dealing with diseases and abnormalities of the mind: abbreviated **psychopathol.**
psy·chop·a·thy (sī-kop'ə-thi), *n.* [*psycho-* + *-pathy*], 1. mental disorder. 2. loosely, psychotherapy.
psy·cho·phys·i·cal (sī'kō-fiz'i-k'l), *adj.* of psychophysics.
psy·cho·phys·i·cist (sī'kō-fiz'ə-sist), *n.* a student of or specialist in psychophysics.
psy·cho·phys·ics (sī'kō-fiz'iks), *n.pl.* [construed as sing.], [*psycho-* + *physics*], the branch of psychology dealing with the functional relations between the body and the mind.
psy·cho·sis (sī-kō'sis), *n.* [*pl.* PSYCHOSES (-sēz)], [Mod. L.; Gr. *psychōsis*, a giving of life < *psychoun*, to animate, give life to < *psychē*, soul], 1. in *psychiatry*, any mental disorder in which the personality is very seriously disorganized: psychoses are of two sorts, *a*) functional (characterized by lack of apparent organic cause, and principally of a schizophrenic or manic-depressive type), and *b*) organic (characterized by a pathological organic condition, such as general paresis, brain tumor, alcoholism, etc.). 2. in *psychology*, any mental state or process. —*SYN.* see **insanity.**
psy·cho·so·mat·ic (sī'kō-sō-mat'ik), *adj.* [*psycho-* + *somatic*], 1. designating or of a physical disorder of the body originating in or aggravated by the psychic or emotional processes of the individual. 2. designating the branch of medicine using a psychological approach to the study of the causes and treatment of physical disorders.
psy·cho·ther·a·peu·tics (sī'kō-ther'ə-pū'tiks), *n.pl.* [construed as sing.], the science of psychotherapy.
psy·cho·ther·a·py (sī'kō-ther'ə-pi), *n.* [*psycho-* + *therapy*], the application of various forms of mental treatment, as hypnosis, suggestion, psychoanalysis, etc., to nervous and mental disorders.
psy·chot·ic (sī-kot'ik), *adj.* 1. of, or having the nature of, a psychosis. 2. having a psychosis. *n.* a person who has a psychosis.
psy·chro- (sī'krō, sī'krə), [< Gr. *psychros*, cold], a combining form meaning *cold*, as in *psychrometer*.
psy·chrom·e·ter (sī-krom'ə-tēr), *n.* [*psychro-* + *-meter*; orig., a thermometer], an instrument with wet and dry bulb thermometers, for measuring the amount of moisture in the air.
Pt, in *chemistry*, platinum.
Pt., 1. Point. 2. Port.
pt., [*pl.* PTS.], 1. part. 2. payment. 3. pint. 4. point.
P.T., 1. Pacific Time. 2. pupil teacher.
p.t., 1. past tense. 2. pro tempore.
P.T.A., Parent-Teacher Association.
Ptah (p'tä, p'täkh), *n.* [Egypt. *Ptaḥ*], the chief god of ancient Memphis, in Egypt, creator of gods and men.
ptar·mi·gan (tär'mə-gən), *n.* [*pl.* PTARMIGANS (-gənz), PTARMIGAN; see PLURAL, II, D, 1], [earlier *termigan*, *termigant* < Scot. *tarmachan*; wrongly spelled with a *p* because of supposed Gr. origin], any of several varieties of northern grouse, having feathered legs and feet and undergoing seasonal changes of color.
PT boat, patrol torpedo boat.
pter·i·dol·o·gy (ter'ə-dol'ə-ji), *n.* [< Gr. *pteris*, *pteridos*, a fern; + *-logy*], that branch of botany dealing with ferns.
pter·i·do·phyte (ter'ə-dō-fīt'), *n.* [< Gr. *pteris*, *pteridos*, a fern; + *-phyte*], a fern or related plant having no seeds.
pter·i·do·phyt·ic (ter'ə-dō-fit'ik), *adj.* of or belonging to the pteridophytes.
pter·i·doph·y·tous (ter'ə-dof'ə-təs), *adj.* having the nature of a pteridophyte.
pter·o- (ter'ō, ter'ə), [< Gr. *pteron*, feather, wing; IE. base *pet-, to go, fly, seen also in Eng. *feather*], a combining form meaning *feather*, *wing*, as in *pterodactyl*.
pter·o·dac·tyl (ter'ə-dak't'l, ter'ə-dak'til), *n.* [Mod. L. *Pterodactylus*; see PTERO- & DACTYL], any of a number of related flying reptiles, extinct at the end of the Mesozoic Era, having wings of skin stretched along the body between the hind limb and a very long digit of the forelimb.

PTERODACTYL
(18 ft. across wings)

pter·o·pod (ter'ə-pod'), *adj.* [*ptero-* + *-pod*], of a group of small mollusks that swim about by means of winglike lobes on the foot. *n.* any member of this group.
pte·rop·o·dan (ti-rop'ə-dən), *adj.* & *n.* pteropod.
pter·o·saur (ter'ə-sôr'), *n.* [Mod. L. *Pterosaurus* < *ptero-* + Gr. *sauros*, a lizard], a pterodactyl.
-pter·ous (tēr-əs), [see PTERO- & -OUS], a combining form meaning *having* (a specified number or kind of) *wings*, as in *homopterous*.
pter·y·goid (ter'ə-goid'), *adj.* [< Gr. *pteryx*, *pterygos*, a wing, fin; + *-oid*], 1. winglike. 2. designating, of, or near either of two winglike processes in the skull that descend from the sphenoid bone. *n.* a pterygoid bone.
ptis·an (tiz'ən, ti-zan'), *n.* [Fr. *ptisane*, *tisane*; LL. *tisana*, for L. *ptisana*, barley groats, drink made from barley groats < Gr. *ptisanē*, peeled barley < *ptissein*, to peel], 1. a drink made by boiling down barley with water and other ingredients; barley water. 2. any similar decoction, as of herbs.
p.t.o., P.T.O., please turn over (leaf).
Ptol·e·ma·ic (tol'ə-mā'ik), *adj.* [Gr. *Ptolemaïkos*], 1. of Ptolemy, the astronomer. 2. of the Ptolemies of the Greco-Egyptian dynasty (323–30 B.C.).
Ptolemaic system, the theory systematized by Ptolemy, according to whom the earth was the center or fixed point of the universe, around which the heavenly bodies moved.
Ptol·e·ma·ist (tol'ə-mā'ist), *n.* an adherent or supporter of the Ptolemaic system of astronomy.
Ptol·e·my (tol'ə-mi), *n.* (*Claudius Ptolemaeus*), Alexandrian astronomer, mathematician, and geographer; lived 2d century A.D.
Ptolemy I, 367?–285 B.C.; king of Egypt (323–285 B.C.); first of the Greco-Egyptian dynasty; founder of the library at Alexandria: called *Ptolemy Soter* (*Savior*).
Ptolemy II, 309–246 B.C.; son of Ptolemy I; king of Egypt (285–246 B.C.): called *Ptolemy Philadelphus*.
pto·maine, pto·main (tō'mān, tō-mān'), *n.* [It. *ptomaina* < Gr. *ptōma*, a corpse, dead body < *piptein*, to fall], any of a class of alkaloid substances, some of which are poisonous, found in decaying animal or vegetable matter.
ptomaine poisoning, an acute digestive disorder caused by the eating of putrid or rancid food containing certain toxic bacilli (formerly believed to be ptomaines).
pto·sis (tō'sis), *n.* [Mod. L.; Gr. *ptōsis*, a fall, falling < *piptein*, to fall], a prolapse, or falling of some organ or part; especially, the permanent drooping of the upper eyelid, caused by the paralysis of its muscle.
pto·tic (tō'tik), *adj.* of or having ptosis.
pty·a·lin (tī'ə-lin), *n.* [< Gr. *ptyalon*, spittle < *ptyein*, to spit; + *-in*], an enzyme in the saliva of man (and some lower animals) that converts starch into dextrin and maltose.
pty·a·lism (tī'ə-liz'm), *n.* [Gr. *ptyalismos*, a spitting < *ptyalizein*, to spit often < *ptyalon*; see PTYALIN], excessive secretion of saliva.
Pu, in *chemistry*, plutonium.
pub (pub), *n.* [contr. < *public* (*house*)], [British Slang], 1. a bar; tavern. 2. a hotel; inn.
pub., 1. public. 2. publication. 3. published. 4. publisher. 5. publishing.
pu·ber·ty (pū'bēr-ti), *n.* [< Fr. or L.; Fr. *puberté*; L. *pubertas* < *pubes*, *puber*, of ripe age, adult], the state of physical development when it is first possible to beget or bear children: in most places the legal age of puberty is fixed at fourteen for boys and twelve for girls.
pu·bes (pū'bēz), *n.* [L., pubic hair, groin, adult], 1. the hair appearing on the body at puberty; especially, the hair at the lower part of the abdomen surrounding the external genitals. 2. the region of the abdomen covered by such hair.
pu·bes (pū'bēz), *n.* plural of **pubis.**
pu·bes·cence (pū-bes''ns), *n.* [Fr.], 1. the reaching of the state of puberty. 2. the soft down that covers the surface of many plants and insects.
pu·bes·cent (pū-bes''nt), *adj.* [Fr.; L. *pubescens*, ppr. of *pubescere*, to reach puberty < *pubes*, adult; see PUBES], 1. reaching or having reached the state of puberty. 2. covered with a soft down, as many plants and insects.
pu·bic (pū'bik), *adj.* of or in the region of the pubis or the pubes.
pu·bis (pū'bis), *n.* [*pl.* PUBES (-bēz)], [Mod. L. < L.; see PUBES], that part of either hipbone forming, with the corresponding part of the other, the front arch of the pelvis: see **skeleton,** illus.
publ., 1. published. 2. publisher.
pub·lic (pub'lik), *adj.* [ME. *publique*; L. *publicus*, altered by association with *pubes*, adult < *poplicus*, contr. of *populicus*, public < *populus*, the people], 1. belonging to, or concerning the people as a whole; of the community at large. 2. for the use or benefit of all, as, a *public* building. 3. acting in an official capacity on behalf of the people as a whole: as, a *public* prosecutor. 4. known by, or open to the knowledge of, all or most people: as, he will make this information *public*. *n.* 1. the people as a whole; community at large. 2. a specific part of the people; those people conside

together because of some common interest or purpose: as, the sporting *public*. Abbreviated **pub.**

in public, in open view; not in private or in secrecy.

ub·lic-ad·dress system (pub′lik-ə-dres′), an electronic amplification system, used in auditoriums, theaters, or the like, so that announcements, music, etc. can be easily heard by a large audience: abbreviated **P.A.**

ub·li·can (pub′li-kən), *n.* [ME.; OFr. *publicain;* L. *publicanus* < *publicus;* see PUBLIC], 1. in ancient Rome, a collector of public revenues, tolls, etc. 2. [British], a saloonkeeper; innkeeper.

ub·li·ca·tion (pub′li-kā′shən), *n.* [ME. *publicacioun;* L. *publicatio* < *publicare;* see PUBLISH], 1. a publishing or being published; public notification. 2. the printing and distribution, usually for sale, of books, magazines, newspapers, etc. 3. something published, as a book, periodical, article, etc. Abbreviated **pub.**

ublic domain, 1. public lands. 2. the condition of being free from copyright or patent: as, Shakespeare's works are in the *public domain.*

ublic enemy, 1. a government with which one's country is at war. 2. a hardened criminal or other person who is a menace to society.

ublic house, [British], 1. a bar; tavern. 2. an inn.

ub·li·cist (pub′li-sist), *n.* [Fr. *publiciste* < L. *publicum,* commonwealth], 1. a student of or specialist in international law. 2. a journalist who writes about politics and public affairs. 3. a publicity agent.

ub·lic·i·ty (pub-lis′ə-ti), *n.* [Fr. *publicité*], 1. the state of being public, or commonly known. 2. any information, usually printed, which brings a person, place, thing, or cause to the notice or attention of the public. . notice by or attention of the public. 4. any procedure or act that seeks to gain this.

ub·li·cize (pub′li-sīz′), *v.t.* [PUBLICIZED (-sīzd′), PUBLICIZING], to give publicity to.

ub·lic·ly (pub′lik-li), *adv.* 1. in a public or open manner. 2. by, or by consent or agency of, the public.

ublic opinion, the opinion of the people generally, especially as a force in determining social conduct and political action.

ublic relations, relations with the general public through publicity; those functions of a corporation, organization, branch of military service, etc. concerned with informing the public of its activities, policies, etc. and attempting to create favorable public opinion.

ub·lic-school (pub′lik-skōōl′), *adj.* of or for public schools.

ublic school, 1. in the United States, an elementary or secondary school that is part of a system of schools maintained by public taxes and supervised by municipal, county, or State authorities, offering education, usually free, to the children and youth of the district. in England, *a)* originally, any nonprofit grammar school endowed for the general use of the public. *b)* now, any of several private, expensive, endowed boarding schools for boys, offering instruction preparatory to college or the public service, as Eton and Rugby.

blic servant, a person who serves the people, as in civil service or elective office.

b·lic-serv·ice corporation (pub′lik-sūr′vis), a privately owned corporation that supplies certain common needs of the public, as water, electricity, gas, or transportation.

b·lic-spir·it·ed (pub′lik-spir′i-tid), *adj.* having or showing zeal for the public welfare.

blic utility, 1. an organization supplying water, electricity, transportation, etc. to the public, operated by a private corporation under a government franchise, or by the government directly. 2. *usually pl.* shares of stock issued by public utilities.

blic works, works constructed by the government for public use or service, as highways or dams.

b·lish (pub′lish), *v.t.* [ME. *publisen, publisshen* < base of OFr. *puplier, publier;* L. *publicare,* to make public < *publicus;* see PUBLIC], 1. to make publicly known; announce, proclaim, divulge, or promulgate. to issue (a printed work, etc.) to the public, as for sale. —*SYN.* see **declare.**

b·lish·er (pub′lish-ēr), *n.* a person or firm that publishes, especially one whose business is the publishing of books, newspapers, magazines, etc.: abbreviated **publ., pub.**

c·ci·ni, Gia·co·mo (jä′kô-mô′ pōōt-chē′nē), 1858–1924; Italian operatic composer.

c·coon (pə-kōōn′), *n.* [see POKE (plant)], 1. any of a number of North American plants that yield a red or yellow dye, as the bloodroot. 2. the dye.

ce (pūs), *n.* [Fr. *puce,* lit., a flea < L. *pulex,* a flea], brownish purple. *adj.* of the color puce.

ck (puk), *n.* [< dial. *puck,* to strike; akin to POKE], *ice hockey,* the hard rubber disk which the players strike with their sticks and try to drive into the opponents' goal.

k (puk), *n.* [ME. *puke;* AS. *puca;* akin to ON. *puki,* a devil; for IE. base see POD], 1. a mischievous sprite; goblin; elf. 2. [P-], the mischievous sprite in Shakespeare's *Midsummer Night's Dream;* Robin Goodfellow.

puck·a (puk′ə), *adj.* [Hind. *pakkā,* ripe, of full weight, cooked], [Anglo-Indian], 1. good or first-rate of its kind. 2. genuine; real. Also spelled **pukka.**

puck·er (puk′ēr), *v.t. & v.i.* [freq. form of *poke* (bag)], to draw up or gather into wrinkles or small folds. *n.* a wrinkle or small fold, or a number of these running together.

puck·er·y (puk′ēr-i), *adj.* of, causing, or characterized by puckering.

puck·ish (puk′ish), *adj.* [*puck* (sprite) + *-ish*], full of mischief; impish: also **Puckish.**

pud·ding (pood′iŋ), *n.* [ME. *poding;* prob. a blend of MFr. *boudin,* black pudding & the AS. base seen in *puduc,* a swelling; for IE. base see POD], 1. [Scot. & Dial.], a sausage made of intestine stuffed with meat, suet, etc., and boiled. 2. a soft, sweetened food, usually made with flour or some cereal as a base and variously containing eggs, milk, fruit, meat, etc. 3. anything like this in appearance or consistency.

pudding stone, conglomerate, a kind of rock in which pebbles are embedded like plums in a pudding.

pud·dle (pud′'l), *n.* [ME. *podel,* dim. < AS. *pudd,* a ditch; for IE. base see POD], 1. a small pool of water, especially stagnant or spilled water. 2. a thick mixture of clay, and sometimes sand, with water. *v.t.* [PUDDLED (-'ld), PUDDLING], 1. to make muddy. 2. to make a thick mixture of (wet clay and sand). 3. to keep water from penetrating by the use of such a mixture. 4. to treat (iron) by puddling. 5. in *agriculture,* to work (soil) while it is wet, as in rice cultivation. *v.i.* to dabble or wallow in dirty or muddy water.

pud·dler (pud′lēr), *n.* a person who puddles clay or iron.

pud·dling (pud′liŋ), *n.* [< *puddle* + *-ing*], 1. the process of working clay or a similar substance with water so as to make a mixture which moisture cannot penetrate. 2. the process of making wrought iron from pig iron by heating and stirring it in the presence of oxidizing agents.

pud·dly (pud′li, pud′'l-i), *adj.* [PUDDLIER (-li-ēr, -i-ēr), PUDDLIEST (-li-ist, -i-ist)], 1. having puddles. 2. like a puddle.

pu·den·cy (pū′d'n-si), *n.* [LL. *pudentia* < L. *pudens,* ppr. of *pudere,* to be ashamed], modesty; embarrassment; bashfulness.

pu·den·dum (pū-den′dəm), *n.* [*pl.* PUDENDA (-də)], [L., neut. of *pudendus,* (something) to be ashamed of < *pudere;* see PUDENCY], 1. the external genitals of the female; vulva. 2. *pl.* the external genitals of either sex.

pudg·i·ness (puj′i-nis), *n.* a pudgy quality or condition.

pudg·y (puj′i), *adj.* [PUDGIER (-i-ēr), PUDGIEST (-i-ist)], [< Scot. dial.; prob. a deriv. < Scot. *pud,* belly (and hence < same base as *puck, puddle, bud,* etc.)], short and stocky or fat; dumpy.

Pue·bla (pwe′blä), *n.* 1. a state of southern Mexico: area, 13,124 sq. mi.; pop., 1,902,000: abbreviated **Pueb.** 2. its capital: pop., 309,000.

pueb·lo (pweb′lō; *also, for 5 & 6,* Sp. pwe′blô), *n.* [*pl.* PUEBLOS (-lōz; Sp. -blôs); *also, for 2,* PUEBLO], [Sp., village, people < L. *populus,* people], 1. a type of communal village built by certain Indians of the southwestern United States and parts of Latin America, consisting of one or more flat-roofed structures of stone or adobe, arranged in terraces and housing a number of families. 2. [P-], any Indian of the tribes inhabiting such villages, as the Zuñi and the Hopi, characterized by a peaceful agricultural life and a culture related to that of the Aztec, Mayan, and Toltec Indians. 3. an Indian village. 4. [P-], a city in central Colorado: pop., 91,000. 5. in Spanish America, a village or town. 6. in the Philippines, a municipality; town or township. *adj.* [P-], of the Pueblo Indians.

pu·er·ile (pū′ēr-il), *adj.* [< Fr. or L.; Fr. *puéril;* L. *puerilis* < *puer,* boy], childish; silly; immature; trivial. —*SYN.* see **young.**

pu·er·il·ism (pū′ēr-il-iz′m), *n.* childishness, especially, in psychiatry, as a symptom of psychoneurosis.

pu·er·il·i·ty (pū′ēr-il′ə-ti), *n.* [Fr. *puérilité;* L. *puerilitas*], 1. the quality or condition of being puerile; childishness. 2. [*pl.* PUERILITIES (-tiz)], an instance of this.

pu·er·per·al (pū-ūr′pēr-əl), *adj.* [< L. *puerpera,* a woman in labor < *puer,* boy + *parere,* to bear], of or connected with childbirth.

puerperal fever, septic poisoning sometimes occurring during childbirth.

pu·er·pe·ri·um (pū′ēr-pêr′i-əm), *n.* [L., childbirth], the period or state of confinement during and immediately after childbirth.

Puer·to Ri·can (pwer′tə rē′kən), 1. of Puerto Rico, its people, or culture. 2. a native or inhabitant of Puerto Rico. Formerly **Porto Rican.**

Puer·to Ri·co (pwer′tə rē′kō), an island commonwealth in the West Indies, associated with the United States:

area, 3,421 sq. mi.; pop., 2,350,000; capital, San Juan: ceded by Spain in the Treaty of Paris (1898): formerly **Porto Rico**: abbreviated **P.R.**

puff (puf), *n.* [ME. *puf;* prob. < the *v.*], 1. *a)* a short, sudden gust, as of wind, or expulsion, as of breath. *b)* the sound of this. *c)* a bit of vapor, smoke, etc. expelled at one time. 2. a draw at a cigarette, etc. 3. a swelling, or a protuberance caused by swelling. 4. a shell of soft, light pastry filled with whipped cream, etc. 5. a soft, bulging mass of material, full in the middle and gathered in at the edges. 6. a soft roll of hair on the head. 7. a soft pad for dabbing powder on the skin or hair. 8. a quilted bed covering with cotton, wool, or down filling. 9. undue or exaggerated praise, as in the advertisement of a book, etc. *v.i.* [ME. *puffen;* AS. *pyffan;* for IE. base see POD], 1. to blow in puffs. 2. *a)* to give forth puffs of smoke, steam, etc. *b)* to breathe rapidly and hard, as from strenuous exercise. 3. to move, giving forth puffs (with *away, out,* or *in*). 4. to come in puffs. 5. to inflate with air or pride; swell (with *out* or *up*). 6. to take a puff or puffs at a cigarette, etc. *v.t.* 1. to blow, drive, give forth, etc. in or with a puff or puffs. 2. to swell; distend; inflate. 3. to praise unduly. 4. to write or print a puff or puffs of (a book, etc.). 5. to smoke (a cigarette, etc.). 6. to set in soft, round masses or rolls, as the hair.

puff adder, [cf. S. Afr. D. *pofadder*], 1. a large, poisonous African snake which swells out its body when irritated. 2. a harmless North American reptile able to puff out its body; hognose snake. Also **puffing adder.**

puff·ball (puf'bôl'), *n.* 1. any of a number of related round, white-fleshed, mushroomlike plants that burst at the touch and discharge a brown powder. 2. the feathery tuft of the dandelion.

puff·er (puf'ẽr), *n.* 1. a person or thing that puffs. 2. any of various fishes capable of expanding by swallowing air, as the swellfish, globefish, etc.

puff·er·y (puf'ẽr-i), *n.* 1. exaggerated praise, or puffing. 2. publicity or advertising that is characterized by exaggerated praise, or puffing.

puf·fin (puf'in), *n.* [ME. *poffin;* prob. < *puf,* a puff; or altered by folk etymology after *puff,* with reference to the enormous beak or blown-up appearance of the young], any of a number of related northern sea birds, black above and white below, with a short neck, ducklike body, and brightly colored triangular beak.

puff·i·ness (puf'i-nis), *n.* a puffy quality or condition.

puff paste, a rich dough for light, flaky pastries.

puff·y (puf'i), *adj.* [PUFFIER (-i-ẽr), PUFFIEST (-i-ist)], 1. blowing or coming in puffs. 2. panting; short-winded. 3. puffed up; swollen; inflated. 4. fat; obese.

pug (pug), *n.* [Early Mod. Eng., a term of endearment; prob. var. of *puck,* with euphemistic change of consonant], 1. a small, short-haired dog with a wrinkled face, snub nose, and curled tail. 2. a pug nose.

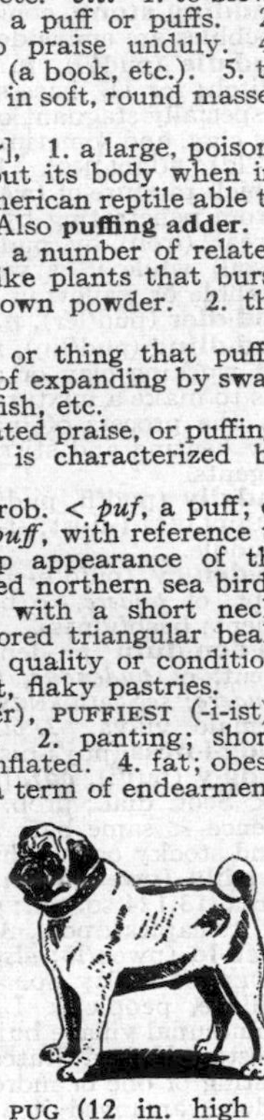

PUG (12 in. high at shoulder)

pug (pug), *v.t.* [PUGGED (pugd), PUGGING], [< dial.; prob. echoic of pounding; orig. sense "to punch, strike"], 1. to mix or fill in with wet, plastic clay. 2. to fill in with clay, mortar, sawdust, etc. for soundproofing. *n.* wet, plastic clay used for making bricks, earthenware, etc.

pug (pug), *n.* [contr. of *pugilist*], [Slang], a pugilist.

pug (pug), *n.* a footprint or trail (of an animal). *v.t.* [PUGGED (pugd), PUGGING], to track or trail (game) by following footprints.

Pu·get Sound (pū'jit), an inlet of the Pacific, with many arms, extending southward into the State of Washington.

pug·ga·ree (pug'ə-rē'), *n.* a puggree.

pug·ging (pug'iŋ), *n.* [< *pug* (to mix) + *-ing*], 1. the mixing of wet clay for making bricks, pottery, etc. 2. clay, mortar, sawdust, etc. used for soundproofing.

pug·gree, pug·gry (pug'ri), *n.* [Hind. *pagrī,* a turban], a light scarf wrapped around the crown of a sun helmet and hanging behind to protect the back of the neck.

pugh (pōō, poo; *conventionalized pronun.*), *interj.* an exclamation of disgust or contempt.

pu·gil·ism (pū'jə-liz'm), *n.* [L. *pugil,* boxer, pugilist < same base as *pugnare,* to fight, *pugnus,* a fist; + *-ism;* cf. PUGNACIOUS], the art or practice of fighting with the fists; boxing; prize fighting.

pu·gil·ist (pū'jə-list), *n.* [see PUGILISM], a person who fights with his fists; prize fighter; boxer.

pu·gil·is·tic (pū'jə-lis'tik), *adj.* of or connected with pugilism or pugilists.

pug·na·cious (pug-nā'shəs), *adj.* [< L. *pugnax* < *pugnare,* to fight; + *-ous;* cf. PUGILISM], given to fighting; quarrelsome; combative. —*SYN.* see **belligerent.**

pug·nac·i·ty (pug-nas'ə-ti), *n.* [L. *pugnacitas*], the state or quality of being pugnacious.

pug nose, a short, thick, turned-up nose.

pug-nosed (pug'nōzd'), *adj.* having a pug nose.

pug·ree (pug'ri), *n.* a puggree.

puis·ne (pū'ni), *adj.* [OFr.; *puis,* afterward + *nē,* born], in *law,* of lower rank; junior. *n.* a puisne judge.

pu·is·sance (pū'i-s'ns, pū-is''ns, pwis''ns), *n.* [ME. *puissaunce;* Late OFr. < *puissant;* see PUISSANT], [Archaic or Poetic], power; strength; might.

pu·is·sant (pū'i-s'nt, pū-is''nt, pwis''nt), *adj.* [ME. Late OFr., powerful; formed as if from a participle *possens* < L. *posse,* to be able], [Archaic or Poetic], powerful; strong; mighty.

puke (pūk), *n., v.i. & v.t.* [PUKED (pūkt), PUKING], [prob. akin to G. *spucken,* to spit, hence < an unrecorded ME. **spuken* < the base of AS. *spiwan* (cf. SPEW)], vomit.

puk·ka (puk'ə), *adj.* pucka.

Pu·las·ki, Cas·i·mir (kaz'i-mir poo-las'ki, poo-las'ki; Pol. pōō-lä'ski), Count, 1748?–1779; Polish soldier and patriot; general in the American Revolutionary army.

pul·chri·tude (pul'krə-tōōd', pul'krə-tūd'), *n.* [ME. L. *pulchritudo* < *pulcher,* beautiful], physical beauty.

pul·chri·tu·di·nous (pul'krə-tōō'd'n-əs, pul'krə-tū'd'n-əs), *adj.* [< L. *pulchritudo, pulchritudinis* (see PULCHRITUDE); + *-ous*], possessing physical beauty.

pule (pūl), *v.i.* [PULED (pūld), PULING], [echoic], to whimper or whine, as a sick or fretful child.

pul·ing (pūl'iŋ), *adj.* whimpering; whining.

Pul·it·zer, Joseph (pool'it-sẽr; *now commonly* pū'lit-sẽr), 1847–1911; American journalist, newspaper owner, and philanthropist, born in Hungary.

Pulitzer Prize, any of a number of yearly prizes for outstanding work in various departments of journalism and literature, established by Joseph Pulitzer.

Pulj (pōōl'y'), *n.* a seaport in northwestern Yugoslavia, formerly in Italy: pop., 29,000: Italian name *Pola.*

pull (pool), *v.t.* [ME. *pullen;* AS. *pullian,* to pluck, snatch with the fingers; ? akin to MLG. *pull, poll,* husk, shell < IE. base **bol-, *bul-,* a lump, knob, seen also in L. *bulla,* a bud, etc.; basic sense would then be "to pluck (fruit, etc.)"], 1. to exert force on in such a way as to cause to move toward or after the source of the force; drag, tug, draw, attract, etc. 2. *a)* to draw, or pluck, out: as, he had two teeth *pulled.* *b)* to pluck and gather: as, she *pulled* several roses. 3. to draw apart; rip; tear: as, the seam of her dress is *pulled.* 4. to stretch (taffy, etc.) back and forth repeatedly. 5. to stretch or strain to the point of injury: as, he *pulled* a muscle in the game. 6. [Dial. or Rare], to draw the entrails from (a fowl). 7. [Colloq.], to put into effect; perform; do: as, the police *pulled* a raid. 8. [Colloq.], to hold back the force of deliberately; restrain: as, he's *pulling* his punches. 9. [Slang], *a)* to arrest (someone). *b)* to make a police raid on. 10. in *baseball, golf,* etc., to hit (the ball) so as to cause it to curve to the left or, if the player is left-handed, to the right. 11. in *horse racing,* to rein in, or restrain (a horse), to keep it from winning. 12. in *printing,* to take (a proof) on a hand press. 13. in *rowing,* *a)* to work (an oar) by drawing it toward one. *b)* to transport by rowing. *c)* to be rowed normally by: as, this boat *pulls* four oars. *v.i.* 1. to exert force in or for dragging, tugging, or attracting something. 2. to take a deep draft of a drink or puff at a cigarette, etc. 3. to be capable of being pulled. 4. to move (*away, ahead,* etc.). *n.* 1. the act, force, or result of pulling (in various senses); specifically, *a)* a dragging, tugging, attracting, etc. *b)* the act or an instance of rowing. *c)* a drink. *d)* a puff at a cigarette, etc. *e)* the effort used in climbing, etc.; hence, *f)* any difficult, continuous effort. *g)* in *sports,* the act or an instance of pulling a ball. 2. something to be pulled, as the handle of a drawer, etc. 3. [Slang], influence or special advantage.

pull apart, to find fault with; criticize.

pull down, 1. to tear down, demolish, or overthrow. 2. to degrade; humble. 3. to reduce.

pull for, [Colloq.], to cheer on, or hope for the success of.

pull off, [Colloq.], to bring about or accomplish.

pull oneself together, to collect one's faculties; regain one's poise, courage, etc.

pull over, [Colloq.], to move to or toward the curb, as a motor vehicle.

pull through, [Colloq.], to get through or over (an illness, difficulty, etc.).

pull up, 1. to uproot. 2. to bring or come to a stop. 3. to move ahead.

SYN.—**pull** is the broad, general term of this list, as defined in sense 1 of the *v.t.* above; **draw** suggests a smoother, more even motion than **pull** (he *drew* his sword from its scabbard); **drag** implies the slow pulling of something heavy, connoting great resistance in the thing pulled (he *dragged* the desk across the floor); **tug** suggests strenuous, persistent effort in pulling but does not necessarily connote success in moving the object (he *tugged* at the rope to no avail); **haul** implies sustained effort in transporting something heavy, often mechanically (to *haul* furniture in a truck); **tow** implies pulling by means of a rope or cable (to *tow* a stalled automobile).—*ANT.* push, shove.

pull·back (pool'bak'), *n.* 1. a pulling back. 2. a retarding or hindering force, situation, etc. 3. a device for pulling something back.

ıl·let (pool′it), *n.* [ME. *pulete, poullet;* OFr. *polete, oulet(te),* dim. of *poule,* hen; L. *pullus,* chicken, young nimal; for IE. base see FOAL; cf. POULTRY], a young en, usually not more than a year old.

ıl·ley (pool′i), *n.* [*pl.* PULLEYS (-iz)], [ME. & OFr. *olie;* ML. *poleia;* prob. < Gr. *polidion,* dim. of *polos,* pulley, inge], 1. a small wheel, someımes turning in a block, with a rooved rim in which a rope ıns, as to raise weights by being ulled down. 2. a combination f such wheels, used to increase ıe applied power. 3. a wheel ıat turns or is turned by a belt ɔ as to transmit or apply ower.

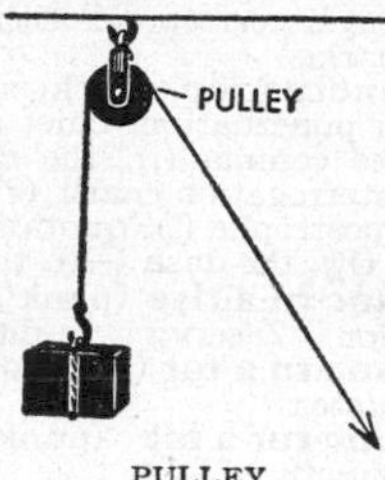

PULLEY

ıll·man car (pool′mən), [after eorge M. *Pullman* (1831–897), Am. inventor], a railroad ar with private compartments r chairs that can be made up into berths for sleeping: lso **Pullman,** *n.*

ıl·lor·um disease (pə-lôr′əm), [L. *pullorum,* genit. pl. *pullus,* chicken], a highly destructive bacterial disıse of poultry, often transmitted in the egg.

ıll-out (pool′out′), *n.* a maneuver in which an airlane levels out into horizontal flight after a dive.

ıll-o·ver (pool′ō′vẽr), *adj.* that is put on by being ulled over the head. *n.* a pull-over sweater, shirt, c.

ı·lu·late (pul′yoo-lāt′), *v.i.* [PULLULATED (-id), PULLATING], [< L. *pullulatus,* pp. of *pullulare,* to spread ıt, sprout < *pullulus,* dim. of *pullus;* see PULLET], to sprout out; germinate; bud. 2. to breed quickly. to spring up in abundance; teem or swarm.

ı·lu·la·tion (pul′yoo-lā′shən), *n.* a pullulating.

ıll-up (pool′up′), *n.* a maneuver in which an airplane ɔes into a short, sudden climb from level flight.

ı·mo·nar·y (pul′mə-ner′i), *adj.* [L. *pulmonarius* < ılmo, *pulmonis,* a lung], 1. of, like, or affecting the ngs. 2. having lungs or lunglike organs. 3. desnating the artery conveying blood from the heart the lungs, and the vein conveying blood from the ngs to the heart.

ı·mo·nate (pul′mə-nāt′, pul′mə-nit), *adj.* [Mod. L. *ılmonatus* < L. *pulmo, pulmonis,* a lung], in *zoology,* having lungs or lunglike organs. 2. belonging to a oup of mollusks having a sort of lung or air sac, as ost snails and slugs. *n.* any member of this group.

ı·mon·ic (pul-mon′ik), *adj.* [Fr. *pulmonique*], 1. ılmonary. 2. of pneumonia; pneumonic.

ı·mo·tor (pul′mō′tẽr, pool′mō′tẽr), *n.* [< L. *pulmo,* lung; + *motor*], an apparatus used in applying tificial respiration to persons who are in danger of ath from drowning, suffocation, etc.: a trade-mark ulmotor).

ıp (pulp), *n.* [Fr. *pulpe;* L. *pulpa,* flesh, pulp of ıit], 1. a soft, moist, formless mass that sticks tother. 2. the soft, juicy part of a fruit. 3. the soft, ongy pith inside the stem of a plant. 4. the soft, ısitive substance underneath the enamel and dentine a tooth. 5. a mixture of ground-up, moistened cellue material, as wood, linen, rags, etc., from which per is made. 6. ore ground to a powder and mixed th water. 7. *usually in pl.* [Slang], a magazine printed rough, inferior paper stock made from wood pulp, ıally containing sensational stories of love, crime, .: cf. **slick.** *v.t.* 1. to reduce to pulp. 2. to remove pulp from. *v.i.* to become pulp.

p·i·ness (pul′pi-nis), *n.* a pulpy quality or condition.

·pit (pool′pit), *n.* [ME.; OFr. *pulpite;* L. *pulpitum,* stage, scaffold], 1. a raised platform from which a rgyman preaches in a church. 2. preachers coltively; (*the*) ministry. 3. preaching.

·pit·eer (pool′pi-têr′), *n.* [*pulpit* + *-eer*], a preacher: ıtemptuous term.

p·ous (pul′pəs), *adj.* [L. *pulposus*], pulpy.

p·wood (pulp′wood′), *n.* 1. soft wood used in king paper. 2. wood ground to pulp for paper.

p·y (pul′pi), *adj.* [PULPIER (-pi-ẽr), PULPIEST (-pi-], of, having the nature of, or like pulp.

que (pool′ki; Sp. pōōl′ke), *n.* [Sp.; prob. of Mex. l. origin], a fermented drink, popular in Mexico, de from the juice of an agave.

sate (pul′sāt), *v.i.* [PULSATED (-id), PULSATING], [< *pulsatus,* pp. of *pulsare,* to beat], 1. to beat or throb thmically, as the heart. 2. to vibrate; quiver; thrill.

sa·tile (pul′sə-t'l, pul′sə-til), *adj.* [ML. *pulsatilis*], ɔulsating. 2. played by beating, as a drum.

sa·tion (pul-sā′shən), *n.* 1. a pulsating; rhythmical ting or throbbing. 2. a beat; throb; vibration.

sa·tive (pul′sə-tiv), *adj.* pulsating.

sa·tor (pul-sā′tẽr), *n.* [L.], any device or machine t that pulsates.

pul·sa·to·ry (pul′sə-tôr′i, pul′sə-tō′ri), *adj.* characterized by pulsation; throbbing.

pulse (puls), *n.* [ME. *pous, pouce;* OFr. *pous, pouls;* L. *pulsus* (*venarum*), beating (of the veins) < *pulsus,* pp. of *pellere,* to beat], 1. the regular beating in the arteries, caused by the contractions of the heart. 2. any beat that is regular or rhythmical. 3. the perceptible underlying feelings of the public, group of people, etc. *v.i.* [PULSED (pulst), PULSING], to pulsate; throb.

pulse (puls), *n.* [ME. *pous;* OFr. *pols, pouls;* L. *puls, pultis,* a pottage made of meal or pulse], 1. the edible seeds of peas, beans, lentils, and similar plants having pods. 2. any plant producing pulse.

pulse·jet (puls′jet′), *n.* an aeropulse (jet engine).

pul·sim·e·ter (pul-sim′ə-tẽr), *n.* [see -METER], an instrument that measures the rate and force of the pulse.

pul·som·e·ter (pul-som′ə-tẽr), *n.* [< *pulse* (to beat) + *-meter*], 1. a type of pistonless pump for raising water by the intermittent condensation of steam: also called *vacuum pump.* 2. a pulsimeter.

pul·ver·a·ble (pul′vẽr-ə-b'l), *adj.* pulverizable.

pul·ver·iz·a·ble (pul′və-rīz′ə-b'l), *adj.* that can be pulverized, or ground to a powder.

pul·ver·i·za·tion (pul′vẽr-i-zā′shən, pul′vẽr-ī-zā′shən), *n.* a pulverizing or being pulverized.

pul·ver·ize (pul′və-rīz′), *v.t.* [PULVERIZED (-rīzd′), PULVERIZING], [Fr. *pulveriser;* LL. *pulverizare* < L. *pulvis,* dust, powder], 1. to crush, grind, etc. into a powder or dust. 2. to break down completely; demolish. *v.i.* to be crushed, ground, etc. into powder or dust.

pul·ver·u·lence (pul-ver′yoo-ləns, pul-ver′oo-ləns), *n.* the quality or condition of being pulverulent.

pul·ver·u·lent (pul-ver′yoo-lənt, pul-ver′oo-lənt), *adj.* [L. *pulverulentus* < *pulvis, pulveris,* dust], 1. consisting of or covered with a powder; powdery. 2. crumbling to powder or dust.

pul·vil·lus (pul-vil′əs), *n.* [*pl.* PULVILLI (-ī)], [L., contr. < *pulvinulus,* dim. of *pulvinus,* a cushion], in *zoology,* the cushionlike part of an insect's foot.

pul·vi·nate (pul′vi-nāt′), *adj.* [L. *pulvinatus* < *pulvinus,* a cushion], 1. cushion-shaped. 2. in *botany,* having a leafstalk with a swollen base.

pul·vi·nat·ed (pul′vi-nā′tid), *adj.* pulvinate.

pul·vi·nus (pul-vī′nəs), *n.* [L., a pillow, elevation], the swollen base of a leafstalk.

pu·ma (pū′mə), *n.* [*pl.* PUMAS (-məz), PUMA; see PLURAL, II, D, 1], [Sp.; Peruv.], 1. a long-tailed, slender, tawny-brown animal of the cat family, found in North and South America; cougar; mountain lion. 2. its fur.

pum·ice (pum′is), *n.* [ME. *pomis, pomeis;* OFr. *pomis, pumis;* L. *pumex,* pumice], a spongy, light, porous, volcanic rock, used in solid or powdered form for removing stains, smoothing, and polishing: also **pumice stone.** *v.t.* [PUMICED (-ist), PUMICING], to clean, polish, etc. with pumice.

pu·mi·ceous (pyoo-mish′əs), *adj.* [L. *pumiceus*], of, having the nature of, or like pumice.

pum·mel (pum′'l), *n.* & *v.t.* [PUMMELED or PUMMELLED (-'ld), PUMMELING or PUMMELLING], pommel.

pump (pump), *n.* [ME. *pumpe, pompe;* MD. *pompe;* Sp. *bomba;* prob. of echoic origin], any of various machines that force a liquid or gas into, or draw it out of, something, as by suction or pressure. *v.t.* 1. to raise or move (fluids) with a pump. 2. to remove water, etc. from. 3. to inflate (a rubber tire) by pumping air into it. 4. to force or draw out, move up and down, pour forth, eject, etc. in the manner of a pump: as, her eyes were *pumped* dry of tears. 5. to question closely and persistently. 6. to get (information) out of a person in this way. 7. to work with the same action as a pump handle or piston does. *v.i.* 1. to work a pump. 2. to raise or move water, etc. with a pump. 3. to move up and down like a pump handle or piston.

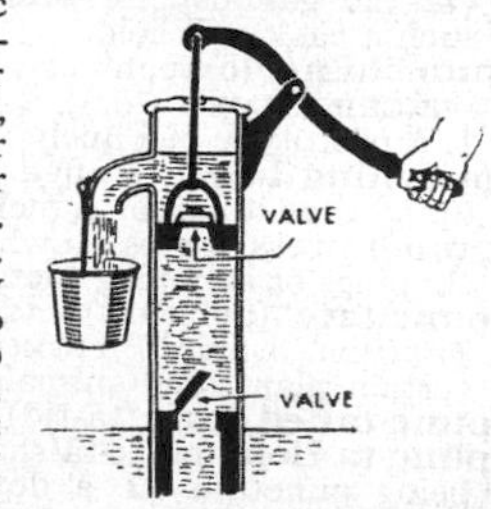

PUMP

pump (pump), *n.* [prob. < Fr. *pompe,* an ornament], a low-cut shoe without straps or ties.

pump box, 1. the chamber in which the piston of a pump works. 2. the piston of a pump.

pump·er·nick·el (pum′pẽr-nik′'l), *n.* [G., Westphalian rye bread; earlier, a booby < *pumpern,* to pass wind + *Nickel,* a goblin < *Niklaus,* Nicholas], a coarse, dark bread made of unsifted rye.

pump·kin (pump′kin; *also commonly* puŋ′kin), *n.* [earlier *pumpion, pompion;* MFr. *pompon, popon;* L. *pepo;* Gr. *pepōn,* lit., cooked by the sun, ripe, hence a gourd or melon not eaten until ripe], 1. a large, round, orange-yellow, gourdlike fruit with many seeds. 2. the vine on which it grows.

pump·kin·seed (pump′kin-sēd′, puŋ′kin-sēd′), *n.* 1. the seed of the pumpkin. 2. any of a number of related small fresh-water fishes of North America, greenish-olive above and orange-yellow below; sunfish.

pun (pun), *n.* [17th-c. clipped form (cf. CHUM, MOB); ? < It. *puntiglio*, fine point, hence verbal quibble (cf. PUNCTILIO)], the humorous use of a word, or of words which are formed or sounded alike but have different meanings, in such a way as to play on two or more of the possible applications; a play on words. *v.i.* [PUNNED (pund), PUNNING], to make a pun or puns. *v.t.* to bring to a specified state by punning.

‡**pu·na** (po͞o′nä), *n.* [Sp.; Quechua], 1. a high, cold, arid plateau, as in the Andes. 2. mountain sickness.

Punch (punch), *n.* [contr. < *Punchinello*, earlier *Polichinello*: from the name of a character in a Neapolitan puppet play], the hero of the puppet show *Punch and Judy*, a hook-nosed, humpbacked figure.
pleased as Punch, greatly pleased or gratified.

punch (punch), *n.* [contr. of earlier *punchon;* see PUNCHEON (a die)], a tool driven or pressed against a surface that is to be pierced, shaped, or stamped, or a nail, bolt, etc. that is to be worked in or out. *v.t.* to pierce, shape, stamp, etc. with a punch.

punch (punch), *v.t.* [ME. *punchen;* prob. var. of *pouncen;* see POUNCE], 1. to prod or poke with a stick. 2. to herd (cattle) by or as by prodding. 3. to strike with the fist. 4. to pierce or perforate with a punch. 5. to make (a hole) with a punch. 6. to cut *out* (a piece) by punching. *n.* 1. a thrusting blow with the fist. 2. [Colloq.], effective force; vigor. —*SYN.* see **strike.**
pull one's punches, [Slang], 1. in *boxing*, to deliver blows that are intentionally ineffective. 2. to attack, criticize, etc. in an intentionally ineffective manner.

punch (punch), *n.* [Hind. *pāc*, five; Sans. *pañca* (cf. FIVE): so named from orig. consisting of five ingredients], a sweetened drink flavored with fruit juices, spices, etc., often mixed with wine or liquor.

Punch-and-Ju·dy show (punch″n-jo͞o′di), a puppet show in which the quarrelsome Punch constantly fights with his wife, Judy.

punch bowl, a large bowl in which punch is served.

punch-drunk (punch′druŋk′), *adj.* 1. having or showing a condition resulting from numerous blows on the head and marked by an unsteady gait, slow muscular movements, hesitant speech, mental confusion, etc.; hence, 2. [Colloq.], acting in a hazy, bewildered manner; thoroughly dazed.

pun·cheon (pun′chən), *n.* [ME. *punchoun;* OFr. *poinçon, poinchon;* LL. **punctio* < *punctiare*, to prick < L. *punctus*, pp. of *pungere*, to prick], 1. a short, upright wooden post used in framework. 2. a heavy, broad piece of roughly dressed timber with one side hewed flat. 3. any of various devices for punching, perforating, or stamping; especially, a figured die used by goldsmiths, etc.

pun·cheon (pun′chən), *n.* [Late ME. *pwncion;* OFr. *ponçon, poinchon;* identical in form with *puncheon* (punch, die, etc.)], 1. a large cask of varying capacity (72-120 gallons), for beer, wine, etc. 2. as much as such a cask will hold.

pun·chi·nel·lo (pun′chə-nel′ō), *n.* [*pl.* PUNCHINELLOS, PUNCHINELLOES (-ōz)], [see PUNCH (the character)], 1. a prototype of Punch. 2. a buffoon; clown.

punching bag, a stuffed or inflated leather bag hung up so that it can be punched for exercise.

punch press, a press in which dies are fitted for cutting, shaping, or stamping metal.

punc·tate (puŋk′tāt), *adj.* [Mod. L. *punctatus* < L. *punctum*, a point], marked with dots or tiny spots, as certain plants and animals.

punc·tat·ed (puŋk′tā-tid), *adj.* punctate.

punc·ta·tion (puŋk-tā′shən), *n.* 1. the condition of being punctate. 2. a dot. 3. a marking with many dots. 4. a statement of points to be negotiated.

punc·til·i·o (puŋk-til′i-ō′), *n.* [*pl.* PUNCTILIOS (-ōz′)], [Sp. *puntillo;* It. *puntiglio* < *punto;* L. *punctum*, a point], 1. a nice point of conduct, manners, ceremony, or honor. 2. observance of petty formalities.

punc·til·i·ous (puŋk-til′i-əs), *adj.* [Fr. *pointilleux* < It. *puntiglio;* see PUNCTILIO], 1. careful in the observance of the nice points of behavior and ceremony. 2. very exact; scrupulous.

punc·tu·al (puŋk′cho͞o-əl), *adj.* [ME.; ML. *punctualis* < L. *punctus*, a point], 1. of or like a point; minute. 2. punctilious. 3. carefully observant of an appointed time; on time; prompt.

punc·tu·al·i·ty (puŋk′cho͞o-al′ə-ti), *n.* 1. the quality or condition of being punctual, or on time. 2. [*pl.* PUNCTUALITIES (-tiz)], an instance of this.

punc·tu·ate (puŋk′cho͞o-āt′), *v.t.* [PUNCTUATED (-id), PUNCTUATING], [< ML. *punctuatus*, pp. of *punctuare* < L. *punctus*, a point], 1. to insert punctuation marks in (written or printed matter) in order to clarify the meaning. 2. to interrupt from time to time. 3. to emphasize. *v.i.* to use punctuation marks.

punc·tu·a·tion (puŋk′cho͞o-ā′shən), *n.* [ML. *punctuatio* < pp. of *punctuare;* see PUNCTUATE], 1. the act, practice, or system of using certain standardized marks and signs in writing and printing, as to separate sentences, independent clauses, parenthetical phrases, etc., in order to make the meaning more easily understood: the marks of punctuation, originally conventionalized from normal speech patterns of pause, pitch, and stress, no longer correspond with these in detail. 2. punctuation marks.

punctuation mark, any of the marks and signs used in punctuation, chief among which are the period (.), the comma (,), the colon (:), the semicolon (;), the interrogation mark (?), the exclamation mark (!), the apostrophe ('), quotation marks (" "), (' '), parentheses (()), the dash (—), the hyphen (-), and brackets ([]).

punc·tu·a·tive (puŋk′cho͞o-ā′tiv), *adj.* 1. of punctuation. 2. serving to punctuate.

punc·tu·a·tor (puŋk′cho͞o-ā′tẽr), *n.* a person who punctuates.

punc·tur·a·ble (puŋk′chẽr-ə-b'l), *adj.* that can be punctured.

punc·ture (puŋk′chẽr), *n.* [ME.; LL. *punctura*, a pricking < L. *pungere*, to pierce], 1. a perforating or piercing. 2. a hole made by a sharp point, as in an automobile tire, the skin, etc. *v.t.* [PUNCTURED (-chẽrd), PUNCTURING], 1. to perforate or pierce with a sharp point. 2. to reduce or put an end to, as if by a puncture, as, his pride was *punctured*. *v.i.* to be punctured.

pun·dit (pun′dit), *n.* [Hind. *pandit;* Sans. *pandita*], 1. in India, a Brahman who is learned in Sanskrit and Hindu philosophy, law, and religion. 2. a person of great learning; an authority: often used humorously.

pung (puŋ), *n.* [< earlier *tom pung*, altered < *toboggan* or its Am. Ind. source], [Dial.], a boxlike sleigh drawn by one horse.

pun·gen·cy (pun′jən-si), *n.* the quality or condition of being pungent.

pun·gent (pun′jənt), *adj.* [L. *pungens*, ppr. of *pungere*, to prick, puncture], 1. producing a sharp sensation of taste and smell; acrid. 2. sharp and piercing; poignant; painful. 3. sharply penetrating; expressive; biting, as, *pungent* language. 4. keenly clever; stimulating.
SYN.—**pungent** literally applies to taste or smell, suggesting a sharp, stinging quality (*pungent* spices), and figuratively implies a penetrating or stimulating quality (*pungent* humor); **piquant** implies an agreeable pungency, tartness, or zest (*piquant* salad dressing, *piquant* wit); **racy** suggests the piquancy and tang of something in its natural and freshest condition (*racy* fruit) and figuratively implies a spirited, vigorous quality (*racy* slang); **spicy** suggests the pungent taste or fragrant aroma of spices (a *spicy* drink) and figuratively, an exciting, often risqué quality (*spicy* stories).—*ANT.* bland, insipid.

Pu·nic (pū′nik), *adj.* [L. *Punicus*, earlier *Poenicus*, Carthaginian, properly Phoenician < *Poeni*, the Carthaginians], 1. of ancient Carthage or its people. 2. like or characteristic of the Carthaginians, regarded by the Romans as faithless and treacherous. *n.* the West Semitic language of ancient Carthage, closely related to Phoenician: it consists of Old Punic, spoken from about the 5th century B.C. to 146 B.C., and Neo-Punic, spoken in parts of the Western Roman Empire from 146 B.C. until about 550 A.D.

Punic Wars, three wars between Rome and Carthage (264–241 B.C., 218–201 B.C., and 149–146 B.C.), which Rome was finally victorious.

pu·ni·ness (pū′ni-nis), *n.* a puny quality or condition.

pun·ish (pun′ish), *v.t.* [ME. *punischen* < inflectional base of OFr. *punir;* L. *punire*, to punish < *poena*, punishment, penalty], 1. to cause (a person) to undergo pain, loss, or suffering for a crime or wrongdoing. 2. to impose a penalty on a criminal or wrongdoer for (an offense). 3. [Colloq.], to treat in a harsh or greedy manner; deplete in quantity, as food or drink. *v.i.* to deal out punishment.
SYN.—**punish** implies the infliction of some penalty on a wrongdoer and generally connotes retribution rather than correction (to *punish* a murderer by hanging him); **discipline** suggests punishment that is intended to control or to establish habits of self-control (to *discipline* a naughty child); **correct** suggests punishment for the purpose of overcoming faults (to *correct* unruly pupils); **chastise** implies usually corporal punishment and connotes both retribution and correction; **castigate** now implies punishment by severe public criticism or censure (to *castigate* a corrupt official); **chasten** implies the infliction of tribulation in order to make obedient, meek, etc. and is used especially in a theological sense (He *chastens* and hasteneth His will to make known).

pun·ish·a·bil·i·ty (pun′ish-ə-bil′ə-ti), *n.* the quality or condition of being punishable.

pun·ish·a·ble (pun′ish-ə-b'l), *adj.* liable to or deserving punishment.

pun·ish·ment (pun′ish-mənt), *n.* 1. a punishing or being punished. 2. a penalty imposed on an offender for a crime or wrongdoing. 3. [Colloq.], rough handling.

pu·ni·tive (pū′nə-tiv), *adj.* [ML. *punitivus* < L. *punitus*, pp. of *punire;* see PUNISH], 1. inflicting punishment. 2. concerned with or directed toward punishment.

pu·ni·to·ry (pū′nə-tôr′i, pū′nə-tō′ri), *adj.* punitive.

Pun·jab (pun-jäb′, pun′jäb), *n.* a former province of British India: in 1947, divided into a state of India (area, 37,378 sq. mi.; pop., 12,641,000; capital, Chan garh), and a province of Pakistan (area 63,134 sq. mi.; pop., 18,814,000; capital, Lahore): each division is called *Punjab*.

Pun·ja·bi (pun-jä'bi), *n.* [see PANJABI], 1. a native of Punjab: also spelled **Panjabi.** 2. Panjabi, the Indic language spoken in the Punjab.

Punjab States, a former agency including a number of small native states in British India.

punk (puŋk), *n.* [< Am. Ind. (Algonquian); cf. Lenape *punk*, fine ashes], 1. decayed wood or dried fungus used for tinder. 2. any substance that smolders when ignited, usually in the form of a stick used to light fireworks, etc.

punk (puŋk), *n.* [Early Mod. Eng. slang; ? < D. *Punken-diek*, name of a dike near Bremen notorious for its red-light district; ? var. of *punch* (to perforate), in slang use], 1. [Obs.], a prostitute. 2. [Slang], *a)* a catamite. *b)* a young hoodlum. *c)* any person, especially a youngster, regarded as inexperienced, insignificant, etc. *adj.* [Slang], poor or bad in quality.

pun·kah, pun·ka (puŋ'kə), *n.* [Hind. *pankhā*], in India, a large fan made from the palmyra leaf, or a large, swinging fan consisting of canvas stretched over a rectangular frame and hung from the ceiling.

punk·ie (puŋ'ki), *n.* [D. *punki* < Am. Ind. (Algonquian); cf. Lenape *punk*, *ponk*, fine ashes], a tiny fly with piercing and sucking mouth parts, found in some mountain regions of the United States.

pun·ner (pun'ẽr), *n.* a punster.

pun·ster (pun'stẽr), *n.* a person who habitually makes, or is fond of making, puns.

punt (punt), *n.* [< slang of Rugby School, England; prob. a form of dial. *bunt*, to strike, kick (cf. BUNT)], in *football*, a type of kick in which the ball is dropped from the hands and then kicked before it strikes the ground. *v.t. & v.i.* to kick (a football) in a punt.

punt (punt), *n.* [AS.; L. *ponto*, a punt, pontoon < *pons*, *pontis*, a bridge], a flat-bottomed boat with broad, square ends, usually propelled by a single long pole. *v.t.* 1. to propel (a punt) by pushing with a pole against the bottom of a shallow river or lake. 2. to carry in a punt. *v.i.* to go in a punt.

punt (punt), *v.i.* [Fr. *ponter* < *ponte*, a point; Sp. *punto* < L. *punctum*, a point], 1. in certain card games, to bet against the dealer or banker. 2. to gamble.

Pun·ta A·re·nas (pōōn'tä ä-re'näs), Magallanes, a city in Chile: the former name.

pun·ty (pun'ti), *n.* [*pl.* PUNTIES (-tiz)], [Fr. *pontil*; It. *pontello*, dim. of *punto*, a point], a metal rod on which the molten glass is handled in glassmaking; pontil.

pu·ny (pū'ni), *adj.* [PUNIER (-ni-ẽr), PUNIEST (-ni-ist)], [Fr. *puîné*, born later; OFr. *puisné*; *puis*, after + *né* (L. *natus*), born], 1. of inferior size, strength, or importance; weak; slight. 2. [Obs.], puisne.

pup (pup), *n.* [contr. of *puppy*], 1. a young dog. 2. a young seal. *v.i.* [PUPPED (pupt), PUPPING], to give birth to pups.

pu·pa (pū'pə), *n.* [*pl.* PUPAE (-pē), PUPAS (-pəz)], [Mod. L.; L., a girl, doll, puppet], an insect in the stage of development between the larval and adult forms.

PUPA OF MOTH

pu·pal (pū'p'l), *adj.* of a pupa.

pu·pate (pū'pāt), *v.i.* [PUPATED (-id), PUPATING], to become a pupa.

pu·pa·tion (pū-pā'shən), *n.* 1. a pupating. 2. the stage in insects between the larval and adult forms.

pu·pil (pū'p'l), *n.* [ME. & OFr. *pupille*; L. *pupillus* (dim. of *pupus*, boy), *pupilla* (dim. of *pupa*, girl), orphan, ward], 1. a person, especially a young person, who is being taught under the supervision of a teacher or tutor, as in school. 2. in *civil law*, a minor under the care of a guardian.

SYN.—**pupil** is applied either to a child in school or to a person who is under the personal supervision of a teacher (Heifetz was a *pupil* of Leopold Auer); **student** is applied either to one who attends an institution of higher learning or to one who is making a study of a particular problem (a *student* of social problems); **scholar**, originally equivalent to **pupil**, is now usually applied to one who has general erudition or who is highly versed in a particular branch of learning (a linguistics *scholar*).

pu·pil (pū'p'l), *n.* [Fr. *pupille*; L. *pupilla*, figure reflected in eye, hence pupil of the eye; special use of *pupilla*; see PUPIL (learner)], the contractile circular opening, apparently black, in the center of the iris of the eye: see **eye**, illus.

pu·pil·age (pū'p'l-ij), *n.* [see -AGE], the state or period of being a pupil.

pu·pil·lar·i·ty, pu·pi·lar·i·ty (pū'pə-lar'ə-ti), *n.* [Fr. *pupilarité*; see PUPIL], in *Scottish law*, the period before puberty (the age of fourteen for boys and twelve for girls).

pu·pil·lar·y (pū'pə-ler'i), *adj.* [Fr. *pupillaire*; L. *pupillaris* < *pupilla*, pupil], of a person who is a pupil.

pu·pil·lar·y (pū'pə-ler'i), *adj.* of the pupil of the eye.

Pu·pin, Michael Id·vor·sky (id-vôr'ski pyoo-pēn'), 1858–1935; American inventor and physicist, born in Yugoslavia.

pu·pip·a·rous (pū-pip'ẽr-əs), *adj.* [< *pupa* + *-parous*], designating or of a group of insects bearing young already developed to the pupal stage, as the horse tick, bee louse, etc.

pup·pet (pup'it), *n.* [ME. *popet*; OFr. *poupette*, dim. < LL. **puppa* < L. *pupa*, a girl, doll, puppet], 1. a small figure that is a likeness of the human form; doll. 2. such a figure moved by attached strings or wires, or by the hands, in a puppet show. 3. a person whose actions, ideas, etc. are controlled by another.

pup·pet·eer (pup'i-têr'), *n.* a person who operates, designs, or costumes puppets, or produces puppet shows.

pup·pet·oon (pup'i-tōōn'), *n.* [*puppet* + *-oon* as in *cartoon*], a motion picture made by arranging jointed puppets into the successive stages of some motion and photographing each stage separately.

pup·pet·ry (pup'it-ri), *n.* 1. puppets or their actions; mummery. 2. the art of producing puppet shows.

puppet show, a play or performance with puppets.

Pup·pis (pup'is), *n.* [L., stern or poop of a ship], a subdivision of the constellation Argo, near Canis Major: see **constellation**, chart.

pup·py (pup'i), *n.* [*pl.* PUPPIES (-iz)], [Fr. *poupée*, a doll, puppet; LL. **puppa*; see PUPPET], 1. a young dog. 2. the young of the shark and some other animals. 3. a silly, conceited, or insolent young man.

pup·py·ish (pup'i-ish), *adj.* of or like a puppy.

puppy love, calf love.

pup tent, a shelter tent.

pur (pũr), *n.*, *v.i.* & *v.t.* [PURRED (pũrd), PURRING], purr.

pur·blind (pũr'blīnd'), *adj.* [ME. *pur blind*; *pur*, quite + *blind*, blind], 1. [Archaic], completely blind. 2. partly blind. 3. slow in perceiving or understanding.

Pur·cell, Henry (pũr's'l), 1659–1695; English composer.

pur·chas·a·ble (pũr'chis-ə-b'l), *adj.* 1. that can be purchased; hence, 2. open to bribery.

pur·chase (pũr'chis), *v.t.* [PURCHASED (-chist), PURCHASING], [ME. *purchacen*; OFr. *pourchacier*, *porchacier*, to pursue; *pour*, for + *chacier*, to chase], 1. to obtain for money or by paying a price; buy. 2. to obtain at a cost or sacrifice. 3. to move or raise by applying mechanical power. 4. in *law*, to acquire (land, buildings, etc.) by means other than inheritance or descent. *n.* 1. anything obtained by buying. 2. the act of buying. 3. income; return: as, worth a decade's *purchase*. 4. a fast hold applied to move something mechanically or to keep from slipping. 5. any apparatus with which such a hold is applied. 6. in *law*, the acquisition of land, buildings, etc. by means other than inheritance or descent.

purchasing power, the value of a specified monetary unit in terms of the amount of commodities or services that can be bought with it.

pur·dah (pũr'də), *n.* [Hind. & Per. *pardah*, a veil], 1. in India, a curtain used to screen off the part of the house where women are secluded; hence, 2. the Hindu system of secluding women.

pure (pyoor), *adj.* [ME. & OFr. *pur*; L. *purus*, pure; IE. base **peu-*, **pū-*, to purify, cleanse, seen also in L. *putare*, to cleanse], 1. free from anything that adulterates, taints, impairs, etc.; unmixed; clear. 2. simple; mere. 3. utter; absolute; sheer. 4. free from defects; perfect; faultless. 5. free from sin or guilt; blameless. 6. virgin or chaste. 7. of unmixed stock; pure-blooded. 8. restricted to the abstract or theoretical aspects: as, *pure* physics: contrasted with *applied*. 9. in the *Bible*, ceremonially undefiled. 10. in *biology*, conforming accurately to the parental type with respect to certain characters; homozygous. 11. in *Kantian philosophy*, free from empiricism. 12. in *phonetics*, having an unchanging sound made by keeping the oral speech organs in a fixed position for the duration of the sound. *n.* [Poetic], that which is pure (with *the*). —*SYN.* see **chaste**.

pure·bred (pyoor'bred'), *adj.* belonging to a breed with recognized characteristics maintained through generations of unmixed descent. *n.* a purebred plant or animal.

pure culture, a culture medium containing only organisms of the particular species required.

pu·rée (pyoo-rā', pyoor'ā), *n.* [Fr. < OFr. *purer*, to strain; L. *purare*, to purify < *purus*, pure], 1. food prepared by straining the boiled pulp through a sieve. 2. a thick soup. *v.t.* to prepare a purée from.

pure line, in *genetics*, a breed or strain of animals or plants that maintains a high degree of consistency in certain characteristics as a result of continued inbreeding for generations.

pure·ly (pyoor'li), *adv.* 1. in a pure manner; unmixed with anything else. 2. merely. 3. innocently. 4. entirely.

pur·fle (pũr'f'l), *v.t.* [PURFLED (-f'ld), PURFLING], [ME. *purfilen*; OFr. *pourfiler* < *pour* (L. *pro*), for + *fil* (L.

filum), a thread], 1. to decorate the border of. 2. to adorn or edge with metallic thread, beads, lace, etc. *n.* an ornamental border or trimming.

pur·fling (pũr′fliŋ), *n.* [< *purfle* + *-ing*], the inlaid border of a violin.

pur·ga·tion (pũr-gā′shən), *n.* [ME. *purgacioun;* OFr. *purgacion;* L. *purgatio*], a purging.

pur·ga·tive (pũr′gə-tiv), *adj.* [ME. *purgatyf;* LL. *purgativus*], 1. purging. 2. causing bowel movement. *n.* 1. a substance that purges. 2. a cathartic. —*SYN.* see **physic.**

pur·ga·to·ri·al (pũr′gə-tôr′i-əl, pũr′gə-tō′ri-əl), *adj.* [< LL. *purgatorius* (see PURGATORY); + *-al*], 1. serving to atone for sins; expiatory. 2. of or like purgatory.

pur·ga·to·ry (pũr′gə-tôr′i, pũr′gə-tō′ri), *n.* [*pl.* PURGATORIES (-iz, -riz)], [ME. *purgatorie* < OFr. & ML.; OFr. *purgatoire;* ML. *purgatorium* < LL. *purgatorius,* cleansing < L. *purgare;* see PURGE], 1. in *Roman Catholic theology,* a state or place in which those who have died in the grace of God expiate their sins by suffering. 2. any state or place of temporary punishment, expiation, or remorse. *adj.* purgative.

purge (pũrj), *v.t.* [PURGED (pũrjd), PURGING], [ME. *purgen;* OFr. *purgier;* L. *purgare,* to cleanse < *purus,* clean + *agere,* to do, act], 1. to cleanse or rid of impurities, foreign matter, or undesirable elements. 2. to cleanse of guilt, sin, or ceremonial defilement. 3. to remove by cleansing; clear *away, off,* or *out.* 4. to clear or rid (a nation, political party, etc.) of individuals held to be disloyal or undesirable. 5. in *law,* to free from a charge or imputation of guilt. 6. in *medicine, a)* to empty (the bowels). *b)* to cause (a person) to empty his bowels. *v.i.* 1. to become clean, clear, or pure. 2. to have or effect a thorough bowel movement. *n.* 1. a purging. 2. that which purges; especially, a purgative, or cathartic. 3. the process of ridding a nation, political party, etc. of individuals held to be disloyal or undesirable.

pu·ri·fi·ca·tion (pyoor′ə-fi-kā′shən), *n.* [ME. *purificacioun;* OFr.; L. *purificatio*], a purifying or being purified.

pu·rif·i·ca·to·ry (pyoo-rif′i-kə-tôr′i, pyoo-rif′i-kə-tō′ri), *adj.* [LL. *purificatorius*], having a purifying effect.

pu·ri·fi·er (pyoor′ə-fi′ẽr), *n.* a person or thing that purifies.

pu·ri·fy (pyoor′ə-fi′), *v.t.* [PURIFIED (-fīd′), PURIFYING], [ME. *purifien;* OFr. *purifier;* L. *purificare* < *purus,* pure + *facere,* to make], 1. to rid of impurities or polluting matter. 2. to free from guilt, sin, or ceremonial uncleanness. 3. to free from foreign or corrupting elements. 4. to purge (*of* or *from*). *v.i.* to be purified.

Pu·rim (poo-rēm′, poor′im, pyoor′im), *n.pl.* [construed as sing.], [Heb. *pūrim,* lit., lots], a Jewish holiday, the Feast of Lots, commemorating the deliverance of the Jews by Esther from a general massacre inspired by Haman: Esth. 9:21: see **Jewish holidays.**

pur·in (pyoor′in), *n.* purine.

pu·rine (pyoor′ēn, pyoor′in), *n.* [G. *purin* < L. *purus,* pure + Mod. L. *uricum,* uric acid], 1. a colorless, crystalline compound, $C_5H_4N_4$, the parent substance of which many of the uric-acid group of compounds are derivatives. 2. any of several basic substances produced by the decomposition of nucleoproteins.

pur·ism (pyoor′iz′m), *n.* [Fr. *purisme* < *pur;* see PURE], 1. strict observance of or insistence upon precise usage or purity in language, style, etc. 2. an instance of this.

pur·ist (pyoor′ist), *n.* [Fr. *puriste*], a person who practices or advocates purism.

pu·ris·tic (pyoo-ris′tik), *adj.* of purism or purists.

Pu·ri·tan (pyoor′ə-t′n), *n.* [< LL. *puritas;* see PURITY], 1. a member of a group in England and the American colonies who, in the 16th and 17th centuries, wanted a greater reformation of the Church of England than that established by Elizabeth, in order further to purify it from elaborate ceremonies and forms. 2. [p-], a person regarded as extremely or excessively strict in matters of morals and religion. *adj.* 1. of the Puritans or Puritanism. 2. [p-], puritanical.

pu·ri·tan·ic (pyoor′ə-tan′ik), *adj.* puritanical.

pu·ri·tan·i·cal (pyoor′ə-tan′i-k′l), *adj.* 1. [P-], of the Puritans or Puritanism. 2. extremely or excessively strict in matters of morals and religion.

pu·ri·tan·i·cal·ly (pyoor′ə-tan′i-k′l-i), *adv.* in a puritanical manner.

Pu·ri·tan·ism (pyoor′ə-t′n-iz′m), *n.* 1. the doctrines and practices of Puritans. 2. [p-], extreme or excessive strictness in matters of morals and religion.

pu·ri·ty (pyoor′ə-ti), *n.* [ME. *purete, purte;* OFr. *purté, pureté;* LL. *puritas* < L. *purus,* pure], the quality or condition of being pure; specifically, *a)* freedom from adulterating matter. *b)* cleanness; clearness. *c)* freedom from evil or sin; innocence; chastity. *d)* freedom from foreign elements: said of language, style, etc. *e)* freedom from mixture with white; color saturation.

purl (pũrl), *v.i.* [echoic], 1. to move in ripples or with a murmuring sound. 2. to move in eddies; swirl. *n.* 1. a purling stream or rill. 2. the murmuring sound of purling water.

purl (pũrl), *v.t.* & *v.i.* [< the *n.*], 1. to purfle. 2. to edge (lace) with a chain of small loops. 3. to invert (stitches) in knitting. Also spelled **pearl** (in senses 2 & 3). *n.* [earlier *pyrle* < a Romance source; cf. It. *pirlare,* to twirl < *pirolo,* a top; cf. PIROUETTE], 1. twisted metal thread, as of gold or silver, used in embroidery. 2. a small loop, or a chain of loops, made on the edge of lace. 3. an inversion of stitches in knitting to produce a ribbed effect. Also spelled **pearl** (in senses 2 & 3).

pur·lieu (pũr′lōō), *n.* [altered (after Fr. *lieu,* a place) < Anglo-Fr. *puralee, puraley;* OFr. *puralée, poralée* < *puraler,* to go through < *pur-, por-* (< L *pro-,* for, but used for L. *per-,* through) + *aler,* to go], 1. an outlying part of a forest, exempted from forest laws and returned to private owners. 2. a place that one visits often or habitually; haunt. 3. *pl.* bounds; limits. 4. an outlying part, as of a city. 5. *pl.* environs.

pur·lin, pur·line (pũr′lin), *n.* [ME. *purlyn;* prob. < OFr.], a piece of timber laid horizontally to support the common rafters of a roof.

pur·loin (pũr-loin′), *v.t.* & *v.i.* [ME. *purlognen;* OFr. *porloignier, purloignier* < *pur-* (L. *pro-*), for + *loin* (L. *longe*), far], to steal; filch. —*SYN.* see **steal.**

pur·ple (pũr′p′l), *n.* [ME. *purpel, purpre;* AS. (Northumbrian) *purpl(e),* dissimilated var. of W.S. *purpur(e)* < L. *purpura,* purple; Gr. *porphyra,* shellfish yielding purple dye], 1. a dark color that is a blend of red and blue. 2. in ancient times, crimson cloth or clothing especially as an emblem of royalty or high rank. 3. the rank or office of a cardinal. *adj.* 1. of the color purple. 2. imperial; royal. 3. ornate; elaborate: as, a *purple* passage in a book. *v.t.* [PURPLED (-p′ld), PURPLING], to make purple. *v.i.* to become purple.

born to (or **in**) **the purple,** being of royal or high birth.
the purple, royal or high rank.

pur·ple-fringed orchis (pũr′p′l-frinjd′), either of two North American orchids with purple-fringed flowers.

Purple Heart, a medal of the Order of the Purple Heart: see **Order of the Purple Heart.**

purple martin, a large American swallow with bluish black plumage.

purple medic, alfalfa, a plant with small, purple flowers.

pur·plish (pũr′plish, pũr′p′l-ish), *adj.* having a purple tinge; somewhat purple.

pur·ply (pũr′pli, pũr′p′l-i), *adj.* [PURPLIER (-pli-ẽr, -i-ẽr), PURPLIEST (-pli-ist, -i-ist)], purplish.

pur·port (pũr-pôrt′, pũr-pōrt′; *also, and for n. always* pũr′pôrt, pũr′pōrt), *v.t.* [Anglo-Fr. *purporter;* OFr. *pourporter, porporter* < *pur-, por-* (L. *pro-*), forth + *porter* (L. *portare*), to bear], 1. to profess or claim as its meaning. 2. to give the appearance, often falsely, of being, intending, etc. *n.* 1. meaning; tenor; sense. 2. intention; object. —*SYN.* see **meaning.**

pur·pose (pũr′pəs), *v.t.* & *v.i.* [PURPOSED (-pəst), PURPOSING], [ME. *purposen;* OFr. *porposer; por, pour* (L. *pro*), for + *poser,* to place; see POSE (to place)], to aim, intend, resolve, or plan. *n.* 1. something one intends to get or do; intention; aim. 2. resolution; determination. 3. the object for which something exists or is done; end in view. —*SYN.* see **intend, intention.**

of set purpose, with determination.
on purpose, with a purpose; intentionally.
to good purpose, with good effect.
to little (or **no**) **purpose,** with little or no effect.
to the purpose, relevant; pertinent.

pur·pose·ful (pũr′pəs-fəl), *adj.* 1. having a purpose; determined. 2. full of meaning.

pur·pose·ly (pũr′pəs-li), *adv.* with a definite purpose; intentionally; deliberately.

pur·pos·ive (pũr′pəs-iv), *adj.* 1. serving some purpose. 2. having a purpose.

pur·pu·ra (pũr′pyoo-rə), *n.* [L.; see PURPLE], a disease characterized by purplish patches on the skin or mucous membranes, caused by the subcutaneous escape of blood from its vessels.

pur·pure (pũr′pyoor), *n.* [ME.; see PURPLE], purple as a tincture in heraldic bearings: represented in engravings by diagonal lines downward from sinister to dexter.

pur·pu·ric (pũr-pyoor′ik), *adj.* of or having purpura.

purr (pũr), *n.* [echoic], 1. a low, vibratory sound made by a cat when it seems to be pleased. 2. any sound resembling this. *v.i.* to utter such a sound. *v.t.* to show or express by purring. Also spelled **pur.**

purse (pũrs), *n.* [ME.; AS. *purs;* LL. *bursa;* Gr. *byrsa,* a skin, hide], 1. a small bag or pouch in which money is carried. 2. finances; money. 3. a sum of money collected as a present or given as a prize. 4. a woman's handbag. 5. anything like a purse in shape, use, etc. *v.t.* [PURSED (pũrst), PURSING], 1. [Archaic], to put in a purse. 2. to gather into small folds; pucker; knit.

purse-proud (pũrs′proud′), *adj.* overbearing or proud because of one's wealth.

purs·er (pũr′sẽr), *n.* [ME., a purse-bearer, treasurer], a ship's officer in charge of the accounts, freight, tickets, etc., especially on a passenger vessel.

purse strings, strings drawn to close a purse.

hold the purse strings, to be in control of the money.
tighten (or **loosen**) **the purse strings,** to reduce (or increase) the amount of money spent.

pur·si·ness (pũr′si-nis), *n.* the quality or condition of being pursy.

purs·lane (pũrs′lin, pũrs′lān), *n.* [ME. *purcelane;* OFr. *porcelaine;* L. *porcilaca,* purslane; cf. PORCELAIN], any of a number of related weeds with pink, fleshy stems and small, round leaves.

pur·su·a·ble (pẽr-sōō′ə-b'l, pẽr-sū′ə-b'l), *adj.* capable of being pursued.

pur·su·ance (pẽr-sōō′əns, pẽr-sū′əns), *n.* [< *pursuant*], a pursuing, or carrying out, as of a project, plan, etc.

pur·su·ant (pẽr-sōō′ənt, pẽr-sū′ənt), *adj.* [ME. & OFr. *poursuiant,* ppr. of *poursuir;* see PURSUE], carrying out; following.

pursuant to, 1. following upon. 2. in accordance or compliance with.

pur·su·ant·ly (pẽr-sōō′ənt-li, pẽr-sū′ənt-li), *adv.* so as to carry out, conform, or accord (with *to*).

pur·sue (pẽr-sōō′, pẽr-sū′), *v.t.* [PURSUED (-sōōd′, -sūd′), PURSUING], [ME. *pursuen;* OFr. *poursuir, porsiore;* LL. *prosequere,* for L. *prosequi; pro-,* forth + *sequi,* to follow], 1. to follow in order to overtake, capture, or kill; chase. 2. to proceed along or follow, as a specified course, action, plan, etc. 3. to try to find; strive for; seek. 4. to follow as an occupation, profession, or study. 5. to continue; carry on. 6. to continue to annoy or distress. *v.i.* 1. to go in pursuit. 2. to go on.

pur·suit (pẽr-sōōt′, pẽr-sūt′), *n.* [ME. *purseute;* OFr. *poursuite*], 1. a pursuing. 2. the thing pursued; occupation or the like ordinarily followed.

pursuit plane, a fast, maneuverable military plane.

pur·sui·vant (pũr′swi-vənt), *n.* [ME. *pursevante;* OFr. *poursuivant,* ppr. of *poursuivre* < *poursuir;* see PURSUE], 1. in the British College of Heralds, an officer ranking below a herald. 2. a follower; attendant.

pur·sy (pũr′si), *adj.* [PURSIER (-si-ẽr), PURSIEST (-si-ist)], [earlier *pursive;* ME. *purcyfe;* Anglo-Fr. *pursif,* for OFr. *polsif* < *poulser, polser,* to push, also breathe, pant < L. *pulsare,* to beat], 1. short-winded. 2. fat.

pur·te·nance (pũr′tə-nəns), *n.* [ME.; OFr.; see APPURTENANCE], [Archaic], the viscera of an animal.

pu·ru·lence (pyoor′ə-ləns, pyoor′yoo-ləns), *n.* 1. a purulent quality or condition. 2. pus.

pu·ru·len·cy (pyoor′ə-lən-si, pyoor′yoo-lən-si), *n.* purulence.

pu·ru·lent (pyoor′ə-lənt, pyoor′yoo-lənt), *adj.* [L. *purulentus* < *pus, puris,* matter, pus], of, like, containing, or discharging pus.

Pu·rús (pōō-rōōs′), *n.* a river in Peru and Brazil flowing into the Amazon: length, 1,850 mi.

pur·vey (pẽr-vā′), *v.t.* [ME. *pourveien;* Anglo-Fr. *purveier;* OFr. *porveir* < L. *providere;* see PROVIDE], to furnish or supply (food or provisions).

pur·vey·ance (pẽr-vā′əns), *n.* [ME. *purve(i)aunce;* OFr. *purveance, porveance*], 1. a purveying. 2. the things purveyed; provisions. 3. formerly, the right of the British sovereign to exact provisions, transport, etc. at a rate fixed by his agent: abolished in 1660.

pur·vey·or (pẽr-vā′ẽr), *n.* [ME. *purveiour;* Anglo-Fr. *purveour;* OFr. *pourveor*], 1. a person who purveys, or supplies provisions, etc. 2. in *English history,* an officer who exacted or supplied provisions for the sovereign, under purveyance (sense 3).

pur·view (pũr′vū), *n.* [Anglo-Fr., for OFr. *pourvoü,* provided, pp. of *pourveir* (see PURVEY); n. use < occurring in legal phrases "*purveu est,*" it is provided, "*purveu que,*" provided that], 1. the body and scope of an act or bill. 2. the extent or range of control, activity, or concern; province. 3. range of sight or understanding.

pus (pus), *n.* [L.; IE. base **pū-,* **pu-,* to rot, stink, seen also in L. *putridus,* putrid, Sans. *pūyati,* it rots], the yellowish-white matter produced by an infection, consisting of bacteria, white corpuscles, serum, etc.

Pu·sey·ism (pū′zi-iz'm), *n.* [after E. B. *Pusey* (1800–1882), Brit. leader of the movement], Tractarianism.

Pu·sey·ite (pū′zi-īt′), *n.* an adherent of Puseyism.

push (poosh), *v.t.* [ME. *posshen;* Early Fr. *pousser;* OFr. *poulser;* L. *pulsare,* to beat, freq. < *pellere, pulsum,* to beat, drive; cf. PULSE], 1. to thrust or press against (a thing) so as to move it away. 2. to move by exerting force in this way. 3. to thrust, shove, or drive up, down, in, out, forward, etc. 4. to urge forward or on; impel; press. 5. to follow up vigorously, as a campaign, claim, etc. 6. to extend; expand: as, the Genoese *pushed* their trade to the Far East. 7. to press hard upon: as, he was *pushed* for time. 8. to urge or promote the use, sale, success, etc. of. *v.i.* 1. to press against a thing so as to move it. 2. to press or thrust forward vigorously. 3. to put forth great effort. 4. to advance against opposition. *n.* 1. a pushing; shove, thrust, etc. 2. a thing to be pushed in order to work a mechanism. 3. a vigorous effort. 4. an advance against opposition. 5. pressure of affairs or of circumstances. 6. an emergency. 7. [Colloq.], aggressiveness; enterprise; drive; force. 8. [Slang], a crowd or clique.

push off, [Colloq.], to set out; depart.

push on, to proceed.

SYN.—**push** implies the exertion of force or pressure by a person or thing in contact with the object to be moved ahead, aside, etc. (to *push* a baby carriage); **shove** implies a pushing of something so as to force it to slide along a surface, or it suggests roughness in pushing (*shove* the box in the corner); to **thrust** is to push with sudden, often violent force, sometimes so as to penetrate something (he *thrust* the knife into his victim's back); **propel** implies a driving forward by a force that imparts motion (the wind *propelled* the sailboat).—*ANT.* pull, draw.

push·ball (poosh′bôl′), *n.* 1. a game, played by two teams, in which a large ball about six feet in diameter is to be pushed across the opponent's goal. 2. the ball used in this game.

push button, a small knob or button which when pushed makes or breaks an electric circuit.

push-but·ton tuning (poosh′but″n), a method of tuning a radio receiver to any of several stations by pushing the proper button.

push·cart (poosh′kärt′), *n.* a cart pushed by hand; used by street peddlers or venders.

push·er (poosh′ẽr), *n.* 1. a person or thing that pushes. 2. an airplane with the propeller mounted behind the engine, usually at the trailing edge of the wing: also **pusher airplane.**

push·ing (poosh′iŋ), *adj.* [ppr. of *push*], 1. aggressive; enterprising; energetic. 2. forward; officious. —*SYN.* see **aggressive.**

Push·kin, A·le·ksan·dr Ser·ge·ye·vich (å′lyek-sän′dẽr syer-gyā′ye-vich pōōsh′kin; Eng. poosh′kin), 1799–1837; Russian poet.

push-o·ver (poosh′ō′vẽr), *n.* [Slang], 1. anything very easy to accomplish. 2. a person, group, etc. easily persuaded, defeated, seduced, etc.

push·pin (poosh′pin′), *n.* 1. a child's game played with pins. 2. anything trivial. 3. a tacklike pin with a prominent head, used as a map marker, etc.

Push·tu (push′tōō), *n.* an Iranian language, the principal one spoken in Afghanistan: also **Pashto.**

pu·sil·la·nim·i·ty (pū′s'l-ə-nim′ə-ti), *n.* the quality or condition of being pusillanimous.

pu·sil·lan·i·mous (pū′s'l-an′ə-məs), *adj.* [LL. *pusillanimis* < L. *pusillus,* tiny + *animus,* the mind], 1. cowardly; irresolute; fainthearted. 2. proceeding from or showing a lack of courage. —*SYN.* see **cowardly.**

puss (poos), *n.* [prob. echoic of the spitting of a cat; cf. D. *poes,* Sw. dial. *pus,* LG. *puus,* a cat, etc.], 1. a cat: pet name or child's term. 2. a girl or young woman: term of affection. 3. [British], a hare.

puss (poos), *n.* [Slang], 1. the face. 2. the mouth.

puss·ley, puss·ly (pus′li), *n.* purslane.

pus·sy (pus′i), *adj.* containing or like pus.

puss·y (poos′i), *n.* [*pl.* PUSSIES (-iz)], [dim. of *puss*], 1. a cat. 2. [Colloq.], a catkin, as of the pussy willow.

puss·y·foot (poos′i-foot′), *v.i.* [Slang], 1. to move with stealth or caution, as a cat does. 2. to avoid committing oneself or making one's position clear. *n.* [Slang], a person who pussyfoots.

pussy willow, a willow having on its branches silvery, velvetlike catkins, which appear before the leaves.

pus·tu·lant (pus′choo-lənt), *adj.* [LL. *pustulans,* ppr.], causing pustules to form. *n.* a pustulant medicine, etc.

pus·tu·lar (pus′choo-lẽr), *adj.* 1. of, or having the nature of, pustules. 2. covered with pustules.

pus·tu·late (pus′choo-lāt′; *for adj.,* pus′choo-lit), *v.t. & v.i.* [PUSTULATED (-id), PUSTULATING], [< L. *pustulatus* < *pustulare,* to blister < *pustula,* a blister, pimple], to form into pustules. *adj.* covered with pustules.

pus·tu·la·tion (pus′choo-lā′shən), *n.* [LL. *pustulatio*], 1. the formation of pustules. 2. a pustule.

pus·tule (pus′chool), *n.* [L. *pustula,* a blister, pimple], 1. a small, inflamed elevation of the skin, containing pus. 2. any small elevation like a blister or pimple.

pus·tu·lous (pus′choo-ləs), *adj.* pustular.

put (poot), *v.t.* [PUT, PUTTING], [ME. *putten, puten;* AS. *putian,* to push, thrust; the mod. senses are prob. < ON. (cf. Dan. *putte,* to place); akin to AS. *pyttan,* to sting, goad; other cognates not known], 1. to thrust; push; drive; impel. 2. to throw or fling with an overhand thrust from the shoulder: as, *put* the shot. 3. to urge on; force: as, he *put* the dog through his tricks. 4. to cause to be in a specified or understood position or place; place; set; lay. 5. to cause to be in a specified condition, situation, relation, etc.: as, *put* her at ease. 6. to impose: as, *put* a tax on luxuries. 7. to direct with steady attention; bring to bear; apply: as, *put* your heart into your work. 8. to attribute; ascribe: as, *put* the proper interpretation on the clause of a contract. 9. to express; state: as, *put* it in plain language. 10. to present for consideration, decision, etc.: as, *put* the question. 11. to place in estimation; appraise. 12. to adapt or fit, as words to music. 13. to wager; bet. *v.i.* to take one's course; move; go (with *in, out, for, back, to,* etc.). *n.* 1. a throw; cast; thrust. 2. in *commerce,* the right or option that one party buys of another to deliver to him a certain amount of a commodity or stock at a specified price, within or at a stipulated time: opposed to *call*. *adj.* [Colloq.], fixed: as, stay *put*.

put about, 1. to change a vessel's course from one tack to another. 2. to move in another direction.

put across, [Slang], 1. to cause to be understood or accepted. 2. to carry out with success. 3. to perpetrate.

put aside, 1. to reserve for later use. 2. to give up; discard. Also **put away** (or **by**).

put away, 1. [Colloq.], to consume (food or drink). 2. [Slang], to kill.

put down, 1. to crush; repress. 2. to deprive of authority, power, or position; degrade; humble. 3. to write down; record. 4. to attribute (to).

put forth, 1. to grow (leaves, shoots, etc.). 2. to bring into action; exert. 3. to propose; offer. 4. to publish; circulate. 5. to set out from port.

put forward, to advance or present, as a plan.

put in, 1. to enter a port or haven. 2. to interpose; insert. 3. [Colloq.], to spend (time) in a specified manner.

put it on, [Slang], to make a pretentious show; pretend; exaggerate.

put it (or **something**) **over on,** [Colloq.], to deceive; trick.

put it there, [Slang], to shake hands, as in expressing agreement, reconciliation, etc.

put off, 1. to postpone; delay. 2. to discard. 3. to evade; divert.

put on, 1. to clothe, adorn, or cover oneself with. 2. to assume or pretend. 3. to apply, as a brake. 4. to stage (a play). 5. to attribute to; impute. 6. to impose on, as a tax.

put out, 1. to expel; dismiss. 2. to gouge out (an eye). 3. to extinguish (a fire or light). 4. to disconcert; confuse. 5. to distress; vex. 6. to inconvenience. 7. to publish. 8. in *baseball*, to retire (a batter or runner).

put over, 1. to postpone; delay. 2. [Colloq.], to accomplish (something) against odds or by craft.

put through, 1. to perform successfully; carry out. 2. to cause to do or undergo.

put (up) to, to present to for consideration or decision.

put to it, to place in a difficult situation; press hard.

put up, 1. to offer; show. 2. to offer as a candidate. 3. to preserve or can, as fruits, vegetables, etc. 4. to erect; build. 5. to lodge, or provide lodgings for. 6. to advance, provide, or stake (money). 7. to pack in containers. 8. [Colloq.], to incite (a person) *to* some action. 9. [Colloq.], to plan secretly beforehand. 10. [Archaic], to sheathe (one's sword).

put upon, to impose on; victimize.

put up with, to bear or suffer patiently; tolerate.

pu·ta·men (pū-tā′mən), *n.* [L., that which falls off in pruning, waste < *putare*, to prune, cleanse; see PURE], the hard stone of certain fruits, as of the peach.

pu·ta·tive (pū′tə-tiv), *adj.* [ME. *putative;* L. *putativus* < *putare*, to suppose, reckon], generally considered or deemed; reputed; supposed.

put·log (poot′lôg′, poot′log′), *n.* [earlier also *, tlock* < *put, v.*], any of the horizontal timbers which support the flooring of a scaffolding.

Put·nam, Israel (put′nəm), 1718–1790; American general in the Revolutionary War.

put-out (poot′out′), *n.* in *baseball*, a play in which the batter or runner is retired, or put out.

pu·tre·fac·tion (pū′trə-fak′shən), *n.* [ME. *putrifaccioun;* L. *putrefactio* < *putrefacere;* see PUTREFY], 1. the decomposition of organic matter by bacteria, fungi, and oxidation, resulting in the formation of foul-smelling products; a rotting. 2. rotting or putrid matter.

pu·tre·fac·tive (pū′trə-fak′tiv), *adj.* 1. causing putrefaction. 2. of or characterized by putrefaction.

pu·tre·fi·er (pū′trə-fī′ẽr), *n.* anything that causes putrefaction.

pu·tre·fy (pū′trə-fī′), *v.t. & v.i.* [PUTREFIED (-fīd′), PUTREFYING], [ME. *putrifien* (prob. via OFr.) < L. *putrefacere* < *putris*, putrid + *facere*, to make], to make or become putrid or rotten; decompose. —*SYN.* see **decay**.

pu·tres·cence (pū-tres′′ns), *n.* 1. the condition of being putrescent. 2. putrescent matter.

pu·tres·cent (pū-tres′′nt), *adj.* [L. *putrescens*, ppr. of *putrescere* < *putrere* < *puter*, *putris*, rotten], 1. putrefying; rotting. 2. of or connected with putrefaction.

pu·tres·ci·ble (pū-tres′ə-b′l), *adj.* liable to undergo putrefaction. *n.* a putrescible substance.

pu·trid (pū′trid), *adj.* [Fr. *putride;* L. *putridus* < *putrere;* see PUTRESCENT; cf. PUS], 1. decomposed; rotten and foul-smelling. 2. causing, showing, or proceeding from decay. 3. morally corrupt; depraved. 4. [Colloq.], very disagreeable or unpleasant. —*SYN.* see **stinking**.

pu·trid·i·ty (pū-trid′ə-ti), *n.* 1. the state or quality of being putrid. 2. putrid matter.

‡**Putsch** (pooch), *n.* [G. < Swiss dial.; lit., a push, blow], an uprising or rebellion, especially an unsuccessful or minor one.

putt (put), *n.* [< *put, v.*], in *golf*, a light stroke made on the putting green in an attempt to get the ball into the hole. *v.t. & v.i.* to hit (the ball) with such a stroke.

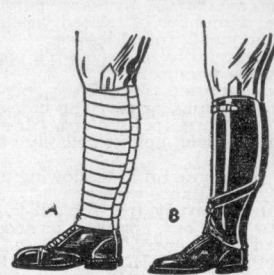

put·tee (pu-tē′, put′i), *n.* [Hind. *paṭṭī*, a bandage; Sans. *paṭṭa*, a strip of cloth], a covering for the lower leg, in the form of a cloth or leather gaiter or a cloth strip wound spirally: also **puttie, putty.**

PUTTEES
A, spiral cloth; B, leather

put·ter (poot′ẽr), *n.* a person or thing that puts.

putt·er (put′ẽr), *n.* 1. in *golf*, a short, straight-faced club used in putting: see **golf club**, illus. 2. a person who putts.

put·ter (put′ẽr), *v.i.* [var. of *potter*], to busy oneself or proceed in a trifling, ineffective, or aimless way; dawdle (often with *over*, *along*, *around*, etc.). *v.t.* to dawdle or fritter (with *away*). *n.* a puttering. Also **potter.**

put·ti·er (put′i-ẽr), *n.* a person who works with putty, as a glazier.

putt·ing green (put′iŋ), in *golf*, the area of smooth, closely mowed turf in which the hole is sunk.

put·ty (put′i), *n.* [Fr. *potée*, calcined tin, brass, lit., potful < *pot*, a pot], 1. a soft, plastic mixture of finely powdered chalk and linseed oil, used in fixing glass panes, filling small cracks, etc. 2. any substance like this in consistency, use, etc. 3. putty powder. 4. a cement of quicklime and water, mixed with plaster of Paris or sand for use as a finishing coat in plastering. *v.t.* [PUTTIED (-id), PUTTYING], to cement, fix, cover, or fill with putty.

put·ty (put′i), *n.* [*pl.* PUTTIES (-iz)], a puttee.

putty knife, a knife for applying putty.

putty powder, powdered oxide of tin, or of tin and lead, used for polishing glass or metals.

put·ty·root (put′i-rōōt′, put′i-root′), *n.* an orchid with yellowish-brown flowers, one leaf at the base of the stem, and a sticky substance in its bulbs.

Pu·tu·ma·yo (pōō′tōō-mä′yô), *n.* a river flowing between Colombia and Peru, through Brazil, into the Amazon: length, 975 mi.: Brazilian name, *Içá*.

put-up (poot′up′), *adj.* [< phrase *put up* (sense 9)], [Colloq.], planned beforehand in an underhand manner as, a *put-up* job.

Pu·vis de Cha·vannes, Pierre (pyâr′ pü′vē′ də shá′vän′), 1824–1898; French painter.

Pu-yi, Henry (pōō′yē′), (*Hsüan T'ung*), 1906– ; last emperor of China (1908–1912); abdicated; ruler of Manchukuo (1932–1945); abdicated.

puz·zle (puz′′l), *v.t.* [PUZZLED (-′ld), PUZZLING], [ME **poselen* (inferred < pp. *poselet*), to bewilder, confuse prob. freq. < *posen*, to pose (a question, etc.); cf. POSE] to perplex; confuse; nonplus. *v.i.* 1. to be perplexed etc. 2. to exercise one's mind, as over the solution of a problem. *n.* 1. the state of being puzzled; bewilderment. 2. a question, problem, etc. that puzzles. 3. a toy or problem for exercising mental ingenuity.

puzzle out, to solve by deep thought, study, etc.

puzzle over, to give deep thought to; concentrate on

SYN.—**puzzle** implies such a baffling quality or such intricacy as of a problem, situation, etc., that one has great difficulty in understanding or solving it; **perplex**, in addition, implies uncertainty or even worry as to what to think, say, or do; **confuse** implies a mixing up mentally to a greater or lesser degree; **confound** implies such confusion as completely frustrates or greatly astonishes one; **bewilder** implies such utter confusion that the mind is staggered beyond the ability to think clearly; to **nonplus** is to cause such perplexity or confusion that one is utterly incapable of speaking, acting, or thinking further; **dum(b)-found** specifically implies as its effect a nonplussed or confounded state in which one is momentarily struck speechless See also **mystery.**

puz·zle·ment (puz′′l-mənt), *n.* the state of being puzzled; bewilderment; perplexity.

puz·zler (puz′lẽr), *n.* a person or thing that puzzles.

Pvt., Private.

PWA, P.W.A., Public Works Administration.

P.W.D., Public Works Department.

pwt., pennyweight.

PX (pē′eks′), post exchange.

pxt., *pinxit*, [L.], he (or she) painted it.

py- (pī), pyo-.

py·ae·mi·a (pī-ē′mi-ə), *n.* pyemia.

py·ae·mic (pī-ē′mik), *adj.* pyemic.

pyc·nid·i·um (pik-nid′i-əm), *n.* [*pl.* PYCNIDIA (-ə)] [Mod. L. < Gr. *pyknos*, thick + dim. suffix *-idion* (L. *-idium*)], the spore case of certain fungi.

pyc·nom·e·ter (pik-nom′ə-tẽr), *n.* [< Gr. *pyknos*, thick dense; + *-meter*], a vessel used to measure the density of liquids or solids.

Pyd·na (pid′nə), *n.* an ancient city in Macedonia: scene of a battle (168 B.C.) in which the Romans defeated the Macedonians.

pye (pī), *n.* a pie (table).

py·e·li·tis (pī′ə-lī′tis), *n.* [Mod. L. < Gr. *pyelos*, basin (cf. PELVIS); + *-itis*], inflammation of the pelvis of the kidney.

py·e·lo·gram (pī′ə-lə-gram′), *n.* an X-ray picture taken by pyelography.

py·e·lo·graph (pī′ə-lə-graf′, pī′ə-lə-gräf′), *n.* a pyelogram.

py·e·log·ra·phy (pī′ə-log′rə-fi), *n.* [< Gr. *pyelos*, basin; + *-graphy*], the art of taking X-ray pictures of the kidney and ureter after filling them with some radio-opaque solution.

py·e·mi·a (pī-ē′mi-ə), *n.* [Mod. L.; *py-* + *-emia* < Gr. *-aimia* < *haima*, blood], a condition of infection caused by the presence in the blood of pus-producing micro-organisms that are carried to various parts of the body, producing abscesses, fever, chill, etc.: also spelled **pyaemia.**

py·e·mic (pī-ē′mik), *adj.* of, characterized by, or having pyemia: also spelled **pyaemic.**

py·gid·i·um (pi-jid′i-əm), *n.* [*pl.* PYGIDIA (-ə)], [Mod. L. < Gr. *pygidion*, dim. of *pygē*, rump], in *zoology*, the end division of the body of an insect or a trilobite.

pyg·mae·an, pyg·me·an (pig-mē′ən), *adj.* [L. *pygmaeus*], pygmy.

Pyg·ma·li·on (pig-māl′yən, pig-mā′li-ən), *n.* [L.; Gr. *Pygmaliōn*], 1. in *Greek legend*, a king of Cyprus, and a sculptor, who fell in love with his statue of a maiden, Galatea, later brought to life by Aphrodite at his prayer. 2. a comedy (1912) by G. B. Shaw.

Pyg·my (pig′mi), *n.* [*pl.* PYGMIES (-miz)], [ME. *pigmey*; L. *pygmaeus*; Gr. *pygmaios*, of the length of the *pygmē*, forearm and fist], 1. any of several races of African and Asiatic dwarfs described in ancient history and legend. 2. a person belonging to any of several modern races of African (*Negrillo*) and Asiatic (*Negrito*) dwarfs. 3. [p-], any person, animal, or plant abnormally undersized; a dwarf. 4. [p-], an insignificant person or thing. *adj.* 1. of the Pygmies. 2. [p-], very small. 3. [p-], insignificant. Also spelled **Pigmy.** —*SYN.* see **dwarf.**

py·ic (pī′ik), *adj.* [*py-* + *-ic*], of pus; purulent.

py·in (pī′in), *n.* [*py-* + *-in*], a protein substance found in pus.

py·ja·mas (pə-jam′əz, pə-jä′məz), *n.pl.* pajamas: British spelling.

pyk·nic (pik′nik), *adj.* [< Gr. *pyknos*, compact, solid; + *-ic*], in *psychology*, designating or having a body type characterized by roundness of contour, squatness, fleshiness, etc. *n.* a person of the pyknic type.

Pyle, Er·nie (ũr′ni pīl), (*Ernest Taylor Pyle*), 1900–1945; American newspaper correspondent, killed in World War II.

Pyle, Howard, 1853–1911; American illustrator, painter, and writer.

py·lon (pī′lon), *n.* [Gr. *pylōn*, gateway], 1. a gateway. 2. a truncated pyramid, or two of these, serving as a gateway to an Egyptian temple. 3. any slender, towering structure flanking an entranceway, supporting telegraph wires, marking a course in an air race, etc.

py·lo·rec·to·my (pī′lə-rek′tə-mi), *n.* [see -ECTOMY], the surgical removal of the pylorus.

py·lor·ic (pī-lôr′ik, pə-lor′ik), *adj.* of the pylorus.

py·lo·rus (pī-lôr′əs, pə-lō′rəs), *n.* [*pl.* PYLORI (-ī, -rī)], [LL.; Gr. *pylōros*, gatekeeper < *pylē*, a gate + *ouros*, watchman], the opening from the stomach into the duodenum, the first part of the small intestine: see **pancreas,** illus.

Pym, John (pim), 1584–1643; English statesman; upheld the rights of Parliament against Charles I.

py·o- (pī′ō, pī′ə), [< Gr. *pyon*, pus], a combining form meaning: 1. *pus*, as in *pyogenic*. 2. *suppurative*, as in *pyosis*. Also **py-,** as in *pyemia*.

py·o·gen·e·sis (pī′ə-jen′ə-sis), *n.* [*pyo-* + *-genesis*], in *medicine*, the formation of pus; pyosis.

py·o·gen·ic (pī′ə-jen′ik), *adj.* [*pyo-* + *-genic*], producing pus.

py·oid (pī′oid), *adj.* [*py-* + *-oid*], of or like pus.

Pyong·yang (pyŏŋ′yäŋ′), *n.* a capital of Korea (see **Korea**): pop., 235,000.

py·or·rhe·a, py·or·rhoe·a (pī′ə-rē′ə), *n.* [Mod. L.; see PYO- & -RRHEA], a discharge of pus; especially, pyorrhea alveolaris.

pyorrhea al·ve·o·la·ris (al-vē′ə-lâr′is), an infection of the gums and tooth sockets, characterized by the formation of pus and, usually, by loosening of the teeth.

py·or·rhe·al, py·or·rhoe·al (pī′ə-rē′əl), *adj.* of, having the nature of, or characterized by pyorrhea.

py·o·sis (pī-ō′sis), *n.* [Mod. L.; Gr. *pyōsis*], the formation or discharge of pus; suppuration.

pyr-, pyro-.

py·ral·i·dan (pī-ral′i-dən), *adj.* & *n.* pyralidid.

py·ral·i·did (pī-ral′i-did), *adj.* [< Mod. L. *Pyralididae*, name of the family < L. *pyralis*, *pyralidis*, kind of flying insect; Gr. *pyralis* < *pyr*, a fire: because supposed to live in or on fire], of a family of small moths with narrow, triangular forewings, broader hind wings, and long legs. *n.* a moth of this family.

pyr·a·mid (pir′ə-mid), *n.* [Fr. *pyramide*; L. *pyramis*; Gr. *pyramis*, *pyramidos*, a pyramid; ME. had *piramis* < L.], 1. a huge structure with a square base and four triangular sides meeting at a point, built by the ancient Egyptians as a royal tomb. 2. an object or formation shaped like a pyramid. 3. in *crystallography*, a form in which the faces intersect the vertical and lateral axes. 4. in *geometry*, a solid figure having a polygonal base, the sides of which form the bases of triangular surfaces meeting at a common vertex. 5. a tree grown or trained in pyramidal form. *v.i.* & *v.t.* 1. to build up in the form of a pyramid; collect in a mass or heap. 2. to engage in (a series of buying or selling operations) during an upward or downward trend in the stock market, working on margin with the profits made in the transactions.

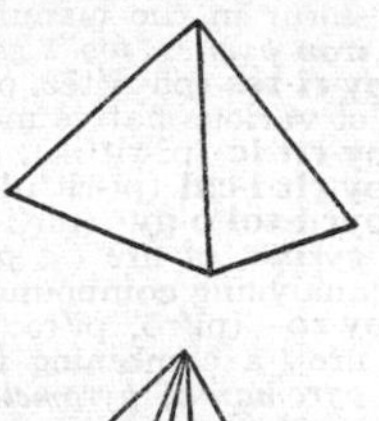

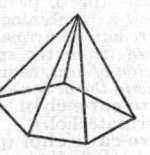

PYRAMIDS

the (Great) Pyramids, the three large pyramids at El Gîza, Egypt: the largest is the Pyramid of Cheops.

py·ram·i·dal (pi-ram′ə-d'l), *adj.* [ML. *pyramidalis*], 1. of a pyramid. 2. having the shape of a pyramid.

py·ram·i·dal·ly (pi-ram′ə-d'l-i), *adv.* in a pyramidal form.

pyr·a·mid·ic (pir′ə-mid′ik), *adj.* pyramidal.

pyr·a·mid·i·cal (pir′ə-mid′i-k'l), *adj.* pyramidal.

Pyr·a·mus and This·be (pir′ə-məs 'n thiz′bi), [L.; Gr. *Pyramos* & L.; Gr. *Thisbē*], Babylonian lovers whose story is told in Ovid's *Metamorphoses*: Pyramus, believing Thisbe killed by a lion when he finds her blood-stained veil at their trysting place, kills himself; and Thisbe, when she finds him dying, kills herself.

py·ran (pī′ran, pī-ran′), *n.* [< *pyrone*], any of a group of closed-chain compounds, C_5H_6O, the ring of which contains one oxygen atom and five carbon atoms.

py·rar·gy·rite (pī-rär′jə-rīt′), *n.* [< Gr. *pyr*, a fire + *argyros*, silver; + *-ite*], a lustrous, dark-red or black mineral, $3Ag_2S \cdot Sb_2S_3$, a sulfide of silver and antimony.

pyre (pīr), *n.* [L. *pyra*; Gr. *pyra* < *pyr*, a fire], a pile of wood on which a dead body is burned; funeral pile.

py·rene (pī′rēn), *n.* [Mod. L. *pyrena* < Gr. *pyrēn*, stone of a fruit], the seed or stone of apples, pears, etc.

Pyr·e·ne·an (pêr′ə-nē′ən), *adj.* of the Pyrenees.

Pyr·e·nees (pêr′ə-nēz′), *n.pl.* a mountain range between France and Spain: highest point, Pico de Aneto.

py·re·thrum (pī-rē′thrəm), *n.* [L.; Gr. *pyrethron*, feverfew < *pyr*, a fire], 1. a kind of chrysanthemum with long stems, finely cut leaves, and white, purplish, or red flowers. 2. an insect powder made from certain chrysanthemums.

py·ret·ic (pī-ret′ik), *adj.* [Mod. L. *pyreticus* < Gr. *pyretos*, burning heat, fever < *pyr*, a fire], 1. of or causing fever. 2. feverish.

pyr·e·tol·o·gy (pir′ə-tol′ə-ji, pī′rə-tol′ə-ji), *n.* [< Gr. *pyretos* (see PYRETIC); + *-logy*], the branch of medicine which deals with fevers.

py·rex (pī′reks), *n.* [< *pie* + L. *rex*, king; spelled as if < Gr. *pyr*, a fire, *pyra*, hearth], a heat-resistant glassware for cooking, etc.: a trade-mark (**Pyrex**).

py·rex·i·a (pī-rek′si-ə), *n.* [Mod. L. < Gr. *pyrexis*, feverishness < *pyressein*, to be feverish < *pyretos*; see PYRETIC], fever.

py·rex·i·al (pī-rek′si-əl), *adj.* of or having pyrexia.

py·rex·ic (pī-rek′sik), *adj.* pyrexial.

pyr·he·li·om·e·ter (pir-hē′li-om′ə-tẽr, pir-hē′li-om′ə-tẽr), *n.* [*pyr-* + *helio-* + *-meter*], an instrument for measuring the amount of energy given off by the sun.

pyr·i·din (pir′ə-din), *n.* pyridine.

pyr·i·dine (pir′ə-dēn′, pir′ə-din), *n.* [*pyrrol* + *-id* + *-ine*], a colorless or pale-yellow liquid, C_5H_5N, having a sharp, penetrating odor, produced in the distillation of coal tar or bone oil and used as a solvent, alcohol denaturant, antiseptic, etc.

pyr·i·dox·ine (pir′ə-dok′sēn, pir′ə-dok′sin), *n.* [< *pyridine* + *oxy-* + *-ine*], a complex pyridine compound, one of the B complex vitamins, found in various foods and prepared synthetically, usually as the hydrochloride: known to prevent nutritional dermatitis in rats: also called *vitamin* B_6.

pyr·i·form (pir′ə-fôrm′), *adj.* [Mod. L. *pyriformis* < ML. *pyrum*, for L. *pirum*, pear; see -FORM], pear-shaped.

py·rim·i·dine (pi-rim′ə-dēn′, pir′im-ə-din), *n.* [after G. *pyrimidin* < *pyridin* (cf. PYRIDINE)], a colorless, crystalline organic compound, $C_4H_4N_2$, the fundamental form of a group of bases, some of which are constituents of nucleic acid.

py·rite (pī′rīt), *n.* [*pl.* PYRITES (pə-rī′tēz, pī-rī′tēz, pī′rīts)], [L. *pyrites* < Gr. *pyritēs*, flint or millstone < *pyritēs* (*lithos*), fire (stone) < *pyr*, a fire], iron sulfide,

fat, āpe, bâre, cär; ten, ēven, hêre, ovẽr; is, bīte; lot, gō, hôrn, tōōl, look; oil, out; up, ūse, fũr; get; joy; yet; chin; she; thin, then; zh, leisure; ŋ, ring; ə for *a* in *ago*, *e* in *agent*, *i* in *sanity*, *o* in *comply*, *u* in *focus*; ' as in *able* (ā′b'l); Fr. bál; ë, Fr. coeur; ö, Fr. feu; Fr. mon; ô, Fr. coq; ü, Fr. duc; H, G. ich; kh, G. doch. See pp. x–xii. ‡ foreign; * hypothetical; < derived from.

FeS_2, a lustrous, yellow mineral occurring abundantly as a native ore and serving principally as a source of sulfur in the manufacture of sulfuric acid: also called *iron pyrites, fool's gold.*

py·ri·tes (pə-rī′tēz, pī-rī′tēz, pī′rīts), *n.* [see PYRITE], any of various native metallic sulfides, as pyrite.

py·rit·ic (pī-rit′ik), *adj.* of, like, or containing pyrites.

py·rit·i·cal (pī-rit′i-k'l), *adj.* pyritic.

pyr·i·tol·o·gy (pir′i-tol′ə-ji, pī′ri-tol′ə-ji), *n.* [< Gr. *pyritēs*, of fire (< *pyr*, a fire); + *-logy*], the science of analyzing compounds by means of the blowpipe.

py·ro- (pī′rō, pī′rə; *occas.* pir′ə), [< Gr. *pyr*, *pyros*, a fire], a combining form meaning: 1. *fire, heat*, as in *pyromania*, *pyrometer*. 2. in *chemistry, a substance derived* (from the specified substance) *by* or *as if by the action of heat*, as in *pyrogallol*. 3. in *geology, a formation due to the action of heat*, as in *pyroxenite*. Also **pyr-**.

py·ro·cat·e·chin (pī′rə-kat′ə-chin, pī′rə-kat′ə-kin), *n.* pyrocatechol.

py·ro·cat·e·chol (pī′rə-kat′ə-kōl′, pī′rə-kat′ə-chōl′, pī′-rə-kat′ə-kol′), *n.* [*pyro-* + *catechu* + *-ol*], a white, crystalline substance, $C_6H_4(OH)_2$, occurring naturally in plants or produced by dry distillation of catechu, etc.

py·ro·chem·i·cal (pī′rə-kem′i-k'l), *adj.* of chemistry at high temperatures.

py·ro·clas·tic (pī′rə-klas′tik), *adj* [*pyro-* + *clastic*], made up of rock material broken into fragments through volcanic or igneous action.

py·ro·con·duc·tiv·i·ty (pī′rə-kon′duk-tiv′ə-ti), *n.* conductivity effected in certain electric insulators when they are subjected to high temperatures.

py·ro·crys·tal·line (pī′rə-kris′t'l-in, pī′rə-kris′t'l-īn′), *adj.* crystallized from molten rock material.

py·ro·e·lec·tric (pī′rō-i-lek′trik), *adj.* of or showing pyroelectricity. *n.* a pyroelectric substance.

py·ro·e·lec·tric·i·ty (pī′rō-i-lek′tris′ə-ti), *n.* the development of electric polarity in certain crystals by a change of temperature: abbreviated **pyroelec.**

py·ro·gal·late (pī′rə-gal′āt), *n.* a salt or ether of pyrogallol.

py·ro·gal·lic acid (pī′rə-gal′ik), pyrogallol.

py·ro·gal·lol (pī′rə-gal′ōl, pī′rə-gal′ol), *n.* [*pyro-* + *gallic* + *-ol*], a white, crystalline phenol, $C_6H_3(OH)_3$, produced by heating gallic acid, and used in medicine, as a developer in photography, etc.

py·ro·gen·ic (pī′rə-jen′ik), *adj.* [*pyro-* + *genic*], 1. producing, or produced by, heat or fever. 2. in *geology*, igneous.

py·rog·e·nous (pī-roj′ə-nəs), *adj.* pyrogenic.

py·rog·nos·tics (pī′rog-nos′tiks), *n.pl.* [< *pyro-* + Gr. *gnōstikos*, knowing], the characteristics of a mineral, including fusibility, flame coloration, etc., as determined by the use of a blowpipe.

py·rog·ra·pher (pī-rog′rə-fẽr), *n.* a person skilled in pyrography.

py·ro·graph·ic (pī′rə-graf′ik), *adj.* of pyrography.

py·rog·ra·phy (pī-rog′rə-fi), *n.* [*pyro-* + *-graphy*], 1. the art or process of burning designs on wood or leather by the use of heated tools. 2. a design so made.

py·ro·lig·ne·ous (pī′rə-lig′ni-əs), *adj.* [Fr. *pyroligneux* < *pyro-* + L. *lignum*, wood], 1. produced by the destructive distillation of wood. 2. designating or of a reddish-brown liquid (*pyroligneous acid*), chiefly acetic acid and methyl alcohol, obtained by the destructive distillation of wood. 3. designating or of methyl alcohol, especially when obtained from wood.

py·rol·o·gy (pī-rol′ə-ji), *n.* pyritology.

py·ro·lu·site (pī′rə-lōō′sit, pī′rə-lū′sit, pī-rol′yoo-sīt′), *n.* [< *pyro-* + Gr. *lousis*, a washing (< *louein*, to wash); + *-ite*], native manganese dioxide, MnO_2, a gray or black, lustrous mineral, used in glassmaking, etc.

py·rol·y·sis (pī-rol′ə-sis), *n.* [Mod. L.; *pyro-* + *-lysis*], chemical decomposition by heat.

py·ro·lyt·ic (pī′rə-lit′ik), *adj.* of pyrolysis.

py·ro·mag·net·ic (pī′rō-mag-net′ik), *adj.* of or produced by the combined action of heat and magnetism.

py·ro·man·cy (pī′rə-man′si), *n.* [ME. & OFr. *piromance*; LL. *pyromantia*; cf. PYRO- & -MANCY], a foretelling of the future by the interpretation of flames.

py·ro·ma·ni·a (pī′rə-mā′ni-ə), *n.* [Mod. L.; *pyro-* + *-mania*], a persistent compulsion to start destructive fires.

py·ro·ma·ni·ac (pī′rə-mā′ni-ak′), *n.* a person having pyromania. *adj.* of or affected with pyromania.

py·ro·ma·ni·a·cal (pī′rō-mə-nī′ə-k'l), *adj.* pyromaniac.

py·rom·e·ter (pī-rom′ə-tẽr), *n.* [*pyro-* + *-meter*], an instrument with which unusually high temperatures, beyond the range of ordinary thermometers, are measured, as by the change of electric current.

py·ro·met·ric (pī′rə-met′rik), *adj.* of or registered on a pyrometer.

py·ro·met·ri·cal (pī′rə-met′ri-k'l), *adj.* pyrometric.

py·rom·e·try (pī-rom′ə-tri), *n.* [*pyro-* + *-metry*], the branch of physics which treats of the measurement of temperatures over 1500° C.

py·ro·mor·phite (pī′rə-môr′fit), *n.* [G. *pyromorphit*; see PYRO- & -MORPH & -ITE], a lead chloride and phosphate, $3Pb_3(PO_4)_2 \cdot PbCl_2$, occurring naturally in any of various colors.

py·rone (pī′rōn, pī-rōn′), *n.* [G. *pyron*; contr. < *pyrokoman*], an unsaturated, closed-chain compound, $C_5H_4O_2$, from which several yellow dyes are derived.

py·rope (pī′rōp), *n.* [ME.; OFr. *pirope*; L. *pyropus*, red bronze; Gr. *pyrōpus*, lit., fiery-eyed < *pyr*, fire + *ōps*, the eye], a variety of garnet, deep red to black in color, containing aluminum and used as a gem.

py·ro·pho·bi·a (pī′rə-fō′bi-ə), *n.* [*pyro-* + *-phobia*], an irrational fear of fire.

py·ro·phor·ic (pī′rə-fôr′ik, pī′rə-for′ik), *adj.* [< Gr. *pyrophoros* < *pyr*, a fire + *pherein*, to bear], capable of igniting spontaneously when exposed to air.

py·ro·phos·phor·ic acid (pī′rō-fos-fôr′ik, pī′rō-fos-for′-ik), [*pyro-* + *phosphoric*], a viscous liquid acid, $H_4P_2O_7$, which crystallizes when left standing at ordinary temperatures and is easily converted to orthophosphoric acid upon dilution with water.

py·ro·pho·tom·e·ter (pī′rō-fō-tom′ə-tẽr), *n.* [*pyro-* + *photometer*], an optical instrument for the measurement of extremely high temperatures.

py·ro·phyl·lite (pī′rə-fil′īt), *n.* [*pyro-* + *phyll-* + *-ite*] a hydrous aluminum silicate, $Al_2O_3 \cdot 4SiO_2 \cdot H_2O$, resembling talc in structure and color, used for polishing rice, as a filler for slate pencils, etc.

py·ro·sis (pī-rō′sis), *n.* [Mod. L.; Gr. *pyrōsis*, a burning < *pyroun*, to burn < *pyr*, a fire], a condition characterized by a burning sensation in the stomach and esophagus and the belching of an acid fluid; heartburn.

py·ro·stat (pī′rə-stat′), *n.* [*pyro-* + *-stat*], 1. a device that automatically puts into action a mechanism sounding an alarm when a fire breaks out near by. 2. a thermostat for high temperatures.

py·ro·sul·fate (pī′rə-sul′fāt), *n.* a salt of pyrosulfuric acid: also called *disulfate.*

py·ro·sul·fur·ic acid (pī′rō-sul-fyoor′ik), [*pyro-* + *sulfuric*], a strong, crystalline acid, $H_2S_2O_7$, prepared commercially as a heavy, oily, fuming liquid: also called *disulfuric acid.*

py·ro·tech·nic (pī′rə-tek′nik), *adj.* [Fr. *pyrotechnique* < *pyro-* + Gr. *technē*, art], 1. of fireworks. 2. brilliant dazzling: as, *pyrotechnic* wit.

py·ro·tech·ni·cal (pī′rə-tek′ni-k'l), *adj.* pyrotechnic.

py·ro·tech·nics (pī′rə-tek′niks), *n.pl.* [construed as sing.], [see PYROTECHNIC], 1. the art of making and using fireworks. 2. a display of fireworks. 3. a dazzling display, as of eloquence, wit, etc.

py·ro·tech·nist (pī′rə-tek′nist), *n.* a person skilled in pyrotechnics.

py·ro·tech·ny (pī′rə-tek′ni), *n.* [Fr. *pyrotechnie*], pyrotechnics (senses 1 & 2).

py·ro·tox·in (pī′rə-tok′sin), *n.* a toxin that induces fever.

py·rox·ene (pī′rok-sēn′), *n.* [Fr. *pyroxène* < *pyro-* + Gr. *xenos*, a stranger: so named (by Haüy, Fr. mineralogist) as being foreign to igneous rocks], a complex silicate mineral, containing iron, magnesium, and calcium, found in igneous rocks.

py·rox·en·ic (pī′rok-sen′ik), *adj.* of or containing pyroxene.

py·rox·e·nite (pī-rok′sə-nīt′), *n.* a dark-colored, granular, igneous rock composed mainly of pyroxene.

py·rox·y·lin, py·rox·y·line (pī-rok′sə-lin), *n.* [Fr. *pyroxyline* < Gr. *pyr*, *pyros*, a fire + *xylon*, wood], nitrocellulose, especially in less highly nitrated and explosive forms than guncotton, used in the manufacture of paints, lacquers, collodion, celluloid, etc.

Pyr·rha (pir′ə), *n.* [L.; Gr. *Pyrrha*], in *Greek mythology* a survivor of a great deluge: see **Deucalion.**

pyr·rhic (pir′ik), *n.* [L. *pyrrhicha*; Gr. *pyrrhichē*, war dance: said to be after *Pyrrhichus*, inventor of the dance] a war dance of the ancient Greeks.

pyr·rhic (pir′ik), *n.* [L. *pyrrhichius*; Gr. *pyrrhichios* (*pous*), pyrrhic (foot)], a metrical foot of two short or unstressed syllables. *adj.* of or composed of pyrrhics

Pyr·rhic victory (pir′ik), [Gr. *Pyrrhikos*], a too costly victory: in reference to the victory of Pyrrhus, king of Epirus, over the Romans at Asculum in 279 B.C., in which the losses were extremely heavy.

Pyr·rho·nism (pir′ə-niz'm), *n.* 1. the doctrine taught by Pyrrho (365–275 B.C.), the Greek Skeptic, that all knowledge, including the testimony of the senses, is uncertain; hence, 2. extreme skepticism.

pyr·rho·tine (pir′ə-tin), *n.* pyrrhotite.

pyr·rho·tite (pir′ə-tīt′), *n.* [< Gr. *pyrrhotēs*, redness (< *pyrrhos*, flame-colored < *pyr*, a fire); + *-ite*], any of several bronze-colored, lustrous native sulfides of iron, often containing small amounts of copper, cobalt, and nickel.

Pyr·rhus (pir′əs), *n.* 1. king of Epirus (295–272 B.C.) lived 318–272 B.C. 2. in *Greek legend*, Achilles' son

pyr·role, pyr·rol (pī-rōl′, pī′rōl), *n.* [G. *pyrrol* < Gr. *pyrros*, fiery + L. *oleum*, oil], a colorless, pungent slightly basic liquid, C_4H_5N, found in bile pigments chlorophyll, and hematin, and obtained from coal tar bone oil, etc. by distillation.

py·ru·vic acid (pī-rōō′vik, pi-rōō′vik), [< *pyr-* + L. *uva*, grape; + *-ic*], a colorless, liquid organic acid CH_3COCO_2H, obtained by the dry distillation of racemic acid or ether.

Py·thag·o·ras (pi-thag′ẽr-əs), *n.* Greek philosopher and mathematician; lived 6th century B.C.

Py·thag·o·re·an (pi-thag′ə-rē′ən), *adj.* of Pythagoras, his philosophy and teachings, or his followers. *n.* a follower of Pythagoras.

Py·thag·o·re·an·ism (pi-thag′ə-rē′ən-iz′m), *n.* the philosophy of Pythagoras, the main tenets of which were the transmigration of the soul and the belief in numbers as the ultimate elements of the universe.

Pyth·i·a (pith′i-ə), *n.* [Gr.], in ancient Greece, the high priestess of the oracle of Apollo at Delphi.

Pyth·i·ad (pith′i-ad′), *n.* [< Gr. *Pythios;* see PYTHIAN], the period of four years from one celebration of the Pythian games to the next.

Pyth·i·an (pith′i-ən), *adj.* [L. *Pythius;* Gr. *Pythios,* of *Pytho,* older name for Delphi and its environs], 1. of Apollo as patron of Delphi and the oracle located there. 2. designating or of the games held at Delphi every four years by the ancient Greeks in honor of Apollo.

Pythias, see **Damon and Pythias.**

Pyth·ic (pith′ik), *adj.* of Pythia or her prophecies.

Py·thon (pī′thon; *for 2 a & b, usually* pī′thən), *n.* [L.; Gr. *Pythōn* < *Pytho;* see PYTHIAN], 1. in *Greek mythology,* an enormous serpent that lurked in the cave of Mount Parnassus and was slain by Apollo. 2. [p-], *a)* any of a group of very large, nonpoisonous snakes of Burma, Indo-China, etc. that crush their prey to death. *b)* any large snake that crushes its prey, as the boa.

py·tho·ness (pī′thə-nis), *n.* [ME. *phitonesse;* OFr. *phitonise;* ML. *phytonissa;* LL. *pythonissa* < Gr. *Pytho,* familiar spirit], 1. the priestess of Apollo at Delphi. 2. any woman soothsayer; prophetess.

py·thon·ic (pi-thon′ik), *adj.* [LL. *pythonicus,* prophetic; Gr. *pythōnikos* < *Pytho,* familiar spirit], of or like an oracle; oracular; prophetic.

py·thon·ic (pi-thon′ik), *adj.* of or like a python.

py·u·ri·a (pi-yoor′i-ə), *n.* [*py-* + *uria*], the presence of pus in the urine.

pyx (piks), *n.* [ME. *pixe;* L. *pyxis;* Gr. *pyxis,* a box < *pyxos,* the box tree], 1. *a)* the container in which the consecrated wafer of the Eucharist is kept. *b)* a small container for carrying the Eucharist to the sick. 2. a box in the British mint, in which specimen coins are placed until the annual test for purity and weight. Also spelled **pix.**

pyx·id·i·um (pik-sid′i-əm), *n.* [*pl.* PYXIDIA (-ə)], [Mod. L.; Gr. *pyxidion,* dim. of *pyxis,* a box; see PYX], in *botany,* a seedcase with two parts, the upper acting as a lid.

PYXIDIUM

pyx·ie (pik′si), *n.* [prob. < the botanical name, *Pyxidanthera barbulata*], a creeping evergreen plant with small, leathery leaves and white, star-shaped flowers.

Pyx·is (pik′sis), *n.* [L., box (mariner's)], formerly, in *astronomy,* a subdivision of the constellation Argo: see **constellation,** chart.

pyx·is (pik′sis), *n.* [*pl.* PYXIDES (-sə-dēz′)], [ME.; see PYX], 1. a vase with a cover, used by the ancient Greeks and Romans. 2. a small box or case. 3. in *botany,* a pyxidium.

Q

Q, q (kū), *n.* [*pl.* Q's, q's, Qs, qs (kūz)], 1. the seventeenth letter of the English alphabet: from the Roman adoption of the early Greek *koppa,* a borrowing from the Phoenician: see **alphabet,** table. 2. the sound of Q or q: normally, in English, *q* is followed by *u,* and is pronounced (*kw*), as in *queen* (kwēn), or occasionally (*k*), as in *conquer* (koŋ′kẽr). 3. a type or impression for Q or q. 4. *a symbol for* the seventeenth in a sequence or group (or the sixteenth if J is omitted). *adj.* 1. of Q or q. 2. seventeenth (or sixteenth if J is omitted) in a sequence or group.

Q (kū), *n.* 1. an object shaped like Q. 2. a medieval Roman numeral for 500. *adj.* shaped like Q.

Q (kū), see **Quiller-Couch, Sir Arthur.**

Q, in *chess,* queen.

Q., 1. Quebec. 2. Queen. 3. Question.

q., 1. *quadrans,* [L.], farthing. 2. quart. 3. quarter. 4. quarterly. 5. quarto. 6. quasi. 7. queen. 8. query. 9. question. 10. quintal. 11. quire. 12. quotient.

Qa·ra Qum (kä-rä′ koom′), *n.* Kara Kum.

QB, in *chess,* queen's bishop.

Q.B., Queen's Bench.

Q.B., q.b., qb, in *football,* quarterback.

Q.C., Queen's Counsel.

q.e., *quod est,* [L.], which is.

Q.E.D., *quod erat demonstrandum,* [L.], which was to be proved.

Q.E.F., *quod erat faciendum,* [L.], which was to be done.

q.i.d. *quater in die,* [L.], four times a day.

Qishm (kish′'m), *n.* an island of Iran, in the Strait of Hormuz: area, 516 sq. mi.; pop., 30,000.

Qiz·il Qum (kiz′il koom′), Kizil Kum.

ql., quintal.

Q.M., Quartermaster.

Q.M.C., Quartermaster Corps.

Q.M.G., Quartermaster General.

qoph (kôf), *n.* koph.

q.pl., *quantum placet,* [L.], as much as you please.

qq. v., *quae vide,* [L.], which (words, etc.) see.

QR, in *chess,* queen's rook.

qr., [*pl.* QRS.], 1. *quadrans,* [L.], farthing. 2. quarter: also **qtr.** 3. quire.

q.s., 1. *quantum sufficit,* [L.], enough. 2. quarter section (of land).

qt., [*pl.* QTS.], 1. quantity. 2. quart.

Q.T., [Slang], quiet: usually in *on the Q.T.,* in secret.

qto., quarto.

qu., 1. quart. 2. quarter. 3. quarterly. 4. queen. 5. query. 6. question.

qua (kwā, kwä), *adv.* [L., abl. sing. fem. of *qui,* who; for IE. base see WHO], as; in the function, character, or capacity of: as, he will testify *qua* official.

quack (kwak), *v.i.* [echoic], to utter the sound or cry made by a duck, or a sound like it. *n.* the sound made by a duck, or any sound like it.

quack (kwak), *n.* [short for *quacksalver*], 1. an untrained person who practices medicine fraudulently. 2. a person who, with little or no foundation, pretends to have knowledge or skill in a particular field; charlatan. *adj.* 1. characterized by pretentious claims with little or no foundation. 2. dishonestly claiming to effect a cure. *v.i.* 1. to engage in quackery. 2. to talk with a pretension to knowledge one does not have.

***SYN.*—quack** and **charlatan** both apply to a person who unscrupulously pretends to knowledge or skill he does not possess, but **quack** almost always is used of a fraudulent or incompetent practitioner of medicine; **mountebank,** in modern use, applies to a person who resorts to cheap and degrading methods in his work, etc.; **impostor** applies especially to a person who fraudulently impersonates another and, more generally, to anyone who pretends to be what he is not; **faker** is a colloquial term for a person who falsely represents himself as being (in character, work, etc.) what he is not.

quack·er·y (kwak′ẽr-i), *n.* [*pl.* QUACKERIES (-iz)], the actions, claims, or methods of a quack.

quack grass, couch grass.

quack·ish (kwak′ish), *adj.* 1. like or characteristic of a quack. 2. boastfully pretentious.

quack·sal·ver (kwak′sal′vẽr), *n.* [Late MD. (D. *kwaksalver*) < *quacken,* to quack, brag, boast + *zalf,* salve], a quack; charlatan.

quad (kwäd), *n.* [Colloq.], a quadrangle (of a college).

quad (kwäd), *n.* in *printing,* a quadrat.

quad (kwäd), *n.* [Chiefly British Slang], a quod.

quad., quadrangle.

quadr-, quadri-.

quad·ra·ge·nar·i·an (kwäd′rə-ji-nâr′i-ən), *adj.* [L. *quadragenarius* < *quadrageni,* forty each < *quadraginta;* see next entry], forty years old, or between the ages of forty and fifty. *n.* a person of this age.

Quad·ra·ges·i·ma (kwäd′rə-jes′i-mə), *n.* [LL. < L. *quadragesimus*, fortieth < *quadraginta*, forty < base of *quattuor*, four], 1. [Obs.], the forty days of Lent. 2. the first Sunday in Lent: also **Quadragesima Sunday.**

quad·ra·ges·i·mal (kwäd′rə-jes′i-m'l), *adj.* [ML. *quadragesimalis;* see prec.], 1. lasting forty days: said of Lent. 2. [Q-], Lenten; of or suitable for Lent.

quad·ran·gle (kwäd′raŋ′g'l), *n.* [Fr.; LL. *quadrangulum* < L. *quadr-* < *quattuor*, four + *angulus*, an angle], 1. in *geometry*, a plane figure with four angles and four sides. 2. an area surrounded on its four sides by buildings. 3. the buildings surrounding a quadrangle. 4. the area of land charted on each of the atlas sheets published by the United States Geological Survey. Abbreviated **quad.**

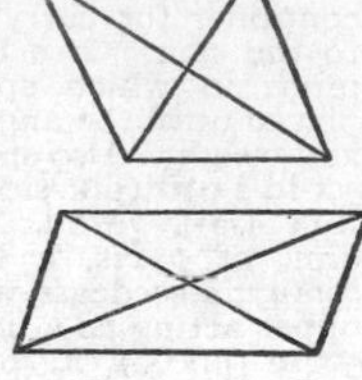

QUADRANGLES

quad·ran·gu·lar (kwäd-raŋ′gyoo-lẽr), *adj.* [LL. *quadrangularis*], having the form of a quadrangle; having four angles and four sides.

quad·rant (kwäd′rənt), *n.* [ML.; L. *quadrans*, fourth part; see QUADRI-], 1. a fourth part of the circumference of a circle; an arc of 90°. 2. a quarter section of a circle. 3. any piece or part shaped like a quarter section of a circle. 4. an instrument for measuring altitudes or angular elevations in astronomy and navigation: it consists of a graduated arc of 90° with a movable index and a sight. 5. in *analytic geometry*, any of the four parts formed by rectangular co-ordinate axes on a plane surface: the quadrants are designated as first, second, third, and fourth in counterclockwise order, starting with the upper right-hand section.

quad·ran·tal (kwäd-ran′t'l), *adj.* [L. *quadrantalis*], 1. shaped like a quadrant. 2. of a quadrant.

quad·rat (kwäd′rat), *n.* [ME.; var. of *quadrate, n.*], in *printing*, a piece of type metal lower than the face of the type, used for spacing, to fill blank lines, etc.: commonly shortened to **quad.**

quad·rate (kwäd′rāt; *also, for adj. & n.*, kwäd′rit), *adj.* [L. *quadratus*, pp. of *quadrare*, to make square < *quadrus*, a square < *quattuor*, four], 1. square or nearly square; rectangular. 2. in *zoology*, designating a bone or cartilage of the skull in birds, fishes, and reptiles, to which the lower jaw is joined. 3. in *astrology*, designating an aspect of heavenly bodies in which they are 90° distant from each other. *n.* [Late ME.; L. *quadratum* < *quadratus*], 1. a square or rectangle. 2. a square or rectangular space, thing, etc. 3. in *zoology*, the quadrate bone. *v.i.* [QUADRATED (-id), QUADRATING], to square; agree (followed by *with*). *v.t.* to make square; make (something) conform (*to*).

quad·rat·ic (kwäd-rat′ik), *adj.* [< *quadrate* + *-ic*], 1. square. 2. in *algebra*, involving a quantity or quantities that are squared but none that are raised to a higher power. *n.* in *algebra*, a quadratic term, expression, or equation.

quadratic equation, in *algebra*, an equation in which the second power, or square, is the highest to which the unknown quantity is raised.

quad·rat·ics (kwäd-rat′iks), *n.pl.* [construed as sing.], the branch of algebra dealing with quadratic equations.

quad·ra·ture (kwäd′rə-chẽr), *n.* [LL. *quadratura* < L. *quadratus;* see QUADRATE], 1. the act of squaring. 2. the determining of the dimensions of a square equal in area to a given surface, as in "the *quadrature* (or squaring) of the circle," a geometrically insoluble problem. 3. in *astronomy*, the relative position of two heavenly bodies when 90° distant from each other: as, the moon is in *quadrature* with the sun when, at either of two points in its orbit, it is half illumined.

quad·ren·ni·al (kwäd-ren′i-əl), *adj.* [< L. *quadriennium;* see QUADRENNIUM], 1. lasting four years. 2. occurring once every four years. *n.* a quadrennial event.

quad·ren·ni·al·ly (kwäd-ren′i-əl-i), *adv.* once every four years.

quad·ren·ni·um (kwäd-ren′i-əm), *n.* [*pl.* QUADRENNIA (-ə)], [L. *quadriennium* < *quadri-* (see QUADRI-) + *annus*, a year], a period of four years.

quad·ri- (kwäd′ri), [L. < base of *quattuor*, four; for IE. base and cognates see FOUR], a combining form meaning *four times, fourfold*, as in *quadrilingual:* also, before a vowel, **quadr-.**

quad·ric (kwäd′rik), *adj.* [< L. *quadra*, a square; + *-ic*], in *mathematics*, of the second degree: used of a function with more than two variables. *n.* a quantic of the second degree.

quad·ri·cen·ten·ni·al (kwäd′ri-sen-ten′i-əl), *n.* [*quadri-* + *centennial*], a 400th anniversary or its celebration. *adj.* of a quadricentennial.

quad·ri·ceps (kwäd′ri-seps′), *n.* [Mod. L.; *quadri-* + L. *-ceps* < *caput*, the head], a muscle with four heads, or points of origin; especially, the large muscle at the front of the thigh, which functions to extend the leg when contracted.

quad·ri·cy·cle (kwäd′rə-sī′k'l), *n.* a four-wheeled cycle, or velocipede.

quad·ri·fid (kwäd′rə-fid), *adj.* [L. *quadrifidus* < *quadri-*, four + *findere*, to divide], divided into four parts, as a leaf or petal.

quad·ri·ga (kwäd-rī′gə), *n.* [*pl.* QUADRIGAE (-jē)], [L., sing. of *quadrigae*, team of four < *quadri-* (see QUADRI-) + *jugum*, a yoke], in ancient Rome, a two-wheeled chariot drawn by four horses abreast.

quad·ri·lat·er·al (kwäd′rə-lat′ẽr-əl), *adj.* [< L. *quadrilaterus* (see QUADRI- & LATERAL); + *-al*], four-sided. *n.* 1. in *geometry*, a plane figure having four sides and four angles. 2. a four-sided area. 3. such an area protected by four fortresses.

quad·ri·lin·gual (kwäd′rə-liŋ′gwəl), *adj.* [< *quadri-* + L. *lingua*, the tongue; + *-al*], 1. written in, or involving, four languages. 2. using or speaking four languages.

QUADRILATERALS

qua·drille (kwə-dril′, kə-dril′), *n.* [Fr.; Sp. *cuadrilla*, dim. < *cuadro*, four-sided battle square < L. *quadra*, a square < *quadrus*, square; see QUADRI-], 1. a square dance of French origin, performed by four couples. 2. music for this dance.

qua·drille (kwə-dril′, kə-dril′), *n.* [Fr., altered (after *quadrille*, the dance) < Sp. *cuartillo*, dim. < *cuarto*, fourth < L. *quartus;* see QUART], a game of cards, popular in the 18th century, played by four persons.

quad·ril·lion (kwäd-ril′yən), *n.* [Fr.; *quadri-* (see QUADRI-) + *million*], 1. in the United States and France, the number represented by 1 followed by 15 zeros. 2. in Great Britain and Germany, the number represented by 1 followed by 24 zeros. *adj.* amounting to one quadrillion in number.

quad·ri·no·mi·al (kwäd′rə-nō′mi-əl), *n.* [*quadri-* + *binomial*], in *algebra*, an expression of four terms (e.g., $x^2 + xy - 3y + 2y^2$). *adj.* in *algebra*, consisting of four terms.

quad·ri·par·tite (kwäd′rə-pär′tīt), *adj.* [ME.; L. *quadripartitus*, pp. of *quadripartire*, to divide into four parts; see QUADRI- & PART], 1. made up of or divided into four parts. 2. shared in or formulated by four persons, nations, etc.: as, a *quadripartite* pact.

quad·ri·sect (kwäd′rə-sekt′), *v.t.* [< *quadri-* + L. *sectus*, pp. of *secare*, to cut], to divide into four equal parts.

quad·ri·syl·lab·ic (kwäd′rə-si-lab′ik), *adj.* of, or having the nature of, a quadrisyllable.

quad·ri·syl·la·ble (kwäd′rə-sil′ə-b'l), *n.* a word of four syllables.

quad·ri·va·lence (kwäd′rə-vā′ləns), *n.* the quality or state of being quadrivalent.

quad·ri·va·len·cy (kwäd′rə-vā′lən-si), *n.* quadrivalence.

quad·ri·va·lent (kwäd′rə-vā′lənt, kwäd-riv′ə-lənt), *adj.* 1. having four valences. 2. having a valence of four. Also, especially for 2, **tetravalent.**

quad·riv·i·al (kwäd-riv′i-əl), *adj.* [< L. *quadrivium*, meeting of four roads < *quadri-* (see QUADRI-) + *via*, road], 1. having four roads meeting in a point. 2. leading in four directions: said of roads or ways.

quad·riv·i·um (kwäd-riv′i-əm), *n.* [ML.; L.; see QUADRIVIAL], in the Middle Ages, the higher division of the seven liberal arts, consisting of arithmetic, geometry, astronomy, and music: cf. **trivium.**

quad·roon (kwäd-ro͞on′), *n.* [Sp. *cuarterón* < *cuarto* (L. *quartus*), a fourth], a person who has one Negro grandparent; child of a mulatto and a white.

quad·ru·mane (kwäd′roo-mān′), *n.* a quadrumanous animal; any of the primates except man.

quad·ru·ma·nous (kwäd-ro͞o′mə-nəs), *adj.* [formed (after *quadruped*) < L. *quadru-* (see QUADRUPED) + *manus*, a hand], in *zoology*, 1. having all four feet adapted to function as hands. 2. of a group of such primates, including monkeys, baboons, apes, etc.

quad·ru·ped (kwäd′roo-ped′), *n.* [L. *quadrupes; quadru-* (used for *quadri-*, especially before p), four + *pes*, a foot], an animal, especially a mammal, with four feet. *adj.* having four feet.

quad·ru·pe·dal (kwäd-ro͞o′pi-d'l, kwäd′roo-ped′'l), *adj.* 1. having four feet. 2. of a quadruped.

quad·ru·ple (kwäd′roo-p'l, kwäd-ro͞o′p'l), *adj.* [Fr.; L. *quadruplus; quadru-*, four (see QUADRUPED) + *-plus* as in *duplus;* see DOUBLE], 1. consisting of or including four. 2. four times as much or as many; fourfold. 3. in *music*, having four beats to the measure, the first and third beats being accented. *adv.* four times as much or as many. *n.* an amount four times as much or as many. *v.t. & v.i.* [QUADRUPLED (-p'ld), QUADRUPLING], to make or become four times as much or as many; multiply by four.

quad·ru·plet (kwäd′roo-plit, kwäd-ro͞o′plit), *n.* [< *quadruple*], 1. *a)* any of four offspring born at a single birth. *b)* *pl.* four offspring born at a single birth. 2. a collection or group of four, usually of one kind.

quadruple time (or **measure**), in *music*, 1. a measure having four beats, of which the first and third are accented. 2. the rhythm resulting from this.

quad·ru·plex (kwäd′roo-pleks′), *adj.* [L.; *quadru-* (see QUADRUPED) + *-plex*, -fold < base of *plaga*, region; see DUPLEX], 1. fourfold. 2. designating or of a system of telegraphy in which four messages can be sent simultaneously over one wire, two in either direction.

quad·ru·pli·cate (kwäd-rōō′plə-kāt′; *for adj. & n., usually* kwäd-rōō′plə-kit), *v.t.* [QUADRUPLICATED (-id), QUADRUPLICATING], [< L. *quadruplicatus*, pp. of *quadruplicare*, to quadruple; *quadru-* (see QUADRUPED) + *plicare*, to fold], to quadruple; make four identical copies of. *adj.* 1. fourfold. 2. in *mathematics*, raised to the fourth power. *n.* any of four copies that are exactly the same.

quad·ru·pli·ca·tion (kwäd-rōō′plə-kā′shən), *n.* [LL. *quadruplicatio*], 1. a quadruplicating. 2. the result of this; something quadruplicated.

‡**quae·re** (kwē′ri), *v. imperative* [L., imperative of *quaerere*, to ask, inquire], inquire; find out: used to express doubt or to suggest that certain information be sought. *n.* a query; question.

quaes·tor (kwes′tẽr, kwēs′tẽr), *n.* [L., contr. < *quaesitor* < *quaesitus*, pp. of *quaerere*, to inquire], in ancient Rome, 1. originally, an official who judged certain criminal cases. 2. later, any of certain state treasurers. Also **questor**.

quaes·to·ri·al (kwes-tôr′i-əl, kwēs-tō′ri-əl), *adj.* of a quaestor.

quaes·tor·ship (kwes′tẽr-ship′, kwēs′tẽr-ship′), *n.* [see -SHIP], the position, rank, or duties of a quaestor.

quaff (kwäf, kwaf), *v.t. & v.i.* [Early Mod. Eng.; prob. a ghost word < LG. *quassen*, to overindulge (in food and drink), printed *ss* being misread as *ff*; earlier forms *quaft*, *quaught* point to an unfamiliar word], to drink or swallow in large quantities and with pleasure. *n.* 1. a quaffing. 2. what is quaffed; a drink.

quag (kwag, kwäg), *n.* [var. of *quake*], a quagmire.

quag·ga (kwag′ə), *n.* [*pl.* QUAGGA, QUAGGAS (-əz); see PLURAL, II, D, 2], [< the native (Hottentot) name], a striped animal of South Africa, now extinct, resembling the donkey and the zebra.

quag·gy (kwag′i, kwäg′i), *adj.* [QUAGGIER (-i-ẽr), QUAGGIEST (-i-ist)], 1. like a quagmire; boggy; soft and miry. 2. soft; flabby.

quag·mire (kwag′mīr′, kwäg′mīr′), *n.* [earlier also *quakemire; quag* + *mire*], 1. wet, boggy ground, yielding under the feet. 2. a difficult position, as of one sinking or stuck in a quagmire.

qua·hog, qua·haug (kwô′hôg, kwə-hôg′), *n.* [Am. Ind. (Narraganset)], a kind of clam having a very hard, solid shell.

Quai d'Or·say (kā′ dôr′sā′; Fr. ke′ dôr′se′), [Fr., lit., quay of Orsay (former Fr. general)], 1. a quay on the Seine in Paris, toward which the building housing the French Foreign Office faces; hence, 2. the French Foreign Office.

quail (kwāl), *v.i.* [ME. *quailen;* prob. < OFr. *coaillier* (L. *coagulare*), to coagulate], to draw back in fear; lose heart or courage; cower. —*SYN.* see **recoil**.

quail (kwāl), *n.* [*pl.* QUAILS (kwālz), QUAIL; see PLURAL, II, D, 1], [ME. *quaile;* OFr. *quaille, caille;* ML. *cuacula;* prob. < Gmc. echoic name (cf. D. *kwakkel*)], any of various game birds of America, Europe, Asia, and Africa, resembling domestic fowls: also called *partridge* or *bobwhite* in certain parts of the United States.

quaint (kwānt), *adj.* [ME. *cointe, queint;* OFr. *cointe, queinte* < L. *cognitus*, known; see COGNITION], 1. [Obs.], clever. 2. [Archaic], wrought with skill. 3. pleasingly odd and antique. 4. singular; unusual; curious. 5. fanciful; whimsical. —*SYN.* see **strange**.

quake (kwāk), *v.i.* [QUAKED (kwākt), QUAKING], [ME. *quaken, quakien;* AS. *cwacian;* prob. of Gmc. echoic origin & akin to Dan. *kvakle*, G. *quackeln*, D. *kwakkelen*, etc., to be sick, shiver with illness], 1. to tremble; shake; quiver, as land in an earthquake. 2. to shudder or shiver, as with fear or cold. *n.* 1. a shaking or tremor. 2. an earthquake. —*SYN.* see **shake**.

Quak·er (kwāk′ẽr), *n.* [orig. derisive: so called from Fox's admonition to "quake" at the word of the Lord], a member of a religious sect, the Society of Friends, founded by George Fox, an Englishman, about 1650: Friends believe in plainness of dress, manners, and religious worship, and are opposed to military service and the taking of oaths; they do not use the term *Quaker* of themselves.

Quak·er·ess (kwāk′ẽr-is), *n.* a Quaker girl or woman.

Quaker gun, a dummy gun or cannon, as of wood: so called from the Quaker opposition to militarism.

Quak·er·ish (kwāk′ẽr-ish), *adj.* like a Quaker in manner, dress, principles, etc.

Quak·er·ism (kwāk′ẽr-iz′m), *n.* the principles and ways of the Quakers.

Quak·er-la·dies (kwāk′ẽr-lā′diz), *n.pl.* the small, blue flowers of the bluet.

Quak·er·ly (kwāk′ẽr-li), *adj.* like Quakers. *adv.* in the manner of Quakers.

Quaker meeting, 1. a religious meeting of Quakers, characterized by long periods of silence. 2. [Colloq.], any meeting or assembly in which there are many silent moments.

quak·i·ly (kwāk′ə-li), *adv.* in a quaky manner.

quak·i·ness (kwāk′i-nis), *n.* the quality or condition of being quaky.

quaking aspen, a kind of poplar with small, flat-stemmed leaves that tremble with the gentlest breeze: also called *trembling aspen*.

quak·y (kwāk′i), *adj.* [QUAKIER (-i-ẽr), QUAKIEST (-i-ist)], inclined to quake; shaky.

qual·i·fi·a·ble (kwäl′ə-fī′ə-b′l), *adj.* that can be qualified.

qual·i·fi·ca·tion (kwäl′ə-fi-kā′shən), *n.* [ML. *qualificatio* < pp. of *qualificare*], 1. a qualifying or being qualified. 2. a modification; restriction; limiting condition. 3. any quality, knowledge, ability, experience, or acquirement that fits a person for a position, office, profession, etc.; a requisite. 4. a condition that must be met in order to exercise certain rights.

qual·i·fi·ca·tor (kwäl′ə-fi-kā′tẽr), *n.* [ML. < pp. of *qualificare;* see QUALIFY], in the *Roman Catholic Church*, a person appointed to prepare cases for trial in an ecclesiastical court.

qual·i·fied (kwäl′ə-fīd′), *adj.* [pp. of *qualify*], 1. having met conditions or requirements set. 2. having the necessary or desirable qualities; fit; competent. 3. limited; modified: as, he gave only *qualified* approval. —*SYN.* see **able**.

qual·i·fi·er (kwäl′ə-fī′ẽr), *n.* 1. a person or thing that qualifies. 2. a word, as an adjective or adverb, that modifies or limits the meaning of another word.

qual·i·fy (kwäl′ə-fī′), *v.t.* [QUALIFIED (-fīd′), QUALIFYING], [Fr. *qualifier;* ML. *qualificare* < L. *qualis*, of what kind + *facere*, to make], 1. to describe by giving the qualities or characteristics of. 2. to render fit for an office, occupation, exercise of a right, etc. 3. to render legally capable. 4. to modify; restrict; limit. 5. to moderate; soften. 6. to change the strength of (a liquor, etc.). 7. in *grammar*, to limit or modify the meaning of (a word). *v.i.* to be or become qualified.

qual·i·ta·tive (kwäl′ə-tā′tiv), *adj.* [LL. *qualitativus*], having to do with quality or qualities: distinguished from *quantitative*.

qualitative analysis, the branch of chemistry dealing with the determination of the elements or ingredients of which a substance is composed: distinguished from *quantitative analysis*.

qual·i·ty (kwäl′ə-ti), *n.* [*pl.* QUALITIES (-tiz)], [ME. & OFr. *qualite;* L. *qualitas* < *qualis*, of what kind], 1. that which makes something what it is; characteristic element; attribute. 2. basic nature; character; kind. 3. the degree of excellence which a thing possesses; hence, 4. excellence; superiority. 5. character; position: as, the attorney advised him in the *quality* of a friend, not professionally. 6. [Archaic], position in society. 7. [Archaic or Dial.], people of high social position. 8. in *acoustics*, the property of a tone, apart from pitch and intensity, determined by its overtones; timbre. 9. in *logic*, the affirmative or negative character of a proposition. 10. in *phonetics*, the character of a vowel sound as determined by the resonance of the vocal chords and the shape of the passage above the larynx when the sound is produced.

SYN.—**quality**, the broadest in scope of these terms, refers to a characteristic (physical or nonphysical, individual or typical) that constitutes the basic nature of a thing or is one of its distinguishing features (the *quality* of mercy); **property** applies to any quality that belongs to a thing by reason of the essential nature of the thing (elasticity is a *property* of rubber); **character** is the scientific or formal term for a distinctive or peculiar quality of an individual or of a class, species, etc. (a hereditary *character*); an **attribute** is a quality assigned to a thing, especially one that may reasonably be deduced as appropriate to it (omnipotence is regarded as an *attribute* of God); **trait** specifically applies to a distinguishing quality of a personality (enthusiasm is one of his outstanding *traits*).

qualm (kwäm, kwôm), *n.* [ME. *qualme, quelme;* AS. *cwealm*, death, disaster, etc. < base of *cwellan*, to kill (see QUELL); all the extant senses show melioration of the orig. meaning], 1. a sudden fit of sickness, faintness, or nausea. 2. a sudden feeling of uneasiness or doubt; misgiving. 3. a scruple; twinge of conscience.

SYN.—**qualm** implies a painful feeling of uneasiness arising from a consciousness that one is or may be acting wrongly (he had *qualms* about having cheated on the test); **scruple** implies doubt or hesitation arising from difficulty in deciding what is right, proper, just, etc. (to break a promise without *scruple*); **compunction** implies a twinge of conscience for wrongdoing, now often for a slight offense (I have no *compunctions* about telling a white lie); **misgiving** implies a disturbed state of mind resulting from a loss of confidence as to whether one is doing what is right (*misgivings* of conscience).

qualm·ish (kwäm′ish, kwôm′ish), *adj.* 1. having qualms. 2. having the nature of a qualm. 3. of such a nature as to produce qualms.

quam·ash (kwäm′ash, kwə-mash′), *n.* a camass.
quan·da·ry (kwän′dri, kwän′də-ri), *n.* [*pl.* QUANDARIES (-driz, -riz)], [origin obscure; prob. < scholastic L. < L. *quando*, when (interrogative)], a state of uncertainty; perplexing situation or position; dilemma. —*SYN.* see **predicament.**
‡**quand même** (kän′ mem′), [Fr.], even if; nevertheless.
quan·dong, quan·dang (kwän′doŋ′), *n.* [native name], 1. a small Australian tree. 2. the edible fruit of this tree, having a single stone, or seed. 3. the stone of this fruit, having an edible kernel. Also **quantong.**
quant (kwant, kwänt), *n.* [? < L. *contus* < Gr. *kontos*, boat pole], [British], a pole with a disk near the end, for propelling a small boat: the disk prevents sinking in the mud. *v.t. & v.i.* [British], to propel (a boat) with a quant.
quan·ta (kwän′tə), *n.* plural of **quantum.**
quan·tic (kwän′tik), *n.* [< L. *quantus*, how much], in *mathematics*, a homogeneous integral function of two or more variables.
quan·ti·fi·ca·tion (kwän′tə-fi-kā′shən), *n.* a quantifying.
quan·ti·fy (kwän′tə-fī′), *v.t.* [QUANTIFIED (-fīd′), QUANTIFYING], [ML. *quantificare* < L. *quantus*, how much, how many + *facere*, to make], 1. to determine or express the quantity of; indicate the extent of. 2. in *logic*, to make the quantity of (a term) clear and explicit, as by using *all*, *none*, or *some*.
quan·ti·ta·tive (kwän′tə-tā′tiv), *adj.* [ML. *quantitativus*], 1. having to do with quantity: distinguished from *qualitative*. 2. capable of being measured. 3. having to do with the quantity of a speech sound.
quantitative analysis, the branch of chemistry dealing with the accurate measurement of the amounts or percentages of the various components of a substance or compound: distinguished from *qualitative analysis*.
quan·ti·ty (kwän′tə-ti), *n.* [*pl.* QUANTITIES (-tiz)], [ME. & OFr. *quantite*; L. *quantitas* < *quantus*, how great < *quam*, to what a degree], 1. an amount; portion. 2. any indeterminate bulk, weight, or number. 3. the exact amount of a particular thing. 4. a great amount or number. 5. that property of anything which can be determined by measurement. 6. in *logic*, that character which is determined by the extension of the subject of a proposition as universal or particular. 7. in *mathematics*, *a*) a thing that has the property of being measurable in dimensions, amounts, etc., or in extensions of these which can be expressed in numbers or symbols. *b*) a number or symbol used to express a mathematical quantity. 8. in *music*, the relative length of a tone. 9. in *philosophy*, that aspect of things to which measure applies and according to which they can be compared with one another. 10. in *phonetics & prosody*, the relative length or brevity of a vowel, continuant consonant, or syllable, with reference to the time needed to utter it. Abbreviated **qt.**
quan·tong (kwän′toŋ′), *n.* a quandong.
quan·tum (kwän′təm), *n.* [*pl.* QUANTA (-tə)], [L., neut. sing. of *quantus*, how much], 1. quantity, or amount. 2. a specified quantity; portion. 3. in the quantum theory, an (or the) elemental unit of energy.
‡**quan·tum suf·fi·cit** (kwän′təm suf′ə-sit), [L., lit., as much as suffices], enough: abbreviated **q.s.**
quantum theory, the theory that energy is not absorbed nor radiated continuously but discontinuously, in definite units called *quanta*.
qua·qua·ver·sal (kwā′kwə-vũr′s′l), *adj.* [< LL. *quaquaversus* (< L. *quaqua*, in all directions + *versus*, pp. of *vertere*, to turn); + *-al*], in *geology*, directed from a common center toward all points of the compass; turning or dipping in all directions.
quar., 1. quarter. 2. quarterly.
quar·an·tin·a·ble (kwôr′ən-tēn′ə-b′l, kwär′ən-tēn′ə-b′l), *adj.* subject to quarantine.
quar·an·tine (kwôr′ən-tēn′, kwär′ən-tēn′), *n.* [It. *quarantina*, lit., space of forty days < *quaranta* < L. *quadraginta*, forty < base of *quattuor*, four], 1. the period, originally forty days, during which an arriving vessel suspected of carrying contagious disease is detained in port in strict isolation. 2. the place where such a vessel is stationed. 3. any isolation or restriction on travel or passage imposed to keep contagious diseases, insect pests, etc. from spreading. 4. a place where persons, animals, or plants having contagious diseases, insect pests, etc. are kept in isolation, or beyond which they are prohibited from travel or passage. 5. a period of forty days. *v.t.* [QUARANTINED (-tēnd′), QUARANTINING], 1. to place under quarantine. 2. to isolate politically, commercially, etc., as an aggressor nation or an armed struggle.
Quarles, Francis (kwôrlz, kwärlz), 1592–1644; English poet.
Quar·ne·ro, Gulf of (kwär-ne′rô), an arm of the Adriatic, between Italy and Yugoslavia.
quar·rel (kwôr′əl, kwär′əl), *n.* [ME. & OFr. *quarel*; ML. *querellus*; LL. **quadrellum*, dim. of L. *quadrus*, a square], 1. a square-headed missile or arrow used in ancient crossbows. 2. any of the small diamond-shaped or square panes of glass in a latticed window. 3. anything with a square-headed part, as a stonemason's chisel.
quar·rel (kwôr′əl, kwär′əl), *n.* [ME. *quarel*, *quarell*, *querel*; OFr. *querele*; L. *querela*, *querella*, complaint < *queri*, to complain, lament], 1. a cause for dispute. 2. a dispute or disagreement, especially one marked by anger and deep resentment. 3. a falling out; breaking up of friendly relations. *v.i.* [QUARRELED or QUARRELLED (-əld), QUARRELING or QUARRELLING], 1. to find fault; complain. 2. to dispute heatedly. 3. to have a breach in friendship.
SYN.—**quarrel** implies heated verbal strife marked by anger and resentment and often suggests continued hostility as a result; **wrangle** suggests a noisy dispute in which each person is vehemently insistent on his views; **altercation** implies verbal contention which may or may not be accompanied by blows; **squabble** implies undignified, childish wrangling over a small matter; **spat** is the colloquial term for a petty quarrel and suggests a brief outburst that does not have a significant effect on a relationship.—*ANT.* agreement, harmony.
quar·rel·er, quar·rel·ler (kwôr′əl-ẽr, kwär′əl-ẽr), *n.* a person who quarrels.
quar·rel·some (kwôr′əl-səm, kwär′əl-səm), *adj.* [see -SOME], inclined to quarrel. —*SYN.* see **belligerent.**
quar·ri·er (kwôr′i-ẽr, kwär′i-ẽr), *n.* [ME. *quaryere*; OFr. *quarrieur* < *quarrer*, to quarry; L. *quadrare*; see QUARRY (of stones)], a person who works in a quarry.
quar·ry (kwôr′i, kwär′i), *n.* [var. of first *quarrel* (in sense 2)], a flat, square or diamond-shaped piece of glass, tile, etc.
quar·ry (kwôr′i, kwär′i), *n.* [*pl.* QUARRIES (-iz)], [ME. *querre*, orig., parts of a slain animal placed on the hide and given to dogs; OFr. *cuiree*; altered (after *cuir*, a skin, hide) < *curée*, pp. of *curer*, to clean, eviscerate < L. *curare*, to attend to], 1. an animal that is being hunted down. 2. anything being hunted or pursued.
quar·ry (kwôr′i, kwär′i), *n.* [*pl.* QUARRIES (-iz)], [ME. *quarey*; ML. *quarreia*, contr. of *quarreria*, *quarraria*, lit., place where stones are squared < L. *quadrare*, to square], a place where stone or slate is excavated, as by cutting or blasting, for building purposes, etc. *v.t.* [QUARRIED (-id), QUARRYING], 1. to excavate or take from a quarry. 2. to make a quarry in (land).
quar·ry·man (kwôr′i-mən, kwär′i-mən), *n.* [*pl.* QUARRYMEN (-mən)], a man who works in a quarry.
quart (kwôrt), *n.* [ME.; OFr. *quarte*, fourth part; L. *quarta*, fem. of *quartus*, fourth < base of *quattuor*, four], 1. a liquid measure, equal to 1/4 gallon (57.75 cubic inches). 2. a dry measure, equal to 1/8 peck. 3. any container with a capacity of one quart. Abbreviated **qt., q., qu.**
quart (kärt), *n.* [Fr. *quarte*; see prec.], 1. carte, a position in fencing: also **quarte.** 2. in *card games*, a sequence of four cards of the same suit.
quar·tal (kwôr′t′l), *adj.* [< *quarter* + *-al*], in *music*, designating or of harmony based on intervals of fourths instead of the usual thirds.
quar·tan (kwôr′t′n), *adj.* [ME. *quartaine*; OFr. (*fièvre*) *quartaine*; L. (*febris*) *quartana*, (fever) occurring every fourth day, fem. of *quartanus* < *quartus*, fourth], occurring every fourth day, counting both days of occurrence: said of a fever. *n.* a type of malaria in which the paroxysms occur every fourth day.
quarte (kärt; Fr. kȧrt), *n.* [Fr.], carte, a position in fencing: also **quart.**
quar·ter (kwôr′tẽr), *n.* [ME. *quartre*; OFr. *quartier*; L. *quartarius*, fourth part < *quartus*, fourth], 1. any of the four equal parts of something; fourth. 2. a measure of grain, equal to 8 bushels (1/4 ton). 3. one fourth of a hundredweight: 25 pounds in the United States, 28 pounds in England. 4. one fourth of a yard, or 9 inches; span. 5. one fourth of a mile. 6. one fourth of a year; three months. 7. a school or college term of instruction, usually one fourth of a school year. 8. *a*) one fourth of an hour; 15 minutes. *b*) the moment marking the end of each fourth of an hour. 9. *a*) one fourth of a dollar; 25 cents. *b*) a silver coin of the United States and Canada equal to 25 cents. 10. one leg of a four-legged animal, with the adjoining parts. 11. *a*) any of the four main points of the compass. *b*) any of the four divisions of the horizon as marked off by the four main compass points. *c*) any of the regions thought of as under these divisions; any part or region of the earth. 12. a particular district or section in a city: as, the Chinese *quarter*. 13. *pl.* lodgings; place of abode. 14. a particular person or group of persons, or a previously identified place, direction, point, etc.: as, this information comes from the highest *quarters*. 15. the part forming the side of a shoe from the heel to the vamp. 16. in *astronomy*, *a*) the period of time in which the moon makes one fourth of its revolution around the earth. *b*) the phase of the moon when it is half lighted. 17. in *football*, etc., any of the four periods into which a game is divided. 18. in *heraldry*, *a*) any of the four equal divisions into which a shield is divided. *b*) the charge occupying such a division. 19. in *military usage*, etc., mercy granted to a surrendering foe. 20. in *nautical usage*, *a*) the afterpart of a ship's side

b) the post or station assigned to one on a ship. *c*) one fourth of a fathom. *d*) one fourth of the distance between any two of the 32 points on the compass: also **quarter point.** Abbreviated **qtr., qr., q., qu., quar.** *v.t.* 1. to divide into four equal parts. 2. loosely, to separate into any number of parts. 3. to defile (the body of a person put to death) by dismembering it into four parts. 4. to provide lodgings for; specifically, to assign (soldiers) to lodgings. 5. to cover (an area) by passing back and forth over it in many directions: said of hounds searching for game. 6. in *heraldry, a*) to place or bear, as different coats of arms, on the quarters of a shield. *b*) to add (a coat of arms) to a shield in a quarterly arrangement. 7. in *mechanics*, to set (a crank, etc.) at right angles to the connecting part. *v.i.* 1. to be lodged or stationed (with *at* or *with*). 2. to range over a field, etc. in search of game: said of hounds in hunting. 3. in *nautical usage*, to blow on the quarter of a ship: said of the wind. *adj.* constituting a quarter; equal to a quarter.
at close quarters, at close range; close together.
cry quarter, to beg for mercy.

quar·ter·age (kwôr′tẽr-ij), *n.* [ME.; OFr.; see -AGE], 1. a payment made or received every quarter of the year. 2. the quarters provided for troops, etc. 3. *a*) the provision of quarters. *b*) the expense of this.

quar·ter·back (kwôr′tẽr-bak′), *n.* in *football*, 1. the player whose position is behind the line of scrimmage together with the fullback and halfbacks, and who generally calls the signals. 2. the position played by a quarterback. Abbreviated **Q.B., q.b., qb.**

quarter crack, a fissure in the lateral part of the wall of a horse's hoof, usually causing lameness.

quarter day, any of the four days regarded as beginning a new quarter of the year, when quarterly payments on rents, etc. are due.

quar·ter-deck, quar·ter·deck (kwôr′tẽr-dek′), *n.* [so called because orig. half the length of the half deck], the afterpart of the upper deck of a ship, usually reserved for officers: it was originally between the poop and the mainmast.

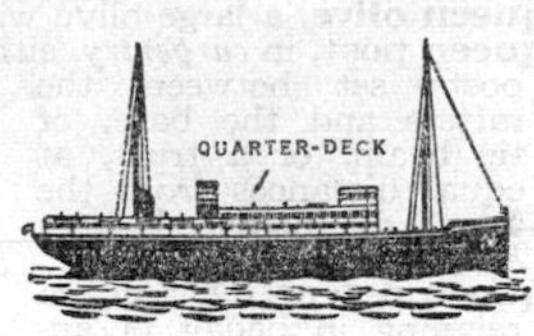

QUARTER-DECK

quar·tered (kwôr′tẽrd), *adj.* [pp. of *quarter*], 1. divided into fourths. 2. provided with quarters or lodgings. 3. quartersawed. 4. in *heraldry*, divided into quarters.

quar·ter-fi·nal (kwôr′tẽr-fi′n'l), *adj.* in *sports*, designating or of the round of matches immediately preceding the semifinals in a tournament. *n.* a quarter-final match.

quar·ter-fi·nal·ist (kwôr′tẽr-fi′n'l-ist), *n.* in *sports*, a person or team competing in a tournament and qualifying for the quarter-final round.

quarter grain, the grain of quartersawed lumber.

quar·ter-hour (kwôr′tẽr-our′), *n.* 1. fifteen minutes. 2. the point on a clock marking the first quarter or third quarter of an hour. Also **quarter hour.**

quar·ter·ing (kwôr′tẽr-iŋ), *adj.* blowing on the afterpart of a ship's side: said of the wind. *n.* 1. a dividing into quarters. 2. the providing of quarters for soldiers, etc. 3. in *heraldry, a*) the division of a shield into quarters. *b*) any of these, or the coat of arms on it.

quar·ter·ly (kwôr′tẽr-li), *adj.* 1. occurring or appearing at regular intervals four times a year. 2. consisting of a quarter. *adv.* 1. once every quarter of the year. 2. in *heraldry*, in or by quarters, as a shield. *n.* [*pl.* QUARTERLIES (-liz)], a publication issued every three months. Abbreviated **q., qu., quar.**

quar·ter·mas·ter (kwôr′tẽr-mas′tẽr, kwôr′tẽr-mäs′-tẽr), *n.* 1. in *military usage, a*) an officer whose duty it is to assign quarters to troops and provide them with clothing, equipment, etc. *b*) any member of the Quartermaster Corps. 2. in *nautical usage*, a petty officer who attends to the steering, ship's compass, signals, etc. Abbreviated **Q.M.** (as a title).

Quartermaster Corps, that branch of the United States Army concerned with supplying food, clothing, etc. to soldiers: abbreviated **Q.M.C.**

quartermaster general, [*pl.* QUARTERMASTERS GENERAL, QUARTERMASTER GENERALS], in the *United States Army*, the general heading the Quartermaster Corps: abbreviated **Q.M.Gen.** (as a title).

quar·tern (kwôr′tẽrn), *n.* [ME. *quarteroun;* OFr. *quarteron* < *quart;* see QUART], 1. a fourth part; quarter. 2. one fourth of a pint; gill. 3. one fourth of a peck. 4. one fourth of a stone, or 3 1/2 pounds. 5. a loaf of bread weighing about four pounds.

quarter note, in *music*, a note (♩) having one fourth the duration of a whole note: also called *crotchet.*

quar·ter-phase (kwôr′tẽr-fāz′), *adj.* in *electricity*, generating, carrying, or run by, two alternating currents whose phases differ by 90 degrees: also called *diphase.*

quarter round, a convex molding, in cross section a quarter of a circle: often called *ovolo.*

quar·ter·saw (kwôr′tẽr-sô′), *v.t.* to saw (a log) into quarters lengthwise and then into boards, in order to show the grain of the wood to advantage.

quarter section, one fourth of a section of land, approximately 1/4 sq. mi., or 160 acres: abbreviated **q.s.**

quarter sessions, 1. in England, a local court that sits quarterly and has limited criminal jurisdiction along with authority in ordinary civil proceedings. 2. in the United States, any of various courts that sit every three months.

quar·ter·staff (kwôr′tẽr-staf′, kwôr′tẽr-stäf′), *n.* [*pl.* QUARTERSTAVES (-stāvz′)], 1. a stout, iron-tipped wooden staff, six to eight feet long, formerly used in England as a weapon: it was held by one hand at the middle and the other at a point about halfway between the middle and the end. 2. fighting or play with such a staff.

quarter step (or **tone**), in *music*, an interval of one quarter of a whole tone.

quar·tet, quar·tette (kwôr-tet′), *n.* [Fr. *quartette;* It. *quartetto*, dim. of *quarto* < L. *quartus*, a fourth], 1. any group of four persons or things. 2. in *music, a*) a composition for four voices or four instruments. *b*) the four performers of such a composition.

quar·tic (kwôr′tik), *adj.* [< L. *quartus*, fourth; + *ic*], in *mathematics*, of the fourth degree. *n.* a quantic of the fourth degree.

quar·tile (kwôr′tīl, kwôr′t'l), *adj.* [ML. *quartilis* < L. *quartus*, a fourth], 1. in *astrology*, designating an aspect of heavenly bodies in which they are 90° distant from each other. 2. in *statistics, a*) designating any of the values in a series dividing the distribution of the individuals in the series into four groups of equal frequency. *b*) designating any of these groups. *n.* 1. in *astrology*, a quartile aspect. 2. in *statistics*, a quartile point or group.

quar·to (kwôr′tō), *n.* [*pl.* QUARTOS (-tōz)], [L., short for *in quarto; in*, in + *quarto*, abl. of *quartus*, a fourth], 1. the page size of a book made up of sheets each of which is folded into four leaves, or eight pages, about nine by twelve inches in size. 2. a book made of pages folded in this way. Abbreviated **4to, 4°, qto., q.** *adj.* having four (quarto) leaves to the sheet.

quartz (kwôrts), *n.* [G. *quarz*, orig. dim. of *zwerg*, dwarf; cf. COBALT, NICKEL], a brilliant, crystalline mineral, silicon dioxide, SiO_2, occurring in abundance, most often in a colorless, transparent form, but also sometimes as variously colored semiprecious stones.

quartz·if·er·ous (kwôrt-sif′ẽr-əs), *adj.* [*quartz* + *-(i)ferous*], consisting of or yielding quartz.

quartz·ite (kwôrts′īt′), *n.* [*quartz* + *-ite*], a massive, hard, light-colored rock with a flinty sheen: it is a metamorphosed sandstone.

quartz lamp, a mercury-vapor lamp with a quartz tube that transmits most of the ultraviolet rays.

quartz plate, in *electricity*, a piece of quartz crystal having electric polarity.

quash (kwäsh), *v.t.* [OFr. *quasser* < LL. *cassare*, to annihilate, destroy < L. *cassus*, empty; form influenced in OFr. by association with L. *quassare;* see next entry], in *law*, to annul or set aside, as an indictment.

quash (kwäsh), *v.t.* [ME. *quashen;* OFr. *quasser;* L. *quassare*, to shake, shatter, shiver, intens. < *quassus*, pp. of *quatere*, to shake, break], to quell; put down; suppress, as an uprising.

qua·si (kwā′si, kwā′zī, kwä′si), *adv.* [L., as if, as it were, just as < *quamsi; quam*, as, how + *si*, if, whether], as if; in a sense or manner; seemingly. *adj.* seeming: as, a *quasi* wisdom. Often hyphenated as a prefix to a noun, adjective, or adverb, as in *quasi-judicial*. Abbreviated **q.**

quasi contract, in *law*, an obligation to do something imposed upon someone by law but bearing the force of a contract and subject to legal action as a contract: now imposed chiefly to prevent unfair gain at the expense of another.

qua·si-ju·di·cial (kwā′si-jōō-dish′əl, kwä′si-jōō-dish′-əl), *adj.* having to do with powers that are to some extent judicial, as those of certain boards and commissions of the Federal government.

quass (kväs), *n.* kvass, a Russian fermented drink.

quas·si·a (kwäsh′i-ə, kwäsh′ə), *n.* [Mod.L. < Graman *Quassi*, Surinam Negro who prescribed it as a remedy for fever, c. 1730], 1. any of a number of related tropical plants. 2. the wood of any of these plants. 3. a bitter drug extracted from this wood.

qua·ter·na·ry (kwə-tũr′nə-ri), *adj.* [L. *quaternarius* < *quaterni*, four together, four each], 1. consisting of four; in sets of four. 2. [Q-], designating or of the geological period following the Tertiary in the Cenozoic Era, comprising the Pleistocene and Recent Epochs.

n. [*pl.* QUATERNARIES (-riz)], 1. the number four. 2. a set of four.

the Quaternary, the Quaternary Period or its rocks: see **geology,** chart.

qua·ter·ni·on (kwə-tũr′ni-ən), *n.* [ME.; LL. *quaternio* < L. *quaterni;* see QUATERNARY], 1. a set of four. 2. in *mathematics, a*) a factor which, by multiplication, changes one vector into another: it is expressible by a quadrinomial. *b*) *pl.* the form of calculus using the quaternion.

Quath·lam·ba (kwät-läm′bä), *n.* the Drakensberg Mountains, a mountain range in South Africa.

qua·torze (kə-tôrz′), *n.* [Fr., fourteen; L. *quattuordecim*], in *piquet,* the four aces, kings, queens, jacks, or tens, scored as fourteen points for the holder.

quat·rain (kwät′rān), *n.* [Fr. < *quatre;* L. *quattuor,* four], a stanza or poem of four lines, usually rhyming *abab* or *abba.*

qua·tre (kä′tẽr; Fr. kȧ′tr′), *n.* [Fr.; L. *quattuor,* four], a card, domino, or die marked with four spots.

quat·re·foil (kat′ẽr-foil′, kat′rə-foil′), *n.* [ME. *quaterfoyle;* OFr. *quatrefeuille; quatre* (L. *quattuor*), four + *feuille* (L. *folium*), a leaf], 1. a flower with four petals. 2. a leaf with four leaflets. 3. in *architecture,* a leaflike ornament having four lobes.

‡**quat·tro·cen·to** (kwät′trō-chen′tô), *n.* [It., lit., four hundred; short for *mille quattrocento,* one thousand four hundred], the 15th century as a period in Italian art and literature.

qua·ver (kwā′vẽr), *v.i.* [ME. *quaveren,* freq. of Early ME. *cwafien,* to shake, tremble (prob. < AS. **cwafian;* cf. QUAKE); the Gmc. echoic base, prob. in basic senses "wabbly, slimy," is seen also in G. *quappe,* tadpole, eelpout, D. *kwabbe,* tadpole, belly], 1. to shake or tremble. 2. to be tremulous: said of the voice. 3. in *music,* to make a trill or trills in singing or playing. *v.t.* 1. to utter in a tremulous voice. 2. in *music,* to sing or play with a trill or trills. *n.* 1. a tremulous quality in a voice or tone. 2. in *music,* an eighth note; half of a crotchet.

qua·ver·y (kwā′vẽr-i), *adj.* quavering; shaky; tremulous.

quay (kē), *n.* [ME. *kei;* OFr. *cai, caie* < Celt. base seen also in W. *cae,* enclosure, field, Bret. *kai,* enclosure; Eng. sp. influenced by Fr. *quai* (OFr. *cai*)], a wharf, usually of concrete or stone, with facilities for loading and unloading ships.

quay·age (kē′ij), *n.* [Fr.; see -AGE], 1. the charge made for using a quay. 2. space on a quay. 3. quays collectively.

quean (kwēn), *n.* [ME. *quene, queyne;* AS. *cwene;* akin to *cwen* (see QUEEN) & Goth. *qino,* woman, etc.; IE. **gwenā,* woman, seen also in Sans. *ganā,* goddess & prob. in L. *genetrix,* mother], 1. a bold, brazen, or impudent girl or woman. 2. an immoral woman; slut. 3. [Scot.], a girl or unmarried woman.

quea·si·ly (kwē′z′l-i), *adv.* in a queasy manner.

quea·si·ness (kwē′zi-nis), *n.* a queasy quality or state.

quea·sy (kwē′zi), *adj.* [QUEASIER (-zi-ẽr), QUEASIEST (-zi-ist)], [Late ME. *qwesye;* akin to, prob. < base of, ON. *kveisa,* ulcer, boil, lit., contusion, Ice. *kveisa,* colic, Norw. *kveis,* hangover, etc. (< IE. base **gwej-,* to overpower, etc.); the immediate source may be either ON. or LG.], 1. causing nausea. 2. affected with nausea. 3. squeamish; qualmish; easily nauseated. 4. uncomfortable; embarrassed. 5. difficult to please; fastidious. 6. troublous; hazardous.

Que·bec (kwi-bek′), *n.* 1. a province of eastern Canada: area, 594,860 sq. mi.; pop., 4,628,000: abbreviated **Que., Q.:** formerly called *Lower Canada.* 2. its capital, on the St. Lawrence River: pop., 171,000 (with suburbs, 310,000).

que·bra·cho (kā-brä′chō), *n.* [Sp., contr. < *quiebrahacha,* lit., ax breaker (because of the hardness of the wood) < *quebrar,* to break + *hacha,* an ax], 1. any of a number of related tropical American trees, whose bark and hard wood are variously used in medicine, tanning, and dyeing. 2. the bark or wood.

Quech·ua (kech′wä), *n.* [Sp. < the native name], 1. a member of any of a group of South American Indian tribes dominant in the former Inca Empire. 2. any of these tribes. 3. the language of these tribes, dialects of which are still in existence among the Indians of Peru and Ecuador. Also spelled **Kechua.**

Quech·uan (kech′wən), *adj.* of the Quechuas, their language, or culture. *n.* Quechua (senses 1 & 3). Also spelled **Kechuan.**

queen (kwēn), *n.* [ME. *quen;* AS. *cwen* (akin to OS. *quān,* ON. *kvæn,* Goth. *qēns,* woman, etc.) < **kwōni-* < ablaut var. of IE. **gwenā* (see QUEAN) found also in Gr. *gynē* (cf. GYNECOLOGY)], 1. the wife of a king. 2. a woman who rules over a monarchy in her own right; female counterpart of a king. 3. a woman foremost among others in certain attributes or accomplishments, as beauty, etc. 4. a place or thing that is regarded as the best or most beautiful of its kind: as, Cuba is called the *Queen* of the Antilles. 5. the fully developed, reproductive female in a colony of bees, ants, or termites: see **bee,** illus. 6. in *cards,* a playing card with a conventionalized picture of a queen on it. 7. in *chess,* the most powerful piece, permitted to move any number of unoccupied spaces in a straight or diagonal direction. Abbreviated **Q., q., qu.** *v.t.* 1. to make (a girl or woman) a queen. 2. in *chess,* to make a queen of (a pawn that has been moved to the opponent's end of the board). *v.i.* to reign as queen.

queen it, to play the queen; domineer.

Queen Anne's lace, a wild plant of the carrot family, with fine leaves and small, delicate, white flowers in flat-topped clusters.

Queen Anne style, 1. a style of architecture developed in England during the early 18th century, characterized by construction in red brick, the modification of classical architecture to meet domestic needs, and the use of simple, dignified ornamentation. 2. a style of furniture developed in the same period, characterized by simple lines and the use of upholstery.

Queen Charlotte Islands, a group of islands in the Pacific, off the coast of British Columbia, Canada.

queen consort, the wife of a reigning king.

queen·dom (kwēn′dəm), *n.* [see -DOM], 1. the rule or realm of a queen. 2. queenhood.

queen dowager, the widow of a king.

queen·hood (kwēn′hood′), *n.* [see -HOOD], the state, rank, or dignity of a queen.

queen·ing (kwēn′iŋ), *n.* a kind of apple.

queen·li·ness (kwēn′li-nis), *n.* the quality or state of being queenly.

queen·ly (kwēn′li), *adj.* [QUEENLIER (-li-ẽr), QUEENLIEST (-li-ist)], 1. of or like a queen. 2. suitable to a queen. *adv.* in a queenly manner.

Queen Mab (mab), in *English folklore,* a fairy queen who governs people's dreams.

Queen Maud Range, a mountain range in Antarctica, south of Ross Shelf Ice.

queen mother, a queen dowager who is mother of a reigning sovereign.

queen olive, a large olive with a long, slender pit.

queen post, in *carpentry,* either of a pair of two vertical posts set between the rafters and the base, or tie beam, of a truss, at equal distances from the apex: distinguished from *king post.*

QUEEN POSTS

queen regent, 1. a queen reigning in behalf of another. 2. [Rare], a queen regnant.

queen regnant, a queen reigning in her own right.

Queens (kwēnz), *n.* a borough of New York City, on western Long Island: pop., 1,810,000.

queen's English, queen's evidence, etc., see **king's English, king's evidence,** etc.

Queens·land (kwēnz′land′, kwēnz′lənd), *n.* a state of eastern Australia: area, 667,000 sq. mi.; pop., 1,472,000; capital, Brisbane: abbreviated **Queensld.**

Queens·town (kwēnz′toun′), *n.* Cóbh, a seaport in Ireland: the former name.

queen truss, in *carpentry,* a truss with queen posts.

queer (kwêr), *adj.* [North Eng. & Scot. dial., prob via beggars' cant < G. *quer,* crosswise, in the orig. sense (MHG. *twer*) "crooked"], 1. differing from what is usual or ordinary; odd; singular; strange 2. slightly ill; qualmish; giddy. 3. [Colloq.], doubtful; suspicious. 4. [Colloq.], having mental quirks; eccentric. 5. [Slang], counterfeit; not genuine. 6. [Slang], homosexual. *v.t.* [Slang], 1. to spoil, as the smooth operation or success of. 2. to put (oneself) into an unfavorable position. *n.* [Slang], 1. counterfeit money. 2. a homosexual. —*SYN.* see **strange.**

queer·ness (kwêr′nis), *n.* 1. the condition or quality of being queer. 2. something queer.

quell (kwel), *v.t.* [ME. *quellen;* AS. *cwellan,* to kill (cf QUALM); akin to G. *qualen,* to torture; IE. base **gwel-,* to let fall, make fall], 1. to crush; subdue; put an end to. 2. to quiet; allay.

Quel·part Island (kwel′pärt′), Saishu, an island south of Korea: a former name.

‡**quel·que chose** (kel′kə shōz′), [Fr., lit., something anything], a trifle.

quench (kwench), *v.t.* [ME. *quenchen;* AS. *cwencan* to extinguish (a fire, etc.), caus. of *cwincan,* to go out akin to Fris. *kwinka,* MHG. *verquinen,* to pass away IE. base **gwej-,* to overpower (cf. QUEASY)], 1. to extinguish; put out: as, water *quenched* the fire. 2. to satisfy; slake: as, he *quenched* his thirst. 3. to cool suddenly, as hot steel, by plunging into water, oil, etc

quench·less (kwench′lis), *adj.* that cannot be quenched

que·nelle (kə-nel′), *n.* [Fr. < G. *knödel,* dumpling < *knoten,* a knot], a ball of minced chicken, beef, or veal fried in fat.

Quen·tin (kwen′tin), a masculine name: see **Quintin**

quer·cet·ic (kwẽr-set′ik, kwẽr-sē′tik), *adj.* of or derived from quercetin.

quer·ce·tin (kwũr′si-tin), *n.* [< L. *quercus,* oak; + *-in*], the yellow, crystalline dyestuff, $C_{15}H_{10}O_7$, extracted from the inner bark of the black oak and also produced synthetically.

quer·cine (kwũr′sin, kwũr′sĩn), *adj.* [LL. *quercinus* < L. *quercus*, oak], of the oak.
quer·cit·ron (kwũr′sit-rən), *n.* [G. < L. *quercus*, oak + Fr. *citron;* see CITRON], 1. the black oak. 2. its bark. 3. the yellow dye made from this bark.
Que·ré·ta·ro (ke-re′tä-rô′), *n.* 1. a state of central Mexico: area, 4,432 sq. mi.; pop., 245,000. 2. its capital: pop., 34,000.
que·rist (kwêr′ist), *n.* one who queries, or questions.
quern (kwũrn), *n.* [ME. *querne;* AS. *cweorn*, hand mill; akin to Dan. *kværn*, etc.; IE. **gwerān*, millstone < base **gwer-*, heavy, seen also in L. *gravis* (cf. GRAVE, *adj.*, GRAVID)], 1. a primitive hand mill for grinding grain, consisting of two stone disks, one upon the other. 2. a small hand mill in which spices are ground.
quer·u·lous (kwer′ə-ləs, kwer′yoo ləs), *adj.* [LL. *querulosus*, for L. *querulus* < *queri*, to complain], 1. inclined to find fault; complaining; fretful; peevish. 2. characterized by complaining.
que·ry (kwêr′i), *n.* [*pl.* QUERIES (-iz)], [< L. *quaere*, 2d pers. sing., imperative, of *quaerere*, to ask, inquire], 1. a question; inquiry. 2. a doubt. 3. a question mark (?), placed at the end of a question or used to express doubt as to the correctness, accuracy, etc. of written or printed matter. Abbreviated **qy., q.** *v.t.* [QUERIED (-id), QUERYING], 1. to call in question; ask about. 2. to question (a person). 3. to express doubt as to the correctness, etc. of (written or printed matter) by marking with question marks. *v.i.* 1. to ask questions. 2. to express doubt. —*SYN.* see **ask.**
Ques·nay, Fran·çois (frän′swȧ′ ke′nā′), 1694–1774; French physician and economist.
quest (kwest), *n.* [ME. & OFr. *queste;* ML. *questa;* LL. **quaesita*, thing sought for < L. *quaesitus*, pp. of *quaerere*, to seek, ask, inquire], 1. a seeking; hunt; pursuit. 2. a journey in search of adventures, as those undertaken by knights-errant in medieval times; heroic expedition in search of a particular object: as, the *quest* of the Golden Fleece. 3. the group of persons participating in a quest. 4. [Rare], a jury of inquest. *v.i.* 1. to follow the track of game, or to bay in pursuit of game, as hounds do. 2. [Rare], to go in search.
ques·tion (kwes′chən), *n.* [ME. *questioun;* Anglo-Fr. *questiun;* OFr. *question;* L. *quaestio* < pp. of *quaerere*, to ask, inquire], 1. an asking; inquiry. 2. something that is asked; interrogative sentence; query. 3. doubt; uncertainty: as, there is no *question* of his veracity. 4. something in controversy before a court. 5. a problem; matter open to discussion or inquiry. 6. a matter or case of difficulty: as, it's not a *question* of money. 7. a point being debated or a resolution brought up for approval or rejection before an assembly. 8. the procedure of putting such a matter to a vote. Abbreviated **q., Q., ques., qu.** *v.t.* 1. to ask questions of; interrogate; put queries to. 2. to doubt; express uncertainty about. 3. to dispute; challenge. *v.i.* to ask a question or questions. —*SYN.* see **ask.**
beside the question, not related to the subject under discussion.
beyond (all) question, beyond dispute.
call in question, 1. to take exception to; challenge. 2. to cast doubt on.
in question, under consideration, debate, etc.
out of the question, impossible; not to be considered.
ques·tion·a·ble (kwes′chən-ə-b'l), *adj.* 1. that can be questioned; open to doubt. 2. of dubious repute; suspected of being immoral, not respectable, etc. —*SYN.* see **doubtful.**
ques·tion·a·bly (kwes′chən-ə-bli), *adv.* in a questionable manner.
ques·tion·ar·y (kwes′chən-er′i), *adj.* [ML. *questionarius*], questioning; inquiring. *n.* [*pl.* QUESTIONARIES (-iz)], a questionnaire.
ques·tion·less (kwes′chən-lis), *adj.* 1. unquestionable; indubitable. 2. asking no questions; unquestioning. *adv.* beyond question; unquestionably.
question mark, the interrogation mark (?).
ques·tion·naire (kwes′chən-âr′), *n.* [Fr.; see QUESTION], a written or printed form used in gathering information on some subject or subjects, consisting of a list of questions to be submitted to one or more persons.
ques·tor (kwes′tẽr, kwēs′tẽr), *n.* a quaestor.
Quet·ta (kwet′ä), *n.* the capital of Baluchistan, Pakistan: pop., 60,000.
quet·zal (ket-säl′), *n.* [Sp.; Nahuatl *quetzaltototl* < *quetzalli*, tail feather], 1. a crested bird of Central America, usually brilliant green above and red below, with long, streaming tail feathers (in the male). 2. [*pl.* QUETZALES (-sä′les)], the gold monetary unit of Guatemala, equal to about one dollar. Also **quezal.**
queue (kū), *n.* [Fr.; OFr. *coue;* L. *cauda*, tail], 1. a plait of hair worn hanging from the back of the head; pigtail. 2. a line or file of persons or things waiting to be served or brought into service. *v.i.* [QUEUED (kūd), QUEUING], [Chiefly British], to form in a line or file while waiting to be served, etc. (often with *up*).
que·zal (ke-säl′), *n.* a quetzal.
Que·zon, Ma·nuel Lu·is (mä-nwel′ lōō-ēs′ ke′sôn; Eng. kā′zon), 1878–1944; Philippine statesman; first president of the Philippine Commonwealth (1935–1944).
Que·zon City (ke′sôn; Eng. kā′zon), the capital of the Philippines, on Luzon: it is a suburb of Manila: pop., 108,000.
quib·ble (kwib′'l), *n.* [dim. < *quib* < L. *quibus*, abl. pl. of *qui*, who, which: *quibus* was common in legal documents and suggested sharp legal practice], 1. [Rare], a play on words. 2. a petty evasion or cavil. *v.i.* [QUIBBLED (-'ld), QUIBBLING], to evade the truth of a point under discussion by caviling; resort to a quibble.
Qui·be·ron Bay (kē′brôn′), a bay of the Atlantic, off northwestern France: scene of a British naval victory over France, in 1759.
quick (kwik), *adj.* [ME. *quik*, lively, alive; AS. *cwicu*, living; akin to ON. *kvikr*, OHG. *quëk*, etc.; IE. base **gwigw-* < **gwei-*, to live, be alive], 1. [Archaic], living. 2. *a)* rapid; swift: as, a *quick* walk. *b)* done with promptness; prompt: as, a *quick* reply. 3. occurring in a brief space of time: as, a *quick* look. 4. prompt to understand or learn; sharp in discernment: as, a *quick* mind. 5. sensitive; acutely perceptive: as, a *quick* sense of smell. 6. easily stirred; fiery: as, a *quick* temper. 7. pregnant. 8. sharply curved. 9. fresh; invigorating. *adv.* quickly; rapidly. *n.* 1. the living, especially in *the quick and the dead.* 2. the sensitive flesh under a toenail or fingernail; hence, 3. the center of the feelings: as, her sarcasm cut him to the *quick.* *v.t.* [Archaic], to animate; invigorate.
SYN.—**quick** implies ability to respond rapidly as an innate rather than a developed faculty (a *quick* mind); **prompt** stresses immediate response to a demand as resulting from discipline, practice, etc. or from willingness (*prompt* to obey, a *prompt* acceptance); **ready** also implies preparation or willingness and, in another sense, connotes fluency, expertness, etc. (a *ready* sympathy, jest, etc.); **apt,** in this connection, implies superior intelligence or a special talent as accountable for quickness of response (an *apt* pupil). See also **agile, fast.**—*ANT.* slow.
quick assets, in *accounting*, cash on hand and all readily marketable merchandise.
quick bread, any bread, as muffins, cornbread, etc., leavened with baking powder, soda, etc., so that it may be baked as soon as the batter is mixed.
quick·en (kwik′ən), *v.t.* [ME. *cwicien;* AS. *cwician* < *cwicu*, alive; see QUICK], 1. to animate; enliven; revive. 2. to arouse; stimulate; stir. 3. to cause to move more rapidly; hasten. *v.i.* 1. to become enlivened; revive. 2. *a)* to begin to show signs of life, as a fetus in the womb. *b)* to enter the stage of pregnancy in which the movement of the fetus can be felt. 3. to move more rapidly: as, the pulse *quickens* with fear. —*SYN.* see **animate.**
quick-fire (kwik′fīr), *adj.* firing, or designed for firing, in quick succession.
quick fire, shots fired in quick succession.
quick-fir·ing (kwik′fīr′iŋ), *adj.* quick-fire.
quick-freeze (kwik′frēz′), *v.t.* [QUICK-FROZE (-frōz′), QUICK-FROZEN (-frō′z'n), QUICK-FREEZING], to subject (raw or freshly cooked food) to such sudden freezing that the flavor and natural juices are retained and the food can be stored at low temperatures for a long time.
quick grass, couch grass.
quick·ie (kwik′i), *n.* [Slang], anything done or made quickly and cheaply; especially, a motion picture made in this way.
quick·lime (kwik′līm′), *n.* [ME. *quykke lyme*, after L. *calx viva*], calcium oxide; unslaked lime.
quick·ly (kwik′li), *adv.* 1. [Obs.], in a living or lively manner. 2. with haste or speed; rapidly.
quick·sand (kwik′sand′), *n.* [ME. *quykkesand;* prob. < MD. or MLG.], a loose, wet, deep sand deposit in which a person or heavy object may easily be engulfed.
quick·set (kwik′set′), *n.* 1. a live slip or cutting, as of hawthorn, planted in a hedge. 2. any plant growing in a hedge. 3. a hedge, as of hawthorn.
quick·sil·ver (kwik′sil′vẽr), *n.* [AS. *cwicseolfor* < *cwicu*, living + *seolfor*, silver; transl. of L. *argentum vivum*, lit., living silver: so called from its liquid form], mercury (the metal). *v.t.* to cover with mercury.
quick·step (kwik′step′), *n.* 1. the step used for marching in quick time. 2. in *music*, a march in the rhythm of quick time. 3. a spirited dance step.
quick-tem·pered (kwik′tem′pẽrd), *adj.* easily angered.
quick time, the normal rate of marching (in the United States Army), 120 (30-inch) paces a minute.
quick-wit·ted (kwik′wit′id), *adj.* nimble of mind.
quid (kwid), *n.* [var. of *cud*], a piece, as of tobacco, to be chewed.
quid (kwid), *n.* [*pl.* QUID], [? orig. slang use of L. *quid*, something, esp. in *quid pro quo*], [British Slang], a sovereign, or one pound sterling.
quid·di·ty (kwid′ə-ti), *n.* [*pl.* QUIDDITIES (-tiz)], [ML.

quidditas < L. *quid*, what, neut. of *quis*, who], 1. the essential quality of a thing. 2. a trifling distinction.

quid·nunc (kwid′nuŋk′), *n.* [L., lit., what now?], a person who is inquisitive about the latest news or gossip; busybody.

‡**quid pro quo** (kwid′ prō kwō′), [L., something for something], 1. one thing in return for another; hence, 2. something equivalent; substitute.

‡**¿quién sa·be?** (kyen sä′be), [Sp.], who knows?

qui·es·cence (kwī-es′′ns), *n.* [LL. *quiescentia* < L. *quiescens*], the quality or state of being quiescent.

qui·es·cen·cy (kwī-es′′n-si), *n.* quiescence.

qui·es·cent (kwī-es′′nt), *adj.* [L. *quiescens*, ppr. of *quiescere*, to become quiet], quiet; still; inactive; in repose. —*SYN.* see **latent.**

qui·et (kwī′ət), *adj.* [ME. & OFr. *quiete;* L. *quietus*, pp. of *quiescere*, to keep quiet < *quies, quietis*, rest; IE. base **kwejē-*, rest, seen also in AS. *hwil*, time; see WHILE], 1. still; calm; motionless. 2. *a*) not noisy; hushed. *b*) not speaking; silent. 3. not agitated in motion; gentle: as, a *quiet* sea. 4. not easily excited or disturbed: as, a *quiet* disposition. 5. not ostentatious or pretentious: as, *quiet* furnishings. 6. not forward; unobtrusive: as, a *quiet* manner. 7. secluded: as, a *quiet* den. 8. serving to relax and soothe: as, a *quiet* evening at home. 9. in *commerce*, not busy: as, a *quiet* day on the stock exchange. *n.* 1. a quiet state or condition; calmness, stillness, inactivity, freedom from noise, etc. 2. a quiet or peaceful quality; freedom from turmoil or agitation. *v.t.* to make quiet; calm or pacify, bring (something in motion) to rest, etc. *v.i.* to become quiet (usually with *down*). *adv.* in a quiet manner. —*SYN.* see **still.**

qui·et·en (kwī′ə-t′n), *v.t. & v.i.* [*quiet* + *-en*, verbalizing suffix], [British or Dial.], to make or become quiet.

qui·et·ism (kwī′ət-iz′m), *n.* [It. *quietismo* < L. *quietus;* see QUIET & -ISM], 1. a form of religious mysticism that involves complete extinction of the human will, drawing away from worldly things, and passive contemplation of God and divine things: it was taught by the 17th-century Spanish priest Molinos. 2. any religious mysticism of this sort. 3. tranquillity of the spirit or quietness of life.

qui·et·ist (kwī′ət-ist), *n.* a person who believes in or practices quietism. *adj.* of quietism or quietists.

qui·e·tude (kwī′ə-tōōd′, kwī′ə-tūd′), *n.* [Fr. *quiétude;* LL. *quietudo*], a state of being quiet; rest; calmness.

qui·e·tus (kwī-ē′təs), *n.* [ML., quit (in the formula *quietus est*, he is quit; L., he is quiet); cf. QUIET, QUIT], 1. discharge or release from debt, obligation, or office. 2. discharge or release from life; death. 3. anything that kills. 4. anything that serves to quiet, curb, or end an activity.

quill (kwil), *n.* [ME. *quil*, hollow stalk, weaver's quill; prob. < MLG. or MD.; cf. LG. *quiele*, quill of a feather (G. *federkiel*); IE. base **gwel-*, to stick, stab], 1. any of the large, stiff wing or tail feathers of a bird. 2. the hollow, horny stem of a feather; calamus. 3. any of the spines of a porcupine or hedgehog. 4. any of various things made from the quill of a feather, as a pen for writing or a plectrum for plucking the strings of certain musical instruments. 5. a musical pipe made of a hollow stem, reed, or cane. 6. a weaver's spindle. 7. in *pharmacy*, a small roll of dried bark, as of cinchona, cinnamon, etc. *v.t.* 1. to plait or form with quillings. 2. to wind on a quill (sense 6).

quil·lai (ki-lī′), *n.* [Sp. < the Chilean (Araucan) native name], 1. a Chilean tree whose inner bark is used as soap. 2. its inner bark: also **quillai bark.**

Quil·ler-Couch, Sir **Arthur Thomas** (kwil′ẽr-kōōch′), (pseudonym *Q*), 1863–1944; English poet and writer.

quil·let (kwil′it), *n.* [? altered < L. *quidlibet*, anything you please; *quid*, what, anything + *libet*, it pleases], [Archaic], a quibble; subtlety.

quill·ing (kwil′iŋ), *n.* a band of material fluted into small ruffles so as to resemble a row of quills.

quill·wort (kwil′wũrt′), *n.* any of a number of related water plants with short, fleshy stems and tufts of long, narrow leaves resembling quills.

quilt (kwilt), *n.* [ME. *quilte;* OFr. *cuilte, coutre, coultre* < L. *culcitra, culcita*, a bed, mattress, pillow; akin to Sans. *kūrcaḥ*, a bundle, roll; IE. base **qweleq-*], 1. a bedcover made of two layers of cloth filled with down, cotton, wool, etc. and stitched together in lines or patterns. 2. anything used as a quilt. 3. any material made up like a quilt. *v.t.* 1. to stitch together, as two pieces of cloth, with a soft material between. 2. to stitch in lines or patterns like those used in quilts. 3. to sew up or fasten between two pieces of material. 4. to line or pad like a quilt. *v.i.* to make a quilt or quilts.

quilt·ing (kwil′tiŋ), *n.* 1. the act or process of making quilts. 2. material for making quilts; quilted work. 3. a quilting bee.

quilting bee, a social gathering of women at which they work together sewing quilts.

quin·a·crine (kwin′ə-krēn′), *n.* [*quin*ine + *ac*rid + *-ine*], atabrine, a synthetic drug: in full, **quinacrine hydrochloride.**

qui·na·ry (kwī′nə-ri), *adj.* [L. *quinarius* < *quini*, five each < *quinque*, five], consisting of five; in sets of five. *n.* [*pl.* QUINARIES (-riz)], a set of five.

quince (kwins), *n.* [orig. pl. of ME. *quine, quyne, coin;* OFr. *cooin;* L. *cotonea, cydonia;* Gr. *kydōnia, kydōnion mēlon*, lit., Cydonian apple < *Kydōnia*, Cydonia, town on the northern coast of Crete], 1. a golden or greenish-yellow, apple-shaped fruit with a hard flesh, used in preserves. 2. the tree that bears it.

quin·cun·cial (kwin-kun′shəl), *adj.* [L. *quincuncialis*], having the form or arrangement of a quincunx.

quin·cunx (kwin′kuŋks), *n.* [*pl.* QUINCUNXES (-iz)], [L., lit., five twelfths < *quinque*, five + *uncia*, a twelfth, ounce], 1. an arrangement of five objects in a square, with one at each corner and one in the middle. 2. in *botany*, an arrangement of the petals in five-petaled flowers.

Quin·cy (*for 1*, kwin′zi; *for 2*, kwin′si), *n.* 1. a city in Massachusetts, near Boston: pop., 87,000. 2. a city in central Illinois, on the Mississippi: pop., 44,000.

Quin·cy, Josiah (kwin′zi, kwin′si), 1744–1775; American patriot.

quin·dec·a·gon (kwin-dek′ə-gon′), *n.* [< L. *quindecim*, fifteen; + *-agon* as in *decagon*], in *geometry*, a plane figure with fifteen angles and fifteen sides.

quin·de·cen·ni·al (kwin′di-sen′i-əl), *adj.* [< L. *quindecim*, fifteen; + *-ennial* as in *biennial*], 1. happening once in a period of fifteen years. 2. lasting for fifteen years. *n.* 1. a fifteenth year of existence or duration; fifteenth anniversary. 2. the celebration of this.

quin·i·a (kwin′i-ə), *n.* [Mod.L. < Sp. *quina*], quinine.

quin·ic acid (kwin′ik), [< *quina* (see QUININE) + *-ic*], a colorless, crystalline acid, $C_6H_7(OH)_4 \cdot COOH$, prepared from cinchona bark, coffee beans, etc.

quin·i·din (kwin′ə-din), *n.* quinidine.

quin·i·dine (kwin′ə-dēn′, kwin′ə-din), *n.* [< *quina* (see QUININE) + *-id* + *-ine*], a colorless, crystalline alkaloid, $C_{20}H_{24}N_2O_2$, isomeric with and resembling quinine, extracted from cinchona bark.

quin·in (kwin′in), *n.* quinine.

qui·ni·na (ki-nē′nə), *n.* quinine.

qui·nine (kwī′nīn, kwi-nēn′), *n.* [< *quina*, cinchona bark (Sp. *quina* < Quechua *quinquina*) + *-ine*], 1. a bitter, crystalline alkaloid, $C_{20}H_{24}N_2O_2$, extracted from cinchona bark. 2. any compound of this, as quinine sulfate, used in medicine for various purposes, especially in the treatment of malaria.

quin·nat salmon (kwin′at), [< the Am. Ind. (upper Chinook) name], chinook salmon.

quin·oid (kwin′oid), *n.* [*quin*one + *-oid*], a substance resembling quinone in structure, properties, etc.

qui·noi·din (kwi-noi′din), *n.* quinoidine.

qui·noi·dine (kwi-noi′dēn, kwi-noi′din), *n.* [*quinoid* + *-ine*], a brownish substance containing a mixture of alkaloids formed in the process of extracting quinine from cinchona, used as a substitute for quinine.

quin·o·lin (kwin′ə-lin), *n.* quinoline.

quin·o·line (kwin′ə-lēn′, kwin′ə-lin), *n.* [*quin*ine + *-ol* + *-ine*], a colorless, liquid compound, C_9H_7N, obtained by the destructive distillation of bones, coal tar, and various alkaloids, or by synthesis: it is used in making antiseptics, dyes, etc.

qui·none (kwi-nōn′, kwin′ōn), *n.* [*quin*ic acid + *-one*] 1. either of two isomeric compounds, $C_6H_4O_2$, especially the yellow, crystalline isomer used in making dyes. 2. any of a series of compounds of this type

qui·non·i·mine (kwi-non′ə-mēn′, kwi-non′ə-min), *n* [< *quinone* + *imine*], a crystalline compound, C_6H_5NO derived from a quinone by the replacement of an oxygen atom by an imino group.

quin·o·noid (kwin′ə-noid′, kwi-nō′noid), *adj.* [< *quinone* + *-oid*], like quinone in structure, properties, etc

quin·qua·ge·nar·i·an (kwiŋ′kwə-ji-nâr′i-ən), *adj.* [< L *quinquagenarius* < *quinquageni*, fifty each < *quinquaginta*, fifty], fifty years old, or between the ages of fifty and sixty. *n.* a person of this age.

Quin·qua·ges·i·ma (kwiŋ′kwə-jes′ə-mə), *n.* [ME. LL. *quinquagesima* (*dies*), fiftieth (day), i.e., before Easter, fem. of L. *quinquagesimus*, fiftieth], the Sunday before Lent: also **Quinquagesima Sunday.**

quin·que- (kwiŋ′kwə), [< L. *quinque*, five], a combining form meaning *five* or *a multiple of five*, as in *quinquevalent:* also, before a vowel, **quinqu-.**

quin·que·fo·li·o·late (kwiŋ′kwə-fō′li-ə-lit), *adj.* [*quinque-* + *foliolate*], in *botany*, having five leaves or leaflets

quin·quen·ni·ad (kwiŋ-kwen′i-ad′), *n.* a quinquennium.

quin·quen·ni·al (kwiŋ-kwen′i-əl), *adj.* [< L. *quinquennis*, of five years < *quinque*, five + *annus*, year], 1. lasting five years. 2. taking place every five years *n.* a quinquennial event.

quin·quen·ni·um (kwiŋ-kwen′i-əm), *n.* [*pl.* QUINQUENNIA (-ə)], [L. < *quinquennis;* see QUINQUENNIAL] a period of five years.

quin·que·reme (kwiŋ′kwə-rēm′), *n.* [L. *quinqueremis* < *quinque*, five + *remus*, oar], a galley having five banks of oars.

quin·que·va·lence (kwiŋ′kwə-vā′ləns, kwiŋ-kwev′ə-ləns), *n.* the quality or state of being quinquevalent

quin·que·va·len·cy (kwiŋ'kwə-vā'lən-si), *n.* quinquevalence.

quin·que·va·lent (kwiŋ'kwə-vā'lənt, kwiŋ-kwev'ə-lənt), *adj.* 1. having five valences. 2. having a valence of five. Also, especially for 2, **pentavalent.**

quin·sy (kwin'zi), *n.* [ME. *quinaci, quynsy;* altered < ML. *quinancia* < LL. *cynanche;* Gr. *kynanchē,* inflammation of the throat, lit., dog-choking < *kyōn,* dog + *anchein,* to choke], an inflammation of the tonsils, accompanied by the formation of pus.

quint (kwint, kint), *n.* [Fr. *quinte;* L. *quinta,* fem. of *quintus,* a fifth < base of *quinque,* five], 1. in *music,* *a)* an interval of a fifth. *b)* an organ stop producing tones a fifth above those sounded by the keys that are pressed. *c)* the E string of a violin. 2. in *piquet,* a sequence of five cards in the same suit.

quint (kwint), *n.* [Colloq.], a quintuplet.

quin·tain (kwin'tin), *n.* [OFr. *quintaine;* ML. *quintana;* prob. < L. *quintana (via),* street in the camp intersecting the legions so as to separate the fifth maniple from the sixth; later, market place < *quintanus,* fifth, belonging to the fifth < *quintus,* fifth], in *medieval sports,* an object supported by a crosspiece on an upright post, used as a target in tilting.

quin·tal (kwin't'l), *n.* [Fr.; ML. *quintale;* Ar. *qinṭār* < L. *centenarius;* see CENTENARY], 1. a hundredweight (100 pounds in the United States, 112 pounds in Great Britain). 2. a metric unit of weight, equal to 100 kilograms (220.46 pounds). Abbreviated **ql., q.**

quin·tan (kwin'tən), *adj.* [L. *quintanus* < *quintus,* fifth], occurring every fifth day (counting both days of occurrence). *n.* a quintan fever, etc.

Quin·te·ro, Joa·quín Ál·va·rez (hwä-kēn' äl'vä-reth' kēn-te'rô), 1873–1944; Spanish playwright; collaborated with his brother Serafín (se'rä-fēn'), 1871–1938.

quin·tes·sence (kwin-tes''ns), *n.* [ME. *quynte(n)cense;* ML. *quinta essentia*], 1. the fifth essence, or ultimate substance, of which the heavenly bodies were thought to be composed, in ancient and medieval philosophy: distinguished from the four elements, air, fire, water, and earth. 2. the pure, concentrated essence of anything. 3. the most perfect manifestation or embodiment of a quality or thing.

quin·tes·sen·tial (kwin'tə-sen'shəl), *adj.* of the quintessence; purest; most perfect.

quin·tet, quin·tette (kwin-tet'), *n.* [< Fr. or It.; Fr. *quintette;* It. *quintetto,* dim. of *quinto* (L. *quintus*), a fifth], 1. any group or set of five persons or things. 2. in *music, a)* a composition for five voices or five instruments, as for string quartet and piano. *b)* the five performers of such a composition.

quin·tile (kwin'til, kwin'tīl), *adj.* [< L. *quintus,* a fifth; + *-ile*], in *astrology,* designating an aspect of heavenly bodies in which they are 72 degrees, or one fifth of a circle, distant from each other. *n.* a quintile aspect.

Quin·til·ian (kwin-til'yən, kwin-til'i-ən), *n.* (*Marcus Fabius Quintilianus*), Roman rhetorician and critic; lived 1st century A.D.

quin·til·lion (kwin-til'yən), *n.* [< L. *quintus,* a fifth; + *million*], 1. in the United States and France, a number represented by 1 followed by 18 zeros. 2. in Great Britain and Germany, a number represented by 1 followed by 30 zeros. *adj.* amounting to one quintillion in number.

Quin·tin (kwin'tin), [Fr. *Quentin;* L. *Quintinus* < *Quintus,* Roman praenomen < *quintus, quinctus,* the fifth], a masculine name: variant, *Quentin.*

quin·tu·ple (kwin'too-p'l, kwin-tū'p'l), *adj.* [Fr.; L. *quintuplex* < *quintus,* a fifth + *plicare,* to fold], 1. consisting of or including five. 2. five times as much or as many; fivefold. *n.* a number, etc. five times as great as another. *v.t. & v.i.* [QUINTUPLED (-p'ld), QUINTUPLING], to make or become five times as much or as many; multiply by five.

quin·tu·plet (kwin'too-plit, kwin-tū'plit, kwin-tup'-lit), *n.* [< *quintuple*], 1. *a)* any of five offspring born at a single birth. *b) pl.* five offspring born at a single birth. 2. a collection or group of five, usually of one kind.

quip (kwip), *n.* [contr. < earlier *quippy* < L. *quippe,* indeed, forsooth], 1. a witty or sarcastic expression or allusion; gibe; jest. 2. a quibble. 3. something curious or odd. *v.t.* [QUIPPED (kwipt), QUIPPING], to direct quips at. *v.i.* to utter quips. —*SYN.* see **joke.**

quip·ster (kwip'stẽr), *n.* a person who quips.

qui·pu (kē'pōō, kwip'ōō), *n.* [Sp. *quipo* < Peruv. (Quechua) *quipu,* a knot], a device consisting of an arrangement of cords variously colored and knotted, used by the ancient Peruvians to keep accounts, record events, send messages, etc.

quire (kwīr), *n., v.t. & v.i.* [QUIRED (kwīrd), QUIRING], [Archaic], choir.

quire (kwīr), *n.* [ME. *quair;* OFr. *quaer,* book of loose pages; LL. *quaternum,* paper packed in lots of four pages < L. *quattuor,* four], a set of 24 or 25 sheets of paper of the same size and stock, the twentieth part of a ream: abbreviated **qr., q.**

in quires, unbound: said of a book.

Quir·i·nal (kwir'i-n'l), *n.* [L. *Quirinalis* < *Quirinus;* see next entry], 1. one of the seven hills on which Rome was built: site of a papal palace, used as a royal residence of Italy since 1871. 2. the Italian civil government, as distinguished from the Vatican, or papal government. *adj.* 1. of or situated on the Quirinal. 2. of Quirinus.

Qui·ri·nus (kwi-rī'nəs), *n.* [L.; akin to *Quirites*], in *Roman mythology,* an early god of war: identified by the Romans with Romulus.

Qui·ri·tes (kwi-rī'tēz), *n.pl.* [L., pl. of *Quiris,* orig., inhabitant of *Cures* (a Sabine town); later, Roman citizen], in ancient Rome, the people as civilians.

quirk (kwũrk), *n.* [? < ON. *kuerk,* a crop, bird's neck (via dial.)], 1. a sudden twist, turn, or stroke, as a flourish in writing. 2. an evasion, subterfuge, quibble, or equivocation. 3. a clever turn of speech; sally; quip. 4. a peculiarity, peculiar trait, or mannerism. 5. in *architecture,* a groove running lengthwise in a molding. *v.t.* in *architecture,* to form with a quirk.

quirk·y (kwũr'ki), *adj.* [QUIRKIER (-ki-ẽr), QUIRKIEST (-ki-ist)], having quirks.

quirt (kwũrt), *n.* [Mex. Sp. *cuarta,* a quirt, long whip < *cuarta,* guide mule, lit., fourth (of a four-mule team), fem. of Sp. *cuarto* (L. *quartus*), fourth], a riding whip with a braided leather lash and a short handle. *v.t.* to strike with a quirt.

quis·ling (kwiz'liŋ), *n.* [after Vidkun *Quisling* (1887–1945), Norw. politician who betrayed his country to the Nazis and became its puppet ruler], a person who betrays his own country by helping an enemy to invade and occupy it; traitor.

quit (kwit), *v.t.* [QUIT, QUITTED (-id), QUITTING], [ME. *quiten;* OFr. *quiter;* ML. *quittare* < LL. *quietare,* to set free < L. *quietus,* quiet, at rest, satisfied], 1. to free (oneself) *of.* 2. to discharge (a debt or obligation); repay. 3. to stop having, using, or doing (something); give up. 4. to let go (something held). 5. to leave; depart from. 6. to stop or discontinue, as work. 7. [Archaic], to conduct (oneself). *v.i.* 1. to go away. 2. to stop or discontinue doing something; give up an undertaking. 3. [Colloq.], to give up one's position of employment; resign. *adj.* clear; free; rid. —*SYN.* see **abandon, go, stop.**

quitch (kwich), *n.* [AS. *cwice* < base of *cwicu,* alive (cf. QUICK): so named supposedly from the great vitality of the plant], a long-rooted grass, growing in lawns, etc. as a weed: also **quitch grass.**

quit·claim (kwit'klām'), *n.* [ME. *quitclayme;* Anglo-Fr. *quiteclame* < the *v.*], 1. the release or relinquishment of a claim. 2. a deed or other legal paper in which a person relinquishes to another a claim to some property or right. *v.t.* [Anglo-Fr. & OFr. *quiteclamer;* *quite,* quit + *clamer,* to call, declare], to give up a claim to (some property or right).

quite (kwīt), *adv.* [ME. *quite;* see QUIT, *adj.*], 1. completely; entirely. 2. really; truly; positively. 3. [Colloq.], to a considerable degree or extent; very.

quite a few, [Colloq.], more than a few.

Qui·to (kē'tô), *n.* the capital of Ecuador: pop., 150,000.

quit·rent (kwit'rent'), *n.* a rent paid in lieu of required feudal services: also **quit rent.**

quits (kwits), *adj.* [< *quit, adj.*], on even terms, as by discharge of a debt, retaliation in vengeance, etc.

cry quits, to declare oneself even with another; agree to stop competing.

quit·tance (kwit''ns), *n.* [ME.; OFr. *quitance* < *quiter;* see QUIT], 1. discharge from a debt or obligation. 2. a document certifying this; receipt. 3. recompense; repayment; reprisal.

quit·ter (kwit'ẽr), *n.* [Colloq.], a person who quits or gives up easily, without trying hard.

quit·tor (kwit'ẽr), *n.* [ME.; OFr. *cuiture,* cooking], any of various foot diseases of horses, mules, etc., characterized by tissue degeneration and the formation of a slough.

‡qui va là? (kē' vå' lå'), [Fr.], who goes there?: a sentry's challenge.

quiv·er (kwiv'ẽr), *v.i.* [ME. *quivere(n);* prob. < base of *quaver;* cf. MD. *quiveren*], to shake with a tremulous motion; tremble. *n.* the act or condition of quivering; tremor; tremble. —*SYN.* see **shake.**

quiv·er (kwiv'ẽr), *n.* [ME. *quyver(e);* Anglo-Fr. *quiveir* (OFr. *quivre, queuvre, cuivre,* etc.) < Gmc.; cf. OHG. *kochar,* AS. *cocer,* arrow case, sheath], 1. a case for holding arrows. 2. its contents.

quiv·er (kwiv'ẽr), *adj.* [ME. *cwyuer;* AS. *cwifer-*], [Obs. or Dial.], nimble; quick.

‡qui vive? (kē' vēv'), [Fr., lit., who lives?], who goes there?: a sentry's challenge.

on the qui vive, on the lookout; on the alert.

Quixote, Don, see **Don Quixote.**

quix·ot·ic (kwik-sot′ik), ***adj.*** 1. [sometimes Q-], like or befitting Don Quixote. 2. extravagantly chivalrous or romantically idealistic; visionary; impractical or impracticable.

quix·ot·i·cal (kwik-sot′i-k'l), ***adj.*** quixotic.

quix·ot·i·cal·ly (kwik-sot′i-k'l-i, kwik-sot′ik-li), ***adv.*** in a quixotic manner.

quix·ot·ism (kwik′sə-tiz'm), ***n.*** 1. quixotic character or practice. 2. a quixotic act or idea.

quiz (kwiz), ***n.*** [*pl.* QUIZZES (-iz)], [prob. an arbitrary formation; ? suggested by L. *quis*, who, which, what, *quid*, how, why, wherefore], 1. [Rare], a queer or eccentric person. 2. a practical joke; hoax. 3. a questioning; especially, an informal oral or written examination to test one's knowledge. ***v.t.*** [QUIZZED (kwizd), QUIZZING], 1. to make fun of (someone or something). 2. to ask questions of (a person) to test his knowledge. —***SYN.*** see **ask.**

quiz program, a type of radio or television program in which a group of experts or members of the audience compete in answering questions.

quiz section, in some colleges and universities, a small group of students who meet with an instructor to discuss and be examined on the content of lectures.

quiz·zer (kwiz′ẽr), ***n.*** a person who quizzes.

quiz·zi·cal (kwiz′i-k'l), ***adj.*** [< *quiz* + *-ic* + *-al*], 1. odd; comical. 2. given to making fun of others; bantering. 3. perplexed; questioning.

‡**quo·ad hoc** (kwō′ad hok′), [L.], 1. to this extent. 2. with respect to this.

‡**quo a·ni·mo?** (kwō an′ə-mō′), [L., lit., with what mind?], with what intent?

quod (kwod), ***n.*** [a form of *quad* < *quadrangle* (of a prison)], [Chiefly British Slang], prison: also **quad.**

‡**quod e·rat de·mon·stran·dum** (kwod er′at dem′ən-stran′dəm), [L.], which was to be demonstrated or proved: abbreviated **Q.E.D.**

‡**quod e·rat fa·ci·en·dum** (kwod er′at fā′shi-en′dəm), [L.], which was to be done: abbreviated **Q.E.F.**

‡**quod est** (kwod est), [L.], which is: abbreviated **q.e.**

‡**quod vi·de** (kwod vī′di), [L.], which see: abbreviated **q.v.**

quoin (koin, kwoin), ***n.*** [var. of *coin*], 1. the external corner of a building; especially, any of the large, squared stones by which the corner of a building is marked. 2. a wedgelike piece of stone, etc., such as the keystone or one of the pieces of an arch. 3. a wedge-shaped wooden or metal block used to lock up type in a galley or form, to keep casks from rolling, to fix the position of a gun breech, etc. ***v.t.*** 1. to secure with a quoin. 2. to furnish with quoins, or corners.

QUOINS

quoit (kwoit, koit), ***n.*** [ME. *coite, coyte;* Anglo-Fr. *jeu de coytes;* prob. < OFr. *coite* (Fr. *couette*), a cushion; ? orig. applied to a cushion target (but note Fr. *coussinet*, flat stone disk, as adduced by Weekley)], 1. a ring of rope or flattened metal, used in the game of quoits. 2. *pl.* a game in which players throw such rings at a peg in the ground, the object being to encircle it or come as close to it as possible. ***v.i.*** [Rare], to play quoits. ***v.t.*** to throw like a quoit.

‡**quo ju·re?** (kwō jōō′ri), [L.], by what right?

‡**quo mo·do** (kwō mō′dō), [L.], 1. in what manner? 2. in the manner that.

quon·dam (kwon′dəm), ***adj.*** [L.], that was at one time; former: as, my *quondam* companion.

Quon·set hut (kwon′sit), [< *Quonset*, R.I., where first manufactured], a prefabricated shelter made of corrugated metal, shaped like a longitudinal half of a cylinder resting on its flat surface: it is similar to the British Nissen hut and was first used by the U.S. Army in World War II.

quo·rum (kwôr′əm, kwō′rəm), ***n.*** [L., genit. pl. of *qui*, who: from use in court commissions], 1. *a*) originally, the number of justices of the peace required to be present at sessions of English courts. *b*) later, English justices of the peace, collectively. 2. a select group or company. 3. the minimum number of members required to be present at an assembly before it can validly proceed to transact business.

quo·ta (kwō′tə), ***n.*** [*pl.* QUOTAS (-təz)], [ML. < L., fem. of *quotus*, how many], a share or proportion which each of a number is called upon to contribute, or which is assigned to each; proportional share.

quot·a·bil·i·ty (kwō′tə-bil′ə-ti), ***n.*** the quality or state of being quotable.

quot·a·ble (kwō′tə-b'l), ***adj.*** that can be quoted; suited for quotation.

quo·ta·tion (kwō-tā′shən), ***n.*** [ML. *quotatio*], 1. the act or practice of quoting. 2. the words or passage quoted. 3. in *commerce*, *a*) a statement of the current price of a stock, bond, commodity, etc. *b*) the price itself. Abbreviated **quot.**

quotation mark, either of a pair of punctuation marks (". . . .") used to enclose a direct quotation: a quotation within a quotation is enclosed in single marks (' . . . .'): in British usage, this procedure is usually reversed.

quote (kwōt), ***v.t.*** [QUOTED (-id), QUOTING], [ME. *coten;* Late OFr. *coter;* ML. *quotare*, to mark the number of, divide into chapters < L. *quotus*, of what number], 1. to reproduce or repeat a passage from or statement of: as, the teacher *quoted* Chaucer. 2. to reproduce or repeat (a passage from a book, a statement, etc.). 3. to cite; refer to as authority or an example. 4. in *commerce*, to state (the price of something). 5. in *printing*, to enclose in quotation marks. ***n.*** [Colloq.], 1. a quotation. 2. a quotation mark.

quoth (kwōth), ***v.t.*** [ME.; AS. *quæth*, pret. of *cwethan*, to speak, say], [Archaic], said: used in the past tense, followed by a subject of the first or third person, and taking as its object the words being repeated.

quoth·a (kwōth′ə), ***interj.*** [phonetic alteration of *quoth he*, used ironically], [Archaic], indeed! forsooth!

quo·tid·i·an (kwō-tid′i-ən), ***adj.*** [ME. *quotidien;* OFr. *cotidian;* L. *quotidianus* < *quotidie*, daily < *quotus*, how many + *dies*, day], daily; recurring every day. ***n.*** anything, especially a fever, that recurs daily.

quo·tient (kwō′shənt), ***n.*** [ME. *quocient;* L. *quoties, quotiens*, how often, how many times < *quot*, how many], in *arithmetic*, the number obtained when one quantity is divided by another: abbreviated **q.**

quo war·ran·to (kwō wô-ran′tō), [*pl.* QUO WARRANTOS (-tōz)], [ML., by what warrant < L. *quo*, abl. of *qui*, who, which + ML. *warrantus*, a warrant], 1. originally, a writ ordering a person to show by what right he exercises an office, franchise, or privilege. 2. *a*) a legal proceeding undertaken to recover an office, franchise, or privilege from the person in possession, initiated upon an information. *b*) the information.

q.v., [L.], 1. *quantum vis*, as much as you will. 2. *quod vide*, which see.

qy., query.

R

R, r (är), ***n.*** [*pl.* R's, r's, Rs, rs (ärz)], 1. the eighteenth letter of the English alphabet: from the Greek *rho*, a borrowing from the Phoenician: see **alphabet**, table. 2. the sound of R or r: in English, it is basically a vowellike, voiced, alveolar, retroflex continuant; but it is also variously heard in British and American dialects as a flipped lingual continuant: in standard varieties of British and some varieties of Eastern and Southern American English, the sound of *r* has been lost in certain positions, as in *bird, sir, father*, etc. 3. a type or impression for R or r. 4. *a symbol for* the eighteenth in a sequence or group (or the seventeenth if J is omitted). ***adj.*** 1. of R or r. 2. eighteenth (or seventeenth if J is omitted) in a sequence or group.

R (är), ***n.*** 1. an object shaped like R. 2. a medieval Roman numeral for 80: with a superior bar ($\bar{R}$), 80,000. 3. in *chemistry, the symbol for* radical, especially organic radical. 4. in *electricity, the symbol for* resistance. 5. in *mathematics, the symbol for* radius or ratio. 6. in *physics & chemistry, the symbol for* gas constant. ***adj.*** shaped like R.

the three R's, reading, writing, and arithmetic, regarded as the basic elementary studies and the fundamentals of an education: so called from the

humorous spelling *reading*, *'riting*, and *'rithmetic*.
R, in *chess*, rook.
r, 1. roentgen(s). 2. royal. 3. ruble. 4. in *electricity*, resistance.
R., 1. Radical. 2. Reaumur. 3. Republic(an). 4. in *ecclesiastical usage*, respond or response: also ℟.
R., r., 1. rabbi. 2. radius. 3. railroad. 4. railway. 5. *recipe*, [L.], take: used in prescriptions: also ℞. 6. *Regina*, [L.], queen. 7. *Rex*, [L.], king. 8. right. 9. river. 10. road. 11. royal. 12. ruble. 13. [*pl.* Rs., Rs, ₨, rs.], rupee.
r., 1. range. 2. rare. 3. received. 4. residence. 5. resides. 6. retired. 7. rises. 8. rod; rods. 9. rubber. 10. in *baseball* & *cricket*, run; runs. 11. in *law*, rule.
Ra (rä), *n.* [Egypt. *Rā*, *Rē'*, sun], the sun god, principal god of the ancient Egyptians, usually depicted as having the head of a hawk and wearing the solar disk as a crown: also **Re.**
Ra, in *chemistry*, radium.
RA, R.A., Regular Army.
R.A., 1. Rear Admiral. 2. Rear Artillery. 3. Royal Academician. 4. Royal Academy. 5. Royal Artillery. 6. in *astronomy*, right ascension.
Ra·bat (rä-bät', rə-bät'), *n.* the capital of Morocco, on the west coast: pop., 156,000.
ra·ba·to (rə-bā'tō, rə-bä'tō), *n.* [*pl.* RABATOS (-tōz)], [Fr. *rabat* < *rabattre;* see REBATE], formerly, a large collar of linen, lace, etc., worn turned down so as to fall over the shoulders.
Ra·baul (rä-boul', rä'boul), *n.* the chief city of New Britain, Bismarck Archipelago: capital of the Territory of New Guinea: pop., 4,700.
Rab·bath Am·mon (rab'əth am'ən), Amman, the capital of Jordan: the Biblical name.
rab·bet (rab'it), *n.* [ME. *rabet;* OFr. *rabat, rabbat* < *rabattre;* see REBATE], 1. a groove or cut made in the edge of a board, etc. in such a way that another piece may be fitted into it to form a joint. 2. a joint made in this way. *v.t.* 1. to cut a rabbet in. 2. to join in a rabbet (joint). *v.i.* to be joined by a rabbet.

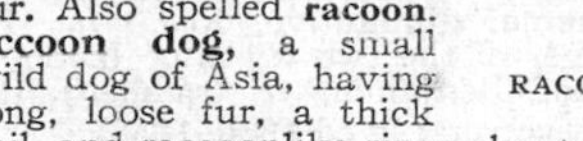
RABBETS

rab·bi (rab'ī), *n.* [*pl.* RABBIS, RABBIES (-īz)], [ME.; AS.; LL.; Gr. *rhabbi;* Heb. *rabbī*, my master, my lord < *rabh*, master, great one], an ordained teacher of the Jewish law, authorized to decide questions of law and ritual and to perform marriages, etc., now usually the spiritual head of a congregation: the term is also used in respectful address: abbreviated **R., r.**
rab·bin (rab'in), *n.* [Fr.; ML. *rabbinus*], a rabbi.
rab·bin·ate (rab'in-it), *n.* 1. the position or office of rabbi. 2. rabbis collectively.
Rab·bin·ic (rə-bin'ik), *n.* the Hebrew language as used in the writings of rabbis of the Middle Ages.
rab·bin·ic (rə-bin'ik), *adj.* rabbinical.
rab·bin·i·cal (rə-bin'i-k'l), *adj.* [< ML. *rabbinus;* + *-ical*], of the rabbis, their doctrines, learning, language, etc., especially in the early Middle Ages.
rab·bin·ist (rab'in-ist), *n.* [< ML. *rabbinus;* + *-ist*], a follower of the Talmudic teachings and traditions of the rabbis.
rab·bin·is·tic (rab'in-is'tik), *adj.* of, or in the tradition of, the rabbis.
rab·bit (rab'it), *n.* [*pl.* RABBITS (-its), RABBIT; see PLURAL, II, D, 1], [ME. *rabette*, young of the cony; akin to MD. *robbe*, Fl. *robbe*, Walloon *rabbett;* these forms, Brit. dial. *robert*, and surname *Rabbetts* suggest etymon < *Rob*, dim. of *Robert*, but may represent folk etym.], 1. a burrowing rodent of the hare family, smaller than most hares and characterized by soft fur, long ears, and a bobbed tail. 2. its fur. 3. loosely, any hare. 4. a dish made of melted cheese and toast: see **Welsh rabbit.** *v.i.* to hunt rabbits.
rabbit fever, tularemia.
rabbit punch, in *boxing*, a short, sharp blow to the back of the neck.
rab·bit·ry (rab'it-ri), *n.* [*pl.* RABBITRIES (-riz)], a place where domesticated rabbits are kept; rabbit hutch.
rabbit's (or **rabbit**) **foot,** the hind foot of a rabbit, used superstitiously as a talisman, or good-luck charm.
rab·ble (rab''l), *n.* [ME. *rabel;* prob. < *rabble* (iron bar, etc.), either *n.* or *v.;* for sense development cf. RASCAL], a noisy, disorderly crowd; mob. *v.t.* [RABBLED (-'ld), RABBLING], to attack with a mob.
the rabble, the common people; the masses: a term of contempt.
rab·ble (rab''l), *n.* [Fr. *râble* < OFr. *roable;* ML. *rotabulum*, poker, shovel; L. *rutabulum*, stirrer, shovel < *ruere*, to rake up], an iron bar used to stir and skim molten iron in puddling. *v.t.* [RABBLED (-'ld), RABBLING], to stir or skim with such a bar.
rab·ble·ment (rab''l-mənt), *n.* a noisy disturbance like that made by a rabble, or mob.
rabble rouser, a person who tries to arouse people to violent action by appealing to their emotions, prejudices, etc.; demagogue.
Rab·e·lais, Fran·çois (frän'swȧ' rȧ'ble'; Eng. rab'ə-lā', rab'ə-lā'), 1494?–1553; French satirist and humorist.
Rab·e·lai·si·an (rab'ə-lā'zhən, rab'ə-lā'zi-ən), *adj.* of or like Rabelais or his works; broadly and coarsely humorous, satirical, etc. *n.* a person who imitates, admires, or studies Rabelais.
rab·id (rab'id), *adj.* [L. *rabidus* < *rabere*, to rage; prob. IE. base **rab-*, violent, raging, seen also in Sans. *râbhas-*, violence, force], 1. violent; raging. 2. excessive in beliefs or opinions; too zealous; fanatical. 3. of or having rabies.
ra·bid·i·ty (rə-bid'ə-ti), *n.* rabid state or quality.
ra·bies (rā'bēz, rā'bi-ēz'), *n.* [L., madness; see RAGE], an infectious virus disease of the central nervous system in dogs and other flesh-eating animals: it can be transmitted to man by the bite of an infected animal and is characterized by choking, convulsions, inability to swallow liquids, etc.; it is fatal if not treated immediately: also called *hydrophobia.*
rac·coon (ra-kōōn'), *n.* [*pl.* RACCOONS (-kōōnz'), RACCOON; see PLURAL, II, D, 1], [altered < Am. Ind. (Algonquian) *arakunem*, lit., hand-scratcher], 1. a small, tree-climbing, flesh-eating mammal of North America, active largely at night and characterized by long, yellow-black fur, black masklike markings across the eyes, and a long, black-ringed tail. 2. its fur. Also spelled **racoon.**

RACCOON (34 in. long)

raccoon dog, a small wild dog of Asia, having long, loose fur, a thick tail, and raccoonlike rings about the eyes.
race (rās), *n.* [ME. (North) *ras(e)* < ON. *rās*, a running, rush; akin to AS. *ræs*, swift movement, attack, etc.; IE. base **eras-*, to flow, move rapidly, trickle, etc. (seen also in L. *rorarii*, skirmishing troops); prob. < **er-*, to set in swift motion (cf. ERRANT)], 1. a competition of speed in running, skating, riding, etc. 2. *pl.* a series of such competitions for horses, on a regular course. 3. *a*) any contest of speed in acting, thinking, etc.: as, a *race* for power. *b*) any contest: as, the *race* for mayor. 4. a steady onward movement or course. 5. the span of life: as, the old man's *race* was run. 6. *a*) a swift current of water. *b*) the channel for a current of water, especially one built to use the water industrially: as, a mill*race.* 7. a channel or groove for the moving parts of a machine, as the groove for the balls in a ball bearing. 8. in *aeronautics*, the slip stream. *v.i.* [RACED (rāst), RACING], 1. to take part in a competition of speed. 2. to go or move swiftly. 3. to move or revolve too swiftly because of less resistance or a lighter load: said of machinery. *v.t.* 1. to compete with in a competition of speed. 2. to cause (a horse, airplane, etc.) to engage in a race. 3. *a*) to cause to go swiftly. *b*) to cause (an engine) to run too swiftly without engaging the gears.
race (rās), *n.* [Fr.; It. *razza;* ? < L. *generatio*, a begetting; see GENERATION], 1. *a*) any of the major biological divisions of mankind, distinguished by color and texture of hair, color of skin and eyes, stature, bodily proportions, etc.: many ethnologists now consider that there are only three primary divisions, the Caucasian (loosely, *white race*), Negroid (loosely, *black race*), and Mongoloid (loosely, *yellow race*), each with various subdivisions: the term has acquired so many unscientific connotations that in this sense it is often replaced in scientific usage by *ethnic stock* or *group*. *b*) mankind. 2. a population that differs from others in the relative frequency of some gene or genes: a modern scientific use. 3. any geographical, national, or tribal ethnic grouping. 4. *a*) the state of belonging to a certain ethnic stock, group, etc. *b*) the qualities, traits, etc. belonging, or supposedly belonging, to such a division. 5. any group of people having the same ancestry; family; clan; lineage. 6. any group of people having the same activities, habits, ideas, etc.: as, the *race* of dramatists. 7. *a*) a group of plants or animals with distinguishing traits that are passed on to the offspring; breed. *b*) in *zoology*, a subspecies, or variety. 8. [Rare], distinctive flavor, taste, etc., as of wines, or quality, especially piquancy, as of speech. *adj.* [of recent origin, with euphemistic intent], Negro.
race·course (rās'kôrs', rās'kōrs'), *n.* a race track, especially one for horse races.

race horse, a horse bred and trained for racing.
ra·ceme (rā-sēm′, rə-sēm′), *n.* [L. *racemus*, cluster of grapes], a variety of flower cluster in which single flowers grow individually on small stems arranged at intervals along a single larger stem, as in the lily of the valley.

RACEME (of common red currant)

ra·ce·mic (rā-sē′mik, rə-sem′ik), *adj.* [< *raceme* + *-ic*], 1. designating or of an optically inactive form of tartaric acid. 2. *a*) consisting of an optically inactive, equimolecular mixture of the dextrorotatory and levorotatory forms of certain substances. *b*) designating or of a compound formed of such a mixture.
rac·e·mif·er·ous (ras′ə-mif′ẽr-əs), *adj.* bearing racemes.
rac·e·mism (ras′ə-miz′m, rə-sē′miz′m), *n.* racemization.
rac·e·mi·za·tion (ras′ə-mi-zā′shən), *n.* the conversion of an optically active substance into a racemic form.
rac·e·mose (ras′ə-mōs′), *adj.* [L. *racemosus*], 1. having the nature of a raceme. 2. bearing a raceme or racemes.
rac·er (rās′ẽr), *n.* 1. any person, animal, airplane, etc. that takes part in races or is capable of great speed. 2. any of several snakes; especially, the American blacksnake. 3. a revolving turntable on certain gun carriages, by which the gun can be aimed.
race riot, fighting and violence between different groups in a community, as between Negroes and whites, characterized by racist hostility.
race suicide, the gradual dying out of a people as a result of the deliberate failure of its members to maintain a birth rate equal to the death rate.
race track, a course prepared for racing; racecourse.
race·way (rās′wā′), *n.* 1. a narrow channel for water. 2. a tube for carrying and protecting electric wires.
Ra·chel (rā′chəl), [LL.; Gr. *Rhachēl;* Heb. *rāḥēl*, lit., ewe], a feminine name: diminutive, *Rae.* *n.* 1. in the *Bible*, the younger of the two wives of Jacob, and mother of Joseph and Benjamin. 2. (rå′shel′), (born *Élisa Félix*), French actress; lived 1820–1858.
ra·chis (rā′kis), *n.* [*pl.* RACHISES (-iz), RACHIDES (rak′ə-dēz′, rā′kə-dēz′)], [Mod. L.; Gr. *rhachis;* IE. base **wrāĝh-*, thorn, point], 1. in *anatomy*, the spinal column. 2. in *botany*, the principal stem of a raceme. 3. in *zoology*, the shaft of a feather, especially that part bearing the barbs. Also spelled **rhachis.**
ra·chit·ic (rə-kit′ik), *adj.* of or having rachitis.
ra·chi·tis (rə-kī′tis), *n.* [Mod. L.; Gr. *rhachitis*, inflammation of the spine < *rhachis*, the spine], rickets.
Rach·ma·ni·noff, Ser·ge·i Vas·sil·ie·vich (syer-gyā′i vå-sēl′ye-vich räkh-mä′nü-nôf; Eng. rak-mä′ni-nôf′), 1873–1943; Russian composer, conductor, and pianist: also spelled **Rachmaninov.**
ra·cial (rā′shəl), *adj.* of or characteristic of a race (ethnic group), races, or race.
ra·cial·ism (rā′shəl-iz′m), *n.* a doctrine or feeling of racial differences or antagonisms, especially with reference to supposed racial superiority, inferiority, or purity; racial prejudice, hatred, or discrimination.
ra·cial·ly (rā′shəl-i), *adv.* in regard to race.
rac·i·ly (rās′′l-i), *adv.* in a racy manner.
Ra·cine (rə-sēn′), *n.* a city in southeastern Wisconsin, on Lake Michigan: pop., 89,000.
Ra·cine, Jean Bap·tiste (zhän bå′tēst′ rå′sēn′; Eng. rə-sēn′), 1639–1699; French poet and writer of tragedies.
rac·i·ness (rās′i-nis), *n.* the quality of being racy.
rac·ism (rās′iz′m), *n.* 1. racialism. 2. program or practice of racial discrimination, segregation, persecution, and domination, based on racialism.
rac·ist (rās′ist), *adj.* of or characterized by racism. *n.* a person who believes in the doctrine of racialism or who advocates or practices racism.
rack (rak), *n.* [ME. *racke;* prob. < MD. *rek*, framework < *recken*, to stretch (akin to Eng. *reach*)], 1. a framework, grating, case, stand, etc. for holding or displaying various articles; specifically, *a*) a grating for holding hay, etc. to feed cattle. *b*) a frame for holding hay, straw, etc. on a wagon. *c*) a frame with hooks for hanging clothes. *d*) a row of pigeonholes for holding sorted papers, etc. *e*) a framework for holding aerial bombs in an airplane. *f*) a frame for arranging billiard balls in a triangle at the beginning of a game. *g*) in *printing*, a frame for holding cases of type. 2. a toothed bar into which a toothed gear wheel, worm gear, etc. meshes. 3. an instrument of torture having a frame on which the victim is bound and stretched until his limbs are pulled out of place. 4. any great mental or physical torment, or its cause. 5. a wrenching or upheaval, as by a storm. *v.t.* [prob. < MD. *recken*], 1. to arrange in or on a rack. 2. to torture by stretching on a rack so as to pull the limbs out of place. 3. to torment physically or mentally: as, a body racked with pain. 4. *a*) to oppress by unfair demands, especially by exacting exorbitant rents. *b*) to raise (rents) to an exorbitant degree. —*SYN.* see **torment.**

RACK (sense *n.* 2)

on the rack, in a very difficult or painful situation.
rack one's brains (or **memory,** etc.), to try very hard to remember or think of something.
rack (rak), *n.* [? var. of *track* with loss of *-t;* cf. RANKLE, RUFF], either of two gaits used by horses, the single foot or the pace. *v.i.* to move with either of these.
rack (rak), *n.* [var. of *wrack*], destruction; wreckage: now only in *go to rack and ruin*, to become ruined.
rack (rak), *n.* [ME. *rac, rakke;* prob. < ON.; cf. ON. *reka*, to drive, Norw., Sw. dial. *rak*, a wreck], a broken mass of clouds blown by the wind. *v.i.* to be blown by the wind: said of clouds. Also spelled **wrack.**
rack (rak), *v.t.* [Late ME.; Pr. *arracar* < *raca*, husk and stems of grapes, thick dregs], to draw off (cider, wine, etc.) from the dregs.
rack·et (rak′it), *n.* [prob. echoic], 1. a noisy confusion; loud and confused talk or activity; uproar. 2. a period of gay, exciting merrymaking or revelry. 3. [Slang], *a*) an obtaining of money illegally, as by bootlegging, fraud, or, especially, threats of violence. *b*) any dishonest scheme or practice; hence, *c*) any business, profession, or occupation: as, selling is a good *racket*: used humorously. *v.i.* 1. to make a racket; take part in a noisy activity. 2. to frolic noisily; revel. —*SYN.* see **noise.**
rack·et (rak′it), *n.* [Fr. *raquette;* ult. < Ar. *rāḥah* (pl. *rāḥāt*), palm of the hand], 1. a light bat for tennis, badminton, etc., with a network of catgut, silk, nylon, etc. in an oval or round frame attached to a handle. 2. a snowshoe. 3. *pl.* a variety of tennis played in a walled enclosure. Also spelled **racquet.**
rack·et·eer (rak′ə-têr′), *n.* [*racket* (uproar), sense 3 + *-eer*], a person who obtains money illegally, as by bootlegging, fraud, or, especially, threats of violence. *v.i.* to obtain money in any of these ways.
rack·et·eer·ing (rak′ə-têr′iŋ), *n.* the practice or method of a racketeer.
rack·et·y (rak′ə-ti), *adj.* 1. making a racket; very noisy. 2. fond of or engaging in frequent revelry, etc.
Rack·ham, Arthur (rak′əm), 1867–1939; English painter and book illustrator.
rack railway, a railway for climbing an inclined plane, as a mountain, having a toothed rail (*rack rail*) between the regular rails for engaging with cogwheels on the locomotive.
rack-rent (rak′rent′), *v.t.* to exact rack rent from.
rack rent, [*rack* (to stretch) + *rent*], a rent whose annual amount is equal, or almost equal, to the value of the property; excessive rent.
rack·work (rak′wũrk′), *n.* a mechanical device having a rack (toothed bar).
rac·on·teur (rak′on-tũr′; Fr. rå′kōn′tẽr′), *n.* [Fr. < *raconter*, to recount], a person skilled at telling stories or anecdotes.
ra·coon (ra-kōōn′), *n.* a raccoon.
rac·quet (rak′it), *n.* a racket (bat).
rac·y (rās′i), *adj.* [RACIER (-i-ẽr), RACIEST (-i-ist)], [*race* (tribe) + *-y*], 1. having the characteristic taste, flavor, or quality associated with the original or genuine type: as, *racy* fruit. 2. lively; spirited; vigorous. 3. piquant; pungent; hence, 4. somewhat indecent; suggestive; risqué: as, a *racy* novel. —*SYN.* see **pungent.**
rad., 1. radial. 2. radical. 3. radius. 4. radix.
ra·dar (rā′där), *n.* [*ra*dio *d*etecting *a*nd *r*anging], a radio detecting instrument consisting of a transmitter that sends out high-frequency radio waves and a receiver that picks them up after they have been reflected by a land mass, ship, etc.: it indicates the direction and distance of the reflecting object.
rad·dle (rad′′l), *v.t.* [RADDLED (-′ld), RADDLING], [Anglo-Fr. *reidele*, cart rail, stout pole (OFr. *reddalle*); MHG. *reidel, reitel*, a cudgel, bar], to interweave.
rad·dle (rad′′l), *n.* [var. of *ruddle*], red ocher. *v.t.* [RADDLED (-′ld), RADDLING], to color with red ocher. Also **ruddle, reddle.**
Ra·dek, Karl (kärl rä′dyek; Eng. rä′dək), 1885–; Soviet Russian writer and politician; convicted of treason (1937).
ra·di·al (rā′di-əl), *adj.* [Fr., or < ML. *radialis;* see RADIUS], 1. *a*) of or like a ray or rays; branching out in all directions from a common center. *b*) having or characterized by parts that branch out in this way. 2. of or situated like a radius. 3. in *anatomy*, of or near the radius or forearm. Abbreviated **rad.**
radial engine, an internal-combustion engine with cylinders arranged radially like wheel spokes.
ra·di·al·ly (rā′di-əl-i), *adv.* so as to be radial.
ra·di·an (rā′di-ən), *n.* [< *radius*], 1. an arc of a circle equal in length to the radius. 2. the angle at the center of a circle formed by two radii cutting off such an arc, equal to 57.295+ degrees.
ra·di·ance (rā′di-əns), *n.* [< *radiant*], the quality or state of being radiant; brightness.
ra·di·an·cy (rā′di-ən-si), *n.* radiance.
ra·di·ant (rā′di-ənt), *adj.* [L. *radians*, ppr. of *radiare*

see RADIATE], 1. sending out rays of light; shining brightly. 2. filled with light; bright: as, the *radiant* morning. 3. showing pleasure, joy, well-being, etc.; beaming: as, a *radiant* smile. 4. issuing (from a source) in or as in rays; radiated: as, *radiant* energy. *n.* 1. in *astronomy,* the point in the heavens from which a shower of meteors appears to come. 2. in *optics,* the point or object from which light proceeds. —*SYN.* see **bright.**

radiant energy, any form of energy radiating from a source, as electromagnetic waves, sound, heat, light, X rays, gamma rays, etc.

radiant heating, a method of heating a building by means of electric coils, hot-water or steam pipes, etc. installed in the floors or walls.

ra·di·ate (rā′di-āt′), *v.i.* [RADIATED (-id), RADIATING], [< L. *radiatus,* pp. of *radiare,* to radiate < *radius;* see RADIUS], 1. to send out rays of heat, light, etc. 2. to come forth or spread out in rays: as, heat *radiates* from the stove. 3. to branch out in lines from a center: as, highways *radiate* from the city. *v.t.* 1. to send out (heat, light, etc.) in rays. 2. to give out or spread (happiness, love, etc.) as if from a center. *adj.* 1. having rays or parts like rays; radial. 2. in *zoology,* having radial symmetry, or balanced arrangement around a central axis. *n.* in *zoology,* an animal having radial symmetry, as a jellyfish.

ra·di·a·tion (rā′di-ā′shən), *n.* [L. *radiatio*], 1. the act or process of radiating; specifically, the process in which energy in the form of rays of light, heat, etc. is sent out from atoms and molecules as they undergo internal change. 2. the rays sent out; radiant energy. 3. the treatment of disease by radium or other radioactive material. 4. radial arrangement of parts.

ra·di·a·tive (rā′di-ā′tiv), *adj.* of, capable of, or characterized by radiation.

ra·di·a·tor (rā′di-ā′tẽr), *n.* anything that radiates; specifically, *a)* a series of pipes or coils through which hot water or steam circulates so as to radiate heat into a room, etc. *b)* loosely, a hot-air register. *c)* a water-filled apparatus, as in an automobile, for radiating superfluous heat and thus cooling the engine.

rad·i·cal (rad′i-k'l), *adj.* [ME.; LL. *radicalis* < L. *radix, radicis,* a root], 1. of or from the root or roots; going to the center, foundation, or source of something; fundamental; basic: as, a *radical* principle. 2. *a)* favoring fundamental or extreme change; specifically, favoring such change of the social structure; very leftist. *b)* [R-], designating or of any of various modern political parties, especially in Europe, ranging from mildly leftist to conservative in program. 3. in *botany,* of or coming from the root. 4. in *mathematics,* having to do with the root or roots of a number or quantity. *n.* 1. *a)* a basic or root part of something. *b)* a fundamental. 2. *a)* a person having radical views. *b)* [R-], a member or adherent of a Radical political party. 3. in *chemistry,* a group of two or more atoms that acts as a single atom and goes through a reaction unchanged, or is replaced by a single atom: symbol, R (no period). 4. in *linguistics,* a word, or part of a word, serving as a base, or root, on which other words have been or can be formed. 5. in *mathematics, a)* any quantity from which the root is to be extracted. *b)* the radical sign. Abbreviated **R., rad.** —*SYN.* see **liberal.**

rad·i·cal·ism (rad′i-k'l-iz'm), *n.* 1. the quality or state of being radical, especially in politics. 2. radical principles, ideals, methods, or practices.

rad·i·cal·ly (rad′i-k'l-i, rad′ik-li), *adv.* 1. *a)* as regards root or origin: as, English is *radically* a Germanic language. *b)* from the very origin or foundation; fundamentally; basically; completely: as, *radically* mistaken. 2. in a manner characterized by radicalism.

radical sign, in *mathematics,* the sign ($\sqrt{}$ or $\sqrt{}$) used before a quantity to indicate that its root is to be extracted: derived from the *r* in Latin *radix,* root.

rad·i·cel (rad′ə-sel′), *n.* [Mod. L. *radicella,* dim. of L. *radix, radicis,* a root], in *botany,* a small root.

rad·i·ces (rad′ə-sēz′, rā′də-sēz′), *n.* alternative plural of **radix.**

rad·i·cle (rad′i-k'l), *n.* [L. *radicula,* dim. of *radix, radicis,* a root], 1. in *anatomy,* the rootlike beginning of a nerve, vein, etc. 2. in *botany, a)* the lower part of the axis of an embryo seedling; strictly, the root part; often, the hypocotyl, sometimes together with the root. *b)* a radicel or rudimentary root. 3. in *chemistry,* a radical.

ra·di·i (rā′di-ī′), *n.* alternative plural of **radius.**

ra·di·o (rā′di-ō′), *n.* [*pl.* RADIOS (-ōz′)], [contr. of *radiotelegraphy, radiotelephony,* etc.], 1. the practice or science of communicating over a distance by converting sounds or signals into electromagnetic waves and transmitting these directly through space, without connecting wires, to a receiving set, which changes them into sounds; wireless telephony or telegraphy. 2. such a receiving set, especially one adapted for receiving the waves of the assigned frequencies of certain transmitters or broadcasting stations. 3. *a)* broadcasting by radio as a business, entertainment, art, etc. *b)* all the facilities and related activities of such broadcasting. 4. a message sent by radio; radiogram. *adj.* 1. of, using, used in, sent by, or operated by radio. 2. having to do with electric frequencies of more than 15,000 cycles per second. *v.t. & v.i.* [RADIOED (-ōd′), RADIOING], to send (a message, etc.) or communicate with (a person, etc.) by radio.

ra·di·o- (rā′di-ō, rā′di-ə), [< L. *radius;* see RADIUS], a combining form meaning: 1. *ray, raylike,* as in *radiolarian.* 2. *by radio,* as in *radiotelegraphy.* 3. in *anatomy, the radius and.* 4. in *medicine, by means of radiant energy,* as in *radiotherapy.* 5. in *physics & chemistry, radioactive,* as in *radiothorium.*

ra·di·o·ac·tive, ra·di·o-ac·tive (rā′di-ō-ak′tiv), *adj.* [*radio-* + *active*], giving off, or capable of giving off, radiant energy in the form of particles or rays, as alpha, beta, and gamma rays, by the disintegration of atomic nuclei: said of certain elements, as radium, thorium, and uranium, and their products.

radioactive series, the series of isotopes of various elements successively formed by a radioactive substance before it comes to a stable state.

ra·di·o·ac·tiv·i·ty (rā′di-ō-ak-tiv′ə-ti, rā′di-ō′ak-tiv′ə-ti), *n.* the property or process of being radioactive.

ra·di·o·au·to·graph (rā′di-ō-ô′tə-graf′, rā′di-ō-ô′tə-gräf′), *n.* [*radio-* + *autograph*], a picture produced on photographic film, etc. by the rays from a radioactive substance in the thing being photographed.

radio beacon, a radio transmitter that gives off special signals to help ships or aircraft determine their positions or come in safely, as at night or in a fog.

radio beam, a constant stream of radio signals sent in a given direction from a radio beacon to serve as a course for incoming airplanes, etc.: also **beam.**

ra·di·o·bi·ol·o·gy (rā′di-ō-bi-ol′ə-ji), *n.* [*radio-* + *biology*], the branch of biology that investigates the effect of radiation on living organisms.

ra·di·o·broad·cast (rā′di-ō-brôd′kast′, rā′di-ō-brôd′-käst′), *v.t. & n.* broadcast by radio.

ra·di·o·chem·is·try (rā′di-ō-kem′is-tri), *n.* the branch of chemistry dealing with radioactive phenomena.

radio compass, a device for determining the direction of incoming radio waves, used in navigation, etc.

ra·di·o·con·duc·tor (rā′di-ō-kən-duk′tẽr), *n.* [*radio-* + *conductor*], any substance or instrument whose conductivity is affected by electric waves, so that it can be used to determine their presence and strength, as a coherer in radio: also **radio conductor.**

radio control, the directional control of pilotless aircraft, missiles, etc. by means of radio waves.

ra·di·o·el·e·ment (rā′di-ō-el′ə-mənt), *n.* a radioactive element.

ra·di·o-fre·quen·cy (rā′di-ō-frē′kwən-si), *adj.* of or using a radio frequency: abbreviated **R.F., r.f.**

radio frequency, in *electricity,* a frequency of more than 10,000 cycles per second.

ra·di·o·gen·ic (rā′di-ō-jen′ik), *adj.* [*radio-* + *-genic*], produced by radioactivity.

ra·di·o·gram (rā′di-ō-gram′), *n.* 1. a message sent by radio: also **radiotelegram.** 2. a radiograph.

ra·di·o·graph (rā′di-ō-graf′, rā′di-ō-gräf′), *n.* [*radio-* + *-graph*], a picture produced on a sensitized film or plate by rays other than light rays, especially by X rays; X-ray picture. *v.t.* to make a radiograph of.

ra·di·og·ra·pher (rā′di-og′rə-fẽr), *n.* a person who makes, or is an expert in, radiographs.

ra·di·o·graph·ic (rā′di-ō-graf′ik), *adj.* of radiography.

ra·di·o·graph·i·cal·ly (rā′di-ō-graf′i-k'l-i, rā′di-ō-graf′-ik-li), *adv.* by means of radiographs or radiography.

ra·di·og·ra·phy (rā′di-og′rə-fi), *n.* the act, process, or art of making radiographs.

ra·di·o·i·so·tope (rā′di-ō-ī′sə-tōp′), *n.* an artificially created radioactive isotope of a chemical element that is normally nonradioactive, used in medical therapy, biological research, etc.

ra·di·o·lar·i·an (rā′di-ə-lâr′i-ən), *n.* [< Mod. L. *Radiolaria,* name of the order < *radiolus,* dim. of L. *radius;* see RADIUS: so named from the radiating pseudopodia], any of a large group of one-celled sea animals with long, slender pseudopodia and a perforated outer skeleton of silica.

ra·di·o·lo·ca·tion (rā′di-ō-lō-kā′shən), *n.* the use of radar or radiolocators in finding the location and direction of enemy aircraft, etc.

ra·di·o·lo·ca·tor (rā′di-ō-lō′kā-tẽr, rā′di-ō-lō-kā′tẽr), *n.* a British device similar to the American radar.

ra·di·ol·o·gy (rā′di-ol′ə-ji), *n.* [*radio-* + *-logy*], the branch of science dealing with radiant energy and its uses, as in the treatment of disease by X rays.

ra·di·o·me·te·or·o·graph (rā′di-ō-mē′ti-ẽr-ə-graf′, rā′-di-ō-mē′ti-ẽr-ə-gräf′), *n.* a radiosonde.

ra·di·om·e·ter (rā'di-om'ə-tẽr), *n.* [*radio-* + *-meter*], an instrument for detecting, and measuring the intensity of, radiant energy, as by exposing to sunlight a set of vanes blackened on one side and suspended on an axis in a vacuum, and measuring their speed of rotation (i.e., the mechanical energy into which the radiant energy has been converted).

RADIOMETER

ra·di·om·e·try (rā'di-om'ə-tri), *n.* the act or art of using a radiometer.

ra·di·o·phone (rā'di-ō-fōn'), *n.* 1. a wireless telephone; telephone operated by radio. 2. in *physics*, any instrument for transforming radiant energy into sound. *v.t. & v.i.* to send (a message) by radiophone (sense 1). Also (for *n.* 1 & *v.*) **radiotelephone.**

ra·di·os·co·py (rā'di-os'kə-pi), *n.* [*radio-* + *-scopy*], the direct examination of the inside structure of opaque objects by means of X rays or rays from radioactive substances.

ra·di·o·sonde (rā'di-ō-sond'), *n.* [Fr.; *radio* (see RADIO) + *sonde*, depth sounding (cf. ME. *sonde*, AS. *sond*, messenger)], a device consisting of a miniature radio transmitter with instruments attached to it, sent into the upper atmosphere in a small balloon and then automatically dropped by parachute, for transmitting recordings of temperature, pressure, and humidity to ground observers by means of special radio signals: also called *radiometeorograph.*

radio spectrum, the complete range of frequencies or wave lengths of electromagnetic waves, specifically those used in radio and television.

radio station, a broadcasting station.

ra·di·o·tel·e·gram (rā'di-ō-tel'ə-gram'), *n.* a radiogram (sense 1).

ra·di·o·tel·e·graph (rā'di-ō-tel'ə-graf', rā'di-ō-tel'ə-gräf'), *n.* an instrument for sending radiotelegrams. *v.t. & v.i.* to send (a message) by a radiotelegraph.

ra·di·o·tel·e·graph·ic (rā'di-ō-tel'ə-graf'ik), *adj.* of or by a radiotelegraph or radiotelegraphy.

ra·di·o·te·leg·ra·phy (rā'di-ō-tə-leg'rə-fi), *n.* the sending of messages by a radiotelegraph.

ra·di·o·tel·e·phone (rā'di-ō-tel'ə-fōn'), *n., v.t. & v.i.* radiophone (*n.* 1 & *v.*).

ra·di·o·tel·e·phon·ic (rā'di-ō-tel'ə-fon'ik), *adj.* of or by a radiotelephone or radiotelephony.

ra·di·o·te·leph·o·ny (rā'di-ō-tə-lef'ə-ni), *n.* telephony by radio, without connecting wires.

ra·di·o·ther·a·py (rā'di-ō-ther'ə-pi), *n.* [*radio-* + *therapy*], the treatment of disease by the use of X rays or rays from a radioactive substance, as radium.

ra·di·o·ther·mics (rā'di-ō-thũr'miks), *n.pl.* [construed as sing.], [< *radio-* + Gr. *thermē*, heat; + *-ics*], the science of heat generation by radio-frequency currents.

ra·di·o·ther·my (rā'di-ō-thũr'mi), *n.* the treatment of disease or alleviation of pain by using the heat given off by radioactive substances; short-wave diathermy.

ra·di·o·tho·ri·um (rā'di-ō-thôr'i-əm, rā'di-ō-thō'ri-əm), *n.* [Mod. L.], a radioactive isotope of thorium, formed from mesothorium 2.

radio tube, a vacuum tube for use in radio, etc.

rad·ish (rad'ish), *n.* [Fr. *radis;* It. *radice;* L. *radix, radicis*, a root; see RADIX; AS. had *rædic* < L.], 1. any of a group of plants of the mustard family, with an edible red or white root. 2. the pungent root, eaten raw as a relish or in a salad.

ra·di·um (rā'di-əm), *n.* [Mod. L. < L. *radius*, a ray], a radioactive metallic chemical element, found in very small amounts in pitchblende and certain other uranium minerals, which undergoes spontaneous atomic disintegration through several stages (see **radon, radium A**), finally forming an isotope of lead: it was discovered by Pierre and Marie Curie in 1898 and is used in the treatment of cancer and some skin diseases: symbol, Ra, formerly Rd; at. wt., 226.05; at. no., 88.

radium A, a substance formed from radon by atomic disintegration: by further disintegration it gives rise to **radium B** (an isotope of lead), which in turn gives rise to **radium C** (an isotope of bismuth), followed successively by the forms **C', D, E, F** (polonium), and **G** (an isotope of lead).

radium emanation, radon.

ra·di·um·ther·a·py (rā'di-əm-ther'ə-pi), *n.* [*radium* + *therapy*], the treatment of cancer or other diseases by the use of radium: also **radium therapy.**

ra·di·us (rā'di-əs), *n.* [*pl.* RADII (-ī'), RADIUSES (-iz)], [L., a rod, spoke (of a wheel), hence radius, ray (of light); for IE. base see RADIX], 1. a ray or raylike part; specifically, *a)* any of the rays of a composite flower. *b)* the pivoted arm of a quadrant, sextant, etc. *c)* a spoke of a wheel. 2. any straight line extending from the center to the periphery of a circle or sphere: symbol, R: abbreviated **R., r., rad.** 3. the circular area or distance limited by the sweep of such a line: as, there was no house within a *radius* of five miles. 4. any limited extent, scope, range, etc.: as, within the *radius* of my experience. 5. *a)* the shorter and thicker of the two bones of the forearm on the same side as the thumb: see **skeleton,** illus. *b)* a corresponding bone of the forelimb of a four-legged animal.

radius vector, [*pl.* RADII VECTORES (vek-tôr'ēz, vek-tō'rēz), RADIUS VECTORS], 1. the distance, or a straight line representing this distance, from a fixed point to a variable point on a curve or curved surface. 2. in *astronomy*, the line joining the center of an attracting body, as the sun, with the center of each of the bodies revolving around it.

ra·dix (rā'diks), *n.* [*pl.* RADICES (rad'ə-sēz', rā'də-sēz'), RADIXES (-iz)], [L.; IE. base **w(e)rād-*, **wṛed-*, twig, root, seen also in L. *ramus*, a branch, *radius*, rod (cf. RAMIFY, RADIUS), Eng. *root, wort, orchard*], 1. the root of a plant. 2. in *linguistics*, a root, base, or etymon. 3. in *mathematics*, a number made the base of a system of numbering: abbreviated **rad.**

Rad·nor (rad'nẽr), *n.* Radnorshire.

Rad·nor·shire (rad'nẽr-shir'), *n.* a county of eastern Wales: pop., 21,000.

ra·don (rā'don), *n.* [*radium* + *-on* as in *neon, argon*], a radioactive gaseous chemical element formed, together with alpha rays, as a first product in the atomic disintegration of radium, and used in the treatment of cancer: also called *radium emanation:* symbol, Rn; at. wt., 222; at. no., 86.

rad·u·la (raj'oo-lə), *n.* [*pl.* RADULAE (-lē')], [L., scraper < *radere*, to scrape], in most mollusks, a ribbonlike part with rows of very small, rudimentary teeth, used to tear up food and take it into the mouth.

Rae (rā), a feminine name: see **Rachel.**

Rae·burn, Sir **Henry** (rā'bẽrn), **1756–1823;** Scottish portrait painter.

R.A.F., RAF, Royal Air Force.

raff (raf), *n.* [ME. *raf;* OFr. *raffe;* cf. RAFT (large number), RIFFRAFF], 1. a large number, collection, or quantity. 2. [Scot. or British Dial.], rubbish; trash; hence, 3. the rabble; riffraff: contemptuous term.

raf·fi·a (raf'i-ə), *n.* [< Malagasy native name], 1. a palm tree of Madagascar, with large, pinnate leaves: also **raffia palm.** 2. fiber from its leaves, woven into baskets, hats, etc. 3. a related palm tree. 4. its fiber.

raf·fi·nose (raf'ə-nōs'), *n.* [< Fr. *raffiner*, to refine; + *-ose*], a sweetish, crystalline trisaccharide, $C_{18}H_{32}O_{16} \cdot 5H_2O$, derived from sugar beets, cottonseed, etc.

raff·ish (raf'ish), *adj.* [*raff* + *-ish*], 1. disreputable; disgraceful. 2. tawdry; flashy; cheap.

raf·fle (raf''l), *n.* [ME. & OFr. *rafle*, dice game < **rafler*, to snatch < D. *rafelen*, to snatch away], a lottery in which each participant buys a chance to win the prize. *v.t.* [RAFFLED (-'ld), RAFFLING], to offer as a prize in a raffle (often with *off*). *v.i.* to conduct a raffle.

raf·fle·si·a (ra-flē'zhi-ə, ra-flē'zi-ə), *n.* [Mod. L., after Sir T. Stamford *Raffles* (1781–1826), Brit. governor in Sumatra, who discovered them], any of a number of related varieties of bad-smelling Malaysian plants with large, stemless flowers and no leaves, growing parasitic on certain vines.

raft (raft, räft), *n.* [ME. *rafte*, a beam, rafter; ON. *raptr*, a log; cf. RAFTER], a number of logs, boards, barrels, etc. fastened together into a sort of platform and floated on water, used as a means of transportation or as a device for conveying the component logs, boards, etc. *v.t.* 1. to transport on a raft. 2. to make into a raft. *v.i.* to travel, work, etc. on a raft.

raft (raft, räft), *n.* [< *raff*, 2 (with unhistoric *-t*)], [Colloq.], a large number, collection, or quantity; lot.

raft·er (raf'tẽr, räf'tẽr), *n.* [ME. *rafter;* AS. *ræfter*, akin to ON. *raptr;* see RAFT (floating platform)], any of the beams that slope from the ridge of a roof to the eaves and serve to support the roof.

rafts·man (rafts'mən, räfts'mən), *n.* [*pl.* RAFTSMEN (-mən)], a man who operates, or works on, a raft.

rag (rag), *n.* [ME. *ragge;* AS. *ragg-* (in *raggig*, ragged) < ON. *rögg*, tuft of hair (cf. Norw. dial. *rugga*, piece of rough cloth); IE. base **reu-*, to tear, tear off, seen also in L. *rutabulum*, shovel (cf. RABBLE, a bar)], 1. a waste piece of cloth, especially one that is torn or uneven. 2. a small piece of cloth for dusting, cleaning, washing, etc. 3. anything more or less resembling a rag, considered of little value: used contemptuously or humorously. 4. *pl.* old, worn clothes; hence, 5. *pl.* any clothes: used humorously: see **glad rags.** 6. the axis and white, tough membrane of citrus fruits. *adj.* made of rags: as, a *rag* doll.

chew the rag, [Slang], to chat or converse.

rag (rag), *v.t.* [RAGGED (ragd), RAGGING], [< 19th-c. Brit. university slang; prob. < phr. *like a red rag to a bull* & derivatives *bullyrag*, etc.], [Slang], 1. to tease. 2. to scold. 3. [British], to play a practical joke or jokes on. *n.* [British Slang], a ragging.

rag (rag), *n.* [prob. var. of *rag* (torn piece)], a kind of slate with one rough surface, used in roofing.

rag (rag), *n.* [Slang], ragtime. *v.t.* [RAGGED (ragd), RAGGING], [Slang], to play in the style of ragtime.

rag·a·muf·fin (rag'ə-muf'in), *n.* [ME. *Ragamofin*, a demon in mystery plays: demons were often described as *ragged*, i.e., shaggy], a dirty, ragged person; tatterdemalion; especially, a dirty, ragged child.

rage (rāj), *n.* [ME.; OFr.; LL. **rabia* < L. *rabies*, rage, madness; akin to *rabere*, to rave, be mad; see RABID], 1. [Obs.], insanity; amentia. 2. a furious, uncontrolled anger; raving fury. 3. a great force, violence, or intensity, as of the wind. 4. strong emotion, enthusiasm, or desire. 5. anything arousing general enthusiasm or desire; craze; fad. *v.i.* [RAGED (rājd), RAGING], 1. to show violent anger in action or speech. 2. to be forceful, violent, agitated, etc.: as, the sea *raged*. 3. to spread unchecked, as a disease. —*SYN.* see **anger, fashion.**

rag·ged (rag′id), *adj.* [< *rag* (torn piece) + *-ed*], 1. shabby or torn from wear: as, a *ragged* shirt. 2. dressed in shabby or torn clothes. 3. uneven; rough; jagged: as, a *ragged* edge. 4. shaggy; unkempt: as, *ragged* hair. 5. not finished; imperfect: as, a *ragged* style. 6. harsh; strident: as, a *ragged* voice.

ragged edge, the extreme edge, as of a precipice; verge: as, on the *ragged edge* of poverty.
on the ragged edge, precariously close to loss of self-control, mental stability, etc.

ragged robin, a plant of the pink family, with loose clusters of pink or red flowers.

rag·gee (rag′i), *n.* [Hind. *rāgī*; Sans. *rāgin*, red], a cereal grass of the East Indies whose grain is a staple food in parts of Asia: also spelled **raggi, raggy, ragi.**

rag·lan (rag′lən), *n.* [after Lord *Raglan* (1788–1855), Brit. commander in chief in the Crimean War; cf. MELTON, SPENCER, etc.], a loose overcoat or topcoat with sleeves that continue in one piece to the collar, so that there are no shoulder seams. *adj.* designating or of such a sleeve.

rag·man (rag′man′, rag′mən), *n.* [*pl.* RAGMEN (-men′, -mən)], a man who collects, buys, and sells rags, old paper, etc.

Rag·na·rok (räg′nə-rok′), *n.* [ON. *ragna rök*, judgment of the gods; *ragna*, genit. pl. of *regin*, god + *rök*, judgment, reason; confused with *ragnarøkkr*, twilight of the gods (G. *götterdämmerung*)], in *Norse mythology*, the destruction of the world in the last great conflict between the gods and the forces of evil.

Rag·na·rök (räg′na-rök′), *n.* Ragnarok.

ra·gout (ra-gōō′), *n.* [Fr. *ragoût* < *ragoûter*, to revive the appetite of < *re-*, re- + *à* (< L. *ad*), to + *goût* (< L. *gustus*), taste], a stew of highly seasoned meat and vegetables. *v.t.* [RAGOUTED (-gōōd′), RAGOUTING (-gōō′iŋ)], to make into a ragout.

rag·pick·er (rag′pik′ẽr), *n.* a person who makes his living by picking up and selling rags and junk.

rag·tag (rag′tag′), *n.* [*rag* (torn piece) + *tag*], the lowest classes; rabble: in *ragtag and bobtail*: contemptuous term.

rag·time (rag′tīm′), *n.* [< *ragged time*, term first applied (c. 1890) to New Orleans music as played by Negro orchestras on Mississippi river boats], 1. a type of American dance music, popular from about 1890 to 1915, characterized by strong syncopation in fast, even time: it is regarded as an early form or predecessor of jazz. 2. its syncopated rhythm.

Ra·gu·sa (rä-gōō′zä), *n.* 1. a city in southeastern Sicily: pop., 50,000. 2. Dubrovnik, a city in Yugoslavia: the Italian name.

rag·weed (rag′wēd′), *n.* [so named from the tattered appearance of the leaves], any of a number of related common weeds with divided leaves and small, yellow-green flowers: the pollen is a cause of hay fever.

rag·wort (rag′wũrt′), *n.* [see RAGWEED], any of a number of tall, related plants with irregularly toothed leaves and yellow flowers.

rah (rä, rô), *interj.* hurrah.

ra·ia (rä′yə), *n.* [Fr. < Turk. *ra'āya* < Ar. *ra'āya*, collective sing. of *ra'īyah*, flock, herd], a non-Moslem inhabitant of a Moslem country, as formerly in Turkey: also spelled **rayah.**

raid (rād), *n.* [North Eng. form of *road*, preserving etym. sense, "a riding"; used orig. of an incursion along the Border; popularized by Scott], 1. a sudden, hostile attack, especially by troops, military aircraft, etc., or by armed, usually mounted, bandits intent on looting. 2. any sudden invasion of some place by police, for discovering and dealing with violations of the law. 3. a deliberate attempt by one or more operators to cause a quick, unexpected fall in stock-market prices. *v.t.* to make a raid or raids on. *v.i.* to take part in or conduct a raid or raids.

raid·er (rād′ẽr), *n.* a person or thing that makes a raid; specifically, *a)* a ship or airplane making a quick, unexpected attack. *b)* [often R-], a member of any of various battalions of the United States Marine Corps especially trained in close combat.

rail (rāl), *n.* [ME.; OFr. *reille*; L. *regula*, a rule; see RULE], 1. a bar of wood, metal, etc. placed horizontally between upright posts to serve as a guard or support. 2. a fence or railing. 3. any of a series of parallel metal bars laid upon crossties or in the ground to make a track for railroad cars, streetcars, etc. 4. a railroad as a means of transportation: as, he went by *rail*. 5. a horizontal piece of wood separating the panels in doors or wainscoting. 6. in *nautical usage*, a narrow wooden piece at the top of a ship's bulwarks. *v.t.* to supply with rails or a railing; fence.
ride on a rail, to place on a rail and carry out of the community: extralegal punishment in which the victim was usually tarred and feathered beforehand.

rail (rāl), *v.i.* [Fr. *railler*, to banter < LL. **ragulare*, to bray], to speak bitterly or reproachfully; complain violently (with *against* or *at*). *v.t.* [Rare], to have an effect on by railing; force, remove, etc. by railing.

rail (rāl), *n.* [*pl.* RAILS (rālz), RAIL; see PLURAL, II, D, 1], [Late ME.; OFr. *raale*; prob. < prec.], any of a number of small wading birds resembling the cranes and living in marshes, characterized by short wings and tail, long toes, and a harsh cry.

rail·head (rāl′hed′), *n.* 1. the farthest point to which rails have been laid in a railroad under construction. 2. in *military usage*, the point on a railroad in a theater of operations at which supplies are unloaded and sent to troops at the front by other means of transportation.

rail·ing (rāl′iŋ), *n.* 1. material for rails. 2. rails collectively. 3. a fence or balustrade made of rails and posts.

rail·ler·y (rāl′ẽr-i; *now rarely* ral′ẽr-i), *n.* [*pl.* RAILLERIES (-iz)], [Fr. *raillerie*; see RAIL (to complain)], 1. light, good-natured ridicule or satire; banter. 2. a teasing act or remark.

rail·road (rāl′rōd′), *n.* 1. a road laid with parallel steel rails along which cars carrying passengers or freight are drawn by locomotives. 2. a complete system of such roads, including land, rolling stock, stations, etc.: abbreviated **R.R., R., r.** 3. the persons or corporation owning and managing such a system. *v.t.* 1. to transport by railroad. 2. to furnish with railroads. 3. [Colloq.], to rush through quickly, especially so quickly as to prevent careful consideration: as, he *railroaded* the motion through the committee. 4. [Slang], to cause to go to prison on a trumped-up charge or with too hasty a trial. *v.i.* to work on a railroad.

rail·road·ing (rāl′rōd′iŋ), *n.* 1. the building or operation of railroads. 2. the act or process of one that railroads (in various senses).

rail-split·ter (rāl′split′ẽr), *n.* a person who splits logs into rails, as for fences.
the Rail-Splitter, Abraham Lincoln.

rail·way (rāl′wā′), *n.* 1. a railroad for light vehicles: as, a street *railway*. 2. [British], any railroad. 3. any track with rails for guiding wheels. Abbreviated **Ry., Rwy., R., r.**

rai·ment (rā′mənt), *n.* [contr. of *arrayment*; see ARRAY], [Archaic or Poetic], clothing; wearing apparel; attire.

rain (rān), *n.* [ME. *rein, raine*; AS. *regn*; akin to G. *regn*; IE. base **reĝ-, *req-*, damp, moist, wet, prob. seen also in L. *rigare*, to wet, moisten (cf. IRRIGATE)], 1. water falling to earth in drops that have been condensed from the moisture in the atmosphere. 2. the falling of such drops; shower or rainstorm. 3. *a)* rainy weather. *b)* *pl.* seasonal rainfalls; the rainy season (preceded by *the*). 4. a rapid falling or propulsion of many small particles or objects: as, a *rain* of ashes. *v.i.* 1. to fall: said of rain, and usually in an impersonal construction, as, it is *raining*. 2. to fall like rain: as, bullets *rained* about him. 3. to cause rain to fall: said of the heavens, God, etc. *v.t.* 1. to pour down (rain or something likened to rain). 2. to give in large quantities: as, they *rained* praises on him.
rain cats and dogs, [Colloq.], to rain heavily.

rain·band (rān′band′), *n.* a dark band in the yellow part of the solar spectrum, due to water vapor in the atmosphere.

rain·bow (rān′bō′), *n.* [AS. *regnboga*; see RAIN & BOW (arc)], the arc containing the colors of the spectrum in consecutive bands, formed in the sky by the refraction, reflection, and dispersion of the sun's rays in falling rain or mist. *adj.* of many colors.

Rainbow Bridge, a natural stone bridge in southern Utah: span, 278 ft.

rainbow trout, any of several varieties of game trout native to the mountain streams and coastal waters of the Pacific States: so called from their coloring.

rain check, the stub of a ticket to a baseball game or other outdoor event, entitling the holder to be admitted at a future date if the original event is halted because of rain: also used figuratively.

rain·coat (rān′kōt′), *n.* a waterproof coat for giving protection from rain.

rain·drop (rān′drop′), *n.* a single drop of rain.

rain·fall (rān′fôl′), *n.* 1. a falling of rain; shower. 2. the amount of water falling in the form of rain, snow, etc. over a given area in a given period of time, usually a year: it is stated in terms of the inches in

fat, āpe, bâre, cär; ten, ēven, hêre, ovẽr; is, bīte; lot, gō, hôrn, tōōl, look; oil, out; up, ūse, fũr; get; joy; yet; chin; she; thin, then; zh, leisure; ŋ, ring; ə for *a* in *ago*, *e* in *agent*, *i* in *sanity*, *o* in *comply*, *u* in *focus*; ′ as in *able* (ā′b'l); Fr. bål; ë, Fr. coeur; ö, Fr. feu; Fr. mon; ô, Fr. coq; ü, Fr. duc; H, G. ich; kh, G. doch. See pp. x–xii. ‡ foreign; * hypothetical; < derived from.

depth of water that has fallen into a rain gauge.

rain gauge, an instrument for measuring the rainfall of a given area: also called *pluviometer, udometer.*

Rai·nier, Mount (rā-nêr′, rā′nir), a mountain of the Cascade Range, in Washington: height, 14,408 ft.: Indian name, *Tacoma.*

rain·i·ness (rān′i-nis), *n.* the quality or condition of being rainy.

rain·proof (rān′prōōf′; *also, and for v. always,* rān′-prōōf′), *adj.* [see -PROOF], not permitting rain to come through; shedding rain. *v.t.* to make rainproof.

rain·storm (rān′stôrm′), *n.* a storm with a heavy rain.

rain water, water that is falling or has fallen as rain, containing relatively little soluble mineral matter.

rain·y (rān′i), *adj.* [RAINIER (-i-ẽr), RAINIEST (-i-ist)], 1. characterized by rain, especially by much rain: as, the *rainy* season. 2. wet with rain. 3. bringing rain: as, *rainy* winds.

rainy day, a possible future time of difficulty or need.

raise (rāz), *v.t.* [RAISED (rāzd), RAISING], [ME. *reisen;* ON. *reisa,* exactly akin to AS. *ræran* (see REAR), caus. of *risan,* to rise (see RISE); IE. base **erei-* (< **er-,* to set in motion, bring up, stir up, etc.), seen also in L. *origo,* source, commencement (cf. ORIGIN) & prob. in L. *irritare* (cf. IRRITATE)], 1. to cause to rise; move to a higher level; lift; elevate. 2. to construct or erect (a building, etc.). 3. to stir up; arouse; incite: as, the Indians *raised* a revolt. 4. to increase in size, value, amount, etc.: as, he *raised* his prices. 5. to increase in degree, intensity, strength, etc.: as, she *raised* her voice. 6. to improve the position, rank, or situation of: as, hard work *raised* the man from poverty. 7. to advance or enhance (fame, reputation, etc.). 8. to cause to arise, appear, come, etc.; especially, to bring back from death; reanimate: as, her cries could *raise* the dead. 9. to cause to come about; provoke; inspire: as, the remark *raised* a laugh. 10. to bring forward for consideration: as, he succeeded in *raising* the question. 11. to collect, gather, or procure (an army, money, etc.). 12. to give forth; utter (a cry, shout, etc.). 13. to bring to an end; remove: as, we have *raised* the siege. 14. to cause to become light; leaven (bread, etc.). 15. *a)* to cause to grow; breed: as, he *raises* corn; hence, *b)* to rear (children); bring up. 16. [Scot.], to make angry or excited; madden. 17. in *commerce,* to increase by fraud the face value of (a check, etc.). 18. in *nautical usage,* to cause (land, another ship, etc.) to appear to rise over the horizon by coming nearer; come within sight of. 19. in *poker,* etc., *a)* to bet more than (the highest preceding bet). *b)* to bet more than (the preceding better). *v.i.* 1. [Dial.], to rise or arise. 2. [Colloq.], to cough up phlegm. 3. in *poker,* etc., to increase the bet. *n.* 1. an act of raising. 2. an increase in amount; specifically, an increase in salary or wages. —*SYN.* see **lift.**

raise Cain (or **the devil, hell, a rumpus, the roof,** etc.), [Slang], to create a disturbance; cause trouble.

raised (rāzd), *adj.* [pp. of *raise*], 1. made in low relief; embossed. 2. made light and fluffy with yeast or other leavening agent: said of bread, etc.

rai·sin (rā′z'n), *n.* [ME. & OFr. *reisin;* LL. **racimus* < L. *racemus,* cluster of grapes], any of various kinds of sweet, dried grapes, usually seedless.

‡rai·son d'é·tat (re′zōn′ dā′tȧ′), [Fr.], reason of state; diplomatic reason.

‡rai·son d'·être (re′zōn′ de′tr′; Eng. rā′zôn det′), [Fr.], reason for being; justification for existence.

‡rai·son·né (re′zô′nā′), *adj.* [Fr., pp. of *raisonner;* see REASON, *v.*], logically or systematically arranged.

raj (räj), *n.* [see RAJAH], in India, rule; sovereignty.

ra·jah, ra·ja (rä′jə), *n.* [Hind. *rājā;* Sans. *rājan* < *rāj,* to rule; akin to L. *rex;* see REGAL], a prince or chief in India, the East Indies, etc.

Ra·ja·sthan (rä′jə-stän′), *n.* a state of northwest central India, including the Rajputana region and the former Ajmer-Merwara province: area, 132,227 sq. mi.; pop., 15,970,000; capital, Jaipur.

Raj·put (räj′pōōt), *n.* [Hind. *rājpūt,* prince < Sans. *rājaputra* < *rājan,* a king (see RAJAH) + *putra,* son], a member of a strong Hindu military and ruling caste of northern India.

Raj·pu·ta·na (räj′poo-tä′nə), *n.* a region in northwest central India: since 1950, included in Rajasthan.

rake (rāk), *n.* [ME. *rake;* AS. *raca;* akin to ON. *reka,* a spade & indirectly to G. *rechen,* a rake; basic sense in Goth. *rikan* (OHG. *rehhan*), to gather, heap up; IE. base as in *right, rich, reckon*], any of various long-handled tools with teeth or prongs at one end, used for gathering loose grass, hay, leaves, etc., or for smoothing broken ground. *v.t.* [RAKED (rākt), RAKING], [< the *n.;* also in part < ON. *raka,* to scrape, shave], 1. to gather or scrape together with or as with a rake. 2. to gather with great care. 3. to scratch or smooth with a rake, as in leveling broken ground. 4. to search through minutely; scour. 5. to direct gunfire along the length of (a line of troops, the deck of a ship, etc.): often used figuratively. *v.i.* 1. to use a rake. 2. to search as if with a rake. 3. to scrape or sweep (with *over, across,* etc.).

rake (rāk), *n.* [contr. of *rakehell*], a dissolute, debauched man; roué.

rake (rāk), *v.i.* [RAKED (rākt), RAKING], [akin to Sw. *raka,* to project, G. *ragen,* Eng. *rock;* prob. < a Scand. word used in the international language of the sea], to be slightly inclined; slant, as a ship's masts, etc. *v.t.* to give a slant to. *n.* 1. a slanting or inclination from the perpendicular. 2. the angle made by the edge of a cutting tool and a plane perpendicular to the surface that is being worked. 3. a cutting away of the outer tip of the trailing edge of an airplane wing so that it is shorter than the leading edge.

rake (rāk), *v.i.* [RAKED (rākt), RAKING], [ME. *raken,* AS. *racian,* to speed forward; akin to MLG. *reken,* to hit, reach; IE. base as in *right,* etc.; cf. RAKE (garden tool)], in *hunting,* 1. to fly after game: said of a hawk. 2. to run after game with the nose to the track instead of in the wind: said of a hunting dog.

rake·hell (rāk′hel′), *n.* [altered, after *rake* (to gather) + *hell* (as if so evil as to be found only by raking hell), < ME. *rakel,* rash, wild; ON. *reikal,* vagrant, reckless], a dissolute, debauched man; rake. *adj.* immoral; dissolute; debauched.

rake·hell·y (rāk′hel′i), *adj.* rakehell.

rake-off (rāk′ôf′), *n.* [*rake* (to gather) + *off*], [Slang], a commission, rebate, or share, especially when received in an illegitimate transaction.

ra·ki (rə-kē′, rak′i), *n.* [Turk. *rāqi;* Ar. *'araq;* see ARRACK], an intoxicating liquor made from grape juice, grain, etc. in southern Europe and the Near East: also spelled **rakee.**

rak·ish (rāk′ish), *adj.* [< *rake* (to slant) + *-ish*], 1. having a trim, neat appearance, suggesting speed: said of a ship; hence, 2. dashing; jaunty.

rak·ish (rāk′ish), *adj.* like a rake; dissolute.

râle (räl), *n.* [Fr. < *râler,* to rattle; prob. akin to *râle* rail (the bird)], in *medicine,* an abnormal rattling or bubbling sound accompanying the normal sound of breathing, and usually indicating a diseased condition of the lungs or bronchi.

Ra·leigh (rô′li), *n.* the capital of North Carolina: pop. 94,000.

Ra·leigh, Sir **Walter** (rô′li, rä′li), 1552?–1618; English explorer, statesman, courtier, historian, and poet: beheaded: also spelled **Ralegh.**

ral·len·tan·do (räl′en-tän′dō, ral′ən-tan′dō), *adj.* & *adv.* [It., ppr. of *rallentare,* to slow down], in *music,* gradually slower: a direction to the performer: abbreviated **rall.**

ral·li·er (ral′i-ẽr), *n.* a person who rallies.

ral·li·form (ral′ə-fôrm′), *adj.* [< Mod. L. *rallus,* a rail (bird); + *-form*], like the rails (birds) in appearance, structure, etc.

ral·line (ral′in, ral′in), *adj.* [< Mod.L. *rallus* < Fr. *râle;* + *-ine*], of or like the rails (birds).

ral·ly (ral′i), *v.t.* [RALLIED (-id), RALLYING], [Fr. *rallier* < *re-,* again + *allier,* to join; see ALLY], 1. to bring back together and put in a state of order, as retreating troops. 2. to summon or bring together for a common purpose: as, the leader *rallied* the workers. 3. to bring back to action; revive: as, he *rallied* his energy. *v.i.* 1. to come back to a state of order: as, the soldiers *rallied.* 2. to come together for a common purpose; hence, 3. to come in order to help: as, he *rallied* to his defeated friend. 4. to come back to action, normal strength, etc.; revive: as, the patient *rallied* from the coma. 5. in *badminton, tennis,* etc., to take part in a rally. 6. in *commerce,* to rise in price after having fallen: said of stocks, etc. *n.* [*pl.* RALLIES (-iz)], a rallying or being rallied; specifically, *a)* a gathering of people for a common purpose; mass meeting. *b)* in *badminton, tennis,* etc., an exchange of several strokes before the point is won. —*SYN.* see **stir.**

ral·ly (ral′i), *v.t.* & *v.i.* [RALLIED (-id), RALLYING], [Fr. *rallier;* see RAIL (to complain)], to tease or mock in mild derision; ridicule; banter.

Ralph (ralf, rälf; Brit. rāf), [ON. *Rathulfr* (akin to AS. *Rædwulf*) < *rath,* counsel + *ulfr,* a wolf], a masculine name: equivalent, Fr. *Raoul.*

ram (ram), *n.* [ME. *ramme;* AS. *ramm, romm;* akin to D. *ram;* Gmc. **ramma;* prob. < **rama-,* strong, sharp, bitter, with reference to the strong smell in the mating season (cf. ON. *rammr,* strong, bitter, sharp)], 1. a male sheep. 2. a battering-ram. 3. *a)* formerly, a sharp metal beak on the prow of a ship, used to batter against or pierce enemy vessels. *b)* a ship with such a beak. 4. a pump that raises water by the force of the water itself falling through a pipe: also called *hydraulic ram.* 5. the weight, or striking part, of a pile driver. 6. the plunger of a force pump. 7. [R-], *a)* the constellation Aries. *b)* the zodiacal sign of this constellation. *v.t.* [RAMMED (ramd), RAMMING], 1. to strike against with great force; drive into. 2. to force into place; press or drive down: as, *ram* the charge into the gun. 3. to stuff or cram (*with* something).

R.A.M., Royal Academy of Music.

Ra·ma (rä′mə), *n.* [Sans. *Rāma*], any of three of the incarnations of the Hindu god Vishnu, especially the seventh.

Ra·ma·chan·dra (rä'mə-chun'drə), ***n.*** [Sans. *Rāma-candra;* see RAMA], Rama, the seventh incarnation of the Hindu god Vishnu: he is the hero of the Ramayana.
Ram·a·dan (ram'ə-dän'), ***n.*** [Ar. *ramaḍān*, lit., the hot month < *ramaḍa*, to be hot], 1. the ninth month of the Moslem year, a period of daily fasting from sunrise to sunset. 2. the fasting.
Ra·ma·ya·na (rä-mä'yə-nə), ***n.*** [Sans. *Rāmāyaṇa*], one of the two great epics of India, written in Sanskrit some time after the Mahabharata.
Ram·a·zan (ram'ə-zän'), ***n.*** [Turk. & Per. < Ar. *ramaḍan*], Ramadan.
ram·ble (ram'b'l), ***v.i.*** [RAMBLED (-b'ld), RAMBLING], [var. of ME. *romblen*, freq. of *romen*, to roam (see ROAM); prob. under influence of D. *rammelen*], 1. to move, especially to walk, about idly, without any special goal; stroll; roam. 2. to talk or write aimlessly, without connection of ideas. 3. to grow or spread in all directions: as, vines *rambled* over the fence. ***n.*** a rambling; aimless stroll. —***SYN.*** see **roam.**
ram·bler (ram'blẽr), ***n.*** a person or thing that rambles; especially, any of certain climbing roses.
ram·bling (ram'bliŋ, ram'b'l-iŋ), ***adj.*** [ppr. of *ramble*], that rambles; disconnected, straggling, wandering, etc.
Ram·bouil·let (ram'boo-lā'; Fr. rän'bōō'yā'), ***n.*** [after *Rambouillet*, France], a variety of merino sheep originally bred in France, now raised in the western United States for both its wool and mutton.
ram·bunc·tious (ram-buŋk'shəs), ***adj.*** [earlier *rambustious, rumbustious;* altered (? after *rum*, from the effect) < *robustious*], [Colloq.], wild, disorderly, boisterous, unruly, etc.
ram·bu·tan (ram-bōō'tən), ***n.*** [Malay < *rambut*, hair], 1. the red, spiny, egg-shaped, edible fruit of a Malayan tree of the soapberry family. 2. the tree.
Ra·meau, Jean Phi·lippe (zhän' fē'lēp' rȧ'mō'), 1683–1764; French composer and organist.
ram·e·kin, ram·e·quin (ram'ə-kin), ***n.*** [Fr. *ramequin;* D. **ramkin*, cheese cake, dish composed largely of cheese < G. *rahm*, cream], 1. a kind of hash made chiefly of bread crumbs, cheese, and eggs, and baked in individual baking dishes. 2. such a baking dish. 3. any food mixture prepared or served in such a dish.
Ram·e·ses (ram'ə-sēz'), ***n.*** see **Ramses.**
ra·mi (rā'mī), ***n.*** plural of **ramus.**
ram·ie (ram'i), ***n.*** [Malay *rami*], 1. an Asiatic plant with many rodlike stems and heart-shaped flowers. 2. the fiber from this plant, used in making fine cloth.
ram·i·fi·ca·tion (ram'ə-fi-kā'shən), ***n.*** [< pp. of ML. *ramificare*], 1. a ramifying or being ramified; specifically, the arrangement of branches or offshoots, as on a plant. 2. the result of ramifying; specifically, *a*) a branch or offshoot. *b*) a subdivision, consequence, or result: as, the ***ramifications*** of an act.
ram·i·form (ram'ə-fôrm'), ***adj.*** [< L. *ramus*, a branch; + *-form*], branched or branchlike.
ram·i·fy (ram'ə-fī'), ***v.t. & v.i.*** [RAMIFIED (-fīd'), RAMIFYING], [Fr. *ramifier;* ML. *ramificare* < L. *ramus*, a branch + *facere*, to make], to divide or spread out into branches or branchlike divisions.
Ra·mil·lies (rȧ'mē'yē'), ***n.*** a village in central Belgium: scene of a French defeat (1706) by the British under Marlborough in the War of the Spanish Succession.
ram·jet (ram'jet'), ***n.*** a jet engine in which the air is continuously compressed by being rammed into the open front end: also called *athodyd.*
ram·mer (ram'ẽr), ***n.*** a person or thing that rams; specifically, a ramrod.
ram·mish (ram'ish), ***adj.*** of or like a ram, or male sheep; specifically, *a*) having a rank smell. *b*) lustful.
Ra·mo·na (rə-mō'nə), [? Sp.; prob. ult. < G. *Raimunda, Reimunda;* see RAYMOND], a feminine name.
ra·mose (rā'mōs, rə-mōs'), ***adj.*** [L. *ramosus* < *ramus*, a branch], 1. bearing many branches. 2. branching.
ra·mous (rā'məs), ***adj.*** 1. ramose. 2. branchlike.
ramp (ramp), ***n.*** [Fr. *rampe* < *ramper;* see RAMP, *v.*], 1. a sloping passage, usually curved, joining different levels of a building, road, etc. 2. a concave bend or curve where a handrail or coping changes its direction, as at a staircase landing. 3. any sloping roadway or passage.

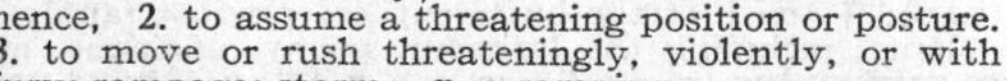
RAMP

ramp (ramp), ***v.i.*** [ME. *rampen, raumpen;* OFr. *ramper*, to climb, clamber], 1. to stand upright on the hind legs, as a lion in heraldry; hence, 2. to assume a threatening position or posture. 3. to move or rush threateningly, violently, or with fury; rampage; storm. ***n.*** a ramping.
ram·page (ram-pāj'; *also, and for n. always,* ram'pāj), ***v.i.*** [RAMPAGED (-pājd', -pājd), RAMPAGING], [orig. Scot. & North Eng. dial. < *ramp, v.* + *rage*], to rush violently about; rage; act wildly. ***n.*** an outbreak of violent, raging behavior: usually in *on the* (or *a*) *rampage.*
ram·pa·geous (ram-pā'jəs), ***adj.*** rampaging; unruly or boisterous; not easily controlled.
ramp·an·cy (ram'pən-si), ***n.*** the quality or state of being rampant.
ramp·ant (ram'pənt), ***adj.*** [ME.; OFr., ppr. of *ramper;* see RAMP, *v.*], 1. growing luxuriantly; flourishing: as, *rampant* plants. 2. spreading unchecked; widespread; rife. 3. violent and uncontrollable in action, manner, speech, etc. 4. in *architecture*, having one abutment higher than the other: said of an arch. 5. in *heraldry*, rearing up on the hind legs, usually in profile, with one forepaw raised above the other, as a lion, etc.
ram·part (ram'pärt, ram'pẽrt), ***n.*** [Fr. *rempart* < *remparer*, to fortify a place < *re-*, again + *emparer* (Pr. *amparer*), to prepare < L. *ante*, before + *parare*, to prepare], 1. an embankment of earth surmounted by a parapet and encircling a castle, fort, etc., for defending it from attackers. 2. anything that defends or protects: as, courage forms a ***rampart*** against troubles. ***v.t.*** to protect with or as with a rampart.
ram·pi·on (ram'pi-ən), ***n.*** [? altered < Fr. *raiponce*, It. *raponzolo* < ML. *rapunculus*, dim. < L. *rapa;* see RAPE (the plant)], a variety of European bellflower with thick, fleshy, white roots that are used in salads.
ram·rod (ram'rod'), ***n.*** 1. a metal rod used for ramming down the charge in a gun that is loaded through the muzzle. 2. a rod for cleaning a rifle bore.
Ram·say, Allen (ram'zi), 1686–1758; Scottish poet and bookseller.
Ramsay, Sir **William,** 1852–1916; Scottish chemist; received Nobel prize in chemistry, 1904.
Ram·ses (ram'sēz), ***n.*** any of twelve Egyptian monarchs who ruled from 1500 to 1000 B.C.; especially, *a*) **Ramses I** (1324?–1258 B.C.). *b*) **Ramses II** (1292–1225 B.C.), believed to be the pharaoh of Exodus. *c*) **Ramses III** (1198–1167 B.C.). Also **Rameses.**
Rams·gate (ramz'gāt'; Brit. ramz'git), ***n.*** a seaport in Kent, southeastern England: pop., 34,000: resort.
ram·shack·le (ram'shak''l), ***adj.*** [back-formation < *ramshackled*, for earlier *ransackled*, pp. of *ransackle*, freq. of *ransack*], loose and rickety; likely to fall to pieces; shaky: as, a *ramshackle* old building.
ram·son (ram'z'n, ram's'n), ***n.*** [ME. *ramsin;* Late AS. *hrameson*, pl. of *hramsa*, wild garlic (construed as sing.); akin to G. *rams*], 1. a kind of garlic with broad leaves. 2. *usually in pl.* its root, used in salads.
ram·til (ram'til), ***n.*** [Hind. *rāmtil* < Sans. *rāma*, Rama + *tila*, sesame], a tropical plant of India, with seeds from which an oil is extracted.
ram·u·lose (ram'yoo-lōs'), ***adj.*** [L. *ramulosus* < *ramulus*, dim. of *ramus*, a branch], having many small branches.
ra·mus (rā'məs), ***n.*** [*pl.* RAMI (-mī)], [L.], in *biology*, a branch or branchlike projecting part.
Ran (rän), ***n.*** [ON. *Rān*], in *Norse mythology*, the goddess of the sea and of drowning persons.
ran (ran), past tense of **run.**
also ran, 1. competed without placing first, second, or third: said of a race horse, etc.; hence, 2. competed without winning: said of a contestant, candidate, etc.
rance (rans), ***n.*** [Fr.], a kind of dull-red marble with markings of pale blue and white, found in Belgium.
ranch (ranch), ***n.*** [< Sp. *rancho*, small farm, group of people who eat together, mess], 1. a large farm, with its buildings, lands, etc., for the raising of cattle, horses, or sheep in great numbers: term used especially in the western United States. 2. any large farm devoted to the raising of a particular crop or livestock: as, a fruit *ranch.* 3. all the people living and working on a ranch. ***v.i.*** to work on or manage a ranch. ***v.t.*** to put (an animal) to graze on a ranch.
ranch·er (ran'chẽr), ***n.*** 1. a person who owns or manages a ranch. 2. a cowboy. Also **ranchman.**
ran·che·ro (ran-chā'rō; Sp. rän-che'rô), ***n.*** [*pl.* RANCHEROS (-rōz; Sp. -rôs)], [Sp.], in the southwestern United States and Mexico, a rancher.
ranch·man (ranch'mən), ***n.*** [*pl.* RANCHMEN (-mən)], a rancher.
ran·cho (ran'chō, rän'chō), ***n.*** [*pl.* RANCHOS (-chōz)], [Sp.], in Spanish America, 1. a hut or group of huts for ranch workers. 2. a ranch.
ran·cid (ran'sid), ***adj.*** [L. *rancidus* < *rancere*, to be rank], having the bad smell or taste of stale fats or oils; not fresh; spoiled. —***SYN.*** see **stinking.**
ran·cid·i·ty (ran-sid'ə-ti), ***n.*** the quality or condition of being rancid.
ran·cor (raŋ'kẽr), ***n.*** [ME. *rancour;* OFr. *rancor;* L. *rancor* < *rancere*, to be rank], a continuing and bitter hate or ill will; deep spite or malice. —***SYN.*** see **malice.**

at, āpe, bâre, cär; ten, ēven, hêre, ovẽr; is, bīte; lot, gō, hôrn, tōōl, look; oil, out; up, ūse, fũr; get; joy; yet; chin; she; thin, then; zh, leisure; ŋ, ring; ə for *a* in *ago*, *e* in *agent*, *i* in *sanity*, *o* in *comply*, *u* in *focus;* ' as in *able* (ā'b'l); Fr. bàl; ë, Fr. coeur; ö, Fr. feu; Fr. mon; ô, Fr. coq; ü, Fr. duc; H, G. ich; kh, G. doch. See pp. x–xii. ‡ foreign; * hypothetical; < derived from.

ran·cor·ous (raŋ′kẽr-əs), *adj.* full of or showing rancor.
ran·cour (raŋ′kẽr), *n.* rancor: British spelling.
rand (rand), *n.* [ME. *rande*, a border, strip; AS. *rand*, *rond*, a brink, shield; akin to ON. *rönd*, shield rim; prob. IE. base **rem-*, to support, etc., as also in Eng. *rim*], 1. [Rare or Dial.], an edge, border, or margin, as the unploughed strip around a field. 2. in *shoemaking*, a leather strip used to level off the back part of a sole before the heel is put on.
Rand, the, Witwatersrand.
Ran·dal, Ran·dall (ran′d'l), [< AS. *Randwulf* (or cognate ON. *Ranthulfr*) < *rand*, a shield + *wulf*, a wolf (ON. *ranth* + *ulfr*)], a masculine name.
Ran·dolph (ran′dolf, ran′dôlf), [ML. *Randulfus* < AS. *Randwulf;* see RANDAL], a masculine name.
Ran·dolph, John (ran′dolf, ran′dôlf), 1773–1833; American statesman and orator.
ran·dom (ran′dəm), *n.* [ME. *randoun*, etc.; OFr. *randon*, violence, speed (in *a randon*, violently); prob. < Frank. **rando* (OHG. *rant*), a shield, edge of a shield; see RAND], impetuous and haphazard movement or course of action: now only in *at random*, without careful choice, aim, plan, etc.; haphazardly. *adj.* lacking aim or method; purposeless; haphazard.
SYN.—**random** applies to that which occurs or is done without careful choice, aim, plan, etc. (a *random* remark); **haphazard** applies to that which is done, made, or said without regard for its consequences, relevancy, etc. and therefore stresses the implication of accident or chance (a *haphazard* selection of books); **casual** implies a happening or seeming to happen by chance without intention or purpose and often connotes nonchalance, indifference, etc. (a *casual* acquaintance); **desultory** suggests a lack of method or system, as in jumping from one thing to another (his *desultory* reading in the textbook); **chance** emphasizes accidental occurrence without prearrangement or planning (a *chance* encounter).—*ANT.* deliberate.
rand·y (ran′di), *adj.* [prob. < *rand*, dial. var. of *rant* + *-y*], [Scot.], coarse; crude; vulgar. *n.* [*pl.* RANDIES (-diz)], [Scot.], 1. an impudent, threatening beggar. 2. a coarse, vulgar, quarrelsome woman; shrew.
ra·nee (rä′ni), *n.* a rani.
rang (raŋ), past tense of **ring** (to sound, as a bell).
range (rānj), *v.t.* [RANGED (rānjd), RANGING], [ME. (North) *rangen;* OFr. *ranger*, var. of *renger*, *rengier* (whence ME. *rengen*) < *renc*, *ranc* < OHG. *hring* (Goth. *hrings*), a ring; cf. RING, RANK, *n.*], 1. to arrange in a certain order; especially, to set in a row or rows. 2. to put into the proper classification or classifications; systematize. 3. to place (oneself or another) with others in a cause, party, etc.: as, he *ranged* himself with the rebels. 4. to put in a line with the target or object, at a proper angle of elevation; train (a gun, telescope, etc.). 5. to travel over or through; roam about: as, they *ranged* the woods. 6. to put out (cattle, etc.) to graze on a range. 7. to uncoil (the cable of an anchor) and arrange on deck. *v.i.* 1. to extend, reach, or lie in a given direction: as, the mountains *range* toward the south. 2. to wander about; roam. 3. to roam through an area, as in searching or hunting: as, the dogs *ranged* through the woods. 4. to have a specified range; be able to project over a specified distance: as, the gun *ranged* five miles. 5. to vary between stated limits: as, the children *ranged* in age from two to five years. 6. in *botany & zoology*, to live or grow in a specified region. 7. in *gunnery*, to determine the range of a target by firing alternate rounds beyond and before it. *n.* [ME. *reng;* OFr. *renc*], 1. a row, line, or series; rank. 2. a class, kind, or order. 3. a series of connected mountains considered as a single system. 4. a line of direction: as, the tree is in *range* with the house. 5. *a)* the maximum effective horizontal distance that a gun can fire its projectile. *b)* the horizontal distance from a gun to its target. 6. a place for shooting practice. 7. the full extent over which something moves or is heard, seen, understood, effective, etc.; scope: as, the *range* of my voice. 8. a wandering or roaming. 9. a large, open area of land over which livestock can wander and graze. 10. the limits of possible variations of amount, degree, etc.: as, the *range* of price was narrow. 11. a cooking stove. 12. in U.S. public surveying, a row of townships between two meridian lines six miles apart. 13. in *botany & zoology*, the region in which a plant or animal is normally found. 14. in *statistics*, the difference between the greatest and smallest values in a series of variable quantities. *adj.* of a range, or open grazing place: as, *range* livestock. Abbreviated **r.**
SYN.—**range** refers to the full extent over which something is perceivable, effective, etc. (the *range* of his knowledge); **reach** refers to the furthest limit of effectiveness, influence, etc. (beyond the *reach* of my understanding); **scope** implies considerable room and freedom of range, but within prescribed limits (does it fall within the *scope* of this dictionary?); **compass** also suggests completeness within limits regarded as a circumference (he did all within the *compass* of his power); **gamut**, in this connection, refers to the full range of shades, tones, etc. between the limits of something (the full *gamut* of emotions). See also **roam.**
range finder, any of various instruments for determining the distance of a target or object from an observer, from a gun, etc.
Range·ley Lakes (rānj′li), a chain of lakes in western Maine.
rang·er (rān′jẽr), *n.* [ME. *raunger;* see RANGE], 1. a wanderer. 2. *a)* any of a group of mounted troops for patrolling a region. *b)* [often R-], any of a group of American soldiers trained for raiding and close combat behind enemy lines. 3. *a)* in England, the chief official of a royal park or forest. *b)* in the United States, a warden who patrols government forests.
Ran·goon (raŋ-gōōn′), *n.* the capital of Burma, at the mouth of the Irawaddy River: pop., 400,000.
rang·y (rān′ji), *adj.* [RANGIER (-ji-ẽr), RANGIEST (-ji-ist)], 1. able or inclined to range about; hence, 2. long-limbed and slender: as, *rangy* cattle.
ra·ni (rä′ni), *n.* [Hind. *rānī;* Sans. *rājñī*, fem. of *rajan;* see RAJAH], in India, 1. the wife of a rajah, king, or prince. 2. a reigning queen or princess. Also spelled **ranee.**
Ran·jit Singh (run′jit sin′hə), 1780–1839; maharajah of the Punjab; founded the Sikh kingdom.
rank (raŋk), *n.* [ME. *renk;* OFr. *ranc*, *renc;* see RANGE], 1. a row, line, or series; range. 2. an orderly arrangement. 3. a social division or class; stratum of society: as, men came from all *ranks* of life. 4. a high position in society; high degree; eminence: as, a man of *rank*. 5. an official grade or position: as, the *rank* of captain. 6. a relative position; degree of quality: as, a poet of the first *rank*. 7. any of the horizontal rows of squares on a chessboard. 8. in *military usage*, *a)* a row of soldiers, vehicles, etc. placed side by side, or abreast of one another: opposed to *file*. *b)* *pl.* an army. *c)* *pl.* the body of soldiers of an army, as distinguished from the officers: as, he rose from the *ranks*. *v.t.* 1. to place in a rank or ranks. 2. to assign a certain rank or position, to: as, he *ranks* football above baseball. 3. to have a higher rank than; take precedence over; outrank: as, a colonel *ranks* a major. *v.i.* 1. to hold a certain rank, or position: as, he *ranks* third on the list. 2. to hold the highest rank, or grade: as, the *ranking* member of the embassy.
pull one's rank on, [Military Slang], to take advantage of one's rank in enforcing commands to (a subordinate).
rank and file, 1. the body of soldiers of an army, as distinguished from the officers; hence, 2. the ordinary people forming the large part of some group; common people, as distinguished from leaders, etc.
rank (raŋk), *adj.* [ME. *ranke;* AS. *ranc*, strong, proud; akin to MLG. *rank*, slender, erect, long and thin; IE. base **reĝ-*, high, upright, to stretch up, etc. (cf. RIGHT); basic sense "stretched, extended"], 1. growing or grown vigorously and coarsely; overly luxuriant: as, *rank* grass. 2. producing a luxuriant crop, often to excess; extremely fertile: as, *rank* soil. 3. strong and offensive in smell or taste; rancid; hence, 4. in bad taste; coarse; indecent. 5. complete; extreme; utter; as, *rank* deceit: used contemptuously. 6. [Obs.] in sexual heat. —*SYN.* see **flagrant, stinking.**
Ran·ke, Le·o·pold von (lā′ô-pōlt′ fôn räŋ′kə), 1795–1886; German historian.
rank·er (raŋk′ẽr), *n.* 1. a person who ranks. 2. [British], *a)* a soldier in the ranks. *b)* a commissioned officer promoted from the ranks.
ran·kle (raŋ′k'l), *v.i.* [RANKLED (-k'ld), RANKLING], [ME. *ranclen;* OFr. *rancler* < *raoncle*, *draoncle;* ML. *dracunculus*, a fester, ulcer < L. *dracunculus*, dim. of *draco*, dragon, snake], 1. to fester; become inflamed or cause inflammation. 2. to cause continual mental pain, resentment, etc.: as, the scornful words *rankled*.
ran·sack (ran′sak), *v.t.* [ME. *ransaken;* ON. *rannsaka* < *rann*, a house + *-saka* < *sækja*, to seek, search; cf. SEEK], 1. to search thoroughly; examine every part of in searching. 2. to search through for plunder; pillage.
ran·som (ran′səm), *n.* [ME. *ranson*, *ransom*, etc.; OFr. *rançon*, *raençon;* L. *redemptio* < pp. of *redimere;* see REDEEM], 1. the redeeming or release of a captive or of seized property by payment of money or compliance with other demands. 2. the price thus paid or demanded. 3. in *theology*, a means of freeing from sin; redemption. *v.t.* 1. to obtain the release of (a captive, property, etc.) by paying the demanded price. 2. to release after such payment. 3. in *theology*, to free from sin; redeem. —*SYN.* see **rescue.**
rant (rant), *v.i.* [MD. *ranten*, to rave; cf. G. *ranzen*, to frolic], 1. to talk in a loud, wild, extravagant way; declaim violently; rave. 2. [British Dial.], to be boisterously merry. *v.t.* to say or declaim in a ranting manner (often with *out*): as, he *ranted* out his denunciation. *n.* 1. loud, wild, extravagant speech. 2. [British Dial.], a boisterous merrymaking.
ra·nun·cu·la·ceous (rə-nuŋ′kyoo-lā′shəs), *adj.* [< Mod. L. *Ranunculaceae*, name of the family (see RANUNCULUS); + *-ous*], of the buttercup or crowfoot family of plants, including the larkspur, peony, anemone, etc.
ra·nun·cu·lus (rə-nuŋ′kyoo-ləs), *n.* [*pl.* RANUNCULUSES (-iz), RANUNCULI (-lī′)], [L., little frog, tadpole, medicinal plant, dim. of *rana*, a frog], any of a large group of plants of the buttercup or crowfoot family.
rap (rap), *v.t.* [RAPPED (rapt), RAPPING], [ME. *rappen*

prob. Gmc.], 1. to strike quickly and sharply; tap. 2. to say sharply (with *out*): as, he *rapped* out an oath. *v.i.* to knock quickly and sharply. *n.* 1. a quick, sharp knock; tap. 2. [Slang], blame or punishment; specifically, a judicial sentence, as to a prison term: usually in *beat* (escape) or *take* (receive) *the rap*.

rap (rap), *n.* [cf. G. *rappe*, small coin], 1. originally, a counterfeit Irish halfpenny; hence, 2. [Colloq.], the least bit: now usually in *not care* (or *give*) *a rap*, not care (or give) anything at all.

rap (rap), *v.t.* [RAPPED or RAPT (rapt), RAPPING], [prob. back-formation < *rapt*], [Obs. or Rare], 1. to seize; snatch. 2. to transport with rapture: now only in the past participle.

ra·pa·cious (rə-pā′shəs), *adj.* [< L. *rapax, rapacis* < *rapere*, to seize; + *-ous*], 1. taking by force; plundering. 2. greedy; voracious; ravenous. 3. living on captured prey: said of animals or birds.

ra·pac·i·ty (rə-pas′ə-ti), *n.* [L. *rapacitas*], the quality, fact, or practice of being rapacious.

Ra·pal·lo (rä-päl′lô), *n.* a seaport in Italy, near Genoa: pop., 14,000.

Ra·pa Nu·i (rä′pä no͞o′i), Easter Island: native name.

rape (rāp), *n.* [Late ME.; Anglo-Fr. *rap, rape;* prob. back-formation < L. *rapere*, to take by force; cf. RAPACIOUS], 1. the crime of having sexual intercourse with a woman or girl forcibly and without her consent: *statutory rape* is the crime of having sexual intercourse with a girl below the age of consent (see **age of consent**). 2. the act of seizing and carrying away by force. 3. the plundering or violent destruction (*of* a city, etc.), as in warfare. *v.t.* [RAPED (rāpt), RAPING], 1. to commit rape on (a woman or girl); ravish; violate. 2. to seize and carry away by force. 3. to plunder or destroy (a city, etc.), as in warfare.

rape (rāp), *n.* [ME.; L. *rapa, rapum*, turnip; IE. base **rap-*, seen also in G. *rübe*, beet, Gr. *rhapys, rhaphys*], a plant of the mustard family, whose seeds yield an oil and whose leaves are used for fodder.

rape (rāp), *n.* [Fr. *râpe;* ML. *raspa;* ult. < OHG. *raspon*, to scrape together; see RASP], the crushed pulp of grapes after the juice has been extracted.

rape oil, the thick oil extracted from rapeseed, used for lubricating, etc.; colza oil: also **rapeseed oil.**

rape·seed (rāp′sēd′), *n.* 1. the seed of the rape plant. 2. the plant.

Raph·a·el (raf′i-əl; *also, for masc. name & n. 1,* rā′fi-əl), [LL.; Gr. *Rhaphaēl;* Heb. *rephā'ēl*, lit., God hath healed], a masculine name. *n.* 1. an archangel mentioned in the Apocrypha. 2. (*Raffaello Sanli*), Italian painter and architect; lived 1483–1520.

ra·phe (rā′fē), *n.* [Mod. L. < Gr. *rhaphē*, a seam < *rhaptein*, to stitch together], 1. in *anatomy*, a seamlike joining of the two lateral halves of an organ, as of the tongue, etc. 2. in *botany*, *a*) a cord of tissue forming a seam along the body of certain ovules. *b*) a median line, rib, or slot on a diatom valve or cell wall.

raph·i·des (raf′ə-dēz′), *n.pl.* [Mod.L. < Gr. *rhaphis, rhaphidos*, a needle], the needle-shaped crystals developed in plant cells.

rap·id (rap′id), *adj.* [Fr. *rapide;* L. *rapidus* < *rapere*, to seize, rush], 1. swift; quick; moving, progressing, or done with speed. 2. steep; abrupt: as, a *rapid* rise in the highway. *n. usually in pl.* a part of a river where the water moves swiftly, as because of a sudden drop in the river bed. —*SYN.* see **fast.**

Rap·i·dan (rap′ə-dan′), *n.* a river in Virginia, flowing eastward into the Rappahannock River.

rap·id-fire (rap′id-fīr′), *adj.* 1. firing or capable of firing shots in rapid succession: said of guns: abbreviated **R.F., r.f.** 2. done, delivered, proceeding, or carried on swiftly and sharply: as, a *rapid-fire* talk.

rap·id-fir·ing (rap′id-fīr′iŋ), *adj.* rapid-fire.

ra·pid·i·ty (rə-pid′ə-ti), *n.* [Fr. *rapidité;* L. *rapiditas*], the quality or condition of being rapid; speed; swiftness.

ra·pi·er (rā′pi-ẽr, rāp′yẽr), *n.* [Fr. *rapière;* orig. used as adj., in OFr. *espee* (sword) *rapiere;* cf. Fr. *râpe*, grater (see RAPPEE), *raspière*, rasper, poker], 1. originally, a slender, two-edged sword with a large cup hilt, used chiefly for thrusting. 2. later, a light, sharp-pointed sword used only for thrusting.

rap·ine (rap′in), *n.* [Fr.; L. *rapina* < *rapere*, to snatch, seize; cf. RAPID], the act of seizing and carrying off by force the property of others; plunder; pillage.

rap·ist (rāp′ist), *n.* a person who has committed rape.

Rap·pa·han·nock (rap′ə-han′ək), *n.* a river in northeastern Virginia, flowing into Chesapeake Bay: length, 155 mi.

rap·pa·ree (rap′ə-rē′), *n.* [Ir. *rapaire*, orig., pikeman < *rapaire*, half-pike], 1. formerly, an Irish freebooting soldier; hence, 2. a plunderer or robber.

rap·pee (ra-pē′), *n.* [Fr. (*tabac*) *râpé*, grated (tobacco), pp. of *râper*, to rasp; ult. < OHG. *raspon*, to scrape together; see RASP], a strong snuff made from the coarser, darker tobacco leaves.

rap·per (rap′ẽr), *n.* a person or thing that raps; specifically, a door knocker.

rap·port (ra-pôrt′, ra-pōrt′; Fr. rȧ′pôr′), *n.* [Fr. < *rapporter*, to refer < *re-*, again + *apporter* < L. *apportare*, to bring < *ad-*, to + *portare*, to carry], relationship; especially, a close or sympathetic relationship; agreement; harmony: see also **en rapport.**

‡rap·proche·ment (rȧ′prôsh′män′), *n.* [Fr. < *rapprocher*, to bring together; see RE-, APPROACH, & -MENT], an establishing or, especially, a restoring of harmony and friendly relations.

rap·scal·lion (rap-skal′yən), *n.* [< earlier *rascallion*, extension of *rascal*], a rascal; rogue.

rapt (rapt), *adj.* [L. *raptus*, pp. of *rapere*, to snatch, seize; cf. RAP (to seize)], 1. carried away in body or spirit (*to* heaven, etc.). 2. carried away with joy, love, etc.; enraptured. 3. completely absorbed or engrossed (*in* meditation, study, etc.). 4. resulting from or showing rapture: as, a *rapt* look.

rap·to·ri·al (rap-tôr′i-əl, rap-tō′ri-əl), *adj.* [L. *raptor*, plunderer < pp. of *rapere*, to snatch; + *-ial*], 1. adapted for seizing prey: as, *raptorial* claws. 2. of or belonging to a group of birds of prey with a strong notched beak and sharp talons, as the eagle, hawk, owl, vulture, etc.

rap·ture (rap′chẽr), *n.* [*rapt* + *-ure*], 1. the state of being carried away with joy, love, etc.; ecstasy. 2. an expression of great joy, pleasure, etc. 3. [Rare], a carrying away or being carried away in body or spirit. *v.t.* [RAPTURED (-chẽrd), RAPTURING], [Poetic], to enrapture; fill with ecstasy. —*SYN.* see **ecstasy.**

rap·tur·ous (rap′chẽr-əs), *adj.* feeling or showing rapture; ecstatic.

‡ra·ra a·vis (râ′rə ā′vis), [*pl.* RARAE AVES (râ′rē ā′vēz)], [L., lit., strange bird], an unusual or extraordinary person or thing; rarity.

rare (râr), *adj.* [Fr.; L. *rarus*, loose, thin, scattered, scarce], 1. not frequently found; scarce; uncommon; unusual; hence, 2. unusually good; remarkably fine; excellent: as, a *rare* scholar. 3. of thin texture; not dense: as, the *rare* atmosphere far above the earth. 4. [Obs.], not close together; scattered. Abbreviated **r.**
SYN.—**rare** is applied to something of which there are not many instances or specimens and usually connotes, therefore, great value (a *rare* gem); **infrequent** applies to that which occurs only at long intervals (his *infrequent* trips); **uncommon** and **unusual** refer to that which does not ordinarily occur and is therefore exceptional or remarkable (her *uncommon* generosity, this *unusual* heat); **scarce** applies to something of which there is, at the moment, an inadequate supply (potatoes are *scarce* these days).—*ANT.* frequent, common, abundant.

rare (râr), *adj.* [earlier *rear;* ME. *rere;* AS. *hrere*, lightly boiled (basic sense prob. "disturbed, moved") < base of *hreran*, to move, shake], not completely cooked; underdone; partially raw: said especially of meat: abbreviated **r.**

rare·bit (râr′bit), *n.* [altered < (*Welsh*) *rabbit*], Welsh rabbit; dish of melted cheese over toast.

rare earth, any of certain basic oxides much alike in physical and chemical properties; specifically, any of the oxides of the rare-earth metals.

rare-earth metals (râr′ũrth′), a group of rare metallic chemical elements with consecutive atomic numbers of 57 to 71 inclusive: also **rare-earth elements.**

rar·ee show (râr′ē), [< pronun. (by Savoyard showmen) of *rare show*], 1. a portable peep show; hence, 2. any street show.

rar·e·fac·tion (râr′ə-fak′shən), *n.* [< pp. of L. *rarefacere*], a rarefying or being rarefied.

rar·e·fac·tive (râr′ə-fak′tiv), *adj.* characterized by or causing rarefaction.

rar·e·fy (râr′ə-fī′), *v.t. & v.i.* [RAREFIED (-fīd′), RAREFYING], [Fr. *raréfier;* L. *rarefacere* < *rarus*, rare + *facere*, to make], 1. to make or become thin, or less dense. 2. to make or become purer, or more refined.

rare·ly (râr′li), *adv.* 1. infrequently; seldom. 2. beautifully, skillfully, excellently, etc. 3. uncommonly; exceptionally; extremely.

rare·ripe (râr′rīp′), *adj.* [*rare*, dial. var. of ME. *rathe*, swiftly, early; + *ripe*], ripening early. *n.* a fruit or vegetable that ripens early; especially, any of a variety of such peaches.

rar·i·ty (râr′ə-ti), *n.* [L. *raritas*], 1. the quality or condition of being rare; specifically, *a*) uncommonness; scarcity. *b*) excellence. *c*) lack of density; thinness. 2. [*pl.* RARITIES (-tiz)], something remarkable or valuable because of its scarcity.

Ra·ro·ton·ga (rä′rô-tôŋ′gə), *n.* one of the Cook Islands, in the South Pacific: pop., 3,900.

ras·cal (ras′k'l), *n.* [ME. *rascaile;* OFr. *rascaille*, scrapings, dregs, rabble < *rasque*, filth, scurf; prob. < LL. *rasicare*, to scrape < L. *radere*, to shave, scrape], 1. a scoundrel; rogue; scamp: often used jokingly or affectionately, as in addressing a mischievous child. 2. [Obs.], one of the rabble. *adj.* 1. [Rare], low; dishonest; base. 2. [Obs.], of the rabble.

ras·cal·i·ty (ras-kal′ə-ti), *n.* 1. the character or behavior of a rascal. 2. [*pl.* RASCALITIES (-tiz)], a low, mean, or dishonest act.

ras·cal·ly (ras′k'l-i), *adj.* of or like a rascal; base; dishonest; mean. *adv.* in a rascally manner.

rase (rāz), *v.t.* [RASED (rāzd), RASING], to raze.

rash (rash), *adj.* [ME. *rasch;* prob. < AS. **ræsc;* akin to ON. *röskr,* G. *rasch,* etc.; for prob. IE. base see RACE (a running)], 1. too hasty in acting or speaking; reckless. 2. characterized by too great haste or recklessness: as, a *rash* act. 3. [Obs.], acting quickly.

rash (rash), *n.* [OFr. *rasche, rasque;* see RASCAL], an eruption of red spots on the skin, usually temporary.

rash·er (rash′ēr), *n.* [? < obs. *rash.* to cut < Fr. *raser;* see RAZE], a thin slice of bacon or, rarely, ham, to be fried or broiled.

Ras·mus·sen, Knud (k'nōōth räs′moo-s'n), (*Knud Johan Victor Rasmussen*), 1879–1933; Danish arctic explorer and author.

ra·so·ri·al (rə-sôr′i-əl, rə-sō′ri-əl), *adj.* [< Mod.L. *Rasores,* lit., scratchers < L. *rasus,* pp. of *radere,* to scrape; + *-ial*], characteristically scratching the ground to find food, as a chicken; gallinaceous.

rasp (rasp, räsp), *v.t.* [ME. *raspere;* OFr. *rasper;* OHG. *raspon,* to scrape together; akin to AS. *hrespan,* to strip, spoil], 1. to scrape or rub with or as with a file. 2. to utter in a rough, grating tone. 3. to grate upon; irritate: as, the baby's crying *rasped* her nerves. *v.i.* 1. to scrape roughly; grate. 2. to make a rough, grating sound. *n.* 1. a type of rough file with raised points instead of lines. 2. a rough, grating sound. 3. a rasping.

rasp·ber·ry (raz′ber′i, raz′bēr-i), *n.* [*pl.* RASPBERRIES (-iz)], [earlier *raspis berry* < *rasp, raspis,* raspberry; prob. same word as ME. *raspis,* kind of wine; cf. OFr. *vin raspé,* ML. *raspecia;* see RAPE (of grapes)], 1. any of a group of prickly shrubs of the rose family. 2. its small, juicy, edible fruit, consisting of a cluster of red, purple, or black drupelets. 3. [< rhyming slang *raspberry tart*], [Slang], a sound of derision, contempt, etc. made by expelling air forcibly so as to vibrate the tongue between the lips.

Ras·pu·tin, Gri·go·ri E·fi·mo·vich (gri-gô′ri ye-fē′mô-vich räs-pōō′tin; Eng. ras-pū′t'n), 1871?–1916; notorious Russian monk who exercised great control over Czar Nicholas II and the Czarina; assassinated.

rasp·y (ras′pi, räs′pi), *adj.* [RASPIER (-pi-ēr), RASPIEST (-pi-ist)], 1. rasping; grating. 2. easily irritated.

ras·sle (ras′'l), *n., v.i. & v.t.* [RASSLED (-'ld), RASSLING], [Dial. or Colloq.], to wrestle: also spelled **wrastle, wrassle, rassel, rastle.**

ras·ter (ras′tēr), *n.* [G., a screen], in *television,* the group of closely spaced parallel lines appearing on the cathode-ray tube when there is no incoming signal: the image is formed by modulating the brightness of the different parts of these lines.

rat (rat), *n.* [ME. *ratte;* AS. *ræt;* akin to G. *ratz, ratte*], 1. any of several kinds of black, brown, or gray, long-tailed rodents, resembling, but larger than, the mouse: popularly applied also to certain other rodents, as the muskrat. 2. [Colloq.], a small pad used in certain styles of women's coiffures to make the hair look thicker. 3. [Slang], a sneaky, contemptible person; specifically, *a)* an informer; stool pigeon. *b)* a worker who betrays or scabs on his fellow workers. *v.i.* [RATTED (-id), RATTING], 1. to hunt for rats, especially with dogs. 2. [Slang], *a)* to desert one's companions, especially one's fellow workers, as rats are reputed to desert a sinking ship. *b)* to act as a stool pigeon.

rats! [Slang], an exclamation of disgust, scorn, disappointment, etc.

smell a rat, to suspect a trick, plot, etc.

rat·a·ble (rāt′ə-b'l), *adj.* 1. that can be rated, or estimated, etc. 2. figured at a certain rate; proportional. 3. [British], taxable. Also spelled **rateable.**

rat·a·bly (rāt′ə-bli), *adv.* proportionally; by rate.

rat·a·fee (rat′ə-fē′), *n.* a ratafia.

rat·a·fi·a (rat′ə-fē′ə), *n.* [Fr.; ? of Creole origin], 1. a cordial or liqueur flavored with almond or fruit kernels. 2. [British], a macaroon: in full, **ratafia biscuit.**

rat·al (rāt′'l), *n.* [< *rate* + *-al* (after *rental*)], the amount at which a person or property is assessed for taxation.

ra·tan (ra-tan′), *n.* rattan.

rat·a·plan (rat′ə-plan′), *n.* [Fr.; echoic of drumming], the beating of a drum, or a sound like this. *v.i.* [RATAPLANNED (-pland′), RATAPLANNING], to make such a sound. *v.t.* to make such a sound on.

rat·bite fever (or **disease**), (rat′bīt′), an infectious disease caused by certain spirochetes and transmitted by the bite of a rat: it is characterized by a bluish-red rash, attacks of fever, and muscular pain.

ratch (rach), *n.* [var. of *ratchet*], a ratchet.

ratch·et (rach′it), *n.* [Fr. *rochet* < It. *rochetto,* bobbin, spindle, dim. of *rocca,* distaff < Goth. **rukka;* akin to OHG. *roccho,* a spindle, distaff], 1. a hinged catch, or pawl, arranged so as to engage with a toothed wheel or bar whose teeth slope in one direction, thus preventing backward movement. 2. such a wheel or bar. 3. such a catch and wheel (or bar) as a unit.

ratchet wheel, a toothed wheel with a catch, or pawl, that keeps it from turning backward; ratchet.

RATCHET WHEEL

rate (rāt), *n.* [ME.; OFr.; L. *rata* (*pars*), reckoned (part), fem. of *ratus,* pp. of *reri,* to reckon], 1. the amount, degree, etc. of anything in relation to units of something else: as, the *rate* of pay per month, *rate* of speed per minute. 2. a fixed ratio; proportion: as, the *rate* of exchange: see **exchange,** *n.* 7. 3. a price or value; specifically, the cost per unit of some commodity, service etc.: as, an electricity *rate,* insurance *rate.* 4. speed of movement or action: as, he read at a moderate *rate.* 5. the amount of time gained or lost by a timepiece. 6. a class; rank: as, of the first *rate.* 7. [British] a local property tax. 8. [Obs.], amount; quantity *v.t.* [RATED (-id), RATING], 1. to estimate the value of appraise. 2. to put into a particular class or rank 3. to consider; esteem: as, he is *rated* as an important national figure. 4. to determine the rates for shipping (goods), as by rail or air. 5. [Colloq.], to deserve: as he *rates* the best. *v.i.* 1. to be classed or ranked 2. to have value, status, or rating. —*SYN.* see **estimate**

at any rate, 1. in any event; whatever happens. 2. a least; anyway.

rate (rāt), *v.t. & v.i.* [RATED (-id), RATING], [ME. *raten araten;* prob. < OFr. *rater, areter,* to scold, accuse < L. *ad-,* to + *reputare,* to count (see REPUTE); but cf Sw. *rata,* to find fault, blame], to scold severely; chide

rate·a·ble (rāt′ə-b'l), *adj.* ratable.

rate·a·bly (rāt′ə-bli), *adv.* ratably.

ra·tel (rā′təl, rä′təl), *n.* [S.Afr.D., short for *rateldas* < D. *raat,* a honeycomb + *das,* a badger], a burrowing animal of India and Africa, somewhat like a badger

rate·pay·er (rāt′pā′ēr), *n.* [British], a person who pays rates, or local taxes.

-rat·er (rāt′ēr), a combining form used in hyphenated compounds, meaning *one of a* (specified) *rate,* or *class* as in *second-rater.*

rath (rath, räth), *adj. & adv.* [Obs. or Poetic], rathe

rathe (rāth), *adj.* [ME.; AS. *hræth,* var. of *hræd,* quick speedy, after *hræthe, hrathe, adv.,* speedily; prob. IE base **qret-,* to shake], [Obs. or Poetic], 1. quick prompt; eager. 2. coming or happening early in the day, year, etc.; especially, blooming or ripening early in the season: said of flowers, plants, etc. *adv.* [Obs or Poetic], 1. quickly; promptly. 2. early, or too early, in the day, season, etc.

Ra·the·nau, Wal·ther (väl′tēr rä′tə-nou′), 1867–1922 German industrialist and statesman; assassinated.

rath·er (rath′ēr; *less often* rä′thēr), *adv.* [ME., compar of *rathe,* quickly; AS. *hrathe, hræthe* (compar. *hrathor*) basic sense "more quickly," hence "preferably" 1. [Obs. or British Dial.], more quickly; sooner; hence 2. more willingly; preferably: as, he would *rather* go than stay. 3. with more justice, logic, reason, etc. as, I, *rather* than you, should take the risk. 4. more accurately; more precisely: as, it was in the morning or *rather,* the early afternoon. 5. on the contrary quite conversely: as, we have not lost; *rather,* we have won. 6. somewhat; to some degree: as, I *rather* enjoy singing. 7. [Chiefly British Colloq.], certainly; assuredly: used as an answer.

had rather, would choose to; would prefer that.

raths·kel·ler (räts′kel′ēr; *now sometimes* rath′skel′ēr *n.* [G. < *rat,* council, town hall + *keller,* cellar], restaurant of the German type that serves beer whisky, wine, etc., usually below the street level.

rat·i·fi·ca·tion (rat′ə-fi-kā′shən), *n.* [Fr.; ML. *ratificatio* < pp. of *ratificare*], a ratifying or being ratified approval; sanction; confirmation.

rat·i·fi·er (rat′ə-fī′ēr), *n.* a person or group that ratifies

rat·i·fy (rat′ə-fī′), *v.t.* [RATIFIED (-fīd′), RATIFYING [Fr. *ratifier;* ML. *ratificare* < L. *ratus* (see RATE, *n.*) *facere,* to make], to approve or confirm; especially, to give formal sanction to. —*SYN.* see **approve.**

ra·ti·né (rat′ə-nā′), *n.* [Fr., frizzed, tufted: of the nap a coarse, loosely woven fabric of cotton, wool, rayon etc., with a nubby or knotty surface.

rat·ing (rāt′iŋ), *n.* [see RATE (to appraise)], 1. a rank class, or grade, as of enlisted men in an army or navy 2. a placement in a certain rank or class. 3. an expression in horsepower, etc. of the working power of an engine or other machine. 4. an evaluation of the credit or financial standing of a businessman, firm etc. 5. an amount determined as a rate, or grade

rat·ing (rāt′iŋ), *n.* [see RATE (to scold)], a scolding sharp reprimand.

ra·tio (rā′shō, rā′shi-ō′), *n.* [*pl.* RATIOS (-shōz, -ōz′) [L.; see REASON], 1. a fixed relation in degree, number etc. between two similar things; proportion: as, in our class there is a *ratio* of three boys to two girls. 2. in *finance,* the relative value of gold and silver in a currency system based on both. 3. in *mathematics* the quotient of one quantity divided by another of the same kind, and usually expressed as a fraction. Symbol, R (no period).

ra·ti·oc·i·nate (rash'i-os'ə-nāt'), ***v.i.*** [RATIOCINATED (-id), RATIOCINATING], [< L. *ratiocinatus*, pp. of *ratiocinari* < *ratio;* see REASON], to reason; especially, to reason using formal logic.

ra·ti·oc·i·na·tion (rash'i-os'ə-nā'shən), ***n.*** 1. a ratiocinating, or reasoning. 2. an instance of reasoning.

ra·ti·oc·i·na·tive (rash'i-os'ə-nā'tiv), ***adj.*** [L. *ratiocinativus*], of or characterized by ratiocination.

ra·tion (rash'ən, rā'shən), ***n.*** [Fr.; ML. *ratio*, ration; L. *ratio;* see REASON], 1. a fixed portion; share; allowance. 2. a fixed allowance or allotment of food or provisions. 3. a fixed daily allowance of food for one person (or one animal) in an army or navy. 4. *pl.* [Military Slang], something to eat; food. ***v.t.*** 1. to give a ration or rations to. 2. to distribute (food, clothing, etc.) in rations, as in times of scarcity.

ra·tion·al (rash'ən-'l), ***adj.*** [L. *rationalis* < *ratio;* see REASON], 1. of, based on, or derived from reasoning: as, *rational* powers. 2. able to reason; reasoning: as, an infant is not yet *rational.* 3. showing reason; not foolish or silly; sensible: as, a *rational* argument. 4. in *mathematics*, designating a number or quantity expressible without a radical sign as an integer or as a quotient of an integer.

SYN.*—rational** implies the ability to reason logically, as by drawing conclusions from inferences, and often connotes the absence of emotionalism (man is a *rational* creature); **reasonable** is a less technical term and suggests the use of practical reason in making decisions, choices, etc. (that sounds like a *reasonable* solution); **sensible**, also a non-technical term, implies the use of common sense or sound judgment (you made a *sensible* decision).—ANT.*** irrational, absurd.

ra·tion·a·le (rash'ə-nal', rash'ə-nā'li, rash'ə-nā'li), ***n.*** [L., neut. of *rationalis*, rational], 1. the fundamental reasons, or rational basis, of something. 2. a statement, exposition, or explanation of reasons or principles.

ra·tion·al·ism (rash'ən-'l-iz'm), ***n.*** [*rational* + *-ism*], 1. the principle or practice of accepting reason as the only authority in determining one's opinions or course of action. 2. in *philosophy*, the theory that the reason, or intellect, is the true source of knowledge, rather than the senses. 3. in *theology*, the doctrine that rejects revelation and the supernatural, and makes reason the sole source of knowledge.

ra·tion·al·ist (rash'ən-'l-ist), ***n.*** a person who believes in or practices rationalism.

ra·tion·al·is·tic (rash'ən-'l-is'tik), ***adj.*** of rationalism or rationalists.

ra·tion·al·is·ti·cal·ly (rash'ən-'l-is'ti-k'l-i, rash'ən-'l-is'tik-li), ***adv.*** in a rationalistic manner.

ra·tion·al·i·ty (rash'ə-nal'ə-ti), ***n.*** [LL. *rationalitas*], 1. the quality or condition of being rational; reasonableness, or the possessing or using of reason. 2. [*pl.* RATIONALITIES (-tiz)], a rational act, belief, etc.

ra·tion·al·i·za·tion (rash'ən-'l-i-zā'shən, rash'ən-'l-ī-zā'shən), ***n.*** a rationalizing or being rationalized.

ra·tion·al·ize (rash'ən-'l-īz'), ***v.t.*** [RATIONALIZED (-īzd'), RATIONALIZING], 1. to make rational; make conform to reason. 2. to explain or interpret on rational grounds. 3. to apply modern methods of efficiency to (an industry, agriculture, etc.). 4. in *mathematics*, to remove the radical signs from (an equation) without changing the value. 5. in *psychology*, to devise superficially rational, or plausible, explanations or excuses for (one's acts, beliefs, desires, etc.), usually without being aware that these are not the real motives. ***v.i.*** 1. to think in a rational or rationalistic manner. 2. to rationalize one's acts, beliefs, etc.

Rat·is·bon (rat'is-bon', rat'iz-bon'), ***n.*** Regensburg.

rat·ite (rat'īt), ***adj.*** [< L. *ratis*, a raft; + *-ite*], of a group of large, flightless birds having a flat breastbone without the keellike ridge of flying birds. ***n.*** any bird of this group, as the cassowary, ostrich, etc.

rat·line (rat'lin), ***n.*** [folk-etym. form; earlier also *ratling;* Late ME. *radeling;* prob. < *raddle* (to interlace), with reference to the appearance of the shrouds; cf. D. *weveling* (LG. *weveline*), ratline, lit. a weaving], 1. any of the small, relatively thin pieces of rope which join the shrouds of a ship and serve as a ladder for climbing the rigging: see **shroud**, illus. 2. the light, tarred rope used for this. Also spelled **ratlin.**

ra·toon (ra-tōōn'), ***n.*** [Sp. *retoño;* Hind. *ratun*], a shoot growing from the root of a plant (especially the sugar cane) that has been cut down. ***v.i.*** to grow new shoots, or grow as a new shoot, from the root of a plant that has been cut down. Also spelled **rattoon.**

rat race, [Slang], a frantic scurry or mad scramble.

rats·bane (rats'bān'), ***n.*** [earlier *rats bane;* see BANE], rat poison; especially, trioxide of arsenic.

rat·tan (ra-tan'), ***n.*** [Malay *rotan* < *raut*, to strip, pare], 1. any of a number of related climbing palms with long, slender, tough stems. 2. a stem of any of these trees, used in making wickerwork, etc. 3. a cane or switch made from this. Also spelled **ratan.**

rat·teen (ra-tēn'), ***n.*** [Fr. *ratine*], [Obs.], a heavy, twilled, woolen cloth like frieze.

rat·ten (rat''n), ***v.t. & v.i.*** [It., to play a rat's trick on < dial. *ratten*, a rat; ME. *ratton*, dim. of *ratte;* see RAT], [British Slang], to destroy or remove machinery, tools, etc. in order to compel (an employer) to agree to certain trade-union demands.

rat·ter (rat'ẽr), ***n.*** 1. *a)* a person hired to catch or destroy rats. *b)* a dog that is especially skilled at catching rats. 2. [Slang], a betrayer or deserter.

rat·tish (rat'ish), ***adj.*** 1. of or infested with rats. 2. like or characteristic of a rat (especially in sense 3).

rat·tle (rat''l), ***v.i.*** [RATTLED (-'ld), RATTLING], [ME. *ratelen;* prob. of WGmc. echoic origin; akin to G. *rasseln*], 1. to make a series of sharp, short sounds in quick succession: as, the window *rattles* in the wind. 2. to go or move with such sounds: as, the wagon *rattled* over the stones. 3. to talk rapidly and incessantly; chatter (often with *on*). ***v.t.*** 1. to cause to rattle: as, he *rattled* the handle. 2. to utter or perform rapidly. 3. [Colloq.], to confuse or upset; disconcert: as, the applause *rattled* the speaker. ***n.*** 1. a quick succession of sharp, short sounds. 2. a rattling noise made by air passing through the mucus of a partly closed throat, often heard in a dying person. 3. a noisy uproar; loud chatter. 4. *a)* a series of horny rings at the end of a rattlesnake's tail, used to produce a rattling sound. *b)* any of these. 5. a device, especially a baby's toy, intended to rattle when shaken. —***SYN.*** see **embarrass.**

rat·tle·brain (rat''l-brān'), ***n.*** a silly, talkative person.

rat·tle·brained (rat''l-brānd'), ***adj.*** of, or having the nature of, a rattlebrain; silly; frivolous; harebrained.

rat·tle·pate (rat''l-pāt'), ***n.*** a rattlebrain.

rat·tle·pat·ed (rat''l-pāt'id), ***adj.*** rattlebrained.

rat·tler (rat'lẽr), ***n.*** a person or thing that rattles; specifically, a rattlesnake.

rat·tle·snake (rat''l-snāk'), ***n.*** any of various poisonous American snakes having an interlocking series of horny rings at the end of the tail that produce a rattling sound when shaken.

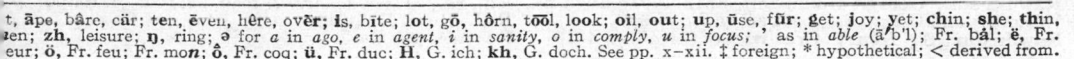

RATTLESNAKE (2–8 ft. long)

rattlesnake plantain, a variety of orchid with spotted leaves and yellowish-white flower spikes.

rattlesnake root, any of a number of related plants with composite flowers of various colors and a thick, bitter root, formerly considered a cure for snake bite.

rattlesnake weed, 1. any of a number of related plants, especially a variety of the hawkweed with one purple-veined leaf to a stem. 2. a rattlesnake plantain.

rat·tle·trap (rat''l-trap'), ***n.*** [*rattle* + *trap* (carriage)], 1. anything worn out, rickety, or rattling, especially such a wagon, automobile, etc. 2. [Slang], *a)* a person who talks much. *b)* the mouth: now usually *trap.*

rat·tling (rat'liŋ), ***adj.*** 1. that rattles. 2. [Colloq.], very fast, good, lively, etc.: as, a *rattling* pace, a *rattling* time. ***adv.*** [Colloq.], very: as, *rattling* good.

rat·tly (rat''l-i, rat'li), ***adj.*** that rattles or tends to rattle; noisy.

rat·toon (ra-tōōn'), ***n. & v.i.*** ratoon.

rat·trap (rat'trap'), ***n.*** 1. a trap for catching rats; hence, 2. a hopeless situation; desperate predicament.

rat·ty (rat'i), ***adj.*** [RATTIER (-i-ẽr), RATTIEST (-i-ist)], 1. of or like rats. 2. full of rats. 3. [Slang], dilapidated.

rau·ci·ty (rô'sə-ti), ***n.*** a raucous quality or condition.

rau·cous (rô'kəs), ***adj.*** [L. *raucus*], hoarse; rough-sounding: as, a *raucous* shout.

rav·age (rav'ij), ***n.*** [Fr. < *ravir;* see RAVISH], 1. the act or practice of violently destroying; destruction. 2. ruin; havoc; devastating damage: as, the *ravages* of time. ***v.t.*** [RAVAGED (-ijd), RAVAGING], [Fr. *ravager* < the *n.*], to destroy violently; devastate; ruin: as, the soldiers *ravaged* the town. ***v.i.*** to commit ravages.

***SYN.*—ravage** implies violent destruction, usually in a series of depredations or over an extended period of time, as by an army, a plague, etc.; **devastate** stresses the total ruin and desolation resulting from a ravaging; **plunder** refers to the forceful taking of loot by an invading or conquering army; **sack** and **pillage** both specifically suggest violent destruction and plunder by an invading or conquering army, **sack** implying the total stripping of all valuables in a city or town; **despoil** is equivalent to **sack** but is usually used with reference to buildings, institutions, etc.

rave (rāv), ***v.i.*** [RAVED (rāvd), RAVING], [ME. *raven;* OFr. *raver*, var. of *rever*, to rave, revel (Fr. *rêver*, to dream)], 1. to talk incoherently or wildly, as a delirious or demented person. 2. to talk with excessive enthusiasm (*about* someone or something). 3. to rage or roar, as a storm. *v.t.* to utter incoherently or with excessive enthusiasm. *n.* 1. the act or condition of raving. 2. a raving action or speech. 3. [Slang], *a)* an excessively enthusiastic commendation: often used attributively, as, *rave* reviews. *b)* an infatuation.

rav·el (rav′'l), *v.t.* [RAVELED or RAVELLED (-'ld), RAVELING or RAVELLING], [MD. *ravelen* (D. *rafelen;* cf. RAFFLE); akin to LG. *rabbeln*], 1. originally, to make complicated or tangled; involve. 2. to separate the parts, especially threads, of; untwist; unweave; unravel. 3. to make clear; disentangle. *v.i.* 1. to become separated into its parts, especially threads; fray (usually with *out*). 2. [Rare], to become complicated or tangled. *n.* 1. a raveled part, especially a thread; raveling. 2. a tangled mass or complication.

Ra·vel, Mau·rice Jo·seph (mô′rēs′ zhō′zef′ rá′vel′; Eng. ra-vel′), 1875–1937; French composer.

rave·lin (rav′lin), *n.* [Fr. *ravelin* < It. *ravellino, revellino*], a detached fortification having two faces projecting outward from the main structure to form a salient angle.

rav·el·ing, rav·el·ling (rav′'l-iŋ, rav′liŋ), *n.* 1. the act of something that ravels or is raveled. 2. anything raveled; especially, a thread raveled from a knitted or woven material.

rav·el·ment (rav′'l-mənt), *n.* a raveling or becoming raveled; especially, entanglement or complication.

rav·en (rā′vən), *n.* [ME. *rauen;* AS. *hræfn;* akin to ON. *hrafn* & less directly to G. *rabe;* IE. echoic base **ker-, *kor-*, imitative of harsh sounds, seen also in L. *crepitare*, to rattle, crackle (cf. CREPITATION): so named from its cry], a large bird of the crow family, with lustrous black feathers and a straight, sharp beak. *adj.* black and lustrous.

rav·en (rav′ən), *v.t.* [OFr. *raviner* < *ravine* (L. *rapina*); see RAPINE], 1. to devour greedily. 2. [Obs.], to seize forcibly. *v.i.* 1. to prowl hungrily; search for prey or plunder. 2. to devour food or prey greedily. 3. to have a voracious appetite. Also spelled **ravin.** *n.* ravin.

rav·en·ing (rav′ən-iŋ), *adj.* [ppr. of *raven*], 1. greedily searching for prey. 2. demented; mad. *n.* ravin.

Ra·ven·na (rə-ven′ə; It. rä-ven′nä), *n.* a city in northeastern Italy: pop., 92,000.

rav·e·nous (rav′ən-əs), *adj.* [OFr. *ravinos* < *ravine;* see RAVEN, *v.*], 1. greedily hungry; voracious. 2. very eager for gratification of some desire: as, *ravenous* for praise. 3. very rapacious. —*SYN.* see **hungry.**

rav·in (rav′ən), *n.* [ME. & OFr. *ravine;* see RAVEN, *v.*], 1. a violent preying or plundering; rapine. 2. anything captured; prey or plunder. Also spelled **raven.** *v.t. & v.i.* to raven.

ra·vine (rə-vēn′), *n.* [Fr., violent rush, flood; see RAVEN, *v.*], a long, deep hollow in the earth's surface, worn by the action of a stream; large gully; gorge.

rav·ing (rāv′iŋ), *adj.* 1. raging; delirious; frenzied. 2. [Colloq.], exciting raving admiration or praise; notable: as, a *raving* beauty. *adv.* so as to cause raving: as, he's *raving* mad. *n.* delirious, incoherent speech.

ra·vi·o·li (rav′i-ō′li; It. rä-vyô′lē), *n.pl.* [usually construed as sing.], [It., pl. of *ravi(u)olo* < dial. *rava;* ult. < L. *rapum*, turnip, beet], small casings of dough, often square, containing highly seasoned chopped meat and, sometimes, spinach, cooked and served usually in a savory sauce.

rav·ish (rav′ish), *v.t.* [ME. *ravissen* < inflectional stem of OFr. *ravir*, to carry away < L. *rapere*, to seize; cf. RAPE, *v. & n.*], 1. to seize and carry away forcibly. 2. to rape. 3. to carry away with emotion; fill with great joy or delight; enrapture.

rav·ish·ing (rav′ish-iŋ), *adj.* [ppr. of *ravish*], causing great joy or delight; charming; enchanting.

rav·ish·ment (rav′ish-mənt), *n.* [OFr. *ravissement*], a ravishing or being ravished; specifically, *a)* a seizing and carrying away forcibly. *b)* rape. *c)* a being carried away with delight or joy; ecstasy; rapture.

raw (rô), *adj.* [ME. *rawe;* AS. *hreaw;* akin to G. *roh;* IE. base **qreu-*, clotted blood, bloody flesh, etc., seen also in L. *crusta*, lit., congealed blood on a wound (cf. CRUST), *crudus* (cf. CRUDE), *crudelis* (cf. CRUEL)], 1. uncooked. 2. in its natural condition; not changed by art, dilution, manufacture, aging, etc.: as, *raw* silk, *raw* whisky. 3. inexperienced; not yet developed or trained: as, a *raw* recruit. 4. with the skin rubbed or torn off; sore and inflamed: as, a *raw* cut. 5. uncomfortably cold and damp; bleak: as, a *raw* wind. 6. [Colloq.], indecent; bawdy; somewhat obscene. 7. [Slang], harsh or unfair: as, he received *raw* treatment. *n.* a raw or inflamed spot on the body.
in the raw, 1. in the natural or original state; without cultivation, refinement, etc. 2. naked; nude.

Ra·wal·pin·di (rä′wəl-pin′di), *n.* the capital of Pakistan, in the northwestern part: pop., 237,000.

raw·boned (rô′bōnd′), *adj.* having little flesh or fat covering the bones; lean; gaunt.

raw·hide (rô′hīd′), *n.* 1. an untanned or only partially tanned cattle hide. 2. a whip made of this.

Raw·lin·son, George (rô′lin-s'n), 1812–1902; English historian and Orientalist; brother of *Sir Henry.*

Rawlinson, Sir **Henry Cres·wicke** (krez′ik), 1810–1895; English archaeologist, soldier, and diplomat.

raw material, material still in its natural or original state, before processing or manufacture.

raw silk, silk reeled from the cocoon but not yet spun.

Ray (rā), a masculine name: see **Raymond.**

ray (rā), *n.* [OFr. *rai;* L. *radius;* see RADIUS], 1. *a)* any of the thin lines, or beams, of light that appear to come from a bright source. *b)* a graphic representation of one of these, as in heraldry. 2. any of several lines radiating from a center; radius. 3. a disclosure of mental or spiritual enlightenment: as, a *ray* of intelligence. 4. a tiny amount; slight trace: as, a *ray* of hope. 5. in *botany*, *a)* a ray flower. *b)* any of the pedicels, or flower stalks, of an umbel. *c)* a medullary ray. 6. in *physics*, *a)* a stream of particles given off by a radioactive substance. *b)* a straight line along which any part of a wave of radiant energy is regarded as traveling from its source to any given point. 7. in *zoology*, *a)* any of the bony spines supporting the fin membrane of a fish. *b)* a radiating limb, as the arm of a starfish. *v.i.* 1. to shine forth in rays. 2. to radiate. *v.t.* 1. to send out in rays; emit. 2. to subject to the action of X rays, radium rays, etc., as in the treatment of disease. 3. to irradiate. 4. to supply with radiating lines.

ray (rā), *n.* [ME. & OFr. *raie;* L. *raia*], any of several fishes, as the electric ray, skate, etc., with a horizontally flat body, both eyes on the upper surface, widely expanded fins at each side, and a slender, whiplike tail.

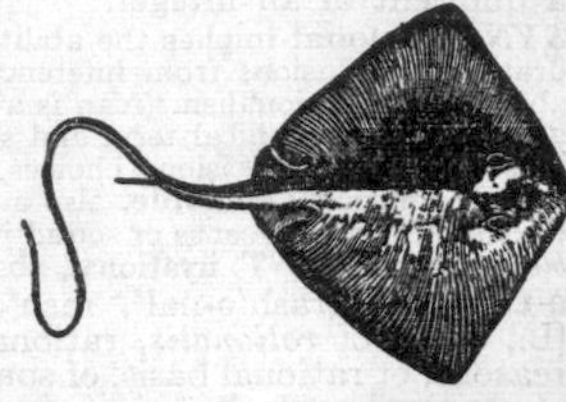

STING RAY (3 ft. wide)

ra·yah (rä′yə), *n.* a raia.

ray flower, any of the flowers around the margin of the head of certain composite flowers, as the daisy: also **ray floret.**

Ray·leigh (rā′li), third Baron, (*John William Strutt*) 1842–1919; English physicist; received Nobel prize in physics, 1904.

ray·less (rā′lis), *adj.* without rays; specifically, without rays of light; dark; gloomy.

Ray·mond, Ray·mund (rā′mənd), [ONorm.Fr. *Raimund, Reimund;* Frank. *Raginmund*, lit., wise protection < Gmc. **ragina-*, counsel (seen in Goth. *ragin*, judgment) + **mund-*, hand, protection (seen in OHG. *munt*)], a masculine name: diminutive, *Ray.*

ray·on (rā′on), *n.* [arbitrary coinage suggested by *ray* (cf. Fr. *rayon*, a ray) as descriptive of its sheen], 1. any of various textile fibers synthetically produced by pressing cellulose acetate or some other cellulose solution through very small holes and solidifying it in the form of filaments. 2. any of various woven or knit fabrics made of such fibers.

raze (rāz), *v.t.* [RAZED (rāzd), RAZING], [Fr. *raser;* LL. **rasare*, to shave, scrape, freq. < L. *rasus*, pp. of *radere*, to scrape], 1. originally, to scrape or graze; wound slightly. 2. to scrape or shave off; erase. 3. to tear down completely; level to the ground; demolish: the current sense. Also spelled **rase.** —*SYN.* see **destroy.**

ra·zee (rā-zē′), *n.* [Fr. *rasé* (as in *vaisseau rasé*, leveled vessel), pp. of *raser*, to level; see RAZE], [Obs.], a ship made smaller and thus reduced in rating by the removal of the upper deck or decks. *v.t.* [RAZEED (-zēd′), RAZEEING], to remove the upper deck or decks of (a ship).

ra·zor (rā′zẽr), *n.* [ME. & OFr. *rasour* < *raser;* see RAZE], a sharp-edged cutting instrument for shaving: see also **safety razor, shaver.**

ra·zor·back (rā′zẽr-bak′), *n.* 1. a wild or semiwild hog of the southern United States, with a slender body, a ridged back, and long legs. 2. a finback; rorqual whale.

razz (raz), *v.t. & v.i.* [contr. < *raspberry*], [Slang], to tease, ridicule, deride, heckle, etc. *n.* [Slang], raspberry (derisive sound).

raz·zle-daz·zle (raz′'l-daz′'l), *n.* [Slang], a state or event of confusion, bewilderment, bustling, etc.

Rb, in *chemistry*, rubidium.

r.b.i., rbi, RBI, in *baseball*, run(s) batted in.

R.C., 1. Red Cross. 2. Roman Catholic.

R.C.A.F., RCAF, Royal Canadian Air Force.

R.C.Ch., Roman Catholic Church.

rcd., received.

R.C.M.P., Royal Canadian Mounted Police.

r-col·or (är′kul′ẽr), *n.* in *phonetics*, the acoustic quality produced by retroflex articulation: also **r-quality.**

R.C.P., Royal College of Physicians.

rcpt., receipt.

R.C.S., Royal College of Surgeons.

Rd, in *chemistry*, radium: now generally **Ra** (no period).

R/D, R.D., in *banking*, refer to drawer.

Rd., rd., 1. rix-dollar. 2. road. 3. rod. 4. round.

R.D., Rural Delivery.

Re (rā), *n.* Ra.

re (rā), ***n.*** [It. < L. *re*sonare; see GAMUT], in *music,* a syllable representing the second tone of the diatonic scale: see **solfeggio.**

re (rē), ***prep.*** [L., abl. of *res,* thing], in the case or matter of; as regards: used in law, etc., for *in re.*

re- (rē; *unstressed* ri), [< Fr. or L.; Fr. *re-, ré-;* L. *re-, red-,* back, backward], a prefix meaning: 1. *back,* as in *repay, restore.* 2. *again, anew, over again,* as in *reappear, retell.* When hyphenated, it is used: 1) to distinguish between a word in which the prefix means simply *again* or *anew* and a word of similar form having a special meaning or meanings (e.g., *re-sound, resound*); 2) to avoid ambiguity in forming nonce words, as in *re-urge;* and 3) before elements beginning with *e,* as in *re-edit, re-elect* (such words are also written *reedit, reëlect,* etc.). The list at the bottom of the following pages contains some of the more common words in which *re-* means simply *again* or *anew.* Words with special meanings are entered in their proper alphabetical places in the vocabulary.

Re, in *chemistry,* rhenium.

R.E., 1. Reformed Episcopal. 2. Right Excellent.

re., 1. in *football,* right end. 2. rupee: also **Re.**

REA, R.E.A., Rural Electrification Administration.

reach (rēch), ***v.t.*** [ME. *rechen;* AS. *ræcan;* akin to G. *reichen;* IE. base **rēig-,* to stretch out, extend the hand, etc., prob. seen also in L. *rigere,* to stiffen (cf. RIGOR, RIGID)], 1. to thrust out; extend (the hand, etc.). 2. to touch; extend to by thrusting out, throwing something, etc. 3. to obtain and hand over to someone else: as, *reach* me the salt. 4. to go as far as; attain: as, we shall *reach* town by night. 5. to carry as far as; penetrate to: as, the news *reached* me late. 6. to have influence on; affect. 7. to get in touch with, as by telephone. ***v.i.*** 1. to thrust out the hand, foot, etc. 2. to stretch, or be extended, in amount, influence, space, time, etc.: as, his power *reaches* into other lands. 3. to carry; penetrate, as sight, sound, etc. 4. to try to obtain something; make an attempt. 5. in *nautical usage,* to sail on a reach. ***n.*** 1. the act of stretching or thrusting out. 2. the power of stretching, obtaining, etc. 3. the distance or extent covered in stretching, obtaining, influencing, etc. 4. a continuous, uninterrupted extent or stretch, especially of water. 5. a pole joining the forward part of a wagon to the rear axle. 6. in *nautical usage,* a tack sailed with the wind coming more or less from abeam: it may be a *close reach,* with the wind forward of the beam; a *beam reach,* with the wind abeam; or a *broad reach,* with the wind abaft the beam.

SYN.—**reach,** the broadest of these terms, implies an arriving at some goal, destination, point in development, etc. (he's *reached* the age of 60); **gain** suggests the exertion of considerable effort to reach some goal (they've *gained* the top of the hill); **achieve** suggests the use of skill in reaching something (we've *achieved* a great victory); **attain** suggests a being goaded on by great ambition to gain an end regarded as beyond the reach of most men (he has *attained* great fame in his profession); **accomplish** implies success in completing an assigned task (to *accomplish* an end). See also **range.**

re·act (ri-akt′), ***v.i.*** [*re-* + *act*], 1. to act in return or reciprocally. 2. to act in opposition. 3. to act in a reverse way; go back to a former condition, stage, etc. 4. to respond to a stimulus; be affected by some influence, event, etc. 5. in *chemistry,* to act with another substance in producing a chemical change.

re-act (rē′akt′), ***v.t.*** to act or do again.

re·act·ance (ri-ak′təns), ***n.*** [*react* + *-ance*], in *electricity,* the opposition to the flow of alternating current made by an induction coil or a condenser.

re·act·ant (ri-ak′tənt), ***n.*** any of the substances involved in a chemical reaction.

re·ac·tion (ri-ak′shən), ***n.*** 1. a return or opposing action, influence, etc. 2. a response, as to a stimulus or influence. 3. a movement back to a former or less advanced condition, stage, etc.; countertendency; especially, such a movement or tendency in economics or politics; extreme conservatism. 4. a chemical change. 5. in *medicine, a*) an action induced by resistance to another action. *b*) a depression or exhaustion of energy following nervous tension, overstimulation, etc. *c*) an increased activity following depression. 6. in *physiology & psychology,* an organic response to a stimulus.

re·ac·tion·ar·y (ri-ak′shən-er′i), ***adj.*** of, characterized by, or advocating reaction, especially in politics. ***n.*** [*pl.* REACTIONARIES (-iz)], a reactionary person; advocate of reaction, especially in politics.

re·ac·tion·ist (ri-ak′shən-ist), ***n. & adj.*** reactionary.

reaction time, in *psychology,* the lapse of time between the application of a stimulus and the beginning of the response: also called *response time.*

re·ac·tive (ri-ak′tiv), ***adj.*** 1. tending to react. 2. of, caused by, or showing reaction.

re·ac·tor (ri-ak′tẽr), ***n.*** 1. a person or thing that reacts or undergoes a reaction. 2. in *electricity,* a device inserted in a circuit to add reactance. 3. in *medicine,* a person or animal having a positive reaction to a particular foreign substance. 4. in *nuclear physics,* an atomic pile in which there is control of the atomic energy produced.

read (rēd), ***v.t.*** [READ (red), READING (rēd′iŋ)], [ME. *reden,* to explain, hence to read; AS. *rædan,* to counsel, interpret; akin to G. *raten,* to counsel, advise (cf. REDE); IE. **rē-dh, *rə-dh* < base **(a)rē-,* to join, fit, seen also in L. *ratio,* a reckoning, thinking (cf. RATIO, RATIONAL, REASON, etc.)], 1. to get the meaning of (something written, printed, etc.) by interpreting its characters or signs. 2. to utter aloud (printed or written matter). 3. to learn the true meaning of; understand the nature or significance of as if by reading: as, you *read* a person's character in his face. 4. to interpret, as dreams, signs, etc. 5. to foretell (the future). 6. to interpret or understand (a printed passage, etc.) as having a particular meaning. 7. to have or give as a reading in a certain passage: as, this edition *reads* "show," not "shew." 8. to get knowledge of; learn from printed matter: as, he *read* the account yesterday. 9. to apply oneself to; study: as, he *read* a subject for examination. 10. to record and show; register: as, the speedometer *reads* fifty miles per hour. 11. to put into a (specified) state by reading. ***v.i.*** 1. to read something written, printed, etc., as words, music, books, etc. 2. to utter or repeat aloud the words of written or printed matter. 3. to learn by reading (with *about* or *of*). 4. to study. 5. to have or give a particular meaning when read: as, the paragraph *reads* to the effect that all men are equal. 6. to contain, or be drawn up in, certain words: as, the sentence *reads* as follows. 7. to admit of being read: followed by *well, poorly,* etc.

read into (or **in**), to attribute a particular meaning to; interpret in a certain way.

read out of, to dismiss or expel from (a political party, society, etc.) by public reading of dismissal.

read (red), past tense and past participle of **read.** ***adj.*** full of knowledge got from reading; informed; learned: usually in hyphenated compounds, as *well-read.*

read·a·bil·i·ty (rēd′ə-bil′ə-ti), ***n.*** the quality or state of being readable.

read·a·ble (rēd′ə-b'l), ***adj.*** 1. that can be read; legible. 2. agreeable and attractive in style; interesting to read.

read·a·bly (rēd′ə-bli), ***adv.*** so as to be readable.

re·ad·dress (rē′ə-dres′), ***v.t.*** 1. to address or occupy (oneself) anew. 2. to change the address on (a letter, etc.).

Reade, Charles (rēd), 1814–1884; English novelist.

read·er (rēd′ẽr), ***n.*** 1. a person who reads. 2. a reciter of literary works in public; one who reads aloud and interprets by gesture and tone of voice. 3. a person who reads lessons, prayers, etc. aloud in church. 4. a person who reads manuscripts for a publisher and advises as to their merit. 5. a person who corrects proofs for a printer. 6. a person who records the readings of meters, etc., as for a public utilities company. 7. a book with selected passages for practice and instruction in reading. 8. [Chiefly British], a lecturer or instructor in a university. 9. an assistant who corrects examinations, themes, etc. for a professor.

read·i·ly (red′'l-i), ***adv.*** [ME. *redili;* see READY & -LY], 1. without hesitation; willingly. 2. without delay; quickly. 3. without difficulty.

read·i·ness (red′i-nis), ***n.*** a ready quality or state.

Read·ing (red′iŋ), ***n.*** 1. a city in southeastern Pennsylvania: pop., 98,000. 2. a city in Berkshire, south central England: pop., 118,000.

Read·ing (red′iŋ), first Marquis of, (*Rufus Daniel Isaacs*), 1860–1935; English jurist; lord chief justice of England (1913–1921); viceroy and governor general of India (1921–1926).

read·ing (rēd′iŋ), ***adj.*** 1. inclined to read or study. 2. made or used for reading. ***n.*** 1. the act or practice of a person who reads; perusal, as of books. 2. the act of repeating aloud the words of printed or written matter, especially for public entertainment. 3. the study of books; academic learning. 4. any material printed or written to be read. 5. a recording of information by figures, signs, etc., as on a barometer, thermometer, etc. 6. the form of a specified word, sentence, etc. in a particular edition of a literary work: as, there were several *readings* for the passage. 7. a particular interpretation, as of something written.

reading desk, 1. a desk with a sloping top on which

reabsorb
reabsorption
reaccommodate
reaccompany
reaccusation
reaccuse
reacquire
reacquisition

a book is supported while being read. 2. a lectern.
reading room, a room (in a club, library, etc.) for reading and writing.
re·ad·just (rē'ə-just'), *v.t.* to adjust again; rearrange.
re·ad·just·ment (rē'ə-just'mənt), *n.* 1. a readjusting or being readjusted. 2. in *finance*, rearrangement of the structure of a corporation: often distinguished from *reorganization*.
re·ad·mis·sion (rē'əd-mish'ən), *n.* a readmitting or being readmitted.
re·ad·mit (rē'əd-mit'), *v.t.* to admit again.
read·y (red'i), *adj.* [READIER (-i-ẽr), READIEST (-i-ist)], [ME. *redie;* AS. *geræde*, prepared (for riding) < base of *rad*, p.t. of *ridan*, to ride; cf. RIDE, ROAD; the ME. form is unique but akin to G. *bereit*, ready, ON. *greithr*, prepared, etc. < the same base as, and of equivalent formation with, the AS. word], 1. prepared or equipped to act immediately; waiting to be used: as, she is *ready* to sing, the house is *ready* for occupancy. 2. prepared in mind; unhesitant; willing. 3. *a)* likely or liable immediately (usually with an infinitive). *b)* apt; inclined (usually with an infinitive): as, he is always *ready* to blame us. 4. clever and skillful mentally or physically; dexterous. 5. done or made without delay; prompt: as, a *ready* reply. 6. convenient or handy to use; available immediately: as, *ready* cash. 7. [Obs.], at hand; present: used in response to a roll call. *v.t.* [READIED (-id), READYING], to prepare; get or make ready (often used reflexively). *n.* 1. [Colloq.], ready money; cash at hand (usually with *the*). 2. in *military science*, the position of a rifle just before aiming and firing. —*SYN.* see **quick.**
make ready, 1. to prepare; get in order. 2. to dress.
read·y-made (red'i-mād'), *adj.* 1. made so as to be ready for immediate use or for sale to any buyer, rather than to individual order: as, *ready-made* suits: opposed to *custom-made*. 2. commonplace; stock; not original: as, *ready-made* opinions.
read·y-to-wear (red'i-tə-wâr'), *adj.* ready-made: said of clothes.
read·y-wit·ted (red'i-wit'id), *adj.* mentally quick; quick in thought or understanding.
re·af·firm (rē'ə-fũrm'), *v.t.* to affirm again.
re·af·fir·ma·tion (rē'af-ẽr-mā'shən), *n.* a reaffirming or being reaffirmed.
re·a·gent (rē-ā'jənt), *n.* [*re-* + *agent;* cf. REACT], in *chemistry*, a substance used to detect or measure another substance or to convert one substance into another by means of the reaction which it causes.
re·al (rē'əl, rēl), *adj.* [OFr.; ML. *realis* < L. *res*, thing], 1. existing or happening as or in fact; actual, true, objectively so, etc.; not merely seeming, pretended, imagined, fictitious, nominal, or ostensible. 2. authentic; genuine. 3. in *law*, of or relating to permanent, immovable things: as, *real* property: opposed to *personal*. 4. in *mathematics*, not imaginary: said of a number or quantity. 5. in *optics*, of or relating to an image made by the actual meeting of light rays at a point. 6. in *philosophy*, existing objectively; actual (not merely possible or ideal), or essential, absolute, ultimate (not relative, derivative, phenomenal, etc.). *n.* anything that actually exists, or reality in general (with *the*). *adv.* [Colloq. or Dial.], very. —*SYN.* see **true.**
re·al (rē'əl; Sp. re-äl'), *n.* [*pl.* REALS (-əlz); Sp. REALES (re-ä'les)], [Sp. & Port., lit., royal < L. *regalis;* see REGAL], 1. a former monetary unit and silver coin of Spain, equal to about 12 1/2 cents: it is still used in some Latin-American countries. 2. a former Spanish monetary unit, equal to about one quarter of a peseta.
re·al (re-äl'), *n.* singular of **reis.**
re·al-es·tate (rēl'ə-stāt', rē'əl-ə-stāt'), *adj.* having to do with real estate or dealing in real estate.
real estate, 1. land, including the buildings or improvements on it and its natural assets, as minerals, water, etc. 2. ownership of or property in land, etc.
re·al·gar (ri-al'gẽr), *n.* [ME.; ML. *realgar;* ult. < Ar. *rahj al-ghār* < *rahj*, powder + *al*, the + *ghār*, a cave, mine: so named because obtained by mining], an orange-red mineral, arsenic sulfide, with a resinous luster, used for making fireworks.
re·al·ism (rē'əl-iz'm), *n.* 1. a tendency to face facts and be practical rather than imaginary or visionary. 2. in *art & literature*, the attempted picturing of people and things as they really are; effort at faithful reproduction of nature: see also **naturalism.** 3. in *philosophy*, *a)* the doctrine that universals have objective reality: opposed to *nominalism*. *b)* the doctrine that material objects exist in themselves, apart from the mind's consciousness of them: opposed to *idealism*.
re·al·ist (rē'əl-ist), *n.* 1. a person concerned with real things and practical matters rather than those that are imaginary or visionary. 2. a believer in or advocate of realism. 3. an artist or writer whose work is characterized by realism.
re·al·is·tic (rē'ə-lis'tik), *adj.* 1. of, having to do with, or in the style of, realism or realists. 2. tending to face facts; practical rather than visionary.
re·al·is·ti·cal·ly (rē'ə-lis'ti-k'l-i, rē'ə-lis'tik-li), *adv.* in a realistic manner.
re·al·i·ty (ri-al'ə-ti), *n.* [*pl.* REALITIES (-tiz)], [Fr. *réalité;* ML. *realitas*], 1. the quality or state of being real. 2. a person or thing that is real; fact. 3. the quality of being true to life; fidelity to nature. 4. in *philosophy*, that which is real: see **real,** *adj.*, sense 6.
in reality, in fact; actually.
re·al·iz·a·ble (rē'ə-līz'ə-b'l), *adj.* that can be realized.
re·al·i·za·tion (rē'əl-i-zā'shən, rē'əl-ī-zā'shən), *n.* 1. a realizing or being realized. 2. something realized.
re·al·ize (rē'ə-līz'), *v.t.* [REALIZED (-līzd'), REALIZING], [Fr. *réaliser*], 1. to make real; bring into being; achieve. 2. to make appear real. 3. to understand fully; apprehend: as, I *realize* the difficulties. 4. to convert (assets, rights, etc.) into money. 5. to gain; obtain: as, the company *realized* a profit. 6. to be sold for; bring as profit: said of property. *v.i.* to sell property, a right, etc. for ready money.
re·al·ly (rē'əl-i, rēl'i), *adv.* 1. in reality; in fact; actually. 2. indeed: as, *really*, you mustn't say that. 3. truly or genuinely: as, a *really* hot day.
realm (relm), *n.* [ME. *reame, realme;* OFr. *reaume, realme;* LL. **regalimen* < L. *regalis;* see REGAL], 1. a kingdom. 2. a region; sphere; territory: as, the *realm* of thought. 3. in *botany & zoology*, a division of animals or plants according to their geographical location.
‡Re·al·po·li·tik (rā-äl'pô-li-tēk'), *n.* [G.], practical politics: usually a euphemism for *power politics*.
re·al·tor (rē'əl-tẽr, rē'əl-tôr'), *n.* [< *realty* + *-or;* coined by C. N. Chadbourn of Minneapolis], a real-estate broker who is a member of the National Association of Real Estate Boards.
re·al·ty (rē'əl-ti), *n.* [*real, adj.* + *-ty*], 1. real estate. 2. [Obs.], fidelity; honesty.
real wages, wages measured by how much they can buy, rather than by monetary value: cf. **nominal wages.**
ream (rēm), *n.* [ME. *rem;* OFr. *raime, rayme;* Sp. *resma* < Ar. *rizmah*, a bale, packet < *razama*, to pack together], 1. a quantity of paper varying from 480 sheets (20 quires) to 516 sheets (*printer's ream*): abbreviated **rm.** 2. *pl.* [Colloq.], a great amount.
ream (rēm), *v.t.* [prob. < ME. (South Eastern) *remen;* AS. *ryman*, lit., to make roomy < base of *rum;* see ROOM], 1. *a)* to enlarge (a hole) in something. *b)* to enlarge the bore of (a gun). Often with *out*. 2. to countersink or taper (a hole): with *out*. 3. to get rid of (a defect) by reaming (with *out*). 4. to remove the juice from (a lemon, orange, etc.).
ream·er (rēm'ẽr), *n.* a person or thing that reams: specifically, *a)* a sharp-edged tool for enlarging or tapering holes. *b)* a device for squeezing the juice from lemons, oranges, etc. *c)* an implement for reaming pipe bowls.

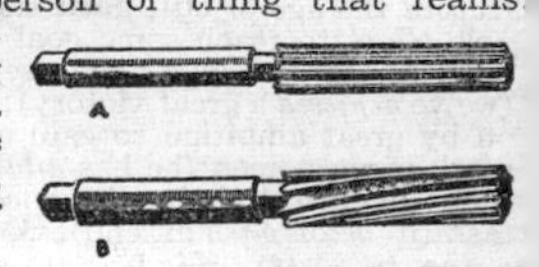

REAMERS
A, with straight fluting; B, with spiral fluting

re·an·i·mate (rē-an'ə-māt'), *v.t.* 1. to animate again; restore to life; revive. 2. to restore spirit to; give fresh courage, strength, etc. to.
re·an·i·ma·tion (rē-an'ə-mā'shən), *n.* a reanimating or being reanimated.
reap (rēp), *v.t.* [ME. *repen, ripen;* AS. *ripan, reopan*, akin to Eng. *ripe;* IE. base **reib-* < **rei-*, to tear, pull out, rend, seen also in AS. *rifter*, sickle, Eng. *ripple*, to break flax], 1. to cut (grain) with a scythe, sickle, or reaping machine. 2. to collect or gather (a crop, harvest, etc.) by cutting. 3. to cut or harvest grain from (a field). 4. to gain or obtain as the reward of action, conduct, work, etc. *v.i.* 1. to reap grain; a harvest, etc. 2. to get a return or reward.
reap·er (rēp'ẽr), *n.* [ME. *reper;* AS. *ripere*], 1. a person who reaps. 2. a reaping machine.
the (Grim) Reaper, death.
reaping machine, a machine for reaping grain, often with an apparatus that automatically expels bundles of the cut grain.
rear (rêr), *n.* [short for *arrear*], 1. the back part of something: as, the *rear* of a house. 2. the place or position behind or at the back: as, he was at the *rear* of the house. 3. the part of an army, navy, etc. farthest away from the battle front: opposed to *van*. *adj.* of, at, or in the rear: as, a *rear* view, a *rear* entrance.
bring up the rear, to come at the end (of a procession); be last in order.
rear (rêr), *v.t.* [ME. *reren;* AS. *ræran*, caus. of *risan* to rise; see RISE], 1. to put upright; elevate. 2. to build; erect. 3. to grow; breed, as animals or plants. 4. to bring to maturity by educating, nourishing, etc.: as, to *rear* children. *v.i.* 1. to rise or stand on

readopt	**reannex**	**reappearance**	**reappoint**
readorn	**reanoint**	**reapplication**	**reappointment**
re-ally	**reappear**	**reapply**	**reapportion**

the hind legs, as a horse. 2. to rise up in anger, etc. (usually with *up*). 3. to rise high, as a mountain peak. —*SYN.* see **lift.**

rear admiral, a naval officer next in rank above a captain and below a vice-admiral: abbreviated **Rear Adm., R.A.** (as a title).

rear guard, in *military science,* a detachment of troops to protect an army's rear.

re·arm (rē-ärm′), *v.t. & v.i.* 1. to arm again. 2. to arm with new or more effective weapons.

re·ar·ma·ment (rē-ärm′ə-mənt), *n.* a rearming or being rearmed.

rear·most (rêr′mōst′), *adj.* farthest in the rear; last.

re·ar·range (rē′ə-rānj′), *v.t.* 1. to arrange again. 2. to arrange in a different manner.

re·ar·range·ment (rē′ə-rānj′mənt), *n.* 1. a rearranging or being rearranged. 2. a new arrangement. 3. in *chemistry,* a redistribution of atoms or atomic groups within a molecule, forming the molecule of a different substance.

rear sight, the sight on a firearm nearest the breech, often with a movable part that can be adjusted to the desired range of fire.

rear·ward (rêr′wôrd′), *n.* [ME. *rerewarde;* Anglo-Fr. *rerewarde;* see REAR, *n.* & WARD (a guard)], 1. [Rare], a position in the rear. 2. [Archaic], the rear (sense 3).

rear·ward (rêr′wẽrd), *adj.* [see -WARD], at, in, or toward the rear. *adv.* backward; toward the rear.

rear·wards (rêr′wẽrdz), *adv.* rearward.

rea·son (rē′z′n), *n.* [ME. *raison;* OFr. *reson, raisun* < L. *ratio,* a reckoning, reason, plan < *ratus,* pp. of *reri,* to think; IE. base **rē-, *rĕ-, *ar-,* to fit, join, seen also in Eng. *arm,* L. *ars,* art], 1. an explanation or justification of an act, idea, etc. 2. a cause; motive. 3. the ability to think, form judgments, draw conclusions, etc. 4. sound thought or judgment; good sense. 5. normal mental powers; a sound mind; sanity. 6. in *logic,* one of the premises of an argument, especially the minor. *v.i.* 1. to think coherently and logically; draw inferences or conclusions from facts known or assumed. 2. to argue or talk in a logical way. *v.t.* 1. to analyze; think logically about; think out systematically. 2. to argue; discuss. 3. to support, justify, etc. with reasons. 4. to persuade or bring by reasoning (with *into* or *out of*). —*SYN.* see **cause, think.**

bring to reason, to make reasonable.

by reason of, because of.

in reason, 1. justifiably. 2. reasonable.

out of all reason, unreasonable.

reason that, to conclude or infer that.

stand to reason, to be logical or reasonable.

with reason, justifiably; rightly.

rea·son·a·bil·i·ty (rē′z′n-ə-bil′ə-ti), *n.* the quality or condition of being reasonable; reasonableness.

rea·son·a·ble (rē′z′n-ə-b′l), *adj.* [ME. *raisonable;* OFr. *raisonable;* L. *rationabilis*], 1. able to reason. 2. amenable to reason; just. 3. not extreme; sensible; sane. 4. not expensive. —*SYN.* see **rational.**

rea·son·a·bly (rē′z′n-ə-bli), *adv.* 1. in a reasonable manner. 2. to a reasonable degree.

rea·son·ing (rē′z′n-iŋ), *n.* 1. the drawing of inferences or conclusions from known or assumed facts; use of reason. 2. the proofs or reasons resulting from this.

rea·son·less (rē′z′n-lis), *adj.* 1. not able to reason. 2. not reasonable; illogical or senseless.

re·as·sur·ance (rē′ə-shoor′əns), *n.* a reassuring or being reassured.

re·as·sure (rē′ə-shoor′), *v.t.* 1. to assure again or anew. 2. to restore to confidence. 3. to reinsure.

Re·au·mur, Ré·au·mur (rā′ə-myoor′), *n.* [after R. A. *Réaumur,* the inventor], a thermometer which registers the boiling point of water at 80° and the freezing point at 0°. *adj.* of this thermometer. Abbreviated **R., Reaum.**

Ré·au·mur, Re·né An·toine Fer·chault de (rə-nā′ än′twän′ fâr′shō′ də rā′ō′mür′; Eng. rā′ə-myoor′), 1683–1757; French physicist, biologist, and inventor.

reave (rēv), *v.t.* [REAVED (rēvd) or REFT (reft), REAVING], [ME. *refen, reven;* AS. *reafian;* akin to G. *rauben,* to rob; for the base see ROB], [Archaic], to take away by violence; seize; bereave.

Re·ba (rē′bə), a feminine name: see **Rebecca.**

re·bap·tism (rē′bap′tiz′m), *n.* a rebaptizing or being rebaptized.

re·bap·tize (rē′bap-tīz′), *v.t.* [LL. *rebaptizare*], 1. to baptize again. 2. to give a new name to.

re·bate (rē′bāt, ri-bāt′), *v.t.* [REBATED (-id), REBATING], [ME. *rebaten* < OFr. *rabattre* < *re-,* re- + *abattre;* see ABATE], 1. *a)* to give back (part of an amount paid). *b)* to make a deduction from (a bill). 2. [Rare], to reduce; lessen. 3. [Archaic], to make dull. *n.* [Fr. *rabat* < the *v.*], a deduction; return of part of an amount paid, as for goods.

re·bate (rab′it, rē′bāt), *n. & v.t.* [REBATED (-id), REBATING], rabbet.

re·ba·to (rə-bä′tō), *n.* a rabato.

re·bec (rē′bek), *n.* [Fr.; altered (? after *bec,* beak) < OFr. *rebebe, rubebe* (ME. *ribibe*) < Ar. *rabāb*], a stringed musical instrument played with a bow, a kind of violin used during the Middle Ages: also spelled **rebeck.**

Re·bec·ca (ri-bek′ə), [LL.; Gr. *Rhebekka;* Heb. *ribbqāh,* lit., noose], a feminine name: diminutives, *Becky, Reba. n.* in the *Bible,* the wife of Isaac and mother of Jacob and Esau: also spelled **Rebekah.**

reb·el (reb′′l; *for v.,* ri-bel′), *n.* [ME.; OFr. *rebelle;* L. *rebellis,* rebel, rebellious < *rebellare;* see the *v.*], a person who openly resists authority or opposes any control. *adj.* 1. rebellious. 2. of rebels. *v.i.* [REBELLED (-beld′), REBELLING], [ME. *rebellen;* OFr. *rebeller;* L. *rebellare; re-,* again + *bellare,* to wage war < *bellum,* war], 1. to resist authority, government, etc. openly and by force. 2. to oppose any authority or control. 3. to feel or show strong aversion: as, his mind *rebels* at the prospect of such drudgery.

reb·el·dom (reb′′l-dəm), *n.* [see -DOM], 1. any area held by rebels. 2. rebels collectively. 3. the actions and behavior of rebels.

re·bel·lion (ri-bel′yən), *n.* [ME. *rebellioun;* OFr.; L. *rebellio;* see REBEL], 1. an act or state of armed, open resistance to authority, government, etc. 2. a defiance of or opposition to any control. 3. a rebelling.

SYN.—**rebellion** implies organized, armed, open resistance to the authority or government in power, and, when applied historically, connotes failure (Shays' *Rebellion*); **revolution** applies to a rebellion that succeeds in overthrowing an old government and establishing a new one (the American *Revolution*) or to any movement that brings about a drastic change in society (the Industrial *Revolution*); **insurrection** suggests a less extensive or less organized outbreak than rebellion (the Philippine *Insurrection*); **revolt** stresses a casting off of allegiance or a refusal to submit to established authority (the *revolt* of the angels led by Lucifer); **mutiny** applies to a forcible revolt of soldiers, or especially sailors, against their officers (*mutiny* on the Bounty); **uprising** is a simple, direct term for any outbreak against a government and applies to small, limited actions or to initial indications of a general rebellion (local *uprisings* against the Stamp Act).

re·bel·lious (ri-bel′yəs), *adj.* 1. resisting authority; engaged in rebellion. 2. of or like rebels or rebellion. 3. opposing any control; defiant. 4. in *medicine,* difficult to treat; resisting cure: as, a *rebellious* growth.

re·birth (rē-bũrth′, rē′bũrth′), *n.* 1. a new or second birth. 2. a reawakening; renaissance; revival.

reb·o·ant (reb′ō-ənt), *adj.* [L. *reboans,* ppr. of *reboare,* to resound, re-echo; *re-,* back + *boare,* to bellow, roar, cry aloud], [Poetic], loudly re-echoing.

re·born (rē-bôrn′), *adj.* born again; having new life, spirit, etc.

re·bound (ri-bound′; *for n., usually* rē′bound′), *v.i.* [ME. *rebounden, rebonden;* OFr. *rebondir*], 1. to bound back; spring back upon impact with something. 2. [Rare or Obs.], to re-echo; reverberate. 3. [Rare or Obs.], to leap; shoot up: as, his spirits *rebounded. v.t.* [Rare], 1. to make bound or spring back. 2. to return (a sound). *n.* a rebounding; recoil: sometimes figurative, as, he married Jane on the *rebound* when Betty jilted him.

re·broad·cast (rē-brôd′kast′, rē-brôd′käst′), *v.t. & v.i.* [see BROADCAST], 1. to broadcast again. 2. to broadcast (a program, etc. received in a relay system from another station). *n.* 1. a rebroadcasting. 2. a program, etc. that is being or has been rebroadcast.

re·buff (ri-buf′), *n.* [MFr. *rebuffe;* It. *ribbufo, rabuffo* < *rabuffare,* to disarrange < *baruffare,* to scuffle < OHG. *biroufan,* to tussle, pluck out], 1. an abrupt, blunt refusal of offered advice, help, etc. 2. any check or repulse. *v.t.* 1. to refuse bluntly; snub. 2. to check; repulse. 3. [Rare], to blow or drive back.

re·buke (ri-būk′), *v.t.* [REBUKED (-būkt′), REBUKING], [Anglo-Fr. *rebuker;* OFr. *rebuchier; re-,* back + *buchier, buschier,* to beat < *busche,* a log; see AMBUSH], 1. to address in sharp and severe disapproval; reprimand. 2. [Obs.], to force back; check. *n.* a sharp reprimand.

re·bus (rē′bəs), *n.* [L., abl. pl. of *res,* a thing; lit., by things: so named because the meaning is indicated by things rather than by words], a kind of puzzle consisting of pictures of objects, signs, etc. which by

re-argue
reascend
reassemble
reassembly
reassert
reassertion
reassess
reassign
reassimilate
reassimilation
reassume
reassumption
reattach
reattachment
reattack
reattempt
reawaken
rebind
rebloom
reblossom
reboil
rebuild
rebuilt
rebury

the sound of their names suggest words or phrases: as, a picture of a bedspring followed by a picture of a meadow is a *rebus* for Springfield.

re·but (ri-but′), ***v.t.*** [REBUTTED (-id), REBUTTING], [ME. *rebuten;* Anglo-Fr. *reboter;* OFr. *rebuter, rebouter* < *re-*, back + *bouter*, to push, thrust; see BUTT (to thrust)], 1. to contradict, refute, or oppose, especially in a formal manner by argument, proof, etc. 2. [Obs.], to force back; repel. —***SYN.*** see **disprove.**

re·but·tal (ri-but′'l), ***n.*** a rebutting, especially in law.

re·but·ter (ri-but′ẽr), ***n.*** 1. a person or thing that rebuts. 2. [n. use of Anglo-Fr. *reboter;* see REBUT], in *law*, a defendant's reply to a plaintiff's surrejoinder.

rec., 1. receipt. 2. received. 3. recipe. 4. record. 5. recorded. 6. recorder. 7. recording.

re·cal·ci·trance (ri-kal′si-trəns), ***n.*** 1. the quality or state of being recalcitrant. 2. recalcitrant action or conduct.

re·cal·ci·tran·cy (ri-kal′si-trən-si), ***n.*** recalcitrance.

re·cal·ci·trant (ri-kal′si-trənt), ***adj.*** [L. *recalcitrans*, ppr. of *recalcitrare*, to kick back; *re-*, back + *calcitrare*, to kick < *calx*, a heel], refusing to obey authority, custom, regulation, etc.; stubbornly defiant. ***n.*** a recalcitrant person. —***SYN.*** see **unruly.**

re·cal·ci·trate (ri-kal′si-trāt′), ***v.i.*** [RECALCITRATED (-id), RECALCITRATING], [L. *recalcitrare;* see RECALCITRANT], to refuse to obey; be stubborn in opposition.

re·cal·ci·tra·tion (ri-kal′si-trā′shən), ***n.*** a recalcitrating.

re·ca·les·cence (rē′kə-les′'ns), ***n.*** [< L. *recalescens*, ppr. of *recalescere*, to grow warm again; *re-*, again + *calescere*, to grow warm < *calere*, to be warm], a sudden and temporary increase in glow and temperature of hot iron or steel when it reaches a particular stage in the cooling process.

re·ca·les·cent (rē′kə-les′'nt), ***adj.*** [L. *recalescens*], having or showing recalescence.

re·call (ri-kôl′; *for n., usually* rē′kôl′), ***v.t.*** 1. to call back; bid return. 2. to remember. 3. to take back; cancel; annul; revoke; withdraw. 4. to bring back in awareness or attention, as to the immediate situation. 5. [Poetic], to revive. ***n.*** 1. a recalling. 2. in *military science*, a signal, as on a bugle, drum, etc., calling soldiers back to camp or ranks. 3. in *nautical usage*, a signal flag ordering a ship to return to a squadron. 4. in *political science*, the process of removing, or right to remove, an official from office by popular vote. —***SYN.*** see **remember.**

Ré·ca·mier, Jeanne Fran·çoise Ju·lie A·dé·la·ïde (zhän frän′swȧz′ zhü′lē′ ȧ′dā′lȧ′ēd′ rā′kȧ′myā′), (*Madame Récamier;* born *Bernard*), 1777–1849; French social and literary leader.

re·cant (ri-kant′), ***v.t.*** [L. *recantare; re-*, back, again + *cantare*, freq. of *canere*, to sing], to withdraw or renounce (beliefs, statements, etc. formerly held), especially in a formal or public manner. ***v.i.*** to make a formal or public withdrawal or renunciation of beliefs, statements, etc. formerly held.

re·can·ta·tion (rē′kan-tā′shən), ***n.*** a recanting.

re·cap (rē-kap′; *also, and for n. always,* rē′kap′), ***v.t.*** [RECAPPED (-kapt′, -kapt′), RECAPPING], [*re-* + *cap*], to cement, mold, and vulcanize a strip of rubber on the outer surface of (a worn pneumatic tire). ***n.*** a recapped tire. Cf. **retread.**

re·cap·i·tal·ize (rē-kap′ə-t'l-īz′), ***v.t.*** to capitalize again; specifically, in *commerce*, to change the capital or capitalization of.

re·ca·pit·u·late (rē′kə-pich′oo-lāt′), ***v.i. & v.t.*** [RECAPITULATED (-id), RECAPITULATING], [LL. *recapitulare;* see RE- & CAPITULATE], to summarize; repeat briefly or in outline. —***SYN.*** see **repeat.**

re·ca·pit·u·la·tion (rē′kə-pich′oo-lā′shən), ***n.*** [ME. *recapitalacion* < OFr. or LL.; OFr. *recapitulation;* LL. *recapitulatio*], 1. a recapitulating. 2. a summary, or brief restatement. 3. in *biology*, the repeating in an individual's development, especially in the embryo, of the evolutionary stages of the species. 4. in *music*, reprise.

re·ca·pit·u·la·tive (rē′kə-pich′oo-lā′tiv), ***adj.*** 1. of recapitulation. 2. recapitulating.

re·ca·pit·u·la·to·ry (rē′kə-pich′oo-lə-tôr′i, rē′kə-pich′-oo-lə-tō′ri), ***adj.*** like or containing recapitulation.

re·cap·ture (rē-kap′chẽr), ***v.t.*** 1. to capture again; retake; get back by capture; reacquire. 2. to get by recapture (sense 2). 3. to remember. ***n.*** 1. a recapturing or being recaptured. 2. the taking by the government of a fixed portion of all earnings exceeding a certain percentage of property value. 3. that which is recaptured.

re·cast (rē-kast′, rē-käst′; *for n.,* rē′kast′, rē′käst′), ***v.t.*** [RECAST, RECASTING], 1. to cast, or mold, again or anew. 2. to improve the form of; reconstruct: as, he *recast* the sentence. 3. to calculate or count again. 4. to provide a new cast for (a play). ***n.*** 1. a recasting. 2. a new form produced by recasting.

recd., rec'd., received.

re·cede (ri-sēd′), ***v.i.*** [RECEDED (-id), RECEDING], [L. *recedere;* see RE- & CEDE], 1. to go or move back: as, the high water *receded.* 2. to withdraw (usually with *from*): as, he *receded* from his bargain. 3. to slope backward. 4. to become more distant, and hence indistinct: as, memories of childhood *recede.*

re·cede (rē′sēd′), ***v.t.*** to cede back.

re·ceipt (ri-sēt′), ***n.*** [< ME. *receite*, with Renaissance Latinate *-p-* (cf. DECEIT, CONCEIT); OFr. *recete;* L. *recepta*, fem. of *receptus*, pp. of *recipere;* see RECEIVE], 1. a recipe. 2. a receiving or being received. 3. a written acknowledgment that something has been received, as goods, money, etc. 4. *a)* that which is received. *b) pl.* the amount received. ***v.t.*** 1. to mark (a bill) paid. 2. to write a receipt for, as goods, etc. ***v.i.*** to write a receipt. Abbreviated **rcpt., rec., rect.**

re·ceipt·or (ri-sē′tẽr), ***n.*** a person who receipts; specifically, in *law*, a person who receipts as bailee for property seized by the sheriff.

re·ceiv·a·bil·i·ty (ri-sēv′ə-bil′ə-ti), ***n.*** the quality or state of being receivable.

re·ceiv·a·ble (ri-sēv′ə-b'l), ***adj.*** [ME. *resceyuable;* Anglo-Fr.; OFr. *recevable;* also < *receive* + *-able*], 1. that can be received. 2. due; requiring payment. 3. suitable for acceptance. ***n. pl.*** accounts or bills receivable.

re·ceive (ri-sēv′), ***v.t.*** [RECEIVED (-sēvd′), RECEIVING], [ME. *receiven;* Anglo-Fr. *receivre;* OFr. *receivre, recevoir;* L. *recipere* < *re-*, back + *capere*, to take], 1. to take into one's possession (something given, offered, sent, etc.); get; accept; acquire. 2. to encounter; experience: as, she *received* much acclaim. 3. to undergo; submit to; suffer; have inflicted on one: as, he *received* punishment. 4. to bear; take the effect or force of: as, all four wheels *receive* the weight equally. 5. to take from another by hearing or listening: as, his confession was *received* by the priest. 6. to apprehend mentally; get knowledge of or information about; learn: as, they *received* the news. 7. to accept mentally as authentic, valid, etc. 8. *a)* to let enter; admit; hence, *b)* to have room for; hold; contain: as, a cistern *receives* rain water. 9. to give admittance to or greet (visitors, guests, etc.). ***v.i.*** 1. to get, accept, take, or acquire something; be a recipient. 2. to receive guests or visitors; be a host. 3. in *radio & television*, to convert incoming electromagnetic waves into sound or light, thus reproducing the sounds or images being transmitted. 4. in *religious usage*, to receive the Eucharist. 5. in *tennis*, etc., to return, or prepare to return, a served ball; be the striker.

SYN.—**receive** means to get by having something given, told, absorbed, etc. and may or may not imply the consent of the recipient (to *receive* a gift, a blow, etc.); **accept** means to receive willingly or favorably, but it sometimes connotes acquiescence rather than explicit approval (he was *accepted* as a member, to *accept* the inevitable); **admit** stresses permission or concession on the part of the one that receives (I will not *admit* him in my home); **take,** in this connection, means to accept something offered, presented, etc. (we can't *take* money from you).—***ANT.*** give.

re·ceiv·er (ri-sēv′ẽr), ***n.*** 1. a person who receives; specifically, *a)* a person who officially receives money, etc. for others; collector; treasurer. *b)* a person who knowingly receives stolen goods for gain or concealment; fence. *c)* in *baseball*, a catcher. *d)* in *law*, a person appointed by a court to administer or hold in trust property in bankruptcy or in a lawsuit. 2. a thing that receives; specifically, *a)* a receptacle; especially in *chemistry*, a receptacle connected with a retort tube, etc., into which a distilled product passes. *b)* an apparatus or device for receiving electrical waves, signals, etc. and converting them into sound or light, as a radio or television receiving set, or that part of a telephone which is held to the ear: see **telephone,** illus.

re·ceiv·er·ship (ri-sēv′ẽr-ship′), ***n.*** [see -SHIP], in *law* 1. the duties or office of a receiver. 2. the state of being administered or held by a receiver.

receiving set, in *radio & television*, an apparatus for converting incoming electromagnetic waves into sound or light, thus reproducing the sounds or images being transmitted; receiver.

re·cen·cy (rē′s'n-si), ***n.*** [ML. *recentia*], the quality or state of being recent.

re·cen·sion (ri-sen′shən), ***n.*** [< Fr. or L.; Fr. *recension;* L. *recensio* < *recensere; re-*, again + *censere*, to value; see CENSURE], 1. a revision of a text, based on critical examination of sources. 2. a version so produced.

re·cent (rē′s'nt), ***adj.*** [Fr. *récent* < L. *recens* < *re-* again + base seen also in Gr. *kainos*, new], 1. done, made, etc. just before the present time; modern; new. 2. of a time just before the present. 3. [R-], in *geology*, designating or of the present epoch, extending from the close of the Pleistocene.

the Recent, the Recent Epoch: see **geology,** chart.

re·cent·ly (rē′s'nt-li), ***adv.*** at a recent time; lately.

re·cept (rē′sept), ***n.*** [*re-*, again + *-cept* as in *concept*], in *psychology*, a mental image formed by successive sense impressions of the same or closely allied objects.

re·cep·ta·cle (ri-sep′tə-k'l), ***n.*** [ME.; L. *receptaculum* < *receptare*, freq. of *recipere;* see RECEIVE], 1. anything used to contain or hold something else; container; vessel. 2. in *botany*, the enlarged part of the stalk on which the flower grows: also called *torus*.

re·cep·ti·bil·i·ty (ri-sep'tə-bil'ə-ti), *n.* the quality or state of being receptible.

re·cep·ti·ble (ri-sep'tə-b'l), *adj.* [LL. *receptibilis* < L. *receptus*, pp. of *recipere*], able to receive or be received.

re·cep·tion (ri-sep'shən), *n.* [ME. *recepcion;* OFr.; L. *receptio* < pp. of *recipere;* see RECEIVE], 1. a receiving or being received. 2. the manner of this: as, a very hearty *reception*. 3. a social function, often formal, for the receiving of guests. 4. the act of mentally accepting or approving. 5. in *radio & television*, the manner of receiving, with reference to the relative quality of reproduction: as, the storm caused poor *reception*.

re·cep·tion·ist (ri-sep'shən-ist), *n.* a person employed in an office to receive callers, make appointments, give information, etc.

reception room, a room in a house, office, etc. for receiving visitors as they arrive.

re·cep·tive (ri-sep'tiv), *adj.* [ML. *receptivus* < L. *receptus;* see RECEIPT], 1. receiving or tending to receive, take in, admit, or contain. 2. inclined to the favorable reception of a request, suggestion, etc. 3. able or ready to receive new ideas, etc. 4. of reception or receptors.

re·cep·tiv·i·ty (ri-sep'tiv'ə-ti, rē'sep-tiv'ə-ti), *n.* the quality or state of being receptive.

re·cep·tor (ri-sep'tēr), *n.* [OFr. *receptour;* L. *receptor* < *receptus;* see RECEIPT], 1. a receiver (in various senses). 2. in *physiology*, a sense organ; nerve ending specialized for the reception of stimuli.

re·cess (ri-ses'; *also, for n., esp. in sense 3,* rē'ses), *n.* [L. *recessus*, pp. of *recedere;* see RECEDE, *v.i.*], 1. a receding or hollow place, as in a surface, wall, etc.; niche. 2. *usually in pl.* a secluded, withdrawn, or inner place: as, subterranean *recesses*, the *recesses* of the subconscious. 3. *a*) a temporary withdrawal from or halting of work or business, as at school. *b*) the state or time of this: as, the court was in *recess*. 4. in *anatomy*, a small cavity, hollow, indentation, etc. in an organ or part. *v.t.* 1. to place or set in a recess. 2. to form a recess in. *v.i.* to take a recess.

re·ces·sion (ri-sesh'ən), *n.* [L. *recessio* < pp. of *recedere;* see RECEDE, *v.i.*], 1. a going back or backward; receding; withdrawal. 2. the procession of the clergy and choir from the chancel to the vestry at the end of the service. 3. a receding part, as of a wall. 4. in *economics*, a temporary falling off of business activity during a period when such activity has been generally increasing, as during that after a depression: cf. **depression.**

re·ces·sion (rē'sesh'ən), *n.* [*re-* + *cession*], a ceding, or giving, back, as to a former owner.

re·ces·sion·al (ri-sesh'ən-'l), *adj.* 1. of a recession. 2. [British], of a parliamentary recess. *n.* 1. a recessional hymn. 2. music for such a hymn.

recessional hymn, a hymn sung at the end of a church service during the recession (sense 2).

re·ces·sive (ri-ses'iv), *adj.* [< L. *recessus* (see RECESS); + *-ive*], 1. receding or tending to recede. 2. tending to move from the last toward the first syllable of a word: said of stress, or accent. 3. in *genetics*, designating or relating to that one of any pair of opposite Mendelian characters which, when factors for both are present in the germ plasm, remains latent: opposed to *dominant*. *n.* in *genetics*, 1. a recessive character or factor. 2. an organism having such characters.

re·charge (rē-chärj'; *for n.,* rē'chärj'), *v.t. & v.i.* to charge again (in various senses). *n.* a recharging.

‡ré·chauf·fé (rā'shô'fā'), *n.* [*pl.* RÉCHAUFFÉS (-fā')], [Fr., pp. of *réchauffer*, to warm over < *ré-*, again + *échauffer*, to heat < LL. **excalefare* < L. *ex-*, intens. + **calefare;* see CHAFE], 1. a dish of left-over food reheated. 2. any used or old material, especially literary material, worked up in a new form; rehash.

re·cher·ché (rə-shâr'shā, rə-shâr'shā'), *adj.* [Fr., pp. of *rechercher;* see RESEARCH], 1. sought out with care; rare; choice; uncommon. 2. having refinement or studied elegance; hence, 3. too refined; too studied.

re·cid·i·vism (ri-sid'ə-viz'm), *n.* [< L. *recidivus* < *recidere*, to fall back < *re-*, back + *cadere*, to fall; + *-ism*], habitual or chronic relapse, or tendency to relapse, into crime or antisocial behavior patterns.

re·cid·i·vist (ri-sid'ə-vist), *n.* [Fr. *récidiviste*], a person characterized by recidivism; habitual criminal.

re·cid·i·vous (ri-sid'ə-vəs), *adj.* characterized by or tending to recidivism.

Re·ci·fe (re-sē'fə), *n.* a seaport in central Brazil: pop., 323,000: also called *Pernambuco.*

rec·i·pe (res'ə-pi), *n.* [L., imperative of *recipere;* see RECEIVE], 1. a formula for a medical prescription: symbol, ℞: now usually called *prescription*. 2. a medicine made up according to such a formula; prescription. 3. a list of materials and directions for preparing a dish or drink; receipt. 4. anything proposed as a remedy, for doing something, or for producing a desired result. Abbreviated **R., r., rec.**

re·cip·i·ence (ri-sip'i-əns), *n.* 1. a receiving. 2. the condition of being recipient; receptiveness.

re·cip·i·en·cy (ri-sip'i-ən-si), *n.* recipience.

re·cip·i·ent (ri-sip'i-ənt), *n.* [< L. *recipiens*, ppr. of *recipere;* see RECEIVE], a person or thing that receives. *adj.* receiving, or ready, willing, or able to receive.

re·cip·ro·cal (ri-sip'rə-k'l), *adj.* [< L. *reciprocus*, returning, reciprocal (cf. *re*, back & *pro*, forward); + *-al*], 1. done, felt, given, etc. in return: as, *reciprocal* tolerance. 2. on both sides; each to the other; mutual: as, they felt a *reciprocal* affection. 3. corresponding but reversed or inverted. 4. corresponding; equivalent or interchangeable; complementary. 5. in *grammar*, *a*) expressing mutual action or relation: as, *each other* is a *reciprocal* pronoun. *b*) formerly, reflexive. 6. in *mathematics*, of the reciprocals of quantities, or their relations. *n.* 1. anything that has a reciprocal action on or relation to another; complement, counterpart, equivalent, etc. 2. in *mathematics*, the quantity (with reference to a given quantity) resulting from the division of 1 by the given quantity: as, the *reciprocal* of 7 is 1/7. —*SYN.* see **mutual.**

re·cip·ro·cal·i·ty (ri-sip'rə-kal'ə-ti), *n.* the condition or quality of being reciprocal.

re·cip·ro·cate (ri-sip'rə-kāt'), *v.t.* [RECIPROCATED (-id), RECIPROCATING], [< L. *reciprocatus*, pp. of *reciprocare* < *reciprocus;* see RECIPROCAL], 1. to cause to move alternately back and forth. 2. to give and get, do, feel, etc. reciprocally; interchange: as, they *reciprocate* enmity. 3. to give, do, feel, etc. in return; return in kind or degree: as, we *reciprocate* her affection. 4. [Rare], to make correspondent or equivalent. *v.i.* 1. to move alternately back and forth; interchange position. 2. to give and get reciprocally; interchange. 3. to make some sort of return for something done, given, etc. 4. to be correspondent or equivalent.

reciprocating engine, any engine in which the pistons move back and forth in a straight line in the cylinders: distinguished from *rotary engine.*

re·cip·ro·ca·tion (ri-sip'rə-kā'shən), *n.* [L. *reciprocatio*], the act or fact of reciprocating (in various senses).

re·cip·ro·ca·tive (ri-sip'rə-kā'tiv), *adj.* 1. reciprocating or tending to reciprocate. 2. characterized by reciprocation.

re·cip·ro·ca·tor (ri-sip'rə-kā'tēr), *n.* a person or thing that reciprocates.

re·ci·proc·i·ty (res'ə-pros'ə-ti), *n.* [Fr. *réciprocité*], 1. reciprocal state or relationship; mutual action, dependence, etc. 2. a reciprocating; interchange; mutual exchange; especially, exchange of special privileges between two countries, to the advantage of both, as mutual reduction of tariffs.

re·ci·sion (ri-sizh'ən), *n.* a rescinding, or annulling.

re·cit·al (ri-sī't'l), *n.* [< *recite* + *-al*], 1. a reciting; specifically, a telling of facts, events, etc. in detail. 2. what is so told; account, story, or description. 3. a detailed statement, as of facts or events. 4. a musical program given by a soloist, soloists, or small ensemble.

rec·i·ta·tion (res'ə-tā'shən), *n.* [L. *recitatio*], 1. a reciting, as of facts, events, etc.; recital. 2. an account, story, etc. 3. *a*) the speaking aloud in public of something memorized. *b*) a piece of prose or verse so memorized and spoken. 4. *a*) a reciting by pupils of answers to questions on a prepared lesson, etc. *b*) a class meeting or period in which this occurs.

rec·i·ta·tive (res'ə-tā'tiv, ri-sīt'ə-tiv), *adj.* [< *recite* + *-ative*], reciting; of, or having the nature of, recital, as of facts, events, etc.

rec·i·ta·tive (res'ə-tə-tēv'), *n.* [It. *recitativo* < L. *recitare;* see RECITE], in *music*, 1. a type of declamatory singing, free in rhythm and tempo, used in the prose parts and dialogue of operas and oratorios. 2. a work or passage in this style. 3. music for such passages. *adj.* having the nature, or in the style or manner, of recitative or declamation. Abbreviated **recit.**

re·cite (ri-sīt'), *v.t.* [RECITED (-id), RECITING], [Fr. *réciter;* L. *recitare;* see RE- & CITE], 1. to repeat or speak aloud from or as from memory, especially in a formal way, as lessons in class or a poem, speech, etc. before an audience. 2. to tell in detail; give an account of; narrate; relate. 3. to enumerate. *v.i.* 1. to repeat or speak aloud something memorized. 2. to recite a lesson or part of a lesson before a teacher; answer questions orally in class.

reck (rek), *v.i. & v.t.* [ME. *recken, retchen;* AS. *reccan;* akin to OHG. *-ruohhen;* base as in *reckon, right*], [Archaic], 1. to have care or concern (for) or take heed (of): as, he *recks* not of the peril. 2. to concern or be of concern; matter (to): as, it *recks* him not.

recharter **recheck** **rechoose** **recircle**

reck·less (rek′lis), ***adj.*** [ME. *reckeles*, AS. *recceleas;* see RECK & -LESS], 1. careless; heedless. 2. not regarding consequences; headlong and irresponsible.

reck·on (rek′ən), ***v.t.*** [ME. *rekkenen*, etc.; AS. *-recenian;* akin to G. *rechnen*, to count; IE. base **reĝ-*, to stretch up, extend, etc., seen also in L. *rigere*, to stiffen (cf. RIGOR, RIGID); cf. REACH, RIGHT; basic sense "to bring together"], 1. to count; figure up; compute. 2. to consider as; regard as being: as, I *reckon* him an enemy. 3. to judge; consider; estimate. 4. [Colloq. or Dial.], to think; suppose. ***v.i.*** 1. to count up; figure. 2. to depend; rely (with *on*). —***SYN.*** see **calculate, rely.**

reckon with, 1. to balance or settle accounts with. 2. to take into consideration.

reck·on·er (rek′ən-ẽr), ***n.*** a person or thing that reckons; especially, a book of mathematical tables, etc. (*ready reckoner*) for help in calculating.

reck·on·ing (rek′ən-iŋ), ***n.*** 1. the act of one who reckons; count or computation; hence, 2. a measuring of possibilities for the future; calculated guess. 3. *a*) the settlement of an account. *b*) the settlement of rewards or penalties for any action. 4. a bill, as at an inn. 5. in *nautical usage*, *a*) the determination of the position of a ship. *b*) the position so determined. See **dead reckoning.**

day of reckoning, 1. a time when accounts must be settled; hence, 2. the Last Judgment.

re·claim (ri-klām′), ***v.t.*** [ME. *reclaimen;* OFr. *reclamer;* L. *reclamare;* see RE- & CLAIM], 1. to rescue or bring back (a person or people) from error, vice, savagery, etc. to ways of living or thinking regarded as right; reform. 2. to make (wasteland, desert, etc.) capable of being cultivated or lived on, as by filling, ditching, or irrigating. 3. to obtain (useful materials, etc.) from waste products. 4. [Obs.], to tame, subdue, as a hawk. ***v.i.*** [Obs.], to exclaim, as in protest. ***n.*** reclamation: as, he's past *reclaim.* —***SYN.*** see **recover.**

re-claim (rē′klām′), ***v.t.*** to claim back; demand the return or restoration of; try to get back.

re·claim·ant (ri-klām′ənt), ***n.*** a person who reclaims.

rec·la·ma·tion (rek′lə-mā′shən), ***n.*** [Fr. *réclamation;* L. *reclamatio*], 1. a reclaiming or being reclaimed; recovery or restoration to a better or useful state, as of wasteland, desert, etc. by ditching, filling, or irrigating. 2. the process or industry of obtaining useful materials from waste products.

‡ré·clame (rā′klâm′), ***n.*** [Fr. < *réclamer;* see RECLAIM], 1. publicity. 2. a seeking for publicity.

re·cline (ri-klīn′), ***v.t.*** [RECLINED (-klīnd′), RECLINING], [ME. *reclynen;* L. *reclinare; re-*, back + *clinare*, to lean], to lay back; cause to lean or lie back or down. ***v.i.*** to lie back or down; lean back; rest or repose lying down (often with *on* or *upon*).

re·cluse (ri-klo͞os′; *for n., usually* rek′lo͞os), ***adj.*** [ME. & OFr. *reclus* < L. *reclusus* (for *n.*, via ML.), pp. of *recludere*, to shut off < *re-*, back + *claudere*, to shut, close], shut away from the world; secluded; solitary. ***n.*** 1. a person who lives apart from the world for religious contemplation; anchorite or anchoress. 2. a person who lives a secluded, solitary life.

re·clu·sion (ri-klo͞o′zhən), ***n.*** 1. the condition or fact of becoming or being a recluse. 2. the condition or fact of being in solitary confinement.

re·clu·sive (ri-klo͞o′siv), ***adj.*** 1. giving reclusion. 2. living in reclusion; recluse.

rec·og·ni·tion (rek′əg-nish′ən), ***n.*** [Fr. *récognition;* L. *recognitio* < *recognitus*, pp. of *recognoscere;* see RECOGNIZANCE], 1. a recognizing or being recognized; acknowledgment; admission, as of a fact; acknowledgment and approval, gratitude, etc.: as, in *recognition* of your services. 2. formal acceptance by a government of the independence and sovereignty of a state newly created, as by secession, or of a government newly set up, as by revolution, in another state. 3. identification of something as having been known before or as being of a certain kind; identification of a person as being known to one; hence, 4. notice, as in passing; greeting; salutation.

re·cog·ni·to·ry (ri-kog′nə-tôr′i, ri-kog′nə-tō′ri), ***adj.*** having to do with recognition, or acknowledgment.

rec·og·niz·a·ble (rek′əg-nīz′ə-b'l), ***adj.*** that can be recognized.

rec·og·niz·a·bly (rek′əg-nīz′ə-bli), ***adv.*** 1. in a recognizable manner. 2. to a recognizable degree or extent.

re·cog·ni·zance (ri-kog′ni-zəns, ri-kon′i-zəns), ***n.*** [ME. *reconissance;* OFr. *reconaissance, recognoissance* < *reconnoisant*, ppr. of *reconoistre* < L. *recognoscere*, to recall to mind; *re-*, again + *cognoscere*, to know; see COGNITION], 1. in *law*, *a*) a bond or obligation of record entered into before a court or magistrate, binding a person to do or not do something, be in court at a certain time, etc. *b*) a sum of money pledged and subject to forfeit if this obligation is not fulfilled. 2. recognition. 3. [Obs.], a symbol, token, or badge.

rec·og·nize (rek′əg-nīz′), ***v.t.*** [RECOGNIZED (-nīzd′), RECOGNIZING], [back-formation < *recognizance*], 1. to know again; identify as known before, or as the same as that known; hence, 2. to know by some detail, as of appearance: as, *recognize* dachshunds by their short legs; hence, 3. to perceive; identify: as, *recognize* the omens of defeat. 4. to acknowledge the existence, validity, or genuineness of: as, *recognize* a claim. 5. to accept as a fact; admit; accept: as, *recognize* defeat. 6. to acknowledge as worthy of appreciation or approval: as, *recognize* devotion. 7. to acknowledge the legal standing of, as a government or state, by some formal action or by entering into dealings with it. 8. to show acquaintance with (a person) by greeting. 9. to grant (a person) the right of speaking in a meeting, assembly, etc.

rec·og·niz·er (rek′əg-nī′zẽr), ***n.*** a person who recognizes.

re·cog·ni·zor (ri-kog′ni-zôr′, ri-kon′i-zôr′), ***n.*** in *law*, a person who enters into a recognizance.

re·coil (ri-koil′; *for n. 1, of weapons, & 3, usually* rē′koil′), ***v.i.*** [ME. *recoilen;* OFr. *reculer* < L. *re-*, back + *culus*, the buttocks], 1. to retreat; draw back, fall back, or stagger back. 2. to start or shrink back, as in fear, surprise, disgust, etc. 3. to fly back when released, as a spring, or kick back when fired, as a gun. 4. to return to or as to the starting point or source; react (with *on* or *upon*): as, our acts *recoil* upon ourselves. ***n.*** 1. a recoiling. 2. the state of having recoiled; reaction. 3. the distance through which a gun, spring, etc. recoils.

SYN.—**recoil** implies a startled reaction or movement in fear, surprise, disgust, etc. (she *recoiled* in horror); **shrink** implies a drawing back, literally or figuratively, from that which is distressing, terrifying, etc. (she *shrank* from telling him); **flinch** implies a show of weakness or faintheartedness in shrinking from anything difficult, dangerous, or painful (he will not *flinch* from duty); **wince** suggests an involuntary manifestation of pain or distress, as by facial distortion (she *winced* at the blow); **quail** suggests a cowering abjectly in the face of anything that menaces one (he *quailed* as the bully approached).

re-coil (rē′koil′), ***v.t. & v.i.*** to coil anew or again.

re-coin (rē-koin′), ***v.t.*** to coin anew or again.

re-coin·age (rē-koin′ij), ***n.*** [see -AGE], 1. a recoining. 2. something recoined.

rec·ol·lect (rek′ə-lekt′), ***v.t.*** [< L. *recollectus;* see next entry], 1. to call back to mind; recall; remember, especially with some effort. 2. to recall to (oneself) something temporarily forgotten: as, "Now I know!" he exclaimed, *recollecting* himself. Cf. **re-collect**, 2*b*. ***v.i.*** to have a recollection; remember.—***SYN.*** see **remember.**

re-col·lect (rē′kə-lekt′), ***v.t.*** [orig. < L. *recollectus*, pp. of *recolligere* (see RE- & COLLECT); later felt as < *re-* + *collect*], 1. to gather together again (what has been scattered). 2. *a*) to collect or rally (one's thoughts, strength, courage, etc.). *b*) to recover or compose (oneself): in this sense sometimes written **recollect.**

rec·ol·lec·tion (rek′ə-lek′shən), ***n.*** [Fr. *récollection;* ML. *recollectio*], 1. the act or power of recollecting, or calling back to mind; remembrance. 2. what is recollected: as, *recollections* of youth. —***SYN.*** see **memory.**

rec·ol·lec·tive (rek′ə-lek′tiv), ***adj.*** of or characterized by recollection.

re-com·mence (rē′kə-mens′), ***v.t. & v.i.*** [Fr. *recommencer*], to commence, or begin, again or anew.

re-com·mence·ment (rē′kə-mens′mənt), ***n.*** a recommencing or being recommenced.

rec·om·mend (rek′ə-mend′), ***v.t.*** [ME. *recomenden;* ML. *recommendare;* see RE- & COMMEND], 1. to give in charge or care; commit; entrust: as, I *recommend* him to your care. 2. to name or speak of favorably as suited for some use, function, position, etc.: as, *recommend* a book. 3. to make acceptable or pleasing: as, his diligence *recommends* him. 4. to advise; counsel: as, *recommend* that something be done.

rec·om·men·da·tion (rek′ə-men-dā′shən), ***n.*** [ME. *recomendacion;* ML. *recommendatio*], 1. a recommending; calling attention to a person or thing as suited for some purpose. 2. anything that recommends; specifically, a letter recommending a person or thing. 3. qualities, abilities, etc. that make a person or thing acceptable or pleasing. 4. advice; counsel.

rec·om·mend·a·to·ry (rek′ə-men′də-tôr′i, rek′ə-men′də-tō′ri), ***adj.*** 1. recommending or serving to recommend. 2. having the nature of recommendation.

re-com·mit (rē′kə-mit′), ***v.t.*** 1. to commit again. 2. to refer to a committee, as a question, bill, etc.

re-com·mit·ment (rē′kə-mit′mənt), ***n.*** a recommitting or being recommitted.

re-com·mit·tal (rē′kə-mit′'l), ***n.*** recommitment.

rec·om·pense (rek′əm-pens′), ***v.t.*** [RECOMPENSED (-penst′), RECOMPENSING], [ME. *recompensen;* OFr. *recompenser;* LL. *recompensare;* see RE- & COMPENSATE], 1. to repay (a person, etc.); reward; compensate. 2. to make repayment or requital for; compensate, as a loss. ***n.*** 1. something given or done in return for something else; repayment, remuneration, requital, or reward. 2. something given or done to make up for a loss, injury, etc.; compensation. —***SYN.*** see **pay.**

---

reclasp	**reclean**	**recolonize**	**recombination**
reclassify	**reclothe**	**recolor**	**recombine**

re·com·pose (rē'kəm-pōz'), *v.t.* 1. to compose again; rearrange, recombine, or reconstitute. 2. to restore to composure.

re·com·po·si·tion (rē'kom-pə-zish'ən), *n.* a recomposing or being recomposed.

rec·on·cil·a·bil·i·ty (rek'ən-sīl'ə-bil'ə-ti), *n.* the quality or condition of being reconcilable.

rec·on·cil·a·ble (rek'ən-sīl'ə-b'l, rek'ən-sīl'ə-b'l), *adj.* that can be reconciled.

rec·on·cil·a·bly (rek'ən-sīl'ə-bli, rek'ən-sīl'ə-bli), *adv.* in a reconcilable manner; so as to be reconcilable.

rec·on·cile (rek'ən-sīl'), *v.t.* [RECONCILED (-sīld'), RECONCILING], [ME. *reconsilen*, OFr. *reconciler;* L. *reconciliare;* see RE- & CONCILIATE], 1. to make friendly again or win over to a friendly attitude. 2. to settle (a quarrel, etc.) or compose (a difference, etc.). 3. to make (arguments, ideas, texts, etc.) consistent, compatible, etc.; bring into harmony. 4. to make content, submissive, or acquiescent (*to*): as, we became *reconciled* to our lot.

rec·on·cile·ment (rek'ən-sīl'mənt, rek'ən-sīl'mənt), *n.* reconciliation.

rec·on·cil·i·a·tion (rek'ən-sil'i-ā'shən), *n.* a reconciling or being reconciled (in various senses).

rec·on·cil·i·a·to·ry (rek'ən-sil'i-ə-tôr'i, rek'ən-sil'i-ə-tō'ri), *adj.* reconciling or tending to reconcile.

rec·on·dite (rek'ən-dīt', ri-kon'dīt), *adj.* [L. *reconditus*, pp. of *recondere*, to put back, hide; *re-*, back + *condere*, to put together, store up, hide; *con-*, together + *-dere* < IE. base **dhē-*, seen also in L. *facere*, to do (cf. FACT, DO)], 1. beyond the grasp of the ordinary mind or understanding; profound; abstruse. 2. dealing with abstruse or difficult subjects. 3. obscure; concealed.

re·con·di·tion (rē'kən-dish'ən), *v.t.* to put back in good condition by cleaning, patching, repairing, etc.

re·con·nais·sance, re·con·nois·sance (ri-kon'ə-səns), *n.* [Fr., earlier *reconnoissance;* see RECOGNIZANCE], 1. in *military science*, the act or process of obtaining information about an enemy area, the troops in it, etc., by examination or survey. 2. a survey of a region for some other purpose, as, in engineering, to prepare for triangulation, or, in geology, to learn its features.

rec·on·noi·ter (rek'ə-noi'tẽr, rē'kə-noi'tẽr), *v.t.* [Fr. *reconnoître*, old form of *reconnaître;* OFr. *reconoistre;* see RECOGNIZANCE], 1. in *military science*, to inspect or survey (an enemy position, etc.). 2. to make an examination or survey of (an area, region, etc.); hence, 3. to survey; examine; explore. *v.i.* to make a reconnaissance. Also spelled **reconnoitre.**

rec·on·noi·ter·er (rek'ə-noi'tẽr-ẽr, rē'kə-noi'tẽr-ẽr), *n.* a person who reconnoiters.

rec·on·noi·tre (rek'ə-noi'tẽr, rē'kə-noi'tẽr), *v.t. & v.i.* [RECONNOITRED (-tẽrd), RECONNOITRING], to reconnoiter.

rec·on·noi·trer (rek'ə-noi'trẽr, rē'kə-noi'trẽr), *n.* a reconnoiterer.

re·con·sid·er (rē'kən-sid'ẽr), *v.t.* 1. to consider again; think over. 2. to think or argue over again with a view to changing a decision. 3. to take up again in a meeting (a matter discussed before and settled). *v.i.* to reconsider a matter.

re·con·sid·er·a·tion (rē'kən-sid'ẽ-rā'shən), *n.* a reconsidering or being reconsidered.

re·con·sign·ment (rē'kən-sīn'mənt), *n.* 1. a consigning again or anew. 2. in *commerce*, a change (made in transit) in the route, destination, or consignee as indicated in the original bill of lading.

re·con·struct (rē'kən-strukt'), *v.t.* 1. to construct again; rebuild; make over. 2. to build up, from remaining parts and other evidence, an image of what something was in its original and complete form.

re·con·struc·tion (rē'kən-struk'shən), *n.* 1. a reconstructing. 2. [R-], *a)* the process, after the Civil War, of reorganizing the Southern States which had seceded and re-establishing them in the Union. *b)* the period of this (1867–1877). 3. something reconstructed.

re·con·struc·tive (rē'kən-struk'tiv), *adj.* reconstructing or tending to reconstruct.

re·con·ver·sion (rē'kən-vũr'zhən, rē'kən-vũr'shən), *n.* 1. a reconverting or being reconverted; especially, the changing (of a nation, industry, etc.) back from a wartime to a peacetime basis. 2. the period during which this goes on.

re·con·vert (rē'kən-vũrt'), *v.t. & v.i.* [*re-* + *convert*], 1. to change back, as to a former status, religion, opinion, etc. 2. to change, as a nation or industry, back from a wartime to a peacetime basis.

re·con·vey (rē'kən-vā'), *v.t.* to convey again or back, as to a former owner or place.

re·con·vey·ance (rē'kən-vā'əns), *n.* a reconveying or being reconveyed.

re·cord (ri-kôrd'; *for n. & adj.*, rek'ẽrd), *v.t.* [ME. *recorden;* OFr. *recorder;* L. *recordari*, to call to mind, remember < *re-*, again + *cor*, *cordis*, heart, mind], 1. to set down, as in writing; preserve an account of: as, *record* the day's events. 2. to register in some permanent form, as on a graph or chart, an indication of (a motion or event) as it occurs: as, a seismograph *records* earthquakes. 3. to serve as evidence of; tell of: as, the marks on the houses *record* the height of the flood waters. 4. *a)* to transform (sound) by electrical or mechanical means and register it in some permanent form, as the grooved track of a phonograph record, the magnetization of fine wire, etc., so that it can be reproduced at will by a reverse process. *b)* to register thus the performance of (a singer, orchestra, piece of music, etc.). 5. to show; indicate. 6. to set down or have set down in a register: as, *record* a vote. *v.i.* 1. to record something. 2. to admit of being recorded. *n.* [ME.; OFr. < the *v.*], 1. a recording or being recorded; preservation in or as in writing. 2. anything that is written down and preserved as evidence; account of events; anything that serves as evidence of an event, etc. 3. anything that the written evidence is put on or in, as a register, monument, etc. 4. an official written report of public proceedings, as in a legislature or court of law; documents preserved as evidence of proceedings, as of court. 5. the known or recorded facts about anything, as about conduct, performance, one's career, etc. 6. a flat disk, cylinder, paper roll, etc. on which sound has been recorded. 7. the best performance, as the highest speed, greatest amount, highest rate, etc., reached and publicly recorded. *adj.* making a record; being the largest, fastest, etc. of its kind: as, a *record* audience, *record* crop. Abbreviated **rec.**

break a record, to excel the best previous performance.
go on record, to state one's opinions publicly.
off the record, not for publication.
on record, recorded; publicly declared.

re·cord·er (ri-kôr'dẽr), *n.* [ME. & Anglo-Fr. *recordour*], 1. an officer appointed or elected to keep records of deeds or other official papers. 2. in some cities, a judge who has the same criminal jurisdiction as a police judge. 3. *a)* a machine that records. *b)* the part of a machine that records what goes on in the rest of the machine. 4. an early form of flute, with eight finger holes and a fipple, held straight up and down when played. 5. one who records. Abbreviated **rec.**

re·cord·er·ship (ri-kôr'dẽr-ship'), *n.* [see -SHIP,] the position or term of office of a recorder.

re·cord·ing (ri-kôr'diŋ), *adj.* that records. *n.* 1. the act of one that records. 2. what is recorded, as on a phonograph record. 3. the record itself. 4. the registering of sound, as on a phonograph record, with reference to the relative quality of reproduction afforded. Abbreviated **rec.**

re·count (ri-kount'), *v.t.* [Late ME. *recounten;* Anglo-Fr. *reconter;* see RE- & COUNT, *v.*], 1. to tell in detail; give an account of; relate; narrate. 2. to tell in order or one by one: as, she *recounted* her sins. —***SYN.*** **see tell.**

re-count (rē'kount'; *for n.*, rē'kount', rē-kount'), *v.t.* to count again. *n.* a second or additional count, as of votes: also written **recount.**

re·count·al (ri-koun't'l), *n.* a recounting.

re·coup (ri-kōōp'), *v.t.* [Fr. *recouper; re-*, again + *couper*, to cut; cf. COUP], 1. to get back an equivalent for; make up for: as, *recoup* a loss. 2. to pay back; reimburse. 3. in *law*, to deduct or hold back (a part of what is due), having some reasonable claim to do so. *n.* a recouping. —***SYN.*** see **recover.**

re·coup·ment (ri-kōōp'mənt), *n.* 1. a recouping or being recouped. 2. something recouped.

re·course (rē'kôrs, ri-kōrs'), *n.* [ME. & OFr. *recours* < L. *recursus*, a running back; see RE- & COURSE], 1. a turning or seeking for aid, protection, safety, etc.: as, he had *recourse* to the law. 2. that to which one turns seeking aid, safety, etc.: as, his one *recourse* was the law. 3. [Obs.], access; admission (to a person). 4. in *commerce & law*, the right to demand payment from the maker or endorser of a commercial paper, as a bill of exchange: usually in *without recourse*, without obligation to pay (added by the endorser to a bill of exchange to protect himself from liability).

re·cov·er (ri-kuv'ẽr), *v.t.* [ME. *recoveren;* OFr. *recovrer;* L. *recuperare;* see RECUPERATE], 1. to get back (something lost, stolen, etc.); regain (health, consciousness, etc.). 2. to compensate for; make up for: as, *recover* losses. 3. to get back for (oneself) a state of control, balance, good physical or mental health, etc.: as, he *recovered* himself quickly in the hospital. 4. to catch

reconcentrate
recondensation
recondense
reconduct
reconfirm
reconquer
reconquest
reconsecrate
reconsecration
reconsign
reconsolidate
reconsolidation
reconstitute
reconvene
recopy
recoronation

or save (oneself) from a slip, stumble, betrayal of feeling, tactless remark, etc. 5. to reclaim, as land from the sea, useful substances from waste, or a person from a bad state. 6. in *law*, to get or get back by final judgment in a court: as, *recover* damages, *recover* judgment against someone. 7. in *sports*, to get back to (a position, as of guard, balance, or readiness). ***v.i.*** 1. to get well again. 2. to catch or save oneself from a slip, stumble, self-betrayal, etc. 3. in *law*, to succeed in a claim; receive judgment in one's favor. 4. in *sports*, to get back to a position of guard, readiness, etc., as after a lunge in fencing or a stroke in rowing.

SYN.—**recover** implies a finding or getting back something that one has lost in any manner (to *recover* stolen property, one's self-possession, etc.); **regain** more strongly stresses a winning back of something that has been taken from one (to *regain* a military objective); **retrieve** suggests diligent effort in regaining something (he was determined to *retrieve* his honor); **recoup** implies recovery of an equivalent in compensation (I tried to *recoup* my losses); **reclaim** implies recovery or restoration to a better or useful state (to *reclaim* wasteland).

re-cov·er (rē'kuv'ẽr), ***v.t.*** to cover again or anew.

re·cov·er·y (ri-kuv'ẽr-i), ***n.*** [*pl.* RECOVERIES (-iz)], [Anglo-Fr. *recoverie*], 1. a recovering, getting back, regaining, or reclaiming. 2. a getting well again, coming or bringing back to consciousness, revival of a person from weakness, etc. 3. a regaining of balance, of former position or condition, etc.; return to soundness. 4. the time needed for recovering. 5. the thing or amount gained in recovering. 6. in *sports*, a return to a position of guard, readiness, etc., as after a lunge in fencing or a stroke in rowing.

rec·re·ance (rek'ri-əns), ***n.*** recreancy.

rec·re·an·cy (rek'ri-ən-si), ***n.*** [*pl.* RECREANCIES (-siz)], [< *recreant*], 1. a cowardly giving up; cowardice. 2. an abject failure to keep faith; treason or disloyalty.

rec·re·ant (rek'ri-ənt), ***adj.*** [ME.; OFr., ppr. of *recreire*, to surrender allegiance; ML. *recredere*, to give in or up; L. *re-*, back, again + *credere*, to believe], 1. *a)* crying for mercy; hence, *b)* cowardly; craven. 2. failing to keep faith; disloyal; traitorous; apostate. ***n.*** 1. a coward; craven. 2. a disloyal person; traitor.

rec·re·ate (rek'ri-āt'), ***v.t.*** [RECREATED (-id), RECREATING], [< L. *recreatus*, pp. of *recreare*, to restore, refresh, create anew; see RE- & CREATE], to put fresh life into; refresh or restore in body or mind, especially after work, by some form of play, amusement, or relaxation. ***v.i.*** to take recreation.

re-cre·ate (rē'kri-āt'), ***v.t.*** to create anew.

rec·re·a·tion (rek'ri-ā'shən), ***n.*** [ME. *recreacioun;* OFr.; L. *recreatio;* see RECREATE], 1. refreshment in body or mind, as after work, by some form of play, amusement, or relaxation. 2. any form of play, amusement, or relaxation used for this purpose, as games, sports, hobbies, reading, walking, etc.

re-cre·a·tion (rē'kri-ā'shən), ***n.*** 1. a re-creating or being re-created. 2. something re-created.

rec·re·a·tion·al (rek'ri-ā'shən-'l), ***adj.*** of, having the nature of, or providing recreation.

recreation room, a room, as in the basement of a home, equipped for amusement and relaxation.

rec·re·a·tive (rek'ri-ā'tiv), ***adj.*** providing, or serving as, recreation.

rec·re·ment (rek'rə-mənt), ***n.*** [< Fr. or L.; Fr. *récrément;* L. *recrementum* < *re-*, back + *cernere*, to separate], 1. the worthless part of anything; waste; dross. 2. in *physiology*, any substance, as saliva, secreted in the body by a gland, etc. and then reabsorbed into the blood.

rec·re·men·tal (rek'rə-men't'l), ***adj.*** of, or having the nature of, recrement.

re·crim·i·nate (ri-krim'ə-nāt'), ***v.i.*** [RECRIMINATED (-id), RECRIMINATING], [< ML. *recriminatus;* see RE- & CRIMINATE], to reply to an accusation by accusing, or charging some fault, in return.

re·crim·i·na·tion (ri-krim'ə-nā'shən), ***n.*** [ML. *recriminatio*], 1. a recriminating; accusation in return. 2. a counteraccusation; countercharge.

re·crim·i·na·tive (ri-krim'ə-nā'tiv), ***adj.*** recriminatory.

re·crim·i·na·to·ry (ri-krim'ə-nə-tôr'i, ri-krim'ə-nə-tō'ri), ***adj.*** 1. recriminating. 2. of, having the nature of, or involving recrimination.

rec room (rek), [Colloq.], a recreation room.

re·cru·desce (rē'kroo-des'), ***v.i.*** [RECRUDESCED (-dest'), RECRUDESCING], [L. *recrudescere; re-*, again + *crudescere*, to become harsh or raw < *crudus*, raw, crude], to break out afresh after a period of latency or relative inactivity; become active again, as a disease.

re·cru·des·cence (rē'kroo-des''ns), ***n.*** [< *recrudescent*], a breaking out afresh; renewal of activity.

re·cru·des·cen·cy (rē'kroo-des''n-si), ***n.*** recrudescence.

re·cru·des·cent (rē'kroo-des''nt), ***adj.*** [L. *recrudescens*, ppr.], recrudescing; breaking out afresh.

re·cruit (ri-kroot'), ***v.t.*** [Fr. *recruter* < *recrute*, a recruit, lit. new growth < *recrû*, pp. of *recroître*, to grow again < L. *re-*, again + *crescere*, to grow, increase], 1. to raise or strengthen (an army, navy, etc.) by enlisting personnel. 2. to enlist (personnel) into an army or navy. 3. to enlist (new members) for a party, organization, etc. 4. [Rare], to increase, strengthen, or maintain by supplying anew. 5. to revive or restore, as health, strength, etc. ***v.i.*** 1. to enlist new personnel for a military force. 2. to get new supplies of something, as in replacement. 3. to regain health, strength, etc. ***n.*** 1. a recently enlisted soldier, sailor, etc.; specifically, in the *United States Army*, formerly, the seventh, or lowest, grade of enlisted man (now *private*). 2. a new member of any group, body, or organization.

re·cruit·ment (ri-kroot'mənt), ***n.*** a recruiting or being recruited.

Rec. Sec., rec. sec., recording secretary.

rect., 1. receipt. 2. rector. 3. rectory.

rec·tal (rek't'l), ***adj.*** of, for, or near the rectum.

rec·tan·gle (rek'taŋ'g'l), ***n.*** [Fr.; LL. *rectiangulum;* see RECTI- & ANGLE (a corner)], any four-sided plane figure with four right angles.

rec·tan·gu·lar (rek-taŋ'gyoo-lẽr), ***adj.*** 1. shaped like a rectangle; having four sides and four right angles. 2. having right-angled corners, or a base in the form of a rectangle, as a building. 3. right-angled.

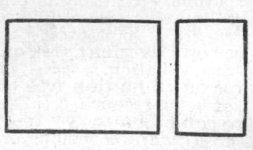

RECTANGLES

rec·tan·gu·lar·i·ty (rek-taŋ'gyoo-lar'ə-ti), ***n.*** the quality or condition of being rectangular.

rec·ti- (rek'tə, rek'ti), [LL. < L. *rectus*, straight], a combining form meaning *straight, right*, as in *rectilinear:* also, before a vowel, **rect-.**

rec·ti·fi·a·ble (rek'tə-fī'ə-b'l), ***adj.*** that can be rectified.

rec·ti·fi·ca·tion (rek'tə-fi-kā'shən), ***n.*** [Fr.; LL. *rectificatio*], a rectifying or being rectified.

rec·ti·fi·er (rek'tə-fī'ẽr), ***n.*** 1. a person or thing that rectifies, as by correction or adjustment. 2. in *electricity*, any device, as a commutator or vacuum tube, which changes alternating current into direct current.

rec·ti·fy (rek'tə-fī'), ***v.t.*** [RECTIFIED (-fīd'), RECTIFYING], [ME. *rectifien;* OFr. *rectifier;* LL. *rectificare* < L. *rectus*, right + *facere*, to make], 1. to put or set right; correct; amend. 2. to adjust, as in movement or balance; adjust by calculation. 3. in *chemistry*, to refine or purify by distillation, especially by distilling again and again. 4. in *electricity*, to change (alternating current) to direct current. 5. in *mathematics*, to find the length of (a curve).

rec·ti·lin·e·al (rek'tə-lin'i-əl), ***adj.*** rectilinear.

rec·ti·lin·e·ar (rek'tə-lin'i-ẽr), ***adj.*** [*recti-* + *linear*], 1. moving in a straight line. 2. forming a straight line. 3. bounded or formed by straight lines. 4. characterized by straight lines. 5. in *optics*, corrected so as not to distort straight lines: said of a type of lens.

rec·ti·tude (rek'tə-tood', rek'tə-tūd'), ***n.*** [ME.; Fr.; LL. *rectitudo* < L. *rectus*, right, straight], 1. conduct according to moral principles; strict honesty; uprightness of character. 2. correctness of judgment or method. 3. [Rare], straightness.

rec·to (rek'tō), ***n.*** [*pl.* RECTOS (-tōz)], [L., abl. of *rectus*, right], in *printing*, any right-hand page of a book; front side of a leaf: opposed to *verso;* abbreviated **ro.**

rec·to·cele (rek'tə-sēl'), ***n.*** [*recto-* (comb. form of *rectum*) + *-cele*], a hernial protrusion of the rectum into the vagina.

rec·tor (rek'tẽr), ***n.*** [ME. *rectour;* L. *rector* < pp. of *regere*, to rule], 1. in the *Protestant Episcopal Church*, a minister in charge of a parish. 2. in the *Church of England*, a clergyman who holds the rights and tithes of his parish: distinguished from *vicar*. 3. in the *Roman Catholic Church*, *a)* the head priest of a parish. *b)* the head of a religious institution or school. 4. in certain schools, colleges, and universities, the head or headmaster. Abbreviated **R., r., rect.**

rec·tor·ate (rek'tẽr-it), ***n.*** [ML. *rectoratus*], the position, office, or term of office of a rector.

rec·to·ri·al (rek-tôr'i-əl, rek-tō'ri-əl), ***adj.*** of a rector or rectors.

rec·to·ry (rek'tẽr-i), ***n.*** [*pl.* RECTORIES (-iz)], [ML. *rectoria*], 1. the house in which an Episcopal minister lives. 2. in the *Church of England*, *a)* a benefice held by a rector. *b)* the house in which a rector lives: distinguished from *vicarage*. Abbreviated **rect.**

rec·trix (rek'triks), ***n.*** [*pl.* RECTRICES (rek-trī'sēz)], [L., fem. of *rector*, a director], in *zoology*, any of the large tail feathers of a bird.

rec·tum (rek'təm), ***n.*** [*pl.* RECTA (-tə)], [L. *rectum* (*intestinum*), lit., straight (intestine)], the lowest segment of the large intestine, extending, in man, from the sigmoid flexure to the anus: see **alimentary canal,** illus.

rec·tus (rek'təs), ***n.*** [*pl.* RECTI (-tī)], [L. *rectus* (*musculus*), lit., straight (muscle)], any of various straight muscles, as of the eye, neck, abdomen, thigh, etc.

re·cum·ben·cy (ri-kum'bən-si), ***n.*** the state or position of being recumbent.

re·cum·bent (ri-kum′bənt), *adj.* [L. *recumbens*, ppr. of *recumbere; re-*, back + *cumbere*, to lie down], 1. lying down; reclining; leaning; specifically, in *biology*, designating a part that leans or lies. 2. resting; inactive. —*SYN.* see **prone**.

re·cu·per·ate (ri-kōō′pə-rāt′, ri-kū′pə-rāt′), *v.t.* [RECUPERATED (-id), RECUPERATING], [< L. *recuperatus*, pp. of *recuperare*, to recover], 1. to restore to health, strength, etc.; make well again. 2. to get back; recover (losses, health, etc.). *v.i.* 1. to be restored to health, strength, etc.; get well again; recover. 2. to recover losses, etc.

re·cu·per·a·tion (ri-kōō′pə-rā′shən, ri-kū′pə-rā′shən), *n.* [L. *recuperatio*], a recuperating; recovery from disease, surgery, financial loss, etc.

re·cu·per·a·tive (ri-kōō′pə-rā′tiv, ri-kū′pə-rā′tiv), *adj.* [L. *recuperativus*], of or promoting recuperation.

re·cu·per·a·tor (ri-kōō′pə-rā′tẽr, ri-kū′pə-rā′tẽr), *n.* a person who recuperates.

re·cu·per·a·to·ry (ri-kōō′pẽr-ə-tôr′i, ri-kū′pẽr-ə-tō′ri), *adj.* recuperative.

re·cur (ri-kũr′), *v.i.* [RECURRED (-kũrd′), RECURRING], [L. *recurrere; re-*, back + *currere*, to run], 1. to return, as in thought, talk, or memory: as, *recurring* to an earlier question. 2. to occur again, as in talk or memory; come up again for consideration. 3. to happen or occur again, especially after some lapse of time; appear at intervals. —*SYN.* see **return**.

re·cur·rence (ri-kũr′əns), *n.* [< *recurrent*], 1. a bringing up again, as in thought or discussion (with *to*). 2. a coming up or back; reappearance; return; repetition. 3. [Rare], resort; recourse.

re·cur·rent (ri-kũr′ənt), *adj.* [L. *recurrens*, ppr.], 1. recurring; appearing or occurring again or periodically. 2. in *anatomy*, turning back in the opposite direction: said of certain arteries and nerves. *n.* in *anatomy*, a recurrent artery or nerve. —*SYN.* see **intermittent**.

recurring decimal, a decimal in which two or more consecutive figures are repeated indefinitely, as .278278278. . .; circulating decimal.

re·cur·vate (ri-kũr′vit, ri-kũr′vāt), *adj.* [L. *recurvatus*, pp.], recurved; bent back.

re·curve (ri-kũrv′), *v.t. & v.i.* [L. *recurvare*], to curve or bend back or backward.

rec·u·san·cy (rek′yoo-z′n-si, ri-kū′z′n-si), *n.* [< *recusant*], the condition of being recusant; refusal to obey or conform, especially in religious matters.

rec·u·sant (rek′yoo-z′nt, ri-kū′z′nt), *n.* [L. *recusans*, ppr. of *recusare*, to reject < *re-*, against + *causa*, a cause], 1. a person who refuses to obey or conform to an established authority or its regulations. 2. in *English history*, a person, especially a Roman Catholic, who refused to attend the services of the Church of England or recognize its authority. *adj.* 1. disobedient of authority, especially in religious matters; dissenting; nonconformist. 2. in *English history*, refusing to attend the services or recognize the authority of the Church of England.

re·cuse (ri-kūz′), *v.t.* [RECUSED (-kūzd′), RECUSING], [ME. *recusen*; L. *recusare*; see RECUSANT], in *law*, [Rare], to challenge (a judge, juror, or court) as prejudiced or otherwise incompetent to act.

red (red), *n.* [ME. *rede, redde*; AS. *read*; akin to G. *rot*, ON. *rauthr*; IE. base **reudh-*, red, seen in L. *ruber, rufus*, red, *rubere*, to be red, etc. (cf. RUBRIC, RUBY, RUBICUND, ROUGE, etc.)], 1. a primary color, or any of a spread of colors at the lower end of the visible spectrum, varying in hue from that of blood to pale rose or pink: see **color**. 2. a pigment producing this color. 3. [often R-], [senses *a* & *b* from the red flag symbolizing revolutionary socialism], *a*) a political radical or revolutionary; especially, a communist. *b*) a citizen of the Soviet Union. *c*) *pl.* North American Indians. 4. a red object, as a red space on the board or wheel used in various games of chance, a red chessman, or a red piece in checkers. *adj.* [REDDER (-ẽr), REDDEST (-ist)], 1. having or being of the color red or any of its hues. 2. having red hair. 3. having, or considered to have, a reddish or coppery skin, as the North American Indians. 4. [often R-], *a*) politically radical or revolutionary; especially, communist. *b*) of the Soviet Union.

in the red, 1. losing money, as a business. 2. in debt.

paint the town red, [Slang], to have a noisy good time, as by visiting bars, night clubs, etc.

see red, [Colloq.], to be or become angry.

re·dact (ri-dakt′), *v.t.* [< L. *redactus*, pp. of *redigere*, to bring into a certain condition, reduce to order; see RE- & ACT], 1. to write out or draw up; frame (a proclamation, government order, etc.). 2. to arrange in proper form for publication; edit.

re·dac·tion (ri-dak′shən), *n.* [< Fr. & LL.; Fr. *rédaction*; LL. *redactio*], 1. the preparation of written work for publication; editing, re-editing, or revision. 2. an edited work; especially, a reissue; new edition.

re·dac·tor (ri-dak′tẽr), *n.* [Fr. *redacteur* < L. *redactus*; see REDACT], an editor: abbreviated **R., r.**

red admiral, [cf. ADMIRAL], a purplish-black European and North American butterfly with white spots near the tips of the forewings and bright-orange bands across the forewings and bordering the hind wings.

red algae, a group of red, brownish-red, purple, or greenish seaweeds, ranging from delicately filamentous to coarse forms.

re·dan (ri-dan′), *n.* [Fr.; OFr. *redent* < L. *re-*, back + *dens, dentis*, a tooth: from its shape], in *military science*, a fortification consisting of two walls or parapets set at an angle pointed toward the enemy and open at the back: two or more are often joined by walls or trenches.

Red Army, the army of the Soviet Union.

red·bait (red′bāt′), *v.t. & v.i.* [< *red, adj.*, 4 + *bait, v.t.*, 2], to make verbal attacks on or utter denunciations of (a person or group) as being red, or communist.

red·bird (red′bũrd′), *n.* 1. the American cardinal. 2. the scarlet tanager. 3. the European bullfinch.

red blood cell, a red corpuscle; erythrocyte.

red-blood·ed (red′blud′id), *adj.* 1. high-spirited and strong-willed; vigorous: said of persons. 2. full of action; exciting; said of novels, etc.

red·breast (red′brest′), *n.* [ME. *redbrest*, robin], 1. any of several birds with a reddish breast; especially, *a*) the robin (American or European). *b*) the knot, an American sandpiper. 2. the red-breasted bream.

red-breast·ed bream (red′bres′tid), a kind of sunfish with a red belly, found in the eastern United States.

red·bud (red′bud′), *n.* any of a number of related trees with small, pink, budlike flowers and heart-shaped leaves; Judas tree.

red·bug (red′bug′), *n.* [from the inflamed red spots that it produces on the human skin], a chigger.

red·cap (red′kap′), *n.* 1. a porter in a railway station, bus station, etc. 2. the European goldfinch. 3. [British Colloq.], a military policeman.

red cedar, 1. any of a number of related evergreen trees with small needle-shaped or scalelike leaves, reddish berrylike fruit, and red wood. 2. this wood.

red cent, [Colloq.], a cent; penny: especially in *not worth a red cent, not give a red cent*, etc.

red clover, a kind of clover with flowers in reddish, ball-shaped heads, grown for fodder.

red·coat (red′kōt′), *n.* a British soldier (of the period when a red coat was part of the British uniform, as during the American Revolution).

Red Crescent, in Turkey, an organization equivalent to the Red Cross, giving medical and other aid in time of war or disaster: its symbol is a red crescent.

red cross, 1. St. George's cross, red on a white ground, the national emblem of England. 2. [R- C-], a red Greek cross on a white ground (*Geneva Cross*), emblem of neutrality in war, adapted from the Swiss flag, with colors reversed, and used since 1864 to mark hospitals, ambulances, etc. in time of war; hence, 3. [R- C-], *a*) an international society for the relief of suffering in time of war or disaster. *b*) any national branch of this. Abbreviated **R.C.** (sense 3).

redd (red), *v.t.* [REDD or REDDED (-id), REDDING], [ME. (North & Scot.) *redden*; akin to & prob. < MLG. *redden* in the same sense; cf. obs. *redd*, to free (< AS. *hreddan*), obs. *rede*, to put in order (< AS. *rædan*), & READY], [Colloq. or Dial.], to put in order; make tidy (often with *up*).

red deer, 1. a kind of deer native to Europe and Asia. 2. the Virginia, or American, deer (in its reddish summer coloring).

red·den (red′′n), *v.t.* to make red. *v.i.* to become red; especially, to blush or flush.

Red Desert, Nefud, a desert in Arabia.

red·dish (red′ish), *adj.* somewhat red.

red·dle (red′′l), *n.* [var. of *ruddle*], red ocher. *v.t.* [REDDLED (-′ld), REDDLING], to color with red ocher. Also **ruddle, raddle.**

red·dle·man (red′′l-mən), *n.* [*pl.* REDDLEMEN (-mən)], a person who sells reddle.

red drum (or **drumfish**), a large, edible drumfish of the Atlantic coast of the United States.

rede (rēd), *n.* [ME. *rede*; AS. *ræd* (akin to G. *rat*) < base of *rædan*, to interpret (see READ, *v.*); the *v.t.* is the same word as *read, v.*, with retained ME. sp.], [Archaic, Poetic, or Dial.], 1. counsel; advice. 2. a plan; scheme. 3. a story; tale. 4. an interpretation. *v.t.* [REDED (-id), REDING], [Archaic, Poetic, or Dial.], 1. to advise; counsel. 2. to explain; interpret, as dreams. 3. to narrate; tell.

redamage **redeceive** **redecorate** **rededicate**
redare **redecide** **redecoration** **rededication**

re·deem (ri-dēm′), *v.t.* [Fr. *rédimer;* L. *redimere* < *re(d)-*, back + *emere*, to get, buy], 1. to buy back. 2. to get back; recover, as by paying a fee. 3. to pay off (a mortgage or note). 4. to convert (paper money) into coin. 5. *a)* to set free; ransom; rescue. *b)* to deliver from sin and its penalties, as by a sacrifice made for the sinner. 6. to fulfill, as a promise. 7. to make amends for; atone or compensate for. —*SYN.* see **rescue.**
re·deem·a·ble (ri-dēm′ə-b'l), *adj.* 1. that can be redeemed. 2. that will be bought back, as bonds, stock, etc.
re·deem·er (ri-dēm′ẽr), *n.* 1. a person who redeems. 2. [R-], Jesus Christ.
re·de·liv·er (rē′di-liv′ẽr), *v.t.* 1. to deliver again. 2. to deliver back; return.
re·de·mand (rē′di-mand′, rē′di-mänd′), *v.t.* 1. to demand again. 2. to demand back; demand the return of. *n.* [Rare], a redemanding.
re·demp·ti·ble (ri-demp′tə-b'l), *adj.* redeemable.
re·demp·tion (ri-demp′shən), *n.* [ME. *redempcion;* OFr.; L. *redemptio* < pp. of *redimere;* see REDEEM], 1. a redeeming or being redeemed (in various senses). 2. something that redeems.
re·demp·tion·er (ri-demp′shən-ẽr), *n.* [*redemption* + *-er*], in Colonial days, a person who paid for his passage from Europe by a stipulated period of service as a bond-servant in America.
re·demp·tive (ri-demp′tiv), *adj.* 1. serving to redeem. 2. of redemption.
Re·demp·tor·ist (ri-demp′tẽr-ist), *n.* [Fr. *rédemptoriste* < L. *redemptor*, redeemer < pp. of *redimere;* see REDEEM], a member of the Congregation of the Most Holy Redeemer, a Roman Catholic order founded in 1732 by St. Alphonsus Liguori, for working and teaching among the poor.
re·demp·to·ry (ri-demp′tə-ri), *adj.* redemptive.
re·de·ploy (rē′di-ploi′), *v.t.* to move (troops) from one front to another, as from Europe to the Pacific.
re·de·pos·it (rē′di-poz′it), *v.t.* to deposit again. *n.* something deposited again.
re·de·vel·op (rē′di-vel′əp), *v.t.* 1. to develop again. 2. in *photography*, to intensify or tone (a developed negative or image) by a second developing process. *v.i.* to develop again.
re·de·vel·op·ment (rē′di-vel′əp-mənt), *n.* a redeveloping or being redeveloped.
red·eye (red′ī′), *n.* 1. any of several fishes with red eyes, as the rudd. 2. the red-eyed vireo. 3. [Slang], strong whisky, especially if inferior. Also **red eye.**
red·fin (red′fin′), *n.* any of a group of fresh-water food fishes of the carp family, with the lower fins red or orange, found in the east central States.
red fir, 1. any of various evergreen trees with cones, needlelike leaves, and reddish wood, including the red silver fir and the California red fir. 2. the wood of any of these trees. 3. the Douglas fir.
red fire, any of various substances, especially one containing strontium nitrate, which burn with a bright red light and are used in fireworks, flares, etc.
red flag, 1. the flag symbolizing revolution, revolutionary socialism, etc.: often used figuratively. 2. a danger signal: from the use of a red flag as a signal at railroad crossings. 3. anything that arouses anger.
red fox, 1. the common European fox, with reddish fur. 2. the similar related fox of North America. 3. the fur of either of these.
red-hand·ed (red′han′did), *adj.* 1. having hands red with blood; hence, 2. in the act, or fresh from the scene, of a crime. 3. bloody; violent: said of actions.
red hat, 1. the official hat, or biretta, of a cardinal, the symbol of his rank. 2. the rank or position of a cardinal. 3. a cardinal.
red·head (red′hed′), *n.* 1. a person with red hair. 2. a North American diving duck the male of which has a red head: it resembles the related canvasback. 3. the redheaded woodpecker.
red·head·ed (red′hed′id), *adj.* having red hair, as a person, or a red head, as a bird.
redheaded woodpecker, a North American woodpecker with a bright-red head and neck, black back, and white underparts.
red heat, 1. the temperature at which a substance is red-hot. 2. the state of being at this temperature.
red herring, 1. a smoked herring. 2. something used to confuse, or to divert attention from something else: from the practice of drawing a herring across the trace in hunting, to distract the hounds.
red hind, the cabrilla, a serranoid food fish.
red-hot (red′hot′), *adj.* 1. hot enough to glow; very hot. 2. very excited, as with anger or enthusiasm. 3. very new; up-to-the-minute: said of news, etc.
red Indian, a North American Indian, having reddish or coppery skin.
red·in·gote (red′iŋ-gōt′), *n.* [Fr.; altered < Eng. *riding coat*], 1. formerly, a man's full-skirted, double-breasted overcoat. 2. a long, unlined, lightweight coat, open down the front, worn by women.

TYPES OF REDINGOTE

red·in·te·grate (ri-din′tə-grāt′), *v.t.* [REDINTEGRATED (-id), REDINTEGRATING], [ME. *redintegraten* < L. *redintegratus*, pp. of *redintegrare;* see RE- & INTEGRATE], to make whole or perfect again; reunite; re-establish.
red·in·te·gra·tion (ri-din′tə-grā′shən), *n.* 1. a redintegrating or being redintegrated. 2. in *psychology*, the tendency to respond to a later stimulus in the same way as to an earlier complex stimulus of which the later one was a part.
re·di·rect (rē′də-rekt′, rē′dī-rekt′), *v.t.* to direct again. *adj.* in *law*, of the questioning of one's own witness again, after his cross-examination by the opposing lawyer.
re·di·rec·tion (rē′də-rek′shən, rē′dī-rek′shən), *n.* a redirecting.
re·dis·count (rē-dis′kount), *v.t.* to discount again. *n.* 1. a rediscounting. 2. *usually pl.* rediscounted commercial paper.
re·dis·trict (rē-dis′trikt), *v.t.* to divide anew into districts, especially in order to reapportion electoral representatives.
red lattice, [Archaic], an alehouse, or tavern: formerly marked by red lattices on the windows.
red lead, red oxide of lead, Pb_3O_4, derived from massicot, used in making paint, in glassmaking, etc.; minium.
red lead ore, crocoite, a red chromate of lead.
red-let·ter (red′let′ẽr), *adj.* memorable; happy: as, a *red-letter* day: from the custom of marking church holidays on the calendar in red ink.
red light, 1. a danger signal. 2. a signal used to bring trains, automobiles, etc. to a stop; stop light.
red-light district (red′līt′), a district (in a town or city) containing many houses of prostitution, sometimes indicated by red lights.
red man, a North American Indian.
red meat, beef or mutton, as distinguished from pork, veal, etc.
Red·mond, John Edward (red′mənd), 1856–1918; Irish political leader; follower of Parnell.
red mullet, see **mullet.**
red oak, 1. any of several oaks whose foliage is dark red in the autumn. 2. the hard wood of such a tree.
red ocher, an earthy hematite, red in color, used as a pigment: also called *ruddle, reddle, raddle.*
red·o·lence (red′ə-ləns), *n.* the quality or state of being redolent. —*SYN.* see **scent.**
red·o·len·cy (red′ə-lən-si), *n.* redolence.
red·o·lent (red′ə-lənt), *adj.* [ME.; OFr.; L. *redolens*, ppr. of *redolere*, to emit a scent; *re(d)-*, intens. + *olere*, to smell], 1. sweet-smelling; fragrant. 2. smelling (*of*): as, *redolent* of flowers; hence, 3. suggestive (*of*).
red osier, a kind of dogwood with dark-red branches and white or bluish fruit.
re·dou·ble (rē-dub′'l), *v.t.* [REDOUBLED (-'ld), REDOUBLING], [Fr. *redoubler;* see RE- & DOUBLE], 1. to make twice as much or twice as great; increase twofold. 2. to repeat; do or say again. 3. to echo or re-echo. 4. to refold; double back. 5. in *bridge*, to double the doubled bid of (one's opponent). *v.i.* 1. to become twice as great or twice as much. 2. to re-echo; resound. 3. in *bridge*, to double a bid that an opponent has already doubled. *n.* in *bridge*, a redoubling.
re·doubt (ri-dout′), *n.* [Fr. *redoute;* It. *ridotto;* ML. *reductus*, a refuge, orig. pp. of L. *reducere;* see REDUCE], 1. in *military science*, *a)* a temporary outlying fortification or breastwork, used to secure hilltops, passes, or the flanks of entrenchments. *b)* in permanent fortifications, a breastwork surrounded by a parapet and dominated by guns from the heavier fortifications behind it. 2. a stronghold.
re·doubt·a·ble (ri-dout′ə-b'l), *adj.* [ME. *redowtable;* OFr. < *redouter*, to fear, dread < L. *re-*, intens. + *dubitare*, to doubt], 1. formidable; fearsome; dread. 2. deserving of respect: as, a *redoubtable* opponent.
re·doubt·a·bly (ri-dout′ə-bli), *adv.* in a redoubtable manner; so as to be redoubtable.
re·doubt·ed (ri-dout′id), *adj.* [Archaic], redoubtable.
re·dound (ri-dound′), *v.i.* [Fr. *redonder;* L. *redundare*, to overflow; *re(d)-*, intens. + *undare*, to surge, swell < *unda*, a wave], 1. to have a result or effect (*to* the credit or discredit, etc. of someone or something): as, this work will *redound* to his credit. 2. to come

redemonstrate
redeny
redescend
redescribe
redetermine
redigest
rediscover
rediscovery
redispose
redissolve
redistill
redistribute
redistribution
redivide
redivision
redo

back; react; recoil (*upon*): said of honor or disgrace. 3. [Obs.], to flow back, as waves.

red·o·wa (red'ə-wə, red'ə-və), *n.* [Fr. & G. < Czech. *rejdovák* < *rejdovati*, to whirl around, turn], 1. either of two ballroom dances of the 19th century, one like a polka, the other like a waltz. 2. music for these.

red pepper, 1. a plant with a red, many-seeded fruit, as the sweet pepper or cayenne. 2. the fruit. 3. the ground fruit or seeds, used for seasoning.

red·poll (red'pōl'), *n.* [*red* + *poll* (the head)], any of a number of finches the males of which usually have a red patch on the head.

Red Polled (pōld), any of a British breed of hornless, reddish dairy and beef cattle: also **Red Poll.**

re-draft (rē'draft', rē'dräft'; *for v.,* rē-draft', rē-dräft'), *n.* 1. a second or later draft or framing, as of a legislative bill. 2. a draft on the drawer or endorser of a protested bill of exchange, for the amount of the bill plus charges and costs. *v.t.* to draft again or anew.

re·dress (ri-dres'; *for n., usually* rē'dres), *v.t.* [ME. *redressen;* OFr. *redrecier;* see RE- & DRESS], 1. to correct and compensate for, as evils, abuses, afflictions, etc. 2. to correct; remedy, as a fault. 3. to compensate; make amends to. 4. to adjust: as, *redress* the balances. *n.* 1. compensation; satisfaction, as for a wrong done. 2. a redressing. —*SYN.* see **reparation.**

re-dress (rē'dres'), *v.t.* to dress again.

re·dress·er, re·dres·sor (ri-dres'ẽr), *n.* a person who redresses.

Red River, 1. a river flowing through Texas and Louisiana into the Mississippi: length, 1,018 mi. 2. a river flowing between North Dakota and Minnesota into Lake Winnipeg, Canada: length, 550 mi.: also called *Red River of the North.* 3. Song Koi, a river in China: the English name.

red·root (red'ro͞ot', red'root'), *n.* a plant with a red root, sword-shaped leaves, and orange-yellow flowers.

Red Sea, a sea between Africa and Arabia, connected with the Mediterranean Sea by the Suez Canal and with the Indian Ocean by the Gulf of Aden: length, 1,450 mi.; area, 169,000 sq. mi.

red-short (red'shôrt'), *adj.* [Sw. *rödskört,* neut. of *rödskör; röd,* red + *skör,* brittle], in *metallurgy,* brittle when red-hot: said of iron or steel with too much sulfur in it.

red·skin (red'skin'), *n.* a North American Indian.

red snapper, a salt-water food fish with a reddish, blue-streaked, oblong body, found in the Gulf of Mexico and off the east coasts of Florida and Georgia.

red squirrel, a common North American squirrel with reddish fur.

red·start (red'stärt'), *n.* [*red* + *start* (< AS. *steort*), tail], 1. a small European bird of the warbler family, with a reddish tail and peculiar darting flight. 2. an American fly-catching warbler, red, black, and white.

red-tape (red'tāp'), *adj.* of or characterized by red tape.

red tape, [after the tape commonly used to tie official papers], 1. official forms and routines; hence, 2. rigid application of regulations and routines, resulting in delays and exasperations in getting business done.

red·top (red'top'), *n.* [from the reddish panicle of some forms], a grass grown in eastern North America for hay and pasturage.

re·duce (ri-do͞os', ri-dūs'), *v.t.* [REDUCED (-do͞ost', -dūst'), REDUCING], [ME. *reducen;* L. *reducere,* to lead back; *re-,* back + *ducere,* to lead], 1. to lessen in any way, as in size, weight, amount, value, price, etc.; diminish. 2. to bring into a certain order; classify; hence, 3. to break up into constituent elements by analysis. 4. *a*) to change to a different form, as by putting something said into writing. *b*) to change to a different physical form, as by melting, crushing, grinding, etc. 5. to lower, as in rank or position; degrade. 6. to bring to order, attention, obedience, etc., as by persuasion or force. 7. to subdue or conquer, as a city or fort by siege or attack; bring under control. 8. *a*) to bring into difficult or wretched circumstances: as, *reduced* to poverty. *b*) to compel by need to do something: used in the passive, as, he was *reduced* to stealing. 9. to weaken in bodily strength; make thin: as, *reduced* to skin and bones. 10. to thin (paint), as with oil. 11. in *arithmetic,* to change in denomination or form without changing in value: as, *reduce* fractions to their lowest terms. 12. in *biology,* to cause (a cell) to undergo meiosis. 13. in *chemistry, a*) to decrease the positive valence of (an element or radical). *b*) to increase the negative valence of (an element or radical). *c*) to remove the oxygen from; deoxidize. *d*) to combine with hydrogen. *e*) to bring into the metallic state by removing nonmetallic elements. 14. in *photography,* to make less dense, as a negative. 15. in *surgery,* to restore (a broken bone, displaced organ, etc.) to its normal position or condition. *v.i.* 1. to become reduced. 2. to lose weight, as by dieting. —*SYN.* see **decrease.**

re·duc·er (ri-do͞os'ẽr, ri-dūs'ẽr), *n.* 1. a person or thing that reduces. 2. in *mechanics,* a pipe fitting threaded to connect two different sizes of pipe. 3. in *photography, a*) a developing agent. *b*) an oxidizing solution for reducing negatives.

re·duc·i·bil·i·ty (ri-do͞os'ə-bil'ə-ti, ri-dūs'ə-bil'ə-ti), *n.* the condition or quality of being reducible.

re·duc·i·ble (ri-do͞os'ə-b'l, ri-dūs'ə-b'l), *adj.* that can be reduced.

re·duc·i·bly (ri-do͞os'ə-bli, ri-dūs'ə-bli), *adv.* in a reducible manner; so as to be reducible.

reducing agent, in *chemistry,* any substance that reduces another substance, or brings about reduction, and is itself oxidized in the process.

reducing glass, a double-concave lens used for reducing the visual size of something viewed through it.

re·duc·tase (ri-duk'tās, ri-duk'tāz), *n.* [*reduction* + *-ase*], any enzyme that speeds up chemical reduction.

‡re·duc·ti·o ad ab·sur·dum (ri-duk'shi-ō' ad ab-sũr'dəm), [L., lit., reduction to absurdity], in *logic,* the proof of a proposition by showing its opposite to be foolish or impossible, or the disproof of a proposition by showing its consequences to be impossible or absurd when it is carried to its logical conclusion.

re·duc·tion (ri-duk'shən), *n.* [Fr. *réduction;* L. *reductio* < *reductus,* pp. of *reducere*], 1. a reducing or being reduced. 2. anything made or brought about by reducing, as a smaller copy, lowered price, etc. 3. the amount by which anything is reduced. 4. in *biology,* meiosis.

re·duc·tion·al (ri-duk'shən-'l), *adj.* of reduction.

re·duc·tive (ri-duk'tiv), *adj.* 1. of reduction. 2. reducing or tending to reduce.

re·duc·tor (ri-duk'tẽr), *n.* in *chemistry,* any apparatus for carrying out the reduction of a metallic solution for purposes of analysis; specifically, a long tube filled with granular zinc for reducing a ferric solution to its ferrous salt.

re·dun·dance (ri-dun'dəns), *n.* redundancy.

re·dun·dan·cy (ri-dun'dən-si), *n.* 1. the state or quality of being redundant. 2. [*pl.* REDUNDANCIES (-siz)], something redundant, as a part or quantity.

re·dun·dant (ri-dun'dənt), *adj.* [L. *redundans,* ppr. of *redundare;* see REDOUND], 1. more than enough; overabundant; excessive. 2. excess; superfluous: as, a *redundant* foot in a line of verse. 3. wordy: as, a *redundant* literary style. 4. unnecessary to the meaning: said of words. 5. in *grammar,* designating or of a verb having alternative forms, as for the past tense or participle (e.g., *awake, dive*). —*SYN.* see **wordy.**

redupl., 1. reduplicate. 2. reduplication. 3. reduplicative.

re·du·pli·cate (ri-do͞o'plə-kāt', ri-dū'plə-kāt'; *for adj. & n., usually* ri-do͞o'plə-kit, ri-dū'plə-kit), *v.t.* [< ML. *reduplicatus,* pp. of *reduplicare;* see RE- & DUPLICATE], 1. to redouble, double, or repeat. 2. in *linguistics, a*) to double (a root syllable or other element) so as to form an inflected or derived form of a word, sometimes with certain changes, as of the vowel (e.g., *chitchat, helter-skelter, tom-tom*). *b*) to form (words) by such repetition. *v.i.* to be or become reduplicated. *adj.* 1. reduplicated; doubled. 2. in *botany,* valvate; having the edges folded back so that they project outward. *n.* something reduplicated.

re·du·pli·ca·tion (ri-do͞o'plə-kā'shən, ri-dū'plə-kā'shən), *n.* [LL. *reduplicatio*], 1. a reduplicating or being reduplicated. 2. something produced by reduplicating, as a word containing a reduplicated element. 3. the element added in a reduplicated word form.

re·du·pli·ca·tive (ri-do͞o'plə-kā'tiv, ri-dū'plə-kā'tiv), *adj.* 1. reduplicating or tending to reduplicate. 2. of or characterized by reduplication. 3. in *botany,* reduplicate. Abbreviated **redupl.**

red·ware (red'wâr'), *n.* [*red* + *ware* (ME. & AS. *war*), seaweed], a large, brown, leathery seaweed.

red·wing (red'wiŋ'), *n.* 1. any of a species of north European songbirds, the smallest of the thrushes, with an orange-red patch on the underside of the wings. 2. the red-winged blackbird.

red-winged blackbird (red'wind'), any of a species of North American blackbirds with a bright-red patch on each wing near the shoulder.

red·wood (red'wood'), *n.* 1. a giant evergreen of the Pacific coast; sequoia. 2. any of a number of trees with reddish wood. 3. the wood of any of these trees.

red-yel·low (red'yel'ō), *n.* a color between red and yellow in the spectrum; orange. *adj.* of this color.

re-ech·o, re·ëch·o (rē-ek'ō), *v.t. & v.i.* to echo back or again; resound. *n.* [*pl.* RE-ECHOES, REËCHOES (-ōz)], the echo of an echo.

redraw redrive redrop redry

reed (rēd), *n.* [ME. *rede, reed;* AS. *hreod;* akin to G. *riet;* prob. IE. base **qreut-*, to shake, tremble: from the plants' motion in the wind], 1. any of a number of related grasses with jointed, hollow stems. 2. a mass of these, growing or dried. 3. a rustic musical instrument made from a hollow stem or stalk and played by blowing through it: used as the symbol of pastoral poetry. 4. [Poetic], an arrow. 5. in *architecture*, a small, rounded molding. 6. in the *Bible*, a unit of length equal to 6 cubits: Ezek. 40: 3, 5. 7. in *music, a)* in certain wind instruments, as the clarinet, a thin strip of some flexible substance, placed against the opening of the mouthpiece so as to leave a narrow opening: when vibrated by the breath, it produces a musical tone. *b)* an instrument with a reed or reeds. *c)* in an organ, a similar contrivance that vibrates in a current of air. 8. in *weaving*, a device on a loom, by means of which threads are drawn between the separated threads of the warp. *v.t.* 1. to thatch with reeds. 2. to decorate with reeds.

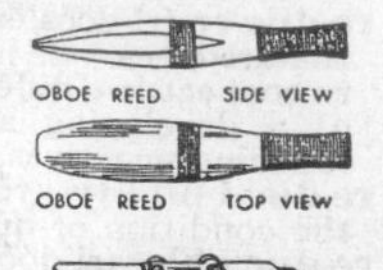

REEDS

Reed, John (rēd), 1887–1920; American journalist and poet.

Reed, Stanley For·man (fôr′mən), 1884– ; American jurist; associate justice, United States Supreme Court (1938–1957).

Reed, Walter, 1851–1902; American army surgeon and bacteriologist.

reed·bird (rēd′bũrd′), *n.* the bobolink.

reed·buck (rēd′buk′), *n.* [*pl.* REEDBUCK, REEDBUCKS (-buks′); see PLURAL, II, D, 2], [transl. of D. *rietbok*], any of several small, marsh-dwelling African antelopes with widely spread hooves and, in the males, backward-sloping, ringed horns turned inward and forward near the tips.

reed bunting, a European bird of the bunting family, having a black head, brown back, and white under parts, and living in marshes and swamps.

reed·i·ly (rēd′′l-i), *adv.* in a reedy manner.

reed·i·ness (rēd′i-nis), *n.* the quality of being reedy.

reed·ing (rēd′iŋ), *n.* [*reed* + *-ing*], 1. *a)* a small, rounded molding resembling a reed. *b)* a set of such moldings, as on a column. 2. ornamentation consisting of such moldings. 3. decoration by the use of woven reeds.

reed instrument, any instrument whose sound is produced by the vibration of a reed, or thin strip of flexible substance: reed instruments include the oboe, clarinet, saxophone, English horn, and bassoon.

reed·ling (rēd′liŋ), *n.* [*reed* + *-ling*], a small European bird with a long tail and orange-brown, black, and white plumage, found in reedy places, as marshes: the male has a black tuft on each side of the face.

reed mace, the cattail.

reed organ, an organ with a set of free metal reeds instead of pipes to produce the tones: cf. **reed pipe.**

reed pipe, an organ pipe in which the tone is produced by a current of air striking a vibrating reed in an opening in the pipe: distinguished from *flue pipe.*

reed stop, 1. a set of reed pipes (in an organ) operated by one knob. 2. the knob.

re·ed·u·cate, re·ëd·u·cate (rē-ej′oo-kāt′), *v.t.* to educate again or anew; especially, to rehabilitate (a handicapped person, etc.) by special training or schooling.

reed warbler, any of various small warblers of Europe and Asia living in marshes and swamps.

reed·y (rēd′i), *adj.* [REEDIER (-i-ẽr), REEDIEST (-i-ist)], 1. full of reeds. 2. made of reed or reeds. 3. like a reed. 4. sounding like a reed instrument; thin; piping.

reef (rēf), *n.* [ME. *riff;* ON. *rif*, lit., a rib], 1. a line or ridge of rock or sand lying at or near the surface of the water. 2. in *mining*, a bed of ore; lode; vein. —*SYN.* see **shoal.**

reef (rēf), *n.* [Early Mod. Eng. phonetic sp. of ME. *riff;* cf. LEECH (of a sail)], in *nautical usage,* 1. a part of a sail which can be folded together and tied down in order to reduce the area exposed to the wind. 2. the act of reefing. *v.t.* 1. to cut down the size of (a sail) by taking in and tying down part of it. 2. to lower (a spar); shorten (a mast or bowsprit) by taking part of it in, lowering it, etc.

reef·er (rēf′ẽr), *n.* 1. a person who reefs: formerly a slang term for a midshipman. 2. a short, thick, double-breasted coat, worn especially by sailors. 3. a woman's form-fitting, double-breasted coat, similar to this. 4. [from the rolled appearance of a *reef* (of a sail)], [Slang], a marijuana cigarette.

reef knot, a common square knot: see **knot,** illus.

reek (rēk), *n.* [ME. *reke;* AS. *rec;* akin to G. *rauch;* only Gmc.], 1. vapor; fume. 2. a strong, unpleasant smell. 3. [Dial.], smoke. *v.i.* [ME. *reken* < the *n.*], 1. to give off steam or smoke. 2. to have a strong, offensive smell. 3. to be permeated with anything very unpleasant. *v.t.* 1. to expose to the action of smoke, etc. 2. to emit or exude (vapor, fumes, etc.).

reek·y (rēk′i), *adj.* [REEKIER (-i-ẽr), REEKIEST (-i-ist)], full of or giving off reek.

reel (rēl), *v.i.* [ME. *relen* < the *n.*: from the sensation of whirling], 1. to give way; fall back; sway, swing, or stagger from shock: as, the line of battle *reeled.* 2. to stagger; lurch violently in moving; swing; sway, as from drunkenness. 3. to go around and around; whirl. 4. to be dizzy; have a sensation of spinning or whirling. *v.t.* to cause to reel. *n.* [ME. *rele;* AS. *hreol;* see next entry], a reeling; whirl; swaying motion; stagger. —*SYN.* see **stagger.**

reel (rēl), *n.* [< *reel* (a whirl): from the movement], 1. a lively Scottish dance, forerunner of many others. 2. the Virginia reel. 3. music for any of these dances.

reel (rēl), *n.* [ME. *rel, rele;* AS. *hreol* < Gmc. **hrehulaz;* prob. IE. base **grek-*, to strike, hence to weave, make a weaving motion], 1. any frame or spool on which thread, wire, film, nets, etc. may be wound: it usually turns on an axle, often by the power of a hand crank. 2. such a frame set on the handle of a fishing rod, to wind up or let out the line. 3. the quantity of wire, thread, etc. usually wound on one reel. 4. about one thousand feet of motion-picture film. *v.t.* 1. to wind on or off a reel (with *in* or *out*). 2. to pull in (a fish) by winding a line on a reel (with *in*). 3. to tell, write, produce, etc. fluently and easily (with *off*).

off the reel, fluently; easily; without hesitation.

re-en·force, re·ën·force (rē′in-fôrs′, rē′in-fōrs′), *v.t. & n.* reinforce.

re-en·ter, re·ën·ter (rē-en′tẽr), *v.t. & v.i.* to enter again (in various senses).

re-entering angle, an angle in a geometric figure with its point turning back into the figure rather than out from it.

re-entering polygon, a polygon with one or more re-entering angles.

re-en·trance, re·ën·trance (rē-en′trəns), *n.* a re-entering; re-entry.

re-en·trant, re·ën·trant (rē-en′trənt), *adj.* re-entering; pointed inward: said of angles, etc. *n.* a re-entrant angle or part.

re-en·try, re·ën·try (rē-en′tri), *n.* 1. a re-entering. 2. a second or repeated entry. 3. in *bridge & whist*, a card that will win a trick and recover the lead. 4. in *law*, a coming into possession again under a right reserved in a prior transfer of property.

reeve (rēv), *n.* [ME. *refe*, earlier *irefe;* AS. *gerefa;* prob. < base of *refan*, to call out; cf. SHERIFF], 1. in *English history, a)* the chief officer, under the king, of a town or district. *b)* the overseer of a manor; steward; bailiff. 2. in Canada, the president of a village or town council.

reeve (rēv), *v.t.* [REEVED (rēvd) or ROVE (rōv); also, for pp., ROVEN (rōv′′n); REEVING], [prob. < D. *reven*, to reef, in sense "use a rope in or as in reefing"], in *nautical usage,* 1. to slip (a rope end, etc.) through a block, ring, or cleat. 2. *a)* to pass in, through, or around something. *b)* to fasten by so doing. 3. to pass a rope through (a block or pulley).

reeve (rēv), *n.* [also *ree;* prob. < dial. *ree, reeve*, to sift or winnow corn; etymologically unconnected with *ruff*], the female of the ruff (sandpiper).

re-ex·am·i·na·tion, re·ëx·am·i·na·tion (rē′ig-zam′ə-nā′shən), *n.* 1. a second or repeated examination. 2. in *law*, the questioning of a witness by the side for which he has been testifying, after, and about what has been said in, the cross-examination.

re-ex·am·ine, re·ëx·am·ine (rē′ig-zam′in), *v.t.* 1. to examine again. 2. in *law*, to subject to re-examination.

re-ex·port, re·ëx·port (rē′iks-pôrt′, rē′iks-pōrt′; *for n.,* rē-eks′pôrt, rē-eks′pōrt), *v.t.* to export again, as imported goods. *n.* 1. a re-exporting. 2. what is re-exported.

ref., 1. referee. 2. reference. 3. referred. 4. reformation. 5. reformed. 6. reformer.

re·face (rē-fās′), *v.t.* [REFACED (-fāst′), REFACING], to put a new face, facing, or surface on.

Ref. Ch., Reformed Church.

re·fect (ri-fekt′), *v.t.* [Late ME., partly back-formation < *refection*, partly < L. *reficere*, lit., to remake], [Obs.], to refresh with food or drink.

re-edit
re-elect
re-election
re-elevate
re-embark
re-embody
re-embrace
re-emerge
re-emergence
re-emigrate
re-emphasize
re-enact
re-enaction
re-enactment
re-encourage
re-endow
re-engage
re-engagement
re-enjoy
re-enlist
re-enlistment
re-enslave
re-erect
re-erection
re-establish
re-establishment
re-exhibit
re-expel
re-experience
re-explain
refashion
refasten

re·fec·tion (ri-fek′shən), *n.* [ME.; OFr.; L. *refectio* < pp. of *reficere* < *re-*, again + *facere*, to make], 1. food or drink taken after a period of hunger or fatigue; refreshment. 2. a light meal; lunch; repast.

re·fec·to·ry (ri-fek′tə-ri), *n.* [*pl.* REFECTORIES (-riz)], [ML. *refectorium* < pp. of L. *reficere;* see REFECTION], a dining hall in a monastery, convent, college, etc.

refectory table, 1. a long, narrow, rectangular table used in a dining hall, especially of a monastery or convent. 2. a dinner table of similar shape, now usually with extensible leaves at both ends.

re·fer (ri-fũr′), *v.t.* [REFERRED (-fũrd′), REFERRING], [OFr. *referer;* L. *referre; re-*, back + *ferre*, to bear], 1. to assign (*to*); regard as caused by or originated in: as, he *referred* his troubles to the war. 2. to assign, or regard or name as belonging (*to* a kind, class, date, etc.). 3. to submit (a quarrel, question, etc.) for determination or settlement. 4. to send or direct (a person) *to* someone or something for aid, information, etc. *v.i.* 1. to relate, or be concerned (with): used with *to*, as, the book *referred* only to fish. 2. to direct attention, or make reference or allusion (with *to*): as, he *referred* lightly to his wound. 3. to turn for information, aid, authority, etc. (with *to*): as, *refer* to a map. *SYN.*—**refer** implies deliberate, direct, and open mention of something (he *referred* in detail to their corrupt practices); **allude** implies indirect, often casual mention, as by a hint, a figure of speech, etc. (although he used different names, he was *alluding* to his co-workers).

ref·er·a·ble (ref′ẽr-ə-b'l), *adj.* that can be referred.

ref·er·ee (ref′ə-rē′), *n.* 1. a person to whom anything is referred for decision. 2. in *law*, a person appointed by a court to study, take testimony in, and report his judgment on, a matter. 3. in *sports*, an umpire; judge of a game, as of a boxing match. *v.t.* [REFEREED (-rēd′), REFEREEING], to act as referee in. *v.i.* to act as referee. Abbreviated **ref.** —*SYN.* see **judge.**

ref·er·ence (ref′ẽr-əns), *n.* 1. a referring or being referred; submission of a problem, dispute, etc. to a person, committee, or authority for settlement. 2. relation; regard: as, with *reference* to his reply. 3. the directing of attention to a person or thing; hence, 4. a mention or allusion. 5. an indication, as in a book or article, of some other work or passage to be consulted; hence, 6. the work or passage so indicated. 7. the mark or sign, as a number or letter, directing the reader to a footnote, etc. 8. *a*) the giving of the name of another person who can offer information or recommendation. *b*) the person so indicated. 9. a written statement of character, qualification, or ability; testimonial. 10. use or consultation to get information, as an aid in research, etc.: often attributive, as, *reference* books. Abbreviated **ref.**

make reference to, to refer to; mention.

reference mark, any symbol used in printing and writing to mark a reference, as *, †, ‡, ¶, §.

ref·er·en·dum (ref′ə-ren′dəm), *n.* [*pl.* REFERENDUMS (-dəmz), REFERENDA (-də)], [L., a carrying back, gerund or neut. gerundive of *referre;* see REFER], 1. the submission of a law, proposed or already in effect, to a direct vote of the people. 2. the right of the people to vote directly on such laws, superseding or overruling the legislature. 3. the vote itself. 4. a note sent by a diplomatic agent to his own government, asking for specific instructions.

ref·er·ent (ref′ẽr-ənt), *n.* [L. *referens*, ppr.], what is referred to; especially, in *semantics*, the object referred to by a term.

ref·er·en·tial (ref′ə-ren′shəl), *adj.* [< *reference* (as if < L. **referentia*) + *-al*], 1. having reference (*to* something). 2. containing a reference or references. 3. used for reference.

re·fer·ra·ble, re·fer·ri·ble (ri-fũr′ə-b'l), *adj.* referable.

re·fer·ral (ri-fũr′əl), *n.* a referring or being referred, as for professional service, etc.

re·fer·rer (ri-fũr′ẽr), *n.* a person who refers.

re·fill (rē-fil′; *for n.*, rē′fil′), *v.t.* to fill again. *n.* a new filling or charge; especially, a unit made to replace the contents of a container that is not itself discarded after use: as, a *refill* for a ball-point pen.

re·fine (ri-fīn′), *v.t.* [*re-* + *fine*, to make fine, after Fr. *raffiner*, to purify], 1. to make fine or pure; free from impurities, dross, alloy, sediment, etc.; purify; clarify. 2. to free from imperfection, vulgarity, commonness, etc.; make more elegant or cultivated; impart polish to; improve, as language. 3. to remove in purifying; take out (with *out* or *away*). *v.i.* 1. to become fine or pure; become free from impurities, etc. 2. to become more polished or elegant. 3. to use niceties and fine distinctions; be subtle, as in language.

refine on (or **upon**), to improve, as by adding refinements.

re·fined (ri-fīnd′), *adj.* [pp. of *refine*], 1. made free from other matter, or from impurities; purified. 2. characterized by cultivation or elegance; free from vulgarity or coarseness: said of manners, speech, character, etc. 3. characterized by more than ordinary subtlety, exactness, precision, etc.

re·fine·ment (ri-fīn′mənt), *n.* 1. a refining or being refined. 2. the result of this; hence, 3. delicacy or elegance of language, speech, manners, etc.; polish; cultivation. 4. a development; improvement; elaboration: as, his solicitude was a *refinement* of cruelty.

re·fin·er·y (ri-fīn′ẽr-i), *n.* [*pl.* REFINERIES (-iz)], [< *refine* + *-ery*, after Fr. *raffinerie*], an establishment or plant for refining, or purifying, materials such as oil, metal, sugar, fats, etc.

re·fit (rē-fit′; *also, for n.*, rē′fit′), *v.t. & v.i.* [REFITTED (-id), REFITTING], to make or be made ready or fit for use again, as by repairing, re-equipping, or re-supplying. *n.* a refitting.

refl., 1. reflection. 2. reflective. 3. reflex. 4. reflexive.

re·flate (ri-flāt′), *v.i. & v.t.* [REFLATED (-id), REFLATING], to reinflate.

re·flect (ri-flekt′), *v.t.* [ME. *reflecten;* OFr. *reflecter;* L. *reflectere; re-*, back + *flectere*, to bend], 1. to bend or throw back, as light, heat, or sound. 2. to give back an image of; mirror or reproduce. 3. to cast or bring back as a consequence (with *on*): as, his deeds *reflect* honor on the nation. 4. [Rare], to fold or turn back. *v.i.* 1. to be bent or thrown back: as, the light *reflected* from the water into his eyes. 2. to bend or throw back light, heat, sound, etc. 3. *a*) to give back an image or likeness. *b*) to be mirrored. 4. to think seriously; contemplate; ponder (with *on* or *upon*). 5. to cast blame or discredit (with *on* or *upon*). —*SYN.* see **consider, think.**

reflecting telescope, a telescope with a concave mirror at the lower end of the tube, which receives the light from the object and reflects it to a focus near the top of the tube.

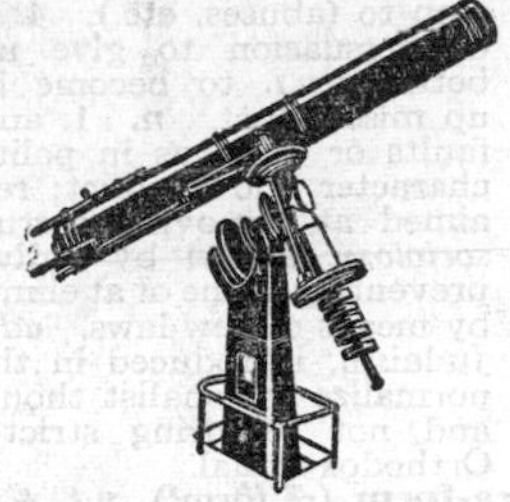
REFLECTING TELESCOPE

re·flec·tion (ri-flek′shən), *n.* [ME. *reflexion;* OFr. *reflexion;* LL. *reflexio*], 1. a reflecting or being reflected. 2. the throwing back by a surface of sound, light, heat, etc. 3. anything reflected. 4. an image; likeness. 5. the fixing of the mind on some subject; serious thought; contemplation. 6. the result of such thought; idea or conclusion, especially if expressed in words. 7. blame; discredit. 8. a remark or statement imputing discredit or blame. 9. an action bringing discredit. 10. in *anatomy & zoology*, a turning or bending back on itself. Also spelled **reflexion.** Abbreviated **refl.**

re·flec·tion·al (ri-flek′shən-'l), *adj.* of reflection.

re·flec·tive (ri-flek′tiv), *adj.* 1. reflecting. 2. of or produced by reflection. 3. meditative; thoughtful. Abbreviated **refl.** —*SYN.* see **pensive.**

re·flec·tiv·i·ty (rē′flek-tiv′ə-ti), *n.* the quality or condition of being reflective.

re·flec·tor (ri-flek′tẽr), *n.* 1. a person or thing that reflects; especially, a surface, object, etc. that reflects light, sound, heat, or the like, as a piece of glass or metal, highly polished and usually concave, which reflects and directs rays or a beam of light. 2. a reflecting telescope. 3. in *photography*, an adjustable, movable screen used to reflect and control light.

‡re·flet (rə-fle′), *n.* [Fr., reflection; see REFLECT], luster or iridescence, as a metallic glaze on pottery.

re·flex (rē′fleks; *for v.*, ri-fleks′), *n.* [< L. *reflexus*, reflected, pp. of *reflectere;* see REFLECT], 1. *a*) reflection, as of light. *b*) light or color resulting from reflection. 2. a reflected image, likeness, or reproduction. 3. in *art*, light reflected from a lighted to a shaded surface. 4. in *physiology*, a reflex action. 5. in *radio*, a reflex apparatus. *adj.* 1. turned, bent, or reflected back. 2. coming in reaction or reflection: as, a *reflex* effect; especially, in *physiology*, designating or of an involuntary action, as a sneeze, resulting when a stimulus is carried by an afferent nerve to a nerve center and the response is reflected along an efferent nerve to some muscle or gland. 3. in *geometry*, designating an angle greater than a straight angle. 4. in *radio*, designating or of an apparatus in which some device functions in a double capacity, as a receiving set in which the same

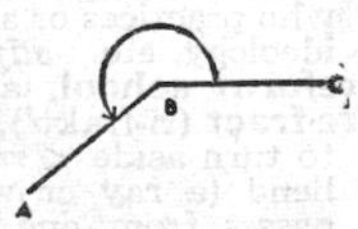

REFLEX ANGLE

tube is both audio-frequency and radio-frequency amplifier. ***v.t.*** 1. to bend, turn, or fold back. 2. to cause to undergo a reflex process. Abbreviated **refl.**

reflex arc, in *physiology,* the entire nerve path involved in a reflex action.

reflex camera, a camera in which the image formed by the lens is reflected by a mirror onto a ground-glass plate to help in focusing the lens.

re·flex·ion (ri-flek′shən), ***n.*** 1. reflection. 2. in *anatomy,* etc., a bending or folding back on itself, as of a part.

re·flex·ive (ri-flek′siv), ***adj.*** 1. reflex. 2. reflective. 3. in *grammar, a)* expressing an action turned back upon the subject; designating a verb whose subject and direct object are identical (e.g., *wash* in "I wash myself"). *b)* designating a pronoun used as the direct object of such a verb, as *myself* in the above example. ***n.*** a reflexive verb or pronoun. Abbreviated **refl.**

re·flex·iv·i·ty (rē′flek-siv′ə-ti), ***n.*** the condition or quality of being reflexive.

ref·lu·ence (ref′lo͞o-əns), ***n.*** [< *refluent*], reflux.

ref·lu·ent (ref′lo͞o-ənt), ***adj.*** [L. *refluens,* ppr. of *refluere,* to flow back; see RE- & FLUENT], flowing back; ebbing, as the tide to the sea.

re·flux (rē′fluks′), ***n.*** [ME.; ML. *refluxus,* pp. of L. *refluere;* see REFLUENT], a flowing back; ebbing, as of a tide: as, the flux and *reflux* of the sea.

re·for·est (rē-fôr′ist, rē-for′ist), ***v.t. & v.i.*** to plant new trees on (land once forested).

re·for·est·a·tion (rē′fôr-is-tā′shən, rē′for-is-tā′shən), ***n.*** a reforesting or being reforested.

re·form (ri-fôrm′), ***v.t.*** [ME. *reformen;* OFr. *reformer;* L. *reformare;* see RE- & FORM], 1. to make better by removing faults and defects; correct. 2. to make better by putting a stop to abuses or malpractices, or by introducing better procedures, etc. 3. to put a stop to (abuses, etc.). 4. to bring (a person) by force or persuasion to give up misconduct and behave better. ***v.i.*** to become better; behave better; give up misconduct. ***n.*** 1. an improvement; correction of faults or evils, as in politics. 2. an improvement in character and conduct; reformation. 3. a movement aimed at removing corruption from politics. 4. in *sociology,* action by individuals or groups aimed at preventing crime or at eliminating or mitigating poverty by means of new laws. ***adj.*** [R.], designating a form of Judaism, introduced in the 19th century, seeking to normalize rationalist thought with historical Judaism and not requiring strict observance of traditional Orthodox ritual.

re-form (rē′fôrm′), ***v.t. & v.i.*** to form again.

ref·or·ma·tion (ref′ẽr-mā′shən), ***n.*** [ME. *reformacion;* L. *reformatio*], 1. a reforming or being reformed. 2. [R-], the 16th-century religious movement that aimed at reforming the Roman Catholic Church and resulted in establishing the Protestant churches.

ref·or·ma·tion·al (ref′ẽr-mā′shən-'l), ***adj.*** of reformation.

re·form·a·tive (ri-fôr′mə-tiv), ***adj.*** [ML. *reformativus*], reforming or tending to reform.

re·form·a·to·ry (ri-fôr′mə-tôr′i, ri-fôr′mə-tō′ri), ***adj.*** reforming or aiming at reform. ***n.*** [*pl.* REFORMATORIES (-iz, -riz)], an institution to which young offenders convicted of lesser crimes are sent for training and discipline intended to reform rather than punish them.

re·formed (ri-fôrmd′), ***adj.*** [pp. of *reform*], 1. improved or corrected, as in behavior or morals, or made better by the removal of errors, abuses, etc. 2. [R-], designating a Protestant church or churches, especially Calvinist as distinguished from Lutheran. 3. [R-], loosely, Reform.

re·form·er (ri-fôr′mẽr), ***n.*** 1. a person who reforms, or tries to reform, something, as morals, institutions, etc. 2. any of the leaders of the Reformation.

re·form·ist (ri-fôrm′ist; *occas.* ref′ẽr-mist), ***n.*** a person who practices or advocates reform, as of some doctrine, ideology, etc. ***adj.*** of or characteristic of reformists.

reform school, a reformatory.

re·fract (ri-frakt′), ***v.t.*** [< L. *refractus,* pp. of *refringere,* to turn aside < *re-,* back + *frangere,* to break], 1. to bend (a ray or wave of light, heat, or sound) as it passes from one medium into another: said of the medium, as, glass *refracts* light. 2. in *optics,* to measure the degree of refraction of (an eye or lens).

refracting telescope, 1. a telescope in which a large double-convex lens (*object glass*) causes light rays to converge to a focus, forming an image magnified by a double-convex eyepiece. 2. a similar telescope, in which the converging rays are intercepted by a double-concave eyepiece.

re·frac·tion (ri-frak′shən), ***n.*** [LL. *refractio*], 1. a refracting or being refracted; bending of a ray or wave of light, heat, or sound, as it passes obliquely from one medium to another of different density, in which its speed is different, or through layers of different density in the same medium; hence, 2. in *astronomy,* the bending of the rays of light from a star or planet, greatest when the star or planet is lowest in the sky, so that it seems higher than it really is. 3. in *optics, a)* the ability of the eye to refract light entering it, so as to form an image on the retina. *b)* the measuring of the degree of refraction of the eye.

re·frac·tion·al (ri-frak′shən-'l), ***adj.*** of refraction.

re·frac·tive (ri-frak′tiv), ***adj.*** 1. refracting or having power to refract. 2. of or caused by refraction.

re·frac·tiv·i·ty (rē′frak-tiv′ə-ti), ***n.*** the condition or quality of being refractive.

re·frac·tom·e·ter (rē′frak-tom′ə-tẽr), ***n.*** [see -METER], an instrument for measuring refraction, as of the eye.

re·frac·tor (ri-frak′tẽr), ***n.*** 1. something that refracts. 2. a refracting telescope.

re·frac·to·ri·ly (ri-frak′tə-rə-li), ***adv.*** in a refractory manner.

re·frac·to·ri·ness (ri-frak′tə-ri-nis), ***n.*** the quality or state of being refractory.

re·frac·to·ry (ri-frak′tə-ri), ***adj.*** [altered < obs. form *refractary;* L. *refractarius* < *refractus;* see REFRACT], 1. stubborn; obstinate; hard to manage: said of a person or animal. 2. resistant to heat; hard to melt or work: said of ores or metals. 3. not yielding to treatment, as a disease. 4. able to resist disease. —***SYN.*** see **unruly.**

re·frain (ri-frān′), ***v.i.*** [ME. *refreinen;* OFr. *refrener;* L. *refrenare; re-,* back + *frenare,* to curb < *frenum,* a rein], to hold back; keep oneself (*from*); forbear (often with *from*). ***v.t.*** [Archaic], to hold back; curb.

SYN.—**refrain** usually suggests the curbing of a passing impulse in keeping oneself from saying or doing something (although provoked, he *refrained* from answering); **abstain** implies voluntary self-denial or the deliberate giving up of something (to *abstain* from liquor); **forbear** suggests self-restraint manifesting a patient endurance under provocation (to *forbear* venting one's wrath).

re·frain (ri-frān′), ***n.*** [ME. *refreine;* OFr. *refrain* < *refraindre,* to restrain, modulate < LL. **refrangere,* for L. *refringere,* to break off < *re-,* back + *frangere,* to break], 1. a phrase or verse repeated at intervals in a song or poem. 2. music for this.

re·fran·gi·bil·i·ty (ri-fran′jə-bil′ə-ti), ***n.*** the state or quality of being refrangible.

re·fran·gi·ble (ri-fran′jə-b'l), ***adj.*** [< *re-* + L. *frangere,* to break; + *-ible*], that can be refracted, as light rays.

re·fresh (ri-fresh′), ***v.t.*** [ME. *refreschen;* OFr. *refrescher, refreschier;* see RE- & FRESH], 1. to make fresh by cooling, wetting, or airing, as a room, etc. 2. to make (a person) feel cooler, stronger, more energetic, etc. than before, as by food, drink, or sleep: also used reflexively. 3. to renew; replenish, as by new supplies, etc.; revive, as the memory. ***v.i.*** 1. to become fresh again; revive. 2. to take refreshment, as food or drink. 3. to lay in fresh supplies. —***SYN.*** see **renew.**

re·fresh·er course (ri-fresh′ẽr), a course of study reviewing material previously studied.

re·fresh·ing (ri-fresh′iŋ), ***adj.*** 1. that refreshes. 2. pleasingly new or different.

re·fresh·ment (ri-fresh′mənt), ***n.*** [OFr. *refreschement*], 1. a refreshing or being refreshed. 2. something that refreshes, as food, drink, rest, etc.; hence, 3. *pl.* food or drink or both, especially as a light meal.

re·frig·er·ant (ri-frij′ẽr-ənt), ***adj.*** [L. *refrigerans,* ppr.], 1. refrigerating; cooling or freezing something. 2. reducing heat or fever. ***n.*** 1. a medicine used to reduce fever. 2. a substance used in refrigeration, as ice or solid carbon dioxide. 3. any of various liquids that vaporize at a low temperature, used in mechanical refrigeration.

re·frig·er·ate (ri-frij′ə-rāt′), ***v.t.*** [REFRIGERATED (-id), REFRIGERATING], [< L. *refrigeratus,* pp. of *refrigerare,* to make cool or cold; *re-,* intens. + *frigerare,* to cool < *frigus,* cold], 1. to make or keep cool or cold; chill. 2. to preserve (food, etc.) by keeping cold or freezing.

re·frig·er·a·tion (ri-frij′ə-rā′shən), ***n.*** [L. *refrigeratio*], a refrigerating or being refrigerated; making or keeping cold or freezing for preservation, as food.

re·frig·er·a·tive (ri-frij′ə-rā′tiv), ***adj.*** refrigerating or serving to refrigerate.

re·frig·er·a·tor (ri-frij′ə-rā′tẽr), ***n.*** something that refrigerates; especially, a box, room, etc. in which food, drink, and the like are kept cool, as by ice or mechanical refrigeration.

refrigerator car, a railroad car built and equipped to keep perishable foods, etc. refrigerated in transit.

re·frig·er·a·to·ry (ri-frij′ẽr-ə-tôr′i, ri-frij′ẽr-ə-tō′ri), ***adj.*** [L. *refrigeratorius*], refrigerating.

re·frin·gent (ri-frin′jənt), ***adj.*** [L. *refringens,* ppr. of *refringere;* see REFRACT], refracting; refractive.

Ref. Sp., Reformed Spelling.

reft (reft), alternative past tense and past participle of **reave.** ***adj.*** robbed or bereft (*of* something).

re·fu·el (rē-fū′əl), ***v.t.*** to supply again with fuel. ***v.i.*** to take on a fresh supply of fuel.

ref·uge (ref′ūj), ***n.*** [ME.; OFr.; L. *refugium* < *refugere,*

reflourish
reflower
refold
reforge
reformulate
reformulation
refortify
refreeze

to retreat; *re-*, back + *fugere*, to flee], 1. shelter or protection from danger, difficulty, etc. 2. a person or thing that gives shelter, help, or comfort. 3. a place of safety; shelter; safe retreat. 4. an expediency; shift; action taken to escape consequences.—*SYN.* see **shelter.**

ref·u·gee (ref'yoo-jē'; *occas.* ref'yoo-jē'), *n.* [Fr. *réfugié*, pp. of *réfugier*, L. *refugere*; see REFUGE], a person who flees from his home or country to seek refuge elsewhere, as in a time of war, political or religious persecution, etc.

re·ful·gence (ri-ful'jəns), *n.* [L. *refulgentia*], the state or quality of being refulgent.

re·ful·gen·cy (ri-ful'jən-si), *n.* refulgence.

re·ful·gent (ri-ful'jənt), *adj.* [L. *refulgens*, ppr. of *refulgere*, to reflect light; see RE- & FULGENT], shining; radiant; glowing; resplendent.

re·fund (ri-fund'; *for n.*, rē'fund'), *v.t.* [ME. *refunden* < OFr. or L.; OFr. *refunder*; L. *refundere*; *re-*, back + *fundere*, to pour], 1. to give back or pay back (money, etc.); repay. 2. to make repayment to; reimburse (a person). *v.i.* to make repayment. *n.* a refunding or the amount refunded; repayment.

re·fund (rē'fund'), *v.t.* to fund again or anew; specifically, in *finance*, *a)* to use borrowed money, especially the proceeds from the sale of a bond issue, to pay back (a loan). *b)* to replace (an old bond issue) with a new bond issue, usually at a lower rate of interest.

re·fund·ment (ri-fund'mənt), *n.* repayment.

re·fur·bish (rē-fūr'bish), *v.t.* [*re-* + *furbish*], to brighten, freshen, or polish up again; renovate.

re·fus·al (ri-fū'z'l), *n.* 1. a refusing. 2. the right or chance to accept or refuse something before it is offered to another; option.

re·fuse (ri-fūz'), *v.t.* [REFUSED (-fūzd'), REFUSING], [ME. *refusen*; OFr. *refuser*; LL. **refusare* < L. *refusus*, pp. of *refundere*; see REFUND (to repay)], 1. to decline to accept; reject. 2. *a)* to decline to do, give, or grant. *b)* to decline (*to* do something): as, *refuse* to go. 3. to decline to accept or submit to (a command, etc.); decline to undergo. 4. to stop short at (a fence, etc.), without jumping it: said of a horse. 5. [Obs.], to renounce. 6. in *military usage*, to bring back out of line (the center or a flank) to protect against possible enemy attack from that sector. *v.i.* to decline to accept, agree to, or do something. —*SYN.* see **decline.**

ref·use (ref'ūs, ref'ūz), *n.* [ME.; OFr. *refus*, pp. of *refuser*; see REFUSE, *v.*], anything thrown away or rejected as worthless or useless; waste; trash; rubbish. *adj.* thrown away or rejected as worthless or useless.

ref·u·ta·ble (ref'yoo-tə-b'l, ri-fū'tə-b'l), *adj.* [LL. *refutabilis*], that can be refuted.

ref·u·ta·bly (ref'yoo-tə-bli, ri-fū'tə-bli), *adv.* in a refutable manner; so as to be refutable.

re·fut·al (ri-fū't'l), *n.* a refuting; refutation.

ref·u·ta·tion (ref'yoo-tā'shən), *n.* [L. *refutatio* < *refutatus*, pp.], 1. a refuting, or proving false or wrong; disproof. 2. something that refutes, as an argument.

re·fute (ri-fūt'), *v.t.* [REFUTED (-id), REFUTING], [L. *refutare*, to repel, repress, check; see RE- & CONFUTE], 1. to prove (a person) to be wrong; confute. 2. to prove (an argument or statement) to be false or wrong, by argument or evidence. —*SYN.* see **disprove.**

Reg., 1. *Regina*, [L.], Queen. 2. Regiment.

reg., 1. regent. 2. regiment. 3. region. 4. register. 5. registered. 6. registrar. 7. registry. 8. regular. 9. regulation. 10. regulator.

re·gain (ri-gān'), *v.t.* [MFr. *regaigner*; see RE- & GAIN], 1. to get into one's possession again; recover. 2. to get back to; succeed in reaching again. —*SYN.* see **recover.**

re·gal (rē'g'l), *adj.* [ME. < OFr. or L.; OFr. *regal*; L. *regalis* < *rex*, *regis*, a king; IE. base **reĝ-*, straight, lead, direct, direction, seen also in L. *regere*, to rule, Sans. *rāj* (cf. RAJAH), AS. *riht* (cf. RIGHT), *rice* (cf. RICH)], 1. of a king; royal. 2. characteristic of, like, or fit for a king; splendid, stately, magnificent, etc.

re·gale (ri-gāl'), *v.t.* [REGALED (-gāld'), REGALING], [Fr. *régaler* < the *n.*], 1. to entertain; provide a splendid feast for. 2. to delight with something pleasing. *v.i.* to feast. *n.* [Fr. *régal*, earlier *régale* < *ré-* (see RE-) + OFr. *gale*, joy, pleasure (see GALLANT)], [Obs.], 1. a feast. 2. a choice food; delicacy. 3. refreshment.

re·gale·ment (ri-gāl'mənt), *n.* a regaling or being regaled.

re·ga·li·a (ri-gā'li-ə, ri-gāl'yə), *n.pl.* [L., neut. pl. of *regalis*; see REGAL], 1. rights or privileges belonging to a king; prerogatives of sovereignty. 2. the emblems and insignia of kingship, as a crown, scepter, etc. 3. the insignia or decorations of any rank or position, or of an order or society. 4. splendid clothes; finery.

re·gal·i·ty (ri-gal'ə-ti), *n.* [*pl.* REGALITIES (-tiz)], [OFr. *regalité*; see REGAL & -ITY], 1. kingship; royalty; sovereignty. 2. a country or area subject to the authority of a king; kingdom. 3. a right or privilege belonging to a king.

Re·gan (rē'gən), *n.* in Shakespeare's *King Lear*, the younger of Lear's two wicked daughters, married to the Duke of Cornwall: see **Goneril, Cordelia.**

re·gard (ri-gärd'), *n.* [ME.; Fr. < *regarder*; see RE- & GUARD], 1. a firm, fixed look; gaze. 2. consideration; attention; concern: as, with special *regard* for your safety. 3. respect and affection; esteem: as, he had high *regard* for his teachers. 4. reference; respect; relation: as, in *regard* to your question. 5. *pl.* good wishes; respects; affection: often used as a complimentary close to a letter. 6. [Obs.], aspect; appearance. *v.t.* 1. to observe or look at with a firm, steady gaze; look at attentively. 2. to take into account; consider. 3. to give attentive heed or respect to. 4. to hold in affection and respect: as, he *regards* his brothers highly. 5. to consider in a certain light or as being something: as, I *regard* this as a nuisance. 6. to have relation to; concern; have reference to: as, this proposal *regards* your welfare. 7. [Obs.], to care for. *v.i.* 1. to look; gaze. 2. to pay heed or attention.

as regards, concerning.

without regard to, not taking into account.

SYN.—**regard** is the most neutral of the terms here, in itself usually implying evaluation of worth rather than recognition of it (the book is highly *regarded* by authorities); **respect** implies high valuation of worth, as shown in deference or honor (a jurist *respected* by lawyers); **esteem,** in addition, suggests that the person or object is highly prized or cherished (a friend *esteemed* for his loyalty); **admire** suggests a feeling of enthusiastic delight in the appreciation of that which is superior (one must *admire* such courage).

re·gard·ant (ri-gär'dənt), *adj.* [Fr., ppr. of *regarder*; see REGARD], in *heraldry*, looking backward, with the face in profile.

re·gard·ful (ri-gärd'fəl), *adj.* 1. observant; heedful; attentive; mindful (often with *of*). 2. showing regard; respectful or considerate.

re·gard·ing (ri-gär'diŋ), *prep.* in (or with) regard to; concerning; about.

re·gard·less (ri-gärd'lis), *adj.* without regard; heedless; unmindful; careless (often with *of*): as, *regardless* of the cost. *adv.* [Colloq.], without regard for, or in spite of, objections, difficulties, etc.; anyway.

re·gard·less·ly (ri-gärd'lis-li), *adv.* in a regardless manner.

re·gat·ta (ri-gat'ə), *n.* [It. (Venetian) *regata*, *regatta* (whence also Fr. *régate*), gondola race, lit. a striving for mastery < *regatar*, to compete], 1. originally, a gondola race in Venice; hence, 2. *a)* any boat race. *b)* a series of such races.

re·ge·late (rē'jə-lāt', rē'jə-lāt'), *v.i.* [REGELATED (-id), REGELATING], to undergo regelation.

re·ge·la·tion (rē'jə-lā'shən), *n.* [see RE- & GELATION], a refreezing or freezing together, as of pieces of moist ice under pressure at a temperature above the freezing point.

re·gen·cy (rē'jən-si), *n.* [*pl.* REGENCIES (-siz)], [ME. *regencie*], 1. the position, function, or authority of a regent or group of regents. 2. a group of men appointed to carry on the government while a king or other hereditary ruler is out of the country, too young, or mentally or physically unable to do so himself. 3. a country or district so governed. 4. the time during which a regent or regency governs; hence, 5. [R-], *a)* in England, the period between 1811 and 1820. *b)* in France, the period between 1715 and 1723. *adj.* [R-], designating or of a style of furniture developed in France between 1715 and 1723, characterized by scrollwork combined with natural forms, many curves, and strict balance and proportion.

re·gen·er·a·cy (ri-jen'ēr-ə-si), *n.* the condition of being regenerate.

re·gen·er·ate (ri-jen'ēr-it; *for v.*, ri-jen'ə-rāt'), *adj.* [< L. *regeneratus*, pp. of *regenerare*, to generate again; see RE- & GENERATE], 1. spiritually reborn. 2. renewed; restored; made better, especially after a decline to a low or abject condition. *v.t.* [REGENERATED (-id), REGENERATING], 1. to cause to be spiritually reborn, as by a religious conversion. 2. to cause to be completely reformed or improved. 3. to form or bring into existence again; re-establish on a new basis. 4. in *electricity & radio*, to amplify by feeding energy back from the output into the input circuit. 5. in *mechanics*, to make use in any way of (heat, energy, pressure, etc. which would otherwise be wasted). 6. in *botany & zoology*, to grow (a part) anew, as a replacement for one hurt or lost. *v.i.* 1. to form again; be made anew. 2. to be regenerated; be reborn spiritually; be reformed or reconstituted. 3. to have a regenerative effect.

re·gen·er·a·tion (ri-jen'ə-rā'shən), *n.* [ME. *regener-*

acioun; OFr.; LL. *regeneratio*], 1. a regenerating or being regenerated; a being renewed, reformed, or reconstituted. 2. a spiritual rebirth or conversion. 3. in *botany & zoology,* the renewal or replacement of any hurt or lost organ or part, as the arm of a starfish or claw of a lobster. 4. in *radio,* the amplification of a radio signal by feeding energy from the output back into the input circuit.

re·gen·er·a·tive (ri-jen′ə-rā′tiv, ri-jen′ẽr-ə-tiv), *adj.* [Fr. *régénératif;* ML. *regenerativus*], 1. regenerating or tending to regenerate. 2. of regeneration.

re·gen·er·a·tor (ri-jen′ə-rā′tẽr), *n.* 1. a person or thing that regenerates. 2. a device used in a furnace or engine to preheat incoming air or gas by exposing it to the heat of exhaust gases.

Re·gens·burg (rā′gəns-boorkh′; Eng. rā′gənz-bũrg′), *n.* a city in Bavaria, Germany, on the Danube River: pop., 125,000 (est. 1946): formerly called *Ratisbon.*

re·gent (rē′jənt), *adj.* [ME. < Fr. or L.; Fr. *régent;* L. *regens,* ppr. of *regere,* to rule; for base see REGAL], 1. acting in place of a king or ruler: as, prince *regent.* 2. [Rare], acting as ruler; ruling. *n.* 1. a person appointed to carry on a government while a king or other hereditary ruler is out of the country, too young, or mentally or physically unable to do so himself. 2. a member of a board appointed to govern a university or other institution, usually educational. 3. any of certain other university officers. 4. [Obs.], a ruler; governor. Abbreviated **Reg., reg., Regt.**

re·gent·ship (rē′jənt-ship′), *n.* [see -SHIP], the position or term of a regent.

Reg·gio di Ca·la·bri·a (red′jô dē kä-lä′brē-ä′), a city in southwestern Italy, on the Strait of Messina: pop., 137,000 (est. 1947): also **Reggio Calabria.**

Reg·gio nell'E·mi·lia (redj′ô nel′e-mēl′yä), *n.* a city in north central Italy: pop., 106,000 (est. 1947): also **Reggio Emilia.**

reg·i·cid·al (rej′ə-sīd′'l), *adj.* of a regicide.

reg·i·cide (rej′ə-sīd′), *n.* [< L. *rex, regis,* a king; + *-cide*], 1. a person who kills, or is responsible for the killing of, a king, especially of his own country; specifically, [R-], any of those who tried and executed Charles I of England. 2. the killing of a king.

re·gime, ré·gime (ri-zhēm′, rā-zhēm′), *n.* [Fr. *régime;* L. *regimen;* see REGIMEN], 1. a political system. 2. a social system; social order. 3. a course of treatment, as of diet and rest; regimen.

reg·i·men (rej′ə-men′, rej′ə-mən), *n.* [L., rule, government < *regere,* to rule], 1. [Archaic], *a)* government; administration; rule. *b)* a particular system of government; regime. 2. a regulated system of diet, exercise, rest, and general hygiene, intended to maintain or improve the health or to have some specific result. 3. [Rare], in *grammar,* government; the influence of one word over the case or mood of another.

reg·i·ment (rej′ə-mənt; *for v.,* rej′ə-ment′), *n.* [Fr. *régiment,* military division; OFr. *regiment, regement,* government; LL. *regimentum* < L. *regere,* to rule; for base see REGAL], 1. a military unit, now usually consisting of three battalions and service and administrative units: it is normally commanded by a colonel and is the basic component of a division: abbreviated **regt., reg.** 2. a large number (of persons, etc.). 3. [Obs.], rule; government. *v.t.* 1. to form into a regiment or regiments. 2. to assign to a regiment or group. 3. to form into an organized or uniform group or groups; organize systematically. 4. to organize and subject to strict discipline and control.

reg·i·men·tal (rej′ə-men′t'l), *adj.* of a regiment.

reg·i·men·tals (rej′ə-men′t'lz), *n.pl.* 1. the uniform and insignia worn by a particular regiment; hence, 2. military uniform.

reg·i·men·ta·tion (rej′ə-men-tā′shən), *n.* a regimenting or being regimented.

Re·gi·na (ri-jī′nə; *for the fem. name, also* ri-jē′nə), [L., queen], a feminine name. *n.* 1. [also r-], queen: the official title of a reigning queen, as, Victoria *Regina:* abbreviated **Reg., R., r.** 2. the capital of Saskatchewan, Canada: pop., 71,000.

re·gi·nal (ri-jī′n'l), *adj.* [ML. *reginalis* < L. *regina,* a queen], of, like, or characteristic of a queen; queenly: equivalent to *regal.*

Reg·i·nald (rej′i-nəld), [ML. *Reginaldus;* OG. *Raganald, Raginold* < Gmc. **ragina-, *ragna-,* judgment, counsel + **waldan,* to rule], a masculine name: diminutive, *Reggie;* variant, *Reynold;* equivalents, Fr. *Regnault, Renaud,* G. *Reinhold,* It. *Rinaldo,* Sp. *Reynaldos.*

re·gion (rē′jən), *n.* [ME. *regioun;* Anglo-Fr. *regiun* (OFr. *regium*); L. *regio* < *regere,* to rule; for base see REGAL], 1. a large and indefinite part of the surface of the earth; district. 2. an area; place; space. 3. a particular part of the world or universe. 4. a sphere; realm, as of art or science. 5. a division or part of an organism, often called after its main part or organ: as, the abdominal *region.* 6. any of the levels into which the atmosphere or ocean is thought of as being divided. 7. a division of the world according to the plants or animals found there. Abbreviated **reg.**

re·gion·al (rē′jən-'l), *adj.* 1. of a whole region, not just a locality. 2. of some particular region, district, etc.; local; sectional.

re·gion·al·ism (rē′jən-'l-iz'm), *n.* 1. *a)* the division of a country into small administrative regions. *b)* the principle of this. 2. regional quality or character. 3. in *literature, a)* the use of a particular region of a country as the setting of stories, plays, etc., representing it as affecting the lives of the characters. *b)* the tendency to emphasize and value the qualities of life in a particular region, especially an agrarian region as opposed to an urban and industrial one.

reg·is·ter (rej′is-tẽr), *n.* [ME. & OFr. *registre;* ML. *registrum,* altered form of *regestum* < LL. *regesta,* records, neut. pl. of L. *regestus,* pp. of *regerere,* to record], 1. *a)* a record or list of events, items, etc., often kept by an official appointed to do so. *b)* a book in which this is kept. 2. an entry in such a book or record. 3. a person who keeps such a record, especially one legally appointed; registrar. 4. registration; registry; enrollment. 5. a device for recording; meter or counter, as of fares paid, money deposited, etc.: as, a cash *register.* 6. *a)* a device in a stove or furnace for controlling the draft, etc. *b)* an opening into a room by which the amount of warm or cold air passing, as through a pipe leading from a furnace or ventilator, can be controlled. 7. in *music,* a musical range or compass, or a particular portion of the compass of an instrument or voice, of which all the tones are produced in the same manner or are similar in quality: as, head *register.* 8. in *photography,* exact matching in position of the focusing screen and the sensitive film or plate which replaces it. 9. in *printing, a)* exact matching in position of pages, lines, etc. on opposite sides of a single sheet. *b)* exact placing of successive colors as they are printed over each other. *v.t.* 1. to enter in a record or list; enroll; record officially. 2. to indicate on or as on a scale: as, the thermometer *registers* 50 degrees. 3. to show, as by facial expression: as, *register* surprise, anger, etc. 4. to safeguard (mail) by having its committal to the postal system recorded, on payment of a fee. 5. in *printing,* etc., to cause to be in register. *v.i.* 1. to enter one's name in a register, as of a hotel. 2. to have one's name placed on the list of those eligible to vote in an election, by making application in the prescribed way. 3. [Colloq.], to make an impression. 4. in *printing,* etc., to be in register. Abbreviated **reg.** —***SYN.*** see **list.**

reg·is·tered (rej′is-tẽrd), *adj.* [pp. of *register*], officially recorded or enrolled; specifically, *a)* designating bonds, etc. having the owner's name listed in a register. *b)* designating dogs, horses, etc. having pedigrees certified and listed by authorized breeders' associations. *c)* legally certified or authenticated. Abbreviated **reg.**

registered nurse, a nurse who has completed her training and has passed a State examination which qualifies her as a nurse in that State: abbreviated **R.N.**

reg·is·tra·ble (rej′is-trə-b'l), *adj.* that can be registered.

reg·is·trant (rej′is-trənt), *n.* [Fr.; ML. *registrans,* ppr.], a person who registers.

reg·is·trar (rej′i-strär′, rej′i-strär′), *n.* [ME. *registrer;* ML. *registrarius*], 1. a person charged with keeping a register; especially, a person responsible for the records in a college, court, etc. 2. a trust company charged with keeping the records of stock transfers, etc. Abbreviated **regr., reg.**

reg·is·tra·tion (rej′i-strā′shən), *n.* [ML. *registratio*], 1. a registering or being registered. 2. an entry in a register. 3. the number of persons registered.

reg·is·try (rej′is-tri), *n.* [*pl.* REGISTRIES (-triz)], 1. registration. 2. an office where registers are kept. 3. a register. Abbreviated **reg.**

re·gi·us (rē′ji-əs), *adj.* [L. < *rex, regis,* a king], 1. royal: designating certain British and Scottish university professorships founded or appointed by royal command. 2. designating a professor holding such a professorship. Abbreviated **R., Reg.**

reg·let (reg′lit), *n.* [Fr. *réglet* < *règle,* a rule; L. *regula;* see RULE], 1. in *architecture,* a flat, narrow molding, used to separate panels, etc. 2. in *printing,* a flat strip of wood or metal, lower than the type face, used to separate lines of type. 3. *a)* reglets collectively. *b)* material used in making these.

reg·ma (reg′mə), *n.* [*pl.* REGMATA (-mə-tə)], [Mod. L.; Gr. *rhēgma,* a fracture < *rhēgnynai,* to break], a dry fruit formed of three or more carpels that burst when ripe.

reg·nal (reg′nəl), *adj.* [ML. *regnalis* < L. *regnum,* reign], of a sovereign, sovereignty, or reign.

reg·nan·cy (reg′nən-si), *n.* the state of being regnant.

reg·nant (reg′nənt), *adj.* [L. *regnans,* ppr. of *regnare;* see REIGN], 1. reigning; ruling. 2. predominant. 3. prevalent; widespread.

re·gorge (ri-gôrj′), *v.t.* [REGORGED (-gôrjd′), REGORGING],

---

regerminate	**regild**	**regive**	**reglorify**
regermination	**regird**	**reglaze**	**reglue**

[Fr. *regorger;* see RE- & GORGE, *v.*], 1. to throw up or back; vomit up. 2. [Rare], to swallow again. *v.i.* to flow back; gush back, as water.

regr., registrar.

re·grant (rē-grant′), *v.t.* to grant again; renew the grant of. *n.* a renewed or second grant.

re·grate (ri-grāt′), *v.t.* [REGRATED (-id), REGRATING], [ME. *regraten;* OFr. *regrater;* ? < *re-*, again + *grater*, to scrape], 1. to buy up (commodities, especially marketable foods) for resale at a profit in the same or a near-by market. 2. to sell (commodities so bought) again.

re·gress (rē′gres; *for v.*, ri-gres′), *n.* [ME. *regresse;* L. *regressus*, pp. of *regredi*, to go back, return < *re-*, back + *gradi*, to go], 1. a going or coming back. 2. the right or privilege of this. 3. backward movement; retrogression. *v.i.* to go back; return; move backward.

re·gres·sion (ri-gresh′ən), *n.* [L. *regressio*], 1. a regressing; a going back; return; movement backward. 2. retrogression. 3. in *biology*, reversion to an earlier or simpler form, or to a general or common type. 4. in *psychoanalysis*, reversion to earlier behavior patterns, as to escape from an unpleasant situation.

re·gres·sive (ri-gres′iv), *adj.* 1. regressing or tending to regress. 2. of, like, or characteristic of regression.

re·gres·sor (ri-gres′ẽr), *n.* a person or thing that regresses.

re·gret (ri-gret′), *v.t.* [REGRETTED (-id), REGRETTING], [ME. *regretten, regreten;* OFr. *regreter* (later *regretter*), to bewail the dead; prob. < Gmc. base in AS. *gretan*, to weep (cf. GREET)], 1. to feel sorrow over; mourn for (a person or thing gone, lost, etc.). 2. to feel sorrow or remorse over (something that has happened, one's own acts, etc.). *n.* 1. sorrow or remorse over something that has happened, especially over something that one has done or left undone. 2. sorrow over a person or thing gone, lost, etc. —*SYN.* see **penitence.**
regrets, 1. feelings of sorrow over what has happened, something gone or lost, etc. 2. a polite expression of regret, as at declining an invitation.

re·gret·ful (ri-gret′fəl), *adj.* feeling or expressing regret.

re·gret·ta·ble (ri-gret′ə-b'l), *adj.* to be regretted; unfortunate.

re·gret·ta·bly (ri-gret′ə-bli), *adv.* 1. in a regrettable manner. 2. to a regrettable extent.

re·gret·ter (ri-gret′ẽr), *n.* a person who regrets.

re·group (rē-grōōp′), *v.t. & v.i.* to group again; specifically, in *military usage*, to reassemble or reorganize (one's forces), as after a battle.

Regt., 1. Regent. 2. Regiment.

reg·u·la·ble (reg′yoo-lə-b'l), *adj.* that can be regulated.

reg·u·lar (reg′yoo-lẽr), *adj.* [ME. *reguler;* OFr. *regulier;* L. *regularis* < *regula;* see RULE], 1. conforming in form, build, or arrangement to a rule, principle, type, standard, etc.; orderly; symmetrical: as, *regular* ranks, *regular* features. 2. characterized by conformity to a fixed principle or procedure. 3. usual; customary: as, he sat in his *regular* place. 4. consistent or habitual in action: as, a *regular* customer, *regular* in one's coming and going. 5. not changing; uniform: as, *regular* speed, a *regular* pulse. 6. conforming to a standard or to a generally accepted rule or mode of conduct; proper. 7. properly qualified: as, a *regular* doctor. 8. [Colloq.], thorough; complete: as, a *regular* nuisance. 9. [Colloq.], pleasant, amiable, dependable, etc. 10. in *botany*, having all similar parts of the same shape and size; symmetrical: said of flowers. 11. in *ecclesiastical usage*, being of a religious order or monastic community and adhering to its rule: opposed to *secular*. 12. in *grammar*, conforming to the usual type in inflection, formation, etc.; having no forms peculiar to itself or to only a few similar words: said mainly of verbs. 13. in *international law*, designating soldiers recognized as legitimate combatants in warfare. 14. in *mathematics*, *a*) having all angles and sides equal, as a polygon. *b*) having all faces exactly the same, as a polyhedron. *c*) governed by one law throughout, as an equation. 15. in *military usage*, designating or of the permanently constituted, or standing, army of a country. 16. in *politics*, designating, of, or loyal to the recognized party leadership, candidates, etc. *n.* 1. one of the regular clergy; member of a religious order, as a monk, friar, etc. 2. a regular soldier. 3. [Colloq.], one who is regular, as in habits. 4. in *politics*, a person who is loyal to the recognized party leadership, candidates, etc. Abbreviated **reg.** —*SYN.* see **normal, steady.**

Regular Army, the permanent, or standing, army of the United States; the United States Army: abbreviated **RA, R.A.:** cf. **Army of the United States.**

reg·u·lar·i·ty (reg′yoo-lar′ə-ti), *n.* [*pl.* REGULARITIES (-tiz)], state, quality, or instance of being regular.

reg·u·lar·ize (reg′yoo-lə-rīz′), *v.t.* [REGULARIZED (-rīzd′), REGULARIZING], to make regular.

reg·u·lar·ly (reg′yoo-lẽr-li), *adv.* 1. in a regular manner. 2. at regular times or intervals.

reg·u·late (reg′yoo-lāt′), *v.t.* [REGULATED (-id), REGULATING], [< L. *regulatus*, pp. of *regulare*, to rule, direct, regulate < *regula*, a rule; see RULE], 1. to control, direct, or govern according to a rule, principle, or system. 2. to adjust to a particular standard, rate, degree, amount, etc.: as, *regulate* the heat. 3. to adjust so as to make operate accurately, as a clock. 4. to make uniform, methodical, orderly, etc.

reg·u·la·tion (reg′yoo-lā′shən), *n.* 1. a regulating or being regulated. 2. a rule, ordinance, or law by which conduct, etc. is regulated. *adj.* 1. ordered or required by regulation; prescribed: as, a *regulation* uniform. 2. usual; normal; ordinary; regular. Abbreviated **reg.** —*SYN.* see **law.**

reg·u·la·tive (reg′yoo-lā′tiv), *adj.* regulating or tending to regulate.

reg·u·la·tor (reg′yoo-lā′tẽr), *n.* a person or thing that regulates; specifically, *a*) a mechanism for controlling or governing the movement of machinery, the flow of liquids, gases, electricity, steam, etc.; governor. *b*) the part of the works of a watch or clock by which its speed is adjusted. *c*) an accurate timepiece serving as a standard by which others are regulated. Abbreviated **reg.**

reg·u·la·to·ry (reg′yoo-lə-tôr′i, reg′yoo-lə-tō′ri), *adj.* regulating or tending to regulate.

Reg·u·lus (reg′yoo-ləs), *n.* (*Marcus Atilius Regulus*), Roman general and consul; lived ?–250? B.C.

reg·u·lus (reg′yoo-ləs), *n.* [*pl.* REGULUSES (-iz), REGULI (-lī′)], [L., little king, dim. < *rex, regis*, a king], 1. [R-], in *astronomy*, a star of the first magnitude in the constellation Leo. 2. in *chemistry* & *metallurgy*, *a*) metallic antimony: formerly so called because of its ready combination with gold, the "king of metals." *b*) impure metal produced by the smelting or reduction of various ores. *c*) partly purified metal that sinks by its weight to the bottom of a crucible when ore is smelted.

re·gur·gi·tant (rē-gũr′jə-tənt), *adj.* regurgitating; characterized by regurgitation.

re·gur·gi·tate (rē-gũr′jə-tāt′), *v.i.* [REGURGITATED (-id), REGURGITATING], [< ML. *regurgitatus*, pp. of *regurgitare*, to regurgitate; *re-*, back + LL. *gurgitare*, to flood], to rush, surge, or flow back. *v.t.* to cause to surge or flow back; specifically, to bring (partly digested food) from the stomach back to the mouth.

re·gur·gi·ta·tion (rē-gũr′jə-tā′shən), *n.* [ML. *regurgitatio*], a regurgitating; specifically, *a*) the return of partly digested food from the stomach to the mouth, as in a ruminant animal. *b*) a backward flow of blood due to the imperfect closure of a heart valve.

re·ha·bil·i·tate (rē′hə-bil′ə-tāt′, rē′ə-bil′ə-tāt′), *v.t.* [REHABILITATED (-id), REHABILITATING], [< ML. *rehabilitatus*, pp. of *rehabilitare*, to restore; see RE- & HABILITATE], 1. to restore to rank, privileges, or property which one has lost. 2. to restore the good name or reputation of; reinstate in good repute. 3. to put back in good condition; re-establish on a firm, sound basis. 4. in *sociology*, to restore (a dependent, defective, or criminal) to a state of physical, mental, and moral health through treatment and training.

re·ha·bil·i·ta·tion (rē′hə-bil′ə-tā′shən, rē′ə-bil′ə-tā′shən), *n.* a rehabilitating or being rehabilitated.

re·hash (rē-hash′; *for n.*, rē′hash′), *v.t.* [*re-* + *hash*], to work up again, as old materials for publication, or go over again, as old, familiar arguments. *n.* 1. a rehashing. 2. something rehashed.

re·hears·al (ri-hũr′s'l), *n.* 1. a rehearsing; reciting; recounting; repeating in order: as, a *rehearsal* of her troubles. 2. a drilling or repeating for practice and future performance. 3. a practice performance of a play, concert, etc., or of part of it, in preparation for a public or formal performance.
in rehearsal, being rehearsed, as a play.

re·hearse (ri-hũrs′), *v.t.* [REHEARSED (-hũrst′), REHEARSING], [ME. *rehersen, rehercen;* OFr. *rehercer, reherser; re-*, again + *hercer, herser*, to harrow < *herce, herse*, a harrow], 1. to repeat aloud as heard or read; recite. 2. to tell in detail; narrate or describe in sequence and at length. 3. to perform for practice, as a play, etc., in preparation for a public or formal performance. 4. to drill or train (a person) by practice in what he is to do. *v.i.* to rehearse a play, etc.

rei (rā), *n.* occasional, but erroneous, singular of **reis.**

Reich (rīk; G. rīH), *n.* [G.; akin to AS. *rice*, L. *rex;* for IE. base see RICH, REGAL], 1. the Holy Roman Empire, from its establishment in the 9th century to its dissolution in 1806 (**First Reich**). 2. Germany or

regrade **regraft** **regrasp** **rehandle** **reharden** **rehear** **reheat** **rehire**

the German government; specifically, *a*) the German Empire, from 1871 to 1919 (**Second Reich**). *b*) the German republic from 1919 to 1933 (**Weimar Republic**). *c*) the German fascist state under the Nazis from 1933 to 1945 (**Third Reich**).

Reichs·bank (rīks′baŋk′; G. rīHs′bäŋk′), ***n.*** [G.; see REICH & BANK], the national bank of Germany.

reichs·mark (rīks′märk′; G. rīHs′märk′), ***n.*** [*pl.* REICHSMARKS (-märks′), REICHSMARK], [G.; see REICH & MARK (coin)], the monetary unit of Germany, reconstituted and issued in November, 1924, equal to 23.8 cents; mark: see **Deutschemark, Ostmark**: abbreviated **RM., r.m.**

reichs·pfen·nig (rīks′fen′ig; G. rīHs′pfen′iH), ***n.*** [*pl.* REICHSPFENNIGS (-igz), G. REICHSPFENNIGE (-i-gə)], [G.; see REICH & PENNY], a minor bronze coin of Germany, equal to 1/100 reichsmark; pfennig.

‡**Reichs·rat, Reichs·rath** (rīHs′rät′), ***n.*** [G., genit. of *Reich* (see REICH) + *rat, rath,* council], the appointive upper house of the German legislature under the Weimar Republic.

Reichs·tag (rīks′täg′; G. rīHs′täkh′), ***n.*** [G. < *Reich,* empire + *tag,* session, meeting, lit. day; cf. DIET (assembly)], 1. formerly, the legislative assembly, or parliament, of Germany. 2. the building in Berlin where it met, destroyed by bombing in World War II.

‡**Reichs·wehr** (rīHs′vâr′), ***n.*** [G., lit., the empire's defense], the German army.

re·i·fy (rē′ə-fī′), ***v.t.*** [REIFIED (-fīd′), REIFYING], [< L. *res,* thing; + *-fy*], to treat (an abstraction) as substantially existing, or as a concrete material object.

reign (rān), ***n.*** [ME. *regne;* OFr. *regne, reigne;* L. *regnum* < *regere;* for base see REGAL], 1. royal power; authority; supreme rule. 2. dominance; prevalence; sway: as, the *reign* of fashion. 3. the period or time of ruling of a sovereign. 4. [Rare], a kingdom. ***v.i.*** [ME. *regnen;* OFr. *regner;* L. *regnare,* to rule < *regnum*], 1. to rule as king or queen; wield royal authority. 2. to hold sway; prevail; predominate: as, peace *reigns.*

Reign of Terror, the period of the French Revolution from 1793 to 1794, during which many persons were beheaded.

re·im·burse (rē′im-bũrs′), ***v.t.*** [REIMBURSED (-bũrst′), REIMBURSING], [*re-* + archaic *imburse,* after Fr. *rembourser* < *re-,* again + *embourser,* to pay < *en-,* in + *bourse,* a purse], 1. to pay back (money spent). 2. to pay back to (a person) money spent; compensate (a person) for damages, time lost, etc. —***SYN.*** see **pay.**

re·im·burse·ment (rē′im-bũrs′mənt), ***n.*** a reimbursing or being reimbursed; repayment (of money spent) or compensation (for time lost, damage suffered, etc.).

re·im·port (rē′im-pôrt′, rē′im-pōrt′; *for n.,* rē-im′pôrt, rē-im′pōrt), ***v.t.*** to import again; especially, to import as finished products (goods previously exported as raw materials). ***n.*** 1. a reimporting or being reimported. 2. something reimported.

re·im·por·ta·tion (rē′im-pôr-tā′shən, rē′im-pōr-tā′shən), ***n.*** 1. a reimporting or being reimported. 2. something reimported.

re·im·pres·sion (rē′im-presh′ən), ***n.*** a second impression; specifically, a reprint, as of a book, from the original, unchanged plates.

Reims (rēmz; Fr. rans), ***n.*** a city in northern France: pop., 111,000 (1946): also spelled **Rheims.**

rein (rān), ***n.*** [ME. *rene;* OFr. *resne;* < LL. **retina* < L. *retinere;* see RETAIN], 1. *usually in pl.* a narrow strap of leather attached to each end of the bit in the mouth of a horse, and held by the rider or driver to control the animal: see **harness,** illus. 2. *pl.* a means of guiding, controlling, checking, or restraining: as, the *reins* of government. ***v.t.*** 1. to put a rein or reins on. 2. to guide, control, check, or restrain with or as with reins. ***v.i.*** 1. to cause to stop or slow down with or as with reins (with *in* or *up*). 2. [Rare], to submit to or be controlled by reins: said of a horse.

draw rein, 1. to tighten the reins. 2. to slacken speed; stop. Also **draw in the reins.**

give (free) rein to, to allow to act without restraint.

keep a rein on, to check or control.

re·in·car·nate (rē′in-kär′nāt), ***v.t.*** to incarnate again; give another or different body to (a soul or spirit).

re·in·car·na·tion (rē′in-kär-nā′shən), ***n.*** [see prec.], 1. rebirth (of the soul) in another body. 2. a new incarnation. 3. the doctrine that the soul reappears after death in another and different bodily form.

rein·deer (rān′dêr′), ***n.*** [*pl.* REINDEER; *occas.,* REINDEERS], [ON. *hreindýri* < *hreinn,* reindeer + *dýr,* deer, animal (cf. DEER); *rein-* appears in AS. as *hran,* a phonetic rendering of the then Norw. form], any of several species of large deer with branching antlers (in both sexes), found in northern regions, where they are domesticated as beasts of burden and as a source of milk, meat, and hides.

Reindeer Lake, a lake in northeastern Saskatchewan, Canada: area, 2,435 sq. mi.

re·in·force (rē′in-fôrs′, rē′in-fōrs′), ***v.t.*** [REINFORCED (-fôrst′, -fōrst′), REINFORCING], [*re-* + *inforce,* var. of *enforce*], 1. to strengthen (a military or naval force) by sending new troops or ships. 2. to increase the number or amount of. 3. to strengthen or make stronger, as by patching, propping, adding new material, etc. 4. to make stronger or more compelling: as, he *reinforced* his arguments. ***n.*** anything that strengthens, as the thicker part of a gun barrel, where the explosion occurs. Also spelled **re-enforce, reënforce.**

reinforced concrete, concrete masonry containing steel bars or mesh to increase its strength.

re·in·force·ment (rē′in-fôrs′mənt, rē′in-fōrs′mənt), ***n.*** 1. a reinforcing or being reinforced. 2. anything that reinforces; specifically, *pl.* additional troops, warships, etc. to reinforce those already sent.

Rein·hardt, Max (mäks rīn′härt), 1873–1943; German theatrical director, producer, and actor, born in Austria.

reins (rānz), ***n.pl.*** [ME. *reines;* OFr. *reins;* L. *renes,* pl. of *ren,* kidney], [Archaic], 1. the kidneys, region of the kidneys, or loins. 2. the loins as the seat of the emotions and affections; hence, 3. the emotions and affections.

re·in·state (rē′in-stāt′), ***v.t.*** to instate again; restore to a former condition, position, etc.

re·in·state·ment (rē′in-stāt′mənt), ***n.*** a reinstating or being reinstated.

re·in·sur·ance (rē′in-shoor′əns), ***n.*** 1. renewed insurance. 2. insurance taken out by an insurer to protect himself against loss. 3. the amount of this.

re·in·sure (rē′in-shoor′), ***v.t.*** to insure again, especially under a contract by which the first insurer transfers all or part of the risk to another insurer.

reis (rās), ***n.pl.*** [*sing.* REAL (re-äl′)], [Port.; see REAL (coin)], a former Portuguese and Brazilian money of account, equal to 1/9 cent and 1/18 cent respectively: abbreviated **Rs.**: cf. **milreis.**

re·it·er·ate (rē-it′ə-rāt′), ***v.t.*** [REITERATED (-id), REITERATING], [< L. *reiteratus,* pp. of *reiterare; re-,* again + *iterare,* to say again, repeat < *iterum,* again], to repeat (something done or said); say or do again or repeatedly. —***SYN.*** see **repeat.**

re·it·er·a·tion (rē-it′ə-rā′shən, rē′it-ə-rā′shən), ***n.*** [L. *reiteratio*], a reiterating or being reiterated; repetition.

re·it·er·a·tive (rē-it′ə-rā′tiv), ***adj.*** repetitious.

re·ject (ri-jekt′; *for n.,* rē′jekt), ***v.t.*** [< L. *rejectus,* pp. of *reicere, rejicere,* to throw or fling back < *re-,* back + *jacere,* to throw], 1. to refuse to take, agree to, accede to, use, believe, etc. 2. to discard; throw out or away as worthless, useless, or substandard; cast off or out. 3. to throw up (food); vomit. 4. to rebuff. ***n.*** something rejected. ***SYN.*** see **decline.**

re·jec·ta·men·ta (ri-jek′tə-men′tə), ***n.pl.*** [Mod.L. < L. *rejectare,* freq. of *rejicere;* see REJECT], 1. things thrown away as worthless or useless. 2. excrement.

re·jec·tion (ri-jek′shən), ***n.*** [L. *rejectio*], 1. a rejecting or being rejected. 2. something rejected.

re·joice (ri-jois′), ***v.i.*** [REJOICED (-joist′), REJOICING], [ME. *rejoissen* < inflectional stem of OFr. *rejoïr* < *re-* + *ējouir* (earlier *esjoïr*) < L. *ex-,* out of + *gaudere,* to rejoice], to be glad, happy, or delighted; be full of joy (often with *at* or *in*). ***v.t.*** to make glad; delight.

re·joic·ing (ri-jois′iŋ), ***n.*** 1. the act of one who rejoices. 2. the feeling or expressing of joy or gladness. 3. an occasion for joy.

re·join (rē-join′), ***v.t.*** [prob. *re-* + *join*], 1. to come into the company of again: as, I will *rejoin* you soon. 2. to join together again; reunite. ***v.i.*** to become joined together again; be reunited.

re·join (ri-join′), ***v.t.*** [Late ME. *rejoyne;* prob. < Anglo-Fr. *rejoyner* (Fr. *rejoindre*); see RE- & JOIN], to say in answer. ***v.i.*** 1. to answer. 2. in *law,* to answer the plaintiff's replication. —***SYN.*** see **answer.**

re·join·der (ri-join′dẽr), ***n.*** [Late ME. *rejoyner;* Anglo-Fr. substantive use of Fr. inf. *rejoindre;* see REJOIN (to answer)], 1. *a*) an answer to a reply. *b*) a reply;

reidentify
reignite
reimplant
reimpose
reimpregnate
reimpress
reimprint
reimprison
reimprisonment
reinaugurate
reincite
reincorporate
reincrease
reincur
reinduce
reinfect
reinfection
reinflame
reinform
reinfuse
reinhabit
reinoculate
reinscribe
reinsert
reinsertion
reinsist
reinspect
reinspection
reinspire
reinstall
reinstruct
reintegrate
reintegration
reinter
reinterment
reinterrogate
reintrench
reintroduce
reintroduction
reinvent
reinvest
reinvestigate
reinvestment
reinvigorate
reinvite
reinvolve
reissue
rejudge

answer. 2. in *law*, the defendant's answer to the plaintiff's replication: cf. **surrejoinder.**

re·ju·ve·nate (ri-jōō'və-nāt'), *v.t.* [REJUVENATED (-id), REJUVENATING], [< *re-* + L. *juvenis*, young; + *-ate*], 1. to make young or youthful again; bring back to youthful strength, appearance, etc. 2. in *geology*, *a*) to increase the grade and speed of flow of (a stream), usually by uplift of the surrounding land. *b*) to give youthful land forms to (a region), as steep slopes.

re·ju·ve·na·tion (ri-jōō'və-nā'shən), *n.* a rejuvenating or being rejuvenated.

re·ju·ve·na·tor (ri-jōō'və-nā'tēr), *n.* a person or thing that rejuvenates.

re·ju·ve·nes·cence (ri-jōō'və-nes''ns), *n.* [< L. *re-*, again + *juvenescens*, ppr. of *juvenescere*, to become young < *juvenis*, young], renewal of youth.

re·ju·ve·nes·cent (ri-jōō'və-nes''nt), *adj.* [see REJUVENESCENCE], becoming or making youthful again.

re·ju·ve·nize (ri-jōō'və-nīz'), *v.t.* [REJUVENIZED (-nīzd'), REJUVENIZING], to rejuvenate.

rel., 1. relating. 2. relative(ly). 3. religion. 4. religious.

re-laid (rē-lād'), past tense and past participle of **re-lay.**

re·lapse (ri-laps'), *v.i.* [RELAPSED (-lapst'), RELAPSING], [< L. *relapsus*, pp. of *relabi*, to slip or slide back; see RE- & LAPSE], to slip or fall back into a former condition, especially after improvement or seeming improvement; specifically, *a*) to fall back into illness after recovery or seeming recovery. *b*) to fall back into bad habits, wrongdoing, error, etc.; backslide. *n.* 1. the act or an instance of relapsing. 2. the recurrence of a disease after apparent recovery.

relapsing fever, any of various acute infectious diseases caused by certain spirochetes transmitted by ticks or lice, and characterized by alternate attacks of fever and chills.

re·late (ri-lāt'), *v.t.* [RELATED (-id), RELATING], [Fr. *relater* < L. *relatus*, pp. of *referre*, to bring back; see REFER], 1. to tell the story of; narrate; recount. 2. to connect or associate, as in thought or meaning; show as having to do with; show a relation between: as, *relate* theory and practice. *v.i.* 1. to have some connection or relation (*to*). 2. to have reference (*to*). —*SYN.* see **tell.**

re·lat·ed (ri-lāt'id), *adj.* [pp. of *relate*], 1. narrated; recounted; told. 2. connected; associated. 3. connected by origin, kinship, marriage, etc.; of the same kind, family, etc. 4. in *music*, closely connected melodically or harmonically: said of tones, chords, etc.

SYN.—**related,** applied to persons, implies close connection through consanguinity or, less often, through marriage (we are *related* through our mothers), applied to things, close connection through common origin, interdependence, etc. (*related* subjects); **kindred** basically suggests blood relationship but in extension connotes close connection as because of similar nature, tastes, goals, etc. (we are *kindred* souls); **cognate** now usually applies to things and suggests connection because of a common source (*cognate* languages); **allied,** applied to persons, suggests connection through voluntary association, applied to things, connection through inclusion in the same category (*allied* sciences); **affiliate** usually suggests alliance of a smaller or weaker party with a larger or stronger one as a branch or dependent (several companies are *affiliated* with this corporation).

re·la·tion (ri-lā'shən), *n.* [ME. *relacion* < OFr. or L.; OFr. *relation*; L. *relatio*; see RELATE], 1. a narrating, recounting, or telling. 2. what is narrated or told; narrative; account; recital. 3. connection or mode of connection, as in thought, meaning, etc.: as, the *relation* of theory and practice, the *relation* of the individual to society. 4. connection of persons by blood or marriage; kinship. 5. a person connected with another or others by blood or marriage; member of the same family; relative; kinsman or kinswoman. 6. *pl.* the connections between or among persons in business or private affairs: as, his *relations* with his friends are good. 7. *pl.* the connections between or among groups, peoples, nations, states, etc.: as, foreign and trade *relations*. 8. reference; regard: as, this work was outlined with *relation* to available funds. 9. in *law*, *a*) the statement of a relator at whose complaint an action is begun. *b*) the referring of an act or proceeding to a time before its completion or enactment, as the time of its taking effect.

in (or **with**) **relation to,** concerning; regarding; about.

re·la·tion·al (ri-lā'shən-'l), *adj.* 1. of relation or relations. 2. showing or specifying relation. 3. in *grammar*, *a*) showing relations of syntax: said of conjunctions, prepositions, relative pronouns, etc. *b*) having to do with grammatical relations that frequently recur: as, the dative, genitive, etc. are *relational* cases.

re·la·tion·ship (ri-lā'shən-ship'), *n.* [*relation* + *-ship*], 1. connection; a being related. 2. connection by blood or marriage; kinship.

rel·a·tive (rel'ə-tiv), *adj.* [< OFr. or L.; OFr. *relatif*; L. *relativus* < L. *relatus*; see RELATE], 1. related each to the other; dependent upon or referring to each other: as, we ended in the same *relative* positions. 2. having to do with; pertinent; relevant: as, his letter was *relative* to this matter. 3. regarded in relation to something else; comparative: as, *relative* wages. 4. involving or expressing relations; meaningful only in relationship: as, cold is a *relative* term. 5. in *grammar*, *a*) designating a word that introduces a subordinate clause and refers to an antecedent: as, *which* is a *relative* pronoun in "the hat which you bought." *b*) introduced by such a word: as, a *relative* clause. *n.* 1. a relative word or thing. 2. a person connected by blood or marriage; kinsman or kinswoman. Abbreviated **rel.**

relative to, 1. relevant to; concerning; about. 2. corresponding to; in proportion to.

rel·a·tive·ly (rel'ə-tiv-li), *adv.* 1. in a relative manner; in relation to or compared with something else; not absolutely: as, a *relatively* unimportant matter. 2. in relation or proportion (*to*). Abbreviated **rel.**

relative major, in *music*, the major key whose tonic is the third degree of a specified minor key.

relative minor, in *music*, the minor key whose tonic is the sixth degree of a specified major key.

rel·a·tiv·ism (rel'ə-tiv-iz'm), *n.* the theory of ethics or knowledge which maintains that the basis of judgment is relative, differing according to events, persons, etc.

rel·a·tiv·ist (rel'ə-tiv-ist), *n.* 1. a person who believes in relativism. 2. a person who believes in relativity.

rel·a·tiv·i·ty (rel'ə-tiv'ə-ti), *n.* 1. the condition, fact, or quality of being relative. 2. the close dependence of one occurrence, value, quality, etc. on another. 3. in *philosophy*, existence only in relation to a thinking mind. 4. in *physics*, the fact, principle, or theory of the relative, rather than absolute, character of motion, velocity, mass, etc., and the interdependence of matter, time, and space: as developed and mathematically formulated by Albert Einstein and H. A. Lorentz in the *special* (or *restricted*) *theory of relativity* and by Einstein in the *general theory of relativity* (an extension covering the phenomena of gravitation), the theory of relativity includes the statements that: 1) there is no observable absolute motion, only relative motion; 2) the velocity of light is constant and not dependent on the motion of the source; 3) no energy can be transmitted at a velocity greater than that of light; 4) the mass of a body in motion is a function of the energy content and varies with the velocity; 5) time is relative; 6) space and time are interdependent and form a four-dimensional continuum; 7) the presence of matter results in a "warping" of the space-time continuum, so that a body in motion passing near by will describe a curve, this being the effect known as gravitation, as evidenced by the deflection of light rays passing through a gravitational field.

relativity of knowledge, in *philosophy*, the theory that all knowledge is relative to the mind, or that things can be known only through their effects on the mind, and that consequently there can be no knowledge of reality as it is in itself.

re·la·tor (ri-lā'tēr), *n.* [L.], 1. a person who relates, or tells; narrator. 2. in *law*, a private person at whose prompting or complaint a public action is begun to bring in question the exercise of an office, franchise, etc.

re·lax (ri-laks'), *v.t.* [L. *relaxare*; *re-*, back + *laxare*, to loosen, widen < *laxus*, loose; cf. LAX], 1. to make looser, or less firm or tense: as, he *relaxed* his hold. 2. to make less strict or severe; soften down: as, she *relaxed* her discipline of the child. 3. to abate; reduce; slacken: as, he *relaxed* his efforts. 4. to reduce the concentration or application of; give rest to: as, *relax* the mind. *v.i.* 1. to become looser or less firm, as the muscles. 2. to become less tense or stern, as one's features. 3. to become less strict; become milder, as discipline. 4. to become easier in manner; become less stiff. 5. to rest from effort, application, or work.

re·lax·a·tion (rē'lak-sā'shən), *n.* [L. *relaxatio* < pp. of *relaxare*], 1. a relaxing or being relaxed; loosening, lessening of severity, etc. 2. permission not to pay part of a penalty, duty, tax, etc. 3. a lessening of or rest from work or effort. 4. recreation; amusement.

re·lax·ed·ly (ri-lak'sid-li), *adv.* in a relaxed manner.

re·lay (rē'lā; *also, and for v. usually*, ri-lā'), *n.* [OFr. *relais*, *pl.*, orig., hounds kept as reserves at points along the course of a hunt < *relaier*, to leave behind; *re-* (see RE-) + *laier*, to leave, let], 1. a fresh supply of dogs, horses, etc. kept in readiness to relieve others in a hunt, on a journey, etc. 2. a crew of workers relieving others at work; shift. 3. a device operated by a relatively weak force but capable of producing a stronger force, used to control a relatively powerful apparatus. 4. in *electricity*, a device by means of which a change of current or a variation in conditions of an electric circuit causes a change in conditions of another circuit

rekindle relabel relaunch relaunder

fat, āpe, bâre, cär; ten, ēven, hêre, ovēr; is, bīte; lot, gō, hôrn, tōōl, look; oil, out; up, ūse, fūr; get; joy; yet; chin; she; thin, *then*; zh, leisure; ŋ, ring; ə for *a* in *ago*, *e* in *agent*, *i* in *sanity*, *o* in *comply*, *u* in *focus*; ' as in *able* (ā'b'l); Fr. bål; ë, Fr. coeur; ö, Fr. feu; Fr. mo*n*; ô, Fr. coq; ü, Fr. duc; H, G. ich; kh, G. doch. See pp. x–xii. ‡ foreign; * hypothetical; < derived from.

or operates another or other devices in the same or another circuit; used in telegraphy, etc. 5. in *sports*, *a*) a relay race. *b*) any of the legs, or laps, of a relay race. *v.t.* [RELAYED (-lād′, -lād), RELAYING], 1. to convey by relays. 2. to convey as if by relays; receive and pass on (a message, news, etc.). 3. to supply or replace with a relay or relays. 4. in *electricity*, to control, operate, or send on by a relay.

re-lay (rē′lā′), *v.t.* [RE-LAID (-lād′), RE-LAYING], to lay again or anew: also written **relay.**

relay race, a race between two or more teams, each member of which goes a certain part of the distance.

re·lease (ri-lēs′), *v.t.* [RELEASED (-lēst′), RELEASING], [ME. *relessen;* OFr. *relesser, relaisser; re-,* again + *laisser,* to leave < L. *laxare,* to loosen < *laxus,* loose, lax], 1. to set free, as from prison; set at liberty, as from work. 2. to unfasten and let go, as something snagged, a bomb, arrow, etc. 3. to grant freedom from a tax, penalty, obligation, etc. 4. to set free from pain, cares, etc.; relieve. 5. to permit to be issued, shown, published, etc. 6. in *law,* to give up or surrender to someone else (a claim, right, etc.). *n.* 1. a setting free; deliverance; liberation. 2. a freeing or being freed from a tax, obligation, etc. 3. a written discharge, as from an obligation, from prison, etc. 4. a letting go of something caught, held in position, etc. 5. a device, as for starting or stopping a machine, used to release some other device. 6. *a*) a releasing to the public, as of a book, film, news, etc. *b*) the book, film, etc. released. 7. in *jazz music,* the third group of four measures in a common form of sixteen-bar chorus, which supplies a bridge between repetitions of the melody. 8. in *law, a*) a giving up or surrender to someone else, as of a claim or right. *b*) the document by which this is done. —*SYN.* see **free.**

re-lease (rē′lēs′), *v.t.* to lease again.

rel·e·gate (rel′ə-gāt′), *v.t.* [RELEGATED (-id), RELEGATING], [< L. *relegatus,* pp. of *relegare,* to send away; *re-,* away, back + *legare,* to send], 1. to exile; banish, usually to a specified place. 2. to consign or assign to an inferior position. 3. to assign to a class, sphere, realm, etc.; classify (something) as belonging to a certain order of things. 4. to refer, commit, or hand over for decision, as to a person. —*SYN.* see **commit.**

rel·e·ga·tion (rel′ə-gā′shən), *n.* [L. *relegatio*], a relegating or being relegated.

re·lent (ri-lent′), *v.i.* [ME. *relente,* to melt < L. *re-lentescere,* to become soft < *re-,* again + *lentus,* flexible, pliant, slow], 1. to soften in temper, resolution, etc.; become less severe, stern, or stubborn. 2. [Obs.], to melt. *v.t.* [Obs.], to cause to relent. —*SYN.* see **yield.**

re·lent·less (ri-lent′lis), *adj.* 1. not relenting; harsh; pitiless. 2. persistent; unremitting.

rel·e·vance (rel′ə-vəns), *n.* the state or quality of being relevant; pertinence.

rel·e·van·cy (rel′ə-vən-si), *n.* relevance.

rel·e·vant (rel′ə-vənt), *adj.* [ML. *relevans,* ppr. of *relevare,* to bear upon (in L., to lift up); see **RELIEVE**], bearing upon or relating to the matter in hand; pertinent; to the point: opposed to *irrelevant.*

SYN.—**relevant** implies close logical relationship with, and importance to, the matter under consideration (*relevant* testimony); **germane** implies such close natural connection as to be highly appropriate or fit (your reminiscences are not truly *germane* to this discussion); **pertinent** implies an immediate and direct bearing on the matter in hand (a *pertinent* suggestion); **apposite** applies to that which is both relevant and happily suitable or appropriate (an *apposite* analogy); **applicable** refers to that which can be brought to bear upon a particular matter or problem (your description is *applicable* to several people); **apropos** is used of that which is opportune as well as relevant (that remark was most *apropos*).—*ANT.* inappropriate, extraneous.

re·li·a·bil·i·ty (ri-lī′ə-bil′ə-ti), *n.* the state or quality of being reliable.

re·li·a·ble (ri-lī′ə-b'l), *adj.* that can be relied on; dependable; trustworthy.

SYN.—**reliable** is applied to a person or thing that can be counted upon to do what is expected or required (his *reliable* assistant); **dependable** refers to a person or thing that can be depended on as in a need or emergency and often connotes level-headedness or steadiness (she is a *dependable* friend); **trustworthy** applies to a person, or, sometimes, a thing, whose truthfulness, integrity, discretion, etc. can be relied on (a *trustworthy* source of information); **trusty** applies to a person or thing which continued experience has shown to be completely trustworthy or dependable (his *trusty* steed).

re·li·a·bly (ri-lī′ə-bli), *adv.* 1. in a reliable manner. 2. to a reliable degree.

re·li·ance (ri-lī′əns), *n.* 1. a relying. 2. trust, dependence, or confidence. 3. what is relied on.

re·li·ant (ri-lī′ənt), *adj.* 1. relying; having or showing trust, dependence, or confidence. 2. self-reliant.

rel·ic (rel′ik), *n.* [ME. *relike;* OFr. *relique;* L. *reliquiae, pl.* < *relinquere;* see **RELINQUISH**], 1. an object, custom, etc. that has survived, wholly or partially, from the past; often, something that has historic interest because of its age and associations with the past, or that serves as a keepsake, or souvenir. 2. *pl.* remaining fragments; surviving parts; ruins. 3. *pl.* [Obs. or Poetic], the body, or parts of the body, of a dead person; remains. 4. in *ecclesiastical usage,* the body or part of the body of, or an object kept and reverenced as a memorial of, a saint, martyr, etc., as in the Roman Catholic and Orthodox Eastern churches.

rel·ict (rel′ikt; *for adj.,* ri-likt′), *n.* [L. *relicta,* fem. of *relictus,* pp. of *relinquere;* see **RELINQUISH**], 1. [Rare], a widow. 2. a plant or animal living on in a particular area as a survival from an earlier period. *adj.* [Archaic], surviving the death of another; especially, widowed.

re·lief (ri-lēf′), *n.* [ME. *relef;* OFr. *relief* < *relever;* see **RELIEVE**], 1. an easing, as of pain, discomfort, or anxiety; setting free from some cause of distress in body or mind; lightening of a burden, as of taxation, oppression, etc. 2. anything that lessens tension or strain, or offers a pleasing change, as to the mind or eye: as, the lakes were a *relief* after the dry countryside. 3. aid in the form of goods or money given by an agency, or by the state, city, county, etc., to persons out of work or in need. 4. any aid given in times of need or danger, as supplies sent into a besieged area or troops sent to take the place of tired forces. 5. *a*) release from work or duty. *b*) the person or persons bringing such release by taking over a post. 6. [It. *rilievo* < *rilevare,* to raise; see **RELIEVE**], in *architecture & sculpture, a*) the projection of figures and forms from a flat surface, so that they stand wholly or partly free. *b*) a work of art so made. Also **relievo, rilievo.** 7. in *feudal law,* a payment made by the heir of a vassal to the overlord on taking over an estate. 8. in *physical geography, a*) the differences in height, collectively, of land forms in any particular area. *b*) these differences as shown by lines or colors on a map. 9. in *literature & drama, a*) sharp contrast, as of ideas, actions, or events. *b*) comic scenes in a serious drama or motion picture: in full, **comic relief.** 10. in *painting,* the apparent solidity or projection of objects, obtained by modeling and gradation in color, etc.; hence, 11. distinctness of outline; contrast.

in relief, carved or molded so as to project from a surface.

on relief, totally or partially supported by a temporary government allowance, as when unemployed.

relief map, a map showing by lines, shading, or color the different heights of land forms, as hills and valleys.

re·liev·a·ble (ri-lēv′ə-b'l), *adj.* that can b,e relieved.

re·lieve (ri-lēv′), *v.t.* [RELIEVED (-lēvd′) RELIEVING], [ME. *releven;* OFr. *relever* < L. *relevare,* to lift up again; *re-,* again + *levare,* to raise < *levis,* light], 1. to ease; lighten; reduce, as pain, anxiety, etc. 2. *a*) to free (a person) from pain, discomfort, anxiety, etc. *b*) to restore (a part of the body, the mind, etc.) to well-being. 3. to give aid or assistance to: as, *relieve* the poor; bring or send help to: as, *relieve* a besieged city. 4. *a*) to set free from a burden, obligation, grievance, etc. *b*) to remove (a burden, etc.). 5. to set free from duty, work, or responsibility by sending someone, or coming oneself, to take it over: as, she *relieved* the nurse. 6. to make less tedious, monotonous, or unpleasant by being or providing a pleasing change. 7. to set off by contrast; make sharply distinct or prominent. 8. to ease (oneself) by passing bodily waste matter.

SYN.—**relieve** implies the reduction of misery, discomfort, or tediousness sufficiently to make it bearable (they played a game to *relieve* the monotony of the trip); **alleviate** implies temporary relief, suggesting that the source of the misery remains unaffected (drugs to *alleviate* the pain); **lighten** implies a cheering or gladdening as by reducing the weight of oppression or depression (nothing can *lighten* the burden of her grief); **assuage** suggests a softening or pacifying influence in lessening pain, calming passion, etc. (her kind words *assuaged* his resentment); **mitigate** implies a moderating or making milder of that which is likely to cause pain (to *mitigate* a punishment); **allay** suggests an effective, although temporary or incomplete, calming or quieting (we've *allayed* his suspicions). See also **comfort.**

re·lie·vo (ri-lē′vō), *n.* [*pl.* RELIEVOS (-vōz)], a relief (sense 6).

relig., religion.

‡**re·li·gieuse** (rə-lē′zhyöz′), *n.* [*pl.* RELIGIEUSES (-zhyöz′)], [Fr.], a woman member of a religious order; nun.

‡**re·li·gieux** (rə-lē′zhyö′), *adj.* [Fr.], religious; pious. *n.* [*pl.* RELIGIEUX (-zhyö′)], a man who has taken monastic vows; member of a religious order; monk.

re·li·gion (ri-lij′ən), *n.* [ME. *religioun;* OFr.; L. *religio;* ? < *religare,* to bind back; *re-,* back + *ligare,* to bind, bind together; or ? < *re-* + base **lig-* (< IE. **leg-,* to be concerned), seen also in Gr. *alegein,* to pay heed to, L. *diligens,* diligent], 1. belief in a divine or superhuman power or powers to be obeyed and worshiped as the creator(s) and ruler(s) of the universe. 2. expression of this belief in conduct and ritual. 3. *a*) any specific system of belief, worship, conduct, etc., often involving a code of ethics and a philosophy: as, the Christian *religion,* the Buddhist *religion,* etc. *b*) loosely, any system of beliefs, practices, ethical values, etc.

relearn relend relet relight

resembling, suggestive of, or likened to such a system: as, humanism is his *religion.* 4. a state of mind or way of life expressing love for and trust in God, and one's will and effort to act according to the will of God, especially within a monastic order or community: as, he achieved *religion.* 5. any object of conscientious regard and pursuit: as, cleanliness was a *religion* to him. 6. [Obs.], *a*) the practice of religious observances or rites. *b*) *pl.* religious rites. Abbreviated **rel., relig.**

re·li·gion·ism (ri-lij'ən-iz'm), ***n.*** 1. excessive religious zeal. 2. pretended or affected religious zeal.

re·li·gion·ist (ri-lij'ən-ist), ***n.*** a religious zealot or enthusiast; fanatic.

re·lig·i·os·i·ty (ri-lij'i-os'ə-ti), ***n.*** [ME. *religiosite;* LL. *religiositas*], 1. the quality of being religious, especially of being extremely or excessively religious. 2. an affectation of this.

re·li·gious (ri-lij'əs), ***adj.*** [ME. *religius;* OFr. *religious;* L. *religiosus*], 1. characterized by adherence to religion; devout; pious; godly. 2. of, concerned with, appropriate to, or teaching religion: as, *religious* books. 3. belonging to a monastic order. 4. careful; conscientiously exact; scrupulous. ***n.*** [*pl.* RELIGIOUS], a person belonging to a monastic order; monk or nun. Abbreviated **rel.** —***SYN.*** see **devout.**

the religious, religious people collectively.

re·lin·quish (ri-liŋ'kwish), ***v.t.*** [Late ME. *relinquisse;* OFr. *relinquir;* L. *relinquere; re-,* from + *linquere,* to leave], 1. to give up; abandon, as a plan, policy, etc. 2. to renounce or surrender (something owned, a right, etc.). 3. to let go (a grasp, etc.).

SYN.—**relinquish** implies a giving up of something desirable and connotes compulsion or the force of necessity (he will not *relinquish* his advantage); **abandon,** in this connection, implies a complete and final relinquishment, as because of weariness, discouragement, etc. (do not *abandon* hope); **waive** suggests a voluntary relinquishing by refusing to insist on one's right or claim to something (to *waive* a jury trial); **forgo** implies the denial to oneself of something, as for the sake of expediency or altruism (I must *forgo* the pleasure of your company this evening). See also **surrender.**—***ANT.*** keep, retain.

re·lin·quish·ment (ri-liŋ'kwish-mənt), ***n.*** a relinquishing or being relinquished.

rel·i·quar·y (rel'ə-kwer'i), ***n.*** [*pl.* RELIQUARIES (-iz)], [Fr. *rêliquaire* < L. *reliquiae;* see RELIC], a small box, casket, or shrine in which a relic or relics are kept and shown.

rel·ique (rel'ik, ri-lēk'), ***n.*** [Archaic], a relic.

re·liq·ui·ae (ri-lik'wi-ē'), ***n.pl.*** [L.; see RELIC], remains, as of fossil organisms.

rel·ish (rel'ish), ***n.*** [ME. *reles;* OFr. *reles, relais,* something remaining < *relaisser;* see RELEASE], 1. *a*) a flavor; taste. *b*) distinctive or characteristic flavor: as, a *relish* of garlic in the stew. 2. a trace or touch (of some quality); hint or suggestion: as, there was a *relish* of malice in his action. 3. an appetizing flavor; pleasing taste. 4. pleasure; enjoyment; zest: as, he eats with *relish.* 5. anything that gives pleasure, zest, or enjoyment; attractive quality. 6. pickles, chutney, or the like, served with meat, etc. to make it more appetizing. ***v.t.*** 1. to give flavor to. 2. to enjoy; like. ***v.i.*** 1. to taste or have the flavor (*of* something). 2. to have a pleasing taste. 3. to please.

rel. pron., relative pronoun.

re·lu·cent (ri-lōō's'nt, ri-lū's'nt), ***adj.*** [L. *relucens,* ppr. of *relucere;* see RE- & LUCENT], reflecting light; bright.

re·luct (ri-lukt'), ***v.i.*** [L. *reluctari* (see RELUCTANT); in later use prob. back-formation < *reluctance, reluctant*], [Rare], 1. to struggle (*against*); revolt (*at*). 2. to offer opposition; show reluctance.

re·luc·tance (ri-luk't'ns), ***n.*** [< *reluctant*], 1. a feeling of not wanting to do or agree to something; being reluctant; unwillingness. 2. [Rare], opposition; revolt. 3. in *electricity,* resistance to the passage of magnetic lines of force; magnetic resistance.

re·luc·tan·cy (ri-luk't'n-si), ***n.*** reluctance.

re·luc·tant (ri-luk't'nt), ***adj.*** [L. *reluctans,* ppr. of *reluctari,* to resist; *re-,* against + *luctari,* to struggle], 1. unwilling; opposed in mind; disinclined. 2. marked by unwillingness: as, a *reluctant* answer. 3. [Rare], struggling against; resisting; opposing.

SYN.—**reluctant** implies an unwillingness to do something, as because of distaste, irresolution, etc. (she was *reluctant* to marry); **disinclined** suggests a lack of desire for something, as because it fails to suit one's taste or because one disapproves of it (I feel *disinclined* to argue); **hesitant** implies a refraining from action, as because of fear, indecision, etc. (don't be *hesitant* about asking this favor); **loath** suggests strong disinclination that amounts almost to repugnance (I am *loath* to accompany him); **averse** suggests a sustained, although not extreme, disinclination (she is *averse* to borrowing money).—***ANT.*** inclined, disposed, eager.

rel·uc·tiv·i·ty (rel'ək-tiv'ə-ti), ***n.*** in *electricity,* specific resistance to magnetization; reluctance exhibited by a one-centimeter cube of a given material.

re·lume (rē-lōōm', rē-lūm'), ***v.t.*** [RELUMED (-lōōmd', -lūmd'), RELUMING], [*re-* + *illume;* cf. Fr. *rallumer*], [Archaic or Poetic], 1. to light again; rekindle. 2. to light up again; illuminate or shine on again.

re·ly (ri-lī'), ***v.i.*** [RELIED (-līd'), RELYING], [ME. *relien,* to rally; OFr. *relier, ralier;* L. *religare;* see RELIGION], to trust; depend; have confidence (with *on* or *upon*).

SYN.—to **rely** (*on* or *upon*) a person or thing is to have confidence, usually on the basis of past experience, that he or it will do what is expected (he can be *relied* on to keep the secret); to **trust** is to have complete faith or assurance that one will not be let down by another (to *trust* in God); to **depend** (*on* or *upon*) a person or thing is to rely on him or it for support or aid (he can *depend* on his wife for sympathy); to **count** (*on*) or, colloquially, to **reckon** (*on*) something is to consider it in one's calculations as certain (they *counted,* or *reckoned,* on my going); to **bank** (*on*), a colloquial term, is to have the confidence of one who is willing to risk money on something (don't *bank* on his help).

re·main (ri-mān'), ***v.i.*** [OFr. *remaindre, remanoir;* L. *remanere; re-,* back, behind + *manere,* to stay], 1. to be left or left over when the rest has been taken away, destroyed, or disposed of in some way. 2. to stay; stay while others go; stay in the same place: as, he *remained* in the house. 3. to continue; go on being: as, he *remained* a cynic. 4. to continue to exist; endure; persist; last: as, the old house still *remains.* 5. to be left to be dealt with, done, said, etc. —***SYN.*** see **stay.**

re·main·der (ri-mān'dẽr), ***n.*** [Anglo-Fr. substantive use of OFr. inf. *remaindre;* see REMAIN], 1. those remaining. 2. the rest; what is left when a part is taken away: as, he ate the *remainder* of the candy. 3. a copy or copies of a book still held by a publisher when the sale has fallen off, usually disposed of very cheaply. 4. in *law,* an estate in expectancy but not in possession, as when land is conveyed by the same deed to one person during his lifetime, and at his death to another and his heirs: distinguished from *reversion.* 5. in *mathematics, a*) what is left when a smaller number is subtracted from a larger. *b*) what is left undivided when one number is divided by another that is not one of its factors. ***adj.*** remaining; left over. ***v.t.*** to sell (books, etc.) as remainders.

SYN.—**remainder** is the general word applied to what is left when a part is taken away (the *remainder* of a meal, one's life, etc.); **residue** and **residuum** apply to what remains at the end of a process, as after the evaporation or combustion of matter or after the settlement of claims, etc. in a testator's estate; **remnant** is applied to a fragment, trace, or any small part left after the greater part has been removed (*remnants* of cloth from the ends of bolts); **balance** is used colloquially in place of **remainder,** but in strict use it implies the amount remaining on the credit or debit side (a bank *balance*).

re·mains (ri-mānz'), ***n. pl.*** 1. what is left; what is left after use, destruction, etc.; remainder; remnant. 2. vestiges; traces. 3. objects, buildings, monuments, etc. surviving from the past. 4. the dead body of a person. 5. writings left unpublished at the death of an author. 6. surviving works, as of an ancient writer.

re·make (rē-māk'; *for n.,* rē'māk'), ***v.t.*** [REMADE (-mād'), REMAKING], to make again or anew. ***n.*** 1. a remaking. 2. something remade, as a motion picture.

re·man (rē-man'), ***v.t.*** [REMANNED (-mand'), REMANNING], 1. to man again, as a boat. 2. to give new manliness or courage to.

re·mand (ri-mand'), ***v.t.*** [ME. *remaunden;* Late OFr. *remander;* LL. *remandare;* L. *re-,* back + *mundare,* to order], 1. to send back; order to go back. 2. in *law, a*) to send (a prisoner or accused person) back to jail, as to investigate the charges against him further. *b*) to send (a case) back to a lower court, with directions concerning additional proceedings. ***n.*** 1. a remanding or being remanded. 2. a person remanded.

rem·a·nent (rem'ə-nənt), ***adj.*** [ME. *remanente;* L. *remanens,* ppr.], remaining; left over.

re·mark (ri-märk'), ***v.t.*** [Fr. *remarquer;* see RE- & MARK, *v.*], 1. to notice; observe; perceive. 2. to comment; say or write as an observation or comment. 3. [Obs.], to mark; distinguish; indicate. ***v.i.*** to make an observation or comment (with *on* or *upon*). ***n.*** 1. a noticing, perceiving, or observing: as, a person worthy of *remark.* 2. something said briefly; comment; casual observation. 3. in *engraving,* remarque.

SYN.—**remark** applies to a brief, more or less casual statement of opinion, etc., as in momentarily directing one's attention to something (a *remark* about her clothes); an **observation** is an expression of opinion on something to which one has given some degree of special attention and thought (the warden's *observations* on prison reform) a **comment** is a remark or observation made in explaining, criticising, or interpreting something (*comments* on a novel); **commentary** is usually applied as a collective noun to a series of explanatory notes or annotations (a *commentary* on Aristotle's *Politics*).

reline **relive** **reloan** **remade**
relisten **reload** **relocate** **remap**

re·mark·a·ble (ri-mär′kə-b'l), *adj.* 1. worthy of remark. 2. unusual; extraordinary. —*SYN.* see **noticeable.**

re·mark·a·bly (ri-mär′kə-bli), *adv.* in a remarkable manner or to a remarkable extent; notably.

re·marque (ri-märk′), *n.* [Fr.; see REMARK], in *engraving,* 1. any mark made on the margin of a plate and appearing only on proofs, to identify a particular stage of the plate. 2. a small design or sketch etched on the margin of a plate, to be removed after a number of early proofs have been taken. 3. a plate, print, or proof bearing such a mark.

Re·marque, E·rich Ma·ri·a (ā′riH mä-rē′ä rə-märk′), 1897- ; German novelist.

Rem·brandt (rem′bränt; Eng. rem′brant), *n.* (*Rembrandt Harmenszoon van Rijn* or *Ryn*), Dutch painter and etcher; lived 1606–1669.

re·me·di·a·ble (ri-mē′di-ə-b'l), *adj.* [Fr. *remédiable;* L. *remediabilis*], that can be remedied.

re·me·di·a·bly (ri-mē′di-ə-bli), *adv.* in a remediable manner; so as to be remediable.

re·me·di·al (ri-mē′di-əl), *adj.* [LL. *remedialis*], providing, or intended to provide, a remedy.

re·me·di·al·ly (ri-mē′di-əl-i), *adv.* so as to remedy.

rem·e·di·less (rem′ə-di-lis; *still occas.* ri-med′ə-lis), *adj.* that cannot be remedied; incurable or irreparable.

rem·e·dy (rem′ə-di), *n.* [*pl.* REMEDIES (-diz)], [ME. & Anglo-Fr. *remedie;* OFr. *remede;* L. *remedium* < *re-,* again + *mederi,* to heal], 1. any medicine or treatment that cures, heals, or relieves a disease or bodily disorder, deadens pain, or tends to restore health. 2. something that corrects, counteracts, or removes an evil or wrong; relief; redress. 3. in *coinage,* variation allowed at the mint in weight and fineness of metal of a coin; tolerance. 4. in *law,* a means, as court action, by which violation of a right is prevented or compensated for; legal redress. *v.t.* [REMEDIED (-did), REMEDYING], 1. to cure or heal, as with medicine. 2. to put right; put back in proper condition. 3. to correct or remove (an evil, etc.). —*SYN.* see **cure.**

re·mem·ber (ri-mem′bẽr), *v.t.* [ME. *remembren;* OFr. *remembrer, se remembrer* < LL. *rememorare;* L. *re-,* back, again + *memorare,* to bring to remembrance < *memor,* mindful; cf. MEMORY], 1. to have (an event, thing, person, etc.) come to mind again; think of again: as, he suddenly *remembered* an appointment. 2. to bring back to mind by an effort; recollect; recall: as, he tried to *remember* the name. 3. to bear in mind; keep in the memory; be careful not to forget. 4. to keep (a person) in mind with some feeling, as of pleasure, gratitude, etc. 5. *a*) to keep (a person) in mind for a present, legacy, etc. *b*) to give a present or tip to: as, *remember* the waiter. 6. to mention (a person) to another as sending regards or greetings: as, *remember* me to your mother. 7. [Obs.], to remind. *v.i.* 1. to bear in mind or call back to mind. 2. to have memory; have the use of one's memory.

SYN.—**remember** implies a putting oneself in mind of something, often suggesting that the thing is kept alive in the memory so that it can be called to conscious thought without effort (he'll *remember* this day); **recall** and **recollect** both imply some effort or will to bring something back to mind, **recall,** in addition, often connoting an imparting of what is brought back (let me *recall* what was said, to *recollect* the days of one's childhood); **remind** implies an agent as the cause of or stimulus for remembering (your story *reminds* me of another); **reminisce** now usually implies the remembering and telling of past events or experiences in one's own life (they *reminisced* about school days).—*ANT.* forget.

re·mem·brance (ri-mem′brəns), *n.* 1. a remembering or being remembered. 2. the power to remember. 3. the extent of time over which one can remember. 4. an object that serves to bring to mind or keep in mind some person, event, etc.; souvenir; keepsake; memento. 5. *pl.* greetings. —*SYN.* see **memory.**

re·mem·branc·er (ri-mem′brən-sẽr), *n.* [Anglo-Fr.; see REMEMBRANCE & -ER], 1. a person who reminds another of something; especially, one engaged or appointed to do so. 2. [usually R-], in England, *a*) formerly, any of several officers of the Court of Exchequer. *b*) an officer of the Supreme Court who is responsible for collecting debts due to the king or queen: also called the *King's* (or *Queen's*) *Remembrancer.* *c*) an officer of the corporation of the City of London. 3. a reminder; souvenir; memento.

rem·i·ges (rem′ə-jēz′), *n.pl.* [*sing.* REMEX (rē′meks)], [L., pl. of *remex,* oarsman], the large quill feathers of a bird's wing; flight feathers.

re·mig·i·al (ri-mij′i-əl), *adj.* of the remiges.

re·mind (ri-mīnd′), *v.t.* & *v.i.* [*re-* + *mind, v.*], to put (a person) in mind (*of* something); cause (a person) to remember: as, *remind* me of it. —*SYN.* see **remember.**

re·mind·er (ri-mīn′dẽr), *n.* a person or thing that reminds; thing to help one remember something else.

re·mind·ful (ri-mīnd′fəl), *adj.* 1. mindful; remembering. 2. reviving memory; reminding; reminiscent.

Rem·ing·ton, Frederic (rem′iŋ-tən), 1861–1909; American painter, sculptor, and illustrator.

rem·i·nisce (rem′ə-nis′), *v.i.* [REMINISCED (-nist′), REMINISCING], [back-formation < *reminiscence*], 1. to call past events or experiences to mind. 2. to talk or write about remembered events or experiences. —*SYN.* see **remember.**

rem·i·nis·cence (rem′ə-nis′'ns), *n.* [< Fr.; see REMINISCENT], 1. a remembering; recollecting; recalling to mind. 2. memory; recollection. 3. *pl.* an account, written or spoken, of remembered events. 4. something that suggests or recalls something else; reminder. —*SYN.* see **memory.**

rem·i·nis·cent (rem′ə-nis′'nt), *adj.* [L. *reminiscens,* ppr. of *reminisci* < *re-,* again + *memini,* to remember], 1. having the nature of or characterized by reminiscence; remembering. 2. recalling the past and telling about it; given to dwelling on the past. 3. bringing to mind something else; suggestive (*of*).

re·mise (ri-mīz′), *v.t.* [REMISED (-mīzd′), REMISING], [Fr., restoration, fem. pp. of *remettre,* to send back; L. *remittere;* see REMIT], in *law,* to give up a claim to; surrender or release by deed.

re·miss (ri-mis′), *adj.* [L. *remissus,* pp. of *remittere;* see REMIT], 1. careless or negligent at work; irresponsible; lax in the performance of duty. 2. characterized by carelessness or negligence; poorly or shoddily done. 3. not energetic; languid; sluggish.

SYN.—**remiss** implies the culpable omission or the extremely careless or indifferent performance of a task or duty (*remiss* in one's obligations); **negligent** and **neglectful** both imply failure to attend to something sufficiently or properly, but **negligent** often stresses this as a habit or trait (*negligent* in dress) and **neglectful** carries an implication of intentional and culpable disregard (a mayor *neglectful* of his pledges to the voters); **derelict** implies flagrant neglect of a duty or obligation; **lax** implies looseness in satisfying or enforcing requirements, observing standards or rules, etc. (*lax* discipline); **slack,** in this connection, implies lack of necessary diligence, efficiency, etc., as because of laziness or indifference (*slack* service in a restaurant).

re·mis·si·ble (ri-mis′ə-b'l), *adj.* [Fr. *rémissible;* LL. *remissibilis* < pp. of L. *remittere*], that can be remitted.

re·mis·sion (ri-mish′ən), *n.* [ME.; OFr.; L. *remissio* < pp. of *remittere;* see REMIT], 1. forgiveness; pardon, as of sins or crimes. 2. cancellation of or release from a debt, tax, penalty, etc. 3. a lessening; abating; diminution, as of heat or cold. 4. a temporary lessening of a disease or pain. 5. a remitting (in various senses). 6. [Obs.], a lessening of tension; relaxation.

re·mit (ri-mit′), *v.t.* [REMITTED (-id), REMITTING], [ME. *remytten;* L. *remittere* (pp. *remissus*), to send back; *re-,* back + *mittere,* to send], 1. to forgive or pardon (sins, etc.). 2. *a*) to refrain from exacting (a payment, tax, etc.). *b*) to refrain from inflicting (a punishment) or enforcing (a sentence); cancel. 3. to decrease; let slacken: as, he *remitted* his efforts. 4. to submit or refer (a matter) for consideration, judgment, or action, especially to someone whose business it is to look after such things. 5. to put back, as into a state or position. 6. to put off; postpone. 7. to send or pay (money). 8. [Rare], to send back to jail; recommit. 9. [Obs.], to give up; surrender. 10. in *law,* to send back (a case) to a lower court for further action. *v.i.* 1. to slacken; moderate in force or intensity. 2. to send money, as in payment; pay.

re·mit·ta·ble (ri-mit′ə-b'l), *adj.* that can be remitted.

re·mit·tal (ri-mit′'l), *n.* remission.

re·mit·tance (ri-mit′'ns), *n.* [< *remit* + *-ance*], 1. the sending of money, as by mail. 2. the money sent.

remittance man, a man who lives abroad supported by remittances from home.

re·mit·tent (ri-mit′'nt), *adj.* [L. *remittens*], remitting; slackening for a while or at intervals, but not quite going away, as a fever. *n.* a remittent fever.

re·mit·ter (ri-mit′ẽr), *n.* 1. a person who remits. 2. restoration, as to a previous state or right. 3. in *law, a*) the transfer of a case to another court, usually a lower one, for decision. *b*) the principle or act of adjudging a person to hold property by an earlier and more valid title to it than the later but defective one by which he took it over.

re·mit·tor (ri-mit′ẽr), *n.* in *law,* a person who makes a remittance.

rem·nant (rem′nənt), *n.* [contr. < ME. *remenant, remanent;* OFr. *remenant, remenaunt,* orig. ppr. of *remaindre;* see REMAIN], 1. what is left over; remainder; residue. 2. a small remaining part, quantity, or number; fragment left over. 3. a trace; last remaining indication of what has been: as, a *remnant* of his former pride. 4. a piece of cloth, ribbon, etc. left over or unsold, as at the end of a bolt. —*SYN.* see **remainder.**

re·mod·el (rē-mod′'l), *v.t.* [REMODELED OR REMODELLED (-'ld), REMODELING OR REMODELLING], 1. to model again. 2. to make over; rebuild.

re·mo·lade (rā′mə-läd′), *n.* rémoulade.

remarriage
remarry
remasticate
remeasure
remelt
remerge
remigrate
remilitarize
remix
remodification
remodify
remold

re·mon·e·ti·za·tion (rē-mon'ə-ti-zā'shən, rē-mun'ə-ti-zā'shən), *n.* a remonetizing or being remonetized.
re·mon·e·tize (rē-mon'ə-tīz', rē-mun'ə-tīz'), *v.t.* [REMONETIZED (-tīzd'), REMONETIZING], to reinstate as legal tender, or lawful money: as, silver was *remonetized.*
re·mon·strance (ri-mon'strəns), *n.* [Late ME.; OFr.; ML. *remonstrantia*], act or instance of remonstrating; protest, complaint, or expostulation.
re·mon·strant (ri-mon'strənt), *adj.* [ML. *remonstrans,* ppr.], remonstrating; expostulatory. *n.* 1. a person who remonstrates. 2. [R-], one of the Arminians in Holland who presented a remonstrance in 1610 setting forth their differences from strict Calvinism.
re·mon·strate (ri-mon'strāt), *v.t.* [REMONSTRATED (-id), REMONSTRATING], [< ML. *remonstratus,* pp. of *remonstrare,* to demonstrate; L. *re-,* again + *monstrare,* to show], 1. to say or plead in protest, objection, complaint, etc. 2. [Obs.], to point out; show; demonstrate. *v.i.* to present and urge reasons in opposition or complaint; protest; object; expostulate. —*SYN.* see **object.**
re·mon·stra·tion (rē'mon-strā'shən, rem'ən-strā'shən), *n.* a remonstrating.
re·mon·stra·tive (ri-mon'strə-tiv), *adj.* remonstrating.
re·mon·stra·tor (ri-mon'strā-tēr), *n.* a person who remonstrates.
re·mon·tant (ri-mon'tənt), *adj.* [Fr., ppr. of *remonter;* see REMOUNT], flowering more than once in a season: said of some roses. *n.* a remontant rose.
rem·o·ra (rem'ə-rə), *n.* [L., lit., hindrance; *re-,* back + *mora,* a delay], any of a group of small ocean fishes with a sucking disk on top of the head, by which they cling to sharks and other larger fishes, turtles, passing ships, etc.: also called *shark sucker.*
re·morse (ri-môrs'), *n.* [ME. & OFr. *remors;* LL. *remorsus,* in L., pp. of *remordere; re-,* again + *mordere,* to bite], 1. a deep, torturing sense of guilt felt for one's actions; regret. 2. pity; compassion: now only in *without remorse,* pitilessly. —*SYN.* see **penitence.**
re·morse·ful (ri-môrs'fəl), *adj.* full of remorse; feeling, expressing, or caused by remorse.
re·morse·less (ri-môrs'lis), *adj.* without remorse; pitiless; merciless; ruthless; cruel.
re·mote (ri-mōt'), *adj.* [ME.; L. *remotus,* pp. of *removere,* to remove], 1. distant in space; far off; far away. 2. far off and hidden away; secluded. 3. far off in (past or future) time: as, the *remote* past. 4. distant in connection, relation, bearing, or the like (*from* some matter): as, a question *remote* from the subject. 5. distantly related by blood or marriage: as, a *remote* cousin. 6. distant in human relations; aloof: as, *remote* and cold in his manner. 7. slight; faint: as, a *remote* resemblance, a *remote* chance. 8. not immediate or primary; far removed in influence: as, the *remote* causes of the depression. —*SYN.* see **far.**
remote control, control of aircraft, missiles, or other apparatus from a distance, as by radio waves.
re·mo·tion (ri-mō'shən), *n.* 1. the act of removing; removal. 2. [Obs.], the act of departing; departure.
ré·mou·lade (rā'mə-läd'; Fr. rā'moo'låd'), *n.* [Fr. < It. *remolata*], a spicy sauce made with the yolks of hard-boiled eggs, vinegar, oil, etc., and served with cold dishes or as a salad dressing: also **remolade.**
re·mount (rē-mount'; *for n., usually* rē'mount'), *v.t. & v.i.* [ME. *remounten;* OFr. *remonter*], to mount again (in various senses). *n.* a fresh horse, or a supply of fresh horses, to replace another or others.
re·mov·a·bil·i·ty (ri-mōōv'ə-bil'ə-ti), *n.* the quality or fact of being removable.
re·mov·a·ble (ri-mōōv'ə-b'l), *adj.* that can be removed.
re·mov·a·bly (ri-mōōv'ə-bli), *adv.* so as to be removable.
re·mov·al (ri-mōōv''l), *n.* a removing or being removed; especially, *a)* a taking away or being taken away. *b)* dismissal from an office or position. *c)* a change of place, residence, etc.
re·move (ri-mōōv'), *v.t.* [REMOVED (-mōōvd'), REMOVING], [ME. *remouen;* OFr. *remouvoir;* L. *removere;* see RE- & MOVE], 1. to move (something) from where it is; lift, push, or carry away, or from one place to another. 2. to take off: as, *remove* your coat. 3. to take (a person) away by death; kill; assassinate. 4. to dismiss, as from an office or position. 5. to wipe out; get rid of; eliminate: as, *remove* the causes of war. 6. to take, extract, separate, or withdraw (*from*). *v.i.* 1. [Poetic], to go away. 2. to move away, as to another residence or place of business; move. *n.* 1. a removing. 2. the space or distance across which, or interval of time in which, a move is made; hence, 3. a step; space; interval: as, we are but one short *remove* from war. 4. [British], a change or transfer of one's furnishings to another residence or place of business; move. 5. [British], a dish or course following another at a meal. —*SYN.* see **move.**
re·moved (ri-mōōvd'), *adj.* [pp. of *remove*], 1. distant by (a specified number of degrees of relationship): as, one's cousin once *removed* is the child of one's first cousin. 2. remote; distant; unconnected (with *from*).
re·mov·er (ri-mōōv'ēr), *n.* 1. a person or thing that removes something: as, a paint *remover.* 2. in *law,* the transfer of a suit from one court to another by a writ of error.
Rem·sen, I·ra (rem's'n), 1846–1927; American chemist and teacher.
re·mu·ner·ate (ri-mū'nə-rāt'), *v.t.* [REMUNERATED (-id), REMUNERATING], [< L. *remuneratus,* pp. of *remunerari, remunerare,* to reward, remunerate < *re-,* again + *munus, muneris,* a gift], 1. to give or pay (a person) something for some work or service done, loss incurred, etc.; reward; recompense. 2. to make up for; compensate: as, his efforts were *remunerated.* —*SYN.* see **pay.**
re·mu·ner·a·tion (ri-mū'nə-rā'shən), *n.* [L. *remuneratio*], 1. a remunerating. 2. that which remunerates; reward; pay; recompense; compensation.
re·mu·ner·a·tive (ri-mū'nə-rā'tiv, ri-mū'nēr-ə-tiv), *adj.* 1. remunerating. 2. affording remuneration; profitable.
Re·mus (rē'məs), *n.* [L.], in *Roman mythology,* the twin brother of Romulus: see **Romulus.**
ren·ais·sance (ren'ə-säns', ren'ə-zäns', ri-nā's'ns), *n.* [Fr. < *renaître,* to be born anew; *re-,* again + *naître,* to be born; LL. **nascere,* for L. *nasci,* to be born], 1. a new birth; rebirth; revival; renascence. 2. [R-], *a)* the great revival of art, literature, and learning in Europe in the 14th, 15th, and 16th centuries, which began in Italy and spread gradually to other countries: it marked the transition from the medieval world to the modern. *b)* the period during which this revival occurred. *c)* the style and forms of art, literature, architecture, etc. of this period. *d)* any similar revival or period of art, literature, or learning: as, the Provençal *Renaissance.* *adj.* [R-], 1. of, characteristic of, or in the style of, the Renaissance: as, *Renaissance* painting, the *Renaissance* mind. 2. designating or of a style of architecture developed in Italy and western Europe between 1400 and 1600, characterized by the revival and adaptation of classical orders and design, harmonious repetition of details, the use of horizontal lines, and delicate carving.
re·nal (rē'n'l), *adj.* [< Fr. or L.; Fr. *rénal;* L. *renalis* < *renes,* kidneys], of or near the kidneys.
renal capsules (or **glands**), adrenal glands.
Re·nan, Jo·seph Er·nest (zhō'zef' âr'nest' rə-nän'; Eng. ri-nan'), 1823–1892; French historian, philologist, and critic.
Ren·ard (ren'ērd), *n.* Reynard (the fox).
re·nas·cence (ri-nas''ns), *n.* [< *renascent*], 1. a new birth; revival; renaissance. 2. [R-], the Renaissance.
re·nas·cent (ri-nas''nt), *adj.* [L. *renascens;* see RE- & NASCENT], being reborn; springing up again; showing new life and strength; reviving.
ren·con·tre (ren-kon'tēr; Fr. rän'kōn'tr'), *n.* [Fr.], a rencounter.
ren·coun·ter (ren-koun'tēr), *v.t. & v.i.* [Fr. *rencontrer;* see RE- & ENCOUNTER], [Rare], 1. to meet in or as in battle. 2. to meet casually. *n.* 1. a hostile meeting; conflict or contest, as a battle, duel, or debate. 2. a casual meeting, as with a friend.
rend (rend), *v.t.* [RENT (rent), RENDING], [ME. *renden;* AS. *rendan;* akin to OFris. *renda, randa;* latter form suggests connection with AS. *rand, rond,* shield, border, with basic sense "to tear the edges off"], 1. to tear, pull, or rip with violence (with *from, off, away,* etc.): as, will they *rend* the child from his mother? 2. to tear, pull apart, rip up, or split with violence: often used figuratively, as, a roar *rends* the air. *v.i.* to tear; burst; split apart. —*SYN.* see **tear.**
rend·er (ren'dēr), *v.t.* [ME. *rendren;* Anglo-Fr. *render;* OFr. *rendre;* LL. **rendere,* for L. *reddere,* to restore < *re(d)-,* back + *dare,* to give], 1. to give, hand over, deliver, present, or submit, as for approval, consideration, payment, etc.: as, *render* an account of your actions, *render* a bill. 2. to give up; surrender (often with *up*): as, they *rendered* up the city to the enemy. 3. to give in return or requital: as, *render* good for evil. 4. to give back; restore (often with *back*): as, I *render* back your gold. 5. to give or pay, as something due or owed: as, *render* thanks, *render* obedience. 6. to cause to be or become; make: as, the heat *renders* me helpless. 7. *a)* to give or provide (aid, etc.). *b)* to do (a service, etc.). 8. to represent; depict. 9. to perform or interpret by performance; recite (a poem, etc.), play (music), treat (a subject, as in painting), act out (a role), etc. 10. to express in other words, as in another language; translate. 11. to melt the fat from (bacon, etc.); clarify, as lard. 12. in *law,* to make (a payment) in money, goods, or service. 13. in *plastering,* to cover (brickwork, etc.) with a first coat

remultiply **rename** **renationalize** **renavigate**

of plaster. *n.* 1. a payment, sometimes in money but usually in goods or services, as for rent. 2. a first coat of plaster applied to brickwork, etc.

ren·dez·vous (rän'də-vōō'; Fr. rän'dā'vōō'), *n.* [*pl.* RENDEZVOUS (-vōōz'; Fr. -vōō')], [Fr.; substantive use of *rendez vous*, betake or present yourself (or yourselves)], 1. a place for a meeting or assembling, as of troops, ships, etc. 2. a place where people are in the habit of meeting or gathering. 3. *a*) an agreement or appointment between two or more persons to meet at a certain time or place. *b*) the meeting itself. 4. [Obs.], a refuge. *v.i.* [RENDEZVOUSED (-vōōd'), RENDEZVOUSING], to meet or assemble at a certain time or place. *v.t.* to assemble (troops, etc.) at a certain time or place.

ren·di·tion (ren-dish'ən), *n.* [obs. Fr.; after L. *redditio* (< pp. of *reddere*) with *-n-* < Fr. *rendre;* see RENDER], a rendering or result of rendering; specifically, *a*) a performance or interpretation (of a piece of music, a role, etc.). *b*) a translation or version. *c*) [Archaic], a surrender; giving up.

ren·e·gade (ren'ə-gād'), *n.* [Sp. *renegado*, pp. of *renegar*, to deny < ML. *renegare;* L. *re-*, again + *negare*, to deny; the word replaces ME. *renagat* < ML. *renegatus*, of the same ult. origin], 1. a person who abandons his religion for another; apostate. 2. a person who abandons his party, principles, people, etc. for another or others; traitor; turncoat; deserter.

ren·e·ga·do (ren'ə-gā'dō), *n.* [*pl.* RENEGADOES (-dōz)], [Archaic], a renegade.

re·nege (ri-nig', ri-nēg'), *v.i.* [RENEGED (-nigd', -nēgd'), RENEGING], [ML. *renegare;* see RENEGADE], 1. in *card games*, to play a card of another suit, against the rules of the game, when holding any of the suit called for. 2. [Colloq.], to back out of an agreement; go back on a promise. *v.t.* [Archaic], to deny; renounce. *n.* in *card games*, a failure to follow suit; reneging.

re·new (ri-nōō', ri-nū'), *v.t.* [ME. *renewen* < *re-* + *newe* (see NEW), after L. *renovare* (see RENOVATE)], 1. to make new or as if new again; make young, fresh, or strong again; bring back into good condition. 2. to give new spiritual strength to; make better in spirit. 3. to cause to exist again; re-establish. 4. to begin again; take up again; resume. 5. to go over again; say again; repeat: as, *renew* one's objections, *renew* a promise. 6. to replace by something new of the same kind; put in a fresh supply of: as, *renew* provisions. 7. to refill with a fresh supply. 8. to give or get an extension of: as, *renew* a lease. *v.i.* 1. to become new again; be renewed. 2. to begin again; start over.

SYN.—**renew** is the most direct but also the broadest term here, implying a making new again by replacing what is old, worn, exhausted, etc. (to *renew* a stock of goods); to **renovate** is to clean up, replace or repair worn parts, etc. so as to bring back to good condition; to **restore** is to bring back to an original or unimpaired condition after exhaustion, illness, dilapidation, etc. (to *restore* an old castle); **refresh** implies a restoring of depleted strength, vigor, etc. by furnishing something needed (a *refreshing* sleep); **rejuvenate** implies a restoring of youthful appearance, vigor, etc. (she looked *rejuvenated* after the plastic surgery).

re·new·al (ri-nōō'əl, ri-nū'əl), *n.* a renewing or being renewed.

re·new·ed·ly (ri-nōō'id-li, ri-nū'id-li), *adv.* again; anew.

Ren·frew (ren'frōō), *n.* 1. a county of western Scotland, on the Clyde: pop., 335,000: also **Renfrewshire.** 2. its county seat: pop., 17,000.

Ren·frew·shire (ren'frōō-shir'), *n.* Renfrew (county).

ren·i- (ren'i, rē'ni), [< L. *ren*, *renis*], a combining form meaning *kidney*, *kidneys*, as in *reniform:* also **reno-**.

Re·ni, Gui·do (gwē'dô re'nē), 1575–1642; Italian painter.

ren·i·form (ren'i-fôrm', rē'ni-fôrm'), *adj.* [Mod. L. *reniformis;* see RENI- & -FORM], shaped like a kidney.

re·nin (rē'nin), *n.* [< L. *ren*, kidney], a protein formed in the kidneys and thought to be associated with some forms of hypertension in man.

re·ni·ten·cy (ri-nī't'n-si, ren'ə-t'n-si), *n.* state, quality, or instance of being renitent.

re·ni·tent (ri-nī't'nt, ren'ə-t'nt), *adj.* [< Fr. or L.; Fr. *rénitent;* L. *renitens*, ppr. of *reniti*, to resist; *re-*, back + *niti*, to struggle], 1. resisting pressure; resistant. 2. opposing stubbornly; recalcitrant; obstinate.

Rennes (ren), *n.* a city in northwestern France: pop., 124,000.

ren·net (ren'it), *n.* [ME. < *rennen*, to run + *-et* (AS. *-el*), n. suffix: so called because rennet causes milk to run, or coagulate; cf. dial. var. *runnet*], 1. the membrane that lines the fourth stomach of a calf or the stomach of some other young animals. 2. *a*) a preparation or extract of this membrane, used to curdle milk, as in making cheese or junket. *b*) anything used to curdle milk. 3. a substance containing rennin, found in the stomach of a calf. 4. rennin.

ren·nin (ren'in), *n.* [*rennet* + *-in*], a coagulating enzyme that can curdle milk, found in the gastric juice of the calf, etc.: cf. **rennet.**

Re·no (rē'nō), *n.* a city in western Nevada: pop., 51,000.

ren·o- (ren'ə, rē'nə), reni-.

Re·noir, Pierre Au·guste (pyâr ô'güst' rə-nwär'), 1841–1919; French painter.

re·nounce (ri-nouns'), *v.t.* [RENOUNCED (-nounst'), RENOUNCING], [ME. *renouncen;* OFr. *renoncer;* L. *renuntiare, renunciare; re-*, back + *nuntiare, nunciare*, to tell < *nuntius*, messenger; see NUNCIO], 1. to give up, usually by a formal public statement (a claim, right, opinion, etc.). 2. to give up, as a habit, practice, etc.; cease to have or show (a feeling, etc.): as, he *renounced* all honor. 3. to cast off; disown; deny all responsibility for or allegiance to (a person): as, *renounce* a son. 4. in *card games*, to indicate a lack of (a certain suit) by playing a card from another. 5. in *law*, to give up formally (a right, claim, or trust, especially one bestowed by a will). *v.i.* 1. in *card games*, to fail to follow suit, having no cards of the suit led. 2. in *law*, to give up a right, trust, etc. *n.* in *card games*, failure to play the suit led. —***SYN.*** see **abdicate.**

re·nounce·ment (ri-nouns'mənt), *n.* a renouncing.

ren·o·vate (ren'ə-vāt'), *v.t.* [RENOVATED (-id), RENOVATING], [< L. *renovatus*, pp. of *renovare*, to renew; *re-*, again + *novare*, to make new < *novus*, new], 1. to make new or like new; clean up, replace worn and broken parts in, repair, etc. 2. to refresh; revive. *adj.* [Archaic], renovated. —***SYN.*** see **renew.**

ren·o·va·tion (ren'ə-vā'shən), *n.* a renovating or being renovated.

ren·o·va·tor (ren'ə-vā'tẽr), *n.* [L.], a person or thing that renovates.

re·nown (ri-noun'), *n.* [ME. & Anglo-Fr. *renoun* < OFr. *renom(m)er*, to name again or often, make famous; *re-*, again + *nom(m)er*, to name; L. *nominare* < *nomen*, a name], 1. fame; great reputation; celebrity. 2. [Obs.], report or rumor. *v.t.* [Obs.], to make famous.

re·nowned (ri-nound'), *adj.* having renown; famous. —***SYN.*** see **famous.**

rens·se·laer·ite (ren'sə-lẽr-īt', ren'sə-lâr'īt), *n.* [after Stephen Van *Rensselaer* (1764–1839), American general and statesman], a variety of talc found in New York State and Canada: it can be worked on a lathe.

rent (rent), *n.* [ME.; OFr. *rente;* LL. **rendita* (pp. of **rendere;* see RENDER), for L. *reddita* (*pecunia*), paid (money)], 1. a stated return or payment for the temporary possession or use of a house, land, or other property, made, usually at fixed intervals, by the tenant or user to the owner. 2. [Obs.], *a*) real estate or other property yielding an income. *b*) income; revenue. 3. in *economics*, *a*) income from the ownership of real estate; return yielded by land under cultivation minus the cost of production. *b*) a return or profit realized from a differential advantage in production, as the difference in yield between relatively good land and the poorest land under cultivation in similar conditions. *v.t.* 1. to get temporary possession and use of (a house, land, etc.) in return for stated payments, usually at fixed intervals. 2. to give temporary possession and use of in return for such payments; lease or let for rent (often with *out*). *v.i.* to be leased or let for rent: as, the room *rents* for $7. —***SYN.*** see **hire.**
for rent, available to be rented.

rent (rent), past tense and past participle of **rend.** *adj.* torn or split.

rent (rent), *n.* [n. use of obs. or dial. *rent*, var. of *rend*], 1. a hole or gap made by rending or tearing, as a torn place in cloth, a fissure in the earth, etc. 2. a breach of relations, as between persons or in an organized group; schism.

rent·al (ren't'l), *n.* [ME.; Anglo-Fr.; Anglo-L. *rentale*], 1. an amount paid or received as rent. 2. an income from rents received. 3. a list, or schedule, of rents. 4. a house, apartment, etc. offered for rent. *adj.* of, in, or for rent.

rental library, a collection of popular books any of which can be borrowed for a small fee.

‡rente (ränt), *n.* [*pl.* RENTES (ränt)], [Fr.; see RENT (payment)], 1. annual income or revenue; annuity. 2. *usually pl. a*) the bonds, stocks, etc. representing the consolidated governmental debt of France. *b*) interest paid on this.

rent·er (ren'tẽr), *n.* 1. a person who pays rent for the use of another's property. 2. a person who owns and rents out property.

rent-free (rent'frē'), *adj. & adv.* without payment of rent.

‡ren·tier (rän'tyā'), *n.* [Fr. < *rente;* see RENTE], a person who has a fixed income from land, bonds, etc.

re·nun·ci·a·tion (ri-nun'si-ā'shən, ri-nun'shi-ā'shən), *n.* [ME.; OFr. *renonciation;* L. *renuntiatio* < *renuntiatus*, pp. of *renuntiare;* see RENOUNCE], 1. a renouncing; giving up formally or voluntarily, often at a sacrifice, as of a right, claim, title, etc. 2. a written statement or declaration of this.

re·nun·ci·a·to·ry (ri-nun'si-ə-tôr'i, ri-nun'shi-ə-tō'ri), *adj.* of or characterized by renunciation.

re·o·pen (rē-ō′p'n), *v.t.* & *v.i.* 1. to open again. 2. to begin again; resume.

re·or·der (rē-ôr′dẽr), *n.* a second or repeated order for the same goods from the same dealer. *v.t.* 1. to give a reorder for; order again. 2. to put in order again. *v.i.* to order goods again.

re·or·gan·i·za·tion (rē′ôr-gən-i-zā′shən, rē-ôr′gən-ī-zā′-shən), *n.* 1. a reorganizing or being reorganized. 2. in *finance*, a thorough reconstruction of a business corporation, comprising a considerable change in capital structure, as effected after, or in anticipation of, a failure and receivership: cf. **readjustment.**

re·or·gan·ize (rē-ôr′gə-nīz′), *v.t.* & *v.i.* to organize again or anew; effect a reorganization (of).

re·o·ri·ent (rē-ôr′i-ent′, rē-ō′ri-ent′; *for adj.*, rē-ôr′i-ənt, rē-ō′ri-ənt), *v.t.* & *v.i.* to orient again or anew. *adj.* [Rare], rising again.

re·o·ri·en·ta·tion (rē-ôr′i-en-tā′shən, rē′ō-ri-en-tā′shən), *n.* a reorienting or being reoriented; new orientation.

rep (rep), *n.* [Fr. *reps;* prob. < Eng. *ribs*], a fabric of silk, wool, cotton, rayon, etc., with a ribbed or corded surface: also **repp, reps.**

Rep., 1. Representative. 2. Republic. 3. Republican.

rep., 1. repeat. 2. report. 3. reported. 4. reporter.

re·paid (ri-pād′), past tense and past participle of **repay.**

re·paint (rē-pānt′; *also, for n.*, rē′pānt′), *v.t.* & *v.i.* to paint again. *n.* 1. anything repainted, as a part of a picture, a car, etc. 2. a repainting.

re·pair (ri-pâr′), *v.t.* [ME. *reparen;* OFr. *reparer;* L. *reparare; re-*, again + *parare*, to prepare, get ready], 1. to put back in good condition after damage, decay, etc.; mend; fix. 2. to renew; restore; revive: as, *repair* one's health. 3. to amend; set right; remedy: as, *repair* the mistake. 4. to make amends for; make up for; compensate for (a wrong, injury, etc.). *n.* 1. the act, process, or work of repairing. 2. *usually in pl.* an instance, piece, or result of repairing. 3. the state of being repaired, or fit for use: as, the car was kept in *repair*. 4. state with respect to repairing: as, the house is in bad *repair*. —*SYN.* see **mend.**

re·pair (ri-pâr′), *v.i.* [ME. *repairen;* OFr. *repairer;* LL. *repatriare* < L. *re-*, back + *patria*, one's native country], 1. to go (*to* a place); betake oneself. 2. to go often, customarily, or in numbers: as, they *repaired* daily to the park. 3. [Obs.], to return. *n.* [Archaic], a place to which a person or persons go often or customarily; resort; haunt.

re·pair·a·ble (ri-pâr′ə-b'l), *adj.* that can be repaired.

re·pair·man (ri-pâr′man′, ri-pâr′mən), *n.* [*pl.* REPAIRMEN (-men′, -mən)], a man whose work is repairing things.

re·pand (ri-pand′), *adj.* [L. *repandus*, bent backward; *re-*, back + *pandus*, pp. of *pandare*, to bend, curve], in *botany*, having a wavy margin, as some leaves.

rep·a·ra·ble (rep′ẽr-ə-b'l), *adj.* [Fr. *réparable;* L. *reparabilis*], that can be repaired, mended, remedied, etc.

rep·a·ra·bly (rep′ẽr-ə-bli), *adv.* in a reparable manner; so as to be reparable.

rep·a·ra·tion (rep′ə-rā′shən), *n.* [OFr. *reparacion;* LL. *reparatio* < pp. of L. *reparare;* see REPAIR (to mend)], 1. a repairing or being repaired; restoration to good condition. 2. repairs. 3. a making of amends; making up for a wrong or injury. 4. anything paid or done to make up for something else; compensation; specifically, *usually pl.*, compensation by a defeated nation for damage done to civilians and their property in a war, payable in money, labor, goods, etc.

SYN.—**reparation** refers to the making of amends, specifically the paying of compensation, for some wrong or injury (war *reparations*); **restitution** implies return to the rightful owner of something that has been taken away, or of an equivalent (he made *restitution* for the libel); **redress** suggests retaliation or resort to the courts to right a wrong (to seek *redress* for an injury); **indemnification** refers to reimbursement, as by an insurance company, for loss, damage, etc.

re·par·a·tive (ri-par′ə-tiv), *adj.* 1. repairing or tending to repair; mending, etc. 2. of or involving reparation.

rep·ar·tee (rep′ẽr-tē′, rep′är-tē′), *n.* [Fr. *repartie*, pp. of *repartir*, to return quickly a thrust or a blow, reply; *re-*, back + *partir* (L. *partire*), to part; see PART], 1. a quick, witty reply. 2. quick, witty conversation. 3. skill in making such replies. —*SYN.* see **wit.**

re·par·ti·tion (rē′pär-tish′ən, rē′pẽr-tish′ən), *n.* 1. a partitioning; distribution. 2. a partitioning again; redistribution. *v.t.* to effect a repartition of.

re·pass (rē-pas′, rē-päs′), *v.i.* & *v.t.* [Fr. *repasser*], to pass back or again.

re·pas·sage (rē-pas′ij), *n.* [ME.; Late OFr.], 1. a repassing. 2. the right or privilege of repassing.

re·past (ri-past′, ri-päst′), *n.* [ME.; OFr.; ML. *repastum* < LL. *repascere*, to feed again; *re-*, again + *pascere*, to feed], 1. *a*) food and drink for a meal. *b*) a meal. 2. [Archaic], *a*) the eating of food, as at a meal. *b*) mealtime. 3. [Obs.], food.

re·pa·tri·ate (rē-pā′tri-āt′), *v.t.* & *v.i.* [REPATRIATED (-id), REPATRIATING], [< LL. *repatriatus*, pp. of *repatriare* < L. *re-*, back + *patria*, native land], to send back or return to the country of birth, citizenship, or allegiance: as, prisoners of war were *repatriated.*

re·pa·tri·a·tion (rē-pā′tri-ā′shən, rē′pā-tri-ā′shən), *n.* [ML. *repatriatio*], a repatriating or being repatriated.

re·pay (ri-pā′), *v.t.* [REPAID (-pād′), REPAYING], [OFr. *repaier*], 1. to pay back (money); refund. 2. to pay back (a person). 3. to make some return for; compensate: as, *repay* a kindness. 4. to give or make some return or recompense to (a person), as for some service. 5. to do or give (the same as has been received): as, *repay* a visit. *v.i.* 1. to make a repayment or return; hence, 2. to reward or punish. —*SYN.* see **pay.**

re·pay·a·ble (ri-pā′ə-b'l), *adj.* that can or must be repaid.

re·pay·ment (ri-pā′mənt), *n.* 1. a repaying or being repaid. 2. the thing or amount repaid.

re·peal (ri-pēl′), *v.t.* [ME. *repelen;* OFr. *rapeler;* see RE- & APPEAL], 1. to withdraw officially or formally; revoke; cancel; annul: as, the law was *repealed.* 2. [Obs.], to call back, as from exile. *n.* a repealing; revocation, abrogation, etc. —*SYN.* see **abolish.**

re·peal·er (ri-pēl′ẽr), *n.* a person or thing that repeals.

re·peat (ri-pēt′), *v.t.* [ME. *repeten;* OFr. *repeter;* L. *repetere; re-*, again + *petere*, to seek, demand, attack], 1. to say or utter again; reiterate: as, *repeat* a remark. 2. to say over or through; recite, as a poem. 3. to say after someone else. 4. to tell to someone else: as, *repeat* a secret. 5. *a*) to do or make again; do over again: as, *repeat* an operation. *b*) to make happen again or undergo again: as, *repeat* an adventure. 6. to say again what has been said before by (oneself): as, he *repeats* himself. 7. to present (itself or themselves) again: as, these things have a way of *repeating* themselves. *v.i.* 1. to say or do again what has been said or done before. 2. to recur: as, experiences *repeat.* 3. to vote more than once in an election: an illegal and punishable act. *n.* 1. a doing or saying again; repetition. 2. anything said, done, or occurring again. 3. in *music*, *a*) a passage repeated in playing. *b*) the symbol for this (:||), placed after, and often before, (||:), a passage to be repeated. Abbreviated **rep.**

SYN.—**repeat** is the common, general word meaning to say, do, make, present, etc. over again (will you *repeat* that question, please?); **iterate** and **reiterate** both suggest a repeating, either once or several times, but **reiterate** strongly implies insistent repetition over and over again (he keeps *reiterating* his innocence); **recapitulate** suggests a repeating briefly of the main points in a discourse in summarizing (he will *recapitulate* his account of the ball game at 8:00 o'clock).

re·peat·ed (ri-pēt′id), *adj.* [pp. of *repeat*], said, made, done, or happening again, or again and again.

re·peat·ed·ly (ri-pēt′id-li), *adv.* more than once; again and again; frequently.

re·peat·er (ri-pēt′ẽr), *n.* 1. a person or thing that repeats. 2. a watch or clock, especially a watch, which can be made to strike whatever hour (or, sometimes, quarter-hour) it has struck last. 3. a repeating rifle or pistol. 4. a person who has been in jail for the same crime, or in the same jail, more than once. 5. a person who fraudulently votes more than once in the same election. 6. in *education*, a student who takes again a course or courses in which he has previously failed. 7. in *mathematics*, a repeating decimal. 8. in *telegraphy*, an automatic relay, for switching a message from a weak to a strong circuit.

repeating decimal, 1. a decimal in which one digit is repeated infinitely (e.g., .23333 . . .). 2. a circulating decimal: see **circulate** (sense 4).

repeating rifle, a rifle that can fire a number of shots without reloading.

re·pel (ri-pel′), *v.t.* [REPELLED (-peld′), REPELLING], [ME. *repellen;* L. *repellere*, to drive back; *re-*, back + *pellere*, to drive], 1. to drive back; force back; hold or ward off: as, *repel* an attack, *repel* a blow. 2. to refuse; reject: as, *repel* advances. 3. to refuse to accept (a person); spurn: as, *repel* a suitor. 4. to cause distaste or dislike in: as, the odor *repels* me. 5. to be resistant to, or present an opposing force to: as, a plastic coating *repels* moisture. 6. to fail to mix with: as, water *repels* oil. Opposed to *attract* (in senses 4, 5, 6). *v.i.* 1. to drive off, or offer an opposing force to, something. 2. to cause distaste, dislike, or aversion.

re·pel·lence (ri-pel′əns), *n.* 1. the quality or state of being repellent. 2. capacity of repelling.

re·pel·len·cy (ri-pel′ən-si), *n.* repellence.

re·pel·lent (ri-pel′ənt), *adj.* [L. *repellens*], 1. repelling; pushing away or driving back. 2. causing distaste,

reoppose **reordain** **reordination** **repacify** **repack** **repaper** **repave** **re-pay**

dislike, or aversion; repulsive. 3. waterproof. *n.* something that repels; specifically, *a*) a waterproof fabric. *b*) any substance, as lime, oil, etc., used to drive away plant pests or other insects. *c*) in *medicine*, anything used to reduce a tumor, swelling, etc.

re·pel·ler (ri-pel′ẽr), *n.* a person or thing that repels.

re·pent (ri-pent′), *v.i.* [ME. *repenten;* OFr. *repentir* < L. *re-*, again + *poenitere*, to repent (used impersonally) < *poena*, punishment], 1. to feel sorry or self-reproachful for what one has done or not done; be conscience-stricken or contrite (often with *of*). 2. to feel such regret or dissatisfaction over some past action, intention, etc. as to change one's mind about it: as, he *repented* of his generosity. 3. in *religious usage*, to feel so contrite over one's sins as to change, or decide to change, one's ways; be penitent. *v.t.* 1. to feel sorry or self-reproachful for (an error, sin, etc.). 2. to feel such regret or dissatisfaction over as to change one's mind about: as, he *repented* his generosity.

re·pent (rē′pənt), *adj.* [L. *repens*, ppr. of *repere*, to creep; see REPTILE], 1. in *botany*, creeping. 2. in *zoology*, reptant; crawling.

re·pent·ance (ri-pen′təns), *n.* a repenting; penitent state; feeling of sorrow, etc., especially for wrongdoing; compunction; contrition; remorse.—*SYN.* see **penitence**.

re·pent·ant (ri-pen′tənt), *adj.* [ME.; OFr., ppr.], 1. repenting; penitent. 2. characterized by or indicative of repentance.

re·peo·ple (rē-pē′p'l), *v.t.* [Fr. *repeupler*], 1. to people anew; provide with new inhabitants. 2. to restock with animals.

re·per·cus·sion (rē′pẽr-kush′ən), *n.* [< Fr. or L.; Fr. *répercussion;* L. *repercussio* < pp. of *repercutere*, to rebound, strike back; see RE- & PERCUSSION], 1. a driving back or being driven back by something resistant; rebound; recoil; hence, 2. reflection, as of light or sound; reverberation; echo. 3. a reaction; action set in motion by an event or action, often very remote: as, the explosion of the first atomic bomb had *repercussions* all over the world. 4. in *medicine*, *a*) the action of a repellent in reducing a swelling, tumor, etc. *b*) ballottement. 5. in *music*, *a*) reiteration of a tone or chord. *b*) reappearance of the subject and answer after an episode in a fugue.

re·per·cus·sive (rē′pẽr-kus′iv), *adj.* [Fr. *répercussif*], causing, caused by, or having the nature of, repercussion; reverberating or reverberated.

rep·er·toire (rep′ẽr-twär′, rep′ẽr-twôr′), *n.* [Fr. *répertoire* < LL. *repertorium;* see REPERTORY], the stock of plays, operas, parts, songs, etc. that a company, actor, singer, etc. is familiar with and ready to perform.

rep·er·to·ry (rep′ẽr-tôr′i, rep′ẽr-tō′ri), *n.* [*pl.* REPERTORIES (-iz, -riz)], [LL. *repertorium*, an inventory < L. *repertus*, pp. of *reperire*, to find out, discover < *re-*, again + *parire*, to produce, invent, acquire], 1. a storehouse; repository for useful things. 2. the things stored; stock; collection. 3. a repertoire.

repertory theater, a theater in which a permanent acting company presents a varied selection of plays.

rep·e·tend (rep′ə-tend′, rep′ə-tend′), *n.* [L. *repetendus*, to be repeated, gerundive of *repetere*, to repeat], 1. in *mathematics*, the digit or digits repeated indefinitely in a repeating or circulating decimal. 2. in *music*, a repeated sound or phrase, as a refrain.

rep·e·ti·tion (rep′ə-tish′ən), *n.* [Fr. *répétition;* L. *repetitio*], 1. a repeating; a doing or saying again, or again and again. 2. recitation, as of something memorized. 3. something repeated or made by repeating; specifically, a reproduction, copy, or replica.

rep·e·ti·tious (rep′ə-tish′əs), *adj.* full of or characterized by repetition, especially tiresome or boring repetition.

re·pet·i·tive (ri-pet′ə-tiv), *adj.* of or characterized by repetition.

re·phrase (rē-frāz′), *v.t.* to phrase again, anew, or in a different way.

re·pine (ri-pīn′), *v.i.* [*re-* + *pine*, *v.*], to feel or express discontent; complain; fret (often with *at*).

re·place (ri-plās′), *v.t.* 1. to place again; put back in a former place, position, condition, etc. 2. to take the place of; supplant: as, the automobile has *replaced* the horse. 3. to provide a substitute or equivalent for: as, *replace* a worn tire. 4. to put back or pay back; restore; return: as, *replace* embezzled funds.

SYN.—**replace** implies a taking the place of someone or something that is now lost, gone, destroyed, worn out, etc. (we *replace* defective tubes); **displace** suggests that the person or thing to be replaced has first been dislodged or ousted (he had been *displaced* in her affections by another man); **supersede** implies a replacing with something superior, more up-to-date, etc. (the steamship *superseded* the sailing ship); **supplant** suggests a displacing through force, fraud, treachery, etc. (the prince had been *supplanted* by an impostor).

re·place·ment (ri-plās′mənt), *n.* 1. a replacing or being replaced. 2. a person or thing that takes the place of another, especially of one that has worn out, broken down, etc. 3. a member of the armed forces who is available for assignment to fill a vacancy or complete a quota; reinforcement. 4. in *crystallography*, the replacing of an angle or edge by one face or more.

re·plead·er (rē-plēd′ẽr), *n.* [*re-* + obs. *pleader* (see PLEAD & -ER); cf. Fr. *replaider*, OFr. *repledoier*], in *law*, 1. a second pleading. 2. the right or privilege of pleading again. 3. a court order requiring the parties to plead again from that point in the pleading where an error first occurred.

re·plen·ish (ri-plen′ish), *v.t.* [ME. *replenissen* < ppr. stem of OFr. *replenir* < L. *re-*, again + *plenus*, full], 1. to make full or complete again, as by furnishing a new supply: as, *replenish* the stock of goods. 2. to supply again with fuel or the like. 3. to repeople.

re·plen·ish·ment (ri-plen′ish-mənt), *n.* 1. a replenishing or being replenished. 2. a fresh supply.

re·plete (ri-plēt′), *adj.* [ME.; OFr. *replet;* L. *repletus*, pp. of *replere; re-*, again + *plere*, to fill], 1. well filled; plentifully supplied. 2. stuffed, as with food; gorged.

re·ple·tion (ri-plē′shən), *n.* the state of being replete; a being full or too full: as, he ate to *repletion*.

re·plev·i·a·ble (ri-plev′i-ə-b'l), *adj.* in *law*, that can be replevied.

re·plev·in (ri-plev′in), *n.* [Anglo-Fr. *replevine* < OFr. *replevir*, to warrant, pledge; *re-*, again + *plevir*, to pledge < Gmc. **plegjan;* see PLEDGE], in *law*, 1. the recovery by a person of goods claimed to be his, on his promise to test the matter in court and give the goods up again if defeated. 2. the writ by which he takes over the goods. *v.t.* to replevy.

re·plev·i·sa·ble (ri-plev′i-sə-b'l), *adj.* repleviable.

re·plev·y (ri-plev′i), *v.t.* [REPLEVIED (-id), REPLEVYING], [OFr. *replevir;* see REPLEVIN], in *law*, 1. to seize or take back (goods) under a writ of replevin. 2. [Rare], to release (a man) from prison when he has found bail to guarantee his return later. *n.* replevin.

rep·li·ca (rep′li-kə), *n.* [It., a reply, repetition < It. & L. *replicare;* see REPLY], 1. a reproduction or copy of a work of art; especially, a copy made by the maker of the original. 2. any very close reproduction or copy; facsimile. —*SYN.* see **copy**.

rep·li·cate (rep′li-kit; *for v.*, rep′li-kāt′), *adj.* [L. *replicatus;* see RE- & PLICATE], in *botany*, folded back on itself, as a leaf. *n.* in *music*, a tone repeated one or more octaves higher or lower than another. *v.t.* [REPLICATED (-id), REPLICATING], 1. to fold; bend back. 2. [Rare], to repeat. 3. [Rare], to reply.

rep·li·cat·ed (rep′li-kāt′id), *adj.* replicate.

rep·li·ca·tion (rep′li-kā′shən), *n.* [ME. *replicacioun;* OFr.; L. *replicatio* < pp. of *replicare;* see REPLY], 1. a folding back; fold. 2. a reply; answer; especially, a reply to an answer. 3. repetition of a sound; echo. 4. a copying. 5. a copy; reproduction. 6. in *law*, the plaintiff's answer to the plea of the defendant.

re·pli·er (ri-plī′ẽr), *n.* a person who replies.

re·ply (ri-plī′), *v.i.* [REPLIED (-plīd′), REPLYING], [ME. *replyen;* OFr. *replier;* L. *replicare*, to fold back, make a reply; *re-*, back + *plicare*, to fold], 1. to answer in words; respond in speech or writing. 2. to respond by some action: as, they *replied* to the enemy's fire. 3. to echo. 4. in *law*, to answer a defendant's plea. *v.t.* to say in answer: as, she *replied* that her mind was made up. *n.* [*pl.* REPLIES (-plīz′)], 1. an answer in words; response in speech or writing. 2. a response by some action. —*SYN.* see **answer**.

‡ré·pon·dez s'il vous plaît (rā′pōn′dā′ sēl′ vōō′ ple′), [Fr.], please reply: placed on formal invitations: abbreviated **R.S.V.P., r.s.v.p.**

re·port (ri-pôrt′, ri-pōrt′), *v.t.* [ME. *reporten;* OFr. *reporter*, to carry back; L. *reportare; re-*, back + *portare*, to carry], 1. to give an account of, often at regular intervals; give information about, as something seen or investigated; say. 2. to carry and repeat (a message, etc.). 3. to write an account of for presentation to others or for publication, as in a newspaper. 4. to give a formal statement or account of; announce formally, as the results of an investigation. 5. to present or return (something referred for study, action, etc.) with the conclusions reached or recommendations made (often with *out*): as, the committee *reported* the bill out. 6. to complain about; denounce to a person in authority: as, *report* a rudeness, *report* a salesgirl to the manager. *v.i.* 1. to make a report. 2. to work as a reporter. 3. to present oneself or make one's presence known: as, *report* for duty. *n.* 1. rumor; gossip; common talk: as, *report* has it that you are married. 2. reputation: as, a man of good *report*. 3. a statement or account brought in and presented, often for publication: as, a *report* of a battle. 4. a formal or official presentation of facts or of the record of something, as an investigation. 5. *pl.* books containing a record of court cases, decisions, etc. 6. the noise made by an explosion: as, the *report* of a gun. Abbreviated **rep., rpt.** —*SYN.* see **tell**.

---

repenalize	**replaster**	**replunge**	**repopularize**
rephotograph	**replay**	**repolish**	**repopulate**
replant	**repledge**	**reponder**	**repopulation**

re·port·a·ble (ri-pôr′tə-b'l, ri-pōr′tə-b'l), *adj.* that can be, or is worth being, reported.
report card, a written report of a pupil's grades, deportment, etc., sent to his parents or guardian at regular intervals.
re·port·er (ri-pôr′tẽr, ri-pōr′tẽr), *n.* [ME. *reportour;* OFr. *reporteur*], a person who reports; especially, *a)* a person authorized to report legal or legislative proceedings: as, a court *reporter. b)* a person who gathers information and writes reports for publication in a newspaper, magazine, etc. Abbreviated **rep.**
rep·or·to·ri·al (rep′ẽr-tôr′i-əl, rep′ẽr-tō′ri-əl), *adj.* of, characteristic of, or like a reporter.
re·pos·al (ri-pōz″l), *n.* a reposing, as of trust, etc.
re·pose (ri-pōz′), *v.t.* [REPOSED (-pōzd′), REPOSING], [Late ME.; OFr. *reposer;* LL. *repausare* < L. *re-*, again + *pausare*, to pause, rest], to lay or put to rest: often reflexive, as, *repose* yourself on the bed. *v.i.* 1. to lie at rest. 2. to rest from work, travel, exercise, etc. 3. to rest in a grave: as, he *reposes* at Arlington Cemetery. 4. to depend; rely (with *in*). 5. to lie quiet and calm: as, the land *reposes* in the dusk. 6. to lie, rest, or be supported: as, the shale *reposes* on a bed of limestone. *n.* 1. a reposing, or resting. 2. *a)* rest. *b)* sleep. 3. peace of mind; freedom from worry or troubles. 4. calm or ease of manner; composure. 5. calm; tranquillity; peace. 6. harmony of form or color, giving an effect of tranquillity, as in a painting.
re·pose (ri-pōz′), *v.t.* [REPOSED (-pōzd′), REPOSING], [ME. *reposen* < L. *repositus* (see REPOSITORY), after verbs in *-pose*, as *dispose*], 1. [Rare], to place; put. 2. to place (trust, confidence, etc. *in* someone).
re·pose·ful (ri-pōz′fəl), *adj.* full of repose; tranquil.
re·pos·it (ri-poz′it), *v.t.* [< L. *repositus;* see REPOSITORY], 1. to put away or deposit (*in* some place), as for safekeeping. 2. [Rare], to replace.
re·po·si·tion (rē′pə-zish′ən, rep′ə-zish′ən), *n.* a repositing or being reposited; specifically, replacement, as of a part of the body by a surgical operation.
re·pos·i·to·ry (ri-poz′ə-tôr′i, ri-poz′ə-tō′ri), *n.* [*pl.* REPOSITORIES (-iz, -riz)], [L. *repositorium* < *repositus*, pp. of *reponere*, to put back; *re-*, back + *ponere*, to place], 1. a box, chest, closet, or room in which things may be placed for safekeeping. 2. [Rare], a building for safekeeping; museum. 3. a warehouse or shop. 4. a burial vault; sepulcher. 5. anything thought of as a place of accumulation or storage. 6. a person to whom something is entrusted or confided; confidant.
re·pos·sess (rē′pə-zes′), *v.t.* 1. to possess again; take or get possession of again. 2. to put in possession again: as, they *repossessed* him of his house.
re·pos·ses·sion (rē′pə-zesh′ən), *n.* a repossessing or being repossessed.
‡re·pous·sé (rə-pōō′sā′), *adj.* [Fr., pp. of *repousser*, to push back; *re-*, back + *pousser;* see PUSH], 1. formed in relief, as a pattern on thin metal beaten up from the underside. 2. shaped or decorated with patterns made in this way. *n.* 1. a pattern or surface made in this way. 2. the art or process of hammering metal in this way.
repp (rep), *n.* rep (fabric).
Rep·plier, Agnes (rep′lẽr), 1855–1950; American essayist.
repr., 1. represented. 2. representing. 3. reprint.
rep·re·hend (rep′ri-hend′), *v.t.* [L. *reprehendere; re-*, back + *prehendere;* see PREHENSILE], 1. to reprimand; rebuke; reprove. 2. to find fault with; censure; blame. —*SYN.* see **criticize.**
rep·re·hen·si·bil·i·ty (rep′ri-hen′sə-bil′ə-ti), *n.* the state or quality of being reprehensible.
rep·re·hen·si·ble (rep′ri-hen′sə-b'l), *adj.* [ME. *reprehensyble;* LL. *reprehensibilis*], deserving to be reprehended.
rep·re·hen·si·bly (rep′ri-hen′sə-bli), *adv.* 1. in a reprehensible manner. 2. to a reprehensible degree.
rep·re·hen·sion (rep′ri-hen′shən), *n.* [ME. *reprehencion;* L. *reprehensio*], a reprehending; reproof or censure.
rep·re·hen·sive (rep′ri-hen′siv), *adj.* [Now Rare], having the nature of, or conveying, reprehension; reproving; censuring.
rep·re·sent (rep′ri-zent′), *v.t.* [ME. *representen;* OFr. *representer;* L. *repraesentare; re-*, again + *praesentare;* see RE- & PRESENT, *v.*], 1. to present or picture to the mind; put clearly before the mind. 2. *a)* to present a likeness or image of; portray; depict. *b)* to be a likeness or image of, as a picture or statue is. 3. to present in words; describe, state, or set forth; often, to do so forcibly or earnestly, so as to influence action, persuade hearers, make effective protest, etc.: as, he *represented* the war as already lost. 4. *a)* to be a sign for; stand for; denote; designate; symbolize: as, x *represents* the unknown. *b)* to denote or express by symbols, characters, etc.: as, *represent* mathematical quantities by letters. 5. to be the equivalent of; correspond to, as in a different place or time: as, a cave *represented* home to these people. 6. *a)* to present, produce, or perform (a play, etc.). *b)* to play the part of; impersonate (a character), as in a drama. 7. to act or stand in place of; be an agent, proxy, or substitute for. 8. to speak and act for by duly conferred authority, as an ambassador for his country or a legislator for his constituents. 9. to serve as a specimen, example, type, or instance of; exemplify or typify.
re·pre·sent (rē′pri-zent′), *v.t.* to present again.
rep·re·sen·ta·tion (rep′ri-zen-tā′shən), *n.* [ME. *representacyon;* Late OFr. *représentation;* L. *repraesentatio*], 1. act or instance of representing, or the state, fact, or mode of being represented (in various senses). 2. a likeness, image, picture, etc. 3. *often in pl.* a description, account, or statement of facts, allegations, or arguments, especially one intended to influence action, persuade hearers, make protest, etc. 4. presentation, production, or performance of a play, etc. 5. representatives collectively. 6. in *law*, a statement or implication of fact, oral or written, as made by one party to induce another to enter into a contract.
rep·re·sen·ta·tion·al (rep′ri-zen-tā′shən-'l), *adj.* of or characterized by representation.
rep·re·sent·a·tive (rep′ri-zen′tə-tiv), *adj.* [ME. < Late OFr. or ML.; Late OFr. *représentatif;* ML. *repraesentativus*], 1. representing or serving to represent; specifically, *a)* picturing; portraying; reproducing. *b)* acting or speaking, especially by due authority, in the place, or on behalf, of another or others; serving as an agent, deputy, or delegate, especially in a legislative assembly. 2. composed of persons duly authorized, as by election, to act and speak for others: as, a *representative* assembly. 3. of, characterized by, or based on representation of the people by elected delegates: as, *representative* government. 4. being an example or type of a certain class or kind of thing; typical: as, Detroit is a *representative* American city. 5. in *botany & zoology*, corresponding to, or taking the place of, some other form of plant or animal, as in a different area. *n.* 1. a person or thing enough like the others in its class or kind to serve as an example or type of the class or kind. 2. a person duly authorized to act or speak for another or others; agent, delegate, deputy, etc., as a member of an elected legislative body. 3. [R-], a member of the lower house of Congress (*House of Representatives*) or of a State legislature: abbreviated **Rep.**
re·press (ri-pres′), *v.t.* [ME. *repressen* < L. *repressus*, pp. of *reprimere;* see RE- & PRESS (to squeeze)], 1. to keep down; hold back; restrain: as, *repress* a sigh. 2. to put down; subdue. 3. to prevent the natural development or expression of; control too strictly or severely: as, the parents *repressed* their child. 4. in *psychiatry*, *a)* to force (ideas, impulses, etc. painful to the conscious mind) into the unconscious, where they still modify behavior or remain dynamic. *b)* to prevent (unconscious ideas, impulses, etc.) from reaching the level of consciousness. Cf. **suppress.**
re·pressed (ri-prest′), *adj.* [pp. of *repress*], affected by, showing, or resulting from repression.
re·press·i·ble (ri-pres′ə-b'l), *adj.* that can be repressed.
re·pres·sion (ri-presh′ən), *n.* 1. a repressing or being repressed. 2. in *psychiatry*, what is repressed.
re·pres·sive (ri-pres′iv), *adj.* tending or serving to repress.
re·prieve (ri-prēv′), *v.t.* [REPRIEVED (-prēvd′), REPRIEVING], [earlier *repry* < Fr. *repris*, pp. of *reprendre*, to take back; altered by association with ME. *repreven* < OFr. *reprover*, to reprove], 1. to postpone the punishment of (a person); especially, to postpone the execution of (a person condemned to death). 2. to give temporary relief to, as from pain. 3. to postpone; defer (something evil). *n.* a reprieving or being reprieved; specifically, *a)* postponement of a penalty, especially that of death, or a warrant ordering this. *b)* a temporary relief or escape, as from pain or evil.
rep·ri·mand (rep′rə-mand′, rep′rə-mänd′; *also, for v.*, rep′rə-mand′, rep′rə-mänd′), *n.* [Fr. *réprimande* < L. *reprimenda*, fem. of *reprimendus*, that is to be repressed < *reprimere*, to repress; see RE- & PRESS (to squeeze)], a severe or formal rebuke, especially by a person in authority. *v.t.* to rebuke severely or formally.
re·print (rē-print′; *for n., usually* rē′print′), *v.t.* to print again; print a new or further impression or edition of, usually without change. *n.* 1. something reprinted; specifically, *a)* a new or further impression or edition, usually without change, of something previously printed, as a book, pamphlet, etc.; especially, such an impression or edition issued by another publisher and intended for sale at a lower price. *b)* a separately printed excerpt, as of an article published

in a magazine; offprint. *c)* in *philately*, a stamp, not to be used for postage, printed from the original plate, often with different paper and ink, after the issue of the stamps has ceased. 2. a reprinting.

re·pris·al (ri-prī′z'l), ***n.*** [OFr. *reprisaille* < *repris*, pp. of *reprendre*, to take back < L. *reprehendere;* see REPREHEND], 1. originally, the forcible seizure of property or subjects in retaliation for an injury inflicted by another country. 2. the act or practice of using force, short of war, against another nation to obtain redress of grievances. 3. injury done, or the doing of injury, in return for injury received, with intent to inflict at least as much harm as has been suffered; retaliation or an act of retaliation, especially in war, as the killing of prisoners.

re·prise (ri-prīz′; *also, for 2,* rə-prēz′), ***n.*** [ME.; OFr., fem. of *repris;* see REPRISAL], 1. *usually pl.* in *English law,* deductions and payments, as for annuities, out of income from lands. 2. in *music,* repetition: now usually restricted to the repetition of or return to the first subject, or theme, of a sonata movement, after the development; recapitulation.

re·proach (ri-prōch′), ***v.t.*** [OFr. *reprochier;* LL. **repropiare* < L. *re-*, back + *prope*, near], 1. to accuse of and blame for a fault; rebuke; reprove; censure; upbraid. 2. to bring shame and disgrace upon; be a cause of discredit to: as, this crime will *reproach* him. ***n.*** 1. a source or cause of shame, disgrace, discredit, or blame. 2. shame, disgrace, discredit, or blame incurred. 3. a blaming or reproving; censure; rebuke. 4. an expression of blame, reproof, or censure. 5. an object of blame, censure, scorn, etc.

re·proach·ful (ri-prōch′fəl), ***adj.*** 1. full of or expressing reproach, or blame, censure, etc. 2. [Obs.], shameful.

re·proach·less (ri-prōch′lis), ***adj.*** without reproach; irreproachable.

rep·ro·bate (rep′rə-bāt′), ***adj.*** [LL. *reprobatus*, pp. of *reprobare;* see REPROVE], 1. depraved; vicious; unprincipled. 2. in *theology*, rejected by God; excluded from salvation and lost in sin. ***n.*** a depraved, vicious person. ***v.t.*** [REPROBATED (-id), REPROBATING], 1. to disapprove; condemn. 2. to reject. 3. in *theology*, to reject and abandon as beyond saving; foreordain (a person) to damnation: said of God.

rep·ro·ba·tion (rep′rə-bā′shən), ***n.*** 1. a reprobating. 2. disapproval; censure. 3. rejection as worthless. 4. in *theology*, rejection by God, as beyond saving.

rep·ro·ba·tive (rep′rə-bā′tiv), ***adj.*** of or expressing reprobation, or disapproval.

re·proc·essed wool (rē-pros′est), wool cloth that has been respun and rewoven from the raveled fibers of cloth previously woven but never used, as the waste or clippings from a garment factory.

re·pro·duce (rē′prə-dōōs′, rē′prə-dūs′), ***v.t.*** to produce again; make, form, or bring into existence again or anew in some way; specifically, *a)* to produce by generation or propagation; bring forth one or more other individuals of (the kind or species) by sexual or asexual processes. *b)* to make grow again, as a lost part or organ. *c)* to bring about or promote the reproduction of (plants or animals). *d)* to make a copy, close imitation, duplication, etc. of (a picture, sound, or the like). *e)* to bring before the mind again, as a past scene; re-create mentally by imagination or memory. *f)* to repeat. *g)* to put (a play, etc.) on again; repeat the performance or presentation of. ***v.i.*** 1. to produce offspring; bring forth others of its kind. 2. to undergo reproduction, or copying, etc.

re·pro·duc·i·ble (rē′prə-dōōs′ə-b'l, rē′prə-dūs′ə-b'l), ***adj.*** that can be reproduced.

re·pro·duc·tion (rē′prə-duk′shən), ***n.*** 1. a reproducing or being reproduced. 2. something made by reproducing; copy, close imitation, duplication, etc. 3. the process, sexual or asexual, by which animals and plants produce new individuals. —***SYN.*** see **copy.**

re·pro·duc·tive (rē′prə-duk′tiv), ***adj.*** 1. reproducing or tending to reproduce. 2. of or for reproduction.

re·proof (ri-prōōf′), ***n.*** [ME. *reprove;* OFr. *reprouve*], 1. a reproving; rebuking; censuring. 2. an expression of censure; rebuke.

re·prov·a·ble (ri-prōōv′ə-b'l), ***adj.*** [ME. *reprouable;* OFr. *reprouvable*], deserving reproof; blameworthy.

re·prov·al (ri-prōōv′'l), ***n.*** reproof.

re·prove (ri-prōōv′), ***v.t.*** [REPROVED (-prōōvd′), REPROVING], [ME. *repreven, reproven;* OFr. *reprover;* LL. *reprobare;* see RE- & PROVE], 1. to speak to in disapproval; rebuke. 2. to express disapproval of; find fault with; censure. 3. [Obs.], to refute; disprove. 4. [Obs.], to convince or convict.

rep·tant (rep′tənt), ***adj.*** [L. *reptans*, ppr. of *reptare*, to crawl, creep; cf. REPTILE], in *biology*, creeping or crawling; repent.

rep·tile (rep′til, rep′tīl), ***n.*** [LL., neut. of L. *reptilis*, crawling < *reptus*, pp. of *repere*, to creep; IE. base **rēp-*, to creep, crawl, seen also in Lith. *rėplioti*, to creep], 1. any of a group of cold-blooded vertebrates that crawl on their bellies, as snakes, or creep on short, stubby legs, as lizards, crocodiles, alligators, and turtles. 2. a person who is sneaky, mean, groveling, malignant, etc. ***adj.*** [L. *reptilis*], 1. of, characteristic of, or like a reptile or reptiles. 2. creeping or crawling. 3. sneaky, mean, groveling, malignant, etc.

rep·til·i·an (rep-til′i-ən), ***adj.*** 1. of the reptiles. 2. like or characteristic of a reptile. 3. sneaky, mean, groveling, malignant, etc. ***n.*** a reptile.

re·pub·lic (ri-pub′lik), ***n.*** [Fr. *république;* L. *respublica; res*, thing, affair, interest + *publica*, fem. of *publicus*, public], 1. *a)* a state or nation in which the supreme power rests in all the citizens entitled to vote (the *electorate*) and is exercised by representatives elected, directly or indirectly, by them and responsible to them. *b)* the form of government of such a state or nation. Cf. **democracy.** 2. any group whose members are regarded as having a certain equality, common aims, etc.: as, the *republic* of letters. 3. a state or nation with a president as its titular head: distinguished from *monarchy*. Abbreviated **Rep., Repub., R.**

re·pub·li·can (ri-pub′li-kən), ***adj.*** 1. of, characteristic of, or having the nature of, a republic. 2. favoring, or in accord with the nature of, a republic. 3. [R-], having to do with the Republican Party. ***n.*** 1. a person who favors a republican form of government. 2. [R-], a member or adherent of the Republican Party. Abbreviated **R., Rep., Repub.**

re·pub·li·can·ism (ri-pub′li-kən-iz'm), ***n.*** 1. republican form of government. 2. republican principles, doctrines, etc. 3. adherence to these. 4. [R-], the principles, policies, etc. of the Republican Party.

re·pub·li·can·ize (ri-pub′li-kən-īz′), ***v.t.*** [REPUBLICANIZED (-īzd′), REPUBLICANIZING], to make republican.

Republican Party, 1. one of the two major political parties in the United States, organized in 1854 to oppose the extension of slavery. 2. a former political party in the United States, organized by Thomas Jefferson: see **Democratic Party.**

Republican River, a river flowing eastward from Colorado and joining the Smoky Hill River to form the Kansas River: length, 445 mi.

re·pub·li·ca·tion (rē′pub-li-kā′shən), ***n.*** 1. publication anew. 2. a book, pamphlet, etc. published again.

republic of letters, 1. literary or learned people as a group. 2. the sphere of literature.

re·pu·di·ate (ri-pū′di-āt′), ***v.t.*** [REPUDIATED (-id), REPUDIATING], [< L. *repudiatus*, pp. of *repudiare*, to put away, divorce < *repudium*, separation, a divorce < *re-*, away, back + base of *pudere*, to feel shame], 1. to refuse to have anything to do with; disown; cast off publicly, as a son, or divorce, as a wife. 2. to refuse to accept or acknowledge; deny the validity or authority of. 3. to refuse to acknowledge or pay, as a debt. 4. to refuse to recognize as due; refuse to pay (an obligation): said of a government. —***SYN.*** see **decline.**

re·pu·di·a·tion (ri-pū′di-ā′shən), ***n.*** [L. *repudiatio*], a repudiating or being repudiated.

re·pu·di·a·tor (ri-pū′di-ā′tẽr), ***n.*** one who repudiates.

re·pugn (ri-pūn′), ***v.t. & v.i.*** [ME. *repugnen;* OFr. *repugner;* L. *repugnare; re-*, back + *pugnare*, to fight], [Rare or Obs.], to oppose; resist.

re·pug·nance (ri-pug′nəns), ***n.*** [ME. *repugnaunce;* OFr.; L. *repugnantia* < *repugnans*, ppr.; see REPUGN], 1. inconsistency; incongruity; contradictoriness. 2. extreme dislike or distaste; strong aversion; antipathy. —***SYN.*** see **aversion.**

re·pug·nan·cy (ri-pug′nən-si), ***n.*** repugnance.

re·pug·nant (ri-pug′nənt), ***adj.*** [ME. *repugnaunt;* OFr.; L. *repugnans*, ppr.; see REPUGN], 1. contradictory; inconsistent: as, actions *repugnant* to his words. 2. offering resistance; opposed; antagonistic: as, *repugnant* forces. 3. causing repugnance; distasteful; offensive; disagreeable: as, a *repugnant* odor. —***SYN.*** see **hateful.**

re·pulse (ri-puls′), ***v.t.*** [REPULSED (-pulst′), REPULSING], [< L. *repulsus*, pp. of *repellere;* see REPEL], 1. to drive back; repel, as an attack. 2. to repel with discourtesy, coldness, indifference, etc.; refuse, reject, or rebuff. ***n.*** [L. *repulsa* < *repulsus*], 1. a repelling or being repelled. 2. a refusal, rejection, or rebuff.

re·pul·sion (ri-pul′shən), ***n.*** 1. a repelling or being repelled; repulse. 2. strong dislike, distaste, or aversion; repugnance. 3. in *physics*, the mutual action by which bodies, particles, etc. tend to repel each other: opposed to *attraction*.

re·pul·sive (ri-pul′siv), ***adj.*** 1. tending to repel. 2. causing strong dislike or aversion; disgusting; offensive. 3. characterized by, or having the nature of, repulsion.

re·pur·chase (rē-pũr′chəs), ***v.t.*** to purchase again; buy back. ***n.*** a repurchasing.

rep·u·ta·bil·i·ty (rep′yoo-tə-bil′ə-ti), ***n.*** the state or quality of being reputable.

rep·u·ta·ble (rep′yoo-tə-b'l), ***adj.*** 1. in good repute; having a good reputation; well thought of; respectable. 2. in good usage; not substandard: said of words.

reproceed **reproclaim** **reprune** **repurify**
reprocess **re-prove** **republish** **repursue**

rep·u·ta·bly (rep′yoo-tə-bli), *adv.* in a reputable manner.
rep·u·ta·tion (rep′yoo-tā′shən), *n.* [ME. *reputacioun;* L. *reputatio* < *reputatus,* pp. of *reputare;* see REPUTE], 1. estimation in which a person or thing is commonly held, whether favorable or not; character in the view of the public, the community, etc.; repute. 2. such estimation when favorable; good repute; good name: as, she has lost her *reputation.* 3. fame; distinction. 4. the estimation of doing something specified, having specified qualities, etc.: as, he has the *reputation* of being a thief.
re·pute (ri-pūt′), *v.t.* [REPUTED (-id), REPUTING], [Late ME. < OFr. or L.; OFr. *reputer;* L. *reputare; re-,* again + *putare,* to think], to consider, esteem, or account (a person or thing) to be as specified; generally suppose or regard: usually in the passive, as, he is *reputed* to be stingy. *n.* 1. reputation. 2. good reputation; public esteem: opposed to *disrepute.*
re·put·ed (ri-pūt′id), *adj.* [pp. of *repute*], generally accounted or supposed to be such: as, the *reputed* owner of a house.
re·put·ed·ly (ri-pūt′id-li), *adv.* supposedly.
req., 1. required. 2. requisition.
re·quest (ri-kwest′), *n.* [ME. & OFr. *requeste;* ML. *requisita* < L. *requisitus,* pp. of *requirere;* see REQUIRE], 1. an asking for, or expressing a desire for, something; solicitation or petition. 2. what is asked for: as, he granted the *request.* 3. the state of being asked for; demand: as, this style is in great *request.* *v.t.* 1. to express a wish or desire for; ask for, usually in a polite way. 2. to ask (a person) to do something.
by request, in response to someone's requesting, or to a demand: as, he played an encore *by request.*
Re·qui·em, re·qui·em (rē′kwi-əm, rek′wi-əm), *n.* [ME.; L., acc. of *requies,* rest (*re-,* again + *quies,* rest): first word of the Introit in the Latin Mass for the Dead], 1. in the *Roman Catholic Church, a)* a Mass for the repose of the soul or souls of the dead. *b)* a celebration of this. *c)* a musical setting for this. 2. any musical service, hymn, or dirge for the repose of the dead. 3. a dirgelike song, chant, or poem.
‡re·qui·es·cat (rek′wi-es′kat), *n.* [L., for *requiescat in pace* (see next entry); subj. of *requiescere;* see RE- & QUIESCENT], a prayer or wish for the repose of the dead.
‡re·qui·es·cat in pa·ce (rek′wi-es′kat in pā′si), [L.], may he (or she) rest in peace: often inscribed on tombstones: abbreviated **R.I.P.**
re·quire (ri-kwīr′), *v.t.* [REQUIRED (-kwīrd′), REQUIRING], [ME. *requiren* < base of OFr. *requerre;* L. *requirere* < *re-,* again + *quaerere,* to ask], 1. to ask or insist upon, as by right or authority; demand: as, they *require* obedience. 2. to order; command: as, he *required* them to be present. 3. to demand as necessary or appropriate; need: as, a hungry man *requires* food. *v.i.* to compel or demand. —*SYN.* see **demand, lack.**
re·quire·ment (ri-kwīr′mənt), *n.* 1. a requiring. 2. something required; something obligatory or demanded, as a condition: as, the *requirements* for college entrance. 3. something needed; a necessity; need.
req·ui·site (rek′wə-zit), *adj.* [L. *requisitus,* pp. of *requirere;* see REQUIRE], required, as by circumstances; necessary for some purpose; indispensable: as, the *requisite* supplies for a journey. *n.* something requisite. —*SYN.* see **essential, need.**
req·ui·si·tion (rek′wə-zish′ən), *n.* [L. *requisitio* < *requisitus,* pp. of *requirere;* see REQUIRE], 1. a requiring; demanding, as by right or authority; formal demand. 2. a formal written order, request, or application, as for equipment, tools, etc. 3. the state of being demanded or put to service or use: as, horses were in *requisition.* 4. a requirement; indispensable condition. 5. in *law,* a demand by one State government upon another for the surrender of a fugitive criminal. *v.t.* 1. to demand or take, as by authority: as, *requisition* food for troops. 2. to demand from; make demands on: as, *requisition* a town for food. Abbreviated **req.**
re·quit·al (ri-kwīt′'l), *n.* 1. a requiting or being requited. 2. something given or done in return; repayment, reward, retaliation, or compensation.
re·quite (ri-kwīt′), *v.t.* [REQUITED (-id), REQUITING], [*re-* + *quite,* obs. var. of *quit*], 1. to make return or repayment for (a benefit, service, etc., or an injury, wrong, etc.). 2. to make return or repayment to for a benefit, injury, etc.; reward or retaliate on. 3. to compensate for; make up for. 4. to give or do in return.
re·ra·di·a·tion (rē′rā-di-ā′shən), *n.* in *physics,* radiation that results from a prior absorption of radiation.
rere·dos (rêr′dos), *n.* [ME. *rerdos;* < Anglo-Fr. *rere-* (see REAR) + *dos,* back (see DOSSER)], an ornamental screen or partition wall behind an altar in a church.
re·route (rē-rōōt′, rē-rout′), *v.t.* to send by a new or different route.
re·run (rē-run′; *for n., usually* rē′run′), *v.t.* [for prin. pts. see RUN], to run again. *n.* a rerunning; especially, a showing of a motion picture after the first showing.
res., 1. research. 2. reserve. 3. residence. 4. resides. 5. residue. 6. resistance. 7. resolution.
re·sal·a·ble (rē-sāl′ə-b'l), *adj.* that can be sold again.
re·sale (rē-sāl′, rē′sāl′), *n.* a selling again.
re·scind (ri-sind′), *v.t.* [OFr. *rescinder;* L. *rescindere* (pp. *rescissus*), to cut off; *re-,* back + *scindere,* to cut], to abrogate; annul; cancel, as a law. —*SYN.* see **abolish.**
re·scis·si·ble (ri-sis′ə-b'l), *adj.* that can be rescinded.
re·scis·sion (ri-sizh′ən, ri-sish′ən), *n.* a rescinding.
re·scis·so·ry (ri-sis′ə-ri, ri-siz′ə-ri), *adj.* [LL. *rescissorius*], rescinding.
re·script (rē′skript), *n.* [L. *rescriptum* < *rescriptus,* pp. of *rescribere; re-,* back + *scribere,* to write], 1. an order or decree issued by a Roman emperor or by the Pope in answer to some difficulty or point of law presented to him, and having the force of law; hence, 2. any official decree or order. 3. *a)* a rewriting. *b)* something rewritten; copy. 4. in *law,* an order, as from a court to its clerk, or from an appellate court to a trial court, giving the disposition of a case.
res·cue (res′kū), *v.t.* [RESCUED (-kūd), RESCUING] [ME. *rescouen, rescowen;* OFr. *rescourre, rescoure* < *re-,* again + *escorre,* to shake, move < L. *excutere,* to shake off, drive away < *ex-,* off + *quatere,* to shake], 1. to free or save from danger, imprisonment, evil, etc. 2. in *law,* to take (a person or thing) out of legal custody by force. *n.* 1. a freeing or saving from danger, imprisonment, evil, etc.; deliverance. 2. in *law,* removal by force from legal custody.
SYN.—**rescue** implies prompt action in freeing someone or something from imminent danger or destruction or in releasing someone from captivity (he *rescued* the drowning child); **deliver** implies a setting free from confinement or from some restricting situation (*deliver* me from his interminable sermons); **redeem** suggests a freeing from bondage or from the consequences of sin, or a reclaiming, as from pawn, deterioration, etc. (how can I *redeem* my good name?); **ransom** specifically implies the payment of what is demanded in order to free one held captive; **save,** in this connection, is a general, comprehensive synonym for any of the preceding terms.
re·search (ri-sũrch′, rē′sũrch), *n.* [MFr. *recerche* (Fr. *recherche*); see RE- & SEARCH], *often in pl.* careful, systematic, patient study and investigation in some field of knowledge, undertaken to establish facts or principles. *v.i.* to do research; make researches; study. Abbreviated **res.** —*SYN.* see **investigation.**
re·seat (rē-sēt′), *v.t.* 1. to seat again. 2. to supply with a new seat or seats.
re·seau, ré·seau (rā-zō′), *n.* [*pl.* RESEAUX, RÉSEAUX (-zō′)], [Fr., dim. < OFr. *roiz* < L. *rete,* net], 1. a network; specifically, in *astronomy,* a network of fine lines on a glass plate, forming little squares of a standard size: used in photographic telescopes to produce a similar network on photographs of stars, for aid in measurement. 2. a netted ground or meshed foundation in lace. 3. a filter screen used in making color films.
re·sect (ri-sekt′), *v.t.* [< L. *resectus,* pp. of *resecare,* to cut off; *re-* (see RE-) + *secare,* to cut], in *surgery,* to perform a resection of (some part): cf. **excise.**
re·sec·tion (ri-sek′shən), *n.* [L. *resectio* < *resectus;* see RESECT], the surgical removal of part of an organ, bone, etc.
re·se·da (ri-sē′də), *n.* [L., a plant; said (by Pliny) to be orig. imperative of *resedare,* to allay, assuage, used in charm accompanying medicinal use of the plant], 1. any of a number of related plants with dense, fragrant spikes of flowers, including the mignonette. 2. the greenish-white color of some mignonette flowers. *adj.* of this color.
res·e·da·ceous (res′ə-dā′shəs), *adj.* [< *reseda* + *-aceous*], of the mignonette family of plants.
re·sem·blance (ri-zem′bləns), *n.* [ME.; Anglo-Fr.], 1. the state, fact, or quality of resembling; similarity of appearance, or, sometimes, of character; likeness. 2. a point, degree, or sort of likeness. 3. something that resembles; likeness or semblance of someone or something. 4. [Obs.], characteristic appearance. 5. [Obs.], likelihood; probability. —*SYN.* see **likeness.**
re·sem·ble (ri-zem′b'l), *v.t.* [RESEMBLED (-b'ld), RESEMBLING], [ME. *resemblen;* OFr. *resembler; re-,* again + *sembler* < L. *simulare;* see SIMULATE], 1. to be like or similar to in appearance or nature. 2. [Archaic], to liken or compare.

requicken
reradiate
reread
rerise
reroll
resaddle
resail
resalute
reseal
re-search
reseed
reseek
resegregate
reseize
reseizure
resell

re·send (rē-send′), *v.t.* [RESENT (-sent′), RESENDING], 1. to send again. 2. to send back.

re·sent (ri-zent′), *v.t.* [Fr. *ressentir* (in *se ressentir de,* to be affected by) < L. *re-*, again + *sentire,* to feel, perceive by the senses], to feel or show displeasure and indignation at (some act, remark, etc.) or toward (a person), from a sense of being injured or offended.

re·sent·ful (ri-zent′fəl), *adj.* feeling or showing resentment.

re·sent·ment (ri-zent′mənt), *n.* [< Fr.; see RESENT], a feeling of displeasure and indignation, from a sense of being injured or offended. —*SYN.* see **offense.**

re·ser·pine (ri-sũr′pēn), *n.* a crystalline alkaloid extracted from the root of an Indian shrub (*Rauwolfia serpentina*), used in the treatment of hypertension and experimentally in psychotherapy.

res·er·va·tion (rez′ẽr-vā′shən), *n.* [ME. *reseruacioun;* OFr.; LL. *reservatio*], 1. a reserving; withholding. 2. something reserved or withheld. 3. *a)* a withholding of a right, interest, etc. *b)* that part of a deed or contract which provides for this. 4. a limiting condition or qualification, tacit or expressed, as in an agreement: as, she accepted the invitation, with mental *reservations.* 5. public land set aside for some special use: as, an Indian *reservation,* military *reservation.* 6. *a)* an arrangement by which a hotel room, theater or train ticket, etc. is set aside and held until called for. *b)* anything so reserved in advance. *c)* the promise or record of such an arrangement.

re·serve (ri-zũrv′), *v.t.* [RESERVED (-zũrvd′), RESERVING], [ME. *reserven;* OFr. *reserver;* L. *reservare;* see RE- & SERVE], 1. to keep back, store up, or set apart for later use or for some special purpose. 2. to hold over to a later time. 3. to set aside or have set aside for a special person, etc.: as, *reserve* a seat on a train. 4. to keep back or retain for oneself: as, I *reserve* the right to come and go freely. *n.* 1. something kept back or stored up, as for later use or for a special purpose. 2. a limitation; reservation; exception. 3. the practice of keeping one's thoughts, feelings, etc. to oneself; self-restraint or avoidance of intimacy in speech and manner. 4. reticence; silence. 5. restraint and control in artistic expression; freedom from exaggeration or extravagance. 6. *pl.* troops held out of action for use in an emergency, for following up an advantage, or for replacing active units. 7. *pl.* men or units in the armed forces not on active duty but subject to call; militia. 8. cash, or assets easily turned into cash, held out of use by a bank or company to meet expected or unexpected demands. 9. land set apart for a special purpose: as, a forest *reserve.* *adj.* being, or having the nature of, a reserve: as, a *reserve* supply. Abbreviated **res.** —*SYN.* see **keep.**
 in reserve, reserved for later use or for some person.
 without reserve, 1. subject to no limitation. 2. without any minimum or asking price: said of goods offered at auction.

reserve bank, any of the twelve main Federal Reserve Banks.

re·served (ri-zũrvd′), *adj.* [pp. of *reserve*], 1. kept in reserve; set apart or kept back for some purpose or use, or for some person, etc. 2. keeping one's thoughts, feelings, etc. to oneself; self-restrained and withdrawn in speech and manner; not effusive; reticent. 3. characterized by reticence, etc. —*SYN.* see **silent.**

re·serv·ist (ri-zũr′vist), *n.* a member of a country's military reserves, or militia.

res·er·voir (rez′ẽr-vwär′, rez′ẽr-vwôr′, rez′ẽr-vôr′), *n.* [Fr. *réservoir* < *réserver;* see RESERVE], 1. a place where anything is collected and stored, generally in large quantity; especially, a natural or artificial lake or pond in which water is collected and stored for use, as to supply the needs of a community. 2. a receptacle or part (in an apparatus) for holding a fluid, as oil, ink, etc. 3. a part, sac, or cavity (in an animal or plant) in which a fluid collects or is secreted. 4. a large supply or store of something.

re·set (rē-set′; *for n., usually* rē′set′), *v.t.* [RESET, RESETTING], to set again, as a broken arm, type, a gem, etc. *n.* 1. a resetting. 2. something reset. 3. a plant that is planted again.

‡**res ges·tae** (rēz jes′tē), [L.], 1. things done; deeds; exploits. 2. in *law,* attendant facts and circumstances.

resh (räsh), *n.* [Heb. *rēsh,* lit., the head], the twentieth letter of the Hebrew alphabet (ר), corresponding to English *R, r:* see **alphabet,** table.

re·ship (rē-ship′), *v.t.* [RESHIPPED (-shipt′), RESHIPPING], 1. to ship again. 2. to transfer to another ship. *v.i.* 1. to go on a ship again; embark again. 2. to sign up (as a member of a ship's crew) for another voyage.

re·ship·ment (rē-ship′mənt), *n.* 1. a reshipping. 2. something reshipped.

Resht (resht), *n.* a city in northwestern Iran: pop., 122,000.

re·side (ri-zīd′), *v.i.* [RESIDED (-id), RESIDING], [Fr. *résider;* L. *residere* < *re-*, back + *sedere,* to sit], 1. to dwell for a long time; have one's residence; live (*in* or *at*): as, he still *resides* in the same house. 2. to be present or inherent; exist (*in*): said of qualities, etc. 3. to be vested (*in*): said of rights, powers, etc.

res·i·dence (rez′i-dəns), *n.* [ME.; OFr.; ML. *residentia*], 1. the act or fact of residing: as, his *residence* in Europe matured him. 2. the fact or status of living or staying in a place while working, going to school, carrying out official duties, etc. (usually preceded by *in*): as, students are required to be in *residence* two years. 3. the place in which a person or thing resides; dwelling place; abode; especially, a house. 4. a large or imposing house; mansion. 5. the time during which a person resides in a place.

res·i·den·cy (rez′i-dən-si), *n.* [*pl.* RESIDENCIES (-siz)], 1. residence. 2. the official residence of a diplomatic officer or representative of a governor general at a foreign court, as in the East Indian native states.

res·i·dent (rez′i-dənt), *adj.* [L. *residens*], 1. residing; living in a place for a long time; having a residence (*in*). 2. living or staying in a place while working, carrying on official duties, etc.: as, a *resident* physician of a hospital. 3. present; inherent; intrinsic. 4. not migratory: said of birds, etc. *n.* 1. a person who lives in a place, as distinguished from a visitor or transient. 2. a diplomatic representative living at a foreign court or capital, as in a protectorate. 3. a bird or animal that is not migratory.

res·i·den·tial (rez′i-den′shəl), *adj.* 1. of or connected with residence: as, a *residential* requirement for students. 2. of, characterized by, or suitable for residences, or homes: as, a *residential* neighborhood.

res·i·den·ti·ar·y (rez′ə-den′shi-er′i, rez′ə-den′shə-ri), *adj.* [ML. *residentarius*], 1. living in a place; resident. 2. required to live in a place; officially resident. *n.* [*pl.* RESIDENTIARIES (-iz, -riz)], 1. a resident. 2. in *ecclesiastical usage,* a clergyman required to live for some time in his official residence.

re·sid·u·al (ri-zij′oo-əl), *adj.* 1. of, or having the nature of, a residue or residuum; left over after part is taken away; remaining. 2. in *mathematics, a)* left by the subtraction of one number from another: as, a *residual* quantity. *b)* designating the difference (called *error*) between observed results and results obtained by formular computation. *c)* designating the deviation (called *error*) of any of a series of values from the mean of the series. *n.* 1. what is left at the end of a process; remainder. 2. in *geology,* an elevated rock mass remaining where erosion has leveled most of the surrounding territory; monadnock. 3. in *mathematics, a)* a residual quantity. *b)* a residual error.

re·sid·u·ar·y (ri-zij′oo-er′i), *adj.* 1. of, or having the nature of, a residue or residuum; remaining; left over. 2. in *law, a)* receiving the residue of an estate: as, a *residuary* legatee. *b)* giving the disposition of the residue of an estate: as, the *residuary* clause in a will.

res·i·due (rez′ə-dōō′, rez′ə-dū′), *n.* [ME.; OFr. *residu;* L. *residuum,* neut. of *residuus,* remaining < *residere;* see RESIDE], 1. that which is left after part is taken away; remainder; rest. 2. a residuum (sense 2). 3. in *law,* that part of a testator's estate which is left after all claims, charges, and bequests have been satisfied. Abbreviated **res.** —*SYN.* see **remainder.**

re·sid·u·um (ri-zij′oo-əm), *n.* [*pl.* RESIDUA (-ə)], [L.], 1. residue. 2. in *chemistry,* the matter remaining at the end of a process, as after evaporation, combustion, filtration, etc.; residual product. —*SYN.* see **remainder.**

re·sign (ri-zīn′), *v.t.* [ME. *resignen;* OFr. *resigner;* L. *resignare; re-*, back + *signare,* to sign], 1. to give up possession of; relinquish, as a claim. 2. to give up (an office, position, etc.). *v.i.* to give up an office, position of employment, etc., especially by formal notice (often with *from*).—*SYN.* see **abdicate, surrender.**
 resign oneself, to submit; accept something passively.

re-sign (rē-sīn′), *v.t.* to sign again.

res·ig·na·tion (rez′ig-nā′shən), *n.* 1. the act of resigning. 2. formal notice of this, especially in writing. 3. patient submission; acquiescence; passive acceptance.

re·signed (ri-zīnd′), *adj.* feeling or showing resignation; submissive; yielding and uncomplaining.

re·sign·ed·ly (ri-zīn′id-li), *adv.* in a resigned manner.

re·sile (ri-zīl′), *v.i.* [RESILED (-zīld′), RESILING], [MFr. *resiler;* L. *resilire* < *re-*, back + *salire,* to jump], to bounce or spring back; rebound; specifically, to come back into shape or position after being pressed or stretched: said of elastic bodies.

re·sil·i·ence (ri-zil′i-əns, ri-zil′yəns), *n.* 1. the quality of being resilient; ability to bounce or spring back into shape, position, etc. after being pressed or stretched; elasticity. 2. the ability to recover strength, spirits, good humor, etc. quickly; buoyancy.

re·sil·i·en·cy (ri-zil′i-ən-si, ri-zil′yən-si), *n.* resilience.

re·sil·i·ent (ri-zil′i-ənt, ri-zil′yənt), *adj.* [L. *resiliens,* ppr. of *resilire;* see RESILE], 1. bouncing or springing back into shape, position, etc.; elastic. 2. recovering

re-serve **resettlement** **reshape** **reshuffle**
resettle **reshake** **resharpen** **resift**

strength, spirits, good humor, etc. quickly; buoyant. —*SYN.* see **elastic.**

res·in (rez′'n), *n.* [ME. & OFr. *resine;* L. *resina* < Gr. *rhētinē*], 1. any of various solid or semisolid organic substances exuded from various plants and trees or prepared synthetically: resins are soluble in ether, alcohol, etc., are nonconductors of electricity, and are used in medicines, varnish, etc. 2. a substance prepared by distilling the resin of certain pine trees; rosin. *v.t.* to treat or rub with resin.

res·in·ate (rez′'n-āt′), *v.t.* [RESINATED (-id), RESINATING], to impregnate with resin.

res·in·if·er·ous (rez″'n-if′ẽr-əs), *adj.* [see -FEROUS], yielding resin: said of trees, etc.

res·in·oid (rez′'n-oid′), *adj.* like resin; resinous. *n.* 1. a resinoid substance, as a synthetic resin. 2. gum resin.

res·in·ous (rez′'n-əs), *adj.* 1. of, having the nature of, characteristic of, or like resin. 2. obtained from resin. 3. containing resin. 4. [Now Rare], electronegative.

res·in·y (rez′'n-i), *adj.* resinous.

re·sist (ri-zist′), *v.t.* [ME. *resisten;* OFr. *resister;* L. *resistere; re-*, back + *sistere*, to set, caus. of *stare*, to stand], 1. to withstand; oppose; fend off; stand firm against; withstand the action of. 2. to oppose actively; fight, argue, or work against. 3. to keep from yielding to, being affected by, or enjoying: as, she tried to *resist* temptation. *v.i.* to oppose or withstand something; offer resistance. *n.* a substance that resists, as a protective coating on a fabric that makes it unaffected by a dye. —*SYN.* see **oppose.**

re·sist·ance (ri-zis′təns), *n.* [ME. & OFr. *resistence;* LL. *resistentia*], 1. a resisting; opposing; withstanding. 2. power or capacity to resist; specifically, the ability of an organism to ward off disease. 3. opposition of some force, thing, etc. to another or others. 4. in *electricity*, *a*) the property of opposing the passage of a current, causing electric energy to be transformed into heat: also called *true* (or *ohmic*) *resistance.* *b*) something, as a coil or length of wire, that offers such resistance; resistor. *c*) impedance: also called *apparent resistance.* 5. [often R-], the organized movement, often underground, of resistance to a government or occupying power regarded as oppressive and unjust, as in France during the Nazi occupation. Symbol, R (sense 4).

re·sist·ant (ri-zis′tənt), *adj.* [L. *resistens*], offering resistance; resisting. *n.* a person or thing that resists.

re·sist·i·bil·i·ty (ri-zis′tə-bil′ə-ti), *n.* the quality or state of being resistible.

re·sist·i·ble (ri-zis′tə-b'l), *adj.* that can be resisted.

re·sis·tive (ri-zis′tiv), *adj.* resisting, tending to resist, or capable of resistance.

re·sis·tiv·i·ty (rē′zis-tiv′ə-ti), *n.* 1. property of, capacity for, or tendency toward resistance. 2. in *electricity*, the resistance between opposite faces of a centimeter cube of a substance: also called *specific resistance.*

re·sist·less (ri-zist′lis), *adj.* 1. that cannot be resisted; irresistible. 2. without power to resist; unresisting.

re·sis·tor (ri-zis′tẽr), *n.* in *electricity*, a device used in a circuit primarily to provide resistance.

‡res ju·di·ca·ta (rēz jōō′di-kā′tə), [L., thing decided], in *law*, a case already decided by judicial authority.

re·sole (rē-sōl′), *v.t.* [RESOLED (-sōld′), RESOLING], to put a new sole on (a shoe, etc.).

res·o·lu·bil·i·ty (rez′ə-loo-bil′ə-ti, rez″'l-yoo-bil′ə-ti), *n.* the quality or state of being resoluble.

res·o·lu·ble (rez′ə-loo-b'l, rez′'l-yoo-b'l), *adj.* [LL. *resolubilis*], that can be resolved.

res·o·lute (rez′ə-lōōt′, rez′'l-ūt′), *adj.* [L. *resolutus*, pp. of *resolvere;* see RE- & SOLVE], having or showing a fixed, firm purpose; determined; resolved; unwavering. —*SYN.* see **faithful.**

res·o·lu·tion (rez′ə-lōō′shən, rez″'l-ū′shən), *n.* [ME. *resolucioun*, dissolution; Late OFr. *résolution;* L. *resolutio* < *resolutus;* see RESOLUTE], 1. *a*) the act or process of resolving something or breaking it up into its constituent parts or elements. *b*) the result of this. 2. *a*) a resolving; determining; deciding. *b*) the thing resolved or determined upon; decision as to future action; resolve. 3. a resolute quality of mind. 4. a formal statement of opinion or determination adopted by an assembly or other group of persons. 5. a solving, as of a puzzle; answering, as of a question; solution. 6. in *medicine*, the subsidence or disappearance of an inflammation, swelling, or fever. 7. in *music*, *a*) the passing of a dissonant tone (in a chord), as an appoggiatura, to a consonant tone. *b*) the passing of a dissonant chord to a consonant chord or, sometimes, to another dissonant chord. *c*) a tone or chord to which such passing occurs. Abbreviated **res.**

re·solv·a·bil·i·ty (ri-zol′və-bil′ə-ti), *n.* the quality or state of being resolvable.

re·solv·a·ble (ri-zol′və-b'l), *adj.* that can be resolved.

re·solve (ri-zolv′), *v.t.* [RESOLVED (-zolvd′), RESOLVING], [ME. *resolven;* L. *resolvere;* see RE- & SOLVE], 1. to break up into separate, constituent elements or parts; analyze. 2. to change; transform (with *into*): used reflexively, as, the discussion *resolved* itself into an argument. 3. to cause (a person) to decide or make up his mind: as, the flood *resolved* him to sell. 4. to determine; reach as a decision or intention (usually followed by an infinitive): as, we *resolved* to go. 5. *a*) to solve or explain; make clear, as a problem. *b*) to remove (doubt, etc.). 6. to decide by vote; make a formal decision about; express by resolution: said of a legislative assembly, etc. 7. [Obs.], to cause to dissolve or melt. 8. in *medicine*, to cause (a swelling, inflammation, etc.) to subside without the formation of pus. 9. in *music*, to cause (a tone or chord) to undergo resolution. 10. in *optics*, to make visible the individual parts of (an image). *v.i.* 1. to be resolved, as by analysis (with *into* or *to*). 2. to determine; come to a decision; make a resolution. 3. in *music*, to undergo resolution. *n.* 1. fixed purpose or intention; firm determination. 2. a formal resolution, as of an assembly. —*SYN.* see **decide.**

re·solved (ri-zolvd′), *adj.* firm and fixed in purpose; determined; resolute.

re·solv·ed·ly (ri-zol′vid-li), *adv.* in a resolute manner; with determination.

re·sol·vent (ri-zol′vənt), *adj.* [L. *resolvens*, ppr.], resolving; causing solution or resolution; solvent. *n.* something resolvent; specifically, a medicine that can cause resolution of a swelling.

res·o·nance (rez′ə-nəns), *n.* [OFr.; L. *resonantia*, an echo], 1. the quality or state of being resonant. 2. reinforcement and prolongation of a sound by reflection or by vibration of other bodies. 3. in *chemistry*, the property of certain molecules of having two or more structures in which only the positions of electrons differ. 4. in *electricity*, the condition of adjustment of a circuit that allows the greatest flow of current of a certain frequency. 5. in *medicine*, the sound produced in the percussion of some part of the body, especially of the chest. 6. in *phonetics*, relative audibility: it rises in inverse proportion to the amount of stricture during articulation. 7. in *physics*, the reinforced vibration of a body exposed to the vibration, at about the same frequency, of another body.

res·o·nant (rez′ə-nənt), *adj.* [L. *resonans*, ppr. of *resonare*, to resound; see RE- & SOUND, *v.*], 1. resounding; re-echoing: as, a *resonant* sound. 2. increasing the intensity of sounds by sympathetic vibration: as, *resonant* walls. 3. full of, or intensified by, resonance: as, a *resonant* voice. 4. of resonance.

res·o·nate (rez′ə-nāt′), *v.i.* [RESONATED (-id), RESONATING], [< L. *resonatus*, pp. of *resonare*, to resound], 1. to be resonant; resound. 2. to produce resonance.

res·o·na·tor (rez′ə-nā′tẽr), *n.* [Mod. L. < pp. of L. *resonare*, to resound], 1. a device for producing resonance or increasing sound by resonance. 2. an instrument for detecting a specific frequency by the use of resonance. 3. in *radio*, the high-frequency circuits of a receiving set.

re·sorb (ri-sôrb′), *v.t.* [L. *resorbere; re-*, again + *sorbere*, to suck up], to absorb again.

res·or·cin (rez-ôr′sin), *n.* resorcinol.

res·or·cin·ol (rez-ôr′si-nōl′, rez-ôr′si-nol), *n.* [*resin* + *orcinol*], a colorless, crystalline compound, $C_6H_4(OH)_2$, prepared synthetically or by fusing certain resins with caustic alkalis: it is used in the manufacture of dyes, celluloid, and hair tonics, and as a medicinal astringent.

re·sorp·tion (ri-sôrp′shən), *n.* [< *resorb*, after *absorption*], a resorbing or being resorbed.

re·sort (ri-zôrt′), *v.i.* [ME. *resorten;* OFr. *resortir; re-*, again + *sortir*, to go out], 1. to go; especially, to go often, customarily, or generally: as, people *resort* to parks and beaches in summer. 2. to have recourse; go or turn for use, help, support, etc.: as, he *resorted* to harsh measures. *n.* [ME.; OFr. < the *v.*], 1. a place to which people go often, customarily, or generally; especially, a place to which people go for rest or relaxation, as on a vacation. 2. a frequent, customary, or general going, gathering together, or visiting: as, a place of general *resort.* 3. a person or thing that one goes or turns to for help, support, etc. 4. a going or turning for help, support, etc.; recourse: as, he had *resort* to his brother. —*SYN.* see **resource.**

re·sound (ri-zound′), *v.i.* [ME. *resounen;* OFr. *resoner;* L. *resonare;* see RE- & SOUND, *v.*], 1. to echo or be filled with sound; reverberate: said of places, etc. 2. to make a loud, echoing, or prolonged sound. 3. to be echoed; be repeated or prolonged: said of sounds; hence, 4. to be celebrated; be extolled: as, his act *resounded* through the nation. *v.t.* 1. to give back

resolder **resolidify** **re-solve** **re-sort**

fat, āpe, bâre, cär; ten, ēven, hêre, ovẽr; is, bīte; lot, gō, hôrn, tōōl, look; oil, out; up, ūse, fũr; get; joy; yet; chin; she; thin, *then;* zh, leisure; ŋ, ring; ə for *a* in *ago*, *e* in *agent*, *i* in *sanity*, *o* in *comply*, *u* in *focus;* ′ as in *able* (ā′b'l); Fr. bàl; ë, Fr. coeur; ö, Fr. feu; Fr. mo*n*; ô, Fr. coq; ü, Fr. duc; H, G. ich; kh, G. doch. See pp. x–xii. ‡ foreign; * hypothetical; < derived from.

(sound); echo. 2. to give forth, utter, or repeat loudly; hence, 3. to celebrate or extol (someone's praises, etc.).

re·sound (rē'sound'), *v.t. & v.i.* to sound again or anew.

re·source (ri-sôrs', rē'sôrs), *n.* [Fr. *ressource* < OFr. *resourdre,* to arise anew; *re-,* again + *sourdre,* to spring up < L. *surgere;* see SURGE], 1. something that lies ready for use or can be drawn upon for aid; supply of something to take care of a need. 2. *pl.* wealth; assets; available money or property: opposed to *liabilities.* 3. *usually in pl.* something that a country, state, etc. has and can use to its advantage: as, our natural *resources* include coal and petroleum. 4. a means of accomplishing something; measure or action that can be resorted to, as in an emergency; expedient: as, his only remaining *resource* was flight. 5. *in pl.* a means of spending one's leisure time; amusement; recreation. 6. ability to deal promptly and effectively with problems, difficulties, etc.; resourcefulness.

SYN.—**resource** applies to any thing, person, action, etc. to which one turns for aid in time of need or emergency (what *resource* is left us?); **resort** is usually used of a final resource, qualified as by *last* (we'll take the train as a last *resort*); **expedient** refers to something used to effect a desired end, specifically to something used as a substitute for the usual means (the day bed was an excellent *expedient* for unexpected guests); **makeshift** applies to a quick expedient and, as a somewhat derogatory term, connotes an inferior substitute, carelessness, etc. (she served sandwiches as a *makeshift* for dinner); **stopgap** refers to a temporary expedient, to be replaced when the usual means is again available (he's just a *stopgap* until a new manager is appointed).

re·source·ful (ri-sôrs'fəl, ri-sōrs'fəl), *adj.* full of resource; able to deal promptly and effectively with problems, difficulties, etc.

resp., 1. respective(ly). 2. respiration. 3. respondent.

re·spect (ri-spekt'), *v.t.* [< L. *respectare,* freq. (or *respectus,* pp.) of *respicere,* to look at, look back on, respect < *re-,* back + *specere,* to look at, see, spy], 1. to feel or show honor or esteem for; consider or treat with deference or courtesy. 2. to show consideration for; avoid intruding upon or molesting: as, *respect* his privacy. 3. to concern; relate to. *n.* [ME. *respecte;* L. *respectus,* a looking at, respect, regard; pp. used as n.], 1. a feeling of deference, honor, or esteem: as, lawyers have great *respect* for him. 2. a state of being held in honor or esteem: as, he died without the *respect* of his countrymen. 3. consideration; courteous regard: as, one must have *respect* for the feelings of others. 4. *pl.* courteous expressions of respect; regards: as, he paid his *respects* to the mayor. 5. a particular point or detail: as, in this *respect* you are wrong. 6. reference; relation: as, with *respect* to your problem. —*SYN.* see **regard.**

in respect of, with reference to; as regards.

in respect that, because of the fact that; considering.

re·spect·a·bil·i·ty (ri-spek'tə-bil'ə-ti), *n.* [*pl.* RESPECTABILITIES (-tiz)], 1. the quality or state of being respectable. 2. respectable character, reputation, or social status. 3. respectable people as a group. 4. *usually in pl.* something accepted or regarded as respectable.

re·spect·a·ble (ri-spek'tə-b'l), *adj.* [ML. *respectabilis*], 1. worthy of respect or esteem; estimable. 2. having, or appropriate to, good social status, reputation, etc.; decent, honest, proper, etc.: as, a *respectable* hotel, *respectable* behavior. 3. fairly good in quality; of moderate excellence: as, his work was *respectable* but not outstanding. 4. fairly large in size, number, or amount. 5. good enough to be seen, used, etc.; presentable: as, a *respectable* suit of clothes.

re·spect·a·bly (ri-spek'tə-bli), *adv.* 1. in a respectable manner. 2. to a respectable extent or degree.

re·spect·er (ri-spek'tẽr), *n.* a person who respects.

respecter of persons, one whose behavior toward people is influenced by their social status, prestige, etc.

re·spect·ful (ri-spekt'fəl), *adj.* full of or characterized by respect; showing deference.

re·spect·ing (ri-spek'tiŋ), *prep.* [see RESPECT], concerning; about; regarding.

re·spec·tive (ri-spek'tiv), *adj.* [ML. *respectivus* < L. *respectus;* see RESPECT], 1. relating individually to each of two or more persons or things; several: as, he described the *respective* weaknesses of the various arguments. 2. [Obs.], favoring one over others; partial; discriminative. 3. [Obs.], worthy of respect. 4. [Obs.], heedful; attentive. Abbreviated **resp.**

re·spec·tive·ly (ri-spek'tiv-li), *adv.* with respect to each of two or more, in the order named or mentioned: as, the first, second, and third prizes went to John, Mary, and George, *respectively:* abbreviated **resp.**

re·spell (rē-spel'), *v.t.* to spell again; specifically, to spell (a word) in a different, usually phonetic, system so as to indicate the pronunciation.

Re·spi·ghi, Ot·to·ri·no (ôt'tô-rē'nô re-spē'gē), 1879–1936; Italian composer.

re·spir·a·ble (ri-spīr'ə-b'l, res'pẽr-ə-b'l), *adj.* [Fr.], 1. that can be respired; fit to be breathed. 2. that can respire; capable of breathing.

res·pi·ra·tion (res'pə-rā'shən), *n.* [ME. *respiracioun;* L. *respiratio* < *respiratus,* pp.], 1. act or process of respiring; breathing; inhaling and exhaling air. 2. the processes by which a living organism or cell takes in oxygen from the air or water, distributes and utilizes it in oxidation, and gives off products of oxidation, especially carbon dioxide. Abbreviated **resp.**

res·pi·ra·tor (res'pə-rā'tẽr), *n.* 1. a contrivance, as of gauze, worn over the mouth, or the mouth and nose, to prevent the inhaling of harmful substances, to warm the air breathed, etc. 2. an apparatus for giving artificial respiration. 3. [British], a gas mask.

re·spir·a·to·ry (ri-spīr'ə-tôr'i, res'pẽr-ə-tō'ri), *adj.* of or for respiration.

re·spire (ri-spīr'), *v.i.* [RESPIRED (-spīrd'), RESPIRING], [ME. *respiren;* OFr. *respirer;* L. *respirare; re-,* back + *spirare,* to breathe; cf. SPIRIT], 1. to breathe; inhale and exhale air. 2. to breathe freely or easily again, as after exertion or anxiety; enjoy a breathing space. *v.t.* 1. to breathe; inhale and exhale. 2. [Rare], to breathe out; exhale; give off (an odor, etc.).

res·pite (res'pit), *n.* [ME. & OFr. *respit;* L. *respectus;* see RESPECT], 1. a delay or postponement, especially of something disagreeable; specifically, in *law,* postponement of the carrying out of a death sentence; reprieve. 2. an interval of temporary relief or rest, as from pain, work, duty, etc.; lull. *v.t.* [RESPITED (-id), RESPITING], 1. to give a respite to. 2. to delay or postpone the carrying out of (a punishment, etc.).

re·splend·ence (ri-splen'dəns), *n.* [ME.; LL. *resplendentia*], the quality or state of being resplendent.

re·splend·en·cy (ri-splen'dən-si), *n.* resplendence.

re·splend·ent (ri-splen'dənt), *adj.* [L. *resplendens,* ppr. of *resplendere;* see RE- & SPLENDENT], shining brightly; full of splendor; dazzling; splendid.

re·spond (ri-spond'), *v.i.* [ME. *responden;* OFr. *respondre;* L. *respondere; re-,* back + *spondere,* to pledge], 1. to answer; reply. 2. to act in return, as if in answer: as, he *responded* to the insult with a blow. 3. [Rare or Obs.], to correspond (*to*). 4. in *law,* to be answerable or liable. 5. in *physiology & psychology,* to react. *v.t.* to say in answer; reply. *n.* 1. in *architecture,* an engaged column, pilaster, etc. supporting an arch. 2. in *ecclesiastical usage,* a response or responsory. Abbreviated **R., ℟.** —*SYN.* see **answer.**

re·spond·ence (ri-spon'dəns), *n.* a responding.

re·spond·en·cy (ri-spon'dən-si), *n.* respondence.

re·spond·ent (ri-spon'dənt), *adj.* [L. *respondens,* ppr.], responding; answering. *n.* 1. a person who responds. 2. in *law,* a defendant, especially in equity, admiralty, appellate, and divorce proceedings. Abbreviated **resp.**

re·sponse (ri-spons'), *n.* [ME. *respounse;* OFr. *respons* (masc.), *response* (fem.); L. *responsum,* neut. of *responsus,* pp. of *respondere;* see RESPOND], 1. something said or done in answer to something else; answer; reply. 2. in *ecclesiastical usage, a*) words, phrases, etc. sung or spoken by the congregation or choir in answer to the officiating clergyman or priest. *b*) a responsory. 3. in *physiology & psychology,* any behavior resulting from the application of a stimulus; reaction. Abbreviated **R., ℟.** (in sense 2).

re·spon·si·bil·i·ty (ri-spon'sə-bil'ə-ti), *n.* [*pl.* RESPONSIBILITIES (-tiz)], 1. condition, quality, fact, or instance of being responsible; obligation. 2. a thing or person for whom one is responsible. —*SYN.* see **duty.**

re·spon·si·ble (ri-spon'sə-b'l), *adj.* [obs. Fr. < L. *responsus,* pp. of *respondere;* see RESPOND & -IBLE], 1. expected or obliged to account (*for* something, *to* someone); answerable; accountable: as, he is *responsible* for the car. 2. involving accountability, obligation, or duties: as, he has a *responsible* position. 3. answerable or accountable as being the cause, agent, or source of something (with *for*): as, who is *responsible* for this state of affairs? 4. able to distinguish between right and wrong and to think and act rationally, and hence accountable for one's behavior. 5. *a*) trustworthy; dependable; reliable: as, she is a *responsible* person. *b*) able to pay debts or meet business obligations.

SYN.—**responsible** applies to one who has been delegated some duty or responsibility by one in authority and who is subject to penalty in case of default (he is *responsible* for making out the reports); **answerable** implies a legal or moral obligation for which one must answer to someone sitting in judgment (he is not *answerable* for the crimes of his parents); **accountable** implies liability for something of value, or responsibility for one's own actions, for which one may be called to account (he will be held *accountable* for anything he may say).

re·spon·si·bly (ri-spon'sə-bli), *adv.* in a responsible manner.

re·spon·sion (ri-spon'shən), *n.* 1. a responding; answering. 2. *pl.* the first of three examinations for the B.A. degree at Oxford University, England.

re·spon·sive (ri-spon'siv), *adj.* [< Fr. or LL.; Fr. *responsif;* LL. *responsivus*], 1. responding; answering. 2. reacting easily or readily to suggestion or appeal: as, a *responsive* audience. 3. containing or consisting of responses: as, *responsive* reading in church.

re·spon·so·ry (ri-spon′sə-ri), *n.* [*pl.* RESPONSORIES (-riz)], [ME. *responsorye;* ML. *responsorium*], in *ecclesiastical usage,* an anthem or series of responses sung in alternation by a soloist and choir after a lection.

res pu·bli·ca (rēz pub′li-kə), [L., lit., public thing; cf. REPUBLIC], the state; commonwealth; republic.

rest (rest), *n.* [ME. *reste;* AS. *rest(e), ræst(e);* akin to G. *rast;* IE. base **erē-*, **rē-*, rest, peace, seen also in Goth. *razn* (and, by metathesis, in AS. *ærn*), house; the Gmc. cognates show the basic sense "rest after traveling"], 1. *a)* peace, ease, and refreshment as produced by sleep. *b)* sleep or repose. 2. refreshing ease or inactivity after work or exertion. 3. a period or occasion of inactivity, as during work or on a journey. 4. *a)* relief from anything distressing, disturbing, annoying, tiring, etc. *b)* peace of mind; mental and emotional calm; tranquillity. 5. the repose of death. 6. absence of motion; state of being still; immobility. 7. a resting or stopping place; shelter; lodging place, as for travelers, sailors, etc. 8. a device for supporting something; support, as for a gun or billiard cue. 9. in *music, a)* an interval of silence between tones. *b)* any of various symbols indicating the length of such an interval: see illus. 10. in *prosody,* a short pause in a line of verse; caesura. *v.i.* [ME. *restan;* AS. *ræstan* < the *n.;* influenced in some senses (esp. 5) by L. *restare,* to stop, stand, and the derived Fr. *rester*], 1. *a)* to get peace, ease, and refreshment by sleeping, lying down, etc. *b)* to sleep. 2. to get ease and refreshment by ceasing from work or exertion. 3. to be at ease or peace; be tranquil. 4. to have the repose of death; be dead. 5. to be, become, or remain quiet, still, or inactive for a while. 6. to remain without change or further action: as, let the matter *rest.* 7. to be, or seem to be, supported; specifically, *a)* to lie, sit, or lean. *b)* to be placed, based, or founded (*in, on, upon,* etc.). 8. to be placed or imposed as a burden or responsibility (*on* or *upon*). 9. to be or lie (where specified): as, the fault *rests* with him. 10. to be directed or fixed (*on* or *upon*): as, his eyes *rested* on the picture. 11. to rely (*on* or *upon*); depend. 12. to remain; stay; abide. 13. in *agriculture,* to remain unploughed or uncropped; lie fallow: said of land. 14. in *law,* to end voluntarily the introduction of evidence in a case. *v.t.* 1. to give rest to; refresh by rest. 2. to place, put, or lay for ease, support, etc.: as, *rest* your head on the pillow. 3. to base; ground: as, he *rested* his argument on trivialities. 4. to direct or fix (the eyes, etc.). 5. to bring to rest; stop. 6. in *law,* to end voluntarily the introduction of evidence in (a case): as, the State *rests* its case.

at rest, in a state of rest; specifically, *a)* asleep. *b)* immobile. *c)* free from distress, care, etc. *d)* dead.

lay to rest, to bury (a dead person).

RESTS (in music) A, whole; B, half; C, quarter rests; D, eighth; E, sixteenth; F, thirty-second

rest (rest), *n.* [ME. & Late OFr. *reste* < *rester,* to rest, remain < L. *restare,* to stop, stand, rest, remain; *re-,* back + *stare,* to stand], 1. *a)* what is left after part is taken away; remainder: as, the *rest* of the candy belongs to George. *b)* [construed as pl.], those that are left; the others: as, all the *rest* of us had finished. 2. [British], surplus or reserve funds. *v.i.* [ME. *resten;* Late OFr. *rester*], 1. to go on being; continue to be; remain (as specified): as, *rest* assured that we will go. 2. [Obs.], to be left over. *v.t.* [Obs.], to cause to remain; keep: as, God *rest* you merry, gentlemen.

rest (rest), *n.* [ME. aphetic var. of *arest,* an arrest], a support for the butt of a lance, projecting from the side of the breastplate in medieval armor.

re·state (rē-stāt′), *v.t.* 1. to state again. 2. to state (something previously stated) in a new form.

re·state·ment (rē-stāt′mənt), *n.* 1. a restating or being restated. 2. a statement made again. 3. a statement (of something stated before) in a new form.

res·tau·rant (res′tə-rənt, res′tə-ränt′), *n.* [Fr., substantive use of ppr. of *restaurer;* see RESTORE], a place where meals can be bought and eaten.

res·tau·ra·teur (res′tə-rə-tũr′; Fr. res′tô′rä′tėr′), *n.* [Fr.], a person who owns or operates a restaurant.

rest cure, a treatment, as for nervous disorders, consisting of complete rest, often with special diet, etc.

rest·ful (rest′fəl), *adj.* 1. full of or giving rest. 2. at rest; quiet; peaceful. —*SYN.* see **comfortable.**

rest·har·row (rest′har′ō), *n.* [ME. *rest,* contr. < *arest* (see ARREST); + *harrow*], any of a number of related plants of the pea family, with clusters of white, pink, or yellow flowers.

res·ti·form (res′tə-fôrm′), *adj.* [Mod. L. < L. *resti(s),* rope + *-form*], ropelike or cordlike; specifically, designating either of two cordlike bundles of nerve fibers (*restiform bodies*) connecting the medulla oblongata with each hemisphere of the cerebellum.

rest·ing (res′tiŋ), *adj.* [ppr. of *rest* (to sleep)], in *botany,* dormant: said of spores, etc.

res·ti·tu·tion (res′tə-to͞o′shən, res′tə-tū′shən), *n.* [ME.; OFr.; L. *restitutio* < *restitutus,* pp. of *restituere,* to set up again, restore < *re-,* again + *statuere,* to set up], 1. a giving back to the rightful owner of something that has been lost or taken away; restoration. 2. a making good for loss or damage; reimbursement. 3. a return to a former condition or situation. 4. in *physics,* the recovery of its shape by an elastic body after pressure or strain is released. —*SYN.* see **reparation.**

res·tive (res′tiv), *adj.* [ME. & OFr. *restif* < OFr. *rester;* see REST (to remain)], 1. refusing to go forward; balky: said of a horse, etc.; hence, 2. hard to control; unruly; refractory. 3. nervous or impatient under pressure or restraint; restless. —*SYN.* see **contrary.**

rest·less (rest′lis), *adj.* 1. characterized by inability to rest or relax; uneasy; unquiet. 2. having or giving no rest or relaxation; disturbed or disturbing: as, a *restless* night, *restless* sleep. 3. never or almost never quiet or still; always active or inclined to action. 4. seeking change; discontented.

restless cavy, the wild guinea pig of South America.

re·stock (rē-stok′), *v.t. & v.i.* to stock again or provide with a new stock, as a store or farm.

res·to·ra·tion (res′tə-rā′shən), *n.* [ME. *restauration;* OFr. *restauration;* LL. *restauratio*], 1. a restoring or being restored; reinstatement. 2. a putting or bringing back into a former, normal, or unimpaired state or condition. 3. a representation of the original form or structure, as of a building, fossil animal, etc.; reconstruction. 4. something restored.

the Restoration, 1. the re-establishment of the monarchy in England in 1660 under Charles II. 2. the period of the reign of Charles II (1660–1685): sometimes taken as including the reign of James II (1685–1688).

re·stor·a·tive (ri-stôr′ə-tiv, ri-stō′rə-tiv), *adj.* [ME. & OFr. *restoratif*], 1. of restoration. 2. tending to restore or capable of restoring; especially, capable of restoring health, strength, consciousness, etc. *n.* something that restores; especially, something that restores to consciousness, as smelling salts.

re·store (ri-stôr′, ri-stōr′), *v.t.* [RESTORED (-stôrd′, -stōrd′), RESTORING], [ME. *restoren;* OFr. *restorer* (Fr. *restaurer*) < L. *restaurare; re-,* again + *staurare* (in comp.), to make strong; cf. RESTAURANT], 1. to give back (something taken away, lost, etc.); make restitution of. 2. to bring back to a former or normal condition, as by repairing, rebuilding, altering, etc.: as, *restore* a building, painting, etc. 3. to put (a person) back in a place, position, rank, etc.: as, *restore* a king. 4. to bring back to health, strength, etc. 5. to reestablish something which has passed away, as a custom, system of government, etc. —*SYN.* see **renew.**

re·strain (ri-strān′), *v.t.* [ME. *restreynen;* OFr. *restraindre;* L. *restringere; re-,* back + *stringere,* to draw tight], 1. to hold back from action; check; suppress; curb. 2. to keep under control. 3. to deprive of physical liberty, as by putting in prison or in an asylum. 4. to limit; restrict.

SYN.—**restrain,** the term of broadest application in this list, suggests the use of strong force or authority either in preventing, or in suppressing and controlling, some action (try to *restrain* your zeal); **curb, check,** and **bridle** derive their current implications from the various uses of a horse's harness, **curb** implying a sudden, sharp action to bring something under control (*curb* your lying tongue), **check** implying a slowing up of action or progress (to *check* inflationary trends), and **bridle** suggesting a holding in of emotions, feelings, etc. (to *bridle* one's envy); **inhibit,** as used in psychology, implies a suppressing or repressing of some action, thought, or emotion (her natural verve had become *inhibited*).

re·strain·ed·ly (ri-strān′id-li, ri-strānd′li), *adv.* in a restrained manner; with restraint.

re·strain·er (ri-strān′ẽr), *n.* a person or thing that restrains; specifically, in *photography,* potassium bromide, etc. added to a developer to retard its action.

re·straint (ri-strānt′), *n.* [ME. *restreinte, restrainte;* OFr. *restrainte*], 1. a restraining or being restrained. 2. something that restrains, as an influence or action. 3. a means or instrument of restraining. 4. a loss or limitation of liberty; confinement. 5. control of emotions, impulses, etc.; reserve; constraint.

restraint of trade, interruption of the free movement of goods in commerce; restriction or prevention of business competition.

re·strict (ri-strikt′), *v.t.* [< L. *restrictus,* pp. of *restringere;* see RESTRAIN], to keep within limits; hold down; limit; confine. —*SYN.* see **limit.**

respread **restart** **re-strain** **restrengthen**

re·strict·ed (ri-strik′tid), *adj.* [pp. of *restrict*], 1. limited; confined. 2. limited to a certain group or groups; especially, limited to white Christians: racist euphemism, as, a *restricted* hotel.
re·stric·tion (ri-strik′shən), *n.* [ME. *restriccion* < Late OFr. or L.; Late OFr. *restriction;* L. *restrictio*], 1. a restricting or being restricted. 2. something that restricts; limitation.
re·stric·tive (ri-strik′tiv), *adj.* [ME.; Late OFr. *restrictif*], 1. restricting or tending to restrict; limiting: as, *restrictive* regulations. 2. in *grammar*, designating a subordinate clause, phrase, or term felt as limiting the application of the word or words that it modifies, as a relative clause (usually not set off by commas) that identifies the person or thing designated by the antecedent (e.g., in "automobiles that have bad brakes are dangerous," *that have bad brakes* is a restrictive relative clause; in "go when the bell rings," *when the bell rings* is a restrictive adverbial clause; in "a man with money is needed," *with money* is a restrictive phrase): opposed to *nonrestrictive, descriptive*.
rest-room (rest′ro͞om′, rest′room′), *n.* 1. a room or rooms (in a public building) equipped with toilets, washbowls, couches, and the like, for the convenience of patrons, employees, etc.; hence, 2. a toilet or lavatory, as in a theater, etc.
re·sult (ri-zult′), *v.i.* [ME. *resulten;* ML. *resultare;* L. *resultare*, to spring back, rebound, freq. of *resilire*, to leap back; see RESILE], 1. to happen or issue as a consequence or effect of some cause (often with *from*): as, learning *results* from study. 2. to end as a consequence (*in* something): as, the discussion *resulted* in new action. *n.* 1. anything that comes about as a consequence or outcome of some action, process, etc. 2. the number, quantity, etc. obtained by mathematical calculation; answer to a problem. —*SYN.* see **effect, follow.**
re·sult·ant (ri-zul′t′nt), *adj.* [L. *resultans*], 1. resulting; being a result; following as a consequence. 2. resulting from two or more forces or agents acting together. *n.* 1. something that results; result. 2. in *physics*, a force, velocity, etc. with an effect equal to that of two or more such forces, etc. acting together.
re·sum·a·ble (ri-zo͞om′ə-b'l, ri-zūm′ə-b'l), *adj.* that can be resumed.
re·sume (ri-zo͞om′, ri-zūm′), *v.t.* [RESUMED (-zo͞omd′, -zūmd′), RESUMING], [ME. *resumen*, to put on, assume; L. *resumere; re-*, again + *sumere*, to take], 1. *a)* to take, get, or occupy again: as, *resume* your seat. *b)* to take back or take on again: as, *resume* a former name. 2. to begin again or go on with again after interruption: as, we *resumed* the conversation. *v.i.* to begin again or go on again after interruption.
ré·su·mé (rā′zoo-mā′, rez′yoo-mā′, rez′o͞o-mā′), *n.* [Fr., pp. of *résumer;* see RESUME], a summing up; summary.
re·sump·tion (ri-zump′shən), *n.* [ME. *resumpcioun;* L. *resumptio* < *resumptus*, pp. of *resumere*], a resuming.
re·su·pi·nate (ri-so͞o′pə-nāt′, ri-sū′pə-nāt′), *adj.* [L. *resupinatus*, pp. of *resupinare*, to bend back < *re-*, back + *supinus*, supine], in *botany*, having an upside-down appearance, as the flower of an orchid; inverted.
re·su·pi·na·tion (ri-so͞o′pə-nā′shən, ri-sū′pə-nā′shən), *n.* the condition of being resupinate.
re·su·pine (rē′soo-pīn′, rē′syoo-pīn′), *adj.* [L. *resupinus;* see RE- & SUPINE], lying on the back; supine.
re·sur·face (rē-sũr′fis), *v.t.* [RESURFACED (-fist), RESURFACING], to put a new or different surface on.
‡re·sur·gam (ri-sũr′gam), [L.], I shall rise again.
re·surge (ri-sũrj′), *v.i.* [L. *resurgere*], 1. to rise again; be resurrected; revive. 2. to surge back again.
re·sur·gence (ri-sũr′jəns), *n.* [< *resurgent*], a rising again; resurging.
re·sur·gent (ri-sũr′jənt), *adj.* [L. *resurgens*, ppr.], rising or tending to rise again; resurging.
res·ur·rect (rez′ə-rekt′), *v.t.* [back-formation < *resurrection*], 1. to raise from the dead or the grave; bring back to life. 2. to bring back into notice, practice, use, etc. *v.i.* to rise from the dead; come back to life.
res·ur·rec·tion (rez′ə-rek′shən), *n.* [ME. *resur(r)eccioun;* OFr.; LL. *resurrectio* < L. *resurrectus*, pp. of *resurgere;* see RESURGE], 1. a rising from the dead, or coming back to life. 2. a coming back into notice, practice, use, etc.; restoration or revival, as of old customs. 3. the state of having risen from the dead.
the Resurrection, in *Christian theology*, 1. the rising of Jesus from the dead after his death and burial. 2. the rising of all the dead at the Last Judgment.
res·ur·rec·tion·al (rez′ə-rek′shən-'l), *adj.* of, or having the nature of, resurrection.
res·ur·rec·tion·ar·y (rez′ə-rek′shən-er′i), *adj.* 1. resurrectional. 2. of resurrectionism.
res·ur·rec·tion·ism (rez′ə-rek′shən-iz'm), *n.* the stealing of bodies from graves, especially for dissection.
res·ur·rec·tion·ist (rez′ə-rek′shən-ist), *n.* 1. a person who steals bodies from graves, especially for dissection. 2. a person who brings something back into use or notice again. 3. a person who believes in resurrection.
re·sur·vey (rē′sẽr-vā′; *for n., usually* rē-sũr′vā), *v.t.* 1. to survey again. 2. to make a new survey of. *n.* a second or new survey.
re·sus·ci·tate (ri-sus′ə-tāt′), *v.t. & v.i.* [RESUSCITATED (-id), RESUSCITATING], [< L. *resuscitatus*, pp. of *resuscitare*, to revive; *re-*, again + *suscitare*, to raise up, revive], to revive; especially, to bring or come back to life or consciousness: said of someone apparently dead, in a faint, etc.
re·sus·ci·ta·tion (ri-sus′ə-tā′shən), *n.* [LL. *resuscitatio*], a resuscitating or being resuscitated; revival.
re·sus·ci·ta·tive (ri-sus′ə-tā′tiv), *adj.* serving or tending to resuscitate.
re·sus·ci·ta·tor (ri-sus′ə-tā′tẽr), *n.* [LL.], a person or thing that resuscitates.
Resz·ke, Jean de (zhän də resh′ke), (*Jan Mieczislaw*), 1850–1925; Polish operatic tenor.
ret (ret), *v.t.* [RETTED (-id), RETTING], [ME. *retten, reten;* MD. *reten, reeten;* ? IE. base **qret-*, to shake, as in OHG. *redan*, to sieve, G. *retten*, to save, etc.; cf. REDD], to dampen or soak (flax, hemp, timber, etc.) in water in order to soften by causing to rot.
ret., 1. retired. 2. returned.
re·ta·ble (ri-tā′b'l), *n.* [Fr., contr. < **reretable; rere* (see REAR) + *table* (see TABLE)], a raised shelf or ledge above an altar for holding altar lights, flowers, etc.
re·tail (rē′tāl; *also, for v.t. 2,* ri-tāl′), *n.* [Late ME. *retaylen;* OFr., lit., a cutting < *retailler*, to cut up; *re-*, again + *tailler*, to cut; see TAILOR], the sale of goods or articles individually or in small quantities directly to the consumer: opposed to *wholesale*. *adj.* of, connected with, or engaged in the sale of goods at retail. *v.t.* 1. to sell individually or in small quantities; sell directly to the consumer. 2. to repeat or pass on to others, as gossip; tell in detail. *v.i.* to be sold at retail: as, these books *retail* at a dollar.
re·tail·er (rē′tāl-ẽr; *also, for 2,* ri-tāl′ẽr), *n.* 1. a retail merchant or dealer. 2. a circulator, as of gossip, etc.
re·tain (ri-tān′), *v.t.* [ME. *reteynen;* OFr. *retenir;* LL. **retenere;* L. *retinere* < *re-*, back + *tenere*, to hold], 1. to hold or keep in possession. 2. to keep in a fixed state or condition. 3. to continue to practice, use, etc. 4. to keep in mind. 5. to hire, or arrange in advance for the services of, by paying a fee: as, *retain* a lawyer. —*SYN.* see **keep.**
retained object, in *grammar*, an object in passive constructions that is the same as the direct or indirect object in the corresponding active constructions (e.g., *money* in "John was given the *money* by me"; corresponding active construction, "I gave John the money").
re·tain·er (ri-tān′ẽr), *n.* 1. a person or thing that retains. 2. a person serving someone of rank, as in feudal times, and owing him occasional service; attendant or adherent, as of a lord. 3. a groove, frame, etc. within which roller bearings are held.
re·tain·er (ri-tān′ẽr), *n.* [substantive use of OFr. *retenir*], 1. a retaining or being retained in one's service. 2. in *law, a)* the act of engaging the services of a lawyer, counselor, etc. *b)* a fee paid to get such services.
retaining wall, 1. a wall built to keep a bank of earth from sliding or water from flooding. 2. a revetment.
re·tain·ment (ri-tān′mənt), *n.* a retaining or being retained.
re·take (rē-tāk′; *for n.,* rē′tāk′), *v.t.* [RETOOK (-took′), RETAKEN (-tā′k'n), RETAKING], 1. to take again, take back, or recapture. 2. in *motion pictures & photography*, to photograph again. *n.* 1. a retaking. 2. a picture, scene, etc. rephotographed or to be rephotographed.
re·tal·i·ate (ri-tal′i-āt′), *v.i.* [RETALIATED (-id), RETALIATING], [< L. *retaliatus*, pp. of *retaliare*, to require, retaliate < *re-*, back + *talio*, punishment in kind < *talis*, such], to return like for like; especially, to return evil for evil; pay back injury for injury: as, if he is hurt, he will *retaliate*. *v.t.* to return an injury, wrong, etc. for (an injury, wrong, etc. given); requite in kind.
re·tal·i·a·tion (ri-tal′i-ā′shən), *n.* a retaliating; reprisal.
re·tal·i·a·tive (ri-tal′i-ā′tiv), *adj.* retaliating; retaliatory.
re·tal·i·a·to·ry (ri-tal′i-ə-tôr′i, ri-tal′i-ə-tō′ri), *adj.* 1. of, having the nature of, or involving retaliation. 2. retaliating or tending to retaliate.
re·tard (ri-tärd′), *v.t.* [Fr. *retarder;* L. *retardare; re-*, back + *tardare*, to make slow < *tardus*, slow], to hinder, delay, or slow the advance or progress of. *v.i.* to be delayed. *n.* a retarding; delay. —*SYN.* see **delay.**
re·tar·da·tion (rē′tär-dā′shən), *n.* [ME. *retardacion;* L. *retardatio*], 1. a retarding or being retarded. 2. something that retards. 3. [Rare], in *music*, a suspension, especially one that resolves upward.
re·tard·a·tive (ri-tär′də-tiv), *adj.* retarding; retardatory.
re·tard·a·to·ry (ri-tär′də-tôr′i, ri-tär′də-tō′ri), *adj.* 1. of, or having the nature of, retardation. 2. retarding or tending to retard.
re·tard·ment (ri-tärd′mənt), *n.* retardation.
retch (rech), *v.i.* [AS. *hræcan*, to clear the throat,

restrike **restrive** **restuff** **resummon**
restring **restudy** **resubject** **resupply**

hawk, spit < *hraca*, clearing of the throat, spittle], to make a straining, involuntary effort to vomit.

retd., 1. retained. 2. returned.

re·te (rē′tē), *n.* [*pl.* RETIA (rē′shi-ə, -ti-ə)], [ME. *riet;* L., a net], in *anatomy*, a network or plexus, as of blood vessels or nerve fibers.

re·tem (rē′tem), *n.* [Ar. *ratam*, pl. of *ratamah*], a desert shrub of the bean family, with small, white flowers: the juniper of the Old Testament.

re·tene (rē′tēn, ret′ēn), *n.* [< Gr. *rhētinē*, resin], a hydrocarbon, $C_{18}H_{18}$, obtained from resinous woods and fossil resins.

re·ten·tion (ri-ten′shən), *n.* [ME. *retencioun;* OFr.; L. *retentio*], 1. a retaining or being retained. 2. power of or capacity for retaining. 3. *a)* a remembering; memory. *b)* ability to remember.

re·ten·tive (ri-ten′tiv), *adj.* [OFr. *retentif*], 1. retaining or tending to retain. 2. having the power of or capacity for retaining. 3. *a)* tenacious: as, a *retentive* memory. *b)* having a good memory.

re·ten·tiv·i·ty (rē′ten-tiv′ə-ti), *n.* 1. the power of or capacity for retaining. 2. in *electricity*, the power of remaining magnetized after the force of magnetization has stopped.

re·te·pore (rē′ti-pôr′, rē′ti-pōr′), *n.* [< Mod. L. *Retepora*, name of the genus < L. *rete*, a net + *porus*, a pore], any of a large group of tiny sea mollusks that live in colonies, their skeletons fusing to form coral-like masses.

re·ti·a·ri·us (rē′shi-âr′i-əs), *n.* [*pl.* RETIARII (-ī′)], [L. < *rete*, a net], in ancient Rome, a gladiator armed with a net and a trident.

re·ti·ar·y (rē′shi-er′i), *adj.* [< L. *rete*, *retis*, a net; + *-ary*], 1. of or like nets or netmaking. 2. building nets, as certain spiders. 3. armed with a net.

ret·i·cence (ret′ə-s′ns), *n.* [< Fr. or L.; Fr. *réticence;* L. *reticentia*], quality, state, or instance of being reticent; reserve.

ret·i·cen·cy (ret′ə-s′n-si), *n.* reticence.

ret·i·cent (ret′ə-s′nt), *adj.* [L. *reticens*, ppr. of *reticere*, to be silent < *re-*, again + *tacere*, to be silent], habitually silent or uncommunicative; disinclined to speak readily; reserved; taciturn. —*SYN.* see **silent.**

ret·i·cle (ret′i-k′l), *n.* [L. *reticulum;* see RETICULE], in *optics*, a network of very fine lines, wires, etc. in the focus of the eyepiece of an optical instrument.

re·tic·u·lar (ri-tik′yoo-lẽr), *adj.* [Mod. L. *reticularis* < L. *reticulum*], 1. netlike. 2. intricate; entangled.

re·tic·u·late (ri-tik′yoo-lit; *also, and for v. always,* ri-tik′yoo-lāt′), *adj.* [L. *reticulatus* < *reticulum;* see RETICULE], like a net or network; netlike; specifically, in *botany*, having the veins arranged like the threads of a net: said of leaves. *v.t.* [RETICULATED (-id), RETICULATING], to divide or mark so as to look like network. *v.i.* to be divided or marked like network.

re·tic·u·la·tion (ri-tik′yoo-lā′shən), *n.* a reticulate arrangement, formation, or pattern; network.

ret·i·cule (ret′i-kūl′), *n.* [Fr. *réticule;* L. *reticulum*, double dim. of *rete*, a net], 1. a small handbag carried by women, originally made of network. 2. a reticle.

re·tic·u·lum (ri-tik′yoo-ləm), *n.* [*pl.* RETICULA (-lə)], [L.; see RETICULE], 1. network; netlike pattern or structure. 2. [R-], in *astronomy*, a southern constellation: see **constellation**, chart. 3. in *biology*, a netlike structure found in the protoplasm of cells. 4. in *zoology*, the second division of the stomach, or second stomach, of cud-chewing animals, as cows: also called *honeycomb bag:* see **ruminant**, illus.

re·ti·form (rē′ti-fôrm′, ret′i-fôrm′), *adj.* [Mod. L. *retiformis* < L. *rete*, *retis*, a net + *-formis*, -form], having criss-crossed lines; netlike in form; reticulate.

ret·i·na (ret′'n-ə, ret′i-nə), *n.* [*pl.* RETINAS (-əz, -nəz), RETINAE (-ē′, -nē′)], [ML.; prob. < L. *rete*, *retis*, a net], the innermost coat of the back part of the eyeball, a layer of cells sensitive to light, in part an expansion of the optic nerve fibers: the image formed by the lens on the retina is carried to the brain by the optic nerve: see **eye**, illus.

ret·i·nal (ret′'n-əl, ret′i-nəl), *adj.* of or on the retina.

ret·in·ene (ret″'n-ēn′, ret′i-nēn′), *n.* [< *retina* + *-ene*], visual yellow.

ret·i·nite (ret″'n-īt′, ret′i-nīt′), *n.* [Fr. *rétinite* < Gr. *rhētinē*, resin; see RESIN & -ITE], any of several fossil resins, especially one derived from lignite.

ret·i·ni·tis (ret″'n-ī′tis, ret′i-nī′tis), *n.* inflammation of the retina.

ret·i·nol (ret″'n-ōl′, ret′i-nol′), *n.* [< Gr. *rhētinē*, resin; + *-ol*], a yellowish liquid hydrocarbon, $C_{32}H_{16}$, obtained by the distillation of resin: it is used as a lubricant, a solvent, an antiseptic, etc.

ret·in·o·scope (ret″'n-ə-skōp′, ret′i-nə-skōp′), *n.* a skiascope.

ret·i·no·scop·ic (ret″'n-ə-skop′ik, ret′i-nə-skop′ik), *adj.* of or by retinoscopy.

ret·i·nos·co·py (ret″'n-os′kə-pi, ret′i-nos′kə-pi), *n.* [< *retina* + *-scopy*], a method for determining the refraction of the eye: also called *skiascopy*.

ret·i·nue (ret′'n-ōō′, ret′i-nū′), *n.* [ME. & OFr. *retenue*, fem. of *retenu*, pp. of *retenir;* see RETAIN], a group of persons in the service of, or in attendance on, a person of rank; body of retainers; escort.

re·tire (ri-tīr′), *v.i.* [RETIRED (-tīrd′), RETIRING], [Fr. *retirer; re-*, back + *tirer*, to draw], 1. to go away or withdraw to a private, sheltered, or secluded place; hence, 2. to go to bed. 3. to give ground, as in battle; retreat; withdraw. 4. to withdraw oneself from business, active service, or public life, especially because of advanced age. 5. to move back or away, or seem to do so. *v.t.* 1. to take or lead away; withdraw: as, *retire* troops from an action. 2. to take out of circulation, as money; take up or pay off (stocks, bonds, bills, etc.). 3. to remove from a position or office: as, they *retired* several generals. 4. in *baseball*, etc., to put out (a batter, side, etc.). —*SYN.* see **go.**

re·tired (ri-tīrd′), *adj.* [pp. of *retire*], 1. withdrawn or apart from the world; in seclusion; secluded. 2. withdrawn from business, active service, etc. 3. of or for a person or persons so withdrawn: as, a *retired* list. 4. withdrawn in space; bent or drawn back.

re·tire·ment (ri-tīr′mənt), *n.* 1. a retiring or being retired; withdrawal, removal, etc. 2. privacy; seclusion. 3. a place of privacy or seclusion.

re·tir·ing (ri-tīr′iŋ), *adj.* [ppr. of *retire*], 1. that retires. 2. drawing back from contact with others, from publicity, etc.; reserved; modest; shy.

re·took (rē-took′), past tense of **retake.**

re·tool (rē-tōōl′), *v.t.* & *v.i.* to adapt the machinery of (a factory) to the manufacture of a different product by changing the tools and dies.

re·tor·sion (ri-tôr′shən), *n.* retortion (sense 2).

re·tort (ri-tôrt′), *v.t.* [< L. *retortus*, pp. of *retorquere*, to twist back; *re-*, back + *torquere*, to twist], 1. to turn (an insult, epithet, deed, etc.) back upon the person from whom it came. 2. to answer (an argument, etc.) in kind. *v.i.* to make a sharp or witty reply; reply in kind or in the same terms as the previous speaker. *n.* 1. a quick, sharp, or witty reply, especially one that turns the words of the previous speaker back upon himself. 2. the act or practice of making such reply. —*SYN.* see **answer.**

re·tort (ri-tôrt′), *n.* [Fr. *retorte;* ML. *retorta* (in L., fem. of *retortus*, pp. of *retorquere*); see prec.], a container, generally of glass and with a long tube, in which substances are distilled or decomposed by heat.

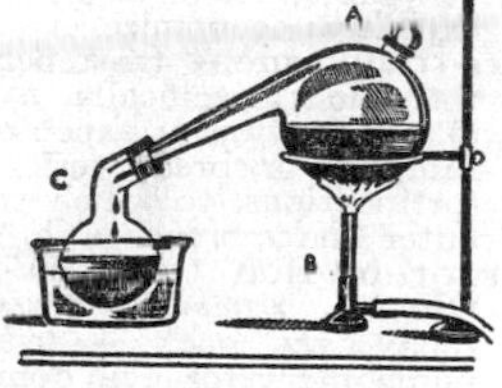

RETORT
A, retort; B, Bunsen burner; C, flask for receiving distilled liquids

re·tor·tion (ri-tôr′shən), *n.* [ML. *retortio*, *retorsio* < L. *retortus*, pp. of *retorquere;* see RETORT, *v.*], 1. a turning, bending, or twisting back or being turned, bent, or twisted back. 2. in *law*, a retaliation; reprisal; especially, in *international law*, mistreatment by one country of the citizens or subjects of another in retaliation for similar mistreatment received from the latter country: also spelled **retorsion.**

re·touch (rē-tuch′; *also, for n.*, rē′tuch′), *v.t.* [Fr. *retoucher;* see RE- & TOUCH], 1. to touch up or change details in (a painting, piece of writing, etc.) in order to improve it. 2. in *photography*, to change (a negative or print) by adding details or removing blemishes, as with a pencil or knife. *n.* 1. a retouching. 2. a detail added or removed in retouching. 3. a photograph, etc. that has been retouched.

re·trace (ri-trās′), *v.t.* [RETRACED (-trāst′), RETRACING], [Fr. *retracer;* see RE- & TRACE], 1. to go back over again, especially in the reverse direction: as, he *retraced* his steps. 2. to trace again the story of, from the beginning. 3. to go over again with the eyes or in memory.

re-trace, re·trace (rē′trās′), *v.t.* to trace over again, as a drawing.

re·tract (ri-trakt′), *v.t.* & *v.i.* [in sense "draw back" < L. *retractus*, pp. of *retrahere*, to draw back; *re-*, back + *trahere*, to draw; in sense "withdraw" < Fr. *rétracter* < L. *retractare*, to draw back, withdraw; *re-*, back + *tractare*, to pull, draw, freq. of *trahere*], 1. to draw back or in. 2. to withdraw or disavow (a state-

reteach
retear
retell
retemper
retest
rethink
retie
retold

ment, promise, offer, charge, etc.); recant or revoke.
re·trac·ta·tion (rē'trak-tā'shən), *n.* a retraction.
re·trac·tile (ri-trak't'l), *adj.* [Fr. *rétractile*], 1. that can be retracted, or drawn back or in, as claws. 2. of retraction: as, *retractile* power.
re·trac·til·i·ty (rē'trak-til'ə-ti), *n.* the quality or state of being retractile.
re·trac·tion (ri-trak'shən), *n.* [ME. *retraccion;* prob. via OFr. < LL. *retractio*], 1. a retracting or being retracted; specifically, *a)* withdrawal, as of a statement, promise, charge, etc. *b)* a drawing or being drawn back or in. 2. power of retracting.
re·trac·tive (ri-trak'tiv), *adj.* [ME. & OFr. *retractif*], retracting or tending to retract.
re·trac·tor (ri-trak'tẽr), *n.* a person or thing that retracts; especially, *a)* a muscle that retracts an organ, protruded part, etc. *b)* a surgical instrument or device for drawing back a part or organ, as the flesh at the edge of an incision.
re·tral (rē'trəl), *adj.* [< L. *retro,* backward; + *-al*], at, near, or toward the back; posterior.
re·tread (rē'tred'; *for n.,* rē'tred'), *v.t.* to put a new tread on (a worn pneumatic tire), especially by cementing, molding, and vulcanizing a whole new rubber tread on the bare underlayer of fabric: cf. **recap.** *n.* a retreaded tire.
re-tread (rē-tred'), *v.t.* [RE-TROD (-trod'), RE-TROD or RE-TRODDEN (-trod''n), RE-TREADING], to tread again: also spelled **retread.**
re·treat (ri-trēt'), *n.* [ME. *retret;* OFr. *retrete, retraite* < pp. of *retraire,* to draw back; L. *retrahere;* see RETRACT], 1. a going back or backward; withdrawal; giving ground before opposition. 2. withdrawal to a safe or private place. 3. a safe, quiet, or secluded place; hiding place. 4. a period of retirement or seclusion, especially one devoted to religious contemplation away from the pressures of ordinary life. 5. an asylum or sanitarium for the mentally ill, for alcoholics, etc. 6. in *military usage, a)* the withdrawal of troops, ships, etc. from a position, especially when forced by enemy attack. *b)* a signal for such a withdrawal. *c)* a signal given by drum or bugle at sunset for lowering the national flag. *d)* the ceremony at which this is done. *v.i.* 1. to withdraw; go back; retire. 2. to slope backward. *v.t.* in *chess,* to move (a piece) back. —*SYN.* see **shelter.**
beat a retreat, 1. in *military usage,* to signal for retreat by beating a drum; hence, 2. to retreat.
re·trench (ri-trench'), *v.t.* [MFr. *retrencher* (Fr. *retrancher*); see RE- & TRENCH, *v.*], 1. to cut down; lessen; curtail; reduce, as expenses. 2. to cut off or out; omit; delete, as a portion of a book. *v.i.* to reduce expenses; economize.
re·trench·ment (ri-trench'mənt), *n.* [MFr.], 1. a retrenching; specifically, *a)* a cutting down, off, or out. *b)* a reduction of expenses. 2. in *military usage, a)* a rampart or breastwork within or behind the main fortifications, to which troops can retreat in case the outer line is breached. *b)* entrenchment.
ret·ri·bu·tion (ret'rə-bū'shən), *n.* [ME. *retribucioun;* OFr.; L. *retributio* < *retributus,* pp. of *retribuere,* to repay; *re-,* back + *tribuere,* to pay], 1. deserved punishment for evil done, or, sometimes, reward for good done; merited requital. 2. in *theology,* reward or punishment in another life for things done in this.
re·trib·u·tive (ri-trib'yoo-tiv), *adj.* of, having the nature of, characterized by, or involving retribution.
re·trib·u·to·ry (ri-trib'yoo-tôr'i, ri-trib'yoo-tō'ri), *adj.* retributive.
re·triev·a·ble (ri-trēv'ə-b'l), *adj.* that can be retrieved.
re·triev·al (ri-trēv''l), *n.* 1. a retrieving; recovery; restoration. 2. possibility of recovery or restoration.
re·trieve (ri-trēv'), *v.t.* [RETRIEVED (-trēvd'), RETRIEVING], [ME. *retreven* < inflected stem of OFr. *retrouver; re-,* again + *trouver,* to find], 1. to get back; recover. 2. to restore; revive: as, he *retrieved* his spirits. 3. to make good; set right; make amends for (a loss, error, etc.). 4. to recall to mind. 5. in *hunting,* to find and bring back (killed or wounded game): said of dogs. *v.i.* in *hunting,* to retrieve game. *n.* retrieval. —*SYN.* see **recover.**
re·triev·er (ri-trēv'ẽr), *n.* 1. a person who retrieves. 2. a dog trained to retrieve game; specifically, any of several breeds of dog developed for this purpose.
ret·ro- (ret'rō; *occas.* rē'trō), [< L. *retro,* backward], a combining form meaning *backward, back, behind,* as in *retroact, retroflex.*
ret·ro·act (ret'rō-akt'), *v.i.* 1. to act backward or in opposition; react. 2. to have reference or application to or influence on things done in the past.
ret·ro·ac·tion (ret'rō-ak'shən), *n.* 1. opposed, reverse, or reciprocal action. 2. effect, as of a law, on things done prior to its enactment or effectuation.
ret·ro·ac·tive (ret'rō-ak'tiv), *adj.* retroacting or tending to retroact; having application to or effect on things prior to its enactment or effectuation: as, a *retroactive* law or agreement.
ret·ro·cede (ret'rō-sēd'), *v.i.* [RETROCEDED (-id), RETROCEDING], [L. *retrocedere; retro-,* back + *cedere,* to go], to go back; recede.
ret·ro·cede (ret'rō-sēd'), *v.t.* [*retro-* + *cede*], to cede back; give back; restore.
ret·ro·ces·sion (ret'rō-sesh'ən), *n.* [LL. *retrocessio*], a retroceding, or going back.
ret·ro·ces·sion (ret'rō-sesh'ən), *n.* a retroceding, or giving back.
ret·ro·choir (ret'rə-kwīr', rē'trō-kwīr'), *n.* [*retro-* + *choir,* after ML. *retrochorus*], that part of a church which lies behind the choir or the main altar.
ret·ro·flex (ret'rə-fleks'), *adj.* [LL. *retroflexus,* pp. of *retroflectere:* see RETRO- & FLEX], 1. bent or turned backward. 2. in *phonetics, a)* having the tip raised and bent backward: said of the tongue. *b)* formed with the tongue in this position: said of sounds.
ret·ro·flexed (ret'rə-flekst'), *adj.* retroflex.
ret·ro·flex·ion (ret'rə-flek'shən), *n.* 1. the condition of being retroflex; bending backward; specifically, in *medicine,* the bending backward of an organ, especially of the body of the uterus, upon itself. 2. in *phonetics, a)* retroflex articulation. *b)* the acoustic quality produced by this: also called *r-color.*
ret·ro·gra·da·tion (ret'rō-grā-dā'shən), *n.* [LL. *retrogradatio;* see RETRO- & GRADATION], 1. backward movement. 2. decline; deterioration.
ret·ro·grade (ret'rə-grād'), *adj.* [ME. *retrograd;* L. *retrogradus* < *retrogradi;* see RETRO- & GRADE], 1. moving or directed backward; retiring or retreating. 2. inverse or reverse: said of order. 3. going back or tending to go back to an earlier or worse condition; retrogressive. 4. in *astronomy, a)* designating motion, real or apparent, in a direction contrary to the order of the signs of the zodiac, or from east to west. *b)* moving in an orbit in a direction opposite to that of the earth as it revolves around the sun. 5. [Obs.], opposed; contrary. *v.i.* [RETROGRADED (-id), RETROGRADING], [L. *retrogradi*], 1. to go, or seem to go, backward. 2. to become worse; decline; deteriorate; degenerate. 3. in *astronomy,* to have a retrograde motion.
ret·ro·gress (ret'rə-gres', ret'rə-gres'), *v.i.* [L. *retrogressus,* pp. of *retrogradi;* see RETROGRADE], to move backward, especially into an earlier, less complex, or worse condition; decline; degenerate.
ret·ro·gres·sion (ret'rə-gresh'ən), *n.* a retrogressing; especially, in *biology,* a return to a lower, less complex stage or state; degeneration.
ret·ro·gres·sive (ret'rə-gres'iv), *adj.* retrogressing or showing retrogression; degenerative.
re·trorse (ri-trôrs'), *adj.* [L. *retrorsus,* contr. of *retroversus,* bent backward; *retro,* back + *versus,* pp. of *vertere,* to turn], bent or turned backward or downward.
ret·ro·spect (ret'rə-spekt'), *n.* [< L. **retrospectus,* pp. of *retrospicere,* to look back < *retro-,* back + *specere,* to look], a looking back on or thinking about things past; contemplation or survey of the past. *v.i.* [Rare], 1. to look back in thought; think about the past. 2. to refer back (*to*). *v.t.* [Rare], to look back on or think about (things past).
in retrospect, in reviewing the past.
ret·ro·spec·tion (ret'rə-spek'shən), *n.* [see RETROSPECT & -ION], 1. act, instance, or faculty of looking back on or reviewing past events, experiences, etc. 2. [Rare], *a)* a looking back or referring (*to*). *b)* reference or allusion to past events.
ret·ro·spec·tive (ret'rə-spek'tiv), *adj.* [see RETROSPECT & -IVE], 1. looking back on or directed to the past, past events, etc. 2. looking or directed backward. 3. applying to the past; retroactive.
ret·rous·sé (ret'roo-sā'; Fr. rə-troo'sā'), *adj.* [Fr., pp. of *retrousser,* to turn up; see RE- & TRUSS], turned up at the tip: said of a nose.
ret·ro·ver·sion (ret'rə-vũr'zhən, ret'rə-vũr'shən), *n.* [< L. *retro-,* back + *versus,* pp. of *vertere,* to turn; + *-ion*], 1. a looking or turning back. 2. a turning or tilting, or being turned or tilted, backward, as of an organ or part: as, *retroversion* of the uterus.
re·turn (ri-tũrn'), *v.i.* [ME. *returnen, retournen;* OFr. *returner, retorner;* see RE- & TURN], 1. to go or come back, as to a former place, condition, etc. 2. to go back in thought or speech: as, let's *return* to the subject. 3. to revert to a former owner. 4. to answer; reply; respond. *v.t.* 1. to bring, send, carry, or put back; restore or replace. 2. to give, send, or do (something of the same sort as, or equivalent to, what has been given, sent, or done); give, visit, or do in requital or reciprocation: as, *return* a visit. 3. to produce, as a profit or revenue; yield. 4. *a)* to report or announce officially or formally. *b)* to turn in (a writ, account, or statement) to a judge or other official. 5. to elect or re-elect, as to a legislature. 6. to replace (a weapon) in its holder. 7. to turn back; turn in the opposite direction. 8. to turn away from, or cause to continue on at an angle to, the previous line of direction. 9. to render (a verdict, etc.). 10. in *card games,* to respond

retrain	**retranslate**	**re-treat**	**retry**
retransfer	**retraverse**	**retrial**	**retune**

to (a partner's lead) with a lead of the same suit. *n.* [ME. *retorn* < the *v.*], 1. a coming or going back, as to a former place, condition, etc. 2. a bringing, sending, carrying, or putting back; restoration or replacement. 3. something returned. 4. a coming back again; reappearance; recurrence: as, on his birthday they wished him many happy *returns* of the day. 5. something done or given as an equivalent for that received; repayment; requital; reciprocation. 6. *a)* profit made on an exchange of goods. *b) often in pl.* yield, profit, or revenue, as from labor, investments, etc. *c)* yield per unit as compared to cost per unit, as in the manufacture of a given product; rate of yield. 7. *a)* a bend or turn, as in a line, wall, etc. *b)* the section between two such bends. 8. an answer; reply; response. 9. a report; especially, *a)* an official or formal report, as of the financial condition of a company. *b) usually in pl.* a report on a count of votes at polling places: as, election *returns*. 10. in *architecture*, etc., the continuation, as of a molding, colonnade, etc., in a different direction, often at a right angle. 11. in *card games*, a lead in response to a partner's lead. 12. in *law*, *a)* the bringing or sending back of a writ, subpoena, summons, etc. to the proper court or official, usually with a short report endorsed on it. *b)* a certified report by an election official, assessor, etc. *c)* a certificate or report endorsed on any such document. 13. in *tennis*, etc., *a)* a batting or throwing back of a ball. *b)* a ball so returned. *adj.* 1. of or for a return or returning: as, a *return* ticket. 2. given, sent, done, etc., in return: as, a *return* visit. 3. returning. 4. returned. 5. changing or reversing direction or formed by a change or reversal in direction, as a bend in a road.

in return, as a return; as an equivalent, response, etc.

SYN.—**return** is the common word meaning to go or come back, as to a former place, person, or condition (let us *return* home); **revert** implies a return to an earlier, usually more primitive, condition, or to the original owner, to a former topic of discussion, etc. (they have *reverted* to savagery); **recur** suggests the return of some action, occurrence, experience, etc. and often connotes its repeated return at intervals (malaria is characterized by a *recurring* fever).

e·turn·a·ble (ri-tũr'nə-b'l), *adj.* 1. that can be returned. 2. that must be returned.

eturn ticket, 1. a ticket for the trip back to the original starting point. 2. a round-trip ticket.

e·tuse (ri-tōōs', ri-tūs'), *adj.* [L. *retusus*, dull, pp. of *retundere*, to beat back], in *botany*, having a blunt or rounded apex with a small notch, as some leaves.

e·type (rē-tīp'; *for n.*, rē'tīp'), *v.t.* to type over again. *n.* something retyped.

Reu·ben (rōō'bin), [Heb. *rĕ'ūbēn*, lit., behold, a son], a masculine name; diminutives, *Rube, Ruby*. *n.* in the *Bible*, 1. the eldest son of Jacob: Gen. 29. 2. the tribe of Israel descended from him: Numb. 32.

Reuch·lin, Jo·hann (yō'hän roiH'lēn, roiH-lēn'), 1455–1522; German scholar of Greek and Hebrew.

Ré·un·ion (rā'ü'nyōn'; Eng. rē-ūn'yən), *n.* a French island in the Indian Ocean, east of Madagascar: area, 970 sq. mi.; pop., 242,000 (est. 1947); capital, St. Denis: former name, *Bourbon*.

e·un·ion (rē-ūn'yən), *n.* [*re-* + *union*; cf. Fr. *réunion*], 1. a bringing or coming together again; reuniting. 2. a gathering of persons after separation, as of members of a college class or of a family.

e·un·ion·ist (rē-ūn'yən-ist), *n.* an advocate of reunion; specifically, an advocate of the reunion of the Anglican Church with the Roman Catholic Church.

e·u·nite (rē'yoo-nīt'), *v.t.* & *v.i.* [< ML. *reunitus*, pp.], to unite again; bring or come together again.

Reu·ters (roi'tẽrz), *n.* [after Baron Paul Julius von *Reuter* (1821–1899), the founder], a private British agency for gathering and distributing news among member newspapers: also **Reuter's News Agency.**

Reu·ther, Walter Philip (rōō'thẽr), 1907– ; American labor leader; president of the C.I.O. (1952–1955).

ev (rev), *n.* [Colloq.], a revolution, as of an engine. *v.t.* [REVVED (revd), REVVING], [Colloq.], to change the speed of (an engine, motor, etc.): usually in *rev up*, to accelerate. *v.i.* [Colloq.], to undergo revving.

Rev., 1. Revelation. 2. [*pl.* REVS.], Reverend.

ev., 1. revenue. 2. reverse. 3. review. 4. revise. 5. revised. 6. revision. 7. [*pl.* REVS.], revolution. 8. revolving.

Re·val (rā'väl), *n.* Tallinn, the capital of the Estonian S.S.R.: the German name.

e·vamp (rē-vamp'), *v.t.* to vamp again or anew; specifically, *a)* to put a new vamp on (a shoe or boot). *b)* to renovate; patch up; redo.

e·veal (ri-vēl'), *v.t.* [ME. *reuelen*; OFr. *reveler* (Fr. *révéler*); L. *revelare*, lit., to draw back the veil < *re-*, back + *velum*, a veil (see VEIL)], 1. to make known (something hidden or kept secret); disclose; divulge. 2. to expose to view; show; exhibit; display.

SYN.—**reveal** implies a making known of something hidden or secret, as if by drawing back a veil (to *reveal* one's identity); **disclose** suggests a laying open, as to inspection, of what has previously been concealed (he refuses to *disclose* his intentions); **divulge** suggests that what has been disclosed should properly have been kept secret or private (do not *divulge* the contents of this letter); **tell** may also imply a breach of confidence (kiss and *tell*) but more commonly suggests the making known of necessary or requested information (*tell* me what to do); **betray** implies either faithlessness in divulging something (*betrayed* by an informer) or inadvertence in revealing something (her blush *betrayed* embarrassment).—*ANT.* conceal, hide.

re·veal (ri-vēl'), *n.* [< ME. *revalen*, to bring down; OFr. *revaler*; *re-*, back + *valer* (see VAIL)], 1. that part of the side of an opening for a window or door which is between the outer edge of the opening and the frame of the window or door. 2. the entire side of such an opening; jamb.

revealed religion, any religion based on the belief that a deity has revealed himself and his will to his creatures.

re·veal·ment (ri-vēl'mənt), *n.* a revealing or being revealed; disclosure; revelation.

re·veil·le (rev'ə-li), *n.* [< Fr. *réveillez* (*-vous*), imperative of (*se*) *réveiller*, to wake up; *ré-* (< L. *re-*) + *veiller* (< L. *vigilare*, to watch)], in *military usage*, 1. a signal on a bugle, drum, etc. at some fixed time early in the morning to waken soldiers or sailors or call them to first assembly. 2. the first assembly of the day.

Re·vel (rev'əl; Russ. re'vel'y'), *n.* Tallinn, the capital of the Estonian S.S.R.: the Russian name.

rev·el (rev''l), *v.i.* [REVELED or REVELLED (-'ld), REVELING or REVELLING], [ME. *revelen*; OFr. *reveler*; L. *rebellare*; see REBEL], 1. to make merry; be noisily festive. 2. to take much pleasure; delight (with *in*): as, he *revels* in sports. *n.* 1. merrymaking; boisterous festivity; revelry. 2. *often pl.* an occasion of merrymaking or boisterous festivity; celebration.

rev·e·la·tion (rev'ə-lā'shən), *n.* [ME. *reuelacioun*; OFr.; LL. *revelatio* < pp. of L. *revelare*], 1. a revealing, or disclosing. 2. something disclosed; disclosure; especially, a striking disclosure, as of something not previously known or realized. 3. in *Christian theology*, *a)* God's disclosure or manifestation to his creatures of himself and his will. *b)* an instance of this. *c)* what is so disclosed or manifested. *d)* something, as the Bible, containing such disclosure or manifestation. 4. [R-], *also pl.* the last book of the New Testament, ascribed to John (in full, **The Revelation of Saint John the Divine**); Apocalypse; abbreviated **Rev.**

rev·e·la·tion·ist (rev'ə-lā'shən-ist), *n.* 1. a person who believes in divine revelation. 2. [also R-], the author of Revelation.

rev·e·la·tor (rev'ə-lā'tẽr), *n.* [LL.; see REVEAL], a person who reveals something.

rev·el·er, rev·el·ler (rev''l-ẽr), *n.* a person who revels or takes part in a revel; merrymaker.

rev·el·ry (rev''l-ri), *n.* [*pl.* REVELRIES (-riz)], reveling; noisy merrymaking; boisterous festivity.

rev·e·nant (rev'ə-nənt), *n.* [Fr., ppr. of *revenir*, to come back < L. *re-*, back + *venire*, to come], 1. a person who returns, as after a long absence. 2. a person who returns as a spirit after death; ghost.

re·venge (ri-venj'), *v.t.* [REVENGED (-venjd'), REVENGING], [OFr. *revenger*, *revenchier* < *re-*, again + *venger*, older *vengier*, to take vengeance < L. *vindicare*; see VINDICATE], 1. to inflict damage, injury, or punishment in return for (an injury, insult, etc.); take vengeance for; retaliate for. 2. to take vengeance in behalf of (a person, oneself, etc.); avenge. *v.i.* [Obs.], to take vengeance. *n.* 1. a revenging; vengeance. 2. what is done in revenging. 3. desire to take vengeance; vindictive spirit. 4. a chance to retaliate or get satisfaction, as by a return match after defeat in a previous one. —*SYN.* see **avenge.**

be revenged, to get revenge; take vengeance.

re·venge·ful (ri-venj'fəl), *adj.* full of revenge; feeling or showing a desire for revenge. —*SYN.* see **vindictive.**

rev·e·nue (rev'ə-nōō', rev'ə-nū'), *n.* [ME. & OFr. *revenu* (Fr. *revenue*, fem.), pp. of *revenir*, to return, come back; *re-*, back + *venir* < L. *venire*, to come], 1. the return from property or investment; income. 2. *a)* an item or source of income. *b) pl.* items or amounts of income collectively. 3. the income from taxes, duties, etc. of a unit of government, as a city, county, state, nation, etc. 4. the governmental department or bureau that handles the collection of such income. Abbreviated **rev.**

revenue cutter, see **cutter** (sense 3*b*).

revenue stamp, a stamp placed on an article to show that a tax has been paid on it.

retwist
re-use
revaluate
revaluation
revalue
revarnish
revegetate
revegetation

re·ver·ber·ant (ri-vũr′bẽr-ənt), ***adj.*** [L. *reverberans*, ppr.], reverberating; re-echoing; resonant.

re·ver·ber·ate (ri-vũr′bə-rāt′), ***v.t.*** [REVERBERATED (-id), REVERBERATING], [< L. *reverberatus*, pp. of *reverberare*, to beat back, repel; *re-*, again + *verberare*, to beat < *verber*, a lash, whip], 1. to throw back (sound); cause (a sound) to re-echo. 2. *a*) to reflect (light, etc.). *b*) to deflect (heat, flame, etc.), as in a reverberatory furnace. 3. to subject to treatment in a reverberatory furnace or the like. ***v.i.*** 1. to re-echo; resound. 2. *a*) to be reflected, as light or sound waves. *b*) to be deflected, as heat or flame in a reverberatory furnace. 3. to recoil; rebound.

re·ver·ber·a·tion (ri-vũr′bə-rā′shən), ***n.*** 1. a reverberating or being reverberated; specifically, *a*) a re-echoing or being re-echoed. *b*) reflection, as of light or sound waves. *c*) deflection of heat or flame, as in a reverberatory furnace. *d*) subjection to treatment in a reverberatory furnace, etc. 2. something reverberated; re-echoed sound, reflected light, etc. 3. in *physics*, multiple reflection of sound waves in a confined area so that the sound persists for some time after the source is cut off.

re·ver·ber·a·tive (ri-vũr′bə-rā′tiv, ri-vũr′bẽr-ə-tiv), ***adj.*** 1. reverberating or tending to reverberate. 2. having the nature of reverberation.

re·ver·ber·a·tor (ri-vũr′bə-rāt′ẽr), ***n.*** something that produces reverberation, as a reflecting lamp or a reverberatory furnace.

re·ver·ber·a·to·ry (ri-vũr′bẽr-ə-tôr′i, ri-vũr′bẽr-ə-tō′ri), ***adj.*** 1. operating, characterized, or produced by reverberation. 2. deflected, as flame or heat. 3. designating a furnace, kiln, or the like in which ore, metal, etc. is heated by a flame deflected downward from the roof. ***n.*** such a furnace, kiln, etc.

Re·vere (ri-vêr′), ***n.*** a city near Boston, Massachusetts, on Boston Bay: pop., 40,000.

re·vere (ri-vêr′), ***v.t.*** [REVERED (-vêrd′), REVERING], [< Fr. or L.; Fr. *révérer;* L. *revereri; re-*, again + *vereri*, to fear, feel awe], to regard with deep respect, love, and awe, as something sacred; venerate.

***SYN.*—revere** implies a regarding with great respect, affection, honor, deference, etc. (a poet *revered* by all); **reverence**, more or less equivalent to **revere**, is usually applied to a thing or abstract idea rather than to a person (they *reverence* the memory of their parents); **venerate** implies a regarding as sacred or holy (to *venerate* saints, relics, etc.); **worship**, in strict usage, implies the use of ritual or verbal formula in paying homage to a divine being but broadly suggests intense love or admiration of any kind (he *worshiped* his wife); **adore**, in strict usage, implies a personal or individual worshiping of a deity, but in broad usage, it suggests a great love for someone and, colloquially, a great liking for something (I *adore* your hat).

re·vere (ri-vêr′), ***n.*** a revers.

Re·vere, Paul (ri-vêr′), 1735–1818; American silversmith and patriot; rode to Lexington at night to warn the colonists that British troops were coming (1775).

rev·er·ence (rev′ẽr-əns), ***n.*** [ME. < OFr. *reverence* or L. *reverentia* < *reverens*, ppr. of *revereri;* see REVERE], 1. a feeling or attitude of deep respect, love, and awe, as for something sacred; veneration. 2. a manifestation of this; specifically, a bow, curtsy, or similar gesture of respect; obeisance. 3. the state of being revered. 4. [R-], a title used in speaking to or of a clergyman: preceded by *your* or *his*. ***v.t.*** [REVERENCED (-ənst), REVERENCING], to treat or regard with reverence; venerate. —***SYN.*** see **awe, honor, revere.**

rev·er·end (rev′ẽr-ənd), ***adj.*** [L. *reverendus*, gerundive of *revereri;* see REVERE], 1. worthy of reverence; deserving to be revered: used [usually R-] as a title of respect for a clergyman, often prefixed to the name; hence, 2. of or characteristic of the clergy. ***n.*** [Colloq.], a clergyman. Abbreviated **Rev.**

rev·er·ent (rev′ẽr-ənt), ***adj.*** [Late ME.; L. *reverens*, ppr.], feeling, showing, or characterized by reverence.

rev·er·en·tial (rev′ə-ren′shəl), ***adj.*** [ML. *reverentialis*], reverent.

rev·er·ie (rev′ẽr-i), ***n.*** [ME. *reuerye*, rejoicing; OFr.; as now used < Fr. *rêverie* < *rêver*, to dream], 1. dreamy thinking or imagining, especially of agreeable things; fanciful musing; daydreaming. 2. a dreamy, fanciful, or visionary notion or daydream. 3. an instrumental musical composition expressing a dreamy or musing mood. Also spelled **revery.**

re·vers (rə-vêr′, rə-vâr′), ***n.*** [*pl.* REVERS (-vêrz′, -vârz′)], [Fr. < L. *reversus;* see REVERSE], 1. a part (of a garment) turned back to show the reverse side, lining, or facing, as a lapel. 2. a piece of trimming used in simulation of such a part. Also **revere.**

re·ver·sal (ri-vũr′s'l), ***n.*** 1. a reversing or being reversed. 2. in *law*, annulment, change, or revocation, as of a lower court's decision.

re·verse (ri-vũrs′), ***adj.*** [ME. & OFr. *revers;* L. *reversus*, pp. of *revertere;* see REVERT], 1. turned backward; opposite or contrary, as in position, direction, order, etc. 2. acting in a way or direction opposite or contrary to the usual, as a machine. 3. causing movement backward or in the opposite direction: as, a *reverse* gear ratio. ***n.*** 1. the opposite or contrary of something. 2. the back or rear of something; specifically, the side of a coin, medal, etc. that does not have the main design: opposed to *obverse*. 3. a reversing; change to the opposite. 4. a change from good fortune to bad; defeat, check, or misfortune. 5. a mechanism, etc. for reversing, as a gear or gear ratio that causes a machine to run backward or in the opposite direction: as, the car was in *reverse*. 6. a reversing movement. ***v.t.*** [REVERSED (-vũrst′), REVERSING], 1. to turn backward, in an opposite position or direction, upside down, or inside out. 2. to change to the opposite; alter completely. 3. to cause to go or move backward or in an opposite direction. 4. to exchange or transpose. 5. in *law*, to revoke or annul (a decision, judgment, etc.). ***v.i.*** 1. to move, go, or turn backward or in the opposite direction: as, the dancers *reversed*. 2. to put a motor, engine, etc. in reverse; reverse the action of the mechanism. Abbreviated **rev.**

***SYN.*—reverse**, the general term, implies a changing to a contrary position, direction, order, etc. (to *reverse* an automobile, a trend, etc.); **invert**, in strictest application, implies a turning upside down or, less commonly, inside out (the image is *inverted* by the lens); **transpose** implies the reversing of the order of elements in a sequence (to *transpose* words in a sentence). See also **opposite.**

re·verse·ly (ri-vũrs′li), ***adv.*** 1. in a reverse manner, position, order, or direction. 2. on the contrary; on the other hand; contrariwise.

re·vers·i·bil·i·ty (ri-vũr′sə-bil′ə-ti), ***n.*** the quality or state of being reversible.

re·vers·i·ble (ri-vũr′sə-b'l), ***adj.*** 1. that can be reversed; specifically, made so that either side can be used as the right side; finished on both sides: said of cloth, coats, etc. 2. that can reverse; specifically, that can change and then go back to the original condition by a reversal of the change: said of a chemical reaction, etc. ***n.*** a reversible coat, jacket, etc.

re·vers·i·bly (ri-vũr′sə-bli), ***adv.*** in a reversible manner; so as to be reversible.

re·ver·sion (ri-vũr′zhən, ri-vũr′shən), ***n.*** [ME.; OFr.; L. *reversio* < *reversus;* see REVERSE], 1. a turning or being turned the opposite way; reversal. 2. a return, as to a former state, custom, or belief; a reverting. 3. in *biology*, *a*) a return to a former or primitive type; atavism. *b*) the return, or reappearance, of characteristics present in early ancestral generations but not in those that have intervened. *c*) an individual or organism with such characteristics. 4. [Obs.], a residue; remainder. 5. in *law*, *a*) the right of succession, future possession, or enjoyment. *b*) the return of an estate to the grantor and his heirs after the period of grant is over. *c*) an estate so returning.

re·ver·sion·al (ri-vũr′zhən-'l, ri-vũr′shən-'l), ***adj.*** reversionary.

re·ver·sion·ar·y (ri-vũr′zhən-er′i, ri-vũr′shən-er′i), ***adj.*** of, involving, or having the nature of, reversion.

re·ver·sion·er (ri-vũr′zhən-ẽr, ri-vũr′shən-ẽr), ***n.*** in *law*, a person who has a reversion or a right to receive an estate in reversion.

re·vert (ri-vũrt′), ***v.i.*** [ME. *reuerten;* OFr. *revertir;* LL. **revertire;* L. *revertere; re-*, back + *vertere*, to turn], 1. to go back in action, thought, speech, etc.; return, as to a former practice, opinion, state, or subject. 2. in *biology*, to return to a former or primitive type; show ancestral characteristics no longer present in the species. 3. in *law*, to go back to a former owner or his heirs. ***n.*** a person or thing that reverts; especially, one who returns to his previous faith. —***SYN.*** see **return.**

re·vert·i·ble (ri-vũr′tə-b'l), ***adj.*** that can revert.

rev·er·y (rev′ẽr-i), ***n.*** [*pl.* REVERIES (-iz)], a reverie.

re·vest (rē-vest′), ***v.t.*** [ME. *revesten;* OFr. *revestir* (Fr. *revêtir*); LL. *revestire*, to reclothe; L. *re-*, again + *vestire*, to clothe], 1. to vest again, as with possession, power, or office; reinvest; reinstate. 2. to vest (office, powers, etc.) again. ***v.i.*** to become vested again (*in*); revert to a former owner or holder.

re·vet (ri-vet′), ***v.t.*** [REVETTED (-id), REVETTING], [Fr. *revêtir;* OFr. *revestir;* see REVEST], to face (a wall, bank of earth, etc.) with a layer of stone, brick, etc.

re·vet·ment (ri-vet′mənt), ***n.*** [see REVET & -MENT], 1. a facing of stone, cement, sandbags, etc., as to protect a wall or a bank of earth. 2. a retaining wall.

re·view (ri-vū′), ***n.*** [MFr. *reveue* (Fr. *revue*) < *revu*, pp. of *revoir;* L. *revidere; re-*, again + *videre*, to see], 1. a viewing again; a looking at, looking over, or studying again. 2. a general survey, report, or account. 3. a looking back on; retrospective view or survey, as of past events, experiences, etc. 4. re-examination; specifically, judicial re-examination, as of the decision of a lower court. 5. a critical discussion or article, as in a newspaper or magazine, dealing with a book, play, concert, etc., especially with a recent one. 6. a magazine containing articles of criticism and appraisal, often in a specific field: as, a scientific *review*, literary *review*. 7. act or process of going over a lesson or subject again, as in recitation. 8. a revue. 9. an examination or inspection; specifically, a formal inspection, as of troops on parade, ships, etc., by a high-ranking officer. ***v.t.*** [*re-* + *view;* also < the *n.*], 1. to view again; look at, look over, or study again. 2. to look back on; view in retrospect. 3. to survey in thought, speech, or writing; make or give a survey of. 4. to examine or inspect; specifically, to inspect formally, as troops. 5. to give or write a critical discussion of (a book, play, etc.). 6. to re-examine; specifically, to re-examine judicially, as a lower court's decision. 7. to go over (lessons, etc.) again, as in recitation. ***v.i.*** to review books, plays, etc., as for a newspaper. Abbreviated **rev.**

re·view·al (ri-vū′əl), ***n.*** a reviewing; review.

re·view·er (ri-vū′ẽr), ***n.*** a person who reviews; especially, a person who writes reviews of books, plays, etc. for a newspaper or magazine.

re·vile (ri-vīl′), ***v.t.*** [REVILED (-vīld′), REVILING], [ME. *revilen;* OFr. *reviler,* to regard or treat as vile; see RE- & VILE], to use abusive or contemptuous language in speaking to or about; call bad names. ***v.i.*** to use abusive language. —***SYN.*** see **scold.**

re·vile·ment (ri-vīl′mənt), ***n.*** 1. a reviling, or abusing in words. 2. an instance of this; abusive speech.

re·vis·al (ri-vīz′'l), ***n.*** 1. a revising or being revised. 2. a revision.

re·vise (ri-vīz′), ***v.t.*** [REVISED (-vīzd′), REVISING], [Fr. *reviser;* L. *revisere; re-,* back + *visere,* to survey, freq. of *videre,* to see], 1. to read over carefully, as a manuscript, published book, etc., to correct and improve, or bring up-to-date. 2. to change or amend: as, they have *revised* the tax rates. ***n.*** 1. a revising or a revised form of something; revision. 2. in ***printing,*** a proof taken after corrections have been made, for looking over or correcting again. Abbreviated **rev.**

Revised Standard Version, a revised translation of the Bible in contemporary English by a group of American scholars: the complete version was published in the United States in 1952.

Revised Version, a revision, or recension, of the Authorized, or King James, Version of the Bible, made by a committee of American and British scholars: the New Testament was published in 1881, the Old Testament in 1885: abbreviated **R.V., Rev. Ver.**

re·vis·er (ri-vīz′ẽr), ***n.*** a person who revises: also spelled **revisor.**

re·vi·sion (ri-vizh′ən), ***n.*** 1. act, process, or work of revising. 2. the result of this; revised form or version, as of a book, manuscript, etc. Abbreviated **rev.**

re·vi·sion·al (ri-vizh′ən-'l), ***adj.*** of or involving revision.

re·vi·sion·ism (ri-vizh′ən-iz'm), ***n.*** the policy or practice of revisionists.

re·vi·sion·ist (ri-vizh′ən-ist), ***n.*** a person who revises, or favors the revision of, some accepted theory, doctrine, etc. ***adj.*** of revisionists or revisionism.

re·vi·sor (ri-vī′zẽr), ***n.*** a reviser.

re·vi·so·ry (ri-vī′zə-ri), ***adj.*** of, or having the nature or power of, revision: as, a *revisory* committee.

re·viv·al (ri-vī′v'l), ***n.*** 1. a reviving or being revived. 2. a bringing or coming back into use, attention, or being, after a decline. 3. a new presentation of a play, motion picture, etc. some time after it has first been presented. 4. restoration to vigor or activity. 5. a bringing or coming back to life or consciousness. 6. a stirring up of religious faith among those who have been indifferent, usually by dramatic, fervid preaching and meetings. 7. *a)* a meeting characterized by fervid preaching, public confession of sins, professions of renewed faith, etc., aimed at arousing religious belief. *b)* a series of such meetings. 8. in *law,* renewal of validity, as of a judgment or contract.

re·viv·al·ism (ri-vī′v'l-iz'm), ***n.*** 1. the fervid spirit or methods characteristic of religious revivals; evangelical enthusiasm. 2. the tendency or desire to revive former ways, customs, institutions, etc.

re·viv·al·ist (ri-vī′v'l-ist), ***n.*** 1. a person who promotes or conducts religious revivals. 2. a person who revives former ways, customs, institutions, etc.

Revival of Learning (or **Letters, Literature**), the Renaissance as related to learning and literature.

re·vive (ri-vīv′), ***v.i.*** [REVIVED (-vīvd′), REVIVING], [ME. *reviven;* Late OFr. *revivre;* L. *revivere; re-,* again + *vivere,* to live], 1. to come back to life; live again after dying. 2. to come back to consciousness. 3. to come back to health and vigor. 4. to flourish again after a decline. 5. to come back into use or attention. 6. to become valid, effective, or operative again. ***v.t.*** 1. to bring back to life. 2. to bring back to consciousness. 3. to bring back to a healthy, vigorous, or flourishing condition after a decline. 4. to bring back into use or attention. 5. to make valid, effective, or operative again. 6. to bring to mind again. 7. to produce (a play, etc.) again after an interval.

re·viv·i·fi·ca·tion (ri-viv′ə-fi-kā′shən), ***n.*** [LL. *revivificatio*], a revivifying or being revivified.

re·viv·i·fy (ri-viv′ə-fī′), ***v.t.*** [REVIVIFIED (-fīd′), REVIVIFYING], [Fr. *revivifier;* LL. *revivificare;* see RE- & VIVIFY], to put new life or vigor into; cause to revive. ***v.i.*** to revive.

rev·i·vis·cence (rev′ə-vis′'ns), ***n.*** [< *reviviscent*], act of reviving or state of being revived; revival or renewal.

rev·i·vis·cen·cy (rev′ə-vis′'n-si), ***n.*** reviviscence.

rev·i·vis·cent (rev′ə-vis′'nt), ***adj.*** [L. *reviviscens,* ppr. of *reviviscere;* see REVIVE], coming or bringing back to life or vigor; reviving.

rev·o·ca·bil·i·ty (rev′ə-kə-bil′ə-ti), ***n.*** the state or quality of being revocable.

rev·o·ca·ble (rev′ə-kə-b'l), ***adj.*** [Late ME.; OFr. (Fr. *révocable*); L. *revocabilis*], that can be revoked: cf. **revokable.**

rev·o·ca·bly (rev′ə-kə-bli), ***adv.*** so as to be revocable.

rev·o·ca·tion (rev′ə-kā′shən), ***n.*** [ME. & OFr. *revocacion;* L. *revocatio* < pp. of *revocare*], a revoking or being revoked; cancellation; repeal; annulment; specifically, in *law,* nullification of an offer to contract.

rev·o·ca·to·ry (rev′ə-kə-tôr′i, rev′ə-kə-tō′ri), ***adj.*** [ME.; LL. *revocatorius*], revoking or tending to revoke; containing or expressing a revocation.

re·voice (rē-vois′), ***v.t.*** [REVOICED (-voist′), REVOICING], 1. to voice again, or in answer, as an echo. 2. to restore the proper tone to (an organ pipe, etc.).

re·vok·a·ble (ri-vōk′ə-b'l), ***adj.*** that can be revoked: cf. **revocable.**

re·voke (ri-vōk′), ***v.t.*** [REVOKED (-vōkt′), REVOKING], [ME. *revoken;* OFr. *revoquer;* L. *revocare; re-,* back + *vocare,* to call], 1. to withdraw, repeal, rescind, cancel, or annul, as a law, permit, etc. 2. [Rare], to recall (something past). ***v.i.*** in *card games,* to fail to follow suit when required and able to do so; renege. ***n.*** in *card games,* a revoking. —***SYN.*** see **abolish.**

re·volt (ri-vōlt′), ***n.*** [Fr. *révolte* < *révolter,* to revolt; It. *rivoltare;* LL. **revolutare* < L. *revolvere;* see REVOLVE], 1. a rising up against the government; rebellion; insurrection. 2. any refusal to submit to or accept authority. 3. the state of a person or persons revolting: as, they are in *revolt.* ***v.i.*** [Fr. *révolter*], 1. to rise up against the government. 2. to refuse to submit to authority; rebel; mutiny. 3. to turn in revulsion from a group or opinion that one has adhered to. 4. to be disgusted or shocked; feel repugnance (with *at, against,* or *from*). ***v.t.*** to disgust; fill with revulsion. —***SYN.*** see **rebellion.**

re·volt·ing (ri-vōl′tiŋ), ***adj.*** [ppr. of *revolt*], 1. engaged in revolt; rebellious. 2. causing revulsion; disgusting; repulsive; offensive; loathsome.

rev·o·lute (rev′ə-lōōt′, rev′ə-lūt′), ***adj.*** [L. *revolutus,* pp. of *revolvere;* see REVOLVE], in *biology,* rolled backward or downward at the tips or margins, as some leaves.

rev·o·lu·tion (rev′ə-lōō′shən, rev′ə-lū′shən), ***n.*** [ME. & OFr. *revolucion;* LL. *revolutio* < *revolutus,* pp. of *revolvere;* see REVOLVE], 1. movement of a body, as a star or planet, in an orbit or circle: in this sense, distinguished from *rotation.* 2. apparent movement of the sun and stars around the earth. 3. the time taken for a body to go around an orbit and return to its original position. 4. a turning or spinning motion of a body around a center or axis; rotation. 5. a single turn of such a rotating body. 6. a complete cycle of events: as, the *revolution* of the seasons. 7. a complete or drastic change of any kind: as, a *revolution* in modern physics. 8. overthrow of a government, form of government, or social system, with another taking its place: as, the English *Revolution* (1688), the American *Revolution* (1775), the French *Revolution* (1789), the Chinese *Revolution* (1911), the Russian *Revolution* (1917). Abbreviated **rev.** —***SYN.*** see **rebellion.**

rev·o·lu·tion·ar·y (rev′ə-lōō′shən-er′i, rev′ə-lū′shən-er′i), ***adj.*** 1. of, having the nature of, characterized by, tending toward, or causing a revolution, or drastic change, especially in a government or social system. 2. revolving or rotating. ***n.*** [*pl.* REVOLUTIONARIES (-iz)], a revolutionist.

Revolutionary Calendar, the official calendar of first French republic: see **French Revolutionary Calendar.**

Revolutionary War, the war (1775–1783), by which the American colonies won their independence from England; American Revolution.

rev·o·lu·tion·ist (rev′ə-lōō′shən-ist, rev′ə-lū′shən-ist), ***n.*** a person who favors or engages in a revolution.

rev·o·lu·tion·ize (rev′ə-lōō′shən-iz′, rev′ə-lū′shən-iz′), ***v.t.*** [REVOLUTIONIZED (-īzd′), REVOLUTIONIZING], 1. to make a complete and basic change in; alter drastically or radically: as, the automobile has *revolutionized* American life. 2. [Rare], to bring about a political revolution in.

revindicate **revindication** **revisit** **revitalize**

re·volv·a·ble (ri-vol′və-b'l), *adj.* that can revolve or be revolved.

re·volve (ri-volv′), *v.t.* [REVOLVED (-volvd′), REVOLVING], [ME. *reuoluen;* OFr. *revolver;* L. *revolvere; re-*, back + *volvere*, to roll], 1. to turn over in the mind; reflect on. 2. to cause to travel in a circle or orbit. 3. to cause to rotate, or spin around an axis. *v.i.* 1. to move in a circle or orbit around a point. 2. to spin or turn around a center or axis; rotate. 3. to recur at intervals; occur periodically. —*SYN.* see **turn.**

re·volv·er (ri-vol′vẽr), *n.* 1. a pistol with a revolving cylinder containing several cartridges so that it can be fired in quick succession without reloading. 2. a person or thing that revolves.

re·volv·ing (ri-vol′viŋ), *adj.* that revolves; specifically, designating or of a radial engine with cylinders revolving around a stationary crankshaft: abbreviated **rev.**

revolving door, a door consisting of four vanes hung on a central axle and so arranged in a wall that a person using it turns it around by pushing on one of the vanes: used to keep out drafts of air.

revolving fund, a sum of money kept for making loans and maintained by putting back into it the money that has been lent, as it is repaid.

re·vue (ri-vū′), *n.* [Fr.; see REVIEW], a type of musical show consisting of several loosely connected skits, songs, and dances, often parodying recent events, plays, etc.: also spelled **review.**

re·vul·sion (ri-vul′shən), *n.* [< Fr. or L.; Fr. *révulsion;* L. *revulsio* < *revulsus*, pp. of *revellere*, to pluck away; *re-*, back + *vellere*, to pull], 1. a drawing or being drawn back or away; withdrawal. 2. a sudden, complete, and violent change of feeling; abrupt, strong reaction in sentiment. 3. in *medicine*, a lessening of disease in, or drawing away of blood from, a diseased part of the body by counterirritation. —*SYN.* see **aversion.**

re·vul·sive (ri-vul′siv), *adj.* of or causing revulsion. *n.* in *medicine*, a revulsive drug or agent.

Rev. Ver., Revised Version.

re·ward (ri-wôrd′), *n.* [ME.; ONorm.Fr., for OFr. *regarde;* see REGARD], 1. something given in return for good or, sometimes, evil, or for service or merit. 2. money offered, as for the capture of a criminal, the return of something lost, etc. 3. compensation; profit; return. *v.t.* 1. to give a reward to. 2. to give a reward for (service, etc.).

SYN.—**reward** usually refers to something given in recompense for a good deed, for merit, etc. (he received a *reward* for saving the child); **prize** applies to something won in competition or, often, in a lottery, game of chance, etc. (she won first *prize* in the golf tournament); **award** implies a decision by judges but does not connote overt competition (he received an *award* for the best feature story of the year); **premium,** in this connection, applies to a reward offered as an inducement to greater effort, production, etc. (he will pay a *premium* for advance delivery).

re·wire (rē-wīr′), *v.t. & v.i.* to wire again or anew; specifically, *a)* to put new wires or wiring in or on (a house, motor, etc.). *b)* to telegraph again.

re·word (rē-wũrd′), *v.t.* 1. to state or express again in other words; change the wording of. 2. to state again in the same words; repeat.

re·write (rē-rīt′; *for n.,* rē′rīt′), *v.t. & v.i.* [REWROTE (-rōt′), REWRITTEN (-rit′'n), REWRITING], 1. to write again. 2. to write in different words or a different form; revise. 3. in *journalism*, to write (news turned in by a reporter) in a form suitable for publication. *n.* an article written this way.

Rex (reks), [L., a king; see REGAL], a masculine name. *n.* 1. [also r-], [*pl.* REGES (rē′jēz)], king: the official title of a reigning king, as, George *Rex:* abbreviated **R., r.** 2. [< *Christus Rex* (L., Christ the King), a publication of Young People's Catholic Action Society], a Belgian fascist political party (founded 1935).

Rex·ist (rek′sist), *adj.* of Rex, Belgian fascist political party. *n.* a member or supporter of this party.

Rey·kja·vik (rā′kyȧ-vēk′), *n.* seaport and capital of Iceland: pop., 54,000 (1947).

Rey·mont, Wla·dy·slaw Sta·ni·slaw (vlä-di′släf stä-nē′släf rā′mônt), (*Ladislas Regmont*), 1868–1925; Polish novelist; received Nobel prize in literature, 1924.

Reyn·ard (ren′ẽrd, rā′nẽrd, rā′närd), *n.* [OFr. *Renard, Renart* < OHG. *Reginhart* < Gmc. **ragina*, counsel, judgment + *hard-*, bold, brave], the fox in the medieval beast epic *Reynard the Fox;* hence, a proper name for the fox in fable and folklore: also **Renard.**

Rey·naud, Paul (pôl rā′nō′), 1878– ; French statesman; premier of France (1940).

Reyn·old (ren′əld), a masculine name: see **Reginald.**

Reyn·olds, Sir **Joshua** (ren′əldz), 1723–1792; English portrait painter.

rf., in *baseball*, right fielder.

R.F., Reserve Force.

R.F., r.f., 1. radio-frequency. 2. rapid-fire.

RFC, R.F.C., Reconstruction Finance Corporation.

RFD, R.F.D., Rural Free Delivery.

rg., in *football*, right guard.

Rh, in *chemistry*, rhodium.

R.H., 1. Royal Highlanders. 2. Royal Highness.

r.h., in *music*, right hand.

rhab·do·man·cy (rab′də-man′si), *n.* [LL. *rhabdomantia;* Gr. *rhabdomanteia* < *rhabdos*, a rod + *manteia*, divination], divination by a rod or wand; especially, the supposed art of finding underground water, ores, etc. by means of a divining rod; dowsing.

rhab·do·my·o·ma (rab′dō-mī-ō′mə), *n.* [Mod. L. < Gr. *rhabdos*, rod + Mod. L. *myoma*, myoma], in *medicine*, a tumor composed of striated muscular fibers.

rha·chis (rā′kis), *n.* a rachis.

Rhad·a·man·thine (rad′ə-man′thin), *adj.* of or like Rhadamanthus; inflexibly just.

Rhad·a·man·thus (rad′ə-man′thəs), *n.* [L.; Gr. *Rhadamanthos*], in *Greek mythology*, a son of Zeus and Europa, rewarded for the exemplary justice that he showed during his life by being made, after his death, one of the three judges of the dead in the lower world, with Aeacus and Minos.

Rhad·a·man·thys (rad′ə-man′this), *n.* Rhadamanthus.

Rhae·ti·a (rē′shi-ə, rē′shə), *n.* an ancient Roman province in the region of modern eastern Switzerland and western Austria.

Rhae·tian (rē′shən), *adj.* of ancient Rhaetia or its people. *n.* a native of Rhaetia.

Rhaetian Alps, a mountain range in southeastern Switzerland, Italy, and Austria: highest peak, Bernina.

Rhae·tic (rē′tik), *adj.* [L. *Rhaeticus*, Rhaetian], in *geology*, designating or of a group of strata of the European Triassic system, prominent in the Rhaetian Alps: also spelled **Rhetic.**

Rhae·to-Ro·man·ic (rē′tō-rō-man′ik), *adj.* designating or of a group of several closely associated Romance dialects spoken in southern Switzerland, the Tyrol, and northern Italy. *n.* this group of dialects as a distinct Romanic language. Cf. **Ladin, Romansh.**

-rhage, -rhagia, see **-rrhage.**

rham·na·ceous (ram-nā′shəs), *adj.* [< Gr. *rhamnos*, prickly shrub; + *-aceous*], in *botany*, of the buckthorn family.

rhap·sod·ic (rap-sod′ik), *adj.* rhapsodical.

rhap·sod·i·cal (rap-sod′i-k'l), *adj.* [Gr. *rhapsōidikos*], of, characteristic of, or having the nature of, rhapsody; extravagantly enthusiastic; ecstatic.

rhap·so·dist (rap′sə-dist), *n.* 1. in ancient Greece, a person who recited rhapsodies; especially, one who recited epic poems as a profession. 2. a person who rhapsodizes.

rhap·so·dize (rap′sə-dīz′), *v.i.* [RHAPSODIZED (-dīzd′), RHAPSODIZING], 1. to speak or write in an extravagantly enthusiastic manner. 2. to recite or write rhapsodies. *v.t.* to recite or utter as a rhapsody.

rhap·so·dy (rap′sə-di), *n.* [*pl.* RHAPSODIES (-diz)], [Fr. *r(h)apsodie;* L. *rhapsodia;* Gr. *rhapsōidia* < *rhapsōdos*, one who stitches or strings songs together, reciter of epic poetry < *rhaptein*, to stitch together + *ōidē*, song], 1. *a)* in ancient Greece, an epic poem, or a part of one, suitable for a single uninterrupted recitation. *b)* a similar modern literary work. 2. any ecstatic or extravagantly enthusiastic utterance in speech or writing. 3. [Obs.], a miscellany. 4. in *music*, an instrumental composition of free, irregular form, suggesting improvisation: abbreviated **rhap.**

rhat·a·ny (rat′ə-ni), *n.* [*pl.* RHATANIES (-niz)], [Sp. *ratania, ratañа* < Peruv. (Quechua) *ratañа*], 1. *a)* a South American leguminous plant (*Peruvian,* or *knotty, rhatany*) with a thick, fleshy root used in medicine as an astringent and tonic, etc. *b)* a related plant; especially, *Brazilian rhatany.* 2. the dried root of any such plant.

Rhe·a (rē′ə), *n.* [L.; Gr. *Rhea*], 1. in *Greek mythology*, the daughter of Uranus and Gaea, wife of Cronus, and mother of Zeus, Poseidon, Hades, Demeter, Hera, and Hestia: called *Mother of the Gods* and identified with Cybele. 2. [r-], any of a group of large South American nonflying birds comprising the American ostriches, resembling the African ostriches but smaller and having three toes instead of two, and a feathered head and neck.

-rhe·a (rē′ə), -rrhea.

Rhe·a Sil·vi·a (rē′ə sil′vi-ə), in *Roman legend*, a vestal virgin who broke her vows and became by Mars the mother of Romulus and Remus.

Rheims (rēmz; rans), *n.* Reims.

Rhein (rīn), *n.* the Rhine: the German name.

Rhein·gold (rīn′gōld′; G. rīn′gôlt′), *n.* [G., Rhine gold], in *Germanic mythology*, the hoard of gold guarded by the Rhine maidens and afterward owned by the Nibelungs and Siegfried: the story is told in varying forms in the *Volsunga Saga, Nibelungenlied,* and Wagner's *Ring of the Nibelung*: also **Rhinegold:** see **Ring of the Nibelung.**

revote
rewarm
rewash
rewater
reweigh
rewin
rewind
rework

Rhein·land (rīn'länt'), *n.* Rhine Province: German name.
rhe·mat·ic (ri-mat'ik), *adj.* [Gr. *rhēmatikos* < *rhēma*, *rhēmatos*, a word, verb], 1. of word formation. 2. of or derived from a verb.
rhe·nic (rē'nik), *adj.* of or containing rhenium.
Rhen·ish (ren'ish), *adj.* [< L. *Rhenus*, Rhine; + *-ish;* replacing ME. *Rinische*, etc. < MHG. (G. *rheinisch*)], of the Rhine or the regions around it. *n.* 1. Rhine wine. 2. the German dialects spoken along the Rhine.
rhe·ni·um (rē'ni-əm), *n.* [Mod. L. < L. *Rhenus*, Rhine; + *-ium* as in *cadmium, radium*], a rare metallic chemical element resembling manganese: symbol, Re; at. wt., 186.31; at. no., 75.
rhe·o- (rē'ō, rē'ə), [< Gr. *rheos*, current], a combining form meaning *a flow, current*, as in *rheoscope, rheostat*.
rhe·om·e·ter (ri-om'ə-tẽr), *n.* [*rheo-* + *-meter*], an instrument for measuring velocity of flow, as of the blood in circulation or of an electric current.
rhe·o·scope (rē'ə-skōp'), *n.* [*rheo-* + *-scope*], a device for indicating the presence of an electric current.
rhe·o·stat (rē'ə-stat'), *n.* [< *rheo-* + Gr. *statos*, standing still < *histanai*, to stand], a device for regulating strength of an electric current by varying the resistance without opening the circuit: abbreviated **rheo.**
rhe·o·stat·ic (rē'ə-stat'ik), *adj.* of or by a rheostat.
rhe·o·tax·is (rē'ə-tak'sis), *n.* [Mod. L. < *rheo-* + Gr. *taxis*, an arranging], the tendency of a living organism or cell to respond to the mechanical stimulus of a current of water by some movement.
rhe·o·tron (rē'ə-tron'), *n.* [*rheo-* + elec*tron*], a betatron.
rhe·o·trope (rē'ə-trōp'), *n.* [*rheo-* + *-trope*], a device for reversing the direction of an electric current; commutator.
rhe·ot·ro·pism (ri-ot'rə-piz'm), *n.* [*rheo-* + *-tropism*], the tendency of a living organism, especially a plant, to respond to the mechanical stimulus of a current of water by some change in the direction of growth.
Rhe·sus (rē'səs), *n.* [L.; Gr. *Rhēsos*], in *Greek legend*, a king of Thrace and ally of Troy, whose horses were stolen by Diomedes and Odysseus: an oracle had said that Troy would not be captured if Rhesus' horses drank from the Xanthus River.
rhe·sus (rē'səs), *n.* [Mod. L.; arbitrary use of L. *Rhesus* (Gr. *Rhēsos*), proper name], a small, short-tailed, brownish-yellow monkey of India; Indian macaque: in full, **rhesus monkey.**
Rhesus factor, Rh factor.
Rhe·tic (rē'tik), *adj.* Rhaetic.
rhe·tor (rē'tẽr, rē'tôr), *n.* [ME. *rethor;* L.; Gr. *rhētōr*], 1. a master or teacher of rhetoric. 2. an orator.
rhet·o·ric (ret'ə-rik), *n.* [ME. *rethorike* < OFr. or L.; OFr. *rethorique* (Fr. *rhétorique*); L. *rhetorica;* Gr. *rhētorikē* (*technē*), rhetorical (art) < *rhētōr*, orator], 1. the art or science of using words effectively in speaking or writing, so as to influence or persuade; especially, now, the art or science of literary composition, particularly in prose, including the use of figures of speech: abbreviated **rhet.** 2. a treatise or book on this. 3. artificial eloquence; showiness and elaboration in language and literary style.
rhe·tor·i·cal (ri-tôr'i-k'l, ri-tor'i-k'l), *adj.* 1. of, having the nature of, or according to rhetoric. 2. using or characterized by mere rhetoric, or artificial eloquence; showy and elaborate in style. Abbreviated **rhet.**
rhe·tor·i·cal·ly (ri-tôr'i-k'l-i, ri-tor'ik-li), *adv.* 1. in a rhetorical manner. 2. according to, or from the standpoint of, rhetoric.
rhetorical question, a question asked, as in oratory or writing, only for rhetorical effect, to emphasize a point, introduce a topic, etc., no answer being expected.
rhet·o·ri·cian (ret'ə-rish'ən), *n.* [ME. & OFr. *rethoricien* (Fr. *rhétoricien*)], 1. a person skilled in rhetoric. 2. a teacher of rhetoric. 3. a person who writes or speaks in a rhetorical, or showy, elaborate manner.
rheum (rōōm), *n.* [ME. & OFr. *reume;* L. *rheuma;* Gr. *rheuma*, a flow, moist discharge; akin to *rheein*, to flow], 1. any watery or catarrhal discharge from the mucous membranes, as of the mouth, eyes, or nose; hence, 2. a cold; rhinitis; catarrh.
rheu·mat·ic (rōō-mat'ik), *adj.* [ME. *reumatike;* OFr. *reumatique;* L. *rheumaticus;* Gr. *rheumatikos;* see RHEUM], 1. of or caused by rheumatism. 2. having or subject to rheumatism. *n.* 1. a person who has, or is subject to, rheumatism. 2. *pl.* [Dial.], rheumatism.
rheumatic fever, an infectious disease associated with the presence of streptococci in the body: it most commonly attacks children, and is characterized by fever, pain and swelling of the joints, inflammation of the heart valves, etc.
rheu·ma·tism (rōō'mə-tiz'm), *n.* [L. *rheumatismus*, rheum, catarrh; Gr. *rheumatismos;* see RHEUM], 1. any of various painful conditions of the joints and muscles; especially, a disease believed to be caused by a microorganism and characterized by inflammation and pain of the joints. 2. rheumatic fever.
rheu·ma·toid (rōō'mə-toid'), *adj.* 1. of, like, or characteristic of rheumatism. 2. having rheumatism.
rheu·ma·toi·dal (rōō'mə-toi'd'l), *adj.* rheumatoid.
rheumatoid arthritis, a chronic disease characterized by inflammation, stiffness, and often deformity, of the joints.
rheum·ic (rōōm'ik), *adj.* of or characterized by rheum.
rheum·y (rōōm'i), *adj.* [RHEUMIER (-i-ẽr), RHEUMIEST (-i-ist)], of, full of, or causing rheum.
Rh factor (är'āch'), [< *rh*esus: from having been discovered first in the blood of rhesus monkeys], an agglutinating factor, usually present in human blood, which may cause hemolytic reactions during pregnancy or after transfusion of blood containing this factor into someone lacking it: individuals who have this factor are *Rh positive;* those who do not have it are *Rh negative:* also **Rhesus factor.**
rhig·o·lene (rig'ə-lēn'), *n.* [< Gr. *rhigos*, cold + L. *oleum*, oil; + *-ene*], a colorless, volatile liquid distilled from petroleum and used as a local anesthetic.
Rhin (ran), *n.* the Rhine: the French name.
rhin- (rīn), rhino-.
rhi·nal (rī'n'l), *adj.* [*rhin-* + *-al*], of the nose; nasal.
Rhine (rīn), *n.* a river flowing through Switzerland and Germany into the North Sea: length, 700 mi.: in German, *Rhein;* in French, *Rhin;* in Dutch, *Rijn.*
Rhine·gold (rīn'gōld'), *n.* [Anglicized form], Rheingold.
Rhine·land (rīn'land', rīn'lənd), *n.* 1. the Rhine Province. 2. that part of Germany west of the Rhine.
rhi·nen·ceph·a·lon (rī'nen-sef'ə-lon'), *n.* [*pl.* RHINENCEPHALA (-lə)], [Mod. L.; see RHINO- & ENCEPHALON], the part of the brain concerned with the sense of smell.
Rhine Palatinate, see **Palatinate, the.**
Rhine Province, a former province of Prussia, Germany, west of the Rhine: area, 9,459 sq. mi.: also called *Rhineland:* German name, *Rheinland.*
rhine·stone (rīn'stōn'), *n.* [transl. of Fr. *caillou du Rhin:* so called because orig. made at Strasbourg], a colorless, bright, artificial gem made of glass or paste, often cut in imitation of a diamond.
Rhine wine, 1. any of various wines produced in the Rhine Valley, especially of the light, dry white wines. 2. a wine of this type produced elsewhere.
rhi·ni·tis (rī-nī'tis), *n.* [Mod. L.; see RHINO- & -ITIS], inflammation of the nose, especially of the nasal mucous membrane.
rhi·no (rī'nō), *n.* [*pl.* RHINOS (-nōz)], [Colloq.], a rhinoceros.
rhi·no (rī'nō), *n.* [< ?], [British Slang], money; cash.
rhi·no- (rī'nō, rī'nə), [< Gr. *rhis*, *rhinos*, the nose], a combining form meaning *nose*, as in *rhinology:* also, before a vowel, **rhin-**.
rhi·noc·er·os (rī-nos'ẽr-əs), *n.* [*pl.* RHINOCEROSES (-iz), RHINOCEROS; see PLURAL, II, D, 1], [ME. *rinoceros;* LL.; Gr. *rhinokerōs*, lit., nose-horned < *rhis, rhinos*, the nose + *keras*, horn], any of various large, heavy, thick-skinned, plant-eating mammals of tropical Africa and Asia, with one or two upright horns on the snout.

INDIAN RHINOCEROS (5–5 3/4 ft. high at shoulder)

rhi·nol·o·gy (rī-nol'ə-ji), *n.* [*rhino-* + *-logy*], the branch of medicine dealing with the nose and its diseases.
rhi·no·plas·tic (rī'nə-plas'tik), *adj.* of rhinoplasty.
rhi·no·plas·ty (rī'nə-plas'ti), *n.* [*rhino-* + *-plasty*], plastic surgery of the nose.
rhi·no·scope (rī'nə-skōp'), *n.* [*rhino-* + *-scope*], an instrument for examining the internal structures of the nose.
rhi·nos·co·py (rī-nos'kə-pi), *n.* examination of the internal structures of the nose, as with a rhinoscope.
rhi·zo- (rī'zō, rī'zə), [< Gr. *rhiza*, a root], a combining form meaning *root*, as in *rhizomorphous, rhizopod:* also, before a vowel, **rhiz-**.
rhi·zo·bi·um (rī-zō'bi-əm), *n.* [*pl.* RHIZOBIA (-ə)], [Mod. L. < *rhizo-* + Gr. *bios*, life], any of a genus of rod-shaped, nitrogen-fixing bacteria found in nodules on the roots of certain plants, as the bean and clover.
rhi·zo·car·pous (rī'zə-kär'pəs), *adj.* [*rhizo-* + *-carpous*], having perennial roots but annual stems and leaves: said of perennial plants.
rhi·zo·ceph·a·lous (rī'zə-sef'ə-ləs), *adj.* [see RHIZO- & CEPHALOUS], of a group of hermaphroditic crustaceans that live as parasites on crabs, etc.
rhi·zo·gen·ic (rī'zə-jen'ik), *adj.* [*rhizo-* + *-genic*], in *botany*, producing roots, as certain cells.
rhi·zog·e·nous (rī-zoj'ə-nəs), *adj.* rhizogenic.
rhi·zoid (rī'zoid), *adj.* [*rhiz-* + *-oid*], rootlike. *n.* any of the rootlike filaments in a moss, fern, etc. that attach the plant to the substratum.
rhi·zoi·dal (rī-zoi'd'l), *adj.* rhizoid.

rhi·zom·a·tous (rī-zom′ə-təs, rī-zō′mə-təs), ***adj.*** having, or having the nature of, a rhizome or rhizomes.

rhi·zome (rī′zōm), ***n.*** [Mod. L. *rhizoma;* Gr. *rhizōma* < *rhizousthai,* to take root < *rhiza,* a root], a rootlike stem under or along the ground, ordinarily in a horizontal position, which usually sends out roots from its lower surface and leafy shoots from its upper surface.

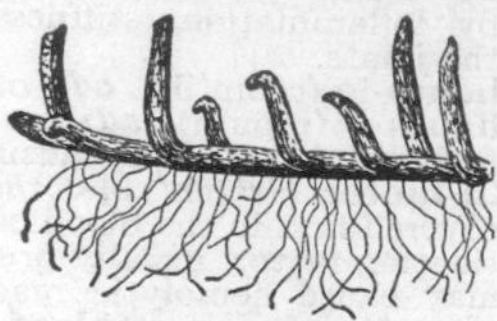

RHIZOME (of sensitive fern)

rhi·zo·mor·phous (rī′zə-môr′fəs), ***adj.*** [*rhizo-* + *-morphous*], in *botany,* formed like a root; root-shaped.

rhi·zoph·a·gous (rī-zof′ə-gəs), ***adj.*** [*rhizo-* + *-phagous*], feeding on roots.

rhi·zo·pod (rī′zə-pod′), ***n.*** [*rhizo-* + *-pod*], any of a group of one-celled animals with rootlike pseudopods.

rhi·zop·o·dan (rī-zop′ə-dən), ***adj.*** of, like, or characteristic of the rhizopods. ***n.*** a rhizopod.

rhi·zop·o·dous (rī-zop′ə-dəs), ***adj.*** rhizopodan.

rhi·zo·pus (rī′zə-pəs), ***n.*** [Mod. L. < *rhizo-* + Gr. *pous,* foot], any fungus of a group including that of bread mold.

rhi·zot·o·my (rī-zot′ə-mi), ***n.*** [*rhizo-* + *-tomy*], in *surgery,* a cutting of the spinal nerve roots, especially of the posterior nerves, as for relieving pain.

Rh negative, see **Rh factor.**

rho (rō), ***n.*** [Gr. *rhō*], the seventeenth letter of the Greek alphabet (P, ρ), corresponding to English *R, r:* see **alphabet,** table.

Rho·da (rō′də), [L. *Rhode;* Gr. *Rhodē* < *rhodon,* a rose], a feminine name.

rho·da·min (rō′də-min), ***n.*** rhodamine.

rho·da·mine (rō′də-mēn′, rō′də-min), ***n.*** [*rhod(o)-* + *amine*], any of a group of synthetic dyes ranging in color from red to pink, obtained by condensation of phthalic anhydride with an amino derivative of phenol.

Rhode Island (rōd), a New England State of the United States: area, 1,214 sq. mi.; pop., 859,000; capital, Providence: one of the thirteen original States; the smallest of all the States: abbreviated **R.I.**

Rhode Islander, a native or inhabitant of Rhode Island.

Rhode Island Red, any of a breed of American chickens with reddish-brown feathers and a black tail.

Rhodes (rōdz), ***n.*** 1. one of the Dodecanese Islands, southwest of Turkey: area, 545 sq. mi.; pop., 55,000. 2. a seaport on this island: capital of the Dodecanese Islands: pop., 24,000. Italian name, *Rodi.*

Rhodes, Cecil John (rōdz), 1853–1902; British capitalist and administrator in South Africa; established Rhodes scholarships.

Rhodes, James Ford, 1848–1927; American historian.

Rho·de·si·a (rō-dē′zhi-ə, rō-dē′zhə), ***n.*** a region including Northern Rhodesia and Southern Rhodesia.

Rhodesia and Nyasaland, Federation of, a federation in the British Commonwealth of Nations, in southern Africa: it comprises the self-governing territory of Southern Rhodesia and the protectorates of Northern Rhodesia and Nyasaland: area, 486,000 sq. mi.; pop., 8,330,000; capital, Salisbury.

Rho·de·sian (rō-dē′zhən), ***adj.*** of Rhodesia or its people. ***n.*** a native or inhabitant of Rhodesia.

Rhodes scholarship, any of a number of scholarships for a three-year period of study at Oxford University, England, established by the will of Cecil John Rhodes for selected students (*Rhodes scholars*) from certain British colonies and dominions and the United States.

Rho·di·an (rō′di-ən), ***adj.*** of Rhodes, its people, or culture. ***n.*** a native or inhabitant of Rhodes.

rho·dic (rō′dik), ***adj.*** of or containing rhodium, especially tetravalent rhodium.

rho·di·um (rō′di-əm), ***n.*** [Mod. L. < Gr. *rhodon,* a rose: so called because of the color of its salts], a hard, gray-white metallic chemical element of the platinum group, used as an alloy with platinum and gold to make the nibs of writing pens and in unalloyed form to electroplate silverware and jewelry: symbol, Rh; at. wt., 102.91; at. no., 45.

rho·do- (rō′dō, rō′də), [< Gr. *rhodon,* a rose], a combining form meaning *rose, rose-red,* as in *rhodolite:* also, before a vowel, **rhod-.**

rho·do·chro·site (rō′də-krō′sīt), ***n.*** [G. *rhodochrosit* < Gr. *rhodochrōs,* rose-colored (< *rhodon,* a rose + *chrōsis,* a coloring < *chrōs, chroos,* color) + G. *-it,* -ite], a glassy, generally rose-red mineral, mainly manganese carbonate, $MnCO_3$, often with some calcium and iron.

rho·do·den·dron (rō′də-den′drən), ***n.*** [L.; Gr. *rhododendron* < *rhodon,* a rose + *dendron,* a tree], any of a number of related trees and shrubs, mainly evergreen, with showy flowers of pink, white, or purple.

rho·do·lite (rō′də-līt′), ***n.*** [*rhodo-* + *-lite*], a pink or rose-red variety of garnet, often used as a gem.

rho·do·nite (rō′də-nīt′), ***n.*** [G. *rhodonit* < Gr. *rhodon,* a rose + G. *-it,* -ite], a glassy, crystalline mineral, a native manganese silicate, $MnSiO_3$, generally found in rose-red masses, sometimes used as an ornamental stone: also called *manganese spar, red manganese.*

Rhod·o·pe, Rhod·o·pi (rod′ə-pi), ***n.*** a mountain range in southwestern Bulgaria: highest peak, 9,596 ft.

rho·dop·sin (rō-dop′sin), ***n.*** [< Gr. *rhodon,* rose + *opsis,* appearance], visual purple.

rho·do·ra (rō-dôr′ə, rō-dō′rə), ***n.*** [L., kind of plant; said to be of Gallic origin], any of a group of shrubs related to the rhododendron, with pink or rose-red flowers that appear before or with the leaves.

-rhoe·a (rē′ə), -rrhea.

rhomb (romb, rom), ***n.*** [Fr. *rhombe* < L.], a rhombus.

rhom·ben·ceph·a·lon (rom′ben-sef′ə-lon′), ***n.*** [Mod. L.; see RHOMB & ENCEPHALON], the part of the brain consisting of the cerebellum, pons, and medulla oblongata; hindbrain.

rhomb·ic (rom′bik), ***adj.*** 1. of, or having the form of, a rhombus. 2. having a rhombus as the base or cross section: said of solid figures. 3. bounded by rhombuses. 4. orthorhombic, as some crystals.

rhom·bi·cal (rom′bi-k'l), ***adj.*** rhombic.

rhom·bo·he·dral (rom′bə-hē′drəl), ***adj.*** of, or having the form of, a rhombohedron.

rhom·bo·he·dron (rom′bə-hē′drən), ***n.*** [*pl.* RHOMBOHEDRONS (-drənz), RHOMBOHEDRA (-drə)], [< Gr. *rhombos* (see RHOMBUS); + *-hedron*], a six-sided prism each face of which is a rhombus.

rhom·boid (rom′boid), ***n.*** [Fr. *rhomboide;* LL. *rhomboides;* Gr. *rhomboeidēs,* rhomboid-shaped; see RHOMBUS & -OID], a parallelogram with oblique angles and only the opposite sides equal. ***adj.*** 1. shaped like a rhomboid. 2. shaped somewhat like a rhombus.

RHOMBOIDS

rhom·boi·dal (rom-boi′d'l), ***adj.*** [cf. Fr. *rhomboïdal*], rhomboid.

rhom·bus (rom′bəs), ***n.*** [*pl.* RHOMBUSES (-iz), RHOMBI (-bī)], [L.; Gr. *rhombos,* object that can be turned; akin to *rhembein,* to turn, whirl], 1. an equilateral parallelogram with oblique angles. 2. a rhombohedron.

RHOMBUS

rhon·chal (roŋ′k'l), ***adj.*** of, or having the nature of, a rhonchus.

rhon·chi·al (roŋ′ki-əl), ***adj.*** rhonchal.

rhon·chus (roŋ′kəs), ***n.*** [*pl.* RHONCHI (-kī)], [L., a snoring < unrecorded Gr. var. of *rhenchos,* a snoring], a rattling sound, somewhat like snoring, heard on auscultation of the chest when there is a partial bronchial obstruction; dry râle.

Rhon·dda (ron′də), ***n.*** a city in southeastern Wales: pop., 106,000.

Rhone, Rhône (rōn), ***n.*** a river flowing through southern Switzerland and southeastern France into the Mediterranean: length, 505 mi.

Rh positive, see **Rh factor.**

rhu·barb (rōō′bärb), ***n.*** [ME. *rubarbe;* OFr. *rheubarbe;* ML. *rheubarbarum,* altered < LL. *rha barbarum* < Gr. *rhēon barbaron,* foreign rhubarb; *rhēon,* plant from the *Rha,* the Volga River + *barbaron,* foreign, barbarous: the drug was orig. imported from Russia], 1. any of a number of related plants with large leaves and fleshy, acid leafstalks used as food. 2. the leafstalks of one variety made into a sauce or baked in a pie. 3. the roots or rhizomes of one variety used in medicine as a cathartic and tonic. 4. [? from the practice in radio broadcasts of repeating "rhubarb" in simulating crowd noises], [Slang], a heated discussion or argument, as in a baseball game.

rhumb (rum, rumb), ***n.*** [< Fr. *rumb* or Port. & Sp. *rumbo;* prob. < L. *rhombus;* see RHOMBUS], 1. a rhumb line. 2. any of the points of a mariner's compass.

rhum·ba (rum′bə), ***n.*** a rumba.

rhumb line, the course of a ship that keeps a constant compass direction, drawn as a line on a map, chart, or globe and cutting across all meridians at the same angle: also called *loxodromic curve.*

rhyme (rīm), ***n.*** [ME. *rime;* associated in ME. with AS. *rim,* a number, but < OFr. *rime;* prob. < L. *rhythmus* (see RHYTHM); Eng. sp. influenced by association with *rhythm:* in ML., *rithmus* meant "accentual verse," which was usually rhymed; hence the mod. sense], 1. a piece of verse, or poem, in which there is a regular recurrence of corresponding sounds, especially at the ends of lines. 2. such verse or poetry in general. 3. correspondence of end sounds in lines of verse or in words: cf. **assonance, consonance.** 4. a word that corresponds with another in end sound (e.g., *love* & *above, witty* & *pretty*). ***v.i.*** [RHYMED (rīmd), RHYMING], 1. to make verse, especially rhyming verse. 2. to form a rhyme: as, "more" *rhymes* with "door." 3. to be composed in metrical form with rhymes: said of verses. ***v.t.*** 1. to put into rhyme. 2. to compose in metrical form with rhymes. 3. to use as a rhyme or rhymes. Also spelled **rime.**

neither rhyme nor reason, neither order nor sense.

rhym·er (rīm′ẽr), *n.* a maker of rhymes, or poems; especially, a rhymester. —*SYN.* see **poet.**

rhyme royal, a stanza of seven lines in iambic pentameter rhyming *ababbcc,* first used in English by Chaucer.

rhyme scheme, the pattern of rhymes used in a piece of verse, usually indicated by letters, as in the above definition for *rhyme royal.*

rhyme·ster (rīm′stẽr), *n.* a maker of rhyme, or verse (in a derogatory sense); poetaster. —*SYN.* see **poet.**

rhyn·cho·ce·pha·li·an (riŋ′kō-sə-fā′li-ən), *adj.* [< Gr. *rhynchos,* snout + *kephalē,* head; + *-ian*], designating or of an almost extinct order of lizardlike reptiles. *n.* a member of this order.

rhy·o·lite (rī′ə-līt′), *n.* [G. *rhyolit* < Gr. *rhyax,* stream (of lava) + *lithos,* stone], a kind of volcanic rock containing much silica and resembling granite in composition but having a texture that shows flow.

rhythm (rith′'m, rith′əm), *n.* [< Fr. or L.; Fr. *rhythme;* L. *rhythmus;* Gr. *rhythmos,* measure, measured motion < base of *rheein,* to flow; cf. RHYME], 1. *a*) flow, movement, procedure, etc. characterized by basically regular recurrence of elements or features, as beat, or accent, in alternation with opposite or different elements or features: as, the *rhythm* of speech, of the heart, of an engine, of dancing, of the seasons, etc. *b*) such recurrence; pattern of flow or movement. 2. in *art,* aesthetic relation of part to part and of parts to the whole; pattern of arrangement: as, the *rhythm* of a picture, of a statue, of a building, etc. 3. in *music, a*) regular (or, occasionally, somewhat irregular) recurrence of grouped strong and weak beats, or heavily and lightly accented tones, in alternation; arrangement of successive tones, usually in measures, according to their relative accentuation and duration. *b*) form or pattern of this: as, rumba *rhythm,* triple *rhythm.* Cf. **time, tempo, meter.** 4. in *prosody, a*) basically regular recurrence of grouped, stressed and unstressed, long and short, or high-pitched and low-pitched syllables in alternation; arrangement of successive syllables, as in metrical units (*feet*) or cadences, according to their relative stress, quantity, and pitch: in English, rhythm depends on accent as composed of interconnected stress, quantity, pitch, and pause. *b*) form or pattern of this: as, iambic *rhythm.*

rhyth·mic (rith′mik), *adj.* [< Fr. or L.; Fr. *rhythmique;* L. *rhythmicus*], rhythmical. *n.* rhythmics.

rhyth·mi·cal (rith′mi-k'l), *adj.* of, having, or using rhythm.

rhyth·mi·cal·ly (rith′mi-k'l-i, rith′mik-li), *adv.* 1. in a rhythmical manner. 2. as regards rhythm.

rhyth·mics (rith′miks), *n.pl.* [construed as sing.], science or system of rhythm and rhythmical forms.

rhyth·mist (rith′mist), *n.* 1. a person expert in, or having a good sense of, rhythm. 2. a (specified) user of rhythm: as, a poor *rhythmist.*

R.I., 1. *Regina et Imperatrix,* [L.], Queen and Empress. 2. *Rex et Imperator,* [L.], King and Emperor. 3. Rhode Island.

ri·al (rī′əl), *n.* [OFr. *rial, real,* lit., royal; cf. REAL (coin)], the monetary unit and a silver coin of Iran, valued at about 3 cents in 1950.

Ri·al·to (ri-al′tō; *also, for 1 & 2,* It. rē-äl′tô), *n.* 1. an island in Venice, formerly the business and trading center. 2. a bridge over the Grand Canal, connecting this island with San Marco island. 3. the theater district in New York City: sometimes applied to theater districts in other cities. 4. [r-], a market or trading place.

ri·ant (rī′ənt), *adj.* [Fr., ppr. of *rire;* L. *ridere,* to laugh], laughing; smiling; gay; cheerful.

ri·a·ta (ri-ä′tə), *n.* [Sp. *reata* < *reatar,* to tie again; *re-* (see RE-) + *atar,* to tie < L. *aptare,* to fit], a lariat.

rib (rib), *n.* [ME. *ribbe;* AS. *rib;* indirectly akin to G. *rippe;* IE. base **rebh-,* to arch over, roof over, seen also in OSlav. *rebro,* a rib: so called from arching over the chest cavity], 1. any of the arched bones attached posteriorly to the vertebral column and enclosing the chest cavity: in man there are twelve pairs of such bones, the upper seven pairs (*true ribs*) being attached by cartilage to the sternum, the next three pairs (*false ribs*) being attached each to the rib above, and the last two pairs (*floating ribs*) being unattached anteriorly: see **skeleton,** illus. 2. a cut of meat having one or more ribs. 3. a wife: in humorous reference to the Biblical creation of Eve from Adam's rib (Gen. 2:21–22). 4. a raised ridge in cloth, especially in knitted material. 5. any of the curved crosspieces extending from the keel to the top of the hull in a ship, forming its framework. 6. any of the short transverse pieces placed at intervals along the length of, and giving shape to, an airplane wing. 7. any narrow riblike piece used to form, strengthen, or shape something: as, a *rib* of an umbrella. 8. in *architecture, a*) a long curved piece in an arch. *b*) any of the transverse and intersecting arches of a vault. 9. in *botany,* any of the main veins in a leaf. *v.t.* [RIBBED (ribd), RIBBING], 1. to provide, form, or strengthen with a rib or ribs. 2. to put ribs in; mark with ribs. 3. [prob. < *rib-tickle*], [Slang], to tease or make fun of.

rib·ald (rib′əld), *adj.* [ME. *ribault;* OFr. *ribaut, ribauld,* etc.; prob. specialized use of personal name *Ribaud* (< Gmc. *Ric-bald,* mighty bold) under influence of OFr. *riber,* to wanton, dissipate (< MHG. *riben,* to copulate; cf. MD. *ribe,* whore)], characterized by coarse joking or mocking; offensive, irreverent, or vulgar in language. *n.* a ribald person. —*SYN.* see **coarse.**

rib·ald·ry (rib′əld-ri), *n.* [ME. *ribawdrye, ribaudrye;* OFr. *ribauderie*], ribald language or humor.

rib·and (rib′ənd, rib′ən), *n.* [Archaic], a ribbon.

rib·band, rib-band (rib′band′, rib′ənd, rib′ən), *n.* [*rib* + *band*], a long, flexible piece of wood or metal fastened across the ribs of a ship to hold them in place while the outside planking or plating is being put on.

Rib·ben·trop, Jo·a·chim von (yō′ä-khim fôn rib′ən-trôp′), 1893–1946; German Nazi leader; minister of foreign affairs (1938–1945); executed for war crimes.

rib·bing (rib′iŋ), *n.* ribs collectively; arrangement or collection of ribs, as in cloth, a ship, etc.

rib·bon (rib′ən), *n.* [Early Mod. Eng. var. of ME. *riban(d)* < OFr. *riban, ruban*], 1. *a*) a narrow strip of satin, silk, rayon, velvet, etc., finished at the edges and of various widths, used for decoration, tying things, etc. *b*) material in such strips. 2. anything like or suggesting such a strip: as, a *ribbon* of blue sky; specifically, a long, thin, flexible metal band, as for a measuring tape, bandsaw, etc. 3. *pl.* torn, ribbonlike strips or shreds; tatters: as, a garment torn to *ribbons.* 4. a narrow strip of cloth inked for use on a typewriter or similar device. 5. *a*) a small strip of colored cloth worn as a badge or awarded as a symbol of honor, achievement, etc.: as, he won a blue *ribbon. b*) in *military usage,* a similar strip worn on the left breast of the uniform to indicate an award of a decoration or medal. 6. *pl.* [Colloq.], reins used in driving. 7. a ribband. *v.t.* 1. to decorate, trim, or mark with or as with a ribbon or ribbons. 2. to split or tear into ribbonlike strips or shreds. *v.i.* to extend or form in a ribbonlike strip or strips.

rib·bon·fish (rib′ən-fish′), *n.* [RIBBONFISH, RIBBONFISHES (-iz); see FISH], any of several sea fishes having an elongated, compressed body suggestive of a ribbon in shape, as the dealfish.

Ri·be·ra, Jo·sé (hô-se′ rē-be′rä), 1588–1656; Spanish painter in Italy: called *Lo Spagnoletto.*

ri·bo·fla·vin (rī′bə-flā′vin), *n.* [*ribose* + *flavin*], a factor of the vitamin B complex, $C_{17}H_{20}O_6N_4$, found in milk, eggs, liver, kidney, grass, fruits, leafy vegetables, yeast, etc.: lack of riboflavin in the diet causes stunted growth, loss of hair, etc.: also called *lactoflavin, vitamin B_2, vitamin G.*

ri·bose (rī′bōs), *n.* [G. *ribonsäure,* a tetrahydroxy acid, $C_5H_{10}O_6$, arbitrarily altered < Eng. *arabinose* < L. *Arabicus,* Arabic; + *-ose* as in *pentose*], a pentose sugar, $C_5H_{10}O_5$, derived from some nucleic acids.

rib·wort (rib′wûrt′), *n.* 1. a plantain with a long stem and ribbed, narrow leaves. 2. any of a number of similar plantains. Also **ribwort plantain.**

-ric (rik), [ME. *-riche, -ricke,* realm, power < AS. *rice,* reign, dominion], a combining form meaning *jurisdiction, realm,* as in *bishopric.*

Ri·car·do, David (ri-kär′dō), 1772–1823; English economist.

Ric·ci·o, David (rich′i-ō′; It. rēt′chô), see **Rizzio, David.**

rice (rīs), *n.* [ME. *rys, ris;* OFr. *ris;* It. *riso;* LL. **oryzum,* for L. *oryza;* Gr. *oryza, oryzon;* of Oriental origin], 1. a cereal grass grown widely in warm climates, especially in the Orient. 2. the starchy seeds or grains of this grass, used as food. *v.t.* [RICED (rīst), RICING], to reduce (potatoes, etc.) to a ricelike consistency.

RICE PLANT

Rice, Elmer (rīs), (born *Elmer Reizenstein*), 1892– ; American playwright.

rice·bird (rīs′bûrd′), *n.* 1. the Java sparrow. 2. in the southern United States, the bobolink.

rice paper, 1. a thin paper made from the straw of the rice grass. 2. a fine, delicate paper made in China by cutting and pressing the pith of certain plants.

ric·er (rīs′ẽr), *n.* a utensil for ricing cooked potatoes, etc. by forcing them through small holes.

rich (rich), *adj.* [ME. *riche;* AS. *rice,* noble, powerful; influenced by OFr. *riche,* rich < OHG. *richi,* powerful, rich; for IE. base see REGAL, RIGHT], 1. having wealth; owning much money or property; wealthy. 2. having abundant natural resources: as, a *rich* country. 3. well supplied; abounding (with *in* or *with*): as, *rich* in minerals. 4. valuable: as, a *rich* prize. 5. of valuable materials or fine, elaborate workmanship; costly and elegant: as, *rich* gifts. 6. elaborate; luxurious; sumptuous: as, a *rich* banquet. 7. having an abundance of good constituents or qualities; specifically, *a)* full of nutritious or choice ingredients, as butter, sugar, cream, seasoning, etc.: often implying an excess of such ingredients: as, *rich* pastries. *b)* full of strength and flavor; full-bodied: as, *rich* wine. 8. *a)* full, deep, and mellow: said of sounds, the voice, etc. *b)* deep; intense; vivid: said of colors. *c)* very fragrant: said of odors. 9. having a high proportion of gasoline to air: as, a *rich* carburetor mixture. 10. abundant; plentiful; ample: as, a *rich* fund of adventures. 11. yielding or producing in abundance, as soil, mines, ores, etc. 12. [Colloq.], *a)* abounding in humor; very amusing; hence, *b)* absurd; preposterous.

the rich, wealthy people collectively.

SYN.—**rich** is the general word for one who has more money or income-producing property than is necessary to satisfy his normal needs; **wealthy** adds to this connotations of grand living, influence in the community, a tradition of richness, etc. (a *wealthy* banker); **affluent** suggests a continuing increase of riches and a concomitant lavish spending (to live in *affluent* circumstances); **opulent** suggests the possession of great wealth as displayed in luxurious or ostentatious living (an *opulent* mansion); **well-to-do** implies sufficient prosperity for easy living.—***ANT.*** poor.

Rich·ard (rich′ẽrd), [ME. *Rycharde, Ricard;* OFr. *Richard;* OHG. *Richart* < Gmc. ***rik-**, king (see RICH) + **harthuz*, strong], a masculine name: diminutive, *Dick;* equivalents, It. *Riccardo*, Sp. *Ricardo*.

Richard I, 1157–1199; king of England (1189–1199); one of the leaders of the Third Crusade: called *Richard Coeur de Lion* (*Richard the Lion-Hearted*).

Richard II, 1367–1400; son of Edward, the Black Prince; king of England (1377–1399); last of the Plantagenet kings; deposed.

Richard III, 1452–1485; king of England (1483–1485).

Richard Coeur de Li·on (kũr də lē′ən; Fr. kër′ də lē′ōn′), Richard I.

Rich·ards, Theodore William (rich′ẽrdz), 1868–1928; American chemist; received Nobel prize in chemistry, 1914.

Rich·ard·son, Henry Han·del (han′d'l rich′ẽrd-s'n), (pseudonym of *Ethel Florence Lindesay Robertson*, nee *Richardson*), 1880?–1946; Australian novelist.

Richardson, Henry Hob·son (hob′s'n), 1838–1886; American architect.

Richardson, Sir Owen Wil·lans (wil′ənz), 1879–1959; English physicist; received Nobel prize in physics, 1928.

Richardson, Samuel, 1689–1761; English novelist.

Ri·che·lieu, Duc de (də rē′shə-lyö′; Eng. rish′ə-lōō′, rish′ə-lōō′), (*Armand Jean du Plessis*), 1585–1642; French cardinal and statesman; leading minister of Louis XIII (1624–1642).

rich·es (rich′iz), *n.pl.* [orig. sing.], [ME. *richess;* OFr. *richesse, richece;* see RICH], valuable possessions; much money, real estate, jewels, etc.; wealth.

rich·ly (rich′li), *adv.* 1. in a rich manner. 2. abundantly; amply; fully.

Rich·mond (rich′mənd), *n.* 1. the capital of Virginia: port on the James River: pop., 220,000. 2. a borough of New York City, including all of Staten Island: pop., 222,000. 3. a city in eastern Indiana: pop., 44,000. 4. a city in California, near San Francisco: pop., 72,000. 5. a city in Surrey, England, on the Thames: pop., 42,000.

rich rhyme, see **perfect rhyme.**

Rich·ter, Jean Paul Frie·drich (zhän poul frē′driH riH′tẽr; Eng. rik′tẽr), (pseudonym *Jean Paul*), 1763–1825; German author.

ri·cin (rī′sin, ris′in), *n.* [< L. *ricinus*, castor-oil plant], a toxic protein found in the castor bean and isolated as a white powder: it agglutinates red blood corpuscles.

ric·in·o·le·ic (ris′i-nə-lē′ik, ris′i-nō′li-ik), *adj.* [< L. *ricinus*, castor-oil plant; + *oleic*], designating or of an unsaturated organic acid, $C_{17}H_{34}O_3$, found as an ester of glycerin in castor oil.

ric·in·o·le·in (ris′i-nō′li-in), *n.* the glycerol ester of ricinoleic acid: it is the main constituent of castor oil.

rick (rik), *n.* [ME. *rec, reek;* AS. *hreac;* akin to D. *rook;* IE. **qreu-q*, that bends, curves < base *(*s*)*qer-*, to bend, seen also in L. *curvus*, bent, curved (see CURVE), Eng. *ridge*], a stack of hay, straw, etc., especially one covered or thatched for protection from rain. *v.t.* to form into a rick or ricks.

Rick·en·back·er, Edward Vernon (rik′ən-bak′ẽr), 1890– ; American aviator and aviation executive.

rick·et·i·ness (rik′i-ti-nis), *n.* the quality or condition of being rickety.

rick·ets (rik′its), *n.* [? altered < Gr. *rhachitis*, rachitis], a disease of the skeletal system, chiefly of children, resulting from a deficiency of calcium salts or vitamin D in the diet, or from lack of sunlight, and characterized by a softening and, often, bending of the bones.

rick·ett·si·a (ri-ket′si-ə), *n.* [after Howard T. *Ricketts* (1871–1910), Am. pathologist], 1. [*pl.* RICKETTSIAE (-ē′)], any of a genus of Gram-negative microorganisms that are the causative agents of certain diseases, as typhus or Rocky Mountain spotted fever: they are transmitted to animals and man by the bite of certain lice and ticks in whose bodies they live as parasites. 2. [R-], [construed as pl.], this genus of microorganisms.

rick·ett·si·al (ri-ket′si-əl), *adj.* of or caused by any rickettsia.

rick·et·y (rik′i-ti), *adj.* 1. having rickets. 2. of or like rickets: as, *rickety* symptoms, *rickety* diseases. 3. weak in the joints; tottering; feeble. 4. liable to fall or break down because weak; shaky. 5. irregular: said of motion, action, etc.

rick·ey (rik′i), *n.* [said to be after a Col. *Rickey;* for discussion see H. L. Mencken, *Am. Lang., Suppl. I*, pp. 252–254], a drink made of carbonated water, lime juice, and an alcoholic liquor, especially gin (*gin rickey*).

rick·rack (rik′rak′), *n.* [dissimilated redupl. of *rack* (to stretch)], 1. flat, zigzag braid used as trimming for dresses, etc. 2. trimming made with such braid.

rick·shaw, rick·sha (rik′shô), *n.* a jinrikisha.

ric·o·chet (rik′ə-shā′, rik′ə-shet′), *n.* [Fr.; used first in *fable du ricochet* (story in which the narrator constantly evades the hearers' questions), altered < OFr. *fable du rouge cokelet* (lit., story of the red cockerel); *cokelet* apparently dim. of *coq*, but prob. altered (with *rouge*, red) < dial. *ricoucà*, to hop < LL. **recalcare*, to tread anew < L. *re-*, again + *calx, calcis*, the heel], the motion made by an object that rebounds or skips one or more times in moving over a flat surface, as a pebble thrown along the surface of a body of water. *v.i.* [RICOCHETED (-shād′), or RICOCHETTED (-shet′id), RICOCHETING (-shā′iŋ), or RICOCHETTING (-shet′iŋ)], [Fr. *ricocher* < the *n.*], to move with such a motion: as, the bullet *ricocheted* from the wall. —***SYN.*** see **skip.**

ric·tus (rik′təs), *n.* [L., open mouth < pp. of *ringi*, to open the mouth wide], 1. a gaping, as of the mouth of an animal or the beak of a bird. 2. the mouth opening.

rid (rid), *v.t.* [RID or RIDDED (-id), RIDDING], [ME. *ruden, ryden;* ON. *rythja, hrythja*, to empty, clear (land); prob. akin to *redd*], 1. to free, clear, relieve, or disencumber, as of something undesirable (usually with *of*): as, *rid* yourself of superstitions. 2. [Obs.], to save or deliver, as from danger, difficulty, etc.; rescue (with *from, out of*, etc.).

be rid of, to be freed from or relieved of (something undesirable).

get rid of, 1. to get free from or relieved of (something undesirable). 2. to do away with; destroy; kill.

rid (rid), archaic past tense and past participle of **ride.**

rid·a·ble (rīd′ə-b'l), *adj.* 1. that can be ridden: as, a *ridable* horse. 2. that can be ridden over, through, etc.: as, a *ridable* path.

rid·dance (rid′'ns), *n.* a ridding or being rid; clearance or removal, as of something undesirable, or deliverance, as from something oppressive.

good riddance, welcome relief or deliverance: often used as an exclamation of approval at getting rid of someone or something.

rid·den (rid′'n), past participle of **ride.** *adj.* dominated or obsessed (by the thing specified): used in hyphenated compounds, as *hag-ridden, fear-ridden*.

rid·dle (rid′'l), *n.* [ME. *redels;* AS. *rædels* < *rædan*, to read, guess; akin to G. *rätsel*, a puzzle], 1. a problem or puzzle in the form of a question, statement, etc. so formulated that some ingenuity is required to solve or answer it; conundrum. 2. any puzzling, perplexing, or apparently inexplicable person or thing, as a difficult problem or enigmatic saying; enigma. *v.t.* [RIDDLED (-'ld), RIDDLING], to give a solution or explanation of (a riddle); unriddle. *v.i.* to propound riddles; speak enigmatically or obscurely. —***SYN.*** see **mystery.**

rid·dle (rid′'l), *n.* [ME. *ridil;* AS. *hriddel*, earlier *hridder* < base of *hridrian*, to sift, winnow; akin to G. *reiter;* IE. **qrei-dhrom* < base *(*s*)*qer-*, to cut, seen also in L. *caro, carnis*, flesh (cf. CARNAL), *cernere*, to sift, separate, distinguish (cf. DISCERN), etc.], a coarse sieve for cinders, gravel, etc. *v.t.* [RIDDLED (-'ld), RIDDLING], 1. to sift through a riddle. 2. to make holes in; perforate: as, bullets *riddled* the automobile. 3. to find and show flaws in; criticize and disprove.

ride (rīd), *v.i.* [RODE (rōd) or *archaic* RID (rid), RIDDEN (rid′'n) or *archaic* RID or RODE, RIDING], [ME. *riden;* AS. *ridan;* akin to G. *reiten;* IE. base **reidh-*, to go, be in motion; seen also in L. *reda*, four-wheel carriage (< Gaul.), etc.; cf. ROAD], 1. to sit on and be carried along by a horse or other animal; especially, to sit on and control a horse in motion. 2. to be carried along on or in a vehicle or conveyance. 3. to be carried on something as if on a horse, etc. 4. to move along; be carried or supported in motion (*on* or *upon*): as, the automobile *rode* on the rims. 5. *a)* to move or float on the water. *b)* to lie at anchor: as, the ship *rode* close to shore. 6. to seem to be floating in space. 7. to be fit for riding or admit of being ridden: as, the car *rides* smoothly. 8. to overlap, as bones in a joint. 9. to move out of place (with *up*): as, his collar *rode* up constantly. 10. in *jazz music*, to improvise freely. 11. [Slang], to continue undisturbed, with no action taken: as, I'll let the matter *ride* a few months. *v.t.* 1. to sit on or in and control so as to move along: as, *ride* a horse, a bicycle, etc. 2. *a*) to move along on or be mounted, carried, or supported on: as, the ship *rides* the waters, the child *rode* the merry-go-round. *b*) to rest on, as by overlapping. 3. to move over, along, or through (a road, area, etc.) by horse, automobile, etc. 4. to engage in or do by riding: as, he *rode* a race with me. 5. to cause to ride. 6. to carry (a person) on something as if riding on horseback: as, the mob *rode* him on a rail. 7. to keep (a ship) at anchor. 8. to control, dominate, tyrannize over, or oppress: often in the past participle, as, *ridden* by doubts. 9. [Colloq.], to torment, harass, or tease by making the butt of ridicule, criticism, etc. 10. in *jazz music*, to improvise freely on (a theme). *n.* 1. a riding; especially, a journey by horseback, automobile, bicycle, etc. 2. a road, track, etc. for riding, especially on horseback. —*SYN.* see **bait.**

ride down, 1. to hit and knock down by riding against. 2. to overtake by riding. 3. to overcome. 4. to exhaust (a horse, etc.) by riding too long or hard.

ride out, 1. to stay afloat or aloft during (a storm, etc.) without too much damage. 2. to withstand or endure successfully.

take for a ride, [Slang], 1. to take somewhere, as in an automobile, and kill, in the manner of gangsters. 2. to hoax; deceive.

ri·dent (rī'd'nt), *adj.* [L. *ridens*, ppr. of *ridere*, to laugh], [Rare], laughing, smiling, or grinning.

rid·er (rīd'ẽr), *n.* 1. a person who rides; especially, one who rides a horse or other animal, or a bicycle, motorcycle, etc. 2. an addition or amendment to a document, etc. 3. a clause, usually dealing with some unrelated matter, added to a legislative bill when it is being considered for passage. 4. any of various devices or pieces moving along, or resting or mounted on, something else, as the top rail of a rail fence or a sliding weight on the beam of a balance.

ridge (rij), *n.* [ME. *rigge*, etc.; AS. *hrycg*; akin to G. *rücken*; prob. < IE. **qreu-q*, that bends < base *(*s*)*qer-*, to bend, seen also in L. *curvus*, bent, arched (cf. CURVE); basic sense "the back"], 1. an animal's back. 2. the long, narrow top or crest of something, as of an animal's back, a wave, an elevation of ground, etc. 3. a long, narrow elevation of land or range of hills or mountains. 4. any narrow raised strip on or in something, as on fabric. 5. the horizontal line formed by the meeting of two sloping surfaces: as, the *ridge* of a roof. 6. a narrow high-pressure area on a weather chart. *v.t. & v.i.* [RIDGED (rijd), RIDGING], 1. to mark with or as with a ridge or ridges. 2. to form into or furnish with a ridge or ridges.

idge·piece (rij'pēs'), *n.* a ridgepole.

idge·pole (rij'pōl'), *n.* the horizontal timber or beam at the ridge of a roof, to which the upper ends of the rafters are attached: also **ridge pole, ridge beam,** etc.

idg·y (rij'i), *adj.* [RIDGIER (-i-ẽr), RIDGIEST (-i-ist)], having, or rising in, a ridge or ridges.

id·i·cule (rid'i-kūl'), *n.* [Fr. < L. *ridiculum*, a jest, laughable (thing), neut. of *ridiculus*, laughable, comical < *ridere*, to laugh], 1. *a*) the act or practice of making someone or something the object of contemptuous laughter by joking, mocking, caricaturing, etc.; derision. *b*) words or actions intended to produce such laughter. 2. [Rare or Obs.], ridiculous thing, character, or quality; absurdity. *v.t.* [RIDICULED (-kūld'), RIDICULING], to make the object of contemptuous laughter; make fun of; deride; mock.

SYN.—**ridicule** implies a making fun of someone or something but does not necessarily connote malice or hostility (he *ridiculed* her new hair-do); **deride** suggests scorn or malicious contempt in ridiculing (to *deride* another's beliefs); **mock** implies a contemptuous ridiculing, especially by caricaturing another's peculiarities (it is cruel to *mock* his lisp); **taunt** implies insulting ridicule especially by jeering and repeatedly calling attention to some humiliating fact (they *taunted* him about his failure).

i·dic·u·lous (ri-dik'yoo-ləs), *adj.* [L. *ridiculosus* or *ridiculus*], deserving ridicule; absurd. —*SYN.* see **absurd.**

id·ing (rīd'iŋ), *adj.* 1. that rides. 2. used in or for riding or traveling: as, a *riding* costume, *riding* horses. *n.* the act of a person or thing that rides.

id·ing (rīd'iŋ), *n.* [ME. (*t*)*riding*; AS. *-thrithing*, a third part (only in L. contexts) < ON. *thrithjungr* < *thrithi*, third; initial *t* was lost to the preceding sound in compounds formed with *North-*, *East-*, and *West-*], 1. any of the three administrative divisions (*North Riding*, *East Riding*, and *West Riding*) of Yorkshire, England. 2. any similar division elsewhere, as of counties in England, Canada, etc.

riding crop, a short whip with a loop on one end for carrying it: used by horseback riders.

riding habit, any costume designed to be worn by horseback riders, especially such a one for women.

riding master, a person who teaches horseback riding.

riding school, a school in which horseback riding is taught.

Rid·ley, Nicholas (rid'li), 1500?–1555; English bishop and Protestant reformer; burned at the stake for heresy.

ri·dot·to (ri-dot'ō), *n.* [*pl.* RIDOTTOS (-ōz)], [It., a festival, redoubt; see REDOUBT], a public entertainment or social gathering, often in masquerade, with music and dancing, popular in 18th-century England.

Rie·ka (rye'kä), *n.* Fiume: the Yugoslavian name.

Rie·mann, Ge·org Fried·rich Bern·hard (gā-ôrkh' frē'driH bern'härt rē'män), 1826–1866; German mathematician.

Rien·zi, Co·la di (kô'lä dē ryen'tsē; Eng. ri-en'zi), (born *Niccolo Gabrini*), 1313?–1354; Italian orator and popular leader: also **Rienzo** (ryen'tsô; Eng. ri-en'zō).

Rif (rif), *n.* a hilly region along the Mediterranean coast of Morocco: also **Er Rif** (er), **Riff.**

‡**ri·fa·ci·men·to** (rē-fä'chē-men'tô; Eng. ri-fä'chi-men'-tō), *n.* [*pl.* RIFACIMENTI (-tē; Eng. -ti)], [It., lit., a remaking < *rifare*, to make over; *ri-*, re- + *fare* (< L. *facere*), to make], a remaking, recasting, or adaptation, as of a piece of writing or music.

rife (rīf), *adj.* [ME. *rif*; AS. *rife*; akin to MD. *rijf*; IE. base **rei-*, to tear, tear off, as also in *ripe*, *reap*; basic notion is of harvest], 1. frequently or commonly occurring; widespread; prevalent; current: as, gossip was *rife*. 2. *a*) abundant; plentiful. *b*) abounding; replete (followed by *with*): as, a thesis *rife* with error. —*SYN.* see **prevailing.**

Riff (rif), *n.* 1. a member of a Berber people living in the Rif and near-by regions. 2. the Rif.

riff (rif), *n.* [prob. back-formation < *riffle*, *n.* 3; ? < *refrain*, *n.*], in *jazz music*, a melodic phrase, repeated again and again, often used as the main theme, as in a final chorus, or as background.

Rif·fi·an (rif'i-ən), *adj.* of Rif or the Riffs. *n.* a Riff.

rif·fle (rif''l), *n.* [< the *v.*], 1. *a*) a shoal, reef, or rocky obstruction in a stream, producing a ripple or a stretch of shallow, rapid, or choppy water. *b*) such a ripple or stretch of water. 2. in *gold mining*, *a*) a contrivance, as of bars, slats, blocks, or stones, put across the bottom of a sluice, etc. to catch or hold the particles of gold in the grooves or channels left between the bars, slats, etc. *b*) any of the bars, slats, etc. *c*) any of the grooves or channels. 3. the act or method of riffling cards. *v.t. & v.i.* [RIFFLED (-'ld), RIFFLING], [prob. var. of *ripple* merged with Canad. Fr. *riffler*, var. of Fr. *rifler*, to scratch, scrape; cf. RIFLE (to cut grooves in)], 1. to form, become, or flow over or through, a riffle. 2. to leaf rapidly through (a book, etc.), as by letting the edges or corners of the pages slip lightly across the thumb. 3. to shuffle (playing cards) by holding part of the deck in each hand, raising the corners or edges slightly, and letting the cards fall alternately together.

riff·raff (rif'raf'), *n.* [earlier *rif and raf*, every scrap; OFr. *rif et raf*, *rifle et rafle*; see RIFLE (to rob) & RAFFLE], 1. those people or that segment of society regarded as of no consequence or merit; mob. 2. [Dial.], trash.

ri·fle (rī'f'l), *v.t.* [RIFLED (-f'ld), RIFLING], [Fr. *rifler*, to scrape, scratch; prob. < OLG. *rifeln*, to groove, furrow < *rive*, *riefe*, a groove, furrow, etc.; akin to AS. *rifelede*, wrinkled], to cut spiral grooves within (a gun barrel, etc.). *v.i.* [Rare], to use or fire a rifle. *n.* [short for *rifled gun*], 1. *a*) a firearm having spiral grooves cut into the inner surface of the barrel to make the bullet spin when fired, thus giving it greater accuracy and distance; especially, such a firearm to be fired from the shoulder: military rifles are distinguished from carbines in that they are longer and heavier and are designed to hold a bayonet. *b*) such a groove. 2. an artillery piece or naval gun with such grooves. 3. *pl.* troops armed with rifles.

ri·fle (rī'f'l), *v.t.* [RIFLED (-f'ld), RIFLING], [ME. *riflen*; OFr. *rifler* (cf. RIFLE, to cut grooves in); of Gmc. origin; cf. obs. D. *rijffelen*, to plunder], 1. *a*) to ransack and rob; pillage; plunder: as, the troops *rifled* the captured city. *b*) to search and rob (a person). 2. to strip bare (usually with *of*): as, the thieves *rifled* the safe of valuables. 3. to take as plunder; steal.

rifle grenade, a grenade designed to be attached to the muzzle of a military rifle and fired by a special device: it explodes on contact.

ri·fle·man (rī'f'l-mən), *n.* [*pl.* RIFLEMEN (-mən)], 1. a soldier, especially an infantry man, armed with a rifle. 2. a man who uses, or is skilled in using, a rifle.

rifle pit, a pit or short trench dug to protect riflemen firing at the enemy.

ri·fler (rī'flẽr), *n.* a person who rifles, or plunders; robber.

rifle range, 1. the distance covered by a bullet fired from a rifle. 2. a place for target practice with a rifle.
ri·fling (rī′fliŋ), *n.* 1. the act or operation of cutting spiral grooves within a gun barrel. 2. a series or system of such grooves.
rift (rift), *n.* [ME.; Dan. < ON. *ript* < *ripta*, to break (a bargain); for the base see RIVE], an opening caused by or as if by splitting; cleft; fissure; crack. *v.t. & v.i.* to burst open; split; crack.
rig (rig), *v.t.* [RIGGED (rigd), RIGGING], [? < ON. *rigga*, to wrap around, whence Norw. *rigga*, to bind, wrap up; IE. base ***reiĝ-*, to bind], 1. *a)* to fit (a ship, mast, etc.) with sails, shrouds, braces, etc. *b)* to fit (a ship's sails, shrouds, etc.) to the masts, yards, etc. 2. to assemble and adjust the wings, fuselage, etc. of (an aircraft). 3. to fit out; equip (often with *out* or *up*). 4. to put together, prepare for use, or arrange, especially in a makeshift or hurried fashion (often with *up*). 5. to arrange in a dishonest way for selfish advantage; manipulate fraudulently: as, speculators *rigged* the market. 6. [Colloq.], to dress; clothe; attire (often with *out* or *up*). *n.* 1. the distinctive arrangement of sails, masts, shrouds, etc. on a vessel. 2. any apparatus for a special purpose; equipment; gear; tackle. 3. equipment for drilling an oil well. 4. a carriage, cart, etc. with its horse or horses. 5. [Colloq.], dress; costume, especially if odd or showy.
Ri·ga (rē′gä; Eng. rē′gə), *n.* seaport and capital of the Latvian S.S.R.: pop., 393,000.
Riga, Gulf of, an arm of the Baltic Sea, between the Latvian S.S.R. and the Estonian S.S.R.: length, c. 100 mi.; width, c. 60 mi.
rig·a·doon (rig′ə-dōōn′), *n.* [Fr. *rigodon, rigaudon;* said to be < *Rigaud*, surname of its reputed 17th-c. inventor], 1. a lively dance for one couple, with a peculiar jumping step: it is no longer popular. 2. music for this, usually in duple time.
Ri·gel (rī′g'l, rī′jəl), *n.* [Ar. *rijl*, foot: so called because in the left foot of Orion], a bluish first-magnitude star, the brightest star in the constellation Orion: see **constellation**, chart.
rig·ger (rig′ẽr), *n.* 1. a person who rigs; specifically, *a)* a person whose work is fitting the rigging of ships, or one who works with hoisting tackle and the like. *b)* a person whose work is assembling and adjusting the fuselage, wings, etc. of aircraft. 2. a protective scaffold used, as on a building under construction, to catch tools or materials that might accidentally fall.
rig·ging (rig′iŋ), *n.* [< *rig* + *-ing*], 1. the chains, ropes, etc. used for supporting and working the masts, sails, yards, etc. of a vessel. 2. equipment; gear.
Rigg's disease (rigz), [after John M. *Riggs* (1810–1885), Am. dentist], pyorrhea alveolaris.
right (rīt), *adj.* [ME. & AS. *riht*, straight, direct, right; akin to G. *recht;* IE. base ***reĝ-*, straight, put in order, etc., as also in L. *rex* (cf. REGAL), *regula* (cf. RULE, REGULAR)], 1. not curved; straight: as, a *right* line. 2. *a)* formed by, or with reference to, a straight line or plane perpendicular to a base: as, a *right* angle. *b)* having the axis perpendicular to the base: as, a *right* cylinder. 3. in accordance with justice, law, morality, etc.; upright; virtuous: as, *right* conduct. 4. *a)* in accordance with fact, reason, some set standard, etc.; correct: as, the *right* answer. *b)* correct in thought, statement, or action: as, he was *right* in his answer. 5. *a)* fitting; appropriate; suitable. *b)* most convenient or favorable. 6. designating the side, surface, etc. meant to be seen; designating the finished, principal, or upper side or surface: as, the *right* side of cloth. 7. *a)* sound; normal: said of the mind, etc. *b)* mentally sound or normal; sane: said of a person. 8. having sound health or good spirits. 9. in a satisfactory condition, or in good order: as, make things *right* again. 10. *a)* designating or of that side of one's body which is toward the east when one faces north, usually the side of the more used hand. *b)* designating or of the corresponding side of anything. *c)* closer to the right side of a person directly before and facing the thing mentioned or understood: as, the top *right* drawer of a desk. Opposed to *left*. 11. of the political right; conservative or reactionary. 12. [Archaic], not spurious or sham; genuine; real. *n.* 1. what is right, or just, lawful, morally good, proper, correct, etc. 2. that which a person has a just claim to; power, privilege, etc. that belongs to a person by law, nature, or tradition: as, it was his *right* to say what he thought. 3. *a)* all or part of the right side. *b)* what is on the right side. 4. in *boxing*, *a)* the right hand. *b)* a blow delivered with the right hand. 5. in *finance*, *a)* the privilege given to a company's stockholders of buying additional stock or shares in a new issue of stock, usually at par or a price below the current market price. *b)* the negotiable certificate indicating this privilege. *c)* *often pl.* a privilege of subscribing for some stock or bond. 6. [often R-], in *politics*, a conservative or reactionary position, party, or group: so called from the position of the seats occupied in some European legislatures. *adv.* [ME. & AS. *rihte*], 1. in a straight line; straight; directly (often with *to, into, through,* etc.): as, go *right* home. 2. *a)* properly; fittingly. *b)* favorably, conveniently, or well. 3. completely; thoroughly: as, the cold penetrated *right* through his clothes. 4. exactly; precisely: as, *right* here. 5. without pause or delay; immediately: as, come *right* now. 6. according to law, justice, etc.; in an upright way. 7. correctly or accurately. 8. on or toward the right hand or side. 9. very; extremely: as, he knows *right* well: dialectal or colloquial except in certain titles, as, the *right* honorable, the *right* reverend. *v.t.* 1. to put in or restore to an upright or proper position: as, we *righted* the boat and started rowing. 2. to correct; make conform with fact, etc. 3. to put in order; set right: as, the maid *righted* the room. 4. to do justice to (a person); make amends to. 5. to make amends for; redress or avenge (a wrong, etc.). *v.i.* to get into or resume an upright or proper position. Abbreviated **rt., R., r.**
by right (or **rights**), in justice; properly.
in one's own right, through one's own authority, ability, etc.; without dependence on another or others.
in the right, right; correct.
right away (or **off**), without delay or pause; at once.
to rights, [Colloq.], in or into good or proper condition or order.
right·a·bout (rīt′ə-bout′), *n.* 1. a rightabout-face. 2. the direction directly opposite, as faced after turning completely about. *adv. & adj.* with, in, or by a rightabout-face.
right·a·bout-face (rīt′ə-bout′fās′), *n.* 1. a turning directly about so as to face in the opposite direction. 2. a complete reversal of belief, conduct, etc. *interj.* a military command to perform a rightabout-face.
right angle, an angle of 90 degrees; angle made by the meeting of two straight lines perpendicular to each other.
right-an·gled (rīt′aŋ′g'ld), *adj.* having or forming one or more right angles; rectangular.
right ascension, in *astronomy*, 1. the rising of a star or point above the horizon on the celestial sphere. 2. the angular distance of a heavenly body from the vernal equinox, measured eastward along the celestial equator and expressed in degrees or hours, minutes, and seconds: abbreviated **R.A.**
Æ.: symbol, α (alpha).

RIGHT ANGLE

right·eous (rī′chəs), *adj.* [altered, by analogy with adjectives in *-eous* < ME. & AS. *rihtwis;* see RIGHT & -WISE], 1. acting in a just, upright manner; doing what is right; virtuous: as, a *righteous* man. 2. morally right or justifiable: as, a *righteous* act. —*SYN.* see **moral**
right·eous·ness (rī′chəs-nis), *n.* 1. the quality or condition of being righteous or just; rectitude or justice. 2. a righteous act, quality, etc.
right field, in *baseball*, the right-hand part of the outfield (as viewed from home plate).
right·ful (rīt′fəl), *adj.* 1. right; just; fair; equitable. 2. having a just, lawful claim, or right: as, the *rightfu[l]* owner. 3. belonging or owned by just or lawful claim or by right: as, a *rightful* rank. 4. [Rare or Obs.] righteous; virtuous.
right-hand (rīt′hand′), *adj.* 1. being on or directe[d] toward the right. 2. of, for, or with the right hand. 3. most helpful or reliable: as, my *right-hand* man. 4. plain-laid: said of a rope.
right-hand·ed (rīt′han′did), *adj.* 1. using the righ[t] hand more skillfully than and in preference to the left. 2. done with the right hand. 3. made for use with the right hand. 4. turning left to right; clockwise. 5. spiraling from left to right, as most shells.
right·ism (rīt′iz'm), *n.* in *politics*, conservative or re[actionary] ideas or actions.
right·ist (rīt′ist), *n.* in *politics*, a person whose politica[l] position is conservative or reactionary. *adj.* in *politics* conservative or reactionary.
right·ly (rīt′li), *adv.* [see RIGHT & -LY], 1. with justice fairly. 2. properly; suitably; fitly. 3. correctly.
right-mind·ed (rīt′mīn′did), *adj.* thinking or believin[g] what is right; having correct views or principles.
right·o (rīt′ō′), *interj.* [British Colloq.], yes; all right certainly: exclamation expressing affirmation or assent
right of search, in *maritime law*, the right of a natio[n] at war to stop the ships of neutral nations on the hig[h] seas and search them for contraband or the like the finding of which makes the ship liable to seizure also **right of visit** (or **visitation**) **and search.**
right-of-way (rīt′əv-wā′), *n.* right of way.
right of way, 1. the right, established by commo[n] or statutory law, of one ship, automobile, etc. to cros[s] in front of another; precedence in moving, as at inter[-]sections. 2. right of passage, as over another's property 3. a route that it is lawful to use. 4. *a)* a strip o[f] land acquired or used by a railroad for its tracks *b)* land over which a public road, an electric powe[r] line, etc. passes.
right triangle, a triangle with one right angle.
right whale, [? "true (i.e., typical) whale" or "righ

whale to hunt for" (because rich in oil)], a large-headed whalebone whale without teeth or dorsal fin.

right-wing (rīt′wiŋ′), *adj.* in *politics*, of the right wing.

right wing, [see RIGHT, *n.* 6], in *politics*, the more conservative or reactionary section of a party, etc.

Ri·gi (rē′gē), *n.* a mountain in central Switzerland, near the Lake of Lucerne: height, 5,905 ft.

rig·id (rij′id), *adj.* [L. *rigidus* < *rigere*, to be stiff; base as in *right, regal*], 1. not bending or flexible; unyielding; stiff: as, a *rigid* metal girder. 2. not moving; firmly fixed; set. 3. severe; strict: as, a *rigid* taskmaster. 4. not deviating or relaxing; rigorous: as, *rigid* regulations. 5. in *aeronautics*, having a rigid framework that encloses containers for the gas: said of a dirigible or airship. —*SYN.* see **stiff, strict.**

ri·gid·i·ty (ri-jid′ə-ti), *n.* [*pl.* RIGIDITIES (-tiz)], [L. *rigiditas*], quality, state, or instance of being rigid.

rig·ma·role (rig′mə-rōl′), *n.* [altered < *ragman roll; ragman* < ME. *rageman*, a document, roll used in a game; cf. RAG, RAGAMUFFIN], a succession of foolish, rambling, or incoherent statements; nonsense.

rig·or (rig′ẽr), *n.* [ME. & OFr. *rigour;* L. *rigor* < *rigere*, to be rigid; base as in *right, regal*], 1. extreme harshness or severity; specifically, *a*) strictness or inflexibility: as, the *rigor* of martial law. *b*) hardship or difficulty: as, the *rigors* of life. *c*) inclemency, as of weather. 2. a severe, harsh, or oppressive act, etc. 3. stiffness; rigidity; specifically, a condition of rigidity in body tissues or organs, in which they are not responsive to stimuli. 4. a shivering or trembling, as in the chill preceding a fever. —*SYN.* see **difficulty.**

rig·or·ism (rig′ẽr-iz′m), *n.* [*rigor* + *-ism*], strictness and austerity, as in living, religion, artistic style, etc.

rig·or·ist (rig′ẽr-ist), *n.* a person who believes in or practices rigorism.

‡ri·gor mor·tis (rī′gôr môr′tis, rig′ẽr), [L., stiffness of death], the progressive stiffening of the muscles that occurs several hours after death as a result of the coagulation of the muscle protein.

rig·or·ous (rig′ẽr-əs), *adj.* [OFr. *rigoureux*, earlier *rigorous;* ML. *rigorosus*], 1. characterized by rigor; very strict or harsh: said of rules, persons, etc. 2. very severe or sharp: said of climate or weather. 3. rigidly precise; thoroughly accurate or exact: as, *rigorous* scholarship. —*SYN.* see **strict.**

rig·our (rig′ẽr), *n.* rigor: British spelling.

Rigs·dag (rigz′däg′), *n.* [Dan. < *rige*, kingdom + *dag*, session, lit., day; cf. REICHSTAG], formerly, the legislature of Denmark, made up of the *Landsting* and the *Folketing*: it was replaced in 1953 by a unicameral Folketing.

rigs·da·ler (rigz′dä′lẽr), *n.* [Dan.; see RIX-DOLLAR], an obsolete Danish silver coin; rix-dollar.

Rig-Ve·da (rig-vā′də, rig-vē′də), *n.* [Sans. *Ṛgveda* < *ric*, praise, hymn + *veda*, knowledge], the Veda of Verses (Psalms), the oldest and most important of the Hindu sacred books, or Vedas.

Riis, Jacob August (rēs), 1849–1914; American journalist and social reformer.

Rijn (rīn), *n.* the Rhine: the Dutch name.

Rijs·wijk (rīs′wīk), *n.* Ryswick: the Dutch name.

rile (rīl), *v.t.* [RILED (rīld), RILING], [pronun. var. of *roil*], [Colloq. or Dial.], 1. to make (a liquid) thick and muddy by stirring the dregs. 2. to anger; irritate.

Ri·ley, James Whit·comb (hwit′kəm rī′li), 1853?–1916; American poet: called the *Hoosier poet.*

‡ri·lie·vo (rē-lye′vô), *n.* [*pl.* RILIEVI (-vē)], [It.; see RELIEF], in *sculpture*, etc., relief (sense 6).

Ril·ke, Rai·ner Ma·ri·a (rī′nẽr mä-rē′ä ril′kə), 1875–1926; German poet and fiction writer, born in Prague.

rill (ril), *n.* [cf. D. & Fris. *ril*, LG. & G. *rille*], a little brook or rivulet.

rill, rille (ril), *n.* [G. *rille*, a groove, furrow; see prec.], in *astronomy*, any of several long, narrow trenches or valleys seen on the moon's surface.

rill·et (ril′it), *n.* [dim. of *rill*], a little rill; brooklet.

rim (rim), *n.* [ME. *rime;* AS. *rima*, an edge, border; akin to ON. *rimi*, a ridge; IE. base **rem-*, to support, etc.], 1. the edge, border, or margin, especially of something circular; often, a raised or projecting edge or border. 2. *a*) the outer, circular part of a wheel. *b*) a circular strip of metal, often removable, on which the tire is mounted on the wheel of an automobile, etc. *v.t.* [RIMMED (rimd), RIMMING], 1. to put a rim or rims on or around. 2. to roll around the rim of: as, the golf ball *rimmed* the hole. *SYN.* see **border.**

Rim·baud, Ar·thur (år′tür′ ran′bō′), 1854–1891; French symbolist poet.

rime (rīm), *n., v.t. & v.i.* [RIMED (rīmd), RIMING], [sp. preferred by many for historical reasons, supposed association with AS. *rim*, number, reckoning, etc.; see RHYME], rhyme.

rime (rīm), *n.* [ME. *rim(e);* AS. *hrim;* akin to ON. *hrim;* IE. base **qrei-*, to touch lightly, as also in AS. *hrinan*, to touch], a white, icy coating formed on grass, leaves, etc. from atmospheric moisture; hoarfrost. *v.t.* RIMED (rīmd), RIMING], to coat with rime.

rim·fire (rim′fīr′), *adj.* 1. designating a cartridge with the primer set in the rim of the base. 2. designating or of a firearm taking a rimfire cartridge. Cf. **centerfire.**

Ri·mi·ni (rē′mē-nē′; Eng. rim′ə-ni), *n.* a city in northeastern Italy, on the Adriatic Sea: pop., 72,000 (est. 1947): ancient name, *Ariminum.*

ri·mose (rī′mōs, rī-mōs′), *adj.* [L. *rimosus* < *rima*, a chink, fissure], full of chinks, fissures, or crevices.

rim·ous (rī′məs), *adj.* rimose.

rim·ple (rim′p′l), *n., v.t. & v.i.* [RIMPLED (-p′ld), RIMPLING], [ME. *rimpyl*, etc.; prob. < AS. **hrympol;* akin to MD., MLG. *rimpe*], wrinkle; rumple; crease.

Rim·ski-Kor·sa·kov, Ni·ko·lai An·dre·e·vich (nē-kô-lī′ än-dryā′ye-vich rēm′ski-kôr′sä-kôf′; Eng. rim′ski-kôr′sə-kôf′), 1844–1908; Russian composer.

rim·y (rīm′i), *adj.* [RIMIER (-i-ẽr), RIMIEST (-i-ist)], covered with rime; frosty.

rind (rīnd), *n.* [ME. *rinde;* AS. *rind, rinde;* prob. < base of *rendan*, to tear; see REND], a hard or firm outer layer or coating: as, the *rind* of cheese, of fruit, of a side of bacon, etc. —*SYN.* see **skin.**

rin·der·pest (rin′dẽr-pest′), *n.* [G. *rinder*, pl. of *rind*, horned beast + *pest*, a plague], an acute infectious disease of cattle and, often, sheep and goats, characterized by fever and inflammation of the mucous membrane of the intestines; cattle plague.

Rine·hart, Mary Roberts (rīn′härt), 1876–1958; American novelist and playwright.

ring (riŋ), *v.i.* [RANG (raŋ) or *rarely* RUNG (ruŋ), RUNG, RINGING], [ME. *ringen;* AS. *hringan;* IE. echoic base **ker-*, **kor-*, seen also in *creak, raven, scream*, etc.], 1. to give forth a clear, resonant sound when struck or otherwise caused to vibrate, as a bell. 2. to produce, as by sounding, a specified impression on the hearer: as, her promises *rang* false. 3. to cause a bell or bells to sound. 4. to sound a bell as a summons (usually with *for*): as, she *rang* for the maid. 5. to sound loudly or be full of sound; be resonant; resound: as, the room *rang* with merriment: also used figuratively, as, the nation *rang* with praise for his deeds. 6. to have a sensation as of ringing, humming, etc.: said of the ears or head. *v.t.* 1. to cause (a bell, etc.) to ring. 2. to sound (a peal, knell, etc.) by or as by ringing a bell or bells. 3. to signal, proclaim, announce, summon, usher (*in* or *out*), etc. by or as by ringing: as, the chimes *rang* the hours. 4. to test (coins, etc.) by the sound produced in striking on something hard. 5. to call by telephone (often with *up*). *n.* 1. the sound of a bell. 2. *a*) any similar sound: as, the *ring* of laughter. *b*) any loud sound, especially when repeated, continued, or reverberated. 3. a characteristic sound or quality: as, the *ring* of pride. 4. a set of bells. 5. act of ringing a bell, etc. 6. a telephone call.

ring down the curtain, 1. to signal for a theater curtain to be lowered; hence, 2. to end something.

ring in, 1. to mark the time of one's arrival at work by means of a time clock. 2. [Slang], to bring in or put in by fraud or trickery.

ring out, to mark the time of one's departure from work by means of a time clock.

ring the bell, [Colloq.], to achieve a success: in allusion to strength-testing devices, as at amusement parks, in which a bell rings to indicate a successful effort.

ring up, to record or enter (a specified amount) in a cash register.

ring up the curtain, 1. to signal for a theater curtain to be raised; hence, 2. to begin something.

ring (riŋ), *n.* [ME.; AS. *hring;* akin to G. *ring;* IE. **(s)qren-gh* < base **(s)qer-*, to bend, as also in L. *circus* (cf. CIRCLE, CIRCUS, etc.), *circa* (cf. CIRCA); cf. RUNG, *n.*], 1. a small, circular band of metal, etc., especially of precious metal, often set with gems, to be worn on the finger as an ornament or a symbol of betrothal, marriage, etc. 2. any of various circular bands or objects, as of metal, plastic, etc., used for some special purpose: as, a key *ring*, napkin *ring*. 3. a circular line, mark, or figure. 4. the outer edge or border of something circular; rim, as of a wheel. 5. a circular cut made, or a circle of bark cut from, around the trunk or a branch of a tree. 6. any of the concentric, roughly circular marks seen in cross sections of the trunks of exogenous trees, resulting from the yearly addition of layers of wood: in full, **annual ring.** 7. any of the turns in a helix or spiral. 8. a circular course, as in dancing. 9. a number of people or things grouped in a circle. 10. a group of people working together to advance their own selfish interests by manipulation and control, as in business, politics, etc. 11. an enclosed area, often circular, for contests, exhibitions, etc.: as, the *ring* of a circus. 12. an enclosure, now usually a square, canvas-covered area set off by stakes and ropes, in which boxing and wrestling matches are held; hence, 13. the sport or profession of boxing; prize fighting (with *the*). 14. an enclosed space for betting at a race; hence, 15. bookmakers collectively. 16. a contest or competition, especially a political one: now usually in *toss one's hat in the ring*, to announce publicly that one is a candidate, as for political nomination. 17. in *chemistry*, a closed chain of atoms; number of atoms united in such a way that they can be represented graphically as a ring. 18. in *geometry*, the space between two concentric circles. ***v.t.*** [RINGED (riŋd), RINGING], 1. to surround or encircle with or as with a ring. 2. to form into a ring or rings. 3. to furnish with a ring or rings. 4. to put a ring in the nose of (an animal), as to prevent rooting or fighting. 5. to circle about (animals) so as to hem them in. 6. in some games, to toss a ring, horseshoe, quoit, etc. so that it encircles (a peg). 7. to cut a circle of bark from (a tree). ***v.i.*** 1. to form or gather in a ring or rings. 2. to move in a circular or curving course; run, fly, etc. in circles or spirals; specifically, in *falconry*, to fly upward in spirals.

run rings around, [Colloq.], 1. to run much faster than; hence, 2. to excel greatly.

ring·bolt (riŋ′bōlt′), ***n.*** a bolt with a ring at the head.

ring·bone (riŋ′bōn′), ***n.*** any pathological bony growth on the pastern bones of a horse, often causing lameness.

ring·dove (riŋ′duv′), ***n.*** 1. the European wood pigeon, with whitish markings on each side of the neck. 2. a European and Asiatic dove resembling the turtledove: also **ringed turtledove.**

ringed (riŋd), ***adj.*** 1. wearing or having a ring or rings; hence (with reference to a wedding or engagement ring), married or engaged. 2. decorated or marked with a ring or rings. 3. encircled or surrounded by a ring or rings. 4. formed like a ring or of rings

rin·gent (rin′jənt), ***adj.*** [L. *ringens*, ppr. of *ringi*, to gape], 1. gaping. 2. in *botany*, having the lips widely separated, as some corollas.

ring·er (riŋ′ẽr), ***n.*** a person or thing that rings, or encircles, etc.; specifically, *a*) a horseshoe, quoit, etc. thrown so that it encircles the peg. *b*) such a throw.

ring·er (riŋ′ẽr), ***n.*** 1. a person or thing that rings a bell, chime, etc. 2. [< *ring in*], [Slang], *a*) a player, horse, etc. dishonestly entered in some competition by falsifying or concealing the facts of identity, status, age, record, etc. *b*) a person or thing that very much resembles another: as, he's a *ringer* for his father.

ring finger, the third finger (next to the little finger), especially of the left hand: the wedding ring is usually worn on this finger.

ring·lead·er (riŋ′lēd′ẽr), ***n.*** [*ring* (a group) + *leader*], a person who leads others, especially in unlawful acts, opposition to authority, etc.

ring·let (riŋ′lit), ***n.*** [dim. of *ring* (a circle)], 1. a little ring or circle. 2. a curl, especially a long one: as, yellow *ringlets* hung down her back.

ring·let·ed (riŋ′lit-id), ***adj.*** having or set in ringlets.

ring·mas·ter (riŋ′mas′tẽr, riŋ′mäs′tẽr), ***n.*** a man who directs the performances in a circus ring.

ring-neck (riŋ′nek′), ***n.*** any of various ring-necked birds, as the ring-necked duck, pheasant, etc.

ring-necked (riŋ′nekt′), ***adj.*** having a distinctive colored stripe or stripes around the neck, as certain animals and birds.

Ring of the Nibelung, 1. in *German legend*, the ring made from the Rheingold by Alberich, leader of a race of dwarfs called the Nibelungs. 2. the tetralogy of music dramas by Richard Wagner, *Das Rheingold, Die Walküre, Siegfried*, and *Götterdämmerung*, telling the story of this ring.

ring ouzel, a small European bird of the thrush family, with a white band on its neck and breast.

ring·side (riŋ′sīd′), ***n.*** 1. the space or place just outside the ring, as at a boxing match or circus; hence, 2. any place that provides a close view of something.

ring snake, 1. a small, grayish-green, nonpoisonous North American snake with a yellow stripe around its neck. 2. a similar European snake; grass snake.

ring·ster (riŋ′stẽr), ***n.*** [Colloq.], a member of a ring, especially of a political ring.

ring-straked (riŋ′strākt′), ***adj.*** [Archaic], ring-streaked.

ring-streaked (riŋ′strēkt′), ***adj.*** having streaks or stripes of color around the body.

ring·toss (riŋ′tôs′), ***n.*** a game in which rings made of rope, etc. are thrown to encircle a peg.

ring·worm (riŋ′wũrm′), ***n.*** any of various contagious skin diseases, as athlete's foot, caused by several related varieties of fungus and characterized by itching and the formation of ring-shaped, discolored patches covered with scales or vesicles.

rink (riŋk), ***n.*** [Scot., earlier *renk* < OFr. *renc*, rank; see RANK, *n.*], 1. a smooth expanse of ice marked off for the game of curling. 2. a part of a bowling green large enough for a match to be played on it. 3. the players on one side in a game of curling, bowling, or quoits. 4. a smooth expanse of ice, often artificially prepared and enclosed, for skating. 5. a smooth floor, usually of wood, for roller skating. 6. a building or enclosure containing a surface for ice skating or roller skating.

rinse (rins), ***v.t.*** [RINSED (rinst), RINSING], [ME. *rincen;* OFr. *rincer*, earlier *reïncier* < LL. **recentiare*, to renew, rinse, purify < L. *recens*, fresh, new; see RECENT], 1. to wash lightly, as by dipping into water or letting water run over, into, or through. 2. to remove soap, dirt, or impurities from by using clean water in this way as a last process in cleansing. 3. to remove (soap, dirt, etc.) in this way. ***n.*** 1. a rinsing. 2. the water used in rinsing.

rins·ing (rin′siŋ), ***n.*** 1. *usually pl. a*) the liquid in or with which anything has been rinsed; hence, *b*) dregs. 2. the act of one that rinses; rinse.

Ri·o (rē′ō), ***n.*** Rio de Janeiro.

Rí·o Bra·vo (rē′ô brä′vô), Rio Grande: Mexican name.

Ri·o de Ja·nei·ro (rē′ō də jə-nêr′ō, rē′ō dā zhə-nā′rō; Port. rē′oo di zhə-nā′roo), a seaport in Brazil: its former capital: pop., 2,303,000: often shortened to **Rio.**

Rí·o de O·ro (rē′ô de ô′rô), 1. a territory on the northwestern coast of Africa: it is part of the Spanish colony of Spanish Sahara: area, c. 73,000 sq. mi.; capital, Villa Cisneros. 2. Spanish Sahara: the former name.

Ri·o Grande (rē′ō grand′, rē′ō gran′di, rē′ō grän′dā; *also, for 2 & 3*, Port. rē′oo grän′di), 1. a river flowing from southern Colorado to the Gulf of Mexico: the boundary between Texas and Mexico: length, 1,800 mi.: Mexican name, *Río Bravo*. 2. a river in southern Brazil, flowing into the Paraná River: length, 650 mi. 3. a city on the coast of southern Brazil: pop., 64,000: formerly called *São Pedro de Rio Grande do Sul*.

Rí·o Mu·ni (rē′ô mōō′nē), a district of Spanish Guinea, on the west central African mainland: area, 9,470 sq. mi.; pop., 157,000; chief city, Bata.

Río Negro, see **Negro, Río.**

ri·ot (rī′ət), ***n.*** [ME. & OFr. *riote* (akin to It. *riota*) < *rioter, rihoter*, to make a disturbance; said to be dim. of *ruir*, to make an uproar < L. *rugire*, to roar], 1. wild or violent disorder, confusion, or disturbance; tumult; uproar. 2. a wild, violent public disturbance, or disturbance of the peace, by a number of persons (in *law*, three or more) assembled together. 3. an unrestrained outburst, as of laughter. 4. a brilliant, vivid display (*of* color). 5. *a*) wild, loose living; debauchery. *b*) unrestrained revelry. *c*) a wild, noisy feast or revel. ***v.i.*** [ME. *rioten;* OFr. *rioter*], 1. to take part in a tumult or disturbance of the peace. 2. *a*) to live in a wild, loose manner. *b*) to engage in unrestrained revelry. 3. to indulge without restraint; revel (*in* something). ***v.t.*** to waste (money, time, etc.) in riotous living (usually with *away*).

run riot, [orig. of dogs barking on the wrong scent], 1. to run wild; act without restraint, control, or discipline. 2. to grow in luxuriance or profusion.

Riot Act, an English law, passed in 1715, providing that if twelve or more persons are unlawfully assembled to the disturbance of the public peace they must disperse on proclamation (*reading the Riot Act*) or be held guilty of felony.

read the riot act to, to command to stop doing something regarded as wrong, warning that disobedience will bring punishment.

ri·ot·ous (rī′ət-əs), ***adj.*** [ME.; OFr. *rioteus*], 1. having the nature of a riot, or disturbance of the peace. 2. engaging in or inciting to riot. 3. loud and disorderly; boisterous; uproarious. 4. loose and wild; dissolute; profligate. 5. luxuriant, as growth.

rip (rip), ***v.t.*** [RIPPED (ript), RIPPING], [Late ME.; prob. < MD. or LG.; cf. Fl. *rippen*, Fris. *rippe* in same sense; prob. IE. base **rei-*, to tear, tear off; cf. REAP, RIPE], 1. to cut or tear apart roughly or vigorously, often, as cloth, along a seam. 2. to remove by or as by cutting or tearing roughly or vigorously (with *off, out, away*, etc.). 3. to produce a rip in; tear. 4. to saw or split (wood) along the grain. ***v.i.*** 1. to become torn or split apart, often, as in cloth, along a seam. 2. [Colloq.], to move with speed or violence. ***n.*** 1. a torn place or burst seam, as in cloth. 2. the act of ripping or tearing. —***SYN.*** see **tear.**

rip into, [Colloq.], to attack violently or sharply, often with words.

rip out, [Colloq.], to utter violently or sharply, as in angry exclamation.

rip (rip), ***n.*** [Early Mod. Eng.; prob. < *rip, v.*; cf. RIPPLE], an extent of rough, broken water caused by the meeting of cross currents or tides.

rip (rip), ***n.*** [var. of *rep*, prob. abbrev. of *reprobate*], [Colloq.], 1. a dissolute, dissipated person. 2. an old, worthless horse. 3. a worthless thing.

R.I.P., [L.], 1. *Requiescat in pace*, may he (or she) rest in peace. 2. *Requiescant in pace*, may they rest in peace.

ri·par·i·an (ri-pâr′i-ən, rī-pâr′i-ən), ***adj.*** [< L. *riparius* < *ripa*, a bank; + *-an*], of, relating to, or living on the bank of a river, lake, etc.: as, fishing and other *riparian* rights belong to owners of *riparian* land.

rip cord, 1. a cord fastened to the gas bag of a balloon or dirigible so that pulling it will open the bag, releasing the gas and causing a rapid descent. 2. a cord, etc. for opening a parachute during descent.

ripe (rīp), *adj.* [ME.; AS.; akin to G. *reif;* for IE. base see RIP, *v.*], 1. *a*) ready to be harvested and used for food, as grain or fruit. *b*) fully grown or developed, as animals ready to be slaughtered for food. 2. like ripe fruit, as in being ruddy and full: as, *ripe* lips. 3. sufficiently advanced, as by being kept in storage or subjected to treatment, to be ready for use: as, *ripe* wine, *ripe* cheese. 4. fully or highly developed, as by study, experience, etc.; mature as in judgment, knowledge, etc.: as, *ripe* wisdom. 5. *a*) characterized by full physical or mental development: as, a person of *ripe* years. *b*) advanced in years: as, the *ripe* age of ninety. 6. ready to do, receive, or undergo something; fully prepared: as, *ripe* for trouble. 7. ready for some operation, treatment, or process. 8. ready to open or be lanced, as a boil. 9. sufficiently advanced; far enough along (*for* some purpose): said of time.

SYN.—**ripe,** in its basic applications, implies readiness to be harvested, eaten, used, etc. (*ripe* apples, cheese, etc.) and, in extended use, full readiness for action, etc. (*ripe* for change); **mature** implies full growth or development, as of living organisms, the mind, etc. (a *mature* tree, *mature* judgment); **mellow** suggests the qualities typical of ripe fruit, such as softness, sweetness, etc. and therefore stresses the absence of sharpness, harshness, etc. (a *mellow* flavor, mood, etc.); **adult** is applied to a person who has reached complete physical or mental maturity, or his legal majority, and to ideas, etc. that show mature thinking.—*ANT.* unripe, immature.

rip·en (rīp'ən), *v.i. & v.t.* to become or make ripe; mature.

ri·poste, ri·post (ri-pōst'), *n.* [Fr. *riposte;* It. *risposta* < *rispondere* < L. *respondere;* see RESPOND], 1. in *fencing,* a sharp, swift thrust made after parrying an opponent's lunge; hence, 2. a sharp, swift return or retort. *v.i.* [RIPOSTED (-id), RIPOSTING], to make a riposte.

rip·per (rip'ẽr), *n.* 1. a person who rips. 2. a thing that rips; device or tool for ripping. 3. a double-ripper. 4. [Chiefly British Slang], some person or thing extraordinarily good or effective of its kind.

rip·ping (rip'iŋ), *adj.* 1. that rips. 2. [Chiefly British Slang], excellent; fine; splendid.

rip·ple (rip''l), *v.i.* [RIPPLED (-'ld), RIPPLING], [Early Mod. Eng.; orig. of stormy, dangerous water; hence prob. < *rip, v.* + *-le,* freq. suffix], 1. to form or have little waves or undulating movements on the surface, as water or grass stirred by a breeze. 2. to flow with such waves or movements on the surface. 3. *a*) to make a sound like that of rippling water. *b*) to proceed with an effect like that of rippling water: said of sound. *v.t.* 1. to cause to ripple. 2. to give a wavy or undulating form or appearance to. *n.* 1. a small wave or undulation, as on the surface of water. 2. a movement, appearance, or formation resembling or suggesting this. 3. a sound like that of rippling water. 4. a small rapid. —*SYN.* see **wave.**

rip·ple (rip''l), *v.t.* [RIPPLED (-'ld), RIPPLING], [ME. **rypelen* (inferred < *rypelinge*) < MLG. or MD.; cf. MD. *repelen,* Fris. *ripelje,* etc.; IE. base prob. as in *reap, rip*], to remove the seeds from (flax, etc.) with a toothed implement resembling a comb. *n.* [prob. < the *v.;* akin to MLG. *repel,* Fris. *ripel,* flax comb], such an implement.

ripple mark, any of the ripply lines on the surface of sand, mud, etc. caused by waves, wind, or both.

rip·plet (rip'lit), *n.* a little ripple.

rip·ply (rip'li), *adj.* [RIPPLIER (-li-ẽr), RIPPLIEST (-li-ist)], characterized by ripples; rippling.

rip·rap (rip'rap'), *n.* [redupl. echoism formed on *rap* with usual vowel dissimilation], 1. a foundation or wall made of broken stones thrown together irregularly or loosely, as in water or on a soft bottom. 2. stones used for this. *v.t.* [RIPRAPPED (-rapt'), RIPRAPPING], to make a riprap in or on; strengthen with riprap.

rip-roar·ing (rip'rôr'iŋ, rip'rōr'iŋ), *adj.* [Slang], very lively and noisy; boisterous; uproarious.

rip·saw (rip'sô'), *n.* [*rip, v.* + *saw*], a saw with coarse teeth, for cutting wood along the grain.

rip·snort·er (rip'snôr'tẽr), *n.* [Slang], 1. a very noisy, violent person or thing, as a violent storm. 2. a very striking or remarkable person or thing.

rip·tide (rip'tīd'), *n.* [see RIP (rough water)], a tide opposing another tide or other tides, thus producing a violently disturbed area of water.

Rip·u·ar·i·an (rip'ū-âr'i-ən), *adj.* [< ML. *ripuarius* (prob. < L. *ripa,* river bank); + *-an*], designating or of a group of Franks who settled along the Rhine near Cologne in the 4th century A.D. *n.* a Ripuarian Frank.

Rip van Win·kle (rip' van wiŋ'k'l), the main character of a story of the same name by Washington Irving, published in the *Sketch Book* in 1819: Rip sleeps in the Catskill Mountains for twenty years and finds everything changed when he wakes.

rise (rīz), *v.i.* [ROSE (rōz), RISEN (riz''n), RISING], [ME. *risen;* AS. *risan;* G. *reisen* (of the sun); IE. base **er-,* to set in motion, etc., in extension **erei-s*], I. *to get up* 1. to stand or assume a vertical or more nearly vertical position, after sitting, kneeling, or lying. 2. to get up after sleeping or resting. 3. to return to life after dying: as, he *rose* from the grave. 4. to rebel; revolt: as, the people *rose* against the king. 5. to end an official assembly or meeting; adjourn: as, the legislature *rose* for vacation. II. *to go up* 1. to go to a higher place or position; ascend. 2. to appear above the horizon: as, the moon *rose.* 3. to attain greater height or a higher level: as, the river *rose* rapidly. 4. to ascend or advance in social status, rank, importance, etc.; become rich, famous, successful, etc. 5. to become erect or rigid. 6. to make an elevation; extend upward: as, the building *rose* high above the trees. 7. to have an upward incline or slant: as, the hills *rise* steeply. 8. to swim to the surface of the water in order to take a fly, bait, etc.: said of a fish. 9. to go up in pitch (of sound). III. *to increase in some way* 1. to increase in amount, degree, quantity, price, etc. 2. to increase in volume (of sound); become louder. 3. to become stronger, more vivid, more buoyant, etc.: as, his spirits *rose.* 4. to become larger and puffier, as dough containing yeast. IV. *to appear by or as by rising* 1. to protrude; stick out; stand out. 2. to originate, begin, or spring up. 3. to have a source: said of a stream. 4. to happen; occur. 5. to become apparent to the eye or mind: as, land *rose* ahead of the ship, doubts *rose* to disturb him. 6. to become apparent to the ear or nose. 7. to be built: as, a house is *rising* on the hill. *v.t.* 1. to cause to rise, as birds from cover or a fish to the surface of the water. 2. in *nautical usage,* to cause to appear above the horizon by coming nearer. *n.* 1. the appearance of the sun, moon, etc. above the horizon. 2. upward motion; ascent. 3. an ascent or advance in social status, rank, importance, etc. 4. the appearance of a fish at the water's surface. 5. a return to life. 6. a piece of high or rising ground; hill. 7. a slope upward. 8. the vertical height of something, as of a flight of stairs or a single step. 9. an increase in height, as of water level. 10. an increase in volume or pitch of a sound. 11. an increase in degree, amount, price, value, etc. 12. a beginning, origin, springing up, etc. 13. [British], a raise (in wages, etc.).

get a rise out of, [Slang], to draw a desired response or retort from by teasing or provoking.

give rise to, to cause to appear or come into existence.

rise to, to show oneself capable of coping with: as, he *rose to* the occasion.

SYN.—**rise** and **arise** both imply a coming into being, action, notice, etc., but **rise** carries an added implication of ascent (empires *rise* and fall) and **arise** is often used to indicate a causal relationship (accidents *arise* from carelessness); **spring** implies sudden emergence (weeds *sprang* up in the garden); **originate** is used in indicating a definite source, beginning, or prime cause (psychoanalysis *originated* with Freud); **derive** implies a proceeding or developing from something else that is the source (this word *derives* from the Latin); **flow** suggests a streaming from a source like water ("Praise God, from whom all blessings *flow*"); **issue** suggests emergence through an outlet (not a word *issued* from his lips); **emanate** implies the flowing forth from a source of something that is nonmaterial or intangible (rays of light *emanating* from the sun); **stem** implies outgrowth as from a root or a main stalk (modern detective fiction *stems* from Poe).

ris·er (rīz'ẽr), *n.* 1. a person or thing that rises. 2. any of the vertical pieces between the steps in a stairway.

ris·i·bil·i·ty (riz'ə-bil'ə-ti), *n.* [*pl.* RISIBILITIES (-tiz)], 1. the quality or state of being risible; ability or inclination to laugh. 2. *usually pl.* a sense of the ridiculous or amusing; appreciation of what is laughable.

ris·i·ble (riz'ə-b'l), *adj.* [Fr.; LL. *risibilis* < L. *risus,* pp. of *ridere,* to laugh], 1. able or inclined to laugh. 2. of or connected with laughter. 3. causing laughter; laughable; funny; amusing; ludicrous.

ris·ing (rīz'iŋ), *adj.* 1. that rises; going up, ascending, mounting, advancing, sloping upward, etc. 2. advancing to adult years; growing; maturing: as, the *rising* generation. *prep.* 1. [Colloq.], somewhat over, or more than. 2. [Dial.], approaching; nearing: as, he was *rising* fifty. *n.* 1. the act or process of a person or thing that rises; especially, an uprising; revolt; insurrection. 2. something that rises; specifically, *a*) a projection or prominence. *b*) [Dial.], a morbid swelling; boil; abscess, etc.

risk (risk), *n.* [Fr. *risque;* It. *risco, risico,* earlier *risigo* (Sp. *riesgo*)], 1. the chance of injury, damage, or loss; dangerous chance; hazard. 2. in *insurance, a*) the chance of loss. *b*) the degree of probability of loss. *c*) the amount of possible loss to the insuring company: in full, **amount at risk.** *d*) a person or thing with reference to the risk involved in insuring him or it. *e*) the type of loss that a policy covers, as life, fire, etc. *v.t.* [Fr. *risquer* < the *n.*], 1. to expose to the

chance of injury, damage, or loss; hazard: as, we *risked* our lives. 2. to incur the risk of; take the chance of: as, he *risked* a fight. —*SYN.* see **danger.**
run (or **take**) **a risk,** to expose oneself to the chance of injury or loss; endanger oneself; take a chance.

risk·y (ris′ki), *adj.* [RISKIER (-ki-ẽr), RISKIEST (-ki-ist)], involving risk; hazardous; dangerous.

‡Ri·sor·gi·men·to (rē-sôr′jē-men′tô), *n.* [It., lit., resurrection], the period of or movement for liberation, reform, and unification of Italy from the latter part of the 18th century to c. 1870.

‡ri·sot·to (rē-sôt′tô), *n.* [It. < *riso*, rice], rice cooked with gravy, grated cheese, etc.

ris·qué (ris-kā′; Fr. rēs′kā′), *adj.* [Fr., pp. of *risquer*, to risk; see RISK], very close to being improper or indecent; daring; suggestive: as, a *risqué* anecdote.

ris·sole (ris′ōl; Fr. rē′sôl′), *n.* [Fr.; ult. < LL. *russeolus*, reddish < L. *russus*, red], a small ball or roll of minced meat or fish mixed with bread crumbs, egg, etc., enclosed in a thin pastry and fried.

Ri·ta (rē′tə), [It.], a feminine name.

ri·tar·dan·do (rē′tär-dän′dō, rē′tär-dan′dō), *adj.* [It., gerund of *ritardare*, to delay; see RETARD], in *music*, becoming gradually slower: a direction to the performer: abbreviated **rit., ritard.**

rite (rīt), *n.* [ME.; L. *ritus*], 1. a ceremonial or formal, solemn act, observance, or procedure in accordance with prescribed rule or custom, as in religious use. 2. any formal, customary observance or procedure: as, the *rites* of courtship. 3. *a)* a prescribed form or particular system of ceremonial procedure, religious or otherwise; ritual: as, the Scottish *rite*. *b)* [often R-], liturgy; especially, any of the historical forms of the Eucharistic service: as, the Anglican *rite*. 4. [often R-], a division of (Eastern and Western) churches according to the liturgy used; specifically, a patriarchate. —*SYN.* see **ceremony.**

rit·u·al (rich′ōō-əl), *adj.* [L. *ritualis*], of, having the nature of, or done as a rite or rites: as, *ritual* dances. *n.* 1. a set form or system of rites, religious or otherwise. 2. the observance of set forms or rites, as in public worship. 3. a book containing rites or ceremonial forms. 4. a ritual service or procedure. 5. ritual acts or procedures collectively. —*SYN.* see **ceremony.**

rit·u·al·ism (rich′ōō-əl-iz′m), *n.* 1. the observance or use of, insistence on, or devotion to ritual. 2. the study of religious ritual.

rit·u·al·ist (rich′ōō-əl-ist), *n.* 1. a student of or expert in matters of ritual. 2. a person who practices or advocates ritualism. *adj.* ritualistic.

rit·u·al·is·tic (rich′ōō-ə-lis′tik), *adj.* 1. of ritual or ritualism. 2. devoted to or practicing ritual.

rit·u·al·is·ti·cal·ly (rich′ōō-ə-lis′ti-k′l-i, rich′ōō-ə-lis′-tik-li), *adv.* in a ritualistic manner.

rit·u·al·ly (rich′ōō-əl-i), *adv.* by or according to a ritual.

ritz·y (rit′si), *adj.* [RITZIER (-si-ẽr), RITZIEST (-si-ist)], [< the *Ritz* hotels founded by César Ritz (1850–1918), Swiss hotelkeeper], [Slang], luxurious, fashionable, elegant, etc.: often ironic.

riv·age (riv′ij), *n.* [ME.; OFr. < *rive* < L. *ripa;* see RIPARIAN & -AGE], [Archaic], a bank, coast, or shore.

ri·val (rī′v′l), *n.* [Fr.; L. *rivalis*, orig., one living near or using the same stream as another; associated in L. with *rivus*, a brook, but influenced from another (unknown) source], 1. a person who tries to get or do the same thing as another, or to equal or surpass another; competitor. 2. a person or thing that can reasonably be said to equal or surpass another in some way; person or thing that can bear comparison: as, plastics have become *rivals* of many metals. 3. [Obs.], an associate or companion in some duty. *adj.* acting as a rival; competing. *v.t.* [RIVALED or RIVALLED (-v′ld), RIVALING or RIVALLING], 1. to try to equal or surpass. 2. to equal in some way; be a match for: as, he *rivaled* his father in intelligence. *v.i.* [Archaic], to be a rival or rivals; compete (*with*).

ri·val·ry (rī′v′l-ri), *n.* [*pl.* RIVALRIES (-riz)], act of rivaling or fact or condition of being a rival or rivals; competition; emulation. —*SYN.* see **competition.**

rive (rīv), *v.t.* [RIVED (rīvd), RIVED or RIVEN (riv′′n), RIVING], [ME. *riven;* ON. *rifa;* IE. base **rei-*, to tear; cf. RIFT, REAP], 1. to tear apart; rend. 2. to split; cleave. 3. to break or dismay (the heart, spirit, etc.). *v.i.* to be or become rived.

riv·en (riv′′n), alternative past participle of **rive.** *adj.* torn apart or split.

riv·er (riv′ẽr), *n.* [ME. *rivere;* OFr. *riviere;* LL. *riparia* < L. *riparius;* see RIPARIAN; for IE. base see RIVE, etc.], 1. a natural stream of water larger than a creek and emptying into an ocean, a lake, or another river: abbreviated **R., r., riv.** 2. any similar or plentiful stream or flow: as, a *river* of lava.
sell down the river, to betray, deceive, abuse, etc.: from the former selling of Negro slaves into harsh servitude on the plantations of the lower Mississippi.
up the river, [Slang], (sent) to or confined in a penitentiary: from the sending of convicts up the Hudson river from New York to Sing Sing.

riv·er (riv′ẽr), *n.* a person or thing that rives.

Ri·ve·ra, Die·go (dye′gô rē-ve′rä), 1886–1957; Mexican painter, known especially for murals.

Rivera, Miguel Primo de, see **Primo de Rivera, Miguel.**

river basin, the area drained by a river and its tributaries.

riv·er·head (riv′ẽr-hed′), *n.* the source of a river.

river horse, a hippopotamus.

riv·er·ine (riv′ẽr-in′, riv′ẽr-in), *adj.* 1. on or near the banks of a river; riparian. 2. of, like, or produced by a river or rivers.

Riv·ers, William Halse (hôls riv′ẽrz), 1864–1922; English anthropologist and physiologist.

Riv·er·side (riv′ẽr-sīd′), *n.* a city in southern California: pop., 84,000.

riv·er·side (riv′ẽr-sīd′), *n.* the bank of a river. *adj.* on or near the bank of a river.

riv·et (riv′it), *n.* [ME. *ryvette;* OFr. < *river*, to clinch; ? < LL. **ripare*, to make firm, fasten (orig., to the shore) < L. *ripa*, a bank, shore], 1. a metal bolt or pin with a head on one end, used to fasten plates or beams together by being inserted through holes: the plain end is then hammered into a head, to lock it into place. 2. a similar device used to fasten or strengthen seams, as on work clothes. *v.t.* 1. to fasten with a rivet or rivets. 2. to hammer or spread the end of (a bolt, etc.) into a head, for fastening something. 3. to fasten firmly. 4. to fix or hold (the eyes, attention, etc.) firmly.

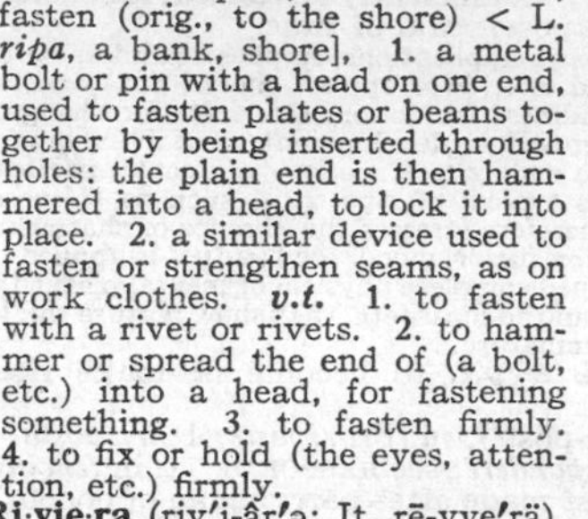

RIVET
A, rivet holding steel beams together; B, C, D, rivets

Ri·vie·ra (riv′i-âr′ə; It. rē-vye′rä), *n.* the Mediterranean coast of France and Italy, from Nice to La Spezia: a famous resort area.

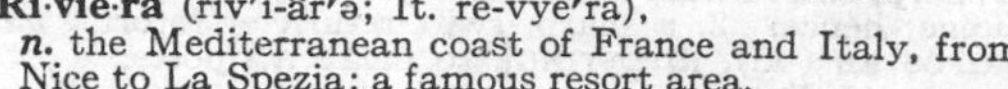

ri·vière (rē-vyer′), *n.* [Fr., lit., a stream, river], a necklace, usually in several strands, of diamonds or other precious stones.

RIVIERA

riv·u·let (riv′yoo-lit), *n.* [earlier *rivolet* < It. *rivoletto*, dim. of *rivolo*, dim. of *rivo*, a stream < L. *rivus*, a brook, stream], a little stream; brook.

rix·dol·lar (riks′dol′ẽr), *n.* [< obs. D. *rijcksdaler*, lit., dollar of the realm < *rijck*, realm (akin to G. *reich*) + *daler* (see DOLLAR); cf. RIGSDALER], formerly, in the Netherlands, Germany, Denmark, etc., any of several silver coins worth about a dollar: abbreviated **Rd., rd.**

Ri·yadh (rē-yäd′), *n.* a city in central Arabia, the capital of Nejd and one of the capitals of Saudi Arabia: pop., 150,000.

Ri·zal, Jo·sé (hô-se′ rē-säl′), 1861–1896; Filipino patriot, physician, novelist, and poet; shot for alleged conspiracy against Spain: *Rizal Day* (December 30) is observed in the Philippines in his memory.

Riz·zi·o, David (rit′si-ō′; It. rēt′tsyô), 1533?–1566; Italian musician; secretary and favorite of Mary, Queen of Scots; assassinated: also **Riccio.**

RM., r.m., reichsmark.

rm., [*pl.* RMS.], 1. ream. 2. room.

R.M.A., 1. Royal Marine Artillery. 2. Royal Military Academy. 3. Royal Military Asylum.

R.M.C., Royal Military College.

R.M.S., 1. Railway Mail Service. 2. Royal Mail Service. 3. Royal Mail Steamship.

r.m.s., root mean square.

Rn, in *chemistry*, radon.

R.N., 1. registered nurse. 2. Royal Navy.

R.N.W.M.P., Royal Northwest Mounted Police.

ro., 1. recto. 2. roan. 3. rood.

R.O., 1. Receiving Office. 2. Receiving Officer. 3. Regimental Order. 4. Royal Observatory.

roach (rōch), *n.* a cockroach.

roach (rōch), *n.* [*pl.* ROACH, ROACHES (-iz); see **PLURAL,** II, D, 2], [ME. & OFr. *roche;* prob. of Gmc. origin], 1. a fresh-water fish of the carp family, found in the rivers of northern Europe. 2. any of various similar fishes, as the American sunfish and golden shiner.

road (rōd), *n.* [ME. *rode, rade*, a riding; AS. *rad*, a ride, passing or traveling on horseback, way < *ridan*, to ride; see RIDE], 1. a way made for traveling between places, especially distant places, by automobile, horseback, etc.; highway. 2. a way; path; course: as, the *road* to fortune. 3. a railroad. 4. *often in pl.* a protected place near shore, not so enclosed as a harbor, where ships can ride at anchor; roadstead. Abbreviated **Rd., rd., R., r.**
on the road, 1. traveling, especially as a salesman. 2. on tour, as a troupe of actors.
take to the road, 1. to start traveling. 2. [Archaic], to become a highwayman.

the road, all the cities and towns generally visited by touring theatrical companies.

road agent, a highwayman, especially as on former stagecoach routes in the western United States.

road·bed (rōd′bed′), *n.* 1. *a*) the foundation laid to support the ties and rails of a railroad. *b*) a layer of crushed rock, cinders, etc. immediately under the ties. 2. the foundation and surface of a road, or highway.

road·block (rōd′blok′), *n.* 1. in *military usage*, a blockade of logs, wire, cement, etc., for holding up enemy vehicles at a point covered by heavy fire. 2. any somewhat similar blockade, often of squad cars, set up by police, as for cutting off the escape route of a fugitive from justice.

road hog, a driver who keeps his car, truck, etc. in or near the middle of the road so that it is hard or impossible for others to pass.

road·house (rōd′hous′), *n.* a tavern, inn, or, especially, night club at the side of a road in the country.

road metal, crushed rock, cinders, etc., used for making and repairing roads and roadbeds.

road runner, a long-tailed desert bird of the southwestern United States, characterized by running swiftly instead of flying; chaparral cock (or hen): it is related to the cuckoo.

road·side (rōd′sīd′), *n.* the side of a road. *adj.* on or at the side of a road.

road·stead (rōd′sted′), *n.* [*road* + *stead* (a place)], a protected place near shore, not so enclosed as a harbor, where ships can ride at anchor: also **road.**

road·ster (rōd′stẽr), *n.* 1. an open automobile with a single seat for two or three persons: many roadsters have a rumble seat as well. 2. a horse for riding or driving on the road. 3. formerly, a bicycle or tricycle for road use.

road·way (rōd′wā′), *n.* 1. a road. 2. that part of a road used by cars, trucks, etc.; traveled part of a road.

roam (rōm), *v.i.* [ME. *romen;* akin to AS. *aræman*, to rise; IE. base **erei-* < **er-*, to set in motion; cf. RISE], to travel without purpose, direction, or plan; go aimlessly; wander; rove; ramble. *v.t.* to wander over or through: as, he *roamed* the fields. *n.* a roaming; ramble.

SYN.—**roam** implies a traveling about without a fixed goal over a large area and carries suggestions of freedom, pleasure, etc. (to *roam* about the country); **ramble** implies an idle moving or walking about and connotes carelessness, aimlessness, etc. (we *rambled* through the woods); **rove** suggests extensive wandering, but it usually implies a special purpose or activity (a *roving* reporter); **range** stresses the extent of territory covered and sometimes suggests a search for something (buffalo *ranging* the plains); **stray** implies a wandering from a given place, fixed course, etc. (sheep *straying* from the fold); **meander** is used of streams, paths, etc., and, in extension, of people and animals, that follow a winding, seemingly aimless course.

roan (rōn), *adj.* [OFr.; Sp. *ruano, roano*, color of a horse having a mixture of bay and gray hairs; prob. ult. < L. *ravidus*, grayish < *ravus*, grayish-yellow, tawny], grayish-yellow or reddish-brown with a thick sprinkling of gray or white: said chiefly of horses. *n.* 1. a roan color. 2. a roan horse or other animal. Abbreviated **ro.**

roan (rōn), *n.* [MScot.; ? < *Rouen*, France], a soft, flexible sheepskin used in bookbinding, often treated to look like morocco. *adj.* made of or bound in roan.

Ro·a·noke (rō′ə-nōk′), *n.* 1. a river in Virginia and North Carolina, flowing into Albemarle Sound: length, 240 mi. 2. a city in southwestern Virginia, on this river: pop., 97,000. 3. an island off the northeastern coast of North Carolina, between Albemarle and Pamlico Sounds: Walter Raleigh tried to start a colony there (1585–1587) but failed.

roar (rôr, rōr), *v.i.* [ME. *roren, raren;* AS. *rarian;* akin to G. *rehren;* IE. echoic base **rei-*, to cry, etc., as also in Sans. *rāyati*, to bellow], 1. to utter a loud, deep sound, as in excitement, pain, anger, etc. 2. to utter a loud, deep, rumbling sound, as a lion. 3. to breathe with a loud, hoarse, rasping noise, as a horse affected with the disease called *roaring.* 4. to talk or laugh loudly and boisterously. 5. to make a loud noise in moving, operating, etc., as a motor or gun. 6. to resound with a noisy din. *v.t.* 1. to utter in or express with a loud, deep sound: as, he *roared* a welcome. 2. to make, put, force, etc. by roaring: as, the spectators *roared* themselves hoarse. *n.* 1. a loud, deep sound, as of a bull, lion, person shouting, etc.; sound of roaring. 2. a loud burst of laughter. 3. a loud noise, as of waves, a storm, a motor, etc.; din.

roar·ing (rôr′iŋ, rōr′iŋ), *n.* 1. the act of an animal, person, etc. that roars. 2. the loud, deep sound made by an animal, etc. that roars. 3. a disease of horses characterized by loud, hoarse, rasping breathing under exertion. *adj.* 1. that roars; loud; noisy. 2. [Colloq.], very active or successful; brisk: as, a *roaring* business.

roast (rōst), *v.t.* [ME. *rosten;* OFr. *rostir;* OHG. *rosten* < *rost*, gridiron, roast], 1. originally, to cook (meat, etc.) over an open fire or in hot ashes, etc. 2. to cook (meat, etc.), as in an oven, with little moisture; bake. 3. to dry, parch, or brown, as coffee, by exposure to heat. 4. to expose to great heat. 5. to heat (ore, etc.) with access of air in a furnace in order to remove impurities or cause oxidation. 6. to warm (oneself), as at a fireplace. 7. [Colloq.], to criticize severely or ridicule without mercy. *v.i.* 1. to roast meat, etc. 2. to undergo roasting; be cooked by being roasted; be baked. 3. to become very hot. *n.* 1. something roasted; especially, roasted meat or a piece of roasted meat. 2. a cut of meat for roasting. 3. a roasting or being roasted. 4. [Colloq.], a picnic, or out-of-door entertainment, at which food is roasted and eaten: as, a steak *roast.* *adj.* roasted: as, *roast* pork.

roast·er (rōs′tẽr), *n.* 1. a person or thing that roasts. 2. a special pan, oven, or apparatus for roasting meat, etc. 3. a young pig, chicken, etc. suitable for roasting.

rob (rob), *v.t.* [ROBBED (robd), ROBBING], [ME. *robben;* OFr. *rober;* OHG. *roubon;* akin to AS. *reafian;* see REAVE], 1. to take property from unlawfully by using or threatening force and violence; commit robbery upon: as, the thief *robbed* me of my money. 2. to deprive of something legally belonging or due, or take or withhold something from unjustly or injuriously, as by stealth or fraud. 3. to plunder; rifle. 4. [Rare], to take as plunder; steal. *v.i.* to commit robbery; be a robber. Cf. **steal.**

rob·a·lo (rob′ə-lō′, rō′bə-lō′), *n.* [*pl.* ROBALOS (-lōz′), ROBALO; see PLURAL, II, D, 1], [Sp. *róbalo* or Port. *robalo* < Catal. *elobarro;* ult. < L. *lupus*, a wolf], any of a family of tropical American sea fishes, especially the largest species, valued as a food fish.

rob·and (rob′ənd), *n.* [earlier *raband* & *robbin;* ult. < ON. *rābenda*, to bend a sail on a yard; *rā*, sailyard + *benda*, to bend, bind; cf. Fr. *raban*, D. *raband*], a short piece of spun yarn or rope, used to fasten the head of a sail to a yard, gaff, etc.

rob·ber (rob′ẽr), *n.* a person who robs.

robber baron, a nobleman of feudal times who robbed people traveling through his domain.

robber fly, any of a group of flies, generally large, that prey on other insects.

rob·ber·y (rob′ẽr-i), *n.* [*pl.* ROBBERIES (-iz)], [ME. & OFr. *roberie*], act or practice of robbing; specifically, in *law*, the felonious taking of another's property from his person or in his immediate presence by the use of violence or intimidation. —*SYN.* see **theft.**

Rob·bia, Lu·ca del·la (lōō′kä del′lä rôb′byä), 1400?–1482; Italian (Florentine) sculptor and worker in enameled terra cotta.

robe (rōb), *n.* [ME.; OFr., a robe, orig. booty, spoils < OHG. *roub, raub*, plunder; see ROB], 1. a long, loose, or flowing garment, especially an outer garment; specifically, *a*) such an outer garment worn on formal occasions, to show rank or office, etc., as by a judge or bishop. *b*) a bathrobe or dressing gown. *c*) a woman's dress or gown, especially an elegant or elaborate one. 2. *pl.* clothes; costume; dress; apparel. 3. a covering or wrap, as of fur, cloth, etc.: as, a lap *robe.* *v.t.* & *v.i.* [ROBED (rōbd), ROBING], to dress in a robe or robes.

‡robe de cham·bre, robe-de-cham·bre (rôb′ də shän′br′), [Fr., lit., robe of (the) chamber], a dressing gown.

Rob·ert (rob′ẽrt), [Fr.; OHG. *Hrodebert, Hruodperht, Ruprecht* < *hruod-, ruod-*, fame + *beraht, perht*, bright, gleaming], a masculine name: diminutives, *Bob, Rob, Robin;* variant, *Rupert;* feminine, *Roberta.*

Robert I, 1. ?–1035; Duke of Normandy; father of William the Conqueror: called *the Devil.* 2. 1274–1329; king of Scotland (1306–1329); won independence of Scotland from England by his victory at Bannockburn (1314): called *Robert (the) Bruce.*

Ro·ber·ta (rə-bũr′tə, rō-bũr′tə), [fem. of *Robert*], a feminine name.

Rob·erts, Elizabeth Mad·ox (mad′əks rob′ẽrts), 1886–1941; American novelist and poet.

Roberts, Frederick Sleigh (slā), Earl Roberts of Kandahar, Pretoria, and Waterford; 1832–1914; British field marshal: called *Bobs.*

Roberts, Owen Josephus, 1875–1955; American jurist; associate justice, United States Supreme Court (1930–1945).

Rob·ert·son, William (rob′ẽrt-sən), 1721–1793; Scottish historian.

Robertson, Sir **William Robert,** 1860–1933; British field marshal; chief of British general staff (1915–1918).

Robert (the) Bruce, see **Robert I.**

Robe·son, Paul (rōb′s'n, rō′bi-s'n), 1898– ; American singer and actor.

Ro·bes·pierre, Max·i·mi·lien Fran·çois Ma·rie I·si·dore de (mák′sē′mē′lyan′ frän′swá′ má′rē′ ē′zē′dôr′ də rô′bes′pyâr′; Eng. rōbz′pyer, rōbz′pêr), 1758–1794; French lawyer and revolutionist; Jacobin leader; executed: called *the Incorruptible.*

rob·in (rob′in), *n.* [< OFr. *Robin*, dim. of *Robert*], 1. a large North American thrush with a dull-red breast and belly. 2. a small European thrush with a yellowish-red breast. Also **robin redbreast.**

Robin Good·fel·low (good′fel′ō), in *English folklore,* a mischievous elf or fairy believed to play tricks on people: identified with Puck.

Robin Hood, in *English legend,* a traditional outlaw of the 12th century who lived with his followers in Sherwood Forest and robbed the rich to help the poor: he is the hero of many ballads and tales, celebrated for his courage, gaiety, courtesy, skill as an archer, etc.

rob·in's-egg blue (rob′inz-eg′), a light greenish blue.

Rob·in·son, Edwin Arlington (rob′in-s'n), 1869–1935; American poet.

Robinson, James Harvey, 1863–1936; American historian and teacher.

Robinson Cru·soe (kro͞o′sō), the hero of Daniel Defoe's novel (1719) of the same name, an English sailor who, when shipwrecked on a tropical island, manages to live for years by various ingenious contrivances until he is rescued: cf. **man Friday.**

ro·ble (rō′blā), *n.* [Sp. & Port. < L. *robur,* hard variety of oak], 1. the California white oak. 2. any of several other trees of the oak family, beech family, etc.

ro·bomb (rō′bom′), *n.* a robot bomb.

rob·o·rant (rob′ə-rənt), *adj.* [L. *roborans,* ppr. of *roborare,* to strengthen < *robur, roboris;* see ROBUST], strengthening. *n.* a roborant medicine or drug; tonic.

ro·bot (rō′bət, rob′ət), *n.* [< Czech *robotnik,* serf, or *robota,* compulsory service < *robotiti,* to drudge; akin to G. *arbeit,* work, AS. *earfoth,* hardship], 1. any of the manlike mechanical beings in Karel Čapek's play *R.U.R.* (Rossum's Universal Robots), who were built to do routine manual work for human beings; hence, 2. *a)* an automaton. *b)* a person who acts or works mechanically and without thinking for himself.

robot bomb, a small, jet-propelled airplane steered by a gyropilot and loaded with high explosives: it falls as a bomb when its fuel is used up.

robot pilot, a device that serves as an automatic pilot, as in an airplane.

Rob·son, Mount (rob′s'n), a mountain in eastern British Columbia: height, 12,972 ft.: highest peak of the Canadian Rockies.

ro·bur·ite (rō′bə-rīt′), *n.* [L. *robur,* strength; + *-ite*], a very powerful, flameless explosive containing chlorinated dinitrobenzene and ammonium nitrate.

ro·bust (rō-bust′, rō′bust), *adj.* [L. *robustus,* oaken, hard, strong < *robur,* hard variety of oak, hardness, strength], 1. *a)* strong and healthy; full of vigor; hardy. *b)* strongly built; muscular; sturdy. 2. suited to or requiring physical strength or stamina: as, *robust* work. 3. rough; coarse; boisterous.—*SYN.* see **healthy.**

ro·bus·tious (rō-bus′chəs), *adj.* [see ROBUST], [Archaic or Humorous], 1. strong; sturdy; stout. 2. rough; rude; coarse; boisterous.

roc (rok), *n.* [Ar. *rukhkh;* Per. *rukh*], in *Arabian & Persian legend,* a fabulous bird of prey, so huge and strong that it could carry off the largest of animals.

Ro·ca, Cape (rô′kä), a cape in Portugal, near Lisbon: it is the westernmost point of continental Europe.

roc·am·bole (rok′əm-bōl′), *n.* [Fr. < G. *rockenbolle; rocken,* rye + *bolle,* bulb], a European leek, a plant used like garlic for seasoning.

Ro·cham·beau, Comte **de** (də rô′shän′bō′), (*Jean Baptiste Donatien de Vimeur*), 1725–1807; French general and marshal; commanded French forces against the British in the American Revolutionary War.

Roch·dale (roch′dāl), *n.* a city in Lancashire, western England: pop., 85,000: one of the earliest English co-operative stores was established there in 1844.

Rochdale principles, principles for the operation of a consumers' co-operative store, as formulated in Rochdale, England: they include selling for cash at current market prices, distribution of profits among members, and democratic control.

Ro·chelle powder (rō-shel′), Seidlitz powder.

Rochelle salt, [after *Rochelle,* France], a colorless, crystalline compound, potassium sodium tartrate, $KNaC_4H_4O_6 \cdot 4H_2O$, used as a laxative.

‡**roche mou·ton·née** (rôsh′ mo͞o′tô′nā′), [Fr., lit., sheep-shaped rock], a rock worn into a smooth, rounded form by glacial action.

Roch·es·ter (ro′ches′tẽr; roch′is-tẽr), *n.* 1. a city in western New York: pop., 319,000. 2. a city in southeastern Minnesota: pop., 41,000. 3. a city in northern Kent, England: pop., 44,000.

roch·et (roch′it), *n.* [ME.; OFr. < *roc,* a cloak; MHG. *roc;* OHG. *hroc, roch;* cf. FROCK], a vestment of lawn or linen, like a surplice, worn by bishops and some other church dignitaries.

rock (rok), *n.* [ME. *rokke, roche;* OFr. *roche;* cf. AS. *-rocc,* ML. *rocca*], 1. a large mass of stone forming a peak or cliff. 2. *a)* stone in the mass. *b)* broken pieces of such stone. 3. *a)* mineral matter variously composed, formed in masses or large quantities in the earth's crust by the action of heat, water, etc. *b)* a particular kind or mass of this. 4. anything like or suggesting a rock, as in strength or stability; especially, a firm support, basis, refuge, etc. 5. the rockfish. 6. the rock dove. 7. [Chiefly British], a type of hard candy. 8. [Colloq. or Dial.], a stone, whether large or small. 9. [Slang], *a) usually in pl.* a piece of money. *b)* a diamond or other gem.

on the rocks, [Colloq.], 1. in or into a condition of ruin or catastrophe. 2. without money; bankrupt. 3. served unmixed over ice cubes, as whisky.

rock (rok), *v.t.* [ME. *rocken;* AS. *roccian;* prob. akin to G. *rücken,* to pull, push; IE. base **req-*, pole, to push with a pole], 1. to move or sway back and forth or from side to side, especially in a gentle, quieting manner, as a cradle, or a child in the arms; hence, 2. to bring into a specified condition by moving or swaying in this way: as, she *rocked* the baby asleep: also used figuratively, as *rocked* into a false sense of security. 3. to move or sway strongly; shake; cause to tremble or vibrate: as, the explosion *rocked* the house. 4. in *mezzotint engraving,* to prepare the surface of (a plate) by roughening with a rocker (sense 5). 5. in *mining,* to wash (sand or gravel) in a rocker (sense 4). *v.i.* 1. to move or sway back and forth or from side to side in or as in a cradle. 2. to move or sway strongly; shake; vibrate. 3. to be rocked, as ore. *n.* 1. the act of rocking. 2. a rocking motion.

rock-and-roll, rock 'n' roll (rok″n-rōl′), *n.* 1. a kind of commercial jazz music based on the blues and characterized by strong, regular beat. 2. a lively dance performed to this music.

rock·a·way (rok′ə-wā′), *n.* [< *Rockaway,* N.J., where formerly made], a light horse-drawn carriage with four wheels, open sides, and a standing top.

rock bass, a fresh-water food fish of the sunfish family, found in eastern North America.

rock-bot·tom (rok′bot′əm), *adj.* at rock bottom; lowest possible.

rock bottom, the lowest level; very bottom.

rock-bound (rok′bound′), *adj.* surrounded or hemmed in by rocks: as, a *rock-bound* inlet.

rock brake, any of several kinds of fern; especially, the parsley fern.

rock candy, large, hard, clear crystals of sugar.

rock cod, a small cod found around rocks; kind of rockfish.

rock crystal, a transparent quartz, especially when colorless.

rock dove, the European wild pigeon: also **rock pigeon.**

Rock·e·fel·ler, John Da·vi·son (dā′vi-s'n rok′ə-fel′ẽr), 1. 1839–1937; American capitalist and philanthropist. 2. 1874–1960; his son; American capitalist and philanthropist.

rock·er (rok′ẽr), *n.* 1. a person who rocks, as a cradle. 2. either of the curved pieces on the bottom of a cradle, rocking chair, etc. 3. a rocking chair. 4. a cradle for washing sand or gravel in gold mining. 5. a device consisting of a small steel plate with a toothed and curved edge, for roughening and thus preparing the surface of a plate to be engraved. 6. a skate with a curved blade.

rocker arm, an armlike piece attached to a rockshaft.

rock·er·y (rok′ẽr-i), *n.* [*pl.* ROCKERIES (-iz)], rocks and soil arranged for growing plants; rock garden.

rock·et (rok′it), *n.* [It. *rocchetta,* a spool or bobbin, rocket, orig. dim. of *rocca,* a distaff; OHG. *roccho,* a distaff: from the resemblance in shape], a projectile consisting of a cylinder filled with a combustible substance which when ignited produces gases that escape through a vent in the rear and drive their container forward by the principle of reaction: some rockets are made to burst in the air with a shower of sparks or stars and are used as fireworks or signals; others are used as weapons: cf. **jet propulsion.** *v.i.* 1. to go like a rocket; dart ahead swiftly. 2. to fly swiftly and almost straight up when flushed: said of game birds.

V-2 ROCKET BOMB AND DIAGRAM

rock·et (rok′it), *n.* [Fr. *roquette;* Pr. *rouqueto,* dim., ult. < L. *eruca,* kind of colewort], 1. a European plant grown like spinach and used in salads: also **rocket salad.** 2. any of a number of related ornamental plants with white, pink, yellow, or purple flowers. 3. a weed found in some parts of the United States.

rocket gun, any weapon that launches a rocket projectile; especially, a bazooka.

rocket launcher, a device for launching rockets; specifically, in *military usage,* a bazooka.

Rock fever, [< the *Rock* of Gibraltar, where the disease is prevalent], undulant fever.

rock·fish (rok′fish′), *n.* [*pl.* ROCKFISH, ROCKFISHES (-iz); see FISH], any of various fishes that stay among rocks offshore or in rocky beds; specifically, *a)* the striped bass. *b)* any of various food fishes of the North Pacific.

as the rock cod. *c)* any of several groupers of the waters around Bermuda, Florida, etc.

Rock·ford (rok′fẽrd), *n.* a city in northern Illinois: pop., 127,000.

rock garden, a garden with flowers and plants growing on rocky ground or among rocks variously arranged.

Rock·ies (rok′iz), *n.pl.* the Rocky Mountains.

rock·i·ness (rok′i-nis), *n.* a rocky quality or state.

rocking chair, a chair mounted on rockers or springs, so as to allow a rocking movement.

rocking horse, a toy horse of wood, etc., set on rockers or springs, and big enough for a child to ride.

Rock Island, a city in northwestern Illinois, on the Mississippi River: pop., 52,000.

Rock·ne, Knute (no͞ot rok′ni), 1888–1931; American football coach, born in Norway.

rock oil, [Chiefly British], petroleum.

rock pigeon, the rock dove.

rock rabbit, a hyrax.

rock-ribbed (rok′ribd′), *adj.* 1. having rocky ridges or elevations: as, *rock-ribbed* coasts; hence, 2. firm; rigid; unyielding: as, a *rock-ribbed* policy.

rock·rose (rok′rōz′), *n.* 1. any of a number of related plants with large, roselike flowers of white, purple, or red. 2. the flower of any of these plants.

rock salt, common salt (sodium chloride) occurring in solid form, especially in rocklike masses.

rock·shaft (rok′shaft′, rok′shäft′), *n.* a machine shaft designed to rock back and forth on its journals rather than to revolve.

rock·weed (rok′wēd′), *n.* any of a number of seaweeds that grow on rocks.

rock wool, a fibrous material that looks like spun glass, made from molten rock or slag by passing a blast of steam through the fluid; mineral wool: it is used for insulation, especially in buildings.

rock·y (rok′i), *adj.* [ROCKIER (-i-ẽr), ROCKIEST (-i-ist)], 1. full of or containing rocks. 2. consisting of rock. 3. like or suggesting a rock; specifically, *a)* firm; stable. *b)* hard; unfeeling: as, a *rocky* heart.

rock·y (rok′i), *adj.* [ROCKIER (-i-ẽr), ROCKIEST (-i-ist)], 1. inclined to rock, or sway; unsteady; shaky. 2. [Slang], weak and dizzy, as from dissipation.

Rocky Mount, a city in eastern North Carolina: pop., 32,000.

Rocky Mountain goat, a white, goatlike antelope of the mountains of northwestern North America, with a thick, shaggy coat and a pair of black horns.

Rocky Mountain National Park, a national park in north central Colorado, including Longs Peak and other snow-covered mountains: area, 405 sq. mi.

Rocky Mountains, a mountain system in western North America, extending from New Mexico to Alaska: highest peaks, Mt. McKinley (in Alaska), 20,300 ft. and Mt. Elbert (in Colorado), 14,431 ft.: also called *Rockies, Great Divide.*

Rocky Mountain sheep, the bighorn.

Rocky Mountain spotted fever, an acute infectious disease caused by Rickettsia transmitted by ticks, and characterized by fever, muscular pains, and skin eruptions: first discovered in the Rocky Mountains, it is also endemic in other parts of the United States.

ro·co·co (rə-kō′kō; *occas.* rō′kə-kō′), *n.* [Fr. < *rocaille,* rockwork, shellwork < *roc* (OFr. *roche*), a rock], 1. a style of architecture and decoration developed in France from the baroque and characterized primarily by elaborate and profuse ornamentation imitating foliage, rockwork, shellwork, scrolls, etc., often done with much delicacy and refinement: it was popular especially in the first half of the 18th century. 2. a style of literature, etc. regarded, often disparagingly, as like this. ***adj.*** 1. of or in rococo. 2. too profuse and elaborate in ornamentation; florid and tasteless.

rod (rod), *n.* [ME. *rodde;* akin to *rode* (see ROOD); Late AS. *rodd*], 1. a straight, slender shoot or stem cut from, or still part of, a bush or tree; hence, 2. in Biblical use, an offshoot or branch of a family or tribe; stock or race: as, the *rod* of Isaiah. 3. any straight, or almost straight, stick, shaft, bar, staff, etc., of wood, metal, or other material. 4. *a)* a stick or switch, or a bundle of sticks or switches, for whipping or beating as punishment; hence, *b)* punishment; chastisement. 5. *a)* a staff, wand, scepter, etc. carried as a symbol of office, rank, power, etc.; hence, *b)* power; authority; often, tyrannical rule. 6. a pole for fishing or angling. 7. a stick used to measure something. 8. *a)* a measure of length equal to 16 1/2 feet, or 5 1/2 yards: also called *perch, pole.* *b)* a square perch, or pole; 30 1/4 square yards. 9. [Slang], a pistol or revolver. 10. in *anatomy,* any of the rod-shaped cells in the retina of the eye that are sensitive to dim light. 11. in *bacteriology,* any microorganism shaped like a rod: see **bacteria,** illus. Abbreviated **rd., Rd., r.**

spare the rod, to refrain from punishing.

rode (rōd), past tense and archaic past participle of **ride.**

ro·dent (rō′d'nt), ***adj.*** [L. *rodens,* ppr. of *rodere,* to gnaw], 1. gnawing. 2. of or like a rodent or the rodents. ***n.*** any of several mammals, as rats, mice, rabbits, squirrels, beavers, etc., characterized by constantly growing incisors adapted for gnawing or nibbling; especially, in popular usage, a rat or mouse.

ro·de·o (rō′di-ō′; ***esp. in the western U.S.***, rō-dā′ō), ***n.*** [*pl.* RODEOS (-ōz′, -ōz)], [Sp., a going around, cattle ring < *rodear,* to go around, surround; L. *rotare;* see ROTATE], 1. a roundup of cattle; hence, 2. a place for enclosing cattle that have been rounded up. 3. an exhibition or competition of the skills of cowboys, as horsemanship, lassoing, etc., for public entertainment.

Rod·er·ic, Rod·er·ick (rod′ə-rik, rod′rik), [ML. *Rodericus;* OHG. *Hrodrich, Ruodrich* < *hruod-, ruod-,* fame + Gmc. **rik-,* a king], a masculine name.

Ro·di (rô′dē), *n.* Rhodes: the Italian name.

Ro·din, Au·guste (ô′güst′ rô′da*n*′; Eng. rō-dan′), 1840–1917; French sculptor.

rod·man (rod′mən), *n.* [*pl.* RODMEN (-mən)], a person who carries or works with a rod; specifically, in *surveying,* the man who carries the leveling rod.

Rod·ney (rod′ni), [< surname *Rodney* < place name *Rodney Stoke,* England], a masculine name: diminutive, *Rod.*

Rod·ney, George Brydg·es (brij′iz rod′ni), Baron Rodney, 1718–1792; British admiral.

Ro·dolph (rō′dolf), a masculine name: see **Rudolph.**

rod·o·mon·tade (rod′ə-mon-tād′, rod′ə-mon-täd′), *n.* [Fr.; It. *rodomontata* < *Rodomonte,* boastful leader of the Saracens, in Ariosto's *Orlando Furioso,*] arrogant boasting, vainglorious bragging, or blustering, ranting talk. ***adj.*** arrogantly boastful or bragging. ***v.i.*** [RODOMONTADED (-id), RODOMONTADING], to boast; brag.

roe (rō), *n.* [dial. also *roan;* ME. *rowne;* prob. < ON. *hrogn* (akin to G. *rogen*); the prevailing form seems to be a new formation on the supposition that ME. *rowne* was an *-n* pl., but traces of a *rowe, roge* (akin to MD. *roge,* OHG. *rogo,* etc.) are found in ME.], 1. fish eggs, especially when still massed in the ovarian membrane: called *hard roe.* 2. fish sperm; milt: called *soft roe.* 3. the spawn of certain crustaceans, as the coral of the lobster.

roe (rō), *n.* [*pl.* ROE, ROES (rōz); see PLURAL, II, D, 2], [ME. *ro;* AS. *ra, raha;* akin to G. *reh* (OHG. *rēho*); IE. **roi-ko* < base **rei-, *roi-,* striped, spotted, seen also in Sans. *riçya-,* antelope], a small, agile, graceful European and Asiatic deer: also **roe deer.**

roe·buck (rō′buk′), *n.* [*pl.* ROEBUCKS (-buks′), ROEBUCK, see PLURAL, II, D, 1], the male of the roe (deer).

roent·gen (rent′gən), *n.* [after W. K. *Roentgen*], the unit used in measuring radiation, as of X rays.

Roent·gen, Wil·helm Kon·rad (vil′helm kôn′rät ront′gən; Eng. rent′gən), 1845–1923; German physicist; discoverer of X rays; received Nobel prize in physics, 1901: also spelled **Röntgen.**

roent·gen·ize (rent′gə-nīz′), *v.t.* [ROENTGENIZED (-nīzd′), ROENTGENIZING], to subject to the action of X rays.

roent·gen·o- (rent′gən-ō, rent′gən-ə), a combining form meaning *Roentgen rays, X rays,* as in *roentgenology.*

roent·gen·o·gram (rent′gən-ō-gram′), *n.* [*roentgeno-* + *-gram*], a photograph taken with X rays.

roent·gen·og·ra·phy (rent′gən-og′rə-fi), *n.* photography by the use of X rays.

roent·gen·ol·o·gy (rent′gə-nol′ə-ji), *n.* [*roentgeno-* + *-logy*], the study and use of X rays, especially in connection with the diagnosis and treatment of disease.

roent·gen·o·ther·a·py (rent′gən-ō-ther′ə-pi), *n.* [*roentgeno-* + *therapy*], the treatment of disease by means of X rays.

Roentgen rays, [also r-], X rays.

ro·ga·tion (rō-gā′shən), *n.* [ME. *rogacioun* < OFr. or L.; OFr. *rogation;* L. *rogatio* < *rogare,* to ask], 1. *usually in pl.* a prayer or supplication, especially as chanted in church ceremonies during Rogation days. 2. in ancient Rome, *a)* a consul's or tribune's proposal of a law to be passed or rejected by the people. *b)* such a proposed law.

Rogation days, the three days before Ascension Day, during which supplications were chanted.

ro·ga·to·ry (rog′ə-tôr′i, rog′ə-tō′ri), ***adj.*** [< L. *rogatus,* pp. of *rogare,* to ask; + *-ory*], questioning or appointed to question for facts, as at law.

Rog·er (roj′ẽr), [< AS. *Hrothgar* & (via. Fr.) cognate OHG. *Hrodger, Rothger* < *hruod-, ruod-,* fame + **ger,* spear], a masculine name. ***interj.*** [< conventional name of international signal flag for *R*], [also r-], 1. received: term used in radiotelephony to indicate reception of a message; hence, 2. [Slang], right! O.K.!

Rog·ers, Will (roj′ẽrz), (***William Penn Adair Rogers***), 1879–1935; American humorist and actor.

rogue (rōg), *n.* [< 16th-c. thieves' slang; ? < L. *rogare,* to ask (see ROGATION)], 1. formerly, a wandering beggar or tramp; vagabond. 2. a rascal; scoundrel. 3. a fun-loving, mischievous person: used affectionately. 4. an animal, as an elephant, that wanders apart from the herd and is fierce and wild. 5. in *biology*, an individual varying markedly from the standard, especially an inferior one. *v.t.* [ROGUED (rōgd), ROGUING], 1. to cheat. 2. to destroy (plants, etc.) as biological rogues. 3. to remove such plants, etc. from (land, etc.). *v.i.* to live or act like a rogue.

ro·guer·y (rō'gə-ri), *n.* [*pl.* ROGUERIES (-riz)], the behavior or act of a rogue; specifically, *a*) trickery; cheating; fraud. *b*) playful mischief.

rogues' gallery, a collection of the photographs of criminals, as used by police in identification.

rogue's march, 1. music played in a jeering manner when a soldier is dishonorably discharged from his regiment. 2. any jeering and noisy expulsion of a person from a community, group, etc.

ro·guish (rō'gish), *adj.* of, characteristic of, or having the nature of, a rogue; specifically, *a*) dishonest; unscrupulous. *b*) fun-loving; playfully mischievous.

roil (roil), *v.t.* [Fr. *rouiller* < OFr. *rouil, roille,* rust, mud; ult. < L. *robigo,* rust], 1. to make (a liquid) cloudy, muddy, unsettled, etc. by stirring up the sediment. 2. to make angry or irritable; displease; vex.

roil·y (roi'li), *adj.* [ROILIER (-li-ẽr), ROILIEST (-li-ist)], [*roil* + *-y*], 1. turbid; muddy. 2. angry; irritable.

roist·er (rois'tẽr), *v.i.* [< earlier *roister,* loud bully; OFr. *ruistre, ruiste* < L. *rusticus;* see RUSTIC], 1. to swagger. 2. to be lively and noisy; revel boisterously.

roist·er·ous (rois'tẽr-əs), *adj.* roistering.

Ro·land (rō'lənd), [Fr.; OHG. *Hruodland, Hrodland* < *hruod-,* fame + *land, lant,* land], a masculine name: It. *Orlando:* also spelled **Rowland.** *n.* a legendary hero of the *Chanson de Roland* and other stories of the Charlemagne cycle, famous for his strength, courage, and chivalrous spirit: he was killed while fighting the Saracens at Roncesvalles in 778 A.D.

a Roland for an Oliver, one thing in full return for another; tit for tat: in allusion to a legendary five-day fight between the hero Roland and his friend Oliver, which neither won.

role, rôle (rōl), *n.* [Fr. *rôle,* lit., a roll: from roll containing actor's part], 1. a part, or character, that an actor plays in a performance; hence, 2. a function or office assumed by someone: as, an advisory *role.*

Rolf (rolf), a masculine name: see **Rudolph.**

roll (rōl), *v.i.* [ME. *rollen;* OFr. *roller, roler, rouler;* LL. **rotulare* < L. *rotula,* dim. of *rota,* a wheel; cf. ROTATE], 1. to move by turning on an axis or over and over. 2. to move or be moved on wheels. 3. to travel about; wander. 4. to pass; elapse: as, the years *rolled* by. 5. to move in a periodical revolution: said of stars, planets, etc., as, the moon *rolls* in its course. 6. to flow, as water, in a full swelling or sweeping motion: as, the waves *rolled* against the boat. 7. to extend in gentle swells. 8. to make a loud, continuous rising and falling sound: as, thunder *rolls.* 9. to rise and fall in a full, mellow cadence, as sound, speech, etc. 10. to form a ball or cylinder by turning over and over on itself or something else: as, the string *rolled* into a tight ball. 11. to turn in a circular motion: as, her eyes *rolled.* 12. to move in a rocking, swaying motion: as, the ship *rolled;* hence, 13. to walk by swaying. 14. to become flattened or spread under a roller. 15. to make progress; advance: as, now we're *rolling.* *v.t.* 1. to move by turning on an axis or over and over: as, she *rolls* a hoop. 2. to move or send on wheels or rollers. 3. to move or send in a full, sweeping motion: as, the ocean *rolls* its waves against the cliff. 4. to beat (a drum) with blows in rapid, light succession. 5. to utter with full, flowing sound: as, he *rolled* his words. 6. to pronounce or say with a trill: as, he *rolls* his r's. 7. to give a swaying motion to: as, the waves *rolled* the ship along. 8. to move gently around and around or from side to side: as, she *rolled* her eyes. 9. to make into a ball or cylinder by winding over and over itself or something else: as, he *rolled* a cigarette. 10. to wrap or enfold, as in a covering: as, she *rolled* the child in a blanket. 11. to make flat, smooth, or spread out by using a roller, rolling pin, etc. 12. to throw (the dice) as in the game of craps. 13. to iron (sleeves, etc.) without forming a crease. 14. [Slang], to rob (a drunken or helpless person). 15. in *printing,* to spread ink on, as type, a form, etc., with a roller. *n.* [ME. & OFr. *rolle;* L. *rotulus, rotula;* in some senses directly < the *v.*], 1. a rolling. 2. a paper, parchment, etc. that is rolled up; scroll. 3. a register; catalogue. 4. a list of names for checking attendance; muster roll. 5. a measure of something rolled into a cylinder: as, a *roll* of wallpaper. 6. a cylindrical mass of something: as, a sausage *roll.* 7. *a*) any of variously shaped, small cakes of bread. *b*) thin cake covered with fruit, nuts, etc. and rolled: as, a jelly *roll.* *c*) beef, veal, etc. rolled and cooked. 8. a roller. 9. a swaying or rolling motion. 10. a rapid succession of light blows on a drum. 11. a loud, reverberating sound; peal, as of thunder. 12. a full, cadenced flow of words. 13. a slight swell or rise on the surface of something, as land. 14. [Slang], money; especially, a wad of paper money. 15. in *aeronautics,* a maneuver in which an airplane in flight performs one complete rotation around its longitudinal axis. 16. in *bookbinding,* a revolving tool used in making an impression or pattern. —*SYN.* see **list.**

roll back, to reduce (prices) to a previous or standard level by government action and control.

roll in, 1. to assemble or arrive, usually in large numbers. 2. [Colloq.], to have much of; abound in.

roll out, 1. to flatten into a sheet by rolling. 2. to spread out by unrolling.

roll round, to recur, as in a cycle: as, winter *rolled round* again.

roll up, 1. to make or put into the form of a roll. 2. to wrap up by turning over and over. 3. to accumulate; increase. 4. [Colloq.], to arrive in or as if in an automobile, carriage, etc.

strike off the rolls, to expel from membership.

Rol·land, Ro·main (rô'man' rô'län'), 1866–1945; French novelist, biographer, dramatist, and music critic; received Nobel prize in literature, 1915.

roll·a·way (rōl'ə-wā'), *adj.* having rollers for easy moving and storing when not in use: as, a *rollaway* bed.

roll·back (rōl'bak'), *n.* a reduction of prices to a previous level by government action and control.

roll call, 1. the reading aloud of a roll, or list of names, as in classrooms, military formations, etc., to find out who is absent. 2. the fixed time, or a signal (as on a bugle), for such a reading.

roll·er (rōl'ẽr), *n.* 1. a person or thing that rolls (in various senses). 2. any of various rolling cylinders or wheels; specifically, *a*) a cylinder of metal, wood, etc. over which something is rolled for easier movement. *b*) a cylinder on which something is rolled up or wound: as, the *roller* of a window blind. *c*) a heavy cylinder of metal, stone, etc. used to crush or smooth something. *d*) in *printing,* a cylinder, usually of hard rubber, for spreading ink on the form just before the paper is impressed. 3. a long bandage in a roll. 4. a heavy, swelling wave that breaks on the shoreline. 5. in *ornithology,* *a*) a tumbler pigeon. *b*) a canary that rolls, or trills, its notes. *c*) a European bird, related to the kingfisher, which rolls and tumbles in flight. —*SYN.* see **wave.**

roller bearing, a bearing in which the shaft turns with rollers, generally of steel, arranged lengthwise in a ring-like track: used to reduce friction.

roller coaster, an amusement device in which small, open cars move on tracks that dip sharply up and down, make sharp turns, etc., so as to thrill the riders.

roll·er-skate (rōl'ẽr-skāt'), *v.i.* to move on roller skates.

roller skate, a skate having small wheels, usually four, instead of a runner, for use on a smooth surface.

roller towel, a long towel sewed together at the ends and suspended on a roller.

roll film, a strip of photographic film rolled on a spool for a series of consecutive exposures.

rol·lick (rol'ik), *v.i.* [prob. blend of *romp* (or *roll*) & *frolic*], to be gay, carefree, and hilarious in play; romp.

rol·lick·ing (rol'ik-iŋ), *adj.* [see prec.], carefree and gay; lively and hilarious.

rol·lick·some (rol'ik-səm), *adj.* [see -SOME], rollicking.

roll·ing (rōl'iŋ), *adj.* [ppr. of *roll*], 1. moving by turning over and over. 2. moving on wheels or rollers. 3. recurring: as, the *rolling* seasons. 4. rotating or revolving on or as on an axis. 5. moving up and down or sideways: as, *rolling* eyes. 6. folded over or back: as, a *rolling* collar. 7. swaying: as, a *rolling* walk. 8. surging up or on in strong waves: as, *rolling* smoke, *rolling* waters. 9. resounding or reverberating: as, *rolling* thunder. 10. trilled: as, a *rolling* note. 11. dipping up and down in gentle slopes: as, *rolling* land. *n.* the action, motion, or sound of something that rolls or is rolled.

rolling hitch, a knot in which one or more turns are made between two hitches: see **knot,** illus.

rolling mill, 1. a factory in which metal bars, sheets, etc. are rolled out. 2. a machine used for such rolling.

rolling pin, a heavy, smooth cylinder of wood, glass, etc. used to roll out dough.

rolling stock, locomotives, freight and passenger cars, and other wheeled railroad vehicles, collectively.

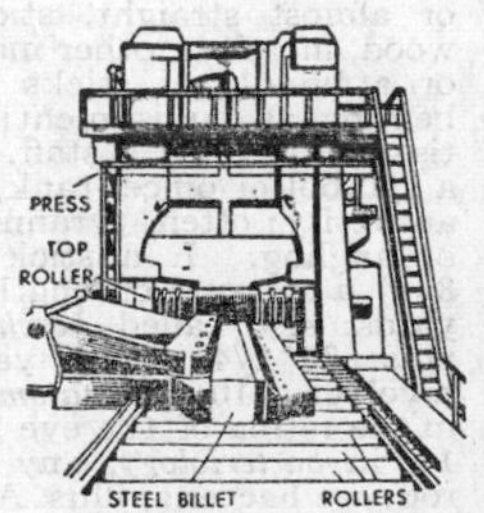

ROLLING MILL

Rol·lo (rol'ō), a masculine name: see **Rudolph.** *n.* Norse viking chieftain; first duke of Normandy; 860?–931? A.D.: also **Hrolf.**

roll-top (rōl'top'), *adj.* made with a flexible top of parallel slats that slides back, as a desk.

roll·way (rōl'wā'), *n.* 1. any place or path along which round or cylindrical objects can be rolled; specifically, a natural or artificial chute down which logs can be rolled or slid into a river, etc. for transportation.

2. a pile of logs on the bank of a river awaiting removal.

Röl·vaag, O·le Ed·vart (ō′lə ed′värt rōl′väg; Norw. röl′vôg), 1876–1931; American novelist, born in Norway.

ro·ly-po·ly (rō′li-pō′li), *adj.* [redupl. on *roll*], short and plump; pudgy; dumpy. *n.* [*pl.* ROLY-POLIES (-liz)], 1. a roly-poly person or thing; especially, such a child. 2. [Chiefly British], a kind of pudding made of rich pastry dough spread with fruit or jam, rolled up, and boiled, steamed, etc.

Rom, rom (rum), *n.* [see ROMANY], a gypsy man or boy.

Rom., 1. Roman. 2. Romance. 3. Romanic. 4. Romans (Epistle to the Romans).

rom., roman (type).

Ro·ma (rô′mä), *n.* Rome: the Italian name.

Ro·ma·ic (rō-mā′ik), *adj.* [Gr. *Rhōmaïkos*, Roman (of the Eastern empire)], 1. of modern Greece. 2. designating or of the language of modern Greece. *n.* this language; Modern Greek.

ro·maine (rō-mān′), *n.* [Fr., fem. adj., Roman], a kind of lettuce with leaves that form a long, slender head: also **romaine lettuce.**

Ro·mains, Jules (zhül rô′man′), (pseudonym of *Louis Farigoule*), 1885– ; French novelist, poet, and dramatist.

Ro·man (rō′mən), *adj.* [AS.; L. *Romanus* < *Roma*, Rome; replacing ME. *Romain* < OFr.], 1. of, characteristic of, or derived from ancient or modern Rome, its people, etc. 2. of the Roman Catholic Church, or the Latin Rite. 3. [usually r-], designating or of the style of printing types most common in modern use, upright, light-faced, and with serifs. *n.* 1. a native, citizen, or inhabitant of ancient or modern Rome. 2. the Italian spoken in Rome. 3. Latin. 4. loosely, a member of the Roman Catholic Church. 5. [usually r-], roman type or characters. Abbreviated **Rom.**, (for *n.* 5) **rom.**

‡ro·man (rô′män′), *n.* [Fr.; OFr. *Romain* (< L. *Romanus*), lit., of Rome; cf. ROMANCE], 1. a type of metrical narrative developed in France in the Middle Ages. 2. popularly, any romantic novel.

‡ro·man à clef (rô′män′ nä klā′), [Fr., lit., novel with a key], a novel in which real persons appear under fictitious names.

Roman alphabet, the alphabet used by the ancient Romans, from which most modern European alphabets are derived: it consisted of twenty-three letters (*J*, *U*, and *W* were added later).

Roman arch, a semicircular arch.

Roman architecture, the style of architecture used by the ancient Romans, characterized by the rounded arch and vault, thick, massive walls, and the use of much brick and concrete.

Roman calendar, the calendar used by the ancient Romans, from which the modern calendar is derived: it consisted originally of ten months, later twelve.

Roman candle, a kind of firework consisting of a long tube that sends out balls of fire, sparks, etc.

Roman Catholic, 1. of the Roman Catholic Church. 2. a member of the Roman Catholic Church. Abbreviated **R.C., Rom. Cath.**

Roman Catholic Church, the Christian church headed by the Pope (Bishop of Rome): abbreviated **R.C.Ch.**

Roman Catholicism, the beliefs, practices, organization, etc. of the Roman Catholic Church.

Ro·mance (rō-mans′, rō′mans), *adj.* [< obs. Fr. (*langue*) *romance*, Romance language; OFr. *romanz*; see ROMANCE (tale)], designating, of, or speaking any of the languages derived from Low Latin; Portuguese, Spanish, Catalan, Provençal, French, Rhaeto-Romanic, Italian, and Romanian. *n.* these languages.

ro·mance (rō-mans′; *also, for n.*, rō′mans), *n.* [ME.; OFr. *romans*, *romanz* < *romanz* (*escrire*), (to write) in Roman (i.e., the vernacular, not Latin); LL. *Romanice* (*scribere*) < L. *Romanicus*; see ROMANIC], 1. formerly, a long narrative in verse or prose, originally written in one of the Romance dialects, about the adventures of knights and other chivalric heroes. 2. later, a fictitious tale of wonderful and extraordinary events, characterized by much imagination and idealization. 3. a type of novel in which the emphasis is on love, adventure, etc. 4. the type of literature comprising such stories. 5. real happenings or adventures as exciting and unusual as those of such literature. 6. the quality or characteristic of excitement, love, and adventure found in such literature. 7. the tendency to derive great pleasure from romantic adventures. 8. an exaggeration or falsehood. 9. a love affair. 10. in *music*, a short, lyrical, usually sentimental piece, suggesting a love song. *v.i.* [ROMANCED (-manst′), ROMANCING], 1. to write or tell romances. 2. to be fanciful or imaginative in thinking and talking. 3. [Colloq.], to make love; court; woo. *v.t.* [Colloq.], to make love to; court.

Roman Curia, in the *Roman Catholic Church*, the papal court: see **Curia Romana.**

Roman Empire, the empire of ancient Rome, established by Augustus in 27 B.C.: it continued until 395 A.D.: see also **Eastern Roman Empire, Western Roman Empire.**

ROMAN EMPIRE

Ro·man·esque (rō′mə-nesk′), *adj.* [Fr.; It. *romanesco*, *romanzesco* < *romanzo*, a romance; OFr. *romanz*; see ROMANCE], 1. of one of the Romance languages, especially Provençal. 2. designating or of a style of European architecture of the 11th and 12th centuries, based on the Roman and characterized by the use of the round arch and vault, thick, massive walls, interior bays, etc. 3. designating or of a style of painting, sculpture, etc. corresponding to this. *n.* 1. the Romanesque style of architecture, painting, etc. 2. a Romance language.

Roman holiday, entertainment or gain acquired at the expense of others' suffering: so called from the gladiatorial contests waged as entertainment in ancient Rome.

Ro·ma·ni·a, Ro·mâ·ni·a (rô-mu′nyä; Eng. rō-mā′ni-ə, rō-mān′yə), *n.* a country in south central Europe, on the Black Sea: area, 91,669 sq. mi.; pop., 18,360,000; capital, Bucharest: also **Rumania, Roumania.**

Ro·ma·ni·an (rō-mā′ni-ən, rō-mān′yən), *adj.* of Romania, its people, their language, etc. *n.* 1. a native or inhabitant of Romania. 2. the Romance language of the Romanians. Also **Rumanian, Roumanian.**

Ro·man·ic (rō-man′ik), *adj.* [L. *Romanicus*], derived from ancient Rome or from vernacular Latin. *n.* in *linguistics*, Romance. Abbreviated **Rom.**

Ro·man·ism (rō′mən-iz′m), *n.* 1. Roman Catholicism: hostile usage. 2. the spirit and influence of ancient Rome.

Ro·man·ist (rō′mən-ist), *n.* [Mod. L. *Romanista*], 1. a Roman Catholic: hostile usage. 2. a person who studies or is expert in Roman law, antiquities, etc.

Ro·man·i·za·tion (rō′mən-i-zā′shən, rō′mən-ī-zā′shən), *n.* a Romanizing or being Romanized.

Ro·man·ize (rō′mən-īz′), *v.t.* [ROMANIZED (-īzd′), ROMANIZING], 1. to make Roman in character, spirit, etc. 2. to make Roman Catholic or convert to Roman Catholicism. 3. to respell in the Roman alphabet. *v.i.* 1. to follow or be influenced by Roman customs, law, etc. 2. to conform or become converted to Roman Catholicism.

Roman law, the code of laws of the ancient Romans: it forms the basis for the modern legal system in many countries.

Roman nose, a nose with a high, prominent bridge.

Roman numerals, the Roman letters used as numerals until the 10th century A.D.: in Roman numerals I = 1, V = 5, X = 10, L = 50, C = 100, D = 500, and M = 1,000. Other numbers are formed from these by adding or subtracting: the value of a symbol following another of the same or greater value is added (e.g., III = 3, XV = 15); the value of a symbol preceding one of greater value is subtracted (e.g., IX = 9); and the value of a symbol standing between two of greater value is subtracted from that of the second, the remainder being added to that of the first (e.g., XIX = 19). Roman numerals are commonly written in capitals, though they may be written in lower-case letters. A bar over a letter indicates multiplication by 1,000 (e.g., $\overline{\text{V}}$ = 5,000).

Ro·ma·nov (rô-mä′nôf; Eng. rō′mə-nôf′), *n.* the Russian ruling family (1613–1917) founded by Mikhail Feodorovich Romanov: also spelled **Romanoff.**

Ro·ma·nov, Mi·kha·il Fe·o·do·ro·vich (mi-khä-ēl′ fyô′dô-rô′vich), 1596–1645; first Romanov czar of Russia (1613–1645).

Roman punch, a frozen dessert made with lemon juice, rum, etc.

Roman rite, in the *Roman Catholic Church*, 1. the customary and authentic form or use of the Latin Rite. 2. loosely, the Latin Rite.

Ro·mans (rō′mənz), *n.pl.* [construed as sing.], the Epistle to the Romans, a book of the New Testament, which was a message from the Apostle Paul to the Christians of Rome: abbreviated **Rom.**

Ro·mansh, Ro·mansch (rō-mansh′, rō-mänsh′), *n.*

[Romansh *rumansch, rumonsch* < LL. *romanice;* see ROMANCE], the language, derived from vernacular Latin, that is spoken in the Grisons or eastern part of Switzerland and in contiguous regions of the Tyrol and Italy; Ladin; Rhaeto-Romanic.

ro·man·tic (rō-man′tik), ***adj.*** [OFr. *romant* (see ROMAUNT); + *-ic:* Fr. *romantique* & G. *romantisch* are both < late 18th-c. Eng., in sense 5], 1. of, having the nature of, characteristic of, or characterized by romance. 2. without a basis in fact; fanciful, fictitious, or fabulous. 3. not practical; visionary or quixotic: as, a *romantic* scheme. 4. full of or dominated by thoughts, feelings, and attitudes characteristic of or suitable for romance: as, a *romantic* youth. 5. of, characteristic of, or supposedly characteristic of romanticism and the Romantic Movement: now often used in a derogatory sense, with implications of unrestrained sensuousness, vague imagery, lack of logical precision, escape from the realities of life, etc.; in literature, the term originally meant "suggestive of romances, Gothic": contrasted with *classical, realistic,* etc. 6. suitable for romance. ***n.*** 1. a romantic person. 2. a romanticist. 3. *pl.* romantic characteristics, thoughts, ways, etc. —***SYN.*** see **sentimental.**

ro·man·ti·cal·ly (rō-man′ti-k′l-i, rō-man′tik-li), ***adv.*** in a romantic manner.

ro·man·ti·cism (rō-man′tə-siz′m), ***n.*** 1. romantic spirit, outlook, tendency, etc. 2. *a)* the Romantic Movement. *b)* the spirit, attitudes, style, etc. of, or adherence to, the Romantic Movement or a similar movement: contrasted with *classicism, realism,* etc.

ro·man·ti·cist (rō-man′tə-sist), ***n.*** an adherent of romanticism in literature, painting, music, etc.

ro·man·ti·cize (rō-man′tə-sīz′), ***v.t.*** [ROMANTICIZED (-sīzd′), ROMANTICIZING], to treat or regard romantically; give a romantic character to or interpretation of.

Romantic Movement, the revolt in the 18th and early 19th centuries against the artistic, political, and religious principles that had become associated with neoclassicism: characterized in literature and the arts by liberalism in form and subject matter, emphasis on feeling and originality, the use of imaginative suggestion, and sympathetic interest in primitive nature, medievalism, and the mystical.

Rom·a·ny (rom′ə-ni), ***n.*** [Gypsy *romani,* fem. & pl. of *romano,* gypsy < *rom,* a man, husband, gypsy < Sans. *doma,* man of low caste], 1. [*pl.* ROMANY, ROMANIES (-niz)], a gypsy. 2. the Indic language of the gypsies, which occurs with many local modifications. ***adj.*** of the gypsies, their language, etc. Also spelled **Rommany.**

Romany rye (rī), [Gypsy *romani* (see ROMANY) + *rei, rai,* a lord < Sans. *rājan,* king; see RAJAH], a person not a gypsy who associates with the gypsies, speaks their language, etc.

ro·maunt (rō-mänt′, rō-mônt′), ***n.*** [OFr. *romant* (Fr. *roman*), var. of *romanz;* see ROMANCE], [Archaic], a romantic poem or story; romance.

Rom. Cath., Roman Catholic.

Rome (rōm), ***n.*** 1. the capital of Italy, on the Tiber River: pop., 1,702,000: formerly the capital of the Roman Republic, the Roman Empire, and the States of the Church: Italian name, *Roma.* 2. a city in central New York: pop., 52,000. 3. a city in northwestern Georgia: pop., 32,000. 4. *a)* the Roman Catholic Church. *b)* Roman Catholicism.

Ro·me·o (rō′mi-ō′), ***n.*** [It. < *Romolo* < L. *Romulus*], 1. the hero of Shakespeare's tragedy *Romeo and Juliet* (c. 1595), son of Montague and lover of Juliet, daughter of Capulet: at the death of the lovers their feuding families become reconciled; hence, 2. [*pl.* ROMEOS (-ōz′)], a lover.

Rom·ish (rōm′ish), ***adj.*** Roman Catholic: hostile usage.

Rom·ma·ny (rom′ə-ni), ***n.*** [*pl.* ROMMANY, ROMMANIES (-niz)], Romany.

Rom·mel, Er·win (er′vēn rôm′əl), **1891–1944;** German field marshal in World War II.

Rom·ney, George (rom′ni, rum′ni), 1734–1802; English painter.

romp (romp), ***n.*** [< earlier *ramp,* vulgar woman, hussy, prob. < ME. *rampen;* OFr. *ramper;* see RAMPANT], 1. a person who romps, especially a girl. 2. [< the *v.*], boisterous, lively play or frolic. 3. [Slang], an easy, winning gait in a race: as, the horse won in a *romp.* ***v.i.*** 1. to play or frolic in a boisterous, lively way. 2. [Slang], to win with ease in a race, contest, etc.: as, the horse *romped* home. —***SYN.*** see **play.**

romp·er (rom′pēr), ***n.*** 1. a person who romps. 2. *pl.* a type of loose-fitting outer garment worn by young children, combining a waist with bloomerlike pants.

romp·ish (rom′pish), ***adj.*** inclined to romp; playful and lively.

Rom·u·lus (rom′yoo-ləs), ***n.*** [L.], in *Roman mythology,* a son of Mars and founder and first king of Rome, deified as Quirinus: he and his twin brother Remus, left to die in the Tiber when they were babies, were reared by a she-wolf; later Romulus killed Remus.

Ron·ald (ron′′ld), [Scot. < ON. *Rögnvaldr;* akin to OG. *Raganald;* see REGINALD], a masculine name.

Ron·ces·valles (ron′sə-valz′; Sp. rôn′thes-vä′lyes), ***n.*** a village in the Pyrenees, in northern Spain: also **Roncevaux:** see **Roland.**

Ronce·vaux (rōns′vō′), ***n.*** Roncesvalles: French name.

ron·deau (ron′dō, ron-dō′), ***n.*** [*pl.* RONDEAUX (-dōz, -dōz′)], [Fr., earlier *rondel* < *rond,* round], 1. a short lyrical poem of thirteen (or sometimes ten) lines with only two rhymes, and an unrhymed refrain that consists of the opening words and is used in two places: also **roundel.** 2. in *music,* a rondo.

ron·del (ron′d'l, ron′del), ***n.*** [ME.; OFr.; see RONDEAU], a kind of rondeau, usually with fourteen lines, two rhymes, and the first two lines used as a refrain in the middle and at the end (the second line occasionally being omitted at the end): also **roundel.**

ron·de·let (ron′d'l-et′), ***n.*** [ME.; OFr., dim. of *rondel*], a short rondel, usually of five or seven lines in one stanza and a refrain consisting of the opening words.

ron·do (ron′dō, ron-dō′), ***n.*** [*pl.* RONDOS (-dōz, -dōz′)], [It.; Fr. *rondeau;* see RONDEAU], in *music,* a composition or movement, often the last movement of a sonata, having its principal theme stated three or more times in the same key, interposed with subordinate themes.

ron·dure (ron′jēr), ***n.*** [Fr. *rondeur;* see ROUND & -ER], [Poetic], a circle or sphere; roundness.

Ron·sard, Pierre de (pyâr də rōn′sâr′), **1524–1585;** French poet.

Röntgen, Wilhelm Konrad, see **Roentgen, Wilhelm.**

Röntgen rays, [also r-], Roentgen rays; X rays.

rood (rōōd), ***n.*** [ME. *rode;* AS. *rod,* a cross, measure; akin to G. *rute,* a rod, pole, Eng. *rod;* IE. base **rēt-, *rōt-,* a pole, thin branch; cf. ROD], 1. originally, the cross on which Jesus was crucified; hence, 2. any cross representing this; crucifix, especially a large one at the entrance to the chancel or choir of a medieval church, often supported on a rood beam or rood screen. 3. a cross as used in crucifixion. 4. in England, a measure of length varying from 5 1/2 to 8 yards, according to locality; sometimes, 1 rod. 5. a measure of area usually equal to 1/4 acre (40 square rods). Abbreviated **ro.**

rood beam, a beam across the entrance to the chancel or choir of a church, usually constituting the head of the rood screen and used to support the rood.

rood loft, a loft or gallery over a rood screen.

rood screen, an ornamental screen, usually with a rood above it, serving as a partition between the nave and the chancel or choir of a church.

roof (rōōf, roof), ***n.*** [*pl.* ROOFS (rōōfs, roofs)], [ME. *rof;* AS. *hrof;* akin to MD. *roef* (D., deckhouse, etc.); IE. base **krapo-,* roof], 1. the outside top covering of a building; hence, 2. figuratively, a house or home. 3. the top or peak of anything: as, the *roof* of the world. 4. anything like a roof in position or use: as, the *roof* of the mouth. ***v.t.*** to provide or cover with or as with a roof.

raise the roof, [Slang.], 1 to be very noisy, as in applause, anger, celebration, etc. 2. to complain loudly.

roof·er (rōōf′ēr, roof′ēr), ***n.*** a person who builds or repairs roofs.

roof garden, 1. a garden on the flat roof of a building. 2. the roof or top floor of a high building, decorated as a garden and used as a restaurant, etc.

roof·ing (rōōf′iŋ, roof′iŋ), ***n.*** 1. the act of covering with a roof. 2. material for a roof or roofs. 3. a roof.

roof·less (rōōf′lis, roof′lis), ***adj.*** 1. having no roof. 2. having no house or shelter; homeless.

roof·tree (rōōf′trē′, roof′trē′), ***n.*** 1. the large horizontal beam extending along the top of a roof; ridgepole; hence, 2. a roof. 3. a home or shelter.

rook (rook), ***n.*** [ME. *roc;* AS. *hroc;* akin to G. *ruch;* IE. echoic base **ker-, *kor-,* orig. of the bird's cry; cf. RAVEN], 1. a gregarious European crow that builds its nest in trees around buildings. 2. a swindler; cheat, especially in gambling. ***v.t. & v.i.*** [prob. from the bird's thievishness], to swindle; cheat.

rook (rook), ***n.*** [ME. & OFr. *roc;* Per. *rukh*], in *chess,* either of the two corner pieces shaped like a castle tower: it can move in a vertical or horizontal direction over any number of consecutive, unoccupied squares: abbreviated **R., r.:** also called *castle.*

rook·er·y (rook′ēr-i), ***n.*** [*pl.* ROOKERIES (-iz)], 1. a breeding place or colony of rooks. 2. a breeding place or colony of other gregarious animals or birds, as seals, penguins, etc. 3. a building or group of buildings that are old and dilapidated and house many people; tenement house or tenement district.

rook·ie (rook′i), ***n.*** [altered < *recruit*], [Slang], 1. an inexperienced recruit in the army. 2. any novice.

rook·y (rook′i), ***adj.*** full of or consisting of rooks.

room (rōōm, room), ***n.*** [ME. & AS. *rum;* akin to G. *raum;* IE. base **rewos,* wide, broad, seen also in L. *rus, ruris,* land (cf. RUSTIC, RURAL)], 1. a space that holds or can hold something: as, *room* for one more. 2. suitable scope or opportunity: as, *room* for doubt. 3. interior space enclosed by walls or separated from other similar spaces by walls or partitions. 4. *pl.* living quarters; lodgings; apartment. 5. the people gathered together in a room: as, the whole *room* was silent. 6. [Obs.], a position or office. *v.i.* to occupy living quarters; have lodgings; lodge. *v.t.* to provide with a room or lodgings. Abbreviated **rm.**

room and board, sleeping accommodations and meals.

room·er (ro͞om′ẽr, room′ẽr), *n.* a person who rents a room or rooms to live in; lodger.

room·ette (ro͞om-et′, room-et′), *n.* a small, private room in some railroad sleeping cars, furnished with a bed that folds into the wall, a toilet, washbasin, etc.

room·ful (ro͞om′fool′, room′fool′), *n.* 1. as much or as many as will fill a room. 2. the people or objects in a room, collectively.

room·i·ly (ro͞om′ə-li, room′ə-li), *adv.* with plenty of room; amply.

room·i·ness (ro͞om′i-nis, room′i-nis), *n.* the quality or state of being roomy.

rooming house, a house with furnished rooms for renting; lodging house.

room·mate (ro͞om′māt′, room′māt′), *n.* the person, or any of the persons, with whom one shares a room or rooms.

room·y (ro͞om′i, room′i), *adj.* [ROOMIER (-i-ẽr), ROOMIEST (-i-ist)], having plenty of room; spacious.

roor·back, roor·bach (roor′bak), *n.* [after the supposed author of a group of alleged selections from a (nonexistent) book, *Roorback's Tour through the Western and Southern States in 1836*, containing spurious charges against James K. Polk, then a presidential candidate], a false or slanderous story devised for political effect, especially against a candidate for election.

roose (ro͞oz; Scot. röz), *n., v.t. & v.i.* [ROOSED (ro͞ozd; Scot. rözd), ROOSING], [Scot.], praise.

Roo·se·velt, Eleanor (rō′zə-velt′, rō′zə-vəlt, rōz′velt; *by some,* ro͞o′zə-velt′), (born *Anna Eleanor Roosevelt*), 1884–1962; wife of *Franklin Delano;* United States delegate to the United Nations (1945–1953).

Roosevelt, Franklin Del·a·no (del′ə-nō′), 1882–1945; thirty-second president of the United States (1933–1945).

Roosevelt, Theodore, 1858–1919; twenty-sixth president of the United States (1901–1909).

Roosevelt Dam, a dam on the Salt River, in central Arizona: height, 284 ft.; length, 1,080 ft.

roost (ro͞ost), *n.* [ME.; AS. *hrost;* akin to MD. *roest;* IE. **krodsto* < base **qred-*, timberwork, beams, as also in Goth. *hrot,* roof], 1. a perch on which birds, especially domestic fowls, can rest or sleep. 2. a place with perches for birds; hence, 3. a place for resting, sleeping, etc. *v.i.* 1. to rest, sit, sleep, etc. on a perch. 2. to stay or settle down, as for the night.

come home to roost, to have repercussions, especially disagreeable ones; boomerang.

rule the roost, to be master.

roost·er (ro͞os′tẽr), *n.* [*roost* + *-er*], the male of the chicken; cock.

root (ro͞ot, root), *n.* [ME. & Late AS. *rote;* ON. *rot:* akin to LG. *rut;* IE. base **wrād-*, etc., branch, root, stick, as also in L. *radix* (cf. RADICAL), AS. *wyrt* (see WORT)], 1. the part of a plant, usually below the ground, that holds the plant in position, draws water and nourishment from the soil, and stores food. 2. any underground part of a plant, as a rhizome. 3. the attached or embedded part of a bodily structure, as of the teeth, hair, nails, etc. 4. the source or origin of an action, quality, etc. 5. a person or family that has many descendants; ancestor. 6. a lower or supporting part; base; hence, 7. an essential part; core: as, the *root* of the matter. 8. in *mathematics, a)* a quantity that, multiplied by itself a specified number of times, produces a given quantity: as, 4 is the square *root* (4 x 4) of 16 and the cube *root* (4 x 4 x 4) of 64. *b)* a quantity that, when substituted for an unknown quantity, will satisfy an equation. 9. in *music,* the basic tone of a chord, on which the chord is constructed; often, the fundamental. 10. in *linguistics,* a base; morpheme to which prefixes, suffixes, etc. are added. *v.i.* 1. to begin to grow by putting out roots. 2. to become fixed, settled, etc. *v.t.* 1. to fix the roots of in the ground. 2. to establish; settle. —*SYN.* see **origin.**

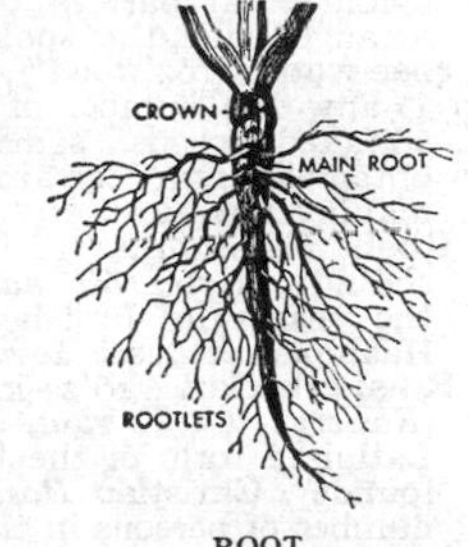

ROOT

root and branch, completely; entirely.

root up (or **out, away**), to pull out by the roots; remove completely; destroy entirely.

take root, 1. to begin growing by putting out roots; hence, 2. to become settled or established.

root (ro͞ot, root), *v.t.* [formerly also *wrote, rout* < AS. *wrotan, wrotian,* to root up < *wrot,* snout; IE. base **wer-*, to tear up, as also in AS. *writan* (cf. WRITE)], to dig or turn up with the snout, as a pig. *v.i.* 1. to search by rummaging (usually with *through*). 2. [Colloq.], to work hard, as for a living; plug; hence, 3. [Slang], to support or encourage a contestant or team, as by applauding and cheering.

Root, Elihu (ro͞ot, root), 1845–1937; American lawyer and statesman; secretary of state (1905–1909); received Nobel peace prize, 1912.

root·age (ro͞ot′ij, root′ij), *n.* [see -AGE], 1. a taking root or being firmly fixed by means of roots. 2. the roots of a plant, collectively.

root beer, a carbonated drink made of root extracts from certain plants, as sassafras, etc.

root hair, in *botany,* one of the thin-walled, hairlike tubular outgrowths from a growing root, which serve to absorb water and minerals from the soil.

root·i·ness (ro͞ot′i-nis, root′i-nis), *n.* the quality of being rooty.

root·let (ro͞ot′lit, root′lit), *n.* a little root or small branch of a root; radicel: see **root,** illus.

root·stalk (ro͞ot′stôk′, root′stôk′), *n.* a rhizome; rootstock.

root·stock (ro͞ot′stok′, root′stok′), *n.* 1. a rhizome; hence, 2. an origin or source. 3. a root used as a stock in the propagation of plants.

root·y (ro͞ot′i, root′i), *adj.* [ROOTIER (-i-ẽr), ROOTIEST (-i-ist)], 1. having many roots. 2. like a root or roots.

rope (rōp), *n.* [ME. *rop, rope;* AS. *rap;* akin to G. *reif* (Goth. *raip*); IE. **reip-*, rag, piece of cloth < **rei-*, to tear (cf. REAP, RIPE); prob. basic sense "what is torn off and twisted"], 1. a thick, strong cord made of intertwisted strands of fiber, thin wires, leather strips, etc. 2. *pl.* such cords strung between posts to enclose a boxing ring. 3. such a cord, or a noose made of it, for hanging a person; hence, 4. death by hanging. 5. a lasso. 6. a ropelike string of things put together by or as by twisting, twining, or braiding: as, a *rope* of pearls. 7. a ropelike, sticky formation in a liquid, as wine. *v.t.* [ROPED (rōpt), ROPING], 1. to fasten, tie, or confine with or as with a rope. 2. to connect or tie together by a rope, as mountain climbers. 3. to separate, mark off, or enclose with a rope (usually with *in, off,* or *out*). 4. to catch or throw with a lasso. *v.i.* to become ropelike and sticky: as, some candy is cooked until it *ropes.*

give one rope, [Colloq.], to allow one freedom of action in the expectation that he will overreach himself.

know the ropes, [Colloq.], to be fully acquainted with the details of a business or procedure.

on the ropes, 1. in *boxing,* knocked against the ropes; hence, 2. [Slang], near collapse or ruin.

rope in, [Slang], to entice; persuade; lure; inveigle.

the end of one's rope, the end of one's actions, means, etc. in a desperate situation.

rope·danc·er (rōp′dan′sẽr, rōp′dän′sẽr), *n.* a performer who dances, walks, or does tricks on a rope stretched between poles high above the ground.

rop·er·y (rōp′ẽr-i), *n.* [*pl.* ROPERIES (-iz)], 1. a place for the manufacture of ropes. 2. [Archaic], roguery.

rope·walk (rōp′wôk′), *n.* a long, low, narrow building, shed, etc. in which ropes are made.

rope·walk·er (rōp′wôk′ẽr), *n.* a ropedancer.

rop·i·ness (rōp′i-nis), *n.* a ropy quality or condition.

rop·y (rōp′i), *adj.* [ROPIER (-i-ẽr), ROPIEST (-i-ist)], 1. forming sticky, stringy threads, as some liquids; glutinous. 2. like a rope or ropes.

roque (rōk), *n.* [< *croquet*], a kind of croquet played on a hard court with special equipment, and requiring more skill than ordinary croquet.

Roque·fort cheese (rōk′fẽrt; Fr. rôk′fôr′), [< *Roquefort,* town in southern France where it was orig. made], a strong cheese with a bluish mold, made from goats' and ewes' milk: also **Roquefort.**

roq·ue·laure (rok′ə-lôr′, rok′ə-lōr′; Fr. rôk′lôr′), *n.* [Fr., after the Duc de *Roquelaure* (1656–1738)], a heavy cloak, usually knee-length, often fur-trimmed and silk-lined, worn by men in the 18th century.

ro·quet (rō-kā′), *v.t. & v.i.* [ROQUETED (-kād′), ROQUETING], [< *croquet*], in *croquet* & *roque,* to hit (another player's ball): said of either a player or his ball. *n.* a roqueting.

ror·qual (rôr′kwəl), *n.* [Fr.; Norw. *röyrkval;* ON. *reytharhvalr,* lit., red whale: so called from the reddish streaks in the skin], any of the whalebone whales with a dorsal fin; finback: some are very large.

Ror·schach test (rôr′shäkh), [after Hermann *Rorschach* (1884–1922), Swiss psychiatrist], in *psychology,* a test for the analysis of personality, in which the person being tested tells what is suggested to him by a series of ink-blot designs of various shapes: his responses are then analyzed and interpreted.

Ro·sa, Mon·te (môn′te rô′zä), a mountain of the

Pennine Alps on the border between Switzerland and Italy: height, 15,196 ft.

ro·sa·ceous (rō-zā′shəs), *adj.* [L. *rosaceus*], 1. of the rose family of plants, including also the strawberry, blackberry, agrimony, etc. 2. having a corolla of five petals, like that of the rose. 3. like a rose. 4. rose-colored; rosy.

Ros·a·lie (roz′ə-lē′, rō′zə-lē′), [Fr.; prob. < L. *rosalia*, annual ceremony of hanging garlands of roses on tombs < *rosa*, a rose], a feminine name.

Ros·a·lind (roz′ə-lind, roz′ə-līnd′), [Sp. *Rosalinda*, as if from *rosa linda*, pretty rose; but prob. ult. < OHG. *Roslindis* < Gmc. **hro-*, fame + *lind-*, linden, shield made of linden wood], a feminine name. *n.* the heroine of Shakespeare's comedy *As You Like It*.

Ros·a·mond (roz′ə-mənd, rō′zə-mənd), [ME. *Rosamunda* < OFr. *Rosamonde* or Sp. *Rosamunda;* LL. *Rosamunda*, as if < L. *rosa munda*, clean rose; but ult. < OHG. *Hrosmund* < Gmc. **hro-*, fame + *mund-*, hand, protection], a feminine name.

ros·an·i·lin (rō-zan′ə-lin), *n.* rosaniline.

ros·an·i·line (rō-zan′ə-lin, rō-zan′ə-līn′, rō-zan′ə-lēn′), *n.* [< *rose* + *aniline*], a crystalline base, $C_{20}H_{21}N_3O$, made by heating aniline and toluidine with nitrobenzene: many aniline dyes are derivatives of it.

Ro·sa·ri·o (rô-sä′ryô), *n.* a city in east central Argentina, on the Paraná River: pop., 522,000 (est. 1944).

ro·sa·ry (rō′zə-ri), *n.* [*pl.* ROSARIES (-riz)], [ME. *rosarie;* L. *rosarium*, rose garden (ML., rosary, garland of roses), neut. of *rosarius*, of roses < *rosa*, a rose], 1. a bed of roses or rose garden. 2. in the *Roman Catholic Church*, *a)* a string of beads used to keep count in saying prayers: it contains sets, five or fifteen, of ten small beads and one large bead; each set (*decade*) is associated with a mystery of the Faith, or happening in the life of Jesus and the Virgin Mary. *b)* [also R-], the prayers said with these beads: a paternoster (large bead), followed by ten Aves (small beads) and a Gloria Patri (large bead) for each set. 3. a string of beads used in a similar way among other religious groups.

Ros·coe (ros′kō), [? < N.Brit. (Celtic) place name], a masculine name.

Rose (rōz), [see ROSE, *n.*], a feminine name: diminutive, *Rosie;* variant, *Rosita;* equivalent, It. & Sp. *Rosa*.

rose (rōz), *n.* [ME.; AS.; L. *rosa* < Gr. *rhodon;* of Oriental origin], 1. any of a number of related plants, characteristically with prickly stems and five-petaled, usually fragrant flowers of red, pink, white, yellow, etc. having many stamens. 2. the flower of any of these plants. 3. any of several similar or related plants. 4. rose color; pinkish red or purplish red. 5. erysipelas: with *the*. 6. a perfume made from or having the fragrance of roses. 7. a rosette. 8. a round, perforated nozzle for a hose, sprinkling can, etc. 9. a form in which gems are often cut so that the upper surface has many small facets. 10. a gem, especially a diamond, cut in this way. 11. a rose window. 12. in *nautical usage*, a compass card or a representation of this, as on maps. *v.t.* [ROSED (rōzd), ROSING], 1. to make rose-colored; specifically, to flush (the cheeks, etc.). 2. to make rose-scented. *adj.* rose-colored.

bed of roses, a comfortable, easy state or position; luxury or idleness.

under the rose, [transl. of L. *sub rosa*], secretly; privately; confidentially.

rose (rōz), past tense of **rise**.

rose acacia, a shrub of the pea family, with large, rose-colored flowers: it grows in the region of the southern Alleghenies: also called *bristly locust*.

ro·se·ate (rō′zi-it, rō′zi-āt′), *adj.* [< L. *roseus*, rosy < *rosa*, a rose; + *-ate*], 1. rose-colored; rosy. 2. made or consisting of roses. 3. bright, cheerful, or optimistic.

rose·bay (rōz′bā′), *n.* 1. any rhododendron. 2. the oleander. 3. [British], the willow herb.

rose beetle, a copper-colored, hard-shelled beetle living in and destructive to rosebushes: also called *rose bug*.

Rose·ber·y (rōz′bĕr-i), fifth Earl of, (*Archibald Philip Primrose*), 1847–1929; English statesman, orator, and author; prime minister (1894–1895).

rose-breast·ed grosbeak (rōz′bres′tid), a North American bird of the finch family, the male of which has a rose-colored triangular patch on the breast.

rose·bud (rōz′bud′), *n.* the bud of a rose.

rose·bush (rōz′boosh′), *n.* a vine or shrub that bears roses.

rose campion, 1. a plant of the pink family, with white, woolly leaves and clusters of small, red or white flowers; mullein pink. 2. the corn cockle.

rose cold (or **fever**), a kind of hay fever believed to be caused by the pollen of roses.

rose color, pinkish red or purplish red.

rose-col·ored (rōz′kul′ẽrd), *adj.* 1. pinkish-red or purplish-red. 2. bright, cheerful, or optimistic.

Rose·crans, William Starke (stärk rōz′krans′, rō′zikranz′), 1819–1898; Union general in the Civil War.

rose·fish (rōz′fish′), *n.* [*pl.* ROSEFISH, ROSEFISHES (-iz); see FISH], a North Atlantic food fish that is orange to red in color when grown: also called *Norway haddock*.

rose geranium, any of several geraniums; especially, a pelargonium with small, pinkish flower clusters and lobed, fragrant leaves, much cultivated in South Africa.

rose hip, the fleshy, bright-colored fruit of the rose.

rose leaf, the petal of a rose.

rose mallow, 1. any of various related plants with large, rose-colored flowers; hibiscus. 2. the hollyhock.

Rose·mar·y (rōz′mâr′i, rōz′mĕr-i), [see ROSEMARY (shrub)], a feminine name.

rose·mar·y (rōz′mâr′i, rōz′mĕr-i), *n.* [altered (after *rose & Mary*) < earlier *rosmarine;* L. *ros marinus* (also *ros maris*), lit., dew of the sea], an evergreen shrub of the mint family, native to the Mediterranean region, with clusters of small, light-blue flowers and leaves that yield a fragrant essential oil, used in making perfume, in cookery, etc.: rosemary is conventionally a symbol of remembrance and constancy.

rose moss, portulaca, especially the garden variety.

rose of Jericho, an Asiatic plant of the mustard family, with oval leaves and spikes of small, white flowers: it curls up when dry and expands again when moistened.

rose of Sharon, 1. the althea, a tall shrub of the mallow family. 2. a St.-John's-wort, with evergreen leaves and large, yellow flowers. 3. a plant mentioned in the Bible: S. of Sol. (Cant.) 2:1.

ro·se·o·la (rō-zē′ə-lə), *n.* [Mod. L., dim. < L. *roseus*, rosy], any rose-colored rash; especially, German measles, or rubella: also called *rose rash*.

Ro·set·ta stone (rō-zet′ə), a tablet of black basalt found in 1799 at Rosetta, a town in Egypt at one of the mouths of the Nile: because it bore parallel inscriptions in Greek and in ancient Egyptian demotic and hieroglyphic characters, it provided a key to the deciphering of ancient Egyptian writing.

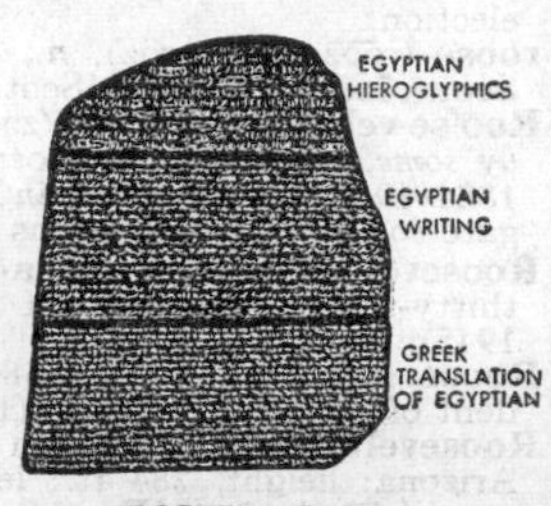

ROSETTA STONE

ro·sette (rō-zet′), *n.* [Fr., dim. of *rose*, a rose], 1. an ornament made of ribbons, threads, etc. gathered or tufted in the shape of a rose. 2. any formation, arrangement, etc. resembling or suggesting a rose. 3. in *architecture*, a painted or sculptured ornament, usually circular, having petals and leaves radiating symmetrically from the center. 4. in *botany*, a circular cluster of leaves, petals, or other organs.

rose-wa·ter (rōz′wô′tẽr, rōz′wät′ẽr), *adj.* 1. like, made with, or having the odor of, rose water; hence, 2. delicate, fine, etc. in an affected or sentimental way.

rose water, a preparation consisting of water and oil of roses, used as a perfume.

rose window, a decorative circular window with a symmetrical pattern of roselike tracery or mullions arranged like the spokes of a wheel.

rose·wood (rōz′wood′), *n.* [so called from its odor], 1. any of a number of valuable hard, reddish, black-streaked woods, sometimes with a roselike odor, obtained from certain tropical trees and used in making furniture, etc. 2. a tree yielding such wood.

Rosh Ha·sha·na (rōsh′ hä-shä′nə; Heb. rōsh′ hä-shô′nô), [Heb. *rōsh hashānāh*, lit., head (or first) of the year], the Jewish New Year: also spelled **Rosh Hashona**, etc.: see **Jewish holidays**.

Ro·si·cru·cian (rō′zə-krōō′shən, roz′ə-krōō′shən), *n.* [*Rosicruc-* (< L. *rosa*, a rose + *crux*, *crucis*, a cross), Latinized form of the G. pseudonym of the supposed founder, Christian *Rosenkreuz;* + *-ian*], 1. any of a number of persons in the 17th and 18th centuries who professed to be members of a secret society said to have various sorts of occult lore and power, and holding esoteric religious doctrines: its symbol was a cross with a red rose in the center. 2. a member of any of several later groups with doctrines and practices said to be based on those of these persons; especially, the Rosicrucian Order, or the Ancient Mystic Order Rosae Crucis (AMORC). *adj.* of or characteristic of the Rosicrucians or Rosicrucianism.

Ro·si·cru·cian·ism (rō′zə-krōō′shən-iz′m, roz′ə-krōō′shən-iz′m), *n.* the doctrines and practices of the Rosicrucians.

ros·i·ly (rō′z′l-i), *adv.* 1. in a rosy manner; brightly; cheerfully; optimistically. 2. with a rosy color.

ros·in (roz′′n, roz′in), *n.* [ME.; OFr. *rosine;* var. of *resine;* see RESIN], resin; specifically, the hard, brittle resin, light-yellow to almost black in color, remaining after oil of turpentine has been distilled from crude turpentine: it is rubbed on violin bows, used in making varnish, etc. *v.t.* to rub with rosin; put rosin on.

Ros·i·nan·te (roz′ə-nan′ti), *n.* [Sp. *rocinante* < *rocin*, a jade, hack; ult. < ML. *runcinus*, sturdy, low-grade horse], 1. Don Quixote's old, bony, broken-down horse; hence, 2. any old, broken-down horse; jade.

ros·i·ness (rō′zi-nis), *n.* a rosy quality or state.

ros·in·weed (roz′'n-wēd′, roz′in-wēd′), *n.* any of a number of related coarse, resinous North American plants of the composite family; especially, the compass plant.

ros·in·y (roz′'n-i, roz′in-i), *adj.* full of, like, or covered with rosin.

Ro·si·ta (rō-zē′tə), a feminine name: see **Rose.**

ro·so·lio (rō-zōl′yō), *n.* [It., earlier *rosoli* < ML. *rossolis*, sun dew (< L. *ros*, dew + *sol, solis*, sun), the plant from which flavor for the drink was orig. extracted], a sweet cordial made from raisins, drunk especially in southern Europe.

Ross, Betsy (rôs), (*Mrs. Elizabeth Griscom Ross*), 1752–1836; American woman who made the first American flag.

Ross, Sir **James Clark,** 1800–1862; nephew of Sir *John;* British naval officer and polar explorer.

Ross, Sir **John,** 1777–1856; British naval officer and arctic explorer.

Ross, Sir **Ronald,** 1857–1932; English physician; known for investigation of malaria-bearing mosquitoes; received Nobel prize in medicine, 1902.

Ross and Crom·ar·ty (rôs 'n krom′ẽr-ti, krum′ẽr-ti), a county of northern Scotland: pop., 61,000 (est. 1946); county seat, Dingwall.

Ross Dependency, a region in Antarctica, including the coasts of the Ross Sea and a number of islands, claimed by Great Britain and administered by New Zealand; area, c. 175,000 sq. mi.

Ros·set·ti, Christina Georgina (rō-set′i, rō-zet′i), 1830–1894; sister of *Dante Gabriel;* English poet.

Rossetti, Dante Gabriel, 1828–1882; English Pre-Raphaelite poet and painter.

Ros·si·ni, Gio·ac·chi·no An·to·nio (jô′ä-kē′nô än-tô′nyô rôs-sē′nē; Eng. rō-sē′ni), 1792–1868; Italian composer of operas.

Ros·si·ya (rô-sē′yä), *n.* Russia: the Russian name.

Ross Sea, an arm of the Antarctic Ocean, between Victoria Land and King Edward VII Land, Antarctica.

Ross Shelf Ice, an ice barrier filling the southern part of the Ross Sea: also called *Ross Barrier.*

Ros·tand, Ed·mond (ed′mōn′ rôs′tän′; Eng. ros′tand), 1868–1918; French dramatist and poet.

ros·tel·late (ros′tə-lāt′, ros′tə-lit), *adj.* [Mod. L. *rostellatus* < L. *rostellum;* see ROSTELLUM], having a rostellum or rostella.

ros·tel·lum (ros-tel′əm), *n.* [*pl.* ROSTELLA (-ə)], [L., dim. of *rostrum*], 1. a small, beaklike process or part. 2. a modification of the stigma in certain orchids.

ros·ter (ros′tẽr), *n.* [D. *rooster*, orig., gridiron (< *roosten*, to roast), hence a grating, list (from the ruled paper used in making lists)], 1. a list of military or naval personnel or groups, with their regular assignments and periods of duty; hence, 2. any list; roll.

Ros·tock (rôs′tôk; Eng. ros′tok), *n.* a city in Mecklenburg, northern Germany: Baltic seaport: pop. (with Warnemünde), 122,000.

Ros·tov (rô-stôf′; *often Anglicized to* ros′tov), *n.* a city in the southern R.S.F.S.R.: seaport at the mouth of the Don: pop., 510,000: also **Rostov-on-Don.**

Ro·stov·tzeff, Mi·chael I·va·no·vich (mī′k'l i-vän′ə-vich rə-stôf′tsef), 1870–1952; American historian, born in Russia.

ros·tra (ros′trə), *n.* alternative plural of **rostrum.**

ros·tral (ros′trəl), *adj.* [LL. *rostralis*], 1. of, in, or on a rostrum. 2. decorated with rostrums, or beaks of ships: as, *rostral* pillars.

ros·trate (ros′trāt), *adj.* [L. *rostratus*], having a rostrum.

ros·trum (ros′trəm), *n.* [*pl.* ROSTRUMS (-trəmz), ROSTRA (-trə)], [L., beak, in pl., speakers' platform (see 1*b*) < *rosus*, pp. of *rodere*, to gnaw, peck], 1. in ancient Rome, *a*) a curved, beaklike projection at the prow of a ship; especially, such a projection on a war galley, used for ramming enemy vessels: also called *beak. b*) the speakers' platform in the Forum, decorated with such beaks taken from captured ships; hence, 2. *a*) any platform, stage, etc. for public speaking. *b*) a pulpit. *c*) public speaking, or public speakers collectively. 3. in *biology*, a beak or beaklike process or part.

ros·y (rō′zi), *adj.* [ROSIER (-zi-ẽr), ROSIEST (-zi-ist)], 1. like a rose, especially in color; rose-red or pink; often, blushing or flushed with a healthy, blooming red: as, *rosy* cheeks. 2. made or consisting of, or adorned with, roses. 3. bright, promising, cheerful, or optimistic: as, a *rosy* future, *rosy* expectations.

SYN.—**rosy** suggests the warm pink or red characterizing a rose in bloom (*rosy* cheeks); **rubicund** implies a flushed, unnatural redness of the face that results from intemperance in food, drink, etc. (a *rubicund* nose); **ruddy** implies such healthy redness as results from an outdoor life (the *ruddy* face of the ranger); **florid** implies the deep, often uneven facial redness of one suffering from hypertension, strong emotional agitation, etc. (his face grew *florid* as he shouted).

rot (rot), *v.i.* [ROTTED (-id), ROTTING], [ME. *rotien;* AS. *rotian;* akin to D. *rotten*, ME. *reten*, to soak (cf. RET); for IE. base see ROTTEN], 1. to decompose gradually; decay; spoil. 2. to fall or pass (*off, away,* etc.) by decaying. 3. to decay morally; become corrupt; degenerate. *v.t.* 1. to cause to decay. 2. to soften the fibers of (flax, etc.) by soaking; ret. *n.* [ME. < ON.; akin to AS. *rotian*], 1. a rotting or being rotten; decay, decomposition, or putrefaction. 2. something rotting or rotten. 3. any of various diseases, especially a parasitic disease of sheep and other domestic animals, characterized by decay, emaciation, etc. 4. any of various plant diseases caused by fungi or bacteria and characterized by decay. 5. [Slang], nonsense; rubbish; twaddle; bosh. *interj.* an exclamation expressing disgust, contempt, annoyance, etc. —*SYN.* see **decay.**

rot., 1. rotating. 2. rotation.

ro·ta (rō′tə), *n.* [L., a wheel], 1. [Chiefly British], a round, as of duties; routine. 2. a roster. 3. [R-], in the *Roman Catholic Church*, a high tribunal consisting of ten prelates (called *auditors*) that serves especially as a court of appeal, as from diocesan courts in matrimonial cases or from the civil and criminal courts of the Vatican City: in full, **Sacra Romana Rota,** or **Sacred Roman Rota.**

Ro·tar·i·an (rō-târ′i-ən), *n.* a member of a Rotary Club. *adj.* of Rotarians or Rotary Clubs.

Ro·tar·i·an·ism (rō-târ′i-ən-iz′m), *n.* the principles and practices of Rotarians.

ro·ta·ry (rō′tə-ri), *adj.* [LL. *rotarius* < L. *rota*, a wheel], 1. turning around a central point or axis, as a wheel; rotating. 2. having a rotating part or parts: as, a *rotary* press. 3. occurring around an axis: as, *rotary* motion. *n.* 1. [*pl.* ROTARIES (-riz)], a rotary machine or engine. 2. [R-], Rotary International.

Rotary Club, any local organization of Rotary International.

rotary engine, 1. an engine in which rotary motion is produced directly, without reciprocating parts, as a steam turbine: distinguished from *reciprocating engine.* 2. an internal-combustion engine with radially arranged cylinders rotating around a stationary crankshaft, used in many airplanes.

Rotary International, [from the fact that meetings were originally held in rotation at the members' offices], an international association of business and professional men, founded in Chicago in 1905, with the aim of serving their communities and fostering understanding among nations: also **Rotary.**

rotary press, a printing press with one or more curved plates mounted on cylinders that rotate against and impress paper moving in a continuous sheet over rotating cylinders.

ro·tat·a·ble (rō′tāt-ə-b'l), *adj.* that can be rotated.

ro·tate (rō′tāt; *also occas., for the v.,* rō-tāt′), *v.i. & v.t.* [ROTATED (-id), ROTATING], [< L. *rotatus*, pp. of *rotare*, to turn < *rota*, a wheel], 1. to turn around or cause to turn around, as a wheel on its axis. 2. to go or cause to go in a regular and recurring succession of changes; take, or cause to take, turns: as, the farmer *rotated* crops. *adj.* [< L. *rota*, a wheel; + *-ate*], shaped like a wheel, with radiating parts, as the corolla of some flowers. —*SYN.* see **turn.**

ro·ta·tion (rō-tā′shən), *n.* [L. *rotatio*], 1. a rotating or being rotated: as, the daily *rotation* of the earth. 2. regular and recurring succession of changes: as, a *rotation* of duties. Abbreviated **rot.**

ro·ta·tion·al (rō-tā′shən-'l), *adj.* of or in rotation.

rotation of crops, a system of rotating in a fixed order the kinds of crops, as grain, grass, etc., grown in the same field, to maintain soil fertility.

ro·ta·tive (rō′tə-tiv), *adj.* 1. rotating or occurring in rotation. 2. of, causing, or caused by rotation.

ro·ta·tor (rō′tā-tẽr, rō-tā′tẽr), *n.* [L.], a person or thing that rotates; specifically, in *anatomy*, [*pl.* ROTATORES (rō′tə-tôr′ēz, rō′tə-tō′rēz)], a muscle that serves to rotate a part of the body.

ro·ta·to·ry (rō′tə-tôr′i, rō′tə-tō′ri), *adj.* 1. of, or having the nature of, rotation. 2. rotary. 3. going or following in rotation, or in succession. 4. causing rotation.

R.O.T.C., Reserve Officers' Training Corps.

rotche, rotch (roch), *n.* [for earlier *rotge;* D. *rotje*, petrel, brant goose], the dovekie, a small arctic auk.

rote (rōt), *n.* [ME., var. of *route* (traveled way)], a fixed, mechanical way of doing something; routine.
by rote, by memory alone, without understanding or thought: as, he repeated the lesson *by rote.*

rote (rōt), *n.* [prob. via ME. dial. < ON. *rōt*, breaking of waves], the sound of the surf beating on the shore.

rote (rōt), *n.* [ME.; OFr.; OHG. *hrotta* < or akin to Celt. *chrotta*, seen also in W. *crwth;* see CROWD (the instrument)], a medieval stringed musical instrument, variously supposed to have been a kind of lyre or lute: also **rotte.**

ro·te·none (rō′tə-nōn′), *n.* [< ?], a white, odorless,

crystalline substance, $C_{23}H_{22}O_6$, obtained from the roots of certain plants and used in insecticides.
rot·gut (rot′gut′), *n.* [*rot* + *gut* (bowel)], [Slang], raw, low-grade whisky.
Roth·er·ham (roth′ēr-əm), *n.* a city in Yorkshire, central England, near Sheffield: pop., 76,000.
Roth·schild, Mey·er Anselm (mī′ēr än′zelm rōt′shilt; Eng. rôth′chīld′, roths′chīld′), 1743–1812; German banker; founded the banking house of Rothschild.
Rothschild, Nathan Meyer, 1777–1836; son of *Meyer Anselm;* banker in Great Britain.
ro·ti·fer (rō′ti-fēr), *n.* [Mod. L. < L. *rota*, a wheel + *ferre*, to bear], any of a group of microscopic, structurally complex water animals with one or more rings of cilia on a disc at the anterior end of the body; wheel animalcule: so called because in some varieties the cilia, when active, look like rotating wheels.
ro·tif·er·al (rō-tif′ēr-əl), *adj.* of a rotifer.
ro·tif·er·ous (rō-tif′ēr-əs), *adj.* rotiferal.
ro·ti·form (rō′tə-fôrm′), *adj.* [< L. *rota*, a wheel; + *-form*], shaped like a wheel.
ro·tis·ser·ie (rō-tis′ēr-i; Fr. rô′tēs′rē′), *n.* [Fr. < *rôtir*, to roast], 1. a shop or restaurant where meats are roasted and sold. 2. a portable electric grill with a turning spit.
rot·l (rot′′l), *n.* [*pl.* ARTAL (är′täl)], [Ar. *raṭl*], 1. a unit of weight used in Moslem regions, varying from about one to about five pounds, according to locality. 2. a varying unit of dry measure used in these regions.
ro·to·gra·vure (rō′tə-grə-vyoor′, rō′tə-grā′vyoor), *n.* [< L. *rota*, a wheel; + *gravure*], 1. a process of printing pictures, letters, etc. on a rotary press using copper cylinders etched from photographic plates: clear, smooth reproductions are thus obtained. 2. a picture or print made by this process. 3. a newspaper pictorial section printed by this process: also called *roto section.*
ro·tor (rō′tēr), *n.* [contr. of *rotator*], 1. the rotating part of a motor, dynamo, etc.: cf. **stator.** 2. a system of rotating airfoils, as of a helicopter. 3. one of the tall, revolving cylinders of a rotor ship.
rotor ship, a kind of sailing ship propelled by the action of the wind on one or more tall, vertical cylinders (*rotors*) that are rotated by a small electric motor.
ro·to section (rō′tō), a rotogravure (sense 3).
rot·te (rot′ə), *n.* a rote (musical instrument).
rot·ten (rot′′n), *adj.* [ME. *roten;* ON. *rotinn;* IE. base **reud-* < **reu-*, to tear, rip open, used orig. of flax left to soak and rot; cf. ROT], 1. decayed; decomposed; spoiled; putrefied; tainted. 2. having a bad odor because of decomposition or decay; putrid; foul-smelling. 3. morally corrupt or offensive; characterized by dishonesty, open to bribery, etc. 4. unsound or weak, as if decayed within. 5. soft or easily broken because of decomposition; friable: said of rocks, etc. 6. [Slang], very bad, unsatisfactory, nasty, etc.
rotten borough, 1. in England (before the Reform Act of 1832), a borough with only a few voters but with the right to send a representative to Parliament; hence, 2. any electoral district or political unit with greater representation than its population warrants.
rot·ten·stone (rot′′n-stōn′), *n.* a siliceous limestone decomposed to a friable state, used for polishing metals.
rot·ter (rot′ēr), *n.* [< *rot*], [Chiefly British Slang], a despicable or objectionable person.
Rot·ter·dam (rot′ēr-dam′; D. rôt′ēr-däm′), *n.* a seaport in the southwestern Netherlands: pop., 648,000 (1947).
ro·tund (rō-tund′), *adj.* [L. *rotundus;* akin to *rota*, a wheel], 1. round or rounded out; plump: as, a *rotund* little man. 2. full-toned; sonorous: as, *rotund* speech.
ro·tun·da (rō-tun′də), *n.* [It. *rotonda* < L. *rotunda*, fem. of *rotundus;* see ROTUND], a round building, hall, or room, especially one with a dome.
ro·tun·di·ty (rō-tun′də-ti), *n.* [LL. *rotunditas*], 1. the condition or quality of being rotund. 2. [*pl.* ROTUNDITIES (-tiz)], something rotund.
‡ro·tu·rier (rô′tü′ryā′), *n.* [*pl.* ROTURIERS (-ryā′)], [Fr. < *roture*, plebeian rank, orig. newly cleared field < ML. *ruptura*, in same sense (in L., a breaking); see RUPTURE], a person not of noble rank; commoner.
Rou·ault, Georges (zhôrzh′ roo-ō′), 1871–1958; French expressionist painter.
Rou·baix (roo′be′), *n.* a city in northern France: pop., 101,000 (1946).
rou·ble (roo′b′l), *n.* a ruble.
rouche (roosh), *n.* a ruche.
rou·é (roo-ā′), *n.* [Fr., pp. of *rouer*, to break on the wheel < L. *rota*, a wheel; orig. a nickname given (c. 1720) to the dissolute male friends of the Duc d'Orléans], a dissipated man; debauchee; rake.
Rou·en (roo-än′; Fr. rwän), *n.* a city on the Seine, in northern France, noted for its cathedral: Joan of Arc was executed here (1431): pop., 108,000 (1946).
rouge (roozh), *n.* [Fr., rouge, red < L. *rubeus;* see RUBY], 1. any of various red or reddish cosmetics, in powder, paste, or liquid form, used for coloring the cheeks and lips. 2. a reddish powder, mainly ferric oxide, used for polishing jewelry, metal, etc. *v.t.* [ROUGED (roozhd), ROUGING], to color with rouge. *v.i.* to use cosmetic rouge.
rouge (roozh), *v.t.* [ROUGED (roozhd), ROUGING], [< ?], in *Canadian football*, to tackle a runner between his goal line and a line 25 yards behind it: the tackler scores one point for his side by doing this. —*n.* 1. in *Canadian football*, a rouging. 2. Canadian football.
rouge et noir (roozh′ ā nwär′), [Fr., red and black], a gambling card game played at a table having two red and two black diamond-shaped marks on which bets are placed.
Rou·get de Lisle, Claude Jo·seph (klōd zhô′zef′ roo′zhā′ də lēl′), 1760–1836; French soldier, poet, and composer; wrote "Marseillaise": also spelled **de l'Isle.**
rough (ruf), *adj.* [ME. *ruh, rugh;* AS. *ruh;* akin to G. *rauh;* IE. **reuk* < base **reu-*, to tear, tear out (cf. ROTTEN); prob. basic sense "hairy, woolly"], 1. not smooth or level; having bumps, projections, etc.; uneven: as, a *rough* surface, *rough* country. 2. shaggy: as, an animal with a *rough* coat. 3. characterized by violent action, motion, agitation, disturbance, or irregularity; specifically, *a*) stormy; tempestuous: as, *rough* weather. *b*) boisterous, disorderly, or riotous: as, *rough* play. 4. harsh; rude; surly; unmannerly; not gentle or mild: as, *rough* manners, a *rough* temper. 5. sounding harsh; discordant; jarring. 6. tasting harsh, sharp, or astringent: as, *rough* wine. 7. coarse, as texture, cloth, food, etc. 8. coarse in manner, tastes, etc.; lacking refinement or culture: as, *rough* men. 9. lacking refinements and luxuries or comforts and conveniences: as, the *rough* life of the pioneers. 10. not refined, polished, or prepared; natural, crude, unwrought, etc.: as, *rough* jewels. 11. not finished, elaborated, perfected, etc.: as, a *rough* sketch; hence, 12. not carefully or thoroughly worked out; without claim to be exact, complete, or detailed; approximate: as, a *rough* estimate. 13. needing strength instead of skill, intelligence, etc.: as, *rough* labor. 14. [Colloq.], difficult, severe, or disagreeable: as, they had a *rough* time of it. 15. in *phonetics*, pronounced with an aspirate; having the sound of *h*. *n.* 1. rough ground. 2. rough material or condition. 3. the rough part, aspect, etc. of something. 4. [Chiefly British], a rough person; rowdy; tough; ruffian. 5. in *golf*, any part of the course where grass, weeds, etc. are allowed to grow uncut, forming a hazard or obstacle. *adv.* in a rough manner; roughly. *v.t.* 1. to make rough; roughen. 2. to handle or treat roughly; specifically, in *football*, etc., to subject (an opponent) to intentional and unnecessary roughness (often with *up*). 3. to make, fashion, sketch, shape, or cut roughly (usually with *in* or *out*): as, *rough* out a scheme. 4. to apply some preparatory or preliminary process or treatment to. *v.i.* 1. to become rough. 2. to behave roughly.
in the rough, in a rough or crude state.
rough it, to live without customary comforts and conveniences, as in camping.
SYN.—**rough** applies to any surface covered with projections, points, ridges, bumps, etc. (*rough* skin, ground, etc.); **harsh** applies to anything disagreeably rough to the touch (a *harsh* texture); that is **uneven** which is not uniform in height, breadth, etc. (an *uneven* floor, hem, etc.); **rugged** implies a roughness of surface in which the sharp, irregular projections are obstacles to travel (*rugged* country) or a roughness of countenance suggestive of strength (a *rugged* jaw); **jagged** suggests uneven, sharp-pointed projections or notches along an edge, as of broken glass, ragged cloth, etc. Most of these words have extended uses suggested by their basic meanings (*rough* weather, *harsh* sounds, an *uneven* performance, a *rugged* life).—*ANT.* smooth.
rough·age (ruf′ij), *n.* [see -AGE], rough material; coarse substance; specifically, coarse food or fodder, as bran, straw, vegetable peel, etc., containing a relatively high proportion of cellulose and other indigestible constituents and serving in the diet as a stimulus to peristalsis.
rough-and-read·y (ruf′′n-red′i), *adj.* 1. rough, or crude, rude, unpolished, etc., but effective enough: as, *rough-and-ready* methods. 2. characterized by rough vigor and prompt action rather than refinement, formality, or nicety: as, a *rough-and-ready* fellow.
rough-and-tum·ble (ruf′′n-tum′b′l), *adj.* violent and disorderly, with no concern for rules: as, a *rough-and-tumble* fight. *n.* a fight or struggle of this kind.
rough breathing, [transl. of L. *spiritus asper*], in *Greek grammar*, the mark (ʽ) placed over initial vowels or ρ (rho) to indicate a preceding *h* sound, or aspirate.
rough·cast (ruf′kast′, ruf′käst′), *n.* 1. a coarse plaster for covering outside surfaces, as walls. 2. a rough pattern or form, or crudely made model. *v.t.* [ROUGHCAST, ROUGHCASTING], 1. to cover (walls, etc.) with roughcast. 2. to make or shape in a rough form.
rough-cut (ruf′kut′), *adj.* cut into small, chopped irregular pieces: said of tobacco: opposed to *fine-cut.*
rough-dry (ruf′drī′), *v.t.* [ROUGH-DRIED (-drīd′), ROUGH-DRYING], to dry (washed laundry) without ironing: also **roughdry.** *adj.* washed and dried but not ironed.
rough·en (ruf′′n), *v.t. & v.i.* to make or become rough.
rough-hew (ruf′hū′), *v.t.* [ROUGH-HEWED (-hūd′), ROUGH-HEWED or ROUGH-HEWN (-hūn′), ROUGH-HEWING], 1. to hew (timber, stone, etc.) roughly, or without finishing or smoothing. 2. to form roughly; give crude shape or outline to. Also **roughhew.**
rough·house (ruf′hous′), *n.* [Slang], rough, boisterous

or rowdy play, fighting, etc., especially indoors. ***v.t.*** [Slang], to treat (a person) roughly and boisterously, usually in fun. ***v.i.*** [Slang], to take part in roughhouse.
rough·ish (ruf′ish), ***adj.*** somewhat rough.
rough·ly (ruf′li), ***adv.*** 1. in a rough manner. 2. approximately.
rough·neck (ruf′nek′), ***n.*** [Slang], a person whose actions and manners are rough and crude; rowdy.
rough·rid·er (ruf′rīd′ẽr), ***n.*** 1. a person who breaks horses so that they can be ridden. 2. a person who does much hard, rough riding. 3. [R-], a member of a volunteer cavalry regiment organized by Theodore Roosevelt and Leonard Wood for service in the Spanish-American War (1898): also **Rough Rider.**
rough·shod (ruf′shod′), ***adj.*** shod with horseshoes that have calks, or metal points, to prevent slipping.
ride roughshod over, to treat in a harsh, arrogant, inconsiderate manner; domineer over.
roul., in *philately*, roulette.
rou·lade (ro͞o-läd′), ***n.*** [Fr. < *rouler*, to roll], 1. a musical ornament consisting of a rapid succession of tones sung to one syllable. 2. a slice of meat rolled with a filling of minced meat and cooked.
rou·leau (ro͞o-lō′), ***n.*** [*pl.* ROULEAUX (-lōz′), ROULEAUS (-lōz′)], [Fr., dim. of *rôle*, roll], 1. a small roll of something; especially, a roll of coins, generally of the same denomination, stacked in a paper wrapper. 2. a roll or fold, as of ribbon, used for trimming hats, etc.
Rou·lers (ro͞o′lâr′), ***n.*** a city in northwestern Belgium: pop., 32,000 (est. 1945).
rou·lette (ro͞o-let′), ***n.*** [Fr., dim. of *rouelle*, small wheel; ML. *rotella*, dim. < L. *rota*, a wheel], 1. a gambling game played by rolling a small ball or marble around a shallow bowl with an inner disk (*roulette wheel*) revolving in the opposite direction: the ball finally comes to rest in one of the numbered, alternately red and black compartments into which this disk is divided, thus determining the winning and losing bets. 2. a small toothed wheel or disk attached to a handle, for making rows of marks or dots, as in engraving, or incisions, as between postage stamps; hence, 3. in *philately*, small, consecutive incisions made in the paper between the stamps in a sheet of stamps, to facilitate their separation: it is unlike perforation in that no paper is removed: abbreviated **roul.** ***v.t.*** [ROULETTED (-id), ROULETTING], to make marks, dots, or perforations in or on with a roulette.
Roum., 1. Roumania. 2. Roumanian.
Rou·ma·ni·a (ro͞o-mā′ni-ə, ro͞o-mān′yə), ***n.*** Romania.
Rou·ma·ni·an (ro͞o-mā′ni-ən, ro͞o-mān′yən), ***adj. & n.*** Romanian.
Rou·me·li·a (ro͞o-mē′li-ə), ***n.*** Rumelia.
round (round), ***adj.*** [ME. *rond, round;* OFr. *roond, reont;* L. *rotundus;* see ROTUND], 1. shaped like a ball; spherical; globular. 2. shaped like a circle, ring, disk, or part of a circle; circular or curved. 3. shaped like a cylinder (in having a circular cross section); cylindrical. 4. curved in shape like part of a sphere. 5. not angular; plump: as, a *round* little person. 6. involving, or done in, by, or with, a circular motion: as, a *round* dance. 7. pronounced with the lips forming an approximately circular or oval opening; rounded: as, a *round* vowel. 8. *a*) not lacking part; full; entire; complete: as, a *round* dozen. *b*) completed; perfected. 9. completed or accomplished by progressing through a course which, as if circular, finally returns to the starting point: as, a *round* trip. 10. constituting, or expressed by, a whole number, or integer; not fractional. 11. expressed in tens, hundreds, thousands, etc.: as, 500 is a *round* number for 498, 503, etc. 12. approximately accurate; rough: as, a *round* guess. 13. large in amount, size, etc.; considerable: as, a *round* sum. 14. having a finish or polish: as, a *round* style of writing. 15. mellow and full in tone; sonorous: said of a sound, the voice, etc. 16. brisk; vigorous and rapid: as, a *round* pace. 17. outspoken; plain and blunt; straightforward; frank; candid. 18. not qualified or modified: as, a *round* oath. ***n.*** 1. something round or rounded; thing or part that is spherical, globular, circular, curved, annular, or cylindrical; hence, 2. a rung of a ladder, or a crossbar connecting the legs of a chair. 3. the rounded part of the thigh of a beef animal, between the rump and the leg: in full, **round of beef:** see **beef,** illus. 4. a kind of sculpture in which the figures are full and completely rounded, not projecting from a background (with *the*): distinguished from *relief*. 5. the state of being round. 6. an assembly or group of people. 7. movement in a circular course or about an axis. 8. a round dance. 9. a course, series, or succession of actions, events, operations, etc. that is complete or ends at a point corresponding to that where it began, as if circular: as, a *round* of parties. 10. the complete extent; whole range: as, the *round* of human beliefs. 11. *often in pl.* a regular, customary course or circuit: as, the watchman made his *rounds.* 12. a single distribution, as of drinks, to each of the members of a group. 13. a single shot from each of a number of rifles, artillery pieces, etc. fired together, or from a single gun: cf. **salvo.** 14. ammunition for such a shot; cartridge, shell, etc. 15. a single outburst, as of applause, cheering, etc.; salvo. 16. [British], a slice (of bread). 17. in *archery*, a specified number of arrows shot at the target from a specified distance according to the rules. 18. in *games & sports*, a single period or division of action, usually one of a series: as, a *round* of poker; specifically, *a*) in *boxing*, any of the timed periods of a fight: a round is now generally limited to three minutes, and the interval between rounds to one minute. *b*) in *golf*, a number of holes or a period of play in a match. 19. in *music*, a short song to be repeated several times, the musical phrases of which are of equal length and harmonize with one another: one singer or group begins the song, and, when starting on the second phrase, is joined by another beginning the first phrase, etc. ***v.t.*** 1. to make round. 2. to pronounce with rounded lips; labialize. 3. to deprive of angularity or make plump. 4. to complete; finish; perfect. 5. to make a circuit of; pass around: as, we *rounded* the island. 6. to make a turn about: as, he *rounded* the corner. 7. to encircle; surround. 8. to cause to move in a circular course. ***v.i.*** 1. to make a complete or partial circuit; move in a curved or circular course. 2. to turn; reverse direction: as, the fleeing cat suddenly *rounded.* 3. to become round. 4. to lose angularity or become plump. 5. to develop (with *into*): as, the talk *rounded* into a plan. ***adv.*** 1. in a circle; along or throughout a circular course or circumference. 2. through a recurring period of time, or from beginning to end: as, the autumn came *round* once more, he worked the whole year *round.* 3. in or through a course or circuit, as from one person or place to another: as, the peddler went *round* with his goods. 4. for each of several; to include all in a group: as, not enough candy to go *round.* 5. so as to encircle, surround, or envelop, or be encircled, surrounded, or enveloped. 6. in circumference: as, his waist measures forty inches *round.* 7. on all sides; in every direction: as, the meadows extended *round.* 8. about; near: as, he visited all the people *round.* 9. by a circuitous course; in a roundabout way. 10. in various places; here and there: as, the child played *round.* 11. with a rotating or revolving movement: as, the wheel spun *round.* 12. in or to the opposite direction: as, he turned *round;* hence, 13. in or to an opposite belief, viewpoint, etc. ***prep.*** 1. so as to encircle, surround, or envelop; about: as, the rope was tied *round* the tree. 2. on the circumference, border, or outer part of. 3. on all sides of; in every direction from: as, the mob shrieked *round* him. 4. in the vicinity of; somewhat close to: as, farms *round* Cleveland. 5. to or through every part or various parts of; in a circuit or course through: as, we went *round* the museum. 6. from the beginning to the end of (a period of time); throughout: as, he worked *round* the day. 7. in various places in or on; here and there in; all about: as, the child played *round* the room. 8. *a*) so as to make a curve or partial circuit about, or turn to the other side of: as, the traffic flowed *round* the obstruction in the road. *b*) located at a point reached by making such a circuit about: as, a store *round* the corner. 9. so as to rotate or revolve about (a center or axis): as, the wheel goes *round* an axle. Abbreviated **rd.** *Round* (*adv.* & *prep.*) and *around* are used interchangeably in colloquial and informal usage; formal usage tends to prefer *round* for "in a circle," "with a rotating movement," etc. and *around* for "on all sides," "here and there." Cf. **around** for special senses. See also phrases under **bring, come, get,** etc.
go the round (or **rounds**), 1. to be circulated among a number of people, as a story, rumor, etc. 2. to walk one's regular course or circuit, as a watchman.
in the round, in an arena theater: see **arena,** sense 4.
round about, 1. in or to the opposite direction. 2. in every direction around.
round in, in *nautical usage*, to haul in.
round off (or **out**), 1. to make or become round or rounded. 2. to complete; finish.
round to, in *nautical usage*, to turn so that the prow is toward the wind.
round up, 1. to drive (cattle, etc.) together; collect in a herd, group, etc.; hence, 2. [Colloq.], to gather, collect, or assemble.
SYN.—**round,** the most inclusive of these words, applies to anything shaped like a circle, sphere, or cylinder, or like a part of any of these; **spherical** applies to a round body or mass having the surface equally distant from the center at all points; **globular** is used of things that are ball-shaped but not neces-

sarily perfect spheres; **circular** is applied to round lines, or round flat surfaces, in the shape of a ring or disk, and it may or may not imply correspondence in form with a perfect circle; **annular** applies to ringlike forms or structures, as the markings in a cross section of a tree.

round (round), *v.t. & v.i.* [ME. *rounen* (+ unhistoric *-d*); AS. *runian*, to whisper; base as in *rune*], [Obs.], to whisper (to).

round·a·bout (round'ə-bout'), *adj.* 1. not straight or straightforward; indirect; circuitous: as, *roundabout* methods, a *roundabout* trip. 2. encircling; enclosing; surrounding. *n.* 1. something, as a path, speech, etc., that is indirect or circuitous. 2. a short, tight jacket or coat worn by men and boys. 3. [Chiefly British], a merry-go-round.

round dance, 1. originally, a dance with the dancers arranged or moving in a circle. 2. any of several dances, as the waltz, polka, fox trot, etc., performed by couples and characterized by revolving or circular movements. Distinguished from *square dance.*

round·ed (roun'did), *adj.* 1. made round. 2. in *phonetics*, pronounced with the lips forming an approximately circular or oval opening; labialized.

roun·del (roun'd'l), *n.* [ME. *rondel;* OFr. *rondel*, orig. dim. of *roond*, round; see ROUND, *adj.*], 1. something round, or circular. 2. a round ornamental panel, plate, niche, etc. 3. a small, round window or pane. 4. *a)* a rondel. *b)* a rondeau. *c)* an English modification of the rondeau, with three stanzas of three lines each and two refrains. 5. a round dance; roundelay.

roun·de·lay (roun'də-lā'), *n.* [OFr. *rondelet*, dim. of *rondel;* see ROUNDEL], 1. a simple song in which some phrase, line, etc. is continually repeated. 2. music for such a song. 3. a dance in which the dancers move in a circle; roundel.

round·er (roun'dẽr), *n.* 1. a person who makes a round or rounds, as a policeman, watchman, etc. 2. a person or thing that rounds; specifically, a tool for rounding corners or edges. 3. *pl.* [construed as sing.], a game somewhat like baseball, played chiefly by the British. 4. [R-], [British], a Methodist preacher who travels a circuit among his congregations. 5. [from the idea of making the rounds of disreputable resorts], [Colloq.], a dissolute spendthrift, drunkard, or habitual criminal.

round hand, careful handwriting in which the letters are rounded, distinct, full, and almost vertical: distinguished from *running hand.*

Round·head (round'hed'), *n.* a member or supporter of the Parliamentary, or Puritan, party in England during the English civil war (1642–1652): originally a derisive term, with reference to the Puritans' close-cropped hair in contrast to the Cavaliers' long hair.

round·house (round'hous'), *n.* [orig., a lockup, after D. *rondhuis*, guardhouse], 1. a building, generally circular or semicircular, with a turntable in the center, used for storing, repairing, and switching locomotives. 2. a cabin on the after part of a ship's quarter-deck.

round·ish (roun'dish), *adj.* somewhat round.

round·let (round'lit), *n.* [ME. *roundelet;* OFr. *rondelet;* see ROUNDELAY], a small circle or circular thing.

round·ly (round'li), *adv.* 1. in a round form; circularly, spherically, etc. 2. in a round manner; specifically, *a)* vigorously, bluntly, severely, etc.: as, he was *roundly* rebuked. *b)* fully; completely.

round of beef, see **round,** *n.* (sense 3).

round robin, [*round* + pers. name *Robin*], 1. a document, as a petition, protest, etc., with the signatures written in a circle to conceal the order of signing. 2. a contest or tournament, as in tennis, chess, etc., in which every entrant is matched with every other one.

round-shoul·dered (round'shōl'dẽrd), *adj.* having the shoulders bent forward, so that the upper back has a rounded form.

rounds·man (roundz'mən), *n.* [*pl.* ROUNDSMEN (-mən)], a person who makes rounds of inspection or the like; especially, a police inspector in charge of a number of patrolmen.

round steak, a cut from a round of beef.

round-ta·ble (round'tā'b'l), *adj.* at or as if at a round table: as, a *round-table* discussion.

Round Table, 1. the large table around which, according to legend, King Arthur and his knights sat: it was made circular to avoid disputes about precedence. 2. King Arthur and his knights, collectively. 3. [r- t-], *a)* a group of persons gathered together for an informal discussion, conference, etc., at or as if at a circular table. *b)* such a discussion, conference, etc.

round-trip (round'trip'), *adj.* of or for a round trip.

round trip, a trip to a place and back to the starting point: also called *return trip.*

round·up (round'up'), *n.* 1. the act of driving cattle, etc. together on the range and collecting them in a herd, as for branding, inspection, or shipping. 2. the herd of cattle, etc. thus collected. 3. the cowboys, horses, etc. that do this work. 4. any similar driving together, collecting, or gathering: as, a *roundup* of suspected persons.

round·worm (round'wûrm'), *n.* any of a large group of round, unsegmented worms, as the pinworm, hookworm, etc.; nematode, especially one living as a parasite in the intestines of man or other animals.

roup (ro͞op), *n.* [prob. < ME. *roupen*, to cry, shout < ON., but akin to AS. *hropan*, G. *rufen*, to call], 1. a poultry disease characterized by hoarseness and a catarrhal discharge from the eyes and nasal passages. 2. hoarseness; huskiness.

roup·y (ro͞op'i), *adj.* [ROUPIER (-i-ẽr), ROUPIEST (-i-ist)], 1. of, like, or having roup. 2. [Chiefly Scot.], hoarse.

rouse (rouz), *v.t.* [ROUSED (rouzd), ROUSING], [orig. technical term in hawking & hunting, hence prob. of Anglo-Fr. or OFr. origin; cf. AROUSE], 1. to cause (game) to rise from cover, come out of a lair, etc.; stir up to flight or attack. 2. to stir up, as to anger or action; excite. 3. to cause to come out of a state of sleep, repose, unconsciousness, etc.; wake. 4. in *nautical usage*, to pull with force; haul. *v.i.* 1. to rise from cover, etc.: said of game. 2. to come out of a state of sleep, repose, etc.; wake. 3. to become active. *n.* 1. a rousing. 2. a signal for rousing; reveille. —*SYN.* see **stir.**

rouse (rouz), *n.* [aphetic for *carouse* (from mistaking *drink carouse* as *drink a rouse*)], [Archaic], a carouse.

rous·ing (rouz'iŋ), *adj.* 1. that rouses; stirring: as, a *rousing* speech. 2. very active or lively; vigorous; brisk: as, a *rousing* business. 3. [Colloq.], astonishing, extraordinary, or outrageous, as a lie.

Rous·seau, Hen·ri (än'rē' ro͞o'sō'), 1844–1910; French painter: called *Le Douanier.*

Rousseau, Jean Jacques (zhän zhäk), 1712–1778; French philosopher, writer, and social theorist.

Rousseau, Pierre É·tienne Thé·o·dore (pyâr ā'tyen' tā'ô'dôr'), 1812–1867; French landscape painter.

roust (roust), *v.t.* [dial. form of *rouse* with unhistoric *-t*], [Colloq.], 1. to rouse or stir (someone or something): usually with *up.* 2. to rout or drive out (someone or something): usually with *out.*

roust·a·bout (roust'ə-bout'), *n.* [*roust*, dial. var. of *rouse* (to stir) + *about*], 1. a deck hand or water-front laborer, as on the Mississippi. 2. a laborer in a circus. 3. an unskilled or transient laborer, especially one who does odd jobs, as a man of all work on a ranch.

rout (rout), *n.* [ME. & OFr. *route*, lit., portion broken off or separated < L. *rupta;* see ROUTE (road)], 1. a disorderly crowd; noisy mob; hence, 2. the rabble. 3. a disorderly flight or retreat, as of defeated troops: as, the enemy was put to *rout.* 4. an overwhelming defeat. 5. [Archaic or Poetic], *a)* a group of people; company; band. *b)* a band of followers; retinue; entourage. 6. [Archaic], a large, fashionable social gathering or party, usually in the evening. 7. in *law*, a disturbance of the peace by three or more persons with intent to create a riot. *v.t.* 1. to put to disorderly flight. 2. to defeat overwhelmingly.—*SYN.* see **conquer.**

rout (rout), *v.i.* [var. of *root* (to dig)], 1. to dig for food with the snout, as a pig. 2. to search by poking and rummaging. *v.t.* 1. to dig up or turn over with the snout. 2. to find or get by turning up, poking about, etc.; expose to view (with *out*). 3. to scoop, gouge, or hollow out. 4. to force out. 5. to make (a person) get out or up (with *out* or *up*).

route (ro͞ot; *also, and for n. 3 usually*, rout), *n.* [ME.; OFr. *route, rote* < L. *rupta* (*via*), broken (path) < *ruptus*, pp. of *rumpere*, to break], 1. a road, way, or course traveled or to be traveled in going from one place to another or in delivering something, as mail, milk, or newspapers. 2. *a)* a set of customers to whom one regularly delivers something, as newspapers or milk. *b)* a job or business of delivering newspapers, etc.: as, the boy sold his newspaper *route.* 3. in *military usage*, an order specifying the course of travel to be followed by troops taking up a new position, the location of the new command posts, etc. *v.t.* [ROUTED (-id), ROUTING], 1. to send, forward, or transport by a specified route: as, *route* the goods through Pittsburgh. 2. to arrange the route for; fix the order of procedure of (a series of operations, etc.): as, he *routed* the orders through the sales department.

go the route, [Colloq.], in *baseball*, to pitch an entire game.

rout·er (rout'ẽr), *n.* a person or thing that routs or a tool for routing; specifically, a plane for gouging out recesses and smoothing the bottoms of grooves.

rou·tine (ro͞o-tēn'), *n.* [Fr. < *route;* see ROUTE], 1. a regular, more or less unvarying procedure, customary, prescribed, or habitual, as of business or daily life. 2. such procedure in general: as, he dislikes *routine.* *adj.* having the nature of, using, or by routine.

rou·tin·ism (ro͞o-tēn'iz'm), *n.* adherence to or prevalence of routine.

roux (ro͞o), *n.* [Fr. *roux* (*beurre*), reddish-brown (butter) < L. *russus;* see RUSSET], a mixture of melted butter (or other fat) and browned flour, used for thickening sauces, soups, gravies, etc.

rove (rōv), *v.i.* [ROVED (rōvd), ROVING], [ME. *rove(n)*, orig. an archery term as *v.t.;* prob. < base of AS. *arafian*, to set free, unloose; IE. base *rep-, to snatch; influenced by *rover* (a pirate)], to wander about; go from place to place, especially over an extensive area, with no particular course or destination; roam. *v.t.* to wander over; roam through: as, he *roved* the woods. *n.* a roving; ramble. —*SYN.* see **roam.**

rove (rōv), *v.t.* [ROVED (rōvd), ROVING], [< same base as prec.], 1. to put (fibers, etc.) through a small opening. 2. to card (wool). 3. to extend and twist (fibers) before spinning. *n.* 1. an extended, twisted fiber of cotton, silk, wool, etc. 2. such fibers in cloth.

rove (rōv), alternative past tense and past participle of **reeve.**

rove beetle, any of a group of swiftly moving beetles with a long, slender body, common in decomposing organic matter.

rov·en (rōv′'n), alternative past participle of **reeve.**

rove-o·ver (rōv′ō′vẽr), *adj.* [term coined by G. M. Hopkins], in *prosody*, having a rhythm continued without pause from one line to the next. *n.* rove-over verse.

rov·er (rōv′ẽr), *n.* [sense 2 < ME. *rovere;* MD. *rover*, a robber < *roven*, to rob; other senses < *rove* (to wander); later use shows some merging of the senses "pirate" & "wanderer"], 1. a person who roves, or wanders. 2. [Archaic], *a*) a pirate. *b*) a pirate ship. 3. in *archery*, *a*) a mark, or target, chosen at random. *b*) any of several set marks for distance shooting. *c*) an archer who starts from a distance. 4. in *croquet*, *a*) a ball that has been knocked through all the wickets and needs only to hit the stake to go out: also **rover ball.** *b*) the player of such a ball.

rov·er (rōv′ẽr), *n.* 1. a person who operates a machine for roving fibers. 2. such a machine.

row (rō), *n.* [ME. *rowe;* AS. *raw, ræw;* prob. IE. **roikwa*, line < base **rei-*, to scratch, split (cf. REAP, RIPE)], 1. a number of people or things arranged so as to form a line, especially a straight line. 2. any of the lines of seats in a theater or auditorium, usually numbered or lettered consecutively from front to rear. 3. a street with a line of buildings on either side. *v.t.* to arrange or put in a row or rows (often with *up*).

hard (or **long**) **row to hoe,** anything difficult or wearisome to do.

row (rō), *v.t.* [ME. *rowen;* AS. *rowan;* akin to ON. *rōa;* IE. base **erē-*, to row, oar, seen also in L. *remus* (**retsmos*), oar (cf. TRIREME), Eng. *rudder*], 1. to propel (a boat, etc.) on water by or as by using oars. 2. to carry in or on a boat, etc. propelled in this way. 3. to propel or carry in a way suggestive of using oars. 4. to use (a specified number of oars): said of a boat. 5. to use (a person or action) in rowing, especially in a race: as, the team *rowed* two new men, he *rowed* a powerful stroke. 6. to engage in (a race) by rowing. 7. to row against in a race. *v.i.* 1. to use oars in propelling a boat. 2. to be propelled by means of oars: said of a boat. *n.* 1. a rowing. 2. *a*) a trip made by rowboat. *b*) the distance of such a trip.

row (rou), *n.* [prob. back-formation < *rouse*, with loss of *s*, as in *pea, cherry, sherry*], [Colloq.], 1. a noisy quarrel, dispute, or disturbance; squabble, brawl, or commotion. 2. noise; clamor. *v.i.* [Colloq.], to make, or take part in, a noisy quarrel or disturbance. *v.t.* [Colloq.], to scold or criticize severely.

row·an (rō′ən, rou′ən), *n.* [< Scand.; cf. Norw. *rogn, raun*, ON. *reynir*], 1. the European mountain ash, a tree with white flowers and red berries. 2. either of two American mountain ashes. 3. a rowanberry.

row·an·ber·ry (rō′ən-ber′i, rou′ən-ber′i), *n.* [*pl.* ROWANBERRIES (-iz)], the reddish, berrylike fruit of the rowan.

row·boat (rō′bōt′), *n.* a boat designed to be rowed.

row·di·ly (rou′də-li), *adv.* in a rowdy manner.

row·di·ness (rou′di-nis), *n.* a rowdy quality or state.

row·dy (rou′di), *n.* [*pl.* ROWDIES (-diz)], [? < *row* (quarrel)], a person whose behavior is rough, quarrelsome, and disorderly; hoodlum. *adj.* [ROWDIER (-di-ẽr), ROWDIEST (-di-ist)], having the nature of or characteristic of a rowdy; rough, quarrelsome, etc.

row·dy·ish (rou′di-ish), *adj.* like or characteristic of a rowdy; rough, quarrelsome, and disorderly.

row·dy·ism (rou′di-iz′m), *n.* the behavior of a rowdy; rough, quarrelsome, disorderly conduct.

row·el (rou′əl), *n.* [ME. *rowelle, rewelle*, etc.; OFr. *rouelle;* see ROULETTE], 1. a small wheel with sharp projecting points, forming the end of a spur. 2. something like or suggestive of a rowel; specifically, a hair, piece of leather, etc. inserted under the skin of a horse or other animal to produce or facilitate a discharge, as of pus. *v.t.* [ROWELED or ROWELLED (-əld), ROWELING or ROWELLING], 1. to spur or prick with or as with a rowel. 2. to insert a rowel in.

ROWEL (on a spur)

row·en (rou′ən), *n.* [ME. *rewayn;* ONorm.Fr. **rewain;* akin to OFr. *regain* < *rewainer, regainer;* see RE- & GAIN], the second growth or crop of grass or hay in one season; aftermath.

Ro·we·na (rō-ē′nə), [? < AS. **Hrothwina* < *hroth*, fame + *wina*, a friend], a feminine name.

row·er (rō′ẽr), *n.* a person who rows a boat.

Row·land (rō′lənd), a masculine name: see **Roland.**

row·lock (rō′lok′, rul′ək), *n.* [altered (after *row, v.t.*) < earlier *oarlock*], [Chiefly British], an oarlock.

Rox·an·a (rok-san′ə), [L. *Roxane;* Gr. *Rhōxanē;* Per. *Roschana*, lit., dawn of day], a feminine name: diminutive, *Roxy;* equivalent, Fr. *Roxane.*

Ro·xas, Man·u·el (mä-nwel′ rô′häs), (*Manuel Roxas y Acuna*), 1892–1948; Philippine statesman; first president of the Philippine Republic (1946–1948).

Rox·burgh (roks′bũr′ō; Brit. roks′brə), *n.* a county of Scotland, on the English border: pop., 45,000; county seat, Jedburgh.

Rox·burgh·shire (roks′bũr′ō-shir′; Brit. roks′brə-shir′), *n.* Roxburgh.

Roy (roi), [as if < OFr. *roy* (Fr. *roi*), a king; but prob. < Gael. *rhu*, red], a masculine name.

roy·al (roi′əl), *adj.* [ME. *roial;* OFr. *roial, real;* L. *regalis* < *rex, regis*, a king; cf. REGAL], 1. of, from, or by a king or queen or kings and queens: as, the *royal* household, the *royal* family, a *royal* edict. 2. having the rank of a king or queen. 3. of a kingdom, its government, etc.: as, the *royal* fleet. 4. founded, chartered, or helped by, or under the patronage of, a king or queen: as, the *Royal* Society. 5. suitable for a king or queen; magnificent; splendid; princely; regal: as, *royal* robes. 6. like or characteristic of a king or queen; majestic; stately; noble: as, a *royal* bearing. 7. unusually large, fine, etc. *n.* 1. a large size of paper, 20 by 25 inches (for printing) or 19 by 24 inches (for writing). 2. a small sail set on the royal mast: see **sail**, illus. Abbreviated **R., r.**

royal blue, a deep, vivid reddish blue.

royal fern, a fern with large, tall, upright fronds.

royal flush, the highest poker hand, consisting of the ace, king, queen, jack, and ten of the same suit.

roy·al·ism (roi′əl-iz′m), *n.* 1. the principles of royal government; monarchism. 2. adherence to a monarch or monarchy.

roy·al·ist (roi′əl-ist), *n.* an adherent of royalism; person who supports a monarch or a monarchy, especially in times of revolution, civil war, etc.; specifically, [R-], *a*) a supporter of Charles I of England; Cavalier. *b*) a supporter of the British in the American Revolution; Tory. *c*) a supporter of the Bourbons in France. *adj.* of royalists or royalism.

royal mast, the small mast next above the topgallant mast.

Royal Oak, a city in southeastern Michigan, near Detroit: pop., 81,000.

royal palm, any of several tall, ornamental palm trees.

royal purple, 1. a dark, bluish purple. 2. originally, crimson: cf. **purple** (sense 2).

roy·al·ty (roi′əl-ti), *n.* [*pl.* ROYALTIES (-tiz)], [ME. *roialte, royaltie;* OFr. *roialté*, etc.], 1. the rank, status, or power of a king or queen; royal position, dignity, etc.; sovereignty. 2. a royal person or, collectively, royal persons. 3. a royal domain or realm; kingdom. 4. royal quality or character; kingliness; nobility, magnanimity, etc. 5. *usually pl.* a right, privilege, or prerogative of a monarch. 6. *a*) a royal right, as over some natural resource, granted by a monarch to a person, corporation, etc. *b*) payment for such a right. 7. a share of the proceeds or product paid to the owner of a right, as a patent, for permission to use it or operate under it. 8. a share of the proceeds from his work, usually a specified percentage, paid to an author, composer, etc.

Royce, Josiah (rois), 1855–1916; American philosopher and educator.

R.P., 1. Reformed Presbyterian. 2. Regius Professor.

r.p.m., revolutions per minute.

R.P.O., Railroad (or Railway) Post Office.

r.p.s., revolutions per second.

rpt., report.

R.Q., respiratory quotient.

R.R., 1. railroad. 2. Right Reverend.

-rrha·gi·a (rā′ji-ə), [Mod. L.; Gr. *-rrhagia* < *rhēgnynai*, to burst], a combining form meaning *abnormal discharge, excessive flow*, as in *menorrhagia:* also **-rhagia, -rrhage, -rhage, -rrhagy.**

-rrhe·a, -rrhoe·a (rē′ə), [Mod. L.; Gr. *-rrhoia* < *rhein*, to flow], a combining form meaning *a flow, discharge*, as in *gonorrhea, diarrhea:* also spelled **-rhea, -rhoea.**

Rs., 1. reis. 2. rupees: also **Rs, Rs, rs.**

R.S., 1. Recording Secretary. 2. Reformed Spelling.

r.s., right side.

R.S.F.S.R., RSFSR, Russian Soviet Federated Socialist Republic.

RSV, R.S.V., Revised Standard Version (of the Bible).

R.S.V.P., r.s.v.p., *répondez s'il vous plaît,* [Fr.], please reply.
rt., right.
r.t., in *football,* right tackle.
Rt. Hon., Right Honorable.
Rt. Rev., Right Reverend.
Rts., in *finance,* rights.
Ru, in *chemistry,* ruthenium.
Ru·an·da-U·run·di (ro͞o-än′dä-oo-roon′di), *n.* a former Belgian-administered UN trust territory in east central Africa: see **Rwanda** and **Burundi.**
rub (rub), *v.t.* [RUBBED (rubd), RUBBING], [ME. *rubben;* prob. < MLG. or MD.; cf. E.Fris. *rubben,* LG. *rubben,* etc.; IE. base **reup-* < **reu-,* to tear, etc.; see ROTTEN], 1. to move one's hand, a cloth, etc. over (a surface or object) with pressure and friction, in a circular or back-and-forth motion. 2. to move (one's hand, a cloth, etc.) over, or spread or apply (polish, etc.) on or over, a surface or object in this way. 3. to move (a thing) against something else, or move (things) over each other with pressure and friction (often followed by *together,* etc.). 4. to apply pressure and friction to, for cleaning, polishing, smoothing, etc. 5. to put into a specified condition by applying pressure and friction: as, he *rubbed* himself dry. 6. to make sore or chafed by rubbing. 7. to force, cause to go, etc. (*in, into,* etc.) by rubbing. 8. to remove by rubbing (with *out, off, away,* etc.). *v.i.* 1. to move with pressure and friction (*on, against,* etc. something): as, the tire *rubs* against the fender. 2. to rub something; exert pressure and friction on something. 3. to admit of being rubbed or removed by rubbing (often with *off, out,* etc.). 4. to go, keep going, manage, etc. with exertion or difficulty, by or as if by rubbing (with *along, on, through,* etc.). *n.* 1. a rubbing. 2. an obstacle, hindrance, or difficulty. 3. a place or spot that has been rubbed until rough or sore. 4. something that irritates, annoys, hurts the feelings, etc., as a jeer or rebuke.
rub down, 1. to massage. 2. to smooth, polish, wear down, etc. by rubbing.
rub it in, [Slang], to keep on mentioning to someone his failure or mistake, often with some malice.
rub out, 1. to erase or be erased by rubbing; hence, 2. [Slang], to kill.
rub the wrong way, to be displeasing, irritating, etc. to; annoy.
rub-a-dub (rub′ə-dub′), *n.* [echoic], a sound of or as of a drum being beaten.
Ru·bái·yát, The (ro͞o′bī-yät′, ro͞o′bi-yät′, ro͞o′bī-yät′), [lit., the quatrains; Ar. *rubā'īyāt,* pl. of *rubā'īyah,* quatrain, fem. of *rubā'ī,* composed of four < *rubā,* four], a long poem in quatrains (rhyming *aaba*), written by Omar Khayyám and known in English chiefly through the translation by Edward FitzGerald.
Rub' al Kha·li (roob′ äl khä′lē), a large desert of southern and eastern Arabia: also called *Great Sandy Desert, Ar Rimal.*
ru·basse (ro͞o-bas′, ro͞o-bäs′), *n.* [< Fr. *rubace;* see RUBY], a variety of crystalline quartz containing bits of iron oxide that produce a ruby-red color.
ru·ba·to (ro͞o-bä′tō), *adj.* [It. < (*tempo*) *rubato,* stolen (time)], in *music,* having some notes arbitrarily lengthened (or shortened) in performance and, often, others correspondingly changed in length; intentionally and temporarily deviating from a strict tempo. *n.* [*pl.* RUBATOS (-tōz)], 1. rubato modification or execution. 2. a rubato passage, phrase, etc. *adv.* with rubato; in a rubato manner.
rub·ber (rub′ẽr), *n.* 1. *a*) a person who rubs, as in polishing something. *b*) a person who rubs down, or massages; masseur. 2. an instrument, tool, etc. used in or for rubbing, as a coarse file, pad, etc. 3. [so named from use as an eraser], an elastic substance produced from the milky sap (*latex*) of various tropical plants, or synthetically: in pure form it is a white, unsaturated hydrocarbon having the formula $(C_5H_8)_n$: crude rubber is treated by vulcanization, etc., for use in making automobile tires, raincoats, electrical insulation, etc. 4. something made of this substance; specifically, *a*) an elastic band for holding small objects together, etc.: in full, **rubber band.** *b*) an eraser. *c*) *usually in pl.* an overshoe; especially, a low-cut overshoe. *d*) in *baseball,* an oblong piece of whitened rubber set in the pitcher's mound and serving as a mark that must not be overstepped in pitching. Abbreviated **r.** *adj.* made of rubber. *v.i.* [cf. RUBBERNECK], [Slang], to stretch one's neck or turn one's head to look at something.
rub·ber (rub′ẽr), *n.* [earlier *a rubbers* (applied to the deciding game at bowls) suggests ME. *at rebours, robours* < OFr. *a rebours,* backward], 1. in *bridge, whist, backgammon,* etc., a series of games, usually three, sometimes five, the majority of which must be won to win the whole series. 2. the odd, or deciding, game in such a series. Abbreviated **r.**
rubber check, [from the notion that it "bounces": see BOUNCE (*v.i.* 4)], [Slang], a check that is worthless because of insufficient funds in the drawer's account.
rub·ber·ize (rub′ẽr-īz′), *v.t.* [RUBBERIZED (-īzd′), RUBBERIZING], to coat or impregnate with rubber or some preparation or solution of rubber.
rub·ber·neck (rub′ẽr-nek′), *n.* [Slang], a person who stretches his neck or turns his head to look at things; one who gazes about in curiosity, as a sightseer. *adj.* [Slang], of or for sightseers: as, a *rubberneck* bus. *v.i.* [Slang], to look at things or gaze about in this way.
rubber plant, 1. any plant yielding a milky sap (*latex*) from which crude rubber is formed. 2. a plant with large, glossy, leathery leaves, native to India, the East Indies, etc. and used as an ornamental house plant in America and Europe.
rub·ber-stamp (rub′ẽr-stamp′), *v.t.* 1. to put the impression of a rubber stamp on; hence, 2. [Colloq.], to approve or endorse (a plan, proposal, etc.) in a routine manner, without thought.
rubber stamp, 1. a stamp made of rubber, pressed on an inking pad and used for printing signatures, dates, etc. 2. [Colloq.], a person, bureau, legislature, etc. that approves or endorses something in a routine manner, without thought.
rub·ber·y (rub′ẽr-i), *adj.* like rubber in appearance, elasticity, toughness, etc.
rub·bish (rub′ish), *n.* [ME. *robous, robys;* Anglo-Fr. *rubbous* (ML. *rubbosa*), rubble; for base see RUB], 1. any material rejected or thrown away as worthless; trash; refuse: often distinguished from *garbage.* 2. worthless, foolish ideas, statements, etc.; nonsense.
rub·bish·y (rub′ish-i), *adj.* like or full of rubbish; worthless.
rub·ble (rub′'l), *n.* [ME. *robel;* prob. < same source as *rubbish*], 1. rough, irregularly broken pieces of stone, brick, etc. 2. masonry made of such pieces; rubblework. 3. crumbling stone fragments forming the top layer of rock deposits.
rub·ble·work (rub′'l-wûrk′), *n.* masonry made of rubble or roughly dressed, irregular stones.
rub·bly (rub′li), *adj.* [RUBBLIER (-li-ẽr), RUBBLIEST (-li-ist)], of, like, or full of rubble.
rub·down (rub′doun′), *n.* a brisk rubbing of the body; massage.
rube (ro͞ob), *n.* [< given name *Reuben*], [Slang], a person who lives in or comes from a rural region and lacks polish and sophistication; rustic.
ru·be·fa·cient (ro͞o′bə-fā′shənt), *adj.* [L. *rubefaciens,* ppr. of *rubefacere,* to redden < *rubeus,* red + *facere,* to make], causing redness, as of the skin. *n.* in *medicine,* any external application, as a salve or plaster, causing redness of the skin.
ru·be·fac·tion (ro͞o′bi-fak′shən), *n.* 1. a making red, as with a rubefacient. 2. redness of the skin, especially as caused by a rubefacient.
ru·bel·la (ro͞o-bel′ə), *n.* [Mod. L., neut. pl. of L. *rubellus,* reddish < *ruber,* red], German measles.
ru·bel·lite (ro͞o-bel′īt), *n.* [< L. *rubellus* (see RUBELLA); + *-ite*], a red variety of tourmaline, used as a gem.
Ru·bens, Pe·ter Paul (pā′tẽr poul rü′bəns; Eng. ro͞o′bənz), 1577–1640; Flemish painter.
ru·be·o·la (ro͞o-bē′ə-lə), *n.* [Mod. L., neut. pl. dim. of L. *rubeus,* red], 1. measles. 2. German measles.
ru·bes·cence (ro͞o-bes′'ns), *n.* the condition or quality of being rubescent.
ru·bes·cent (ro͞o-bes′'nt), *adj.* [L. *rubescens,* ppr. of *rubescere,* to grow red < *rubere,* to redden < *ruber,* red], becoming red; specifically, blushing or flushing.
ru·bi·a·ceous (ro͞o′bi-ā′shəs), *adj.* [< L. *rubia,* madder; + *-aceous*], of the madder family of plants, chiefly tropical shrubs, trees, and herbs, including the coffee, ipecac, and cinchona plants, the gardenia, etc.
Ru·bi·con (ro͞o′bi-kon′), *n.* [L. *Rubico, Rubiconis*], a small river in northern Italy that formed the southern boundary of Cisalpine Gaul: when Caesar crossed it at the head of his army to march on Rome in 49 B.C., he began the civil war with Pompey.
cross (or **pass**) **the Rubicon,** to start on a course of action from which there is no turning back; take a final, irrevocable step.
ru·bi·cund (ro͞o′bi-kund′), *adj.* [Fr. *rubicond;* L. *rubicundus* < *ruber,* red], reddish; ruddy. —*SYN.* see **rosy.**
ru·bi·cun·di·ty (ro͞o′bi-kun′də-ti), *n.* [ML. *rubicunditas*], the quality or state of being rubicund.
ru·bid·i·um (ro͞o-bid′i-əm), *n.* [Mod. L. < L. *rubidus,* red (from the red lines in its spectrum)], a soft, silvery-white metallic chemical element, resembling potassium: symbol, Rb; at. wt., 85.48; at. no., 37.
ru·bied (ro͞o′bid), *adj.* colored like a ruby; deep-red.
ru·big·i·nous (ro͞o-bij′ə-nəs), *adj.* [LL. *rubiginosus* < L. *rubigo,* rust], rust-colored; reddish-brown.
Ru·bin·stein, An·ton (än-tôn′ roo-bin-shtin′; Eng. ro͞o′bin-stīn′), 1829–1894; Russian pianist and composer.
ru·bi·ous (ro͞o′bi-əs), *adj.* [Rare], ruby-colored; red.
ru·ble (ro͞o′b'l), *n.* [Russ. *rubl';* prob. < same source as Hind. *rūpiya,* rupee], the monetary unit and a silver coin of the Soviet Union, equal to about $1.10 in 1961: one ruble is equivalent to 100 kopecks: also spelled **rouble:** abbreviated **R., r.**
ru·bric (ro͞o′brik), *n.* [ME. *rubryke;* OFr. *rubriche,*

rubrique; L. *rubrica,* red earth (for coloring) < L. *ruber,* red], 1. in early books and manuscripts, a chapter heading, initial letter, specific sentence, etc. printed or written in red, decorative lettering, etc.; hence, 2. a heading, title, etc., as of a chapter or section of a book. 3. a direction in a prayer book, etc. for conducting religious services, usually printed in red. 4. the title or a heading of a law or part of a legal code, originally written or printed in red. 5. [Archaic], red ocher. ***adj.*** 1. inscribed in red. 2. [Archaic], red or reddish.

ru·bri·cal (rōō′bri-k'l), ***adj.*** of, prescribed by, or according to rubrics, especially liturgical rubrics.

ru·bri·cate (rōō′bri-kāt′), ***v.t.*** [RUBRICATED (-id), RUBRICATING], [< L. *rubricatus,* pp. of *rubricare,* to redden < *rubrica;* see RUBRIC], 1. to mark, color, or illuminate (a book, etc.) with red; write or print in red letters. 2. to provide with or regulate by rubrics.

ru·bri·ca·tion (rōō′bri-kā′shən), ***n.*** 1. a rubricating or being rubricated. 2. something written or printed in red.

ru·bri·ca·tor (rōō′bri-kā′tẽr), ***n.*** a person who puts rubrics in books, etc.

ru·bri·cian (rōō-brish′ən), ***n.*** an expert in or adherent of liturgical rubrics.

Ru·by (rōō′bi), [see RUBY (gem)], a feminine name.

ru·by (rōō′bi), ***n.*** [*pl.* RUBIES (-biz)], [ME. & OFr. *rubi;* ult. < L. *rubeus,* red; cf. ROUGE], 1. a clear, deep-red variety of corundum, valued as a precious stone: also called *Oriental ruby, true ruby.* 2. something made of this stone, as a watch jewel. 3. deep red. 4. something deep red, as wine. 5. [British], in *printing,* a size of type, 5 1/2 point, corresponding to agate. ***adj.*** deep-red.

ruche (rōōsh), ***n.*** [Fr., lit., beehive; OFr. *rusche* < ML. *rusca,* bark; prob. of Celt. origin], a frilling or pleating of lace, ribbon, muslin, net, etc. for trimming women's dresses: also spelled **rouche.**

ruch·ing (rōōsh′iŋ), ***n.*** 1. ruches collectively; trimming made of a ruche or ruches. 2. material used to make a ruche or ruches.

ruck (ruk), ***n.*** [ME. *ruke,* a heap; prob. < ON.; cf. Norw. *ruka,* little heap; IE. base as in *rick*], 1. originally, a heap or stack, as of fuel; hence, 2. a large number or quantity; multitude, mass, or crowd. 3. *a)* the horses left behind by the leaders in a race. *b)* the multitude or mass of undistinguished, ordinary people or things; common run.

ruck (ruk), ***n., v.t. & v.i.*** [prob. via dial. < ON. *hrukka*], crease, fold, wrinkle, or pucker.

ruck·sack (ruk′sak′; G. rook′zäk′), ***n.*** [G. < dial. form of *rücken,* the back + *sack,* a sack], a kind of knapsack strapped over the shoulders.

ruck·us (ruk′əs), ***n.*** [prob. a merging of *rumpus* & *ruction*], [Dial. or Colloq.], noisy confusion; uproar; row; disturbance.

ruc·tion (ruk′shən), ***n.*** [altered < *insurrection,* orig. with reference to the Irish Insurrection of 1798], [Colloq.], a riotous outbreak or uproar; noisy disturbance or quarrel.

rud·beck·i·a (rud-bek′i-ə), ***n.*** [Mod. L., after Olaus *Rudbeck* (1630–1702), Swed. botanist], any of a group of composite flowers with showy blossoms, mainly yellow, as the black-eyed Susan; coneflower.

rudd (rud), ***n.*** [akin to ME. *rude, rode;* AS. *rudu,* red; for base see RED], a European fresh-water fish of the carp family: also called *red-eye.*

rud·der (rud′ẽr), ***n.*** [ME. & AS. *rother,* a paddle; for IE. base see ROW (to propel with oars)], 1. a broad, flat, movable piece of wood or metal hinged vertically at the stern of a boat or ship, used for steering. 2. a piece like this in an aircraft, etc., used for steering to the left or right: see **airplane,** illus. 3. something serving to guide, direct, or control.

rud·der·post (rud′ẽr-pōst′), ***n.*** 1. a rudderstock. 2. in some ships, an added sternpost, to which the rudder is fastened.

rud·der·stock (rud′ẽr-stok′), ***n.*** the part of a ship's rudder by which it is pivoted to the sternpost or rudderpost.

rud·di·ness (rud′i-nis), ***n.*** a ruddy quality or state.

rud·dle (rud′'l), ***n.*** [< AS. *rudu,* red; cf. RUDD], red ocher. ***v.t.*** [RUDDLED (-'ld), RUDDLING], to color with red ocher. Also **reddle, raddle.**

rud·dle·man (rud′'l-mən), ***n.*** [*pl.* RUDDLEMEN (-mən)], a person who sells ruddle.

rud·dock (rud′ək), ***n.*** [ME. *ruddok;* AS. *rudduc* < base of *rudu,* red + *-ock*], the European robin.

rud·dy (rud′i), ***adj.*** [RUDDIER (-i-ẽr), RUDDIEST (-i-ist)], [ME. *rudi;* AS. *rudig* < *rudu,* red; for base see RED], 1. having a healthy red color: as, a *ruddy* complexion. 2. red or reddish. —***SYN.*** see **rosy.**

ruddy duck, a North American duck the adult male of which has a brownish-red neck and upper body, black crown, and white cheeks.

rude (rōōd), ***adj.*** [ME.; OFr.; L. *rudis*], 1. coarse or rough in form or workmanship; crude. 2. barbarous or ignorant: as, *rude* savages. 3. lacking refinement, culture, or elegance; uncouth; boorish. 4. discourteous; unmannerly: as, a *rude* reply. 5. rough; violent; harsh: as, *rude* winds blew. 6. harsh in sound; discordant; not musical: as, *rude* tones. 7. having or showing little skill, accuracy, method, etc.: as, *rude* drawings. 8. not carefully worked out or finished; rough: as, a *rude* plan. 9. sturdy; robust; rugged.

SYN.—**rude,** in this comparison, implies a deliberate lack of consideration for others' feelings and connotes, especially, insolence, impudence, etc. (it was *rude* of you to ignore your uncle); **ill-mannered** connotes ignorance of the amenities of social behavior rather than deliberate rudeness (a well-meaning but *ill-mannered* fellow); **impolite** implies merely a failure to observe the forms of polite society (it would be *impolite* to leave so early); **discourteous** suggests a lack of dignified consideration for others (a *discourteous* reply); **uncivil** implies a disregarding of even the most elementary of good manners (her *uncivil* treatment of the waiter).—***ANT.*** polite, civil.

ru·di·ment (rōō′də-mənt), ***n.*** [L. *rudimentum* < *rudis;* see RUDE], 1. *usually in pl.* a first principle, element, or fundamental, as of a subject to be learned: as, the *rudiments* of art. 2. a first slight beginning or appearance, or undeveloped form or stage, of something. 3. in *biology,* an incompletely developed organ or part, as one in an embryonic condition; specifically, a vestigial organ or part with no functional activity; vestige.

ru·di·men·tal (rōō′də-men′t'l), ***adj.*** rudimentary.

ru·di·men·ta·ri·ly (rōō′də-men′tẽr-ə-li), ***adv.*** 1. in a rudimentary manner. 2. so as to be rudimentary.

ru·di·men·ta·ri·ness (rōō′də-men′tẽr-i-nis), ***n.*** the quality or condition of being rudimentary.

ru·di·men·ta·ry (rōō′də-men′tẽr-i, rōō′də-men′tri), ***adj.*** of, or having the nature of, a rudiment or rudiments; specifically, *a)* elementary. *b)* incompletely or imperfectly developed. *c)* vestigial.

Ru·dolf, Lake (rōō′dolf), ***n.*** a lake in northwestern Kenya Colony, Africa: area, 3,475 sq. mi.; length, c. 180 mi.

Ru·dolph (rōō′dolf, rōō′dôlf), [G. *Rudolf;* OHG. *Rudolf, Hrodulf* < *hruod-,* fame + *wolf,* a wolf], a masculine name: variants, *Rodolph, Rolf, Rollo;* equivalents, Fr. *Rodolphe,* G. *Rudolf,* It. & Sp. *Rodolfo.*

Rudolph I, 1218–1291; German king and emperor of the Holy Roman Empire (1273–1291); founder of the House of Hapsburg: also spelled **Rudolf.**

rue (rōō), ***v.t.*** [RUED (rōōd), RUING], [ME. *reowen;* AS. *hreowan;* akin to G. *reuen;* IE. base **qreu-,* matted blood, raw flesh, etc. (cf. CRUST, CRUDE, CRUEL, RAW); basic sense "to shudder with horror"], 1. to feel remorse or repentance for (a sin, fault, etc.). 2. to wish (an act, agreement, etc.) undone, unmade, etc.; regret. ***v.i.*** to be sorrowful or regretful. ***n.*** [Archaic], 1. sorrow, repentance, or regret. 2. pity; compassion.

rue (rōō), ***n.*** [ME. *ruwe;* OFr.; L. *ruta;* Gr. *rhytē*], any of a group of strong-scented herbs, especially one with yellow flowers and bitter-tasting leaves formerly much used in medicine: traditional symbol of grief, regret, etc. (with punning allusion to *rue,* regret).

rue anemone, a small North American herb with white or pinkish flowers.

rue·ful (rōō′fəl), ***adj.*** 1. causing sorrow or pity; pitiable; lamentable. 2. feeling, expressing, or showing sorrow or pity; mournful.

ru·fes·cence (rōō-fes′'ns), ***n.*** the quality or condition of being rufescent.

ru·fes·cent (rōō-fes′'nt), ***adj.*** [L. *rufescens,* ppr. of *rufescere,* to become red < *rufus,* red], having a red tinge; reddish.

ruff (ruf), ***n.*** [contr. of *ruffle* (a pleat)], 1. a high, frilled or pleated collar of starched muslin, etc., worn by men and women in the 16th and 17th centuries. 2. something circular like this collar; specifically, a collar of prominent or colored feathers or fur on a bird or beast. 3. a European or Asiatic sandpiper the male of which grows a large ruff during the breeding season: the female is called a *reeve.* 4. a kind of pigeon with a ruff.

ruff (ruf), ***n.*** [OFr. *roffle, rouffle, ronfle;* ? altered < *triomphe;* see TRUMP; cf. It. *ronfa,* a card game], 1. [Obs.], an old card game somewhat like whist. 2. [< the *v.*], in *card games,* the act of trumping. ***v.t. & v.i.*** in *card games,* to trump.

ruff, ruffe (ruf), ***n.*** [prob. < *rough*], a small, spotted European fresh-water fish of the perch family.

ruffed (ruft), ***adj.*** having a ruff or ruffs.

ruffed grouse, a North American game bird with a feathered ruff: also called *partridge* (in the northern United States), *pheasant* (in the southern United States), *birch partridge* (in Canada).

ruf·fi·an (ruf′i-ən, ruf′yən), ***n.*** [Fr. *rufian;* It. *ruffiano,* a pander; Eng. sense influenced by *rough*], a brutal, violent, lawless person; tough. ***adj.*** brutal, violent, and lawless.

ruf·fi·an·ism (ruf′i-ən-iz'm, ruf′yən-iz'm), *n.* ruffianly behavior or character.

ruf·fi·an·ly (ruf′i-ən-li, ruf′yən-li), *adj.* like or characteristic of a ruffian; brutal, violent, and lawless.

ruf·fle (ruf′'l), *v.t.* [RUFFLED (-'ld), RUFFLING], [ME. *ruffelen* < ON. or MLG.; cf. LG. *ruffelen*, ON. *hrufla*, to scratch], 1. to take away the smoothness or regularity of; wrinkle; ripple: as, the wind *ruffles* the surface of the water. 2. to fold or draw (cloth, etc.) into ruffles. 3. to put ruffles on as trimming. 4. to make (feathers, etc.) stand up in or as in a ruff, as a bird in fright. 5. to disturb, irritate, or annoy: as, nothing *ruffles* her. 6. *a*) to turn over (the pages of a book, etc.) rapidly. *b*) to shuffle (cards). *v.i.* 1. to become uneven, wrinkled, etc. 2. to become disturbed, irritated, etc. *n.* 1. a narrow ornamental pleat or trimming of cloth, lace, etc. 2. something like this, as a bird's ruff. 3. a disturbance; irritation. 4. a break in surface smoothness; ripple.

ruf·fle (ruf′'l), *n.* [also earlier *ruff;* prob. echoic], a low, continuous beating of a drum, not so loud as a roll. *v.i.* & *v.t.* [RUFFLED (-'ld), RUFFLING], to beat (a drum, etc.) with a ruffle.

ruf·fle (ruf′'l), *v.i.* [RUFFLED (-'ld), RUFFLING], [ME. *ruffelen;* prob. specialized use of prec.], 1. to make a noisy disturbance. 2. to be arrogant; swagger. *n.* a noisy disturbance; brawl.

ruf·fly (ruf′li), *adj.* [RUFFLIER (-li-ẽr), RUFFLIEST (-li-ist)], of, in, or like a ruffle or ruffles.

ru·fous (rōō′fəs), *adj.* [L. *rufus*, red, reddish], brownish-red or yellowish-red; rust-colored.

Ru·fus (rōō′fəs), [L., red, red-haired], a masculine name.

rug (rug), *n.* [of Scand. origin; cf. Norw. *rugga*, coarse covering, *skinnrugga*, skin rug; akin to ON. *rögg*, long rough fleece; IE. base **reu-*, to tear; cf. RUB], 1. a piece of thick, often napped fabric, woven strips of rag, an animal skin, etc. used as a floor covering: usually distinguished from *carpet* in being a single piece of definite shape, not intended to cover the entire floor. 2. [Chiefly British], a piece of heavy, warm cloth used as a lap robe, wrap, etc.

ru·ga (rōō′gə), *n.* [*pl.* RUGAE (-jē)], [L.], *usually in pl.* in *botany, zoology*, etc., a wrinkle, fold, or crease.

ru·gate (rōō′gāt, rōō′git), *adj.* [L. *rugatus*, pp. of *rugare* < *ruga*, a wrinkle], wrinkled, folded, or creased.

Rug·by (rug′bi), *n.* 1. a town in Warwickshire, central England: pop., 38,000. 2. a famous boys' school there, founded in 1567. 3. a kind of football, first played at this school, in which each team consists of 15 players and the oval ball may be passed, dribbled with the feet, or carried: the American game of football developed from this: in full, **Rugby football.**

rug·ged (rug′id), *adj.* [ME.; of Scand. origin (cf. Sw. *rugga*, to roughen); < base of *rug* + *-ed*], 1. having irregular surface projections and depressions; not smooth or regular in surface or contour; uneven; rough; wrinkled: as, *rugged* ground, *rugged* mountains. 2. *a*) heavy, strong, and irregular, as facial features. *b*) having such features: as, a *rugged* face. 3. stormy; tempestuous: as, *rugged* weather. 4. sounding harsh: as, *rugged* tones. 5. severe; harsh; hard; stern: as, a *rugged* life, a *rugged* climate. 6. not polished, cultivated, refined, or elegant; rude: as, *rugged* manners. 7. strong; robust; sturdy; vigorous. —*SYN.* see **rough.**

Rug·ger (rug′ẽr), *n.* [British Slang], Rugby football.

ru·gose (rōō′gōs, rōō-gōs′), *adj.* [L. *rugosus* < *ruga*, a wrinkle], having or full of wrinkles; corrugated; ridged: as, a *rugose* leaf.

ru·gos·i·ty (rōō-gos′ə-ti), *n.* [< Fr. or LL.; Fr. *rugosité;* LL. *rugositas*], 1. the state or quality of being rugose. 2. [*pl.* RUGOSITIES (-tiz)], a wrinkle or corrugation.

ru·gous (rōō′gəs), *adj.* rugose.

Ruhr (roor; G. rōōr), *n.* 1. a river in western Germany, flowing into the Rhine: length, 144 mi. 2. the important mining and industrial region centered in the valley of this river.

ru·in (rōō′in, rōō′'n), *n.* [ME. & OFr. *ruine;* L. *ruina* < *ruere*, to fall], 1. [Rare], a falling down, as of a building, wall, etc.; hence, 2. *pl.* the remains of a fallen building, city, etc., or of something destroyed, devastated, decayed, etc. 3. *a*) anything that has fallen to pieces, been destroyed, become decayed through age, etc.: as, the bombed city was a *ruin. b*) a person regarded as being physically, mentally, or morally a wreck of what he was. 4. the state of having fallen to pieces or of being destroyed, devastated, decayed, etc. 5. downfall, complete destruction, overthrow, devastation, decay, etc., as of a thing or person, or in general; specifically, *a*) complete loss of means, solvency, position, etc. *b*) moral downfall, or loss of chastity, of a woman. 6. anything that causes downfall, destruction, decay, etc.: as, gambling was his *ruin. v.t.* to bring or reduce to ruin; specifically, *a*) to destroy, damage greatly or irreparably, spoil, etc. *b*) to impoverish or make bankrupt. *c*) to deprive (a woman) of chastity. *v.i.* to go or come to ruin.

SYN.—**ruin** implies a state of decay, disintegration, etc. especially through such natural processes as age and weather (the barn is in a state of *ruin*); **destruction** implies annihilation or demolition, as by fire, explosion, flood, etc. (the *destruction* of the village in an air raid); **havoc** suggests total destruction or devastation, as following an earthquake or hurricane; **dilapidation** implies a state of ruin or shabbiness resulting from neglect (the *dilapidation* of a deserted house).

ru·in·ate (rōō′ə-nāt′), *v.t.* & *v.i.* [RUINATED (-id), RUINATING], [< ML. *ruinatus*, pp. of *ruinare*, to ruin < L. *ruina;* see RUIN], [Archaic], to ruin. *adj.* ruined.

ru·in·a·tion (rōō′ə-nā′shən), *n.* [< *ruinate, v.*], 1. a ruining or being ruined. 2. anything that ruins; ruin (sense 6).

ru·in·ous (rōō′in-əs, rōō′'n-əs), *adj.* [OFr. *ruineux;* L. *ruinosus*], 1. falling or fallen into ruin; dilapidated; decayed. 2. bringing or tending to bring ruin; very destructive or harmful; disastrous: as, *ruinous* floods.

Ruis·dael, Ja·cob van (yä′kôp vän rois′dȧl), 1628?–1682; Dutch landscape painter: also spelled **Ruysdael, Ruijsdael.**

rule (rōōl), *n.* [ME. *reule, rewle;* OFr. *reule, riule;* L. *regula*, straight piece of wood, ruler, rule < *regere*, to lead straight, rule; for IE. base see REGAL], 1. an established guide or regulation for action, conduct, method, arrangement, etc. 2. a complete set or code of regulations in a religious order: as, the Benedictine *rule.* 3. a fixed principle that determines conduct; habit; custom: as, morning prayer was a *rule* of the household. 4. a criterion or standard. 5. something that usually or normally happens or obtains; the customary or ordinary course of events: as, famine and disease are the *rule* following war. 6. government; reign; control: as, the *rule* of Elizabeth. 7. a ruler (sense 2). 8. [Obs.], way of acting; behavior. 9. in *law*, a decision, order, etc. made by a judge or court in regard to a specific question: abbreviated **r.** 10. in *mathematics*, a method or procedure prescribed for computing or solving a problem. 11. in *printing*, a thin strip of metal, usually brass, as high as type, used to print lines between columns, make decorative borders, etc. *v.t.* [RULED (rōōld), RULING], 1. to have an influence over; guide: as, he was *ruled* by his friends. 2. to lessen; restrain: as, reason *ruled* his fear. 3. to have authority over; govern; direct: as, the king *ruled* the country. 4. to be the most important element of: as, action *rules* the plot. 5. to settle by decree; determine: as, the court *ruled* the validity of the point. 6. to mark lines on with or as with a ruler. 7. to mark (a line) with or as with a ruler. *v.i.* 1. to have absolute authority; govern. 2. to be at a specified rate or level; prevail: said of prices, commodities, etc., as, prices *rule* low. 3. to issue a formal decree about a question: as, the court will *rule* on the matter. —*SYN.* see **govern, law.**

as a rule, usually.

rule out, to exclude by decision.

rule of three, in *mathematics*, the method of finding the fourth term of a proportion when three terms are given.

rule of thumb, [from the method of measuring by the thumb], 1. a rule based on experience or practice rather than on scientific knowledge. 2. any way of doing things that is practical though crude.

rul·er (rōōl′ẽr), *n.* 1. a person or thing that rules or governs. 2. a thin strip of wood, metal, etc. with a straight edge and markings in inches or centimeters and their fractional parts, used in drawing straight lines, measuring length, etc.; straightedge. 3. a person or device that rules lines on paper, etc.

rul·er·ship (rōōl′ẽr-ship′), *n.* [see -SHIP], the position, power, jurisdiction, or term of a ruler; sovereignty.

rul·ing (rōōl′iŋ), *adj.* that rules; specifically, *a*) governing. *b*) predominating. *c*) prevalent. *n.* 1. the act of governing; control. 2. a decision made by a court or judge. 3. the act of drawing or measuring with a ruler. 4. a line or lines so drawn.

Rum (rōōm), *n.* Rome: the Arabic name, formerly used to designate the Byzantine Empire.

rum (rum), *n.* [short for *rumbullion*, name associated with the Fr. place name *Rambouillet* (with reference to peaches & gooseberries); cf. Fr. *rebouillir*, to boil again], 1. an alcoholic liquor distilled from fermented molasses, sugar cane, etc. 2. any alcoholic liquor; intoxicating drink in general.

rum (rum), *adj.* [< obs. *rum*, good, great; ? < *Rom*, a Gypsy; see ROMANY], [Slang], 1. [Archaic], good; excellent. 2. [Chiefly British], odd; strange; queer. 3. bad, poor, etc.: as, a *rum* joke.

rum (rum), *n.* rummy (card game).

Rum., 1. Rumania. 2. Rumanian.

Ru·ma·ni·a (rōō-mā′ni-ə, rōō-mān′yə), *n.* Romania.

Ru·ma·ni·an (rōō-mā′ni-ən, rōō-mān′yən), *adj.* & *n.* Romanian.

rum·ba (rum′bə; Sp. rōōm′bä), *n.* [Sp.; prob. of Afr. origin], 1. a dance of Cuban Negro origin and complex rhythm. 2. a modern ballroom adaptation of this, characterized by emphasized rhythmic movements of the lower part of the body. 3. music for, or in the rhythm of, this dance. Also spelled **rhumba.**

rum·ble (rum′b'l), *v.i.* [RUMBLED (-b'ld), RUMBLING], [ME. *romblen, romlen;* prob. < MD. *rommelen* < Gmc.

echoic base], 1. to make a deep, heavy, continuous, rolling sound: as, thunder *rumbles*. 2. to move or go with such a sound: as, the truck *rumbled* down the street. *v.t.* 1. to cause to make, or move with, such a sound. 2. to utter or say with such a sound. 3. to polish, mix, etc. in a rumble, or tumbling box. *n.* 1. a deep, heavy, continuous, rolling sound. 2. a space for luggage or a small extra seat, as for servants, in the rear of a carriage. 3. a rumble seat. 4. a tumbling box. 5. [Slang], a gang fight.

rumble seat, in some automobiles, especially formerly, an extra, open seat in the rear, behind the roofed seat: it can be folded shut when not in use.

rum·bly (rum'bli), *adj.* rumbling, or causing or characterized by a rumbling sound.

Ru·me·li·a (roo-mē'li-ə), *n.* the area of the former Turkish empire in the Balkans, including Macedonia, Thrace, and Albania: also spelled **Roumelia.**

ru·men (roo'min), *n.* [*pl.* RUMINA (-mi-nə)], [L., throat, gullet], 1. the first stomach of a ruminant. 2. the cud of a ruminant.

ru·mi·nant (roo'mə-nənt), *adj.* [L. *ruminans*, ppr. of L. *ruminare*, to ruminate], 1. chewing the cud. 2. of the cud-chewing animals. 3. meditative. *n.* any of a group of four-footed, hoofed, even-toed, and cud-chewing mammals, as the cattle, buffalo, bison, goat, deer, antelope, camel, giraffe, llama, etc., which have a stomach consisting of four divisions or chambers, the rumen, reticulum, omasum (or manyplies, psalterium), and abomasum: the grass, etc. that they eat is swallowed unchewed and passes into the rumen or reticulum, from which it is regurgitated, chewed and mixed with saliva, again swallowed, and then passed through the reticulum and omasum into the abomasum, where it is acted on by the gastric juice.

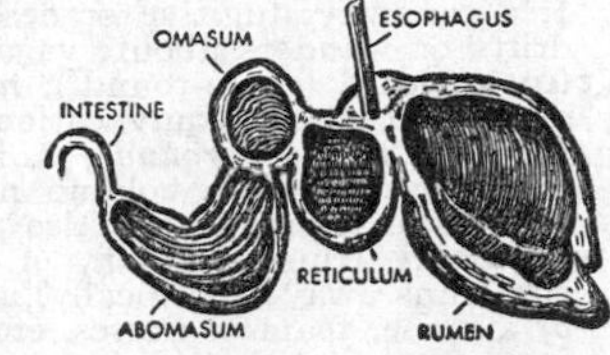

STOMACH OF A RUMINANT

ru·mi·nate (roo'mə-nāt'), *v.i. & v.t.* [RUMINATED (-id), RUMINATING], [< L. *ruminatus*, pp. of *ruminare*, to ruminate], 1. to chew (the cud), as a cow does. 2. to turn (something) over in the mind; meditate or reflect (on). —*SYN.* see **ponder.**

ru·mi·na·tion (roo'mə-nā'shən), *n.* 1. the act of chewing the cud. 2. meditation; reflective consideration.

ru·mi·na·tive (roo'mə-nā'tiv), *adj.* ruminating or inclined to ruminate; meditative.

ru·mi·na·tor (roo'mə-nā'tēr), *n.* [LL.], a person who ruminates.

rum·mage (rum'ij), *n.* [MFr. *arrumage* < *arrumere*, to stow cargo in the hold < *aruner*, to arrange < *run*, *rum*, ship's hold < AS. *rum*, room], 1. miscellaneous articles; odds and ends. 2. a rummaging, or thorough search. 3. a rummage sale. 4. [Obs.], *a*) the arrangement of cargo in a ship's hold. *b*) a stowage or storage place. *v.t.* [RUMMAGED (-ijd), RUMMAGING], 1. to search through (a place, receptacle, etc.) diligently and thoroughly, especially by moving the contents about, turning them over, etc.; ransack. 2. to get, turn up, or bring to light by or as by searching thoroughly (with *up* or *out*). *v.i.* to search diligently and thoroughly, as through the contents of a receptacle.

rummage sale, 1. a sale of contributed miscellaneous articles, used or new, as clothing, household furnishings, etc., to raise money for charitable purposes or for some organization. 2. a sale of miscellaneous merchandise at a shop, as for clearance before restocking, or of unclaimed articles at a warehouse, etc.

rum·mer (rum'ēr), *n.* [D. *roemer*, *romer* < *roemen*, to praise: hence, orig., a glass used for drinking toasts in praise of someone], a large drinking glass or cup.

rum·my (rum'i), *adj.* [RUMMIER (-i-ēr), RUMMIEST (-i-ist)], [*rum* (queer) + *-y*], [Chiefly British Slang], odd; strange; queer. *n.* [prob. < the *adj.*], a card game, played in many variations, in which the object is to match cards into sets of the same denomination or sequences of the same suit. Also **rum.**

rum·my (rum'i), *n.* [*pl.* RUMMIES (-iz)], [< *rum* (alcoholic liquor) + *-y*], [Slang], a drunkard. *adj.* of or like rum.

ru·mor (roo'mēr), *n.* [ME. *rumour;* OFr.; L., noise], 1. general talk not based on definite knowledge; mere gossip; hearsay. 2. an unconfirmed report, story, or statement in general circulation. 3. [Obs.], loud disapproval, protest, clamor, or uproar. *v.t.* to tell, report, or spread by rumor or as a rumor.

ru·mour (roo'mēr), *n. & v.t.* rumor: British spelling.

rump (rump), *n.* [ME. *rumpe;* ON. *rumpr;* akin to G. *rumpf*, trunk (of the body); IE. base **qremb-*, to turn, bend], 1. the hind part of the body of an animal, where the legs and the back come together. 2. a cut of meat, usually beef, from this part, behind the loin and above the round: see **beef**, illus. 3. the buttocks. 4. the last and unimportant or inferior part; fag end; mere remnant; hence, 5. a legislature, etc. having only a remnant of its former membership, as because of expulsions, and hence regarded as unrepresentative and without authority.

Rum·pel·stilts·kin (rum'p'l-stilt'skin), *n.* in *German folklore*, a deformed dwarf who made an agreement with the young bride of a king to spin for her the large quantity of flax required by the king: in return she was to give the dwarf her first child unless she guessed his name within a month, but she succeeded and the dwarf disappeared.

rum·ple (rum'p'l), *n.* [MD. *rompel* < *rompe*, a wrinkle], an uneven fold or crease; wrinkle. *v.t. & v.i.* [RUMPLED (-p'ld), RUMPLING], to make rumples (in); crumple.

Rump Parliament, in *English history*, 1. the part of the Long Parliament remaining after the purge of 1648 until disbanded by Cromwell in 1653. 2. the same body recalled in 1659 and disbanded in 1660.

rum·pus (rum'pəs), *n.* [said to be < Swiss G. student slang], [Colloq.], noisy or violent disturbance; uproar.

rumpus room, a room, usually in the basement of a house, for games, dancing, etc.; recreation room.

rum·run·ner (rum'run'ēr), *n.* a person, ship, etc. engaged in smuggling alcoholic liquor across a border.

run (run), *v.i.* [RAN (ran) or *dial.* RUN, RUN, RUNNING], [ME. *rinnen* (pp. *runnen*) < ON. *rinna*, *renna*, to run, with vowel influence < pp.; akin to G. *rinnen;* IE. base (**re-nw-ō*) < **er-*, to set in motion, etc., seen also in L. *origo* (cf. ORIGIN)], 1. to go by moving the legs rapidly, faster than in walking, and (in a two-legged animal) in such a way that for an instant both feet are off the ground. 2. to go rapidly; move swiftly: as, we *ran* to her aid, the ship *ran* before the wind. 3. to go, move, grow, etc. easily and freely, without hindrance or restraint; be unchecked. 4. to go away rapidly; flee. 5. to make a quick trip (*up to, down to, over to*, etc. a specified place) for a brief stay. 6. *a*) to take part in a contest or race. *b*) to be a candidate in an election. 7. to finish a contest or race in a specified numerical position: as, my horse *ran* last. 8. to swim in migration, as upstream or inshore for spawning, etc.: said of fish, as, the salmon *run* every year. 9. to go, as on a schedule; ply between two points: as, the bus *runs* between Chicago and New York. 10. to go or pass lightly and rapidly: as, a breeze *ran* through the trees. 11. to be current; circulate: as, the story *runs* that the bank will close. 12. to climb or creep: said of plants, as, the vine *runs* over the porch. 13. to extend in time; extend through the years: as, his family line *runs* back to the Conquest. 14. to move continuously: as, his tongue *ran* on and on. 15. to become loosened and ravel: as, her stocking *ran*. 16. to revolve or move with or as with parts that revolve, slide, etc.; operate: as, the machine is *running*. 17. to return constantly to the mind; be remembered: as, thoughts *ran* in his head. 18. to flow: as, blood *runs* in the veins. 19. to melt and flow: as, the butter *ran*. 20. *a*) to spread when put on a surface, as a liquid. *b*) to spread over or be diffused through cloth, etc. when moistened, as colors. 21. to be wet or covered with a flow: as, the gutters *ran* with blood, her eyes *ran* with tears. 22. to give passage to a fluid; specifically, *a*) to discharge pus, mucus, etc. *b*) to leak, as a faucet. 23. to elapse: as, the days *ran* into weeks. 24. to appear or be presented continuously or in a continuing series: as, the play *ran* for a year. 25. to continue in effect or force: as, the law *runs* for twenty years. 26. to extend in or as in a continuous line: as, the fence *runs* through the woods. 27. to proceed or pass into a specified condition, situation, etc.: as, he always *ran* into trouble. 28. to sail or float (aground, etc.): said of a ship. 29. to be written, expressed, played, etc. in a specified way: as, the proverb *runs* like this. 30. to be or continue at a specified size, price, amount, etc.: as, the apples *run* large this year. *v.t.* 1. to run along or follow (a specified course or route). 2. to travel over; cover by running, driving, etc.: as, wild horses *ran* the range. 3. to do or perform by or as by running: as, he *ran* a race. 4. to subject oneself to or be subjected to (a risk, etc.); incur. 5. to get past or escape by going through: as, the ship *ran* the blockade. 6. to sew with a rapid, continuous succession of stitches. 7. to pursue, or hunt (game, etc.). 8. to compete with in or as in a race; vie with. 9. *a*) to enter (a horse, etc.) in a race. *b*) to put up as a candidate for election. 10. to make run, move, operate, etc. 11. to bring, lead, or force into a specified condition, situation, etc. by or as by running: as, he *ran* me breathless, his action *ran* us into difficulties. 12. *a*) to carry or convey, as in a ship or vehicle; transport. *b*) to carry (taxable or outlawed goods) in or out illegally; smuggle. 13. to drive, force, or thrust (an object) into or against (something). 14. to allow to continue in force: as, he *ran* a bill at the store. 15. to make move or pass rapidly, flow, etc. in a specified way, direction, place, etc.: as, *run* water into a glass. 16. *a)* to be in charge of; manage: as, she *runs* the household. *b)* to perform the steps of (an experiment, test, etc.). 17. to mark, draw, or trace, as boundary lines on a map. 18. to extend or trace in a specified way or direction: as, *run* the rope taut, *run* the story back to its source. 19. to undergo or be affected by, as a fever, etc. 20. to flow with, discharge, or pour forth: as, the gutters *ran* blood. 21. to melt, fuse, or smelt (ore). 22. to cast or mold, as from molten metal; found. 23. to publish (an advertisement or story) in a newspaper. 24. in *billiards*, etc., to complete successfully (a specified number of strokes, shots, etc.) in uninterrupted sequence. *n.* 1. *a)* an act or period of running or moving rapidly. *b)* a running pace; rapid gait. *c)* capacity for running. 2. the distance covered or time spent in running. 3. a trip; journey; especially, *a)* a single, customary, or regular trip, as of a train, ship, etc. *b)* a quick trip for a brief stay at a place: as, take a *run* up to Detroit. 4. a route: as, the milkman finished his *run*. 5. *a)* movement onward, progression, or course, especially when quick, easy, or smooth. *b)* the direction, as of the grain of wood, or tendency, as of events. 6. a continuous course or period of a specified condition, action, etc.: as, a *run* of good luck. 7. a continuous course of performances, etc.: as, the play had a *run* of a year. 8. continued demand, call, etc. or series of sudden, urgent demands, etc., as on a bank for payment of deposits. 9. a period of being in public demand or favor. 10. a continuous series or sequence, as of cards in one suit. 11. a continuous extent of something. 12. a flow or rush of water, etc., as of the tide. 13. a small, swift stream, as a brook, rivulet, etc. 14. *a)* a period during which some fluid flows readily. *b)* the amount of flow. 15. *a)* a period of operation of a machine or machinery. *b)* the amount of something produced during such a period; output. 16. *a)* a kind, sort, or class, as of goods. *b)* the ordinary, usual, or average kind. 17. something in, on, or along which something else runs or can run; specifically, *a)* a way, track, channel, trough, pipe, runway, etc. *b)* an enclosed area in which domestic animals or fowls can move about freely: as, a chicken *run;* hence, 18. freedom to move about at will through all the parts or to use all the facilities (*of* a place): as, we had the *run* of his grounds. 19. a number of animals in motion together. 20. a well-defined track made by some animals in migration, etc.: as, a buffalo *run*. 21. *a)* a large number of fish migrating together, as upstream or inshore for spawning. *b)* such migration of fish. 22. a ravel in something knitted, as in a stocking. 23. the bower of a bowerbird. 24. in *aviation*, the approach to the target made by a bombing plane: in full, **bombing run.** 25. in *baseball*, a scoring point, made by a successful circuit of the bases: abbreviated **r.** (*sing. & pl.*). 26. in *billiards*, etc., an uninterrupted sequence of successful strokes, shots, etc. 27. in *cricket*, a scoring point, made by a successful running of both batsmen from one wicket to the other. 28. in *music*, a rapid succession of tones, as a roulade. 29. in *nautical usage*, the extreme after part of a ship's bottom, from where it starts to curve up and in toward the stern. *adj.* 1. melted; made liquid. 2. poured or molded while in a melted state: as, *run* metal. 3. drained or extracted, as honey. 4. [Colloq.], illegally transported; smuggled; contraband.

a run for one's money, 1. powerful competition. 2. some satisfaction for what one has expended, as in betting on a near winner in a race.

in the long run, over the whole range, or in the final outcome, of some sequence of events; ultimately.

on the run, 1. running. 2. hurrying from place to place or task to task. 3. running away; in retreat.

run across, to encounter by chance.

run after, 1. to pursue or follow. 2. [Colloq.], to seek the company or companionship of.

run away with, 1. to deprive of self-control, balance, etc., as anger or enthusiasm. 2. *a)* to outdo greatly all other contestants or performers in. *b)* to get (a prize, honors, etc.) in this way.

run down, 1. to cease to run, or stop operating, as a mechanical device, through lack of power. 2. to run, ride, or drive against so as to knock down. 3. to pursue and capture or kill. 4. to speak of slightingly or injuriously; disparage. 5. to lessen or lower in worth, quality, etc., as a house through lack of repairs, or in health, strength, etc., as a person through overwork; make or become run-down. 6. to read through rapidly. 7. in *baseball*, to cause (a runner trapped between two bases) to be put out.

run for it, to run in order to escape or avoid something.

run in, 1. to include or insert, as something additional. 2. [Slang], to take into custody by the authority of the law; arrest. 3. in *printing*, to make continuous without a break or paragraph.

run into, 1. to encounter by chance. 2. to run, ride, or drive against so as to hit; collide with.

run off, 1. to print, typewrite, etc. 2. to cause to be run, performed, played, etc. 3. to decide the winner of (a race, etc.) by a runoff.

run on, 1. to continue or be continued; specifically, in *printing*, to continue without a break or new paragraph. 2. to talk continuously.

run out, 1. to come to an end; expire or become used up, exhausted, etc. 2. to force to leave; drive out.

run out of, to use up a supply of (something).

run over, 1. to ride or drive over. 2. to overflow. 3. to examine, rehearse, etc. rapidly or casually.

run through, 1. to use up, spend, etc. quickly or recklessly. 2. to pierce. 3. to run over (sense 3).

run up, to raise, rise, or make rapidly.

run·a·bout (run'ə-bout'), *n.* 1. a person who runs about from one place to another. 2. a light, one-seated, open carriage. 3. a light, one-seated, open automobile; roadster. 4. a light motorboat.

run·a·gate (run'ə-gāt'), *n.* [altered (after *run* + obs. *agate*, on the way) < ME. *renegat*, apostate, villain < OFr. *renegat* < ML. *renegatus;* see RENEGADE], [Archaic], 1. a runaway; fugitive or deserter. 2. a person who drifts or wanders about; vagabond.

run-a·round (run'ə-round'), *n.* 1. [Slang], a series of evasive excuses, equivocations, etc.: usually in *get* (or *give*) *the run-around*. 2. in *printing*, an arrangement of type in a column narrower than usual, as around an illustration. Also **runround.**

run·a·way (run'ə-wā'), *n.* 1. a person, animal, etc. that runs away; specifically, *a)* a fugitive or deserter. *b)* a horse, team of horses, etc. that has broken loose from control of the rider or driver. 2. a running away. 3. a runaway race or victory. *adj.* 1. running away or having run away; escaping, eloping, or breaking loose from control: as, *runaway* lovers, a *runaway* horse. 2. of or done by runaways or running away: as, a *runaway* marriage. 3. easily won, as a race, or decisive, as a victory. 4. *a)* rising rapidly, as prices. *b)* characterized by such prices: as, a *runaway* inflation.

run·back (run'bak'), *n.* in *football*, 1. a running back with the ball, as after receiving the kickoff. 2. the distance so run.

run·ci·ble spoon (run'sə-b'l), [prob. coined < *runcinate* + *-ible;* used by E. Lear in "The Owl and the Pussycat"], a kind of fork with two broad prongs and one sharp-edged, curved prong.

run·ci·nate (run'si-nit, run'si-nāt'), *adj.* [L. *runcinatus*, pp. of *runcinare*, to plane off < *runcina*, a plane (formerly understood as "saw")], irregularly saw-toothed, with the teeth or lobes curved backward as some leaves: see **leaf**, illus.

run·dle (run'd'l), *n.* [ME. *rundel*, var. of *roundel*] 1. a rung, or round, as of a ladder. 2. one of the bars in a lantern pinion. 3. something that rotates, as a wheel or the drum of a capstan.

rund·let (rund'lit), *n.* [OFr. *rondelet*, dim. of *rondelle* little tun or barrel, round shield], [Archaic], 1. a small barrel or cask of varying capacity. 2. the amount of liquor contained in this: an old British liquid measure, usually taken as equal to about 18 wine gallons. Also **runlet.**

run-down (run'doun'), *adj.* 1. not wound and therefore not running, as a spring-operated clock or watch. 2. in poor physical condition, as from overwork; weak and exhausted; debilitated. 3. fallen into disrepair; dilapidated. *n.* 1. in *baseball*, the act of running down a base runner. 2. a concise summary or outline.

rune (rōōn), *n.* [ME. *roun;* AS. *run*, a secret, mystery, runic character; readopted in 17th c. in form of ON. *rūn;* IE. echoic base **reu-*, hoarse sound; cf. ROUND (to whisper); in sense 4 < Finn. *runo*, poem, canto < ON. *rūn*], 1. any of the characters of an alphabet used by the ancient Scandinavians and other ancient Germanic peoples. 2. something inscribed or written in such characters. 3. any similar character or mark having some mysterious meaning or magical powers attributed to it. 4. *a)* a Finnish poem or canto. *b)* loosely, any ancient Scandinavian poem. *c)* [Poetic], any poem, verse, or song.

rung (ruŋ), *n.* [ME. *rong;* AS. *hrung*, a staff, rod, pole; akin to G. *runge;* for IE. base see RING (a circlet)], any sturdy stick, bar, or rod, especially a rounded one used as a crossbar, strengthening part, etc.; specifically, *a)* any of the crosspieces constituting the steps of a ladder. *b)* a supporting crosspiece between the legs of a chair, or across the back, etc. *c)* a spoke of a wheel.

rung (ruŋ), past participle and rare past tense of **ring** (to make the sound of a bell).

ru·nic (rōō'nik), *adj.* [< Mod. L. *runicus* < ON. *rūn* a rune], 1. of, consisting of, characterized by, or set down in runes. 2. like or suggestive of runes in decorative interlaced effect, as knots and other figures on the monuments, etc. of ancient peoples of northern Europe. *n.* in *printing*, a style of decorative type having almost uniformly thick lines.

run-in (run'in'), *adj.* in *printing*, that is run in. *n.* 1. run-in matter. 2. [Colloq.], a quarrel, fight, etc.

run·let (run′lit), *n.* [*run, n.* + *-let*], a runnel, or rivulet.
run·let (run′lit), *n.* a rundlet.
run·nel (run′'l), *n.* [ME. *rinel, runel;* AS. *rynel* < base of *rinnan,* to run; cf. RUN], 1. a small stream; little brook or rivulet. 2. a small channel or watercourse.
run·ner (run′ẽr), *n.* 1. a person, animal, or thing that runs, as a racer. 2. a person who runs errands, carries messages, etc., as for a bank or brokerage house. 3. an agent, collector, etc., as for a bank or broker. 4. a person whose work is to solicit patronage or business, as for a hotel or store. 5. *a)* a smuggler. *b)* a smuggling ship. 6. a person who operates or manages something, as a machine. 7. *a)* a long, narrow, decorative cloth put across a table, chest of drawers, etc. *b)* a long, narrow rug, as for a hall or corridor. 8. a long ravel, as in hose; run. 9. *a)* a long, slender, trailing stem that puts out roots along the ground at its nodes or end, thus producing new plants. *b)* any plant that spreads in this way, as the strawberry. 10. any of various twining plants: as, the scarlet *runner.* 11. something on or in which something else moves, as a sliding part in machinery. 12. either of the long, narrow pieces of metal or wood on which a sled or sleigh slides. 13. the blade of a skate. 14. a sharp, curved blade for opening a furrow in seeding. 15. in *metallurgy,* a channel through which molten metal is poured into a mold; gate. 16. in *zoology,* the jurel, a food fish.

RUNNER
(strawberry plant)

runner bean, [British], a string bean.
run·ner-up (run′ẽr-up′), *n.* a person or team that finishes second in a race, contest, etc., especially in the final round of a tournament.
run·ning (run′iŋ), *n.* 1. the act of a person or thing that runs (in various senses); racing, management, etc. 2. power or ability to run. 3. *a)* that which runs, or flows. *b)* the amount or quantity that runs. *adj.* 1. moving, passing, or advancing rapidly. 2. *a)* run at a rapid gait: as, a *running* race. *b)* trained to race at this gait: said of a horse. 3. flowing: as, *running* water. 4. cursive: said of handwriting. 5. melting; becoming liquid or fluid. 6. discharging liquid; especially, discharging pus, etc.: as, a *running* sore. 7. creeping or climbing: said of plants. 8. going, or in operation, as machinery. 9. in a straight line; linear: said of measurement, as, a *running* foot. 10. going on, extending, etc. without interruption; continuous: as, a *running* commentary, a *running* design. 11. in succession; successive: placed after the noun, as, for five days *running.* 12. prevalent. 13. in progress; current: as, a *running* account. 14. moving or going easily or smoothly. 15. slipping or sliding easily: as, a *running* knot. 16. moving when pulled, as a rope. 17. done in, with, or by a run: as, a *running* jump. 18. of the normal run (of a train, bus, etc.): as, the *running* time is two hours.
in (or **out of**) **the running,** in (or out of) the competition; having (or having lost) a chance to win.
running board, especially formerly, a footboard, or step, extending along the lower part of the side of an automobile, etc.
running fire, 1. a rapid succession of shots, as from soldiers in ranks; hence, 2. a rapid succession, as of remarks, questions, etc.
running gear, the working parts of a machine; especially, the wheels, axles, transmission, etc. of a locomotive, automobile, or the like, together with their attachments, as distinguished from the body.
running hand, rapid handwriting, sometimes almost illegible, in which the letters are slanted and close together, formed without often lifting the pen or pencil from the paper: distinguished from *round hand.*
running head (or **title**), a descriptive heading or title printed at the top of every page or, sometimes, every other page, usually the left-hand ones.
running knot, a knot so tied as to slide along the rope, thus forming a noose (*running noose*) that tightens as the rope is pulled: see **knot,** illus.
running mate, 1. *a)* a horse that is a teammate for another horse. *b)* a horse used to set the pace for another horse in a race. 2. a candidate for the lesser of two closely associated offices, as for the vice-presidency, regarded as running for election together with his party's candidate for the greater.
Run·ny·mede (run′i-mēd′), *n.* a meadow on the south bank of the Thames, west of London, where King John is thought to have met his barons in 1215 and signed the Magna Charta.
run-off (run′ôf′), *n.* 1. something that runs off, as rain in excess of the amount absorbed by the ground. 2. waste products eliminated in manufacturing. 3. a deciding, final race, game, etc., as in case of a tie.
run-of-the-mill (run′əv-thə-mil′), *adj.* [see RUN, *n.,* 16*b*], not selected or special; ordinary; average: also **mill-run.**
run-on (run′on′), *adj.* in *printing,* that is run on. *n.* run-on matter.
run·round (run′round′), *n.* a run-around (sense 2).
runt (runt), *n.* [prob. akin to AS. *hrindan,* to thrust (cf. AS. *Hrunting,* ON. *Hrotter,* sword names of this same origin); senses 2 & 3*a* may be influenced by a homophonous word akin to D. *rund,* an ox], 1. *a)* a stunted, undersized, or dwarfish animal, plant, thing, or (usually in a contemptuous sense) person. *b)* the smallest animal of a litter. 2. an ox or cow of a small breed or size. 3. [Scot. or British Dial.], *a)* an old cow or ox. *b)* a withered old woman. *c)* an old or decayed tree stump. *d)* the hardened stem of a cabbage or other plant.
runt·i·ness (run′ti-nis), *n.* a runty quality or state.
runt·y (run′ti), *adj.* [RUNTIER (-ti-ẽr), RUNTIEST (-ti-ist)], stunted; undersized; dwarfish.
run·way (run′wā′), *n.* 1. a way, as a channel, track, chute, groove, trough, etc., in, on, or along which something runs, or moves; specifically, *a)* the channel or bed of a stream. *b)* a strip of leveled ground, often paved, for use by airplanes in taking off and landing. *c)* a track or ramp for wheeled vehicles. *d)* a beaten path made by deer or other animals. *e)* in *bowling,* a track along which the bowls are returned to the bowlers. 2. an enclosed area in which chickens, etc. can move about freely: also **run.**
ru·pee (ro͞o-pē′), *n.* [Hind. *rūpiyah* < Sans. *rūpya,* wrought silver], 1. the monetary unit and a silver coin of India, valued at about 20 cents in 1950. 2. the monetary unit of Pakistan, valued at about 30 cents in 1950. Abbreviated **R., r., Re.** (*pl.* **Rs., Rs, Rs, rs.**).
Ru·pert (ro͞o′pẽrt), [G. *Ruprecht, Rupprecht;* see ROBERT], a masculine name.
rup·tur·a·ble (rup′chẽr-ə-b'l), *adj.* that can be ruptured.
rup·ture (rup′chẽr), *n.* [Fr.; L. *ruptura* < *ruptus,* pp. of *rumpere,* to break; IE. base **reu(p)-,* to tear out, tear apart, break, seen also in Eng. *reave, rob*], 1. the act of breaking apart or bursting, or the state of being broken apart or burst; breach. 2. a breaking off of friendly or peaceful relations, as between countries or individuals. 3. in *medicine,* hernia; especially, abdominal or inguinal hernia. *v.t. & v.i.* [RUPTURED (-chẽrd), RUPTURING], 1. to break apart or burst. 2. to affect with, undergo, or suffer a rupture.
ru·ral (roor′əl), *adj.* [ME.; LL. *ruralis* < L. *rus, ruris,* the country < IE. **rewos,* space, wide, seen also in Goth. *rums,* room, space, Eng. *room*], 1. of or characteristic of the country (as distinguished from cities or towns), country life, or country people; rustic: opposed to *urban.* 2. living in the country. 3. having to do with farming; agricultural.
SYN.*—rural** is the comprehensive, nonspecific word referring to life on the farm or in the country as distinguished from life in the city (*rural* schools); **rustic** stresses the contrast between the supposed crudeness and unsophistication of the country and the polish and refinement of the city (*rustic* humor); **pastoral** suggests the highly idealized primitive simplicity of rural life, originally among shepherds; **bucolic,** a somewhat contemptuous term, emphasizes the alleged boorishness of rural persons (her *bucolic* suitor).—ANT.*** urban.
rural free delivery, free delivery of mail by carriers on routes in rural areas: abbreviated **RFD, R.F.D.**
ru·ral·ism (roor′əl-iz'm), *n.* 1. rural quality or character. 2. a rural idiom.
ru·ral·ist (roor′əl-ist), *n.* a person who leads or advocates a rural life.
ru·ral·i·ty (roo-ral′ə-ti), *n.* [*pl.* RURALITIES (-tiz)], 1. ruralism. 2. *usually in pl.* a rural characteristic, feature, scene, etc.
ru·ral·i·za·tion (roor′əl-i-zā′shən, roor′əl-ī-zā′shən), *n.* a ruralizing or being ruralized.
ru·ral·ize (roor′əl-iz′), *v.t.* [RURALIZED (-īzd′), RURALIZING], to make rural. *v.i.* to live or stay for a time in the country; rusticate.
Ru·rik (roor′ik), *n.* a Scandinavian chief of the 9th century A.D. who is regarded as the founder of the Russian monarchy; died 879 A.D.
Rus., 1. Russia. 2. Russian.
ruse (ro͞oz), *n.* [ME.; Late OFr. < *ruser,* to dodge; OFr. *reüsser,* to get out of the way; ? < L. *recusare,* to refuse, or LL. **refusare,* to deny; see REFUSE, *v.*], a stratagem, trick, or artifice. —***SYN.*** see **trick.**
rush (rush), *v.i.* [ME. *ruschen;* OFr. *reüsser;* cf. RUSE], 1. to move or go swiftly or impetuously; dash. 2. to make a swift, sudden attack or assault (*on* or *upon*); charge. 3. to dash recklessly or rashly (often with *into*). 4. to pass, come, go, come into view, act, etc. swiftly, suddenly, or hastily: as, the stars *rushed*

out, a terrible thought *rushed* into her mind. *v.t.* 1. to move, send, push, drive, etc. swiftly, violently, or hastily: as, they *rushed* him out of the room, the resolution was *rushed* through the Senate. 2. to do, make, or cause to move, go, or act, with unusual or excessive speed or haste; hurry: as, I don't like to *rush* my work, don't *rush* me. 3. *a*) to make a swift, sudden attack or assault on; charge. *b*) to overcome or capture by such an attack or assault. 4. [Slang], to lavish attentions on, as in courting. 5. in *football*, to advance (the ball) by a rush or series of rushes. *n.* 1. a rushing. 2. an eager movement of many people to get to a place, as to a new territory or a region where gold has recently been found. 3. busyness; haste; hurry: as, the *rush* of modern life. 4. a sudden, swift attack or assault; onslaught. 5. in many American colleges, a kind of scrimmage between groups of students, as between freshmen and sophomores, held as a contest, often for the temporary possession of some trophy. 6. a press, as of business or traffic, necessitating unusual haste or effort. 7. in *football*, *a*) an attempt to carry the ball through the opponent's line, as by plunging. *b*) in former usage, any of certain players in the forward line (*rush line*): as, center *rush*. 8. *usually in pl.* in *motion pictures*, a first print, as of a scene photographed on the previous day, projected for inspection by the director, etc. *adj.* 1. necessitating haste: as, *rush* orders. 2. characterized by a rush (sense 6): as, *rush* hours.

with a rush, suddenly and forcefully.

rush (rush), *n.* [ME. *rusche, rische;* AS. *rysce;* akin to MD. *risch*, G. *rusch;* IE. base **rezg-*, to plait, twist], 1. any of various grasslike plants with hollow or pithy stems, growing usually in wet or marshy places. 2. a stem of such a plant, used for making baskets, mats, chair seats, etc. 3. something of little or no value.

Rush, Benjamin (rush), 1745–1813; American physician; signer of the Declaration of Independence.

rush candle, a candle made with the pith of a rush as the wick; rushlight.

rush·er (rush'ẽr), *n.* a person or thing that rushes; specifically, in *football*, a player in the rush line.

rush hour, a time of the day when business, traffic, etc. are especially heavy.

rush·light (rush'līt'), *n.* a rush candle: also **rush light.**

rush line, in *football*, the forward line, normally including the ends, tackles, guards, and center.

rush·y (rush'i), *adj.* [RUSHIER (-i-ẽr), RUSHIEST (-i-ist)], 1. consisting or made of rushes (plants). 2. full of or covered with rushes. 3. rushlike.

ru·sine antler (rōō'sin, rōō'sīn), [< Mod. L. *Rusa* (< Malay *rusa*, deer), name of the genus; + *-ine*], a type of antler with a single tine at the brow and a simple, two-pronged fork at the tip.

‡rus in ur·be (rus' in ũr'bi), [L.], the country in the city: said of a city, town, or city home characterized by trees, lawns, etc.

rusk (rusk), *n.* [Sp. *rosca*, twisted roll of bread, lit., a spiral, screw < LL. **rosicare*, to gnaw], 1. *a*) sweet, raised bread or cake toasted in an oven, or baked a second time, until browned and crisp. *b*) a piece of this. 2. a light, soft, sweetened biscuit or bread.

Rus·kin, John (rus'kin), 1819–1900; English writer, art critic, and social reformer.

Russ (rus), *adj. & n.* [*pl.* RUSS], [cf. Fr. *Russe*, Russ, *Rusi*], Russian.

Russ (roos), *n.* the Niemen, a river in Byelorussia and Lithuania: so called at its mouth.

Russ., 1. Russia. 2. Russian.

Rus·sel, Rus·sell (rus''l), [< surname *Russell*, orig. dim. of Fr. *roux*, red], a masculine name: diminutive, *Russ.*

Rus·sell, Bertrand (rus''l), (*Bertrand Arthur William Russell*), third Earl Russell, 1872– ; English philosopher, mathematician, and writer: received Nobel prize in literature, 1950.

Russell, Charles Edward, 1860–1941; American journalist and author.

Russell, Elizabeth Mary, (pseudonym *Elizabeth;* born *Mary Annette Beauchamp*), Countess Russell, 1866–1941; English novelist.

Russell, George William (pseudonym *Æ*), 1867–1935; Irish poet, essayist, and painter.

Russell, Lord **John,** first Earl Russell of Kingston Russell, 1792–1878; English statesman; prime minister (1846–1852; 1865–1866).

Russell, Lillian, (born *Helen Louise Leonard*), 1861–1922; American singer and actress.

Rus·sell·ite (rus''l-īt'), *n.* a Jehovah's Witness: former name.

rus·set (rus'it), *n.* [ME.; OFr. *rousset*, dim. of *rous* < L. *russus*, reddish (akin to *ruber*, red)], 1. yellowish brown or reddish brown. 2. a coarse homespun cloth, reddish-brown or brownish, formerly made and used for clothing by country people. 3. a winter apple with a rough, mottled skin. *adj.* 1. yellowish-brown or reddish-brown. 2. made of russet (cloth); hence, 3. [Rare], rustic, simple, etc.

Rus·sia (rush'ə), *n.* 1. before 1917, an empire (*Russian Empire*) in eastern Europe and northern Asia, ruled by a czar: capital, St. Petersburg (Petrograd). 2. now, *a*) the Union of Soviet Socialist Republics; Soviet Union: popularly so called. *b*) the Russian Soviet Federated Socialist Republic, a part of the Soviet Union. Russian name, *Rossiya.* 3. [r-], Russia leather.

Russia leather, a fine, smooth leather, usually dyed dark red, originally made in Russia of hides treated with oil from birch bark: used in bookbinding, etc.

Rus·sian (rush'ən), *adj.* of Russia, its people, their language, etc. *n.* 1. a native or inhabitant of Russia. 2. a member of the chief Slavic people of Russia: cf. **Great Russian, Little Russian, White Russian.** 3. the East Slavic language of the Russians, especially the form spoken by the Great Russians: the principal language of the Soviet Union.

Russian dressing, mayonnaise mixed with chili sauce, chopped pickles, pimientos, etc.: used on salads.

Rus·sian·ize (rush'ən-īz'), *v.t.* [RUSSIANIZED (-īzd'), RUSSIANIZING], to make Russian in character.

Russian (Orthodox) Church, a branch of the Orthodox Eastern Church: it was the national church of czarist Russia.

Russian Revolution, 1. the revolution of 1917 in which the government of the Czar was overthrown by Russian workers, peasants, soldiers, and sailors: it consisted of two distinct revolutions, the first (*February Revolution*) being the uprising of March (February, Old Style), in which a parliamentarian government headed by Kerensky came to power, the second (*October Revolution*) being the uprising of November (October, Old Style), in which this government was replaced by the Soviet government led by the Bolsheviks (Communists) under Lenin. 2. the October Revolution.

Russian Soviet Federated Socialist Republic, a republic in Europe and Asia, forming the largest division of the Soviet Union: a federation of Regions, Territories, Autonomous Soviet Socialist Republics, and Autonomous Regions: area, 6,322,350 sq. mi.; pop., 114,337,000; capital, Moscow: abbreviated **R.S.F.S.R., RSFSR:** also called (*Soviet*) *Russia.*

Russian thistle, a large weed with spiny branches and small leaves, which matures into a tumbleweed.

Russian wolfhound, any of a breed of large dog with a narrow head, long legs, and silky coat; borzoi: so called because of Russian origin.

RUSSIAN WOLFHOUND (32 in. high at shoulder)

Rus·so- (rus'ō, rus'ə), a combining form meaning: 1. *Russia* or *Russian*, as in *Russophobe*. 2. *Russian and*, as in *Russo-Japanese.*

Rus·so·phile (rus'ō-fīl'), *n.* [*Russo-* + *-phile*], a person who admires or is extremely fond of Russia, its people, customs, influence, etc. *adj.* of Russophiles.

Rus·so·phobe (rus'ō-fōb'), *n.* a person who has Russophobia. *adj.* of Russophobes.

Rus·so·pho·bi·a (rus'ō-fō'bi-ə), *n.* [*Russo-* + *-phobia*], hatred or fear of Russia, its people, customs, influence, etc.

rust (rust), *n.* [ME.; AS.; akin to G. *rost;* base **rudh-s-to* < IE. base **reudh-*, red, seen also in AS. *read* (cf. RED), *rudu* (cf. RUDD)], 1. the reddish-brown or reddish-yellow coating formed on iron or steel by oxidation, as during exposure to air and moisture: it consists mainly of ferric oxide, Fe_2O_3, and ferric hydroxide, $Fe(OH)_3$: also **iron rust.** 2. any coating or film formed on any other metal by oxidation or corrosion. 3. any stain or formation resembling iron rust. 4. any habit, influence, growth, etc. injurious to usefulness, to the mind or character, etc. 5. disuse of mental or moral powers; inactivity; idleness. 6. the color of iron rust; reddish brown or reddish yellow. 7. in *botany*, *a*) any of a number of plant diseases caused by parasitic fungi and characterized by a spotted reddish or brownish discoloration of stems and leaves. *b*) any fungus causing such a disease: also **rust fungus.** *v.i. & v.t.* 1. to have or cause to have such a disease. 2. to become or cause to be coated with rust, as iron. 3. to deteriorate or spoil, as through disuse, inactivity, etc.: as, his mind had *rusted.* 4. to become or make rust-colored.

rust-col·ored (rust'kul'ẽrd), *adj.* having the color of iron rust; reddish-brown or reddish-yellow.

rus·tic (rus'tik), *adj.* [Late ME. *rustyk;* L. *rusticus* < *rus*, the country; see RURAL], 1. of or living in the country, as distinguished from cities or towns; rural. 2. lacking refinement, elegance, polish, or sophistication; specifically, *a*) simple, plain, or artless. *b*) rough, awkward, uncouth, or boorish. 3. made of rough, bark-covered branches or roots: as, *rustic* furniture. 4. in *masonry*, having a rough surface or irregular, deeply sunk, deliberately conspicuous joints; rusticated. *n.* a country person, especially one regarded as unsophisticated, simple, awkward, uncouth, etc. —*SYN.* see **rural.**

rus·ti·cal (rus'ti-k'l), *adj. & n.* [Archaic or Rare], rustic.

rus·ti·cal·ly (rus′ti-k'l-i, rus′tik-li), ***adv.*** in a rustic manner.

rus·ti·cate (rus′ti-kāt′), ***v.i.*** [RUSTICATED (-id), RUSTICATING], [< L. *rusticatus*, pp. of L. *rusticari*, to rusticate < *rusticus;* see RUSTIC], 1. to go to the country. 2. to live or stay in the country; lead a rural life. ***v.t.*** 1. to send to, or cause to live or stay in, the country. 2. [British], to suspend (a student) from a university or college for a specified time as punishment. 3. to make (a person, etc.) rustic. 4. to make or finish (masonry, etc.) in the rustic style.

rus·ti·ca·tion (rus′ti-kā′shən), ***n.*** [L. *rusticatio*], 1. a rusticating or being rusticated. 2. a period of this.

rus·ti·ca·tor (rus′ti-kā′tẽr), ***n.*** a person who rusticates.

rus·tic·i·ty (rus-tis′ə-ti), ***n.*** [*pl.* RUSTICITIES (-tiz)], [Fr. or L.; Fr. *rusticité;* L. *rusticitas*], 1. quality, state, or instance of being rustic; awkwardness, ignorance, inelegance, simplicity, etc. 2. rustic, or rural, life or character. 3. a rural characteristic.

rust·i·ly (rus′t'l-i), ***adv.*** in a rusty manner or state; in a way suggestive of rustiness.

rust·i·ness (rus′ti-nis), ***n.*** rusty quality or state.

rus·tle (rus″l), ***v.i. & v.t.*** [RUSTLED (-'ld), RUSTLING], [with unhistoric *-t-* < ME. *rouslen*, etc.; akin to earlier Fl. *ruysselen;* W.Gmc. echoic base], to make, or move, stir, etc. so as to produce, an irregular succession of soft, rubbing sounds, as of leaves, papers, cloth, etc. being moved about. ***n.*** such a succession of sounds.

rus·tle (rus′'l), ***v.i. & v.t.*** [RUSTLED (-'ld), RUSTLING], [? < *rush, v.* + *hustle*], 1. [Colloq.], to work or proceed with, or move, bring, or get by, energetic or vigorous action. 2. *a)* originally, in the western United States, to round up (cattle, etc.), especially as a professional cowboy; hence, *b)* [Colloq.], to steal (cattle, etc.).
rustle up, [Colloq.], to collect or get together, as by foraging around.

rus·tler (rus′lẽr), ***n.*** a person or thing that rustles; especially, [Colloq.], *a)* an active, energetic person. *b)* a cattle thief.

rust·less (rust′lis), ***adj.*** 1. free from rust. 2. rustproof.

rust·proof (rust′proof′), ***adj.*** resistant to rust.

rust·y (rus′ti), ***adj.*** [RUSTIER (-ti-ẽr), RUSTIEST (-ti-ist)], [ME. *rusti;* AS. *rustig*], 1. coated with rust, as a metal, or affected with the disease of rust, as a plant. 2. consisting of or caused by rust. 3. not working freely or easily because of, or as if because of, rust; stiff in operation. 4. *a)* impaired by disuse, neglect, idleness, etc.: as, his geometry is *rusty*. *b)* having lost facility through lack of practice: as, I'm a little *rusty* in chess. 5. having the color of rust. 6. faded, old-looking, or shabby.

rut (rut), ***n.*** [OFr. *route;* see ROUTE], 1. a groove, furrow, or track, especially one made in the ground by the passage of wheeled vehicles. 2. a fixed, routine procedure or course of action, thought, etc. ***v.t.*** [RUTTED (-id), RUTTING], to make a rut or ruts in.

rut (rut), ***n.*** [ME. *rutte;* OFr. *ruit;* L. *rugitus*, a roaring (as of deer in rut) < *rugire*, to roar], 1. the periodic sexual excitement of male deer, camels, sheep, goats, etc., corresponding to *estrus* in the female; heat. 2. the period during which this occurs. ***v.i.*** [RUTTED (-id), RUTTING], to be in rut. ***v.t.*** [Rare], to copulate with (the female); cover.

ru·ta·ba·ga (roo′tə-bā′gə), ***n.*** [Sw. dial. *rotabagge*], a turnip with a large, yellow root; Swedish turnip.

ru·ta·ceous (roo tā′shəs), ***adj.*** [L. *rutaceus* < *ruta;* see RUE (plant)], 1. of or like rue (the plant). 2. of the rue family of plants, including the rue, lemon, orange, lime, fraxinella, etc., often having a strong scent.

Ruth (rooth), [LL. < Heb. *rūth*, prob. contr. < *rĕ'ūth*, companion], a feminine name. ***n.*** in the *Bible*, *a)* the Moabite woman who left her own people to become the wife of Boaz of Bethlehem: she is celebrated for her devotion to her mother-in-law, Naomi. *b)* a book of the Old Testament that tells the story of Ruth.

ruth (rooth), ***n.*** [ME. *reuthe* < base of AS. *hreowian*, to rue (cf. RUE, *v.*) + *-th*], [Archaic], 1. pity; compassion. 2. sorrow; grief; remorse.

Ruth, George Herman (rooth), (*"Babe" Ruth*), 1895–1948; American baseball player.

Ru·the·ni·a (roo-thē′ni-ə), ***n.*** the Carpatho-Ukraine, a part of the Ukrainian S.S.R.: the former name.

Ru·the·ni·an (roo-thē′ni-ən), ***n.*** 1. a member of a group of Ukrainians, or Little Russians, living in Ruthenia and eastern Czechoslovakia. 2. their East Slavic language, closely related to Ukrainian. ***adj.*** 1. of Ruthenia or the Ruthenians. 2. of Ruthenian.

ru·then·ic (roo-then′ik, roo-thē′nik), ***adj.*** designating or of chemical compounds containing ruthenium with a higher valence than in the corresponding ruthenious compounds.

ru·the·ni·ous (roo-thē′ni-əs), ***adj.*** designating or of chemical compounds containing ruthenium with a lower valence than in the corresponding ruthenic compounds.

ru·the·ni·um (roo-thē′ni-əm), ***n.*** [Mod. L. < ML. *Ruthenia*, Russia: so named because first found in ores from the Urals], a rare metallic chemical element of the platinum group, very hard and brittle, and silvery-gray in color: symbol, Ru; at. wt., 101.7; at. no., 44.

Ruth·er·ford, Ernest (ruth′ẽr-fẽrd), first Baron Rutherford of Nelson, 1871–1937; British physicist, born in New Zealand; received Nobel prize in chemistry, 1908.

ruth·ful (rooth′fəl), ***adj.*** [Archaic], full of ruth; feeling, showing, or arousing pity or sorrow.

ruth·less (rooth′lis), ***adj.*** without ruth; pitiless. —***SYN.*** see **cruel.**

ru·ti·lant (roo′ti-lənt), ***adj.*** [L. *rutilans*, ppr. of *rutilare*, to have a reddish glow < *rutilus;* see RUTILE], [Rare], glowing, gleaming, or glittering.

ru·ti·lat·ed (roo′ti-lā′tid), ***adj.*** containing rutile needles, as a kind of quartz.

ru·tile (roo′tēl, roo′til), ***n.*** [Fr.; G. *rutil;* L. *rutilus*, red, akin to *rufus*, *rubeus*, red], a lustrous, dark-red mineral, titanium dioxide, TiO_2, commonly found in prismatic crystals and usually containing some iron.

Rut·land (rut′lənd), ***n.*** 1. a city in western Vermont: pop., 18,000. 2. Rutlandshire.

Rut·land·shire (rut′lənd-shir′), ***n.*** a county of east central England: pop., 24,000; county seat, Oakham: also **Rutland.**

Rut·ledge, Edward (rut′lij), 1749–1800; brother of *John;* American lawyer and statesman.

Rutledge, John, 1739–1800; American jurist and statesman; associate justice, United States Supreme Court (1789–1791); appointed chief justice (1795), but not confirmed by the Senate.

Rutledge, Wi·ley Blount (wī′li blount), 1894–1949; American jurist; associate justice, United States Supreme Court (1943–1949).

rut·ti·ness (rut′i-nis), ***n.*** a rutty quality or state.

rut·tish (rut′ish), ***adj.*** in or inclined to rut (sexual heat); lustful.

rut·ty (rut′i), ***adj.*** [RUTTIER (-i-ẽr), RUTTIEST (-i-ist)], having or full of ruts: as, a *rutty* road.

Ru·wen·zo·ri Mountains (roo′wen-zō′ri), a small group of mountains in central Africa, on the boundary between the Belgian Congo and Uganda: probably the "Mountains of the Moon" referred to by ancient writers: highest peak, Mt. Stanley, 16,787 ft.

Ruysdael, Jacob van, see **Ruisdael, Jacob van.**

Ruy·ter, Mi·chel A·dri·aans·zoon de (mi′khəl ȧ′drē-ȧn′sən də roi′tẽr), 1607–1676; Dutch admiral.

R.V., Revised Version (of the Bible).

R.V.S.V.P., *répondez vite s'il vous plaît,* [Fr.], please reply immediately.

R.W., 1. Right Worshipful. 2. Right Worthy.

Rwan·da (ẽr-wän′dä), ***n.*** a country in east central Africa, east of Congo (sense 2): formerly part of the UN trust territory of Ruanda-Urundi: area, 10,169 sq. mi.; pop., 2,725,000; capital, Kigali.

Rwy., Railway: also **Ry.**

Rx, Rx, rx, tens of rupees.

-ry (ri), -ery: shortened form, as in *dentistry, jewelry.*

Ry., Railways.

Ry·der, Albert Pink·ham (piŋk′əm rī′dẽr), 1847–1917; American painter.

rye (rī), ***n.*** [see PLURAL, II, D, 3], [ME.; AS. *ryge;* akin to G. *roggen;* IE. base **rughio-*, rye, seen also in Lith. *rugŷs*, rye grain], 1. a hardy cereal grass widely grown for its grain and straw. 2. the grain or seeds of this plant, used for making flour and whisky, and as feed for livestock. 3. whisky distilled from this grain.

rye (rī), ***n.*** [Gypsy *rei*, *rai*, a lord < Sans. *rājan*, a king; see REGAL], a gentleman: as, Romany *rye*.

rye grass, any of a number of quick-growing grasses.

rynd (rīnd, rind), ***n.*** [ME.; akin to & prob. < MD. *rijn*, with unhistoric *-d*], an iron bar running across the under face of an upper millstone, which it supports on the spindle.

Ryo·jun (ryô′joon′), ***n.*** Ryojunko.

Ryo·jun·ko (ryô′joon-kô′), ***n.*** Port Arthur, a city in Manchuria: the Japanese name.

ry·ot (rī′ət), ***n.*** [Hind. *raiyat* < Ar. *ra'īyah*, a flock, herd], in India, a peasant or tenant farmer.

Rys·wick (riz′wik), ***n.*** a village in the Netherlands, near The Hague: pop., 16,000: Dutch name, *Rijswijk*.

Ryu·kyu (rū′kū′), ***n.*** a chain of islands in the western Pacific, between Kyushu and Taiwan: area, 921 sq. mi.; pop., 833,000 (est. 1947): formerly a Japanese possession.

S

S, s (es), *n.* [*pl.* S's, s's, Ss, ss (es′iz)], 1. the nineteenth letter of the English alphabet: from the Greek *sigma*, a borrowing from the Phoenician: see **alphabet**, table. 2. a sound of S or s, usually a voiceless fricative, IPA [s], formed by the apex of the tongue. 3. a type or impression for S or s. 4. *a symbol for* the nineteenth in a sequence or group (or the eighteenth if J is omitted). *adj.* 1. of S or s. 2. the nineteenth (or eighteenth if J is omitted) in a sequence or group.

S (es), *n.* 1. an object shaped like S. 2. a medieval Roman numeral for 7 or 70: with a superior bar (S̄), 70,000. 3. in *chemistry, the symbol for* sulfur. *adj.* shaped like S.

-s, [alternate form of *-es* assimilated to prec. voiceless sounds as (s) and to prec. voiced sounds as (z) when those sounds are not sibilants; cf. slip(*s*), need(*z*), glas(*iz*); < ME. *-es, -is, -s*, representing: 1) AS. *-as*, masc. pl. inflection, reinforced by Anglo-Fr. *-(e)s*, pl. suffix; 2) ME. *-(e)s*, 3d pers. sing., pres. indic. inflection < Northern and North East Midland dial. (cf. -ETH, -TH); 3) AS. *-es*, masc. & neut. genit. sing. inflection (cf. -'s)], 1. the inflectional ending used to form the plural of most nouns, as in *hips, shoes*, etc. 2. the inflectional ending used to form the third person singular of verbs in the present tense, indicative mood, as in *gives, runs*, etc. 3. a suffix used to form some adverbs, as in *betimes, towards*, etc.

-'s, [assimilated contr. < ME. *-es;* AS. *-es*, masc. & neut. genit. sing. inflection], the inflectional ending used to form the possessive singular of nouns (and some pronouns) and the possessive plural of nouns not ending in *s*: as, boy'*s*, one'*s*, women'*s*.

-'s, the unstressed and assimilated form of: 1. *is*, as in *he's here*. 2. *has*, as in *she's spoken*. 3. *us*, as in *let's go*.

S., 1. Sabbath. 2. Saturday. 3. Saxon. 4. Senate. 5. September. 6. [It.], *Signor*. 7. Socialist. 8. Sunday.

S, S., s, s., south.

S., s., 1. [*pl.* SS., ss.], saint. 2. school. 3. society.

s., 1. second; seconds. 2. section. 3. see. 4. series. 5. shilling; shillings. 6. sign. 7. silver. 8. singular. 9. sire. 10. son. 11. steamer. 12. substantive.

Sa, in *chemistry*, samarium.

Sa., Saturday.

S.A., 1. Salvation Army. 2. South Africa. 3. South America. 4. South Australia. 5. *Sturmabteilung*, [G.], storm troops. 6. [Slang], sex appeal.

s.a., 1. semiannual. 2. small arms.

Saar (sär; G. zär), *n.* 1. a river in France and Germany, flowing northward into the Moselle River: length, 125 mi. 2. a state of West Germany, in the valley of the Saar River: administered by France under League of Nations supervision from 1919 to 1935, when it was returned to Germany: from 1948 to 1957, an autonomous government having a customs union with France: area, 991 sq. mi.; pop., 976,000; capital, Saarbrücken: German name, *Saarland*: former name, *Saar Basin Territory*.

SAAR BASIN

Saar·brück·en (zär′brük′ən; Eng. sär′brook′ən), *n.* the capital of the Saar: pop., 119,000.

Saar·land (zär′länt), *n.* the Saar: German name.

Sab., Sabbath.

Sa·ba (sā′bə), *n.* an ancient kingdom of southern Arabia: Biblical name, *Sheba*.

sab·a·dil·la (sab′ə-dil′ə), *n.* [Sp. *cebadilla*, dim. of *cebada*, barley < L. *cibare*, to feed], 1. a plant of the lily family, with dark, barleylike seeds used in medicine and insect poison. 2. its seeds.

Sa·bae·an (sə-bē′ən), *adj.* [< L. *Sabaeus;* Gr. *Sabaios*], of Saba (Biblical Sheba), its people, their language, etc. *n.* 1. a member of the Semitic people of Saba. 2. the South Arabic language of the Sabaeans, known only from inscriptions. Also spelled **Sabean.**

Sa·ba·ism (sā′bi-iz'm), *n.* [< Heb. *tsābhā*, host (of heaven), army; + *-ism*], the worship of stars.

Sa·ba·ist (sā′bi-ist), *n.* an adherent of Sabaism.

Sab·a·oth (sab′i-oth′, sab′i-ôth′, sə-bā′ôth), *n.pl.* [ME. LL.; Gr. *Sabaōth;* Heb. *tsebhāōth*, pl. of *tsābhā*, host, army], in the *Bible*, armies; hosts: chiefly in *the Lord of Sabaoth:* Rom. 9:29, James 5:4.

Sab·a·ti·ni, Raf·a·el (raf′i-əl sab′ə-tē′ni; It. sä′bä-tē′nē), 1875–1950; Italian novelist (in English).

Sab·ba·tar·i·an (sab′ə-târ′i-ən), *adj.* [L. *sabbatarius*], 1. of the Sabbath and its observance. 2. of the doctrines of the Sabbatarians. *n.* 1. a person who observes the Sabbath (Saturday). 2. a person who believes in observing Sunday as the Sabbath, especially one who favors rigid observance.

Sab·ba·tar·i·an·ism (sab′ə-târ′i-ən-iz'm), *n.* 1. observance of the Sabbath (Saturday). 2. rigid observance of Sunday as the Sabbath.

Sab·bath (sab′əth), *n.* [ME. *sabat* < OFr. & AS. *sabat;* both < L. *sabbatum;* Gr. *sabbaton;* Heb. *shabbāth* < *shābath*, to rest], 1. the seventh day of the Jewish week, set aside by the fourth Commandment for rest and worship; Saturday. 2. Sunday: name applied by most Protestant denominations. 3. [s-], a period of rest. *adj.* of the Sabbath. Abbreviated **S., Sab.**

Sabbath school, 1. Sunday school. 2. among Seventh Day Adventists, a similar school held on Saturday.

Sab·bat·ic (sə-bat′ik), *adj. & n.* [Fr. *sabbatique;* Gr. *sabbatikos* < *sabbaton;* see SABBATH], Sabbatical.

Sab·bat·i·cal (sə-bat′i-k'l), *adj.* [*Sabbatic* + *-al*], 1. of or suited to the Sabbath. 2. [s-], bringing a period of rest that recurs in regular cycles: as, a *sabbatical* leave. *n.* [s-], a sabbatical year.

sabbatical year, 1. among the ancient Jews, every seventh year, in which, according to Mosaic law, the land and vineyards were to remain fallow and debtors were to be released. 2. a year or half year of absence for study, rest, or travel, given at intervals, originally every seven years, to teachers, in some colleges and universities.

Sa·be·an (sə-bē′ən), *adj. & n.* Sabaean.

sa·ber (sā′bẽr), *n.* [Fr. *sabre;* MHG. *sabel;* of Slav. origin], 1. a heavy cavalry sword with a slightly curved blade. 2. in *fencing*, a type of weapon, heavier than a foil, used with a slashing as well as thrusting movement: a touch may be scored with the edge or point. *v.t.* to strike, wound, or kill with a saber. Also spelled **sabre.**

saber rattling, a threatening of war, or a menacing show of armed force.

sa·ber-toothed (sā′bẽr-tōōtht′), *adj.* designating various animals with long, curved canine teeth in the upper jaw: also spelled **sabre-toothed.**

saber-toothed tiger, any of a group of extinct animals of the cat family, closely resembling the tiger, but with a more massive body, shorter legs and tail, and long, curved upper canine teeth: found from the Oligocene to the Pleistocene, and of wide distribution.

Sa·bine (sā′bīn), *n.* [L. *Sabinus*], 1. a member of an ancient tribe living chiefly in the Apennines of central Italy, conquered by the Romans in the 3d century B.C. 2. their Italic language. *adj.* of the Sabines or their language.

Sa·bine (sə-bēn′), *n.* 1. a river flowing between Texas and Louisiana into Sabine Lake: length, 500 mi. 2. a lake (in full, **Sabine Lake**) formed by a widening of the Sabine River just before it empties into the Gulf of Mexico.

sa·ble (sā′b'l), *n.* [*pl.* SABLES (-b'lz), SABLE; see PLURAL, II, D, 1], [ME.; OFr.; ML. *sabelum;* MD. *sabel;* OHG. *zobel;* Russ. *sobol';* of Oriental origin], 1. a flesh-eating weasellike mammal of northern Europe and parts of Asia, related to the marten and valued for its glossy dark fur. 2. a related animal of North America. 3.

the costly fur or pelt of the sable. 4. *pl.* a coat, neckpiece, etc. made of this. 5. *pl.* mourning clothes. 6. in *heraldry*, the color black, represented in engraving by crossing vertical and horizontal lines to produce a dark shading. *adj.* 1. made of or with the fur of the sable. 2. black; dark.

Sa·ble, Cape (sā'b'l), 1. a cape at the southern tip of Nova Scotia, Canada. 2. a cape at the southern tip of Florida.

sable antelope, any of a variety of large antelopes found in South Africa, with long, scimitar-shaped horns.

sa·ble·fish (sā'b'l-fish'), *n.* [*pl.* SABLEFISH, SABLEFISHES (-iz); see FISH], an edible fish of the North Pacific, resembling the mackerel; beshow.

sa·bot (sab'ō, sab'ət; Fr. sȧ'bō'), *n.* [Fr.; altered (after *bot*, a boot) < *savate*, old shoe; via Turk. < Ar. *sabbât*, sandal], 1. a kind of shoe shaped and hollowed from a single piece of wood, worn by peasants in Europe. 2. a heavy leather shoe with a wooden sole. 3. a small sailing dinghy whose hull somewhat resembles such a shoe. 4. in *military usage*, a wooden disk or soft metal clip fastened to a projectile, formerly used in muzzle-loading cannon.

SABOTS
A, wood; B, leather

sab·o·tage (sab'ə-täzh', sab'ə-tij; Fr. sȧ'bô'tȧzh'), *n.* [Fr. < *saboter*, to work badly, damage < *sabot*; see SABOT & -AGE; from damage done to machinery by wooden shoes], 1. intentional destruction of machines, waste of materials, etc., as by employees during labor disputes. 2. intentional obstruction of or damage to some productive process, organized activity or effort, etc. 3. *a*) destruction of railroads, bridges, machinery, etc. by enemy agents in time of war; hence, *b*) any deliberate obstruction of a nation's war work. *v.t.* (sab'ə-täzh'), [SABOTAGED (-täzhd'), SABOTAGING], to injure or destroy by sabotage. *v.i.* to engage in sabotage.

sab·o·teur (sab'ə-tūr'; Fr. sȧ'bô'tër'), *n.* [Fr.], a person who engages in sabotage.

sa·bre (sā'bēr), *n.* & *v.t.* [SABRED (-bērd), SABRING], saber.

sa·bre·tache (sā'bēr-tash', sab'ēr-tash'), *n.* [Fr.; G. *säbeltasche; säbel*, saber + *tasche*, a pouch or pocket], a square leather case hung from the saber belt, sometimes worn by cavalrymen.

sa·bre-toothed (sā'bēr-tōōtht'), *adj.* saber-toothed.

sab·u·los·i·ty (sab'yoo-los'ə-ti), *n.* the state or quality of being sabulous.

sab·u·lous (sab'yoo-ləs), *adj.* [L. *sabulosus* < *sabulo*, sand], sandy; gritty.

Sac (sak, sôk), *n.* [*pl.* SAC], any member of a tribe of North American Indians of Algonquian linguistic stock living originally in Michigan, Wisconsin, and Illinois, and now settled on reservations in Oklahoma and Iowa: also **Sauk.**

sac (sak), *n.* [Fr.; L. *saccus;* see SACK (bag)], a pouchlike part in a plant or animal, often filled with fluid.

sac·a·ton (sak'ə-tōn'), *n.* [Sp. *zacatón* < *zacate, sacate* < Nahuatl *çacatl*, kind of grass], a coarse grass, used for hay or pasture in the southwestern United States.

sac·cate (sak'āt), *adj.* [ML. *saccatus* < L. *saccus*, a bag], 1. shaped like a sac; pouchlike. 2. having a sac.

sac·char-(sak'ēr), saccharo-.

sac·cha·rate (sak'ə-rāt'), *n.* [*sacchar*ic + *-ate*], 1. a salt or ester of saccharic acid. 2. a compound of sugar with the oxide of calcium, strontium, or a similar metal.

sac·char·ic (sə-kar'ik), *adj.* [*sacchar*in + *-ic*], 1. of or derived from saccharine compounds. 2. designating or of a diacid, $(CHOH)_4(COOH)_2$, obtained by oxidizing dextrose and other hexoses.

sac·cha·ride (sak'ə-rīd', sak'ə-rid), *n.* [*sacchar*in + *-ide*], 1. a compound of sugar with an organic base. 2. any of the carbohydrates; especially, a monosaccharide. 3. a saccharate.

sac·cha·rif·er·ous (sak'ə-rif'ēr-əs), *adj.* [*sacchar*(*i*)- + *-ferous*], containing or producing sugar.

sac·char·i·fi·ca·tion (sə-kar'ə-fi-kā'shən), *n.* a saccharifying or being saccharified.

sac·char·i·fy (sə-kar'ə-fī'), *v.t.* [SACCHARIFIED (-fīd'), SACCHARIFYING], [*sacchar*(*i*)- + *-fy*], to convert (starch or dextrin) into sugar, as by chemical means.

sac·cha·rim·e·ter (sak'ə-rim'ə-tēr), *n.* [Fr. *saccharimètre;* see SACCHARO- & -METER], any instrument used to find out the amount of sugar in a solution, as a form of polariscope.

sac·cha·rin (sak'ə-rin), *n.* [< ML. *saccharum*, sugar; L. *saccharon;* Gr. *sakcharon;* ult. < Sans. *śarkarā*, grit, gravel, sugar (cf. SUGAR); + *-in*], a white, crystalline coal-tar compound, $C_7H_5O_3NS$, about 400 times sweeter than cane sugar, used as a sugar substitute in diabetic diets, etc.

sac·cha·rine (sak'ə-rin, sak'ə-rīn'), *adj.* [*sacchar-* + *-ine*], 1. of, having the nature of, containing, or producing sugar. 2. very sweet or sirupy: as, a *saccharine* voice: used derisively. *n.* saccharin.

sac·cha·rin·i·ty (sak'ə-rin'ə-ti), *n.* the quality or condition of being saccharine.

sac·cha·ri·za·tion (sak'ə-ri-zā'shən), *n.* a saccharizing or being saccharized.

sac·cha·rize (sak'ə-rīz'), *v.t.* [SACCHARIZED (-rīzd'), SACCHARIZING], [*sacchar-* + *-ize*], to convert into sugar; ferment; saccharify.

sac·cha·ro- (sak'ə-rō, sak'ə-rə), [< Gr. *sakcharon*, sugar; see SACCHARIN], a combining form meaning: 1. *sugar*, as in *saccharometer*. 2. *saccharine and.* Also, before a vowel, **sacchar-.**

sac·cha·roid (sak'ə-roid'), *adj.* [*sacchar-* + *-oid*], having a texture suggestive of loaf sugar; crystalline and granular: said of stone.

sac·cha·roi·dal (sak'ə-roi'd'l), *adj.* saccharoid.

sac·cha·rom·e·ter (sak'ə-rom'ə-tēr), *n.* [*saccharo-* + *-meter*], a form of hydrometer for finding out the amount of sugar in a solution.

sac·cha·rose (sak'ə-rōs'), *n.* [*sacchar-* + *-ose*], cane or beet sugar; sucrose.

Sac·co, Ni·co·la (nē-kô'lä säk'kô; Eng. sak'ō), 1891–1927; Italian anarchist in America; together with B. Vanzetti, charged with murder and payroll theft in 1920; their conviction and execution aroused international protest, being regarded by many as the result of political bias.

sac·cu·late (sak'yoo-lāt'), *adj.* [< L. *sacculus*, dim. of *saccus*, a sack; + *-ate*], formed of or divided into saccules or a series of saclike expansions.

sac·cu·lat·ed (sak'yoo-lā'tid), *adj.* sacculate.

sac·cule (sak'ūl), *n.* [L. *sacculus*, dim. of *saccus*, a sack], a small sac; especially, the smaller of the two divisions of the membranous labyrinth of the inner ear.

sac·cu·lus (sak'yoo-ləs), *n.* [*pl.* SACCULI (-lī')], [L., dim. of *saccus*, a sack], a saccule.

sac·er·do·tal (sas'ēr-dō't'l), *adj.* [ME. *sacerdotale;* Late OFr.; L. *sacerdotalis* < *sacerdos*, priest < *sacer*, holy + base of *dare*, to give], 1. of priests or the office of priest; priestly. 2. characterized by belief in the divine authority of the priesthood.

sac·er·do·tal·ism (sas'ēr-dō't'l-iz'm), *n.* [*sacerdotal* + *-ism*], the character, system, methods, or practices of the priesthood; priestcraft: often in a hostile sense.

sa·chem (sā'chəm), *n.* [< Am. Ind. (Algonquian) *sâchimau*, chief], 1. among some North American Indian tribes, the chief (of the tribe or of a confederation). 2. any of the leading officials of the Tammany Society.

sa·chet (sa-shā'; *also, esp.* Brit., sash'ā), *n.* [Fr., dim. of *sac*, a bag], 1. a small bag, pad, etc. filled with perfumed powder, used to scent clothing. 2. powder for such a bag: also **sachet powder.**

Sachs, Hans (häns zäkhs), 1494–1576; German Meistersinger and playwright, a cobbler by trade.

Sach·sen (zäkh'sən), *n.* Saxony: the German name.

sack (sak), *n.* [ME. *sac, sak;* AS. *sacc;* L. *saccus*, Gr. *sakkos* < Heb. *saq*, sackcloth, grain sack], 1. a bag, especially a large one of coarse cloth, for holding grain, foodstuffs, etc. 2. such a bag with its contents. 3. the quantity contained in such a bag: a measure of weight of varying amounts. 4. a short, loose-fitting jacket worn by women or babies: also spelled **sacque.** 5. [Slang], dismissal; discharge (with *the*). 6. [Slang], *a*) a sleeping bag. *b*) a bed. 7. in *baseball*, a base. *v.t.* 1. to put into a sack or sacks. 2. [Slang], to dismiss (a person) from service; discharge. Abbreviated **sk.**

sack (sak), *n.* [Fr. *sac;* It. *sacco*, orig., plunder (cf. hunting use of *bag*) < ML. *saccare*, to sack < L. *saccus;* see prec.], the plundering or looting, especially by soldiers, of a captured city or town. *v.t.* to plunder or loot (a captured city, etc.). —***SYN.*** see **ravage.**

sack (sak), *n.* [earlier (*wyne*)*seck;* Fr. (*vin*)*sec*, dry (wine) < L. *siccus*, dry], any of various dry white wines from Spain or the Canary Islands, popular in England during the 16th and 17th centuries.

sack·but (sak'but'), *n.* [Fr. *saquebute*, sackbut; earlier, hooked lance for fighting on horseback < OFr. *saquer*, to draw, pull + *bouter*, to push, butt], 1. a medieval wind instrument, forerunner of the trombone. 2. [false transl. of Aram. *sabbĕkha;* see SAMBUKE], in the *Bible*, a stringed instrument resembling a lyre: Dan. 3:5.

sack·cloth (sak'klôth', sak'kloth'), *n.* 1. sacking. 2. coarse, rough cloth worn as a symbol of penitence or mourning: it was originally made of goats' hair.
in sackcloth and ashes, 1. in the *Bible*, wearing sackcloth and sprinkling ashes on one's head to express mourning or penitence. 2. in a state of great mourning, penitence, or remorse.

sack coat, a man's short, loose-fitting, straight-backed coat, usually part of a business suit.
sack·er (sak'ẽr), *n.* a person who sacks; plunderer.
sack·er (sak'ẽr), *n.* a person who makes or fills sacks.
sack·ful (sak'fool'), *n.* [*pl.* SACKFULS (-foolz')], 1. the amount that a sack will hold. 2. a large quantity.
sack·ing (sak'iŋ), *n.* coarse cloth woven of flax, hemp, jute, etc., used for making sacks and bags.
sack race, a race in which each contestant ties his legs in a sack and moves by jumping.
Sack·ville, Thomas (sak'vil), first Earl of Dorset and Baron Buckhurst, 1536–1608; English statesman and poet.
sacque (sak), *n.* a sack (jacket).
sa·cral (sā'krəl), *adj.* [< L. *sacrum*, neut. of *sacer*, sacred; + *-al*], of or for religious rites or observances.
sa·cral (sā'krəl), *adj.* [Mod. L. *sacralis;* see SACRUM], of, or in the region of, the sacrum.
sac·ra·ment (sak'rə-mənt), *n.* [ME.; OFr. *sacrement;* L. *sacramentum*, sum deposited by the two parties to a suit (so named prob. from being deposited in a sacred place), oath (in LL., the gospel, a mystery; used as transl. of Gr. *mystērion*) < *sacrare*, to consecrate < *sacer*, sacred], 1. in *Christianity*, any of certain rites ordained by Jesus: baptism, confirmation, the Eucharist, penance, holy orders, matrimony, and extreme unction are the seven recognized by the Roman Catholic and Orthodox Eastern churches; Protestants generally recognize only baptism and the Lord's Supper. 2. [sometimes S-], the Eucharist: often with *the.* 3. *a)* the consecrated bread and wine used in the Eucharist. *b)* the bread alone. Often with *blessed* or *holy.* 4. something regarded as having a sacred character or mysterious meaning. 5. a symbol or token. 6. a solemn oath or pledge, as one ratified by a rite.
sac·ra·men·tal (sak'rə-men't'l), *adj.* [ME. *sacramentale;* LL. *sacramentalis*], 1. of or used in a sacrament. 2. bound by a sacrament. *n.* in the *Roman Catholic Church*, a ceremony or sacred object like a sacrament, but instituted by the Church, as the use of holy water.
sac·ra·men·tal·ism (sak'rə-men't'l-iz'm), *n.* the doctrine that the sacraments are necessary to salvation.
sac·ra·men·tal·ist (sak'rə-men't'l-ist), *n.* a believer in sacramentalism.
sac·ra·men·tal·ly (sak'rə-men't'l-i), *adv.* in, by, or in the manner of, a sacrament.
sac·ra·men·tar·i·an (sak'rə-men-târ'i-ən), *adj.* [LL. *sacramentarius*], 1. of the sacraments. 2. [S-], of the Sacramentarians. *n.* 1. [S-], a person who believes that the sacraments are the symbolic rather than corporeal manifestation of Christ: used by Luther of Zwingli and his followers. 2. a sacramentalist.
Sac·ra·men·to (sak'rə-men'tō), *n.* 1. a river in California, flowing southward and westward into San Francisco Bay: length, 382 mi. 2. the capital of California, on this river: pop., 192,000.
sa·crar·i·um (sə-krâr'i-əm), *n.* [*pl.* SACRARIA (-ə)], [L. < *sacer*, holy], 1. in ancient Rome, a shrine or place to keep sacred things, as household gods. 2. the sanctuary in a Christian church; part surrounding the altar.
sa·cred (sā'krid), *adj.* [pp. of obs. *sacre*, to consecrate; ME. *sacren;* OFr. *sacrer;* L. *sacrare* < *sacer*, holy], 1. consecrated to or belonging to a god or deity; holy. 2. of a religion or religious rites and practices: as, a *sacred* song: opposed to *profane, secular.* 3. regarded with the same respect and reverence accorded holy things; venerated; hallowed. 4. set apart for, and dedicated to, some person, place, purpose, sentiment, etc., rather than to a god: as, *sacred* to his memory. 5. secured by a religious feeling or sense of justice against any defamation or violation; inviolate. —*SYN.* see **holy.**
Sacred College, in the *Roman Catholic Church*, the College of Cardinals: it elects and advises the Pope.
sacred cow, any person or thing regarded as above criticism or attack: used humorously.
sac·ri·fice (sak'rə-fis'), *n.* [ME. *sacrfiise;* OFr.; L. *sacrificium* < *sacer*, sacred + *facere*, to make], 1. *a)* an offering of the life of a person or animal, or of an object, as propitiation or homage to a deity. *b)* something so offered. 2. *a)* a giving up, destroying, permitting injury to, or foregoing of some valued thing for the sake of something of greater value or having a more pressing claim. *b)* a thing so given up, etc. 3. *a)* a selling or giving up of something at less than its supposed value. *b)* goods sold at a loss. *c)* the loss incurred. 4. in *baseball*, a sacrifice bunt or sacrifice fly. *v.t.* [SACRIFICED (-fist'), SACRIFICING], 1. to offer to a god or deity in homage or propitiation. 2. to give up, destroy, permit injury to, or forego (a valued thing) for the sake of something of greater value or having a more pressing claim. 3. to sell at less than the supposed value; incur a loss in selling. 4. in *baseball*, to advance (a base runner) by means of a sacrifice. *v.i.* 1. to offer or make a sacrifice. 2. to make a sacrifice bunt or sacrifice fly.
the supreme sacrifice, the giving of one's life, as for a cause or an ideal.
sacrifice bunt, in *baseball*, a play in which the batter intentionally bunts the ball in such a manner that he can be put out but a base runner will be advanced.
sacrifice fly, in *baseball*, a play in which the batter, when there are fewer than two outs, intentionally flies out in order to score a runner from third base.
sac·ri·fi·cial (sak'rə-fish'əl), *adj.* of, having the nature of, used in, or offering a sacrifice.
sac·ri·lege (sak'rə-lij), *n.* [ME.; OFr.; L. *sacrilegium* < *sacrilegus*, temple robber < *sacer*, sacred + *legere*, to gather up, take away], 1. the crime of appropriating to oneself, or to secular use, what is consecrated to God or religion: as, robbery of a church is a *sacrilege.* 2. the intentional desecration or disrespectful treatment of persons, places, things, or ideas held sacred.
SYN.—**sacrilege** implies a violation of something sacred, as by appropriating to oneself or to a secular use something that has been dedicated to a religious purpose; **profanation** suggests a lack of reverence or a positive contempt for things regarded as sacred; **desecration** implies a removal of the sacredness of some object or place, as by defiling or polluting it.
sac·ri·le·gious (sak'ri-lē'jəs, sak'ri-lij'əs), *adj.* 1. injurious or disrespectful to things held sacred; profane. 2. guilty of sacrilege.
sa·cring (sā'kriŋ), *n.* [ME.; see SACRED], [Archaic], consecration of the bread and wine of the Eucharist.
sacring bell, a bell rung during the Mass at the elevation of the bread and wine after consecration.
sa·crist (sā'krist), *n.* [OFr. *sacriste;* ML. *sacrista* < L. *sacer*, sacred], a sacristan.
sac·ris·tan (sak'ris-tən), *n.* [ME. *sacristane;* ML. *sacristanus* < *sacrista*, sacrist], 1. an official in charge of the sacristy of a church. 2. a sexton.
sac·ris·ty (sak'ris-ti), *n.* [*pl.* SACRISTIES (-tiz)], [Fr. *sacristie;* ML. *sacristia* < *sacrista*, sacrist], a room or small apartment in a church, where the sacred vessels, vestments, etc. are kept; vestry.
sa·cro- (sā'krō, sā'krə), [< *sacrum*], a combining form meaning: 1. *the sacrum.* 2. *sacral* (of the sacrum) *and*, as in *sacroiliac.*
sac·ro·il·i·ac (sā'krō-il'i-ak'), *adj.* [*sacro-* + *iliac*], of the sacrum and the ilium; especially, designating the joint between them.
sac·ro·sanct (sak'rō-saŋkt'), *adj.* [L. *sacrosanctus* < *sacer*, sacred + *sanctus*, holy], very sacred, holy, or inviolable.
sac·ro·sanc·ti·ty (sak'rō-saŋk'tə-ti), *n.* the state or quality of being sacrosanct.
sa·cro·sci·at·ic (sā'krō-sī-at'ik), *adj.* [*sacro-* + *sciatic*], in *anatomy*, of the sacrum and the ischium.
sa·crum (sā'krəm), *n.* [*pl.* SACRA (-krə), SACRUMS (-krəmz)], [Mod. L.; L. (*os*) *sacrum*, lit., sacred (bone): ? so called from being used formerly in sacrifices], a thick, triangular bone situated at the lower end of the spinal column, where it joins both hipbones to form the dorsal part of the pelvis: it is formed in man of five fused sacral vertebrae: see **skeleton**, illus.
sad (sad), *adj.* [SADDER (-ẽr), SADDEST (-ist)], [ME.; AS. *sæd*, sated, full, hence having feelings associated with satiety; akin to G. *satt*, satisfied (with food, etc.); IE. base **sā-*, satisfied, sated, seen also in L. *satis*, enough (cf. SATISFY, SATIETY)], 1. having, expressing, or showing low spirits or sorrow; unhappy; mournful; sorrowful. 2. causing or characterized by dejection, melancholy, or sorrow. 3. dark-colored; dull. 4. [Colloq.], very bad; deplorable: often used as an intensive. 5. [Dial.], heavy, compact, or soggy: said of earth, pastry, etc. 6. [Archaic], sober; trustworthy; firm; constant.
SYN.—**sad** is the simple, general term, ranging in implication from a mild, momentary unhappiness to a feeling of intense grief; **sorrowful** implies a sadness caused by some specific loss, disappointment, etc. (the death of his dog left him *sorrowful*); **melancholy** suggests a more or less chronic mournfulness or gloominess, or, often, merely a wistful pensiveness (his *melancholy* thoughts about the future); **dejected** implies discouragement or a sinking of spirits, as because of frustration; **depressed** suggests a mood of brooding despondency, as because of fatigue or a sense of futility (the novel left him feeling *depressed*); **doleful** implies a mournful, often lugubrious, sadness (the *doleful* look on a lost child's face).—*ANT.* happy, cheerful.
sad·den (sad''n), *v.t. & v.i.* to make or become sad.
sad·dle (sad''l), *n.* [ME. *sadel;* AS. *sadol;* akin to G. *sattel;* IE. **sod-tlo* < base **sed-*, to sit, seen also in L. *sedere*, to sit (cf. SEDENTARY), Eng. *sit*], 1. a padded leather seat for a rider on a horse, bicycle, etc. 2. the position of a person riding in such a seat. 3. a padded part of a harness worn over a horse's back to hold the shafts: see **harness**, illus. 4. the part of an animal's back where a saddle is placed. 5. anything shaped like or suggestive of a saddle. 6. a ridge between two peaks or summits. 7. *a)* a cut of mutton, etc. including part of the backbone and the two loins. *b)* the rear part of the back of a fowl. *c)* such a cut or part prepared for eating. *v.t.* [SADDLED (-'ld), SADDLING], 1. to put a saddle upon. 2. to load or encumber, as with a burden. 3. to impose as a burden, obligation, etc.
in the saddle, in a position of control.
sad·dle·back (sad''l-bak'), *n.* something saddle-backed.
sad·dle-backed (sad''l-bakt'), *adj.* 1. having a low, hollow back curved like a saddle, as some horses. 2. having a concave outline, as a ridge between peaks.
sad·dle·bag (sad''l-bag'), *n.* a large bag, usually one of

a pair, carried on either side of the back of a horse, etc., just behind the saddle.
sad·dle·bow (sad″l-bō′), *n.* the arched front part, or bow, of a saddle, the top of which is the pommel.
sad·dle·cloth (sad″l-klôth′, sad″l-kloth′), *n.* a thick cloth placed under a saddle on an animal's back.
saddle horse, a horse trained or suitable for riding.
sad·dler (sad′lẽr), *n.* [ME. *sadelere*], a person whose work is making, repairing, or selling saddles.
saddle roof, a roof with two gables and a ridge.
sad·dler·y (sad′lẽr-i), *n.* [*pl.* SADDLERIES (-iz)], [ME. *sadelarie*], 1. the work or craft of a saddler. 2. the articles, as harnesses, bridles, saddles, etc., made by a saddler. 3. the shop where such articles are sold.
saddle shoes, flat-heeled sport shoes having a band of leather in a contrasting color across the instep: they are usually brown on white or black on white.
saddle soap, a preparation, usually of mild soap and neat's-foot oil, for cleaning and softening leather.
saddle stitch, a simple overcasting stitch, sometimes made with strips of leather.
sad·dle·tree (sad″l-trē′), *n.* [ME. *sadeltre*], 1. the frame of a saddle. 2. the North American tulip tree.
Sad·du·ce·an (saj′oo-sē′ən, sad′yoo-sē′ən), *adj.* of or like the Sadducees or their doctrines.
Sad·du·cee (saj′oo-sē′, sad′yoo-sē′), *n.* [LL. *Sadducaei*, Sadducees; Gr. *Saddukaioi;* Heb. *tsaddūqīm;* prob. < *tsādhōq*, Zadok; cf. Ezek. 40:46], any member of a strict sect of Jews at the time of Jesus that denied resurrection of the dead and the existence of angels and rejected those parts of the law handed down by oral tradition: opposed to *Pharisee*.
sa·dhe (sä-dā′, tsä′di), *n.* [Heb. *tsādē*], the eighteenth letter of the Hebrew alphabet: see **tsadi.**
Sa·die (sā′di), a feminine name: see **Sarah.**
sad·i·ron (sad′ī′ẽrn), *n.* [*sad* (in obs. sense of heavy) + *iron*], a heavy flatiron.
sad·ism (sad′iz'm, sā′diz'm), *n.* [after Count Donatien de *Sade* (1740–1814), whose writings describe various sexual aberrations], 1. the getting of sexual pleasure from dominating, mistreating, or hurting one's partner, physically or otherwise. 2. popularly, the getting of pleasure of any sort from mistreating or hurting another or others. Distinguished from *masochism*.
sad·ist (sad′ist, sā′dist), *n.* a sadistic person.
sa·dis·tic (sa-dis′tik, sā-dis′tik), *adj.* of or characterized by sadism.
sa·dis·ti·cal·ly (sa-dis′ti-k'l-i, sā-dis′tik-li), *adv.* in a sadistic manner.
Sa·do·wa (sä′dô-vä′), *n.* Königgrätz, Czechoslovakia.
sad sack, [Slang], a soldier or other person who means well but is incompetent, ineffective, etc. and is consistently mistreated or in trouble.
sa·fa·ri (sə-fä′ri, suf′ə-rē′), *n.* [*pl.* SAFARIS (-riz, -rēz′)], [Swahili < Ar. *safara*, to travel], 1. a journey or hunting expedition, especially in eastern Africa. 2. the caravan of such an expedition.
safe (sāf), *adj.* [SAFER (sāf′ẽr), SAFEST (sāf′ist)], [ME. & OFr. *sauf;* L. *salvus;* akin to *salus*, health, sound condition, Goth. *hails*, whole, Sans. *sarva*, unharmed, whole], 1. free from damage, danger, or injury; secure. 2. having escaped danger or injury; unharmed. 3. *a*) giving protection. *b*) involving no risk. *c*) trustworthy. 4. no longer dangerous; unable to cause trouble or damage: as, *safe* in jail. 5. taking no risks; prudent; cautious: said of persons. 6. in *baseball*, designating a batter or base runner who reaches a base without being put out. *n.* [earlier *save* < *save, v.*], 1. an air-cooled compartment for storing food: as, a meat *safe*. 2. a locking container or box, usually of metal, in which to store valuables. 3. any box in which articles are kept to protect them from dust, moths, water, etc.
SYN.—**safe** implies freedom from damage, danger, or injury or from the risk of damage, etc. (is it *safe* to leave?); **secure,** often interchangeable with **safe,** is now usually applied to something about which there is no need to feel apprehension (he is *secure* in his job).—*ANT.* dangerous, precarious, unsure.
safe·blow·er (sāf′blō′ẽr), *n.* a person who uses explosives to open and rob safes.
safe·blow·ing (sāf′blō′iŋ), *n.* the use of explosives to open safes for robbing them.
safe·break·er (sāf′brā′kẽr), *n.* a person who breaks open safes to rob them.
safe-con·duct (sāf′kon′dukt), *n.* [ME. & OFr. *sauf-conduit*], 1. permission to travel through foreign or enemy regions, protected against arrest or harm. 2. a written pass giving such permission. 3. a guard or convoy accompanying the holder of such a pass. *v.t.* (*also* sāf′kən-dukt′), 1. to grant safe-conduct to. 2. to escort or protect through hostile territory.
safe·crack·er (sāf′krak′ẽr), *n.* a person who breaks open safes, as with a chisel, etc., and robs them.
safe·crack·ing (sāf′krak′iŋ), *n.* the breaking open and robbing of safes.
safe-de·pos·it box (sāf′di-poz′it), a strong metal container for storing valuable papers, jewels, or keepsakes, as in a bank or safe-deposit company vault.
safe-deposit company, a business firm which provides a vault for the safekeeping of valuables.
safe·guard (sāf′gärd′), *n.* [ME. & OFr. *sauvegarde*], any person or thing that protects or guards against loss or injury; specifically, *a*) a precaution or protective stipulation. *b*) a permit or pass allowing safe passage. *c*) a convoy or guard. *d*) a mechanical contrivance for the prevention of accident. *v.t.* to protect or guard.
safe hit, in *baseball*, a hit allowing a batter to reach first base without the aid of an error.
safe·keep·ing (sāf′kēp′iŋ), *n.* a keeping or being kept in safety; protection.
safe·ty (sāf′ti), *n.* [*pl.* SAFETIES (-tiz)], [ME. *sauvete;* Early Fr. *sauveté* < ML. *salvitas*, safety < L. *salvus;* see SAFE], 1. the quality or condition of being safe; freedom from danger, injury, or damage; security. 2. any of certain devices for preventing accident. 3. in *baseball*, a safe hit. 4. in *football*, a play in which a player grounds the ball behind his own goal line when the ball was caused to pass the goal line by his own team: it scores as two points for the opponents: distinguished from *touchback*. *adj.* giving safety; reducing danger or harm.
safety belt, 1. a life belt. 2. a belt worn by telephone linesmen, window washers, etc., attached as to a telephone pole or window sill, to prevent falling. 3. a seat belt securing a passenger in an airplane or automobile to give protection against sudden bumps, as in landing, or in a collision.
safety fuse, a long fuse that can be lighted at a distance from the explosive for increased safety.
safety glass, 1. glass made by fastening together two sheets of glass with a transparent, plastic substance; it is shatterproof and is used for automobile windshields, etc. 2. glass reinforced with wire.
safety island, a slightly raised concrete platform or a marked area in a street, where passengers may get on or off streetcars, busses, etc. in relative safety.
Safety Islands, a group of three islands off the coast of French Guiana.
safety lamp, 1. a miner's lamp in which a protective enclosure, as of wire gauze, surrounds the flame. 2. any lamp constructed to avoid explosion, fire, etc.

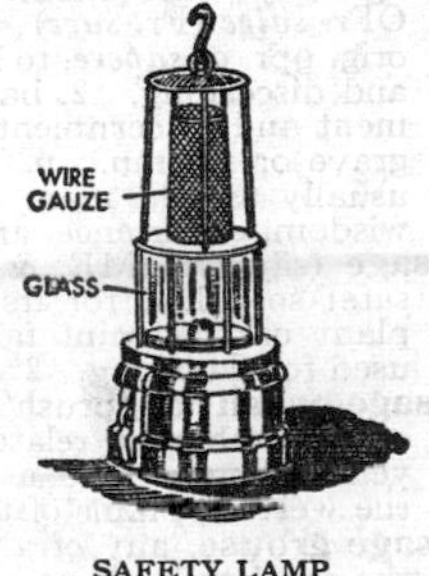

SAFETY LAMP

safety lock, 1. a lock for a door, etc., which can be opened only by its own key, and which is designed to prevent picking. 2. a safety catch on a firearm.
safety match, a match that will light only when it is struck on a prepared surface.
safety pin, a pin bent back on itself so as to form a spring, and having the point covered and held with a guard which prevents accidental unfastening and possible scratches.
safety razor, a razor with a detachable blade fitted into a holder provided with guards and set at an angle which minimizes the danger of cutting the skin.
safety valve, 1. an automatic valve for a steam boiler, etc., which opens and releases steam if the pressure becomes excessive. 2. anything which serves as an outlet for the release of strong emotion, excess energy, anxiety, etc.

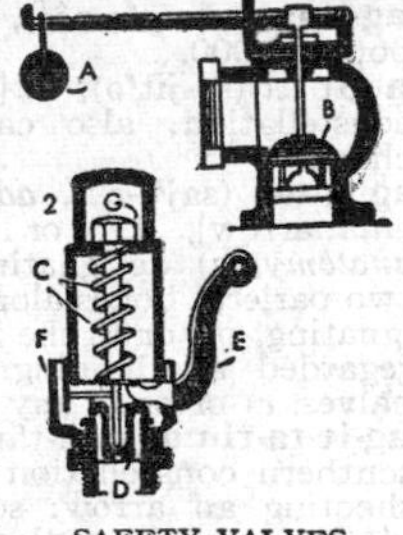

SAFETY VALVES
1. Weighted Valve: A, weight; B, valve 2. Pop Valve: C, spring; D, valve; E, hand lever; F, exhaust vent; G, adjusting nut

safety zone, a safety island.
saf·flow·er (saf′lou′ẽr), *n.* [D. *saffloer;* OFr. *saffleur;* It. *saffiore;* influenced in form by *flower*], 1. a thistlelike plant with large, orange flowers. 2. the dyestuff and drug prepared from its flowers.
saf·fron (saf′rən), *n.* [ME. *saffran;* OFr. *safran;* via It. *zafferano* or Sp. *azafran* < Ar. *za'farān*], 1. a plant with purplish flowers and orange stigmas yielding a dye, seasoning, and medicine. 2. its dried stigmas. 3. orange yellow: also **saffron yellow.** *adj.* orange-yellow.
Sa·fid Rud (sa-fēd′ rōōd′), a river in northwestern Iran, flowing into the Caspian: length, 450 mi.
S. Afr., 1. South Africa. 2. South African.
saf·ra·nin (saf′rə-nin), *n.* safranine.

saf·ra·nine (saf′rə-nēn′, saf′rə-nin), *n.* [Fr. *safran,* saffron; + *-ine*], 1. a yellowish-red aniline dye, $C_{20}H_{19}N_4Cl$, or any of several dyes closely related in structure to this. 2. any mixture of the various salts of the safranine dyes, used as a dye and as a stain in microscopy.

S. Afr. D., South African Dutch.

saf·rol (saf′rōl, saf′rol), *n.* safrole.

saf·role (saf′rōl), *n.* [< Fr. *safran,* saffron; + *-ole* (for *-ol*)], a clear, colorless oil, $C_{10}H_{10}O_2$, found in sassafras oil, camphor wood, etc., and used in perfumes.

sag (sag), *v.i.* [SAGGED (sagd), SAGGING], [ME. *saggen* (also 16th-c. *sacke*); prob. < ON. nautical language, either directly or via MLG.; cf. Sw. *sacka,* Norw. dial. *sakka, sagga,* in same senses; IE. base **sēk-,* to slacken, as also in L. *segnis,* tired, sleepy], 1. to sink, bend, or curve, especially in the middle, from weight or pressure. 2. to hang down unevenly or loosely. 3. to lose firmness or strength; weaken through weariness, age, etc.; droop. 4. to decline in price or value. 5. in *nautical usage,* to drift. ***v.t.*** to cause to sag. ***n.*** 1. a sagging. 2. the degree or amount of sagging. 3. a place of sagging; sunken or depressed place. 4. in *nautical usage,* drift to leeward; leeway.

sa·ga (sä′gə), *n.* [ON., thing said, tale, story; akin to AS. *sagu* (cf. SAW, a saying); for IE. base see SAY], 1. a medieval Scandinavian story of battles, customs, and legends, narrated in prose and generally telling the traditional history of an important Norse family. 2. any long story of adventure or heroic deeds.

sa·ga·cious (sə-gā′shəs), *adj.* [< L. *sagax, sagacis,* wise, foreseeing; akin to *sagire,* to perceive acutely; cf. SAKE], 1. keenly perceptive or discerning; shrewd; farsighted in judgment. 2. [Archaic], having a keen sense of smell. —***SYN.*** see **shrewd.**

sa·gac·i·ty (sə-gas′ə-ti), *n.* [*pl.* SAGACITIES (-tiz)], [Fr. *sagacité;* L. *sagacitas*], quality or instance of being sagacious; penetrating intelligence, keen perception, and sound judgment.

sag·a·more (sag′ə-môr′, sag′ə-mōr′), *n.* [< Am. Ind. (Algonquian); see SACHEM], a chief of second rank among certain tribes of North American Indians: sometimes equivalent to *sachem.*

saga novel, a long, rambling chronicle novel telling the story of several generations of a family.

sage (sāj), *adj.* [SAGER (sāj′ẽr), SAGEST (sāj′ist)], [ME.; OFr. *saige* (Fr. *sage*) < LL. **sapius* < L. *sapiens,* wise, orig. ppr. of *sapere,* to know, taste], 1. wise, perceptive, and discerning. 2. based upon wisdom; showing judgment and discernment: as, a *sage* comment. 3. [Obs.], grave or solemn. ***n.*** 1. a very wise man. 2. a man, usually an old man, venerated and respected for his wisdom, experience, and judgment. —***SYN.*** see **wise.**

sage (sāj), *n.* [ME. & OFr. *sauge;* L. *salvia* < *salvus,* safe: so called for its reputed healing powers], 1. a plant of the mint family, with grayish-green leaves used for flavoring. 2. any related plant. 3. sagebrush.

sage·brush (sāj′brush′), *n.* [*sage* (plant) + *brush*], any of a number of related shrubs with small, white or yellow flowers and a sagelike odor, found chiefly on the western plains of the United States.

sage grouse, any of a variety of large grouse living on the sagebrush plains of western North America.

sage hen, the sage grouse, especially the female.

sag·ger, sag·gar (sag′ẽr), *n.* [dial. *saggard,* contr. < *safeguard*], in *ceramics,* 1. a protective case of fire clay for baking finer or more delicate articles in the kiln. 2. the clay of which it is made. ***v.t.*** to bake in a sagger. Also **seggar.**

Sa·gha·lien (sä′gä-lyen′), *n.* Sakhalin.

Sag·i·naw (sag′ə-nô′), *n.* a city in central Michigan: pop., 98,000.

Sa·git·ta (sə-jit′ə), *n.* [L., lit., arrow], a small northern constellation: also called *Arrow:* see **constellation,** chart.

sag·it·tal (saj′i-t′l), *adj.* [Mod. L. *sagittalis* < L. *sagitta,* arrow], 1. of or like an arrow or arrowhead. 2. in *anatomy, a*) designating or of the suture between the two parietal bones along the length of the skull. *b*) designating, of, or in the longitudinal plane of this suture, regarded as dividing the body into right and left halves. *c*) of or in any plane parallel to this.

Sag·it·ta·ri·us (saj′i-târ′i-əs), *n.* [ME.; L., archer], 1. a southern constellation supposedly outlining a centaur shooting an arrow: see **constellation,** chart. 2. the ninth sign of the zodiac (♐), which the sun enters about November 23: see **zodiac,** illus.

sag·it·tar·y (saj′i-ter′i), *adj.* [L. *sagittarius* < *sagitta,* arrow], 1. of an arrow or archery. 2. like an arrow. ***n.*** in *mythology,* a centaur.

sag·it·tate (saj′i-tāt′), *adj.* [Mod. L. *sagittatus* < L. *sagitta,* arrow], in the shape of an arrowhead, as some leaves: see **leaf,** illus.

sa·git·ti·form (sə-jit′ə-fôrm′, saj′i-tə-fôrm′), *adj.* sagittate.

sa·go (sā′gō), *n.* [*pl.* SAGOS (-gōz)], [Malay *sāgū*], 1. a kind of starch prepared from the pith of certain palm trees, used in making puddings, etc. 2. any of the varieties of palm from which it is obtained.

Sa·guache (sə-wäch′), *n.* the Sawatch Range.

sa·gua·ro (sə-gwä′rō, sə-wä′rō), *n.* [*pl.* SAGUAROS (-rōz)] [Sp. < the Piman native name], a giant cactus with thick, spiny stem and white flowers.

Sag·ue·nay (sag′ə-nā′), *n.* a river in southern Quebec Canada, flowing into the St. Lawrence: length, 125 mi

Sa·ha·ra (sə-hâr′ə, sə-hä′rə), *n.* [Ar. *ṣahra,* a desert] a vast desert region of plateaus and lowlands extendin over northern Africa: area, 3,500,000 sq. mi.

Sa·ha·ran·pur (sə-hä′rən-poor′), *n.* a city in Uttar Pra desh, India: pop., 148,000.

sa·hib (sä′ib), *n.* [Hind. *sāhib* < Ar. *ṣāhib,* master, lit friend], sir; master: title used, until recently, b natives in India when speaking to or of a European

said (sed), past tense and past participle of **say.** ***adj*** aforesaid; named before.

sa·id (sä′id), *n.* sayid.

Sa·i·da (sä′ē-dä′), *n.* a seaport in Lebanon, built on th site of ancient Sidon: pop., 22,000.

sai·ga (sī′gə), *n.* [Russ. *saĭga*], a small, stocky, sheep like antelope native to the steppes of southeaster Russia and southwestern Siberia.

Saï·gon (sī-gŏn′, sī-gon′; Fr. sá′ē′gōn′), *n.* seaport an capital of South Vietnam: pop. (with Cholon), 1,300,000

sail (sāl), *n.* [ME. *seil,* sail; AS. *segl;* akin to G. *segel* IE. **seq-lóm* < base **seq-,* to cut, seen also in L. *secar* (cf. SECTION), *secula* (cf. SICKLE), *segmentum* (cf. SEG MENT)], 1. any of the shaped sheets of canvas or othe strong material spread to catch or deflect the wind by means of which some vessels and some land vehicle are driven forward. 2. sails collectively. 3. a sailin vessel or vessels. 4. a short or long trip in any vessel 5. anything like a sail, as an arm of a windmill. ***v.i*** [ME. *seilen;* AS. *seglian* < the *n.*], 1. to be move forward by means of a sail or sails, or by mechanica means such as a propeller. 2. to move upon or trave by water: said of a vessel or its passengers. 3. t begin a trip by water: said of a vessel or its passengers 4. to glide, float, or move steadily through the air. 5. t move smoothly and with dignity, like a ship in ful sail. 6. [Colloq.], to pass quickly. 7. [Colloq.], to mov vigorously into action (with *in*): as, he *sailed* in an finished the job. ***v.t.*** 1. to move through or upo (a body of water) in a boat or ship. 2. to handle steer, or manage (a boat or ship). 3. to guide throug water according to a compass, charts, etc.; navigate.

in sail, with sails set.

make sail, 1. to spread out a ship's sail. 2. to begi a trip by water.

sail against the wind, 1. to sail a course that slant slightly away from the true direction of the wind; sai close-hauled. 2. to work under difficulties or agains direct opposition. Also **sail near (to) the wind.**

sail into, [Colloq.], 1. to begin vigorously; ente upon with energy or force. 2. to attack, criticize or reprimand severely.

set sail, 1. to hoist the sails in preparation for depar ture; hence, 2. to start out on a voyage by water

take in sail, to lower sails, either at the end of a voyage or to reduce the area of sail set.

under sail, sailing; with sails set.

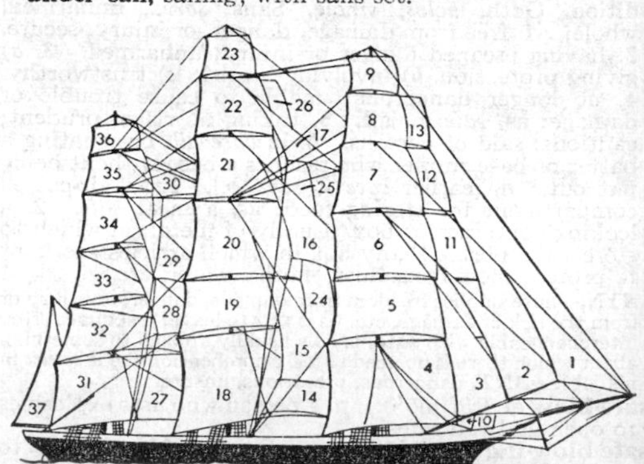

SAILS ON A FULL-RIGGED SHIP

1. flying jib; 2. jib; 3. fore-topmast staysail; 4. foresail 5. lower fore-topsail; 6. upper fore-topsail; 7. fore-topgallant sail; 8. foreroyal; 9. fore-skysail; 10. lowe studding sail; 11. fore-topmast studding sail; 12. fore topgallant studding sail; 13. foreroyal studding sail 14. main staysail; 15. main-topmast staysail; 16. main topgallant staysail; 17. main-royal staysail; 18. mainsail 19. lower main topsail; 20. upper main topsail; 21. main topgallant sail; 22. main royal; 23. main skysail; 24 main-topmast studding sail; 25. main-topgallant studding sail; 26. main-royal studding sail; 27. mizzen staysail; 28. mizzen-topmast staysail; 29. mizzen topgallant staysail; 30. mizzen-royal staysail; 31 mizzen sail; 32. lower mizzen topsail; 33. uppe mizzen topsail; 34. mizzen-topgallant sail; 35. mizze royal; 36. mizzen skysail; 37. spanker

sail·boat (sāl′bōt′), *n.* a boat having a sail or sails by means of which it is propelled.
sail·cloth (sāl′klôth′, sāl′kloth′), *n.* 1. long-fibered canvas or other cloth used in making sails. 2. heavy textile material like that used in making sails. 3. a piece of such material used as a covering, etc.
sail·er (sāl′ẽr), *n.* 1. a boat equipped with or propelled by sails: used with special reference to speed or manner of sailing, as, a swift *sailer*. 2. a fast vessel of any kind.
sail·fish (sāl′fish′), *n.* [*pl.* SAILFISH, SAILFISHES (-iz); see FISH], 1. any of a group of large tropical marine fishes related to the swordfish, but with scales and a large saillike dorsal fin in addition to the sword-shaped upper jaw. 2. a basking shark.
sail·ing (sāl′iŋ), *n.* 1. the act of a thing or person that sails. 2. the art of navigation. 3. progression, in terms of speed or manner, of a vessel. 4. the start of a vessel or person on a trip by water. *adj.* 1. driven forward by the action of wind on sails. 2. concerned with ships and shipping: as, *sailing* orders.
sail·or (sāl′ẽr), *n.* [ME. *sailer*], 1. a person who makes his living by sailing; mariner; seaman. 2. *a)* an enlisted man in the navy. *b)* any person in the navy. 3. a person sailing on a vessel, with reference to susceptibility to seasickness: as, he is a good *sailor*. 4. a straw hat with a shallow, flat crown and flat brim. *adj.* like a sailor's: as, a boy's *sailor* suit.
sail·or·ing (sāl′ẽr-iŋ), *n.* the work and life of a sailor.
sail·or·ly (sāl′ẽr-li), *adj.* like, suited for, or characteristic of sailors.
sail·or's-choice (sāl′ẽrz-chois′), *n.* [*pl.* SAILOR'S-CHOICE], 1. a small porgy. 2. a pigfish.
sailor's knot, any of a number of knots used by sailors.
sain (sān), *v.t.* [ME. *seinen, sainen;* AS. *segnian;* L. *signare;* see SIGN, *v.*], [Archaic or Dial.], 1. to make the sign of the cross on or over. 2. to bless, as a protection against evil. 3. to protect by prayer.
sain·foin (sān′foin), *n.* [Fr.; *sain,* wholesome < L. *sanus,* healthy (confused in Fr. with *saint*) + *foin* (L. *faenum*), hay], a beanlike plant used for fodder.
saint (sānt), *n.* [ME.; OFr. *seint, saint;* L. *sanctus,* holy, consecrated], 1. a holy person. 2. a person who is exceptionally meek, charitable, patient, etc. 3. [S-], a member of any of certain religious groups calling themselves *Saints.* 4. in certain churches, a person officially recognized as having lived an exceptionally holy life, and thus as being in heaven and capable of interceding for sinners; canonized person. *adj.* holy; sacred; blessed. *v.t.* to canonize; make a saint of. Abbreviated **St., S., s.** Names of saints are entered in this dictionary under the given name (see **John, Paul,** etc.); for some other entries, see **St.** & ff.
Saint Agnes's Eve, the night of January 20, when a girl was supposed to have a revelation of her future husband if she performed certain superstitious rites.
Saint Anthony's cross, a cross shaped like the Greek letter *tau* (T).
Saint Ber·nard (bẽr-närd′), a large, reddish-brown and white dog of a breed kept by the monks of the hospice of the Great St. Bernard Pass, in the Swiss Alps, trained to look for and rescue travelers in the snow.
Sainte-Beuve, Charles Au·gus·tin (shàrl′ ō′güs′tan′ sant′böv′), 1804–1869; French critic and writer.
saint·ed (sān′tid), *adj.* 1. of, like, or suitable for a saint; saintly. 2. regarded or venerated as a saint. 3. holy; sacred; hallowed.
Saint-Gau·dens, Augustus (sānt-gô′d′nz), 1848–1907; American sculptor, born in Ireland.
saint·hood (sānt′hood′), *n.* [see -HOOD], 1. the status or rank of a saint. 2. saints collectively.
Saint-Just, Lou·is An·toine Lé·on de (lwē′ än′twån′ lā′ōn′ də san′zhüst′), 1767–1794; French revolutionist; guillotined.
saint·li·ness (sānt′li-nis), *n.* the quality of being saintly.
saint·ly (sānt′li), *adj.* [SAINTLIER (-li-ẽr), SAINTLIEST (-li-ist)], like or suitable for a saint.
Saint Patrick's Day, March 17, observed by the Irish in honor of the patron saint of Ireland.
Saint-Pierre, Jacques Hen·ri Ber·nar·din de (zhäk′ än′rē′ ber′nàr′dan′ də san′pyâr′), 1737–1814; French writer.
Saint-Saëns, Charles Ca·mille (shàrl′ kȧ′mē′y′ san′-sän′), 1835–1921; French composer.
Saints·bur·y, George Edward Bate·man (bāt′mən sānts′bẽr-i), 1845–1933; English writer and critic.
saint·ship (sānt′ship), *n.* [see -SHIP], sainthood.
Saint-Si·mon, Comte **de,** (də san′sē′mōn′), (*Claude Henri de Rouvroy*), 1760–1825; French social philosopher; advocated a form of socialism.
Saint Valentine's Day, February 14, observed in honor of a martyr of the 3d century: the customary sending of valentines, candy, etc. to sweethearts on this day is not connected with the saint.
Sai·pan (sī′pän′, sī′pan′), *n.* one of the Marianas Islands, in the western Pacific: formerly a Japanese mandate, in 1946 it became a trust territory of the United States.
Sa·is (sā′is), *n.* an ancient city in the Nile delta: capital of Lower Egypt (663–525 B.C.).
Sa·i·shu Island (sä′i-shōō′), a Japanese island in the Yellow Sea, south of Korea: area, 710 sq. mi.: English name, *Quelpart Island.*
saith (seth), archaic third person singular, present indicative of **say.**
sake (sāk), *n.* [ME.; AS. *sacu,* cause or suit at law, contention; akin to G. *sache,* thing, affair; IE. base **săg-*, to investigate, seen also in L. *sagire,* to perceive, find, etc., *sagax,* sharply discerning (cf. SAGACIOUS); basic sense "judicial investigation"], 1. motive; purpose; end; cause: as, for the *sake* of money. 2. advantage; behalf; benefit; account: as, for my *sake.*
sa·ke (sä′ki), *n.* [Japan.], a Japanese alcoholic beverage made from fermented rice.
sa·ker (sā′kẽr), *n.* [Fr. *sacre;* Sp. *sacro;* Ar. *saqr*], a large falcon of southern Europe, used in falconry.
Sa·kha·lin (sä-khä-lēn′; Eng. sak′ə-lēn′), *n.* an island off eastern Siberia, north of Japan: area, 24,560 sq. mi.: formerly, the northern part belonged to the U.S.S.R., the southern, to Japan; in 1946, the entire island was granted to the U.S.S.R.: also **Saghalien:** Japanese name, *Karafuto.*
Sa·ki (sä′ki), *n.* (pseudonym of *Hector Hugh Munro*), 1870–1916; English author, born in Burma.
Sak·ti (sak′ti), *n.* Shakti.
Sak·tism (sak′tiz′m), *n.* Shaktism.
sal (sal), *n.* [ME.; L.], in *pharmacy,* etc., salt.
sa·laam (sə-läm′), *n.* [Ar. *salām,* health, peace; akin to Heb. *shālōm,* peace], 1. an Oriental greeting or ceremonial compliment, made by bowing low with the palm of the right hand placed on the forehead. 2. an obeisance or respectful greeting. *v.t.* to greet with a salaam. *v.i.* to make a salaam.
sal·a·bil·i·ty (sāl′ə-bil′ə-ti), *n.* the condition or quality of being salable: also spelled **saleability.**
sal·a·ble (sāl′ə-b'l), *adj.* that can be sold; marketable: also spelled **saleable.**
sa·la·cious (sə-lā′shəs), *adj.* [L. *salax, salacis* < *salire,* to leap, (of animals) cover sexually], 1. lecherous; lustful; hence, 2. pornographic; obscene.
sa·lac·i·ty (sə-las′ə-ti), *n.* [L. *salacitas*], the quality or condition of being salacious.
sal·ad (sal′əd), *n.* [ME. *salat, salad;* OFr. *salade;* Pr. *salada;* L. *salata,* pp. of *salare,* to salt < *sal,* salt], 1. a dish, usually cold, of sea food, chicken, eggs, raw or cooked fruits or vegetables, especially lettuce, etc., in various combinations, prepared with a dressing of oil, vinegar, and spices or mayonnaise, etc. 2. any green plant or herb used for such a dish or eaten raw; especially, [Dial.], lettuce.
salad days, [after Shakespeare, *Antony and Cleopatra,* I, v], time of youth and inexperience.
salad dressing, a preparation similar to a sauce, usually some combination of oil, vinegar, spices, or vegetable products, served on a salad or mixed with it.
Sal·a·din (sal′ə-din), *n.* sultan of Egypt (1174–1193); lived 1138–1193; captured Jerusalem: opposed the Crusades.
Sa·la·do, Río (sä-lä′thô), 1. a river in northern Argentina, flowing southeastward into the Paraná River: length, 1,100 mi. 2. a river in central Argentina: length, 850 mi.
Sal·a·man·ca (sal′ə-maŋ′kə; Sp. säl′ä-mäŋ′kä), *n.* a city in west central Spain: pop., 54,000: scene of a battle (1812) of the Peninsular War, in which the English under Wellington defeated the French.
sal·a·man·der (sal′ə-man′dẽr), *n.* [ME. & OFr. *salamandre;* L. *salamandra* < Gr.], 1. a mythological reptile resembling the lizard, supposed to be able to endure or live in fire. 2. a spirit supposed to live in fire; an elemental spirit in Paracelsus' theory of elementals. 3. a person who enjoys and can endure great heat. 4. any of various articles used in fire or able to withstand heat, as an iron poker, a plate for browning pastry, etc. 5. any of a group of scaleless, lizardlike animals related to the frogs and toads, with soft, moist skins and a tail.

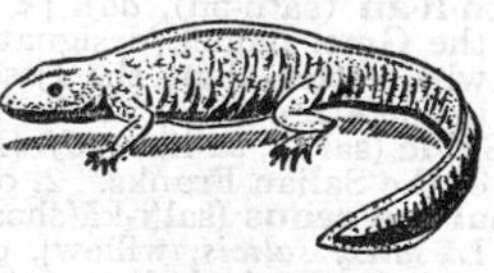

SALAMANDER
(about 4 in. long)

sal·a·man·drine (sal′ə-man′drin), *adj.* of or like a salamander.
Sa·lam·bri·a (sä-läm′brē-ä′; Eng. sə-lam′bri-ə), *n.* a river in Thessaly, Greece, flowing into the Gulf of Salonika: length, 125 mi.: Modern Greek name, *Pēneios;* ancient name, *Peneus.*
sa·la·mi (sə-lä′mi), *n.* [It., *pl.,* preserved meat, salt pork < L. *sal,* salt], a highly spiced, salted sausage, originally Italian.

Sal·a·mis (sal'ə-mis; Gr. sä-lä-mēs'), *n.* 1. a Greek island in the Gulf of Aegina, near Athens: area, 36 sq. mi.; pop., 15,000: scene of a naval battle (480 B.C.) of the Persian War, in which the Greeks defeated the Persians. 2. an ancient city of Cyprus.

sal-am·mo·ni·ac (sal'ə-mō'ni-ak, sal'ə-mōn'yak), *n.* sal ammoniac.

sal ammoniac, [ME. *sal armoniak;* L. *sal Ammoniacum,* lit., salt of Ammon: said to have been prepared originally from camel dung near the shrine of Jupiter *Ammon*], ammonium chloride.

sal·a·ried (sal'ə-rid), *adj.* 1. receiving a salary. 2. yielding a salary: as, a *salaried* position.

sal·a·ry (sal'ə-ri), *n.* [*pl.* SALARIES (-riz)], [ME. *salarie;* OFr. *salaire;* L. *salarium,* orig., salt money (i.e., money given to buy salt, as part of Roman soldiers' pay), hence pay < *sal,* salt], a fixed payment at regular intervals for services, usually other than manual or mechanical: distinguished from *wages, fees.* —*SYN.* see **wage.**

sale (sāl), *n.* [ME.; Late AS. *sala* < ON. *sala;* for IE. base see SELL], 1. the exchange of property of any kind, or of some services, for an agreed sum of money or other valuable consideration; selling. 2. a market; opportunity to sell: as, will there be any *sale* for these tiger skins? 3. the act of offering goods to the highest bidder; auction. 4. a special offering of goods at reduced prices, usually for some special reason or occasion: as, a rummage *sale.*
for (or **on**) **sale,** to be sold; offered for purchase.

sale·a·bil·i·ty (sāl'ə-bil'ə-ti), *n.* salability.

sale·a·ble (sāl'ə-b'l), *adj.* salable.

Sa·lem (sā'ləm), *n.* 1. a city on the coast of northern Massachusetts: pop., 39,000. 2. a city in northwestern Oregon: the capital: pop., 49,000. 3. a city in Madras, India: pop., 202,000.

sal·ep (sal'ep), *n.* [Fr.; Sp.; Ar. *saḥlab,* altered & contr. < *khuṣa al-tha'lab,* fox's testicles; cf. ORCHID], the dried tubers of various orchids, ground up and used as food.

sal·e·ra·tus (sal'ə-rā'təs), *n.* [Mod. L. *sal aeratus,* aerated salt], sodium (or sometimes potassium) bicarbonate; baking soda, as used in cooking.

Sa·ler·no (sä-ler'nô; Eng. sə-lũr'nō), *n.* an Italian seaport near Naples: pop., 87,000.

Sa·ler·num (sə-lũr'nəm), *n.* Salerno: the ancient name.

sales·clerk (sālz'klũrk'), *n.* a person employed to sell goods in a store.

sales·girl (sālz'gũrl'), *n.* a saleslady.

sales·la·dy (sālz'lā'di), *n.* [*pl.* SALESLADIES (-diz)], [Colloq.], a girl or woman employed to sell goods, especially in a store.

sales·man (sālz'mən), *n.* [*pl.* SALESMEN (-mən)], a man employed to sell goods, either in a store or as a traveling agent or representative.

sales·man·ship (sālz'mən-ship'), *n.* [see -SHIP], 1. the work of a salesman. 2. ability or skill at selling.

sales·peo·ple (sālz'pē'p'l), *n.pl.* salespersons.

sales·per·son (sālz'pũr's'n), *n.* a person employed to sell goods, especially in a store.

sales resistance, resistance of potential customers to efforts and inducements aimed at getting them to buy.

sales·room (sālz'rōōm', sālz'room'), *n.* a room in which goods are offered for sale.

sales talk, 1. persuasion or argument used in an attempt to sell something; hence, 2. any argument aimed at persuading one to do something.

sales tax, a tax on sales or on receipts from sales, usually added to the price by the seller.

sales·wom·an (sālz'woom'ən), *n.* [*pl.* SALESWOMEN (-wim'in)], a saleslady.

Sal·ford (sôl'fẽrd, sal'fẽrd), *n.* a city in England, near Manchester: pop., 162,000.

Sa·li·an (sā'li-ən), *adj.* [< LL. *Salii,* Salian Franks < the Gmc. name], designating or of a tribe of Franks who settled along the Ijssel River, in the Netherlands, in the 4th century A.D. *n.* a Salian Frank.

Sal·ic (sal'ik, sā'lik), *adj.* [Fr. *Saliqueé;* ML. *Salicus*], 1. of the Salian Franks. 2. of the Salic law. Also **Salique.**

sal·i·ca·ceous (sal'i-kā'shəs), *adj.* [Mod. L. *salicaceus* < L. *salix, salicis,* willow], of the willow family of trees and shrubs, including the willows and poplars.

sal·i·cin (sal'ə-sin), *n.* [Fr. *salicine* < L. *salix,* willow], a white, crystalline glucoside, $C_{13}H_{18}O_7$, obtained from the bark of certain poplars and willows, and used in medicine as a tonic and to reduce fever.

Salic law, 1. a code of laws of Germanic tribes, including the Salian Franks; especially, the provision of this code excluding women from inheriting land; hence, 2. the law excluding women from succeeding to the throne in the French and Spanish monarchies. 3. any law of similar purport.

sal·i·cyl·ate (sal'ə-sil'āt, sə-lis'ə-lāt', sal'ə-sil'āt), *n.* any salt or ester of salicylic acid.

sal·i·cyl·ic acid (sal'ə-sil'ik), [see SALICIN, -YL, & -IC], a white, crystalline compound, $C_6H_4(OH)COOH$, prepared from salicin or phenol and used as a food preservative and mild antiseptic, and, in the form of its salts, to treat rheumatism, relieve pain, etc.

sa·li·ence (sā'li-əns, sāl'yəns), *n.* 1. the quality of being salient. 2. a salient part, feature, detail, etc.

sa·li·en·cy (sā'li-ən-si, sāl'yən-si), *n.* [*pl.* SALIENCIES (-siz)], salience.

sa·li·ent (sā'li-ənt, sāl'yənt), *adj.* [L. *saliens,* ppr. of *salire,* to leap], 1. *a*) leaping; jumping; capering. *b*) gushing; jetting forth. 2. pointing outward; jutting; projecting, as an angle. 3. standing out from the rest; noticeable; conspicuous; prominent. *n.* 1. the part of a battle line, trench, fort, etc. which projects farthest toward the enemy. 2. a salient angle, part, etc.

sa·li·en·ti·an (sā'li-en'shi-ən, sā'li-en'shən), *adj.* [Mod. L. *Salientia,* name of the order (< L. *saliens;* see SALIENT); + *-an*], of a group of animals that live both on land and in water, with a broad body, no tail, and hind legs which are helpful in jumping: it includes frogs, toads, and tree toads. *n.* an animal of this group.

sa·lif·er·ous (sə-lif'ẽr-əs), *adj.* [< L. *sal,* salt; + *-ferous*], producing or containing salt.

sal·i·fy (sal'ə-fī'), *v.t.* [SALIFIED (-fīd'), SALIFYING], [Fr. *salifier* < L. *sal,* salt + *facere,* to make], to make salty; specifically, *a*) to impregnate with salt. *b*) to form a salt with; convert into a salt. *c*) to combine with a salt.

Sa·li·na (sə-lī'nə), *n.* a city in central Kansas, on the Smoky Hill River: pop., 43,000.

sa·li·na (sə-lī'nə), *n.* [Sp. < L. *salinae,* salt pits < *sal,* salt], 1. a salt marsh, pond, or lake, not connected with the sea. 2. a saltworks.

sa·line (sā'līn), *adj.* [Fr. *salin;* LL. **salinus* < L. *sal,* salt], 1. of, characteristic of, or containing common salt, or sodium chloride; salty. 2. of or containing any of the salts of the alkali metals or magnesium. *n.* 1. a salt spring, lick, marsh, mine, etc. 2. any of the metallic salts, especially a salt of magnesium or of an alkali metal, often used in medicine as cathartics. 3. a saline solution, especially one that is isotonic, used in medical treatment or for biological experiments.

sa·lin·i·ty (sə-lin'ə-ti), *n.* a saline quality or state.

sal·i·nom·e·ter (sal'i-nom'ə-tẽr), *n.* [see SALINE & -METER], an instrument for measuring the amount of salt in a solution.

Sa·lique (sə-lēk', sal'ik, sā'lik), *adj.* Salic.

Salis·bur·y (sôlz'ber'i, sôlz'bẽr-i), *n.* 1. the county seat of Wiltshire, England, noted for its 13th-century cathedral: pop., 33,000. 2. the capital of Southern Rhodesia, and of the Federation of Rhodesia and Nyasaland: pop., 125,000.

Salisbury, third Marquis of (*Robert Arthur Talbot Gascoyne-Cecil*), 1830–1903; English statesman.

Salisbury Plain, a large tract of land in Wiltshire, England: site of Stonehenge.

Salisbury steak, Hamburg steak.

Sa·lish (sā'lish), *n.* a Salishan Indian, especially a Flathead.

Sa·lish·an (sā'lish-ən, sal'ish-ən), *adj.* [< Am. Ind. (Salishan) *sälst,* people], designating or of an American Indian linguistic family of the northwestern United States and southwestern Canada, including Flathead and Coeur d'-Alêne. *n.* this linguistic family.

sa·li·va (sə-lī'və), *n.* [L.], the thin, watery, slightly viscid fluid secreted by the salivary glands: it serves as an aid to digestion by moistening and softening food, and contains an enzyme, ptyalin, which converts starch to maltose.

sal·i·var·y (sal'ə-ver'i), *adj.* of or secreting saliva.

sal·i·vate (sal'ə-vāt'), *v.t.* [SALIVATED (-id), SALIVATING], [< L. *salivatus,* pp. of *salivare,* salivate], to produce an excessive flow of saliva in. *v.i.* to secrete saliva.

sal·i·va·tion (sal ə-vā'shən), *n.* [L. *salivatio*], 1. the act or process of salivating. 2. an excessive flow of saliva, as because of mercurial poisoning.

sal·i·va·tor (sal'ə-vā'tẽr), *n.* in *medicine,* any substance that stimulates the flow of saliva.

Salk, Jonas Edward (sôlk), 1914—; American physician; developed a vaccine to prevent poliomyelitis.

‡salle (sål), *n.* [Fr.], a hall or room.

‡salle à man·ger (sål' å' män'zhā'), [Fr.], a room for eating; dining room.

sal·len·ders (sal'ən-dẽrz), *n.pl.* [Fr. *solandres,* pl. of *solandre*], a dry eruption on the hock of a horse.

sal·let (sal'it), *n.* [OFr. *salade;* It. *celata* < L. *caelata* (*cassis*), engraved (helmet) < *caelare,* to engrave: so called from the figures cut on it], a light, rounded helmet with a projecting neckguard and, often, a visor, worn in the 15th century.

sal·low (sal'ō), *adj.* [ME. *salou;* AS. *salu, salowig, sealwe,* sallow, dark; akin to OHG. *salo* (G. dial. *sal*); IE. base **sal-,* dirty gray, seen also in L. *saliva,* spittle (cf. SALIVA), *salix,* willow (cf. next entry)], of a sickly pale-yellowish complexion. *v.t.* to make sallow.

sal·low (sal'ō), *n.* [ME. *salhe, salwe;* AS. *sealh* < same base as *sallow, adj.*], 1. a kind of willow with large spikes of flowers which appear before the leaves; goat willow. 2. a willow twig.

sal·low·ish (sal'ō-ish), *adj.* somewhat sallow.

sal·low·y (sal'ō-i), *adj.* full of sallows (willows).

Sal·lust (sal'əst), *n.* (*Gaius Sallustius Crispus*), Roman historian and statesman; lived 86–34 B.C.

Sal·ly (sal'i), a feminine name: see **Sarah.**

sal·ly (sal'i), *n.* [*pl.* SALLIES (-iz)], [Fr. *saillie* < *saillir,* to come forth suddenly, rush out, leap < L. *salire,* to leap, spring], 1. a sudden rushing forth, as of troops to attack besieging forces. 2. any sudden start into activity. 3. a quick witticism; bright retort; quip. 4. an excursion or unusual side trip; jaunt. *v.i.* [SALLIED (-id), SALLYING], 1. to rush out suddenly. 2. *a)* to start suddenly. *b)* to come or go out of doors. *c)* to set out on a trip. Used with *forth* or *out*. —***SYN.*** see **joke.**

Sally Lunn (lun), [said to be name of 18th-c. Eng. woman who first made these at Bath], a variety of sweetened teacake, usually served hot: also **sally lunn.**

sal·ma·gun·di (sal′mə-gun′di), *n.* [Fr. *salmigondis;* prob. < It. *salame conditi,* preserved pickled meat; *salame* < *sal,* salt + *conditi* < pp. of *condire,* to flavor; L. *condire,* to preserve, pickle], 1. a dish of chopped meat, eggs, etc. flavored with onions, anchovies, pepper, vinegar, and oil. 2. any mixture or medley.

sal·mi, sal·mis (sal′mi; Fr. sȧl′mē′), *n.* [Fr.; prob. contr. < *salmigondis;* see SALMAGUNDI], a highly seasoned dish of partly roasted game or fowl, stewed in wine.

salm·on (sam′ən), *n.* [*pl.* SALMON, SALMONS (-ənz); see PLURAL, II, D, 2], [ME. *salmon, saumoun;* OFr. *saumon;* L. *salmo, salmonis;* prob. < *salire,* to leap], 1. any of several varieties of game and food fishes of the North Atlantic, with silver scales and flesh that is yellowish-pink when cooked: they live in salt water and spawn in fresh water, though some varieties are landlocked in lakes. 2. any of several closely related varieties, especially those of the North Pacific. 3. the color of cooked salmon flesh; yellowish pink or pale red.

salm·on·ber·ry (sam′ən-ber′i), *n.* [*pl.* SALMONBERRIES (-iz)], 1. a bramble with purple or pinkish flowers and orange-pink berries. 2. the berry.

sal·mo·noid (sal′mə-noid′), *adj.* 1. like a salmon. 2. of the suborder that includes the salmons. *n.* a salmonoid fish; specifically, any of the salmons.

salmon pink, yellowish pink or pale red.

salmon trout, 1. a European sea trout. 2. a Great Lakes trout; namaycush. 3. any large trout resembling a salmon; specifically, the steelhead.

sal·ol (sal′ōl, sal′ol), *n.* [*salicylic* + *-ol*], a colorless, crystalline compound, $C_{13}H_{10}O_3$, the phenyl ester of salicylic acid, used in medicine as an internal antiseptic.

Sa·lo·me (sə-lō′mi; G. zä′lô-mā′), *n.* [LL.; Gr. *Salōmē;* Heb. *shālōm,* peace], 1. in the *Bible,* the daughter of Herodias: her dancing pleased Herod so much that he granted her request, made at her mother's instigation, for the head of John the Baptist: Matt. 14:8. 2. *a)* a play (1894) written in French by Oscar Wilde, based on the story of Salome. *b)* a one-act opera (1905) by Richard Strauss, based on this play.

Sa·lo·mé (sȧ′lô′mā′), *n.* [Fr.], Salome.

Sal·o·mon, Haym (hīm sal′ə-mən), 1740?–1785; American merchant and patriot, born in Poland; helped finance the Revolutionary War.

sa·lon (sə-lon′; Fr. sȧ′lôn′), *n.* [*pl.* SALONS (-lonz′; Fr. -lôn′)], [Fr.; see SALOON], 1. a large reception hall or room for receiving guests, especially a public room in a hotel or on a ship; saloon. 2. a drawing room of a private home in French-speaking countries. 3. a regular gathering of distinguished guests such as might meet in a drawing room; especially, a meeting of literary or artistic people in a celebrity's home. 4. a room or gallery for the exhibition of paintings or other works of art. 5. an exhibition of works of art; especially, [S-], an annual art show of the work of living French artists, held in Paris. 6. a commercial establishment for performing some service: as, a beauty *salon.*

Sa·lo·ni·ka (sal′ə-nē′kə, sal′ə-nī′kə, sə-lon′i-kə; Gr. sä′lô-nē′kä), *n.* a seaport in Macedonia, Greece: pop., 217,000: Greek name, *Thessalonike;* ancient names, *Therma, Thessalonica.*

Salonika, Gulf of, an arm of the Aegean Sea, off northeastern Greece.

sa·loon (sə-lōōn′), *n.* [Fr. *salon;* It. *salone* < *sala,* a room, hall < OHG. *sal,* a room, dwelling], 1. any large room or hall designed for receptions, exhibitions, entertainments, etc.; specifically, the main social cabin of a passenger ship. 2. any large public room used for some specific purpose: as, a dining *saloon.* 3. a place where alcoholic drinks are sold to be drunk on the premises; public bar. 4. [British], a sedan (automobile).

sa·loon·keep·er (sə-lōōn′kēp′ẽr), *n.* a person who operates a saloon (sense 3).

sa·loop (sə-lōōp′), *n.* [var. of *salep*], a hot drink made from powdered salep or from sassafras.

Sal·op (sal′əp), *n.* Shropshire.

Sa·lo·pi·an (sə-lō′pi-ən), *adj.* of Shropshire or its people. *n.* a native or inhabitant of Shropshire.

sal·pa (sal′pə), *n.* [Mod. L.; L. *salpa,* kind of stockfish; Gr. *salpē*], any of a group of free-swimming tunicates characterized by a barrel-shaped body ringed with muscle and open at both ends.

sal·pin·go- (sal-piŋ′gō, sal-piŋ′gə), [< Gr. *salpinx, salpingos,* a trumpet], a combining form meaning: 1. *of a Fallopian tube.* 2. *of a Eustachian tube.* Also, before a vowel, **salping-.**

sal·pinx (sal′piŋks), *n.* [*pl.* SALPINGES (sal-pin′jēz)], [Mod. L.; Gr. *salpinx,* a trumpet], in *anatomy,* 1. a Fallopian tube. 2. a Eustachian tube.

sal·si·fy (sal′sə-fī′), *n.* [Fr. *salsifis;* It. *sassefrica* (as if < L. *fricare,* to rub)], a plant with long, white, fleshy roots having an oysterlike flavor; oyster plant.

sal so·da (sal′sō′də), *n.* sal soda.

sal soda, crystallized sodium carbonate.

salt (sôlt), *n.* [ME.; AS. *sealt;* akin to G. *salz;* IE. base **sal-,* salt, as also in L. *sal* (see SAL), prob. in *-sul-* in *insula* (cf. INSULAR), Gr. *hāls, hālos* (cf. HALOGEN)], 1. sodium chloride, NaCl, a white, crystalline substance with a characteristic taste, found in natural beds, in sea water, etc., and used for seasoning and preserving food, etc. 2. a chemical compound derived from an acid by replacing hydrogen, wholly or partly, with a metal or an electropositive radical: the salt of an *-ous* acid is usually indicated by the suffix *-ite,* the salt of an *-ic* acid by the suffix *-ate.* 3. that which gives a tang or piquancy to anything. 4. sharp, pungent humor or wit. 5. something that preserves, purifies, or corrects. 6. a saltcellar. 7. *pl. a)* any mineral salts used for medicinal purposes, as for moving the bowels. *b)* smelling salts. 8. [Colloq.], a sailor, usually an experienced one. *adj.* 1. containing salt. 2. preserved with salt. 3. tasting or smelling of salt. 4. pungent; lively; witty. 5. *a)* flooded with salt water. *b)* growing in salt water. *v.t.* 1. to sprinkle or season with salt. 2. to preserve with salt or in a salt solution. 3. to treat with salt in chemical processes. 4. to season or give tang to: as, he *salted* his conversation with wit. 5. to give artificial value to; specifically, *a)* to alter (books, prices, etc.) in order to give false value. *b)* to scatter minerals or ores in (a mine), put oil in (a well), etc. in order to deceive prospective buyers.

salt away (or **down**), 1. to pack and preserve with salt. 2. [Colloq.], to store or save (money, etc.).

salt of the earth, [after Matt. 5:13], any person or persons regarded as the finest, noblest, etc.

salt out, to separate (a dissolved substance) from a solution by adding salt.

with a grain (or **pinch**) **of salt,** [Latinized as *cum grano salis*], with allowance or reserve; skeptically.

worth one's salt, worth one's wages, sustenance, etc.

sal·tant (sal′tənt), *adj.* [L. *saltans,* ppr. of *saltare,* to leap < *salire,* to leap], leaping; dancing; jumping.

sal·ta·rel·lo (sal′tə-rel′ō), *n.* [It. < L. *saltare,* to leap], 1. a lively Italian dance with a hopping, skipping step. 2. music for this dance.

sal·ta·tion (sal-tā′shən), *n.* [L. *saltatio,* a dancing, dance < *saltatus,* pp. of *saltare,* to leap], 1. a leaping, jumping, or dancing. 2. sudden change, movement, or development, as if by leaping. 3. palpitation or throbbing, as of an artery. 4. in *biology,* mutation.

sal·ta·to·ri·al (sal′tə-tôr′i-əl, sal′tə-tō′ri-əl), *adj.* 1. of saltation. 2. in *zoology,* having the nature of, characterized by, or adapted for leaping.

sal·ta·to·ry (sal′tə-tôr′i, sal′tə-tō′ri), *adj.* [L. *saltatorius* < *saltare,* to leap], 1. of, characterized by, or adapted for leaping or dancing. 2. proceeding by abrupt movements or changing by sudden variation.

salt·cel·lar (sôlt′sel′ẽr), *n.* [ME. *salt saler; salt,* salt + Fr. *salière,* saltcellar < L. *sal,* salt], a small dish, or a container with a perforated top, for holding salt.

salt·ed (sôl′tid), *adj.* 1. treated, especially preserved, with salt. 2. [Colloq.], experienced or proficient in some occupation, work, etc.

salt·er (sôl′tẽr), *n.* 1. a person who makes or sells salt. 2. a person who salts meat, fish, etc.

salt·ern (sôl′tẽrn), *n.* [AS. *sealtærn; sealt,* salt + *ærn,* a building], a saltworks.

sal·ti·grade (sal′ti-grād′), *adj.* [< L. *saltus,* a leap + *gradi,* to walk], having legs adapted for leaping.

Sal·til·lo (säl-tē′yô), *n.* the capital of Coahuila, Mexico: pop., 70,000.

salt·i·ly (sôl′t′l-i), *adv.* in a salty manner.

salt·i·ness (sôl′ti-nis), *n.* salty quality or state.

sal·tire (sal′tẽr), *n.* [ME. *sawtire, sautire;* OFr. *sautoir,* stirrup loop; ML. *saltatorium* < L. *saltatorius;* see SALTATORY], in *heraldry,* a bearing in the form of a St. Andrew's cross, formed by a bend and a bend sinister crossing: also spelled **saltier.**

salt·ish (sôl′tish), *adj.* somewhat salty.

Salt Lake City, the capital of Utah, east of Great Salt Lake: pop., 189,000: center of Mormonism.

salt lick, an exposed natural deposit of mineral rock salt which animals come to lick.

salt marsh, grassland over which salt water flows at intervals.

Sal·ton Sea (or **Sink**) (sôl′t′n), a depression, 287 ft. below sea level, in the Imperial Valley, southern California, filled with water from the Colorado River: 40 mi. by 10 mi.

salt·pe·ter, salt·pe·tre (sôlt′pē′tẽr), *n.* [ME. & OFr. *salpetre;* ML. *sal petrae*, salt of rock < L. *sal*, salt + *petra*, a rock], 1. potassium nitrate. 2. sodium nitrate: also called *Chile saltpeter*.
salt pit, a pit where salt is obtained.
salt pork, pork cured in salt; especially, the fatty parts from the back, side, or belly of a hog.
salt rheum, any of various skin diseases, especially eczema.
Salt River, 1. a river in central Arizona, flowing into the Gila River: length, 200 mi.: site of Roosevelt Dam. 2. a river in northeastern Missouri, flowing into the Mississippi: length, 200 mi.
salt shaker, a container for salt, with a perforated top.
salt-wat·er (sôlt′wô′tẽr, sôlt′wät′ẽr), *adj.* of, consisting of, or living in salt water.
salt water, water containing much salt; sea water.
salt·works (sôlt′wũrks′), *n.* [*pl.* SALTWORKS], a place where salt is made, as by evaporation, etc.
salt·wort (sôlt′wũrt′), *n.* [? after D. *zoutkruid*], 1. any of a number of related plants used in making soda ash. 2. the glasswort.
salt·y (sôl′ti,) *adj.* [SALTIER (-ti-ẽr), SALTIEST (-ti-ist)], 1. of, tasting of, or containing salt. 2. smelling of the sea. 3. pungent; sharp; piquant; witty.
sa·lu·bri·ous (sə-lōō′bri-əs, sə-lū′bri-əs), *adj.* [L. *salubris* < *salus*, health], healthful; wholesome; salutary.
sa·lu·bri·ty (sə-lōō′brə-ti, sə-lū′brə-ti), *n.* [ME. *salubrite;* L. *salubritas*], the quality of being salubrious.
Sa·lu·ki (sə-lōō′ki), *n.* [Ar. *salūqi* <*Salūq*, an ancient Arabian city], any of a breed of dog of the greyhound family, with long ears and silky hair.
Sa·lus (sā′ləs), *n.* the Roman goddess of health and prosperity: identified with the Greek Hygeia.
sal·u·tar·i·ly (sal′yoo-ter′ə-li), *adv.* in a salutary manner.
sal·u·tar·i·ness (sal′yoo-ter′i-nis), *n.* the quality of being salutary.
sal·u·tar·y (sal′yoo-ter′i), *adj.* [< Fr. or L.; Fr. *salutaire;* L. *salutaris* < *salus, salutis*, health], 1. promoting or conducive to health; healthful. 2. promoting or conducive to some good purpose; beneficial or wholesome.
sal·u·ta·tion (sal′yoo-tā′shən), *n.* [ME. *salutacioun;* OFr.; L. *salutatio* < *salutatus*, pp. of *salutare;* see SALUTE], 1. the act of greeting, paying respect, addressing, or welcoming by gestures or words. 2. a form of words serving as a greeting or welcome; especially, the "Dear Sir," etc. of a letter.
sa·lu·ta·to·ri·an (sə-lōō′tə-tôr′i-ən, sə-lū′tə-tō′ri-ən), *n.* [< *salutatory* + *-an*], in some schools and colleges, the student, usually second highest in scholastic rank, who gives the salutatory: cf. **valedictorian.**
sa·lu·ta·to·ry (sə-lōō′tə-tôr′i, sə-lū′tə-tō′ri), *adj.* [L. *salutatorius*], of or expressing a salutation. *n.* [*pl.* SALUTATORIES (-iz, -riz)], an opening or welcoming address, as at school or college commencement exercises.
sa·lute (sə-lōōt′, sə-lūt′), *v.t.* [SALUTED (-id), SALUTING], [ME. *saluten;* L. *salutare*, to salute, wish health to < *salus, salutis*, health, greeting < *salvus*, safe, well], 1. to greet or welcome in a friendly manner or by ceremonial gesture, such as bowing, tipping the hat, etc.; welcome with customary actions or words. 2. to honor by performing a prescribed act or gesture, such as dipping the flag, firing cannon, raising the hand, etc., as a mark of military, naval, or official respect. 3. to present itself to, as if in greeting: as, laughter *saluted* us. *v.i.* to make a salute. *n.* [OFr. *salut;* L. *salus*], an act, words, or gesture made to express welcome, honor, respect, etc.; specifically, *a)* a formal kiss as a gesture of greeting or respect. *b)* a prescribed formal gesture such as raising the hand in a certain way to the head, in military and naval practice. *c)* a firing of cannon. *d)* a dipping of a flag or flags.
Salv., Salvador.
sal·va·ble (sal′və-b′l), *adj.* [< LL. *salvare;* see SAVE], that can be saved or salvaged.
Sal·va·do·ran (sal′və-dôr′ən, sal′və-dō′rən), *adj.* of El Salvador, its people, or culture. *n.* a native or inhabitant of El Salvador.
Sal·va·do·ri·an (sal′və-dôr′i-ən, sal′və-dō′ri-ən), *adj.* & *n.* Salvadoran.
sal·vage (sal′vij), *n.* [Fr. < OFr. *salver*, to save; see SAVE], 1. the rescue of a ship, crew, and cargo at sea from peril such as fire, shipwreck, capture, etc. 2. compensation given by the owners or insurers to persons who assist in the rescue operations. 3. the ship, cargo, or crew which is so rescued. 4. the restoration of a sunken or wrecked ship and its cargo by divers and special apparatus. 5. in *insurance*, *a)* the rescue of goods or property from damage by fire. *b)* the property so rescued. *c)* the amount paid for rescue. *d)* the value of the goods. *e)* proceeds from the sale of such goods. 6. utilization of any sort of damaged or waste material. *v.t.* [SALVAGED (-vijd), SALVAGING], 1. to save from shipwreck, capture, fire, flood, etc. 2. to restore (sunken or wrecked ships) by divers and special apparatus. 3. to utilize (waste, damaged goods, etc.).
sal·var·san (sal′vẽr-san′), *n.* [G. < L. *salvare*, to save + G. *arsen*, arsenic], arsphenamine, a compound of arsenic used in the treatment of syphilis, etc.: a trademark (**Salvarsan**): originally called *606*.
sal·va·tion (sal-vā′shən), *n.* [ME. *salvacioun;* OFr. *sauvation;* L. *salvatio* < *salvatus*, pp. of *salvare*, to save] 1. a saving or being saved; preservation from destruction; rescue. 2. a person or thing which is a means, cause, or source of preservation or rescue. 3. in *theology* spiritual rescue from sin and death; saving of the soul through the atonement of Jesus; redemption.
Salvation Army, an international organization on semimilitary lines, founded in England by William Booth in 1865 for religious and philanthropic purposes among the very poor: name adopted in 1878: abbreviated **S.A.**
Sal·va·tion·ist (sal-vā′shən-ist), *n.* a member of the Salvation Army.
salve (sav, säv), *n.* [ME. *salf, save;* AS. *sealf;* akin to G. *salbe;* IE. base *selp-, a fat, butter, as also in Sans. *sarpis-*, melted butter], 1. any medicinal ointment applied to wounds, skin irritations, burns, etc. for purposes of soothing or healing. 2. something that soothes or heals; balm: as, her kind words were a *salve* for his tender conscience. 3. flattery. *v.t.* [SALVED (savd, sävd), SALVING], [AS. *sealfian* < the *n.*], 1. [Archaic], to apply salve to (wounds, etc.). 2. to soothe; smooth over; palliate; assuage. 3. to flatter.
sal·ve (sal′vi), *interj.* [L.; see SALVO (a volley)], hail!
salve (salv), *v.t.* [SALVED (salvd), SALVING], [back-formation < *salvage*], to salvage.
sal·ver (sal′vẽr), *n.* [Fr. *salve;* Sp. *salva*, the tasting of food before serving to see that it is wholesome, hence tray on which food was placed, salver < *salvar*, to taste, save; L. *salvare;* see SAVE], a tray on which letters, visiting cards, refreshments, etc. are presented.
sal·vi·a (sal′vi-ə), *n.* [L.; see SAGE (plant)], any of a variety of garden plants of the mint family, especially the scarlet sage, grown for its brilliant red flowers.
Sal·vi·ni, Tom·ma·so (tôm-mä′zô säl-vē′nē), 1829-1916; Italian actor of tragedies.
sal·vo (sal′vō), *n.* [*pl.* SALVOS, SALVOES (-vōz)], [It. *salvo* < L. *salve*, hail, imperative of *salvere*, to be safe], 1. a discharge of a number of pieces of artillery or small arms, in regular succession or at the same time, either as a salute or, especially in naval battles, as a hostile broadside. 2. a burst of cheers or applause.
sal·vo (sal′vō), *n.* [*pl.* SALVOS (-vōz)], [< ML. legal phr. *salvo jure*, right being reserved (< L. *salvus;* see SAFE)] 1. a dishonest mental reservation; excuse or quibbling evasion. 2. in *law*, a saving clause; reservation.
sal vo·la·ti·le (vō-lat′′l-ē′), [Mod. L., volatile salt], a mixture of ammonium bicarbonate and ammonium carbonate, especially in aromatic solution for use as smelling salts.
sal·vor (sal′vẽr), *n.* a person or ship that helps in the salvage of a ship, its cargo, etc.
Sal·ween (sal′wēn′), *n.* a river flowing through Tibet and Burma into the Gulf of Martaban: length, 1,750 mi.
Salz·burg (zälts′boorkh; Eng. sôlz′bẽrg), *n.* a city in central Austria: pop., 107,000 (est. 1948): scene of annual music festivals.
Sam., 1. Samaritan. 2. Samuel.
S. Am., 1. South America. 2. South American.
Sa·mar (sä′mär), *n.* one of the Philippine Islands, southeast of Luzon: area, 5,124 sq. mi.; pop., 471,000; chief city, Catbalogan.
Sa·ma·ra (sä-mä′rä), *n.* Kuibyshev: the former name.
sam·a·ra (sam′ə-rə, sə-mâr′ə), *n.* [L. *samara, samera*, seed of the elm], a dry, hard, winged fruit, as of the elm or ash; key fruit.
Sa·ma·rang (sə-mär′äŋ), *n.* Semarang.
Sam·ar·cand (sam′ẽr-kand′), *n.* Samarkand.
Sa·mar·i·a (sə-mâr′i-ə), *n.* 1. an ancient kingdom of Palestine, between Judea and Galilee. 2. a city in Samaria: the ancient capital of Israel.

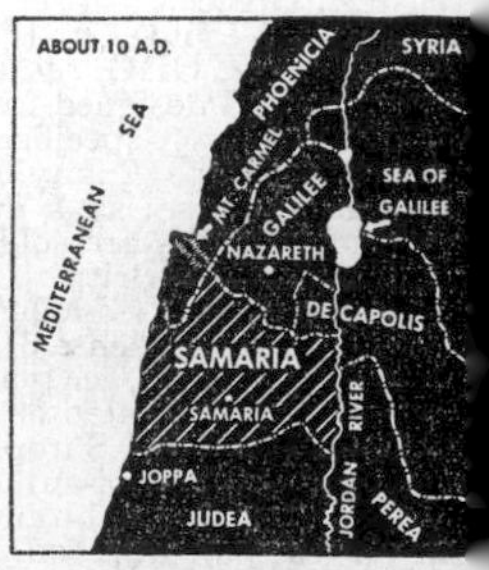

SAMARIA

Sa·mar·i·tan (sə-mar′ə-t′n), *n.* [ME.; AS.; LL. *Samaritanus;* Gr. *Samareitēs* < *Samareia*, Samaria], 1. a native or inhabitant of Samaria. 2. a person who comes to the aid of another: see **good Samaritan.** *adj.* of Samaria or its people. Abbreviated **Sam.**
sa·ma·ri·um (sə-mâr′i-əm), *n.* [Mod. L. < Eng. *samarskite*], a metallic chemical element of the rare-earth group: symbols, Sm, Sa; at. wt., 150.43; at. no., 62.
Sam·ar·kand (sam′ẽr-kand′; Russ. sä′mär-känt′), *n.* a city of the Uzbek S.S.R., in central Asia: pop. 134,000: ancient name, *Maracanda.*
sa·mar·skite (sə-mär′skīt), *n.* [G. *samarskit*, after Col. Samarski, Russ. mining official],a lustrous, velvet-black mineral containing iron, thorium, uranium, and some of the rare-earth metals, as samarium, cerium, etc.

sam·ba (sam′bə, säm′bə), *n.* [Port.; of Afr. origin], a Brazilian dance of African origin. *v.i.* to dance the samba.

sam·bar (sam′bẽr, säm′bẽr), *n.* [*pl.* SAMBARS (-bẽrz), SAMBAR; see PLURAL, II, D, 1], [Hind. *sābar;* Sans. *śambara*], a large Asiatic deer with a mane and three-pointed antlers.

sam·bo (sam′bō), *n.* [*pl.* SAMBOS (-bōz)], [Sp. *zambo*], a person of American Indian (or mulatto) and Negro descent.

Sam·bre (säṅ′br′), *n.* a river flowing through northern France and southern Belgium: length, c. 100 mi.

Sam Browne belt (sam broun), [after Gen. Sir *Samuel J. Browne* (1824–1901), Brit. army officer], a military belt with one or two diagonal shoulder straps, usually one across the right shoulder: it is designed to carry the weight of a pistol or sword and is worn by officers.

sam·buke (sam′būk), *n.* [L. *sambuka;* Gr. *sambykē;* Aram. *sabbĕkhā*], an ancient stringed instrument similar to a harp.

sam·bur (sam′bẽr, säm′bẽr), *n.* [*pl.* SAMBURS (-bẽrz), SAMBUR; see PLURAL, II, D, 1], a sambar.

same (sām), *adj.* [ME.; ON. *samr, sami;* akin to Goth. *sama;* IE. base **som-* < **sem-*, in one together, seen also in Gr. *homōs*, the same, *homoios*, like (cf. HOMO-), L. *similis* (< **semelis*), like (cf. SIMILAR); AS. had *same, adv.*, of this origin], 1. being the very one; identical. 2. alike in kind, quality, amount, or degree; corresponding. 3. unchanged; not different: as, he looks the *same* as ever. 4. before-mentioned; just spoken of. *Same* is rarely used without *the*. *pron.* the same person or thing (usually with *the, this,* or *that*). *adv.* in the same way; in like manner (usually with *the*).

all the same, 1. nevertheless. 2. of no importance.

just the same, 1. in the same way. 2. nevertheless.

SYN.—**same,** in one sense, agrees with **selfsame** and **very** in implying that what is referred to is one thing and not two or more distinct things (that is the *same*, or *selfsame* or *very*, house we once lived in) and, in another, implies reference to things that are really distinct but without any significant difference in kind, appearance, amount, etc. (I eat the *same* food every day); **identical,** in one sense, also expresses the first idea (this is the *identical* bed where he slept) and, in another, implies exact correspondence in all details, as of quality, appearance, etc. (the signatures are *identical*); **equal** implies the absence of any difference in quantity, size, value, degree, etc. (*equal* weights, an *equal* advantage); **equivalent** implies of things that they amount to the same thing in value, force, meaning, etc. ($5 or its *equivalent* in merchandise).—*ANT.* different.

sa·mekh, sa·mech (sä′mekh, sä′mek), *n.* [Heb.], the fifteenth letter of the Hebrew alphabet (ס), corresponding to English *S, s:* see **alphabet**, table.

same·ness (sām′nis), *n.* 1. the state or quality of being the same; identity or uniformity. 2. lack of change or variety; monotony.

S. Amer., 1. South America. 2. South American.

Sam Hill (sam hil), [Slang], hell: a euphemism.

Sa·mi·an (sā′mi-ən), *adj.* of Samos or its people. *n.* a native or inhabitant of Samos.

sam·iel (sam′yel), *n.* [Turk. *samyel* < *sam,* poison (< Ar. *samm*) + *yel,* wind], the simoom.

sam·i·sen (sam′i-sen′), *n.* [Japan. < Chin. *san hsien,* three strings], a Japanese musical instrument somewhat like a banjo, but with three strings.

sam·ite (sam′īt, sā′mīt), *n.* [ME. & OFr. *samit;* ML. *samitum* < MGr. *hexamiton* < *hexamitos,* woven with six threads < Gr. *hex,* six + *mitos,* a thread], a heavy silk fabric worn in the Middle Ages: it was sometimes interwoven with gold.

Saml., Sam'l, Samuel.

sam·let (sam′lit), *n.* [< *salmon* + *-let;* prob. after earlier *salmonet*], a young or small salmon.

Sam·my (sam′i), *n.* [*pl.* SAMMIES (-iz)], [< Uncle *Sam*], [Slang], a United States soldier in World War I: nickname used especially by Europeans.

Sam·nite (sam′nīt), *n.* a member of a pre-Roman people, descended from the Sabines, who lived in Samnium. *adj.* of Samnium or the Samnites.

Sam·ni·um (sam′ni-əm), *n.* an ancient country in south central Italy.

Sa·mo·a (sə-mō′ə), *n.* a group of islands in the South Pacific, north of Tonga: former name, *Navigators Islands:* see **American Samoa, Western Samoa.**

Sa·mo·an (sə-mō′ən), *adj.* of Samoa, its people, their language, etc. *n.* 1. a native or inhabitant of Samoa. 2. the Polynesian language of the Samoans.

Sa·mos (sā′mos; Gr. sä′môs), *n.* a Greek island off Asia Minor: area, 180 sq. mi.; pop., 60,000.

Sam·o·thrace (sam′ə-thrās′), *n.* a Greek island in the northern Aegean: area, 68 sq. mi.; pop., 4,000: Greek name, *Samothrake.*

Sam·o·thra·cia (sam′ə-thrā′shə), *n.* Samothrace.

Sam·o·thra·cian (sam′ə-thrā′shən), *adj.* of Samothrace, its people, or culture. *n.* a native of Samothrace.

Sa·mo·thra·ke (sä′mô-thrä′kē), *n.* Samothrace.

sam·o·var (sam′ə-vär′, säm′ə-vär′), *n.* [Russ., lit., self-boiler], a metal urn with an internal tube for heating water in making tea: used especially in Russia.

SAMOVAR

Sam·o·yed, Sam·o·yede (sam′ə-yed′), *n.* [Russ., lit., self-eater], 1. any of a Uralic people living in Siberia. 2. their Uralic language, which has five distinct dialects. 3. any of a powerful breed of Siberian dog, with a thick, white coat. *adj.* of the Samoyeds (sense 1) or Samoyed.

Sam·o·yed·ic (sam′ə-yed′ik), *adj.* Samoyed.

samp (samp), *n.* [< Am. Ind. (Algonquian) *nasaump*, softened by water], 1. coarse meal of Indian corn. 2. a porridge of this.

sam·pan (sam′pan), *n.* [Chin. *san-pan* < Port. *champão, champana;* Sp. *champán,* canoe; prob. of S. Am. Indian origin], any of various small boats used in the harbors and rivers of China and Japan, rowed with a scull from the stern, and often having a sail and an awning.

SAMPAN

sam·phire (sam′fīr′), *n.* [earlier *sampire, sainpere,* altered < Fr. (*herbe de*) *Saint Pierre,* St. Peter's (herb)], 1. a fleshy plant of the parsley family, with cut leaves and small clusters of flowers: it is used in salads. 2. a kind of glasswort.

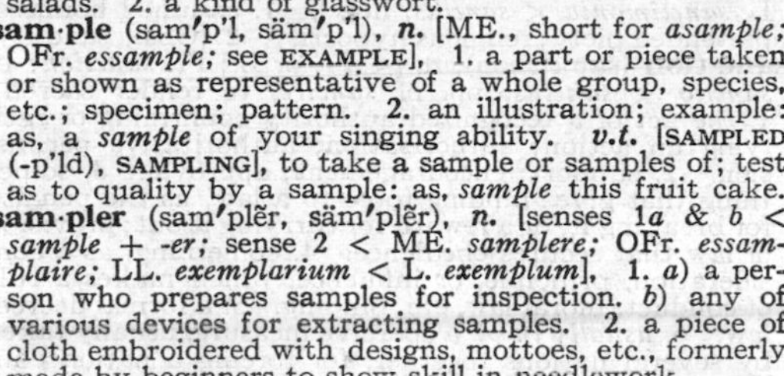

sam·ple (sam′p'l, säm′p'l), *n.* [ME., short for *asample;* OFr. *essample;* see EXAMPLE], 1. a part or piece taken or shown as representative of a whole group, species, etc.; specimen; pattern. 2. an illustration; example: as, a *sample* of your singing ability. *v.t.* [SAMPLED (-p'ld), SAMPLING], to take a sample or samples of; test as to quality by a sample: as, *sample* this fruit cake.

sam·pler (sam′plẽr, säm′plẽr), *n.* [senses 1*a* & *b* < *sample* + *-er;* sense 2 < ME. *samplere;* OFr. *essamplaire;* LL. *exemplarium* < L. *exemplum*], 1. *a*) a person who prepares samples for inspection. *b*) any of various devices for extracting samples. 2. a piece of cloth embroidered with designs, mottoes, etc., formerly made by beginners to show skill in needlework.

sam·pling (sam′pliŋ), *n.* 1. the act or process of taking a small part or quantity of something as a sample for testing or analysis. 2. the sample so taken.

Samp·son (sam′s'n, samp′s'n), see **Samson.**

Samp·son, William Thomas (samp′sən), 1840–1902; American naval officer in the Spanish-American War.

Sam·son (sam′s'n), [LL.; Gr. *Sampsōn;* Heb. *shimshōn* < *shemesh,* sun; interpretation of name uncertain], a masculine name: variant, *Sampson. n.* 1. in the *Bible,* an Israelite distinguished for his great strength: he was betrayed to the Philistines by Delilah, his mistress: Judges 13–16. 2. any very strong man.

Sam·u·el (sam′ū-əl, sam′yool), [LL.; Gr. *Samouēl;* Heb. *shĕmūēl,* lit., name of God], a masculine name: diminutive, *Sam. n.* in the *Bible,* 1. a Hebrew judge and prophet. 2. either of two books (I Samuel, II Samuel) of the Old Testament. Abbreviated **Sam., Saml., Sam'l.**

sam·u·rai (sam′oo-rī′), *n.* [*pl.* SAMURAI], [Japan.], 1. *a*) a member of a military class in feudal Japan, consisting of the retainers of the daimios, or great nobles: a samurai wore two swords. *b*) *pl.* this class. 2. *a*) a Japanese army officer or member of the military caste. *b*) *pl.* the Japanese military caste.

San (sän), *n.* a river in southern Poland, flowing northward to the Vistula River: length, 275 mi.

San (san, sän), *n.* [Sp. & It.], Saint.

Sa·n'a, Sa·naa (sä-nä′), *n.* the capital of Yemen, Arabia: pop., 50,000.

San An·ge·lo (san an′jə-lō′), a city in central Texas: pop., 59,000.

San An·to·ni·o (san′ ən-tō′ni-ō′, san′ an-tō′ni-ō′), a city in south central Texas: pop., 588,000: site of the Alamo.

san·a·tive (san′ə-tiv), *adj.* [ME. *sanatyf;* OFr. *sanatif;* ML. *sanativus* < L. *sanatus,* pp. of *sanare,* to heal], [Rare], having the power to heal or cure; curative.

san·a·to·ri·um (san′ə-tôr′i-əm, san′ə-tō′ri-əm), *n.* [*pl.* SANATORIUMS (-əmz), SANATORIA (-ə)], [Mod. L. < LL. *sanatorius,* giving health < L. *sanare,* to heal], a sanitarium.

fat, āpe, bâre, cär; ten, ēven, hêre, ovẽr; is, bīte; lot, gō, hôrn, tōōl, look; oil, out; up, ūse, fũr; get; joy; yet; **chin; she; thin,** *th*en; **zh,** leisure; **ŋ,** ring; **ə** for *a* in *ago*, *e* in *agent*, *i* in *sanity*, *o* in *comply*, *u* in *focus;* ′ as in *able* (ā′b'l); Fr. bål; ë, Fr. coeur; ö, Fr. feu; Fr. mon; ô, Fr. coq; ü, Fr. duc; **H,** G. ich; **kh,** G. doch. See pp. x–xii. ‡ foreign; * hypothetical; < derived from.

san·a·to·ry (san′ə-tôr′i, san′ə-tō′ri), *adj.* [LL. *sanatorius;* see SANATORIUM], conducive to health; curative.

san·be·ni·to (san′bə-nē′tō), *n.* [*pl.* SANBENITOS (-tōz)], [Sp. *sambenito* < *San Benito,* Saint Benedict: so named from resembling a Benedictine scapular], 1. a yellow penitential garment resembling a scapular in shape, and having a red St. Andrew's cross in front and in back, worn by a confessed, penitent heretic. 2. a similar black garment painted with flames, devils, etc., worn by a condemned heretic at an auto-da-fé.

San Ber·nar·di·no (san′ bũr′nẽr-dē′nō), 1. a city in southern California: pop., 92,000. 2. a mountain pass in the Lepontine Alps, southeastern Switzerland: height, 6,768 ft. 3. a mountain range in southern California: in full, **San Bernardino Mountains**: highest peak, San Gorgonio, 11,485 ft. 4. a mountain of this range: height, 10,630 ft.

San·cho Pan·za (saŋ′kō pan′zə; Sp. sän′chô pän′thä), the simple, credulous peasant acting as a squire to Don Quixote in Cervantes' romance, whose practical, rustic common sense serves as a contrast to the visionary idealism of his master.

sanc·ti·fi·ca·tion (saŋk tə-fi-kā′shən), *n.* [LL. *santificatio*], a sanctifying or being sanctified.

sanc·ti·fied (saŋk′tə-fīd′), *adj.* [pp. of *sanctify*], 1. dedicated; consecrated. 2. sanctimonious.

sanc·ti·fi·er (saŋk′tə-fī′ẽr), *n.* a person or thing that sanctifies.

sanc·ti·fy (saŋk′tə-fī′), *v.t.* [SANCTIFIED (-fīd′), SANCTIFYING], [Latinized form replacing ME. *seintifien;* OFr. *saintifier;* LL. *sanctificare* < L. *sanctus,* holy + *facere,* to make], 1. to make holy; specifically, *a*) to make free from sin; purify. *b*) to set apart as holy; consecrate. *c*) to make (a person) holy. 2. to give sanction to; cause to be respected; make sacred, or inviolable. 3. to make productive of spiritual blessing.

sanc·ti·mo·ni·ous (saŋk′tə-mō′ni-əs), *adj.* [< *sanctimony* + *-ous*], pretending to be very holy or pious; affecting sanctity. —*SYN.* see **devout.**

sanc·ti·mo·ny (saŋk′tə-mō′ni), *n.* [OFr. *sanctimonie;* L. *sanctimonia* < *sanctus,* holy], 1. assumed holiness; pretended piety; religious hypocrisy. 2. [Obs.], sanctity.

sanc·tion (saŋk′shən), *n.* [< Fr. or L.; Fr. *sanction;* L. *sanctio* < *sanctus,* pp. of *sancire,* to render sacred], 1. the act of a recognized authority confirming or ratifying an action; authorization; authoritative permission. 2. support; encouragement; approval. 3. something that gives binding force to a law, as the penalty for breaking it, or a reward for carrying it out; provision of law that secures obedience. 4. something, as a consideration, principle, or influence, which makes a rule of conduct, moral law, etc. binding. 5. a formal decree; law. 6. *usually in pl.* a coercive measure, usually taken by several nations together, for forcing a nation considered to have violated international law to stop the violation: as, *sanctions* may consist in withholding loans, limiting relations, imposing a blockade, etc. *v.t.* to give sanction to; specifically, *a*) to authorize; ratify; confirm. *b*) to approve; encourage; support; countenance; permit. —*SYN.* see **approve.**

sanc·ti·ty (saŋk′tə-ti), *n.* [*pl.* SANCTITIES (-tiz)], [L. *sanctitas* < *sanctus,* holy], 1. saintliness; holiness; purity. 2. the state of being consecrated to a deity; sacredness. 3. the quality of being regarded as sacred; binding force; inviolability. 4. anything held sacred.

sanc·tu·ar·y (saŋk′chōō-er′i), *n.* [*pl.* SANCTUARIES (-iz)], [ME. & OFr. *saintuaire;* LL. *sanctuarium* < L. *sanctus,* sacred], 1. a holy place; building or place set aside for worship of a god or gods; specifically, *a*) the Temple at Jerusalem. *b*) a Christian church. *c*) any church or temple. *d*) a particularly holy place within a church or temple, as the part around the altar, the holy of holies in the Jewish Temple, etc. 2. a place of refuge or protection: originally fugitives from justice were immune from arrest in churches or other sacred places. 3. refuge or protection; immunity from punishment or the law, as by taking refuge in a church, etc. 4. a reservation where animals or birds are sheltered for breeding purposes and may not be hunted or otherwise molested. —*SYN.* see **shelter.**

sanc·tum (saŋk′təm), *n.* [*pl.* SANCTUMS (-təmz), SANCTA (-tə)], [short for *sanctum sanctorum,* holy of holies, neut. of L. *sanctus,* pp. of *sancire,* to consecrate], 1. a sacred or private place. 2. a study or private room where one is not to be disturbed.

sanc·tum sanc·to·rum (saŋk′təm saŋk-tôr′əm, saŋk-tō′rəm), [ME.; L., orig., transl. of Heb. *qodhesh haqqodhōshim,* holy of holies, via Gr.], 1. a most holy place. 2. in the Jewish Temple, the place where the Ark of the Covenant was placed; the holy of holies. 3. a place of utmost privacy: often used humorously.

Sanc·tus (saŋk′təs), *n.* [ME.; L., holy], 1. the hymn constituting the culmination of the preface of the Mass or Communion service, beginning *Sanctus, sanctus, sanctus* (Holy, holy, holy). 2. a musical setting for this.

Sanctus bell, a small bell rung at various parts of the Mass, the first ringing being three times at the Sanctus.

sand (sand), *n.* [ME.; AS.; akin to G. *sand,* ON. *sandr*], 1. loose, gritty particles of worn or disintegrated rock, usually deposited along the shores of bodies of water, in river beds, or in deserts. 2. *usually pl.* a tract or area of sand; beach, etc. 3. the sand in an hourglass. 4. *pl.* moments; particles of time: as, the *sands* of life. 5. [Slang], grit; courage. 6. the reddish-yellow color characteristic of sand. *v.t.* 1. to sprinkle with sand. 2. to smooth or polish with sand or sandpaper. 3. to mix or adulterate with sand. 4. to beach on the sand. 5. to cover with sand. 6. to fill up with sand.

Sand, George (sand; Fr. sänd), (pseudonym of *Baronne Dudevant;* born *Amandine Aurore Lucie Dupin*), 1803–1876; French novelist.

san·dal (san′d'l), *n.* [ME. *sandalie;* L. *sandalium;* Gr. *sandalion,* dim. of *sandalon*], 1. a kind of shoe made of a sole fastened in various ways to the foot by straps over the instep, toes, or ankle. 2. a similar shoe for women, having the upper slashed with openwork or made of straps. 3. a low-cut rubber overshoe not covering much more than the sole of the shoe. 4. a strap for holding a low shoe or slipper on the foot.

san·dal (san′d'l), *n.* sandalwood.

san·daled, san·dalled (san′d'ld), *adj.* provided with or wearing sandals.

san·dal·wood (san′d'l-wood′), *n.* [ME. *sandell;* OFr. *sandal;* ML. *sandalum;* Ar. *çandal;* ult. < Sans. *çandana*], 1. the hard, light-colored, close-grained, sweet-smelling heartwood of any of several allied trees of the Asiatic area, used for carving and cabinetmaking or burned as incense. 2. any of these trees, especially an evergreen (*white sandalwood*) growing in India. 3. *a*) any of a number of similar or related trees, especially an East Indian tree (*red sandalwood*) with a heavy, dark-red dyewood. *b*) the wood of any of these. Also **sandal.**

Sandalwood Island, Sumba: the English name.

san·da·rac (san′də-rak′), *n.* [L. *sandaraca;* Gr. *sandarakē;* of Oriental origin], 1. *a*) the resin of the sandarac tree, used in varnish and as incense. *b*) the tree. 2. realgar.

sandarac tree, a North African tree of the pine family, with hard, fragrant wood, yielding a brittle, slightly aromatic, somewhat transparent, yellow resin.

sand·bag (sand′bag′), *n.* 1. a bag filled with sand and used for ballast in ships, military fortifications, levee protection against floods, etc. 2. a small, narrow bag filled with sand and used as a weapon. *v.t.* [SANDBAGGED (-bagd′), SANDBAGGING], 1. to place sandbags in or around. 2. to strike or stun with a sandbag; hence, 3. [Colloq.], to force into doing something.

sand bar, a ridge or narrow shoal of sand formed in a river or along a shore by the action of currents or tides.

sand·blast (sand′blast′, sand′bläst′), *n.* 1. a current of air or steam carrying sand at a high velocity, used in etching glass and in cleaning the surfaces of metals, stone, buildings, etc. 2. the machine used to apply this blast. 3. any strong destructive force. *v.t.* to engrave or clean with a sandblast.

sand-blind (sand′blīnd′), *adj.* [ME.; altered < AS. **samblind; sam,* half (akin to L. *semi-*) + *blind,* blind], weak-sighted; partially blind.

sand·box (sand′boks′), *n.* a box or similar receptacle filled with sand, as for children to play in or, on locomotives, etc., for dropping sand on slippery rails.

sandbox tree, a tropical tree with small, roundish, woody fruit that bursts with a loud noise when dry.

sand·bur, sand·burr (sand′bũr′), *n.* any of a number of harmful weeds with burlike fruit.

Sand·burg, Carl (sand′bẽrg, san′bẽrg), 1878– ; American poet, writer, and ballad collector.

sand-cast (sand′kast′, sand′käst′), *v.t.* to make (a casting) by pouring metal in a mold of sand.

sand crack, a lesion in the horn of a horse's hoof, often causing lameness.

sand dab, any of various small, edible flatfishes.

sand dollar, any of several flat, round, disklike sea urchins, about three inches in diameter, which live on sandy ocean beds.

sand·ed (san′did), *adj.* 1. covered, filled, or clogged with sand. 2. of a sandy color; speckled.

sand eel, a sand launce.

sand·er (san′dẽr), *n.* 1. a person who sands or sandpapers. 2. a device for sanding or sandpapering.

sand·er·ling (san′dẽr-liŋ), *n.* [prob. < *sand* + AS. *yrthling,* farmer, kind of bird, lit. earthling], a small, gray-and-white sandpiper, common on sandy beaches.

sand flea, 1. any of various fleas that live in sandy places. 2. the chigoe. 3. a beach flea.

sand fly, any of various small, biting flies found near the seashore: some varieties transmit certain diseases.

sand·glass (sand′glas′, sand′gläs′), *n.* an instrument consisting of two glass globes with a connecting passage, used for measuring time by the flowing of sand from one globe to the other; hourglass.

sand grouse, any of certain pigeonlike birds found in sandy regions of southern Europe, Asia, and Africa.

san·dhi (san′di, sän′di), *n.* [Sans. < *sandhī-,* a placing together], in *linguistics,* 1. a context in which a word is phonetically modified by assimilation to contiguous words: as, *'s* is the form of *is* occurring in *sandhi.*

2. the assimilations, etc. shown by a word in such a context: as, in *won't*, *n't* occurs instead of *not* by *sandhi*. 3. the phonetic form assumed by a word in such a context. *adj.* showing the effects of sandhi: as, *'ll* is the *sandhi* form of *will* in *he'll*.

sand·hog (sand'hôg', sand'hog'), *n.* 1. a laborer who works or digs in sand. 2. a laborer employed in underground or underwater construction projects, working under compressed air, as in a caisson. Also **sand hog.**

sand hopper, a sand flea.

Sand·hurst (sand'hẽrst), *n.* a village in Berkshire, England: site of the royal military and staff colleges.

San Diego (san' di-ā'gō), a city on the coast of southern California: pop., 573,000.

sand·i·ness (san'di-nis), *n.* a sandy state or quality.

sand launce, [*sand* + *launce*, var. of *lance* (weapon)], any of various small, elongated sea fishes that can dig themselves into the sand: also **sand lance** (or **eel**).

sand lily, a plant of the lily family, with narrow, grasslike leaves and clusters of white, star-shaped flowers.

sand-lot (sand'lot'), *adj.* of or having to do with a sandy lot or field in or near a city: applied to games played in such lots, as, *sand-lot* baseball.

sand·man (sand'man'), *n.* [prob. < G. *sandmann*], a mythical person, as in fairy tales, supposed to make children sleepy by throwing sand in their eyes.

sand·pa·per (sand'pā'pẽr), *n.* paper having one side covered with a sand coating, used for smoothing and polishing. *v.t.* to smooth or polish with sandpaper.

sand·pip·er (sand'pīp'ẽr), *n.* [*pl.* SANDPIPERS (-ẽrz), SANDPIPER; see **PLURAL, II, D, 1**], any of several shore birds related to the plovers and snipes but distinguished by the length of the soft-tipped bill: the European *common sandpiper* and the American *spotted sandpiper* are two varieties.

San·dra (san'drə), a feminine name: see **Alexandra.**

sand·stone (sand'stōn'), *n.* a common sedimentary rock ranging in color from yellow to red and brown, and consisting of sand grains, usually quartz, cemented together by silica, lime, etc.: much used for building.

sand·storm (sand'stôrm'), *n.* a windstorm in which large quantities of sand are blown about in clouds.

sand trap, a pit or trench filled with sand, serving as a hazard on a golf course.

San·dus·ky (san-dus'ki, sən-dus'ki), *n.* a city in Ohio: port on Lake Erie: pop., 32,000.

sand verbena, any of a number of related trailing plants with fragrant, pink, white, or yellow flowers.

sand viper, 1. the horned viper. 2. the hognose.

Sand·wich (sand'wich), *n.* one of the Cinque Ports, in Kent, England: pop., 4,000.

sand·wich (sand'wich, san'wich), *n.* [after John Montagu, 4th Earl of *Sandwich* (1718–1792), said to have eaten these in order not to leave the gaming table for meals], 1. two or more slices of bread with a filling of meat, fish, eggs, vegetables, etc. between them. 2. anything like a sandwich in arrangement. *v.t.* to place or squeeze between two other persons, places, or things.

Sandwich Islands, the Hawaiian Islands: former name.

sandwich man, 1. a man who walks the street displaying two advertising boards hung from his shoulders, one in front and one behind. 2. a man who makes or sells sandwiches.

sand·wort (sand'wũrt'), *n.* any of a number of related low, tufted, mat-forming plants, growing in sandy soil.

sand·y (san'di), *adj.* [SANDIER (-di-ẽr), SANDIEST (-di-ist)], 1. composed of, full of, or covered with sand. 2. like sand; shifting; unstable. 3. of the color of sand; pale reddish-yellow: usually said of hair.

Sandy Hook, a peninsula in eastern New Jersey, south of Manhattan Island.

sane (sān), *adj.* [L. *sanus*, healthy], 1. mentally healthy; sound of mind; rational. 2. (of the mind) sound; not diseased. 3. showing good sense; sound; sensible; reasonable: as, a *sane* policy.

San·ford, Mount (san'fẽrd), a mountain of the Wrangell range, eastern Alaska: height, 16,206 ft.

San·for·ize (san'fə-rīz'), *v.t.* [SANFORIZED (-rīzd'), SANFORIZING], [back-formation from *Sanforized*, a trademark applied to fabrics so treated: after *Sanford* L. Cluett, the inventor], to preshrink (cotton or linen cloth) permanently by a patented process before making it into shirts, dresses, etc.

San Fran·cis·co (san' frən-sis'kō), a city on the coast of central California: pop., 740,000; with Oakland and suburbs, 2,783,000: often colloquially shortened to **Frisco.**

San Francisco Bay, an arm of the Pacific, off San Francisco and Oakland.

San Francisco Mountain, an extinct volcano in central Arizona: height, 12,611 ft.

sang (saŋ), alternative past tense of **sing.**

san·ga·ree (saŋ'gə-rē'), *n.* [Sp. *sangría*, lit., bleeding < *sangre* < L. *sanguis*, blood], a cold drink of wine, spices, and sweetened water.

San·ger, Margaret (saŋ'gẽr), (born *Margaret Higgins*), 1883– ; American advocate of birth-control education.

‡sang-froid (säŋ'frwà'), *n.* [Fr., lit., cold blood], composure; imperturbability. —*SYN.* see **equanimity.**

San·graal (saŋ'grāl'), *n.* [< OFr. *Saint Graal;* see SAINT & GRAIL], the Holy Grail.

San·gre·al (saŋ'gri-əl), *n.* the Sangraal.

San·gre de Cris·to (säŋ'gre de krēs'tô), a mountain range in southern Colorado and northern New Mexico: highest point, Blanca Peak, 14,390 ft.

san·gui- (saŋ'gwi), [< L. *sanguis*, blood], a combining form meaning *blood*.

san·guif·er·ous (saŋ-gwif'ẽr-əs), *adj.* [*sangui-* + *-ferous*], carrying or conducting blood.

san·gui·na·ri·a (saŋ'gwi-nâr'i-ə), *n.* [Mod. L. < L. (*herba*) *sanguinaria*, (herb) that stanches blood < *sanguis*, blood], a plant of the poppy family, with lobed leaves, white flowers, and large roots used in medicine; bloodroot.

san·gui·nar·i·ly (saŋ'gwi-ner'ə-li), *adv.* in a sanguinary manner.

san·gui·nar·i·ness (saŋ'gwi-ner'i-nis), *n.* the quality or state of being sanguinary.

san·gui·nar·y (saŋ'gwi-ner'i), *adj.* [L. *sanguinarius* < *sanguis, sanguinis*, blood], 1. accompanied by much bloodshed, murder, or carnage. 2. flowing with blood; bloodstained. 3. bloodthirsty.

san·guine (saŋ'gwin), *adj.* [ME. *sanguin;* Late OFr. *sanguin;* L. *sanguineus* < *sanguis, sanguinis*, blood], 1. of the color of blood; ruddy: said especially of complexions. 2. in *medieval physiology*, having the warm, passionate, cheerful temperament and the healthy, ruddy complexion of one in whom the blood is the predominant humor of the four; hence, 3. cheerful; confident; optimistic; hopeful. 4. sanguinary.

san·guin·e·ous (saŋ-gwin'i-əs), *adj.* [L. *sanguineus* < *sanguis, sanguinis*, blood], 1. of or containing blood. 2. having the color of blood; red. 3. of bloodshed; sanguinary. 4. sanguine; confident; hopeful.

san·guin·o·lent (saŋ-gwin'ə-lənt), *adj.* [Fr.; L. *sanguinolentus* < *sanguis, sanguinis*, blood], of, containing, or tinged with blood.

San·he·drim (san'hi-drim, san'i-drim; Heb. sän-hed'rim), *n.* the Sanhedrin.

San·he·drin (san'hi-drin, san'i-drin; Heb. sän-hed'rin), *n.* [L. Heb. *sanhedrin;* Gr. *synedrion*, a sitting together, assembly < *syn-*, together + *hedra*, seat], the highest court and council of the ancient Jewish nation, having religious and civil functions: it was composed of 71 members, presided over by the high priest, and was abolished with the destruction of Jerusalem in 70 A.D.: also **Great Sanhedrin.**

san·i·cle (san'i-k'l), *n.* [ME. *sanycle;* OFr.; ML. *sanicula;* prob. dim. < L. *sanus*, healthy], any of a number of related plants of the parsley family, with long-stalked leaves and clusters of small, white or yellowish flowers: formerly regarded as having healing powers.

sa·ni·es (sā'ni-ēz'), *n.* [L.; akin to *sanguis*, blood], a thin, often greenish, discharge of pus and blood from a wound or ulcer.

sa·ni·ous (sā'ni-əs), *adj.* 1. of, or having the nature of, sanies. 2. characterized by or discharging sanies.

san·i·tar·i·an (san'ə-târ'i-ən), *adj.* of the laws of health, sanitation, or hygiene; sanitary. *n.* a person who is interested in and has knowledge of public health and sanitary studies; an advocate of sanitary measures.

san·i·tar·i·ly (san'ə-ter'ə-li), *adv.* in a sanitary manner.

san·i·tar·i·ness (san'ə-ter'i-nis), *n.* the quality or state of being sanitary.

san·i·tar·i·um (san'ə-târ'i-əm), *n.* [*pl.* SANITARIUMS (-əmz), SANITARIA (-ə)], [Mod. L. < *sanitas*, health], 1. a quiet, restful resort, as in the mountains, where people go to rest and regain health. 2. an institution for the care of invalids or convalescents, especially one making use of local natural resources, as mineral springs, or one treating a specific disease, as tuberculosis. Also **sanatorium.**

san·i·tar·y (san'ə-ter'i), *adj.* [Fr. *sanitaire* < L. *sanitas;* see SANITY & -ARY], 1. of health or the rules and conditions of health; especially, of absence of dirt and agents of infection or disease; tending to promote health and healthful conditions. 2. in a clean, healthy condition; hygienic. *n.* [*pl.* SANITARIES (-iz)], a public toilet, water closet, or urinal. Abbreviated **Sn.**

sanitary belt, a narrow elastic belt for holding a sanitary napkin in place.

sanitary engineering, the branch of civil engineering having to do with sewage disposal, water supply, etc.

sanitary napkin, an absorbent pad of cotton, etc. worn by women during menstruation.

san·i·ta·tion (san'ə-tā'shən), *n.* [*sanitary* + *-ation*], 1. the science and practice of effecting healthful and hygienic conditions; study and use of hygienic measures such as drainage, ventilation, pure water supply, etc. 2. drainage and disposal of sewage.

san·i·ty (san'ə-ti), *n.* [ME. *sanite;* L. *sanitas,* health], 1. the condition of being sane; soundness of mind; mental health. 2. soundness of judgment.

San Ja·cin·to (san'jə-sin'tō), a river in eastern Texas, flowing into Galveston Bay: in a battle (1836) near its mouth, troops led by Sam Houston won Texas from Mexico.

san·jak (sån'jak'), *n.* [Turk. *sanjāq,* lit., a banner], formerly, an administrative subdivision of a vilayet, or province, in Turkey.

San Joa·quin (san'wô-kēn', san'wä-kēn'), a river in central California, flowing into the Sacramento River: length, 350 mi.

San Jo·se (san' hō-zā', san' ə-zā'), a city in west central California: pop., 204,000.

San Jo·sé (sän hô-se'), the capital of Costa Rica: pop., 134,000.

San Jo·se scale (san' hō-zā'), [< *San Jose,* California, where first observed in the United States], a scale insect very destructive to fruit trees.

San Juan (san hwän', san wôn'; Sp. sän hwän'), 1. seaport and capital of Puerto Rico: pop., 452,000. 2. a river flowing between Nicaragua and Costa Rica into the Caribbean: length, 100 mi.

San Juan Hill, a hill near Santiago de Cuba: scene of a battle (1898) of the Spanish-American War, in which American troops defeated the Spaniards.

San Juan Islands, a group of islands off northwestern Washington.

San Juan Mountains, a mountain range in southwestern Colorado: highest point, 14,306 ft.

sank (saŋk), alternative past tense of **sink.**

San·khya (säŋ'kyə), *n.* [Sans. *sāṃkhya*], one of the six major systems of Hindu philosophy, dualistic in metaphysics, involving two ultimate principles of matter and spirit.

Sankt Mo·ritz (zäŋkt mō'rits), St. Moritz.

San Le·an·dro (san' li-an'drō), a city in central California, near Oakland: pop., 66,000.

San Lu·is Po·to·sí (sän'lōō-ēs' pô'tô-sē'), 1. a state in east central Mexico: area, 24,415 sq. mi.; pop., 1,048,000. 2. its capital: pop., 160,000.

San Ma·ri·no (sän' mä-rē'nô; Eng. san' mə-rē'nō), 1. an independent republic within eastern Italy: area, 38 sq. mi.; pop., 17,000. 2. its capital.

San Mar·tín, Jo·sé de (hô-se' de sän' mär-tēn'), 1778–1850; South American soldier and hero: leader in the fight for independence of Argentina, Chile, and Peru.

San Ma·te·o (san' mə-tā'ō), a city in central California, near San Francisco: pop., 70,000.

san·nup (san'up), *n.* [< Am. Ind. (Algonquian)], a married male American Indian.

San Re·mo (sän re'mô; Eng. san rē'mō), a seaport and resort town in northwestern Italy: pop., 32,000.

sans (sanz; Fr. sän), *prep.* [ME. *saun;* OFr. *sanz* (Fr. *sans*); altered < L. *absentia,* absence (under influence of *sine,* without)], [Archaic or Poetic], without.

Sans., Sanskrit.

San Sal·va·dor (san sal'və-dôr'; Sp. sän' säl'vä-*th*ôr'), 1. the capital of El Salvador, Central America: pop., 253,000. 2. one of the eastern Bahama Islands: area, 60 sq. mi.; pop., 700: first New World land sighted by Columbus (1492): also called *Watling Island.*

San·scrit (san'skrit), *n.* Sanskrit.

sans-cu·lotte (sanz'koo-lot', sanz'kyoo-lot'; Fr. sän'kü'lôt'), *n.* [Fr., lit., without breeches], 1. a revolutionary: term of contempt applied by the aristocrats to the republicans of the poorly clad French Revolutionary army, who substituted pantaloons for knee breeches; hence, 2. any radical or revolutionary.

sans-cu·lot·tic (sanz'koo-lot'ik, sanz'kyoo-lot'ik), *adj.* of the sans-culottes or sans-culottism.

sans-cu·lot·tide (sanz'koo-lot'id, sanz'kyoo-lot'id; Fr. sän'kü'lô'tēd'), *n.* [Fr. < *sans-culotte*], 1. one of the five extra days (six in leap year) of the regular year in the French Revolutionary Calendar, added to the month Fructidor. 2. *pl.* the festivities held during these days. Also **sans-culottid.**

sans-cu·lot·tism (sanz'koo-lot'iz'm, sanz'kyoo-lot'iz'm), *n.* the principles and methods of sans-culottes.

‡sans doute (sän' dōōt'), [Fr.], without doubt; certainly.

San Se·bas·tián (sän' se-bäs-tyän'; Eng. san' si-bas'chən), a city in Spain, on the Bay of Biscay: pop., 135,000.

san·sei (san'sā, sän'sā), *n.* [*pl.* SANSEI, SANSEIS (-sāz)], [Japan., third generation; cf. NISEI], [also S-], a native American citizen whose grandparents were Japanese immigrants to the United States.

san·se·vi·e·ri·a (san'sə-vi-ē'ri-ə), *n.* [Mod. L., after the Prince of *Sanseviero* (1710–1771), a learned Neapolitan], any of a number of related plants of the lily family, with stiff, thick, lance-shaped leaves.

‡sans gêne (sän' zhen'), [Fr.], without embarrassment or constraint; in or with an easy, casual manner.

San·skrit (san'skrit), *n.* [< Sans. *saṃskṛta,* lit., made together, hence (with reference to its formalized literary and religious nature) well arranged, properly regulated; *sam-,* together (base as in *same*) + *-kṛta,* made: so called in distinction to ***Prākrit,*** lit., the common (spoken) language, dialect], 1. the classical Old Indic literary language, as cultivated from the 3d century B.C. onward and still used in the ritual of the Northern Buddhist Church: because of the antiquity of its written expression and the detailed descriptive analysis in the *Sutras* of the Hindu grammarian Pānini (end of the 4th century B.C.), Sanskrit has provided the chief clue in the discovery of Indo-European and fostered the modern science of descriptive linguistics. 2. loosely, any written form of Old Indic, including Vedic. *adj.* of or written in Sanskrit. Abbreviated **Sans., Sansk., Skrt., Skt., Skr.** Also spelled **Sanscrit.**

San·skrit·ic (san-skrit'ik), *adj.* Sanskrit.

San·skrit·ist (san'skrit-ist), *n.* a scholar of Sanskrit or the Sanskritic languages.

‡sans pa·reil (sän' pä're'y'), [Fr.], without equal.

‡sans peur et sans re·proche (sän' pēr' ā' sän' rə-prôsh'), [Fr.], without fear and without reproach.

sans-ser·if (san-ser'if, sanz'ser'if), *n.* [Fr. *sans* + Eng *serif*], a style of printing type with no serifs.

‡sans sou·ci (sän' sōō'sē'), [Fr.], 1. without care or worry; gay. 2. [S- S-], the palace built (1745–1747) by Frederick the Great near Potsdam, Germany.

San Ste·fa·no (sän ste'fä-nô'), a town in European Turkey, near Istanbul, where a treaty was made between Russia and Turkey in 1878, at the end of the Russo-Turkish War: Turkish name, *Yeşilköy.*

San·ta (san'tə, san'ti; *for adj., also* sän'tä), *n.* Santa Claus. *adj.* [Sp. or It., fem. of *santo* < L. *sanctus,* holy], holy or saint: used in combinations, as *Santa Fé:* abbreviated **Sta.**

San·ta An·a (san'tə an'ə; *also, for 2,* Sp. sän'tä ä'nä), 1. a city in southwestern California: pop., 100,000. 2. a city in El Salvador, Central America: pop., 119,000.

San·ta An·na, An·to·nio Ló·pez de (än-tô'nyô lô'pes de sän'tä ä'nä), 1795–1876; Mexican revolutionist, general, president, and dictator.

San·ta Bar·ba·ra (san'tə bär'bə-rə), a city on the coast of southwestern California: pop., 59,000.

Santa Barbara Islands, a chain of islands off the coast of southern California.

San·ta Cat·a·li·na (san'tə kat'ə-lē'nə), an island off the coast of southern California: a tourist resort: area, 7[illegible] sq. mi.: also **Catalina.**

San·ta Cla·ra (sän'tä klä'rä), 1. a city in central Cuba: pop., 142,000. 2. (san'tə klâr'ə), a city in west central California: pop., 59,000.

San·ta Claus, San·ta Klaus (san'tə klôz', san'ti klôz'), [dial. D. *Sante Klaas* < *Sant Nikolaas,* St. Nicholas], in *folklore,* a fat, white-bearded, jolly old man in a red suit, who lives at the North Pole, makes toys for children, and distributes gifts at Christmas time: also called *Saint Nicholas, Saint Nick.*

San·ta Cruz (san'tə-krōōz'; Sp. sän'tä krōōth'), 1. St. Croix, one of the Virgin Islands. 2. one of the Santa Barbara Islands.

Santa Cruz de Ten·er·ife (də ten'ə-rif'; Sp. de te'ne-rē'fe), a seaport in the Canary Islands: pop., 135,000.

San·ta Fe (san'tə fā', san'tə fē'), the capital of New Mexico: pop., 35,000.

San·ta Fé (sän'tä fe'; Eng. san'tə fā'), a city in eastern Argentina: pop., 220,000.

Santa Fe Trail, a trade route between Santa Fe, New Mexico, and Independence, Missouri: important from 1821 to 1880.

san·ta·la·ceous (san'tə-lā'shəs), *adj.* [< Mod. L. *Santalaceae,* name of the family < ML. *santalum,* sandalwood + *-ous*], of the sandalwood family of plants.

San·ta Ma·ri·a (sän'tä mä-rē'ä), 1. the flagship that Columbus used in his voyage of 1492. 2. an active volcano in western Guatemala: height, 12,500 ft.

San·ta Mon·i·ca (san'tə mon'i-kə), a suburb of Los Angeles, California, on the Pacific: pop., 83,000.

San·tan·der (sän'tän-dâr'), *n.* a city in Spain, on the Bay of Biscay: pop., 118,000.

San·ta·ya·na, George (san'ti-an'ə, san'ti-ä'nə; Sp. sän'tä-yä'nä), 1863–1952; American philosopher and poet, born in Spain; in Italy (1923–1952).

San·tee (san-tē'), *n.* a river in central South Carolina, flowing into the Atlantic: length, 143 mi.

San·ti·a·go (sän'tē-ä'gô; Eng. san'ti-ā'gō), *n.* the capital of Chile: pop., 1,169,000.

Santiago de Cu·ba (de kōō'bä), 1. a seaport of southern Cuba: pop., 163,000. 2. Oriente: former name.

San·to Do·min·go (sän'tô *th*ô-miŋ'gô; Eng. san'tō də-miŋ'gō), 1. the Dominican Republic: the former name. 2. the capital of the Dominican Republic: pop., 478,000.

san·ton (san'tən, sän-tōn'), *n.* [Sp. < *santo;* see SANTA], a Moslem monk or hermit.

san·ton·i·ca (san-ton'i-kə), *n.* [Mod. L.; L. (*herba*) *santonica* < *Santoni,* a people of Aquitania], 1. a European wormwood tree. 2. a drug made of its dried flowers, containing santonin.

san·to·nin, san·to·nine (san'tə-nin), *n.* [Fr. < Mod. L. *santonica*], a colorless, crystalline compound, $C_{15}H_{18}O_3$, obtained from certain species of wormwood and used in medicine for expelling intestinal worms.

San·tos (sän'toos, sän'tōs), *n.* a seaport in southern Brazil: pop., 207,000: coffee-exporting center.

São Fran·cis·co (soun′ frän-sēs′koo), a river in eastern Brazil, flowing into the Atlantic: length, 1,800 mi.

São Lu·iz do Ma·ra·nhão (soun lwēs′ doo mä′rə-nyoun′), a seaport of Brazil, on an island off its northern coast: pop., 89,000: also **São Luiz.**

São Mi·guel (soun′ mē-gel′), the largest island of the Azores: area, 297 sq. mi.; pop., 117,000.

Saône (sōn), *n.* a river in east central France, flowing southward into the Rhone River: length, 300 mi.

São Pau·lo (soun pou′loo), 1. a state of southeastern Brazil; area, 91,310 sq. mi.; pop., 8,522,000 (est. 1948). 2. its capital: pop., 1,323,000.

São Paulo de Lo·an·da (də lô-än′dä), Loanda, Africa.

São Pe·dro de Ri·o Gran·de do Sul (soun pe′droo də rē′oo grän′de doo sōōl′), Rio Grande, a city in Brazil.

Saor·stat Eir·eann (sâr′stôt′ âr′ən), [Ir. *saor*, free + *stat*, state; see Eire], the Irish Free State: the Gaelic name: also **Saorstat.**

São Sal·va·dor (soun säl′və-dôr′), Bahía, a city in Brazil.

São To·mé, São Tho·mé (soun′ tô-me′), a Portuguese island in the Gulf of Guinea, off Africa: area, 326 sq. mi.; pop., 52,000: English name, *St. Thomas.*

sap (sap), *n.* [ME.; AS. *sæp;* akin to G. *saft;* IE. base **sab-*, var. of **sap-*, to taste, perceive, seen also in L. *sapere*, to taste of (cf. sapient)], 1. the juice which circulates through a plant, especially a woody plant, bearing water, food, etc. to the tissues. 2. any fluid considered vital to the life or health of an organism. 3. vigor; energy; vitality. 4. sapwood. 5. [< dial. *sapskull* & *saphead*], [Slang], a stupid person; fool. *v.t.* [sapped (sapt), sapping], to drain of sap.

sap (sap), *n.* [OFr. *sappe* < the *v.*], an extended, narrow trench for approaching or undermining an enemy position or a besieged place. *v.t.* [sapped (sapt), sapping], [Fr. *saper*, *sapper* < *sappe*, a spade; It. *zappe* < *zappa*, goat: the handle resembled a goat's horns], 1. to undermine by digging away foundations; dig beneath. 2. to undermine in any way; weaken; exhaust; devitalize. *v.i.* 1. to dig saps. 2. to approach an enemy's position by saps. —*SYN.* see **weaken.**

sap·a·jou (sap′ə-jōō′; Fr. så′på′zhōō′), *n.* [Fr. < Tupi name], a small South American monkey; capuchin.

sa·pan·wood (sə-pan′wood′), *n.* [D. *sapanhout* < Malay *sapan*], 1. a wood yielding a red dye, obtained from an East Indian tree of the senna family. 2. the tree. Also spelled **sappanwood.**

sap·head (sap′hed′), *n.* [Colloq.], a stupid person; fool.

sap·head·ed (sap′hed′id), *adj.* [Colloq.], stupid; foolish.

sa·phe·na (sə-fē′nə), *n.* [ML.; Ar. *ṣāfin*], either of two large superficial veins of the leg.

sa·phe·nous (sə-fē′nəs), *adj.* of or associated with a saphena.

sap·id (sap′id), *adj.* [L. *sapidus* < *sapere*, to have a taste, taste of; cf. sap (juice)], 1. savory; having a pleasing taste. 2. having interest; engaging.

sa·pid·i·ty (sə-pid′ə-ti), *n.* the quality of being sapid.

sa·pi·ence (sā′pi-əns), *n.* [ME.; OFr.; L. *sapientia* < *sapiens;* see sapient], wisdom.

sa·pi·en·cy (sā′pi-ən-si), *n.* sapience.

sa·pi·ent (sā′pi-ənt), *adj.* [L. *sapiens*, ppr. of *sapere*, to taste, know; cf. sap (juice)], wise; sagacious; full of knowledge; discerning: often ironical. —*SYN.* see **wise.**

sa·pi·en·tial (sā′pi-en′shəl), *adj.* [LL. *sapientialis* < L. *sapiens*], having, providing, or expounding wisdom.

sap·in·da·ceous (sap′in-dā′shəs), *adj.* [< Mod. L. *Sapindaceae*, name of the family < *Sapindus*, the type genus < L. *sapo*, soap + *Indicus*, Indian; + *-ous*], of the soapberry family of plants.

sap·less (sap′lis), *adj.* 1. without sap; dry; withered. 2. without vigor or energy; devitalized; insipid.

sap·ling (sap′liŋ), *n.* [ME. *sappelynge;* see sap (juice) & -ling], 1. a young tree. 2. a youth.

sap·o·dil·la (sap′ə-dil′ə), *n.* [Sp. *sapotilla*, *zapotilla*, dim. of *sapote*, *zapote* < Nahuatl *tzapotl*], 1. a tropical American evergreen tree yielding chicle and having a brown, rough-skinned fruit with a sweet, yellowish pulp; sapota. 2. the fruit: also **sapodilla plum.**

sap·o·na·ceous (sap′ə-nā′shəs), *adj.* [Mod. L. *saponaceus* < L. *sapo*, *saponis*, soap], soapy.

sa·pon·i·fi·a·ble (sə-pon′ə-fī′ə-b′l), *adj.* that can be saponified.

sa·pon·i·fi·ca·tion (sə-pon′ə-fi-kā′shən), *n.* [Fr. < *saponifier;* see saponify], chemical conversion of fats into soap.

sa·pon·i·fi·er (sə-pon′ə-fī′ẽr), *n.* a chemical agent used in saponification.

sa·pon·i·fy (sə-pon′ə-fī′), *v.t.* [saponified (-fīd′), saponifying], [Fr. *saponifier* < L. *sapo*, *saponis*, soap + *facere*, to make], to convert (a fat) into soap by reaction with an alkali. *v.i.* to undergo conversion to soap.

sap·o·nin (sap′ə-nin), *n.* [Fr. *saponine* < L. *sapo*, *saponis*, soap; see -in], any of a group of glucosides, found in soapwort, soapbark, etc., which form a soapy foam when dissolved in water.

sap·o·nine (sap′ə-nin, sap′ə-nēn′), *n.* saponin.

sap·o·nite (sap′ə-nīt′), *n.* [Sw. *saponit* < L. *sapo*, *saponis*, soap; see -ite], a hydrous silicate of aluminum and magnesium, occurring in soft, soapy masses in veins and cavities of rock formations.

sa·por (sā′pẽr, sā′pôr), *n.* [L. < *sapere*, to taste; cf. sap (juice)], that quality in a substance which produces taste or flavor; savor; relish: British spelling, **sapour.**

sa·por·ous (sā′pẽr-əs), *adj.* [see sapor], of or having taste or flavor.

sa·po·ta (sə-pō′tə), *n.* [Mod. L.; Sp. *sapota*, *sapote;* see sapodilla], a sapodilla.

sap·o·ta·ceous (sap′ə-tā′shəs), *adj.* [< Mod. L. *Sapotaceae*, name of the family < *sapota* (see sapota); + *-ous*], of the sapodilla family of plants.

sap·pan·wood (sə-pan′wood′), *n.* sapanwood.

sap·per (sap′ẽr), *n.* 1. a soldier employed in digging saps, repairing fortifications, etc. 2. a person or thing that saps.

Sap·phic (saf′ik), *adj.* [L. *Sapphicus;* Gr. *Sapphikos* < *Sapphō*], 1. of Sappho. 2. designating or of certain meters or a form of stanza or strophe used by or named after Sappho, especially a stanza of three five-stress lines followed by a short line. *n.* a Sapphic verse.

Sap·phi·ra (sə-fī′rə), *n.* [Gr. *Sappheirē* < Aram. word akin to Gr. *sappir*, beautiful], in the *Bible*, the wife of Ananias, who was struck dead with her husband for lying: Acts 5:1–10.

sap·phire (saf′īr), *n.* [ME. & OFr. *saphir;* L. *sapphirus;* Gr. *sappheiros;* via Sem. (cf. Heb. *sappīr*) < Sans. *śanipriya*, lit., dear to Saturn], 1. a hard, transparent precious stone of a clear, deep-blue corundum. 2. its color. 3. a hard, translucent or transparent variety of corundum, varying in color. 4. a gem made of this: as, white, yellow, or purple *sapphire.* *adj.* deep-blue.

sap·phir·ine (saf′ẽr-in, saf′ə-rīn′), *adj.* of or like sapphire. *n.* 1. a blue or green silicate of magnesium and aluminum, $Mg_5Al_{12}Si_2O_{27}$. 2. a blue variety of spinel.

sap·phism (saf′iz′m), *n.* [< *Sappho*, *Sapphic*, etc. + *-ism*], lesbianism.

Sap·pho (saf′ō), *n.* a woman poet of ancient Greece, who lived on Lesbos; fl. c. 600 B.C.: known for love lyrics.

sap·pi·ness (sap′i-nis), *n.* a sappy state or quality.

Sap·po·ro (sä′pô-rô′), *n.* the capital of Hokkaido, Japan: pop., 314,000.

sap·py (sap′i), *adj.* [ME. *sapy;* AS. *sæpig*], 1. full of sap; juicy. 2. energetic; vigorous. 3. [< *sap*, *n.* 5], [Slang], foolish; silly; fatuous.

sapr-, sapro-.

sa·pre·mi·a, sa·prae·mi·a (sə-prē′mi-ə), *n.* [Mod. L. < *sapr-* + *-emia*], a form of blood poisoning caused by the products of putrefactive microorganisms in the blood.

sap·ro- (sap′rō, sap′rə), [< Gr. *sapros*, rotten; akin to *sēpein*, to rot], a combining form meaning *dead, putrefying, decaying*, as in *saprogenic.*

sap·ro·gen·ic (sap′rə-jen′ik), *adj.* [*sapro-* + *-genic*], producing, or produced by, putrefaction.

sa·prog·e·nous (sə-proj′ə-nəs), *adj.* saprogenic.

sap·ro·lite (sap′rə-līt′), *n.* [*sapro-* + *-lite*], decomposed rock.

sa·proph·a·gous (sə-prof′ə-gəs), *adj.* [*sapro-* + *-phagous*], feeding on decaying organic matter.

sap·ro·phyte (sap′rə-fīt′), *n.* [*sapro-* + *-phyte*], any organism that lives on decaying organic matter, as some fungi and bacteria.

sap·ro·phyt·ic (sap′rə-fit′ik), *adj.* of, or having the nature of, a saprophyte.

sap·sa·go (sap′sə-gō′), *n.* [altered < G. *schabzieger* < *schaben*, to scrape + *zieger*, whey], a variety of hard cheese made in Switzerland, flavored with melilot.

sap·suck·er (sap′suk′ẽr), *n.* any of a group of small, insect-eating American woodpeckers that drill holes in maples, apple trees, etc. and drink the sap.

sap·wood (sap′wood′), *n.* the soft wood just beneath the bark of a tree; alburnum.

Sar., 1. Sardinia. 2. Sardinian.

S.A.R., Sons of the American Revolution.

Sar·a (sâr′ə), a feminine name: see **Sarah.**

sar·a·band (sar′ə-band′), *n.* [Fr. *sarabande;* Sp. *zarabanda;* ult. < Per. *sarband*, kind of dance and song; *sar*, head + *band*, pres. stem of *bastan*, to bind], 1. a graceful, stately, slow Spanish dance in triple time, developed from an earlier lively dance. 2. music for, or in the tempo of, this dance, with decided emphasis on the second beat of the measure, often constituting one of the movements of the classical suite.

Sar·a·cen (sar′ə-s′n), *n.* [ME. *Sarasene;* OFr. *Sarazin;* LL. *Saracenus* < Late Gr. *Sarakēnos*], 1. originally, any member of the nomadic tribes of Syria and near-by regions. 2. later, an Arab. 3. any Moslem, especially as opposed to the Crusaders. *adj.* of the Saracens.

Sar·a·cen·ic (sar′ə-sen′ik), *adj.* Saracen.

Sa·ra·gos·sa (sar′ə-gos′ə), *n.* a city in northeastern Spain, on the Ebro River: pop., 284,000 (est. 1946): Spanish name, *Zaragoza.*

Sar·ah (sâr′ə), [Heb. *sārāh*, princess], a feminine name:

fat, āpe, bâre, cär; ten, ēven, hêre, ovẽr; is, bīte; lot, gō, hôrn, tōōl, look; oil, out; up, ūse, fũr; get; joy; yet; chin; she; thin, then; zh, leisure; ŋ, ring; ə for *a* in *ago*, *e* in *agent*, *i* in *sanity*, *o* in *comply*, *u* in *focus;* ′ as in *able* (ā′b′l); Fr. bål; ë, Fr. oeur; ö, Fr. feu; Fr. mon; ô, Fr. coq; ü, Fr. duc; H, G. ich; kh, G. doch. See pp. x–xii. ‡ foreign; * hypothetical; < derived from.

diminutives, *Sadie, Sal, Sally*: also spelled **Sara.** *n.* in the *Bible*, the wife of Abraham and the mother of Isaac.

Sa·rai (sâr'ī), *n.* in the *Bible*, Sarah: so called before God's covenant with Abraham.

Sa·ra·je·vo (sä-rä'ye-vô; Eng. sä'rə-yā'vō), *n.* a city formerly in Austria-Hungary, now in central Yugoslavia: pop., 136,000: scene of the assassination of Archduke Francis Ferdinand (June 28, 1914), which precipitated World War I: also **Serajevo.**

sa·ran (sə-ran'), *n.* any of various thermoplastic resins obtained by the polymerization or copolymerization of certain vinyl compounds: it is used in extruded or molded form in making various fabrics, acid-resistant pipes and fittings, wrapping film, etc.

Sar·a·nac Lake (sar'ə-nak'), 1. any of three lakes (*Upper, Middle,* and *Lower*) in northern New York. 2. a resort town on Lower Saranac Lake: pop., 6,000.

Sar·a·to·ga (sar'ə-tō'gə), *n.* 1. a county in east central New York, on the Hudson River: pop., 89,000. 2. a town in this county: scene of a battle (1777) of the American Revolution, in which Burgoyne surrendered to Gates: now called *Schuylerville.*

Saratoga Springs, a town in east central New York: pop., 17,000: site of mineral springs and racecourse.

Saratoga trunk, [after *Saratoga* Springs], a large trunk, formerly much used by women.

Sa·ra·tov (sä-rä'tôf), *n.* 1. a region of the R.S.F.S.R. in southeast central European Russia: pop., 2,167,000. 2. its capital, on the Volga: pop., 581,000.

Sa·ra·wak (sə-rä'wäk), *n.* a territory in British Borneo, occupying the northwestern coast of Borneo: area, 47,000 sq. mi.; pop., 744,000.

sar·casm (sär'kaz'm), *n.* [Fr. *sarcasme;* L. *sarcasmos;* Gr. *sarkasmos* < *sarkazein*, to tear flesh like dogs, speak bitterly < *sarx, sarkos*, flesh], 1. a taunting, sneering, cutting, or caustic remark; gibe or jeer, generally ironical. 2. the making of such remarks. 3. the characteristic quality of such remarks.

sar·cas·tic (sär-kas'tik), *adj.* 1. of, having the nature of, or characterized by sarcasm; sneering; caustic; cutting; taunting. 2. using, or fond of using, sarcasm. ***SYN.***—**sarcastic** implies intent to hurt by taunting with mocking ridicule, veiled sneers, etc. (a *sarcastic* reminder that work begins at 8:00 A.M.); **satirical** implies as its purpose the exposing or attacking of the vices, follies, stupidities, etc. of others and connotes the use of ridicule, sarcasm, etc. (Swift's *satirical* comments); **ironical** applies to a humorous or sarcastic form of expression in which the intended meaning of what is said is directly opposite to the usual sense ("My, you're early," was his *ironical* taunt to the latecomer); **sardonic** implies sneering or mocking bitterness in a person, or, more often, in his expression, remarks, etc. (a *sardonic* smile); **caustic** implies a cutting, biting, or stinging wit or sarcasm (a *caustic* tongue).

sar·cas·ti·cal·ly (sär-kas'ti-k'l-i, sär-kas'tik-li), *adv.* in a sarcastic manner.

sarce·net (särs'net), *n.* [Anglo-Fr. *sarzinett*, dim. < ME. *Sarsin, Sarasene*, Saracen], a soft silk cloth, used for ribbons, linings, etc.

sar·co- (sär'kō, sär'kə), [< Gr. *sarx, sarkos*, flesh], a combining form meaning *flesh*, as in *sarcology*: also, before a vowel, **sarc-.**

sar·co·carp (sär'kə-kärp'), *n.* [*sarco-* + *-carp*], in *botany*, 1. the fleshy part of a stone fruit, as in the plum. 2. loosely, any fleshy fruit.

sar·col·o·gy (sär-kol'ə-ji), *n.* [*sarco-* + *-logy*], the branch of anatomy that deals with the soft tissues of the body.

sar·co·ma (sär-kō'mə), *n.* [*pl.* SARCOMAS (-məz), SARCOMATA (-mə-tə)], [Mod. L.; Gr. *sarkōma* < *sarx*, flesh], any of various malignant tumors that begin in connective tissue, or in tissue developed from the mesoblast and not epithelial: cf. **carcinoma.**

sar·co·ma·toid (sär-kō'mə-toid'), *adj.* sarcomatous.

sar·co·ma·to·sis (sär-kō'mə-tō'sis), *n.* a condition characterized by a spread of sarcomas through the body.

sar·co·ma·tous (sär-kō'mə-təs, sär-kom'ə-təs), *adj.* of, or having the nature of, a sarcoma.

sar·coph·a·gus (sär-kof'ə-gəs), *n.* [*pl.* SARCOPHAGI (-jī'), SARCOPHAGUSES (-gəs-iz)], [L.; Gr. *sarkophagos* < *sarx, sarkos*, flesh + *phagein*, to eat: so named because the limestone caused rapid disintegration of the contents], 1. among the ancient Greeks and Romans, a limestone coffin or tomb, often inscribed and elaborately ornamented. 2. any stone coffin, especially one exposed to view in the open air or in a large or monumental tomb.

sar·cous (sär'kəs), *adj.* [< *sarco-* + *-ous*], of or composed of flesh or muscle.

sard (särd), *n.* [ME. *saarde;* L. *sarda;* Gr. *sardios, sardion*, sard, lit. Sardian stone < *Sardeis*, Sardis], 1. a very hard, deep orange-red variety of chalcedony, used in jewelry, etc. 2. a piece of this. Also **sardine.**

sar·dine (sär-dēn'), *n.* [*pl.* SARDINES (-dēnz'), SARDINE; see PLURAL, II, D, 1], [Fr. < L. *sardina;* Gr. *sardēnē* < *sarda*, kind of fish; prob. < Gr. *Sardō*, Sardinia], 1. a small pilchard of the herring family, suitable for eating when preserved in oil. 2. any of a variety of small fishes preserved for eating in tightly packed tins.

sar·dine (sär'din, sär'dīn), *n.* sard.

Sar·din·i·a (sär-din'i-ə, sär-din'yə), *n.* 1. an Italian island in the Mediterranean, south of Corsica: area, 9,300 sq. mi.; pop., 1,276,000; chief city, Cagliari. 2. a former kingdom, including this island, Piedmont, Savoy, and Genoa, ruled by the House of Savoy.

Sar·din·i·an (sär-din'i-ən, sär-din'yən), *adj.* of Sardinia or its people. *n.* 1. a native or inhabitant of Sardinia. 2. the Romance dialect of Sardinia.

Sar·dis (sär'dis), *n.* the capital of ancient Lydia.

sar·di·us (sär'di-əs), *n.* [ME.; LL.; Gr. *sardios* < *Sardeis*, Sardis, capital of Lydia], 1. a sard. 2. one of the twelve precious stones worn in the breastplate of the Jewish high priest, said to have been a ruby: Ex. 28:17.

sar·don·ic (sär-don'ik), *adj.* [Fr. *sardonique* < L. *sardonius;* Gr. *sardonios*, altered after *Sardō*, Sardinia < *sardanios*, bitter, scornful (used of smiles or laughter); prob. akin to *sairein*, to grin, sneer, but explained in ancient etymologies as derived < *sardanē*, Sardinian plant whose bitter taste caused facial contortion], disdainfully or bitterly sneering, ironical, or sarcastic: as, a *sardonic* smile. —***SYN.*** see **sarcastic.**

sar·don·i·cal·ly (sär-don'i-k'l-i, sär-don'ik-li), *adv.* in a sardonic manner.

sar·do·nyx (sär'də-niks), *n.* [ME.; L.; Gr. *sardonyx* < *sardios, sardion*, sard + *onyx*, onyx], a variety of onyx made up of alternating layers of white chalcedony and sard, used as a gem, especially in making cameos.

Sar·dou, Vic·to·rien (vēk'tô'ryan' sår'dōō'), 1831–1908; French dramatist.

Sarg, Tony (särg), (*Anthony Frederick Sarg*), 1882–1942; U.S. puppeteer and illustrator from Germany.

sar·gas·so (sär-gas'ō), *n.* [Port. *sargaço, sargasso* < *sarga, sargo*, kind of grape], any of a number of related floating, brown seaweeds with berrylike air sacs; gulfweed: also **sargasso weed.**

Sar·gas·so Sea (sär-gas'ō), a region of calms and mixing ocean currents in the Atlantic, northeast of the West Indies, famous for its sargasso.

sar·gas·sum (sär-gas'əm), *n.* [Mod. L.; Port. *sargasso;* see SARGASSO], any of a number of related seaweeds, the gulfweeds, found in the warmer seas.

Sar·gent, John Singer (sär'jənt), 1856–1925; American painter.

Sar·gon II (sär'gon), ?–705 B.C.; Assyrian warrior; king of Assyria (722–705 B.C.).

sa·ri (sä'rē), *n.* [*pl.* SARIS (-rēz)], [Hind. *sarī, sarhī;* Sans. *śāṭī*], the principal outer garment of a Hindu woman, consisting of a long piece of cloth worn wrapped around the body with one end over the head.

sark (särk), *n.* [< ME. *serke* with Late ME. vowel change; < AS. *serc* & cognate ON. *serkr*], [Scot. or Archaic], a shirt or chemise.

Sar·ma·ti·a (sär-mā'shi-ə, sär-mā'shə), *n.* the region between the Vistula and the Volga, now part of Poland and the Soviet Union: the ancient name.

Sar·ma·tian (sär-mā'shən), *adj.* of Sarmatia. *n.* any of an ancient people who lived in Sarmatia.

sar·men·tose (sär-men'tōs), *adj.* [L. *sarmentosus*, full of twigs < *sarmentum*, a twig < *sarpere*, to trim, cut off], producing long, slender stems which take root along the ground, as the strawberry plant.

sa·rong (sə-rôŋ', sä'rôŋ'), *n.* [Malay *sāroṅ*], 1. the principal garment of men and women in the Malay Archipelago, the East Indies, etc., consisting of a long strip of cloth, often brightly colored and printed, worn around the lower part of the body like a skirt. 2. cotton cloth for such garments.

Sa·roy·an, William (sə-roi'ən), 1908– ; American short-story writer and playwright.

Sar·pe·don (sär-pē'd'n, sär-pē'don), *n.* [L.; Gr. *Sarpēdōn*], in *Greek mythology*, 1. a son of Zeus and Europa, who became king of Lycia and was allowed to live three generations. 2. in one version, a son of Zeus and Laodamia, killed by Patroclus in the Trojan War.

sar·ra·ce·ni·a (sar'ə-sē'ni-ə), *n.* [Mod. L., after D. *Sarrazin* of Quebec], any of a number of related American plants with nodding flowers, yellow to purple, and mottled, pitcherlike leaves which attract insects.

sar·ra·ce·ni·a·ceous (sar'ə-sē'ni-ā'shəs), *adj.* belonging to the sarracenia family of plants.

sar·sa·pa·ril·la (särs'pə-ril'ə, sär'sə-pə-ril'ə, sas'pə-ril'ə), *n.* [Sp. *zarzaparrilla; zarza*, bramble + *parrilla*, dim. of *parra*, vine], 1. any of a number of tropical American plants with large, fragrant roots and toothed, heart-shaped leaves. 2. the dried roots of any of these plants, used as a tonic and for flavoring. 3. an extract of this. 4. a carbonated drink flavored with sarsaparilla.

sarse·net (särs'net), *n.* sarcenet.

Sar·to, An·dre·a del (än-dre'ä del sär'tô), (born *Andrea d'Agnolo*), 1486–1531; Florentine painter.

sar·tor (sär'tẽr), *n.* [LL. < L. *sartus*, pp. of *sarcire*, to patch, mend], a tailor: literary and humorous.

sar·to·ri·al (sär-tôr'i-əl, sär-tō'ri-əl), *adj.* [LL. *sartor* (see SARTOR); + *-ial*], 1. of tailors or their work; hence, 2. of clothing or dress, especially men's. 3. in *anatomy*, of the sartorius.

sar·to·ri·us (sär-tôr'i-əs, sär-tō'ri-əs), *n.* [Mod. L. < LL. *sartor*, a tailor; see SARTOR: in reference to the cross-legged position traditionally ascribed to tailors at work], a narrow muscle of the thigh, the longest in the human body, that passes obliquely across the front of the thigh

and assists in rotating the leg to the position assumed in sitting cross-legged.
Sar·tre, Jean-Paul (zhän′ pôl′ sär′tr′), 1905– ; French philosopher, playwright, and novelist.
Sa·rum use (sâr′əm), [ML. *Sarum;* said to be < abbrev. of L. *Sarisburia* < Late AS. *Searesburh* (earlier *Searobyrg*); prob. directly via L. *Sorviodunum* < Brit. name], the form or order of divine service used in the churches of Sarum (Salisbury) before the Reformation.
Sa·se·bo (sä′se-bô′), *n.* a city on the western coast of Kyushu, Japan: pop., 258,000.
sash (sash), *n.* [Ar. *shāsh,* turban], an ornamental band, ribbon, or scarf worn over the shoulder or around the waist, often (by men) as a symbol of distinction.
sash (sash), *n.* [taken as sing. of earlier *shashes* < Fr. *châsse, châssis,* a frame, sash; see CHASSIS], a frame for holding the glass pane or panes of a window or door, especially a sliding frame. *v.t.* to furnish with sashes.
sa·shay (sa-shā′), *v.i.* [altered < *chassé* (dance)], [Colloq.], to glide, move around, or go.
sash cord (or **line**), a cord attached to either side of a sliding sash, having balancing weights so that the window can be raised or lowered easily.
sa·sin (sā′sin), *n.* [< the native name], the India antelope, or black buck.
Sas·katch·e·wan (sas-kach′ə-wän′), *n.* 1. a province of south central Canada: area, 251,700 sq. mi.; pop. 881,000; capital, Regina: abbreviated **Sask.** 2. a river in Canada, flowing eastward into Lake Winnipeg: length, 1,200 mi.
Sas·ka·toon (sas′kə-to͞on′), *n.* a city in central Saskatchewan, Canada: pop., 82,000.
sas·ka·toon (sas′kə-to͞on′), *n.* [< Am. Ind. (Cree) *misâskwatomin* < *misâskwat,* shadbush, lit. tree with much wood + *min,* berry], a small bush of the rose family, with purple fruit; shadbush.
sass (sas), *n.* [var. of *sauce*], 1. *a)* [Dial.], garden vegetables. *b)* stewed fruit or preserves served as a dessert. 2. [Colloq.], impudent talk. *v.t.* [Colloq.], to talk impudently or disrespectfully to.
sas·sa·by (sas′ə-bi), *n.* [*pl.* SASSABIES (-biz)], [Sechuana *tsèsèbè*], any of a group of large South African antelopes related to the hartebeest.
sas·sa·fras (sas′ə-fras′), *n.* [Sp. *sasafras;* ? < earlier Sp. *sassifragia,* saxifrage; influenced by native Am. name], 1. any of a number of related trees with yellow flowers and bluish fruit. 2. the dried root bark of any of these trees, used in medicine and for flavoring. 3. the flavor.
Sas·sa·ni·an (sa-sā′ni-ən), *n. & adj.* Sassanid.
Sassanian Dynasty, ruling family of the Persian Empire (226–641 A.D.).
Sas·sa·nid (sas′ə-nid), *adj.* of the Sassanian Dynasty. *n.* [*pl.* SASSANIDS (-nidz), SASSANIDAE (sa-san′ə-dē′)], any member of the Sassanian Dynasty.
Sas·se·nach (sas′ə-nak′, sas′′n-əkh), *n.* [Ir. *Sasanach* or Gael. *Sasunnach* < Gael. *Sasunn,* Saxon], a Saxon, Englishman, or Lowlander: term used by Irish and Scots.
Sas·soon, Sieg·fried (sēg′frēd sə-so͞on′), 1886– ; English writer and poet.
sass·y (sas′i), *adj.* [SASSIER (-i-ẽr), SASSIEST (-i-ist)], [dial. var. of *saucy*], [Dial. or Colloq.], impudent; saucy.
sas·sy (sas′i), *n.* [W. Afr.; ? < Eng. *saucy*], an African tree with poisonous bark and wood: also **sassy bark.**
sas·sy·wood (sas′i-wood′), *n.* a sassy.
sat (sat), past tense and past participle of **sit.**
Sat., 1. Saturday. 2. Saturn.
Sa·tan (sā′t'n), *n.* [Heb. *ṣāṭān,* enemy < *sātan,* to be adverse, plot against], in *Christian theology,* the great enemy of man and of goodness; the Devil: usually identified with Lucifer, the chief of the fallen angels, cast out of heaven by Michael, according to the Talmud.
sa·tang (sä-taŋ′), *n.* [*pl.* SATANG], [Siamese *satāŋ*], a bronze coin and money of account in Thailand, equal to 1/100 of a baht.
sa·tan·ic (sā-tan′ik, sə-tan′ik), *adj.* of, characteristic of, or like Satan; devilish; wicked; infernal; diabolical.
sa·tan·i·cal (sā-tan′i-k'l, sə-tan′i-k'l), *adj.* satanic.
sa·tan·i·cal·ly (sā-tan′i-k'l-i, sə-tan′ik-li), *adv.* in a satanic manner.
Sa·tan·ism (sā′t'n-iz'm), *n.* [chiefly after Fr. *satanisme*], worship of Satan; especially, the principles and rites of a cult which travesties Christian ceremonies.
satch·el (sach′əl), *n.* [ME. & OFr. *sachel;* L. *saccellus,* dim. of *saccus,* a sack, bag], a small bag for carrying clothes, books, etc., sometimes having a shoulder strap.
sate (sāt), *v.t.* [SATED (-id), SATING], [prob. shortened form < L. *satiare,* to fill full, satisfy; cf. SAD], 1. to satisfy (an appetite, desire, etc.) to the full; gratify completely. 2. to gratify with more than enough, so as to weary or disgust; surfeit; glut. —*SYN.* see **satiate.**
sate (sat, sāt), archaic past tense and past participle of **sit.**
sa·teen (sa-tēn′), *n.* [< *satin,* after *velveteen*], a smooth, glossy, cotton cloth made to imitate satin.
sat·el·lite (sat′ə-līt′), *n.* [Fr.; L. *satelles, satellitis,* an attendant, guard], 1. a follower or attendant attached to a prince or other person of importance; hence, 2. an obsequious or fawning follower or dependent. 3. a small planet revolving around a larger one; moon. 4. a man-made object put into orbit around the earth, the sun, or some other heavenly body. 5. a small state that is economically dependent on, and hence adjusts its policies to, a larger, more powerful state.
sa·ti·a·bil·i·ty (sā′shi-ə-bil′ə-ti, sā′shə-bil′ə-ti), *n.* the quality of being satiable.
sa·ti·a·ble (sā′shi-ə-b'l, sā′shə-b'l), *adj.* [ML. *satiabilis*], that can be sated or satiated.
sa·ti·a·bly (sā′shi-ə-bli, sā′shə-bli), *adv.* in a satiable manner.
sa·ti·ate (sā′shi-āt′), *adj.* [L. *satiatus,* pp. of *satiare,* to fill full, satisfy < *sat, satis,* sufficient; cf. SAD], having had enough or more than enough; sated. *v.t.* [SATIATED (-id), SATIATING], 1. [Rare], to satisfy to the full; gratify completely. 2. to gratify with more than enough, so as to weary or disgust; sate; glut; surfeit; cloy.
SYN.—**satiate** and **sate** in their basic sense mean to satisfy to the full, but in current use **satiate** almost always implies, as **sate** often does, a being filled or stuffed so full that all pleasure or desire is lost (*satiated,* or *sated,* with food, success, etc.); **surfeit** implies a being filled or supplied to nauseating or disgusting excess (*surfeited* with pleasure); **cloy** stresses the distaste one feels for something too sweet, rich, etc. that one has indulged in to excess (*cloying,* sentimental music); **glut** implies an overloading by filling or supplying to excess (to *glut* the market).
sa·ti·a·tion (sā′shi-ā′shən), *n.* a satiating or being satiated.
sa·ti·e·ty (sə-tī′ə-ti), *n.* [Fr. *satiété;* L. *satietas*], the state of being satiated.
sat·in (sat′′n), *n.* [ME.; OFr.; Sp. *setuni;* Ar. (*aṭlas*) *zaitūnī,* (satin) of *Zaitūn,* Med. name of Chuanchow, China], a silk, nylon, or rayon cloth having a smooth finish, glossy on the face, dull on the back. *adj.* made of or like satin; smooth, soft, and glossy.
sat·i·net, sat·i·nette (sat′′n-et′), *n.* [Fr. < *satin*], 1. thin or inferior satin. 2. a strong cloth of cotton and wool, made to resemble satin.
sat·in·wood (sat′′n-wood′), *n.* 1. any of several very smooth woods used in fine furniture. 2. any of a number of trees yielding such a wood; especially, an East Indian tree of the mahogany family.
sat·i·ny (sat′′n-i), *adj.* of or like satin; lustrous.
sat·ire (sat′īr), *n.* [Fr. < L. *satira,* or *satura,* a satire, poetic medley, orig. a dish of various fruits < *satur,* full; for IE. base see SAD], 1. *a)* a literary work in which vices, follies, stupidities, abuses, etc. are held up to ridicule and contempt. *b)* such literary works collectively, or the art of writing them. 2. the use of ridicule, sarcasm, irony, etc. to expose, attack, or deride vices, follies, etc. —*SYN.* see **caricature, wit.**
sa·tir·ic (sə-tir′ik, sa-tir′ik), *adj.* satirical.
sa·tir·i·cal (sə-tir′i-k'l, sa-tir′i-k'l), *adj.* 1. of, having the nature of, or containing satire. 2. indulging in, or fond of indulging in, satire. —*SYN.* see **sarcastic.**
sa·tir·i·cal·ly (sə-tir′i-k'l-i, sa-tir′ik-li), *adv.* in a satirical manner.
sat·i·rist (sat′ə-rist), *n.* 1. a writer of satires. 2. a person who is fond of indulging in satire.
sat·i·rize (sat′ə-rīz′), *v.t.* [SATIRIZED (-rīzd′), SATIRIZING], [Fr. *satiriser*], to attack or criticize with satire.
sat·is·fac·tion (sat′is-fak′shən), *n.* [ME. *satisfaccioun;* OFr. *satisfaction;* L. *satisfactio*], 1. a satisfying or being satisfied. 2. something which satisfies; specifically, *a)* in *theology,* atonement for sin. *b)* reparation for injury or insult. *c)* settlement of debt; payment or discharge of obligation. *d)* anything that brings gratification, pleasure, or contentment.
give satisfaction, 1. to satisfy. 2. to accept a challenge to duel or fight.
sat·is·fac·to·ri·ly (sat′is-fak′tẽr-ə-li), *adv.* in a satisfactory manner.
sat·is·fac·to·ri·ness (sat′is-fak′tẽr-i-nis), *n.* the state or quality of being satisfactory.
sat·is·fac·to·ry (sat′is-fak′tẽr-i), *adj.* [Fr. *satisfactoire;* ML. *satisfactorius*], satisfying; fulfilling all needs, expectations, wishes, desires, requirements, etc.
sat·is·fi·er (sat′is-fī′ẽr), *n.* a person or thing that satisfies.
sat·is·fy (sat′is-fī′), *v.t.* [SATISFIED (-fīd′), SATISFYING], [ME. *satisfyen;* OFr. *satisfier;* L. *satisfacere* < *satis,* enough + *facere,* to make], 1. to fulfill the needs, expectations, wishes, or desires of; content; gratify. 2. to suffice, fulfill, or answer the requirements or conditions of. 3. to comply with (rules, standards, or obligations). 4. *a)* to free from doubt or anxiety; convince. *b)* to answer (a doubt, objection, etc.) adequately or convincingly; solve. 5. *a)* to give what is due to. *b)* to discharge (an obligation, debt, etc.); settle in full. 6. to make reparation to or for. *v.i.* to give satisfaction.
SYN.—**satisfy** implies complete fulfillment of one's wishes, needs, expectations, etc.; **content** implies a filling of require-

ments to the degree that one is not disturbed by a desire for something more or different (some persons are *satisfied* only by great wealth, others are *contented* with a modest, but secure income).

sa·trap (sā′trap, sat′rəp), *n.* [ME.; L. *satrapes;* Gr. *satrapēs;* OPer. *shathrapavan*, lit., protector of the land], 1. the governor of a province in ancient Persia. 2. a ruler of a dependency, often a despotic, subordinate official; petty tyrant.

sa·trap·y (sā′trə-pi, sat′rə-pi), *n.* [*pl.* SATRAPIES (-piz)], [Fr. *satrapie;* L. *satrapia;* Gr. *satrapeia*], 1. the government or authority of a satrap. 2. the province ruled by a satrap.

Sat·su·ma (sat′soo-mä′, sat-soo′mə), *n.* [< Japan. *Satsuma*, province in Kyushu, where made], a variety of Japanese pottery.

sat·u·ra·bil·i·ty (sach′ēr-ə-bil′ə-ti), *n.* the state or quality of being saturable.

sat·u·ra·ble (sach′ēr-ə-b'l), *adj.* [L. *saturabilis*], that can be saturated.

sat·u·rant (sach′ēr-ənt), *adj.* [L. *saturans*], saturating. *n.* a substance that saturates.

sat·u·rate (sach′oo-rāt′), *v.t.* [SATURATED (-id), SATURATING], [< L. *saturatus*, pp. of *saturare*, to fill up, saturate < *satur*, full], 1. to cause to be thoroughly soaked, imbued, or penetrated. 2. to cause (something) to be so completely filled, charged, or treated with something else that no more can be taken up. 3. in *chemistry*, to cause (a substance) to combine to the full extent of its combining capacity with another. *adj.* (*usually* sach′ēr-it), 1. [Chiefly Poetic], saturated. 2. deep; intense: said of colors. —*SYN.* see **soak.**

sat·u·rat·ed (sach′oo-rāt′id), *adj.* [pp. of *saturate*], 1. filled to capacity; having absorbed all that can be taken up. 2. soaked through with moisture; wet. 3. undiluted with white: said of colors. 4. in *geology*, containing as much combined silica as is possible: said of rocks and minerals.

saturated compound, an organic compound containing no double or triple bonds and having no free valence.

saturated solution, a solution in equilibrium at a definite temperature with the undissolved solute; solution containing so much dissolved substance that no more can be dissolved at the given temperature.

sat·u·rat·er (sach′oo-rāt′ēr), *n.* a person or thing that saturates: also **saturator.**

sat·u·ra·tion (sach′oo-rā′shən), *n.* [LL. *saturatio*], 1. a saturating or being saturated. 2. the degree of intensity of a color, as measured by its freedom from mixture with white. 3. the condition of a magnetic substance that has been magnetized to the highest possible degree.

saturation bombing, the practice of dropping an intense concentration of bombs almost simultaneously from a number of bombers in close formation, in order to destroy virtually everything in a given target area.

saturation point, the point at which the greatest possible amount of a substance has been absorbed.

sat·u·ra·tor (sach′oo-rā′tēr), *n.* a saturater.

Sat·ur·day (sat′ēr-di), *n.* [ME. *Saterdai;* AS. *Sæterdæg* or *Sæternes-dæg* < *Sætern* (< L. *Saturnus*), Saturn + *dæg*, day], the seventh and last day of the week: abbreviated **Sat., S., Sa., Stdy.**

Sat·urn (sat′ērn), *n.* [ME. *Satourn, Saturnus;* AS. *Sætern-, Saturnus;* L. *Saturnus*, akin to *satus*, pp. of *serere*, to sow], 1. in *Roman mythology*, the god of agriculture: identified with the Greek Cronus. 2. the second largest planet in the solar system, sixth in distance from the sun, notable for the three concentric rings which revolve around it in the plane of its equator: diameter, 72,000 mi.; diurnal rotation, 10 hrs., 14 min.; period of revolution, 29.5 years; symbol, ♄. Abbreviated **Sat.** 3. [ML. use of L. *Saturnus*], in *alchemy*, lead (the metal).

Sat·ur·na·li·a (sat′ēr-nā′li-ə), *n.pl.* [L., neut. pl. of *Saturnalis*, of Saturn], 1. the ancient Roman festival of Saturn, held about December 17, with general feasting and revelry in celebration of the winter solstice. 2. [s-], [sometimes construed as sing.], a period or occasion of unrestrained, often orgiastic, revelry.

Sat·ur·na·li·an (sat′ēr-nā′li-ən), *adj.* 1. of the Saturnalia. 2. [s-], riotously merry or orgiastic.

Sa·tur·ni·an (sə-tũr′ni-ən), *adj.* [< L. *Saturnius*, of Saturn; + *-an*], 1. of the Roman god Saturn, whose reign was called "the golden age"; hence, 2. prosperous, contented, happy, or peaceful: said of a period, age, etc. 3. of the planet Saturn.

sa·tur·ni·id (sə-tũr′ni-id), *n.* [< Mod. L. *Saturniidae*, name of the family < *Saturnia*, type genus < L. *Saturnius*, Saturnian], any of a family of large moths with a small head, broad wings, and hairy body.

sat·ur·nine (sat′ēr-nīn′), *adj.* [OFr. *saturnin*, of Saturn (also of lead, heavy < ML. *Saturnus*, lead) < L. *Saturnus*, Saturn], 1. in *astrology*, born under the supposed influence of the planet Saturn. 2. sluggish; gloomy; morose; grave; taciturn. 3. *a*) of or like lead. *b*) having lead poisoning.

sat·ur·nism (sat′ēr-niz'm), *n.* chronic lead poisoning.

‡Sat·ya·gra·ha (sut′yə-gru′hə), *n.* [< Hind.; lit., a grasping for truth; Sans. *satya*, truth + *graha*, grasping], the political doctrine of Mohandas K. Gandhi, which favored passive resistance and non-co-operation in opposing British rule in India.

sat·yr (sat′ēr, sā′tēr), *n.* [Fr. *satyre;* L. *satyrus;* Gr. *satyros*], 1. in *Greek mythology*, a woodland deity, attendant on Bacchus, usually represented as having pointed ears, short horns, the head and body of a man and legs of a goat, and thought of as fond of riotous merriment and lechery: see also **faun.** 2. a man of lustful nature; lecherous man. 3. a man having satyriasis. 4. any of a group of butterflies with gray or brown wings often marked with eyelike spots.

sat·y·ri·a·sis (sat′ə-rī′ə-sis), *n.* [Mod. L.; Gr. *satyriasis;* see SATYR], excessive and uncontrollable sexual desire in a man: see also **nymphomania.**

sa·tyr·ic (sə-tir′ik), *adj.* [L. *satyricus;* Gr. *satyrikos*], 1. of satyrs. 2. designating or of a type of ancient Greek drama having a chorus of satyrs.

sa·tyr·i·cal (sə-tir′i-k'l), *adj.* satyric.

sa·tyr·o·ma·ni·ac (sə-tir′ō-mā′ni-ak′), *n.* [< Gr. *satyros*, satyr; + *-maniac*], a man having satyriasis.

Sau (sou), *n.* Sava: the German name.

sauce (sôs), *n.* [ME. *sause;* OFr. *sause, saulse* < LL. *salsa* < L. *salsus*, salted < *salire*, to salt > *sal*, salt; cf. SALT], 1. a liquid or soft dressing served with food to improve its taste. 2. mashed, stewed fruit. 3. something that adds interest, zest, or flavor. 4. [Colloq.], impertinence; impudence. 5. [Dial.], any green vegetable. *v.t.* [SAUCED (sôst), SAUCING], 1. to flavor or season with sauce; add sauce to. 2. to give flavor or relish to. 3. [Colloq.], to be impudent or saucy to.

sauce·box (sôs′boks′), *n.* [Colloq.], a saucy person; especially, an impertinent child.

sauce·pan (sôs′pan′), *n.* a small metal pot with a long handle, used for cooking.

sau·cer (sô′sēr), *n.* [ME. *sawsere;* OFr. *saussier* (Fr. *saucière*) < *sauce;* see SAUCE], 1. *a*) a small, round, shallow dish designed to hold a cup and catch any spilled liquid. *b*) any small, round, shallow dish. 2. anything round and shallow like a saucer.

sau·ci·ly (sô′sə-li), *adv.* in a saucy or impudent manner.

sau·ci·ness (sô′si-nis), *n.* the quality of being saucy.

sau·cy (sô′si), *adj.* [SAUCIER (-si-ēr), SAUCIEST (-si-ist)], [*sauce* + *-y;* cf. SASSY], 1. rude; impudent. 2. pert; sprightly: as, a *saucy* smile. —*SYN.* see **impertinent.**

Sa·u·di Arabia (sä-oo′di), *n.* a kingdom in central Arabia: area, c. 597,000 sq. mi.; pop., c. 6,000,000; capitals, Riyadh and Mecca: abbreviated **Sau. Ar.**

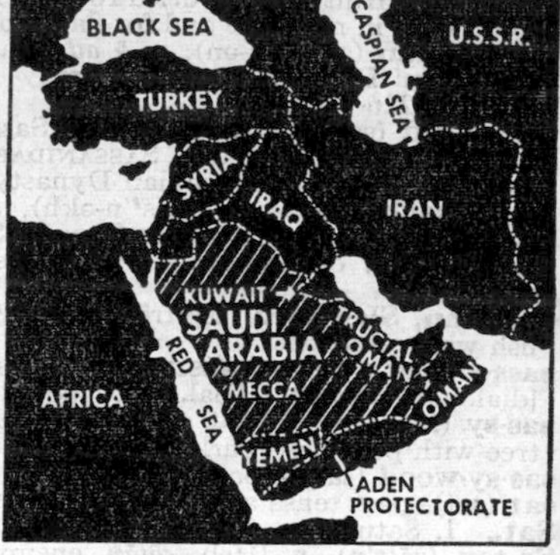

SAUDI ARABIA

sau·er·bra·ten (sou′ēr-brä′t'n; G. zou′ēr-brä′-tən), *n.* [G.; *sauer*, sour + *braten*, roast], a dish made of beef or pork marinated in vinegar before cooking.

sauer·kraut (sour′krout′), *n.* [G., *sauer*, sour + *kraut*, cabbage], chopped cabbage fermented in a brine of its own juice with salt.

sau·ger (sô′gēr), *n.* [prob. Am. Ind.], a small American pike perch not valued as a game or food fish.

Sauk (sôk), *n.* Sac.

Saul (sôl), [LL. *Saul*, first king of Israel (< Gr. *Saoul*) & *Saulus*, Saul of Tarsus (< Gr. *Saulos*), both < Heb. *shā'ūl*, lit., asked (i.e., of God)], a masculine name. *n.* in the *Bible*, 1. the first king of Israel. 2. the original name of the Apostle Paul: see **Paul,** Saint.

Sault Sainte Ma·rie, Sault Ste. Ma·rie (soo′sānt′-mə-rē′), 1. a city in northern Michigan, on St. Marys River: pop., 19,000. 2. a city opposite it, in Ontario, Canada: pop., 32,000.

Sault Sainte Marie Canals, three ship canals (two U.S., one Canadian) in the waterway connecting Lake Superior with Lake Huron: also **the Soo (Canals).**

sau·na (sou′nä), *n.* [Finn.], 1. a Finnish steam bath, accompanied by light beating of the skin with birch or cedar boughs. 2. the bathhouse.

saun·ter (sôn′tēr), *v.i.* [Late ME. *santre(n)*, to muse, meditate; prob. via OFr. (cf. mod. form) < some Romance form of *saint;* for possible base of mod. sense, "to wander, as to saints' shrines," cf. ROAM], 1. to walk about idly; stroll. 2. to loiter. *n.* 1. a leisurely and aimless walk. 2. a careless, slow gait.

Sau·rash·tra (sou′rush-trə), *n.* a former state of western India: merged into the state of Bombay, 1956: area, 21,742 sq. mi.

sau·rel (sô′rəl), *n.* [Fr. & Pr. < Gr. *sauros*, horse

mackerel], a common salt-water food fish of Europe and America: also called *scad*.
sau·ri·an (sô'ri-ən), *adj.* [*saur-* + *-ian*], of, or having the characteristics of, lizards, crocodiles, or dinosaurs. *n.* any of a group of reptiles including the lizards and, in former classifications, crocodiles, dinosaurs, etc.
sau·ro- (sô'rō, sô'rə), [< Gr. *saura, sauros*, a lizard], a combining form meaning *lizard*, as in *sauropod*: also, before a vowel, **saur-**.
sau·ro·pod (sô'rə-pod'), *n.* [*sauro-* + *-pod*], any of a group of dinosaurs, consisting of those which ate plants and had a long neck and tail, five-toed limbs, and a small head. *adj.* of the sauropods.
sau·rop·o·dous (sô-rop'ə-dəs), *adj.* of the sauropods.
-sau·rus (sô'rəs), [< Gr. *sauros*, a lizard], a combining form meaning *lizard*, used to form the genus names of certain reptiles, as in *ichthyosaurus*.
sau·ry (sô'ri), *n.* [*pl.* SAURIES (-riz)], [prob. < Mod. L. *saurus*, a fish < Gr. *saura*, a lizard], any of a group of sea fishes with a long, slender body and a projecting beak, found in temperate Atlantic waters.
sau·sage (sô'sij), *n.* [ME. *sausige;* ONorm.Fr. *saussiche;* OFr. *saulsage, saucisse, saulcisse;* LL. *salsicia* < L. *salsus;* see SAUCE], 1. meat, usually pork, chopped fine, highly seasoned, and ordinarily stuffed into or enclosed in a tube of thin prepared intestine or other membranous tissue. 2. any object shaped like a sausage, as a captive observation balloon.
sau·té (sō-tā'), *adj.* [Fr., pp. of *sauter*, to leap], fried quickly and turned frequently in a little fat. *v.t.* [SAUTÉED (-tād'), SAUTÉING], to fry quickly and turn frequently in a little fat. *n.* a sautéed dish.
sau·terne (sō-tũrn'; Fr. sô'târn'), *n.* [< *Sauternes*, town in the department of Gironde, in France], a white table wine, usually sweet: also spelled **sauternes**.
‡**sauve qui peut** (sōv' kē' pö'), [Fr., lit., save (himself) who can], a disorganized retreat; rout.
Sa·va (sä'vä), *n.* a river in northern Yugoslavia, flowing eastward into the Danube: length, 450 mi.: French name, *Save;* German name, *Sau*.
sav·a·ble (sāv'ə-b'l), *adj.* that can be saved.
sav·age (sav'ij), *adj.* [ME. *savage, sauvage;* OFr. *savaige, salvage;* LL. *salvaticus*, wild; L. *silvaticus*, belonging to a wood, wild < *silva*, a wood], 1. wild; uncultivated; in a state of nature; rugged: as, a *savage* forest. 2. fierce; ferocious; untamed: as, a *savage* tiger. 3. without civilization; primitive; barbarous: as, a *savage* tribe. 4. lacking polish; crude; rude. 5. cruel; pitiless. 6. furious; ill-tempered. *n.* 1. a human being living somewhat like an animal, in an uncivilized, primitive way. 2. a fierce, brutal person. 3. a crude, boorish person. —*SYN.* see **barbarian**.
Savage Island, Niue, an island in the South Pacific.
sav·age·ry (sav'ij-ri), *n.* [*pl.* SAVAGERIES (-riz)], [Fr. *sauvagerie*], 1. the condition of being savage, wild, primitive, or uncultivated: said of men, animals, or nature. 2. savage act, behavior, or disposition; barbarity. 3. savage creatures collectively.
sav·ag·ism (sav'ij-iz'm), *n.* savagery.
Sa·vai·i (sä-vī'ē), *n.* an island of Western Samoa, in the Pacific: area, 703 sq. mi.; pop. (with Upolu), 97,000.
sa·van·na, sa·van·nah (sə-van'ə), *n.* [Sp. *sabana*, earlier *zavana* < the Carib name], 1. a treeless plain or relatively flat, open region, especially in lands of seasonal rains near the tropics. 2. a grassland characterized by scattered trees, especially in tropical or subtropical regions.
Sa·van·nah (sə-van'ə), *n.* 1. a river flowing between South Carolina and Georgia into the Atlantic: length, 314 mi. 2. a seaport in Georgia, on this river: pop., 149,000.
sa·vant (sə-vänt', sav'ənt; Fr. så'vän'), *n.* [*pl.* SAVANTS (-vänts', -ənts; Fr. -vän')], [Fr., orig. ppr. of *savoir* < L. *sapere*, to know], a learned person; scholar; person famous for his knowledge and wisdom.
Save (såv), *n.* Sava: the French name.
save (sāv), *v.t.* [SAVED (sāvd), SAVING], [ME. *saven, sauven;* OFr. *sauver, salver;* L. *salvare* < *salvus*, safe], 1. to rescue or preserve from harm or danger; keep or remove from damage or injury; make or keep safe. 2. to keep in health and well-being: formerly used in greeting, as, *save* you, sir. 3. to preserve for future use; lay by (often with *up*). 4. to prevent or guard against expense, loss, or waste of; gain advantage of: as, this train *saves* hours. 5. to help (one) to avoid loss or waste of: as, it *saves* me time. 6. to avoid, prevent, lessen, or guard against: as, *save* expense. 7. to treat carefully in order to preserve, lessen wear, etc. 8. in *theology*, to deliver (a person, soul, etc.) from sin and punishment; redeem from spiritual death. *v.i.* 1. to avoid expense, loss, waste, etc.; be economical. 2. to keep something or someone from danger, harm, etc. 3. to hoard; put by money or goods. 4. to keep; last. 5. in *theology*, to exercise power to redeem from evil and sin. —*SYN.* see **rescue**.
save (sāv), *prep.* [ME. *sauf, safe;* OFr. *sauf-* (Fr. *sauf*), safe < L. *salvus*], except; but. *conj.* 1. except; but. 2. [Archaic], unless.
save·a·ble (sāv'ə-b'l), *adj.* savable.
save-all (sāv'ôl'), *n.* any of a number of devices which prevent waste or damage, save time, etc.; specifically, *a*) a strip of canvas added to a sail to catch the wind. *b*) overalls. *c*) a pinafore. *d*) a child's savings bank.
sav·e·loy (sav'ə-loi'), *n.* [altered < Fr. *cervelas;* It. *cervellata* < *cervello*, the brains; L. *cerebellum;* see CEREBELLUM], a highly seasoned, dried sausage.
sav·er (sāv'ẽr), *n.* a person or thing that saves: usually in hyphenated compounds, as *labor-saver*.
sav·in, sav·ine (sav'in), *n.* [AS. *safine;* OFr. *savine;* L. (*herba*) *Sabina*, lit., Sabine (herb), savin], 1. a low, spreading kind of juniper tree. 2. an oily drug from this tree, used in medicine. 3. the red cedar.
sav·ing (sāv'iŋ), *adj.* that saves; specifically, *a*) rescuing; preserving. *b*) economizing or economical. *c*) containing an exception; making a reservation: as, a *saving* clause. *d*) compensating; redeeming. *n.* 1. the act of one that saves. 2. any reduction in expense, time, labor, etc., or the result of such reduction: as, a *saving* of 10%. 3. what is saved; especially, *pl.* sums of money saved. 4. in *law*, a reservation; exception.
sav·ing (sāv'iŋ), *prep.* 1. with due respect for. 2. with the exception of; except; save. *conj.* save.
savings account, an account in a savings bank.
savings bank, a bank in which savings may be deposited; especially, a banking establishment whose business is to receive and invest depositors' savings, on which it pays interest.
sav·ior, sav·iour (sāv'yẽr), *n.* [ME. & OFr. *sauveour;* LL. *salvator* < L. *salvare*, to save], 1. a person who saves. 2. [usually Saviour], Jesus Christ: with *the*.
Sa·voie (så'vwå'), *n.* Savoy: the French name.
sa·voir-faire (sav'wär-fâr'; Fr. så'vwår'fâr'), *n.* [Fr., to know (how) to do], ready knowledge of what to do or say, and of when and how to do or say it; tact. —*SYN.* see **tact**.
‡**sa·voir-vi·vre** (så'vwår'vē'vr'), *n.* [Fr., to know (how) to live], good breeding; good manners.
Sav·o·na·ro·la, Gi·ro·la·mo (jē-rô'lä-mô' sä'vô-nä-rô'lä; Eng. sav'ə-nə-rō'lə), 1452–1498; Italian monk and religious reformer; burned at the stake for heresy.
sa·vor (sā'vẽr), *n.* [ME. & OFr. *savour;* L. *sapor;* cf. SAP (juice)], 1. *a*) that quality of something which acts on the sense of taste or of smell. *b*) a particular taste or smell. 2. characteristic quality; distinctive property. 3. perceptible trace; tinge. 4. power to excite interest, zest, etc. 5. [Archaic], repute. *v.i.* 1. to have the particular taste or smell: as, Italian cooking *savors* of garlic. 2. to have the characteristic quality; smack (*of*). 3. to show traces or signs: as, this work *savors* of hatred. *v.t.* 1. to season or flavor; give flavor or scent to. 2. to have the particular flavor or smell of. 3. to have the characteristic quality of. 4. to show traces or signs of. 5. to taste or smell, especially with relish; hence, 6. to enjoy with appreciation; relish. Also (British spelling) **savour**.
sa·vor·i·ly (sā'vẽr-ə-li), *adv.* in a savory manner.
sa·vor·i·ness (sā'vẽr-i-nis), *n.* the quality of being savory, or pleasing to the taste or smell.
sa·vor·y (sā'vẽr-i), *adj.* [SAVORIER (-i-ẽr), SAVORIEST (-i-ist)], [ME. *savouri;* OFr. *savouré*, pp. of *savourer*, to taste < *savour*, savor], 1. pleasing to the taste or smell; appetizing. 2. agreeable; pleasing. 3. morally pleasing; respectable. 4. salty or piquant, not sweet, as a relish. *n.* [*pl.* SAVORIES (-iz)], [British], a small, highly seasoned portion of food served at the end or beginning of dinner. Also (British spelling) **savoury**.
sa·vor·y (sā'vẽr-i), *n.* [ME. *saverey;* OFr. *savoreie*, altered, prob. by association with *savour*, savor < L. *satureia*, savory (whence AS. *sætherie*, via OFr.)], an aromatic variety of mint, used in cooking.
Sa·voy (sə-voi'), *n.* 1. a former duchy of the kingdom of Sardinia, ceded to France (1860): French name, *Savoie*. 2. a European ruling family of Piedmont and Savoy (1000?–1718) and of Italy (1720–1946).
sa·voy (sə-voi'), *n.* [Fr. (*chou de*) *Savoie*, (cabbage of) Savoy], a kind of cabbage with crinkled leaves and a compact head.
Sa·voy·ard (sə-voi'ẽrd; Fr. så'vô'yår'), *n.* 1. a native or inhabitant of Savoy. 2. [< the *Savoy*, London theater where the operas were first produced], an actor, producer, or enthusiastic admirer, of Gilbert and Sullivan operas. *adj.* of Savoy, its people, or culture.
sav·vy (sav'i), *v.i.* [SAVVIED (-id), SAVVYING], [altered < Sp. *sabe* (*usted*), do (you) know? < *saber*, to know; L. *sapere;* cf. SAPIENT], [Slang], to understand; get the idea. *n.* [Slang], common sense; understanding. *adj.* [Slang], shrewd, wise, or discerning.
saw (sô), *n.* [ME. *sawe;* AS. *saga;* akin to G. *sage;* IE. base **seq-*, to cut, as also in L. *secare*, to cut (see SECTION), *segmentum* (see SEGMENT); cf. SAXON], 1.

a) a cutting tool, of various shapes and sizes, consisting essentially of a thin blade of metal, usually steel, the edge of which is a series of sharp teeth, and which may be worked by hand or machinery. *b*) any of various tools or devices somewhat like this but with a sharp edge instead of teeth. 2. a machine having such a tool or tools. ***v.t.*** [SAWED (sôd), SAWED or SAWN (sôn), SAWING], 1. to cut or divide with a saw. 2. to shape or form with a saw. 3. to make sawlike cutting motions through (the air, etc.). 4. to operate or produce with a to-and-fro motion suggestive of that used in working a saw: as, *saw* your knife through the meat, *saw* a tune out on the fiddle. ***v.i.*** 1. to cut with or as with a saw. 2. to cut: said of a saw itself. 3. to be cut with a saw: as, this plank *saws* easily.

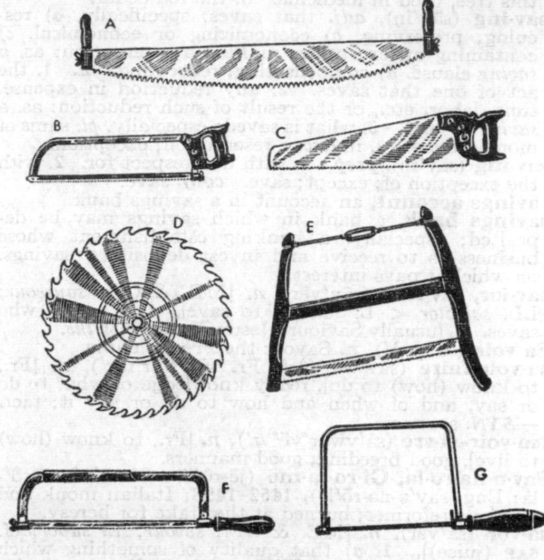

SAWS

A, crosscut saw; B, butcher's saw; C, handsaw; D, circular saw; E, bucksaw; F, hack saw; G, coping saw

saw (sô), ***n.*** [ME. *sawe;* AS. *sagu;* cf. SAGA, SAY], a saying; maxim; proverb. —***SYN.*** see **saying.**

saw (sô), past tense of **see.**

Sa·watch (sə-wäch′), ***n.*** a mountain range of the Rocky Mountains, in central Colorado: highest peak, Mt. Elbert, 14,431 ft.: also spelled **Saguache.**

saw·bones (sô′bōnz′), ***n.*** [Slang], a surgeon.

saw·buck (sô′buk′), ***n.*** [D. *zaagbuk*], 1. a sawhorse, especially one with the legs projecting above the crossbar. 2. [from the resemblance of the crossed legs of a carpenter's sawbuck to an X (the Roman numeral for *10*)], [Slang], a ten-dollar bill.

saw·dust (sô′dust′), ***n.*** minute particles of wood resulting as a by-product of sawing wood.

saw·fish (sô′fish′), ***n.*** [*pl.* SAWFISH, SAWFISHES (-iz); see FISH], any of a group of tropical giant rays which have the upper jaw prolonged into a long, flat, sawlike snout edged with teeth on both sides.

saw·fly (sô′flī′), ***n.*** [*pl.* SAWFLIES (-flīz′)], any of a group of four-winged insects the female of which is provided with a pair of sawlike organs that cut into plants, the eggs being then deposited in the cuts.

saw grass, [cf. SEDGE], any of a number of related grasslike plants with saw-edged leaves.

saw·horse (sô′hôrs′), ***n.*** a rack on which wood is placed for sawing.

saw log, a log large enough for sawing.

saw·mill (sô′mil′), ***n.*** 1. a factory or place where logs are sawed into boards. 2. a large sawing machine.

sawn (sôn), alternative past participle of **saw.**

saw set, an instrument used to set, or bend slightly outward, the teeth of a saw.

saw-toothed (sô′tōōtht′), ***adj.*** having teeth like those of a saw; serrate.

saw·yer (sô′yẽr), ***n.*** [ME. *sawier* for *sawere,* with *-ier* after OFr. suffix *-ier;* cf. CLOTHIER, LAWYER], 1. a person whose work is sawing wood, as into planks and boards. 2. a log or tree caught in a river so that its branches saw back and forth with the water. 3. any of a group of beetles whose larvae burrow in wood.

sax (saks), ***n.*** [Colloq.], a saxophone.

Sax., 1. Saxon. 2. Saxony.

sax·a·tile (sak′sə-til), ***adj.*** [L. *saxatilis* < *saxum,* a rock; prob. akin to *secare,* to cut; for IE. base see SAW (tool)], living or growing on or among rocks; saxicoline.

Saxe, Comte **Her·mann Mau·rice de** (er′män′ mô′rēs′ də säks′), 1696–1750; French general; marshal of France (1744–1750).

Saxe-Al·ten·burg (säks′äl′tən-bŭrg′), ***n.*** a former duchy of central Germany: now a part of Thuringia, Germany.

Saxe-Co·burg-Go·tha (säks′kō′bŭrg-gō′thə), ***n.*** a former duchy of central Germany: now divided between Bavaria and Thuringia, Germany: former name (1901–1917) of British royal house of Windsor.

Saxe-Mei·ning·en (säks′mī′niŋ-ən), ***n.*** a former duchy of central Germany: now a part of Thuringia, Germany.

Saxe-Wei·mar-Ei·sen·ach (säks′vī′mär-ī′zə-näkh), ***n.*** a former grand duchy of central Germany: now a part of Thuringia, Germany.

sax·horn (saks′hôrn′), ***n.*** [after A. J. *Sax* (1814–1894), Belgian inventor], any of a group of valved brass-wind instruments, with a full, even tone and a wide range.

sax·ic·o·line (sak-sik′ə-līn′, sak-sik′ə-lin), ***adj.*** [< L. *saxum,* a rock (cf. SAXATILE) + *colere,* to dwell; + *-ine*], living or growing on or among rocks.

sax·ic·o·lous (sak-sik′ə-ləs), ***adj.*** saxicoline.

sax·i·fra·ga·ceous (sak′si-frə-gā′shəs), ***adj.*** in ***botany,*** of the saxifrage family.

sax·i·frage (sak′si-frij), ***n.*** [ME.; OFr.; L. *saxifraga* < *saxum,* a rock (cf. SAXATILE) + base of *frangere,* to break; so named prob. from growing in rock crevices; cf. SASSAFRAS], any of a group of related plants with white, yellow, purple, or pinkish, small flowers, and leaves massed usually at the base of the plant; rockfoil.

Sax·o Gram·mat·i·cus (sak′sō grə-mat′i-kəs), 1150?–1220?; Danish historian.

Sax·on (sak′s′n), ***n.*** [ME.; OFr.; LL. *Saxo,* pl. *Saxones* < W.Gmc. **Saxon-* (whence AS. *Seaxan*) < base akin to OHG. *sahs,* sword, knife & L. *saxum,* rock, stone, *secare,* to cut], 1. a member of an ancient Germanic people that lived in northern Germany: some Saxons invaded and conquered parts of England in the 5th and 6th centuries A.D. 2. an Anglo-Saxon (senses 1 & 3). 3. a native or inhabitant of modern Saxony. 4. the Low German dialect of the early Continental Saxons; Old Saxon. 5. the German dialect of modern Saxony. ***adj.*** 1. of the early Continental Saxons, their language, etc. 2. English or Anglo-Saxon. 3. of modern Saxony. Abbreviated **S., Sax.**

Sax·on·ism (sak′s′n-iz′m), ***n.*** a word, phrase, idiom, etc. of English or Anglo-Saxon origin.

Sax·o·ny (sak′sə-ni), ***n.*** 1. a former kingdom of Germany. 2. a division of southern Germany: area, 5,789 sq. mi.; pop., 5,207,000; capital, Dresden. 3. a province of Prussia: area, 9,755 sq. mi.; pop., 3,623,-000; capital, Magdeburg. German name, *Sachsen.* 4. [so called because first produced in Saxony, Germany], *a*) a fine wool fabric with a glossy surface. *b*) a closely twisted yarn used for knitting. Abbreviated **Sax.**

sax·o·phone (sak′sə-fōn′), ***n.*** [after A. J. *Sax,* inventor (see SAXHORN) + Gr. *phōnē,* sound], any of a group of single-reed, keyed wind instruments somewhat like the clarinet but having a curved metal body and a deeper, mellower tone.

SAXOPHONE

sax·o·phon·ist (sak′sə-fōn′ist), ***n.*** a saxophone player.

sax·tu·ba (saks′tōō′bə, saks′tū′-bə), ***n.*** [< *sax-* as in *saxhorn* + *tuba*], a large, deep-toned saxhorn.

say (sā), ***v.t.*** [SAID (sed), SAYING; 3d pers. sing., pres. indic., SAYS (sez), *archaic* SAITH (seth)], [ME. *seien* (< orig. 3d pers. sing., pres. indic.), *seggen;* AS. *secgan* (< **sagjan-*); akin to G. *sagen;* prob. IE. base **seqw-,* to see, hence cause to see, say, tell, seen in L. *inseque,* tell!, Eng. *see;* cf. SAW (a saying)], 1. to utter, pronounce, or speak. 2. to state; declare; tell; express in words. 3. to state positively, with assurance, or as an opinion: as, I wish I could *say* when it will happen. 4. to recite; repeat: as, *say* your prayers. 5. to estimate; assume; hypothesize: as, he is, *say,* forty. 6. to allege; report: as, people *say* he's angry. ***v.i.*** to make a statement; speak; express an opinion. ***n.*** 1. what a person says; dictum. 2. a chance to speak: as, you've had your *say.* 3. power or authority, as to make a final decision: often with *the.*

go without saying, to be too obvious to need explanation; be self-evident.

that is to say, in other words; that means.

Sa·yan Mountains (sä-yän′), a mountain range in north central Asia, between the Tuvinian Autonomous Region and Krasnoyarsk Territory, U.S.S.R.

sa·yid, say·yid (sä′yid), ***n.*** [Ar. *sayyid*], lord: a Moslem title applied to those who claim to be descendants of Mohammed through his daughter Fatima: also **said.**

say·ing (sā′iŋ), ***n.*** 1. the act of one who says. 2. something said; especially, an adage, proverb, or maxim.

SYN.—**saying** is the simple, direct term for any pithy expression of wisdom or truth; a **saw** is an old, homely saying that is well worn by repetition (the preacher filled his sermon with wise *saws*); a **maxim** is a general principle drawn from practical experience and serving as a rule of conduct (Ex.: "Keep thy shop and thy shop will keep thee"); an **adage** is a saying that has been popularly accepted over a long period of time (Ex.: "Where there's smoke, there's fire"); a **proverb** is a piece of practical wisdom expressed in homely, concrete terms (Ex.: "A penny saved is a penny earned"); a **motto** is a maxim accepted as a guiding principle or as an ideal of behavior (Ex.: "Honesty is the best policy"); an **aphorism** is a terse saying embodying a general truth or principle (Ex.: "He is a fool that cannot conceal his wisdom"); an **epigram** is a terse, witty, pointed statement that gains its effect by ingenious antithesis (Ex.: "The only way to get rid of a temptation is to yield to it").

says (sez), third person singular, present indicative, of **say.**

say-so (sā′sō′), *n.* [Colloq.], 1. an unsupported statement or assertion. 2. right of decision. 3. a dictum.

Sb, *stibium,* [L.], in *chemistry,* antimony.

sb., substantive.

S.B., 1. *Scientiae Baccalaureus,* [L.], Bachelor of Science. 2. South Britain (England and Wales).

s.b., sb, stolen base(s).

SbE, south by east.

'sblood (zblud), *interj.* [Archaic], God's blood: a euphemistic oath expressing anger, surprise, etc.

SbW, south by west.

Sc, in *chemistry,* scandium.

Sc., 1. Scotch. 2. Scots. 3. Scottish.

sc., 1. scale. 2. scene. 3. scilicet. 4. screw. 5. scruple.

S.C., 1. Sanitary Corps. 2. Signal Corps. 3. South Carolina. 4. Staff Corps. 5. Supreme Court.

s.c., 1. in *printing,* small capitals. 2. supercalendered.

scab (skab), *n.* [ME. *scabbe* < AS. *sceabb* & the cognate ON. **skabbr;* prob. influenced in form and sense by L. *scabies;* see SCABIES], 1. a crust which forms over a sore or wound during healing. 2. a skin disease of animals, especially sheep; mange. 3. *a)* a plant disease caused by certain fungi. *b)* one of the roundish, roughened spots marking this disease. 4. [Slang], a low, contemptible fellow; scoundrel; hence, 5. in the *labor movement, a)* a worker who refuses to join a union, or who works for less pay or under different conditions than those accepted by the union. *b)* a worker who refuses to strike, or who takes the place of a striking worker. *v.i.* [SCABBED (skabd), SCABBING], 1. to become covered with a scab; form a scab. 2. to work or act as a scab.

scab·bard (skab′ẽrd), *n.* [ME. *scauberd, scauberk, scaberge;* OFr. *escalberc;* prob. < OHG. *scar,* sword, cutting tool (akin to *shear*) + *bergan,* to hide, protect], a sheath or case to hold the blade of a sword, dagger, or bayonet. *v.t.* to put into a scabbard; sheathe.

scab·bi·ly (skab′ə-li), *adv.* in a scabby manner.

scab·bi·ness (skab′i-nis), *n.* a scabby quality or state.

scab·ble (skab′'l), *v.t.* [SCABBLED (-'ld), SCABBLING], [earlier *scapple* < OFr. *escapeler,* to dress timber], in *stonework,* to shape roughly.

scab·by (skab′i), *adj.* [SCABBIER (-i-ẽr), SCABBIEST (-i-ist)], 1. covered with or consisting of scabs. 2. having scab (skin disease). 3. low; base; mean; scurvy.

sca·bi·es (skā′bi-ēz′, skā′bēz), *n.* [L., roughness, itch < *scabere,* to scratch; cf. SHAVE], a contagious skin disease caused by certain mites that burrow under the skin and deposit eggs, causing intense itching; the itch.

sca·bi·et·ic (skā′bi-et′ik), *adj.* of or having scabies.

sca·bi·o·sa (skā′bi-ō′sə), *n.* [ML. *scabiosa* (*herba*) < L. *scabies;* see SCABIES: so called because considered a remedy for the itch], any of a number of related plants having showy, variously colored flowers with knobbed, protruding stamens: also **scabious.**

sca·bi·ous (skā′bi-əs), *adj.* [< Fr. or L.; Fr. *scabieux;* L. *scabiosus*], 1. scabby. 2. of or like scabies.

sca·bi·ous (skā′bi-əs), *n.* a scabiosa.

sca·brous (skā′brəs), *adj.* [LL. *scabrosus* < L. *scabere,* to scratch], 1. rough with small points or knobs, like a file; scaly; scabby. 2. full of difficulties. 3. lacking in delicacy; risqué; salacious; improper.

scad (skad), *n.* [*pl.* SCAD, SCADS (skadz); see PLURAL, II, D, 2], [akin to *shad*], a saurel.

scads (skadz), *n.pl.* [prob. for *scat* (< AS. *sceat* & ON. *skattr,* a treasure, tribute, tax in money); the U.S. popularity of the term may be due to a dial. refashioning of the cognate G. *schatz,* a treasure], [Colloq.], a very large number or amount: as, *scads* of money.

Sca·fell Pike (skô′fel′), a peak of the Cumbrian Mountains: highest point in England, 3,210 ft.

scaf·fold (skaf′'ld, skaf′ōld), *n.* [ME. *scafald;* OFr. *escafalt* < *es-* (L. *ex-,* out) + LL. **catafalcum;* see CATAFALQUE], 1. a temporary wooden or metal framework for supporting workmen and materials during the erecting, repairing, or painting of a building, etc. 2. a raised platform on which criminals are executed, as by hanging, etc. 3. a temporary wooden stage or platform for exhibition purposes. 4. any raised framework. 5. scaffolding. *v.t.* to furnish or support with, or put on, a scaffold.

scaf·fold·ing (skaf′'l-diŋ), *n.* 1. the poles, planks, and other materials which form a scaffold. 2. a scaffold or system of scaffolds.

scagl·io·la (skal-yō′lə), *n.* [It. *scagliuola,* dim. of *scaglia,* a shell], an ornamental plasterwork of gypsum and glue, made in imitation of granite or marble.

scal·a·ble (skāl′ə-b'l), *adj.* that can be scaled.

sca·lade (skə-lād′), *n.* [It. *scalada* < *scalare,* to scale < *scala,* ladder; see SCALE (ladder)], [Obs.], an escalade.

scal·age (skāl′ij), *n.* [< *scale* + *-age*], 1. the percentage by which anything is scaled down to allow for shrinkage, etc. 2. the estimate of lumber in a log being scaled.

sca·lar (skā′lẽr), *adj.* [L. *scalaris,* of a ladder < *scalae,* steps, ladder], in *mathematics,* designating or of a quantity that has magnitude but no direction in space, as volume or temperature. *n.* a scalar quantity. Distinguished from *vector.*

sca·lar·i·form (skə-lar′ə-fôrm′), *adj.* [< L. *scalaris,* like a ladder (see SCALE, ladder); + *-form*], shaped like a ladder; having markings like the rungs of a ladder.

scal·a·wag (skal′ə-wag′), *n.* [? < *Scalloway,* Shetland Islands, place of origin of a small breed of ponies, yielding early sense of "undersized horse, runt"; ? < OFr. *escaulevage,* toll paid by merchants; cf. SCAVENGER], 1. a scamp; rascal. 2. a white Southerner who was a Republican during the Reconstruction, following the Civil War: an opprobrious term used by Southern Democrats. Also **scallawag, scallywag.**

scald (skôld), *v.t.* [ME. *scalden;* ONorm.Fr. *escalder;* OFr. *eschalder, eschauder;* LL. *excaldare* < L. *ex-,* intens. + *caldus, calidus,* hot], 1. to burn or injure with hot liquid or steam. 2. to heat almost to the boiling point. 3. to use boiling liquid on; specifically, *a)* to sterilize by the use of boiling liquid. *b)* to loosen the skins of (fruits, etc.) by the use of boiling water. *v.i.* to be or become scalded. *n.* 1. a burn or injury caused by scalding. 2. in *botany, a)* a disease of cranberries. *b)* a whitening or browning of plant tissues, caused by certain fungi or too much sun.

scald (skôld, skäld), *n.* a skald (poet).

scald·ic (skôl′dik, skäl′dik), *adj.* skaldic.

scale (skāl), *n.* [< It. or L.; It. *scala;* L. *scala* (usually *scalae, pl.*), a flight of stairs, ladder], 1. *a)* originally, a ladder; flight of stairs; hence, *b)* a means of ascent. 2. a series of marks along a line, at regular or graduated distances, used in measuring or computing: as, the *scale* of a thermometer. 3. any instrument marked in this manner. 4. *a)* the proportion that a map, model, etc. bears to the thing that it represents; ratio between the dimensions of a representation and those of the object: as, a *scale* of one inch to a mile. *b)* a divided line, on a map, indicating this ratio or proportion. 5. *a)* a system of grouping or classifying in a series of steps or degrees according to a standard of relative size, amount, importance, perfection, etc.; progressive graduated series: as, the social *scale,* wage *scale. b)* any point, grade, level, or degree in such a series. 6. a system of numerical notation in which the value of a figure is determined by its place in the order according to the constant fixed as the basis of the system; basis for a numerical system: as, the decimal *scale.* 7. an escalade. 8. in *music,* a series of tones arranged in a sequence of rising or falling pitches in accordance with any of various systems of intervals; especially, all of such a series contained in one octave: see also **chromatic, diatonic, major scale, minor scale.** *v.t.* [SCALED (skāld), SCALING], 1. to climb up or over; go up by or as by a ladder or by clambering. 2. to regulate or make according to a scale. 3. to reduce according to a fixed ratio or proportion: as, prices were *scaled* down 5 per cent. 4. to measure by or as by a scale. 5. to measure (logs) or estimate the board feet of (timber). *v.i.* 1. to climb; go up. 2. to go up in a graduated series.

on a large (or **small,** etc.) **scale,** to a relatively large (or small, etc.) degree or extent.

scale (skāl), *n.* [ME.; aphetic form < OFr. *escale* (Fr. *écale*), husk, cup & OFr. *escaille* (Fr. *écaille*), fish scale, oyster shell; both < Gmc. base of OHG. *scala,* ON. *skāl* (cf. SCALE, a dish)], 1. one of the thin, flat, overlapping, horny plates forming the outer protective covering of many fishes and reptiles. 2. one of the structurally similar thin plates on birds' legs or certain insects' wings. 3. any thin, flaky or platelike layer or piece, such as a thin flake of skin. 4. a flaky film of oxide which forms on metals when heated or rusted. 5. a coating which forms on the inside of boilers, kettles, or other metal containers when heated. 6. any scalelike leaf or bract; especially, such a leaf covering the bud of a seed plant. 7. any of a number of related sucking insects that attack plants. *v.t.* [SCALED (skāld), SCALING], 1. to strip or scrape scales from. 2. to remove in thin layers; pare down. 3. to cause scales to form on; cover with scales. 4. to throw (a thin, flat object) so that its edge cuts the air, or so that it skips along the surface of water. *v.i.* 1. to flake or peel off in scales. 2. to become covered with scales.

scale (skāl), *n.* [ME.; ON. *skāl*, bowl, weighing balance; akin to OHG. *scala* (G. *schale*, a shell) & AS. *scealu*, a shell, cup (cf. SHALE); IE. base *(*s*)*qel-*, to cut, seen also in L. *silex*, a pebble (cf. SILICA, SILICATE); cf. prec. SCALE], 1. either of the shallow dishes or pans of a balance. 2. *usually pl.* *a*) a balance itself. *b*) any weighing machine. *v.t.* [SCALED (skāld), SCALING], 1. to weigh in scales. 2. to have a weight of. 3. to balance; compare. *v.i.* to be weighed. Abbreviated **sc.**
the Scales, Libra (constellation or sign of the zodiac).
turn the scales, to determine; decide.

scale·board (skāl′bôrd′, skāl′bōrd′, skab′ẽrd), *n.* [*scale* (thin plate) + *board*], 1. a very thin board or sheet of wood, as for backing a framed picture or mirror, or for use as veneer. 2. in *printing*, a very thin slip of wood or pasteboard used (formerly) in justifying.

scale insect, any of a group of small insects destructive to plants, the females of which secrete a round scale under which they live and lay their eggs.

scale moss, any of a number of related mosslike plants with small, scalelike leaves; thalloid liverwort.

sca·lene (skā-lēn′), *adj.* [LL. *scalenus*; Gr. *skalēnos*, uneven, odd], 1. in *anatomy*, designating or of any of a group of deeply set muscles extending from the first two ribs to the cervical vertebrae, and serving to bend the neck. 2. in *geometry*, *a*) having unequal sides and angles: said of a triangle. *b*) having the axis not perpendicular to the base; oblique: said of a cone, etc.

sca·le·nus (skā-lē′nəs), *n.* [LL.], a scalene muscle.

scal·i·ness (skāl′i-nis), *n.* a scaly quality or condition.

scaling ladder, a ladder used for climbing walls of fortified places, etc.

scall (skôl), *n.* [ME.; ON. *skalli*, bald head], any scaly, or scabby, disease of the skin; scurf.

scal·la·wag (skal′ə-wag′), *n.* a scalawag.

scal·lion (skal′yən), *n.* [ME. *scalon*; ONorm.Fr. *escalogne* (for OFr. *eschaloigne*) < LL. **escalonia* < L. (*caepa*) *Ascalonia*, (onion of) Ascalon (a city in Philistia)], any of three varieties of onion; specifically, *a*) the shallot. *b*) the leek. *c*) a green onion with a long, thick stem and an almost bulbless root.

scal·lop (skäl′əp, skal′əp), *n.* [ME. *scalop*; OFr. *escalope*; of Gmc. origin; cf. SCALE (thin plate)], 1. any of numerous related mollusks with two curved shells deeply grooved, ridged, and hinged together. 2. the large muscle of such a mollusk, used as food. 3. one of the two shells; specifically, *a*) one worn as a badge by pilgrims returning from the Holy Land. *b*) one used as a baking dish. 4. a small dish in which fish or other food is baked and served. 5. one of a series of curves, circle segments, projections, etc. forming an ornamental edge on cloth, lace, etc. *v.t.* 1. to cut the edge or border of in scallops. 2. to bake until brown in a casserole, etc. with a milk sauce and bread crumbs; escalop. Also **scollop.**

scal·ly·wag (skal′i-wag′), *n.* a scalawag.

scalp (skalp), *n.* [ME. *scalp*, *scalpe*; prob., in specialized sense < ON. *skālpr*, sheath; IE. base **sqel-b-* < **sqel-*, to cut (cf. SCALE, a balance)], 1. the skin on the top and back of the head, usually covered with hair. 2. a part of this, cut or torn off from the head of an enemy by North American Indians and preserved as a trophy. 3. a trophy. 4. the skin on the top of the head of a dog, wolf, etc. 5. [Colloq.], a small profit made by scalping. *v.t.* 1. to cut or tear the scalp from; hence, 2. to cheat, defeat, or rob. 3. [Colloq.], to buy and sell in order to make small, quick profits. 4. [Colloq.], to buy and sell (theater tickets, etc.) as a scalper. *v.i.* [Colloq.], to scalp bonds, tickets, etc.

scal·pel (skal′pəl), *n.* [L. *scalpellum*, dim. of *scalprum*, a knife < *scalpere*, to cut], a small, light, straight knife with a very sharp blade, used by surgeons and in anatomical dissections.

SCALPEL

scalp·er (skal′pẽr), *n.* a person who scalps; especially, [Colloq.], a person who buys up quantities of theater tickets, etc. at relatively low prices and sells them at prices in excess of established rates.

scalp lock, a lock or tuft of hair left on the shaven crown of the head by North American Indians as a challenge to their enemies.

scal·y (skāl′i), *adj.* [SCALIER (-i-ẽr), SCALIEST (-i-ist)], 1. having, covered with, composed of, or resembling a scale or scales. 2. shedding or yielding scales or flakes. 3. full of or infested with scale insects. 4. [Slang], mean; low; despicable.

scaly anteater, a pangolin.

Sca·man·der (skə-man′dẽr), *n.* the Menderes (sense 2), a river in Asia Minor: the ancient name.

scam·mo·ny (skam′ə-ni), *n.* [ME. *skamonye*; L. *scammonia*; Gr. *skammōnia*], 1. a climbing plant with thick roots, arrowhead-shaped leaves, and white flowers. 2. the resin from its roots, used as a cathartic.

scamp (skamp), *n.* [< obs. *scamp*, to roam, contr. of *scamper*], a worthless fellow; rogue; rascal.

scamp (skamp), *v.t.* [< dial. *scamp*, in same sense; akin to or < ON. *skammr*, short (cf. *skemma*, to shorten); cf. SCANT], to do or perform in a careless, inadequate way.

scam·per (skam′pẽr), *v.i.* [ONorm.Fr. *escamper* (for OFr. *eschamper*) < LL. **excampere*, to escape < L. *ex*, out + *campus*, a plain, field of battle; lit., to decamp], to run or go hurriedly or quickly. *n.* a scampering.

scam·pi (skam′pi), *n.* [*pl.* SCAMPIES (-piz)], [It. pl.], a large, greenish prawn, valued as food.

scamp·ish (skam′pish), *adj.* of or like a scamp.

scan (skan), *v.t.* [SCANNED (skand), SCANNING], [ME. *scannen*, also formerly written *scand* < L. *scandere*, to climb, mount, scan; cf. SCALE (to climb)], 1. to analyze (verse) into its rhythmic components; determine the rhythm of; count accents and syllables, and determine metrical feet of. 2. to read or recite (verse) aloud in order to demonstrate its rhythmic structure. 3. to look at closely; scrutinize. 4. to glance at quickly; consider hastily. 5. in *television*, to traverse (a surface) rapidly with a beam of light or electrons in transmitting or reproducing a picture. *v.i.* 1. to scan verse. 2. to conform to metrical principles: said of verse. 3. in *television*, to scan a surface. *n.* 1. a scanning. 2. scope of vision. —***SYN.*** see **scrutinize.**

Scan., Scand., 1. Scandinavia. 2. Scandinavian.

scan·dal (skan′d'l), *n.* [Fr. *scandale* < LL. *scandalum*; also ME. *scandle* < OFr. *escandle* < LL. *scandalum*, cause for stumbling < Gr. *skandalon*, a snare; prob. akin to L. *scandere*, to climb; cf. SCAN], 1. any act, person, or thing that offends or shocks moral feelings of the community and leads to disgrace: as, those slums are a *scandal*. 2. a reaction of shame, disgrace, outrage, etc. caused by such an act, person, or thing. 3. ignominy; disgrace. 4. malicious gossip; defamatory talk; backbiting; slanderous reports. *v.t.* [SCANDALED or SCANDALLED (-d'ld), SCANDALING or SCANDALLING], 1. [Dial. or Archaic], to slander; defame. 2. [Obs.], to scandalize. 3. [Obs.], to disgrace. —***SYN.*** see **disgrace.**

scan·dal·ize (skan′d'l-īz′), *v.t.* [SCANDALIZED (-īzd′), SCANDALIZING], [Fr. *scandaliser*; LL. *scandalizare* < Gr. *skandalizein*, to snare < *skandalon*; see SCANDAL], to shock or outrage the moral feelings of; offend by some improper or unconventional conduct; shock.

scan·dal·mon·ger (skan′d'l-muŋ′gẽr), *n.* a person who gossips maliciously and spreads scandal.

scan·dal·ous (skan′d'l-əs), *adj.* [Fr. *scandaleux*; ML. *scandalosus*], 1. causing scandal; offensive and shocking to the moral feelings of the community; of such a nature as to outrage a sense of decency; shameful. 2. consisting of evil and malicious reports; libelous; defamatory; spreading slander. 3. fond of scandal.

scan·dent (skan′dənt), *adj.* [L. *scandens* < *scandere*, to climb], climbing by attaching itself, as a vine.

Scan·der·beg (skan′dẽr-beg′), *n.* Albanian leader and national hero (born *George Castriota*); lived 1403?–1468.

scan·di·a (skan′di-ə), *n.* [Mod. L.; see SCANDIUM], the oxide of scandium, Sc_2O_3, a white, amorphous powder.

Scan·di·an (skan′di-ən), *adj.* of the Scandinavian Peninsula.

scan·dic (skan′dik), *adj.* of scandium.

Scan·di·na·vi·a (skan′də-nā′vi-ə), *n.* 1. the ancient Norse lands: now, Sweden, Norway, Denmark, and Iceland. 2. the Scandinavian Peninsula.

Scan·di·na·vi·an (skan′də-nā′vi-ən), *adj.* of Scandinavia, its people, their language, etc. *n.* 1. one of the people of Scandinavia. 2. the subbranch of the Germanic languages spoken by them; North Germanic; Norse. 3. Anglo-Norse.

Scandinavian Peninsula, a large peninsula of northern Europe, containing Norway and Sweden.

scan·di·um (skan′di-əm), *n.* [Mod. L. < ML. *Scandia*, Scandinavia < L. *Scandia*, northern European lands], a rare metallic chemical element found in combination with various elements of the rare-earth group: symbol, Sc; at. wt., 45.10; at. no., 21.

scan·na·ble (skan′ə-b'l), *adj.* that can be scanned.

scan·sion (skan′shən), *n.* [Fr. < L. *scansio*], the analysis of verse into its rhythmic components; act of scanning: the marks of scansion used in this dictionary are: for an accented syllable, ′; for an unaccented syllable, ˘; for a foot division, |.

scan·so·ri·al (skan-sôr′i-əl, skan-sō′ri-əl), *adj.* [< L. *scansus*, pp. of *scandere*, to climb], in *zoology*, 1. of or adapted for climbing, as the feet of a bird. 2. that climbs or can climb.

scant (skant), *adj.* [ME.; ON. *skamt* < *skammr*, short; prob. IE. base **sqep-*, etc., to handle a sharp tool, seen also in L. *capo* (cf. CAPON)], 1. inadequate in size or amount; not enough; meager. 2. lacking a small part of the whole; not quite up to full measure. *v.t.* 1. to limit in size or amount; stint. 2. to fail to give full measure of. 3. to treat in an inadequate manner. *adv.* [Dial.], scarcely; barely. —***SYN.*** see **meager.**
scant of, short of; having an insufficient supply of.

scant·i·ly (skan′t'l-i), *adv.* in a scanty manner.

scant·i·ness (skan′ti-nis), *n.* the quality of being scanty.

scant·ling (skant′liŋ), *n.* [< obs. *scantillon*; OFr. *eschantillon*, specimen, pattern, orig. corner piece, chip], 1. a small quantity or amount. 2. dimensions of building material. 3. a small beam or timber, especially one of small cross section, as a 2×4. 4. a small, upright timber, as in the frame of a structure. 5. small beams or timbers collectively.

scant·y (skan′ti), *adj.* [SCANTIER (-ti-ẽr), SCANTIEST (-ti-ist)], [< *scant*], 1. barely sufficient; not ample; meager. 2. insufficient; not enough. 3. narrow; small; close. —*SYN.* see **meager.**

Scap·a Flow (skap′ə, skä′pə), a channel in the Orkney Islands, northern Scotland: British naval base: see **Orkney Islands,** map.

scape (skāp), *n.* [L. *scapus*], 1. a leafless flower stalk growing from the crown of the root, as that of the tulip, dandelion, etc. 2. something like a stalk, as the shaft of a feather, the shaft of a column, etc.

'scape, scape (skāp), *n., v.t. & v.i.* ['SCAPED, SCAPED (skāpt), 'SCAPING, SCAPING], [ME. *scapien, scapen*], [Archaic], escape.

scape·goat (skāp′gōt′), *n.* [*scape*, contr. of *escape* + *goat*], 1. a goat over the head of which the high priest of the ancient Jews confessed the sins of the people on the Day of Atonement, after which it was allowed to escape: Lev. 16:8–22; hence, 2. a person, group, or thing that bears the blame for the mistakes or crimes of others, or for some misfortune due to another agency.

scape·grace (skāp′grās′), *n.* [see SCAPEGOAT], a graceless, unprincipled fellow; scamp; rogue; rascal.

cape wheel, the notched wheel in the escapement of a clock or watch: cf. **escapement.**

scaph·oid (skaf′oid), *adj.* [Gr. *skaphoeidēs* < *skaphē*, a boat + *eidos*, a shape], boat-shaped; especially, designating a small, boat-shaped bone of the wrist or ankle. *n.* a scaphoid bone.

sca·pi- (skā′pi), [< L. *scapus*, a stalk], a combining form meaning *stalk, shaft.*

scap·o·lite (skap′ə-līt′), *n.* [< Gr. *skāpos*, rod; + *-lite*], any of a group of minerals composed of silicates of aluminum, calcium, and sodium; wernerite.

sca·pose (skā′pōs), *adj.* [< *scape* + *-ose*], in *botany*, 1. bearing scapes. 2. resembling a scape. 3. consisting of a scape.

. caps., in *printing*, small capitals.

cap·u·la (skap′yoo-lə), *n.* [*pl.* SCAPULAE (-lē′), SCAPULAS (-ləz)], [LL., the shoulder; L. *scapulae*, the shoulder blades], the shoulder blade; either of two flat, triangular bones in the back of the shoulder in man, or a similar bone in other vertebrates: see **skeleton,** illus.

cap·u·lar (skap′yoo-lẽr), *adj.* [Mod. L. *scapularis* < LL. *scapula*], of the shoulder, scapula, or scapulae. *n.* 1. a sleeveless outer garment falling from the shoulders, worn as part of a monk's habit. 2. two small pieces of cloth joined by strings, worn on the chest and back, under the clothes, by some Roman Catholics as a token of religious devotion. 3. in *anatomy & zoology, a)* a scapula. *b)* a feather growing from a bird's scapular region. 4. in *surgery*, a bandage passed over the shoulder to support it or to keep another bandage in place.

cap·u·lar·y (skap′yoo-ler′i), *adj. & n.* [*pl.* SCAPULARIES (-iz)], scapular.

cap·u·lo- (skap′yoo-lō, skap′yoo-lə), [< LL. *scapula*; see SCAPULA], a combining form meaning *scapula* or *scapula and:* also **scapul-.**

car (skär), *n.* [ME. *skarre, skerre;* OFr. *escare;* L. *eschara* < Gr. *eschara*, fireplace, brazier, scar of a burn], 1. a mark left on the skin or other tissue after a wound, burn, ulcer, pustule, lesion, etc. has healed; cicatrix. 2. any blemish or mark resembling this, as on the stem of a plant where a leaf was attached. 3. *a)* the result left on the mind by suffering or anguish. *b)* the physical sign of suffering, such as a line on the face. *v.t.* [SCARRED (skärd), SCARRING], to mark with or as with a scar. *v.i.* to form a scar in healing.

car (skär), *n.* [ME. *scarre, sker;* ON. *sker;* for IE. base see SHEAR, *v.;* cf. SKERRY], [British], 1. a precipitous rocky place or cliff. 2. a projecting or isolated rock, as in the sea.

car·ab (skar′əb), *n.* [Fr. *scarabée;* L. *scarabeus*], 1. a beetle, especially the black, winged dung beetle, held sacred by the ancient Egyptians. 2. an image of this beetle, cut from a stone or gem, often engraved with symbols on the flat underside, and formerly worn as a charm.

TOP BOTTOM

EGYPTIAN SCARAB

car·a·bae·an (skar′ə-bē′ən), *n. & adj.* scarabaeid.

car·a·bae·id (skar′ə-bē′id), *adj.* [< Mod. L. *Scarabaeidae*, name of the family < L. *scarabaeus;* akin to Gr. *karabos*, a beetle], of or belonging to a large family of true beetles with a squat, stout body and antennae made up of small plates (lamellated). *n.* a beetle of this family, as the dung beetle or tumble bug, Japanese beetle, rose chafer, scarab, etc.

car·a·bae·oid (skar′ə-bē′oid), *adj.* scarabaeid.

scar·a·bae·us (skar′ə-bē′əs), *n.* [*pl.* SCARABAEUSES (-iz), SCARABAEI (-ī)], [L.], a scarab.

scar·ab·oid (skar′ə-boid′), *adj.* of, like, or having the nature of, a scarab.

Scar·a·mouch (skar′ə-mouch′, skar′ə-mōōsh′), *n.* [Fr. *Scaramouche;* It. *Scaramuccia*, lit., a skirmish], 1. a stock character in old Italian comedy, depicted as a braggart and poltroon; hence, 2. [s-], a boastful coward, poltroon, or rascal.

Scar·bor·ough (skär′bũr′ō, skär′bə-rə), *n.* a resort town in Yorkshire, on the northeastern coast of England: pop., 42,000 (est. 1946).

scarce (skârs), *adj.* [ME. *scars;* ONorm.Fr. *escars* (for OFr. *eschars*); LL. **escarpsus*, for L. *excerptus*, pp. of *excerpere*, to pick out, select (see EXCERPT); hence, that which is picked out and therefore scarce], 1. not common; rarely seen. 2. not plentiful; not equal to the demand; hard to get. *adv.* scarcely: a literary usage. —*SYN.* see **rare.**

make oneself scarce, [Colloq.], to go or stay away.

scarce·ly (skârs′li), *adv.* 1. hardly; not quite; only just. 2. probably not or certainly not: as, *scarcely* true.

scarce·ment (skârs′mənt), *n.* [ME. (Anglo-L.); prob. *scarce* + *-ment*], a ledge or offset in a wall, etc.

scar·ci·ty (skâr′sə-ti), *n.* [*pl.* SCARCITIES (-tiz)], [ME. *scarsite;* ONorm.Fr. *escarseté*], 1. the condition or quality of being scarce; inadequate supply; deficiency; lack. 2. rarity; uncommonness.

scare (skâr), *v.t.* [SCARED (skârd), SCARING], [ME. *skerren* < *sker*, shy, afraid; ON. *skiarr*, shy, timid; prob. IE. base *(*s*)*qer-*, to jump, jump about, as also in L. *scurra*, buffoon (cf. SCURRILOUS)], 1. to startle; fill with sudden terror; strike fear into. 2. to drive (*away* or *off*) by frightening. *v.i.* to be frightened; take sudden fright: as, nervous people *scare* easily. *n.* [ME. *skerre* < the *v.*], a sudden fear or panic; attack of fright, often unreasonable. —*SYN.* see **frighten.**

scare up, [Colloq.], to produce or gather quickly.

scare·crow (skâr′krō′), *n.* 1. anything set up in a field to scare crows, etc. away from crops, usually a crude figure of a man roughly dressed; hence, 2. anything that frightens one but is actually not harmful. 3. a person dressed in very old and ragged clothes.

scare·head (skâr′hed′), *n.* [Colloq.], an exceptionally large newspaper headline, for sensational news.

scare·mon·ger (skâr′muŋ′gẽr), *n.* a person who circulates alarming rumors.

scarf (skärf), *n.* [*pl.* SCARFS, SCARVES (skärvz)], [ONorm. Fr. *escarpe* < OFr. *escreppe*, a purse suspended from the neck, wallet; ON. *skreppa*, wallet], 1. a long, broad piece of silk or other cloth worn about the neck, head, or shoulders as an ornament or to give warmth and protection from the wind. 2. any neckerchief or necktie with hanging ends. 3. a long, narrow covering for a table, bureau top, etc. 4. in *military usage*, a sash. *v.t.* 1. to cover or wrap with or as with a scarf or scarfs. 2. to wrap or put on loosely, as a scarf.

scarf (skärf), *n.* [prob. < ON. *skarfr*, notch in a timber (via nautical language); IE. base *(*s*)*qer-p-* (< **sqer-*, to cut), as also in L. *carpere*, to pluck off (cf. CARPET)], 1. a joint made by notching, grooving, or otherwise cutting the ends of two piecesandfasteningthem so that they lap over and join firmly into one continuous piece: also **scarf joint.** 2. the ends of a piece cut in this fashion. 3. a groove along a whale's body. *v.t.* 1. to join by a scarf. 2. to make a scarf in the end of. ‡ 3. to cut scarfs in and remove the skin and blubber of (a whale).

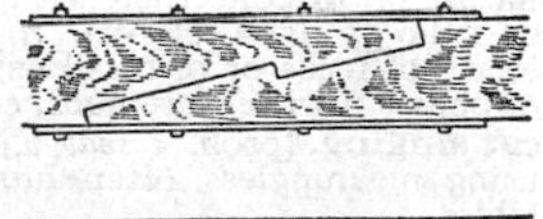

SCARF JOINTS

scarf·skin (skärf′skin′), *n.* [*scarf* (cloth covering) + *skin*], the outermost layer of skin; epidermis.

scar·i·fi·ca·tion (skar′ə-fi-kā′shən), *n.* [L. *scarificatio*], 1. a scarifying. 2. scratches or cuts made by scarifying.

scar·i·fi·ca·tor (skar′ə-fi-kā′tẽr), *n.* [Mod. L.], a surgical instrument for scarifying the skin.

scar·i·fi·er (skar′ə-fī′ẽr), *n.* 1. an agricultural machine for loosening the soil without turning it over. 2. a scarificator.

scar·i·fy (skar′ə-fī′), *v.t.* [SCARIFIED (-fīd′), SCARIFYING], [Fr. *scarifier;* L. *scarificare, scarifare* < Gr. *skariphasthai*, to scratch an outline, sketch < *skariphos*, a pencil, stylus; akin to L. *scribere*, to write], 1. to make a series of small, superficial incisions or punctures in (the skin), as in surgery. 2. to criticize sharply; make cutting remarks about. 3. in *agriculture, a)* to loosen or stir (the topsoil). *b)* to make incisions in the coats of (seeds) in order to hasten germination.

scar·i·ous (skâr′i-əs), *adj.* [Fr. *scarieux;* Mod. L. *scariosus* < L. *scaria*, thorny shrub], in *botany*, dry, thin, membranous, and not green, as some bracts.

t, āpe, bâre, cär; ten, ēven, hêre, ovẽr; is, bīte; lot, gō, hôrn, tōōl, look; oil, out; up, ūse, fũr; get; joy; yet; chin; she; thin, hen; zh, leisure; ŋ, ring; ə for *a* in *ago*, *e* in *agent*, *i* in *sanity*, *o* in *comply*, *u* in *focus*; ′ as in *able* (ā′b'l); Fr. bål; ë, Fr. eur; ö, Fr. feu; Fr. mon; ô, Fr. coq; ü, Fr. duc; H, G. ich; kh, G. doch. See pp. x–xii. ‡ foreign; * hypothetical; < derived from.

scar·la·ti·na (skär'lə-tē'nə), *n.* [Mod. L.; It. *scarlattina* < *scarlatto*, scarlet], scarlet fever: term used popularly for a mild form of the disease.

scar·la·ti·noid (skär'lə-tē'noid, skär-lat'ə-noid'), *adj.* resembling scarlatina, or scarlet fever, or its rash.

Scar·lat·ti, A·les·san·dro (ä'les-sän'drô skär-lät'tē; Eng. skär-lä'ti), 1659–1725; Italian composer.

Scarlatti, Do·me·ni·co (dô-me'nē-kô'), 1683–1757; son of *Alessandro;* Italian composer.

scar·let (skär'lit), *n.* [ME. *scarlat;* OFr. *escarlate* < ML. *scarlatum;* of Per. or Ar. origin], 1. very bright red with a slightly orange tinge. 2. cloth or clothing of this color. *adj.* 1. of this color. 2. of sin; sinful; specifically, whorish (cf. **Scarlet Woman**).

scarlet fever, an acute contagious disease, especially of children, caused by certain streptococci and characterized by sore throat, fever, and a scarlet rash.

scarlet hat, in the *Roman Catholic Church,* a cardinal's hat, especially as a symbol of rank.

scarlet letter, a scarlet letter A, which women condemned of adultery were formerly forced to wear.

scarlet runner, a climbing bean plant of tropical America, having scarlet flowers, and pods with large, edible, red-and-black seeds: also **scarlet runner bean.**

scarlet tanager, any of a group of songbirds related to the finch and native to the United States, with a scarlet body and black wings and tail.

Scarlet Woman, the Roman Catholic Church: an opprobrious term based on the reference in Rev. 17:1–6.

scarp (skärp), *n.* [Fr. *escarpe* < It. *scarpa,* a scarp, slope; cf. ESCARPMENT], 1. a steep slope; abrupt declivity. 2. ground formed into a steep slope as part of a fortification; steep slope on the inner face of a ditch below the rampart. *v.t.* 1. to make or cut into a steep slope. 2. to provide with a scarp.

Scar·ron, Paul (pôl skà'rôn'), 1610–1660; French humorous writer of poems, plays, and novels.

scarves (skärvz), *n.* alternative plural of **scarf** (cloth).

scar·y (skâr'i), *adj.* [SCARIER (-i-ēr), SCARIEST (-i-ist)], [< *scare* + *-y*], [Colloq.], 1. causing alarm; frightening. 2. easily frightened; very timid.

scat (skat), *n.* [< ON. *skattr;* cf. SCADS], a tax, especially a land tax in the Shetland Islands: also spelled **scatt.**

scat (skat), *v.i.* [SCATTED (-id), SCATTING], [? a hiss + *cat*], [Colloq.], to go away: usually in the imperative.

scath (skath), *n.* & *v.t.* [Dial.], scathe.

scathe (skāth), *v.t.* [SCATHED (skāthd), SCATHING], [ME. *scathen;* ON. *skatha* < *skathi,* harm; akin to G. *schaden,* to harm; IE. base **skēth-,* **skəth-,* to injure, seen also in Gr. (*a*)*skēthēs,* unharmed], 1. [Archaic or Dial.], *a*) to injure or hurt. *b*) to blast; wither; sear. 2. to denounce fiercely. *n.* [Archaic or Dial.], injury or harm.

scath·ing (skāth'iŋ), *adj.* [ppr. of *scathe*], searing; blasting; withering: usually figurative, as, *scathing* remarks.

scat·o- (skat'ō, skat'ə), [< Gr. *skōr, skatos,* excrement], a combining form meaning *feces, excrement,* as in *scatology.*

scat·o·log·i·cal (skat'ə-loj'i-k'l), *adj.* of, having the nature of, or concerned with scatology.

sca·tol·o·gy (skə-tol'ə-ji), *n.* [*scato-* + *-logy*], 1. the study of feces or of fossil excrement. 2. the study of or obession with excrement, excretion, etc. in literature.

scat singing, [prob. < *scat, v.*], jazz vocal improvisation using meaningless, often humorously suggestive, syllables.

scatt (skat), *n.* a scat.

scat·ter (skat'ēr), *v.t.* [Early ME. *scateren, schateren;* prob. a freq. (cf. -ER) based on AS. *sceat* & ON. *skattr,* money, treasure; cf. SCAT, *n.,* SCADS], 1. *a*) to throw about; sprinkle here and there; strew loosely. *b*) to sprinkle over with something. 2. to separate and drive in several directions; rout; disperse. 3. to waste; dissipate. 4. in *physics, a*) to reflect or refract in an irregular, diffuse manner. *b*) to diffuse or deflect in an irregular manner. *v.i.* to separate and go in several directions: as, the crowd *scattered. n.* 1. a scattering. 2. what is scattered.

SYN.—**scatter** implies a strewing around loosely (to *scatter* seeds) or a forcible driving apart in different directions (the breeze *scattered* the papers); **disperse** implies a scattering which completely breaks up an assemblage and spreads the individuals far and wide (a people *dispersed* throughout the world); **dissipate** implies complete dissolution, as by crumbling, wasting, etc. (to *dissipate* a fortune); **dispel** suggests a scattering that drives away something that obscures, confuses, troubles, etc. (to *dispel* fears). See also **sprinkle.** —*ANT.* assemble, gather, collect.

scat·ter·brain (skat'ēr-brān'), *n.* a person who is incapable of concentrated thinking; giddy, frivolous, flighty person.

scat·ter·brained (skat'ēr-brānd'), *adj.* giddy; flighty; frivolous.

scat·ter·brains (skat'ēr-brānz'), *n.* a scatterbrain.

scat·ter·good (skat'ēr-good'), *n.* a person who wastes money, possessions, etc.; spendthrift.

scat·ter·ing (skat'ēr-iŋ), *adj.* 1. distributed over a wide area; found or occurring at irregular intervals. 2. cast so as to be distributed in small numbers among several or many candidates: said of votes.

scatter rug, any of various types of small rug for covering only part of a floor.

scaup (skôp), *n.* [*pl.* SCAUPS (skôps), SCAUP; see PLURAL, II, D, 1], [< *scaup,* obs. var. of *scalp*], any of several northern wild ducks related to the canvasback and redhead. Also **scaup duck.**

scav·enge (skav'inj), *v.t.* [SCAVENGED (-injd), SCAVENGING], [back-formation < *scavenger*], 1. to clean up, as streets, alleys, etc.; collect rubbish, dirt, or garbage from. 2. to remove burned gases from (the cylinder of an internal-combustion engine). 3. in *metallurgy,* to clean (molten metal) by using a substance that will combine chemically with the impurities present. *v.i.* 1. to act as a scavenger. 2. to look for food.

scav·eng·er (skav'in-jēr), *n.* [ME. *scavager* < Anglo-Fr. *scawage,* inspection < ONorm.Fr. *escauwer,* to inspect < Fl. *scauwen,* to see; for IE. base see SHOW; for *-n-* cf. MESSENGER], 1. a person who is employed to clean the streets, removing filth, garbage, etc. 2. any animal that eats refuse and decaying organic matter. 3. anything that removes impurities, refuse, etc.

Sc.B., *Scientiae Baccalaureus,* [L.], Bachelor of Science.

Sc.D., *Scientiae Doctor,* [L.], Doctor of Science.

sce·na·ri·o (si-nâr'i-ō', si-nä'ri-ō'), *n.* [*pl.* SCENARIOS (-ōz')], [It. < LL. *scenarius,* of stage scenes < L. *scena;* see SCENE], 1. an outline or synopsis of the plot of a drama, opera, etc., indicating scenes, characters, etc. 2. the outline of a motion picture, indicating the action in the order of its development, the scenes, the cast of characters and their appearances, etc.

sce·na·rist (si-nâr'ist, si-nä'rist), *n.* one who writes scenarios for motion pictures.

scend (send), *n.* [< *send,* assumed to be a contr. of *ascend*], the upward heaving of a ship: correlative of *pitch. v.i.* to be heaved upward, as by a wave: said of a ship. Also spelled **send.**

scene (sēn), *n.* [Fr. *scène;* L. *scena, scaena;* Gr. *skēnē,* covered place, tent, stage], 1. the place in which any event, real or imagined, occurs: as, London was the *scene* of his troubles. 2. the setting or locale of the action of a play, opera, story, etc.: as, the *scene* of *Hamlet* is Denmark. 3. a division of a play, usually part of an act, in which the action is continuous and there is no shift of place. 4. a part of a play, motion picture, story, etc. that constitutes a unit of development or action, as a passage between certain characters. 5. the painted screens, backdrops, and properties which represent the place of action in a play, motion picture, opera, or the like: as, change the *scenes.* 6. a view of people or places; picture or spectacle. 7. a display of strong or excited feeling before others: as, the women made a painful *scene* in court. 8. an episode, situation, or event, real or imaginary, especially as described or represented. 9. [Obs.], a theater stage. Abbreviated **sc.** —*SYN.* see **view.**

scen·er·y (sēn'ēr-i), *n.* [*pl.* SCENERIES (-iz)], [It. *scenario* < LL.; see SCENARIO], 1. painted screens, backdrops, hangings, flats, etc., used on the stage to represent places and surroundings. 2. the general aspect or appearance of a place; features of a landscape.

sce·nic (sē'nik, sen'ik), *adj.* [Fr. *scénique;* L. *scenicus;* Gr. *skēnikos* < *skēnē,* scene], 1. *a*) of the stage; dramatic; theatrical. *b*) relating to stage effects or stage scenery. 2. of natural scenery; affording many beautiful views; picturesque. 3. representing an action, event, situation, etc.

sce·ni·cal (sē'ni-k'l, sen'i-k'l), *adj.* scenic.

scenic railway, a roller coaster.

sce·no·graph·ic (sē'nə-graf'ik, sen'ə-graf'ik), *adj.* of scenography.

sce·no·graph·i·cal (sē'nə-graf'i-k'l, sen'ə-graf'i-k'l), *adj.* scenographic.

sce·nog·ra·phy (sē-nog'rə-fi), *n.* [Fr. *scénographie;* L. *scaenographia;* Gr. *skēnographia* < *skēnē,* scene + *graphein,* to write], 1. the art of drawing in perspective. 2. scene painting, especially in ancient Greece.

scent (sent), *v.t.* [ME. *senten;* OFr. *sentir* < L. *sentire,* to feel], 1. to smell; perceive by the olfactory sense. 2. to get a hint of; have a suspicion of. 3. to fill with an odor; perfume; give fragrance to. *v.i.* to hunt by the sense of smell. *n.* 1. a smell; odor. 2. the sense of smell. 3. a manufactured fluid preparation used to give fragrance; perfume. 4. an odor left by an animal, by which it is tracked in hunting; hence, 5. a track followed in hunting. 6. any clue by which something is followed or detected. 7. an intuitive capacity for discovering or detecting: as, a *scent* for news.

SYN.—**scent,** in this comparison, implies a relatively faint but pervasive smell, especially one characteristic of a particular thing (the *scent* of apple blossoms); **perfume** suggests a relatively strong, but usually pleasant, smell, either natural or manufactured (the rich *perfume* of carnations); **fragrance** always implies an agreeable, sweet smell, especially of growing things (the *fragrance* of a freshly mown lawn); **bouquet** is specifically applied to the fragrance of a wine or brandy; **redolence** implies a rich, pleasant combination of smells (the *redolence* of a grocery store). See also **smell.**—*ANT.* stench, stink.

scep·ter (sep'tēr), *n.* [ME. *sceptre, ceptre;* OFr. *ceptre,* *sceptre;* L. *sceptrum;* Gr. *skēptron,* staff to lean on < base of *skēptesthai,* to prop oneself, lean on something], 1. a rod or staff, highly ornamented, held by rulers on ceremonial occasions as a symbol of authority and sovereignty; hence, 2. royal or imperial authority; sovereignty. *v.t.* to furnish with a scepter; invest with royal or imperial authority. Also spelled **sceptre.**

scep·tic (skep′tik), *n. & adj.* skeptic.

scep·ti·cal (skep′ti-k'l), *adj.* skeptical.

scep·ti·cism (skep′tə-siz'm), *n.* skepticism.

scep·tre (sep′tẽr), *n. & v.t.* [SCEPTRED (-tẽrd), SCEPTRING], scepter: chiefly British spelling.

sch., 1. school. 2. schooner.

Schacht, Hjal·mar (yäl′mär shäkht), 1877– ; German financier; minister of national economy (1934–1937): tried at Nuremburg for war crimes but acquitted (1947).

schat·chen (shät′khən), *n.* [Yid. < Heb. *shadhkhān*], a man who arranged marriages among European Jews; marriage broker.

Schaum·burg-Lip·pe (shoum′boorkh-lip′ə), *n.* a former division of northwestern Germany: earlier, a principality.

sched·ule (skej′ool; Brit. shed′yool), *n.* [altered (after ML. *schedula*) < ME. *sedule;* OFr. *cedule;* LL. *scedula,* dim. of L. *sceda, scheda,* a leaf of paper < Gr. *schidē,* splinter of wood, split piece < *schizein,* to split], 1. a list, catalogue, or inventory of details, often as an explanatory supplement to a will, bill of sale, deed, etc. 2. a list of times of recurring events, projected operations, arriving and departing trains, etc.; timetable; hence, 3. a timed plan for a procedure or project. *v.t.* [SCHEDULED (-oold; Brit. -yoold), SCHEDULING], 1. to place or include in a schedule. 2. to make a schedule of. 3. to appoint or plan for a certain time or date.

scheel·ite (shēl′īt), *n.* [after K. W. *Scheele* (1742–1786), Swed. chemist], native calcium tungstate, $CaWO_4$, an important ore of tungsten.

schef·fer·ite (shef′ẽr-īt′), *n.* [after H. T. *Scheffer* (1710–1759), Swed. mineralogist], a brownish or blackish pyroxene containing manganese and sometimes much iron.

Sche·he·ra·za·de (shə-hâr′ə-zä′də, shə-hêr′ə-zä′də), *n.* in *The Arabian Nights,* the Sultan's bride, teller of the tales, who saves her life by keeping the Sultan interested in them.

Schel·de (skhel′də), *n.* Scheldt.

Scheldt (skelt), *n.* a river in France, Belgium, and the Netherlands, flowing into the North Sea: length, 270 mi.: also **Schelde:** French name, *Escaut.*

Schel·ling, Fried·rich Wil·helm Jo·seph von (frē′driH vil′helm yō′zef fôn shel′iŋ), 1775–1854; German philosopher and writer.

sche·ma (skē′mə), *n.* [*pl.* SCHEMATA (-mə-tə)], [L.; see SCHEME], an outline, systematic arrangement, diagram, scheme, or plan.

sche·mat·ic (skē-mat′ik), *adj.* [Mod. L. *schematicus*], of, or having the nature of, a scheme or schema; diagrammatic.

sche·mat·i·cal·ly (skē-mat′i-k'l-i, skē-mat′ik-li), *adv.* in a schematic manner.

sche·ma·tism (skē′mə-tiz'm), *n.* [Mod. L. *schematismus* < Gr. *schēmatismos* < *schēmatizein,* to form; see SCHEME], a set form for classification or exposition; arrangement of parts according to a scheme; design.

sche·ma·ti·za·tion (skē′mə-ti-zā′shən, skē′mə-tī-zā′shən), *n.* a schematizing or being schematized.

sche·ma·tize (skē′mə-tīz′), *v.i. & v.t.* [SCHEMATIZED (-tīzd′), SCHEMATIZING], [Gr. *schēmatizein*], to form, form into, or arrange according to, a scheme or schemes.

scheme (skēm), *n.* [L. *schema;* Gr. *schēma, schēmatos,* a form, appearance, plan; akin to *schein, echein,* to hold, have < IE. base **segh-,* to hold, hold fast, conquer, seen also in Sans. *sáhas,* power, victory, Goth. *sigis,* G. *sieg,* victory], 1. a carefully arranged and systematic program of action; systematic plan for attaining some object. 2. an orderly combination of things on a definite plan; system. 3. a plot; underhand intrigue. 4. a visionary plan or project. 5. an outline or diagram showing different parts or elements of an object or system. 6. an astrological diagram. *v.t.* [SCHEMED (skēmd), SCHEMING], 1. to make a scheme for; plan as a scheme; devise; contrive. 2. to plan in an underhand way; plot. *v.i.* 1. to make schemes; form plans. 2. to plot; intrigue. —*SYN.* see **plan.**

schem·ing (skēm′iŋ), *adj.* crafty; tricky; given to forming crafty schemes or plots.

Sche·nec·ta·dy (skə-nek′tə-di), *n.* a city in east central New York: pop., 82,000.

scher·zan·do (sker-tsän′dō, sker-tsan′dō), *adj.* [It., ppr. of *scherzare,* to play < *scherzo;* see SCHERZO], in *music,* playful; sportive. *adv.* in *music,* playfully; sportively: a direction to the performer.

scher·zo (sker′tsō), *n.* [*pl.* SCHERZOS (-tsōz), SCHERZI (-tsē)], [It., a jest, sport < G. *scherz,* a jest], a lively, playful movement in 3/4 time, usually following a slow one, and often constituting the third section of a sonata, symphony, or quartet.

Schia·pa·rel·li, Gio·van·ni Vir·gi·nio (jô-vän′nē vêr-jē′nyô skyä′pä-rel′lē), 1835–1910; Italian astronomer.

Schick, Bé·la (bā′lə shik), 1877– ; American pediatrician, born in Hungary; devised Schick test.

Schick test (shik), [after B. *Schick*], a test to determine immunity to diphtheria, made by injecting dilute diphtheria toxin under the skin: if an area of inflammation results, the patient is not immune.

schil·ler (shil′ẽr), *n.* [G., color play < *schillern,* to change color], a peculiar bronzelike luster in certain minerals, often iridescent, caused by internal reflection.

Schil·ler, Jo·hann Chri·stoph Fried·rich von (yō′hän kris′tôf frē′driH fôn shil′ẽr), 1759–1805; German poet and dramatist.

schil·ler·ize (shil′ẽr-īz′), *v.t.* [SCHILLERIZED (-īzd′), SCHILLERIZING], to give schiller to (a mineral) by the formation of minute cavities in the faces of crystals in parallel planes.

schil·ling (shil′iŋ), *n.* [G.; see SHILLING], 1. the monetary unit and a coin of Austria, originally equal to about 14 cents, but valued at about 4 cents in 1956. 2. a former minor coin of Germany.

schip·per·ke (skip′ẽr-ki), *n.* [D. dial., little skipper], any of a Belgian breed of small, black, short-haired dog with a foxlike head, erect ears, a broad chest, and no tail, originally used as watchdogs on boats.

schism (siz''m), *n.* [ME. *scisme;* OFr. *cisme, scisme;* LL. *schisma;* Gr. *schisma* < Gr. *schizein,* to cleave, cut], 1. a split or division in an organized group or society, as the result of difference of opinion, of doctrine, etc.; especially, a formal split or division in the Christian church. 2. the offense of causing or trying to cause a split or division in the church or in religion. 3. a sect formed by such a split or division.

schis·mat·ic (siz-mat′ik), *adj.* [ME. *scismatike;* OFr. *scismatique;* LL. *schismaticus;* Gr. *schismatikos*], 1. of, characteristic of, or having the nature of, schism. 2. tending to, causing, or guilty of schism. *n.* a person who causes or participates in schism.

schis·mat·i·cal (siz-mat′i-k'l), *adj.* schismatic.

schist (shist), *n.* [Fr. *schiste* < L. *schistos,* split; Gr. *schistos,* easily cleft < *schizein,* to cleave], a crystalline rock that can be easily split into layers.

schist·ose (shis′tōs), *adj.* of, or having the nature or form of, schist.

schis·to·some (shis′tə-sōm′), *n.* [Mod. L. *Schistosoma* < Gr. *schistos,* cleft + *sōma,* body], any of a group of flukes that live as parasites in the blood of mammals and birds, causing a disease that affects the intestines, liver, spleen, etc.

schis·to·so·mi·a·sis (shis′tə-sō-mī′ə-sis), *n.* [< *schistosome* + *-iasis*], the disease caused by schistosomes.

schist·ous (shis′təs), *adj.* schistose.

schiz·o- (skiz′ō, skiz′ə), [< Gr. *schizein,* to cleave, cut], a combining form meaning *split, cleavage, division,* as in *schizocarp, schizophrenia:* also, before a vowel, **schiz-.**

schiz·o·carp (skiz′ə-kärp′), *n.* [*schizo-* + *-carp*], in *botany,* a dry fruit, as of the maple, that splits at maturity into two or more one-seeded carpels which remain closed.

schiz·o·car·pous (skiz′ə-kär′pəs), *adj.* of, or having the nature of, a schizocarp.

schiz·o·gen·e·sis (skiz′ə-jen′ə-sis), *n.* [Mod. L.; *schizo-* + *-genesis*], in *biology,* reproduction by fission.

schiz·oid (skiz′oid), *n.* [*schiz-* + *-oid*], a person who has schizophrenia. *adj.* of, like, or having schizophrenia.

schiz·o·my·cete (skiz′ō-mī-sēt′), *n.* [*schizo-* + *-mycete*], any of the class of vegetable microorganisms comprising the bacteria; bacterium.

schiz·o·my·co·sis (skiz′ō-mī-kō′sis), *n.* [Mod. L.; *schizo-* + *mycosis*], any disease caused by schizomycetes.

schiz·o·phrene (skiz′ə-frēn′), *n.* [< *schizophrenia*], a person who has schizophrenia.

schiz·o·phre·ni·a (skiz′ə-frē′ni-ə), *n.* [Mod. L. < *schizo-* + Gr. *phrēn,* the mind], a mental disorder characterized by indifference, withdrawal, hallucinations, and delusions of persecution and omnipotence, often with unimpaired intelligence: a more inclusive term than *dementia praecox,* avoiding the implications of age and deterioration.

schiz·o·phren·ic (skiz′ə-fren′ik), *adj.* of or having schizophrenia. *n.* a person having schizophrenia.

schiz·o·phyte (skiz′ə-fīt′), *n.* [*schizo-* + *-phyte*], in *botany,* any of a group of plants, including the schizomycetes, which consist of a single cell, or a chain or colony of cells, and reproduce only by simple fission or by asexual spores.

schiz·o·pod (skiz′ə-pod′), *n.* [< Mod. L. *Schizopoda* < Gr. *schizopous,* having parted toes; see SCHIZO- & -POD], any of a group of crustaceans, formerly considered an order, resembling the shrimp but having a soft shell. *adj.* of the schizopods.

schiz·o·thy·mi·a (skiz'ə-thī'mi-ə), *n.* [Mod. L. < *schizo-* + Gr. *thymos*, spirit], a mild form of schizophrenia, characterized by introversion, withdrawal, etc.
schiz·o·thy·mic (skiz'ə-thī'mik), *adj.* of or characterized by schizothymia.
Schle·gel, Au·gust Wil·helm von (ou'goost vil'helm fôn shlā'g'l), 1767–1845; German poet and critic.
Schlegel, Fried·rich von (frē'driH), 1772–1829; brother of *August;* German philosopher, poet, and critic.
Schlei·er·ma·cher, Fried·rich Ernst Da·ni·el (frē'driH ernst dä'ni-el shlī'ẽr-mä'khẽr), 1768–1834; German theologian and philosopher.
schle·mihl, schle·miel (shlə-mēl'), *n.* [Yid. < Heb. proper name *Shelumiēl* (lit., my peace is God); current meaning prob. developed by metonymy and partly popularized after Peter *Schlemihl*, title character of a novel by Adelbert von Chamisso (1814)], [Slang], an inefficient, bungling person who habitually fails or is easily victimized.
Schle·si·en (shlā'zi-ən), *n.* Silesia: the German name.
Schles·wig (shles'wig; G. shläs'viH), *n.* a former duchy of Denmark: now a part of Schleswig-Holstein: Danish name, *Slesvig*: see **Holstein**, map.
Schles·wig-Hol·stein (shles'wig-hōl'stīn; G. shläs'viH-hōl'shtīn), *n.* a province of Prussia, on the border of Denmark: area, 5,420 sq. mi.; pop., 2,651,000 (est. 1946); capital, Kiel: formed from the former Danish duchies of Lauenburg, Holstein, and part of Schleswig.
Schley, Win·field Scott (win'fēld slī), 1839–1911; American naval officer; victor in battle of Santiago (1898).
Schlie·mann, Hein·rich (hīn'riH shlē'män), 1822–1890; German archaeologist.
schlie·ren (shlêr'ən), *n.pl.* [*sing.* SCHLIERE (-ə)], [G., lit., streaks], small streaks or masses in igneous rocks, differing in composition from the main rock but blending gradually into it.
schmaltz (shmälts), *n.* [via Yid. < G. *schmalz*, lit., melted fat; akin to *schmelzen*, to melt], [Slang], 1. anything very sentimental and unctuous, as certain music, literature, etc. 2. unctuous sentimentalism.
Schmitt, Ber·na·dotte Ev·er·ly (bũr'nə-dot' ev'ẽr-li shmit), 1886– ; American historian.
schnap·per (shnap'ẽr, snap'ẽr), *n.* [altered (after G. *schnapper*) < *snapper*], a snapper (kind of fish) of Australia and New Zealand.
schnapps (shnäps, shnaps), *n.* [G., a dram, nip < D. *snaps*, lit., a gulp, mouthful; cf. SNAP], 1. Holland gin. 2. any strong alcoholic liquor. Also spelled **schnaps.**
schnau·zer (shnou'zẽr), *n.* [G. < *schnauzen*, to snarl, growl], any of a breed of small active terrier with a close, wiry coat, originally bred in Germany: also called *wire-haired pinscher.*

SCHNAUZER (18–20 in. high at shoulder)

schnit·zel (shnit's'l), *n.* [G.], a cutlet of meat, usually of veal.
Schnitz·ler, Ar·thur (är'toor shnits'lẽr), 1862–1931; Austrian novelist, dramatist, and physician.
schnor·rer (shnôr'ẽr), *n.* [Yid.; G. *schnurrer* < *schnurren*, to whir, purr (of echoic origin): because of the sound made by the musical instruments carried by the beggars], a beggar.
schnoz·zle (shnoz''l), *n.* [via Yid. < G. *schnauze;* akin to Eng. *snout*], [Slang], the nose.
Scho·field, John Mc·Al·lis·ter (mək-al'is-tẽr skō'fēld), 1831–1906; American general and statesman.
schol·ar (skol'ẽr), *n.* [ME. *scoler* < AS. *scolere* or OFr. *escoler;* both < LL. *scholaris*, relating to a school < L. *schola*, a school], 1. a learned person; one trained in a special branch of learning, as literature, arts, etc.; advanced student. 2. a student who is given money or other aid, as by some institution, to continue his studies. 3. a student; person attending a school. 4. a person who can read and write. —*SYN.* see **pupil.**
schol·arch (skol'ärk), *n.* [Gr. *scholarchēs* < *scholē*, a school + *archein*, to rule], 1. the head of a school. 2. the head of a school of philosophy in ancient Athens.
schol·ar·ly (skol'ẽr-li), *adj.* 1. of or characteristic of scholars. 2. having or showing much knowledge, accuracy, and critical ability. 3. studious; devoted to learning. 4. orderly and thorough in methods of study. *adv.* like a scholar.
schol·ar·ship (skol'ẽr-ship'), *n.* [*scholar* + *-ship*], 1. the quality of knowledge and learning shown by a student; standard of work done in school. 2. the systematized knowledge of a learned man, exhibiting accuracy, critical ability, and thoroughness; erudition. 3. a specific gift of money or other aid, as by an institution, to help a student continue his studies. 4. a foundation to supply such aid.
scho·las·tic (skə-las'tik), *adj.* [L. *scholasticus;* Gr. *scholastikos* < *scholazein*, to devote one's leisure to study, be at leisure < *scholē;* see SCHOOL (institution)], 1. of schools, colleges, universities, students, teachers, and studies; educational; academic. 2. of or characteristic of medieval schoolmen and their methods. 3. pedantic, dogmatic, formal, etc. 4. of secondary schools: as, *scholastic* football games. *n.* 1. a student; scholar. 2. a schoolman (sense 1). 3. a person who is devoted to logical subtleties and quibblings; pedant. 4. a person who favors scholasticism. Abbreviated **schol.** Also **Scholastic** (for *n.* 2 & 4, *adj.* 2).
scho·las·ti·cal (skō-las'ti-k'l), *adj.* scholastic.
scho·las·ti·cism (skə-las'tə-siz'm), *n.* 1. [often S-], the system of logic, philosophy, and theology of medieval university scholars, or schoolmen, from the 10th to the 15th century, based upon Aristotelian logic and the writings of the early Christian fathers. 2. an insistence upon traditional doctrines and methods.
scho·li·ast (skō'li-ast'), *n.* [LL. *scholiasta;* LGr. *scholiastēs* < *scholiazein*, to comment < Gr. *scholion*, a comment < *scholē;* see SCHOOL (institution)], one who writes notes and comments in the margins of books and manuscripts; especially, an ancient interpreter and annotator of the classics.
scho·li·as·tic (skō'li-as'tik), *adj.* of a scholiast or scholiasts.
scho·li·um (skō'li-əm), *n.* [*pl.* SCHOLIA (-ə)], [ML. < Gr. *scholion* < *scholē;* see SCHOOL (institution)], 1. a marginal note or commentary, especially on the text of a Greek or Latin writer. 2. a note following or with a proof or demonstration, as in mathematics.
Schön·berg, Arnold (shōn'bẽrg; G. shön'berkh), 1874–1951; Austrian composer and conductor in America.
school (sko͞ol), *n.* [ME. *scole;* AS. *scol;* L. *schola*, school < Gr. *scholē*, leisure, that in which leisure is employed, discussion, philosophy, place where spare time is employed, school], 1. a place or institution for teaching and learning; establishment for education; specifically, *a*) an institution for teaching children: see **grammar school, high school, secondary school,** etc. *b*) a place for training and instruction in some special field, skill, etc.: as, a dancing *school. c*) a college or university. *d*) in the Middle Ages, a seminary of logic, metaphysics, and theology. 2. the building or buildings, classrooms, laboratories, etc. of any such establishment. 3. all the students, or pupils, and teachers at any such establishment: as, the *school* was given a holiday. 4. the period of instruction at any such establishment; regular session of teaching: as, *school* begins in September. 5. the process of being educated; formal training and instruction; formal education: as, he never finished *school.* 6. any situation, set of circumstances, or experiences through which a person gains knowledge, training, or discipline: as, the *school* of hard knocks. 7. a particular division of an institution of learning; special department of a college or university: as, the junior *school*, the *school* of liberal arts. 8. a group of people held together by the same teachings, beliefs, opinions, methods, etc.; followers or disciples of a teacher, leader, or creed: as, the French Impressionist *school.* 9. a way of life; style of customs, manners, etc.: as, a gentleman of the old *school.* 10. formerly, the regulations and drill instructions governing duties and training of any branch of the army or navy: as, the *school* of the soldier. *v.t.* 1. to train; teach; instruct; educate. 2. to discipline; control. 3. [Archaic], to reprimand. *adj.* 1. of a school or schools. 2. [Obs.], of the schoolmen (sense 1). Abbreviated **sch., S., s.** —*SYN.* see **group, teach.**
school (sko͞ol), *n.* [D., a crowd, school of fish; see SHOAL (a crowd)], a large number of fish or water animals of the same kind swimming together. *v.i.* to swim together in a school, as fish, whales, etc.
school age, 1. the age at which a child may or must be sent to school. 2. the years during which attendance at school is required or customary.
school board, a group of people, elected or appointed, who are in charge of local public schools.
school·book (sko͞ol'book'), *n.* a book used for study in schools; textbook.
school·boy (sko͞ol'boi'), *n.* a boy attending school. *adj.* characteristic of a boy attending school.
school day, 1. a day on which school is in session. 2. the time, in any day, when school is in session.
school·fel·low (sko͞ol'fel'ō), *n.* a person educated at the same school and at the same time as another.
school·girl (sko͞ol'gũrl'), *n.* a girl attending school. *adj.* characteristic of a girl attending school.
school·house (sko͞ol'hous'), *n.* a building used as a school.
school·ing (sko͞ol'iŋ), *n.* 1. formal instruction at school; education. 2. cost of instruction and living at school. 3. [Archaic], disciplinary correction; reprimand.
school·ma'am (sko͞ol'mäm', sko͞ol'mam'), *n.* [Colloq.], a schoolmarm.
school·man (sko͞ol'mən), *n.* [*pl.* SCHOOLMEN (-mən)], 1. [often S-], one of the medieval university teachers of philosophy, logic, and theology; scholastic. 2. (sko͞ol'man'), [*pl.* SCHOOLMEN (-men')], a professional teacher, educator, or scholar.
school·marm (sko͞ol'mäm', sko͞ol'märm'), *n.* [Colloq.], a woman schoolteacher, especially one who tends to be old-fashioned, prudish, and pedantic: often humorous or satirical.

school·mas·ter (sko͞ol′mas′tẽr, sko͞ol′mäs′tẽr), *n.* 1. a man who teaches in a school. 2. a man who is manager, head, or principal of a school. 3. a person or thing that disciplines or instructs. 4. a snapper (kind of fish).

school·mate (sko͞ol′māt′), *n.* a person educated at the same school and at the same time as another.

school·mis·tress (sko͞ol′mis′tris), *n.* 1. a woman who teaches in a school. 2. a woman principal of a school.

school·room (sko͞ol′ro͞om′, sko͞ol′room′), *n.* a room in which pupils are instructed, usually in a school.

school·teach·er (sko͞ol′tēch′ẽr), *n.* a person who teaches in a school.

school·yard (sko͞ol′yärd′), *n.* the ground around or near a school, especially when used for games and sports.

school year, the part of a year when school is in session, usually from September to June.

schoon·er (sko͞on′ẽr), *n.* [< New England word *scoon,* to skim or skip upon the water], 1. a ship with two or more masts, rigged fore and aft. 2. [Colloq.], a covered wagon: in full, **prairie schooner.** 3. a large beer glass, usually holding a pint. Abbreviated **sch.**

schoon·er-rigged (sko͞on′ẽr-rigd′), *adj.* rigged like a schooner, fore and aft.

Scho·pen·hau·er, Ar·thur (är′toor shō′pən-hou′ẽr), 1788–1860; German philosopher.

Scho·pen·hau·er·ism (shō′pən-hou′ẽr-iz′m), *n.* the pessimistic philosophy of Schopenhauer, which holds that ultimate reality is "will," an all-impelling force expressing itself in the individual as the will to live, and that only by renouncing desire can the will be allayed.

schorl (shôrl), *n.* [G. *schörl*], tourmaline, especially the black variety.

schot·tische, schot·tish (shot′ish), *n.* [< G. (*der*) *schottische* (*tanz*), (the) Scottish (dance)], 1. a form of round dance in 2/4 time, similar to the polka, but with a slower tempo. 2. music for this dance.

Schrö·ding·er, Er·win (er′vēn shrö′diŋ-ẽr), 1887–1961; German physicist; Nobel prize in physics, 1933.

Schu·bert, Franz Peter (fränts sho͞o′bẽrt; G. sho͞o′-bert), 1797–1828; Austrian composer.

Schu·mann, Robert (sho͞o′män), 1810–1856; German composer.

Schu·mann-Heink, Ernestine (sho͞o′mən-hīnk′), 1861–1936; American contralto, born in Austria.

Schurz, Carl (shoorts), 1829–1906; American statesman, Union general, editor, and lawyer, born in Germany.

‡**Schutz·staf·fel** (shoots′shtä′fəl), *n.* [G., protective rank], the personal bodyguard of Adolf Hitler; later, the Elite Guard of the Nazi militia, used to suppress opposition in Germany and conquered countries: also called *Black Shirts*: abbreviated **S.S., SS.**

Schuy·ler, Philip John (skī′lẽr), 1733–1804; American general and statesman.

Schuy·ler·ville (skī′lẽr-vil′), *n.* a village in New York: pop., 1,400: former name, *Saratoga.*

Schuyl·kill (sko͞ol′kil), *n.* a river in southeastern Pennsylvania, flowing into the Delaware River at Philadelphia: length, 130 mi.

schwa (shwä; G. shvä), *n.* [G. < Heb. *sh'wa*], 1. the unstressed, central vowel sound of most unstressed syllables in English; neutralized sound of *a* in *ago, e* in *agent, i* in *sanity,* etc. 2. the symbol (ə) used to represent this sound, as in the International Phonetic Alphabet and this dictionary.

Schwab, Charles Michael (shwäb, shwôb), 1862–1939; American steel manufacturer and financier.

Schwa·ben (shvä′bən), *n.* Swabia: the German name.

Schwarz·wald (shvärts′vält′), *n.* the Black Forest: the German name.

Schweit·zer, Al·bert (äl′bert shvīt′sẽr; Eng. shwīt′sẽr), 1875– ; Alsatian theologian, musician, and medical missionary in Africa.

Schweiz (shvīts), *n.* Switzerland: the German name.

schwei·zer·kä·se (shvīt′sẽr-ke′zə, swīt′sẽr-kā′zə), *n.* [G.], Swiss cheese.

Schwe·rin (shvā-rēn′), *n.* the capital of Mecklenburg, in northern Germany: pop., 94,000.

Schwyz (shvēts), *n.* 1. a canton of central Switzerland: pop., 78,000. 2. its capital: pop., 11,000.

sci., 1. science. 2. scientific.

sci·ae·noid (sī-ē′noid), *adj.* [< L. *sciaena,* kind of fish (Gr. *skiaina*); + *-oid*], of a group of fishes most of which have a large air bladder used in producing various noises. *n.* a fish of this group, as the drumfish.

sci·a·gram (sī′ə-gram′), *n.* a skiagram.

sci·a·graph (sī′ə-graf′, sī′ə-gräf′), *n.* & *v.t.* skiagraph.

sci·am·a·chy (sī-am′ə-ki), *n.* [Gr. *skiamachia* < *skia,* a shadow + *machein,* to fight], 1. a sham fight. 2. a fighting with shadows or imaginary enemies.

sci·at·ic (sī-at′ik), *adj.* [Fr. *sciatique;* ML. *sciaticus;* altered < L. *ischiadicus;* Gr. *ischiadikos* < *ischion,* the hip, hip joint], of, in the region of, or affecting the hip or its nerves.

sci·at·i·ca (sī-at′i-kə), *n.* [Mod. L. < ML. *sciaticus*], any painful condition in the region of the hip and thighs; especially, neuritis of the long nerve (*sciatic nerve*) passing down the back of the thigh.

sci·ence (sī′əns), *n.* [ME. *sciens;* Late OFr.; L. *scientia* < *sciens,* ppr. of *scire,* to know], 1. originally, state or fact of knowing; knowledge, often as opposed to *intuition, belief,* etc. 2. systematized knowledge derived from observation, study, and experimentation carried on in order to determine the nature or principles of what is being studied. 3. a branch of knowledge or study, especially one concerned with establishing and systematizing facts, principles, and methods, as by experiments and hypotheses: as, the *science* of music. 4. *a*) the systematized knowledge of nature and the physical world. *b*) any branch of this. See **natural science.** 5. skill based on training: often humorous, as, the *science* of boxing. 6. [S-], Christian Science.

science fiction, imaginative stories centered about some projected, often fantastic, scientific development.

sci·en·tial (sī-en′shəl), *adj.* 1. of or producing science, or knowledge. 2. having efficient knowledge.

sci·en·tif·ic (sī′ən-tif′ik), *adj.* [Fr. *scientifique;* ML. *scientificus* < L. *scientia,* knowledge + *facere,* to make; orig. used as transl. of Gr. *epistēmonikos,* making knowledge], 1. of or dealing with science: as, *scientific* study. 2. used in or for natural science: as, *scientific* apparatus. 3. *a*) based on, using, or in accordance with, the principles and methods of science; systematic and exact: as, *scientific* classification. *b*) trained in following or observing the principles and methods of science: as, a *scientific* thinker. 4. *a*) done according to methods gained by training: as, *scientific* boxing. *b*) having or showing skill and training; skillful.

sci·en·tif·i·cal·ly (sī′ən-tif′i-k'l-i, sī′ən-tif′ik-li), *adv.* in a scientific manner.

sci·en·tism (sī′ən-tiz′m), *n.* 1. the techniques, beliefs, or attitudes characteristic of scientists. 2. the principle that scientific methods can be applied in all fields of investigation: often a disparaging usage.

sci·en·tist (sī′ən-tist), *n.* 1. a specialist in science, especially natural science. 2. [S-], a Christian Scientist.

scil·i·cet (sil′i-set′), *adv.* [ME.; L., contr. of *scire licet,* it is permitted to know], namely; to wit; that is to say: abbreviated **sc., scil., SS., ss.**

Scil·ly Isles (sil′i), a group of numerous small islands off Cornwall, England: pop., 1,700.

scim·i·tar, scim·i·ter (sim′ə-tẽr), *n.* [It. *scimitarra;* ? Continental borrowing < *smiler,* used for *scimitar* in the 16th & 17th c.], a short, curved sword with an edge on the convex side, used by Turks, Arabs, etc.

scin·coid (siŋ′koid), *adj.* [Mod. L. *scincoides* < L. *scincus* (see SKINK); + *-oid*], of or like the skinks. *n.* a scincoid lizard.

scin·til·la (sin-til′ə), *n.* [L.], 1. a spark; hence, 2. a particle; the least trace: used only figuratively.

scin·til·lant (sin′tə-lənt), *adj.* scintillating; sparkling.

scin·til·late (sin′tə-lāt′), *v.i.* [SCINTILLATED (-id), SCINTILLATING], [< L. *scintillatus,* pp. of *scintillare,* to sparkle < *scintilla,* a spark], 1. to give off sparks; flash; sparkle. 2. to sparkle intellectually; be brilliant and witty. 3. to twinkle, as a star. *v.t.* to give off (sparks, flashes, etc.); sparkle with.

scin·til·lat·ing (sin′tə-lāt′iŋ), *adj.* that scintillates.

scin·til·la·tion (sin′tə-lā′shən), *n.* 1. the act of scintillating; sparkling. 2. a spark; flash. 3. a brilliant display of wit. 4. in *astronomy,* the twinkling of the stars. 5. in *nuclear physics,* the flash of light made by a ray or particle from a radioactive material upon striking a crystal detector.

scintillation counter, an instrument for detecting and measuring radioactivity: it utilizes a photoelectric cell in converting scintillations into a signal.

sci·o·graph (sī′ə-graf′, sī′ə-gräf′), *n.* a skiagraph.

sci·o·lism (sī′ə-liz′m), *n.* [< L. *sciolus,* smatterer, dim. of *scius,* knowing < *scire,* to know; cf. SCIENCE], surface knowledge; shallow learning; quackery; charlatanism.

sci·o·list (sī′ə-list), *n.* [see SCIOLISM], a person whose knowledge is on the surface; pretender to learning.

sci·o·lis·tic (sī′ə-lis′tik), *adj.* of or showing sciolism.

sci·on (sī′ən), *n.* [ME. *sioun, ciun;* OFr. *cion;* prob. < L. *sectio;* see SECTION], 1. a shoot or bud of a plant, especially one for planting or grafting: also spelled **cion.** 2. a descendant.

Sci·o·to (sī-ō′tə, sī-ō′tō), *n.* a river in central Ohio, flowing southward into the Ohio River: length, 237 mi.

Scip·i·o (sip′i-ō′), *n.* 1. (*Publius Cornelius Scipio Africanus*), Roman general; lived 237–183 B.C.; defeated Hannibal (202 B.C.): called *the Elder* (or *Major*). 2. (*Publius Cornelius Scipio Aemilianus Africanus*), grandson (through adoption) of the above; Roman general; lived 185–129 B.C.; destroyed Carthage (146 B.C.): called *the Younger* (or *Minor*).

‡**sci·re fa·ci·as** (sī′rē fā′shi-as′), [L., that you cause to know], in *law,* 1. a writ, founded on a record, requiring the person against whom it is issued to appear and show cause why the record should not be enforced or an-

nulled. 2. a proceeding begun by issuing such a writ.

scir·rhoid (skir′oid), *adj.* like a scirrhus.

scir·rhos·i·ty (ski-ros′ə-ti), *n.* the quality or condition of being scirrhous.

scir·rhous (skir′əs), *adj.* [Mod. L. *scirrhosus* < *scirrhus*], of, or having the nature of, a scirrhus.

scir·rhus (skir′əs), *n.* [*pl.* SCIRRHI (-ī), SCIRRHUSES (-iz)], [Mod. L. < L. *scirros;* Gr. *skirrhos,* hardened swelling, tumor < *skiros,* hard], a hard cancer or cancerous tumor made up of much fibrous connective tissue.

scis·sile (sis′il), *adj.* [L. *scissilis* < *scissus,* pp. of *scindere,* to cut], that can be cut or split smoothly and easily, as into plates or laminae.

scis·sion (sizh′ən, sish′ən), *n.* [Fr.; LL. *scissio* < L. *scissus,* pp. of *scindere,* to cut], the act of cutting, dividing, or splitting, or the state of being cut, divided, or split; division; separation; fission.

scis·sor (siz′ẽr), *v.t.* [< *scissors*], to cut, cut off, or cut out with scissors.

scis·sors (siz′ẽrz), *n.pl.* [ME. *sisoures;* OFr. *cisoires* < LL. *cisoria,* pl. of *cisorium,* cutting tool < *caedere,* to cut; Eng. sp. altered by association with L. *scissor,* one who cuts < *scissus,* pp. of *scindere,* to cut], 1. a cutting instrument, smaller than shears, with two opposing blades, each having a looped handle, which are pivoted together in the middle so that they can slide over each other as the instrument is closed: also called *pair of scissors.* 2. [construed as sing.], *a)* a gymnastic feat or exercise in which the legs are moved in a way suggestive of the opening and closing of scissors. *b)* a scissors hold.

scissors hold, a wrestling hold in which one contestant clasps the other with his legs.

scissors kick, a form of swimming kick (used especially with a side stroke) in which one leg is bent back at the knee, the other swung forward, then both brought together with a snap.

scis·sor·tail (siz′ẽr-tāl′), *n.* a variety of flycatcher found in the southern United States and Mexico, having a forked tail: also **scissor-tailed flycatcher.**

scis·sure (sizh′ẽr, sish′ẽr), *n.* [ME.; L. *scissura* < *scindere,* to cut], a cleft or opening, natural or made by cutting.

sci·u·rine (sī′yoo-rin′, sī′yoo-rin), *adj.* [< L. *sciurus* (Gr. *skiouros,* squirrel < *skia,* a shadow + *oura,* a tail); + *-ine*], designating or of a family of rodents consisting of squirrels, ground squirrels, marmots, etc.

sci·u·roid (sī-yoor′oid), *adj.* [< L. *sciurus* (see SCIURINE); + *-oid*], 1. like a squirrel. 2. in *botany,* like a squirrel's tail, as the spikes of barley.

sclaff (sklaf, skläf), *v.i.* [< Scot. *sclaf,* to shuffle; of echoic origin], in *golf,* to strike or scrape the ground before hitting the ball. *v.t.* in *golf,* 1. to scrape (a club) along the ground before hitting the ball. 2. to make (a stroke) in this way. 3. to hit (the ball) in this way. *n.* a sclaffing stroke.

scler-, sclero-.

scle·ra (sklêr′ə), *n.* [Mod. L. < Gr. *sklēros,* hard], a tough, white, fibrous membrane covering all of the eyeball except the area covered by the cornea.

scle·ren·chy·ma (skli-reŋ′ki-mə), *n.* [Mod. L. < Gr. *sklēros,* hard + *enchyma,* infusion; cf. PARENCHYMA], in *botany,* plant tissue of thick-walled cells, as in the stems of palms, shells of nuts, etc.

scle·ri·a·sis (skli-rī′ə-sis), *n.* [Mod. L.; Gr. *sklēriasis* < *sklēria,* hardness < *sklēros,* hard], a hardening, or induration, of tissue.

scle·rite (sklêr′īt), *n.* [*scler-* + *-ite*], one of the hard plates or spicules forming the shell-like covering of certain invertebrates.

scle·rit·ic (skli-rit′ik), *adj.* of or having scleritis: also **sclerotitic.**

scle·rit·is (skli-rī′tis), *n.* [see -ITIS], inflammation of the sclera: also **sclerotitis.**

scle·ro- (sklêr′ō, skler′ə), [< Gr. *sklēros,* hard], a combining form meaning: 1. *hard,* as in *sclerometer.* 2. *of the sclera.* Also, before a vowel, **scler-.**

scler·o·der·ma (sklêr′ə-dũr′mə, skler′ə-dũr′mə), *n.* [Mod. L.; *sclero-* + *derma*], a chronic disease in which the skin becomes hard and rigid.

scler·o·der·ma·tous (sklêr′ə-dũr′mə-təs, skler′ə-dũr′mə-təs), *adj.* 1. of or having scleroderma. 2. in *zoology,* covered with a hard outer tissue, as of horny scales or plates.

scler·oid (sklêr′oid), *adj.* [*scler-* + *-oid*], in *biology,* hard; hardened; indurated.

scle·ro·ma (skli-rō′mə), *n.* [*pl.* SCLEROMATA (-mə-tə)], [Gr. *sklērōma,* a hardening < *sklēros,* hard], a hardening of body tissue; tumorlike induration.

scle·rom·e·ter (skli-rom′ə-tẽr), *n.* [*sclero-* + *-meter*], an instrument for measuring the relative hardness of metals or minerals.

scle·ro·sal (skli-rō′s'l), *adj.* of, or having the nature of, sclerosis.

scle·rosed (skli-rōst′, sklêr′ōzd), *adj.* [< *sclerosis*], hardened, or indurated, as by sclerosis.

scle·ro·sis (skli-rō′sis), *n.* [*pl.* SCLEROSES (-sēz)], [Mod. L.; Gr. *sklērōsis,* a hardening < *sklēros,* hard], 1. in *botany,* a hardening of the cell wall of a plant, as by the formation of wood. 2. in *medicine,* a hardening of body tissues or parts, as by an excessive growth of fibrous connective tissue.

scle·ro·tial (skli-rō′shəl), *adj.* of sclerotium.

scle·rot·ic (skli-rot′ik), *adj.* [Mod. L. *scleroticus* < Gr. *sklērotēs,* hardness], 1. of, characterized by, or having sclerosis. 2. of the sclera. *n.* the sclera: see **eye,** illus.

scler·o·tit·ic (sklêr′ə-tit′ik, skler′ə-tit′ik), *adj.* scleritic.

scle·ro·ti·tis (sklêr′ə-tī′tis, skler′ə-tī′tis), *n.* scleritis.

scle·ro·ti·um (skli-rō′shi-əm), *n.* [*pl.* SCLEROTIA (-ə)], [Mod. L. < Gr. *sklēros,* hard], in certain fungi, a hardened, weblike, black or reddish-brown mass of threads in which food material is stored.

scle·rot·o·my (skli-rot′ə-mi), *n.* [*pl.* SCLEROTOMIES (-miz)], [*sclero-* + *-tomy*], surgical incision into the sclera.

scle·rous (sklêr′əs), *adj.* [Gr. *sklēros,* hard], hard; bony.

Sc. M., Master of Science.

scoff (skôf, skof), *n.* [ME. *scof;* prob. via dial. < ON. **skof,* a taunt < base seen in AS. *scop* (OHG. *scof*), poet (orig., composer of taunting verses); IE. base **sqeub-,* var. of **sqeubh-,* to throw, push away, seen also in AS. *scufan,* to push (cf. SHOVE)], 1. an expression of mocking contempt, scorn, or derision; jeer. 2. an object of mocking contempt, scorn, etc. *v.t.* to mock at or deride. *v.i.* to show mocking contempt, scorn, or derision, especially by language; jeer (often with *at*).

SYN.—**scoff** implies a showing of scorn or contempt as a manifestation of doubt, cynicism, irreverence, etc. (they *scoffed* at his diagnosis of the disease); **sneer** implies a display of contempt, disparagement, etc., as by a derisive smile or scornful insinuating tone of voice ("You call this a dinner?" he *sneered*); **jeer** suggests openly insulting, coarse remarks or mocking laughter (the crowd *jeered* at the speaker); **gibe** implies a taunting or mocking, either in amiable teasing or in sarcastic reproach (he kept *gibing* at me for my clumsiness); **flout** suggests a treating with contempt or disdain, especially by ignoring or rejecting (to *flout* the law).

scold (skōld), *n.* [ME. *scolde;* apparently < ON. *skald,* poet (prob. because of satirical verses); cf. SKALD, SCOFF], a person, especially a woman, who habitually uses abusive language. *v.t.* [ME. *scolden* < the *n.*], to find fault with angrily; rebuke or chide severely. *v.i.* 1. to find fault angrily; rebuke or chide severely. 2. to use angry, abusive language.

SYN.—**scold** is the common term meaning to find fault with or rebuke in angry, irritated, often nagging language (a mother *scolds* a naughty child); **upbraid** implies bitter reproach or censure and usually connotes justification for this (she *upbraided* me for my carelessness); **berate** suggests continuous, heated, even violent reproach, often connoting excessive abuse (the old shrew continued *berating* them); **revile** implies the use of highly abusive and contemptuous language and often connotes deliberate defamation or slander (he *reviled* his opponent unmercifully); **vituperate** suggests even greater violence in the attack (*vituperating* each other with foul epithets).

scol·e·cite (skol′ə-sīt′, skō′lə-sīt′), *n.* [G. *scolezit* < Gr. *skōlēx,* a worm], a hydrous silicate of calcium and aluminum, $CaAl_2Si_3O_{10}·3H_2O$.

sco·lex (skō′leks), *n.* [*pl.* SCOLECES (skə-lē′sēz), SCOLICES (skol′ə-sēz′, skō′lə-sēz′)], [Mod. L.; Gr. *skōlēx,* a grub, worm], the round segment forming the head of a tapeworm, provided with hooks or suckers.

sco·li·o·sis (skō′li-ō′sis, skol′i-ō′sis), *n.* [Mod. L.; Gr. *skoliōsis,* crookedness < *skolios,* crooked], in *medicine,* lateral curvature of the spine.

scol·lop (skol′əp), *n. & v.t.* scallop.

scol·o·pen·drid (skol′ə-pen′drid), *n.* [< Mod. L. *Scolopendridae,* name of family < L. *scolopendra* (Gr. *skolopendra*), kind of multiped], any of a large group of many-legged arthropods including the centipedes.

scom·broid (skom′broid), *adj.* [< L. *scomber,* mackerel (< Gr. *skombros*); + *-oid*], 1. of the mackerel family or a larger group including it and related fishes. 2. like a mackerel. *n.* a mackerel or related fish.

sconce (skons), *n.* [ME. *sconse;* OFr. *esconse,* dark lantern; ML. *sconsa,* contr. of *absconsa* < L. *absconsus,* pp. of *abscondere,* to hide], a bracket attached to a wall for holding a candle, candles, or the like.

sconce (skons), *n.* [D. *schans,* a fortress, orig. wickerwork, wicker basket], 1. a protection, cover, or shelter, as a hut or shed. 2. a protection for the head, as a helmet. 3. [Colloq.], *a)* the head or skull. *b)* good sense; brains. 4. in *military usage,* a small fort; detached bulwark or defense work. *v.t.* [SCONCED (skonst), SCONCING], 1. to protect or provide with a sconce (sense 4). 2. to fortify, shelter, or screen.

sconce (skons), *v.t.* [SCONCED (skonst), SCONCING], [< ?], to fine; especially, at Oxford University, to fine lightly for a breach of manners. *n.* such a fine.

Scone, the Stone of (sko͞on, skōn), the stone upon which the Scottish kings before 1296 were crowned at Scone, Scotland: stolen (1950) from under the coronation chair at Westminster Abbey; restored (1951).

scone (skōn), *n.* [Scot., contr. < MD. *schoonbrot,* fine bread; *schoon* (akin to G. *schön,* AS. *scene*), beautiful + *brot* (akin to Eng. *bread*)], a kind of tea cake, often resembling a baking powder biscuit, usually baked over a hot fire on a griddle, and served with butter.

scoop (sko͞op), *n.* [ME. *scope* < MD. *schope,* bailing vessel + *schoppe*, a shovel], 1. any of various ladles or other utensils like small, deep shovels; specifically, *a*) one used for dipping or bailing liquids. *b*) a kitchen utensil used to take up sugar or flour. *c*) a small coal shovel. *d*) a ladle. *e*) a small, spoonlike surgical instrument. *f*) a small, hemispherical utensil for dishing up ice cream. 2. the deep shovel of a dredge or steam shovel, which takes up sand, dirt, etc. 3. the act of taking up with a scoop. 4. the amount taken up at one time by a scoop. 5. a hollowed-out place; bowl-shaped depression. 6. a motion as of scooping. 7. [Colloq.], a large profit made by speculation or by a business transaction. 8. [Newspaper Slang], a beat. ***v.t.*** 1. to take up or out with or as with a scoop. 2. to empty by bailing. 3. to dig out; hollow out. 4. to make by digging or hollowing out. 5. [Colloq.], to gather (*in*) as if with a scoop. 6. [Newspaper Slang], to get and publish a piece of news before (a rival or rivals); get a beat on.

scoop·ful (sko͞op′fool′), ***n.*** as much as a scoop will hold.

scoot (sko͞ot), ***v.i.*** [prob. via dial. < ON. *skiōta*, to shoot, hence akin to AS. *sceotan* (cf. SHOOT)], [Colloq.], to go quickly; scurry off; dart. ***n.*** [Colloq.], a quick departure; a scurrying off; a darting.

scoot·er (sko͞ot′ẽr), ***n.*** [< *scoot, v.*], 1. a child's vehicle, consisting of a low, narrow footboard with a wheel at each end, the front one attached to a handlebar for steering: it is moved by a series of pushes made by one foot against the ground. 2. a somewhat similar vehicle equipped with a seat and propelled by a small internal-combustion engine: in full, **motor scooter.** 3. a flat-bottomed sailboat with runners, for use on water or ice. 4. a swift motorboat that skims over the water.

scoot·er (sko͞ot′ẽr), ***n.*** a scoter.

scop (skop, skōp), ***n.*** [Late AS., poet, minstrel, lit. maker of taunting verses; for IE. base see SCOFF; cf. SHOVE], an Old English poet; bard.

scope (skōp), ***n.*** [It. *scopo;* L. *scopus;* Gr. *skopos*, a mark, spy, watcher < base of *skopein*, to see; IE. base **spek-*, to peer, look carefully, seen also in L. *specere*, to see, OHG. *spehon*, to spy], 1. the area that the mind can cover; range of view; extent of perception or intellectual grasp: as, beyond the *scope* of a child's understanding. 2. the area or field within which any activity goes on; range or extent of action, observation, inquiry, etc.: as, the *scope* of a history book. 3. room for free outlook or liberty of action; opportunity. 4. the range of a missile. 5. length, extent, or sweep, as of a cable. 6. [Archaic], end; purpose. —***SYN.*** see **range.**

-scope (skōp), [Mod. L. *-scopium* < Gr. *-skopion* < *scopein*, to see, view], a combining form meaning (an instrument, etc. for) *seeing* or *observing*, as in *telescope.*

sco·pol·a·min (skō-pol′ə-min, skō′pə-lam′in), ***n.*** scopolamine.

sco·pol·a·mine (skō-pol′ə-mēn′, skō′pə-lam′in), ***n.*** [G. *scopolamin* < Mod. L. *Scopolia*, genus of plants in which the alkaloid appears (after G. A. *Scopoli* (1723–1788), of Pavia, Italy) + G. *amin*, amine], an alkaloid, $C_{17}H_{21}O_4N$, obtained from certain plants of the nightshade family and used in producing twilight sleep.

sco·po·line (skō′pə-lēn′, skō′pə-lin), ***n.*** [cf. SCOPOLAMINE], a colorless, crystalline compound, $C_8H_{13}NO_2$, derived from scopolamine and used as a narcotic.

scop·u·late (skop′yoo-lit), ***adj.*** [< L. *scopulae*, little broom, orig. pl. of *scopula*, broom twig, dim. of *scopa*, thin branch, shoot; + *-ate*], in *zoology*, brushlike.

-sco·py, [< Gr. *skopein*, to see, view], a combining form meaning *a seeing, observing, examination*, as in *bioscopy.*

scor·bu·tic (skôr-bū′tik), ***adj.*** [Mod. L. *scorbuticus* < ML. *scorbutus*, scurvy < MD. *scorft;* akin to Eng. *scurf*], of, like, or having scurvy.

scor·bu·ti·cal (skôr-bū′ti-k'l), ***adj.*** scorbutic.

scorch (skôrch), ***v.t.*** [ME. *scorchen* < OFr. *escorcher* (Fr. *écorcher*), to flay, take skin off; L. *excorticare* < *ex-* + *cortex*, bark], 1. to burn slightly; char and discolor the surface of. 2. to parch or shrivel by heat; cause to wither. 3. to affect painfully; wound the feelings of by verbal attack or sarcasm. 4. to burn and destroy everything in (a given area) before giving it up to the enemy. ***v.i.*** 1. to be burned slightly; be singed. 2. [Colloq.], to ride or drive at very high speed. ***n.*** a superficial mark or burn. —***SYN.*** see **burn.**

scorched-earth policy (skôrcht′ũrth′), the policy of burning and destroying all property in a given area before giving it up to an advancing enemy.

scorch·er (skôr′chẽr), ***n.*** a person or thing that scorches; specifically, [Colloq.], *a*) an extremely hot day. *b*) a severe or withering rebuke, sarcastic remark, etc. *c*) a person who drives at an excessive rate of speed.

score (skôr, skōr), ***n.*** [ME.; Late AS. *scoru;* ON. *skor* < base as in SHEAR], 1. *a*) a scratch, mark, incision, etc.: as, the *scores* made on ice by skates. *b*) a line drawn or scratched, often to mark a starting point, etc. *c*) notches made in wood, chalk marks, or any marks made to keep tally or account; hence, 2. an amount or sum due; account; debt; hence, 3. figuratively, a grudge; grievance: as, pay off an old *score.* 4. anything offered as a reason or motive: as, on the *score* of poverty. 5. the number of points made in a game or contest by a player or team, or the record of these points: as, the *score* is 2 to 0. 6. grade or rating, as on a test or examination. 7. *a*) twenty people or objects; a set of twenty. *b*) *pl.* very many. 8. [Colloq.], a successful move, stroke, remark, etc. 9. [Colloq.], the actual facts; realities of a situation or of life: often in *know the score.* 10. in *music*, *a*) a written or printed copy of a composition, showing all the parts for the instruments or voices. *b*) the music for a musical comedy or motion picture, usually when distinguished from the lyrics, dialogue, etc. ***v.t.*** [SCORED (skôrd, skōrd), SCORING], [ME. *scoren*], 1. to mark with notches, scratches, cuts, etc. 2. to mark with lines, as with a pen or pencil: as, the page is *scored* with underlinings. 3. to cancel or mark out by lines drawn (with *out*). 4. to mark with lines or notches in keeping account. 5. to keep account of by or as by lines or notches; reckon; tally; mark. 6. *a*) to make (runs, hits, etc.) in a game and so add to the number of points made for oneself or one's team: as, he *scored* a hit. *b*) to count toward the number of points: as, a safety *scores* two. *c*) to record or enter the score of. *d*) to record or add (points) to one's score: as, John *scores* five for that play. 7. *a*) to scourge. *b*) to criticize severely; upbraid. 8. to grade (an examination, etc.); rate or evaluate, as in testing. 9. to gain or achieve, as a success. 10. in *cookery*, to cut superficial gashes in (meat, etc.). 11. in *music*, to orchestrate, arrange, or write out in a score. ***v.i.*** 1. to make a point or points, as in a game. 2. to run up a score. 3. to keep the score, as of a game. 4. *a*) to gain an advantage. *b*) to achieve credit or success. 5. to make notches, lines, gashes, etc.

score card, 1. a card for recording the score of a game, match, etc., as in golf. 2. a card printed with players' names, weights, positions, etc. at a sports event.

sco·ri·a (skôr′i-ə, skō′ri-ə), ***n.*** [*pl.* SCORIAE (-ē′)], [ME.; L.; Gr. *skōria*, refuse, dross < *skōr*, dung], 1. the slag or refuse left after the metal has been smelted from the ore. 2. loose, cinderlike lava.

sco·ri·a·ceous (skôr′i-ā′shəs, skō′ri-ā′shəs), ***adj.*** having the nature of scoria.

sco·ri·fi·ca·tion (skôr′ə-fi-kā′shən, skō′rə-fi-kā′shən), ***n.*** the process of scorifying.

sco·ri·fy (skôr′ə-fī′, skō′rə-fī′), ***v.t.*** [SCORIFIED (-fīd′), SCORIFYING], [see -FY], to reduce to scoria, or slag.

scorn (skôrn), ***n.*** [ME. *scorn, scarn;* OFr. *escarn, escharn* < *escarnir, escharnir*, to scorn < Frank. base akin to OHG. *skernon*, to mock; affected in OFr. by association with *escorner*, to disgrace, lit. to unhorn < L. *ex-*, from + *cornu*, a horn], 1. a feeling that a person or thing is mean and contemptible; disdain; extreme contempt. 2. the expression of this feeling in words or manner; contemptuous treatment or disdainful utterance. 3. an object of this feeling; person or thing held in contempt or disdain. ***v.t.*** 1. to regard with scorn; consider mean and contemptible; despise. 2. to refuse or reject as mean and contemptible; spurn with scorn. ***v.i.*** [Obs.], to scoff; mock; jeer.—***SYN.*** see **despise.**
laugh to scorn, to treat derisively.

scorn·ful (skôrn′fəl), ***adj.*** full of scorn; having or showing contempt and disdain.

scor·pae·noid (skôr-pē′noid), ***adj.*** [< L. *scorpaena*, kind of fish < Gr. *skorpaina;* + *-oid*], designating or of a family of spiny-finned sea fishes. ***n.*** a scorpaenoid fish.

Scor·pi·o (skôr′pi-ō′), ***n.*** [L., lit., scorpion], 1. a southern constellation between Libra and Sagittarius, supposedly resembling a scorpion in shape: see **constellation,** chart: also **Scorpius.** 2. in *astrology*, the eighth sign of the zodiac (♏), which the sun enters about October 24: see **zodiac,** illus.

scor·pi·oid (skôr′pi-oid′), ***adj.*** [Gr. *skorpioeidēs*], 1. like a scorpion. 2. of the order consisting of the true scorpions. 3. with a curved end, like a scorpion's tail.

scor·pi·on (skôr′pi-ən), ***n.*** [ME.; OFr.; L. *scorpio;* Gr. *skorpios*], 1. any of an order of arachnids found in warm regions, with a front pair of nipping claws and a long, slender, jointed tail ending in a curved, poisonous sting. 2. in the *Bible*, a variety of whip or scourge, perhaps inset with spikes: I Kings 12:11. 3. [S-], Scorpio.

SCORPION
(1–8 in. long)

scorpion fly, any of a group of insects whose abdomen, in the male, curls up at the end and resembles a scorpion's sting.

Scor·pi·us (skôr′pi-əs), ***n.*** the constellation Scorpio: see **constellation,** chart.

Scot (skot), ***n.*** [< AS. *Scottas, pl.* < LL. *Scotus, Scottus*], 1. a member of a Gaelic tribe of northern Ireland that migrated to Scotland in the 5th century A.D. 2. a native or inhabitant of Scotland: cf. **Scotsman, Scotchman.**

scot (skot), *n.* [ME.; merging of ON. *skot* & OFr. *escot* (< the same Gmc. base); akin to *shot*], money assessed or paid; tax; levy.

scot and lot, 1. an old parish tax in Great Britain, assessed according to ability to pay. 2. in full: in the phrase *pay scot and lot.*

Scot., 1. Scotch. 2. Scotland. 3. Scottish.

Scotch (skoch), *adj.* [< *Scottish*], 1. of Scotland, its people, their language, etc.; Scottish. 2. [Slang], tight-fisted; stingy: opprobrious usage, from the vulgarized notion of the Scottish character. *n.* 1. any of the dialects of English spoken by the people of Scotland. 2. Scotch whisky. Cf. **Scottish.**

the Scotch, the Scottish people.

scotch (skoch), *v.t.* [ME. *scocchen;* prob. < Anglo-Fr. *escoche* < OFr. etymon of Fr. *coche,* a notch, nick], 1. to cut; scratch; score; notch; hence, 2. [< Theobald's emendation of *scorch* in Shakespeare's *Macbeth,* III, iii, 13], to wound without killing; maim; crush. 3. to put down; stifle; stamp out: as, he *scotched* the rumor.

scotch (skoch), *v.t.* [prob. < prec. in specialized sense], to block (a wheel, log, etc.) with a wedge, block, etc. to prevent movement. *n.* a block, wedge, etc. put under a wheel or log to prevent rolling, slipping, etc.

Scotch broth, mutton broth thickened with barley.

Scotch-I·rish (skoch'ī'rish), *adj.* 1. designating or of a group of people living in Northern Ireland who are descended from Scottish settlers. 2. of Scottish and Irish descent. *n.* a person of Scottish and Irish descent.

Scotch·man (skoch'mən), *n.* [*pl.* SCOTCHMEN (-mən)], a Scot; Scotsman: often considered an opprobrious form.

Scotch tape, a thin, paperlike adhesive tape: a trademark.

Scotch terrier, a Scottish terrier.

Scotch whisky, whisky, often having a smoky flavor, distilled in Scotland from malted barley.

Scotch woodcock, eggs cooked and served on toast or crackers spread with anchovies or anchovy paste.

sco·ter (skō'tẽr), *n.* [*pl.* SCOTERS (-tẽrz), SCOTER; see PLURAL, II, D, 1], [prob. dial. var. < *scoot;* cf. SCOOTER], any of several large sea ducks found along the arctic coasts of Europe and America: also **scooter.**

scot-free (skot'frē'), *adj.* 1. free from payment of scot, or tax; hence, 2. unharmed or unpunished; clear; safe.

Sco·tia (skō'shə, skō'shi-ə), *n.* [LL.], [Poetic], Scotland.

sco·ti·a (skō'shə, skō'shi-ə), *n.* [L.; Gr. *skotia,* lit., darkness: so called from the shadow within the cavity], a deep concave molding, usually at the base of a column.

Sco·tism (skō'tiz'm), *n.* the scholastic philosophy of John Duns Scotus and his followers: see **Duns Scotus.**

Scot·land (skot'lənd), *n.* a division of Great Britain, north of England: area, 30,405 sq. mi.; pop., 5,241,000; capital, Edinburgh.

Scotland Yard, 1. a short street in London, off Whitehall, originally the site of the police headquarters. 2. the headquarters of the London police, on the Thames embankment since 1890: in full, **New Scotland Yard.** 3. the London police, especially the detective bureau.

scot·o- (skōt'ō, skō'tə), [< Gr. *skotos,* darkness; akin to Eng. *shade*], a combining form meaning *darkness.*

sco·to·ma (skə-tō'mə), *n.* [*pl.* SCOTOMATA (-mə-tə)], [LL. < Gr. *skotōma* < *skotos,* darkness + *-ōma,* -oma], a dark area in the visual field; blind spot.

Scots (skots), *adj.* [ME. (northern) *Scottis*], Scottish. *n.* the Scottish dialect of English. Cf. **Scottish.**

Scots·man (skots'mən), *n.* [*pl.* SCOTSMEN (-mən)], a Scot: the current term in Scotland.

Scott, Robert Fal·con (fôl'kən skot), 1868–1912; English naval officer and antarctic explorer.

Scott, Sir Walter, 1771–1832; Scottish poet and novelist.

Scott, Win·field (win'fēld), 1786–1866; American general; commander in Mexican War.

Scot·ti·cism (skot'ə-siz'm), *n.* a Scottish idiom, expression, word, pronunciation, etc.

Scot·tish (skot'ish), *adj.* of Scotland, its people, their English dialect, etc. *n.* the English spoken by the people of Scotland. *Scottish,* the original form, is preferred to *Scotch* and *Scots* in American and British formal and literary usage with reference to the people, the country, and its institutions and characteristics, and in Scotland has replaced *Scotch,* the colloquial form prevailing in the United States and England; but with some words, *Scotch* is almost invariably used (e.g., tweed, whisky), with others, *Scots* (e.g., law, mile).

the Scottish, the Scottish people.

Scottish Gaelic, see **Gaelic.**

Scottish terrier, any of a breed of terrier with short legs, a squarish muzzle, rough, wiry hair, and pointed, erect ears.

scoun·drel (skoun'drəl), *n.* [prob. a disparaging dim. (cf. -LE) < Anglo-Fr. *escoundre* (OFr. *escondre*), to abscond, evade < L. *ex-* + *condere,* to hide (cf. ABSCOND)], a person without principles or moral scruples; rascal; villain. *adj.* characteristic of a scoundrel; base.

scoun·drel·ly (skoun'drəl-i), *adj.* 1. having the character of a scoundrel. 2. of or like a scoundrel.

scour (skour), *v.t.* [ME. *scouren;* MD. *schuren;* OFr. *escurer;* LL. **excurare,* to take great care of; L. *ex-,* intens. + *curare,* to take care of < *cura,* care], 1. to clean by vigorous rubbing, as with abrasives, soap and water, etc.; make clean and bright; polish thoroughly. 2. to remove dirt and grease from (wool, etc.). 3. *a)* to wash by flowing through or over; flush. *b)* to wash away; remove from by rapid flow of water. 4. to clear the intestines of; purge. 5. to clean (wheat). 6. to remove from as if by cleaning; sweep away; get rid of. *v.i.* 1. to clean things by vigorous rubbing and polishing. 2. to become clean and bright by rubbing and polishing. *n.* 1. the act of scouring. 2. a cleansing agent used in scouring. 3. a scoured place, as a part of a channel where mud has been washed away. 4. *pl.* dysentery in cattle, etc.

scour (skour), *v.t.* [ME. *scouren;* prob. < OFr. *escourre,* to run forth; L. **excurrere; ex-,* out + *currere,* to run], to pass over quickly, or range over or through, as in search or pursuit: as, he *scoured* the library for the book. *v.i.* to run or move quickly, or range about, as in search or pursuit.

scourge (skũrj), *n.* [ME.; OFr. *escorgie* < L. *ex,* off, from + *corrigia,* a strap, whip], 1. a whip; instrument for flogging. 2. any means of inflicting severe punishment, suffering, or vengeance. 3. the punishment or affliction itself. 4. any cause of serious trouble or affliction: as, the *scourge* of war. *v.t.* [SCOURGED (skũrjd), SCOURGING], 1. to whip; flog severely. 2. to punish, chastise, or afflict severely; torment.

scour·ing rush (skour'iŋ), any of a number of related plants with hollow, jointed stems and scalelike leaves, used to polish metal and wood; horsetail.

scour·ings (skour'iŋz), *n.pl.* 1. dirt, refuse, or remains removed by or as if by scouring. 2. refuse removed from grain before milling.

scouse (skous), *n.* [contr. < *lobscouse*], a sailors' dish of sea biscuit and vegetables, with or without meat.

scout (skout), *n.* [ME. *scoute;* OFr. *escoute* < *escouter, escolter,* to hear (Fr. *écouter*) < L. *auscultare,* to listen], 1. a person, ship, or plane sent out to discover what the enemy is doing, how much strength he has, etc. 2. a person who is a member of the Boy Scouts or Girl Scouts. 3. the act of scouting. 4. [Slang], fellow; guy. 5. in *sports,* etc., a person sent out to observe the tactics of a competitor, to find new talent, etc. *v.t.* 1. to spy upon; follow closely. 2. to look for; watch. *v.i.* 1. to go in search of military or naval information about the enemy; reconnoiter. 2. to go in search of something; prowl: as, *scout* around for some firewood. 3. to be an active member of the Boy Scouts or Girl Scouts.

scout (skout), *v.t.* [via dial. < ON. *skúta, skúti,* a taunt, allied to *skota,* to shove; cf. SCOFF, SCOP], to reject as absurd; flout; scoff at.

scout·craft (skout'kraft', skout'kräft'), *n.* the art or practice of scouting; especially, the activities of the Boy Scouts or Girl Scouts.

scout·hood (skout'hood'), *n.* [*scout* + *-hood*], 1. the state of being a Boy Scout or Girl Scout. 2. the character or characteristics of Boy Scouts or Girl Scouts.

scout·ing (skout'iŋ), *n.* the activities of scouts.

scout·mas·ter (skout'mas'tẽr, skout'mäs'tẽr), *n.* the adult leader of a troop of Boy Scouts.

scow (skou), *n.* [< D. *schouw,* lit., boat which is poled along; akin to LG. *schalde,* punt pole, scow, OS. *scaldan,* to shove (a boat)], a large, flat-bottomed boat with square ends, used for carrying freight, and now generally towed by a tug.

scowl (skoul), *v.i.* [ME. *scoulen, sculen;* prob. < ON.; cf. Dan. *skule,* in same sense; see SKULK], 1. to wrinkle the forehead and lower the eyebrows in displeasure; look angry, irritated, or sullen. 2. to look threatening; lower. *v.t.* to affect, influence, or express with a scowl or scowls. *n.* 1. a wrinkling of the forehead and lowering of the eyebrows in displeasure; angry frown. 2. a threatening or gloomy aspect. —***SYN.*** see **frown.**

scr., scruple.

scrab·ble (skrab''l), *v.i.* [SCRABBLED (-'ld), SCRABBLING], [D. *schrabbelen* < *schrabben,* to scrape], 1. to scratch, scrape, or paw as though looking for something. 2. to struggle. 3. to scribble; make meaningless marks. *v.t.* 1. to scrape together quickly. 2. to scribble. *n.* 1. a scraping with the hands or paws. 2. a scramble. 3. a scribble; scrawl. 4. a struggle.

scrag (skrag), *n.* [prob. < ON.; cf. Norw. *skragg,* feeble, stunted person, Dan. *skrog,* ON. *skröggr,* a fox (nickname); IE. base **s(q)er-,* to shrivel, shrink], 1. a lean, scrawny person or animal. 2. a thin, stunted tree or plant. 3. the neck, or back of the neck, of mutton, veal, etc. 4. [Slang], the human neck. *v.t.* [SCRAGGED (skragd), SCRAGGING], [Slang], to twist or wring the neck of; hang; throttle; garrote.

scrag·gi·ly (skrag'ə-li), *adv.* in a scraggy shape or form.

scrag·gi·ness (skrag'i-nis), *n.* the quality or condition of being scraggy.

scrag·gly (skrag'li), *adj.* [SCRAGGLIER (-li-ẽr), SCRAGGLIEST (-li-ist)], [see SCRAGGY & -LY], unkempt; rough,

as a beard; jagged; irregular; splintered, as rocks.
scrag·gy (skrag'i), *adj.* [SCRAGGIER (-i-ẽr), SCRAGGIEST (-i-ist)], [< *scrag*], 1. scraggly. 2. lean; bony; skinny.
scram (skram), *v.i.* [SCRAMMED (skramd), SCRAMMING], [contr. of *scramble*], [Slang], to go away or out: usually in the imperative.
scram·ble (skram'b'l), *v.i.* [SCRAMBLED (-b'ld), SCRAMBLING], [? a fusion of *scamper* + *scrabble*], 1. to climb, crawl, or clamber with the hands and feet. 2. to scuffle and fight for something, as for coins scattered on the ground; struggle roughly with others. 3. to struggle to get something highly prized: as, they *scrambled* for office. *v.t.* 1. to throw together haphazardly; mix in a confused way. 2. to gather haphazardly; collect without method (often with *up*). 3. to cook (eggs) after mixing the white and yolk together, as with milk or butter. *n.* 1. a hard climb or advance, as over rough, difficult ground. 2. a disorderly struggle, as to get something prized.
scran·nel (skran''l), *adj.* [popularized by Milton (*Lycidas*, l. 124); prob. via dial. < ON. (cf. Sw. dial. *skran*, miserable, Norw. *skrann*) < nasalized form of base seen in *scrag;* cf. SCRAWNY], [Archaic], 1. thin; lean; slight; scrawny. 2. harsh and feeble: said of sound.
Scran·ton (skran'tən), *n.* a city in northeastern Pennsylvania: pop., 111,000.
scrap (skrap), *n.* [ME. *scrappe;* ON. *skrap*, scraps, trifles < *skrapa*, to scrape; cf. SCRAPE], 1. a small piece; little bit; fragment. 2. a bit of something written or printed; brief extract. 3. discarded metal in the form of machinery, auto parts, etc. suitable only for reprocessing. 4. discarded articles or fragments of rubber, leather, cloth, paper, etc. 5. *pl.* bits of food. 6. *pl.* the remnants of animal fat after the oil has been removed by rendering. 7. *pl.* souvenirs, pictures, clippings, etc. pasted as mementos into a book. *adj.* 1. in the form of fragments, pieces, odds and ends, or leftovers. 2. used and discarded. *v.t.* [SCRAPPED (skrapt), SCRAPPING], 1. to make into scrap; break up. 2. to treat as useless; discard; junk.
scrap (skrap), *n.* [prob. < *scrape*, orig., nefarious scheme; cant term], [Slang], a fight or quarrel. *v.i.* [SCRAPPED (skrapt), SCRAPPING], [Slang], to fight or quarrel.
scrap·book (skrap'book'), *n.* a book of blank pages for pasted clippings, pictures, and souvenirs; memory book.
scrape (skrāp), *v.t.* [SCRAPED (skrāpt), SCRAPING], [ME. *scrapien, scrapen;* ON. *skrapa;* akin to D. *schrapen;* IE. base **squereb-* (as in L. *scrobis*, a pit) < **squer-*, to cut; see SHARP], 1. to rub over the surface of with something rough or sharp. 2. to make smooth or clean with a tool or abrasive. 3. to remove by rubbing with something sharp or rough (with *off, out, from*, etc.). 4. to bring into contact with something rough so as to scratch or graze: as, I *scraped* my knee on the stone. 5. to rub with a harsh sound; draw along or over so as to cause a grating sound: as, the bow *scrapes* the fiddle. 6. to dig, especially with the hands and nails. 7. to collect or gather slowly and with difficulty: as, he *scraped* together some money. *v.i.* 1. to scrape something so as to remove dirt, etc. 2. to rub against something harshly; grate. 3. to give out a harsh, grating noise. 4. to collect or gather goods or money slowly and with difficulty. 5. to manage to live; exist with difficulty. 6. to draw the foot back along the floor when bowing. *n.* 1. the act of scraping. 2. a scraped place; abrasion or scratch on a surface. 3. the noise of scraping; harsh, grating sound. 4. a disagreeable or embarrassing situation; predicament, usually caused by one's own conduct.
scrap·er (skrāp'ẽr), *n.* 1. any of various tools designed for scraping. 2. a person or thing that scrapes.
scrap·ing (skrāp'iŋ), *n.* 1. the act of a person or thing that scrapes. 2. the sound of this. 3. *usually pl.* something scraped off, together, or up.
scrap iron, discarded or waste pieces of iron, to be recast or reworked.
scrap·per (skrap'ẽr), *n.* a person or thing that scraps.
scrap·per (skrap'ẽr), *n.* [Slang], a person who engages in or is fond of scrapping, or fighting, especially a plucky, hard boxer.
scrap·ple (skrap''l), *n.* [dim. of *scrap*], corn meal or flour boiled with scraps of pork, allowed to set, sliced, and fried.
scrap·py (skrap'i), *adj.* [SCRAPPIER (-i-ẽr), SCRAPPIEST (-i-ist)], 1. made of scraps; consisting of odds and ends. 2. disconnected; disjointed: as, *scrappy* thinking.
scrap·py (skrap'i), *adj.* [SCRAPPIER (-i-ẽr), SCRAPPIEST (-i-ist)], [< *scrap* (fight) + *-y*], [Slang], fond of fighting.
Scratch (skrach), *n.* [ME. *skratte* (< ON. *skratti*, monster, devil, sorcerer), altered after *scratch;* akin to G. *schrat*, goblin; IE. base **sqer-*, to shrivel, shrink; cf. SCRAG], [sometimes s-], the Devil: usually **Old Scratch.**
scratch (skrach), *v.t.* [said to be < ME. *scratten* (< ON.), fused with *cracchen*, to scratch < MD. *cratsen*, to scratch], 1. to mark, break, or cut the surface of slightly with something pointed or sharp. 2. to tear or dig with the nails or claws. 3. *a)* to rub or scrape lightly, as with the fingernails, to relieve itching, etc. *b)* to chafe. 4. to rub or scrape with a grating noise: as, he *scratched* a match on the wall. 5. to write or draw hurriedly or carelessly. 6. to strike out or cancel (writing, etc.). 7. to gather or collect with difficulty; scrape (with *up*). 8. in *politics, a)* to signify refusal to vote for (a candidate) by striking out his name. *b)* to strike out a certain name or names on (the regular party ticket). *c)* to divide (one's vote) or mark (one's ballot) so as to support mainly one party. 9. in *sports*, to mark off (a competitor's name); especially, to withdraw (an entry) in horse racing. *v.i.* 1. to use nails or claws in digging or wounding. 2. to rub or scrape the skin lightly, as with the fingernails, to relieve itching, etc. 3. to get along with difficulty. 4. to give out a harsh, scraping noise. 5. to withdraw from a race or contest. 6. in *billiards & pool*, to commit a scratch. *n.* 1. the act of scratching. 2. a mark or tear made in a surface by something sharp or rough. 3. a slight wound inflicted by nails, claws, or something pointed. 4. a grating sound; scraping. 5. a hasty mark, as of a pen; scribble. 6. a mark or line made to indicate the starting point of a race or the place where boxers formerly stood to begin fighting. 7. in *billiards*, a chance shot. 8. in *billiards & pool, a)* a shot that results in a penalty. *b)* a miss. 9. in *sports, a)* the starting point or time of a contestant who receives no handicap. *b)* such a contestant. *adj.* 1. used for hasty notes, preliminary or tentative figuring, etc.: as, *scratch* paper. 2. starting from scratch; having no handicap or allowance, as a contestant. 3. done or made by chance, as a shot. 4. put together in haste and without much selection: as, a *scratch* team.
 from (or at, on) scratch, 1. from the starting line, as in a race. 2. from nothing; without advantage.
 up to scratch, 1. toeing the mark in a prize fight or a race; ready to start a race, contest, etc. 2. [Colloq.], ready to meet difficulties, start on an enterprise, etc. 3. [Colloq.], up to a standard.
scratch·es (skrach'iz), *n.pl.* [often construed as sing.], a skin disease of horses, characterized by the formation of dry scabs near the fetlock or behind the knee.
scratch hit, in *baseball*, a chance hit credited to the batter, which normally would have been an out.
scratch test, a test for determining the substances to which a person is allergic, made by rubbing allergens into small scratches or punctures in the skin.
scratch·y (skrach'i), *adj.* [SCRATCHIER (-i-ẽr), SCRATCHIEST (-i-ist)], 1. having the appearance of being drawn roughly, hurriedly, etc.; made with scratches. 2. making a scraping, scratching noise. 3. scratched together; haphazard. 4. that scratches, scrapes, tears, chafes, etc.; irritating; itching: as, *scratchy* cloth.
scrawl (skrôl), *v.t. & v.i.* [ME. *scrawlen*, to shamble; prob. altered form of *crawl* with echoic *scr-* cluster], to write, draw, or mark awkwardly, hastily, or carelessly; especially, to write with sprawling, shapeless handwriting. *n.* 1. shapeless, sprawling, often illegible handwriting. 2. something scrawled.
scrawl·y (skrôl'i), *adj.* [SCRAWLIER (-i-ẽr), SCRAWLIEST (-i-ist)], consisting of or characterized by a scrawl.
scraw·ni·ness (skrô'ni-nis), *n.* the quality or condition of being scrawny.
scraw·ny (skrô'ni), *adj.* [SCRAWNIER (-ni-ẽr), SCRAWNIEST (-ni-ist)], [prob. < ON. **skrannig-;* cf. SCRANNEL], lean; thin; scraggy; scrubby. —*SYN.* see **lean.**
screak (skrēk), *v.i.* [ON. *skraekja;* cf. SHRIEK, SCREECH], to screech or creak. *n.* a screech or creak.
scream (skrēm), *v.i.* [ME. *scremen, screamen;* ON. *skraema*, to terrify, lit. to make jump < IE. base *(*s*)*quer-*, to jump, jump about, seen also in L. *scurra*, buffoon (cf. SCURRILOUS)], 1. *a)* to utter a shrill, loud, piercing cry in anger, pain, or fright. *b)* to make a shrill, piercing sound. 2. to laugh loudly or hysterically. 3. to have a startling effect; leave a vivid impression. 4. to use heated, intense, or hysterical language. *v.t.* 1. to utter with or as with a scream or screams. 2. to bring into a specified state by screaming: often reflexive. *n.* 1. *a)* a sharp, piercing cry; wail; shriek. *b)* a shrill, piercing sound. 2. [Colloq.], a hilariously entertaining person or thing.
SYN.—**scream** is the general word for a loud, high, piercing cry, as in anger, pain, or fear; **shriek** suggests a sharper, more sudden cry than **scream** and connotes either great terror or pain or loud, high-pitched, unrestrained laughter; **screech** suggests an unpleasantly shrill or harsh cry that is painful to the hearer.
scream·er (skrēm'ẽr), *n.* 1. a person who screams. 2. [Slang], a person or thing of remarkable size, strength, excellence, etc. 3. [Slang], a person or thing that makes one scream with laughter or thrills; especially, a very thrilling or funny story, etc. 4. [Slang], an exclamation point: printer's term. 5. [Slang], a sensational headline.

6. any of a group of long-toed South American birds.

scream·ing (skrēm′iŋ), ***adj.*** 1. that screams. 2. having the nature of a scream; violent or startling in effect. 3. causing screams of laughter; very funny; hilarious.

scree (skrē), ***n.*** [back-formation < pl. *screes* < earlier *screethes* < ON. *skritha*, a landslide < *skritha*, to slide (akin to G. *schreiten*, to stride)], [British], 1. a pebble; stone. 2. an accumulation of small or broken stones, as at the foot of a steep slope.

screech (skrēch), ***v.i.*** [ME. *scriken, scrichen;* ON. *skraekja*, of Gmc. echoic origin; cf. SHRIEK], to utter a shrill, high-pitched, harsh cry or shriek. ***v.t.*** to utter with a shriek. ***n.*** a shrill, high-pitched, harsh cry or shriek. —***SYN.*** see **scream.**

screech owl, 1. any of a group of small owls with feathered ear tufts and an eerie, wailing screech instead of a hoot. 2. a barn owl.

screech·y (skrēch′i), ***adj.*** [SCREECHIER (-i-ẽr), SCREECHIEST (-i-ist)], screeching; loud and shrill.

screed (skrēd), ***n.*** [ME. *screde;* var. of *shred;* sense from "long list on a strip of paper"], 1. a long, tiresome, noisy speech on any subject; harangue. 2. a long passage of prose, usually argumentative. 3. a wooden strip, etc. placed at intervals along a wall to be plastered, to gauge the thickness of the plastering.

screen (skrēn), ***n.*** [ME. *skrene*, a sieve, curtain; OFr. *escran, escren;* prob. < OHG. *scerm* (G. *schirm*), a guard, protection, screen; cf. SCRIM], 1. *a*) a light, movable, covered frame or series of frames hinged together, serving as a portable partition which separates, conceals, shelters, or protects. *b*) any partition or curtain serving the same purpose. 2. anything that functions to shield, protect, conceal, or shelter in the manner of a curtain: as, a smoke *screen*, a *screen* of trees. 3. a coarse mesh of wire, etc., used to separate finer from coarser parts, as of sand, earth, or coal; sieve. 4. a frame covered with a mesh, as of wire, plastic, or cloth, used for protection, as on a window. 5. a large sheet, curtain, or surface upon which lantern slides, motion pictures, etc. are projected. 6. motion pictures collectively; the film industry or art. 7. in *military usage*, *a*) a body of troops sent out to protect an area or cover troop movements. *b*) a protective formation of light vessels, as destroyers, about heavier ones, as carriers. 8. in *photoengraving*, a transparent plate, as of optical glass, ruled with two sets of parallel lines running in opposite directions, used in the half-tone process. 9. in *physics*, a device used as a shield to prevent interference of some sort. 10. in *psychoanalysis*, a form of concealment, as, in a dream, a person who stands for another or others with whom he has some characteristics in common. ***v.t.*** 1. to shut off from view, or to shelter or protect, with or as with a screen. 2. to sift by means of a sieve; pass through a coarse mesh; separate finer from coarser parts of. 3. *a*) to interview or test in order to separate according to skills, personality, aptitudes, etc. *b*) to separate in this way (usually with *out*). 4. to show (a motion picture); project (pictures, etc.) upon a screen, as with a motion-picture or slide projector. 5. to photograph with a motion-picture camera. 6. to adapt (a story, play, etc.) for motion pictures. ***v.i.*** to be screened or suitable for screening, as in motion pictures.

screen·ings (skrēn′iŋz), ***n.pl.*** 1. refuse left after screening; rubbish. 2. material that has been screened.

screen·play (skrēn′plā′), ***n.*** a story written in a form suitable to production as a motion picture or adapted to this form from a novel, stage play, etc.

screw (skrōō), ***n.*** [ME. *screwe;* OFr. *escroue*, hole in which the screw turns < L. *scrofa*, sow, influenced by *scrobis*, vulva], 1. a mechanical device used for fastening things together, consisting of a naillike cylinder of metal grooved in an advancing spiral, and usually having a slotted head: it penetrates only by being turned: **male** (or **external**) **screw.** 2. anything like such a device. 3. a hollow cylinder equipped with a spiral groove on its inner surface into which the male screw fits: **female** (or **internal**) **screw.** 4. the act of turning or twisting; turn of a screw. 5. a screw propeller. 6. [Chiefly British], *a*) a stingy person; miser. *b*) a crafty bargainer. 7. [Chiefly British], a bit of tobacco, etc. (in a twisted paper). 8. [Chiefly British], a worn-out horse. 9. [Slang], a prison guard. 10. [British Slang], salary. ***v.t.*** 1. to twist; turn; tighten. 2. to fasten, make secure, tighten, press, insert, etc. with or as with a screw or screws. 3. to contort; squeeze; twist out of natural shape: as, *screw* one's face up. 4. to force to do something; compel, as if by using screws. 5. to extort or practice extortion on: as, he *screwed* me out of money. ***v.i.*** 1. to come apart or go together by being turned or twisted in the manner of a screw: as, the lid *screws* on. 2. to be fitted for being put together or taken apart by a screw or screws. 3. to twist; turn; wind; have a motion like that of a screw. 4. to practice extortion. Abbreviated **sc.**

MACHINE SCREW

MACHINE SCREW

WOOD SCREW

LAG SCREW

SET SCREW

SCREWS

have a screw loose, [Slang], to be eccentric, odd, etc.

put the screws on (or **to**), to subject to force; exert pressure upon, as in exacting payment.

screw·ball (skrōō′bôl′), ***n.*** 1. in *baseball*, a pitched ball that wobbles or moves erratically. 2. [Slang], a person who seems erratic, irrational, unconventional, or unbalanced. ***adj.*** [Slang], peculiar; irrational; erratic.

screw bean, 1. the spirally twisted pod growing on a mesquite tree of the southwestern United States and used for fodder. 2. this tree.

screw·driv·er (skrōō′driv′ẽr), ***n.*** a tool shaped like a chisel, with a blunt end which fits into the slot in the head of a screw, used for tightening, loosening, or turning screws: also **screw driver.**

screwed (skrōōd), ***adj.*** 1. having threads like a screw. 2. twisted. 3. [Chiefly British Slang], drunk.

screw eye, a screw with a loop instead of a head.

screw hook, a screw with a hook instead of a head.

screw jack, a jackscrew, kind of lifting jack.

screw pine, any of a group of shrubs and trees of the Malay Peninsula and tropical islands, with leaves arranged in spirals and aerial roots.

screw propeller, a revolving hub fitted with radiating blades arranged in a spiral, used for propelling ships, aircraft, etc.

SCREW PROPELLER

screw thread, the spiral ridge of a screw.

screw·y (skrōō′i), ***adj.*** [SCREWIER (-i-ẽr), SCREWIEST (-i-ist)], [Slang], 1. unbalanced; irrational. 2. peculiar; eccentric. 3. impractical. 4. misleading.

Scria·bin, A·lek·san·dr Ni·ko·la·ye·vich (ä′lyek-sän′dẽr nē′kô-lä′ye-vich skryä′bĕn; Eng. skri-ä′bin), 1872–1915; Russian composer and pianist.

scrib·al (skrīb′'l), ***adj.*** 1. of scribes, or writers. 2. arising from the process of writing: as, a *scribal* error.

scrib·ble (skrib′'l), ***v.t.*** [SCRIBBLED (-'ld), SCRIBBLING], [ML. *scribillare* < L. *scribere*, to write], 1. to write carelessly or illegibly. 2. to cover with meaningless or illegible marks. 3. to compose hastily, without regard to style. ***v.i.*** 1. to write in a careless or illegible way. 2. to make meaningless or illegible marks. ***n.*** 1. illegible or careless handwriting; scrawl. 2. meaningless marks. 3. an inferior literary work.

scrib·bler (skrib′lẽr), ***n.*** a person who scribbles; specifically, *a*) a person who writes illegibly or carelessly. *b*) a hack writer; inferior and unimportant author.

scribe (skrīb), ***n.*** [ME.; Early Fr.; L. *scriba* < *scribere*, to write], 1. a writer; author. 2. a professional penman; person who copied manuscripts before the invention of printing. 3. a clerk; public writer or secretary. 4. a pointed instrument for marking a line on stone, brick, wood, etc. to show where it is to be cut. 5. formerly, a teacher or doctor of the Jewish law. ***v.t.*** [SCRIBED (skrībd), SCRIBING], 1. to mark (wood, bricks, etc.) with a scribe. 2. to mark (a line) with a scribe. ***v.i.*** to work as a scribe.

Scribe, Au·gus·tin Eu·gène (ō′güs′tan′ ë′zhen′ skrĕb), 1791–1861; French dramatist and librettist.

scrib·er (skrīb′ẽr), ***n.*** a scribe (sense 4).

scrim (skrim), ***n.*** [form & sense suggest cognate of G. *schirm*, a screen, protection (OHG. *scerm;* cf. SCREEN), via Walloon Fr. or LG.], a light, loosely woven cotton or linen cloth, used for curtains, upholstery linings, etc.

scrim·mage (skrim′ij), ***n.*** [altered < *skirmish*], 1. a rough-and-tumble fight; tussle; confused struggle. 2. in *football*, *a*) the play that follows the pass from center when the two teams are lined up. *b*) football practice in the form of actual play. 3. in *Rugby*, scrummage. ***v.i.*** [SCRIMMAGED (-ijd), SCRIMMAGING], to take part in a scrimmage.

line of scrimmage, in *football*, an imaginary line on which the ball rests at the beginning of each play and along which the two teams line up.

scrim·mag·er (skrim′ij-ẽr), ***n.*** in *Rugby*, a forward.

scrimp (skrimp), ***v.t.*** [prob. < AS. *scrimman*, to shrink, merged with an ON. cognate (cf. Sw. *skrympa*, to shrink); IE. base *(*s*)*qremb-*, to bow, bend, bow down], 1. to make too small, little, short, or narrow; skimp. 2. to treat stingily; stint. ***v.i.*** to be sparing and frugal; try to make ends meet. ***adj.*** curtailed; scanty.

scrimp·i·ly (skrim′pə-li), ***adv.*** in a scrimpy manner.

scrimp·i·ness (skrim′pi-nis), ***n.*** a scrimpy quality.

scrimp·y (skrim′pi), ***adj.*** [SCRIMPIER (-pi-ẽr), SCRIMPIEST (-pi-ist)], 1. skimpy; scanty; meager. 2. stingy.

scrim·shaw (skrim′shô′), ***n.*** [earlier also *scrimshander;* the base is prob. a nautical adaptation of Fr. *escrimer* (OFr. *scrimir*), to fight (with a sword), either in sense "to make flourishes," or, like Fr. *s'escrimer*, "to work hard for small results"; the 2d element ? influenced by the personal name *Scrimshaw* or by *-shaws* in *kickshaws*], 1. careful decoration and carving of shells, bone, ivory, etc. by sailors on long voyages. 2. a product of such handicraft. 3. any neat piece of mechanical work. ***v.t.*** to decorate (shells, etc.) by carving. ***v.i.*** to do this kind of work.

scrip (skrip), ***n.*** [ME. *scrippe;* prob. < ON. *skreppa* (base as in SCARF, band), but influenced by OFr. *escrepe* in phr. *escrepe et bordon*, wallet and staff], [Archaic], a small bag, wallet, or satchel.

scrip (skrip), ***n.*** [altered < *script*], 1. a writing; list, receipt, etc. 2. a small piece or scrap, especially of paper. 3. a certificate of a right to receive something; specifically, *a*) a certificate representing fractions of shares of stock. *b*) a temporary certificate given for part payment of a stock subscription or a bond, to be exchanged later when full payment is made. *c*) a temporary paper to be exchanged for money, goods, land, etc. *d*) a certificate of indebtedness, issued as currency. 4. paper money in amounts of less than a dollar, formerly issued in the United States; fractional currency.

Scripps, Edward Wyl·lis (wil'is skrips), 1854–1926; American newspaper publisher.

‡scrip·sit (skrip'sit), [L.], he (or she) wrote (it): placed after the author's name on a manuscript, etc.

script (skript), ***n.*** [ME.; OFr. *escript;* L. *scriptum*, neut. of *scriptus*, pp. of *scribere*, to write], 1. handwriting; written words, letters, or figures. 2. printing or printers' type which imitates handwriting. 3. a style of handwriting; manner or method of forming letters or figures. 4. a written document; original manuscript: opposed to *copy*. 5. *a*) a manuscript or typewritten copy of a play, radio show, role, or motion-picture screenplay. *b*) the written part of a play, radio show, etc., excluding performance, music, scenery, etc.: as, the acting was poor, but I liked the *script*.

scrip·to·ri·um (skrip-tôr'i-əm, skrip-tō'ri-əm), ***n.*** [*pl.* SCRIPTORIA (-ə)], [ML. < L. *scriptus;* see SCRIPT], a writing room; especially, a room in a monastery reserved for copying manuscripts, writing, and studying.

scrip·tur·al (skrip'chẽr-əl), ***adj.*** [often S-], of, contained in, or according to the Scriptures; Biblical.

scrip·ture (skrip'chẽr), ***n.*** [ME.; OFr. *escripture;* L. *scriptura* < *scriptus*, pp. of *scribere*, to write], 1. originally, anything written; a writing, manuscript, document, etc. 2. [S-], *usually pl.* the Bible; books of the Old and New Testaments or of either: also **(the) Holy Scripture, (the) Holy Scriptures.** 3. [S-], [Rare], a passage or text of the Bible. 4. any sacred or religious writing or books. Abbreviated **Script.**

scrive·ner (skriv'nẽr, skriv''n-ẽr), ***n.*** [ME. *scriveyner;* extended <obs. *scrivein;* OFr. *escrivain;* It. *scrivano* < LL. **scribanus* < L. *scribere*, to write], [Archaic], 1. a public clerk, draftsman, or copyist; scribe. 2. a notary.

scro·bic·u·late (skrō-bik'yoo-lit), ***adj.*** [< L. *scrobiculus*, dim. of *scrobis*, a pit; + *-ate*], having many small depressions; pitted; furrowed.

scrod (skrod), ***n.*** [prob. < MD. *schrode*, piece cut off, strip; cf. cognate SHRED], a young codfish, split and prepared for cooking.

scrof·u·la (skrof'yoo-lə), ***n.*** [ML.; L. *scrofulae*, pl., swellings of the neck glands < *scrofa*, a sow, ? because supposed to be subject to the disease], tuberculosis of the lymphatic glands, especially of the neck, characterized by the enlargement and degeneration of the glands; king's evil.

scrof·u·lous (skrof'yoo-ləs), ***adj.*** 1. of, like, or having scrofula. 2. morally corrupt; degenerate.

scroll (skrōl), ***n.*** [altered (by association with *roll*) < ME. *scrowe, scroue;* OFr. *escroue* (cf. ESCROW); of Gmc. origin], 1. a roll of parchment or paper, usually with writing upon it. 2. an ancient book in the form of a rolled manuscript. 3. a list or schedule: as, the *scroll* of Fame. 4. anything having the form of a partly unrolled or loosely rolled sheet of paper; specifically, *a*) an ornament or ornamental design in coiled or spiral form: as, the volute of an Ionic capital is a *scroll*. *b*) a flourish added to a signature, or to special words, figures, etc. ***v.t.*** 1. to form into a scroll. 2. to decorate with spiral designs. ***v.i.*** to roll or curl up into a spiral.

scroll saw, a thin, ribbonlike saw for cutting thin wood into spiral or ornamental designs.

scroll·work (skrōl'wũrk'), ***n.*** 1. ornamental work with a scroll or scrolls as the basic design. 2. ornamental work cut out with a scroll saw.

Scrooge (skrōōj), ***n.*** 1. the hard, miserly old man in Dickens' story *A Christmas Carol*, who is made kindly and gentle by the revelations of spirits that visit him on Christmas Eve; hence, 2. any miserly, stingy person.

scroop (skrōōp), ***v.i.*** [echoic, after *scrape*], [Dial.], to make a strident, grating sound; creak; grate. ***n.*** [Dial.], a strident, grating sound.

scroph·u·lar·i·a·ceous (skrof'yoo-lâr'i-ā'shəs), ***adj.*** [< Mod. L. *Scrophularia*, the type genus (from supposed power to cure scrofula); + *-ous*], in *botany*, of the figwort family, composed chiefly of medicinal herbs.

scro·tal (skrō't'l), ***adj.*** of the scrotum.

scro·tum (skrō'təm), ***n.*** [*pl.* SCROTA (-tə), SCROTUMS (-təmz)], [L.; for IE. base see SHRED], in most male mammals, the pouch of skin containing the testicles and related structures.

scrouge (skrouj, skrōōj), ***v.t.*** [SCROUGED (skroujd, skrōōjd), SCROUGING], [earlier *scruze;* prob. echoic, suggested by *screw, squeeze*, etc.], [British Dial.], to crowd; squeeze; press.

scrounge (skrounj), ***v.t. & v.i.*** [SCROUNGED (skrounjd), SCROUNGING], [prob. echoic extension, suggested by *scrouge*], [Slang], to look around for and take (something) without permission; pilfer.

scrub (skrub), ***n.*** [dial. var. of *shrub*, influenced by ON.; collective senses < Australia], 1. *a*) originally, a straggly, inferior tree or shrub. *b*) short, stunted trees, bushes, or shrubs growing thickly together. *c*) land covered with such growth. 2. any person or thing smaller than the usual, or inferior in quality, breed, etc. 3. in *sports*, *a*) a player not on the varsity squad or regular team. *b*) *pl.* a team made up of such players. ***adj.*** 1. mean; poor; inferior. 2. undersized; undernourished; small. 3. of or for players not on the varsity squad or regular team; hence, 4. impromptu; hastily got up: as, a *scrub* game.

scrub (skrub), ***v.t.*** [SCRUBBED (skrubd), SCRUBBING], [ME. *scrobben;* prob. < ON.; cf. Dan. *skrubbe*, Norw. dial. *skrubba*, to rub hard; akin to MLG. *schrubben;* prob. IE. base **sqer-*, to cut, as also in Early Dan. *skrub*, unevenness], 1. to clean or wash by rubbing or brushing hard. 2. to remove by brushing or rubbing. 3. to rub hard. 4. to cleanse (a gas) of impurities. ***v.i.*** to clean something by rubbing, as by using brush, water, and soap. ***n.*** 1. the act of scrubbing. 2. a person who works hard and lives meanly; drudge.

scrub·ber (skrub'ẽr), ***n.*** a person or thing that scrubs; specifically, *a*) a person who scrubs floors, decks, etc. *b*) a stiff brush. *c*) any of various devices for cleansing gas of impurities.

scrub·by (skrub'i), ***adj.*** [SCRUBBIER (-i-ẽr), SCRUBBIEST (-i-ist)], 1. stunted in growth; undersized or inferior. 2. covered with or consisting of brushwood, or scrub. 3. paltry, shabby, etc.

scrub oak, any of various American dwarf oaks.

scruff (skruf), ***n.*** [altered < earlier *scuff* (< ON. *skopt*, the hair), after *scruff*, var. of *scurf;* IE. base **sqeu-p-*, **sqeu-bh-*, a tuft, wisp], the nape, or back, of the neck.

scrum (skrum), ***n.*** [British Colloq.], a scrummage.

scrum·mage (skrum'ij), ***n.*** [dial. var. of *scrimmage*], in *Rugby*, a formation around the ball in which the two sets of forwards compactly pressed together try to push their opponents away from the ball and restart the play by breaking away with it or kicking it out. ***v.t. & v.i.*** [SCRUMMAGED (-ijd), SCRUMMAGING], to play or place (the ball) in a scrummage.

scrump·tious (skrump'shəs), ***adj.*** [altered < *sumptuous* with emphatic initial *scr-*], [Slang], very fine; very nice; first-rate; splendid.

scrunch (skrunch), ***v.t. & v.i.*** [< *crunch*, with emphatic initial *scr-*], to crunch; crush; chew noisily and with force. ***n.*** a sound or act of crunching.

scru·ple (skrōō'p'l), ***n.*** [ME.; OFr. *scrupule;* L. *scrupulus*, small sharp stone, hence small stone used as weight, small weight; also a sharp stone, as in a man's shoe, uneasiness, difficulty, small trouble, doubt], 1. a very small quantity or amount; very small part. 2. an ancient Roman weight, 1/288 of an as (1/24 ounce). 3. an apothecaries' weight, equal to 1/3 dram (20 grains, or 1/24 ounce). 4. a feeling of hesitancy, doubt, or uneasiness arising from difficulty in deciding what is right, proper, expedient, etc.; qualm; misgiving. ***v.t. & v.i.*** [SCRUPLED (-p'ld), SCRUPLING], to hesitate (at) from doubt or uneasiness; be unwilling because of conscientious motives; have scruples (about): usually followed by an infinitive. Abbreviated **sc., scr.** (in senses 2 & 3). —***SYN.*** see **qualm.**

scru·pu·los·i·ty (skrōō'pyoo-los'ə-ti), ***n.*** [< Fr. or L.; Fr. *scrupulosité;* L. *scrupulositas*], 1. the quality of being scrupulous. 2. [*pl.* SCRUPULOSITIES (-tiz)], an instance of this.

scru·pu·lous (skrōō'pyoo-ləs), ***adj.*** [< Fr. or L.; Fr. *scrupuleux;* L. *scrupulosus*], 1. having or showing scruples; characterized by careful attention to what is right or proper; conscientiously honest and upright. 2. *a*) careful of details; precise, accurate, and correct; exact. *b*) demanding, or characterized by, precision, care, and exactness. —***SYN.*** see **careful, upright.**

scru·ti·nize (skrōō't'n-īz'), ***v.t.*** [SCRUTINIZED (-īzd'), SCRUTINIZING], [< *scrutiny* + *-ize*], to look at very carefully; examine closely; inspect minutely.

SYN.—**scrutinize** implies a looking over carefully and searchingly in order to observe the minutest details (he slowly *scrutinized* the bank note); **inspect** implies a close, critical observation, especially in order to detect errors, flaws, etc. (he *inspected* the building for fire hazards); **examine** suggests a close observation or investigation in order to determine the condition, quality, validity, etc. of something (the doctor *examined* me thoroughly); **scan**, in its earlier, stricter sense, implies a close scrutiny and analysis, but in current, popular usage, it more frequently connotes a quick, rather superficial survey (he *scanned* the headlines).

scru·ti·ny (skrōō′t'n-i), *n.* [*pl.* SCRUTINIES (-iz)], [OFr. *scrutinie;* LL. *scrutinium* < L. *scrutari*, to search into carefully], a close examination; minute inspection; careful, lengthy look.

scu·ba (skōō′bə), *n.* [*s*elf-*c*ontained *u*nderwater *b*reathing *a*pparatus], an apparatus including tanks of compressed air, worn by divers for breathing under water: also written **Scuba, SCUBA.**

scud (skud), *v.i.* [SCUDDED (-id), SCUDDING], [orig. said of a hare; hence prob. < dial. *scut*, a tail, especially of a hare; influenced by *scoot*], 1. to run or move swiftly; glide or skim along easily. 2. to be driven or run before the wind. *n.* 1. the act of scudding. 2. clouds or spray driven by the wind.

Scu·dé·ry, Mag·de·leine de (måg′də-len′ de skü′dā′-rē′), 1607–1701; French writer: also spelled **Scudéri.**

scu·do (skōō′dō), *n.* [*pl.* SCUDI (-dē)], [It., orig., a shield; L. *scutum*, a shield: so named from bearing a shield], a former monetary unit and gold or silver coin of Italy and Sicily, valued at about one dollar.

scuff (skuf), *v.t.* [prob. a merged word going back to ON. *skūfa*, to shove, push (cf. Sw. *skuffa*, to push); akin to *shove* & dial. *scuff*, a light blow, to touch lightly < *scuff*, hair, nape of the neck; see SCRUFF], 1. to scrape (the ground, floor, etc.) with the feet. 2. to wear a rough place or places on the surface of. 3. to touch or brush lightly in passing. 4. to move (the feet) with a dragging motion. *v.i.* to walk without lifting the feet; shuffle. *n.* 1. a noise or act of scuffing. 2. a worn or rough spot. 3. a loose-fitting house slipper without a heel or counter.

scuf·fle (skuf′'l), *v.i.* [SCUFFLED (-'ld), SCUFFLING], [< *scuff* + *-le*, freq. suffix], 1. to struggle or fight in rough confusion. 2. to drag the feet; shuffle; scuff. *n.* 1. a rough, confused fight; close, haphazard struggle. 2. a shuffling: as, the *scuffle* of feet.

scull (skul), *n.* [ME. *skulle, sculle;* prob. < ON. & akin to *skull* but with more basic etym. meaning; cf. Early Sw. *skolle*, thin plate; IE. base ***sqel-*, to cut (cf. SHIELD, SKILL, SKULL)], 1. an oar twisted from side to side over the stern of a boat to move it forward. 2. one of a pair of light oars with concave blades, used, one on each side of a boat, by a single rower. 3. a light, narrow racing boat for one or more rowers. *v.i. & v.t.* to propel (a boat) with a scull or sculls.

scul·ler·y (skul′ẽr-i), *n.* [*pl.* SCULLERIES (-iz)], [OFr. *escuelerie*, care of dishes and kitchen utensils < *escuelier*, maker or keeper of plates and dishes < *escuelle*, a dish < L. *scutella*, salver, tray], a room adjoining the kitchen, where pots and pans are cleaned and stored or where the rough, dirty kitchen work is done.

scul·lion (skul′yən), *n.* [OFr. *escouillon*, a mop, cloth < *escouve*, a broom < L. *scopa*, a broom], [Archaic], 1. a servant who does the rough work of a kitchen. 2. a low, miserable fellow; wretch.

sculp., 1. sculptor. 2. sculptural. 3. sculpture.

scul·pin (skul′pin), *n.* [prob. altered < Fr. *scorpene* < L. *scorpaena*, sea scorpion], 1. any of a group of spiny, generally scaleless sea fishes with a large head and wide mouth. 2. the bullhead, a related fresh-water fish.

‡**sculp·sit** (skulp′sit), [L.], he (or she) carved (it): placed after the artist's name on a sculpture, etc.: abbreviated **sculp., sculpt.**

sculp·tor (skulp′tẽr), *n.* [L. < *sculpere*, to carve in stone], a person who models or carves figures of clay, stone, metal, wood, etc.; artist who creates three-dimensional representations: abbreviated **sculp.**

sculp·tress (skulp′tris), *n.* [Rare], a woman sculptor.

sculp·tur·al (skulp′chẽr-əl) *adj.* of or like sculpture.

sculp·ture (skulp′chẽr), *n.* [ME.; OFr.; L. *sculptura* < *sculptus*, pp. of *sculpere*, to carve in stone], 1. the art of carving wood, chiseling stone, casting metal, modeling clay or wax, etc. into three-dimensional representations, as statues, figures, ornaments, etc. 2. any product or products of this art; a work or works of sculpture. *v.t.* [SCULPTURED (-chẽrd), SCULPTURING], 1. to cut, carve, chisel, cast, or mold into statues, figures, etc. 2. to represent or portray by means of sculpture. 3. to make or form by means of sculpture. 4. to decorate with sculpture. 5. to change in form by erosion: as, the river has *sculptured* the rock.

sculp·tur·esque (skulp′chə-resk′), *adj.* like or suggesting sculpture; shapely, statuelike, etc.

scum (skum), *n.* [ME. *scum, scume;* MD. *schum;* akin to G. *schaum*, foam, scum (cf. MEERSCHAUM); IE. base ***(s)qeu-*, to cover, hide, seen also in L. *obscurus* (cf. OBSCURE); basic sense "that covers"], 1. a thin layer of impurities which forms on the top of liquids or bodies of water, often as the result of boiling or fermentation. 2. the dross or refuse on top of molten metals. 3. refuse; worthless parts of anything. 4. a low, despicable, worthless person, or such people collectively. *v.t.* [SCUMMED (skumd), SCUMMING], to skim; remove from the surface. *v.i.* to form scum; become covered with scum.

scum·ble (skum′b'l), *v.t.* [SCUMBLED (-b'ld), SCUMBLING], [< *scum*], 1. in *painting*, *a*) to soften the outlines or color of by applying a thin coat of opaque color. *b*) to apply (color) in this manner. 2. in *drawing*, to soften the outlines of by rubbing or blurring. 3. to make by either of these processes. *n.* 1. a coat of color added in scumbling. 2. the softening of outline produced by scumbling.

scum·my (skum′i), *adj.* [SCUMMIER (-i-ẽr), SCUMMIEST (-i-ist)], 1. covered with scum. 2. of or like scum. 3. despicable; low; worthless; mean.

scup (skup), *n.* [*pl.* SCUP, SCUPS (skups); see PLURAL, II, D, 2], [< Am. Ind. (Narragansett), lit., close (scaled)], any of a group of marine food fishes related to the grunts and snappers, found on the Atlantic coast of the United States: also called *porgy*.

scup·per (skup′ẽr), *n.* [prob. for *scupper hole* < OFr. *escope*, bailing scoop < Gmc. base seen in *scoop*], an opening in a ship's side to allow water to run off the deck. *v.t.* [British Slang], to disable; put in great difficulty; annihilate, as by a surprise attack.

scup·per·nong (skup′ẽr-nôŋ′, skup′ẽr-noŋ′), *n.* [< the *Scuppernong* River in North Carolina], 1. a yellowish-green grape with a plumlike flavor. 2. the wine made from this grape.

scurf (skũrf), *n.* [ME. *scurf, scorf, scrof;* AS. < Scand.; cf. Dan. *skurv;* akin to AS. *sceorf*], 1. little, dry scales shed by the skin, as dandruff. 2. any scaly coating.

scurf·y (skũr′fi), *adj.* [SCURFIER (-fi-ẽr), SCURFIEST (-fi-ist)], of, like, or covered with scurf.

scur·rile, scur·ril (skũr′il), *adj.* [L. *scurrilis* < *scurra*, buffoon], [Archaic], scurrilous.

scur·ril·i·ty (skə-ril′ə-ti), *n.* [L. *scurrilitas*], 1. the quality of being scurrilous; coarseness or indecency of language, especially in invective or joking. 2. [*pl.* SCURRILITIES (-tiz)], a scurrilous act or remark.

scur·ril·ous (skũr′i-ləs), *adj.* [< L. *scurrilis*, buffoonlike < *scurra*, buffoon; + *-ous*], 1. coarse; vulgar; foul-mouthed; using indecent or abusive language. 2. containing coarse vulgarisms or indecent abuse.

scur·ry (skũr′i), *v.i.* [SCURRIED (-id), SCURRYING], [< *hurry-scurry; ?* a fusion of *scour* + *hurry*], to run hastily; scamper. *n.* 1. a hasty running; scampering. 2. the sound of hasty running. 3. a short run or race.

scur·vi·ly (skũr′v'l-i), *adv.* in a scurvy manner; meanly.

scur·vi·ness (skũr′vi-nis), *n.* the quality of being scurvy.

scur·vy (skũr′vi), *adj.* [SCURVIER (-vi-ẽr), SCURVIEST (-vi-ist)], [< *scurf*], 1. originally, scurfy. 2. low; mean; vile; contemptible. *n.* [< the *adj.*], a disease resulting from a deficiency of vitamin C in the body, characterized by weakness, anemia, spongy gums, bleeding from the mucous membranes, etc.

scurvy grass, a plant of the mustard family, with heart-shaped leaves, small white flowers, and a tarlike flavor, used in salads and medicine.

scut (skut), *n.* [ME., a tail, hare (see SCUD); prob. < ON.; cf. Ice. *skott*, tail of a fox, ON. *skot*, something projecting, *skutr*, stern of a boat; for IE. base see **shoot**], a short, stumpy tail, as of a hare or deer.

scu·ta (skū′tə), *n.* plural of **scutum.**

scu·tage (skū′tij), *n.* [ML. *scutagium* < L. *scutum*, a shield], in *feudal law*, a tax paid by the holder of a knight's fee, usually in lieu of military service.

Scu·ta·ri (skōō′tä-ri), *n.* 1. a city in northwestern Albania: the former capital: pop., 41,000: Albanian name, *Shkodër*. 2. Üsküdar, a section of Istanbul.

Scutari, Lake, a lake between southwestern Yugoslavia and northwestern Albania: area, c. 130 sq. mi.

scu·tate (skū′tāt), *adj.* [L. *scutatus* < *scutum*, a shield], 1. in *botany*, shaped like a shield: said especially of leaves joined to the stalk at about the center of the lower surface instead of at the base. 2. in *zoology*, covered or protected by bony or horny plates or scales.

scutch (skuch), *v.t.* [prob. < OFr. ***escoucher** < LL. ***excussare**, to shake much], to free the fibers of (flax, cotton, etc.) from woody parts by beating. *n.* an instrument for doing this.

scutch·eon (skuch′ən), *n.* [ME. *scochoun*, etc.; contr. of *escutcheon*], 1. an escutcheon. 2. any metal shield or plate, as for a keyhole, nameplate, etc. 3. a scute.

scute (skūt), *n.* [L. *scutum*, a shield], an external bony or horny plate; scutum.

scu·tel·late (skū′t'l-āt′, skūt′'l-it), *adj.* [Mod. L. *scutellatus* < *scutellum;* see SCUTELLUM], covered or protected with scutella, or small scales or plates.

scu·tel·late (skū′t'l-āt), *adj.* [< L. *scutella*, a salver, dim. of *scutra*, a tray; + *-ate;* Eng. meaning affected by association with L. *scutum*, a shield], in *botany* & *zoology*, shaped like a shield or platter; round.

scu·tel·la·tion (skū′t'l-ā′shən), *n.* [< *scutellate* (covered with scales)], the entire covering or arrangement of small scales or plates, as on a bird's leg.

scu·tel·lum (skū-tel′əm), *n.* [*pl.* SCUTELLA (-ə)], [Mod. L., for L. *scutulum*, dim. of *scutum*, a shield], 1. in *botany*, any of various parts shaped like a shield. 2. in *zoology*, a small horny scale or plate.

scu·ti·form (skū′ti-fôrm′), *adj.* [< L. *scutum*, a shield; + *-form*], shaped like a shield; scutate.

scut·ter (skut′ẽr), *v.i.* [var. of *scuttle*, *v.* + *-er*, freq. suffix], [British Colloq. or Dial.], to scurry about; bustle. *n.* [British Colloq. or Dial.], a scurrying or bustling about.

scut·tle (skut′'l), *n.* [ME. & AS. *scutel*, a dish < L. *scutella;* pronun. influenced by the L.], 1. a basket with a narrow base and a wide mouth, used for carrying grain, vegetables, etc. 2. a kind of bucket, usually with a wide, covered pouring spout, used for pouring coal on a fire.

scut·tle (skut′'l), *v.i.* [SCUTTLED (-'ld), SCUTTLING], [< dial. *scut*, var. of *scud* + *-le*, freq. suffix], to run or move quickly; scurry, especially away from danger, trouble, etc. *n.* a scurry or scamper; hasty flight or departure.

scut·tle (skut′'l), *n.* [OFr. *escoutille*, hatchway (Fr. *écoutille*); Sp. *escotilla;* prob. < Gmc. base of *shove*], 1. an opening in a wall or roof, fitted with a lid or cover. 2. an opening or hatchway in the outer hull or deck of a ship, fitted with a lid or cover. 3. the lid or cover for such an opening. *v.t.* [SCUTTLED (-'ld), SCUTTLING], 1. to cut a hole or holes through the hull of (a ship or boat) below the water line. 2. to sink (a ship or boat) by this means.

scut·tle·butt (skut′'l-but′), *n.* [orig. < *scuttled butt*, lidded cask, a butt or cask on shipboard with fresh drinking water], [Slang], 1. a drinking fountain on shipboard. 2. rumor or gossip.

scu·tum (skū′təm), *n.* [*pl.* SCUTA (-tə)], [L.; IE. base **(s)geu-t-*, to cover, seen also in Gr. *skutos*, a hide, leather], 1. the long, leather-covered, wooden shield carried by infantrymen in the Roman legions. 2. [S-], in *astronomy*, a small constellation in the Milky Way supposedly resembling a shield in shape: see **constellation**, chart. 3. in *zoology*, a heavy, horny scale or platelet, as on the bodies of certain reptiles.

Scyl·la (sil′ə), *n.* [L.; Gr. *Skylla* < *skylax*, a dog: Scylla is said to have barked like a dog], a dangerous rock on the Italian side of the Straits of Messina, opposite the whirlpool Charybdis: in classical mythology both Scylla and Charybdis were personified as female monsters.

between Scylla and Charybdis, facing difficulty or danger on either hand; between two perils or evils, neither of which can be evaded without risking the other.

scy·phi- (sī-fi), [< L. *scyphus;* see SCYPHUS], a combining form meaning *scyphus* or *cup*, as in *scyphiform*.

scy·phi·form (sī′fi-fôrm′), *adj.* [*scyphi-* + *-form*], in *zoology*, cup-shaped.

scy·pho·zo·an (sī′fə-zō′ən), *n.* [< Gr. *skyphos*, a cup + *zoion*, an animal], any of a number of sea coelenterates, chiefly jellyfishes.

scy·phus (sī′fəs), *n.* [*pl.* SCYPHI (-fī)], [L. < Gr. *skyphos*], 1. a form of ancient Greek cup with two flat-topped handles and no foot. 2. in *botany*, a cup-shaped part, as that between the petals and stamens in some flowers.

scythe (sīth), *n.* [altered (in error, after L. *scindere*, to cut) < ME. *sithe;* AS. *sithe*, *sigthe*, a scythe; akin to LG. *seged;* IE. base **seq-*, to cut, seen also in L. *sica*, dagger; cf. SEDGE, SICKLE, etc.], a tool with a long, single-edged blade set at an angle on a bent wooden shaft fitted with two handles, used in cutting long grass, grain, etc. by hand. *v.t.* [SCYTHED (sīthd), SCYTHING], to cut with a scythe.

SCYTHE

Scyth·i·a (sith′i-ə), *n.* an ancient region in southeastern Europe and Asia: its exact boundaries have not been determined.

Scyth·i·an (sith′i-ən), *adj.* of ancient Scythia, its people, their language, etc. *n.* 1. one of a nomadic and warlike people who lived in ancient Scythia. 2. their Iranian language.

S/D, sight draft.

S.D., 1. *Scientiae Doctor*, [L.], Doctor of Science. 2. Senior Deacon. 3. South Dakota: also **S. Dak.**

S.D., s.d., in *mathematics*, standard deviation.

s.d., sine die.

S. Dak., South Dakota.

'sdeath (zdeth), *interj.* [Archaic], God's death: a euphemistic oath expressing anger, surprise, emphasis, etc.

Se, in *chemistry*, selenium.

SE, S.E., s.e., southeast.

S.E., Southeastern (postal district).

sea (sē), *n.* [ME. *se, see;* AS. *sæ;* akin to D. *zee* (cf. ZUIDER ZEE) & G. *see;* IE. base **sē(i)-*, to drip, wet, etc.], 1. the continuous body of salt water covering the greater part of the earth's surface; ocean. 2. a large body of salt water wholly or partly enclosed by land: as, the Red *Sea*, Irish *Sea*. 3. a large body of fresh water: as, *Sea of Galilee*. 4. the state of the surface of the ocean with regard to waves or swells: as, a calm *sea*, light *sea*. 5. a heavy swell or wave; as, we shall be swamped by the next *sea*. 6. something like or suggesting the sea in extent or vastness; very great amount or number: as, lost in a *sea* of debt.

at sea, 1. on the open sea. 2. uncertain; bewildered.

follow the sea, to make one's living by serving on ocean-going ships.

go to sea, 1. to become a sailor. 2. to embark on a voyage.

put to sea, to sail away from land.

sea anchor, a large, canvas-covered frame, usually conical, let out from a ship as a drag or float to reduce drifting or to keep the ship heading into the wind.

sea anemone, any of various sea polyps having a firm, gelatinous body topped with petallike tentacles: they are often brightly colored and live attached to rocks.

sea bass, 1. a dark-brown or black marine food fish with large scales and a wide mouth, found along the Atlantic coast. 2. any of various similar marine fishes.

Sea·bee (sē′bē′), *n.* [< *C*onstruction *B*attalion], a member of any of the construction battalions of the Civil Engineer Corps of the United States Navy: they build and defend harbor facilities, airfields, and the like.

sea bird, a bird living on or near the sea.

sea biscuit, a type of hard biscuit formerly eaten by sailors; hardtack.

sea·board (sē′bôrd′, sē′bōrd′), *n.* [*sea* + *board* (border) or Fr. *bord*, an edge, side], land near or bordering on the sea; seacoast. *adj.* bordering on the sea.

sea-born (sē′bôrn′), *adj.* 1. born in or of the sea: as, Aphrodite, the *sea-born* goddess. 2. produced by or originating in the sea.

sea-borne, sea·borne (sē′bôrn′, sē′bōrn′), *adj.* 1. carried on or by the sea. 2. afloat: said of ships.

sea bread, ship biscuit; hardtack.

sea breeze, a breeze blowing inland from the sea.

sea calf, the common seal; harbor seal.

sea·coast (sē′kōst′), *n.* land bordering on or near to the sea; seashore.

sea cow, 1. any of several sea mammals, as the dugong and manatee. 2. the walrus. 3. the hippopotamus.

sea cucumber, [cf. Fr. *coucombre de mer*], any of a group of echinoderms with a cucumber-shaped body, leathery skin, and long, branched tentacles around the mouth; holothurian.

sea devil, 1. the devilfish. 2. the angelfish (shark).

sea dog, [cf. G. *seehund*], 1. the dogfish. 2. the common seal; sea calf. 3. a sailor, especially an experienced one.

sea duck, any of a group of ducks inhabiting salt water, especially the American eider duck.

sea eagle, 1. any of several fish-eating birds related to the bald eagle. 2. the osprey.

sea elephant, any of several very large seals that are hunted for oil: the males have a short trunk, or proboscis, somewhat like that of the elephant.

sea fan, any of several fan-shaped corals.

sea·far·er (sē′fâr′ẽr), *n.* a person who travels on the sea.

sea·far·ing (sē′fâr′iŋ), *adj.* of or engaged in life at sea. *n.* 1. the business or profession of a sailor. 2. travel by sea.

sea fight, a battle fought between ships at sea.

sea·flow·er (sē′flou′ẽr), *n.* a sea anemone or a similar polyp.

sea foam, 1. foam or froth on sea water. 2. meerschaum.

sea food, food prepared from or consisting of salt-water fish or shellfish.

sea·fowl (sē′foul′), *n.* any bird living on or near the sea.

sea fox, a kind of shark with a long tail fin; thresher shark.

sea front, the part of a town or other built-up area facing on the sea.

sea gauge, 1. the draft, or depth, of water needed to float a ship. 2. a gauge used in measuring sea depths.

sea·girt (sē′gũrt′), *adj.* surrounded by the sea.

sea·go·ing (sē′gō′iŋ), *adj.* 1. made for use on the open sea: as, a *seagoing* schooner. 2. seafaring.

sea-green (sē′grēn′), *adj.* pale bluish-green.

sea green, a sea-green color.

sea gull, a bird with long wings and webbed feet, living near and feeding from the water; gull.

sea hog, the porpoise.

fat, āpe, bâre, cär; ten, ēven, hêre, ovẽr; is, bīte; lot, gō, hôrn, tōōl, look; oil, out; up, ūse, fũr; get; joy; yet; chin; she; thin, *then*; zh, leisure; ŋ, ring; ə for *a* in *ago*, *e* in *agent*, *i* in *sanity*, *o* in *comply*, *u* in *focus;* ' as in *able* (ā′b'l); Fr. bål; ë, Fr. coeur; ö, Fr. feu; Fr. mo*n*; ô, Fr. coq; ü, Fr. duc; H, G. ich; kh, G. doch. See pp. x-xii. ‡ foreign; * hypothetical; < derived from.

sea holly, a small plant with pale-blue flowers and spiny, bluish leaves.

sea horse, 1. the walrus. 2. the hippocampus, a small, semitropical fish with a slender tail, plated body, and a head and foreparts somewhat like those of a horse. 3. a mythical sea creature, half fish and half horse.

SEA HORSE (3–10 in. long)

sea-is·land (sē′ī′lənd), ***adj.*** of or from the Sea Islands.

sea-island cotton, a fine kind of long-fibered cotton grown originally in the Sea Islands and now in other areas.

Sea Islands, a chain of islands off the coasts of South Carolina, Georgia, and Florida.

sea kale, [from growing near the coast], a fleshy mustard plant whose young shoots are used like asparagus.

sea king, [after ON. *sækonungr* (AS. *sæ-kyning*)], a Norse pirate chief of the Middle Ages.

seal (sēl), ***n.*** [ME. *seel;* OFr. *seel* < L. *sigillum,* a seal, mark, lit. little mark < *signum;* see SIGN], 1. a design, initial, or other device placed on a letter, document, etc. as a signature or proof of authenticity: letters were formerly closed with a wafer of molten wax into which was pressed the distinctive seal of the sender. 2. a stamp, signet ring, etc. used for making such an impression. 3. a wax wafer, piece of paper, etc. bearing the impression of some design recognized, usually by law, as official. 4. something that seals, closes, or fastens tightly. 5. something that confirms, authenticates, or guarantees; pledge: as, his fear was a *seal* of secrecy. 6. an indication; sign; token: as, their handshake was a *seal* of friendship. 7. any device, as a looped trap filled with water, preventing the passage of gas through a pipe. 8. an ornamental paper stamp: as, a Christmas *seal.* ***v.t.*** [ME. *selen;* OFr. *seeler* < the *n.*], 1. to mark with a seal; fix a seal to; hence, 2. to secure the contents of (a letter, envelope, etc.), originally by closing with a sealed wax wafer, now usually with mucilage, tape, etc. 3. to ratify, confirm, or authenticate (a document, etc.) by marking with a seal. 4. to attest to or confirm the truth or genuineness of (a promise, etc.). 5. to certify as being accurate, exact, of a given size, quality, capacity, etc. by fixing a stamp or seal to: as, have these scales been *sealed?* 6. to grant, assign, or designate with a seal, pledge, etc.: as, he has *sealed* his estate to his son. 7. to settle, determine, or decide finally or irrevocably. 8. to close completely, especially so as to make airtight; close, shut, or fasten with or as with a seal: as, *seal* the doors before fumigating, *seal* the cracks in the wall. 9. in *Mormonism, a*) to make formal and binding; solemnize: said of a marriage, adoption, etc. *b*) to give (a woman) in marriage. 10. in *electricity,* to bring into full, interlocking contact, as a plug and jack.

set one's seal to, 1. to mark or stamp with one's seal; hence, 2. to endorse; approve.

the seals, [British], symbols or marks of office, especially of public office.

seal (sēl), ***n.*** [*pl.* SEALS (sēlz), SEAL; see PLURAL, II, D, 1], [ME. *sele;* AS. *seolh;* akin to OHG. *selah;* prob. IE. base *selk-, to pull, draw (with reference to the seal's labored movements on land)], 1. a sea mammal with a torpedo-shaped body, a doglike head, and four webbed feet or flippers: it lives in cold or temperate waters and eats fish; *fur seals* are hunted for the valuable fur. 2. *a*) this fur; sealskin. *b*) a similar fur used as a substitute for this. 3. leather made from sealskin. ***v.i.*** to hunt seals.

FUR SEAL (5–6 ft. long)

sea lavender, any of a number of related stiff plants with white, pink, lavender, or yellow flowers and many branches.

sea lawyer, [Colloq.], a contentious sailor, who likes to argue points of sea law, usually on the basis of slight or inaccurate knowledge.

seal brown, a rich, dark brown.

sealed orders, written orders or instructions, as to the captain of a ship informing him of his destination, mission, etc., given in a sealed envelope not to be opened until a specified time or place is reached.

sea legs, the ability to walk without loss of balance on board ship, especially in a rough sea.

seal·er (sēl′ẽr), ***n.*** 1. a person or thing that seals. 2. an officer whose duty is to inspect, test, and certify weights and measures.

seal·er (sēl′ẽr), ***n.*** 1. a hunter of seals. 2. a ship used in seal hunting.

seal·er·y (sēl′ẽr-i), ***n.*** [*pl.* SEALERIES (-iz)], 1. the work of hunting seals. 2. a place where seals are hunted.

sea lettuce, any of a number of related seaweeds with edible, leaflike parts.

sea level, the level of the surface of the sea, especially when halfway between high and low tide: used as a standard in measuring heights and depths.

sea lily, a crinoid.

sealing wax, a combination of resin and turpentine used for sealing letters, dry batteries, etc.: it is hard at normal temperatures but softens when heated.

sea lion, a large seal with ears, of the North Pacific.

seal ring, a signet ring.

seal·skin (sēl′skin′), ***n.*** 1. the skin or pelt of the seal, especially with the coarse outer hair removed and the soft undercoat dyed dark-brown or black. 2. a garment made of this. ***adj.*** made of sealskin.

sea lungwort, a fleshy plant with egg-shaped, white-spotted leaves and white, purple, or blue flowers.

Sea·ly·ham terrier (sē′li-ham′, sē′li-əm), [so named from being bred at *Sealyham,* an estate in Pembrokeshire, Wales], any of a small, long-bodied breed of terrier with short legs, a shaggy white coat, and a head like that of a Scottish terrier.

seam (sēm), ***n.*** [ME. *seme;* AS. *seam;* akin to G. *saum;* IE. base **sū-, sēw-,* to sew, seen also in L. *suere, sutum* (cf. SUTURE), Eng. *sew*], 1. a line formed by sewing together two pieces of material. 2. any line formed by the joining together of separate pieces; line marking adjoining edges, as of boards. 3. a mark, line, ridge, etc. like this, as a scar, wrinkle, mold line on glass, etc. 4. a thin layer or stratum of ore, coal, etc. ***v.t.*** 1. to join together so as to form a seam. 2. to mark with a seamlike line, crack, wrinkle, etc. 3. in *knitting,* to purl. ***v.i.*** 1. to crack open. 2. [Dial.], to sew. 3. in *knitting,* to purl.

sea maid, [Obs. or Poetic], 1. a mermaid. 2. a sea nymph or goddess.

sea·man (sē′mən), ***n.*** [*pl.* SEAMEN (-mən)], [ME. *seeman;* cf. G. *seemann*], 1. a sailor; mariner. 2. an enlisted man ranking below a petty officer in the navy.

sea·man·like (sē′mən-līk′), ***adj.*** like or characteristic of a good seaman; having or showing seamanship.

sea·man·ly (sē′mən-li), ***adj.*** seamanlike.

sea·man·ship (sē′mən-ship′), ***n.*** [*seaman* + *-ship*], skill in sailing or working a ship; ability of a good seaman.

sea·mark (sē′märk′), ***n.*** 1. a line marking the upper limit of the tide. 2. any prominent object on shore, as a lighthouse, serving as a guide for a ship's course.

sea mew, [ME. *semewe;* cf. MEW], a sea gull.

sea mouse, a segmented sea worm with a flat, oval body covered with scales and iridescent bristles.

seam·stress (sēm′stris), ***n.*** [ME. *seamestre,* man or woman who sews; AS. *seamestre* < *seam,* a seam; + additional fem. suffix *-ess*], a woman who is expert at sewing, especially one who makes her living by sewing: also **sempstress.**

seam·y (sēm′i), ***adj.*** [SEAMIER (-i-ẽr), SEAMIEST (-i-ist)], having or showing seams, especially with rough, unfinished edges, as the underside of a garment.

the seamy side, the least attractive aspect.

‡Sean·ad Eir·eann (san′äd âr′ən), [Ir.], the Senate, or upper house, of the legislature (*Oireachtas*) of Ireland.

sé·ance (sā′äns; Fr. sā′äns′), ***n.*** [Fr., lit., a sitting < OFr. *seoir;* L. *sedere,* to sit], 1. a meeting or session. 2. a meeting at which a group of spiritualists try to communicate with the spirits of the dead.

sea onion, a plant of the lily family, with wide leaves, dense clusters of small, whitish flowers, and a bulb used in medicine; squill.

sea otter, a web-footed sea mammal of the otter family, found along the North Pacific coast: its dark-brown fur is very valuable.

sea pen, a kind of polyp that forms colonies having the shape of a feather.

sea·plane (sē′plān′), ***n.*** any airplane designed to land on and take off from water.

sea·port (sē′pôrt′, sē′pōrt′), ***n.*** 1. a port or harbor used by ocean ships. 2. a town or city having such a port or harbor. Abbreviated **spt.**

sea power, 1. naval strength. 2. a nation having great naval strength. Distinguished from *land power.*

sea purse, a horny case or capsule produced by certain skates, rays, and sharks, serving to hold their eggs.

sea·quake (sē′kwāk′), ***n.*** an earthquake on the floor of the sea.

sear (sêr), ***adj.*** [ME. *seer;* AS.; var. of SERE], dry; withered; faded. ***v.t.*** [ME. *seeren;* AS. *searian* < *sear;* see the *adj.*], 1. to dry up; wither. 2. to scorch or burn the surface of so as to make dry or hard. 3. to brand or cauterize with a hot iron. 4. to make callous or unfeeling; harden. ***v.i.*** to become sear; wither. ***n.*** any mark or condition produced by searing. —***SYN.*** see **burn.**

sear (sêr), ***n.*** [Fr. *serre,* a grasp < OFr. *serrer,* to close, press; LL. **serrare,* (as if < *serrare,* to saw, but with meaning of *serare,* to bolt, bar) < L. *sera,* a bar, bolt], the catch in a gunlock that holds the hammer cocked or half-cocked.

sea raven, a kind of sculpin found in the North Atlantic.

search (sũrch), *v.t.* [ME. *serchen, cerchen;* OFr. *cercher* (Fr. *chercher*) < L. *circare*, to go round, go about, explore < *circus*, a ring], 1. to go over or look through for the purpose of finding something; explore; rummage; examine: as, they *searched* the house for weapons, he *searched* his records in vain. 2. to examine (a person) for something concealed, by running one's hands over the clothing, through the pockets, etc. 3. to examine closely and carefully; test and try; probe: as, he *searched* his soul for the answer. 4. to pierce; penetrate; go through: as, the wind *searched* her ragged clothing. *v.i.* to try to find something; make a search. *n.* 1. an act of searching; scrutiny, inquiry, or examination in an attempt to find something, gain knowledge, etc. 2. [Rare], a person or group that searches. 3. the act of a belligerent in stopping and searching a neutral ship for contraband: see **right of search.**

in search of, making a search for; trying to find, learn, etc. by searching.

search out, to seek or find by searching.

search·ing (sũr′chiŋ), *adj.* 1. examining or exploring thoroughly; scrutinizing; thorough; vigorous. 2. keen; sharp; piercing; penetrating: as, the *searching* wind.

search·light (sũrch′lit′), *n.* 1. an apparatus containing a source of light and a reflector that projects the light produced in a concentrated, far-reaching beam: it is usually mounted on a swivel so that the beam can be directed. 2. the beam of light projected.

search party, a group of people taking part in a search.

search warrant, a legal document authorizing or directing a peace officer to search a specified person, premises, dwelling, etc., as for stolen or contraband articles, items to be used in evidence, suspected criminals, etc.

sea risk, the danger or risk involved in traveling or transporting by water.

sea robber, a pirate.

sea robin, a fish of the gurnard family, especially the American species having reddish coloring.

sea room, enough open space for maneuvering a ship.

sea rover, 1. a pirate. 2. a pirate ship.

sea·scape (sē′skāp′), *n.* [*sea* + land*scape*], 1. a view of the sea. 2. a picture of this.

sea serpent, 1. any large, unidentified serpentlike animal living, or thought to live, in the sea. 2. any of several poisonous sea snakes.

sea shell, the shell of any salt-water mollusk.

sea·shore (sē′shôr′, sē′shōr′), *n.* land along the sea; seacoast; specifically, in *law*, the ground lying between the usual high-water and low-water marks.

sea·sick (sē′sik′), *adj.* suffering from seasickness.

sea·sick·ness (sē′sik′nis), *n.* nausea, dizziness, etc. caused by the rolling and pitching of a ship at sea.

sea·side (sē′sīd′), *n.* land along the sea; seashore; seacoast. *adj.* at or of the seaside.

sea snake, 1. any of a number of poisonous snakes living in tropical seas. 2. a sea serpent.

sea·son (sē′z'n), *n.* [ME. *sesoun, seson;* OFr. *seson, seison, saison;* LL. *satio*, sowing time (in L., a sowing) < base of L. *serere*, to sow; cf. SEMEN, SEED, SOW], 1. any one of the four arbitrary divisions of the year, characterized chiefly by differences in temperature, weather, number of hours of daylight, and growth of plants; spring, summer, fall, or winter. 2. a time or part of the year during which a specified kind of agricultural work is done: as, the planting *season*, harvest *season*, etc. 3. the time when something specified flourishes, develops, takes place, is popular, permitted, or at its best: as, the opera *season*, orange *season*, fishing *season*, etc. 4. a period of time, especially a relatively short one. 5. the suitable, fitting, or convenient time: often for something specified, as, this is the topcoat *season*. 6. the time of a specified festival: as, the Christmas *season*. 7. [< the *v.*], [Obs.], something that seasons. *v.t.* 1. to add to or change the flavor of (food); flavor. 2. to add zest or interest to. 3. *a)* to make more suitable for use; improve the quality of, as by aging, exposure to air, etc.; cure; mature. *b)* to give (an athlete) experience to improve his play. 4. to make used to; accustom; inure; acclimatize: as, he was *seasoned* to the hard life. 5. to make less harsh or severe; temper; soften: as, *season* your remarks with discretion. *v.i.* to become seasoned, or more suitable for use.

for a season, for a while.

in good season, early enough.

in season, 1. available fresh for use as food: said of fruits, vegetables, sea food, etc., usually of a locality specified or understood. 2. at the legally established time for being hunted or caught: said of game, etc. 3. in or at the suitable or proper time. 4. in good season; early enough. 5. ready to mate or breed: said of animals.

in season and out of season, at any time; at all times.

out of season, not in season.

sea·son·a·ble (sē′z'n-ə-b'l), *adj.* [ME. *sesonable;* Anglo-Fr. < OFr. *saison;* see SEASON], 1. suitable to or usual for the time of year. 2. coming or done at the right time; opportune; timely. —*SYN.* see **timely.**

sea·son·a·bly (sē′z'n-ə-bli), *adv.* in a seasonable manner; at the right time or season.

sea·son·al (sē′z'n-əl), *adj.* 1. of or characteristic of the season or seasons. 2. affected by or depending on a season; hence, 3. coming at regular intervals.

sea·son·al·ly (sē′z'n-əl-i), *adv.* 1. with or at a given season. 2. in a seasonal manner; periodically.

sea·son·ing (sē′z'n-iŋ), *n.* [*season* + *-ing*], 1. any flavoring added to food; condiment. 2. anything that adds zest, interest, or variety.

season ticket, a ticket that entitles the holder to use or service, usually unlimited, for a given period or series of events: season tickets are sold for railroad travel, play on golf courses, entertainments, etc.

sea squirt, a small sea animal with a flabby body that contracts to shoot out jets of water; ascidian; tunicate.

sea swallow, 1. any bird of the tern family. 2. the stormy petrel.

seat (sēt), *n.* [ME. *sete;* ON. *sæti* < base seen in *sit*], 1. the manner of sitting, as on horseback. 2. the place or space where a person sits; place to sit: as, I can't find a *seat*. 3. a thing to sit on; chair, bench, stool, etc. 4. the buttocks. 5. the part of a garment covering the buttocks. 6. the part of a chair, bench, etc. that supports the buttocks. 7. the right to sit as a member; position of a member; membership: as, he has a *seat* on the commission. 8. a part or surface upon which the base of something rests. 9. the place where something is carried on, settled, or established; center; location; place: as, the *seat* of government, *seat* of learning. 10. the town where a king, bishop, etc. makes his home. 11. a home; residence; especially, a large house that is part of a country estate. *v.t.* 1. to put or set in or on a seat. 2. to help or settle into a seat. 3. to have a seat or seats for; accommodate with a seat or seats: as, the stadium *seats* 50,000 people. 4. to put a seat in or on; patch or renew the seat of; reseat. 5. to put, fix, or establish in a particular place, position of authority, etc.

be seated, 1. to take a seated position; sit down. 2. to be sitting. 3. to be located, settled, or situated.

sea tangle, any of various seaweeds.

seat belt, a restraining device, usually consisting of anchored straps that buckle across the hips, to protect a seated passenger from abrupt jolts, as in a collision.

seat·er (sēt′ēr), *n.* something having (a specified number of) seats: used, in hyphenated compounds, of automobiles, airplanes, etc., as in *two-seater, four-seater*.

seat·ing (sēt′iŋ), *n.* 1. the act of providing with a seat or seats. 2. material for covering chair seats, etc. 3. the arrangement of seats or of persons seated. 4. *a)* a seat (sense 8). *b)* a part that rests on this.

SEATO (sē′tō), Southeast Asia Treaty Organization.

sea trout, 1. any of several salt-water trouts related to the salmon. 2. any of several weakfishes.

Se·at·tle (sē-at′'l), *n.* a seaport on Puget Sound, in Washington: pop., 557,000.

sea urchin, any of several sea animals of the echinoderm family, having a flattened globular body of fused plates covered with a spiny skin.

sea wall, a wall or embankment made to break the force of the waves and to protect the shore from erosion.

sea·wan (sē′wən), *n.* sewan.

sea·want (sē′wənt), *n.* sewan.

sea·ward (sē′wērd), *n.* a direction or position away from the land and toward the sea. *adj.* 1. directed, going, or situated toward the sea. 2. from the sea: said of a wind. *adv.* toward, or in the direction of, the sea.

sea·wards (sē′wērdz), *adv.* seaward.

sea·ware (sē′wâr′), *n.* [via dial. < AS. *sæware*, seaweed; *sæ*, sea + *ware*, alga], seaweed; especially, large, coarse seaweed tossed up on shore.

sea·way (sē′wā′), *n.* 1. a way or route by sea; sea as a means of travel. 2. the movement of a ship through the water. 3. the open sea. 4. a rough sea. 5. an inland waterway to the sea for ocean-going ships.

sea·weed (sē′wēd′), *n.* any sea plant or plants; especially, any marine alga.

sea wolf, 1. any of several large, ferocious sea fishes, as the sea bass, blenny, etc. 2. a pirate.

sea·wor·thi·ness (sē′wũr′*thi*-nis), *n.* the quality or condition of being seaworthy.

sea·wor·thy (sē′wũr′*thi*), *adj.* fit to travel in on the open sea; safe in rough weather; sturdy: said of a ship.

sea wrack, seaweed, especially of the large kinds.

se·ba·ceous (si-bā′shəs), *adj.* [Mod. L. *sebaceus* < L. *sebum*, tallow], of or like fat, tallow, or sebum; especially, designating certain skin glands that secrete sebum.

se·bac·ic (si-bas′ik, si-bās′ik), *adj.* [< L. *sebaceus*, tallow candle < *sebum*, tallow; + *-ic*], designating or of a white, crystalline acid, $C_{10}H_{18}O_4$, obtained by the distillation of oleic acid.

Se·bas·tian (si-bas′chən), [L. *Sebastianus;* Gr. *Sebastianos*, lit., a man of Sebastia (Gr. *Sebasteia*), ancient

name of Sivas, or a man of Sebaste (Gr. *Sebastē*), name of the city of Samaria after the time of Herod the Great; both < Gr. *Sebastos*, lit., venerable, august, epithet of the emperor Augustus], a masculine name.
Se·bas·to·pol (si-bas′tə-pōl′), *n.* Sevastopol.
SEbE, southeast by east.
se·bi- (sē′bi), [< L. *sebum*, tallow], a combining form meaning *tallow, wax*, as in *sebiferous*.
se·bif·er·ous (si-bif′ẽr-əs), *adj.* [*sebi-* + *-ferous*], 1. in *botany*, secreting a fatty or waxlike substance. 2. in *physiology*, sebaceous.
seb·or·rhe·a, seb·or·rhoe·a (seb′ə-rē′ə), *n.* [< L. *sebum*, tallow; + *-rrhea*], an excessive discharge from the sebaceous glands resulting in an abnormally oily skin, often with yellowish, greasy scales.
SEbS, southeast by south.
se·bum (sē′bəm), *n.* [L., tallow], the semiliquid, greasy secretion of the sebaceous glands.
‡**sec** (sek), *adj.* [Fr.], dry; not sweet: said of wine.
SEC, S.E.C., Securities and Exchange Commission.
sec., 1. secant. 2. second; seconds. 3. secondary. 4. secretary. 5. section; sections. 6. sector. 7. security.
se·cant (sē′kənt, sē′kant), *adj.* [L. *secans*, ppr. of *secare*, to cut], cutting; intersecting. *n.* 1. any straight line intersecting a curve at two or more points. 2. in *trigonometry*, *a*) a straight line extending from the center of a circle through the end of an arc of its circumference to another straight line that is tangent to the radius at the other end of the arc. *b*) the length of this. *c*) the ratio of the length of this line to the length of the radius; hence, *d*) the ratio of the length of the hypotenuse of any right-angled triangle to the length of either of the other two sides with reference to the enclosed angle. Abbreviated **sec.**

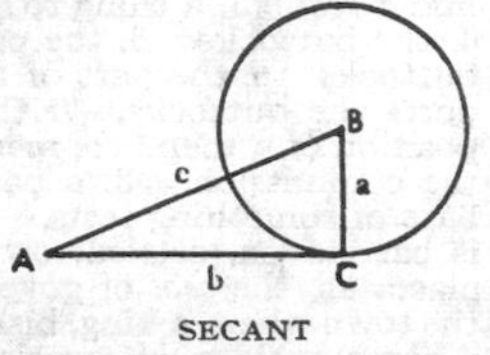

SECANT

$\frac{c}{a}$, secant of angle ABC; $\frac{c}{b}$, secant of angle BAC

‡**sec·co** (sek′kô), *adj.* [It.; L. *siccus*], dry. *n.* tempera painting done on dry plaster: distinguished from *fresco*.
se·cede (si-sēd′), *v.i.* [SECEDED (-id), SECEDING], [L. *secedere; se-*, apart + *cedere*, to go], to withdraw formally from membership in a group, association, organization, etc.; break off one's connection with others, as in a political or religious group.
se·cern (si-sũrn′), *v.t.* [L. *secernere*, to sunder, separate; *se-*, aside + *cernere*, to separate], 1. to discriminate, or distinguish. 2. [Rare], in *physiology*, to secrete.
se·cern·ent (si-sũrn′ənt), *adj.* secreting.
se·cern·ment (si-sũrn′mənt), *n.* a secerning or being secerned.
se·ces·sion (si-sesh′ən), *n.* [L. *secessio*], 1. an act of seceding; formal withdrawal or separation. 2. [often S-], the withdrawal of a State from the Federal Union.
se·ces·sion·al (si-sesh′ən-′l), *adj.* of or constituting secession.
se·ces·sion·ist (si-sesh′ən-ist), *n.* a person who favors or takes part in secession, or upholds the right to secede; specifically [often S-], one favoring the secession of the Southern States at the start of the Civil War.
Se·chua·na (se-chwä′nä), *n.* any of a group of Bantu dialects spoken in the southern part of Northern Rhodesia.
Seck·el (sek′′l), *n.* [after the Penn. fruitgrower who originated the variety], a small, sweet, juicy, reddish-brown variety of pear: also **Seckel pear.**
sec. leg., *secundum legem*, [L.], according to law.
se·clude (si-klōōd′, si-klūd′), *v.t.* [SECLUDED (-id), SECLUDING], [L. *secludere* < *se-*, apart + *claudere*, to shut], 1. to keep away or apart from others; bar or shut off from the view of or relations with others; isolate. 2. to make private or hidden; screen.
se·clud·ed (si-klōōd′id, si-klūd′id), *adj.* [pp. of *seclude*], shut off or kept apart from others; isolated; remote; withdrawn: as, a *secluded* meeting place.
se·clu·sion (si-klōō′zhən, si-klū′zhən), *n.* [ML. *seclusio*], 1. a secluding or being secluded; retirement; isolation; privacy. 2. a secluded spot. —*SYN.* see **solitude.**
se·clu·sive (si-klōō′siv, si-klū′siv), *adj.* [< L. *seclusus*, pp. of *secludere* (see SECLUDE); + *-ive*], 1. tending to seclude. 2. fond of or seeking seclusion.
sec·ond (sek′ənd), *adj.* [ME. *secunde;* OFr. < L. *secundus*, following, second < *sequi*, to follow; cf. SEQUENT, SEQUEL], 1. coming next after the first in order of place or time; 2d. 2. another; other; additional; supplementary: as, we all took a *second* helping. 3. being of the same kind as another; resembling a given original: as, there has been no *second* Shakespeare. 4. next below the first in rank, power, value, merit, excellence, etc.; hence, 5. inferior; subordinate; secondary. 6. in *music*, *a*) lower in pitch. *b*) playing or singing a part that is lower in pitch. *n.* 1. a person or thing that is second. 2. the next after the first. 3. an article of merchandise that falls below the standard set for first quality. 4. *pl. a*) a kind of coarse flour. *b*) bread made from this. 5. a person who acts as an aid or official assistant to another, especially to one of the principals in a duel or boxing match. 6. in *music*, *a*) the interval between consecutive diatonic tones. *b*) a tone separated from another by this interval. *c*) the combination of two such tones in harmony. *d*) the second part in a harmonized composition; especially, the alto. *e*) an instrument or voice taking this part. Abbreviated **sec., s.** *v.t.* 1. to act as an aid or second to; aid; support; assist. 2. to give support or encouragement to; further; reinforce. 3. to indicate one's approval or support of (a motion, etc.) as a necessary preliminary to discussion of or vote on it. *adv.* in the second place, rank, group, etc.
sec·ond (sek′ənd), *n.* [Fr. *seconde;* ML. *secunda minuta*, lit., second minute: so called from being a further division (i.e., beyond the minute) < L. *secundus;* see SECOND, *adj.*], 1. 1/60 of a minute of time. 2. a very short time; moment; instant. 3. 1/60 of a minute of angular measurement; 1/3600 of a degree of arc; symbol ″, as, 20°10′30″. Abbreviated **sec., s.** (*sing. & pl*).
Second Advent, in the theology of some Christian sects, the expected return of Christ to earth to sit in judgment of both the living and the dead; millennium.
Second Adventist, a person who expects the Second Advent, especially a member of a sect having a belief in the millennium as part of its doctrine.
sec·ond·ar·i·ly (sek′ən-der′ə-li, sek′ən-der′ə-li), *adv.* so as to be secondary; in a secondary manner.
sec·ond·ar·i·ness (sek′ən-der′i-nis), *n.* the state or quality of being secondary.
sec·ond·ar·y (sek′ən-der′i), *adj.* [ME. *secoundarie*, etc.; L. *secundarius*], 1. second, or below the first, in rank, importance, class, place, etc.; subordinate; minor; not primary. 2. derived or resulting from something considered primary or original; dependent; derivative. 3. coming after that which is first in a series of processes, events, stages, etc., as of growth or development. 4. coming next in sequence after the primary or elementary level: as, *secondary* school, *secondary* flight training. 5. in *chemistry*, *a*) formed by the replacement of two atoms or radicals in the molecule: as, *secondary* sodium phosphate, Na_2HPO_4. *b*) characterized by or designating a carbon atom that is directly attached to two other atoms or radicals in a closed or open chain. 6. in *electricity*, *a*) designating or of an induced current or its circuit. *b*) having current produced by induction: as, a *secondary* coil. 7. [S-], in *geology*, Mesozoic. 8. in *zoology*, designating or of the second joint or segment of a bird's wing or the quills attached to this. *n.* [*pl.* SECONDARIES (-iz)], 1. a person or thing that is secondary, subordinate, or inferior. 2. in *electricity*, a secondary circuit or coil. 3. in *zoology*, a quill growing from the second joint or segment of a bird's wing. Abbreviated **sec.**
secondary accent, 1. in a word with two or more syllables accented, or stressed, any accent that is weaker than the full, or primary, accent. 2. any symbol (in this dictionary, ′), indicating such an accent.
secondary color, a color formed by the mixture of two primary colors in equal quantities.
secondary education, education, as in a high school, between the primary and collegiate levels.
secondary school, a school, especially a high school, giving a secondary education.
second base, in *baseball*, the base between first base and third base, located behind the pitcher.
sec·ond-best (sek′ənd-best′), *adj.* of quality next below the first; next to the best.
second best, something second-best.
second childhood, senility; dotage.
sec·ond-class (sek′ənd-klas′, sek′ənd-kläs′), *adj.* 1. of the class, rank, excellence, etc. next below the highest; of secondary quality. 2. designating or of accommodations next below the best: as, a *second-class* railway carriage. 3. designating or of a class of mail consisting of newspapers, periodicals, etc.: such mail carries lower postage rates than first-class mail. 4. inferior, inadequate, etc. *adv.* 1. with accommodations next below the best: as, we traveled to Europe *second-class*. 2. as or by second-class mail.
Second Coming, the Second Advent.
second cousin, the child of one's parent's first cousin.
se·conde (si-kond′; Fr. sə-gōnd′), *n.* [Fr., fem. of *second*, second], a parrying position in fencing.
second estate, see **estate** (sense 2).
second fiddle, 1. *a*) the part played by the second violin section of an orchestra. *b*) any member of this section; hence, 2. a person, part, or position of secondary importance.
second floor, 1. the floor above the ground floor of a building. 2. in Europe and Great Britain, the floor two stories above the ground floor: sometimes used in this sense in hotels, etc. in the United States.
second growth, tree growth on land stripped of virgin forest.
sec·ond-guess (sek′ənd-ges′), *v.t. & v.i.* [Colloq.], to use hindsight in criticizing or advising (someone), re-solving (a past problem), remaking (a decision), etc.

sec·ond·hand (sek′ənd-hand′), *adj.* [cf. Fr. *de seconde main*], 1. not direct from the original source; not original. 2. used or worn previously by another; not new. 3. of or dealing in merchandise that is not new.
second hand, 1. the hand (of a clock or watch) that indicates the seconds and moves around the dial once every minute. 2. one who or that which is intermediate: now only in *at second hand,* indirectly.
Second International, an international organization of Socialist (Social-Democratic) parties, founded in Paris in 1889: it later became the Labor and Socialist International.
second lieutenant, a commissioned officer of the lowest rank in the United States Army or Marine Corps.
sec·ond·ly (sek′ənd-li), *adv.* in the second place; second: used chiefly in enumerating topics.
second mate, a ship's officer next in rank below the first mate.
second mortgage, an additional mortgage placed on property already mortgaged: the holder of a second mortgage may present his claim only after the conditions of the first mortgage have been fulfilled.
second nature, a habit, characteristic, etc. acquired and fixed so deeply as to seem part of a person's nature.
‡**se·con·do** (se-kôn′dô), *n.* [*pl.* SECONDI (-dē)], [It.; L. *secundus,* second], in *music,* 1. the second, usually the lower, part in a concerted piece, especially in a piano duet. 2. a person performing such a part.
second papers, the final application of an alien for United States citizenship; petition for naturalization.
second person, that form of a pronoun or verb which refers to the person spoken to: in *you do, you* and *do* are said to be in the second person.
sec·ond-rate (sek′ənd-rāt′), *adj.* 1. second in quality or other rating; second-class. 2. inferior; mediocre.
Second Republic, the republic established in France in 1848, when Louis Philippe was deposed and Louis Napoleon was elected president, lasting until 1852, when the Second Empire was established.
second self, a person so intimately associated with another as to have taken on many of his personality traits, attitudes, beliefs, etc.
second sight, the supposed ability to see that which cannot normally be seen, as future events, supernatural objects, etc.
sec·ond-sto·ry (sek′ənd-stôr′i, sek′ənd-stō′ri), *adj.* of, on, or in the second story, or floor.
sec·ond-sto·ry man, [Slang], a burglar, especially one who enters a building through an upstairs window.
second wind, 1. the return of relatively normal ease in breathing following the exhaustion that occurs during severe exertion or exercise, as in running: it is due to improved action of the heart; hence, 2. the recovered capacity for continuing any sort of effort.
Second World War, see **World War II.**
sec·par (sek′pär′), *n.* parsec, a unit of measure.
se·cre·cy (sē′krə-si), *n.* [*pl.* SECRECIES (-siz)], [ME. *secretee;* repatterned after *secret* + *-cy*], 1. the quality or condition of being secret, or concealed. 2. the ability to keep things from the knowledge of others; power to keep secrets. 3. a tendency to keep things secret; quality or habit of being secretive.
se·cret (sē′krit), *adj.* [ME.; OFr. < L. *secretus,* pp. of *secernere,* to set apart; *se-,* apart + *cernere,* to sift, distinguish, discern, perceive], 1. kept from public knowledge or from the knowledge of certain persons. 2. retired; remote; secluded. 3. keeping one's affairs to oneself; secretive; close. 4. beyond general knowledge or understanding; incomprehensible; deeply mysterious. 5. concealed from sight or notice; hidden: as, a *secret* drawer. 6. acting in secret: as, a *secret* society, *secret* agent. *n.* 1. something known only to a certain person or persons and purposely kept from the knowledge of others. 2. something not revealed, understood, or explained; mystery: as, the *secrets* of Egyptian embalming. 3. the true cause or explanation, regarded as not obvious: as, *secrets* of success. 4. [S-], a prayer said in a low voice after the Offertory in the Mass.
in secret, without the knowledge of others; secretly.
SYN.—**secret,** the general term, implies a concealing or keeping from the knowledge of others, for whatever reason (my *secret* opinion of him); **covert** implies a concealing as by disguising or veiling (a *covert* threat); **clandestine** suggests that what is being kept secret is of an illicit, immoral, or proscribed nature (their *clandestine* meetings in the park); **stealthy** implies a slow, quiet secrecy of action in an attempt to elude notice and often connotes deceit (the *stealthy* advance of the panther); **furtive** adds to this connotations of slyness or watchfulness and suggests a reprehensible objective (the *furtive* movement of his hand toward my pocket); **surreptitious** connotes a feeling of guilt in the one who is acting in a furtive or stealthy manner (she stole a *surreptitious* glance at him); **underhand** implies a stealthiness characterized by fraudulence or deceit (*underhand* business dealings). —***ANT.*** open, obvious.
secret agent, a person who carries on espionage or similar work of a secret nature, as for a government.
‡**se·cré·taire** (sek′rə-târ′), *n.* [Fr.], a writing desk; secretary.
sec·re·tar·i·al (sek′rə-târ′i-əl), *adj.* of a secretary.
sec·re·tar·i·at, sec·re·tar·i·ate (sek′rə-târ′i-it), *n.* [Fr. *secrétariat;* ML. *secretariatus*], 1. the office or position of a secretary. 2. the office or place where a secretary does his work. 3. a staff or department headed by a secretary. 4. a staff or group of secretaries.
sec·re·tar·y (sek′rə-ter′i), *n.* [*pl.* SECRETARIES (-iz)], [ML. *secretarius,* one entrusted with secrets < L. *secretum;* see SECRET], 1. a person employed to keep records, take care of correspondence and other writing tasks, etc. for an organization or individual. 2. a general official in over-all charge of such work. 3. an official in charge of a department of government. 4. a writing desk, especially one topped with a small bookcase. Abbreviated **sec., secy., sec'y.**
secretary bird, [so named because the crest resembles pens stuck over the ear], a large African bird of prey with a long neck, long legs, and a bunch of penlike feathers sticking out from the back of its head: it feeds on insects, snakes, and other reptiles.
sec·re·tar·y-gen·er·al (sek′rə-ter′i-jen′ẽr-əl), *n.* [*pl.* SECRETARIES-GENERAL], a secretary having authority over others; head of a secretariat.
sec·re·tar·y·ship (sek′rə-ter′i-ship′), *n.* [see -SHIP], the position, term, or work of a secretary.
se·crete (si-krēt′), *v.t.* [SECRETED (-id), SECRETING], [< L. *secretus,* pp. of *secernere;* see SECRET], 1. to put or keep in a secret place; hide; conceal. 2. in *biology* & *physiology,* to separate (a substance) from the blood or sap and elaborate as a new substance to be used by the organism or excreted as waste. —***SYN.*** see **hide.**
se·cre·tin (si-krē′tin), *n.* [*secret*ion + *-in*], a hormone produced in the small intestine to stimulate the secretion of pancreatic juice and bile.
se·cre·tion (si-krē′shən), *n.* [OFr.; L. *secretio,* a separation < *secretus,* pp. of *secernere;* see SECRET], 1. the act or process of secreting; specifically, *a*) a hiding or concealing. *b*) the separation and elaboration of a substance from the blood or sap. 2. a substance so secreted by an animal or plant.
se·cre·tive (si-krē′tiv; *for 1, often* sē′krə-tiv), *adj.* [*secret* + *-ive*], 1. tending to conceal one's thoughts, feelings, affairs, etc. from others; reticent; not frank or open. 2. secretory. —***SYN.*** see **silent.**
se·cre·tor (si-krēt′ẽr), *n.* a duct, gland, etc. that secretes.
se·cre·to·ry (si-krē′tə-ri), *adj.* of, or having the function of, secretion; secreting. *n.* a secretory gland, etc.
se·cret-serv·ice (sē′krit-sũr′vis), *adj.* of or having to do with the secret service.
secret service, 1. a government service organized to carry on secret investigation and the like; specifically, [S- S-], a division of the United States Treasury Department concerned with the discovery and arrest of counterfeiters, the protection of the President, etc. 2. espionage service, as conducted by the armed forces.
secret society, any organized group that conceals some of its rituals and other activities from nonmembers.
sect (sekt), *n.* [ME. & Fr. *secte;* L. *secta* < *sequi,* to follow; cf. SEQUEL], 1. a group of people having a common leadership, set of opinions, philosophical doctrine, etc.; school; following. 2. any group holding certain views, political principles, etc. in common. 3. a religious denomination, especially a small group that has broken away from an established church.
sect (sekt), *n.* [< L. *sectus,* pp. of *secare,* to cut; cf. SEGMENT], a part or section.
sect., section.
sec·tar·i·an (sek-târ′i-ən), *adj.* [< ML. *sectarius* < L. *secta* (see SECT, group); + *-an*], 1. of or characteristic of a sect. 2. devoted to, or prejudiced in favor of, some sect; hence, 3. narrow-minded; bigoted. *n.* 1. originally, an apostate from an established church. 2. a member of any religious sect. 3. a person who is blindly and narrow-mindedly devoted to a sect.
sec·tar·i·an·ism (sek-târ′i-ən-iz′m), *n.* the beliefs and practices of sectarians, especially those of a narrow, bigoted nature.
sec·tar·i·an·ize (sek-târ′i-ən-īz′), *v.t.* [SECTARIANIZED (-īzd′), SECTARIANIZING], to make sectarian in spirit; fill with sectarian feelings or principles.
sec·ta·ry (sek′tə-ri), *n.* [*pl.* SECTARIES (-riz)], [< Fr. or ML.; Fr. *sectaire;* ML. *sectarius* < L. *secta;* see SECT (group)], 1. a sectarian. 2. [often S-], a dissenter from an established church, especially a Protestant nonconformist.
sec·tile (sek′til), *adj.* [Fr.; L. *sectilis* < *secare,* to cut; cf. SAW], capable of being cut smoothly with a knife.
sec·til·i·ty (sek-til′ə-ti), *n.* the condition of being sectile.
sec·tion (sek′shən), *n.* [Fr.; L. *sectio* < *sectus,* pp. of *secare,* to cut; cf. SAW], 1. the act or process of cutting or separating by cutting. 2. a part separated or removed by cutting; slice; division. 3. a very thin slice of matter used for microscopic study. 4. a part or

division of something written. 5. any distinct or separate part: as, a bookcase in five *sections*, various *sections* of society. 6. a division of public lands constituting 640 acres, or 1/36 of a township. 7. a loose subdivision of a biological genus, group, family, etc. 8. a drawing, description, or remaining part of something as it would appear if cut straight through in a given plane. 9. any of several subdivisions of military or naval forces. 10. in *railroading*, *a*) part of a sleeping car containing an upper and lower berth. *b*) the smallest administrative division of the right of way, usually several miles of track under the care of a single maintenance crew. *c*) any train running on the same schedule as another. ***v.t.*** 1. to cut or divide into sections. 2. to arrange by or represent in sections, as by shading in mechanical drawing. Abbreviated **sec.**, **s.**, **sect.** —***SYN.*** see **part.**

sec·tion·al (sek'shən-'l), ***adj.*** 1. of or characteristic of a given section or district. 2. made up of or divided into sections or parts, especially separable sections.

sec·tion·al·ism (sek'shən-'l-iz'm), ***n.*** undue concern for or devotion to the interests of a particular section of the country; sectional spirit, bias, etc.

sec·tion·al·ize (sek'shən-'l-īz'), ***v.t.*** [SECTIONALIZED (-īzd'), SECTIONALIZING], 1. to make sectional. 2. to divide into sections, especially geographical sections.

sec·tion·al·ly (sek'shən-'l-i), ***adv.*** in a sectional manner; in or according to sections.

section gang, a crew of men who do the maintenance work on a railroad section.

section mark, the mark (§) used to indicate a section in a book, etc.

sec·tor (sek'tẽr), ***n.*** [LL.; L., cutter < *sectus*, pp. of *secare*, to cut], 1. part of a circle bounded by any two radii and the arc included between them. 2. a mathematical instrument consisting of two rulers marked with various scales and jointed together at one end, used in solving problems, measuring angles, etc. 3. any of the districts into which an area is divided for military operations. Abbreviated **sec.** ***v.t.*** to divide into sectors.

sec·to·ri·al (sek-tôr'i-əl, sek-tō'ri-əl), ***adj.*** [< Mod. L. *sectorius* (< L. *sector*, a cutter); + *-al*], 1. of a sector. 2. adapted for cutting or shearing: said especially of the premolar teeth of carnivorous mammals. ***n.*** a sectorial tooth.

sec·u·lar (sek'yoo-lẽr), ***adj.*** [ME. *seculer*, *seculere*; OFr. *seculer*; LL. *saecularis* (L., belonging to an age) < L. *saeculum*, generation, age], 1. of or belonging to the world and worldly things as distinguished from the church and religious affairs; not sacred or religious; temporal; worldly: as, *secular* music, *secular* schools. 2. living in the outside world; not bound by a monastic vow or rule: as, the *secular* clergy: opposed to *regular*. 3. coming or happening only once in an age or century. 4. lasting for an age or ages; continuing for a long time or from age to age. 5. secularistic. ***n.*** 1. a member of the secular clergy. 2. [Obs.], a layman.

sec·u·lar·ism (sek'yoo-lẽr-iz'm), ***n.*** [*secular* + *-ism*], 1. secular spirit, views, or the like; especially, a system of doctrines and practices that rejects any form of religious faith and worship. 2. the belief that religion and ecclesiastical affairs should not enter into the functions of the state, especially into public education.

sec·u·lar·ist (sek'yoo-lẽr-ist), ***n.*** an adherent of secularism.

sec·u·lar·is·tic (sek'yoo-lə-ris'tik), ***adj.*** of or according to secularism.

sec·u·lar·i·ty (sek'yoo-lar'ə-ti), ***n.*** [ME. *seculerte*; Early Fr. *sécularité*; ML. *saecularitas*], 1. the state or quality of being secular. 2. secularism. 3. [*pl.* SECULARITIES (-tiz)], a secular concern, matter, etc.

sec·u·lar·i·za·tion (sek'yoo-lẽr-i-zā'shən, sek'yoo-lẽr-ī-zā'shən), ***n.*** a secularizing or being secularized.

sec·u·lar·ize (sek'yoo-lə-rīz'), ***v.t.*** [SECULARIZED (-rīzd'), SECULARIZING], [Fr. *séculariser* < L. *saecularis*; see SECULAR], 1. to convert from religious to civil ownership or use. 2. to free from monastic vows or rules. 3. to deprive of any religious character, influence, or significance. 4. to convert to secularism.

se·cund (sē'kənd, sek'ənd), ***adj.*** [L. *secundus*, following], in *botany*, growing on one side only, as the flowers in the lily of the valley.

Se·cun·der·a·bad (sē-kun'dẽr-ä-bäd', si-kun'drə-bad'), ***n.*** a city in India, near the city of Hyderabad: pop., 225,000: also **Sikandarabad.**

sec·un·dine (sek'ən-dīn', sek'ən-din), ***n.*** [LL. *secundinae*, pl., the afterbirth < L. *secundus*, following; see SECOND], 1. in *botany*, the second, or inner, coat of an ovule. 2. *pl.* the afterbirth.

se·cun·dum (si-kun'dəm), ***prep.*** [L.], according to, as in *secundum usum* (ū'səm), according to usage.

se·cur·a·ble (si-kyoor'ə-b'l), ***adj.*** that can be secured.

se·cure (si-kyoor'), ***adj.*** [L. *securus* < *se-*, free from + *cura*, care], 1. free from fear, care, doubt, or anxiety; not worried, troubled, or apprehensive. 2. free from danger; not exposed to damage, attack, etc.; safe. 3. in safekeeping or custody. 4. not likely to fail or give way; firm; strong; stable: as, make the knot *secure*. 5. sure; certain; to be relied upon. 6. [Archaic], overconfident; careless. ***v.t.*** [SECURED (-kyoord'), SECURING], 1. to make secure, or safe; guard; protect: as, *secure* your position against attack. 2. to make sure or certain; guarantee; ensure, as with a pledge: as, someone must *secure* the loan. 3. to make firm, fast, tight, etc.: as, *secure* the catch on the window. 4. to get hold or possession of; obtain; acquire: as, we have *secured* a cottage for the summer. ***v.i.*** to be or become secure, or safe; have or give security: as, we must *secure* against possible obstacles. —***SYN.*** see **get, safe.**

se·cu·ri·ty (si-kyoor'ə-ti), ***n.*** [*pl.* SECURITIES (-tiz)], [ME. *securite*; L. *securitas* < *securus*; see SECURE], 1. the state or feeling of being free from fear, care, danger, etc.; safety or a sense of safety. 2. freedom from doubt; certainty. 3. overconfidence; carelessness. 4. something that gives or assures safety; protection; safeguard. 5. something given as a pledge of repayment, fulfillment of a promise, etc.; guarantee. 6. a person who agrees to make good the failure of another to pay, perform a duty, etc.; surety. 7. *usually in pl.* any evidence of debt or ownership of property, especially a bond or stock certificate. Abbreviated **sec.**

Security Council, the organ of the United Nations responsible for maintaining international peace and security.

secy., sec'y., secretary.

Se·da·li·a (si-dā'li-ə, si-dāl'yə), ***n.*** a city in west central Missouri: pop., 24,000.

Se·dan (si-dan'; Fr. sə-dän'), ***n.*** a city in northeastern France, on the Meuse River: pop., 18,000: scene of a battle (1870) of the Franco-Prussian War, in which the Prussians defeated the French.

se·dan (si-dan'), ***n.*** [earlier also *sidan*; prob. coined < L. *sedere*, to sit, by Sir S. Duncombe (1634); orig., a sedan chair], 1. a type of closed automobile having two or four doors, and two seats, front and rear. 2. a sedan chair.

sedan chair, an enclosed chair for one person, carried on poles by two men.

se·date (si-dāt'), ***adj.*** [L. *sedatus*, pp. of *sedare*, to settle, caus. of *sedere*, to sit], 1. calm; quiet; composed. 2. serious; sober; dignified; grave. —***SYN.*** see **serious.**

se·da·tion (si-dā'shən), ***n.*** in *medicine*, the act or process of reducing excitement, irritation, or pain, especially by means of a sedative.

sed·a·tive (sed'ə-tiv), ***adj.*** [Fr. *sédatif*; ML. *sedativus* < L. *sedatus*; see SEDATE], tending to soothe or quiet; specifically, in *medicine*, having the property of lessening excitement, irritation, or pain. ***n.*** a sedative medicine or treatment.

sed·en·tar·i·ly (sed''n-ter'ə-li), ***adv.*** in a sedentary manner.

sed·en·tar·i·ness (sed''n-ter'i-nis), ***n.*** the quality or state of being sedentary.

sed·en·tar·y (sed''n-ter'i), ***adj.*** [Fr. *sédentaire*; L. *sedentarius* < *sedens*, ppr. of *sedere*, to sit], 1. characterized by or involving sitting: as, a *sedentary* task. 2. accustomed to sit much of the time. 3. remaining in one locality; not migratory: said of birds, etc. 4. in *zoology*, fixed to one spot, as a barnacle.

Se·der (sā'dẽr), ***n.*** [*pl.* SEDARIM (sə-där'im)], [Heb. *sedher*, arrangement, service, lection], in ***Judaism***, the feast commemorating the exodus of the Jews from Egypt, observed in the home on the eve of the first day (and by orthodox Jews also the eve of the second day) of Passover.

sedge (sej), ***n.*** [ME., also *segge*; AS. *secg*; IE. base **seq-*, to cut, as also in L. *secare* (cf. SECTION, SECTOR, etc.), Eng. *saw*, *scythe*: the leaves have three sharp edges], any of several coarse, grasslike plants usually growing in tufts or clumps in wet ground.

sedg·y (sej'i), ***adj.*** [SEDGIER (-i-ẽr), SEDGIEST (-i-ist)], 1. covered or bordered with sedge. 2. like sedge.

se·dil·i·a (si-dil'i-ə), ***n.pl.*** [*sing.* SEDILE (-dī'lē)], [L., *pl.* of *sedile*, a seat], a set of seats, usually three, along the south side of a church, for the use of the clergy when not officiating.

sed·i·ment (sed'ə-mənt), ***n.*** [Fr. *sédiment*; L. *sedimentum* < *sedere*, to sit], 1. any matter that settles to the bottom of a liquid. 2. in *geology*, any matter or mass deposited by water or wind.

sed·i·men·tal (sed'ə-men't'l), ***adj.*** sedimentary.

sed·i·men·ta·ri·ly (sed'ə-men'tẽr-ə-li), ***adv.*** so as to be sedimentary.

sed·i·men·ta·ry (sed'ə-men'tẽr-i), ***adj.*** 1. of, having the nature of, or containing sediment. 2. formed by the deposit of sediment, as rocks.

sed·i·men·ta·tion (sed'ə-men-tā'shən), ***n.*** the depositing of sediment.

se·di·tion (si-dish'ən), ***n.*** [OFr. *sedition*; L. *seditio* < *sed-*, apart + *itio*, a going < *ire*, to go], 1. the stirring up of discontent, resistance, or rebellion against the government in power. 2. [Rare], rebellion; insurrection.

SYN.—**sedition** applies to anything regarded by a government as stirring up resistance or rebellion against it and implies that the evidence is not overt or absolute; **treason** implies an overt act in violation of the allegiance owed to one's state, specifically, a levying war against it or giving aid or comfort to its enemies.

se·di·tion·ar·y (si-dish′ən-er′i), *adj.* seditious. *n.* [*pl.* SEDITIONARIES (-iz)], a person charged with or convicted of sedition.

se·di·tious (si-dish′əs), *adj.* [OFr. *seditieux;* L. *seditiosus*], 1. of or constituting sedition. 2. stirring up discontent, resistance, or rebellion. 3. having a tendency to sedition.

se·duce (si-dōōs′, si-dūs′), *v.t.* [SEDUCED (-dōōst′, -dūst′), SEDUCING], [L. *seducere,* to lead apart; *se-,* apart + *ducere,* to lead], 1. to persuade to do something disloyal, disobedient, etc. 2. to persuade to do wrong, as by offering something; tempt to evil or wrongdoing; lead astray. 3. to persuade to engage in unlawful sexual intercourse, especially for the first time; induce to give up chastity. —*SYN.* see **lure.**

se·duce·ment (si-dōōs′mənt, si-dūs′mənt), *n.* seduction.

se·duc·er (si-dōōs′ẽr, si-dūs′ẽr), *n.* a person or thing that seduces; especially, a man who seduces a woman.

se·duc·i·ble (si-dōōs′ə-b'l, si-dūs′ə-b'l), *adj.* that can be seduced.

se·duc·tion (si-duk′shən), *n.* [Fr. *séduction;* L. *seductio*], 1. the act of seducing or the state of being seduced. 2. something that seduces.

se·duc·tive (si-duk′tiv), *adj.* [< L. *seductus,* pp. of *seducere* (see SEDUCE); + *-ive*], tending to seduce, or lead astray; tempting; strongly attractive; enticing.

se·du·li·ty (si-dū′lə-ti, si-dōō′lə-ti), *n.* [L. *sedulitas*], the quality or fact of being sedulous.

sed·u·lous (sej′oo-ləs), *adj.* [L. *sedulus*], working hard and steadily; diligent and persistent. —*SYN.* see **busy.**

se·dum (sē′dəm), *n.* [L., houseleek], any of a large group of mainly perennial herbs with fleshy stalks and leaves and white, yellow, or pink flowers.

see (sē), *v.t.* [SAW (sô), SEEN (sēn), SEEING], [ME. *seen, sen;* AS. *seon* (< **sehwan*); akin to G. *sehen,* Goth. *saihwan;* IE. base **seqw-,* to observe, show, see, tell, as also in L. *inseque;* cf. SAY], 1. to get knowledge or an impression of through the eyes and the sense of sight; perceive visually; look at; view. 2. *a*) to get a clear mental impression of; grasp by thinking; understand: as, I can't *see* your point. *b*) to accept as right or proper: as, I can't *see* him as president. 3. to learn; discover; find out: as, *see* what they want. 4. to have personal knowledge of; experience; witness: as, she had *seen* better days, they have *seen* the results of three wars. 5. to look over; inspect; examine: as, the doctor had better *see* your incision. 6. to take care; make sure: as, *see* that he does the job properly. 7. to escort; accompany; attend: as, I'll *see* you to the door, he will *see* her to her home. 8. to encounter; meet; come in contact with: as, have you *seen* your brother recently? 9. to call on; have an interview with; consult: as, you had better *see* a lawyer. 10. to admit to one's presence; receive: as, he is too ill to *see* you. 11. to be a spectator at; visit; attend: as, have you *seen* the new musical? 12. in *card games, a*) to meet (a bet) by staking an equal sum. *b*) to meet the bet of (another) in this way. *v.i.* 1. to have the power of sight. 2. to discern objects, colors, etc. by using the eyes: as, I can't *see* that far. 3. to comprehend; understand. 4. to look for the purpose of finding out something. 5. to think over a given matter; reflect: as, let me *see,* where did I put it? *interj.* behold! look! Abbreviated **s.**

see about, 1. to find out about; investigate; inquire into. 2. to attend to.

see after, to take care of; look after.

see double, to see two of every object, through inability to focus the eyes, as from drunkenness.

see into, 1. to investigate; look into. 2. to understand or perceive the true meaning, character, or nature of.

see off, to go with (another) to the place from which he is to leave, as on a journey.

see out, 1. to carry out; finish; go through with. 2. to wait till the end of.

see through, 1. to understand or perceive the true meaning, character, or nature of. 2. to carry out to the end; finish. 3. to help out or carry through a time of difficulty.

see to, to attend to; look after.

SYN.—**see,** the most simple and direct of these terms, is the basic term for the use of the organs of sight; **behold** implies a directing of the eyes on something and holding it in view, usually stressing the strong impression made (he never *beheld* a sight more beautiful); **espy** and **descry** both imply a catching sight of with some effort, **espy** suggesting the detection of that which is small, partly hidden, etc. (he *espied* the snake crawling through the grass) and **descry** the making out of something from a distance or through darkness, mist, etc. (he *descried* the distant steeple); **view** implies a seeing or looking at what lies before one, as in inspection or examination (the jury *viewed* the body at the inquest).

see (sē), *n.* [ME. *se;* OFr. *sie, sied* < L. *sedes,* a seat], 1. the official seat, or center of authority, of a bishop. 2. the position, authority, or jurisdiction of a bishop. 3. [Obs.], a seat of authority, especially a throne.

see·catch (sē′kach′), *n.* [Russ. *sekach*], the adult male of the fur seal of Alaskan waters.

see·catch·ie (sē′kach′i), *n.* a seecatch.

seed (sēd), *n.* [*pl.* SEEDS (sēdz), SEED], [ME. *sede, seed;* AS. *sæd;* akin to G. *saat;* IE. base **sei-,* to cast, let fall, seen also in L. *serere,* to sow, plant, *sator,* sower, etc.], 1. the part of a flowering plant that contains the embryo and will develop into a new plant if sown; fertilized and mature ovule. 2. any part from which a new plant will grow: as, a potato *seed.* 3. seeds collectively: as, we must buy *seed* for the lawn. 4. the source, origin, or beginning of anything: as, oppression sows the *seeds* of revolt. 5. family stock; ancestry. 6. descendants; posterity. 7. seed oysters. 8. sperm; semen. *v.t.* 1. to plant with seed. 2. to sow (seeds). 3. to remove the seeds from. 4. to sprinkle particles of dry ice, silver iodide, etc. into (clouds) in an attempt to induce rainfall. 5. in *sports, a*) to distribute the names of the ranking contestants in (the draw for position in a tournament) so that those with the greatest skill are not matched together in the early rounds. *b*) to treat (a player) as a ranking contestant in this way. *v.i.* 1. to become ripe and produce seed. 2. to go to seed; shed seed. 3. to sow seed.

go to seed, 1. to shed seeds after the time of flowering or bearing has passed. 2. to deteriorate; become weak, useless, unprofitable, etc.

seed·bed (sēd′bed′), *n.* a bed of soil, usually covered with glass, in which small plants are grown from seed for transplanting.

seed·cake (sēd′kāk′), *n.* any cake or cookie containing spicy seeds, as of caraway.

seed·case (sēd′kās′), *n.* a seed vessel.

seed coat, the skin or coating of a seed.

seed coral, fragments of coral used in ornaments.

seed corn, corn used for sowing a new crop.

seed·er (sēd′ẽr), *n.* 1. a person or thing that sows seeds. 2. a device used for removing seeds, as from raisins.

seed·i·ly (sēd′'l-i), *adv.* in a seedy manner.

seed·i·ness (sēd′i-nis), *n.* the state or quality of being seedy.

seed leaf, an embryo leaf within a seed; cotyledon.

seed·ling (sēd′liŋ), *n.* 1. a plant grown from a seed, as distinguished from one grown from a cutting, bud graft, etc. 2. a young tree less than three feet high.

seed·man (sēd′mən), *n.* [*pl.* SEEDMEN (-mən)], a seedsman.

seed oysters, oyster spat; very young oysters, especially at the stage suitable for transplanting.

seed pearl, a very small pearl, often imperfect.

seed plant, any seed-bearing plant.

seeds·man (sēdz′mən), *n.* [*pl.* SEEDSMEN (-mən)], 1. a person whose work is sowing seeds. 2. a person whose business is selling seeds.

seed·time (sēd′tīm′), *n.* the season for sowing seeds.

seed vessel, any dry, hollow fruit, as a pod, containing seeds; pericarp: also called *seed capsule.*

seed·y (sēd′i), *adj.* [SEEDIER (-i-ẽr), SEEDIEST (-i-ist)], 1. containing much seed: as, this orange is too *seedy.* 2. gone to seed. 3. containing small bubbles: said of glass. 4. shabby, shabbily dressed, etc. 5. [Colloq.], feeling or looking physically bad or low in spirits.

See·ger, Alan (sē′gẽr), 1888–1916; American poet.

see·ing (sē′iŋ), *n.* [ME.; cf. SEE & -ING], 1. the sense or power of sight; vision. 2. the act of using the eyes to see. *adj.* [ppr. of *see*], having the sense of sight. *conj.* in view of the fact; considering; inasmuch as.

Seeing Eye, an institution near Morristown, New Jersey, which breeds and trains dogs (*Seeing Eye dogs*) as guides and companions for blind people.

seek (sēk), *v.t.* [SOUGHT (sôt), SEEKING], [ME. *seken, sechen;* AS. *secan* (< **sōkjan*); akin to OS. *sōkian,* G. *suchen;* IE. base **sag-,* to track down, trace, as also in L. *sagire,* to scent out, perceive (cf. SAGE)], 1. to try to find; search for; look for. 2. to go to; resort to: as, he *sought* the woods for peace. 3. to search; explore. 4. to ask or inquire for; try to learn or discover: as, he *sought* the answer in many places. 5. to try to get or acquire; aim at; pursue. 6. to try; attempt: used with an infinitive, as, he *sought* to appease his enemies. *v.i.* 1. to try to find someone or something; make a search or investigation. 2. [Obs.], to go; resort; pay a visit (*to*).

seel (sēl), *v.t.* [OFr. *ciller, siller* < *cil;* L. *cilium,* eyelash], 1. in *falconry,* to sew together the eyelids of (a young hawk). 2. to close (the eyes). 3. to blind or hoodwink.

See·land (sē′lənd), *n.* Zealand, an island of Denmark.

seem (sēm), *v.i.* [ME. *semen;* prob. < ON. *sæma,* to conform to (akin to AS. *seman,* to bring to agreement); for IE. base see SAME], 1. to appear to be; give the impression of being; appear: as, he *seems* glad to see us. 2. to appear to one's own mind: as, I *seem* to hear voices. 3. to appear to exist: as, there *seems* no point in going. 4. to be apparently true: as, it *seems* he was not there.

seem·ing (sēm′iŋ), *adj.* apparent, especially as dis-

tinguished from *actual*. ***n.*** outward form or appearance; especially, deceptive or specious appearance.
seem·ing·ly (sēm′iŋ-li), ***adv.*** so far as can be observed.
seem·li·ness (sēm′li-nis), ***n.*** the quality of being seemly.
seem·ly (sēm′li), ***adj.*** [SEEMLIER (-li-ẽr), SEEMLIEST (-li-ist)], [ME. *semlich;* ON. *sœmiligr* < *sœmr*, fitting; cf. SEEM], 1. [Archaic or Dial.], pleasing in appearance; fair; handsome. 2. suitable, proper, fitting, or becoming, especially with reference to conventional standards of conduct or good taste; decent; decorous. ***adv.*** in a seemly manner; properly, fittingly, etc.
seen (sēn), past participle of **see**.
seep (sēp), ***v.i.*** [ME. *sepen* < AS. *sipian*, to soak; akin to MLG. *sīpen*, to drip; IE. base **seip-*, to run out, drip], to leak through small openings or pores; ooze; percolate. ***n.*** a place where water or petroleum oozes from the ground to form a pool.
seep·age (sēp′ij), ***n.*** [see -AGE], 1. the act or process of seeping; leakage; oozing. 2. liquid that seeps.
seer (*for 1*, sē′ẽr; *for 2*, sêr), ***n.*** 1. a person who sees. 2. a person who foretells the future; prophet.
seer (sêr, sâr), ***n.*** a ser.
seer·ess (sêr′is), ***n.*** a female seer; prophetess.
seer·suck·er (sêr′suk′ẽr), ***n.*** [Hind. *shirshaker* < Per. *shir u shakar*, lit., milk and sugar, also a kind of striped linen cloth], a light, crinkled fabric of linen or cotton, usually with a striped pattern.
see·saw (sē′sô′), ***n.*** [redupl. of *saw:* from the action of sawing], 1. a plank balanced on a support at the middle, used by children at play, one sitting at either end and causing his end to rise and fall alternately with the other. 2. the act of playing in this way. 3. any back-and-forth or up-and-down motion, action, or tendency, likened to that of a seesaw: as, the *seesaw* of pitched battle. 4. in *whist*, a crossruff. ***adj.*** moving back and forth or up and down. ***v.t. & v.i.*** to move up and down or back and forth on or as on a seesaw.
seethe (sēth), ***v.t.*** [SEETHED (sēthd), SEETHING; *obs.* past tense SOD (sod), pp. SODDEN (sod′'n)], [ME. *sethen;* AS. *sēothan;* akin to G. *sieden;* prob. IE. base **sew-*, to cook, boil], 1. to cook by boiling. 2. to soak, steep, or saturate in liquid. ***v.i.*** 1. to boil; be boiling hot. 2. to surge, bubble, or foam, as boiling liquid. 3. to be violently agitated, excited, or disturbed. ***n.*** the act or condition of seething. —***SYN.*** see **boil**.
seg·gar (seg′ẽr), ***n. & v.t.*** sagger.
seg·ment (seg′mənt), ***n.*** [L. *segmentum* < *secare*, to cut], 1. any of the parts into which a body is separated or separable; division; section. 2. in *geometry*, *a)* a part of a figure, especially of a circle or sphere, marked off or made separate by a line or plane, as a part of a circular area bounded by an arc and its chord. *b)* any of the finite sections of a line. 3. in *zoology*, *a)* any of the sections that form the body of an arthropod. *b)* the part of a limb between the joints. ***v.t. & v.i.*** to divide into segments. —***SYN.*** see **part**.
seg·men·tal (seg-men′t'l), ***adj.*** 1. having the form of a segment of a circle. 2. of, or having the nature of, a segment or segments. 3. composed of segments.
seg·men·tal·ly (seg-men′t'l-i), ***adv.*** in or by segments.
seg·men·tar·y (seg′mən-ter′i), ***adj.*** segmented.
seg·men·ta·tion (seg′mən-tā′shən), ***n.*** 1. a dividing or being divided into segments. 2. in *biology*, the progressive growth and cleavage of a single cell into many others to form a new organism.
segmentation cavity, the central cavity of a blastula; blastocoele.
‡se·gno (se′nyô), ***n.*** [*pl.* SEGNI (-nyē)], [It. < L. *signum*, a sign], in *music*, a sign, especially the one (𝄋 or :S:) at the beginning or end of a repeat.
se·go (sē′gō), ***n.*** [< Am. Ind. (Shoshonean); cf. Ute *sígo*], a perennial bulb plant with trumpet-shaped flowers, found in western North America: also **sego lily**.
Se·go·via (se-gô′vyä), ***n.*** a city in central Spain: pop., 18,000.
seg·re·gate (seg′ri-gāt′; *for adj., usually* seg′ri-git), ***adj.*** [ME. *segregat;* L. *segregatus*, pp. of *segregare*, to set apart, lit. to set apart from the flock < *se-*, apart + *grex, gregis*, a flock], separate; set apart; segregated. ***v.t.*** [SEGREGATED (-id), SEGREGATING], to set apart from others or from the main mass or group; isolate; specifically, to compel (racial groups) to live, go to school, etc. apart from each other. ***v.t.*** 1. to separate from the main mass and collect together in a new body: said of crystals. 2. to separate from others; be segregated. 3. in *biology*, to separate in accordance with Mendel's law; undergo segregation.
seg·re·gat·ed (seg′ri-gāt′id), ***adj.*** conforming to a system that segregates racial groups.
seg·re·ga·tion (seg′ri-gā′shən), ***n.*** [LL. *segregatio*], 1. a segregating or being segregated. 2. a segregated part, group, number, etc. 3. in *biology*, the separation of allelomorphic genes or characters, as in meiosis.
seg·re·gat·ive (seg′ri-gā′tiv), ***adj.*** 1. tending to segregate. 2. characterized by unsociability or disunity.
‡se·gue (sā′gwā), [It., 3d pers. sing., pres. indic. of *seguire*, to follow], in *music*, continue without break into the next section, piece, etc.: a direction to the performer.
‡se·gui·dil·la (se′gē-dē′lyä), ***n.*** [Sp. < *seguida*, a following, sequence < *seguir*, to follow], 1. a fast Spanish dance, danced and sung to the accompaniment of castanets. 2. the music for this dance, in 3/4 time. 3. a stanza of four to seven short lines, partly assonant, with a distinctive rhythm, sung to this music.
‡sei·cen·to (se-chen′tô), ***n.*** [It.; cf. CINQUECENTO], the 17th century, with reference to the Italian art and literature produced then.
seiche (sāsh), ***n.*** [< Swiss Fr.; ? ult. < L. *siccus*, dry], a movement back and forth of the water in a lake or other land-locked body of water, varying in duration and resulting in fluctuation of the water level.
sei·del (zī′d'l, sī′d'l), ***n.*** [*pl.* SEIDEL], [G.], [often S-], a large beer mug, sometimes with a hinged lid.
Seid·litz powders (sed′lits), [so called (1815) because their properties are said to resemble those of natural waters from the spring at *Seidlitz*, Czechoslovakia], a laxative composed of two powders, one of sodium bicarbonate and Rochelle salt, the other of tartaric acid: the two are separately dissolved in water, combined, and drunk while effervescing: also **Seidlitz powder**.
sei·gneur (sān′yẽr; Fr. sān′yër′), ***n.*** [Fr.; L. *senior;* see SENIOR], a feudal lord or noble; seignior.
seign·ior (sēn′yẽr), ***n.*** [ME. *segnour;* Anglo-Fr. *segnour;* OFr. *seignor;* L. *senior;* see SENIOR], 1. originally, the lord of a fee or manor. 2. a lord; noble; gentleman. 3. a title of respect corresponding to *Sir*.
seign·ior·age (sēn′yẽr-ij), ***n.*** [OFr. *seignorage* < *seignor;* see SEIGNIOR], 1. something claimed or taken by a sovereign or other superior as his just right or due. 2. any profits or charges arising from the minting of gold and silver coins from bullion, usually the difference between face value and intrinsic value.
seign·ior·al (sēn′yer-əl), ***adj.*** seignorial.
seign·ior·y (sēn′yẽr-i), ***n.*** [*pl.* SEIGNIORIES (-iz)], [ME. & OFr. *seignorie*], 1. the dominion, rights, or authority of a seignior, or feudal lord. 2. the extent or territory covered by this. 3. a body of lords, especially those of a medieval Italian republic. Also spelled **signory**.
sei·gno·ri·al (sēn-yôr′i-əl, sēn-yō′ri-əl), ***adj.*** of or having to do with a seignior.
Seine (sān; Fr. sen), ***n.*** a river in France, flowing through Paris into the English Channel: length, 480 mi.
seine (sān), ***n.*** [ME. *seyne;* AS. *segne;* L. *sagena;* Gr. *sagēnē*], a large fishing net with floats along the top edge and weights along the bottom. ***v.t. & v.i.*** [SEINED (sānd), SEINING], to fish with a seine.
seise (sēz), ***v.t.*** [SEISED (sēzd), SEISING], [var. of *seize*], in *law*, to take possession of; possess; seize.
sei·sin (sē′zin), ***n.*** seizin.
seis·mal (sīz′məl, sīs′məl), ***adj.*** seismic.
seis·mic (sīz′mik, sīs′mik), ***adj.*** [< Gr. *seismos*, an earthquake < *seiein*, to shake], 1. of or having to do with an earthquake or earthquakes. 2. caused by an earthquake. 3. subject to earthquakes.
seis·mi·cal (sīz′mi-k'l, sīs′mi-k'l), ***adj.*** seismic.
seis·mism (sīz′miz'm, sīs′miz'm), ***n.*** [< Gr. *seismos*, earthquake; + *-ism*], the phenomena of earthquakes, collectively.
seis·mo- (sīz′mə, sīs′mə), [< Gr. *seismos*, earthquake < *seiein*, to shake], a combining form meaning ***earthquake***, as in *seismogram:* also, rarely, *sismo-*.
seis·mo·gram (sīz′mə-gram′, sīs′mə-gram′), ***n.*** [*seismo-* + *-gram*], the chart of an earthquake as recorded on a seismograph.
seis·mo·graph (sīz′mə-graf′, sīs′mə-gräf′), ***n.*** [*seismo-* + *-graph*], an instrument that records the direction, intensity, and time of earthquakes.
seis·mo·graph·ic (sīz′mə-graf′ik, sīs′mə-graf′ik), ***adj.*** 1. of or recorded by a seismograph. 2. of seismography.
seis·mog·ra·phy (sīz-mog′rə-fi, sīs-mog′rə-fi), ***n.*** the use of the seismograph in recording earthquakes.
seismol., 1. seismological. 2. seismology.
seis·mo·log·ic (sīz′mə-loj′ik, sīs′mə-loj′ik), ***adj.*** seismological.
seis·mo·log·i·cal (sīz′mə-loj′i-k'l, sīs′mə-loj′i-k'l), ***adj.*** of or having to do with seismology.
seis·mo·log·i·cal·ly (sīz′mə-loj′i-k'l-i, sīs′mə-loj′ik-li), ***adv.*** in accordance with the principles of seismology.
seis·mol·o·gy (sīz-mol′ə-ji, sīs-mol′ə-ji), ***n.*** [*seismo-* + *-logy*], the study of earthquakes and related matters.
seis·mom·e·ter (sīz-mom′ə-tẽr, sīs-mom′ə-tẽr), ***n.*** [*seismo-* + *-meter*], a seismograph.
seis·mo·met·ric (sīz′mə-met′rik, sīs′mə-met′rik), ***adj.*** seismographic.
seis·mo·scope (sīz′mə-skōp′, sīs′mə-skōp′), ***n.*** [*seismo-* + *-scope*], an instrument indicating only the occurrence and time of earthquakes.
seis·mo·scop·ic (sīz′mə-skop′ik, sīs′mə-skop′ik), ***adj.*** of or recorded by a seismoscope.
seiz·a·ble (sēz′ə-b'l), ***adj.*** that can be seized.
seize (sēz), ***v.t.*** [SEIZED (sēzd), SEIZING], [ME. *saisen, seisen;* OFr. *saisir, seisir;* LL. *sacire;* prob. < Gmc. base of *set*], 1. originally, to put in legal possession of a feudal holding. 2. to take legal possession of. 3. to take possession of suddenly and by force. 4. to have a sudden and drastic effect upon; attack; strike: as, his mind was *seized* with a sudden paralysis. 5. to

capture; take prisoner; catch; arrest. 6. to grasp suddenly with the hand; take hold of forcibly. 7. to grasp with the mind; comprehend; understand. 8. to take advantage of (an opportunity, etc.) quickly. 9. in *nautical usage*, to fasten together (ropes, etc.), as by lashings; bind; lash. —*SYN.* see **take**.

seize on (or **upon**), 1. to take hold of suddenly and with force. 2. to take possession of.

seiz·er (sēz′ẽr), *n.* a person or thing that seizes.

sei·zin (sē′zin), *n.* [Fr. *saisine* < *saisir;* see SEIZE], in *law*, 1. legal possession, especially of a freehold estate. 2. property so possessed. Also spelled **seisin**.

seiz·ing (sēz′iŋ), *n.* 1. seizure. 2. in *nautical usage*, *a)* the act of binding or fastening together, as with lashings. *b)* lashings or cordage used for this. *c)* a fastening made in this way.

sei·zor (sē′zẽr, sē′zôr), *n.* [< *seize* + *-or*], in *law*, a person who takes possession of a freehold estate.

sei·zure (sē′zhẽr), *n.* 1. a seizing or being seized. 2. a sudden attack, as of disease.

se·jant, se·jeant (sē′jənt), *adj.* [Anglo-Fr. *seiant*, ppr. of *seier* (OFr. *seoir*), to sit; L. *sedere*], in *heraldry*, sitting with the forelegs upright.

‡**Sejm** (sām), *n.* [Pol., assembly], 1. formerly, the lower chamber of the Polish Parliament. 2. the Polish Parliament, now consisting of only one chamber.

sel., 1. selected. 2. selection; selections.

se·la·chi·an (si-lā′ki-ən), *adj.* [< Mod. L. *Selachii*, name of the group (< Gr. *selachos*, cartilaginous fish, shark); + *-an*], of or belonging to an order of fishes including the sharks, dogfishes, and rays: now sometimes restricted to the division of this order containing the sharks and dogfishes. *n.* a selachian fish.

sel·a·gi·nel·la (sel′ə-ji-nel′ə), *n.* [Mod. L., dim. < L. *selago, selaginis*, kind of plant], any of a group of ferns with a mosslike appearance.

se·lah (sē′lə; Heb. sel′ô), *n.* [Heb. *selāh;* meaning not known; prob. a musical or liturgical direction], a Hebrew word found frequently at the end of a verse in the Psalms: its meaning is unknown, but it is often interpreted as an indication of a musical pause or rest.

se·lam·lik (se-läm′lik), *n.* [Turk. *selāmliq* < Ar. *salam* (see SALAAM) + Turk. suffix *-liq*], 1. that part of a Turkish house set apart for men, in which guests are received. 2. formerly, the ceremonial visit of the Turkish sultan to a mosque every Friday.

Se·lan·gor (se-läŋ′gôr), *n.* a state of the Federation of Malaya: area, 3,160 sq. mi.; pop., 672,000.

sel·dom (sel′dəm), *adv.* [ME. *selden;* AS. *seldum, seldan*, dat. pl. of *seld-*, strange, rare; akin to G. *selten;* for IE. base see SELF], rarely; infrequently; not often.

se·lect (sə-lekt′), *adj.* [L. *selectus*, pp. of *seligere*, to choose, pick out < *se-*, apart + *legere*, to choose], 1. chosen in preference to another or others; picked out, especially for excellence or some special quality; picked. 2. choice; excellent; outstanding. 3. careful in choosing or selecting; fastidious; hence, 4. exclusive: as, a *select* company of critics. *v.t.* to choose or pick out from among others, as for excellence, desirability, etc. *v.i.* to make a selection; choose. —*SYN.* see **choose**.

se·lect·ee (sə-lek′tē′), *n.* a person inducted into the armed forces under selective service.

se·lec·tion (sə-lek′shən), *n.* [L. *selectio*], 1. a selecting or being selected. 2. that or those selected. 3. in *biology*, any process, whether natural or artificial, by which certain organisms or characteristics are permitted or favored to survive and reproduce in, or as if in, preference to others: cf. **natural selection**. Abbreviated **sel.** (*sing.* & *pl.*). —*SYN.* see **choice**.

se·lec·tive (sə-lek′tiv), *adj.* 1. of, having to do with, or characterized by selection. 2. having the power of selecting; tending to select. 3. in *radio*, excluding oscillations on all frequencies except the one desired.

selective service, compulsory military training and service according to age, physical fitness, ability, etc.

se·lec·tiv·i·ty (sə-lek′tiv′ə-ti), *n.* 1. the state or quality of being selective. 2. the degree to which a radio receiver will reproduce the signals of a given transmitter while rejecting the signals of the others.

se·lect·man (sə-lekt′mən; *locally, also* sē′lekt-man′), *n.* [*pl.* SELECTMEN (-mən, -men′)], [*select* + *man*], one of a board of officers chosen annually in New England towns to manage municipal affairs.

se·lec·tor (sə-lek′tẽr), *n.* [LL.], a person or thing that selects.

sel·e·nate (sel′ə-nāt′), *n.* [*selenic* + *-ate*], a salt of selenic acid.

Se·le·ne (si-lē′nē), *n.* [Gr. *Selēnē* < *selēnē*, the moon], the Greek goddess of the moon: cf. **Luna, Artemis, Hecate.**

se·le·nic (si-lē′nik, si-len′ik), *adj.* 1. designating or of compounds in which selenium has a higher valence than in corresponding selenious compounds. 2. designating or of a colorless, crystalline acid, H_2SeO_4.

se·le·ni·ous (si-lē′ni-əs), *adj.* 1. designating or of compounds in which selenium has a lower valence than in corresponding selenic compounds. 2. designating or of a colorless, crystalline acid, H_2SeO_3.

sel·e·nite (sel′ə-nīt′), *n.* [L. *selenites;* Gr. *selēnitēs* (*lithos*), lit., moon (stone) < *selēnē*, the moon: so named because thought to wax and wane with the moon], a kind of gypsum found in crystallized or foliated form.

se·le·ni·um (si-lē′ni-əm), *n.* [Mod. L. < Gr. *selēnē*, the moon: so named from its being associated with *tellurium* < L. *tellus*, the earth], a chemical element of the sulfur group: it is used in photoelectric devices because its electrical conductivity varies with the intensity of light: symbol, Se; at. wt., 78.96; at. no., 34.

selenium cell, a photoelectric cell containing selenium plates.

sel·e·nog·ra·pher (sel′ə-nog′rə-fẽr), *n.* an expert in selenography.

se·le·no·graph·ic (si-lē′nə-graf′ik), *adj.* of or having to do with selenography.

sel·e·nog·ra·phy (sel′i-nog′rə-fi), *n.* [Mod. L. *selenographia* < Gr. *selēnē*, the moon; + *-graphy*], the study of the surface and physical features of the moon.

sel·e·nol·o·gy (sel′i-nol′ə-ji), *n.* [< Gr. *selēnē*, the moon; + *-logy*], the branch of astronomy dealing with the moon.

Se·leu·ci·a (sə-lōō′shi-ə, sə-lōō′shə), *n.* 1. an ancient city in Babylonia, on the Tigris River, built by Seleucus I. 2. any of several ancient cities in Syria.

Se·leu·cid (si-lōō′sid), *adj.* Seleucidan. *n.* any of the Seleucidae.

Se·leu·ci·dae (si-lōō′si-dē′), *n.pl.* [*sing.* SELEUCID (-sid)], [< *Seleucus* + *-id*], the members of the dynasty founded by Seleucus Nicator, general of Alexander the Great, in 312 B.C.: they ruled most of Asia Minor, Syria, Persia, and Bactria till 64 B.C.

Se·leu·ci·dan (si-lōō′si-dən), *adj.* of or having to do with a Seleucid or the dynasty of Seleucidae.

Se·leu·cus I (si-lōō′kəs), (*Seleucus Nicator*), 358?–280 B.C.; Macedonian general; king of Babylon (312–280 B.C.); first of the Seleucid dynasty.

self (self), *n.* [*pl.* SELVES (selvz)], [ME.; AS. *self, seolf, sylf;* IE. **se-lo* < base **se-*, reflexive pronoun (as in L. *sibi, se*) + *(*o*)*lo*, pronoun; basic sense "itself, by itself"], 1. the identity, character, or essential qualities of any person or thing. 2. the identity, personality, individuality, etc. of a given person; one's own person as distinct from all others. 3. one's own welfare, interest, or advantage; selfishness: as, people concerned only with thought of *self*. *pron.* [Colloq.] myself, himself, herself, or yourself: as, tickets for *self* and wife. *adj.* 1. being uniform or the same throughout. 2. of the same kind, nature, color, material, etc. as the rest: as, a *self* lining, *self* trim, etc.

self- (self), [ME.; AS. *self*, *sylf-* < *self, n.*], a prefix used in hyphenated compounds, meaning: 1. *of oneself* or *itself:* the object of the action, as in *self-appraisal, self-restraint*. 2. *by oneself* or *itself:* the subject of the action, as in *self-appointed, self-starting*. 3. *in oneself* or *itself*, as in *self-centered*. 4. *to* or *with oneself* or *itself*, as in *self-addressed, self-content*.

self-a·base·ment (self′ə-bās′mənt), *n.* abasement or humiliation of oneself.

self-ab·ne·ga·tion (self′ab-ni-gā′shən), *n.* lack of consideration for oneself or one's own interests; self-denial.

self-ab·sorp·tion (self′əb-sôrp′shən, self′ab-zôrp′shən), *n.* absorption in one's own interests, affairs, etc.

self-a·buse (self′ə-būs′), *n.* 1. misuse of one's own abilities, talents, etc. 2. masturbation: a euphemism.

self-act·ing (self′ak′tiŋ), *adj.* acting without outside influence or stimulus; working by itself; automatic.

self-ad·dressed (self′ə-drest′), *adj.* addressed to oneself: as, please enclose a *self-addressed* envelope.

self-ap·point·ed (self′ə-poin′tid), *adj.* appointed or chosen by oneself and not by others.

self-as·ser·tion (self′ə-sũr′shən), *n.* the act of demanding recognition for oneself or of asserting or insisting upon one's rights, claims, etc.

self-as·ser·tive (self′ə-sũr′tiv), *adj.* characterized by self-assertion; forward; pushing.

self-as·sur·ance (self′ə-shoor′əns), *n.* confidence in oneself; assurance in one's own ability, talent, etc.

self-as·sured (self′ə-shoord′), *adj.* having or showing self-assurance; self-confident; composed.

self-cen·tered (self′sen′tẽrd), *adj.* 1. stationary or unmoving, as a center or point about which other things move. 2. occupied or concerned only with one's own affairs; egocentric; selfish.

self-col·lect·ed (self′kə-lek′tid), *adj.* self-possessed.

self-col·ored (self′kul′ẽrd), *adj.* 1. having only one color. 2. having the natural color; with original color unchanged, as a fabric.

self-com·mand (self′kə-mand′, self′kə-mänd′), *n.* self-control.

self-com·pla·cen·cy (self′kəm-plā′s′n-si), *n.* the state or quality of being self-complacent.

self-com·pla·cent (self′kəm-plā′s′nt), *adj.* self-satisfied; pleased with oneself, one's abilities, actions, etc.

self-com·posed (self'kəm-pōzd'), *adj.* having or showing composure; calm; cool.

self-con·ceit (self'kən-sēt'), *n.* too high an opinion of oneself; conceit; vanity.

self-con·ceit·ed (self'kən-sēt'id), *adj.* showing or having self-conceit.

self-con·fi·dence (self'kon'fə-dəns), *n.* the quality of being self-confident; belief in or reliance on oneself or one's abilities, etc. —*SYN.* see **confidence.**

self-con·fi·dent (self'kon'fə-dənt), *adj.* confident of one's own ability; sure of oneself; self-reliant.

self-con·scious (self'kon'shəs), *adj.* 1. unduly conscious of oneself as an object of notice; awkward or embarrassed in the presence of others; ill-at-ease; shy. 2. showing embarrassment, etc.: as, a *self-conscious* cough. 3. in *philosophy & psychology*, having or showing awareness of one's own existence, actions, etc., as distinguished from those of others; conscious of oneself or one's own ego.

self-con·sist·ent (self'kən-sis'tənt), *adj.* consistent with oneself or itself.

self-con·tained (self'kən-tānd'), *adj.* 1. keeping one's affairs to oneself; reserved; uncommunicative. 2. showing self-command or self-control. 3. having all working parts, complete with motive power, in an enclosed or covered unit: said of machinery. 4. having within oneself or itself all that is necessary; functioning independently; self-sufficient, as a community.

self-con·tent (self'kən-tent'), *adj.* satisfied with what one has or is. *n.* self-satisfaction.

self-con·tent·ment (self'kən-tent'mənt), *n.* self-satisfaction.

self-con·tra·dic·tion (self'kon'trə-dik'shən), *n.* 1. contradiction of oneself or itself. 2. any statement or idea containing elements that contradict each other.

self-con·tra·dic·to·ry (self'kon'trə-dik'tēr-i), *adj.* characterized by self-contradiction; inconsistent.

self-con·trol (self'kən-trōl'), *n.* control of oneself, or of one's own emotions, desires, actions, etc.

self-de·ceit (self'di-sēt'), *n.* a deceiving of oneself or being deceived by oneself; self-deception.

self-de·cep·tion (self'di-sep'shən), *n.* self-deceit.

self-de·fense (self'di-fens'), *n.* 1. defense of oneself or of the things that are one's own, as property, security, rights, reputation, etc. 2. the art of boxing: usually in *manly art of self-defense.* 3. in *law*, the right to preserve oneself with whatever force is reasonably necessary against actual violence or the threat of violence.

self-de·fen·sive (self'di-fen'siv), *adj.* of or constituting self-defense.

self-de·lu·sion (self'di-lōō'zhən, self'di-lū'zhən), *n.* self-deception.

self-de·ni·al (self'di-nī'əl), *n.* denial or sacrifice of one's own desires or pleasures, often for the sake of others.

self-de·ny·ing (self'di-nī'iŋ), *adj.* of or exercising self-denial.

self-de·struc·tion (self'di-struk'shən), *n.* destruction of oneself or itself; specifically, suicide.

self-de·ter·mi·na·tion (self'di-tūr'mə-nā'shən), *n.* 1. determination or decision according to one's own mind or will, without outside influence; free will. 2. the right of a people to decide upon its own form of government, without coercion or outside influence.

self-de·ter·mined (self'di-tūr'mind), *adj.* determined or decided by oneself or itself.

self-de·ter·min·ing (self'di-tūr'min-iŋ), *adj.* characterized by, or having the power of, self-determination.

self-de·vo·tion (self'di-vō'shən), *n.* devotion of oneself to the interests of others; self-sacrifice.

self-dis·ci·pline (self'dis'ə-plin), *n.* planned control and training of oneself for the sake of development.

self-dis·trust (self'dis-trust'), *n.* lack of confidence in oneself or one's abilities.

self-driv·en (self'driv''n), *adj.* containing its own drive or motive power; automotive.

self-ed·u·cat·ed (self'ej'oo-kāt'id), *adj.* educated or trained by oneself, without teachers or financial aid.

self-ef·face·ment (self'i-fās'mənt), *n.* the practice of avoiding the notice or attention of others by keeping oneself in the background and minimizing one's own actions; modest, retiring behavior.

self-es·teem (self'ə-stēm'), *n.* 1. belief in oneself; self-respect. 2. undue pride in oneself. —*SYN.* see **pride.**

self-ev·i·dent (self'ev'i-dənt), *adj.* evident without need of proof or discussion; clearly apparent; axiomatic.

self-ex·am·i·na·tion (self'ig-zam'ə-nā'shən), *n.* examination or study of one's own qualities, thoughts, conduct, motives, etc.; analysis of oneself; introspection.

self-ex·e·cut·ing (self'ek'sə-kūt'iŋ), *adj.* making provision for its own execution; coming into effect automatically when specified, without further provision being made, as a death clause in a contract.

self-ex·ist·ence (self'ig-zis'təns), *n.* the quality or state of being self-existent.

self-ex·ist·ent (self'ig-zis'tənt), *adj.* having independent existence; existing of or by itself without external cause or agency.

self-ex·plain·ing (self'ik-splān'iŋ), *adj.* self-explanatory.

self-ex·plan·a·to·ry (self'ik-splan'ə-tôr'i, self'ik-splan'ə-tō'ri), *adj.* explaining itself; furnishing its own explanation; needing no explanation; obvious.

self-ex·pres·sion (self'ik-spresh'ən), *n.* the expression of one's own personality or emotions, especially through some art form.

self-feed·ing (self'fēd'iŋ), *adj.* automatically supplying itself with what is needed, as a machine.

self-fer·til·i·za·tion (self'fūr't'l-i-zā'shən, self'fūr't'l-ī-zā'shən), *n.* fertilization by its own pollen or seed, as in some plants and animals: cf. **cross-fertilization.**

self-for·get·ful (self'fēr-get'fəl), *adj.* forgetful or inconsiderate of oneself; selfless; unselfish.

self-ful·fill·ment (self'fəl-fil'mənt), *n.* fulfillment of one's aspirations, hopes, etc. through one's own efforts.

self-gov·erned (self'guv'ērnd), *adj.* having self-government; independent.

self-gov·ern·ing (self'guv'ērn-iŋ), *adj.* self-governed.

self-gov·ern·ment (self'guv'ēr-mənt), *n.* 1. [Rare], self-control. 2. the governing of a group by the action of its own members, as in electing representatives to make its laws. 3. the state of being self-governed.

self-hard·ened (self'här'd'nd), *adj.* self-hardening.

self-hard·en·ing (self'här'd'n-iŋ), *adj.* designating or of any steel that will harden if air-cooled after being heated above red heat.

self·heal (self'hēl'), *n.* any of various plants supposed to have healing properties, as the allheal, sanicle, etc.

self-help (self'help'), *n.* the act of taking care of oneself without outside help, as in improving the mind or abilities through study.

self·hood (self'hood), *n.* [*self* + *-hood*], 1. all the things that make a person what he is; personality; individuality. 2. the condition of being self-centered; selfishness.

self-i·den·ti·ty (self'ī-den'tə-ti), *n.* the identity of a thing with itself, or the awareness of this identity in the self.

self-im·por·tance (self'im-pôr't'ns), *n.* an exaggerated opinion of one's own importance, especially as shown in behavior; pompous or officious conceit.

self-im·por·tant (self'im-pôr't'nt), *adj.* having or showing self-importance; pompously or officiously conceited.

self-im·posed (self'im-pōzd'), *adj.* imposed or inflicted on oneself by oneself, as a penalty.

self-im·prove·ment (self'im-prōōv'mənt), *n.* improvement of one's condition, mind, abilities, etc. through one's own efforts.

self-in·clu·sive (self'in-klōō'siv), *adj.* including oneself or itself.

self-in·duced (self'in-dōōst', self'in-dūst'), *adj.* 1. induced by oneself or itself. 2. produced by self-induction.

self-in·duc·tion (self'in-duk'shən), *n.* the induction of an electric current in a circuit by the variation of current in that circuit.

self-in·dul·gence (self'in-dul'jəns), *n.* indulgence of one's own desires, impulses, etc.

self-in·dul·gent (self'in-dul'jənt), *adj.* practicing or showing self-indulgence.

self-in·flict·ed (self'in-flik'tid), *adj.* inflicted on oneself by oneself, as an injury.

self-in·i·ti·at·ed (self'i-nish'i-āt'id), *adj.* initiated by oneself or itself.

self-in·sur·ance (self'in-shoor'əns), *n.* insurance of oneself or one's property, usually by providing a fund out of current income.

self-in·ter·est (self'in'tēr-ist, self'in'trist), *n.* 1. one's own interest or advantage. 2. an exaggerated regard for this, usually at the expense of others; selfishness.

self·ish (sel'fish), *adj.* 1. having such regard for one's own interests and advantage that the happiness and welfare of others become of less concern than is considered right or just; too much concerned with one's own welfare. 2. showing or caused by such regard, as an action.

self-knowl·edge (self'nol'ij), *n.* knowledge of one's own qualities, character, abilities, etc.

self·less (self'lis), *adj.* without regard for oneself or one's own interests; unselfish.

self-liq·ui·dat·ing (self'lik'wə-dāt'iŋ), *adj.* providing profit in a short time; converting itself into cash in the normal course of business.

self-load·ing (self'lōd'iŋ), *adj.* loading again by its own action, as a gun.

self-love (self'luv'), *n.* love of self; regard for or interest in oneself and one's happiness.

self-lov·ing (self'luv'iŋ), *adj.* having or showing self-love.

self-made (self'mād'), *adj.* 1. made by oneself or itself. 2. successful, rich, etc. through one's own efforts.

self-mas·ter·y (self'mas'tēr-i, self'mäs'tēr-i), *n.* self-command; self-control.

self-mov·ing (self'mōōv'iŋ), *adj.* moving or able to move under its own power, or of itself.

self-o·pin·ion (self'ə-pin'yən), *n.* 1. one's opinion of himself; especially, high opinion of oneself. 2. high regard for, or stubbornness in, one's own opinion.

self-o·pin·ion·at·ed (self'ə-pin'yən-āt'id), *adj.* 1. without regard for the opinion of others; stubborn in holding to one's own opinions. 2. conceited.

self-or·dained (self'ôr-dānd'), *adj.* ordained or appointed by oneself and not by others.
self-pit·y (self'pit'i), *n.* pity for oneself.
self-pol·li·nat·ed (self'pol'ə-nāt'id), *adj.* pollinated by the transfer of pollen from stamen to pistil in the same flower.
self-pol·lu·tion (self'pə-lōō'shən), *n.* masturbation: a euphemism.
self-pos·sessed (self'pə-zest'), *adj.* having or showing self-possession; calm; undisturbed; composed.
self-pos·ses·sion (self'pə-zesh'ən), *n.* the full possession or control of one's faculties or feelings; presence of mind; self-command; composure. —*SYN.* see **confidence.**
self-pres·er·va·tion (self'prez-ẽr-vā'shən), *n.* 1. preservation of oneself from danger, injury, or death. 2. the urge to preserve oneself, regarded as an instinct.
self-pro·duced (self'prə-dōōst', self'prə-dūst'), *adj.* produced by oneself or itself.
self-pro·nounc·ing (self'prə-noun'siŋ), *adj.* having diacritical marks or other aids to pronunciation directly applied to the original spelling instead of being rewritten in phonetic transcription: as, a Bible with *self-pronouncing* proper names.
self-pro·pelled (self'prə-peld'), *adj.* producing its own power of movement or propulsion; propelled of itself.
self-pro pel·ling (self'prə-pel'iŋ), *adj.* self-propelled.
self-pro·tec·tion (self'prə-tek'shən), *n.* self-defense.
self-re·al·i·za·tion (self'rē-əl-i-zā'shən, self'rē-əl-ī-zā'shən), *n.* the complete fulfillment or development of the self and all its possibilities.
self-re·cord·ing (self'ri-kôr'diŋ), *adj.* making an automatic record of its own functions or operations, as a machine; autographic.
self-re·gard (self'ri-gärd'), *n.* regard or concern for oneself and one's interests.
self-re·la·tion (self'ri-lā'shən), *n.* self-identity.
self-re·li·ance (self'ri-lī'əns), *n.* reliance upon or confidence in one's own judgment, abilities, etc.
self-re·li·ant (self'ri-lī'ənt), *adj.* having or showing self-reliance.
self-re·nun·ci·a·tion (self'ri-nun'si-ā'shən), *n.* renunciation of one's own interests or desires, usually for the benefit of others; self-sacrifice.
self-re·proach (self'ri-prōch'), *n.* accusation or blame of oneself; guilt feeling.
self-re·proach·ful (self'ri-prōch'fəl), *adj.* reproachful of oneself.
self-re·spect (self'ri-spekt'), *n.* a proper respect for oneself, one's character, and one's behavior.
self-re·spect·ing (self'ri-spek'tiŋ), *adj.* having or showing self-respect.
self-re·straint (self'ri-strānt'), *n.* restraint imposed on oneself by oneself; self-control.
self-right·eous (self'rī'chəs), *adj.* 1. righteous, proper, moral, etc. in one's own opinion; pharisaical. 2. characteristic of a self-righteous person.
self-ris·ing (self'rīz'iŋ), *adj.* rising by itself; specifically, rising without the addition of a ferment, as certain flour.
self-sac·ri·fice (self'sak'rə-fīs'), *n.* the sacrifice of oneself or one's interests, usually for the supposed advantage of others; self-denial.
self-sac·ri·fic·ing (self'sak'rə-fīs'iŋ), *adj.* having or showing self-sacrifice.
self·same (self'sām'), *adj.* exactly the same; identical; (the) very same. —*SYN.* see **same.**
self-sat·is·fac·tion (self'sat-is-fak'shən), *n.* the quality or state of being self-satisfied.
self-sat·is·fied (self'sat'is-fīd'), *adj.* feeling or showing satisfaction with oneself or one's accomplishments.
self-seal·ing (self'sēl'iŋ), *adj.* made with a substance that automatically seals bullet holes, punctures, etc.: as, a *self-sealing* gas tank or pneumatic tire.
self-seek·er (self'sēk'ẽr), *n.* a person who seeks only or mainly to further his own interests.
self-seek·ing (self'sēk'iŋ), *n.* the behavior or traits of a self-seeker. *adj.* characteristic of a self-seeker; selfish.
self-serv·ice (self'sũr'vis), *n.* the act or practice of serving oneself in a cafeteria, store, etc. *adj.* designating an establishment characterized by this practice.
self-sown (self'sōn'), *adj.* sown by such means as wind, water, or other natural agency, as some weeds, rather than by man or an animal.
self-start·er (self'stär'tẽr), *n.* any device, other than a hand crank or auxiliary engine, used for automatically starting an internal-combustion engine.
self-styled (self'stīld'), *adj.* named (as such) by oneself: as, he is a *self-styled* guardian of democracy.
self-suf·fi·cien·cy (self'sə-fish'ən-si), *n.* the quality or state of being self-sufficient.
self-suf·fi·cient (self'sə-fish'ənt), *adj.* 1. able to get along without help; independent. 2. having too much confidence in one's own abilities, powers, etc.; conceited.
self-suf·fic·ing (self'sə-fīs'iŋ), *adj.* self-sufficient.
self-sup·port (self'sə-pôrt', self'sə-pōrt'), *n.* support of oneself or itself without aid or reinforcement.
self-sup·port·ed (self'sə-pôr'tid, self'sə-pōr'tid), *adj.* supported by oneself or itself.
self-sup·port·ing (self'sə-pôr'tiŋ, self'sə-pōr'tiŋ), *adj.* supporting oneself or itself.
self-sur·ren·der (self'sə-ren'dẽr), *n.* the surrender of oneself or one's will to an influence, emotion, etc.
self-sus·tain·ing (self'sə-stān'iŋ), *adj.* supporting or able to support oneself or itself.
self-taught (self'tôt'), *adj.* taught through one's own efforts without help from others; self-educated.
self-tor·ture (self'tôr'chẽr), *n.* any mental or physical distress inflicted upon oneself.
self-will (self'wil'), *n.* a persistent carrying out of one's own will or wishes, especially when in conflict with others; stubbornness; obstinacy.
self-willed (self'wild'), *adj.* exercising or showing self-will; stubborn; obstinate.
self-wind·ing (self'wīn'diŋ), *adj.* wound automatically, as some wrist watches, clocks, etc.
self-wrong (self'rôŋ'), *n.* any wrong done to oneself.
Se·li·na (sə-lē'nə, sə-lī'nə), [prob. < Fr. *Céline;* L. *Coelina* < *coelum,* heaven], a feminine name.
Sel·juk (sel-jōōk'), *n.* [Turk. *Seljūq,* legendary ancestor of the dynasties], a member of any of several Turkish dynasties ruling over western Asia from the 11th to the 13th centuries. *adj.* 1. of these dynasties. 2. of the Seljuk Turks.
Sel·juk·i·an (sel-jōōk'i-ən), *adj.* of or characteristic of a Seljuk or the Seljuks. *n.* a Seljuk.
Seljuk Turks, a branch of Turkic peoples that expanded westward from Turkestan in the 11th century.
Sel·kirk (sel'kẽrk), *n.* 1. a county of southern Scotland: pop., 21,000 (est. 1946): also **Selkirkshire.** 2. its county seat: pop., 5,500.
Selkirk Mountains, a mountain range in southeastern British Columbia, Canada.
Sel·kirk·shire (sel'kẽrk-shir'), *n.* Selkirk.
sell (sel), *v.t.* [SOLD (sōld), SELLING], [ME. *sellen;* AS. *sellan,* to give, offer; akin to Goth. *saljan,* to offer (sacrifice); caus. formation in sense "to cause to take" < IE. base **sel-,* to take, grasp], 1. to give up, deliver, or exchange (goods, services, etc.) for money or its equivalent; part with for a price. 2. to make a practice of offering or stocking for sale; have or offer regularly for sale; deal in: as, a department store *sells* many things. 3. *a)* to give up or deliver (a person) to his enemies or into slavery, bondage, etc. *b)* to betray (a country, cause, etc.); hence, 4. to give up (one's honor, trust, etc.) for profit. 5. to bring about, help in, or promote the sale of; cause to be sold: as, radio *sells* many products. 6. [Colloq.], to establish faith, confidence, or belief in: as, he couldn't *sell* the scheme even to his friends. 7. [Colloq.], to persuade (a person) of the value of; convince (with *on*): as, he was *sold* on the idea. 8. [Slang], to cheat; dupe; hoax. *v.i.* 1. to exchange goods or services for money, etc.; engage in selling. 2. to be a popular item on the market; attract buyers. 3. to be sold (*for*): as, belts *sell* for one dollar. 4. [Colloq.], to be widely approved or accepted: as, do you think the idea will *sell?* *n.* [Slang], 1. a trick or hoax. 2. salesmanship, as in *hard sell* (high-pressure salesmanship).
sell off, to get rid of by selling, especially at low prices.
sell oneself, 1. to exchange one's services for a price, especially for a dishonorable or sexual purpose. 2. [Colloq.], to convince another of one's worth.
sell out, 1. to get rid of completely by selling. 2. [Colloq.], to sell or betray (someone, one's trust, etc.).
sell up, 1. to sell all of. 2. [British], *a)* to sell all of, as land or household goods, to satisfy debts, as in bankruptcy. *b)* to sell all the goods of (a person).
SYN.—**sell** implies a transferring of the ownership of something to another for money (to *sell* books, a house, etc.); **barter** implies an exchange of goods or services without using money (to *barter* food for clothes); **trade,** in transitive use, also implies the exchange of articles (let's *trade* neckties), and, intransitively, implies the carrying on of a business in which one buys and sells a specified commodity (to *trade* in wheat); **auction** implies the public sale of items one by one, each going to the highest of the competing bidders (to *auction* off unclaimed property); **vend** applies especially to the selling of small articles, as by peddling, slot machine, etc. (*vending* machines). —*ANT.* buy.
sell·er (sel'ẽr), *n.* 1. a person who sells; vendor. 2. something that sells, usually with reference to its rate of sale: as, a good *seller.*
sell·ing (sel'iŋ), *adj.* 1. of sale: as, *selling* price. 2. engaged in the business of offering something for sale. 3. easily salable; in great demand.
selling race, a horse race in which the horses entered are for sale at a specified price: each horse's price determines the weight he shall carry.
sell·out, sell-out (sel'out'), *n.* [Colloq.], 1. a selling out. 2. an entertainment for which all the seats or tickets are sold.

Sel·ma (sel′mə), [? < Gr. *selma*, a ship, vessel], a feminine name.
Selt·zer (selt′sẽr), *n.* [altered < G. *Selterser* < *Nieder Selters*, a town near Wiesbaden, Germany], 1. natural spring water of high mineral content and effervescent quality. 2. [often s-], any similar water prepared artificially. Also **Seltzer water.**
sel·vage, sel·vedge (sel′vij), *n.* [< *self* + *edge*, after MD. *selfegge, selfegghe*], 1. a specially woven edge which prevents cloth or fabric from raveling. 2. the edge plate or receptacle of a lock into which the bolt fits.
selves (selvz), *n.* plural of **self.**
Sem., 1. Seminary. 2. Semitic.
sem., semicolon.
se·man·tic (sə-man′tik), *adj.* [Gr. *sēmantikos*, significant < *sēmainein*, to show], 1. of meaning, especially meaning in language: as, syllable stress is a *semantic* factor. 2. of or according to the science of semantics.
se·man·tics (sə-man′tiks), *n.pl.* [construed as sing.], [< *semantic*, after Fr. *sémantique* (of the same origin), as adopted in 1887], 1. the branch of linguistics concerned with the nature, structure, and, especially, the development and changes, of the meanings of speech forms; semasiology. 2. the scientific study of the relations between signs, or symbols, and what they mean, or denote, and of behavior in its psychological and sociological aspects as it is influenced by signs.
sem·a·phore (sem′ə-fôr′, sem′ə-fōr′), *n.* [Fr. *sémaphore* < Gr. *sēma*, a sign + *pherein*, to bear], 1. any apparatus for signaling, as by an arrangement of lights, flags, and mechanical arms on railroads. 2. a system of signaling by the use of two flags, one held in each hand: the letters of the alphabet are represented by the various positions of the arms. 3. any system of signaling by semaphore. *v.t. & v.i.* [SEMAPHORED (-fôrd′, -fōrd′), SEMAPHORING], to signal by semaphore.
sem·a·phor·ic (sem′ə-fôr′ik, sem′ə-for′ik), *adj.* of, by, or like a semaphore.
Se·ma·rang (sə-mä′räŋ), *n.* a city on the northern coast of Java: pop., 218,000: also spelled **Samarang.**
se·ma·si·o·log·i·cal (si-mā′si-ə-loj′i-k'l), *adj.* semantic.
se·ma·si·ol·o·gy (si-mā′si-ol′ə-ji), *n.* [< Gr. *sēmasia*, signification of a word; + *-logy*], in *linguistics*, semantics.
se·mat·ic (si-mat′ik), *adj.* [< Gr. *sēma, sēmatos*, a sign; + *-ic*], in *biology*, serving as a warning or sign of danger, as the color of some poisonous snakes.
sem·bla·ble (sem′blə-b'l), *adj.* [ME.; OFr. < *sembler;* see SEMBLANCE], [Archaic], 1. similar; like. 2. suitable. 3. apparent or seeming but not real. *n.* [Archaic], 1. something similar. 2. resemblance; likeness.
sem·blance (sem′bləns), *n.* [ME.; OFr. < *sembler*, to seem, appear < L. *similare, simulare*, to make like < *similis*, like], 1. outward form or appearance; aspect. 2. the look or appearance of something else; resemblance. 3. a likeness, image, representation, or copy. 4. false, assumed, or deceiving form or appearance. 5. mere empty show; pretense. —*SYN.* see **appearance.**
Sem·brich, Mar·cel·la (mär-tsel′ä zem′briH; Eng. mär-sel′ə sem′brik), (born *Praxede Marcelline Kochańska*), 1858–1935; American operatic soprano, born in Austria.
se·mé (sə-mā′), *adj.* [Fr., orig. pp. of *semer*, to sow; L. *seminare* < *semen*, a seed], in *heraldry*, having a design of many small figures; dotted, as with stars.
se·mei·ol·o·gy (sē′mī-ol′ə-ji), *n.* semiology.
se·mei·ot·ic (sē′mī-ot′ik), *adj.* semiotic.
Sem·e·le (sem′ə-lē′), *n.* [L.; Gr. *Semelē*], in *Greek mythology*, the daughter of Cadmus, and mother of Zeus's son Dionysus: when she desired to see Zeus as he appeared to the gods, she was destroyed by his lightning.
se·men (sē′mən), *n.* [*pl.* SEMINA (sem′i-nə)], [L., a seed], the thick, whitish fluid secreted by the male reproductive organs and containing the spermatozoa.
se·mes·ter (sə-mes′tẽr), *n.* [G.; L. (*cursus*) *semestris*, half-yearly (period) < *sex*, six + *mensis*, month], 1. a six-month period; half year. 2. one of the two (or three) terms, of fifteen to eighteen weeks each, which make up a school or college year in most American educational institutions.
sem·i- (sem′i, sem′ə; *now sometimes* sem′ī), [L.; akin to Gr. *hēmi-*, Sans. *sāmi-*, AS. *sām-*], a prefix meaning: 1. *half*, as in *semidiameter*. 2. *partly, not fully, imperfectly*, as in *semicivilized*. 3. *twice in a* (specified period), as in *semiannually*.
sem·i·an·nu·al (sem′i-an′ū-əl), *adj.* 1. happening, prepared, presented, etc. every half year. 2. lasting half a year, as some plants. Abbreviated **s.a.**
sem·i·an·nu·al·ly (sem′i-an′ū-əl-i), *adv.* every six months; twice yearly.
sem·i·au·to·mat·ic (sem′i-ô′tə-mat′ik), *adj.* 1. partly automatic and partly hand-controlled: said of machinery. 2. having an automatic chambering mechanism but requiring a trigger pull for each round fired: said of repeating firearms.
sem·i·breve (sem′ə-brēv′), *n.* [It.], in *music*, a whole note (𝅝), equal to four crotchets: see **neume**, illus.
sem·i·cen·ten·ni·al (sem′i-sen-ten′i-əl), *adj.* [*semi-* + *centennial*], 1. happening once in a period of 50 years. 2. lasting for 50 years. *n.* 1. a 50th year of existence or duration; 50th anniversary. 2. the celebration of this.
sem·i·cir·cle (sem′ə-sũr′k'l), *n.* [L. *semicirculus;* see SEMI- & CIRCLE], 1. a half circle. 2. any object or grouping in the form of a half circle.
sem·i·cir·cu·lar (sem′ə-sũr′kyoo-lẽr), *adj.* [ML. *semicircularis*], having the form of a semicircle.
semicircular canal, any of the three loop-shaped, tubular structures of the inner ear that serve to maintain balance in the organism: see **ear**, illus.
sem·i·civ·i·lized (sem′ə-siv′′l-īzd′), *adj.* partly civilized.
sem·i·co·lon (sem′ə-kō′lən), *n.* a mark of punctuation (;) indicating a degree of separation greater than that marked by the comma and less than that marked by the period, etc.: conventionally used chiefly to separate units that contain elements separated by commas, and to separate co-ordinate clauses having a relationship in meaning not explicitly stated: abbreviated **sem.**
sem·i·con·scious (sem′ə-kon′shəs), *adj.* not fully conscious or awake; half-conscious.
sem·i·dai·ly (sem′ə-dā′li), *adj.* twice daily.
sem·i·de·tached (sem′i-di-tacht′), *adj.* partly separate or detached, as a pair of houses joined with a common wall but not connected with other buildings.
sem·i·de·vel·oped (sem′i-di-vel′əpt), *adj.* partly developed.
sem·i·di·am·e·ter (sem′i-dī-am′ə-tẽr), *n.* half a diameter; radius.
sem·i·di·ur·nal (sem′i-dī-ũr′n'l), *adj.* 1. of, lasting, or performed in half a day; specifically, designating or of half the arc traveled by a heavenly body between the times of its rising and setting. 2. coming twice a day, or about every twelve hours, as the tides.
sem·i·di·vine (sem′i-di-vīn′), *adj.* in *theology*, not having full divinity.
sem·i·dome (sem′ə-dōm′), *n.* a curved ceiling or roof covering a semicircular room, bay, etc.; half dome.
sem·i·el·lip·ti·cal (sem′i-i-lip′ti-k'l), *adj.* 1. having the form of a half ellipse. 2. nearly or imperfectly elliptical.
sem·i·fi·nal (sem′ə-fī′n'l), *adj.* coming just before the final: said of the divisions of a contest or tournament. *n.* a semifinal round, match, etc.
sem·i·fi·nal·ist (sem′ə-fī′n'l-ist), *n.* a person taking part in a semifinal round, match, etc.
sem·i·flu·id (sem′ə-flo͞o′id), *adj.* neither liquid nor solid; heavy or thick but capable of flowing; viscous but fluid. *n.* a substance of this nature.
sem·i·lu·nar (sem′i-lo͞o′nẽr), *adj.* [*semi-* + *lunar*], shaped like a half-moon; crescent-shaped.
semilunar valve, either of the two crescent-shaped valves, one at the junction of the right ventricle and pulmonary artery (*pulmonary valve*), the other at the junction of the left ventricle and aorta (*aortic valve*), which function to prevent blood from flowing back into the ventricles.
sem·i·month·ly (sem′ə-munth′li), *adj.* coming, happening, done, etc. twice a month. *n.* something coming, appearing, etc. twice a month, especially a magazine. *adv.* twice monthly; every half month.
sem·i·nal (sem′ə-n'l), *adj.* [ME.; Late OFr.; L. *seminalis* < *semen, seminis*, a seed], 1. of or containing seed or semen. 2. of reproduction: as, *seminal* power. 3. like seed; constituting a source; germinal; originative.
sem·i·nar (sem′ə-när′, sem′ə-när′), *n.* [G.; L. *seminarium;* see SEMINARY], 1. a group of supervised students doing research or advanced study. 2. *a*) a course for such a group. *b*) the room where it meets.
sem·i·nar·y (sem′ə-ner′i), *n.* [*pl.* SEMINARIES (-iz)], [L. *seminarium*, seed plot, nursery, neut. of *seminarius*, of seed < *semen*, a seed], 1. a place where something develops, grows, or is cultivated: as, slums are *seminaries* of crime. 2. a school, especially a private school for young women. 3. a school or college where priests, ministers, etc. are trained. 4. a seminar. Abbreviated **Sem.**
sem·i·na·tion (sem′ə-nā′shən), *n.* [L. *seminatio* < *seminare*, to sow < *semen*, a seed], 1. a spreading or propagation; dissemination. 2. in *botany*, the act or process of sowing seed.
sem·i·nif·er·ous (sem′ə-nif′ẽr-əs), *adj.* [< L. *semen, seminis*, a seed; + *-ferous*], 1. seed-bearing. 2. containing or conveying semen.
sem·i·niv·o·rous (sem′ə-niv′ẽr-əs), *adj.* [< L. *semen, seminis*, a seed; + *-vorous*], seed-eating.
Sem·i·nole (sem′ə-nōl′), *n.* [*pl.* SEMINOLE, SEMINOLES (-nōlz′)], [Am. Ind. (Creek) *Simanóle*, lit., separatist, runaway], a member of a tribe of Muskhogean Indians who settled in Florida: a branch of the Creek tribe. *adj.* of this tribe of Indians.
sem·i·of·fi·cial (sem′i-ə-fish′′l), *adj.* having some, but not full, official authority; partly official.
se·mi·ol·o·gy (sē′mī-ol′ə-ji), *n.* [< Gr. *sēmeion;* + *-logy*], 1. the science of signs or sign language. 2. the branch of medicine having to do with symptoms; symptomatology. Also **semeiology.**
se·mi·ot·ic (sē′mī-ot′ik), *adj.* [Gr. *sēmeiōtikos* < *sēmeion*, a sign], 1. of signs or sign language. 2. in *medicine*, *a*) of symptoms. *b*) symptomatic. Also **semeiotic.**
se·mi·ot·i·cal (sē′mī-ot′i-k'l), *adj.* semiotic.

sem·i·o·vip·a·rous (sem'i-ō-vip'ẽr-əs), *adj.* producing young whose natal development is incomplete, as marsupials.

sem·i·pal·mate (sem'ə-pal'māt, sem'ə-pal'mit), *adj.* in *zoology*, with only a half web connecting the anterior toes; not fully palmate.

sem·i·par·a·sit·ic (sem'ə-par'ə-sit'ik), *adj.* 1. in *biology*, ordinarily parasitic but capable of a saprophytic life. 2. in *botany*, taking part of its food from the host and making the rest by itself, as the mistletoe; both parasitic and photosynthetic.

sem·i·per·me·a·ble (sem'ə-pũr'mi-ə-b'l), *adj.* allowing some substances to pass; permeable to smaller molecules but not to larger ones, as a membrane in osmosis.

sem·i·plas·tic (sem'ə-plas'tik), *adj.* partly plastic.

sem·i·po·lit·i·cal (sem'i-pə-lit'i-k'l), *adj.* political in some respects only.

sem·i·por·ce·lain (sem'ə-pôr'sə-lin), *n.* an opaque porcelain with a finish like that of earthenware.

sem·i·pre·cious (sem'ə-presh'əs), *adj.* designating gems of lower value than those classified as precious: said of the garnet, turquoise, etc.

sem·i·pri·vate (sem'ə-prī'vit), *adj.* partly but not completely private; specifically, designating or of a hospital room having two, or sometimes three or four, beds.

sem·i·pro (sem'i-prō'), *n.* [contr. < *semiprofessional*], [Colloq.], a person who engages in a sport for pay but not as a regular occupation.

sem·i·pub·lic (sem'ə-pub'lik), *adj.* partly but not completely public.

sem·i·qua·ver (sem'ə-kwā'vẽr), *n.* a sixteenth note (♬).

Se·mir·a·mis (si-mir'ə-mis), *n.* Assyrian queen; fl. c. 800 B.C.; legendary founder of Babylon, noted for her beauty, wisdom, and sexual excesses.

sem·i·rig·id (sem'ə-rij'id), *adj.* designating an airship having a rigid internal keel but no other supporting framework.

sem·i·round (sem'ə-round'), *adj.* generally round but with one flat surface. *n.* anything having this shape.

sem·i·skilled (sem'ə-skild'), *adj.* 1. partly skilled. 2. of or doing manual work that requires some but not extensive training.

sem·i·sol·id (sem'ə-sol'id), *adj.* not fluid but capable of changing shape, as gelatin. *n.* a semisolid substance.

sem·i·spher·i·cal (sem'ə-sfer'i-k'l), *adj.* in the shape of a half sphere; hemispherical.

Sem·ite (sem'īt, sē'mīt), *n.* [Mod. L. *Semita* < LL. *Sem*, Shem; Gr. *Sēm;* Heb. *shēm*], a member of any of the peoples whose language is Semitic, including the Hebrews, Arabs, Assyrians, Phoenicians, Babylonians, etc.; now, specifically, a Jew: also **Shemite.**

Se·mit·ic (sə-mit'ik), *adj.* 1. of, characteristic of, or like a Semite or the Semites. 2. designating or of a major group of languages of southwestern Asia and northern Africa, related to the Hamitic languages and divided into *East Semitic* (Akkadian), *North West Semitic* (Phoenician, Punic, Aramaic, Hebrew, Modern Hebrew, etc.) and *South West Semitic* (Arabic, Ethiopic, Amharic): abbreviated **Sem.**

Se·mit·ics (sə-mit'iks), *n.pl.* [construed as sing.], the study of Semitic culture, languages, literature, etc.

Sem·i·tism (sem'ə-tiz'm, sē'mə-tiz'm), *n.* 1. a Semitic word or idiom. 2. characteristics of the Semites; especially, the ideas, cultural qualities, etc. originating with the Jews.

sem·i·tone (sem'ə-tōn'), *n.* 1. in *music*, a tone at an interval of a half step from another in a diatonic scale; half tone. 2. such an interval.

sem·i·ton·ic (sem'ə-ton'ik), *adj.* of or constituting a semitone.

sem·i·trail·er (sem'ə-trāl'ẽr), *n.* a large trailer with four or more wheels that is attached to a tractor cab for hauling and can be detached, as for loading.

sem·i·trop·i·cal (sem'ə-trop'i-k'l), *adj.* having some of the characteristics of the tropics; partly tropical.

sem·i·vow·el (sem'ə-vou'əl), *n.* a vowel used as a consonant: the English semivowels *w, y* are phonetically vowels (ōō, ē) used as consonants, as in *wall, yoke.*

sem·i·week·ly (sem'ə-wēk'li), *adj.* coming, happening, done, etc. twice a week or every half week. *n.* something that comes, happens, is done, etc. twice weekly or every half week, as a newspaper published twice a week. *adv.* twice weekly; every half week.

sem·i·year·ly (sem'ə-yêr'li), *adj.* coming, happening, done, etc. twice a year or every half year. *n.* something that comes, happens, is done, etc. twice yearly or every half year. *adv.* twice yearly; every half year.

sem·o·li·na (sem'ə-lē'nə), *n.* [It. *semolino*, dim. of *semola*, bran], meal consisting of the hard, coarse kernels of wheat, a by-product in the manufacture of fine flour: used in making macaroni, puddings, etc.

‡sem·per (sem'pẽr), *adv.* [L.], always.

‡semper fi·de·lis (fi-dē'lis, fi-dā'lis), [L.], always faithful: the motto of the United States Marine Corps.

‡semper i·dem (ī'dem), [L.], always the same.

‡semper par·a·tus (pə-rā'təs), [L.], always prepared: the motto of the United States Coast Guard.

sem·pi·ter·nal (sem'pi-tũr'n'l), *adj.* [ME.; Late OFr. *sempiternel;* ML. *sempiternalis* < L. *sempiternus* < *semper*, always + *eternus*, eternal], everlasting; perpetual; eternal.

sem·pi·ter·ni·ty (sem'pi-tũr'nə-ti), *n.* [< L. *sempiternus* (see SEMPITERNAL); + *-ity*], the state or quality of being sempiternal; eternity.

semp·stress (sem'stris, semp'stris), *n.* [var. of *seamstress*], a seamstress.

sen (sen), *n.* [*pl.* SEN], [Japan.; Chin. *ch'ien*, coin], a Japanese copper or bronze coin equal to 1/100 of a yen.

Sen., sen., 1. Senate. 2. Senator. 3. senior.

sen·a·ry (sen'ẽr-i), *adj.* [L. *senarius* < *seni*, six each < base of *sex*, six], of six; on the basis of six.

sen·ate (sen'it), *n.* [ME. *senat, senas;* OFr. *senat, senaz* (Fr. *sénat*); L. *senatus* < *senex, senis*, old, aged], 1. literally, a council of elders. 2. the supreme council of the ancient Roman state, originally only of patricians but later including the plebeians. 3. a lawmaking assembly; state council; hence, 4. [S-], a legislative group, generally the smaller, and called the *upper*, of the two houses forming certain national and State legislatures: in the United States Senate there are two senators from each State, regardless of its size: see also **House of Representatives.** 5. a governing or advisory council in a college or university. Abbreviated **Sen., S.**

sen·a·tor (sen'ə-tẽr), *n.* [ME. & OFr. *senatour;* L. *senator*], a member of a senate: abbreviated **Sen., sen.**

sen·a·to·ri·al (sen'ə-tôr'i-əl, sen'ə-tō'ri-əl), *adj.* [< L. *senatorius* (< *senator*); + *-al*], 1. of or suitable for a senator or a senate. 2. composed of senators. 3. entitled to elect a senator: said of an electoral district.

sen·a·tor·ship (sen'ə-tẽr-ship'), *n.* [*senator* + *-ship*], the position, term of office, etc. of a senator.

‡se·na·tus con·sul·tum (si-nā'təs kən-sul'təm), [L.], a decree of the ancient Roman senate.

send (send), *v.t.* [SENT (sent), SENDING], [ME. *senden;* AS. *sendan;* akin to G. *senden*, Goth. *sandjan;* caus. formation in sense "to cause to go"; IE. base **sent-*, to go, find out, discover, seen also in L. *sentire*, to feel, sense; cf. SENSE], 1. *a)* to cause to go or be carried; dispatch; transmit: as, food, medicine, and doctors were *sent* by plane. *b)* to dispatch (a letter, telegram, etc.) by mail, messenger, etc. 2. to cause (a person) to go from one place to another, especially by asking, directing, or commanding: as, *send* the man to me, the storm *sent* them hurrying to their homes. 3. to arrange for the going of; enable to go or attend: as, his father *sent* him to college. 4. to cause to move, as by releasing, hitting, discharging, throwing, etc.: as, the explosion *sent* a cloud of smoke high in the air, he *sent* the ball over the trees. 5. to bring or drive into some state or condition: as, the noise will *send* him out of his mind. 6. to cause to happen, come, etc.; give: as, a crop *sent* to reward our toil. 7. [Slang], to perform jazz music in such a way as to cause great excitement or exhilaration in (the listener or performer). *v.i.* to send a message or messenger.

send flying, 1. to dismiss or cause to depart hurriedly. 2. to stagger or repel, as with a blow. 3. to put to flight; rout. 4. to scatter abruptly in all directions.

send for, 1. to ask for the arrival of; summon. 2. to place an order for; make a request for delivery of.

send forth, to be a source of; cause to appear; give out or forth; produce; emit.

send in, to dispatch, hand in, or send to a central point.

send off, 1. to mail, dispatch, or send away, as a letter, gift, etc. 2. to dismiss. 3. to give a send-off to.

send out, 1. to dispatch, distribute, issue, mail, etc. from a central point. 2. to send forth.

send packing, to dismiss abruptly; drive (another) away, as in disgrace.

send up, 1. to cause to rise, climb, or go up. 2. [Colloq.], to sentence to imprisonment.

send (send), *n.* [prob. < *send* (to dispatch) but influenced by *scend* (< *ascend, descend*, etc.)], 1. the driving motion of a wave or the sea. 2. a scend. *v.i.* 1. to be plunged forward, as by a wave. 2. to scend.

Sen·dai (sen'dī'), *n.* a city in eastern Honshu, Japan: pop., 294,000 (est. 1947).

sen·dal (sen'd'l), *n.* [ME. & OFr. *cendal, sendal;* ult. < Gr. *sindōn*, fine linen], 1. a light silk fabric used in the Middle Ages for costumes, flags, etc. 2. anything made of this material.

send·er (sen'dẽr), *n.* a person or thing that sends, as a telegraphic transmitter.

send-off (send'ôf'), *n.* [Colloq.], 1. an expression or demonstration of friendly feeling toward someone starting out on a trip, career, etc. 2. a start or beginning given to someone or something.

Sen·e·ca (sen'i-kə), *n.* [< D. *Sennacaas*, the Five Nations < Am. Ind. (Mohegan) *A'sinnika*, transl. of Iroquois *Onĕñiute'*, short for *onĕñiute' roñ non*, Oneida, lit. people of the standing rock], a member of a tribe of Iroquoian Indians who lived in the area of the Genesee River, New York: see **Five Nations.** *adj.* of this tribe.

Sen·e·ca (sen'i-kə), *n.* (*Lucius Annaeus Seneca*), Roman statesman, writer, and Stoic philosopher; lived 4 B.C.–65 A.D.: his tragedies influenced Elizabethan drama.

sen·e·ga (sen'i-gə), *n.* [< *Senega*, var. of *Seneca*], 1. a North American plant of the milkwort family. 2. its dried root, used as an expectorant.

Sen·e·gal, Sé·né·gal (sen'i-gôl'; Fr. sā'nā'gȧl'), *n.* 1. a country in western Africa, on the Atlantic: a former French colony, it is now a member of the French Community: area, 76,124 sq. mi.; pop., 2,550,000; capital, Dakar. 2. a river flowing between Senegal and Mauritania into the Atlantic: length, 1,000 mi.

Sen·e·gal·ese (sen'i-gô-lēz', sen'i-gə-lēz'), *adj.* of Senegal or its people. *n.* [*pl.* SENEGALESE], 1. one of the native Moors or Negroes of Senegal. 2. their language.

Sen·e·gam·bi·a (sen'ə-gam'bi-ə), *n.* a region in western Africa between the Senegal and Gambia Rivers, in Senegal, Mali, and Gambia.

se·nes·cence (sə-nes''ns), *n.* [< *senescent*], the process or state of growing old; onset of old age.

se·nes·cent (sə-nes''nt), *adj.* [L. *senescens*, ppr. of *senescere*, to grow old < *senex*, old], growing old; aging.

sen·es·chal (sen'ə-shəl), *n.* [ME. & OFr. *seneschal;* OHG. *siniskalk*, oldest servant; **sini*, old + *skalk*, servant], a powerful official in the household of a medieval noble: he was in charge of administering justice and managing the domestic affairs of the estate, and he represented his lord in court.

‡sen·hor (se-nyôr'), *n.* [Port. < L. *senior* (see SENIOR); cf. Sp. *señor*, It. *signor*], a man; gentleman: Portuguese title equivalent to *Mr.* or *Sir:* abbreviated **Sr.**

‡sen·ho·ra (se-nyô'rä), *n.* [Port., fem. of *senhor*], a married woman; lady: Portuguese title equivalent to *Mrs.* or *Madam:* abbreviated **Sra.**

‡sen·ho·ri·ta (se'nyô-rē'tä), *n.* [Port., dim. of *senhora*], an unmarried woman or girl; young lady: Portuguese title equivalent to *Miss:* abbreviated **Srta.**

se·nile (sē'nīl, sē'nil), *adj.* [L. *senilis* < *senex*, old], 1. of old age. 2. showing signs of old age; elderly; weak in mind and body. 3. resulting from old age. 4. in *physical geography*, nearing the end of an erosion cycle.

se·nil·i·ty (sə-nil'ə-ti, sē-nil'ə-ti), *n.* 1. the condition or quality of being senile; old age. 2. the characteristics of old age; weakness; infirmity of mind and body.

sen·ior (sēn'yẽr), *adj.* [ME.; L. *senior*, compar. of *senex*, old], 1. of the greater age; older: often indicating the older of two having the same name, as a father and son: abbreviated **Sr.** 2. of higher rank or standing, or longer in service. 3. of or belonging to the graduating class in a high school or college. *n.* 1. a person older than another or others. 2. a person of greater rank, standing, or length of service. 3. a person in the graduating class of a high school or college. Abbreviated **Sen., sen.**

senior high school, high school: usually the tenth, eleventh, and twelfth grades: distinguished from *junior high school.*

sen·ior·i·ty (sēn-yôr'ə-ti, sēn-yor'ə-ti), *n.* [*pl.* SENIORITIES (-tiz)], 1. the state or quality of being senior; precedence in birth, rank, etc. 2. status, priority, or precedence achieved by length of service in a given job, as in determining an employee's eligibility for promotion.

Sen·lac (sen'lak), *n.* a hill in southeastern England, near Hastings: site of the battle of Hastings (1066).

sen·na (sen'ə), *n.* [ML. *senna, sena;* Ar. *sanā*], 1. any of a number of related plants of the pea family, with pods and yellow or pinkish flowers. 2. the dried leaves of some of these plants, used in medicine as a laxative.

Sen·nach·er·ib (sə-nak'ẽr-ib), *n.* son of Sargon II; lived ?–681 B.C.; king of Assyria (705–681 B.C.).

sen·net (sen'it), *n.* [OFr. *senet, sinet, signet*, dim. of *signe*, a sign; cf. SIGNET], [Archaic], a trumpet call used as a signal for ceremonial entrances and exits: a stage direction in Elizabethan drama.

sen·night, se'n·night (sen'īt, sen'it), *n.* [< *seven night*], [Archaic], a week.

sen·nit (sen'it), *n.* [prob. < *seven* + *knit*], 1. a flat braided material made by plaiting strands of rope yarn. 2. plaited grass or palm leaves used for making hats.

‡se·ñor (se-nyôr'), *n.* [*pl.* SEÑORES (-nyô'res)], [Sp. < L. *senior;* see SENIOR], a man; gentleman: Spanish title equivalent to *Mr.* or *Sir:* abbreviated **Sr.**

‡se·ño·ra (se-nyô'rä), *n.* [Sp., fem. of *señor*], a married woman; lady: Spanish title equivalent to *Mrs.* or *Madam:* abbreviated **Sra.**

‡se·ño·ri·ta (se'nyô-rē'tä), *n.* [Sp., dim. of *señora*], an unmarried woman or girl; young lady: Spanish title corresponding to *Miss:* abbreviated **Srta.**

sen·sate (sen'sāt), *adj.* [LL. *sensatus*, intelligent < L. *sensus*, sense], 1. having the power of physical sensation. 2. registering on the senses; felt by the senses.

sen·sa·tion (sen-sā'shən), *n.* [LL. *sensatio* < *sensatus;* see SENSATE], 1. the power or process of receiving conscious sense impressions through direct stimulation of the bodily organism or of the sense organs: as, hearing, seeing, touching, tasting, and smelling are *sensations.* 2. an immediate reaction to external stimulation of a sense organ; conscious feeling or sense impression: as, a *sensation* of cold. 3. a generalized feeling or reaction, often vague and without reference to immediate stimulus: as, a *sensation* of happiness. 4. a state or feeling of excitement and interest caused in a group, community, etc.: as, the play caused a *sensation.* 5. the action, event, etc. causing such a feeling.

sen·sa·tion·al (sen-sā'shən-'l), *adj.* 1. of the senses or sensation. 2. of, or in accordance with, philosophical sensationalism. 3. arousing intense interest and excitement; startling; exciting. 4. using or having effects intended to startle, shock, thrill, or arouse interest and intense excitement.

sen·sa·tion·al·ism (sen-sā'shən-'l-iz'm), *n.* 1. the use of subject matter, style, language, or artistic expression that is intended to shock, startle, excite, or arouse intense interest; addiction to what is sensational (sense 4) in literature, art, public speaking, etc.; sensational methods. 2. in *ethics*, sensualism. 3. in *philosophy*, the belief that all knowledge is acquired through the use of the senses.

sen·sa·tion·al·ist (sen-sā'shən-'l-ist), *n.* 1. a sensational artist, reporter, speaker, etc.; person who practices sensationalism. 2. a believer in philosophical sensationalism.

sen·sa·tion·al·is·tic (sen-sā'shən-'l-is'tik), *adj.* of sensationalists or sensationalism.

sense (sens), *n.* [Fr. *sens;* L. *sensus* < *sentire*, to feel, perceive; for IE. base see SEND], 1. the ability of the nerves and the brain to receive and react to stimuli, as light, sound, impact, constriction, etc.: formerly confined to denoting any of five faculties of receiving impressions through specific bodily organs and the nerves associated with them (sight, touch, taste, smell, and hearing): as, not perceptible to the *senses:* see also **sixth sense.** 2. the senses considered as a total function of the bodily organism, as distinguished from intellect, movement, etc. 3. feeling, impression, perception, or recognition, either through the senses or through the intellect; awareness: as, a *sense* of warmth, an uneasy *sense* of guilt. 4. an ability to judge, distinguish, discriminate, or estimate external conditions, sounds, etc.: as, a *sense* of direction, pitch, etc. 5. an ability to feel, appreciate, understand, or comprehend some quality, as humor, honor, etc. 6. the ability to think or reason soundly; normal intelligence and judgment, often as reflected in behavior. 7. meaning; especially, any of several meanings conveyed by or attributed to the same word or phrase. 8. essential signification; gist: as, few people grasped the *sense* of his remarks. 9. soundness of judgment or reasoning; evidence of normal intelligence or understanding: as, there is some *sense* in what he says. 10. something wise, sound, or reasonable: as, there's no *sense* in going. 11. the general opinion, sentiment, or attitude of a group. 12. direction; tendency. *v.t.* [SENSED (senst), SENSING], 1. to be or become aware of; perceive: as, he *sensed* our hostility. 2. [Colloq.], to comprehend; understand. —*SYN.* see **meaning.**

in a sense, from one aspect; to some extent or degree.

make sense, to be intelligible or logical.

senses, normal ability to think or reason soundly: as, come to your *senses.*

sense·less (sens'lis), *adj.* 1. unconscious. 2. not having good sense; stupid; foolish. 3. arising from a lack of judgment or intelligence; unreasonable; meaningless.

sense organ, any organ or structure, as an eye or taste bud, specialized to receive specific stimuli and transmit them as sensations to the brain; receptor.

sense perception, 1. perception or the knowing of facts from stimuli received and responded to by the senses. 2. the process of obtaining such knowledge. 3. the ability to gain such knowledge.

sen·si·bil·i·ty (sen'sə-bil'ə-ti), *n.* [*pl.* SENSIBILITIES (-tiz)], [ME. & Late OFr. *sensibilite;* LL. *sensibilitas* < L. *sensibilis;* see SENSIBLE], 1. the capacity for physical sensation; power of responding to stimuli; ability to feel. 2. *often pl.* the capacity for being affected emotionally or intellectually, whether pleasantly or unpleasantly; receptiveness to impression; mental or emotional responsiveness. 3. *often pl.* the capacity to respond intelligently and perceptively to intellectual, moral, or aesthetic events or values, especially those which are considered higher or refined; delicate, sensitive awareness or responsiveness; keen intellectual perception. 4. [Rare], responsiveness, as of a plant, thermometer, etc., to changing conditions. 5. [Archaic], readiness to respond to suffering or to the pathetic.

sen·si·ble (sen'sə-b'l), *adj.* [ME.; OFr.; L. *sensibilis* < *sensus*, pp. of *sentire*, to feel, perceive], 1. that can cause physical sensation; perceptible to the senses. 2. perceptible to the intellect. 3. easily perceived; marked; striking; appreciable. 4. having senses; capable of sensation; sensitive. 5. having appreciation or understanding; cognizant; aware; emotionally or intellectually conscious: as, he was *sensible* of their grief. 6. having or showing good sense or sound judgment; intelligent; reasonable; wise. —*SYN.* see **aware, material, perceptible, rational.**

sen·si·bly (sen'sə-bli), *adv.* 1. so as to be sensible or noticeable; appreciably. 2. in a sensible manner; intelligently; wisely.

sen·si·tive (sen′sə-tiv), ***adj.*** [ME. *sensitife;* OFr. *sensitif;* ML. *sensitivus* < L. *sensus,* pp. of *sentire,* to feel, perceive], 1. of the senses or sensation; especially, connected with the reception or transmission of sense impressions; sensory. 2. receiving and responding to stimuli from outside objects or agencies; having sensation. 3. responding or feeling readily and acutely; very keenly susceptible to stimuli: as, a *sensitive* ear; hence, 4. tender; raw; easily hurt, as a healing wound. 5. having or showing keen sensibilities. 6. easily offended, disturbed, shocked, irritated, etc., as by the actions of others; high-strung, tense, and touchy. 7. changing easily or quickly in the presence of some force or agency; very responsive to external conditions, as to light, heat, etc.: as, photographic film is *sensitive* to light. 8. showing, or liable to show, unusual variation; fluctuating: as, a *sensitive* stock market.

sensitive plant, a tropical American plant with a spiny stem and purplish flowers, whose leaflets fold and leafstalks droop at the slightest touch: it is often cultivated in hothouses.

sen·si·tiv·i·ty (sen′sə-tiv′ə-ti), ***n.*** the condition or quality of being sensitive.

sen·si·ti·za·tion (sen′sə-ti-zā′shən, sen′sə-tī-zā′shən), ***n.*** a sensitizing or being sensitized.

sen·si·tize (sen′sə-tīz′), ***v.t.*** [SENSITIZED (-tīzd′), SENSITIZING], to make sensitive or susceptible; specifically, *a*) in ***photography,*** to make (a film or plate) sensitive to light, etc. *b*) in ***immunology,*** to make sensitive or hypersensitive to a serum by repeated injection.

sen·si·tom·e·ter (sen′sə-tom′ə-tẽr), ***n.*** an instrument used for measuring sensitivity, as of the eyes.

sen·so·ri·al (sen-sôr′i-əl, sen-sō′ri-əl), ***adj.*** sensory.

sen·so·ri·um (sen-sôr′i-əm, sen-sō′ri-əm), ***n.*** [*pl.* SENSORIUMS (-əmz), SENSORIA (-ə)], [LL. < L. *sensus,* sense], 1. the whole sensory apparatus of the body. 2. the supposed seat of physical sensation in the gray matter of the brain.

sen·so·ry (sen′sẽr-i), ***adj.*** [< *sense* + *-ory*], 1. of the senses or sensation. 2. connected with the reception and transmission of sense impressions.

sen·su·al (sen′sho͞o-əl), ***adj.*** [< Fr. or L.; Fr. *sensuel;* L. *sensualis* < *sensus,* sense, feeling], 1. [Rare], sensory or sensuous. 2. of the body and the senses as distinguished from the intellect: as, *sensual* pleasures. 3. *a*) connected or preoccupied with bodily or sexual pleasures; voluptuous. *b*) lustful; licentious; lewd. 4. resulting from, or showing preoccupation with, bodily or sexual pleasure: as, a *sensual* expression. 5. of the doctrine of sensationalism. —***SYN.*** see **carnal, sensuous.**

sen·su·al·ism (sen′sho͞o-əl-iz′m), ***n.*** 1. frequent or excessive indulgence in sensual pleasures. 2. the belief that the pleasures of the senses constitute the greatest good. 3. the expression of this belief, as in art; emphasis on what is sensuous. 4. in ***philosophy,*** sensationalism.

sen·su·al·ist (sen′sho͞o-əl-ist), ***n.*** 1. a person who indulges excessively in sensual pleasures; voluptuary. 2. a person who believes in sensualism.

sen·su·al·is·tic (sen′sho͞o-əl-is′tik), ***adj.*** sensual.

sen·su·al·i·ty (sen′sho͞o-al′ə-ti), ***n.*** [ME. & OFr. *sensualite;* LL. *sensualitas*], 1. the state or quality of being sensual; fondness for or indulgence in sensual pleasures. 2. lasciviousness; lewdness.

sen·su·al·i·za·tion (sen′sho͞o-əl-i-zā′shən, sen′sho͞o-əl-ī-zā′shən), ***n.*** a sensualizing or being sensualized.

sen·su·al·ize (sen′sho͞o-əl-īz′), ***v.t.*** [SENSUALIZED (-īzd′), SENSUALIZING], to make sensual; instill with sensualism.

sen·su·ous (sen′sho͞o-əs), ***adj.*** [< L. *sensus,* sense; + *-ous*], 1. of, derived from, based on, affecting, appealing to, or perceived by the senses. 2. readily susceptible through the senses; enjoying the pleasures of sensation.

SYN.—**sensuous** suggests the strong appeal of that which is pleasing to the eye, ear, touch, etc. and, of a person, implies susceptibility to the pleasures of sensation (soft, *sensuous* music); **sensual** refers to the gratification of the grosser bodily senses or appetites (*sensual* excesses); **voluptuous** implies a tending to excite, or giving oneself up to the gratification of, sensuous or sensual desires (her *voluptuous* charms); **luxurious** implies a reveling in that which lavishly provides a high degree of physical comfort or satisfaction (a *luxurious* feeling of drowsiness); **epicurean** implies delight in luxury and sensuous pleasure, especially that of eating and drinking.

sent (sent), past tense and past participle of **send.**

sen·tence (sen′təns), ***n.*** [ME.; OFr.; L. *sententia,* way of thinking, opinion, sentiment; prob. for *sentientia* < stem of *sentiens,* ppr. of *sentire,* to feel, perceive], 1. a decision, opinion, or judgment, as of a court. 2. the determination or declaration by a court of the punishment of a convicted person. 3. the punishment itself. 4. a word or group of words stating, asking, commanding, requesting, or exclaiming something; conventional unit of connected speech or writing, usually containing a subject and predicate, beginning with a capital letter, and ending with an end mark (period, question mark, exclamation point, or points of suspension); linguistically, as much of a speaker's expression as he places between definite final pitches and pauses. 5. [Archaic], a meaningful saying; maxim. 6. in *music,* a period. ***v.t.*** [SENTENCED (-tənst), SENTENCING], to pronounce judgment or punishment upon (a convicted person).

sentence stress, the voice stress given to certain words in a sentence to emphasize the meaning: in English it normally falls on the noun elements in the subject and on the object or complement.

sen·ten·tial (sen-ten′shəl), ***adj.*** [L. *sententialis*], 1. of a grammatical sentence. 2. of, or having the nature of, a decision, judgment, or judicial sentence.

sen·ten·tious (sen-ten′shəs), ***adj.*** [L. *sententiosus* < *sententia;* see SENTENCE], 1. expressing much in words; pointed, compact, and terse; short and pithy. 2. full of, or fond of using, maxims, proverbs, and axioms; aphoristic; often, ponderously trite and moralizing.

sen·tience (sen′shəns, sen′shi-əns), ***n.*** 1. a sentient state or quality; capacity for feeling or perceiving; consciousness. 2. mere awareness or sensation that does not involve thought or perception.

sen·tien·cy (sen′shən-si, sen′shi-ən-si), ***n.*** sentience.

sen·tient (sen′shənt, sen′shi-ənt), ***adj.*** [L. *sentiens,* ppr. of *sentire,* to perceive by the senses], of, having, or capable of feeling or perception; conscious. ***n.*** 1. a person or thing that is sentient. 2. the mind.

sen·ti·ment (sen′tə-mənt), ***n.*** [ME. & OFr. *sentement;* ML. *sentimentum* < L. *sentire,* to feel, perceive], 1. a complex combination of feelings and opinions as a basis for action or judgment; general emotionalized attitude: as, patriotism has been called a noble *sentiment.* 2. a thought, opinion, judgment, or attitude, usually a result of deliberation, but often colored with emotion: as, what are his ***sentiments*** about prohibition? 3. sensibility; delicacy of feeling; susceptibility to feeling or to emotional appeal; tendency to be influenced by emotions, not reason. 4. appeal to the emotions in literature or art; expression of delicate, sensitive feeling. 5. sentimentality; maudlin emotion. 6. a short sentence expressing some trite thought, as in a toast. 7. the thought or meaning behind something said, as distinct from the words used. —***SYN.*** see **feeling, opinion.**

sen·ti·men·tal (sen′tə-men′t′l), ***adj.*** 1. having or showing tenderness, emotion, delicate feeling, etc., as music, poetry, etc. 2. affectedly or superficially emotional; pretending but lacking true depth of feeling; maudlin; mawkish. 3. influenced more by emotion than reason; acting from feeling rather than from practical and utilitarian motives; moved by emotional factors. 4. of or caused by sentiment: as, a *sentimental* reason.

SYN.—**sentimental** suggests emotion of a kind that is felt in a nostalgic or tender mood (*sentimental* music) or emotion that is exaggerated, affected, foolish, etc. (a trashy, *sentimental* novel); **romantic** suggests emotion aroused by that which appeals to the imagination as it is influenced by the idealization of life in literature, art, etc. (a ***romantic*** girl waiting for her Prince Charming); that is **mawkish** which is sentimental in a disgustingly weak, insincere, or exaggerated way (a *mawkish* soap opera); that is **maudlin** which is tearfully or weakly sentimental in a foolish way (an intoxicated, *maudlin* guest); **gushy,** an informal word, implies an effusive display of sentiment or enthusiasm (*gushy* congratulations).

sen·ti·men·tal·ism (sen′tə-men′t′l-iz′m), ***n.*** 1. the habit, quality, or condition of being sentimental. 2. any expression of this.

sen·ti·men·tal·ist (sen′tə-men′t′l-ist), ***n.*** a person showing or indulging in sentimentalism; sentimental person.

sen·ti·men·tal·i·ty (sen′tə-men-tal′ə-ti), ***n.*** 1. the quality, character, or condition of being sentimental. 2. [*pl.* SENTIMENTALITIES (-tiz)], any expression of this.

sen·ti·men·tal·ize (sen′tə-men′t′l-īz′), ***v.i.*** [SENTIMENTALIZED (-īzd′), SENTIMENTALIZING], to be sentimental; think or behave in a sentimental way. ***v.t.*** 1. to make sentimental. 2. to regard or treat sentimentally; be sentimental about: as, he *sentimentalized* the war.

sen·ti·nel (sen′ti-n′l), ***n.*** [Fr. *sentinelle;* It. *sentinella;* prob. (via LL. *sentinare,* to avoid danger by wise means) < L. *sentire,* to feel], a person or animal that guards a group against surprise; sentry. ***v.t.*** [SENTINELED or SENTINELLED (-n′ld), SENTINELING or SENTINELLING], 1. to guard or watch over as a sentinel. 2. to furnish or protect with a sentinel. 3. to post as a sentinel.

stand sentinel, to serve as a sentinel.

sen·try (sen′tri), ***n.*** [*pl.* SENTRIES (-triz)], [prob. a merged word based on Late ME. *centry,* form of *sanctuary,* but influenced by Early Mod. Eng. *centrenel,* form of *sentinel;* cf. dial. *sentuary, century*], 1. a sentinel, especially each of the men of a military guard who are posted to guard against, and give warning of, danger. 2. guard or watch: as, to keep *sentry.*

sentry box, a small, boxlike structure serving as a shelter for a sentry on duty during bad weather.

Se·nu·si, Se·nus·si (se-no͞o′si), ***n.*** a religious brotherhood of North African Moslems: during and after World

War I their tribes were attacked and finally subjugated by French, British, and Italian forces.

Se·nu·si·an (se-nōō′si-ən), *adj.* of or like the Senusi.

Se·oul (sā-ōōl′, sōl; Kor. syö-ool′), *n.* a capital of Korea (see **Korea**): pop., 935,000: Japanese name, *Keijo.*

Sep., 1. September. 2. Septuagint.

se·pal (sē′p'l, sep′'l), *n.* [Fr. *sépale;* Mod. L. *sepalum,* coined (1790) by H. J. de Necker < L. *separatus,* separate + *petalum,* petal], in *botany,* any of the leaf divisions of the calyx: abbreviated **sep.**

-sep·al·ous (sep′'l-əs), [*sepal* + *-ous*], a combining form meaning *having* (a specified number or kind of) *sepals,* as in *trisepalous.*

sep·a·ra·bil·i·ty (sep′ẽr-ə-bil′ə-ti), *n.* the state or quality of being separable.

sep·a·ra·ble (sep′ẽr-ə-b'l), *adj.* [ME.; L. *separabilis*], that can be separated.

sep·a·ra·bly (sep′ẽr-ə-bli), *adv.* so as to be separable.

sep·a·rate (sep′ə-rāt′; *for adj. & n.,* sep′ẽr-it, sep′rit), *v.t.* [SEPARATED (-id), SEPARATING], [ME. *separaten* < L. *separatus,* pp. of *separare,* to separate; *se-,* apart + *parare,* to arrange, provide], 1. to set or put apart (two or more things) into parts, groups, sets, etc.; cause to part; divide; disunite; sever. 2. to see the differences between; distinguish or discriminate between. 3. to cause (two people) to cease associating or living together, as through legal action: as, how long have the Parkers been *separated?* 4. to keep apart by being between; divide: as, the wall *separates* the houses. 5. to single out or set apart from others for a special purpose; sort; segregate. 6. to take away (a part or ingredient) from a combination or mixture. 7. to discharge or release from active duty in the armed forces. *v.i.* 1. to withdraw or secede (with *from*): as, he has *separated* from the party. 2. to part, come or draw apart, or become disconnected. 3. to part company; go in different directions; cease to associate. 4. to stop being together as man and wife. 5. to become distinct or disengaged: as, cream *separates* from milk. *adj.* 1. set apart or divided from the rest or others; not joined, united, or connected; severed. 2. not associated with others; having its own existence; distinct; individual; independent. 3. thought of or regarded as having its own individual form or function: as, the *separate* parts of the body. 4. withdrawn from the company or association of others; solitary; isolated; secluded. 5. of or peculiar to one; not shared or held in common: as, they wanted *separate* rooms. *n.* 1. anything separate. 2. a separate publication, as a single article from a book. Abbreviated **sep.**

SYN.—**separate** implies the putting apart of things previously united, joined, or assembled (to *separate* machine parts, a family, etc.); **divide** implies a separation into parts, pieces, groups, etc. by or as by cutting, splitting, branching, etc., often for purposes of apportionment (to *divide* the profits into equal shares); **part** is now usually applied to the separation of persons or things that have been closely connected or associated ("till death us do *part*"); **sever** implies a forcible and complete separation, as by cutting off a part from a whole (to *sever* a branch from a tree); **sunder,** now a literary term, implies a violent splitting, tearing, or wrenching apart. —*ANT.* unite, combine.

sep·a·ra·tion (sep′ə-rā′shən), *n.* 1. a separating or being separated. 2. the place where a separating occurs; break; division. 3. something that separates. 4. a divorce. 5. an arrangement by which a man and wife live apart by agreement or by court decree.

separation center, a center where men and women in the armed forces are discharged or released from active duty, or where their records are processed.

sep·a·ra·tion·ist (sep′ə-rā′shən-ist), *n.* a separatist.

sep·a·ra·tist (sep′ə-rā′tist), *n.* 1. a person who withdraws or secedes, especially one who is a member of a group that has seceded from a larger group; dissenter; nonconformer. 2. a person who advocates political or religious separation.

sep·a·ra·tive (sep′ə-rā′tiv), *adj.* [< Fr. or LL.; Fr. *séparatif;* LL. *separativus*], tending to separate or cause separation.

sep·a·ra·tor (sep′ə-rā′tẽr), *n.* [LL.], 1. a person or thing that separates. 2. any of several devices for separating one substance from another, as cream from milk.

sep·a·ra·to·ry (sep′ẽr-ə-tôr′i, sep′ẽr-ə-tō′ri), *adj.* separative.

Se·phar·dic (si-fär′dik), *adj.* of the Sephardim, their characteristics, or culture.

Se·phar·dim (si-fär′dim), *n.pl.* [*sing.* SEPHARD (si-färd′)], [Heb. *sĕphārādhim* < *Sĕphārādh,* a region mentioned in Ob. 3:20, often identified with Spain, but prob. orig. an area in Asia Minor], 1. the Jews of Spain and Portugal before the Inquisition. 2. their descendants. Distinguished from *Ashkenazim.*

se·pi·a (sē′pi-ə), *n.* [L.; Gr. *sēpia*], 1. any of several cuttlefishes with an internal shell. 2. a dark-brown pigment prepared from the inky fluid secreted by cuttlefish. 3. a dark reddish-brown color. 4. a photographic print in this color. *adj.* 1. of sepia. 2. dark reddish-brown.

se·pi·o·lite (sē′pi-ə-līt′), *n.* [G. *sepiolith* < Gr. *sēpion,* cuttlefish + *-lith* (see -LITE)], meerschaum.

se·poy (sē′poi), *n.* [Port. *sipae;* Hind. & Per. *sipāhī* < *sipāh,* army], a native of India serving in a European army, especially the British army.

sep·pu·ku (se′pōō′koo), *n.* [Japan.], in Japan, suicide by disembowelment; hara-kiri.

seps (seps), *n.* [L.; Gr. *sēps* < *sēpein,* to rot: from the reputed effect of its bite], 1. a poisonous snake mentioned frequently in classical literature. 2. a skink.

sep·sis (sep′sis), *n.* [Mod. L.; Gr. *sēpsis,* putrefaction < *sēpein,* to make putrid], poisoning caused by the absorption into the blood of pathogenic microorganisms, as from putrefying material; blood poisoning.

sept (sept), *n.* [OFr. *septe,* var. of *secte,* sect], 1. an old Irish clan or tribe ruled by a patriarch. 2. any similar group, especially one localized and based on common descent in both male and female lines: properly distinguished from *sib.*

Sept., 1. September. 2. Septuagint.

sep·ta (sep′tə), *n.* plural of **septum.**

sep·tal (sep′t'l), *adj.* of or forming a septum or septa.

sep·tar·i·an (sep-târ′i-ən), *adj.* of or like septarium.

sep·tar·i·um (sep-târ′i-əm), *n.* [*pl.* SEPTARIA (-ə)], [Mod. L. < L. *septum;* see SEPTUM], a cementlike mass, as of limestone, shot through with fissures filled with some other material, as calcite.

sep·tate (sep′tāt), *adj.* [Mod. L. *septatus*], having or divided by a septum or septa.

sep·ta·va·lent (sep′tə-vā′lənt), *adj.* [Rare], heptavalent.

sep·tec·to·my (sep-tek′tə-mi), *n.* [*septum* + *-ectomy*], the surgical removal of part of the nasal septum.

sep·tem- (sep′tem), [< L. *septem,* seven], a combining form meaning *seven* or *seventh,* as in *septempartite:* also **sept-.**

Sep·tem·ber (sep-tem′bẽr, səp-tem′bẽr), *n.* [ME. *Septembre;* L. *September,* name of the seventh month of the Roman year < *septem,* seven; the orig. name was AS. *hærfestmonath,* harvest month], the ninth month of the year, having 30 days: abbreviated **Sept., Sep., S.**

September massacre, the massacre of the Royalists in Paris, September 2 to 6, 1792, during the Revolution.

Sep·tem·brist (sep-tem′brist), *n.* a person who took part in the September massacre.

sep·tem·par·tite (sep′tem-pär′tīt), *adj.* divided into seven parts.

sep·tem·vir (sep-tem′vẽr), *n.* [L.; *septem,* seven + *vir,* a man], each of a group of seven men, especially in ancient Rome, associated in some office or work.

sep·te·nar·y (sep′tə-ner′i), *adj.* [L. *septenarius* < *septem,* seven], 1. of the number seven. 2. consisting of or forming a group of seven. 3. septennial. *n.* [*pl.* SEPTENARIES (-iz)], 1. the number seven. 2. a group or set of seven, especially seven years. 3. a line of verse of seven feet.

sep·ten·ni·al (sep-ten′i-əl), *adj.* [< L. *septennium,* a period of seven years < *septem,* seven + *annus,* year; + *-al*], 1. lasting seven years. 2. coming, happening, etc. every seven years.

sep·ten·ni·al·ly (sep-ten′i-əl-i), *adv.* every seven years.

sep·ten·tri·o·nal (sep-ten′tri-ə-n'l), *adj.* [OFr.; L. *septentrionalis* < *septentriones,* the seven stars near the north pole, lit. seven plowing oxen < *septem,* seven + *triones,* plowing oxen], [Archaic], northern; boreal.

sep·tet, sep·tette (sep-tet′), *n.* [G. < L. *septem,* seven + G. *duet*], 1. a group of seven persons or things. 2. in *music, a)* a composition for seven voices or seven instruments. *b)* the seven performers of such a composition.

sep·ti- (sep′ti), a combining form of various origins and meanings: 1. [< L. *septem,* seven], *seven* or *seventh,* as in *septilateral.* 2. [< Gr. *septos,* putrid], *decomposed, vitiated,* as in *septicemia.* 3. [< L. *septum,* partition, fence], *a dividing wall,* as in *septifragal.* Also, before a vowel, **sept-.**

sep·tic (sep′tik), *adj.* [L. *septicus;* Gr. *sēptikos* < *sēpein,* to make putrid], 1. causing sepsis or putrefaction; infective. 2. of or resulting from sepsis or putrefaction. *n.* a septic substance or agent.

sep·ti·ce·mi·a, sep·ti·cae·mi·a (sep′tə-sē′mi-ə), *n.* [Mod. L. *septicemia* < Gr. *sēptikos,* putrefactive + *haima,* blood], blood poisoning caused by the presence of pathogenic microorganisms and their toxic products in the blood.

sep·ti·ce·mic, sep·ti·cae·mic (sep′tə-sē′mik), *adj.* of or having septicemia.

sep·ti·cid·al (sep′tə-sī′d'l), *adj.* [< *septi-* (dividing wall) + L. *caedere,* to cut; + *-al*], in *botany,* breaking open at a natural dividing line: said of a form of dehiscence.

sep·tic·i·ty (sep-tis′ə-ti), *n.* 1. a septic quality. 2. a tendency to be or become septic or to cause infection.

septic sore throat, an acute, severe infection of the throat, caused by certain hemolytic streptococci and characterized by fever, inflammation of the tonsils, etc.

septic tank, a tank in which waste matter is putrefied and decomposed through bacterial action.

sep·tif·ra·gal (sep-tif′rə-gəl), *adj.* [*septi-* (dividing wall) + base of L. *frangere,* to break; + *-al*], in *botany,* breaking away from a natural dividing line: said of a method of dehiscence.

sep·ti·lat·er·al (sep′tə-lat′ẽr-əl), *adj.* having seven sides.

sep·til·lion (sep-til′yən), *n.* [Fr. < L. *septem,* seven +

Fr. *million*], 1. in the United States and France, the number represented by 1 followed by 24 zeros. 2. in Great Britain and Germany, the number represented by 1 followed by 42 zeros. *adj.* amounting to one septillion in number.

sep·ti·mal (sep′ti-məl), *adj.* [< L. *septimus*, seventh (< *septem*, seven); + *-al*], of the number seven.

sep·time (sep′tēm), *n.* [< L. *septimus*, seventh], parry, the seventh position in fencing.

sep·tu·a·ge·nar·i·an (sep′cho͞o-ə-ji-nâr′i-ən), *adj.* [< L. *septuagenarius;* see SEPTUAGENARY], seventy years old or between seventy and eighty. *n.* a person of this age.

sep·tu·ag·e·nar·y (sep′cho͞o-aj′ə-ner′i), *adj. & n.* [*pl.* SEPTUAGENARIES (-iz)], [L. *septuagenarius* < *septuageni*, seventy each < *septuaginta*, seventy], [Rare], septuagenarian.

Sep·tu·a·ges·i·ma (sep′cho͞o-ə-jes′i-mə), *n.* [ME. *Septuagesme;* L., fem. of *septuagesimus*, seventieth], the third Sunday before Lent: also **Septuagesima Sunday.**

Sep·tu·a·gint (sep′to͞o-ə-jint′, sep′cho͞o-ə-jint′), *n.* [< L. *septuaginta*, seventy: because of the ancient tradition that it was completed in 70 (or 72) days by 72 Palestinian Jews in the 3d century B.C., for Ptolemy II, king of Egypt], a Greek translation of the Old Testament: abbreviated **Sep., Sept.**

sep·tum (sep′təm), *n.* [*pl.* SEPTA (-tə)], [L. *septum, saeptum*, enclosure, hedge < *sepire, saepire*, to enclose, fence < *saepes*, a hedge], a part that separates; dividing wall; partition: as, the nostrils are divided by a *septum*.

sep·tu·ple (sep′to͞o-p'l, sep-tū′p'l), *adj.* [LL. *septuplus* < L. *septem*, seven], 1. consisting of or including seven. 2. seven times as much or as many; sevenfold. *v.t.* [SEPTUPLED (-p'ld), SEPTUPLING], to make seven times as much or as many; multiply by seven.

sep·ul·cher (sep′'l-kẽr), *n.* [ME. & OFr. *sepulcre;* L. *sepulcrum* < *sepelire*, to bury], 1. a vault for burial; grave; tomb. 2. a place for the safekeeping of relics, as in an altar. *v.t.* to place in a sepulcher; bury.

se·pul·chral (sə-pul′krəl), *adj.* [L. *sepulcralis*], 1. of sepulchers, burial, the grave, etc. 2. suggestive of the grave or burial; tomblike; dismal; gloomy. 3. deep and melancholy: said of sound.

sep·ul·chre (sep′'l-kẽr), *n. & v.t.* [SEPULCHRED (-kẽrd), SEPULCHRING], sepulcher: British spelling.

sep·ul·ture (sep′'l-chẽr), *n.* [ME.; OFr.; L. *sepultura* < *sepelire*, to bury], 1. burial; interment. 2. [Archaic], a burial place; sepulcher.

seq., 1. sequel. 2. *sequentes* or *sequentia*, [L.], the following.

se·qua·cious (si-kwā′shəs), *adj.* [L. *sequax* < *sequi*, to follow], 1. tending to follow any leader; lacking individuality, as in thought; dependent; servile; compliant. 2. showing or following logical or smooth sequence.

se·quel (sē′kwəl), *n.* [ME.; OFr. *sequelle;* L. *sequela* < *sequi*, to follow], 1. something that follows; anything subsequent or succeeding; continuation. 2. something that comes as a result of something else; aftermath; effect; consequence. 3. any literary work complete in itself but continuing a story started in an earlier work.

se·que·la (si-kwē′lə), *n.* [*pl.* SEQUELAE (-lē)], [L. < *sequi*, to follow], a person or thing that follows; specifically, in *medicine*, a diseased condition resulting from a previous disease.

se·quence (sē′kwəns), *n.* [Fr. *séquence;* LL. *sequentia* < L. *sequens;* see SEQUENT; in sense 7, ME. had *sequens*], 1. the following or coming of one thing after another; succession. 2. the order in which this occurs. 3. a continuous or related series, often of uniform things: as, a sonnet *sequence*. 4. three or more playing cards in the same suit and in unbroken order; run. 5. a resulting event; consequence; sequel. 6. in *motion pictures*, a part of a film story treating an episode without any interruptions of continuity. 7. in *music*, a succession of phrases based on the same melodic pattern but repeated at different pitches, sometimes in different keys. 8. in the *Roman Catholic Church*, a hymn coming between the gradual and the gospel; a prose. —*SYN.* see **series.**

se·quent (sē′kwənt), *adj.* [L. *sequens*, ppr. of *sequi*, to follow], 1. following in time or order; subsequent. 2. following as a result or effect; consequent. *n.* something that follows, as a result; consequence.

se·quen·tial (si-kwen′shəl), *adj.* 1. sequent. 2. characterized by or forming a regular sequence of parts.

se·ques·ter (si-kwes′tẽr), *v.t.* [ME. *sequestren;* OFr. *sequestrer* < LL. *sequestrare*, to remove, lay aside, separate < L. *sequester*, trustee], 1. to set off or apart; separate; segregate. 2. to take possession of (property) as security for a debt, claim, etc. 3. to take over; confiscate; seize, especially by authority. 4. [Rare], to withdraw; seclude: sometimes used reflexively.

se·ques·tered (si-kwes′tẽrd), *adj.* [pp. of *sequester*], removed from others; isolated; secluded; retired.

se·ques·trate (si-kwes′trāt), *v.t.* [SEQUESTRATED (-id), SEQUESTRATING], [< LL. *sequestratus*, pp.; see SEQUESTER], 1. to confiscate. 2. [Archaic], to sequester.

se·ques·tra·tion (sē′kwes-trā′shən, si-kwes′trā′shən), *n.* [ME. *sequestracyoun;* OFr.; LL. *sequestratio*], 1. a sequestering or being sequestered; seclusion; separation. 2. *a)* the legal seizure of property for security. *b)* confiscation of property, as by court or government action.

se·ques·tra·tor (sē′kwes-trā′tẽr, si-kwes′trā′tẽr), *n.* [LL.], 1. a person who sequestrates. 2. a person appointed to administer sequestrated property.

se·ques·trec·to·my (sē′kwes-trek′tə-mi), *n.* [*pl.* SEQUESTRECTOMIES (-miz)], [see SEQUESTRUM & -ECTOMY], the surgical removal of a sequestrum or sequestra.

se·ques·trum (si-kwes′trəm), *n.* [*pl.* SEQUESTRA (-trə)], [Mod. L.; see SEQUESTER], in *medicine*, a piece of dead tissue, especially bone, which has become separated from the surrounding healthy tissue.

se·quin (sē′kwin), *n.* [Fr. < It. *zecchino* < *zecca*, a mint < Ar. *sikkah, sekkah*, a stamp, die], 1. an obsolete Italian gold coin, equal to about $2.25. 2. a small, shiny ornament or spangle, as a metal disk, especially one of many sewn on fabric for decoration.

se·quoi·a (si-kwoi′ə), *n.* [Mod. L. < *Sikwâyi*, Cherokee who invented the Cherokee syllabary], either of two species of related giant evergreen trees with small, oval cones and hard wood, found in California (the redwood and the big tree).

Sequoia National Park, a national park in east central California, containing giant sequoias: area, 604 sq. mi.

ser (sêr), *n.* [Hind. *sēr*], in India, a unit of weight of a little over two pounds, equal to about 1/40 of a maund: also **seer.**

ser- (sêr), sero-.

ser., 1. series. 2. sermon.

se·ra (sêr′ə), *n.* alternative plural of **serum.**

‡sé·rac (sā′räk′), *n.* [Swiss-Fr., orig., name of a type of white cheese], a pointed mass or pinnacle of ice left standing among the crevasses of a glacier.

se·rag·lio (si-ral′yō, se-räl′yō), *n.* [*pl.* SERAGLIOS (-yōz)], [It. *serraglio*, enclosure, paddock, also (by association with Turk. *serai*, palace) palace, seraglio < LL. **serraculum*, enclosure < **serrare*, for L. *serare*, to lock, bar < *sera*, a lock], 1. the place where a Moslem keeps his wives or concubines; harem. 2. the palace of a Turkish sultan or noble.

se·ra·i (sə-rä′i), *n.* [Turk., palace, inn, etc.; Per. *sarāī*], in the Orient, an inn for travelers; caravansary.

Se·ra·je·vo (ser′ə-yā′vō), *n.* Sarajevo.

Se·rang (se-räng′), *n.* Ceram.

se·ra·pe (se-rä′pi; Sp. se-rä′pe), *n.* [Mex. Sp. *serape, sarape*], a woolen blanket, often brightly colored, used as a garment in Spanish-American countries.

ser·aph (ser′əf), *n.* [*pl.* SERAPHS (-əfs), SERAPHIM (-ə-fim′)], [ML., back-formation < LL. *seraphim*, *pl.* < Heb. *śĕrāphīm*, *pl.*], in *theology*, a member of the highest of the nine orders of angels, represented in the Bible as the celestial beings with three pairs of wings.

se·raph·ic (sə-raf′ik), *adj.* [ML. *seraphicus*], of, like, or suitable for a seraph; angelic.

se·raph·i·cal (sə-raf′i-k'l), *adj.* seraphic.

se·raph·i·cal·ly (sə-raf′i-k'l-i, sə-raf′ik-li), *adv.* in a seraphic manner.

ser·a·phim (ser′ə-fim′), *n.* alternative plural and, formerly, alternative singular of **seraph.**

Se·ra·pis (sə-rā′pis), *n.* [L.; Gr.], in *Egyptian, Greek & Roman mythology*, a god of the lower world.

Serb (sûrb), *n.* [Serb. *Srb*], 1. one of a Slavic people of the Balkans. 2. their language. *adj.* Serbian.

Serb., 1. Serbia. 2. Serbian.

Ser·bi·a (sûr′bi-ə), *n.* a former kingdom in the Balkans: now a federated republic of Yugoslavia, in the eastern part: capital, Belgrade: formerly called *Servia.*

SERBIA

Ser·bi·an (sûr′bi-ən), *adj.* of Serbia, the Serbs, or their language. *n.* 1. a native or inhabitant of Serbia; especially, one of the Slavic people of Serbia; Serb. 2. Serbo-Croatian as spoken in Serbia.

Ser·bo- (sûr′bō), a combining form meaning *Serbian:* also **Servo-.**

Ser·bo-Cro·a·tian (sũr′bō-krō-ā′shən), *n.* the South Slavic language spoken in Yugoslavia: it is generally written with Roman characters in Croatia but with Cyrillic characters in Serbia. *adj.* of this language or the people who speak it.

Ser·bo·ni·an (sẽr-bō′ni-ən), *adj.* [< Gr. *Serbōnis* (*limen*), the Serbonian (lake)], designating or of Lake Serbonis in ancient Egypt, a bog, now dry, in which whole armies were said to have sunk.

sere (sêr), *n.* [back-formation < *series*], in *ecology*, the complete series of changes occurring in the cycle of a plant formation.

sere (sêr), *adj.* [var. of *sear*], [Poetic], dried up; withered.

‡**se·rein** (sə-ran′), *n.* [Fr. < LL. **seranum*, evening, twilight < L. *sera* (*hora*), evening (hour) < *serus*, late], a misty rain falling from a clear sky just after sunset.

ser·e·nade (ser′ə-nād′), *n.* [Fr. *sérénade;* It. *serenata* < *sereno*, serene, open air < L. *serenus*, clear, serene; meaning influenced by association with L. *sera;* see SEREIN], 1. a vocal or instrumental performance of music outdoors at night, especially by a lover under the window of his sweetheart. 2. a piece of music suitable for this. *v.t. & v.i.* [SERENADED (-id), SERENADING], to play or sing a serenade (to).

ser·e·na·ta (ser′ə-nä′tə), *n.* [*pl.* SERENATAS (-təz), SERENATE (-te)], [It.; see SERENADE], in *music*, 1. a type of dramatic or pastoral secular cantata. 2. an orchestral composition having several movements, intermediate between the suite and the symphony.

ser·en·dip·i·ty (ser′ən-dip′ə-ti), *n.* [coined by Horace Walpole (c. 1754) after his tale *The Three Princes of Serendip* (i.e., Ceylon), who made such discoveries], an apparent aptitude for making fortunate discoveries accidentally.

se·rene (sə-rēn′), *adj.* [L. *serenus*], 1. clear; bright; unclouded: as, a *serene* sky. 2. undisturbed; calm; tranquil; quiet. 3. [S-], exalted; honorable; high-ranking: used in the titles of members of certain European royal families, as, His *Serene* Highness. *n.* [Rare or Poetic], a serene expanse, as of sky or water. —*SYN.* see **calm.**

se·ren·i·ty (sə-ren′ə-ti), *n.* [*pl.* SERENITIES (-tiz)], [Fr. *sérénité;* L. *serenitas*], 1. the quality or state of being serene; calmness; tranquillity; repose. 2. clearness; brightness. 3. [S-], a title of honor used in speaking to or of members of certain royal families, etc.: preceded by *His*, *Her*, or *Your*. —*SYN.* see **equanimity.**

Se·reth (zā′rət), *n.* Siret: the German name.

serf (sũrf), *n.* [OFr.; L. *servus*, a slave], 1. originally, a slave. 2. a person in feudal servitude, bound to his master's land and transferred with it to a new owner. 3. any person who is oppressed or without freedom.

serf·age (sũr′fij), *n.* [see -AGE], serfdom.

serf·dom (sũrf′dəm), *n.* the condition or status of a serf; bondage.

serf·hood (sũrf′hood′), *n.* [*serf* + *-hood*], serfs collectively.

serge (sũrj), *n.* [ME. & OFr. *sarge;* LL. **sarica;* L. *serica* (*lana*), (wool of the) *Seres*, an Oriental people, prob. the Chinese; cf. SERICEOUS], 1. a twilled, worsted fabric used for suits, etc. 2. a twilled silk, rayon, etc., used for linings.

ser·gean·cy (sär′jən-si), *n.* [*pl.* SERGEANCIES (-siz)], the position or rank of a sergeant.

ser·geant (sär′jənt), *n.* [ME. *serjaunt, sergant;* OFr. *serjent, sergant* < L. *serviens*, serving < *servire*, to serve], 1. formerly, a feudal servant who attended his master in battle. 2. a sergeant-at-arms. 3. a sergeant-at-law: also spelled **serjeant.** 4. a police officer ranking next below a captain or a lieutenant. 5. in the *United States armed forces*, a noncommissioned officer ranking just above a corporal: in the Army, formerly the fourth grade of enlisted man (now *corporal*) and now the third grade (formerly *staff sergeant*); in the Marine Corps and Air Force, the fourth grade. Abbreviated **Sgt., Sergt., Serg., sgt., sergt., serg.**

ser·geant-at-arms (sär′jənt-ət-ärmz′), *n.* [*pl.* SERGEANTS-AT-ARMS], an officer appointed to keep order in a legislature, court, social club, etc.

ser·geant-at-law (sär′jənt-ət-lô′), *n.* [*pl.* SERGEANTS-AT-LAW], a member of a former group of high-ranking British barristers having certain special privileges in the king's courts: also spelled **serjeant-at-law.**

sergeant first class, in the *United States Army*, the second grade of enlisted man (formerly *technical sergeant*), ranking just below master sergeant.

sergeant fish, 1. a large, striped, sea fish related to the mackerel. 2. the robalo.

sergeant major, [*pl.* SERGEANTS MAJOR], 1. in the *United States Army*, an enlisted man, usually a master sergeant, who is assistant to an adjutant, as of a regiment: an occupational title and not a rank. 2. in the *United States Marine Corps*, the highest ranking noncommissioned officer. Abbreviated **Sgt. Maj.**

ser·geant·ship (sär′jənt-ship′), *n.* [*sergeant* + *-ship*], the rank, position, or duties of a sergeant.

Sergt., sergt., sergeant.

se·ri·al (sêr′i-əl), *adj.* [Mod. L. *serialis* < L. *series*, a row, order, sequence; cf. SERIES], 1. of, arranged in, or forming a series: as, *serial* numbers. 2. appearing, published, etc. in a series or succession of continuous parts at regular intervals. 3. of a serial or serials: as, the magazine has the *serial* rights to the story. *n.* 1. any novel, story, etc. published or presented in serial form. 2. a periodical.

se·ri·al·ize (sêr′i-ə-līz′), *v.t.* [SERIALIZED (-līzd′), SERIALIZING], to put or publish in serial form, as a story.

se·ri·al·ly (sêr′i-əl-i), *adv.* 1. in series: as, we were numbered *serially* in order of application. 2. in a succession of parts; as a serial.

serial number, a number, usually one of a series, used to identify: as, *serial numbers* are given to soldiers at enlistment, to engines at the time of manufacture, etc.

se·ri·ate (sêr′i-it), *adj.* [ML. *seriatus*, pp. of *seriare*, to arrange in a series], arranged or occurring in a series.

se·ri·a·tim (sêr′i-ā′tim, ser′i-ā′tim), *adv.* [ML. < L. *series*, after *gradatim*], one after another in order; point by point; serially.

se·ri·ceous (si-rish′əs), *adj.* [LL. *sericeus* < L. *sericus* < *sericum*, silk, lit., Seric stuff < *Sericus*, of the *Seres* (Gr. *Sēres*), a people of eastern Asia; cf. Fr. *sériciculture*], 1. of or like silk; downy; silky. 2. in *botany*, having a covering of short, straight, silky hairs.

ser·i·cul·ture (ser′i-kul′chẽr), *n.* [< L. *sericus* (see SERICEOUS); + *culture*], the art or process of raising and keeping silkworms for the production of raw silk.

ser·i·e·ma (ser′i-ē′mə, ser′i-ā′mə), *n.* [Mod. L. < Tupi *seriema*, lit., crested], 1. a crested Brazilian bird of the crane family, with gray and umber coloring and long legs and neck. 2. an Argentinian bird similar to this bird but smaller.

se·ries (sêr′iz), *n.* [*pl.* SERIES], [L. < *serere*, to join or weave together], 1. a group or number of similar or related things arranged in a row: as, a *series* of arches. 2. a group or number of related or similar persons, things, or events coming one after another; sequence; succession. 3. a number of things produced as a related group; set, as of novels by one author dealing with the same characters. 4. in *mathematics*, a succession of terms, each related to a preceding term by some law; especially, the indicated sum of such a set of terms. 5. in *rhetoric*, a group of successive coordinate elements of a sentence. Abbreviated **ser., s.**
in series, in *electricity*, connected in a series circuit.
SYN.—**series** applies to a number of similar, more or less related things following one another in time or place (a *series* of concerts); **sequence** emphasizes a closer relationship between the things, such as logical connection, numerical order, etc. (the *sequence* of events); **succession** merely implies a following of one thing after another, without any necessary connection between them (a *succession* of errors); **chain** refers to a series in which there is a definite relationship of cause and effect or some other logical connection (a *chain* of ideas).

series circuit, an electrical circuit in which the parts are connected end to end, positive pole to negative pole, so that current flows from part to part in succession: opposed to *parallel circuit*.

se·ries-wound (sêr′iz-wound′), *adj.* in *electricity*, designating a dynamo or motor in which the armature and the field magnet coil are connected in series with the outer circuit: opposed to *shunt-wound*.

ser·if (ser′if), *n.* [D. *schreef*, a stroke, line < *schrijve*, to write < L. *scribere*], in *printing*, a fine line projecting from a main stroke of a letter, especially one of the fine cross strokes at the top or bottom: see **type,** illus.

ser·i·graph (ser′i-graf′, ser′i-gräf′), *n.* [< L. *sericum* (see SERICEOUS); + *-graph*], a color print made by the silk-screen process and printed by the artist himself.

ser·i·graph·er (sə-rig′rə-fẽr), *n.* a person who makes serigraphs.

ser·i·graph·y (sə-rig′rə-fi), *n.* the art of making serigraphs.

ser·in (ser′in), *n.* [Fr.; origin prob. echoic], a small yellow or yellowish-green European bird of the finch family, related to the canary.

ser·in (ser′in, sêr′in), *n.* serine.

ser·ine (ser′ēn, sêr′in), *n.* [< L. *sericus*, silken; + *-ine*], a colorless crystalline compound, $C_3H_7NO_3$, present in many proteins.

se·rin·ga (sə-riŋ′gə), *n.* [Fr. & Port.; see SYRINGA], any of several Brazilian rubber trees.

se·ri·o·com·ic (sêr′i-ō-kom′ik), *adj.* partly serious and partly comic.

se·ri·o·com·i·cal (sêr′i-ō-kom′i-k′l), *adj.* seriocomic.

se·ri·ous (sêr′i-əs), *adj.* [Fr. *sérieux;* ML. *seriosus* < L. *serius*, grave, orig., prob. weighty, heavy < IE. base **swer-*, seen also in AS. *swær*, heavy, sad, grievous, Goth. *swers*, honored, important, orig., heavy], 1. of, showing, having, or caused by earnestness or deep thought; earnest, grave, sober, or solemn: as, a *serious* man. 2. of a grave or solemn aspect: as, a frivolous mind behind a *serious* face. 3. *a*) meaning what one says or does; not joking or trifling; sincere. *b*) not thought, said, or done in play. 4. concerned or dealing with grave or important matters, problems, etc.; weighty; important. 5. requiring careful consideration or thought; involving difficulty, effort, or considered action. 6. giving cause for anxiety; critical; dangerous.
SYN.—**serious** implies absorption in deep thought or involve-

ment in something really important as distinguished from something frivolous or merely amusing (he takes a *serious* interest in the theater); **grave** implies the dignified weightiness of heavy responsibilities or cares (a *grave* expression on his face); **solemn** suggests an impressive or awe-inspiring seriousness (a *solemn* ceremony); **sedate** implies a dignified, proper, sometimes even prim seriousness (a *sedate* clergyman); **earnest** suggests a seriousness of purpose marked by sincerity and enthusiasm (an *earnest* desire to help); **sober** implies a seriousness marked by temperance, self-control, emotional balance, etc. (a *sober* criticism). —*ANT.* frivolous, flippant.

se·ri·ous-mind·ed (sêr'i-əs-mīn'did), *adj.* of, having, or showing earnestness or seriousness of purpose, method, etc.; characterized by preoccupation with serious matters and not by levity, joking, etc.

ser·jeant (sär'jənt), *n.* [Esp. British], sergeant.

ser·mon (sũr'mən), *n.* [ME.; OFr.; L. *sermo*], 1. a speech given as instruction in religion or morals, usually by a clergyman in a pulpit using a text from Scripture. 2. any lecture or serious talk on behavior, responsibility, etc., especially a long, tedious, annoying one. Abbreviated **ser.** —*SYN.* see **speech.**

ser·mon·ic (sũr-mon'ik), *adj.* of, or having the nature of, a sermon; solemn; moralizing.

ser·mon·ize (sũr'mə-nīz'), *v.i.* [SERMONIZED (-nīzd'), SERMONIZING], 1. to preach, especially in a dogmatic, moralizing way; lecture. 2. to deliver a sermon or sermons. *v.t.* to preach to; exhort; lecture.

Sermon on the Mount, the sermon delivered by Jesus to his disciples: Matt. 5–7, Luke 6:20–49: it contains the essentials of Christian belief.

se·ro- (sêr'ō, sêr'ə), [< *serum*], a combining form meaning *serum*, as in *serology*: also, before a vowel, **ser-.**

se·rol·o·gy (si-rol'ə-ji), *n.* [*sero-* + *-logy*], the science dealing with the properties or use of serums.

se·ros·i·ty (si-ros'ə-ti), *n.* [*pl.* SEROSITIES (-tiz)], [Fr. *sérosité*], 1. a thin, watery fluid, as that found in the joints of the body. 2. a serous quality or condition.

ser·o·tine (ser'ə-tin, ser'ə-tīn'), *adj.* [Fr. *sérotine;* L. *serotinus* < *serus*, late], late or delayed in development: said especially of late-flowering plants.

se·rot·i·nous (si-rot'ə-nəs), *adj.* serotine.

se·rous (sêr'əs), *adj.* [Fr. *séreux;* Mod. L. *serosus* < *serum;* see SERUM], 1. of or containing serum. 2. like serum; thin and watery.

serous fluid, any of several serumlike fluids in the body cavities, especially in those lined with serous membrane.

serous membrane, a thin membrane that lines most of the closed cavities of the body: the peritoneum is the serous membrane lining the abdominal cavity.

ser·ow (ser'ō), *n.* [native (Tibet or Sikkim) name], any of a group of goat antelopes of eastern Asia, found especially in the Himalayas.

Ser·pens (sũr'penz), *n.* a northern constellation supposedly like a snake in shape: see **constellation,** chart.

ser·pent (sũr'pənt), *n.* [ME.; OFr.; L. *serpens, serpentis* < *serpens*, ppr. of *serpere*, to creep], 1. a snake, especially a large or poisonous one. 2. a sly, sneaking, treacherous person. 3. a firework which, as it burns, lengthens out and writhes like a snake. 4. in the *Bible*, Satan; the Devil, in the form he assumed to tempt Eve: Gen. 3:1–5. 5. in *music*, an obsolete, coiled, bass wind instrument of wood covered with leather.

ser·pen·ti·form (sũr-pen'tə-fôrm'), *adj.* [< L. *serpens, serpentis;* + *form*], shaped like a serpent.

ser·pen·tine (sũr'pən-tēn'; *for adj., also* sũr'pən-tīn'), *adj.* [Fr. *serpentin;* LL. *serpentinus*], of or like a serpent; especially, *a*) evilly cunning or subtle; devilishly sly; treacherous. *b*) coiled or twisted; winding; turning often. *n.* [from resemblance to a serpent's skin], a mineral, magnesium silicate, $Mg_3Si_2O_7 \cdot 2H_2O$, usually green or brownish red and often mottled.

ser·pig·i·nous (sẽr-pij'ə-nəs), *adj.* like a serpigo.

ser·pi·go (sẽr-pī'gō), *n.* [ME.; ML. < L. *serpere*, to creep], any spreading skin disease, as ringworm.

ser·ra·noid (ser'ə-noid'), *adj.* [Mod. L. *Serranus*, type genus < L. *serra*, a saw; + *-oid*], designating or of a family of carnivorous fishes including the sea bass and related types. *n.* a serranoid fish.

ser·rate (ser'āt, ser'it), *adj.* [L. *serratus* < *serra*, a saw], having sawlike notches along the edge, as some leaves.

ser·rat·ed (ser'ā-tid), *adj.* serrate.

ser·ra·tion (se-rā'shən), *n.* 1. the condition of being serrate. 2. a single tooth or notch in a serrate edge. 3. a formation or set of these.

ser·ra·ture (ser'ə-chẽr), *n.* [L. *serratura*], serration.

ser·ried (ser'id), *adj.* [pp. of obs. *serry* < Fr. *serrer*, to crowd < LL. *serare*, to bolt, lock < *sera*, a bar], placed close together; crowded; compact, as soldiers in ranks.

ser·ri·form (ser'ə-fôrm'), *adj.* [< L. *serra*, a saw; + *-form*], shaped like a saw; serrate.

ser·ru·late (ser'oo-lāt', ser'yoo-lit), *adj.* [< L. *serrula*, dim. of *serra*, a saw; + *-ate*], having small, fine teeth or notches along the edge; finely serrate.

ser·ru·la·tion (ser'oo-lā'shən, ser'yoo-lā'shən), *n.* 1. the condition of being serrulate. 2. a single tooth or notch in a serrulate edge. 3. a formation or set of these.

Ser·to·ri·us, Quin·tus (kwin'təs sẽr-tôr'i-əs, sẽr-tō'ri-əs), ?–72 B.C.; Roman general and statesman; assassinated.

ser·tu·lar·i·an (sũr'choo-lâr'i-ən), *n.* [< Mod. L. *Sertularia* (dim. < L. *serta*, a garland), name of the genus; + *-an*], a hydroid made up of double-rowed branches of cupped polyps.

se·rum (sêr'əm), *n.* [*pl.* SERUMS (-əmz), SERA (-ə)], [L., whey], 1. any watery animal fluid, especially blood serum, the clear, yellowish fluid which separates from the clot when blood coagulates. 2. blood serum containing agents of immunity, taken from an animal made immune to a specific disease by inoculation: it is used as an antitoxin. 3. the whey of milk. 4. watery vegetable fluid.

ser·val (sũr'vəl), *n.* [Fr. < Port. (*lobo*) *cerval; lobo* (< L. *lupus*), a wolf + *cerval* (< L. *cervus*), a stag], a South African wildcat with a black-spotted tawny coat, long legs, and a ringed tail.

ser·vant (sũr'vənt), *n.* [ME.; OFr., ppr. of *servir;* L. *servire*, to serve], 1. a person employed to perform services, especially household duties, for another or others. 2. a slave. 3. a person employed by a government; public servant; civil servant. 4. a person ardently devoted to another or to a cause, creed, etc. Abbreviated **serv.**

serve (sũrv), *v.t.* [SERVED (sũrvd), SERVING], [ME. *servien;* OFr. *servir* < L. *servire*, to serve], 1. to work for; be a servant to. 2. *a*) to do services or duties for; give service to; aid; assist; help: as, he *served* his country as a great statesman. *b*) to give obedience and reverent honor to, as God. 3. to fight for; do military or naval service for. 4. to go through or spend (a term of imprisonment, service, etc.): as, he *served* four years in the navy. 5. to carry out the duties connected with (a position, office, etc.). 6. to wait on (customers), as in a store. 7. to provide (customers or users) with goods or services. 8. to provide (goods) for customers; supply. 9. to prepare and offer (food, etc.) in a certain way, to others, etc.: as, she *served* cocktails to us, he *served* the chicken with chestnut dressing. 10. to offer or set food, etc. before (a person); help (a person) to food, etc. 11. to meet the needs or satisfy the requirements of; be sufficient for: as, one nail will *serve* my purpose. 12. to be used by: as, one hospital *serves* the entire city. 13. to function or perform for: as, my memory *serves* me well. 14. to behave toward; treat: as, she was cruelly *served.* 15. to deliver (a legal instrument), as a summons. 16. to deliver a legal instrument to; present with a writ, etc. 17. to hit (a ball, etc.) to one's opponent in order to start play, as in tennis, badminton, etc. 18. to operate or tend (a large gun). 19. in *animal husbandry*, to copulate with (a female). 20. in *nautical usage*, to put a binding around in order to protect or strengthen (rope, etc.). *v.i.* 1. to work as or be a servant. 2. to be in service; do service: as, he *served* in the navy. 3. to carry out the duties connected with an office or position. 4. to be used or usable; be of service; function. 5. to meet needs; satisfy requirements; be adequate or sufficient: as, this nail is too short to *serve.* 6. to provide guests with something to eat, drink, or smoke; wait on table. 7. to be suitable or favorable: as, the weather hardly *serves* for strolling. 8. to start play by hitting the ball, etc. to one's opponent, as in tennis. 9. to act as server at Mass. *n.* in *tennis, badminton,* etc., 1. the act or manner of serving the ball, etc. 2. the flight of the ball, etc. in service. 3. a turn at serving the ball, etc.

serve one right, to bring evil or misfortune to one deservedly; give one his just deserts.

serv·er (sũr'vẽr), *n.* 1. a person who serves, as an altar assistant at Mass, a tennis player who serves the ball, a waiter, etc. 2. a thing used in serving, as a tray or salver for dishes.

Ser·ve·to, Mi·guel (mē-gel' ser-ve'tô), Michael Servetus: Spanish name.

Ser·ve·tus, Michael (sẽr-vē'təs), 1511–1553; Spanish physician and theologian; burned at the stake in Geneva on the charge of heresy.

Ser·vi·a (sũr'vi-ə), *n.* Serbia: the former name.

serv·ice (sũr'vis), *n.* [ME. *servise;* OFr. *servise, service;* L. *servitium* < *servus*, a slave], 1. the occupation or condition of a servant. 2. employment, especially public employment. 3. a branch or department of this, including the people working in it; specifically, 4. the United States armed forces; Army, Navy, Marine Corps, or Air Force: as, he was in the *service* for three years. 5. work done for a master or superior; hence, 6. work done or duty performed for another or others: as, professional *services*, repair *service*, a life devoted to public *service.* 7. [Rare or Archaic], respect; attention; devotion, as of a lover to his lady. 8. the serving of God, as through good works, prayer, etc. 9. any religious ceremony, usually public worship: as, church *service*, marriage *service*, etc. 10. a musical setting for such a ceremony, as a canticle. 11. helpful, beneficial, or friendly action or conduct; act giving assistance or advantage to another. 12. the result of this; benefit; advantage. 13. the act or manner of serving food: as, the food was of even worse quality than the *service*. 14. a set of utensils or articles used in serving: as, silver tea *service*, breakfast *service*, etc. 15. an activity carried on to provide people with the use of something, as electric power, water, transportation, mail delivery, telephones, etc. 16. the act or method of providing these. 17. the quality of that which is provided: as, our electric *service* is poor. 18. anything useful, as maintenance, supplies, installation, repairs, etc., provided by a dealer or manufacturer for people who have bought things from him. 19. *a*) an act, manner, or turn of serving in tennis, badminton, etc. *b*) the ball, etc. as served. 20. in *animal husbandry*, the covering of a female by the male. 21. in *law*, notification of legal action, especially through the serving of a writ, etc. 22. in *nautical usage*, any material, as wire, used in serving (ropes, etc.). ***adj.*** 1. of, for, or in service. 2. of, for, or used by servants, tradespeople, etc.: as, a *service* entrance. 3. for use during active service: as, a *service* uniform: distinguished from *dress, full-dress*. ***v.t.*** [SERVICED (-vist), SERVICING], 1. to furnish with a service: as, one power company *services* the entire valley. 2. to make fit for service, as by inspecting, adjusting, repairing, refueling, etc.

at one's service, 1. ready to serve or co-operate with one. 2. ready for one's use.

of service, giving aid or assistance; helpful; useful.

serv·ice (sũr'vis), ***n.*** [ME. *serves*, pl. of obs. *serve;* AS. *syrfe;* LL. **sorbea* < L. *sorbus*, service tree], 1. a European tree of the rose family, resembling the mountain ash and having small, edible fruit: also **service tree.** 2. a small tree or bush similar to this: also **wild service tree.** 3. a shadbush. 4. the fruit of any of these.

Ser·vice, Robert William (sũr'vis), 1874?–1958; Canadian writer.

serv·ice·a·bil·i·ty (sũr'vis-ə-bil'ə-ti), ***n.*** the quality or degree of being serviceable.

serv·ice·a·ble (sũr'vis-ə-b'l), ***adj.*** [ME. *servisable;* OFr. *servisable*], 1. that can be of service; ready for use; useful; usable. 2. that will give good service, especially in long, hard use; durable: as, a *serviceable* fabric. 3. beneficial; profitable; helpful. 4. [Archaic], willing to serve; attentive and obliging.

serv·ice·a·bly (sũr'vis-ə-bli), ***adv.*** in a serviceable manner.

serv·ice·ber·ry (sũr'vis-ber'i), ***n.*** [*pl.* SERVICEBERRIES (-iz)], 1. the fruit of any service tree. 2. the shadbush or Juneberry.

service cap, a military cap with a round, flat top and a visor.

service club, any of various clubs, as Rotary, Kiwanis, etc., organized to provide various services for its own members and to promote the community welfare.

service elevator, an elevator used by servants and tradespeople and for carrying goods, baggage, etc.

service entrance, an entrance used by tradespeople, employees, etc. rather than by the general public.

serv·ice·man (sũr'vis-man'), ***n.*** [*pl.* SERVICEMEN (-men')], 1. a member of the armed forces. 2. a person whose work is servicing or repairing something: as, a radio *serviceman*. Also **service man, service-man.**

service station, 1. a place providing maintenance service, parts, supplies, etc. for mechanical or electrical equipment: as, a radio *service station*. 2. a place providing such service for automobiles, trucks, and motorcycles; gas station.

service stripe, a stripe, or one of a number of stripes, worn on the lower sleeve of a uniform to indicate the number of years spent as a soldier, policeman, etc.

ser·vi·ette (sũr'vi-et'), ***n.*** [Fr. < *servir*, to serve], a table napkin.

ser·vile (sũr'v'l), ***adj.*** [ME. *servylle* < L. *servilis* < *servus*, a slave], 1. of a slave or slaves. 2. like that of slaves or servants: as, *servile* employment. 3. like or characteristic of a slave; humbly yielding or submissive; cringing. 4. [Archaic], held in slavery; not free.

SYN.—**servile** suggests the cringing, submissive behavior characteristic of a slave (*servile* flattery); **subservient** applies to one who occupies an inferior or subordinate position that furthers another's ends, and may or may not connote servility (a faculty *subservient* to the board of trustees); **slavish** implies utter abjectness and submissiveness in obeying, depending on, or following another (*slavish* adherence to the rules of grammar); **menial** applies to such work or position that is regarded as low or degrading (restricted to the *menial* job of a porter); **obsequious** implies a servile, fawning attitude toward someone regarded as one's superior (an *obsequious* courtier). —***ANT.*** domineering, imperious.

ser·vil·i·ty (sẽr-vil'ə-ti), ***n.*** [*pl.* SERVILITIES (-tiz)], servile attitude, character, or conduct; humble yielding or submissiveness; cringing humility.

ser·vi·tor (sũr'və-tẽr), ***n.*** [ME. & OFr. *servitour;* LL.], 1. a person who serves another; servant or attendant. 2. a follower; adherent.

ser·vi·tude (sũr'və-tōōd', sũr'və-tūd'), ***n.*** [Fr.; L. *servitudo* < *servus*, a slave], 1. the condition of a slave; subjection to a master; slavery; bondage. 2. work imposed as punishment for crime. 3. in *law*, easement.

SYN.—**servitude** refers to compulsory labor or service for another, often, specifically, such labor imposed as punishment for crime; **slavery** implies absolute subjection to another person who owns and completely controls one; **bondage** originally referred to the condition of a serf bound to his master's land, but now implies any condition of subjugation or captivity. —***ANT.*** freedom, liberty.

Ser·vo- (sũr'vō), Serbo-.

ser·vo·mech·a·nism (sũr'vō-mek'ə-niz'm), ***n.*** [< L. *servus*, slave; + *mechanism*], in *automation*, the device, as an electric motor, a pump, or a stoker, activated by electrical or mechanical impulses, that automatically operates a machine, a tool, etc.

ses·a·me (ses'ə-mē'), ***n.*** [Fr. *sésame;* L. *sesamum, sesama;* Gr. *sēsamon, sēsamē*], 1. an East Indian plant whose flat seeds yield an oil and are used for food. 2. its seeds. See also **open sesame.**

ses·a·moid (ses'ə-moid'), ***adj.*** [Gr. *sēsamoeidēs* < *sēsamon*, sesame + *eidos*, a form], shaped like a sesame seed; specifically, designating or of any of certain small bony or cartilaginous nodules developing in tendons, as at a joint. ***n.*** a sesamoid bone or cartilage.

ses·qui- (ses'kwi), [L., more by a half < *semis*, half + *que*, and], a combining form meaning *one and a half*, as in *sesquicentennial*.

ses·qui·cen·ten·ni·al (ses'kwi-sen-ten'i-əl), ***adj.*** [*sesqui-* + *centennial*], of or ending a period of 150 years. ***n.*** a 150th anniversary or its celebration.

ses·qui·ox·ide (ses'kwi-ok'sīd), ***n.*** [*sesqui-* + *oxide*], an oxide in which three atoms or equivalents of oxygen are combined with two of some other element or radical.

ses·quip·e·dal (ses-kwip'i-d'l, ses'kwi-pē'd'l), ***adj.*** sesquipedalian.

ses·qui·pe·da·li·an (ses'kwi-pə-dā'li-ən), ***adj.*** [< L. *sesquipedalis*, of a foot and a half; *sesqui-*, more by a half + *pedalis* < *pes, pedis*, a foot], 1. measuring a foot and a half. 2. very long: said of words. 3. using long words. ***n.*** a long word.

ses·sile (ses'il), ***adj.*** [L. *sessilis* < *sessus*, pp. of *sedere*, to sit], 1. in *anatomy & zoology*, *a*) attached directly by its base. *b*) permanently fixed; immobile. 2. in *botany*, having no pedicel or peduncle; attached directly to the main stem, as some flowers and leaves.

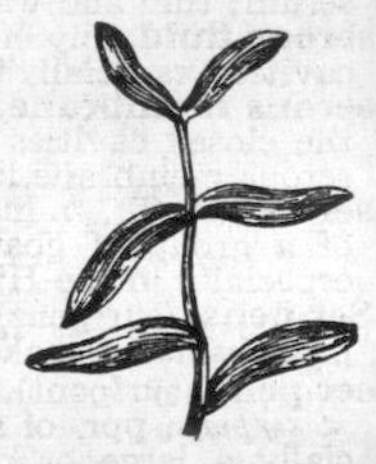

SESSILE LEAVES

ses·sion (sesh'ən), ***n.*** [Fr.; L. *sessio* < *sedere*, to sit], 1. the sitting together or meeting of a group; assembly, as of a court, legislature, council, etc. 2. a continuous, day-to-day series of such sittings. 3. the term or period of either of these. 4. a school term or period of study, classes, etc. 5. [Colloq.], a period of activity of any kind, especially one that is trying or burdensome: as, he had quite a *session* with the policeman. Abbreviated **sess.**

in session, meeting; assembled.

ses·sion·al (sesh'ən-'l), ***adj.*** 1. of a session or sessions. 2. taking place each session.

ses·terce (ses'tũrs), ***n.*** [L. *sestertius* (*nummus*), for *semis tertius*, two and a half, because equal in value to two and a half asses], an old Roman coin, originally of silver, later of brass or copper, equal to 1/4 denarius or about five cents.

ses·ter·ti·um (ses-tũr'shi-əm), ***n.*** [*pl.* SESTERTIA (-shiə)], [L. < *mille sestertium*, a thousand sesterces], an old Roman monetary unit, equal to 1,000 sesterces.

ses·tet (ses-tet', ses'tet), ***n.*** [It. *sestetto*, dim. of *sesto*, sixth; L. *sextus*, sixth < *sex*, six], 1. in *music*, a sextet. 2. the final six lines of a sonnet.

ses·ti·na (ses-tē'nə), ***n.*** [*pl.* SESTINAS (-nəz), SESTINE (-ni)], [It. < *sesto* (L. *sextus*), sixth], a kind of poem having six six-line stanzas and a three-line envoy: the end words of the first stanza are repeated with progressively changed order in the other five stanzas and are included, medially and finally, in the envoy.

Set (set), ***n.*** [Gr. *Sēth* < Egypt. *Setesh*], an Egyptian god of evil, represented with an animal's head and a pointed snout: also **Seth.**

set (set), ***v.t.*** [SET, SETTING], [ME. *setten;* AS. *settan* (akin to G. *setzen* & Goth. *satjan*), causative formation "to cause to sit" < base of *sit*], 1. to place in a sitting position; cause to sit; seat. 2. *a*) to cause (a fowl) to sit on eggs in order to hatch them. *b*) to put (eggs) under a fowl or in an incubator to hatch them. 3. to put in some place or position; cause to be, lie, stand, etc. in a place: as, *set* the book on the table. 4. to put in the place designed or meant to receive or hold it; put in the right place: as, he *set* the wheel on the axle. 5. to put or move (a part of the body) into or on a specified place: as, he *set* his hand on my shoulder. 6. to bring (something) into contact with something else;

cause to be next or applied to something: as, she *set* a match to the paper. 7. *a*) to put down on paper, in a record book, etc.; write down; record. *b*) to put or affix (one's signature, seal, etc.) on a document. 8. to cause to be in a condition or relation specified by a following adverbial expression; specifically, *a*) to cause to be or become: as, he *set* the house on fire. *b*) to cause to take a certain physical position: as, he *set* the book on end. 9. to cause to be in working or proper condition; put in order; arrange; fix; adjust; specifically, *a*) to fix (a net, trap, etc.) in a position to catch animals. *b*) to fix (a sail) in a position to catch the wind. *c*) to put (a movable part of an instrument or machine) in position to work, as a chuck on a lathe. *d*) to adjust so as to be in a desired position for use; regulate: as, *set* a radio dial, clock, etc. *e*) to put an edge on (a knife, razor, etc.). *f*) to adjust (teeth of a saw). *g*) to arrange (a table) with knives, forks, plates, etc. for a meal. *h*) to put (a joint or bone) into normal position for healing, mending, etc. when dislocated or fractured. 10. to cause to be in a settled or rigid position; specifically, *a*) to put or press into a fixed or rigid position: as, he *set* his jaw. *b*) to cause (one's mind, purpose, etc.) to be fixed, unyielding, determined, etc. *c*) to cause to become firm or hard in consistency: as, pectin *sets* jelly. *d*) to make (a color) fast in dyeing. *e*) to mount, embed, or fix (gems) in rings, bracelets, etc. *f*) to cover, encrust, or decorate (gold, watches, etc.) with gems; fix gems in. *g*) to fix firmly in a frame: as, *set* the glass in the window. *h*) to put curls or waves temporarily in (hair) by arranging it with lotions, hairpins, etc. and letting it dry. 11. to cause to take a particular direction; specifically, *a*) to cause to move in a certain direction; propel: as, the current *set* them northward. *b*) to point, direct, or face in a certain direction: as, he *set* his face toward home. *c*) to direct (one's desires, hopes, heart, etc.) with serious attention *in* or *on* someone or something. 12. to appoint; institute; establish; ordain; specifically, *a*) to post or station (a person) for certain duties: as, we *set* sentries at all the gates. *b*) to place in a position of authority. *c*) to fix (limits or boundaries). *d*) to fix or appoint (a time) for something to happen: as, he *set* September 30 as the deadline. *e*) to fix a time for (an event). *f*) to establish (a regulation, law, etc.); prescribe (a form, order, etc.). *g*) to give or furnish (an example, pattern, etc.) for others. *h*) to introduce (a fashion, style, etc.). *i*) to allot or assign (a task, lesson, etc.) for work or study. *j*) to fix (an amount of work, quota, etc.) for a given period. *k*) to begin to apply (oneself) to a task, etc. 13. to estimate or fix; place mentally; specifically, *a*) to fix (the amount of a price, fine, rent ceiling, etc.): as, the judge *set* fifty dollars as the fine. *b*) to fix the amount of (a price, fine, rent ceiling, etc.): as, the judge *set* the fine at fifty dollars. *c*) to estimate or value (a person or thing) in some specified way: as, I *set* at nothing what once I loved. *d*) to have (a certain estimate of a person or thing): as, I *set* little store by him. 14. in *baking*, to put aside (leavened dough) to rise. 15. in *hunting*, to point toward the position of (game): said of dogs. 16. in *music*, *a*) to write or fit (words) to music. *b*) to write or fit (music) to words. 17. in *printing*, *a*) to compose (type). *b*) to put (manuscript) into type. 18. in the *theater*, *a*) to place (a scene) in a given locale: as, Shakespeare *set* the scene in Venice. *b*) to make up or put together (scenery) on the stage; arrange (items of scenery) in a certain way. *c*) to arrange the scenery and properties on (the stage). *v.i.* 1. to sit on eggs: said of a fowl. 2. to become firm or hard in consistency: as, the cement *set* after several hours. 3. to become fast: said of a dye, color, etc. 4. to begin to move, travel, etc. (with *out*, *forth*, *on*, *off*, or *forward*). 5. to have a certain direction; tend: as, the wind *sets* to the south. 6. to make an apparent descent toward and below the horizon; go down; hence, 7. to wane; decline. 8. to hang, fit, or suit in a certain way: as, the jacket *sets* well. 9. [Now Dial.], to sit. 10. in *botany*, to begin to develop after pollination; form fruit in the blossom. 11. in *hunting*, to point toward the position of game: said of a dog. *adj.* 1. fixed or appointed in advance: as, a *set* time. 2. established; prescribed, as by authority. 3. deliberate; intentional; purposeful. 4. conventional; stereotyped; not spontaneous: as, a *set* speech. 5. fixed; motionless; rigid; immovable. 6. resolute; obstinate; unyielding. 7. firm or hard in consistency. 8. ready: as, get *set*. 9. formed; put together; built. *n.* 1. a setting or being set; specifically, *a*) the act of a dog in setting game. *b*) a becoming hard or firm in consistency. 2. the way or position in which a thing is set; specifically, *a*) direction; course, as of a current; hence, *b*) tendency; inclination. *c*) change of form resulting from pressure, twisting, strain, etc.; warp; bend; also, sidewise deflection of saw teeth. *d*) the way in which an article of clothing fits or hangs. *e*) the position or attitude of a limb or part of the body: as, the *set* of her head. *f*) in *psychology*, an adjustment of an organism in preparation for a certain definite kind of activity. 3. something which is set; specifically, *a*) a twig or slip for planting or grafting. *b*) a number of backdrops, flats, properties, etc. constructed and assembled for a scene in a play or motion picture; formal, constructed scenery. 4. a group of persons; specifically, *a*) a company or group with common habits, occupations, interests, etc.: as, a *set* of smugglers. *b*) an exclusive or select group; clique; coterie. *c*) the number of couples needed for a country or square dance. 5. a collection of things belonging, issued, used, or growing together; specifically, *a*) a number of tools or instruments used for the same purpose: as, a carpentry *set*. *b*) the collection of objects necessary for playing a game, especially a parlor game. *c*) a collection or group of books, magazines, etc. by one author, in one series, on one subject, etc. *d*) a matching collection of china, silverware, etc. *e*) the complement of natural or artificial teeth of a person or animal. *f*) a clutch of eggs. *g*) the figures that make up a country or square dance. *h*) receiving equipment for radio or television assembled, as in a cabinet, for use. *i*) in *tennis*, a group of six or more games won before the other side wins five or by a margin of two if the score is tied at more than four games each. *j*) in *squash*, etc., a similar group of games. —***SYN.*** see **coterie.**

all set, [Colloq.], prepared; ready.

set about, to begin; start doing.

set against, 1. to balance. 2. to compare. 3. to make hostile toward; make an enemy of.

set apart, to separate and keep for a purpose; reserve.

set aside, 1. to set apart. 2. to discard; dismiss; reject. 3. to annul; declare void.

set back, 1. to put (a clock or its hands) to an earlier time, especially to standard time. 2. to reverse or hinder the progress of.

set down, 1. to place so as to rest upon a surface; put down; let alight. 2. to put in writing or print; record. 3. to consider; estimate; ascribe; attribute.

set forth, 1. to publish. 2. to express in words; state.

set in, 1. to begin. 2. to blow or flow towards the shore: said of wind, current, etc.

set off, 1. to start (a person) doing something. 2. to set in relief; make prominent by contrast. 3. to show to advantage; enhance. 4. to cause to explode.

set on, 1. to incite; urge on. 2. to attack.

set out, 1. to limit; define; mark out. 2. to plan; lay out (a town, garden, etc.). 3. to display, as for sale; exhibit. 4. to plant.

set to, 1. to make a beginning; get to work; begin. 2. to begin fighting.

set up, 1. *a*) to place in an upright position. *b*) to place in a high position. *c*) to raise to power. *d*) to raise. 2. to put together or erect (a tent, machine, etc.). 3. to establish; found. 4. to begin. 5. to provide with money, etc., as for a business; fit out. 6. to cause to feel stimulated, exhilarated, etc. 7. to advance or propose (a theory, etc.). 8. to cause. 9. to put (drinks, etc.) before customers. 10. to treat.

set upon, to attack, especially with violence.

se·ta (sē'tə), *n.* [*pl.* SETAE (-tē)], [L.], in *botany* & *zoology*, a bristle or bristlelike part or organ.

se·ta·ceous (si-tā'shəs), *adj.* [Mod. L. *setaceus* < L. *seta*, a bristle], 1. having bristles. 2. bristlelike.

set·back (set'bak'), *n.* 1. a reversal, check, or interruption in progress; relapse; upset. 2. a steplike indentation or recessed section, as in a wall or the upper parts of a building; offset. 3. a current running opposite to the main flow of water; eddy.

set chisel, a broad-pointed chisel used in cutting the heads from rivets, bolts, etc.

Seth (seth), [LL.; Gr. *Sēth*; Heb. *shēth*, lit., appointed], a masculine name. *n.* in the *Bible*, the third son of Adam: Gen. 4:25.

Seth (sāt), *n.* Set, an Egyptian god.

se·ti- (sē'ti), [< L. *seta*, a bristle], a combining form meaning *bristle*, as in *setiferous*.

se·tif·er·ous (si-tif'ẽr-əs), *adj.* [*seti-* + *-ferous*], having, forming, or covered with bristles.

se·ti·form (sē'tə-fôrm'), *adj.* [*seti-* + *-form*], resembling a seta, or bristle, in shape.

se·tig·er·ous (si-tij'ẽr-əs), *adj.* [*seti-* + *-gerous*], setiferous.

set·off (set'ôf'), *n.* 1. a thing that makes up for or sets off something else; counterbalance; compensation. 2. *a*) the settlement of a debt through the debtor's establishment of a counterclaim against his creditor. *b*) a claim so established. 3. in *architecture*, an offset.

se·ton (sē't'n), *n.* [ME. *ceton*, *seton*; ML. *seto*, *setonis* < L. *seta*, bristle], in *medicine*, 1. one or more threads, horsehairs, etc. introduced beneath the skin to cause or to maintain a discharge. 2. the discharge.

Se·ton, Ernest Thompson (sē't'n), 1860–1946; American writer and painter; known for stories and pictures of animals: also called *Ernest Seton-Thompson*.

se·tose (sē'tōs, si-tōs'), *adj.* [L. *setosus*], setaceous.

set·screw (set'skrōō'), *n.* 1. a machine screw passing through one part and against or into another to prevent movement, as of a ring around a shaft. 2. a screw used in regulating or adjusting the tension of a spring, etc. See **screw**, illus.

‡**set·te·cen·to** (set'te-chen'tô), *n.* [It.; cf. CINQUECENTO], the 18th century, with reference to the Italian art and literature produced then.

set·tee (se-tē'), *n.* [< *set;* regarded as dim. of *seat*], 1. a seat or bench with a back, usually for two or three people. 2. a small or medium-sized sofa.

set·ter (set'ẽr), *n.* 1. a person who sets or a thing used in setting: as, a *setter* of rules, a mechanical *setter* for bowling pins. 2. any of a breed of long-haired bird dog of which there are three varieties (***English, Irish,*** and ***Gordon setters***): they are trained to find the game and point out its position by standing rigid (formerly by crouching).

set·ting (set'iŋ), *n.* 1. the act of a person or thing that sets. 2. a thing in or upon which something, especially a gem, is set. 3. time and place, environment, background, or surroundings, as of a story, poem, person's life, etc. 4. actual physical surroundings or scenery whether real, as of a garden, or artificial, as on a stage. 5. the music or the composing of music for a set of words, as a poem. 6. the eggs in the nest of a setting hen.

set·tle (set''l), *n.* [ME. *settle, settel;* AS. *setl* (akin to G. *sessel*) < base of *sit*], a long wooden bench with a back, arm rests, and sometimes a chest beneath the seat.

set·tle (set''l), *v.t.* [SETTLED (-'ld), SETTLING], [ME. *setlen;* AS. *setlan* < *setl*, a seat; cross-influenced in ME. by several homonymous words], 1. to put in order; arrange or adjust as desired, as clothing, a room, one's affairs, etc. 2. to put, plant, or set in place so as to be firmly or comfortably situated. 3. to establish as a resident or residents: as, the firm has *settled* its employees in near-by houses. 4. to migrate to and set up residence or a community in; colonize: as, New York was *settled* by the Dutch. 5. to cause to sink and become more dense and compact: as, he *settled* the ashes by shaking them, the rain will *settle* the dust; hence, 6. to clarify (a liquid) by settling the sediment. 7. to free from disturbance, as the mind, nerves, stomach, etc. 8. [Colloq.], to prevent from creating a disturbance or interfering, as by a reprimand or a blow. 9. to make stable or permanent; establish: as, experience has *settled* the system by which they work. 10. to establish in business, office, work, marriage, etc. 11. to fix definitely; determine; decide (something in doubt or question). 12. to end (a dispute). 13. to pay (a bill, debt, account, etc.). 14. to decide (a legal dispute) by agreement without court action. ***v.i.*** 1. to stop moving and stay in one place; come to rest: as, the bird *settled* on the wire, his gaze *settled* on the latest arrival. 2. to cast itself over the landscape, as darkness, fog, etc. or over a person or group, as gloom or silence; descend. 3. to become localized or fixed in a given part of the body: said of pain or disease. 4. to take up permanent residence; make one's home: as, they *settled* in Canada. 5. to move downward; sink, especially gradually, as by its own weight: as, the car *settled* in the soft ground, the bridge *settled* at one end. 6. to become more dense or compact by sinking, as sediment or loose soil when shaken. 7. to become clearer by the settling of sediment or dregs: said of liquid. 8. to become more stable or composed; stop fluctuating or changing; settle down. 9. to reach an agreement or decision (usually with ***with, on,*** or ***upon***). 10. to pay what is owing: as, he won't *settle* without court action. —***SYN.*** see **decide.**

settle down, 1. to take up permanent residence, a regular job, etc.; lead a more routine, settled life, as after marriage. 2. to become less nervous, restless, or erratic. 3. to apply oneself steadily or attentively.

settle upon (or **on**), 1. to make up one's mind about; decide; resolve. 2. to make over (property, etc.) to by legal action.

set·tle·ment (set''l-mənt), *n.* 1. a settling or being settled. 2. establishment in life, business, marriage, etc. 3. an inhabiting or colonizing, as of a new land. 4. a group of people or a place concerned in this; colony. 5. a small or isolated community; village. 6. an agreement, arrangement, or understanding. 7. payment or adjustment, as of a claim. 8. the conveyance or disposition of property for the benefit of a person. 9. the amount of property thus conveyed. 10. a community center offering social and educational activities: the services are usually free and directed at the underprivileged element of the population. 11. the gradual subsidence of all or part of a structure.

settlement house, a settlement (sense 10).

settlement worker, a social welfare worker associated with a settlement house.

set·tler (set'lẽr), *n.* 1. a person or thing that settles. 2. a person who settles in a new country or colony.

set·tlings (set'liŋz), *n.pl.* the solid matter that settles to the bottom of a liquid; sediment.

set·tlor (set'lẽr), *n.* in *law*, a person who makes a settlement of property.

set-to (set'tōō'), *n.* [*pl.* SET-TOS (-tōōz')], [< phr. *set to*], [Colloq.], 1. a fight or struggle, especially a fist fight. 2. any sharp contest or argument; bout.

set·up (set'up'), *n.* 1. the way in which something is set up; plan, make-up, or arrangement, as of equipment, an organization, etc. 2. bodily posture; carriage. 3. soda water, ice, etc. for mixing with alcoholic liquor. 4. [Slang], *a*) a contest in which the contestants are so unevenly matched that the outcome is certain; contest deliberately arranged to result in an easy victory; hence, *b*) any undertaking that is, or is purposely made, very easy.

Seu·rat, Georges (zhôrzh sö'rà'), 1859–1891; French neoimpressionist painter.

Se·vas·to·pol (si-vas'tə-pōl'; Russ. se'väs-tô'pôl-y'), *n.* a city in the Crimea, on the Black Sea: pop., 112,000: also spelled **Sebastopol.**

sev·en (sev''n), *adj.* [ME. *seoven;* AS. *seofon, seofan;* akin to G. *sieben;* IE. base ***septṁ*, as also in Sans. *sapta*, L. *septem* (cf. SEPT-), Gr. *heptă* (cf. HEPT-), etc.], totaling one more than six. ***n.*** 1. the cardinal number between six and eight; 7; VII. 2. a person or thing numbered seven, as a contestant, a playing card, etc.

Seven against Thebes, in *Greek legend*, the story of the expedition of seven heroes to help Polynices recover the throne of Thebes from his brother Eteocles, who had agreed to share it with him but refused to give it up after his turn: subject of a tragedy by Aeschylus.

seven deadly sins, see **deadly sins.**

sev·en·fold (sev''n-fōld'), *adj.* [see -FOLD], 1. having seven parts. 2. having seven times as much or as many. ***adv.*** seven times as much or as many.

Seven Hills of Rome, the seven hills on and about which the city of Rome was built; the Palatine, Capitoline, Quirinal, Caelian, Aventine, Esquiline, and Viminal.

seven seas, all the oceans of the world.

sev·en·teen (sev''n-tēn'), *adj.* [ME. *seventene;* AS. *seofentyne;* see SEVEN & -TEEN], seven more than ten. ***n.*** the cardinal number between sixteen and eighteen; 17; XVII.

sev·en·teenth (sev''n-tēnth'), *adj.* [ME. *sevententhe;* AS. *seofon-teotha;* see SEVENTEEN & -TH], 1. preceded by sixteen others in a series; 17th. 2. designating any of the seventeen equal parts of something. ***n.*** 1. the one following the sixteenth. 2. any of the seventeen equal parts of something; 1/17.

sev·en·teen-year locust (sev''n-tēn'yêr'), a cicada which lives underground as a larva for from thirteen to seventeen years before emerging as an adult to live in the open for a brief period.

sev·enth (sev''nth), *adj.* [ME. *seventhe*, a new formation on *seven* + *-th*, replacing AS. *seofande, seofende* (akin to G. *siebente*) & *seofotha*], 1. preceded by six others in a series; 7th. 2. designating any of the seven equal parts of something. ***n.*** 1. the one following the sixth. 2. any of the seven equal parts of something; 1/7. 3. in *music*, *a*) a note seven degrees above or below another in the diatonic scale. *b*) the interval between these. *c*) the seventh note of the diatonic scale; leading note; subtonic. *d*) the chord formed by any tone and the third, fifth, and seventh of which it is the fundamental: also **seventh chord.**

sev·enth-day (sev''nth-dā'), *adj.* 1. of the seventh day (Saturday). 2. [often S-], observing the Sabbath on Saturday: as, *Seventh-day* Adventists.

seventh heaven, 1. the seventh, usually highest, of the concentric spheres in which the stars are supposed to be fixed, according to various ancient systems of astronomy, or in which God and his angels are, according to certain theologies; hence, 2. a condition of perfect happiness.

sev·enth·ly (sev''nth-li), *adv.* in the seventh place.

sev·en·ti·eth (sev''n-ti-ith), *adj.* [ME. *seventithe;* see SEVENTY & -TH], 1. preceded by sixty-nine others in a series; 70th. 2. designating any of the seventy equal parts of something. ***n.*** 1. the one following the sixty-ninth. 2. any of the seventy equal parts of something; 1/70.

sev·en·ty (sev''n-ti), *adj.* [ME. *seofentig;* AS. (*hund*)-*seofontig;* see SEVEN & -TY (tens)], seven times ten. ***n.*** [*pl.* SEVENTIES (-tiz)], the cardinal number between sixty-nine and seventy-one; 70; LXX.

the seventies, the years from seventy through seventy-nine (of a century or a person's age).

sev·en·ty-five (sev''n-ti-fiv'), *n.* a seventy-five millimeter gun, especially the French artillery piece of this bore used in World War I.

sev·en-up (sev''n-up'), *n.* a card game for two, three, or four persons in which seven points constitute a game.

Seven Wonders of the World, seven remarkable objects of ancient times: traditionally, they are the Egyptian pyramids, the walls and hanging gardens of Babylon, the Mausoleum at Halicarnassus, the temple of Artemis at Ephesus, the Colossus of Rhodes, the statue of Zeus by Phidias at Olympia, and the Pharos (or lighthouse) at Alexandria.

Seven Years' War, 1756–1763; a war in which England and Prussia defeated Austria, France, Russia, Sweden, and Saxony: Prussia established her power in Europe and England seized French colonies in America and India.

sev·er (sev'ẽr), *v.t. & v.i.* [ME. *severen;* OFr. *sevrer, severer;* LL. **seperare;* L. *separare*], 1. to separate; make or become distinct; divide: as, a river *severs* Ohio from West Virginia. 2. to part or break off, as by cutting or with force; cut in two: as, the cable *severed* under the strain, *severing* all relationship. —***SYN.*** see **separate.**

sev·er·a·ble (sev'ẽr-ə-b'l), *adj.* that can be severed or divided; specifically, in *law,* separable into distinct, independent obligations: said of a contract.

sev·er·al (sev'ẽr-əl, sev'rəl), *adj.* [ME.; OFr. < LL. *separalis* < L. *separ,* separate], 1. separate; distinct; individual; hence, 2. different; respective; diverse: as, the *several* opinions of the different people. 3. more than two but not many; of an indefinite but small number; few. *n.* several persons or things; a few.

sev·er·al·ly (sev'ẽr-əl-i, sev'rəl-i), *adv.* 1. separately; distinctly. 2. respectively: as, the proposals which the parties have *severally* made.

sev·er·al·ty (sev'ẽr-əl-ti, sev'rəl-ti), *n.* [*pl.* SEVERALTIES (-tiz)], [Anglo-Fr. *severauté* < OFr. *several*], 1. the condition or character of being several or distinct. 2. property owned by individual right. 3. the condition of property so owned.

sev·er·ance (sev'ẽr-əns), *n.* [ME. < OFr. *sevrance,* via Anglo-Fr.], a severing or being severed.

se·vere (sə-vêr'), *adj.* [Fr. *sévère* < L. *severus*], 1. harsh or strict, as in treatment; unsparing; stern. 2. serious; grave; forbidding, as in expression or manner. 3. conforming strictly to a rule, method, standard, etc.; rigidly accurate. 4. extremely plain or simple; unornamented; restrained: said of style, as, a dress with *severe* lines. 5. keen; violent; extreme; intense, as pain, heat, etc. 6. difficult; rigorous; trying, as a rule, test, etc.

SYN.—**severe** applies to a person or thing that is strict and uncompromising and connotes a total absence of softness, laxity, frivolity, etc. (a *severe* critic, hair-do, etc.); **stern** implies an unyielding firmness, especially as manifested in a grim or forbidding aspect or manner (a *stern* guardian); **austere** suggests harsh restraint, self-denial, stark simplicity (the *austere* diet of wartime), or an absence of warmth, passion, ornamentation, etc. (an *austere* bedroom); **ascetic** implies extreme self-denial and self-discipline or even, sometimes, the deliberate self-infliction of pain and discomfort, as by religious fanatics (an *ascetic* hermit). —***ANT.*** mild, lax, indulgent.

se·ver·i·ty (sə-ver'ə-ti), *n.* [Fr. *sévérité;* L. *severitas*], 1. the quality or condition of being severe; specifically, *a)* strictness; harshness; sternness. *b)* gravity, as of expression or manner; seriousness. *c)* rigid accuracy or exactness. *d)* extreme plainness or restraint, as in style. *e)* violence; intensity; acuteness, as of cold, illness, etc. *f)* rigorous or trying character. 2. [*pl.* SEVERITIES (-tiz)], something severe, as a punishment.

Sev·ern (sev'ẽrn), *n.* a river in Wales and England, flowing into the Bristol Channel: length, 210 mi.

Se·ver·us (si-vêr'əs), *n.* (*Lucius Septimius Severus*), Roman emperor (193–211 A.D.); lived 146–211 A.D.

Sé·vi·gné, Marquise **de** (də sā'vē'nyā'), (born *Marie de Rabutin-Chantal*), 1626–1696; French writer.

Se·vil·la (sā-vē'lyä), *n.* Seville.

Se·ville (sə-vil'; *esp.* Brit. sev'il), *n.* a city in southern Spain, on the Guadalquivir River: pop., 370,000 (est. 1946): Spanish name, *Sevilla.*

Sè·vres (sev'rə, sev'ẽrz; Fr. sevr'), *n.* 1. a town in France near Paris: pop., 15,000 (1946). 2. a fine porcelain made there.

sew (sō), *v.t.* [SEWED (sōd), SEWED or SEWN (sōn), SEWING], [ME. *sewen, souwen;* AS. *siwan, siwian, siowian,* etc.; akin to Goth. *siujan;* IE. base **siw-,* to sew, seen also in L. *suere* (*sutum*), to sew, sew together; cf. SUTURE], 1. to join, mend, or fasten with stitches made with needle and thread; put stitches into. 2. to make, mend, fasten, close, etc. by sewing. *v.i.* to work with needle and thread or at a sewing machine.

sew up, 1. to close or bring together the edges of with stitches. 2. to enclose in something by sewing. 3. [Colloq.], to get or have absolute control of or right to; monopolize.

sew·age (sōō'ij, sū'ij), *n.* [*sewer* + *-age*], the waste matter carried off by sewers or drains.

Sew·all, Samuel (sōō'əl, sū'əl), 1652–1730; American jurist born in England; presided over witchcraft trials at Salem.

se·wan (sē'wən), *n.* [Am. Ind.], shells used as money by the Algonquian Indians: also **seawan, seawant.**

Sew·ard, William Henry (sōō'ẽrd, sū'ẽrd), 1801–1872; American statesman; secretary of state (1861–1869).

Sew·ard Peninsula (sōō'ẽrd, sū'ẽrd), an Alaskan peninsula, on Bering Strait.

sew·er (sōō'ẽr, sū'ẽr), *n.* [ME.; OFr. *seuwiere;* LL. **exaquaria* < **exaquare,* to drain off < L. *ex,* out + *aqua,* water], an underground pipe or drain used to carry off water and waste matter.

sew·er (sō'ẽr), *n.* a person or thing that sews.

sew·er (sōō'ẽr, sū'ẽr), *n.* [contr. < Anglo-Fr. *asseour;* OFr. *asseoir,* to seat, cause to sit; L. *assidere,* to sit by < *ad-,* to + *sedere,* to sit], a medieval servant of high rank in charge of serving the meals.

sew·er·age (sōō'ẽr-ij, sū'ẽr-ij), *n.* [see -AGE], 1. removal of surface water and waste matter by sewers. 2. a system of sewers. 3. sewage.

sew·ing (sō'iŋ), *n.* 1. the act or occupation of a person who sews. 2. material for sewing; needlework.

sewing circle, a group of women who make a social event of sewing.

sewing machine, a machine with a mechanically driven needle used for sewing and stitching.

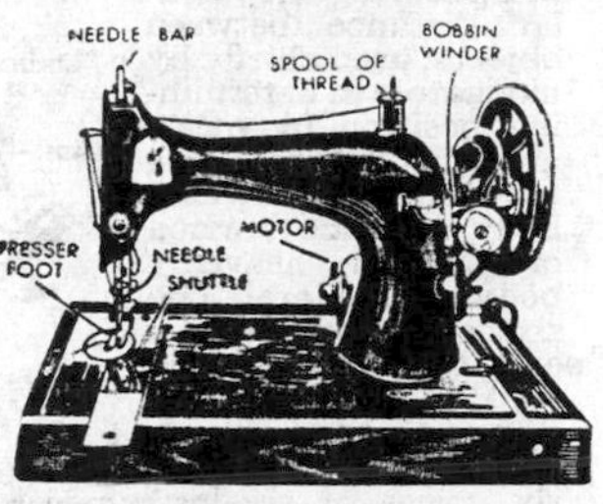

SEWING MACHINE

sewn (sōn), alternative past participle of **sew.**

sex (seks), *n.* [ME.; Late OFr. *sexe;* L. *sexus;* prob. < base of *secare,* to cut, divide], 1. either of the two divisions of organisms distinguished as male or female; males or females (especially men or women) collectively. 2. the character of being male or female; all of the things which distinguish a male from a female. 3. anything connected with sexual gratification or reproduction or the urge for these, especially the attraction of individuals of one sex for those of the other.

the fair (or **gentle, weaker**) **sex,** women.

the sterner (or **stronger**) **sex,** men.

sex- (seks), [< L. *sex,* six], a combining form meaning *six:* also **sexi-.**

sex·a·ge·nar·i·an (sek'sə-ji-nâr'i-ən), *adj.* [< L. *sexagenarius,* of sixty < *sexageni,* sixty each; + *-an*], sixty years old or between sixty and seventy. *n.* a person of this age.

sex·ag·e·nar·y (seks-aj'ə-ner'i), *adj.* [L. *sexagenarius;* see SEXAGENARIAN], 1. designating or of the number sixty. 2. proceeding by sixties. 3. sexagenarian. *n.* [*pl.* SEXAGENARIES (-iz)], a sexagenarian.

Sex·a·ges·i·ma (sek'sə-jes'i-mə), *n.* [ME. *sexagesime;* L., fem. of *sexagesimus,* sixtieth], the second Sunday before Lent: also **Sexagesima Sunday.**

sex·a·ges·i·mal (sek'sə-jes'i-m'l), *adj.* [ML. *sexagesimalis* < L. *sexagesimus,* sixtieth], of or based on the number sixty. *n.* a fraction whose denominator is sixty or a power of sixty.

sex appeal, the physical attractiveness and personal charm that attract members of the opposite sex.

sex·cen·te·nar·y (seks-sen'tə-ner'i, seks'sen-ten'ə-ri), *adj.* [*sex-* + *centenary*], of six hundred, especially six hundred years. *n.* [*pl.* SEXCENTENARIES (-iz, -riz)], a six-hundredth anniversary.

sex chromosome, a sex-determining chromosome in the germ cells of most plants and animals: fertilized eggs containing two X chromosomes (one from each parent germ cell) develop into females, those containing one X and one Y chromosome (male germ cells carry either one or the other) develop into males.

sexed (sekst), *adj.* 1. of or having sex or sexual differentiation. 2. having (a specified degree of) sexuality.

sex·en·ni·al (sek-sen'i-əl), *adj.* [< L. *sexennium,* six years < *sex,* six + *annus,* year], 1. lasting six years. 2. coming, happening, etc. every six years. *n.* a sexennial event.

sex hygiene, the branch of hygiene dealing with sex and sexual behavior as they relate to the welfare of both the individual and the community.

sex·i- (sek'si), sex-.

sex·i·ly (sek'si-li), *adv.* in a sexy manner.

sex·i·ness (sek'si-nis), *n.* the state or quality of being sexy.

sex·i·va·lent (sek'sə-vā'lənt), *adj.* 1. having six valences. 2. having a valence of six. Also, esp. for 2, **hexavalent.**

sex·less (seks'lis), *adj.* 1. lacking the characteristics of sex; asexual. 2. apparently lacking in normal sexual passion or drive; without love; sexually cold.

sex-linked (seks'liŋkt'), *adj.* in *genetics,* designating or of any factor linked to the sex chromosomes of either parent, or any character dependent on such a factor.

sex·ol·o·gy (sek-sol'ə-ji), *n.* the science dealing with human sexual behavior.

sex·par·tite (seks-pär'tīt), *adj.* [*sex-* + *partite*], of or divided into six parts.

sext (sekst), *n.* [ME. *sexte;* LL. *sexta* < L. *sexta* (*hora*), sixth (hour), fem. of *sextus,* sixth], [often S-], in *ecclesiastical usage,* 1. the fourth of the seven canonical hours: it falls at or shortly before noon, the sixth hour of the day. 2. a service held daily at this time.

sex·tain (seks′tān), *n.* [< L. *sextus*, sixth, after Eng. *quatrain*; cf. SESTINA], a stanza having six lines.

sex·tan (seks′tən), *adj.* [Mod. L. *sextanus* < L. *sextus*, sixth], occurring every sixth day, counting from the first day of occurrence. *n.* a sextan fever, etc.

Sex·tans (seks′tənz), *n.* [L.; see SEXTANT], a small southern constellation near the equator.

sex·tant (seks′tənt), *n.* [L. *sextans*, a sixth < *sex*, six: meaning an arc of the sixth part of a circle], 1. an instrument used in measuring the angular distance between objects: used chiefly by navigators in determining position by measurement of the angle between a heavenly body and the horizon or another heavenly body. 2. [Rare], one sixth of a circle.

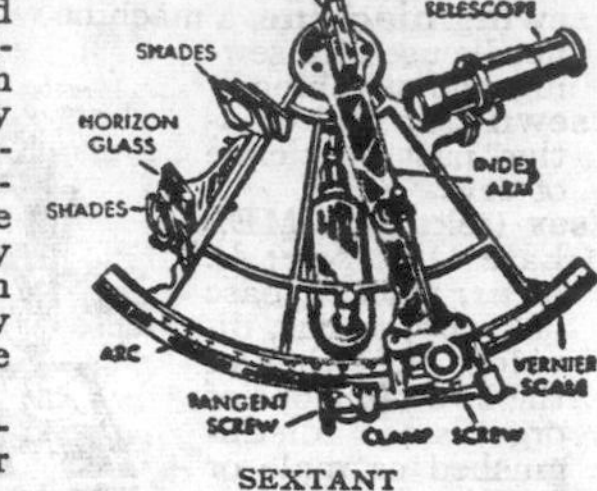

SEXTANT

sex·tet, sex·tette (seks-tet′), *n.* [altered, after L. *sex*, six < *sestet*], 1. any group of six. 2. in *music*, *a)* a composition for six voices or six instruments. *b)* the six performers of such a composition. Also **sestet**.

sex·tile (seks′t'l), *n.* [L. *sextilis* < *sex*, six], in *astrology*, the position or aspect of two heavenly bodies sixty degrees distant from each other. *adj.* in *astrology*, designating such an aspect.

sex·til·lion (seks-til′yən), *n.* [Fr. < L. *sex*, six + Fr. sep*tillion*], 1. in the United States and France, the number represented by 1 followed by 21 zeros. 2. in Great Britain and Germany, the number represented by 1 followed by 36 zeros. *adj.* amounting to one sextillion in number.

sex·to·dec·i·mo (seks′tō-des′ə-mō′), *n.* [*pl.* SEXTODECIMOS (-mōz′)], [L., abl. of *sextusdecimus*, sixteenth], 1. the page size of a book made up of printer's sheets folded into sixteen leaves, each leaf being approximately 4 1/2 by 6 3/4 inches. 2. a book consisting of pages of this size: also called *sixteenmo*, and written *16mo* or *16°*. *adj.* consisting of pages of this size.

sex·ton (seks′tən), *n.* [ME. *sextein*, altered < OFr. *secrestain*, ML. *sacristanus*; see SACRISTAN], a church official in charge of the maintenance of church property: he usually rings the church bells and sometimes digs the graves in the churchyard.

sex·tu·ple (seks′too-p'l, seks-tū′p'l), *adj.* [< L. *sextus*, sixth, after Eng. *quadruple*, *quintuple*], 1. consisting of or including six. 2. six times as much or as many; sixfold. 3. in *music*, having six beats to the measure. *n.* an amount six times as much or as many. *v.t. & v.i.* [SEXTUPLED (-p'ld), SEXTUPLING], to make or become six times larger in amount; multiply by six.

sex·tu·plet (seks′too-plit, seks-tū′plit, seks-tup′lit), *n.* [< *sextuple*], 1. *a)* one of six offspring born at a single birth. *b)* *pl.* six offspring born at a single birth. 2. a collection or group of six, usually of one kind.

sex·u·al (sek′shōō-əl), *adj.* [LL. *sexualis*], 1. of, characteristic of, or affecting sex, the sexes, the organs of sex and their functions, or sex instincts or drives. 2. in *biology*, *a)* having sex. *b)* designating or of reproduction by the union of male and female germ cells.

sex·u·al·i·ty (sek′shōō-al′ə-ti), *n.* 1. the state or quality of being sexual. 2. interest in or concern with sex.

sex·u·al·ly (sek′shōō-əl-i), *adv.* 1. in a sexual manner. 2. by means of sex. 3. with reference to sex.

sexual selection, the selection of mates, especially in the higher animals, on the basis of certain structural or functional characters, resulting in the preservation of these characters in the population.

sex·y (sek′si), *adj.* [SEXIER (-si-ēr), SEXIEST (-si-ist)], [Slang], exciting or intended to excite sexual desire; erotic; lascivious.

Sey·chelles (sā-shel′, sā-shelz′), *n.* a group of British islands in the Indian Ocean, northeast of Madagascar: area, 156 sq. mi.; pop., 35,000; capital, Victoria.

Sey·mour (sē′mōr, sē′mōr), [after Eng. family name *Seymour*; prob. < AS. *sæ*, sea, lake + *mor*, a hill], a masculine name.

Sey·mour, Jane (sē′mōr, sē′mōr), 1509?–1537; third wife of Henry VIII; mother of Edward VI.

sf., sforzando.

Sfax (sfäks), *n.* a city in Tunisia, on the Mediterranean: pop., 43,000.

Sfor·za, Count **Car·lo** (kär′lō sfôr′tsä), 1873–1952; Italian anti-Fascist statesman.

Sforza, Fran·ces·co (frän-ches′kō), Duke of Milan, 1401–1466; son of *Giacomuzzo;* Italian soldier.

Sforza, Gia·co·muz·zo (or **Mu·zi·o**) **At·ten·do·lo** (jä′kō-mōō′tsō, *or* mōō′tzi-ō, ä-ten′dō-lō′), 1369–1424; Italian soldier.

Sforza, Lu·do·vi·co (lōō′dō-vē′kō), Duke of Milan, 1451–1508; son of *Francesco;* patron of Leonardo da Vinci: called *the Moor*.

‡**sfor·zan·do** (sfôr-tsän′dō), *adj. & adv.* [It. < *sforzare*, to force], in *music*, with force or emphasis: a direction to the performer: symbol, >, ∧: abbreviated **sf.**, **sfz.**

‡**sfor·za·to** (sfôr-tsä′tō), *adj. & adv.* sforzando.

sfz., sforzando.

s.g., specific gravity.

sgd., signed.

's-Gra·ven·ha·ge (skhrä′vən-hä′khə), *n.* The Hague; a city in the Netherlands: the Dutch name.

Sgt., **sgt.**, Sergeant.

Sgt. Maj., Sergeant Major.

sh., 1. sheet. 2. shilling; shillings. 3. in *bookbinding*, sheep.

shab·bi·ly (shab′'ə-li), *adv.* in a shabby manner.

shab·bi·ness (shab′i-nis), *n.* 1. shabby quality or state. 2. shabby conduct or treatment.

shab·by (shab′i), *adj.* [SHABBIER (i-ēr), SHABBIEST (-i-ist)], [< dial. var. *shab* < AS. *sceabb*, a scab, scale; see SCAB, SCABBY], 1. broken down; worn out; unkempt; deteriorated: as, *shabby* surroundings. 2. showing much wear; old; ragged; threadbare: said of clothing. 3. wearing such clothing; seedy. 4. beggarly; mean; unworthy: as, a *shabby* offering. 5. disgraceful; shameful: as, *shabby* treatment of one's parents.

shab·by-gen·teel (shab′i-jen-tēl′), *adj.* shabby but trying to give an appearance of dignity and self-respect.

Sha·bu·oth (shä-vōō′ōth, shə-vōō′ōs), *n.pl.* [construed as sing.], [Heb. *shebuōth*, lit., weeks], a Jewish holiday, the Feast of Weeks, or Pentecost, originally celebrating the spring harvest, but now also associated with the revelation of the Law at Mount Sinai: see **Jewish holidays**.

shack (shak), *n.* [said to be contr. < Mex. *jacal* < Aztec *xacalli*, wooden hut (the transition form *shackle* was formerly in U.S. use), but influenced by & ? < *ramshack*, contr. < *ramshackle*], a small house or cabin that is crudely built and furnished; hut; shanty.

shack up, [Slang], 1. to spend the night. 2. to cohabit (*with*).

shack·le (shak′'l), *n.* [ME. *schakel;* AS. *sceacul;* akin to D. *schakel*, chain link; IE. base *(*s*)*kenk-*, to gird, bind; the AS. sense may be influenced by *sceacan*, to shake (cf. SHAKE)], 1. a metal fastening, usually one of a linked pair, for the wrists or ankles of a person kept prisoner; fetter; manacle. 2. anything that restrains freedom of expression or action. 3. any of several devices used in fastening or coupling. *v.t.* [SHACKLED (-'ld), SHACKLING], 1. to put shackles on; fetter. 2. to fasten or connect with a shackle or shackles. 3. to restrain in freedom of expression or action. —*SYN.* see **hamper**.

SHACKLES

Shack·le·ton, Sir **Ernest Henry** (shak′'l-tən), 1874–1922; British antarctic explorer.

shad (shad), *n.* [*pl.* SHAD, SHADS (shadz); see PLURAL, II, D, 2], [AS. *sceadd;* akin to Norw. dial. *skadd;* prob. IE. base **sqat-*, to leap, spring up], any of several salt-water fishes related to the herring but having a deeper body and spawning in rivers: the common shad found along the North Atlantic coast is a valuable food fish.

shad·ber·ry (shad′ber′i, shad′bēr-i), *n.* [*pl.* SHADBERRIES (-iz)], 1. a shadbush. 2. its fruit.

shad·blow (shad′blō′), *n.* a shadbush.

shad·bush (shad′boosh′), *n.* [so named from flowering when the shad appear in U.S. rivers], any of a number of related plants of the rose family, with white flowers and purple-black berries; shad-blow; Juneberry.

shad·dock (shad′ək), *n.* [after Capt. *Shaddock*, who first carried this fruit from the East to the West Indies], 1. a large, yellow, coarse-grained, pear-shaped fruit resembling a grapefruit. 2. the tree it grows on.

shade (shād), *n.* [ME. *schade;* AS. *sceadu* (genit. & dat. *sceadwe*); akin to Goth. *skadus;* IE. base **skot-*, darkness, shadow, as also in Gr. *skotos*, darkness; see SHADOW], 1. comparative darkness caused by a more or less opaque object cutting off rays of light, as from the sun. 2. an area less brightly lighted than its surroundings. 3. [Archaic or Poetic], a shadow. 4. *chiefly pl.* a retired or secluded place. 5. an indication or representation of darkness in painting, drawing, photography, etc. 6. degree of darkness of a color; gradation of a color with reference to its mixture with black: as, various *shades* of blue: cf. **tint**. 7. *a)* a small difference or variation: as, *shades* of opinion. *b)* a slight amount or degree; trace; touch; suggestion: as, a *shade* of humor in his voice. 8. [Poetic], *a)* anything lacking substance or reality; phantom. *b)* a ghost; specter; spirit. 9. any of various devices used to protect or screen from light: as, a window *shade*. *v.t.* [SHADED (-id), SHADING], 1. to protect or screen from light or heat: as, *shade* your eyes from the sun. 2. to hide or screen with or as with a shadow. 3. to darken; dim; obscure. 4. *a)* to represent the effects of shade in (a painting, photograph, etc.); add shading to. *b)* to depict in, or mark with, gradations of light or color. 5. to change by very slight degrees or gradations. 6. to lessen or reduce slightly, as a price. *v.i.* to change or vary slightly or by degrees. —*SYN.* see **color.**

in (or **into**) **the shade,** 1. in darkness or shadow. 2. in comparative obscurity: as, an author put *in the shade* by brilliant, new writers.

the shades, 1. the increasing darkness, as of evening. 2. *a)* the world of the dead; nether world; Hades. *b)* the disembodied spirits of the dead, collectively.

shad·i·ly (shād'ə-li), *adv.* in a shady manner.

shad·i·ness (shād'i-nis), *n.* a shady state or quality.

shad·ing (shād'iŋ), *n.* 1. protection or shielding against light or heat. 2. the representation of light or shade in a picture. 3. any small difference or variation, as in quality, kind, etc.

sha·doof (shä-dōōf'), *n.* [Ar. *shādūf*], a device consisting of a long, pivoted pole with a bucket on one end and a weight on the other, used in the East for raising water, especially in irrigating land.

shad·ow (shad'ō), *n.* [ME. *schadwe* < the indirect cases (dat. & genit. *sceadwe*) of AS. *sceadu,* shade (cf. SHADE)], 1. a definite area of shade cast upon a surface by a body intercepting the light rays. 2. the dark image made by such a body. 3. *pl.* the growing darkness after sunset. 4. *a)* gloom, sadness, or depression. *b)* that which casts gloom, etc. over something. 5. the shaded area of a picture. 6. a mirrored image; reflection. 7. *a)* something without reality or substance; imaginary vision. *b)* a ghost; apparition. 8. a vague indication; symbol; omen; prefiguration: as, coming events cast their *shadows* before. 9. *a)* a faint suggestion or appearance; trace: as, there's not a *shadow* of hope. *b)* remnant; vestige: as, the power of the Crown was reduced to a *shadow.* 10. a close or constant companion. 11. a person who trails another closely, as a detective or spy. 12. [Rare], protection or shelter. *v.t.* 1. [Archaic], *a)* to shelter from light or heat. *b)* to shelter; protect. 2. to throw a shadow upon; cover with shadow. 3. to make dark or gloomy; cloud. 4. to represent vaguely, mystically, or prophetically; prefigure (often with *forth*). 5. to shade in painting, drawing, etc. 6. to stay close to or follow, especially in secret so as to observe the movements and activities of: as, the detective *shadowed* the suspect.

in the shadow of, very close to; verging upon.

under the shadow of, 1. very close to; verging upon. 2. in danger of; apparently fated for.

shad·ow·box·ing (shad'ō-bok'siŋ), *n.* sparring with an imaginary opponent: an exercise used by boxers.

shad·ow·graph (shad'ō-graf', shad'ō-gräf'), *n.* [*shadow* + *-graph*], 1. an image or silhouette produced by throwing a shadow upon a lighted surface. 2. an X-ray photograph; radiograph.

shad·ow·i·ness (shad'ō-i-nis), *n.* the state or quality of being shadowy.

shad·ow·less (shad'ō-lis), *adj.* 1. casting no shadow. 2. without shade or shadow, as a lighted surface.

shad·ow·y (shad'ō-i), *adj.* 1. resembling, or of the nature of, a shadow; specifically, *a)* without reality or substance; fleeting or illusory. *b)* dim; indistinct. 2. covered with or producing shade or shadow; shaded. 3. [Obs.], vaguely indicative; symbolic.

Sha·drach (shā'drak), *n.* [Heb. *shadhrakh;* of Bab. origin], in the *Bible,* one of the three Jewish captives in Babylonia who were cast into a blazing furnace by Nebuchadnezzar and came out miraculously unharmed: Dan. 3:12: see also **Meshach, Abednego.**

Shad·well, Thomas (shad'wel, shad'wəl), 1642?–1692; English poet and playwright; poet laureate (1688–1692).

shad·y (shād'i), *adj.* [SHADIER (-i-ẽr), SHADIEST (-i-ist)], 1. giving shade. 2. shaded, as from the sun; full of shade. 3. of darkness, secrecy, or concealment; hence, 4. [Colloq.], of questionable character or honesty.

keep shady, [Slang], to stay in hiding or out of sight.

on the shady side of, beyond (a given age); older than.

SHAEF (shāf), Supreme Headquarters Allied Expeditionary Forces, in World War II.

shaft (shaft), *n.* [ME. *scheft, schaft;* AS. *sceaft;* akin to G. *schaft;* IE. base **sqep-,* etc., to cut with a sharp tool, seen also in L. *scapus,* shaft, stalk], 1. the long stem or body of an arrow or spear. 2. an arrow or spear. 3. a missile or something compared to a missile; bolt: as, *shafts* of lightning, derision, etc. 4. a cone or column of light; ray; beam. 5. a long, slender part or object, specifically, *a)* [Rare], the trunk of a tree or stem of a plant. *b)* the stem or rib of a feather. *c)* the mid section of a long bone. *d)* the supporting stem of a branched candlestick. *e)* a column or obelisk; also, the main, usually cylindrical, part between the ends of a column or pillar: see **column,** illus. *f)* a flagpole. *g)* a tall, slender building or part of a building; spire. *h)* the long, slender handle of any of several tools or implements. *i)* either of the two poles between which an animal is harnessed to a vehicle; thill. *j)* a bar supporting, or transmitting motion to, a mechanical part: as, the drive *shaft* of an engine. 6. a long, narrow opening or passage sunk into the earth, usually vertical or slanting: as, a mine *shaft:* see **mine,** illus. 7. a vertical opening passing through the floors of a building, as for an elevator. 8. a tube or conduit for the passage of air, as used in heating or ventilating.

Shaftes·bur·y (shafts'ber'i, shafts'bẽr-i, shäfts'bẽr-i), first Earl of (*Anthony Ashley Cooper*), 1621–1683; English statesman; lord chancellor (1672–1673).

shaft·ing (shaf'tiŋ), *n.* 1. a system or group of shafts, as for transmitting motion, conveying air, etc. 2. material for making shafts.

shag (shag), *n.* [< AS. *sceacga,* via ME. dial.; akin to ON. *skegg,* a beard; IE. base **(s)qeq-,* to spring forth, as also in Eng. *shake*], 1. [Rare], heavily matted wool or hair. 2. a heavy, rough nap, as on some woolen cloth. 3. cloth with such a nap. 4. any disordered or tangled mass. 5. coarsely shredded tobacco. *v.t.* [SHAGGED (shagd), SHAGGING], 1. to make shaggy or rough. 2. [Slang], in *baseball,* to chase after and catch (balls) in batting practice.

shag (shag), *n.* [specialized use of prec. word with reference to the rough crest], a small cormorant, a sea bird having a crest during the breeding season.

shag (shag), *n.* [< dial. *shag* < ME. *schaggen, schoggen,* to shake, toss; prob. < base of *shake*], a dance step, popular in the late 1930's, consisting of a fast hopping step first with one foot and then the other. *v.i.* [SHAGGED (shagd), SHAGGING], to dance the shag.

shag·bark (shag'bärk'), *n.* 1. a hickory tree with gray, shredding bark and roundish nuts. 2. its wood. 3. its nut. Also **shellbark.**

shag·gi·ly (shag'ə-li), *adv.* in a shaggy manner.

shag·gi·ness (shag'i-nis), *n.* a shaggy state or quality.

shag·gy (shag'i), *adj.* [SHAGGIER (-i-ẽr), SHAGGIEST (-i-ist)], 1. covered with or having long, coarse hair or wool. 2. carelessly groomed; unkempt: said of a person. 3. of tangled, coarse growth; straggly; scrubby. 4. having a rough nap or surface.

shaggy dog, [< such an anecdote involving a shaggy dog], [Slang], a humorous anecdote with a surprise ending involving ludicrously unreal or irrational behavior.

sha·green (shə-grēn'), *n.* [Fr. *chagrin,* Venetian *sagrin* < Turk. *saghri,* horse's back, hide], 1. rawhide with a rough, granular surface, made from the skin of the horse, camel, seal, etc. 2. the hard, rough skin of the shark or dogfish, sometimes used as a polisher.

shah (shä), *n.* [Per. *shāh,* short for *pādshāh;* see PADISHAH], a title of the ruler of Iran and the rulers of certain other Eastern lands.

Sha·hap·ti·an (shä-hap'ti-ən), *n.* a member of a subgroup of the Oregonian family of American Indians, formerly living in the upper Columbia River Valley. *adj.* designating or of this group.

Shah Ja·han (shä' jə-hän'), 1592–1666; Mogul emperor of Hindustan (1628–1658); builder of the Taj Mahal: also spelled **Shah Jehan.**

Shah·ja·han·pur (shä'jə-hän-pōōr'), *n.* a city in United Provinces, northern India: pop., 79,000.

shai·tan (shī-tän'), *n.* [Ar. *shaiṭān* < Heb. *sāṭān;* see SATAN], 1. [often S-], in *Moslem usage,* the Devil; Satan. 2. an evil being; fiend. Also spelled **sheitan.**

Shak., Shakespeare.

shake (shāk), *v.t.* [SHOOK (shook), SHAKEN (shāk''n), SHAKING], [ME. *schaken;* AS. *sceacan, scacan;* akin to LG. *schacken;* for IE. base see **SHAG** (matted wool)], 1. to cause to move up and down, back and forth, or from side to side with short, quick movements. 2. to bring, force, throw, stir up, dislodge, etc. by or as by abrupt, brisk movements. 3. to cause to quiver or tremble; vibrate: as, the wind *shook* the building. 4. *a)* to cause to totter or become unsteady. *b)* to unnerve; weaken: as, he was visibly *shaken* by the news. 5. to brandish; flourish; wave. 6. to clasp (another's hand), as in greeting. 7. [Slang], to get away from or rid of: as, he *shook* his pursuers. 8. in *dice,* to rattle (the dice) just before casting them. 9. in *music,* to trill. *v.i.* 1. to move or be moved quickly and irregularly up and down, back and forth, or from side to side; vibrate. 2. to tremble, quake, or quiver, as from cold or fear. 3. to become unsteady; totter; reel. 4. to shake hands, as in greeting. 5. in *music,* to trill. *n.* 1. an act of shaking; back-and-forth movement. 2. an unsteady or trembling movement; tremor. 3. a natural split or fissure in rock or timber. 4. [Colloq.], an earthquake. 5. [Slang], a very short time; moment: as, I'll be there in two *shakes.* 6. in *music,* a rapid alternation between two notes; trill.

give (a person or thing) the shake, [Slang], to avoid or get rid of (an undesirable person or thing).

no great shakes, [Colloq.], not of outstanding ability, importance, etc.; not unusual; ordinary.

shake down, 1. to bring down or cause to fall by

shaking, as an apple from a tree. 2. to cause to settle or become lower by shaking. 3. to condition (new equipment, etc.). 4. [Slang], to extort money from, as by blackmail.
shake hands, to clasp each other's hands as a token of agreement or friendship, or in parting or greeting.
shake off, to get away from or rid of (an undesirable person or thing).
shake out, 1. to cause to fall out by shaking, as salt from a shaker. 2. to clean or empty by shaking, as a shoe with gravel in it, a rug, etc. 3. to straighten out by shaking, as a folded or wrinkled cloth.
shake up, 1. to shake, especially so as to mix or blend. 2. to disturb or rouse by or as by shaking. 3. to jar or shock. 4. to redistribute by or as by shaking.
the shakes, [Colloq.], a convulsive trembling, often accompanying intermittent fever, alcoholism, etc.
SYN.—**shake** is the general word for a moving up and down or back and forth with quick, short motions; **tremble** implies such an involuntary shaking of the body as to suggest a loss of co-ordination or control, as from fear, fatigue, etc. (she *trembled* at the lion's roar); **quake** usually suggests a relatively violent trembling, as in great agitation (to *quake* in one's boots with dread); **quiver** suggests a slight, tremulous vibration, as of a taut string that has been plucked (the leaves *quivered* in the breeze); **shiver** implies a slight, momentary quivering of the body, as from cold or in fearful apprehension (he *shivered* at the thought of facing them); **shudder** implies a sudden, convulsive quivering, as in horror or revulsion (she *shuddered* at the grisly sight); **wobble** suggests a shaking or tottering that connotes instability (the chair *wobbled* on its unsteady legs).

shake·down (shāk′doun′), *n.* 1. a crude, makeshift bed, as of straw on the floor. 2. [Slang], an extortion of money, as by blackmail. *adj.* [Colloq.], for testing the performance or operational characteristics or acclimating the personnel: as, the *shakedown* cruise of a new battleship.

shak·en (shāk′ən), past participle of **shake.**

Shak·er (shāk′ẽr), *n.* [so called by others from movements of a dance constituting a part of their ritual], a member of a religious sect observing a doctrine of celibacy, common property, and community living.

shak·er (shāk′ẽr), *n.* 1. a person or thing that shakes. 2. a device used in shaking, especially in mixing or blending.

Shaker Heights, a city in northeastern Ohio: suburb of Cleveland: pop., 36,000.

Shak·er·ism (shāk′ẽr-iz′m), *n.* the doctrines or practices of the Shakers.

Shake·speare, William (shāk′spêr′), 1564–1616; English poet and dramatist: called the *Bard of Avon:* also spelled **Shakspere, Shaksper, Shakespere,** etc.: abbreviated **Shak., Shaks., Sh.**

Shake·spear·e·an, Shake·spear·i·an (shāk-spêr′i-ən), *adj.* of or like Shakespeare, his works, or style. *n.* a scholar specializing in Shakespeare and his works.

Shake·spear·e·an·ism, Shake·spear·i·an·ism (shāk-spêr′i-ən-iz′m), *n.* 1. Shakespearean style. 2. a Shakespearean expression.

Shakespearean sonnet, a sonnet composed of three groups of four lines each (*quatrains*) typically with the rhyme scheme *abab cdcd efef,* and a final couplet with the rhyme *gg:* also called *Elizabethan sonnet.*

shake-up (shāk′up′), *n.* a shaking up; specifically, a reorganization of a drastic or extensive nature, as in policy or personnel.

shak·i·ly (shāk′ə-li), *adv.* in a shaky manner; insecurely; weakly; tremblingly.

shak·i·ness (shāk′i-nis), *n.* a shaky quality or state.

shak·ing (shāk′iŋ), *n.* 1. the act of a person or thing that shakes. 2. the ague or a chill.

shaking palsy, a chronic degenerative disease of the central nervous system, characterized by tremors, muscular rigidity, weakness, and a masklike expression.

shak·o (shak′ō), *n.* [*pl.* SHAKOS (-ōz)], [Fr. *schako;* Hung. *csákó* < G. *zacke,* a peak, point], 1. a stiff, cylindrical military dress hat, usually with a flat top and a plume. 2. a large military dress hat made of fur.

Shaks., Shakespeare.

Shak·spere, Shak·sper (shāk′spêr), *n.* Shakespeare.

Shak·sper·i·an (shāk-spêr′i-ən), *adj.* Shakespearian.

Shak·ti (shuk′ti), *n.* [Sans. *śakti*], in *Hinduism,* 1. [s-], power. 2. the female principle or generative power. 3. Devi. Also **Sakti.**

Shak·tism (shuk′tiz′m), *n.* Shakti worship: also **Saktism.**

shak·y (shāk′i), *adj.* [SHAKIER (-i-ẽr), SHAKIEST (-i-ist)], 1. not firm, substantial, or secure; weak; unsound; unsteady, as a structure. 2. shaking; trembling; tremulous. 3. not dependable or reliable; questionable, as a person or his word.

shale (shāl), *n.* [a use of obs. *shale,* a shell < AS. *scealu,* a shell], a kind of fine-grained rock formed by the hardening of clay: it splits into thin layers when broken.

SHAKO

shale oil, a dark mineral oil derived from bituminous shale or brown coal.

shall (shal), *v.* [past tense SHOULD (shood); *archaic* 2d pers. sing., present tense, SHALT (shalt); *archaic* 2d pers. sing., past tense, SHOULDEST (shood′ist), SHOULDST (shoodst); no other forms now in use], [ME. *schal,* pl. *schullen;* AS. *sceal,* inf. *sceolan;* akin to G. *soll* (*sollen*); IE. base **sqel-,* to be indebted, obligated, guilty, which may be a special sense < **squel-,* to cut, with basic sense "to be liable to fine for killing, i.e., cutting"], an auxiliary used in formal speech: 1. to express futurity in the first person, and determination, compulsion, obligation, or necessity in the second and third persons. 2. in a question expecting *shall* in the answer. 3. in laws and resolutions: as, the fine *shall* not exceed $100. 4. in subordinate clauses introduced by *if, when,* etc. These formal conventions, however, do not reflect prevailing usage in which *shall* and *will* are used interchangeably, with *will* predominating in all persons. See also **will, should, would.**

shal·loon (sha-lōōn′, shə-lōōn′), *n.* [Fr. *chalon* < *Châlons-sur-Marne,* France], a twilled woolen fabric used largely for linings.

shal·lop (shal′əp), *n.* [Fr. *chaloupe;* D. *sloep,* sloop; cf. JALOPY], a small open boat fitted with oars or sails or both; dinghy.

shal·lot (shə-lot′), *n.* [obs. Fr. *eschalotte,* altered < *eschaloigne;* see SCALLION], 1. an onionlike plant whose clustered bulbs, resembling garlic but milder, are used for flavoring. 2. a small onion.

shal·low (shal′ō), *adj.* [ME. *schalowe;* prob. < the stem **scealw-* of AS. *scealu* < base of *sceald,* shallow (cf. SHOAL)], 1. not deep: as, a *shallow* stream. 2. lacking depth of character, intellect, or meaning; superficial. *n.* a shallow place in a body of water; shoal. *v.t. & v.i.* to make or become shallow. —***SYN.*** see **superficial.**

shalt (shalt), archaic second person singular, present indicative, of **shall:** used with *thou.*

shal·y (shāl′i), *adj.* [SHALIER (-i-ẽr), SHALIEST (-i-ist)], of, like, or containing shale.

sham (sham), *n.* [prob. < a northern dial. var. of *shame*], 1. formerly, a trick or fraud. 2. an imitation that is meant to deceive; counterfeit; deception; fake. 3. a person who falsely affects a certain character. 4. an ornamental cover simulating some piece of personal or household linen: as, a pillow *sham.* *adj.* not genuine or real; false; counterfeit. *v.t.* [SHAMMED (shamd), SHAMMING], 1. [Rare], to cheat or trick. 2. to be or make an imitation or false show of; counterfeit; feign. *v.i.* to pretend to be what one is not; make false pretenses. —***SYN.*** see **false.**

sha·man (shä′mən, sham′ən, shā′mən), *n.* [*pl.* SHAMANS (-mənz, -ənz)], [Russ.; Tungusic *samān;* Prakrit *śamana,* Buddhist monk < Sans. *śramaṇa,* orig., ascetic; cf. *śram,* to exhaust, fatigue], a priest or medicine man of shamanism.

sha·man·ic (shə-man′ik), *adj.* of a shaman or shamanism.

sha·man·ism (shä′mən-iz′m, sham′ən-iz′m, shā′mən-iz′m), *n.* 1. the religion of certain peoples of northeast Asia, based on the doctrine that the workings of good and evil spirits can be influenced only by the shamans. 2. any similar religion, as of some American Indians.

sha·man·is·tic (shä′mən-is′tik, sham′ən-is′tik, shā′mən-is′tik), *adj.* of or like shamanism.

Sha·mash (shä′mäsh), *n.* [Assyr.], in *Assyro-Babylonian religion,* the sun god, responsible for summer warmth and the success of crops, and a symbol for justice.

sham·ble (sham′b'l), *v.i.* [SHAMBLED (-b'ld), SHAMBLING], [< obs. *shamble, adj.,* in *shamble legs;* prob. < *shamble, n.,* in obs. sense of stool, bench], to walk in a lazy or clumsy manner, barely lifting the feet. *n.* a shambling walk or gait.

sham·bles (sham′b'lz), *n.pl.* [construed as sing.], [ME. *schamel,* a bench; AS. *scamel, sceamul,* a bench or stool; ult. < L. *scamellum,* dim. < *scamnum,* a bench; present meaning derives from the use of a bench in the sale of meat], 1. *a*) a place where meat is sold; butcher's shop. *b*) [British], *in sing.* a bench or stall for the sale of meat. 2. a slaughterhouse. 3. a place where much killing has been done; scene of bloodshed or carnage: sometimes extended to mean any scene or condition of great destruction or disorder, as, the children left the house a *shambles.*

shame (shām), *n.* [ME. *schame;* AS. *scamu;* akin to G. *scham;* IE. base *(*s*)*kam-,* to hide, cover; basic sense "a covering up"; base seen also in L. *camisia,* shirt (cf. CAMISADO, CHEMISE)], 1. a disturbed or painful feeling of guilt, incompetence, indecency, or blameworthiness. 2. a tendency to have feelings of this kind. 3. dishonor; disgrace: as, he brings *shame* upon his name. 4. a person or thing that brings shame, dishonor, or disgrace. 5. something regrettable, unfortunate, or outrageous: as, it's a *shame* that they were cheated. *v.t.* [SHAMED (shāmd), SHAMING], 1. to cause to feel shame; make ashamed. 2. to dishonor; disgrace. 3. to drive, force, or impel by a sense of shame: as, he was

shamed out of his prejudice. —*SYN.* see **disgrace.**
for shame! you ought to be ashamed!; here is cause for shame!
put to shame, 1. to cause to feel shame. 2. to do much better than; surpass; outshine.
shame on, shame should be felt by; this is shameful of.

shame·faced (shām′fāst′), *adj.* [altered, by folk etym. < ME. *schamfast;* AS. *scam-fæst; scam,* shame + *fæst,* fast, firm], 1. extremely modest; bashful; shy. 2. showing a feeling of shame or guilt; ashamed.

shame·fac·ed·ly (shām′fās′id-li, shām′fāst′li), *adv.* in a shamefaced manner.

shame·fac·ed·ness (shām′fās′id-nis, shām′fāst′nis), *n.* the state of being shamefaced.

shame·ful (shām′fəl), *adj.* 1. bringing or causing shame or disgrace; disgraceful. 2. violating what is considered to be just, moral, or decent; offensive.

shame·less (shām′lis), *adj.* 1. having no feeling of shame, modesty, or decency; brazen; impudent. 2. showing such lack of feeling, as an action.

sham·mer (sham′ẽr), *n.* a person who shams.

sham·my (sham′i), *n.* [*pl.* SHAMMIES (-iz)], [Fr. *chamois*], chamois.

Sha·mo (shä′mō′), *n.* the Gobi desert: Chinese name.

sham·poo (sham-pōō′), *v.t.* [SHAMPOOED (-pōōd′), SHAMPOOING], [Hind. *chāmpo,* imperative of *chāmpnā,* to press, knead, shampoo], 1. to massage. 2. to wash (the hair and scalp), usually with a specially prepared soap, etc. 3. to wash the hair and scalp of. *n.* 1. the washing of the hair and scalp. 2. a preparation, as of soap, used for shampooing.

sham·rock (sham′rok), *n.* [Ir. *seamrog,* dim. of *seamar,* clover], any of certain clovers or cloverlike plants with leaflets in groups of three, used as the emblem of Ireland.

SHAMROCK

Shan (shän, shan), *n.* 1. a member of a group of Mongoloid tribes who live in Indo-China. 2. their Thai language.

shan·dry·dan (shan′dri-dan′), *n.* [< North West Brit. dial. *shandry,* a cart], [Dial.], 1. a two-wheeled chaise or cart. 2. any decrepit vehicle.

shan·dy·gaff (shan′di-gaf′), *n.* [prob. a university alteration of Cockney *shanti o' gaffer,* pot of beer < *shanty* in the Cockney sense "beer house"], a beverage of ale or beer mixed with ginger ale or ginger beer.

Shang·hai (shaŋ′hī′, shäŋ′hī′), *n.* a seaport in Kiangsu province, east central China, near the mouth of the Yangtze River: pop., 4,301,000 (est. 1947).

Shang·hai (shaŋ′hī; *also, for v.,* shaŋ-hī′), *n.* [< *Shanghai,* China], a kind of chicken with long, feathered legs: ancestor of the Cochin and Brahma. *v.t.* [SHANGHAIED (-hīd, -hīd′), SHANGHAIING], [s-], 1. [orig. said of sailors thus kidnapped for crew duty on the China run], to kidnap, usually by drugging, for service aboard ship. 2. [Slang], to induce (another) to do something through force or underhanded methods.

Shan·gri-La (shaŋ′gri-lä′), *n.* [< the scene of James Hilton's novel, *Lost Horizon*], 1. any imaginary, idyllic utopia or hidden paradise. 2. *a)* the mythical starting place of the bombing raid over Tokyo and other cities, April 18, 1942; hence, *b)* any secret starting place of bombing raids or other military operations: the term was first used in this sense by Franklin Roosevelt.

Shan·hai·kwan (shän′hī′gwän′), *n.* a city in Hopeh, China, at eastern end of Chinese Wall: pop., 80,000.

shank (shaŋk), *n.* [ME. *schanke;* AS. *scanc, sceanca;* akin to base of G. *schenkel,* thigh; IE. base **sqeng-,* to squat, stoop, bend], 1. the lower part of the leg; part between the knee and the ankle in man or a corresponding part in ‡animals. 2. the whole leg. 3. a cut of beef from the upper foreleg or hind leg. 4. the part, usually straight or stemlike, between the top or handle and the working part; shaft: said of instruments, tools, etc. 5. the whole of a piece of type exclusive of the printing surface; body. 6. *a)* the narrow part of a shoe sole in front of the heel. *b)* the piece of metal, etc. that gives it form. 7. [Colloq.], the end or latter part of anything: as, the *shank* of the journey. 8. in *botany,* a footstalk. *v.i.* in *botany,* to decay and fall off a diseased footstalk, as a flower.
ride (or **go**) **on shank's mare,** to walk.
shank of the evening, [Colloq.], 1. originally, the end or latter part of the evening (afternoon); twilight. 2. the beginning or early part of the evening (night).

Shan·non (shan′ən), *n.* a river in Ireland, flowing southwestward into the Atlantic: length, 250 mi.

shan·ny (shan′i), *n.* [< Brit. dial. *shan*], a mottled green salt-water fish; European smooth blenny.

Shan·si (shan′sē′; Chin. shän′sē′), *n.* a province of northeastern China: area, 66,265 sq. mi.; pop., 15,222,000 (est. 1947); capital, Taiyuan.

Shan States, native states of northeastern Burma, including the *Northern* and *Southern Shan States*: area, c. 60,000 sq. mi.; pop., 1,506,000.

shan't (shant, shänt), shall not.

shant·ey (shan′ti, shän′ti), *n.* [*pl.* SHANTIES (-tiz)], a chantey, a sailor's work song: also **shanty.**

Shan·tung (shan′tuŋ′, shän′dooŋ′), *n.* 1. a province of northeastern China, on the Yellow Sea: area, 57,851 sq. mi.; pop., 39,289,000 (est. 1947); capital, Tsinan. 2. a peninsula in the eastern part of this province. 3. [sometimes s-], a silk fabric made from the silk of wild silkworms: it is usually undyed. 4. [sometimes s-], a somewhat similar rayon or cotton fabric.

shan·ty (shan′ti), *n.* [*pl.* SHANTIES (-tiz)], [< Canad. Fr. *chantier,* workshop, applied to lumberers' living quarters], a small, shabby dwelling; shack; hut.

shan·ty·town (shan′ti-toun′), *n.* 1. the section of a city where there are many shanties or ramshackle houses. 2. the inhabitants of such a section.

Shao·hing (shou′shiŋ′), *n.* a city in Chekiang province, eastern China: pop., 300,000.

shape (shāp), *n.* [ME. *schap(e);* AS. *(ge)sceap,* created thing < *scieppan,* to create, form; IE. base *(*s*)*qep-,* etc., to make with a sharp tool, as also in L. *capo* (cf. CAPON), Eng. *shaft*], 1. the quality of a thing that depends on the relative position of all points composing its outline or external surface; physical or spatial form. 2. the form characteristic of a particular person or thing. 3. the contour of the body, exclusive of the face; figure. 4. assumed or feigned appearance; guise: as, an enemy in the *shape* of a friend. 5. an imaginary or spectral form; phantom. 6. something having a particular shape, used as a mold or basis for shaping or fashioning; form, as for making hats, molding gelatin, etc. 7. any of the forms, structures, etc. in which a thing may exist or be embodied: as, dangers of every *shape.* 8. definite, regular, or suitable form; orderly arrangement: as, his story began to take *shape.* 9. [Colloq.], condition; state, especially of health: as, the injured man was in bad *shape.* *v.t.* [SHAPED (shāpt), SHAPED or *archaic* SHAPEN (-'n), SHAPING], 1. to give definite shape to; make, as by cutting or molding material. 2. to arrange, fashion, express, or devise in definite form, as a plan, answer, etc. 3. to adapt or adjust: as, *shape* your plans to your abilities. 4. to direct or conduct, as one's life, the course of events, etc. 5. [Obs.], to appoint; decree; ordain. *v.i.* 1. [Rare], to become suited; conform. 2. [Rare], to come about; happen. 3. [Colloq.], to take shape or form (often with *into*). —*SYN.* see **form, make.**
shape up, [Colloq.], 1. to develop to a definite form, condition, etc. 2. to develop satisfactorily or favorably.
take shape, to come to have definite form, condition, etc.; show distinct development.

shape·less (shāp′lis), *adj.* 1. without distinct or regular shape or form; hence, 2. not pleasing to the eye; without symmetry; unshapely.

shape·li·ness (shāp′li-nis), *n.* the state or quality of being shapely.

shape·ly (shāp′li), *adj.* [SHAPELIER (-li-ẽr), SHAPELIEST (-li-ist)], having good shape or form; pleasing to the eye; well-proportioned.

shap·er (shāp′ẽr), *n.* a person or thing that shapes material, etc.

Shap·ley, Har·low (här′lō shap′li), 1885– ; American astronomer.

Sha·ra (shär′ə), *n.* Sharra.

shard (shärd), *n.* [ME. *scheard;* AS. *sceard* < *scieran, sceran,* to shear, separate; cf. SHEAR], 1. a fragment or broken piece, especially of pottery; potsherd. 2. the thin, hard wing cover of a beetle or weevil. 3. any thin, hard covering; shell; plate. Also **sherd.**

share (shâr), *n.* [ME. *schare;* AS. *scearu* < *sceran,* to cut; cf. SHEAR], 1. a part or portion which is alloted or belongs to an individual; part contributed by one. 2. a just, due, reasonable, or full share: as, everyone has done his *share* of work, we had our *share* of laughs. 3. any of the parts or portions into which the ownership of a piece of property is divided; especially, any one of the equal parts into which the capital stock of a corporation is divided. Abbreviated **shr.** (*sing. & pl.*). *v.t.* [SHARED (shârd), SHARING], 1. to distribute in shares; divide in portions; apportion. 2. to have a share of together with others; use, experience, enjoy, endure, etc. in common (sometimes with *with*): as, *share* the candy with your playmates. *v.i.* to have or take a share or part; participate (often with *in*).
go shares, to take part jointly; be equally concerned, as in an enterprise.

on shares, with each person concerned taking a (usually equal) share of the profit or loss.

SYN.—**share** means to use, enjoy, possess, etc. in common with others and generally connotes a giving or receiving a part of something (to *share* expenses, glory, etc.); **participate** implies a taking part with others in some activity, enterprise, etc. (to *participate* in the talks); **partake** implies a taking one's share, as of a meal, responsibility, etc. (to *partake* of a friend's hospitality).

share (shâr), *n.* [ME. *schar;* AS. *scear* < *sceran,* to cut; cf. SHEAR], the part of a plow or other agricultural tool that cuts the soil; plowshare.

share·crop (shâr′krop′), *v.i. & v.t.* [SHARECROPPED (-kropt′), SHARECROPPING], to work (land) as a sharecropper.

share·crop·per (shâr′krop′ẽr), *n.* a tenant farmer who works the land for a share of the crop.

share·hold·er (shâr′hōl′dẽr), *n.* a person who holds or owns a share or shares.

Sha·ri (shä′ri), *n.* a river in central Africa, flowing northwestward into Lake Chad: length, 1,400 mi.: French name, *Chari.*

shark (shärk), *n.* [prob. < G. *schurke,* scoundrel, rogue, sharper], 1. a viciously dishonest person; swindler; cheat. 2. [Slang], a person having great ability in a given activity; adept; expert. *v.t.* [Archaic], to get by fraud or strategems. *v.i.* to live by such methods.

shark (shärk), *n.* [prob. same word as prec.], any of several large fishes, mostly marine, with a tough, spiny, slate-gray skin, separate lateral gill openings, and a slender, rounded body with the mouth on the underside: most sharks are fish-eaters and the larger ones will attack man.

shark·skin (shärk′skin′), *n.* 1. leather made from the skin of a shark. 2. a cloth of cotton or rayon, with a smooth, silky surface, used for summer suits, etc. 3. *a)* a small, pebbly pattern woven into fabric. *b)* fabric woven with such a pattern.

Shar·on (shâr′ən), [< *Sharon* (in Palestine); ? contr. of *Rose of Sharon*], a feminine name.

Shar·on (shâr′ən), *n.* 1. a city in western Pennsylvania: pop., 25,000. 2. a plain along the coast of Israel, between Mt. Carmel and Jaffa.

sharp (shärp), *adj.* [ME. *scherpe, scharpe;* AS. *scearp;* akin to G. *scharf;* IE. base **(s)qereb-* < **(s)qer-,* to cut, seen also in L. *caro* (*carnis*), flesh, orig., cut-off piece of flesh (cf. CARNAL)], 1. suitable for use in cutting or piercing; having a thin edge or fine point; keen. 2. having a point or edge; not rounded or obtuse; peaked: as, a *sharp* ridge, features, etc.; hence, 3. not gradual; abrupt; acute: as, a *sharp* turn or rise; hence, 4. clearly defined; distinct; clear: as, a *sharp* difference. 5. made up of hard, angular particles, as sand. 6. quick, acute, or penetrating in perception or intellect; clever; shrewd. 7. showing or having a keen awareness; attentive; vigilant: as, *sharp* eyes, *sharp* lookout. 8. crafty; designing; underhanded. 9. harsh; biting; severe, as language, temper, criticism, etc. 10. violent or impetuous, as an attack. 11. brisk; active; vigorous: as, a *sharp* run, encounter, etc. 12. having a keen effect on the senses or emotions; specifically, *a)* cold; cutting, as the wind. *b)* severe; intense; acute; keen, as pain, grief, appetite, etc. *c)* strong; biting; pungent, as in taste or smell. *d)* high-pitched; shrill; piercing: said of sound. *e)* brilliant; intense: as, a *sharp* flash of light. 13. [Slang], attractively dressed or groomed; good-looking; handsome; beautiful. 14. in *music, a)* raised in pitch by a semitone or half step: as, A *sharp* (A♯). *b)* out of tune by being above true pitch. *c)* with the signature in sharps: as, a *sharp* key. Opposed to *flat.* 15. in *phonetics,* voiceless. *n.* 1. *usually in pl.* a sewing needle with an extremely fine point. 2. [Colloq.], an expert or adept. 3. [Colloq.], a sharper. 4. in *music, a)* a note or tone one half step above another. *b)* the symbol (♯) indicating such a note: opposed to *flat.* *v.t.* in *music,* to make sharp; raise a half step or semitone. *v.i.* in *music,* to sing or play above true pitch. *adv.* 1. in a sharp manner; specifically, *a)* abruptly or briskly. *b)* attentively or alertly. *c)* so as to have a sharp point or edge. *d)* keenly; piercingly. *e)* in *music,* above the true pitch. 2. precisely; promptly; exactly: as, they came at one o'clock *sharp.*

SYN.—**sharp** and **keen** both apply to that which is cutting, biting, incisive, or piercing, as because of a fine edge, but **sharp** more often implies a harsh cutting quality (a *sharp* pain, tongue, flavor, etc.) and **keen,** a pleasantly biting or stimulating quality (*keen* wit, delight, etc.); **acute** literally implies sharp-pointedness and figuratively suggests a penetrating or poignant quality (*acute* hearing, distress, etc.). —*ANT.* dull.

Sharp, William (shärp), (pseudonym *Fiona Macleod*), 1856?–1905; Scottish poet, scholar, and novelist.

sharp-cut (shärp′kut′), *adj.* 1. cut or shaped so as to be sharp. 2. clearly outlined or defined; clear; distinct.

sharp-eared (shärp′ẽrd′), *adj.* 1. having pointed ears. 2. having keenly sensitive hearing.

sharp-edged (shärp′ejd′), *adj.* having a fine edge or edges; cutting; sharp.

sharp·en (shär′p'n), *v.t. & v.i.* to make or become sharp or sharper.

sharp·er (shär′pẽr), *n.* a person, usually a gambler, who is dishonest in dealing with others; cheat; swindler.

sharp-eyed (shärp′īd′), *adj.* seeing things that are hard to see; having keen sight or perception.

sharp·ie (shär′pi), *n.* [< *sharp,* with reference to the sharp lines and fast sailing qualities], a long, narrow, flat-bottomed, New England fishing boat: it has a centerboard and one or two masts, each rigged with a triangular sail.

sharp-nosed (shärp′nōzd′), *adj.* 1. having a thin, pointed nose. 2. having a sharp, projecting front. 3. having a keen sense of smell.

sharp-set (shärp′set′), *adj.* 1. intensely desirous; having a keen appetite or longing, as for food. 2. set so as to be sharp or at an acute angle.

sharp·shoot·er (shärp′shōōt′ẽr), *n.* 1. a person who shoots with great accuracy; good marksman. 2. in the *United States Army, a)* a rating of proficiency of a rifleman, ranking above a marksman and below an expert. *b)* a soldier with this rating.

sharp-sight·ed (shärp′sīt′id), *adj.* 1. having keen sight; sharp-eyed. 2. sharp-witted; keenly observant.

sharp-tongued (shärp′tuŋd′), *adj.* using or characterized by severe, sharp, or harshly critical language.

sharp-wit·ted (shärp′wit′id), *adj.* having or showing keen intelligence or discernment; thinking quickly and effectively.

Shar·ra (shär′ə), *n.* 1. [*pl.* SHARRA], one of a Mongoloid people living in Outer Mongolia. 2. the East Mongolic language of the Sharra. Also spelled **Shara.**

Shas·ta, Mount (shas′tə), a mountain in northern California: height, 14,162 ft.

Shasta daisy, [after Mt. *Shasta,* California], 1. a kind of daisylike chrysanthemum. 2. its flower.

Shatt-al-A·rab (shat′əl-ä′räb, shät′əl-ä-räb′), *n.* the confluence of the Tigris and Euphrates Rivers, flowing 120 mi. to the Persian Gulf.

shat·ter (shat′ẽr), *v.t.* [ME. *schateren,* var. of *scateren,* to scatter], 1. to break or burst into pieces suddenly, as with a blow. 2. to damage severely, as a structure, one's health or nerves, etc.; destroy; wreck; disable. 3. [Obs.], to scatter. *v.i.* to break or burst into pieces; be damaged; smash. *n. pl.* broken pieces; fragments: chiefly in *in* or *into shatters.* —*SYN.* see **break.**

shat·ter·proof (shat′ẽr-prōōf′), *adj.* that will not shatter.

shave (shāv), *v.t.* [SHAVED (shāvd), SHAVED or SHAVEN (shāv′'n), SHAVING], [ME. *schaven;* AS. *sceafan;* akin to G. *schaben;* IE. base **sqebh-,* etc., to cut, as also in L. *scabere,* to shave; cf. SHAPE], 1. to cut or scrape away a thin slice or slices from, as the edge of a plank; hence, 2. to cut or scrape into thin sections, as ice. 3. to cut off (hair, especially the beard) at the surface of the skin (often with *off* or *away*). 4. to cut the hair to the surface of (an area of the body); cut the beard of (a person). 5. to pass close to or skim the surface of; graze. 6. to cut short or trim closely, as grass; hence, 7. [Colloq.], to lower by a slight margin, as a price. 8. [Colloq.], in *commerce,* to purchase (a note, draft, etc.) at a discount greater than the legal rate of interest. *v.i.* 1. to cut off hair or beard with a razor or shaver; shave oneself. 2. to be hard or grasping in bargaining or dealing. *n.* 1. a tool used for shaving, paring, slicing, etc. 2. something shaved or sliced off; shaving. 3. the act of shaving the beard or the result of this: as, a sharp razor means a good *shave.* 4. [Colloq.], a near approach without actual encounter or contact; narrow miss or escape: as, a close *shave.*

shave·ling (shāv′liŋ), *n.* 1. a person whose head is entirely or partly shaved, especially a priest or monk: used contemptuously. 2. a youth.

shav·en (shāv′'n), alternative past participle of **shave.** *adj.* 1. shaved or tonsured. 2. closely trimmed.

shav·er (shāv′ẽr), *n.* 1. a person who shaves. 2. an instrument used in shaving: as, an electric *shaver.* 3. a person who is hard or grasping in bargaining. 4. [Colloq.], a boy; youngster; lad.

shave·tail (shāv′tāl′), *n.* [orig., an unbroken mule; hence ? in allusion to the new, untrained mules formerly sent to the Quartermaster Corps with closely bobbed tails], [Slang], a second lieutenant, especially one recently appointed.

Sha·vi·an (shā′vi-ən), *adj.* [< Mod. L. *Shavius,* Latinized < *Shaw*], of or characteristic of George Bernard Shaw or his work. *n.* an admirer of Shaw or his work.

shav·ing (shāv′iŋ), *n.* 1 .the action of a person or thing that shaves. 2. something shaved off, especially a thin slice of wood or metal.

shaving brush, a short, cylindrical brush used to spread lather on the face, etc. in shaving.

shaving cream, a creamy salve used to moisten and soften the beard in shaving.

shaw (shô), *n.* [ME. *shawe;* AS. *sceaga;* akin to ON. *skagi;* for IE. base see SHAG (matted wool)], [Archaic or Dial.], a clump of bushes or trees; thicket; copse.

Shaw, George Bernard (shô), 1856–1950; Irish dramatist and critic; received Nobel prize in literature, 1925.

Shaw, Henry Wheel·er (hwēl′ẽr), (pseudonym *Josh Billings*), 1818–1885; American humorist.

Shaw, Thomas Edward, see **Lawrence, T.E.**

shawl (shôl), *n.* [Per. *shāl,* via Urdu], an oblong or square cloth worn, especially by women, as a covering for the head or shoulders.

shawm (shôm), *n.* [ME. *shalmeye, schalme,* etc.; OFr. *chalemie,* altered < *chalamel;* LL. *calamellus,* dim. of L. *calamus,* a reed], a double-reed wind instrument resembling the oboe: now obsolete.

Shaw·nee (shô-nē′, shô′nē), *n.* [*pl.* SHAWNEE, SHAWNEES (-nēz′)], [< Am. Ind. (Algonquian); cf. Shawnee *Shawunogi,* southerners < *shawun,* south], 1. a member of a tribe of Algonquian Indians that migrated from the Savannah River Valley into Ohio and Indiana and now live in Oklahoma. 2. a city in central Oklahoma: pop., 24,000.

shay (shā), *n.* [back-formation < *chaise,* assumed as pl.], [Colloq.], a light carriage; chaise.

Shays, Daniel (shāz), 1747?–1825; American soldier; leader of a popular insurrection (*Shays' Rebellion*) in western Massachusetts in 1786–1787.

she (shē; *unstressed* shi), *pron.* [for *pl.* see THEY], [ME. *sche, scho;* prob. formed after AS. *seo,* fem. def. article; orig. replacing AS. *heo,* she, only in those East Midland & Northern dialects of ME. in which phonetic change had leveled AS. *eo* under *e,* hence, *heo,* she, with *he,* he; later generalized; Brit. Western dialects still have (*h*)*u* < AS. *heo* as the regular fem. pron.], the girl, woman, or female animal (or, sometimes, the object regarded as female) previously mentioned: *she* is the nominative case form, *her* the objective, *her* or *hers* the possessive, and *herself* the intensive and reflexive, of the feminine third personal pronoun. *n.* a girl, woman, or female animal: as, our dog is a *she.*

she- (shē), a combining form meaning *female,* used in hyphenated compounds, as *she-bear.*

shea (shē), *n.* [Mandingo *si, se*], an African tree whose seeds yield a thick, white fat (*shea butter*) used as a food, etc.

sheaf (shēf), *n.* [*pl.* SHEAVES (shēvz)], [ME. *schefe;* AS. *sceaf;* akin to G. *schaub(e);* IE. **sqeup-,* **sqeubh-,* a clump, bundle], 1. a bunch of cut stalks of grain, etc. bound up in a bundle. 2. a quiverful of arrows, usually 24 in number. 3. a collection of things set or bound together; bundle, as of papers. *v.t.* to arrange or bind in a sheaf or sheaves, as grain.

shear (shêr), *v.t.* [SHEARED (shêrd), SHEARED or SHORN (shôrn), SHEARING], [ME. *scheren;* AS. *sceran;* akin to G. *scheren;* IE. base **sqer-,* to cut; cf. SHIRE], 1. to cut with shears or a similar sharp-edged instrument. 2. to remove (the hair, wool, etc.) by cutting or clipping. 3. to cut or clip the hair, wool, etc. from. 4. to strip or divest (*of* a power, right, etc.). 5. [Dial.], to reap with a sickle. *v.i.* 1. *a*) to use a cutting tool, as shears, in trimming or cutting wool, shrubbery, metal, etc. *b*) [Dial.], to use a sickle in reaping. 2. to come apart or break under the action of shearing stress. 3. to move by or as if by cutting: as, the plane *sheared* through the clouds. *n.* [ME. *schere;* AS. *scear*], 1. *a*) [Rare], a pair of large scissors; shears. *b*) a single blade of such a pair. 2. any machine used in cutting metal, especially sheet metal. 3. the action, process, or result of shearing. 4. something shorn or removed by shearing, as a sheep or its wool. 5. a shearing: used in designating a sheep's age: as, a sheep of three *shears.* 6. *a*) shearing stress. *b*) any strain or distortion in shape resulting from the action of shearing stress.

shear·ing (shêr′iŋ), *n.* 1. the action or process of cutting with or as with shears. 2. something cut off with shears, as the amount of wool cut from sheep.

shearing stress, the action or force causing two contacting parts or layers to slide upon each other, moving apart in opposite directions parallel to the plane of their contact.

shear·ling (shêr′liŋ), *n.* [see SHEAR & -LING], a sheep that has been sheared once, usually a yearling.

shears (shêrz), *n.pl.* 1. large scissors. 2. any of several large tools or machines used to cut metal, etc. by the action of two opposed cutting edges working against each other upon the material being cut. 3. a device used in hoisting, consisting of two or more guyed poles or legs spread at the base and joined at the top to hold hoisting tackle: also **shear** (or **sheer**) **legs.**

shear·wa·ter (shêr′wô′tẽr, shêr′wot′ẽr), *n.* [*shear* + *water:* so named from skimming or shearing the water], any of several black-and-white sea birds that skim the water in flight: they are about the size of a pigeon and are related to the petrels and albatrosses.

sheat·fish (shēt′fish′), *n.* [*pl.* SHEATFISH, SHEATFISHES (-iz); see FISH], [prob. < AS. *sceota,* recorded as "trout" < base of *sceotan,* to shoot, dart (cf. SHOOT)], an extremely large freshwater catfish of eastern and central Europe: some specimens weigh over 300 pounds.

sheath (shēth), *n.* [*pl.* SHEATHS (shēthz, shēths)], [ME. *schethe;* AS. *sceath;* akin to G. *scheide;* IE. base **sqēi-,* to cut, split, divide; the earliest form of sheath was prob. a split stick], 1. a case for the blade of a knife, sword, etc. 2. a covering or receptacle resembling this, as the membrane around a muscle, a leaf base enveloping a stem of grass, etc. *v.t.* to sheathe.

sheath·bill (shēth′bil′), *n.* either of two white-plumed antarctic sea birds distinguished by a horny, saddlelike sheath at the upper base of the beak.

sheathe (shēth), *v.t.* [SHEATHED (shēthd), SHEATHING], [ME. *schethen* < *schethe*], 1. to put into a sheath or scabbard. 2. to enclose in or protect with a case or covering: as, wood *sheathed* with tin. 3. to thrust or sink into flesh, as a sword. 4. to retract (claws).

sheath·ing (shēth′iŋ), *n.* 1. the act of placing in or encasing with a sheath. 2. something that sheathes or encases; covering; casing; specifically, *a*) the inner covering of boards or waterproof material on the roof or outside wall of a frame house. *b*) the protective covering of a ship's bottom or hull. *c*) the material for either of these.

sheath knife, a knife carried in a sheath.

sheave (shēv), *n.* [< ME. *schive,* with lowered vowel; var. of *shive*], a wheel with a grooved rim, such as is mounted in a pulley block to guide the rope or cable; pulley wheel or any similarly grooved wheel.

sheave (shēv), *v.t.* [SHEAVED (shēvd), SHEAVING], [< *sheaf*], to gather and fix (grain, papers, etc.) in a sheaf or sheaves.

sheaves (shēvz), *n.* 1. plural of **sheaf.** 2. plural of **sheave.**

She·ba (shē′bə), *n.* Saba: the Biblical name.

Sheba, Queen of, in the *Bible,* the queen who visited King Solomon to investigate his reputed wisdom and greatness: I Kings 10:1–13.

she·bang (shə-baŋ′), *n.* [prob. a var. of *shebeen*], [Slang], a particular matter of concern; affair, business, establishment, contrivance, thing, etc.

She·bat (shə-bät′, shə-vät′), *n.* [Heb.], the fifth month of the Jewish year: see **Jewish calendar.**

she·been (shi-bēn′), *n.* [Anglo-Ir. < Ir. *sībīn,* little mug], [Chiefly Irish & Scot.], a house or establishment where liquor is sold without a license.

She·be·li, We·bi (wā′bi shā-bel′i), *n.* a river in Ethiopia and Somalia, flowing into the Juba River: length, 700 mi.: Italian name, *Uebi Scebeli.*

She·boy·gan (shi-boi′gən), *n.* a city in east central Wisconsin, on Lake Michigan: pop., 46,000.

shed (shed), *n.* [earlier *shad* (ME. *shadde*), var. of *shade* < AS. *scead,* in sense "protection"], 1. a small, roughly built shelter, storage place, or workshop, built either as a separate structure or as a lean-to. 2. a large, strongly built, barnlike or hangarlike structure, as for storage, often with open front or sides.

shed (shed), *v.t.* [SHED, SHEDDING], [ME. *scheden;* AS. *sceadan, scadan,* to separate, distinguish; akin to G. *scheiden,* to cut, separate; IE. base **sqēi-,* to cut, seen also in L. *scire,* to distinguish, know, Gr. *schizein,* to split; cf. SCIENCE, SCHISM, SCHIZO-, etc.], 1. to pour out; give off; emit. 2. to cause to flow in a stream or fall in drops; let flow or drop: as, she *shed* tears. 3. to send forth or spread about; radiate; diffuse; impart: as, he *sheds* confidence wherever he goes. 4. to cause to flow off without penetrating; throw off; repel: as, oilskin *sheds* water. 5. to cast off or lose (a natural growth or covering, as leaves, skin, hair, etc.). *v.i.* 1. to shed a natural growth or covering: as, our dog is *shedding* badly. 2. to drop off or fall out, as leaves, seeds, etc. *n.* [ME. *schede,* division], a line or ridge from which water flows in two directions; watershed.

shed blood, to kill by violent means; take life.

she'd (shēd), 1. she had. 2. she would.

shed·der (shed′ẽr), *n.* 1. a person or thing that sheds. 2. a lobster, crab, etc. that is shedding or has just shed its shell.

shed·ding (shed′iŋ), *n.* 1. the action of a person or thing that sheds. 2. something shed.

sheen (shēn), *n.* [earlier used as adj. < ME. *schene;* AS. *scene, sciene,* beautiful, splendid (akin to G. *schön*); meaning influenced by association with *shine*], 1. brightness; shininess; luster. 2. bright or shining attire. *adj.* [Poetic], of shining beauty; bright. *v.i.* [Dial. or Poetic], to shine; gleam.

sheen·y (shēn′i), *adj.* [SHEENIER (-i-ẽr), SHEENIEST (-i-ist)], having a sheen; bright; shining.

sheep (shēp), *n.* [*pl.* SHEEP], [ME. *schep;* AS. *sceap, scæp;* akin to G. *schaf;* known only in W.Gmc.], 1. any of a wide variety of cud-chewing mammals related to the goats, with heavy wool, edible flesh called mutton, and skin used in making leather, parchment, etc. 2. leather made from the skin of the sheep, as for bookbinding: abbreviated **sh.** 3. a person who is meek, stupid, timid, defenseless, submissive, etc.

make sheep's eyes at, to look at with great or exaggerated tenderness; look shyly and lovingly at.

sheep·ber·ry (shēp′ber′i, shēp′bẽr-i), *n.* [*pl.* SHEEPBERRIES (-iz)], a large shrub with white flowers and blue-black berries.

sheep·cot (shēp′kot′), *n.* a sheepcote.

sheep·cote (shēp′kōt′), *n.* [cf. COTE], a sheepfold.
sheep-dip (shēp′dip′), *n.* any chemical preparation used as a bath to free sheep from vermin and sheep scab or to clean the fleece and skin before shearing.
sheep dog, a dog trained to herd and protect sheep; specifically, *a*) a collie. *b*) a large, gentle dog with a short tail and long, rough hair covering the face and eyes: also called *old English sheep dog.*
sheep·fold (shēp′fōld′), *n.* [ME.; Late AS. *sceapa fald;* cf. FOLD], a yard or enclosure for sheep.
sheep·herd·er (shēp′hũr′dẽr), *n.* a person who herds or tends a large flock of sheep grazing in open pasture.
sheep·ish (shēp′ish), *adj.* [ME. *shepisse,* like a sheep], 1. bashful or embarrassed in manner; shy; awkward. 2. resembling sheep in meekness, timidity, etc.
sheep·kill (shēp′kil′), *n.* sheep laurel.
sheep laurel, a small shrub with pinkish flowers, and leaves supposed to be poisonous to sheep.
sheep·man (shēp′man′, shēp′mən), *n.* [*pl.* SHEEPMEN (-men′, -mən)], 1. a person who makes a business of raising sheep. 2. a sheepherder or shepherd.
sheep run, a sheepwalk.
sheep·shank (shēp′shaŋk′), *n.* 1. the shank of a sheep. 2. something thin, scrawny, or weak. 3. a knot used for shortening a rope: see **knot,** illus.
sheeps·head (shēps′hed′), *n.* 1. a sheep's head prepared as food. 2. a foolish or stupid person. 3. [*pl.* SHEEPSHEAD, SHEEPSHEADS (-hedz′); see PLURAL, II, D, 2], a large, salt-water food fish with massive head and forepart, two sets of teeth, and a striped body: it is common along the Atlantic coast of the United States.
sheep·shear·er (shēp′shêr′ẽr), *n.* 1. one who shears sheep. 2. any tool or machine used in sheering sheep.
sheep·shear·ing (shēp′shêr′iŋ), *n.* 1. the act of shearing sheep. 2. the time when sheep are sheared. 3. a traditional feast held at this time.
sheep·skin (shēp′skin′), *n.* 1. the skin of a sheep, especially one dressed with the fleece on it. 2. parchment or leather made from the skin of a sheep: the parchment is often used for documents, as diplomas; hence, 3. [Colloq.], a diploma.
sheep sorrel, a weed with fleshy, acid-tasting leaves, found in dry places.
sheep·walk (shēp′wôk′), *n.* a pasture or range for sheep.
sheer (shêr), *v.i.* [a form of *shear,* prob. influenced by cognate D. or LG. *scheren,* to cut, deviate, warp away], to turn aside from a course; swerve; deviate. *v.t.* to cause to turn or sheer. *n.* 1. deviation from a course; abrupt turn; swerve. 2. the oblique heading or position of a ship riding at a single bow anchor. 3. the upward curve of a ship's hull or deck lines as seen from the side.
sheer (shêr), *adj.* [ME. *schere, skere;* ON. *skiær,* bright, clear, pure; for IE. base see SHIMMER], 1. very thin; transparent; diaphanous: said of textiles. 2. not mixed or mingled with anything else; pure; undiluted. 3. absolute; downright; unqualified; utter: as, *sheer* persistence, etc. 4. perpendicular or extremely steep, as the face of a cliff. *adv.* 1. completely; utterly; outright. 2. perpendicularly or very steeply. *n.* thin, fine material, or a garment made of it. —*SYN.* see **steep.**
sheer legs, a kind of hoisting apparatus; shears.
sheet (shēt), *n.* [ME. *schete;* AS. *sceat,* piece of cloth, lappet, region; akin to G. *schoss,* bosom, ON. *skaut,* lappet; for prob. IE. base see SHOOT; basic sense "what projects"], 1. a large, rectangular piece of cotton, linen, etc., used in pairs as bedding, one above and one below the body. 2. [Poetic], a sail. 3. *a*) a rectangular piece of paper, especially one of a number of pieces cut to a definite, uniform size, as for use in writing, printing, etc. *b*) *pl.* the leaves of a book, magazine, etc., especially when unbound. *c*) a newspaper. 4. a broad continuous surface, layer, or expanse, as of flame, water, ice, etc. 5. a broad, thin, usually rectangular piece of any material, as glass, plywood, tin, etc. 6. in *geology,* any layer or deposit of rock, gravel, soil, ice, etc. that is broad in extent and comparatively thin. 7. in *philately,* the unseparated block of stamps printed by a single impression of a plate. *v.t.* to cover or provide with a sheet or sheets. Abbreviated **sh.**
sheet (shēt), *n.* [as if < AS. *sceata,* lower corner of a sail, but actually < comp. *sceatline,* line attached to that part of a sail], 1. a rope or chain attached to a lower corner of a sail: it is shortened or slackened to control the set of the sail. 2. *pl.* [< use in *stern sheets, foresheets*], the spaces not occupied by thwarts, or cross seats, at the bow and stern of an open boat.
a sheet in (or to) **the wind,** [Slang], slightly drunk.
sheet home, to tighten the sheets of (a square sail) so as to extend it against the wind.
three sheets in (or to) **the wind,** [Slang], very drunk.
sheet anchor, [earlier also *shute anchor* < ME. *scheten, schuten* (AS. *sceotan*), to shoot, fall, rush, hence one that can be shot out rapidly], 1. a large anchor carried amidships and used only in emergencies. 2. a person or thing to be relied upon in danger or emergency.
sheet bend, in *nautical usage,* a knot used in fastening a rope to the bight of another rope or to an eye: see **knot,** illus.
sheet·ing (shēt′iŋ), *n.* 1. cotton or linen material used for making sheets. 2. material used in covering or lining a surface: as, copper *sheeting.* 3. the action or process of covering with or forming into sheets.
sheet iron, iron rolled thin to the form of a sheet.
sheet lightning, a sheetlike illumination caused by lightning reflected and diffused by clouds, etc.
sheet metal, metal rolled thin to the form of a sheet.
sheet music, music printed on unbound sheets of paper.
Shef·field (shef′ēld), *n.* a city in Yorkshire, England: pop., 476,000 (est. 1946).
sheik, sheikh (shēk; *rarely,* shāk), *n.* [Ar. *shaikh,* lit. old man < *shakha,* to grow old], 1. the chief of an Arab family, tribe, or village: used as a title of respect. 2. an official in the Moslem religious organization. 3. [< E. M. Hull's novel, *The Sheik*], [Slang], a masterful man to whom women are irresistibly attracted.
sheik·dom, sheikh·dom (shēk′dəm), *n.* the territory ruled by a sheik.
Shei·la (shē′lə), [Ir.], a feminine name: see **Cecilia.**
shei·tan (shī-tän′), *n.* a shaitan.
shek·el (shek′′l), *n.* [Heb. *sheqel* < *shāqal,* to weigh], 1. an ancient weight unit used by the Hebrews, Babylonians, etc., equal to about half an ounce. 2. a half-ounce gold or silver coin of the ancient Hebrews. 3. *pl.* [Slang], money, especially coins.
She·ki·nah (shi-kī′nə; Heb. shə-khē′nô), *n.* [Heb. *shekhinah* < *shakhan,* to dwell], in *Hebrew theology,* the manifestation of the presence of God; Divine Presence.
shel·drake (shel′drāk′), *n.* [*pl.* SHELDRAKES (-drāks′), SHELDRAKE; see PLURAL, II, D, 1], [ME. *sheldedrake,* either < *sheld,* a shield, hence emblazoned, varicolored, + *drake,* or < a ME. cognate of MD. *schillede,* variegated < *schillen,* to make different], 1. any of several large European wild ducks that feed on fish, shellfish, etc. and nest in burrows: the plumage is variegated and often brightly colored. 2. any of several other ducks, especially the merganser.
shelf (shelf), *n.* [*pl.* SHELVES (shelvz)], [ME. *schelfe,* MLG. *schelf,* set of shelves; AS. *scylf,* prob., rock shelf is basically the same word], 1. a thin, flat length of wood or other material set horizontally at right angles to a wall and used for holding things. 2. a similar support built into a frame, as in a bookcase or cupboard: usually one of a set. 3. the contents or capacity of a shelf. 4. something like a shelf, as a flat ledge jutting out from a cliff. 5. a sandbar or reef. 6. in *mining,* bedrock, as under deposits of soil, gravel, etc.
on the shelf, out of use, activity, or circulation.
shell (shel), *n.* [ME. *schelle;* AS. *sciel, scell;* akin to MD. *schelle;* IE. base **sqel-,* to cut, divide, as also in Eng. *scale, shale,* etc.], 1. a hard outer covering, as of an animal, egg, fruit, seed, etc. 2. material of or like animal shell, used in manufacturing, decorating, etc. 3. something like or suggestive of a shell in being hollow, empty, or simply a covering or framework, as the hull of a boat, an unfilled pie crust, etc. 4. mere empty show or outward appearance without real substance, content, or meaning. 5. a long, narrow, thin-hulled racing boat rowed usually by a team of oarsmen. 6. a hollow, explosive missile of the kind fired from a large gun: the more common kinds of shell contain high explosives, shrapnel, or chemicals producing gas, smoke, fire, etc. 7. a small arms cartridge consisting of a metal or paper case holding the primer, the powder charge, and the bullet or shot. 8. a pyrotechnic cartridge which explodes high in the air. 9. a mollusk. 10. in *chemistry, a*) one of the spherical layers of electrons contained in an atom. *b*) the space taken up by such a layer. *v.t.* 1. to remove the shell or covering from; take out of the shell: as, it is easier to *shell* peas than oysters. 2. to separate (kernels of corn, wheat, etc.) from the cob or ear. 3. to fire shells at from a large gun or guns; bombard. *v.i.* 1. to separate or become freed from the shell or covering: as, peanuts *shell* easily. 2. to fall, slough, or peel off, as a shell.
come out of one's shell, to become more sociable and less shy or reserved.
retire into one's shell, to become less sociable and more shy or reserved.
shell out, [Colloq.], to hand over; pay out (money).
she'll (shēl), 1. she shall. 2. she will.
shel·lac, shel·lack, shell-lac (shə-lak′), *n.* [*shell* + *lac,* used as transl. of Fr. *laque en écailles,* lac in fine sheets], 1. refined lac, a resin usually produced in thin, flaky layers or shells and used in making varnish, phonograph records, insulating materials, etc. 2. a thin, usually clear kind of varnish containing shellac resin and alcohol. *v.t.* [SHELLACKED, SHELL-LACKED (-lakt′), SHELLACKING, SHELL-LACKING], 1. to apply shellac to; cover or treat with shellac. 2. [Slang], *a*) to beat. *b*) to defeat decisively.
shel·lack·ing (shə-lak′iŋ), *n.* [Slang], 1. a whipping; flogging; beating. 2. a thorough defeat.
shell·back (shel′bak′), *n.* [*shell* + *back;* prob. with reference to the shell of the sea turtle], 1. an old, experienced sailor. 2. anyone who has crossed the equator by ship.
shell·bark (shel′bärk′), *n.* the shagbark.
shell bean, any bean, as the lima, of which only the

seeds are used as food: distinguished from *string bean.*

-shelled (sheld), a combining form meaning *having a* (specified kind of) *shell,* as in *soft-shelled.*

Shel·ley, Mary Woll·stone·craft (wool′stən-kraft′ *or* wool′stən-kräft′ shel′i), (born *Mary Wollstonecraft Godwin*), 1797–1851; second wife of *Percy Bysshe;* English novelist.

Shelley, Per·cy Bysshe (pũr′si bish), 1792–1822; English poet.

shell·fire (shel′fir′), *n.* bombardment with shells; artillery attack.

shell·fish (shel′fish′), *n.* [*pl.* SHELLFISH, SHELLFISHES (-iz); see FISH], [ME. *shellfyssche;* AS. *scilfisc*], any aquatic animal with a shell, as the lobster, clam, etc.

shell game, 1. a swindling game in which spectators are challenged to bet on the location of a small object ostensibly concealed under one of three cups or nutshells manipulated by a sleight-of-hand operator; thimblerig; hence, 2. any game or scheme in which the customers are victimized.

shell jacket, a close-fitting semiformal jacket; mess jacket.

shell·proof (shel′prōōf′), *adj.* proof against damage from shells or bombs.

shell shock, combat fatigue: formerly so called because thought to be a direct result of the continued concussion of artillery fire.

shell·shocked (shel′shokt′), *adj.* suffering from shell shock.

shel·ly (shel′i), *adj.* [SHELLIER (-i-ẽr), SHELLIEST (-i-ist)], 1. covered with or having many shells: as, a *shelly* patch of sea bottom. 2. of, like, or having a shell or shells.

shel·ta (shel′tə), *n.* [earlier *sheldru, shelter,* prob. a repatterning of OIr. *bēlre,* speech], an esoteric jargon based in part on the systematic alteration of Irish and Gaelic and still spoken in some parts of England and Ireland by tinkers, vagrants, etc.

shel·ter (shel′tẽr), *n.* [altered < ME. *scheltroun,* earlier *scheltrum* < AS. *sceldtruma,* lit., shield troop, body of men protected by interlocked shields; *sceld* (cf. SHIELD) + *truma,* an array, troop (cf. TRIM); basic sense "shielding"], 1. something that covers, protects, or defends; protection, or place affording protection, as from the elements, danger, etc.; a place of refuge. 2. the state of being covered, protected, or defended; protection; refuge. *v.t.* to provide shelter or refuge for; protect; defend. *v.i.* to find protection or refuge; take cover.

SYN.—**shelter** implies the protection of something that covers, as a roof or other structure that shields one from the elements, danger, etc. (to find *shelter* from the rain); **refuge** suggests a place of safety that one flees to in escaping danger, difficulties, etc. (he sought political *refuge* in France); **retreat** implies retirement from that which threatens one's peace, etc. and withdrawal to a safe, quiet, or secluded place (a country *retreat*); **asylum** is applied to a refuge where one is immune from seizure or harm, as because it is beyond a particular legal jurisdiction (the convict sought *asylum* abroad); a **sanctuary** is an asylum that has a sacred or inviolable character (the former right of *sanctuary* in churches).

shelter tent, a small, portable tent large enough to shelter two men: it consists of two sections (*shelter halves*), each of which is carried by a soldier as part of his field equipment: also called *pup tent.*

shel·ty, shel·tie (shel′ti), *n.* [*pl.* SHELTIES (-tiz)], [prob. < Orkney pronun. of ON. *hjalti,* Shetlander], 1. a Shetland pony. 2. a Shetland sheep dog.

shelve (shelv), *v.i.* [SHELVED (shelvd), SHELVING], [prob. < *shelf*], to incline or slope gradually. *v.t.* [< *shelves,* pl. of *shelf*], 1. to furnish or equip with shelves. 2. to put on a shelf or shelves; hence, 3. *a*) to put away as if on a shelf; lay aside; defer: as, let's *shelve* the discussion. *b*) to retire from active service.

shelves (shelvz), *n.* plural of **shelf.**

shelv·ing (shel′viŋ), *n.* 1. material for shelves: as, wood *shelving.* 2. shelves collectively.

Shem (shem), *n.* [Heb. *shēm*], in the *Bible,* the eldest of the three sons of Noah and traditional ancestor of the Semitic people.

Shem·ite (shem′it), *n.* Semite.

Shem·it·ic (shem-it′ik), *adj.* Semitic.

Shen·an·do·ah (shen′ən-dō′ə), *n.* 1. a river in Virginia, flowing northeastward into the Potomac River: length, 200 mi. 2. its valley, between the Blue Ridge and Allegheny Mountains. 3. a town in east central Pennsylvania: pop., 11,000.

Shenandoah National Park, a national park in the Blue Ridge Mountains of northern Virginia.

she·nan·i·gan (shi-nan′i-gən), *n.* [? altered < Ir. *sionnachuighim,* I play the fox; ? G. dial. *schinageln, schinegeln, schineckeln,* to work at hard labor; hence, by pejoration, to use trickery to avoid such work], *now usually pl.* [Colloq.], nonsense; trickery; mischief; often, a treacherous or deceitful trick.

Shen·si (shen′sē′; Chin. shun′shē′), *n.* a province of north central China: area, 76,382 sq. mi.; pop., 15,881,000; capital, Sian.

Shen·stone, William (shen′stən, shen′stōn′), 1714–1763; English poet.

shent (shent), *adj.* [ME. *schent* < pp. of *schenden,* to put to shame, harm; akin to G. *schänden*], [Archaic & Dial.], 1. disgraced. 2. lost, ruined, or defeated, as a cause. 3. injured; damaged. 4. reproached.

She·ol (shē′ōl), *n.* [Heb. *shĕ'ōl* < *shā'al,* to dig], 1. in the *Old Testament,* a place in the depths of the earth where the dead are supposed to go; underworld. 2. [s-], [Colloq.], hell.

shep·herd (shep′ẽrd), *n.* [ME. *shephirde;* AS. *sceaphyrde, scephyrde;* see SHEEP & HERD], 1. a person who herds and takes care of sheep. 2. a religious leader; minister; pastor. 3. a sheep dog. *v.t.* to tend, herd, guard, lead, etc. as or like a shepherd.

the Good Shepherd, Jesus of Nazareth.

shepherd dog, a sheep dog.

shep·herd·ess (shep′ẽrd-is), *n.* a girl or woman shepherd: a stock character in pastoral poetry.

Shepherd Kings, see **Hyksos.**

shep·herd's-purse (shep′ẽrdz-pũrs′), *n.* a weed with small, white flowers and triangular, pouchlike pods.

Sher·a·ton (sher′ə-t′n), *adj.* designating or of furniture made by, or in the style of, Thomas Sheraton (1751–1806), an English cabinetmaker: it is characterized by simplicity and lightness of form, straight lines, and classically chaste decoration.

sher·bet (shũr′bət), *n.* [Turk. *sharbat* < Ar. *sharbah,* a drink], 1. [British], a beverage made of watered fruit juice and sugar: it is served cold. 2. a frozen dessert of fruit juice, sugar, and water, milk, or egg white.

Sher·brooke (shũr′brook), *n.* a city in southern Quebec, Canada: pop., 59,000.

sherd (shũrd), *n.* shard.

she·reef (shə-rēf′), *n.* a sherif.

Sher·i·dan, Philip Henry (sher′i-d'n), 1831–1888; Union general in the Civil War.

Sheridan, Richard Brins·ley (brinz′li), 1751–1816; Irish dramatist and politician.

she·rif (shə-rēf′), *n.* [Ar. *sharīf,* noble], 1. a descendant of Mohammed through his daughter Fatima: a title of nobility inheritable through either parent. 2. an Arab prince or chief. 3. the chief magistrate of Mecca.

sher·iff (sher′if), *n.* [ME. *schirreve;* AS. *scirgerefa; scir,* shire (cf. SHIRE, SHEAR) + *gerefa,* reeve (cf. REEVE)], 1. the chief law-enforcement officer of a county, charged in general with the keeping of the peace and the execution of court orders. 2. in England before the Norman Conquest, the chief administrative and judicial officer of a shire.

sher·iff·dom (sher′if-dəm), *n.* 1. the district within which a sheriff has authority or jurisdiction. 2. the office of sheriff.

Sher·man, John (shũr′mən), 1823–1900; brother of *William Tecumseh;* American statesman.

Sherman, Roger, 1721–1793; American statesman.

Sherman, William Tecumseh, 1820–1891; Union general in the Civil War.

Sher·ring·ton, Sir **Charles Scott** (sher′iŋ-tən), 1861–1952; English physiologist; shared Nobel prize in physiology, 1932.

sher·ris (sher′is), *n.* [Archaic], sherry.

sher·ry (sher′i), *n.* [taken as sing. of earlier *sherris* < *Xeres* (now Jerez), Spain, where first obtained], 1. a strong, nonsparkling Spanish wine: its color varies from light yellow to dark brown. 2. any similar wine.

sherry cobbler, a drink made with sherry, citrus juice, sugar, and cracked ice.

Sher·wood, Robert Em·met (em′it shũr′wood), 1896–1955; American playwright.

Sher·wood Forest (shũr′wood), a forest in the region of Nottinghamshire, England: made famous in the Robin Hood legends.

she's (shēz), 1. she is. 2. she has.

Shet·land (shet′lənd), *n.* 1. the Shetland Islands. 2. a Shetland pony. 3. Shetland wool.

Shetland Islands, a group of islands northeast of the Orkney Islands, forming a county of Scotland: area, 551 sq. mi.; pop., 18,000: also called *Zetland Islands.*

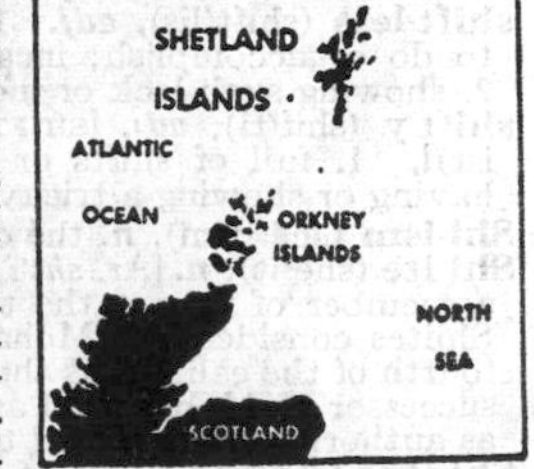

SHETLAND ISLANDS

Shetland pony, any of a breed of sturdy ponies with rough coats and long tails and manes, originally from the Shetland Islands.

Shetland sheep dog, any of a breed of dogs closely resembling collies but only 13 to 16 inches high: originally from the Shetland Islands.

Shetland wool, a kind of soft, fine, loosely twisted wool yarn.

She·vu·oth (shə-vōō′ōth, shə-vōō′ōs), *n.* [Heb.], Shabuoth: see **Jewish holidays.**

shew (shō), *n., v.t. & v.i.* show.

shew·bread (shō′bred′), *n.* [*shew*, older var. of *show* + *bread*, after G. *shaubrot*, Luther's transl. for Heb. *leḥem pānīm*, lit., bread of faces, presence bread], the twelve loaves of unleavened bread placed at the altar before Jehovah every Sabbath by the ancient Hebrew priests and eaten by them alone at the end of the week: also spelled **showbread.**

Shi·ah (shē′ə), *n.* a Shiite.

shib·bo·leth (shib′ə-ləth), *n.* [ME. *sebolech*, after L. (Vulgate) *sciboleth;* Heb., a stream, flood: present meaning from the use of the word as a test word], 1. in the *Bible*, the test word used by the Gileadites to distinguish the escaping Ephraimites, who could not pronounce the initial *sh*: Judg. 12:6; hence, 2. any test word or password. 3. any phrase, formula, custom, etc. considered distinctive, as of a party, class, faction, etc.

shied (shīd), past tense and past participle of **shy.**

shield (shēld), *n.* [ME. *schelde;* AS. *scield, sceld;* akin to G. *schild;* for IE. base see SHELL; prob. basic sense "what is cut, is split"], 1. a broad piece of protective armor carried in the hand or worn on the forearm to ward off blows or missiles. 2. any person or thing that guards, protects, or defends. 3. a heraldic escutcheon. 4. anything shaped like a shield, as a plaque or trophy. 5. a movable canopy protecting workers from cave-ins in mines, tunnels, etc. 6. a heavy metal screen attached to an artillery piece for the protection of the gunners. 7. a guard or safety screen, as over the moving parts of machinery. 8. a device worn inside a part of a garment, as at the armpits, to prevent the fabric from being soiled by perspiration. 9. in *zoology*, a hard surface covering or shell; protective plate, as on a turtle. *v.t.* 1. to be or provide a shield for; defend; protect; guard. 2. [Archaic], to prevent or forbid: as, heaven *shield* that it should happen. *v.i.* to act as a shield; serve as protection. —*SYN.* see **defend.**

shield-bear·er (shēld′bâr′ẽr), *n.* an attendant who carried the shield of a knight.

shi·er (shī′ẽr), *n.* a horse that shies easily.

shift (shift), *v.t.* [ME. *schiften;* AS. *sciftan*, to divide, separate; akin to G. *schichten;* for IE. base see SHIP], 1. to move or transfer from one person, place, or position to another: as, don't *shift* the responsibility. 2. to put another or others in place of; replace by another of the kind; change. 3. to change (gears) from one arrangement to another. 4. to change phonetically, as by Grimm's law. 5. [Archaic or Dial.], to change (clothes). *v.i.* 1. to change position, direction, form, character, etc. 2. to get along; manage: as, you must *shift* for yourself now. 3. to use tricky or fraudulent methods; practice evasion. 4. to change from one gear to another: as, our new car *shifts* automatically. 5. [Archaic or Dial.], to change one's clothing. *n.* 1. a means or plan of conduct, especially one followed in an emergency or difficulty; expedient; stratagem; hence, 2. a fraudulent scheme or method; evasion; trick. 3. the act of shifting from one person, place, position, etc. to another; change; transfer; substitution. 4. a set or group of employees working in relay with another or others: as, three members of the night *shift* were absent. 5. the daily working period of such a group. 6. a change in direction, as of the wind. 7. [Archaic or Dial.], a change of clothing. 8. [Now Rare], a chemise. 9. in *football*, a lateral movement or regrouping of the offensive backfield just before the ball is put in play. 10. in *geology*, a fault or displacement, as in a vein. 11. in *linguistics*, a phonetic change: see **Great Vowel Shift.** 12. in *music*, a change in the position of the hand, as on the finger board of a violin. —*SYN.* see **move.**

make shift, 1. to do as well as one can under unsatisfactory or difficult conditions; use the means, however inadequate, at one's disposal. 2. to do one's best (*with*).

shift·i·ly (shif′tə-li), *adv.* in a shifty manner.

shift·i·ness (shif′ti-nis), *n.* a shifty quality.

shift·less (shift′lis), *adj.* 1. lacking the will or ability to do or accomplish; incapable, inefficient, lazy, etc. 2. showing such lack or incapacity.

shift·y (shif′ti), *adj.* [SHIFTIER (-ti-ẽr), SHIFTIEST (-ti-ist)], 1. full of shifts or expedients; resourceful. 2. having or showing a tricky nature; evasive.

Shi·ism (shē′iz′m), *n.* the doctrine of the Shiites.

Shi·ite (shē′īt), *n.* [Ar. *shī'i*, a follower, partisan; + *-ite*], a member of one of the two great sects of Moslems: Shiites consider Ali, Mohammed's son-in-law and the fourth of the caliphs, as the first Imam and the rightful successor of Mohammed and do not accept the Sunna as authoritative: opposed to *Sunnite*: also called *Shiah.*

Shi·it·ic (shē-it′ik), *adj.* of the Shiites or their doctrine.

shi·kar (shi-kär′), *n.* [Pers. *shikār*], in India, hunting. *v.t. & v.i.* in India, to hunt.

shi·ka·ri, shi·ka·ree (shi-kä′rē), *n.* [Pers. *shikāri* < *shikār*, a hunt, via Urdu], in India, a hunter, especially a native hunter who serves as a guide.

Shi·ko·ku (shē′kô-kōō′), *n.* an island of Japan, south of Honshu: area, 7,246 sq. mi.; pop., 3,310,000.

shill (shil), *n.* [if, as apparently, contr. < *shillaber* prob. ult. < *shillibeer* (< G. *Shillibeer*, Eng. coac owner, 1797–1866), a combined hearse and mournin coach], [Slang], the confederate of a gambler, barker or peddler, as at a carnival, who pretends to bu something, make a bet, etc. in order to lure onlooker into participating.

shil·le·lagh, shil·la·lah (shi-lā′lə, shə-lā′li), *n.* [< th village of *Shillelagh*, near Arklow, in County Wicklow Ireland, famous for its oaks and blackthorns], a clu or cudgel: also spelled **shillelah, shillala.**

shil·ling (shil′iŋ), *n.* [ME. *schilling;* AS. *scylling;* aki to G. *schilling;* for IE. base see SHELL; prob. basi sense "what is cut off (from a piece of metal) to serv as money"], 1. a British money of account and silve coin, equal to 12 pence or 1/20 of a pound: symbol, / 2. any of several coins or moneys of account of differen values used in other countries. 3. a coin of colonia America, varying in value from about 12 to 16 cent Abbreviated **s., sh.** (*sing. & pl.*).

shil·ly-shal·ly (shil′i-shal′i), *adv.* [a redupl. of *shall I* meaning shall I or shall I not?], in a vacillating manne hesitantly; irresolutely. *adj.* vacillating; hesitant; i resolute. *n.* indecision; vacillation; irresolution, espe cially of a trifling kind. *v.i.* [SHILLY-SHALLIED (-id) SHILLY-SHALLYING], 1. to be irresolute; vacillate hence, 2. to concern oneself with trifles.

Shi·loh (shī′lō), *n.* 1. a national military park a Pittsburg Landing, southwestern Tennessee, on th Tennessee River: scene of a battle (1862) of the Civ War. 2. an ancient town in central Palestine.

shi·ly (shī′li), *adv.* shyly.

shim (shim), *n.* [prob. via dial. < an AS. cognate Norw. dial. *skeima*, thin plate; for IE. base see SHELL a thin, usually wedge-shaped piece of wood, metal, et used for filling space, leveling, etc., as in masonry. *v.* to fit with a shim or shims.

shim·mer (shim′ẽr), *v.i.* [ME. *schimeren;* AS. *scymrian* akin to G. *schimmern*, freq. formation on base of AS *scima*, a ray, light; IE. base **skāi-*, to glimmer, as als in Eng. *shine*], to shine with an unsteady light; glimme *n.* a shimmering light; glimmer. —*SYN.* see **flash.**

shim·mer·y (shim′ẽr-i), *adj.* shimmering.

shim·mey (shim′i), *n.* [*pl.* SHIMMIES (-iz)], a shimmy

shim·my (shim′i), *n.* [< Fr. *chemise*, a chemise], 1. marked shaking, vibration, or wobble, as in automobi wheels. 2. a jazz dance, popular in the 1920's, cha acterized by much shaking of the body. 3. [Dial. c Colloq.], a chemise. *v.i.* [SHIMMIED (-id), SHIMMYING 1. to shake, vibrate, or wobble. 2. to dance th shimmy.

Shi·mo·no·se·ki (shē′mô-nô-sä′ki), *n.* a city on th coast of southwestern Honshu, Japan: pop., 177,00 (est. 1947).

shin (shin), *n.* [ME. *schine;* AS. *scinu;* G. *schiene*, thi plate; *schien-*, shin; for IE. base see SHELL; basic sens "thin place"], 1. the front part of the leg between th knee and the ankle. 2. the lower part of the foreleg i beef cattle: distinguished from *shank*, the upper forele *v.t. & v.i.* [SHINNED (shind), SHINNING], 1. to climb (rope, pole, etc.) using both hands and legs for grippin 2. to kick (another) in the shins.

shin (shēn), *n.* [Heb. *ṣin, shīn*, lit., tooth], the twenty second letter of the Hebrew alphabet (ש), correspon ing phonetically to English *sh*: see **alphabet,** table.

Shi·nar (shī′när), *n.* Babylonia or its southern divisio Sumer: the Biblical name.

shin·bone (shin′bōn′), *n.* the inner bone of the lowe leg; tibia: also **shin bone.**

shin·dig (shin′dig), *n.* [folk-etym. form of *shindy*, unde stood as shin-dig, jovial kick in the shin], [Colloq.], 1. dance. 2. any social affair; party.

shin·dy (shin′di), *n.* [*pl.* SHINDIES (-diz)], [prob. < *shi* in sense "show, hence merrymaking"], [Colloq.], 1. noisy disturbance; commotion; row. 2. a shindig.

shine (shīn), *v.i.* [SHONE (shōn), or, esp. for *v.t.* 2 SHINED (shīnd), SHINING], [ME. *schinen;* AS. *scinan* akin to G. *scheinen;* for IE. base see SHIMMER], 1. t emit, give, or reflect light; be radiant or bright wi light; gleam; glow. 2. to stand out; excel; be eminen conspicuous, or brilliant. 3. to exhibit itself clearly o brightly; appear conspicuously: as, happiness *shon* from her face. *v.t.* 1. to cause to shine: as, *shine* you flashlight over here. 2. to make shiny or bright b polishing, as shoes. *n.* 1. brightness; radiance. 2. lus ter; polish; gloss. 3. a shoeshine. 4. splendor; bri liance; show. 5. [Slang], a disturbance; commotio 6. [Slang], a trick or prank. —*SYN.* see **polish.**

rain or shine, regardless of whether it is raining o fair weather.

shine up to, [Slang], to try to become friendly with

take a shine to, [Slang], to develop a liking for.

shin·er (shīn′ẽr), *n.* 1. a person or thing that shines 2. [*pl.* SHINERS (-ẽrz), SHINER; see PLURAL, II, D, 1], fresh-water carp minnow with silvery scales: often use as fish bait. 3. [Slang], a black eye resulting from bruise.

shin·gle (shiŋ′g'l), *n.* [Norw. *singel;* of echoic origin] 1. large, coarse, waterworn gravel, as found on

beach. 2. an area, as a beach, covered with this.
shin·gle (shiŋ'g'l), *n.* [ME. *schingle*, altered < *schindle* < L. *scindula*, a shingle < *scindere*, to split, divide], 1. a thin, wedge-shaped slat or board laid with others in a series of overlapping rows as a covering for roofs and the sides of houses. 2. a piece of any kind of material, as asbestos, used in the same way. 3. a woman's short haircut in which the hair in back is cropped close. 4. [Colloq.], a small signboard, especially that of a physician or lawyer. *v.t.* [SHINGLED (-g'ld), SHINGLING], 1. to cover (a roof, etc.) with shingles. 2. [orig. applied to shearing sheep], to cut (hair) in shingle style.
hang out one's shingle, [Colloq.], to open an office for professional consultation: used especially of physicians and lawyers.
shin·gles (shiŋ'g'lz), *n.* [altered < ML. *cingulus* < L. *cingulum*, a belt, girdle < *cingere*, to gird: used in ML. as transl. of Gr. *zōnē*, a girdle, shingles], herpes zoster; an acute virus disease characterized by the eruption of small blisters on the skin along the course of a nerve, usually about the waist.
shin·gly (shiŋ'gli), *adj.* [SHINGLIER (-gli-ẽr), SHINGLIEST (-gli-ist)], of, like, or covered with shingle (gravel).
shin guard, a heavily padded or stiffened guard worn to protect the shins in certain games, as hockey, baseball, etc.
shin·i·ness (shīn'i-nis), *n.* the state or quality of being shiny; luster; polish.
shin·ing (shīn'iŋ), *adj.* 1. giving off or reflecting light; radiant; bright. 2. brilliant; remarkable; eminent: as, a *shining* example of generosity. —*SYN.* see **bright.**
shin·leaf (shin'lēf'), *n.* any of a number of related plants with slender stalks having small, rounded evergreen leaves at the base.
shin·ny (shin'i), *n.* [*pl.* SHINNIES (-iz)], [prob. < cry *shin ye*, used in game; origin obscure], 1. a simple form of hockey, popular especially with children. 2. the crooked stick or club used in this game. *v.i.* [SHINNIED (-id), SHINNYING], to play shinny. Also spelled **shinney.**
shin·ny (shin'i), *v.i.* [SHINNIED (-id), SHINNYING], [Colloq.], to climb by using the shins for gripping (usually with *up*).
shin·plas·ter (shin'plas'tẽr, shin'pläs'tẽr), *n.* 1. any of several kinds of plasters and poultices used on sore shins. 2. a piece of paper money made almost worthless, as by inflation or inadequate security. 3. a piece of paper money of small face value, usually less than a dollar, especially one formerly issued by some private banks.
Shin·to (shin'tō), *n.* [Japan. < Chin. *shin*, god or spirit + *tao*, way or law], a principal religion of Japan: chief emphasis is upon the worship of ancestors and ancient heroes and upon the divinity of the emperor: prior to 1945, the state religion.
Shin·to·ism (shin'tō-iz'm), *n.* 1. the principles of Shinto. 2. a belief in Shinto.
shin·y (shīn'i), *adj.* [SHINIER (-i-ẽr), SHINIEST (-i-ist)], 1. bright; shining. 2. smoothly polished; glossy.
ship (ship), *n.* [ME. *schippe;* AS. *scip;* akin to G. *schiff;* IE. base **sqei-b-* < **sqēi-*, to cut, divide, etc.; basic sense "hollowed-out tree trunk"; cf. SKIFF], 1. any vessel of considerable size navigating deep water and not propelled by oars, paddles, or the like: distinguished from *boat.* 2. a sailing vessel with a bowsprit and at least three square-rigged masts, each composed of lower, top, and topgallant members. 3. a ship's officers and crew. 4. any aircraft: as, a B-29 is a large *ship.* *v.t.* [SHIPPED (shipt), SHIPPING], 1. to put or take on board a ship. 2. to send or transport by any carrier: as, we *shipped* the cattle by rail. 3. to take in (water) over the gunwale or side, as in a heavy sea. 4. to put or fix (an object) in its proper place on a ship or boat: as, *ship* the oars. 5. to engage (a person or persons) for work on a ship. 6. [Colloq.], to send away; get rid of. *v.i.* 1. to go aboard ship; embark. 2. to engage to serve on a ship.
about ship! turn the ship (onto a new tack)!: a command to the helmsman.
when one's ship comes home (or **in**), when one's fortune has been made or one's expectations have been realized.
-ship (ship), [ME. *-schipe;* AS. *-scipe* < base of *sceppan*, to create, make & hence of Eng. *shape;* akin to G. *-schaft*], a suffix added to nouns (or, rarely, adjectives) to form nouns meaning: 1. *the quality, condition,* or *state of,* as in *fellowship, friendship.* 2. *a) the rank, status,* or *office of,* as in *kingship, governorship.* *b) a person having the rank* or *status of,* as in *lordship.* 3. *ability* or *skill in,* as in *penmanship, leadership.*
ship biscuit, a kind of hard biscuit that will not spoil easily; hardtack: it is used on long voyages.
ship·board (ship'bôrd', ship'bōrd'), *n.* 1. a ship. 2. [Obs.], the side of a ship.
on shipboard, on or in a ship.
ship·build·er (ship'bil'dẽr), *n.* a person whose business is the designing and building of ships.
ship·build·ing (ship'bil'diŋ), *n.* the construction of ships. *adj.* of or used in ship construction.
ship canal, a canal large enough to allow the passage of ships.
ship chandler, a person who deals in ship supplies.
Ship·ka Pass (ship'kä), a pass in the Balkan Mountains of Bulgaria: height, 4,376 ft.
ship·load (ship'lōd'), *n.* a full load for a ship; cargo.
ship·man (ship'mən), *n.* [*pl.* SHIPMEN (-mən)], 1. [Archaic], a seaman; sailor. 2. a shipmaster.
ship·mas·ter (ship'mas'tẽr, ship'mäs'tẽr), *n.* the officer in command of a merchant ship; captain.
ship·mate (ship'māt'), *n.* a sailor on the same ship; fellow sailor.
ship·ment (ship'mənt), *n.* 1. the shipping or transporting of goods; consignment for transportation. 2. goods shipped or consigned. Abbreviated **shpt.**
ship money, a tax levied on English ports, maritime counties, etc. to provide money for the construction of warships: it was abolished in 1640.
ship of the line, formerly, a warship of the largest class, carrying at least seventy-four guns: such ships had a position in the line of battle.
ship·own·er (ship'ōn'ẽr), *n.* an owner or part owner of a ship or ships.
ship·pa·ble (ship'ə-b'l), *adj.* that can be shipped.
ship·per (ship'ẽr), *n.* a person or agent who ships goods.
ship·ping (ship'iŋ), *n.* 1. the act or business of sending or transporting goods. 2. ships collectively, as of a nation, port, industry, etc., especially with reference to tonnage.
shipping clerk, an employee who prepares and enters goods for shipment.
shipping room, a room or department, as in a factory, from which goods are taken by a carrier for shipment.
ship-rigged (ship'rigd'), *adj.* rigged as a ship, with three or more masts and square sails.
ship·shape (ship'shāp'), *adj.* having everything neatly in place, as on board ship; trim; orderly. *adv.* in a shipshape manner.
ship's papers, all the documents that a merchant ship must carry to meet the requirements of port authorities, international law, etc.
ship·way (ship'wā'), *n.* 1. the supporting structure or track on which a ship is built and from which it is launched. 2. a ship canal or channel.
ship·worm (ship'wũrm'), *n.* any of a number of small, valved mollusks with wormlike bodies: they burrow into and damage submerged wood.
ship·wreck (ship'rek'), *n.* 1. the remains of a wrecked ship; wreckage. 2. the loss or destruction of a ship through storm, collision, going aground, etc. 3. any ruin, failure, or destruction. *v.t.* 1. to cause to undergo shipwreck (sense 2). 2. to destroy, ruin, or wreck.
ship·wright (ship'rīt'), *n.* a man whose work is the construction and repair of ships.
ship·yard (ship'yärd'), *n.* a place where ships are built and repaired.
Shi·raz (shē-räz', shẽr'az), *n.* a city in southern Iran: pop., 129,000.
Shi·ré (shē're), *n.* a river in southeastern Africa, flowing from Lake Nyasa into the Zambezi River: length, 370 mi.
shire (shīr), *n.* [ME. *schire;* AS. *scire*, office, charge; thought by some to be akin to AS. *sceran*, to shear, divide, in sense "what is cut off," but vowel phonology is obscure; akin to OHG. *scīra*, official charge; cf. SHERIFF], 1. formerly, a district or region in Great Britain, generally coinciding with the modern county. 2. any of the counties of Great Britain with a name containing the terminal combining form *-shire.*
shire horse, any of a breed of large, powerful draft horses, originally raised in the shires, or midland counties, of England.
shirk (shũrk), *v.t.* [< *shirk, n.;* prob. < G. *schurke*, scoundrel, rascal; cf. SHARK], to neglect or evade doing (something that should be done). *v.i.* to practice evasion; neglect an obligation. *n.* a person who shirks.
Shir·ley (shũr'li), [< the surname *Shirley* < the place name *Shirley* (England) < AS. *scir*, shire + *leah*, meadow, lea, hence lea where the shire moot was held], a feminine name: diminutive, *Shirl.*
Shir·ley, James (shũr'li), 1596–1666; English dramatist.
shirr (shũr), *n.* [< ?], a series of parallel rows of short, running stitches with gatherings between rows. *v.t.* 1. to make a shirr or shirrs in (cloth). 2. to bake (eggs) with crumbs in small buttered dishes.
shirr·ing (shũr'iŋ), *n.* a shirr or shirrs.
shirt (shũrt), *n.* [ME. *schirte, schurte;* AS. *scyrte* < **skurti* < base of *scort*, short (cf. SHORT); akin to G. *schürze*, apron, doublet of Eng. *skirt* (cf. SKIRT); basic sense "short garment"], 1. any of various cloth garments

worn by men on the upper part of the body, often under a coat or jacket. 2. an undershirt. 3. a woman's shirtwaist.

in one's shirt sleeves, not wearing a coat or jacket over one's shirt.

keep one's shirt on, [Slang], to be patient or calm.

lose one's shirt, [Slang], to lose all of one's possessions.

shirt·band (shûrt′band′), *n.* a strip of cloth sewn into a shirt, as on the collar, for stiffening.

shirt front, the front of a man's shirt; especially, a heavily starched panel sewn into the front of a dress shirt.

shirt·ing (shûr′tiŋ), *n.* material used in making shirts.

shirt-sleeve (shûrt′slēv′), *adj.* 1. simple; plain; informal. 2. homespun; unpolished; plebeian: as, *shirt-sleeve* philosophy.

shirt·waist (shûrt′wāst′), *n.* a woman's tailored blouse, usually worn with a separate, unmatching skirt.

shit·tah (shit′ə), *n.* [Heb. *shiṭṭāh*, pl. *shiṭṭīm*], a kind of Asiatic acacia tree with close-grained, yellowish-brown wood: also **shittah tree.**

shit·tim (shit′im), *n.* [Heb., pl. of *shiṭṭāh*], the wood of the shittah, used in making the ark of the covenant and parts of the Jewish tabernacle: also **shittim wood.**

Shi·va (shē′və), *n.* Siva.

shiv·a·ree (shiv′ə-rē′), *n.* [altered < *charivari*], a noisy demonstration or celebration; especially, a mock serenade with kettles, horns, etc. to a couple on their wedding night; charivari. *v.t.* [SHIVAREED (-rēd′), SHIVAREEING], to serenade with a shivaree.

shive (shīv), *n.* [ME. *schive;* AS. **scife;* akin to G. *scheibe*, anything round and flat; for IE. base see SHEAVE], 1. a piece split off; splinter. 2. a stiff piece of flax husk. 3. *pl.* refuse consisting of such pieces. 4. a thin or shallow cork for a wide-mouthed bottle.

shiv·er (shiv′ẽr), *n.* [ME. *schivere*, freq. formation (cf. -ER) < base of SHEAVE, SHIVE], a fragment or splinter of something broken, as glass. *v.t. & v.i.* [ME. *schiveren*], to break into many fragments or splinters; shatter.

shiv·er (shiv′ẽr), *v.i.* [ME. *chiueren, cheveren;* prob. altered < *chivelen* in same sense < AS. *ceafl*, a jaw (cf. JOWL); prob. basic sense "to have chattering teeth"], to shake, quiver, or tremble, as from fear or cold. *v.t.* to cause (a sail) to flutter by presenting the edge to the wind. *n.* a shaking, quivering, or trembling, as from fear or cold. —***SYN.*** see **shake.**

shiv·er·y (shiv′ẽr-i), *adj.* easily broken into shivers, or fragments; brittle.

shiv·er·y (shiv′ẽr-i), *adj.* 1. shivering or inclined to shiver; suffering from cold, fear, etc. 2. causing or likely to cause shivering; chilly; chilling; terrifying.

Shi·zu·o·ka (shē′zōō-ô′kä), *n.* a city on the coast of southern Honshu, Japan: pop., 206,000 (est. 1947).

Shko·dër (shkô′dẽr), *n.* Scutari: the Albanian name.

shoal (shōl), *n.* [AS. *scolu* via dial.; akin to D. *school* (of fish); IE. base **sqel-*, to divide (cf. SHALE, SHELL)], 1. a large group; mass; crowd; specifically, 2. a large school of fish. *v.i.* to come together in or move about as a shoal or school.

shoal (shōl), *n.* [< earlier *shoal, adj.*, shallow; ME. *scholde, scheald;* AS. *sceald*, shallow; for IE. base see SHALLOW], 1. a place, as in a river, sea, etc., where the water is shallow; shallow. 2. a sand bar or piece of rising ground forming a shallow place, especially one visible at low water. *v.i.* to become shallow. *v.t.* 1. to make shallow. 2. to sail into a shallow or shallower part of (water): said of a ship.

***SYN.*—shoal** applies to any place in a sea, river, etc. where the water is shallow and difficult to navigate; **bank,** in this connection, applies to a shallow place, formed by an elevated shelf of ground, that is deep enough to be safely navigated by lighter vessels; a **reef** is a ridge of rock, coral, etc. lying at or very close to the surface of the sea, just offshore; **bar** applies to a ridge of sand, etc. silted up across the mouth of a river or harbor and hindering navigation.

shoal·y (shōl′i), *adj.* full of shoals, or shallows.

shoat (shōt), *n.* [Late ME. *schote;* prob. < LG.; cf. W. Fl. *schote;* U.S. use prob. via D.], a young pig, especially when able to feed alone: also spelled **shote.**

shock (shok), *n.* [Fr. *choc* < *choquer;* see the *v.*], 1. the impact of persons or forces in combat. 2. *a)* a sudden, powerful concussion; violent blow, shake, or jar: as, the *shock* of an earthquake. *b)* the result or effect of such concussion. 3. *a)* any sudden disturbance or agitation of the mind or emotions, as through great loss or surprise. *b)* something causing this. 4. an extreme stimulation of the nerves accompanying the passage of electric current through the body. 5. [Colloq.], a paralytic stroke. 6. in *medicine*, a condition of disorder of the circulatory system, resulting from injury or a sudden psychic disturbance, and characterized by a decrease in blood pressure, a weak and rapid pulse, and, often, unconsciousness. *v.t.* [Fr. *choquer* < MD. *schokken*, to collide], 1. to disturb the mind or emotions of; affect with great surprise, distress, disgust, etc. 2. to affect with physical shock. 3. to produce electrical shock in (a body). *v.i.* [Archaic or Poetic], to come together violently; collide.

***SYN.*—shock** suggests the violent impact on the mind or emotions of an unexpected, overwhelming event that comes a a blow (*shocked* by her sudden death); **startle** implies a shoc of surprise or fright of a kind that literally causes one to jum or shrink (*startled* by the outburst of criticism against him **paralyze** implies such extreme shock as causes one to b temporarily helpless (*paralyzed* with fear); to **stun** is to shoc with such impact as to stupefy or daze (*stunned* by the disaste

shock (shok), *n.* [ME. *schokke;* prob. < MD. or MLG cf. MD., MLG. *schok*, corn shock; IE. base **(s)qeu-* (as also in Lith. *kúgis*, heap of hay) < **qeu-*, to ben curve; basic sense "rounded heap"], a bunch of grai sheaves stacked together to cure and dry. *v.t. & v.i.* t gather and pile in shocks.

shock (shok), *n.* [prob. back-formation < *shock dog* 1. a thick, bushy or tangled mass, as of hair. 2. shock dog.

shock absorber, a mechanical device for lessening, b absorbing, the force of shocks and jarring, as on th springs of an automobile.

shock dog, [< *shough*, lap dog from Iceland], [Obs any dog with long, bushy hair, as a poodle.

shock·er (shok′ẽr), *n.* 1. a person or thing that shock 2. [British], a sensational piece of writing.

shock-head (shok′hed′), *adj.* shockheaded.

shock·head·ed (shok′hed′id), *adj.* having a thic bushy head of hair.

shock·ing (shok′iŋ), *adj.* 1. having an effect like th of a heavy blow or shock; staggering: as, the *shocki* news of his death. 2. highly offensive or revoltin disgusting, as to good taste, propriety, etc.: sometim used as a mere intensive meaning "very bad."

shock tactics, in *military science*, an attack procedu usually of a surprise nature, carried out by a hea concentration of forces.

shock therapy, in *psychiatry*, a method of treati certain psychotic conditions by injecting such dru as insulin or metrazol or by applying electric curre to the brain, in order to induce shock artificially: al **shock treatment.**

shock troops, troops especially chosen, trained, a equipped to lead an attack.

shock worker, a worker who has excelled in volunta increase of production, usually under an efficiency sy tem: see **Stakhanovism.**

shod (shod), past tense and past participle of **sh**

shod·dy (shod′i), *n.* [*pl.* SHODDIES (-iz)], [19th-c. Yorkshire dial., orig., inferior quarry stone or co prob. < *shode, shoad*, loose pieces < AS. *scadan*, to vide, separate; cf. SHED, *v.*], 1. an inferior woolen ya made from fibers taken from used fabrics and repr essed. 2. cheap woolen cloth made from this. 3. an thing of less worth or quality than it appears or claimed to have; sham. *adj.* [SHODDIER (-i-ẽr), SHO DIEST (-i-ist)], 1. made of shoddy or of any infer material. 2. lacking the worth or quality that it a pears or is claimed to have; sham.

shoe (shōō), *n.* [*pl.* SHOES (shōōz), *archaic* or *di* SHOON (shōōn)], [ME. *sho, scho;* AS. *scoh, sceoh;* akin G. *schuh;* IE. base **squ-*, to cover, hide, seen also in *obscurus* (cf. OBSCURE)], 1. an outer covering for t human foot, having a light upper part and a stiff or thi sole and heel: sometimes restricted to footwear th does not cover the ankle, as distinguished from a bo 2. a horseshoe. 3. something having a shape or u like that of a shoe; specifically, *a)* a metal cap ferrule fitted over the end of a cane, pole, staff, e *b)* the curved part of a brake that presses against wheel to create friction and retard or stop motio *c)* a part forming a base for the supports of a sup structure, as a roof, bridge, etc. *d)* the metal st along the bottom of a sled runner. *e)* the outer coveri or casing of a pneumatic rubber tire. *f)* the slidi contact plate by which an electric train picks current from the third rail. *g)* a metal protecting pl upon which a mechanical part moves. *v.t.* [SH (shod), SHOEING (shōō′iŋ)], 1. to furnish or fit with shoe or shoes. 2. to cover, tip, sheathe (a stick, weari surface, etc.) with a metal plate, ferrule, etc.

fill one's shoes, to take one's place.

in another's shoes, in another's position.

the shoe is on the other foot, the situation is co pletely reversed.

where the shoe pinches, the source of trouble, gri difficulty, etc.

shoe·bill (shōō′bil′), *n.* a large wading bird of the her family, with long legs and a heavy shoelike bill: fou along the White Nile in central Africa.

shoe·black (shōō′blak′), *n.* a person whose work cleaning and polishing shoes; bootblack.

shoe·horn (shōō′hôrn′), *n.* an implement of metal, ho etc. with a troughlike blade, inserted at the back of shoe to aid in slipping it on.

shoe·lace (shōō′lās′), *n.* a length of cord, leather, e used for lacing and fastening a shoe.

shoe·mak·er (shōō′māk′ẽr), *n.* a person whose busine is making or repairing shoes.

shoe·mak·ing (shōō′māk′iŋ), *n.* the business of maki or repairing shoes.

sho·er (shōō′ẽr), *n.* a person who shoes horses.

shoe·shine (shōō′shīn′), *n.* 1. the cleaning and polishing of a pair of shoes. 2. the polished surface resulting from this. 3. a shoeblack.
shoe·string (shōō′striŋ′), *n.* a shoelace.
on a shoestring, with little capital and resources, as in starting a business.
shoe tree, a shoe-shaped form inserted in a shoe to stretch it or preserve its shape.
sho·far (shō′fär, shō′fẽr), *n.* a shophar.
sho·gun (shō′gōōn′, shō′gun′), *n.* [Japan. < Chin. *chiang-chun*, leader of an army], any of the military governors of Japan who, until 1868, constituted a quasi-dynasty exercising absolute rule and relegating the emperors to a nominal position.
sho·gun·ate (shō′gōōn-āt′, shō′gun-it), *n.* 1. the rank, position, or office of a shogun. 2. government by a shogun or shoguns.
Sho·la·pur (shō′lə-poor′), *n.* a city in eastern Bombay, India: pop., 212,000.
shone (shōn), alternative past tense and past participle of **shine**.
shoo (shōō), *interj.* [a natural cry], 1. an exclamation used in scaring away chickens and other animals; hence, 2. go away! get out! *v.i.* [SHOOED (shōōd), SHOOING], to cry "shoo". *v.t.* to drive away abruptly, as by crying "shoo."
shook (shook), *n.* [prob. var. of *shock* (bunch of sheaves)], 1. a set of the pieces used in assembling a single box, barrel, cask, etc. 2. a shock of grain sheaves.
shook (shook), past tense of **shake**.
shoon (shōōn), *n.pl.* [Archaic or Dial.], shoes.
shoot (shōōt), *v.t.* [SHOT (shot), SHOT or *obs.* SHOTTEN (-′n), SHOOTING], [ME. *schoten, scheten;* AS. *sceotan;* akin to G. *schiessen;* IE. base *(*s*)*qeud-*, to throw, cast], 1. to pass swiftly over, by, across, etc.: as, he *shot* the rapids in his canoe. 2. to pour or empty out; dump, as down a chute. 3. to throw or hurl out or forth; cast (an anchor, fish net, etc.). 4. to slide (a door bolt) into or out of its fastening. 5. to variegate, streak, fleck, etc. with another color or substance; as, a blue sky *shot* with white clouds. 6. to put or thrust out or forth, as a branch, leaves, etc. 7. *a*) to send forth (a missile or projectile); discharge or fire (a bullet, arrow, etc.). *b*) to discharge or emit (rays) with force. 8. to send forth swiftly, dartingly, or with force or feeling, as a question, reply, glance, fist, etc. 9. to discharge or fire (a gun, bow, charge of explosive, etc.). 10. to hunt game in or on (a tract of land). 11. to take the altitude of, as a star, with a transit, sextant, etc. 12. to hit, wound, or kill with a missile discharged from a weapon. 13. to take a picture of with a camera; photograph; film. 14. [Slang], to send; hand; give: as, *shoot* the salt to me. 15. in *games & sports*, *a*) to throw, drive, or propel (a ball, marble, etc.) toward the objective. *b*) to make or score (a goal, points, total strokes, etc.). *c*) to play, as golf, pool, craps, etc. *v.i.* 1. to move swiftly, as an arrow from a bow; rush; dart. 2. to be felt suddenly and keenly, as heat, pain, etc. 3. to grow or sprout, especially rapidly. 4. to jut out; project. 5. to send forth a missile or projectile, especially from a gun. 6. to discharge bullets, arrows, etc.; go off; fire: as, the gun won't *shoot* until it is cocked. 7. *a*) to photograph a scene or subject. *b*) to start the cameras working in photographing a motion-picture scene. 8. to hunt game with a gun: as, he fishes but he doesn't *shoot*. 9. in *sports*, *a*) to propel a ball, etc. toward the objective. *b*) to play golf, pool, etc.: as, he's been *shooting* poorly for some time. *n.* 1. a shooting trip, party, or contest: as, a turkey *shoot*. 2. the action of growing or sprouting; hence, 3. a new growth; sprout; twig. 4. action or motion like that of something shot, as of water from a hose. 5. a sloping trough or channel; chute. 6. a twinge or spasm of pain. 7. [Archaic], the act of shooting. 8. in *rowing*, the interval between strokes. *interj.* [Slang], an exclamation expressing disgust, disappointment, etc.
shoot at, [Colloq.], to try to reach, gain, or accomplish; strive for.
shoot down, to bring down by hitting with a shot or shots.
shoot off one's (or **at the**) **mouth**, [Slang], to speak without caution or discretion; blab.
shoot up, 1. to grow or rise rapidly. 2. to hit with several or many shots; hence, 3. [Colloq.], to spread terror and destruction throughout by lawless and wanton shooting.
shot through with, having too much or too many; filled with (something unwanted, dangerous, etc.).
shoot·ing (shōōt′iŋ), *n.* the act of a person or thing that shoots.
shooting box, a small house or lodge used by sportsmen during the shooting season.
shooting gallery, a place, as at an amusement park, for practice shooting at enclosed targets.
shooting iron, [Slang], any firearm.
shooting star, 1. a meteor. 2. any of a number of related plants with oblong leaves and clusters of rose, white, and purple flowers whose petals are turned back.
shop (shop), *n.* [ME. *schoppe;* AS. *sceoppa*, booth, stall; akin to G. *schopf*, porch, lean-to; IE. base *(*s*)*qeup-*, *(*s*)*qeub-h-*, a bundle, wisp; prob. basic meaning "roof made of straw bundles"], 1. a place where things are offered for sale; store. 2. a place where a particular kind of work is done: as, a carpenter *shop*. *v.i.* [SHOPPED (shopt), SHOPPING], to visit shops in order to look at, price, or buy things that are for sale.
set up shop, to open or start a business.
shut up shop, 1. to close a place of business, as for the night. 2. to go out of business.
talk shop, to discuss one's work or things related to one's work.
shop·girl (shop′gũrl′), *n.* a young woman who works as a clerk in a store.
sho·phar (shō′fär, shō′fẽr), *n.* [Heb. *shōphār*], a ram's horn formerly used as a signaling trumpet by the Jews in battle and still blown in synagogues on the New Year and the Day of Atonement: also spelled **shofar**.
shop·keep·er (shop′kēp′ẽr), *n.* a person who operates a shop, or store.
shop·lift·er (shop′lif′tẽr), *n.* a person who steals articles exposed for sale in a shop.
shop·lift·ing (shop′lif′tiŋ), *n.* the stealing of articles exposed for sale in a shop.
shop·man (shop′mən), *n.* [*pl.* SHOPMEN (-mən)], 1. a shopkeeper. 2. a salesperson in a store; clerk.
shop·per (shop′ẽr), *n.* 1. a person who shops. 2. a person hired by a store to shop for others. 3. a person hired by a store to compare competitors' merchandise and prices.
shop·ping (shop′iŋ), *n.* the act of visiting a shop or store to look at, price, or buy goods offered for sale.
shop steward, a person elected by his fellow workers in the local branch of a labor union to represent them in dealing with the employer and to see that union rules are enforced.
shop·talk (shop′tôk′), *n.* 1. the specialized or technical vocabulary and idioms of those in the same work, way of life etc.: see **slang**. 2. conversation about one's work or business, especially after hours.
shop·walk·er (shop′wôk′ẽr), *n.* a person hired by a store to supervise clerks and direct customers; floorwalker.
shop·win·dow (shop′win′dō), *n.* a show window.
shop·worn (shop′wôrn′, shop′wōrn′), *adj.* wrinkled, soiled, worn, etc. from having been displayed in a shop.
Shor·an, shor·an (shôr′an, shō′ran), *n.* [< *Short Range Navigation*], a radar system by which positions on the earth's surface are located by means of high-frequency radio waves transmitted from a plane to ground stations.
shore (shôr, shōr), *n.* [ME. *schore;* prob. < MLG. or MD.; cf. MLG. (Late MD.) *schore*, in same sense; IE. base **sqeū-*, to separate, divide; prob. basic sense "point of division (between land and water)"], 1. land at or near the edge of a body of water, especially a large body. 2. land as opposed to water. 3. in *law*, the land area between the marks of high and low water.
in shore, near, nearer, or toward the shore.
off shore, 1. away from the shore and toward the water. 2. close to shore.

SYN.—**shore** is the general word applied to an edge of land directly bordering on the sea, a lake, a river, etc.; **coast** applies only to land along the sea; **beach** applies to a level stretch of sandy or pebbly seashore or lake shore, usually one that is washed by high water; **strand** is a poetic word for **shore** or **beach**; **bank** applies to the rising or steep land at the edge of a stream.

shore (shôr, shōr), *n.* [Late ME. *schore* < MD. or MLG. *schōre;* prob. < base of SHEAR], a prop, as a beam, placed under or against something for support or stability; specifically, any of the timbers used to support a boat or ship that is out of water. *v.t.* [SHORED (shôrd, shōrd), SHORING], to support or make stable with a shore or shores; prop (usually with *up*).

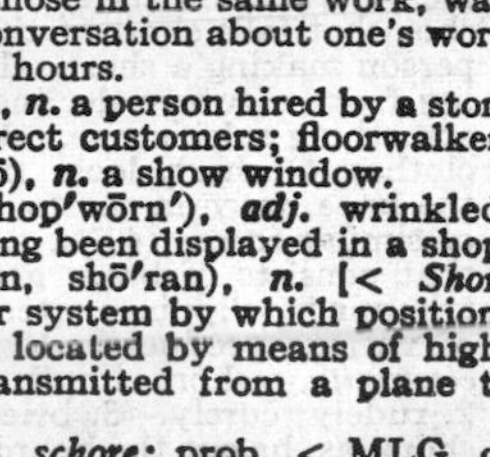

SHORES

shore (shôr, shōr), archaic or dialectal past tense and past participle of **shear**.
Shore, Jane (shôr, shōr), 1445?–1527?; mistress of Edward IV of England.
shore-based (shôr′bāst′, shōr′bāst′), *adj.* designating aircraft that operate from bases on shore rather than from aircraft carriers.
shore bird, any of a number of birds that nest on the shore: the group includes the curlews, snipes, sandpipers, ruffs, etc.

shore dinner, a meal consisting of freshly caught sea food.
shore leave, leave granted to a ship's crew members for going ashore.
shore·less (shôr′lis, shōr′lis), *adj.* [Poetic], having no shore; extending without end; boundless.
shore line, a line marking the edge of a body of water.
shore patrol, a detail of the United States Navy, Coast Guard, or Marine Corps acting as military police on shore: abbreviated **SP, S.P.**
shore·ward (shôr′wẽrd, shōr′wẽrd), *adv.* toward the shore. *adj.* moving toward the shore.
shor·ing (shôr′iŋ, shōr′iŋ), *n.* 1. the act of supporting with or as with shores. 2. a system of shores used for support.
shorn (shôrn, shōrn), alternative past participle of **shear.**
short (shôrt), *adj.* [ME. *schort;* AS. *scort, sceort* (cf. SHIRT); akin to OHG. *scurz,* ON. *skort,* short piece of clothing; IE. ***sqer-d** < base ***sqer-**, to cut, seen also in L. *caro, carnis,* lit., cut-off piece of flesh; cf. CARNAL], 1. not extending far from end to end; not long. 2. not great in span, range, or scope, as a distance, journey, throw, view, etc. 3. low in height; not tall. 4. lasting but a little time; brief. 5. not retentive for long: said of memory. 6. condensed; concise; brief, as a literary style, story, speech, etc. 7. brief or abrupt to the point of rudeness; curt; hence, 8. short-tempered. 9. less than or lacking a sufficient or correct amount: as, a *short* measure, the loss of my laundry has left me *short,* we are *short* ten dollars. 10. not far enough to reach the mark, objective, etc.: as, a shot that fell *short.* 11. having a tendency to break or crumble; friable, as clay, pastry, etc. 12. in *commerce, a)* not having in possession at the time of sale the commodities or securities one is selling. *b)* of or designating a sale of commodities or securities not in the possession of the seller. 13. in *phonetics & prosody,* comparatively brief in duration: said of sounds, syllables, etc. *n.* 1. something that is short; specifically, *a)* a short sound or syllable contrasted with one that is long, as in prosody. *b)* a motion-picture short subject. *c)* a fish, etc. that is below the size that may be legally taken. *d)* a shot that falls short of the target or objective. 2. *a)* a person making a short sale with the intention of profiting from a future decline in price. *b)* a short sale or something sold in one. 3. *pl. a)* knee breeches; smallclothes. *b)* short, loose trousers reaching part way to the knee, worn in sports, etc. *c)* a man's undergarment of similar form. 4. *pl.* a by-product of wheat milling that consists of bran, germ, and coarse meal. 5. *pl.* trimmings, clippings, etc. left over in the manufacture of various products. 6. in *baseball,* shortstop. 7. in *electricity,* a short circuit. *adv.* 1. abruptly; suddenly. 2. rudely; curtly. 3. briefly; concisely. 4. so as to be short: as, he cut the board off too *short.* 5. on the near side of a given point; so as not to reach a given condition, etc.: as, we were stopped just *short* of disaster. 6. without having possession (of that which is sold). *v.t. & v.i.* in *electricity,* to short-circuit.—*SYN.* see **brief.**
fall (or **come**) **short,** 1. to be lacking or insufficient. 2. to fail to reach or attain.
for short, by way of abbreviation or contraction.
in short, 1. in summing up; to summarize. 2. in a few words; briefly.
make short work of, to deal with or dispose of quickly.
run short, to have less than enough.
short and sweet, brief, usually unexpectedly so.
short for, being a shortened form of; being an abbreviation or nickname for.
short of, 1. not equaling; less than. 2. without a sufficient or correct amount of; lacking. 3. not far enough to reach (the mark, objective, etc.).
short account, 1. the account of a person who sells securities or commodities short. 2. the total short sales in a particular commodity or in the market as a whole.
short·age (shôr′tij), *n.* [*short* + *-age*], a deficiency in the quantity or amount needed; deficit; insufficiency: abbreviated **shtg.**
short-armed (shôrt′ärmd′), *adj.* 1. having disproportionately short arms. 2 having a short reach. 3. struck with the arm bent, as a blow.
short·bread (shôrt′bred′), *n.* a rich, crumbly cake or cooky made with shortening.
short·cake (shôrt′kāk′), *n.* 1. a crisp, light biscuit served with fruit, whipped cream, etc. as a dessert. 2. any sweet cake, as spongecake, served in this way. 3. a dessert made with either of these: as, strawberry *shortcake.*
short·change (shôrt′chānj′), *v.t. & v.i.* [SHORTCHANGED (-chānjd′), SHORTCHANGING], [Colloq.], 1. to give less money than is due in change. 2. to cheat.
short-cir·cuit (shôrt′sũr′kit), *v.t. & v.i.* to make a short circuit (in).
short circuit, 1. a side circuit of very low relative resistance connecting two points in an electric circuit of higher resistance so as to deflect most of the current; hence, 2. loosely, a disrupted electric circuit resulting from this.
short·com·ing (shôrt′kum′iŋ), *n.* a coming short of what is expected or required; fault; deficiency; inadequacy; defect, as in character.
short commons, a scanty food ration.
short covering, the buying of securities or commodities to close out a short sale.
short cut, 1. a shorter way to get to the same place; hence, 2. any way of saving time, effort, expense, etc.
short division, division, usually by any number up to twelve, without written indication of the process used.
short·en (shôr′t'n), *v.t.* 1. to make short or shorter; reduce in length, amount, or extent. 2. to furl or reef (a sail) so that less canvas is exposed to the breeze. 3. to add shortening to (pastry, etc.). *v.i.* to become short or shorter.
SYN.—**shorten** implies reduction in length, extent, or duration (to *shorten* a rope, a visit, one's life, etc.); **curtail** implies a making shorter than was originally intended, as because of necessity or expediency (expenditures *curtailed* because of reduced income); **abridge** implies reduction in compass by condensing, omitting parts, etc. but usually connotes that what is essential is kept (to *abridge* a dictionary); **abbreviate** usually refers to the shortening of a word or phrase by contraction or by substitution of a symbol, but also has extended, sometimes jocular applications (an *abbreviated* costume). —*ANT.* lengthen, extend, expand.
short·en·ing (shôr′t'n-iŋ, shôrt′niŋ), *n.* 1. the act of making or becoming short or shorter. 2. fat used in baked goods to make them crisp or flaky.
Shorter Catechism, a catechism adopted by the Westminster Assembly in 1647: used chiefly by the Presbyterians.
short-haired (shôrt′hârd′), *adj.* having short hair or fur.
short·hand (shôrt′hand′), *n.* any system of speed writing using symbols that can be made quickly to represent letters, words, and phrases. *adj.* 1. using shorthand. 2. written in shorthand.
short-hand·ed (shôrt′han′did), *adj.* short of workers or helpers; needing more hands.
short·head (shôrt′hed′), *n.* 1. a head with a cephalic index of 80 or more. 2. a person having such a head; brachycephalic person.
short-head·ed, short·head·ed (shôrt′hed′id), *adj.* having a shorthead.
short·horn (shôrt′hôrn′), *n.* any of a breed of heavy, well-formed cattle with short, curved horns: they are raised for both beef and milk and vary widely in color.
shor·ti·a (shôr′ti-ə), *n.* [Mod. L. *Shortia,* after C. W. *Short* (1794–1863), Am. horticulturist], any of a number of related evergreen plants with nodding, bell-shaped white flowers on long stalks.
short·ish (shôr′tish), *adj.* rather short.
short-leg·ged (shôrt′leg′id, shôrt′legd′), *adj.* having short legs.
short-lived (shôrt′līvd′; *also, esp. Brit.,* shôrt′livd′), *adj.* 1. living only a short time. 2. lasting or continuing only a short time.
short·ly (shôrt′li), *adv.* 1. in a few words; briefly. 2. in a short time; soon. 3. abruptly. 4. rudely; curtly.
short-or·der (shôrt′ôr′dẽr), *adj.* [< *in short order*], offering or cooking short orders.
short order, any food quickly prepared after it has been ordered in a restaurant.
in short order, quickly.
short-range (shôrt′rānj′), *adj.* limited in range; carrying or reaching only a short distance.
short sale, a sale of securities or commodities which the seller does not yet have but expects to buy at a lower price before the date of delivery as contracted.
short short story, a story so short that it can usually be printed complete on one page of a magazine: characteristically it conveys a single mood, is concise, fast moving, and has a surprise ending.
short shrift, 1. originally, a very brief period of confession and absolution before death. 2. very little care or attention, as from lack of patience or sympathy. 3. little or no mercy or respite.
make short shrift of, to make short work of; dismiss summarily: also **give short shrift.**
short·sight·ed (shôrt′sīt′id), *adj.* 1. unable to see clearly at a distance; nearsighted; myopic. 2. having or showing a lack of foresight.
short snort, [Slang], a quick drink of liquor.
short snorter, [< *short snort*], a member of an informal organization composed of passengers or pilots who have made transoceanic flights and who carry, as a token of membership, a dollar bill or pound note autographed by three or more other members.
short-spo·ken (shôrt′spō′k'n), *adj.* 1. using only a few words to express one's thoughts; laconic; hence, 2. brief to the point of rudeness; curt.
short·stop (shôrt′stop′), *n.* in *baseball,* the infielder stationed between second and third base.
short story, a kind of story varying widely in length but shorter than the novel or novelette: characteristically it develops a single central theme or impression and is limited in scope and number of characters.
short subject, any short presentation shown along with

the featured picture in a motion-picture program: animated cartoons and travelogues are *short subjects.*
short-tem·pered (shôrt'tem'pẽrd), *adj.* having a tendency to lose one's temper; easily or quickly angered.
short-term (shôrt'tũrm'), *adj.* requiring payment or coming due in a short time, as a loan.
short ton, a unit of weight, equal to 2,000 pounds avoirdupois: abbreviated **sh. tn.**: cf. **ton.**
short-waist·ed (shôrt'wās'tid), *adj.* unusually short between shoulders and waistline; with a high waistline.
short-wave (shôrt'wāv'), *adj.* in *radio,* of, by, or using short wave.
short wave, a radio wave sixty meters or less in length.
short-wind·ed (shôrt'win'did), *adj.* 1. easily put out of breath by exercise. 2. breathing with quick, labored breaths.
short·y (shôr'ti), *n.* [*pl.* SHORTIES (-tiz)], [Colloq.], a person or thing of less than average height or size.
Sho·sho·ne (shō-shō'ni), *n.* 1. a member of a group of Shoshonean Indians originally scattered over Montana, Wyoming, and Oregon: also spelled **Shoshoni.** 2. an American Indian language spoken by this group. 3. a river in northwestern Wyoming, flowing into the Big Horn River: length, 135 mi.
Sho·sho·ne·an (shō-shō'ni-ən, shō'shə-nē'ən), *adj.* designating or of a subbranch of the Uto-Aztecan linguistic family of North American Indians: it includes the Shoshone, Comanche, Ute, Paiute, Hopi, etc.
Shoshone Cavern, a large cave in northwestern Wyoming: area, 210 acres: a national monument.
Shoshone Dam, a dam on the Shoshone River: height, 328 ft.
Shoshone Falls, a waterfall of the Snake River, southern Idaho: height, 210 ft.
Sho·sta·ko·vich, Dmi·tri (d'mē'tri shô'stä-kô'vich; Eng. shos'tə-kō'vich), 1906– ; Russian composer.
shot (shot), *n.* [ME. *schotte;* AS. *sceot* < base of *sceotan* (cf. SHOOT); akin to G. *schoss*], 1. the act of shooting; discharge of a missile, especially from a gun. 2. *a*) the distance over which a missile travels. *b*) figuratively, range; reach; scope. 3. an attempt to hit with a missile; hence, 4. *a*) any attempt; try. *b*) a guess; conjecture. 5. a pointed, critical remark. 6. a stroke, throw, drive, etc. in any of several games. 7. *a*) a projectile designed to be discharged from a firearm or cannon, especially a solid ball or bullet as distinguished from an explosive shell. *b*) such projectiles collectively. 8. *a*) lead in small pellets, of which a quantity is used for a single charge of a shotgun. *b*) a single pellet of this kind. 9. a heavy metal ball cast for distance by contestants. 10. a blast or the amount of explosive used for a blast, as in mining. 11. a marksman: as, he's a fair *shot.* 12. a photographic record; a single photograph, or a sequence in motion-picture film. 13. [cf. SCOT], an amount due, especially for drinks or entertainment, or one's share of payment. 14. [Colloq.], a dose, as of vaccine, given by hypodermic injection. 15. [Colloq.], a drink of liquor; specifically, a jigger. 16. [Colloq.], something to bet on, considered from the standpoint of odds or chances of winning: as, that horse is a twenty-to-one *shot. v.t.* [SHOTTED (-id), SHOTTING], to load or weight with shot.
a long shot, 1. an attempt not likely to succeed. 2. [Colloq.], a bet against heavy odds; hence, 3. [Colloq.], someone or something considered to have little chance of winning or succeeding.
have (or **take**) **a shot at,** [Colloq.], to make a try at.
like a shot, 1. quickly; rapidly. 2. suddenly.
not by a long shot, [Slang], not even by the slightest chance; not at all; never.
put the shot, to heave or throw a heavy metal ball with an overhand pushing motion in a field contest for distance.
shot (shot), past tense and past participle of **shoot.** *adj.* 1. variegated, streaked, flecked, etc. with another color or substance. 2. woven with threads of different colors so as to appear iridescent. 3. [Colloq.], no longer usable; ruined; worn out. 4. [Colloq.], destined for, or having met with, failure, defeat, frustration, etc.: as, his chances are *shot.*
shote (shōt), *n.* [dial. *shoot, shot;* cf. SHOAT], a young pig: also spelled **shoat.**
shot effect, an irregularity in the emission of thermions from the electron tube filament, resulting in popping noises upon amplification.
shot·gun (shot'gun'), *n.* a smoothbore gun used for firing a charge of small shot at short range, as in hunting small game.
shot-put (shot'poot'), *n.* 1. a contest in which athletes put the shot. 2. a single throw of the shot.
shot·ten (shot''n), obsolete past participle of **shoot.** *adj.* [in specialized sense (esp. applied to herrings), prob. influenced by D. *schoten*], 1. that has recently spawned and so become of inferior food value: said of fish; hence, 2. [Archaic], undesirable; worthless.
should (shood), *v.* [ME. *scholde, shold;* AS. *sceolde, scolde,* p.t. of *sceal, scal,* I am obliged; see SHALL], 1. past tense of **shall.** 2. an auxiliary used to express *a*) obligation, duty, propriety, necessity, etc.: e.g., children *should* get hot lunches. *b*) expectation or probability: e.g., since they left Saturday they *should* be here by Monday: equivalent to *ought to* and not replaceable by *would. c*) futurity from the standpoint of the past in indirect quotations where *shall* and *will* were used in the direct quotations: replaceable by *would*: e.g., I said I *should* (or *would*) be home by nine. *d*) futurity in polite or unemphatic requests or in statements with implications of uncertainty or doubt: replaceable by *would*: e.g., *should* (or *would*) you like some tea? I *should* (or *would*) think he'd like it. *e*) a future condition: e.g., if I *should* go, would you be there?: in this sense *would* is considered colloquial or, by some, substandard. *f*) a past condition, real or unreal: replaceable by *would*: e.g., I *should* (or *would*) have gone, but you never asked me. N.B. In formal speech the distinctions between *should* and *would* are the same as those between *shall* and *will.*
shoul·der (shōl'dẽr), *n.* [ME. *schuldere;* AS. *sculdor;* akin to G. *schulter;* prob. < IE. **sql-dhra,* shoulder blade used as a spade < base **sqel-,* to cut; cf. SHELL, SHILLING, SKULL, etc.], 1. *a*) the joint connecting the arm or forelimb with the body. *b*) the part of the body including this joint and extending along the top (in quadrupeds, the side) of the trunk to the base of the neck. 2. *pl.* the two shoulders and the part of the back between them: often used figuratively with reference to this region of the body as a place where burdens are often carried. 3. a cut of meat consisting of the upper foreleg and attached parts: see **pork,** illus. 4. the part of a garment that covers the shoulder. 5. the part of a hide anterior to the butt, corresponding to the animal's shoulders. 6. something like a shoulder in shape or position; shoulderlike projection. 7. the angle between the face and flank of a bastion in a fortification. 8. the part of the top of a piece of type which extends beyond the base of the raised letter or character. 9. either edge of a road or highway. *v.t.* 1. to push or thrust along or through, with or as with the shoulder: as, he *shouldered* his way through the crowd. 2. to take or carry upon the shoulder; hence, 3. to assume the burden of. *v.i.* to push with the shoulder or shoulders.
cry on someone's shoulder, to seek comfort or sympathy in someone; tell one's troubles to someone.
put one's shoulder to the wheel, to set to work vigorously; put forth vigorous effort.
rub shoulders with, to associate or mingle with (famous or prominent people, etc.).
shoulder arms, to rest a rifle against the (right or left) shoulder, supporting the butt with the hand on the same side.
shoulder to shoulder, 1. side by side and close together. 2. working together; with common effort.
straight from the shoulder, 1. moving straight forward from the shoulder: said of a blow. 2. without reserve or evasion; frankly.
turn (or **give**) **a cold shoulder to,** 1. to treat with coldness or disdain; show dislike for. 2. to avoid; shun.
shoulder blade, either of the two flat bones in the upper back articulated with the humerus; scapula.
shoulder knot, a knot of ribbon or lace worn on the shoulder as an insigne, decoration, etc.
shoulder strap, 1. a strap worn over the shoulder to support the garment, etc. to which it is attached. 2. a piece of cloth fixed to the shoulder of a uniform to hold insignia.
should·est (shood'ist), alternative archaic second person singular of **should**: used with *thou.*
should·n't (shood''nt), should not.
shouldst (shoodst), alternative archaic second person singular of **should**: used with *thou.*
shout (shout), *n.* [ME. *schoute;* prob. < an AS. cognate of ON. *skūta,* a taunt, via dial.; IE. base *(*s*)*qeud-,* to cry out], 1. a loud sound made with the voice; loud, sudden cry or call. 2. any sudden, loud outburst or uproar. *v.t.* to utter in a loud voice; say or express in a shout. *v.i.* to utter a shout; cry out loudly.
shout (someone) down, to silence or overwhelm (someone) by loud shouting; shout louder than (another).
shove (shuv), *v.t.* & *v.i.* [SHOVED (shuvd), SHOVING], [ME. *schouven, schoven;* AS. *scufan;* akin to Goth. *-skiuban,* G. *schieben;* IE. base **sqeubh-,* to push, thrust, throw; cf. SHOVEL], 1. to push or thrust, as along a surface. 2. to push roughly. *n.* the act of shoving; a push or thrust. —*SYN.* see **push.**
shove off, 1. to push (a boat) away from shore, as in departing. 2. [Colloq.], to start off; leave; depart.
shov·el (shuv''l), *n.* [ME. *schovele;* AS. *sceofol, sceofl* < base of *scufan,* to shove; cf. SHOVE], 1. a tool with a broad, deep scoop or blade and a long handle: used in

lifting and moving loose material, as earth, snow, gravel, etc. 2. a shovelful. 3. a shovel hat. ***v.t.*** [SHOVELED or SHOVELLED (-'ld), SHOVELING or SHOVELLING], 1. to lift and move with a shovel. 2. to clean or dig out with a shovel, as a path. 3. to put or throw in large quantities: as, he *shoveled* sugar into his coffee.

shov·el·bill (shuv″'l-bil′), ***n.*** a river duck; shoveler.

shov·el·board (shuv″'l-bôrd′, shuv″'l-bōrd′), ***n.*** shuffleboard.

shov·el·er (shuv″'l-ẽr), ***n.*** 1. a person or thing that shovels. 2. a kind of river duck with a very long, broad, flattened bill. Also spelled **shoveller.**

shov·el·ful (shuv″'l-fool′), ***n.*** [*pl.* SHOVELFULS (-foolz′)], as much as a shovel will hold.

shovel hat, a stiff, low-crowned hat with a broad brim turned up at the sides: worn by some English clergymen.

shov·el·head (shuv″'l-hed′), ***n.*** 1. a small shark related to the hammerhead: its head resembles the blade of a shovel. 2. the shovel-nosed sturgeon.

shov·el·ler (shuv″'l-ẽr), ***n.*** a shoveler.

shov·el-nosed (shuv″'l-nōzd′), ***adj.*** having a broad, flattened nose, head, or bill.

shovel-nosed shark, either of two flat-headed sharks found along the California coast.

shovel-nosed sturgeon, a kind of fresh-water sturgeon of the Mississippi Valley, valued as a food fish.

show (shō), ***v.t.*** [SHOWED (shōd), SHOWN (shōn) or SHOWED, SHOWING], [ME. *schowen, schewen;* AS. *sceawian;* akin to G. *schauen,* to look at; IE. base **qeu-,* to notice, seen also in L. *cavere,* to beware (cf. CAUTION)], 1. to bring or put in sight or view; cause or allow to appear or be seen; make visible; exhibit; display. 2. to enter (animals, flowers, paintings, etc.) in a show or exhibition. 3. to guide; conduct: as, the bellboy *showed* him to his room. 4. to direct a person's observation or attention to; point out: as, we *showed* him the sights. 5. to reveal, manifest, or make evident (an emotion, condition, quality, etc.) by behavior or outward sign: as, he *showed* his anger without meaning to, the judge *showed* mercy to the prisoners. 6. to exhibit or manifest (oneself or itself) in a given character, condition, etc.: as, the group has *shown* itself to be reliable. 7. to make known, manifest, or clear; reveal; explain: as, he has *shown* the difference between them. 8. to make evident by logical procedure; prove; demonstrate: as, scientists have *shown* that it is possible. 9. to register; indicate: as, a barometer *shows* the air pressure. 10. to grant or bestow (favor, grace, etc.). 11. in *law,* to allege; plead: as, *show* cause. ***v.i.*** 1. to be or become seen or visible; appear. 2. to be apparent or noticeable: as, the scratch won't *show.* 3. to have a given appearance; appear: as, it *shows* poorly in this light. 4. to finish third or better in a horse or dog race. 5. in the *theater,* to give a performance; appear. ***n.*** 1. a showing, demonstration, or manifestation: as, a *show* of passion. 2. a display or appearance, specifically a colorful or striking one: as, the costumed dancers made quite a *show.* 3. spectacular, pompous display; ostentation. 4. an indication of the presence of metal, coal, oil, etc. in the earth; trace. 5. something false or superficial; semblance; pretense: as, her sympathy was mere *show.* 6. a person or thing looked upon as peculiar, ridiculous, laughable, etc.; spectacle; sight. 7. a public display or exhibition, as of art, animals, flowers, etc. 8. a presentation of entertainment, especially of a theatrical nature: as, the *show* begins at eight o'clock, who sponsors this radio *show?* 9. [Colloq.], any undertaking, matter, or affair: as, his political career was a disgraceful *show.* 10. [Military Slang], a battle, campaign, etc.

for show, in order to attract notice or attention.

show in, to usher or conduct into a given place.

show off, 1. to make a display of; exhibit in a showy manner. 2. to behave in a manner intended to attract attention; make a vain display.

show out, to usher or conduct out of a given place.

show up, 1. to bring or come to light; expose or be exposed, as faults. 2. to be clearly seen; be prominent or apparent. 3. to come; arrive; make an appearance. 4. [Colloq.], to be far superior to.

stand (or **have**) **a show,** [Colloq.], to have a chance, especially a remote one.

SYN.—**show** implies a putting or bringing something into view so that it can be seen or looked at (*show* us the garden); to **display** something is to spread it out before one so that it is shown to advantage (jewelry ***displayed*** on a sales counter); **exhibit** implies prominent display, often for the purpose of attracting public attention or inspection (to ***exhibit*** products at an exposition); **expose** implies the laying open and displaying of something that has been covered or concealed (this bathing suit *exposes* her scar); **flaunt** implies an ostentatious, impudent, or defiant display (to *flaunt* one's riches, vices, etc.).

show bill, a sheet or placard containing a notice or advertisement: also **show card.**

show·boat (shō′bōt′), ***n.*** a boat containing a theater and carrying a troupe of actors who play river towns.

show·bread (shō′bred′), ***n.*** shewbread.

show business, the theater, vaudeville, motion pictures, circuses, etc. as a business or industry.

show·case (shō′kās′), ***n.*** a glass-enclosed case for protecting things on display, as in a store or exhibition.

show·down (shō′doun′), ***n.*** [Colloq.], 1. in *poker,* the laying down of the cards face up. 2. a revelation or disclosure, as of the true nature of a situation.

show·er (shō′ẽr), ***n.*** a person who shows, exhibits, demonstrates, etc.

show·er (shou′ẽr), ***n.*** [ME. *schoure;* AS. *scur;* akin to G. *schauer,* shower, squall; IE. base **(s)qeu-,* to cover, cover over, as also in L. *obscurus* (see OBSCURE)], 1. a brief fall of rain, hail, or sleet. 2. a sudden, abundant fall or discharge, as of tears, meteors, rays, sparks, etc. 3. an abundant flow; rush: as, a *shower* of complaints. 4. a party during which a number of gifts are presented to the guest of honor: as, a bridal *shower.* 5. a shower bath. ***v.t.*** 1. to make wet with water or other liquid; sprinkle; spray. 2. to pour forth in a shower; scatter or distribute abundantly: as, he *showered* gifts upon us. ***v.i.*** 1. to fall or come in a shower. 2. to take a shower bath.

shower bath, 1. a bath in which the body is sprayed with fine streams of water from small jets. 2. an apparatus or room used for such a bath.

show·er·y (shou′ẽr-i), ***adj.*** 1. raining in showers; raining briefly and frequently. 2. of or like a shower.

show·i·ly (shō′ə-li), ***adv.*** in a showy manner.

show·i·ness (shō′i-nis), ***n.*** the quality or condition of being showy.

show·ing (shō′iŋ), ***n.*** 1. the act of presenting or bringing to view or notice: as, a *showing* of evidence. 2. an exhibition; formal display.

show·man (shō′mən), ***n.*** [*pl.* SHOWMEN (-mən)], 1. a person who makes a business of producing or managing shows. 2. a person who is skilled at this or at presenting anything in an interesting or dramatic manner.

show·man·ship (shō′mən-ship′), ***n.*** [*showman* + *-ship*], the art of being a showman; skill as a showman.

shown (shōn), alternative past participle of **show.**

show-off (shō′ôf′), ***n.*** 1. the act of showing off; vain or showy display. 2. [Colloq.], one who shows off.

show of hands, a display or raising of hands, as in voting, volunteering, etc.

show·piece (shō′pēs′), ***n.*** 1. something displayed or exhibited; hence, 2. something that is a fine example of its kind.

show place, 1. a place that is displayed or exhibited to the public for its beauty, etc.; hence, 2. any place that is beautiful, lavishly furnished, etc.

show·room (shō′rōōm′, shō′room′), ***n.*** a room where merchandise is displayed, as for advertising or sale.

show window, a store window in which goods are displayed.

show·y (shō′i), ***adj.*** [SHOWIER (-i-ẽr), SHOWIEST (-i-ist)], 1. of striking or attractive appearance; making a show. 2. attracting attention in a cheap or artificial way; flashy; ostentatious. —***SYN.*** see **gaudy.**

shpt., shipment.

shr., share; shares.

shrank (shraŋk), alternative past tense of **shrink.**

shrap·nel (shrap′nəl), ***n.*** [after Gen. H. *Shrapnel* (1761–1842), of the British Army, who invented it], 1. an artillery shell filled with an explosive charge and many small metal balls, set to explode in the air over the objective. 2. such shells collectively, or the metal balls scattered by the explosion of such shells. 3. shell fragments scattered by any exploding shell.

DIAGRAM OF SHRAPNEL SHELL
C, cartridge; F, fuse; P, powder charge; S, shrapnel

shred (shred), ***n.*** [ME. *schrede;* AS. *screada;* akin to G. *schrot;* IE. base **sqreut-* (whence also L. *scrotum;* cf. SCROTUM) < **sqer-,* to cut; cf. SHROUD], 1. an irregular strip or long, narrow piece cut or torn off. 2. a very small piece or amount; fragment; particle: as, there's not a *shred* of truth in it. ***v.t.*** [SHREDDED (-id) or SHRED, SHREDDING], to cut or tear into shreds.

shred·der (shred′ẽr), ***n.*** a person or thing that shreds.

Shreve·port (shrēv′pôrt′, shrēv′pōrt′), ***n.*** a city in northwestern Louisiana, on the Red River: pop., 164,000.

shrew (shrōō), ***n.*** [sense 2 only in ME. *schrewe,* malicious person; AS. *screawa;* sense 1 may be a special application of this in view of the malignant reputation of the mammal; cf. MHG. *schröuwel,* devil; the AS. form would then be a nickname; cf. SHREWD], 1. a small, mouselike mammal with soft, brown fur and a long snout: it feeds on insects and worms and was once thought venomous. 2. a scolding, nagging, evil-tempered woman.

shrewd (shrōōd), ***adj.*** [ME. *shrewed, schrewed,* pp. of *schrewen,* to curse < *schrewe;* see SHREW], 1. keen-witted, clever, or sharp in practical affairs; astute. 2. [Archaic], *a)* keen; sharp. *b)* artful; cunning. 3. [Obs.],

a) evil; bad; wicked. *b*) sly; mischievous. *c*) shrewish.
SYN.—**shrewd** implies keenness of mind, sharp insight, and a cleverness or sharpness in practical matters (a *shrewd* comment, businessman, etc.); **sagacious** implies keenness of discernment and farsightedness in judgment (a *sagacious* counselor); **perspicacious** suggests the penetrating mental vision or discernment that enables one clearly to see and understand what is obscure, hidden, etc. (a *perspicacious* judge of character); **astute** implies shrewdness combined with sagacity and sometimes connotes, in addition, artfulness or craftiness (an *astute* politician). See also **clever**.

shrew·ish (shrōō′ish), *adj.* like a shrew in disposition; evil-tempered; nagging; scolding.

shrew·mouse (shrōō′mous′), *n.* [*pl.* SHREWMICE (-mīs′)], a shrew.

Shrews·bur·y (shrōōz′ber′i, shrōz′bĕr-i), *n.* the county seat of Shropshire, England: pop., 38,000.

shriek (shrēk), *v.i.* [ME. *schriken*, var. of *scriken*; prob. < ON. **skrīka*, to cry, parallel with *skrīkia*, cry of birds & Norw. *skrīka*, to cry; IE. echoic base **ker-*, etc. (as also in L. *corvus;* cf. CORVINE), but prob. with direct echoic refashioning in Gmc. languages; cf. SHRIKE, SCREECH], to make a loud, sharp, piercing cry or sound, as certain birds and beasts, persons in terror, anger, pain, or laughter, or inanimate things that produce sound; screech. *v.t.* to utter with a shriek. *n.* a loud, sharp, piercing cry or sound. —*SYN.* see **scream**.

shriev·al·ty (shrēv′′l-ti), *n.* [*pl.* SHRIEVALTIES (-tiz)], 1. a sheriff's office or term of office. 2. the district served by a sheriff.

shrieve (shrēv), *n.* [Obs.], a sheriff.

shrift (shrift), *n.* [ME. *schrift;* AS. *scrift* < *scrifan*, to receive confession < L. *scribere*, to write, draw up a law; cf. SHRIVE], [Archaic], 1. confession to and absolution by a priest. 2. the act of shriving. See also **short shrift**.

shrike (shrīk), *n.* [< AS. (via dial.) *scric*, bird of shrill cry < same base as *shriek* with reference to the cry], any of several shrill-voiced birds with hooked beaks, gray, black, and white plumage, and long tails: most types feed on insects, some on small birds, frogs, etc.: also called *butcher bird*.

shrill (shril), *adj.* [ME. *schrille, schril;* akin to LG. *schrell*, G. *schrill*; echoic, but prob. < same ult. base as SHRIEK], 1. having or producing a high, thin, piercing tone; high-pitched. 2. characterized or accompanied by shrill sounds. 3. [Archaic or Poetic], keen; sharp; biting; poignant. *adv.* shrilly. *v.i.* to make a shrill noise or sound. *v.t.* to utter shrilly.

shril·ly (shril′li), *adv.* in or with a shrill tone, voice, or sound. *adj.* (shril′i), [Poetic], shrill.

shrimp (shrimp), *n.* [*pl.* SHRIMPS (shrimps), SHRIMP; see PLURAL, II, D, 1], [ME. *schrimpe*, shrimp, puny person < base of AS. *scrimman* (akin to G. *schrimpfen*), to shrink, dry up (cf. SCRIMP); basic sense "shrunken creature"], 1. a small, slender, long-tailed crustacean, valued as food. 2. [Colloq.], a small or insignificant person.

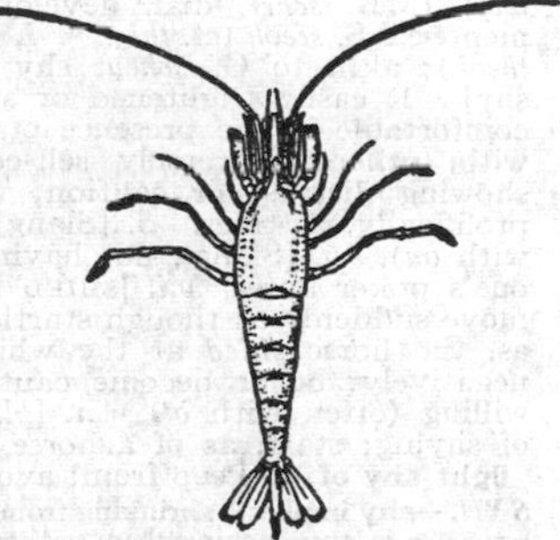
SHRIMP (2 in. long)

shrine (shrīn), *n.* [ME. *schrin;* AS. *scrin;* L. *scrinium*, chest, box], 1. a case or other container holding sacred relics, as the bones of a saint. 2. the tomb of a saint or other person held sacred. 3. a place of worship, usually one centered around some sacred object or scene. 4. a place or thing endowed with a sacred character because of its history or associations. *v.t.* [SHRINED (shrīnd), SHRINING], to enshrine.

shrink (shriŋk), *v.i.* [SHRANK (shraŋk) or SHRUNK (shruŋk), SHRUNK or SHRUNKEN (shruŋk′′n), SHRINKING], [ME. *schrynken;* AS. *scrincan;* akin to Sw. *skrynka*, to wrinkle; prob. < IE. **sqrenq* < base **sqer-*, to bend, curve (as in L. *curvus;* cf. CURVE), in basic sense "to bend up, draw together"], 1. to contract, as from heat, cold, moisture, etc. 2. to lessen, as in amount, worth, etc. 3. to draw back; turn away; cower, as from fear. 4. to avoid or wish to avoid taking action; be reluctant; withdraw: as, I *shrink* from going to the city. *v.t.* to cause to shrink or contract. *n.* a shrinking; shrinkage. —*SYN.* see **contract, recoil**.

shrink·a·ble (shriŋk′ə-b′l), *adj.* that can shrink or be shrunk.

shrink·age (shriŋk′ij), *n.* [see -AGE], 1. the act or process of shrinking; contraction in size, as of a fabric in washing. 2. decrease in value; depreciation. 3. the total loss in weight of livestock from the time of shipment to the final processing as meat. 4. the amount of such contraction, decrease, or loss.

shrive (shrīv), *v.t.* [SHRIVED (shrīvd) or SHROVE (shrōv), SHRIVEN (shriv′′n) or SHRIVED, SHRIVING], [ME. *shriven;* AS. *scrifan* < L. *scribere*, to write, whence also G. *schreiben*, to write; sense development: to write down—to prescribe—to prescribe penance], 1. [Archaic], to hear the confession of and, usually after penance, give absolution to. 2. [Archaic or Rare], to get absolution for (oneself) by confessing and doing penance. *v.i.* [Archaic], 1. to make confession; go to confession. 2. to hear confessions.

shriv·el (shriv′′l), *v.t. & v.i.* [SHRIVELED or SHRIVELLED (-′ld), SHRIVELING or SHRIVELLING], [Early Mod. Eng. dial.; the form suggests an etymon either < AS. or < LG.; akin to Sw. dial. *skryvla*, to wrinkle], 1. to curl up or wrinkle; wither. 2. to make or become helpless, useless, or inefficient. —*SYN.* see **wither**.

shriv·en (shriv′′n), alternative past participle of **shrive**.

shroff (shrof), *n.* [Anglo-Ind. *sharaf;* Ar. *sarrāf*], in the Orient, 1. a banker or moneychanger. 2. an expert in testing coins.

Shrop·shire (shrop′shir), *n.* 1. a county of England, on the border of Wales: pop., 257,000 (est. 1945); county seat, Shrewsbury: also called *Salop*. 2. a kind of large, black-faced, hornless sheep originally developed in Shropshire, England.

shroud (shroud), *n.* [ME. *schroude;* AS. *scrud;* akin to ON. *skrud*, accouterments, cloth < var. of the base of *shred;* basic sense "a fragment, cut-off piece (of cloth)"], 1. a cloth used to wrap a corpse for burial; winding sheet. 2. something that covers, protects, or screens; veil; shelter. 3. one of a set of ropes stretched from a ship's side to a masthead to offset lateral strain on the mast. *v.t.* 1. to hide; cover; screen. 2. to wrap (a corpse) in a shroud. 3. [Archaic], to shelter and protect. *v.i.* [Archaic], to take shelter.

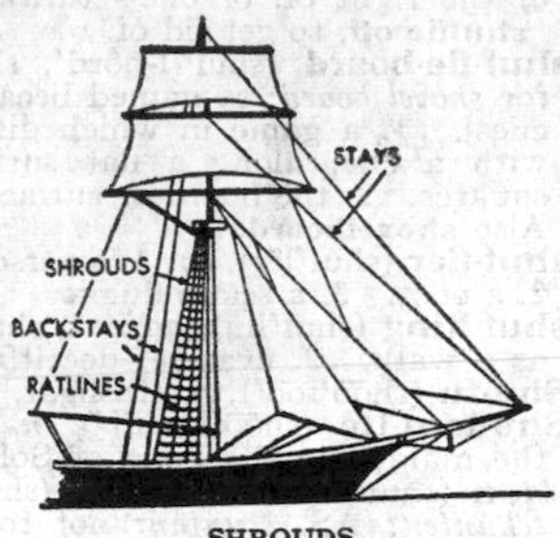

SHROUDS

shroud knot, an overhand knot: see **knot**, illus.

shroud-laid (shroud′lād′), *adj.* made up of four strands plain-laid on a core: said of rope.

shrove (shrōv), alternative past tense of **shrive**.

Shrove·tide (shrōv′tīd′), *n.* [ME. *schroffetide;* prob. (as also with *Shrove Monday*, etc.) a 15th-c. formation in which the 1st element (< *shrive*) replaces earlier *fast-, fasten-*], the three days before Ash Wednesday (*Shrove Sunday, Monday*, and *Tuesday*), formerly set aside as a special period for going to confession and a season of festivity just before Lent.

shrub (shrub), *n.* [Early ME. *schrubbe*, either < a var. of AS. *scrybb*, brushwood, or < a blending of this with *scrub;* cf. SCRUB], a bushy, woody plant with several permanent stems instead of a single trunk; bush.

shrub (shrub), *n.* [var. of *shrab* < Ar. *sharab, shurb*, drink; cf. SHERBET], a drink made of acid fruit juice, sugar, and, usually, rum or brandy.

shrub·ber·y (shrub′ēr-i), *n.* [*pl.* SHRUBBERIES (-iz)], 1. shrubs collectively. 2. a place where many shrubs are grown.

shrub·bi·ness (shrub′i-nis), *n.* the condition or quality of being shrubby.

shrub·by (shrub′i), *adj.* [SHRUBBIER (-i-ēr), SHRUBBIEST (-i-ist)], 1. covered with shrubs. 2. like a shrub.

shrug (shrug), *v.t. & v.i.* [SHRUGGED (shrugd), SHRUGGING], [ME. *schruggen*, orig., to shiver (as with cold)], to draw up (the shoulders), as in expressing indifference, doubt, disdain, contempt, etc. *n.* the gesture so made.

shrunk (shruŋk), alternative past tense and past participle of **shrink**.

shrunk·en (shruŋk′′n), alternative past participle of **shrink**. *adj.* contracted in size; shriveled.

shtg., shortage.

shuck (shuk), *n.* [? perhaps a metathesis of *husk*, arising orig. in such compounds as *cornshucking* < *cornhusking*], 1. a shell, pod, or husk. 2. the shell of an oyster or clam. 3. *pl.* [Colloq.], something valueless: as, not worth *shucks*. *v.t.* 1. to remove the shucks of. 2. to remove like a shuck: as, he *shucked* his clothes.

shucks (shuks), *interj.* [based on *shuck*], an exclamation expressing disappointment or disgust.

shud·der (shud′ēr), *v.i.* [ME. *schoderen* < or akin to

MLG. *schōderen* or MD. *schūderen;* akin to G. *schaudern,* freq. of the base in OS. *skuddian,* to shake; IE. base *(s)qut-, to shake, as also in AS. *scudan,* to hurry], to shake or tremble suddenly and violently, as in horror or extreme disgust. *n.* the act of shuddering; convulsive tremor of the body, as in horror, etc. —*SYN.* see **shake.**

shuf·fle (shuf''l), *v.t.* [SHUFFLED (-'ld), SHUFFLING], [Early Mod. Eng.; prob. < LG. *schuffeln,* to walk clumsily, shuffle cards < base of *shove*], 1. *a)* to move (the feet) along the ground or floor with a dragging or shoving gait. *b)* to perform (a dance) with such steps. 2. to mix (playing cards) so as to change their order or arrangement. 3. to push or mix together in a jumbled or disordered mass. 4. to shift from one place to another. 5. to bring, put, or thrust (*into* or *out of*) clumsily or trickily. *v.i.* 1. to move with a dragging gait without lifting the feet, as in walking or dancing. 2. to get into or out of a situation or condition by trickery, evasion, lies, etc.: as, he has *shuffled* out of responsibility time and again; hence, 3. to act in a shifty, dishonest manner; practice deceit, trickery, evasion, etc. 4. to change or shift repeatedly from one position or place to another. 5. to shuffle cards. 6. to make clumsy, fumbling motions in getting into or out of clothing. *n.* 1. the act of shuffling. 2. a tricky or deceptive action; evasion or inconsistency; trick. 3. a shuffling of the feet; hence, 4. a gait, dance, motion, etc. characterized by this. 5. *a)* the act of rearranging the order of a pack of playing cards. *b)* the right of, or one's turn at, shuffling the cards.
shuffle off, to get rid of.

shuf·fle·board (shuf''l-bôrd', shuf''l-bōrd'), *n.* [prob. for *shovel board:* so named because of the shape of the cues], 1. a game in which disks are slid, or pushed with a cue, along a flat surface toward numbered squares. 2. the board or surface on which it is played. Also **shovelboard.**

shuf·fler (shuf'lẽr), *n.* 1. a person or thing that shuffles. 2. a coot. 3. a scaup duck.

shuf·fling (shuf'liŋ), *adj.* 1. characterized by a shuffle, as a walk. 2. evasive; deceitful; shifty.

Shu·fu (shōō'fōō'), *n.* Kashgar, a city in western China.

Shu·lam·ite (shōō'lə-mīt'), *n.* an epithet applied to the maiden in the Song of Solomon, 6:13.

shun (shun), *v.t.* [SHUNNED (shund), SHUNNING], [ME. *schunien;* AS. *scunian:* not found outside Eng., but ? < same base as *shunt*], to keep away from; avoid scrupulously or consistently.

shun·ner (shun'ẽr), *n.* a person who shuns.

shunt (shunt), *v.t. & v.i.* [Early ME. *schunten;* prob. a blending of AS. *scyndan,* to hasten, with a LG. cognate of OHG. *scunten;* for IE. base see SHUDDER], 1. to move or turn to one side or away; turn off or out of the way. 2. to shift or switch, as a train, car, etc., from one track to another. 3. in *electricity,* to divert or be diverted by a shunt: said of a current. 4. to provide or connect with a shunt. *n.* 1. the act of shunting. 2. a railroad switch. 3. in *electricity,* a conductor connecting two points in a circuit and serving to divert part of the current from the main circuit.

shunt-wound (shunt'wound'), *adj.* in *electricity,* designating a dynamo or motor in which a part of the armature current is shunted through the field magnet coils: opposed to *series-wound.*

shush (shush), *interj.* [echoic], hush! be quiet! *v.t.* to say "shush" to; tell (another) to be quiet; hush.

Shu·shan (shōō'shăn), *n.* Susa: the Biblical name.

shut (shut), *v.t.* [SHUT, SHUTTING], [ME. (West Midland) *schutten;* AS. *scyttan* < base of *sceotan,* to cast (cf. SHOOT)], 1. to move (a door, window, curtain, lid, etc.) into a position that closes the opening to which it is fitted. 2. to fasten (a door, etc.) securely, as with a bolt or catch. 3. to close (an opening, passage, container, etc.). 4. to prevent or forbid entrance to or exit from; close; bar. 5. to fold up or bring together the parts of, as an umbrella, the hand, lips, etc. *v.i.* to move to a closed position; be or become shut. *adj.* 1. closed, fastened, or secured. 2. in *phonetics,* checked. *n.* 1. the act or time of shutting or closing; close. 2. the connecting line between two pieces of welded metal.
shut down, 1. to close by lowering; push or pull down, as a lid. 2. to lower and darken the view; overhang darkly or dimly, as night, fog, etc. 3. to cease operating; close, usually temporarily, as a factory. 4. [Colloq.], to bring to an end or restrict severely (with *on* or *upon*).
shut in, to surround or enclose; confine by enclosing.
shut of, [Dial. or Colloq.], rid of; free from.
shut off, 1. to prevent the passage of (electricity, steam, etc.). 2. to prevent passage through (a road, faucet, etc.).
shut out, 1. to deny entrance or admission to; exclude (sound, a view, etc.). 2. to prevent (an opposing side or team) from scoring.
shut up, 1. to put in an enclosure, receptacle, or place of confinement; enclose or confine; imprison. 2. to close all the entrances to. 3. [Colloq.], to stop or cause to stop talking.

shut·down (shut'doun'), *n.* a shutting down or stoppag[e] of activity, especially of work in a factory temporaril[y].

shut-eye (shut'ī'), *n.* [Slang], sleep.

shut-in (shut'in'), *n.* an invalid who is unable to g[o] out. *adj.* 1. unable to go out; confined, as by illnes[s] etc. 2. in *psychiatry,* inclined to shun others; abno[r]mally introverted.

shut·off (shut'ôf'), *n.* 1. something that shuts off flow or movement, as of a liquid. 2. a condition o[f] being shut off; stoppage.

shut·out (shut'out'), *n.* 1. a lockout of employee[s]. 2. in *sports, a)* a preventing of the opposing team fro[m] scoring. *b)* a game in which one team is shut out.

shut·ter (shut'ẽr), *n.* 1. a person or thing that shut[s]. 2. a movable screen or cover for a window, usuall[y] hinged and fitted with louvers. 3. anything used t[o] cover an opening, as a slide or door on a lantern. 4. [a] device for opening and closing the aperture of a len[s] in a camera to expose the film or plate. *v.t.* to clos[e] or furnish with a shutter or shutters.

shut·tle (shut''l), *n.* [ME. *schytel;* AS. *scytel,* missile [<] base of *sceotan,* to shoot; so called because shot to an[d] fro with the thread in weaving], 1. an instrumen[t] containing a reel or spool of the woof thread, used i[n] weaving to carry the thread back and forth betwee[n] the warp threads: see **weaving,** illus. 2. a smaller bu[t] similar thread holder used in tatting, etc. 3. a devic[e] that carries the lower thread back and forth in makin[g] a lock stitch on a sewing machine. 4. any of sever[al] devices having a similar to-and-fro action. 5. [a] shuttle train or shuttle bus. *v.t. & v.i.* [SHUTTLE[D] (-'ld), SHUTTLING], to move rapidly to and fro, like [a] shuttle.

shuttle bus, a motorbus making short, regular trip[s] between an outlying district and some point on a mai[n] transportation line.

shut·tle·cock (shut''l-kok'), *n.* 1. a rounded piece [of] cork having a flat end stuck with feathers: it is struck back and forth across a net by players with rackets in badminton or with paddles in battledore and shuttlecock: also called *bird.* 2. the game of battledore and shuttlecock.

SHUTTLECOCK

shuttle train, a train making regular and frequent trips back and forth over a short route.

Shver·nik, Ni·ko·lai (ni-kô-lī' shver'nik), 1888– ; president of the Soviet Union (1946–1953).

shy (shī), *adj.* [SHIER or SHYER (shī'ẽr), SHIEST or SHYEST (shī'ist)], [ME. *schei,* dial. development < AS. *sceoh* (cf. *thigh* < AS. *theoh*); akin to G. *scheu,* shy & base in *schüchter[n],* shy], 1. easily frightened or startled; timid. 2. u[n]comfortable in the presence of, and avoiding conta[ct] with, others; extremely self-conscious; bashful. [3.] showing distrust or caution; wary. 4. not bearin[g] prolifically, as trees. 5. [Slang], lacking; short (ofte[n] with *on*). 6. [Slang], not having paid money due, [as] one's poker ante. *v.i.* [SHIED (shīd), SHYING], 1. [to] move suddenly as though startled; jump; start; recoi[l]: as, the horse *shied* at the white stone. 2. to rea[ct] negatively; be or become cautious, doubtful, or u[n]willing (often with *at*). *n.* [*pl.* SHIES (shīz)], an a[ct] of shying; start, as of a horse.
fight shy of, to keep from; avoid; evade.

SYN.—**shy** implies a shrinking from the notice of others and reticence in approaching them, either as an inherent trait or [as] resulting from inexperience; **bashful** implies such shyness as displayed in awkward behavior and embarrassed timidit[y]; **diffident** implies a self-distrust and lack of self-confidence th[at] makes one reluctant to assert oneself; **modest** implies [an] unassuming manner in one who, because of his ability, achiev[e]ments, etc., might be expected to assert himself strongl[y]; **demure,** in current usage, suggests a decorously mode[st] manner, often one that is affectedly so. —*ANT.* bold, confiden[t].

shy (shī), *v.t. & v.i.* [SHIED (shīd), SHYING], [prob. [<] *cockshy,* to throw at a cock < *shy cock,* a cock that w[ould] not fight unless tormented into doing so; hence, ult., th[e] same word as *shy, adj.*], to throw or fling, especiall[y] sidewise with a jerk: as, he *shied* a stone over th[e] wall. *n.* [*pl.* SHIES (shīz)], 1. a shying; throw [or] fling. 2. [Colloq.], a try or attempt. 3. [Colloq.], [a] verbal fling; gibe.

Shy·lock (shī'lok'), *n.* 1. the relentless moneylender [in] Shakespeare's *Merchant of Venice;* hence, 2. a perso[n] without sentiment in business matters; exactin[g] creditor.

shy·ly (shī'li), *adv.* in a shy manner.

shy·ster (shī'stẽr), *n.* [also earlier *shuyster;* understoo[d] as *shy* (in earlier sense of "disreputable") + *-ster,* bu[t] ? < G. *scheisser,* defecator], [Slang], a person, especial[ly] a lawyer, who uses unethical or tricky methods; pett[i]fogger.

Si (sē), *n.* Si-Kiang.

si (sē), *n.* [arbitrary modification of *sol*], in *music,*

syllable representing the seventh tone of the diatonic scale: see also **ti.**
sí (sē), *adv.* [It. & Sp.], yes.
i, in *chemistry,* silicon.
.I., 1. Sandwich Islands. 2. Staten Island.
i·a·la·gog·ic (sī′ə-lə-goj′ik), *adj.* stimulating the flow of saliva. *n.* a sialagogue.
i·al·a·gogue (sī-al′ə-gog′), *n.* [< Gr. *sialon,* saliva; + *-agogue*], anything, especially a medicine, that stimulates the flow of saliva.
i·a·lid (sī′ə-lid), *adj.* [< Mod. L. *Sialidae,* name of the family < Gr. *sialis,* a kind of bird], of a group of insects including the dobson fly. *n.* a sialid insect.
i·al·i·dan (sī-al′i-dən), *adj. & n.* sialid.
i·al·kot (sī-äl′kōt), *n.* a city in West Punjab, Pakistan: pop., 138,000.
i·a·loid (sī′ə-loid′), *adj.* [< Gr. *sialon,* saliva; + *-oid*], resembling saliva.
i·am (sī-am′, sī′am), *n.* Thailand: official name until 1939, and from 1945 to 1949.
iam, Gulf of, an arm of the South China Sea, bounded by the Malay Peninsula, Thailand, and French Indo-China.
i·a·mang (sē′ə-maŋ′, syä′maŋ), *n.* [*pl.* SIAMANGS (-maŋz′, -maŋz)], [Malay *siămaṅ* < *āmaṅ,* black], a Sumatran gibbon with long black hair: it is the largest of all gibbons.
i·a·mese (sī′ə-mēz′), *n.* 1. [*pl.* SIAMESE], a native of Siam: the Siamese are of Thai stock. 2. the Sino-Tibetan language of the Siamese; Thai. *adj.* of Siam, its people, their language, etc.
iamese cat, a breed of short-haired cat characterized by a fawn-colored coat shading to brown at the face, paws, and tail.
i·a·mese twins (sī′ə-mēz′, sī′ə-mēz′), 1. a set of twin Siamese boys, Chang and Eng (1811–1874), born with chests joined by a thick band of cartilage and flesh. 2. any pair of twins born with bodies joined.
i·an (sē′än′; Chin. shē′än′), *n.* the capital of Shensi province, China, on the Yellow River: pop., 591,000 (est. 1947): also called *Singan.*
iang·tan (syäŋ′tän′), *n.* a city in Hunan province, China: pop., 300,000.
ib (sib), *n.* [ME. *sibb,* kinship; AS. *sib(b)*; akin to G. *sippe,* kinship, lineage; IE. base **s(w)e-bh-,* of the same kind (as also in *Swabian,* etc.) < **se-,* reflexive pronoun], 1. a person's blood relatives; kin. 2. a blood relative; kinsman or kinswoman; especially, a brother or sister. 3. in *anthropology,* a unilinear, usually exogamous kin group based on traditional common descent, whether patrilineal or matrilineal, and often having a common totem: usually distinguished from *clan, sept.* *adj.* 1. related by blood. 2. [Rare], closely related; akin.
i·be·li·us, Jean (zhän si-bā′li-oos; Eng. sə-bāl′yəs), 1865–1957; Finnish composer.
i·ber·i·a (sī-bêr′i-ə), *n.* the region of the Soviet Union in northern Asia, extending from the Ural Mountains to the Pacific: abbreviated **Sib.**
i·ber·i·an (sī-bêr′i-ən), *adj.* of Siberia or its people. *n.* a native or inhabitant of Siberia: abbreviated **Sib.**
ib·i·lance (sib′′l-əns), *n.* 1. the condition or quality of being sibilant. 2. a sibilant sound; hissing.
ib·i·lan·cy (sib′′l-ən-si), *n.* [*pl.* SIBILANCIES (-siz)], a sibilance.
ib·i·lant (sib′′l-ənt), *adj.* [L. *sibilans* < *sibilare,* to hiss], having or making a hissing sound. *n.* a hissing sound or the symbol for it: *s, sh, z, zh, j,* and *ch* are sibilants.
ib·i·late (sib′′l-āt′), *v.t. & v.i.* [SIBILATED (-id), SIBILATING], [< L. *sibilatus,* pp.; see SIBILANT], to hiss; pronounce with a hissing sound.
ib·i·la·tion (sib′′l-ā′shən), *n.* [LL. *sibilatio* < L. *sibilare,* to hiss], 1. the making or uttering of a hissing sound. 2. a hissing sound.
ib·ling (sib′liŋ), *n.* [*sib* (cf. SIB) < AS. *sib(b)*; + *-ling;* ME. & AS. *sibling* meant "a relative"], *often in pl.* one of two or more persons born at different times of the same parents; brother or sister.
ib·yl (sib′′l), [L. *Sibylla;* see SIBYL (soothsayer)], a feminine name: also spelled **Sybil.**
ib·yl (sib′′l), *n.* [ME. *sibil;* L. *sibylla;* Gr. *sibylla*], 1. any of certain women consulted as prophetesses or oracles by the ancient Greeks and Romans. 2. a witch; sorceress; fortuneteller.
·byl·ic, si·byl·lic (si-bil′ik), *adj.* sibylline.
ib·yl·line (sib′′l-īn′, sib′′l-in), *adj.* [L. *sibyllinus*], 1. of or like the sibyls or their prophecies; hence, 2. prophetic; oracular; mysterious.
ibylline Books, a number of manuscripts of prophecy and wisdom consulted regularly by the ancient Romans and thought to have been written by the sibyl of Cumae.
ic (sik), *adv.* [L.], thus; so: used within brackets, [*sic*], to show that a quoted passage, often containing some error, is precisely reproduced.
c (sik), *adj.* [Dial.], such.

sic (sik), *v.t.* [SICKED (sikt), SICKING], to sick; attack.
Sic., 1. Sicilian. 2. Sicily.
Si·ca·ni·an (si-kā′ni-ən), *adj.* Sicilian.
sic·ca·tive (sik′ə-tiv), *adj.* [LL. *siccativus* < L. *siccatus,* pp. of *siccare,* to dry < *siccus,* dry], causing to dry; drying. *n.* a substance that promotes drying, especially one used in painting; drier.
Si·ci·lia (si-sil′i-ə, si-sil′yə; It. sē-chēl′yä), *n.* Sicily.
Si·cil·i·an (si-sil′i-ən, si-sil′yən), *adj.* of Sicily, its people, their dialect, etc. *n.* 1. a native or inhabitant of Sicily. 2. the Italian dialect of the Sicilians.
Sicilian Vespers, a popular uprising of the Sicilian people in April, 1282, against French oppression under Charles of Anjou: the ringing of a Palermo vesper bell was the signal for the revolution, in which thousands of French were killed.
Sicilies, Two, see **Two Sicilies.**
Sic·i·ly (sis′′l-i), *n.* an island of Italy, off its southwestern tip: area, 9,926 sq. mi.; pop., 4,256,000 (est. 1943); chief city, Palermo: Italian name, ***Sicilia.***
sick (sik), *adj.* [< ME. *seke* with shortened vowel (cf. RICK); AS. *seoc;* akin to G. *siech;* IE. base **seug-,* to be troubled or grieved], 1. suffering from disease or illness; unwell; ill: this sense is rare or literary in England. 2. having nausea; vomiting or ready to vomit: the predominant sense in England. 3. characteristic of or accompanying sickness: as, a *sick* expression, *sick* headache. 4. of or for sick people: as, *sick* bed, *sick* leave. 5. deeply disturbed or distressed; extremely upset, as by grief, disappointment, disgust, failure, etc. 6. disgusted by reason of excess; surfeited (usually with *of*): as, he is *sick* of their puns. 7. impaired; unsound. 8. having a great longing (with *for*): as, he is *sick* for the hills. 9. of sickly color; pale. 10. mentally ill. 11. in *agriculture, a*) incapable of producing an adequate yield of a certain crop: as, wheat-*sick* soil. *b*) infested with harmful microorganisms: as, a *sick* field. *n.* sick people (with *the*).
SYN.—**sick** and **ill** both express the idea of being in bad health, affected with disease, etc. (for differences in American and British usage, see definition above), but **sick** is more commonly used than **ill,** which is somewhat formal (he's a *sick* person, he is *sick,* or *ill,* with the flu); **ailing** usually suggests prolonged or even chronic poor health (she has been *ailing* ever since her operation); **indisposed** suggests a slight, temporary illness or feeling of physical discomfort (*indisposed* with a headache). —*ANT.* well, healthy.
sick (sik), *v.t.* [var. of *seek*], 1. to set upon; pursue and attack: said especially of or to a dog. 2. to urge or incite to attack: as, he *sicked* his dog on us. Also spelled **sic.**
sick bay, a ship's hospital and dispensary.
sick·bed (sik′bed′), *n.* a bed upon which a sick person lies.
sick call, in *military usage,* 1. a daily formation made up of those men who wish to receive medical attention. 2. a signal for or the time of such a formation.
sick·en (sik′′n), *v.i.* [ME. *sekenen* < *seke,* sick], to become sick. *v.t.* to make sick.
sick·en·ing (sik′′n-iŋ), *adj.* 1. causing sickness or nausea. 2. completely disgusting or revolting.
sick headache, 1. any headache accompanied by or resulting from nausea. 2. migraine.
sick·ish (sik′ish), *adj.* 1. somewhat sick or nauseated. 2. somewhat sickening or nauseating.
sick·le (sik′′l), *n.* [ME. *sikel;* AS. *sicol* < L. *secula* < *secare,* to cut], 1. a cutting tool consisting of a crescent-shaped blade with a short handle: used for cutting down tall grasses and weeds. 2. [S-], a sickle-shaped group of six stars in the constellation Leo.

SICKLE

sick leave, leave granted for illness: often a fixed number of days.
sick·le·bill (sik′′l-bil′), *n.* any bird with a sharply curved bill resembling a sickle.
sickle feather, any long, curving feather, as in the tail of a rooster.
sick·li·ness (sik′li-nis), *n.* the state or quality of being sickly.
sick·ly (sik′li), *adj.* [SICKLIER (-li-ẽr), SICKLIEST (-li-ist)], 1. in poor health; chronically sick or prone to sickness; not strong or robust. 2. of or produced by sickness: as, a *sickly* pallor. 3. characterized by the prevalence of disease or sickness; producing illness; unhealthy. 4. sickening; nauseating, as an odor. 5. faint; feeble; pale, as light or color. 6. weak; mawkish; insipid. *adv.* in a sick manner. *v.t.* [SICKLIED (-lid), SICKLYING], to make sickly, as in color, vigor, etc.

sick·ness (sik'nis), *n.* 1. the condition of being sick or diseased; illness. 2. a malady or disease. 3. nausea.

sick·room (sik'ro͞om', sik'roo͝m'), *n.* a room in which a person lies sick.

‡**sic pas·sim** (sik pas'im), [L., lit., so everywhere], thus throughout (the book, passage, etc.).

‡**sic sem·per ty·ran·nis** (sik sem'pẽr ti-ran'is), [L.], thus ever to tyrants.

‡**sic trans·it glo·ri·a mun·di** (sik tran'sit glō'ri-ə mun'dī), [L.], thus passes away the glory of the world; thus vanishes earthly fame.

Si·cy·on (sish'i-ən), *n.* a city of ancient Greece, in the northern Peloponnesus, near Corinth.

Sid·dhar·tha (sid-där'tə), see **Buddha.**

Sid·dons, Sarah (sid''nz), (born *Sarah Kemble*), 1755–1831; English actress.

sid·dur (sid'oor), *n.* [Heb. *siddūr*, arrangement, order], the Jewish prayer book containing prayers for week-days and the Sabbath.

side (sīd), *n.* [ME.; AS.; akin to G. *seite;* prob. < the base of AS. *sid*, ample, broad, with basic sense "the long side"; IE. base *sēi-, to stretch out (cf. SOW, *v.*)], 1. the right or left half of a human or animal body, especially either half of the trunk. 2. a position or space beside one. 3. *a)* any of the lines or surfaces that bound or limit something: as, a square has four *sides*, a cube six. *b)* any bounding line or surface of an object other than the ends or top and bottom. *c)* either of the two bounding surfaces of an object that are distinguished from the front, back, top, and bottom. 4. either of the two surfaces of a thing having no appreciable thickness, as paper, cloth, etc. 5. a surface or part of a surface having a specified aspect: as, the inner *side* of a vase, the visible *side* of the moon. 6. any aspect or phase as contrasted with another or others: as, the cruel *side* of him. 7. either of the two lateral surfaces of a ship from stem to stern above the water line. 8. the slope of a hill, bank, or other incline. 9. the shore of a river or other body of water. 10. any location, area, space, direction, etc. considered with reference to its position in relation to an observer or to a point or line thought of as central. 11. the action, position, or attitude of one person or faction opposing another: as, explain your *side* of the argument. 12. one of the parties in a contest, conflict, etc.; faction. 13. line of descent through either parent; maternal or paternal lineage. 14. [British Slang], assumed superiority; arrogance. 15. [British], in *billiards*, English. *adj.* 1. of, at, or on a side or sides: as, *side* entrances. 2. to or from one side: as, a *side* glance. 3. not of primary importance; minor; secondary, as an interest or consideration. *v.t.* [SIDED (-id), SIDING], 1. to furnish with sides or siding. 2. [Colloq.], to put or thrust aside.
  on the side, [Colloq.], 1. as a secondary or part-time occupation. 2. in addition to the primary issue.
  side by side, beside each other; together.
  side with, to sympathize with or support (one party, faction, etc.) in opposition to another.
  take sides, to be in sympathy with or give support to one of the parties in a discussion, dispute, etc.

side arms, weapons of the kind that may be worn at the side or at the waist, as sword, bayonet, pistol, etc.

side·board (sīd'bôrd', sīd'bōrd'), *n.* 1. a piece of dining-room furniture for holding linen, silver, china, etc. 2. a board that forms or is part of a side: as, the *sideboards* of a wagon.

side·burns (sīd'bũrnz'), *n.pl.* [reversed < *burnsides*, after Gen. A. E. *Burnside*, who wore them], 1. short whiskers grown only on the cheeks. 2. the hair growing on the sides of a man's face, near the ears, when the rest of the beard is cut off.

side·car (sīd'kär'), *n.* a small car attached to the side of a motorcycle, for carrying a passenger.

sid·ed (sīd'id), *adj.* having sides: usually in combination, as, six-*sided*.

side dish, 1. any food served in addition to the chief course and usually in a separate dish. 2. a small dish used for this.

side-kick (sīd'kik'), *n.* [Slang], 1. a companion; close friend. 2. a partner; confederate.

side light, 1. a light coming from the side; hence, 2. chance or incidental knowledge or information. 3. a window or opening in or at the side of a wall, door, etc. 4. a lamp or light carried on the side: a ship carries a red *side light* on the port side and a green one on the starboard.

side line, a line at or along the side; specifically, *a)* either of two lines marking the side limits of a playing field, court, etc., as in hockey or tennis. *b) pl.* the space just outside such lines, usually occupied by spectators. *c)* a small line branching off the main line, as of a railroad, pipeline, etc. *d)* a hobble attached to an animal's foreleg and hind leg on the same side. *e)* a line, as of merchandise or business, in addition to one's main line: as, the carpenter does wood carving as a *side line.*

side·line (sīd'līn'), *v.t.* [SIDELINED (-līnd'), SIDELINING], to remove from active participation: as, he was *sidelined* by his injury.

side·ling (sīd'liŋ), *adv.* [ME. *sydelinge;* cf. SIDE & -LIN sidelong; sideways; obliquely. *adj.* 1. directed moving to the side: as, a stealthy, *sideling* approac 2. inclined; sloping.

side·long (sīd'lôŋ'), *adv.* 1. toward the side; laterall obliquely. 2. on the side; side downward. *adj.* inclined; slanting; sloping. 2. directed to the side, a glance; hence, 3. indirect; subtle, as a remark.

side meat, [Dial.], meat from the side of a pig; bac or salt pork.

side·piece (sīd'pēs'), *n.* a piece forming or attached the side of something.

si·de·re·al (sī-dêr'i-əl), *adj.* [< L. *sidereus* < *sidu sideris*, a star], 1. of the stars or constellations; starr stellar. 2. measured by the apparent motion of fix stars: a *sidereal day*, the interval between two successi transits of a star over the meridian, equals 23 hou 56 minutes, 4.09 seconds of mean solar time; a *sidere hour* equals 1/24 of a sidereal day.

sid·er·ite (sid'ẽr-īt'), *n.* [< Fr. or L.; Fr. *sidérite; sideritis*, fem., or *siderites*, masc.; Gr. *sidēritis, sideri* < *sidēros*, iron], 1. a valuable ore of iron, $FeCO_3$, ir carbonate, usually yellowish to light-brown in col 2. a meteorite consisting chiefly of iron.

sid·er·it·ic (sid'ə-rit'ik), *adj.* of siderite.

sid·er·o- (sid'ẽr-ō, sid'ẽr-ə), [< Gr. *sidēros*], a combini form meaning *iron*, as in *siderolite:* also, before a vow **sider-.**

sid·er·o- (sid'ẽr-ō, sid'ẽr-ə), [< L. *sidus, sideris*, a star] combining form meaning *star*, as in *siderostat:* als before a vowel, **sider-.**

sid·er·o·lite (sid'ẽr-ə-līt'), *n.* [*sidero-* (iron) + *-lite*], a meteorite containing large proportions of both ir and silicates.

sid·er·o·sis (sid'ə-rō'sis), *n.* [Mod. L. < *sider-* + *-osi* 1. any disease of the lungs caused by the inhaling particles of iron or other metal. 2. an abnormal depo of iron in the body tissues.

sid·er·o·stat (sid'ẽr-ō-stat'), *n.* [*sidero-* + *-stat*], a mirr which turns with the apparent motion of a star so to keep the star constantly within the field of a fix telescope or similar instrument.

side·sad·dle (sīd'sad''l), *n.* a saddle upon which t rider sits with both legs on the same side of the anim designed for women wearing skirts while riding.

side show, 1. a small show run in connection with t main show or attraction, as of a circus. 2. something minor or secondary importance; subordinate event.

side·slip (sīd'slip'), *v.i.* 1. to slip or skid sideways, on skis. 2. in *aeronautics*, to perform a sideslip. *v* to cause to sideslip. *n.* 1. a slip or skid to the side. in *aeronautics*, a maneuver in which an airplane is ma to fall sideways and slightly forward by holding t control stick forward and to one side while depressi the rudder control on the opposite side: a standa method of reducing altitude.

side·split·ting (sīd'split'iŋ), *adj.* 1. very hearty; co vulsive: said of laughter. 2. causing hearty laught as, a *sidesplitting* account of the evening.

side-step (sīd'step'), *v.t.* [SIDE-STEPPED (-stept'), SID STEPPING], to avoid by or as by stepping aside; dod as, he cannot *side-step* this difficulty. *v.i.* to step to o side; take a side step.

side step, 1. a step to one side, as to avoid somethi 2. a step or stair located at the side.

side stroke, a swimming stroke performed, while lyi sideways in the water, by working the arms alternate backward and forward while executing a scissors ki with the legs.

side·swipe (sīd'swīp'), *v.t.* & *v.i.* [SIDESWIPED (-swīpt SIDESWIPING], to hit along the side in passing. *n.* glancing blow of this kind.

side·track (sīd'trak'), *v.t.* & *v.i.* 1. to switch, as train, from a main line to a siding. 2. to turn aw from the main issue or course; divert or be divert *n.* a railroad siding.

side·walk (sīd'wôk'), *n.* a path or area, usually pav at the side of a street, for pedestrians.

side·ward (sīd'wẽrd), *adv.* & *adj.* directed or movi toward one side.

side·wards (sīd'wẽrdz), *adv.* sideward.

side·way (sīd'wā'), *adj.* & *adv.* sideways. *n.* a byw also **side way.**

side·ways (sīd'wāz'), *adv.* 1. from the side. 2. so as present a side; with one side forward. 3. toward o side; laterally; obliquely. *adj.* turned or moving ward or from one side.

side-wheel (sīd'hwēl'), *adj.* designating a steamb having a paddle wheel on each side.

side-wheel·er (sīd'hwēl'ẽr), *n.* a side-wheel steambo cf. **stern-wheeler.**

side whiskers, whiskers growing at the side of the fa

side wind, 1. a wind blowing from or against the si cross-wind. 2. an indirect manner, source, influen etc.: as, the announcement reached us by a *side wi*

side·wind·er (sīd'wīn'dẽr), *n.* 1. a kind of small ratt snake. 2. [Colloq.], a powerful swinging blow of t fist, delivered from the side.

side·wise (sīd'wīz'), *adj.* & *adv.* sideways.

sid·ing (sīd′iŋ), *n.* 1. boarding or shingles forming the outside covering of a frame building. 2. a short railway track connected with a main track by a switch and used for unloading, bypassing, etc.; sidetrack.

si·dle (sī′d'l), *v.i.* [SIDLED (-d'ld), SIDLING], [prob. back-formation < *sideling*], to move sideways, especially in a shy, fearful, or stealthy manner. *n.* a sidling movement.

Sid·ney (sid′ni), [< the surname *Sidney;* prob. reduced < *St. Denis*], 1. a masculine name: diminutive, *Sid:* also spelled **Sydney.** 2. a feminine name.

Sid·ney, Sir Philip (sid′ni), 1554–1586; English soldier, poet, and statesman.

Si·don (sī′d'n), *n.* the capital of ancient Phoenicia: site of modern Saïda.

Si·do·ni·an (sī-dō′ni-ən), *adj.* of Sidon, its people, or culture. *n.* a native or inhabitant of Sidon.

siè·cle (sye′kl'), *n.* [*pl.* SIÈCLES (-kl')], [Fr.], a century; period; age.

siè·cle d'or (sye′kl' dôr′), [Fr.], (the) golden age: said of the reign of Louis XIV of France.

Sieg·bahn, Karl Man·ne Ge·org (kärl män′ne yā′ôr-y' sēg′bän), 1886– ; Swedish physicist; received Nobel prize in physics, 1924.

siege (sēj), *n.* [ME. *sege;* OFr. *sege, siege;* LL. ***sedium,** seen in *obsidium,* the sitting down before a town, siege < *sedere,* to sit], 1. the encirclement of a fortified place by an opposing armed force intending to take it, usually by blockade and bombardment. 2. any persistent attempt to gain control, overcome opposition, etc. 3. [Obs.], a seat; throne. 4. [Obs.], rank; position. 5. [Colloq.], a long, distressing or wearying period: as, a *siege* of illness. *v.t.* [SIEGED (sējd), SIEGING], to lay siege to; besiege.

lay siege to, to subject to a siege; attempt to win, gain, overcome, etc.

Siege Perilous, a seat at King Arthur's Round Table, fatal to all occupants except the knight destined to find the Holy Grail.

Sieg·fried (sēg′frēd; G. zēk′frēt′), *n.* [G. < Gmc. ***segu-,** power, victory + ***frith-,** peace, protection], the hero of a Germanic legend having several versions: in the *Nibelungenlied,* he wins the treasure of the Nibelungs, kills a dragon, rescues and betroths Brunhild only to secure her as wife for Gunther, whose sister Kriemhild he then marries: see also **Sigurd, Nibelungenlied, Ring of the Nibelung.**

Siegfried line, a heavily fortified defense line built along the French border in Germany between 1933 and 1938: also called *Westwall.*

Sie·mens, Sir William (sē′mənz; G. zē′məns), (born *Karl Wilhelm von Siemens*), 1823–1883; British engineer and inventor, born in Germany.

Si·e·na (si-en′ə; It. sye′nä), *n.* 1. a city in west central Italy: pop., 52,000. 2. a former republic surrounding this city; annexed to Tuscany in 1557.

Sien·kie·wicz, Hen·ryk (hen′rik shen-kye′vich), 1846–1916; Polish novelist; received Nobel prize in literature, 1905.

Si·en·na (si-en′ə), *n.* [It. *terra di Siena* (*Sienna*), lit., earth of Siena (Italy), where it was first obtained], 1. an earth pigment containing iron and manganese, yellowish-brown in the natural state. 2. a reddish-brown pigment made by burning this; burnt sienna. 3. the color of either of these.

Si·er·ra (si-er′ə), *n.* [Sp. < L. *serra,* a saw], 1. a range of hills or mountains having a saw-toothed appearance from a distance. 2. any of several salt-water game and food fishes resembling the mackerel: also called *pintado, kingfish.*

Si·er·ra Le·o·ne (si-er′ə lē-ō′ni), a country in western Africa, on the Atlantic, between Guinea and Liberia: a former British colony and protectorate, it is now a member of the British Commonwealth of Nations: area, 27,925 sq. mi.; pop., 2,500,000; capital, Freetown.

Si·er·ra Ma·dre (si-er′ə mä′drā; Sp. sye′rä mä′dre), a large mountain system of Mexico, made up of three main ranges, Sierra Madre Occidental, Sierra Madre Oriental, and Sierra Madre del Sur.

Si·er·ra Ne·va·da (si-er′ə nə-vad′ə, nə-vä′də; *also, for* 2, Sp. sye′rä ne-vä′*th*ä), 1. a mountain range in eastern California: highest peak, Mt. Whitney, 14,501 ft. 2. a range in southern Spain: highest peak, Mulhacén.

Si·es·ta (si-es′tə), *n.* [Sp. < L. *sexta* (*hora*), sixth (hour), noon, hottest part of the day], a brief nap or rest, especially as taken at midday or after the noon meal in Spain, some Latin American countries, etc.

sieur (syẽr), *n.* [Fr.; contr. < *seigneur* < L. *senior;* see SENIOR], [Archaic], sir: a French title of respect.

sieve (siv), *n.* [ME. *sive;* AS. *sife;* akin to G. *sieb;* prob. IE. base ***seip-,** to drip, run in drops, etc., seen also in Eng. *seep*], a utensil having many small meshed or perforated openings of a size allowing passage only to liquids or to the finer particles of loose or pulverized matter; sifter; strainer. *v.t. & v.i.* [SIEVED (sivd), SIEVING], to sift.

sieve tube, in *botany,* one of the tubes made of thin-walled cells in the inner bark of a tree or shrub, serving to conduct food substances.

sift (sift), *v.t.* [ME. *siften;* AS. *siftan* < *sife,* a sieve; akin to G. *sichten;* cf. SIEVE], 1. to pass through a sieve so as to separate the coarse from the fine particles. 2. to scatter (a pulverized substance) by or as by the use of a sieve. 3. to inspect or examine with care, as by testing or questioning; weigh (evidence, etc.). 4. to separate; screen; distinguish: as, he *sifted* fact from fable. *v.i.* 1. to sift something. 2. to pass through or as through a sieve.

sif·ter (sif′tẽr), *n.* a thing used for sifting; sieve.

sift·ings (sif′tiŋz), *n.pl.* 1. something sifted: as, *siftings* of snow beside the door. 2. something removed by sifting; residue.

Sig., sig., 1. signal. 2. signature. 3. [It.], *a*) *signor.* *b*) *signore; signori.*

sigh (sī), *v.i.* [ME. *sighen,* back-formation < *sihten,* p.t. of *siken* < AS. *sican,* to sigh; prob. echoic], 1. to take in and let out a long, deep, audible breath, especially in expressing sorrow, relief, fatigue, longing, etc. 2. to make a sound like that of a sigh: as, trees *sighing* in the wind. 3. to feel longing or grief; yearn or lament (often with *for*). *v.t.* 1. to express with a sigh. 2. to spend (time) in sighing: as, he *sighed* his youth away. 3. [Rare], to lament with sighing. *n.* the act or sound of sighing.

sight (sīt), *n.* [ME. *siht;* AS. (*ge*)*siht* < base of *seon,* to see + *-th;* akin to G. *sicht*], 1. *a*) something seen; view. *b*) a remarkable or spectacular view; spectacle: as, the dawn was a *sight* to behold. *c*) *chiefly pl.* a thing worth seeing: as, the *sights* of the city. 2. the act of seeing; perception by the eyes. 3. inspection or examination: as, we were allowed first *sight* of the new contract. 4. a view; look; glimpse. 5. aim or an observation taken with mechanical aid, as on a sextant, gun, etc. 6. the faculty or power of seeing; vision; eyesight. 7. mental vision or perception. 8. range or field of vision. 9. *a*) mental view; opinion; judgment: as, he can do no wrong in her *sight.* *b*) [Obs.], insight. 10. any of various devices used to aid the eyes in lining up a gun, optical instrument, etc. on its objective. 11. [Colloq.], anything having a strikingly unpleasant or unusual appearance: as, our house was a *sight* after the party, she's a *sight* without her make-up. 12. [Colloq.], a large number or amount: as, it'll need a *sight* of fixing. *v.t.* 1. to observe or examine by taking a sight: as, he *sighted* their movements carefully. 2. to catch sight of; see. 3. to bring into the sights of a rifle, etc.; aim at. 4. to furnish with sights or a sighting device. 5. to adjust the sights of (a gun, etc.). *v.i.* 1. to take aim or an observation with a sight. 2. to look carefully in a specified direction: as, *sight* along the line.

a sight for sore eyes, [Colloq.], a person or thing that is pleasant to see; welcome sight.

at first sight, when seen for the first time; without further study or deliberation.

at (or on) sight, 1. when or as soon as seen. 2. in *commerce,* upon demand or presentation.

by sight, by appearance; not through being acquainted.

catch sight of, 1. to make out by means of the eyes; discern; see. 2. to see briefly; glimpse.

lose sight of, 1. to fail to keep in sight; see no longer. 2. to fail to keep in mind; forget.

not by a long sight, 1. not nearly. 2. not at all.

out of sight, 1. not in sight. 2. far off; remote; hence, 3. [Colloq.], beyond reach; unattainable; extremely high, as in standards, price, etc.

out of sight of, 1. not in sight of. 2. not close or near to; remote from.

out of sight, out of mind, persons or things not seen or present are forgotten or neglected.

sight unseen, without seeing (the thing mentioned) beforehand.

sight draft, a draft payable on presentation: abbreviated **S/D.**

sight·ed (sīt′id), *adj.* having (a) sight: usually in combination, as in *farsighted, quick-sighted.*

sight·hole (sīt′hōl′), *n.* a hole for seeing or sighting through, as on a quadrant.

sight·less (sīt′lis), *adj.* 1. blind. 2. unseen; invisible.

sight·li·ness (sīt′li-nis), *n.* the condition of being sightly.

sight·ly (sīt′li), *adj.* [SIGHTLIER (-li-ẽr), SIGHTLIEST (-li-ist)], 1. pleasant to the sight; comely. 2. providing a fine view.

sight reading, the act or skill of playing or singing readily upon sight written music unfamiliar to one.

sight-see·ing (sīt′sē′iŋ), *n.* the act of going to visit places and things of interest, for pleasure, education, etc. *adj.* for or engaged in seeing sights.

sight-se·er (sīt′sē′ẽr), *n.* a person engaged in sight-seeing.

sig·il (sij′əl; *occas.* sig′əl), *n.* [LL. *sigillum,* dim. of L. *signum,* a sign], 1. a seal; signet. 2. in *magic & astrol-*

ogy, an image or sign having some mysterious power.

sigill., *sigillum*, [L.], seal (signet).

sig·il·late (sij'ə-lāt'), *adj.* [LL. *sigillatus*, pp. of *sigillare* < *sigillum;* see SIGIL], 1. having a pressed-in pattern, as earthenware. 2. in *botany*, having markings resembling those made by a seal, or signet.

Sig·is·mund (sij'is-mənd, sig'is-mənd; G. zē'gis-moont'), [G.; Goth. *Sigismunth* < *sigis*, victory + + Gmc. **mund-*, hand, protection], a masculine name: variant, *Sigmund*. *n.* Holy Roman emperor (1411–1437); lived 1368–1437.

sig·ma (sig'mə), *n.* [Gr.], the eighteenth letter of the Greek alphabet (Σ, σ, s), corresponding to English *S*, *s*: see **alphabet**, table.

sig·mate (sig'māt), *adj.* shaped like a sigma or an S.

sig·moid (sig'moid), *adj.* [Gr. *sigmoeidēs;* see SIGMA & -OID], 1. having a double curve like the letter S. 2. of the sigmoid flexure of the colon.

sig·moi·dal (sig-moi'd'l), *adj.* sigmoid.

sigmoid flexure, 1. in *anatomy*, the last curving part of the colon, ending in the rectum. 2. in *zoology*, an S-shaped curve.

Sig·mund (sig'mənd), [< G. *Siegmund* & ON. *Sigmundr* < Gmc. **sig-*, victory + *mund-*, hand, protection], a masculine name: see **Sigismund.**

sign (sīn), *n.* [ME. *sygne;* OFr. *signe;* L. *signum;* the orig. AS. word was *tacen* (cf. TOKEN)], 1. something that indicates a fact, quality, etc.; indication; token: as, a black arm band is a *sign* of mourning. 2. a gesture or motion that conveys information, gives a command, etc.: as, he nodded a *sign* of approval. 3. a mark or symbol having an accepted and specific meaning: as, the *sign* ? indicates a question, the *sign* 𝄇 means "repeat" in music, the *sign* + means "add" in mathematics. 4. a publicly displayed board, placard, etc. bearing some information or advertisement. 5. anything marking the trail of an animal, as droppings, a track, etc.: as, deer *signs* were plentiful. 6. any visible trace or indication; vestige: as, he showed no *sign* of friendship. 7. *a)* an act or happening regarded as a miraculous demonstration of divine power. *b)* an omen; portent. 8. in *astrology*, any of the twelve divisions or houses of the zodiac, each represented by a symbol: see **zodiac.** 9. in *medicine*, an objective indication of a disease, apparent to someone other than the patient. *v.t.* 1. to mark with a sign, especially with the sign of the cross, as in blessing or consecrating. 2. to write one's name on, as in acknowledging authorship, authorizing action, etc. 3. to write (one's name) as a signature. 4. to hire or engage by written contract; sign on. 5. to express, indicate, or signify with a sign: as, he *signed* his approval with a nod. *v.i.* 1. to write one's signature, as in attesting or confirming something. 2. to make a sign; signal. Abbreviated **s.**

sign away (or **over**), to abandon or transfer title to (something) by or as by signing a document; convey.

sign off, 1. in *radio*, to stop broadcasting after making station identification. 2. [Slang], to stop talking.

sign on, to engage (oneself or others) for employment; hire or be hired, especially by a signed agreement.

sign up, 1. to sign on; specifically, 2. to enlist in some branch of military service.

SYN.—**sign,** the broadest in scope of these terms, applies to an action, condition, quality, occurrence, or visible object that points to a fact or conveys a meaning (a *sign* of spring, good will, the zodiac, etc.); **mark** suggests that which is imprinted on, or is intrinsically characteristic of, something (suffering left its *mark* on his face); **token** suggests something given or serving as a symbol or sign of some quality, feeling, value, etc. (a *token* of good will); a **symptom** is an outward, recognizable sign of the existence of a disease, disorder, etc. (prejudice is a *symptom* of social maladjustment); **indication** is the general word, interchangeable with any of the preceding words.

sig·nal (sig'n'l), *n.* [ME.; OFr.; LL. *signale*, neut. of *signalis* < L. *signum*, a sign], 1. a sign; token; indication. 2. a sign or event fixed or understood as the occasion for prearranged combined action: as, a *signal* for a fire drill. 3. anything which incites to action. 4. a sign given by gesture, mechanical device, etc. to convey command, warning, or other information: as, a red light is a stop *signal*. 5. in *card games*, a bid or play designed to give information to one's partner. 6. in *telegraphy, radio, television*, etc., the electrical impulses, sound or picture elements, etc. received or transmitted. *adj.* 1. not average or ordinary; conspicuous; remarkable; notable. 2. used as a signal or in signaling. *v.t.* [SIGNALED or SIGNALLED (-n'ld), SIGNALING or SIGNALLING], 1. to make a signal or signals to. 2. to make known or communicate (information) by signals. *v.i.* to make a signal or signals. Abbreviated **Sig., sig.**

Signal Corps, in the *United States Army*, the combat arm in charge of most forms of communication and many meteorological, photographic, and range-finding services: abbreviated **S.C., Sig. C.**

sig·nal·er (sig'n'l-ẽr), *n.* a person or thing that signals.

sig·nal·ize (sig'n'l-īz'), *v.t.* [SIGNALIZED (-īzd'), SIGNALIZING], 1. to make signal, remarkable, or noteworthy; distinguish. 2. to point out; call attention t

sig·nal·ler (sig'n'l-ẽr), *n.* a signaler.

sig·nal·ly (sig'nəl-i), *adv.* in a signal, or striking, manne remarkably; notably.

sig·nal·man (sig'n'l-man', sig'n'l-mən), *n.* [*pl.* SIGNAL MEN (-men', -mən)], a man responsible for operatin sending, or receiving signals.

sig·nal·ment (sig'n'l-mənt), *n.* [*signal* + *-ment*], description giving distinguishing or identifying mark as of someone wanted by the police.

sig·na·to·ry (sig'nə-tôr'i, sig'nə-tō'ri), *adj.* [L. *signat rius* < *signore;* see SIGN], joining or taking part in t signing of something. *n.* [*pl.* SIGNATORIES (-iz)], person, agency, government, etc., usually one of severa whose signature is attached to a document.

sig·na·ture (sig'nə-chẽr), *n.* [ML. *signatura* < L. *signar* to sign], 1. a person's name written by himself, or representation of this in a mark, stamp, deputy handwriting, etc. 2. the act of signing one's nam 3. that part of a doctor's prescription telling t patient how to use the medicine prescribed: usual marked *S* or *Sig.* 4. a musical number or sound effe which opens or closes a radio program. 5. in *mus* a sign or signs placed at the beginning of a staff show key or time. 6. in *printing*, *a)* a large she upon which are printed four, or some multiple of fou pages and which, when folded and bound, forms o section of a book or pamphlet. *b)* a letter or numb at the bottom of the first page in such a sheet showi in what order the sheet is to be bound. Abbreviat **Sig., sig.**

sign·board (sīn'bôrd', sīn'bōrd'), *n.* a board beari a sign or notice, especially one advertising a busine

sig·net (sig'nit), *n.* [ME.; OFr., dim. of *signe*, a sig 1. a seal, especially one used as a signature in marki documents as official, etc. 2. a mark or impressi made by or as by a signet. *v.t.* to stamp or make offic with a signet.

signet ring, a finger ring containing a signet, often the form of an initial.

sig·nif·i·cance (sig-nif'ə-kəns), *n.* [L. *significantia significans;* see SIGNIFICANT], 1. that which is si nified; meaning. 2. the quality of being significar suggestiveness; expressiveness. 3. importance; co sequence; moment. —*SYN.* see **importance, meaning**

sig·nif·i·can·cy (sig-nif'ə-kən-si), *n.* significance.

sig·nif·i·cant (sig-nif'ə-kənt), *adj.* [L. *significans*, p of *significare*, to signify], 1. *a)* having or expressi a meaning. *b)* full of meaning. 2. important; m mentous. 3. having or conveying a special or hidd meaning; suggestive. *n.* [Archaic], something that h significance; sign.

sig·ni·fi·ca·tion (sig'nə-fi-kā'shən), *n.* [ME. *signific cioun;* OFr. *significaciun;* L. *significatio*], 1. signi cance; meaning. 2. the act of signifying; indicatio —*SYN.* see **meaning.**

sig·nif·i·ca·tive (sig-nif'ə-kā'tiv), *adj.* significant.

sig·ni·fi·er (sig'nə-fī'ẽr), *n.* a person or thing that s nifies.

sig·ni·fy (sig'nə-fī'), *v.t.* [SIGNIFIED (-fīd'), SIGNIFYIN [ME. *signifien;* Late OFr. *signifier;* L. *significare signum*, a sign + *facere*, to make], 1. to be a sign indication of; mean: as, his rags *signify* his poverty. to show or make known, as by a sign, words, etc.: *signify* "yes" by raising your hand. *v.i.* to have so meaning or importance; be significant; matter.

si·gnior (sēn'yôr, sēn'yōr), *n.* signor: English spelling

sign language, communication of thoughts or ideas means of manual signs and gestures.

sign manual, a personal signature, especially that o monarch on an official document.

sign of the zodiac, any of the twelve divisions or hou of the zodiac, each represented by a symbol: see **zodi**

‡**si·gnor** (sē-nyôr'; Eng. sēn'yôr, sēn'yōr), *n.* [It.; duced form of *signore;* see SIGNORE], 1. [S-], M Italian title of respect, used before the name. 2. gentleman; man. Abbreviated **Sig., sig., S.**

‡**si·gno·ra** (sē-nyô'rä), *n.* [*pl.* SIGNORE (-re)], [It., fe of *signor*], woman; lady: Italian title equivalent to *M* or *Madam.*

‡**si·gno·re** (sē-nyô're; Eng. sēn-yôr'ā, sēn-yō'rā), *n.* [SIGNORI (-rē)], [It.; L. *senior;* cf. SENIOR, SEÑOR], gentleman; man. 2. sir: Italian title of respect, us in direct address but not before the name (cf. **signo** Abbreviated **sig., Sig.**

‡**si·gno·ri·na** (sē'nyô-rē'nä), *n.* [*pl.* SIGNORINE (-ne [It., dim. of *signora*], an unmarried woman or gi young lady: Italian title equivalent to *Miss.*

‡**si·gno·ri·no** (sē'nyô-rē'nô), *n.* [*pl.* SIGNORINI (-nē [It., dim. of *signore*], a young man; young gentlema Italian title equivalent to *Master.*

si·gno·ry (sēn'yẽr-i), *n.* [*pl.* SIGNORIES (-iz)], seignio

sign·post (sīn'pōst'), *n.* 1. a post bearing a sign; gui post. 2. a clear indication; obvious clue, symptom, e

Sigs·bee, Charles Dwight (sigz'bi), 1845–1923; Ame can admiral who commanded the *Maine* in 1898.

Si·gurd (sig'ẽrd), *n.* in *Norse legend*, the hero of t Volsunga Saga: identified with the German Siegfri

Si·kan·dar·a·bad (sē-kun'dẽr-ä-bäd'), *n.* Secunderab

·i·kang (sē'kaŋ'; Chin. shē'käŋ'), *n.* a Chinese province in Nearer Tibet: area, 164,991 sq. mi.; pop., 1,651,000 (est. 1947); capital, Kangting.

ikh (sēk), *n.* [Hind., a disciple], a believer in Sikhism *adj.* of or belonging to the Sikhs.

ikh·ism (sēk'iz'm), *n.* the doctrines of a Hindu religious sect founded in northern India about 1500: belief in one god and rejection of the caste system are the main principles.

i-kiang (sē'kyäŋ'; Chin. shē'jyäŋ'), *n.* a river in southern China, flowing into the South China Sea: length, 1,250 mi.: also called *Si.*

ik·kim (sik'im), *n.* a state of northeastern India: area, 2,818 sq. mi.; pop., 122,000; capital, Gangtok.

i·kor·sky, I·gor (ē'gôr si-kôr'ski), 1889– ; American aeronautical engineer, born in Russia.

i·lage (sī'lij), *n.* [< *ensilage*, after *silo*], in *agriculture*, green fodder preserved in a silo.

i·las (sī'ləs), [LL.; Gr. *Silas;* prob. of Sem. origin], a masculine name: diminutive, *Si.*

i·le·na·ceous (sī'lə-nā'shəs), *adj.* [< Mod. L. *Silene*, a genus of plants (< L. *Silenus*, Silenus); + *-aceous*], in *botany*, caryophyllaceous.

i·lence (sī'ləns), *n.* [ME.; OFr. *scilence, silence;* L. *silentium* < *silens;* see SILENT], 1. the state or fact of keeping silent; a refraining from speech or the making of noise. 2. absence of any sound or noise; stillness. 3. a withholding of knowledge; omission of mention: as, we noted the author's *silence* on that point. 4. failure to communicate, write, keep in touch, etc. 5. oblivion or obscurity. *v.t.* [SILENCED (-lənst), SILENCING], 1. to cause to be silent. 2. to put down; repress; overcome. 3. to put (enemy guns) out of action. *interj.* be silent!

i·lenc·er (sī'lən-sēr), *n.* 1. a person or thing that silences. 2. a device for deadening the sound of a gun. 3. [Chiefly British], a muffler for an internal-combustion engine.

i·lent (sī'lənt), *adj.* [L. *silens* < *silere*, to be silent], 1. making no vocal sound; not speaking; speechless; mute. 2. seldom speaking; saying little; not talkative. 3. free from or making no sound or noise; quiet; still; noiseless. 4. not spoken, uttered, or expressed; tacit: as, *silent* longing. 5. withholding knowledge; omitting mention; uncommunicative: as, the report was *silent* on this matter. 6. inactive: as, the machines had been *silent* for six months. 7. designating or of motion pictures that do not have an accompanying synchronized speech and sound recording: printed captions are used to present dialogue in silent films.

SYN.—**silent** is the simple, direct word for one who is temporarily not speaking or one who seldom speaks; **taciturn** applies to a person who is habitually uncommunicative; **reserved** implies a habitual disposition to be withdrawn in speech and self-restrained or aloof in manner; **reticent** implies a disinclination, sometimes temporary as from embarrassment, to express one's feelings or impart information; **secretive** suggests the furtive or evasive reticence of one who conceals things unnecessarily. See also **still.** —***ANT.*** talkative, voluble.

ilent butler, an ornamental dish with a hinged cover and handle, in which to empty ash trays, etc.

ilent partner, a partner who shares in financing but not in managing a business, firm, etc.

·le·nus (sī-lē'nəs), *n.* [*pl.* SILENI (-nī)], [L.; Gr. *Seilēnos*, Silenus], in *Greek mythology*, 1. [S-], the foster father and tutor of Bacchus and leader of the satyrs, traditionally pictured as a fat, drunken, jovial old man with pointed ears and goat's legs. 2. any of a group of woodland deities resembling the satyrs.

i·le·sia (sī-lē'shi-ə, sə-lē'shə), *n.* a region of central Europe, in the upper valley of the Oder River, divided before World War II among Germany which held the largest part), Czechoslovakia, and Poland: in 1945, by the terms of the Potsdam agreement, German Silesia was given to Poland: Polish name, *Śląsk;* Czech name, *Slezsko;* German name, *Schlesien.*

SILESIA
(1815–1867)

·le·si·a (sī-lē'shi-ə, sə-lē'shə), *n.* a strong, lightweight linen or twilled cotton cloth used for linings: the linen was originally made in Silesia.

Si·le·sian (sī-lē'shi-ən, sə-lē'shən), *adj.* of Silesia, its people, or culture. *n.* a native or inhabitant of Silesia.

si·lex (sī'leks), *n.* [L.], 1. silica, especially in the form of flint or quartz. 2. heat-resistant glass made of fused quartz. 3. a device of such glass used for making coffee: a trade-mark (**Silex**).

sil·hou·ette (sil'oo-et', sil'ə-wet'), *n.* [after Étienne de *Silhouette*, Fr. minister of finance in 1759], 1. an outline drawing, especially a profile portrait, filled in with a solid color: silhouettes are usually cut from black paper and fixed on a light background. 2. any dark shape or outline seen against a light background. *v.t.* [SILHOUETTED (-id), SILHOUETTING], to show or project in a silhouette. —***SYN.*** see **outline.**

SILHOUETTE

sil·i·ca (sil'i-kə), *n.* [Mod. L. < L. *silex, silicis*, flint], the dioxide of silicon, SiO_2, a hard, glassy mineral found in a variety of forms, as in quartz, sand, opal, etc.

silica gel, a colloidal form of silica used as a drying agent in air-conditioning equipment, as a carrier of catalysts in chemical reactions, etc.

sil·i·cate (sil'i-kit; *esp. by chemists* sil'i-kāt'), *n.* a salt or ester derived from silica or a silicic acid.

si·li·ceous (sə-lish'əs), *adj.* [L. *siliceus*], 1. of, containing, or like silica. 2. growing in soil that has a large proportion of silica in it.

si·lic·ic (sə-lis'ik), *adj.* [*silicon* + *-ic*], of, like, or derived from silica or silicon.

silicic acid, any of several hypothetical acids of which the different mineral silicates may be regarded as salts.

sil·i·cide (sil'i-sīd', sil'i-sid), *n.* a binary compound of silicon.

sil·i·cif·er·ous (sil'i-sif'ēr-əs), *adj.* [< L. *silex, silicis*, a flint; + *-ferous*], containing, producing, or in combination with silica.

si·lic·i·fy (sə-lis'ə-fī'), *v.t.* [SILICIFIED (-fīd'), SILICIFYING], [< L. *silex, silicis*, a flint; + *-fy*], to convert into or impregnate with silica. *v.i.* to become silicified, as wood.

si·li·cious (sə-lish'əs), *adj.* siliceous.

si·li·ci·um (sə-lish'i-əm, sə-lis'i-əm), *n.* [Mod. L. < L. *silex, silicis*, a flint], silicon.

sil·i·cle (sil'i-k'l), *n.* [< Fr. or L.; Fr. *silicule;* L. *silicula*, dim. of *siliqua*, a pod], in *botany*, a short, broad silique.

sil·i·co- (sil'i-kō, sil'i-kə), [< *silicon*], a combining form meaning *silicon, silica,* as in *silicosis:* also, before a vowel, **silic-.**

sil·i·con (sil'i-kən), *n.* [< L. *silex, silicis*, flint], a nonmetallic chemical element found always in combination and more abundant in nature than any other element except oxygen, with which it combines to form silica: symbol, Si; at. wt., 28.06; at. no., 14.

sil·i·cone (sil'ə-kōn'), *n.* [< *silicon*], any of a group of synthetic resins, oils, greases, plastics, etc., in which the carbon has been replaced by silicon: such compounds are characterized by relatively high resistance to temperature changes, to water, etc. and are used in lubricants, synthetic rubber, polishes, and the like.

sil·i·co·sis (sil'ə-kō'sis), *n.* [Mod. L. < *silic-* + *-osis*], a chronic disease of the lungs caused by the continued inhaling of silica dust, as in quarrying stone.

si·lic·u·lose (sə-lik'yoo-lōs'), *adj.* 1. having silicles. 2. having the form of a silicle.

si·lique (si-lēk', sil'ik), *n.* [Fr.; L. *siliqua*], the pod of plants of the mustard family, with two valves which fall away from a frame bearing the seeds.

sil·i·quose (sil'ə-kwōs'), *adj.* [Mod. L. *siliquosus* < L. *siliqua*, a pod], 1. having siliques. 2. having the form of a silique.

sil·i·quous (sil'ə-kwəs), *adj.* siliquose.

silk (silk), *n.* [see PLURAL, II, D, 3], [ME. *silke, selke;* AS. *seoluc* (for *siluc); ult. < L. *sericus*, fabric of the *Seres*, the Chinese (cf. SERGE); the change of *r* to *l* is due to roundabout transmission via northern Europe], 1. the fine, soft, shiny fiber produced by silkworms to form their cocoons. 2. thread or fabric made from this material. 3. a garment made of this fabric. 4. *pl.* the distinctive silk uniform of a jockey, prize fighter, acrobat, etc. 5. the silk gown worn by a king's (or queen's) counsel in British law courts. 6. any silklike filament or substance, as that within a milkweed pod,

on the end of an ear of corn, etc. *adj.* of or like silk; silken. *v.i.* to bloom: said of Indian corn.
hit the silk, [Slang], to leave an aircraft by means of a parachute.
silk·a·line, silk·a·lene (sil′kə-lēn′), *n.* a thin, soft, cotton fabric with a silky luster.
silk cotton, the silky fibers covering the seeds of various bombacaceous trees, used to stuff cushions, etc.: also called *kapok.*
silk-cot·ton tree (silk′kot″n), any bombacaceous tree, especially one from which silk cotton is obtained, as the ceiba, or kapok tree.
silk·en (sil′k'n), *adj.* [ME. *silken, selken;* AS. *seolcen;* cf. SILK & -EN], 1. made of silk. 2. dressed in silk. 3. silklike in appearance, texture, etc.; soft; smooth; glossy; hence, 4. *a)* smooth and ingratiating: as, *silken* flattery. *b)* elegant; luxurious: as, *silken* ease. *c)* soft; gentle; delicate: as, a *silken* caress.
silk hat, a tall, cylindrical hat covered with silk or satin, worn by men in dress clothes.
silk·i·ness (sil′ki-nis), *n.* a silky state or quality.
silk-screen print (silk′skrēn′), a print made by the silk-screen process: cf. **serigraph.**
silk-screen process, a stencil method of printing a flat color design through a piece of silk or other fine cloth on which all parts of the design not to be printed have been stopped out by an impermeable substance.
silk-stock·ing (silk′stok′iŋ), *adj.* 1. fashionably or richly dressed; elegant. 2. wealthy; aristocratic: as, the *silk-stocking* trade. *n.* 1. a member of the wealthy, aristocratic class. 2. [Colloq.], a Federalist or Whig.
silk·weed (silk′wēd′), *n.* milkweed.
silk·worm (silk′wũrm′), *n.* any of certain moth caterpillars that produce cocoons of silk fiber: they feed chiefly on mulberry leaves and are cultivated as the source of commercial silk.
silk·y (sil′ki), *adj.* [SILKIER (-ki-ẽr), SILKIEST (-ki-ist)], 1. of or like silk; soft; smooth; lustrous. 2. having fine, soft, silklike hairs, as some leaves.
sill (sil), *n.* [ME. *sille, sylle;* AS. *syl, syll;* akin to G. *schwelle;* IE. base **sel-*, a beam, plank], 1. a heavy, horizontal timber or line of masonry supporting a house wall, etc. 2. a horizontal piece forming the bottom frame of a door or window.
sil·la·bub (sil′ə-bub′), *n.* [prob. a var. of dial. *sillibouk,* lit., silly (i.e., happy) stomach, in which *-bub* shows influence of *bub,* breast; Eng. dial. has also *merribowk,* lit., merry stomach, for the term], a dessert or beverage made of sweetened milk or cream mixed with wine or cider and beaten to a froth: also spelled **syllabub.**
Sil·lan·pää, Frans Ee·mil (fråns e′mil sil′lån-pa′), 1888– ; Finnish writer; received Nobel prize in literature, 1939.
sil·ler (sil′ẽr), *n.* [Scot.], silver; money.
sil·li·ly (sil′ə-li), *adv.* in a silly manner.
sil·li·ness (sil′i-nis), *n.* 1. the quality of being silly. 2. something silly; silly behavior.
sil·ly (sil′i), *adj.* [SILLIER (-i-ẽr), SILLIEST (-i-ist)], [ME. *seli, sili* (with shortened vowel), good, blessed, innocent; AS. *sælig,* happy, prosperous, blessed (akin to G. *selig,* blessed) < *sæl,* time; sense development: happy—blessed—innocent—(deserving pity)—unworldly—foolish; cf. INNOCENT, CRETIN], 1. feeble-minded; imbecile. 2. having or showing little sense, judgment, or sobriety; foolish, stupid, absurd, ludicrous, etc. 3. [Colloq.], dazed; senseless, as from a blow. 4. [Dial.], helpless; weak. 5. [Archaic], feeble; infirm. 6. [Archaic], simple; plain; innocent. *n.* [Colloq.], a silly person.
SYN.—**silly** implies ridiculous or irrational behavior that seems to demonstrate a lack of common sense, good judgment, or sobriety (it was *silly* of you to lock the door); **stupid** implies a dull-wittedness or lack of normal intelligence or understanding (he is not so *stupid* as to believe that); **fatuous** suggests stupidity, inanity, or obtuseness coupled with a smug complacency (a *fatuous* babbitt); **asinine** implies the extreme stupidity conventionally attributed to an ass (an *asinine* argument). See also **absurd.** —*ANT.* wise, intelligent.
si·lo (sī′lō), *n.* [*pl.* SILOS (-lōz)], [Fr.; Sp.; L. *sirus;* Gr. *siros*], an airtight pit or tower in which green fodder is preserved. *v.t.* to store in a silo.
Si·lo·am (si-lō′əm, sə-lōm′), *n.* [Heb. *shiloah,* lit., sending forth], in the *Bible,* a spring and pool outside Jerusalem: John 9:7.
silt (silt), *n.* [ME. *sylte;* prob. < ON. (cf. Dan. *sylt,* Norw. *sylta,* sea beach, sea marsh); akin to G. *sülze,* salt marsh; for IE. base see SALT], any earthy material composed of fine particles, as soil or sand, suspended in or deposited by water. *v.t. & v.i.* to fill or choke up with silt. —*SYN.* see **wash.**
silt·y (sil′ti), *adj.* [SILTIER (-ti-ẽr), SILTIEST (-ti-ist)], 1. of or like silt. 2. full of or clouded with silt.
Si·lun·dum (si-lun′dəm), *n.* [*silicon* + *carborundum*], silicon carbide, SiC, produced in an electric furnace and used as an abrasive for electric resistors, etc.: a trademark.
Sil·u·res (sil′yoo-rēz′), *n.pl.* an ancient, warlike tribe of southeastern Wales, conquered by the Romans about 80 A.D.
Si·lu·ri·an (sə-loor′i-ən, sī-lyoor′i-ən), *adj.* 1. of the Silures or the territory held by them. 2. designatin or of the geological period after the Ordovician an before the Devonian in the Paleozoic Era, char acterized by the appearance of scorpions (the firs land animals) and extensive coral reefs: so called be cause its rocks were first found in an area occupied b the Welsh, assumed to be descendants of the Silures.
the Silurian, the Silurian Period or its rocks: se **geology,** chart.
si·lu·rid (sə-loor′id, sī-lyoor′id), *n.* [< Mod. L. *Siluridae* name of the family < L. *silurus,* a kind of river fish Gr. *silouros*], any of a number of fresh-water catfishe found in Europe and Asia.
sil·va (sil′və), *n.* [*pl.* SILVAS (-vəz), SILVAE (-vē)], [L., forest], 1. the forest trees of a certain area. 2. a boo or treatise describing the trees of a certain region. Als spelled **sylva.**
Sil·van (sil′vən), a masculine name: see **Sylvan.**
sil·van (sil′vən), *adj. & n.* sylvan.
Sil·va·nus (sil-vā′nəs), a masculine name: see **Sylvanu** *n.* Roman god of the woods and farming.
sil·ver (sil′vẽr), *n.* [ME. *sylver, selfer;* AS. *seolfer;* aki to G. *silber,* Goth. *silubr,* etc.; cf. also Russ. *serebr* prob. a loan word < outside IE.], 1. a white, preciou metallic chemical element that is extremely ductile an malleable, capable of a high polish, and an exceller conductor of heat and electricity: symbol, Ag; a wt., 107.880; at. no., 47. 2. the metal regarded as commodity or medium of exchange, as in the form ingots, coins, etc.; hence, 3. money of any kin 4. something, especially tableware, made of or plate with silver; silverware. 5. a lustrous, grayish-whi color; silvery color. 6. something having this colo as the material used in coating the back of a mirro 7. a salt of silver, as used in photography, etc. *adj.* made of, containing, or plated with silver: as, *silv* thread. 2. of, based on, or having to do with silver: a the *silver* standard. 3. of or advocating the adoptio of silver as a standard of currency: as, the *silver* blo 4. having the color or luster of silver; silvery. 5. havir a silvery tone or sound. 6. eloquent: as, a *silver* tongu 7. marking or celebrating the twenty-fifth year: as, *silver* wedding anniversary. *v.t.* 1. to cover or co with silver or something like silver. 2. to cause to r semble silver in color or luster: as, trees *silvered* wit snow. *v.i.* to become silvery in color. Abbreviated **s.**
Silver Age, 1. the period of Latin literature comin between 14 and 180 A.D., distinguished by the writing of Martial, Juvenal, Tacitus, etc. 2. in *classic mythology,* the second age of the world, inferior to t first or Golden Age.
silver bell, any of a number of related trees with droo ing, bell-shaped, white flowers.
sil·ver-bell tree (sil′vẽr-bel′), a silver bell.
sil·ver·ber·ry (sil′vẽr-ber′i), *n.* [*pl.* SILVERBERRIES (-iz) a shrub with fragrant flowers and silvery leaves an fruit.
silver birch, the white birch.
silver bromide, a yellow-white crystalline compoun AgBr, which becomes dark when exposed to light: use in photography.
silver certificate, a piece of paper money issued on t basis of a government's possession of silver in t amount of the face value of the certificate, payable the bearer on demand: a United States silver certifica is legal tender for all debts, public and private.
silver chloride, a white crystalline compound, Ag which becomes dark when exposed to light: used photography.
sil·ver·fish (sil′vẽr-fish′), *n.* 1. [*pl.* SILVERFISH, SILVE FISHES (-iz); see FISH], any of various fishes of silve color, as the tarpon, silversides, etc. 2. a wingle insect with silvery scales, long feelers, and a bristly ta it thrives in dampness and darkness and lives chiefly starches and sugars.
silver foil, silver beaten into thin sheets.
silver fox, 1. a fox with black fur in which the individu hairs are banded with white near the tips. 2. the fu
silver gilt, 1. silver with a thin coating of gold. 2. imitation of this made with silver leaf coated wi yellow lacquer.
sil·ver-gray (sil′vẽr-grā′), *adj.* gray with a silvery luste *n.* a silver-gray color.
sil·ver-haired (sil′vẽr-hârd′), *adj.* having silvery-wh or gray hair.
sil·ver·i·ness (sil′vẽr-i-nis), *n.* the quality or state being silvery.
sil·ver·ing (sil′vẽr-iŋ), *n.* 1. the act of covering wi silver or a silvery substance. 2. a coating of silver or substance like silver; hence, 3. a silvery sheen appearance.
silver leaf, very thin silver foil.
silver lining, some basis for hope in the midst of despa misfortune, etc.
sil·ver·ly (sil′vẽr-li), *adv.* with a silvery appearance sound.
sil·vern (sil′vẽrn), *adj.* [ME. *silveren;* AS. *seolfren;* SILVER & -EN], [Archaic], of or like silver.
silver nitrate, a colorless crystalline salt, $AgNO_3$, pr

pared by dissolving silver in dilute nitric acid and used in silver plating, photography, as an antiseptic, etc.

ilver plate, tableware made of silver.

ilver screen, 1. a screen on which motion pictures are projected in theaters. 2. motion pictures collectively: with *the.*

il·ver·side (sil'vẽr-sīd'), *n.* silversides.

il·ver·sides (sil'vẽr-sīdz'), *n.* [*pl.* SILVERSIDES], any of a number of small fishes or minnows with silver stripes along the sides.

il·ver·smith (sil'vẽr-smith'), *n.* a person who makes and repairs silver articles.

ilver standard, a monetary standard in which the basic currency unit is equal to a specified quantity of silver.

ilver Star Medal, a United States military decoration in the form of a bronze star with a small silver star at the center, awarded for gallantry in action.

l·ver-tongued (sil'vẽr-tuŋd'), *adj.* eloquent.

l·ver·ware (sil'vẽr-wâr'), *n.* articles, especially tableware, made of or plated with silver.

lver wedding, a twenty-fifth wedding anniversary.

l·ver·weed (sil'vẽr-wēd'), *n.* 1. a plant with long stems, yellow flowers, and leaves which are silvery underneath. 2. any of a number of related plants of he morning-glory family, with similar leaves.

l·ver·y (sil'vẽr-i), *adj.* 1. having the appearance of silver; like silver in color or luster. 2. softly and clearly inging: as, a *silvery* tone. 3. covered with or containing silver.

il·ves·ter (sil-ves'tẽr), a masculine name: see **Sylvester.**

il·vi·a (sil'vi-ə), a feminine name: see **Sylvia.**

l·vi·cul·ture (sil'vi-kul'chẽr), *n.* [< L. *silva,* forest; + *culture*], the art of cultivating a forest; forestry.

'il vous plaît (sēl' vōō' ple'), [Fr., lit., if it pleases you], if you please; please.

·mar (si-mär'), *n.* [Fr. *simarre;* It. *cimarra* < Ar. *sammur,* sable], a loose robe or jacket for women.

m·a·rou·ba (sim'ə-rōō'bə), *n.* [Mod. L.; Carib], 1. any of a number of related tropical American trees with bitter bark, large-disked flowers, and pulpy fruit. 2. the bark, used in pharmacy.

m·a·rou·ba·ceous (sim'ə-rōō-bā'shəs), *adj.* [< Mod. L. *Simaroubaceae,* name of the family (< *simarouba*); + *-ous*], in *botany,* of the ailanthus family.

m·chath To·rah (sim-khäth' tō-rä', sim'khäs tō'rô), [Heb. *simhath torah,* lit., rejoicing in the Torah, or Law], a Jewish holiday, the Rejoicing in the Law: also spelled **Simhath Torah:** see **Jewish holidays.**

m·e·on (sim'i-ən), [LL.; Gr. *Symeōn;* Heb. *shim'ōn,* lit., heard], a masculine name. *n.* in the *Bible,* 1. a son of Jacob; hence, 2. a tribe of Israel descended from him. 3. a pious man who, on seeing the infant Jesus in the Temple, spoke the words later set to the canticle "Nunc Dimittis": Luke 2:25.

meon Styl·i·tes, Saint (stī-lī'tēz), 390?–459 A.D.; Syrian monk who lived and preached on the top of a pillar: his day is September 2.

m·fe·ro·pol (sim'fe-rô'pôl-y'), *n.* a city in the Crimea: pop., 143,000.

m·i·an (sim'i-ən), *adj.* [< L. *simia,* an ape], of or like an ape or monkey, especially an anthropoid ape. *n.* an ape or monkey, especially an anthropoid ape.

m·i·lar (sim'ə-lẽr), *adj.* [Fr. *similaire* < L. *similis*], 1. nearly but not exactly the same or alike; having a general resemblance. 2. in *geometry,* having the same shape, but not the same size or position.

m·i·lar·i·ty (sim'ə-lar'ə-ti), *n.* [*similar* + *-ity;* cf. Fr. *similarité*], 1. the state or quality of being similar; resemblance or likeness. 2. [*pl.* SIMILARITIES (-tiz)], a point, feature, or instance in which things are similar. —*SYN.* see **likeness.**

m·i·lar·ly (sim'ə-lẽr-li), *adv.* so as to be similar; in like manner; likewise.

n·i·le (sim'ə-lē'), *n.* [*pl.* SIMILES (-lēz')], [ME.; L. < *similis,* like], a figure of speech in which one thing is likened to another, dissimilar thing by the use of *like, as,* etc. (e.g., a heart as big as a whale, her tears flowed like wine): distinguished from *metaphor,* in that the comparison is made explicit.

mil·i·tude (sə-mil'ə-tōōd', sə-mil'ə-tūd'), *n.* [ME.; OFr.; L. *similitudo*], 1. a person or thing resembling another; counterpart; facsimile. 2. form; image. 3. a) [Rare], a simile. *b*) a parable or allegory. 4. similarity; likeness; resemblance.

n·i·ous (sim'i-əs), *adj.* simian.

n·i·tar (sim'ə-tẽr), *n.* a scimitar.

m·la (sim'lə), *n.* a city in East Punjab, India: pop., 18,000: former summer capital of India under British government.

n·mer (sim'ẽr), *v.i.* [earlier *simper;* of echoic origin], 1. to boil gently with a low, murmuring sound; be or stay at or just below the boiling point. 2. to be about to break out, as in anger, revolt, etc. *v.t.* to keep at or just below the boiling point. *n.* the state of simmering: as, keep the water at a *simmer.* —*SYN.* see **boil.**

simmer down, 1. to simmer, as a liquid, until the volume is reduced or condensed. 2. to cease simmering; subside; cool off; abate.

sim·nel (sim'nəl), *n.* [OFr. *simenel, seminel;* ML. *simila,* small wheat bread; L., fine wheat flour; akin to Gr. *semidalis,* finest wheat flour; ult. prob. < Bab. *samīdu,* fine flour], [Archaic], 1. a rich fruitcake prepared at Christmas, Easter, etc. 2. a crisp bread or biscuit made of fine flour, and often boiled before baking.

si·mo·le·on (sə-mō'li-ən), *n.* [Slang], a dollar.

Si·mon (sī'mən), [L.; Gr. *Simōn, Seimōn;* Heb. *shim'ōn,* lit., heard], a masculine name: diminutive, *Sim. n.* 1. in the *Bible,* one of the twelve apostles (called Peter): see **Peter.** 2. a brother or relative of Jesus: Mark 6:3.

Si·mon, Sir **John Allse·brook** (ôls'brook sī'mən), Viscount Simon, 1873–1954; English lawyer and statesman.

si·mo·ni·ac (si-mō'ni-ak'), *n.* [ME. *symoniak;* ML. *simoniacus*], a person who practices simony.

sim·o·ni·a·cal (sī'mə-nī'ə-k'l, sim'ə-nī'ə-k'l), *adj.* 1. of or constituting simony. 2. guilty of simony.

Si·mon·i·des (sī-mon'ə-dēz'), *n.* a Greek lyric poet who died in the 5th century B.C.

sim·o·nist (sī'mə-nist, sim'ə-nist), *n.* a simoniac.

Si·mon·ize (sī'mə-nīz'), *v.t.* [SIMONIZED (-nīzd'), SIMONIZING], [< *Simoniz,* trade-mark for a preparation used for this purpose], to clean and wax the enameled surface of (an automobile body, etc.).

Simon Le·gree (lə-grē'), 1. the villainous slave overseer in Harriet Beecher Stowe's *Uncle Tom's Cabin;* hence, 2. any relentless taskmaster.

Simon Ma·gus (mā'gəs), in the *Bible,* a Samaritan magician who offered money for instruction in the rite of imparting the Holy Ghost by the laying on of hands: Acts 8:9–24.

Simon Peter, see **Peter** (apostle).

si·mon-pure (sī'mən-pyoor'), *adj.* [after *Simon Pure,* a Quaker in Susanna Centlivre's play *A Bold Stroke for a Wife* (1718), who must prove his identity against an impostor's claims], genuine; real; authentic.

sim·o·ny (sī'mə-ni, sim'ə-ni), *n.* [ME. & OFr. *simonie;* ML. *simonia* < *Simon Magus*], the buying or selling of sacred or spiritual things, as ecclesiastical pardons, church offices, etc.

si·moom (si-mōōm'), *n.* [Ar. *samūm* < *samma,* to poison], a hot, violent, sand-laden wind of the African and Asiatic deserts: also called *samiel.*

si·moon (si-mōōn'), *n.* a simoom.

simp (simp), *n.* [Slang], a simpleton.

sim·per (sim'pẽr), *v.i.* [Early Mod. Eng.; prob. akin to MD. *simper, simperlije,* dainty, affected, etc.; origin prob. echoic of pursed lips, etc.], to smile in a silly, affected, or self-conscious way; smirk. *v.t.* to say or express with a simper. *n.* a silly, affected, or self-conscious smile; smirk. —*SYN.* see **smile.**

sim·ple (sim'p'l), *adj.* [SIMPLER (-plẽr), SIMPLEST (-plist)], [ME.; OFr.; L. *simplex*], 1. having or consisting of only one part, feature, substance, etc.; not compounded or complex; single. 2. having few parts or features; not complicated or involved: as, a *simple* pattern; hence, 3. easy to do, solve, or understand, as a task, question, etc. 4. without additions or qualifications; mere; bare: as, here are the *simple* facts. 5. *a*) not ornate; unembellished; unadorned: as, *simple* clothes. *b*) not luxurious or elegant; plain: as, *simple* tastes. 6. without guile or deceit; innocent; artless. 7. without ostentation or affectation; unpretending; natural. 8. of low rank or position; specifically, *a*) humble; lowly. *b*) common; ordinary. 9. lacking significance; unimportant. 10. having or showing little sense or reasoning ability; easily misled or deceived; foolish; stupid; hence, 11. [Dial.], feeble-minded. 12. in *chemistry, a*) elementary. *b*) unmixed. 13. in *law,* unconditional; absolute: as, in fee *simple.* 14. in *music, a*) not compound: said of time or measure. *b*) not having overtones: as, a *simple* tone. *c*) not elaborated: as, *simple* harmony. 15. in *zoology,* not divided into or made up of parts; not compounded: as, a *simple* tunicate. *n.* 1. a person who is ignorant or easily misled. 2. *a*) a medicinal plant or herb. *b*) a medicine made from such a plant. 3. something having only one part, substance, etc. 4. [Archaic], a person of humble parentage or position. —*SYN.* see **easy.**

simple equation, an equation in which the expressions of the unknown are stated in the first power only: $x + y = z$ is a simple equation, $x^2 + y^3 = 31$ is not.

simple fraction, a fraction in which both the numerator and denominator are whole numbers, as 1/2.

simple fruit, any fruit developing from a single pistil.

sim·ple-heart·ed (sim'p'l-här'tid), *adj.* artless or unsophisticated in nature; sincere.

simple honors, three honor cards in trump held by the same side in auction bridge.

simple interest, interest paid only on the principal lent and not on previously accumulated interest.
simple machine, any one of the simple devices, including the lever, wheel and axle, pulley, wedge, screw, and inclined plane, once believed to constitute the basic features of all machines.
sim·ple-mind·ed (sim'p'l-mīn'did), *adj.* 1. simple-hearted; unsophisticated. 2. having little sense; foolish; stupid. 3. feeble-minded.
simple sentence, a sentence having one main clause and no subordinate clauses (e.g., "The boy ran.").
Simple Simon, 1. a foolish character in a nursery rhyme of the same name. 2. [Colloq.], any simpleton.
sim·ple·ton (sim'p'l-tən), *n.* [< *simple*, after names ending in *-ton*], a person who is silly, stupid, or easily deceived; fool.
sim·plex (sim'pleks), *adj.* [L., simple], 1. having only one part; not complex or compounded. 2. relating to simplex telegraphy.
simplex telegraphy, a system of telegraphy in which only one message may be sent over a wire at one time.
sim·pli·ci·den·tate (sim'plə-si-den'tāt), *adj.* [< Mod. L. *Simplicidentata*, name of the group < L. *simplex*, simple + *dens*, a tooth], belonging to the group of rodents having only one pair of upper incisors, including all but the rabbits, hares, and pikas.
sim·plic·i·ty (sim-plis'ə-ti), *n.* [*pl.* SIMPLICITIES (-tiz)], [ME. *simplicite;* OFr. *simplicité;* L. *simplicitas*], 1. a simple state or quality, as of form or composition; freedom from intricacy or complexity. 2. absence of luxury, elegance, embellishment, or the like. 3. freedom from affectation, subtlety, etc.; artlessness. 4. plainness or naturalness, as of behavior, way of life, etc. 5. lack of sense or reasoning ability; foolishness; dullness.
sim·pli·fi·ca·tion (sim'plə-fi-kā'shən), *n.* [Fr.], 1. a simplifying or being simplified. 2. any result of this, as a simpler form, process, or device.
sim·pli·fi·er (sim'plə-fī'ẽr), *n.* a person or thing that simplifies.
sim·pli·fy (sim'plə-fī'), *v.t.* [SIMPLIFIED (-fīd'), SIMPLIFYING], [Fr. *simplifier;* ML. *simplificare*], to make more simple; render less complex; make easy or easier.
Sim·plon (sim'plon; Fr. san'plōn'), *n.* 1. a pass in the Alps between Switzerland and Italy: a road built by Napoleon crosses it. 2. a railway tunnel near this pass: length, 12 1/4 mi.
sim·ply (sim'pli), *adv.* 1. in a simple manner; so as to be simple; with simplicity. 2. merely; only; just: as, his answer was *simply* this. 3. absolutely; completely: as, this is *simply* ridiculous.
sim·u·la·crum (sim'yoo-lā'krəm), *n.* [*pl.* SIMULACRA (-krə)], [L. < *simulare;* see SIMULATE], 1. an image. 2. a mere pretense or semblance; vague representation; counterfeit; travesty; sham.
sim·u·lant (sim'yoo-lənt), *adj.* [L. *simulans*, ppr.; see SIMULATE], in *biology*, exhibiting simulation.
sim·u·lar (sim'yoo-lẽr), *n.* a simulator. *adj.* 1. simulated; feigned. 2. simulative (*of* something).
sim·u·late (sim'yoo-lāt'), *v.t.* [SIMULATED (-id), SIMULATING], [< L. *simulatus*, pp. of *simulare*, to feign < *simul*, together with, likewise], 1. to give a false indication or appearance of; pretend; feign: as, *simulate* an interest. 2. to have the external characteristics of; look or act like: as, the insect *simulated* a twig. *adj.* simulated; pretended; feigned. —*SYN.* see **assume.**
sim·u·la·tion (sim'yoo-lā'shən), *n.* [ME. & OFr. *simulacion;* L. *simulatio*], 1. the act of simulating; pretense; feigning. 2. false resemblance, as through imitation.
sim·u·la·tive (sim'yoo-lā'tiv), *adj.* practicing or characterized by simulation.
sim·u·la·tor (sim'yoo-lāt'ẽr), *n.* a person or thing that simulates.
si·mul·cast (sī'məl-kast', sī'məl-käst'), *v.t.* [SIMULCAST, SIMULCASTING], [< *simul*taneous + broad*cast*], to transmit (a program, event, etc.) simultaneously by radio and television. *n.* a program, etc. so transmitted.
si·mul·ta·ne·i·ty (sī'm'l-tə-nē'ə-ti, sim''l-tə-nē'ə-ti), *n.* a being simultaneous; occurrence together.
si·mul·ta·ne·ous (sī'm'l-tā'ni-əs, sim''l-tā'ni-əs), *adj.* [< L. *simul*, at the same time, after *momentaneous*], occurring, done, existing, etc. together or at the same time. —*SYN.* see **contemporary.**
simultaneous equations, two or more equations used together in the same problem and having unknowns of the same value.
sin (sēn), *n.* [Heb.], the twenty-first letter of the Hebrew alphabet (ש), corresponding to English *S, s:* see **alphabet,** table.
sin (sin), *n.* [ME. (East Midland) *sinne;* AS. *synne* (for **sunjo*); akin to G. *sünde;* ? < IE. base **sn̥tā-*, **sn̥tī-*, sin], 1. the breaking of religious law or a moral principle, especially through a willful act. 2. any offense, misdemeanor, or fault: as, a social or aesthetic *sin. v.i.* [SINNED (sind), SINNING], 1. to break a religious law or moral principle; commit sin. 2. to commit an offense or fault of any kind; do wrong. *v.t.* 1. to commit sinfully. 2. to spend, bring about, etc. by sinning.
sin, sine.
Si·nai, Mount (sī'nī; *occas.* sī'nə-ī'), in the *Bible*, the mountain (probably in the southern part of the Sinai peninsula but not identified) where Moses received the law from God: Ex. 19.
Si·na·ic (sī-nā'ik), *adj.* Sinaitic.
Sinai Peninsula, a peninsula in northeastern Egypt projecting into the Red Sea: it is east of the Suez Canal and west of Palestine.
Si·na·it·ic (sī'nə-it'ik), *adj.* of or from Mount Sinai or the Sinai Peninsula.
sin·al·bin (sin-al'bin), *n.* [< L. *sinapis*, mustard + *alba*, fem. of *albus*, white; + *-in*], a pale-yellow crystalline glucoside, $C_{30}H_{42}O_{15}N_2S_2$, obtained from white mustard seed.
Si·na·lo·a (sē'nä-lô'ä), *n.* a state of western Mexico area, 22,580 sq. mi.; pop., 493,000; capital, Culiacán.
sin·a·pin (sin'ə-pin), *n.* sinapine.
sin·a·pine (sin'ə-pēn', sin'ə-pin), *n.* [< L. *sinapis* mustard; + *-ine*], an alkaloid derivative of sinalbin $C_{16}H_{25}O_6N$, known only in the form of its salts.
sin·a·pism (sin'ə-piz'm), *n.* [L. *sinapismus* < Gr. *sinapismos* < *sinapi*, mustard], a mustard plaster.
sin·ar·chism, sin·ar·quism (si-När'kiz'm), *n.* [< Sp. *sin-*, syn- + Eng. *anarchism*, Sp. *anarquismo*], an armed fascist movement in Mexico, formed in 1937 to fight for the establishment of a totalitarian clerical state.
sin·ar·chist (si-när'kist), *n.* a follower of sinarchism.
sin·ar·quis·ta (sin'är-kis'tə), *n.* a sinarchist.
Sin·bad the Sailor (sin'bad), a merchant in *The Arabian Nights* who made seven adventurous voyages: also **Sindbad.**
since (sins), *adv.* [ME. *sins, sinnes, sithens, sithence* all genit. forms < AS. *siththan*, for earlier **siththon sith*, after, since + *thon*, instrumental form of *thæt*, the that, demonstrative article], 1. from then until now as, he came last Tuesday and has been here ever *since.* 2. at some or any time between then and now: as, he was injured a year ago but has *since* fully recovered. 3. before the present time; before now; ago: as, he disappeared many years *since. prep.* 1. continuously or without exception or interruption from (the time given) until now: as, we have been walking *since* one o'clock. 2. during the period between (the time given) and now subsequently to: as, he's written twice *since* his departure. *conj.* 1. during the period following the time when: as, they've seen each other often *since* they met. 2. continuously or without exception or interruption from the time when: as, she has been unhappy *since* she left home. 3. inasmuch as; because: as, *since* he was king he could do no wrong.
long since, long before now; a long time ago.
sin·cere (sin-sêr'), *adj.* [SINCERER (-ẽr), SINCEREST (-ist)], [Fr. *sincère;* L. *sincerus*, clean, pure, sincere < *sine* without + base of *caries* (cf. CARIES), decay, rottenness hence, orig., undecayed], 1. without deceit, pretense or hypocrisy; truthful; faithful; straightforward; honest: as, he gave a *sincere* statement of his feelings. 2. being the same in actual character as in outward appearance; genuine; real: as, a life of *sincere* devotion. 3. [Archaic], not mixed or adulterated: as, *sincere* wine. 4. [Obs.], uninjured; whole.
SYN.—**sincere** implies an absence of deceit, pretense, or hypocrisy and an adherence to the simple, unembellished truth (a *sincere* desire to help); **unaffected** implies a natural, genuine simplicity and a freedom from artificial behavior (an *unaffected* prose style); **unfeigned** suggests behavior that is honest and spontaneous (she looked at him with *unfeigned* admiration); **heartfelt** stresses depth as well as sincerity of feeling, especially as expressed in warm words, acts, etc. (he extended his *heartfelt* sympathy); **hearty** adds to this connotations of exuberance and geniality (my *hearty* congratulations). —*ANT.* false.
sin·cer·i·ty (sin-ser'ə-ti), *n.* [*pl.* SINCERITIES (-tiz)], [Fr. *sincérité;* L. *sinceritas*], the quality or state of being sincere; honesty; genuineness; good faith; truth.
sin·cip·i·tal (sin-sip'ə-t'l), *adj.* of the sinciput.
sin·ci·put (sin'si-put'), *n.* [L., half a head; *semi*, half + *caput*, the head], the upper part of the skull or head especially, the forehead.
Sin·clair, Up·ton (up't'n sin-klâr'), 1878– ; American novelist and socialist.
Sind (sind), *n.* a province of Pakistan, in northwestern India: area, 48,136 sq. mi.; pop., 4,535,000; capital Karachi.
Sind·bad (sind'bad, sin'bad), *n.* see **Sinbad the Sailor.**
sine (sīn), *n.* [L. *sinus*, a bending, curve, used as translation of Ar. *jaib*, bosom of a garment, sine], in *mathematics*, 1. originally, the length of a perpendicular dropped from one end of an arc of a circle to the diameter passing through the other end of the arc. 2. the ratio of this line to the radius of the circle. 3. the ratio of the side opposite an acute angle of a right triangle to the hypotenuse. Abbreviated **sin** (no period).

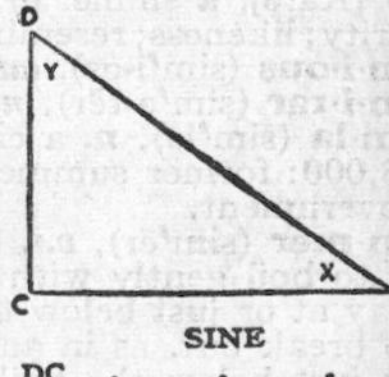

SINE
$\frac{DC}{DB}$, sine of angle X
$\frac{CB}{DB}$, sine of angle Y

‡si·ne (sī'ni), *prep.* [L.], without.
si·ne·cure (sī'ni-kyoor', sin'ə-kyoor'), *n.* [< L. *sine*, without

+ *cura*, cure, care], 1. a church office that pays a salary without involving cure (care) of souls. 2. any office or position that brings profit or advantage without involving much work, responsibility, etc.

si·ne·cur·ism (sī'ni-kyoor-iz'm, sin'ə-kyoor-iz'm), *n.* 1. a system in which sinecures are available. 2. the policy or principle of giving or taking sinecures.

si·ne·cur·ist (sī'ni-kyoor'ist, sin'ə-kyoor'ist), *n.* a person who holds or seeks a sinecure.

si·ne di·e (sī'ni dī'ē), [L.], without (a) day (being set for meeting again); for an indefinite period: as, the assembly adjourned *sine die:* abbreviated **s.d.**

‡**si·ne pro·le** (sī'ni prō'li), [L.], in *law*, without offspring; childless: abbreviated **s.p.**

‡**si·ne qua non** (sī'ni kwā non'), [L., without which not], an essential condition, qualification, etc.; indispensable thing; absolute prerequisite.

sin·ew (sin'ū), *n.* [ME. *sinewe;* AS. *seonwe*, oblique form < nom. *sinu, seonu;* akin to D. *zenew* & (via the nom.) G. *sehne;* IE. base **sēi-*, to bind, what binds or connects], 1. a tendon. 2. muscular power; strength; force. 3. any source of power or strength; means of supplying strength. *v.t.* to strengthen with or as with sinews; provide with sinews.

sin·ew·y (sin'yoo-wi), *adj.* 1. of or like sinew; tough; strong. 2. having many or large sinews, as a cut of meat. 3. having good muscular development: as, *sinewy* shoulders; hence, 4. vigorous; powerful; robust: as, a *sinewy* style of writing.

sin·fo·ni·a (sin'fə-nē'ə; It. sēn'fô-nē'ä), *n.* [*pl.* SINFONIE (-nē'e)], [It.], a symphony.

sin·ful (sin'fəl), *adj.* full of or characterized by sin; wicked; immoral.

sing (siŋ), *v.i.* [SANG (saŋ) or *now rarely* SUNG (suŋ), SUNG, SINGING], [ME. *singen;* AS. *singan;* akin to G. *singen;* IE. base **sengwh-* (which, outside Gmc., is found only in Gr. *omphē*, a voice, oracle)], 1. *a*) to produce musical sounds or notes with the voice, especially in a connected series, as in voicing a song. *b*) to deliver musical selections vocally, especially as a professional. 2. to use song or verse in description, praise, etc.: as, of thee I *sing*. 3. to sound somewhat like the singing of a human voice; produce a musical note or notes, as a songbird, steaming teakettle, wind, etc. 4. to buzz, hum, ring, etc., as the ears, an insect, flying missile, etc. 5. to admit of being sung. 6. to be exultant; rejoice: as, a sight to make one's heart *sing*. 7. [Slang], to confess to a crime, especially so as to implicate others. *v.t.* 1. to render or deliver (a song, musical role, etc.) by singing; utter with musical inflections. 2. to chant or intone (part of a church service, etc.). 3. to describe, proclaim, extol, celebrate, etc. in or as in song or verse: as, they all *sing* his praises. 4. to bring to a given state, as sleep, by singing. 5. to accompany, escort, etc. with singing. *n.* 1. a shrill buzzing, whistling, or humming sound: as, the *sing* of arrows overhead. 2. [Colloq.], *a*) group singing. *b*) a gathering of people for group singing.

sing out, [Colloq.], to speak or call out loudly; shout.

sing., singular.

sing·a·ble (siŋ'ə-b'l), *adj.* 1. that can be sung. 2. easy to sing; tuneful; lyrical; melodic.

Si·ngan (sē'n'gän'), *n.* Sian.

Sin·ga·pore (siŋ'gə-pôr', siŋ'gə-pōr'), *n.* 1. an island off the tip of the Malay Peninsula: area, 217 sq. mi.; pop., 1,467,000: it is a self-governing state under British protection, and was a British crown colony until June, 1959: official name, *the State of Singapore*. 2. the capital of this state: pop., 729,296.

singe (sinj), *v.t.* [SINGED (sinjd), SINGEING], [with nasalized vowel (cf. HINGE, WING) < ME. *sengen;* AS. *sengan* < **sangjan*, caus. < base of *sing;* orig. meaning "to make sing; hence, to hiss"; akin to G. *sengen*], 1. to burn superficially or slightly. 2. to expose (an animal carcass) to flame in removing bristles or feathers. 3. to burn the nap from (cloth) as a process of manufacture. 4. to burn the ends of (hair) after cutting. *n.* 1. a singeing. 2. a superficial or slight burn. —*SYN.* see **burn**.

sing·er (siŋ'ẽr), *n.* 1. a person who sings, especially one who sings professionally. 2. a bird that sings. 3. a poet.

sing·er (sin'jẽr), *n.* a person or thing that singes.

Sing·er, Isaac Mer·ritt (mer'it siŋ'ẽr), 1811–1875; American inventor; improved the sewing machine.

Singh., Singhalese.

Sin·gha·lese (siŋ'gə-lēz'), *adj.* [< Sans. *Siṅhala*, Ceylon; + *-ese*], of Ceylon, its principal race, their language, etc. *n.* 1. [*pl.* SINGHALESE], a member of the Singhalese people. 2. their Indic language. Also **Sinhalese**.

sin·gle (siŋ'g'l), *adj.* [ME. & OFr. *single, sengle;* LL. *singulus* (in L. only in pl. *singuli*) single < base seen also in *semel*, once, *simplex*, simple], 1. one only; one and no more; individual. 2. without another or others; alone; solitary. 3. of or for one person, as a bed, room, etc., or one family, as a house. 4. [British], weak in quality: said of beer, ale, etc. 5. between two persons only; with only one on each side: as, *single* combat. 6. *a*) unmarried. *b*) of or characteristic of the unmarried state. 7. having only one part; not double, compound, multiple, etc. 8. having only one row or set of petals: said of flowers and plants. 9. honest; sincere. 10. seeing justly: as, judge with a *single* eye. 11. in *telegraphy*, simplex. *v.t.* [SINGLED (-g'ld), SINGLING], to select or distinguish from others (now usually with *out*). *v.i.* 1. to move with a single-foot gait: said of horses. 2. in *baseball*, to make a single. *n.* 1. a single person or thing. 2. in *baseball*, a hit by which the batter reaches no farther than first base. 3. in *cricket*, a hit by which one run is scored. 4. in *golf*, a match between two persons; twosome: distinguished from *foursome*. 5. *pl.* in *tennis*, etc., a game with only one player on each side. Abbreviated **sgl.**

SYN.—**single** simply refers to one that is not united with or accompanied by another (a *single* chair in the room, a *single* man); **sole** applies to the only one of its kind under consideration or in a particular situation (my *sole* dependent, his *sole* contribution); **unique** strictly applies to the only one of its kind in existence (a *unique* bronze statue), but in popular usage often implies mere rareness or unusualness (a *unique* experience); **solitary** adds to the sense of singleness connotations of isolation or separation (a *solitary* tree in the meadow); **individual** refers to every one of a group or class as distinguished from all the others (an *individual* listing of members); **particular** applies to a single, distinct instance, example, etc. of a group or class (must you have this *particular* seat?).

sin·gle-act·ing (siŋ'g'l-ak'tiŋ), *adj.* acting in or impelled from one direction only; not reciprocating: as, a *single-acting* engine.

sin·gle-ac·tion (siŋ'g'l-ak'shən), *adj.* designating a firearm whose hammer must be cocked by hand before the weapon can be fired.

sin·gle-breast·ed (siŋ'g'l-bres'tid), *adj.* covering the front of the body with only one thickness, overlapping just enough to fasten: said of coats, vests, etc.: opposed to *double-breasted*.

sin·gle-en·try (siŋ'g'l-en'tri), *adj.* having to do with bookkeeping by single entry.

single entry, a system of bookkeeping in which the only account kept is a single one consisting of debts owed to and by the concern in question.

single file, 1. a single column of persons or things placed or moving one directly behind another. 2. in such a column: as, the men are marching *single file*.

sin·gle-foot (siŋ'g'l-foot'), *n.* the gait of a horse in which the legs move in lateral pairs, each foot falling singly and the body being supported alternately upon one foot and two feet. *v.i.* to move with this gait. Also called *rack*.

sin·gle-hand·ed (siŋ'g'l-han'did), *adj.* 1. having only one hand or one person. 2. using or requiring the use of only one hand: as, a *single-handed* sword. 3. without help: done or working alone; unaided.

sin·gle-heart·ed (siŋ'g'l-här'tid), *adj.* honest; faithful; sincere.

sin·gle-mind·ed (siŋ'g'l-mīn'did), *adj.* 1. single-hearted. 2. with only one aim or purpose.

sin·gle-phase (siŋ'g'l-fāz'), *adj.* of or having a single, independent alternating current, as a circuit, winding, etc.

single standard, a moral code establishing one standard of behavior for men and women alike, especially in matters of sex.

sin·gle-stick (siŋ'g'l-stik'), *n.* 1. a swordlike stick fitted with a guard and used for fencing. 2. the sport of fencing with such sticks.

sin·gle-stick·er (siŋ'g'l-stik'ẽr), *n.* [Colloq.], a sailboat, especially a sloop, having but a single mast.

sin·glet (siŋ'glit), *n.* [British], a man's undershirt or jersey.

sin·gle-tax (siŋ'g'l-taks'), *adj.* advocating or having to do with single tax.

single tax, 1. a system of taxation in which all revenue is derived from a tax on a single object, specifically on land. 2. a tax of this kind.

sin·gle·ton (siŋ'g'l-tən), *n.* [< *single*, after proper names ending in *-ton*], 1. a playing card that is the only one of its suit held by a given player. 2. a single thing, as distinguished from one of a pair, several, etc.

sin·gle-track (siŋ'g'l-trak'), *adj.* 1. having only one set of rails: as, a *single-track* trolley or railroad. 2. having a limited scope; narrow: as, a *single-track* mind. Also **one-track**.

sin·gle·tree (siŋ'g'l-trē'), *n.* [altered < earlier *swingletree* < ME. *swingle*, a rod, whip + *tre;* see TREE], a wooden bar swung at the center from a hitch on a plow, wagon, etc. and hooked at either end to the traces of a horse's harness: also called *whiffletree, whippletree*.

sin·gly (siŋ'gli), *adv.* 1. as a single, separate person or thing; alone. 2. individually and in sequence; one by one. 3. single-handed; unaided; alone.

Sing Sing (siŋ′siŋ′), a New York State penitentiary at Ossining.
sing·song (siŋ′sôŋ′, siŋ′soŋ′), *n.* 1. a rising and falling tone in a monotonous cadence. 2. verse, sound, voice, etc. characterized by such tone or cadence. *adj.* characterized by such tone or cadence. *v.t. & v.i.* to speak, sing, etc. in a singsong manner.
sin·gu·lar (siŋ′gyoo-lẽr), *adj.* [ME. *singuler;* OFr. *singuler, singulaire;* L. *singularis* < *singulus*, single], 1. being the only one of its kind; sole; single; unique: as, a *singular* item or specimen. 2. *a*) individual; separate. *b*) [Obs.], of or having to do with an individual. *c*) [Obs.], peculiar to one; private. 3. strange; unusual; queer: as, what a *singular* remark! 4. exceptional; extraordinary; remarkable: as, *singular* beauty. 5. in *grammar*, of or denoting only one: opposed to *plural*. 6. in *logic*, of an individual or particular thing considered by itself. *n.* 1. in *grammar*, *a*) the singular number. *b*) the singular form of a word. Opposed to *plural*. 2. in *logic*, a thing considered apart from all others. Abbreviated **sing.**, **s.** (in *grammar*).
sin·gu·lar·i·ty (siŋ′gyoo-lar′ə-ti), *n.* [*pl.* SINGULARITIES (-tiz)], 1. the condition or quality of being singular. 2. a singular person or thing; peculiar feature or characteristic.
sin·gu·lar·ize (siŋ′gyoo-lə-rīz′), *v.t.* [SINGULARIZED (-rizd′), SINGULARIZING], to make singular.
Sin·ha·lese (sin′hə-lēz′), *adj. & n.* Singhalese.
Sin·i·cism (sin′ə-siz′m), *n.* [< LL. *Sinae*, an Oriental people, prob. the Chinese], something, as a custom or a language trait, peculiar to the Chinese.
sin·i·grin (sin′i-grin), *n.* [< Mod. L. *Sinapis nigra*, black mustard (< L. *sinapis*, mustard + *nigra*, fem. of *niger*, black); + *-in*], a glucoside salt, $C_{10}H_{16}KNO_9S_2$, found in the seeds of black mustard.
sin·is·ter (sin′is-tẽr), *adj.* [ME. & OFr. *sinistre;* L. *sinister*, left, left hand], 1. originally, on, to, or toward the left-hand side; left. 2. forming, or placed on, the left half of a coat of arms, regarded from the bearer's point of view (the right, from the observer's). 3. suggesting the approach of disaster, misfortune, etc.; threatening harm or evil; ominous; portentous. 4. wicked, evil, or dishonest, especially in some dark, mysterious way: as, it is somehow to their own *sinister* interest. 5. disastrous; unfortunate (often with *to*).
SYN.—**sinister**, in this connection, applies to that which can be interpreted as presaging imminent danger or evil (a *sinister* smile); **baleful** refers to that which is inevitably deadly, destructive, pernicious, etc. (a *baleful* influence); **malign** is applied to that which is regarded as having an inherent tendency toward evil or destruction (a *malign* doctrine).
sin·is·tral (sin′is-trəl), *adj.* [OFr. < L. *sinistra*, left hand; see SINISTER], 1. of or having to do with the left side. 2. having whorls that rise to the apex in clockwise spirals: said of sea shells. 3. left-handed.
sin·is·tro- (sin′is-trō, sin′is-trə), [< L. *sinister;* see SINISTER], a combining form meaning *of, at, toward,* or *using the left*, as in *sinistrodextral*: also, before a vowel, **sinistr-**.
sin·is·tro·dex·tral (sin′is-trō-deks′trəl), *adj.* [*sinistro-* + *dextral*], going or directed from left to right, as the movement of the hand in writing.
sin·is·tror·sal (sin′is-trôr′səl), *adj.* sinistrorse.
sin·is·trorse (sin′is-trôrs′, sin′is-trôrs′), *adj.* [L. *sinistrorsus*, contr. of *sinistrovorsus* < *sinister*, to the left + *versus, vorsus*, pp. of *vertere*, to turn], in *botany*, twining upward to the left, as the stems of some vines: opposed to *dextrorse*.
sin·is·trous (sin′is-trəs), *adj.* 1. threatening or accompanied by misfortune or disaster; unfortunate. 2. sinistral.
Si·nit·ic (si-nit′ik), *n.* [see SINO-, -ITE, -IC], a branch of the Sino-Tibetan languages, including Chinese and its dialects. *adj.* of China, the Chinese, or their language.
sink (siŋk), *v.i.* [SANK (saŋk) or SUNK (suŋk), SUNK or *obs.* SUNKEN (-′n), SINKING], [ME. *sinken;* AS. *sincan;* akin to G. *sinken;* IE. base **sengw-*, to fall, sink], 1. to go beneath the surface of water, deep snow, soft ground, etc. so as to be partly or completely covered. 2. to go down slowly; fall or descend gradually: as, the balloon *sank* to earth, she *sank* wearily into a chair. 3. to appear to fall or descend: as, the moon *sank* behind a cloud. 4. to become lower in level; diminish in height or depth: as, the lake has *sunk* three inches, brace the center of the floor or it will *sink*, the land *sinks* gradually to the river's edge. 5. to become less intense; diminish or decrease in degree or volume; subside, as wind, flames, sound of a voice, etc. 6. to become lower in value or amount; lessen, as the price of stock, a total figure, cost, etc. 7. to seem or become hollow or shrunken; recede, as the cheeks or eyes. 8. to pass gradually (*into* a given condition), as sleep, despair, lethargy, etc. 9. to become increasingly and dangerously ill; approach death; fail: as, he is *sinking* rapidly. 10. to undergo decline in social, moral, or economic state; lose position, prestige, etc. 11. to penetrate: as, water *sinks* rapidly through topsoil. 12. to make an enduring impression; enter and have lasting effect, as upon the mind or heart. *v.t.* 1. to cause to submerge or go beneath the surface: as, high waves *sank* the boat, he *sank* his spade in the ground. 2. to cause or allow to fall or go down; lower: as, she *sank* her head in her hands. 3. to make (a well, mine, engraved design, etc.) by digging, drilling, or cutting. 4. to reduce the volume, degree, or intensity of (the voice, etc.). 5. to invest. 6. to lose by investing: as, he has *sunk* a fortune in that fraud. 7. to hold back, suppress, or conceal (evidence, identity, personal interests, etc.). 8. to pay up (a debt). 9. to debase (character, dignity, etc.). 10. to defeat; undo; ruin: now usually in the passive, as, if they see us we are *sunk*. *n.* [ME. *sinke* < the *v.*], 1. a cesspool or sewer. 2. any place or thing considered morally filthy or corrupted. 3. any of various basins or receptacles, as in a kitchen, connected with a drainpipe and, usually, a water supply. 4. in *geology*, an area of sunken land, especially one in which water collects without a natural outlet, often forming a salt lake.
sink in, [Colloq.], to be grasped by the mind, especially with difficulty; be recognized or understood in full.
sink·er (siŋk′ẽr), *n.* 1. a worker whose job is to sink something: as, a die *sinker*. 2. a thing that sinks, as a lead weight used in fishing. 3. [Colloq.], a doughnut.
sink·hole (siŋk′hōl′), *n.* 1. an opening, as the down pipe to a sewer, made for the drainage of water, sewage, etc. 2. a hollow or hole into which surface water drains, especially such a hole worn through rock and leading to an underground channel.
Sin·kiang (sin′kyaŋ′; Chin. shin′jyän′), *n.* a large province of northwestern China: area, 706,000 sq. mi.; pop., 4,047,000 (est. 1947); capital, Urumchi.
sinking fund, a fund made up of sums of money set aside at intervals, usually invested at interest, to pay a debt, meet depreciation expenses, etc.: abbreviated **S.F.**
sin·less (sin′lis), *adj.* without sin; innocent.
sin·ner (sin′ẽr), *n.* a person who sins; wrongdoer.
Sinn Fein (shin fān), [Ir., we ourselves], a revolutionary society and movement founded in Ireland about 1905 to establish political and economic independence and to revive Irish culture: abbreviated **S.F.**
Sin·o- (sī′nō, sin′ō), [< Gr. *Sinai*, an Oriental people], a combining form meaning: 1. *of the Chinese people or language*, as in *Sinology*. 2. *Chinese and*, as in *Sino-Japanese*.
Sin·o-Jap·a·nese (sī′nō-jap′ə-nēz′, sin′ō-jap′ə-nēz′), *adj.* having to do with both China and Japan.
Sin·o·log·i·cal (sī′nə-loj′i-k′l, sin′ə-loj′i-k′l), *adj.* of Sinology.
Sin·o·logue (sī′nə-lôg′, sin′ə-lôg′), *n.* [Fr. *sinologue* < Gr. *Sinai*, the Chinese + *logos*, discourse], a student of or expert in Sinology.
Si·nol·o·gy (sī-nol′ə-ji, si-nol′ə-ji), *n.* [*Sino-* + *-logy*], the study of Chinese language, literature, art, customs, etc.
Sin·o-Ti·bet·an (sī′nō-ti-bet′′n, sin′ō-ti-bet′′n), *adj.* designating or of a family of Eastern Asiatic languages spoken in Tibet, China, Burma, and Thailand: it comprises Tibeto-Burman, Chinese, Thai, etc.
sin·ter (sin′tẽr), *n.* [G., akin to Eng. *cinder;* cf. CINDER], 1. a crust or deposit of silica or calcium carbonate formed by water from some mineral springs, geysers, etc. 2. a fused conglomerate of heated non-metallic material. *v.i. & v.t.* to become or make into a sinter (sense 2).
sin·u·ate (sin′ū-it; *also, and for v. always,* sin′ū-āt′), *adj.* [L. *sinuatus*, pp. of *sinuare*, to bend < *sinus*, bend], 1. bending or winding in and out; wavy; sinuous. 2. in *botany*, having a wavy margin, as some leaves. *v.i.* [SINUATED (-id), SINUATING], to bend or wind in and out; be sinuous or wavy.
sin·u·a·tion (sin′ū-ā′shən), *n.* 1. a sinuating. 2. sinuosity.
sin·u·os·i·ty (sin′ū-os′ə-ti), *n.* [Fr. *sinuosité*], 1. the state or quality of being sinuous. 2. [*pl.* SINUOSITIES (-tiz)], a turn, bend, or curve, especially one of a series.
sin·u·ous (sin′ū-əs), *adj.* [L. *sinuosus* < *sinus*, a bend], 1. bending, winding, or curving in and out; wavy; serpentine. 2. devious; crooked; not straightforward or honest. 3. in *botany*, sinuate.
si·nus (sī′nəs), *n.* [*pl.* SINUSES (-iz), SINUS], [L., a bent surface, curve, fold], 1. a bend or curve. 2. any cavity or hollow formed by a bending or curving. 3. in *anatomy & zoology*, any of various cavities, hollows, or passages; especially, *a*) any of the air cavities in the skull opening into the nasal cavities. *b*) a large channel for venous blood. *c*) a dilated part in a blood vessel, etc. 4. in *botany*, the rounded depression between two consecutive lobes, as of a leaf. 5. in *medicine*, a narrow channel leading from a pus-filled cavity. 6. popularly, sinusitis.
si·nus·i·tis (sī′nəs-ī′tis), *n.* [see -ITIS], inflammation of a sinus or sinuses, especially of the skull.
Si·on (sī′ən), *n.* Zion.
-sion (shən, zhən), [L. *-sio, -sionis*], a suffix meaning *the act, quality, condition, or result of*, as in *revulsion, confusion*: see also **-tion**.
Siou·an (sōō′ən), *adj.* designating or of a linguistic family of North American Indians formerly inhabiting the west central United States, central Canada, and parts of Virginia and Carolina: it includes Catawba, Iowa, Winnebago, Omaha-Osage, Dakota, Crow, etc.

Sioux (sōō), *n.* [*pl.* SIOUX (sōō, sōōz)], [Fr., contr. < *Nadowessioux* < Am. Ind. (Ojibway) *Nâdowessi*, lit., little snake < *Nâdowe*, Iroquois, lit., big snake], a member of a confederation of Siouan Indian tribes that lived in the northern plains of the United States: Indian name, *Dakota*. *adj.* of these tribes.

Sioux City, a city in western Iowa, on the Missouri River: pop., 89,000.

Sioux Falls, a city in southeastern South Dakota: pop., 65,000.

sip (sip), *v.t. & v.i.* [SIPPED (sipt), SIPPING], [ME. *sippen*; prob. < AS. *sypian*, to drink in, absorb; influenced by the cognate *sup*], to drink only a little at a time; drink little by little. *n.* 1. the act of sipping. 2. a small quantity sipped.

si·phon (sī′fən), *n.* [Fr.; L. *sipho*, *siphonis*; Gr. *siphōn*, a tube, pipe, siphon], 1. a bent tube used for carrying liquid out over the top edge of a container through the force of atmospheric pressure upon the surface of the liquid: one end of the tube is placed in the liquid, the other, the longer end, outside the container at a point below the surface level of the liquid: the tube must be filled, as by suction, before flow will start. 2. a siphon bottle. 3. a tubelike organ in some animals, as cuttlefishes, used for drawing in or ejecting liquids. *v.t.* to draw off or carry through or as through a siphon. *v.i.* to pass through a siphon. Also spelled **syphon.**

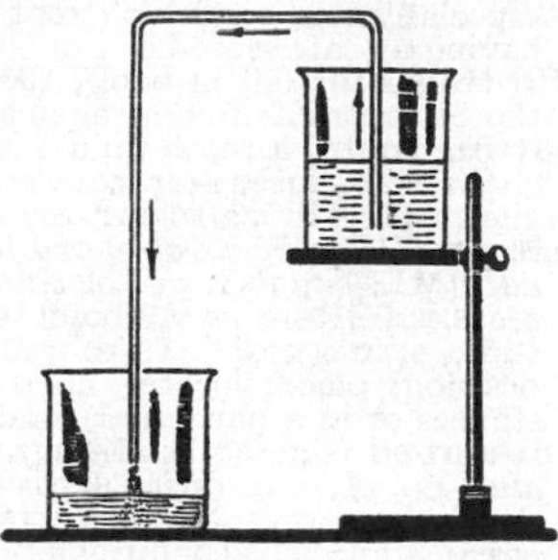

SIPHON

si·phon·age (sī′fən-ij), *n.* [see -AGE], a siphoning.

si·phon·al (sī′fən-'l), *adj.* of, or having the form of, a siphon.

siphon bottle, a heavy, sealed bottle with a tube on the inside connected at the top with a nozzle and valve which, when opened, allows the flow of pressurized, carbonated water contained within.

si·phon·ic (sī-fon′ik), *adj.* siphonal.

si·pho·no·phore (sī′fən-ə-fôr′, sī-fon′ə-fôr′), *n.* [< Gr. *siphōn*, a tube, siphon; + *-phore*], any of a number of small swimming or floating sea hydrozoans budding into colonies of many different shapes and colors.

si·pho·no·ste·le (sī′fən-ə-stē′li, sī′fən-ə-stēl′), *n.* [< Gr. *siphōn*, a tube, siphon; + *stele*], in *botany*, a hollow tube of vascular tissue in certain stems, as that of a fern.

sip·id (sip′id), *adj.* [back-formation < *insipid*], [Rare], having a fine flavor, or taste; savory.

sip·pet (sip′it), *n.* [prob. dim. of *sop*], 1. a small piece of toast soaked in soup, gravy, etc. 2. a small piece of toasted or fried bread used as a garnish. 3. any small piece; fragment.

sir (sũr), *n.* [ME. < *sire*; see SIRE], 1. [sometimes S-], a respectful term of address used to a man; not followed by the given name or surname. 2. [S-], the title used before the given name or full name of a knight or baronet: as, *Sir* Walter Raleigh. 3. [Archaic], a term of address used with the title of a man's office, rank, or profession: as, *sir* priest, *sir* judge, *sir* knight; hence, 4. a title used humorously or derisively: as, *sir* grouch. 5. [Obs.], a man of rank; lord. Abbreviated **Sr.**

Si·ra·cu·sa (sē′rä-kōō′zä), *n.* Syracuse, a seaport in Sicily: the Italian name.

sir·dar (sẽr-där′, sũr′där), *n.* [Hind. & Per. *sardār*, leader; *sar*, the head + *dār*, holding], 1. in India, *a*) a native chief or noble. *b*) a high military officer. *c*) a head servant, especially a litter bearer. 2. formerly, in Egypt, the British commander in chief of the army.

sire (sīr), *n.* [ME.; OFr. *sire*, *sieur*, a master < L. *senior*; see SENIOR], 1. formerly, a person of authority; man of high rank: now used only as a title of respect in addressing a king, equivalent to "your majesty." 2. [Poetic], a father or forefather. 3. the male parent of a quadruped. *v.t.* [SIRED (sīrd), SIRING], to beget: said especially of quadrupeds. Abbreviated **s.**

si·ren (sī′rən), *n.* [ME. *siren*, *seiren*; L. < Gr. *seirēn*], 1. in *Greek & Roman mythology*, any of several sea nymphs, represented as part bird and part woman, who lured sailors to their death on rocky coasts by seductive singing. 2. a woman who makes obvious use of her charms to entice or allure; seductive woman. 3. *a*) an acoustical instrument in which steam or air is driven against a rotating, perforated disk so as to generate sound. *b*) a similar device used as a warning signal, foghorn, factory whistle, etc. 4. a small, slime-coated, lizard-shaped animal with no hind legs, two short front legs, internal lungs, and external gills: it lives in water or moist mud. *adj.* of or like a siren; charmingly seductive; tempting.

si·re·ni·an (sī-rē′ni-ən), *n.* [< Mod. L. *Sirenia*, name of the order (< L. *siren*; see SIREN); + *-an*], any of several large, vegetarian sea mammals, as the dugong and the manatee, or sea cow, with a cigar-shaped body, a blunt snout, large, mobile lips, flipperlike forelimbs, and a large tail fluke.

Si·ret (si-ret′), *n.* a river flowing from the Carpathians in southwestern U.S.S.R. through Romania, into the Danube: length, 270 mi.: German name, *Sereth*.

Sir·i·us (sir′i-əs), *n.* [ME.; L. < Gr. *Seirios*, the scorcher], the brightest star in the heavens, located in the constellation Canis Major: also called *Dog Star*: see **constellation**, chart.

sir·loin (sũr′loin), *n.* [OFr. **surloigne* < *sur*, over + *longe*, loin: sp. after *sir* from legend that the cut was knighted for its excellence], a choice cut of beef from the loin end between the rump and the porterhouse.

si·roc·co (sə-rok′ō), *n.* [*pl.* SIROCCOS (-ōz)], [It. < Ar. *sharq*, the east < *sharaqa*, to rise (of the sun)], 1. a hot, steady, oppressive wind blowing from the Libyan deserts across the Mediterranean into southern Europe, where it is sometimes accompanied by rain. 2. any hot, oppressive wind, especially one blowing toward a center of low barometric pressure.

sir·rah (sir′ə), *n.* [< *sir*], [Archaic], a contemptuous term of address used to a man.

sir-rev·er·ence (sũr′rev′ẽr-əns), *interj.* [confused form for *sa'reverence*, shortened < *save reverence*, saving your reverence; cf. L. *salva reverentia*], [Obs.], begging your pardon: an expression of apology formerly used before a word or expression regarded as indelicate or coarse.

sir·up (sir′əp, sũr′əp), *n.* [ME. *sirupe*; OFr. *sirop*; ML. *sirupuum*; Ar. *sharāb* < *shariba*, to drink; cf. SHRUB (a drink), SHERBET], any sweet, thick liquid; specifically, *a*) a solution made by boiling sugar with water and, often, fruit juices, artificial flavoring, etc. *b*) any solution of sugar used in pharmacy as a vehicle for medicines. *c*) the sweet, thick liquid obtained in the process of manufacturing cane sugar or glucose. *d*) maple sirup, corn sirup, etc. Also spelled **syrup.**

sir·up·y (sir′əp-i, sũr′əp-i), *adj.* 1. of sirup. 2. like sirup in sweetness or thickness.

sis (sis), *n.* [contr. of *sister*], [Colloq.], sister.

si·sal (sī′s'l, sis′'l), *n.* [after *Sisal*, Yucatán, a former seaport (< Maya *Sisal*, lit., cold waters)], 1. a strong fiber obtained from the leaves of an agave of Yucatán, used for making rope. 2. the plant yielding this fiber. Also **sisal hemp.**

Sis·er·a (sis′ẽr-ə), *n.* [Heb. *shīsherā'*; prob. of Hittite origin], in the *Bible*, a military leader of the Canaanites against the Israelites, murdered by Jael, who drove a nail through his head while he slept: Judges 4, 5.

sis·kin (sis′kin), *n.* [via Fl. < G. *sisschen*, dial. var. of *zeischen*, dim. of *zeizig* < Czech *čížek*, dim. of *číž* (akin to Pol *czyz*), of echoic origin], 1. a European and Asiatic finch with green plumage and black and yellow markings. 2. a North American finch with a gray breast, yellow back, and brown markings.

sis·mo- (sis′mō, sis′mə), [Rare], seismo-.

Sis·mon·di, Jean Charles Lé·o·nard Si·monde de (zhäṅ shárl′ lā′ô′nár′ sē′mônd′ də sēs′môn′dē′; Eng. sis-mon′di), 1773–1842; Swiss historian and economist.

sis·si·fy (sis′ə-fī′), *v.t.* [SISSIFIED (-fīd′), SISSIFYING], [Colloq.], to cause (a boy or man) to be a sissy.

sis·sy (sis′i), *n.* [*pl.* SISSIES (-iz)], [dim. of *sis*], [Colloq.], a boy or man whose behavior, tastes, interests, etc. seem more feminine than masculine.

sis·sy·ish (sis′i-ish), *adj.* [Colloq.], of, like, or like that of a sissy.

sis·ter (sis′tẽr), *n.* [ME.; ON. *systir* (akin to AS. *sweoster*, whence dial. *suster*, etc.); akin to G. *schwester*; IE. base **swesor-*, sister, seen also in Sans. *svasar*, L. *soror* (cf. SORORITY), etc.], 1. *a*) a woman or girl related to one by having the same parents: sometimes also used of animals. *b*) a woman or girl related to one by having one parent in common; half sister. *c*) a stepsister. *d*) a foster sister. 2. *a*) a friend thought of as a sister. *b*) a female fellow member of the same race, creed, profession, or organization. 3. a member of a female religious order; nun: as, *Sisters* of Mercy nurse the sick and give aid to the poor. 4. a thing thought of as feminine and associated with some kindred thing; one of the same kind, model, etc. 5. ‡[British], a nurse, especially a head nurse. 6. [Colloq.], any woman: often used as a familiar term of address. *adj.* related or seeming to be related as sisters; sisterly.

sis·ter·hood (sis′tẽr-hood′), *n.* 1. the state or fact of being a sister; relationship of sisters. 2. a group of women having some interest, belief, etc. in common, as the women's auxiliary of an organization. 3. an association of women forming a religious order.

sis·ter-in-law (sis′tẽr-in-lô′), *n.* [*pl.* SISTERS-IN-LAW], 1. the sister of one's husband or wife. 2. the wife of

one's brother. 3. occasionally, the wife of one's husband's or wife's brother.
sis·ter·ly (sis'tẽr-li), *adj.* of, like, or befitting a sister. *adv.* as a sister should.
Sis·tine (sis'tēn, sis'tin), *adj.* [It. *Sistino* < *Sisto* (L. *Sextus*, lit., sixth)], of or having to do with any pope named Sixtus: also **Sixtine.**
Sistine Chapel, the principal chapel in the Vatican at Rome, famous for its frescoes by Michelangelo and other artists: built by order of Sixtus IV.
Sistine Madonna, the Madonna painted by Raphael in 1515 for the Church of St. Sixtus at Piacenza, Italy.
sis·troid (sis'troid), *adj.* [< ?], in *mathematics*, designating the angle formed by the convex sides of two intersecting curves: opposed to *cissoid.*
sis·trum (sis'trəm), *n.* [*pl.* SISTRUMS (-trəmz), SISTRA (-trə)], [ME.; L. < Gr. *seistron* < *seiein*, to shake], a metal rattle or noisemaker consisting of a handle and a frame fitted with loosely held rods, jingled by the ancient Egyptians in the worship of Isis.

SISTRUM

Sis·y·phe·an (sis'ə-fē'ən), *adj.* [< L. *Sisypheius;* Gr. *Sisypheios* < *Sisyphos;* + *-an*], 1. of or like that of Sisyphus; hence, 2. endless and difficult: as, a *Sisyphean* labor.
Sis·y·phus (sis'ə-fəs), *n.* [L.; Gr. *Sisyphos*], in *Greek mythology*, the shrewd and greedy king of Corinth who was doomed forever in Hades to roll uphill a heavy stone which always rolled down again.
sit (sit), *v.i.* [SAT (sat) or *archaic* SATE (sat, sāt), SITTING; *obs.* pp. SITTEN (-'n)], [ME. *sitten;* AS. *sittan;* akin to G. *sitzen;* IE. base **sed-*, to sit, seen also in L. *sedere;* cf. SET, SEAT, SEDENTARY, etc.], 1. to rest the weight of the body upon the buttocks and the backs of the thighs, as on a chair, rock, etc.; be seated. 2. to rest on the haunches with the forelegs braced: said of quadrupeds. 3. to perch or roost: said of birds. 4. to cover and warm eggs for hatching; set; brood. 5. to occupy a seat in the capacity of judge, legislator, etc. 6. to be in session: as, the court will not *sit* this month. 7. to pose: as, he is *sitting* for his portrait, she won't *sit* for any other painter. 8. [British], to take a formal examination, as for an academic degree, scholarship, etc. (usually with *for*). 9. to be inactive or out of use. 10. to be located or have a place: as, the old barn has been *sitting* here for two centuries. 11. to fit: as, this hat doesn't *sit* well, the beam must *sit* solidly in the notch. 12. to rest or lie in any condition or position: as, responsibility *sits* lightly upon him. 13. to baby-sit. *v.t.* 1. to place in a seat; cause to sit; seat (often used reflexively): as, *sit* yourself in that chair. 2. to keep one's seat on (a horse, etc.).
sit down, 1. to lower oneself to a sitting position; take a seat. 2. to settle down or take up a place or position, as in the siege of a town.
sit in, to take part; participate; attend (often with *on*).
sit on (or **upon**), 1. to be a member of; be on (a jury, committee, etc.). 2. to confer on or investigate. 3. [Colloq.], to put down; suppress; repress. 4. [Colloq.], to reprimand or rebuke severely.
sit out, 1. to stay until the end of. 2. to stay longer than (another); outsit. 3. to remain seated during or take no part in (a dance, game, etc.).
sit up, 1. to rise to a sitting position. 2. to sit erect. 3. to sit on the haunches with the forelegs drawn up before the chest: said of animals. 4. to postpone the time of going to bed until a late hour. 5. [Colloq.], to become suddenly alert; be surprised or startled.
sit-down strike (sit'down'), a strike in which the strikers stay inside a factory or other place of employment, refusing to work or leave until agreement is reached: also **sit-down.**
site (sīt), *n.* [ME.; OFr.; L. *situs*, position, situation, seat], 1. a piece of land considered from the standpoint of its use for some specified purpose: as, a good *site* for a picnic. 2. the place where something is, is to be, or was located: as, we stood on the *site* of an ancient city.
sith (sith), *adv., conj., prep.* [ME.; AS. *siththa*, contr. form of *siththan* (cf. SINCE)], [Archaic], since.
sit-in (sit'in'), *n.* the organized act of occupying seats in a restaurant, bus station, etc. that practices racial discrimination, in seeking to integrate it.
Sit·ka (sit'kə), *n.* a town in southeastern Alaska, on Baranof Island: pop., 3,000.
si·to- (sī'tō, sī'tə), [< Gr. *sitos*, food, grain], a combining form meaning *food* or *eating*, as in *sitophobia:* also **sitio-.**
si·tol·o·gy (sī-tol'ə-ji), *n.* [*sito-* + *-logy*], the study of foods, food values, nutrition, diet, etc.; dietetics.
si·to·ma·ni·a (sī'tə-mā'ni-ə), *n.* [*sito-* + *-mania*], an abnormally great desire for food: also **sitiomania.**
si·to·pho·bi·a (sī'tə-fō'bi-ə), *n.* [*sito-* + *-phobia*], fear of food.
si·tos·ter·in (sī-tos'tẽr-in), *n.* sitosterol.
si·tos·ter·ol (sī-tos'tẽr-ōl', sī-tos'tẽr-ol), *n.* [*sito-* + chole*sterol*], a crystalline alcohol, $C_{27}H_{45}OH$, found in wheat, corn, Calabar beans, etc.
Si·tsang (sē'tsäŋ'), *n.* Tibet: the Chinese name.
sit·ten (sit''n), obsolete past participle of **sit.**
sit·ter (sit'ẽr), *n.* a person or thing that sits; specifically, *a*) a person hired to sit with a child or children when the parents are out, as for the evening: also **baby sitter.** *b*) a brooding hen.
Sit·ter, Wil·lem de (vil'əm də sit'ẽr), 1872–1934; Dutch astronomer.
sit·ting (sit'iŋ), *n.* 1. the act or position of one that sits. 2. a session or meeting, as of a committee. 3. a period of being seated at some activity: as, he read the story in two *sittings.* 4. *a*) the number of eggs upon which a hen sits for a single hatching. *b*) a brooding upon eggs, as by a hen. 5. a seat in a church, especially one for which rent is paid. *adj.* that sits; having a seat; seated.
Sit·ting Bull (sit'iŋ bool), 1834?–1890; Indian chief of the Sioux tribe; fought against General Custer (1876).
sitting room, a room (in a home) furnished with sofas, chairs, etc., used for conversation, entertainment of guests, etc.; living room: sometimes called *parlor.*
sit·u·ate (sich'ōō-it; *also, and for v. always*, sich'ōō-āt'), *adj.* [ML. *situatus*, pp. of *situare*, to place < L. *situs;* see SITE], [Rare or Archaic], situated. *v.t.* [SITUATED (-id), SITUATING], 1. to put in a certain place or position; place; locate. 2. to place in given circumstances or in a particular condition.
sit·u·at·ed (sich'ōō-āt'id), *adj.* [pp. of *situate* < L. *situatus*, pp. of *situare;* see SITUATION], 1. having a given site or location; placed; located. 2. subject to certain circumstances or conditions.
sit·u·a·tion (sich'ōō-ā'shən), *n.* [Fr.; ML. *situatio* < L. *situare*, to place < *situs*, a place, site], 1. manner in which a thing is situated; place of an object in relation to its surroundings; location; position. 2. a place; locality. 3. position or condition with regard to circumstances. 4. *a*) the combination of circumstances at any given moment; state of affairs. *b*) any significant combination of circumstances developing in the course of a novel, play, etc. 5. a position of employment. —*SYN.* see **position, state.**
si·tus (sī'təs), *n.* [L.; see SITE], position or location; especially, the normal position, as of an organ of the body or a plant part.
Sit·well, Edith (sit'wəl), 1887– ; sister of *Osbert* and *Sacheverell;* English poet and critic.
Sitwell, Os·bert (oz'bẽrt), 1892– ; English poet, dramatist, and novelist.
Sitwell, Sa·chev·er·ell (sə-shev'ẽr-əl), 1900– ; English poet and critic.
sitz bath (sits), [partial transl. of G. *sitzbad; sitz*, a seat + *bad*, bath], 1. a bath in which only the hip area is immersed, usually as a medical treatment. 2. a tub or basin used for such a bath.
Si·va (sē'və, shē'və), *n.* [Hind.; Sans., auspicious], Hindu god of destruction and reproduction, a member of the supreme Hindu trinity: also **Shiva:** see **Brahma, Vishnu.**
Si·va·ism (sē'və-iz'm, shē'və-iz'm), *n.* worship of Siva.
Si·va·is·tic (sē'və-is'tik, shē'və-is'tik), *adj.* of Sivaism.
Si·van (si-vän', siv'ən), *n.* [Heb.], the ninth month of the Jewish year: see **Jewish calendar.**
Si·vas (sē-väz'), *n.* a city in central Turkey: pop., 65,000.
six (siks), *adj.* [ME.; AS. *sex, six*, etc.; akin to G. *sechs*, Goth. *saihs;* IE. base **sweks-*, **seks-*, etc., seen also in L. *sex* (cf. SEX-), Gr. *hex* (cf. HEXA-), etc.], totaling one more than five. *n.* 1. the cardinal number between five and seven; 6; VI. 2. a person or thing numbered six or something having six units as its essential characteristic, as a playing card with six pips.
at sixes and sevens, [Colloq.], 1. in confusion or disorder. 2. at odds; disagreeing.
six·fold (siks'fōld'), *adj.* [AS. *sixfeald;* see -FOLD], 1. having six parts. 2. having six times as much or as many. *adv.* six times as much or as many.
six-foot·er (siks'foot'ẽr), *n.* [Colloq.], a person six feet tall.
Six Nations, the confederation of the Five Nations and the Tuscarora tribe.
six·pence (siks'pəns), *n.* 1. the sum of six pence (pennies). 2. a small British silver coin of this value.
six·pen·ny (siks'pen'i, siks'pən-i), *adj.* 1. worth or costing sixpence; hence, 2. of small worth; cheap. 3. designating a size of nails, usually two inches.
six-shoot·er (siks'shōōt'ẽr), *n.* [Colloq.], a revolver firing six shots without reloading.
six·teen (siks'tēn'), *adj.* [ME. *sixtene;* AS. *syxtene;* see SIX & -TEEN], six more than ten. *n.* the cardinal number between fifteen and seventeen; 16; XVI.
six·teen·mo (siks-tēn'mō), *n.* [*pl.* SIXTEENMOS (-mōz)], sextodecimo; 16mo.: a size of book.
six·teenth (siks'tēnth'), *adj.* [ME. *sixtenthe*, replacing AS. *syxteotha*, etc.; see SIXTEEN & -TH], 1. preceded by fifteen others in a series; 16th. 2. designating any of the sixteen equal parts of something. *n.* 1. the

one following the fifteenth. 2. any of the sixteen equal parts of something; 1/16. 3. in *music,* a sixteenth note.
ixteenth note, in *music,* a note (♪) having one sixteenth the duration of a whole note; semiquaver.
ixth (siksth), *adj.* [AS. *sixta;* akin to G. *sechste;* see SIX & -TH], 1. preceded by five others in a series; 6th. 2. designating any of the six equal parts of something. *n.* 1. the one following the fifth. 2. any of the six equal parts of something; 1/6. 3. in *music, a*) an interval of six degrees in a diatonic scale. *b*) a tone six degrees above or below a given tone. *c*) the combination of two tones separated by this interval. *d*) the sixth note of a diatonic scale; submediant; superdominant.
ixth chord, in *music,* an inverted triad, as e g-c.
ixth·ly (siksth'li), *adv.* in the sixth place.
ixth sense, a power of perception which seems as strong as any of the five senses; intuition.
ix·ti·eth (siks'ti-ith), *adj.* [AS. *sixteogotha* < *sixtig:* see SIXTY & -TH], 1. preceded by fifty-nine others in a series; 60th. 2. designating any of the sixty equal parts of something. *n.* 1. the one following the fifty-ninth. 2. any of the sixty equal parts of something; 1/60.
ix·tine (siks'tin), *adj.* Sistine.
ix·tus IV (siks'təs), 1414–1484; Pope (1471–1484).
ixtus, Saint, 1. (*Sixtus I*), Pope (116?–125? A.D.): his day is April 6. 2. (*Sixtus II*), Pope (257–258 A.D.) and martyr: his day is August 6. 3. (*Sixtus III*), Pope (432–440 A.D.): his day is March 28.
ix·ty (siks'ti), *adj.* [ME. *sixti;* AS. *sixtig;* see SIX & -TY (tens)], ten times six. *n.* [*pl.* SIXTIES (-tiz)], the cardinal number between fifty-nine and sixty-one; 60; LX.
the sixties, the years from sixty through sixty-nine (of a century or a person's age).
ix·ty-four dollar question (siks'ti-fôr'), [Colloq.], the most important, or principal, question: so called from the award given for answering correctly the final one of a series of questions on a radio quiz program.
ix·ty-fourth note (siks'ti-fôrth', siks'ti-fōrth'), in *music,* a note (𝅘𝅥𝅱) having one sixty-fourth the duration of a whole note.
iz·a·ble (sīz'ə-b'l), *adj.* of considerable size or bulk; large: also spelled **sizeable.**
iz·a·bly (sīz'ə-bli), *adv.* so as to be sizable.
iz·ar (siz'ẽr), *n.* [< *size* (standard ration)], a student receiving a scholarship allowance at Cambridge University or Trinity College, Dublin: also spelled **sizer.**
ize (sīz), *n.* [ME.; OFr. *sise,* contr. of *assise;* see ASSIZE], 1. that quality of a thing which determines how much space it occupies; dimensions or magnitude of a thing. 2. any of a series of graded classifications into which merchandise is divided according to this: as, jumbo *size* peanuts, *size* nine shoes. 3. *a*) extent, magnitude, amount, etc.: as, the *size* of this undertaking is incredible. *b*) sizable amount, dimensions, etc. 4. character with regard to ability to meet requirements: as, the governorship is too big for the *size* of him. 5. [Colloq.], actual condition; true state of affairs: as, that's the *size* of it. 6. [Obs.], standard ration or allowance, as of food. *v.t.* [SIZED (sīzd), SIZING], 1. to make or shape in accordance with a given size. 2. to arrange or grade according to size.
of a size, of one or the same size.
size up, [Colloq.], 1. to make an estimate or judgment of. 2. to meet requirements or specifications.
ize (sīz), *n.* [contr. of Fr. *assise,* layer; see ASSIZE], any thin, pasty substance used as a glaze or filler on porous materials, as on plaster, paper, or cloth. *v.t.* [SIZED (sīzd), SIZING], to apply size to; fill, stiffen, or glaze with size.
size (sīz), -sized.
ize·a·ble (sīz'ə-b'l), *adj.* sizable.
sized (sīzd), a combining form, usually in hyphenated compounds, meaning *having* (a specified) *size,* as in *small-sized:* also **-size,** as in *life-size.*
z·er (siz'ẽr), *n.* a sizar.
z·ing (sīz'iŋ), *n.* 1. size (glaze or filler). 2. the act or process of applying this.
z·y (sīz'i), *adj.* having the nature of or resembling size; viscous; glutinous.
z·zle (siz''l), *v.i.* [SIZZLED (-'ld), SIZZLING], [echoic word], to make a hissing sound when in contact with heat, as a drop of water on hot metal. *n.* such a sound.
z·zling (siz'liŋ), *adj.* that sizzles; extremely hot.
J., Society of Jesus.
æl·land (shel'län), *n.* Zealand Island: Danish name.
., sack.
a·gen, Cape (skä'gən), The Skaw.
ag·er·rak, Skag·e·rak (skag'ə-rak'), *n.* an arm of the North Sea between Norway and Denmark: length, 50 mi.; width, 80 mi.
ald (skôld, skäld), *n.* [ME.; ON. *skāld;* akin to Eng. *scold*], any ancient Scandinavian poet, specifically one of the Viking period, writing in the complex late Old Norse style: also spelled **scald.**
ald·ic (skôl'dik, skäl'dik), *adj.* of the skalds or their poetry: also spelled **scaldic.**

skat (skät), *n.* [G. < It. *scartare,* to discard], a card game for three people, played with thirty-two cards.
skate (skāt), *n.* [taken as sing. of earlier *skates* < D. *schaats,* a skate, stilt; OFr. *escache,* of Gmc. origin; cf. LG. *shake,* a leg], 1. *a*) a bladelike metal runner mounted in a frame having clamps and straps for fastening it to the sole of a shoe and used for gliding on ice. *b*) a shoe with such a runner permanently attached. Also **ice skate.** 2. a similar frame or shoe with small wheels instead of a runner, for gliding on a hardwood floor or other smooth surface: also **roller skate.** *v.i.* [SKATED (-id), SKATING], to move along or glide on or as on skates.
skate on thin ice, to be in a difficult, insecure, or dangerous situation.
skate (skāt), *n.* [*pl.* SKATES (skāts), SKATE; see PLURAL, II, D, 1], [ME. *scate;* ON. *skata;* said to be < L. *squatus,* flat fish], a salt-water food fish of the ray family, with a broad, flat body.
skate (skāt), *n.* [Slang], 1. a worn-out old horse. 2. a person regarded with condescension, contempt, etc.
skating rink, a surface or area specially prepared or set aside for skating.
skat·ol (skat'ōl, skat'ol), *n.* skatole.
skat·ole (skat'ōl), *n.* [< Gr. *skōr, skatos,* dung; + *-ol*], a foul-smelling, colorless, crystalline compound, C_9H_9N, formed by the decomposition of proteins, as in the intestine.

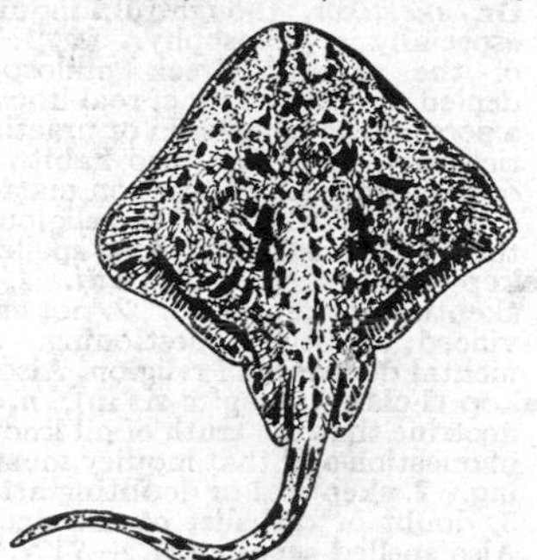

WINTER SKATE (4 ft. long)

Skaw, The (skô), a cape of northern Denmark: also **Cape Skagen.**
skean (skēn), *n.* [Gael. & Ir. *sgian*], a kind of dagger or short sword formerly used in Scotland and Ireland.
Skeat, Walter William (skēt), 1835–1912; English philologist and lexicographer.
ske·dad·dle (ski-dad''l), *v.i.* [SKEDADDLED (-'ld), SKEDADDLING], [popularized in military slang of Civil War period; said to be < north. Brit. dial., but prob. a fanciful formation], [Colloq.], to run away; get away in a hurry. *n.* [Colloq.], a running or scurrying away.
skee (skē), *n.* & *v.i.* [SKEED (skēd), SKEEING], ski.
skeet (skēt), *n.* a form of trapshooting in which the shooter fires from eight different angles at clay targets thrown from traps to simulate birds in flight.
skeg (skeg), *n.* [D. *schegge* < ON. *skegg,* a beard; basic sense "a projection"], in *nautical usage,* the after-part of the keel, or an extension of this upon which the rudder post is mounted.
skein (skān), *n.* [ME. *skeyn;* OFr. *esca(i)gne*], 1. a quantity of thread or yarn wound in a coil. 2. something like this, as a coil of hair. 3. a flock of wild fowl.
skel·e·tal (skel'ə-t'l), *adj.* of, or having the nature of, a skeleton.
skel·e·ton (skel'ə-t'n), *n.* [Mod. L.; Gr. *skeleton* (*sōma*), dried (body), mummy < *skeletos,* dried up; akin to *sklēros,* dry, hard], 1. the hard framework of an animal body for supporting the tissues and protecting the organs; specifically, all the bones collectively, or the bony framework, of a human being or other vertebrate animal. 2. anything like a skeleton in any of various ways; specifically, *a*) a very lean or emaciated person or animal. *b*) a supporting framework, as of a ship. *c*) an outline or preliminary sketch, as of a novel. *d*) the meager or devitalized remains of something. *adj.* of or like a skeleton; specifically, of, or having the nature of, the main or essential outline, framework, etc.: as, a *skeleton* force.

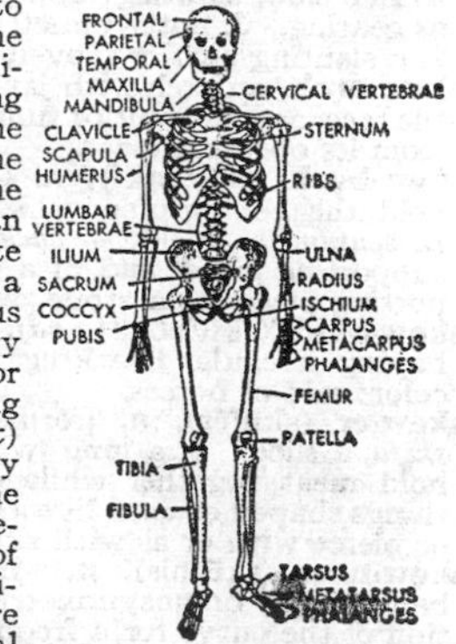

HUMAN SKELETON

skeleton at the feast, a person or event that brings gloom or sadness to an occasion of joy or celebration.
skeleton in the closet, some fact about a member of a family, etc. kept secret because of shame or fear of disgrace.

, āpe, bâre, cär; ten, ēven, hêre, ovẽr; is, bīte; lot, gō, hôrn, tōōl, look; oil, out; up, ūse, fũr; get; joy; yet; chin; she; thin, en; zh, leisure; ŋ, ring; ə for *a* in *ago, e* in *agent, i* in *sanity, o* in *comply, u* in *focus;* ' as in *able* (ā'b'l); Fr. bál; ë, Fr. ur; ö, Fr. feu; Fr. mon; ô, Fr. coq; ü, Fr. duc; H, G. ich; kh, G. doch. See pp. x–xii. ‡ foreign; * hypothetical; < derived from.

skel·e·ton·ize (skel'ə-t'n-iz'), *v.t.* [SKELETONIZED (-izd'), SKELETONIZING], 1. to reduce (a body) to a skeleton. 2. to outline; sketch briefly. 3. to reduce greatly in number or size, as an office force.

skeleton key, a key having a large part of the bit filed away so that it can be used to open a number of locks as a master key.

skel·lum (skel'əm), *n.* [Early Mod. Eng. < D. *schelm* < G. *schelm*, rascal (OHG. *scelmo*)], [Archaic or British Dial.], a rascal; rogue; scamp.

Skel·ton, John (skel't'n), 1460?–1529; English poet, clergyman, and satirist.

skep (skep), *n.* [ME. *skeppe;* ON. *skeppa*], 1. a kind of round basket of wicker or wood. 2. the amount held by such a basket. 3. a beehive, especially one of straw.

skep·tic (skep'tik), *adj.* [OFr. *sceptique;* L. *scepticus;* Gr. *skeptikos*, thoughtful, inquiring], skeptical: used especially in philosophy. *n.* 1. [S-], a member of any of the ancient Greek philosophical schools which denied the possibility of real knowledge of any kind. 2. a person who believes in or practices philosophical skepticism. 3. a person who habitually doubts, questions, or suspends judgment upon matters generally accepted. 4. a person who doubts religious doctrines, especially those of Christianity. Also spelled **sceptic.**

skep·ti·cal (skep'tə-k'l), *adj.* 1. of or characteristic of skeptics or skepticism. 2. not easily persuaded or convinced; doubting; questioning. 3. doubting the fundamental doctrines of religion. Also spelled **sceptical.**

skep·ti·cism (skep'tə-siz'm), *n.* 1. the philosophical doctrine that the truth of all knowledge must always be in question and that inquiry must be a process of doubting. 2. skeptical or doubting attitude or state of mind. 3. doubt or disbelief of the doctrines of Christianity. Also spelled **scepticism.** —*SYN.* see **uncertainty.**

sker·ry (sker'i), *n.* [*pl.* SKERRIES (-iz)], [via Orkney dial. < ON. *sker;* IE. base *-sqer-*, to cut, as also in Eng. *shear, share, scar* (a rock), etc.], [Scot.], an isolated rock or reef in the sea.

sketch (skech), *n.* [earlier *schitz;* D. *schets;* It. *schizzo;* L. *schedium*, extempore poem < Gr. *schedios*, extempore, sudden], 1. a simple, rough drawing or design, done rapidly and without much detail. 2. a brief plan or description of major parts or points; outline. 3. a short, light, informal story, description, play, or piece of music. *v.t.* to draw or describe quickly or in outline; make a sketch of. *v.i.* to make a sketch or sketches.

sketch·book (skech'book'), *n.* 1. a book of drawing paper for making sketches. 2. a book of literary sketches. Also **sketch book.**

sketch·i·ly (skech'ə-li), *adv.* in a sketchy manner.

sketch·i·ness (skech'i-nis), *n.* the quality or condition of being sketchy.

sketch·y (skech'i), *adj.* [SKETCHIER (-i-ẽr), SKETCHIEST (-i-ist)], 1. having the form of a sketch; presenting only major parts or points; not detailed. 2. lacking completeness or thoroughness; rough; inadequate.

skete (skēt), *n.* [Gr. *skētē* < *skētis*, lower Egyptian desert renowned for its hermits], a community of monks or hermits of the Greek Church.

skew (skū), *v.i.* [ONorm.Fr. *eskiuer, escuer*, varied < OFr. *eschiuver;* see ESCHEW], 1. to take a slanting or oblique course or direction; move aside or sideways; swerve or twist. 2. [Dial.], to squint or glance sideways (with *at*). *v.t.* 1. to make slanting or oblique. 2. to bias, distort, or pervert. *adj.* 1. turned aside or to one side; slanting; oblique. 2. having such a part, as gearing. 3. not symmetrical. *n.* 1. a slant or twist. 2. a slanting part or movement.

skew arch, an arch with jambs not at right angles with the face, as in a vault or tunnel which narrows or widens from its opening.

skew·back (skū'bak'), *n.* [*skew*, sloping stone cut to hold the coping of a gable < ME. *scuwe;* OFr. *escu;* L. *scutum*, a shield; + *back*], 1. the slanting surface supporting either end of a segmental arch. 2. a supporting piece, as a stone, with such a surface.

skew·bald (skū'bôld'), *adj.* [< ME. *skewed*, piebald], having irregular markings of white and some other color: said of horses.

skew·er (skū'ẽr), *n.* [formerly written *skiver* < ON. *skifa*, a slice], 1. a long, wooden or metal pin used to hold meat together while cooking. 2. any of several things shaped or used like a meat skewer. *v.t.* to fasten or pierce with or as with skewers.

skew·ness (skū'nis), *n.* 1. the fact or condition of being skew, or unsymmetrical. 2. in *statistics*, deviation of the curve for a frequency distribution from the symmetrical curve for such a distribution.

ski (skē; *also* Norw., shē), *n.* [*pl.* SKIS (skēz, shēz), SKI], [Norw.; ON. *skith*, snowshoe; akin to *skid*], one of a pair of long, thin, wood runners that can be fastened to the feet for traveling on snow. *v.i.* [SKIED (skēd), SKIING], 1. to travel on skis by gliding over the snow. 2. to engage in the sport of gliding down snow-covered inclines on skis. Also **skee.**

ski·a·gram (skī'ə-gram'), *n.* [Gr. *skia*, a shadow; + *-gram*], a skiagraph: also spelled **sciagram, skiogram.**

ski·a·graph (skī'ə-graf', skī'ə-gräf'), *n.* [Gr. *skia*, a shadow; + *-graph;* cf. SKIAGRAPHY], a picture consisting of shadows, especially those cast on a sensitized surface by X rays. *v.t.* to make a skiagraph of. Also spelled **sciagraph, sciograph, skiograph.**

ski·ag·ra·phy (skī-ag'rə-fi), *n.* [Gr. *skiagraphia* < *skiagraphos*, drawing in light and shade < *skia*, a shadow + *graphein*, to draw], the art or practice of making skiagraphs, especially by X ray.

ski·a·scope (skī'ə-skōp'), *n.* the instrument used in skiascopy; retinoscope.

ski·as·co·py (skī-as'kə-pi), *n.* [Gr. *skia*, a shadow; + *-scopy*], a method for refracting an eye by illuminating the retina with a skiascope and observing the movements of light and shadow on the pupil; retinoscopy.

skid (skid), *n.* [Early Mod. Eng. < ON. *skith*, wooden billet (cf. SKI); akin to *sheath, shed*], 1. a plank, log, etc., often one of a pair or set, used as a support or as a track upon which to slide or roll a heavy object. 2. a low, wooden platform for holding loads or stacks. 3. *pl.* a wooden structure placed against the side of a ship to protect it from damage, as when unloading. 4. a runner used in place of a wheel on an aircraft landing gear. 5. a sliding wedge or drag used to check the motion of a vehicle by pressure against a wheel. 6. the act of skidding. *v.t.* [SKIDDED (-id), SKIDDING], 1. to brake or lock (a wheel) with a skid. 2. to support with or slide on a skid or skids. 3. to cause (a wheel, vehicle, etc.) to slide or skid, as on ice. *v.i.* 1. to slide without turning, as a wheel when skids or brakes are applied on a slippery surface. 2. to slide or slip sideways, as a vehicle when not gripping the road on ice or in a fast turn. 3. in *aeronautics*, to move sideways and outward while turning, as a result of failing to bank sufficiently. —*SYN.* see **slide.**

on the skids, [Slang], about to meet with some misfortune; falling from power, losing prestige, etc.

skid doo (ski-dōō'), *v.i.* [< *skedaddle*], [Slang], to go away; leave: usually in the imperative.

skid fin, in *aeronautics*, a longitudinal fin placed edge upright, usually along the top wing of a biplane, to reduce skidding.

skid·proof (skid'prōōf'), *adj.* that prevents skidding, as an automobile tire, a road surface, etc.

skid row, [Slang], a section of a city frequented by hobos, vagrants, derelicts, etc.

ski·er (skē'ẽr), *n.* a person who skis.

skiff (skif), *n.* [OFr. *esquif;* It. *schifo;* OHG. *scif;* cf. SHIP], 1. any light rowboat. 2. a long, narrow rowboat, especially one with a centerboard, outrigger, and a small sail.

ski·ing (skē'iŋ), *n.* the act or sport of traveling or gliding on skis.

ski·jor·ing (skē'jôr'iŋ, skē-jō'riŋ), *n.* [Norw. *skigjöring*, lit., ski-doing], a sport in which people on skis are drawn over snow or ice by a horse, tractor, etc.

ski jump, 1. a jump made by a person wearing skis. 2. an incline or track used for such jumping, especially as a competitive sport.

skil·ful (skil'fəl), *adj.* skillful.

skill (skil), *n.* [ME., discernment, reason; ON. *skil*, distinction, etc., akin to *skilja*, to cut apart, separate, etc.; IE. base **sqel-*, to cut (cf. SHIELD, SHILLING); basic sense "ability to separate," hence "discernment"], 1. great ability or proficiency; expertness: as, his *skill* in mathematics is well known. 2. an art, craft, or science, especially one involving the use of the hands or body; hence, 3. ability in such an art, craft, or science. 4. [Obs.], knowledge; understanding; judgment. *v.* [Archaic], to matter, avail, or make a difference: as, what *skills* it that we suffer? —*SYN.* see **art.**

skilled (skild), *adj.* 1. having skill; skillful. 2. having or requiring an ability, as in a particular industrial occupation, machine operation, etc., gained by special experience or a regular program of training or apprenticeship: as, a toolmaker is a *skilled* workman.

skil·let (skil'it), *n.* [ME. *skelett;* ? < OFr. *escuellette*, dim. of *escuelle*, porringer, basin < L. *scutella*, dim. of *scutra*, a dish; considered by some to be dim. of Eng. dial. *skeel*, pail (< ON. *skjōla*, pail)], 1. a deep, heavy stewing pan with a long handle and, sometimes, legs. 2. a frying pan.

skill·ful (skil'fəl), *adj.* having or showing skill; accomplished; expert: also spelled **skilful.**

skil·ling (skil'iŋ), *n.* [Norw., Dan., Sw., etc.; akin to *shilling*], in certain Scandinavian countries, a former copper coin and money of account, equal to less than a cent.

skim (skim), *v.t.* [SKIMMED (skimd), SKIMMING], [ME. *skemen, skimen* < OFr. *escumer*, lit., to scum (< OHG. *scum;* cf. G. *schaum*, scum, foam) or < the cognate ON. *skūm* (cf. SCUM) via **skȳmja, v.*], 1. to clear (a liquid) of floating matter: as, he *skimmed* the milk of its cream. 2. to remove (floating matter) from a liquid: as, *skim* cream from the milk. 3. to coat or cover with a thin layer: as, a pond *skimmed* with ice. 4. to look at hastily or carelessly; glance through a book, etc. without reading word for word. 5. to glide or pass swiftly and lightly over. 6. to cause to move in this way: as, he *skimmed* a flat stone across the creek. *v.i.*

1. to move along swiftly and lightly over a surface, through space, etc.; glide; sail. 2. to make a rapid or careless examination, as of a book (usually with *over* or *through*). 3. to become thinly coated, as with scum. ***n.*** 1. something skimmed off; specifically, skim milk. 2. the act of skimming. 3. [Obs.], scum.

kim·ble-scam·ble (skim′b'l-skam′b'l, skim″'l-skam″'l), ***adj.*** rambling, incoherent, nonsensical, etc.

kim·mer (skim′ẽr), ***n.*** [ME. *skemour, skemere* < OFr. *escumoir* (in sense 2) & < Eng. *skim*], 1. a person or thing that skims. 2. any utensil used in skimming liquids. 3. any of several long-winged sea birds that skim the water in search of food: also called *scissorbill.*

kim milk, milk from which cream has been removed.

kim·ming (skim′iŋ), ***n.*** *usually pl.* anything that has been skimmed from a liquid.

kimp (skimp), ***adj.*** [prob. altered < *scrimp*, but cf. ON. *skemma*, to shorten; akin to *scant, scamp, v.*], [Colloq.], scanty. ***v.i.*** [Colloq.], 1. to give or allow too little; be stingy; scrimp. 2. to keep expenses very low: as, we *skimped* to save money. ***v.t.*** [Colloq.], 1. to do poorly or carelessly. 2. to be stingy in or toward.

kimp·i·ly (skim′pə-li), ***adv.*** in a skimpy manner.

kimp·i·ness (skim′pi-nis), ***n.*** skimpy quality or state.

kimp·y (skim′pi), ***adj.*** [SKIMPIER (-pi-ẽr), SKIMPIEST (-pi-ist)], [Colloq.], 1. barely or not quite enough; somewhat less in size, fullness, etc. than is needed; scanty. 2. stingy.

kin (skin), ***n.*** [ME. *skynn;* ON. *skinn;* akin to G. *schinden*, to flay, peel; IE. base **sqen-*, to split off; prob. < **seq-*, to cut], 1. the outer covering or integument of the animal body. 2. such a covering, especially that of a small animal, when removed from the body and prepared for use; pelt. 3. something resembling skin in appearance or function; any outer layer, as fruit rind, the shell or plating of a ship, a film or scum, the outermost nacreous layer in a pearl, etc. 4. a container for liquids made of skin. 5. [Slang], a miserly person; skinflint. 6. [Slang], a swindler or cheat. ***v.t.*** SKINNED (skind), SKINNING], 1. to cover with or as with skin; grow skin on. 2. to remove skin from. 3. to strip or peel off, as or like skin. 4. [Colloq.], to defraud or cheat; swindle. ***v.i.*** 1. to become covered with skin. 2. to lose the skin; shed. 3. [Slang], to escape; get away.

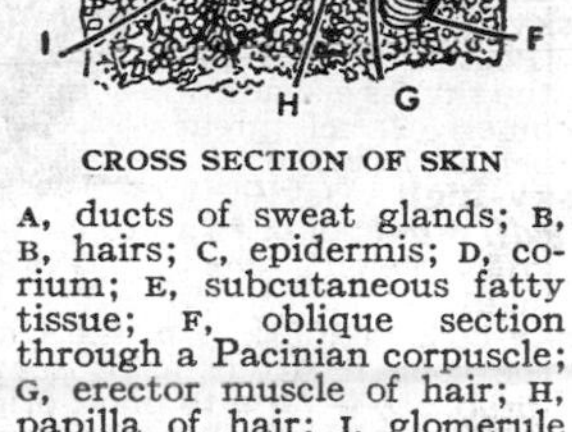

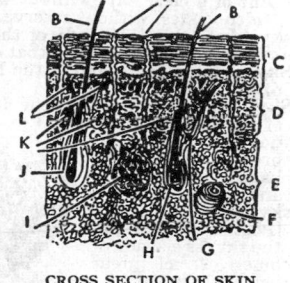

CROSS SECTION OF SKIN

A, ducts of sweat glands; B, B, hairs; C, epidermis; D, corium; E, subcutaneous fatty tissue; F, oblique section through a Pacinian corpuscle; G, erector muscle of hair; H, papilla of hair; I, glomerule of sweat gland; J, hair follicle; K, sebaceous glands; L, papillae of corium

be no skin off one's back, [Slang], to affect one not at all; be of no concern to one.
by the skin of one's teeth, [Colloq.], by the smallest possible margin; barely.
get under one's skin, [Slang], to anger or irritate one.
have a thick skin, to be undisturbed by criticism, insults, etc.; be callous or insensitive.
have a thin skin, to be acutely sensitive to blame, criticism, insults, etc.
in (or with) a whole skin, [Colloq.], without injury.
save one's skin, [Colloq.], to avoid death or injury.
skin alive, 1. to remove the skin from (a living person or animal). 2. [Colloq.], to scold or punish severely. 3. [Colloq.], to overcome or defeat decisively.

YN.—**skin** is the general term for the outer covering of the animal body and for the covering, especially if thin and tight, of certain fruits and vegetables (human *skin*, the *skin* of a peach); **hide** is used of the tough skins of certain large animals, as of a horse, cow, elephant, etc.; **pelt** refers to the skin, especially the untanned skin, of a fur-bearing animal, as of a mink, ox, sheep, etc.; **rind** applies to the thick, tough covering of certain fruits, as of a watermelon, or of cheeses, bacon, etc.; **peel** is used of the skin or rind of fruit that has been removed, as by stripping (potato *peel*, lemon *peel*); **bark** applies to the hard covering of trees and woody plants.

in·bound (skin′bound′), ***adj.*** 1. with skin drawn tight over the flesh. 2. suffering from scleroderma.

in-deep (skin′dēp′), ***adj.*** 1. penetrating no deeper than the skin. 2. without real depth or significance; superficial; shallow. ***adv.*** so as to be only skin-deep.

in diving, underwater diving in which the swimmer, without lines to the surface, is variously equipped with goggles, flipperlike foot attachments, a skintight rubber garment, portable compressed-air equipment, etc.

skin·flint (skin′flint′), ***n.*** [< thieves' slang; lit., one who would skin a flint for the sake of gain or economy], a niggardly person; miser.

skin·ful (skin′fool′), ***n.*** [*pl.* SKINFULS (-foolz′)], 1. as much liquid as a skin container can hold. 2. [Colloq.], as much as the stomach can hold; bellyful.

skin game, [Colloq.], 1. a crooked or fraudulent game of chance. 2. any cheating, swindling trick.

skin grafting, the surgical transplanting of skin from another part of the body or from another person to replace skin destroyed, as by burning.

skink (skiŋk), ***n.*** [L. *scincus;* Gr. *skinkos*], any of a number of tropical lizards having thick, shiny bodies, heavy scales, and short legs.

skinned (skind), ***adj.*** having a (specified kind of) skin: usually in hyphenated compounds, as *dark-skinned.*

skin·ner (skin′ẽr), ***n.*** 1. a person who strips skins or processes them for market. 2. a swindler. 3. [Colloq.], a (mule) driver.

Skin·ner, Cornelia O·tis (ō′tis skin′ẽr), 1901– ; daughter of *Otis;* American actress and writer.

Skinner, Otis, 1858–1942; American actor.

skin·ni·ness (skin′i-nis), ***n.*** skinny quality or state.

skin·ny (skin′i), ***adj.*** [SKINNIER (-i-ẽr), SKINNIEST (-i-ist)], 1. of or like skin. 2. without much flesh; emaciated; thin. —***SYN.*** see **lean.**

skin·tight (skin′tīt′), ***adj.*** clinging closely to the skin; tight-fitting, as a garment.

ski·o·gram (skī′ə-gram′), ***n.*** a skiagram.

ski·o·graph (skī′ə-graf′, skī′ə-gräf′), ***n.*** a skiagraph.

skip (skip), ***v.i.*** [SKIPPED (skipt), SKIPPING], [ME. *skippen* (prob. < ON.); cf. earlier Sw. *scuppa, scoppa*, in the same senses; prob. IE. base **sqeubh-*, to throw, cast; cf. SHOVE], 1. to leap, jump, or spring lightly; move along with quick steps and jumps: as, the girls *skipped* gaily by. 2. to be deflected from a surface; ricochet. 3. to pass, or direct the attention, from one point to another, omitting what lies between. 4. to be promoted in school beyond the next regular grade. 5. [Colloq.], to leave hurriedly, especially under questionable circumstances; abscond. ***v.t.*** 1. to jump or leap lightly over. 2. to pass over without noticing, reading, mentioning, doing, etc. 3. to cause to skip or ricochet. 4. [Colloq.], to leave (a place) hurriedly. ***n.*** 1. *a*) an act of skipping; leap; spring. *b*) a skipping gait in which hops and steps are alternated. 2. a passing over or omitting. 3. in *music*, a passing from one note to another at an interval greater than a second.

SYN.—**skip** suggests a springing forward lightly and quickly, leaping on alternate feet, and of inanimate things, deflection from a surface in a series of jumps; **bound** implies longer, more vigorous leaps, as in running, or by an elastic object thrown along the ground; **hop** suggests a single short jump, as on one leg, or a series of short, relatively jerky jumps; **ricochet** is used of an inanimate object that has been thrown or shot and that bounds or skips in glancing deflection from a surface.

ski pants, loose-cut slack trousers that fit tightly around the ankle: used in skiing and other winter sports.

skip-bomb (skip′bom′), ***v.i.*** & ***v.t.*** to fly low and drop bombs so that they explode under water against the side of (a ship or other target).

skip distance, in *radio*, the distance along the surface of the earth between the farthest point reached by the ground wave of a transmitting station and the nearest point at which the radio wave is reflected back to the earth from the ionosphere.

skip·jack (skip′jak′), ***n.*** [*pl.* SKIPJACKS (-jaks′), SKIPJACK; see PLURAL, II, D, 1], 1. any of several kinds of fish that leap out of, or play at the surface of, the water. 2. a beetle that can snap itself back onto its feet when turned on its back.

skip·per (skip′ẽr), ***n.*** 1. a person or thing that skips. 2. the saury. 3. a small, swift-flying butterfly with club-shaped antennae. 4. any skipping insect.

skip·per (skip′ẽr), ***n.*** [ME.; MD. *schipper* < *schip*, a ship], 1. the captain of a ship, especially of a small ship. 2. any person who leads or directs.

skip·pet (skip′it), ***n.*** [dim. of *skep*], a small box or envelope used to protect a seal tied to a document.

skirl (skũrl), ***v.t.*** & ***v.i.*** [ME. (northern) *skrille, skyrle;* prob. < ON.; cf. Norw. dial. *skrylla*, to scream; for IE. base see SHRILL], [Scot. & Dial.], to sound out in shrill, piercing tones: said especially of a bagpipe. ***n.*** a shrill sound, specifically that of a bagpipe.

skir·mish (skũr′mish), ***n.*** [ME. *scarmishe, skrymishe;* OFr. *escarmuche* (cf. SCARAMOUCHE); It. *scaramuccia* < Gmc. **skirmjan*, to protect < *scirm*, a guard, protection; see SCRIMMAGE], 1. a brief fight or encounter carried on between small groups, usually part of a battle or war. 2. any slight, unimportant conflict; brush. ***v.i.*** [ME. *scarmishen, skirmishen* < an inflectional stem of OFr. *eskirmir* < Gmc. **skirmjan;* see the *n.*], to take part in a skirmish. —***SYN.*** see **battle.**

skir·mish·er (skũr′mish-ẽr), ***n.*** 1. a person who skirmishes. 2. any of a group of soldiers taking part in a skirmish or spread out in extended order for attack.

skirr (skūr), *v.i.* [of echoic origin], to move, run, fly, etc. swiftly and, especially, with a whirring sound. *v.t.* [Dial.], 1. to cover or pass through in searching; scour. 2. to cause to skim or glide, as by throwing. *n.* a whirring sound.

skir·ret (skir′it), *n.* [ME. *skirwhit,* altered < OFr. *eschervis;* ult. < Ar. *karawya;* see CARAWAY], a plant with clusters of small flowers and white, edible roots.

skirt (skūrt), *n.* [ME.; ON. *skyrt,* shirt, *kirtle,* exactly cognate with AS. *scyrte* (cf. SHIRT); for IE. base see SHORT], 1. that part of a garment, as of a robe, dress, etc., that hangs below the waist. 2. a woman's garment that hangs from the waist to cover the lower part of the body. 3. something like a skirt, as a flap hanging from the side of a saddle. 4. *pl.* the outer parts; border; edge; fringe; outskirts, as of a city. 5. [Slang], a girl or woman. *v.t.* 1. to lie along or form the border or edge of. 2. to move along the border or edge of; pass around instead of across or through, as a woods. 3. to border or edge (*with* something). *v.i.* to be on, or move along, the edge or border: as, the path *skirts* along the edge of the pond.

skit (skit), *n.* [< dial. v., to be skittish, taunt; prob. < Anglo-N. *skytja, var. of ON. *skjota,* to shoot (akin to Eng. *shoot*)], 1. a verbal slap; gibe. 2. a short piece of satirical or humorous writing. 3. a comic theatrical sketch, as in a revue.

skit·ter (skit′ẽr), *v.i.* [freq. of dial. *skit,* to dart about; of Scand. origin; ult. akin to *shoot*], 1. to skip or move along quickly and lightly, especially over water. 2. to draw a fish bait or lure over the surface of the water with a skipping motion. *v.t.* to cause to skitter.

skit·tish (skit′ish), *adj.* [< base of *skit* + *-ish*], 1. spirited; lively; playful, especially in a coy manner. 2. easily frightened; nervous; excitable; jumpy: as, a *skittish* horse. 3. fickle; undependable.

skit·tle (skit′′l), *n.* [prob. < the ON. cognate of *shuttle* with reference to the ball or projectile: cf. Dan. *skyttel,* a shuttle, marble, etc.], 1. the game of ninepins. 2. any of the pins used in this game.

(not) all beer and skittles, (not) pure pleasure and enjoyment.

skive (skīv), *v.t.* [SKIVED (skīvd), SKIVING], [ON. *skifa;* akin to Eng. *shive*], to slice or cut off (leather, rubber, etc.) in thin layers; shave; pare.

skiv·er (skīv′ẽr), *n.* 1. a soft, thin leather made from the outer half of split sheepskin and used for bookbindings, hat linings, etc. 2. a person who skives leather. 3. a cutting device used in skiving leather.

skiv·vy (skiv′i), *n.* [*pl.* SKIVVIES (-iz)], [< dial. *skivie,* silly, awry; Scot. Gael. *skaivie,* askew; ON. *skeifr,* crooked], [Slang], a man's, especially a sailor's, undershirt or, *pl.,* underwear.

skoal (skōl), *interj.* [Dan. & Norw. *skaal,* a cup < ON. *skāl,* a bowl], to your health!: a toast.

Skop·lje (skôp′lye), *n.* a city in southeastern Yugoslavia: pop., 68,000: Turkish name, *Üsküb.*

Skr., Skrt., Skt., Sanskrit.

sku·a (skū′ə), *n.* [adapted (c. 1604) < Faroese *skūgver* < ON. *skūfr;* prob. so called from the dark color], any of several large, brown, northern sea birds related to the gulls; jaeger: they rob other birds of their food: also **skua gull.**

skul·dug·ger·y (skul-dug′ẽr-i), *n.* [Early Mod. Scot. *sculdudrie;* formation < OFr. *escoulourgie, a slipping < *escoulourgier* (LL. *excollubricare; cf. LUBRICATE), to slip; sense development: fornication—obscenity—rascality—trickery], [Colloq.], mean trickery; craftiness.

skulk (skulk), *v.i.* [ME. *sculken* (prob. < ON.); cf. Dan. *skulke,* to skulk; for prob. IE. base see SCOWL], 1. to move or lurk about in a stealthy, craven manner; slink. 2. to avoid work or responsibility; shirk; malinger. *n.* a person who skulks. —*SYN.* see **lurk.**

skull (skul), *n.* [ME. *scolle* < Scand.; cf. Norw. dial. *skol, skul,* shell (of an egg or nut)], 1. the bony framework of the head, enclosing and protecting the brain. 2. the head regarded as the seat of thought or intelligence: usually with allusion to stupidity, dullness, etc., as, thick *skull,* empty *skull.*

PARIETAL
FRONTAL
SPHENOID
NASAL
OCCIPITAL BONE
SUPERIOR MAXILLARY
TEMPORAL BONE
INFERIOR MAXILLARY
AUDITORY CANAL
MALAR
MASTOID

SKULL

skull and cross-bones, a human skull facing forward with two long bones crossed beneath it, as formerly pictured on pirates' flags: now used as a warning sign, as in labeling poisons.

skull·cap (skul′kap′), *n.* a light, close-fitting, brimless cap, usually worn indoors.

skunk (skuŋk), *n.* [contr. < Am. Ind. (Abnaki) *segonku*] 1. [*pl.* SKUNKS (skuŋks), SKUNK; see PLURAL, II, D, 1], a bushy-tailed mammal about the size of a cat: it has glossy black fur, usually with white stripes down its back, and ejects an offensive-smelling, musky liquid when molested. 2. [Colloq.], a despicable offensive person. *v.t.* [Slang], to defeat overwhelmingly and keep from scoring in a game or contest.

SKUNK (about 2 ft. long)

skunk cabbage, a plant with thick roots, wide leaves and a disagreeable smell.

skunk·weed (skuŋk′wēd′), *n.* skunk cabbage.

sky (skī), *n.* [*pl.* SKIES (skiz)], [ME. *ski, skei;* ON. *sky* cloud; akin to AS. *sceo,* a cloud; IE. base *squeu-, to cover, hide, seen also in L. *obscurus* (cf. OBSCURE), Eng. *shower*], 1. *often pl.* the upper atmosphere, especially with reference to its appearance: as, blue *skies,* a cloudy *sky.* 2. the expanse of the heavens, apparently arching over the earth; firmament. 3. heaven; celestial regions. 4. climate; weather: as, the balmy southern *sky.* 5. [Obs.], a cloud. *v.t.* [SKIED or SKYED (skīd), SKYING], [Colloq.], 1. to hit, throw, shoot, etc. high in the air. 2. to hang (a picture) high up on the wall, especially in an exhibition.

out of a clear sky, without warning; suddenly.

to the skies, without reserve; extravagantly.

sky-blue (skī′blōō′), *adj.* of the color sky blue.

sky blue, a blue color like that of the sky on a clear day.

Skye (skī), *n.* an island in the Hebrides, Scotland: area 670 sq. mi.; pop., 9,900.

Skye terrier (skī), [after the Isle of *Skye,* off the coast of Scotland], a small dog of the terrier breed, with shaggy hair, a long body, and short legs.

SKYE TERRIER (9 in. high at shoulder)

sky·ey (skī′i), *adj.* [Poetic], 1. of or like the sky, as a shade of blue. 2. of great height; lofty.

sky-high (skī′hī′), *adj. & adv.* of or to a great height; very high.

sky·lark (skī′lärk′), *n.* the Old World lark, famous for the song it utters as it soars toward the sky. *v.i.* [prob. *sky* + *lark,* to play: orig. naut., of playing in the rigging], to play about boisterously; frolic.

sky·light (skī′līt′), *n.* a window in a roof or ceiling.

sky·line (skī′līn′), *n.* 1. the line along which the sky seems to touch the earth; visible horizon. 2. the outline, as of a city, seen against the sky. Also **sky line.**

sky pilot, [Slang], 1. a clergyman, chaplain, or missionary. 2. an aviator.

sky·rock·et (skī′rok′it), *n.* a firework rocket that explodes in mid-air, giving off a display of colored flames, sparks, etc. *v.i.* [Colloq.], to rise rapidly, as a driven ball, prices, etc.

Sky·ros (skē′rôs), *n.* an island in the northern Sporades in the Aegean Sea: area, 80 sq. mi.; pop., 3,000.

sky·sail (skī′sāl′, skī′s′l), *n.* the small sail set above the royal at the top of a square-rigged mast: see **sail,** illus.

sky·scrap·er (skī′skrāp′ẽr), *n.* a very tall building.

sky·ward (skī′wẽrd), *adv.* toward the sky. *adj.* moving or leading toward the sky.

sky·wards (skī′wẽrdz), *adv.* skyward.

sky·ways (skī′wāz′), *n.pl.* routes of air travel; air lanes.

sky·writ·er (skī′rīt′ẽr), *n.* an aviator skilled in sky writing.

sky·writ·ing (skī′rīt′iŋ), *n.* the act or process of tracing words, figures, etc. in the sky by trailing smoke from an airplane in flight.

s.l., *sine loco,* [L.], without place.

slab (slab), *n.* [ME. *sclabbe* (prob. a blend of OFr. *esclape,* a splinter + a word connected with *slab, adj.*)], 1. a piece that is flat, broad, and fairly thick: as, a *slab* of concrete. 2. a half-curved piece cut from the outside of a log in sawing planks. 3. [Slang], in *baseball,* the pitcher's plate. *v.t.* [SLABBED (slabd), SLABBING], 1. to make into a slab or slabs. 2. to cut the slabs from (a log). 3. to pave or cover with slabs.

slab (slab), *adj.* [prob. < ON. *slabb,* mud, mire; cf. prec.], [Archaic], thick and heavy; viscid: as, *slab* porridge.

slab·ber (slab′ẽr), *v.i. & v.t., n.* slobber.

slab-sid·ed (slab′sīd′id), *adj.* [Colloq.], 1. flat-sided. 2. tall and slender; lank.

slack (slak), *adj.* [ME. *slakke;* AS. *slæc;* akin to ON. *slak;* IE. base *(s)lēg-, etc., loose, slack, seen also in L. *laxus* (cf. LAX)], 1. slow; idle; sluggish. 2. barely moving: said of a current, as of air or water. 3. characterized by little work, trade, or business; not busy or active; dull: as, a *slack* period. 4. loose; relaxed; n tight, taut, or firm; hence, 5. easily changed or influenced; weak; lax. 6. careless; neglectful; indifferent: as, a *slack* workman, *slack* bookkeeping. *v.t.* 1. to make slack; slacken. 2. to slake. *v.i.* to be or become slack; slacken. *adv.* in a slack manner; so as to be slack. *n.* 1. a part that is slack or hangs loose. 2. a lack of tension or tautness; looseness: as, there was *slack* in the rope. 3. a stoppage of movement in a current. 4. a time of little activity; dull period; lull. 5. in *prosody*, the unstressed syllable or syllables within a foot, especially in sprung rhythm. —*SYN.* see **remiss.**

slack off, to slacken.

slack up, to go more slowly.

slack (slak), *n.* [ME. *sleck, slacke* < MLG. or MD.; cf. D. *slak*, earlier Fl. *slecke*, dross; see SLAG], a mixture of small pieces of coal, coal dust, and dirt left from the screening of coal.

slack (slak), *n.* [ON. *slakki*], [Scot. & British Dial.], 1. *a)* a small valley; dell. *b)* a hollow in the ground or in a hillside. 2. a boggy hollow; morass.

slack·en (slak'ən), *v.i.* [< *slack, adj.*], 1. to become less active, intense, etc. 2. to become slower or less brisk, as trade, etc. 3. to become less tense; loosen, as rope. *v.t.* 1. to reduce the intensity or severity of; retard; abate; moderate. 2. to reduce the tension of; relax; loosen. —*SYN.* see **delay.**

slack·er (slak'ẽr), *n.* a person who evades duties and responsibilities; especially, one who evades military service in time of war.

slacks (slaks), *n.pl.* full-cut trousers for casual wear by men and women.

slack water, 1. the period between tides when the water is neither in ebb nor flood. 2. any stretch of water having little or no current.

slag (slag), *n.* [< MLG. *slagge;* akin to G. *schlacke* & var. of *slack, n.;* prob. IE. base ***slak-**, to strike, seen also in Eng. *slay;* prob. basic sense "what is struck away (in metalworking)"], 1. the fused refuse or dross separated from a metal in the process of smelting. 2. lava resembling this. *v.t.* & *v.i.* [SLAGGED (slagd), SLAGGING], to change or form into slag.

slag·gy (slag'i), *adj.* of or like slag.

slain (slān), past participle of **slay.**

slake (slāk), *v.t.* [SLAKED (slākt), SLAKING], [ME. *slakien;* AS. *slacian* < *slæc*, slack; cf. SLACK, *adj.*], 1. to allay or make less active or intense by satisfying, as thirst, desire, etc.; assuage; satisfy. 2. to cause (a fire) to die down or go out. 3. to produce a chemical change in (lime) by combination with water: slaked lime is calcium hydroxide. 4. [Obs.], to lessen, reduce, or relieve. 5. [Obs.], to lessen the tension of. *v.i.* 1. to become slaked or undergo slaking, as lime, thirst, etc. 2. to become less active or intense; slacken.

sla·lom (slä'lŏm), *n.* [Norw.], a downhill skiing race over a zigzag course marked by posts, etc. *v.i.* to ski in or as in a slalom.

slam (slam), *v.t.* [SLAMMED (slamd), SLAMMING], [prob. < ON. via Brit. dial.; cf. Norw. dial. *slamra, slemma*], 1. to shut or allow to shut with force and noise: as, don't *slam* the door. 2. to hit, throw, or put in place with force and noise: as, he *slammed* the box into the cupboard. 3. [Colloq.], to criticize severely. *v.i.* to shut, go into place, etc. with force and noise. *n.* 1. a heavy, noisy impact, shutting, etc. 2. the noise made by this. 3. [Colloq.], severe criticism.

slam (slam), *n.* [< prec., with reference to its finality in the game], in *card games*, 1. the winning of all the tricks in one deal, as in whist: in bridge, called *grand slam*, or when one trick short of this, *little slam*. 2. an old card game resembling ruff.

slam-bang (slam'baŋ'), *adv.* [Colloq.], swiftly or abruptly and with loud noise.

slan·der (slan'dẽr), *n.* [ME. *sclaunder;* Anglo-Fr. *esclaundre* (OFr. *esclandre, escandle*); LL. *scandalum;* see SCANDAL], 1. the utterance or spreading of a false statement or statements, harmful to another's character or reputation: legally, *slander* is spoken, as distinguished from *libel*, which is written. 2. such a statement. *v.t.* to make a slanderous statement about.

slan·der·ous (slan'dẽr-əs), *adj.* [ME. *sclaunderous;* cf. OFr. *esclandreux*], 1. characterized by or constituting slander. 2. uttering or spreading slander.

slang (slaŋ), *n.* [< 18th-c. cant; Norw. *slengjeord*, slang term & *slengjenamn*, nickname, suggest deriv. < Continental cognate of Eng. *sling;* cf. phr. *sling language;* a cant clipped form < sling *language*], 1. originally, the specialized vocabulary and idioms of criminals, tramps, etc., the purpose of which was to disguise from outsiders the meaning of what was said: now usually called *cant*. 2. the specialized vocabulary and idioms of those in the same work, way of life, etc.: now usually called *shoptalk, argot, jargon*. 3. colloquial language that is outside of conventional or standard usage and consists of both coined words (*blurb, whoopee*) and those with new or extended meanings (*rubberneck, sap*): slang develops from the attempt to find fresh and vigorous, colorful, pungent, or humorous expression, and generally either passes into disuse or comes to have a more formal status. *v.i.* to use slang or abusive talk. *v.t.* to address with slang or abusive talk.

slang (slaŋ), dialectal and archaic past tense of **sling.**

slang·i·ly (slaŋ'ə-li), *adv.* in a slangy manner; with slang.

slang·i·ness (slaŋ'i-nis), *n.* the quality of being slangy.

slang·y (slaŋ'i), *adj.* [SLANGIER (-i-ẽr), SLANGIEST (-i-ist)], 1. of, having the nature of, or containing slang. 2. given to using slang.

slank (slaŋk), archaic past tense of **slink.**

slant (slant), *v.t.* & *v.i.* [ME. *slenten*, to glide, slope; prob. < ON.; cf. Norw. *slenta*, to fall sideways], 1. to incline or turn from a direct line or course, especially one that is perpendicular or level; slope. 2. [Colloq.], to write or tell so as to express a particular bias or attitude. *n.* 1. an oblique or inclined surface, line, direction, etc.; slope; incline. 2. [Colloq.], a point of view; attitude; opinion; bias. 3. [Colloq.], a glance; quick look. *adj.* [prob. short for *on slante*, aslant, hence of same origin as the *v.*], oblique; sloping; inclined.

slant·ways (slant'wāz'), *adv.* slantwise.

slant·wise (slant'wīz'), *adv.* so as to slant or slope; slantingly; obliquely. *adj.* slanting; oblique.

slap (slap), *n.* [LG. *sklapp;* of echoic origin], 1. a blow or smack, especially with something flat, as the palm of the hand. 2. an injury to pride, self-respect, etc.; insult; rebuff. *v.t.* [SLAPPED (slapt), SLAPPING], 1. to strike with something flat, as the palm of the hand. 2. to put, throw, hit, etc. carelessly or with force: as, she *slapped* the butter into the pan. *adv.* [Colloq.], 1. suddenly; abruptly. 2. straight; directly: as, he ran *slap* into the wall. —*SYN.* see **strike.**

slap-bang (slap'baŋ'), *adj.* & *adv.* [Colloq.], slapdash.

slap·dash (slap'dash'), *n.* 1. carelessness; abruptness. 2. something done carelessly and hastily: as, his book is mere *slapdash*. *adv.* in a hasty, careless manner; haphazardly. *adj.* hasty, careless, impetuous, etc.

slap-hap·py (slap'hap'i), *adj.* [Slang], 1. dazed or mentally impaired by or as by blows on the head; punch-drunk. 2. foolish; silly.

slap·jack (slap'jak'), *n.* 1. a pancake or griddlecake; flapjack. 2. a simple card game.

slap·per (slap'ẽr), *n.* a person or thing that slaps.

slap·stick (slap'stik'), *n.* 1. an implement made of two flat pieces of wood that slap together loudly when hit against something: formerly used by stage comedians to increase the sound of a blow. 2. crude comedy in which the humor depends upon violent activity, horseplay, etc. *adj.* characterized by such comedy.

slash (slash), *v.t.* [ME. *slaschen;* ? < OFr. *esclachier*, to break, but influenced by *lash*], 1. to cut or wound with sweeping strokes or blows, as of a knife. 2. to gash: as, he fell on the broken glass and *slashed* his arm. 3. to whip viciously; lash; scourge. 4. to cut slits in (a fabric, dress, etc.), especially so as to expose underlying material, usually of another color. 5. to reduce drastically: as, our budget has been *slashed*. 6. to criticize severely. *v.i.* to make a sweeping stroke or strokes with or as with something sharp; cut or criticize violently. *n.* 1. a sweeping stroke made with a knife, etc. 2. a cut made by or as by such a stroke; gash; slit. 3. an ornamental slit in a fabric, dress, etc. 4. *a)* an open place in a forest, cluttered with branches, chips, or other debris, as from the cutting of timber. *b)* such debris or trimmings.

slash (slash), *n.* [< Brit. dial. *slash*, boggy hollow & *slashy*, swampy; prob. < AS. *slæc*, slack, with palatalized final consonant, but associated with *slosh* & *slush* via echoism], a low, swampy area, usually covered with brush.

slash·ing (slash'iŋ), *adj.* 1. severe; merciless; violent. 2. dashing; spirited. 3. [Colloq.], immense; tremendous: as, a *slashing* success. *n.* a slash.

slash pine, 1. *a)* a kind of pine growing in slashes, or swamps. *b)* its wood. 2. the loblolly pine.

Śląsk (shlônsk), *n.* Silesia: the Polish name.

slat (slat), *n.* [ME. *sclat;* OFr. *esclat*, a fragment < *esclater*, to splinter], a thin, narrow strip of wood, metal, etc.; lath: as, *slats* of a bedstead. *v.t.* [SLATTED (-id), SLATTING], to provide or make with slats.

slat (slat), *v.i.* [SLATTED (-id), SLATTING], [ME. *sclatten*, as if < *sclat* (cf. SLAT, *n.*); prob. partly echoic], to flap or beat vigorously, as clothes blowing on a line. *v.t.* [Dial.], 1. to throw forcefully. 2. to beat; strike. *n.* [Dial.], a sharp blow.

S. Lat., south latitude.

slate (slāt), *n.* [OFr. *esclate*, fem. of *esclat;* see SLAT (lath)], 1. a kind of hard, fine-grained rock that cleaves naturally into thin, smooth-surfaced layers. 2. a thin piece of slate or slatelike material, especially one used as a roofing tile or as a tablet for writing on with chalk. 3. the bluish-gray color of most slate.

4. a list of candidates proposed for nomination or election. *v.t.* [SLATED (-id), SLATING], 1. to cover with slate. 2. to put on a list or designate, as for candidacy, appointment, theatrical engagement, etc.

a clean slate, a record showing no marks of discredit, dishonor, etc.; clean record.

slate (slāt), *v.t.* [SLATED (-id), SLATING], [Anglo-Ir. < the notion of hurling slate, or rocks], [Colloq.], 1. to punish severely; abuse. 2. to scold or criticize harshly.

slat·er (slāt'ẽr), *n.* 1. a person who lays slate roofs, etc. 2. a wood louse.

slath·er (sla*th*'ẽr), *n.* [dial., to slither; var. of north Brit. dial. *slither*, large quantity of loose stones < *slither*, to slip], *usually in pl.* [Dial. or Colloq.], a large quantity; lot. *v.t.* [Dial. or Colloq.], to use a lot of.

slat·ing (slāt'iŋ), *n.* 1. the act or craft of laying slates. 2. slates collectively, as a material for roofing, etc.

slat·tern (slat'ẽrn), *n.* [prob. < dial. *slatter*, to spill, slop, waste], a woman who is careless and untidy in her habits, appearance, work, etc.; slut.

slat·tern·li·ness (slat'ẽrn-li-nis), *n.* a slatternly state or quality.

slat·tern·ly (slat'ẽrn-li), *adj.* 1. having the habits of a slattern; dirty; slovenly; untidy. 2. characteristic of or fit for a slattern. *adv.* in a slatternly manner.

slat·ting (slat'iŋ), *n.* 1. slats collectively. 2. material for making slats.

slat·y (slāt'i), *adj.* [SLATIER (-i-ẽr), SLATIEST (-i-ist)], 1. of or like slate. 2. slate-colored.

slaugh·ter (slô'tẽr), *n.* [ME. *slahter;* ON. *slātr*, lit., slain flesh < base seen in Eng. *slay*], 1. the killing of an animal or animals for food; butchering. 2. the killing of a human being, especially in a brutal manner. 3. the killing of people in large numbers, as in battle. *v.t.* 1. to kill (an animal or animals) for food; butcher. 2. to kill (people), especially brutally or in large numbers.

SYN.—**slaughter,** as applied to people, suggests extensive and brutal killing, as in battle or by deliberate acts of wanton cruelty; **massacre** implies the indiscriminate and wholesale slaughter of those who are defenseless or helpless to resist; **butchery** adds implications of extreme cruelty and of such cold-blooded heartlessness as one might display in the slaughtering of animals; **carnage** stresses the result of bloody slaughter and suggests the accumulation of the bodies of the slain; **pogrom** refers to an organized, often officially inspired, massacre of a minority group, specifically of the Jews in Czarist Russia.

slaugh·ter·house (slô'tẽr-hous'), *n.* a place where animals are butchered for food; abattoir.

slaugh·ter·ous (slô'tẽr-əs), *adj.* brutally destructive or murderous.

Slav (släv, slav), *n.* [G. *Slave*, ML. *Slavus;* see SLAVE], a member of any of a group of peoples of eastern, southeastern, and central Europe, generally divided into Eastern Slavs (Great Russians, Ukrainians, and Byelorussians), Southern Slavs (Serbs, Croats, Bulgars, Slovenes, Slavonians, etc.), and Western Slavs (Czechs, Poles, Slovaks, Moravians, etc.). *adj.* Slavic.

Slav., 1. Slavic. 2. Slavonian. 3. Slavonic.

slave (slāv), *n.* [OFr. *esclave;* ML. *Sclavus, Slavus*, Slav < LGr. *Sklabos;* ult. < OSlav. *Slověne, slovo*, a word: first applied to captives of Slavic origin in southeastern Europe], 1. a human being who is owned by and absolutely subject to another human being, as by capture, purchase, or birth; bond servant divested of all freedom and personal rights. 2. a person who is completely dominated by some influence, habit, etc.: as, *slaves* to fashion. 3. a person who slaves; drudge. 4. a slave ant. *v.i.* [SLAVED (slāvd), SLAVING], to work like a slave; drudge; toil. *v.t.* [Rare], to enslave.

slave ant, any ant captured by and forced to work for ants of other species.

Slave Coast, the west African coast between the Volta and Benin rivers, on the Gulf of Guinea: former center of the African slave trade.

slave driver, 1. a person who directs or oversees the work of slaves. 2. any merciless taskmaster.

slave·hold·er (slāv'hōl'dẽr), *n.* a person who owns slaves.

slave·hold·ing (slāv'hōl'diŋ), *adj.* that has or owns slaves. *n.* possession or ownership of slaves.

slave-mak·ing ant (slāv'māk'iŋ), an ant belonging to a species that enslaves other ants: also **slave maker.**

slav·er (slav'ẽr), *v.i.* [ME. *slaveren;* prob. < ON. *slafra;* akin to *slobber*], to let saliva, etc. run or dribble from the mouth; drool. *v.t.* to slobber on or cover with saliva. *n.* 1. saliva drooling from the mouth. 2. nonsense; humbug; drivel.

slav·er (slāv'ẽr), *n.* 1. a slave ship. 2. a person who deals in slaves; slave hunter or trader.

slav·er·y (slāv'ẽr-i), *n.* 1. the owning or keeping of slaves as a practice or institution; slaveholding. 2. the condition of a slave; bondage; servitude. 3. a condition of submission to or domination by some influence, habit, etc. 4. hard, continuous work like that done by slaves; drudgery. —*SYN.* see **servitude.**

slave ship, a ship for carrying people to a place where they are to be sold as slaves.

Slave States, Alabama, Arkansas, Delaware, Florida, Georgia, Kentucky, Louisiana, Maryland, Mississippi, Missouri, North Carolina, South Carolina, Tennessee, Texas, and Virginia: in these fifteen states slavery was legal before the Civil War.

slave trade, traffic in slaves; specifically, the former transportation of African Negroes to America for sale as slaves.

slav·ey (slāv'i), *n.* [*pl.* SLAVEYS (-iz)], [British Colloq.], a woman or girl who is a domestic servant, especially one who does hard, menial work.

Slav·ic (släv'ik, slav'ik), *adj.* of the Slavs, their languages, etc.; Slavonic. *n.* a major subbranch of the Indo-European family of languages, generally divided into West Slavic (Polish, Sorbian, Czech, and Slovak), South Slavic (Old Church Slavonic, Bulgarian, Serbo-Croatian, and Slovene), and East Slavic (Russian, or Great Russian; Ukrainian, or Little Russian; and Byelorussian, or White Russian).

Slav·i·cism (släv'ə-siz'm, slav'ə-siz'm), *n.* Slavism.

slav·ish (slāv'ish), *adj.* 1. of or characteristic of a slave or slaves; hopelessly submissive; servile. 2. of or characteristic of slavery; oppressive; despotic. 3. blindly dependent or imitative: as, *slavish* adherence to a model. —*SYN.* see **servile.**

Slav·ism (släv'iz'm, slav'iz'm), *n.* the characteristics, interests, culture, etc. common to all Slavs.

Sla·vo- (slä'vō, slav'ə), a combining form meaning *Slav*

slav·oc·ra·cy (slāv-ok'rə-si), *n.* [*pl.* SLAVOCRACIES (-siz)], [< *slave* + *-cracy*], in the United States before 1865 slaveholders and pro-slavery forces as a dominant or powerful class.

Sla·vo·ni·a (slə-vō'ni-ə), *n.* a region of the Balkans, now in northern Yugoslavia.

Sla·vo·ni·an (slə-vō'ni-ən), *adj.* 1. of Slavonia or its people. 2. Slavic. *n.* 1. a native or inhabitant of Slavonia. 2. a Slav. 3. the Slavic language group.

SLAVONIA

Sla·von·ic (slə-von'ik), *adj.* 1. Slavonian. 2. Slavic. *n.* the Slavic language group.

Slav·o·phil (släv'ə-fil, slav'ō-fil), *n.* a Slavophile.

Slav·o·phile (släv'ə-fīl', slav'ə-fil), *n.* [*Slavo-* + *-phile*], a person who admires or is very fond of th[e] Slavs, their customs, culture, etc. *adj.* of Slavophile[s].

Slav·o·phobe (släv'ə-fōb', slav'ə-fōb'), *n.* a person wh[o] has Slavophobia. *adj.* of Slavophobes.

Slav·o·pho·bi·a (släv'ə-fō'bi-ə, slav'ə-fō'bi-ə), *n.* [*Slav[o-]* + *phobia*], hatred or fear of the Slavs, their cultur[e,] influence, etc.

Sla·voph·o·bist (slə-vof'ə-bist), *n.* a Slavophobe.

slaw (slô), *n.* [D. *sla, slaa*, contr. of Fr. *salade*, salad] shredded cabbage served as a salad.

slay (slā), *v.t.* [SLEW (slōō), SLAIN (slān), SLAYING], [M[E.] *slayn, sleen;* AS. *slean, slan* < **slahan;* akin to G. *schlagen;* IE. base **slak-*, to hit, as also in MIr. *slac[-]* sword], 1. to kill by violent means; bring death upo[n;] destroy. 2. [Obs.], to strike or hit. —*SYN.* see **kill.**

sld., 1. sailed. 2. sealed.

sleave (slēv), *n.* [< AS. *-slǣfan*, to separate; IE. ba[se] **sqel-*, to cut, as also in Eng. *slit*], 1. *a)* a fine si[lk] thread separated from a larger thread. *b)* untwiste[d] silk that tends to mat or tangle; floss. 2. any tangle, [as] of ravelings. *v.t.* [SLEAVED (slēvd), SLEAVING], to se[p]arate or pull apart, as twisted or tangled threads.

slea·zi·ness (slē'zi-nis, slā'zi-nis), *n.* a sleazy quality [or] condition.

slea·zy (slē'zi, slā'zi), *adj.* [SLEAZIER (-zi-ẽr), SLEAZIE[ST] (-zi-ist)], [< obs. *Sleasie*, cloth made in Silesia, Ge[r]many], flimsy or thin in texture or substance; lackin[g] firmness: as, a *sleazy* rayon fabric.

sled (sled), *n.* [ME. *sledde;* MLG. or MFl. *sledde;* akin [to] G. *schlitten;* for IE. base see SLIDE], any of several kin[ds] of vehicle mounted on runners for use on snow, ic[e,] etc.: small sleds are used in the sport of coasting, lar[ger] ones (also called *sledges*), for carrying loads. *v[.t.]* [SLEDDED (-id), SLEDDING], to carry on a sled. *v.i.* ride on a sled.

sled·der (sled'ẽr), *n.* 1. a person who rides or drives [a] sled. 2. an animal used for drawing a sled.

sled·ding (sled'iŋ), *n.* 1. a riding or carrying on a sle[d.] 2. the condition of the ground with reference to the u[se] of sleds; the going for sleds: often used figuratively, a[s,] the work was hard *sledding.*

sledge (slej), *n.* [ME. *slegge;* AS. *slecge* < base of *slea[n],* *slan*, to strike, slay; see SLAY], a long, heavy hamme[r,] usually used with both hands. *v.t. & v.i.* [SLEDG[ED]] (slejd), SLEDGING], to strike with or as with a sledg[e.]

sledge (slej), *n.* [MD. *sleedse;* akin to D. *slede*, ML[G.] *sledde;* but of Fris. origin], a sled or sleigh for carryi[ng] passengers or loads over ice, snow, etc. *v.i. & v*

[**SLEDGED** (slejd), **SLEDGING**], to go or take by sledge.
sledge-ham·mer (slej'ham'ẽr), ***v.t.*** 1. to hit with a sledge hammer. 2. to attack with force so as to have an overpowering effect upon. ***adj.*** crushingly destructive; forceful; powerful.
sledge hammer, a sledge (heavy hammer).
sleek (slēk), ***adj.*** [var. of *slick*, with Early Mod. Eng. lengthening of vowel; cf. CREEK], 1. smooth and shiny; glossy, as a highly polished surface, well-kept hair or fur, etc. 2. of well-fed or well-groomed appearance: as, fat, *sleek* pigeons. 3. polished in speech and behavior, especially in a way that does not seem genuine; unctuous; oily. ***v.t.*** to make sleek; smooth; polish.
sleek·y (slēk'i), ***adj.*** sleek.
sleep (slēp), ***n.*** [ME. *slep*; AS. *slæp*; akin to G. *schlaf*, sleep, *schlaff*, loose, lax; IE. **slab* < base **leb-*, *lab-*, etc., loose, slack, seen also in L. *labor* (*lapsus*), to slip, sink (cf. LAPSE)], 1. *a*) a natural, regularly recurring condition of rest for the body and mind, during which there is little or no conscious thought, sensation, or movement. *b*) a period or occasion of sleeping. 2. any condition resembling sleep, as death, unconsciousness, hibernation, etc. 3. in *botany*, the tendency, as of petals or leaves, to assume a different position at night; nyctitropism. ***v.i.*** [**SLEPT** (slept), **SLEEPING**], 1. to be in the state of sleep; slumber. 2. to be in a condition resembling sleep, as that of death, quiescence, hibernation, etc. 3. in *botany*, to assume a different position at night, as petals or leaves. ***v.t.*** 1. to slumber in (a specified kind of sleep): as, he *slept* the sleep of the just. 2. [Colloq.], to provide sleeping accommodations for: as, this cabin will *sleep* four.
last sleep, death.
sleep away, 1. to spend in sleeping; sleep during. 2. to get rid of by sleeping.
sleep in, to sleep at the place where one is employed as a household servant.
sleep off, to rid oneself of by sleeping.
leep·er (slēp'ẽr), ***n.*** [ME. *slepere*; AS. *slæpere*], 1. a person or animal that sleeps, especially in a specified way: as, the man is a sound *sleeper*. 2. a timber or beam laid horizontally, as on the ground, to support something above it. 3. [British], a tie supporting a railroad track. 4. a railroad sleeping car. 5. a race horse, book, etc. that unexpectedly achieves a striking success.
leep·i·ly (slēp'ə-li), ***adv.*** in a sleepy or drowsy manner.
leep·i·ness (slēp'i-nis), ***n.*** a sleepy quality or state.
leeping bag, a large, warmly lined bag made to sleep in, especially out of doors.
leeping car, a railway car equipped with berths, compartments, etc. for passengers to sleep in.
leeping partner, [British], a silent partner.
leeping sickness, 1. an infectious disease, especially common in tropical Africa, caused by certain species of trypanosome that are transmitted by the bite of certain flies, especially the tsetse fly: it is characterized by fever, weakness, tremors, lethargy, and finally prolonged coma ending in death. 2. inflammation of the brain, caused by a virus and characterized by apathy, drowsiness, and lethargy: also called *encephalitis lethargica, epidemic encephalitis*.
leep·less (slēp'lis), ***adj.*** 1. with little or no sleep; wakeful; restless; unquiet. 2. alert at all times; constantly watchful. 3. constantly in action or motion; never at rest: as, the *sleepless* wind.
leep·walk·er (slēp'wôk'ẽr), ***n.*** a person who walks while asleep; somnambulist.
leep·walk·ing (slēp'wôk'iŋ), ***n.*** the act or practice of walking while asleep; somnambulism.
leep·y (slēp'i), ***adj.*** [**SLEEPIER** (-i-ẽr), **SLEEPIEST** (-i-ist)], 1. ready or inclined to sleep; needing sleep; drowsy. 2. characterized by an absence of activity; dull; idle; lethargic: as, a *sleepy* river town. 3. causing drowsiness; inducing sleep. 4. of or exhibiting drowsiness.
SYN.—**sleepy** applies to a person who is overcome by a desire o sleep and, figuratively, suggests either the power to induce leepiness or a resemblance to this state (a *sleepy* town, ong, etc.); **drowsy** stresses the sluggishness or lethargic heaviness accompanying sleepiness (the *drowsy* sentry fought ff sleep through his watch); **somnolent** is a formal equivalent f either of the preceding (the *somnolent* voice of the speaker); **lumberous,** a poetic equivalent, in addition sometimes sugests latent powers in repose (a *slumberous* city).
eep·y·head (slēp'i-hed'), ***n.*** a sleepy person.
eet (slēt), ***n.*** [ME. *slete*, *slet*; AS. **sliete*, **slete*; akin to G. *schlosse*, hail; IE. base **sleu-*, loose, lax; basic sense "soft, yielding"], 1. partly frozen rain, or rain that reezes as it falls. 2. a mixture of rain with snow or ail. 3. the icy coating formed when rain freezes on rees, streets, etc. ***v.i.*** to shower in the form of sleet.
eet·i·ness (slēt'i-nis), ***n.*** a sleety quality or condition.
eet·y (slēt'i), ***adj.*** [**SLEETIER** (-i-ẽr), **SLEETIEST** (-i-ist)], f, like, or characterized by sleet.
eeve (slēv), ***n.*** [ME. *sleve*; AS. *sliefe*, *slefe*; akin to MFris. *slēf*, *slīf*, sleeve; IE. base **sleub-*, to slide, slip, seen also in L. *lubricus* (cf. LUBRICATE)], 1. that part of a garment that covers an arm or part of an arm. 2. a tube or tubelike part fitting over or around another part. ***v.t.*** [**SLEEVED** (slēvd), **SLEEVING**], to provide or fit with a sleeve or sleeves.
laugh up (or **in**) **one's sleeve,** to laugh secretly to oneself while being outwardly serious.
up one's sleeve, hidden or secret but ready at hand.
sleeved (slēvd), ***adj.*** fitted with sleeves: often in hyphenated compounds, as *short-sleeved*.
sleeve·less (slēv'lis), ***adj.*** having no sleeves: as, a *sleeveless* sweater.
sleeve valve, a rotating, reciprocating sleeve between the piston and cylinder wall of some internal-combustion engines: the sleeve has two slots which open and close the fuel intake and exhaust ports in the cylinder wall.
sleigh (slā), ***n.*** [D. *slee*, contr. of *slede*, a sled or sledge], a light passenger vehicle on runners, used for travel on snow and ice. ***v.i.*** to ride in or drive a sleigh.
sleigh bells, a number of small bells fixed to the harness straps of an animal drawing a sleigh.
sleigh·ing (slā'iŋ), ***n.*** 1. a riding or carrying in a sleigh. 2. the condition of the snow that makes this possible: as, good *sleighing*.
sleight (slīt), ***n.*** [ME. *slehthe*; ON. *slœgth* < *slœgr*, crafty, clever (cf. SLY); hence *sleight* equals *sly* + *-th* (for the change *-t* < *-th* cf. HEIGHT)], 1. [Rare or Archaic], cunning or craft used in deceiving. 2. a clever act of deception; skillful trick or stratagem. 3. skill; deftness; dexterity.
sleight of hand, 1. skill with the hands, especially in confusing or deceiving onlookers, as in magic; legerdemain. 2. a trick or series of tricks thus performed.
slen·der (slen'dẽr), ***adj.*** [ME. *slendre*, *sclendre*; prob. < Anglo-Fr. *esclendre*, either < or via MD.; cf. obs. D. *slinder*], 1. small in width or girth for the length or height; long and thin; slim. 2. small or limited in amount, size, extent, etc.; meager: as, *slender* earnings. 3. of little force or validity; having slight foundation; feeble: as, *slender* hope. 4. lacking volume or fullness, as sound. 5. in *phonetics*, close. —***SYN.*** see **thin.**
slen·der·ize (slen'dẽr-īz'), ***v.t.*** & ***v.i.*** [**SLENDERIZED** (-īzd'), **SLENDERIZING**], to make or become slender.
slept (slept), past tense and past participle of **sleep.**
Sles·vig (sles'vikh), ***n.*** Schleswig: the Danish name.
sleuth (slōōth), ***n.*** [ME. *sloth* (mod. sp. < northern dial.); ON. *sloth*, a track, trail], 1. a sleuthhound. 2. [Colloq.], a detective. ***v.i.*** to act as a detective.
sleuth·hound (slōōth'hound'), ***n.*** 1. a dog, especially a bloodhound, that can follow a trail by scent. 2. [Colloq.], a detective.
slew (slōō), ***n.*** a slough (swamp).
slew (slōō), ***n.***, ***v.t.*** & ***v.i.*** slue (turn).
slew (slōō), ***n.*** [? akin to Ir. *sluagh*, a host], [Colloq.], a large number, group, or amount; lot: also spelled **slue.**
slew (slōō), past tense of **slay.**
Slez·sko (sles'kô), ***n.*** Silesia: the Czech name.
SLIC, S.L.I.C., (Federal) Savings and Loan Insurance Corporation.
slice (slīs), ***n.*** [ME.; OFr. *esclice* < *esclicier*, to slice < OHG. *slizan*, to split; akin to Eng. *slit*], 1. a relatively thin, broad piece cut from an object having some bulk or volume: as, a *slice* of apple. 2. a part, portion, or share: as, he spent a large *slice* of his winnings. 3. any of various implements with a flat, broad blade, used for turning food in a skillet, serving fish, etc. 4. a spatula for spreading printing ink. 5. in *golf*, a sliced stroke. ***v.t.*** [**SLICED** (slīst), **SLICING**], 1. to cut into slices. 2. *a*) to cut as a slice or slices (with *off*, *from*, *away*, or *out*). *b*) to cut across or through like a knife: as, the plow *sliced* the land. 3. to separate into parts or shares. 4. to use a slice (implement) or slice bar to work at, spread, remove, etc. 5. in *golf*, to cause (a ball) to curve to the right (for a right-handed player) or to the left (for a left-handed player) by hitting it with a glancing stroke. ***v.i.*** in *golf*, to slice a ball.
slice bar, an iron bar with a broad, thin end, used in a coal furnace to loosen coals, clear out ashes, etc.
slic·er (slīs'ẽr), ***n.*** 1. a tool or device used for slicing: as, a bread *slicer*. 2. a person who slices.
slick (slik), ***v.t.*** [ME. *slikien*; ? < ON. (cf. Ice. *slīkja*, to make smooth) but prob. < AS. *-slician*, lit., to smooth by hammering < *slic*, a mallet, hammer; IE. base **sleig-*, to strike, cut, seen also in L. *ligo*, hatchet], 1. to make sleek, glossy, or smooth. 2. [Colloq.], to make smart, neat, or tidy (usually with *up*). ***adj.*** [ME. *slike* < the *v.*], 1. sleek; glossy; smooth. 2. slippery; oily, as a surface. 3. accomplished; adept; clever; smart; ingenious. 4. [Colloq.], clever in deception or trickery; deceptively plausible; smooth: as, a *slick* alibi. 5. [Colloq.], having or showing skill in composition or technique but little depth or literary significance: as, a *slick* book, a *slick* style of writing. 6. [Slang], excellent; fine; enjoyable: as, it was a *slick*

meal. 7. [Slang], having a pleasing appearance; attractive. *n.* 1. a smooth area on the surface of water, as resulting from a film of oil. 2. something used for smoothing and polishing, as a kind of broad, flat chisel. 3. [Slang], a magazine printed on paper with a glossy finish: distinguished from *pulp*. *adv.* smoothly, cleverly, deftly, easily, etc.

slick·en·side (slik′'n-sīd′), *n.* [dial. *slicken*, var. of *slick* + *side*], *often in pl.* a smooth, polished rock surface produced by friction, pressure, or cleavage.

slick·er (slik′ẽr), *n.* [*slick, v.* or *adj.* + *-er*], 1. a loose, waterproof coat made of oil-treated cloth. 2. [Colloq.], a tricky, cleverly deceptive person.

slid (slid), past tense and alternative past participle of **slide.**

slid·den (slid′'n), alternative past participle of **slide.**

slide (slīd), *v.i.* [SLID (slid), SLID or SLIDDEN (slid′'n), SLIDING], [ME. *sliden;* AS. *slidan;* IE. base **(s)leidh*, slippery, prob. a deriv. < **(s)lei-*, slimy, as also in Eng. *slime*], 1. to move along in constant frictional contact with some surface or substance: as, the boxes *slide* across the deck, the car *slid* to a stop. 2. to move in this manner on a sled, the feet, etc. in contact with a smooth surface, as ice. 3. to move quietly and smoothly; glide. 4. to move stealthily or secretly: as, the cat *slid* around the corner. 5. to slip: as, the sword *slid* from his hand. 6. to slip or pass gradually into or out of some condition, habit, situation, etc. 7. in *baseball*, to drop down and slide along the ground toward a base to avoid being tagged out by the baseman. *v.t.* 1. to cause to slide; make move with a smooth, gliding motion. 2. to move, place, or introduce quietly or dexterously (usually with *in* or *into*). *n.* 1. an act of sliding. 2. a smooth, usually inclined track, surface, or trough used for sliding; chute: as, the children made a *slide* on the snow bank. 3. something that operates by sliding; sliding part. 4. a transparent plate bearing a picture for projection on a screen, as by a magic lantern. 5. a small glass plate used as a mounting for objects to be examined under a microscope. 6. *a*) the fall of a mass of rock, snow, earth, etc. down a slope. *b*) the mass that falls. 7. in *music*, *a*) a portamento. *b*) a U-shaped section of tubing which is moved to change the pitch of certain brass-wind instruments, especially the trombone. *c*) a grace or ornamentation made up of two or more notes leading to a main note.

let slide, to fail to take care of; neglect.

SYN.—**slide** implies easy movement, as over a smooth surface, and usually suggests continuous contact with it (to *slide* on ice, to *slide* back into old habits); **slip** more often implies that the surface is frictionless and the contact not continuous, therefore suggesting an involuntary movement or an accident (to *slip* and fall on the ice, her name *slipped* from his mind); **glide** suggests a flowing, smooth, easy, usually silent movement and continuous or intermittent contact with a surface (*gliding* dancers); **skid** means to slide or slip sideways and out of control, as a vehicle when not gripping an icy road.

slide fastener, a device used to fasten together or unfasten two adjoining edges of material, as on the fly of a sweater, the placket of a dress, etc.: it consists of two rows of small interlocking tabs which are joined or separated by the action of a part that slides up and down: also called *zipper*: cf. **zipper.**

slide knot, a kind of slipknot: see **knot,** illus.

Slide Mountain (slīd), the highest peak of the Catskills: height, 4,204 ft.

slide rule, an instrument consisting of a ruler with a central sliding piece, both being marked with logarithmic scales: used in making rapid mathematical calculations.

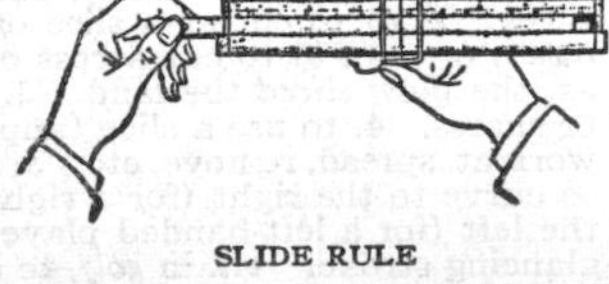

SLIDE RULE

slide trombone, a long brass-wind instrument having, instead of valves, a U-shaped tube which slides in and out, so that the length of the air column can be adjusted to vary the tone: see also **trombone.**

slide valve, a valve which opens and closes a passageway, as the cylinder port of a steam engine, by sliding back and forth across it.

slide·way (slīd′wā′), *n.* an inclined ramp, chute, etc. used as a slide.

slid·ing (slīd′iŋ), *adj.* 1. varying in accordance with given conditions; adjustable: as, a *sliding* rate of liability. 2. operating or moving on the principle of a slide, as a door or panel.

sliding scale, 1. a standard or schedule, as of rates, wages, etc., which varies with other conditions or standards. 2. a slide rule.

slight (slīt), *adj.* [ME. (northern dial.) *sliht, sleht* < Anglo-N. **sleht* (ON. *slēttr*); akin to G. *schlicht*, smooth; basic sense "sleek"], 1. light in form or build; not stout or heavy; slender. 2. frail; fragile. 3. lacking weight, strength, substance, or significance. 4. small in amount or extent; not great or intense: as, a *slight* fever. *v.t.* 1. to do carelessly or poorly; neglect. 2. to treat with disrespect or indifference; be discourteous toward. 3. to treat as unimportant. *n.* a slighting or being slighted by pointedly indifferent, disrespectful, or supercilious treatment. —*SYN.* see **neglect, thin.**

slight·ing (slīt′iŋ), *adj.* constituting or imparting a slight; discourteous; contemptuous.

slight·ly (slīt′li), *adv.* 1. in a slight manner. 2. to a slight degree.

Sli·go (slī′gō), *n.* 1. a county in northwestern Ireland, in Connaught province: area, 694 sq. mi.; pop., 67,000. 2. seaport and county seat of Sligo: pop., 13,000.

sli·ly (slī′li), *adv.* slyly.

slim (slim), *adj.* [SLIMMER (-ẽr), SLIMMEST (-ist)], [earlier, useless, bad, weak < D. *slim*, crafty, bad; akin to G. *schlimm*, bad; IE. base **slemb-*, fallen awry, crooked], 1. small in girth in proportion to height or length; slender. 2. small in amount, degree, or extent; slight; scant; meager: as, *slim* pickings, a *slim* possibility. 3. [Dial.], sly; crafty. *v.t. & v.i.* [SLIMMED (slimd), SLIMMING], to make or become slim. —*SYN.* see **thin.**

slime (slīm), *n.* [ME.; AS. *slim;* akin to G. *schleim;* IE. base **(s)lei-*, slimy, sticky; cf. SLIDE], 1. any soft, moist, slippery, sometimes sticky matter, as thin mud, the mucous coating on fish, etc. 2. any moist or sticky substance that is considered filthy or disgusting. *v.t.* [SLIMED (slīmd), SLIMING], 1. to cover with slime. 2. to clean slime from.

slime mold, any of the myxomycetes, a class of primitive organisms: also **slime fungus.**

slim·i·ly (slīm′ə-li), *adv.* in a slimy manner.

slim·i·ness (slīm′i-nis), *n.* the condition or quality of being slimy.

slimp·sy (slimp′si), *adj.* [SLIMPSIER (-si-ẽr), SLIMPSIEST (-si-ist)], slimsy.

slim·sy (slim′zi), *adj.* [SLIMSIER (-zi-ẽr), SLIMSIEST (-zi-ist)], [< *slim*, after *flimsy*], [Colloq.], slight; flimsy.

slim·y (slīm′i), *adj.* [SLIMIER (-i-ẽr), SLIMIEST (-i-ist)], 1. of or like slime. 2. covered with or composed of slime. 3. disgusting; repulsive; filthy.

sling (sliŋ), *n.* [ME. *slinge* < the *v.*], 1. a primitive instrument for throwing stones, etc., consisting of a piece of leather tied to cords that are whirled by hand for releasing the missile. 2. a slingshot. 3. the act of throwing with or as with a sling; cast; throw; fling. 4. a device, usually a supporting band or strap, used in raising and lowering a heavy object or for carrying something, as a rifle, from the shoulder. 5. a wide piece of cloth looped under an injured arm for support. *v.t.* [SLUNG (sluŋ), SLINGING; *dial. and archaic p.t.* SLANG (slaŋ)], [ME. *slingen;* AS. *slingan*, to twist oneself, worm along; present senses from twisting motion used in manipulating a sling; akin to G. *schlingen*, to twist; cf. SLINK (to move)], 1. to throw (stones, etc.) with a sling. 2. to throw, cast, fling, or hurl. 3. to raise, lower, or carry in a sling. 4. to hang loosely or in a sling; suspend, especially by several attachments, as a hammock.

sling (sliŋ), *n.* [cf. LG. *slingen*, G. *schlingen*, to swallow], an iced drink made with alcoholic liquor, water, sugar, and, usually, lemon juice.

sling·er (sliŋ′ẽr), *n.* 1. a man using a sling for throwing missiles, as in ancient warfare. 2. a person who throws or slings. 3. a person operating, or supervising the use of, a sling, as in loading.

sling·shot (sliŋ′shot′), *n.* a Y-shaped piece of wood, metal, etc. with an elastic band attached to the upper tips for shooting stones, etc.

slink (sliŋk), *v.i.* [SLUNK sluŋk), SLINKING; *archaic p.t.* SLANK (slaŋk)], [ME. *slinken;* AS. *slincan*, to creep, crawl along; akin to LG. *slinken;* IE. base **sleng-*, to wind, twist, turn, var. of **slenq-* seen in SLING, *v.*], to move in a quiet, furtive, or sneaking manner, as from fear, guilt, etc.; sneak. —*SYN.* see **lurk.**

slink (sliŋk), *v.t.* [SLINKED (sliŋkt) or SLUNK (sluŋk), SLINKING], [prob. < *sling*, to cast, fling], to give birth to before the normal time; expel (a fetus) prematurely: said of animals. *n.* an animal, especially a calf, born before the normal time. *adj.* born prematurely.

slink·y (sliŋ′ki), *adj.* [SLINKIER (-ki-ẽr), SLINKIEST (-ki-ist)], [*slink* (to move) + *-y*], 1. sneaking; stealthy; furtive. 2. [Slang], sinuous and graceful in movement, line, etc.

slip (slip), *v.i.* [SLIPPED or *archaic* or *poetic* SLIPT (slipt), SLIPPING], [ME. & MLG. *slippen;* akin to G. *schlüpfen*; IE. base **(s)leib-*, slimy, slippery < **lei-*, slimy, sliding (cf. LIME)], 1. to go quietly or secretly· move without attracting notice: as, he *slipped* out of the house. 2. *a*) to go, move, pass, etc. smoothly, quickly, or easily. *b*) to go imperceptibly; pass unmarked: as, time *slipped* by. 3. to pass gradually into or out of some condition, activity, habit, opinion, etc. 4. to escape or pass from a person's memory, mind, power, grasp, etc.: as, here is a chance you mustn't allow to *slip*. 5. to move out of place by sliding; shift or slide from position: as, the plate *slipped* from his hand, the child *slipped* off my knee. 6. to slide accidentally on a slippery surface, lose footing, etc. 7. to make a mistake; fall into error; err. 8. to become worse; lose strength, ability, mental keenness, etc.: as, he has been *slipping* for several years. 9. [Colloq.], to declin slightly; fall off: as, the market has *slipped.* ***v.t.*** 1. to cause to slip or move with a smooth, sliding motion: as, he *slipped* the bolt through the hole. 2. to put (*on*) or take (*off*) quickly or easily, as an article of clothing. 3. to put, pass, insert, etc. quickly, deftly, or stealthily: as, she *slipped* a pill into her mouth, he *slipped* in a cutting remark. 4. *a*) to escape or pass from (the mind or memory). *b*) to let pass unheeded; overlook; miss. 5. to get loose from; become free of (some restraining device): as, the prisoner has *slipped* his bonds. 6. to let loose: said of hounds freed for the pursuit of game. 7. to transfer (a stitch) from one needle to another without knitting it, as in forming patterns in, or decreasing the width of, a knitted piece. 8. to slink (a fetus). ***n.*** 1. *a*) a pier or platform sloping into the water to serve as a landing place. *b*) an inclined plane leading down to water, on which ships are built or repaired. *c*) a space between piers or wharves, used for the docking of ships. 2. the difference between the actual speed of a vessel and the speed at which it would move if the propeller were acting against a solid. 3. a leash for a dog or other animal. 4. a woman's undergarment, generally about the length of a dress. 5. a child's dress or pinafore. 6. a covering, as for a pillow, that can be easily put on or taken off. 7. an act of slipping, sliding, or falling down. 8. a deviation or turning aside, especially from a practice, course of conduct, etc. considered beneficial or proper; hence, 9. an error or mistake, especially one made inadvertently in speaking, writing, etc. 10. an accident or mishap. 11. the amount or degree of operative inefficiency of a mechanical device, expressed in terms of the difference between theoretical and actual output. 12. movement of one part upon another where no movement is meant to exist; play. 13. a cleavage and displacement in a rock mass or strata. 14. in *cricket,* a fielder placed behind the wickets on the off side of the batter. —***SYN.*** see **error, slide.**

give one the slip, to evade or escape from one.

let slip, to say or tell without intending to.

slip a cog, [Colloq.], 1. to make a mistake. 2. to undergo a mishap; go wrong; miscarry.

slip over, to pass over (a matter, etc.) superficially or without adequate attention.

slip one over on, [Colloq.], to trick; hoodwink; cheat.

slip up, [Colloq.], 1. to make a mistake; be in error. 2. to undergo a mishap; miscarry.

slip (slip), *n.* [ME. *slippe;* MD. *slippe* < *slippen,* to cut], 1. a stem, root, twig, etc. cut or broken off a plant and used for planting or grafting; cutting; scion. 2. a young person, especially one who is small or slender. 3. any slender person: as, she's a mere *slip* of a woman. 4. a long, thin piece or strip, as of wood. 5. a small piece of paper, especially one prepared for a specific use: as, an order *slip.* 6. a narrow church pew. ***v.t.*** [SLIPPED (slipt), SLIPPING], to take a slip from (a plant) for planting or grafting.

slip (slip), *n.* [ME.; AS. *slypa,* a paste, slime; IE. base **sleub-,* to glide, slip, seen also in L. *lubricus,* slippery (cf. LUBRICATE), Eng. *sloove*], in *ceramics,* clay thinned to the consistency of cream for use in decorating or casting, or as a cement or coating.

slip cover, a removable, fitted cloth cover for an armchair, sofa, etc.

slip·knot (slip'not'), *n.* a knot made so that it will slip along the rope, etc. around which it is tied; running knot: also **slip knot:** see **knot,** illus.

slip noose, a noose made with a slip knot.

slip-on (slip'on'), *adj.* 1. easily put on or taken off. 2. to be put on and taken off over the head: said of garments. *n.* a slip-on garment, as a sweater.

slip·o·ver (slip'ō'vẽr), *n. & adj.* slip-on.

slip·page (slip'ij), *n.* [see -AGE], 1. a slipping, as of one gear past another. 2. the amount of this. 3. the resulting loss of motion or power, as in a chain drive.

slip·per (slip'ẽr), *n.* a kind of light, low shoe that may be easily slipped on: as, bedroom *slippers.*

slip·pered (slip'ẽrd), *adj.* wearing slippers.

slip·per·i·ness (slip'ẽr-i-nis, slip'ri-nis), *n.* the state or quality of being slippery.

slip·per·y (slip'ẽr-i, slip'ri), *adj.* [SLIPPERIER (-i-ẽr, -ri-ẽr), SLIPPERIEST (-i-ist, -ri-ist)], [Early Mod. Eng. < ME. *sliper,* slippery; AS. *slipur;* prob. after MD. or MLG.; cf. LG. *slipperig;* for IE. base see SLIP, *v.*], 1. causing or liable to cause sliding or slipping, as wet, waxed, or greasy surfaces. 2. tending to slip away, as from a grasp or hold. 3. evasive; shifty; deceitful; not reliable or trustworthy. 4. [Obs.], immoral.

slippery elm, 1. a wide-spreading hardwood tree with fragrant, sticky inner bark. 2. the bark, used as a demulcent.

slip·py (slip'i), *adj.* [Dial. or Colloq.], slippery.

slip ring, one of two or more continuous rings by means of which current is conducted to or from the brushes in a motor or dynamo.

slip·sheet (slip'shēt'), *n.* a blank sheet of paper inserted between freshly printed sheets to prevent offset. ***v.t. & v.i.*** to insert slipsheets between (printed sheets).

slip·shod (slip'shod'), *adj.* [*slip, v.* + *shod,* after dial. or obs. *slip-shoe,* a slipper], 1. wearing shoes with worn-down heels. 2. generally careless, as in appearance, performance of duty, style, etc. —***SYN.*** see **slovenly.**

slip·slop (slip'slop'), *n.* [redupl. of *slop*], [Colloq.], 1. cheap, weak liquor; slops. 2. shallow, pointless talk or writing; twaddle.

slip stream, the current of air thrust backward by the spinning propeller of an aircraft; propeller wash.

slipt (slipt), archaic or poetic past tense of **slip.**

slip-up (slip'up'), *n.* [Colloq.], an error; oversight.

slip·way (slip'wā'), *n.* a slope or incline leading into the water, as in a shipyard.

slit (slit), *v.t.* [SLIT, SLITTING], [ME. *slitten,* new formation < *sliten* < AS. *slitan,* to cut; IE. **sqlei-d* < base *(*s*)*qel-,* to cut, seen also in Eng. *skill, shield,* etc.], 1. to cut or split open, especially by a straight, lengthwise incision. 2. to cut lengthwise into strips. ***n.*** 1. a cut or tear, especially one that is long and straight. 2. a narrow opening: as, the *slit* under the door lets in light.

slith·er (sli*th*'ẽr), *v.i.* [< dial. *slidder,* to slip, slide; ME. *slideren;* AS. *sliderian;* freq. < base of *slidan* (cf. SLIDE)], 1. to slip or slide on or as on a gravelly slope or a similar loose, broken surface. 2. *a*) to move along by sliding, slipping, or gliding, as a snake. *b*) to walk with a sliding motion. ***v.t.*** to cause to slide or slither. ***n.*** a sliding, slithering motion.

slith·er·y (sli*th*'ẽr-i), *adj.* 1. slippery. 2. like or characterized by a slither: as, a *slithery* walk.

slit·ter (slit'ẽr), *n.* 1. a person who slits. 2. any of several knifelike devices used for cutting or slitting.

slit trench, a narrow, relatively shallow trench for protecting the individual soldier from shellfire, etc.

sliv·er (sliv'ẽr), *n.* [< dial. *slive,* to cut; ME. *sliven,* to cut, cleave; AS. *slifan;* for IE. base see SLEAVE], 1. a thin, often pointed piece that has been cut, split, or broken off; splinter. 2. a loose, thin, continuous fiber, as of wool or flax, ready to be drawn and twisted. ***v.t. & v.i.*** to form, cut, split, or break into slivers.

sli·vo·vitz (sliv'ə-vits'), *n.* [Russ. < *sliva* (OSlav. *sliva*), a plum; akin to Eng. *sloe;* cf. SLOE], a kind of plum brandy drunk especially in Slavic countries.

Sloan, John (slōn), 1871–1951; American painter and etcher.

slob (slob), *n.* [Ir. *slab*], 1. [Dial.], mud. 2. any soft, sloppy surface. 3. [Colloq.], a sloppy, stupid, clumsy person.

slob·ber (slob'ẽr), *v.i.* [prob. < D. *slobberen,* to slobber < base seen in *slaver, v.*], 1. to let saliva run from the mouth; slaver. 2. to indulge in extreme sentimentality, as in speaking. ***v.t.*** to wet, smear, or dribble on with saliva. ***n.*** 1. saliva running from the mouth; slaver. 2. extreme sentimentality in talk, etc. Also **slabber.**

slob·ber·y (slob'ẽr-i), *adj.* 1. unpleasantly wet; sloppy; slimy. 2. characterized by slobber or slobbering.

sloe (slō), *n.* [ME. *slo, sla;* AS. *sla, slah;* akin to G. *schlehe;* IE. base **sli-,* **sloi-,* etc., bluish, livid, as also in OSlav. & Russ. *sliva,* plum (cf. SLIVOVITZ)], 1. a small, blue-black, plumlike fruit. 2. the plant it grows on; blackthorn. 3. any of various wild plums.

sloe-eyed (slō'īd'), *adj.* having large, dark eyes.

sloe gin, alcoholic liquor distilled from grain and flavored with fresh sloes.

slog (slog), *v.t. & v.i.* [SLOGGED (slogd), SLOGGING], [var. of *slug, v.*], to hit hard; slug.

slog (slog), *v.t. & v.i.* [SLOGGED (slogd), SLOGGING], [ME. *sloggen;* prob. < ON.; cf. Sw. dial. *slogga,* to be slow; base reappears in *sluggish, sluggard*], to make (one's way) heavily and with great effort; plod; toil.

slo·gan (slō'gən), *n.* [Gael. *sluggh-ghairm* < *sluagh,* a host + *gairm,* a call], 1. a cry used by Scottish Highland and Irish clans in battle or as an assembly signal. 2. a catchword or rallying motto distinctly associated with a political party or other group. 3. a catch phrase used to advertise a product.

slog·ger (slog'ẽr), *n.* [< *slog* (to hit)], one who slogs.

sloid, slojd (sloid), *n.* sloyd.

sloop (slōōp), *n.* [D. *sloep;* LG. *sluup* < *slupen* (akin to AS. *slupan*), to glide (cf. SLOPE); base as in *lubricate,* etc.], a small, one-masted vessel originally rigged fore-and-aft with a jib, mainsail, and often topsails and staysails: the modern sloop usually has a jib-headed mainsail and is distinguished from the cutter in having the mast further forward and only a single headsail.

sloop of war, 1. originally, a sailing vessel rigged in any of several ways and mounting from 10 to 32 guns. 2. later, any war vessel larger than a gunboat, having guns mounted on one deck only.

sloop-rigged (slōōp'rigd'), *adj.* having rigging like that of a sloop.

slop (slop), *n.* [ME. *sloppe;* AS. *sloppe* (only in comp.) < base of *slypa* (cf. SLIP, a kind of clay)], 1. watery snow or mud; slush. 2. a splash or puddle of spilled liquid. 3. any liquid or semiliquid food that is unappetizing or of poor quality. 4. *often pl.* *a*) liquid waste of any kind. *b*) kitchen waste or swill, used for feeding animals. 5. *pl.* distillery mash after the alcohol has been removed. 6. [Slang], a sloppy, careless, or slovenly person. See also **slops.** *v.i.* [SLOPPED (slopt), SLOPPING], 1. to spill or splash. 2. to walk or splash through slush or mud. *v.t.* 1. to spill liquid on. 2. to spill.

slop over, 1. to overflow or spill, as a liquid when its container is tilted. 2. [Colloq.], to make a display of sentimentality; gush.

slope (slōp), *n.* [contr. of *aslope* < AS. *aslopen*, pp. of *aslupan*, to slip away < *slupan*, to glide (cf. SLOOP)], 1. a piece of ground that is not flat or level; rising or falling ground. 2. any inclined line, surface, position, etc.; slant. 3. deviation from the horizontal or vertical. 4. the amount or degree of this. 5. the land area that drains into a given ocean. *v.i.* [SLOPED (slōpt), SLOPING], to have an upward or downward inclination; take an oblique direction; incline; slant. *v.t.* to cause to slope. *adj.* [Poetic], sloping.

slop·ing (slōp'iŋ), *adj.* that slopes or slants; inclined.

slop·pi·ly (slop'ə-li), *adv.* in a sloppy manner.

slop·pi·ness (slop'i-nis), *n.* a sloppy state or quality.

slop·py (slop'i), *adj.* [SLOPPIER (-i-ẽr), SLOPPIEST (-i-ist)], 1. consisting of or covered with slop; wet and splashy; muddy; slushy. 2. splashed or spotted with liquids. 3. [Colloq.], *a*) very untidy; showing lack of care; slovenly; messy. *b*) careless; slipshod. 4. [Colloq.], gushingly sentimental. —*SYN.* see **slovenly.**

slops (slops), *n.pl.* [ME. *sloppes*, pl. of *slop*, *sloppe;* AS. *slop* in *overslop;* akin to ON. *yfirsloppr;* prob. < base of *slip;* for sense cf. SLEEVE], 1. loose-fitting garments, especially trousers or breeches. 2. cheap, ready-made clothing. 3. the clothes, bedding, and other equipment issued to a ship's crew.

slop·shop (slop'shop'), *n.* a store selling slops, or cheap, ready-made clothing.

slop·work (slop'wũrk'), *n.* 1. the manufacture of slops, or cheap clothing. 2. any work that is carelessly done or of poor quality.

slosh (slosh), *v.t.* [var. of dial. *slush*, *v.* < *slush*, *n.*], to shake or agitate (a liquid or something in a liquid). *v.i.* to splash or move clumsily through water, mud, etc. *n.* slush.

slot (slot), *n.* [ME.; OFr. *esclot*, the hollow between the breasts], 1. a narrow notch, groove, or opening, as a keyway in a piece of machinery, a slit for a coin in a vending machine, etc. 2. a nozzle-shaped passage through a wing of an airplane near the leading edge, formed by a main and an auxiliary airfoil and designed to minimize wind drag. *v.t.* [SLOTTED (-id), SLOTTING], to make a slot or slots in.

slot (slot), *n.* [OFr. *esclot;* ON. *slōth;* cf. SLEUTH], 1. a track or trail of an animal, especially a deer. 2. any track, trace, or trail. *v.t.* [SLOTTED (-id), SLOTTING], to follow the trail of.

sloth (slōth, slôth, sloth), *n.* [ME. *slouthe* < *slou*, slow, used for older *slewthe*, *sleuthe* < AS. *slæwth*, sloth < *slaw*, slow; see SLOW & -TH], 1. disinclination to work or exert oneself; sluggishness; indolence; laziness. 2. slowness; delay. 3. any of several slow-moving, tree-dwelling South American mammals, one species (*three-toed sloth*) having three toes on each front foot, another, (*two-toed sloth*), having two toes on each front foot.

SLOTH (24 in. long)

sloth bear, a bear with shaggy black fur, a flexible snout, and long white claws: it is found in India and Ceylon.

sloth·ful (slōth'fəl, slôth'fəl, sloth'fəl), *adj.* characterized by sloth; disinclined to activity; indolent; lazy.

slot machine, a vending machine, gambling device, etc. fitted with a slot in which a coin must be inserted before the mechanism will work.

slouch (slouch), *n.* [akin to ON. *slōkr*, lazy fellow < *slōka*, to hang down, droop; prob. via a lost AS. cognate; base as in *slack*, *slink*], 1. a person who is awkward, lazy, or (in colloquial usage and usually with a negative) incompetent: as, he's no *slouch* at tennis. 2. *a*) a drooping or bending forward of the head and shoulders. *b*) slovenly posture in general. 3. a hanging down or drooping, as of a hat brim. *v.i.* 1. to have a drooping, slovenly posture; sit, stand, walk, etc. in a slouch. 2. to droop, as a hat brim. *v.t.* to cause to slouch.

slouch hat, a soft hat with a broad, drooping brim.

slouch·i·ly (slouch'ə-li), *adv.* in a slouchy manner.

slouch·i·ness (slouch'i-nis), *n.* the state or quality of being slouchy.

slouch·y (slouch'i), *adj.* [SLOUCHIER (-i-ẽr), SLOUCHIEST (-i-ist)], slouching, especially in posture.

slough (sluf), *n.* [ME. *slouh;* akin to G. *schlauch*, a skin, bag; IE. base **sleuĝ-*, to glide, slip; prob. < LG. source], 1. the skin of a snake, especially the outer layer that is periodically cast off. 2. any castoff layer or covering: often used figuratively. 3. in *medicine*, a mass of dead tissue that separates from the surrounding tissue. *v.i.* [< the *n.*], 1. to be shed, cast off, or discarded; come off; fall away. 2. to shed skin or other covering: often used figuratively. 3. in *medicine*, to separate from the surrounding tissue: said of dead tissue. Often with *off* or *away*. *v.t.* 1. to throw off; shed; discard; get rid of (often with *off*). 2. in *bridge*, to get rid of (a card considered valueless).

slough (slou; *for 4*, slōō), *n.* [ME. *slogh*, *slo;* AS. *sloh;* akin to MLG. *slōch*, a swamp; IE. base **sklēq-*, etc., as also in Eng. *slag*], 1. a place, as a hollow, full of soft, deep mud. 2. [< *slough of despond*, in Bunyan's *Pilgrim's Progress*], deep, hopeless dejection or discouragement. 3. moral degradation. 4. a swamp, bog, or marsh, especially one that is part of an inlet or backwater: also spelled **slew, slue.**

slough·y (sluf'i), *adj.* [SLOUGHIER (-i-ẽr), SLOUGHIEST (-i-ist)], of or like slough, or dead tissue.

slough·y (slou'i), *adj.* [SLOUGHIER (-i-ẽr), SLOUGHIEST (-i-ist)], of or like a slough; miry; boggy.

Slo·vak (slō'vak, slō-vak', slō'väk), *n.* 1. any of a Slavic people living chiefly in Slovakia. 2. the West Slavic language of the Slovaks, closely related to Czech. *adj.* of Slovakia, the Slovaks, their language, etc.

Slo·va·ki·a (slō-vä'ki-ə, slō-vak'i-ə), *n.* a province in eastern Czechoslovakia: area, 18,921 sq. mi.; pop., 3,402,000 (est. 1947); capital, Bratislava.

Slo·va·ki·an (slō-vä'ki-ən, slō-vak'i-ən), *n.* & *adj.* Slovak.

slov·en (sluv'ən), *n.* [ME. *slovein;* prob. < MD. *slof* (< *sloffen*, to neglect) + Anglo-Fr. *-ain*, *-ein*], a person who is careless in his habits, behavior, appearance, or methods of work; dirty or untidy person.

Slo·vene (slō-vēn', slō'vēn), *n.* 1. any of a Slavic people living chiefly in Slovenia. 2. their South Slavic language. *adj.* of Slovenia, the Slovenes, their language, etc. Also **Slovenian.**

Slo·ve·ni·a (slō-vē'ni-ə), *n.* a federated republic of Yugoslavia, in the northwestern part: area, 6,265 sq. mi.; pop., 1,144,000; capital, Ljubljana.

Slo·ve·ni·an (slō-vē'ni-ən), *adj.* & *n.* Slovene.

slov·en·li·ness (sluv'ən-li-nis), *n.* the state or quality of being slovenly.

slov·en·ly (sluv'ən-li), *adj.* [SLOVENLIER (-li-ẽr), SLOVENLIEST (-li-ist)], 1. characteristic of a sloven. 2. careless in habits, behavior, appearance, or methods of work; untidy; slipshod. *adv.* in a slovenly manner.

SYN.—**slovenly** implies a general carelessness or shiftlessness as characterized by a want of attention to cleanliness, orderliness, etc. (a *slovenly* housewife); **slipshod** suggests a carelessness about details and a resulting lack of precision, accuracy, thoroughness, etc. (*slipshod* work); **untidy** implies a lack of neatness in appearance or arrangement (an *untidy* room); **unkempt**, basically meaning uncombed, stresses untidiness as resulting from neglect (an *unkempt* ragamuffin, lawn, etc.); **sloppy**, a colloquial word in this connection, suggests a carelessness spilling over of something loose and therefore implies messiness, lack of restraint, etc. (a *sloppy* eater, *sloppy* thinking, etc.). —*ANT.* neat, tidy, fastidious.

Slo·ven·sko (slô'ven-skô'), Slovakia: the Czech name.

slow (slō), *adj.* [ME. *slowe;* AS. *slaw;* akin to D. *sleeuw;* often, but doubtfully, derived < IE. base **laiwo-*, left side, wrong side, seen also in L. *laevus*, left hand], 1. not quick or clever in understanding; dull; obtuse. 2. *a*) taking a longer time than is expected or usual to act, move, go, happen, etc. *b*) not quick, ready, or prompt: as, a *slow* retort, *slow* to appreciate. 3. making relatively little progress for the time spent; marked by low speed, rate of rhythm, etc.; not fast or rapid. 4. holding back fast progress, development, etc.; making speed difficult or impossible: as, a *slow* growing season, *slow* track. 5. showing a time that is behind the correct time: said of a timepiece. 6. passing slowly or tediously; dull; not interesting: as, a *slow* afternoon. 7. characterized by little activity; slack: as, *slow* trading. 8. lacking in energy; sluggish. 9. behind the times; out of fashion. 10. burning so as to give off a low or moderate heat: as, a *slow* fire. 11. gradual, as growth. *v.t.* 1. to make slow or slower. 2. to retard; delay. Often with *up* or *down*. *v.i.* to go or become slow or slower (often with *up* or *down*). *adv.* slowly. —*SYN.* see **stupid.**

slow·down (slō'doun'), *n.* a slowing down or being slowed down; specifically, a planned slowing down of industrial production on the part of labor or management.

slow match, a match, or fuse, that burns slowly, used for setting off blasting charges.

slow-mo·tion (slō'mō'shən), *adj.* 1. moving or operating below usual or normal speed. 2. denoting a motion picture photographed by exposing more pictures per minute than is usual, so that the action on the screen, when the film is projected at the normal speed, appears much slower than the original action.

slow-mov·ing (slō′mōōv′iŋ), *adj.* 1. moving slowly; showing little progress or activity. 2. selling in a relatively small quantity, as merchandise, stocks, etc.

slow·poke (slō′pōk′), *n.* [Slang], a person who acts or moves slowly.

slow time, [Colloq.], standard time, as distinguished from daylight-saving time, war time, etc.

slow-wit·ted (slō′wit′id), *adj.* having a mind that works slowly and ineffectively; not bright or alert; dull.

slow·worm (slō′wũrm′), *n.* [AS. *slawyrm;* from its supposed deadly sting], the blindworm, a legless lizard.

sloyd (sloid), *n.* [Sw. *slöjd,* skill], a system of manual training originating in Sweden, based upon the use of hand tools in wood carving and joining: also spelled **sloid, slojd.**

S.L.P., Socialist Labor Party.

slub (slub), *n.* [prob. < the *v.*, which is ? a specialized technical use < MD. *slubbe,* thick mud, ooze (Eng. dial. *slub*); cf. SLUBBER], 1. a roll of fiber, as of wool or cotton, twisted slightly for use in spinning. 2. yarn with fibers that are untwisted at intervals. *v.t.* [SLUBBED (slubd), SLUBBING], to draw out and twist slightly for use in spinning, as wool, cotton, etc.

slub·ber (slub′ẽr), *v.t.* [prob. var. of *slobber;* sense 2 corresponds with LG. *slubbern* (G. *schluppern*), to scamp in working, orig., to wade through mud], [Dial.], 1. to smear, stain, or daub over. 2. to do carelessly or awkwardly; botch.

sludge (sluj), *n.* [dial. var. of *slutch,* belonging to the word group *slutch, slitch, slike, sleek,* mud; ME. had *sluche, slike* & the v. *sluchchen,* to daub with mud; prob. < AS. **slyce* (akin to D. *slijk,* G. dial. *schleich,* etc.) < IE. base **sleuĝ-,* to slip, glide, as in Eng. *slough,* a skin], 1. mud, mire, or ooze covering the ground or forming a deposit at the bottom of bodies of water. 2. finely broken drift ice. 3. any heavy, slimy deposit, sediment, or mass, as the waste resulting from oil refining, the mud brought up by a mining drill, the precipitate in a sewage tank, the sediment in a steam boiler, etc.

sludg·y (sluj′i), *adj.* [SLUDGIER (-i-ẽr), SLUDGIEST (-i-ist)], of or like sludge; muddy; oozy.

slue (slōō), *v.t. & v.i.* [SLUED (slōōd), SLUING], [Early Mod. Eng. < nautical use; prob. akin to or < obs. D. *slooien,* to drag, tug; IE. base **sleu-,* loose, lax, as also in Eng. *sleuth*], to turn or swing around a pivot or fixed point. *n.* 1. the act of sluing. 2. the position to which a thing has been slued. Also spelled **slew.**

slue (slōō), *n.* a slough (swamp).

slue (slōō), *n.* a slew (large number).

slug (slug), *n.* [ME. *slugge,* slow, clumsy person or thing; IE. base **sleu-,* to hang loosely, lax, seen also in Eng. *slack, slumber;* cf. SLUGGARD], 1. a small mollusk resembling and moving like a land snail, but having only a rudimentary internal shell or none at all. 2. any of several caterpillars that resemble slugs. 3. an animal, vehicle, etc. that moves sluggishly.

slug (slug), *n.* [Early Mod. Eng.; prob. < LG.; meaning suggests derivation < p.t. base of MD. *slaen,* or MLG. *slan,* to strike, with sense "what is struck off"; cf. SLAG], 1. a small piece or lump of metal; specifically, a bullet. 2. a piece of metal shaped like and used in place of a coin in automatic coin machines. 3. in *printing, a*) a strip of nonprinting metal used to space between lines or as a temporary marker. *b*) a line of type made in one piece or strip, as by a linotype machine.

slug (slug), *n.* [D. *sluck,* a swallow], [Slang], a single drink, especially of straight alcoholic liquor.

slug (slug), *v.t.* [SLUGGED (slugd), SLUGGING], [< dial.; immediate origin doubtful, but prob. akin to & derived < the p.t. base seen in & stem of AS. *slean,* to strike. kill (cf. SLAY)], [Colloq.], to hit hard, especially with the fist. *n.* [Colloq.], a hard blow or hit.

slug·a·bed (slug′ə-bed′), *n.* [< ME. *slugge,* a lazy person or thing; cf. SLUG (mollusk)], a lazy person who stays in bed after others are up.

slug·gard (slug′ẽrd), *n.* [ME. *slugarde, slogarde < sluggen, sloggen,* to be lazy, go slowly + *-ard;* cf. SLOG, SLUG], a person who is habitually lazy or idle; indolent or slothful person. *adj.* lazy; idle; sluggish.

slug·ger (slug′ẽr), *n.* [Colloq.], a person who slugs; specifically, *a*) a prize fighter. *b*) a baseball player with a high percentage of extra-base hits.

slug·gish (slug′ish), *adj.* [< *slug* (mollusk) + *-ish*], 1. lacking in energy, alertness, or vigor; indisposed to exertion; lazy; slothful. 2. slow or slow-moving; not active; dull. 3. not functioning with normal vigor: as, a *sluggish* digestive system.

sluice (slōōs), *n.* [ME. *scluse;* OFr. *escluse;* LL. *exclusa,* fem. pp. < L. *excludere,* to shut out, exclude < *ex-,* out + *claudere,* to shut], 1. an artificial channel or passage for water, having a gate or valve at its head to regulate the flow, as in a canal or millstream. 2. the water held back by or passing through such a gate. 3. a gate or valve used in opening or closing a sluice; floodgate: also **sluice gate.** 4. any channel, especially one for excess water. 5. a sloping trough or flume through which water is run, as in washing gold ore, carrying logs, etc. *v.t.* [SLUICED (slōōst), SLUICING], 1. to draw off by or as by means of a sluice. 2. *a*) to wash with water flowing in or from a sluice. *b*) to wash off with a rush of water: as, the sailors *sluiced* the deck with hoses. 3. to carry (logs, etc.) in a sluice. *v.i.* to run or flow in or as in a sluice.

sluice·way (slōōs′wā′), *n.* an artificial channel for water, with or without a floodgate; sluice.

slum (slum), *n.* [c. 1800 < cant; orig. sense, a room; ? cant perversion of the word *room*], a heavily populated area in which housing and other living conditions are extremely poor. *v.i.* [SLUMMED (slumd), SLUMMING], to visit slums: as, they *slummed* out of curiosity.

slum·ber (slum′bẽr), *v.i.* [ME. *slumeren;* AS. *slumerian* < *sluma,* slumber; for IE. base see SLUG (mollusk)], 1. to sleep. 2. to be dormant, negligent, or inactive. *v.t.* to spend in sleeping. *n.* 1. sleep. 2. an inactive or quiescent state.

slum·ber·ous (slum′bẽr-əs), *adj.* 1. inclined to slumber; sleepy; drowsy. 2. suggestive of or characterized by slumber. 3. causing sleep or drowsiness; soporific. 4. tranquil; calm; quiet: as, a *slumberous* little desert town. — ***SYN.*** see **sleepy.**

slum·brous (slum′brəs), *adj.* slumberous.

slum·mer (slum′ẽr), *n.* 1. a person who slums. 2. a person living in a slum.

slump (slump), *v.i.* [prob. < LG. *slumpen,* to come about by accident; akin to G. *schlumpen;* U.S. use prob. via. D.], 1. to fall, sink, or collapse, especially suddenly or heavily. 2. to fall or sink into a bog or through a crust of ice or snow. 3. to decline suddenly, as in value, activity, etc. 4. to have a drooping posture or gait. *n.* 1. a sudden or sharp fall. 2. a decline in business activity, prices, etc.

slung (sluŋ), past tense and past participle of **sling.**

slung shot, a small, heavy weight attached to a strap or thong, for use as a weapon.

slunk (sluŋk), past tense and past participle of **slink** (to move).

slunk (sluŋk), alternative past tense and past participle of **slink** (to give birth).

slur (slũr), *v.t.* [SLURRED (slũrd), SLURRING], [prob. < MD. *sleuren, slooren,* to drag, move slowly, trail in mud; cf. ME. *sloor,* thin mud, MD. *slore,* in the derived sense, a slut], 1. to pass over quickly and carelessly; make little of (often with *over*). 2. to pronounce (a syllable, etc.) rapidly and indistinctly. 3. [Dial.], to stain, smirch, or sully. 4. to blur or smear, as in printing. 5. to disparage or discredit; cast aspersions on. 6. in *music, a*) to sing or play (different and successive notes) by gliding from one to another without a break. *b*) to mark (notes) with a slur. *n.* 1. the act or process of slurring. 2. something slurred, as a pronunciation. 3. a blot, stain, or smear. 4. anything harmful or intended to be harmful to a person's reputation; aspersion, reproach, stigma, etc. 5. in *music, a*) a combination of slurred notes. *b*) a mark (‿) or (⁀) connecting such notes.

slur·ry (slũr′i), *n.* [*pl.* SLURRIES (-iz)] [< ME. *sloor,* cf. SLUR, *n.*], a thin mixture of water and any of several fine, insoluble materials, as clay, cement, soil, etc.

slush (slush), *n.* [prob. via dial. < ON.; cf. obs. Dan. *slus* of the same origin], 1. partly melted snow or ice. 2. soft mud; mire. 3. refuse fat or grease from cooking on board ship. 4. any of several greasy compounds used as lubricants or rust preventives for machinery. 5. overly sentimental talk or writing; drivel. *v.t.* 1. to splash or cover with slush, especially in lubricating or protecting. 2. to patch with mortar or cement.

slush fund, 1. a fund established aboard ship from the sale of refuse fat, etc. and used to buy small luxuries; hence, 2. money used for bribery, political pressure, or other corrupt purposes.

slush·y (slush′i), *adj.* [SLUSHIER (-i-ẽr), SLUSHIEST (-i-ist)], 1. full of or covered with slush. 2. of or like slush.

slut (slut), *n.* [ME. *slutte, slotte* (akin to G. dial. *schlutte, schlutz*) < ON. or MLG.; basic sense in cognate MLG. *slōt,* a puddle (cf. SLUR, *n.*); for IE. base see SLEET], 1. a woman who is careless of her appearance; dirty, slovenly woman; slattern. 2. a woman of loose character. 3. a bold or impudent girl: a humorous usage. 4. a female dog; bitch.

slut·tish (slut′ish), *adj.* 1. like a slut; carelessly dirty or untidy. 2. having the morals of a slut.

sly (slī), *adj.* [SLIER or SLYER (slī′ẽr), SLIEST or SLYEST (slī′ist)], [ME. *slye, slege;* ON. *slægr,* clever, cunning, lit., able to strike < base of *slā* & AS. *slean,* to strike

(cf. SLAY)], 1. [Dial.], skillful or clever. 2. skillful at trickery or deceit; crafty; wily. 3. showing a secretive, crafty, or wily nature; cunningly underhanded. 4. mischievous in a playful or waggish way; roguish.
on the sly, secretly; stealthily.

SYN.—**sly** implies a working to achieve one's ends by evasiveness, insinuation, furtiveness, duplicity, etc. (a *sly* bargain); **cunning** implies a cleverness or shrewd skillfulness at deception and circumvention (a *cunning* plot); **crafty** implies an artful cunning in contriving stratagems and subtle deceptions (a *crafty* diplomat); **tricky** suggests a shifty, unreliable quality rather than cleverness at deception (*tricky* subterfuges); **foxy** suggests slyness and craftiness that have been sharpened by experience (a *foxy* old trader); **wily** implies the deceiving or ensnarement of others by subtle stratagems and ruses (*wily* blandishments).

sly·ly (slī′li), *adv.* in a sly manner: also spelled **slily.**

slype (slīp), *n.* [prob. < LG.; cf. Fl. *slijpe,* covered or secret path < base seen in AS. *slūpan,* to glide, slip], a covered passage between the transept and chapter house of a cathedral or monastic church.

Sm, in *chemistry,* samarium.

S.M., 1. *Scientiae Magister,* [L.], Master of Science. 2. Sergeant Major. 3. State Militia.

smack (smak), *n.* [ME. *smac, smak;* AS. *smæc;* akin to G. *(ge)schmack;* IE. base **smeg(h)-,* to taste, represented outside Gmc. only in Lith.], 1. a distinctive taste or flavor, especially one that is faint or slight. 2. a small amount; touch; trace; suggestion. 3. a taste, bit, or mouthful. *v.i.* to have a smack (usually with *of*): as, diction that *smacks* of the stage.

smack (smak), *n.* [of Gmc. echoic origin; akin to MD. *smack,* D. *smak,* LG. *smacke,* one of which may be source of the Eng. word], 1. a sharp noise made by pressing the lips together and parting them suddenly, as in gusto. 2. a loud kiss. 3. a sharp blow with the hand or any flat object; slap; crack. 4. the sound of such a blow. *v.t.* 1. to press (the lips) together and part them suddenly so as to make a smack. 2. to kiss or slap loudly. *v.i.* to make a loud, sharp noise, as on impact: as, the snowball *smacked* against the wall. *adv.* 1. with or as with a smack; violently; sharply. 2. directly; fully: as, he ran *smack* into trouble.

smack (smak), *n.* [prob. < D. & LG. *smak* (whence also Dan. *smakke,* etc., Sp. *esmaque*); in origin prob. a nickname (cf. SMACK, *v.*)], 1. a small sailboat, usually rigged as a sloop. 2. a fishing vessel fitted with a well for keeping fish alive.

smack·ing (smak′iŋ), *adj.* [ppr. of *smack*], brisk; sharp; lively; vigorous.

small (smôl), *adj.* [ME. *smal,* narrow, slender; AS. *smæl;* akin to G. *schmal,* narrow; connected with IE. base **mēlo-,* young animal, ? seen also in L. *malus,* bad, lit., small, hence worthless (cf. MALEFICENT)], 1. little in size, especially when compared with others of the same kind; not large or big; limited in size. 2. *a*) little in quantity, extent, numbers, value, duration, etc.: as, a *small* income. *b*) of slight intensity; of limited degree or scope. *c*) consisting of relatively few units; numerically low. 3. of little importance or significance; trivial. 4. having only a little investment, capital, etc.; doing business on a small scale: as, a *small* tradesman. 5. small-minded; mean; petty. 6. of low or inferior rank; ordinary; not notable. 7. gentle and low; soft: said of sound or the voice. 8. diluted; light; weak: as, *small* ale. *adv.* 1. in small pieces. 2. in a low, faint tone; softly. 3. in a small manner. *n.* 1. something small; small part: as, the *small* of the back. 2. *pl.* small things or articles collectively. 3. *pl.* knee breeches; smallclothes.
feel small, to feel shame or humiliation.
sing small, to become humble or timid after having been arrogant, boastful, etc.

SYN.—**small** and **little** are often used interchangeably, but **small** is preferred with reference to something concrete of less than the usual quantity, size, amount, value, importance, etc. (a *small* man, tax, audience, matter, etc.) and **little** more often applies to absolute concepts (he has his *little* faults), in expressing tenderness, indulgence, etc. (the *little* woman), and in connoting insignificance, meanness, pettiness, etc. (of *little* importance); **diminutive** implies extreme, sometimes delicate smallness or littleness (the *diminutive* Lilliputians); **minute** and the more informal **tiny** suggest that which is extremely diminutive, often to the degree that it can be discerned only by close scrutiny (a *minute,* or *tiny,* difference); **miniature** applies to a copy, model, representation, etc. on a very small scale (*miniature* painting); **petite** has specific application to a girl or women who is small and trim in figure. —*ANT.* large, big, great.

small·age (smôl′ij), *n.* [ME. *smalache* < *smal* (see SMALL) + Fr. *ache,* smallage; L. *apium,* parsley], a kind of wild celery.

small arms, firearms of small caliber, carried by hand, as pistols, carbines, rifles, etc.: abbreviated **s.a.**

small beer, 1. weak or inferior beer. 2. a person or thing of little importance or significance; trivial matters.

small calorie, see **calorie** (sense 1).

small capital, a capital letter of smaller size than the regular capital letter used. These are the regular capitals used in this dictionary: A, B, C, D; these are the small capitals: A, B, C, D.

small change, 1. coins, especially those of low denomination. 2. something of little value or importance.

small·clothes (smôl′klōz′, smôl′klōthz′), *n.pl.* [Archaic], close-fitting knee breeches of the kind worn during the 18th century.

small fry, 1. young or small fish. 2. small children; youngsters. 3. persons or things regarded as unimportant or insignificant.

small hours, the first few hours following midnight.

small intestine, the narrow, convoluted upper part of the intestines, extending from the pyloric end of the stomach to the large intestine.

small·ish (smôl′ish), *adj.* somewhat small; not large.

small letter, any letter that is not a capital.

small-mind·ed (smôl′mīn′did), *adj.* blindly selfish, prejudiced, vindictive, etc.; petty; mean; narrow.

small of the back, the concave part of the back just above the hips.

small pica, a size of type, about 11 point. This is in small pica.

small potatoes, [Colloq.], 1. a person or thing of little importance. 2. petty or insignificant people or things.

small·pox (smôl′poks′), *n.* [*small* + *pox*], an acute, infectious virus disease characterized by fever, vomiting, and pustular eruptions that often leave pitted scars, or pockmarks, when healed: also called *variola.*

small stores, small miscellaneous articles, as tobacco, soap, etc., stocked by a ship's store for sale to the crew.

small·sword (smôl′sôrd′, smôl′sōrd′), *n.* a light, tapering, straight sword, used especially in fencing.

small talk, light conversation about common, everyday things; chitchat.

small-time (smôl′tīm′), *adj.* [Slang], limited, minor, or petty; not large-scale, extensive, or significant: opposed to *big-time.*

small-town (smôl′toun′), *adj.* of or characteristic of a small town as opposed to a city.

smalt (smôlt), *n.* [Fr.; It. *smalto* < Gmc. **smalt* < base of OHG. *smelzan,* to melt; cf. SMELT, *v.*], 1. deep-blue glass prepared from silica, potash, and oxide of cobalt: used, when pulverized, as a pigment. 2. pigment made in this way. 3. the deep-blue color of this pigment.

smalt·ine (smôl′tin, smôl′tēn), *n.* smaltite.

smalt·ite (smôl′tīt), *n.* [*smalt* + *-ite*], a white to gray native cobalt arsenide, $CoAs_2$, crystalline or granular in form and used as a blue pigment in coloring glass and ceramics.

‡**smal·to** (zmäl′tô), *n.* [*pl.* SMALTI (-tē)], [It. < Gmc. base seen also in Eng. *smelt,* MD. *smalt,* melted fat], 1. a kind of colored glass or enamel used in mosaics. 2. a piece of this.

smar·agd (smar′agd), *n.* [ME. & OFr. *smaragde;* L. *smaragdus;* see EMERALD], an emerald.

sma·rag·dine (smə-rag′din), *adj.* [ME. *smaragdyn;* L. *smaragdinus;* see EMERALD], 1. of emerald. 2. emerald in color. *n.* smaragd.

sma·rag·dite (smə-rag′dīt), *n.* [Fr.; see SMARAGD & -ITE], a bright-green kind of amphibole or hornblende.

smart (smärt), *v.i.* [ME. *smerten;* AS. *smeortan;* akin to G. *schmerzen;* IE. **mer-d* < base **mer-,* to rub away, fret, etc., seen also in L. *mordere,* to bite, sting (cf. MORDANT); basic sense "to ache from repeated contact, rubbing, etc."], 1. *a*) to cause sharp, stinging pain, as a slap. *b*) to be the source of such pain, as a wound. *c*) to feel such pain. 2. to feel mental distress or irritation, as in grief, resentment, remorse, etc.; suffer. *v.t.* to cause to smart. *n.* [ME. *smerte* < base of *v.*], a smarting sensation; sharp pain or distress whether physical or mental. *adj.* [ME. *smerte;* AS. *smeart* < base of *v.*], 1. causing keen pain: as, a *smart* blow across the hand. 2. sharp; intense, as pain. 3. brisk; vigorous; lively: as, they started off at a *smart* pace. 4. *a*) alert; clever; capable; quick; witty. *b*) shrewd or sharp, as in one's dealings. 5. neat; clean; fresh. 6. in keeping with the current fashion; stylish. 7. [Dial.], quite strong, intense, numerous, etc.; considerable: as, that's a right *smart* rain. —*SYN.* see **intelligent.**

smart al·eck (al′ik), [*smart* + *Aleck,* nickname for *Alexander*], [Colloq.], a person who is offensively conceited and self-assertive; cocky, bumptious person.

smart·en (smär′t'n), *v.t.* 1. to make smart; improve in appearance or style; spruce up. 2. to make brisk, bright, or alert.

smart money, [< *smart, n.*], 1. money paid as compensation for injuries, wounds, etc. received in the line of duty. 2. money paid to cancel, or compensate for failure to keep the terms of, a contract, agreement, etc. 3. money paid over and above usual damages as an extra penalty for gross negligence, cruelty, etc. 4. [< *smart, adj.* 4], money bet by those thought to have the best chance of picking a winner.

smart set, sophisticated, fashionable people, collectively.

smart·weed (smärt′wēd′), *n.* any of several plants growing in wet places, with spikes of tiny flowers and leaves which cause the skin to smart on contact.

smash (smash), *n.* [prob. < *mash,* with intens. *s-;* but cf. Norw. *smaska* in same sense], 1. a hard, heavy hit or blow; specifically, a hard, overhand tennis stroke that is difficult to return. 2. *a*) a violent, noisy breaking or shattering. *b*) the sound of this. 3. *a*) a violent collision. *b*) a wreck. 4. complete ruin or defeat; total failure, especially in business; smashup. 5. a drink made of mint, sugar, water, and some kind of alcoholic liquor. *v.t.* 1. to break or shatter into pieces with noise or violence. 2. to hit (a tennis ball) with a hard, overhand stroke. 3. to hit with a hard, heavy blow or impact. 4. to ruin completely; defeat utterly; wreck. *v.i.* 1. to break into pieces. 2. to be destroyed; come to ruin. 3. to collide with crushing force. 4. to move by smashing or with force. —*SYN.* see **break.**

go (or **come**) **to smash,** [Colloq.], 1. to become smashed or broken. 2. to fail utterly; be ruined.

smash·up (smash'up'), *n.* 1. a wreck or collision, especially one that does great damage. 2. complete defeat or failure; ruin. 3. any disaster or catastrophe.

smat·ter (smat'ẽr), *v.t.* [ME. *smateren,* to chatter < ON.], 1. to talk or utter with only slight or superficial knowledge. 2. to dabble in; study or learn superficially. *n.* a smattering.

smat·ter·ing (smat'ẽr-iŋ), *n.* [*smatter, v.* + *-ing*], slight or superficial knowledge (usually with *of*).

sm. c., sm. caps., small capitals.

smear (smêr), *v.t.* [ME. *smerien;* AS. *smerian,* to anoint; akin to G. *schmieren;* IE. base **smeru-,* grease, seen also in OIr. *smir,* marrow & prob. in L. *medullae,* marrow], 1. to cover, daub, or soil with something greasy, sticky, or dirty. 2. to apply or daub (something greasy, sticky, or dirty) so as to leave a coating, mark, etc. 3. to make a smear with: as, he *smeared* his hand across the wet paint. 4. to harm the reputation of; malign; defame; slander. 5. [Slang], to overwhelm, defeat, stop, thwart, etc. completely and decisively. *v.i.* to be or become smeared. *n.* 1. a spot or mark made by smearing. 2. a small quantity of some substance, as blood, smeared on a slide for microscopic study, etc. 3. a smearing or slandering of a reputation. 4. *a*) [Obs.], ointment; oily substance. *b*) a substance to be smeared on something.

smear·case (smêr'kās'), *n.* [< G. *schmierkäse* < *schmieren,* to spread (cf. SMEAR) + *käse,* cheese], cottage cheese.

smear·i·ness (smêr'i-nis), *n.* smeary quality or state.

smear·y (smêr'i), *adj.* [SMEARIER (-i-ẽr), SMEARIEST (-i-ist)], 1. covered with or having smears; smeared. 2. tending to smear, as wet ink.

smell (smel), *v.t.* [SMELLED (smeld) or SMELT (smelt), SMELLING], [ME. (southeastern dial.) *smellen;* AS. **smyllan* < base **smul-* (cf. SMOLDER); basic sense "to give off smoke"], 1. to be or become aware of by means of the nose and the olfactory nerves; catch the scent or odor of. 2. to sense the presence or existence of: as, they *smelled* trouble and ran. 3. to test by the scent or odor; sniff: as, *smell* the milk and tell me if it's sour. *v.i.* 1. to use the sense of smell; sniff (often with *at* or *of*). 2. *a*) to have or emit a scent or odor: as, the bread *smells* fresh. *b*) to have or emit an unpleasant odor; be malodorous. 3. to have the odor or a suggestion of something specified (with *of*): as, his breath *smells* of garlic, his offer *smells* of treachery. 4. [Slang], to lack ability, worth, merit, etc.; be of poor quality. *n.* [ME. *smel*], 1. that one of the five senses of the body by which a substance is perceived through the chemical stimulation of nerves (*olfactory nerves*) in the nasal cavity by particles given off by that substance. 2. the characteristic stimulation of any specific substance upon the olfactory nerves; odor; scent. 3. an act of smelling. 4. that which suggests the presence or existence of something; trace; suggestion.

smell out, to look for or find by or as by smelling.

smell up, to fill with a bad odor; cause to stink.

SYN.—**smell** is the most general word for any quality perceived through the olfactory sense (foul and fresh *smells*); **scent** refers to the emanation from the thing smelled, often implying that it can be discriminated only by a sensitive sense of smell (the *scent* of a hunted animal); **odor** suggests a heavier emanation and, therefore, one that is more generally perceptible and more clearly recognizable (chemical *odors*); **aroma** suggests a pervasive, spicy, pleasant odor (the *aroma* of fine tobacco).

smell·er (smel'ẽr), *n.* 1. a person or animal that has or uses the sense of smell. 2. a thing that smells. 3. a person employed to test by the sense of smell: as, a cheese *smeller.* 4. a sensitive hair, bristle, antenna, etc. used as an organ of touch; feeler. 5. [Slang], the nose.

smelling bottle, a bottle containing smelling salts.

smelling salts, an aromatic mixture of carbonate of ammonium with some fragrant scent, used as an inhalant in relieving faintness, headaches, etc.

smell·y (smel'i) *adj.* [SMELLIER (-i-ẽr), SMELLIEST (-i-ist)], having or giving off an unpleasant smell.

smelt (smelt), *n.* [*pl.* SMELTS (smelts), SMELT; see PLURAL, II, D, 1], [ME.; AS.; akin to D. *smelt,* G. *schmelte,* sand eel: since the fish has a peculiar odor, the name is prob. < the base of *smell, v.*], any of a number of small, silvery, troutlike food fishes found in northern seas: they spawn in tidal rivers.

smelt (smelt), *v.t.* [MD. or MLG. *smelten;* akin to G. *schmelzen;* base as in Eng. *malt, melt* with intens. *s-*], 1. to melt or fuse (ore, etc.) so as to separate impurities from pure metal. 2. to refine or extract (metal) in this way. *v.i.* to undergo fusing or smelting.

smelt (smelt), alternative past tense and past participle of **smell.**

smelt·er (smel'tẽr), *n.* 1. a person engaged in the work or business of smelting. 2. an apparatus in which, or a place where, smelting is done.

smelt·er·y (smel'tẽr-i), *n.* [*pl.* SMELTERIES (-iz)], a building, business, etc. in which smelting is done.

Sme·ta·na, Be·dřich (be'dẽr-zhikh sme'tȧ-nȧ; Eng. smet'n-ə), 1824–1884; Czech composer.

Smeth·wick (smeth'ik), *n.* a city in west central England, near Birmingham: pop., 76,000 (est. 1946).

smew (smū), *n.* [unexplained var. of form *smee,* seen also in obs. D. *smeente,* G. *schmeiente,* kind of small duck], the merganser, a duck of Europe and Asia.

smidg·en (smij'in), *n.* [? related to *midge,* seen also in U.S. dial. *smidge, smitch,* with same meaning], [Dial. or Colloq.], a small amount; a bit.

smi·la·ca·ceous (smī'lə-kā'shəs), *adj.* [< Mod. L. *Smilacaceae,* name of the family (see SMILAX); + *-ous*], of or belonging to a family of woody vines with parallel-veined leaves, one-sexed flowers, and round berries.

smi·lax (smī'laks), *n.* [L.; Gr. *smilax,* bindweed], 1. any of a number of related, usually prickly, woody vines, including the sarsaparilla. 2. a greenhouse vine popular for its bright-green leaves.

smile (smīl), *v.i.* [SMILED (smīld), SMILING], [ME. *smilen* < a LG. source; cf. older D. *smuylen,* to smile; IE. base **smei-,* to smile, be astonished, seen also in L. *mirus,* wonderful (cf. ADMIRE)], 1. to have or take on a facial expression showing pleasure, amusement, affection, friendliness, irony, derision, etc. and characterized by an upward curving of the corners of the mouth and a sparkling of the eyes. 2. to look (*at, on,* or *upon* someone) with a pleasant expression of this kind. 3. [Poetic], to have a favorable, pleasing, or agreeable appearance: as, hillsides *smiling* in the sunlight. *v.t.* 1. to express with a smile. 2. to change or affect by smiling. *n.* 1. the act of smiling. 2. the facial expression made in smiling. 3. a favorable, pleasing, or agreeable appearance; bright, pleasant aspect.

smile away, to drive away or get rid of by a smile or smiling: as, the child *smiled away* his tears.

smile on (or **upon**), to regard with favor or approval; be favorable or encouraging to.

SYN.—**smile** is the general term for a facial expression somewhat resembling that in a laugh but not accompanied by vocal sound (a *smile* that is bright, bitter, tender, etc.); **grin,** applied to a broad smile showing the teeth, implies mischievous amusement, unaffected cheerfulness, foolishness, etc. (an impish *grin,* the *grin* of an idiot); **simper** is applied to a silly, affected, or coy smile (a coquette with a *simper* on her face); a **smirk** is a simpering smile that is conceited, knowing, or annoyingly complacent (a self-satisfied *smirk*). —*ANT.* frown.

smirch (smŭrch), *v.t.* [ME. *smorchen;* prob. < OFr. *esmorcher,* to hurt], 1. to make dirty or discolor, as by smearing or staining with grime. 2. to sully; dishonor (a reputation, good name, etc.). *n.* 1. a smudge; smear; stain. 2. a stain on reputation, etc.

smirk (smŭrk), *v.i.* [ME. *smirken;* AS. *smercian,* to smile < the same base as Eng. *smile*], to smile in a conceited, knowing, or annoyingly complacent way. *n.* a smile of this kind. —*SYN.* see **smile.**

smite (smīt), *v.t.* [SMOTE (smōt) or *obs.* SMIT (smit), SMITTEN (smit''n) or SMIT or SMOTE, SMITING], [ME. *smiten;* AS. *smitan;* akin to G. *schmeissen,* to throw; IE. base **sme-,* to smear, smear on, stroke on], 1. *a*) to hit or strike hard. *b*) to bring into a specified condition by or as by a blow: as, the Lord will *smite* him dead. 2. to defeat, punish, destroy, or kill. 3. to strike or attack with powerful or disastrous effect. 4. to affect strongly and suddenly (*with* some feeling): as, *smitten* with dread. 5. to disquiet mentally; distress: as, *smitten* by conscience. 6. to strike or impress favorably; inspire with love; enamor: as, she has *smitten* him with her charms. *v.i.* 1. to strike hard; deal a heavy blow or blows: as, he *smote* upon the door with his sword. 2. to fall, dash, come, pass, etc. with sudden force. —*SYN.* see **strike.**

smith (smith), *n.* [ME.; AS.; akin to G. *schmied* (older *schmid*); IE. base **smēi-,* etc., to work with a sharp tool, seen also in Gr. *smilē,* a knife], 1. a person who makes or repairs metal objects, especially by shaping the metal while it is hot and soft; metalworker: usually in combination, as *silversmith.* 2. a blacksmith.

Smith, Adam (smith), 1723–1790; Scottish economist.

Smith, Alfred Emanuel, 1873–1944; American political leader.

Smith, Francis Hopkinson, 1838–1915; American writer, painter, and engineer.
Smith, James, 1719?–1806; American patriot; signer of the Declaration of Independence.
Smith Captain **John,** 1580–1631; English colonist in Virginia.
Smith, Joseph, 1805–1844; American founder of the Mormon church.
Smith, Sydney, 1771–1845; English clergyman and essayist.
Smith, William, 1769–1839; English geologist.
smith·er·eens (smith'ə-rēnz'), *n.pl.* [Ir. *smidirin*], [Colloq.], small fragments or broken pieces; bits.
smith·ers (smith'ẽrz), *n.pl.* [Colloq.], smithereens.
smith·er·y (smith'ẽr-i), *n.* [*pl.* SMITHERIES (-iz)], 1. the work or craft of a smith. 2. a smithy.
Smith·son, James (smith's'n), 1765–1829; British mineralogist and chemist.
Smith·so·ni·an Institution (smith-sō'ni-ən), an institution founded in 1846 in Washington, D.C., by a bequest of James Smithson: branches of the Institution cover a wide range of fields in the arts and sciences.
smith·son·ite (smith'sən-it'), *n.* [after James *Smithson* + *-ite*]. 1. native zinc carbonate, $ZnCO_3$. 2. a native silicate of zinc; calamine.
smith·y (smith'i), *n.* [*pl.* SMITHIES (-iz)], [ME. *smithi, smiththe* < AS. *smiththe* or ON. *smithja* < AS. *smith* or ON. *smithr*, smith], the workshop of a smith, especially a blacksmith; forge.
smit·ten (smit''n), alternative past participle of **smite.** *adj.* 1. struck with great force. 2. disastrously or deeply affected; afflicted. 3. [Colloq.], deeply in love.
smock (smok), *n.* [ME. *smoc* < AS. *smoc* or ON. *smokkr*; IE. *(*s*)*meugh* < base **meug-*, slippery, to slip, slip on, seen also in L. *mucus*, slime (cf. MUCOUS), Eng. *smuggle*], 1. a loose, shirtlike, outer garment worn to protect the clothes. 2. [Archaic], a chemise. *v.t.* 1. to dress in a smock. 2. to decorate with smocking.
smock frock, a heavy smock, especially of the kind worn by European farm laborers.
smock·ing (smok'iŋ), *n.* [*smock* + *-ing*], shirred work; decorative stitching used in gathering cloth to make it hang in even folds.
smog (smog), *n.* [*smoke* + *fog*], a mixture of fog and smoke. —*SYN.* see **mist.**
smoke (smōk), *n.* [ME.; AS. *smoca*; akin to G. *schmauch*; IE. base **smeugh-*, etc., to smoke, fume, seen also in Gr. *smykhein*, to smolder], 1. the vaporous matter arising from something burning and made visible by minute particles of carbon suspended in it. 2. any vapor, fume, mist, etc. resembling smoke. 3. an act or period of smoking tobacco, etc.: as, do we have time for a *smoke?* 4. something without substance, significance, or lasting reality; fruitless or insubstantial result: as, our plans went up in *smoke*. 5. something that is beclouding or obscuring. 6. something to smoke, as a cigarette or pipeful of tobacco. 7. in *physical chemistry*, a suspension of solid particles in a gas. *v.i.* [SMOKED (smōkt), SMOKING], 1. to give off smoke or a smokelike substance. 2. to discharge smoke in the wrong place, especially into a room, as a furnace, fireplace, etc. 3. to give off too much smoke, as a lamp, type of fuel, etc. 4. to move very rapidly, especially so as to raise dust. 5. to draw the smoke of tobacco, etc. into the mouth, and often lungs, and blow it out again. *v.t.* 1. to stain or color with smoke. 2. to treat with smoke, as in flavoring or curing some meats, controlling insects, etc. 3. to drive or force out with or as with smoke: as, we *smoked* the woodchuck from his hole. 4. to draw the smoke of or from (tobacco, a pipe, cigar, etc.) into the mouth, and often lungs, and blow it out again. 5. [Archaic], to detect or be suspicious of: as, he *smoked* the trick at once. 6. [Obs.], to tease or mock.
smoke out, to drive or force into the open with or as with smoke; force out of hiding, secrecy, etc.
smoke bomb, a kind of bomb containing chemicals which when ignited give off dense clouds of smoke: used in military operations to make a smoke screen.
smoke·house (smōk'hous'), *n.* a place where meats, fish, etc. are exposed to smoke in order to flavor and cure them.
smoke·jack (smōk'jak'), *n.* [*smoke* + *jack*, *n.* 7], a device which turns a fireplace roasting spit, taking its power from a wheel which is rotated by the heated air rising through the chimney.
smoke·less (smōk'lis), *adj.* having or making little or no smoke.
smokeless powder, a kind of gun powder that makes little or no smoke when it is fired.
smok·er (smōk'ẽr), *n.* 1. a person or thing that smokes: as, that chimney is a bad *smoker*. 2. a person who habitually smokes tobacco. 3. a railroad car or compartment in which smoking is allowed, especially on a train on which smoking is not elsewhere allowed. 4. a social gathering for men only: so called because at one time etiquette forbade smoking in mixed gatherings.
smoke screen, a cloud of artificial smoke spread to screen the movements of troops, ships, etc.
smoke·stack (smōk'stak'), *n.* a pipe for the discharge of smoke from a steamship, locomotive, factory, etc.
smoke tree, any of a number of related small trees with filmy, feathery flower clusters resembling smoke.
smok·i·ly (smōk'ə-li), *adv.* in a smoky manner.
smok·i·ness (smōk'i-nis), *n.* the condition or quality of being smoky.
smoking car, a railroad car in which smoking is allowed; smoker.
smoking jacket, a loose, heavy jacket, usually trimmed with braid and worn for smoking indoors to protect other clothing from the smell of tobacco.
smoking room, a room or lounge set apart for smoking.
smok·y (smōk'i), *adj.* [SMOKIER (-i-ẽr), SMOKIEST (-i-ist)], 1. giving off smoke, especially more than is usual or desirable. 2. like, of, or as of smoke: as, a *smoky* haze. 3. filled with smoke. 4. having the color of smoke. 5. colored, tarnished, or soiled by smoke.
Smoky Hill, a river in Kansas, joining the Republican to form the Kansas River: length, 540 mi.
Smoky Mountains, Great Smoky Mountains, a range in North Carolina and Tennessee.
smoky quartz, cairngorm, a variety of quartz.
smol·der (smōl'dẽr), *v.i.* [Late ME. *smoldren* < Gmc. **smul-* (cf. SMELL); IE. base **smel-*, to burn slowly and smokily, seen also in Lith. *smilkstù*, to give off vapor], 1. to burn and smoke without flame; be consumed by slow combustion. 2. to exist in a suppressed state or with activity stifled. 3. to show signs of suppressed anger or hate: as, his glance *smoldered*. *n.* a smoldering. Also spelled **smoulder.**
Smo·lensk (smo-lensk', smō-lensk'; Russ. smô-lyensk'), *n.* 1. a region of the R.S.F.S.R. in west central European Russia: pop., 2,691,000. 2. its capital, on the Dnepr: pop., 157,000.
Smol·lett, Tobias George (smol'it), 1721–1771; British novelist.
smolt (smōlt), *n.* [special use of dial. *smolt*, shining < AS. *smolt*, *adj.* smooth, with reference to new scales of the fish], a young salmon at the stage during which it first leaves fresh water and descends to the sea.
smooch (smōōch), *v.t.* & *n.* smutch.
smooth (smōōth), *adj.* [ME. *smothe*; AS. (rare) *smoth* < **smanth-*; ? IE. **somo-s*, fitting together, suited, hence even], 1. *a*) having an even or level surface; having no roughness or projections that can be seen or felt. *b*) having its projections leveled by wear: as, a *smooth* tire. 2. having an even consistency; without lumps: as, a *smooth* paste. 3. even, calm, or gentle in flow or movement; untroubled by storm or roughness: as, *smooth* seas, a *smooth* voyage, etc. 4. free from interruptions, irregularities, obstacles, difficulties, etc.: as, *smooth* progress. 5. calm; serene; not easily agitated or ruffled, as a temper, disposition, etc. 6. free from hair, beard, etc.: as, a *smooth* cheek. 7. pleasing to the taste; not harsh or irritating; bland. 8. having an easy, gentle, flowing rhythm or sound. 9. suave, polished, or ingratiating, especially in a flattering, insincere way: as, *smooth* words, a *smooth* manner. 10. [Slang], very pleasant, attractive, or enjoyable: as, a *smooth* time. 11. [Slang], polished; competent; charming: as, a *smooth* dancer. 12. in *mechanics*, frictionless. 13. in *phonetics*, not aspirated. *v.t.* 1. to make level or even. 2. to remove the lumps from. 3. to free from interruptions, difficulties, etc.; make easy. 4. to make calm or serene; soothe. 5. to make less crude; polish; refine. *adv.* in a smooth manner. *n.* 1. something smooth; smooth part. 2. an act of smoothing. —*SYN.* see **easy, level.**
smooth away, to remove (difficulties, obstacles, etc.).
smooth down, to make smooth or calm; soothe.
smooth over, to cause to seem unimportant; make light of; palliate; minimize, as faults.
smooth·bore (smōōth'bôr', smōōth'bōr'), *adj.* having no grooves or ridges on the inner surface of the barrel: said of guns: opposed to *rifled*. *n.* a smoothbore gun.
smooth breathing, [after L. *spiritus lenis*], in Greek, 1. the sound of a vowel beginning a word when it is pronounced without an aspiration, or the sound of *h*, preceding it. 2. the symbol (') placed before such a vowel in writing. Distinguished from *rough breathing*.
smooth·en (smōōth''n), *v.t.* & *v.i.* to make or become smooth.
smooth-faced (smōōth'fāst'), *adj.* 1. having no beard or mustache; smooth-shaven. 2. having a smooth face, or surface: as, a *smooth-faced* tile. 3. having a false semblance of sincerity; plausibly ingratiating.
smooth muscle, muscle controlled by the involuntary nervous system, as that in the uterus, intestines, etc.: also called *nonstriated muscle*.
smooth-shav·en (smōōth'shāv''n), *adj.* wearing no beard or mustache.
smooth-spo·ken (smōōth'spō'k'n), *adj.* speaking in a pleasing, persuasive, or polished manner.
smooth-tongued (smōōth'tuŋd'), *adj.* smooth-spoken, especially in a plausible or flattering way.
smör·gås·bord, smor·gas·bord (smür'gəs-bôrd', smür'gəs-bōrd'; Sw. smẽr'gōs-bōrd'), *n.* [Sw.], 1. hors d'oeuvres or appetizers, especially as served buffet style at a long table. 2. a meal composed of these. 3. a restaurant serving smörgåsbord.

‡smor·zan·do (smôr-tsän'dô), *adj.* [It.], in *music*, dying away: abbreviated **smorz.**

smote (smōt), alternative past tense and past participle of **smite.**

smoth·er (smuth'ẽr), *v.t.* [ME. *smorthren, smothren* < *smorther, smother*, dense smoke; AS. has same base in *smorian*, to suffocate; akin to MLG. *smoren*, to smoke < var. of the IE. base of *smell, smolder*], 1. *a)* to prevent (a person) from breathing or getting air; suffocate; stifle. *b)* to kill by smothering. 2. to cover (a fire), excluding air from it and causing it to smolder or die down. 3. to cover over thickly: as, liver *smothered* in onions. 4. to hide or suppress by or as by covering; stifle: as, he *smothered* a yawn. *v.i.* 1. to be unable to breathe or get air; be suffocated. 2. to be hidden, stifled, or suppressed. 3. [Dial.], to smolder. *n.* 1. dense, suffocating smoke, dust, steam, etc. 2. [Archaic], a smoldering fire. 3. a smoldering state or condition. 4. a confused turmoil; welter.

smoth·er·y (smuth'ẽr-i), *adj.* liable to smother or stifle; suffocating.

smoul·der (smōl'dẽr), *v.i. & n.* smolder.

smudge (smuj), *n.* [Early Mod. Eng.; var. of *smutch;* cf. SLUDGE], 1. a stain, blur, or smear; dirty spot. 2. a fire made to produce dense smoke. 3. dense or suffocating smoke, as used in driving away insects or protecting plants from frost. *v.t.* [SMUDGED (smujd), SMUDGING], [ME. *smogen;* var. of *smutch, v.;* akin to or < source of D. *smotsen*, to besmirch; base as in ME. *smoten* (see SMUT)], 1. to smoke (an orchard, etc.) for protection against frost or insects. 2. to make dirty; soil; smutch. *v.i.* 1. to blur or smear: as, the ink *smudged* when he blotted it. 2. to be smudged.

smudg·i·ly (smuj'ə-li), *adv.* in a smudgy manner.

smudg·i·ness (smuj'i-nis), *n.* the quality or condition of being smudgy.

smudg·y (smuj'i), *adj.* [SMUDGIER (-i-ẽr), SMUDGIEST (-i-ist)], covered with smudges; stained, blurred, etc.

smug (smug), *adj.* [SMUGGER (-ẽr), SMUGGEST (-ist)], [prob. < LG. *smuk*, trim, neat; akin to G. *schmuck*, neat; for IE. base see SMOCK], 1. originally, neat; spruce; trim; smart. 2. narrowly contented with one's own accomplishments, beliefs, morality, etc.; self-satisfied; complacent.

smug·gle (smug''l), *v.t.* [SMUGGLED (-'ld), SMUGGLING], [< D. *smuckeln* or LG. *smuggeln;* akin to AS. *smugan*, to creep; for IE. base see SMOCK], 1. to bring into or take out of a country secretly, under illegal conditions or without paying the required import or export duties. 2. to bring, take, carry, introduce, etc. secretly or stealthily. *v.i.* to practice smuggling; be a smuggler.

smug·gler (smug'lẽr), *n.* [< LG. *smuggeler*], 1. a person engaged in smuggling. 2. a ship used in smuggling.

smut (smut), *n.* [< LG. *smutt;* akin to G. *schmutz*, dirt; AS. had cognate *smitte*], 1. *a)* sooty matter. *b)* a particle of this. 2. a mark made by something dirty; soiled spot. 3. obscene talk or writing. 4. in *botany*, *a)* a plant disease characterized by the appearance of masses of black spores which usually break up into a fine powder. *b)* any of a number of related fungi causing this disease. *v.t.* [SMUTTED (-id), SMUTTING], [later var. of ME. *smoten*, to besmirch; prob. < LG.; cf. D. *smotsen* (akin to G. *schmutzen*); see SMUDGE, SMUTCH], to mark or affect with smut; make smutty. *v.i.* to be marked or affected by smut; become smutty.

smutch (smuch), *v.t.* [< ME. **smuchchen*, **smochchen*, of which the recorded *smogen* (cf. SMUDGE) is a dial. var.; akin to & prob. < the source of D. *smotsen* (G. *schmutzen*) in the same sense; extension of the base of Eng. *smut*], to make dirty; smudge. *n.* 1. a dirty spot or mark; smudge. 2. soot, smut, grime, or dirt.

smutch·y (smuch'i), *adj.* [SMUTCHIER (-i-ẽr), SMUTCHIEST (-i-ist)], smudgy.

Smuts, Jan Chris·ti·aan (yän kris'ti-ȧn smuts), 1870–1950; South African statesman and general; prime minister (1919–1924; 1939–1948).

smut·ti·ly (smut'ə-li), *adv.* in a smutty manner.

smut·ti·ness (smut'i-nis), *n.* the quality or condition of being smutty.

smut·ty (smut'i), *adj.* [SMUTTIER (-i-ẽr), SMUTTIEST (-i-ist)], 1. soiled with smut. 2. affected with plant smut. 3. obscene.

Smyr·na (smũr'nə), *n.* a city in Turkey, on the Aegean Sea: pop., 200,000 (est. 1945): Turkish name, *Izmir.*

Smyr·ne·an (smũr'ni-ən), *adj.* of Smyrna.

Smyth, Sir **Robert Ste·phen·son** (stē'vən-sən smith), see **Baden-Powell.**

Sn, *stannum*, [L.], in *chemistry*, tin.

snack (snak), *n.* [ME. *snake*, a bite < *snaken*, to bite, snap; prob. < MD. *snacken*, to snap], 1. a share or part. 2. a small quantity of food or drink; light meal, usually one taken between regular meals.

snaf·fle (snaf''l), *n.* [short for *snaffle piece;* prob. < D. *snavel*, horse's muzzle; OD. *snabel, snavel*, dim. of *snabbe, snebbe*, bill of a bird; akin to G. *schnabel;* cf. SNAP], a light, jointed bit attached to a bridle and having no curb. *v.t.* [SNAFFLED (-'ld), SNAFFLING], to fit with or control by a snaffle.

sna·fu (sna-fōō', snaf'ōō), *adj.* [< *s*ituation *n*ormal, *a*ll *f*ouled (euphemism) *u*p], [Military Slang], in characteristic disorder or confusion; mixed up as usual. *v.t.* [SNAFUED (-fōōd', -ōōd), SNAFUING], [Military Slang], to throw into confusion; entangle.

snag (snag), *n.* [via. North. dial. < ON.; cf. ON. *snagi*, clothes peg, Norw. *snag*, sharp point, projection; akin to G. *schnake*], 1. a piece, part, or point that sticks out, especially one that is sharp or rough, as the broken end of a tree limb. 2. an underwater tree stump or branch that is dangerous to the navigation of a river, lake, etc. 3. a broken or irregular tooth; snaggletooth. 4. a break or tear, as in cloth, made by a splinter, snag, etc. 5. an obstacle, difficulty, etc. which is unexpected or hidden. *v.t.* [SNAGGED (snagd), SNAGGING], 1. to catch, tear, or damage in any way on a snag. 2. to impede with or as with a snag. 3. to clear (a body of water) of snags.

snag·gle·tooth (snag''l-tōōth'), *n.* [*pl.* SNAGGLETEETH (-tēth')], [< *snag*], 1. a tooth that sticks out beyond the others. 2. a crooked or broken tooth.

snag·gle·toothed (snag''l-tōōtht'), *adj.* having snaggleteeth.

snag·gy (snag'i), *adj.* [SNAGGIER (-i-ẽr), SNAGGIEST (-i-ist)], 1. of, or having the nature of, a snag. 2. full of snags, as a body of water. 3. having snags.

snail (snāl), *n.* [ME. *snaile;* AS. *snegl, snægl;* akin to G. dial. *schnägel*, ON. *snigill;* IE. base **sneg-*, **sneq-*, to creep, seen also in Eng. *snake, sneak*], 1. any of a large number of slow-moving gastropod mollusks living on land or in water and having a short, thick, wormlike body and a protective shell, usually spiral in shape: some kinds of snails are used as food. 2. any lazy, slow-moving person or animal; sluggard.

snail-paced (snāl'pāst'), *adj.* very slow-moving.

snake (snāk), *n.* [ME.; AS. *snaca;* akin to MLG.; for IE. base see SNAIL], 1. any of a wide variety of limbless reptiles with an elongated, scaly body and a tapering tail: some species have a poisonous bite. 2. a person or thing resembling a snake in any of various ways; specifically, *a)* a treacherous or deceitful person. *b)* a plumber's tool consisting of a long, flexible metal rod for removing obstructions from pipes, etc. *v.i.* [SNAKED (snākt), SNAKING], to move, curve, twist, or turn like a snake. *v.t.* [Colloq.], 1. to drag or pull, especially lengthwise and with force. 2. to pull quickly; jerk.

snake·bird (snāk'bũrd'), *n.* a tropical, fish-eating bird with a long, snakelike neck, slender head, and sharp-pointed bill.

snake charmer, a person, especially an Oriental, who charms or hypnotizes snakes by means of music or movements of the hands.

snake dance, 1. a dance forming part of a religious ceremony performed every two years by the Hopi Indians: the participants handle live rattlesnakes as part of the ritual. 2. a kind of informal parade in which the celebrants join hands in a long line, winding back and forth as they progress.

snake fence, a zigzag fence of rails that cross each other at an angle.

snake·head (snāk'hed'), *n.* a kind of American figwort with spikes of white or purple flowers; turtlehead.

snake in the grass, a person or thing that is evil or dangerous and hidden or seemingly harmless.

snake·mouth (snāk'mouth'), *n.* a kind of orchid native to eastern North America, with pink flowers and lance-shaped leaves.

Snake River, a river flowing westward and northward, from Yellowstone National Park into the Columbia: length, 1,038 mi.

snake·root (snāk'rōōt', snāk'root'), *n.* 1. any of a number of plants reputed to be remedies for snake bites. 2. the roots of any of these plants.

snake·skin (snāk'skin'), *n.* 1. a snake's skin. 2. leather made from this.

snake·stone (snāk'stōn'), *n.* 1. an ammonite. 2. a piece of stone or porous material supposed to cure the bite of a snake.

snak·y (snāk'i), *adj.* [SNAKIER (-i-ẽr), SNAKIEST (-i-ist)], 1. of or like a snake or snakes. 2. having a snakelike form; serpentine; winding; twisting. 3. cunningly treacherous or evil. 4. full of or infested with snakes. 5. formed of or entwined with snakes, as the caduceus.

snap (snap), *v.i.* [SNAPPED (snapt), SNAPPING], [MD. or MLG. *snappen;* akin to G. *schnappen;* Gmc. base **snab-*, seen also in Eng. *snaffle*], 1. to bring the jaws together sharply; bite suddenly (often with *at*): as, the animal *snapped* at the meat. 2. to snatch or grasp quickly or eagerly (with *at*): as, we *snapped* at the invitation. 3. to speak sharply, abruptly, or irritably (often with *at*). 4. to break or part suddenly, especially with a sharp, cracking sound; hence, 5. to give way suddenly under strain, as nerves, resistance, etc. 6. to make a sudden, sharp cracking or clicking sound: as, the fire is *snapping*, the whip *snapped* loudly. 7. to close, fasten, go into place, etc. with a snapping sound: as, the lock *snapped* shut. 8. to move or act suddenly and smartly: as, the soldiers *snapped* to attention. 9. to open and shut rapidly so as to appear to flash, as in anger: said of the eyes. ***v.t.*** 1. to grasp or seize suddenly with or as with a bite; take eagerly; snatch (often with *up*). 2. to break or sever suddenly or with a snapping sound. 3. to speak or utter sharply or harshly, as in anger (often with *out*). 4. to cause to make a snapping sound. 5. to close, fasten, put into place, etc. with a snapping sound: as, he *snapped* the safety before putting the gun away. 6. to strike sharply by releasing one end of something held under tension: as, he *snapped* her with a rubber band. 7. to cause to move suddenly and smartly: as, he *snapped* the ball to first base. 8. to take a snapshot of. 9. in *football*, to put (the ball) into play by sending it back to a receiver: said of a center. ***n.*** [MD. *snap*], 1. a sudden bite, grasp, snatch, catch, etc. 2. a sudden breaking or parting. 3. a sudden, sharp cracking or clicking sound: as, we heard the *snap* of the whip. 4. a short, angry utterance or manner of speaking. 5. a brief period or spell: said only of cold weather. 6. any clasp or fastening that closes with a click or snap. 7. a hard, thin cooky, usually flavored with ginger. 8. a snapshot. 9. [Colloq.], alertness, vigor, or energy: as, the performers seemed to have no *snap*. 10. [Slang], something easy, as a task, job, problem, etc.; hence, 11. [Slang], a person who is easy to influence, persuade, control, etc.; tractable person. ***adj.*** 1. made or done quickly or on the spur of the moment without deliberation; impulsive: as, a *snap* decision. 2. that fastens with a snap. 3. [Slang], simple; easy: as, a *snap* assignment. ***adv.*** with a snap.

not a snap, not a bit; not at all.

snap (a person's) head off, to speak sharply or harshly to, as in anger or impatience.

snap one's fingers at, to show lack of concern for; be careless of or indifferent toward.

snap out of it, to change suddenly from a bad condition to a better one; improve or recover quickly.

snap·back (snap′bak′), ***n.*** in *football*, the act of the center in passing the ball back to a receiver.

snap·drag·on (snap′drag′ən), ***n.*** [< *snap* + *dragon:* from the mouth-shaped flowers], 1. any of various related plants with white, yellow, red, or purplish, saclike, two-lipped flowers. 2. *a*) a game in which raisins, etc. are snatched from a bowl of burning brandy; flapdragon. *b*) that which is so snapped.

snap·per (snap′ẽr), ***n.*** [*pl.* SNAPPERS (-ẽrz), SNAPPER; see PLURAL, II, D, 1], 1. a person or thing that snaps. 2. a snapping turtle. 3. any of a group of tropical food fishes resembling the bass; especially, the red snapper. 4. a snapping beetle.

snap·pi·ly (snap′ə-li), ***adv.*** in a snappy manner.

snap·pi·ness (snap′i-nis), ***n.*** the quality or condition of being snappy.

snapping beetle, any of several beetles which jerk their bodies, making a snapping sound, when held in the fingers or turned on their backs.

snapping turtle, a large, fresh-water turtle of the eastern and southern United States, having powerful jaws which snap with great force: it feeds largely on fish and is widely used as food.

snap·pish (snap′ish), ***adj.*** 1. likely to snap or bite. 2. cross; irritable; uncivil; sharp-tongued.

snap·py (snap′i), ***adj.*** [SNAPPIER (-i-ẽr), SNAPPIEST (-i-ist)], 1. snappish; cross. 2. that snaps; snapping. 3. [Colloq.], full of life or vigor; brisk; strong; sharp: as, a *snappy* reply, pace, etc. 4. [Colloq.], stylish; smart.

make it snappy, [Slang], be quick; hurry.

snap roll, a maneuver in which an airplane makes one complete fast roll about its longitudinal axis while keeping its horizontal direction.

snap·shot (snap′shot′), ***n.*** 1. a hurried shot fired with little or no aim; quick, offhand shot. 2. a small photograph taken in an instant by snapping the shutter of a hand camera.

snare (snâr), ***n.*** [for sense 1, Early ME. < ON. *snara;* other senses < MD. & MLG. *snare;* akin to AS. *snearh*, cord, G. *schnur*, string; IE. base *(*s*)*ner-*, to twist, wind, as also in L. *nervus* (cf. NERVE), Eng. *narrow*], 1. a kind of trap for small animals, usually consisting of a noose which jerks tight upon the release of a spring trigger. 2. anything dangerous, risky, etc.

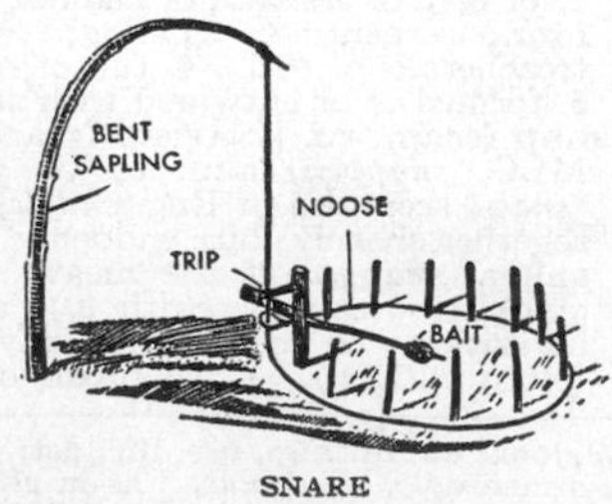

SNARE

that tempts or attracts; thing by which a person is entangled; trap. 3. a length of wire or gut across the bottom of a snare drum; hence, 4. *pl.* a set of snare drums. 5. in *surgery*, a wire noose for removing tumors, etc. ***v.t.*** [SNARED (snârd), SNARING], [ME. *snaren* < the *n.*], 1. to catch in a trap or snare. 2. to tempt or attract into a situation that is dangerous, risky, etc. —***SYN.*** see **catch, trap.**

snare drum, a small, double-headed drum with snares, or lengths of gut, strung across the bottom to increase the resonance.

snark (snärk), ***n.*** [prob. < *sn*ake + sh*ark*], an imaginary animal created by Lewis Carroll in his poem *The Hunting of the Snark.*

snarl (snärl), ***v.i.*** [extended from earlier *snar*, to growl; prob. < a Gmc. echoic base (cf. G. *schnarren*, Sw. *snarra*, to growl)], 1. to growl fiercely or harshly, baring the teeth, as a threatening dog. 2. to speak harshly and sharply, as in anger, impatience, etc. ***v.t.*** to utter or give vent to with a snarl: as, he *snarled* his contempt. ***n.*** 1. a snarling; fierce, angry growl. 2. a harsh utterance expressing anger, impatience, etc.

snarl (snärl), ***v.t.*** [ME. *snarlen* < *snare:* the formation may be ON. (cf. OSw. *snarel*, noose)], 1. to make knotted or tangled, as thread. 2. to make disordered or confused; complicate: as, traffic is *snarled.* 3. to ornament (metalwork) with a raised design, as by hammering. ***v.i.*** to become knotted or tangled. ***n.*** 1. a knotted or tangled mass or tuft; tangle: as, his hair is full of *snarls.* 2. a confused, disordered state or situation; complication; confusion.

snarl·y (snär′li), ***adj.*** [SNARLIER (-li-ẽr), SNARLIEST (-li-ist)], snarling; cross; bad-tempered.

snarl·y (snär′li), ***adj.*** [SNARLIER (-li-ẽr), SNARLIEST (-li-ist)], snarled; tangled; confused.

snatch (snach), ***v.t.*** [ME. *snacchen, snecchen;* prob. var. of *snakken*, to seize (cf. SNACK)], 1. to grasp or seize suddenly, eagerly, or without right, warning, etc.; grab. 2. to remove abruptly or hastily. 3. to take, get, or avail oneself of hastily or while there is a chance: as, he *snatched* a few hours of rest. 4. [Slang], to kidnap. ***n.*** 1. a snatching; sudden seizing or grab. 2. a brief period; short time or spell: as, a *snatch* of sleep. 3. a small portion, especially one that is incomplete or disconnected; fragment; bit: as, *snatches* of gossip. 4. [Slang], a kidnapping. —***SYN.*** see **take.**

snatch at, 1. to attempt to grasp or seize with a sudden movement; grab at. 2. to accept or take advantage of (a chance, etc.) with great eagerness.

snatch·y (snach′i), ***adj.*** [SNATCHIER (-i-ẽr), SNATCHIEST (-i-ist)], done in snatches; irregular; disconnected; not complete or continuous.

snath (snath), ***n.*** [AS. *snæd;* prob. influenced by ON. *sneitha*, to cut], the curved shaft or handle of a scythe.

snathe (snāth), ***n.*** a snath.

sneak (snēk), ***v.i.*** [ME. *sniken;* AS. *snican;* for IE. base see SNAIL], 1. to move quietly and stealthily so as to avoid being seen or heard; go furtively. 2. to be a sneak; behave in a stealthy, underhand, or cowardly manner. ***v.t.*** 1. to give, put, conduct, transfer, etc. secretly or in a stealthy, sneaking manner: as, he *sneaked* the jewels across the border; hence, 2. [Colloq.], to take stealthily; steal. ***n.*** 1. a person who sneaks; stealthy, underhand, contemptible person. 2. an act of sneaking. —***SYN.*** see **lurk.**

sneak out of, to avoid or escape (duty, a task, etc.) by sneaking or stealth.

sneak·er (snēk′ẽr), ***n.*** 1. a person or animal that sneaks. 2. *pl.* [so named from their noiseless tread], [Colloq.], canvas shoes with continuous sole and heel of one piece of soft rubber, used for indoor sports, etc.: also called *tennis shoes.*

sneak·ing (snēk′iŋ), ***adj.*** [ppr. of *sneak*], 1. cowardly; stealthy; underhand; furtive: as, a *sneaking* manner. 2. not admitted or made known to others; secret: as, a *sneaking* fondness for jazz music.

sneaking suspicion, a slight or increasing suspicion.

sneak preview, [Colloq.], an advance, usually unpublicized, showing of a motion picture, as for evaluating audience reaction prior to the regular showing.

sneak thief, a person who commits thefts in a sneaking way, without the use of force or violence.

sneak·y (snēk′i), ***adj.*** [SNEAKIER (-i-ẽr), SNEAKIEST (-i-ist)], of or like a sneak; sneaking; cowardly.

sneer (snêr), ***v.i.*** [ME. *sneren;* akin to Fris. *sneere*, to scorn, Dan. *snaere*, to grin like a dog; prob. < base of Eng. *snarl*], 1. to smile derisively; show scorn or contempt by a smiling grimace. 2. to express derision, scorn, or contempt in speech or writing. ***v.t.*** 1. to utter with a sneer or in a sneering manner. 2. to affect in a particular way by sneering: as, the proposal was *sneered* down. ***n.*** 1. an act of sneering. 2. a sneering expression, insinuation, etc. —***SYN.*** see **scoff.**

sneer·ing (snêr′iŋ), ***adj.*** characterized by a sneer; derisive; scornful.

sneeze (snēz), ***v.i.*** [SNEEZED (snēzd), SNEEZING], [ME. *snesen*, altered < *fnesen* (AS. *fneosan*); prob. < graphic confusion of *f* with long *s;* IE. base **pneu-*, to breathe, seen also in Gr. *pneuma*, breath (cf. PNEUMONIA)], to exhale breath from the nose and mouth in a sudden, involuntary, explosive action, as a result of an irritation of the nasal mucous membrane. *n.* an act of sneezing.

not to be sneezed at, not to be disregarded or considered lightly.

sneeze·weed (snēz′wēd′), *n.* any of a number of related coarse plants with bronze or yellow flowers said to cause sneezing.

sneeze·wort (snēz′wũrt′), *n.* a strong-smelling, white-flowered plant whose leaves are used in snuff.

snell (snel), *adj.* [ME.; AS.; akin to G. *schnell*], [Dial.], 1. quick; active. 2. clever; smart; acute. 3. severe; extreme; harsh. 4. keen; sharp.

snell (snel), *n.* [U.S. dial.; prob. < D. or D. dial.; cf. G. *schnellen*, to snap, spring back < base of prec.], a short length of gut, horsehair, etc. used to attach a fishhook to a fishline; leader.

snick (snik), *n.* [prob. a back-formation < *snick and snee;* see SNICKERSNEE], 1. a small cut or notch; nick. 2. in *cricket*, a glancing blow. *v.t.* 1. to make a snick in; cut slightly; nick. 2. to hit sharply. 3. in *cricket*, to hit (the ball) a glancing blow.

snick (snik), *n., v.t. & v.i.* [echoic], click.

snick·er (snik′ẽr), *v.i.* [echoic], 1. to laugh in a sly, partly stifled manner; giggle; titter: as, the class *snickered* at the teacher's mistake. 2. to neigh; nicker. *v.t.* to utter with a snicker. *n.* a sly, partly stifled laugh. —*SYN.* see **laugh.**

snick·er·snee (snik′ẽr-snē′), *n.* [< *snick and snee*, combat with knives; earlier also *stick or snee* < D. *steken*, to thrust, stab + *snijden*, to cut], a knife designed for use as a thrusting and cutting weapon.

snide (snīd), *adj.* [orig., counterfeit, bogus < thieves' slang; prob. of D. dial. or G. origin < base of G. *schneiden*, to cut, with reference to coin clipping and, later, to cutting, or sarcastic, remarks; cf. G. *schneidend*, sarcastic], [Slang], sly and malicious: as, a *snide* remark.

sniff (snif), *v.i.* [ME. *sniffen* (also *snevien*); akin to Dan. *snive;* ult. origin echoic; cf. SNIVEL, SNUFFLE], 1. to draw in air through the nose with enough force to be heard, as in clearing the nose or smelling something. 2. to express contempt, skepticism, etc. by sniffing. *v.t.* 1. to breathe in forcibly through the nose; inhale sharply. 2. to test the smell of by sniffing. 3. to detect, perceive, or get a suspicion of by or as by sniffing; smell; scent: as, we *sniffed* danger in the man's manner. *n.* 1. an act or sound of sniffing. 2. something sniffed.

snif·fle (snif′'l), *v.i.* [SNIFFLED (-'ld), SNIFFLING], to sniff repeatedly so as to check mucus running from the nose. *n.* an act or sound of sniffling.

the sniffles, [Colloq.], 1. a head cold. 2. the sniffling that accompanies a crying spell.

sniff·y (snif′i), *adj.* [SNIFFIER (-i-ẽr), SNIFFIEST (-i-ist)], [Colloq.], characterized by or having a tendency to sniff, especially as a sign of contempt; scornful; contemptuous; disdainful.

snif·ter (snif′tẽr), *n.* [< *snift*, var. of *sniff*], 1. a liquor glass that tapers to a small opening to concentrate the aroma. 2. [Slang], a small drink of liquor.

snig·ger (snig′ẽr), *n., v.t. & v.i.* [echoic], snicker.

snig·gle (snig′'l), *v.i.* [SNIGGLED (-'ld), SNIGGLING], [< dial. *snig*, an eel < base seen in *snail*], to fish for eels by putting a baited hook into their burrows. *v.t.* to catch (eels) by this method.

snip (snip), *v.t.* [SNIPPED (snipt), SNIPPING], [D. *snippen;* akin to *snap*], 1. to cut with scissors or shears in a short, quick stroke or strokes. 2. to remove by or as by such cutting. *v.i.* to make a short, quick cut or cuts. *n.* 1. a small cut made with scissors, etc. 2. the sound of this. 3. *a)* a small piece cut off. *b)* any small piece; bit. 4. *pl.* heavy hand shears used for cutting sheet metal, etc. 5. [Colloq.], a young, small, or insignificant person, especially one regarded with contempt.

snipe (snīp), *n.* [*pl.* SNIPES (snīps), SNIPE; see PLURAL, II, D, 1], [ME. *snype;* ON. *snipa* (akin to G. *schnepfe*) < base seen in Eng. *snip, snap;* basic sense "bird which snaps up"], 1. any of several wading birds related to the woodcock, living chiefly in marshy places and characterized by a long, flexible bill used in digging for worms, etc. 2. a shot from a hidden position. 3. [Slang], a cigar or cigarette butt. *v.i.* [SNIPED (snīpt), SNIPING], 1. to hunt or shoot snipe. 2. to shoot from a hidden position at separate individuals of an enemy force.

snip·er (snīp′ẽr), *n.* in *military usage*, a sharpshooter concealed to harass the enemy by picking off individual members, usually at long range with a telescopic rifle.

snip·pet (snip′it), *n.* [dim. of *snip*], 1. a small scrap or fragment, especially one snipped or cut off. 2. [Colloq.], a young, small, or insignificant person; snip.

snip·pet·y (snip′it-i), *adj.* 1. made up of scraps or snippets. 2. [Colloq.], snippy.

snip·pi·ly (snip′ə-li), *adv.* in a snippy manner.

snip·pi·ness (snip′i-nis), *n.* a snippy state or quality.

snip·py (snip′i), *adj.* [SNIPPIER (-i-ẽr), SNIPPIEST (-i-ist)], 1. made up of small scraps or snips; fragmentary. 2. [Colloq.], curt, sharp, or snappish, especially in an insolent manner.

snitch (snich), *v.t.* [< 18th-c. thieves' slang; orig. sense "a nose"; cf. SNOUT], [Slang], to steal (usually something of little value). *v.i.* [Slang], 1. to be a petty thief; steal. 2. to be an informer; tell; peach (usually with *on*). *n.* [Slang], an informer.

sniv·el (sniv′'l), *v.i.* [SNIVELED or SNIVELLED (-'ld), SNIVELING or SNIVELLING], [ME. *snivelen;* AS. **snyflan* < base seen in *snofl* & *snyflung*, mucus], 1. to have mucus running from the nose. 2. to sniff repeatedly, as from a head cold, crying, etc.; sniffle; snuffle. 3. to cry and sniffle. 4. to fret or complain in a whining, tearful manner. 5. to make a whining, tearful, often false display of grief, sympathy, disappointment, etc. *n.* 1. nasal mucus. 2. the act of sniveling or sniffling. 3. a sniveling, whining display of grief, etc.

snob (snob), *n.* [orig. dial. "boy, cobbler's boy" < ON. *snāpr*, dolt; other senses via cant, prob. < LG. source; ? akin to *snub*], 1. [Obs.], a person having no wealth or social rank; one of the common people. 2. a person who attaches great importance to wealth, social position, etc., having contempt for and keeping aloof from those whom he considers his inferiors, often one admiring, imitating, and seeking to associate with those whom he considers his superiors. 3. a person who regards himself as better than others in some way and behaves undemocratically: as, an intellectual *snob*.

snob·ber·y (snob′ẽr-i), *n.* [*pl.* SNOBBERIES (-iz)], snobbish behavior or character, or an instance of this.

snob·bish (snob′ish), *adj.* of, like, or characteristic of a snob or snobs.

snood (snōōd), *n.* [< AS. *snod*, via dial.; akin to OSw. *snoth*, string, cord; IE. base **snē-*, etc., to draw together, spin (cf. NEEDLE)], 1. a tie or ribbon formerly worn around the hair, especially by young unmarried women. 2. a netlike bag worn at the back of a woman's head to hold the hair. 3. a hat or part of a hat resembling this. 4. in *fishing*, a snell. *v.t.* to bind or hold up (the hair) with a snood.

snoop (snōōp), *v.i.* [D. *snoepen;* cf. SNOUT], [Colloq.], to look about, in a sneaking, prying way. *n.* [Colloq.], 1. a person who snoops. 2. a snooping.

snoot (snōōt), *n.* [ME. *snute;* see SNOUT], [Colloq.], 1. the nose. 2. the face. 3. a grimace.

snoot·i·ly (snōōt′'l-i), *adv.* [Colloq.], in a snooty manner.

snoot·i·ness (snōōt′i-nis), *n.* [Colloq.], the quality or state of being snooty.

snoot·y (snōōt′i), *adj.* [SNOOTIER (-i-ẽr), SNOOTIEST (-i-ist)], [*snoot*, *n.* + *-y*], [Colloq.], haughty; snobbish.

snooze (snōōz), *n.* [< 18th-c. cant; prob. < LG. *snūsen* (Dan. *snuse*), to sniff, snore; cf. SNOUT], [Colloq.], a brief sleep; nap; doze. *v.i.* [SNOOZED (snōōzd), SNOOZING], [Colloq.], to take a brief sleep; nap; doze; drowse.

Sno·qual·mie Falls (snō-kwol′mi), a waterfall of the Snoqualmie River, Washington: height, 268 ft.

snore (snôr, snōr), *v.i.* [SNORED (snôrd, snōrd), SNORING], [ME. *snoren;* origin echoic], to breathe with a harsh, vibrating sound while asleep, usually with the mouth open. *v.t.* to spend or pass (time) in snoring (with *away*, etc.). *n.* the act or sound of snoring.

snor·kel (snôr′k'l) *n.* [G. *schnörkel*, spiral], a device for submarines, consisting of air intake and exhaust tubes for Diesel engines and for ventilation: it permits submergence for long periods.

snort (snôrt), *v.i.* [ME. *snorten, snurten;* prob. < *snoren*, to snore], 1. to force breath suddenly and violently through the nostrils so as to make a harsh sound: as, the horse *snorted* at our approach. 2. to express anger, contempt, or the like by a snort. 3. to make a noise like a snort: as, the outboard motor *snorted* and stopped. 4. [Colloq.], to laugh with a loud outburst or boisterously. *v.t.* 1. to express or utter with a snort. 2. to expel or emit by or as by a snort. *n.* 1. the act or sound of snorting. 2. a small drink of liquor.

snot (snot), *n.* [ME. *snot, snotte;* AS. (*ge*)*snot*, mucus; akin to G. dial. *schnutz;* for IE. base see SNOUT], 1. nasal mucus: vulgar term. 2. [Slang], an offensive or contemptible person.

snot·ty (snot′i), *adj.* [SNOTTIER (-i-ẽr), SNOTTIEST (-i-ist)], 1. of, like, or dirtied with snot. 2. [Slang], *a)* offensive; contemptible. *b)* impudent, haughty, etc.

snout (snout), *n.* [ME. *snoute, snute;* prob. < MD. *snute, snuite;* akin to G. *schnauze;* IE. base **snā-*, etc., to drip fluid, wetness, seen also in L. *natare* (< **snə-t*), to swim (cf. NATATION), Eng. *snot, snuff*, etc.; basic sense "that drips mucus"], 1. *a)* the projecting nose and jaws, or muzzle, of an animal. *b)* some anterior prolongation of the head resembling this, as in a weevil; rostrum. 2. something like an animal's snout, as a nozzle or spout. 3. [Colloq.], a human nose, especially one that is large, prominent, etc.

snout beetle, a small, scaly weevil with a long beak or snout, living chiefly on grains, fruits, and nuts.

snow (snō), *n.* [ME.; AS. *snaw;* akin to G. *schnee;* IE. base **sneigwh-*, to snow, **snoigwhos*, snow, seen also in OIr. *snechta*, Russ. *snieg*, L. *nix*, *nivis*, etc.], 1. particles of water vapor which when frozen in the upper air fall to earth as soft, white, crystalline flakes. 2. a falling of snow. 3. a mass or accumulation of fallen snow. 4. [Poetic], whiteness. 5. something like snow in whiteness, texture, etc. 6. [Slang], cocaine or heroin. *v.i.* [AS. *sniwian*], to fall as or like snow. *v.t.* 1. to shower or let fall as or like snow. 2. to cover, obstruct, etc. with or as with snow (with *in, up, under*, etc.).

snow·ball (snō'bôl'), *n.* 1. a mass of snow packed together into a ball. 2. a variety of cranberry bush with large, round clusters of small, white flowers; guelder-rose. *v.i.* 1. to increase or accumulate rapidly like a rolling ball of snow. 2. to throw snowballs. *v.t.* to throw snowballs at.

snow·bank (snō'baŋk'), *n.* a large mass of snow, especially a drift on a hillside, in a gully, etc.

snow·ber·ry (snō'ber'i, snō'bẽr-i), *n.* [*pl.* SNOWBERRIES (-iz)], 1. any of a number of plants with round, white berries. 2. the fruit of any of these plants.

snow·bird (snō'bũrd'), *n.* [*snow* + *bird*], 1. an American bird of the finch family, with a gray back and white breast; junco. 2. the snow bunting. 3. [cf. SNOW, 6 & BIRD, 5], [Slang], a person addicted to the use of cocaine or heroin.

snow-blind (snō'blīnd'), *adj.* blinded temporarily by exposure to the rays of the sun reflected from snow.

snow blindness, the condition of being snow-blind.

snow-bound (snō'bound'), *adj.* enclosed or confined by snow.

snow-broth (snō'brôth'), *n.* 1. a mixture of snow and water, or melted snow. 2. ice-cold liquor.

snow bunting, a small finch inhabiting cold regions in the northern hemisphere: also **snowflake.**

snow·bush (snō'boosh'), *n.* any of a number of related California shrubs with many small, white flowers.

snow·cap (snō'kap'), *n.* a cap of snow, as on a mountain.

snow-capped (snō'kapt'), *adj.* having the top covered with snow, as a mountain, tree, etc.

snow-clad (snō'klad'), *adj.* [Poetic], covered with snow.

Snow·don (snō'd'n), *n.* a mountain in northwestern Wales: height, 3,557 ft.

snow·drift (snō'drift'), *n.* 1. a mass or pile of snow formed by the action of the wind. 2. snow carried along by the wind.

snow·drop (snō'drop'), *n.* 1. a low-growing bulb plant with drooping white flowers which appear in early spring. 2. its bulb or flower. 3. the common anemone.

snow·fall (snō'fôl'), *n.* 1. a fall of snow. 2. the amount of snow that falls in a given area or period of time.

snow·flake (snō'flāk'), *n.* 1. a single feathery crystal of snow. 2. the snow bunting. 3. any plant resembling the snowdrop.

SNOWFLAKES
A, star form; B, composite form; C, triangular form; D, tabular form

snow ice, white, opaque ice consisting of frozen slush.

snow·i·ly (snō'ə-li), *adv.* in a snowy manner.

snow·i·ness (snō'i-nis), *n.* the quality or condition of being snowy.

snow lily, a white dogtooth violet of the Rocky Mountains.

snow line (or **limit**), the lower boundary of a high region in which snow never melts.

snow plant, a red, fleshy, parasitic plant with hanging red flowers and no leaves, growing in the pine forests of the Sierra Nevada, and often found in early spring before the snow has melted.

snow·plow (snō'plou'), *n.* any plowlike device or machine used to clear snow off a road, railroad, etc.

snow pudding, a kind of fluffy pudding made with beaten egg whites, sugar, and flavored gelatin.

snow·shed (snō'shed'), *n.* a long shed or shelter covering a section of railroad track which might otherwise become blocked with snow.

snow·shoe (snō'shōō'), *n.* a racket-shaped frame of wood fitted with crosspieces and crisscrossed with strips of leather, etc., worn on the feet to prevent sinking in deep snow. *v.i.* [SNOWSHOED (-shōōd'), SNOWSHOEING], to use snowshoes in walking.

SNOWSHOES

snow·storm (snō'stôrm'), *n.* a snow accompanied by a strong wind.

snow-white (snō'hwīt'), *adj.* white as snow.

snow·y (snō'i), *adj.* [SNOWIER (-i-ẽr), SNOWIEST (-i-ist)], 1. characterized by snow. 2. covered or filled with snow: as, a *snowy* valley. 3. like or suggestive of snow; specifically, *a*) pure; unsoiled; spotless. *b*) white. 4. of or consisting of snow.

snub (snub), *v.t.* [SNUBBED (snubd), SNUBBING], [ME. *snubben;* ON. *snubba*, to chide, rebuke, snub], 1. originally, to check or interrupt with sharp or slighting words. 2. to treat with scorn, contempt, disdain, etc.; behave coldly toward; slight. 3. to stop or check the movement of suddenly: said of a rope, cable, etc., or of something, as a boat, to which this is attached. *n.* 1. scornful, slighting action or treatment; a deliberate discourtesy; affront. 2. a snubbing, or checking. *adj.* short and turned up: said of the nose.

snub·ber (snub'ẽr), *n.* 1. a person who snubs. 2. a thing used for checking motion by snubbing. 3. a kind of automobile shock absorber which operates by restricting the action of the body springs.

snub·by (snub'i), *adj.* [SNUBBIER (-i-ẽr), SNUBBIEST (-i-ist)], 1. turned up; snub. 2. tending to snub or slight.

snub-nosed (snub'nōzd'), *adj.* having a snub nose.

snuff (snuf), *n.* [ME. *snuff;* prob. akin to MHG. *snipfen*, to snip, snap off, G. *schnipfel*, a shred, morsel], the charred end of a candlewick. *v.t.* [ME. *snuffen* < the *n.*], 1. to trim off the charred end of (a candlewick). 2. to put out (a candle) with snuffers or by pinching.

snuff out, 1. to put out (a candle, etc.); extinguish. 2. to bring to an end suddenly or violently; destroy.

snuff (snuf), *v.t.* [MD. *snuffen;* base as in *snout*], 1. to draw in through the nose; inhale strongly; sniff. 2. to smell, sniff, or sniff at. *v.i.* 1. to sniff or snort. 2. [Rare], to take or use powdered tobacco or snuff. *n.* 1. the act or sound of snuffing; sniff. 2. *a*) a preparation of powdered tobacco taken up into the nose by sniffing or applied to the gums with a snuff stick. *b*) a pinch of this. 3. any powder taken by inhaling. 4. smell; scent; odor.

up to snuff, [Colloq.], 1. up to the usual standard, as in health, quality, etc. 2. not easily cheated or deceived; knowing; alert.

snuff·box (snuf'boks'), *n.* a small, usually ornamental box for holding snuff.

snuff·ers (snuf'ẽrz), *n.pl.* an instrument, as a kind of shears, for snuffing a candle: also **pair of snuffers.**

snuf·fi·ness (snuf'i-nis), *n.* a snuffy quality or state.

snuf·fle (snuf''l), *v.i.* [SNUFFLED (-'ld), SNUFFLING], [freq. of *snuff* (to sniff)], 1. to breathe audibly and with difficulty or by constant sniffing, as a dog in trailing; sniff or sniffle. 2. to speak or sing in a nasal tone. 3. [Rare], to speak in a whining, hypocritical manner. *v.t.* to utter by snuffling. *n.* 1. the act or sound of snuffling. 2. a nasal tone or twang. 3. [Rare], whining, hypocritical speech.

the snuffles, a condition in which the nostrils are obstructed by mucus, as in a cold, causing snuffling.

snuff stick, a soft stick chewed at one end and used for dipping snuff and applying it to the gums.

snuff·y (snuf'i), *adj.* [SNUFFIER (-i-ẽr), SNUFFIEST (-i-ist)], 1. like snuff, as in color or texture. 2. having the habit of taking snuff. 3. soiled with snuff. 4. disagreeable; unattractive.

snuff·y (snuf'i), *adj.* [SNUFFIER (-i-ẽr), SNUFFIEST (-i-ist)], [*snuff* (to sniff) + *-y*], sulky; displeased; annoyed.

snug (snug), *adj.* [SNUGGER (-ẽr), SNUGGEST (-ist)], [Early Mod. Eng. < nautical lang.; prob. < LG. (cf. E.Fris. *snugge*, D. *snugger*, smooth, neat, dainty)], 1. protected from the weather or the cold; comfortable; secure; warm; cozy. 2. small but well arranged; compact and convenient; neat; trim: as, a *snug* cottage. 3. large enough to provide ease and comfort: said of an income. 4. tight or close in fit: as, is the coat too *snug?* 5. trim and well-built; seaworthy. 6. hidden: as, the thief kept *snug* behind the door. *adv.* so as to be snug. *v.i.* [SNUGGED (snugd), SNUGGING], [Dial.], to snuggle. *v.t.* to make snug or secure. —***SYN.*** see **comfortable.**

snug down, in *nautical usage*, to make ready for a storm by reducing sail, lashing movable gear, etc.

snug·ger·y (snug'ẽr-i), *n.* [*pl.* SNUGGERIES (-iz)], something snug, as a place, room, position, etc.

snug·gle (snug''l), *v.i.* [SNUGGLED (-'ld), SNUGGLING], [freq. of *snug*], to lie closely and comfortably; nestle; cuddle, as for warmth, in affection, etc. *v.t.* to hold or draw close or in a comfortable position; cuddle; nestle.

so (sō), *adv.* [ME. *so, swo;* AS. *swa*, so, as; akin to Goth. *swa*, OHG. *so;* IE. base **se-*, **swe-*, reflexive particle], 1. in the way or manner shown, expressed, indicated, understood, etc.; as stated or described; in such a manner: as, hold your golf club *so.* 2. *a*) to the degree expressed or understood; to such an extent: as, why are you *so* late? *b*) to a very high degree; very: as, they are *so* happy together. *c*) [Colloq.], very much: as, she *so* wants to go. 3. for the reason specified; therefore; as a result; consequently: as, they were late, and *so* didn't go. 4. more or less; approximately that number, amount, etc.: as, he won fifty dollars or *so*: in this sense, *so* is often regarded as a pronoun. 5. also; likewise: as, she enjoys music, and *so* does he: also used colloquially in contradicting a negative statement, as, I did *so* tell the truth! 6. then: as, *so* you really don't like my hat. *conj.* 1. in order that; with the purpose that: usually followed by *that*, as, he died *so* (that) we might live. 2. [Colloq.], with the result that. 3. if only; as long as; provided that (often followed by *that*). As a conjunction, *so* is sometimes used colloquially as a superfluous element connecting clauses in narration. Example: *So* I told him we would go. *So* he said we shouldn't bother. *So* we didn't. ***pron.*** 1. that which has been specified or named: as, he was a poor man, but he did not remain *so*. 2. see *adv.* sense 4. ***interj.*** an exclamation expressing surprise, approval or disapproval, triumph, etc., or a command to stop.

and so on (or **forth**), and others; and the rest; and in like manner; et cetera (etc.).

so as, 1. with the purpose or result (followed by an infinitive). 2. provided that.

so what? [Colloq.], even if so, what then?: used to express disregard, challenge, contempt, etc.

so (sō), *n.* in *music*, sol.

So., 1. South. 2. southern.

S.O., 1. Signal Officer. 2. Special Order.

soak (sōk), *v.t.* [ME. *soken;* AS. *socian* < base of *sucan;* see SUCK], 1. to saturate or make thoroughly wet, as by placing in liquid for a long period. 2. to take in (liquid) by sucking or absorbing (usually with *up*). 3. to take in mentally, especially with little effort (usually with *up*). 4. [Colloq.], to drink (liquor), especially to excess. 5. [Slang], to give a heavy blow to. 6. [Slang], to charge excessively; make pay too dearly. 7. [Slang], to make (one) drunk. 8. [Slang], to pawn. *v.i.* 1. to remain in long contact with moisture so as to become thoroughly wet or saturated. 2. to pass or penetrate: as, the fact *soaked* into his head. 3. [Colloq.], to drink to excess. *n.* 1. the act or process of soaking. 2. the state of being soaked. 3. liquid used for soaking or steeping. 4. [Slang], a drunkard. 5. [Slang], a drunken spree. 6. [Slang], the state of being pawned: as, in *soak*. 7. [Slang], a hard blow, as with the fist.

soak out, to draw out by or as by soaking.

SYN.—**soak** implies immersion in a liquid, etc. as for the purpose of absorption, thorough wetting, softening, etc. (to *soak* bread in milk); **saturate** implies absorption to a point where no more can be taken up (air *saturated* with moisture); **drench** implies a thorough wetting as by a downpour (a garden *drenched* by the rain); **steep** usually suggests soaking for the purpose of extracting the essence of something (to *steep* tea); **impregnate** implies the penetration and permeation of one thing by another (wood *impregnated* with creosote).

soak·age (sōk'ij), *n.* [see -AGE], 1. a soaking or being soaked. 2. liquid that has seeped out or been absorbed.

soak·ers (sōk'ẽrz), *n.pl.* short knitted pants of absorbent material, especially wool, put on over a baby's diaper for added protection.

so-and-so (sō''n-sō'), *n.* [*pl.* SO-AND-SOS (-sōz')], [Colloq.], some person or thing either not specified or not known: often used euphemistically in place of a stronger epithet.

soap (sōp), *n.* [ME. *sope, sape;* AS. *sape;* akin to G. *seife;* IE. base **seib-*, to trickle, run out, seen also in L. *sebum*, tallow (cf. SEBACEOUS); prob. basic sense "liquid gum or fat"], 1. a substance mixed with water to produce suds for washing or cleaning: soaps are usually produced by the action of an alkali, as caustic soda or potash, on a fat or oil. 2. any metallic salt of a fatty acid. 3. [Slang], money, especially as used for bribery. *v.t.* to rub or treat with soap.

no soap, [Slang], the offer, suggestion, etc. is not acceptable.

soap·bark (sōp'bärk'), *n.* 1. a tree of the rose family, with leathery leaves, white flower clusters, and soaplike inner bark used in cleansing preparations. 2. any of several shrubs of the mimosa family with such bark. Also **soapbark tree.** 3. the bark of any of these trees.

soap·ber·ry (sōp'ber'i, sōp'bẽr-i), *n.* [*pl.* SOAPBERRIES (-iz)], 1. any of a number of related trees with white or yellowish flowers and round fruit containing a soapy material: also **soapberry tree.** 2. the fruit.

soap·box (sōp'boks'), *n.* 1. a box or carton for soap. 2. any box used as a platform by a person making an informal speech to a street audience. *adj.* of or characteristic of such speeches or speakers. *v.i.* to speak informally to a street audience.

soap bubble, 1. a bubble of soapy water; hence, 2. something short-lived, unsubstantial, or ephemeral.

soap flakes, soap in the form of thin flakes or chips: also **soap chips.**

soap·i·ness (sōp'i-nis), *n.* the quality or condition of being soapy.

soap opera, [Colloq.], a daytime radio serial drama of a melodramatic, sentimental nature: so called because many are sponsored by soap manufacturers.

soap·stone (sōp'stōn'), *n.* steatite, a soft talc in rock form, used for griddles, bed warmers, etc.

soap·suds (sōp'sudz'), *n.pl.* soapy water, especially when stirred into a foam.

soap·wort (sōp'wûrt'), *n.* any of a number of related plants with white, pink, or red flowers and thick juice which produces a lather in water.

soap·y (sōp'i), *adj.* [SOAPIER (-i-ẽr), SOAPIEST (-i-ist)], 1. covered with or containing soap. 2. of, like, or characteristic of soap. 3. [Slang], suave; unctuous; oily.

soar (sôr, sōr), *v.i.* [ME. *soren;* OFr. *essorer*, to expose (wings) to the air, hence soar into the air, as a falcon; LL. **exaurare* < L. *ex-*, out + *aura*, air (cf. AURA)], 1. to rise or fly high into the air. 2. to fly, sail, or glide along high in the air. 3. to glide without loss of altitude, as an airplane. 4. to rise above the usual or ordinary level; be elevated. *v.t.* [Poetic], to reach by soaring. *n.* 1. soaring range or scope. 2. the act of soaring. —*SYN.* see **fly.**

sob (sob), *v.i.* [SOBBED (sobd), SOBBING], [ME. *sobben;* AS. **sobbian* < base of *supan*, to swallow, suck in (cf. SUP); IE. base **seu-*, to suck, something soft, seen also in L. *sugere*, to suck, AS. *soppe* (cf. SOP), etc.], 1. to weep aloud with a catch or break in the voice and short, gasping breaths. 2. to make a sound like that of sobbing, as the wind, an animal in pain, etc. *v.t.* 1. to bring (oneself) into a given state, especially sleep, by sobbing. 2. to utter with sobs. *n.* the act or sound of a person or thing that sobs. —*SYN.* see **cry.**

so·be·it (sō-bē'it), *conj.* [Archaic], provided; if it should be that.

so·ber (sō'bẽr), *adj.* [ME. & OFr. *sobre;* L. *sobrius*], 1. temperate or sparing in the use of alcoholic liquor. 2. not drunk. 3. temperate in any way; not extreme or extravagant. 4. serious, solemn, grave, or sedate. 5. quiet; plain; not bright or garish: said of color, clothes, etc. 6. not exaggerated or distorted: as, the *sober* truth. 7. characterized by reason, sanity, or self-control; showing mental and emotional balance. *v.t.* & *v.i.* to make or become sober (often with *up* or *down*). —*SYN.* see **serious.**

so·ber-mind·ed (sō'bẽr-mīn'did), *adj.* of a sober mind.

So·bies·ki, John (sô-byes'ki), see **John III.**

so·bri·e·ty (sō-brī'ə-ti), *n.* [ME. *sobrete;* OFr. *sobriete;* L. *sobrietas* < *sobrius*, sober], the state or quality of being sober; specifically, *a*) temperance or moderation, especially in the use of drink. *b*) seriousness, solemnity, gravity, or sedateness of manner or appearance.

so·bri·quet (sō'bri-kā'), *n.* [Fr.; OFr. *soubz briquet*, chuck under the chin (cf. It. *sottobecco*, nickname, lit. under the beak); prob. *soubz* (Fr. *sous*), under + *briquet*, chest (cf. BRISKET)], 1. a nickname. 2. an assumed name. Also **soubriquet.**

sob sister, [Slang], a woman journalist, especially one who writes sentimental human-interest stories.

sob story, a sentimental account or story intended to arouse pity or compassion.

Soc., Socialist.

Soc., soc., society.

soc·age (sok'ij), *n.* [ME.; Anglo-Fr.; ML. *socagium*, lit., tenure of one over whom his lord had a certain jurisdiction < *soc;* see SOKE], a medieval English system of land tenure in which a tenant held land in return for a fixed payment or for certain stated nonmilitary services to his lord.

so-called (sō'kôld'), *adj.* known or called by this term, but usually inaccurately or improperly so: as, he is a *so-called* liberal.

soc·cer (sok'ẽr), *n.* [altered < *association;* cf. *rugger* for *Rugby football*], a game played with a round ball by two teams of eleven men on a field with a goal at either end: the ball is moved chiefly by kicking or by bunting with the head, the use of the hands and arms being prohibited: also called *association football.*

So·che (sō'che'), *n.* a city in western Sinkiang, China: pop., 70,000: also called *Yarkand.*

so·cia·bil·i·ty (sō'shə-bil'ə-ti), *n.* [*pl.* SOCIABILITIES (-tiz)], quality, fact, or instance of being sociable.

so·cia·ble (sō'shə-b'l), *adj.* [Fr.; L. *sociabilis* < *sociare*, to associate < *socius*, companion], 1. enjoying the company of others; fond of companionship; companionable. 2. friendly; agreeable, especially in an easy, informal way; affable. 3. characterized by pleasant, informal conversation and companionship: as, a *sociable* evening. *n.* a social, especially a church social.

so·cia·bly (sō'shə-bli), *adv.* in a sociable manner.

so·cial (sō'shəl), *adj.* [< Fr. or L.; Fr. *social;* L. *socialis* < *socius*, companion; akin to L. *sequi*, to follow, AS. *secg*, a man, warrior], 1. of or having to do with human beings living together as a group in a situation requiring that they have dealings with one another: as, *social* consciousness, *social* reform, *social* problems. 2. living in this way: as, modern man is *social*, the family is a *social* unit. 3. of or having to do with the ranks or activities of society, especially the more exclusive or fashionable of these: as, a *social* climber, *social* notes. 4. sociable; getting along well with others: as, a *social* nature. 5. of, for, or fond of friends, companionship, etc.: as, a *social* club. 6. offering material aid, vocational advice, etc. to those who need it; of or engaged in welfare work: as, a *social* worker or agency. 7. living or associating in groups or communities: as, the ant is a *social* creature. 8. socialist. 9. in *botany*, growing in clumps or masses. 10. in *history*, of or between allies or confederates, as a war. ***n.*** an informal gathering of people for recreation or amusement; party.

social climber, a person who tries to get acquainted with distinguished or wealthy people.

social contract (or **compact**), the theory, put forward by Hobbes, Locke, and Rousseau, that society had its origin in loose associations of individuals for mutual protection, and that since out of these grew the concepts of law and sovereignty, government cannot be by force alone but must rest upon the consent of the governed.

Social Credit, the theory that the profits of industry are not true earnings and should be returned to the community as a whole, together with all interest, in the form of dividends to consumers: put forward by C. H. Douglas (1879–1952), English engineer.

social dancing, ballroom dancing.

Social Democracy, 1. Social Democratic parties collectively. 2. their doctrines, methods, etc.

Social Democrat, a member or adherent of a Social Democratic party.

So·cial-Dem·o·crat·ic (sō′shəl-dem′ə-krat′ik), ***adj.*** of, characteristic of, or like Social Democracy or Social Democrats.

Social Democratic Party, 1. a German Marxist political party formed in 1875 by the merger of the General German Workers' Association, founded in 1863 by F. Lassalle, with the Social Democratic Workers' Party, founded in 1869 by A. Bebel and W. Liebknecht. 2. any of various similar political parties in other countries, often called *Socialist* parties.

social disease, venereal disease.

social evil, 1. anything that threatens the welfare of the people, as illicit trade in narcotics, slum housing, etc. 2. prostitution: a euphemism.

social insurance, any government measure, as a pension plan, health and accident insurance, etc., protecting people in low-income groups against economic and industrial hazards.

so·cial·ism (sō′shəl-iz′m), ***n.*** [cf. Fr. *socialisme*], 1. the theory or system of the ownership and operation of the means of production and distribution by society or the community rather than by private individuals, with all members of society or the community sharing in the work and the products. 2. [often S-], *a)* political movement for establishing such a system. *b)* the doctrines, methods, etc. of the Socialist parties. 3. in *Communist doctrine*, the stage of society coming between the capitalist stage and the communist stage, in which private ownership of the means of production and distribution has been eliminated, as in the Soviet Union, and the production of goods is sufficient to permit realization of the slogan *from each according to his ability, to each according to his work.* See also **communism.**

so·cial·ist (sō′shəl-ist), ***n.*** 1. an advocate or supporter of socialism. 2. [S-], a member of a Socialist party. ***adj.*** 1. of, characteristic of, or like socialism or socialists. 2. advocating or supporting socialism.

so·cial·is·tic (sō′shə-lis′tik), ***adj.*** socialist.

so·cial·is·ti·cal·ly (sō′shə-lis′ti-k'l-i, sō′shə-lis′tik-li), ***adv.*** in a socialistic manner.

Socialist Party, a political party based on the principles of socialism advocated by Marx and Engels but later extensively modified by various revisionists: abbreviated **S.P.:** see also **Social Democratic Party.**

so·cial·ite (sō′shə-līt′), ***n.*** [Colloq.], a person who is prominent in fashionable society.

so·ci·al·i·ty (sō′shi-al′ə-ti), ***n.*** [< Fr. or L.; Fr. *socialité;* L. *socialitas*], 1. the quality or state of being social or sociable; sociability. 2. [*pl.* SOCIALITIES (-tiz)], the trait or tendency in individuals to join together in groups and associate with each other.

so·cial·i·za·tion (sō′shəl-i-zā′shən, sō′shəl-ī-zā′shən), ***n.*** a socializing or being socialized.

so·cial·ize (sō′shə-līz′), ***v.t.*** [SOCIALIZED (-līzd′), SOCIALIZING], 1. to make social; adjust to or make fit for co-operative group living. 2. to adapt or make conform to the common needs of a social group. 3. to subject to governmental ownership and control; nationalize. 4. to cause to become socialist. ***v.i.*** [Colloq.], to take part in social activity.

socialized medicine, 1. complete medical care, made available through public funds, for all the people in a community, district, or nation. 2. group medicine.

social register, a list of socially prominent people.

social science, 1. the study of people and how they live together as families, tribes, communities, races, etc.; sociology. 2. any of several studies, as history, economics, civics, etc., dealing with the structure of society and the activity of its members.

social security, any system by which a group provides for those of its members who may be in need; specifically, in the United States, a Federal system of old-age, unemployment, or disability insurance for various categories of employed and dependent persons, financed by a fund maintained jointly by employees, employers, and the government.

so·cial-serv·ice (sō′shəl-sûr′vis), ***adj.*** of or having to do with social work.

social service, social work.

social settlement, a settlement (sense 10).

social work, any service or activity designed to promote the welfare of the community and the individual, as through health and psychology clinics, recreation halls and playgrounds, aid for the needy, the aged, the physically handicapped, etc.

social worker, a person who does social work.

so·ci·e·tal (sə-sī′ə-t'l), ***adj.*** of society or a society (senses 1, 2, 3).

so·ci·e·ty (sə-sī′ə-ti), ***n.*** [*pl.* SOCIETIES (-tiz)], [Fr. *société;* L. *societas* < *socius*, companion], 1. a group of animals or plants living together under the same environment and regarded as constituting a homogeneous unit or entity; especially, a group of persons regarded as forming a single community. 2. all people, collectively, regarded as constituting a community of related, interdependent individuals. 3. the system or condition of living together as a community: as, a primitive *society*. 4. company or companionship: as, I do not seek his *society*. 5. one's friends or associates: as, for *society* he had two old aunts. 6. any organized group of people joined together because of some interest in common: as, a medical *society*. 7. the members of the wealthy, fashionable class: as, all *society* attended the concert. 8. the conduct, standards, activities, etc. of this class. Abbreviated **S., s., Soc., soc.**

society column, a newspaper column that reports the social affairs of the wealthy, fashionable class.

Society Islands, a group of islands of French Oceania, in the South Pacific: area, 650 sq. mi.; pop., 31,000; capital, Papeete, on Tahiti.

Society of Friends, a Christian religious sect founded in England c. 1650 by George Fox: the Friends have no formal creed, rites, liturgy, or priesthood, and reject violence in human relations, including war: see **Quakers.**

Society of Jesus, a Roman Catholic religious order: see **Jesuit.**

society verse, [transl. of Fr. *vers de société*], light poetry written to suit the taste of fashionable society.

So·cin·i·an (sō-sin′i-ən), ***n.*** [Mod. L. *Socinianus*], a believer in the doctrines of Socinus. ***adj.*** of or having to do with Socinus or his doctrines.

So·cin·i·an·ism (sō-sin′i-ən-iz′m), ***n.*** the theological doctrines of Faustus Socinus, denying the divinity of Jesus, the Trinity, the natural immortality of man, etc., and explaining sin and salvation rationalistically.

So·ci·nus, Faus·tus (fôs′təs sō-sī′nəs), (born *Fausto Sozzini*), 1539–1604; Italian religious reformer.

so·ci·o- (sō′si-ō, sō′shi-ō), [Fr. < L. *socius*, companion], a combining form meaning *society, social.*

sociol., 1. sociological. 2. sociology.

so·ci·o·log·i·cal (sō′si-ə-loj′i-k'l, sō′shi-ə-loj′i-k'l), ***adj.*** 1. of or having to do with human society, its organization, needs, development, etc. 2. of sociology.

so·ci·o·log·i·cal·ly (sō′si-ə-loj′i-k'l-i, sō′shi-ə-loj′ik-li), ***adv.*** according to or by means of sociology.

so·ci·ol·o·gist (sō′si-ol′ə-jist, sō′shi-ol′ə-jist), ***n.*** an expert or specialist in sociology.

so·ci·ol·o·gy (sō′si-ol′ə-ji, sō′shi-ol′ə-ji), ***n.*** [Fr. *sociologie* (coined by Comte); see SOCIO- & -LOGY], the study of the history, development, organization, and problems of people living together as social groups; social science.

so·ci·om·e·try (sō′si-om′ə-tri, sō′shi-om′ə-tri), ***n.*** [see SOCIO- & -METRY], a science that studies and seeks to evaluate relationships within social groups, especially by means of statistics.

sock (sok), ***n.*** [ME. *sok, socke*; AS. *socc* < L. *soccus*, kind of light low-heeled shoe], 1. a light shoe worn by comic characters in ancient Greek and Roman drama; hence, 2. comedy or the muse of comedy. 3. a kind of short stocking reaching only part way to the knee.

sock (sok), ***v.t.*** [Early Mod. Eng. < cant], [Slang], 1. to hit or strike with force, especially with the fist. 2. to put or place: as, he *socked* all his money in the bank. ***n.*** [Slang], a blow. ***adv.*** [Slang], directly, squarely.

sock·dol·a·ger (sok-dol′ə-jẽr), ***n.*** [< prec. + *doxology* (in the sense of final) + *-er*], [Slang], 1. something so effective or forceful as to be final or decisive, as a heavy blow; finisher. 2. something very large for its kind.

sock·et (sok′it), ***n.*** [ME. & Anglo-Fr. *soket*, spearhead shaped like a small plowshare < OFr. *soc*, plowshare; of Celt. origin], a hollow piece or part into which something fits: as, the *socket* of an electric bulb, of the eye, of the hipbone, etc.: see **ball-and-socket joint,** illus. ***v.t.*** to furnish with or fit into a socket.

sock·eye (sok′ī′), ***n.*** [altered < Salishan *suk-kegh*], a red salmon of the north Pacific, used for canning.

so·cle (sok″l, sō′k'l), ***n.*** [Fr.; It. *zoccolo*, pedestal, wooden shoe; L. *socculus*, dim. of *soccus*, a shoe], in *architecture*, a projecting, ledgelike foundation piece, as for a column, wall, statue, etc.

So·co·tra (sō-kō′trə), ***n.*** an island in the Indian Ocean, south of Arabia: a part of the Aden protectorate: area, 1,400 sq. mi.; pop., 12,000: also spelled **Sokotra.**

Soc·ra·tes (sok′rə-tēz′), ***n.*** Athenian idealist philosopher and teacher; 470?–399 B.C.

So·crat·ic (sō-krat′ik), ***adj.*** [L. *Socraticus;* Gr. *Sōkratikos*], of or having to do with Socrates or his philosophy. ***n.*** 1. a follower of Socrates. 2. any Greek philosopher directly influenced by Socrates.

So·crat·i·cal·ly (sō-krat′i-k'l-i, sō-krat′ik-li), ***adv.*** in a Socratic manner.

Socratic irony, pretense of ignorance in a discussion to expose the fallacies in the opponent's logic.

Socratic method, a method of teaching or discussion, as used by Socrates, in which one asks a series of easily answered questions that inevitably lead the answerer to a logical conclusion foreseen by the questioner.

sod (sod), obsolete past tense of **seethe.**

sod (sod), ***n.*** [ME.; prob. < MD. *sode;* akin to Eng. *seethe, sodden:* the name prob. refers to the wet ground from which fuel turf was cut], 1. a surface layer of earth containing grass plants with their matted roots; turf; sward. 2. a piece of this layer. ***v.t.*** [SODDED (-id), SODDING], to cover with sod or sods.

under the sod, dead and buried.

so·da (sō′də), ***n.*** [ML. *soda* (It. & Sp. *soda,* Fr. *soude*); said to be orig. It. < *sodo,* firm < L. *solidus* (cf. SOLID); first used of ash in glassmaking], 1. sodium carbonate. 2. sodium bicarbonate. 3. sodium hydroxide. 4. sodium oxide. 5. soda water (sense 1). 6. a beverage made of soda water flavored with sirup, fruit, etc., often mixed with ice cream. 7. in *faro,* the card turned face up in the dealing box before the start of play.

soda ash, crude sodium carbonate.

soda biscuit, 1. a bread or biscuit made with baking soda and sour milk or buttermilk. 2. a soda cracker.

soda cracker, a light, crisp cracker, usually salted, prepared from dough made of flour, water, soda, and cream of tartar.

soda fountain, 1. a counter fitted with equipment for making and serving soft drinks, sodas, milkshakes, sundaes, sandwiches, etc. 2. a container for soda water, with faucets by which it is drawn off.

soda jerk, [Slang], a person who works at a soda fountain.

soda lime, a white, powdery mixture of sodium hydroxide and calcium oxide, used as a chemical reagent and as an absorbent for moisture and acid gases.

so·da·lite (sō′də-līt′), ***n.*** [*soda* + *-lite*], a silicate of sodium and aluminum with some chlorine, $Na_4Al_3Si_3O_{12}Cl$: it resembles marble when polished and is used as an ornamental stone.

so·dal·i·ty (sō-dal′ə-ti), ***n.*** [*pl.* SODALITIES (-tiz)], [< Fr. or L.; Fr. *sodalité;* L. *sodalitas* < *sodalis,* companion], 1. fellowship; companionship. 2. an association or brotherhood. 3. in the *Roman Catholic Church,* a lay society formed for devotional or charitable activity.

soda pop, a soft drink made of carbonated water with various, often artificial, flavorings, sold in tightly capped bottles or cans.

soda water, 1. water charged under pressure with carbon dioxide gas, used in making ice-cream sodas, mixed drinks, etc. 2. a solution of water, acid, and sodium bicarbonate, used for the same purposes.

sod·den (sod′'n), obsolete past participle of **seethe.** ***adj.*** 1. filled with moisture; soaked through. 2. moist or heavy as a result of improper baking or cooking; soggy, as bread. 3. dull; stupid; not lively or alert, as from fatigue or overindulgence. 4. [Rare], boiled or steeped. 5. having a boiled, soaked, or bloated look. ***v.t. & v.i.*** to make or become sodden.

so·di·um (sō′di-əm), ***n.*** [Mod. L. < *soda*], a silver-white, alkaline metallic chemical element having a waxlike consistency: it is found in nature only in combined form and is extremely active chemically: symbol, Na (for *natrium*); at. wt., 22.997; at. no., 11.

sodium benzoate, a sweet, odorless, white powder, $NaC_7H_5O_2$, the sodium salt of benzoic acid, used as a food preservative, antiseptic, etc.

sodium bicarbonate, a white, crystalline compound, $NaHCO_3$, used in baking powder, fire extinguishers, as an antacid, etc.: also called ***baking soda.***

sodium bromide, a white, crystalline compound, NaBr, used in medicine as a sedative and in photography to produce silver bromide.

sodium carbonate, 1. the anhydrous sodium salt of carbonic acid, Na_2CO_3: also called *soda ash.* 2. any of the hydrated carbonates of sodium; especially, the colorless, crystalline compound $Na_2CO_3 \cdot 10H_2O$, commonly called *sal soda* or ***washing soda.***

sodium chlorate, a colorless, crystalline salt, $NaClO_3$, used as an oxidizing agent in matches, explosives, etc.

sodium chloride, common salt, NaCl.

sodium cyanide, a white, highly poisonous salt, NaCN, used in electroplating, as an insecticide, etc.

sodium dichromate, a red, crystalline salt, $Na_2Cr_2O_7$, used as an oxidizing agent, antiseptic, etc.

sodium hydroxide, a white substance, NaOH, in the form of powder, flakes, sticks, etc., widely used in chemistry, oil refining, paper and rayon manufacture, etc.: also called ***caustic soda, lye, sodium hydrate.***

sodium hyposulfite, 1. a clear, crystalline salt, $Na_2S_2O_4$, used as a chemical reagent. 2. sodium thiosulfate.

sodium nitrate, a clear, odorless, crystalline salt, $NaNO_3$, used in manufacturing nitric acid, sodium nitrite, explosives, fertilizers, etc., and as a reagent and oxidizing agent in chemistry: also called *Chile saltpeter.*

sodium pentothal, see **pentothal sodium.**

sodium peroxide, a yellowish-white powder, Na_2O_2, used as an antiseptic, bleaching agent, air and water purifier, and oxidizing agent.

sodium phosphate, any of three clear, crystalline sodium salts of phosphoric acid widely used in industry.

sodium sulfate, a white, crystalline salt, Na_2SO_4, used in medicine and in the making of dyes, glass, etc.

sodium sulfite, a white salt, Na_2SO_3, in the form of crystals or powder, used in dyeing, engraving, and photography, and as a bleaching agent, preservative; etc.

sodium thiosulfate, a white, crystalline salt, $Na_2S_2O_3$, used as an antichlor, as a fixing agent in photography, etc.: popularly but incorrectly called (*sodium*) *hyposulfite, hypo.*

so·di·um-va·por lamp (sō′di-əm-vā′pẽr), a globe fitted with two electrodes and filled with sodium vapor, which sheds a yellow, glareless light when electric current is passed through it: also **sodium lamp.**

Sod·om (sod′əm), ***n.*** in the *Bible,* a city destroyed by fire together with a neighboring city, Gomorrah, because of the sinfulness of the people: Gen. 18–19.

Sod·om·ite (sod′əm-īt′), ***n.*** [ME.; OFr.; L. *Sodomita*]. 1. an inhabitant of Sodom. 2. [s-], a person who practices sodomy.

sod·om·y (sod′əm-i), ***n.*** [ME. & OFr. *sodomie* < *Sodom* (Gen. 18–19)], any sexual intercourse regarded as abnormal, as between persons of the same sex, especially males, or between a person and an animal.

Soem·ba (sōōm′bä), ***n.*** Sumba.

Soem·ba·wa (sōōm-bä′wä), ***n.*** Sumbawa.

Soen·da Islands (sōōn′dä), Sunda Islands.

Soe·ra·ba·ja (sōō′rä-bä′yä), ***n.*** Surabaya.

Soe·ra·kar·ta (sōō′rä-kär′tä), ***n.*** Surakarta.

so·ev·er (sō-ev′ẽr), ***adv.*** [*so* + *ever*], 1. in any way; to any extent or degree (usually following *how* and an adjective): as, how dark *soever* the night may be. 2. of any kind; at all; whatever: as, no rest *soever.*

-so·ev·er (sō-ev′ẽr), a combining form added for emphasis or generalization to *who, what, when, where, how,* etc., and meaning ***any*** (person, thing, time, place, or manner) ***of all those possible.***

so·fa (sō′fə), ***n.*** [Fr.; Ar. *ṣuffah,* orig., cushion on a saddle for a camel], an upholstered couch, usually of spring construction, with fixed back and arms.

sofa bed, a type of sofa that can be opened into a full-sized bed.

so·far (sō′fär) ***n.*** [*so*und *f*ixing *a*nd *r*anging], a system for determining the location of underwater sounds as far as 2000 miles from shore, which facilitates the rescue of survivors of sea disasters.

sof·fit (sof′it), ***n.*** [Fr. *soffite;* It. *soffito, soffita* < LL. **suffictus,* for L. *suffixus;* see SUFFIX], in *architecture,* the underside of a structural part, as of a beam, arch, etc.

So·fi·a (sō′fi-ə, sō-fē′ə; Bulg. sô′fē-yä′), ***n.*** the capital of Bulgaria: pop., 401,000: Bulgarian name, *Sofiya.*

S. of Sol., Song of Solomon.

soft (sôft), ***adj.*** [ME.; AS. *softe,* gentle, quiet < **samfto-;* akin to G. *sanft;* IE. base **sem-,* together, together with, seen also in L. *similis* (cf. SIMILE, SIMILAR, etc.), Eng. *seem,* etc.; basic sense "fitting, friendly, suited to"], 1. giving way easily under pressure, as a feather pillow or moist clay; easily shaped or worked. 2. easily cut, marked, or worn away, as pine wood or pure gold. 3. not hard for its kind; not as hard as is normal, desirable, etc.: as, *soft* butter. 4. smooth or fine to the touch; not rough, harsh, or coarse. 5. bland; not acid, sour, or sharp. 6. nonalcoholic: said of drinks. 7. having in solution few or none of the mineral salts that interfere with the lathering and cleansing properties of soap: said of water. 8. mild, gentle, or temperate, as a breeze, the weather, climate, etc. 9. weak; delicate; not strong or vigorous; not able to endure hardship, privation, etc. 10. requiring little effort; not difficult; easy: as, he has a very *soft* job. 11. *a*) kind or gentle, especially to the point of weakness; not severe; lenient or compassionate. *b*) easily impressed, influenced, or imposed upon. 12. subdued; not bright or intense: said of color. 13. showing little contrast or distinctness; not sharp: as, a *soft* etching, a *soft* line or border. 14. gentle; low; not loud or harsh: said of sound. 15. in *phonetics, a*) sibilant: said of *c* and *g,* as in *citrus* and *German. b*) lenis, or lenis and voiced. *c*) palatalized, as certain consonants in Slavic languages. ***adv.*** softly;

gently; quietly. *n.* something soft; soft part. ***interj.*** [Archaic], 1. be quiet! hush! 2. slow up! stop!

SYN.—**soft,** in this connection, implies an absence or reduction of all that is harsh, rough, too intense, etc., so as to be pleasing to the senses (*soft* colors, a *soft* voice); **bland** implies such an absence of irritation, stimulation, pungency, etc. as to be soothing, unexciting, and hence, sometimes, uninteresting (*bland* foods, climate, etc.); **mild** applies to that which is not as rough, harsh, irritating, etc. as it might be (a *mild* cigarette, criticism, etc.); **gentle,** often equivalent to **mild,** carries a more positive connotation of being pleasantly soothing or tranquil (a *gentle* breeze, voice, etc.). —***ANT.*** harsh, rough.

soft·ball (sôft′bôl′), ***n.*** 1. a kind of baseball played on a smaller diamond and with a ball larger and softer than in ordinary baseball. 2. the ball used.

soft-boiled (sôft′boild′), ***adj.*** boiled only a short time so that the yolk is soft: said of eggs.

soft coal, coal that yields pitch and tar when it is burned: soft coal makes more smoke and ashes than hard coal: also called *bituminous coal.*

soft drink, a nonalcoholic drink, especially a carbonated drink.

sof·ten (sôf″n), ***v.t. & v.i.*** [ME. *softnen;* cf. SOFT & -EN], to make or become soft or softer.

softening of the brain, 1. degeneration of the brain tissues into a soft, fatty substance. 2. in popular usage, loss of mind; dementia.

soft-finned (sôft′find′), ***adj.*** in *zoology,* having fins with soft rods or rays instead of hard spines.

soft·head (sôft′hed′), ***n.*** a stupid or feeble-minded person; simpleton.

soft·heart·ed (sôft′här′tid), ***adj.*** 1. full of compassion or tenderness. 2. not strict or severe, as in discipline or authority.

soft·ie (sôf′ti), ***n.*** [*pl.* SOFTIES (-tiz)], [Colloq.], a softy.

soft·ish (sôf′tish), ***adj.*** somewhat soft; not hard.

soft palate, the soft, fleshy part at the rear of the roof of the mouth; velum.

soft-ped·al (sôft′ped″l), ***v.t.*** [SOFT-PEDALLED (-′ld), SOFT-PEDALLING], 1. to soften or dampen the tone of (a musical instrument) by use of a pedal made for this purpose. 2. [Colloq.], to tone down; play down; make less emphatic, less obtrusive, less conspicuous, etc.

soft pedal, a pedal used to soften or dampen the tone of a musical instrument, as a piano or harp.

soft-shell (sôft′shel′; *for n., usually* sôft′shel′), ***adj.*** soft-shelled. ***n.*** a soft-shelled crab.

soft-shelled (sôft′sheld′), ***adj.*** having a soft shell.

soft-shelled crab, a crab at the stage between the shedding of its old shell and the hardening of the new.

soft-shelled turtle, a mud turtle with a soft, leatherlike shell.

soft-shoe (sôft′sho͞o′), ***adj.*** designating a kind of tap dancing done without metal taps on the shoes.

soft shoulder, a soft strip of ground along the edge of a highway.

soft-soap (sôft′sōp′), ***v.t.*** 1. to apply soft soap to. 2. [Colloq.], to flatter.

soft soap, 1. soap in liquid or semifluid form. 2. [Colloq.], flattery.

soft-spo·ken (sôft′spō′k′n), ***adj.*** 1. speaking or spoken with a soft, low voice. 2. smooth; ingratiating; suave.

soft·wood (sôft′wood′), ***n.*** 1. any light, easily cut wood. 2. the wood of any tree with true cones. 3. any tree with soft wood.

soft·y (sôf′ti), ***n.*** [*pl.* SOFTIES (-tiz)], [Colloq.], a person who is soft or weak in body, character, or mind.

Sog·di·an (sog′di-ən), ***n.*** 1. one of an Iranian people who lived in Sogdiana. 2. their extinct Iranian language.

Sog·di·a·na (sog′di-ā′nə), ***n.*** an ancient land in the region of modern Uzbekistan, between the Oxus River and the Syr Darya: it was part of the Persian Empire: capital, Samarkand.

sog·gi·ly (sog′ə-li), ***adv.*** in a soggy manner.

sog·gi·ness (sog′i-nis), ***n.*** the quality or state of being soggy.

sog·gy (sog′i), ***adj.*** [SOGGIER (-i-ẽr), SOGGIEST (-i-ist)], [< obs. *sog,* damp, boggy place; prob. < ON. *sog,* lit., a sucking < base of *suck, soak*], soft and heavy with moisture; sodden; soaked: also used figuratively.

So·ho (sō-hō′, sō′hō), ***n.*** a French, Italian, and Swiss quarter of London, noted for its restaurants.

‡**soi-di·sant** (swȧ′dē′zän′), ***adj.*** [Fr., lit., self-saying], 1. so-called by oneself; self-styled. 2. pretended; would-be: as, he's a *soi-disant* authority in every field.

‡**soi·gné** (swȧ′nyā′), ***adj.*** [Fr.], 1. well-cared for or attended to. 2. neat; tidy; well-groomed.

‡**soi·gnée** (swȧ′nyā′), ***adj.*** [Fr.], feminine of **soigné.**

soil (soil), ***n.*** [ME. *soile;* OFr. *soile, sueil;* L. *solum*], 1. the surface layer of earth, supporting plant life; hence, 2. figuratively, a place for growth or development of any kind. 3. land; country; territory: as, native *soil,* foreign *soil.* 4. ground or earth: as, barren *soil.*

soil (soil), ***v.t.*** [ME. *soilen;* OFr. *soillier;* LL. **suculare* < L. *suculus,* dim. of *sus,* pig], 1. to make dirty, especially on the surface. 2. to smirch or stain. 3. to bring disgrace upon. 4. to corrupt or defile; sully. ***v.i.*** to become soiled or dirty. ***n.*** [OFr. *soil;* L. *suile,* pig sty < *sus,* pig], 1. a soiled spot; stain; smirch. 2. manure used for fertilizing. 3. filth; excrement. 4. a soiling or being soiled.

soil (soil), ***v.t.*** [OFr. *saoler, saouler* < L. *satullare,* to satiate < *satullus,* filled (with food), dim. of *satur;* see SATURATE], 1. to feed (animals) on soilage. 2. to purge (animals) by means of green food.

soil·age (soil′ij), ***n.*** [see SOIL (to feed) & -AGE], green crops cultivated for fodder.

soil bank, a Federal program under which subsidies are paid to farmers who take out of production land used for certain surplus crops and instead improve it by the use of various soil-enrichment methods.

soil pipe, in *plumbing,* a pipe for carrying off liquid waste from toilets: distinguished from *waste pipe.*

soil·ure (soil′yoor), ***n.*** [ME. *soylure;* OFr. *soilleure* (Fr. *souillure*) < *soillier;* see SOIL (to make dirty)], 1. a soiling, dirtying, or sullying. 2. a strain; blot.

soi·ree, soi·rée (swä-rā′), ***n.*** [Fr. *soirée* < *soir,* evening; L. *serum,* late time, late hour, neut. of *serus,* late], an evening party or gathering.

Sois·sons (swȧ′sōn′), ***n.*** a city in northern France, on the Aisne River: pop., 20,000.

so·ja (sō′jə, sō′yə), ***n.*** [Mod. L. < Sp. & D.; see SOY], 1. the soy bean: also **soja bean.** 2. a sauce made from it.

so·journ (sō′jũrn; *also, for v.,* sō-jũrn′), ***v.i.*** [ME. *sojournen;* OFr. *sojorner, sojourner;* LL. **subdiurnare* < L. *sub-,* under + *diurnus,* of a day < *dies,* day], to live somewhere temporarily, as on a visit; stay for a while. ***n.*** a brief or temporary stay; visit.

soke (sōk), ***n.*** [ME.; ML. *soca;* AS. *socn,* jurisdiction, prosecution < base of *secan* (< **sokjan*), to seek; cf. SEEK], in *English history,* 1. the right to hold court and dispense justice within a given territory. 2. the territorial jurisdiction of a court.

So·ko·to (sō′kō-tō′), ***n.*** a former kingdom, now a province of northern Nigeria, Africa: pop., 1,667,000.

So·ko·tra (sō-kō′trə), ***n.*** Socotra.

Sol (sol), ***n.*** [ME.; L. < **sawol,* **saol;* IE. base **sāwel-*], 1. the sun. 2. the sun god of the ancient Romans. 3. in *alchemy,* gold.

sol (sōl; Sp. sôl), ***n.*** [*pl.* SOLS (sōlz); Sp. SOLES (sô′les)], [Sp., lit., sun: from the radiant sun used as a device on one side], 1. the monetary unit of Peru, valued at about 6 cents in 1950. 2. a silver coin of this value.

sol (sōl), ***n.*** [< L. *solve;* see GAMUT], in *music,* a syllable representing the fifth tone of the diatonic scale: see **solfeggio.**

sol (sol, sōl), ***n.*** [< hydro*sol,* but sometimes associated with G. *sole,* brine], a colloidal dispersion in a liquid.

Sol., 1. Solicitor. 2. Solomon.

sol., 1. soluble. 2. solution.

‡**so·la** (sō′lə), ***adj.*** [L.], feminine of **solus.**

sol·ace (sol′is), ***n.*** [ME.; OFr. *solaz;* L. *solacium, solatium* < *solari,* to comfort; ? akin to AS. *sæl,* Goth. *sels;* see SILLY], 1. an easing of grief, loneliness, discomfort, etc. 2. something that eases or relieves; comfort; consolation; relief. ***v.t.*** [SOLACED (-ist), SOLACING], 1. to give solace to; comfort; console. 2. to lessen or allay (grief, sorrow, etc.). —***SYN.*** see **comfort.**

sol·ace·ment (sol′is-mənt), ***n.*** 1. a solacing. 2. that which solaces.

sol·a·na·ceous (sol′ə-nā′shəs), ***adj.*** [< L. *solanum,* nightshade; + *-aceous*], in *botany,* of the nightshade family.

so·lan goose (sō′lən), [Scot.; earlier *soland* < ON. *sūla,* gannet + *-and, ond,* a duck], the common gannet.

so·la·num (sō-lā′nəm), ***n.*** [L., nightshade], any of a number of related plants of the nightshade family.

so·lar (sō′lẽr), ***adj.*** [L. *solaris* < *sol,* the sun], 1. of or having to do with the sun. 2. produced by or coming from the sun: as, *solar* energy. 3. depending upon the sun's light or energy: as, *solar* heating, *solar* telegraphy. 4. fixed or measured by the earth's motion with relation to the sun: as, *solar* time, a *solar* day. 5. in *astrology,* under the influence of the sun.

solar day, 1. the period of the rotation of the earth with relation to the sun; twenty-four hours, measured from noon to noon or from midnight to midnight. 2. in *law,* the period from sunrise to sunset.

so·lar·ism (sō′lẽr-iz′m), ***n.*** [*solar* + *-ism*], the explanation of myths and folklore by reference to the sun or the personification of the sun.

so·lar·i·um (sō-lâr′i-əm), ***n.*** [*pl.* SOLARIA (-ə)], [L., sun dial, place exposed to the sun < *sol,* the sun], a glassed-in porch, room, etc. where people sun themselves, as in treating illness; sunroom.

so·lar·i·za·tion (sō′lẽr-i-zā′shən, sō′lẽr-ī-zā′shən), ***n.*** a solarizing or being solarized.

so·lar·ize (sō′lə-rīz′), ***v.t.*** [SOLARIZED (-rīzd′), SOLARIZING], [*solar* + *-ize*], 1. to affect by exposing to the light and heat of the sun. 2. to overexpose (a photographic film or plate). ***v.i.*** to become injured by overexposure, as a photographic plate.

solar plexus, 1. a network of nerves in the abdominal cavity behind the stomach and in front of the uppermost part of the aorta, containing ganglia that send nerve impulses to the abdominal viscera. 2. [Colloq.], the upper middle part of the abdomen.

solar system, the sun and all the heavenly bodies that revolve around it.

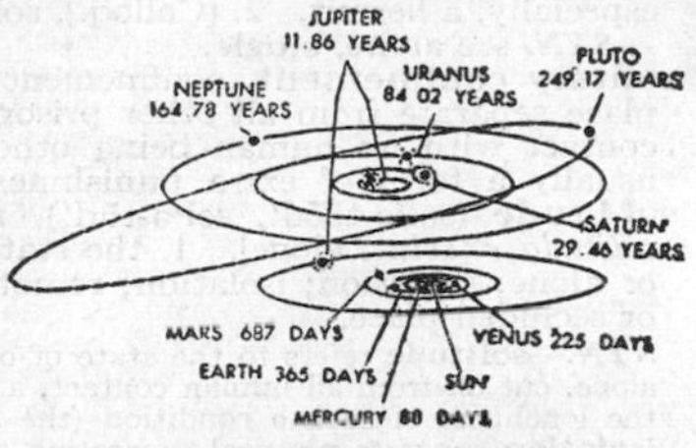

solar year, a period during which any planet makes one complete revolution around the sun: 365 days, 5 hours, 48 minutes, and 46 seconds is the length of the earth's solar year.

so·la·ti·um (sō-lā'shi-əm), *n.* [*pl.* SOLATIA (ə)], [L.; see SOLACE], something given to compensate, as for loss or injury.

sold (sōld), past tense and past participle of **sell.**

SOLAR SYSTEM

The diagram shows the approximate orbits and lengths of the solar years of the nine planets, with the satellites of each. The orbit of Jupiter, shown as the smallest innermost ring in the upper figure, is also reproduced as the outermost ring in the lower figure in order to show the orbits of Mars, Earth, Venus, and Mercury. The broken line in the orbit of Pluto indicates where it lies south of the plane of the ecliptic.

sol·der (sod'ẽr), *n.* [ME. *soudour;* OFr. *soudure, souldure* < *soulder, souder,* to make solid < L. *solidare,* to make firm], 1. a metal alloy used when melted for joining or patching metal parts or surfaces: *soft solders* melt easily; *hard solders* melt only at red heat. 2. figuratively, anything that joins or fuses; bond. *v.t.* 1. to join, patch, etc. with solder. 2. to act as a bond between; hold together; unite. *v.i.* 1. to become joined or united as by solder. 2. to join things with solder.

soldering iron, a pointed metal tool used for melting and applying solder: it must be heated, as in a flame or electrically.

soldering paste, a greaselike flux used in soldering.

sol·dier (sōl'jẽr), *n.* [ME. *soldiour, soudiour;* OFr. *soldier, soudiour* < *soude, solde,* a coin, pay < L. *solidus,* piece of money < *solidus,* firm, solid], 1. a man serving in an army; member of an army. 2. an enlisted man, as distinguished from one holding a warrant or commission. 3. a man of much military experience or military skill. 4. a person who works for a specified cause. 5. a kind of ant or termite having an enlarged head and jaws and serving as a fighter in defense of the colony. *v.i.* 1. to serve as a soldier. 2. to shirk one's duty, as by making a pretense of working, feigning illness, etc.

sol·dier·ly (sōl'jẽr-li), *adj.* of, like, or characteristic of a good soldier.

soldier of fortune, a military adventurer, willing to serve wherever he can get pay, pleasure, etc.

sol·dier·ship (sōl'jẽr-ship'), *n.* [see -SHIP], 1. skill or ability in military matters. 2. military science.

Soldier's Medal, a United States military decoration given for deeds of heroism outside of combat.

sol·dier·y (sōl'jẽr-i), *n.* [*pl.* SOLDIERIES (-iz)], 1. soldiers collectively. 2. a group of soldiers. 3. military science; soldiership.

sol·do (sol'dō; It. sôl'dô), *n.* [*pl.* SOLDI (-di; It. -dē)], [It.; see SOLDIER], an Italian copper coin and unit of money, equal to 1/20 of a lira.

sole (sōl), *n.* [ME. < AS. & Fr.; both < LL. **sola,* for L. *solea,* a sandal, sole < *solum,* a sole, base, ground, bottom], 1. the bottom surface of the foot. 2. the part of a shoe, boot, sock, etc. corresponding to this. 3. the bottom or resting surface of any of several objects, as a golf club, plow, etc. *v.t.* [SOLED (sōld), SOLING], 1. to furnish (a shoe, etc.) with a sole, especially a new one. 2. in *golf,* to put the sole of (a club) on the ground, as in getting ready to hit the ball.

sole (sōl), *adj.* [ME. *sool;* OFr. *sol;* L. *solus;* ? < **swolos* < base of *suus,* his own, one's own], 1. without another or others; single; one and only. 2. of or having to do with only one (specified) person or group. 3. acting, working, etc. automatically or without help. 4. [Archaic], alone; solitary. 5. in *law,* unmarried: only in *feme sole* and *woman sole.* —*SYN.* see **single.**

sole (sōl), *n.* [ME.; OFr.; Pr. *sola;* LL. **sola,* for L. *solea,* sole (a fish), also sole of a shoe: so named from its shape], any of certain sea flatfishes highly valued as food: the name is loosely applied to some species of plaice and halibut.

sol·e·cism (sol'ə-siz'm), *n.* [Fr. *solécisme;* L. *soloecismus;* Gr. *soloikismos* < *soloikos,* speaking incorrectly < corrupt Attic dialect used by colonists in *Soloi,* in Cilicia], 1. a violation of the conventional usage, grammar, etc. of a language; substandard use of words (e.g., "I seen him" for "I saw him"): see also **barbarism, impropriety.** 2. a violation of good manners; breach of etiquette. 3. a mistake or impropriety.

sol·e·cist (sol'ə-sist), *n.* a person who habitually commits solecisms.

sol·e·cis·tic (sol'ə-sis'tik), *adj.* 1. of, like, or constituting a solecism. 2. characteristic of a solecist.

sole·ly (sōl'li), *adv.* 1. alone; without another or others: as, we are *solely* to blame. 2. only, exclusively, merely, or altogether: as, he reads *solely* for enjoyment.

sol·emn (sol'əm), *adj.* [ME. & OFr. *solemne, solempne;* L. *sollemnis, sollennis,* yearly, annual, hence religious, solemn (from association with annual religious festivals) < *sollus,* all, entire + *annus,* year], 1. set aside according to ritual or tradition: said especially of religious ceremonies, festivals, etc.; hence, 2. sacred. 3. according to strict form; formal, as a ceremony. 4. serious; grave; deeply earnest. 5. arousing feelings of awe; very impressive: as, a *solemn* occasion. 6. somber because dark in color. —*SYN.* see **serious.**

so·lem·ni·fy (sə-lem'nə-fī'), *v.t.* [SOLEMNIFIED (-fīd'), SOLEMNIFYING], to make solemn.

so·lem·ni·ty (sə-lem'nə-ti), *n.* [*pl.* SOLEMNITIES (-tiz)], [ME. *solempnete;* OFr. *solemnité;* L. *sollemnitas*], 1. solemn ceremony, formality, ritual, etc.: as, the *solemnity* of the coronation, a feast day marked by many *solemnities.* 2. solemn feeling, character, or appearance; serious or awesome quality; impressiveness; gravity. 3. in *law,* a formality needed to validate an act, etc.

sol·em·ni·za·tion (sol'əm-ni-zā'shən, sol'əm-nī-zā'shən), *n.* a solemnizing or being solemnized.

sol·em·nize (sol'əm-nīz'), *v.t.* [SOLEMNIZED (-nīzd'), SOLEMNIZING], [ME. *solempnisen;* OFr. *solemniser;* ML. *solemnizare* < L. *sollemnis;* see SOLEMN], 1. to celebrate with formal ceremony or according to ritual, as a religious holiday. 2. to perform (a ceremony): as, the marriage was *solemnized.* 3. to make serious or grave. —*SYN.* see **celebrate.**

so·le·noid (sō'lə-noid'), *n.* [Fr. *solénoïde* < Gr. *sōlēn,* a channel + *eidos,* a form], a coil of wire carrying an electric current and having the properties of a magnet: solenoids regulate the timing of aircraft machine guns fired through the propeller arc.

so·le·noi·dal (sō'lə-noi'd'l), *adj.* of or acting as a solenoid.

So·lent, The (sō'lənt), a channel between England and the Isle of Wight.

So·leure (sô'lẽr'), *n.* Solothurn: the French name.

sol-fa (sōl'fä'), *n.* [It. *solfa; sol* + *fa,* two of the notes of the gamut], 1. the syllables *do* (formerly *ut*), *re, mi, fa, sol, la, ti* (formerly *si*), *do* (or *ut*), used to represent the tones of a scale, regardless of its key. 2. the use of these syllables, as in vocal exercises. *v.t. & v.i.* [SOL-FAED (-fäd'), SOL-FAING], to sing (a scale, phrase, or song) to the sol-fa syllables.

sol-fa·ist (sōl'fä'ist), *n.* a person who uses sol-fa.

‡sol·fa·ta·ra (sôl'fä-tä'rä), *n.* [It. < *solfo,* sulfur; L. *sulfur*], a volcanic vent or fissure giving off only vapors, especially sulfurous gases.

sol·feg·gio (sol-fej'ō, sol-fej'i-ō'), *n.* [*pl.* SOLFEGGIOS (-ōz, -ōz'), SOLFEGGI (-fej'i)], [It. < *solfa;* see SOL-FA], 1. voice practice in which scales are sung to the sol-fa syllables; solmization. 2. the use of these syllables in singing, especially in reading a song, etc. at sight.

sol·fe·ri·no (sol'fə-rē'nō), *n.* [< *Solferino,* village in Italy], 1. fuchsin, a red dye. 2. a bright purplish red.

so·lic·it (sə-lis'it), *v.t.* [ME. *soliciten;* OFr. *solliciter;* L. *sollicitare* < *sollicitus;* see SOLICITOUS], 1. to ask or seek earnestly or pleadingly; beg; entreat: as, we *solicit* your support, he *solicited* them for help. 2. to tempt or entice (another) to do wrong. 3. to accost (another) for some immoral purpose, as a prostitute does. *v.i.* to make solicitation. —*SYN.* see **beg.**

so·lic·i·ta·tion (sə-lis'ə-tā'shən), *n.* [L. *sollicitatio*], 1. a soliciting; earnest plea or request; entreaty. 2. temptation or enticement to wrongdoing.

so·lic·i·tor (sə-lis'ə-tẽr), *n.* [ME. *solycitour;* OFr. *solliciteur*], 1. a person who solicits; especially, one who seeks trade, asks for contributions, etc. 2. in England, any lawyer other than a barrister: solicitors are not members of the bar and may not plead cases in superior courts. 3. a lawyer serving as official law officer for a city, department, or other division of government. Abbreviated **Sol.** —*SYN.* see **lawyer.**

solicitor general, [*pl.* SOLICITORS GENERAL, SOLICITOR GENERALS], 1. a law officer serving the national government and ranking next below the attorney general. 2. the chief law officer in some States having no attorney general. Abbreviated **S.G.**

so·lic·i·tous (sə-lis'ə-təs), *adj.* [L. *sollicitus* < *sollus,* whole + *citus,* pp. of *ciere,* to set in motion], 1. showing care, attention, or concern: as, he was *solicitous* for his employees' welfare. 2. showing anxious desire; eager: as, he was *solicitous* to make friends. 3. full of anxiety or apprehension; troubled.

so·lic·i·tude (sə-lis′ə-tōōd′, sə-lis′ə-tūd′), ***n.*** [ME.; L. *sollicitudo*], 1. the state of being solicitous; care, concern, etc.; sometimes, excessive care or concern. 2. *pl.* causes of care or concern. —***SYN.*** see **care.**

sol·id (sol′id), ***adj.*** [ME. & OFr. *solide;* L. *solidus*], 1. offering some resistance to pressure; not easily changed in shape; relatively firm or compact: distinguished from *liquid, gaseous.* 2. filled with matter beneath the surface; not hollow. 3. in or of length, breadth, and thickness; cubic: as, a *solid* yard of concrete. 4. substantial; firm; strong; sound: as, a *solid* structure, *solid* reasoning, a *solid* citizen. 5. serious; not superficial or trivial: as, a *solid* problem. 6. complete; thoroughgoing: as, *solid* satisfaction. 7. having no breaks or divisions: as, a *solid* line of fortifications, a *solid* word. 8. characterized by no pauses or interruptions: as, he talked for two *solid* hours. 9. *a*) of one or the same color, material, or consistency throughout. *b*) containing no more alloy than is specified by law to insure hardness: said of gold, etc. 10. characterized by or showing complete unity; unanimous: as, a *solid* vote for world government. 11. thick or dense in appearance or texture, as fog, etc. 12. real; genuine. 13. [Colloq.], firm or dependable in views, sympathy, partisanship, etc. 14. [Colloq.], having a firmly favorable or good relationship. 15. [Slang], very good; excellent: as, a *solid* dance band. 16. in ***printing,*** having no lead separators between the lines of type: opposed to ***open.*** ***n.*** 1. a substance that offers some resistance to pressure and is not easily changed in shape: distinguished from *gas, liquid.* 2. an object or figure having or represented as having length, breadth, and thickness. —***SYN.*** see **firm.**

sol·i·da·go (sol′i-dā′gō), ***n.*** [Mod. L. < L. *solidare,* to strengthen: in reference to its supposed healing powers], any of a number of related plants with plumelike clusters of tiny, usually yellow flowers; goldenrod.

solid angle, an angle formed at a point where three or more planes meet, as at any corner of a square box.

sol·i·dar·i·ty (sol′ə-dar′ə-ti), ***n.*** [*pl.* SOLIDARITIES (-tiz)], [Fr. *solidarité* < *solidaire* < *solide,* solid], combination or agreement of all elements or individuals, as of a group; complete unity, as of opinion, purpose, interest, feeling, etc. —***SYN.*** see **unity.**

sol·i·dar·y (sol′ə-der′i), ***adj.*** [Fr. *solidaire;* see SOLID & -ARY], having or showing solidarity; completely united.

solid geometry, the geometry of solid figures.

so·lid·i·fi·ca·tion (sə-lid′ə-fi-kā′shən), ***n.*** a solidifying or being solidified.

so·lid·i·fy (sə-lid′ə-fī′), ***v.t. & v.i.*** [SOLIDIFIED (-fīd′), SOLIDIFYING], [after Fr. *solidifier*], 1. to make or become solid, firm, hard, compact, etc. 2. to crystallize.

so·lid·i·ty (sə-lid′ə-ti), ***n.*** [Fr. *solidité;* L. *soliditas*], 1. the quality or condition of being solid; firmness, soundness, compactness, etc. 2. in ***geometry,*** volume.

Solid South, those Southern States traditionally regarded as solidly supporting the Democratic Party.

sol·i·dus (sol′i-dəs), ***n.*** [*pl.* SOLIDI (-dī′)], [LL.], 1. a gold coin of the Late Roman Empire, valued at about three dollars: later called *bezant.* 2. a medieval money of account worth twelve denarii: abbreviated **s** in £ s.d. 3. the slant line (/), originally the old long s (ʃ), used to separate shillings from pence, as 7/6, or as a dividing line in fractions, dates, etc.

sol·i·fid·i·an (sol′ə-fid′i-ən), ***n.*** [< L. *solus,* alone + *fides,* faith], in ***theology,*** a person who believes that faith alone, without works or merit, insures salvation.

so·lil·o·quist (sə-lil′ə-kwist), ***n.*** a person who soliloquizes.

so·lil·o·quize (sə-lil′ə-kwīz′), ***v.i.*** [SOLILOQUIZED (-kwīzd′), SOLILOQUIZING], to talk to oneself; deliver a soliloquy. ***v.t.*** to utter in or as a soliloquy.

so·lil·o·quy (sə-lil′ə-kwi), ***n.*** [*pl.* SOLILOQUIES (-kwiz)], [LL. *soliloquium* < L. *solus,* alone + *loqui,* to speak], 1. an act or instance of talking to oneself. 2. lines in a drama in which a character reveals his thoughts to the audience but not to the other characters by speaking as if to himself.

So·li·mões (sô′lē-môɴzh′), ***n.*** the Amazon River above its juncture with the Rio Negro: Brazilian name.

sol·ip·sism (sol′ip-siz′m), ***n.*** [< L. *solus,* alone + *ipse,* self; + *-ism*], in ***philosophy,*** 1. the theory that the self can be aware of nothing but its own experiences and states; hence, 2. the theory that nothing exists or is real but the self.

sol·ip·sist (sol′ip-sist), ***n.*** a believer in solipsism.

sol·i·taire (sol′ə-târ′, sol′ə-târ′), ***n.*** [< Fr. or L.; Fr. *solitaire;* L. *solitarius;* see SOLITARY], 1. originally, a hermit or recluse. 2. a single gem, especially a diamond, set by itself, as in a ring. 3. any of several games, especially card games, played by one person.

sol·i·tar·i·ly (sol′ə-târ′ə-li), ***adv.*** so as to be solitary.

sol·i·tar·i·ness (sol′ə-ter′i-nis), ***n.*** the state or quality of being solitary.

sol·i·tar·y (sol′ə-ter′i), ***adj.*** [ME. *solitarie;* OFr. *solitaire;* L. *solitarius* < *solus,* alone], 1. living or being alone. 2. without others; single; only: as, a *solitary* case of measles. 3. characterized by loneliness or lack of companions. 4. lonely; remote; unfrequented: as, a *solitary* place. 5. done in solitude. ***n.*** [*pl.* SOLITARIES (-iz)], 1. a person who lives by himself and away from others; especially, a hermit. 2. [Colloq.], solitary confinement. —***SYN.*** see **alone, single.**

solitary confinement, confinement of a prisoner in a place separate from all other prisoners so that he has contact with no human being other than his jailers: usually a form of extra punishment for misconduct.

sol·i·tude (sol′ə-tōōd′, sol′ə-tūd′), ***n.*** [ME.; OFr.; L. *solitudo* < *solus,* alone], 1. the state of being solitary, or alone; seclusion; isolation; remoteness. 2. a lonely or secluded place.

SYN.—**solitude** refers to the state of one who is completely alone, cut off from all human contact, and sometimes stresses the loneliness of such a condition (the *solitude* of a hermit); **isolation** suggests physical separation from others, often an involuntary detachment resulting from the force of circumstances (the *isolation* of a forest ranger); **seclusion** suggests retirement from intercourse with the outside world, as by confining oneself to a home, an asylum, etc.

sol·ler·et (sol′ẽr-et, sol′ẽr-et′), ***n.*** [OFr. *soleret,* dim. of *soler,* a shoe < *sole;* see SOLE (of a shoe)], a kind of shoe worn with a suit of armor and made of overlapping hinged steel plates: see **armor,** illus.

sol·mi·za·tion (sol′mi-zā′shən), ***n.*** [Fr. < *solmiser,* to sol-fa < *sol* + *mi,* two of the notes of the gamut], the act or practice of using a system of syllables, especially the sol-fa syllables, in singing the tones of a scale.

So·lo (sō′lō), ***n.*** Surakarta.

so·lo (sō′lō), ***n.*** [*pl.* SOLOS (-lōz); *rarely* SOLI (-lē)], [It. < L. *solus,* alone], 1. a musical piece or passage to be played or sung by one person, with or without accompaniment. 2. an airplane flight made by a pilot alone, without any passengers or instructor. 3. any performance by one person alone. 4. any card game in which there are no partners. ***adj.*** 1. arranged for or performed by a single voice or instrument. 2. performing a solo. 3. made or done by one person. ***v.i.*** in ***aviation,*** to make a solo flight, especially one's first.

so·lo·ist (sō′lō-ist), ***n.*** a person who performs a solo.

Sol·o·mon (sol′ə-mən), [LL. *Solomon, Salomon;* Gr. *Solomōn, Salōmōn;* Heb. *shĕlōmōh,* lit., peaceful < *shālōm,* peace], a masculine name: diminutive, *Sol.* ***n.*** 1. the son of David and king of Israel in the 10th century B.C.: he built the first Temple and was noted for his wisdom; hence, 2. a very wise man; sage.

Solomon Islands, a group of islands in the Pacific, east of New Guinea: area, 14,800 sq. mi.; pop., 95,000: Bougainville, Buka, and small adjacent islands form part of the Australian Territory of New Guinea; other islands are a British protectorate.

Sol·o·mon's-seal (sol′ə-mənz-sēl′), ***n.*** [transl. of ML. *sigillum Salomonis:* so called prob. from markings on the rootstock], any of a number of related plants with bell-shaped flowers and black or blue fruit.

Solomon's seal, a mystic symbol in the form of a six-pointed star: cf. **Star of David.**

So·lon (sō′lən, sō′lon), ***n.*** 1. Athenian statesman and lawgiver; 638–559 B.C.; framed the democratic laws of Athens; hence, 2. [sometimes s-], a wise man, especially a lawmaker.

so long, [said to be folk etym. < *salaam*], [Colloq.], good-by.

So·lo·thurn (zō′lō-toorn′), ***n.*** a city in northwestern Switzerland, on the Aar River: pop., 15,000: French name, *Soleure.*

sol·stice (sol′stis), ***n.*** [ME.; OFr.; L. *solstitium* < *sol,* the sun + *sistere,* to cause to stand still < *stare,* to stand], 1. either of two points on the sun's ecliptic at which it is farthest north or farthest south of the equator. 2. the time at which the sun reaches either of these two points: see **summer solstice, winter solstice.** 3. a furthest point, turning point, or point of culmination.

sol·sti·tial (sol-stish′əl), ***adj.*** [< Fr. or L.; Fr. *solsticial;* L. *solstitialis*], 1. of or characteristic of a solstice, especially the summer solstice. 2. taking place at or about the time of a solstice.

sol·u·bil·i·ty (sol′yoo-bil′ə-ti), ***n.*** [*pl.* SOLUBILITIES (-tiz)], 1. the quality, condition, or extent of being soluble; capability of being dissolved. 2. the amount of a substance that can be dissolved in a given solvent under specified conditions.

sol·u·ble (sol′yoo-b′l), ***adj.*** [ME.; OFr.; L. *solubilis* < *solvere,* to loosen; see SOLVE], 1. that can be dissolved; capable of passing into solution: as, sugar is *soluble* in water. 2. capable of being solved or explained.

soluble glass, water glass (sodium silicate, etc.).

sol·u·bly (sol′yoo-bli), ***adv.*** so as to be soluble.

‡**so·lus** (sō′ləs), ***adj.*** [L.], alone: a stage direction.

sol·ute (sol′ūt, sō′lōōt), ***n.*** [< L. *solutus,* pp. of *solvere,* to loosen; see SOLVE], the substance dissolved in a solution: distinguished from *solvent.* ***adj.*** 1. dissolved; in solution. 2. in ***botany,*** separate; not adhering.

so·lu·tion (sə-lōō′shən, sə-lū′shən), ***n.*** [ME. *solucioun;* OFr. < L. *solutio* < *solutus,* pp. of *solvere,* to loosen; see SOLVE], 1. the act, method, or process of solving a problem; hence, 2. an explanation, clarification, answer, etc.: as, the *solution* of a mystery. 3. the act or process of dispersing one or more substances in another, usually a liquid, so as to form a homogeneous mixture; a dissolving. 4. the state or fact of being dissolved. 5. a homogeneous molecular mixture, usually a liquid, so produced: as, a *solution* of sugar and water. 6. a separation or breaking up, as into component parts; dissolution; break; breach. 7. in *medicine, a)* the termination of a disease. *b)* the crisis of a disease. *c)* a drug in watery solution; medicine in liquid form. Abbreviated **sol.**

solv·a·bil·i·ty (sol'və-bil'ə-ti), ***n.*** capability of being solved.

solv·a·ble (sol'və-b'l), ***adj.*** 1. that can be solved, as a problem. 2. that can be dissolved.

Sol·vay, Ernest (sol'vā), 1838–1922; Belgian chemist.

Solvay process, a process developed by Solvay for making soda (sodium carbonate) by treating common salt (sodium chloride) with ammonia and carbon dioxide.

solve (solv), ***v.t.*** [SOLVED (solvd), SOLVING], [ME. *solven;* L. *solvere* (for *se-luere*), to loosen, release, free < *se-*, apart + *luere*, to let go, set free], 1. to find or provide a satisfactory answer or explanation for; make clear; explain. 2. to find or provide a satisfactory solution for (a problem).

sol·ven·cy (sol'vən-si), ***n.*** a solvent state or quality.

sol·vent (sol'vənt), ***adj.*** [L. *solvens*, ppr. of *solvere*, to loosen; see SOLVE], 1. able to pay all one's debts; meeting all financial responsibilities. 2. that can dissolve another substance; used for dissolving. ***n.*** 1. a substance used for dissolving another substance. 2. something that solves or explains; solution.

Sol·way Firth (sol'wā fũrth), an arm of the Irish Sea, between England and Scotland: length, 38 mi.

Sol·y·man (sol'i-mən), see **Suleiman.**

so·ma (sō'mə), ***n.*** [*pl.* SOMATA (-mə-tə)], [Mod. L. < Gr. *sōma*, body], the entire body of an animal or plant, with the exception of the germ cells.

So·ma·li (sō-mä'li, sə-mä'li), ***n.*** [*pl.* SOMALI, SOMALIS (-liz)], 1. a member of a group of Hamitic tribes living in and near Somaliland. 2. their Cushitic language.

So·ma·li·a (sō-mä'li-ə, sə-mä'li-ə), ***n.*** a country in eastern Africa, on the Indian Ocean and the Gulf of Aden: formed by the merger of British Somaliland and Italian Somaliland: area, 246,201 sq. mi.; pop., 1,990,000; capital, Mogadishu.

So·ma·li·land (sō-mä'li-land', sə-mä'li-land'), ***n.*** a region in eastern Africa, on the Gulf of Aden and the Indian Ocean: see **French Somaliland** and **Somalia.**

so·mat·ic (sō-mat'ik), ***adj.*** [Gr. *sōmatikos* < *sōma*, the body], 1. of the body, as distinguished from the soul, mind, or psyche; corporeal; physical. 2. in *biology*, of the soma. 3. in *anatomy & zoology*, of the framework or outer walls of the body, as distinguished from the viscera; parietal. —***SYN.*** see **bodily.**

somatic cell, any of the cells of an organism that become differentiated into the tissues, organs, etc. of the body: opposed to *germ cell.*

so·ma·to- (sō'mə-tō, sō'mə-tə), [< Gr. *sōma, sōmatos*, body], a combining form meaning *body*, as in *somatology, somatoplasm*: also, before a vowel, **somat-.**

so·ma·to·log·ic (sō'mə-tə-loj'ik), ***adj.*** of somatology.

so·ma·to·log·i·cal (sō'mə-tə-loj'i-k'l), ***adj.*** somatologic.

so·ma·tol·o·gy (sō'mə-tol'ə-ji), ***n.*** [*somato-* + *-logy*], 1. the science concerned with the properties of organic bodies. 2. the branch of anthropology that deals with the physical nature and characteristics of man.

so·ma·to·plasm (sō'mə-tə-plaz'm), ***n.*** [*somato-* + *-plasm*], the protoplasm of a body cell as distinguished from that of a germ cell.

so·ma·to·pleure (sō'mə-tə-ploor'), ***n.*** [*somato-* + Gr. *pleura*, a side], in *embryology*, the outer of the two layers into which the mesoblast of vertebrates divides, forming the body wall.

som·ber, som·bre (som'bẽr), ***adj.*** [Fr. *sombre* < LL. **subumbrare*, to shade < L. *sub*, under + *umbra*, shade], 1. dark and gloomy; dark and dull. 2. mentally depressed or depressing; gloomy; dismal; melancholy; sad.

som·bre·ro (som-brâr'ō), ***n.*** [*pl.* SOMBREROS (-ōz)], [Sp. < *sombra*, shade; cf. SOMBER], a broad-brimmed hat, usually of felt, worn in Spain, Latin America, etc.

som·brous (som'brəs), ***adj.*** [Archaic], somber.

some (sum), ***adj.*** [ME. *som, some;* AS. *sum*, a certain one; akin to Goth. *sums;* for IE. base see SAME, SOFT], 1. being a certain one or ones not specified or known: as, *some* people never change their minds. 2. being of a certain unspecified (but often considerable) number, quantity, degree, etc.: as, *some* guests are here already, won't you have *some* butter? 3. about: as, *some* twenty of us were injured. 4. [Colloq.], remarkable, striking, etc.: as, that was *some* fight. ***pron.*** 1. a certain one or ones not specified or known; some one or ones: as, *some* will agree, others will not. 2. a certain indefinite or unspecified number, quantity, etc., as distinguished from the rest. ***adv.*** 1. approximately; about: as, *some* twenty persons. 2. [Colloq.], somewhat: as, the snow is *some* deeper than yesterday. 3. [Colloq.], to a great extent or at a great rate: as, you'll have to travel *some* to get there on time.

-some (səm), [AS. *-sum* < base of *same*], a suffix meaning *like, apt* or *tending to* (*be*), as in *lonesome, tiresome.*

-some (səm), [AS. *sum;* see SOME], a suffix meaning *in* (a specified) *number*, as in *threesome.*

-some (sōm), [< Gr. *sōma*, body], a combining form meaning *body*, as in *chromosome.*

some·bod·y (sum'bud'i, sum'bod'i, sum'bəd-i), ***n.*** [*pl.* SOMEBODIES (-iz)], a person of importance. ***pron.*** a person unknown or not named; some person; someone.

some·day (sum'dā'), ***adv.*** at some future day or time.

some·how (sum'hou'), ***adv.*** in a way or by a method not known, stated, or understood: as, *somehow* they have solved the problem.

somehow or other, somehow.

some·one (sum'wun', sum'wən), ***pron.*** somebody.

som·er·sault (sum'ẽr-sôlt'), ***n.*** [altered < OFr. *sombresault, soubresault* < L. *supra*, over + *saltus*, a leap], an acrobatic stunt performed by turning the body one full revolution forward or backward, heels over head: often used figuratively, as of a complete reversal of opinion, sympathies, etc. ***v.i.*** to perform a somersault. Also **summersault, somerset, summerset.**

Som·er·set (sum'ẽr-set'), ***n.*** Somersetshire.

som·er·set (sum'ẽr-set'), ***n. & v.i.*** somersault.

Som·er·set·shire (sum'ẽr-set-shir'), ***n.*** a county of southwestern England, on the Bristol Channel: pop., 551,000; county seat, Taunton.

Som·er·ville (sum'ẽr-vil'), ***n.*** a city in Massachusetts, near Boston: pop., 95,000.

some·thing (sum'thiŋ), ***n.*** 1. a thing not definitely known, understood, or identified; some undetermined thing: as, there's *something* sinister in his laugh. 2. some thing or things, definite but unspecified: as, he has *something* to show for his efforts. 3. an important person or thing. ***adv.*** to some extent; somewhat.

some·time (sum'tīm'), ***adv.*** 1. at some time not known or specified; at some time or other. 2. at some unspecified time in the future. 3. [Rare], sometimes. 4. [Archaic], formerly; at some time in the past. ***adj.*** having been formerly (as specified); former: as, a *sometime* leader of the group.

some·times (sum'tīmz'), ***adv.*** 1. at times; on various occasions; occasionally. 2. [Obs.], formerly; at some time in the past.

some·way (sum'wā'), ***adv.*** in some way or manner: also **some way.**

some·ways (sum'wāz'), ***adv.*** someway.

some·what (sum'hwät', sum'wət), ***n.*** 1. some portion, part, amount, degree, or thing. 2. an important person or thing. ***adv.*** to some extent; in some degree; a little; rather: as, he was *somewhat* tardy.

some·where (sum'hwâr'), ***adv.*** 1. in, to, or at some place not known or specified. 2. at some unspecified point in amount, degree, time, etc. (with *about* or *in*): as, *somewhere* about eight o'clock. ***n.*** an unspecified or undetermined place.

some·wheres (sum'hwârz'), ***adv.*** [Chiefly Dial.], somewhere: in general use, considered solecistic.

some·whith·er (sum'hwith'ẽr), ***adv.*** [Archaic], 1. to some place; somewhere. 2. in some direction.

some·wise (sum'wīz'), ***adv.*** [Archaic], in some way or to some degree (usually preceded by *in*).

so·mi·tal (sō'mi-t'l), ***adj.*** of or characterized by a somite or somites.

so·mite (sō'mīt), ***n.*** [< Gr. *sōma*, body; + *-ite*], 1. any of the longitudinal series of segments into which the body of certain organisms, as the arthropods, is divided. 2. a similar segment in the human embryo.

so·mit·ic (sō-mit'ik), ***adj.*** somital.

Somme (sum; Fr. sôm), ***n.*** a river in northern France, flowing into the English Channel: length, 150 mi.

som·nam·bu·lant (som-nam'byoo-lənt), ***adj.*** having the habit of somnambulating.

som·nam·bu·late (som-nam'byoo-lāt'), ***v.i.*** [SOMNAMBULATED (-id), SOMNAMBULATING], [< L. *somnus*, sleep + *ambulatus*, pp. of *ambulare*, to walk], to get up and move about in a trancelike state while asleep. ***v.t.*** to walk across or through while asleep.

som·nam·bu·la·tion (som-nam'byoo-lā'shən), ***n.*** a somnambulating.

som·nam·bu·la·tor (som-nam'byoo-lāt'ẽr), ***n.*** a somnambulist.

som·nam·bu·lism (som-nam'byoo-liz'm), ***n.*** 1. the habit or act of somnambulating. 2. the characteristic actions of a person who somnambulates.

som·nam·bu·list (som-nam'byoo-list), ***n.*** a person who somnambulates; sleepwalker.

som·nam·bu·lis·tic (som-nam'byoo-lis'tik), ***adj.*** of somnambulism or somnambulists.

som·nif·er·ous (som-nif'ẽr-əs), ***adj.*** [L. *somnifer* <

somnus, sleep + *ferre*, to bring, bear; + *-ous*], inducing sleep; soporific.

som·nif·ic (som-nif'ik), *adj.* [L. *somnificus* < *somnus*, sleep + *facere*, to make], somniferous.

som·nil·o·quist (som-nil'ə-kwist), *n.* [< *somniloquy* + *-ist*], a person who talks while asleep.

som·nil·o·quy (som-nil'ə-kwi), *n.* [< L. *somnus*, sleep + *loqui*, to speak], 1. the habit or act of talking while asleep. 2. the words spoken by a person while asleep.

som·no·lence (som'nə-ləns), *n.* [ME. & OFr. *sompnolence;* L. *somnolentia* < *somnolentus;* see SOMNOLENT], sleepiness; drowsiness.

som·no·len·cy (som'nə-lən-si), *n.* somnolence.

som·no·lent (som'nə-lənt), *adj.* [OFr. *sompnolent;* L. *somnolentus* < *somnus*, sleep], 1. sleepy; drowsy. 2. inducing drowsiness. —*SYN.* see **sleepy.**

Som·nus (som'nəs), *n.* [L., sleep], in *Roman mythology*, the god of sleep.

son (sun), *n.* [ME. *sone, sune;* AS. *sunu;* akin to G. *sohn;* IE. **sunú-s*, lit., the child-bearing, the birth < base **seu-*, to give birth to, produce], 1. a male child in relation to his parents or parent. 2. any male descendant. 3. *a)* a son-in-law. *b)* an adopted male child. 4. any male person considered as the product of a given school, cause, native land, etc. 5. an affectionate or familiar form of address to a boy or man, as used by an older person. Abbreviated **s.**

the Son, Jesus Christ, second person of the Trinity.

so·nance (sō'nəns), *n.* 1. sonant quality or state. 2. [Obs.], *a)* a sound. *b)* a tune. —*SYN.* see **sound.**

so·nant (sō'nənt), *adj.* [L. *sonans*, sounding, ppr. of *sonare*, to sound], 1. of sound. 2. having sound; sounding. 3. in *phonetics*, voiced: opposed to *surd, voiceless.* *n.* in *linguistics*, 1. a voiced speech sound. 2. a speech sound used in any given language as a syllabic: opposed to *consonant.* 3. in Indo-European, a sonorant.

so·nar (sō'när), *n.* [*so*und *na*vigation *r*anging], an apparatus that transmits high-frequency sound waves in water and registers the vibrations reflected back from an object, used in detecting submarines, locating schools of fish, finding depths of oceans, etc.

so·na·ta (sə-nä'tə), *n.* [It., lit., a sounding < L. *sonare*, to sound; orig. applied to an instrumental composition as opposed to *cantata*, lit., something sung; cf. CANTATA], an extended instrumental composition for piano or for some other solo instrument or instruments, often with piano accompaniment: it is usually in three or four movements having a unity of subject and style but differing in tempo, rhythm, and melody.

sonata form, a complex form of musical composition, typically used for the first movement of a sonata, symphony, concerto, etc., and consisting basically of an exposition (or statement), development, and recapitulation (or restatement), usually followed by a coda.

so·na·ti·na (son'ə-tē'nə, sō'nə-tē'nə), *n.* [It., dim. of *sonata*], a short or simplified sonata.

son·der·class (zon'dẽr-klas', zon'dẽr-kläs'), *n.* [< G. *sonder*, separate, special; akin to Eng. *sunder*], any of a class of small, narrow racing yachts of extremely light displacement, limited in dimensions, sail area, etc.

song (sôŋ), *n.* [ME. *songe;* AS. *song, sang* (akin to G. *sang*) < p.t. base of *singan*, to sing (cf. SING)], 1. the act or art of singing: as, he broke into *song.* 2. a piece of music sung or as if for singing. 3. *a)* poetry; verse. *b)* a relatively short metrical composition for, or suitable for, singing, as a ballad or simple lyric. 4. a musical sound like singing: as, the *song* of the lark.

for a song, for very little money; cheaply.

song and dance, 1. singing and dancing, especially in vaudeville. 2. [Colloq.], talk, especially an explanation, that is pointless or evasive.

song·bird (sôŋ'bũrd'), *n.* 1. a bird that makes vocal sounds resembling music. 2. a woman singer.

song·ful (sôŋ'fool), *adj.* full of song; melodious.

Song·ka (soŋ'kä'), *n.* Songkoi.

Song·koi (soŋ'koi'), *n.* a river flowing from Hunnan, southwestern China, into the Gulf of Tonkin: length, c. 500 mi.: also **Songka**: English name, *Red River.*

song·less (sôŋ'lis), *adj.* 1. without singing. 2. unable to sing.

Song of Solomon, a book of the Old Testament consisting of a love poem, dramatic and lyrical in character, traditionally ascribed to Solomon: abbreviated **S. of Sol.**: also called *Canticles, Song of Songs.*

song sparrow, a common North American sparrow known as a songbird.

song·ster (sôŋ'stẽr), *n.* [ME. *songestere;* AS. *sangestre;* cf. SONG & -STER], 1. a singer. 2. a writer of songs or poems. 3. a songbird.

song·stress (sôŋ'stris), *n.* 1. a woman singer. 2. a woman who writes songs or poems.

song thrush, the mavis, a European songbird.

son·ic (son'ik), *adj.* [< L. *sonus*, sound; + *-ic*], 1. of or having to do with sound. 2. designating or of a speed equal to the speed of sound (about 1,087 feet per second or 741 miles per hour).

sonic boom, an explosive sound generated by the accumulation of pressure in a wave preceding an airplane traveling at or above the speed of sound: where this wave touches the ground, the variation in pressure is experienced as a loud report.

so·nif·er·ous (sō-nif'ẽr-əs), *adj.* [< L. *sonus*, a sound; + *-ferous*], carrying or producing sound.

son-in-law (sun''n-lô'), *n.* [*pl.* SONS-IN-LAW], the husband of one's daughter.

son·net (son'it), *n.* [Fr.; It. *sonnetto;* Pr. *sonet*, dim. of *son*, a sound, song < L. *sonus*, a sound], a poem normally of fourteen lines in any of several fixed verse and rhyme schemes, typically in rhymed iambic pentameter: sonnets characteristically express a single theme or idea: see **Petrarchan sonnet, Shakespearean sonnet.** *v.t. & v.i.* to write sonnets (about).

son·net·eer (son'ə-têr'), *n.* [*sonnet* + *-eer*], 1. a person who writes sonnets. 2. any minor or inferior poet: used contemptuously. *v.t. & v.i.* to sonnet.

son·ny (sun'i), *n.* [*pl.* SONNIES (-iz)], little son: used in addressing any young boy in a familiar way.

son of Adam, any man or boy.

son of a gun, [Slang], 1. a person or thing regarded angrily, contemptuously, indulgently, familiarly, etc. 2. an interjection expressing surprise, annoyance, etc.

Son of God (or **Man**), Jesus Christ.

so·nom·e·ter (sō-nom'ə-tẽr), *n.* [< L. *sonus*, a sound; + *-meter*], 1. an instrument used in the study of sound and pitch through measurement of the vibrations of sound-producing bodies. 2. an audiometer.

So·no·ra (sô-nô'rä), *n.* a state of northwestern Mexico, on the Gulf of California: area, 70,477 sq. mi.; pop., 364,000; capital, Hermosillo.

so·no·rant (sō-nôr'ənt, sō-nō'rənt), *n.* in *phonetics*, a voiced consonant that is sufficiently sonorous to be used, like a vowel, as a syllabic sound: *l, m, n*, and *r* are often so used in the final unstressed syllables of English words.

so·nor·i·ty (sə-nôr'ə-ti, sə-nor'ə-ti), *n.* [*pl.* SONORITIES (-tiz)], [< Fr. or LL.; Fr. *sonorité;* LL. *sonoritas*], quality, state, or instance of being sonorous; resonance.

so·no·rous (sə-nôr'əs; *chiefly* Brit. son'ẽr-əs), *adj.* [L. *sonorus* < *sonor*, a sound, din], 1. producing or capable of producing sound, especially sound of full, deep, or rich quality; resonant. 2. full, deep, or rich: said of sound. 3. having a powerful, impressive sound; high-sounding: as, *sonorous* prose.

son·ship (sun'ship), *n.* [see -SHIP], the fact, state, or relation of being a son.

son·sy, son·sie (son'si), *adj.* [< dial. *sonse*, prosperity, plenty < Scot. Gael. *sonas*, good fortune; + *-y*], [Scot., Irish, & N. Eng. Dial.], 1. lucky. 2. buxom; handsome; pleasing. 3. comfortable. 4. good-natured.

Soo (Canals), Sault Sainte Marie Canals.

Soo·chow (sōō'chou'; Chin. sōō'jō'), *n.* a city in Kiangsu province, eastern China: pop., 260,000.

soon (sōōn), *adv.* [ME. *sone;* AS. *sona*, at once; akin to OHG. *sān;* the AS. form is prob. < *son*, as soon as + *a*, ever; cf. Goth. *sunsaiw*, like, equivalent to], 1. in a short time (after a time specified or understood); shortly; before long: as, do come to see us *soon.* 2. promptly; quickly: as, I'll come as *soon* as possible. 3. ahead of time; early: as, but you came so *soon!* 4. readily; willingly: as, I would just as *soon* stay home as go. 5. [Obs.], at once; immediately.

had sooner, would rather; would prefer to.

sooner or later, inevitably; eventually.

soon·er (sōōn'ẽr), *n.* [Slang], 1. any person who occupies homestead land, as in the western United States, before the authorized time for doing so, thus gaining an unfair advantage in choice of location; hence, 2. anyone who gains an unfair advantage over others by doing something before the proper time. 3. [S-], a native or inhabitant of Oklahoma.

Soong (sooŋ), *n.* the name of a prominent Chinese family whose members include Ching-ling (1890–), the widow of Sun Yat-sen, and Mei-ling (1898–), the wife of Chiang Kai-shek.

soot (soot; *less often* sōōt), *n.* [ME. & AS. *sot;* akin to MD. *soet;* IE. base **sed-*, to sit, seen also in L. *sedere*, to sit (cf. SEDILIA); basic sense "what settles"], a black substance consisting chiefly of carbon particles formed by the incomplete combustion of burning matter. *v.t.* to cover, soil, or treat with soot.

sooth (sōōth), *adj.* [ME. & AS. *soth* < **santh* (cf. SOFT); akin to ON. *sannr*, true; IE. base **es-*, to be (cf. AM, IS), in form **sént, *sónt*, seen also in Sans. *sant-*, being, good, basic sense "that is"], 1. [Archaic], true or real. 2. [Poetic], soothing; smooth. *n.* [Archaic], truth; fact.

in sooth, [Archaic], in truth; truly.

soothe (sōōth), *v.t.* [SOOTHED (sōōthd), SOOTHING], [ME. *sothen;* AS. *sothian* < *soth*, truth (cf. SOOTH); orig. sense "to prove to be true"], 1. to make calm or composed, as by gentle treatment, flattery, etc.; appease; mollify. 2. to allay or relieve, as pain; assuage; ease. *v.i.* to have a soothing effect. —*SYN.* see **comfort.**

sooth·fast (sōōth'fast', sōōth'fäst'), *adj.* [ME. *sothfast;* AS. *sothfæst*], [Archaic], 1. truthful, honest, or loyal. 2. true or real.

sooth·ing (sōōth'iŋ), *adj.* [ppr. of *soothe*], tending or intended to soothe; calming; giving ease or relief.

sooth·ly (sōōth'li), *adv.* [Archaic], in sooth; truly.

sooth·say (sōōth′sā′), *v.i.* [SOOTHSAID (-sed′), SOOTHSAYING], to make predictions; foretell. *n.* a prediction.
sooth·say·er (sōōth′sā′ẽr), *n.* [ME. *sothseyere*, one who speaks the truth], 1. a person who predicts or pretends to foretell the future. 2. the mantis.
sooth·say·ing (sōōth′sā′iŋ), *n.* [< *sooth* + *saying*, lit., truth telling], 1. a predicting, or foretelling. 2. a prediction, or prophecy.
soot·i·ness (soot′i-nis; *less often*, sōōt′i-nis), *n.* the quality or condition of being sooty.
soot·y (soot′i; *less often*, sōōt′i), *adj.* [SOOTIER (-i-ẽr), SOOTIEST (-i-ist)], [ME. *soti;* AS. *sotig;* cf. SOOT & -Y], 1. of or like soot. 2. covered or soiled with soot. 3. dark-brown or black; dark; dusky.
sop (sop), *n.* [ME. *soppe;* AS. *sopp* < base of *supan* (cf. SUP)], 1. a piece of food, as bread, soaked in milk, gravy, etc. 2. *a*) something given as a reward, concession, or appeasement. *b*) a bribe. 3. a milksop. *v.t.* [SOPPED (sopt), SOPPING], [AS. *soppian* < the *n.*], 1. to soak, steep, or saturate in or with liquid. 2. to take up, as water, by absorption (usually with *up*). *v.i.* 1. to soak or ooze (with *in*, etc.): said of a liquid. 2. to be or become thoroughly wet.
SOP, S.O.P., in *military usage*, standing (or standard) operating procedure: cf. **standing order.**
sop., soprano.
So·phi·a (sō-fī′ə, sō′fi-ə), [< Gr. *sophia*, skill, intelligence, wisdom < *sophos*, wise], a feminine name: diminutive, *Sophy;* variant, *Sophie.*
So·phie (sō′fi), a feminine name: see **Sophia.**
soph·ism (sof′iz′m), *n.* [ME. *sophime;* OFr. *sophisme;* LL. *sophisma;* Gr. *sophisma* < *sophizesthai*, to play the sophist < *sophos*, clever, skillful, wise], a clever and plausible but fallacious argument or form of reasoning, whether or not intended to deceive; fallacy or sophistry.
soph·ist (sof′ist), *n.* [Fr. *sophiste;* L. *sophista;* Gr. *sophistēs*, wise man: see SOPHISM], 1. [often S-], in ancient Greece, any of a group of teachers of rhetoric, politics, philosophy, etc., some of whom were notorious for their clever, specious arguments. 2. a learned person. 3. any person practicing clever, specious reasoning.
soph·ist·er (sof′is-tẽr), *n.* 1. a sophist. 2. a student in his second year (*junior sophister*) or third year (*senior sophister*) at certain British universities.
so·phis·tic (sə-fis′tik), *adj.* sophistical.
so·phis·ti·cal (sə-fis′ti-k′l), *adj.* [< L. *sophisticus;* Gr. *sophistikos* < *sophistēs*, wise man, sophist], 1. of or characteristic of sophists or sophistry; hence, 2. clever or plausible but unsound and tending to mislead: as, a *sophistical* argument. 3. using sophistry.
so·phis·ti·cal·ly (sə-fis′ti-k′l-i, sə-fis′tik-li), *adv.* so as to be sophistical; in a sophistical manner.
so·phis·ti·cate (sə-fis′tə-kāt′; *also, for n.*, sə-fis′tə-kit), *v.t.* [SOPHISTICATED (-id), SOPHISTICATING], [ME. *sophisticaten* < ML. *sophisticatus*, pp. of *sophisticare* < L. *sophisticus*, sophistical], 1. to change from a natural, simple, or artless state, etc.; make artificial or worldly-wise. 2. to corrupt or mislead. 3. to make impure by mixture or adulteration. 4. to alter (a text, etc.) without authority; falsify. *v.i.* to use sophistical reasoning. *n.* a sophisticated person.
so·phis·ti·cat·ed (sə-fis′tə-kāt′id), *adj.* [pp. of *sophisticate*], 1. characterized by a lack of simplicity or naturalness; refined to the point of artificiality; hence, 2. worldly-wise; not naive. 3. for sophisticates.
so·phis·ti·ca·tion (sə-fis′tə-kā′shən), *n.* [ME. *sophisticacioun;* ML. *sophisticatio*], 1. sophistry. 2. the act or process of sophisticating. 3. the state, quality, or character of being sophisticated.
soph·is·try (sof′is-tri), *n.* [*pl.* SOPHISTRIES (-triz)], [ME. *sophistrie;* OFr. *sophisterie*], 1. unsound or misleading but clever, plausible, and subtle argument or reasoning; sophism. 2. the methods or practices of the Sophists.
Soph·o·cles (sof′ə-klēz′), *n.* Greek tragic dramatist; lived 496?–406 B.C.
soph·o·more (sof′ə-môr′, sof′ə-mōr′), *n.* [altered (after Gr. *sophos*, wise + *mōros*, foolish) < older *sophumer* < *sophum*, sophism; prob. < ME. *sophime;* see SOPHISM], 1. a student in the second year of college or high school. 2. a sophomoric person; know-it-all whose thinking is really immature or foolish. 3. a person in his second year of any enterprise: as, Senator Brown is a *sophomore* in Congress. *adj.* of sophomores. Abbreviated **soph.**
soph·o·mor·ic (sof′ə-môr′ik, sof′ə-mor′ik), *adj.* of, like, or characteristic of a sophomore or sophomores, often regarded as self-assured, opinionated, etc., though immature and inexperienced.
soph·o·mor·i·cal (sof′ə-môr′i-k′l, sof′ə-mor′i-k′l), *adj.* sophomoric.
soph·o·mor·i·cal·ly (sof′ə-môr′i-k′l-i, sof′ə-mor′ik-li), *adv.* in a sophomoric manner.
-so·phy (sə-fi), [< Gr. *sophia*, skill, wisdom], a combining form meaning *knowledge* or *thought*, as in *philosophy, theosophy.*
so·por (sō′pẽr), *n.* [L.], an unnaturally deep sleep; stupor.
so·po·rif·er·ous (sop′ə-rif′ẽr-əs, sō′pə-rif′ẽr-əs), *adj.* [< L. *soporifer* < *sopor*, sleep + *ferre*, to bring], soporific.
so·po·rif·ic (sop′ə-rif′ik, sō′pə-rif′ik), *adj.* [< L. *sopor*, sleep; + *-fic*], 1. causing or tending to cause sleep. 2. of or characterized by sleep or sleepiness. *n.* something, as a drug, that causes sleep.
sop·ping (sop′iŋ), *adj.* [ppr. of *sop*], thoroughly wet; drenched; soaking.
sop·py (sop′i), *adj.* [SOPPIER (-i-ẽr), SOPPIEST (-i-ist)], 1. sopping. 2. rainy. 3. [British Slang], too sentimental.
so·pra·no (sə-pran′ō, sə-prä′nō), *n.* [*pl.* SOPRANOS (-ōz, -nōz), SOPRANI (-prä′nē)], [It. < *sopra* (L. *supra*), above], in *music*, 1. the highest singing voice, of women and boys, usually ranging two octaves or more up from middle C. 2. a singer with such a range. 3. a part for such a voice. *adj.* of, for, or having the range of, a soprano. Abbreviated **sop., S., s.**
so·ra (sō′rə), *n.* [? < Am. Ind. name], a wading bird of the rail family, small and short-billed: also **sora rail.**
So·ra·ta (sô-rä′tä), *n.* Illampu, a mountain in Bolivia.
Sorb (sôrb), *n.* [G. *Sorbe;* of Slav. origin; cf. SERB], one of an old Slavic people, ancestors of the Wends.
sorb (sôrb), *n.* [Fr. *sorbe;* L. *sorbum*, serviceberry, *sorbus*, service tree], 1. any of a number of European trees of the apple family. 2. the fruit: also **sorb apple.**
Sor·bi·an (sôr′bi-ən), *adj.* of the Sorbs or their language. *n.* 1. the West Slavic language of the Sorbs; Wendish. 2. a Sorb.
Sor·bonne (sôr-bon′; Fr. sôr′bôn′), *n.* [Fr., after the founder, Robert de *Sorbon* (1201–1274), chaplain of Louis IX], 1. a former theological college in Paris, established about the middle of the 13th century. 2. the seat of the faculties of letters and science (and until late in the 19th century, of theology) of the University of Paris.
sor·cer·er (sôr′sẽr-ẽr), *n.* [extended < ME. *sorcer;* OFr. *sorcier*, sorcerer < LL. **sortiarius*, one who throws or declares a lot < L. *sors, sortis*, a lot], a person who practices sorcery; magician; wizard.
sor·cer·ess (sôr′sẽr-is), *n.* a female sorcerer; witch.
sor·cer·ous (sôr′sẽr-əs), *adj.* of, having the nature of, characterized by, or practicing sorcery.
sor·cer·y (sôr′sẽr-i), *n.* [*pl.* SORCERIES (-iz)], [ME. & OFr. *sorcerie* < *sorcier;* see SORCERER], the supposed use of an evil supernatural power over people and their affairs; witchcraft; black magic. —***SYN.*** see **magic.**
sor·did (sôr′did), *adj.* [Fr. *sordide;* L. *sordidus* < *sordes*, filth], 1. dirty; filthy. 2. squalid; depressingly wretched. 3. base; ignoble; mean. 4. mercenary, avaricious, grasping, or meanly selfish. —***SYN.*** see **base.**
‡sor·di·no (sôr-dē′nō), *n.* [*pl.* SORDINI (-nē)], [It.], in *music*, a mute.
sore (sôr, sōr), *adj.* [ME. *sor, sar;* AS. *sar;* akin to G. *sehr*, very, lit. sore; IE. base **sai-*, pain, sickness, seen also in L. *saevus* (< **sai-wo-*), raging, terrible, etc.], 1. *a*) giving physical pain; painful; tender: as, a *sore* tooth. *b*) feeling physical pain, as from wounds, bruises, etc. 2. easily irritated or angered; touchy; temperamental; oversensitive. 3. filled with sadness, grief, or sorrow; distressed: as, our hearts are *sore* for them. 4. causing sadness, grief, misery, or distress: as, a *sore* hardship. 5. provocative of irritation or disagreeable feelings. 6. [Colloq.], angry; offended; feeling hurt or resentful. *n.* [AS. *sar*, pain], 1. a place on the body where tissue is injured, as by a bruise, cut, or burn. 2. any source of pain, irritation, grief, distress, etc. *adv.* [Archaic], sorely.
sore·head (sôr′hed′, sōr′hed′), *n.* [*sore* + *head*], [Colloq.], a person who is angry, resentful, disgruntled, vindictive, etc., or one easily made so, as by defeat.
sore·ly (sôr′li, sōr′li), *adv.* [ME. *sorelie;* AS. *sarlice;* see SORE & -LY], 1. grievously; painfully; severely: as, his patience was *sorely* tried. 2. urgently; greatly; extremely: as, help was *sorely* needed.
sor·ghum (sôr′gəm), *n.* [Mod. L.; It. *sorgo* < dial. *soreg* < L. *syricus*, Syrian: hence, orig., Syrian grass], 1. any of a number of related cereal grasses with sweet, juicy stalks, grown for grain, fodder, sirup, etc. 2. a sirup made from the juice of some of these grasses.
sor·go (sôr′gō), *n.* [It.; see SORGHUM], any of several varieties of sorghum grown for sirup or fodder.
so·ri (sō′rī), *n.* plural of **sorus.**
sor·i·cine (sôr′i-sin′, sor′i-sin), *adj.* [L. *soricinus* < *sorex, soricis*, a shrew], 1. of or belonging to a group of small, mouselike animals, the shrews. 2. shrewlike.
so·ri·tes (sō-rī′tēz), *n.* [L.; Gr. *sōreitēs* (*syllogismos*), heaped up (syllogism), a sorites < *sōros*, a heap], in *logic*, a series of premises followed by a conclusion, arranged so that the predicate of the first premise is the subject of the next, and so forth, the conclusion uniting the subject of the first with the predicate of the last in an elliptical series of syllogisms.
so·rit·i·cal (sō-rit′i-k′l), *adj.* of, or having the nature of, sorites.

so·ror·i·cide (sə-rôr′ə-sīd′, sə-ror′ə-sīd′), ***n.*** [LL. *sororicidium* < L. *soror*, sister + *caedere*, to strike, kill], 1. the act of killing one's own sister. 2. [L. *sororicida*], a person who kills his own sister.

so·ror·i·ty (sə-rôr′ə-ti, sə-ror′ə-ti), ***n.*** [*pl.* SORORITIES (-tiz)], [< L. *soror, sororis*, sister, after *fraternity;* cf. ML. *sororitas*], 1. a group of women or girls joined together by common interests, for fellowship, etc., as in a social club. 2. a club or other organization composed of women or girls, as at many colleges.

so·ro·sis (sə-rō′sis), ***n.*** [*pl.* SOROSES (-sēz)], [Mod. L. < Gr. *soros*, a heap], 1. a multiple fruit formed by the merging of many flowers into a fleshy mass, as in the mulberry. 2. a women's club.

sor·rel (sôr′əl, sor′əl), ***n.*** [ME. *sorel;* OFr. *surele* < OHG. *sur*, sour; cf. SOUR], 1. any of a number of related plants with sour, fleshy leaves used in salads. 2. any of various other similar plants, as the wood sorrel.

sor·rel (sôr′əl, sor′əl), ***n.*** [Late ME. < OFr. *sorel* < *sor, sore*, a hawk with red plumage], 1. reddish brown. 2. a reddish-brown horse, etc. ***adj.*** reddish-brown.

sorrel tree, a North American tree with thick bark, white flowers, grayish fruit, and sour evergreen leaves.

Sor·ren·to (sə-ren′tō; It. sôr-ren′tô), ***n.*** a resort town in Italy, on the Bay of Naples: pop., 27,000.

sor·ri·ly (sôr′ə-li, sor′ə-li), ***adv.*** in a sorry manner.

sor·ri·ness (sôr′i-nis, sor′i-nis), ***n.*** the quality or state of being sorry.

sor·row (sor′ō, sôr′ō), ***n.*** [ME. *sorwe, sorowe, seorwe;* AS. *sorg, sorh;* akin to G. *sorge;* IE. base **s(w)ergh-*, to be ill, be sorrowful, seen also in Sans. *serg*, illness], 1. mental suffering caused by loss, disappointment, etc.; sadness, grief, or regret. 2. that which produces such suffering; trouble, loss, affliction, etc. 3. the outward expression of such suffering; mourning; lamentation. ***v.i.*** to feel sorrow; grieve.

SYN.—**sorrow** refers to the deep, often long-continued mental anguish caused by a sense of loss, disappointment, etc. (her secret, life-long *sorrow*); **grief** suggests a more painfully intense anguish, usually of relatively shorter duration, for some specific misfortune, disaster, etc. (his *grief* over the stricken child); **sadness** refers to a condition of low spirits or mournfulness, resulting either from a specific cause or from a general feeling of depression, hopelessness, etc.; **woe** refers to intense unhappiness or sharp grief that cannot be consoled. —***ANT.*** joy, happiness.

sor·row·ful (sor′ō-fəl, sôr′ō-fəl), ***adj.*** [ME. *soruful;* AS. *sorhful*], full of sorrow; specifically, *a)* feeling sorrow. *b)* causing sorrow. *c)* expressing sorrow. —***SYN.*** see **sad.**

sor·ry (sôr′i, sor′i), ***adj.*** [SORRIER (-i-ēr), SORRIEST (-i-ist)], [ME. *sari, sori;* AS. *sarig, sari*, in pain, pained at heart < *sar*, sore], 1. full of sorrow, pity, sympathy, or regret: as, we were *sorry* to hear of his death, we were *sorry* to have missed you: often used as an expression of apology. 2. inferior in worth or quality; poor: as, a *sorry* exhibition of acting. 3. wretched; miserable; dismal; pitiful: as, a slum is a *sorry* place.

sort (sôrt), ***n.*** [ME. & OFr. *sorte;* LL. **sorta* < L. *sors, sortis*, a lot, condition], 1. any group of things related by having something in common; kind; class. 2. quality; type; nature; character: as, remarks of that *sort.* 3. [Archaic], manner; fashion; way: as, he spoke in a queer *sort.* 4. *usually in pl.* in *printing*, any of the kinds of characters in a font of type. ***v.t.*** to place, separate, or arrange according to class or kind (often with *out*). ***v.i.*** [Archaic], 1. to associate; consort. 2. to harmonize or agree; suit. —***SYN.*** see **type.**

of sorts, 1. of various kinds. 2. of a poor or inferior kind: also **of a sort.**

out of sorts, 1. in *printing*, lacking certain sorts of type. 2. [Colloq.], not in a good humor; cross. 3. [Colloq.], not feeling well; slightly ill.

sort of, [Colloq.], somewhat.

sor·tie (sôr′ti), ***n.*** [Fr. < *sortir*, to issue, go out], 1. a sudden attack by forces of a besieged place upon the besiegers; raid. 2. the forces making such an attack. 3. one mission or attack by a single military plane.

sor·ti·lege (sôr′ti-lij), ***n.*** [Fr. *sortilège;* ML. *sortilegium* < LL. *sortilegus*, fortune teller < L. *sors*, a lot + *legere*, to read], 1. divination or prophecy by lots. 2. sorcery.

so·rus (sō′rəs), ***n.*** [*pl.* SORI (-rī)], [Mod. L. < Gr. *sōros*, a heap], a cluster of spore cases on the under surface of a fern frond, or a similar cluster or spot, as of fungus spores.

S O S (es′ō′es′), 1. the standard signal of distress (. . . – – – . . .) used internationally in wireless telegraphy, as by ships, aircraft, etc.; hence, 2. [Colloq.], any call or appeal for help.

Sos·no·wiec (sôs-nô′vyets), ***n.*** a city in southwestern Poland: pop., 78,000 (est. 1946).

so-so (sō′sō′), ***adv.*** indifferently; just tolerably or passably. ***adj.*** not very good or well; rather poor, bad, or unwell. Also **so so.**

sos·te·nu·to (sos′tə-no͞o′tō; It. sôs′te-no͞o′tô), ***adj.*** [It., pp. of *sostenere*, to sustain], in *music*, held for the full indicated time value, or somewhat prolonged in the time value of the tones: abbreviated **sost., sosten.** ***n.*** [*pl.* SOSTENUTOS (-tōz), SOSTENUTI (-tē)], a movement or passage of this kind.

sot (sot), ***n.*** [ME.; Late AS. < OFr. < LL. *sottus*, stupid] a habitual drunkard.

Soth·ern, E. H. (suth′ērn), (*Edward Hugh Sothern*), 1859–1933; American actor.

So·thic (sō′thik, soth′ik), ***adj.*** [Gr. *Sōthiakos* < *Sōthis*, the Dog Star < Egypt. *Septit*], of or having to do with Sirius, the Dog Star.

Sothic cycle, a period of 1,460 Sothic years (1,461 years) in the ancient Egyptian calendar: also **Sothic period.**

so·tol (sō′tōl, sō-tōl′), ***n.*** [Sp. *sotol, zotol* < Nahuatl *tzotolli*], any of a number of related treelike desert plants with dense clusters of whitish, lilylike flowers, growing in the southwestern United States and northern Mexico.

sot·tish (sot′ish), ***adj.*** 1. of or like a sot. 2. stupid or foolish from or as from too much drinking.

sot·to vo·ce (sot′ō vō′chi; It. sôt′tô vô′che), [It., under the voice], in an undertone, so as not to be overheard.

sou (so͞o), ***n.*** [*pl.* SOUS (so͞oz; Fr. so͞o)], [Fr. < L. *solidus* a coin], 1. a small French coin equal to 1/20 of a franc; 5-centime piece. 2. a French 10-centime piece. 3. a former French coin of varying value and composition.

Sou., Southern.

sou·a·ri nut (so͞o-ä′rē), [Fr. *saouari* < the native name in Guiana], the butternut of a number of related South American trees.

sou·bise (so͞o′bēz′), ***n.*** [Fr., after Marshal *Soubise* (1715–1787)], a sauce containing onions and melted butter.

sou·brette (so͞o-bret′), ***n.*** [Fr.; Pr. *soubreto* < *soubret*, affected, sly < *soubra*, to put to one side < L. *superare*, to be above], in the *theater*, 1. a lady's maid or maidservant, especially one involved in intrigue. 2. any pretty, flirtatious, or frivolous young woman character. 3. an actress who plays such characters.

sou·bri·quet (so͞o′bri-kā′), ***n.*** a sobriquet.

sou·car (sou-kär′), ***n.*** [Hind. *sāhūkār* < Sans. *sādhu*, straight], in India, a Hindu banker: also spelled **sowcar.**

sou·chong (so͞o′shôŋ′), ***n.*** [Chin. *hsiao*, small or young + *chung*, kind], a variety of black tea, grown especially in China.

Sou·dan (so͞o′dän′; Eng. so͞o-dan′), ***n.*** Sudan: the French spelling.

Sou·da·nese (so͞o′də-nēz′), ***adj.*** & ***n.*** Sudanese.

souf·fle (so͞o′f′l), ***n.*** [Fr. < *souffler*, to blow; cf. SOUFFLÉ], in *medicine*, a soft, blowing sound heard on auscultation.

souf·flé (so͞o-flā′, so͞o′flā), ***adj.*** [Fr., pp. of *souffler*, to blow], in *cooking*, light and puffy: as, cheese *soufflé.* ***n.*** any of several baked foods made light and puffy by the addition of beaten egg whites before baking.

souf·fléed (so͞o′flād′, so͞o′flād), ***adj.*** soufflé.

sough (suf, sou), ***n.*** [19th c. < Northern dial. < ME. *swough* < AS. *swogan*, to sound], a soft, low, murmuring, sighing, or rustling sound. ***v.i.*** [ME. *swowen, soghen;* AS. *swogan*, to sound], to make a sough.

sought (sôt), past tense and past participle of **seek.**

soul (sōl), ***n.*** [ME. *sowle, sawle;* AS. *sawol;* akin to G. *seele*, Goth. *saiwala;* only in Gmc. languages], 1. an entity which is regarded as being the immortal or spiritual part of the person and, though having no physical or material reality, is credited with the functions of thinking and willing, and hence determining all behavior. 2. the moral or emotional nature of man. 3. spiritual or emotional warmth, force, etc., or evidence of this: as, the painting, like the artist, lacks *soul.* 4. vital or essential part, quality, or principle: as, "brevity is the *soul* of wit." 5. the person who leads or dominates; central figure: as, Cromwell, *soul* of the Commonwealth. 6. embodiment; personification: as, she is the *soul* of kindness. 7. a person: as, I didn't see a *soul* about. 8. the spirit of a dead person, thought of as separate from the body and leading an existence of its own.

upon my soul! 1. originally, "I shall risk eternal damnation if this is not so!" 2. an exclamation of surprise.

soul·ful (sōl′fəl), ***adj.*** full of or showing deep feeling.

soul·less (sōl′lis), ***adj.*** lacking soul, sensitivity, or deepness of feeling; without spirit or inspiration.

sound (sound), ***n.*** [< ME. *soun, son* (+ unhistoric *-d*); OFr. *son;* L. *sonus*], 1. that which is or can be heard; the sensation of hearing, resulting from the stimulation of the auditory nerves by vibrations carried in the air, water, etc. 2. such vibrations (*sound waves*). 3. any auditory effect that is distinctive or characteristic of its source; identifiable noise: as, the *sound* of aircraft overhead. 4. a noise made by the organs of speech. 5. the distance within which a given sound may be heard; earshot: as, within *sound* of the guns. 6. mental impression or effect; meaning; suggestion; implication: as, we liked the *sound* of his report. 7. mere meaningless noise. 8. [Archaic], report; rumor. ***v.i.*** 1. to make a sound. 2. to give a specified mental impression as through sound; be heard or understood; seem; appear: as, her voice *sounds* troubled, the plan *sounds* feasible. 3. in *law*, to be concerned only; have effect or significance: as, an action *sounding* in damages. ***v.t.*** 1. to cause to sound, or to produce the sound of. 2. to express, signal, indicate, or announce: as, *sound* the alarm, the clock *sounds* the hour. 3. to pronounce: as, he doesn't *sound* his *r*'s. 4. to spread abroad; celebrate: as, they *sounded* her praises. 5. to examine, as the chest, by auscultation or percussion.

sound off, 1. to speak in turn, as in counting off for a military formation. 2. [Slang], to start speaking, especially when silence is in order. 3. [Slang], to speak in a loud or offensive way, as in boasting.

SYN.—**sound** is the general term for anything that is or may be heard (the *sound* of footsteps); **noise** usually refers to a sound that is unpleasant or disagreeable because it is too loud, harsh, discordant, etc. (the *noise* of a boiler factory); **tone** is generally applied to a sound regarded as pleasant or musical because it has regularity of vibration resulting in a constant pitch (the range of *tones* in a violin); **sonance**, in its general use, is a relatively rare synonym for **sound,** but in its restricted use in phonetics, applies to the quality of a sound that is voiced, or uttered by vibrating the vocal cords (all vowels have *sonance*). —***ANT.*** silence.

sound (sound), ***adj.*** [ME. *sound, sund;* AS. (*ge*)*sund;* akin to G. *gesund,* Dan. *sund,* etc.; ? < the base seen in Eng. *sooth*], 1. free from defect, damage, or decay; solid; whole and in good condition: as, a *sound* timber. 2. normal and healthy; not weak, diseased, or impaired: as, of *sound* mind and body. 3. firm; safe; stable; secure, especially financially: as, only *sound* banks withstood the crash. 4. based on truth or valid reasoning; reliable; sensible: as, a *sound* method, *sound* judgment. 5. orthodox; conservative. 6. thorough; complete: as, a *sound* investigation. 7. deep and undisturbed: said of sleep. 8. morally strong; honest, honorable, loyal, etc. 9. in *law,* valid. ***adv.*** soundly. —***SYN.*** see **valid, healthy.**

sound (sound), ***n.*** [ME.; partly < AS. *sund,* a swimming, water, strait & partly < the cognate & synonymous ON. *sund;* for IE. base see SWIM], 1. a wide channel or strait linking two large bodies of water or separating an island from the mainland. 2. a long inlet or arm of the sea. 3. the air sac, or swimming bladder, of a fish.

sound (sound), ***v.t.*** [OFr. *sonder* < LL. *subundare,* to submerge < L. *sub,* under + *unda,* a wave], 1. to measure the depth or various depths of (water or a body of water), especially with a weighted line: as, the bay was *sounded* and found navigable. 2. to measure (depth) in this way. 3. to investigate or examine (the bottom of the sea, etc.) with a weighted line that brings up adhering particles. 4. to investigate, examine, or try to find out, as a person's opinions. 5. to try to find out, or to find out, the opinions or feelings of (another or others) on a given matter, as by roundabout questioning or allusive remarks (often with *out*). 6. in *medicine,* to examine with a sound, or probe. ***v.i.*** 1. to sound water or a body of water. 2. to move downward through water; dive. 3. to try to find out something, as by roundabout questioning, etc. ***n.*** 1. a sounding. 2. in *medicine,* a long probe used in examining body cavities.

Sound, The (sound), a strait between Zealand and Sweden: Danish and Swedish name, *Öresund.*

sound·board (sound'bôrd', sound'bōrd'), ***n.*** a sounding board.

sound effects, sounds, as of thunder, blows, animals, traffic, etc., artificially produced to simulate sounds called for in the script of a radio, stage, motion-picture, or television production.

sound·er (soun'dẽr), ***n.*** 1. a person or thing that makes a sound or sounds. 2. a telegraphic device that converts electric code impulses into sound.

sound·er (soun'dẽr), ***n.*** a person or thing that sounds the depth of water, etc.

sound film, a motion-picture film with a sound track.

sound·ing (soun'diŋ), ***adj.*** 1. making or giving forth sound. 2. resonant or sonorous. 3. imposing in sound; high-sounding; bombastic.

sound·ing (soun'diŋ), ***n.*** 1. the act of measuring the depth or examining the bottom of a body of water, etc., with or as with a weighted line. 2. depth so measured. 3. *pl.* a place, usually less than 600 feet in depth, where such measurements can be taken.

sounding board, 1. a thin plate, as of wood, built into a musical instrument to increase its resonance. 2. a structure, as on a rostrum, designed to reflect the sound of a speaker's voice toward the audience.

sounding line, a line or cable weighted at one end and used for measuring the depth of water.

sound·less (sound'lis), ***adj.*** without sound; perfectly quiet; noiseless.

sound·ly (sound'li), ***adv.*** 1. in a sound manner; without weakness or error: as, he reasons *soundly.* 2. so as to be not easily awakened. 3. thoroughly; completely; forcefully: as, they were *soundly* defeated.

sound·man (sound'man'), ***n.*** [*pl.* SOUNDMEN (-men')], a man in charge of sound effects.

sound·proof (sound'prōōf'), ***adj.*** impervious to sound. ***v.t.*** to make soundproof.

sound track, the area along one side of a motion-picture film, carrying the sound record of the film.

soup (sōōp), ***n.*** [Fr. *soupe;* of Gmc. origin; cf. SUP], 1. a liquid food made by cooking meat, vegetables, fish, etc. in water, milk, etc. 2. [Slang], nitroglycerin. 3. [Slang], a heavy overcast, often with rain, that makes aerial navigation difficult. 4. [Slang], capacity for speed: as, his new car has plenty of *soup.*

in the soup, [Slang], in a difficult, disappointing, or hopeless situation.

soup up, [Slang], to increase in capacity for speed, as an engine, by enriching the fuel mixture, supercharging, etc.

soup-and-fish (sōōp''n-fish'), ***n.*** [Slang], clothes worn on a formal occasion; full dress: from the variety and abundance of food served at formal dinners.

soup·çon (sōōp'sōn'), ***n.*** [Fr.; OFr. *sospeçon;* LL. *suspectio,* for L. *suspicio;* see SUSPICION], 1. literally, a suspicion; hence, 2. a very slight amount; suggestion or trace, especially of a given flavor, as onion.

soup kitchen, 1. a place where free food is given to people unable to provide their own. 2. a mobile kitchen, as used by an army in the field.

soup·spoon (sōōp'spōōn'), ***n.*** a spoon with a large bowl, used in eating soup.

soup·y (sōōp'i), ***adj.*** [SOUPIER (-i-ẽr), SOUPIEST (-i-ist)], of or like soup.

sour (sour), ***adj.*** [ME. *sour, sur;* AS. *sur;* akin to G. *sauer;* IE. **sūro-s,* salty, bitter, as also in Lith. *sūras,* salty; cf. SORREL (the plant)], 1. having a sharp, acid taste; tart, as lime or lemon juice, vinegar, green fruit, etc. 2. made acid by fermentation; rank; rancid; spoiled: as, this milk smells *sour.* 3. cross; disagreeable; bad-tempered; peevish; morose; bitter: as, failure made him *sour.* 4. below the usual or desired standard or quality; not satisfactory; poor: as, his game has gone *sour.* 5. distasteful or unpleasant. 6. excessively acid: said of soil. 7. tainted with sulfur compounds: said of gasoline, etc. ***n.*** 1. that which is sour; something sour. 2. an acid drink: as, a whisky *sour.* ***v.t. & v.i.*** to make or become sour (in any sense).

SYN.—**sour** usually implies an unpleasant sharpness of taste and often connotes fermentation or rancidness (*sour* milk); **acid** suggests a sourness that is normal or natural (a lemon is an *acid* fruit); **acidulous** suggests a slightly sour or acid quality (*acidulous* spring water); **tart** suggests a slightly stinging sharpness or sourness and usually connotes that this is pleasant to the taste (a *tart* cherry pie). —***ANT.*** sweet.

source (sôrs, sōrs), ***n.*** [ME. *sours;* OFr. *sourse, surse* < *sourdre,* to rise; L. *surgere;* see SURGE], 1. a spring, fountain, etc. that is the starting point of a stream. 2. that from which something comes or develops; place of origin; prime cause: as, the garden is the *source* of much of his pleasure. 3. a person or thing from which information is or may be gotten: as, the author's *sources* were all recognized authorities. 4. the person or business firm that makes payment of dividends, interest, etc. —***SYN.*** see **origin.**

source material, original or primary sources of information on any given study or subject.

sour·dine (sōōr-dēn'), ***n.*** [Fr.; It. *sordina* < *sordo,* deaf, muted, dull-sounding; L. *surdus;* see SURD], in *music,* 1. originally, any of several instruments of low or soft tone. 2. a mute, especially one for a trumpet.

sour·dough (sour'dō'), ***n.*** 1. [Dial.], leaven; especially, fermented dough saved from one baking so that it can be used in the next, thus avoiding the need for fresh yeast. 2. a prospector or settler in the western United States, Canada, or Alaska, especially one living alone: so called from his using sourdough.

sour gourd, 1. a woody fruit with acid pulp and many large seeds. 2. the Australian or African tree on which it grows.

sour grapes, something scorned only because it cannot be had.

sour gum, any of a number of tall related trees with crooked branches and leaves that turn bright red in the fall; tupelo.

sour·ish (sour'ish), ***adj.*** somewhat sour; not sweet.

sour·puss (sour'poos'), ***n.*** [Slang], a person who has a gloomy or disagreeable expression or nature.

sour·sop (sour'sop'), ***n.*** 1. a tropical American tree with large, pulpy, acid fruit. 2. its fruit.

Sou·sa, John Philip (sōō'zə, sōō'sə), 1854–1932; American composer and bandmaster: called the *March King.*

sou·sa·phone (sōō'zə-fōn', sōō'sə-fōn'), ***n.*** [after John Philip *Sousa,* who suggested it], a brass-wind instrument of the tuba class: it was developed from the helicon and is used especially in military bands.

souse (sous), ***n.*** [ME. *sows;* OFr. *souz, soult;* OHG. *sulza,* brine], 1. a pickled food, especially the feet, ears, and head of a pig. 2. liquid used for pickling; brine. 3. the act of plunging into a liquid, especially into brine for pickling. 4. [Slang], a drunkard. ***v.t. & v.i.*** [SOUSED (soust), SOUSING], 1. to pickle. 2. to plunge or steep in a liquid. 3. to make or become soaking wet. 4. [Slang], to make or become intoxicated.

souse (sous), *n.* [altered < ME. *source* < OFr. *sors*, *source*, in the same sense; cf. SOURCE], in *falconry*, 1. the act of rising in flight: said of a hunted bird. 2. the act of swooping down on a hunted bird: said of a hawk, falcon, etc. *v.t.* & *v.i.* [SOUSED (soust), SOUSING], in *falconry*, to swoop down (on) in attack. *adv.* with a swoop or plunge; suddenly.

soused (soust), *adj.* [pp. of *souse* (to pickle)], [Slang], drunk; intoxicated.

‡sou·tache (so͞o'tȧsh'), *n.* [Fr.; altered < Hung. *szuszak*, a pendant curl of hair], a narrow, flat braid used for trimming and embroidery.

sou·tane (so͞o-tän'), *n.* [Fr.; It. *sottana* < *sotto*, under < L. *subtus*, under, beneath < *sub*, under], a cassock or tunic worn by Roman Catholic priests.

south (south), *n.* [ME. *suth*; AS. *suth* (akin to OHG. *sund*) < **sunth-*; prob. < the base of *sun*], 1. the direction to the left of a person facing the sunset: direction of the South Pole from any other point on the earth's surface. 2. the point on a compass at 180°, directly opposite north. 3. a region or district in or toward this direction. 4. [often S-], the southern part of the earth, especially the antarctic regions. *adj.* 1. in, of, to, toward, or facing the south. 2. blowing from the south: as, a *south* wind. 3. [S-], designating the southern part of a continent, country, etc.: as, *South* America, *South* India. *adv.* in or toward the south; in a southerly direction. Abbreviated **S, S., s, s., So.**
the South, 1. that part of the United States which is bounded on the north by the southern border of Pennsylvania, the Ohio River, and the northern border of Missouri. 2. the Confederacy.

South Africa, a country in southernmost Africa: in the British Commonwealth until 1961: area, 472,359 sq. mi.; pop., 15,983,000; capitals, Cape Town, Pretoria: former name, *Union of South Africa;* abbreviated **S. Afr., S.A.**

South African, 1. of southern Africa. 2. of South Africa. 3. a native or inhabitant of South Africa, especially one of European ancestry.

South African Dutch, 1. the Boers. 2. their language; Afrikaans: abbreviated **S.Afr.D.**

South African Republic, the Transvaal: former name.

South America, a continent in the Western Hemisphere: area, 6,814,000 sq. mi.; pop., 148,000,000.

South American, 1. of South America or its people. 2. a native or inhabitant of South America.

South·amp·ton (sou-thamp'tən, south-hamp'tən), *n.* 1. the mainland division of Hampshire county, southern England: pop., 1,336,000; county seat, Winchester. 2. a seaport in this county: pop., 200,000.

Southampton Island, an island in northern Hudson Bay, Canada: area, 16,114 sq. mi.

South Australia, a state of south central Australia: area, 380,070 sq. mi.; pop., 989,000; capital, Adelaide.

South Bend, a city in northern Indiana: pop., 132,000.

south·bound (south'bound'), *adj.* going southward.

south by east, the direction, or the point on a mariner's compass, halfway between due south and south-southeast; 11° 15' east of due south: abbreviated **SbE** (no period).

south by west, the direction, or the point on a mariner's compass, halfway between due south and south-southwest; 11°15' west of due south: abbreviated **SbW** (no period).

South Carolina, a Southern State of the United States: area, 31,055 sq. mi.; pop., 2,383,000; capital, Columbia: abbreviated **S.C.**

South Carolinian, 1. of South Carolina or its people. 2. a native or inhabitant of South Carolina.

South China Sea, an arm of the Pacific, touching Taiwan, the Philippines, Borneo, the Malay Peninsula, and Indochina.

South Dakota, a Middle Western State of the United States: area, 77,047 sq. mi.; pop., 681,000; capital, Pierre: abbreviated **S.Dak., S.D.**

South Dakotan, 1. of South Dakota or its people. 2. a native or inhabitant of South Dakota.

South·down (south'doun'), *n.* [after *South Downs*], any of a breed of small, hornless English sheep having short wool and bred chiefly for food.

South Downs, a range of hills in Sussex and Hampshire, England.

south·east (south'ēst'; *in nautical usage*, sou-ēst'), *n.* 1. the direction, or the point on a mariner's compass, halfway between south and east; 45° east of due south. 2. a region or district in or toward this direction. *adj.* 1. in, of, to, toward, or facing the southeast. 2. from the southeast: as, a *southeast* wind. *adv.* in, toward, or from the southeast. Abbreviated **SE, S.E., s.e.**
the Southeast, the southeastern part of the United States.

southeast by east, the direction, or the point on a mariner's compass, halfway between southeast and east-southeast; 11°15' east of southeast: abbreviated **SEbE** (no period).

southeast by south, the direction, or the point on a mariner's compass, halfway between southeast and south-southeast; 11°15' south of southeast: abbreviated **SEbS** (no period).

south·east·er (south'ēs'tẽr; *in nautical usage*, sou-ēs'tẽr), *n.* a storm or strong wind from the southeast.

south·east·er·ly (south'ēs'tẽr-li; *in nautical usage*, sou-ēs'tẽr-li), *adj.* & *adv.* 1. in or toward the southeast. 2. from the southeast: as, a *southeasterly* wind.

south·east·ern (south'ēs'tẽrn; *in nautical usage*, sou-ēs'tẽrn), *adj.* 1. in, of, or toward the southeast. 2. from the southeast: as, a *southeastern* wind. 3. [S-], of or characteristic of the Southeast.

south·east·ward (south'ēst'wẽrd; *in nautical usage*, sou-ēst'wẽrd), *adv.* & *adj.* toward the southeast. *n.* a southeastward direction, point, or region.

south·east·ward·ly (south'ēst'wẽrd-li; *in nautical usage*, sou-ēst'wẽrd-li), *adj.* & *adv.* 1. toward the southeast. 2. from the southeast: as, a *southeastwardly* wind.

south·east·wards (south'ēst'wẽrdz; *in nautical usage*, sou-ēst'wẽrdz), *adv.* southeastward.

South·end-on-Sea (south'end'on-sē'), *n.* a seaport in southeastern England, on the Thames estuary: pop., 165,000: resort.

south·er (sou*th*'ẽr), *n.* a storm or wind from the south.

south·er·ly (su*th*'ẽr-li), *adj.* 1. in, of, or toward the south. 2. from the south: as, a *southerly* wind. *adv.* 1. toward the south. 2. from the south.

south·ern (su*th*'ẽrn), *adj.* [ME. & AS. *suthern*], 1. in, of, toward, or facing the south. 2. from the south: as, a *southern* wind. 3. [S-], of or characteristic of the South. *n.* a southerner. Abbreviated **S., s., So., Sou.**

Southern Alps, a mountain range in New Zealand, on South Island: highest peak, Mt. Cook, 12,349 ft.

Southern Cross, a southern constellation in which there are four very bright stars in the form of a cross.

Southern Crown, the southern constellation Corona Australis.

south·ern·er (su*th*'ẽr-nẽr, su*th*'ən-ẽr), *n.* 1. a native or inhabitant of the south. 2. [S-], a native or inhabitant of a Southern State.

Southern Hemisphere, that half of the earth south of the equator.

south·ern·ly (su*th*'ẽrn-li), *adj.* & *adv.* southerly.

south·ern·most (su*th*'ẽrn-mōst'), *adj.* farthest south.

Southern Rhodesia, a British self-governing territory in southern Africa: part of the Federation of Rhodesia and Nyasaland: area, 150,333 sq. mi.; pop., 3,200,000; capital, Salisbury.

Southern Sporades, a group of Greek islands in the Aegean, southwest of Turkey: they belonged to Italy from 1912 to 1947.

south·ern·wood (su*th*'ẽrn-wood'), *n.* [ME. *suthernewode;* AS. *sutherne wudu*: from being native to southern Europe], a shrubby wormwood with yellowish flowers and fragrant leaves, sometimes used in making beer.

Sou·they, Robert (sou'*th*i, su*th*'i), 1774–1843; English poet and writer; poet laureate (1813–1843).

South Gate, a city in southwestern California: suburb of Los Angeles: pop., 54,000.

South Holland, a province of the western Netherlands, on the North Sea: pop., 2,726,000; capital, The Hague.

south·ing (sou*th*'iŋ), *n.* 1. inclination or movement toward the south. 2. in *astronomy*, the distance in degrees that a heavenly body is south of the celestial equator; southern declination. 3. in *navigation*, the variation in latitude toward the south from the last reckoning of position.

South Island, the larger of the two large islands of New Zealand: area, 58,092 sq. mi.

south·land (south'lənd, south'land'), *n.* 1. land lying in the south. 2. the southern part of a country, etc.

south·most (south'mōst), *adj.* southernmost.

South Ossetian Autonomous Region, an autonomous region of the Georgian S.S.R., in the Caucasus: area, 1,428 sq. mi.; pop., 96,000; capital, Stalinir.

south·paw (south'pô'), *n.* [Slang], in *sports*, a left-handed player; especially, a pitcher who throws left-handed. *adj.* [Slang], left-handed.

South Platte, a river in Colorado and Nebraska, joining the North Platte to form the Platte River: length, 424 mi.

South Pole, the southern end of the earth's axis; 90th degree of south latitude.

South·port (south'pôrt', south'pōrt'), *n.* a city in Lancashire, England, on the Irish Sea: pop., 81,000: resort.

south·ron (su*th*'rən), *n.* [altered (prob. after *Briton*, *Saxon*) < *southren*, dial. var. of *southern*], a southerner: applied specifically in Scottish dialect to an Englishman. *adj.* southern.

South Sea Islander, a native or inhabitant of the South Sea Islands.

South Sea Islands, the islands in the South Pacific.

South Seas, 1. the South Pacific. 2. all the seas located south of the equator.

South Shields (shēldz), a seaport in northeastern England: pop., 109,000.

south-south·east (south'south'ēst'; *in nautical usage*, sou'sou-ēst'), *n.* the direction, or the point on a mariner's compass, halfway between due south and southeast; 22°30' east of due south. *adj.* & *adv.* 1. in or toward this direction. 2. from this direction: as, a

south-southeast wind. Abbreviated **SSE, S.S.E., s.s.e.**
south-south·west (south′south′west′; *in nautical usage,* sou′sou-west′), ***n.*** the direction, or the point on a mariner's compass, halfway between due south and southwest; 22°30′ west of due south. ***adj. & adv.*** 1. in or toward this direction. 2. from this direction: as, a *south-southwest* wind. Abbreviated **SSW, S.S.W., s.s.w.**
south·ward (south′wẽrd; *in nautical usage,* suth′ẽrd), ***adj. & adv.*** toward the south. ***n.*** a southward direction, point, or region.
south·ward·ly (south′wẽrd-li; *in nautical usage,* suth′ẽrd-li), ***adj. & adv.*** 1. toward the south. 2. from the south: as, a *southwardly* wind.
south·wards (south′wẽrdz), ***adv.*** southward.
South·wark (suth′ẽrk), ***n.*** a borough of London.
south·west (south′west′; *in nautical usage,* sou-west′), ***n.*** 1. the direction, or the point on a mariner's compass, halfway between south and west; 45° west of due south. 2. a district or region toward this direction. ***adj.*** 1. in, of, to, toward, or facing the southwest. 2. from the southwest: as, a *southwest* wind. ***adv.*** in, toward, or from the southwest. Abbreviated **SW, S.W., s.w.**
the Southwest, the southwestern part of the United States, especially Oklahoma, Texas, New Mexico, Arizona, and southern California.
South West Africa, a territory in southwestern Africa, on the Atlantic: administered by South Africa: area, 317,817 sq. mi.; pop., 525,000; capital, Windhoek: formerly, German Southwest Africa.
southwest by south, the direction, or the point on a mariner's compass, halfway between southwest and south-southwest; 11°15′ south of southwest: abbreviated **SWbS** (no period).
southwest by west, the direction, or the point on a mariner's compass, halfway between southwest and west-southwest; 11°15′ west of southwest: abbreviated **SWbW** (no period).
south·west·er (south′wes′tẽr; *in nautical usage,* sou-wes′tẽr), ***n.*** 1. a storm or strong wind from the southwest. 2. a sailor's waterproof hat of oilskin, canvas, etc., having a brim that broadens in the back to protect the neck in stormy weather. Also **sou'wester, souwester.**
south·west·er·ly (south′wes′tẽr-li; *in nautical usage,* sou-wes′tẽr-li), ***adj. & adv.*** 1. in or toward the southwest. 2. from the southwest: as, a *southwesterly* wind.
south·west·ern (south′wes′tẽrn; *in nautical usage,* sou-wes′tẽrn), ***adj.*** 1. in, of, or toward the southwest. 2. from the southwest: as, a *southwestern* wind. 3. [S-], of or characteristic of the Southwest. Abbreviated **SW, S.W., s.w.**
south·west·ward (south′west′wẽrd; *in nautical usage,* sou-west′wẽrd), ***adv. & adj.*** toward the southwest. ***n.*** a southwestward direction, point, or region.
south·west·ward·ly (south′west′wẽrd-li; *in nautical usage,* sou-west′wẽrd-li), ***adj. & adv.*** 1. toward the southwest. 2. from the southwest: as, a *southwestwardly* wind.
south·west·wards (south′west′wẽrdz; *in nautical usage,* sou-west′wẽrdz), ***adv.*** southwestward.
sou·ve·nir (sōō′və-nêr′, sōō′və-nêr′), ***n.*** [Fr., orig. an inf., to remember < L. *subvenire,* to come to mind], something kept or serving as a reminder of a place, an occasion, or a person; keepsake; memento.
sou'·west·er, sou·west·er (sou-wes′tẽr), ***n.*** a southwester.
sov·er·eign (sov′rin, sov′ẽr-in, suv′rən), ***adj.*** [ME. *soveraine, sovereyn;* OFr. *soverain, souverain;* LL. ***superanus** < L. *super,* above, over], 1. above or superior to all others; chief; greatest; supreme. 2. supreme in power, rank, or authority. 3. of or holding the position of ruler; royal; reigning. 4. independent of all others: as, a *sovereign* state. 5. excellent; very effectual, as a cure or remedy. ***n.*** 1. a person who possesses sovereign authority; monarch; ruler. 2. a group of persons or a state that possesses sovereign authority. 3. a British gold coin valued at 20 shillings or one pound sterling. Also **sovran.** Abbreviated **sov.**
sov·er·eign·ly (sov′rin-li, sov′ẽr-in-li, suv′rən-li), ***adv.*** 1. as a sovereign; royally. 2. supremely; exceedingly.
sov·er·eign·ty (sov′rin-ti, sov′ẽr-in-ti, suv′rən-ti), ***n.*** [*pl.* SOVEREIGNTIES (-tiz)], [ME. *soverainete;* Anglo-Fr. *sovereyneté,* OFr. *souveraineté*], 1. the state or quality of being sovereign. 2. the status, dominion, rule, or authority of a sovereign. 3. supreme and independent political authority: as, state *sovereignty.* 4. a sovereign state or governmental unit.
so·vi·et (sō′vi-it, sō′vi-et′, sō′vi-et′), ***n.*** [Russ., lit., council], 1. a council or body of delegates. 2. in the Soviet Union, any of the various governing councils, local, intermediate, and national, elected by and representing the people: they constitute a pyramidal governmental structure, with the village and town soviets as its base and the Supreme Soviet as its apex. 3. any similar council in various socialist governing systems elsewhere. ***adj.*** 1. of a soviet or soviets. 2. of or connected with government by soviets. 3. [S-], of or connected with the Soviet Union.
so·vi·et·ism (sō′vi-it-iz′m), ***n.*** government by soviets.
so·vi·et·i·za·tion (sō′vi-it-ə-zā′shən, sō′vi-it-ī-zā′shən), ***n.*** a sovietizing or being sovietized.
so·vi·et·ize (sō′vi-ə-tīz′), ***v.t.*** [SOVIETIZED (-tīzd′), SOVIETIZING], to change to a soviet form of government.
Soviet Russia, 1. Union of Soviet Socialist Republics. 2. Russian Soviet Federated Socialist Republic.
Soviet Union, Union of Soviet Socialist Republics.
sov·ran (sov′rən, suv′rən), ***adj. & n.*** [old sp., under influence of It. *sovrano* (< OFr.)], sovereign.
sow (sou), ***n.*** [ME. *sowe, suwe;* AS. *sugu;* akin to G. *sau* (OHG. *su*); IE. base ***sū-*, pig, as also in L. *sus;* cf. SWINE], 1. an adult female pig. 2. *a)* a channel or sluice carrying molten metal from a blast furnace to the molds in which pig bars are cast. *b)* metal solidified in this channel.
sow (sō), ***v.t.*** [SOWED (sōd), SOWN (sōn) or SOWED, SOWING], [ME. *sowen, sawen;* AS. *sawan;* akin to G. *säen;* for IE. base see SEED], 1. to scatter or plant (seed) for growing. 2. to plant (a field, ground, earth, etc.) with seed; plant seed on or in. 3. to spread abroad; broadcast; disseminate; try to propagate. 4. to implant; inculcate. ***v.i.*** to sow seed for growing.
sow·bel·ly (sou′bel′i), ***n.*** [Colloq.], salt pork.
sow bug (sou), a small terrestrial isopod living in damp places, as under rocks or logs: also called *wood louse.*
sow·car (sou-kär′), ***n.*** a soucar.
sow·ens (sō′ənz, sōō′ənz), ***n.pl.*** [Gael. *sūghan,* the liquid used in preparing sowens < *sūgh, sūbh,* sap], [Scot.], a kind of porridge made from fermented oat husks.
sown (sōn), alternative past participle of **sow.**
sow thistle (sou), [Early ME. *sugethistel* (parallel with G. *saudistel*) < AS. *sugu* (see sow, *n.*); + *thistle*], a coarse weed with yellow flowers and spiny leaves.
sox (soks), ***n.pl.*** socks (hose).
soy (soi), ***n.*** [Japan., colloq. for *shōyū;* Chin. *chiang-yu; chiang,* salted bean + *yu,* oil], 1. an oriental sauce used on fish, meat, and some vegetables: it is made from soybeans that have been fermented and steeped in brine. 2. the soybean (plant or seed).
soy·a (soi′ə, sō′yə), ***n.*** [Chiefly British], soy.
soy·bean (soi′bēn′), ***n.*** 1. a plant with white or purple flowers and hairy, brownish pods. 2. its seed, which yields flour, oil, and other commercial products.
Sp., 1. Spain. 2. Spaniard. 3. Spanish.
sp., 1. special. 2. [*pl.* SPP.], species. 3. specific. 4. specimen. 5. spelling. 6. spirit.
S.P., SP 1. Shore Patrol. 2. Submarine Patrol.
s.p., *sine prole,* [L.], childless.
spa (spä), ***n.*** [< *Spa,* celebrated watering place in Belgium], 1. a mineral spring. 2. any place, especially a resort, having a mineral spring.
space (spās), ***n.*** [ME.; OFr. *espace;* L. *spatium*], 1. distance extending without limit in all directions; that which is thought of as a boundless, continuous expanse extending in all directions or in three dimensions, within which all material things are contained. 2. distance, interval, or area between or within things; extent; room: as, leave a wide *space* between the rows; hence, 3. (enough) area or room for some purpose: as, we couldn't find a parking *space,* put your answers in these *spaces.* 4. reserved accommodations, as on a train or ship. 5. interval or length of time: as, too short a *space* between arrival and departure. 6. the universe outside the earth's atmosphere: in full, **outer space.** 7. in *music,* an open place between the lines of a staff. 8. in *printing,* any blank piece of type metal used to separate characters, etc. 9. in *telegraphy,* an interval when the key is open, or not in contact, during the sending of a message. 10. [Obs.], time allotted or available for something. ***v.t.*** [SPACED (spāst), SPACING], to arrange with space or spaces between; divide into or by spaces.
Space Age, the period characterized by the launching of artificial satellites and manned space vehicles: regarded as beginning with the launching of the first sputnik on October 4, 1957.
space·craft (spās′kraft′, spās′kräft′), ***n.sing. & pl.*** any spaceship(s) or satellite(s) designed for travel, exploration, etc. in space outside the earth's atmosphere.
space fiction, novels and stories about interplanetary travel in the future.
space·less (spās′lis), ***adj.*** 1. having no spatial limits. 2. occupying no space.
space·man (spās′mən), ***n.*** [*pl.* SPACEMEN (-mən)], an astronaut or, as in space fiction, any of the crew of a spaceship.
spac·er (spās′ẽr), ***n.*** 1. a device used for making spaces, as in printing. 2. a device used to increase the speed of telegraphic transmission by reversing the current. 3. a person or thing that spaces.
space-sav·ing (spās′sāv′iŋ), ***adj.*** that saves space. ***n.*** the act or practice of saving space.

space·ship (spās′ship′), ***n.*** a rocket-propelled vehicle for travel in outer space.

space time, space-time continuum.

space-time continuum (spās′tīm′), the four-dimensional continuum involving the three dimensions of space and that of time, in which all things exist: see **relativity.**

space writer, a writer, especially a journalist, whose pay is based upon the amount of space occupied by his copy.

spa·cial (spā′shəl), ***adj.*** spatial.

spac·ing (spās′iŋ), ***n.*** 1. the arrangement of spaces. 2. space or spaces, as between printed words. 3. the act of a person or thing that spaces.

spa·cious (spā′shəs), ***adj.*** [OFr. *spacieux;* L. *spatiosus*], 1. having or giving more than enough space or room; vast; extensive. 2. great; large; not confined or limited.

spade (spād), ***n.*** [ME.; AS. *spadu;* akin to G. *spaten;* IE. base **spē-*, etc., long flat piece of wood; cf. SPOON < same base], 1. a heavy, flat-bladed, long-handled tool used for digging: the metal blade is pressed into the ground with the foot. 2. any of several tools resembling a spade. 3. a part of the trail of a gun carriage which digs into the ground to take up recoil. ***v.t. & v.i.*** [SPADED (-id), SPADING], to dig or cut with a spade.
call a spade a spade, to call something by its right name; use plain, blunt words.

spade (spād) ***n.*** [Sp. *espada*, sword (the sign used on Spanish cards) < L. *spatha*, spatula; see SPATHE], 1. the black figure (♠) marking one of the four suits of playing cards. 2. *pl.* the suit of cards so marked. 3. a card of this suit.

spade·fish (spād′fish′), ***n.*** [*pl.* SPADEFISH, SPADEFISHES (-iz); see FISH], 1. a disk-shaped salt-water food fish with sharp-spined fins, found along the Atlantic coast. 2. the paddlefish.

spade·foot (spād′foot′), ***n.*** a kind of toad with a horn-like projection on the hind foot which is used in digging: also **spadefoot toad.**

spade·ful (spād′fool′), ***n.*** the quantity, as of soil, taken up on a spade.

spad·er (spād′ẽr), ***n.*** 1. a person or thing that spades. 2. a digging machine.

spade·work (spād′wûrk′), ***n.*** any difficult or tiresome work necessary to make a beginning.

spa·di·ceous (spā-dish′əs), ***adj.*** [Mod. L. *spadiceus* < L. *spadix*, date-brown color], 1. of a bright-brown color. 2. bearing a spadix. 3. of the nature of a spadix.

spa·dix (spā′diks), ***n.*** [*pl.* SPADIXES (-iz), SPADICES (spā-dī′sēz)], [L., a palm branch broken off together with the fruit; Gr. *spadis*], a fleshy spike of tiny flowers, usually enclosed in a spathe.

spa·ghet·ti (spə-get′i), ***n.*** [It., pl. of *spaghetto*, dim. of *spago*, small cord], 1. a food consisting of long strings of flour paste, cooked by boiling or steaming and served with a sauce: it resembles macaroni except that the strings are solid, not tubular. 2. in *electricity*, an insulating tubing somewhat resembling macaroni, used for sheathing bare wire.

spa·hi, spa·hee (spä′hē), ***n.*** [Turk. & Per. *sipāhī;* see SEPOY], 1. formerly, a member of a corps of Turkish irregular cavalry. 2. a member of a corps of native Algerian cavalry in the French armed forces.

Spain (spān), ***n.*** a country in southwestern Europe, on the Iberian Peninsula: area, 190,050 sq. mi.; pop., 30,128,000; capital, Madrid: declared a monarchy by Franco in 1947: Spanish name, *España.*

SPAIN

spake (spāk), archaic past tense of **speak.**

Spa·la·to (spä′lä-tô′), ***n.*** a seaport in southwestern Yugoslavia: pop., 76,000: Serbian name, *Split.*

spall (spôl), ***n.*** [ME. *spalle;* prob. var. of *spalde*, a chip < *spalden*, to chip, split < MLG. *spalden* (akin to G. *spalten*)], a flake or chip, especially of stone. ***v.t. & v.i.*** to break up, chip, split, or crumble, as ore.

spal·peen (spal-pēn′, spal′pēn), ***n.*** [Ir. *spailpīn*], [Irish], a scamp or rascal.

Sp. Am., 1. Spanish America. 2. Spanish American.

span (span), ***n.*** [ME. *spanne;* AS. *span, sponn;* akin to G. *spanne;* prob. IE. base **spe-*, to extend, as also in L. *spatium* (cf. SPACE)], 1. a measure of length, equal to nine inches, based on the distance between the tip of the thumb and the tip of the little finger when extended. 2. *a)* the full amount or extent between any two limits. *b)* the distance between ends or supports: as, the *span* of an arch. 3. a part between two supports: as, a bridge of four *spans.* 4. the distance between the tips of an airplane's wings; wing length. 5. a short space of time. 6. [prob. influenced by D. *spannen*, to unite], a team of two animals used together. ***v.t.*** [SPANNED (spand), SPANNING], 1. to measure, especially by the hand with the thumb and little finger extended. 2. to encircle with the hand or hands, in or as in measuring. 3. to extend, stretch, reach, or pass over or across: as, the bridge *spans* the river. 4. to furnish with something that extends or stretches over: as, we *spanned* the aisle with an arch. —***SYN.*** see **pair.**

span (span), archaic past tense of **spin.**

Span., 1. Spaniard. 2. Spanish.

Span·dau (shpän′dou), ***n.*** a former city in Germany, now a district of western Berlin: pop., 160,000.

span·drel (span′drəl), ***n.*** [dim. of Anglo-Fr. *spaundre;* prob. < OFr. *espandre*, to expand; L. *expandere*], 1. the triangular space between the exterior curve of an arch and a rectangular frame or mold enclosing it. 2. one of the spaces between a series of arches and a straight cornice running above them.

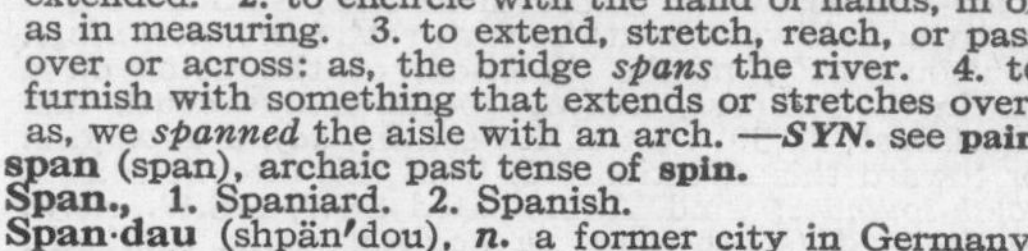

SPANDRELS

spang (spaŋ), ***adv.*** [< dial. *spang*, with a leap < dial. *spang*, to leap], [Colloq.], abruptly; directly.

span·gle (spaŋ′g′l), ***n.*** [ME. *spangel*, dim. of AS. *spang*, a buckle, clasp; akin to G. *spange*], 1. a small piece of bright metal, especially one of many sewn on fabric for decoration. 2. any small, bright object. ***v.t.*** [SPANGLED (-g′ld), SPANGLING], to cover or decorate with spangles or other bright objects. ***v.i.*** to glitter with or as with spangles.

span·gly (spaŋ′gli), ***adj.*** [SPANGLIER (-gli-ẽr), SPANGLIEST (-gli-ist)], of, like, or covered with spangles; glittering.

Span·iard (span′yẽrd), ***n.*** [OFr. *Espaignart* < *Espaigne*, Spain], a native or inhabitant of Spain.

span·iel (span′yəl), ***n.*** [ME. *spainel;* OFr. *espagneul*, lit., Spanish dog; Pr. *espanhol*, Spanish; It. *spagnuolo* < *Spagna*, Spain], 1. any of several breeds of dog characterized by a silky coat, large drooping ears, a small tail, and short legs: the three main classes are *field spaniels* (used for hunting), *water spaniels*, and *toy spaniels* (chiefly pets). 2. a servile, fawning person.

Span·ish (span′ish,) ***adj.*** of Spain, its people, their language, etc. ***n.*** the Romance language of Spain and of Spanish America: its dialects include Aragonese, Asturian, Andalusian (the basis of the Spanish spoken in Spanish America), and Castilian (the standard language of Spain).
the Spanish, the Spanish people.

Spanish America, Mexico and those countries in Central and South America and islands in the Caribbean in which Spanish is the chief language.

Span·ish-A·mer·i·can (span′ish-ə-mer′ə-kən), ***adj.*** 1. of both Spain and America. 2. of Spanish America or its people. ***n.*** a native or inhabitant of Spanish America, especially one of Spanish descent.

Spanish-American war, the war between the United States and Spain (1898).

Spanish Armada, a fleet sent against England in 1588 by Philip II of Spain: defeated by the English fleet.

Spanish bayonet, any of a number of desert plants with stiff, sword-shaped, spine-tipped leaves; yucca.

Spanish cedar, 1. a tree of South and Central America yielding a light, aromatic wood used in making cigar boxes, etc. 2. its wood.

Spanish fly, a bright-green beetle of southern Europe: it is finely ground and used in medicine as a blistering agent, diuretic, or genito-urinary stimulant; cantharides.

Spanish Guinea, a Spanish colony in west Central Africa, including Río Muni on the mainland, the island of Fernando Po, and other small islands in the Gulf of Guinea: area, 10,036 sq. mi.; pop., 213,000; capital, Santa Isabel.

Spanish Inquisition, the Inquisition as reorganized in Spain in 1478 under the control of the Spanish sovereigns: notorious for its cruel and extreme practices against those accused of heresy.

Spanish lace, any lace made in Spain, especially one of black silk in a floral pattern.

Spanish mackerel, any of various edible sea fishes related to the mackerel.

Spanish Main, 1. formerly, the mainland of America adjacent to the Caribbean Sea; especially, the northern coast of South America, from the Isthmus of Panama to the mouth of the Orinoco River. 2. later, the Caribbean Sea, or that part of it adjacent to the northern coast of South America, formerly traveled by Spanish merchant ships sailing between the Eastern and Western hemispheres.

Spanish Morocco, formerly, the Spanish zone of the sultanate of Morocco: see **Morocco.**

Spanish moss, a mosslike plant having small flowers and slender, gray stems with tiny leaves: it usually hangs in long, graceful strands from the branches of trees: also called **Florida moss.**

Spanish needles, 1. any of a number of related plants with small, spiny, hard, dry fruit. 2. the fruit itself.

Spanish onion, a large, mild-flavored kind of onion, often eaten raw.

Spanish paprika, 1. a mild red pepper of Spanish origin. 2. the plant on which it grows.

Spanish Sahara, a Spanish colony on the northwestern coast of Africa: area, 102,702 sq. mi.; pop., 25,000: former name, *Río de Oro*.

spank (spaŋk), ***v.t.*** [echoic], to strike with something flat, as the open hand, especially on the buttocks, as in punishment. ***v.i.*** [< *spanking, adj.*], to move along swiftly or smartly. ***n.*** a smart slap given in spanking.

spank·er (spaŋ'kẽr), ***n.*** 1. a person or thing that spanks. 2. [Colloq.], a swiftly moving horse. 3. in *nautical usage, a*) a fore-and-aft sail, usually hoisted on a gaff, on the aftermast of a square-rigged vessel: also called *driver*: see **sail**, illus. *b*) the aftermast and its sail on a schooner-rigged vessel of more than three masts.

spank·ing (spaŋ'kiŋ), ***adj.*** [< intens. use of *spanking*, ppr. of *spank*], 1. swiftly moving; rapid. 2. brisk; strong: said of a wind, breeze, etc. 3. [Colloq.], exceptionally fine, large, strong, vigorous, etc.

span·ner (span'ẽr), ***n.*** 1. a person or thing that spans. 2. [G. < *spannen*, to stretch], [British], a tool used to turn nuts or bolts; wrench.

span-new (span'nōō', span'nū'), ***adj.*** [ME. *span-newe* < ON. *spān-nȳr* < *spānn*, a chip (akin to Eng. *spoon*) + *nȳr*, new], [Dial.], perfectly new.

span·worm (span'wũrm'), ***n.*** the measuring worm.

Spar, SPAR (spär), ***n.*** [< *s*emper *par*atus (always prepared), L. motto of the U. S. Coast Guard], a member of the United States Coast Guard Women's Reserve (SPARS).

spar (spär), ***n.*** [ME.; MD.; akin to AS. *spæren*, gypsum], any shiny, crystalline mineral that cleaves easily into chips or flakes.

spar (spär), ***n.*** [ME. *sparre* < ON. *sparri, sperra* or MD. *sparre;* IE. base **sper-*, a pole, rod, as also in L. *sparus*, short spear, Eng. *spear*], 1. any pole, as a mast, yard, boom, or gaff, supporting or extending the sails of a ship. 2. a structural member running lengthwise along, and supporting the ribs of, an airplane wing. ***v.t.*** [SPARRED (spärd), SPARRING], to equip with spars.

spar (spär), ***v.i.*** [SPARRED (spärd), SPARRING], [ME. *sparren;* OFr. *esparer;* It. *sparare*, to fling out the hind legs, kick < *parare*, to parry], 1. to fight with the feet and spurs: said of a fighting cock. 2. to box, especially with skill and some caution, landing few heavy blows. 3. to wrangle or dispute. ***n.*** a sparring, boxing match, or dispute.

spar·a·ble (spar'ə-b'l), ***n.*** [altered < *sparrow bill:* from its shape], a small, headless nail used by shoemakers.

spar buoy, a buoy in the shape of a spar, anchored at one end.

spar deck, the upper deck running the full length of a ship.

spare (spâr), ***v.t.*** [SPARED (spârd), SPARING], [ME. *sparien;* AS. *sparian;* akin to G. *sparen*], 1. to treat with mercy or lenience; save; refrain from killing, injuring, troubling, or distressing. 2. to save or free (a person) from (something): as, she was *spared* the agony of seeing the accident, we have *spared* you the trouble. 3. to refrain from, omit, avoid using, or use frugally: as, don't *spare* your efforts. 4. to give up the use or possession of; get along without; dispense with: as, I can't *spare* the money or the time. 5. to part with or give up conveniently. ***v.i.*** 1. to practice close economy; be frugal or sparing. 2. to be merciful or restrained, as in punishing. ***adj.*** 1. not in regular use or immediately needed; extra: as, a *spare* room, a *spare* piece of machinery. 2. not taken up by regular duties; free: said of time. 3. frugal; meager; scanty: as, they lived on *spare* rations. 4. lean; thin; not fleshy. ***n.*** 1. a spare, or extra, part, thing, etc. 2. in *bowling, a*) the act of knocking down all the pins with two consecutive rolls of the ball. *b*) a score so made. —***SYN.*** see **lean, meager.**

spare·ly (spâr'li), ***adv.*** so as to be spare; scantily; poorly.

spare·rib (spâr'rib'), ***n.*** [prob. altered (after *spare, adj.*) < MLG. *ribbespẽr*], a cut of pork consisting of the thin end of the rib with most of the meat cut away: see **pork**, illus.

sparge (spärj), ***v.t. & v.i.*** [SPARGED (spärjd), SPARGING], [OFr. *espargier* < L. *spargere*, to sprinkle], to splash or sprinkle.

spar·ing (spâr'iŋ), ***adj.*** 1. that spares. 2. careful; frugal. 3. scanty, meager, or limited. —***SYN.*** see **thrifty.**

spark (spärk), ***n.*** [ME. *sparke, sperke, spearke;* AS. *spearca;* akin to MD. *sparke;* IE. base **sp(h)er(e)-g-*, to strew, sprinkle, as also in L. *spargere* (cf. SPARGE), etc.; cf. SPARKLE], 1. a small, glowing piece of matter, especially one thrown off by a fire. 2. any flash or sparkle of light like this. 3. a particle or trace: as, a *spark* of interest. 4. a trace of life or animation; particle of vitality. 5. *a*) the small, brief flash of light accompanying the discharge, or arcing, of an electric current from one point to another, as between the points of a spark plug. *b*) such a discharge. *c*) a device controlling such a discharge, as in an internal-combustion engine. ***v.i.*** 1. to produce or give off sparks. 2. to come forth as or like sparks. 3. to form the sparks properly: said of the ignition in an internal-combustion engine. ***v.t.*** to serve as the activating or animating influence of or in; kindle or fire into activity, especially of a vigorous and sustained kind.

spark (spärk), ***n.*** [ON. *sparkr*, lively < the base of prec.], 1. a gay, dashing, gallant young man. 2. a beau or lover. ***v.t. & v.i.*** [Colloq.], to court; woo.

spark arrester, 1. any device used to prevent sparks from escaping, as from a chimney. 2. in *electricity*, a device used to prevent sparking.

spark coil, an electric induction coil producing a spark, as in an internal-combustion engine.

spark gap, a gap made in an electric circuit for the passage of sparks from one terminal to the other.

spark·ish (spär'kish), ***adj.*** [*spark* (gay young man) + *-ish*], of or like a gay, dashing, gallant young man.

spar·kle (spär'k'l), ***v.i.*** [SPARKLED (-k'ld), SPARKLING], [ME. *sparklen*, freq. of *sparken*, to spark], 1. to give off sparks; hence, 2. to gleam or shine intermittently; glitter; glisten, as jewels, wet grass in the sun, etc. 3. to be brilliant and lively: as, her wit *sparkled*. 4. to effervesce. ***v.t.*** to cause to sparkle. ***n.*** 1. a spark; glowing particle. 2. a sparkling, or glittering. 3. brilliance; liveliness; vivacity. —***SYN.*** see **flash.**

spar·kler (spär'klẽr), ***n.*** a person or thing that sparkles; specifically, *a*) a noiseless, sparkling, pencil-shaped firework. *b*) *pl.* [Colloq.], eyes that are clear and brilliant. *c*) a diamond or other sparkling gem.

spar·kling (spär'kliŋ), ***adj.*** 1. that sparkles or sparks; glittering, brilliant, or lively. 2. effervescent.

sparkling water, soda water.

spark plug, a piece fitted into the cylinder of an internal-combustion engine to ignite the fuel mixture within: it carries an electric current into the cylinder, which sparks between two terminals in the presence of the mixture.

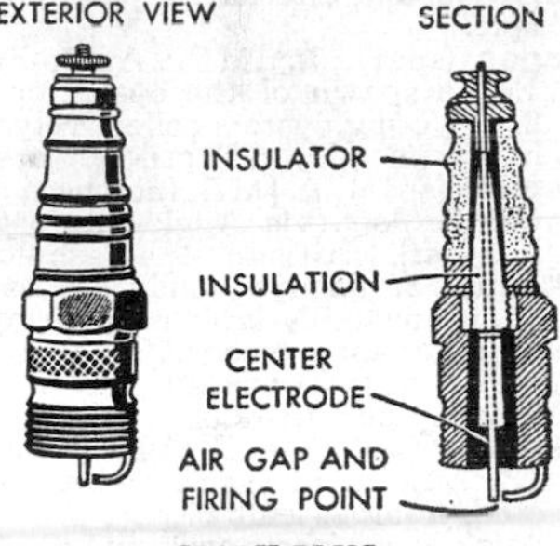

SPARK PLUG

spar·ling (spär'liŋ), ***n.*** [ME. *sperlynge* < OFr. *esperlinge* (Fr. *éperlan*) < Gmc.; akin to G. *spierling*], 1. the European smelt. 2. a young herring.

spar·oid (spâr'oid, spar'oid), ***adj.*** [< L. *sparus*, gilthead; + *-oid*], of the sea breams, a group of marine fishes that includes the porgies, scup, sheepshead, etc. ***n.*** a fish of this group.

sparring partner, any person with whom a prize fighter boxes for practice.

spar·row (spar'ō), ***n.*** [ME. *sparwe;* AS. *spearwa;* akin to MHG. *sparwe;* IE. base **sper-*, bird name, esp. for sparrow, as also in L. *parra*, bird of misfortune, Gr. *sporgilos*, sparrow, etc.], any of several small weaverbirds or birds of the finch family, especially the common small bird (*house sparrow*) usually known in America as the *English sparrow*: others are the European or American *tree sparrow*, the American *song sparrow, chipping sparrow, sage sparrow*, etc.

spar·row·grass (spar'ə-gras'), ***n.*** [altered by popular etym. < *asparagus*], [Colloq.], asparagus.

sparrow hawk, [ME. *sparowhawke*: so named from preying on sparrows], 1. a small European hawk with short wings. 2. a small American falcon that feeds chiefly on insects and small birds and game.

spar·ry (spär'i), ***adj.*** [SPARRIER (-i-ẽr), SPARRIEST (-i-ist)], 1. of or like spar. 2. rich in spar, as land.

sparse (spärs), ***adj.*** [L. *sparsus*, pp. of *spargere*, to scatter; cf. SPARK], thinly spread or distributed; not dense or crowded. —***SYN.*** see **meager.**

spar·si·ty (spär'sə-ti), ***n.*** the condition of being sparse.

Spar·ta (spär'tə), ***n.*** in ancient Greece, the chief city of the Peloponnesus, in Laconia: also called *Lacedaemon*.

Spar·ta·cus (spär'tə-kəs), ***n.*** Thracian slave; ? –71B.C.; leader of a slave revolt against Rome.

Spar·tan (spär't'n), ***adj.*** [L. *Spartanus*], 1. of ancient Sparta, its people, or their culture. 2. like or characteristic of the Spartans; warlike, brave, hardy, stoical, severe, frugal, highly disciplined, etc. ***n.*** 1. a native or citizen of Sparta. 2. a person with Spartan traits.

Spar·tan·burg (spär't'n-bũrg'), ***n.*** a city in northwestern South Carolina: pop., 44,000.

Spar·tan·ism (spär't'n-iz'm), ***n.*** 1. the folkways, strict standards of discipline and fortitude, attitudes, etc. of the ancient Spartans. 2. any similar standards, etc.

spar·te·in (spär'ti-in), ***n.*** sparteine.

spar·te·ine (spär′ti-ēn′, spär′ti-in), *n.* [< Mod. L. *Spartium*, name of the broom genus (< Gr. *spartos*, the broom); + *-ine*], a clear, oily liquid, $C_{15}H_{26}N_2$, obtained from broom and used in medicine as a heart stimulant.

spasm (spaz'm), *n.* [ME.; OFr. *spasme;* L. *spasmus, spasma;* Gr. *spasmos, spasma* < *spān*, to draw, pull, wrench], 1. a sudden, abnormal, involuntary muscular contraction: a *tonic spasm* is persistent and sustained; a *clonic spasm* is one of a series of relatively brief contractions alternating with relaxations. 2. any sudden, violent, temporary activity, feeling, etc.

spas·mod·ic (spaz-mod′ik), *adj.* [Mod. L. *spasmodicus* < Gr. *spasmōdēs* < *spasmos*, spasm + *eidos*, likeness], 1. of, having the nature of, like, or characterized by a spasm or spasms; sudden, violent, and temporary; fitful; intermittent. 2. characterized by emotional outbursts or excitability.

spas·mod·i·cal (spaz-mod′i-k'l), *adj.* spasmodic.

spas·mod·i·cal·ly (spaz-mod′i-k'l-i, spaz-mod′ik-li), *adv.* in a spasmodic manner.

spas·tic (spas′tik), *adj.* [L. *spasticus;* Gr. *spastikos*, drawing, pulling < *spān*, to pull, wrench], of or characterized by spasm; specifically, designating a form of paralysis in which certain muscles are in a state of continuous contraction, causing rigidity of a normally movable part. *n.* a person with spastic paralysis.

spas·ti·cal·ly (spas′ti-k'l-i, spas′tik-li), *adv.* in a spastic manner.

spat (spat), *n.* [prob. echoic], [Colloq.], 1. a slap. 2. a brief, petty quarrel or dispute. *v.i.* [SPATTED (-id), SPATTING], 1. to slap. 2. to engage in a brief, petty quarrel or dispute. *v.t.* to slap.—*SYN.* see **quarrel.**

spat (spat), *n.* [contr. < *spatterdash*], *usually in pl.* a covering for the instep and ankle, usually of heavy cloth; short gaiter.

spat (spat), alternative past tense and past participle of **spit.**

spat (spat), *n.* [ME.; Anglo-Fr.; prob. akin to *spit*], 1. the spawn of the oyster or other bivalve shellfish. 2. *a*) young oysters collectively. *b*) a young oyster. *v.i.* [SPATTED (-id), SPATTING], to spawn: said of oysters.

spate (spāt), *n.* [ME. (northern dial.) *spate;* said to be < OFr. *espoit* (via Anglo-Fr. **espeit*) < Gmc. base seen in *spout*], [British], 1. a flash flood. 2. a sudden, heavy rain. 3. flooded condition: as, the river is in *spate.* 4. an unusually large outpouring, as of words.

spa·tha·ceous (spə-thā′shəs), *adj.* [Mod. L. *spathaceus;* see SPATHE & -ACEOUS], 1. having a spathe. 2. of, or having the nature of, a spathe.

spathe (spāth), *n.* [Fr.; L. *spatha;* Gr. *spathē*, flat blade; IE. base as in *spade, spoon,* etc.], a large, leaflike part or pair of such parts enclosing a flower cluster (especially a spadix).

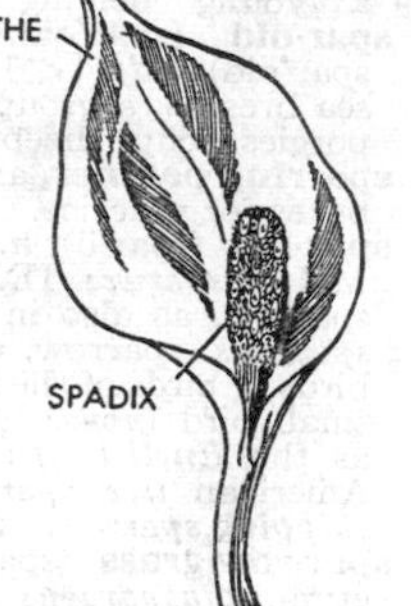

SPATHE

spath·ic (spath′ik), *adj.* [G. *spath, spat* (< MHG. *spat*); + *-ic*], of or like spar.

spa·those (spā′thōs, spath′ōs), *adj.* spathaceous.

spath·ose (spath′ōs), *adj.* spathic.

spa·tial (spā′shəl), *adj.* [< L. *spatium*, space], 1. of space. 2. happening or existing in space. Also spelled **spacial.**

spa·tial·ly (spā′shəl-i), *adv.* 1. with reference or regard to space. 2. in or by means of space.

spa·ti·o·tem·po·ral (spā′shi-ō-tem′pēr-əl), *adj.* existing in both space and time.

spat·ter (spat′ēr), *v.t.* [< LG.; cf. Fris. *spateren*, freq. of *spatten*, to splash, spurt], 1. to scatter in drops or small blobs: said of soft or liquid substances, as, she *spattered* white paint over the red. 2. to splash or spot with such drops or blobs. 3. to injure the name or reputation of; defame. *v.i.* 1. to emit or spurt out in drops or small blobs, as a boiling liquid. 2. to fall or strike in or as in a shower, as raindrops or pellets. *n.* 1. a spattering. 2. the sound of this. 3. a mark or wet spot caused by spattering.

spat·ter·dash (spat′ēr-dash′), *n.* [*spatter* + *dash*], *usually in pl.* a long legging worn to protect the stocking or trouser leg, as in wet weather.

spat·ter·dock (spat′ēr-dok′), *n.* 1. a common pond lily with thick roots, flat heart-shaped leaves, and yellow cup-shaped flowers. 2. any pond lily of the same or a related genus, especially one with yellow flowers.

spat·u·la (spach′oo-lə), *n.* [L., dim. of *spatha;* Gr. *spathē*, broad flat instrument; cf. SPATHE, SPADE], a knifelike implement with a broad, flat, flexible blade, used for spreading or blending foods, paints, etc.

spat·u·lar (spach′oo-lēr), *adj.* of or like a spatula.

spat·u·late (spach′oo-lit, spach′oo-lāt′), *adj.* [Mod. L. *spatulatus*], shaped like a spatula or a spoon, as some leaves: see **leaf,** illus.

spav·in (spav′in), *n.* [ME. *spaveine;* OFr. *esparvain;* prob. < Gmc. base seen in Eng. *sparrow*], a disease of horses in which a deposit of bone (*bone spavin*) or an infusion of lymph (*bog spavin*) develops in the hock joint, usually causing lameness.

spav·ined (spav′ind), *adj.* afflicted with spavin; lame.

spawn (spôn), *v.t. & v.i.* [ME. *spaunnen* (for **spaunden*); Anglo-Fr. *espaundre;* OFr. *espandre*, to shed (Fr. *épandre*) < L. *expandere;* see EXPAND], 1. to produce or deposit (spawn or eggs). 2. to bring forth or be the source of (especially something regarded with contempt and produced prolifically or in great quantity). 3. in *horticulture*, to plant with spawn, or mycelium. *n.* 1. the mass of eggs (or the milt) emitted by fishes, mollusks, crustaceans, amphibians, etc. 2. something produced, especially in great quantity, or some person or thing regarded as a product or offspring: usually contemptuous. 3. the mycelium of fungi, especially of mushrooms grown to be eaten, used for propagation.

spay (spā), *v.t.* [Anglo-Fr. *espeier* < OFr. *espeer*, to cut with a sword < *espee*, sword; L. *spatha*, broad flat instrument; cf. SPATHE, SPADE], to remove the ovaries of (a living animal); sterilize (a female).

S.P.C.A., Society for Prevention of Cruelty to Animals.

S.P.C.C., Society for Prevention of Cruelty to Children.

speak (spēk), *v.i.* [SPOKE (spōk) or *archaic* SPAKE (spāk), SPOKEN (spōk′'n) or *archaic* SPOKE, SPEAKING], [ME. *speken;* Late AS. *specan* < AS. *sprecan;* akin to G. *sprechen;* IE. base **sp(h)er(e)-g-*, etc., to strew, sprinkle, as also in L. *spargere*, to sprinkle (cf. SPARGE), Eng. *spark*, etc.; basic sense "to scatter (words)"], 1. to utter words with the ordinary voice; talk. 2. to express or communicate opinions, feelings, ideas, etc. by or as by talking: as, he would not *speak* in our behalf, actions *speak* louder than words. 3. to make a speech; deliver an address or lecture; discourse. 4. to converse. 5. to make or give out sound: as, the guns *spoke* sharply, they taught their dog to *speak* for food. *v.t.* 1. to express or make known by or as by speaking: as, he *speaks* the sentiments of us all, newspapers often *speak* the truth. 2. to use or be able to use (a given language) in speaking. 3. to utter orally, as words. 4. to speak to; address. 5. [Archaic], to declare or show to be; proclaim: as, his record *speaks* him a blackguard. 6. in *nautical usage*, to hail (a ship).

so to speak, in a manner of speaking; that is to say.

speak for, 1. to speak in behalf of. 2. to ask for; ask to have kept for oneself.

speak of, to talk about; mention.

speak out (or **up**), 1. to speak audibly or clearly. 2. to speak freely, without hesitation.

speak well for, to say or indicate something favorable about.

to speak of, worthy of mention.

SYN.—**speak** and **talk** are generally synonymous, but **speak** often connotes formal address to an auditor or audience (who will *speak* at the dinner?) and **talk** often suggests informal colloquial conversation (we were *talking* at dinner); **converse** suggests a talking together by two or more people so as to exchange ideas, information, etc. (they are *conversing* in the parlor); **discourse** suggests a somewhat formal, detailed, extensive talking to another or others (he was *discoursing* to us on Keats).

speak-eas·y (spēk′ēz′i), *n.* [*pl.* SPEAK-EASIES (-iz)], [*speak* + *easy*: so named because the orders are given quietly], [Slang], a place where alcoholic drinks are sold illegally.

speak·er (spēk′ēr), *n.* 1. a person who speaks; especially, *a*) a person who makes a speech or speeches in public. *b*) a person who speaks effectively in public. *c*) the officer presiding over any of various lawmaking bodies; specifically, [S-], the presiding officer of the United States House of Representatives: in full, **Speaker of the House.** 2. a book of selections for use as exercises in declamation. 3. a loud-speaker.

speak·er·ship (spēk′ēr-ship′), *n.* [see -SHIP], the office or position of speaker, or presiding officer.

speak·ing (spēk′iŋ), *adj.* 1. that speaks or seems to speak; expressive; eloquent; vivid: as, a *speaking* appearance of grief, a *speaking* likeness. 2. used in or for speech. 3. allowing or admitting of speech: as, he approached within *speaking* range, she had a *speaking* acquaintance with him. *n.* 1. the act or art of a person who speaks. 2. that which is spoken; utterance; discourse.

on speaking terms, 1. making a practice of speaking or conversing (with another or each other). 2. having a relationship friendly enough to allow of speech or conversation, as in greeting.

speaking tube, a tube or pipe made to carry the voice, as from one part of a building to another.

spear (spêr), *n.* [ME. & AS. *spere* (akin to G. *speer*); for IE. base see SPAR (pole)], 1. a weapon consisting of a long wooden shaft with a sharp point, usually of metal or stone, for thrusting or throwing. 2. its point. 3. any spearlike, often forked, implement used for thrusting, as in fishing. 4. a spearman. 5. [var. of *spire* (stem); ? influenced by *spear* (weapon)], a long blade or shoot, as of grass. *v.t.* 1. to pierce or stab with something pointed, as a spear. 2. to catch, as fish, with a spear. *v.i.* 1. to pierce, penetrate, or shoot like a spear. 2. [cf. *n.* 5], to sprout into a long stem.

spear·fish (spêr′fish′), *n.* [*pl.* SPEARFISH, SPEARFISHES (-iz); see FISH], a large marine fish with a long, spearlike growth on its upper jaw, related to the swordfish and sailfish.

spear grass, any of several kinds of grass with long, spearlike leaves.

spear·head (spêr′hed′), *n.* 1. the point or head of a spear. 2. the leading person, part, or group in an endeavor, especially in a military attack. *v.t.* to be the leading person, part, or group in (an attack, etc.): as, the Third Army *spearheaded* the invasion.

spear·man (spêr′mən), *n.* [*pl.* SPEARMEN (-mən)], a fighting man armed with a spear.

spear·mint (spêr′mint′), *n.* [prob. so named from the appearance of the flowers on the stem], a fragrant plant of the mint family, used for flavoring.

spear side, [*spear* + *side*: so named in contrast to *distaff side*], the paternal side or male line of a family.

spear·wort (spêr′wûrt′), *n.* any of a number of related plants of the crowfoot family, with spear-shaped leaves.

spec., 1. special. 2. specially. 3. specification.

spe·cial (spesh′əl), *adj.* [ME.; OFr. *especial;* L. *specialis* < *species*, kind, sort], 1. of a kind different from others; distinctive, peculiar, or unique: as, the play requires a *special* stage. 2. unusual; uncommon; exceptional; extraordinary. 3. especial; chief: as, her *special* friend, my *special* hate. 4. of or for a particular person, occasion, purpose, etc.: as, by *special* permission of the publisher, a *special* edition; hence, 5. not general or regular; specific; limited: as, *special* legislation, a *special* tax. 6. specified; definite: as, do you want any *special* kind? *n.* a special person or thing, as a special train, edition, etc. Abbreviated **sp., spec.**

SYN.—**special** and **especial** both imply that the thing so described has qualities, aspects, uses, etc. which differentiate it from others of its class, and the choice of word generally depends on euphony, but **especial** is usually preferred where pre-eminence is implied (a matter of *especial* interest to you); **specific** and **particular** are both applied to something that is singled out for special attention, but **specific** suggests the explicit statement of an example, illustration, etc. (he cited *specific* cases), and **particular** emphasizes the distinctness or individuality of the thing so described (in this *particular* case). —*ANT.* general.

special court-martial, a military court for judging offenses less grave than those judged by a general court-martial: it consists of three or more officers or (since 1948) enlisted men.

special delivery, a postal service through which, for an extra fee, mail is delivered by a special messenger before the regular delivery.

spe·cial·ism (spesh′əl-iz′m), *n.* 1. a specializing in one or more branches or fields of a study, profession, etc. 2. such a branch or field.

spe·cial·ist (spesh′əl-ist), *n.* a person who specializes in a particular field of study, professional work, etc.: as, a *specialist* in gynecology. *adj.* specialistic.

spe·cial·is·tic (spesh′əl-is′tik), *adj.* of a specialist or specialism.

spe·ci·al·i·ty (spesh′i-al′ə-ti), *n.* [*pl.* SPECIALITIES (-tiz)], [ME. *specialite;* OFr. *specialité*], 1. a special or distinctive mark, quality, or characteristic. 2. *pl.* special points or details; particulars. 3. a specialty (in various senses).

spe·cial·i·za·tion (spesh′əl-i-zā′shən, spesh′əl-ī-zā′shən), *n.* a specializing or being specialized.

spe·cial·ize (spesh′ə-līz′), *v.t.* [SPECIALIZED (-līzd′), SPECIALIZING], [Fr. *spécialiser*], 1. to make special, specific, or particular; specify: as, *specialize* your accusation. 2. to direct toward or concentrate on a specific end. 3. to adapt to a special condition, use, or requirement: as, a rooster's spurs are toes *specialized* for fighting. 4. to specify the payee in endorsing (a check, etc.). *v.i.* 1. to follow a special or limited line of endeavor; concentrate on only one part or branch of a subject, etc. 2. to become adapted to meet a special condition, use, etc., as parts of an organism.

spe·cial·ly (spesh′əl-i), *adv.* 1. in a special manner; particularly. 2. for a special purpose. Abbreviated **spec.**

special pleading, 1. in *law*, the allegation that special or new matter exists which will offset matter presented by the opposite side. 2. an argument or presentation that leaves out what is unfavorable and develops only what is favorable to the case.

spe·cial·ty (spesh′əl-ti), *n.* [*pl.* SPECIALTIES (-tiz)], [ME. *specialte;* OFr. *especialte*], 1. a special quality, feature, point, characteristic, etc. 2. a thing specialized in; special interest, field of study or professional work, etc. 3. the state of being special. 4. an article or kind of articles characterized by special features, uncommon or superior quality, novelty, alleged particular attention in production, or the like: as, doughnuts are the *specialty* of this bakery. 5. in *law*, a special contract, obligation, agreement, etc. under seal, or a contract by deed.

spe·cie (spē′shi), *n.* [abl. of L. *species*, and so used as an Eng. word prob. from its occurrence in the phrase *paid in specie*], coin, as distinguished from paper money. **in specie,** 1. in kind. 2. in coin.

spe·cies (spē′shiz), *n.* [*pl.* SPECIES], [L., a seeing, appearance, shape, kind, or quality], 1. a distinct kind; sort; variety; class: as, various *species* of villains. 2. a single, distinct kind of plant or animal, having certain distinguishing characteristics: a category of biological classification: cf. **genus.** 3. [Obs.], outward form, appearance, or mental image. 4. [Obs.], specie. 5. in *logic*, a group of individuals or objects having certain distinguishing attributes in common, given a common name, and comprised with other similar groups in a more comprehensive grouping called a *genus*. 6. in the *Roman Catholic Church*, *a*) the outward form, or appearance of bread or wine, of the respective transubstantiated elements of the Eucharist. *b*) either of these elements. Abbreviated **sp.**
the species, the human race.

specif., specifically.

spec·i·fi·a·ble (spes′ə-fī′ə-b'l), *adj.* that can be specified.

spe·cif·ic (spi-sif′ik), *adj.* [ML. *specificus* < L. *species*, kind, appearance + *facere*, to make], 1. limiting or limited; specifying or specified; precise; definite; explicit: as, a *specific* use of a word, for no *specific* reason. 2. of a species: as, *specific* characteristics. 3. peculiar to or characteristic of something, as traits, etc. 4. of a special, or particular, sort or kind. 5. in *medicine*, *a*) specially indicated as a cure for a particular disease: said of a remedy. *b*) produced by a particular microorganism: said of a disease. *n.* 1. something specially suited for a given use or purpose. 2. a specific cure or remedy. Abbreviated **sp.** —*SYN.* see **explicit, special.**

spe·cif·i·cal (spi-sif′i-k'l), *adj.* specific.

spe·cif·i·cal·ly (spi-sif′i-k'l-i, spi-sif′ik-li), *adv.* in a specific manner; definitely; precisely; particularly.

spec·i·fi·ca·tion (spes′ə-fi-kā′shən), *n.* [ML. *specificatio*], 1. a specifying; detailed mention or definition. 2. *usually pl.* a detailed description of the parts of a whole; statement or enumeration of particulars, as to size, quality, performance, terms, etc.: as, here are the *specifications* for the new building. 3. something specified; specified item, etc. Abbreviated **spec.**

specific gravity, the ratio of the weight or mass of a given volume of a substance to that of an equal volume of another substance (water for liquids and solids, air or hydrogen for gases) used as a standard: abbreviated **sp. gr., s.g., G.**

specific heat, 1. the ratio of the amount of heat required to raise the temperature of a unit mass of a substance one degree to the amount of heat required to raise the temperature of the same mass of water one degree. 2. the number of calories needed to raise the temperature of one gram of a given substance 1° C. Abbreviated **sp. ht.**

spec·i·fic·i·ty (spes′ə-fis′ə-ti), *n.* the quality or state of being specific.

spec·i·fy (spes′ə-fī′), *v.t.* [SPECIFIED (-fīd′), SPECIFYING], [ME. *specifien;* OFr. *specifier;* ML. *specificare* < L. *species* + *facere*, to make], 1. to mention, describe, or define in detail; state definitely: as, he *specified* the reasons for their failure. 2. to include as an item in a set of specifications. 3. to state explicitly as a condition.

spec·i·men (spes′ə-mən), *n.* [L., a mark, token, example < *specere*, to see, behold], 1. a part of a whole, or one individual of a class or group, used as a sample or example of the whole, class, or group; typical part, organism, etc.: abbreviated **sp.** 2. [Colloq.], a (specified kind of) individual or person: as, an unsavory *specimen*. 3. [Colloq.], a sample of urine for analysis.

spe·ci·os·i·ty (spē′shi-os′ə-ti), *n.* [LL. *speciositas*], 1. the state or quality of being specious. 2. [*pl.* SPECIOSITIES (-tiz)], something specious.

spe·cious (spē′shəs), *adj.* [ME. *specius;* L. *speciosus*, showy, beautiful, plausible < *species*, look, show, appearance], 1. seeming to be good, sound, correct, logical, etc. without really being so; plausible but not genuine: as, *specious* logic. 2. [Obs.], pleasing to the sight; fair or showy. —*SYN.* see **plausible.**

speck (spek), *n.* [ME. *specke;* AS. *specca;* for IE. base see SPARK, SPEAK], 1. a small spot, mark, or stain. 2. a very small bit; particle. *v.t.* to mark with specks.

speck·le (spek′'l), *n.* [dim. of *speck*], a small mark of contrasting color; speck. *v.t.* [SPECKLED (-'ld), SPECKLING], to mark with speckles.

specs (speks), *n.pl.* [Colloq.], eyeglasses; spectacles.

spec·ta·cle (spek′tə-k'l), *n.* [ME.; OFr.; L. *spectaculum* < *spectare*, to behold, freq. of *specere*, to see], 1. something to look at, especially some strange or remarkable sight; unusual display: as, the northern lights made quite a *spectacle*. 2. a public show or exhibition on a grand scale. 3. *pl.* a pair of lenses fitted in frames and worn in front of the eyes to aid the vision, shield the eyes from glare, etc.: often **a pair of spectacles.** 4. *pl.* something through which one views things, or something that influences, colors, or biases one's views or ideas. 5. *usually pl.* something like a pair of spectacles, or eyeglasses, in shape, use, etc., as the frame with one red and one green glass in a semaphore.

spec·ta·cled (spek'tə-k'ld), *adj.* 1. wearing spectacles. 2. having markings that resemble spectacles in form: said of animals.

spec·tac·u·lar (spek-tak'yoo-lẽr), *adj.* [< L. *spectaculum* (see SPECTACLE); + *-ar*], 1. of or like a spectacle, or show. 2. unusual to a striking degree; characterized by a great display, as of daring. *n.* an elaborate, extended television program, usually in color.

spec·ta·tor (spek'tā-tẽr, spek-tā'tẽr), *n.* [L. < *spectare*, to behold], a person who sees or watches a given thing or event without taking an active part; onlooker.

the Spectator, an English periodical (1711–1712; 1714), successor to the *Tatler*, published and written by Joseph Addison and Richard Steele: it was composed chiefly of short essays professedly edited by the members of the imaginary Spectator Club, representative types in the social life of the times.

spec·ter (spek'tẽr), *n.* [Fr. *spectre* < L. *spectrum*, an appearance, apparition < *spectare*, to behold], 1. a ghost; apparition. 2. any object of fear or dread.

spec·tra (spek'trə), *n.* alternative plural of **spectrum.**

spec·tral (spek'trəl), *adj.* [< *specter, spectre* + *-al*], 1. of, having the nature of, or like a specter; phantom; ghostly. 2. of or caused by a spectrum or spectra.

spec·tral·i·ty (spek-tral'ə-ti), *n.* the quality or state of being spectral.

spec·tre (spek'tẽr), *n.* specter: British spelling.

spec·tro- (spek'trə, spek'trō), [< *spectrum*], a combining form meaning: 1. *of radiant energy as exhibited in a spectrum*, as in *spectrogram*. 2. *of or by a spectroscope*, as in *spectroheliogram*.

spec·tro·gram (spek'trə-gram'), *n.* [*spectro-* + *-gram*], a photograph of a spectrum.

spec·tro·graph (spek'trə-graf', spek'trə-gräf'), *n.* [*spectro-* + *-graph*], 1. an instrument for dispersing light radiation into a spectrum and recording the spectrum photographically. 2. a photograph of a spectrum.

spec·tro·he·li·o·gram (spek'trə-hē'li-ə-gram'), *n.* [*spectro-* + *helio-* + *-gram*], a photograph of the sun made by monochromatic light, usually showing streaks or prominences on the sun's surface.

spec·tro·he·li·o·graph (spek'trə-hē'li-ə-graf', spek'-trə-hē'li-ə-gräf'), *n.* a device used for making spectroheliograms.

spec·trol·o·gy (spek-trol'ə-ji), *n.* the study of spectra.

spec·trom·e·ter (spek-trom'ə-tẽr), *n.* [G. *spektrometer;* see SPECTRO- & -METER], 1. an instrument used for measuring spectral wave lengths. 2. an instrument used for determining the index of refraction.

spec·tro·pho·tom·e·ter (spek'trō-fə-tom'ə-tẽr), *n.* [*spectro-* + *photometer*], an instrument used for comparing the color intensities of different spectra.

spec·tro·scope (spek'trə-skōp'), *n.* [G. *spektroskop;* see SPECTRO- & -SCOPE], an optical instrument used for forming spectra for study.

SPECTROSCOPE

spec·tro·scop·ic (spek'trə-skop'ik), *adj.* 1. made or performed with a spectroscope. 2. of a spectroscope.

spec·tro·scop·i·cal (spek trə-skop'i-k'l), *adj.* spectroscopic.

spec·tro·scop·i·cal·ly (spek'trə-skop'i-k'l-i), *adv.* by means of a spectroscope.

spec·tros·co·py (spek-tros'kə-pi, spek'trə-skō'pi), *n.* the study of spectra through use of the spectroscope.

spec·trum (spek'trəm), *n.* [*pl.* SPECTRA (-trə), SPECTRUMS (-trəmz)], [Mod. L. < L. *spectrum;* see SPECTER], 1. the series of colored bands diffracted and arranged in the order of their respective wave lengths by the passage of white light through a prism or other diffracting medium and shading continuously from red (produced by the longest wave visible) to violet (produced by the shortest). 2. any of various arrangements of colored bands or lines, together with invisible components at both ends of the spectrum (cf. **infrared, ultraviolet**), similarly formed by light from incandescent gases or other sources of radiant energy, which can be studied by a spectrograph. 3. an afterimage. 4. in *radio*, the range of wave lengths of radio waves, from 3 centimeters to 30,000 meters, or of frequencies of radio waves, from 10 to 10,000,000 kilocycles: also **radio spectrum.**

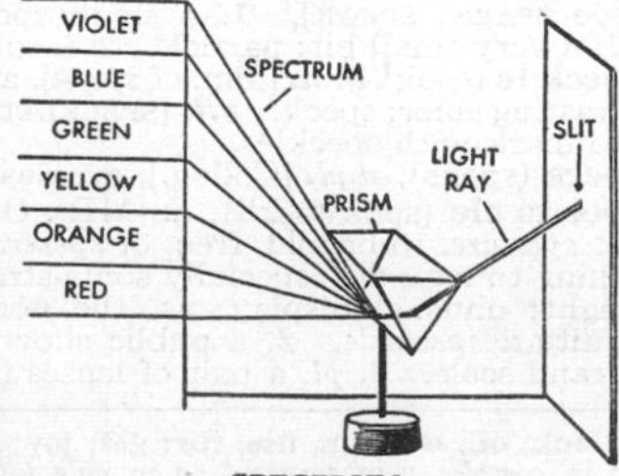

SPECTRUM

spectrum analysis, analysis of substances or bodies through study of their spectra.

spec·u·lar (spek'yoo-lẽr), *adj.* [L. *specularis*], of, like, or by means of, a speculum.

spec·u·late (spek'yoo-lāt'), *v.i.* [SPECULATED (-id), SPECULATING], [< L. *speculatus*, pp. of *speculari*, to view < *specula*, watch tower < *specere*, to see], 1. to think about the various aspects of a given subject; meditate; ponder; especially, to conjecture. 2. to buy or sell stocks, commodities, land, etc., hoping to take advantage of an expected rise or fall in price; take part in any risky business venture or enterprise on the chance of making huge profits. —*SYN.* see **think.**

spec·u·la·tion (spek'yoo-lā'shən), *n.* 1. meditation; pondering; thought; especially, conjecture. 2. the act of speculating in stocks, land, etc. 3. a speculative business venture.

spec·u·la·tive (spek'yoo-lā'tiv, spek'yoo-lə-tiv), *adj.* [ME. & OFr. *speculatif;* L. *speculativus*], 1. of, characterized by, or having the nature of, speculation, or meditation, contemplation, conjecture, etc. 2. theoretical, not practical. 3. of or characterized by financial speculation; hence, 4. risky. 5. indulging in or fond of speculation.

spec·u·la·tor (spek'yoo-lā'tẽr), *n.* a person who speculates, especially in financial operations.

spec·u·la·to·ry (spek'yoo-lə-tôr'i, spek'yə-lə-tō'ri), *adj.* [L. *speculatorius*], speculative.

spec·u·lum (spek'yoo-ləm), *n.* [*pl.* SPECULA (-lə), SPECULUMS (-ləmz)], [L., a mirror < *specere*, to look], 1. a mirror, especially one of polished metal used as a reflector in a telescope, etc. 2. in *medicine & surgery*, an instrument for dilating a passage or cavity to facilitate its examination. 3. in *zoology*, a distinctive, usually iridescent patch of color on the wings of certain birds, especially ducks.

speculum metal, an alloy of copper and tin that will take a mirrorlike polish, used for making specula.

sped (sped), alternative past tense and past participle of **speed.**

speech (spēch), *n.* [ME. *speche;* AS. *spæc, spræc* < base of *sprecan*, to speak (cf. SPEAK); akin to G. *sprache*], 1. the act of speaking; expression or communication of thoughts and feelings by spoken words, vocal sounds, and gestures. 2. the power or ability to speak. 3. the manner of speaking: as, Southern *speech.* 4. that which is spoken; utterance, remark, statement, talk, conversation, etc. 5. a talk or address given in public. 6. the language used by a certain group of people; dialect or tongue. 7. the study of the theory and practice of oral expression and communication: as, a college course in *speech.* 8. [Archaic], rumor; report.

SYN.—**speech** is the general word for a discourse delivered to an audience, whether prepared or impromptu; **address** implies a formal, carefully prepared speech and usually attributes importance to the speaker or the speech (an *address* to a legislature); **oration** suggests an eloquent, rhetorical, sometimes merely bombastic speech, especially one delivered on some special occasion (political *orations* at the picnic); a **lecture** is a carefully prepared speech intended to inform or instruct the audience (a *lecture* to a college class); **talk** suggests informality and is applied either to an impromptu speech or to an address or lecture in which the speaker deliberately uses a simple, conversational approach; a **sermon** is a speech by a clergyman intended to give religious or moral instruction and usually based on Scriptural text.

speech clinic, a school or clinic for correcting speech disorders.

speech community, all the people speaking a particular language or dialect, whether in a single geographical area or dispersed throughout various regions.

speech disorder, any conspicuous speech imperfection, or variation from the accepted speech standards, caused either by a physical defect in the speech organs or by a mental disorder, as aphasia, stuttering, etc.

speech·i·fi·er (spē'chə-fi'ẽr), *n.* a person who speechifies.

speech·i·fy (spē'chə-fi'), *v.i.* [SPEECHIFIED (-fid'), SPEECHIFYING], to make a speech or speeches: used humorously or contemptuously.

speech·less (spēch'lis), *adj.* 1. incapable of speech; unable to speak. 2. not speaking at or for a given time; silent, as from shock. 3. not expressed or expressible in words: as, *speechless* terror. —*SYN.* see **voiceless.**

speech·less·ly (spēch'lis-li), *adv.* without speaking; silently; dumbly.

speech·mak·er (spēch'māk'ẽr), *n.* a person who makes a speech or speeches; orator: often derisive.

speed (spēd), *n.*‡ [ME. *spede;* AS. *sped, spæd,* wealth, power, success < base of *spowan,* to prosper, succeed], 1. the act or state of moving rapidly; swiftness; quick motion. 2. the rate of movement or motion; velocity: as, what was his *speed?* 3. a gear or arrangement of gears for the drive of an engine: as, this truck has five forward *speeds.* 4. [Archaic], luck; success; prosperity: as, she wished him good *speed.* *v.i.* [SPED (sped) or SPEEDED (-id), SPEEDING], 1. to move rapidly, especially more rapidly than is safe or allowed by law. 2. [Archaic], *a)* to get along; fare; hence, *b)* to have fortune, good or bad. *c)* to have good fortune; prosper; succeed. *v.t.* 1. to help (a project) to succeed; aid; promote. 2. to wish Godspeed to: as, *speed* the parting guest. 3. to send, convey, or cause to move, go, etc., swiftly: as, he *sped* the ball on its way. 4. to increase the speed of; make go or work faster. 5. to cause or design (a machine, etc.) to operate at a certain speed or speeds. 6. [Archaic], to cause to succeed or prosper. —*SYN.* see **haste.**

speed up, to increase in speed; accelerate.

speed·boat (spēd'bōt'), *n.* a motorboat built for speed.

speed·er (spēd'ẽr), *n.* a person or thing that speeds; especially, a person who drives a motor vehicle at a higher speed than is safe or legal.

speed·i·ly (spē'd'l-i), *adv.* with speed or promptness; quickly; rapidly.

speed·i·ness (spē'di-nis), *n.* rapidity or promptness; haste; dispatch.

speed·ing (spēd'iŋ), *n.* the act of driving a motor vehicle at a higher speed than is safe or legal.

speed·om·e·ter (spi-dom'ə-tẽr), *n.* [< *speed* + *-meter*], 1. a device attached to an automobile or other vehicle to indicate speed, as in miles per hour; tachometer. 2. a similar device for indicating the distance traveled as well as the speed; odometer.

speed·ster (spēd'stẽr), *n.* 1. a speeder. 2. an open automobile, usually a two-seater, built for speed.

speed trap, a region, municipality, etc. where traffic police are especially on the alert for violations of the speed laws, and where even minor violations are dealt with severely.

speed-up (spēd'up'), *n.* the act of speeding up; increase in speed, output, etc.

speed·way (spēd'wā'), *n.* 1. a track for racing automobiles. 2. a road built for high-speed traffic.

speed·well (spēd'wel), *n.* [< *speed, v.* + *well, adv.;* prob. with basic meaning "prosper well"], any of a number of related plants with tightly packed clusters of white, blue, or violet flowers.

speed·y (spēd'i), *adj.* [SPEEDIER (-i-ẽr), SPEEDIEST (-i-ist)], 1. characterized by speed of motion; rapid; swift. 2. without delay; quick; prompt: as, a *speedy* reply. —*SYN.* see **fast.**

Spei·cher, Eugene Edward (spī'kẽr), 1883– ; American painter.

speiss (spīs), *n.* [G. *speise,* amalgam, lit. food < ML. *spesa,* cost, expense < L. *expendere,* to spend], a mixture of metallic arsenides produced during the smelting of copper, iron, and certain other ores.

spe·lae·an, spe·le·an (spi-lē'ən), *adj.* [< L. *spelaeum;* Gr. *spēlaion,* a cave], 1. of or like a cave. 2. cave-dwelling.

spe·le·ol·o·gy (spē'li-ol'ə-ji), *n.* [< L. *spelaeum;* Gr. *spēlaion,* a cave; + *-logy*], the science of exploring caves.

spell (spel), *n.* [ME. *spel;* AS. *spel, spell,* a saying, tale, charm; akin to Goth. *spill,* recital, tale; IE. base *(*s*)*pel-,* to speak loudly], 1. a word, formula, or form of words supposed to have some magic power. 2. magical power or irresistible influence; charm; fascination.

cast a spell on, to enchant; hence, to win the complete affection of.

under a spell, held in a spell or trance; enchanted.

spell (spel), *v.t.* [SPELLED (speld) or SPELT (spelt), SPELLING], [ME. *spellen;* OFr. *espeler, espeller;* of Gmc. origin; akin to prec.], 1. to name, write, print, or signal the letters which make up (a word, syllable, etc.), especially the right letters in the right order. 2. to make up (a word, etc.): said of specified letters. 3. to signify; mean: as, this chance *spelled* success for him. *v.i.* to spell a word, words, etc.; especially, to do so correctly.

spell out, 1. to read letter by letter or with difficulty. 2. to make out, or discern, as if by close reading.

spell (spel), *v.t.* [SPELLED (speld), SPELLING], [ME. *spelien;* AS. *spelian,* to substitute for; prob. akin to G. *spiel,* play], 1. [Colloq.], to serve or work in place of (another), especially so as to give a period of rest to; relieve. 2. [Chiefly Australian], to relieve, as a horse, by giving a period of rest to. *v.i.* [Chiefly Australian], to take a period of rest or relief. *n.* 1. a turn of serving or working in place of another. 2. a period or turn of work, duty, etc.: as, his *spell* as guard was a short one. 3. a turn, period, or fit of something: as, a *spell* of brooding. 4. a period of a specified sort of weather: as, a cold *spell.* 5. [Colloq.], a period of time that is indefinite, short, or of a specified character. 6. [Colloq.], a short distance. 7. [Colloq.], a period or fit of some illness, indisposition, etc. 8. [Chiefly Australian], a period of rest or relief from activity.

spell·bind (spel'bīnd'), *v.t.* SPELLBOUND (-bound'), SPELLBINDING], [back-formation < *spellbound*], to hold by or as by a spell; fascinate; enchant.

spell·bind·er (spel'bīn'dẽr), *n.* [Colloq.], a speaker who holds his audience spellbound.

spell·bound (spel'bound'), *adj.* [*spell* (charm) + *bound,* pp. of *bind*], held or affected by or as by a spell; fascinated; enchanted.

spell·down (spel'doun'), *n.* a spelling bee, especially one in which a contestant is eliminated from further competition by a specified number of misspellings.

spell·er (spel'ẽr), *n.* 1. a person who spells words, etc. 2. a spelling book.

spell·ing (spel'iŋ), *n.* 1. the act of forming words, etc. by putting letters together. 2. the study of this. 3. the way in which a word is spelled; orthography. Abbreviated **sp.**

spelling bee, a competition in which the person or team spelling the most words correctly is the winner.

spelling book, an exercise book used to teach spelling.

spelt (spelt), alternative past tense and past participle of **spell** (to name the letters of).

spelt (spelt), *n.* [ME.; AS.; LL. *spelta*], a hard-grained kind of wheat, or any of its varieties.

spel·ter (spel'tẽr), *n.* [OFr. *espeautre;* MD. *speauter* (G. *spiauter*); prob. akin to Eng. *pewter*], zinc: term applied in commerce, especially to zinc ingots.

spe·lunk·er (spi-luŋ'kẽr), *n.* [< L. *spelunca,* a cave], a person whose hobby is speleology.

spence (spens), *n.* [ME.; OFr. *despense* (Fr. *dêpense*); see DISPENSE], [Archaic or Dial.], a larder or pantry; also spelled **spense.**

Spen·cer (spen'sẽr), [< the surname *Spencer* < obs. *spencer,* butler, steward; OFr. *despenciser* < *despense,* larder, buttery < *despendre,* to spend (see SPEND)], a masculine name: sometimes spelled **Spenser.**

spen·cer (spen'sẽr), *n.* [after the 2d Earl of *Spencer* (1758–1834)], a short jacket, usually of wool, worn by men or women.

spen·cer (spen'sẽr), *n.* [< pers. name *Spencer*], a trysail on a gaff.

Spen·cer, Herbert (spen'sẽr), 1820–1903; English philosopher.

Spen·ce·ri·an (spen-sêr'i-ən), *adj.* 1. of or having to do with Herbert Spencer or his system of philosophy, which attempted to systematize all the sciences into a coherent whole. 2. of or characteristic of the style of penmanship taught by Platt Rogers Spencer (1800–1864), American teacher, characterized by rounded, well-formed letters. *n.* a follower of Herbert Spencer.

spend (spend), *v.t.* [SPENT (spent), SPENDING], [ME. *spenden;* AS. *spendan* (in comp.) < L. *expendere;* see EXPEND], 1. to use up, exhaust, consume, or wear out: as, he *spent* his energy quickly, his fury was *spent.* 2. to pay out (money); disburse. 3. to give or devote, as time, labor, thought, or effort, to some enterprise or for some purpose. 4. to pass (a period of time): as, they *spent* an hour together. 5. to waste; squander. 6. in *nautical usage,* to lose: as, they *spent* their rudder. *v.i.* 1. to pay out or use up money, etc. 2. [Obs.], to be or become consumed, wasted, or exhausted.

spend·er (spen'dẽr), *n.* a person who spends, especially one who spends freely or lavishly.

Spen·der, Stephen (spen'dẽr), 1909– ; English poet.

spending money, money for miscellaneous personal expenses.

spend·thrift (spend'thrift'), *n.* a person who spends money carelessly or wastefully; squanderer. *adj.* of a spendthrift; wasteful; extravagant; prodigal.

Speng·ler, Oswald (speŋ'lẽr; G. shpeŋ'lẽr), 1880–1936; German philosopher; known for his theory of history.

Spen·ser, Edmund (spen'sẽr), 1552?–1599; English poet.

Spen·se·ri·an (spen-sêr'i-ən), *adj.* of or characteristic of Edmund Spenser or his writing. *n.* 1. a follower or imitator of Spenser. 2. a Spenserian stanza, or a poem in such stanzas.

Spenserian stanza, a stanza consisting of eight lines of iambic pentameter and a final line of iambic hexameter (an alexandrine), with a rhyme scheme *ababbcbcc,* used by Spenser in *The Fairie Queene.*

spent (spent), past tense and past participle of **spend.** *adj.* 1. tired out; physically exhausted; without energy. 2. used up; worn out; without power or force.

sperm (spũrm), *n.* [ME. & OFr. *sperme;* LL. *sperma;* Gr. *sperma,* seed, germ < *speirein,* to sow; base as in Eng. *spray*], 1. the male generative fluid; semen. 2. any of the germ cells in this fluid; spermatozoon.

sperm (spũrm), *n.* 1. spermaceti. 2. sperm oil. 3. a sperm whale.

-sperm (spũrm), [see SPERM (fluid)], a combining form meaning *seed*, as in *gymnosperm*.
sper·ma·ce·ti (spũr'mə-set'i, spũr'mə-sē'ti), *n.* [ML. < LL. *sperma*, sperm + L. *ceti*, genit. of *cetus*, a whale], a white, waxlike substance taken from the oil in the head of a sperm whale, dolphin, etc., used in making cosmetics, ointments, candles, etc.
-sper·mal (spũr'm'l), -spermous.
sper·ma·ry (spũr'mẽr-i), *n.* [*pl.* SPERMARIES (-iz)], [Mod. L. *spermarium* < *sperma;* see SPERM (fluid)], an organ in which male germ cells are formed; male gonad; testis.
sper·mat·ic (spẽr-mat'ik), *adj.* [Fr. *spermatique;* LL. *spermaticus;* Gr. *spermatikos*], 1. of or having to do with sperm or sperm cells; generative. 2. of or having to do with a spermary.
spermatic cord, the cordlike structure suspending a testicle within the scrotum and containing the vas deferens, blood vessels and nerves supplying the testicle, etc.
sper·ma·ti·um (spẽr-mā'shi-əm), *n.* [*pl.* SPERMATIA (-ə)], [Mod. L.; Gr. *spermation*, dim. of *sperma*, a seed], 1. a nonmotile male gamete in red algae. 2. a very small cell thought to be a male gamete, found in some lichens and fungi.
sper·ma·to- (spũr'mə-tō, spũr'mə-tə), [< Gr. *sperma, spermatos*, a seed], a combining form meaning *seed* or *sperm*, as in *spermatogenesis*: also **spermat-, sperm-.**
sper·ma·to·cyte (spũr'mə-tə-sīt'), *n.* [*spermato-* + *-cyte*], a cell that develops through several stages to form spermatozoa or spermatozoids.
sper·ma·to·gen·e·sis (spũr'mə-tə-jen'ə-sis), *n.* [Mod. L.; see SPERMATO- & -GENESIS], the production and development of spermatozoa.
sper·ma·to·ge·net·ic (spũr'mə-tō'jə-net'ik), *adj.* of spermatogenesis.
sper·ma·to·go·ni·al (spũr'mə-tə-gō'ni-əl), *adj.* of or having to do with a spermatogonium.
sper·ma·to·go·ni·um (spũr'mə-tə-gō'ni-əm), *n.* [*pl.* SPERMATOGONIA (-ə)], [Mod. L. < *spermato-* + Gr. *gonē*, offspring], 1. a primitive male germ cell. 2. a spermogonium.
sper·ma·toph·o·ral (spũr'mə-tof'ẽr-əl), *adj.* of or having to do with a spermatophore.
sper·ma·to·phore (spũr'mə-tə-fôr', spũr'mə-tə-fōr'), *n.* [*spermato-* + *-phore*], a case or capsule containing a number of spermatozoa, expelled whole by the male of certain animals, as the segmented worms and mollusks.
sper·ma·to·phyte (spũr'mə-tə-fīt'), *n.* [< *spermato-* + Gr. *phyton*, a plant], any seed-bearing plant.
sper·ma·to·phyt·ic (spũr'mə-tə-fit'ik), *adj.* of or having to do with a spermatophyte.
sper·ma·tor·rhe·a, sper·ma·tor·rhoe·a (spũr'mə-tə-rē'ə), *n.* [*spermato-* + *-rrhea*], the too frequent involuntary discharge of semen without an orgasm.
sper·ma·to·zo·a (spũr'mə-tə-zō'ə), *n.* plural of **spermatozoon.**
sper·ma·to·zo·al (spũr'mə-tə-zō'əl), *adj.* of or having to do with spermatozoa.
sper·ma·to·zo·an (spũr'mə-tə-zō'ən), *adj.* spermatozoal.
sper·ma·to·zo·ic (spũr'mə-tə-zō'ik), *adj.* spermatozoal.
sper·ma·to·zo·id (spũr'mə-tə-zō'id), *n.* [< *spermatozoon* + *-id*], in certain mosses, ferns, etc., a male sex cell, or gamete, that moves by means of cilia: it is usually produced in an antheridium.
sper·ma·to·zo·oid (spũr'mə-tə-zō'oid), *n.* a spermatozoid.
sper·ma·to·zo·on (spũr'mə-tə-zō'on), *n.* [*pl.* SPERMATOZOA (-ə)], [Mod. L. < *spermato-* + Gr. *zōion*, animal, living being], the male germ cell, found in semen, which penetrates the ovum, or egg, of the female to fertilize it: it has a well-defined head, mid-section, and tail, and moves with a swimming action: also **sperm.**
sper·mic (spũr'mik), *adj.* of or having to do with sperm.
sperm·in (spũr'min), *n.* spermine.
sperm·ine (spũr'mēn, spũr'min), *n.* [*sperm* + *-ine*], a basic substance, $C_{10}H_{26}N_4$, found in semen, yeast, and some animal tissue.
sper·mo- (spũr'mə), spermato-: also, before a vowel, **sperm-.**
sper·mo·go·ni·um (spũr'mə-gō'ni-əm), *n.* [*pl.* SPERMOGONIA (-ə)], [Mod. L. < *spermo-* + Gr. *gonē*, offspring], a cup-shaped or flask-shaped organ in certain fungi, lichens, etc., in which spermatia are produced.
sperm oil, a valuable lubricating oil taken from the head of the sperm whale.
sper·mo·phile (spũr'mə-fīl', spũr'mə-fil), *n.* [< Gr. *sperma*, a seed; + *-phile*], any of several burrowing, squirrellike rodents, including the chipmunk, ground squirrel, suslik, and gopher: they can do much damage to crops.
sper·mous (spũr'məs), *adj.* of or like sperm.
-sper·mous (spũr'məs), a combining form meaning *having* (a specified number or kind of) *seed*, as in *monospermous*.
sperm whale, a large, toothed whale inhabiting the warm seas: a closed cavity in its square head contains spermaceti and sperm oil: also called *cachalot*.
Sper·ry, Elmer Ambrose (sper'i), 1860–1930; American inventor, electrical engineer, and manufacturer.
sper·ry·lite (sper'i-līt'), *n.* [after its discoverer, F. L. *Sperry*, of Sudbury, Ontario], a silvery-white granular or crystalline native compound of platinum and arsenic, $PtAs_2$.
spew (spū), *v.t. & v.i.* [ME. *spewen;* AS. *spiwan;* akin to G. *speien*, Goth. *speiwan;* IE. base **sp(h)jēu-*, as also in L. *spuere*, to vomit (cf. SPUTUM)], to throw up from or as from the stomach; vomit; eject: also spelled **spue.** *n.* something spewed; vomit.
Spey·er (shpī'ẽr), *n.* a city in Bavaria, Germany: pop., 27,000: English name, *Spires*.
Spe·zi·a, La (lä spe'tsyä), *n.* a seaport on the Ligurian Sea, in northern Italy: pop., 121,000 (est. 1947).
sp. gr., specific gravity.
Sp. Gui., Spanish Guinea.
sphac·e·late (sfas'ə-lāt'), *v.t. & v.i.* [SPHACELATED (-id), SPHACELATING], [< Mod. L. *sphacelatus*, pp. of *sphacelare*, to mortify < *sphacelus*, gangrene; Gr. *sphakelos*], to make or become gangrenous; mortify.
sphac·e·la·tion (sfas'ə-lā'shən), *n.* the fact or process of becoming sphacelated, or gangrenous.
sphae·ro- (sfêr'ō, sfêr'ə), [< Gr. *sphaira;* see SPHERE], a combining form meaning *a sphere* or *like a sphere:* also, before a vowel, **sphaer-.**
sphag·nous (sfag'nəs), *adj.* of, consisting of, or covered with sphagnum.
sphag·num (sfag'nəm), *n.* [Mod. L. < Gr. *sphagnos*, kind of moss], 1. any of a number of related grayish mosses found in bogs; peat moss. 2. a mass of such mosses, used to make fertilizer, to pack and pot plants, to make surgical dressings, etc.
sphal·er·ite (sfal'ẽr-īt'), *n.* [< Gr. *sphaleros*, deceptive, uncertain; + *-ite*], native zinc sulfide, ZnS, the principal ore of zinc, usually brownish with a resinous luster: also called *zinc blende*.
sphene (sfēn), *n.* [Fr. *sphène* < Gr. *sphēn*, a wedge: so named because of its crystal form], titanite, especially the light-colored variety.
sphe·nic (sfē'nik), *adj.* [< Gr. *sphēn*, a wedge; + *-ic*], 1. wedge-shaped. 2. designating or of a number having three unequal prime factors.
sphe·no- (sfē'nō, sfē'nə), [< Gr. *sphēn*, a wedge], a combining form meaning: 1. *shaped like a wedge*, as in *sphenogram*. 2. *of the sphenoid bone*. Also, before a vowel, **sphen-.**
sphe·no·gram (sfē'nə-gram'), *n.* [*spheno-* + *-gram*], a cuneiform, or wedge-shaped, character.
sphe·nog·ra·phy (sfi-nog'rə-fi), *n.* [*spheno-* + *-graphy*], writing done in wedge-shaped characters; cuneiform writing.
sphe·noid (sfē'noid), *adj.* [Gr. *sphēn*, a wedge; + *-oid*], 1. wedge-shaped. 2. in *anatomy*, designating or of the wedge-shaped compound bone at the base of the skull: see **skull,** illus. *n.* the sphenoid bone.
sphe·noi·dal (sfi-noi'd'l), *adj.* sphenoid.
spher·al (sfêr'əl), *adj.* [LL. *sphaeralis*], 1. of or like a sphere. 2. rounded in form; spherical. 3. symmetrical.
sphere (sfêr), *n.* [ME. *spere;* OFr. *espere;* L. *sphaera;* Gr. *sphaira*], 1. any round body or figure having the surface equally distant from the center at all points; globe; ball. 2. a star or planet. 3. the visible heavens; sky. 4. the apparent globe (*celestial sphere*) formed by the heavens and visible only as a dome extending from horizon to horizon. 5. any of a series of hypothetical spherical shells, transparent, concentric, and postulated as revolving one within another, in which the stars, planets, sun, moon, etc. were supposedly set: a concept of ancient astronomy. 6. the place or range of action or existence; field or extent of knowledge, experience, influence, etc.; province; compass; domain. 7. social stratum; place in society; walk of life. *v.t.* [SPHERED (sfêrd), SPHERING], 1. to put in or as in a sphere. 2. to put among the heavenly spheres. 3. to form into a sphere.
-sphere (sfêr), a combining form meaning *a sphere* or *like a sphere*, as in *blastosphere, stratosphere*.
spher·ic (sfer'ik), *adj.* [LL. *sphaericus;* Gr. *sphairikos*], spherical.
spher·i·cal (sfer'i-k'l), *adj.* [*spheric* + *-al*], 1. shaped like a sphere; globular. 2. of a sphere or spheres. 3. of the heavenly spheres (sometimes with astrological reference). —*SYN.* see **round.**
spherical aberration, optical distortion resulting from spherical form, as in a lens or mirror.
spherical angle (or **triangle,** etc.), an angle (or triangle, etc.) formed by intersecting arcs of great circles of a sphere.
spher·i·cal·ly (sfer'i-k'l-i, sfer'ik-li), *adv.* 1. in the form of a sphere or spherical section. 2. so as to be spherical.
sphe·ric·i·ty (sfi-ris'ə-ti), *n.* the quality or state of being spherical; round form; roundness.
spher·ics (sfer'iks), *n.pl.* [construed as sing.], the geometry and trigonometry of figures formed on the surface of a sphere.
sphe·roid (sfêr'oid), *n.* [L. *sphaeroides;* Gr. *sphairoeidēs*], a body that is almost but not quite a perfect sphere: the earth is a *spheroid*. *adj.* spheroidal.

sphe·roi·dal (sfi-roi′d'l), *adj.* having the form of a spheroid; almost spherical.
sphe·roi·dic·i·ty (sfêr′oi-dis′ə-ti), *n.* the quality or state of being spheroidal.
sphe·roi·di·ty (sfi-roi′də-ti), *n.* spheroidicity.
sphe·rom·e·ter (sfi-rom′ə-tẽr), *n.* [Fr. *sphéromètre;* see SPHERE & -METER], an instrument used for measuring the surface curvature of bodies that are spherical, cylindrical, etc.
spher·u·lar (sfer′oo-lẽr), *adj.* spherical.
spher·ule (sfer′ōōl), *n.* [L. *sphaerula,* dim. of *sphaera;* see SPHERE], a small sphere or spherical body; globule.
spher·u·lite (sfer′oo-līt′), *n.* [< *spherule* + *-ite*], a group of crystals arranged in the shape of a sphere, as in certain volcanic rocks.
spher·u·lit·ic (sfer′oo-lit′ik), *adj.* of or containing spherulites.
spher·y (sfêr′i), *adj.* [SPHERIER (-i-ẽr), SPHERIEST (-i-ist)], [Poetic], 1. of or like a sphere, especially a heavenly body; hence, 2. celestial; starlike.
sphinc·ter (sfiŋk′tẽr), *n.* [LL.; Gr. *sphinktēr* < *sphingein,* to draw close], in *anatomy,* a ring-shaped muscle that surrounds a natural opening in the body and can open or close it by expanding or contracting.
sphinc·ter·al (sfiŋk′tẽr-əl), *adj.* of, or having the nature of, a sphincter.
sphinx (sfiŋks), *n.* [*pl.* SPHINXES (-iz), SPHINGES (sfin′jēz)], [ME.; L.; Gr. *sphinx,* lit., the strangler], 1. any Egyptian statue or figure having, typically, the body of a lion and the head of a man, ram, or hawk. 2. [S-], a huge statue of this kind with the head of a man, at Gîza, near Cairo, Egypt. 3. in *Greek mythology, a)* a winged monster with a lion's body and the head and breasts of a woman; specifically, *b)* [S-], a monster of this kind that perched on a rock near Thebes and asked a riddle of every passer-by, strangling all who could not answer: Oedipus solved the riddle, and the Sphinx killed herself. 4. a person whose manner or expression suggests that his character is deep and mysterious. 5. in *zoology,* a hawk moth.

SPHINX AT GÎZA

sphra·gis·tics (sfrə-jis′tiks), *n.pl.* [construed as sing.], [< Gr. *sphragistikos,* of seals < *sphragis,* a seal], the study of engraved seals.
sp. ht., specific heat.
sphyg·mic (sfig′mik), *adj.* [Mod. L. *sphygmicus;* Gr. *sphygmikos* < *sphygmos,* the pulse], in *physiology,* of the pulse.
sphyg·mo- (sfig′mō, sfig′mə), [< Gr. *sphygmos,* the pulse], a combining form meaning *the pulse,* as in *sphygmograph.*
sphyg·mo·gram (sfig′mə-gram′), *n.* [*sphygmo-* + *-gram*], the record or tracing made by a sphygmograph.
sphyg·mo·graph (sfig′mə-graf′, sfig′mə-gräf′), *n.* [*sphygmo-* + *-graph*], an instrument for recording the rate, force, and variations of the pulse.
sphyg·mo·graph·ic (sfig′mə-graf′ik), *adj.* of or recorded by a sphygmograph.
sphyg·mog·ra·phy (sfig-mog′rə-fi), *n.* the recording of the pulse by means of a sphygmograph.
sphyg·moid (sfig′moid), *adj.* [< *sphygmo-* + *-oid*], like the pulse.
sphyg·mo·ma·nom·e·ter (sfig′mō-mə-nom′ə-tẽr), *n.* [*sphygmo-* + *manometer*], an instrument for measuring arterial blood pressure.
sphyg·mom·e·ter (sfig-mom′ə-tẽr), *n.* [*sphygmo-* + *-meter*], an instrument for measuring the force and rate of the pulse.
sphyg·mus (sfig′məs), *n.* [Mod. L. < Gr. *sphygmos,* the pulse], the pulse.
spi·ca (spī′kə), *n.* [L., ear of grain, orig. a point; cf. SPIKE (nail)], 1. [*pl.* SPICAE (-sē)], in *botany,* a spike, as of a flower. 2. [S-], in *astronomy,* a bright star in the constellation Virgo: see **constellation,** chart.
spi·cate (spī′kāt), *adj.* [L. *spicatus,* pp. of *spicare,* to provide with spikes < *spica,* a point], in *botany & zoology,* 1. spikelike in form. 2. arranged in a spike or spikes.
spi·cat·ed (spī′kā-tid), *adj.* spicate.
spic·ca·to (spi-kä′tō), *adj.* [It., (pp. of *spiccare,* to detach), removed], in *music,* detached; played with the bow wrist relaxed so that the bow rebounds between notes: a direction to the violinist, etc.
spice (spīs), *n.* [ME. *spice, spece;* OFr. *espice, espece;* L. *species,* species; in LL., wares, assorted goods, especially spices and drugs], 1. *a)* any of several vegetable substances, as clove, cinnamon, nutmeg, pepper, etc., used to season food: spices are usually dried for use and have distinctive flavors and aromas. *b)* such substances collectively or as a material. 2. a spicy fragrance or aroma. 3. that which gives zest or piquancy; interesting or flavorful part. 4. a small bit; trace; suggestion: as, a *spice* of envy in her tone. *v.t.* [SPICED (spīst), SPICING], 1. to season or flavor with spice. 2. to add zest or piquancy to; make interesting.
spice·ber·ry (spīs′ber′i), *n.* [*pl.* SPICEBERRIES (-iz)], 1. a Florida tree of the myrtle family, having orange or black fruit. 2. the fruit of this tree. 3. the checkerberry; wintergreen.
spice·bush (spīs′boosh′), *n.* a shrub with leathery leaves, small yellowish flowers, and red fruit.
Spice Islands, the Molucca Islands.
spic·er·y (spīs′ẽr-i), *n.* [*pl.* SPICERIES (-iz)], [ME. *spicerie;* OFr. *espicerie* (Fr. *épicerie*) < *espice* (cf. SPICE)], 1. spices. 2. something spicy; spicy quality, flavor, or aroma. 3. [Obs.], a place where spices are kept.
spice·wood (spīs′wood′), *n.* a spicebush.
spic·i·ly (spīs′′l-i), *adv.* so as to be or make spicy; in a spicy manner.
spic·i·ness (spīs′i-nis), *n.* a spicy quality.
spick-and-span (spik′′n-span′), *adj.* [short for *spick-and-span-new; spick,* var. of *spike,* a nail + *span-new* < ME. *spon-neowe;* ON. *spān-nȳr* < *spānn,* a chip, shaving + *nyr,* new], 1. new; fresh. 2. neat and clean.
spic·u·lar (spik′yoo-lẽr), *adj.* spiculate.
spic·u·late (spik′yoo-lāt′), *adj.* [L. *spiculatus*], 1. shaped like a spicule; needlelike. 2. covered with or consisting of spicules.
spic·ule (spik′ūl), *n.* [Fr.; L. *spiculum,* dim. of *spica,* a point, ear, spike], 1. a small, hard, sharp-pointed, needlelike piece or process, especially of bony or calcareous material, as in the skeleton of the sponge. 2. a small spike of flowers.
spic·u·lum (spik′yoo-ləm), *n.* [*pl.* SPICULA (-lə)], [L.], a spicule; especially, any of several spinelike organs found in lower animals, as the starfish.
spic·y (spī′si), *adj.* [SPICIER (-si-ẽr), SPICIEST (-si-ist)], 1. containing or abounding in spices. 2. having the flavor or aroma of a spice or spices; fragrant; aromatic. 3. piquant; pungent. 4. risqué; racy. —*SYN.* see **pungent.**
spi·der (spī′dẽr), *n.* [ME. *spithre;* AS. **spithra,* for **spinthra* < *spinnan,* to spin; cf. SPIN], 1. any of a number of small, eight-legged animals having a body composed of two divisions, a cephalothorax bearing the legs and an abdomen bearing two or more pairs of spinnerets, whose function is to spin the silk threads from which they make nests, cocoons, or webs for trapping insects: the spider is an arachnid and not an insect. 2. a person thought of as spiderlike in nature or appearance. 3. a trivet. 4. a frying pan, originally one with attached legs for use over an open fire. 5. a device for pulverizing the ground, used with a cultivator.
spider crab, any of several very large sea crabs with a pear-shaped body and long, slender legs.
spider monkey, any of a group of monkeys of South and Central America having long, spidery limbs and long, prehensile tails.
spider web, a netlike web spun by a spider to catch insects.
spi·der·wort (spī′dẽr-wũrt′), *n.* any of a number of related plants with grasslike leaves and blue or purplish flowers.
spi·der·y (spī′dẽr-i), *adj.* 1. like a spider or spiders. 2. long and thin like a spider's legs. 3. infested with spiders.
spie·gel (spē′g'l), *n.* spiegeleisen: also **spiegel iron.**
spie·gel·ei·sen (spē′g'l-ī′z'n), *n.* [G. < *spiegel,* mirror (OHG. *spiagal;* L. *speculum;* cf. SPECULUM) + *eisen,* iron], a kind of hard, white pig iron containing manganese.
spiel (spēl), *n.* [G., play, game], [Slang], a talk or speech. *v.i.* [Slang], to talk, speak, or orate.
spi·er (spī′ẽr), *n.* a person who spies; spy.
spiff·y (spif′i), *adj.* [SPIFFIER (-i-ẽr), SPIFFIEST (-i-ist)], [< dial. *spiff,* well-dressed person; prob. orig. a cant term], [Slang], attractive to the eye; smart; neat; fine; spruce.
spig·ot (spig′ət), *n.* [ME. *spigote;* prob. via OFr. < base of *spike*], 1. a plug or peg used to stop the vent in a barrel, etc. 2. *a)* a faucet. *b)* the valve or plug in a faucet. 3. the end of a pipe that is inserted into an enlarged end of another pipe so as to form a joint.
spike (spīk), *n.* [ME.; prob. < ON. *spikr,* a nail, spike; ult. < L. *spica,* ear of corn (cf. SPICA, SPICULATE); IE. base as in *spoke, spire,* etc.], 1. a sharp-pointed part or projection, usually slender and of metal, as along the top of an iron fence, etc. 2. a long, heavy nail. 3. any long, slender, pointed object, as the single antler of a young deer. 4. *pl.* sharp or pointed metal projections on the soles, and often on the heels, of shoes used for baseball, golf, track, etc., to prevent slipping. 5. a young mackerel not more than six inches long. *v.t.* [SPIKED (spīkt), SPIKING], 1. to

fasten or fit with or as with a spike or spikes. 2. to mark, pierce, cut, etc. with a spike or spikes, or impale on a spike. 3. to make (a cannon) unusable by driving a spike into the touchhole; hence, 4. to thwart, frustrate, or block, as a scheme. 5. [Slang], to add alcohol or strong alcoholic liquor to (a drink). 6. in *baseball*, etc., to injure (an opponent, another player, etc.) with the spikes on one's shoes.

spike (spīk), *n.* [ME. *spik;* L. *spica*], 1. an ear of grain. 2. a long flower cluster with flowers attached directly to the stalk.

spike lavender, a European lavender mint that yields an oil used in art.

spike·let (spīk′lit), *n.* in *botany*, a small spike, as in a flower cluster of grass.

spike·nard (spīk′nẽrd, spīk′närd), *n.* [ME.; ML. *spica nardi* < L. *spica*, an ear of grain + *nardus*, aromatic root, nard], 1. a fragrant ointment used by the ancients. 2. the East Indian plant that yielded it. 3. an American plant with whitish flowers, purplish berries, and fragrant roots.

spik·y (spīk′i), *adj.* [SPIKIER (-i-ẽr), SPIKIEST (-i-ist)], 1. shaped like a spike; long and pointed. 2. having or set with spikes.

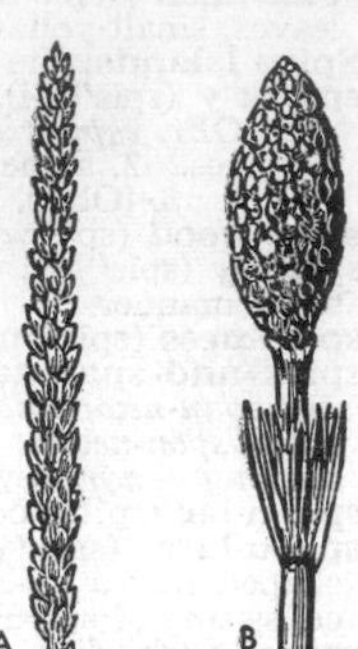

SPIKES
A, spike of plantain; B, spike of horsetail

spile (spīl), *n.* [MD., a splinter, skewer, bar, spindle], 1. a plug or spigot, as for a barrel. 2. a tap or spout driven into a maple tree to draw off sap. 3. a heavy stake or timber driven into the ground as a foundation or support. *v.t.* [SPILED (spīld), SPILING], 1. to furnish or support with spiles, or stakes. 2. to set a spile into (a tree, barrel, etc.); hence, 3. to draw off (liquid) through a spile. 4. to stop up (a hole) with a spile, or plug.

spil·i·kin (spil′i-kin), *n.* [< MD. *spilleken*, dim. of *spille*, a splinter, pin; cf. SPILE], 1. one of a set of pegs or strips, as of bone, used in playing certain games, as jackstraws, cribbage, etc. 2. *pl.* [construed as sing.], a game in which these are used. Also spelled **spillikin.**

spil·ing (spīl′iŋ), *n.* [< *spill*, dial. var. of *spile*], spiles or timbers collectively; piling.

spill (spil), *v.t.* [SPILLED (spild) or SPILT (spilt), SPILLING], [ME. *spillen;* AS. *spillan*, to destroy, squander; akin to G. *(ver)spillen;* IE. base **sp(h)el-*, to split, split off, as also in L. *spolium* (cf. SPOILS), Eng. *spall*, etc.], 1. to allow or cause, especially in an unintentional or accidental manner, to run, fall, or flow over from a receptacle or container, usually with resulting loss or waste: said of a liquid or a loose or granular substance. 2. to shed (blood). 3. to empty the wind from (a sail). 4. to scatter, especially by emptying from a receptacle or container. 5. [Obs.], *a)* to kill. *b)* to destroy or ruin. *c)* to squander; waste. 6. [Colloq.], to make known (something secret or unknown); divulge. 7. [Colloq.], to cause or allow to fall; throw off (a rider, load, etc.). *v.i.* to be spilled from a receptacle or container; overflow; run out; fall out. *n.* 1. a spilling. 2. the amount spilled. 3. a spillway. 4. [Colloq.], a fall or tumble, as from a horse, bicycle, etc.

spill (spil), *n.* [var. of *spile*], 1. a splinter. 2. a slender piece of any substance, especially a thin roll or fold of paper, to be lighted in a fire and used as a match. 3. a small peg or plug for stopping up a hole; spile. 4. a small metal peg, pin, or rod.

spill·way (spil′wā′), *n.* [*spill, v.* + *way*], a passageway or channel to carry off excess water, as from a reservoir.

spilt (spilt), alternative past tense and past participle of **spill.**

spilth (spilth), *n.* [< *spill, v.*], 1. a spilling. 2. that which is spilled; especially, anything spilled profusely.

spin (spin), *v.t.* [SPUN (spun) or *archaic* SPAN (span), SPUN, SPINNING], [ME. *spinnen;* AS. *spinnan* (cf. SPIDER); akin to G. *spinnen;* IE. base **(s)pen-*, to draw, spin; cf. SPINDLE], 1. to draw out and twist fibers of (wool, cotton, etc.) into thread. 2. to make (thread, yarn, etc.) by this process. 3. to make (a web, cocoon, etc.) from a filament of a viscous fluid that is extruded from the body and hardens on exposure to the air: said of spiders, silkworms, etc. 4. to make or produce in a way suggestive of spinning. 5. to carry out to a great length; prolong; protract (a story, etc.): usually with *out*. 6. to tell (a story, yarn, etc.). 7. to cause to whirl or rotate swiftly: as, the boy *spun* the top. *v.i.* 1. to spin thread or yarn. 2. to form a thread, web, etc.: said of spiders, etc. 3. to fish with a spoon or spinner. 4. to whirl or rotate swiftly. 5. to seem to be spinning from dizziness. 6. to move along swiftly and smoothly. *n.* 1. a whirling or rotating action or movement. 2. the act of causing such an action or movement. 3. a moving along swiftly and smoothly. 4. a ride or short trip in a vehicle. 5. any of various maneuvers in which an airplane comes down nose first along a spiral path of large pitch and small radius. —*SYN.* see **turn.**

spi·na·ceous (spi-nā′shəs), *adj.* [< ML. *spinachia;* see SPINACH], of, related to, or resembling spinach or other plants of the goosefoot family.

spin·ach (spin′ich, spin′ij), *n.* [earlier *spynnage, spynache;* OFr. *espinage;* ML. *spinachia;* Sp. *espinaca* < Ar. *isbānah;* influenced by L. *spina* (cf. SPINE) from the prickly seeds], 1. a plant of the goosefoot family, with large, dark-green, juicy, edible leaves, usually eaten cooked. 2. its leaves.

spi·nal (spī′n'l), *adj.* [LL. *spinalis*], 1. of or having to do with the spine or spinal cord. 2. of a spine or needle-shaped process. *n.* spinal anesthesia.

spinal anesthesia, in *surgery*, local anesthesia of the lower half of the body by the injection of an anesthetic into the lumbar portion of the spinal cord.

spinal canal, the canal, or tube, formed by the vertebral arches, containing the spinal cord.

spinal column, the series of joined vertebrae forming the axial support for the skeleton; spine; backbone.

spinal cord, the thick cord of nerve tissue of the central nervous system, extending down the spinal canal from the medulla oblongata.

spin·dle (spin′d'l), *n.* [ME. (with intrusive *-d-*) < AS. *spinel* < *spinnan*, to spin], 1. a slender rod or pin used in spinning; specifically, *a)* in hand spinning, a rounded rod, usually wooden, tapering toward each end, for twisting into thread the fibers pulled from the material on the distaff, and notched at one end so as to hold the thread. *b)* on a spinning wheel, the rod by which the thread is twisted and on which it is then wound. *c)* in a spinning machine, one of the rods holding the bobbins on which the thread is wound as it is spun. See **distaff**, illus. 2. a measure for yarn, equal to 14,400 yards in linen or 15,120 yards in cotton. 3. something having the long, slender shape of a spindle, as the bundle of nuclear fibers formed during one stage of mitosis, or a short turned piece in a baluster. 4. any rod, pin, or shaft that revolves or serves as an axis for a revolving part. 5. a small axis, axle, arbor, mandrel, or shaft. 6. in a lathe, a shaftlike part (*live spindle*) that rotates while holding the thing to be turned, or a similar part (*dead spindle*) that does not rotate. 7. a hydrometer. 8. a metal rod, pipe, etc., usually with a lantern, ball, or other easily visible object at its top, fastened to a rock, shoal, or the like as a warning to vessels. *adj.* 1. of or like a spindle or spindles. 2. designating or of the maternal side or female line of a family. *v.i.* [SPINDLED (-d'ld), SPINDLING], 1. to grow in a long, slender shape. 2. to grow into a long, slender stalk or stem. *v.t.* 1. to form into a spindle. 2. to fit or equip with a spindle.

spin·dle-leg·ged (spin′d'l-leg′id, spin′d'l-legd′), *adj.* having thin legs.

spin·dle·legs (spin′d'l-legz′), *n.pl.* 1. thin legs. 2. [construed as sing.], [Colloq.], a person with thin legs.

spin·dle-shanked (spin′d'l-shaŋkt′), *adj.* spindle-legged.

spindle tree, [cf. G. *spindelbaum*], any of a number of related hardwood trees or shrubs used to make spindles.

spin·dling (spin′dliŋ), *adj.* slender in proportion to length or height. *n.* a spindling person or thing.

spin·dly (spin′dli), *adj.* [SPINDLIER (-dli-ẽr), SPINDLIEST (-dli-ist)], spindling.

spin·drift (spin′drift′), *n.* [altered < *spoondrift* < earlier *spoom drift; spoom* (? < L. *spuma*, foam) + *drift*], spray blown from a rough sea or surf.

spine (spīn), *n.* [ME.; OFr. *espine;* L. *spina*, a thorn, prickle, backbone], 1. any of the short, sharp, woody processes projecting from certain plants, as the cactus. 2. any of the sharp, stiff projections on the bodies of certain animals, as the quill of a porcupine or a ray of a fish's fin. 3. anything resembling either of these projections. 4. the spinal column; backbone. 5. anything regarded as resembling a backbone; specifically, *a)* a ridge of ground, etc. *b)* the back of a bound book, usually bearing the title and author's name.

spi·nel (spi-nel′, spin′'l), *n.* [Fr. *spinelle;* It. *spinella*, dim. < L. *spina*, spine], a hard, crystalline mineral composed chiefly of oxide of aluminum, magnesium, and iron, and found in various colors: a red variety (*spinel ruby*) is used as a gem.

spine·less (spīn′lis), *adj.* 1. having no backbone; invertebrate. 2. having a weak or flexible backbone. 3. lacking moral fiber; without courage or will power. 4. without spines, or thorny processes.

spi·nelle (spi-nel′, spin′'l), *n.* spinel.

spi·nes·cent (spī-nes′'nt), *adj.* [LL. *spinescens*, ppr. of *spinescere*, to grow spiny < L. *spina*, spine], 1. spiny; having spines. 2. becoming spiny or spinelike.

spin·et (spin′it), *n.* [OFr. *espinete;* It. *spinetta;* prob. < Giovanni *Spinetti* (c. 1500), of Venice, said to be the inventor], 1. an obsolete, small variety of harpsichord with a single keyboard. 2. a small upright piano, either of an early oblong form or of modern design.

spi·nif·er·ous (spī-nif′ẽr-əs), *adj.* [L. *spinifer* < *spina*, spine + *ferre*, to bear; + *-ous*], bearing spines.

spin·i·fex (spin′i-feks′), *n.* [Mod. L. < L. *spina*, spine +

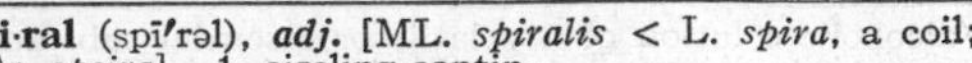

facere, to make], any of a number of related Australian grasses having stiff, pointed leaves and seeds with an elastic spine.

spi·nig·er·ous (spī-nij′ẽr-əs), *adj.* spiniferous.

spin·i·ness (spīn′i-nis), *n.* the quality or condition of being spiny.

spin·na·ker (spin′ə-kẽr), *n.* [said to be formed < *spinx*, altered < *Sphinx*, name of a yacht which carried the sail; prob. an altered form of *spanker*], a large, triangular sail on racing yachts, set from a boom that swings out on the side opposite the main boom and used especially when running before the wind.

spin·ner (spin′ẽr), *n.* a person or thing that spins; specifically, *a)* a person who spins yarn, etc. for a living. *b)* a shiny fish lure that spins like a propeller when drawn through the water. *c)* a domelike cap that fits over the hub of an airplane propeller. *d)* a football play in which the ball carrier whirls around to prevent the opposing team from knowing in which direction he will run.

spin·ner·et (spin′ẽr-et′), *n.* [dim. of *spinner*], an organ used by spiders, caterpillars, etc. in spinning threads of silk.

spin·ner·y (spin′ẽr-i), *n.* [*pl.* SPINNERIES (-iz)], a factory where yarn is spun; spinning mill.

spin·ney (spin′i), *n.* [*pl.* SPINNEYS (-iz)], [ME. (N.W. Midland) *spenne;* OFr. *espinei;* LL. *spinetum* < L. *spina*, thorn, spine], [British], a thicket or grove.

spin·ning (spin′iŋ), *n.* the act of making thread or yarn from fibers or filaments. *adj.* that spins.

spinning jenny, a spinning machine fitted with several spindles, for spinning more than one thread at a time.

spinning wheel, a primitive spinning machine fitted with a single spindle driven by the rotation of a large wheel spun by a foot treadle or by hand.

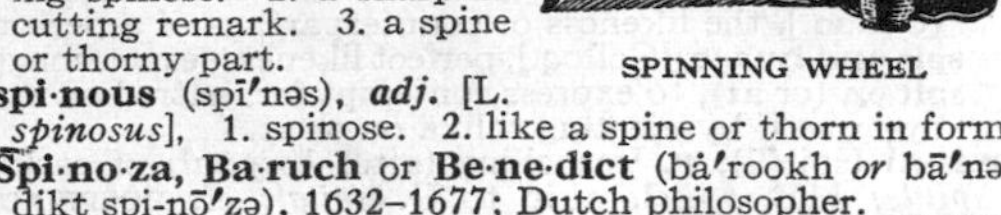

SPINNING WHEEL

spin·ny (spin′i), *n.* [British], a spinney.

spi·nose (spī′nōs), *adj.* [L. *spinosus* < *spina*, spine], full of or covered with spines or thorns.

spi·nos·i·ty (spī-nos′ə-ti), *n.* [LL. *spinositas*], 1. the quality or condition of being spinose. 2. a sharp or cutting remark. 3. a spine or thorny part.

spi·nous (spī′nəs), *adj.* [L. *spinosus*], 1. spinose. 2. like a spine or thorn in form.

Spi·no·za, Ba·ruch or **Be·ne·dict** (bä′rookh *or* bā′nə-dikt spi-nō′zə), 1632–1677; Dutch philosopher.

Spi·no·zism (spi-nō′ziz′m), *n.* the philosophy of Spinoza, who taught that there is but one substance, God, having two aspects, thought and extension.

spin·ster (spin′stẽr), *n.* [ME. *spinnestere* < *spinnen*, to spin; + *-ster*], 1. a woman who spins thread or yarn. 2. an unmarried woman; especially, an elderly woman who has never married; old maid.

spin·ster·hood (spin′stẽr-hood′), *n.* [see -HOOD], the state of being a spinster.

spin·thar·i·scope (spin-thar′i-skōp′), *n.* [< Gr. *spintharis*, a spark; + *-scope*], a small device with a fluorescent screen, for observing the scintillations of the alpha rays given off by a radioactive substance.

spi·nule (spī′nūl, spin′ūl), *n.* [L. *spinula*, dim. of *spina*, spine], a small spine.

spin·u·lose (spin′yoo-lōs′, spīn′yoo-lōs′), *adj.* [Mod. L. *spinulosus*], 1. having or covered with spinules. 2. having the shape of a spinule.

spin·y (spīn′i), *adj.* [SPINIER (-i-ẽr), SPINIEST (-i-ist)], 1. covered with spines, thorns, or prickles. 2. full of difficulties; troublesome; thorny. 3. spine-shaped.

spiny anteater, the echidna, an egg-laying mammal resembling a porcupine.

spin·y-finned (spīn′i-find′), *adj.* having fins in which the membrane is supported by stiff, unbranched, and unsegmented rays.

spiny lobster, any of a group of sea crustaceans, related and similar to the common lobster, but lacking the large pincers.

spi·ra·cle (spī′rə-k′l, spir′ə-k′l), *n.* [ME. *spirakle;* L. *spiraculum* < *spirare*, to breathe], 1. a small opening allowing the outer air to come through into a confined space; air hole. 2. in *zoology*, *a)* an opening through which air or water is taken in and expelled in respiration, as in the whale; blowhole. *b)* any of the small openings of the tracheal respiratory system of certain arthropods, etc., ordinarily along the sides of the body.

spi·rac·u·lar (spī-rak′yoo-lẽr, spi-rak′yoo-lẽr), *adj.* of or consisting of a spiracle.

spi·rae·a (spī-rē′ə), *n.* [L.; Gr. *speiraia*, meadowsweet < *speira*, a spiral, coil], any of a number of related shrubs of the rose family, with dense clusters of small pink or white flowers, as the meadowsweet: also spelled **spirea.**

spi·ral (spī′rəl), *adj.* [ML. *spiralis* < L. *spira*, a coil; Gr. *speira*], 1. circling continuously around a point or center in curves that constantly increase (or decrease) in size; coiled or coiling in one plane. 2. coiled or coiling in constantly changing planes, as the thread of a screw; helical. *n.* 1. a spiral curve occurring in a single plane. 2. a spiral curve occurring in a series of planes, as the thread of a screw; helix. 3. something having a spiral form, as a coiled snake or a bedspring. 4. a spiral path or flight: as, the descending *spiral* of a falling leaf. 5. a section or segment of a spiral. 6. a continuous, widening decrease or increase: as, an inflationary *spiral* is an economic condition in which an increase in prices, etc. results in a series of further increases, to the point of financial collapse. 7. in *football*, a kick or pass in which the ball rotates on its longer axis as it moves through the air. *v.i.* [SPIRALED or SPIRALLED (-rəld), SPIRALING or SPIRALLING], to move in or form a spiral. *v.t.* to cause to move in or form into a spiral: as, the war *spiraled* prices to new heights.

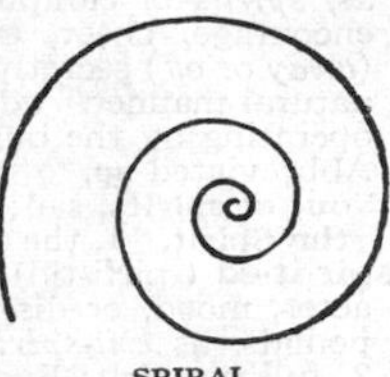

SPIRAL

spi·ral·ly (spī′rəl-i), *adv.* in the form of a spiral.

spiral nebula, a distant galaxy having the visible form of a spiral.

spi·rant (spī′rənt), *n.* [< L. *spirans*, ppr. of *spirare*, to breathe], a consonantal sound, as (sh) or (v), produced by the passage of breath through the partially closed oral cavity; fricative. *adj.* having the nature of a spirant; fricative.

spire (spīr), *n.* [Fr.; L. *spira;* Gr. *speira*], 1. a spiral or coil. 2. any of the convolutions of a spiral or coil. 3. in *zoology*, the upper part of a spiral shell.

spire (spīr), *n.* [ME., a young shoot or blade of grass; AS. *spir;* akin to ON. *spīra;* IE. base **spei-*, a point, pointed wood, as also in L. *spina* (cf. SPINE)], 1. a sprout, spike, or stalk of a plant, a blade of grass, etc. 2. the top part of a pointed, tapering object or structure, as a mountain peak; summit. 3. anything that tapers to a point, as a pointed tower or steeple. *v.i.* [SPIRED (spīrd), SPIRING], to extend upward, tapering to a point; shoot up, rise in, or put forth a spire or spires. *v.t.* to furnish with a spire or spires.

spi·re·a (spī-rē′ə), *n.* spiraea.

spired (spīrd), *adj.* having a spire or spires.

spi·reme (spī′rēm), *n.* [Gr. *speirēma*, a coil < *speira*, a spiral, coil], in *biology*, the nuclear chromatin of a cell, a threadlike form seen in an early stage of mitosis.

Spires (spīrz), *n.* Speyer: the English name.

spi·rif·er·ous (spī-rif′ẽr-əs), *adj.* [< L. *spira* (see SPIRAL); + *-ferous*], in *zoology*, characterized by a spire, or spiral structure, as some shells, or by spiral appendages, as a brachiopod.

spi·ril·lum (spī-ril′əm), *n.* [*pl.* SPIRILLA (-ə)], [Mod. L., dim. of L. *spira* (see SPIRAL)], 1. any of a genus of bacteria having the form of a spiral thread and characterized by flagella: see **bacteria,** illus. 2. any of various other microorganisms having a similar form.

spir·it (spir′it), *n.* [ME.; OFr. *espirit;* L. *spiritus*, breath, courage, vigor, the soul, life < *spirare*, to blow, breathe], 1. *a)* the life principle, especially in man, originally regarded as an animating vapor infused by the breath, or as bestowed by a deity; hence, *b)* the soul. 2. the thinking, motivating, feeling part of man, often as distinguished from the body; mind; intelligence. 3. [also S-], life, will, consciousness, thought, etc., regarded as separate from matter. 4. a supernatural being, especially one thought of as haunting or possessing a person, house, etc., as a ghost, or as inhabiting a certain region, being of a certain (good or evil) character, etc., as an angel, demon, fairy, or elf. 5. an individual person or personality thought of as showing or having some specific quality: as, she was a brave *spirit.* 6. *often pl.* frame of mind; disposition; mood; temper: as, in high *spirits.* 7. vivacity, courage, vigor, enthusiasm, etc.: as, answer with *spirit.* 8. enthusiastic loyalty: as, school *spirit.* 9. real meaning; true intention: opposed to *letter*, as, he followed the *spirit* if not the letter of the law. 10. a pervading animating principle, essential or characteristic quality, or prevailing tendency or attitude: as, the *spirit* of the Renaissance. 11. a divine animating influence or inspiration. 12. *often pl.* a strong alcoholic liquor produced by distillation. 13. [Obs.], *a)* any of certain substances or fluids thought of as permeating organs of the body. *b)* in *alchemy*, sulfur, sal ammoniac, mercury, or orpiment. 14. *also pl.* in *chemistry*, *a)* any liquid produced by the distillation of certain materials, as wood fermentation mixtures, etc.: as, *spirits* of turpentine. *b)* ethanol. 15. in *dyeing*, a solution of a tin salt, etc., used as a mordant. 16. in *pharmacy*, an alcoholic solution of a volatile or essential substance: as, *spirits* of camphor. ***v.t.*** 1. to inspirit, animate, encourage, cheer, etc. (also with *up*). 2. to carry (*away* or *off*) secretly and swiftly, as though in a supernatural manner. ***adj.*** 1. of spirits or spiritualism. 2. operating by the burning of alcohol: as, a *spirit* lamp. Abbreviated **sp.**

out of spirits, sad; depressed.

the Spirit, 1. the Holy Ghost. 2. God.

spir·it·ed (spir′i-tid), ***adj.*** 1. having a (specified) character, mood, or disposition: used in hyphenated compounds, as *evil-spirited, fine-spirited, low-spirited,* etc. 2. full of spirit; lively; vigorous; energetic; animated.

spir·it·ing (spir′i-tiŋ), ***n.*** behavior or activity of a spirit.

spir·it·ism (spir′i-tiz′m), ***n.*** spiritualism.

spir·it·less (spir′it-lis), ***adj.*** lacking spirit, energy, or vigor; not lively or animated; listless; depressed.

spirit level, a glass tube held in a frame and containing a liquid, usually alcohol, with a bubble in it: when the bubble rests at the center of the tube, the frame, or a surface upon which it is placed, is known to be level, or horizontal.

‡**spi·ri·to·so** (spē′rē-tô′sô; Eng. spir′i-tō′sō), ***adj.*** [It.], in *music,* lively; spirited.

spirits of hartshorn, a solution of liquid ammonia, as for household use: also **spirit of hartshorn.**

spirits of turpentine, oil of turpentine; turpentine (sense 2): also **spirit of turpentine.**

spirits of wine, alcohol: also **spirit of wine.**

spir·it·u·al (spir′i-cho͞o-əl, spir′i-chool), ***adj,*** [ME. & OFr. *spirituel;* L. *spiritualis*], 1. of the spirit or the soul, often in a religious or moral aspect, as distinguished from the body. 2. of, from, or concerned with the intellect, or what is often thought of as the better or higher part of the mind. 3. of or consisting of spirit; not corporeal. 4. characterized by the ascendancy of the spirit; showing much refinement of thought and feeling. 5. of religion or the church; sacred, devotional, or ecclesiastical; not lay or temporal. 6. spiritualistic or supernatural. ***n.*** 1. a religious folk song of American Negro origin, often treating Biblical matter in a way suggestive of the folk ballad, with the use of refrain and vigorous rhythm. 2. a spiritual thing or concern; especially, *pl.* church matters.

spiritual incest, in *ecclesiastical usage,* sexual intercourse between persons having a spiritual kinship, as from having been baptized together.

spir·it·u·al·ism (spir′i-cho͞o-əl-iz′m, spir′i-choo-liz′m), ***n.*** 1. the belief that the dead survive as spirits which can communicate with the living, especially with the help of a third party, called a medium. 2. any practice arising from this belief. 3. the philosophical doctrine that all reality is in essence spiritual; idealism. 4. spirituality; spiritual quality, etc. Also **spiritism.**

spir·it·u·al·ist (spir′i-cho͞o-əl-ist, spir′i-chool-ist), ***n.*** 1. a person who believes in or practices spiritualism (senses 1 & 2). 2. a person who believes in the doctrine of philosophical spiritualism. 3. a person concerned with or devoted to spiritual things.

spir·it·u·al·is·tic (spir′i-cho͞o-ə-lis′tik, spir′i-choo-lis′-tik), ***adj.*** of spiritualism or spiritualists.

spir·it·u·al·i·ty (spir′i-cho͞o-al′ə-ti), ***n.*** [*pl.* SPIRITUALITIES (-tiz)], 1. spiritual character, quality, or nature: opposed to *sensuality, worldliness.* 2. *often pl.* the rights, jurisdiction, tithes, etc. belonging to the church or to an ecclesiastic. 3. the fact or state of being incorporeal.

spir·it·u·al·i·za·tion (spir′i-cho͞o-əl-i-zā′shən, spir′i-chool-ī-zā′shən), ***n.*** a spiritualizing or being spiritualized.

spir·it·u·al·ize (spir′i-cho͞o-ə-līz′, spir′i-choo-līz′), ***v.t.*** [SPIRITUALIZED (-līzd′), SPIRITUALIZING], 1. to make spiritual; deprive of materiality or worldliness. 2. to give a spiritual sense or meaning to.

spir·it·u·al·ty (spir′i-cho͞o-əl-ti), ***n.*** [*pl.* SPIRITUALTIES (-tiz)], 1. the clergy. 2. *often pl.* spiritual or ecclesiastical things, as ecclesiastical property, rights, etc.

‡**spi·ri·tu·el** (spē′rē′tü′el′; Eng. spir′i-cho͞o-el′), ***adj.*** [Fr. (fem. *spirituelle*); see SPIRITUAL], 1. having or showing a refined, ethereal nature. 2. having or showing a quick, graceful wit or mind.

spir·it·u·ous (spir′i-cho͞o-əs), ***adj.*** [< L. *spiritus,* spirit; + *-ous*], of, like, or containing alcohol: said especially of distilled as opposed to fermented beverages.

spir·i·tus as·per (spir′i-təs as′pẽr), [L.], in *Greek grammar,* the rough breathing.

spir·i·tus fru·men·ti (spir′i-təs fro͞o-men′tī), [L., lit., spirit of grain], whisky.

spir·i·tus le·nis (spir′i-təs lē′nis), [L.], in *Greek grammar,* the smooth breathing.

spi·ro- (spī′rō, spī′rə), [< L. *spirare,* to breathe], a combining form meaning *respiration,* as in *spirograph.*

spi·ro- (spī′rō, spī′rə), [< Gr. *speira,* a coil], a combining form used to indicate *a spiral* or *coil,* as in *spirochete.*

spi·ro·chete, spi·ro·chaete (spī′rə-kēt′), ***n.*** [Mod. L. *spirochaeta* < Gr. *speira,* a spiral + *chaitē,* hair], any of a group of slender, spiral-shaped bacteria, some varieties of which cause disease.

spi·ro·che·to·sis, spi·ro·chae·to·sis (spī′rə-ki-tō′sis), ***n.*** an infectious disease of chickens, etc., caused by a spirochete and usually fatal.

spi·ro·graph (spī′rə-graf′, spī′rə-gräf′), ***n.*** [*spiro-* + *-graph*], an instrument for recording the movements of breathing.

spi·ro·gy·ra (spī′rə-jī′rə), ***n.*** [Mod. L. < Gr. *speira,* a spiral, coil + *gyros,* a ring], any of a number of related fresh-water algae containing spiral chlorophyll bands.

spi·roid (spī′roid), ***adj.*** [see SPIRE (a spiral) & -OID], like a spiral; having a spiral form.

spi·rom·e·ter (spī-rom′ə-tẽr), ***n.*** [*spiro-* + *-meter*], an instrument for measuring the breathing capacity of the lungs.

spi·rom·e·try (spī-rom′ə-tri), ***n.*** the measurement of lung capacity by means of a spirometer.

spirt (spũrt), ***n., v.t. & v.i.*** spurt.

spir·u·la (spir′yoo-lə, spir′oo-lə), ***n.*** [*pl.* SPIRULAE (-lē′)], [Mod. L., dim. of L. *spira;* see SPIRAL], a two-gilled mollusk related to the squid and cuttlefish, with a flat spiral shell that is partitioned into a series of chambers and is largely internal.

spir·y (spir′i), ***adj.*** [SPIRIER (-i-ẽr), SPIRIEST (-i-ist)], spiral; coiled; curled.

spir·y (spīr′i), ***adj.*** [SPIRIER (-i-ẽr), SPIRIEST (-i-ist)], 1. of, or having the form of, a spire, or pointed, tapering object, slender stalk, steeple, etc. 2. having many spires.

spit (spit), ***n.*** [ME. *spite;* AS. *spitu;* akin to OHG. *spizzi,* a point; IE. base **spei-,* a point (cf. SPIRE)], 1. a thin, pointed rod or bar on which meat is impaled and held to be broiled or roasted over a fire. 2. a narrow point of land extending into a body of water. 3. a long, narrow reef, shoal, or sandbank extending from the shore. ***v.t.*** [SPITTED (-id), SPITTING], to thrust a pointed rod through; fix or impale on or as on a spit.

spit (spit), ***v.t.*** [SPAT (spat) or SPIT, SPITTING], [ME. *spitten;* AS. *spittan;* akin to Dan. *spytte;* IE. echoic base **sp(h)jēu-,* etc., as also in L. *sputum,* Eng. *spew*], 1. to eject from within the mouth. 2. to eject, throw out, emit, or utter explosively: as, the man *spat* an oath. 3. to light (a fuse). ***v.i.*** 1. to eject saliva from the mouth; expectorate. 2. to rain or snow lightly or briefly. 3. to make an explosive hissing noise, as an angry cat. ***n.*** 1. the act of spitting. 2. saliva. 3. something like saliva, as the frothy secretion of certain insects. 4. a light, brief shower of rain or fall of snow. 5. [Colloq.], the likeness or counterpart, as of a person.

spit and image, [Colloq.], perfect likeness; exact image.

spit on (or **at**), to express contempt for, hatred of, etc. by or as if by ejecting saliva on or at.

spit·al (spit′'l), ***n.*** [respelling (after *hospital*) of earlier *spittle;* ME. *spitel;* akin to G. *spital;* cf. HOSPITAL], [Obs.], 1. a hospital, especially one for the very poor and for those having leprosy or other diseases regarded as loathsome. 2. a loathsome place. 3. a shelter for the use of travelers on a road.

spit·ball (spit′bôl′), ***n.*** 1. a piece of paper chewed up into a wad for throwing. 2. in *baseball,* a pitch, now illegal, made to curve by moistening one side of the ball with saliva.

spitch·cock (spich′kok′), ***n.*** [? < *spit* + *cook;* earlier, *spechcoke*], an eel split open or cut up in pieces and broiled or fried. ***v.t.*** to prepare (an eel) in this way.

spit curl, a curled lock of hair dampend, as with spit, and pressed flat against the forehead or temple.

spite (spīt), ***n.*** [ME. *spit,* contr. < *despit;* see DESPITE], 1. a mean or evil feeling toward another, characterized by the inclination to hurt, humiliate, annoy, frustrate, etc.; ill will; malice. 2. an instance of this; a grudge. 3. [Archaic], annoyance or chagrin. ***v.t.*** [SPITED (-id), SPITING], 1. to behave in a spiteful manner toward; vent one's spite upon by hurting, annoying, frustrating, etc. 2. [Archaic], to annoy or offend. —***SYN.*** see **malice.**

cut off one's nose to spite one's face, [Colloq.], to injure or inconvenience oneself in an attempt to injure or annoy another.

in spite of, in defiance of; regardless of; notwithstanding.

spite·ful (spīt′fəl), ***adj.*** full of or showing spite; purposefully annoying; malicious. —***SYN.*** see **vindictive.**

spit·fire (spit′fīr′), ***n.*** a person who is easily aroused to violent outbursts of anger; especially, such a woman or girl.

Spits·ber·gen (spits′bũr′gən), ***n.*** Svalbard, a group of islands in the Arctic Ocean, belonging to Norway.

spit·ter (spit′ẽr), ***n.*** 1. a person or animal that spits saliva, etc. 2. [Colloq.], in *baseball,* a spitball.

spit·ter (spit′ẽr), ***n.*** 1. a person whose work is putting meat on a spit and turning it over a fire. 2. a young deer whose antlers are beginning to sprout.

spitting image, [Colloq.], spit and image; perfect likeness.

spit·tle (spit′'l), ***n.*** [altered < *spattle* (AS. *spatl* < base of *spætan,* to spit; cf. SPIT), after *spit* (to eject)], 1. saliva; spit. 2. the frothy secretion of larval spittle insects.

spittle insect, any of a number of leaping insects whose larvae surround themselves with a frothy secretion.

spit·toon (spi-to͞on′), ***n.*** [< *spit*], a jarlike container to spit into; cuspidor.

spitz dog (spits), [G. < *spitz*, pointed], a variety of small Pomeranian dog, usually white, with sharp-pointed muzzle and ears and a long, silky coat.

SPITZ DOG (14 in. high at shoulder)

spit·zen·burg, spit·zen·berg (spit′s'n-bûrg′), *n.* [also *Esopus Spitzenberg* < D. *spits*, a point, pointed (the apple is pointed) + *berg*, hill, mountain: so named because the seedling was discovered on a hillside near Esopus, New York], [sometimes S-], any of several kinds of winter apples having red and yellow skin and a fine flavor.

spiv (spiv), *n.* [prob. dial. var. of 19th-c. slang *spiff*, person who dresses flashily (cf. SPIFFY); but ? < "suspected *p*ersons and *i*tinerant *v*agrants," police phrase], [British Slang], a person who lives by his wits, without doing any regular work.

splanch·nic (splaŋk′nik), *adj.* [Mod. L. *splanchnicus;* Gr. *splanchnikos* < *splanchnon*, an entrail], of the viscera; visceral.

splanch·no- (splaŋk′nō, splaŋk′nə), [< Gr. *splanchnon*, viscera], a combining form meaning *the viscera*, as in *splanchnology:* also, before a vowel, **splanchn-.**

splanch·nol·o·gy (splaŋk-nol′ə-ji), *n.* [*splanchno-* + *-logy*], the branch of medical study dealing with the structure, functions, and diseases of the viscera.

splash (splash), *v.t.* [intens. extension of *plash*], 1. to cause (a liquid substance) to fly or scatter. 2. to dash or scatter a liquid substance, mud, etc. on, so as to wet or soil. 3. to cause to splash a liquid: as, stop *splashing* your feet in the puddles. 4. to make (one's way) by splashing. 5. to mark or spot by or as by splashing: as, a street *splashed* with sunlight. *v.i.* 1. to cause a liquid substance to fly or scatter. 2. to fall, strike, or scatter with a splash or splashes: as, rain *splashed* against the window. 3. to move with splashes: as, the dog *splashed* eagerly into the water. *n.* 1. the act or sound of splashing. 2. a mass of flying water, mud, etc. 3. a spot or mark made by or as by splashing.
make a splash, [Colloq.], to attract great, often brief attention by doing something striking, spectacular, or ostentatious.

splash·board (splash′bôrd′, splash′bōrd′), *n.* 1. any screen or board protecting riders on a vehicle from being splashed in wet weather; dashboard or mudguard. 2. a screen to keep water from splashing on to the deck of a boat. 3. a trap for closing a sluice or spillway.

splash·er (splash′ẽr), *n.* 1. a person or thing that splashes. 2. anything giving protection from splashes.

splash·y (splash′i), *adj.* [SPLASHIER (-i-ẽr), SPLASHIEST (-i-ist)], 1. splashing; making splashes. 2. liable to splash; wet, muddy, etc. 3. covered or marked with splashes. 4. [Colloq.], attracting much notice or attention; spectacular; striking.

splat (splat), *n.* [via dial. < base of *split*], a thin, flat piece of wood, especially as used in the back of a chair.

splat·ter (splat′ẽr), *n., v.t. & v.i.* [var. of *spatter*], spatter; splash.

splay (splā), *n.* [contr. of *display*], 1. a sloping or beveled surface or angle. 2. a spreading; expansion; enlargement. *adj.* 1. sloping or spreading out. 2. broad and flat. 3. awkward. 4. awry. *v.t.* [ME. *splaien*], 1. to spread, enlarge, or expand. 2. to make beveled or sloping. 3. to dislocate (a bone): said of animals. *v.i.* to spread out, especially so as to slant or slope.

splay·foot (splā′foot′), *n.* [*pl.* SPLAYFEET (-fēt′)], 1. a foot that is flat and turned outward. 2. the physical abnormality characterized by feet of this kind.

splay·foot·ed (splā′foot′id), *adj.* having splayfoot.

spleen (splēn), *n.* [ME. *splen* < OFr. or L.; OFr. *esplen;* L. *splen;* Gr. *splēn*, spleen; akin to Sans. *plīhan*, OSlav. *slezna*, spleen], 1. a large, vascular, ductless organ in the upper left part of the abdominal cavity near the stomach: it has various functions in modifying the structure of the blood, and was formerly regarded as the seat of certain emotions; hence, 2. malice; spite; bad temper. 3. [Archaic], melancholy; low spirits. 4. [Obs.], a whim or caprice.

spleen·ful (splēn′fəl), *adj.* full of spleen; bad-tempered; irritable; peevish; spiteful.

spleen·ish (splēn′ish), *adj.* spleenful.

spleen·wort (splēn′wûrt′), *n.* any of a group of ferns with simple or compound fronds and linear or oblique sori on the upper surface of an oblique veinlet.

spleen·y (splēn′i), *adj.* [SPLEENIER (-i-ẽr), SPLEENIEST (-i-ist)], spleenful.

splen- (splēn, splen), spleno-.

splen·dent (splen′dənt), *adj.* [L. *splendens*, ppr. of *splendere*, to shine], 1. shining; lustrous. 2. brilliant; splendid; magnificent. 3. illustrious.

splen·did (splen′did), *adj.* [L. *splendidus* < *splendere*, to shine], 1. having or showing splendor; specifically, *a*) shining; lustrous; brilliant. *b*) magnificent; gorgeous. 2. worthy of high praise; grand; glorious; illustrious: as, a *splendid* deed of valor. 3. [Colloq.], very good; excellent; fine: as, what *splendid* weather!
***SYN.*—splendid** applies to that which literally or figuratively dazzles or impresses with its brilliance, luster, etc. (a *splendid* uniform, hero, etc.); **gorgeous** applies to that which is striking for its brilliance and variety of color (a *gorgeous* floral display); **glorious** refers to that which is radiantly beautiful or distinctive (a *glorious* sunset); **sublime** implies such an exalted beauty or grandeur as to inspire awe or admiration (the *sublime* Grand Canyon); **superb** is applied to that which exceeds all others in grandeur, splendor, etc. (a *superb* performance of an opera). All of these words are now used hyperbolically, in informal speech, with weakened effect.

splen·dif·er·ous (splen-dif′ẽr-əs), *adj.* [< *splendor* + *-ferous*], [Colloq.], gorgeous; splendid: used humorously.

splen·dor (splen′dẽr), *n.* [OFr. *esplendour;* L. *splendor* < *splendere*, to shine], 1. great luster or brightness; brilliance. 2. magnificent richness or glory; impressiveness; pomp; grandeur.

splen·dor·ous (splen′dẽr-əs), *adj.* characterized by splendor.

splen·dour (splen′dẽr), *n.* splendor: British spelling.

splen·drous (splen′drəs), *adj.* splendorous.

sple·net·ic (spli-net′ik), *adj.* [Fr. *splénétique;* LL. *spleneticus*], 1. of the spleen; splenic. 2. bad-tempered; irritable; peevish; spiteful; spleenful. 3. [Obs.], melancholy. *n.* a spleenful person. —***SYN.*** see **irritable.**

sple·net·i·cal (spli-net′i-k'l), *adj.* splenetic.

sple·net·i·cal·ly (spli-net′i-k'l-i), *adv.* in a splenetic manner.

sple·ni·al (splē′ni-əl), *adj.* of the splenius.

splen·ic (splen′ik, splē′nik), *adj.* [Fr. *splénique;* L. *splenicus;* Gr. *splēnikos*], 1. of or having to do with the spleen. 2. located in or near the spleen.

sple·ni·tis (spli-nī′tis), *n.* [*splen-* + *-itis*], inflammation of the spleen.

sple·ni·us (splē′ni-əs), *n.* [Mod. L. < Gr. *splēnion*, a bandage, dim. of *splēn*, spleen], a large, flat muscle on either side of the back of the neck, serving to rotate the neck and head.

sple·no- (splē′nō, splen′ə), [< Gr. *splēn*, *splēnos*, the spleen], a combining form meaning *the spleen*: also, before a vowel, **splen-.**

spleu·chan (sploo͞′khən), *n.* [< Scot. Gael. *spliuchan*], [Scot. & Irish], a pouch for money or tobacco.

splice (splīs), *v.t.* [SPLICED (splīst), SPLICING], [MD. *splissen;* akin to *splitten*, to split], 1. to join or unite (ropes or rope ends) by weaving together the end strands. 2. to join together pieces, as of wood, by overlapping and binding, especially at the ends. 3. [Slang], to join in marriage. *n.* a joint or joining made by splicing.

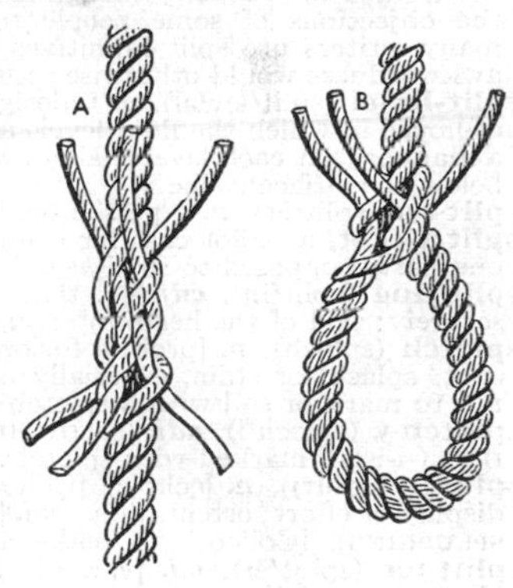

SPLICES
A, short splice; B, eye splice

spline (splīn), *n.* [< East Anglian dial. *splind* < base of *split*], 1. a long, flat, pliable piece, as of wood or metal, especially one used in drawing curves. 2. a flat key or strip that fits into a groove or slot between parts, as between a shaft and a pulley, so as to allow only relative lengthwise motion of the parts. 3. the groove or slot into which it fits. *v.t.* [SPLINED (splīnd), SPLINING], 1. to fit with a spline. 2. to cut a groove or slot in for a spline.

splint (splint), *n.* [Late ME. *splente;* MD. *splinte* < base seen in *split*], 1. a thin strip of wood or cane woven together with others to make baskets, chair seats, etc. 2. a thin strip of metal used in overlapping construction with others to make medieval armor. 3. any device used to hold a broken bone in place or to keep a part of the body in a fixed position, as a thin, rigid strip of wood or metal. 4. a bony growth or tumor on the cannon bone of a horse, mule, etc. 5. [British Dial.], a splinter. *v.t.* to fit, support, or hold in place with or as with a splint or splints.

splint bone, in horses and related animals, either of

two small bones, one on each side of the leg bone between the hock and fetlock.

splin·ter (splin′tẽr), *v.t. & v.i.* [Late ME.; MD. < *splinte;* see SPLINT], to break or split into thin, sharp pieces. *n.* a thin, sharp piece of wood, bone, etc., made by splitting or breaking; sliver. *adj.* designating a group that separates from a main party, church, etc. because of divergent views. —*SYN.* see **break.**

splin·ter·y (splin′tẽr-i), *adj.* 1. easily splintered. 2. of or like a splinter. 3. resulting in splinters, as a fracture. 4. full of splinters; splintered; jagged; rough.

Split (splēt), *n.* Spalato: the Serbian name.

split (split), *v.t.* [SPLIT or *obs.* SPLITTED (-id), SPLITTING], [MD. *splitten;* akin to MHG. *splīzen;* IE. base *(*s*)*plei-*, to split, crack], 1. to separate, cut, or divide into two or more parts; cause to separate along the grain or length; break into layers. 2. to break or tear apart by force; burst; rend. 3. to divide into parts or shares; portion out: as, they *split* the cost of the trip. 4. to cause (a group, political party, etc.) to separate into divisions or factions; disunite. 5. in *chemistry, a*) to break (a molecule) into atoms; separate the components of. *b*) to produce nuclear fission in (an atom or atoms). *v.i.* 1. to separate or divide lengthwise into two or more parts; separate along the grain or length. 2. to break or tear apart; burst; rend. 3. to separate or break up through failure to agree, etc. 4. [Colloq.], to divide something with another or others, each taking a share: as, winners *split.* 5. [19th-c. Slang], to inform on an accomplice; peach. *n.* 1. the act or process of splitting. 2. the result of splitting; specifically, *a*) a break; fissure; crack; tear. *b*) a breach or division in a group, between persons, etc. 3. a splinter; sliver. 4. a single thickness of hide split horizontally. 5. a flexible strip of wood used in basketmaking. 6. a confection made of a split banana or other fruit with ice cream, nuts, sauces, whipped cream, etc. 7. *often pl.* the feat of spreading the legs apart until they lie flat on the floor, the body remaining upright. 8. [Colloq.], *a*) a small bottle of carbonated water, wine, etc., half the usual size, often about six ounces. *b*) a drink or portion half the usual size. *c*) a half pint. 9. [Slang], a share, as of loot or booty. 10. in *bowling,* an arrangement of pins after the first bowl, so separated as to make a spare almost impossible. *adj.* 1. divided or separated along the length or grain; broken into parts. 2. divided; separated. 3. in the *stock market,* given in sixteenths, and not in eighths: said of a quotation smaller than the normal trading unit. —*SYN.* see **break.**
split off, to break off or separate as by splitting.

split infinitive, in *grammar,* an infinitive with the verbal and the *to* separated by an adverb. Example: he decided *to gradually change* his procedure. Despite the objections of some people to this construction, many writers use split infinitives where ambiguity or awkwardness would otherwise result.

split-lev·el (split′lev′əl), *adj.* designating or of a type of house in which the floor levels are staggered in such a manner that each level is about a half story above or below the adjacent one.

split·ter (split′ẽr), *n.* a person or thing that splits.

split ticket, a ballot cast for candidates of more than one party: opposed to *straight ticket.*

split·ting (split′iŋ), *adj.* 1. that splits. 2. *a*) aching severely: said of the head. *b*) severe, as a headache.

splotch (sploch), *n.* [prob. a fusion of *spot* + *blotch*], a spot, splash, or stain, especially one that is irregular. *v.t.* to mark or soil with a splotch or splotches.

splotch·y (sploch′i), *adj.* [SPLOTCHIER (-i-ẽr), SPLOTCHIEST (-i-ist)], marked with splotches.

splurge (splũrj), *n.* [echoic], [Colloq.], any very showy display or effort; ostentation. *v.i.* [SPLURGED (splũrjd), SPLURGING], [Colloq.], to make a splurge; show off.

splut·ter (splut′ẽr), *v.i.* [var. of *sputter*], 1. to make hissing or spitting sounds, or to give off or scatter particles or drops in an explosive way; sputter. 2. to speak hurriedly and confusedly, as when excited or embarrassed. *v.t.* 1. to utter hurriedly and confusedly; sputter. 2. to spatter. *n.* 1. a spluttering sound or utterance; fuss. 2. a loud sputtering or splash.

Spode (spōd), *n.* a fine porcelain or chinaware originated by Josiah Spode at Staffordshire, England, about 1799: also **spode.**

spod·u·mene (spoj′oo-mēn′), *n.* [Fr. *spodumène;* Gr. *spodoumenos,* ppr. of *spodoun,* to burn to ashes < *spodos,* ashes], a crystalline mineral, lithium aluminum silicate, $LiAl(SiO_3)_2$: it is usually light-green or yellow and is sometimes used as a gem.

Spohr, Lou·is (lōō′ē shpôr), 1784–1859; German composer and violinist.

spoil (spoil), *v.t.* [SPOILED (spoild) or SPOILT (spoilt), SPOILING], [ME. *spoilen;* OFr. *espoillier* < L. *spoliare,* to plunder < *spolium,* hide stripped from an animal, arms taken from a defeated foe, plunder], 1. to damage or injure in such a way as to make useless, valueless, etc.; destroy. 2. to mar or impair the enjoyment, quality, or functioning of: as, the rain *spoiled* our picnic. 3. to cause to demand or expect too much by overindulgence. 4. [Archaic], *a*) to strip (a person) of goods, money, etc. by force. *b*) to rob; pillage; plunder. *c*) to seize (goods) by force. *v.i.* 1. to be damaged or injured in such a way as to become useless, valueless, etc.; decay, as food. 2. [Colloq.], to be aggressively eager: as, he's *spoiling* for a fight. 3. [Archaic.], to pillage; plunder. *n.* 1. *usually pl.* goods, territory, etc. taken by force in war; plunder; loot; booty. 2. *usually pl.* public offices to which the successful political party has the power of appointment. 3. an object of plunder; prey. 4. waste material removed in making excavations, etc. 5. [Archaic], the act of plundering; spoliation. 6. [Obs.], damage; impairment.
SYN.—**spoil** (now, more commonly, **spoils**) refers to any property, territory, etc. taken in war by the conqueror; **pillage** suggests violence and destructiveness in the taking of spoils; **plunder** is equivalent to **pillage** but also applies to property taken by bandits, highwaymen, etc; **booty** suggests plunder taken by a band or gang, to be divided among the members; **prize** refers specifically to spoils taken at sea, especially an enemy warship or its cargo; **loot,** a more derogatory equivalent for any of the preceding, emphasizes the immorality or predatory nature of the act. See also **decay, indulge, injure.**

spoil·age (spoil′ij), *n.* [see -AGE], 1. a spoiling or being spoiled. 2. something spoiled or the amount spoiled.

spoils·man (spoilz′mən), *n.* [*pl.* SPOILSMEN (-mən)], a person who aids a political party in order to share in the spoils, or one who advocates the spoils system.

spoil·sport (spoil′spôrt′, spoil′spōrt′), *n.* a person who acts so as to prevent others from enjoying themselves.

spoils system, the system or practice of regarding and treating appointive public offices as the booty of the successful party in an election, to be distributed, with their opportunities for profit, among party workers.

spoilt (spoilt), alternative past tense and past participle of **spoil.**

Spo·kane (spō-kan′), *n.* a city in eastern Washington: pop., 182,000.

spoke (spōk), *n.* [ME.; AS. *spaca;* akin to G. *speiche;* IE. base **spei-*, a point, pointed wood, as also in L. *spina* (cf. SPINE), *spica* (cf. SPICULATE)], 1. any of the braces or bars extending between the hub and the rim of a wheel. 2. a ladder rung. 3. any of the grips or handholds fixed along the rim of a ship's steering wheel. 4. a stick, bar, etc. used to prevent a wheel from turning, as in going down a hill. *v.t.* [SPOKED (spōkt) SPOKING], 1. to equip with spokes. 2. to thrust a spoke, or bar, into (a wheel) to prevent movement.

spoke (spōk), past tense or archaic past participle of **speak.**

spo·ken (spō′kən), past participle of **speak.** *adj.* 1. uttered; oral: opposed to *written.* 2. characterized by or uttered in a (specified) kind of voice: used in hyphenated compounds, as *harsh-spoken.*

spoke·shave (spōk′shāv′), *n.* a cutting or planing tool consisting of a blade with a handle at either end: so called because originally used to shape spokes, but now used for trimming and smoothing rounded surfaces.

spokes·man (spōks′mən), *n.* [*pl.* SPOKESMEN (-mən)], [irregularly formed < *spoke,* p.t. of *speak*], a person who speaks or gives information for another or others.

spoke·wise (spōk′wīz′), *adj.* radiating out from a center as the spokes of a wheel. *adv.* so as to be spokewise.

spo·li·ate (spō′li-āt′), *v.t.* [SPOLIATED (-id), SPOLIATING], [< L. *spoliatus,* pp. of *spoliare;* see SPOIL], to rob, plunder, or despoil.

spo·li·a·tion (spō′li-ā′shən), *n.* [ME. *spoliacioun;* L. *spoliatio*], 1. a spoliating or being spoliated; robbery; plundering: said especially of the authorized seizure of neutral ships in wartime. 2. in *law,* the destruction or alteration of a document by an unauthorized person.

spo·li·a·tive (spō′li-ā′tiv), *adj.* [< *spoliate* + *-ive*], having a reducing or diminishing effect; specifically, in *medicine,* having this effect on the blood.

spo·li·a·tor (spō′li-ā′tẽr), *n.* [L.; see SPOIL], a person who robs or plunders.

spon·da·ic (spon-dā′ik), *adj.* [L. *spondaicus;* Gr. *spondeiakos*], 1. of or characterized by a spondee or spondees. 2. constituting a spondee.

spon·da·i·cal (spon-dā′i-k′l), *adj.* spondaic.

spon·dee (spon′dē), *n.* [Fr. *spondée;* L. *spondeus;* Gr. *spondeios* < *spondē,* solemn libation (because such libations were accompanied by a solemn melody)], a metrical foot consisting of two long syllables or, in English poetry, two heavily accented syllables: most alleged spondees in English really have one secondary accent.

spon·dy·li·tis (spon′də-lī′tis), *n.* [*spondyl-* + *-itis*], inflammation of the vertebrae.

spon·dy·lo- (spon′di-lō, spon′di-lə), [< Gr. *spondylos* joint of the back, vertebra], a combining form meaning *vertebra,* as in *spondylitis:* also, before a vowel, **spondyl-**.

sponge (spunj), *n.* [ME.; Late AS.; L. *spongia;* Gr. *spongia*], 1. a plantlike sea animal having a porous structure and a tough, fibrous skeleton, and growing fixed (except in the larval stage), in large colonies. 2. the skeleton, or a piece of the skeleton, of such animals, which is light in weight, remains somewhat tough while becoming soft when wet, has a characteristic elastic compressibility, and can absorb many times its own weight in water: it is used in washing surfaces, in bathing, etc.

3. any substance like this; specifically, *a*) a pad of gauze or cotton, as used in surgery. *b*) any of several light, porous cakes or puddings. *c*) bread dough. *d*) any of several metals, as platinum, found in a porous mass. *e*) a spongy substance made of rubber, plastic, etc. and used in washing, bathing, etc. 4. *a*) a person having a spongelike capacity, as for drink, knowledge, etc. *b*) [Colloq.], a person who, though able to work, depends on others for food, money, etc. 5. a sponge bath. ***v.t.*** [SPONGED (spunjd), SPONGING], [ME. *spongen* < the *n.*], 1. to use a sponge on so as to dampen, wipe clean, etc. 2. to remove or obliterate with or as with a damp sponge (with *out, off, away,* etc.). 3. to absorb with, as with, or like a sponge (often with *up*). 4. [Colloq.], to get without cost, as by begging, imposition, etc. ***v.i.*** 1. to gather sponges from the sea. 2. to take up liquid like a sponge. 3. [Colloq.], to be a sponge (sense 4*b*): often with *on*. —*SYN.* see **parasite.**

throw, toss, etc. **up** (or **in**) **the sponge,** [Colloq.], to admit defeat; submit; give up: from the practice by a boxer's second of throwing a sponge into the ring to concede defeat.

sponge bath, a bath taken by using a wet sponge or cloth without getting into water.

sponge·cake (spunj'kāk'), ***n.*** a light, porous kind of cake made of flour, beaten eggs, sugar, etc., but no shortening: also **sponge cake.**

spong·er (spun'jẽr), ***n.*** 1. a person or vessel that gathers sponges. 2. a person who cleans, etc. with a sponge. 3. [Colloq.], a person who sponges, or lives upon others; parasite.

spon·gi·ness (spun'ji-nis), ***n.*** the quality or state of being spongy.

sponging house, formerly in England, a place where debtors were held until they either paid their debts or were put in prison for nonpayment.

spon·gy (spun'ji), ***adj.*** [SPONGIER (-ji-ẽr), SPONGIEST (-ji-ist)], 1. like a sponge; specifically, *a*) light, soft, and elastic. *b*) full of holes; porous. *c*) absorbent. 2. of or characteristic of a sponge.

spon·sion (spon'shən), ***n.*** [L. *sponsio* < *spondere,* to promise solemnly], 1. the act of becoming surety for another. 2. a formal promise, pledge, or engagement, especially one made on behalf of another person. 3. in *international law,* an act done or engagement made for a state by an unauthorized agent.

spon·son (spon'sən), ***n.*** [said to be seaman's alteration of *expansion;* orig. applied to the platforms on each side of a steamer's paddlewheels], 1. a structure that projects over the side of a ship or boat; specifically, *a*) a projecting gun platform. *b*) an air chamber built into the gunwale of a canoe. 2. a short, winglike piece attached to the hull of a seaplane just above water level to give stability in the water.

spon·sor[1] (spon'sẽr), ***n.*** [L., surety < *spondere,* to promise solemnly], 1. a person who enters into an agreement to be responsible for some other person, especially in case of the other's default; surety. 2. a godfather or godmother; person who answers for a child at baptism, making the profession of faith and the promises prescribed. 3. a person or agency that gives endorsement to or vouches for some person or thing. 4. a business firm or other agency that pays the costs of a radio or television program (usually a program that combines entertainment with advertising for the benefit of the firm or agency). ***v.t.*** to act as sponsor for.

SYN.—a **sponsor** is one who assumes a certain degree of responsibility for another in any of various ways (the *sponsor* of a television program assumes the costs of production); a **patron** is one who assumes the role of protector or benefactor, now usually in a financial capacity, as of an artist, an institution, etc.; a **backer** is one who lends support, especially financial support, to someone or something but does not necessarily assume any responsibilities (the magazine failed when it lost its *backers*); **angel** is a slang term for the backer of a theatrical enterprise.

spon·so·ri·al (spon-sō'ri-əl), ***adj.*** of or characteristic of a sponsor.

spon·sor·ship (spon'sẽr-ship'), ***n.*** [see **-SHIP**], 1. a sponsoring. 2. the position, policies, etc. of a sponsor.

spon·ta·ne·i·ty (spon'tə-nē'ə-ti), ***n.*** 1. the state or quality of being spontaneous. 2. [*pl.* SPONTANEITIES (-tiz)], spontaneous behavior, movement, action, etc.

spon·ta·ne·ous (spon-tā'ni-əs), ***adj.*** [L. *spontaneus* < *sponte,* of free will], 1. acting in accordance with or resulting from a natural feeling, impulse, or tendency, without any constraint, effort, or premeditation. 2. having no external cause or influence; occurring or produced within of its own energy, force, etc.; self-acting. 3. growing naturally without being planted or tended; indigenous; wild.

SYN.—**spontaneous** applies to that which is done so naturally that it seems to come without prompting or premeditation (a *spontaneous* demonstration); **impulsive** applies to that which is prompted by some external incitement or sudden inner inclination rather than by conscious, rational volition (an *impulsive* retort); **instinctive** suggests an instantaneous, unwilled response to a stimulus, as if prompted by some natural, inborn tendency (he took an *instinctive* liking to her); **involuntary** refers to that which is done without thought or volition, as a reflex action (an *involuntary* flicker of the eyelid); **automatic** suggests an unvarying, machinelike reaction to a given stimulus or situation (an *automatic* response). —***ANT.*** deliberate, voluntary.

spontaneous combustion, the process of catching fire and burning as a result of heat generated by internal chemical action.

spontaneous generation, the theory that living organisms can originate in nonliving matter independently of other living matter; abiogenesis.

spon·toon (spon-tōōn'), ***n.*** [Fr. (*e*)*sponton;* It. *spontone, spuntone* < *punto;* L. *punctum,* a point], a short pike or halberd carried by 18th century infantry officers.

spoof (spōōf), ***n.*** [orig. a game involving hoaxing and nonsense, invented, c. 1889, by Arthur Roberts, Brit. comedian], [Slang], a hoax, joke, or deception. ***v.t. & v.i.*** [Slang], to fool; deceive; trick.

spook (spook), ***n.*** [D.], [Colloq.], a specter; ghost.

spook·ish (spook'ish), ***adj.*** [Colloq.], spooky.

spook·y (spook'i), ***adj.*** [SPOOKIER (-i-ẽr), SPOOKIEST (-i-ist)], [Colloq.], of, like, or suggesting a spook or spooks; ghostly; weird; eerie.

spool (spōōl), ***n.*** [ME. *spole;* MD. *spoele;* akin to G. *spul;* IE. base **sp*(*h*)*el-,* to split, split off, as also in L. *spolium,* lit., skin flayed from an animal (cf. SPOIL)], 1. a rod or cylinder, usually having a hole running from end to end and a rim at either end, upon which thread, wire, etc. is wound. 2. something like a spool. ***v.t.*** to wind on a spool.

spoon (spōōn), ***n.*** [ME. *spon,* a spoon, chip, splinter; AS. *spon,* a chip; influenced by cognate ON. *spōnn,* a spoon; IE. base **spē-,* **spə-,* a flat piece of wood, as also in Eng. *spade, spathe,* etc.], 1. a utensil consisting of a small, shallow, usually oval-shaped bowl and a handle, used in eating and cooking for picking up or stirring food or drink. 2. something shaped like a spoon; specifically, *a*) a shiny, curved fishing bait, usually made of metal, set above a hook or hooks so as to revolve when drawn through the water, as in casting: also **spoon bait.** *b*) an oar or paddle having a curved blade. *c*) a curved projecting part at the top of a torpedo tube, for keeping the torpedo on a horizontal course. 3. a golf club with a wooden head and more loft than a driver or brassie: see **golf club,** illus. ***v.t.*** 1. to take up with or as with a spoon. 2. to push, lift, or hit with a scooping motion, as the ball in some games. 3. to shape or hollow out like a spoon bowl. ***v.i.*** 1. to fish with a spoon bait. 2. to spoon or scoop a ball, etc. 3. [Colloq.], to make love, as by kissing and caressing.

born with a silver spoon in one's mouth, born to good fortune; born rich.

spoon·bill (spōōn'bil'), ***n.*** 1. any of several wading birds with a broad, flat bill that is spoon-shaped at the tip. 2. any of a number of other birds with a bill like this. 3. the paddlefish. 4. a spoon-shaped bill.

spoon bread, a kind of bread, usually of corn meal, that remains doughy after baking and must be served with a spoon.

spoon·drift (spōōn'drift'), ***n.*** spindrift.

spoon·er·ism (spōōn'ẽr-iz'm), ***n.*** [after Rev. W. A. *Spooner* (1844–1930), of New College, Oxford, famous for his spoonerisms], an unintentional interchange of sounds, usually initial sounds, in two or more words. Example: It is kistumary to cuss the bride.

spoon·ey (spōōn'i), ***n.*** [*pl.* SPOONIES (-iz)], ***& adj.*** [SPOONIER (-i-ẽr), SPOONIEST (-i-ist)], spoony.

spoon·fed (spōōn'fed'), ***adj.*** 1. fed with a spoon; hence, 2. *a*) treated with too much indulgence or solicitude; pampered; coddled. *b*) given no chance to develop initiative or independence in action and thought.

spoon·ful (spōōn'fool'), ***n.*** [*pl.* SPOONFULS (-foolz')], as much as a spoon will hold.

spoon·y (spōōn'i), ***n.*** [*pl.* SPOONIES (-iz)], [Colloq.], 1. a person who spoons, or is amorous in a silly, sentimental way. 2. [Chiefly British], a silly, foolish, or simple-minded person. ***adj.*** [SPOONIER (-i-ẽr), SPOONIEST (-i-ist)], [Colloq.], 1. foolishly sentimental or mawkish; amorous in a silly way. 2. [Chiefly British], silly; foolish. Also spelled **spooney.**

spoor (spoor, spôr, spōr), ***n.*** [D.; cf. AS. *spor*], the track or trail of an animal, especially of a wild animal hunted as game. ***v.t. & v.i.*** to trace or track by a spoor.

Spo·ra·des (spôr'ə-dēz', spō'rə-dēz'; Gr. spô-rä'*th*es), ***n.pl.*** two groups of Greek islands (Northern Sporades and Southern Sporades) in the Aegean, off the southwestern coast of Asia Minor.

spo·rad·ic (spō-rad'ik, spō-rad'ik), ***adj.*** [ML. *sporadicus;* Gr. *sporadikos* < *sporas,* scattered; cf. SPORE], 1. happening from time to time; not constant or regular; occasional. 2. widely separated from others, scattered, or isolated in occurrence; appearing singly, apart, or in isolated instances: as, a *sporadic* disease, *sporadic* strikes.

spo·rad·i·cal·ly (spô-rad′i-k′l-i, spō-rad′ik-li), ***adv.*** in a sporadic manner.

spo·ran·gi·al (spô-ran′ji-əl, spō-ran′ji-əl), ***adj.*** 1. of, or having the nature of, a sporangium. 2. characterized by sporangia.

spo·ran·gi·um (spô-ran′ji-əm, spō-ran′ji-əm), ***n.*** [*pl.* SPORANGIA (-ə)], [Mod. L. < Gr. *spora*, a seed + *angeion*, vessel], a spore case or single cell giving rise to spores.

spore (spôr, spōr), ***n.*** [Mod. L. *spora;* Gr. *spora*, a sowing, seed; akin to *speirein*, to sow], 1. in *biology*, any of various small reproductive bodies, often consisting of a single cell, produced by mosses, ferns, certain protozoans, etc. asexually (*asexual spore*) or by the union of gametes (*sexual spore*): they are highly resistant and are capable of giving rise to a new adult individual, either immediately or after an interval of dormancy. 2. any small organism or cell that can develop into a new individual; seed, germ, etc. ***v.i.*** [SPORED (spôrd, spōrd), SPORING], to bear or develop spores.

spore case, a case which contains spores; sporangium.

spore fruit, any specialized structure in which spores are formed.

spo·ro- (spôr′ō, spō′rə), a combining form meaning *spore*, as in *sporocarp*: also, before a vowel, **spor-.**

spo·ro·carp (spôr′ə-kärp′, spō′rə-kärp′), ***n.*** [*sporo-* + *-carp*], a many-celled body produced from a fertilized archicarp, serving for the development of spores in red algae, lichens, and certain fungi.

spo·ro·cyst (spôr′ə-sist′, spō′rə-sist′), ***n.*** [*sporo-* + *-cyst*], 1. in *botany*, a resting cell giving rise to asexual spores. 2. in *zoology*, *a*) a saclike stage in the development of some trematodes which produces daughter sporocysts by asexual means. *b*) a cyst produced by some protozoans before sporulation, or a protozoan in encystment.

spo·ro·gen·e·sis (spôr′ə-jen′ə-sis, spō′rə-jen′ə-sis), ***n.*** [Mod. L.; see SPORO- & -GENESIS], 1. reproduction by means of spores. 2. the formation of spores.

spo·rog·e·nous (spô-roj′ə-nəs, spō-roj′ə-nəs), ***adj.*** characterized by sporogenesis.

spo·ro·go·ni·um (spôr′ə-gō′ni-əm, spō′rə-gō′ni-əm), ***n.*** [*pl.* SPOROGONIA (-ə)], [Mod. L.; see SPORO- & -GONY], the sporophyte in mosses and liverworts, usually a spore-bearing capsule on a stalk.

spo·rog·o·ny (spô-rog′ə-ni, spō-rog′ə-ni), ***n.*** [*sporo-* + *-gony*], the process by which sporozoites are produced from a zygote in the sexual phase of certain sporozoans.

spo·ro·phore (spôr′ə-fôr′, spō′rə-fōr′), ***n.*** [*sporo-* + *-phore*], an organ or branch which bears spores.

spo·ro·phyll, spo·ro·phyl (spôr′ə-fil, spō′rə-fil), ***n.*** [*sporo-* + *-phyll*], a leaf or leaflike part producing spores or sporangia.

spo·ro·phyte (spôr′ə-fīt′, spō′rə-fīt′), ***n.*** [*sporo-* + *-phyte*], the form bearing asexual spores, in plants having alternation of generations: cf. **gametophyte.**

-spor·ous (spôr′əs, spō′rəs), [< *spore* + *-ous*], a combining form meaning *having* (a specified number or kind of) *spores*, as in *monosporous*.

spo·ro·zo·an (spôr′ə-zō′ən, spō′rə-zō′ən), ***adj.*** [< Mod. L. *Sporozoa*, name of the group; see SPORO- & -ZOA], of or belonging to a group of one-celled parasites which pass through phases of both sexual generation and asexual generation, during which sporogenesis takes place: the organisms of malaria and Texas fever belong to this group. ***n.*** an organism of this group.

spo·ro·zo·ite (spôr′ə-zō′īt, spō′rə-zō′īt), ***n.*** [*sporozoan* + *-ite*], an active spore that is the offspring of the passive spores formed by the division of a zygote, in sporozoans.

spor·ran (spor′ən, spôr′ən), ***n.*** [Gael. *sporan* < LL. *bursa*, a purse], a leather pouch or purse, usually covered with fur or hair, worn hanging from the front of the belt in the dress costume of Scottish Highlanders.

sport (spôrt, spōrt), ***n.*** [ME. *sporte;* contr. of *disport*], 1. any activity or experience that gives enjoyment or recreation; pastime; diversion. 2. such an activity requiring more or less vigorous bodily exertion and carried on according to some traditional form or set of rules, whether outdoors, as football, hunting, golf, racing, etc., or indoors, as basketball, bowling, squash, etc. 3. fun; play: as, it was great *sport* to play in the surf. 4. *a*) a thing joked about; object of ridicule; laughingstock. *b*) a thing played with; plaything. 5. [Colloq.], a gambler. 6. [Colloq.], *a*) a person who has sportsmanlike or sporting characteristics: as, be a *sport! b*) a person judged according to his ability to take loss, defeat, teasing, etc.: as, is he a good or a poor *sport?* 7. [Colloq.], a gay, fast, showy person; flashy fellow. 8. [Obs.], amorous trifling or play. 9. in *biology*, a plant or animal showing some marked variation from the normal type. 10. in *botany*, a bud variation. ***v.t.*** 1. [Colloq.], to wear or display, especially with unnecessary show: as, he is *sporting* a loud suit. 2. [Obs.], to amuse (oneself, etc.). ***v.i.*** 1. to play or frolic. 2. to engage in a sport or sports (senses 1 & 2). 3. *a*) to joke or jest. *b*) to make sport; trifle. 4. [Archaic], to engage in amorous trifling or play. 5. in *biology*, to vary markedly from the normal type; mutate. 6. in *botany*, to show bud variation. ***adj.*** 1. of or for sports. 2. suitable for informal, casual wear; not dressy: said of clothes. —***SYN.*** see **play.**

in (or **for**) **sport,** in joke or jest; not in earnest.

make sport of, to mock or ridicule; poke fun at.

sport (or **sports**) **car,** a low, small automobile, typically an open car with a high-compression engine and seats for two.

sport·ful (spôrt′fəl, spōrt′fəl), ***adj.*** full of sport or merriment; playful.

sport·i·ly (spôr′t′l-i, spōr′t′l-i), ***adv.*** in a sporty manner.

sport·i·ness (spôr′ti-nis, spōr′ti-nis), ***n.*** the quality of being sporty.

sport·ing (spôr′tiŋ, spōr′tiŋ), ***adj.*** 1. of or having to do with sports, or athletic games, etc. 2. interested in or taking part in sports, or athletic games, etc. 3. sportsmanlike; fair. 4. interested in or having to do with games, races, etc. characterized by gambling or betting.

sporting chance, [Colloq.], a fair chance, involving loss in case of failure.

sporting house, [Colloq.], 1. a gambling house. 2. a house of prostitution; brothel.

spor·tive (spôr′tiv, spōr′tiv), ***adj.*** 1. fond of or full of sport or merriment; playful. 2. of, or having the nature of, sport, especially outdoor sport. 3. done in fun or playfully, not in earnest. 4. [Obs.], amorous.

sports (spôrts, spōrts), ***adj.*** sport: as, *sports* clothes.

sports·man (spôrts′mən, spōrts′mən), ***n.*** [*pl.* SPORTSMEN (-mən)], 1. a man who is interested in or takes part in sports, especially hunting, fishing, horse racing, etc. 2. a person who can take loss or defeat without complaint, or victory without gloating, and who treats his opponents with fairness, generosity, courtesy, etc.

sports·man·like (spôrts′mən-līk′, spōrts′mən-līk′), ***adj.*** characteristic of or befitting a sportsman.

sports·man·ly (spôrts′mən-li, spōrts′mən-li), ***adj.*** sportsmanlike.

sports·man·ship (spôrts′mən-ship′, spōrts′mən-ship′), ***n.*** [see -SHIP], 1. skill in or fondness for sports. 2. qualities and behavior befitting a sportsman.

sports·wear (spôrts′wâr′, spōrts′wâr′), ***n.*** sport clothes.

sports·wom·an (spôrts′woom′ən, spōrts′woom′ən), ***n.*** [*pl.* SPORTSWOMEN (-wim′ən)], a woman who is interested in or takes part in sports: cf. **sportsman.**

sport·y (spôr′ti, spōr′ti), ***adj.*** [SPORTIER (-ti-ẽr), SPORTIEST (-ti-ist)], [Colloq.], 1. sporting or sportsmanlike. 2. characteristic of a sport or sporting man; hence, 3. loud, flashy, or showy, as clothes.

spor·u·late (spôr′yoo-lāt′), ***v.i.*** [SPORULATED (-id), SPORULATING], to undergo sporulation.

spor·u·la·tion (spôr′yoo-lā′shən), ***n.*** in *biology*, the formation of spores, especially by multiple fission after encystment.

spor·ule (spôr′ūl), ***n.*** [Mod. L. *sporula*, dim. of *spora*] a small spore or, sometimes, any spore.

spot (spot), ***n.*** [ME.; prob. < MD. *spotte;* akin to ON *spotti*, small piece (of ground)], 1. a small area that i[s] different, as in color or texture, from the background o[r] main area of which it is a part; often, a mark made b[y] some foreign matter; stain; mark; blot; speck; patch 2. a flaw or defect, as in character or reputation something blameworthy; fault. 3. a locality; place as, there's a good fishing *spot* in the middle of the lake 4. a salt-water food fish having a black spot behind th[e] shoulders. 5. [British Colloq.], a small quantity bit: as, let's have a *spot* of lunch. 6. [Slang], a spot light. 7. [Slang], position; situation: as, he's got a goo[d] *spot* with that firm; hence, 8. [Slang], position or plac[e] in a schedule or listing: as, he has one of the best *spot* in radio. ***v.t.*** [SPOTTED (-id), SPOTTING], 1. to mar[k] with spots. 2. to sully; stain; blemish. 3. to mark fo[r] future consideration. 4. to place in or on a given spo[t] or spots; locate: as, the officer *spotted* his men at stra tegic points. 5. to remove (individual spots, marks etc.), as in dry cleaning. 6. [Colloq.], to detect; see recognize; pick out: as, I couldn't *spot* her in th[e] crowd. 7. [Colloq.], to allow as an advantage or handi cap: as, I *spotted* him two points. ***v.i.*** 1. to becom[e] marked with spots: as, this fabric will not *spot* in th[e] rain. 2. to cause a spot or spots; make a stain, as ink water, etc. ***adj.*** 1. *a*) that can be paid out or delivere[d] immediately; ready: as, *spot* cash. *b*) involving im mediate payment of cash. *c*) engaged in cash trans actions only. 2. made at random: as, a *spot* check 3. *a*) broadcast from a local radio station. *b*) inserte[d] between regular radio programs: said of advertisement or announcements.

hit the high spots, [Colloq.], to treat only the mai[n] points of a topic, as in a rapid or cursory discussio[n]

hit the spot, [Colloq.], to satisfy a craving or need.

in a spot, [Slang], in a bad situation; in trouble.

on the spot, 1. on or at the locality or place men tioned. 2. at once; immediately. 3. [Slang], i[n] trouble or difficulty. 4. [Slang], in a position wher[e] something, as a reply, is expected of one. 5. [Slang] in danger, especially in danger of death by murde[r]

touch a (or **one's**) **sore spot,** [Colloq.], to touch upon [a] point or subject about which one is sensitive.

spot·less (spot′lis), ***adj.*** 1. having no spots; perfectl[y] clean. 2. having no faults or defects, as in character; irreproachable.

spot·light (spot'līt'), *n.* 1. a strong beam of light used to illuminate prominently a particular person, thing, or group, as on the stage of a theater. 2. a lamp used to project such a beam of light. 3. public notice or prominence. 4. an accessory light with a strong focused beam, attached to an automobile, usually at the side of the windshield, so that the driver can direct the beam in any direction by moving an inward-projecting shaft or handle.

Spot·syl·va·ni·a (spot'sil-vā'ni-ə, spot's'l-vān'yə), *n.* a village in northeastern Virginia: a battle (1864) of the Civil War was fought there between Grant and Lee.

spot·ta·ble (spot'ə-b'l), *adj.* that can be spotted.

spot·ted (spot'id), *adj.* 1. marked with spots. 2. stained; blemished; sullied.

spotted adder, the milk snake.

spotted crake, a small European bird of the rail family, resembling the American sora.

spotted crane's-bill (krānz'bil'), the wild geranium.

spotted fever, any of various febrile diseases accompanied with skin eruptions; especially, typhus, cerebrospinal meningitis, or Rocky Mountain spotted fever.

spot·ter (spot'ẽr), *n.* a person or thing that spots; specifically, *a)* a detective or any person hired to watch for dishonesty among employees, as in a bank. *b)* a person whose duty is to keep a lookout for, and report the position of, the enemy: as, an aircraft *spotter*. *c)* a device used on railroads to mark automatically irregularities in the roadbed. *d)* a person whose duty is to determine for a gunner or gun crew the position of a target and the relative closeness to it of the projectiles fired. *e)* a person whose work is removing spots, etc. in dry cleaning.

spot·ti·ly (spot''l-i), *adv.* in a spotty manner.

spot·ti·ness (spot'i-nis), *n.* the quality or condition of being spotty.

spot·ty (spot'i), *adj.* [SPOTTIER (-i-ẽr), SPOTTIEST (-i-ist)], 1. having, occurring in, or marked with spots. 2. not uniform or consistent; irregular, as in quality; uneven.

spous·al (spou'z'l), *n.* [aphetic for *espousal;* ME. *spousaille;* OFr. *espousaile*], 1. [Obs.], wedlock. 2. *often pl.* [Archaic], a marriage ceremony; nuptials. *adj.* of marriage; nuptial.

spouse (spouz, spous), *n.* [ME. *spus;* OFr. *espous* < L. *sponsus,* betrothed, pp. of *spondere,* to promise solemnly], a partner in marriage; either member of a married couple spoken of in relation to the other. *v.t.* [SPOUSED (spouzd, spoust), SPOUSING], [Archaic], 1. to marry; take as one's spouse. 2. to join or give in marriage.

spout (spout), *n.* [ME. *spute, spoute* < the *v.*], 1. a pipe, orifice, or projection (as on a teapot, sprinkling can, or pitcher) by which a liquid is poured or discharged. 2. a stream, jet, or discharge of or as of liquid from a spout. 3. a waterspout. 4. a small elevator formerly used by pawnbrokers to carry up pawned articles for storage; hence, 5. [Slang], a pawnbroker's establishment. *v.t.* [ME. *sputen, spouten,* to spout, vomit < MD. *spuiten,* to spout; prob. < base of *spit, spew*], 1. to shoot out (liquid, etc.) from or as from a spout: as, a whale *spouted* water high in the air. 2. to speak or utter in a loud, pompous, oratorical manner. 3. [Slang], to pawn. *v.i.* 1. to flow or shoot out with force in a jet: said of liquid, etc. 2. to discharge liquid, etc. from or as from a spout. 3. to spout words or speeches.
  up the spout, [Slang], 1. in pawn. 2. in straits; lost; ruined.

spp., species (*pl.* of **specie**).

S.P.Q.R., *Senatus Populusque Romanus,* [L.], the Senate and the Roman people.

sprad·dle (sprad''l), *v.t. & v.i.* [SPRADDLED (-'ld), SPRADDLING], [< a merging of *spread & straddle*], [Dial. or Colloq.], to spread (the legs) so as to span or straddle.

sprag (sprag), *n.* [via dial.; prob. < ON.; cf. Dan. *sprag,* a twig < base of *sprage,* to crack, crackle; for IE. base see SPARK], 1. a roof prop used in a coal mine. 2. a piece of wood, etc. used to block the wheel of a vehicle or to prevent a vehicle from rolling backward on a grade.

sprain (sprān), *v.t.* [OFr. *espreindre,* to force out, strain; LL. **expremere,* for L. *exprimere;* see EXPRESS], to wrench or twist a ligament or muscle of (a joint, as the ankle) without dislocating the bones. *n.* 1. an act of spraining. 2. an injury resulting from this, characterized by swelling, pain, and disablement of the joint.

sprang (spraŋ), alternative past tense of **spring.**

sprat (sprat), *n.* [< ME. *sprotte;* AS. *sprot;* akin to LG. *sprotte;* prob. < base of AS. *sprytlan,* to come forth, sprout; cf. SPRIT, SPROUT], 1. a small European fish of the herring family. 2. any of several other small herrings.

sprawl (sprôl), *v.i.* [ME. *spraulen;* AS. *spreawlian,* to move convulsively; akin to Norw. dial. *sprala;* prob. IE. base **sp(h)er-,* to strew, sprinkle, scatter, spring forth, etc.; cf. SPRAY (mist)], 1. to spread the limbs in a relaxed, awkward, or unnatural position. 2. to sit or lie in such a position: as, the wounded man *sprawled* in his chair. 3. to crawl in an awkward, ungainly way. 4. to spread awkwardly or without a regular pattern; take up more space than is necessary, as handwriting, a line of men, etc. *v.t.* to cause to sprawl. *n.* a sprawling movement or position.

sprawl·y (sprôl'i), *adj.* [SPRAWLIER (-i-ẽr), SPRAWLIEST (-i-ist)], sprawling or tending to sprawl.

spray (sprā), *n.* [prob. < LG.; cf. *sprei,* spray, drizzle; for IE. base see SPRAWL], 1. a cloud or mist of fine liquid particles, as of water from breaking waves. 2. *a)* a jet of fine liquid particles, as from an atomizer or spray gun. *b)* liquid, as perfume or insecticide, used in such a device. 3. a device for shooting out such a jet or jets. 4. something likened to a spray (senses 1. & 2*a*): as, a *spray* of gunfire. *v.t.* [cf. MD. *sprayen,* to sprinkle], 1. to direct a spray upon; treat with a spray. 2. to shoot out in a spray: as, he *sprayed* paint on the wall. *v.i.* 1. to scatter or shoot out a spray. 2. to scatter or shoot out in a spray.

spray (sprā), *n.* [ME. *sprai, spraye;* for IE. base see SPARK], 1. a small branch or sprig of a tree or plant, with leaves, berries, flowers, etc. 2. a design or ornament like this.

spray gun, a device that shoots out a spray of liquid, as paint or insecticide, by air pressure.

spread (spred), *v.t.* [SPREAD, SPREADING], [ME. *spreden, spredden;* AS. *sprædan;* akin to G. *spreiten;* IE. **sprei-d-,* to sprinkle, strew < base **sp(h)er-,* seen also in Eng. *sprawl,* etc.], 1. to draw out so as to display more fully; open out or expand so as to cover more space; unfold; unfurl. 2. to lay out in display; exhibit. 3. to stretch out (the fingers, arms, legs, wings, etc.); extend. 4. to distribute over a surface or area; scatter; disperse. 5. *a)* to distribute in a thin layer; smear: as, she *spread* butter on the toast. *b)* to cover by smearing with a thin layer of something: as, *spread* this slice with jelly. 6. to extend over a certain period of time; prolong: as, the bank *spread* the payments on the loan over eighteen months. 7. to cause to be widely or more widely known, felt, existent, etc.; disseminate; propagate; diffuse: as, radio *spreads* news quickly, unsanitary conditions *spread* disease. 8. to cover, overlay, or deck with something. 9. *a)* to set (a table) for a meal. *b)* to set (food) on a table. 10. to push apart or farther apart. 11. to record in full; recount. 12. to flatten out, as the end of a rivet by hammering. *v.i.* 1. to extend itself; be extended or expanded. 2. to become distributed or dispersed. 3. to be made widely or more widely known, felt, existent, etc.; be disseminated, propagated, or diffused. 4. to be pushed apart or farther apart. 5. to be of such consistency that it can be distributed in a thin layer, as butter; admit of being smeared. *n.* 1. the act of spreading; extension; expansion; diffusion. 2. the extent to which something is spread or can be spread. 3. an expanse; extent; stretch; compass. 4. *a)* two facing pages of a newspaper, magazine, etc., treated as a single continuous sheet, as in advertising. *b)* printed matter set across the page of a newspaper, magazine, etc., or across several columns. 5. a cloth cover for a table, bed, etc. 6. any soft substance, as jam, butter, etc., used for spreading on bread. 7. [Colloq.], a meal, especially one with a wide variety of food. 8. [Colloq.], a pretentious display. 9. in *aeronautics,* wing span. 10. in *rummy,* etc., a set of three or four cards of the same denomination, or three or more cards of the same suit and consecutive denominations.
  spread oneself, [Colloq.], 1. to exert oneself in order to make a good impression, etc. 2. to show off; brag.
  spread oneself thin, to try to do too many things at once.

spread-ea·gle (spred'ē'g'l), *adj.* 1. having the figure of an eagle with wings and legs spread. 2. [Colloq.], boastful; bombastic: said especially of a type of patriotism. *v.t.* [SPREAD-EAGLED (-g'ld), SPREAD-EAGLING], to stretch out in the form of a spread eagle, as for a flogging. *v.i.* to perform a spread eagle (sense 2).

spread eagle, 1. the figure of an eagle with wings and legs spread, used as an emblem of the United States. 2. something resembling or suggesting such a figure, as an acrobatic figure in fancy skating.

spread·er (spred'ẽr), *n.* a person or thing that spreads; specifically, *a)* a knifelike utensil for spreading butter, etc. *b)* a contrivance for scattering something: as, a manure *spreader*. *c)* a device, as a bar, for keeping apart wires, stays, or the like.

Spree (shprā), *n.* a river in eastern Prussia, Germany, flowing into the Havel River: length, 220 mi.

spree (sprē), *n.* [late 18th-c. slang, for earlier *spray*], 1. a lively, noisy frolic. 2. a drinking bout; period of drunkenness.

sprig (sprig), *n.* [ME. *sprigge;* prob. < base seen in *spray* (sprig), *spark*, etc.], 1. a little twig or spray. 2. a design or ornament like this. 3. a small, headless brad. 4. a small, three-cornered piece of tin or zinc used to hold a pane of glass in the sash. 5. a young fellow; stripling. 6. a person as the offspring or scion of a family, institution, class, etc.: used humorously. *v.t.* [SPRIGGED (sprigd), SPRIGGING], 1. to remove a sprig or sprigs from (a bush, tree, etc.). 2. to mark or decorate with a design of sprigs. 3. to fasten with small, headless brads.

sprig·gy (sprig′i), *adj.* [SPRIGGIER (-i-ẽr), SPRIGGIEST (-i-ist)], 1. having many sprigs, as a plant. 2. suggestive of a sprig or sprigs.

spright·li·ness (sprīt′li-nis), *n.* the quality or state of being sprightly.

spright·ly (sprīt′li), *adj.* [SPRIGHTLIER (-li-ẽr), SPRIGHTLIEST (-li-ist)], [var. of *spritely*], gay; lively; brisk; animated. *adv.* in a sprightly manner. —*SYN.* see **agile, lively.**

spring (spriŋ), *v.i.* [SPRANG (spraŋ) or SPRUNG (spruŋ), SPRUNG, SPRINGING], [ME. *springen;* AS. *springan;* akin to G. *springen;* IE. base **sper^h-*, **sprengh-*, to move quickly, as also in Sans. *spṛhayati*, strive for], 1. to move suddenly and rapidly; specifically, *a)* to move upward or forward from the ground by suddenly contracting the muscles; leap; bound. *b)* to rise suddenly and quickly from or as from a sitting or lying position: as, he *sprang* to his feet. *c)* to move, appear, come, etc. suddenly and quickly; dart: often used figuratively, as, a curse *sprang* to his lips. *d)* to move as a result of resilience; be elastic. 2. to come or arise as from some source; specifically, *a)* to grow or develop: as, the plant *springs* from a seed. *b)* to come as a result: as, this error *springs* from faulty reasoning. *c)* to come into existence: as, cities and towns *sprang* up. *d)* to be descended: as, he *springs* from a famous stock. *e)* [Archaic], to begin to appear, as day; dawn. 3. to explode or discharge: said of a military mine. 4. to become warped, bent, split, cracked, etc.: as, two boards of the siding have *sprung.* 5. to rise up above surrounding objects; tower: as, the church steeple *springs* high above the town. 6. in *architecture,* to rise from the impost with an outward curve. In many senses of the *v.i., spring* is often followed by *up. v.t.* 1. to cause to leap or come forth suddenly: as, we *sprang* a covey of quail. 2. to leap over; vault: as, he *sprang* the wall. 3. to cause to close or snap shut, as by a spring: as, the fox *sprang* the trap. 4. to cause to warp, bend, strain, split, crack, etc., as by force. 5. to cause (a military mine) to explode. 6. to make known or cause to appear suddenly; announce unexpectedly: as, when will you *spring* the news of your marriage? 7. [Slang], to get (someone) released from jail or custody, as by paying bail. *n.* [ME. & AS. *springe*], 1. the act, the ability, an instance, etc. of springing; specifically, *a)* a jump or leap forward or upward, or the distance covered by this. *b)* a sudden darting or flying back. *c)* the ability to do this; resilience; elasticity. 2. a device, as a coil of wire, that returns to its original form after being forced out of shape: springs are used to absorb shock in beds, automobiles, etc., and as the motive power in clocks and similar mechanisms. 3. a flow of water from the ground, the source of a stream; hence, 4. any source, origin, or motive. 5. that season of the year in which plants begin to grow after lying dormant all winter: in the North Temperate Zone, regarded as including the months of March, April, and May: in the astronomical year, that period between the vernal equinox and the summer solstice; hence, 6. any period of beginning or newness: as, the *spring* of his life. 7. a warping, bending, crack, break, etc., as of the mast of a ship. 8. [Archaic], the dawn or dawning, as of day or light. 9. in *architecture,* the line or plane in which an arch rises from its impost. 10. [Scot.], a gay, lively song or dance. *adj.* 1. of, for, appearing in, or planted in the spring. 2. of or acting like a spring; elastic; resilient. 3. having, or supported on, a spring or springs: as, a *spring* mattress. 4. coming from a spring: as, *spring* water. —*SYN.* see **rise.**

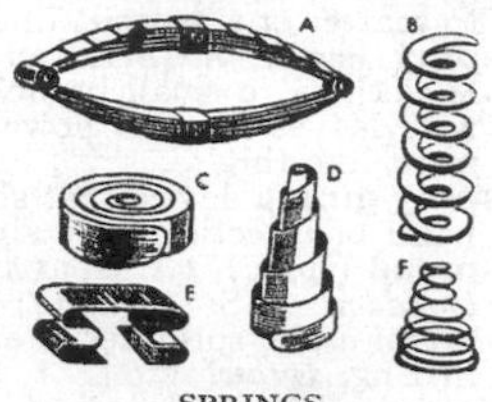

SPRINGS
A, leaf; B, spiral; C, coil; D, volute; E, flat; F, spiral

spring a leak, to begin to leak suddenly.

spring·al (spriŋ′əl), *n.* [Scot. *springel, springald;* prob. < *spring, v.*], [Archaic], an active young man; youth.

spring·ald (spriŋ′əld), *n.* [Archaic], a springal.

spring beauty, any of a number of related small, spring-blooming plants with white or pinkish flowers.

spring·board (spriŋ′bôrd′, spriŋ′bōrd′), *n.* 1. a flexible, springy board used by acrobats, gymnasts, etc. as a take-off in performing various feats of leaping. 2. a somewhat flexible board projecting over water, used as a take-off in diving: usually called *diving board.*

spring·bok (spriŋ′bok′), *n.* [*pl.* SPRINGBOK, SPRINGBOKS (-boks′); see PLURAL, II, D, 2], [D. < *springen,* to spring + *bok,* a buck], a South African gazelle that jumps high into the air when frightened.

spring·buck (spriŋ′buk′), *n.* [*pl.* SPRINGBUCK, SPRINGBUCKS (-buks′); see PLURAL, II, D, 2], a springbok.

spring chicken, 1. a young chicken, especially one only a few months old, used for broiling or frying. 2. [Slang], a person, especially a woman, who is young, inexperienced, naive, etc.

springe (sprinj), *n.* [ME. *sprenge* < AS. *sprengan,* to cause to spring, caus. of *springan,* to spring; cf. SPRING], a snare consisting of a noose attached to something under tension, as a bent tree branch. *v.t.* [SPRINGED (sprinjd), SPRINGEING], to snare in a springe. *v.i.* to set springes.

spring·er (spriŋ′ẽr), *n.* 1. a person or thing that springs. 2. a springer spaniel. 3. a springbok. 4. a grampus. 5. a spring chicken. 6. in *architecture, a)* the support upon which an arch rests; impost. *b)* the lowest stone or lowest part of an arch.

springer spaniel, a breed of large field spaniel, used for flushing, or springing, game.

spring fever, the feeling of laziness and listlessness or restlessness that many people have during the first warm, sunny days of spring.

Spring·field (spriŋ′fēld′), *n.* 1. a city in Massachusetts, on the Connecticut River: pop., 174,000. 2. a city in central Illinois: its capital: pop., 83,000. 3. a city in west central Ohio: pop., 83,000. 4. a city in southwestern Missouri: pop., 96,000.

Springfield rifle, [< *Springfield,* Mass., location of a U. S. armory], a .30-caliber, breech-loading, magazine-fed rifle, operated by a bolt, adopted for use by the United States Army in 1903 and replaced as the standard infantry weapon by the Garand rifle in World War II.

spring·halt (spriŋ′hôlt′), *n.* stringhalt.

spring·head (spriŋ′hed′), *n.* a source or fountainhead.

spring·house (spriŋ′hous′), *n.* a small building enclosing a spring or brook, used for cooling milk, etc.

spring·i·ly (spriŋ′ə-li), *adv.* in a springy manner.

spring·i·ness (spriŋ′i-nis), *n.* the quality or condition of being springy.

spring·let (spriŋ′lit), *n.* a small spring of water.

spring lock, a lock in which the bolt is shot automatically by a spring.

spring·tail (spriŋ′tāl′), *n.* a small, wingless insect with two stiff tail bristles which can be bent under and suddenly straightened out to effect a vaulting leap.

spring·tide (spriŋ′tīd′), *n.* springtime.

spring tide, 1. a tide occurring at or shortly after the new and the full moon: it is normally the highest tide of the month. 2. any great flow, rush, or flood.

spring·time (spriŋ′tīm′), *n.* 1. the season of spring; spring of the year; springtide. 2. a period or time resembling or suggesting spring; earliest period.

spring·y (spriŋ′i), *adj.* [SPRINGIER (-i-ẽr), SPRINGIEST (-i-ist)], 1. having spring; flexible; elastic; resilient. 2. having many springs of water.

sprin·kle (spriŋ′k'l), *v.t.* [SPRINKLED (-k'ld), SPRINKLING], [ME. *sprinklen, sprenklen* < *sprengen,* to scatter (cf. SPRINGE) < base of AS. *springan;* cf. SPRING], 1. to scatter in drops or particles, as water or sand. 2. to scatter drops or particles upon; cover or strew with a sprinkling. *v.i.* 1. to scatter something in drops or particles. 2. to fall in drops or particles; specifically, 3. to rain lightly or infrequently. *n.* 1. the act of sprinkling. 2. a light rain.

SYN.—to **sprinkle** is to cause to fall in small drops or particles (to *sprinkle* water, to *sprinkle* sugar over berries); to **scatter** is to disperse the units of a group in different directions, usually in an irregular distribution (the wind *scattered* the papers on the desk); to **strew** is to scatter, either regularly or irregularly, especially so as to more or less cover a surface (to *strew* sawdust on a floor).

sprin·kler system (spriŋ′klẽr), 1. a system of pipes and attached nozzles or sprinklers carrying water or other extinguishing fluid to the various parts of a building, etc.: the system is usually made to operate automatically in the presence of great heat. 2. a system of pipes and nozzles used for watering a lawn, garden, greenhouse, golf course, etc.

sprin·kling (spriŋ′kliŋ), *n.* 1. a small number, quantity, or amount, especially one that is sprinkled, scattered, or thinly distributed. 2. the act of a person or thing that sprinkles.

sprint (sprint), *v.i.* [ME. *sprenten,* to leap, run < Anglo-N. **sprenta;* cf. ON. *spretta,* to run], to run or race at full speed, especially for a short distance. *v.t.* to traverse by sprinting. *n.* 1. the act of sprinting. 2. a short race at full speed. 3. a brief period of intense activity.

sprit (sprit), *n.* [ME. *spret;* AS. *sprēot,* a sprout or pole; akin to G. *spriet* (< D.); for IE. base see SPREAD], 1. a pole or spar extended diagonally upward from a mast to the topmost corner of a fore-and-aft sail, serving to extend the sail. 2. a bowsprit.

sprite (sprīt), *n.* [ME. *sprit;* OFr. *esprit* or *esperit(e);* L.

spiritus; see SPIRIT], 1. an elf, pixie, fairy, or goblin. 2. [Archaic], a ghost.

sprit·sail (sprit′sāl′; *in nautical usage,* sprit′s'l), *n.* a sail extended by a sprit.

sprock·et (sprok′it), *n.* [Early Mod. Eng.; prob. < a LG. source; base prob. as in *sprag*], 1. any of a number of teeth or points, as on the rim of a wheel, arranged to fit into the links of a chain. 2. a sprocket wheel.

sprocket wheel, a wheel fitted with sprockets on its outer rim, used in a chain drive.

sprout (sprout), *v.i.* [ME. *sprouten, spruten* < AS. *sprutan;* akin to G. *spriessen;* IE. base **spreu-d* < ult. base in *spread,* etc.], 1. to begin to grow or germinate; give off shoots or buds. 2. to grow or develop rapidly. *v.t.* 1. to cause to sprout or grow. 2. to remove sprouts from. *n.* [ME. *sprute* < the *v.*], 1. a young growth on a plant, as a stem or branch; shoot. 2. a new growth from a bud, rootstock, germinating seed, etc. 3. something like or suggestive of a sprout, as an offshoot or scion. 4. *pl.* Brussels sprouts.

SPROCKET WHEEL

spruce (sprōōs), *n.* [ME. *Spruce,* for *Pruce,* Prussia; ML. *Prussia;* prob. so called because the tree was first known as a native of Prussia], 1. any of a number of related evergreen trees with needle-shaped leaves and drooping cones or berrylike fruit. 2. the wood of any of these trees.

spruce (sprōōs), *adj.* [< ME. *Spruce,* for *Pruce,* Prussia, esp. in the phr. *Spruce leather,* this leather having been regarded as particularly fine and elegant], neat; trim; smart; dapper. *v.t. & v.i.* [SPRUCED (sprōōst), SPRUCING], to make or become spruce (usually with *up*).

spruce beer, a fermented beverage made with an extract of spruce leaves and twigs.

sprue (sprōō), *n.* [D. *spruw, sprouw*], a chronic tropical disease characterized by anemia, gastrointestinal disorders, sore throat, etc.; psilosis.

sprue (sprōō), *n.* [< ?], in *founding,* 1. an opening through which molten metal is poured into the mold. 2. the waste piece of metal cast in such an opening.

sprung (spruŋ), past participle and alternative past tense of **spring.**

sprung rhythm, [term invented by G. M. Hopkins (1844–1889), Eng. poet], in *prosody,* a kind of rhythm characterized by different types of feet of equal time length, stressed always on the first syllable: the feet may differ in number of syllables.

spry (sprī), *adj.* [SPRIER or SPRYER (-ẽr), SPRIEST or SPRYEST (-ist)], [< Brit. dial. *sprey, spree, spry,* etc.; of ON. origin; cf. Sw. *sprygg,* lively; base as in Eng. *spark*], full of life; active; nimble; brisk. —*SYN.* see **agile.**

spt., seaport.

spud (spud), *n.* [ME. *spudde;* prob. < ON.; cf. Dan. *spyd,* a spear; base as in *spit* (a rod); sense 3 from the use of the implement in potato digging], 1. a sharp, spadelike tool used for rooting out weeds. 2. a spudder. 3. [Colloq.], a potato. *v.t.* [SPUDDED (-id), SPUDDING], to dig up with a spud.

spud·der (spud′ẽr), *n.* [< *spud* + *-er*], a heavy bar with a chisel point, used for removing bark from trees.

spue (spū), *v.t. & v.i.* [SPUED (spūd), SPUING], to spew.

spume (spūm), *n.* [ME.; OFr. *espume;* L. *spuma* < *spuere,* to spit out], foam, froth, or scum. *v.i. & v.t.* [SPUMED (spūmd), SPUMING], to foam or froth.

spu·mes·cence (spyoo-mes′'ns), *n.* [see SPUMESCENT], the state of being frothy or foamy.

spu·mes·cent (spyoo-mes′'nt), *adj.* [L. *spumescens,* ppr. of *spumescere,* to grow frothy < *spuma;* see SPUME], 1. like froth or foam. 2. frothing; foaming.

spu·mo·ne (spə-mō′ni; It. spōō-mô′ne), *n.* spumoni.

spu·mo·ni (spə-mō′ni), *n.* [It., pl. of *spumone*], an Italian frozen dessert made of various layers of smooth ice cream, often containing candied fruits and pistachio nuts: also **spumone.**

spu·mous (spū′məs), *adj.* [ME.; L. *spumosus* < *spuma;* see SPUME], of, like, or covered with froth or foam.

spum·y (spūm′i), *adj.* [SPUMIER (-i-ẽr), SPUMIEST (-i-ist)], spumous.

spun (spun), past tense and past participle of **spin.** *adj.* formed by or as if by spinning.

spun glass, fine glass fiber, made by forming liquid glass into a thread.

spunk (spuŋk), *n.* [Ir. *sponc,* tinder, touchwood, sponge; Gael. *sponc* < L. *spongia,* a sponge], 1. a kind of wood or fungus that takes fire easily; punk; tinder. 2. [British Dial.], a spark or small flame. 3. [Colloq.], courage; spirit; pluck; mettle. *v.i.* to flare up; kindle.

spunk·i·ly (spuŋ′kə-li), *adv.* [Colloq.], in a spunky manner.

spunk·i·ness (spuŋ′ki-nis), *n.* [Colloq.], the quality or state of being spunky.

spunk·y (spuŋ′ki), *adj.* [SPUNKIER (-ki-ẽr), SPUNKIEST (-ki-ist)], [Colloq.], having spunk; courageous; spirited.

spun silk, a kind of yarn made from silk floss or waste.

spun sugar, melted sugar, usually with coloring added, that is drawn out into threadlike form and gathered into fluffy balls to be eaten as a confection.

spun yarn, in *nautical usage,* a line made of several rope yarns twisted together.

spur (spũr), *n.* [ME. *spure;* AS. *spura, spora;* akin to G. *sporn;* IE. base **sp(h)er-,* to jerk, seen also in Sans. *sphurāti,* (he) kicks away, L. *spernere,* lit., to push away], 1. any of several kinds of pointed devices worn on the heel by horsemen, used to urge the horse forward. 2. anything that urges, impels, or incites; stimulus. 3. something like a spur; specifically, *a)* a spinelike process on the wings or legs of certain birds. *b)* a climbing iron, as used by lumberjacks. *c)* a sharp metal device attached to the leg of a gamecock, for injuring the other bird in a cockfight. *d)* a short, stunted, or projecting branch or shoot of a tree, etc. *e)* ergot of rye. 4. a ridge, range, or lesser elevation projecting in a lateral direction from the main mass of a mountain or mountain range. 5. *a)* a griffe. *b)* a buttress, as of masonry, or any similar offset from a wall or other part of a structure. *c)* a short wooden reinforcing piece; brace; strut. 6. a spur track. 7. in *botany,* a slender, tubelike structure formed by an extension of one or more petals or sepals, as in columbine or larkspur. *v.t.* [SPURRED (spũrd), SPURRING], 1. to strike or prick with a spur or spurs; hence, 2. to urge; incite; stimulate. 3. to provide with a spur or spurs. 4. to strike or injure as with a spur (sense *3c*). *v.i.* 1. to spur a horse. 2. to hurry; hasten.—*SYN.* see **motive.**

HORSEMAN'S SPUR

on the spur of the moment, hastily and abruptly; without forethought or preparation.

win one's spurs, to attain distinction or honor, especially for the first time; establish one's reputation.

spurge (spũrj), *n.* [ME.; OFr. *espurge* < *espurger,* to purge; L. *expurgare;* see EXPURGATE], any of a group of related plants including fleshy, shrubby, and herblike types, all having a milky juice; euphorbia.

spur gear, 1. a gear wheel having radial teeth parallel to the axle. 2. a system of gearing having this kind of gear wheel: also **spur gearing.**

spurge laurel, an evergreen shrub with yellowish-green flowers, oblong leaves, and poisonous berries, found in Europe and Asia.

spu·ri·ous (spyoor′i-əs), *adj.* [L. *spurius*], 1. illegitimate; bastard. 2. false; counterfeit; not genuine. 3. in *botany,* false; like in appearance but unlike in structure or function. —*SYN.* see **artificial.**

spurn (spũrn), *v.t.* [ME. *spurnen;* AS. *spurnan,* to spurn, kick; for IE. base see SPUR], 1. to push or drive away contemptuously with or as with the foot. 2. to refuse or reject with contempt or disdain; scorn. *v.i.* to show contempt or disdain in refusing or rejecting. *n.* 1. a kick. 2. a spurning; scornful refusal.—*SYN.* see **decline.**

SPUR GEAR

spurred (spũrd), *adj.* having, wearing, or fitted with spurs or spurlike parts.

spur·rer (spũr′ẽr), *n.* a person or thing that spurs.

spur·ri·er (spũr′i-ẽr), *n.* a person who makes spurs.

spur·ry, spur·rey (spũr′i), *n.* [D. *spurrie;* ? < ML. *spergula*], 1. a weed with white flowers and threadlike leaves. 2. any of a number of related chickweeds.

spurt (spũrt), *v.t.* [prob. < ME. *sprutten, spritten,* to sprout, spring forth; AS. *spryttan* < base of *sprutan;* see SPROUT], to shoot forth suddenly in a stream or gushing flow; squirt; jet. *v.i.* 1. to gush forth in a stream or jet. 2. to show a sudden, brief burst of energy or spell of activity: as, the runners *spurted* in the last lap. *n.* 1. a sudden gushing or shooting forth; jet. 2. a sudden, brief burst of energy or spell of activity. Also spelled **spirt.**

spur track, a short side track connected with the main track of a railroad: also **spur.**

spur wheel, a spur gear.

sput·nik (spoot′nik, sput′nik), *n.* [Russ.; lit., co-traveler], an artificial satellite of the earth, especially [often S–], any of those put into orbit by the U.S.S.R. beginning in October, 1957.

sput·ter (sput′ẽr), *v.i.* [< *spout* + *-er,* freq. suffix; cf. D. *sputteren*], 1. to spit out drops of saliva, bits of food, etc. in an explosive manner, as when talking excitedly;

splutter. 2. to speak hastily in a confused, explosive manner. 3. to eject bits or drops of something in an explosive manner, with sharp sizzling or spitting sounds, as burning wood, frying fat, etc. ***v.t.*** 1. to spit or throw out (bits or drops) in an explosive manner. 2. to utter by sputtering. ***n.*** 1. a sputtering. 2. the noise of sputtering. 3. bits or drops thrown out in sputtering. 4. hasty, confused, explosive utterance.

spu·tum (spū′təm), ***n.*** [*pl.* SPUTA (-tə)], [L., that which is spit out < *spuus*, pp. of *spuere*, to spit; cf. SPIT], 1. saliva; spit. 2. mucus together with saliva, etc., spat out from the mouth.

Spuy·ten Duy·vil (spī′t'n dī′v'l), a creek between Manhattan island and the mainland, connecting the Hudson and Harlem rivers.

spy (spī), ***v.t.*** [SPIED (spīd), SPYING], [ME. *spien, espien;* OFr. *espier* < OHG. *spehōn, spiohōn*, to search out, examine, investigate], 1. to watch or observe closely and secretly, with unfriendly purpose (usually with *out*). 2. to catch sight of; make out; perceive; see. 3. to examine closely; inspect carefully; scrutinize. 4. to discover by close examination, careful inspection, etc. (with *out*). ***v.i.*** 1. to watch or observe closely and secretly; act as a spy. 2. to keep watch. 3. to make a close examination or careful inspection. ***n.*** [*pl.* SPIES (spīz)], 1. a person who keeps close and secret watch on another or others. 2. a person employed by a government to get secret information about the affairs of another or other governments, especially about the armed forces, armaments, war plans, etc., or one who, in time of war, acts as a secret agent to get information for the enemy. 3. a spying.

spy·glass (spī′glas′, spī′gläs′), ***n.*** a small telescope.

Sq., Squadron.

Sq., sq., square.

sq. ft., square foot; square feet.

sq. in., square inch; square inches.

sq. mi., square mile; square miles.

sqq., *sequentes; sequentia*, [L.], the following ones.

sq. r., square rod; square rods.

squab (skwäb, skwôb), ***n.*** [< dial. *squab, adj.*, short and plump; prob. < ON.; cf. Sw. *sqvabb*, loose flesh], 1. a nestling pigeon, still unfledged. 2. a short, stout person. 3. a cushion. 4. a sofa or couch. ***adj.*** 1. newly hatched or not fully fledged. 2. short and stout.

squab·ble (skwäb′'l, skwôb′'l), ***v.i.*** [SQUABBLED (-'ld), SQUABBLING], [< or akin to the Scand. word represented by Sw. *skvabbel*, a dispute], to quarrel noisily over a small matter; wrangle. ***v.t.*** in *printing*, to disarrange (type that has been set) so that letters or lines become mixed. ***n.*** a noisy, petty quarrel or dispute; wrangle. —***SYN.*** see **quarrel.**

squab·by (skwäb′i, skwôb′i), ***adj.*** [SQUABBIER (-i-ẽr), SQUABBIEST (-i-ist)], short and stout.

squad (skwäd, skwôd), ***n.*** [Fr. *escouade;* Sp. *escuadra* (It. *squadra*), a square < LL. **exquadrare*, to form into a square; see SQUARE], 1. a small group of soldiers assembled for inspection, duty, etc.: the smallest military tactical unit, a subdivision of a platoon, normally led by a sergeant (formerly staff sergeant). 2. any small group of people acting together: an athletic team is often called a *squad*. ***v.t.*** [SQUADDED (-id), SQUADDING], 1. to form into a squad or squads. 2. to assign to a squad.

squad car, a police patrol car, now usually equipped with short-wave radio telephone devices for communicating with headquarters.

squad·ron (skwäd′rən, skwôd′rən), ***n.*** [It. *squadrone* < *squadra*, a square; see SQUAD], 1. a group of warships assigned to some special duty; unit or subdivision of a fleet. 2. a unit of cavalry consisting of from two to four troops, a headquarters troop, and certain auxiliary units. 3. a unit of military aviation consisting of two or more flights. 4. any organized body or group. ***v.t.*** to form into a squadron or squadrons.

squal·id (skwäl′id, skwôl′id), ***adj.*** [L. *squalidus* < *squalere*, to be foul or filthy], 1. foul; unclean. 2. wretched; miserable; sordid.

squa·lid·i·ty (skwä-lid′ə-ti, skwô-lid′ə-ti), ***n.*** [L. *squaliditas*], squalor; squalidness.

squall (skwôl), ***n.*** [prob. of Scand. origin], 1. a brief, violent windstorm, usually with rain or snow. 2. [Colloq.], trouble or disturbance. ***v.i.*** to storm briefly; blow a squall.

squall (skwôl), ***v.i. & v.t.*** [prob. of echoic origin], to cry or scream loudly and harshly. ***n.*** a harsh, shrill cry or loud scream.

squall·y (skwôl′i), ***adj.*** [SQUALLIER (-i-ẽr), SQUALLIEST (-i-ist)], 1. characterized by squalls; gusty. 2. threatening; stormy.

squal·or (skwäl′ẽr, skwôl′ẽr; *occas.* skwā′lẽr), ***n.*** [L., foulness; akin to *squalere*, to be filthy], the quality or condition of being squalid; filth and wretchedness.

squa·ma (skwā′mə), ***n.*** [*pl.* SQUAMAE (-mē)], [L., a scale, husk], a scale or scalelike part of an animal or plant.

squa·mate (skwā′māt), ***adj.*** [LL. *squamatus* < L. *squama*, a scale], having or covered with scales; scaly.

squa·ma·tion (skwə-mā′shən), ***n.*** 1. the condition of being squamate. 2. epidermal scale arrangement.

squa·mo- (skwā′mō, skwā′mə), [< L. *squama*, a scale], a combining form meaning *squama*.

squa·mo·sal (skwə-mō′s'l), ***adj.*** 1. squamous. 2. in *zoology*, designating or of a bone in the skull of lower vertebrates analogous to the squamous portion of the temporal bone in man. ***n.*** a squamosal bone.

squa·mose (skwā′mōs, skwə-mōs′), ***adj.*** squamous.

squa·mous (skwā′məs), ***adj.*** [L. *squamosus* < *squama*, a scale], 1. formed of, like, or covered with scales. 2. in *anatomy*, designating or of the thin, scalelike, upper anterior portion of the temporal bone.

squam·u·lose (skwam′yoo-lōs′, skwā′myoo-lōs′), ***adj.*** [Mod. L. *squamulosus* < L. *squamula*, dim. of *squama*, a scale], having, covered with, or consisting of small scales.

squan·der (skwän′dẽr, skwôn′dẽr), ***v.t.*** [prob. a specialized use of dial. *squander*, to scatter, extinguish (a fire), popularized after Shakespeare's *Merchant of Venice*, I, iii, 22], to spend or use wastefully or extravagantly. ***v.i.*** to be wasteful or extravagant. ***n.*** a squandering; wasteful or extravagant expenditure.

square (skwâr), ***n.*** [ME.; OFr. *esquarre;* LL. **exquadra* < **exquadrare*, to make square; L. *ex*, out + *quadrare*, to square < *quadrus*, a square < *quattuor*, four], 1. a plane figure having four equal sides and four right angles. 2. anything having or approximating this shape: as, a *square* of cloth. 3. an area bounded by streets on four sides. 4. the distance along one side of such an area. 5. *a*) an open area bounded by, or at the intersection of, several streets, usually landscaped and used as a park, memorial, etc. *b*) buildings surrounding such an area. 6. a body of troops formed into a square (sense 2). 7. an instrument having two sides that form an angle of 90 degrees, used for laying out or testing right angles. 8. the product of a number or quantity multiplied by itself: as, 9 is the *square* of 3. 9. [Slang], a person who is square (*adj.* 12). 10. [Obs.], a standard, criterion, rule, principle, etc. ***v.t.*** [SQUARED (skwârd), SQUARING], [ME. *squaren;* OFr. *esquarrer;* LL. **exquadrare;* see the *n.*], 1. to make into a form having four equal sides and four right angles; make square. 2. to make into a form having straight sides and right angles; hence, 3. to make or check with regard to straightness or evenness: as, he *squared* the surface with a straightedge. 4. to bring to or near to the form of a right angle or straight line: as, *square* your shoulders. 5. to settle; adjust; make right or even: as, we have *squared* accounts. 6. to adjust or settle the accounts of: as, this money will *square* him. 7. to make equal: as, his touchdown *squared* the score. 8. to adapt; regulate; reconcile; make conform: as, *square* these figures with the latest information. 9. to mark off (a surface) in a series of connected squares. 10. to bring into the correct position, as with reference to a line, course, etc. 11. to multiply (a number or quantity) by itself. 12. to find the number of square units in (an area). 13. [Slang], to bribe. ***v.i.*** 1. to be or fit at right angles. 2. to fit; agree; accord. 3. in *golf*, to even the scores. ***adj.*** [ME.; OFr. *esquarre*, pp. of *esquarrer*], 1. *a*) having four equal sides and four right angles. *b*) more or less cubical; rectangular and three-dimensional, as a box. 2. forming a right angle, or having a rectangular part or parts. 3. correctly adjusted or positioned; straight, level, even, etc. 4. leaving no balance; balanced; even. 5. just; fair; honest; not crooked. 6. clear; direct; straightforward; unequivocal: as, a *square* refusal. 7. *a*) designating or of a unit of surface measure in the form of a square having sides of a specified length. *b*) given or stated in terms of such surface measure. 8. having a shape broad for its length or height, with a solid, sturdy appearance, and somewhat rectangular. 9. having a square or rectangular section, as some files. 10. designating a number that is the product of another number multiplied by itself. 11. [Colloq.], satisfying; solid; substantial: as, a *square* meal. 12. [Slang], not conversant with the current fads, styles, slang, etc.; old-fashioned or unsophisticated. 13. in *nautical usage*, at right angles to the keel and mast, as the yards of a square-rigged ship. ***adv.*** 1. honestly; fairly; justly. 2. so as to be or form a square; in square shape; at right angles. 3. directly; exactly. 4. so as to face. 5. firmly; solidly. Abbreviated **sq., Sq.**

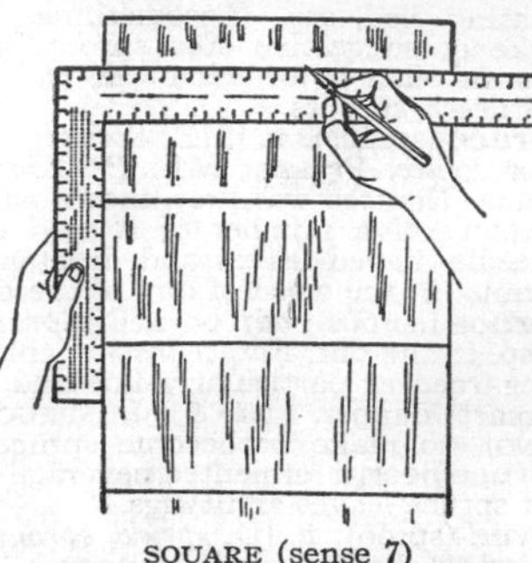

SQUARE (sense 7)

on the square, 1. at right angles (to something specified). 2. [Colloq.], honest; fair; genuine. 3. [Colloq.], honestly; fairly; genuinely.

out of square, 1. not at right angles (with something specified). 2. [Colloq.], not in harmony, order, or agreement. 3. [Colloq.], incorrectly.
square away, 1. to bring a ship's yards around so as to sail directly before the wind. 2. to square off.
square off, to assume a posture of attack or self-defense, as in boxing.
square oneself, [Colloq.], to compensate for a wrong, damage, hurt, etc. done by oneself to another or others; make amends.
square peg in a round hole, a person poorly suited to his job, environment, etc.; misfit.
square the circle, 1. to construct or find a square equal in area to a circle: an insoluble problem. 2. to do or attempt something that seems impossible.
square up, 1. to make a settlement, as by paying, balancing accounts, etc. 2. to assume a posture of opposition (*to* an adversary).

square bracket, in *printing*, a bracket; either of the paired parenthetical marks [ ].

square dance, a dance, as a quadrille, in which the couples are grouped in a given form, as a square.

squared circle, [Colloq.], the boxing ring; prize ring: also **squared ring.**

square deal, [Colloq.], any treatment or dealing that is honest, fair, and just.

square-faced (skwâr′fāst′), *adj.* having a face that is somewhat rectangular in outline.

square·head (skwâr′hed′), *n.* [Slang], 1. a Scandinavian. 2. a German. A vulgar term of contempt.

square knot, a double knot in which the free ends run parallel to the standing parts; reef knot: see **knot,** illus.

square meal, a complete and satisfying meal.

square measure, a system of measuring area, in which 144 square inches = 1 square foot, 9 square feet = 1 square yard, 30 1/4 square yards = 1 square rod, 160 square rods = 1 acre, 640 acres = 1 square mile.

square-rigged (skwâr′rigd′), *adj.* rigged with square sails as the principal sails.

square-rig·ger (skwâr′rig′ẽr), *n.* a square-rigged ship.

square root, the number or quantity which when squared will produce a given number or quantity: as, 3 is the *square root* of 9.

square sail, a four-sided sail rigged on a yard suspended horizontally across the mast.

square shooter, [Colloq.], a person who is honest and just.

square-shoul·dered (skwâr′shōl′dẽrd), *adj.* having an erect posture with the shoulders thrown back.

square-toed (skwâr′tōd′), *adj.* 1. having a broad, square toe: said of a shoe. 2. old-fashioned and narrowly conservative or formal; precise; prim.

square-toes (skwâr′tōz′), *n.* an old-fashioned and narrowly conservative or formal person.

squar·ish (skwâr′ish), *adj.* more nearly square than round; somewhat square.

squar·rose (skwar′ōs, skwä′rōs), *adj.* [L. *squarrosus*], 1. in *botany & zoology*, rough or scaly. 2. in *botany*, stiff and crowded together, as some leaves.

squar·rous (skwar′əs), *adj.* squarrose.

squash (skwäsh, skwôsh), *v.t.* [OFr. *esquasser;* LL. **exquassare* < L. *ex-*, intens. + *quassus*, pp. of *quatere*, to shake, shatter; cf. QUASH, of which the word is often intens.], 1. to beat, press, or squeeze into or as into a soft, flat mass or pulp; crush. 2. to quash; suppress; bring to an abrupt end: as, he tried to *squash* his son's ambition. 3. [Colloq.], to silence or disconcert (another) in a crushing manner. *v.i.* 1. to be squashed, as by a heavy fall, pressure, etc. 2. to make a sound of squashing or splashing. 3. to force one's way; crowd; squeeze. *n.* 1. something easily squashed or crushed. 2. a soft, pulpy mass. 3. a squashing or the fact of being squashed. 4. the sound of squashing. 5. [British], a drink made of fruit juice and other ingredients: as, lemon *squash.* 6. either of two similar games combining elements of both tennis and handball; specifically, *a*) *squash rackets*, played in a walled court with a small racket and a rubber ball. *b*) *squash tennis*, played in a larger court with a larger racket and a livelier ball. *adv.* 1. so as to squash. 2. with a squashing sound.

squash (skwäsh, skwôsh), *n.* [< Am. Ind. (Algonquian); cf. Massachusett *askoot-asquash*, lit., eaten raw], 1. the fleshy fruit of any of various plants of the gourd family, eaten as a vegetable. 2. a plant bearing this fruit.

squash bug, a large, dark-colored insect that attacks squash vines and similar plants.

squash court, a walled court used in playing squash.

squash·i·ly (skwäsh′ə-li, skwôsh′ə-li), *adv.* 1. so as to be squashy. 2. with a squashing sound.

squash·i·ness (skwäsh′i-nis, skwôsh′i-nis), *n.* the quality or condition of being squashy.

squash·y (skwäsh′i, skwôsh′i), *adj.* [SQUASHIER (-i-ẽr), SQUASHIEST (-i-ist)], 1. soft and wet; mushy. 2. easily squashed or crushed. 3. characterized by a squashed appearance.

squat (skwät, skwôt), *v.i.* [SQUATTED (-id), or SQUAT, SQUATTING], [ME. *squatten;* OFr. *esquatir; es-* (L. *ex-*), intens. + *quatir*, to press flat; LL. **coactire* < L. *coactus*, pp. of *cogere*, to force, compress], 1. to sit on the heels with the knees bent. 2. to crouch with the feet drawn in close to the body. 3. to crouch or cower close to the ground, as an animal. 4. to settle on land, especially public or unoccupied land, without right or title. 5. to settle on public land under regulation by the government, in order to get title to it. *v.t.* to cause to squat: usually reflexive. *adj.* 1. seated in a squatting position. 2. short and heavy or thick, as though squatting. *n.* 1. the act of squatting. 2. the position taken in squatting; crouching posture.

squat·ter (skwät′ẽr, skwôt′ẽr), *n.* 1. a person or animal that squats, or crouches. 2. a person who squats (senses 4 & 5).

squat·ty (skwät′i, skwôt′i), *adj.* [SQUATTIER (-i-ẽr), SQUATTIEST (-i-ist)], squat; thickset.

squaw (skwô), *n.* [< Am. Ind. (Algonquian); cf. Massachusett *squas*], 1. an American Indian woman or wife. 2. any woman: chiefly humorous.

squaw·fish (skwô′fish′), *n.* [*pl.* SQUAWFISH, SQUAWFISHES (-iz); see FISH], a long, slender fish of the carp family, found in rivers of the northern Pacific coast of the United States and Canada.

squawk (skwôk), *v.i.* [echoic], 1. to utter a loud, harsh cry, as a parrot or chicken. 2. [Slang], to complain or protest, especially in a loud or raucous voice. *v.t.* to utter in a squawk. *n.* 1. a loud, harsh cry. 2. [Slang], a loud, raucous complaint or protest. 3. the black-crowned night heron.

squaw man, a white man married to or living with an American Indian woman.

squaw·root (skwô′ro͞ot′, skwô′root′), *n.* a yellowish-brown, scaly, leafless plant of eastern North America, parasitic on the roots of some trees, especially of oaks.

squeak (skwēk), *v.i.* [? fusion of *squeal* & *shriek;* but cf. Sw. *sqväka*], 1. to utter or make a thin, sharp, high-pitched cry or sound. 2. [Slang], to act as an informer; squeal. *v.t.* 1. to utter or produce in a squeak. 2. to cause (a door, etc.) to squeak. *n.* 1. a squeaking. 2. a thin, sharp cry or sound, usually short.
narrow squeak, [Colloq.], a narrow escape: also **close** (or **near**) **squeak.**

squeak·i·ly (skwēk′ə-li), *adv.* with a squeaky sound.

squeak·i·ness (skwēk′i-nis), *n.* the quality or state of being squeaky.

squeak·y (skwēk′i), *adj.* [SQUEAKIER (-i-ẽr), SQUEAKIEST (-i-ist)], squeaking.

squeal (skwēl), *v.i.* [ME. *squelen;* prob. echoic], 1. to utter or make a loud, sharp, high-pitched cry or sound. 2. [Slang], to act as an informer; betray a secret. *v.t.* to utter in a squeal. *n.* 1. a squealing. 2. a loud, sharp, high-pitched cry or sound, somewhat prolonged.

squeam·ish (skwēm′ish), *adj.* [ME. *squaimous;* Anglo-Fr. *escoimous*, orig., disdainful, shy, etc.], 1. having a digestive system that is easily upset; easily nauseated; queasy. 2. easily shocked or offended; prudish. 3. excessively fastidious; oversensitive. —*SYN.* see **dainty.**

squee·gee (skwē′jē, skwē-jē′), *n.* [prob. < *squeege*, intens. form of *squeeze*], 1. a T-shaped tool having the crossbar edged with a strip of rubber or the like, used to scrape water from a flat surface, as in washing windows. 2. a rubber roller used for this purpose in photographic development, lithography, etc. *v.t.* [SQUEEGEED (-jēd, -jēd′), SQUEEGEEING], to scrape, press, or treat with a squeegee. Also **squilgee.**

squeez·a·ble (skwēz′ə-b'l), *adj.* 1. that can be squeezed, pressed, compressed, etc. 2. capable of being constrained or forced to yield something.

squeeze (skwēz), *v.t.* [SQUEEZED (skwēzd), SQUEEZING], [intens. of ME. *queisen* (AS. *-cwysan*, to crush) in same sense < IE. base **gwei-*, to overpower, press strongly], 1. to press hard or closely; exert pressure on, especially from two or more sides, often in order to extract liquid, as juice, or the like; compress. 2. to get, bring forth, or extract by pressure: as, she *squeezed* water from the clothes. 3. to get, extract, or extort by force or unfair means. 4. to force or cause to pass by pressing: as, he *squeezed* his hand through the opening. 5. to oppress with exactions, burdensome taxes, or the like. 6. to embrace closely; hug. 7. to make a facsimile impression, or squeeze, of. 8. [Colloq.], to put pressure or bring influence to bear upon (a person or persons) to do a certain thing, as to pay money, etc. 9. in *bridge*, to force (an opponent) to play a potentially winning card in a trick that he cannot win. *v.i.* 1. to yield or give way to pressure. 2. to exert pressure. 3. to force one's way by pushing or pressing (with *in, out, through*, etc.). *n.* 1. a squeezing or being squeezed; hard or close pressure. 2. *a*) a close embrace; hug. *b*) a firm pressing or grasping of another's hand in one's own. 3. the state of being closely pressed or packed; crush. 4. a facsimile impression made by pressing a soft sub-

stance onto something, as a coin or inscription. 5. a small quantity of something extracted by squeezing. 6. [Colloq.], pressure or influence brought to bear, as in extortion. 7. in *bridge*, a play in which one player is squeezed by another.
squeeze play, 1. in *baseball*, a play in which the batter tries to bunt so that a runner on third base, starting to run at the pitcher's first pitching motion, may have a chance to score. 2. in *bridge*, any play that forces an opponent to discard a potentially winning card.
squelch (skwelch), ***n.*** [< earlier *quelch* (fusion of *quell* & *crush*) with *s-* intens.], 1. the sound of liquid, mud, slush, etc. moving under pressure or suction, as in wet shoes. 2. a crushed mass of something. 3. [Colloq.], a crushing retort, answer, rebuke, etc. ***v.t.*** 1. to crush or smash by or as by falling or stamping upon; squash. 2. to suppress, subdue, or silence completely and with a crushing effect. ***v.i.*** 1. to make a squelch (sense 1). 2. to walk heavily, as through mud or slush, or in wet shoes, making such a sound.
sque·teague (skwē-tēg′), ***n.*** [*pl.* SQUETEAGUE], [< the Am. Ind. (Narragansett) name], 1. a food fish of the croaker family, found in the Atlantic off the eastern coast of North America. 2. any of several related fishes.
squib (skwib), ***n.*** [prob. echoic], 1. any firework that burns with a hissing, spurting noise, ending in an explosion. 2. a broken firecracker that burns without exploding, making a hissing noise. 3. a short, sharp, usually witty attack in words; lampoon. 4. [British], any firecracker. ***v.t. & v.i.*** [SQUIBBED (skwibd), SQUIBBING], 1. to burn or shoot off (a squib). 2. to write or utter a squib or squibs (against). 3. to fire or explode with the sound of a squib.
squid (skwid), ***n.*** [*pl.* SQUIDS (skwidz), SQUID; see PLURAL, II, D, 1], [prob. < *squit*, dial. for *squirt*], a long, slender sea mollusk having ten arms, two being much longer than the others: small squid are used as food and for fish bait.
squil·gee (skwil′jē, skwil-jē′), ***n. & v.t.*** squeegee.
squill (skwil), ***n.*** [ME.; Late OFr. *squille;* L. *squilla; scilla;* Gr. *skilla*], 1. the dried bulb of a plant of the lily family, sliced and used in medicine as an expectorant, diuretic, etc. 2. the plant, found in southern Europe and northern Africa: also called *sea onion.* 3. any of a number of related plants of the lily family, with blue, white, or purple flowers.
squill (skwil), ***n.*** a squilla.
squil·la (skwil′ə), ***n.*** [*pl.* SQUILLAS (-əz), SQUILLAE (-ē)], [L. *squilla, scilla*, prawn, shrimp, sea onion; see SQUILL (a plant)], any of several crustaceans that burrow along the seashore; mantis crab.
squil·la·gee (skwil′ə-jē′), ***n. & v.t.*** squilgee; squeegee.
squill·gee (skwil′jē, skwil-jē′), ***n. & v.t.*** squilgee; squeegee.
squinch (skwinch), ***n.*** [altered < earlier *scunch*, contr. of *scuncheon, scoucheon;* OFr. *escoinson, escoisson* < LL. *excussio*, a striking out], an interior corner support, as a small arch, corbeling, or lintel, supporting a weight, as of a spire, resting upon it.
squint (skwint), ***v.i.*** [contr. of *asquint*], 1. to look or peer with the eyes partly closed. 2. to look with the eyes turned to the side; look obliquely or askance. 3. to be cross-eyed. 4. to incline or have a tendency (*toward* a given direction, belief, etc.). 5. to deviate from a given line, tendency, etc. ***v.t.*** 1. to cause to squint. 2. to keep (the eyes) partly closed in looking at something, as when the light is too strong. ***n.*** 1. a squinting. 2. an inclination or tendency. 3. an oblique or perverse tendency or bent. 4. the condition of being cross-eyed; strabismus. 5. [Colloq.], a look or glance, often sidelong, quick, or casual. ***adj.*** 1. squinting; looking obliquely, askance, or sidelong. 2. characterized by strabismus: as, *squint* eyes.
squint-eyed (skwint′id′), ***adj.*** squinting; specifically, *a*) cross-eyed. *b*) looking askance; malicious; prejudiced; spiteful.
squire (skwīr), ***n.*** [contr. of *esquire;* ME. *squier*, etc.], 1. a young man of high birth who served a knight as an attendant or armor-bearer. 2. in England, a title of respect given to a large rural landowner; country gentleman. 3. a title of respect applied commonly to a justice of the peace or similar local dignitary, as in a rural district. 4. an attendant or escort; especially, a man escorting a woman; gallant. ***v.t. & v.i.*** [SQUIRED (skwīrd), SQUIRING], to act as a squire (to).
squire·arch·y (skwīr′är-ki), ***n.*** [*squire* + *-archy*, after *hierarchy*], 1. country gentry or large landowners collectively. 2. government by country gentry or large landowners. Also spelled **squirarchy.**
squir·een (skwīr-ēn′), ***n.*** [*squire* + Ir. dim. suffix *-een;* Gael. *-in*], a small landowner; petty squire.
squire·ling (skwīr′liŋ), ***n.*** a squireen.
squirm (skwũrm), ***v.i.*** [prob. dial. echoism, influenced by *worm*], 1. to twist and turn the body in a snakelike movement; wriggle; writhe. 2. to show or feel distress, as from painful embarrassment, humiliation, etc. ***n.*** 1. the act of squirming. 2. a squirming motion.
squirm·y (skwũr′mi), ***adj.*** [SQUIRMIER (-mi-ẽr), SQUIRMIEST (-mi-ist)], squirming.
squir·rel (skwũr′əl, skwũrl; *esp. Brit.*, skwir′əl), ***n.*** [*pl.* SQUIRRELS (-əlz, skwũrlz), SQUIRREL; see PLURAL, II, D, 1], [ME. *squirel;* OFr. *esquirel, escurel;* LL. **sciuriolus*, dim. of **scurius*, for L. *sciurus;* Gr. *skiouros*, squirrel < *skia*, a shadow + *oura*, tail], 1. any of a group of small, tree-dwelling rodents with heavy fur and a long, bushy tail: common species are the *gray squirrel*, the *red squirrel*, the *fox squirrel*, and the *European squirrel*. 2. any of various other rodents related to these, as the chipmunks, certain flying phalangers of Australia, woodchucks, etc. 3. the fur of some of these animals.

COMMON GRAY SQUIRREL (1 1/2 ft. long)

squirrel corn, a plant with cream-colored flowers, having roots with yellow, grainlike buds.
squirt (skwũrt), ***v.t. & v.i.*** [altered < earlier *swirt* < LG. & D. *swirtjen*, to squirt], 1. to spurt; shoot out, as liquid, in a jet or thin stream. 2. to wet (a person or thing) with liquid so shot out. ***n.*** 1. something used to squirt liquid, as a syringe. 2. the act of squirting. 3. a small amount of squirted liquid; jet or thin stream. 4. [Colloq.], a small or insignificant person, especially one who is impudent or conceited; whippersnapper.
squirt gun, 1. a toy gun that shoots a stream of liquid. 2. a spray gun.
squirting cucumber, a trailing plant with cucumber-shaped fruit which bursts when ripe, ejecting the seeds.
squish (skwish), ***v.t. & v.i., n.*** [Dial.], squash.
sq. yd., square yard; square yards.
Sr, in *chemistry*, strontium.
Sr., 1. Senior. 2. [Port.], *Senhor.* 3. [Sp.], *Señor.* 4. Sir
Sra., 1. [Port.], *Senhora.* 2. [Sp.], *Señora.*
‡sri (shrē), ***n.*** [Hind., lit., glorious, reverent < Sans. *śrī*], a Hindu title of address, equivalent to English *mister:* as, *sri* Jawaharlal Nehru.
Sri·nag·ar (srē-nug′ẽr), ***n.*** the capital of Kashmir state, India: pop., 174,000.
S.R.O., standing room only.
Srta., 1. [Port.], *Senhorita.* 2. [Sp.], *Señorita.*
SS., ss., 1. *Sancti*, [L.], Saints. 2. scilicet. 3. sections.
ss., in *baseball*, shortstop.
S.S., SS., *Schutzstaffel*, [G.], Black Shirts.
S.S., SS, S/S, steamship.
SS.D., *Sanctissimus Dominus*, [L.], Most Holy Lord: a title applied to the Pope.
SSE, S.S.E., s.s.e., south-southeast.
S.S.R., SSR, Soviet Socialist Republic.
SSW, S.S.W., s.s.w., south-southwest.
-st, -est (sense 2).
St., 1. Saint: terms beginning with *St.* are entered in this dictionary as if spelled St-. 2. Strait. 3. Street.
St., st., statute; statutes.
st., 1. stanza. 2. stet. 3. stone (unit of weight).
s.t., short ton.
Sta., 1. Santa. 2. Station.
sta., 1. stationary. 2. stator.
stab (stab), ***v.t.*** [STABBED (stabd), STABBING], [var. of dial. *stob* < ME. *stob*, a stake, stump, a var. of *stub*], 1. to pierce or wound with or as with a knife, dagger, or other pointed weapon. 2. to thrust or plunge (a knife, etc.), as into a thing. 3. to go into in a sharp, thrusting way. ***v.i.*** 1. to make a thrust or cause a wound with or as with a knife, dagger, etc. 2. to give the sensation of a knife wound: said of pain. ***n.*** 1. a wound made by stabbing. 2. a thrust, as with a knife or dagger. 3. a sudden sensation of anguish or pain. 4. [Colloq.], an attempt; try.
‡Sta·bat Ma·ter (stä′bät mä′tẽr, stā′bat mā′tẽr), [L., lit., the mother was standing], 1. a Latin hymn about the sorrows of the Virgin Mary at the crucifixion of Jesus. 2. any musical setting of this hymn.
stab·ber (stab′ẽr), ***n.*** a person or thing that stabs.
sta·bile (stā′bil, stab′il), ***adj.*** [L. *stabilis;* see STABLE, *adj.*], 1. stable; stationary; fixed in position. 2. in *medicine, a*) designating or of a method of applying electricity for therapeutic purposes, in which the active electrode remains fixed over the diseased part: opposed to *labile. b*) somewhat resistant to heat.
sta·bil·i·ty (stə-bil′ə-ti), ***n.*** [*pl.* STABILITIES (-tiz)], [ME. *stablete;* OFr. *stableté* (Fr. *stabilité*); L. *stabilitas*], 1. the state or quality of being stable, or fixed; steadiness. 2. firmness of character, purpose, or resolution. 3. resistance to change; permanence. 4. the capacity of an object to return to equilibrium or to its original position after having been displaced. 5. in the *Roman Catholic Church*, a monk's vow to remain for life in the same monastery.
sta·bi·li·za·tion (stā′b′l-i-zā′shən, stab″l-i-zā′shən), ***n.*** a stabilizing or being stabilized.

sta·bi·lize (stā′bə-līz′, stab′ə-līz′), *v.t.* [STABILIZED (-līzd′), STABILIZING], [Fr. *stabiliser* < L. *stabilis;* see -IZE], 1. to make stable, or firm. 2. to keep from changing or fluctuating, as in price. 3. to equip (an airplane, ship, etc.) with a stabilizer.

sta·bi·liz·er (stā′bə-līz′ẽr, stab′ə-līz′ẽr), *n.* a person or thing that stabilizes; specifically, *a)* any of various parts or devices used to make an airplane steady in flight. *b)* a substance added to an explosive to prevent it from exploding spontaneously.

sta·ble (stā′b'l), *adj.* [ME.; OFr. *estable;* L. *stabilis* < *stare,* to stand], 1. not easily moved or thrown off balance; not likely to break down, fall apart, or give way; firm; steady; fixed. 2. firm in character, purpose, or resolution; steadfast. 3. resisting change; permanent; enduring. 4. capable of returning to equilibrium or original position after having been displaced. 5. in *chemistry,* not easily decomposing.

sta·ble (stā′b'l), *n.* [ME.; OFr. *estable;* L. *stabulum* < *stare,* to stand], 1. a building in which horses or cattle are sheltered and fed. 2. a group of animals kept or belonging in such a building. 3. all the race horses belonging to one owner. 4. the people employed to take care of and train such a group of race horses. *v.t. & v.i.* [STABLED (-b'ld), STABLING], to lodge, keep, or be kept in or as in a stable.

sta·ble·boy (stā′b'l-boi′), *n.* a boy who works in a stable.

sta·ble·man (stā′b'l-man′, stā′b'l-mən), *n.* [*pl.* STABLEMEN (-men′, -mən)], a man who works in a stable.

sta·bling (stā′bliŋ), *n.* 1. a stable or stables. 2. accommodations in a stable or stables, for horses, etc.

stab·lish (stab′lish), *v.t.* [Archaic], to establish.

sta·bly (stā′bli), *adv.* in a stable manner; firmly.

stac·ca·to (stə-kä′tō; It. stäk-kä′tô), *adj.* [It., pp. of *staccare,* short for *distaccare,* to detach], 1. in *music,* with distinct breaks between successive tones; abrupt; detached: as, a series of *staccato* notes, a *staccato* passage: opposed to *legato*: abbreviated **stacc.** 2. made up of abrupt, distinct elements or sounds: as, a *staccato* outburst of rage, gunfire, etc. *adv.* so as to be staccato. *n.* [*pl.* STACCATOS (-tōz)], something, as a speech pattern, that is staccato.

stack (stak), *n.* [ME. *stac;* ON. *stakkr;* IE. base **stāk-,* to stand, be placed < **stā-,* to stand (cf. STAND)], 1. a large pile of straw, hay, etc., especially one symmetrically arranged with a smooth outer surface for outdoor storage. 2. any somewhat orderly pile or heap, as of boxes, poker chips, etc. 3. a number of arms, especially three rifles, leaning against each other on end so as to form a cone. 4. in Great Britain, a unit of solid measure equal to 108 cubic feet, used for cut wood, coal, etc. 5. a chimney; specifically, *a)* a number of flues or pipes arranged together. *b)* a single smoke pipe or chimney, especially one of metal, as on a ship, locomotive, etc. 6. a set of book shelves. 7. *pl.* the section where the books are kept in a library. 8. [Colloq.], a large number or quantity. *v.t.* 1. to pile or arrange in a stack. 2. to load with stacks of something.

stack the cards, 1. to arrange the order of playing cards secretly so that certain cards are dealt to certain players. 2. to prearrange circumstances, usually secretly and unfairly. Also **stack the deck.**

stac·te (stak′tē), *n.* [ME. *stacten* < acc. of L. *stacte,* oil of myrrh; Gr. *staktē* < *stazein,* to drip], a spice used by the ancient Jews in preparing incense: Ex. 30:34.

stad·dle (stad′'l), *n.* [ME. *stadel, stathel;* AS. *stathol;* akin to G. *stadel,* barn; IE. base as in *stand*], a lower part or structure; support; specifically, the base or supporting framework of a stack, as of hay.

Sta·der splint (stā′dẽr), [after Otto *Stader* (1894–), Am. veterinary surgeon], a metal splint consisting of two pins driven through the bone above and below a fracture and held in place by two rods extending between them on the outside of the limb: the splint allows freedom of movement of the fractured limb.

stad·hold·er (stad′hōl′dẽr), *n.* [D. *stadhouder; stad,* a place + *houder,* a holder], 1. formerly, the governor or viceroy of a province of the Netherlands. 2. the chief magistrate of the United Provinces of the Netherlands. Also **stadtholder.**

sta·di·a (stā′di-ə), *n.* [It.; prob. < L. *stadia,* pl. of *stadium* (see STADIUM); sense development obscure], 1. a device used in calculating distance through measurement of angles; specifically, *a)* a surveyor's transit used together with a graduated rod (*stadia rod*). *b)* the rod. *c)* any of several military range finders, as a stick with graduations, used in judging distance by measuring the apparent height of a man viewed from a distance. 2. a method of surveying using a stadia. *adj.* designating or of this method of surveying.

sta·di·a (stā′di-ə), *n.* plural of **stadium** (senses 1 & 3).

sta·di·om·e·ter (stā′di-om′ə-tẽr), *n.* [< Gr. *stadion* (see STADIUM); + *-meter*], 1. an instrument for measuring angles and making a graphic record of their bearings. 2. a device for measuring the length of a curve, broken line, etc., consisting of a toothed wheel that traverses the curve, line, etc., and an index.

sta·di·um (stā′di-əm), *n.* [*pl.* STADIA (-ə)], [ME.; L.; Gr. *stadion,* fixed standard of length < *histanai,* to stand], 1. in ancient Greece, *a)* a track for foot races, usually semicircular, with tiers of seats for spectators. *b)* any of several measures of linear distance, based on the length of such tracks (at Athens, 607 ft.; but the Olympic stadium was slightly over 630 ft., and others varied considerably). 2. [*pl.* STADIUMS (-əmz)], a place used for outdoor games, meetings, etc., partly or completely surrounded by tiers of seats, usually for thousands of spectators. 3. a stage, as of a disease.

stad·le (stad′'l), *n.* a staddle.

stadt·hold·er (stat′hōl′dẽr), *n.* a stadholder.

Staël, Madame **de** (də stäl), Baronne de Staël-Holstein. (born *Anne Louise Germaine Necker*), **1766–1817;** French writer.

staff (staf, stäf), *n.* [*pl.* STAVES (stāvz), STAFFS (stafs, stäfs)], [ME. *staf;* AS. *stæf;* akin to G. *stab;* IE. base **stebh-,* **stabh-,* post, pole, etc., as also in Sans. *stabhnáti,* (he) supports; cf. STEM], 1. a stick, rod, or pole; specifically, *a)* a stick used as a support in walking. *b)* a pole or club used as a weapon. *c)* a pole for supporting a banner or flag. *d)* a rod, wand, etc. used as a symbol of authority. *e)* [Archaic], a shaft, as of a lance. *f)* any of several graduated sticks or rules used for measuring, as in surveying. 2. figuratively, a support: as, he was a *staff* to the whole group. 3. [*pl.* STAFFS], a group of people assisting a chief, manager, president, or other leader. 4. [*pl.* STAFFS], a group of officers serving a military or naval commanding officer in an advisory and administrative capacity without combat duties or command. 5. [*pl.* STAFFS], a specific group of workers or employees: as, a teaching *staff,* office *staff,* maintenance *staff.* 6. in *music,* the five horizontal lines and four intermediate spaces on which music is written or printed. *adj.* of or having to do with a staff (senses 3, 4, 5). *v.t.* [STAFFED (staft, stäft), STAFFING], to provide with a staff, as of workers.

staff (staf, stäf), *n.* [< G. *staffieren,* to fill out, decorate; via D. < OFr. *estoffe,* stuff; see STUFF], a building material consisting of plaster and fiber, used for temporary decorative structures, statues, etc.

staff officer, an officer serving on a staff.

staff of life, bread, regarded as the basic food.

Staf·ford (staf′ẽrd), *n.* 1. Staffordshire. 2. the county seat of Staffordshire: pop., 32,000.

Staf·ford·shire (staf′ẽrd-shir′), *n.* a county of central England: pop., 1,466,000 (est. 1945); county seat, Stafford.

staff sergeant, 1. in the *United States Army,* formerly, the third grade of enlisted man (now *sergeant*). 2. in the *United States Marine Corps & Air Force,* the third grade of enlisted man, ranking just below technical sergeant.

stag (stag), *n.* [*pl.* STAGS (stagz), STAG; see PLURAL, II, D. 1], [ME.; AS. *stagga;* akin to ON. *steggr, steggi,* male bird; IE. base **stegh-,* to stick; prob. basic sense "capable of procreation as male"], 1. *a)* a full-grown male deer: said specifically of the European red deer. *b)* the male of some other animals, as the caribou. 2. a male animal castrated in maturity. 3. *a)* a man who attends a social gathering unaccompanied by a woman. *b)* a social gathering attended by men only. *adj.* for men only: as, a *stag* party. *v.t.* [STAGGED (stagd), STAGGING], [Slang], to observe or follow secretly or furtively; spy on. *v.i.* to go to a party, etc. as a stag (sense 3*a*).

go stag, [Colloq.], to go as a stag (sense 3*a*).

stag beetle, any of several large beetles characterized by branched, antlerlike mandibles in the male.

stage (stāj), *n.* [ME.; OFr. *estage;* LL. *staticum* < L. *status,* pp. of *stare,* to stand], 1. a platform or dock. 2. a scaffold. 3. a level, floor, or story. 4. a shelf attached to a microscope for holding the object to be viewed: see **microscope,** illus. 5. *a)* a platform on which plays, speeches, etc. are presented. *b)* any area, as in an arena theater, in which actors perform. 6. the whole area back of the footlights in a theater. 7. the theater, drama, or acting as a profession. 8. the scene of an event or series of events: as, Central Europe has been the *stage* of many wars. 9. a place where a stop is made on a journey, especially a regular stopping point with accommodations for travelers. 10. the distance or a part of a route between stopping places; leg of a journey. 11. *a)* a stagecoach. *b)* a motor bus. 12. a period, level, or degree in a process of development, growth, or change: as, an advanced *stage* of an insect. 13. one of two or more propulsion systems used in sequence in powering a rocket carrying an artificial satellite, etc. into outer space: when a stage has caused the rocket to reach a certain speed, position, etc., it is usually separated from the remaining part or parts. 14. in *geology,* a division of stratified rocks ranking just below *series,* corresponding to *age* in the scale of chronology. 15. in *radio,* an element or part in some complex arrangement of parts; specifically, a tube with its accessory apparatus in an amplifier made up of a number of tubes. ***v.t.*** [STAGED (stājd), STAGING], 1. to present, represent, or exhibit on or as on a stage. 2. to plan, arrange, and carry out: as, the enemy *staged* a counteroffensive. ***v.i.*** 1. to be suitable for presentation on the stage: as, the play *stages* well. 2. to travel by stagecoach.

by easy stages, 1. traveling only a short distance at a time. 2. working or acting gradually, not hurriedly, with plenty of stops, as for rest.

stage·coach (stāj'kōch'), ***n.*** a horse-drawn coach carrying passengers, parcels, and mail on scheduled trips over a regular route.

stage·craft (stāj'kraft', stāj'kräft'), ***n.*** skill in, or the art of, writing or producing plays.

stage direction, 1. an instruction, written into the text of a play, directing the movements, actions, etc. of the performers. 2. the art or practice of directing the production of a play.

stage door, an outside door leading to the backstage part of a theater, for the use of actors, production staff, etc.

stage-door Johnny (stāj'dôr', stāj'dōr'), [Slang], a man who associates with, or seeks the company of, actresses or chorus girls.

stage effect, an effect or impression created on the stage by action, lighting, scenery, etc.

stage fright, nervousness felt when appearing before an audience, as by an inexperienced performer.

stage·hand (stāj'hand'), ***n.*** a person who does manual work connected with producing a play, as the arrangement of scenery, operation of lights, etc.

stage manager, the person in over-all charge of the production of a play: he superintends the acting company, the stage technicians, and the staging of each performance of the play.

stag·er (stāj'ẽr), ***n.*** [< *stage, n.* + *-er*], 1. a person or animal of much experience; old hand; veteran (usually with *old*): as, the milk horse was an old *stager* and knew the route. 2. [Archaic], an actor.

stage-struck (stāj'struk'), ***adj.*** having an intense desire to become an actor or actress.

stage whisper, 1. a loud whisper by an actor on the stage, intended to be heard by the audience. 2. any similar whisper intended to be heard by others than the person to whom it is addressed.

stag·y (stāj'i), ***adj.*** [STAGIER (-i-ẽr), STAGIEST (-i-ist)], stagy.

stag·gard (stag'ẽrd), ***n.*** [ME. *stagard; stag* + *-ard*], a stag, or male red deer, in its fourth year.

stag·gart (stag'ẽrt), ***n.*** a staggard.

stag·ger (stag'ẽr), ***v.i.*** [ME. *stakeren;* ON. *stakra,* to cause to stumble; akin to & prob. influenced in form by MD. *staggeren*], 1. to move unsteadily, as though about to collapse; totter, sway, or reel, as from a blow, fatigue, drunkenness, etc. 2. to lose determination, strength of purpose, etc.; hesitate; waver. ***v.t.*** 1. to cause to stagger, as with a blow. 2. to affect strongly with astonishment, horror, grief, etc.; overwhelm. 3. to set or incline alternately, as on either side of a line; make zigzag in arrangement: as, the teeth of most saws are *staggered.* 4. to arrange (periods of activity, duties, etc.) so as to eliminate crowding or overconcentration: as, employees' vacation periods have been *staggered.* 5. in *aeronautics,* to set in a stagger. ***n.*** 1. a staggering; reeling, unsteady movement. 2. a staggered or zigzag arrangement. 3. *pl.* [construed as sing.], a nervous disease of horses, cattle, etc., causing the animals to stagger or fall when walking. 4. in *aeronautics, a)* the setting of one wing of an airplane forward of another wing above or below it so that there is a difference in the projection of their leading edges. *b)* the amount of this difference.

***SYN.*—stagger** implies unsteady movement characterized by a loss of equilibrium and failure to maintain a fixed course (to *stagger* under a heavy load); **reel** suggests a swaying or lurching so as to appear on the verge of falling (the drunken man *reeled* down the hall); **totter** suggests the uncertain, faltering steps of a feeble old person or of an infant learning to walk.

stag·ger·bush (stag'ẽr-boosh'), ***n.*** an American shrub with white or pinkish flowers, poisonous to livestock.

stag·hound (stag'hound'), ***n.*** one of a breed of large hounds used in hunting stags, boars, etc.

stag·i·ly (stāj'ə-li), ***adv.*** in a stagy manner.

stag·i·ness (stāj'i-nis), ***n.*** the quality or condition of being stagy.

stag·ing (stāj'iŋ), ***n.*** 1. a temporary structure used for support; scaffolding. 2. the business of operating stagecoaches. 3. travel by stagecoach. 4. the act or process of presenting a play on the stage.

staging area, in *military usage,* the place of embarkation of troops leaving for a combat zone.

Stag·i·rite (staj'ə-rīt'), ***n.*** a native or inhabitant of Stagira, in ancient Macedonia; specifically, Aristotle.

stag·nan·cy (stag'nən-si), ***n.*** the condition or quality of being stagnant.

stag·nant (stag'nənt), ***adj.*** [L. *stagnans,* ppr. of *stagnare,* to cause to stand, stagnate], 1. without motion or current; not flowing or moving; hence, 2. foul from lack of movement: said of water, etc. 3. lacking in activity, interest, etc.; dull; sluggish: as, a *stagnant* mind.

stag·nate (stag'nāt), ***v.i.*** [STAGNATED (-id), STAGNATING], [< L. *stagnatus,* pp. of *stagnare,* to stagnate], to be or become stagnant. ***v.t.*** to make stagnant.

stag·na·tion (stag-nā'shən), ***n.*** 1. a stagnating or being stagnated. 2. a stagnant condition.

stag·y (stāj'i), ***adj.*** [STAGIER (-i-ẽr), STAGIEST (-i-ist)], 1. of or characteristic of the stage; theatrical (usually in an unfavorable sense); hence, 2. affected; not real or genuine: as, a *stagy* type of diction. Also spelled **stagey.**

Stahl·helm (shtäl'helm'), ***n.*** [G., lit., steel helmet; *stahl,* steel + *helm,* helmet], in Germany after World War I, a veterans' organization of a military and nationalist character and of monarchist sympathy.

staid (stād), archaic past tense and past participle of **stay** (to remain). ***adj.*** 1. [Rare], resisting change; fixed; settled. 2. sober; sedate; settled and steady.

stain (stān), ***v.t.*** [contr. of *distain;* OFr. *desteindre,* to discolor, lose color < L. *dis-,* from + *tingere,* to color], 1. to spoil the appearance of by coloring or soiling; discolor; spot. 2. to spoil or spot (a character, reputation, etc.); taint; corrupt; dishonor. 3. to change the appearance of (wood, cloth, glass, etc.) by coloring; dye; tint. 4. to treat (material for microscopic study) with a coloring matter that facilitates study, as by making transparent parts visible or by producing a different effect upon different structures or tissues. ***v.i.*** to impart or take a color or stain. ***n.*** 1. a color, discoloration, or spot resulting from or as from staining. 2. a moral blemish; dishonor; guilt; taint. 3. a substance used to impart color in staining; specifically, *a)* a dye or pigment in solution, for staining wood, cloth, etc. *b)* a dye used to stain material for microscopic study.

stained glass, glass colored in any of various ways, as by fusing metallic oxides into it, by enameling, by burning pigments into its surface, etc.: it is used especially for church windows.

stain·less (stān'lis), ***adj.*** 1. without a mark or stain. 2. that will not become stained or discolored.

stainless steel, steel alloyed with chromium, etc., virtually immune to rust and corrosion.

stair (stâr), ***n.*** [ME. *steire;* AS. *stæger* < base of *stigan,* to climb; cf. STILE], 1. *usually pl.* a flight of steps; staircase. 2. a single step, usually one of a series, leading from one level or floor to another.

stair·case (stâr'kās'), ***n.*** a series or flight of stairs, especially one with a supporting structure and a handrail or balustrade.

stair·head (stâr'hed'), ***n.*** the head, or top, of a staircase.

stair·way (stâr'wā'), ***n.*** a flight of stairs; staircase.

stair·well (stâr'wel'), ***n.*** the vertical shaft (in a building) containing a staircase: also **stair well.**

staith (stāth), ***n.*** [ME. *stathe* < AS. *stæth,* shore, influenced by cognate ON. *stāth,* landing place; for IE. base see STAND], [British Dial.], 1. a stage or wharf with equipment for loading and unloading. 2. *a)* an embankment. *b)* a path or narrow road along an embankment.

stake (stāk), ***n.*** [ME.; AS. *staca;* akin to D. *staak;* base as in *stick*], 1. a length of wood or metal pointed at one end for driving into the ground. 2. the post to which a person is tied for execution by burning. 3. execution by burning. 4. a pole or post fitted upright into a socket, as at the edge of a railway flatcar, truck bed, etc., to help hold a load. 5. a truck having a stake body. 6. *often pl.* something, especially money, risked or hazarded, as in a wager, game, or contest: as, the gamblers were playing for high *stakes.* 7. *often pl.* a reward given a winner, as in a race; prize. 8. a race in which a prize is offered. 9. a share or interest, especially a financial one, in property, a person, a business venture, or the like. 10. [Colloq.], a grubstake. ***v.t.*** [STAKED (stākt), STAKING], 1. to mark the location or boundaries of with or as with stakes, specifically so as to establish a claim (with *out,* etc.). 2. to fasten or support with a stake or stakes. 3. to hitch or tether to a stake. 4. to close (*up* or *in*), shut (*out*), etc. by stakes in the form of a fence or barrier. 5. [influenced by MD. *staken,* to fix, place], to risk or hazard; gamble; bet: as, he *staked* his winnings on the next hand. 6. [Colloq.], to furnish with money or resources, as for a business venture. 7. [Colloq.], to grubstake.

at stake, being risked or hazarded, or dependent upon the outcome (of something specified or implied).

pull up stakes, [Colloq.], to change one's place of residence, business, etc.

stake body, a flat truck body having sockets into which stakes may be fitted, as to support railings.

stake·hold·er (stāk'hōl'dẽr), ***n.*** one who holds money, etc. bet by others and pays it to the winner.

Sta·kha·no·vism (stə-kä'nə-viz'm), ***n.*** [after Aleksei G. *Stakhanov,* Soviet miner who initiated it in 1935], in the Soviet Union, an efficiency system in which workers voluntarily increase their piecework production by improvement of techniques, etc., and are rewarded with bonuses and privileges.

Sta·kha·no·vite (stə-kä'nə-vīt'), ***n.*** in the Soviet

Union, a worker officially declared to have excelled in Stakhanovism. ***adj.*** of Stakhanovism or Stakhanovites.

sta·lac·ti·form (stə-lak′ti-fôrm′), ***adj.*** having the form or position of a stalactite.

sta·lac·tite (stə-lak′tīt, stal′ək-tīt′), ***n.*** [Mod. L. *stalactites* < Gr. *stalaktos*, trickling or dropping < *stalassein*, to let fall drop by drop], 1. an icicle-shaped deposit of carbonate of lime hanging from the roof or sides of a cave, formed, like stalagmites, by the evaporation of dripping water having a high lime content. 2. anything having the form or position of a stalactite.

STALACTITES (A) AND STALAGMITES (B)

stal·ac·tit·ic (stal′ək-tit′ik), ***adj.*** 1. stalactiform. 2. of or covered with stalactites.

stal·ac·tit·i·cal (stal′ək-tit′i-k'l), ***adj.*** stalactitic.

‡sta·lag (shtä′läk; Eng. stal′ag), ***n.*** [G., contr. < *stammlager*; *stamm*, a base, lit. stem + *lager*, a camp], a German prisoner-of-war camp for captured privates and noncommissioned officers.

sta·lag·mite (stə-lag′mīt, stal′əg-mīt′), ***n.*** [Mod. L. *stalagmites* < Gr. *stalagmos*, a dropping < *stalassein*, to drop or drip], a cone-shaped deposit of carbonate of lime extending vertically from the floor of a cave, often forming beneath, and becoming continuous with, a stalactite above: see **stalactite**, illus.

stal·ag·mit·ic (stal′əg-mit′ik), ***adj.*** 1. having the form or position of a stalagmite. 2. of or covered with stalagmites.

stal·ag·mit·i·cal (stal′əg-mit′i-k'l), ***adj.*** stalagmitic.

St. Al·bans (ôl′bənz), ***n.*** a city in Hertfordshire, southeastern England: pop., 44,000: ancient name, *Verulamium*.

stale (stāl), ***adj.*** [ME.; prob. < a LG. source; cf. W.Fl. *stel-* in same sense; for base see STAND], 1. having lost freshness; worsened by having been kept too long; specifically, *a)* flat; vapid; tasteless: as, *stale* beer. *b)* hard and dry: said of bread, etc. *c)* low in oxygen content; stagnant: as, *stale* water or air. *d)* in an early stage of decay, as meat or eggs. 2. having lost originality or newness; lacking in interest through familiarity or overuse; hackneyed; trite: as, a *stale* joke, *stale* gossip. 3. past the peak of mental or physical vigor and keenness; out of condition as a result of either too much or too little activity. 4. in *law*, having lost legal force or effect through lack of use or action, as a claim or lien. ***v.t. & v.i.*** [STALED (stāld), STALING], to make or become stale (in any sense).

stale (stāl), ***v.i.*** [STALED (stāld), STALING], [prob. < MLG. *stal*, urine; akin to prec. *stale*], to urinate: said of horses and cattle. ***n.*** urine of horses or cattle.

stale·mate (stāl′māt′), ***n.*** [ME. *stale*, stalemate < Anglo-Fr. *estale*, fixed location (prob. < OHG. *stal*, a place); + *mate* (to checkmate)], 1. in *chess*, any situation in which it is impossible for one of the players to move without placing his king in check: it results in a draw. 2. any situation making further action impossible; deadlock; draw. ***v.t.*** [STALEMATED (-id), STALEMATING], 1. to subject to or bring into a stalemate; hence, 2. to bring to a standstill.

Sta·lin (stä′lin, stä′lēn), ***n.*** Stalino.

Sta·lin, Joseph (stä′lin, stä′lēn), (born *Iosif Vissarionovich Dzhugashvili*), 1879–1953; Soviet dictator and statesman; general secretary of the Communist Party of the Soviet Union (1922–1953); commander in chief of the Soviet armed forces in World War II; premier (1941–1953).

Sta·lin·a·bad (stä′li-nä-bät′), ***n.*** the capital of the Tadzhik S.S.R., central Asia: pop., 224,000: formerly called *Dyushambe, Diushambe*.

Sta·lin·grad (stä′lin-grad′; Russ. stä′lin-grät′), ***n.*** 1. a region of the R.S.F.S.R., in south central European Russia: pop., 1,849,000. 2. its capital, on the Volga: pop., 591,000: scene of a decisive battle (1942–1943) of World War II, in which the Russians defeated the Germans: formerly called *Tsaritsyn*.

Sta·li·no (stä′li-nô′), ***n.*** a city in the southeastern Ukrainian S.S.R.: pop., 701,000: also **Stalin**: former name, *Yuzovka*.

Sta·linsk (stä′linsk), ***n.*** a city in the southern Siberian U.S.S.R.: pop., 377,000.

stalk (stôk), ***v.i.*** [ME. *stalken*; AS. *stealcian* (in comp.); prob. < *stealc*, high, steep (with allusion to a stalking gait); for IE. base see STALK (a stem)], 1. to walk in a stiff, haughty manner: as, he *stalked* out of the room in anger: sometimes used figuratively, as, plague *stalks* across the land. 2. to pursue or approach game, an enemy, etc. stealthily, as from cover. 3. [Obs.], to walk or move along stealthily or furtively. ***v.t.*** 1. to pursue or approach (game, etc.) stealthily. 2. to stalk through: as, terror *stalked* the streets. ***n.*** 1. a slow, stiff, haughty step or gait. 2. the act of stalking game, an enemy, etc.

stalk (stôk), ***n.*** [ME. *stalke*, dim. of *stale*; AS. *stæla*, a stalk, stem of a plant; akin to G. *stiele*; IE. base **st(h)el-*, to place, put, seen also in L. *stolidus* (cf. STOLID)], 1. the stem or main axis of a plant. 2. any part resembling this, as in some invertebrate animals. 3. in *botany*, any lengthened support on which an organ grows, as the petiole of a leaf or the peduncle of a flower.

stalk·ing-horse (stôk′iŋ-hôrs′), ***n.*** 1. a horse, or a figure of a horse, used as cover by a hunter stalking game; hence, 2. anything used to disguise or conceal intentions, schemes, or activities; blind; pretext. 3. in *politics*, a candidate whose candidacy is a mere maneuver to conceal that of someone more important, or to divide and thus defeat the opposition.

stalk·y (stôk′i), ***adj.*** [STALKIER (-i-ẽr), STALKIEST (-i-ist)], 1. like a stalk; long and slender. 2. having or consisting of stalks.

stall (stôl), ***n.*** [ME. *stal*; AS. *steall*, *stall*, a place, station, stall, stable; for base see STALK (stem)], 1. a stable. 2. a room or compartment for one animal in a stable. 3. a small compartment or booth; specifically, *a)* any of a number of booths, tables, or counters, as at a market or fair, at which goods are sold. *b)* a pew or enclosed seat in the main part of a church or in the choir. *c)* [British], a seat near the stage in a theater, especially one in the front part of the orchestra, separated from adjacent seats by railings or the like. 4. a protective sheath, as of rubber, for a finger or thumb; cot. 5. any of various sheaths or marked-off or enclosed areas. 6. in *aeronautics*, the condition that is the result of stalling. ***v.t.*** 1. to put or keep (an animal) in a stall, sometimes so as to fatten. 2. to cause to stick fast, as in mud. 3. to check or stop the motion or progress of; bring to a standstill, especially unintentionally. 4. to cause (an airplane, motor, etc.) to stall. ***v.i.*** 1. to be kept in, or occupy, a stall. 2. to stick fast, as in mud. 3. to be brought to a standstill, especially unintentionally. 4. to stop operating because of overloading or insufficient fuel supply: said of a motor or engine. 5. in *aeronautics*, to lose the amount of forward speed necessary to maintain altitude and be controlled: as, the plane *stalls* at forty-three miles per hour.

stall (stôl), ***v.i.*** [< *stall*, a decoy, var. of obs. *stale*, person who lures or snares; Anglo-Fr. *estale* < OFr. *estaler*; see STALL (stop)], [Colloq.], to act or speak evasively or hesitantly so as to deceive or delay: as, stop *stalling* and tell us the rest. ***v.t.*** [Colloq.], to put off or delay by stalling (usually with *off*): as, he could no longer *stall* off his creditors. ***n.*** [Colloq.], any action, device, story, etc. used to deceive or delay; evasive trick.

stall-fed (stôl′fed′), ***adj.*** kept and fed in a stall to fatten.

stall-feed (stôl′fēd′), ***v.t.*** [STALL-FED (-fed′), STALL-FEEDING], 1. to feed and keep (an animal) inactive in a stall for fattening. 2. to feed with dry fodder.

stal·lion (stal′yən), ***n.*** [ME. *stalon*; OFr. *estalon* < OHG. *stal*, a stall], an uncastrated male horse, especially one used as a stud.

stal·wart (stôl′wẽrt), ***adj.*** [ME. *stalworthe*; AS. *stælwyrthe*, short for *statholwyrthe*, firm; *stathol*, foundation + *wyrthe*, worth; hence, lit., having a firm foundation], 1. strong; sturdy; robust. 2. valiant. 3. resolute; firm; unyielding. ***n.*** 1. a stalwart person. 2. a person who supports any given cause, especially that of a political party, with firm partisanship. —***SYN.*** see **strong**.

Stam·boul (stäm-bōōl′), ***n.*** 1. the old section of Istanbul, Turkey. 2. sometimes, all of Istanbul.

sta·men (stā′mən), ***n.*** [*pl.* STAMENS (-mənz), *rare* STAMINA (stam′ə-nə)], [L., a warp, thread < *stare*, to stand], a pollen-bearing organ in a flower, made up of a slender stalk (*filament*) and a pollen sac (*anther*); microsporophyll of a seed plant.

Stam·ford (stam′fẽrd), ***n.*** a city in southwestern Connecticut: pop., 93,000.

stam·i·na (stam′ə-nə), ***n.*** [L., pl. of *stamen*; see STAMEN], resistance to fatigue, illness, hardship, etc.; staying power; endurance.

stam·i·na (stam′ə-nə), ***n.*** alternative plural of **stamen**.

stam·i·nal (stam′ə-nəl), ***adj.*** 1. of, showing, or having to do with stamina. 2. in *botany*, of or relating to a stamen or stamens.

stam·i·nate (stam′ə-nit, stam′ə-nāt′), ***adj.*** [L. *staminatus*], in *botany*, 1. bearing stamens but no pistils, as male flowers. 2. having or bearing a stamen or stamens.

sta·min·e·al (stə-min′i-əl), *adj.* in *botany*, staminal.

stam·i·ni- (stam′ə-ni), [< L. *stamen, staminis*], a combining form meaning *stamen*, as in *staminiferous*: also **stamin-**.

stam·i·nif·er·ous (stam′ə-nif′ẽr-əs), *adj.* [*stamini-* + *-ferous*], having or bearing a stamen or stamens.

stam·i·no·di·um (stam′ə-nō′di-əm), *n.* [*pl.* STAMINODIA (-ə)], [Mod. L. < L. *stamen, staminis*, stamen + Mod. L. *-odium* (see -ODE, like)], in *botany*, 1. an abortive or sterile stamen. 2. a structure resembling this.

stam·i·no·dy (stam′ə-nō′di), *n.* [< *stamin-* + Gr. *-ōdia*, a becoming like < *-ōdēs* (see -ODE, like)], the change of other organs of a flower into stamens.

stam·mel (stam′'l), *n.* [OFr. *estamel* < *estame*, woolen thread < L. *stamen;* see STAMEN], 1. a coarse, red cloth of wool, or wool mixed with linen or cotton, used for undergarments. 2. the red color of this cloth.

stam·mer (stam′ẽr), *v.t.* & *v.i.* [ME. *stameren;* AS. *stamerian;* akin to D. *stameren;* freq. formation < IE. base ***stem-**, to stumble in speech, as also in G. *stumm*, dumb, Eng. *stumble*], to speak or say with involuntary pauses and rapid repetitions of syllables and sounds, as from excitement, confusion, embarrassment, etc. *n.* act, instance, or habit of stammering. Cf. **stutter.**

stamp (stamp), *v.t.* [Early ME. *stampen;* akin to G. *stampfen*, AS. *stempan*, to press to pieces; IE. base ***stembh-**, to crush < ***stebh-**, a post, pole (cf. STAFF)], 1. to bring (the foot) down forcibly upon something. 2. *a)* to strike down on forcibly with the foot: as, he *stamped* the floor in anger. *b)* to beat, press, force, crush, drive, etc. with or as with a forcible downward thrust or thrusts of the foot: as, *stamp* out a cigarette, *stamp* out a revolt. 3. to imprint or cut out (a mark, form, device, etc.) by bringing a form forcibly against a material: as, he *stamped* his initials into the leather, these ashtrays are *stamped* from metal sheets. 4. to impress, mark, or imprint with some design, device, characters, etc., as to decorate or show authenticity, ownership, sanction, or the like. 5. to impress or mark distinctly, deeply, or indelibly: as, a face *stamped* with greed, the incident was *stamped* in her memory. 6. to put an official seal or a stamp on (a document, letter, etc.). 7. to characterize or reveal distinctly, as if by imprinting. 8. [Dial.], to pulverize (ore, etc.) by grinding or crushing. *v.i.* 1. to bring down the foot forcibly, as in showing anger or removing mud from the shoe. 2. to walk with loud, heavy steps, as in anger, etc. *n.* 1. the act of stamping. 2. a machine, tool, etc. used for stamping or crushing ore, etc. 3. any tool or implement, as a die, used by being brought forcibly against something to mark or shape it. 4. a mark or form made by such a tool or implement. 5. a mark, seal, impression, etc. used to show officially that a tax has been paid, authority given, service performed, etc. 6. *a)* a small piece of paper, imprinted on the face with a distinctive design or picture, and usually gummed on the back, issued by a government for a specified price and required to be affixed to a letter, parcel, document, commodity subject to duty, etc., as evidence that the prescribed fee, as for carrying mail, has been paid. *b)* any more or less similar piece of paper, issued by an organization, business firm, etc.: as, trading *stamps*. 7. any characteristic sign or impression; indication: as, the book bears the *stamp* of its author's bigotry. 8. character; kind; class; type.

Stamp Act, a law passed by the British Parliament in 1765 requiring that stamps and stamped paper, parchment, etc. be used for all documents and writings in the American colonies: it aroused so much opposition that it was repealed in March, 1766.

stam·pede (stam-pēd′), *n.* [Am. Sp. *estampida*, a crash, uproar < Sp. *estampar*, to stamp], 1. a sudden, headlong running away of a group of frightened animals, especially horses or cattle. 2. a confused, headlong rush or flight of a large group of people. 3. any sudden, impulsive, spontaneous mass movement: as, there developed a *stampede* to support the new candidate. *v.i.* [STAMPEDED (-id), STAMPEDING], to move, or take part, in a stampede (in any sense). *v.t.* to cause to stampede.

stamp·er (stam′pẽr), *n.* a person or thing that stamps; specifically, *a)* a person who cancels stamps, etc. in a post office. *b)* a person who stamps (something specified), as in a factory: as, a metal *stamper*. *c)* any of various machines or tools for stamping, as for pulverizing stone or cleaning textiles in a rotating vessel.

stamp·ing ground (stam′piŋ), [Colloq.], the habitual or favorite gathering place, resort, or haunt (of the animals or persons specified).

stamp mill, a mill or machine for pulverizing ore.

stance (stans), *n.* [OFr. *estance;* LL. **stantia* < L. *stans, stantis*, ppr. of *stare*, to stand], the way a person or animal stands; posture, especially with reference to the position of the feet, as in certain sports. —*SYN.* see **posture.**

stanch (stanch; *also, and for the adj. usually*, stänch), *v.t.* [ME. *stanchen, staunchen;* OFr. *estanchier;* LL. **stanticare*, to bring to a stop < L. *stans, stantis*, ppr. of *stare*, to stand], 1. to stop or check the flow of (blood or other body fluid). 2. to stop or check the flow of blood from (a cut or wound). 3. [Archaic or Dial.], to quench, allay, appease, check, or quell. *v.i.* to stop flowing, as blood. *adj.* [OFr. *estanche*, fem. of *estanc;* akin to *v.*], 1. watertight; seaworthy: as, a *stanch* ship. 2. firm; trustworthy; loyal: as, a *stanch* supporter. 3. strong; solidly made; substantial. Also, especially for the *adj.*, **staunch.** —*SYN.* see **faithful.**

stan·chion (stan′shən), *n.* [ME. *stanchon;* OFr. *estanson, estancon* < *estance;* see STANCE], 1. an upright bar, beam, or post used as a support. 2. one of a pair of linked, upright bars that fit behind an animal's head to confine it in a stall. *v.t.* 1. to provide or support with stanchions. 2. to confine (cattle, etc.) with stanchions.

stand (stand), *v.i.* [STOOD (stood), STANDING], [ME. *standen;* AS. *standan;* akin to MD. *standen;* IE. base **stā-, *stə-*, to stand, be placed, as also in *stable, state, station*, etc.], 1. *a)* to be or remain in an upright position, supported on the feet (or foot): distinguished from *kneel, crouch, lie, sit*, etc.: said of human beings and some animals. *b)* to be or remain in an upright position, supported on its base, bottom, pedestal, etc.: said of physical objects. *c)* to grow upright or erect: said of plants. 2. to take a standing position. 3. *a)* to take, move into, or be in a (specified) standing position: as, he *stood* aloof, *stand* back! *b)* to take or maintain a (specified) position, attitude, or course, as of support, antagonism, responsibility, sponsorship, etc.: as, I *stand* opposed to this act. 4. to have a (specified) height when standing: as, he *stands* six feet. 5. to point: said of a dog. 6. to be placed; be situated. 7. to gather and remain, or be stagnant, as water. 8. to remain unchanged, undestroyed, intact, effective, or valid: as, the law still *stands*. 9. to be in a (specified) condition, relation, or circumstance: as, they *stood* in awe. 10. to be at a (specified) rank, degree, or the like: as, John *stands* first on the honor roll. 11. to maintain one's opinion, viewpoint, adherence, etc.; remain resolute or firm. 12. to agree or accord. 13. [Chiefly British], to be a candidate for election; run, as for a certain office. 14. to make resistance, as to hostile action. 15. *a)* to come to a stop; halt. *b)* to be stationary. 16. to hesitate, as at doing something; scruple. 17. to show the (specified) relative position of those involved: said of a score, account, reckoning, etc. 18. in *nautical usage*, to take or hold a certain course at sea, or go in a certain direction: as, the ship *stood* to sea. *v.t.* 1. to make stand; set or place upright. 2. to endure; tolerate; bear. 3. to remain uninjured or unaffected by; withstand; resist. 4. to be subjected to; undergo: as, they *stood* trial. 5. [Colloq.], to bear the cost of (a dinner, etc.), as when treating. 6. in *military usage*, to stand in formation at (reveille, retreat, etc.). *n.* [AS. *stand* < *standan*, to stand], 1. a standing (in various senses); especially, a stopping; halt or stop; specifically, *a)* a stopping to counterattack, resist, etc., as in a retreat. *b)* a halt made by a touring theatrical company to give a performance, or the place stopped at. 2. the place where a person stands or is supposed to stand; a position; station: as, he took his *stand* at the rear. 3. a view, opinion, or position, as on an issue: as, I have made my *stand* clear. 4. a structure for a person or persons to stand or sit on; specifically, *a)* a raised platform, as for a band or for spectators along the line of march of a parade: as, a reviewing *stand*. *b)* a set of steplike tiers of benches, as for the spectators at an athletic field or stadium. *c)* the place where a witness testifies in a courtroom. 5. a place of business; specifically, *a)* a booth, stall, etc. where goods are sold. *b)* a parking space along the side of a street, reserved for taxicabs, etc. *c)* a business site or location. 6. a rack, small table, etc. for holding certain things: as, a music *stand*. 7. a standing growth of trees or plants. 8. [Obs. or Dial.], a group, set, etc. —*SYN.* see **bear.**

make a stand, 1. to take a position for defense or opposition. 2. to support a definite position, opinion, etc. 3. to come to a stop.

stand a chance (or **show**), to have a chance, as of victory or survival.

stand by, 1. to be near and ready to act if or when needed. 2. to aid or support. 3. to make good (a promise, etc.); keep to; maintain, as a policy. 4. to be near or present, especially in a passive manner or as a mere onlooker. 5. in *radio*, to remain tuned in, as for continuance of a program, or to remain ready to transmit without actually doing so.

stand down, in *law*, to leave the witness stand, as after testifying.

stand for, 1. to be a symbol for or sign of; represent; mean. 2. [Colloq.], to tolerate or endure.

stand in, [Colloq.], 1. to cost. 2. to be on good terms; be friendly (usually followed by *with*).

stand off, 1. to keep at a distance. 2. to fail or refuse to agree or comply. 3. to put off, stave off, or evade, as a creditor or assailant. 4. in *nautical usage*, to take or hold a course away from shore.

stand on, 1. to be based or founded upon; depend on. 2. to insist upon; demand due observance of (ceremony, one's dignity or rights, etc.). 3. in *nautical usage*, to hold the same course or tack.

stand one's ground, to maintain one's position, as against attack.
stand out, 1. to project. 2. to show up clearly; be distinct in appearance. 3. to be prominent, notable, or outstanding; have distinction. 4. to refuse to give in; be firm in resistance. 5. in *nautical usage,* to take or hold a course away from shore.
stand over, to postpone or be postponed; hold over.
stand to, 1. to keep working at without pause. 2. to stand by; be ready. 3. to support; hold to; refuse to abandon; hence, 4. to abide by (a promise, etc.).
stand up, 1. to rise to or be in a standing position. 2. to prove valid, satisfactory, durable, etc. 3. [Slang], to fail to keep an engagement with.
stand up for, to take the side of; defend; support.
stand up to, to confront fearlessly; refuse to be cowed or intimidated by.
take the stand, to sit (or stand) in the designated place in a courtroom and give testimony.

stand·ard (stan'dẽrd), *n.* [ME.; OFr. *estendard;* prob. < Gmc. **standan,* to stand + *ort,* a place; hence, a standing place], 1. any figure or object, especially a flag or banner, used as an emblem or symbol of a people, military unit, etc.; specifically, *a)* in *heraldry,* a long, tapering flag used as an ensign, as by a king. *b)* in *military usage,* the colors of a cavalry unit. 2. something established for use as a rule or basis of comparison in measuring or judging capacity, quantity, content, extent, value, quality, etc.: as, *standards* of weight and measure are fixed by the government. 3. the proportion of pure gold or silver and base metal prescribed for use in coinage. 4. the commodity or commodities used as the basis of a given monetary system: see **gold standard, silver standard.** 5. something used by general agreement to determine whether or not a thing is as it should be; type, model, or example established by usage; pattern; criterion. 6. a level or grade of excellence, attainment, etc., regarded as a goal or measure of adequacy. 7. any upright object used as a support, often a part of the thing it supports; supporting piece; base; stand. 8. in *botany,* the large, upper petal of a butterfly-shaped flower; vexillum. 9. [British], in *education,* a grade or class (in an elementary school). 10. in *horticulture,* a tree or shrub with a tall, erect stem, allowed to grow to full size and form without the support of a trellis, wall, etc. *adj.* 1. used as, or meeting the requirements of, a standard, rule, model, etc.; hence, 2. generally recognized as excellent and authoritative: as, *standard* reference books. 3. having no special or unusual features; ordinary; regular; typical: as, the *standard* model of an automobile. 4. generally used, and regarded as proper for use, in books, periodicals, lectures, speeches, documents, literary compositions of various sorts, and the conduct of public affairs; of a level of linguistic usage that excludes locutions, constructions, pronunciations, etc. considered too informal, vulgar, provincial, mistaken, or otherwise likely to detract from the dignity or prestige of the user: as, *standard* English. 5. in *printing,* of ordinary height, width, or face weight: said of type. Abbreviated **std.**

***SYN.*—standard** applies to some measure, principle, model, etc. with which things of the same class are compared in order to determine their quantity, value, quality, etc. (*standards* of purity for drugs); **criterion** applies to a test or rule for measuring the excellence, fitness, or correctness of something (mere memory is no accurate *criterion* of intelligence); **gauge** literally applies to a standard of measurement (a wire *gauge*), but figuratively, it is equivalent to **criterion** (sales are an accurate *gauge* of a book's popularity); **yardstick** refers to a test or criterion for measuring genuineness or value (time is the only true *yardstick* of a book's merit). See also **model.**

stand·ard-bear·er (stan'dẽrd-bâr'ẽr), *n.* 1. the man assigned to carry the standard, or flag, of a group, especially of a military organization. 2. the leader or chief representative of a movement, political party, etc.

stand·ard·bred, stand·ard-bred (stan'dẽrd-bred'), *adj.* bred to meet certain standards; specifically, designating or of a breed of horses used for harness races.

standard candle, a unit of light equal to the light given off by a candle of a specified material, size, and burning rate, as a 7/8-inch candle of spermaceti burning at the rate of 120 grains per hour.

standard dollar, 1. since January 31, 1934, a United States dollar of 15 5/21 grains of gold, 0.900 fine. 2. prior to 1934, a United States dollar of 25.8 grains of gold, 0.900 fine.

stand·ard-gauge (stand'ẽrd-gāj'), *adj.* of, for, or having the standard gauge.

standard gauge, 1. a width of 4 feet, 8 1/2 inches between the rails of a railroad track, established as standard. 2. a railroad having such a gauge. 3. a locomotive or car for a standard-gauge railroad.

stand·ard·i·za·tion (stan'dẽr-di-zā'shən, stan'dẽr-dī-zā'shən), *n.* a standardizing or being standardized.

stand·ar·dize (stan'dẽr-dīz'), *v.t.* [STANDARDIZED (-dīzd'), STANDARDIZING], 1. to make standard or uniform; cause to be without variations or irregularities. 2. to compare with or test by a standard.

standard of living, a level of subsistence, as of a nation, social class, or person, with reference to the adequacy of necessities and comforts in daily life.

standard time, the official civil time for any given region; mean solar time, determined by distance east or west of Greenwich, England: the earth is divided into twenty-four time zones extending from pole to pole, four of them (*Eastern, Central, Mountain,* and *Pacific*) falling within the borders of the United States and using the civil times of the 75th, 90th, 105th, and 120th meridians respectively; adjacent time zones are one hour apart, but some slight variations occur in legal time, as when a country extending across more than one time zone keeps a uniform legal time nationally.

stand-by (stand'bī'), *n.* [*pl.* STAND-BYS (-bīz')], a person or thing that can always be depended upon or used with good effect: as, that story is an old *stand-by* of his.

stand·ee (stan-dē'), *n.* [Colloq.], a person who stands, usually because there are no vacant seats, as at a concert or play.

stand·fast (stand'fast', stand'fäst'), *n.* 1. a stable, reliable person or thing. 2. a firm, fixed position.

stand-in (stand'in'), *n.* 1. a person who serves as a substitute for a motion-picture actor or actress while lights and cameras are being adjusted, etc. 2. any substitute for another. 3. [Slang], a position of favor and influence, as with an important person.

stand·ing (stan'diŋ), *n.* 1. the act, state, or position of a person or thing that stands. 2. a place to stand; standing room. 3. status, position, rank, or reputation: as, he has lost his *standing* as an authority. 4. duration or length of service, existence, membership, etc.: as, a record of long *standing.* *adj.* 1. that stands; upright or erect, as a position. 2. done or made in or from a standing position: as, a *standing* shot or jump. 3. stagnant; not flowing: said of water. 4. lasting, permanent, or for an unlimited time: as, a *standing* order for a dozen eggs a week. 5. stationary; not movable. 6. not in operation, use, activity, etc., as a machine.

standing army, an army maintained during peacetime, as well as in time of war, on a permanent organizational basis.

standing order, 1. in *military usage,* formerly, a general order always in force in a particular command, establishing a standard or uniform procedure: now called *standing* (or *standard*) *operating procedure.* 2. *pl.* in *parliamentary procedure,* the rules for procedure which continue in force through all sessions until changed or repealed.

standing rigging, the heavy ropes and stays that support the masts and spars of a ship.

standing room, room in which to stand, especially when there are no vacant seats, as in a theater.

stand·ish (stan'dish), *n.* [? < *stand* + *dish*], [Archaic], a stand for writing materials; inkstand.

Stan·dish, Captain Miles (stan'dish), 1584?–1656; English colonist; military leader of Plymouth colony.

stand·off (stand'ôf'), *n.* 1. a standing off or being stood off. 2. a counterbalancing or equalizing effect. 3. a tie or draw in a game or contest. *adj.* standoffish.

stand·off·ish (stand'ôf'ish), *adj.* withdrawn; aloof; reserved.

stand oil, linseed oil thickened by heat treatment, as for use in paint.

stand-out (stand'out'), *n.* [Colloq.], a person who steadfastly refuses to concur in the otherwise unanimous opinion, decision, etc. of the group.

stand·pat (stand'pat'), *adj.* [Colloq.], of or characterized by a tendency to stand pat, or resist change; conservative.

stand·pat·ter (stand'pat'ẽr), *n.* [Colloq.], a person who follows a standpat policy; conservative.

stand·pipe (stand'pīp'), *n.* a large vertical pipe or cylindrical tank for storing water, as to get a desired head or uniform pressure.

stand·point (stand'point'), *n.* [after G. *standpunkt*], 1. position from which something is seen or viewed. 2. figuratively, mental position from which things are viewed and judged; point of view.

St. Andrew's Cross, a cross in the shape of the letter X, blazoned in white on a blue background.

stand·still (stand'stil'), *n.* a stop, halt, or cessation.

stand-up (stand'up'), *adj.* 1. standing upright or erect. 2. done or taken while standing: as, a *stand-up* drink. 3. high, stiff, and without folds: said of a collar.

stane (stān), *n., adj., v.t.* [Scot. & N. Eng. Dial.], stone.

stang (staŋ), archaic past tense and past participle of **sting.**

stang (staŋ), *n., v.t. & v.i.* [< ME. *stangen* < ON. *stanga,* to prick, goad], [Scot. & N. Eng. Dial.], sting; pain.

stan·hope (stan'hōp, stan'əp), *n.* [after Fitzroy *Stan-*

hope (1787–1864), Eng. clergyman for whom the first was built], a light, open carriage with two or four wheels and, usually, a single seat.

Stan·hope, Philip Dor·mer (dôr′mẽr stan′əp), see **Chesterfield,** fourth Earl of.

Stan·is·lau (shtän′is-lou′), *n.* Stanislav.

Sta·ni·slav (stá′ni-släf′), *n.* a city in the southwestern Ukrainian S.S.R.: pop., 60,000: Polish name, *Stanisławów;* German name, *Stanislau.*

Stan·i·slav·sky, Kon·stan·tin (kon′stən-tēn′ stan′i-slaf′ski; Russ. stän′i-släf′ski), (born *Konstantin Sergeyevich Alekseyev*), 1863–1938; Russian actor, director, and producer; cofounder of the Moscow Art Theater.

Sta·ni·sla·wów (stä′nē-slä′voof), *n.* Stanislav.

stank (staŋk), alternative past tense of **stink.**

Stan·ley (stan′li), [< the surname *Stanley* < the place name *Stanley* < AS. *stan leah,* stone lea], a masculine name.

Stan·ley, Sir **Henry Morton** (stan′li), (born *John Rowlands*) 1841–1904; British explorer in Africa.

Stanley, Mount, the highest peak of the Ruwenzori Mountains, in central Africa: height, 16,798 ft.

Stanley Falls, a series of seven cataracts of the Congo River, central Belgian Congo.

stan·na·ry (stan′ẽr-i), *n.* [*pl.* STANNARIES (-iz)], [ML. *stannaria* < LL. *stannum;* see STANNUM], [British], a tin mine or place where tin is smelted.

stan·nate (stan′āt), *n.* a salt of stannic acid.

stan·nic (stan′ik), *adj.* [< LL. *stannum,* tin; + *-ic*], of or containing tin, specifically with a valence of four.

stan·nite (stan′īt), *n.* [< LL. *stannum,* tin; + *-ite*], 1. a gray or black mineral with metallic luster, a native sulfide of tin, copper, and iron: also called *tin pyrites.* 2. a salt formed by the reaction of stannous hydroxide (stannous acid) or stannous oxide with alkali hydroxides.

stan·nous (stan′əs), *adj.* [< LL. *stannum;* + *-ous*], of or containing tin, specifically with a valence of two.

stan·num (stan′əm), *n.* [L. *stannum, stagnum,* an alloy of silver and lead (in LL., tin); ? akin to W. *ystaen,* tin], tin: symbol, Sn (no period).

Sta·no·voi Mountains (stä′nô-voi′), a mountain system in eastern Siberia, extending from the southern border to the Arctic Ocean, made up of the Yablonoi, Kolyma, and Anadyr Ranges: highest peaks, c. 8,000 ft.

St. Anthony's fire, erysipelas.

Stan·ton, Edwin Mc·Mas·ters (mək-mas′tẽrz stan′tən), 1814–1869; American statesman; secretary of war (1862–1867).

Stanton, Elizabeth Ca·dy (kā′di), 1815–1902; American reformer and leader in the struggle for women's rights, especially the right to vote.

stan·za (stan′zə), *n.* [It., lit., stopping place, room < LL. **stantia;* see STANCE], a group of lines of verse forming one of the divisions of a poem: it is usually recurrent, made up of four or more lines, and characterized by a regular pattern with respect to the number of lines and the arrangement of meter and rhyme: abbreviated **st.**

stan·za·ic (stan-zā′ik), *adj.* of, or in the form of, a stanza or stanzas.

sta·pe·di·al (stə-pē′di-əl), *adj.* of the stapes.

sta·pe·li·a (stə-pē′li-ə), *n.* [Mod. L., after Jan Bode van *Stapel* (died 1636), D. botanist and physician], any of a number of related cactuslike plants of the milkweed family, with large, star-shaped, bad-smelling, yellowish or purple flowers.

sta·pes (stā′pēz), *n.* [ML., a stirrup; ? < OHG. *stapf,* a step], a small, stirrup-shaped bone, the innermost of a chain of three bones in the middle ear of mammals: see **ear,** illus.

staph·y·lo- (staf′i-lō, staf′i-lə), [< Gr. *staphylē,* bunch of grapes], a combining form meaning: 1. *uvula,* as in *staphylorrhaphy.* 2. *staphylococcus.* Also, before a vowel, **staphyl-.**

staph·y·lo·coc·cic (staf′i-lə-kok′sik), *adj.* of or caused by staphylococci.

staph·y·lo·coc·cus (staf′i-lə-kok′əs), *n.* [*pl.* STAPHYLOCOCCI (-kok′sī)], [Mod. L.; see STAPHYLO- & -COCCUS], any of a group of spherical, Gram-positive bacteria that generally occur in irregular clusters or short chains and are the cause of pus formation in boils, abscesses, etc.

staph·y·lo·plas·ty (staf′i-lə-plas′ti), *n.* [*staphylo-* + *-plasty*], the use of plastic surgery to repair defects of the soft palate.

staph·y·lor·rha·phy, staph·y·lor·a·phy (staf′ə-lôr′ə-fi, staf′ə-lor′ə-fi), *n.* [< *staphylo-* + Gr. *rhaphē,* a sewing, suture], the operation of uniting a cleft palate by plastic surgery.

sta·ple (stā′p'l), *n.* [ME. *stapel;* OFr. *estaple;* MD. *stapel,* mart, emporium, post, orig. support], 1. the chief commodity, or one of several important commodities, made, grown, or sold in a particular place, region, country, etc. 2. a chief item, part, material, or element in anything. 3. raw material. 4. any chief item of trade, regularly stocked and in constant demand: as, flour, sugar, and salt are *staples.* 5. *a*) the fiber of cotton, wool, flax, etc., with reference to length and fineness. *b*) a particular length and degree of fineness of such fiber. 6. [Archaic], a principal market, trading center, etc. *adj.* 1. regularly found on the market or in stock as a result of a constant demand; hence, 2. produced, consumed, or exported regularly and in quantity. 3. most important; leading; principal: as, *staple* industries, *staple* topics for gossip. *v.t.* [STAPLED (-p'ld), STAPLING], to sort (wool, cotton, etc.) according to the nature of its staple.

sta·ple (stā′p'l), *n.* [ME. *stapel;* AS. *stapol,* a post, pillar; akin to G. *stapel,* stake, beam; for IE. base see STEP], 1. a U-shaped piece of metal with sharp-pointed ends, driven into a surface to hold a hook, hasp, wire, etc. against it. 2. a similar piece of thin wire driven through papers and clinched over as a binding. *v.t.* [STAPLED (-p'ld), STAPLING], to fasten or bind with a staple or staples.

sta·pler (stā′plẽr), *n.* 1. a person who deals in staple goods. 2. a person who staples (wool, etc.).

sta·pler (stā′plẽr), *n.* a machine used for driving wire staples into a material, especially for the purpose of binding papers, pamphlets, booklets, magazines, etc.

star (stär), *n.* [ME. *sterre;* AS. *steorra;* akin to D. *ster, star;* IE. base **ster-,* a star, as also in L. *stella* (dim. < **ster-ela*); cf. STELLAR], 1. any of the heavenly bodies seen as small, fixed points of light in the night sky. 2. any one of these bodies that is a distant sun: distinguished from *moon, planet, meteor, comet,* etc. 3. a conventionalized flat figure having (usually five or six) symmetrical projecting points, regarded as a representation of a star of the sky. 4. any mark, shape, emblem, or the like resembling such a figure. 5. an asterisk (*). 6. any heavenly body, as a planet, meteor, the moon, etc. 7. *a*) in *astrology,* a planet, zodiacal constellation, etc. regarded as influencing human fate or destiny. *b*) *often pl.* fate; destiny; fortune. 8. a person who excels or performs brilliantly in a given activity, especially a sport. 9. a prominent actor or actress, especially one playing a leading role in a given production. *v.t.* [STARRED (stärd), STARRING], 1. to mark or set with stars as a decoration. 2. to mark with one or more stars as a grade of quality. 3. to mark with an asterisk. 4. to present or feature (an actor or actress, etc.) in a leading role. *v.i.* 1. to perform brilliantly; excel. 2. to play a leading role, as in a theatrical production. *adj.* 1. brilliant or outstanding for skill and talent; excelling others; leading: as, a *star* performer. 2. of a star or stars.

see stars, [Colloq.], to experience the sensation of lights brightly flashing before the eyes, as from a blow on the head.

thank one's (lucky) stars, to be thankful for what appears to be good luck.

star apple, 1. a tropical evergreen with shining leaves, whitish flowers, and applelike fruit showing a star-like figure inside when cut across. 2. its fruit.

star·board (stär′bẽrd, stär′bôrd′, stär′bōrd′), *n.* [ME. *sterbord;* AS. *steorbord* < *steoran,* to steer (the old rudder being a kind of large oar used on the right side of the ship)], the right-hand side of a ship or airplane as one faces forward, toward the bow: opposed to *port, larboard.* *adj.* of or on the starboard. *adv.* to or toward the starboard. *v.t.* & *v.i.* to turn (the helm) to the right.

starch (stärch), *n.* [ME. *starche* < *sterchen,* to stiffen < AS. *stercan* < *stearc,* rigid, stiff; cf. STARK], 1. a white tasteless, odorless food substance found in potatoes, cereals, yams, peas, and many other foods: it is a granular solid, chemically a complex carbohydrate $(C_6H_{10}O_5)_n$. 2. a powdered form of this, used in water solution for stiffening cloth fabrics, etc. 3. *pl.* starchy foods. 4. formal, unbending manner or behavior; stiffness. 5. [Colloq.], energy; vigor. *v.t.* to stiffen with or as if with starch.

Star Chamber, [ME. *Sterred Chambre;* Anglo-Fr. *chambre d'estoiles;* Anglo-L. *camera stellata:* so called because the roof was ornamented with stars], 1. formerly, an English court made up of councilors appointed by royal authority, which met in secret session without a jury, used torture to force confessions, and handed down arbitrary judgments that were extremely severe: abolished in 1641. 2. any tribunal, investigating body, etc. similarly unjust, arbitrary, and inquisitorial.

starch·i·ness (stär′chi-nis), *n.* the quality or condition of being starchy.

starch·y (stär′chi), *adj.* [STARCHIER (-chi-ẽr), STARCHIEST (-chi-ist)], 1. of, having the nature of, or like starch. 2. containing starch. 3. stiffened with starch. 4. stiff; formal; unbending.

star·dom (stär′dəm), *n.* 1. the status of a star: as, the young actress finally attained *stardom.* 2. stars of the theater, motion pictures, etc., collectively.

star dust, 1. a patch or cluster of stars too distant to be seen separately with the naked eye. 2. [Colloq.], an enchanting, dreamlike quality, tone, or mood.

stare (stâr), *v.i.* [STARED (stârd), STARING], [ME. *staren* < AS. *starian;* akin to ON. *stara;* Gmc. **stara-,* having fixed eyes, rigid; IE. base **ster-,* rigid, stiff], 1. to gaze or look steadily and intently, as in fear, admiration, wonder, etc. 2. to be glaring or conspicuous said especially of color. 3. to stand on end, as hair, etc. ***v.t.*** 1. to stare at: as, he *stared* the stranger up and down. 2. to affect in a given way by staring: as, we *stared* her into confusion. ***n.*** the act of staring; steady, intent look or gaze. —***SYN.*** see **look.**

stare down, to meet the gaze of (another), causing him to look away by continued staring.

stare one in the face, 1. to look at one steadily and intently. 2. to be imminent, pressing, or inescapable.

stare out of countenance, to stare at (another) until he becomes annoyed, embarrassed, etc.

star·fish (stär′fish′), ***n.*** [*pl.* STARFISH, STARFISHES (-iz); see FISH], a small sea animal with a hard, spiny outer covering and five or more arms or rays arranged like the points of a star; asteroid.

STARFISH (5-6 in. across)

star·flow·er (stär′flou′ẽr), ***n.*** 1. any of a group of related plants of the primrose family, with white or pink, five-petaled, star-shaped flowers. 2. any of various other plants with star-shaped flowers, as the star-of-Bethlehem.

star·gaze (stär′gāz′), ***v.i.*** [back-formation < *stargazer*], 1. to gaze at the stars. 2. to indulge in dreamy, absent-minded thoughts.

star·gaz·er (stär′gāz′ẽr), ***n.*** 1. a person who gazes at the stars; specifically, *a*) an astrologer. *b*) an astronomer: used humorously. 2. any of several marine fishes having eyes in the top of the head.

star·gaz·ing (stär′gāz′iŋ), ***n.*** 1. the act of a person who gazes at the stars. 2. absent-mindedness. 3. dreaminess; impracticality.

star grass, any of a number of grasslike plants with star-shaped flowers.

stark (stärk), ***adj.*** [ME. *starc;* AS. *stearc;* for base see STARE], 1. stiff; rigid: said of the dead. 2. standing out in sharp outline: as, a tree *stark* in the snow. 3. bleak; desolate; barren. 4. stark-naked. 5. sheer; utter; downright: as, *stark* terror. 6. [Archaic], *a*) hard, harsh, or severe. *b*) strong; powerful. ***adv.*** 1. in a stark manner; severely; vigorously. 2. utterly; downright; entirely; quite.

Stark, Harold Rayns·ford (rānz′fẽrd stärk), 1880– ; American admiral in World War II.

Stark, John (stärk), 1728–1822; American general in the Revolutionary War.

stark-nak·ed (stärk′nāk′id), ***adj.*** [altered (by association with *stark*) < ME. *stertnaked,* lit., tail-naked; *stert-* < AS. *steort,* tail, rump; IE. base **ster-,* stiff, rigid; cf. STARE, START], absolutely naked.

star·less (stär′lis), ***adj.*** without stars.

star·let (stär′lit), ***n.*** 1. a small star. 2. [Colloq.], a young motion-picture actress being prepared for starring roles.

star·light (stär′līt′), ***n.*** light given by the stars. ***adj.*** 1. of starlight. 2. lighted by the stars; starlit.

star·like (stär′līk′), ***adj.*** 1. like a star in brilliance. 2. star-shaped; having radial points.

star·ling (stär′liŋ), ***n.*** [ME., dim. of *stare;* AS. *stær,* starling; akin to L. *sturnus*], any of a number of birds with characteristic iridescent plumage: all are native to Europe, but some have been introduced into the United States.

star·lit (stär′lit′), ***adj.*** lighted by the stars.

star-nosed mole (stär′nōzd′), a long-tailed mole having a ring of fleshy tentacles around its nose.

star-of-Beth·le·hem (stär′əv-beth′li-əm, stär′əv-beth′li-hem′), ***n.*** any of a number of related plants of the lily family, with white, star-shaped flowers and long, narrow leaves.

Star of Bethlehem, the bright star which is supposed to have hung low over Bethlehem at the birth of Jesus of Nazareth, guiding the Magi to the manger: Matt. 2:2,9,10.

Star of David, [transl. < Heb. *mogēn dovid,* lit., shield of David], a six-pointed star formed of two (often interlaced) equilateral triangles: a symbol of Judaism and now of the Republic of Israel: as a mystic symbol in the Middle Ages, called *Solomon's Seal.*

STAR OF DAVID

starred (stärd), ***adj.*** 1. marked or decorated with or as with a star or stars. 2. thought to be influenced or affected by the stars. 3. presented as a star, or leading performer.

star·ri·ness (stär′i-nis), ***n.*** the quality or state of being starry.

star·ry (stär′i), ***adj.*** [STARRIER (-i-ẽr), STARRIEST (-i-ist)], 1. set or marked with stars. 2. shining like stars; bright. 3. star-shaped. 4. lighted by or full of stars. 5. of or coming from the stars. 6. consisting of, or having the nature of, stars.

Stars and Bars, the flag first used by the American Confederacy: it had three horizontal bars—one of white between two of red—and in the upper left corner a blue field marked with a circle of white stars, one for each seceded State.

Stars and Stripes, the flag of the United States, consisting of a rectangle with seven red, horizontal stripes alternating with six white ones, and, in the upper left corner, a blue field with 50 white stars, one for each State.

star sapphire, a sapphire cut with a convex surface and seeming, by reflected light, to have a star-shaped figure in it.

star shell, in *military usage,* a shell timed to burst in mid-air in a shower of bright particles that momentarily light up the surrounding terrain.

star-span·gled (stär′spaŋ′g'ld), ***adj.*** studded or spangled with stars.

Star-Spangled Banner, 1. the flag of the United States. 2. the national anthem of the United States: the words were written by Francis Scott Key during the bombardment of Fort McHenry (1814) in the War of 1812.

start (stärt), ***v.i.*** [ME. *sterten* (orig. Kentish & Northern) < AS. *styrtan* & cognate ON. *sterta;* akin to G. *stürzen,* to overthrow; IE. base **sterd-,* < **ster-,* stiff; cf. STARE, STARK-NAKED], 1. to move suddenly, usually involuntarily, as from rest, a given position, etc.; jump, leap, jerk, etc.: as, the backfire made her *start,* the cat *started* back. 2. to be displaced; become loose, warped, etc. 3. to stick out or seem to stick out, as the eyes in fear, surprise, etc. 4. *a*) to begin to do something or go somewhere; go into action or motion. *b*) to make or have a beginning; commence. 5. to be among the beginning entrants in a race; be a starter: as, since two of the horses were scratched, only six *started.* 6. to spring into being, activity, view, or the like. ***v.t.*** 1. to cause to jump or move suddenly; rouse; flush: as, we *started* three birds at one time. 2. to displace, loosen, warp, etc.: as, the collision *started* a seam. 3. to cause or enable to begin; set into motion or action. 4. to introduce (a subject, topic, or discussion). 5. to open and make the contents flow from (a receptacle); tap. 6. to give the starting signal for (a race) or to (the contestants in a race). 7. to cause to be an entrant in a race, etc. 8. [Archaic or Dial.], to startle; cause to start, or move involuntarily. ***n.*** 1. a sudden, brief shock or fright; startled reaction; hence, 2. a sudden, startled movement; jump, leap, jerk, etc. 3. *pl.* sudden, usually brief bursts of activity: usually in the phrase *by fits and starts.* 4. *a*) a part that is loosened, warped, etc. *b*) a break or gap resulting from this. 5. a starting, or beginning; a getting into action or motion; commencement; hence, 6. a place where, or a time when, a beginning is made, as in a race; starting point. 7. a factor or position giving an advantage, as in a race or contest; lead; edge. 8. a signal to begin, as in a race. 9. an opportunity of beginning or entering upon a career, etc. 10. [Archaic], an outburst or fit, as of emotion, or a sally, as of wit. —***SYN.*** see **begin.**

start in, to begin a task, activity, etc.

start out, 1. to start a journey. 2. to make a start on some course of action or procedure, as a career.

start up, 1. to rise up or stand suddenly, as in fright. 2. to come into being suddenly; spring up. 3. to cause (a motor, etc.) to begin running.

start·er (stär′tẽr), ***n.*** a person or thing that starts; specifically, *a*) the first in a series. *b*) a person or animal that starts in a race: as, of the ten *starters* only six finished. *c*) a person who gives the signal to start, as in a race. *d*) a person who supervises the departure of buses, commercial aircraft, etc. *e*) a self-starter.

star thistle, 1. a European weed with spiny leaves and heads of purple flowers. 2. a related weed with yellow flowers; caltrop.

starting post, the place where a horse race starts, usually marked with a post.

star·tle (stär′t'l), ***v.t.*** [STARTLED (-t'ld), STARTLING], [ME. *stertlen,* to rush, stumble along, freq. of *sterten;* see START], 1. to frighten or alarm suddenly or unexpectedly; cause to start, or move involuntarily, as from sudden fright. 2. to cause to feel a shock of surprise: as, he was *startled* at the extent of the uprising. ***v.i.*** to be startled. ***n.*** 1. a start or shock, as of surprise or fright. 2. something that startles. —***SYN.*** see **shock.**

star·tling (stär′tliŋ), ***adj.*** [ppr. of *startle*], causing a shock of fright or surprise.

star·va·tion (stär-vā′shən), ***n.*** 1. the act of starving. 2. the state of being starved.

starve (stärv), ***v.i.*** [STARVED (stärvd), STARVING], [ME. *sterven;* AS. *steorfan,* to die, perish; akin to G. *sterben;*

IE. base *sterbh- < *ster-, stiff, rigid; basic sense "to become stiff"], 1. to die from lack of food. 2. to suffer or become weak from hunger. 3. to suffer from great poverty and need. 4. [Dial.], to suffer or die from cold. 5. [Colloq.], to be very hungry. 6. [Obs.], to die. ***v.t.*** 1. to cause to starve; deprive of food. 2. to force or compel by starvation: as, they *starved* the city into submission. —***SYN.*** see **hungry.**

starve for, to be in great need of; have a strong desire for (affection, etc.).

starve·ling (stärv′liŋ), ***adj.*** [< *starve*], 1. starving; weak and hungry. 2. poverty-stricken. 3. characterized by or suggestive of starvation or poverty. 4. of poor quality or inadequate quantity. ***n.*** a person or animal that is thin and weak from lack of food.

stash (stash), ***v.t. & v.i.*** [prob. a blend of *store* and *cache*], [Slang], to put or hide away (money, valuables, etc.) in a secret or safe pl ace,as for future use.

sta·sis (stā′sis, stas′is), ***n.*** [*pl.* STASES (stā′sēz)], [Mod. L.; Gr. *stasis*, a standing < *histanai*, to stand], a stoppage of the flow of some fluid in the body, as of blood in a blood vessel or feces in the intestines.

-stat (stat), [Gr. *-statēs*], a combining form meaning *stationary, making stationary*, as in *gyrostat, thermostat.*

stat., 1. statuary. 2. statue. 3. statute; statutes.

stat·a·ble (stāt′ə-b'l), ***adj.*** that can be stated.

state (stāt), ***n.*** [ME. *stat;* OFr. *estat;* L. *status*, state, position, standing < *stare*, to stand], 1. a set of circumstances or attributes characterizing a person or thing at a given time; way or form of being; condition: as, his affairs are in a bad *state*, what is his mental *state?* 2. a particular mental or emotional condition: as, a *state* of melancholy. 3. condition as regards physical structure, constitution, internal form, stage or phase of existence, etc. 4. [Obs. or Rare], *a)* condition or position in life; social status, rank, or degree. *b)* high rank or position. 5. the style of living characteristic of people having high rank and wealth; rich, imposing, ceremonious display; dignity and pomp. 6. [sometimes S-], *pl.* legislative bodies in any of several countries; estates. 7. [sometimes S-], the power or authority represented by a body of people politically organized under one government, especially an independent government, within a territory or territories having definite boundaries. 8. [sometimes S-], such a body of people; body politic. 9. [usually S-], one of the territorial and political units constituting a federal government, as in the United States. 10. the territory of a state (senses 8 & 9). 11. the political organization constituting the basis of civil government: as, church and *state.* 12. the sphere of highest governmental authority and administration: as, matters of *state.* ***adj.*** 1. of, for, or characteristic of occasions of great ceremony; formal; ceremonial. 2. [sometimes S-], of or having to do with the body politic, government, or state. ***v.t.*** [STATED (-id), STATING], 1. to set, settle, or establish by specifying. 2. to set forth in words, especially in a specific, definite, or formal way.

in (or **into**) **a state,** [Colloq.], 1. in (or into) a bad condition, as of disorder or difficulty. 2. in (or into) a condition of agitation or excitement.

lie in state, to be displayed formally to the public before burial.

the States, [Colloq.], the United States: often so called abroad.

SYN.—**state** and **condition** both refer to the set of circumstances surrounding or characterizing a person or thing at a given time (what is his mental *state*, or *condition?*), but **condition** more strongly implies some relationship to causes or circumstances (his *condition* will not permit him to travel); **situation** implies a significant interrelationship of the circumstances, and connection between these and the person involved (to be in a difficult *situation*); **status,** basically a legal term, refers to one's state as determined by such arbitrary factors as age, sex, training, mentality, service, etc. (his *status* as a veteran exempts him).

state bank, a bank controlled or chartered by a state.

state capitalism, a form of capitalism in which much of the capital, industry, etc. is state-owned.

state chamber, a room used on formal or ceremonial occasions.

state·craft (stāt′kraft′, stāt′kräft′), ***n.*** the art of, or skill in, the managing of state affairs; statesmanship.

stat·ed (stāt′id), ***adj.*** [pp. of *state*], 1. established; fixed; regular. 2. declared; alleged. 3. formulated.

State Department, the department of the executive branch of the United States government in charge of relations with foreign countries.

State flower, the floral emblem selected for or adopted by a State, often by action of the legislature.

state·hood (stāt′hood), ***n.*** [see -HOOD], the condition of being a state rather than a territory, dominion, etc.

State·house (stāt′hous′), ***n.*** the official meeting place of the legislature of a State of the United States; State Capitol: also **State house.**

state·less (stāt′lis), ***adj.*** having no state or nationality.

state·li·ness (stāt′li-nis), ***n.*** the quality or condition of being stately.

state·ly (stāt′li), ***adj.*** [STATELIER (-li-ēr), STATELIEST (-li-ist)], 1. imposing; dignified; majestic. 2. slow, dignified, and deliberate: as, a *stately* pace. ***adv.*** in a stately manner. —***SYN.*** see **grand.**

state·ment (stāt′mənt), ***n.*** 1. an act of stating, or setting forth in words. 2. something stated, specified, or said; account or declaration. 3. an abstract of a financial account, especially of money due.

Stat·en Island (stat′'n), an island between New Jersey and Long Island, forming the Borough of Richmond, New York City: area, 57 sq. mi.; pop., 222,000.

State prison, a prison maintained by a State.

sta·ter (stā′tēr), ***n.*** [ME.; L.; Gr. *statēr*, orig., a weight; IE. base **stā-*, to stand], any of various gold and silver coins of ancient Greece and Persia.

State rights, States' rights.

state·room (stāt′rōōm′, stāt′room′), ***n.*** 1. a cabin on board ship. 2. a private sleeping room in a railroad car.

State's attorney, a lawyer appointed or elected to prepare cases for the State and represent it in court.

state's evidence, in *law*, evidence given by or for the prosecution in a criminal case, usually evidence given by a criminal against his associates.

turn state's evidence, to give evidence for the prosecution in a criminal case.

States-Gen·er·al (stāts′jen′ēr-əl), ***n.*** [transl. of Fr. *états généraux*, D. *staaten generaal*], 1. the legislative body in France before the Revolution of 1789, made up of representatives of the clergy, the nobility, and the third estate. 2. the legislative assembly of the Netherlands.

state·side (stāt′sīd′), ***adj.*** [Colloq.], of or characteristic of the United States: as, *stateside* newspapers. ***adv.*** [Colloq.], in, to, or toward the United States: as, I haven't been *stateside* for three years.

states·man (stāts′mən), ***n.*** [*pl.* STATESMEN (-mən)], [*state's*, genit. of *state* + *man*, after Fr. *homme d'état*], a person who shows wisdom and skill in conducting state affairs and treating public issues, or one experienced or engaged in the business of government.

states·man·like (stāts′mən-līk′), ***adj.*** 1. of or befitting a statesman. 2. having the qualities considered typical of a statesman.

states·man·ly (stāts′mən-li), ***adj.*** statesmanlike.

states·man·ship (stāts′mən-ship′), ***n.*** [see -SHIP], the ability, character, or methods of a statesman; skill in managing public affairs.

state socialism, the theory, doctrine, or practice of an economy planned and controlled by the state, based on state ownership of public utilities, basic industries, etc.

States of the Church, Papal States, lands formerly ruled by the Church in Italy.

States' rights, all the rights and powers which the Constitution neither grants to the Federal government nor denies to the various State governments; sometimes, all the rights and powers claimed for the States, including the right of secession from the United States: also **State rights.**

State university, a university kept up by a State government as part of its public educational system.

state-wide (stāt′wīd′), ***adj.*** extending throughout a state; over all the state.

stat·ic (stat′ik), ***adj.*** [Mod. L. *staticus;* Gr. *statikos*, causing to stand < *histanai*, to cause to stand], 1. acting through weight only: said of the pressure exerted by a motionless body or mass; hence, 2. of bodies, masses, or forces at rest or in equilibrium: opposed to *dynamic.* 3. not moving or progressing; at rest; inactive; stationary. 4. in *electricity*, designating, of, or producing stationary electrical charges, as those resulting from friction. 5. in *radio*, of or having to do with static. ***n.*** 1. electrical discharges in the atmosphere that interfere with radio reception, etc. 2. interference or noises produced by such discharges.

stat·i·cal (stat′i-k'l), ***adj.*** static.

stat·i·cal·ly (stat′i-k'l-i, stat′ik-li), ***adv.*** in a static manner.

stat·ics (stat′iks), ***n.pl.*** [construed as sing.], [see STATIC & -ICS], the branch of mechanics dealing with bodies masses, or forces at rest or in equilibrium.

sta·tion (stā′shən), ***n.*** [ME. *stacioun;* Late OFr.; L *statio*, a standing, post, station < *status*, pp. of *stare*, to stand], 1. the place where a person or thing stands or is located, especially an assigned post, position, or location; specifically, *a)* the place where a person, as a guard, stands while on duty. *b)* the post, building, base or headquarters assigned to a group of people working together: as, a police *station*, first-aid *station*, postal *station*, military-government *station.* *c)* in Australasia, a sheep or cattle ranch. *d)* a place or region to which a naval fleet, ship, etc. is assigned for duty. *e)* in India formerly, the place of residence of British officials or military officers of a district. 2. *a)* a regular stopping place, as on a bus line or railroad. *b)* the building or buildings at such a place, for passengers, etc. 3. social standing, position, or rank. 4. a place equipped to transmit or receive radio waves; especially, the studios offices, and technical installations collectively of an establishment for radio or television transmission. 5 a fixed point from which measurements are made i surveying. 6. in *biology*, a habitat, especially the characteristic habitat of a given plant or animal. 7. [Archaic], the fact or condition of being stationary. *v.t.* to assign to a station; place; post. Abbreviated **Sta.**

station agent, an official in charge of a small railroad station, or of a department in a larger station.

sta·tion·ar·y (stā'shən-er'i,) *adj.* [ME. *stacionarye;* L. *stationarius* < *statio;* see STATION], 1. not moving; fixed; at rest. 2. unchanging in condition, value, etc.; not increasing or decreasing. 3. not migratory or itinerant. *n.* [*pl.* STATIONARIES (-iz)], a person or thing that is stationary. Abbreviated **sta.**

stationary engine, a steam engine set in a fixed place.

stationary engineer, a person who operates and maintains stationary engines and mechanical equipment, such as steam boilers, ventilating equipment, etc.

sta·tion·er (stā'shən-ẽr), *n.* [ME. *stacionere;* ML. *stationarius,* tradesman with a fixed station or shop (by contrast with a peddler) < L. *stationarius,* stationary], 1. originally, a bookseller or publisher. 2. a person who sells paper, ink, pens, and other writing materials.

sta·tion·er·y (stā'shən-er'i), *n.* [< *stationer*], writing materials; specifically, paper and envelopes used for writing letters.

station house, a building used as a station, especially by a company of police or firemen.

sta·tion·mas·ter (stā'shən-mas'tẽr, stā'shən-mäs'tẽr), *n.* an official in charge of a major railroad station.

stations of the cross, [sometimes S- C-], a series of fourteen images or pictures, as in a church or along a path leading to a shrine, representing the stages of Jesus' sufferings, visited in succession by worshipers.

station wagon, an automobile with folding or removable rear seats and a back end that opens for easy loading of luggage, etc., having a body of wood or metal panels.

stat·ism (stāt'iz'm), *n.* 1. the doctrine of state sovereignty, as in a republic, or adherence to this. 2. the doctrine or practice of vesting economic control, economic planning, etc. in a centralized state government: the current sense. 3. [Obs.], statecraft or politics.

stat·ist (stāt'ist), *n.* 1. a statistician. 2. a person who believes in or advocates statism. *adj.* of, characteristic of, or advocating statism.

sta·tis·tic (stə-tis'tik), *adj.* statistical. *n.* 1. a statistical item or element. 2. [Rare], statistics (sense 2).

sta·tis·ti·cal (stə-tis'ti-k'l), *adj.* [< ML. *statisticus* < **statista,* statesman < L. *status;* see STATE], of, having to do with, consisting of, or based on statistics.

sta·tis·ti·cal·ly (stə-tis'ti-k'l-i, stə-tis'tik-li), *adv.* 1. in the form of statistics. 2. according to statistics. 3. by means of statistics.

stat·is·ti·cian (stat'is-tish'ən), *n.* an expert or specialist in statistics, or a person who assembles, classifies, and tabulates statistical data.

sta·tis·tics (stə-tis'tiks), *n.pl.* [< G. *statistik* < ML. *statisticus;* see STATISTICAL], 1. facts or data of a numerical kind, assembled, classified, and tabulated so as to present significant information about a given subject. 2. [construed as sing.], the science of assembling, classifying, and tabulating such facts or data.

stat·o·cyst (stat'ə-sist'), *n.* [< Gr. *statos,* standing, stationary; + *-cyst*], a sense organ found in many invertebrate animals, consisting typically of a sac filled with fluid and containing small sensory hairs and particles of lime, etc.: it functions as an organ of balance or equilibrium.

sta·tor (stā'tẽr), *n.* [Mod. L.; L., a supporter < pp. of *stare,* to stand], a fixed part forming the pivot or housing for a revolving part (*rotor*), as in a motor, dynamo, etc.

stat·o·scope (stat'ə-skōp'), *n.* [< Gr. *statos,* standing; + *-scope*], 1. a highly sensitive aneroid barometer. 2. such a barometer adapted for use as an altitude indicator for an aircraft.

stat·u·ar·y (stach'ōō-er'i), *n.* [*pl.* STATUARIES (-iz)], [L. *statuaria* < *statuarius,* of statues < *statua;* see STATUE], 1. statues collectively; group of statues. 2. the art of making statues. 3. a sculptor. *adj.* of or suitable for a statue or statues. Abbreviated **stat.**

stat·ue (stach'ōō, stach'oo), *n.* [ME.; OFr.; L. *statua* < *statuere,* to set, place < base of *stare,* to stand], the form of a person or animal carved in wood, stone, etc., modeled in a plastic substance, or cast in plaster, bronze, etc., especially when done in the round rather than in relief: abbreviated **stat.**

stat·ued (stach'ōōd, stach'ood), *adj.* 1. decorated with statues. 2. sculptured.

Statue of Liberty, a bronze statue, over 150 feet high, of a crowned woman, the Goddess of Liberty, holding a torch in her upraised hand: it was given to the United States by France and is located on Liberty Island in New York harbor: official name, *Liberty Enlightening the World.*

stat·u·esque (stach'ōō-esk'), *adj.* [< *statue,* after *picturesque*], of or like a statue; specifically, *a*) tall and well-proportioned: as, a *statuesque* figure. *b*) stately; graceful; showing poise and dignity.

stat·u·ette (stach'ōō-et'), *n.* [Fr., dim. of *statue*], a small statue.

stat·ure (stach'ẽr), *n.* [ME.; OFr.; L. *statura,* height or size of body < *statuere;* see STATUE], 1. the height of the body (of an animal, especially of man) in a natural standing position. 2. [Rare], the height of an object. 3. development, growth, or elevation reached: used figuratively, as, moral *stature.* —***SYN.*** see **height.**

sta·tus (stā'təs, stat'əs), *n.* [*pl.* STATUSES (-iz)], [L.; see STATE], 1. condition or position with regard to law: as, her *status* is that of a married woman. 2. position; rank; standing: as, no one can question his *status* as a scholar. 3. state, or condition, as of affairs. —***SYN.*** see **state.**

‡sta·tus quo (stā'təs kwō', stat'əs kwō'), [L., lit., the state in which], the existing state of affairs (at any specified time), or the existing condition (of anything specified): also **status in quo.**

‡sta·tus quo an·te (stā'təs, *or* stat'əs, kwō an'ti), [L., lit., the state in which before], the previous state of affairs, or the previous condition (of anything specified).

stat·u·ta·ble (stach'oo-tə-b'l), *adj.* statutory.

stat·ute (stach'oot), *n.* [ME. & OFr. *statut;* LL. *statutum,* neut. of L. *statutus,* pp. of *statuere;* see STATUE], 1. an established rule or law: as, the *statutes* of a university. 2. *a*) a law passed by a legislative body and set forth in a formal document. *b*) such a document. Abbreviated **St., st., stat.** (*sing. & pl.*). —***SYN.*** see **law.**

statute book, a book or other record of statutes.

statute law, law established by a legislative body.

statute mile, 5,280 feet.

statute of limitations, a statute limiting the period within which legal action can be taken in a given matter.

stat·u·to·ry (stach'oo-tôr'i, stach'oo-tō'ri), *adj.* 1. of, or having the nature of, a statute or statutes. 2. fixed, authorized, or established by statute. 3. declared by statute to be such, and hence punishable legally: said of an offense. 4. conforming to a statute.

St. Augustine, a seaport in northeastern Florida: oldest city in the United States: pop., 15,000.

staunch (stônch, stänch), *adj., v.t. & v.i.* stanch.

stau·ro·lite (stô'rə-līt'), *n.* [< Gr. *stauros,* a cross; + *-lite*], a dark-colored silicate of iron and aluminum: the crystals are often found twinned in the form of a cross.

stau·ro·lit·ic (stô'rə-lit'ik), *adj.* of, characteristic of, or having the nature of, staurolite.

stau·ro·scope (stô'rə-skōp'), *n.* [< Gr. *stauros,* a cross; + *-scope*], an instrument for finding the position of planes of polarized light vibration in crystals.

Sta·vang·er (stä-van'ẽr), *n.* a seaport in southwestern Norway: pop., 53,000.

stave (stāv), *n.* [ME. *stave,* taken as sing. of *staves,* pl. of *staff*], 1. one of the thin, shaped strips of wood set edge to edge to form the wall of a barrel, wooden bucket, etc. 2. a stick or staff. 3. a rung, as of a ladder. 4. a set of verses, or lines, of a poem or song; stanza. 5. in *music,* a staff. *v.t.* [STAVED (stāvd) or STOVE (stōv), STAVING], 1. to break or puncture, especially by breaking in a stave or staves. 2. to furnish with staves. *v.i.* to be or become stove in, as a boat; break up or in.

stave in, to break a hole in; crush inward.

stave off, to ward off, hold off, or put off, as by force, guile, or evasion.

staves (stāvz), *n.* 1. alternative plural of **staff.** 2. plural of **stave.**

staves·a·cre (stāvz'ā'kẽr), *n.* [OFr. *stafisagre;* ML. *staphisagria* < Gr. *staphis,* raisin + *agrios,* wild], a tall, purple-flowered plant of Europe and Asia, a larkspur with poisonous seeds having strongly emetic and cathartic properties.

stay (stā), *n.* [ME. *staie, steye;* AS. *stæg;* akin to D. *stag, staag;* IE. base **stāk-,* to stand, place], a heavy rope or cable, usually of wire, used as a brace or support, as for the masts of a ship; guy: see **shroud,** illus. *v.t.* 1. to brace or support with a stay or stays. 2. to change the angle of (a mast) by shifting the stays. 3. to put (a ship) on the other tack. *v.i.* to tack: said of a ship.

in stays, in the process of tacking: said of a ship.

stay (stā), *n.* [OFr. *estai* < base of *stay* (rope)], 1. a support; prop; brace. 2. a strip of stiffening material used in a corset, the collar of a shirt, etc. 3. *pl.* a corset, especially one stiffened with whalebone. *v.t.* 1. to support; hold or prop up· 2. to strengthen, comfort, or sustain in mind or spirit. 3. to cause to rest (*on, upon,* or *in*) for support. 4. to support or strengthen with stays.

stay (stā), *v.i.* [STAYED (stād) or *archaic* STAID (stād), STAYING], [ME. *staien;* Anglo-Fr. *estaier;* OFr. *ester;* L. *stare,* to stand], 1. to continue in the place or condition specified; remain; keep: as, *stay* at home, the weather *stayed* bad for three days, these clothes won't *stay* white. 2. to be located for a while, especially as a guest or resident; live, dwell, or reside (for the time specified). 3. to stand still; stop; halt. 4. to pause; tarry; wait; delay: as, *stay* a little before going on with your labors. 5. [Colloq.], to be able to continue or endure; hold out; last: as, he doesn't *stay* well in the mile run. 6. [Colloq.], to keep up, as with another contestant in a race. 7. [Archaic], to cease. 8. [Archaic], to make a stand; stand one's ground. 9. in *poker*, to remain in a hand by seeing, or meeting, a bet, ante, or raise. ***v.t.*** 1. to stop, halt, or check. 2. to hinder, impede, restrain, or detain. 3. to postpone or delay (legal action or proceedings). 4. [Rare], to quell or allay (strife, etc.). 5. to satisfy or appease for a time the pangs or cravings of (thirst, appetite, etc.). 6. to remain through, during, for, or (with *out*) to the end of: as, *stay* the week (out). 7. [Archaic], to await; wait for. ***n.*** 1. *a*) a stopping or being stopped. *b*) a stop, halt, check, or pause. 2. a postponement or delay in legal action or proceedings: as, the man was given a *stay* of execution. 3. *a*) the action of remaining or continuing in a place for a time. *b*) time spent in a place: as, she had a long *stay* in the hospital. 4. [Colloq.], staying power. 5. [Archaic], a standstill. 6. [Obs.], *a*) a hindrance. *b*) restraint or control. *c*) delay.

SYN.*—stay,** the general term, implies a continuing in a specified place (*stay* there until you hear from me); **remain** specifically suggests a staying behind while others go (he alone *remained* at home); **wait** suggests a staying in anticipation of something (*wait* for me at the library); **abide,** now somewhat archaic, implies a staying fixed for a relatively long period, as in settled residence (he came for a visit and has been *abiding* here since); **tarry** and **linger** imply a staying on after the required or expected time for departure, **linger,** especially, implying that this is deliberate, as from reluctance to leave (we *tarried* in town two days, he *lingered* at his sweetheart's door). —ANT.*** go, leave, depart.

staying power, ability to last or endure; endurance.

stay·sail (stā′sāl′; *in nautical usage,* stā′s'l), ***n.*** a sail, especially a triangular sail, fastened on a stay.

S.T.B., *Sacrae Theologiae Baccalaureus,* [L.], Bachelor of Sacred Theology.

St. Ber·nard (bẽr-närd′), 1. either of two mountain passes in the Alps: see **Great St. Bernard, Little St. Bernard.** 2. a Saint Bernard dog.

St. Christopher, St. Kitts, an island in the West Indies.

St. Clair (klâr), 1. a river between Michigan and Ontario, Canada, connecting Lake Huron and Lake St. Clair: length, 41 mi. 2. a lake between Michigan and Ontario: area, 445 sq. mi.

St. Clair Shores, a city in southeastern Michigan: a suburb of Detroit: pop., 77,000.

St.-Cloud (san′klo͞o′), ***n.*** a city in northern France: suburb of Paris: pop., 18,000.

St. Cloud (kloud), a city in central Minnesota, on the Mississippi: pop., 34,000.

St. Croix (kroi), 1. an island of the United States part of the Virgin Islands: area, 82 sq. mi.; pop., 13,000: also called *Santa Cruz.* 2. a river flowing between Wisconsin and Minnesota, into the Mississippi: length, 200 mi. 3. a river flowing between Maine and New Brunswick into Passamaquoddy Bay: length, 75 mi.

std., standard.

S.T.D., *Sacrae Theologiae Doctor,* [L.], Doctor of Sacred Theology.

St. De·nis (san′də-nē′), 1. a city in France, north of Paris: pop., 81,000. 2. seaport and capital of Réunion Island: pop., 42,000.

Ste., *Sainte,* [Fr.], Saint (female).

stead (sted), ***n.*** [ME. & AS. *stede;* akin to G. *statt,* a place, *stadt,* town; IE. base **stā-,* **stə-,* to stand, seen also in L. *status* (cf. STATUS)], 1. the place or position of a person or thing as filled by a replacement, substitute, or successor: as, if you can't come, send her in your *stead.* 2. advantage, service, or avail. 3. [Archaic or Dial.], a place, site, or locality. ***v.t.*** [Archaic], to be of advantage, service, or avail to.

stand (one) in good stead, 1. to give (one) good use or service. 2. to give (one) an advantage.

stead·fast (sted′fast′, sted′fäst′, sted′fəst), ***adj.*** [ME. *stedefast;* AS. *stedefæste;* see STEAD & FAST, *adj.*], 1. firm, fixed, settled, or established. 2. constant; not changing, fickle, or wavering. Also spelled **stedfast.**

stead·i·ly (sted′'l-i), ***adv.*** in a steady manner.

stead·i·ness (sted′i-nis), ***n.*** a steady quality or state.

stead·ing (sted′iŋ), ***n.*** [*stead* + *-ing*], [Scot. & N. Eng. Dial.], 1. the house and other buildings connected with a farm. 2. a site for a building.

stead·y (sted′i), ***adj.*** [STEADIER (-i-ẽr), STEADIEST (-i-ist)], [ME. *stedi;* AS. *stedig* < *stede;* see STEAD], 1. firm; fixed; stable; that does not shake, tremble, totter, etc. 2. constant, regular, uniform, or continuous; not changing, wavering, faltering, etc.: as, a *steady* gaze, a *steady* rise in prices. 3. not given to sudden changes in behavior, loyalty, disposition, etc. 4. not easily agitated, excited, or upset; calm and controlled: as, *steady* nerves. 5. grave; sober; staid; reliable; not frivolous or dissipated. 6. keeping almost upright, as in a rough sea, or keeping headed as it is: said of a ship. ***interj.*** 1. be steady! remain calm and controlled! 2. keep the ship headed as it is: a command to the helmsman. ***v.t. & v.i.*** [STEADIED (-id), STEADYING], to make or become steady. ***n.*** [Slang], one's regular sweetheart.

go steady, [Colloq.], to be sweethearts.

SYN.*—steady** implies a fixed regularity or constancy, especially of movement, and a lack of deviation, fluctuation, faltering, etc. (a *steady* breeze); **even,** often interchangeable with **steady,** emphasizes the absence of irregularity or inequality (an *even* heartbeat); **uniform** implies a sameness or likeness of things, parts, events, etc., usually as the result of conformity with a fixed standard (a *uniform* wage rate); **regular** emphasizes the orderliness or symmetry resulting from evenness or uniformity (*regular* features, attendance, etc.); **equable** implies that the quality of evenness or regularity is inherent (an *equable* temper). —ANT.*** changeable, jerky.

steak (stāk), ***n.*** [ME. *steike;* ON. *steik* < base of *steikja,* to roast on a spit; for IE. base see STICK], 1. a slice of meat, especially beef, or of a large fish, cut thick for broiling or frying. 2. ground beef or other meat cooked in this way: as, Salisbury *steak.*

steal (stēl), ***v.t.*** [STOLE (stōl), STOLEN (stōl′'n), STEALING], [ME. *stelen;* AS. *stælan, stelan;* akin to G. *stehlen;* prob. IE. base **ster-,* to rob], 1. to take or appropriate (another's property, ideas, etc.) without permission, dishonestly, or unlawfully, especially in a secret or surreptitious manner. 2. to get or take slyly, surreptitiously, or without permission: as, he *stole* a look. 3. to take or gain insidiously or artfully: as, the costs of lobbying *stole* his profits, he *stole* her heart. 4. to move, put, carry, or convey surreptitiously or stealthily (with *in, into, from,* etc.). 5. in *baseball,* to gain (a base or bases) safely without the help of a hit or an error: said of a base runner. ***v.i.*** 1. to be a thief; practice theft. 2. to move, pass, etc. stealthily, quietly, or without being noticed. ***n.*** [Colloq.], 1. an act of stealing. 2. something stolen; hence, 3. something obtained at a ludicrously low cost.

***SYN.*—steal** is the general term implying the taking of another's money, possessions, etc. dishonestly or in a secret or surreptitious manner (to *steal* jewelry, a kiss, etc.); **pilfer** implies the stealing of small sums or petty objects (a *pilfering* house guest); **filch** also implies petty theft, but connotes that it is done by surreptitious snatching (to *filch* candy in a store); **purloin,** a literary word interchangeable with any of the preceding, stresses the removal of that which one means to appropriate for his own use (letters *purloined* by a blackmailer); **lift, swipe,** and **pinch** are slang terms meaning to steal, pilfer, or filch, **lift,** in addition, having specific colloquial application to plagiarism.

steal·ing (stēl′iŋ), ***n.*** 1. the act of a person who steals; theft. 2. *usually pl.* things stolen; loot. ***adj.*** that steals.

stealth (stelth), ***n.*** [ME. *stalthe, stelthe* < base of *stelen,* to steal; + *-th*], 1. secret or furtive action or behavior; surreptitious or clandestine procedure. 2. [Obs.], theft. 3. [Obs.], a surreptitious departure.

stealth·i·ly (stel′thə-li), ***adv.*** in a stealthy manner.

stealth·i·ness (stel′thi-nis), ***n.*** the quality or state of being stealthy.

stealth·y (stel′thi), ***adj.*** [STEALTHIER (-thi-ẽr), STEALTHIEST (-thi-ist)], characterized by stealth; done or acting in a secret, furtive manner. —***SYN.*** see **secret.**

steam (stēm), ***n.*** [ME. *steme;* AS.; akin to D. *stoom;* W. Fris. *steam;* only in W. Gmc.], 1. originally, a vapor, fume, or exhalation. 2. water as converted into an invisible vapor or gas by being heated to the boiling point; vaporized water: it is used for heating and cooking and, under pressure, as a source of power. 3. condensed water vapor, seen as a mist on windows, rising from boiling water, etc. 4. steam power: as, many sailing vessels were converted to *steam.* 5. [Colloq.], power; force; energy. ***adj.*** 1. using steam, as for heating or propulsion, or heated, operated, propelled, etc. by steam. 2. containing or conducting steam, as a pipe. 3. treated with, or exposed to the action of, steam. ***v.i.*** 1. to give off steam or a steamlike vapor, especially condensed water vapor. 2. to rise or be given off as steam. 3. to become covered with steam, or condensed water vapor, as a window, etc. 4. to generate steam. 5. to move or travel by steam power. ***v.t.*** 1. to treat with, or expose to the action of, steam, as in cooking, cleaning, etc. 2. to give off (vapor) or emit as steam.

let (or **blow**) **off steam,** [Colloq.], to express strong feeling; release pent-up emotion.

steam·boat (stēm′bōt′), ***n.*** a steamship.

steam boiler, a tank in which water is heated to produce steam and hold it under pressure.

steam chest, a compartment in a steam engine through which steam passes from the boiler to the cylinder also **steam box.**

steam engine, an engine using steam under pressure to supply mechanical energy, usually through the action of a piston sliding in a cylinder.

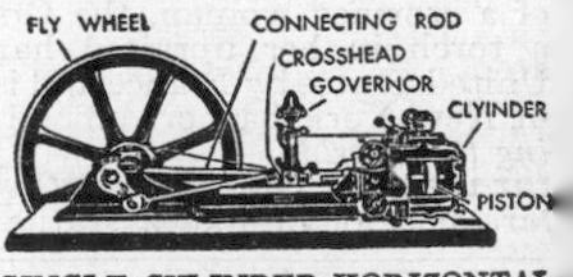

SINGLE-CYLINDER HORIZONTAL STEAM ENGINE

steam·er (stēm′ẽr), ***n.*** 1. something operated by steam power; specifically, *a*) a steamship. *b*) a truck or automobile driven by steam power. *c*) a steam engine. 2. a container in which things are treated with steam. 3. a person or thing that steams. Abbreviated **s., str.**

steamer rug, a coarse woolen blanket of the kind used by passengers in deck chairs on shipboard.

steamer trunk, a broad, low, rectangular trunk, originally designed to fit under a bunk on shipboard.

steam fitter, a mechanic who specializes in the installation and maintenance of the boilers, pipes, etc. in steam pressure systems.

steam fitting, the work of a steam fitter.

steam heat, heat given off by steam in a closed system of pipes and radiators.

steam·i·ly (stēm′ə-li), *adv.* in a steamy manner.

steam·i·ness (stēm′i-nis), *n.* the quality or condition of being steamy.

steam-roll·er (stēm′rōl′ẽr), *v.t.* 1. to bring overwhelming force to bear upon; crush or override as if with a steam roller: as, he *steam-rollered* the opposition. 2. to cause the passage or defeat of (a legislative bill, etc.), or make (one's way, etc.), by crushing the opposition or overriding obstacles. *v.i.* to move with overwhelming, crushing force, or use steam-roller tactics. *adj.* suggestive of a steam roller.

steam roller, 1. a heavy, steam-driven roller used in building and repairing roads. 2. figuratively, an overwhelming power or influence, especially when used relentlessly to force acceptance of a policy, override opposition, etc.

steam·ship (stēm′ship′), *n.* a ship driven by steam power: abbreviated **SS, S/S, S.S.**

steam shovel, a large, mechanically operated digger, powered by steam.

steam table, a type of table or counter, as in restaurants, having a metal top with steam-heated compartments in which food may be kept warm.

STEAM SHOVEL

steam·tight (stēm′tīt′), *adj.* that will prevent the passage or leakage of steam: as, a *steamtight* valve.

steam turbine, a turbine turned by steam moving under great pressure.

steam·y (stēm′i), *adj.* [STEAMIER (-i-ẽr), STEAMIEST (-i-ist)], 1. of or like steam. 2. covered or filled with steam. 3. giving off steam or steamlike vapor.

Ste. Anne de Beau·pré (sānt an′ də bō′prā′; Fr. san′tän′ də bō′prā′), a village on the St. Lawrence River near Quebec: Roman Catholic shrine.

ste·ap·sin (sti-ap′sin), *n.* [G. < *stearin* + *pepsin*], an enzyme present in the pancreatic juice: it converts fats into glycerol and free acids.

ste·a·rate (stē′ə-rāt′), *n.* a salt or ester of stearic acid.

ste·ar·ic (sti-ar′ik, stêr′ik), *adj.* [Fr. *stéarique* < Gr. *stear*, tallow], of, derived from, or like stearin or fat.

stearic acid, a colorless, waxlike fatty acid, $CH_3(CH_2)_{16}CO_2H$, found in many animal and vegetable fats, and used in making candles, stearates, soaps, etc.

ste·a·rin (stē′ə-rin, stêr′in), *n.* [Fr. *stéarine* < Gr. *stear*, stiff fat, tallow, suet], 1. a white, crystalline substance, glyceryl stearate, $(C_{18}H_{35}O_2)_3C_3H_5$, found in the solid portion of most animal and vegetable fats. 2. stearic acid (as used in commerce).

ste·a·rine (stē′ə-rin, stêr′ēn), *n.* stearin.

ste·a·rop·tene (stē′ə-rop′tēn), *n.* [*stear*ic + elae*optene*], the oxygenated, chiefly solid part of an essential oil: distinguished from *elaeoptene*.

ste·a·tite (stē′ə-tīt′), *n.* [L. *steatitis* < Gr. *stear*, tallow, suet], talc occurring in the form of a mass; soapstone.

ste·a·tit·ic (stē′ə-tit′ik), *adj.* of or like steatite.

ste·a·to·py·gi·a (stē′ə-tō-pī′ji-ə, stē′ə-tō-pij′i-ə), *n.* [Mod. L. < Gr. *stear, steatos*, fat + *pygē*, buttocks], enlargement of the hips and buttocks as a result of large deposits of fat: found especially among the Hottentots and certain other African peoples, particularly in the women.

ste·a·to·pyg·ic (stē′ə-tō-pij′ik), *adj.* of or characterized by steatopygia.

ste·a·to·py·gous (stē′ə-tō-pī′gəs), *adj.* steatopygic.

ste·a·top·y·gy (stē′ə-top′ə-ji), *n.* steatopygia.

ste·at·or·rhe·a (stē′ə-tə-rē′ə), *n.* [< Gr. *stear, steatos*, fat; + *-rrhea*], 1. seborrhea. 2. an excessive amount of fat in the feces.

sted·fast (sted′fast′, sted′fäst′, sted′fəst), *adj.* steadfast.

steed (stēd), *n.* [ME. *stede;* AS. *steda*, stud horse, stallion < base of AS. *stod*, stud (see STUD)], 1. a horse, especially a riding horse: literary term. 2. [Archaic], a high-spirited horse.

steel (stēl), *n.* [see PLURAL, II, D, 3], [ME. *stel;* AS. *stiele, stæli;* akin to G. *stahl;* IE. base **sta-*, to stand, be placed, stand fast (cf. STAND)], 1. a hard, tough metal composed of iron alloyed with various small percentages of carbon: steel may be alloyed with other metals, as nickel, chromium, etc., to produce specific properties, as hardness, resistance to rusting, etc. 2. a particular kind of steel: *hard* (or *high*) *steel* has a relatively high carbon content, as distinguished from *soft* (or *mild* or *low*) *steel*, which has a relatively low carbon content, and *medium steel*, which has a medium carbon content. 3. a piece of steel; something made of steel; specifically, *a*) [Poetic], a sword or dagger. *b*) a piece of steel used with flint for making sparks. *c*) a steel strip used for stiffening, as in a corset. *d*) a roughened steel rod used as a knife sharpener. 4. great strength or hardness: as, sinews of *steel*. 5. *often in pl.* the market price of shares in a steel-making company: as, *steels* fell during the week. *adj.* of or like steel. *v.t.* 1. to cover, point, or edge with steel. 2. to make hard, tough, relentless, unfeeling, etc. Abbreviated **s.**

steel-blue (stēl′blōō′), *adj.* of the color steel blue.

steel blue, a metallic blue, as that of tempered steel.

Steele, Sir Richard (stēl), 1672–1729; English essayist and playwright.

steel engraving, 1. an engraving made on a steel plate. 2. a print from such a plate. 3. the process used in making such engravings.

steel-gray (stēl′grā′), *adj.* of the color steel gray.

steel gray, a dark, somewhat bluish gray.

steel·head (stēl′hed′), *n.* [*pl.* STEELHEAD, STEELHEADS (-hedz′); see PLURAL, II, D, 2], a large rainbow trout found along the Pacific coast of North America.

steel·i·ness (stēl′i-nis), *n.* the quality or condition of being steely.

steel mill, a mill where steel is made, processed, and shaped in various forms.

steel wool, long, hairlike shavings of steel, used for cleaning, smoothing, and polishing.

steel·work (stēl′wũrk′), *n.* 1. articles or parts made of steel. 2. a frame or structure made of steel. 3. *pl.* [often construed as sing.], a steel mill.

steel·work·er (stēl′wũr′kẽr), *n.* a worker in a steel mill.

steel·y (stēl′i), *adj.* [STEELIER (-i-ẽr), STEELIEST (-i-ist)], 1. made of steel. 2. like steel, as in color, hardness, etc.

steel·yard (stēl′yärd′; *now less freq.* stil′yẽrd), *n.* [*steel* + *yard* (in obs. sense of rod, bar); a mistransl. of MLG. *stâlhof; stâl*, a sample, pattern + *hof*, a courtyard], a balance or scale consisting of a metal arm suspended off center from above: the object to be weighed is hung from the shorter end, and a sliding weight is moved along the graduated longer end until the whole arm balances.

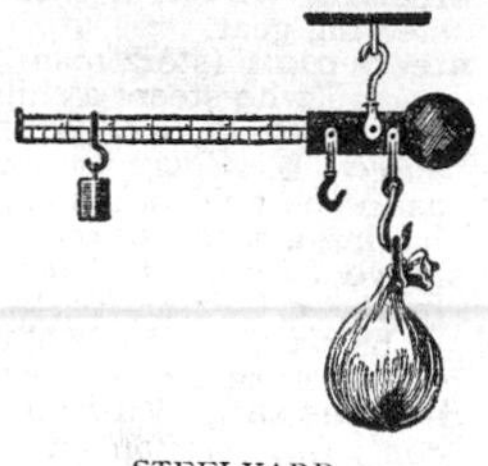

STEELYARD

Steen, Jan (yän stān), 1626–1679; Dutch painter.

steen·bok (stēn′bok′, stān′bok′), *n.* [*pl.* STEENBOK, STEENBOKS (-boks′); see PLURAL, II, D, 2], [D.; *steen*, a stone + *bok*, a buck], a small African antelope: also **steinbok.**

steep (stēp), *adj.* [ME. *step, steep;* AS. *steap*, lofty, high; akin to OFris. *stap, steep*, MHG. *stouf*, cliff (as in G. *Hohenstaufen*); IE. **steu-p* (prob. < base **stā-*, to stand), as also in AS. *stupian* (cf. STOOP)], 1. having a relatively sharp rise or slope; precipitous: as, a *steep* incline. 2. [Colloq.], *a*) unreasonably high or great; exorbitant; excessive: as, his demands seem rather *steep*, a *steep* price. *b*) extreme: as, a *steep* statement. 3. [Obs.], high; lofty. *n.* a steep slope or incline.

SYN.—**steep** suggests such sharpness of rise or slope as to make ascent or descent very difficult (a *steep* hill); **abrupt** implies a sharper degree of inclination in a surface breaking off suddenly from the level (an *abrupt* bank at the river's edge); **precipitous** suggests the abrupt and headlong drop of a precipice (a *precipitous* height); **sheer** applies to that which is perpendicular, or almost so, and unbroken throughout its length (cliffs falling *sheer* to the sea).

steep (stēp), *v.t.* [ME. *stepen;* ON. *steypa*, to overturn, pour out liquids < base seen in Eng. *stoup*], 1. to soak in liquid, in order to soften, clean, extract the essence of, etc. 2. to immerse, saturate, or impregnate. *n.* 1. a steeping or being steeped. 2. liquid in which something is steeped. *v.i.* to undergo the process of being soaked in liquid, as tea. —*SYN.* see **soak.**

steeped in, immersed in; saturated or imbued with.

steep·en (stēp′'n), *v.t. & v.i.* to make or become steep or steeper.

stee·ple (stē′p'l), *n.* [ME. *stepel;* AS. *stypel* < base of *steap*, lofty; see STEEP, *adj.*], 1. a tower rising above the main structure of a building, especially of a church, usually capped with a spire. 2. a church tower with a spire. 3. a spire, as on a church tower.

stee·ple·bush (stē′p'l-boosh′), *n.* the hardhack, a shrub.

stee·ple·chase (stē′p'l-chās′), *n.* [so called because the race usually had as its goal a steeple visible from a considerable distance], 1. originally, a horse race run across country. 2. a horse race run over a prepared course obstructed with artificial ditches, hedges, walls, etc. 3. a foot race run across country or over a prepared course with ditches and other obstacles.

stee·ple·chas·er (stē'p'l-chās'ẽr), *n.* a horse or person taking part in a steeplechase.

stee·pled (stē'p'ld), *adj.* having a steeple or steeples.

stee·ple·jack (stē'p'l-jak'), *n.* a man employed to paint, or make repairs upon, steeples, smokestacks, etc.: also **steeple jack.**

steer (stêr), *v.t.* [ME. *steren;* AS. *stieran;* akin to G. *steuern;* IE. **stēu-ro*, **stəw-ro*, prop, post, steering oar < base **stā-*, to stand], 1. to guide (a ship or boat) by means of a rudder. 2. to direct the course or movement of: as, he *steered* the automobile, she *steered* herself around the corner. 3. to oversee; direct; control: as, she *steered* our efforts in the right direction. 4. to set and follow (a course). *v.i.* 1. to steer a ship, automobile, etc. 2. to be steered or guided: as, the car *steers* easily. 3. to set and follow a course or way. *n.* [Slang], advice or suggestion as to how to proceed; tip. —*SYN.* see **guide.**

steer clear of, to keep clear of or away from; avoid.

steer (stêr), *n.* [ME. *ster;* AS. *steor;* akin to G. *stier;* IE. **steu-ro* (seen also in MPer. *stor*, horse, draft animal) < base **stā-*, to stand (cf. STAND)], 1. a young castrated male of the cattle family; young ox. 2. any male of beef cattle.

steer·age (stêr'ij), *n.* [see -AGE], 1. the act of steering or guiding. 2. in *nautical usage, a*) a ship's reaction to the movement of the helm. *b*) the section of a passenger ship occupied by the passengers paying the lowest fare: originally, the part of the ship containing the steering mechanism.

steer·age·way (stêr'ij-wā'), *n.* the minimum forward speed needed to make a ship react to the helm.

steering committee, a committee, as of a legislative body, appointed to arrange the order of business.

steering gear, any mechanism used for steering, as in a ship, automobile, airplane, etc.

steering wheel, a wheel that is turned to operate a steering gear.

steers·man (stêrz'mən), *n.* [*pl.* STEERSMEN (-mən)], a person who steers a ship or boat.

steeve (stēv), *v.t.* [STEEVED (stēvd), STEEVING], [Fr. *estiver;* L. *stipare*, to compress, cram], to stow (cargo), as in the hold of a ship, by means of a spar or derrick having a block at one end. *n.* such a spar or derrick.

steeve (stēv), *v.i. & v.t.* [STEEVED (stēvd), STEEVING], [prob. < OFr. *estive*, tail of a plough (L. *stiva*)], to set or be set at an angle above the line of the horizon or of the keel: said of a bowsprit. *n.* the angle so formed.

Ste·fans·son, Vil·hjal·mur (vil'hyoul'mẽr ste'fänsson'; Eng. stef'ən-s'n), 1879–1962; arctic explorer and author, born in Canada of Icelandic parents.

Stef·fens, Lincoln (stef'ənz), (*Joseph Lincoln Steffens*), 1866–1936; American author, editor, and lecturer.

steg·o·my·ia (steg'ə-mī'ə), *n.* [Mod. L. < Gr. *stegos*, a roof + *myia*, a fly], the yellow-fever mosquito, *Aëdes aegypti*: the former name.

steg·o·sau·rus (steg'ə-sô'rəs), *n.* [*pl.* STEGOSAURI (-rī)], [Mod. L. < Gr. *stegos*, a roof; + *-saurus*], a reptile of great size found in fossil state in the Upper Jurassic rocks of North America; any of a genus of huge dinosaurs characterized by a small head and heavy bony plates with sharp spines down the backbone.

Stei·chen, Edward (stī'kən), 1879– ; American photographer.

Stei·er·mark (shtī'ẽr-märk'), *n.* Styria: German name.

stein (stīn), *n.* [G.], 1. an earthenware beer mug; hence, 2. popularly, any similar mug, as of glass, etc.

Stein, Gertrude (stīn), 1874–1946; American writer, in France.

Stein·am·ang·er (shtīn'äm-äŋ'ẽr), *n.* Szombathely: the German name.

Stein·beck, John Ernst (ũrnst stīn'bek), 1902– ; American novelist and short-story writer; received Nobel prize in literature, 1962.

stein·bok (stīn'bok'), *n.* [*pl.* STEINBOK, STEINBOKS (-boks')]; see PLURAL, II, D, 2], a steenbok.

Stein·metz, Charles Pro·te·us (prō'ti-əs stīn'mets), 1865–1923; American electrical engineer and inventor, born in Germany.

ste·le (stē'li; *for 2, usually* stēl), *n.* [L. *stela;* Gr. *stēle*, a post or slab, upright stone], 1. an upright stone slab or pillar engraved with an inscription or design and used as a monument, grave marker, etc. 2. in *architecture*, a prepared surface, as on a façade, having an inscription, carved design, etc. 3. in *botany*, a central tube of tissue in the roots and stems of plants which grow by the addition of layers on the outside.

St. Elias, 1. a mountain range near the coast of southern Alaska and Canada: highest peak, Mt. Logan, 19,850 ft. 2. a volcanic mountain in this range, on the border between Alaska and Canada: height, 18,008 ft.

Stel·la (stel'ə), [L. *stella*, a star], a feminine name: see **Estella.**

stel·lar (stel'ẽr), *adj.* [LL. *stellaris* < L. *stella*, a star], 1. of the stars or a star. 2. like a star, as in shape. 3. by or as by a star performer; excellent. 4. leading; chief: as, the *stellar* role in a play.

stel·late (stel'it, stel'āt), *adj.* [L. *stellatus*, pp. of *stellare*, to cover with stars < *stella*, a star], star-shaped; coming out in rays or points from a center.

stel·lat·ed (stel'ā-tid), *adj.* stellate.

stel·lif·er·ous (ste-lif'ẽr-əs), *adj.* [L. *stellifer* (< *stella*, a star + *ferre*, to bear); + *-ous*], [Rare], full of stars.

stel·li·form (stel'i-fôrm'), *adj.* [Mod. L. *stelliformis* < L. *stella*, a star + *forma*, form], stellate.

stel·lu·lar (stel'yoo-lẽr), *adj.* [< LL. *stellula*, dim. of L. *stella*, a star; + *-ar*], 1. stellate. 2. covered with small stars or starlike spots of color.

St. El·mo's fire (el'mōz), [< *Saint Elmo*, patron saint of sailors], an electric discharge, resembling a flame, which is sometimes seen at prominent points of a mast, etc. on a ship at sea: also **St. Elmo's light.**

stem (stem), *n.* [ME.; AS. *stemn, stefn;* akin to G. *stamm*, tree trunk; IE. base **stebh-*, **stəbh-*, etc., post, pole, stub, trunk, as also in *staff*], 1. *a*) the main upward-growing axis of a plant, usually extending in a direction opposite to that of the root and above the ground. *b*) the main stalk or trunk of a tree, shrub, or other plant; main body of the aboveground part of a plant, from which leaves, flowers, and fruit develop. 2. *a*) any stalk or part supporting leaves, flowers, or fruit. *b*) a pedicel, petiole, or peduncle. *c*) a stalk of bananas. 3. a stemlike piece or part: as, the *stem* of a goblet, the *stem* of a tobacco pipe; specifically, *a*) the cylindrical shaft projecting from a watch, with a knurled knob at its end for winding the spring. *b*) the rounded rod in some locks, about which the key fits and is turned. *c*) the main or thick stroke of a letter, as in printing. *d*) the vertical line constituting part of a musical note (other than a whole note or breve). 4. the upright piece to which the side timbers or plates are attached to form the prow of a ship. 5. the forward part of a ship; prow; bow. 6. the part of a word to which inflectional endings are added or in which phonetic changes are made for inflection: cf. **base, root.** 7. *a*) a branch of a family. *b*) lineage; ancestry; stock. *v.t.* [STEMMED (stemd), STEMMING], 1. to remove the stem or stems from (a fruit, etc.). 2. to provide (artificial flowers, etc.) with stems. 3. [< *n.* 4 & 5], to make headway or progress against: as, the small boat could not *stem* the incoming tide. *v.i.* to originate, derive, or be descended. —*SYN.* see **rise.**

from stem to stern, 1. from one end of a ship to the other. 2. through the entire length of anything.

stem (stem), *v.t.* [STEMMED (stemd), STEMMING], [ME. < Scand.; cf. ON. *stemma* (akin to G. *stemmen*), to stop; for base see STAMMER], 1. to stop or check; especially, to dam up (a river, etc.), or to stop or check as if by damming up. 2. to stop up, plug, or tamp, as a hole. *v.i.* to stop or slow down in skiing by turning one ski (*single stemming*) or both skis (*double stemming*) with the heel more or less outward. *n.* in *skiing*, an act or manner of stemming.

stemmed (stemd), *adj.* 1. having a stem, usually of a specified kind: as, a thin-*stemmed* goblet. 2. with the stem or stems removed.

stem·mer (stem'ẽr), *n.* a person or thing that removes stems: as, a fruit *stemmer*, tobacco *stemmer*.

stem·son (stem's'n), *n.* [< *stem*, after *keelson*], a piece of timber connecting the stem and keelson in the frame of a wooden ship.

stem·ware (stem'wâr), *n.* stemmed goblets, glasses, etc., collectively.

stem-wind·er (stem'win'dẽr), *n.* a stem-winding watch.

stem-wind·ing (stem'win'diŋ), *adj.* wound by turning a knurled knob at the outer end of the stem.

stench (stench), *n.* [ME.; AS. *stenc* < base of *stincan*, to smell, stink], an offensive smell or odor; stink.

sten·cil (sten's'l), *v.t.* [STENCILED or STENCILLED (-s'ld), STENCILING or STENCILLING], [< ME. *stansilen*, *stensilen;* OFr. *estenceler*, to ornament with spangles < *estencele*, a spangle, spark; LL. **stincilla*, for L. *scintilla*, a spark], to mark or paint with a stencil. *n.* 1. a thin sheet, as of paper or metal, perforated or cut through in such a way that when ink, paint, etc. is applied to the sheet patterns, designs, letters, etc. form on the surface beneath the sheet. 2. a pattern, design, letters, etc. made by stenciling.

STENCIL

sten·cil·er, sten·cil·ler (sten's'l-ẽr), *n.* a person or thing that makes stencils.

Sten·dhal (stän'dál'), *n.* (pseudonym of *Marie Henri Beyle*), French novelist and essayist; 1783–1842.

Sten gun (sten), [after *S*heppard and *T*urpin, the inventors + *E*ngland], a British light machine gun that can be held when fired: it is capable of firing at the rate of 550 rounds per minute.

sten·o- (sten'ō, sten'ə), [< Gr. *stenos*, narrow], a com bining form meaning *small, thin, narrow, abbreviated,* etc., as in *stenography.*

sten·o·graph (sten′ə-graf′, sten′ə-gräf′), *v.t.* [back-formation < *stenographer*], to write in shorthand. *n.* 1. something written in shorthand. 2. a symbol used in shorthand. 3. a keyboard machine that prints shorthand symbols.

ste·nog·ra·pher (stə-nog′rə-fẽr), *n.* a person skilled in stenography.

sten·o·graph·ic (sten′ə-graf′ik), *adj.* 1. of or having to do with stenography. 2. written in shorthand and, usually, transcribed in typewriting.

sten·o·graph·i·cal (sten′ə-graf′i-k′l), *adj.* stenographic.

sten·o·graph·i·cal·ly (sten′ə-graf′i-k′l-i, sten′ə-graf′ik-li), *adv.* by means of stenography.

ste·nog·ra·phist (stə-nog′rə-fist), *n.* a stenographer.

ste·nog·ra·phy (stə-nog′rə-fi), *n.* [*steno-* + *-graphy*], shorthand writing or, often, the process of taking down dictation in shorthand and later transcribing it in typewriting.

ste·no·sis (sti-nō′sis), *n.* [Mod. L.; Gr. *stenōsis* < *stenos*, narrow], in *medicine*, a narrowing, or constriction, of a passage, duct, opening, etc.

sten·o·type (sten′ə-tīp′), *n.* 1. a symbol or symbols representing a sound, word, or phrase in stenotypy. 2. a keyboard machine that prints such symbols: a trademark (**Stenotype**).

sten·o·typ·y (sten′ə-tīp′i, ste-not′ə-pi), *n.* [< *steno-* + Gr. *typē*, impression], a kind of shorthand using ordinary letters as symbols for sounds, words, and phrases.

Sten·tor (sten′tôr), *n.* [L.; Gr. *Stentōr*], 1. a Greek herald in the Trojan War, described in the *Iliad* as having the voice of fifty men. 2. [usually s-], a person having a very loud voice. 3. [s-], a one-celled animal shaped like a ram's horn.

sten·to·ri·an (sten-tôr′i-ən, sten-tō′ri-ən), *adj.* [*Stentor* + *-ian*], very loud.

step (step), *n.* [ME. *steppe;* AS. *stepe;* akin to (rare) G. *stapf;* IE. base **steb-*, **stəb-*, etc., post, pole; basic sense "to stamp feet"; cf. STAMP], 1. the action of moving the foot once and bringing it to rest again, as in walking or running. 2. the distance covered by such a movement; hence, 3. a short distance: as, the tavern is just a *step* from here. 4. a manner of stepping; gait. 5. the sound of stepping; tread; footfall. 6. a mark or impression made by stepping; footprint. 7. a rest for the foot in climbing, as a stair or the rung of a ladder. 8. *pl. a*) a flight of stairs. *b*) [British], a stepladder. 9. something resembling a stair step; specifically, *a*) an offset in a piece of machinery. *b*) a shelf or ledge cut in mining or quarrying. *c*) a raised frame or platform supporting the butt end of a mast. 10. a degree; rank; level; stage: as, they were one *step* nearer defeat. 11. any of a series of acts, processes, etc.: as, let me explain the next *step*. 12. a sequence of movements in dancing, usually repeated in a set pattern. 13. in *music*, *a*) a degree of the staff or scale. *b*) the interval between two such consecutive degrees. *v.i.* [STEPPED (stept), STEPPING], [ME. *steppen;* AS. *steppan, stapan*], 1. to move forward or backward by executing a step or steps. 2. to walk, especially a short distance: as, *step* here a moment. 3. to move with measured steps, as in dancing. 4. to move quickly or briskly: often with *along*, as, he *stepped* along at a fast clip. 5. to come or enter (*into* a situation, condition, etc.): as, he *stepped* into a small fortune. 6. *a*) to put the foot down (*on* something): as, he accidentally *stepped* on my foot. *b*) to press down with the foot (*on* something): as, he *stepped* on the accelerator. *v.t.* 1. to take (a stride, pace, etc.). 2. to set down (the foot). 3. to execute the steps of (a dance): as, *step* a gavotte together. 4. to measure by taking steps: usually with *off*, as, he *stepped* off twenty paces. 5. to provide with steps; specifically, *a*) to cut steps in: as, he *stepped* the hill leading to his house. *b*) to arrange in a series of degrees or grades. 6. in *nautical usage*, to set and fix (a mast) in its step, or supporting structure.

break step, to stop marching in cadence.

in step, 1. conforming to a rhythm or cadence in marching, dancing, etc.; especially, conforming to the cadence of another marcher or other marchers. 2. in conformity or agreement.

keep step, to stay in step.

out of step, not in step.

step by step, by degrees; gradually.

step down, 1. to resign or abdicate (*from* an office, position, etc.). 2. to decrease or reduce, as in rate, by or as by one or more steps, or degrees.

step in, to start to participate; intervene.

step it, to dance.

step on it, [Colloq.], to go faster; hurry; hasten.

step out, 1. to leave a room, building, etc., especially for a short time. 2. [Colloq.], to go out for a good time; go on a date. 3. to start to walk briskly, especially with long strides.

step up, 1. to go or come near; approach. 2. to advance or progress. 3. to increase or raise, as in rate, by or as by one or more steps, or degrees.

take steps, to adopt certain means or measures.

watch one's step, 1. to exercise care in walking or stepping. 2. [Colloq.], to be careful or cautious.

step·broth·er (step′bruth′ẽr), *n.* [see STEPCHILD], one's stepparent's son by a former marriage.

step·child (step′chīld′), *n.* [*pl.* STEPCHILDREN (-chil′drən)], [ME. *step, steop* < AS. *steop-* < base of *astypan, astepan*, to bereave, make orphan: orig. applied to the orphaned children, but later to those related by remarriage, of a parent], a child of one's husband or wife by a former marriage.

step·dame (step′dām′), *n.* [Archaic], a stepmother.

step·daugh·ter (step′dô′tẽr), *n.* a female stepchild.

step-down (step′doun′), *adj.* that steps down, or decreases; specifically, *a*) designating a transformer that converts an electric current from a higher to a lower voltage. *b*) designating a gear that reduces the ratio. Opposed to *step-up*.

step·fa·ther (step′fä′thẽr), *n.* a male stepparent.

Steph·a·na (stef′ə-nə), [Mod. L., fem. of *Stephen*], a feminine name: variant, *Stephanie*.

Steph·a·nie (stef′ə-ni), a feminine name: see **Stephana**.

Ste·phen (stē′vən; stē′fən *is a sp. pronun.*), [L. *Stephanus;* Gr. *Stephanas* < *stephanos*, a crown], a masculine name: diminutive, *Steve*; feminine, *Stephana;* equivalents, L. *Stephanus*, Fr. *Étienne*, G. *Stephan*, It. *Stefano*, Sp. *Esteban*, Russ. *Stepan*: also spelled **Steven**. *n.* (*Stephen of Blois*), grandson of William the Conqueror; 1097?–1154; king of England (1135–1154).

Stephen, Saint, 1. the first Christian martyr: his day is December 26: Acts 7:60. 2. c. 975–1038 A.D.; first king of Hungary (997–1038 A.D.): also **Stephen I.**

Ste·phens, Alexander Hamilton (stē′vənz), 1812–1883; vice-president of the Confederacy (1861–1865).

Stephens, James, 1882–1950; Irish writer.

Ste·phen·son, George (stē′vən-sən), 1781–1848; English engineer; one of the inventors of the locomotive.

Stephenson, Robert, 1803–1859; son of *George;* English engineer; inventor of the tubular bridge.

step-ins (step′inz′), *n.pl.* 1. women's short, loose-fitting underpants. 2. open-heeled shoes or slippers.

step·lad·der (step′lad′ẽr), *n.* a four-legged ladder, usually hinged at the top for easy storage, and having broad, flat rungs or steps.

step·moth·er (step′muth′ẽr), *n.* a female stepparent.

Step·ney (step′ni), *n.* a borough of London.

step-off (step′ôf′), *n.* a drop to a lower level or plane; drop-off, as from an underwater ledge or shelf.

step·par·ent (step′pâr′ənt), *n.* [see STEPCHILD], the person who has married one's parent after the death or divorce of the other parent; stepfather or stepmother.

steppe (step), *n.* [Fr. or G. < Russ. *step′*], 1. one of the great plains of southeastern Europe and Asia, having few or no trees. 2. any similar plain.

step·per (step′ẽr), *n.* a person or animal that steps, usually in a specified manner, as a horse or a dancer.

step·ping·stone (step′iŋ-stōn′), *n.* 1. a stone, usually one of a series, used to step on, as in crossing a stream, soft turf, etc. 2. something used to better one's position or situation; means or opportunity for advancement. Also **stepping stone**.

step·sis·ter (step′sis′tẽr), *n.* [see STEPCHILD], one's stepparent's daughter by a former marriage.

step·son (step′sun′), *n.* a male stepchild.

step-up (step′up′), *adj.* that steps up, or increases: said of a transformer, gear, etc.: cf. **step-down**.

step·wise (step′wīz′), *adv.* like a series of steps.

-ster (stẽr), [ME. *-stre, -ster;* AS. *-estre*, orig. a fem. agent suffix], a suffix meaning *a person who is, does,* or *creates* (something specified), as in *oldster, punster*: often derogatory, as in *rhymester, trickster*.

ster., sterling.

ster·co·ra·ceous (stũr′kə-rā′shəs), *adj.* [< L. *stercus, stercoris*, dung; + *-aceous*], of, containing, like, or having the nature of feces, or dung.

ster·co·rous (stũr′kə-rəs), *adj.* stercoraceous.

ster·cu·li·a·ceous (stẽr-kū′li-ā′shəs), *adj.* [< L. *Sterculius*, the deity presiding over manuring (< *stercus*, dung); + *-aceous*], designating or of a family of mainly tropical trees and shrubs, as the cacao and the kola.

stere (stêr), *n.* [Fr. *stère* < Gr. *stereos*, solid, cubic], a cubic meter.

ster·e·o (ster′i-ō′, stêr′i-ō′), *a shortened form of* stereophonic, stereoscopic, stereotype, etc.

ster·e·o- (ster′i-ō, stêr′i-ə), [< Gr. *stereos*, hard, firm, solid], a combining form meaning *solid, firm, three-dimensional*, as in *stereoscope, stereography*: also, before some vowels, **stere-**.

stereo., stereotype.

ster·e·o·bate (ster′i-ə-bāt′, stêr′i-ə-bāt′), *n.* [L. *stereobata;* Gr. *stereobatēs* < *stereos*, solid + *batēs*, that which steps or treads], a foundation, as of a building, or a solid substructure or platform of masonry, as used to support columns in classical architecture.

ster·e·o·chem·is·try (ster'i-ə-kem'is-tri, stêr'i-ə-kem'-is-tri), *n.* [*stereo-* + *chemistry*], the branch of chemistry dealing with the spatial arrangement of atoms or groups of atoms that make up molecules.

ster·e·o·chrome (ster'i-ə-krōm', stêr'i-ə-krōm'), *n.* a picture produced by stereochromy.

ster·e·o·chro·mic (ster'i-ə-krō'mik, stêr'i-ə-krō'mik), *adj.* of or produced by stereochromy.

ster·e·o·chro·my (ster'i-ə-krō'mi, stêr'i-ə-krō'mi), *n.* [< *stereo-* + Gr. *chrōma*, color], a process of mural painting using water glass as a fixative, either mixed with the pigment or laid over the finished painting.

ster·e·o·gram (ster'i-ə-gram', stêr'i-ə-gram'), *n.* a stereographic diagram or picture, or a stereograph.

ster·e·o·graph (ster'i-ə-graf', stêr'i-ə-gräf'), *n.* [*stereo-* + *-graph*], a picture or a pair of pictures prepared for use with a stereoscope.

ster·e·o·graph·ic (ster'i-ə-graf'ik, stêr'i-ə-graf'ik), *adj.* of or produced by stereography.

ster·e·o·graph·i·cal (ster'i-ə-graf'i-k'l, stêr'i-ə-graf'i-k'l), *adj.* stereographic.

ster·e·o·graph·i·cal·ly (ster'i-ə-graf'i-k'l-i, stêr'i-ə-graf'ik-li), *adv.* by stereography.

ster·e·og·ra·phy (ster'i-og'rə-fi, stêr'i-og'rə-fi), *n.* [*stereo-* + *-graphy*], the art of representing the forms of solids on a plane surface; branch of solid geometry that deals with the construction of regularly defined solids.

ster·e·o·i·som·er·ism (ster'i-ō-i-som'ẽr-iz'm, stêr'i-ō-i-som'ẽr-iz'm), *n.* [*stereo-* + *isomerism*], isomerism of optically active compounds, the atoms or atomic groups of which have different spatial arrangements.

ster·e·o·met·ric (ster'i-ə-met'rik, stêr'i-ə-met'rik), *adj.* of or produced by stereometry.

ster·e·o·met·ri·cal (ster'i-ə-met'ri-k'l, stêr'i-ə-met'ri-k'l), *adj.* stereometric.

ster·e·o·met·ri·cal·ly (ster'i-ə-met'ri-k'l-i, stêr'i-ə-met'-rik-li), *adv.* by stereometry.

ster·e·om·e·try (ster'i-om'ə-tri, stêr'i-om'ə-tri), *n.* [*stereo-* + *-metry*], the art of determining the dimensions and volume of solids.

ster·e·o·phon·ic (ster'i-ə-fon'ik, stêr'i-ə-fon'ik), *adj.* [*stereo-* + *phonic*], designating or of sound reproduction, as in motion-pictures, phonograph recording, or radio, using two or more channels to carry and reproduce the sounds from the directions in which they were originally picked up by corresponding microphones.

ster·e·op·sis (ster'i-op'sis, stêr'i-op'sis), *n.* [Mod. L.; see STEREO- & -OPSIS], stereoscopic vision.

ster·e·op·ti·con (ster'i-op'ti-kən, stêr'i-op'ti-kən), *n.* [Mod. L.; see STEREO- & OPTIC], a magic lantern having a powerful projection light, especially one using double pictures, each with a separate lens, for producing dissolving views.

ster·e·o·scope (ster'i-ə-skōp', stêr'i-ə-skōp'), *n.* [*stereo-* + *-scope*], an instrument that gives a three-dimensional effect to photographs viewed through it: it has two eyepieces, through which two slightly different views of the same scene are viewed side by side.

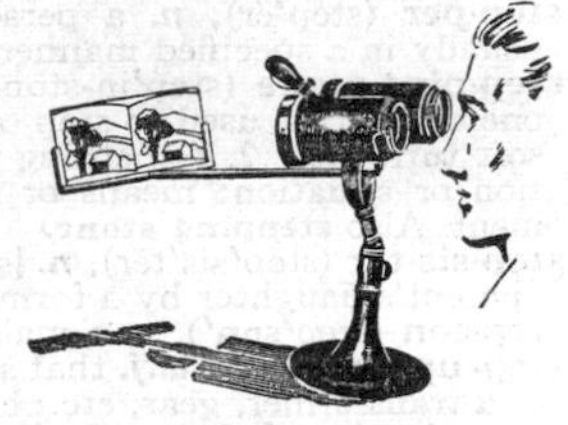

STEREOSCOPE

ster·e·o·scop·ic (ster'i-ə-skop'ik, stêr'i-ə-skop'ik), *adj.* of, like, or used in a stereoscope.

ster·e·o·scop·i·cal (ster'i-ə-skop'i-k'l, stêr'i-ə-skop'i-k'l), *adj.* stereoscopic.

ster·e·o·scop·i·cal·ly (ster'i-ə-skop'i-k'l-i, stêr'i-ə-skop'-ik-li), *adv.* 1. by a stereoscope. 2. so as to appear three-dimensional.

ster·e·os·co·py (ster'i-os'kə-pi, stêr'i-os'kə-pi), *n.* 1. the science of stereoscopic effects and techniques. 2. the viewing of things as in three dimensions.

ster·e·o·tax·is (ster'i-ə-tak'sis, stêr'i-ə-tak'sis), *n.* [see STEREO- & TAXIS], a movement of an organism for which the stimulus is contact with a solid body.

ster·e·ot·ro·pism (ster'i-ot'rə-piz'm, stêr'i-ot'rə-piz'm), *n.* a tropism in which the directing stimulus is contact with something solid.

ster·e·o·type (ster'i-ə-tīp', stêr'i-ə-tīp'), *n.* [Fr. *stéréotype, adj.*; see STEREO- & -TYPE], 1. a one-piece printing plate cast in type metal from a mold taken of a printing surface, as a page of set type. 2. stereotypy. 3. an unvarying form or pattern; fixed or conventional expression, notion, character, mental pattern, etc., having no individuality, as though cast from a mold: as, the Negro is too often portrayed as a *stereotype*. *v.t.* [STEREOTYPED (-tīpt'), STEREOTYPING], 1. to make a stereotype of. 2. to print from stereotype plates.

ster·e·o·typed (ster'i-ə-tīpt', stêr'i-ə-tīpt'), *adj.* 1. having the nature of a stereotype; especially, hackneyed; trite; not original or individualized. 2. printed from stereotype plates. —*SYN.* see **trite.**

ster·e·o·typ·er (ster'i-ə-tīp'ẽr, stêr'i-ə-tīp'ẽr), *n.* a person or thing that stereotypes.

ster·e·o·typ·ic (ster'i-ə-tip'ik, stêr'i-ə-tip'ik), *adj.* 1. of or produced by stereotypy. 2. stereotyped; hackneyed.

ster·e·o·typ·ist (ster'i-ə-tīp'ist, stêr'i-ə-tīp'ist), *n.* a stereotyper.

ster·e·o·typ·y (ster'i-ə-tīp'i, stêr'i-ə-tīp'i), *n.* [Fr. *stéréotypie*], 1. the process of making or printing from stereotype plates. 2. *a*) abnormal repetition of an action, phrase, etc., especially as seen in one phase of dementia praecox. *b*) the abnormal maintenance of a single position, or posture, over an extended period of time, as in some phases of schizophrenia.

ster·ic (ster'ik, stêr'ik), *adj.* [*stereo-* + *-ic*], having to do with the spatial arrangement of the atoms in a molecule.

ster·i·cal (ster'i-k'l, stêr'i-k'l), *adj.* steric.

ster·ile (ster''l, ster'il), *adj.* [L. *sterilis*], 1. incapable of producing others of its kind; barren. 2. producing little or nothing; unfruitful: as, *sterile* soil, a *sterile* policy. 3. lacking in interest or vitality; not stimulating or effective: as, a *sterile* style or presentation. 4. deprived of its usual power or function; ineffective: said of gold (in monetary usage). 5. free from living microorganisms. 6. in *botany*, *a*) unable or failing to bear fruit or spores, as a plant, or to germinate, as a seed. *b*) having stamens only, as a male flower, or having neither pistils nor stamens.

SYN.—**sterile** and **infertile** imply incapability of producing offspring or fruit, as because of some disorder of the reproductive system; **barren** and **unfruitful** are specifically applied to a sterile woman or to plants, soil, etc.; **impotent** is specifically applied to a man who lacks the power to engage in sexual intercourse. All of these words have figurative uses (*sterile* thinking, an *infertile* mind, a *barren* victory, *unfruitful* efforts, *impotent* rage). —*ANT.* fertile.

ste·ril·i·ty (stə-ril'ə-ti), *n.* [*pl.* STERILITIES (-tiz)], the quality or condition of being sterile.

ster·i·li·za·tion (ster'ə-li-zā'shən, ster'ə-lī-zā'shən), *n.* a sterilizing or being sterilized.

ster·i·lize (ster'ə-līz'), *v.t.* [STERILIZED (-līzd'), STERILIZING], to make sterile; specifically, *a*) to make incapable of producing others of its kind, as by removing the organs of reproduction or preventing them from functioning effectively: usually with reference to surgical operations. *b*) to free from living microorganisms, as by subjecting to great heat or chemical action. Also spelled **sterilise.**

ster·i·liz·er (ster'ə-līz'ẽr), *n.* a person or thing that sterilizes, especially a device used to destroy living microorganisms by heat or chemical action.

ster·let (stũr'lit), *n.* [Fr. or G. < Russ. *sterlyad'*], a small sturgeon used as food and as a source of caviar.

ster·ling (stũr'liŋ), *n.* [ME. *sterlinge*, Norman silver penny (whence OHG. *sterlinc*, OFr. *esterlin*, ML. *esterlingus*, etc.); prob. < AS. *_steorling_ < *steor* (cf. STAR) + *-ling*: from the star stamped on it], 1. originally, an early English silver penny: a pound weight of these pennies was later standardized as a money of account. 2. English money having the fineness of quality of the standard silver penny. 3. sterling silver or articles made of it. 4. the standard of fineness of legal British coinage: for silver, 0.500 (0.925 before 1920); for gold, 0.91666 (0.995 formerly). 5. British money. *adj.* 1. of standard quality: said of silver that is at least 92.5 per cent pure; originally said of silver having the quality of that in the sterling (sense 1). 2. of or payable in British money. 3. made of sterling silver. 4. having genuinely high quality or value; excellent: as, a man of *sterling* principles. Abbreviated **ster., stg., stlg.**

stern (stũrn), *adj.* [ME. *sterne;* AS. *styrne*, for *_stierne_; IE. base *_ster-_, stiff, rigid (cf. STARE, STARVE)], 1. hard; severe; unyielding; strict: as, *stern* measures, *stern* treatment. 2. grim; forbidding: as, a *stern* face or manner. 3. relentless; firm; inexorable: as, *stern* purpose, *stern* reality. —*SYN.* see **severe.**

stern (stũrn), *n.* [ME. *steorne;* prob. < ON. *stjorn*, steering < *styra*, to steer; cf. STEER], 1. the rear end of a ship or boat. 2. the rear end of anything.

ster·na (stũr'nə), *n.* alternative plural of **sternum.**

ster·nal (stũr'n'l), *adj.* [Mod. L. *sternalis*], of or near the sternum.

stern chase, in *nautical usage*, a chase in which one ship follows in the wake of, or astern of, another.

stern chaser, a gun mounted on the stern of a ship used for firing to the rear.

Sterne, Laurence (stũrn), 1713–1768; English novelist and clergyman.

stern·fore·most (stũrn'fôr'mōst, stũrn'fôr'məst), *adv.* 1. with the stern foremost; backward: said of a ship hence, 2. in an awkward, cumbersome manner.

stern·most (stũrn'mōst, stũrn'məst), *adj.* 1. nearest the stern. 2. farthest astern; rearmost.

ster·no- (stũr'nō, stũr'nə), [< *sternum*], a combining form meaning *of the sternum and.*

stern·post (stũrn'pōst'), *n.* the main, upright piece at the stern of a vessel, usually supporting the rudder.

stern sheets, the space at the stern of an open boat.

stern·son (stũrn's'n), *n.* [< *stern* (of a ship), after *keelson*], in *nautical usage*, a heavy curved piece connecting the keelson to the sternpost: also **sternson** (or **stern**) **knee.**

ster·num (stũr′nəm), *n.* [*pl.* STERNA (-nə), STERNUMS (-nəmz)], [Mod. L. < Gr. *sternon*, the breastbone], a thin, flat structure of bone and cartilage to which most of the ribs are attached in the front of the chest in most vertebrates; breastbone: see **skeleton,** illus.

ster·nu·ta·tion (stũr′nyoo-tā′shən), *n.* [L. *sternutatio* < *sternutare*, to sneeze, freq. of *sternuere*, to sneeze; IE. base **pster-*, to sneeze, seen also in Gr. *ptarnysthai*], a sneeze or sneezing.

ster·nu·ta·tive (stẽr-nū′tə-tiv), *adj.* [Rare], sternutatory.

ster·nu·ta·to·ry (stẽr-nū′tə-tôr′i, stẽr-nū′tə-tō′ri), *adj.* of or causing sternutation. *n.* [*pl.* STERNUTATORIES (-iz, -riz)], a sternutatory substance, as snuff.

stern·ward (stũrn′wẽrd), *adv.* toward the stern; astern.

stern·way (stũrn′wā′), *n.* backward movement of a ship.

stern-wheel·er (stũrn′hwēl′ẽr), *n.* a steamer propelled by a paddle wheel at the stern.

ster·oid (ster′oid), *n.* [*ster*ol + *-oid*], any of a group of compounds including the sterols, bile acids, sex hormones, etc., characteristically having the carbon ring structure of the sterols.

ster·ol (ster′ōl, ster′ol), *n.* [contr. of *cholesterol*], any of a group of solid cyclic alcohols found in plant and animal tissues, as cholesterol.

ster·tor (stũr′tẽr), *n.* [Mod. L. < L. *stertere*, to snore], a heavy snoring accompanying breathing, as in certain diseases.

ster·to·rous (stũr′tə-rəs), *adj.* characterized by or breathing with stertor, or heavy snoring.

stet (stet), [L., 3d pers. sing., pres. subj., of *stare*, to stand], let it stand: a printer's term used to indicate that matter previously struck out is to remain. *v.t.* [STETTED (-id), STETTING], to cancel a correction or deletion previously made of (a word, character, passage, etc., as in a proof or manuscript) by marking with the word *stet*, and often with a row of dots.

steth·o- (steth′ō, steth′ə), [Gr. *stetho-*, *steth-* < *stēthos*, the chest, breast], a combining form meaning *chest, breast*, as in *stethoscope*: also, before a vowel, **steth-.**

ste·thom·e·ter (ste-thom′ə-tẽr), *n.* [*stetho-* + *-meter*], an instrument for measuring the expansion of the chest or abdomen in respiration.

steth·o·scope (steth′ə-skōp′), *n.* [see STETHO- & -SCOPE], in *medicine*, a hearing instrument used in auscultation, for examining the heart, lungs, etc. by listening to the sounds they make.

steth·o·scop·ic (steth′ə-skop′ik), *adj.* 1. of the stethoscope or its use. 2. made or obtained by the use of the stethoscope.

steth·o·scop·i·cal (steth′ə-skop′i-k'l), *adj.* stethoscopic.

steth·o·scop·i·cal·ly (steth′ə-skop′i-k'l-i, steth′ə-skop′-ik-li), *adv.* by means of the stethoscope.

ste·thos·co·py (ste-thos′kə-pi), *n.* the use of the stethoscope.

St.-É·tienne (san′tā′tyen′), *n.* a city in southeastern France: pop., 182,000.

Stet·tin (shte-tēn′; Eng. stet′in), *n.* a city in northwestern Poland, at the mouth of the Oder River: formerly, the capital of Pomerania, Germany: pop., 249,000: Polish name, *Szczecin.*

Stet·tin·i·us, Edward Riley (stə-tin′i-əs), 1900–1949; American industrialist and statesman; secretary of state (1944–1945).

Steu·ben, Baron **Frederick William von** (von stōō′-bin, stū′bin; G. fôn shtoi′bən), 1730–1794; German general; served as volunteer in the Continental Army during the American Revolution.

Steu·ben·ville (stōō′b'n-vil′, stū′b'n-vil′), *n.* a city in east central Ohio, on the Ohio River: pop., 32,000.

ste·ve·dore (stē′və-dôr′, stē′və-dōr′), *n.* [Sp. *estivador* < *estivar*, to stow, ram tight < L. *stipare*, to cram, stuff], a person employed at loading and unloading ships. *v.t. & v.i.* [STEVEDORED (-dôrd′, -dōrd′), STEVEDORING], to load or unload the cargo of (a ship).

stevedore's knot, a kind of knot: see **knot,** illus.

Ste·ven (stē′vən), a masculine name: see **Stephen.**

Ste·vens, Thaddeus (stē′vənz), 1792–1868; American statesman and antislavery leader.

Ste·ven·son, Robert Louis (stē′vən-s'n), 1850–1894; Scottish novelist, poet, and essayist.

stew (stōō, stū), *v.t. & v.i.* [ME. *stuen, stuwen* < OFr. *estuver*, to stew, bathe; LL. **extufare* < L. *ex*, out + Gr. *typhos*, steam, smoke], 1. to cook by boiling slowly; simmer. 2. [Colloq.], to worry. *n.* 1. [< obs. sense, a public room for hot baths: such rooms were often used for immoral purposes; cf. BAGNIO], *usually in pl.* a brothel. 2. a dish, especially a mixture of meat and several vegetables, cooked by slow boiling. 3. [Colloq.], a state of worry or anxiety. 4. [Obs.], a stewpan. —*SYN.* see **boil.**

stew in one's own juice, to suffer, especially from one's own actions.

stew (stōō, stū), *n.* [ME. *stuwe;* OFr. *estui* (Fr. *étui*), a sheath, case, fish tub < *estuier*, to shut up, enclose], a pond, tank, etc. in which fish or oysters are kept alive for table use.

stew·ard (stōō′ẽrd, stū′ẽrd), *n.* [ME. *stiward;* AS. *stiweard, stigeweard* < *stig, sti*, enclosure, hall, also sty + *weard*, a ward, keeper], 1. a person put in charge of the affairs of a large household or estate, whose duties include supervision of the kitchen and the servants, management of household accounts, etc. 2. one who acts as a supervisor or administrator, as of finances and property, for another or others. 3. a person who buys the provisions, supervises the kitchen, etc. in a club or other institution. 4. a person, usually one of a group, in charge of arrangements for a ball, race, meeting, etc. 5. one of the staff of servants on a passenger ship: as, a deck *steward*. 6. an officer on a ship who is in charge of stores and culinary arrangements. 7. see **shop steward.** *v.i.* to act as a steward.

stew·ard·ess (stōō′ẽr-dis, stū′ẽr-dis), *n.* 1. a woman steward (in any sense). 2. a woman employed to take care of passengers' wants, as on a ship, airplane, etc.

stew·ard·ship (stōō′ẽrd-ship′, stū′ẽrd-ship′), *n.* [see -SHIP], the position, duties, or service of a steward.

Stew·art (stōō′ẽrt, stū′ẽrt), a masculine name: see **Stuart.**

Stew·art, Du·gald (dōō′gəld stōō′ẽrt, dū′gəld stū′ẽrt), 1753–1828; Scottish philosopher.

Stew·art Island (stōō′ẽrt, stū′ẽrt), an island of New Zealand, south of South Island: area, 670 sq. mi.

stewed (stōōd, stūd), *adj.* 1. cooked by stewing, as food. 2. [Slang], drunk; inebriated.

stew·pan (stōō′pan′, stū′pan′), *n.* a pan used for stewing.

stg., sterling.

St. Gal·len (gäl′ən), a city in northeastern Switzerland: pop., 74,000.

stge., storage.

St. George's (jôr′jiz), the capital of the Windward Islands, West Indies Federation: seaport on Grenada: pop., 5,800.

St. George's Channel, the strait between Ireland and Wales, connecting the Irish Sea with the Atlantic.

St. George's cross, a red Greek cross on a white background.

St.-Ger·main (san′zher′man′), *n.* a French town near Paris: pop., 20,000: a treaty was signed there in 1919 between Austria and the Allies.

St.-Ger·main-en-Laye (san′zher′man′än′lā′), *n.* St.-Germain.

St. Gott·hard (got′ẽrd, goth′ẽrd; Fr. san′gô′tärd′), 1. a mountain range of the Alps in southern Switzerland: highest peak, 10,490 ft. 2. a pass through these mountains. 3. a railway tunnel under this pass: length, 9 1/4 mi.

St. He·le·na (he-lē′nə), 1. a British island in the Atlantic, off southern Africa: area, 47 sq. mi.; pop., 4,800: place of Napoleon's exile. 2. a British colony including St. Helena, Ascension, and the Tristan da Cunha islands: area, 119 sq. mi.; pop., 5,400.

ST. HELENA

St. Hel·ens (hel′ənz), a city in Lancashire, northwestern England: pop., 111,000.

St. Hel·ier (hel′yẽr), a town on the island of Jersey, Channel Islands: pop., 19,000.

sthe·ni·a (sthi-nī′ə, sthē′-ni-ə), *n.* [Mod. L. < Gr. *sthenos*, strength], in *medicine*, a condition of great strength or vitality: opposed to *asthenia.*

sthen·ic (sthen′ik), *adj.* of or characterized by sthenia: said especially of diseases characterized by the abnormally vigorous activity of some vital process.

stiac·cia·to (styä-chä′tō), *n.* [It., crushed, flat < *stiacciare*, to crush], 1. the act or process of carving or modeling in very low relief. 2. an object, as the head on a coin, produced in this way. *adj.* in very low relief.

stib·i·al (stib′i-əl), *adj.* [< L. *stibium*, antimony; + *-al*], of or like antimony.

stib·in (stib′in), *n.* stibine.

stib·ine (stib′ēn, stib′in), *n.* [*stibium* + *-ine*], the hydride of trivalent antimony, SbH_3, a colorless, poisonous gas.

stib·i·um (stib′i-əm), *n.* [ME.; L. < Gr. *stibi*], antimony: symbol, Sb (no period).

stib·nite (stib′nīt), *n.* [< *stibine*; + *-ite*], native trisulfide of antimony, Sb_2S_3, a lead-gray, usually crystalline mineral, the chief source of antimony.

stich (stik), ***n.*** [Gr. *stichos*], in *prosody*, a line, or verse.

stich·ic (stik′ik), ***adj.*** 1. of or made up of stichs. 2. made up of lines having the same metrical form.

stich·o·met·ric (stik′ə-met′rik), ***adj.*** of, having to do with, or using stichometry.

stich·o·met·ri·cal (stik′ə-met′ri-k'l), ***adj.*** stichometric.

sti·chom·e·try (sti-kom′ə-tri), ***n.*** [< Gr. *stichos*, a line, verse; + *-metry*], the practice of expressing the successive ideas in a prose composition in single lines of lengths corresponding to natural cadences or sense divisions.

stich·o·myth·i·a (stik′ə-mith′i-ə), ***n.*** [Gr. *stichomythia* < *stichos*, a line + *mythos*, speech, talk], dialogue in single alternate lines, as in ancient Greek drama.

stich·o·myth·ic (stik′ə-mith′ik), ***adj.*** of, or having the form of, stichomythia.

sti·chom·y·thy (sti-kom′ə-thi), ***n.*** stichomythia.

-stich·ous (stik′əs), [< Gr. *stichos*, a line, row; + *-ous*], a combining form meaning *having* (a specified number or kind of) *rows*, as in *tristichous*.

stick (stik), ***n.*** [ME. *stikke;* AS. *sticca;* akin to D. *stek;* IE. base **steig-*, a point, as also in Gr. *stigma* (cf. STIGMA), L. *instigare* (cf. INSTIGATE), etc.], 1. a long, usually slender piece of wood; specifically, *a*) a twig or small branch broken off or cut off, especially a dead and dry one. *b*) a tree branch of any size, used for fuel, etc. *c*) a long, slender, and usually tapering piece of wood shaped for a specific purpose, as a wand, staff, club, baton, cane, rod, etc. 2. a stalk, as of celery. 3. something shaped like a stick. 4. an individual, sticklike piece: as, a *stick* of chewing gum. 5. a sticklike playing implement: as, a hockey *stick*. 6. something made of sticks, as a racing hurdle. 7. a sticking, as with a pointed weapon; stab. 8. the power of adhering or making adhere. 9. an amount of rum, brandy, etc. added to a beverage. 10. a number of bombs dropped from the air in such a way as to fall in a line across a target. 11. [Archaic], a stoppage, delay, or obstacle. 12. [Colloq.], a dull, stupid, or spiritless person. 13. in *aeronautics*, a lever for operating the elevators and ailerons of an airplane, thus controlling its movements lengthwise and sideways: also **joy stick**. 14. in *nautical usage*, a mast or a part of a mast. 15. in *printing*, *a*) a composing stick. *b*) its contents. ***v.t.*** [STUCK (stuk), STICKING], [combination of ME. *steken*, to prick, fasten (< AS. *stecan*) & ME. *stikien* < AS. *stician*, to stick, stab, prick; both are related in origin], 1. to pierce or puncture, as with a pointed instrument. 2. to kill by piercing; stab. 3. to thrust, push, or press (a knife, pin, etc.) so as to pierce. 4. to fasten by making pierce or penetrate: as, *stick* a thumbtack in the board; hence, 5. to decorate with things fastened in this way: as, a coat *stuck* with medals. 6. to set with piercing objects: as, a cushion *stuck* with pins. 7. to thrust or poke: as, *stick* your nose out the door. 8. to fasten or attach as by gluing, pinning, etc.: as, *stick* the poster on the wall. 9. *a*) to transfix or impale. *b*) to impale (insect specimens, etc.), as on a pin, and mount for exhibit. 10. *a*) to obstruct, entangle, bog down, etc. *b*) to detain, delay, etc. Usually used in the passive: as, the wheels were *stuck*, I was *stuck* in town. 11. [STICKED (stikt), STICKING], [< the *n.*], *a*) to prop (a vine, etc.) with a stick or sticks. *b*) in *printing*, to set in a composing stick. 12. [Colloq.], to place; put; set. 13. [Colloq.], to make sticky by smearing. 14. [Colloq.], to puzzle; baffle: as, I'm *stuck* by this question. 15. [Slang], *a*) to make pay, often exorbitantly. *b*) to impose a disagreeable task, burden, etc. upon. *c*) to cheat or defraud. 16. [Slang], to endure or tolerate. ***v.i.*** 1. to be or remain fixed or embedded by a pointed end, as a nail, etc. 2. to be or remain attached by adhesion; adhere; cleave. 3. to remain in the same place; stay; abide: as, they *stick* at home. 4. to remain in close association; be fixed; cling: as, friends *stick* together, the nickname *stuck*. 5. to keep close: as, he *stuck* to the trail. 6. to persevere; persist: as, she *stuck* at (or to) her work. 7. to remain firm and resolute; endure: as, she *stuck* through thick and thin. 8. to become fixed, blocked, lodged, etc., as by an obstacle; specifically, *a*) to become embedded and immovable: as, my shoe *stuck* in the mud. *b*) to become unworkable; jam: as, the gears *stuck*. *c*) to become stopped or delayed; come to a standstill: as, the bill *stuck* in committee. *d*) to remain unsold. 9. to be puzzled. 10. to be reluctant; hesitate; scruple: as, he'll *stick* at nothing. 11. to protrude, project, or extend (with *out*, *up*, *down*, etc.).

stick around, [Slang], to stay near at hand; not go away.

stick by, to remain faithful or loyal to.

stick up, [Slang], to commit armed robbery upon.

stick up for, [Colloq.], to support; uphold; defend.

the sticks, [Colloq.], the rural districts; the country.

SYN.*—stick** is the simple, general term here, implying attachment by gluing or fastening together in any way, by close association, etc. (to *stick* a stamp on a letter, to *stick* to a subject); **adhere** implies firm attachment and, of persons, denotes voluntary allegiance or devotion to an idea, cause, leader, etc. (to *adhere* to a policy); **cohere** implies such close sticking together of parts as to form a single mass (glue made the particles of sawdust *cohere*); **cling** implies attachment by embracing, entwining, or grasping with the arms, tendrils, etc. (a vine *clinging* to the trellis); **cleave** is a poetic or lofty term implying a very close, firm attachment (his tongue *clove* to the roof of his mouth, Ruth *clove* to Naomi). —ANT.*** part, detach, separate.

stick·er (stik′ẽr), ***n.*** a person or thing that sticks; specifically, *a*) a bur, barb, or thorn. *b*) a gummed patch or label. *c*) a tenacious or persistent person. *d*) [Colloq.], something puzzling or difficult to solve.

stick·ful (stik′fool′), ***n.*** in *printing*, the contents or capacity of a composing stick.

stick·i·ly (stik′'l-i), ***adv.*** in a sticky manner.

stick·i·ness (stik′i-nis), ***n.*** the quality or condition of being sticky.

sticking place, the place or degree at which something will stick, or become firm or constant.

sticking plaster, adhesive material for covering a slight wound, usually made of a thin cloth gummed on one side; court plaster.

sticking point, sticking place.

stick insect, any of several insects whose bodies resemble a small stick.

stick-in-the-mud (stik′'n-*th*ə-mud′), ***n.*** [Colloq.], a person who resists change or progress; person lacking imagination, initiative, adaptability, etc.

stick·le (stik′'l), ***v.i.*** [STICKLED (-'ld), STICKLING], [prob. < ME. *stightlen*, to rule, order, dispose, freq. of *stighten*, to dispose, destine; AS. *stihtan*], 1. to raise objections, haggle, or make difficulties, especially in a stubborn, narrow manner, usually about trifles. 2. to have scruples or objections; scruple; demur.

stick·le·back (stik′'l-bak′), ***n.*** [ME. *stykylbak* < AS. *sticel*, a prick, sting < base of *sticca;* see STICK], a small, scaleless salt-water and fresh-water fish with two to five sharp spines in front of the dorsal fin: the male builds a nest for the female's eggs.

stick·ler (stik′lẽr), ***n.*** [cf. STICKLE], 1. a person who insists uncompromisingly on the observance of something specified: usually with *for*, as, a *stickler* for discipline. 2. [Colloq.], a sticker (sense *c*).

stick·pin (stik′pin′), ***n.*** a pin worn as an ornament in a cravat or necktie.

stick·seed (stik′sēd′), ***n.*** any of several plants, especially of the borage group, with barbs or prickles on the seeds or fruit.

stick·tight (stik′tīt′), ***n.*** an herb of the aster family, with flat, needlelike seeds that stick to clothing, fur, etc.: also called *bur marigold*.

stick-to-it·ive·ness (stik′too͞′it-iv-nis), ***n.*** [Colloq.], pertinacity.

stick-up (stik′up′), ***n.*** [Slang], a holdup.

stick·weed (stik′wēd′), ***n.*** ragweed.

stick·y (stik′i), ***adj.*** [STICKIER (-i-ẽr), STICKIEST (-i-ist)], 1. that sticks; adhesive; tending to cling to anything touched. 2. covered with an adhesive substance: as, *sticky* fingers. 3. [Colloq.], humid: as, *sticky* heat.

Stieg·litz, Alfred (stēg′lits), 1864–1946; American photographer.

stiff (stif), ***adj.*** [ME. & AS. *stif;* akin to G. *steif;* IE. base **stip-*, etc., a pole, sticking, pressing, etc., as also in L. *stipes*, a stem, tree trunk, stake (cf. STIPULATE), *stipare* (cf. STIPATE)], 1. hard to bend or stretch; rigid; firm; not flexible or pliant. 2. hard to move or operate; not free or limber: as, the steering gear is *stiff*. 3. stretched tight; taut; tense. 4. sore or limited in movement: said of joints and muscles. 5. having such joints or muscles, as from exertion, cold, etc. 6. not fluid or loose; thick; dense; firm: as, beat the egg whites until *stiff*, this soil is too *stiff* for easy digging. 7. strong; specifically, *a*) moving swiftly, as a breeze or current. *b*) containing much alcohol: said of a drink. *c*) of high potency: as, a *stiff* dose of medicine. 8. harsh: as, *stiff* punishment. 9. difficult: as, a *stiff* assignment, a *stiff* climb. 10. excessively formal, constrained, or awkward; not easy, natural, or graceful. 11. resolute, stubborn, or uncompromising, as a person, a fight, etc. 12. [Colloq.], *a*) resistant to lowering influences; maintaining a firm level. *b*) high. Said of prices, etc. 13. in *nautical usage*, not careening or heeling over much despite the amount of sail carried or the strength of the wind. 14. [Scot. & British Dial.], sturdy; stalwart; robust. ***n.*** [Slang], 1. a corpse. 2. an excessively formal or constrained person. 3. an awkward or rough person: as, you big *stiff!* 4. a hobo. 5. a man: in *working stiff*.

SYN.*—stiff** implies a firmness of texture which makes a substance resist a bending force to a greater or lesser degree and figuratively connotes formality or constraint (a *stiff* collar, manner, etc.); **rigid** implies such stiffness in a thing that it resists a bending force to the breaking point and figuratively connotes strictness or severity (a *rigid* framework, disciplinarian, etc.); **inflexible** is applied to that which cannot be bent or, figuratively, diverted (an *inflexible* rod, will, etc.); **inelastic** implies a lack of resilience and, figuratively, of adaptability (the brittle, *inelastic* bones of the aged, *inelastic* regulations). See also **firm.** —ANT.*** limp, pliant.

stiff·en (stif′'n), ***v.t. & v.i.*** to make or become stiff or stiffer.

stiff-necked (stif′nekt′), *adj.* stubborn; obstinate.
sti·fle (stī′f'l), *v.t.* [STIFLED (-f'ld), STIFLING], [ME. *stufflen*, a freq. formation < OFr. *estouffer* (Fr. *étouffer*), to smother, or < ON. *stīfla*, to stop up], 1. to prevent from breathing; suffocate; smother. 2. to suppress or repress; hold back; check; stop: as, she *stifled* her sobs. *v.i.* 1. to die from lack of air. 2. to suffer from lack of fresh, cool air.
sti·fle (stī′f'l), *n.* [ME. *stifle;* prob. < *stiff* + *-le;* the former common form was *stiffle*], the kneelike joint above the hock in the hind leg of certain animals, as the horse and dog: also **stifle joint.**
sti·fling (stī′fliŋ), *adj.* that stifles; suffocating; choking.
stig·ma (stig′mə), *n.* [*pl.* STIGMAS (-məz); *also, and for 4, 5, and 6 usually,* STIGMATA (-mə-tə)], [L.; Gr., lit., a prick with a pointed instrument < *stizein*, to prick; cf. STICK], 1. a distinguishing mark burned or cut into the flesh, as of a slave or criminal. 2. something that detracts from the character or reputation of a person, group, etc.; mark of disgrace or reproach. 3. a mark, sign, etc. indicating that something is not considered normal or standard. 4. a small mark, scar, or opening on the surface of an animal body: as, a pore is a *stigma.* 5. in *botany*, the upper tip of the pistil of a flower, receiving the pollen. 6. in *medicine, a*) a spot on the skin, especially one that bleeds as the result of certain nervous tensions. *b*) any sign characteristic of a specific disease.
stig·ma·ta (stig′mə-tə), *n.pl.* [Gr., pl. of *stigma*], marks resembling the crucifixion wounds of Jesus, said to have appeared supernaturally on certain persons.
stig·mat·ic (stig-mat′ik), *adj.* 1. of, like, or having a stigma, stigmas, or stigmata. 2. anastigmatic. *n.* a person marked with stigmata.
stig·mat·i·cal (stig-mat′i-k'l), *adj.* stigmatic.
stig·ma·tism (stig′mə-tiz'm), *n.* 1. the condition characterized by the presence of stigmata. 2. the condition of a lens, and the normal condition of the eye, in which rays of light from a single point are focused upon a single point: opposed to *astigmatism.*
stig·ma·ti·za·tion (stig′mə-ti-zā′shən, stig′mə-tī-zā′shən), *n.* a stigmatizing or being stigmatized.
stig·ma·tize (stig′mə-tīz′), *v.t.* [STIGMATIZED (-tīzd′), STIGMATIZING], [ML. *stigmatizare;* Gr. *stigmatizein*, to mark < *stigma*, a mark, brand], 1. to mark with a stigma or stigmas; brand. 2. to characterize or mark as disgraceful. 3. to cause stigmata to appear on.
stil·bene (stil′bēn), *n.* [< Gr. *stilbein*, to glitter; + *-ene*], a crystalline hydrocarbon, $C_6H_5CH{:}CHC_6H_5$, used in the manufacture of dyes.
stil·bes·trol (stil-bes′trōl, stil-bes′trol), *n.* [*stilb*ene + *estr*in + *-ol*], a synthetic hormone, $C_{18}H_{20}O_2$, a source of various estrogens, some of which have greater potency than the natural estrogens.
stil·bite (stil′bīt), *n.* [Fr. < Gr. *stilbein*, to glitter; see -ITE], a native hydrous silicate of sodium, calcium, and aluminum, $Na_2CaAl_2Si_6O_{16}{\cdot}6H_2O$, often found in the form of sheaflike crystalline aggregates.
stile (stīl), *n.* [ME. *stile, stigele;* AS. *stigel* < *stigan*, to climb], 1. a step or set of steps used in climbing over a fence or wall. 2. a turnstile.
stile (stīl), *n.* [D. *stijl*, doorpost], a vertical piece in a panel or frame, as of a door or window.
sti·let·to (sti-let′ō), *n.* [*pl.* STILETTOS, STILETTOES (-ōz)], [It., dim. of *stilo*, dagger < L. *stilus;* see STYLE], 1. a small dagger having a slender, tapering blade. 2. a small, sharp-pointed instrument used for making eyelet holes in cloth, etc. *v.t.* [STILETTOED (-ōd), STILETTOING], to stab, or kill by stabbing, with a stiletto.
still (stil), *adj.* [ME. & AS. *stille;* akin to G. *still;* IE. **stel-nú-s* < base **st(h)el-*, to put in place, set up, as also in Gr. *stelē*, pillar (cf. STELE), *stellein*, to put in order, etc.], 1. without sound; quiet; silent. 2. hushed, soft, or low in sound. 3. stationary; at rest; motionless. 4. characterized by little or no commotion or agitation; tranquil; calm; serene: as, the *still* water of the lake. 5. not effervescent or bubbling; without sparkle: said of wine. 6. in *photography, a*) designating or of an individual, usually posed photograph. *b*) having to do with a single photograph taken from a reel of motion-picture film. *n.* 1. [Poetic], silence; quiet. 2. a still photograph. 3. [Colloq.], *a*) a still-life picture. *b*) a still alarm. *adv.* 1. at or up to the time indicated, whether past, present, or future. 2. even; yet: used as an intensifier with a comparative form, etc., as, it was cold yesterday, but today it is *still* colder. 3. nevertheless; even then; yet: as, he is old and *still* he is able. 4. [Poetic], ever; constantly; continually. *conj.* nevertheless; yet. *v.t.* to make still; quiet; specifically, *a*) to make silent. *b*) to make motionless. *c*) to calm; relieve; allay. *v.i.* to become still.
SYN.—**still** always implies the absence of sound and, almost always, of movement (the *still* hours before dawn, a *still* pool); **quiet** also implies the absence of sound but usually stresses freedom from excitement, commotion, agitation, etc. (a *quiet* town, motor, etc.); **noiseless** stresses the absence of noise or sound and often suggests movement unaccompanied by sound (a *noiseless* typewriter); **hushed** suggests the suppression of noise or sound (the *hushed* corridors of a hospital).—*ANT.* noisy, stirring.
still (stil), *n.* [< obs. *still*, to distill < L. *stillare*, to drop, drip, trickle < *stilla*, a drop], 1. an apparatus used for distilling liquids, especially alcoholic liquors. 2. a distillery. *v.t. & v.i.* [Obs.], to distill.
still alarm, a fire alarm given by telephone or by any means other than the regular signal apparatus.
still·birth (stil′bũrth′), *n.* 1. the birth of a stillborn fetus. 2. a stillborn fetus.
still·born (stil′bôrn′), *adj.* dead when born.

BOILING IMPURE LIQUID
COLD WATER
IN
DISTILLED LIQUID
OUT

STILL

still-hunt (stil′hunt′), *v.t. & v.i.* to hunt or pursue stealthily.
still hunt, 1. a stealthy hunt for game, as by stalking or using cover; hence, 2. [Colloq.], a stealthy or quiet, cautious pursuit of anything.
still-life (stil′līf′), *adj.* of or having to do with still life.
still life, 1. small inanimate objects, as fruit, bottles, flowers, books, etc., used as subjects for a picture. 2. a picture having such a subject.
Still·son wrench (stil′s'n), a wrench having a jaw which moves through a collar pivoted loosely to the shaft, used for turning pipes, etc.: the jaw tightens as pressure is applied to the handle: a trade-mark: see **wrench,** illus.
still·y (stil′i), *adj.* [STILLIER (-i-ẽr), STILLIEST (-i-ist)], [ME. *stillich;* AS. *stillic*], [Poetic], still; silent; quiet; calm. *adv.* (stil′li), [ME. *stilleli*, etc.; AS. *stillice*], in a still manner; silently; quietly; calmly.
stilt (stilt), *n.* [ME. *stilte;* prob. of LG. or Scand. origin; akin to G. *stelze*, stilt], 1. one of a pair of poles fitted with a footrest somewhere along its length and used for walking, as through water or for amusement. 2. a long post or pole used to hold something aboveground or out of the water: as, the henhouse is placed on *stilts.* 3. [*pl.* STILTS (stilts), STILT; see PLURAL, II, D, 1], any of several wading birds of the plover family, with a long, slender bill and three-toed legs, living chiefly in marshes. *v.t.* to set or raise on or as on stilts.
stilt·ed (stil′tid), *adj.* 1. raised or elevated on or as on stilts. 2. artificially formal or dignified; pompous.
Stil·ton cheese (stil′t'n), [orig. sold at *Stilton*, England], a rich, waxy cheese having a blue-green mold: also **Stilton,** *n.*
Stil·well, Joseph W. (stil′wel′, stil′wəl), 1883–1946; American general in World War II.
Stim·son, Henry Lewis (stim′s'n), 1867–1950; American statesman; secretary of state (1929–1933); secretary of war (1911–1913; 1940–1945).
stim·u·lant (stim′yoo-lənt), *adj.* [L. *stimulans*, ppr.], that stimulates; stimulating. *n.* anything that stimulates; specifically, *a*) an alcoholic drink. *b*) in *medicine & physiology*, any drug, etc. that temporarily increases the activity of some vital process or of some organ.
stim·u·late (stim′yoo-lāt′), *v.t.* [STIMULATED (-id), STIMULATING], [< L. *stimulatus*, pp. of *stimulare*, to prick, goad, excite < *stimulus*, a goad], 1. to rouse to action or increased action, as by goading; spur on; excite. 2. to invigorate by an alcoholic drink. 3. in *medicine & physiology*, to excite (an organ, part, etc.) to activity or increased activity. *v.i.* to act as a stimulant or stimulus. —*SYN.* see **animate, provoke.**
stim·u·lat·er (stim′yoo-lāt′ẽr), *n.* a person or thing that stimulates.
stim·u·la·tion (stim′yoo-lā′shən), *n.* [L. *stimulatio*], a stimulating or being stimulated.
stim·u·la·tive (stim′yoo-lā′tiv), *adj.* stimulating or tending to stimulate. *n.* something that stimulates.
stim·u·la·tor (stim′yoo-lā′tẽr), *n.* [L.], a person or thing that stimulates.
stim·u·lus (stim′yoo-ləs), *n.* [*pl.* STIMULI (-lī′)], [L., a goad, sting, torment, pang, spur, incentive], 1. something that rouses or incites to action or increased action; incentive. 2. in *physiology & psychology*, any action or agent that causes or changes an activity in an organism, organ, or part, as something that excites an end organ, starts a nerve impulse, activates a muscle, etc.
sti·my (stī′mi), *n.* [*pl.* STIMIES (-miz)], & *v.t.* [STIMIED (-mid), STIMYING], stymie.
sting (stiŋ), *v.t.* [STUNG (stuŋ) or *archaic* STANG (staŋ), STINGING], [ME. *stingen;* AS. *stingan;* akin to ON.

stinga; IE. base **stengh-*, to pierce], 1. to prick or wound with a sting: said of plants and insects. 2. to cause sharp, sudden, smarting pain to, by or as by pricking with a sharp point: as, the nettles *stung* her legs, salt will *sting* raw flesh. 3. to pain, or cause to suffer, in the mind: as, his conscience *stung* him sharply. 4. to stir up or stimulate suddenly and sharply: as, her words *stung* him into action. 5. [Slang], to get the better of; cheat; dupe: usually in the passive or past participle, as, he got *stung* on that deal. ***v.i.*** 1. to use a sting; prick or wound with a sting. 2. to cause or feel sharp, smarting pain, either physical or mental: as, iodine *stings*, his leg *stung* from the nettles. ***n.*** [AS. *sting*], 1. the act of stinging. 2. a pain or wound resulting from or as from stinging. 3. a thing that urges or stimulates; goad. 4. the ability or power to sting. 5. a sharp-pointed organ in insects and certain other animals, used to prick, wound, or inject poison. 6. in *botany*, any of a number of stinging, hollow hairs on some plants, as nettles.

sting·a·ree (stiŋ'ə-rē', stiŋ'ə-rē'), ***n.*** [altered < *sting ray*], a sting ray.

sting·er (stiŋ'ẽr), ***n.*** 1. a person or thing that stings; specifically, *a*) an animal or plant that stings. *b*) a sharp-pointed organ used for stinging. *c*) [Colloq.], a blow, reply, etc. that stings. 2. an alcoholic drink made with white crème de menthe, brandy, and ice. 3. [British Slang], a highball of whisky and soda.

stin·gi·ly (stin'jə-li), ***adv.*** in a stingy, or miserly, manner.

stin·gi·ness (stin'ji-nis), ***n.*** the quality or condition of being stingy, or miserly.

stinging hair, in *botany*, a sting.

stin·go (stiŋ'gō), ***n.*** [from the sharpness of the taste], [Slang], 1. strong beer or ale. 2. energy; vim; zest.

sting·ray (stiŋ'rā'), ***n.*** a sting ray.

sting ray, a large ray having a whiplike tail with sharp spines capable of inflicting severe wounds: also **stingaree.**

sting·y (stin'ji), ***adj.*** [STINGIER (-ji-ẽr), STINGIEST (-ji-ist)], [< *stinge*, dial. form of *sting;* basic sense "sharp-tongued in bargaining"], 1. giving or spending grudgingly or only through necessity; mean; miserly; close-fisted. 2. less than needed or expected; scanty; meager.

SYN.—**stingy** implies a grudging, mean reluctance to part with anything belonging to one; **close** suggests the keeping of a tight hold on what one has accumulated; **niggardly** implies such closefistedness that one grudgingly spends or gives the least amount possible; **parsimonious** implies unreasonable economy or frugality, often to the point of niggardliness; **penurious** implies such extreme parsimony and niggardliness as to make one seem poverty-stricken or destitute; **miserly** implies the penuriousness of one who is meanly avaricious and hoarding. —***ANT.*** generous, bountiful.

sting·y (stiŋ'i), ***adj.*** stinging or capable of stinging.

stink (stiŋk), ***v.i.*** [STANK (staŋk) or STUNK (stuŋk), STUNK, STINKING], [ME. *stinken;* AS. *stincan;* akin to G. *stinken;* prob. < IE. base **steu-*, to push, in the basic sense "to rise up, rise up like dust"], 1. to have a strong, unpleasant smell. 2. to be very offensive; be hateful or abhorrent. 3. [Slang], to be no good; be of low standard or quality. ***v.t.*** to cause to stink (usually with *up*). ***n.*** a strong, unpleasant smell; stench.

raise a stink, [Slang], to cause trouble through complaint or criticism.

stink out, to drive or force out by a strong, unpleasant smell.

stink·ard (stiŋk'ẽrd), ***n.*** [Obs. or Rare], a stinker.

stink bomb, a device made to burn or explode and give off an offensive smell.

stink·bug (stiŋk'bug'), ***n.*** a bug that stinks; any of various foul-smelling insects, many of which have a broad, flat body.

stink·er (stiŋk'ẽr), ***n.*** a person or thing that stinks; specifically, *a*) a stinkpot. *b*) any of several large petrels. *c*) [Slang], a person regarded with disgust.

stink·horn (stiŋk'hôrn'), ***n.*** any of several foul-smelling fungi.

stink·ing (stiŋk'iŋ), ***adj.*** that stinks; bad-smelling: in vulgar colloquial usage often a general term of condemnation or disapproval, or a mere intensive.

SYN.—**stinking** and the more formal **fetid** both imply foulness of odor (a *stinking* cesspool, a *fetid* gum resin); **malodorous** is the broadest term here, ranging in application from an unpleasant smell to one that is strongly offensive (*malodorous* cheeses); **noisome** stresses the unwholesomeness or harmfulness of that which gives off a foul odor (the *noisome* stench of open sewers); **putrid** suggests the disgusting foul smell of decomposed or rotting organic matter (buzzards feeding on *putrid* corpses); **rank** implies a disagreeably strong odor that offends to a greater or lesser degree (the *rank* smell of a goat); **rancid** specifically suggests the bad smell or taste of stale fats or oils (*rancid* butter); **musty** suggests the stale, moldy smell of a long-closed room, food kept in a damp place, etc.

stinking smut, bunt, a variety of wheat smut.

stink·pot (stiŋk'pot'), ***n.*** a kind of stink bomb formerly used in naval warfare.

stink·stone (stiŋk'stōn'), ***n.*** any stone, as some limestones, which gives off a foul smell when rubbed or struck, as from decayed organic matter contained in it.

stink·weed (stiŋk'wēd'), ***n.*** any of several plants, as the Jimson weed, having a foul or strong smell.

stink·wood (stiŋk'wood'), ***n.*** 1. any of several trees having wood of an offensive odor. 2. the wood of any of these trees.

stint (stint), ***v.t.*** [ME. *stynten, stinten, stenten*, to stint, cease, stop; AS. *styntan, stintan*, to blunt or dull < *stunt*, blunt, dull; cf. STUNTED], 1. to restrict or limit to a certain quantity, number, share, or allotment, often small or scanty. 2. [Archaic], to stop. ***v.i.*** 1. to be sparing or grudging in giving or using. 2. [Archaic & Dial.], to stop. ***n.*** 1. restriction; limit; limitation. 2. a limited or fixed quantity, allotment, share, etc. 3. an assigned task or quantity of work. 4. [Obs.], cessation or pause. —***SYN.*** see **task.**

stint (stint), ***n.*** [< ?], any of various small sandpipers.

stipe (stīp), ***n.*** [Fr.; L. *stipes*, a log, stock, trunk of a tree; akin to Eng. *stiff*], a stalk, as that supporting a pistil, fern frond, cap of a mushroom, etc.

sti·pel (stī'p'l), ***n.*** [Mod. L. *stipella*, dim. of L. *stipula;* see STIPULE], a small or secondary stipule at the base of a leaflet.

sti·pel·late (stī-pel'it, stī'pə-lāt'), ***adj.*** having a stipel.

sti·pend (stī'pend), ***n.*** [ME. & OFr. *stipendie* < L. *stipendium*, a tax, impost, tribute; contr. for *stipipendum* < *stips*, small coin or a contribution in small coin + *pendere*, to weigh out, pay], a regular or fixed payment for services, as a salary, or a periodic payment, as a pension or allowance. —***SYN.*** see **wage.**

sti·pen·di·ar·y (stī-pen'di-er'i), ***adj.*** [L. *stipendiarius*], 1. receiving, or performing services for, a stipend. 2. paid for by a stipend: said of services. 3. of, or having the nature of, a stipend. 4. paying taxes or rendering services, as to a feudal lord. ***n.*** [*pl.* STIPENDIARIES (-iz)], 1. a person who receives a stipend. 2. a tenant paying tribute to a feudal lord.

sti·pes (stī'pēz), ***n.*** [*pl.* STIPITES (stip'ə-tēz')], [L.; see STIPE], 1. a stalk; peduncle; stipe. 2. the second, subbasal segment of a maxilla in the insects and crustaceans.

sti·pi·form (stī'pi-fôrm'), ***adj.*** [< L. *stipes*, *stipitis;* + *-form*], having the form of a stipe.

stip·i·tate (stip'ə-tāt'), ***adj.*** [Mod. L. *stipitatus* < L. *stipes, stipitis;* see STIPE], having, or growing on, a stipe.

stip·i·ti·form (stip'i-tə-fôrm'), ***adj.*** stipiform.

stip·ple (stip''l), ***v.t.*** [STIPPLED (-'ld), STIPPLING], [D. *stippelen* < *stippel*, a speckle, dim. of *stip*, a point], to paint, draw, engrave, or apply in small points or dots rather than in lines or solid areas. ***n.*** 1. the art or method of painting, drawing, or engraving in dots. 2. the effect produced by this, or an effect, as in nature, resembling it. 3. stippled work.

stip·pler (stip'lẽr), ***n.*** 1. a person who works in stipple. 2. a brush, sponge, etc. used in stippling.

stip·pling (stip'liŋ), ***n.*** stipple.

stip·u·lar (stip'yoo-lẽr), ***adj.*** 1. of or like a stipule or stipules. 2. growing on or near a stipule.

stip·u·late (stip'yoo-lāt'), ***v.t.*** [STIPULATED (-id), STIPULATING], [< L. *stipulatus*, pp. of *stipulari*, to bargain < OL. *stipulus*, firm; IE. base **stip-*, a pole, etc.; cf. STIFF], 1. to include specifically in the terms of an agreement, contract, etc.; arrange definitely. 2. to specify as an essential condition of or requisite in an agreement. ***v.i.*** to make a specific demand or arrangement (*for* something) as a condition of or requisite in an agreement.

stip·u·late (stip'yoo-lit, stip'yoo-lāt'), ***adj.*** [Mod. L. *stipulatus*], having stipules.

stip·u·lat·ed (stip'yoo-lā'tid), ***adj.*** stipulate.

stip·u·la·tion (stip'yoo-lā'shən), ***n.*** [L. *stipulatio*], 1. act of stipulating. 2. something stipulated; point or condition agreed upon, as in a contract.

stip·u·la·tor (stip'yoo-lā'tẽr), ***n.*** one who stipulates.

stip·u·la·to·ry (stip'yoo-lə-tôr'i, stip'yoo-lə-tō'ri), ***adj*** of, having the nature of, or characterized by stipulation.

stip·ule (stip'ūl), ***n.*** [Fr.; Mod. L. *stipula;* L. *stipula* a stalk, straw, dim. of *stipes*, trunk], one of two small, leaflike parts at the base of some leafstalks, or leaf petioles.

stir (stũr), ***v.t.*** [STIRRED (stũrd), STIRRING], [ME. *stirien, styrien;* AS. *styrian;* for IE. base see STORM], 1. to move, shake, agitate, etc., especially slightly. 2. to change the position of slightly; displace: as, he *stirred* the log. 3. to rouse from dormancy, lethargy, indifference, etc. 4. to put (oneself, one's limbs, etc.) into motion or activity, often briskly. 5. *a*) to make (a liquid) move with an agitated motion so that the particles change position with relation to one another, as by passing some implement through it. *b*

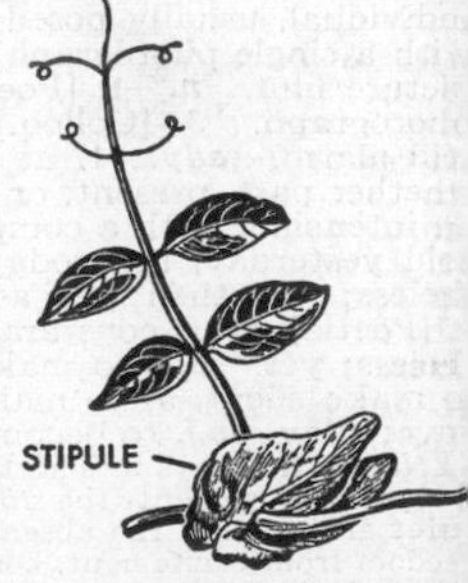

STIPULE (of pea)

to impart a similar motion to (something consisting of separate particles). 6. to excite the feelings of; move strongly. 7. to incite or provoke (often with *up*). *v.i.* 1. to move or change position, especially only slightly: as, the patient hasn't *stirred* for an hour. 2. to be up and about; be busy and active. 3. to be taking place, going on, happening, etc.: as, things are *stirring* in the office. 4. to begin to show signs of activity; begin to come to life: as, a grass-roots movement was *stirring*. 5. to be stirred: as, the mixture *stirs* easily. *n.* 1. a stirring, as with a spoon. 2. movement; activity; agitation. 3. a state of excitement; commotion; tumult: as, the crowd was in a *stir*. 4. a poke; jog; shove. 5. [Archaic], a public disturbance or revolt.

SYN.—**stir** (in this sense, often **stir up**) implies a bringing into action or activity by exciting or provoking (the colonies were *stirred* to rebellion); **arouse** and **rouse** are often used interchangeably, but **arouse** usually implies merely a bringing into consciousness, as from a state of sleep (she was *aroused* by the bell) and **rouse** suggests an additional incitement to vigorous action (the rifle shot *roused* the sleeping guard); **awaken** and **waken** literally mean to arouse from sleep, but figuratively they suggest the elicitation of latent faculties, emotions, etc. (it *awakened*, or *wakened*, her maternal feelings); **rally** implies a gathering of the component elements or individuals so as to stir to effective action (to *rally* troops, one's energy, etc.).

stir (stũr), *n.* [19th-c. thieves' slang, prob. either < dial. *stir*, porridge (with reference to prison fare) or < *stir*, *v.*, with wry allusion to confinement], [Slang], a prison.

stir·a·bout (stũr'ə-bout'), *n.* a porridge of oatmeal or corn meal stirred in boiling water or milk.

stirk (stũrk), *n.* [ME. *stirk;* AS. *styrc, styric*], a bullock or heifer, especially one between one and two years old.

Stir·ling (stũr'liŋ), *n.* 1. a county in central Scotland: pop., 193,000: also **Stirlingshire.** 2. its county seat: pop., 27,000.

Stir·ling·shire (stũr'liŋ-shir'), *n.* Stirling.

stir·pi·cul·ture (stũr'pi-kul'chẽr), *n.* [< L. *stirps*, a stock + *cultura*, culture], selective breeding for the development of strains with certain characteristics.

stirps (stũrps), *n.* [*pl.* STIRPES (stũr'pēz)], [L.], 1. stock; race, family, or branch of a family. 2. in *law*, the person from whom a family or branch of a family is descended. 3. in *biology*, the total number of determinant factors present in a fertilized ovum.

stir·rer (stũr'ẽr), *n.* a person or thing that stirs.

stir·ring (stũr'iŋ), *adj.* 1. active; busy; bustling. 2. moving; rousing; exciting; thrilling: as, *stirring* music.

stir·rup (stũr'əp, stir'əp), *n.* [ME. *stirop;* AS. *stigrap, stigerap* < base of *stigan*, to climb (cf. STILE) + *rap*, a rope (cf. ROPE)], 1. a flat-based ring hung from a saddle and used as a footrest in mounting and riding. 2. any of various supports, clamps, etc. resembling or suggesting such a ring. 3. in *nautical usage*, a rope hung from a yard and supporting a footrope by means of an eye at the end, through which the footrope is passed.

stirrup bone, in *anatomy*, the stapes: see **ear**, illus.

stirrup cup, 1. a farewell drink taken by a rider mounting to depart. 2. any farewell drink.

stirrup leather, a strap connecting a stirrup with the saddle: also **stirrup strap.**

stirrup pump, a hand pump for putting out fires, set in a bucket and held firm by a stirrup, or bracket, for one foot.

stitch (stich), *n.* [ME. *stiche;* AS. *stice*, a puncture, stab; for IE. base see STICK], 1. a single complete in-and-out movement of a threaded needle in sewing, etc. 2. a similar complete movement in knitting, crocheting, etc. 3. a loop, knot, etc. made by stitching. 4. a particular kind of stitch or style of stitching. 5. a sudden, sharp pain in the side or back. 6. [Colloq.], a bit: as, he hasn't done a *stitch* of work, wearing not a *stitch* of clothes. *v.i.* to make stitches; sew. *v.t.* 1. to fasten, join, repair, adorn, or operate upon with or as with stitches; sew. 2. to fasten or unite (cartons, etc.) with staples.

stitch·wort (stich'wũrt'), *n.* [ME. *stichwurt* < AS. *stice*, a stab, puncture (cf. STITCH) + *wort* (a plant)], any of a number of related chickweeds.

stith·y (stith'i, stith'i), *n.* [*pl.* STITHIES (-iz)], [ME. *stethie, stithi;* ON. *stethi*, anvil; for base see STEAD], 1. an anvil. 2. a forge or smithy. *v.t.* [STITHIED (-id), STITHYING], [Archaic], to make on a forge.

sti·ver (stī'vẽr), *n.* [D. *stuiver*], 1. a Dutch coin equal to 1/20 of a guilder. 2. anything of small value, or a small quantity.

St. James's Court (jām'ziz), see **Court of St. James.**

St. James's Palace, the Tudor palace in London where the kings and queens of England lived from the time of Henry VIII to Victoria's accession in 1837.

St. John, 1. the capital of the Leeward Islands, West Indies Federation, on Antigua: pop., 13,000. 2. a seaport on the St. John River, in New Brunswick, Canada: pop., 52,000. 3. an island of the United States, part of the Virgin Islands: area, 20 sq. mi.; pop., 900. 4. a river in northern Maine and New Brunswick, Canada, flowing southeastward into the Bay of Fundy: length, 400 mi. 5. a lake in southern Quebec province, Canada: area, 367 sq. mi.

St. Johns (jonz), a river in eastern Florida, flowing northward to the Atlantic: length, 350 mi.

St. John's (jonz), seaport and capital of Newfoundland: pop., 78,000.

St. John's evil, epilepsy.

St.-John's-wort (sānt-jonz'wũrt'), *n.* any of a number of related plants, as the rose of Sharon, having yellow flowers with many stamens.

St. Joseph, a city in northwestern Missouri, on the Missouri River: pop., 80,000.

St. Kitts (kits), an island of the Leeward group, in the West Indies Federation: area, 68 sq. mi.; pop. (with Nevis), 59,000: also called *St. Christopher.*

St. Lau·rent, Louis Stephen (san'lō'rän'), 1882– ; prime minister of Canada (1948–1957).

St. Lawrence, 1. a river flowing from Lake Ontario northeastward into the Gulf of St. Lawrence: length, 2,100 mi. 2. a gulf off eastern Canada, at the mouth of this river.

St. Lawrence Seaway, an inland waterway for ocean-going ships, connecting the Great Lakes with the Atlantic Ocean: it is made up of the St. Lawrence River, various canals, etc.

stlg., sterling.

St. Lô (san' lō'), a city in northwestern France: almost completely destroyed during World War II.

St. Lou·is (lōō'is, lōō'i), a port on the Mississippi, in eastern Missouri: pop., 750,000.

St. Lu·ci·a (lōō'shi-ə, lū'shə, lōō-sē'ə), an island of the Windward group, in the West Indies Federation: area, 233 sq. mi.; pop., 92,000.

St. Ma·lo (san' mà'lō'), a seaport in Brittany, France: site of a battle (1944) of World War II.

St. Marks (märks), a cathedral in Venice, combining Roman, Gothic, and Byzantine architecture.

St. Marys (mâr'iz), 1. a river flowing from Lake Superior into Lake Huron, forming the boundary between northeastern Michigan and Ontario, Canada: length, 40 mi. 2. a river flowing between eastern Florida and Georgia into the Atlantic: length, 175 mi.

St.-Mi·hiel (san'mē'yel'), *n.* a town on the Meuse River, in northeastern France: scene of a battle (1918) of World War I, in which the Americans defeated the Germans.

St. Mo·ritz (mō'rits), *n.* a town in southeastern Switzerland: pop., 2,500: mountain resort: German spelling, *Sankt Moritz.*

St.-Na·zaire (san'nà'zâr'), a seaport in western France, on the Loire River: site of a battle of World War II.

sto·a (stō'ə), *n.* [*pl.* STOAE (stō'ē), STOAS (-əz)], [Gr. *stoa*], a covered walk or portico having a wall on one side and pillars on the other.

stoat (stōt), *n.* [*pl.* STOATS (stōts), STOAT; see PLURAL, II, D, 1], [ME. *stote;* use of a similar word in dial. for "gadfly" suggests connection with the Gmc. base **staut-*, **stot-*, to thrust, push, etc., but the application is obscure; cf. also dial. *stoat*, *v.*, to bounce; prob. of the same origin], an ermine, especially when in its brown summer coat.

stoc·ca·do (sto-kä'dō, sto-kā'dō), *n.* [< Fr. & It.; Fr. *estocade;* It. *stoccata* < *stocca*, a dagger, sword point < Fr. *estoc* < OFr. *estoquier*, to strike with the edge or point < LG. *stoken*, to stick, prick; cf. STOCK], [Archaic], a stab or thrust with a pointed weapon.

stoc·ca·ta (sto-kä'tə, sto-kā'tə), *n.* stoccado.

stock (stok), *n.* [ME. *stocke;* AS. *stocc;* akin to G. *stock*, a stick; IE. base **steu-*, to push, hit (in the extended form **steu-g*); prob. basic sense "a cut-off trunk or branch"], 1. the trunk of a tree. 2. [Archaic], *a*) a tree stump. *b*) a wooden block or log. 3. *a*) a blockhead. *b*) anything lacking life, motion, or feeling. 4. *a*) a plant stem into which a graft is inserted. *b*) a plant from which cuttings are taken. 5. an underground plant stem; rhizome. 6. any of a number of plants of the mustard family, as the evening stock, the gillyflower, or the Virginia stock. 7. *a*) the first of a line of descent; original progenitor, as of a human line, or type, as of a group of animals or plants. *b*) lineage; descent; ancestry. *c*) a strain, race, or other related group of animals or plants. *d*) an ethnic group or major division of the human race. *e*) a group of related languages or families of languages. 8. a supporting block, as for an anvil. 9. the body, main part, or handle of an implement, weapon, etc., to which the working parts are attached; specifically, *a*) a bitstock or brace. *b*) the butt or handle of a whip, fishing rod, etc. *c*) the block of a plane, in which the cutting blade is inserted. *d*) the frame of a plow, to which the share, handles, etc. are attached. *e*) the wooden or metal piece of a rifle, carbine, or similar firearm, or the corresponding part of a machine gun or other rapid-fire weapon, holding the barrel, etc. *f*) the long beam forming the basic part of the body of a field-gun carriage. *g*) a kind of wrench for holding thread-cutting dies. 10. *pl.* a former instrument of punishment consisting of a heavy wooden frame with holes for confining an offender's ankles and, sometimes, his wrists. 11. *pl.* a frame of timbers supporting a ship during construction. 12. *pl.* a frame in which an animal is held for shoeing, etc. 13. something out of which other things are made; specifically, *a*) raw material: as, paper *stock*. *b*) water in which meat, fish, etc. has been boiled, used as a base for soup or gravy. 14. a store or supply; specifically, *a*) all the animals, equipment, etc. kept and used on a farm. *b*) livestock. *c*) the total amount of goods on hand in a store, etc. *d*) the portion of a pack of playing cards or dominoes not dealt out but left to be drawn from. 15. *a*) formerly, the part of a tally given to the creditor; hence, *b*) a debt represented by a tally or tallies. *c*) a debt owed to persons who have lent their money for interest, or the certificates representing this. *d*) the capital, or fund of invested money, used by a business firm in making its transactions. *e*) shares of corporate capital, or the certificates of ownership representing them. *f*) [Colloq.], a part interest in something. 16. *a*) a stock company (sense 2). *b*) its repertoire. 17. a large, wide, stiff cravat, worn formerly. 18. [Obs.], a stocking. 19. in *zoology*, a colony of connected zooids, forming a compound organism. ***v.t.*** 1. to provide with or attach to a stock, as a firearm, plow, etc. 2. to furnish with stock, as a farm, or a stock, as a shop, etc. 3. to keep or put in a supply of for sale or for future use. 4. to sow (land) with grass, clover, etc. 5. [Obs.], to put in the stocks. ***v.i.*** 1. to put forth new shoots: said of a plant. 2. to put in a stock, or supply (often with *up*). ***adj.*** 1. continually kept in stock: as, *stock* sizes; hence, 2. of the nature of something kept in stock; common, ordinary, hackneyed, or trite: as, a *stock* joke. 3. that deals with stock: as, a *stock* checker. 4. relating to stock or a stock company. 5. for breeding: as, a *stock* mare. 6. of, or for the raising of, livestock: as, *stock* farming. Abbreviated **stk.**

in stock, available for sale or use; on hand.

on the stocks, being built: said of a ship, etc.

out of stock, not immediately available for sale or use; not in stock.

take stock, 1. to inventory the amount of stock on hand. 2. to make an estimate or appraisal, as of available resources, probabilities, etc.

take stock in, 1. to buy a share or shares of stock in (a company, etc.). 2. [Colloq.], to have faith in, give credence to, or attribute real significance to.

Stock, Frederick August (stok), 1872–1942; American conductor and composer, born in Germany.

stock·ade (sto-kād′), ***n.*** [Fr. *estacade* (also *estocade*, by association with OFr. *estoc*, a trunk, log; of Gmc. origin); Pr. *estacado* < *estaca*, a post, stake < Gmc. base akin to Eng. *stake*], 1. a barrier of stakes driven into the ground side by side, for defense against attack. 2. any similar enclosure. ***v.t.*** [STOCKADED (-id), STOCKADING], to surround, protect, or fortify with a stockade.

stock·bro·ker (stok′brō′kẽr), ***n.*** a person who acts as an agent in buying and selling stocks and bonds.

stock·bro·ker·age (stok′brō′kẽr-ij), ***n.*** [see -AGE], a stockbroker's work or business.

stock·bro·king (stok′brō′kiŋ), ***n.*** stockbrokerage.

stock car, 1. a railway car built to carry livestock. 2. any passenger automobile of standard make, but with a supercharged engine, used in professional races with similar automobiles.

stock certificate, a certificate that is evidence of ownership of a specified number of shares in a specified corporation: also **certificate of stock.**

stock company, 1. a company or corporation whose capital is divided into shares. 2. a theatrical company established to present a repertoire of plays, usually at one theater.

stock dove, [ME. *stockdowe*, etc.: the stock dove nests in hollow trees (cf. STOCK, 1)], the European wild pigeon.

stock exchange, 1. a place where stocks and bonds are regularly bought and sold. 2. an association of stockbrokers who meet together for the business of buying and selling stocks and bonds according to fixed regulations. Abbreviated **St. Ex.**

stock farm, a farm mainly for raising livestock.

stock·fish (stok′fish′), ***n.*** [*pl.* STOCKFISH, STOCKFISHES (-iz); see FISH], [ME. *stokfysshe*; prob. < or after MD. *stokvisch*], any fish cured by being split and hung in the open air to dry without salt, as cod, haddock, etc.

stock·hold·er (stok′hōl′dẽr), ***n.*** 1. a person owning a share or shares of stock in a given company. 2. in Australia, a stockman (sense 1).

Stock·holm (stok′hōm′, stok′hōlm′; Sw. stôk′hôlm), ***n.*** the capital of Sweden, on the Baltic Sea: pop., 805,000.

stock·i·ly (stok′′l-i), ***adv.*** so as to be stocky.

stock·i·ness (stok′i-nis), ***n.*** the quality of being stocky.

stock·i·net (stok′i-net′), ***n.*** [prob. for earlier *stocking net*], an elastic, machine-knitted cloth used for making stockings, underwear, etc.

stock·ing (stok′iŋ), ***n.*** [< *stock*, in obs. sense of stocking, leg covering], 1. a closefitting covering, usually knitted, for the leg and foot. 2. something resembling this, as a bandage, patch of color, etc.

in one's stocking feet, without one's shoes on but wearing stockings or socks.

stock in trade, 1. goods kept available for sale at a store or shop. 2. tools, materials, etc. used in carrying on a trade or a business. 3. any resources, practices, or devices characteristically employed by a given person or group.

stock·ish (stok′ish), ***adj.*** like a stock, or block of wood; stupid; dull; thick-headed.

stock·job·ber (stok′job′ẽr), ***n.*** 1. [British], an operator in the stock exchange who deals only with brokers, not with the public. 2. a stockbroker or stock salesman: often contemptuous.

stock·man (stok′mən, stok′man′), ***n.*** [*pl.* STOCKMEN (-mən, -men′)], 1. a man who owns or raises livestock. 2. a man who works in a stockroom or warehouse where goods, materials, etc. are kept. 3. a man who has charge of livestock or works on a stock farm.

stock market, 1. a stock exchange. 2. business carried on at a stock exchange: as, the *stock market* was active today. 3. the prices quoted on stocks and bonds.

stock·pile (stok′pīl′), ***n.*** a reserve supply of goods, raw material, etc., accumulated for use when needed: also **stock pile.** ***v.t.* & *v.i.*** [STOCKPILED (-pīld′), STOCKPILING], to accumulate a stockpile or stockpiles (of).

Stock·port (stok′pôrt′, stok′pōrt′), ***n.*** a city in Cheshire, England, near Manchester: pop., 142,000.

stock·pot (stok′pot′), ***n.*** 1. a pot used for boiling down stock for soup. 2. a pot, etc. containing any mixture.

stock raising, the raising of livestock.

stock·room (stok′rōōm′, stok′room′), ***n.*** a room in which a store of goods, materials, etc. is kept: also **stock room.**

stock-still (stok′stil′), ***adj.*** as still as a stock, or log; perfectly motionless.

Stock·ton (stok′tən), ***n.*** a city in central California: pop., 86,000.

Stock·ton, Frank R. (stok′tən), (*Francis Richard Stockton*), 1834–1902; American author.

Stock·ton-on-Tees (stok′tən-on-tēz′), ***n.*** a seaport in Durham, England: pop., 78,000.

stock·y (stok′i), ***adj.*** [STOCKIER (-i-ẽr), STOCKIEST (-i-ist)], [*stock* (block) + *-y*], heavily built; sturdy; thick-set and relatively short.

stock·yard (stok′yärd′), ***n.*** a yard for livestock; especially, an enclosure, usually with pens, etc., in which cattle, hogs, sheep, or horses are kept temporarily before being slaughtered or sent to market.

stodg·i·ly (stoj′′l-i), ***adv.*** in a stodgy manner.

stodg·i·ness (stoj′i-nis), ***n.*** the quality or condition of being stodgy.

stodg·y (stoj′i), ***adj.*** [STODGIER (-i-ẽr), STODGIEST (-i-ist)], [< dial. *stodge*, heavy food + *-y*], 1. heavy and uninteresting: said of food. 2. heavily built; bulky. 3. crammed full; packed. 4. dull; tedious; uninteresting; philistine: as, a *stodgy* person or book.

stoe·chi·ol·o·gy (stē′ki-ol′ə-ji), ***n.*** stoichiology.

stoe·chi·om·e·try (stē′ki-om′ə-tri), ***n.*** stoichiometry.

sto·gie, sto·gy (stō′gi), ***n.*** [*pl.* STOGIES (-giz)], [for earlier *stoga*, aphetic for *Conestoga*, town in Pennsylvania: said to be so named because favored by drivers of Conestoga wagons], 1. a long, thin, inexpensive cigar. 2. a heavy, roughly made shoe or boot. Also spelled **stogey.**

Sto·ic (stō′ik), ***n.*** [ME. *Stoycis*, *pl.*; L. *stoicus*; Gr. *stōikos* < *stoa*, porch, colonnade: so called because Zeno taught under a colonnade, the Poecile, at Athens], 1. a member of a Greek school of philosophy founded by Zeno about 308 B.C.: the Stoics believed that all happenings were the result of divine will and that therefore man should be calmly accepting and free from passion, grief, or joy. 2. [s-], a stoical person. ***adj.*** 1. of the Stoics or their philosophy. 2. [s-], stoical. —***SYN.*** see **impassive.**

sto·i·cal (stō′i-k′l), ***adj.*** 1. showing austere indifference to joy, grief, pleasure, or pain; calm and unflinching under suffering, bad fortune, etc. 2. [S-], Stoic.

sto·i·cal·ly (stō′i-k′l-i, stō′ik-li), ***adv.*** in a stoical manner.

stoi·chei·ol·o·gy (stoi′ki-ol′ə-ji), ***n.*** stoichiology.

stoi·chei·om·e·try (stoi′ki-om′ə-tri), ***n.*** stoichiometry

stoi·chi·o·log·i·cal (stoi′ki-ə-loj′i-k′l), ***adj.*** of or having to do with stoichiology.

stoi·chi·ol·o·gy (stoi′ki-ol′ə-ji), ***n.*** [< Gr. *stoicheion*; see STOICHIOMETRY; + *-logy*], the physiological study of the component elements of animal tissues.

stoi·chi·o·met·ric (stoi′ki-ə-met′rik), ***adj.*** of or having to do with stoichiometry.

stoi·chi·o·met·ri·cal (stoi′ki-ə-met′ri-k′l), ***adj.*** stoichiometric.

stoi·chi·om·e·try (stoi′ki-om′ə-tri), ***n.*** [< Gr. *stoicheion* a first principle, element, base; + *-metry*], 1. the determination of the atomic weights of elements, the proportions in which they combine, and the weight relations in any chemical reaction. 2. the branch of chemistry dealing with the relationships of elements in combination, especially with quantitative relationships.

Sto·i·cism (stō'i-siz'm), *n.* 1. the philosophical system of the Stoics. 2. [s-], indifference to pleasure or pain; stoical behavior; impassivity. —*SYN.* see **patience.**

stoke (stōk), *v.t. & v.i.* [STOKED (stōkt), STOKING], [back-formation < *stoker;* D. *stoker* < *stoken,* to poke, stir up a fire < *stok,* a stick (cf. STOCK)], 1. to stir up and feed fuel to (a fire, furnace, etc.). 2. to tend (a furnace, boiler, etc.).

stoke·hold (stōk'hōld'), *n.* 1. a room or compartment in which the boilers are stoked on a ship. 2. a stokehole (sense 2).

stoke·hole (stōk'hōl'), *n.* [*stoke* + *hole;* in part transl. of D. *stookgat* < *stoken,* to stoke + *gat,* a hole], 1. the opening in a furnace or boiler through which the fuel is put. 2. a space in front of a furnace or boiler from which the fire is tended, as on a ship. 3. a stokehold (sense 1).

Stoke-on-Trent (stōk'on-trent'), *n.* a city in Staffordshire, England: pop., 270,000 (est. 1946).

stok·er (stōk'ẽr), *n.* [D.; see STOKE], 1. a man who tends a furnace, especially of a steam boiler, as on a ship, locomotive, etc. 2. a mechanical device that feeds coal, etc. into a furnace.

Sto·kow·ski, Le·o·pold An·to·ni Sta·ni·slaw (lē'ə-pōld' än-tô'ni stä-nē'släf stə-kôf'ski; *occas.* stə-kou'ski), 1882– ; American orchestra conductor, born in England.

stole (stōl), *n.* [ME.; AS.; L. *stola;* Gr. *stolē,* a garment, orig., array, equipment < base of *stellein,* to place, array], 1. a long, robelike outer garment worn by matrons in ancient Rome. 2. a long, decorated strip of cloth worn like a scarf by officiating clergymen of various churches. 3. a woman's long scarf of cloth or fur worn with the ends hanging in front.

stole (stōl), past tense of **steal.**

stol·en (stōl'ən), past participle of **steal.**

stol·id (stol'id), *adj.* [L. *stolidus,* firm, slow, stupid; cf. STILL], having or showing little or no emotion or awareness; unexcitable; impassive. —*SYN.* see **impassive.**

sto·lid·i·ty (stə-lid'ə-ti), *n.* [*pl.* STOLIDITIES (-tiz)], [L. *stoliditas*], the quality or condition of being stolid.

sto·lon (stō'lon), *n.* [L. *stolo, stolonis*], 1. in *botany,* a trailing branch or shoot that takes root at the tip to form a new plant; runner or rhizome. 2. in *zoology,* a stemlike part in certain compound organisms, as the coral, giving rise to buds from which new individuals grow.

sto·ma (stō'mə), *n.* [*pl.* STOMATA (-mə-tə, stom'ə-tə)], [Mod. L. < Gr. *stoma,* mouth], 1. a breathing pore in the epidermis of plants. 2. in *zoology,* a mouth or mouthlike opening; especially, an ingestive opening in lower animals.

stom·ach (stum'ək), *n.* [ME. *stomak;* Fr. *estomac;* L. *stomachus,* gullet, esophagus, stomach; Gr. *stomachos,* throat, gullet < *stoma,* a mouth], 1. *a)* the large, saclike organ into which food passes from the esophagus or gullet for storage while undergoing the early processes of digestion: see **alimentary canal,** illus. *b)* any of the separate sections of such a digestive organ, as in ruminants, or all these sections collectively. 2. any digestive cavity, as in invertebrates. 3. the abdomen; belly. 4. appetite. 5. desire or inclination of any kind. 6. [Archaic], character or disposition. 7. [Obs.], *a)* pride. *b)* resentment. *v.t.* 1. to be able to eat or digest. 2. to tolerate; bear; endure. 3. [Obs.], to resent.

stom·ach·ache (stum'ək-āk'), *n.* pain in the stomach or abdomen.

stom·ach·er (stum'ək-ẽr), *n.* [*stomach* + *-er*], an ornamented, triangular piece of cloth formerly worn, especially by women, as an article of dress for covering the chest and abdomen.

sto·mach·ic (stō-mak'ik), *adj.* [L. *stomachicus;* Gr. *stomachikos*], 1. of or having to do with the stomach. 2. acting as a digestive tonic. *n.* a digestive tonic.

sto·mach·i·cal (stō-mak'i-k'l), *adj.* stomachic.

stomach pump, an apparatus, consisting usually of a flexible rubber tube that is introduced into the stomach through the mouth and esophagus, used, as in a case of poisoning, to remove the contents of the stomach by suction.

stomach tooth, either of the canine teeth in the lower jaw of infants: so called because its appearance is sometimes accompanied by gastric disorders.

sto·ma·ta (stō'mə-tə, stom'ə-tə), *n.* plural of **stoma.**

stom·a·tal (stom'ə-t'l, stō'mə-t'l), *adj.* in *botany* & *zoology,* of or having a stoma or stomata.

sto·mat·ic (stō-mat'ik), *adj.* [Mod. L. *stomaticus;* Gr. *stomatikos* < *stomata,* pl. of *stoma,* a mouth; cf. STOMACH], 1. of the mouth. 2. of, or having the nature of, a stoma.

sto·ma·ti·tis (stō'mə-tī'tis, stom'ə-tī'tis), *n.* [*stomat(o)-* + *-itis*], inflammation of the mouth.

stom·a·to- (stom'ə-tō, stō'mə-tə), [< Gr. *stoma, stomatos,* a mouth], a combining form used in medicine and biology to mean *like* or *relating to a mouth,* as in *stomatology:* also, before a vowel, **stomat-.**

sto·ma·tol·o·gy (stō'mə-tol'ə-ji), *n.* [*stomato-* + *-logy*], the branch of medicine dealing with the mouth and its diseases.

stom·a·to·pod (stom'ə-tō-pod', stō'mə-tə-pod'), *n.* [< Mod. L. *Stomatopoda,* name of the order; see STOMATO- & -POD], any of a number of crustaceans, as the squilla, having gills on appendages attached to the abdomen.

stom·a·tous (stom'ə-təs, stō'mə-təs), *adj.* having a stoma or stomata.

-stom·a·tous (stom'ə-təs, stō'mə-təs), -stomous.

-stome (stōm), [< Gr. *stoma,* a mouth], a combining form meaning *mouth,* as in *cyclostome.*

sto·mo·dae·um, sto·mo·de·um (stō'mə-dē'əm, stom'ə-dē'əm), *n.* [*pl.* STOMODAEA, STOMODEA (-ə)], [Mod. L. < Gr. *stoma,* mouth + *hodios,* on the way < *hodos,* way, road], the oral cavity in the digestive tract of an embryo, which develops into the mouth.

-stomous, [< Gr. *stoma,* a mouth; + *-ous*], a combining form meaning *having a* (specified kind of) *mouth.*

stomp (stomp), *n., v.t. & v.i.* [Dial.], stamp.

-stomy, [Gr. *-stomia* < *stomos,* the mouth], a suffix meaning *a surgical opening into* (a specified part or organ).

stone (stōn), *n.* [ME. *ston, stoon;* AS. *stan;* akin to G. *stein;* IE. base **stāi-,* to become thick, compress, stiffen, as also in L. *stilla* (< **stirela*), a drop (cf. DISTILL, STILL)], 1. the hard, solid, nonmetallic mineral matter of which rock is composed. 2. a piece of rock of relatively small size. 3. a piece of rock shaped or finished for some purpose; specifically, *a)* a building block. *b)* a paving block. *c)* a gravestone or memorial. *d)* a boundary mark or milestone. *e)* a grindstone or whetstone. 4. something that resembles a small stone; specifically, *a)* a hailstone. *b)* a testicle. *c)* the stonelike seed of certain fruits; specifically, the hard endocarp of a drupe, as of the peach. 5. a precious stone or gem. 6. [*pl.* STONE], in Great Britain, 14 pounds avoirdupois: abbreviated **st.** 7. in *medicine, a)* a small stony mass abnormally formed in the kidney, bladder, or gall bladder; calculus. *b)* a disease characterized by such formations. 8. in *printing,* a table with a smooth top, originally of stone, on which page forms are composed. *v.t.* [STONED (stōnd), STONING], 1. to throw stones at; pelt or kill with stones. 2. to furnish, pave, line, etc. with stones. 3. to polish, sharpen, etc. with a stone. 4. to remove the stone from (a peach, cherry, etc.). 5. [Obs.], to make like stone; make hard. *adj.* of stone or stoneware.

cast the first stone, to be the first to censure, criticize, or attack.

leave no stone unturned, to do everything possible.

stone- (stōn), [< *stone, n.,* with the sense of "like, or as is, a stone"], a combining form used as an intensive in hyphenated compounds, meaning *very, completely,* as in *stone-broke, stone-blind.*

Stone, Harlan Fiske (stōn), 1872–1946; American jurist; chief justice, United States Supreme Court (1941–1946).

Stone, Lucy, (*Mrs. Henry Brown Blackwell*), 1818–1893; American woman suffragist.

Stone Age, the period in human culture during which stone implements were used: it is divided into the Eolithic, Paleolithic, and Neolithic Periods.

stone-blind (stōn'blīnd'), *adj.* completely blind.

stone-broke (stōn'brōk'), *adj.* [*stone-* + *broke*], [Slang], having no money at all; penniless.

stone bruise, a bruise on the sole of the foot resulting from walking on stones, etc.

stone·chat (stōn'chat'), *n.* [so called because its cry resembles the sound of pebbles being knocked together], a small European bird of the thrush family.

stone·crop (stōn'krop'), *n.* [ME. *stoncroppe;* AS. *stancrop; stan,* stone + *crop,* a sprout], any of various related plants with fleshy leaves and usually yellow or white flowers, found on rocks and walls; sedum.

stone·cut·ter (stōn'kut'ẽr), *n.* a person or machine that cuts and dresses stone.

stone-deaf (stōn'def'), *adj.* completely deaf.

stone fruit, any fruit, as a plum or cherry, containing a stone; drupe.

Stone·henge (stōn'henj), *n.* a prehistoric stone structure on Salisbury Plain, England.

stone lily, a fossil crinoid.

stone marten, 1. a marten of central and southern Europe and Asia having a white patch on its throat and breast. 2. its fur.

stone·ma·son (stōn'mā's'n), *n.* a person who cuts stone to shape and uses it in making walls, buildings, etc.: also **stone mason.**

Stone Mountain, a granite mountain near Atlanta, Georgia, on which is carved a huge memorial to the heroes of the Confederacy.

stone parsley, any of a number of plants of the parsley

family, with cream-colored flowers and fragrant seeds used as seasoning.

ston·er (stōn'ẽr), *n.* 1. a person who cuts stones. 2. an implement used in removing stones from fruit.

Stone River, a river in central Tennessee, flowing north into the Cumberland River: length, c. 60 mi.

stone roller, 1. one of a group of fresh-water carp. 2. a fish of the sucker family.

stone's throw, 1. the distance that a stone can be thrown; hence, 2. a relatively short distance.

stone·wall (stōn'wôl'), *v.i.* in *cricket*, to play only a defensive game in order to gain a draw: said of a batsman.

Stone·wall Jackson (stōn'wôl'), see **Jackson, Thomas Jonathan.**

stone·ware (stōn'wâr'), *n.* a coarse, dense, heavily glazed kind of pottery containing much silica or sand and flint.

stone·work (stōn'wũrk'), *n.* 1. the art or process of working in stone, as in masonry or jewelry. 2. something made or built in stone; specifically, masonry: as, the first story is *stonework*. 3. *pl.* a place where masonry stone is cut and dressed.

stone·wort (stōn'wũrt'), *n.* any of a number of related green algae with jointed stems and curved branches, usually covered with lime.

ston·i·ly (stōn'ə-li), *adv.* so as to be stony.

ston·i·ness (stō'ni-nis), *n.* a stony quality or condition.

ston·y (stō'ni), *adj.* [STONIER (-ni-ẽr), STONIEST (-ni-ist)], [ME. *stoony;* AS. *stanig*], 1. covered with or having many stones. 2. of or like stone; specifically, *a*) hard. *b*) relentless; unfeeling; pitiless. *c*) cold; fixed; rigid. 3. petrifying. 4. [Slang], stone-broke. 5. [Poetic], made or consisting of stone.

ston·y-broke (stō'ni-brōk'), *adj.* [Slang], stone-broke.

ston·y-heart·ed (stō'ni-här'tid), *adj.* hard; unfeeling; pitiless; cruel.

Stony Point, a village in southeastern New York: scene of several battles of the Revolutionary War.

stood (stood), past tense and past participle of **stand.**

stooge (stōōj), *n.* [< ?], [Colloq.], 1. *a*) an actor stationed in the audience to assist a comedian by heckling him. *b*) an actor who assists a comedian by feeding him lines, being the victim of pranks, etc.; hence, 2. any person who acts as a foil, underling, etc. to another: term of contempt. *v.i.* [Colloq.], to be a stooge (*for* someone).

stook (stōōk, stook), *n.* [ME. *stouke;* prob. < a LG. source; cf. MLG. *stūke* & *stūken*, to set up stooks, W.Fl. *stuik* & *stuiken*], [British], a bundle of sheaves of cut grain; shock.

stool (stōōl), *n.* [ME.; AS. *stol;* akin to G. *stuhl;* IE. base **stā-*, to stand, with *-l* suffix as also in OSlav. *stolu*, a seat, throne], 1. a single seat having three or four legs and no back or arms: low stools are sometimes used as a footrest for seated people. 2. a toilet; water closet; privy. 3. a bowel movement. 4. feces. 5. a root or tree stump sending out shoots. 6. a cluster of such shoots. 7. a pole to which a bird is fastened as a decoy for others. 8. a bird or other object so used; stool pigeon; lure; decoy. *v.i.* 1. to put out shoots in the form of a stool. 2. to evacuate the bowels. 3. [Colloq.], to act as a stool pigeon, or informer.

stool pigeon, 1. a pigeon or other bird used as a decoy. 2. a person serving as a decoy. 3. [Colloq.], a spy or informer.

stoop (stōōp), *v.i.* [ME. *stupen;* AS. *stupian;* akin to ON. *stūpa;* IE. **steu-p* < base **steu-*, to push, strike, as also in L. *stupere*, to be struck senseless (cf. STUPENDOUS); see STEEP], 1. to bend the body forward or in a crouch. 2. to carry the head and shoulders or the upper part of the body habitually bent forward. 3. to lower or demean oneself; condescend; deign. 4. [Rare], to yield or submit. 5. to pounce or swoop down, as a bird of prey. *v.t.* 1. to bend forward. 2. [Archaic], to humble or debase. *n.* 1. the act or position of stooping the body, especially habitually. 2. condescension; lowering of dignity or superiority. 3. a swoop.

SYN.—**stoop,** in this connection, implies a descending in dignity, as by committing some shameful or immoral act (to *stoop* to cheating); **condescend** implies a voluntary descent by one high in rank, power, etc. to act graciously or affably toward one regarded as his inferior (the general *condescended* to talk with the private); **deign** is usually used in negative constructions or with such qualifications as *hardly, barely*, etc. and, hence, connotes unwilling or arrogant condescension (she *deigned* to answer me).

stoop (stōōp), *n.* [D. *stoep*], 1. originally, a platform with steps and, usually, seats, at the door of a house. 2. any small porch at the entrance of a house.

stoop (stōōp), *n.* a stoup.

stop (stop), *v.t.* [STOPPED or *poetic* STOPT (stopt), STOPPING], [ME. *stoppen;* AS. *-stoppian* (in comp.) < LL. *stuppare*, to stop up, stuff < L. *stuppa* (Gr. *stuppē*), tow; hence akin to Fr. *étouper*, G. *stopfen*, etc.], I. *to close by filling, shutting off, covering, etc.* 1. to stanch (a cut, wound, etc.). 2. to block up (a passage, road, etc.); make impassable; obstruct. 3. to fill in, plug up, or cover (a hole, cavity, opening, mouth, etc.). 4. to close (a bottle, jug, or other container) with a cork, plug, etc. 5. *a*) to close (a finger hole of a wind instrument) so as to produce a desired tone. *b*) to produce (a tone) in this way. II. *to cause to cease motion, activity, etc.* 1. to prevent the passage or further passage of (water, light, etc.); block; obstruct; intercept. 2. to prevent the movement or further movement of; specifically, *a*) to halt the progress of (a person, animal, vehicle, etc.). *b*) to check (a blow, stroke, or thrust of an opponent); parry; counter. *c*) to defeat (an opponent). *d*) to intercept (a letter, etc.) in transit. 3. to cease; desist from (with a gerund): as, he *stopped* talking. 4. to cause to cease or end: as, *stop* that racket. 5. to cause (an engine, machine, etc.) to cease operation. 6. to press down (a violin string, etc.) against the finger board to produce a desired pitch. 7. to place a stop order on (a stock or other security). 8. in *bridge*, to block future play of (a suit) by holding key cards. 9. in *rhetoric*, to punctuate. III. *to keep from beginning, acting, happening, etc.; prevent* 1. to keep (a person) from doing something contemplated. 2. to prevent the starting, advent, etc. of; preclude. 3. to notify one's bank to withhold payment on (one's check). *v.i.* 1. to cease moving, walking, proceeding, etc.; halt. 2. to leave off doing something, either temporarily or permanently; desist from continuing. 3. to cease operating, as from mechanical failure or lack of fuel. 4. to be able to go no further: as, his arguments *stop* there. 5. to become clogged or choked. 6. to tarry; stay. *n.* 1. a stopping or being stopped; check; arrest; cessation; halt. 2. a coming to an end; finish; end. 3. a stay or sojourn. 4. a place stopped at, as on a bus route, streetcar line, etc. 5. something that stops; an obstruction; obstacle; specifically, *a*) a plug or stopper. *b*) a stop order. *c*) an order to withhold payment on a check. *d*) a mechanical part that stops, limits, or regulates motion, as the pawl in a watch or clock. *e*) a punctuation mark, especially a period. 6. *a*) pressure, as of a finger, on a string of a violin, etc. to produce a desired pitch. *b*) a fret on a guitar, etc. 7. *a*) the closing of a finger hole of a wind instrument to change tone. *b*) a hole in a wind instrument closed by a finger or key. 8. *a*) a tuned set of organ pipes or reeds of the same specific type and tone quality. *b*) a pull, lever, or key for putting such a set or sets into or out of operation. 9. in *nautical usage*, a piece of line used to secure something. 10. in *phonetics*, *a*) the act of completely stopping the outgoing breath, as with the velum, lips, or tongue. *b*) a consonant formed in this way, as *p, b, k, g, t,* and *d*. 11. in *photography*, *a*) the aperture, usually adjustable, of a lens; hence, *b*) the F number.

put a stop to, to cause to cease; stop; end.

stop off, to stop for a short stay en route to a place.

stop over, 1. to stay for a while. 2. to break a journey, as for rest.

SYN.—**stop** implies a suspension or ending of some motion, action, or progress (my watch *stopped*); **cease** implies a suspension or ending of some state or condition or of an existence (the war had *ceased*); **quit** is equivalent to either **stop** or **cease** (to *quit* working means either to stop working, as for the day, or to cease working, i.e., to retire); **discontinue** suggests the suspension of some action that is a habitual practice, an occupation, etc. (he has *discontinued* the practice of law); **desist** implies a ceasing of some action that is annoying, harmful, futile, etc. (*desist* from further bickering). —*ANT.* begin, start, commence.

stop·cock (stop'kok'), *n.* a cock or valve for stopping or controlling the movement of a fluid, as through a pipe; faucet.

stope (stōp), *n.* [akin to *step*], a steplike excavation formed by the removal of ore from around a mine shaft. *v.t.* & *v.i.* [STOPED (stōpt), STOPING], to mine in stopes.

stop·gap (stop'gap'), *n.* a person or thing serving as a temporary substitute for another; makeshift. *adj.* that is a stopgap. —*SYN.* see **resource.**

stop light, 1. a traffic light, usually red, signaling vehicles to stop. 2. a light at the rear of a vehicle, that lights up when the brakes are applied.

stop order, an order, as to a broker, to buy or sell a certain stock when a specified price is reached.

stop·o·ver (stop'ō'vẽr), *n.* 1. a brief stop or stay at a place in the course of a journey. 2. a train ticket, etc. permitting such a stop.

stop·page (stop'ij), *n.* [see -AGE], 1. a stopping or being stopped. 2. an obstructed condition; block.

stop·per (stop'ẽr), *n.* 1. a person or thing that stops or causes a stoppage. 2. something inserted to close an opening; plug. *v.t.* to close with a plug or stopper.

stop·ple (stop''l), *n.* [ME. *stoppel*, dim. < *stoppen*, to stop; cf. -LE], a stopper. *v.t.* [STOPPLED (-'ld), STOPPLING], to stopper.

stop street, a street intersection at which vehicles must come to a complete stop before continuing.

stopt (stopt), poetic past tense and past participle of **stop.**

stop watch, a watch with a hand that can be started

and stopped instantly so as to indicate fractions of seconds, as in timing races, etc.

stor·age (stôr′ij, stō′rij), *n.* [see -AGE], 1. a storing or being stored. 2. a place or space for storing goods. 3. the cost of keeping goods stored. 4. the charging of a storage battery so as to make possible the subsequent generation of electricity. Abbreviated **stge.**

storage battery, a battery of electrochemical cells for generating electric current: the cells can be recharged by passing a current through them in the direction opposite to the discharging flow of current.

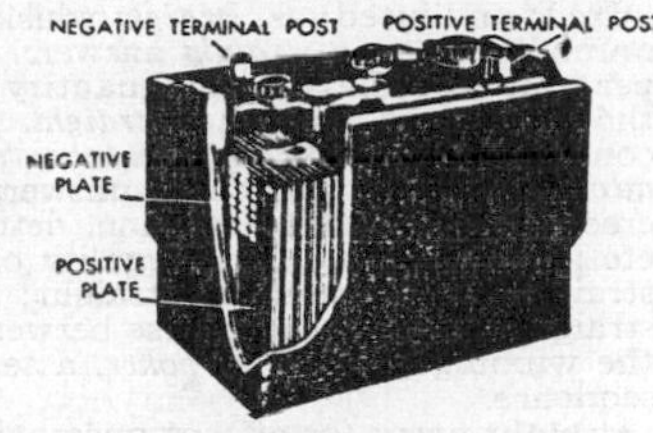

STORAGE BATTERY

sto·rax (stō′raks), *n.* [ME.; L. *storax, styrax;* Gr. *styrax*], 1. the balsam of the Asiatic liquidambar tree, used in medicine and perfumery. 2. a gum resin obtained from certain styracaceous trees.

store (stôr, stōr), *n.* [ME. *stor, stoor;* OFr. *estor* < *estorer,* to erect, furnish, equip, store; L. *instaurare,* to repair, restore, erect], 1. a supply (*of* something) for use when needed; reserve; stock. 2. *pl.* supplies, especially of food, clothing, arms, etc. 3. an establishment where goods are regularly offered for sale. 4. a place where supplies are kept; storehouse; warehouse. 5. a great amount or number; abundance. *v.t.* [STORED (stôrd, stōrd), STORING], [ME. *storen;* OFr. *estorer;* see the *n.*], 1. to put aside or accumulate for use when needed. 2. to fill or furnish with a supply or store: as, a mind *stored* with trivia. 3. to put in a warehouse, etc. for safekeeping.

in store, set aside for the future; in reserve.

set store by, to have regard or esteem for; value.

store·house (stôr′hous′, stōr′hous′), *n.* a place where things are stored; especially, a warehouse.

store·keep·er (stôr′kēp′ẽr, stōr′kēp′ẽr), *n.* a person in charge of a store or stores.

store·room (stôr′rōōm′, stōr′room′), *n.* a room where things are stored.

sto·rey (stôr′i, stō′ri), *n.* [*pl.* STOREYS (-iz, -riz)], [British], a story (of a building).

sto·ried (stôr′id, stō′rid), *adj.* 1. ornamented with designs showing scenes from history, a story, etc. 2. famous in story or history.

sto·ried (stôr′id, stō′rid), *adj.* having (a specified number of) stories: usually in hyphenated compounds, as *three-storied.*

sto·ri·ette (stôr′i-et′, stō′ri-et′), *n.* [dim. of *story* (narrative)], a very short story.

stork (stôrk), *n.* [*pl.* STORKS (stôrks), STORK; see PLURAL, II, D, 1], [ME.; AS. *storc;* akin to G. *storch;* IE. **ster(e)g* < base **ster-,* to be rigid, stiff, as also in *stark, stretch,* etc.: the bird was named from its stiff-legged walk], any of a group of large, long-legged wading birds, having a long neck and bill: it is related to the heron.

stork's-bill (stôrks′bil′), *n.* any of a number of related geraniums with beak-shaped fruit.

storm (stôrm), *n.* [ME.; AS.; akin to G. *sturm;* IE. base **(s)twer-,* to whirl, move or turn quickly, as also in AS. *styrian* (cf. STIR), L. *turbare* (cf. TURBULENT, TURBINE, etc.)], 1. an atmospheric disturbance characterized by a strong wind, usually accompanied by rain, snow, sleet, or hail, and, often, thunder and lightning; hence, 2. any heavy fall of snow, rain, or hail. 3. anything resembling a storm; specifically, *a)* a heavy shower or flight of objects: as, a *storm* of bullets. *b)* a strong outburst of emotion, passion, excitement, etc.: as, a *storm* of criticism. *c)* a strong disturbance or upheaval of a political or social nature. *d)* in *military usage,* a sudden, strong attack on a fortified place. 4. in *meteorology,* any wind ranging in speed from 64–72 miles per hour. *v.i.* 1. to be stormy; blow violently, rain, snow, etc. 2. to be violently angry; rage; rant. 3. to rush or move violently and tumultuously: as, he *stormed* into the office. *v.t.* 1. to attack or assault violently and unceasingly: as they *stormed* him with questions. 2. in *military usage,* to capture or attempt to capture (a fortified place) with a sudden, strong attack. —*SYN.* see **attack.**

Storm, The·o·dor (tā′ô-dôr shtôrm), 1817–1888; German poet and novelist.

storm·bound (stôrm′bound′), *adj.* halted, delayed, or cut off by storms.

storm cellar, an underground shelter used during hurricanes, tornadoes, etc.

storm center, 1. the shifting center of a cyclone, an area of lowest barometric pressure and comparative calm. 2. a center or focus of trouble, turmoil, or disturbance.

storm door, a door placed outside of the regular entrance door as added protection against winter weather.

storm·i·ly (stôr′mə-li), *adv.* in a stormy manner.

storm·i·ness (stôr′mi-nis), *n.* a stormy quality or condition.

storm·proof (stôrm′prōōf′), *adj.* 1. that can withstand a storm. 2. giving protection against storms.

storm trooper, a member of the Sturmabteilung.

storm window, a window placed outside of a regular window as added protection against winter weather.

storm·y (stôr′mi), *adj.* [STORMIER (-mi-ẽr), STORMIEST (-mi-ist)], [ME. *stormi;* AS. *stormig*], 1. of, characteristic of, or affected by storms. 2. having or characterized by storms. 3. violent; raging; passionate.

stormy petrel, 1. any of several small, black-and-white sea birds thought to presage storms. 2. a person thought to presage or bring trouble.

Stor·ting, Stor·thing (stôr′tiŋ′, stōr′tiŋ′), *n.* [Norw. *storting* (earlier *storthing*); *stor,* great + *ting,* assembly (cf. THING, assembly)], the Parliament of Norway.

sto·ry (stôr′i, stō′ri), *n.* [*pl.* STORIES (-iz, -riz)], [ME. *storie;* OFr. *estoire;* L. *historia;* see HISTORY], 1. the telling of a happening or connected series of happenings, whether true or fictitious; account; narration. 2. a fictitious literary composition in prose or poetry, shorter than a novel; narrative; tale. 3. such tales, collectively, as a form of literature. 4. the plot of a novel, play, etc. 5. a report or rumor. 6. [Colloq.], a falsehood; fib. 7. [Archaic], history. 8. in *journalism, a)* a news article. *b)* a person or event considered newsworthy. *v.t.* [STORIED (-id, -rid), STORYING], 1. [Archaic], to describe in a story; tell the story of. 2. to decorate with paintings, etc. representing scenes from history or legend.

SYN.—**story,** the broadest in scope of these words, refers to a series of connected events, true or fictitious, that is written or told with the intention of entertaining or informing; **narrative** is a more formal word and more often implies a true story than a fictitious one; **tale,** a somewhat elevated or poetical term, usually suggests a simple, leisurely story, more or less loosely organized, especially a fictitious or legendary one; **anecdote** applies to a short, entertaining account of a single incident, usually personal or biographical.

sto·ry (stôr′i, stō′ri), *n.* [*pl.* STORIES (-iz, -riz)], [prob. of same origin as *story* (narrative) with sense of "storied" windows or friezes marking the outside of different floors; Anglo-L. *(h)istoria* is actually recorded in this sense], 1. a section or horizontal division of a building extending from the floor to the ceiling or roof lying directly above it: as, a house having only one *story,* a building of many *stories.* 2. all the rooms on the same level of a building. 3. any horizontal section or division. Also spelled **storey.**

sto·ry·tell·er (stôr′i-tel′ẽr, stō′ri-tel′ẽr), *n.* 1. a person who tells stories. 2. [Colloq.], a fibber; liar.

sto·tin·ka (stô-tiŋ′kå), *n.* [*pl.* STOTINKI (-ki)], [Bulg.], a small Bulgarian coin equal to 1/100 lev.

St.-Ouen (san′twän′), *n.* a city near Paris, on the Seine: pop., 45,000 (1946).

stound (stound), *n.* [ME.; AS. *stund;* akin to G. *stunde,* hour], 1. [Archaic or Dial.], a time; moment. 2. [Obs. or Dial.], a pain or pang; shock. *v.i.* [Scot. or British Dial.], to ache, pain, or smart.

stoup (stōōp), *n.* [ME. *stowpe,* bucket < ON. *staup;* sense of "drinking vessel" prob. < MD. *stoop;* akin to G. *stauf;* for IE. base see STEEP, *adj.*] 1. [Archaic or British Dial.], *a)* a drinking cup; tankard. *b)* as much as such a cup will hold. 2. [Scot.], a pail, or bucket. 3. a basin for holy water in a church. Also spelled **stoop.**

stour (stōōr), *n.* [ME. *stoure, sture;* OFr. *estour, estorn* < the base seen in *storm*], [Archaic or Dial.], 1. combat or conflict. 2. turmoil. 3. a storm. 4. wind-blown dust.

stout (stout), *adj.* [ME. *stoute, stowte* < OFr. *estout, estot,* bold; through Gmc.; ult. < L. *stultus,* foolish, simple], 1. courageous; brave; undaunted. 2. *a)* strong in body; sturdy. *b)* strong in construction; firm; substantial: as, a *stout* wall. 3. powerful; forceful. 4. fat; thickset; fleshy; corpulent. *n.* 1. a stout person. 2. a garment for a stout person. 3. strong, dark-brown beer, ale, or porter. —*SYN.* see **strong.**

stout·heart·ed (stout′här′tid), *adj.* courageous; brave.

sto·va·ine, sto·va·in (stō-vā′in), *n.* [< *stove* (transl. of Fr. *Fourneau,* name of the discoverer); + *-aine,* after *cocaine,* etc.], a local anesthetic, usually injected spinally: a trade-mark (**Stovaine**).

stove (stōv), *n.* [MD., a heated room; akin to G. *stube,* sitting room, AS. *stofa,* hot air bath], 1. an apparatus using fuel or electricity for heating a room, cooking, etc. 2. any heated chamber or room, as a kiln, used for drying manufactured articles, raising plants, etc.

stove (stōv), alternative past tense and past participle of **stave.**

stove·pipe (stōv′pīp′), *n.* 1. a metal pipe used to carry off smoke or fumes from a stove, as into a chimney flue. 2. [Colloq.], a stovepipe hat.

stovepipe hat, [Colloq.], a man's tall silk hat.

sto·ver (stō′vẽr), ***n.*** [ME.; OFr. *estover, estovoir;* prob. < L. *est opus,* it is needful], 1. corn stalks, excluding the grain, used as fodder for animals. 2. [British Dial.], fodder of any kind.

stow (stō), ***v.t.*** [ME. *stowen* < AS. *stow,* a place; IE. base **stā-,* to stand (cf. STAND)], 1. to pack or store away; especially, to pack in an orderly, compact manner. 2. to fill by packing in an orderly manner. 3. to hold or receive: said of a room, container, etc. 4. [Obs.], to provide lodging for. 5. [Slang], to stop; cease: as, *stow* the chatter.

stow away, 1. to put or hide away, as in a safe place. 2. to be a stowaway.

stow·age (stō′ij), ***n.*** [see -AGE], 1. a stowing or being stowed. 2. place or room for stowing. 3. something stowed; amount stowed. 4. charges for stowing.

stow·a·way (stō′ə-wā′), ***n.*** a person who hides aboard a ship, train, etc. before it starts out so as to obtain free passage or evade port officials, etc.

Stowe, Harriet Beecher (stō), 1811–1896; sister of Henry Ward Beecher; American writer.

St. Paul, the capital of Minnesota, on the Mississippi: pop., 313,000.

St. Paul's, a cathedral in London, designed by Sir Christopher Wren.

St. Peter's, a cathedral in Rome whose dome was constructed chiefly under the guidance of Michelangelo.

St. Pe·ters·burg (pē′tẽrz-bũrg′), 1. the capital of the former Russian empire: name changed to *Petrograd* in 1914 and *Leningrad* in 1924. 2. a city on the west central coast of Florida: winter resort: pop., 181,000.

St. Pierre (san′ pyâr′), 1. a city on Réunion Island: pop., 28,000. 2. a former city on Martinique, in the West Indies: destroyed (1902) by the eruption of Mount Pelée.

St. Pierre and Miq·ue·lon Islands (mik′ə-lon′; Fr. san′ pyâr′, mēk′lōn′), a French colony in the Atlantic, off the southern coast of Newfoundland: area, 93 sq. mi.; pop., 5,000; capital, St. Pierre.

St.-Quen·tin (san′kän′tan′; Eng. kwen′tən), ***n.*** a city in northern France: pop., 54,000.

str., 1. steamer. 2. in *music,* string; strings.

stra·bis·mal (strə-biz′m'l), ***adj.*** strabismic.

stra·bis·mic (strə-biz′mik), ***adj.*** 1. of or having to do with strabismus. 2. cross-eyed.

stra·bis·mi·cal (strə-biz′mi-k'l), ***adj.*** strabismic.

stra·bis·mus (strə-biz′məs), ***n.*** [Mod. L.; Gr. *strabismos* < *strabizein,* to squint < *strabos,* twisted], a disorder of the eyes, as cross-eye, in which both eyes cannot be focused on the same point at the same time; squint.

Stra·bo (strā′bō), ***n.*** Greek geographer; 63? B.C.–24? A.D.

stra·bot·o·my (strə-bot′ə-mi), ***n.*** [< Gr. *strabos,* squinting; + *-tomy*], the surgical operation of cutting a muscle or muscles of the eyeball to correct strabismus.

Stra·chey, Lyt·ton (lit′'n strā′chi), (*Giles Lytton Strachey*), 1880–1932; English biographer.

strad·dle (strad′'l), ***v.t.*** [STRADDLED (-'ld), STRADDLING], [freq. of *stride*], 1. to place oneself with a leg on either side of; be astride of. 2. to spread (the legs) wide apart. 3. [Colloq.], to appear to take both sides of (an issue); avoid committing oneself on. ***v.i.*** 1. to sit, stand, or walk with the legs wide apart; be astride. 2. [Colloq.], to straddle an issue, argument, etc.; refuse to commit oneself; hedge. ***n.*** 1. the act or position of straddling. 2. the space between straddled legs. 3. [Colloq.], a refusal to commit oneself definitely to either side of an issue, etc. 4. in the *stock exchange,* an option giving the holder the right to buy from the seller, or sell to him, a specified number of shares at a specified price within the stated time.

Stra·di·va·ri, An·to·ni·o (än-tô′nyô strä′dē-vä′rē), (Latin name *Antonius Stradivarius*), 1644–1737; Italian violinmaker of Cremona.

Strad·i·var·i·us (strad′ə-vâr′i-əs), ***n.*** a string instrument, especially a violin, made by Antonio Stradivari.

strafe (strāf, sträf), ***v.t.*** [STRAFED (strāft, sträft), STRAFING], [< G. phr. *Gott strafe England* (God punish England) used in World War I], 1. to attack with gunfire; especially, to attack (ground positions, troops, etc.) with machine-gun fire from low-flying aircraft. 2. to bombard heavily: also used figuratively.

Straf·ford (straf′ẽrd), first Earl of, (*Thomas Wentworth*), 1593–1641; English statesman; adviser of Charles I.

strag·gle (strag′'l), ***v.i.*** [STRAGGLED (-'ld), STRAGGLING], [ME. *straglen,* prob. for **straklen,* freq. of *straken,* to go about, wander, roam], 1. to stray from the path or course or wander from the main group. 2. to wander or be scattered over a wide area; ramble. 3. to leave, arrive, or occur at scattered, irregular intervals.

strag·gly (strag′li), ***adj.*** [STRAGGLIER (-li-ẽr), STRAGGLIEST (-li-ist)], straggling.

straight (strāt), ***adj.*** [ME. *streght* (pp. of *strecchen,* to stretch, used as *adj.*); AS. *streht,* pp. of *streccan,* to stretch; cf. STRETCH], 1. having the same direction throughout its length; having no curvature or angularity: as, a *straight* line. 2. not crooked, bent, bowed, wavy, curly, etc.; upright; erect: as, a *straight* back, *straight* hair. 3. with all cylinders in a direct line: said of some internal-combustion engines. 4. direct; undeviating; continuous; uninterrupted, etc.: as, a *straight* course. 5. following strictly the principles, slate of candidates, etc. of a political party: as, he votes a *straight* ticket. 6. following a direct or systematic course of reasoning, etc.; methodical; accurate. 7. in order; properly arranged, etc.: as, put your room *straight.* 8. *a*) honest; sincere; upright. *b*) [Colloq.], reliable, as information. 9. outspoken; frank. 10. unmixed; undiluted: as, *straight* whisky. 11. unqualified; unmodified: as, a *straight* answer. 12. at a fixed price per unit regardless of the quantity bought or sold: as, the apples are ten cents *straight.* 13. in *card games,* consisting of cards in sequence: as, a *straight* flush. ***adv.*** 1. in a straight line; unswervingly. 2. upright; erectly. 3. without deviation, detour, circumlocution, etc.; directly. ***n.*** 1. the quality or condition of being straight. 2. something straight; specifically, *a*) the straight part of a racecourse between the last turn and the winning post. *b*) in *poker,* a series of five cards in sequence.

straight away (or **off**), at once; without delay.

straight angle, an angle of 180 degrees.

straight-arm (strāt′ärm′), ***v.t.*** in *football,* to push away (a tackler) with the arm outstretched. ***n.*** the act of straight-arming.

straight·a·way (strāt′ə-wā′), ***adj.*** extending in a straight line. ***n.*** a track, or part of a track, that extends in a straight line.

straight·edge (strāt′ej′), ***n.*** a piece or strip of wood, etc. having a perfectly straight edge used in drawing straight lines, testing plane surfaces, etc.

straight·en (strāt′'n), ***v.t. & v.i.*** to make or become straight.

straight-faced (strāt′fāst′), ***adj.*** showing no amusement or other emotion.

straight·for·ward (strāt′fôr′wẽrd), ***adj.*** 1. moving or leading straight ahead; direct. 2. honest; frank; open. ***adv.*** in a straightforward manner; directly.

straight·for·wards (strāt′fôr′wẽrdz), ***adv.*** straightforward.

straight-line (strāt′līn′), ***adj.*** 1. composed of straight lines. 2. having the parts arranged in a straight line or lines. 3. designating a linkage or similar device (*straight-line motion*) used to produce or copy motion in straight lines.

straight man, in the *theater,* an actor who serves as a foil for a comedian.

straight-out (strāt′out′), ***adj.*** [Colloq.], 1. straightforward; direct. 2. unrestrained; outright. 3. thoroughgoing; unqualified.

straight·way (strāt′wā′), ***adv.*** at once; without delay.

strain (strān), ***v.t.*** [ME. *streinen;* OFr. *estraindre,* to strain, wring hard; L. *stringere,* to draw tight; cf. STRINGENT], 1. to draw or stretch tight. 2. to exert, use, or tax to the utmost: as, he *strained* every nerve to get there. 3. to overtax; injure by exertion; sprain: as, he *strained* a muscle climbing. 4. to injure or weaken by force, pressure, etc.: as, the wind *strained* the roof. 5. to stretch or force beyond the normal, customary, or legitimate limits: as, he *strained* the rule to his own advantage. 6. to change the form or size of, by applying external force. 7. *a*) to pass through a screen, sieve, filter, etc.; filter. *b*) to remove or free by filtration, etc. 8. to hug; embrace: now only in *to strain to one's bosom* (or *heart,* etc.). 9. [Obs.], to force; constrain. ***v.i.*** 1. to make violent or continual efforts; strive hard: as, she *strained* to win. 2. to be or become strained. 3. to be subjected to great stress or pressure. 4. to pull with force. 5. to filter, ooze, or trickle. ***n.*** 1. a straining or being strained. 2. great effort, exertion, or tension. 3. a sprain or wrench. 4. change in form or size, or both, resulting from stress or force; hence, 5. stress; force. 6. a great or excessive demand on one's emotions, resources, etc.: as, a *strain* on my imagination.

strain at, 1. to use great effort in trying to move (an object); push or pull hard at. 2. to have unusually great difficulty accepting; balk at.

strain (strān), ***n.*** [ME. *strene, streen, stren;* AS. *streon,* gain, procreation, stock, race < base of *strynan, streonan,* to produce], 1. originally, *a*) a begetting. *b*) offspring. 2. ancestry; lineage; descent. 3. the descendants of a common ancestor; race; stock; line; breed; variety. 4. a line of individuals of a certain species or race, differentiated from the main group by certain, generally superior qualities, especially as the result of artificial breeding. 5. an inherited or natural character or tendency. 6. a trace; streak. 7. the manner, style, or mood of a speech, book, action, etc.: as, he wrote in an angry *strain.* 8. *often pl.* a passage of music; tune; air. 9. a flight or outburst of eloquence, profanity, etc.

strain·er (strān′ẽr), ***n.*** 1. a device for stretching or tightening something. 2. a device for straining, sifting, or filtering; sieve, filter, colander, etc.

strain·ing piece (strān′iŋ), a horizontal brace or beam connected at either end to opposite rafters in a roof truss: also **straining beam.**

strait (strāt), ***adj.*** [ME. *streit;* OFr. *estreit* < L. *strictus,* pp. of *stringere,* to draw tight; cf. STRAIN, *v.* & STRIN-

GENT], 1. [Archaic], restricted or constricted; narrow; tight; confined. 2. [Archaic], strict; rigid; exacting. 3. straitened; difficult; distressing. *n.* 1. [Rare], a narrow passage. 2. *often in pl.* a narrow waterway connecting two large bodies of water. 3. *often in pl.* difficulty; distress. 4. [Rare], an isthmus. Abbreviated **St.** —*SYN.* see **emergency.**

strait·en (strāt''n), *v.t.* 1. to make strait or narrow; limit; contract. 2. [Rare], to restrict or confine; hamper. 3. to bring into difficulties, especially financial hardships; distress: usually in the past participle, especially in the phrase *in straitened circumstances,* lacking sufficient money.

strait jacket, a coatlike device that binds the arms tight against the body: used to restrain mentally deranged persons, criminals, etc. who are violent.

strait-laced (strāt'lāst'), *adj.* 1. [Archaic], *a)* tightly laced, as a corset. *b)* wearing tightly laced garments. 2. narrowly strict or severe in behavior or opinions.

Straits Settlements, a former British colony in the Malay Peninsula, including the settlements of Penang and Malacca, Cocos Island, Christmas Island, and Singapore.

strake (strāk), *n.* [ME.; akin to *stretch* but associated with *streak*], a single line of planking or metal plating extending from one end of a ship to the other.

Stral·sund (shträl'zoont), *n.* a seaport in northeastern Germany: besieged (1628) by Wallenstein: pop., 44,000.

stra·min·e·ous (strə-min'i-əs), *adj.* [L. *stramineus* < *stramen,* straw], 1. of or like straw. 2. straw-colored.

stra·mo·ni·um (strə-mō'ni-əm), *n.* [Mod. L.; ML. *stramonia,* thought by some to be altered from a Tartar word], 1. a poisonous weed of the nightshade family, with toothed leaves, white flowers, and prickly fruit; jimson weed; thorn apple; stinkweed. 2. its dried leaves, used in medicine as a narcotic, etc.

stram·o·ny (stram'ə-ni), *n.* stramonium.

strand (strand), *n.* [ME.; AS.; akin to ON. *strǫnd;* the Gmc. base blends senses < IE. base **ster-,* to extend, stretch out & **ster-,* a stripe, etc.], land at the edge of a body of water; shore, especially ocean shore. *v.t. & v.i.* 1. to run or drive aground, as a ship. 2. to put or come into a difficult, helpless position: used especially in the passive, as, *stranded* in a strange city with no money. —*SYN.* see **shore.**

strand (strand), *n.* [OFr. *estran;* prob. of Gmc. origin], 1. any of the bundles of thread, fiber, wire, etc. that are twisted together to form a length of string, rope, or cable. 2. a string, thread, or other ropelike filament: as, a *strand* of beads. *v.t.* 1. to form (rope, etc.) by twisting together strands. 2. to break a strand or strands of (a rope, etc.).

strand line, a shore line, especially a former one from which the water has receded.

strange (strānj), *adj.* [STRANGER (strān'jẽr), STRANGEST (strān'jist)], [ME.; OFr. *estrange;* L. *extraneus,* that is without < *extra,* on the outside], 1. *a)* [Archaic], foreign; alien. *b)* of another place or locality. 2. not previously known, seen, heard, or experienced; unfamiliar. 3. unusual; uncommon; extraordinary. 4. queer; peculiar; odd. 5. reserved; distant; not familiar. 6. unaccustomed; lacking experience: as, he was *strange* to the job. *adv.* in a strange manner; strangely.

SYN.—**strange,** the term of broadest application here, refers to that which is unfamiliar, as because of being uncommon, unknown, new, etc. (a *strange* voice, idea, device, etc.); **peculiar** applies either to that which puzzles or to that which has unique qualities (a *peculiar* smell, pattern, etc.); **odd** suggests that which differs from the ordinary or conventional, sometimes to the point of being bizarre (*odd* behavior); **queer** adds to this an emphasis of eccentricity, abnormality, or suspicion (a *queer* facial expression); **quaint** suggests an oddness, especially an antique quality, that is pleasing or appealing (a *quaint* costume); **outlandish** suggests an oddness that is decidedly fantastic or bizarre (*outlandish* customs). —*ANT.* familiar, ordinary.

stran·ger (strān'jẽr), *n.* [ME. *strangere, straungere* < OFr. *estrangier* (Fr. *étranger*); cf. STRANGE], 1. an outsider, newcomer, or foreigner. 2. a guest or visitor. 3. a person not known or familiar to one; person who is not an acquaintance. 4. a person unaccustomed (*to* something specified); novice: as, he is a *stranger* to hate. 5. in *law,* a person who is not party (*to* an act, agreement, title, etc.). —*SYN.* see **alien.**

stran·gle (straŋ'g'l), *v.t.* [STRANGLED (-g'ld), STRANGLING], [ME. *strangelen;* OFr. *estrangler;* L. *strangulare* < Gr. *strangalan* < *strangalē,* halter < *strangos,* twisted], 1. to kill by squeezing the throat so as to shut off the breath, as with the hands, a noose, etc.; throttle; choke. 2. to suffocate or choke in any manner. 3. to suppress; stifle; repress. *v.i.* to be strangled; choke; suffocate.

strangle hold, 1. a wrestling hold that chokes off an opponent's breath. 2. figuratively, any force or action that restricts or suppresses freedom.

stran·gles (straŋ'g'lz), *n.* an infectious disease of horses, characterized by a catarrhal inflammation of the mucous membrane of the respiratory tract.

stran·gu·late (straŋ'gyoo-lāt'), *v.t.* [STRANGULATED (-id), STRANGULATING], [< L. *strangulatus,* pp. of *strangulare*], 1. to strangle. 2. in *medicine,* to constrict or obstruct (a tube, vessel, duct, etc.) so as to cut off the flow of some fluid.

stran·gu·la·tion (straŋ'gyoo-lā'shən), *n.* [L. *strangulatio* < *strangulare*], a strangling or strangulating or a being strangled or strangulated.

stran·gu·ry (straŋ'gyoo-ri), *n.* [L. *stranguria;* Gr. *strangouria* < *stranx, strangos,* a drop + *ouron,* urine], slow and painful urination.

strap (strap), *n.* [dial. form of *strop;* ME. *strope, strop* < OFr. *estrop* & AS. *stropp,* both < L. *struppus,* a strap, thong, fillet; Gr. *strophos,* a band, cord], 1. a narrow strip or band of leather or other flexible material, often with a buckle or similar fastener at one end, for binding or securing things. 2. any flat, narrow piece, as of metal, used as a fastening. 3. any of several straplike objects, as a shoulder strap, a loop for pulling on boots, etc. 4. a razor strop. *v.t.* [STRAPPED (strapt), STRAPPING], 1. to fasten with a strap. 2. to beat with a strap. 3. to strop (a razor).

strap·hang·er (strap'haŋ'ẽr), *n.* [Colloq.], a standing passenger, as on a crowded bus or streetcar, who supports himself by holding onto a strap, etc. suspended from above.

strap·pa·do (strə-pā'dō, strə-pä'dō), *n.* [*pl.* STRAPPADOES (-dōz)], [It. *strappata* < *strappare,* to pull], 1. a form of torture in which the victim was tied by his wrists to a long rope, lifted in the air, and suddenly dropped part way to the ground. 2. the instrument used in this torture.

strap·per (strap'ẽr), *n.* 1. a person or thing that straps. 2. [Colloq.], a strapping person.

strap·ping (strap'iŋ), *adj.* [ppr. of *strap,* used (like *thumping, whopping,* expressing violent action) to denote something of large size], [Colloq.], tall and well-built; strong; robust.

Stras·bourg (stras'bẽrg, sträz'bẽrg; Fr. sträz'bōōr'), *n.* a city in northeastern France, on the Rhine: pop., 175,000 (1946): German name, *Strassburg.*

strass (stras), *n.* [G., after the inventor, Josef *Strasser,* G. jeweler], a lustrous lead glass used in making artificial jewels; paste.

Strass·burg (shträs'boorkh), *n.* Strasbourg.

stra·ta (strā'tə, strat'ə), *n.* alternative plural of **stratum.**

strat·a·gem (strat'ə-jəm), *n.* [Fr. *stratagème;* L. *strategema;* Gr. *stratēgēma,* device or act of a general < *stratēgos,* a general < *stratos,* army + *agein,* to lead], 1. a trick, scheme, or device used for deceiving an enemy in war. 2. any trick or deception. —*SYN.* see **trick.**

stra·tal (strā't'l), *adj.* of a stratum or strata.

stra·te·gic (strə-tē'jik), *adj.* 1. of or having to do with strategy. 2. characterized by sound strategy; favorable; advantageous. 3. essential to effective military strategy: as, *strategic* materials.

stra·te·gi·cal (strə-tē'ji-k'l), *adj.* strategic.

stra·te·gi·cal·ly (strə-tē'ji-k'l-i, strə-tē'jik-li), *adv.* 1. in a strategic manner. 2. with reference to strategy.

stra·te·gics (strə-tē'jiks), *n.pl.* [construed as sing.], strategy.

strat·e·gist (strat'ə-jist), *n.* one skilled in strategy.

strat·e·gy (strat'ə-ji), *n.* [*pl.* STRATEGIES (-jiz)], [Fr. *stratégie;* Gr. *stratēgia,* generalship < *stratēgos,* general], 1. the science of planning and directing large-scale military operations, specifically (as distinguished from *tactics*), of maneuvering forces into the most advantageous position prior to actual engagement with the enemy. 2. a plan or action based on this. 3. skill in managing or planning, especially by using stratagem.

Strat·ford-on-A·von (strat'fẽrd-on-ā'vən), *n.* Stratford upon Avon.

Strat·ford up·on A·von (strat'fẽrd ə-pon' ā'vən), a town in Warwickshire, England, on the Avon River: birthplace and burial place of Shakespeare.

strath (strath; Scot. stràth), *n.* [< Scot. Gael. *srath*], a wide river valley.

strath·spey (strath'spā', strath'spā'), *n.* [< *Strathspey,* district in Scotland], 1. a Scottish dance resembling, but slower than, the reel. 2. the music for this dance.

stra·tic·u·late (strə-tik'yoo-lit, strə-tik'yoo-lāt'), *adj.* [< Mod. L. **straticulum,* dim. of L. *stratum;* + *-ate*], in *geology,* arranged in thin layers or strata.

strat·i·fi·ca·tion (strat'ə-fi-kā'shən), *n.* 1. a stratifying. 2. a stratified arrangement or appearance. 3. in *geology, a)* formation in strata. *b)* a stratum.

strat·i·form (strat'ə-fôrm'), *adj.* [< *stratum* + *-form*], having the form of a stratum; showing stratification; specifically, *a)* designating or of clouds arranged in a stratus. *b)* in *anatomy,* designating cartilage occurring in a bone in layers, as a support for tendons.

strat·i·fy (strat'ə-fī'), *v.t.* [STRATIFIED (-fīd'), STRATIFYING], [Fr. *stratifier;* ML. *stratificare* < L. *stratum,* layer, pavement + *facere,* to make], 1. to form or arrange in layers or strata. 2. in *horticulture,* to preserve (seeds) by placing them between layers of soil, peat moss, etc.

strat·i·graph·ic (strat'ə-graf'ik), *adj.* of stratigraphy.

strat·i·graph·i·cal (strat'ə-graf'i-k'l), *adj.* stratigraphic.

stra·tig·ra·phy (strə-tig'rə-fi), *n.* [< *stratum* + *-graphy*], 1. the arrangement of rocks in layers or strata. 2. the branch of geology dealing with such stratification: abbreviated **stratig.**

stra·toc·ra·cy (strə-tok'rə-si), *n.* [< Gr. *stratos*, army; + *-cracy*], government by the military.

stra·to-cu·mu·lus (strā'tō-kū'myoo-ləs), *n.* [*pl.* STRATOCUMULI (-lī')], [Mod. L.; see STRATUS & CUMULUS], a dark cloud formation having the appearance of mounds piled one on top of the other, usually seen in winter.

stra·to·sphere (strat'ə-sfêr', strā'tə-sfêr'), *n.* [Fr. *stratosphère* < L. *stratum*, stratum + Fr. *atmosphère*, atmosphere], the upper part of the earth's atmosphere, beginning at an altitude of about seven miles and continuing to the ionosphere: it is characterized by an almost constant temperature at all altitudes.

strat·o·spher·ic (strat'ə-sfer'ik, strā'tə-sfer'ik), *adj.* of the stratosphere.

stra·tum (strā'təm, strat'əm), *n.* [*pl.* STRATA (-tə, -ə), STRATUMS (-təmz, -əmz)], [L., a covering, quilt, blanket, pavement < *stratus*, pp. of *sternere*, to spread, stretch out, cover], 1. a horizontal layer or section of material, especially any of several lying one upon another; specifically, *a)* in *biology*, a layer of tissue. *b)* in *geology*, a single layer of sedimentary rock representing the deposition of a single geological period. 2. a section, level, or division regarded as like a stratum: as, the highest *stratum* of society.

stra·tus (strā'təs), *n.* [*pl.* STRATI (-tī)], [L., a strewing, pp. of *sternere*, to spread, stretch out, cover], a cloud formation extending in a long, low layer.

STRATUS CLOUDS

Straus, Os·kar (ôs'kär shtrous; Eng. strous), 1870–1954; Austrian composer.

Strauss, Jo·hann (yō'hän shtrous; Eng. strous), 1825–1899; Austrian composer, especially of waltzes.

Strauss, Rich·ard (riH'-ärt), 1864–1949; German composer and conductor.

Stra·vin·sky, I·gor Fe·do·ro·vich (ē'gôr fyô'dô-rô'vich strȧ-vēn'ski; Eng. strə-vin'ski), 1882– ; Russian composer in America.

straw (strô), *n.* [ME. *stra, strea;* AS. *streaw, streow, strea* < base seen in Eng. *strew* (AS. *streowian*); hence akin to L. *stramen*, straw], 1. hollow stalks or stems of grain after threshing: used for fodder, as a stuffing for mattresses, etc. 2. a single one of such stalks. 3. such a stalk or, now especially, a tube of waxed paper, glass, etc. used for sucking beverages. 4. something of little or no value; worthless trifle. *adj.* 1. straw-colored; yellowish. 2. made of straw. 3. of little or no value or significance; worthless; meaningless.

catch (or **clutch, grasp**) **at a straw**, to try anything that offers even the least hope.

straw·ber·ry (strô'ber'i, strô'bẽr-i), *n.* [*pl.* STRAWBERRIES (-iz)], [ME. *strawberi;* AS. *streawberie* < *streaw*, straw + *berige*, berry: prob. so called from the small achenes on the fruit], 1. the small, red, cone-shaped, fleshy fruit of a vinelike plant of the rose family. 2. this plant: also **strawberry vine.**

strawberry bass, the calico bass.

strawberry blonde, reddish blonde.

strawberry bush, a shrub with rough, red pods, and seeds with a red covering; wahoo.

strawberry mark, a small, red birthmark.

strawberry roan, reddish roan.

strawberry shrub, any of a number of related plants with dark-red flowers of a strawberry fragrance.

strawberry tomato, any of a number of related plants with white or yellowish flowers, large bright calyxes, and small, yellow, tomato-flavored fruit.

strawberry tree, a European evergreen with clusters of small, white flowers and red, strawberrylike fruit.

straw·board (strô'bôrd', strô'bōrd'), *n.* a kind of coarse cardboard made of straw and used in making boxes, etc.

straw boss, [? < *straw man*], [Colloq.], a person having subordinate authority, as a foreman's assistant.

straw color, a pale-yellow color.

straw-col·ored (strô'kul'ẽrd), *adj.* pale-yellow.

straw·flow·er (strô'flou'ẽr), *n.* a tall plant with variously colored, paperlike flowers dried for winter bouquets.

straw man, 1. a bundle of straw made to look like a man, as for a scarecrow. 2. a perjured witness. 3. a person of little importance; nonentity.

straw vote, an unofficial vote or poll taken to determine general group opinion on a given issue.

straw wine, a sweet, rich wine made from grapes that have been spread out on straw and dried in the sun.

straw·worm (strô'wũrm'), *n.* 1. the caddis worm, a water larva of the caddis fly. 2. any of several insect larvae which damage the stalks of wheat, etc.

straw·y (strô'i), *adj.* [STRAWIER (-i-ẽr), STRAWIEST (-i-ist)], 1. of or like straw. 2. made or covered with straw or thatching.

stray (strā), *v.i.* [ME. *straien;* OFr. *estraier;* prob. < LL. **estragare* < L. *extra vagare*, to wander outside], 1. to wander from a given place, limited area, direct course, etc., especially aimlessly; roam; rove. 2. to go wrong; be in error; deviate (*from* what is right). 3. to turn aside from the matter at hand; fail to concentrate; be inattentive or digress: as, their thoughts *strayed* as she entered the room. *n.* 1. a person or thing that strays; especially, a domestic animal wandering at large. 2. *usually pl.* an electrical disturbance interfering with radio reception; static. *adj.* 1. having strayed or wandered; lost. 2. isolated; occasional; incidental: as, we caught only a few *stray* words. —*SYN.* see **roam.**

streak (strēk), *n.* [ME. *strike, streke;* AS. *strica* < the base seen in Eng. *strike*], 1. a line or long, thin mark; stripe or smear, generally differing in color or texture from the surrounding area. 2. a vein or stratum of a mineral. 3. a layer, as of fat in meat. 4. a strain, element, or tendency in behavior, temperament, etc.; trait: as, a nervous *streak.* 5. [Colloq.], a period or spell: as, a long *streak* of bad luck. 6. in *mineralogy*, a colored line of powder produced by rubbing a mineral over a hard, white surface: it serves as a distinguishing character. *v.t.* to make streaks on or in; mark with streaks. *v.i.* 1. to form streaks; become streaked. 2. to move at high speed; go fast; hurry.

like a streak, [Colloq.], at high speed; swiftly.

streak·i·ly (strē'kə-li), *adv.* in a streaky manner.

streak·i·ness (strē'ki-nis), *n.* the quality or condition of being streaky.

streak·y (strē'ki), *adj.* [STREAKIER (-ki-ẽr), STREAKIEST (-ki-ist)], 1. marked with or showing streaks. 2. occurring in streaks. 3. uneven or variable, as in quality.

stream (strēm), *n.* [ME. *strem;* AS.; akin to G. *strom;* IE. base **sreu-*, to flow, as also in Gr. *rheein*, to flow (cf. RHEO-)], 1. a current or flow of water or other liquid, especially one running along the surface of the earth; specifically, a small river. 2. a steady movement or flow of any fluid (a *stream* of cold air) or of rays of energy (a *stream* of light). 3. a continuous series or succession: as, a *stream* of cars. 4. a trend or course: as, the *stream* of events. *v.i.* 1. to flow in or as in a stream. 2. to give off a stream; flow (*with*): as, eyes *streaming* with tears. 3. to move steadily or continuously. 4. to move swiftly; rush: as, fire *streamed* up the side of the wall. 5. to extend or stretch out; float; fly, as a flag in the breeze. *v.t.* 1. to cause to flow. 2. to extend (a flag, etc.) out to its length.

stream·er (strēm'ẽr), *n.* 1. a long, narrow, ribbonlike flag or banner. 2. any long, narrow strip of material or ribbon hanging loose at one end. 3. a ray or stream of light extending up from the horizon. 4. a newspaper headline that extends across the full page.

stream·let (strēm'lit), *n.* a small stream; rivulet.

stream·line (strēm'līn'), *n.* 1. the path, or a section of the path, of a fluid moving past a solid object. 2. a shape or contour with reference to its resistance to air, etc. *adj.* designating, of, or having a contour designed to offer the least resistance in moving through air, water, etc. by permitting an unbroken flow of the fluid about it: as, a *streamline* boat. *v.t.* [STREAMLINED (-līnd'), STREAMLINING], to give a streamline form to.

stream·lined (strēm'līnd'), *adj.* 1. having a streamline form. 2. so arranged or fashioned as to secure the greatest progress and efficiency with the least delay and obstruction: as, a *streamlined* office.

stream-of-con·scious·ness (strēm'əv-kon'shəs-nis), *adj.* designating or of a form of novel in which the story is developed through recording the thoughts of one or more of the characters.

stream of consciousness, [term originated by William James (1842–1910)], in *psychology*, individual conscious experience regarded as a continuous series of occurrences rather than as separate, disconnected events.

stream·y (strēm'i), *adj.* [STREAMIER (-i-ẽr), STREAMIEST (-i-ist)], 1. full of streams or currents. 2. like a stream; streaming; flowing; running.

street (strēt), *n.* [ME. *strete;* AS. *stræt;* LL. *strata*, for L. *strata via*, paved road; *strata*, fem. of *stratus*, pp. of *sternere*, to strew, scatter, pave; cf. STRATUM], 1. a public road in a town or city; especially, a paved thoroughfare with the sidewalks and buildings along one or both sides. 2. such a road apart from its sidewalks: as, don't play in the *street.* 3. the people living, working, etc. in the buildings along a given street: as, the whole *street* contributed. Abbreviated **St.**

street Arab, a homeless or neglected child left to roam the streets; gamin; street urchin.

street·car (strēt'kär'), *n.* a large coach or car for public transportation, that follows a regular route along certain streets, usually on rails.

street railway, a railway that runs along the public streets; streetcar line.

street urchin, a homeless or neglected child left to roam the streets; gamin; street Arab.

street·walk·er (strēt'wôk'ẽr), *n.* a person who walks in the streets; especially, a prostitute who seeks trade along the streets.

strength (streŋth, streŋkth), *n.* [ME. *strengthe;* AS. *strengthu* < **strang-ithu;* see STRONG & -TH], 1. the state or quality of being strong; force; power; vigor. 2. the power to resist strain, stress, etc.; toughness; durability. 3. the power to resist attack; impregnability. 4. legal, moral, or intellectual force or effectiveness. 5. *a)* capacity for producing a reaction or effect; potency, as of drugs, liquors, etc. *b)* great capacity for producing such effect. 6. intensity, as of sound, color, odor, etc. 7. force, as measured in numbers: as, the battalion is at full *strength.* 8. a source of strength; that which makes strong; support. 9. in the *stock exchange,* a tendency to rise or remain firm in prices.

on the strength of, based or relying on.

SYN.—**strength** refers to the inherent capacity to act upon or affect something, to endure, to resist, etc. (the *strength* to lift something, tensile *strength*); **power,** somewhat more general, applies to the ability, latent or exerted, physical or mental, to do something (the *power* of the press, of a machine, etc.); **force** usually suggests the actual exertion of power, especially in producing motion or overcoming opposition (the *force* of gravity); **might** suggests great or overwhelming strength or power (with all one's *might*); **energy** specifically implies latent power for doing work or affecting something (the *energy* in an atom); **potency** refers to the inherent capacity or power to accomplish something (the *potency* of a drug). —*ANT.* weakness, impotence.

strength·en (streŋ'thən, streŋk'thən), *v.t. & v.i.* to increase in strength; make or become stronger.

stren·u·os·i·ty (stren'ū-os'ə-ti), *n.* the quality of being strenuous.

stren·u·ous (stren'ū-əs), *adj.* [L. *strenuus,* vigorous, active; allied to Gr. *strēnēs,* strong], 1. requiring or characterized by great effort or energy. 2. vigorous, ardent, zealous, etc.: as, a *strenuous* orator. —*SYN.* see **active.**

strep·to·coc·cal (strep'tə-kok'əl), *adj.* of or caused by streptococci.

strep·to·coc·cic (strep'tə-kok'sik), *adj.* streptococcal.

strep·to·coc·cus (strep'tə-kok'əs), *n.* [*pl.* STREPTOCOCCI (-kok'sī)], [Mod. L. < Gr. *streptos,* bent, twisted + *kokkos,* a grain, seed, berry], any of a group of spherical, Gram-positive bacteria that divide in only one plane, occurring generally in chains: some species cause various serious diseases.

strep·to·my·cin (strep'tə-mī'sin), *n.* [< Gr. *streptos,* twisted + *mykēs,* fungus; + *-in*], an antibiotic drug similar to penicillin, obtained from certain molds and used in the treatment of various diseases.

strep·to·thri·cin (strep'tə-thrī'sin, strep'tə-thris'in), *n.* [< Mod. L. *Streptothrix,* name of the fungus (< Gr. *streptos,* twisted + *thrix,* hair); + *-in*], an antibiotic drug derived from a certain species of fungus.

Stre·se·mann, Gus·tav (goos'täf shtrā'zə-män'), 1878–1929; German statesman.

stress (stres), *n.* [OFr. *estrece;* LL. *estrictia* < L. *strictus,* strict; also, in some senses, contr. of *distress*], 1. strain; pressure; especially, *a)* force exerted upon a body, that tends to strain or deform its shape. *b)* the intensity of such force, usually measured in pounds per square inch. *c)* the resistance or cohesiveness of a body resisting such force. 2. urgency; importance; significance. 3. tension; strained exertion: as, the *stress* of war affected all the people. 4. in *music,* accent. 5. in *phonetics, a)* the relative force with which a syllable is uttered: in English, there are normally *primary* or *strong stress* ('), *secondary* or *light stress* ('), and *zero stress* (lack or reduction of stress). *b)* primary stress. 6. in *prosody, a)* the relative force of utterance given a syllable or word according to the meter. *b)* an accented syllable. *v.t.* [OFr. *estrecer;* LL. **strictiare* < L. *strictus,* strict], 1. to put stress, pressure, or strain on. 2. to give stress or accent to. 3. to emphasize.

-stress (stris), [< *-ster* + *-ess*], a feminine suffix corresponding to *-ster,* as in *songstress.*

stretch (strech), *v.t.* [ME. *strecchen;* AS. *streccan;* akin to G. *strecken;* IE. **ster(e)g* < base **ster-,* to be stiff, rigid, etc., as also in Eng. *stride*], 1. to hold or reach out; extend (an arm, hand, etc.). 2. to cause (the body or limbs) to reach out to full length, as in yawning, relaxing, etc. 3. to pull or spread out to full extent or to greater size: as, *stretch* the carpet out to dry, she *stretched* the sweater to make it fit. 4. to cause to reach or extend over a given space or distance; extend. 5. *a)* to cause to reach or extend farther, especially too far; force beyond normal limits; strain: as, don't *stretch* the material or you'll rip it, they have *stretched* the law; hence, *b)* to exaggerate. 6. to make tense or tight with effort; strain (a muscle, etc.). 7. [Slang], to knock down, especially so as to cause to lie at full length. 8. [Archaic or Dial.], to execute by hanging. 9. [Slang or Dial.], to lay out for burial. *v.i.* 1. *a)* to spread or be spread out to full extent or beyond normal limits. *b)* to extend or continue over a given space or distance. 2. to extend the body or limbs to full length, as in yawning or reaching for something. 3. to become stretched or be capable of being stretched to greater size, as any elastic substance. 4. to lie down at full length (usually with *out*). 5. [Slang], to be executed by hanging; hang. *n.* 1. a stretching or being stretched. 2. an unbroken period; continuous space (*of* time): as, over a *stretch* of three months. 3. [Slang], a prison sentence. 4. the extent to which something can be stretched. 5. an unbroken length, tract, or space; continuous extent or distance: as, a long *stretch* of white beach. 6. one of the sections of a course or track for racing, especially the straight length of track before the finish line in horse racing. 7. a course or direction.

stretch·er (strech'ẽr), *n.* 1. a person or thing that stretches; specifically, *a)* a brace or tie used to extend or support a framework; crosspiece. *b)* a brick or stone laid lengthwise in a wall. *c)* any of several framelike devices used for stretching and shaping cloth, garments, etc. 2. a light frame covered with canvas, etc. and used for carrying the sick, injured, or dead; litter.

stretch·er-bear·er (strech'ẽr-bâr'ẽr), *n.* a person who helps carry a stretcher (sense 2).

stretch·i·ness (strech'i-nis), *n.* the quality of being stretchy.

stretch-out (strech'out'), *n.* [Colloq.], a system of industrial operation in which workers are required to do more work with little or no increase in pay. *adj.* of or designating such a system.

stretch·y (strech'i), *adj.* [STRETCHIER (-i-ẽr), STRETCHIEST (-i-ist)], 1. that can be stretched; elastic. 2. liable to stretch too far.

‡**stret·ta** (stret'tä; Eng. stret'ə), *n.* [*pl.* STRETTE (-te), Eng. STRETTAS (-əz)], [It.], stretto (especially sense 2).

‡**stret·to** (stret'tô; Eng. stret'ō), *n.* [*pl.* STRETTI (-tē), Eng. STRETTOS (-ōz)], [It. < L. *strictus,* tight, narrow, strait, pp. of *stringere,* to draw tight; cf. STRINGENT], in *music,* 1. in a fugue, the following of the voices in close succession, especially in the closing section. 2. any concluding passage performed with a climactic increase in speed: in this sense, usually **stretta.**

strew (strōō), *v.t.* [STREWED (strōōd), STREWED or STREWN (strōōn), STREWING], [ME. *strawen, strewen;* AS. *streowian, streawian, strewian;* akin to G. *streuen;* IE. base **streu-* (< **ster-,* to extend, stretch out, strew), as also in L. *struere,* to pile up (cf. STRUCTURE); see STRAW], 1. to scatter; spread here and there by or as by sprinkling. 2. to cover by or as by scattering or sprinkling. 3. to be scattered or dispersed over (a surface). —*SYN.* see **sprinkle.**

stri·a (strī'ə), *n.* [*pl.* STRIAE (-ē)], [L.], 1. a narrow groove or channel. 2. a ridge or fillet, as between the flutings of a stone column. 3. a fine streak or line; especially, one of a number of parallel lines.

stri·ate (strī'āt; *for adj., usually* strī'it), *v.t.* [STRIATED (-id), STRIATING], [< L. *striatus,* grooved, furrowed, pp. of *striare,* to groove, channel < *stria,* a groove], to mark with striae. *adj.* striated.

stri·at·ed (strī'āt-id), *adj.* [pp. of *striate*], marked with striae.

stri·a·tion (strī-ā'shən), *n.* 1. the condition of having striae; striated pattern, appearance, etc. 2. the arrangement of striae. 3. a stria.

strick·en (strik'ən), occasional past participle of **strike.** *adj.* 1. struck or wounded, as by a missile. 2. afflicted or affected, as by something disagreeable, painful, or overwhelming. 3. having the contents level with the top: said of a measure or container.

strick·le (strik''l), *n.* [ME. *strikile;* AS. *stricel* < base in *strican,* to hit (cf. STRIKE)], 1. a stick used to level the top of a measure of grain. 2. a tool used for sharpening a scythe, etc. 3. in *founding,* a bevel-edged finishing tool used in shaping molds in sand, etc. *v.t.* [STRICKLED (-'ld), STRICKLING], to use a strickle on.

strict (strikt), *adj.* [L. *strictus,* pp. of *stringere,* to draw tight, compress; cf. STRINGENT], 1. exact; accurate; precise; not loose or vague. 2. perfect; absolute; entire. 3. *a)* allowing no difference or deviation; following or enforcing a rule or rules with great care; punctilious. *b)* closely enforced; rigorous. 4. [Obs.], close; tight.

SYN.—**strict,** in this connection, implies exact, undeviating conformity to standards, rules, conditions, etc. (the *strict* interpretation of a law); **rigid** implies an unyielding inflexibility often connoting excessive firmness (*rigid* rules); **rigorous** implies such uncompromising strictness as to impose hardships or difficulties (*rigorous* discipline); **stringent** implies such strictness as to limit, bind, curb, or confine (a *stringent* censorship code). —*ANT.* lax, flexible.

stric·tion (strik'shən), *n.* [L. *strictio;* cf. STRICT], constriction.

stric·ture (strik'chẽr), *n.* [ME. *strictture;* L. *strictura* < *strictus,* pp. of *stringere,* to draw tight, compress], 1. adverse criticism; censure. 2. [Rare], a binding, closing, or contraction. 3. [Obs.], strictness. 4. in *medicine,* a stenosis, or narrowing of a passage in the body.

stride (strīd), ***v.i.*** [STRODE (strōd) or *obs.* STRID (strid), STRIDDEN (strid'n) or *obs.* STRID, STRIDING (strīd'iŋ)], [ME. *striden;* AS. *stridan;* akin to G. *streiten,* to quarrel; IE. base **ster-*, to be stiff, rigid, etc.; cf. STARK, STARVE, STRETCH, etc.], 1. to walk with long steps, especially in a vigorous or pompous manner. 2. to take a single, long step, as in passing over something. 3. [Rare], to sit or stand astride. ***v.t.*** 1. to take a single, long step in passing over (an obstacle, etc.). 2. to stride along or through: as, they *strode* the street. 3. to sit or stand astride of; straddle. ***n.*** 1. the act of striding. 2. a long step. 3. a forward movement by a four-legged animal, completed when the legs return to their original relative positions. 4. the distance covered in such a step. 5. *usually pl.* progress; advancement.

hit one's stride, to reach one's normal speed or level of efficiency.

take in one's stride, to do or cope with easily and without undue effort or hesitation.

stri·dence (strī'd'ns), ***n.*** the quality of being strident or the degree of this.

stri·den·cy (strī'd'n-si), ***n.*** stridence.

stri·dent (strī'd'nt), ***adj.*** [L. *stridens,* ppr. of *stridere,* to make a grating noise, rasp; cf. STRICT], harsh-sounding; shrill; grating; creaking. —***SYN.*** see **vociferous.**

stri·dor (strī'dẽr), ***n.*** [L. < *stridere,* to rasp, whistle], 1. a strident sound. 2. in *medicine,* a harsh, high-pitched whistling sound produced in breathing by an obstruction in the bronchi, trachea, or larynx.

strid·u·lant (strij'oo-lənt), ***adj.*** stridulating.

strid·u·late (strij'oo-lāt'), ***v.i.*** [STRIDULATED (-id), STRIDULATING], [< Mod. L. *stridulatus,* pp. of *stridulare* < L. *stridulus* (see STRIDULOUS)], to make a shrill grating or chirping sound, as certain insects.

strid·u·la·tion (strij'oo-lā'shən), ***n.*** the act or sound of stridulating.

strid·u·lous (strij'oo-ləs), ***adj.*** [L. *stridulus* < *stridere,* to rasp, hiss, rattle; cf. STRIDENT], making a shrill grating or chirping sound.

strife (strīf), ***n.*** [ME. *strif;* OFr. *estrif* < *estriver;* see STRIVE], 1. the act of striving or vying with another; contention; competition. 2. a quarrel; struggle; conflict. 3. [Archaic], strong endeavor. —***SYN.*** see **discord.**

strig·il (strij'əl), ***n.*** [L. *strigilis*], 1. an instrument of bone, metal, etc. used by the ancient Greeks and Romans for scraping the skin after a bath. 2. in *Roman architecture,* one of a series of wavelike decorative flutings.

stri·gose (strī'gōs, stri-gōs'), ***adj.*** [Mod. L. *strigosus* < L. *striga,* a furrow], 1. in *botany,* having stiff hairs or bristles, as some leaves. 2. in *zoology,* having fine, close-set grooves or streaks.

strike (strīk), ***v.t.*** [STRUCK (struk), STRUCK or *occas.* STRICKEN (strik'n) or *obs.* STROOK (strook), STRUCKEN (struk'n), STRIKING], [ME. *striken,* to proceed, flow, strike with rod or sword; AS. *strican,* to go, proceed, advance; akin to G. *streichen;* IE. **streig-*, as also in L. *stringere* (cf. STRINGENT), *strigilis* (cf. STRIGIL)], 1. to hit with the hand or a tool, weapon, etc. in or as in the hand; smite; specifically, *a*) to give a blow to; hit with force: as, he *struck* the nail with a hammer. *b*) to give (a blow, etc.). *c*) to separate, take off, take away, etc. by or as by a blow: as, they *struck* the gun from his hand. *d*) to make or impress by stamping, punching, printing, etc.: as, a mint *strikes* coins. *e*) to harpoon or shoot (a whale). *f*) to hook (a fish that has risen to the bait) by a pull on the line. 2. to produce (a tone, etc.) by hitting a key on a musical instrument. 3. to announce (time), as by causing a hammer to hit a bell: said of clocks, etc. 4. to cause to come into violent or forceful contact; specifically, *a*) to cause to hit something; dash; cast: as, she *struck* her elbow against the door. *b*) to bring forcefully into contact: as, he *strikes* the cymbals together. *c*) to cause to ignite by friction: as, he *struck* a match; hence, 5. to produce (a light, etc.) by friction. 6. to come into violent or forceful contact with; crash into; hit: as, the stone *struck* his head, the lightning *struck* the chimney. 7. to wound with the fangs: said of snakes. 8. to attack. 9. to come into contact with; specifically, *a*) to fall on; shine on: as, the light *struck* the windows. *b*) to catch or reach (the ear): said of a sound. *c*) to come upon; arrive at: as, we *struck* the main road. *d*) to notice, find, or hit upon suddenly or unexpectedly. *e*) to discover; find after drilling or prospecting: as, they *struck* oil. *f*) to appear to: as, what a sight *struck* my eyes. 10. to affect as if by contact, a blow, etc.; specifically, *a*) to come into the mind of; occur to: as, the idea just *struck* me. *b*) to be attractive to; impress (one's fancy, sense of humor, etc.). *c*) to seem to: as, that *strikes* me as rather silly. *d*) to cause to become suddenly: as, he was *struck* dumb. *e*) to influence, inspire, or overcome suddenly with strong feeling: as, they were *struck* with amazement. *f*) to cause (a feeling, emotion, etc.) to come suddenly; arouse: as, the scream *struck* terror to my heart. 11. *a*) to make and ratify (a bargain, agreement, truce, etc.). *b*) to arrive at by figuring, estimating, etc.: as, they *struck* a balance. 12. to lower or haul down (a sail, flag, etc.): sailors formerly *struck* sails in protest of grievances, to prevent a ship from sailing; hence, 13. [derived from the prec. via obs. sense "to put (tools) out of use" in protest of grievances], to refuse to continue to work at (a factory, etc.) until certain demands have been met. 14. *a*) originally, to stroke or smooth; hence, *b*) to level (a measure of grain, sand mold, etc.) by stroking the top with a straight instrument; strickle. 15. to assume (an attitude, pose, etc.), as by a sudden movement. 16. *a*) to send down or put forth (roots): said of plants, etc.; hence, *b*) to cause (cuttings, etc.) to take root. 17. [Slang], to borrow from or make an urgent request of: now usually *hit, touch.* 18. [Obs.], to wage (battle). 19. [cf. 12], in the *theater, a*) to dismantle and remove (a scene). *b*) to remove the scenery of (a play). *c*) to turn (a light) down or off. ***v.i.*** 1. to deliver a blow or blows. 2. to aim a blow or blows: as, I *struck* at the ball, but missed. 3. to attack: as, the enemy *struck* at dawn. 4. *a*) to make a sound or sounds as by being struck: as, the bell, clock, etc. is *striking;* hence, *b*) to be announced by the striking of a bell, etc.: as, three o'clock had *struck.* 5. to make sudden and violent contact; hit; collide (with *against, on,* or *upon*): as, the ball *struck* against the house. 6. to ignite or be capable of igniting: as, this match won't *strike.* 7. to seize or snatch at a bait: said of a fish. 8. to make a darting movement in an attempt to inflict a wound: said of a snake, tiger, etc. 9. to penetrate; pierce: as, the wind *struck* through the cracks. 10. to come suddenly or unexpectedly; fall, light, etc. (with *on* or *upon*): as, we *struck* on the right combination. 11. to lower sail. 12. to haul down one's flag in token of surrender. 13. to refuse to continue to work until certain demands are met; go on strike. 14. to send out roots; take root: said of a plant. 15. to advance or proceed, especially in a new direction; turn: as, they *struck* northward. 16. to move or pass quickly; dart. ***n.*** 1. a striking; blow. 2. a strickle. 3. *a*) a concerted refusal by employees to go on working in an attempt to force an employer to grant certain demands, as for higher wages, better working conditions, collective bargaining, etc. *b*) any similar refusal by a group of people to do something: as, a buyers' *strike.* 4. a finding of a rich deposit of oil, coal, minerals, etc.; hence, 5. any sudden success, especially one bringing large financial return. 6. the act or evidence of a fish's seizing or snatching at bait: as, I just got a *strike!* 7. the number of coins, medals, etc. struck at one time. 8. the metal piece on a doorjamb into which the latch fits when the door is shut. 9. in *baseball,* a pitched ball which is *a*) struck at but missed. *b*) fairly delivered but not struck at. *c*) hit foul but not caught (unless there are already two strikes.) *d*) on a third strike, hit as a foul tip caught by the catcher: three strikes put the batter out. 10. in *bowling, a*) the act of knocking down all the pins on the first bowl. *b*) the score made in this way. 11. in *geology & mining,* the trace of a rock bed, fault, or vein on the horizontal.

be struck with, to be attracted to or impressed by.

have two strikes against one, [Colloq.], to be at a decided disadvantage: from the three strikes permitted a batter in baseball.

(out) on strike, striking (*v.i.* 13).

strike camp, to break up or abandon a camp by taking down tents, etc.

strike down, 1. to cause to fall by a blow, etc.; knock down. 2. to have a disastrous or disabling effect upon: said of illness, etc.

strike dumb, to amaze; astound; astonish.

strike hands, 1. to show agreement by clasping hands; hence, 2. to make a bargain, contract, etc.

strike home, 1. to deliver an effective or crippling blow. 2. to achieve a desired or significant effect.

strike in, to interrupt or interpose.

strike it rich, 1. to discover a rich deposit of ore, oil, etc. 2. to become rich or successful suddenly.

strike off, 1. to separate or remove by or as by a blow. 2. to remove from a record, etc.; erase; expunge. 3. to print from set type.

strike out, 1. to make by hitting or striking. 2. to originate; produce; devise. 3. to aim or strike a blow; hit out. 4. to remove from a record, etc.; erase; expunge. 5. to begin moving or acting; start out. 6. in *baseball, a*) to be put out as the result of three strikes. *b*) to put (a batter) out by pitching three strikes.

strike up, 1. to begin playing, singing, sounding, etc. 2. to begin (a friendship, etc.). 3. to emboss (metal, decorative figures, etc.).

SYN.—**strike** and **hit** are more or less interchangeable in meaning to deliver a blow to or toward someone or something (he *struck,* or *hit,* the boy), but each is more frequently used in certain connections than the other (lightning *struck* the barn, he *hit* the bull's-eye); **punch** implies a hitting with or as with the closed fist (to *punch* one on the jaw); **slap** implies a hitting with or as with the palm of the hand (to *slap* one's face); **smite,** a literary or rhetorical word, emphasizes the force used in striking or hitting (he will *smite* you dead); **knock** implies either a hitting so as to displace (he *knocked* the vase from the table) or a repeated striking (he *knocked* at the window).

strike·break·er (strīk′brāk′ẽr), *n.* a person who engages in strikebreaking, as by working as a scab, supplying scabs for the employer, intimidating strikers, etc.
strike·break·ing (strīk′brāk′iŋ), *n.* the act of trying to break up or frustrate a workers' strike.
strike-out (strīk′out′), *n.* in *baseball*, a striking out.
strik·er (strīk′ẽr), *n.* 1. a person who strikes; specifically, *a*) a worker who is on strike. *b*) an assistant who does the hammering for a blacksmith. *c*) a harpooner. 2. a thing that strikes, as the clapper in a bell, the striking device in a clock, the firing pin in a gun, etc. 3. in the *United States Army*, an enlisted man employed as an officer's servant or orderly.
strik·ing (strīk′iŋ), *adj.* 1. that strikes or is on strike. 2. extraordinary; remarkable. —*SYN.* see **noticeable.**
Strind·berg, Au·gust (ou′gust strin′bar′y′; Eng. strind′bẽrg, strin′bẽrg), 1849–1912; Swedish novelist and dramatist.
string (striŋ), *n.* [ME. *string, streng;* AS. *streng;* akin to G. *strang;* for IE. base see STRONG], 1. *a*) a thin line of twisted fiber, or a very thin strip or length of wire, leather, etc., used for tying, pulling, fastening, etc.; small cord; thick thread; very thin rope; twine. *b*) a narrow strip of leather or cloth for fastening shoes, clothing, etc.; lace: as, an apron *string*, boot *string*. 2. a number of objects threaded, strung, or hung on a string: as, a *string* of pearls. 3. a number of things arranged as though on a string; line of things in succession: as, a *string* of houses. 4. a group of players or athletes arranged according to ability: as, the players of the second *string* will play the varsity. 5. *a*) a slender cord of wire, gut, nylon, etc. stretched on a musical instrument, as a violin, harp, piano, etc., and bowed, plucked, or struck to make a musical sound. *b*) *pl.* all the stringed instruments of an orchestra, especially those played with a bow. *c*) *pl.* the players of such instruments. Abbreviated **str.** (*sing.* & *pl.*). 6. a strong, slender organ, formation, etc. resembling a string; specifically, *a*) [Obs.], an animal nerve or tendon. *b*) a fiber of a plant, especially one connecting the two halves of a pod. 7. [Colloq.], a condition, limitation, or proviso attached to a plan, offer, donation, etc. 8. in *architecture*, *a*) any of the notched sides of a stair, supporting the treads. *b*) a stringcourse. 9. in *billiards*, *a*) a line across the table at one end, from behind which the cue ball must be played after being out of play: in full, **string line.** *b*) the act of stroking the cue ball so that it rebounds from the far cushion to stop as close as possible to the string line, for determining the order of play. 10. in *horse racing*, a number of horses belonging to one owner. *v.t.* [STRUNG (struŋ), STRUNG or *rare* STRINGED (striŋd), STRINGING], 1. to provide with strings. 2. to put on a string; thread or bead on a string. 3. to tie, pull, fasten, hang, lace, etc. with a string or strings. 4. to adjust or tune the strings of (a musical instrument) by tightening, etc.; hence, 5. to tighten; brace; strengthen. 6. to make excited, tense, or nervous. 7. to remove the strings (sense 6*b*) from (beans, etc.). 8. to arrange in a row. 9. to stretch like a string; extend: as, *string* a cable. 10. [Colloq.], to fool; hoax; josh (often with *along*). *v.i.* 1. to form into a string or strings. 2. to stretch out in a line; extend; stretch; move or progress in a string.
on a string, in a completely dependent condition; helpless; under control.
pull strings, 1. to get someone to use influence in one's behalf, often secretly. 2. to direct action of others, often secretly.
string along with, to follow faithfully; adhere to; be faithful to; have confidence in.
string up, [Colloq.], to kill by hanging.
string bean, 1. any of a number of varieties of bean having thick, meaty pods eaten as a vegetable when still unripe. 2. the pod of any of these plants.
string·board (striŋ′bôrd′, striŋ′bōrd′), *n.* a board placed along the side of a staircase to support the ends of the steps.
string·course (striŋ′kôrs′, striŋ′kōrs′), *n.* a decorative, horizontal band or molding set in the wall of a building.
stringed (striŋd), rare past participle of **string.** *adj.* 1. having strings, as certain musical instruments. 2. produced by strings: as, *stringed* music. 3. tied or fastened with strings.
strin·gen·cy (strin′jən-si), *n.* [*pl.* STRINGENCIES (-siz)], the quality or state of being stringent; specifically, *a*) strictness; severity. *b*) scarcity: said of money, as in the market. *c*) a convincing quality, as in debate.
‡**strin·gen·do** (strĕn-jen′dô), *adj.* [It. < L. *stringens;* see STRINGENT], in *music*, accelerating the tempo, as toward a climax: a direction to the performer.
strin·gent (strin′jənt), *adj.* [L. *stringens*, ppr. of *stringere*, to draw tight; cf. STRICT, STRIKE], 1. strict; severe. 2. short in loan or investment money: said of a market. 3. compelling; convincing. —*SYN.* see **strict.**
string·er (striŋ′ẽr), *n.* 1. a person or thing that strings. 2. a long piece of timber used as a support; specifically, *a*) a horizontal timber connecting upright posts in a frame. *b*) a stringpiece. *c*) in *railroading*, a lengthwise timber for supporting a rail.
string·halt (striŋ′hôlt′), *n.* [altered < *springhalt*], a condition in horses causing the hind legs to jerk spasmodically in walking: also **springhalt.**
string·i·ness (striŋ′i-nis), *n.* the quality of being stringy.
string·piece (striŋ′pēs′), *n.* a long, horizontal timber for supporting a framework, as at the edge of a floor.
string quartet, 1. a quartet of players on stringed instruments, usually comprising first and second violins, a viola, and a violoncello. 2. a composition to be performed by such a group.
string tie, a narrow necktie, usually tied in a bow.
string·y (striŋ′i), *adj.* [STRINGIER (-i-ẽr), STRINGIEST (-i-ist)], 1. like a string or strings; long, thin, wiry, etc. 2. consisting of strings or fibers. 3. having tough fibers, as meat, celery, etc.; fibrous. 4. forming strings; viscous; ropy: as, *stringy* molasses.
strip (strip), *v.t.* [STRIPPED or *rare* STRIPT (stript), STRIPPING], [ME. *stripen, strepen;* AS. *strypan* (in comp.), *bestrypan*, to plunder; akin to G. *streipen*, to strip off (OHG. *stroufen*, to flay); IE. base **strei-b-;* cf. Eng. *strike*], 1. *a*) to remove the clothing or covering of (a person); make naked; undress. *b*) to remove (the clothing, covering, etc.) from a person: as, he *stripped* the shirt from his back. 2. *a*) to deprive or dispossess (a person or thing) of honors, titles, attributes, etc. *b*) to remove or take (honors, attributes, etc.) from a person or thing. *c*) to plunder; spoil; make destitute; rob. 3. *a*) to pull, tear, or take off (a covering, skin, etc.). *b*) to pull, tear, or take off the covering, skin, etc. of. 4. to make bare or clear by removing fruit, growth, removable parts, etc.: as, we *stripped* the room of furniture, the locusts *stripped* the fields. 5. to take apart (a firearm, etc.) piece by piece, as for cleaning; dismantle. 6. to break or jam the thread of (a nut, bolt, or screw). 7. to break off the teeth of (a gear). 8. to remove the last milk from (a cow) with a stroking movement of the thumb and forefinger. 9. to remove the large central rib from (tobacco leaves). *v.i.* to take off all clothing; undress.

SYN.—**strip** implies the pulling or tearing off of clothing, outer covering, etc. and often connotes forcible or even violent action and total deprivation (to *strip* paper off a wall, *stripped* of sham); **denude** implies that the thing stripped is left exposed or naked (land *denuded* of vegetation); **divest** implies the taking away of something with which one has been clothed or invested (an official *divested* of authority); **bare** simply implies an uncovering or laying open to view (to *bare* one's head in reverence); **dismantle** implies the act of stripping a house, ship, etc. of all of its furniture or equipment (a *dismantled* factory).

strip (strip), *n.* [altered < *stripe* by association with *strip, v.*], 1. a long, narrow piece, as of land, ribbon, wood, etc. 2. a comic strip. 3. a long narrow runway for the take-off and landing of airplanes, usually laid out in the direction of the prevailing wind: also **airstrip, landing strip.** 4. in *philately*, a vertical or horizontal row of three or more attached stamps. *v.t.* to cut or tear into strips.
strip cropping, crop planting in which strips of heavy-rooted and loose-rooted plants are alternated to lessen erosion, as on a hillside.
stripe (strīp), *n.* [< a LG. source; cf. MLG. & MD. *stripe;* akin to Eng. *strip*], 1. a long, narrow band, mark, or streak, differing in color, texture, or material from the surrounding area. 2. a long welt on the skin, as from a whipping. 3. a stroke with a whip, etc. 4. any of various strips of cloth or braid worn on the sleeve of a military uniform or the like to indicate rank, length of service, wounds, etc. 5. a distinctive mark or color. 6. type; kind; sort. *v.t.* [STRIPED (strīpt), STRIPING], to mark with a stripe or stripes.
striped (strīpt, strī′pid), *adj.* [pp. of *stripe*], having a stripe or stripes.
striped squirrel, a chipmunk.
strip·er (strīp′ẽr), *n.* [Military Slang], any enlisted man, or a naval officer, who wears a stripe or stripes (sense 4): usually in hyphenated compounds, meaning *one wearing* (a specified number of) *stripes*, as a *four-striper.*
strip·ling (strip′liŋ), *n.* [ME. *strypling*, lit., one slim as a strip], a grown boy; youth passing into manhood.
strip mining, a method of mining, especially for coal, by laying bare a mineral deposit near the surface of the earth, instead of by sinking a shaft.
strip·per (strip′ẽr), *n.* a person or thing that strips; specifically, [Slang], a woman who does a strip tease.
strip planting, strip cropping.
stript (stript), rare past tense and past participle of **strip.**
strip tease, a performance, as in burlesque shows, in which a woman takes off her clothes piece by piece, usually to the accompaniment of music.

strip·y (strīp′i), *adj.* [STRIPIER (-i-ẽr), STRIPIEST (-i-ist)], striped.
strive (strīv), *v.i.* [STROVE (strōv) or *less often* STRIVED (strīvd), STRIVEN (striv′′n) or STRIVED, STRIVING], [ME. *striven;* OFr. *estriver*, to quarrel, contend < *estrif*, effort (see STRIFE)], 1. to make great efforts; try very hard: as, they *strove* to win. 2. to be in conflict; struggle; contend; fight: as, *strive* against oppression. 3. [Obs.], to compete; vie. —*SYN.* see **try.**
strob·il (strob′il), *n.* a strobile.
strob·i·la·ceous (strob′ə-lā′shəs), *adj.* in *botany*, 1. relating to or resembling a strobile. 2. having strobiles.
strob·ile (strob′il), *n.* [< Fr. or LL.; Fr. *strobile;* LL. *strobilus;* Gr. *strobilos*, anything twisted, pine cone < base of *strephein*, to twist], 1. a conelike mass of closely packed, scalelike, spore-bearing leaves, as of the horsetail. 2. a seed-bearing cone, as of the pine.
strob·o·scope (strob′ə-skōp′), *n.* [< Gr. *strobos*, a twisting round; + *-scope*], an instrument for studying periodic or varying motion by illuminating a moving body at frequent, rapid intervals.
strob·o·scop·ic (strob′ə-skop′ik), *adj.* of, or having the nature of, a stroboscope.
strob·o·scop·i·cal (strob′ə-skop′i-k′l), *adj.* stroboscopic.
strode (strōd), past tense of **stride.**
stroke (strōk), *n.* [ME. *stroke, strok;* AS. **strac-* < *strican*, to hit, etc. (cf. STRIKE); akin to G. *streich*], 1. a striking of one thing against another; blow or impact of an ax, whip, etc. 2. *a*) a sudden action resulting in a powerful or destructive effect, as if from a blow: as, a *stroke* of lightning. *b*) any action having an immediate effect, often a pleasant one: as, a *stroke* of luck. 3. any sudden attack of disease or illness, especially of apoplexy or paralysis. 4. *a*) a single effort to do, produce, or accomplish something, especially a successful effort. *b*) something accomplished by such an effort. 5. *a*) the sound of striking, as of a clock. *b*) the time indicated by this: as, he arrived at the *stroke* of nine. 6. *a*) a single movement of the arms, hands, etc. or of an instrument in the hands, especially such a movement as for striking the ball in tennis, golf, billiards, etc. *b*) any of a series of repeated rhythmic motions made against water, air, etc.: as, the *stroke* of a swimmer, rower, etc.; hence, *c*) a type, manner, or rate of such movement: as, a slow *stroke*. *d*) a single movement of a pen or similar marking tool. 7. a mark made by or as by a pen or similar marking tool. 8. a beat of the heart. 9. a gentle, caressing motion with the hand. 10. in *mechanics*, any of a series of continuous, often reciprocating, movements; specifically, a single movement of a piston from one end of its range to the other, constituting a half revolution of the engine. 11. in *rowing*, *a*) the rower who sits nearest the stern and sets the rate of rowing for the others. *b*) the position occupied by this rower. *v.t.* [STROKED (strōkt), STROKING], [ME. *stroken, strokien;* AS. *stracian* < p.t. base of *strican* (cf. STRIKE)], 1. to draw one's hand, a tool, etc. gently over the surface of, as in caressing. 2. to set the rate of rowing for (a crew).
keep stroke, to make strokes in rhythm.
stroke oar, 1. the oar set nearest the stern. 2. the oarsman who operates this oar, usually setting the pace for the other oarsmen.
stroll (strōl), *v.i.* [Early Mod. Eng. *stroll, strowl;* prob. < Swiss G. military slang *strollen, strolchen*], 1. to walk in an idle, leisurely manner; saunter. 2. to go idly from place to place; wander. *v.t.* to stroll along or through (the countryside, etc.). *n.* the act of strolling; leisurely walk.
stroll·er (strōl′ẽr), *n.* 1. a person who saunters. 2. a person who wanders from place to place, as an itinerant actor. 3. a vagrant. 4. a small cart with openings for the legs, in which an infant can stand supported while learning to walk. 5. a light baby carriage.
stro·ma (strō′mə), *n.* [*pl.* STROMATA (-mə-tə)], [L., coverlet, bed covering; Gr. *strōma*, mattress, bed], in *anatomy*, 1. the connective tissue forming the framework or matrix of an organ or part. 2. the colorless framework of a red blood corpuscle or other cell.
stro·mat·ic (strō-mat′ik), *adj.* of, or having the nature of, a stroma.
Strom·bo·li (strôm′bô-lē′), *n.* one of the Lipari Islands in the Mediterranean, north of Sicily.
stro·mey·er·ite (strō′mī′ẽr-īt′), *n.* [after Friedrich *Stromeyer*, 19th-c. G. chemist; + *-ite*], a lustrous, steel-gray mineral, $(Ag, Cu)_2S$, sulfide of silver and copper.
strong (strôŋ), *adj.* [ME. *stronge, strang;* AS. *strang, strong;* akin to ON. *strangr*, strong, severe &, more remotely, to G. *streng*, severe; IE. base **strenk-*, **streng-*, tense, taut, as also in L. *stringere*, to draw taut; cf. STRING, STRINGENT], 1. *a*) physically powerful; having great muscular strength; robust. *b*) in a healthy and sound condition; hale; hearty: as, I feel *stronger* today. 2. morally powerful; having strength of character or will. 3. *a*) intellectually powerful; able to think vigorously and clearly. *b*) having special competency or ability (*in* a specified subject or field): as, he's *strong* in chemistry. 4. powerfully made or built; tough; firm; durable: as, a *strong* wall. 5. hard to capture; easily defended; able to resist and endure attack: as, a *strong* fort. 6. having many resources; powerful in wealth, numbers, supplies, etc.: as, a *strong* army. 7. having a specified number or amount; reaching a certain degree in number or strength: as, a task force 6,000 *strong*. 8. having a powerful effect; vigorously effective; drastic: as, *strong* measures. 9. having a large amount of its essential quality; not weak or diluted: as, *strong* coffee. 10. affecting the senses powerfully; intense in taste, flavor, etc.: as, a *strong* light, *strong* smell, etc. 11. having an offensive taste or smell; rank: as, *strong* butter. 12. firm and loud: as, a *strong* voice. 13. intense in degree or quality; not mild; specifically, *a*) ardent; passionate; warm: as, *strong* affection. *b*) forceful; persuasive; cogent. *c*) felt deeply; pronounced; decided: as, a *strong* opinion. *d*) zealous; vigorously active: as, a *strong* Democrat. *e*) vigorous, forthright, and unambiguous, often offensively so: as, *strong* language. *f*) clear; distinct; marked: as, a *strong* resemblance. 14. moving rapidly and with force: as, a *strong* wind. 15. characterized by rapidly rising prices: as, a *strong* market. 16. in English and other Germanic languages, designating or of those verbs expressing variation in tense by internal change of vowel rather than by the addition of inflectional endings, as *swim, swam, swum*: also called *irregular*: opposed to *weak*. *adv.* in a strong manner; greatly; severely; with force.
SYN.—**strong** is the broadest in scope of these terms, implying power that can be exerted actively as well as power that resists destruction (a *strong* body, fortress, etc.); **stout** implies ability to stand strain, pressure, wear, etc. without breaking down or giving way (a *stout* rope, heart, etc.); **sturdy** suggests the strength of that which is solidly developed or built and hence difficult to shake, weaken, etc. (*sturdy* oaks, faith, etc.); **tough** suggests the strength of that which is firm and resistant in consistency or character (*tough* leather, opposition, etc.); **stalwart** stresses staunchness or reliability (a *stalwart* supporter).—*ANT.* weak.
strong-arm (strôŋ′ärm′), *adj.* [Colloq.], using physical force. *v.t.* [Colloq.], to use physical force upon.
strong·bark (strôŋ′bärk′), *n.* a small tree of Florida and the West Indies, with strong, hard, orange-streaked, brown wood.
strong·box (strôŋ′boks′), *n.* a heavily made box or safe for storing valuables.
strong drink, drink containing much alcohol.
strong·hold (strôŋ′hōld′), *n.* a place having strong defenses; fortified place; fortress; secure refuge.
strong-mind·ed (strôŋ′min′did), *adj.* having a strong, unyielding mind or will; determined.
strong·room (strôŋ′rōōm′, strôŋ′room′), *n.* a strongly built room used for the safekeeping of valuables.
strong-willed (strôŋ′wild′), *adj.* strong-minded.
stron·gyle, stron·gyl (stron′jil), *n.* [Mod. L. *Strongylus*, type genus < Gr. *strongylos*, round], any of various roundworms living as parasites in man and animals and causing severe damage or death.
stron·gy·lo·sis (stron′ji-lō′sis), *n.* [Mod. L.], the condition of being infested by strongyles.
stron·ti·a (stron′shi-ə), *n.* [Mod. L. < *strontium*], 1. the oxide of strontium, SrO, a white powder somewhat like lime. 2. loosely, strontium hydroxide, $Sr(OH)_2$.
stron·ti·an (stron′shi-ən, stron′shən), *n.* [see STRONTIUM], strontium, especially in the form of a compound.
stron·ti·an·ite (stron′shi-ən-īt′), *n.* [*strontian* + *-ite*], native strontium carbonate, $SrCO_3$, a white, greenish, or yellowish mineral.
stron·tic (stron′tik), *adj.* of strontium.
stron·ti·um (stron′shi-əm), *n.* [Mod. L. < *Strontian*, Argyllshire, Scotland, where it was first found], a pale-yellow, metallic chemical element resembling calcium in properties and found only in combination: strontium compounds burn with a red flame and are used in fireworks: a deadly radioactive isotope of strontium (**strontium 90**) is present in the fallout of atomic-weapon explosions: symbol, Sr; at. wt. 87.63; at. no., 38.
strook (strook), obsolete past participle of **strike.**
strop (strop), *n.* [ME. *stroppe;* AS. (akin to G. *strüpfe*) < L. *struppus*, band; cf. STRAP], 1. a strip of leather; strap. 2. a device used for putting a fine edge on razors: strops are made of leather, leather-covered wood, or specially treated cloth. *v.t.* [STROPPED (stropt), STROPPING], to sharpen on a strop.
stro·phan·thin (strō-fan′thin), *n.* [< Mod. L. *Strophanthus*, type genus < Gr. *strophē*, a turning (see STROPHE) + *anthos*, flower; + *-in*], a white or pale-yellow poisonous crystalline compound, $C_{31}H_{48}O_{12}$, used as a heart stimulant.
stro·phe (strō′fi), *n.* [Gr. *strophē*, a turning, twist < *strephein*, to turn], 1. in the ancient Greek theater, *a*) the movement of the chorus in turning from right to left of the stage. *b*) that part of a choric song performed during this. 2. in a Pindaric ode, the stanza which is answered by the antistrophe. 3. a stanza; especially, any of the irregular divisions of an ode, etc.
stroph·ic (strof′ik, strō′fik), *adj.* of or like a strophe.
stroph·i·cal (strof′i-k′l, strō′fi-k′l), *adj.* strophic.
stroph·u·lus (strof′yoo-ləs), *n.* [Mod. L., dim. < Gr.

strophos, twisted cord; cf. STROPHE], any of various mild forms of miliaria, especially common in children.
strove (strōv), alternative past tense of **strive**.
strow (strō), *v.t.* [STROWED (strōd), STROWN (strōn) or STROWED, STROWING], [Archaic], to strew.
struck (struk), past tense and past participle of **strike**. *adj.* closed or affected by a labor strike.
struck·en (struk'′n), obsolete past participle of **strike**.
struck jury, in *law*, a jury of 12 drawn from the panel of 24 names remaining after each side has been permitted to strike out 12 of the original list of 48 names.
struc·tur·al (struk′chẽr-əl), *adj.* 1. of, having, or characterized by structure, or formation. 2. of or resulting from changes in the structure of the earth's crust; tectonic. 3. used in construction or building.
struc·tur·al·ly (struk′chẽr-əl-i), *adv.* with reference to structure.
structural steel, steel prepared and shaped for use in the construction of buildings, bridges, etc.
struc·ture (struk′chẽr), *n.* [L. *structura* < *structus*, pp. of *struere*, to heap together, arrange; cf. STREW], 1. manner of building, constructing, or organizing. 2. something built or constructed, as a building or dam. 3. the arrangement or interrelation of all the parts of a whole; manner of organization or construction: as, they studied the *structure* of the atom, the *structure* of society. 4. something composed of parts: as, a plant is a complex *structure*. —*SYN.* see **building**.
stru·del (strōō′d'l; G. shtrōō′dəl), *n.* [G., lit., whirlpool, eddy, pancake], a kind of pastry made of a very thin sheet of dough filled with apples, cherries, cheese, etc. and rolled.
strug·gle (strug′′l), *v.i.* [STRUGGLED (-′ld), STRUGGLING], [ME. *strogelen*, a freq. formation, prob. partly echoic], 1. to contend or fight violently with an opponent. 2. to make great efforts or attempts; strive; labor: as, she *struggled* to overcome her prejudice. 3. to make one's way with difficulty: as, he *struggled* through the thicket. *v.t.* [Rare], to bring about, make, dispute, etc. by struggling. *n.* 1. great effort or series of efforts; violent exertion. 2. conflict; strife; contention. —*SYN.* see **conflict, try**.
struggle for existence, the competition among living organisms to survive in a given environment, especially as a factor in natural selection: see **natural selection**.
strum (strum), *v.t. & v.i.* [STRUMMED (strumd), STRUMMING], [echoic], 1. to pluck (a stringed musical instrument) carelessly, idly, or unskillfully. 2. to play (a tune) in this way. *n.* the act or sound of this.
Stru·ma (strōō′mä), *n.* a river flowing through southwestern Bulgaria and northeastern Greece, into the Aegean: length, 225 mi.
stru·ma (strōō′mə), *n.* [*pl.* STRUMAE (-mē)], [L., a scrofulous tumor < *struere*, to build], 1. in *botany*, a cushionlike swelling at the base of an organ. 2. in *medicine*, *a)* scrofula. *b)* goiter.
strum·mer (strum′ẽr), *n.* a person who strums.
stru·mose (strōō′mōs, strōō-mōs′), *adj.* [L. *strumosus*], 1. strumous. 2. in *botany*, having a struma.
stru·mous (strōō′məs), *adj.* [L. *strumosus*], in *medicine*, of, characteristic of, or having struma.
strum·pet (strum′pit), *n.* [ME.; ? connected with OFr. *strupe* (L. *stuprum*), dishonor], a prostitute; harlot.
strung (struŋ), past tense and alternative past participle of **string**.
strut (strut), *v.i.* [STRUTTED (-id), STRUTTING], [ME. *struten, strouten*, to spread out, swell out; AS. *strutian*, to stand rigid; IE. base **ster-*, to be stiff, rigid], to walk in a vain, stiff, swaggering manner. *v.t.* to provide with a strut or brace. *n.* 1. the act of strutting; vain, swaggering walk or gait. 2. a brace fitted into a framework to resist pressure in the direction of its length.
stru·thi·ous (strōō′thi-əs), *adj.* [< L. *struthio* (< Gr. *strouthion*, sparrow, ostrich); + *-ous*], designating or of any of a group of large, flightless birds including the ostriches, rheas, emus, etc.; specifically, of or like the African ostrich.
strych·ni·a (strik′ni-ə), *n.* [Mod. L. < L. *strychnos*], [Obs.], strychnine.
strych·nic (strik′nik), *adj.* of or resulting from strychnine.
strych·nin (strik′nin), *n.* strychnine.
strych·nine (strik′nin, strik′nēn, strik′nīn), *n.* [Fr. < L. *strychnos*; Gr. *strychnos*, nightshade], a highly poisonous, colorless, crystalline alkaloid, $C_{21}H_{22}N_2O_2$, obtained from nux vomica and related plants: it is used in small doses as a stimulant to the nervous system.
strych·nin·ism (strik′nin-iz'm), *n.* a diseased condition resulting from an overdose or improper use of strychnine.
St. Thomas, 1. an island of the United States in the Virgin Islands, West Indies: area, 32 sq. mi.; pop., 16,000. 2. Charlotte Amalie, the capital of the Virgin Islands: the former name. 3. São Tomé: the English name.
Stu·art (stōō′ẽrt, stū′ẽrt), [< the surname *Stuart*; ? < AS. *stigweard*, chamberlain (cf. STEWARD)], a masculine name: also spelled **Stewart**.
Stu·art (stōō′ẽrt, stū′ẽrt), *n.* the family that ruled in Scotland from 1371 to 1603 and in England and Scotland from 1603 to 1714 except during the Commonwealth (1649–1660).
Stuart, Charles Edward, see **Charles Edward Stuart**.
Stuart, Gilbert Charles, 1755–1828; American portrait painter.
Stuart, James E·well Brown (ū′′l), 1833–1864; American Confederate general: called *Jeb Stuart*.
stub (stub), *n.* [ME. *stubbe*; AS. *stubb, stybb*; akin to ON. *stubbr*; for IE. base see STEEP, *adj.*], 1. a tree stump. 2. a short piece or length remaining after the main part has been removed or used up: as, the *stub* of a tail, cigar, tree root, pencil, etc. 3. any short projection: as, a mere *stub* of a horn. 4. a pen having a short, blunt point. 5. a stub nail. 6. a short piece of a ticket, bank check, etc. kept as a record after the rest has been torn off. *v.t.* [STUBBED (stubd), STUBBING], 1. to dig or pull (weeds, etc.) out by the roots. 2. to clear (land) of stubs, or stumps. 3. to strike (one's foot, toe, etc.) against something by accident.
stubbed (stubd), *adj.* 1. like a stub; short; stubby. 2. covered with stubs or stumps. 3. stocky; hardy.
stub·bi·ness (stub′i-nis), *n.* the quality or condition of being stubby.
stub·ble (stub′′l), *n.* [ME. *stobil*; OFr. *estouble, stuble*; LL. **stupula*, for L. *stipula*, a stalk, stem], 1. the short stumps of grain, corn, etc. left standing after harvesting. 2. any growth like this: as, a *stubble* of beard.
stub·bled (stub′′ld), *adj.* covered with stubble.
stub·bly (stub′li), *adj.* [STUBBLIER (-li-ẽr), STUBBLIEST (-li-ist)], 1. covered with or composed of stubble. 2. like stubble; short and bristly.
stub·born (stub′ẽrn), *adj.* [ME. *stoburn, stiborne*; prob. < AS. *stubb, stybb*, a stub, stump; cf. STUB], 1. refusing to yield, obey, or comply; resisting doggedly; determined; obstinate. 2. done or carried on in a stubborn, obstinate, or persistent manner: as, a *stubborn* campaign. 3. hard to handle, treat, or deal with; intractable: as, a *stubborn* piece of oak.
SYN.—**stubborn** implies an innate fixedness of purpose, course, condition, etc. that is strongly resistant to change, manipulation, etc. (a *stubborn* child, belief, etc.); **obstinate** applies to one who adheres persistently, and often unreasonably, to his purpose, course, etc., against argument or persuasion (a panel hung by an *obstinate* juror); **dogged** implies thoroughgoing determination or, sometimes, sullen obstinacy (the *dogged* pursuit of a goal); **pertinacious** implies a strong tenacity of purpose that is regarded unfavorably by others (a *pertinacious* critic). —*ANT.* compliant, tractable, pliant.
Stubbs, William (stubz), 1825–1901; English historian, educator, and prelate; bishop of Oxford.
stub·by (stub′i), *adj.* [STUBBIER (-i-ẽr), STUBBIEST (-i-ist)], 1. covered with stubs or stubble. 2. short and heavy or dense: as, *stubby* bristles. 3. short and thickset; stocky.
stub nail, 1. a short, thick nail. 2. an old horseshoe nail, especially one broken off or worn down.
stuc·co (stuk′ō), *n.* [*pl.* STUCCOES, STUCCOS (-ōz)], [It.; prob. < OHG. *stucchi*, crust], 1. a kind of fine plaster or cement used for surfacing inside or outside walls, molding relief ornaments, cornices, etc. 2. stuccowork. *v.t.* to cover or decorate with stucco.
stuc·co·work (stuk′ō-wũrk′), *n.* work done in stucco.
stuck (stuk), past tense and past participle of **stick**.
stuck-up (stuk′up′), *adj.* [Colloq.], snobbish; conceited; haughty; arrogant.
stud (stud), *n.* [ME. *stode, stude*; AS. *studu*, column, pillar, post; akin to ON. *stoth*, G. *stützen*, to prop, support; IE. base **stā-*, to stand (cf. STAND)], 1. any of a series of small knobs or rounded nailheads used to ornament a surface, as of leather. 2. a small, double-headed, buttonlike device used as a collar fastener, shirt-front ornament, etc. 3. an upright piece in the frame of a building, to which horizontal boards or laths are nailed. 4. a metal crossbar bracing a link, as in a chain cable. 5. a projecting pin or peg used as a support, pivot, stop, etc. *v.t.* [STUDDED (-id), STUDDING], 1. to set or decorate with studs or studlike objects. 2. to be set thickly on; be scattered over: as, rocks *stud* the hillside. 3. to scatter or cluster (something) thickly: as, jewels *studded* on bracelets. 4. to provide (a building) with studs or upright members.
stud (stud), *n.* [ME. *stod, stode*; AS. *stod*; akin to G. *stute*, mare (OHG. *stuot*, stud of horses); for IE. base see prec.], 1. a collection of horses, especially a group kept for breeding. 2. the place where such horses are kept. 3. a studhorse. *adj.* 1. of or having to do with a stud: as, a *stud* farm. 2. kept for breeding.
at stud, available for breeding: said of male animals.
stud·book (stud′book′), *n.* a register of pedigreed horses, especially of race horses: also **stud book**.

stud·ding (stud′iŋ), *n.* 1. the studs of a building. 2. the material for these.

stud·ding·sail (stud′iŋ-sāl′; *in nautical usage,* stun′s'l), *n.* [? < D. *stooten,* to push, urge on; akin to G. *stossen,* to push; + *sail*], an auxiliary sail, usually of light canvas, set outside the edge of a working sail in light weather by means of an extensible boom: also **studding sail**: see **sail**, illus.

stu·dent (stōō′d'nt, stū′d'nt), *n.* [ME. *studiante, studente* < OFr. *estudiant;* L. *studens,* ppr. of *studere,* to be eager about, study], 1. a person who studies, or investigates: as, a *student* of human behavior. 2. a person who is enrolled for study at a school, college, etc. Abbreviated **stud.** —***SYN.*** see **pupil.**

student lamp, a reading lamp in which the direction of the light rays can be adjusted.

stu·dent·ship (stōō′d'nt-ship′, stū′d'nt-ship′), *n.* [see -SHIP], 1. a scholarship. 2. the state of being a student.

stud·horse (stud′hôrs′), *n.* a male horse kept for breeding; stallion.

stud·ied (stud′id), *adj.* 1. prepared or planned by careful study. 2. deliberate; premeditated: as, *studied* indifference. 3. [Rare], learned.

stu·di·o (stōō′di-ō′, stū′di-ō′), *n.* [*pl.* STUDIOS (-ōz′)], [It., a study], 1. a room, building, etc. in which an artist does his work. 2. a place where motion pictures are professionally produced. 3. a room or rooms especially designed for producing and transmitting radio or television programs.

studio couch, a kind of sofa that can be opened into a full-sized bed.

stu·di·ous (stōō′di-əs, stū′di-əs), *adj.* [ME. *studiouse;* L. *studiosus*], 1. fond of, or often engaged in, study. 2. characterized by careful heed or attention; thoughtful; zealous. 3. [Rare], studied; deliberate. 4. [Poetic], conducive to study.

stud poker, a variety of the game of poker in which each player is dealt five cards, the first face down and the others face up, the betting being done on each round of open cards dealt: sometimes seven cards are dealt, the first two, and often the last, face down.

stud·work (stud′wũrk′), *n.* work done with studs.

stud·y (stud′i), *n.* [*pl.* STUDIES (-iz)], [ME. *studie;* OFr. *estudie;* L. *studium,* a busying oneself about a thing, zeal, study < *studere,* to busy oneself about, apply oneself to, study], 1. the act or process of applying the mind in order to acquire knowledge, as by reading, investigating, etc. 2. careful attention to, and critical examination and investigation of, any subject, event, etc.: as, after *study* of the matter, the judge gave his decision, the *study* of human nature. 3. a branch of learning; department of knowledge. 4. *pl.* education; schooling. 5. a product of study (senses 1 & 2); specifically, *a*) an essay, monograph, or thesis embodying the results of a particular investigation. *b*) a work of literature or art treating a subject in careful detail and made primarily as an instructive exercise for the maker. *c*) a first sketch for a story, picture, etc. *d*) a short musical composition as an exercise in technique; étude. 6. an earnest effort; deliberate intention: as, his constant *study* is to do a job well. 7. abstracted state of mind; deep thought or mental absorption. 8. a room designed for study, writing, reading, etc., usually with books, a desk, and similar furnishings. 9. a person, especially an actor, with reference to his ability to memorize or learn: as, John is a quick *study.* ***v.t.*** [STUDIED (-id), STUDYING], 1. to apply one's mind to attentively; try to learn by reading, thinking, etc.: as, *study* history. 2. *a*) to examine or investigate carefully: as, I shall *study* your problem. *b*) to look at carefully; scrutinize: as, he *studied* the map. 3. to read (a book, lesson, etc.) so as to know and understand it; hence, 4. to memorize. 5. to take a course in, as at a school or college. 6. to pay attention to; give care and thought to: as, he *studies* to do the right thing. ***v.i.*** 1. to apply the mind in order to acquire knowledge. 2. to be a student; take a regular course in some branch of knowledge. 3. to meditate; ponder. —***SYN.*** see **consider.**

study hall, in some schools, a room where groups of students can study during free periods between classes.

stuff (stuf), *n.* [ME. *stoffe;* OFr. *estoffe* (Fr. *étoffe,* material); prob. < L. *stuppa,* tow (cf. STOP)], 1. the material or substance out of which anything is or can be made; raw material. 2. constituent elements; basic parts; essence; character: as, he is made of sterner *stuff* than his brother. 3. any kind of matter, indefinitely. 4. cloth, especially woolen cloth. 5. *a*) household goods. *b*) personal belongings. *c*) objects; things. 6. something to be drunk or swallowed; especially, a medicine or potion. 7. worthless objects; refuse; junk. 8. foolish or worthless ideas, words, etc.; nonsense: often used as an interjection expressing disagreement, derision, irritation, etc. ***v.t.*** [ME. *stoffen;* OFr. *estoffer* < *estoffe*], 1. to fill the inside of (something); pack; specifically, *a*) to fill (a cushion, chair, etc.) with padding or stuffing, as an upholsterer does. *b*) to fill the skin of (a dead animal, bird, etc.) as part of the process of mounting and preserving, as a taxidermist does. *c*) to fill (a chicken, turkey, etc.) with seasoning, bread crumbs, etc. before roasting. 2. *a*) to fill too full; cram; overload: as, the drawer is *stuffed* with papers. *b*) to fill to excess with food. 3. to fill with; pack or cram with; crowd in. 4. to fill with information, ideas, etc.: as, he *stuffed* his head with facts. 5. to put fraudulent votes into (a ballot box). 6. *a*) to plug; block. *b*) to choke; stop up, as with phlegm. 7. to force; push: as, he *stuffed* a handkerchief into his pocket. 8. to treat (leather) with a preparation of oil and tallow for preserving it. ***v.i.*** to eat too much or too quickly.

stuffed shirt (stuft), [Slang], a pompous, pretentious, but actually insignificant person.

stuff·i·ly (stuf′ə-li), *adv.* in a stuffy manner.

stuf·fi·ness (stuf′i-nis), *n.* the quality or condition of being stuffy.

stuff·ing (stuf′iŋ), *n.* 1. the action of filling, packing, or gorging. 2. something used to fill or stuff; specifically, *a*) soft, springy material used as padding in cushions, upholstered furniture, etc. *b*) a mixture, as of bread crumbs, seasoning, etc., for stuffing a fowl, roast, or the like before cooking.

stuffing box, a chamber that holds packing tightly around a moving part, as a piston rod, boat propeller shaft, etc., to prevent leakage of fluid along the part.

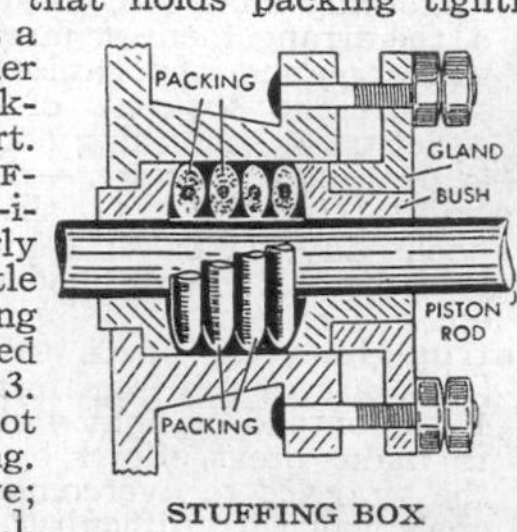

STUFFING BOX

stuf·fy (stuf′i), *adj.* [STUFFIER (-i-ẽr), STUFFIEST (-i-ist)], [*stuff* + *-y*], 1. poorly ventilated; having little fresh air; close. 2. having the nasal passages stopped up, as from a cold. 3. [Colloq.], dull; stodgy; not interesting or stimulating. 4. [Colloq.], conservative; old-fashioned. 5. [Colloq.], prim; strait-laced. 6. (Colloq.), sulky; obstinate.

Stu·ka (stōō′kə; G. shtōō′kä), *n.* [< G. *sturzkampfflugzeug; sturz,* a fall + *kampf,* a battle + *flugzeug,* aircraft], a German dive bomber of World War II.

stull (stul), *n.* [? < G. *stollen,* a support, prop], any of several kinds of supports or frameworks used in mines to prevent cave-ins, support a platform, etc.

stul·ti·fi·ca·tion (stul′tə-fi-kā′shən), *n.* a stultifying or being stultified.

stul·ti·fi·er (stul′tə-fi′ẽr), *n.* a person or thing that stultifies.

stul·ti·fy (stul′tə-fī′), *v.t.* [STULTIFIED (-fīd′), STULTIFYING], [LL. *stultificare* < L. *stultus,* foolish + *facere,* to make], 1. to cause to appear foolish, stupid, inconsistent, etc.; make absurd or ridiculous. 2. to cause to be of no effect; make worthless or useless: as, his present behavior *stultifies* his previous efforts. 3. in *law,* to allege (oneself or another) to be of unsound mind and, hence, not legally responsible.

stum (stum), *n.* [D. *stom,* must < *stom,* dumb; cf. Fr. *vin muet* & G. *stumm,* dumb], 1. grape juice that is unfermented or only partly fermented. 2. wine revived by the addition of stum to increase fermentation. ***v.t.*** [STUMMED (stumd), STUMMING], [D. *stommen;* see the *n.*], to revive (wine) by the addition of stum.

stum·ble (stum′b'l), *v.i.* [STUMBLED (-b'ld), STUMBLING], [ME. *stomblen, stomelen;* prob. < ON. **stumla* (cf. Norw. *stumla,* to stumble in the dark, etc.) < the base seen in *stammer*], 1. to trip or miss one's step in walking, running, etc. 2. to walk or go in an unsteady or awkward manner, as from age, weakness, etc. 3. to speak, act, or proceed in a confused, blundering manner: as, he *stumbled* through his recitation. 4. to fall into sin or error; do wrong. 5. to come by chance; happen: as, I *stumbled* across a clue. ***v.t.*** to cause to stumble. ***n.*** 1. the act of stumbling. 2. a blunder, error, or sin.

stumbling block, something that causes stumbling; obstacle, hindrance, or difficulty.

stump (stump), *n.* [ME. *stumpe, stompe;* prob. < ON. *stumpr* or the cognate MLG. *stump,* MD. *stomp;* base as in STUB], 1. the lower end of a tree or plant remaining in the ground after most of the stem or trunk has been cut off. 2. anything like a stump; specifically, *a*) the part of a limb or tooth left after the rest has been cut off, broken off, etc. *b*) the part of anything left after the main or important part has been removed, worn off, etc.; butt; stub: as, the *stump* of a pencil. 3. a short, stocky person or animal. 4. the place where a political speech is made; political rostrum: so called because speeches were originally made from tree stumps. 5. *a*) the sound of a heavy, clumsy, tramping step. *b*) such a step. 6. a pointed rubber stick or a heavy, pointed roll of paper used for shading charcoal or pencil drawings. 7. [Former Colloq.], a dare; challenge. 8. *pl.* [Slang], the legs. 9. in *cricket,* any of the three upright sticks of a wicket. ***v.t.*** 1. to reduce to a stump; lop. 2. to remove stumps from (land). 3. to canvass, or travel over (a district), making political speeches. 4. to tone down or soften with a stump (sense 6). 5. [Colloq.], to stub (one's toes, etc.). 6. [Colloq.], to puzzle; perplex; baffle; foil. 7. [Colloq.], to challenge; dare. 8. in

cricket, to put (a batsman) out by striking a bail from the wicket with the ball while the batsman is out of his ground: said of the wicketkeeper. *v.i.* 1. to walk with a heavy, clumsy, thumping step, as with a wooden leg. 2. to travel about making political speeches.
up a stump, [Colloq.], unable to act, think, answer, etc.; in a dilemma; perplexed; nonplussed.
stump·age (stump'ij), *n.* [*stump* + *-age*], 1. standing timber, especially with reference to its value. 2. the right to cut such timber.
stump·i·ness (stum'pi-nis), *n.* the quality or condition of being stumpy.
stump·y (stum'pi), *adj.* [STUMPIER (-pi-ẽr), STUMPIEST (-pi-ist)], 1. covered with stumps. 2. like a stump; short and thickset; stubby.
stun (stun), *v.t.* [STUNNED (stund), STUNNING], [ME. *stonien, stunien;* OFr. *estoner*, to stun, resound; L. **extonare; ex-*, intens. + *tonare*, to thunder, crash], 1. to make senseless or unconscious, as by a blow. 2. to daze or stupefy; shock deeply; astound; overwhelm: as, we were *stunned* by the sight. 3. to overpower or bewilder as by a loud noise or explosion. *n.* 1. the condition of being stunned. 2. something that stuns, as a shock or blow. —*SYN.* see **shock.**
stung (stuŋ), past tense and past participle of **sting.**
stunk (stuŋk), past participle and alternative past tense of **stink.**
stun·ner (stun'ẽr), *n.* a person or thing that stuns; specifically, [Colloq.], one who is remarkably beautiful, excellent, etc.
stun·ning (stun'iŋ), *adj.* [ppr. of *stun*], 1. that stuns. 2. [Colloq.], remarkable, especially for beauty, smartness, etc.
stun·sail, stun·s'le (stun's'l), *n.* a studdingsail.
stunt (stunt), *v.t.* [< ME. *stunt*, dull, stupid < AS. *stunt*, stupid, but influenced in meaning by ON. *stuttr*, short], 1. to check the growth or development of; dwarf. 2. to hinder (growth or development). *n.* 1. the act or process of stunting or dwarfing. 2. a stunted creature or thing.
stunt (stunt), *n.* [Late 19th-c. college slang; said to be < G. *stunde* in sense "a lesson" (cf. STOUND), but *stump* was used earlier in the same sense & *stunt*, dial. var. of *stint*, may have influenced the word], [Colloq.], something done for a thrill, to attract attention, etc.; exhibition of skill or daring; feat. *v.i.* [Colloq.], to perform a stunt or stunts. *v.t.* to perform stunts in or with (an airplane, etc.).
stunt man, in *motion pictures*, a professional acrobat, etc. who takes the place of an actor in dangerous scenes involving falls, leaps, or the like.
stu·pa (stōō'pə), *n.* [Sans.], a domelike mound containing a Buddhist shrine.
stupe (stōōp, stūp), *n.* [L. *stupa*, tow; cf. STOP], in *medicine*, a soft cloth dipped in hot water, wrung dry, often medicated, and applied to the body to relieve pain.
stu·pe·fa·cient (stōō'pə-fā'shənt, stū'pə-fā'shənt), *adj.* [L. *stupefaciens*, ppr. of *stupefacere;* see STUPEFY], stupefying. *n.* a drug, etc. that produces stupor.
stu·pe·fac·tion (stōō'pə-fak'shən, stū'pə-fak'shən), *n.* [Fr. *stupéfaction*], 1. a stupefying or being stupefied. 2. great amazement or bewilderment; astonishment.
stu·pe·fac·tive (stōō'pə-fak'tiv, stū'pə-fak'tiv), *adj.* [Fr. *stupéfactif;* ML. *stupefactivus*], stupefacient.
stu·pe·fi·er (stōō'pə-fī'ẽr, stū'pə-fī'ẽr), *n.* a person or thing that stupefies.
stu·pe·fy (stōō'pə-fī', stū'pə-fī'), *v.t.* [STUPEFIED (-fīd'), STUPEFYING], [Fr. *stupéfier;* L. *stupefacere* < *stupere*, to be stunned or amazed + *facere*, to make], 1. to bring into a state of stupor; stun; make dull or lethargic. 2. to astound; amaze; astonish.
stu·pen·dous (stōō-pen'dəs, stū-pen'dəs), *adj.* [L. *stupendus*, gerundive of *stupere*, to be struck, stunned, or amazed], overwhelming; astonishingly great in some quality; especially, amazingly large; immense.
stu·pid (stōō'pid, stū'pid), *adj.* [L. *stupidus* < *stupere*, to be stunned or amazed], 1. in a state of stupor; dazed; stunned; stupefied. 2. lacking normal intelligence or understanding; slow-witted; dull. 3. showing or resulting from a lack of normal intelligence; foolish; irrational: as, what a *stupid* idea. 4. dull and boring; tiresome: as, a very *stupid* party. *n.* a stupid person.
SYN.—**stupid** implies such lack of intelligence or incapacity for perceiving, learning, etc. as might be shown by one in a mental stupor (a *stupid* idea); **dull** implies a mental sluggishness that may be constitutional or may result from overfatigue, disease, etc. (the fever left him *dull* and listless); **dense** suggests thickheadedness or obtuseness (too *dense* to take a hint); **slow** suggests that the quickness, but not necessarily the capacity, to learn is below average (a pupil *slow* in his studies); **retarded** implies a being behind others of the same age or class because of mental deficiency or slowness in learning (a *retarded* pupil). See also **silly.** —*ANT.* intelligent, bright.
stu·pid·i·ty (stōō-pid'ə-ti, stū-pid'ə-ti), *n.* [L. *stupiditas*], 1. the quality or condition of being stupid. 2. [*pl.* STUPIDITIES (-tiz)], something stupid; foolish remark, irrational act, etc.
stu·por (stōō'pẽr, stū'pẽr), *n.* [ME.; L. < *stupere*, to be stunned or amazed], 1. a state in which the mind and senses are dulled; partial or complete loss of sensibility, as from the use of a narcotic. 2. mental or moral dullness or apathy. —*SYN.* see **lethargy.**
stu·por·ous (stōō'pẽr-əs, stū'pẽr-əs), *adj.* of or in a stupor.
stur·died (stũr'did), *adj.* having sturdy (the disease).
stur·di·ly (stũr'də-li), *adv.* in a sturdy manner.
stur·di·ness (stũr'di-nis), *n.* the quality or condition of being sturdy.
stur·dy (stũr'di), *adj.* [STURDIER (-di-ẽr), STURDIEST (-di-ist)], [ME. *stourdi, sturdi;* OFr. *estourdi*, stunned, dazed, reckless (Fr. *étourdi*, thoughtless); basic sense "hard to influence or control"], 1. firm; resolute; that will not yield or compromise: as, *sturdy* defiance, a *sturdy* policy. 2. strong; vigorous; stout; hardy. —*SYN.* see **strong.**
stur·dy (stũr'di), *n.* [OFr. *estourdi*, giddiness; see STURDY, *adj.*], gid (a disease of sheep).
stur·geon (stũr'jən), *n.* [*pl.* STURGEONS (-jənz), STURGEON; see PLURAL, II, D, 1], [ME. *sturgiun;* Anglo-Fr. *sturgeon;* OFr. *esturgeon, estourgeon;* of Gmc. origin; cf. OHG. *sturjo*], any of several large food fishes having rows of spiny plates along the body and a projecting snout: valuable as a source of caviar and isinglass.
‡Sturm·ab·tei·lung (shtoorm'äp'tī'looŋ), *n.* [G., lit., storm division < *sturm*, a storm + *abteilen*, to divide], the Storm Troopers, a political militia of the Nazi party, organized about 1923 to keep order at party demonstrations and carry on propaganda by terrorist methods: after the liquidation of its leaders in 1934, it was reorganized to give premilitary and postmilitary indoctrination to German men: also called *Brown Shirts*: abbreviated **SA, S.A.**
‡Sturm und Drang (shtoorm' oont dräŋ'), [G., lit., storm and stress], a movement in 18th-century German literature away from the influence of French neoclassicism: it is the early phase of German romanticism.
stut·ter (stut'ẽr), *v.t. & v.i.* [freq. of ME. *stutten*, to stutter; akin to G. *stossen*, to knock, push], to speak or say with involuntary pauses, spasms, and repetition or prolongation of sounds and syllables, generally as a symptom of some psychic disturbance. *n.* the act or an instance of stuttering. Cf. **stammer.**
Stutt·gart (stut'gärt; G. shtoot'gärt), *n.* a city in southern Germany: capital of Württemberg: pop., 411,000 (est. 1946).
Stuy·ve·sant, Peter (stī'və-s'nt), 1592–1672; last Dutch governor of New Netherland (1646–1664).
St. Vincent, a British island of the Windward group in the West Indies: area, 150 sq. mi.; pop., 62,000 (1946).
St. Vi·tus's dance (vī'təs-iz), chorea, especially of children: also **St. Vitus' dance.**
sty (stī), *n.* [*pl.* STIES (stīz)], [ME. *stie;* AS. *sti* < same base as *stig*, hall, enclosure (cf. STEWARD)], 1. a pen for pigs. 2. any foul, filthy, or depraved place. *v.t. & v.i.* [STIED (stīd), STYING], to lodge in or as in a sty.
sty, stye (stī), *n.* [*pl.* STIES (stīz)], [< faulty interpretation of obs. *styany* (*styan-eye*) as *sty on eye* < dial. *styan*, rising; AS. *stigend*, ppr. of *stigan*, to climb, rise], a small, inflamed swelling of a sebaceous gland on the rim of the eyelid.
Styg·i·an (stij'i-ən), *adj.* [< L. *Stygius* (< Gr. *Stygios* < base of *Styx*); + *-an*], 1. of or characteristic of the river Styx and the infernal regions; hence, 2. [also s-], infernal; dark; gloomy; hellish. 3. [also s-], inviolable; completely binding, as an oath sworn by the river Styx.
sty·lar (stī'lẽr), *adj.* [< *style* + *-ar*], of or like a style (instrument).
style (stīl), *n.* [ME. *stil, stile;* OFr. *stile, style;* L. *stilus*], 1. a sharp, slender, pointed instrument used by the ancients in writing on wax tablets. 2. any of several devices, etc. similar in shape or use; specifically, *a*) [Obs.], a pen. *b*) an etching needle. *c*) a phonograph needle. *d*) an engraving tool. *e*) the pointer on a dial, chart, etc. *f*) in *botany*, a small pointed process or part, especially the stalklike part of a pistil between the stigma and the ovary. 3. *a*) manner or mode of expression in language; way of putting thoughts into words. *b*) specific or characteristic manner of expression, execution, construction, or design, in any art, period, work, employment, etc.: as, the Byzantine *style*, modern *style*. 4. distinction, excellence, originality, and character in any form of artistic or literary expression: as, this author lacks *style*. 5. the way in which anything is made or done; manner. 6. the way in which people of fashionable society dress, speak, conduct themselves, etc.; current and elegant mode. 7. distinction and elegance of manner and bearing. 8. form of address; title: as, he is entitled to the *style* of Mayor. 9. something stylish; especially, a dress, coat, etc. of current, smart design. 10. sort; kind; variety;

type. 11. a way of reckoning time, dates, etc.: see **Old Style, New Style.** 12. in *printing*, manner of dealing with spelling, punctuation, word division, etc. of any particular press, publisher, etc. *v.t.* [STYLED (stīld), STYLING], 1. to name; call: as, Abraham Lincoln was *styled* the Great Emancipator. 2. to design the style of. 3. to bring into accord with accepted style, as of a printer; normalize spelling, punctuation, etc. —*SYN.* see **fashion.**

style·book (stīl'book'), *n.* a book consisting of examples or rules of style (esp. sense 12).

sty·let (stī'lit), *n.* [Fr.; It. *stiletto;* see STILETTO], 1. a slender, pointed weapon; especially, a stiletto. 2. in *surgery*, a thin probe for examining wounds. 3. in *zoology*, any pointed, bristlelike protrusion.

sty·li·form (stī'li-fôrm'), *adj.* [Mod. L. *styliformis;* see STYLE & -FORM], shaped like a style (instrument).

styl·ish (stīl'ish), *adj.* conforming to current style in dress, decoration, behavior, etc.; smart; fashionable.

styl·ist (stīl'ist), *n.* 1. a writer, etc. whose work has style (sense 4) or is characterized by a particular style. 2. a person who designs, or advises on, current styles, as in dress.

sty·lis·tic (stī-lis'tik), *adj.* [< *style*, after G. *stilistisch*], of or having to do with style, especially literary style.

sty·lis·ti·cal (stī-lis'ti-k'l), *adj.* stylistic.

sty·lis·ti·cal·ly (stī-lis'ti-k'l-i, stī-lis'tik-li), *adv.* with regard to style.

sty·lite (stī'līt), *n.* [Late Gr. *stylitēs* < Gr. *stylos*, a pillar], any of a class of religious ascetics of the early Middle Ages who lived on the tops of pillars.

styl·i·za·tion (stīl'i-zā'shən), *n.* a stylizing or being stylized.

styl·ize (stīl'īz), *v.t.* [STYLIZED (-īzd), STYLIZING], [< *style*, after G. *stilisiren*], to make conform to a given style; specifically, to design or represent according to the rules of a style rather than according to nature; conventionalize.

sty·lo- (stī'lō, stī'lə), [< L. *stylus*, incorrect for *stilus*, pointed instrument], a combining form meaning *pointed, sharp*, as in *stylograph:* also, before a vowel, **styl-.**

sty·lo·bate (stī'lə-bāt'), *n.* [L. *stylobates;* Gr. *stylobatēs* < *stylos*, pillar + *bainein*, to go], in *architecture*, a continuous base or coping for a row of columns.

sty·lo·graph (stī'lə-graf', stī'lə-gräf'), *n.* [*stylo-* + *-graph*], a fountain pen having a pierced conical point, rather than a nib, through which the ink flows.

sty·lo·graph·ic (stī'lə-graf'ik), *adj.* 1. of or like a stylograph. 2. of or used in stylography.

sty·log·ra·phy (stī-log'rə-fi), *n.* [*stylo-* + *-graphy*], drawing, writing, or engraving done with a style or similar instrument.

sty·loid (stī'loid), *adj.* resembling a style; styliform; specifically, in *anatomy*, designating or of any of various long, slender processes, especially that at the base of the temporal bone.

sty·lo·lite (stī'lə-līt'), *n.* [*stylo-* + *-lite*], a small, column-like formation forming part of a rock deposit, usually of limestone.

sty·lo·po·di·um (stī'lə-pō'di-əm), *n.* [*pl.* STYLOPODIA (-ə)], [Mod. L.; see STYLE & -PODIUM], the fleshy support at the base of the style in flowers of the carrot family.

sty·lus (stī'ləs), *n.* [*pl.* STYLUSES (-iz), STYLI (-lī)], [L., for *stilus*, pointed instrument], 1. a style or other needle-like marking device. 2. *a)* a sharp, pointed device for cutting the grooves of a phonograph record. *b)* the needle for reproducing the sound of such a record.

sty·mie (stī'mi), *n.* [prob. a use of earlier Scot. *stymie*, a person partially blind < *styme;* ME. *stime*, in the phr. *not able to see a stime* (coinciding in sense with ON. *skima*), not able to see at all: the reference is to the blind shot caused by a stymie], in *golf*, 1. the condition that exists on a putting green when an opponent's ball lies in a direct line between the player's ball and the hole. 2. a ball lying in such a position. *v.t.* [STYMIED (-mid), STYMIEING], 1. to hinder or obstruct as with a stymie. 2. to block; impede. Also spelled **stimy.**

sty·my (stī'mi), *n.* [*pl.* STYMIES (-miz)], & *v.t.* [STYMIED (-mid), STYMYING], stymie.

styp·sis (stip'sis), *n.* [LL.; Gr. *stypsis;* see STYPTIC], the action or use of a styptic.

styp·tic (stip'tik), *adj.* [Fr. *styptique;* L. *stypticus;* Gr. *styptikos*, astringent < *styphein*, to contract], tending to halt bleeding by contracting the tissues or blood vessels; astringent. *n.* any styptic substance.

styp·ti·cal (stip'ti-k'l), *adj.* styptic.

styp·tic·i·ty (stip-tis'ə-ti), *n.* the quality of being styptic.

styptic pencil, a small stick of a styptic substance used to stop bleeding, as from surface nicks or cuts.

Styr (stir), *n.* a river in the northwestern Ukrainian S.S.R., flowing into the Pripyat River: formerly in Poland: length, c. 300 mi.

sty·ra·ca·ceous (stī'rə-kā'shəs), *adj.* [< Mod. L. *Styracaceae*, name of the family (< L. *styrax, storax*, storax); + *-ous*], of a family of trees and shrubs with a fleshy or dry fruit and clusters of flowers, usually white, whose petals are united all around.

sty·rene (stī'rēn, stêr'ēn), *n.* [< L. *styrax, storax* (see STORAX); + *-ene*], a colorless or yellowish, aromatic liquid, $C_6H_5CH{\cdot}CH_2$, used in organic synthesis, especially in manufacturing synthetic rubber and plastics.

Styr·i·a (stêr'i-ə), *n.* a province of southeastern Austria: German name, *Steiermark.*

sty·ro·foam (stī'rə-fōm'), *n.* [< *styrene* + *foam*], rigid, lightweight, cellular polystyrene, used in boat construction, insulation, commercial displays, etc.: a trademark (**Styrofoam**).

sty·ro·lene (stī'rə-lēn'), *n.* styrene.

Styx (stiks), *n.* [L. < Gr. *Styx*, lit., the Hateful < *stygein*, to hate], in *Greek mythology*, a river encircling the lower world, over which Charon ferried dead souls.

Su., Sunday.

su·a·bil·i·ty (sōō'ə-bil'ə-ti, sū'ə-bil'ə-ti), *n.* the state of being suable.

su·a·ble (sōō'ə-b'l, sū'ə-b'l), *adj.* liable to suit in a court; that may be sued.

sua·sion (swā'zhən), *n.* [ME. *suasioun;* L. *suasio* < *suasus*, pp. of *suadere*, to persuade], persuasion.

sua·sive (swā'siv), *adj.* [< L. *suasus* (see SUASION); + *-ive*], persuasive.

suave (swäv; *occas.* swāv), *adj.* [Fr. < L. *suavis*, sweet], smoothly gracious or polite; polished; blandly ingratiating; urbane.

SYN.—**suave** suggests the smoothly gracious social manner of one who deals with people easily and tactfully (a *suave* sophisticate); **urbane** suggests the social poise of one who is highly cultivated and has had much worldly experience (an *urbane* cosmopolite); **diplomatic** implies adroitness and tactfulness in dealing with people and handling delicate situations, sometimes in such a way as to gain one's own ends (a *diplomatic* answer); **politic** also expresses this idea, often stressing the expediency or opportunism of a particular policy pursued (a *politic* move); **bland** is the least complex of these terms, simply implying a gentle or ingratiating pleasantness (a *bland* disposition).

suav·i·ty (swav'ə-ti, swä'və-ti), *n.* [Fr. *suavité;* L. *suavitas*], 1. the quality of being suave; graceful politeness or polish; urbanity. 2. [*pl.* SUAVITIES (-tiz)], a suave action, speech, etc.

sub (sub), *n.* [Colloq.], *a contracted form of* sublieutenant, submarine, subordinate, subscription, substitute, and other words beginning with *sub-*. *v.i.* [SUBBED (subd), SUBBING], [Colloq.], to be a substitute (*for* someone).

sub- (sub, səb), [< L. *sub*, under, below], a prefix meaning: 1. *under, beneath, below*, as in *submarine, subsoil.* 2. *lower in rank or position than, inferior or subordinate to*, as in *subaltern, subagent.* 3. *to a lesser degree than, somewhat, slightly*, as in *subhuman, subtropical, subconscious.* 4. *a) so as to form a division into smaller or less important parts*, as in *sublet, subdivide. b) forming such a division*, as in *subsection, subdivision.* 5. in *chemistry*, *a) with less than the normal amount of* (the specified substance), as in *subchloride. b) basic*, as in *subcarbonate.* 6. in *mathematics*, *designating a ratio inverse to a given ratio*, as in *subduplicate.* In words of Latin origin, *sub-* assimilates to *suc-* before *c*, as in *succeed; suf-* before *f*, as in *suffer; sug-* before *g*, as in *suggest; sum-* before *m*, as in *summon; sup-* before *p*, as in *supplant; sur-* before *r*, as in *surrender*: *sub-* often changes to *sus-* before *c, p*, and *t*, as in *sustain, suspend.*

sub., 1. subaltern. 2. substitute(s). 3. suburb(an).

sub·ac·id (sub-as'id), *adj.* [L. *subacidus*], 1. slightly acid or sour, as certain fruits. 2. slightly sharp or biting, as a remark.

sub·a·cute (sub'ə-kūt'), *adj.* between acute and chronic with reference to duration: said of a disease.

sub·a·gent (sub-ā'jənt), *n.* a person representing an agent; agent of an agent.

sub·al·pine (sub-al'pīn, sub-al'pin), *adj.* [L. *subalpinus*, lit., lying near the Alps < *sub-*, below + *Alpinus*, Alpine], 1. designating or of regions at the foot of the Alps. 2. designating or of mountain regions at an altitude of between four and six thousand feet, below the timber line.

sub·al·tern (səb-ôl'tērn; *also, esp. for adj. 3 & n. 3,* sub''l-tũrn'), *adj.* [Fr. *subalterne;* LL. *subalternus;* L. *sub-*, under + *alternus*, alternate], 1. subordinate; of lower rank. 2. [Chiefly British], holding an army commission below that of captain. 3. in *logic*, particular, with reference to a universal of which it is part. *n.* 1. a subordinate. 2. [Chiefly British], a subaltern officer. 3. in *logic*, a subaltern proposition.

sub·al·ter·nate (səb-ôl'tēr-nit, səb-al'tēr-nit), *adj.* [ME., ML. *subalternatus*, pp. of *subalternare* < LL. *subalternus;* see SUBALTERN], 1. following in order; successive. 2. in an alternate arrangement, but tending to become opposite: said of leaves.

sub·al·ter·na·tion (səb-ôl'tēr-nā'shən, sub'al-tēr-nā'shən), *n.* the condition of being subalternate.

sub·ant·arc·tic (sub'ant-ärk'tik), *adj.* designating or of the area surrounding the Antarctic Circle.

sub·a·quat·ic (sub'ə-kwat'ik, sub'ə-kwät'ik), *adj.* partly aquatic.

sub·a·que·ous (sub-ā'kwi-əs, sub-ak'wi-əs), *adj.* [*sub-* + *aqueous*], 1. adapted for underwater use or existence; underwater. 2. formed, living, or occurring under water.

sub·arc·tic (sub-ärk'tik), *adj.* designating or of the area immediately surrounding the Arctic Circle.

sub·ar·id (sub-ar'id), *adj.* slightly arid; moderately dry.

sub·at·om (sub-at'əm), *n.* a constituent part of an atom.
sub·au·di·tion (sub'ô-dish'ən), *n.* [LL. *subauditio* < *subaudire*, to understand or supply a word omitted; L. *sub-*, under + *audire*, to hear], 1. the act or process of understanding or mentally filling in a word or thought implied but not expressed. 2. something thus understood or filled in.
sub·au·ric·u·lar (sub'ô-rik'yoo-lẽr), *adj.* situated below the auricle of the ear.
sub·base (sub'bās'), *n.* the lowest horizontal section of a base.
sub·base·ment (sub'bās'mənt), *n.* any floor or room below a basement.
sub·bass (sub'bās'), *n.* in *music*, a pedal stop, of 16 or 32 feet, producing the lowest tones in an organ.
sub·branch (sub'branch'), *n.* a division of a branch.
sub·cal·i·ber (sub-kal'ə-bẽr), *adj.* 1. smaller than the caliber of the firearm from which it is fired: said of a projectile fired through a tube of proper caliber inserted in the barrel. 2. of or having to do with a subcaliber projectile.
sub·car·ti·lag·i·nous (sub'kär-tə-laj'ə-nəs), *adj.* 1. situated beneath cartilage. 2. partly cartilaginous.
sub·ce·les·tial (sub'sə-les'chəl), *adj.* [*sub-* + *celestial*], 1. beneath the heavens; terrestrial; hence, 2. mundane. 3. in *astronomy*, situated exactly beneath the zenith. *n.* a subcelestial being.
sub·cel·lar (sub'sel'ẽr), *n.* a cellar beneath another cellar.
sub·cen·tral (sub-sen'trəl), *adj.* close to or beneath the center.
sub·chlo·ride (sub-klôr'īd, sub-klō'rid), *n.* a chloride containing a relatively small proportion of chlorine.
sub·class (sub'klas', sub'kläs'), *n.* a subdivision of a class.
sub·cla·vi·an (sub-klā'vi-ən), *adj.* situated under the clavicle. *n.* a subclavian vein, artery, etc.
subclavian groove, either of two grooves in the first rib, one for the main artery (*subclavian artery*) and the other for the main vein (*subclavian vein*) of the arm.
sub·clin·i·cal (sub-klin'i-k'l), *adj.* without clinical symptoms, as a disease in its early stages.
sub·com·mit·tee (sub'kə-mit'i), *n.* a subordinate committee chosen from the members of a main committee.
sub·con·scious (sub-kon'shəs), *adj.* 1. occurring without conscious perception, or with only slight perception, on the part of the individual: said of mental processes and reactions. 2. not fully conscious; imperfectly aware. *n.* that portion of mental activity of which the individual has little or no conscious perception.
sub·con·scious·ness (sub-kon'shəs-nis), *n.* 1. the subconscious. 2. a subconscious quality or condition.
sub·con·ti·nent (sub-kon'tə-nənt), *n.* a large land mass, smaller than that usually called a continent.
sub·con·tract (sub-kon'trakt; *for v.*, sub'kən-trakt'), *n.* a secondary contract undertaking some of the obligations of a primary or previous contract: construction companies often let *subcontracts* for the electrical work, plumbing, etc. in a new building. *v.t.* *& v.i.* to make a subcontract (for).
sub·con·trac·tor (sub'kon'trak-tẽr, sub'kən-trak'tẽr), *n.* a person who assumes by secondary contract some of the obligations of an original contractor.
sub·cu·ta·ne·ous (sub'kū-tā'ni-əs), *adj.* [*sub-* + *cutaneous*], being, used, or introduced beneath the skin.
sub·dea·con (sub-dē'kən), *n.* [altered, after *sub-* + *deacon* < ME. *sudeakne*; OFr. *soudiakene*; ML. *subdiaconus*], a minister ranking next below a deacon.
sub·deb (sub-deb', sub'deb'), *n.* [< *sub-* + *debutante*], 1. a girl in the years just preceding her debut into society; hence, 2. any girl of such age. *adj.* of or suitable for a subdeb.
sub·de·part·ment (sub'di-pärt'mənt), *n.* a division of a department.
sub·di·vide (sub'də-vīd'), *v.t. & v.i.* 1. to divide further after previous division has been made. 2. to divide (land) into small parcels for ready sale.
sub·di·vi·sion (sub'də-vizh'ən, sub'də-vizh'ən), *n.* [LL. *subdivisio*], 1. a subdividing or being subdivided. 2. a piece or part, as of land, resulting from this.
sub·dom·i·nant (sub-dom'ə-nənt), *n.* in *music*, the fourth tone of a diatonic scale; tone next below the dominant.
sub·du·a·ble (səb-do͞o'ə-b'l, səb-dū'ə-b'l), *adj.* that can be subdued.
sub·du·al (səb-do͞o'əl, səb-dū'əl), *n.* a subduing or being subdued.
sub·duce (səb-do͞os', səb-dūs'), *v.t.* [SUBDUCED (-do͞ost', -dūst'), SUBDUCING], [L. *subducere; sub-*, from + *ducere*, to lead], [Obs.], to withdraw; take away.
sub·duct (səb-dukt'), *v.t. & v.i.* [< L. *subductus*, pp.; see SUBDUCE], to withdraw; subtract; remove.
sub·due (səb-do͞o', səb-dū'), *v.t.* [SUBDUED (-do͞od', -dūd'), SUBDUING], [ME. *subdewen, soduen;* OFr. *souduire;* L. *subducere*, to draw away, remove], 1. to bring into subjection; conquer; vanquish. 2. to overcome, as by persuasion or training; control. 3. to make less intense; reduce; lower; diminish; soften. 4. to repress (emotions, passions, etc.). 5. to till or cultivate (land). —*SYN.* see **conquer.**
sub·ed·i·tor (sub-ed'i-tẽr), *n.* a subordinate editor.
su·be·re·ous (soo-bêr'i-əs, syoo-bêr'i-əs), *adj.* [L. *subereus* < *suber*, cork, cork tree], in *botany*, of or like cork; suberose.
su·ber·ic (soo-ber'ik, syoo-ber'ik), *adj.* [Fr. *suberique* < L. *suber*, cork tree], 1. of cork. 2. designating a dibasic acid, $(CH_2)_6(CO_2H)_2$, obtained by the oxidation of cork and from other sources.
su·ber·in (so͞o'bẽr-in, sū'bẽr-in), *n.* [Fr. *subérine* < L. *suber*, cork + Fr. *-ine*, -ine], a waxy or fatty substance contained in cork.
su·ber·ine (so͞o'bə-rin', sū'bə-rēn'), *n.* suberin.
su·ber·i·za·tion (so͞o'bẽr-i-zā'shən, sū'bẽr-i-zā'shən), *n.* in *botany*, a suberizing or being suberized.
su·ber·ize (so͞o'bə-rīz', sū'bə-rīz'), *v.t.* [SUBERIZED (-rīzd'), SUBERIZING], [L. *suber*, cork; + *-ize*], in *botany*, to change into cork by the formation of suberin in the cell walls.
su·ber·ose (so͞o'bə-rōs', sū'bə-rōs'), *adj.* [Mod. L. *suberosus* < L. *suber*, cork], corklike in appearance; suberized.
su·ber·ous (so͞o'bẽr-əs, sū'bẽr-əs), *adj.* suberose.
sub·fam·i·ly (sub'fam'ə-li, sub-fam'ə-li), *n.* any of the main subdivisions of a family of plants or animals.
sub·ge·nus (sub-jē'nəs), *n.* [*pl.* SUBGENERA (-jen'ẽr-ə), SUBGENUSES (-iz)], any of the main subdivisions of a genus of plants or animals.
sub·gla·cial (sub-glā'shəl), *adj.* found or formerly deposited at the bottom of a glacier.
sub·grade (sub'grād'), *n.* the surface or grade of a foundation layer, as for a street or sidewalk.
sub·group (sub'gro͞op'), *n.* a subdivision of a group, especially of a group in the periodic table of chemical elements.
sub·gum (sub'gum'), *adj.* [Cantonese, lit., mixed vegetables], designating any of various Chinese or Chinese-American dishes, as chow mein, prepared with water chestnuts, mushrooms, etc.
sub·head (sub'hed'), *n.* 1. the title of a subdivision of a chapter, article, etc. 2. a subordinate heading or title, as of a newspaper article. 3. the assistant to the head of a school, etc.
sub·head·ing (sub-hed'iŋ), *n.* a subhead (senses 1 & 2).
sub·hu·man (sub-hū'mən), *adj.* 1. below the human race in development; less than human. 2. nearly human.
sub·in·dex (sub-in'deks), *n.* [*pl.* SUBINDICES (-də-sēz')], in *mathematics*, a figure or character added below and to the right of a symbol to distinguish it from others: in Y_3 and X_a, *3* and *a* are *subindices.*
sub·in·feu·da·tion (sub'in-fyoo-dā'shən), *n.* 1. the transfer of feudal lands by a vassal lord to a subtenant with all the original privileges and responsibilities falling to the new holder. 2. tenure so established. 3. the lands or fief so held.
sub·ir·ri·gate (sub-ir'ə-gāt'), *v.t.* to irrigate (land) by a system of underground pipes.
‡su·bi·to (so͞o'bē-tô'; Eng. so͞o'bi-tō'), *adv.* [It.; L., suddenly < pp. of *subire*, to approach, spring up; *sub-*, under + *ire*, to go], in *music*, quickly; abruptly: a direction to the performer.
subj., 1. subject. 2. subjective. 3. subjunctive.
sub·ja·cen·cy (sub-jā's'n-si), *n.* a subjacent condition.
sub·ja·cent (sub-jā's'nt), *adj.* [L. *subjacens*, ppr. of *subjacere*, to lie under; *sub-*, under + *jacere*, to lie], 1. situated directly under or below; underlying. 2. being lower but not directly beneath.
sub·ject (sub'jikt; *for v.*, səb-jekt'), *adj.* [ME. *suget;* OFr. *sujet, suject, subject* < L. *subjectus*, pp. of *subjicere*, to place under, put under, subject < *sub-*, under + *jacere*, to throw], 1. under the authority or control of, or owing allegiance to, another: as, *subject* peoples. 2. having a disposition or tendency; liable (with *to*): as, he is *subject* to fits of anger. 3. liable to receive; exposed (with *to*): as, *subject* to censure. 4. contingent or conditional upon (with *to*): as, it is *subject* to my approval. *n.* [ME. *suget;* OFr. *sujet, subgiet;* L. *subjectus;* see the *adj.*], 1. a person under the authority or control of another; especially, a person in his relationship to a ruler, government, etc., to which he owes allegiance. 2. someone or something made to undergo a treatment, experiment, etc.; specifically, a dead body to be dissected for study or experimentation. 3. something dealt with in discussion, study, writing, painting, etc.; theme. 4. the main theme of a musical composition or movement. 5. originating cause; reason; occasion: as, a *subject* for great sorrow. 6. any of the various courses of study in a school or college; branch of learning: as, mathematics is my favorite *subject.* 7. in *grammar*, the word or group of words in a sentence about which some-

thing is said and which serves as the starting point of the action except in passive constructions: subjects are nouns or pronouns or other words functioning as nouns or pronouns. 8. in *logic*, that part of a proposition about which something is said; that which is affirmed or denied. 9. in *philosophy*, *a*) the actual substance of anything as distinguished from its qualities and attributes. *b*) the mind, or ego, that thinks and feels, as distinguished from everything outside of the mind. *v.t.* 1. [Obs.], to place under or below. 2. [Rare], to place before; submit: as, a plan *subjected* for approval. 3. to bring under the authority or control of; cause to owe allegiance. 4. to cause to have a disposition or tendency; expose: with *to*, as, his weakness *subjected* him to many diseases. 5. to cause to undergo or experience some action or treatment: with *to*, as, they *subjected* him to indignities. Abbreviated **subj.**

***SYN.*—subject** is the general word for whatever is dealt with in discussion, study, writing, art, etc. (the *subject* of a talk, painting, etc.); a **theme** is a subject developed or elaborated upon in a literary or artistic work, or one that constitutes the underlying motif of the work (a novel with a social *theme*); a **topic** is a subject of common interest selected for individual treatment, as in an essay, or for discussion by a group of persons (baseball is their favorite *topic* of conversation); **text** is specifically applied to a Biblical passage chosen as the subject of a sermon.

sub·jec·tion (səb-jek′shən), *n.* [ME. *subjeccioun;* OFr.; L. *subjectio*], a subjecting or being subjected.

sub·jec·tive (səb-jek′tiv), *adj.* [L. *subjectivus*, of the subject < *subjectus;* see SUBJECT], 1. of, affected by, or produced by the mind or a particular state of mind; of or resulting from the feelings or temperament of the subject, or person thinking, rather than the attributes of the object thought of: as, a *subjective* judgment. 2. determined by and emphasizing the ideas, thoughts, feelings, etc. of the artist, writer, or speaker. 3. in *grammar*, nominative. 4. in *philosophy*, having to do with any of the elements in apprehension or apperception derived from the limitations of the mind rather than from reality independent of mind. 5. in *medicine*, designating or of a symptom or condition perceptible only to the patient. 6. in *psychology*, *a*) existing or originating within the observer's mind and, hence, incapable of being checked externally or verified by other persons. *b*) introspective. Abbreviated **subj.** Cf. **objective.**

sub·jec·tiv·ism (səb-jek′tiv-iz′m), *n.* 1. the philosophic theory that all knowledge is subjective and relative, never objective. 2. any philosophic theory of knowledge that gives great importance to the subjective or a priori elements of conscious experience. 3. an ethical doctrine that considers the supreme good to be some form of subjective feeling, usually of pleasure, or that measures supreme good by the criterion of such feeling.

sub·jec·ti·vis·tic (səb-jek′ti-vis′tik), *adj.* of or characterized by subjectivism.

sub·jec·tiv·i·ty (sub′jek-tiv′ə-ti), *n.* a subjective quality or state; specifically, *a*) the tendency to consider all things only in the light of one's own personality. *b*) concern with only one's own thoughts and feelings. *c*) the reflection of an artist's character and personality in his work.

subject matter, the thing or things considered in a book, course of instruction, discussion, etc.

sub·join (səb-join′), *v.t.* [OFr. *subjoindre;* L. *subjungere;* see SUB- & JOIN], to add (something) at the end of what has been stated; append.

sub·join·der (səb-join′dẽr), *n.* something subjoined.

‡sub ju·di·ce (sub jo͞o′di-si), [L., lit., under judgment], before the court; under consideration; not yet decided.

sub·ju·gate (sub′joo-gāt′), *v.t.* [SUBJUGATED (-id), SUBJUGATING], [ME. *subiugaten* < L. *subjugatus*, pp. of *subjugere*, to bring under the yoke < *sub-*, under + *jugum*, a yoke], 1. to bring under control or subjection; conquer. 2. to cause to become subservient; subdue. —*SYN.* see **conquer.**

sub·ju·ga·tion (sub′joo-gā′shən), *n.* [ML. *subjugatio*], a subjugating or being subjugated; subjection.

sub·ju·ga·tor (sub′joo-gā′tẽr), *n.* [L.], a person who subjugates.

sub·junc·tive (səb-juŋk′tiv), *adj.* [LL. *subjunctivus* < *subjunctus*, pp. of *subjungere*, to subjoin], designating or of that mood of a verb used to express supposition, desire, hypothesis, possibility, etc., rather than to state an actual fact: distinguished from *indicative*, *imperative*. *n.* 1. the subjunctive mood. 2. a subjunctive verb form. Abbreviated **subj.**

sub·king·dom (sub′kiŋ′dəm, sub-kiŋ′dəm), *n.* a primary division of the plant or animal kingdom: now called a *phylum.*

sub·lap·sar·i·an (sub′lap-sâr′i-ən), *n.* & *adj.* [Mod. L. *sublapsarius* < L. *sub-*, below + *lapsus*, a fall], infralapsarian.

sub·lease (sub′lēs′; *for v.*, sub-lēs′), *n.* a lease granted by a lessee to another person of all or part of the property. *v.t.* 1. to grant a sublease of. 2. to receive or hold a sublease of.

sub·let (sub-let′, sub′let′), *v.t.* [SUBLET, SUBLETTING], 1. to lease or let to another (property leased to oneself). 2. to let out (work) to a subcontractor.

sub·le·thal (sub-lē′thəl), *adj.* not quite lethal; insufficient to cause death: as, a *sublethal* dose of poison.

sub·lieu·ten·ant (sub′lo͞o-ten′ənt, sub′lū-ten′ənt), *n.* in some armies and navies, an officer ranking next below a lieutenant.

sub·li·mate (sub′lə-māt′; *for adj. & n., usually* sub′lə-mit), *v.t.* [SUBLIMATED (-id), SUBLIMATING], [< L. *sublimatus*, pp. of *sublimare;* see SUBLIME], 1. to purify or refine (a substance) by subliming. 2. figuratively, to purify or refine. 3. to express (socially unacceptable impulses or biological drives) in constructive, socially acceptable forms, often unconsciously. *v.i.* to undergo sublimation. *adj.* sublimated. *n.* a product of sublimation.

sub·li·ma·tion (sub′lə-mā′shən), *n.* [ME. *sublimacion;* ML. *sublimatio*], 1. a sublimating or being sublimated. 2. the process of subliming. 3. a product of sublimating.

sub·lime (sə-blīm′), *adj.* [Fr.; L. *sublimis* < *sub-*, up to + *limen*, lintel, hence orig., up to the lintel], 1. noble; exalted; majestic. 2. inspiring awe or admiration through grandeur, beauty, etc. 3. [Poetic], elated; joyful. 4. [Poetic], proud; lofty; haughty. 5. [Archaic], upraised; aloft. *n.* something sublime; sublime quality (with *the*). *v.t.* [SUBLIMED (-blīmd′), SUBLIMING], [ME. *sublimen;* OFr. *sublimer;* L. *sublimare* < the *adj.*], 1. to make sublime. 2. to purify (a solid) by heating directly to a gaseous state and condensing the vapor back into solid form. *v.i.* to go through such a process of purification. —*SYN.* see **splendid.**

sub·lim·i·nal (sub-lim′ə-n'l, sub-lī′mə-n'l), *adj.* [< *sub-* + L. *limen*, threshold; + *-al*], in *psychology*, below the threshold of consciousness or apprehension; subconscious; too slight to be perceived: as, a *subliminal* stimulus. *n.* the subconscious.

sub·lim·i·ty (sə-blim′ə-ti), *n.* [L. *sublimitas*], 1. the state or quality of being sublime, majestic, noble, etc. 2. [*pl.* SUBLIMITIES (-tiz)], something sublime.

sub·lu·nar (sub-lo͞o′nẽr), *adj.* sublunary.

sub·lu·nar·y (sub′loo-ner′i, sub-lo͞o′nẽr-i), *adj.* [Mod. L. *sublunaris* < L. *sub-*, under + *luna*, the moon], 1. situated beneath the moon. 2. earthly; mundane.

sub·ma·chine gun (sub′mə-shēn′), a portable, automatic or semiautomatic firearm with a short barrel and a stock, fired from the shoulder or hip.

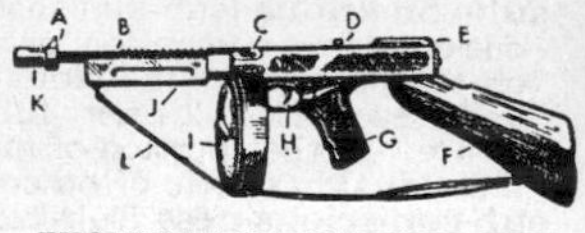

THOMPSON SUBMACHINE GUN
A, front sight; B, barrel; C, breech; D, rear sight; E, wind gauge; F, stock; G, pistol grip; H, trigger; I, magazine; J, hand grip; K, compensator; L, sling

sub·mar·gin·al (sub-mär′ji-n'l), *adj.* 1. considered to be below the standard that yields a satisfactory profit: as, a *submarginal* vein of coal. 2. below the margin. 3. in *biology*, near the margin.

sub·ma·rine (sub′mə-rēn′; *for n. & v., usually* sub′mə-rēn′), *adj.* [*sub-*, under + *marine*], being, living, used, or carried on beneath the surface of the water, especially of the sea. *n.* 1. a submarine plant or animal. 2. a kind of warship that can operate under water. *v.t.* [SUBMARINED (-rēnd′, -rēnd′), SUBMARINING], to attack, especially to torpedo, with a submarine warship.

submarine chaser, a small, fast naval patrol vessel carrying depth charges and light deck guns for use against submarines.

sub·max·il·la (sub′mak-sil′ə), *n.* [*pl.* SUBMAXILLAE (-ē)], [Mod. L.; L. *sub-*, under + *maxilla*, jawbone], the lower jaw or jawbone.

sub·max·il·lar·y (sub-mak′si-ler′i), *adj.* designating, of, or below the submaxilla; especially, designating or of either of two salivary glands, one on each side, below the inside edge of the submaxilla.

sub·me·di·ant (sub-mē′di-ənt), *n.* [*sub-*, under + *mediant*], the sixth tone of a diatonic scale; tone just above the dominant and below the subtonic: also called *superdominant.*

sub·merge (səb-mũrj′), *v.t.* [SUBMERGED (-mũrjd′), SUBMERGING], [L. *submergere; sub-*, under + *mergere*, to plunge], 1. to place under or as under water; plunge into water, etc. 2. to cover over; suppress; hide. *v.i.* to sink or plunge beneath the surface of water, etc.

sub·mer·gence (səb-mũr′jəns), *n.* a submerging or being submerged.

sub·mer·gi·ble (səb-mũr′jə-b'l), *adj.* that can be submerged.

sub·merse (səb-mũrs′), *v.t.* [SUBMERSED (-mũrst′), SUBMERSING], [< L. *submersus*, pp. of *submergere*], to submerge.

sub·mersed (səb-mũrst), *adj.* submerged; specifically, in *botany*, growing under water.

sub·mers·i·ble (səb-mũr′sə-b'l), *n.* [Rare], a submarine. *adj.* that can be submersed, especially so as to continue functioning.

sub·mer·sion (səb-mũr′shən, səb-mũr′zhən), *n.* a submersing or being submersed.

sub·mi·cro·scop·ic (sub'mī-krə-skop'ik), *adj.* too small to be seen through a microscope.
sub·miss (səb-mis'), *adj.* [Archaic], submissive; humble.
sub·mis·sion (səb-mish'ən), *n.* [ME.; OFr.; L. *submissio* < *submissus*, pp. of *submittere*], 1. the act of submitting, yielding, or surrendering. 2. the quality or condition of being submissive; resignation; obedience; meekness. 3. the act of submitting something to another for decision, consideration, etc.
sub·mis·sive (səb-mis'iv), *adj.* [< L. *submissus*, pp. of *submittere* (see SUBMIT); + *-ive*], having or showing a tendency to submit without resistance; docile; yielding.
sub·mit (səb-mit'), *v.t.* [SUBMITTED (-id), SUBMITTING], [ME. *submitten;* L. *submittere; sub-*, under, down + *mittere*, to send], 1. to present or refer to others for decision, consideration, etc. 2. to yield to the action, control, power, etc. of another or others; yield; surrender: often used reflexively. 3. to offer as an opinion; suggest; propose. *v.i.* 1. to yield to the power, control, etc. of another or others; give in. 2. to defer to another's judgment or decision. 3. to be submissive, obedient, humble, etc. —*SYN.* see **surrender.**
sub·mit·tal (səb-mit''l), *n.* the act of submitting.
sub·mon·tane (sub-mon'tān), *adj.* [< *sub-* (below) + L. *montanus*, of a mountain < *mons, montis*, mountain], 1. located at the foot of a mountain or mountains. 2. of or characteristic of foothills. 3. beneath a mountain.
sub·mul·ti·ple (sub-mul'ti-p'l), *n.* [*sub-* (below) + *multiple*], a number or quantity with reference to another which it will divide exactly; aliquot part: as, 3 is a *submultiple* of 12.
sub·nor·mal (sub-nôr'm'l), *adj.* [*sub-* (below) + *normal*], below the normal; less than normal, especially in intelligence. *n.* a subnormal person.
sub·nor·mal·i·ty (sub'nôr-mal'ə-ti), *n.* a subnormal quality or condition.
sub·o·ce·an·ic (sub'ō-shi-an'ik), *adj.* situated or taking place beneath the floor of the ocean.
sub·or·bit·al (sub-ôr'bit-'l), *adj.* 1. designating or of a space flight in which the spacecraft follows a steep, short-range trajectory instead of going into orbit. 2. beneath the orbit of the eye.
sub·or·der (sub'ôr'dẽr, sub-ôr'dẽr), *n.* a subdivision of an order of plants or animals.
sub·or·di·nal (sub-ôr'də-n'l), *adj.* [< Mod. L. *subordo, subordinis* (< L. *sub-*, below + *ordo*, order); + *-al*], of or ranking as a suborder.
sub·or·di·nate (sə-bôr'də-nit; *for v.*, sə-bôr'də-nāt'), *adj.* [ML. *subordinatus*, pp. of *subordinare;* L. *sub-*, under + *ordinare*, to order], 1. inferior to or placed below another in rank, power, importance, etc.; secondary. 2. under the power or authority of another. 3. subservient or submissive. 4. in *grammar*, *a*) designating or of a clause that is dependent upon another clause and does not itself constitute a formal sentence. *b*) introducing such a clause: as, *who, that, which, since, if*, etc. are *subordinate* conjunctions. *n.* a subordinate person or thing. *v.t.* [SUBORDINATED (-id), SUBORDINATING], 1. to place in a subordinate position; treat as inferior or less important. 2. to make obedient or subservient (*to*); control; subdue.
sub·or·di·na·tion (sə-bôr'də-nā'shən), *n.* 1. a subordinating or being subordinate. 2. subjection or submission to rank, power, authority, etc.; obedience.
sub·or·di·na·tion·ism (sə-bôr'də-nā'shən-iz'm), *n.* in *theology*, the doctrine that the second and third persons of the Trinity are subordinate to the first person.
sub·or·di·na·tive (sə-bôr'də-nā'tiv), *adj.* 1. tending to or involving subordination. 2. in *grammar*, introducing a subordinate clause; subordinate.
sub·orn (sə-bôrn'), *v.t.* [Fr. *suborner;* L. *subornare*, to furnish or supply, instigate, incite secretly; *sub-*, under + *ornare*, to furnish], 1. to get or bring about through bribery or other illegal methods. 2. to induce or instigate (another) to do something illegal, especially to commit perjury.
sub·or·na·tion (sub'ôr-nā'shən), *n.* [Fr.], a suborning or being suborned; especially, the crime of inducing another to commit perjury (*subornation of perjury*).
Su·bo·ti·ca, Su·bo·ti·tsa (sōō'bô'ti-tsä), *n.* a city in northeastern Yugoslavia: pop., 75,000: Hungarian name, *Szabadka.*
sub·ox·ide (sub-ok'sīd, sub-ok'sid), *n.* an oxide containing a relatively small proportion of oxygen.
sub·phy·lum (sub-fī'ləm), *n.* any of the principal subdivisions of a phylum.
sub·plot (sub'plot'), *n.* a secondary or subordinate plot in a play, novel, etc.
sub·poe·na (sə-pē'nə, səb-pē'nə), *n.* [ME. *subpena, suppena;* ML.; L. *sub*, under + *poena*, pain, penalty], a written legal order directing a person to appear in court to give testimony, etc. *v.t.* [SUBPOENAED (-nəd), SUBPOENAING], to serve or summon with such an order. Also spelled **subpena.**
‡**sub poe·na** (sub pē'nə), [L.], under penalty.
sub·prin·ci·pal (sub-prin'sə-p'l), *n.* 1. a subordinate principal in a school, etc. 2. a secondary brace or rafter. 3. in *music*, an open diapason subbass in an organ.
sub·re·gion (sub'rē'jən), *n.* any of the divisions of a region, especially with reference to the distribution of plants and animals.
sub·rep·tion (səb-rep'shən), *n.* [L. *subreptio* < *subreptus*, pp. of *subripere*, to take away secretly, steal < *sub*, under + *rapere*, to take away, snatch], 1. the fraudulent concealment or misrepresentation of facts. 2. a false inference drawn from this. 3. the procurement of advantage, property, etc., especially of an ecclesiastical dispensation, by means of such fraudulent concealment of fact.
sub·rep·ti·tious (sub'rep-ti'shəs), *adj.* of, characterized by, or secured by subreption.
sub·ro·gate (sub'rə-gāt'), *v.t.* [SUBROGATED (-id), SUBROGATING], [< L. *subrogatus*, pp. of *subrogare*, to cause to be chosen in place of another; *sub-*, under + *rogare*, to ask], to substitute (one person) for another; especially, to substitute (one creditor) for another.
sub·ro·ga·tion (sub'rə-gā'shən), *n.* [ME. *subrogacioun;* ML. *subrogatio* < L. *subrogatus*], a subrogating; especially, substitution of one creditor for another.
‡**sub ro·sa** (sub rō'zə), [L., lit., under the rose: the rose in ancient times was a symbol of silence or secrecy], secretly; privately; confidentially.
sub·scap·u·lar (sub-skap'yoo-lẽr), *adj.* situated beneath the scapula.
sub·scribe (səb-skrīb'), *v.t.* [SUBSCRIBED (-skrībd'), SUBSCRIBING], [ME.; L. *subscribere; sub-*, under + *scribere*, to write], 1. to sign (one's name) at the end of a document, etc. 2. to write one's signature on (a document, etc.) as an indication of consent, acceptance, etc. 3. to support; consent to; favor; sanction. 4. to promise to pay or contribute (money), especially by signing a pledge. *v.i.* 1. to sign one's name at the end of a document, etc. 2. to give support, sanction, or approval; consent; agree: as, he would not *subscribe* to such a measure. 3. to promise to pay or contribute a sum of money. 4. to agree to receive and pay for a periodical, etc. for a specified period of time (with *to*).
sub·scrib·er (səb-skrīb'ẽr), *n.* a person who subscribes to something.
sub·script (sub'skript), *adj.* [L. *subscriptus*, pp. of *subscribere;* see SUBSCRIBE], written underneath. *n.* a figure, letter, symbol, etc. that is written underneath, as a mathematical subindex.
sub·scrip·tion (səb-skrip'shən), *n.* [L. *subscriptio*], 1. the act of subscribing. 2. something subscribed; specifically, *a*) a written signature. *b*) a signed document, etc. *c*) consent or sanction, especially in writing. *d*) an amount of money subscribed. *e*) a formal agreement to receive and pay for a periodical, books, theater tickets, etc. for a specified period of time. *f*) the right to receive a periodical, etc., as by payment of a fixed sum. 3. in *ecclesiastical usage*, assent to certain doctrines for promoting uniformity; specifically, in the Anglican Church, acceptance of the Thirty-nine Articles of Faith and the Book of Common Prayer.
sub·scrip·tive (səb-skrip'tiv), *adj.* of, for, or indicating subscription.
sub·sec·tion (sub-sek'shən, sub'sek'shən), *n.* a division of a section.
sub·se·quence (sub'si-kwəns, sub'si-kwens'), *n.* 1. the fact or condition of being subsequent. 2. a subsequent happening, etc.
sub·se·quen·cy (sub'si-kwən-si), *n.* subsequence.
sub·se·quent (sub'si-kwənt, sub'si-kwent'), *adj.* [ME.; L. *subsequens*, ppr. of *subsequi*, to follow close after; *sub-*, after + *sequi*, to follow], coming after; following in time, place, or order.
subsequent to, after; following after; following.
sub·se·quent·ly (sub'si-kwənt-li, sub'si-kwent'li), *adv.* at a subsequent time; afterward.
sub·serve (səb-sũrv'), *v.t.* [L. *subservire; sub-*, under + *servire*, to serve], to be useful or helpful to (a purpose, cause, etc.); serve; promote; aid.
sub·ser·vi·ence (səb-sũr'vi-əns), *n.* 1. the state or quality of being subservient. 2. subservient behavior or manner; submissiveness; servility.
sub·ser·vi·en·cy (səb-sũr'vi-ən-si), *n.* subservience.
sub·ser·vi·ent (səb-sũr'vi-ənt), *adj.* [L. *subserviens*, ppr. of *subservire*, to subserve], 1. that is useful, helpful, or of service, especially in an inferior or subordinate capacity. 2. submissive; obsequious. —*SYN.* see **servile.**
sub·shrub (sub'shrub'), *n.* an undershrub.
sub·side (səb-sīd'), *v.i.* [SUBSIDED (-id), SUBSIDING], [L. *subsidere; sub-*, under + *sidere*, to settle < *sedere*, to sit], 1. to sink or fall to the bottom; settle, as sediment. 2. to sink to a lower level. 3. to become less active, violent, intense, etc.; become quiet; abate. —*SYN.* see **wane.**
sub·sid·ence (səb-sīd''ns, sub'si-dəns), *n.* [L. *subsidentia*], the process of subsiding.

sub·sid·i·ar·i·ly (səb-sid′i-er′ə-li), *adv.* in a subsidiary manner or capacity.

sub·sid·i·ar·y (səb-sid′i-er′i), *adj.* [L. *subsidiarius* < *subsidium;* see SUBSIDY], 1. acting as a supplement; giving aid, support, service, etc.; auxiliary, especially in a secondary or subordinate capacity. 2. of, constituting, or maintained by a subsidy or subsidies. *n.* [*pl.* SUBSIDIARIES (-iz)], 1. a person or thing that gives aid, support, or service; auxiliary. 2. a company controlled by another company which owns most of its shares: in full, **subsidiary company.** 3. in *music,* a subordinate theme.

sub·si·di·za·tion (sub′sə-di-zā′shən, sub′sə-dī-zā′shən), *n.* a subsidizing or being subsidized.

sub·si·dize (sub′sə-dīz′), *v.t.* [SUBSIDIZED (-dīzd′), SUBSIDIZING], [< *subsidy* + *-ize*], 1. to support with a subsidy. 2. to buy the aid or support of with a subsidy: now often implying bribery.

sub·si·dy (sub′sə-di), *n.* [*pl.* SUBSIDIES (-diz)], [ME. *subsidie;* Anglo-Fr. *subsidie;* L. *subsidium,* auxiliary forces, reserve troops, aid, support < *subsidere,* to sit down, remain; *sub-,* down + *sidere,* to settle], a grant of money; specifically, *a*) a grant of money from one government to another, especially to aid in carrying on a war against a third. *b*) a government grant to a private enterprise considered of benefit to the public. *c*) in England, formerly, money granted by Parliament to the king.

sub·sist (səb-sist′), *v.i.* [Fr. *subsister;* L. *subsistere,* to stand still, stay, abide; *sub-,* under + *sistere,* to place, stand], 1. to continue to be or exist as a reality or in a given state; abide. 2. to continue to live; remain alive (*on* sustenance, *by* specific means, etc.). 3. to consist or inhere (*in*). 4. in *philosophy,* to be logically conceivable and, hence, to hold true. *v.t.* to maintain with sustenance; support.

sub·sist·ence (səb-sis′təns), *n.* [ME.; LL. *subsistentia* < L. *subsister;* see SUBSIST], 1. existence; being; continuance. 2. the quality of being inherent. 3. the act of providing sustenance. 4. means of support or livelihood. 5. in *philosophy,* the status of something that subsists.

sub·sist·ent (səb-sis′tənt), *adj.* [L. *subsistens*], existing; being; having subsistence, substance, or reality.

sub·soil (sub′soil′), *n.* the layer of soil beneath the surface soil. *v.t.* to stir or turn up the subsoil of.

sub·so·lar (sub-sō′lẽr), *adj.* [*sub-* + *solar*], 1. located under the sun. 2. worldly; terrestrial; mundane. 3. characterized by having the sun in the zenith. 4. being between the tropics; equatorial.

sub·son·ic (sub′son′ik), *adj.* [< *sub-;* + L. *sonus,* sound; + *-ic*], designating or of speeds that are less than that of sound through air (about 738 miles per hour).

‡sub spe·ci·e (sub spē′shi-ē′), [L.], under the aspect (of).

sub·spe·cies (sub-spē′shiz, sub′spē′shiz), *n.* [Mod. L.; see SUB- & SPECIES], a division of a species.

subst., 1. substantive. 2. substitute.

sub·stage (sub′stāj′), *n.* a fixture under the stage of a microscope, used to hold mirrors, etc: see **microscope,** illus.

sub·stance (sub′stəns), *n.* [ME.: OFr.; L. *substantia* < *substare,* to be present, exist], 1. the real or essential part or element of anything; essence; reality; matter. 2. the physical matter of which a thing consists; material. 3. *a*) solid quality; substantial character. *b*) consistency; body. 4. the real content of a statement, speech, etc.; true meaning; purport. 5. matter of a particular kind; stuff. 6. material possessions; property; resources; wealth. 7. in *philosophy,* something that has independent existence and is acted upon by causes or events.
in substance, 1. with regard to essential elements; substantially. 2. actually; really.

sub·stand·ard (sub-stan′dẽrd), *adj.* below standard; specifically, *a*) below a standard established by law. *b*) in *linguistics,* deviating from the standard language patterns of cultivated speakers of the language: as, obscenities, solecisms, slang, etc. are generally considered *substandard.*

sub·stan·tial (səb-stan′shəl), *adj.* [ME. & OFr. *substanciel;* LL. *substantialis*], 1. of or having substance. 2. real; actual; true; not imaginary. 3. strong; solid; firm; stout. 4. considerable; ample; large. 5. of considerable worth or value; important. 6. having property or possessions; wealthy. 7. with regard to essential elements. 8. in *philosophy,* of, or having the nature of, substance. *n. usually pl.* a substantial thing.

sub·stan·tial·ism (səb-stan′shəl-iz′m), *n.* in *philosophy,* 1. the doctrine that substantial realities underlie all phenomena. 2. the doctrine that matter is a real substance.

sub·stan·ti·al·i·ty (səb-stan′shi-al′ə-ti), *n.* [LL. *substantialitas*], 1. the quality or state of being substantial; real existence. 2. genuineness; true worth. 3. physical firmness; solidity.

sub·stan·tial·ly (səb-stan′shə-li), *adv.* 1. in a substantial manner; solidly; firmly; with strength. 2. to a substantial degree; specifically, *a*) truly; really; actually. *b*) largely; essentially; in the main.

sub·stan·ti·ate (səb-stan′shi-āt′), *v.t.* [SUBSTANTIATED (-id), SUBSTANTIATING], [< Mod. L. *substantiatus,* pp. of *substantiare* < L. *substantia;* see SUBSTANCE], 1. to give substance or true existence to. 2. to give concrete form or body to; convert into substance. 3. to show to be true or real by giving evidence; prove; confirm. —*SYN.* see **confirm.**

sub·stan·ti·a·tion (səb-stan′shi-ā′shən), *n.* a substantiating or being substantiated; embodiment.

sub·stan·ti·val (sub′stən-tī′v'l), *adj.* of, or having the nature of, a substantive.

sub·stan·ti·val·ly (sub′stən-tī′v'l-i), *adv.* as a substantive.

sub·stan·tive (sub′stən-tiv), *adj.* [ME. & OFr. *substantif;* LL. *substantivus* < *substantia;* see SUBSTANCE], 1. existing independently; not dependent upon or subordinate to another. 2. of considerable amount; substantial. 3. having a real existence; actual. 4. of or containing the essential elements; essential. 5. of or consisting of legal rights and principles as distinguished from rules of form. 6. of a dye, becoming fixed without the use of a mordant. 7. in *grammar, a*) showing or expressing existence: as, the *substantive* verb "to be." *b*) of or used as a substantive. *n.* 1. something substantive. 2. in *grammar, a*) a noun. *b*) any word or group of words used as an equivalent for a noun. Abbreviated **s., sb., subst.**

sub·sta·tion (sub′stā′shən), *n.* a branch station.

sub·sti·tute (sub′stə-tōōt′, sub′stə-tūt′), *n.* [ME.; L. *substitutus,* pp. of *substituere,* to put instead of < *sub-,* under + *statuere,* to put, place], a person or thing acting or used in place of another; specifically, *a*) formerly, a person who, for a payment, entered military service in another's place. *b*) in *grammar,* any word, as a pronoun, the verb *to do,* etc., used in place of another word or words (e.g., *did* for *shouted* in "she shouted and so did he."). *v.t.* [SUBSTITUTED (-id), SUBSTITUTING], 1. to put or use in place of another. 2. to take the place of. *v.i.* to act or serve in place of another: often with *for.* *adj.* substitutional. Abbreviated **subst.**

sub·sti·tu·tion (sub′stə-tōō′shən, sub′stə-tū′shən), *n.* a substituting or being substituted.

sub·sti·tu·tion·al (sub′stə-tōō′shən-'l, sub′stə-tū′shən-'l), *adj.* 1. of or characterized by substitution. 2. that is a substitute.

sub·sti·tu·tion·ar·y (sub′stə-tōō′shən-er′i, sub′stə-tū′shən-er′i), *adj.* substitutional.

sub·sti·tu·tive (sub′stə-tōō′tiv, sub′stə-tū′tiv), *adj.* [LL. *substitutivus*], 1. of or having to do with substitution. 2. being or capable of being a substitute.

sub·strate (sub′strāt), *n.* 1. a substratum. 2. in *biochemistry,* the substance that is acted upon by an enzyme or ferment.

sub·strat·o·sphere (sub-strat′ə-sfêr′, sub-strā′tə-sfêr′), *n.* the stratum of the atmosphere just below the stratosphere, from about 3 1/2 miles to about 7 miles above the earth's surface.

sub·stra·tum (sub-strā′təm, sub′strat′əm), *n.* [*pl.* SUBSTRATA (-tə, -ə)], [L., neut. of *substratus,* pp. of *substernere,* to strew beneath; *sub-,* under + *sternere,* to strew], 1. a part, substance, element, etc. which lies beneath and supports another; foundation. 2. figuratively, any basis or foundation. 3. in *agriculture,* subsoil. 4. in *biology,* the medium upon which an organism grows. 5. in *metaphysics,* substance, with reference to the events or causes which act upon it.

sub·struc·tion (sub-struk′shən), *n.* a substructure.

sub·struc·tur·al (sub-struk′chẽr-əl), *adj.* of a substructure.

sub·struc·ture (sub-struk′chẽr), *n.* a part or structure acting as a support; base; foundation.

sub·sume (səb-sōōm′, səb-sūm′), *v.t.* [SUBSUMED (-sōōmd′, -sūmd′), SUBSUMING], [Mod. L. *subsumere;* L. *sub-,* under + *sumere,* to take], 1. to include in a class, group, order, etc.; classify. 2. to show (an idea, instance, etc.) to be covered by a rule, principle, etc.

sub·sump·tion (səb-sump′shən), *n.* [Mod. L. *subsumptio* < *subsumptus,* pp. of *subsumere*], 1. a subsuming or being subsumed. 2. something subsumed; especially, a minor concept or premise.

sub·sump·tive (səb-sump′tiv), *adj.* [Mod. L. *subsumptivus*], of, or having the nature of, subsumption.

sub·tan·gent (sub-tan′jənt), *n.* [Mod. L. *subtangens;* see SUB- & TANGENT], that part of the axis of abscissas included between the ordinate of a point on a curve and the tangent at that point.

sub·tem·per·ate (sub-tem′pẽr-it), *adj.* of or occurring in the colder areas of the Temperate Zones.

sub·ten·an·cy (sub-ten′ən-si), *n.* 1. the status or occupancy of a subtenant. 2. the period of such occupancy.

sub·ten·ant (sub-ten′ənt), *n.* a person who rents from a tenant; tenant of a tenant.

sub·tend (səb-tend′), *v.t.* [L. *subtendere; sub-,* under + *tendere,* to stretch], 1. to extend under; be opposite to in position: as, each side of a triangle *subtends* the opposite angle. 2. in *botany,* to enclose in an angle, as between a leaf and its stem.

sub·ter- (sub′tẽr), [< L. *subter,* below, beneath], a prefix meaning *below, under, less than, secretly.*

sub·ter·fuge (sub′tẽr-fūj′), *n.* [Fr.; LL. *subterfugium* < L. *subterfugere*, to flee secretly, escape; *subter-*, below + *fugere*, to flee, escape], any plan or action used to evade something difficult or unpleasant; device; artifice. —*SYN.* see **deception.**

sub·ter·nat·u·ral (sub′tẽr-nach′ẽr-əl), *adj.* below, or less than, what is natural.

sub·ter·ra·ne·an (sub′tə-rā′ni-ən), *adj.* [L. *subterraneus* < *sub-*, under + *terra*, earth], 1. lying beneath the earth's surface; underground. 2. secret; hidden.

sub·ter·ra·ne·ous (sub′tə-rā′ni-əs), *adj.* subterranean.

sub·tile (sut′'l, sub′til), *adj.* [ME. *soubtil;* OFr. *subtil, soutil;* L. *subtilis;* see SUBTLE], subtle (esp. sense 1).

sub·til·i·ty (səb-til′ə-ti), *n.* [*pl.* SUBTILITIES (-tiz)], subtlety.

sub·til·i·za·tion (sut′'l-i-zā′shən, sub′t'l-ī-zā′shən), *n.* [ML. *subtilizatio*], a subtilizing or being subtilized.

sub·til·ize (sut′'l-īz′, sub′t'l-īz′), *v.t. & v.i.* [SUBTILIZED (-īzd′), SUBTILIZING], [ML. *subtilizare* < L. *subtilis*, subtle], to make or become subtle; especially, to discuss or argue with subtle distinctions.

sub·til·ty (sut′'l-ti, sub′t'l-ti), *n.* [*pl.* SUBTILTIES (-tiz)], subtlety.

sub·ti·tle (sub′tī′t'l), *n.* 1. a secondary or explanatory title, as of a book or play. 2. a book title repeated at the top of the first page of text. 3. in *motion pictures*, *a)* descriptive titles or dialogue thrown on the screen between scenes, as in a silent motion picture. *b)* dialogue translated from the original language and superimposed on the film.

sub·tle (sut′'l), *adj.* [ME. *sotil, sutell, soutil;* OFr. *soutil;* L. *subtilis*, fine, thin, precise, orig. closely woven < *sub-*, under + *tela*, web; cf. SUBTILE], 1. thin; rare; tenuous; not dense or heavy. 2. keen; acute; penetrating; discriminating. 3. delicately skillful or clever; deft; ingenious. 4. crafty; artful; wily; designing. 5. strangely suggestive; mysterious; sly: as, a *subtle* wink. 6. hard to solve, detect, or understand; intricate; abstruse: as, a *subtle* problem. 7. acting in an insidious way: as, a *subtle* poison. Also (esp. sense 1) **subtile.**

sub·tle·ty (sut′'l-ti), *n.* [ME. *sutelte;* OFr. *sotillete;* L. *subtilitas*], 1. the quality or condition of being subtle; especially, the ability or practice of making fine distinctions. 2. [*pl.* SUBTLETIES (-tiz)], something subtle; especially, a fine distinction. Also **subtility, subtilty.**

sub·tly (sut′li, sut′'l-i), *adv.* in a subtle manner.

sub·ton·ic (sub-ton′ik), *n.* in *music*, the seventh tone of a diatonic scale; tone next below the upper tonic.

sub·tor·rid (sub-tôr′id, sub-tor′id), *adj.* subtropical.

sub·tract (səb-trakt′), *v.t. & v.i.* [< L. *subtractus*, pp. of *subtrahere*, to draw away underneath, subtract; *sub-*, under + *trahere*, to draw], to take away or deduct, as a part from a whole or one quantity from another.

sub·trac·tion (səb-trak′shən), *n.* a subtracting or being subtracted; especially, the mathematical process of finding the difference between two numbers or quantities.

sub·trac·tive (səb-trak′tiv), *adj.* [ML. *subtractivus*], 1. tending to subtract. 2. capable of or involving subtraction. 3. that is to be subtracted; marked with the minus sign (—).

sub·tra·hend (sub′trə-hend′), *n.* [L. *subtrahendus*, gerundive of *subtrahere;* see SUBTRACT], a number or quantity to be subtracted from another (the *minuend*).

sub·treas·ur·y (sub′trezh′ẽr-i, sub-trezh′ẽr-i), *n.* [*pl.* SUBTREASURIES (-iz)], a branch treasury.

sub·trop·ic (sub-trop′ik), *adj.* subtropical.

sub·trop·i·cal (sub-trop′i-k'l), *adj.* 1. designating or of regions bordering on the tropical zone. 2. characteristic of such regions; nearly tropical.

sub·trop·ics (sub-trop′iks), *n.pl.* subtropical regions.

su·bu·late (sōō′byoo-lit, sū′byoo-lāt′), *adj.* [Mod. L. *subulatus* < L. *subula*, an awl], slender and tapering to a point; awl-shaped.

sub·urb (sub′ẽrb), *n.* [ME.; OFr. *suburbe;* L. *suburbium* < *sub-*, under + *urbs, urbis*, town], 1. a district, especially a residential district, on the outskirts of a city: often a separately incorporated city or town. 2. *pl.* outlying parts, or confines. Abbreviated **sub.**

the suburbs, the residential areas near, or on the outskirts of, a city.

sub·ur·ban (sə-bũr′bən), *adj.* 1. of, in, or residing in a suburb or the suburbs. 2. characteristic of the suburbs or suburbanites: variously connoting a combination of rural and urban features, middle-class conservatism, etc. *n.* a suburbanite. Abbreviated **sub.**

sub·ur·ban·ite (sə-bũr′bən-īt′), *n.* a person living in a suburb.

sub·ur·bi·a (sə-bũr′bi-ə), *n.* the suburbs collectively; usually used to connote the values, attitudes, and activities regarded as characteristic of suburban life.

sub·ur·bi·car·i·an (sə-bũr′bi-kâr′i-ən), *adj.* [< LL. *suburbicarius* < L. *suburbanus* (see SUBURB); + *-an*], being in the suburbs of Rome; specifically, designating or of the six dioceses surrounding Rome, each of which is under the jurisdiction of a cardinal bishop.

sub·vene (səb-vēn′), *v.i.* [SUBVENED (-vēnd′), SUBVENING], [L. *subvenire*, to come to one's assistance, lit., to come up; *sub-*, under + *venire*, to come], to intervene with support or aid; happen or come so as to help, especially by preventing something.

sub·ven·tion (səb-ven′shən), *n.* [ME. *subvencioun;* OFr. *subvencion;* LL. *subventio*], 1. a subvening. 2. money granted, as by a government, in support of a study, institution, or undertaking; subsidy; grant.

‡sub ver·bo (sub vũr′bō), [L.], under the word (specified): with reference to an entry in a dictionary, index, etc.: abbreviated **s.v.**: also **sub voce.**

sub·ver·sion (səb-vũr′zhən, səb-vũr′shən), *n.* [ME.; OFr.; L. *subversio*], 1. a subverting or being subverted; ruin; overthrow. 2. something that subverts; cause of ruin or overthrow.

sub·ver·sive (səb-vũr′siv), *adj.* [< L. *subversus*, pp. of *subvertere* (see SUBVERT); + *-ive*], tending to subvert, overthrow, or destroy (something established). *n.* a person regarded as subversive.

sub·vert (səb-vũrt′), *v.t.* [ME. *subverten;* OFr. *subvertir;* L. *subvertere; sub-*, under + *vertere*, to turn], 1. to overthrow or destroy (something established). 2. to undermine or corrupt, as in character or morals.

‡sub vo·ce (sub vō′si), [L., under the voice], sub verbo.

sub·way (sub′wā′), *n.* 1. an underground way or passage. 2. an underground, metropolitan electric railway or the tunnel through which this runs.

suc- (suk), see **sub-.**

suc·ce·da·ne·um (suk′si-dā′ni-əm), *n.* [*pl.* SUCCEDANEA (-ə)], [Mod. L., neut. sing. < L. *succedaneus*, substituted < *succedere;* see SUCCEED], a substitute.

suc·ceed (sək-sēd′), *v.i.* [OFr. *succeder;* L. *succedere*, to go beneath or under, follow after < *sub-*, under + *cedere*, to go], 1. to come next after another; follow; ensue: as, all *succeeding* laws were null and void. 2. to follow another into office, possession, etc.: as, the vice-president *succeeds* in case of the president's death. 3. to have success; accomplish something planned or attempted; also, formerly, to have (a specified) success: as, he *succeeded* badly. 4. [Obs.], to devolve, as an estate. *v.t.* 1. to take the place left by; follow into office, possession, etc. 2. to come or occur after; follow.

SYN.—**succeed** implies the favorable outcome of an undertaking, career, etc. or the attainment of a desired goal (to *succeed* as a businessman); **prosper** implies continued, often increasing, good fortune or success (the nation *prospered* under his administration); **flourish** more specifically suggests a figurative state of flowering, when a person or thing is at the peak of development, influence, etc. (militarism *flourishes* in a fascist state); **thrive** implies vigorous growth or development, as because of favorable conditions (industry *thrived* in the North). See also **follow.** —*ANT.* fail

suc·cen·tor (sək-sen′tẽr), *n.* [LL. < *succinere*, to accompany < *sub-*, under + *canere*, to sing], the assistant to the leader in certain church choirs.

suc·cess (sək-ses′), *n.* [L. *successus* < *succedere;* see SUCCEED], 1. [Obs.], result; outcome. 2. a favorable or satisfactory outcome or result. 3. extent of succeeding: as, what *success* did he have? 4. the gaining of wealth, fame, rank, etc. 5. a successful person or thing.

suc·cess·ful (sək-ses′fəl), *adj.* 1. coming about, taking place, or turning out to be as was hoped for; having a favorable result: as, a *successful* mission. 2. achieving or having achieved success; specifically, having gained wealth, fame, rank, etc.

suc·ces·sion (sək-sesh′ən), *n.* [ME.; OFr.; L. *successio* < *succedere;* see SUCCEED], 1. the act of succeeding or coming after another in order or sequence or to an office, estate, etc. 2. the right to succeed to an office, estate, etc. 3. a number of persons or things coming one after another in time or space; series; sequence: as, a *succession* of piercing screams. 4. *a)* a series of heirs or rightful successors of any kind. *b)* the order or line of such a series. —*SYN.* see **series.**

in succession, one after another in a regular series or sequence.

suc·ces·sion·al (sək-sesh′ən-'l), *adj.* of, involving, or occurring in a regular sequence or succession.

suc·ces·sive (sək-ses′iv), *adj.* [ME. < L. *successus* (see SUCCESS); + *-ive*], 1. coming in succession; following one after another in sequence without an interruption; consecutive. 2. of or involving succession.

suc·ces·sor (sək-ses′ẽr), *n.* [ME.; OFr. *successur, successour;* L. < *successus*, pp. of *succedere;* see SUCCEED], a person or thing that succeeds, or follows, another; especially, one who succeeds to an office, title, etc.

suc·cinct (sək-siŋkt′), *adj.* [ME., girdled, girded; L. *succinctus*, prepared, short, contracted, pp. of *succingere*, to gird below, tuck up, prepare < *sub-*, under + *cingere*, to gird], 1. clearly and briefly stated; terse. 2. characterized by brevity and conciseness of speech. 3. [Archaic], enclosed as by a girdle. —*SYN.* see **concise.**

suc·cin·ic acid (sək-sin′ik), [Fr. *succinique* < L. *succinum*, amber], a colorless, crystalline dibasic acid,

($(CH_2CO_2H)_2$, found in amber, lignite, and many plants, and produced synthetically or during alcoholic fermentation: it is used in medicine and organic synthesis.

suc·cor (suk'ẽr), *v.t.* [ME. *socouren;* OFr. *sucurre, socorre;* L. *succurrere* < *sub-*, under + *currere*, to run], to give assistance to in time of need or distress; help; aid; relieve. *n.* [ME. & OFr. *sucurs;* ML. *succursus* < the *v.*], 1. aid; help; relief; assistance. 2. a person or thing that succors. —*SYN.* see **help.**

suc·cor·y (suk'ẽr-i), *n.* [altered, after MLG. *suckerie* < older *sycory*, early form of *chicory;* see CHICORY], chicory.

suc·co·tash (suk'ə-tash'), *n.* [< Am. Ind. (Narragansett) *misickquatash*, ear of corn], a dish consisting of beans and corn kernels cooked together.

suc·cour (suk'ẽr), *v.t. & n.* succor: British spelling.

suc·cu·ba (suk'yoo-bə), *n.* [*pl.* SUCCUBAE (-bē')], a succubus.

suc·cu·bus (suk'yoo-bəs), *n.* [*pl.* SUCCUBI (-bī')], [ME.; ML. < *succuba*, strumpet < *succubare*, to lie under < *sub-*, under + *cubare*, to lie], in *folklore*, a female demon thought to have sexual intercourse with sleeping men: cf. **incubus.**

suc·cu·lence (suk'yoo-ləns), *n.* succulent quality or condition; juiciness.

suc·cu·len·cy (suk'yoo-lən-si), *n.* succulence.

suc·cu·lent (suk'yoo-lənt), *adj.* [L. *succulentus* < *sucus*, juice], 1. full of juice; juicy. 2. interesting; not dry or dull. 3. in *botany*, having juicy tissues, as a cactus.

suc·cumb (sə-kum'), *v.i.* [OFr. *succomber;* L. *succumbere* < *sub-*, under + *cumbere*, nasalized form of *cubare*, to lie], 1. to give way; yield; submit (often with *to*): as, he *succumbed* to her persuasion. 2. to die (often with *to*): as, he *succumbed* to cancer. —*SYN.* see **yield.**

suc·cur·sal (sə-kũr's'l), *adj.* [Fr. *succursale* < ML. *succursus;* see SUCCOR], subsidiary; especially, designating a church or monastery that is a branch of a main one.

suc·cuss (sə-kus'), *v.t.* [< L. *succussus*, pp. of *succutere*, to toss up < *sub-*, under + *quatere*, to shake], to shake forcibly; specifically, in *medicine*, to shake (a patient) in order to detect the presence of a liquid in some body cavity, especially in the thorax.

suc·cus·sa·tion (suk'ə-sā'shən), *n.* succussion.

suc·cus·sion (sə-kush'ən), *n.* [L. *succussio*], the act or method of succussing.

suc·cus·sive (sə-kus'iv), *adj.* of succussion.

such (such), *adj.* [ME. *swulc, swilch, swich;* AS. *swylc, swilc, swelc;* akin to G. *solch*, Goth. *swaleiks;* orig. a compound < base of *so* + base of *like*], 1. of this or that kind; of the same or similar kind; like or similar to something mentioned or implied; specifically, *a*) being the same as what was stated before: as, *such* happiness was all he wished. *b*) being the same in quality or kind: as, hats, coats, and *such* objects. 2. not named; indefinite; some; certain: as, on *such* a day as you may go. 3. so extreme, so much, so great, etc.: used, according to the context, for emphasis: as, he never expected *such* honor. *Such* is a term of comparison, although that with which comparison is made is not always expressed. When expressed, *as* or *that* is used as a correlative with *such* (e.g., *such* love *as* his is seldom experienced, we had *such* fun *that* nobody left). It is not preceded by an article, although the article may occur between it and the noun it modifies (e.g., *such* a fellow!). *adv.* [Colloq.], to such a degree; so: as, he was *such* a good man. *pron.* 1. such a person (or persons) or thing (or things): as, *such* as live by the sword. 2. the person or thing mentioned or implied: as, *such* was his nature.

as such, 1. as being what is indicated or suggested. 2. in itself: as, a name, *as such*, means nothing.

such as, 1. for example. 2. like or similar to (something specified).

such and such, being a particular one but not named or specified: as, he went to *such and such* a place.

such·like (such'līk'), *adj.* of such a kind; of like or similar kind. *pron.* persons or things of such a kind.

suck (suk), *v.t.* [ME. *suken;* AS. *sucan;* akin to G. *saugen;* IE. base *seuq-, *suq- < *seu-, damp, sap, moistness, as also in L. *sugere*, to suck; cf. SUP, SOAK], 1. to draw (liquid) into the mouth by forming a partial vacuum with the lips and tongue. 2. to take up or in by or as by sucking; absorb, inhale, etc.: as, he *sucked* air into his lungs, the pumps soon *sucked* the water from the hold. 3. to draw liquid from (a breast, fruit, etc.) by action of the lips and tongue. 4. to dissolve or consume by holding in the mouth or licking, as candy, ice, etc. 5. to hold (the thumb, etc.) in the mouth. 6. to bring into a specified state by sucking: as, he *sucked* the orange dry. *v.i.* 1. to draw in water, air, etc. by creating a partial vacuum; suck something. 2. to suck milk from the breast or udder. 3. to make the sound of sucking. 4. to draw in air instead of liquid: said of a faulty pump. *n.* 1. the act of sucking; sucking action or force; suction. 2. the sound of sucking. 3. something drawn in by sucking; especially, [Colloq.], the amount sucked at one time; sip.

suck in, [Slang], to take advantage of; swindle, etc.

suck·er (suk'ẽr), *n.* 1. a person or thing that sucks. 2. a fish of the carp family, with a mouth adapted for sucking. 3. a part or device used for sucking; specifically, *a*) a pipe or conduit through which something is sucked. *b*) the piston or piston valve of a suction pump. *c*) an organ used by the snail, leech, etc. for sucking or holding fast to a surface by suction. 4. [Slang], a person easily cheated or taken in; dupe; simpleton. 5. [Colloq.], a lollipop. 6. in *botany*, any of the rootlike sucking organs of certain parasitic plants; haustorium. 7. in *horticulture*, a shoot springing from the roots or stem of a plant. *v.t.* to remove suckers, or shoots, from. *v.i.* to bear suckers, or shoots.

suck·fish (suk'fish'), *n.* [*pl.* SUCKFISH, SUCKFISHES (-iz); see FISH], 1. the remora. 2. a small sea fish of the blenny family, having a sucking disk on the underside.

suck·le (suk''l), *v.t.* [SUCKLED (-'ld), SUCKLING], [ME. *suclen, sokelen*, freq. of *suken*, to suck], 1. to cause to suck at the breast or udder; nurse; hence, 2. to bring up; rear; foster. *v.i.* to suck at the breast.

suck·ler (suk'lẽr), *n.* 1. a mammal. 2. a suckling.

suck·ling (suk'liŋ), *n.* [ME. *suklynge*, dim. < *souken, soken*, to suck], an unweaned child or young animal.

Suck·ling, Sir John (suk'liŋ), 1609–1642; English poet.

Su·cre (so͞o'kre), *n.* the nominal capital of Bolivia, in the south central part: pop., 54,000.

su·cre (so͞o'kre), *n.* [Am. Sp., after Antonio José de *Sucre* (1795–1830), S. Am. liberator], the monetary unit of Ecuador, equal to about 4 1/2 cents in 1947.

su·crose (so͞o'krōs, sū'krōs), *n.* [< Fr. *sucre*, sugar], a crystalline sugar, $C_{12}H_{22}O_{11}$, found in sugar cane, sugar beets, etc.

suc·tion (suk'shən), *n.* [OFr.; L. *suctio* < *suctus*, pp. of *sugere*, to suck], 1. the act or process of sucking. 2. the production of a vacuum or partial vacuum in a container or over a surface, so that the external atmospheric pressure forces the surrounding fluid into the space or causes something to adhere to the surface. 3. the sucking force created in this way. *adj.* 1. causing suction. 2. operating by means of suction.

suction pump, a pump that draws water up by suction created by pistons fitted with valves.

suction stop, in *phonetics*, a stop sound made by drawing the breath into the mouth and clicking the lips or tongue: see **click,** 3.

suc·to·ri·al (suk-tôr'i-əl, suk-tō'ri-əl), *adj.* [Mod. L. *suctorius* < L. *suctus*, pp. of *sugere*, to suck], 1. of or adapted for sucking or suction. 2. having organs used for sucking. 3. feeding by sucking fluids.

Su·dan (so͞o-dan'), *n.* 1. a country south of Egypt: formerly under British and Egyptian control, it was proclaimed an independent republic in 1956: area, 967,500 sq. mi.; pop., 11,615,000; capital, Khartoum: former name, *Anglo-Egyptian Sudan.* 2. a vast plains region extending across central Africa: French spelling, *Soudan.*

Su·da·nese (so͞o'də-nēz'), *adj.* of the Sudan or its people. *n.* [*pl.* SUDANESE], a native or inhabitant of the Sudan. Also spelled **Soudanese.**

Sudan grass, [after the *Sudan*, Africa, where it is cultivated], a kind of grass grown for hay.

Su·dan·ic (so͞o-dan'ik), *adj.* designating or of a family of languages, variously spoken across northern Africa, including Yoruba, Mandingo, and Tshi. *n.* this family of languages.

su·dar·i·um (so͞o-dâr'i-əm, sū-dâr'i-əm), *n.* [*pl.* SUDARIA (-ə)], [L. < *sudor*, sweat], a handkerchief or cloth for wiping sweat from the face; specifically, a veronica.

su·da·ry (so͞o'dẽr-i, sū'dẽr-i), *n.* [*pl.* SUDARIES (-riz)], a sudarium.

su·da·to·ri·um (so͞o'də-tôr'i-əm, sū'də-tō'ri-əm), *n.* [*pl.* SUDATORIA (-ə)], [L., neut. of *sudatorius;* SEE SUDATORY], a heated room used for sweat baths.

su·da·to·ry (so͞o'də-tôr'i, sū'də-tō'ri), *adj.* [L. *sudatorius* < *sudor*, sweat], 1. of a sudatorium. 2. sudorific. *n.* [*pl.* SUDATORIES (-iz, -riz)], [L. *sudatorium* < the *adj.*], 1. a sudatorium. 2. a sudorific.

sudd (sud), *n.* [Ar.], floating masses of weeds, reeds, etc. that often obstruct navigation on the White Nile.

sud·den (sud''n), *adj.* [ME. *sodain;* OFr. *sodain, sudain;* LL. *subitanus, for L. *subitaneus*, sudden, extended < *subitus*, pp. of *subire*, to go stealthily; *sub-*, under + *ire*, to go or come], 1. happening, coming, or appearing unexpectedly; not foreseen or prepared for. 2. done, coming, or taking place quickly or abruptly; hasty.

all of a sudden, suddenly; unexpectedly.

SYN.—**sudden** implies extreme quickness or hastiness and, usually, unexpectedness (a *sudden* outburst of temper); **precipitate** adds the implication of rashness or lack of due deliberation (a *precipitate* descision); **abrupt** implies a breaking in or off suddenly and, hence, suggests the lack of any warning, a curtness or lack of ceremony, etc. (an *abrupt* dismissal); **impetuous** implies vehement impulsiveness or extreme eagerness (an *impetuous* suitor). —*ANT.* deliberate.

Su·der·mann, Her·mann (her'män zo͞o'dẽr-män'; Eng. so͞o'dẽr-mən), 1857–1928; German dramatist and novelist.

Su·de·ten (so͞o-dā't'n; G. zo͞o-dā'tən), *n.pl.* [construed as sing. in senses 2 & 3], 1. the Sudetes Mountains. 2. the Sudetenland. 3. a native or inhabitant of the Sudetenland *adj.* of the Sudetenland or its people.

Su·de·ten·land (sōō-dā′t'n-land′; G. zōō-dā′tən-länt′), *n.* a mountainous region in northern Czechoslovakia, including the Sudetes Mountains, annexed by Nazi Germany in October, 1938 after the Munich Pact and returned to Czechoslovakia in 1945: area, 8,721 sq. mi.; pop., 2,945-000.

SUDETENLAND (1938)

Su·de·tes Mountains (sōō-dē′tēz), a mountain range in northern Czechoslovakia and southern Silesia.
‡su·dor (sōō′dôr, sū′dôr), *n.* [L.], sweat; perspiration.
su·dor·if·er·ous (sōō′də-rif′ẽr-əs, sū′də-rif′ẽr-əs), *adj.* [Mod. L. *sudoriferus* < L. *sudor, sudoris*, sweat; see -FEROUS], secreting sweat.
su·dor·if·ic (sōō′də-rif′ik, sū′də-rif′ik), *adj.* [Mod. L. *sudorificus* < L. *sudor, sudoris*, sweat + *facere*, to make], causing or increasing sweating. *n.* a medicine, etc. that causes or increases sweating.
suds (sudz), *n.pl.* [prob. (via East Anglian dial.) < MD. *sudse*, marsh, marsh water], 1. soapy water. 2. a froth on the surface of soapy water; foam. 3. [Slang], beer.
suds·y (sud′zi), *adj.* [SUDSIER (-zi-ẽr), SUDSIEST (-zi-ist)], full of or like suds or froth; foamy.
sue (sōō, sū), *v.t.* [SUED (sōōd, sūd), SUING], [ME. *suen, sewen, suwen;* OFr. *sevre, suir, sivir;* LL. **sequere*, for L. *sequi*, to follow], 1. to appeal to; petition; beseech. 2. [Archaic], to act as suitor to; woo. 3. in *law*, *a)* to petition (a court) for justice or redress through legal action. *b)* to bring civil action against or prosecute in a court of law in seeking redress of wrongs or justice. *c)* to carry (an action) through to its final decision. *v.i.* 1. to make an appeal; petition; plead. 2. [Archaic], to pay suit; woo. 3. to institute legal proceedings in court; bring suit. —*SYN.* see **appeal.**
sue out, to apply for and receive from a court (a writ or other legal process).
Sue, Eu·gène (ö′zhen′ sü; Eng. sōō), (born *Marie Joseph Sue*), 1804–1857; French novelist.
suede, suède (swād), *n.* [Fr. Suède, Sweden, in *gants de Suède*, Swedish gloves], 1. tanned leather, formerly kid, and now usually calf, having the flesh side buffed into a nap. 2. a kind of cloth made to resemble this: also **suede cloth.**
su·et (sōō′it, sū′it), *n.* [ME., dim. of Anglo-Fr. *sue;* OFr. *sieu, seu* < L. *sebum*, fat, tallow], the hard, crumbly fat deposited around the kidneys and loins of cattle and sheep: used in cooking and making tallow.
Sue·to·ni·us (swi-tō′ni-əs), (*Gaius Suetonius Tranquillus*), *n.* Roman historian; fl. c. 100 A.D.
su·et·y (sōō′it-i, sū′it-i), *adj.* of, like, or containing suet.
Su·ez (sōō-ez′, sōō′ez), *n.* a seaport in Egypt, on the Suez Canal and the Gulf of Suez: pop., 50,000.

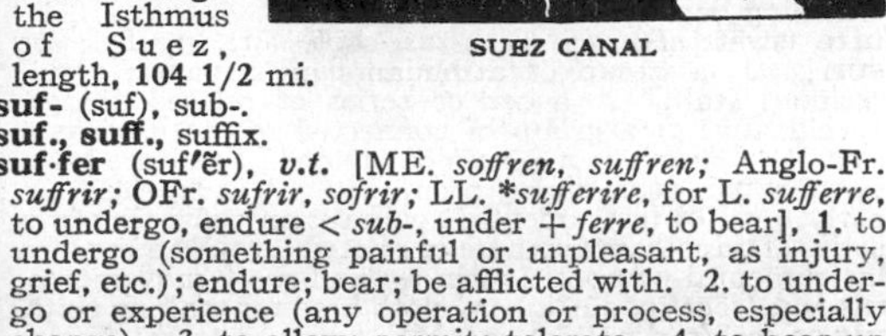

SUEZ CANAL

Suez, Gulf of, a northern arm of the Red Sea.
Suez, Isthmus of, a strip of land connecting Asia and Africa: it is cut by the Suez Canal.
Suez Canal, a ship canal joining the Mediterranean and Red Seas through the Isthmus of Suez, length, 104 1/2 mi.
suf- (suf), sub-.
suf., suff., suffix.
suf·fer (suf′ẽr), *v.t.* [ME. *soffren, suffren;* Anglo-Fr. *suffrir;* OFr. *sufrir, sofrir;* LL. **sufferire*, for L. *sufferre*, to undergo, endure < *sub-*, under + *ferre*, to bear], 1. to undergo (something painful or unpleasant, as injury, grief, etc.); endure; bear; be afflicted with. 2. to undergo or experience (any operation or process, especially change). 3. to allow; permit; tolerate. 4. to bear up under; endure: now only in negative constructions, as, he could not *suffer* criticism. *v.i.* 1. to experience pain, harm, injury, loss, etc. 2. to be punished; receive a penalty, especially death. 3. [Archaic], to tolerate or endure evil, injury, etc. —*SYN.* see **bear, let.**
suf·fer·a·ble (suf′ẽr-ə-b'l, suf′rə-b'l), *adj.* that can be suffered, endured, or allowed; tolerable.
suf·fer·a·bly (suf′ẽr-ə-bli, suf′rə-bli), *adv.* so as to be sufferable.
suf·fer·ance (suf′ẽr-əns, suf′rəns), *n.* [ME. *suffrance;* Anglo-Fr. & OFr. *soffrance, soufrance;* LL. *sufferentia* < L. *sufferens*, ppr.; see SUFFER], 1. the power or capacity to endure or tolerate pain, distress, etc. 2. consent, permission, or sanction implied by failure to interfere or prohibit; toleration. 3. [Archaic], suffering. 4. [Archaic], patient endurance; submission.
on sufferance, allowed or tolerated but not actually supported or encouraged.
suf·fer·ing (suf′ẽr-iŋ, suf′riŋ), *n.* 1. the bearing or undergoing of pain, distress, or injury. 2. something suffered; pain; distress; injury. —*SYN.* see **distress.**
suf·fice (sə-fīs′, sə-fīz′), *v.i.* [SUFFICED (-fīst′, -fīzd′), SUFFICING], [ME. *suffisen* < an inflectional stem of OFr. *suffire*, to suffice; L. *sufficere*, to provide, suffice < *sub-*, under + *facere*, to make], 1. to be enough; be sufficient or adequate. 2. [Obs.], to be competent or able. *v.t.* to be enough for; meet the needs of; satisfy.
suf·fi·cien·cy (sə-fish′ən-si), *n.* 1. sufficient means, ability, or resources; specifically, *a)* an ample amount or quantity (*of* what is needed). *b)* enough wealth or income. 2. the state or quality of being sufficient or adequate; adequacy. 3. self-sufficiency.
suf·fi·cient (sə-fish′ənt), *adj.* [ME.; OFr.; L. *sufficiens*, ppr. of *sufficere;* see SUFFICE], 1. as much as is needed; equal to what is specified or required; enough. 2. [Archaic], competent; well-qualified; efficient; able.
SYN.—**sufficient** and **enough** agree in describing that which satisfies a requirement exactly and is neither more nor less in amount than is needed (a word to the wise is *sufficient, enough* food for a week); **adequate** suggests the meeting of an acceptable (sometimes barely so) standard of fitness or suitability (the supporting players were *adequate*). —*ANT.* deficient, inadequate.
suf·fi·cient·ly (sə-fish′ənt-li), *adv.* so as to be sufficient; to a sufficient degree; enough.
suf·fix (suf′iks; *for v., usually* sə-fiks′), *n.* [Mod. L. *suffixum* < L. *suffixus*, pp. of *suffigere*, to fasten on beneath < *sub-*, under + *figere*, to fix], 1. a sound, syllable, or syllables added at the end of a word or word base to change its meaning, give it grammatical function, or form a new word, as *-ish* in *smallish*, *-ed* in *walked*, and *-ness* in *darkness*. 2. in *mathematics*, a subindex. *v.t.* to add as a suffix. Abbreviated **suf., suff.**
suf·fix·al (suf′ik-s'l), *adj.* of, or having the nature of, a suffix.
suf·fix·ion (sə-fik′shən), *n.* a suffixing or being suffixed.
suf·flate (sə-flāt′), *v.t.* [< L. *sufflatus*, pp. of *sufflare* < *sub-* + *-flare*, to blow], [Obs.], to inflate.
suf·fo·cate (suf′ə-kāt′), *v.t.* [SUFFOCATED (-id), SUFFOCATING], [< L. *suffocatus*, pp. of *suffocare*, to choke < *sub-*, under + *fauces*, gullet, throat], 1. to kill by cutting off the supply of air to the lungs, gills, etc. so as to cause asphyxiation. 2. to hinder the free breathing of; deprive of fresh air. 3. to smother, suppress, extinguish, etc. by, or as by, cutting off the supply of air. *v.i.* 1. to die by being suffocated. 2. to be unable to breathe freely; choke; stifle; smother.
suf·fo·ca·tion (suf′ə-kā′shən), *n.* [L. *suffocatio*], a suffocating or being suffocated.
suf·fo·ca·tive (suf′ə-kā′tiv), *adj.* tending to suffocate.
Suf·folk (suf′ək), *n.* a county on the eastern coast of England, divided into East Suffolk and West Suffolk: pop., 374,000 (est. 1945).
Suf·folk (suf′ek), *n.* [after *Suffolk* County, England]. 1. any of a breed of hornless mutton sheep having a black face and feet: also **Suffolk Down.** 2. any of a breed of English draft horses having a small, heavy body and chestnut-colored coat: also **Suffolk punch.**
suf·fra·gan (suf′rə-gən), *n.* [ME.; OFr.; ML. *suffraganus* < L. *suffragari*, to vote for, support, favor], 1. a bishop appointed to assist the bishop of a diocese. 2. any bishop in his capacity as a subordinate to his archbishop. *adj.* under a higher authority; auxiliary: said especially of a bishop in relation to his archbishop.
suf·frage (suf′rij), *n.* [ME.; Late OFr.; L. *suffragium*], 1. a short prayer of intercession or supplication. 2. a vote or voting; especially, a vote in favor of someone or something. 3. the right to vote, especially in political matters; franchise.
suf·fra·gette (suf′rə-jet′), *n.* [< *suffrage* + *-ette*], a woman who militantly advocates female suffrage.
suf·fra·get·tism (suf′rə-jet′iz'm), *n.* the principles or practices of suffragettes.
suf·fra·gist (suf′rə-jist), *n.* a person who believes in extending political suffrage, especially to women.

suf·fu·mi·gate (sə-fū′mə-gāt′), *v.t.* [< L. *suffumigare;* cf. SUB- & FUMIGATE], to fumigate from below.

suf·fuse (sə-fūz′), *v.t.* [SUFFUSED (-fūzd′), SUFFUSING], [< L. *suffusus,* pp. of *suffundere,* to pour beneath, diffuse beneath or upon < *sub-,* under + *fundere,* to pour], to overspread, as with a liquid, light, color, etc.

suf·fu·sion (sə-fū′zhən), *n.* [ME.; L. *suffusio*], 1. a suffusing or being suffused. 2. something, as a coloring or tint, that suffuses; especially, a flush or blush.

suf·fu·sive (sə-fū′siv), *adj.* that suffuses; suffusing.

Su·fi (so͞o′fi), *n.* [Ar. *ṣūfī,* ascetic, lit., a man of wool < *ṣūf,* wool], a person who believes in or practices Sufism.

Su·fism (so͞o′fiz'm), *n.* a system of Moslem mysticism practiced chiefly in Persia, from which has developed a literature of symbolical poetry.

Su·fis·tic (so͞o-fis′tik), *adj.* of, characteristic of, or practicing Sufism.

sug- (sug), see **sub-**.

sug·ar (shoog′ẽr), *n.* [ME. *sugre;* OFr. *sucre;* ML. *succarum;* Ar. *sakkar, sokkar;* Per. *shakar;* Sans. *śarkarā,* gravel, clayed or candied sugar], 1. a sweet, usually crystalline, substance, $C_{12}H_{22}O_{11}$, extracted chiefly from sugar cane and sugar beets and used as a food and sweetening agent: also called *cane* (or *beet*) *sugar, saccharose, sucrose.* 2. any of a class of sweet, soluble, crystalline carbohydrates, as the disaccharides (sucrose, lactose, and maltose) and the monosaccharides (glucose and fructose). 3. flattery; honeyed words. 4. [Slang], money. *v.t.* 1. to mix (food) with sugar; sprinkle with sugar. 2. to sweeten with sugar. 3. to cause to seem less disagreeable; make pleasant or acceptable with flattery, etc. *v.i.* 1. to form sugar crystals or granules by long, slow boiling (usually with *off*). 2. to make maple sugar.

sugar beet, a variety of beet having a root with white flesh and a high sugar content.

sug·ar·ber·ry (shoog′ẽr-ber′i), *n.* [*pl.* SUGARBERRIES (-iz)], the hackberry.

sugar bowl, a small container of glass, china, etc., usually with a cover, for sugar at the table.

sug·ar·bush (shoog′ẽr-boosh′), *n.* a grove or orchard of sugar maples.

sugar cane, a very tall tropical grass with jointed stems, cultivated as the main source of sugar.

sug·ar-coat (shoog′ẽr-kōt′), *v.t.* 1. to cover or coat with sugar. 2. to make seem more pleasant or attractive, as with flattery, euphemism, etc.

sug·ar-coat·ing (shoog′ẽr-kōt′iŋ), *n.* 1. the act or process of coating with sugar. 2. that which makes something seem more pleasant or attractive, as flattery, etc.

sugar corn, sweet corn.

sug·ar-cured (shoog′ẽr-kyoord′), *adj.* treated with a pickling preparation of sugar, salt, and nitrate or nitrite: said of ham, bacon, etc.

SUGAR CANE
A, plant; B, section of cane

sugar daddy, [Slang], a wealthy, especially older, man who lavishes gifts on young women in return for their attentions.

sug·ared (shoog′ẽrd), *adj.* sweetened with or as with sugar; sugar-coated.

sug·ar·house (shoog′ẽr-hous′), *n.* a place where sugar is processed; especially, a building where maple sap is boiled for producing maple sirup and sugar.

sug·ar·i·ness (shoog′ẽr-i-nis, shoog′ri-nis), *n.* the quality or condition of being sugary.

sug·ar-loaf (shoog′ẽr-lōf′), *adj.* shaped like a sugar loaf.

sugar loaf, 1. a conical mass of crystallized sugar. 2. something shaped like this, as a hill or mound.

sugar maple, a North American maple, valued for its hard wood and for its sap which yields maple sirup and maple sugar.

sugar of lead, lead acetate.

sugar of milk, lactose.

sugar pine, any of a number of tall related pines of the Pacific coast, with soft, reddish-brown wood, large cones, and sugarlike resin.

sug·ar·plum (shoog′ẽr-plum′), *n.* a round or oval piece of sugary candy; bonbon.

sugar tongs, small tongs used for handling lump sugar at the table.

sug·ar·y (shoog′ẽr-i, shoog′ri), *adj.* 1. of or containing sugar. 2. like sugar; specifically, *a)* sweet. *b)* granular. 3. sweetly flattering or pleasant; honeyed.

sug·gest (səg-jest′; *also, esp. Brit.* sə-jest′), *v.t.* [< L. *suggestus,* pp. of *suggerere,* to carry or lay under, furnish < *sub-,* under + *gerere,* to carry], 1. to bring (a thought, problem, desire, etc.) to the mind for consideration. 2. to arouse (a thought) in the mind through association of ideas: as, what does this shape *suggest* to you? 3. to propose (someone or something) as a possibility: as, can you *suggest* a course of study? 4. to show indirectly; imply; intimate: as, her dark skin *suggests* a Latin background. 5. to serve as a motive for; prompt: as, my success *suggested* further attempts.

SYN.—**suggest** implies a putting of something into the mind either intentionally, as by way of a proposal (I *suggest* you leave now), or unintentionally, as through association of ideas (the smell of ether *suggests* a hospital); **imply** stresses the putting into the mind of something involved, but not openly expressed, in a word, a remark, etc. and suggests the need for inference (his answer *implied* a refusal); **hint** connotes faint or indirect suggestion that is, however, intended to be understood (he *hinted* that he would come); **intimate** suggests a making known obliquely by a very slight hint (he only dared to *intimate* his feelings); **insinuate** implies the subtle hinting of something disagreeable or of that which one lacks the courage to say outright (are you *insinuating* that she is dishonest?).

sug·gest·i·bil·i·ty (səg-jes′tə-bil′ə-ti), *n.* the quality or condition of being suggestible.

sug·gest·i·ble (səg-jes′tə-b'l), *adj.* 1. capable of being influenced by suggestion; especially, susceptible to hypnotic suggestion. 2. that can be suggested.

sug·ges·tion (səg-jes′chən), *n.* [ME. & OFr. *suggestioun;* L. *suggestio*], 1. a suggesting or being suggested. 2. something suggested. 3. the process through which an idea is brought to the mind because of its connection or association with an idea already in the mind. 4. a faint hint or indication; small amount; trace: as, there was a *suggestion* of boredom in her tone. 5. in *psychology, a)* the inducing of an idea, decision, etc., by means of a verbal or other stimulus, in another individual, who accepts it uncritically, as in hypnosis. *b)* an idea so induced, or the stimulus by which such uncritical acceptance is effected.

sug·ges·tive (səg-jes′tiv), *adj.* 1. that suggests or tends to suggest thoughts or ideas. 2. tending to suggest something considered improper or indecent.

su·i·cid·al (so͞o′i-sī′d'l, sū′i-sī′d'l), *adj.* 1. of, involving, or leading to suicide. 2. having an urge to commit suicide.

su·i·cide (so͞o′i-sīd′, sū′i-sīd′), *n.* [L. *sui,* of oneself; + *-cide*], 1. the act of killing oneself intentionally. 2. ruin of one's interests or prospects through one's own actions, policies, etc. 3. a person who commits suicide. *v.i.* [SUICIDED (-id), SUICIDING], [Colloq.], to commit suicide.

‡su·i ge·ne·ris (sū′ī jen′ẽr-is, so͞o′ī jen′ẽr-is), [L.], of his (her, or its) own kind; individual; unique.

‡su·i ju·ris (sū′ī jo͞o′ris, so͞o′ī joor′is), [L., in one's own right], in *law,* legally competent to manage one's own affairs, because of legal age and of sound mind.

su·int (so͞o′int, sū′int, swint), *n.* [Fr. < *suer,* to sweat; L. *sudare*], the natural grease found in sheep's wool: a source of potash.

Suisse (swēs), *n.* Switzerland: the French name.

suit (so͞ot, sūt), *n.* [ME. *siute, seute;* OFr. *suite, sieute;* LL. **sequita* < **sequere,* to follow < L. *sequi,* to follow], 1. a set of clothes to be worn together; now, especially, a coat, trousers (or skirt), and, often, a vest, usually all of the same material. 2. a group of similar things forming a set or series. 3. any of the four sets of thirteen playing cards each (*spades, clubs, hearts,* and *diamonds*) forming a pack. 4. historically, the act of following or attending a feudal court in an effort to secure justice. 5. action to secure justice in a court of law; attempt to recover a right or claim through legal action. 6. *a)* an act of suing, pleading, or requesting. *b)* a petition. 7. a wooing. *v.t.* 1. to meet the requirements of; be suitable for or appropriate to; agree with; befit. 2. to make suitable or appropriate; fit; adapt. 3. to please; satisfy: as, nothing *suits* him today. 4. [Rare], to furnish with clothes; dress. *v.i.* 1. [Archaic], to correspond or harmonize (usually with *to* or *with*). 2. to be fit, suitable, or convenient.

bring suit, to institute legal action; sue.

follow suit, 1. to play a card of the same suit as the card led. 2. to do as another or others have done; follow the example set.

suit oneself, to act according to one's own wishes.

suit·a·bil·i·ty (so͞ot′ə-bil′ə-ti, sūt′ə-bil′ə-ti), *n.* the quality of being suitable, fit, appropriate, harmonious, etc.

suit·a·ble (so͞ot′ə-b'l, sūt′ə-b'l), *adj.* that suits a given purpose, occasion, condition, etc.; fitting; appropriate; becoming. —*SYN.* see **fit.**

suit·a·bly (so͞ot′ə-bli, sūt′ə-bli), *adv.* in a suitable manner; so as to be suitable.

suit·case (so͞ot′kās′, sūt′kās′), *n.* a flat, rectangular traveling bag, or valise.

suite (swēt; *also, for 2b, occas.* so͞ot, sūt), *n.* [Fr.; see SUIT], 1. a group of attendants or servants; train; retinue; staff. 2. a set or series of related things; specifically, *a)* a group of connected rooms used as a unit. *b)* a number of pieces of matched furniture for a given room: as, a dining room *suite.* 3. in *music, a)* an early form of instrumental composition consisting of a series of dances in the same or related keys. *b)* a modern instrumental composition in a number of movements.

suit·ing (so͞ot′iŋ, sūt′iŋ), *n.* cloth used for making suits.

suit·or (so͞o′tẽr, sū′tẽr), *n.* [ME. *sutere, sutoure;* Anglo-Fr. *seutor;* L. *secutor*], 1. a person who requests, petitions, or entreats. 2. a person who sues at law; party to a lawsuit. 3. a man who courts or woos a woman.

Sui·yüan (swā′yü-än′), *n.* a province of Inner Mongolia:

area, 113,758 sq. mi.; pop., 2,230,000 (est. 1947); capital, Kweihsui.
su·ki·ya·ki (sōō'ki-yä'ki), ***n.*** [Japan.], a Japanese dish of sliced meat, onions, and other vegetables fried together and seasoned with soya sauce, sake, and sugar.
Suk·kos (sook'ōs), ***n.*** Sukkoth.
Suk·koth (sook-ōth', sook'ōs), ***n.pl.*** [construed as sing.], [Heb. *sūkōth*, lit., tabernacles], a Jewish holiday, the Feast of Tabernacles, celebrating the fall harvest: also **Succos**: see **Jewish holidays.**
sul·cate (sul'kāt), ***adj.*** [L. *sulcatus*, pp. of *sulcare*, to furrow < *sulcus*, a furrow], having deep, parallel furrows or grooves; grooved; fluted.
sul·cat·ed (sul'kā-tid), ***adj.*** sulcate.
sul·ca·tion (sul-kā'shən), ***n.*** [see SULCATE & -ION], any of a series of deep, parallel grooves or furrows.
sul·cus (sul'kəs), ***n.*** [*pl.* SULCI (-sī)], [L.], a groove or furrow; especially, in ***anatomy***, any of the shallow grooves separating the convolutions of the brain.
Su·lei·man (sü'lā-män'), ***n.*** sultan of the Ottoman Empire (1520–1566); lived 1496?–1566: called the *Magnificent*; also **Solyman.**
sulf- (sulf), a combining form meaning *of* or *containing sulfur*: also **sulph-.**
sul·fa (sul'fə), ***adj.*** designating or of a family of drugs of the sulfanilamide type, used in combating certain bacterial infections: words beginning with *sulfa-* may also be spelled **sulpha-.**
sul·fa·di·a·zine (sul'fə-dī'ə-zēn', sul'fə-dī'ə-zin), ***n.*** [*sulfa* + *diazine*], a sulfa drug, $C_{10}H_{10}N_4O_2S$, used in treating certain pneumococcus, streptococcus, and staphylococcus infections.
sul·fa·gua·ni·dine (sul'fə-gwan'ə-dēn', sul'fə-gwä'nə-din), ***n.*** [*sulfa* + *guanidine*], a sulfa drug, $C_7H_{10}N_4O_2S \cdot H_2O$, used in the treatment of various intestinal infections.
sul·fa·mer·a·zine (sul'fə-mer'ə-zēn'), ***n.*** [*sulfa* + *-mer* + *azine*], a sulfa drug, $C_{11}H_{12}N_4O_2S$, a methyl derivative of sulfadiazine that is more rapidly absorbed.
sul·fa·meth·yl·thi·a·zole (sul'fə-meth''l-thī'ə-zōl'), ***n.*** [*sulfa* + *methyl* + *thiazole*], a sulfa drug, $C_{10}H_{12}N_3O_2S$, used especially in treating staphylococcus infections.
sulf·a·nil·a·mide (sul'fə-nil'ə-mīd'), ***n.*** [*sulfanilic* + *amide*], a white crystalline compound, $NH_2C_6H_4SO_2NH_2$, used in treating gonorrhea, septicemia, streptococcus infections, etc.: a synthetic coal-tar product.
sul·fa·pyr·a·zine (sul'fə-pêr'ə-zēn'), ***n.*** [*sulfa* + *pyrazine*], a sulfa drug, $C_{10}H_{10}N_4O_2S$, used in treating certain pneumococcus, streptococcus, and staphylococcus infections.
sul·fa·pyr·i·dine (sul'fə-pêr'ə-dēn', sul'fə-pêr'ə-din), ***n.*** [*sulfa* + *pyridine*], a sulfa drug, $C_{11}H_{11}N_3O_2S$, used especially in the treatment of pneumonia.
sulf·ar·se·nide (sulf-är'sə-nīd', sulf-är'sə-nid), ***n.*** a double salt of sulfide and arsenide.
sul·fa·sux·i·dine (sul'fə-suk'sə-dēn', sul'fə-suk'sə-din), ***n.*** [< *sulfa* + *succinic* (with *-cc-* spelled phonetically as *x*) + *-ide* + *-ine*], a sulfa drug, $C_{16}H_{15}N_3O_5S_2$, used especially in treating infections in the intestinal and urinary tracts: a trade-mark (**Sulfasuxidine**).
sul·fate (sul'fāt), ***n.*** [Fr.; Mod. L. *sulphas*, *sulphatis* < L. *sulphur*, sulfur], a salt of sulfuric acid. ***v.t.*** [SULFATED (-id), SULFATING], 1. to treat with sulfuric acid or a sulfate. 2. to convert into a sulfate. 3. to cause a deposit of sulfates to form on (the plates of a storage battery). ***v.i.*** to become sulfated.
sul·fa·thi·a·zole (sul'fə-thī'ə-zōl'), ***n.*** [*sulfa* + *thiazole*], a sulfa drug, $C_9H_9N_3O_2S_2$, used especially in treating pneumonia and staphylococcus infections.
sul·fa·tize (sul'fə-tīz'), ***v.t.*** [SULFATIZED (-tīzd'), SULFATIZING], to turn (sulfide ores, etc.) into sulfate, as by roasting.
sul·fid (sul'fid), ***n.*** sulfide.
sul·fide (sul'fīd), ***n.*** a compound of sulfur with another element or a radical.
sul·fite (sul'fīt), ***n.*** a salt of sulfurous acid.
sul·fit·ic (sul-fit'ik), ***adj.*** of, like, or using sulfite.
sul·fo- (sul'fō, sul'fə), a combining form used in chemistry, meaning: 1. *having divalent sulfur.* 2. *replacing oxygen with sulfur.* 3. *having the sulfonic or sulfonyl group.* Also **sulpho-.**
sul·fo·nal (sul'fə-nal', sul'fə-nal'), ***n.*** [G. *sulfonal*; *sulfon*, sulfone + *-al*, as in *veronal*], a colorless, crystalline substance, $(CH_3)_2C(SO_2 \cdot C_2H_5)_2$, used in medicine as a soporific.
sul·fo·na·mide (sul-fon'ə-mīd', sul'fən-am'id), ***n.*** [< *sulfonyl* + *amide*], any of the sulfa drugs, as sulfathiazole or sulfapyridine, containing the monovalent radical $-SO_2NH_2$ and used in the treatment of various bacterial diseases.
sul·fo·nate (sul'fə-nāt'), ***n.*** the ester of a sulfonic acid. ***v.t.*** [SULFONATED (-id), SULFONATING], to introduce the sulfonic group into (an aromatic hydrocarbon) by treating with sulfuric acid.
sul·fone (sul'fōn), ***n.*** [G. *sulfon* < *sulfur*, sulfur], any of a group of compounds containing the radical SO_2, the sulfur atom of which is linked chemically with a carbon atom of each of two alkyl groups.
sul·fon·ic (sul-fon'ik), ***adj.*** [< *sulfone* + *-ic*], designating or of the univalent acid group SO_3H.
sulfonic acid, any acid containing the sulfonic group and derived from sulfuric acid by the replacement of an OH group.
sul·fo·ni·um (sul-fō'ni-əm), ***n.*** [Mod. L.; *sulf*ur + ammo*nium*], a univalent electropositive radical made up of three alkyl radicals and one atom of sulfur, as the triethyl sulfonium radical $(C_2H_5)_3S$-.
sul·fon·meth·ane (sul'fōn-meth'ān, sul'fon-meth'ān), ***n.*** [< *sulfone* + *methane*], sulfonal.
sul·fo·nyl (sul'fə-nil, sul'fə-nēl'), ***n.*** [< *sulfone* + *-yl*], the divalent radical SO_2: also **sulfuryl.**
sul·fur (sul'fẽr), ***n.*** [ME. *sulphre*; L. *sulphur*, *sulfur*], a pale-yellow, nonmetallic chemical element found in crystalline or amorphous form: it burns with a blue flame and a stifling odor and is used in vulcanizing rubber, making matches, paper, gunpowder, insecticides, sulfuric acid, etc.: symbol, S; at. wt., 32.06; at. no., 16: see also **sulphur**: see **sulf-.**
sul·fu·rate (sul'fyoo-rit, sul'fə-rit), ***adj.*** [L. *sulphuratus*], of, like, or containing sulfur. ***v.t.*** (sul'fyoo-rāt', sul'fə-rāt'), [SULFURATED (-id), SULFURATING], to combine or treat with sulfur.
sul·fu·ra·tion (sul'fyoo-rā'shən, sul'fə-rā'shən), ***n.*** a sulfurating or being sulfurated.
sul·fu·ra·tor (sul'fyoo-rā'tẽr, sul'fə-rā'tẽr), ***n.*** a device used for bleaching with sulfur fumes.
sulfur dioxide, a heavy, colorless, suffocating gas, SO_2, easily liquefied and used as a bleach, disinfectant, and refrigerant.
sul·fu·re·ous (sul-fyoor'i-əs), ***adj.*** [L. *sulfureus*], 1. of, like, or containing sulfur. 2. greenish-yellow.
sul·fu·ret (sul'fyoo-rit; *for v.*, sul'fyoo-ret'), ***n.*** [Mod. L. *sulphuretum*], a sulfide. ***v.t.*** [SULFURETTED (-id), SULFURETTING], to combine or impregnate with sulfur.
sul·fu·ric (sul-fyoor'ik), ***adj.*** [Fr. *sulfurique*], of or containing sulfur, especially sulfur having a valence of six.
sulfuric acid, an oily, colorless, corrosive liquid, H_2SO_4, used in making dyes, paints, explosives, fertilizers, etc.: also called *oil of vitriol.*
sul·fu·ri·za·tion (sul'fyoo-ri-zā'shən, sul'fẽr-ī-zā'shən), ***n.*** a sulfurizing or being sulfurized.
sul·fu·rize (sul'fyoo-rīz', sul'fẽr-īz'), ***v.t.*** [SULFURIZED (-rīzd', -īzd'), SULFURIZING], [Fr. *sulfuriser*; see SULFUR & -IZE], to combine, treat, or impregnate with sulfur or a compound of sulfur, especially with sulfur dioxide fumes in bleaching or disinfecting.
sul·fu·rous (sul-fyoor'əs, sul'fẽr-əs), ***adj.*** 1. of or containing sulfur, especially sulfur having a valence of four. 2. like burning sulfur in odor, color, etc.: see also **sulphurous.**
sulfurous acid, a colorless acid, H_2SO_3, known only in the form of its salts or in aqueous solution and used as a chemical reagent, a bleach, in medicine, etc.
sul·fur·y (sul'fẽr-i), ***adj.*** of or like sulfur.
sul·fur·yl (sul'fẽr-il, sul'fyoor-il), ***n.*** [*sulfur* + *-yl*], sulfonyl.
sulk (sulk), ***v.i.*** [back-formation < *sulky*], to be sulky. ***n.*** 1. *often pl.* a sulky mood or state. 2. a sulky person.
sulk·i·ly (sul'k'l-i), ***adv.*** in a sulky manner.
sulk·i·ness (sul'ki-nis), ***n.*** sulky manner or behavior.
sulk·y (sul'ki), ***adj.*** [SULKIER (-ki-ẽr), SULKIEST (-ki-ist)], [prob. < AS. *solcen* (in comp.), slothful, remiss; IE. base **selĝ-*, to let go, let loose, as also in OIr. *sleg*, a spear], 1. showing resentment and ill-humor by sullen, withdrawn behavior. 2. gloomy; dismal; sullen: as, a sulky day. ***n.*** [*pl.* SULKIES (-kiz)], [so called < the *adj.*, in the sense of keeping aloof, because the vehicle seated only one person], a light, two-wheeled carriage having a seat for only one person. —***SYN.*** see **sullen.**
Sul·la (sul'ə), ***n.*** (*Lucius Cornelius Sulla*), Roman general and dictator; lived 138–78 B.C.
sul·len (sul'ən), ***adj.*** [ME. *solein*, *solain*, alone, solitary; LL. **solanus*, alone < L. *solus*, alone], 1. showing resentment and ill-humor by morose, unsociable withdrawal; sulky; glum. 2. gloomy; dismal; sad; depressing. 3. somber; dull. 4. slow-moving; sluggish. 5. baleful; threatening: as, *sullen* clouds.
SYN.—**sullen** suggests a gloomy, withdrawn silence, usually connoting resentfulness or ill-humor (the *sullen* prisoners marched along); **glum** implies a dejected silence resulting from low spirits or a feeling of depression (he listened with a *glum* expression); **morose** suggests a sour, unsociable glumness (he took a *morose* view of the future); **surly** suggests a brusque, ill-tempered gruffness (a *surly* answer); **sulky** suggests a sullenness characterized by petulance and discontent (a *sulky* child). —***ANT.*** genial, amiable, good-natured.
Sul·li·van, Sir **Arthur Seymour** (sul'i-vən), 1842–1900; English composer; wrote comic operas in collaboration with Sir William S. Gilbert.
Sullivan, John Lawrence, 1858–1918; American prize

fighter; world heavyweight champion (1882–1892).
Sullivan, Louis Hen·ri (hen′ri), 1856–1924; American architect.
sul·ly (sul′i), *v.t. & v.i.* [SULLIED (-id), SULLYING], [prob. < Fr. *souiller;* ? < LL. **suculare*, to soil < L. *suculus*, dim. of *sus*, a boar, swine; cf. SOIL, *v.*], to make or become soiled, stained, tarnished, or defiled. *n.* [*pl.* SULLIES (-iz)], a stain or tarnish; defilement; blemish.
Sul·ly, Duc de (də sü′lē′; Eng. sul′i), (*Maximilien de Béthune*), 1560–1641; French statesman.
Sul·ly-Pru·dhomme, Re·né Fran·çois Ar·mand (rə-nā′ fräṅ′swȧ′ ȧr′mäṅ′ sü′lē′prü′dôm′), 1839–1907; French poet; received Nobel prize in literature, 1901.
sulph- (sulf), sulf-: for words beginning **sulph-**, see forms under **sulf-**.
sul·pha (sul′fə), *adj.* sulfa.
sul·phur (sul′fẽr), *n.* 1. sulfur. 2. any of a number of small, yellow butterflies. 3. a greenish-yellow color. *adj.* greenish-yellow.
sul·phur-bot·tom (sul′fẽr-bot′əm), *n.* the largest of all whales, bluish gray in color, found in the Antarctic and in the colder parts of the Atlantic and Pacific Oceans.
sul·phu·rous (sul′fẽr-əs; *for 1, usually* sul-fyoor′əs), *adj.* 1. sulfurous. 2. infernal; hellish. 3. violently passionate; heated; fiery.
sul·tan (sul′t′n), *n.* [Fr.; Ar. *sulṭān*, victorious, also a ruler, prince], 1. a Moslem ruler; especially [S-], formerly, the ruler of Turkey. 2. [S-], any of a breed of chicken with heavily feathered feet and legs. 3. a sultana (sense 4).
sul·tan·a (sul-tan′ə, sul-tä′nə), *n.* [It., fem. of *sultano;* Ar. *sulṭān*, sultan], 1. the wife of a sultan. 2. the mother, sister, or daughter of a sultan. 3. a mistress, especially of a king, prince, etc. 4. a game bird of the rail family, with bright blue and green feathers; purple gallinule. 5. a small, white, seedless grape used for raisins and in wine-making.
sul·tan·ate (sul′t′n-it, sul′t′n-āt′), *n.* 1. the authority, position, or reign of a sultan. 2. the territory or jurisdiction of a sultan.
sul·tan·ess (sul′t′n-is), *n.* a sultana (senses 1 & 2).
sul·tan·ship (sul′t′n-ship′), *n.* [see -SHIP], a sultanate.
sul·tri·ly (sul′trə-li), *adv.* so as to be sultry.
sul·tri·ness (sul′tri-nis), *n.* a sultry quality or state.
sul·try (sul′tri), *adj.* [SULTRIER (-tri-ẽr), SULTRIEST (-tri-ist)], [var. of *sweltry* < *swelter;* see SWELTER], 1. oppressively hot and moist; close; sweltering. 2. extremely hot; fiery. 3. hot or inflamed, as with passion or lust.
Su·lu (sōō′lōō), *n.* 1. a member of a Moro tribe of the Sulu Archipelago. 2. the dialect of the Sulus.
Su·lu·an (sōō-lōō′ən), *adj.* of the Sulus or their language. *n.* a Sulu.
Sulu Archipelago, a group of islands in the Philippines, southwest of Mindanao: area, 1,086 sq. mi.
Sulu Sea, an arm of the Pacific, between the Philippines and Borneo: see **Philippine Islands**, map.
sum (sum), *n.* [ME. *summe;* OFr. *somme, sume;* L. *summa*, fem. of *summus*, highest, superl. < base of *super*, above], 1. an amount of money: as, they paid a great *sum* for the painting. 2. the whole amount; total result; aggregate: as, that is the *sum* of our experience. 3. gist; summary; substance. 4. the result obtained by adding together two or more numbers or quantities; total. 5. numbers to be added together. 6. [Colloq.], a problem in arithmetic. 7. [Archaic], the highest degree; height; summit. *v.t.* [SUMMED (sumd), SUMMING], 1. to determine the sum of by adding. 2. to sum up; recapitulate; summarize.
  sum to, to total; add up to.
  sum up, 1. to add up or collect into a whole or total. 2. to state in a few words; summarize; review briefly. 3. to give a brief review or summary; recapitulate.
SYN.—**sum** refers to the number or amount obtained by adding the individual units (the *sum* of three and five is eight); **amount** applies to the result obtained by combining all the sums, quantities, measures, etc. that are involved (he paid the full *amount* of the damages); **aggregate** refers to the whole group or mass of individual items gathered together (the *aggregate* of his experiences); **total** stresses the wholeness or inclusiveness of a sum or amount (the collection reached a *total* of $200).
sum- (sum), see **sub-**.
su·mac, su·mach (shōō′mak, sōō′mak), *n.* [ME. *sumak;* OFr.; ML. *sumach;* Ar. *summaq* < *sumaka*, to be tall], 1. any of a number of related plants with lance-shaped leaves and cone-shaped clusters of hairy, red fruit. 2. the powdered leaves of some of these plants, used in tanning and dyeing. 3. the wood of any of these plants.
Su·ma·tra (soo-mä′trə), *n.* a large island of Indonesia, south of the Malay Peninsula: area, 163,145 sq. mi.; pop., c. 13,600,000; chief cities, Medan and Padang.
Su·ma·tran (soo-mä′trən), *adj.* of Sumatra, its people, or culture. *n.* a native or inhabitant of Sumatra.
Sum·ba (sōōm′bä), *n.* an island of Indonesia, west of Timor: area, 4,272 sq. mi.; pop., 182,000: also spelled **Soemba**: English name, *Sandalwood Island.*
Sum·ba·wa (sōōm-bä′wä), *n.* an island of Indonesia, between Lombok and Flores: area, 5,129 sq. mi.; pop., 316,000: also spelled **Soembawa.**
Su·mer (sōō′mẽr, sū′mẽr), *n.* an ancient region in the lower Euphrates River Valley.
Su·mer·i·an (sōō-mêr′i-ən, sū-mêr′i-ən), *adj.* 1. of Sumer. 2. designating or of an ancient people of Babylonia, probably of non-Semitic origin. *n.* 1. one of the Sumerian people. 2. the language of the Sumerians, of undetermined relationship, extinct since the 3d century B.C.: its tablets and inscriptions date back to 4000 B.C.
Su·mi·ri·an (sōō-mêr′i-ən, sū-mêr′i-ən), *adj. & n.* Sumerian.
‡**sum·ma cum lau·de** (sum′ə kum lô′di, soom′ə koom lou′de), [L.], with the greatest praise: phrase used to signify graduation with the highest honors from a university or college: cf. **cum laude, magna cum laude.**
sum·ma·ri·ly (sum′ə-rə-li, su-mer′ə-li), *adv.* in a summary manner.
sum·ma·ri·ness (sum′ə-ri-nis), *n.* a summary quality.
sum·ma·rist (sum′ə-rist), *n.* a person who makes a summary.
sum·ma·ri·za·tion (sum′ə-ri-zā′shən, sum′ə-rī-zā′shən), *n.* a summarizing or being summarized.
sum·ma·rize (sum′ə-rīz′), *v.t.* [SUMMARIZED (-rīzd′), SUMMARIZING], 1. to make a summary or condensed statement of; state briefly. 2. to be a summary of.
sum·ma·ry (sum′ə-ri), *adj.* [ME.; ML. *summarius* < L. *summa*, a sum], 1. that presents the substance or general idea in brief form; summarizing; concise; condensed. 2. prompt and informal; done without delay or ceremony: as, *summary* punishment, *summary* procedure. *n.* [*pl.* SUMMARIES (-riz)], [L. *summarium;* see the *adj.*], a brief statement or account covering the substance or main points; digest; abridgment; compendium. —*SYN.* see **abridgment.**
summary court-martial, the least formal military court, consisting of one officer, for judging minor offenses.
sum·ma·tion (sum-ā′shən), *n.* [Mod. L. *summatio*], 1. the act or process of summing, or of finding a total. 2. a total or aggregate. 3. a final summing up of arguments, as in a court trial or debate, before the decision is to be rendered.
sum·mer (sum′ẽr), *n.* [ME. *sumer;* AS. *sumor, sumer;* akin to G. *sommer;* IE. base **sem-*, summertime, seen also in Sans. *sắma*, half year, season], 1. the warmest season of the year, regarded in the North Temperate Zone as including the months of June, July, and August: in the astronomical year, that period between the summer solstice and the autumnal equinox. 2. a year as reckoned by this season: as, a youth of sixteen *summers.* 3. any period regarded, like summer, as a time of growth, development, fulfillment, perfection, etc. *adj.* 1. of or characteristic of summer. 2. done, used, played, etc. during the summer: as, *summer* opera. *v.i.* to pass the summer: as, we *summer* on Cape Cod. *v.t.* to keep, feed, or maintain during the summer.
sum·mer (sum′ẽr), *n.* [ME. *sumer, somere;* OFr. *somier*, pack horse < LL. *saumarius*, for *sagmarius*, a pack horse < L. & Gr. *sagma*, pack saddle], 1. a large, horizontal supporting beam or girder. 2. a lintel. 3. the capstone of a column supporting an arch or lintel.
sum·mer·house (sum′ẽr-hous′), *n.* a small, open structure in a garden, park, etc., for providing a shady rest.
summer house, a house or cottage, as in the country, used during the summer.
sum·mer·like (sum′ẽr-līk′), *adj.* summery.
sum·mer·ly (sum′ẽr-li), *adj.* summery.
sum·mer·sault (sum′ẽr-sôlt′), *n. & v.i.* somersault.
summer sausage, dried or smoked, uncooked sausage, that keeps well in warm weather.
sum·mer·set (sum′ẽr-set′), *n. & v.i.* somersault.
summer solstice, the time during the summer when the sun is farthest from the equator: June 21 or 22 in the Northern Hemisphere.
summer squash, any of a number of small squashes grown in summer and eaten before fully ripe.
sum·mer·time (sum′ẽr-tīm′), *n.* the season of summer.
sum·mer·y (sum′ẽr-i), *adj.* of, like, or characteristic of summer; summerlike.
sum·mit (sum′it), *n.* [OFr. *sommette, somet*, dim. of *som*, summit < L. *summum*, highest part < *summus*, highest], 1. the highest point, part, or elevation; top or apex. 2. the highest degree or state; acme. 3. the highest level of officialdom; specifically, in connection with diplomatic negotiations, the level involving heads of government: as, a meeting at the *summit.*
SYN.—**summit** literally refers to the topmost point of a hill or similar elevation and, figuratively, to the highest attainable level, as of achievement; **peak** refers to the highest of a number of high points, as in a mountain range or, figuratively, in a graph; **climax** applies to the highest point, as in interest, force, excitement, etc., in a scale of ascending values; **acme** refers to the highest possible point of perfection in the development or progress of something; **apex** suggests the highest point (literally, of a geometric figure such as a cone, figuratively, of a career, process, etc.) where all ascending lines, courses, etc. ultimately meet; **pinnacle**, in its figurative uses, is equivalent to **summit** or **peak**, but sometimes connotes a giddy or unsteady height; **zenith** literally refers to the highest point in the

heavens and, hence, figuratively suggests fame or success reached by a spectacular rise.

sum·mon (sum′ən), *v.t.* [ME. *somonen;* OFr. *somondre, semondre;* L. *summonere,* to remind privily < *sub-,* under, secretly + *monere,* to advise, warn], 1. to call together; order to meet or convene. 2. to order to come or appear; call or send for with authority. 3. to issue a legal summons against. 4. to call upon to act, especially to surrender. 5. to call forth; rouse; gather; collect (often with *up*): as, *summon* (*up*) your strength. —*SYN.* see **call**.

sum·mon·er (sum′ən-ẽr), *n.* a person who summons; specifically, formerly, an official who served court summonses.

sum·mons (sum′ənz), *n.* [*pl.* SUMMONSES (-iz)], [ME. *somounce, somons,* Anglo-Fr. *somonse;* OFr. *sumunse* < base of *somondre, semondre;* see SUMMON], a call or order to come, attend, appear, or perform some action; specifically, *a*) in *law,* an official order to appear in court; also, the writ containing such an order. *b*) a call, command, knock, or other signal that summons. *v.t.* [Colloq.], to serve a court summons upon.

‡sum·mum bo·num (sum′əm bō′nəm), [L.], highest, or greatest, good.

Sum·ner, Charles (sum′nẽr), 1811–1874; American statesman and abolitionist.

sump (sump), *n.* [ME. *sompe;* MLG. *sump* or MD. *somp, sump;* for IE. base see SWAMP], 1. a pit or well in which liquids collect; specifically, *a*) a cesspool. *b*) an oil trap or reservoir at the bottom of the lubricating system of an internal-combustion engine. 2. in *mining,* a pit or pool at the bottom of a shaft or mine, in which water collects and from which it is pumped: see **mine,** illus.

sump·ter (sump′tẽr), *n.* [ME. *sompter;* OFr. *sometier;* LL. **sagmatarius* (cf. SUMMER, a girder)], a pack horse, mule, or other animal used for carrying baggage.

sump·tion (sump′shən), *n.* [L. *sumptio* < pp. of *sumere,* to take, select], in *logic,* a major premise.

sump·tu·ar·y (sump′chōō-er′i), *adj.* [L. *sumptuarius* < *sumptus,* expense], of or regulating expenses or the spending of money.

sumptuary laws, laws regulating extravagance in food, dress, etc. on religious or moral grounds.

sump·tu·ous (sump′chōō-əs), *adj.* [OFr. *sumptueux;* L. *sumptuosus* < *sumptus,* expense], 1. involving great expense; costly; lavish. 2. magnificent; splendid.

Sumter, Fort, see **Fort Sumter.**

sun (sun), *n.* [ME. & AS. *sunne;* akin to G. *sonne;* IE. **sāu-en, *su-en,* sun < base **sāu-,* seen also in L. *sol* (< **saw-el*); cf. SOL, SOLSTICE, etc.], 1. the incandescent body of gases about which the earth and other planets revolve and which furnishes light, heat, and energy for the solar system: it is the star nearest the earth, whose mean distance from it is nearly 93,000,000 miles: its diameter is about 865,000 miles; its mass is about 322,000 times, and its volume more than 1,300,000 times, that of the earth, and its density, about one fourth that of the earth. 2. the heat or light of the sun: as, don't sit in the direct *sun.* 3. any incandescent heavenly body that is the center of a solar system. 4. something like the sun, as in warmth, brilliance, splendor, etc. 5. [Poetic], a day. 6. [Poetic], a year. 7. [Archaic], sunrise or sunset. *v.t.* [SUNNED (sund), SUNNING], to expose to the sun's rays; warm, dry, bleach, tan, etc. in or as in the sunlight. *v.i.* to sun oneself. Abbreviated **s.**

from sun to sun, [Archaic], from sunrise to sunset.

place in the sun, a prominent or favorable position or situation.

under the sun, on earth; in the world.

Sun., Sunday.

sun bath, exposure of the body to direct sunlight.

sun-bathe (sun′bāth′), *v.i.* [SUN-BATHED (-bāthd′), SUN-BATHING], to expose the body to direct sunlight.

sun·beam (sun′bēm′), *n.* a ray or beam of sunlight.

sun·bird (sun′bũrd′), *n.* 1. a small, brightly colored, tropical songbird resembling the hummingbird. 2. the sun bittern.

sun bittern, either of two wading birds of tropical America, related to the cranes and herons.

sun·bon·net (sun′bon′it), *n.* a bonnet for women and girls, having a large brim and a flap at the back for shading the face and neck from the sun.

sun·bow (sun′bō′), *n.* [Poetic], a rainbow.

sun·burn (sun′bũrn′), *n.* 1. an inflammation of the skin resulting from prolonged exposure to the sun's rays. 2. the reddish color of sunburned skin. *v.t. & v.i.* [SUNBURNED (-bũrnd′) or SUNBURNT (-burnt′), SUNBURNING], to get or cause to get sunburn.

sun·burst (sun′bũrst′), *n.* 1. the sudden appearance of sunlight, as through a break in clouds. 2. a jeweled brooch, etc. representing the sun with spreading rays.

sun-cured (sun′kyoord′), *adj.* cured, as meat, by drying in the sun.

sun·dae (sun′di), *n.* [prob. an invented term; ? < *Sunday;* from being orig. sold only on this day; see also H. L. Mencken, *Am. Lang., Suppl. I.* p. 376], a serving of ice cream covered with a sirup, fruit, nuts, whipped cream, etc.

Sun·da Islands (sun′də; Du. sōōn′dä), a chain of islands in the United States of Indonesia, including Sumatra, Java, Bali, Lombok, Sumbawa, and Flores: also spelled **Soenda.**

sun dance, a religious dance in worship of the sun performed at the summer solstice by certain plains tribes of North American Indians.

Sunda Strait, the narrow strait between Sumatra and Java.

Sun·day (sun′di), *n.* [AS. *sunnan dæg,* day of the sun; used as transl. of LL. *dies solis,* day of the sun], the first day of the week: it is observed as the Sabbath by most Christian denominations: abbreviated **Sun., S., Su.**

Sun·day, Bil·ly (bil′i sun′di), (*Rev. William Ashley Sunday*), 1863–1935; American evangelist.

Sunday best, [Colloq.], one's best clothes.

Sun·day-go-to-meet·ing (sun′di-gō′tə-mēt′iŋ), *adj.* [Colloq.], appropriate to Sunday church services; i.e., best or most presentable, as clothes, manners, etc.

Sunday school, 1. a school, usually affiliated with some church, giving religious instruction on Sunday. 2. its teachers and pupils. Abbreviated **S.S.**

sun deck, an open porch or deck for rest or recreation in the sun.

sun·der (sun′dẽr), *v.t. & v.i.* [ME. *sundren;* AS. *sundrian, syndrian* < *sundor, sunder,* asunder; akin to G. *sonder;* IE. base **seni-,* etc., in **senitar,* away from, by itself; base seen in L. *sine,* without], to break apart; separate; part; split. —*SYN.* see **separate.**

in sunder, into parts or pieces; apart.

sun·der·ance (sun′dẽr-əns, sun′drəns), *n.* a sundering or being sundered; separation.

Sun·der·land (sun′dẽr-lənd), *n.* a seaport on the northeastern coast of England: pop., 182,000.

sun·dew (sun′dōō′, sun′dū′), *n.* [MD. *sondauw,* lit., sun dew], any of a number of related plants with slender stems, leaves covered with sticky hairs, and clusters of pink, red, or white flowers.

sun·di·al (sun′dī′əl, sun′dīl′), *n.* an instrument that indicates time by the position of the shadow of a pointer or gnomon cast by the sun on the face of a dial marked in hours.

GNOMON

SUNDIAL

sun disk, a disk flanked by two serpents and set in a pair of outspread wings, a symbol of the Egyptian sun god, Ra.

sun·dog (sun′dôg′), *n.* 1. a bright, often colored spot near the sun; parhelion. 2. a small halo or rainbow on the parhelic circle.

sun·down (sun′doun′), *n.* [? contr. < *sun go down*], sunset.

sun-dried (sun′drīd′), *adj.* dried by the sun.

sun·dries (sun′driz), *n.pl.* [see SUNDRY], sundry items; miscellaneous things of various sorts.

sun·drops (sun′drops′), *n.pl.* any of a number of related plants with large, usually yellow flowers which remain open during the sunlight hours.

SUN DISK

sun·dry (sun′dri), *adj.* [ME. *sundri, syndri;* AS. *syndrig,* separate < *sunder,* apart; cf. SUNDER & -Y], various; miscellaneous; divers: as, *sundry* items of clothing.

sun·fast (sun′fast′, sun′fäst′), *adj.* that will not fade if exposed to sunlight.

sun·fish (sun′fish′), *n.* [*pl.* SUNFISH, SUNFISHES (-iz); see FISH], 1. any of various small, fresh-water fishes of North America including the crappie, bluegill, and, especially, the pumpkinseed. 2. a large ocean fish having a short, thick, almost tailless body, a small mouth, and very long dorsal and anal fins.

sun·flow·er (sun′flou′ẽr), *n.* any of a number of tall related plants having yellow, daisylike flowers with yellow, brown, purple, or almost black disks that contain edible seeds from which an oil is extracted.

Sunflower State, Kansas.

Sung (sooŋ), *n.* [Chin.], a dynasty (960–1279 A.D.) of the Chinese Empire, famous for achievement in art, literature, and philosophy.

sung (suŋ), past participle and rare past tense of **sing.**

Sun·ga·ri (sōōŋ′gä-rē′), *n.* a river of Manchuria, flowing into the Amur River: length, 1,130 mi.

Sung·kiang (sooŋ′jyäŋ′), *n.* a province of central Manchuria: area, 30,703 sq. mi.; pop., 2,571,000 (est. 1947); capital, Harbin.

sun·glass (sun′glas′, sun′gläs′), *n.* 1. a convex lens used to produce heat by converging the sun's rays at a single point; burning glass. 2. *pl.* eyeglasses having special lenses to protect the eyes from the sun's glare.
sun·glow (sun′glō′), *n.* a colored glow seen in the sky at sunrise or sunset as a result of the diffraction of the sun's rays by particles in the air.
sun god, the sun personified and worshiped as a god.
sunk (suŋk), past participle and alternative past tense of **sink**.
sunk·en (suŋk′ən), obsolete past participle of **sink**. *adj.* 1. sunk in liquid; especially, at the bottom of a body of water: as, a *sunken* ship. 2. situated beneath the surface of the surrounding medium: as, a *sunken* rock. 3. that is below the usual or general level: as, a *sunken* garden. 4. depressed; hollow: as, *sunken* cheeks.
sun lamp, 1. an electric lamp that radiates ultraviolet rays, used therapeutically as a substitute for sunlight. 2. a lamp with parabolic mirrors for intensifying and reflecting light, as in a motion-picture studio.
sun·less (sun′lis), *adj.* without sun or sunlight; dark.
sun·light (sun′līt′), *n.* the light of the sun.
sun·lit (sun′lit′), *adj.* lighted by the sun.
sunn (sun), *n.* [Hind. *san;* Sans. *śaṇa*, hempen], 1. an East Indian plant with silvery, lance-shaped leaves, yellow flowers, and stems yielding fiber used in canvas, rope, etc. 2. its fiber. Also **sunn hemp.**
Sun·na, Sun·nah (soon′ə), *n.* [Ar. *sunnah*, lit., a form, course, tradition], Moslem law based, according to tradition, on the teachings and practices of Mohammed and observed by orthodox Moslems: it is supplementary to the Koran.
sun·ni·ly (sun′ə-li), *adv.* in a sunny manner.
sun·ni·ness (sun′i-nis), *n.* a sunny state or quality.
Sun·nite (soon′īt), *n.* [< Ar. *sunnah* (see SUNNA); + *-ite*], a member of one of the two great sects of Moslems: Sunnites approve the historical order of the first four caliphs as the rightful line of succession to Mohammed and accept the Sunna as an authoritative supplement to the Koran: opposed to *Shiite*.
sun·ny (sun′i), *adj.* [SUNNIER (-i-ẽr), SUNNIEST (-i-ist)], 1. having or full of sunshine; bright with sunlight. 2. of, like, or coming from the sun. 3. warm; cheerful; bright: as, a *sunny* smile or disposition.
sunny side, 1. the side exposed to sunlight. 2. the more pleasing or favorable part, feature, or aspect.
on the sunny side of, somewhat younger than (a specified age).
sun parlor, a sitting room having many large windows to admit much sunlight.
sun·proof (sun′prōōf′), *adj.* impervious to or unaffected by sunlight.
sun·ray (sun′rā′), *n.* 1. a ray of sunlight. 2. a representation of this in art.
sun·rise (sun′rīz′), *n.* [*sun* + *rise*, *v.*, prob. in such phrases as *before the sun rise*], 1. the daily appearance of the sun above the eastern horizon. 2. the varying time of this. 3. the atmospheric phenomena at this time.
sun·room (sun′rōōm′, sun′room′), *n.* a sun parlor.
sun·set (sun′set′), *n.* [ME. *sunne set, sonsette;* see SUNRISE], 1. the daily disappearance of the sun below the western horizon. 2. the varying time of this. 3. atmospheric phenomena at this time; especially, the color of the western sky at sunset. 4. the final phase or decline (*of* a period).
sun·shade (sun′shād′), *n.* a parasol, awning, broad hat, etc. used for protection against the sun's rays.
sun·shine (sun′shīn′), *n.* 1. the shining of the sun. 2. the light and heat given off by the sun. 3. a surface or area on which the sun shines. 4. *a*) cheerfulness, happiness, etc. *b*) a source or cause of cheerfulness, etc.
sun·shin·y (sun′shīn′i), *adj.* 1. bright with sunlight. 2. warm; bright; cheerful.
sun·spot (sun′spot′), *n.* any of the dark spots sometimes seen on the surface of the sun: they are believed to have some connection with magnetic disturbances on earth.
sun·stroke (sun′strōk′), *n.* a form of heatstroke caused by excessive exposure to the sun and characterized by high body temperature, convulsions, and, often, coma: cf. **heat exhaustion.**
sun·struck (sun′struk′), *adj.* having sunstroke.
sun tan, 1. a darkened condition of the skin resulting from exposure to the sun. 2. a yellowish red-brown color.
sun·up (sun′up′), *n.* sunrise.
Sun Valley, a resort town in central Idaho.
sun·ward (sun′wẽrd), *adv.* toward the sun. *adj.* facing the sun.
sun·wards (sun′wẽrdz), *adv.* sunward.
sun·wise (sun′wīz′), *adv.* in the direction of the sun's apparent motion across the sky; clockwise.
Sun Yat-sen (soon′ yät′sen′), (born *Sun Wen*), 1866–1925; Chinese political leader; organized revolution against the Manchus; founded Kuomintang (1911); president of China (1921–1922).
‡**su·o ju·re** (sū′ō jōō′ri), [L.], in one's own right.
‡**su·o lo·co** (sū′ō lō′kō), [L.], in its own (i.e., proper) place.

Su·o·mi (soo-ô′mi), *n.* Finland: the Finnish name.
sup (sup), *v.t.* & *v.i.* [SUPPED (supt), SUPPING], [ME. *soupen, supen;* AS. *supan*, to sup, drink; akin to G. *saufen;* IE. base **seu-*, something damp and soft, sap, as also in L. *sugere*, to suck; cf. SOP, SIP; the Mod. Eng. form is < northern dial.], to take (liquid) into the mouth in small amounts; sip. *n.* a small mouthful of liquid.
sup (sup), *v.i.* [SUPPED (supt), SUPPING], [ME. *soupen, sopen;* OFr. *soper*], to eat the evening meal; have supper. *v.t.* to provide with supper.
sup- (sup), see **sub-**.
sup., 1. superior. 2. superlative. 3. supplement. 4. supplementary. 5. supply. 6. *supra*, [L.], above. 7. supreme.
su·per (sōō′pẽr, sū′pẽr), *n.* [< *super-* as used in numerous Eng. compounds], 1. [Colloq.], an extra person, especially an actor having a small nonspeaking part; supernumerary. 2. [Colloq.], a product of superior grade, extra-large size, etc.: a trade term. 3. [Colloq.], a superintendent. 4. in *bookbinding*, a kind of starched cotton mesh used for reinforcing books. *adj.* superfine; of great excellence: often ironical, as, a *super* patriot. *v.t.* in *bookbinding*, to reinforce with super.
su·per- (sōō′pẽr, sū′pẽr), [L. < *super*, above], a prefix meaning: 1. *over, above, on top of*, as in *superstructure, superscribe*. 2. *higher in rank or position than, superior to*, as in *superintendent, supervisor*. 3. *a*) *greater in quality, amount, or degree than, surpassing*, as in *superfine, superabundance*. *b*) *greater or better than others of its kind*, as in *supermarket*. 4. *to a degree greater than normal*, as in *superheat, supersaturate*. 5. *extra, additional*, as in *supertax*. 6. *to a secondary degree*, as in *superparasite*. 7. *in chemistry, with a large or unusually large amount of* (the specified substance), as in *superphosphate*: an earlier prefix now largely replaced by *bi-*, *di-*, *per-*, etc.
super., 1. superfine. 2. superior.
su·per·a·ble (sōō′pẽr-ə-b'l, sū′pẽr-ə-b'l), *adj.* [L. *superabilis* < *superare*, to overcome < *super*, over], that can be overcome or conquered; surmountable.
su·per·a·bound (sōō′pẽr-ə-bound′, sū′pẽr-ə-bound′), *v.i.* [LL. *superabundare;* see SUPER- & ABOUND], 1. to be very abundant; be in great abundance. 2. to be too abundant; be in excess.
su·per·a·bun·dance (sōō′pẽr-ə-bun′dəns, sū′pẽr-ə-bun′dəns), *n.* 1. the state of being superabundant. 2. more than is usual or needed; surplus; excess.
su·per·a·bun·dant (sōō′pẽr-ə-bun′dənt, sū′pẽr-ə-bun′dənt), *adj.* [LL. *superabundans*, ppr. of *superabundare;* see SUPER- & ABOUND], being more than is usual or needed; surplus; excess; overly abundant.
su·per·add (sōō′pẽr-ad′, sū′pẽr-ad′), *v.t.* [L. *superaddere;* see SUPER- & ADD], to put in as extra; add (something) to what has been added already; add further.
su·per·an·nu·ate (sōō′pẽr-an′ū-āt′, sū′pẽr-an′ū-āt′), *v.t.* [back-formation < *superannuated*], 1. to retire from service, especially with a pension, because of old age or infirmity. 2. to set aside as old-fashioned or obsolete.
su·per·an·nu·at·ed (sōō′pẽr-an′ū-āt′id, sū′pẽr-an′ū-āt′id), *adj.* [< ML. *superannatus* (with *-u-* after L. *annus*) < L. *super annum*, beyond a year], 1. discharged from service, especially on a pension, because of old age or infirmity. 2. obsolete; old-fashioned; outdated. 3. too old or worn for further work, service, etc.
su·per·an·nu·a·tion (sōō′pẽr-an′ū-ā′shən, sū′pẽr-an′ū-ā′shən), *n.* 1. a superannuating or being superannuated. 2. a pension received by a superannuated person.
su·perb (soo-pũrb′, syoo-pũrb′), *adj.* [L. *superbus*, proud, haughty, delicate < *super*, above], 1. noble; grand; majestic: said of buildings, architecture, etc. 2. rich; elegant; luxurious. 3. of the highest quality; extremely fine; excellent. —*SYN.* see **splendid.**
su·per·cal·en·der (sōō′pẽr-kal′ən-dẽr, sū′pẽr-kal′ən-dẽr), *n.* [*super-* + *calender*], a series of polished rollers used to give an extra-high gloss to paper, rubber, etc. *v.t.* to process with a supercalender.
su·per·car·go (sōō′pẽr-kär′gō, sū′pẽr-kär′gō), *n.* [*pl.* SUPERCARGOES, SUPERCARGOS (-gōz)], [earlier *supracargo* < Sp. *sobrecargo*, *supercargo;* see SUPER- & CARGO], an officer on a merchant ship who has charge of the cargo, representing the shipowner in all transactions.
su·per·charge (sōō′pẽr-chärj′, sū′pẽr-chärj′), *v.t.* to increase the power of (an engine), as by the use of a supercharger.
su·per·charg·er (sōō′pẽr-chär′jẽr, sū′pẽr-chär′jẽr), *n.* a blower or compressor used to increase the power of an internal-combustion engine by increasing the supply of air to the cylinders beyond that pumped in by the pistons.
su·per·cil·i·ar·y (sōō′pẽr-sil′i-er′i, sū′pẽr-sil′i-er′i), *adj.* [Mod. L. *superciliarius* < L. *super-*, above + *cilium*, eyelid], of, or in the region of, the eyebrow.
su·per·cil·i·ous (sōō′pẽr-sil′i-əs, sū′pẽr-sil′i-əs), *adj.* [LL. *superciliosus* < L. *supercilium*, eyebrow, hence (with reference to facial expression with raised brows) pride, haughtiness < *super-*, above + *cilium*, eyelid], disdainful or contemptuous; full of or characterized by pride or scorn; haughty; arrogant. —*SYN.* see **proud.**

su·per·class (sōō′pẽr-klas′, sū′pẽr-kläs′), ***n.*** in *biology,* 1. a subdivision of a subphylum. 2. sometimes, a subphylum.

su·per·co·lum·nar (sōō′pẽr-kə-lum′nẽr, sū′pẽr-kə-lum′nẽr), ***adj.*** in *architecture,* having one order of columns above another.

su·per·co·lum·ni·a·tion (sōō′pẽr-kə-lum′ni-ā′shən, sū′pẽr-kə-lum′ni-ā′shən), ***n.*** an architectural plan characterized by one order of columns above another.

su·per·cool (sōō′pẽr-kōōl′, sū′pẽr-kōōl′), ***v.t.* & *v.i.*** to cool, as a liquid, below its freezing point without solidification.

su·per·dom·i·nant (sōō′pẽr-dom′ə-nənt, sū′pẽr-dom′ə-nənt), ***n.*** in *music,* the submediant.

su·per·dread·nought (sōō′pẽr-dred′nôt, sū′pẽr-dred′nôt), ***n.*** [*super-* + *dreadnaught*], a battleship of the dreadnought class, but larger and with greater firepower.

su·per·e·go (sōō′pẽr-ē′gō, sū′pẽr-eg′ō), ***n.*** in *psychoanalysis,* that part of the psyche which controls at an unconscious level the impulses of the id; conscience of the unconscious: distinguished from *ego, id.*

su·per·em·i·nence (sōō′pẽr-em′ə-nəns, sū′pẽr-em′ə-nəns), ***n.*** the quality of being supereminent.

su·per·em·i·nent (sōō′pẽr-em′ə-nənt, sū′pẽr-em′ə-nənt), ***adj.*** [L. *supereminens,* ppr. of *supereminere,* to rise above; see SUPER- & EMINENT], eminent beyond others in rank, dignity, character, etc.

su·per·er·o·gate (sōō′pẽr-er′ə-gāt′, sū′pẽr-er′ə-gāt′), ***v.i.*** [SUPEREROGATED (-id), SUPEREROGATING], [< LL. *supererogatus,* pp. of *supererogare,* to pay out beyond what is expected; *super-,* above + *erogare,* to pay out (after consent by the people); *e-* (for *ex-*), out + *rogare,* to ask], to do more than is required or expected.

su·per·er·o·ga·tion (sōō′pẽr-er′ə-gā′shən, sū′pẽr-er′ə-gā′shən), ***n.*** [LL. *supererogatio* < *supererogatus*], the act or an instance of supererogating.

works of supererogation, in the *Roman Catholic Church,* good works done, as by saints, over and above those commanded by God.

su·per·e·rog·a·to·ry (sōō′pẽr-i-rog′ə-tôr′i, sū′pẽr-i-rog′ə-tō′ri), ***adj.*** [ML. *supererogatorius;* see SUPEREROGATE & -ORY], 1. done or observed beyond the degree required or expected. 2. superfluous; unnecessary.

su·per·fam·i·ly (sōō′pẽr-fam′ə-li, sū′pẽr-fam′ə-li), ***n.*** in *biology,* a category ranking above a family and below an order.

su·per·fe·cun·da·tion (sōō′pẽr-fē′kən-dā′shən, sū′pẽr-fek′ən-dā′shən), ***n.*** [*super-* + *fecundation*], in *physiology,* the fertilization of two ova at separate times during the same menstrual period.

su·per·fe·tate (sōō′pẽr-fē′tāt, sū′pẽr-fē′tāt), ***v.i.*** [SUPERFETATED (-id), SUPERFETATING], [< LL. *superfetatus,* pp. of *superfetare*], in *physiology,* to conceive a second time while still pregnant from an earlier conception.

su·per·fe·ta·tion (sōō′pẽr-fi-tā′shən, sū′pẽr-fi-tā′shən), ***n.*** [see SUPERFETATE], the fertilization of an ovum during a pregnancy already in existence.

su·per·fi·cial (sōō′pẽr-fish′əl, sū′pẽr-fish′əl), ***adj.*** [ME. *superficyall,* etc.; L. *superficialis* < *superficies;* see SUPERFICIES], 1. of or being on the surface. 2. square: said of measurements. 3. concerned with and understanding only the easily apparent and obvious; not profound; shallow. 4. quick and cursory: as, a *superficial* reading. 5. apparent, but not real; external: as, a *superficial* resemblance.

SYN.—**superficial** implies concern with the obvious or surface aspects of a thing (a *superficial* resemblance) and, in a derogatory sense, a lack of thoroughness, profoundness, significance, etc. (*superficial* judgments); **shallow,** in this connection always derogatory, implies a lack of depth of character, intellect, meaning, etc. (*shallow* writing); **cursory,** which may or may not be derogatory, suggests a hasty consideration of something without pausing to note details (a *cursory* reading of a manuscript). —***ANT.*** deep, profound, deliberate.

su·per·fi·ci·al·i·ty (sōō′pẽr-fish′i-al′ə-ti, sū′pẽr-fish′i-al′ə-ti), ***n.*** 1. the state or quality of being superficial. 2. [*pl.* SUPERFICIALITIES (-tiz)], something superficial.

su·per·fi·cial·ly (sōō′pẽr-fish′ə-li, sū′pẽr-fish′ə-li), ***adv.*** 1. in a superficial manner. 2. to a superficial degree.

su·per·fi·ci·es (sōō′pẽr-fish′i-ēz′, sū′pẽr-fish′ēz), ***n.*** [*pl.* SUPERFICIES], [L. < *super-,* above + *facies,* face], 1. a surface; outer area. 2. the outward form or aspect.

su·per·fine (sōō′pẽr-fīn′, sū′pẽr-fīn′), ***adj.*** [Fr. *superfin;* see SUPER- & FINE], 1. too subtle, delicate, or refined; overnice. 2. of exceptionally fine quality; extra fine: said of merchandise, etc. Abbreviated **super.**

su·per·flu·i·ty (sōō′pẽr-flōō′ə-ti, sū′pẽr-flōō′ə-ti), ***n.*** [*pl.* SUPERFLUITIES (-tiz)], [ME. *superfluite;* OFr. *superfluité;* L. *superfluitas*], 1. the state or quality of being superfluous. 2. a quantity or number beyond what is needed; excess; superabundance. 3. *usually in pl.* something superfluous; thing not needed.

su·per·flu·ous (soo-pũr′flōō-əs, syoo-pũr′flōō-əs), ***adj.*** [L. *superfluus* < *superfluere,* to overflow; *super-,* above + *fluere,* to flow], 1. being more than is needed, useful, or wanted; surplus; excessive. 2. not needed; unnecessary: as, a *superfluous* remark.

su·per·fuse (sōō′pẽr-fūz′, sū′pẽr-fūz′), ***v.t.* & *v.i.*** [SUPERFUSED (-fūzd′), SUPERFUSING], [< L. *superfusus,* pp. of *superfundere;* see SUPER- & FUSE, *v.*], 1. to pour or be poured over or on something. 2. in *chemistry,* to supercool.

su·per·fu·sion (sōō′pẽr-fū′zhən, sū′pẽr-fū′zhən), ***n.*** a superfusing or being superfused.

su·per·heat (sōō′pẽr-hēt′, sū′pẽr-hēt′; *for n.,* sōō′pẽr-hēt′, sū′pẽr-hēt′), ***v.t.*** 1. to overheat. 2. to heat (a liquid) above its boiling point without vaporization. 3. to heat (steam not in contact with water) beyond its saturation point, so that a drop in temperature will not cause reconversion to water. ***n.*** the number of degrees by which the temperature of superheated steam exceeds the temperature of the steam at its saturation point.

su·per·heat·er (sōō′pẽr-hēt′ẽr, sū′pẽr-hēt′ẽr), ***n.*** an apparatus used for superheating steam.

su·per·het·er·o·dyne (sōō′pẽr-het′ẽr-ə-dīn′, sū′pẽr-het′ẽr-ə-dīn′), ***adj.*** [*super*sonic + *heterodyne*], designating or of a form of radio reception in which part of the amplification is carried out at an intermediate supersonic frequency produced by beating the frequency of the received carrier waves with that of locally generated oscillations. ***n.*** a radio set for this method of reception.

su·per·high·way (sōō′pẽr-hī′wā′, sū′pẽr-hī′wā′), ***n.*** a highway for high-speed traffic, consisting generally of four or more lanes and connecting with crossroads by means of cloverleaves.

su·per·hu·man (sōō′pẽr-hū′mən, sū′pẽr-hū′mən), ***adj.*** [*super-* + *human*], 1. regarded as having powers or a nature above that of man; divine; supernatural. 2. greater than that of a normal human being.

su·per·im·pose (sōō′pẽr-im-pōz′, sū′pẽr-im-pōz′), ***v.t.*** 1. to impose or lay (something) on top of something else. 2. to add.

su·per·im·po·si·tion (sōō′pẽr-im′pə-zish′ən, sū′pẽr-im′pə-zish′ən), ***n.*** 1. a superimposing or being superimposed. 2. something superimposed.

su·per·in·cum·bence (sōō′pẽr-in-kum′bəns, sū′pẽr-in-kum′bəns), ***n.*** the quality or state of being superincumbent.

su·per·in·cum·ben·cy (sōō′pẽr-in-kum′bən-si, sū′pẽr-in-kum′bən-si), ***n.*** superincumbence.

su·per·in·cum·bent (sōō′pər-in-kum′bənt, sū′pẽr-in-kum′bənt), ***adj.*** [L. *superincumbens,* ppr. of *superincumbere;* see SUPER- & INCUMBENT], 1. lying or resting on something else. 2. suspended above; overhanging.

su·per·in·duce (sōō′pẽr-in-dōōs′, sū′pẽr-in-dūs′), ***v.t.*** [L. *superinducere;* see SUPER- & INDUCE], to introduce or bring in as an addition to something else.

su·per·in·duc·tion (sōō′pẽr-in-duk′shən, sū′pẽr-in-duk′shən), ***n.*** a superinducing or being superinduced.

su·per·in·tend (sōō′pẽr-in-tend′, sū′pẽr-in-tend′), ***v.t.*** [LL. *superintendere;* see SUPER- & INTEND], to act as superintendent of; direct; manage; supervise.

su·per·in·tend·ence (sōō′pẽr-in-ten′dəns, sū′pẽr-in-ten′dəns), ***n.*** [ML. *superintendentia*], the function of a superintendent; direction; management; supervision.

su·per·in·tend·en·cy (sōō′pẽr-in-ten′dən-si, sū′pẽr-in-ten′dən-si), ***n.*** 1. superintendence. 2. the office or rank of a superintendent.

su·per·in·tend·ent (sōō′pẽr-in-ten′dənt, sū′pẽr-in-ten′dənt), ***n.*** [OFr. *superintendant* < LL. *superintendens,* ppr. of *superintendere,* to superintend], a person in charge of a department, institution, project, etc.; director; manager; supervisor. ***adj.*** superintending. Abbreviated **Supt., supt.**

Su·pe·ri·or (sə-pêr′i-ẽr, soo-pêr′i-ẽr), ***n.*** 1. the largest of the Great Lakes, between Michigan and Ontario, Canada, and bordering on Minnesota and Wisconsin: area, 31,810 sq. mi.: usually **Lake Superior.** 2. a port in northwestern Wisconsin, on Lake Superior: pop., 35,000.

su·pe·ri·or (sə-pêr′i-ẽr, soo-pêr′i-ẽr), ***adj.*** [ME.; OFr.; L., compar. of *superus,* that is above], 1. having greater elevation; higher; upper. 2. printed or written above another figure or letter or the rest of the line: in $n^2 = y^x$, *2* and *x* are *superior.* 3. higher in rank, position, authority, etc. 4. greater in value, quality, amount, power, etc. 5. far above the average; of high quality, worth, ability, etc.; excellent. 6. having or showing a feeling that one is better than others; arrogant; haughty; supercilious. 7. more comprehensive or inclusive; generic: said of words, terms, concepts, etc. 8. in *astronomy, a)* farther from the sun than the earth is: said of certain planets. *b)* designating a conjunction that is farther from the earth than the sun is. 9. in *botany, a)* situated over some other organ. *b)* growing free from the calyx: said of an ovary. ***n.*** 1. a person who is superior, as in rank, merit, etc. 2. the head of a

monastery, convent, etc. Abbreviated **sup., super.**
superior to, 1. higher than. 2. greater than. 3. unaffected by; not yielding to or influenced by; indifferent to (something painful, unpleasant, etc.).
su·pe·ri·or·i·ty (sə-pêr'i-ôr'ə-ti, soo-pêr'i-or'ə-ti), ***n.*** the state or quality of being superior.
superiority complex, popularly, a feeling of superiority or exaggerated self-importance, often accompanied by excessive aggressiveness, a domineering attitude, etc. which are actually compensation for feelings of inferiority: see **inferiority complex.**
su·per·ja·cent (sōō'pẽr-jā's'nt, sū'pẽr-jā's'nt), ***adj.*** [L. *superjacens*, ppr. of *superjacere; super-*, over + *jacere*, to lie], lying or resting above or upon.
su·per·la·tive (soo-pũr'lə-tiv, syoo-pũr'lə-tiv), ***adj.*** [ME. & OFr. *superlatif;* LL. *superlativus* < L. *superlatus*, excessive; *super-*, above, beyond + *latus*, pp. of *ferre*, to carry], 1. superior to or excelling all other or others; of the highest kind, quality, degree, etc.; supreme. 2. excessive; exaggerated. 3. in ***grammar,*** expressing the extreme degree of the quality or attribute indicated by the simple, or positive, form of an adjective or adverb: usually indicated by the suffix *-est* (*hardest*) or by the use of *most* with the positive form (*most beautiful*). ***n.*** 1. the highest or utmost degree; acme; height; peak. 2. something superlative. 3. in ***grammar,*** *a)* the superlative degree; extreme degree of comparison of an adjective or adverb. *b)* a word or form in this degree. Abbreviated **superl., sup.**
su·per·lu·nar (sōō'pẽr-lōō'nẽr, sū'pẽr-lū'nẽr), ***adj.*** superlunary.
su·per·lu·na·ry (sōō'pẽr-lōō'nẽr-i, sū'pẽr-lū'nẽr-i), ***adj.*** [< *super-* + L. *luna*, moon; + *-ary*], 1. located above or beyond the moon. 2. celestial; not earthly.
su·per·man (sōō'pẽr-man', sū'pẽr-man'), ***n.*** [*pl.* SUPERMEN (-men')], [*super-* + *man*, transl. of G. *übermensch*], 1. in the philosophy of Nietzsche, an idealized superior, dominating man, regarded as the goal of the evolutionary struggle for survival. 2. a man having apparently superhuman powers.
su·per·mar·ket (sōō'pẽr-mär'kit, sū'pẽr-mär'kit), ***n.*** a large food store or market in which shoppers serve themselves from open shelves and pay for their purchases at the exit: also **super market.**
su·per·nal (sōō-pũr'n'l, sū-pũr'n'l), ***adj.*** [OFr. < L. *supernus*, upper < *super*, above], 1. of, from, or being in the sky or heaven. 2. high in rank, merit, power, etc.; lofty. 3. celestial; ethereal; heavenly; divine.
su·per·na·tant (sōō'pẽr-nā'tənt, sū'pẽr-nā'tənt), ***adj.*** [L. *supernatans*, ppr. of *supernatare*, to swim above; *super-*, over + *natare*, to swim], floating on the surface.
su·per·nat·u·ral (sōō'pẽr-nach'ẽr-əl, sū'pẽr-nach'ẽr-əl), ***adj.*** [ML. *supernaturalis* < L. *super*, above + *natura*, nature], 1. existing or occurring outside the normal experience or knowledge of man; caused by other than the known forces of nature. 2. attributed to hypothetical forces beyond nature; miraculous; divine.
the supernatural, 1. something supernatural. 2. the intervention of supernatural forces in nature.
su·per·nat·u·ral·ism (sōō'pẽr-nach'ẽr-əl-iz'm, sū'pẽr-nach'ẽr-əl-iz'm), ***n.*** 1. the quality or state of being supernatural. 2. belief in the supernatural, especially a belief that some supernatural, or divine, force controls nature and the universe.
su·per·nat·u·ral·ist (sōō'pẽr-nach'ẽr-əl-ist, sū'pẽr-nach'ẽr-əl-ist), ***n.*** a person who believes in the supernatural or in supernaturalism. ***adj.*** supernaturalistic.
su·per·nat·u·ral·is·tic (sōō'pẽr-nach'ẽr-əl-is'tik, sū'pẽr-nach'ẽr-əl-is'tik), ***adj.*** of or characteristic of supernaturalism.
su·per·nat·u·ral·ize (sōō'pẽr-nach'ẽr-əl-īz', sū'pẽr-nach'ẽr-əl-īz'), ***v.t.*** [SUPERNATURALIZED (-īzd'), SUPERNATURALIZING], 1. to make supernatural. 2. to think of or treat as supernatural.
su·per·nor·mal (sōō'pẽr-nôr'm'l, sū'pẽr-nôr'm'l), ***adj.*** better than normal or average, as in intelligence.
su·per·nu·mer·ar·y (sōō'pẽr-nōō'mẽr-er'i, sū'pẽr-nū'mẽr-er'i), ***adj.*** [LL. *supernumerarius* < L. *super*, above + *numerus*, number], 1. that exceeds or is beyond the regular or prescribed number; extra. 2. that is beyond the number or quantity needed or desired; superfluous. ***n.*** [*pl.* SUPERNUMERARIES (-iz)], 1. a supernumerary person or thing. 2. in the *theater*, an actor having a small, nonspeaking part, as in a mob scene.
su·per·or·der (sōō'pẽr-ôr'dẽr, sū'pẽr-ôr'dẽr), ***n.*** in *biology*, a category between an order and a class or subclass.
su·per·or·gan·ic (sōō'pẽr-ôr-gan'ik, sū'pẽr-ôr-gan'ik), ***adj.*** above or beyond the organic.
su·per·par·a·site (sōō'pẽr-pâr'ə-sīt', sū'pẽr-pâr'ə-sīt'), ***n.*** an organism that lives as a parasite upon another parasite.
su·per·phos·phate (sōō'pẽr-fos'fāt, sū'pẽr-fos'fāt), ***n.*** an acid phosphate, especially a mixture of monocalcium phosphate, $CaH_4(PO_4)_2$, and calcium sulfate made by treating bone, phosphate rock, etc. with sulfuric acid and used as fertilizer.
su·per·phys·i·cal (sōō'pẽr-fiz'i-k'l, sū'pẽr-fiz'i-k'l), ***adj.*** above or beyond the physical; not explainable by the known laws of physics.
su·per·pos·a·ble (sōō'pẽr-pōz'ə-b'l, sū'pẽr-pōz'ə-b'l), ***adj.*** that can be superposed.
su·per·pose (sōō'pẽr-pōz', sū'pẽr-pōz'), ***v.t.*** [SUPERPOSED (-pōzd'), SUPERPOSING], [Fr. *superposer;* see SUPER- & POSE (to place)], 1. to lay or place on, over, or above something else. 2. in *geometry*, to make (one figure) coincide with another in all parts, by or as by placing one on top of the other.
su·per·posed (sōō'pẽr-pōzd', sū'pẽr-pōzd'), ***adj.*** [pp. of *superpose*], in *botany*, growing directly above another part or organ.
su·per·po·si·tion (sōō'pẽr-pə-zish'ən, sū'pẽr-pə-zish'ən), ***n.*** [Fr.; LL. *superpositio* < pp. of *superponere*, to place over; *super-*, over + *ponere*, to put, place], a superposing or being superposed.
su·per·pow·er (sōō'pẽr-pou'ẽr, sū'pẽr-pou'ẽr), ***n.*** 1. a state having political power over other powerful states. 2. electrical power secured by linking together a number of electrical power systems in a single area into one main power system, so as to increase the efficiency of distribution.
su·per·sat·u·rate (sōō'pẽr-sach'oo-rāt', sū'pẽr-sach'oo-rāt'), ***v.t.*** [SUPERSATURATED (-id), SUPERSATURATING], [*super-* + *saturate*, after Fr. *sursaturer*], to cause to contain more of a solution than is normally possible; saturate beyond the normal point for the given temperature.
su·per·sat·u·ra·tion (sōō'pẽr-sach'oo-rā'shən, sū'pẽr-sach'oo-rā'shən), ***n.*** a supersaturating or being supersaturated.
su·per·scribe (sōō'pẽr-skrīb', sū'pẽr-skrīb'), ***v.t.*** [SUPERSCRIBED (-skrībd'), SUPERSCRIBING], [L. *superscribere; super-*, above + *scribere*, to write], 1. to write, mark, or engrave (an inscription, name, etc.) on the top or outer surface of something. 2. to write a name, address, etc. on the outside of (a letter, parcel, etc.).
su·per·script (sōō'pẽr-skript', sū'pẽr-skript'), ***adj.*** [L. *superscriptus*, pp.; see SUPERSCRIBE], written above: cf. **subscript.** ***n.*** a number, symbol, letter, etc. written above and to the side of another, as an algebraic exponent.
su·per·scrip·tion (sōō'pẽr-skrip'shən, sū'pẽr-skrip'shən), ***n.*** [ME. *superscripcioun;* L. *superscriptio*], 1. the act of superscribing. 2. something superscribed; especially, an address on a letter, etc. 3. in ***pharmacy,*** the Latin word *recipe* (meaning "take") or its symbol, ℞, on a prescription.
su·per·sede (sōō'pẽr-sēd', sū'pẽr-sēd'), ***v.t.*** [SUPERSEDED (-id), SUPERSEDING], [OFr. *superseder, superceder*, to surcease, leave off, give over; L. *supersedere*, lit., to sit over, preside over, forbear, refrain, desist; *super-*, above + *sedere*, to sit], 1. to cause to be set aside or dropped from use as inferior or obsolete and replaced by something else. 2. to take the place or office of; succeed. 3. to remove or cause to be removed so as to make way for another; supplant. —***SYN.*** see **replace.**
su·per·se·de·as (sōō'pẽr-sē'di-as, sū'pẽr-sē'di-as), ***n.*** [ME.; L., you shall desist < *supersedere;* cf. SUPERSEDE], a legal document issued to halt or delay the action of some process of law, as the execution of a sentence.
su·per·se·dure (sōō'pẽr-sē'jẽr, sū'pẽr-sē'jẽr), ***n.*** a superseding or being superseded.
su·per·sen·si·ble (sōō'pẽr-sen'sə-b'l, sū'pẽr-sen'sə-b'l), ***adj.*** outside or above the range or perception of the senses.
su·per·sen·si·bly (sōō'pẽr-sen'sə-bli, sū'pẽr-sen'sə-bli), ***adv.*** so as to be supersensible.
su·per·sen·si·tive (sōō'pẽr-sen'sə-tiv, sū'pẽr-sen'sə-tiv), ***adj.*** sensitive to an abnormal degree.
su·per·sen·so·ry (sōō'pẽr-sen'sə-ri, sū'pẽr-sen'sə-ri), ***adj.*** beyond or apart from normal sense perception; extrasensory; supersensible.
su·per·sen·su·al (sōō'pẽr-sen'shōō-əl, sū'pẽr-sen'shōō-əl), ***adj.*** 1. supersensory. 2. spiritual.
su·per·serv·ice·a·ble (sōō'pẽr-sũr'vis-ə-b'l, sū'pẽr-sũr'vis-ə-b'l), ***adj.*** too eager to be of service; disagreeably officious.
su·per·ses·sion (sōō'pẽr-sesh'ən, sū'pẽr-sesh'ən), ***n.*** [ML. *supersessio*], a superseding or being superseded.
su·per·son·ic (sōō'pẽr-son'ik, sū'pẽr-son'ik), ***adj.*** [< *super* (above) + L. *sonus*, sound], 1. designating or of vibrations or waves with frequencies higher than those audible to the human ear (above about 20,000 per second). 2. designating or of a speed greater than the speed of sound (above about 1,087 feet per second, or 738 miles per hour). 3. traveling at such a speed.
su·per·son·ics (sōō'pẽr-son'iks, sū'pẽr-son'iks), ***n.pl.*** [construed as sing.], [see SUPERSONIC & -ICS], the science dealing with supersonic phemomena.
su·per·state (sōō'pẽr-stāt', sū'pẽr-stāt'), ***n.*** a state or government having power over other subordinated states.
su·per·sti·tion (sōō'pẽr-stish'ən, sū'pẽr-stish'ən), ***n.*** [OFr.; L. *superstitio*, excessive fear of the gods, superstition, orig., a standing still over < *superstare*, to stand over; *super-*, over + *stare*, to stand], 1. any belief or attitude that is inconsistent with the known laws of science or with what is generally considered in the particular society as true and rational; especially,

such a belief in charms, omens, the supernatural, etc. 2. any action or practice based on such a belief or attitude. 3. such beliefs or attitudes collectively.

su·per·sti·tious (sōō'pẽr-stish'əs, sū'pẽr-stish'əs), ***adj.*** 1. of, characterized by, or resulting from superstition. 2. having or manifesting superstitions.

su·per·stra·tum (sōō'pẽr-strā'təm, sū'pẽr-strā'təm), ***n.*** a stratum lying over another.

su·per·struc·ture (sōō'pẽr-struk'chẽr, sū'pẽr-struk'-chẽr), ***n.*** 1. a structure built on top of another. 2. that part of a building above the foundation. 3. that part of a ship, especially of a warship, above the main deck. 4. the rails and ties of a railroad as distinguished from the ballast or roadbed.

su·per·sub·tle (sōō'pẽr-sut''l, sū'pẽr-sut''l), ***adj.*** too subtle.

su·per·sub·tle·ty (sōō'pẽr-sut''l-ti, sū'pẽr-sut''l-ti), ***n.*** the quality of being supersubtle.

su·per·tax (sōō'pẽr-taks', sū'pẽr-taks'), ***n.*** an additional tax; especially, a surtax.

su·per·ton·ic (sōō'pẽr-ton'ik, sū'pẽr-ton'ik), ***n.*** in *music*, the second tone of a scale, next above the tonic.

su·per·vene (sōō'pẽr-vēn', sū'pẽr-vēn'), ***v.i.*** [SUPERVENED (-vēnd'), SUPERVENING], [L. *supervenire*, to come over or upon, follow; *super-*, over + *venire*, to come], 1. to come or happen as something additional, unexpected, or foreign to the normal course of events. 2. to take place; ensue.

su·per·ven·ient (sōō'pẽr-vēn'yənt, sū'pẽr-vēn'yənt), ***adj.*** [L. *superveniens*, ppr.], supervening.

su·per·ven·tion (sōō'pẽr-ven'shən, sū'pẽr-ven'shən), ***n.*** 1. the act of supervening. 2. a supervening event.

su·per·vise (sōō'pẽr-vīz', sū'pẽr-vīz'), ***v.t. & v.i.*** [SUPERVISED (-vīzd'), SUPERVISING], [< ML. *supervisus*, pp. of *supervidere* < L. *super-*, over + *videre*, to see], to oversee or direct (work, workers, a project, etc.); superintend.

su·per·vi·sion (sōō'pər-vizh'ən, sū'pẽr-vizh'ən), ***n.*** a supervising or being supervised; direction; management.

su·per·vi·sor (sōō'pẽr-vī'zẽr, sū'pẽr-vī'zẽr), ***n.*** [ML.], 1. a person who supervises; superintendent; manager; director. 2. in certain school systems, an official in charge of the courses of study for a particular subject and of all teachers of that subject.

su·per·vi·sor·ship (sōō'pẽr-vī'zẽr-ship', sū'pẽr-vī'zẽr-ship'), ***n.*** [see -SHIP], the position, duties, or administration of a supervisor.

su·per·vi·so·ry (sōō'pẽr-vī'zə-ri, sū'pẽr-vī'zə-ri), ***adj.*** 1. of a supervisor or supervision. 2. supervising.

su·pi·nate (sōō'pə-nāt', sū'pə-nāt'), ***v.t. & v.i.*** [SUPINATED (-id), SUPINATING], [< L. *supinatus*, pp. of *supinare*, to lay backward, throw on the back < *supinus*, backward], in ***anatomy***, to turn (the hand or forelimb) so that the palm is upward or away from the body.

su·pi·na·tion (sōō'pə-nā'shən, sū'pə-nā'shən), ***n.*** [LL. *supinatio*], 1. a supinating or being supinated. 2. the position resulting from this. Opposed to *pronation*.

su·pi·na·tor (sōō'pə-nā'tẽr, sū'pə-nā'tẽr), ***n.*** the muscle in the forearm by which supination is effected.

su·pine (sōō-pīn', sū-pīn'; *for n.*, sōō'pīn, sū'pīn), ***adj.*** [L. *supinus*], 1. lying on the back, face upward: opposed to *prone*. 2. with the palm upward or away from the body: said of the hand. 3. [Poetic], leaning or sloping backward. 4. mentally or morally inactive; sluggish; listless; passive. ***n.*** a Latin verbal noun formed from the stem of the past participle and having only an accusative and an ablative form. —***SYN.*** see **prone.**

supp., 1. supplement. 2. supplementary.

sup·per (sup'ẽr), ***n.*** [ME. *super;* OFr. *soper*, *super*, *souper*, supper, orig. inf., to sup; see SUP], the last meal of the day, eaten in the evening.

sup·per·time (sup'ẽr-tīm'), ***n.*** the time when supper is eaten.

suppl., 1. supplement. 2. supplementary.

sup·plant (sə-plant', sə-plänt'), ***v.t.*** [Fr. *supplanter;* L. *supplantare*, to put something under the sole of the foot, trip up < *sub-*, under + *planta*, sole of the foot], 1. to take the place of; supersede, especially through force, scheming, or treachery. 2. to remove or uproot in order to replace with something else. —***SYN.*** see **replace.**

sup·plan·ta·tion (sup'lan-tā'shən), ***n.*** a supplanting or being supplanted.

sup·ple (sup''l), ***adj.*** [ME. & OFr. *souple;* L. *supplex*, humble, submissive < *supplicare;* see SUPPLICATE], 1. easily bent or twisted; flexible; pliant. 2. lithe; limber: as, a *supple* body. 3. easily changed or influenced; yielding; compliant. 4. yielding too easily; obsequious; servile. 5. adaptable; resilient; elastic: said of the mind, etc. ***v.t. & v.i.*** [SUPPLED (-'ld), SUPPLING], to make or become supple. —***SYN.*** see **elastic.**

sup·ple·jack (sup''l-jak'), ***n.*** 1. a twining plant with tough stems, greenish-white flowers, and dark-purple fruit. 2. a walking stick made from such a stem.

sup·ple·ly (sup''l-li), ***adv.*** in a supple manner; flexibly.

sup·ple·ment (sup'lə-mənt; *for v.*, sup'lə-ment'), ***n.*** [ME.; L. *supplementum* < *supplere;* see SUPPLY], 1. something added, especially to make up for a lack or deficiency. 2. a section added to a book or the like to give additional information, correct errors in the body of the work, etc. 3. a separate section containing feature stories, comic strips, etc., issued with a newspaper. 4. the amount to be added to a given angle or arc to make 180° or a semicircle. ***v.t.*** to provide a supplement to; add to, especially so as to make up for a lack or deficiency. Abbreviated **suppl., supp., sup.**

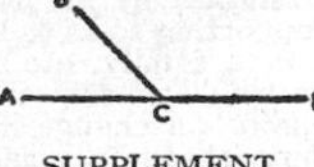

SUPPLEMENT angle BCA supplements angle BCD, and vice versa

sup·ple·men·tal (sup'lə-men't'l), ***adj.*** supplementary.

sup·ple·men·ta·ry (sup'lə-men'tẽr-i), ***adj.*** 1. supplying what is lacking; serving as a supplement; additional. 2. equaling 180° when added together: said of arcs or angles. Abbreviated **suppl., supp., sup.**

sup·ple·tion (sə-plē'shən), ***n.*** [ME. *supplecioun;* OFr.; L. **suppletio* (cf. SUPPLETORY)], 1. a supplementing. 2. in *linguistics*, the supplying of deficient forms of a word by forms drawn from another word. Example: *went*, originally the past tense of *wend*, is used, as a result of *suppletion*, to express the past tense of *go*.

sup·ple·to·ry (sup'lə-tôr'i, sup'lə-tō'ri), ***adj.*** [LL. *suppletorius* < L. *suppletus*, pp. of *supplere;* see SUPPLY], supplementary.

sup·pli·ance (sup'li-əns), ***n.*** [< *suppliant*], [Rare], supplication.

sup·pli·ant (sup'li-ənt), ***n.*** [ME. *suppliaunt;* see the *adj.*], a person who supplicates; petitioner. ***adj.*** [Fr., ppr. of *supplier;* L. *supplicare*, to supplicate], 1. asking humbly; supplicating; entreating; beseeching. 2. expressing supplication: as, *suppliant* words.

sup·pli·cant (sup'lə-kənt), ***adj.*** [L. *supplicans*, ppr. of *supplicare*, to supplicate], supplicating. ***n.*** a person who supplicates; suppliant.

sup·pli·cate (sup'lə-kāt'), ***v.t.*** [SUPPLICATED (-id), SUPPLICATING], [ME. < L. *supplicatus*, pp. of *supplicare*, to kneel down, pray < *sub-*, under + *plicare*, to fold, double up], 1. to ask for humbly and earnestly, as by prayer. 2. to make a humble request of; petition earnestly. ***v.i.*** to make a humble request or supplication, especially in prayer. —***SYN.*** see **appeal.**

sup·pli·ca·tion (sup'lə-kā'shən), ***n.*** [ME. *supplicacioun;* OFr.; L. *supplicatio*], 1. the act of supplicating. 2. a humble request, prayer, petition, etc.

sup·pli·ca·to·ry (sup'li-kə-tôr'i, sup'li-kə-tō'ri), ***adj.*** [ML. *supplicatorius*], supplicating.

sup·pli·er (sə-plī'ẽr), ***n.*** a person or agency that supplies.

sup·ply (sə-plī'), ***v.t.*** [SUPPLIED (-plīd'), SUPPLYING], [ME. *supplyen;* OFr. *supplier;* L. *supplere*, to fill up < *sub-*, under + *plere*, to fill], 1. to give; furnish; provide; yield: as, we *supply* all materials. 2. to compensate for; make good: as, friends have *supplied* their loss, you must *supply* the deficiency. 3. to meet the needs or requirements of; furnish, provide, or equip with what is needed: as, we can *supply* you with materials. 4. to act as a substitute in; fill or serve in temporarily: as, several men have *supplied* his pulpit. ***v.i.*** to serve as a temporary substitute. ***n.*** [*pl.* SUPPLIES (-plīz')], 1. the act of supplying. 2. an amount or quantity available for use; stock; store. 3. the amount of a commodity available for purchase at a given price: opposed to *demand*. 4. *pl.* materials, provisions, etc. for supplying an army, an expedition, a business, etc. 5. *pl.* an amount of money granted for government expenses; appropriation. 6. a temporary substitute, as for a minister or teacher. 7. [Obs.], *a*) aid; assistance. *b*) reinforcements. ***adj.*** 1. having to do with a supply or supplies. 2. serving as a substitute. Abbreviated **sup.**

sup·ply (sup'li), ***adv.*** supplely.

sup·port (sə-pôrt', sə-pōrt'), ***v.t.*** [Fr. *supporter;* L. *supportare*, to carry, bring to a place, hence to endure, sustain < *sub-*, under + *portare*, to carry], 1. to carry the weight of; keep from falling, slipping, or sinking; keep steady or in position. 2. to give courage, faith, or confidence to; help; comfort; strengthen. 3. to give approval to; be in favor of; subscribe to; sanction; uphold. 4. to maintain or provide for (a person, institution, etc.) with money or subsistence. 5. to show or tend to show to be true; help prove, vindicate, or corroborate: as, this evidence *supports* his claim. 6. to bear; endure; submit to; tolerate. 7. to keep up; maintain; sustain: as, the discussion was not well *supported*. 8. in the *theater*, *a*) to act (a part). *b*) to have a subordinate role in the same play with (a specified star). ***n.*** 1. a supporting or being supported. 2. a person or thing that supports. 3. a means of support; subsistence.

SYN.—**support**, the broadest of these terms, suggests a favoring of someone or something, either by giving active aid or merely by approving or sanctioning (to *support* a candidate for office); **uphold** suggests that what is being supported is under attack (to *uphold* civil rights for all); **sustain** implies full active support so as to strengthen or keep from failing (*sustained* by his hope for the future); **maintain** suggests a supporting so as to keep intact or unimpaired (to *maintain* the law, a family, etc.); **advocate** implies support in speech or writing and sometimes connotes persuasion or argument (to *advocate* a change in policy); **back** (often **back up**) suggests support, as financial aid, moral encouragement, etc., given to prevent failure (I'll *back* you *up* in your demands).

sup·port·a·ble (sə-pôr′tə-b′l, sə-pōr′tə-b′l), *adj.* that can be supported; bearable; endurable.

sup·port·er (sə-pôr′tẽr, sə-pōr′tẽr), *n.* 1. a person who supports; advocate; adherent; partisan. 2. a thing that supports; especially, an elastic appliance used to support or bind some part of the body, as a jockstrap. 3. in *heraldry*, either of a pair of figures, as of animals or men, standing one on each side of an escutcheon. —*SYN.* see **follower.**

sup·pos·a·ble (sə-pōz′ə-b′l), *adj.* that can be supposed.

sup·pose (sə-pōz′), *v.t.* [SUPPOSED (-pōzd′), SUPPOSING], [ME. *supposen;* OFr. *supposer*, to put, lay, or set upon; also, to suppose, imagine < L. *sub*, under + OFr. *poser;* see POSE (to place)], 1. to assume to be true, as for the sake of argument or to illustrate a proof: as, *suppose* A equals B. 2. to believe to be; imagine; think; presume. 3. to involve the assumption of; presuppose. 4. to consider as a proposed or suggested possibility: used in the imperative, as, *suppose* I write him first. 5. to expect; obligate: always in the passive, as, I'm *supposed* to be there at eight o'clock. *v.i.* to make a supposition; conjecture.

sup·posed (sə-pōzd′), *adj.* 1. regarded as true, genuine, etc., without actual knowledge. 2. merely imagined.

sup·pos·ed·ly (sə-pōz′id-li), *adv.* according to what is, was, or may be supposed.

sup·po·si·tion (sup′ə-zish′ən), *n.* [OFr.; L. *suppositio*, a putting or placing under, substitution < *suppositus*, pp. of *supponere*, to put, place, or set under < *sub-*, under + *ponere*, to place, put], 1. the act of supposing. 2. something supposed; theory; hypothesis.

sup·po·si·tion·al (sup′ə-zish′ən-′l), *adj.* of, having the nature of, or based on supposition; conjectural.

sup·pos·i·ti·tious (sə-poz′ə-tish′əs), *adj.* [L. *suppositicius* < *suppositus;* see SUPPOSITION], 1. substituted with intent to deceive or defraud; spurious; counterfeit. 2. suppositional.

sup·pos·i·tive (sə-poz′ə-tiv), *adj.* [< L. *suppositus* (see SUPPOSITION); + *-ive*], having the nature of, based on, or involving supposition. *n.* in *grammar*, a conjunction introducing a supposition, as *if, assuming, provided*, etc.

sup·pos·i·to·ry (sə-poz′ə-tôr′i, sə-poz′ə-tō′ri), *n.* [*pl.* SUPPOSITORIES (-iz, -riz)], [LL. *suppositorium*, neut. of *suppositorius*, placed underneath < L. *suppositus;* see SUPPOSITION], a small piece of medicated substance, usually in the shape of a cone or ovoid, introduced into the rectum, vagina, etc., where it is melted and diffused by the body temperature.

sup·press (sə-pres′), *v.t.* [ME. *suppressen* < L. *suppressus*, pp. of *supprimere*, to press under, suppress < *sub-*, under + *premere*, to press], 1. *a)* to put down by force; subdue; quell; crush. *b)* to abolish by authority. 2. to keep from appearing or being known; keep back; restrain; conceal: as, I *suppressed* a laugh, newspapers have *suppressed* the story. 3. to prevent or prohibit the publication of (a book, passage in a book, etc.). 4. to check the flow or discharge of; stop. 5. in *psychiatry*, to conceal or withhold from consciousness.

sup·pres·sion (sə-presh′ən), *n.* [L. *suppressio*], 1. a suppressing or being suppressed. 2. in *psychoanalysis*, the deliberate exclusion of an idea, desire, or feeling from consciousness or overt action.

sup·pres·sive (sə-pres′iv), *adj.* tending to suppress; that suppresses.

sup·pu·rate (sup′yoo-rāt′), *v.i.* [SUPPURATED (-id), SUPPURATING], [< L. *suppuratus*, pp. of *suppurare*, to gather pus underneath < *sup-* (see SUB-) + *pus, puris*, pus, matter], to form or discharge pus; fester.

sup·pu·ra·tion (sup′yoo-rā′shən), *n.* [L. *suppuratio* < *suppuratus;* see SUPPURATE], 1. the formation or discharge of pus. 2. pus.

sup·pu·ra·tive (sup′yoo-rā′tiv), *adj.* of, causing, or characterized by suppuration. *n.* a medicine, etc. inducing suppuration.

supr., supreme.

‡su·pra (soo̅′prə, sū′prə), *adv.* [L.], above: abbreviated **sup.**

su·pra- (soo̅′prə, sū′prə), [< L. *supra*, above, over], a prefix meaning *above, over, beyond*, as in *supramaxillary.*

su·pra·lap·sar·i·an (soo̅′prə-lap-sâr′i-ən, sū′prə-lap-sâr′i-ən), *n.* [< *supra-* + L. *lapsus*, a fall; + *-arian* as in *Unitarian*, etc.], any of the Calvinists who hold that God's plan of salvation for some preceded the fall of man from grace, which had been predestined: opposed to *infralapsarian.*

su·pra·lim·i·nal (soo̅′prə-lim′i-n′l, sū′prə-lim′i-n′l), *adj.* [*supra-* + *liminal*], above the threshold of consciousness; conscious: opposed to *subliminal.*

su·pra·mo·lec·u·lar (soo̅′prə-mə-lek′yoo-lẽr, sū′prə-mə-lek′yoo-lẽr), *adj.* composed of more than one molecule.

su·pra·or·bit·al (soo̅′prə-ôr′bi-t′l, sū′prə-ôr′bi-t′l), *adj.* in *anatomy*, situated above the orbit of the eye.

su·pra·pro·test (soo̅′prə-prō′test, sū′prə-prō′test), *n.* [< It. *sopra protesto*, upon protest; cf. SUPRA- & PROTEST], in *law*, an acceptance or payment of a bill of exchange by someone other than the drawer, after protest for nonacceptance or nonpayment by the drawee.

su·pra·re·nal (soo̅′prə-rē′n′l, sū′prə-rē′n′l), *adj.* [*supra-* + *renal*], situated on or above the kidney; specifically, designating or of an adrenal gland. *n.* an adrenal gland.

su·prem·a·cy (sə-prem′ə-si, soo-prem′ə-si, syoo-prem′ə-si), *n.* [*pl.* SUPREMACIES (-siz)], [< *supreme* + *-acy*], 1. the quality or state of being supreme. 2. supreme power or authority.

su·preme (sə-prēm′, soo-prēm′, syoo-prēm′), *adj.* [Fr. *suprême;* L. *supremus*, superl. of *superus*, that is above, higher], 1. highest in rank, power, authority, etc.; dominant. 2. highest in quality, achievement, etc.; most excellent. 3. highest in degree; utmost: as, a *supreme* fool. 4. final; ultimate.

Supreme Being, God.

Supreme Court, 1. the highest Federal court, consisting of nine judges: its decisions are final and take precedence over those of all other judicial bodies in the country. 2. the highest court in any of the States. Abbreviated **Sup. Ct., Sup. C., S.C.**

supreme sacrifice, the sacrifice of one's life, especially in war.

Supreme Soviet, the parliament of the Soviet Union: it consists of two equal chambers, the Council of the Union (whose members are elected on the basis of population) and the Council of the Nationalities (whose members are elected by the various nationality groups).

Supt., supt., Superintendent.

sur- (sũr), [< Fr. *sur;* OFr. *sur-, sour-;* L. *super, supra*, over, above], a prefix meaning *over, upon, above, beyond*, as in *surcoat, surface.*

sur- (sũr), see **sub-.**

sur., surplus.

su·ra (soor′ə), *n.* [Ar. *surah*, lit., step, degree], any of the main divisions, or chapters, of the Koran.

Su·ra·ba·ya (soo̅′rä-bä′yä), *n.* a seaport and naval base in northeastern Java: pop., 342,000: also spelled **Soerabaja.**

su·rah (soor′ə), *n.* [< *Surat*, India], a soft, twilled fabric of silk or of silk and rayon.

Su·ra·kar·ta (soo̅′rä-kär′tä), *n.* a city in central Java: pop., 165,000: also spelled **Soerakarta**: also called *Solo.*

su·ral (soor′əl, syoor′əl), *adj.* [Mod. L. *suralis* < L. *sura*, calf of the leg], of the calf of the leg.

Su·rat (soo-rat′, soor′ət), *n.* a seaport in Bombay state, western India: pop., 99,000.

sur·base (sũr′bās′), *n.* a molding or cornice along the top of a base, as of a pedestal, baseboard, etc.

sur·based (sũr′bāst′), *adj.* [< *surbase* + *-ed*], 1. having a surbase. 2. [< Fr. *surbaissé; sur-* (< L. *super*), over + *baissé*, pp. of *baisser*, to lower], designating an arch whose rise is less than half its span.

sur·cease (sũr-sēs′), *v.t. & v.i.* [SURCEASED (-sēst′), SURCEASING], [ME. *sursessen* < OFr. *sursis*, masc., *sursise*, fem., pp. of *surseoir*, to pause, leave off, delay; L. *supersedere*, to refrain from, desist], [Archaic], to stop; end. *n.* [Archaic], end; cessation.

sur·charge (sũr-chärj′; *for n., usually* sũr′chärj′), *v.t.* [Fr. *surcharger*], 1. to overcharge. 2. to overload; overburden. 3. to fill to excess or beyond normal capacity. 4. to mark (a postage stamp) with a surcharge. 5. in *law*, to show an omission, as of a credit, in (an account). *n.* 1. *a)* an additional amount added to the usual charge. *b)* an excessive charge; overcharge. 2. an extra or excessive load, burden, etc. 3. a new valuation overprinted on a postage stamp, etc., to change its denomination. 4. in *law*, a surcharging.

sur·cin·gle (sũr′sin′g′l), *n.* [ME. & OFr. *surcengle* < *sur-*, over + L. *cingulum*, a belt], 1. a strap passed around a horse's body to bind on a saddle, blanket, pack, etc. 2. a girdle, especially of a cassock.

sur·coat (sũr′kōt′), *n.* [ME. & OFr. *surcote*], an outer coat or gown; especially, in the Middle Ages, a loose, short cloak worn over armor.

sur·cu·lose (sũr′kyoo-lōs′), *adj.* [L. *surculosus* < *surculus*, a twig, graft, sucker, dim. of *surus*, a twig, branch], in *botany*, having suckers.

surd (sũrd), *adj.* [L. *surdus*, deaf, dull, mute; used to transl. Gr. *alogos*, irrational, lit., without reason], 1. in *mathematics*, that cannot be expressed in rational numbers; irrational: said of a number or quantity. 2. in *phonetics*, voiceless. *n.* 1. in *mathematics*, a surd number or quantity: as, $\sqrt{5}$ is a *surd*. 2. in *phonetics*, a voiceless sound.

sure (shoor), *adj.* [ME. *sur, seur;* OFr. *sur, seür, segur;* L. *securus*], 1. [Rare], secure; safe; stable. 2. that will not fail; always effective: as, a *sure* method. 3. that can be relied or depended upon; trustworthy: as, he is my *sure* lieutenant and adviser. 4. that cannot be doubted, questioned, or disputed; absolutely true. 5. having or showing no doubt or hesitancy; positive; confident; certain: as, he approached with a *sure* step, are you *sure* of your facts? 6. *a*) that can be counted on to be or happen: as, he's heading for *sure* defeat. *b*) having confidence in some future contingency: as, I'm *sure* he'll come. 7. bound or destined to do, experience, or be something specified: as, he is *sure* to lose, it's *sure* to snow. 8. never missing; unerring; steady: as, a *sure* aim. ***adv.*** [Colloq.], 1. surely; inevitably. 2. certainly; indeed: an intensive, often used as an affirmative answer to questions.

for sure, certainly; without doubt.
make sure, to be or cause to be certain.
sure enough, [Colloq.], certainly; without doubt.
to be sure, surely; certainly.

SYN.—**sure,** the simple word, suggests merely an absence of doubt or hesitancy (I'm *sure* you don't mean it); **certain** usually suggests conviction based on specific grounds or evidence (this letter makes me *certain* of his innocence); **confident** stresses the firmness of one's certainty or sureness, especially in some expectation (he's *confident* he'll win); **positive** suggests unshakeable confidence, especially in the correctness of one's opinions or conclusions, sometimes to the point of dogmatism (he's too *positive* in his beliefs). — ***ANT.*** doubtful.

sure-e·nough (shoor′i-nuf′), ***adj.*** [Colloq.], real; actual.

sure-fire (shoor′fīr′), ***adj.*** [Colloq.], sure to be successful or as expected; that will not fail.

sure-foot·ed (shoor′foot′id), ***adj.*** not likely to stumble, slip, fall, or err.

sure·ly (shoor′li), ***adv.*** 1. with assurance or confidence; in a sure, unhesitating manner. 2. without a doubt; assuredly; unquestionably; certainly: often used as an intensive emphasizing belief or supposition, as, *surely* you don't believe that!

sure·ty (shoor′ti, shoor′ə-ti), ***n.*** [*pl.* SURETIES (-tiz)], [ME. & OFr. *seurte* < L. *securitas* < *securus*, sure, secure], 1. the state of being sure; sureness; assurance. 2. something sure; certainty. 3. something that makes sure, protects, or gives assurance, as against loss, damage, or default; guarantee; security. 4. a person who makes himself responsible for another; specifically, in *law*, one who makes himself liable for another's debts, defaults of obligations, etc.

sure·ty·ship (shoor′ti-ship′, shoor′ə-ti-ship′), ***n.*** [see -SHIP], the position or responsibility of a person acting as surety for another.

surf (sũrf), ***n.*** [formerly *suffe* & hence prob. var. of *sough*, but early use for the Indian seas makes possible a native name borrowing], 1. the waves or swell of the sea breaking on the shore or a reef. 2. the foam or spray caused by this.

sur·face (sũr′fis), ***n.*** [Fr. < *sur-* (see SUR-) + *face*, a face, after L. *superficies*], 1. *a*) the outer face, or exterior, of an object. *b*) any of the faces of a solid. 2. superficial features, as of a personality; outward appearance. 3. in *geometry*, an extent or magnitude having length and breadth, but no thickness. 4. in *aeronautics*, an airfoil. ***adj.*** 1. of, on, or at the surface. 2. exterior; superficial. ***v.t.*** [SURFACED (-fist), SURFACING], 1. to treat the surface of; give a specified kind of surface to; especially, to make smooth or level. 2. to bring (a submarine) to the surface of the water. ***v.i.*** 1. to work at or near the surface, as in mining. 2. to rise to the surface of the water: as, the fish *surfaced* and jumped.

surface noise, noise produced by the friction of a phonograph needle in passing along the grooves of a record.

surface plate, a steel plate having a tooled flat surface used as a standard of flatness, as in manufacturing.

surface tension, a property of liquids in which the exposed surface tends to contract to the smallest possible area, as in the spheroidal formation of drops: it is a phenomenon attributed to the attractive forces, or cohesion, between the molecules of the liquid.

surf·bird (sũrf′bũrd′), ***n.*** a shore bird of the plover family, found on the Pacific coast: it has a broad tail, white at the base and black at the tip.

surf·board (sũrf′bôrd′, sũrf′bōrd′), ***n.*** a long, narrow board used in the water sport of riding in toward shore on the crests of waves.

SURFBOARD

surf·boat (sũrf′bōt′), ***n.*** a sturdy, light boat used in heavy surf.

surf duck, the scoter, a kind of sea duck.

sur·feit (sũr′fit), ***n.*** [ME. *surfet*, *surfait*; OFr. *sorfait* < *surfaire*, to overdo; *sur-* (< L. *super*), over + *faire* (< L. *facere*), to make], 1. too great an amount or supply; excess (usually with *of*): as, a *surfeit* of complaints. 2. overindulgence, especially in food or drink. 3. discomfort or disorder resulting from overindulgence in food or drink. 4. disgust, nausea, etc. resulting from any kind of excess; satiety. ***v.t.*** [ME. *sorfeten*], to feed or supply to satiety or excess. ***v.i.*** to indulge or be supplied to satiety or excess; overindulge. —***SYN.*** see **satiate.**

surf fish, any of a group of small, perchlike fishes living in shallow water along the Pacific coast: they bear living young.

surf scoter, any of a group of sea ducks living in northern waters: the males are black with white-marked faces and necks, the females and young are grayish-brown.

surf·y (sũr′fi), ***adj.*** [SURFIER (-fi-ẽr), SURFIEST (-fi-ist)], 1. of, like, or forming surf. 2. having surf, especially heavy surf.

surg., 1. surgeon. 2. surgery. 3. surgical.

surge (sũrj), ***n.*** [prob. via Fr. < L. *surgere*, to rise], 1. *a*) a large mass of or as of moving water; wave; swell; billow. *b*) such waves or billows collectively. 2. a movement of or like that of a mass of water; violent rolling, sweeping, or swelling motion: as, the *surge* of the sea. 3. a short, sudden rush or excess of electric current in a circuit. 4. in *nautical usage*, the concave part of a capstan or windlass, upon which the rope slips, or surges. ***v.i.*** [SURGED (sũrjd), SURGING], 1. to have a heavy, violent swelling motion; move in or as in a surge or surges. 2. to be tossed about on waves, as a vessel. 3. to increase suddenly or oscillate abnormally: said of an electric current. 4. to slip, as a rope or cable on a capstan or windlass. ***v.t.*** to slacken or release (a rope or cable) suddenly.

sur·geon (sũr′jən), ***n.*** [ME. *surgien*; OFr. *cirurgien*, *serurgien* < *cirurgie*, *sirurgie*; see SURGERY], a doctor who practices surgery, as distinguished from a physician: abbreviated **surg.**

sur·geon·cy (sũr′jən-si), ***n.*** the position of a surgeon.

sur·geon·fish (sũr′jən-fish′), ***n.*** [*pl.* SURGEONFISH, SURGEONFISHES (-iz); see FISH], a bright-colored tropical fish with sharp, lancelike spines on either side of the base of the tail.

Surgeon General, [*pl.* SURGEONS GENERAL, SURGEON GENERALS], 1. in the United States Army or Navy, the chief general officer or admiral in charge of the medical department. 2. in the United States Bureau of Public Health, the chief medical officer. 3. [s- g-], in the British Army, a member of the medical staff. Abbreviated **Surg. Gen.**

sur·geon's knot (sũr′jənz), a knot used as by surgeons in tying ligatures, etc.: see **knot,** illus.

sur·ger·y (sũr′jẽr-i), ***n.*** [*pl.* SURGERIES (-iz)], [ME. *surgerie*; OFr. *cirurgie*, *sirurgie*, contr. of *cirurgerie*, *serurgerie*; LL. *chirurgia* < Gr. *cheirourgia*, a working with the hands, handicraft, skill < *cheir*, *cheiros*, the hand + *ergein*, to work], 1. the treatment of disease, injury, or deformity by manual or instrumental operations, as the removal of diseased parts or tissue by cutting. 2. the branch of medicine dealing with this. 3. the laboratory or operating room of a surgeon or hospital. 4. in Great Britain, a doctor's office. Abbreviated **surg.** See also **tree surgery.**

sur·gi·cal (sũr′ji-k'l), ***adj.*** 1. of surgeons or surgery. 2. used in or connected with surgery. 3. resulting from or after surgery. Abbreviated **surg.**

sur·gi·cal·ly (sũr′ji-k'l-i), ***adj.*** 1. by surgery: as, he was cured *surgically*. 2. with reference to surgery.

surg·y (sũr′ji), ***adj.*** [SURGIER (-ji-ẽr), SURGIEST (-ji-ist)], 1. surging; having a surge or surges. 2. characteristic of a surge or surges.

Su·ri·ba·chi (soor′ə-bä′chi), ***n.*** a volcano on Iwo Jima: site of a battle (1945) in World War II.

su·ri·cate (soor′ə-kāt′, syoor′ə-kāt′), ***n.*** [Fr. *surikate*; S.Afr. D., prob. < native name], a small, four-toed, burrowing mammal of South Africa, related to the civet and mongoose.

Su·ri·nam (soor′i-näm′, soor′i-nam′), ***n.*** a Dutch colony in northern South America, on the Atlantic: area, 54,291 sq. mi.; pop., 182,000 (est. 1947); capital, Paramaribo: also called *Netherlands Guiana*, *Dutch Guiana*.

sur·li·ly (sũr′lə-li), ***adv.*** in a surly manner.

sur·li·ness (sũr′li-nis), ***n.*** a surly state or quality.

sur·ly (sũr′li), ***adj.*** [SURLIER (-li-ẽr), SURLIEST (-li-ist)], [earlier *serly*, *sirly*, masterful, imperious < *sir*], 1. bad-tempered; uncivil; sullenly rude. 2. [Rare or Obs.], haughty; arrogant. —***SYN.*** see **sullen.**

sur·mise (sẽr-mīz′; *also, for n.*, sũr′mīz), ***n.*** [ME. *surmyse*; OFr. *surmise*, accusation, fem. of *surmis*, pp. of *surmettre*, lit., to put upon, hence to accuse; *sur-* (< L. *super*), above + *mettre*, to put < L. *mittere*, to send], 1. an idea or opinion formed from evidence that is neither positive nor conclusive; conjecture; guess. 2. the act or process of surmising; conjecture in general. ***v.t. & v.i.*** [SURMISED (-mīzd′), SURMISING], to imagine or infer (something) without conclusive evidence; conjecture; guess. —***SYN.*** see **guess.**

sur·mount (sẽr-mount′), *v.t.* [ME. *surmounten;* OFr. *surmonter;* see SUR- & MOUNT], 1. [Rare], to surpass; exceed; go beyond. 2. to get the better of; conquer; overcome. 3. to be or lie at the top of; be or rise above. 4. to climb up and across; get over (a height, obstacle, etc.). 5. to place something on top of or above.

sur·mul·let (sẽr-mul′it), *n.* [*pl.* SURMULLETS (-its), SURMULLET; see PLURAL, II, D, 1], [Fr. *surmulet;* OFr. *sormulet; sor,* red, sorrel + *mulet,* mullet], a perchlike salt-water food fish with two barbels attached to the lower lip; red mullet.

sur·name (sũr′nām′; *also, for v.,* sũr′nām′), *n.* [altered, after *name* < ME. *surnoun* < OFr. *surnom; sur-* (< L. *super*), over + *nom,* a name], 1. a family name as distinguished from a given or Christian name; last name. 2. a name or epithet added to a person's given name; agnomen: as, King Richard had the *surname* "the Lionhearted." *v.t.* [SURNAMED (-nāmd′, -nāmd′), SURNAMING], to give a surname (especially sense 2) to.

sur·pass (sẽr-pas′, sẽr-päs′), *v.t.* [OFr. *surpasser; sur-* (< L. *super*), beyond + *passer,* to pass], 1. to excel or be superior to. 2. to exceed in quantity, degree, amount, etc. 3. to go beyond the limit, capacity, range, etc. of: as, his luck *surpassed* his wildest dreams. —*SYN.* see **excel.**

sur·pass·ing (sẽr-pas′iŋ, sẽr-päs′iŋ), *adj.* that surpasses the average or usual; exceeding or excelling; unusually excellent. *adv.* [Obs. or Poetic], excellently.

sur·plice (sũr′plis), *n.* [ME. *surplis;* Anglo-Fr. *surpliz;* OFr. *surpliz, sorpeliz;* LL. **superpelliceum; super-,* above + *pelliceum,* fur robe, neut. of L. *pelliceus, pellicius,* made of skins], a loose, white, wide-sleeved cloak or gown worn variously, over the cassock, by the clergy and choir in the Roman Catholic and Anglican churches.

sur·pliced (sũr′plist), *adj.* wearing a surplice.

sur·plus (sũr′plus, sũr′pləs), *n.* [ME.; OFr.; *sur-,* above + L. *plus,* more], 1. a quantity or amount over and above what is needed; something left over; excess. 2. the excess of the assets of a business over its liabilities for a given period. 3. the excess of the total accumulated assets of a business over its liabilities and capital stock outstanding. *adj.* forming a surplus; excess; extra. Abbreviated **s., sur.**

sur·plus·age (sũr′plus-ij), *n.* [ME.; cf. SURPLUS & -AGE], 1. surplus; excess. 2. irrelevant or unnecessary words; specifically in *law,* superfluous allegations in a pleading.

surplus value, in *Marxist economics,* the amount by which the value of the worker's product exceeds that of his pay: regarded as the source of the capitalist's profit.

sur·print (sũr′print′), *v.t.* to print (something new) over matter already printed. *n.* something surprinted.

sur·pris·al (sẽr-prī′z′l), *n.* a surprising or being surprised; surprise.

sur·prise (sẽr-prīz′), *v.t.* [SURPRISED (-prīzd′), SURPRISING], [OFr. *surpris,* pp. of *sorprendre, surprendre,* to surprise, take napping; *sur-* (< L. *super*), above + *prendre* (< L. *prehendere*), to take], 1. to come upon (someone or something) suddenly or unexpectedly; take unawares. 2. to attack or capture suddenly and without warning. 3. to cause to wonder or to be amazed or astonished because unexpected, unusual, etc.; astound. 4. *a)* to cause (someone) by some sudden or unexpected action to do or say something unintended: often with *into. b)* to bring out or elicit (something) by such means: as, we *surprised* an admission from him. *n.* 1. the act of surprising; unexpected seizure or attack. 2. the state of being surprised; feeling aroused by something unusual or unexpected; astonishment. 3. something that surprises; especially, a sudden or unexpected event or unusual thing that causes wonderment or astonishment.

take by surprise, 1. to come upon suddenly or without warning; surprise. 2. to amaze; astonish; astound.

SYN.—**surprise,** in this connection, implies an affecting with wonder because unexpected, unusual, etc. (I'm *surprised* at your concern); **astonish** implies a surprising so greatly as to appear unbelievable (to *astonish* with sleight of hand); **amaze** suggests an astonishing that causes bewilderment or confusion (*amazed* at the sudden turn of events); **astound** suggests a shocking astonishment that leaves one helpless to act or think (I was *astounded* by his proposal); **flabbergast** is a colloquial term suggesting an astounding to the point of speechlessness.

sur·pris·ed·ly (sẽr-prīz′id-li), *adv.* with surprise; in a manner showing surprise.

sur·pris·ing (sẽr-prīz′iŋ), *adj.* causing surprise; amazing.

sur·re·al·ism (sə-rē′əl-iz′m), *n.* [Fr. *surréalisme; sur-* (see SUR-) + *réalisme,* realism], a modern movement in art and literature, in which an attempt is made to portray or interpret the workings of the subconscious mind as manifested in dreams: it is characterized by an irrational, noncontextual arrangement of material.

sur·re·al·ist (sə-rē′əl-ist), *adj.* of, practicing, or characterized by surrealism. *n.* a surrealist painter, writer, etc.

sur·re·al·is·tic (sə-rē′əl-is′tik), *adj.* of surrealism.

sur·re·but·tal (sũr′ri-but′′l), *n.* in *law,* the act of giving evidence in support of a surrebutter.

sur·re·but·ter (sũr′ri-but′ẽr), *n.* in *law,* a plaintiff's reply to a defendant's rebutter.

sur·re·join·der (sũr′ri-join′dẽr), *n.* in *law,* a plaintiff's reply to a defendant's rejoinder.

sur·ren·der (sə-ren′dẽr), *v.t.* [OFr. *surrendre; sur-,* upon, up + *rendre,* to render], 1. to give up possession of or power over; yield to another on demand or compulsion. 2. to give up claim to; give over or yield, especially voluntarily, as in favor of another. 3. to give up or abandon: as, we *surrendered* all hope. 4. to yield or resign (oneself) to an emotion, influence, etc. 5. [Obs.], to give back or in return. *v.i.* to give oneself up to another's power or control, especially as a prisoner; yield. *n.* [Anglo-Fr. < OFr. *surrendre* (see the *v.*); inf. used as *n.*], 1. the act of surrendering, yielding, or giving up. 2. in *insurance,* the voluntary abandonment of a policy by an insured person in return for a cash payment (*surrender value*), thus freeing the company of liability.

SYN.—**surrender** commonly implies the giving up of something completely after striving to keep it (to *surrender* a fort, one's freedom, etc.); **relinquish** is the general word implying an abandoning, giving up, or letting go of something held (to *relinquish* one's grasp, a claim, etc.); to **yield** is to concede or give way under pressure (to *yield* one's consent); to **submit** is to give in to authority or superior force (to *submit* to a conqueror); **resign** implies a voluntary, formal relinquishment and, used reflexively, connotes submission or passive acceptance (to *resign* an office, to *resign* oneself to failure).

sur·rep·ti·tious (sũr′əp-tish′əs), *adj.* [L. *surrepticius* < *surreptus,* pp. of *surripere,* to take away secretly < *sub-,* under + *rapere,* to seize], 1. done, got, made, etc. in a secret, stealthy way; clandestine. 2. acting in a secret, stealthy way. —*SYN.* see **secret.**

Sur·rey (sũr′i), *n.* a county of southeastern England: pop., 1,366,000 (est. 1945); county seat, Guildford.

sur·rey (sũr′i), *n.* [*pl.* SURREYS (-iz)], [said to be after *Surrey,* England], a light, pleasure carriage having four wheels and two seats, both facing forward.

SURREY

Surrey, Earl of, (*Henry Howard*), 1517?–1547; English courtier and poet; executed for treason.

sur·ro·gate (sũr′ə-gāt′; *also, for n.,* sũr′ə-git), *n.* [L. *surrogatus,* pp. of *surrogare,* to elect in place of another, substitute < *sub-,* under, in place of + *rogare,* to ask, elect], 1. a deputy or substitute, especially for an ecclesiastical judge, bishop, or bishop's chancellor. 2. in some States, a probate court judge in charge of probating wills, administering estates, etc. *v.t.* [SURROGATED (-id), SURROGATING], 1. to put in another's place as a substitute or deputy. 2. in *law,* to subrogate.

sur·round (sə-round′), *v.t.* [ME. *sourrounden;* Anglo-Fr. *surounder;* OFr. *suronder,* to overflow; LL. *superundare;* L. *super,* over + *undare,* to move in waves, rise < *unda,* a wave], 1. to cause to be encircled on all or nearly all sides; enclose; encompass: as, we *surrounded* the house with trees. 2. to constitute an enclosure around; encircle: as, a wall *surrounds* the city. 3. to cut off (a fort, military unit, etc.) from communication or retreat by enclosing or shutting in with enemy troops; beset; invest.

sur·round·ing (sə-roun′diŋ), *n.* that which surrounds; especially, *pl.,* the things, conditions, circumstances, influences, etc. that surround a given place or person; environment. *adj.* that surrounds, or encompasses.

‡sur·sum cor·da (sũr′səm kôr′də), [L.], literally, lift up (your) hearts: an incitement to courage, fervor, etc.: opening words of the Preface of the Mass.

sur·tax (sũr′taks′; *also, for v.,* sũr′taks′), *n.* [*sur-* + *tax,* after Fr. *surtaxe*], an extra tax on something already taxed; especially, a graduated tax on the amount by which an income exceeds a given figure. *v.t.* to levy a surtax on.

sur·tout (sẽr-tōōt′, sẽr-tōō′; Fr. sür′tōō′), *n.* [Fr., lit., over-all; *sur,* over + *tout* < L. *totus,* all], a long, close-fitting overcoat or outer garment worn by men.

sur·veil·lance (sẽr-vā′ləns, sẽr-vāl′yəns), *n.* [Fr. < *surveiller,* to watch over; *sur-* (< L. *super*), over + *veiller* < L. *vigilare,* to watch], 1. watch or observation kept over a person, especially one under suspicion or a prisoner. 2. supervision or inspection.

sur·veil·lant (sẽr-vā′lənt, sẽr-vāl′yənt), *n.* a person who watches, observes, or supervises. *adj.* keeping surveillance.

sur·vey (sẽr-vā′; *for n., usually* sũr′vā), *v.t.* [ME. *surveien;* Anglo-Fr. *surveier;* OFr. *surveoir; sur-* (< L. *super*), over + *veoir* < L. *videre,* to see], 1. to examine for some specific purpose; inspect or consider carefully; review in detail. 2. to look at or consider, especially in a general or comprehensive way; view. 3. to determine the location, form, or boundaries of (a tract of land) by measuring the lines and angles in accordance with the principles of geometry and trigonometry. *v.i.* to survey land. *n.* [*pl.* SURVEYS (-vāz, -vāz′)], 1. a general study or inspection: as, the *survey* showed a critical lack of decent housing. 2. a general view; comprehensive study or examination: as, the course presents a *survey* of Italian art. 3. the process of surveying a tract or area of land for determining the location, form, or boundaries. 4. an area that has been surveyed. 5. a plan or written description of this.

sur·vey·ing (sẽr-vā′iŋ), *n.* 1. the act of surveying. 2. the science or occupation of surveying land.

sur·vey·or (sẽr-vā′ẽr), *n.* [ME. *surveior;* OFr. *surveour*], 1. a person who surveys land. 2. an inspector or superintendent, especially a customs official who ascertains the amount and value of imported merchandise.

sur·vey·or·ship (sẽr-vā′ẽr-ship′), *n.* [see -SHIP], the office or position of a surveyor.

surveyor's level, a revolving telescope mounted on a tripod and fitted with cross hairs and a spirit level: used by surveyors in finding points of identical elevation.

surveyor's measure, a system of measurement used in surveying:

7.92 inches	=	1 link
100 links	=	1 chain, or 66 feet
80 chains	=	1 mile
625 square links	=	1 square pole
16 square poles	=	1 square chain
10 square chains	=	1 acre
640 acres	=	1 section, or 1 square mile
36 sections	=	1 township

sur·viv·al (sẽr-vī′v'l), *n.* 1. the act, state, or fact of surviving. 2. something that survives, as an ancient belief, custom, usage, etc.

survival of the fittest, see **natural selection.**

sur·vive (sẽr-vīv′), *v.t.* [SURVIVED (-vīvd′), SURVIVING], [ME. *surviven;* OFr. *survivre;* L. *supervivere; super-*, above + *vivere*, to live], 1. to live or exist longer than or beyond the life or existence of; outlive. 2. to continue to live after or in spite of: as, we *survived* the wreck. *v.i.* to continue living or existing, as after an event or after another's death. —*SYN.* see **outlive.**

sur·viv·er (sẽr-vī′vẽr), *n.* a survivor.

sur·viv·ing (sẽr-vī′viŋ), *adj.* that survives.

sur·vi·vor (sẽr-vī′vẽr), *n.* a person or thing that survives.

sur·vi·vor·ship (sẽr-vī′vẽr-ship′), *n.* [see -SHIP], 1. the state of being a survivor. 2. in *law,* the right of a surviving joint owner or owners to take the share of an owner who dies.

Su·sa (sōō′sä), *n.* a ruined city in western Iran: the capital of ancient Elam: Biblical name, *Shushan:* see **Elam,** map.

Su·san (sōō′z'n, sū′z'n), [Fr. *Susanne;* LL. *Susanna;* Gr. *Sousanna* < Heb. *shōshannāh,* lily], a feminine name: variants, *Susanna, Susannah;* diminutives, *Sue, Susie, Suzy;* equivalents, Fr. *Susanne, Suzanne.*

Su·san·na, Su·san·nah (sōō-zan′ə, sū-zan′ə), a feminine name: see **Susan.**

sus·cep·ti·bil·i·ty (sə-sep′tə-bil′ə-ti), *n.* [*pl.* SUSCEPTIBILITIES (-tiz)], [ML. *susceptibilitas*], 1. the quality or state of being susceptible. 2. *pl.* sensitivities; feelings. 3. a susceptible temperament or disposition; capacity for receiving impressions. 4. the capacity of a substance for being magnetized, expressed in the ratio of the extent of magnetization to the strength of the magnetizing force.

sus·cep·ti·ble (sə-sep′tə-b'l), *adj.* [ML. *susceptibilis* < L. *suscipere,* to receive, undertake < *sus-* (for *sub-*), under + *capere,* to take], easily affected emotionally; having a sensitive nature or feelings; responsive.
susceptible of, that can be affected with; admitting; allowing: as, testimony *susceptible of* error.
susceptible to, easily influenced by or affected with; especially liable to: as, *susceptible to* tuberculosis.

sus·cep·ti·bly (sə-sep′tə-bli), *adv.* so as to be susceptible.

sus·cep·tive (sə-sep′tiv), *adj.* [ML. *susceptivus*], 1. susceptible. 2. receptive.

sus·cep·tiv·i·ty (sus′ep-tiv′ə-ti), *n.* the quality of being susceptive.

sus·lik (sus′lik), *n.* [Russ.], 1. a small gopher or ground squirrel of north central Eurasia; spermophile. 2. its fur.

sus·pect (sə-spekt′; *for adj. & n., usually* sus′pekt), *v.t.* [Fr. *suspecter* < L. *suspectus,* pp. of *suspicere,* to look under, look up to, admire, also to mistrust; *sus-* (for *sub-*), under + *spicere,* to look], 1. to believe (someone) to be guilty of something specified on little or no evidence. 2. to believe to be bad, wrong, harmful, questionable, etc.; distrust. 3. to imagine to be; think probable or likely; suppose; presume; surmise. *v.i.* to be suspicious; have suspicion. *adj.* viewed with suspicion; suspected. *n.* a person who is suspected, especially one suspected of a crime, etc.

sus·pend (sə-spend′), *v.t.* [ME. *suspenden;* OFr. *suspendre* < L. *suspendere,* to hang up; *sus-* (for *sub-*), under + *pendere,* to hang], 1. to bar or exclude from an office, privilege, position, etc., usually for a specified time, as a penalty; debar. 2. to cause to cease or become inoperative for a time; stop or withhold temporarily: as, train service has been *suspended.* 3. to keep undecided or in abeyance; hold back (judgment, sentence, etc.). 4. to hang by a support from above so as to allow free movement. 5. to hold without attachment, as dust in the air; keep in suspension. 6. to keep in suspense, wonder, etc. *v.i.* 1. to stop temporarily. 2. to withhold payment; fail to pay debts or obligations. —*SYN.* see **adjourn, exclude.**

sus·pend·ed animation (sə-spen′did), a temporary cessation of the vital functions resembling death, as in asphyxiation.

sus·pend·ers (sə-spen′dẽrz), *n.pl.* 1. a pair of straps or bands passed over the shoulders to support the trousers. 2. [British], garters.

sus·pense (sə-spens′), *n.* [ME.; Anglo-Fr. & OFr. *suspens, suspense,* delay, deferring; ML. *suspensum* < L. *suspensus,* suspended, uncertain, lit., hung up, pp. of *suspendere,* to suspend], 1. the state of being undecided or undetermined. 2. the state of being uncertain, as in awaiting a decision, usually characterized by some anxiety or apprehension. 3. uncertainty; indecisiveness. 4. [Rare], suspension or interruption, as of a legal right.

suspense account, in *bookkeeping,* an account in which items are temporarily entered until their disposition can be determined.

sus·pen·si·bil·i·ty (sə-spen′sə-bil′ə-ti), *n.* the quality of being suspensible.

sus·pen·si·ble (sə-spen′sə-b'l), *adj.* [< L. *suspensus* (see SUSPENSE); + *ible*], that can be suspended.

sus·pen·sion (sə-spen′shən), *n.* [L. *suspensio* < *suspensus;* see SUSPENSE], 1. a suspending or being suspended; specifically, *a)* a barring from office, etc. *b)* a stoppage of payment, etc. *c)* a holding back of a judgment, etc. 2. a supporting device upon or from which something is suspended. 3. the system of springs, etc. supporting a vehicle upon its undercarriage or axles. 4. the act or means of suspending the balance or pendulum in a timepiece. 5. the condition of a solid whose particles are dispersed through a fluid but not dissolved in it. 6. a substance in this condition. 7. in *music, a)* the holding back of one or more tones in a chord while the others progress, so that a temporary dissonance is created. *b)* the tone or tones so held.

suspension bridge, a bridge suspended from chains or cables which are anchored at either end and supported by towers at regular intervals.

suspension point, any of a series of dots, properly three, indicating the omission of words or sentences, as in something quoted.

SUSPENSION BRIDGE

sus·pen·sive (sə-spen′siv), *adj.* [ML. *suspensivus*], 1. that suspends, defers, or temporarily stops something. 2. tending to suspend judgment; undecided in mind. 3. of, characterized by, or in suspense; apprehensive. 4. expressing or creating suspense: as, a *suspensive* sentence. 5. [Rare], of or characterized by physical suspension.

sus·pen·sor (sə-spen′sẽr), *n.* [ML.], a suspensory.

sus·pen·so·ry (sə-spen′sə-ri), *adj.* [< L. *suspensus* (see SUSPENSE); + *-ory*], 1. suspending, supporting, or sustaining: as, a *suspensory* muscle or bandage. 2. suspending or delaying, especially so as to leave something undecided. *n.* [*pl.* SUSPENSORIES (-riz)], a suspensory muscle, bandage, truss, etc.

suspensory ligament, a ligament supporting the lens of the eye.

sus·pi·cion (sə-spish′ən), *n.* [ME. *suspecion;* Anglo-Fr. *suspecioun;* OFr. *sospeçon;* LL. *suspectio,* orig., a looking up to, esteeming, later with sense of L. *suspicio,* suspicion; L. *suspectus,* pp. of *suspicere,* to look up at, admire; look secretly at, mistrust, suspect; sp. altered after L. *suspicio* from same source], 1. the act or an instance of suspecting; believing of something bad, wrong, harmful, etc. with little or no supporting evidence. 2. the feeling or state of mind of a person who suspects. 3. a very small amount or degree; suggestion; inkling; trace. *v.t.* [Dial. or Colloq.], to suspect.
above suspicion, not to be suspected; honorable.
on suspicion, on the basis of suspicion; because suspected.
under suspicion, suspected.

sus·pi·cious (sə-spish′əs), *adj.* [ME. & OFr. *suspecious;* L. *suspiciosus*], 1. arousing or likely to arouse suspicion in others. 2. showing or expressing suspicion. 3. *a)* suspecting; feeling suspicion. *b)* tending habitually to suspect, especially to suspect fault, evil, etc.

sus·pi·ra·tion (sus′pi-rā′shən), *n.* [L. *suspiratio* < *suspirare,* to suspire], a prolonged sigh.

sus·pire (sə-spīr′), *v.i.* [SUSPIRED (-spīrd′), SUSPIRING], [L. *suspirare,* to breathe out < *sub-,* under + *spirare,*

to breathe], [Poetic], to take a long breath; especially, to sigh.
Sus·que·han·na (sus'kwi-han'ə), *n.* a river flowing through New York, Pennsylvania, and Maryland into Chesapeake Bay: length, 444 mi.
Sus·sex (sus'iks), *n.* 1. a former Anglo-Saxon kingdom of southern England. 2. a county on the southern coast of England, divided into East Sussex and West Sussex: pop., 771,000 (est. 1945).
sus·tain (sə-stān'), *v.t.* [ME. *sustenen, susteinen;* Anglo-Fr. & OFr. *sustenir;* L. *sustinere* < *sus-* (for *sub-*), under + *tenere*, to hold], 1. to maintain; keep in existence; keep going; prolong: as, this pedal *sustains* the tones. 2. to keep supplied with necessities; provide for. 3. to support from or as from below; carry the weight or burden of. 4. to strengthen the spirits, courage, etc. of; comfort; buoy up; encourage. 5. to endure; bear up against; withstand. 6. to undergo; experience; suffer, as an injury or loss. 7. to uphold or support the validity or justice of. 8. to confirm; prove; corroborate.—***SYN.*** see **support.**
sus·tain·ing program (sə-stān'iŋ), any radio program presented and paid for by a radio station or network rather than by a commercial sponsor.
sus·tain·ment (sə-stān'mənt), *n.* a sustaining or being sustained.
sus·te·nance (sus'ti-nəns), *n.* [ME. *sustenaunce;* OFr. *soustenance;* LL. *sustinentia*, patience, endurance < L. *sustinere;* see SUSTAIN], 1. sustainment. 2. maintenance; support; means of livelihood. 3. that which sustains life; nourishment; food.
sus·ten·tac·u·lar (sus'ten-tak'yoo-lẽr), *adj.* [< L. *sustentaculum*, a support (< *sustentare*, to hold up, support, intens. of *sustinere;* see SUSTAIN); + *-ar*], in *anatomy*, supporting: said of connective-tissue cells, etc.
sus·ten·ta·tion (sus'ten-tā'shən), *n.* [ME. *sustentacioun;* OFr. *sustentacion;* L. *sustentatio* < *sustentare;* cf. SUSTAIN], 1. a sustaining or being sustained; maintenance; support; preservation. 2. something that sustains or supports; sustenance.
sus·ten·ta·tive (sus'ten-tā'tiv, sə-sten'tə-tiv), *adj.* that sustains; of or providing sustentation.
sus·ten·tion (sə-sten'shən), *n.* [coined < *sustain* by analogy with *detention, retention*, etc.], a sustaining or being sustained: as, the *sustention* of a musical tone.
su·sur·rant (soo-sũr'ənt, syoo-sũr'ənt), *adj.* [L. *susurrans*, ppr. of *susurrare*, to whisper < *susurrus*, a humming; akin to *surdus;* see SURD], whispering; murmuring; rustling.
su·sur·rate (soo-sũr'āt, syoo-sũr'āt), *v.i.* [SUSURRATED (-id), SUSURRATING], [L. *susurratus*, pp.; see SUSURRANT], to whisper; murmur; rustle.
su·sur·ra·tion (sōō'sə-rā'shən, sū'sə-rā'shən), *n.* [ME. *susurracioun;* L. *susurratio;* cf. SUSURRANT], a whisper; murmur; rustle.
su·sur·rous (soo-sũr'əs, syoo-sũr'əs), *adj.* susurrant.
su·sur·rus (soo-sũr'əs, syoo-sũr'əs), *n.* [L.; see SUSURRANT], a whispering, murmuring, or rustling sound.
Suth·er·land (su*th*'ẽr-lənd), *n.* a county on the northern coast of Scotland: pop., 14,000 (est. 1946); county seat, Dornoch.
Sutherland Falls, a waterfall of South Island, New Zealand: height, 1,904 ft.
Suth·er·land·shire (su*th*'ẽr-lənd-shir'), *n.* Sutherland.
Sut·lej (sut'lej), *n.* a river in southern Tibet and northwestern India, flowing into the Indus River: length, 900 mi.
sut·ler (sut'lẽr), *n.* [MD. *soeteler* (D. *zoetelaar*) < *soetelen*, to perform menial offices or dirty work], a person who follows an army to sell food, liquor, etc. to its soldiers.
su·tra (sōō'trə), *n.* [Sans. *sūtra*, a thread, string], 1. in *Brahmanism*, *a)* a precept or maxim. *b)* a collection of these. 2. in *Buddhism*, scriptural narratives, especially the dialogues of the Buddha.
sut·ta (soot'ə), *n.* a sutra.
sut·tee (su-tē', sut'ē), *n.* [Hind. *sattī;* Sans. *satī*, chaste and virtuous wife < *sat*, good, pure, ppr. of *as*, to be], 1. a Hindu widow who throws herself alive, and is cremated, on the funeral pile of her husband's body. 2. such self-cremation: now rare.
sut·tee·ism (su-tē'iz'm, sut'ē-iz'm), *n.* the custom or practice of suttee.
Sut·ter's Mill (sut'ẽrz), a mill, owned by John Sutter (1803–1880), northeast of Sacramento, California: gold was first discovered near there in 1848.
su·tur·al (sōō'chẽr-əl, sū'chẽr-əl), *adj.* [Fr. *sutural* & Mod. L. *suturalis*], of or located in or near a suture.
su·ture (sōō'chẽr, sū'chẽr), *n.* [Fr.; L. *sutura* < *sutus*, pp. of *suere*, to sew], 1. the act of joining together by or as by sewing. 2. the line along which such a joining is made. 3. in *anatomy*, the joining together, or the line of junction, of two bones, especially of the skull. 4. in *botany*, *a)* a seam formed when two parts unite. *b)* a line along which a fruit, as a pod or capsule, splits. 5. in *surgery*, *a)* the act or method of joining together the two edges of a wound or incision by stitching or similar means. *b)* any of the stitches of gut, thread, wire, etc. so used. *v.t.* [SUTURED (-chẽrd), SUTURING], to join together with or as with sutures.
‡**su·um cui·que** (sū'əm kwī'kwē), [L.], to each his own.
Su·va (sōō'vä), *n.* the capital of the Fiji Islands: seaport on Viti Levu Island: pop., 15,500.
Su·vo·rov, A·le·ksan·dr Va·sil·ie·vich (ä'lyek-sän'dr' vä-sēl'ye-vich soo-vô'rôf), Count Suvorov-Rymnikski, Prince Italiski, 1729–1800; Russian field marshal.
Su·wan·nee (sə-wôn'i, swô'nē), *n.* a river in Georgia and Florida, flowing into the Gulf of Mexico: length, 240 mi.: also spelled **Swanee.**
Su·zanne (sōō-zan', sū-zan'), a feminine name: see **Susan.**
su·ze·rain (sōō'zə-rin, sū'zə-rān'), *n.* [Fr. < *sus*, above < L. *susum, sursum*, upward, above (contr. of *subversum; sub-*, under + *versum*, a turning < pp. of *vertere*, to turn) + ending of *souverain*, sovereign], 1. a ruler, especially a feudal lord. 2. a state in its relation to another over which it has political control.
su·ze·rain·ty (sōō'zə-rin-ti, sū'zə-rān'ti), *n.* [*pl.* SUZERAINTIES (-tiz)], [Fr. *suzeraineté*], the position or power of a suzerain.
S.V., *Sancta Virgo*, [L.], Holy Virgin.
s.v., [L.], *sub verbo* or *sub voce.*
Sval·bard (säl'bär), *n.* a group of Norwegian islands in the Arctic Ocean: area, 24,294 sq. mi.; pop., 1,000 (est. 1947): also called *Spitsbergen.*
svelte (svelt), *adj.* [Fr.; It. *svelto;* Sp. *suelto;* LL. **solvitus*, free, released < L. *solvere;* see SOLVE], slender and graceful; lithe.
Sverd·lovsk (sferd-lôfsk'), *n.* 1. a region of the R.S.F.S.R., in the Ural Mountains of western Siberia: pop., 2,512,000. 2. its capital: pop., 426,000: formerly called *Ekaterinburg.*
Sve·ri·ge (svâr'ye), *n.* Sweden: the Swedish name.
SW, S.W., s.w., 1. southwest. 2. southwestern.
Sw., 1. Sweden. 2. Swedish.
S.W., South Wales.
S.W.A., South West Africa.
swab (swäb), *n.* [back-formation < *swabber*], 1. a mop for cleaning decks, floors, etc. 2. *a)* a small piece of cotton, cloth, sponge, etc. used to apply medicine to, or clean discharged matter from, the throat, mouth, etc. *b)* the matter collected in this way. 3. a long-handled brush for cleaning the barrel of a gun, etc. 4. [Slang], a clumsy, loutish person. *v.t.* [SWABBED (swäbd), SWABBING], to use a swab on; clean, medicate, etc. with a swab. Also **swob.**
Swab., 1. Swabia. 2. Swabian.
swab·ber (swäb'ẽr), *n.* [Early Mod. D. *zwabber* < *zwabben*, to do dirty work], 1. a person who uses a swab. 2. a clumsy, loutish person. 3. a swab.
Swa·bi·a (swā'bi-ə), *n.* a former duchy in southwestern Germany: now a district of southwestern Bavaria: pop., 1,221,000 (est. 1946): German name, *Schwaben.*
Swa·bi·an (swā'bi-ən), *adj.* [< Mod. L. *Suabia*, Latinized < G. *Schwaben*, Swabia < OHG. *Swaba*, a German tribe < IE. **swe-bh*, of the same kind], of Swabia, its people, their language, etc. *n.* 1. a native or inhabitant of Swabia. 2. the High German dialect of the Swabians.
swad·dle (swäd''l), *n.* [ME. *swathil;* AS. *swæthel* < *swathian*, to swathe; cf. SWATHE], a cloth or bandage used for swaddling. *v.t.* [SWADDLED (-'ld), SWADDLING], 1. to wrap (a newborn baby) in long narrow bands of cloth. 2. to bind in or as in bandages; swathe.
swaddling clothes, 1. formerly, the long, narrow bands of cloth wrapped around a newborn baby. 2. baby clothes. 3. the period of infancy or of close parental control. 4. any rigid control or restrictions, as of the immature. Also **swaddling bands, swaddling clouts.**
Swa·de·shi (swə-dā'shi), *n.* [Sans. *svadeśin*, native < *svadeśa*, native land; via Bengali], in India, a policy of boycotting foreign goods to encourage home production.
swag (swag), *v.i.* [SWAGGED (swagd), SWAGGING], [prob. < ON.; cf. Norw. dial. *svagga*, to sway], 1. to sway or lurch. 2. to sink down; sag. 3. in Australia, to travel carrying a swag. *n.* 1. in Australia, a bundle containing the personal belongings of a foot traveler, miner, etc. 2. a swaying or lurching. 3. [Slang], stolen money or property; loot; plunder.
swage (swāj), *n.* [ME.; OFr. *souage* < LL. *soca*, a rope], 1. a kind of tool for bending or shaping metal. 2. a die or stamp for shaping or marking metal by hammering. *v.t.* [SWAGED (swājd), SWAGING], to use a swage on; shape, bend, etc. with a swage.
swage block, a block of metal made with grooves and perforations, used as a form in hammering out bolt heads, etc.
swag·ger (swag'ẽr), *v.i.* [prob. freq. of *swag*], 1. to walk with a bold, arrogant, or lordly stride; strut. 2. to boast, brag, or show off in a loud, superior manner. *v.t.* to influence by blustering; bluff. *n.* swaggering walk, manner, or behavior. —***SYN.*** see **boast.**
swagger stick, a short stick or cane as carried by some army officers, etc.

SWAGES
A, collar swage; B, spring swage

Swa·hi·li (swä-hē′li), *n.* [< Ar. *sawāḥil*, pl. of *sāḥil*, coast + *-i*, belonging to], 1. [*pl.* SWAHILI], one of a Bantu people inhabiting Zanzibar and the near-by mainland, characterized by a large admixture of Arab stock. 2. their Northern Bantu language, used as a lingua franca in east central Africa. *adj.* Swahilian.

Swa·hi·li·an (swä-hē′li-ən), *adj.* of the Swahili or their language.

swain (swān), *n.* [ME. *swein;* ON. *sveinn*, boy, servant; akin to AS. *swan*], [Poetic or Archaic], 1. a country youth. 2. a young rustic lover or gallant. 3. a lover.

swale (swāl), *n.* [prob. akin to ON. *svalr*, cool], a hollow or depression, especially one in wet, marshy ground.

swal·low (swäl′ō), *n.* [ME. *swalu, swalwe;* AS. *swalewe, swealwe;* akin to G. *schwalbe;* IE. **swol-wi* or **swalw-i*, a bird name, as also in Russ. *solovej*, Czech *slavík*, nightingale, etc.], 1. any of a family of small, swift-flying birds with long, pointed wings and forked tails, known for their regular migrations. 2. any of certain swifts resembling swallows.

swal·low (swäl′ō), *v.t.* [ME. *swalwen, swolwen;* AS. *swelgan;* akin to G. *schwelgen;* IE. base **swel-*, to devour; cf. SWILL, *n.*], 1. to pass (food, etc.) from the mouth through the gullet or esophagus into the stomach, usually by a series of muscular actions in the throat. 2. to take in; absorb; engulf; envelop: often with *up*. 3. to take back (words said); retract; withdraw. 4. to put up with; tolerate; bear humbly: as, he had to *swallow* their insults. 5. to refrain from expressing; hold back; suppress: as, *swallow* your pride. 6. [Colloq.], to accept (a statement) as true without question or investigation; receive gullibly. *v.i.* to perform the muscular actions characteristic of swallowing something, especially as in emotion. *n.* 1. the act of swallowing. 2. the amount swallowed at one time. 3. the throat or gullet. 4. the opening in a block or pulley through which the rope runs.

swal·low·tail (swäl′ō-tāl′), *n.* 1. something having a forked shape like that of a swallow's tail. 2. any of various butterflies having the lower wings extended in taillike points. 3. a swallow-tailed coat.

swal·low-tailed (swäl′ō-tāld′), *adj.* having a tail or end extended in forked points like that of a swallow.

swallow-tailed coat, a man's coat that tapers down in two long tails, or skirts, at the back; full-dress coat.

swal·low·wort (swäl′ō-wũrt′), *n.* 1. a celandine. 2. a kind of vine whose root is used in medicine. 3. a plant related to the milkweed.

swam (swam), past tense of **swim** (to move through water).

swam (swam), past tense of **swim** (to be dizzy).

swa·mi (swä′mi), *n.* [*pl.* SWAMIS (-miz)], [Hind. *svāmī;* Sans. *svāmin*, a lord], lord; master: a Hindu title of respect, especially for a Hindu religious teacher.

swamp (swämp, swômp), *n.* [prob. < D. *zwamp*, marsh; akin to Eng. *sump*], a piece of wet, spongy land; marsh; bog. *adj.* of or native to a swamp. *v.t.* 1. to plunge or sink in a swamp, deep water, etc.; hence, 2. to flood or submerge with or as with water. 3. to overcome or overwhelm; ruin: as, heavy debts soon *swamped* them. 4. to sink (a boat) by filling with water. *v.i.* to become swamped; sink in or as in a swamp or water.

swamp fever, malaria.

swamp·land (swämp′land′, swômp′land′), *n.* swampy land.

swamp·y (swäm′pi, swôm′pi), *adj.* [SWAMPIER (-pi-ẽr), SWAMPIEST (-pi-ist)], 1. of or consisting of a swamp or swamps. 2. like a swamp; wet and spongy; marshy.

swa·my (swä′mi), *n.* [*pl.* SWAMIES (-miz)], a swami.

swan (swän, swôn), *n.* [ME.; AS.; akin to G. *schwan;* IE. base **swen-*, to sound, sing, as in L. *sonus* (cf. SOUND)], 1. [*pl.* SWANS (swänz, swônz), SWAN; see PLURAL, II, D, 1], any of several large-bodied, web-footed water birds with long, graceful necks and, usually, pure white feathers: swans are graceful swimmers and strong flyers. 2. a poet or singer of great ability: from the myth that swans sing sweetly just before dying. 3. [S-], the constellation Cygnus.

swan (swän, swôn), *v.i.* [? < Brit. dial. *Is' wan*, I'll warrant], [Dial.], to swear: usually in the phrase *I swan!*, an exclamation of surprise, impatience, etc.

swan dive, a forward dive in which the legs are held straight and together, the back is curved, and the arms are stretched out to the sides.

Swa·nee (swô′nē), *n.* Suwannee.

swang (swaŋ), archaic or dialectal past tense of **swing.**

swan·herd (swän′hũrd′, swôn′hũrd′), *n.* a person who tends swans.

swank (swaŋk), *n.* [orig. in slang < dial. *v.i.;* prob. akin to AS. *swancor*, pliant, supple, with notion of swinging the body; for IE. base see SWING], [Slang], 1. stylish display or ostentation in dress, etc. 2. swaggering, ostentatious behavior, speech, etc. *adj.* 1. [Slang], ostentatiously stylish. 2. [Dial.], active; lively. *v.i.* [Slang], to act in a showy, pretentious manner; swagger.

swank (swaŋk), alternative past tense of **swink.**

swank·i·ly (swaŋ′kə-li), *adv.* [Slang], in a swanky manner.

swank·i·ness (swaŋ′ki-nis), *n.* [Slang], the quality of being swanky.

swank·y (swaŋ′ki), *adj.* [SWANKIER (-ki-ẽr), SWANKIEST (-ki-ist)], [*swank* + *-y*], [Slang], ostentatiously stylish; swaggering; showy.

swan maiden, in various ancient mythologies, a creature with the supernatural power of taking on at will the form of a swan or of a beautiful maiden.

swan·ner·y (swän′ẽr-i, swôn′ẽr-i), *n.* [*pl.* SWANNERIES (-iz)], a place where swans are kept or bred.

swan's-down (swänz′doun′, swônz′doun′), *n.* 1. the soft, fine underfeathers, or down, of the swan, used for trimming clothes, making powder puffs, etc. 2. a soft, thick fabric of wool and silk, rayon, or cotton, used for making baby clothes, etc. Also **swansdown.**

Swan·sea (swän-si, swôn′zi), *n.* a seaport in southern Wales: pop., 152,000 (est. 1946).

swan·skin (swän′skin′, swôn′skin′), *n.* 1. the skin of a swan with feathers on it. 2. any of various soft flannels of wool or cotton.

swan song, 1. the song supposed in ancient fable to be sung by a dying swan. 2. the last act, final creative work, etc. of a person, as before his death.

swan-up·ping (swän′up′iŋ, swôn′up′iŋ), *n.* [< *swan* + *up, prep.*], 1. the marking of young swans with a notch in the upper beak as a sign of ownership. 2. a yearly expedition on the Thames for this purpose.

swap (swäp, swôp), *v.t. & v.i.* [SWAPPED (swäpt, swôpt), SWAPPING], [ME. *swappen*, to strike, move quickly; prob. echoic], [Colloq.], to exchange; trade; barter. *n.* [Colloq.], an exchange, trade, or barter. Also spelled **swop.**

‡**swa·raj** (swə-räj′), *n.* [Hind.; Sans. *svarāj*, self-ruling; *sva-*, own (akin to L. *suus*, own); + *rāj*, rule; cf. RAJAH], in India, home rule; political independence; self-government: during the period of British rule it was [S-] the name of the political party seeking Indian autonomy.

sward (swôrd), *n.* [ME. *swarde;* AS. *sweard*, a skin, hide; akin to G. *schwarte*, rind, hard skin], grass-covered soil; turf. *v.t. & v.i.* to cover or become covered with grass or turf.

sware (swâr), archaic past tense of **swear.**

swarm (swôrm), *n.* [ME.; AS. *swearm;* akin to G. *schwarm;* IE. base **swer-*, to buzz, hum, as also in L. *susurrere*, to hiss (cf. SUSURRANT)], 1. a large number of bees, led by a queen, leaving one hive for another to start a new colony. 2. a colony of bees in a hive. 3. a large, moving mass of insects. 4. a moving crowd or throng. 5. in *biology*, a mass of motile one-celled organisms. *v.i.* 1. to gather and fly off in a swarm: said of bees. 2. to move, collect, be present, etc. in large numbers; throng; abound. 3. to be filled or crowded; teem (usually with *with*). 4. in *biology*, to burst forth in a swarm. *v.t.* to fill with a swarm; crowd; throng. —*SYN.* see **crowd, group.**

swarm (swôrm), *v.i. & v.t.* [orig. nautical word; prob. akin to prec.], to climb (a tree, mast, etc.) using the hands and feet; shin.

swarm·er (swôr′mẽr), *n.* 1. a person or thing that swarms; member of a swarm. 2. in *biology*, a swarm spore.

swarm spore, in *biology*, any of a mass of motile spores; zoospore.

swart (swôrt), *adj.* [ME. *swerte, swarte;* AS. *sweart;* akin to G. *schwarz*, black; IE. **swordos*, dirty, black, as also in L. *sordidus* (cf. SORDID)], [Dial. or Poetic], swarthy.

swarth (swôrth), *n.* [Dial.], sward. *adj.* swarthy.

swarth·i·ly (swôr′*th*ə-li, swôr′thə-li), *adv.* so as to be swarthy.

swarth·i·ness (swôr′*th*i-nis, swôr′thi-nis), *n.* the quality of being swarthy.

swarth·y (swôr′*th*i, swôr′thi), *adj.* [SWARTHIER (-*th*i-ẽr, -thi-ẽr), SWARTHIEST (-*th*i-ist, -thi-ist)], [< dial. *swarth*, var. of *swart* + *-y*], having a dark skin; dusky; dark. —*SYN.* see **dusky.**

swash (swäsh, swôsh), *v.i.* [echoic], 1. to dash, strike, wash, etc. with a splashing sound; splash. 2. to swagger. *v.t.* to splash (a liquid), as in a container. *n.* 1. a body of swift, dashing water; specifically, a channel cutting through or behind a sandbank. 2. a bar washed over by the sea. 3. the splashing of water or the sound of this. 4. a swaggering; blustering.

swash·buck·ler (swäsh′buk′lẽr, swôsh′buk′lẽr), *n.* [*swash* + *buckler*, a shield], a blustering, swaggering fighting man.

swash·buck·ler·ing (swäsh′buk′lẽr-iŋ, swôsh′buk′lẽr-iŋ), *n. & adj.* swashbuckling.

swash·buck·ling (swäsh′buk′liŋ, swôsh′buk′liŋ), *n.* the characteristic behavior of a swashbuckler; loud boasting or bullying. *adj.* of or typical of a swashbuckler.

swash·ing (swäsh′iŋ, swôsh′iŋ), *adj.* [see SWASHBUCK-

LER], 1. swashbuckling. 2. splashing. 3. [Archaic], violent; slashing.
swash letters, italic capital letters formed with long tails and flourishes.
swas·ti·ka, swas·ti·ca (swäs'ti-kə, swas'ti-kə), ***n.*** [Sans. *svastika* < *svasti,* well-being, benediction < *su,* well + *asti,* being, is], 1. a design or ornament of ancient origin in the form of a Greek cross with each arm bent in a right-angle extension: it exists as a mystic symbol among various American Indian tribes and in India, Japan, Persia, etc. 2. this design with the extensions bent in a clockwise direction, used in Nazi Germany as the party emblem and symbol of anti-Semitism.

SWASTIKA

Swat (swät), ***n.*** 1. a district in northwestern Pakistan, on the Indus River. 2. [*pl.* SWATI (-ti)], one of an East Indian people of Moslem faith who live in Swat: also called *Swati.*
swat (swät), ***v.t.*** [SWATTED (-id), SWATTING], [echoic], [Colloq.], to hit with a quick, sharp blow. ***n.*** [Colloq.], a quick, sharp blow. Also **swot.**
swatch (swäch), ***n.*** [< N. dial.; orig., a cloth tally], a sample piece of cloth or other material.
swath (swäth, swôth), ***n.*** [ME. *swathe;* AS. *swathu,* a track; akin to G. *schwad, schwade,* space covered by a scythe swing; cf. SWADDLE, SWATHE], 1. the space or width covered with one cut of a scythe or other mowing device. 2. [Rare], a stroke with a scythe. 3. a line or row of grass, wheat, etc. cut in one course by a scythe, mower, etc. 4. a strip, track, or row.
cut a wide swath, to make an ostentatious display; make a great stir; appear important.
swathe (swāth), ***v.t.*** [SWATHED (swāthd), SWATHING], [ME. *swathen;* AS. *swathian, swethian;* IE. base *sqeudh-, to conceal, hide, as also in Sans. *kuhū-,* the new moon, MIr. *codal,* skin, etc.; cf. SWATH, SWADDLE], 1. to wrap or bind up in a long strip or bandage. 2. to wrap (a bandage, etc.) around something. 3. to surround; envelop; enclose. ***n.*** a bandage or wrapping.
swathe (swāth), ***n.*** a swath.
Swa·ti (swä'ti), ***n.*** [*pl.* SWATI], a Swat.
Swa·tow (swä'tou'), ***n.*** a city on the coast of Kwangtung province, China: pop., 215,000.
swat·ter (swät'ẽr, swôt'ẽr), ***n.*** 1. a person who swats. 2. a device, as of fine wire mesh at the end of a handle, for swatting flies, etc.: in full, **fly swatter.**
sway (swā), ***v.i.*** [ME. *sweigen;* ON. *sveigja* & LG. *swājen,* to be moved from side to side; IE. base *swei-, to bend, curve, swing], 1. to swing or move from side to side or to and fro; fluctuate; oscillate. 2. to lean or incline to one side; veer. 3. to incline or tend in judgment or opinion. 4. to have control or influence; rule. ***v.t.*** 1. to cause to swing or move from side to side. 2. to cause to lean or incline to one side. 3. to cause (a person, one's opinion, etc.) to incline in a particular direction. 4. to cause to turn from a given course; divert: as, his threats will not *sway* us. 5. [Archaic], *a)* to wield (a scepter, etc.). *b)* to rule over or control; dominate. 6. in *nautical usage,* to hoist into place, as a mast: usually with *up.* ***n.*** 1. a swaying or being swayed; movement to the side; a swinging, leaning, fluctuation, etc. 2. impetus; influence; force; control: as, moved by the *sway* of passion. 3. rule; dominion; sovereign power or authority. —***SYN.*** see **affect, power, swing.**
sway-back, sway·back (swā'bak'), ***n.*** the condition of being sway-backed. ***adj.*** sway-backed.
sway-backed (swā'bakt'), ***adj.*** [prob. < ON.; cf. Dan. *sveibaget;* see SWAY], having an abnormal inward curve in the spine, usually as a result of strain or overwork: said of horses, cattle, etc.
swayed (swād), ***adj.*** sway-backed.
Swa·zi (swä'zi), ***n.*** a member of a Bantu tribe of Swaziland.
Swa·zi·land (swä'zi-land'), ***n.*** a British territory in southeastern Africa: area, 6,705 sq. mi.; pop., 237,000; capital, Mbabane: abbreviated **Swaz.**
SWbS, southwest by south.
SWbW, southwest by west.
swear (swâr), ***v.i.*** [SWORE (swôr) or *archaic* SWARE (swâr), SWORN (swôrn), SWEARING], [ME. *swerien;* AS. *swerian;* akin to G. *schwören;* IE. base *swer-, to speak, seen also in L. *sermo* (< *swermo), a speaking (cf. SERMON); see ANSWER], 1. to make a solemn declaration or affirmation with an appeal to God or to someone or something held sacred for confirmation: as, he *swore* by the Bible. 2. to make a solemn pledge or promise; vow. 3. to use profane or blasphemous language; curse. 4. in *law,* to give evidence or state under oath. ***v.t.*** 1. to declare solemnly in the name of God or of someone or something held sacred. 2. to pledge or vow on oath. 3. to assert or promise with great conviction or emphasis: as, I *swear* the man's a fool! 4. to take (an oath) by swearing. 5. to administer a legal oath to.
swear by, 1. to name (a person or thing held sacred) in taking an oath. 2. to have great faith in.
swear in, to administer an oath to (a person taking office, a witness, etc.).
swear off, to promise to give up, leave off, or renounce.
swear out, to obtain (a warrant for someone's arrest) by making a charge under oath.
swear·word (swâr'wūrd'), ***n.*** a word or phrase used in swearing or cursing; profane word.
sweat (swet), ***v.i.*** [SWEAT or SWEATED (-id), SWEATING], [ME. *sweten;* AS. *swætan* < *swat,* sweat; akin to G. *schweissen;* IE. base *sweid-, to sweat, as also in L. *sudor,* sweat (cf. SUDATION)], 1. to give forth a characteristic salty moisture through the pores of the skin; perspire. 2. *a)* to give forth moisture in droplets on its surface: as, a ripening cheese *sweats. b)* to collect and condense water in droplets on its surface: as, he stirred his iced drink until the glass *sweated.* 3. to ferment: said of tobacco leaves, etc. 4. to come forth in drops through pores or a porous surface; ooze. 5. [Colloq.], to work so hard as to cause sweating: often used metaphorically. ***v.t.*** 1. *a)* to give forth (moisture) through its pores or a porous surface. *b)* to collect and condense (moisture) on its surface. 2. to cause to sweat, or perspire, as by drugs, exercise, heat, etc. 3. to cause to give forth moisture; especially, to ferment: as, the tobacco leaves are being *sweated.* 4. to make wet with sweat, or perspiration: as, he *sweated* his shirt. 5. to try to get rid of by sweating: often with *out,* as, he is *sweating* out his cold. 6. to heat (a metal) in order to extract an easily fusible constituent. 7. *a)* to heat (solder) until it melts. *b)* to unite (metal parts) by heating at the point of contact. 8. to remove particles of metal from (a coin) illegally, as by shaking in a bag with other coins. 9. to cause to work so hard as to sweat; overwork; hence, 10. to cause (employees) to work long hours at low wages under poor working conditions; exploit. 11. [Colloq.], to get information from by torture or by long, grueling questioning; subject to the third degree. ***n.*** [altered, after the *v.* < ME. *swat, swote,* sweat; AS. *swat*], 1. the clear, alkaline, salty liquid given forth in drops through the pores of the skin; perspiration. 2. the moisture given forth or collected in droplets on the surface of something. 3. a sweating or being sweated; especially, an artificially induced sweating. 4. a condition of eagerness, anxiety, impatience, etc. regarded as strong enough to cause sweating. 5. hard work; drudgery. 6. exercise, as a run, given a horse before a race.
sweat blood, [Slang], 1. to work very hard; overwork. 2. to be impatient, apprehensive, anxious, etc.
sweat (something) out, [Slang], 1. to wait through (a line, etc.). 2. to anticipate or wait anxiously or impatiently for (something).
sweat·band (swet'band'), ***n.*** a band of leather, etc. inside a hat to protect it against sweat from the brow.
sweat·box (swet'boks'), ***n.*** a box in which hides, etc. are sweated.
sweat·ed (swet'id), ***adj.*** [pp. of *sweat*], 1. soiled, dampened, etc. by sweat. 2. that has been made to sweat; specifically, employed for long hours at low wages under poor working conditions; exploited.
sweat·er (swet'ẽr), ***n.*** 1. a person or thing that sweats, especially to excess. 2. a knitted or crocheted outer garment for the upper part of the body, with or without sleeves and either a pull-over or a jacket. 3. a sudorific. 4. an employer who sweats his employees.
sweat gland, any of the many, very small, coiled, tubular glands in the subcutaneous tissue that secrete sweat through the pores of the skin.
sweat·i·ly (swet'ə-li), ***adv.*** so as to be sweaty.
sweat·i·ness (swet'i-nis), ***n.*** a sweaty condition.
sweating sickness, an acute infectious, rapidly fatal disease that was epidemic in England in the 15th and 16th centuries and was characterized by a high fever and profuse sweating.
sweat shirt, a heavy, long-sleeved cotton jersey, worn as by athletes to absorb sweat during or after exercise.
sweat·shop (swet'shop'), ***n.*** a shop or plant where employees are forced to work long hours at low wages under poor working conditions.
sweat·y (swet'i), ***adj.*** [SWEATIER (-i-ẽr), SWEATIEST (-i-ist)], 1. sweating; covered with sweat. 2. like or like that of sweat: as, a *sweaty* odor. 3. causing sweat. 4. calling for great effort; laborious.
Swed., 1. Sweden. 2. Swedish.
Swede (swēd), ***n.*** a native or inhabitant of Sweden.
Swe·den (swē'd'n), ***n.*** a country in northern Europe, on the Scandinavian Peninsula: area, 173,143 sq. mi.; pop., 7,471,000; capital, Stockholm: Swedish name, *Sverige.*
Swe·den·borg, Emanuel (swē'd'n-bôrg'; Sw. svā'd'n-bôr'y'), 1688–1772; Swedish philosopher, scientist, theologian, and mystic.
Swe·den·bor·gi·an (swē'd'n-bôr'ji-ən), ***n.*** any of the followers of Swedenborg, who claimed special Scriptural revelations from God. ***adj.*** of Swedenborg, his doctrines, or his followers, who constitute the New (Jerusalem) Church.
Swe·den·bor·gi·an·ism (swē'd'n-bôr'ji-ən-iz'm), ***n.*** the religious doctrines of Swedenborg.

Swe·den·borg·ism (swē′d'n-bôrg′iz'm), *n.* Swedenborgianism.
Swed·ish (swē′dish), *adj.* of Sweden, its people, their language, etc. *n.* the North Germanic language of the Swedes.
the Swedish, the Swedish people.
Swedish massage, massage combined with Swedish movements, as in treating certain diseases.
Swedish movements, a set or system of exercises involving various muscle groups of the body, used in the treatment of certain diseases.
Swedish Nightingale, Jenny Lind.
swee·ny (swē′ni), *n.* [< dial. G. *schweine,* atrophy], atrophy of the shoulder muscles of horses.
sweep (swēp), *v.t.* [SWEPT (swept), SWEEPING], [ME. *swepen,* altered < AS. *swapan* after *swepe, n.;* cf. SWOOP], 1. to clear or clean (a surface, room, etc.) as by brushing with a broom. 2. to remove, clear away, or clean up (dirt, debris, etc.) with or as a brush or broom or with a brushing movement. 3. to clear (a space, path, etc.) with or as with a broom. 4. to strip, clear, carry away, or destroy with force of movement. 5. to move or carry along with a sweeping movement: as, he *swept* the cards into a pile, she *swept* her hand through her hair. 6. to touch or brush in moving across: as, his hands *swept* the keyboard, her dress *sweeps* the ground. 7. to pass swiftly over or across; traverse, as in search: as, armed bands *sweep* the countryside, his eyes *swept* the terrain. 8. to drag (*v.t.,* 2). 9. to rake (*v.t.,* 5). 10. [Colloq.], *a)* to win all the games or events of (a series, set, or match); hence, *b)* to win overwhelmingly: as, the Democrats *swept* the election. *v.i.* 1. to clean a surface, room, etc. with or as a broom or the like. 2. to move, pass, or progress steadily or smoothly, especially with speed, force, or gracefulness: as, the planes *sweep* across the sky, her fingers *swept* over the strings, the music *sweeps* to a thrilling close. 3. *a)* to trail one's skirts, etc. in moving. *b)* to trail, as skirts. 4. to reach or extend in a long, graceful curve or line: as, the road *sweeps* up the hill. *n.* 1. the act of sweeping; cleaning, clearing, or removing with or as with a broom. 2. *a)* a steady sweeping or driving movement: as, the *sweep* of a scythe. *b)* a stroke or blow resulting from this. 3. a trailing, as of skirts. 4. range or scope: as, they came within the *sweep* of our guns. 5. a stretch; extent; reach: as, a long *sweep* of meadow. 6. a line, contour, curve, etc. that gives an impression of flow or movement. 7. a person whose work is sweeping: as, a chimney *sweep.* 8. *usually pl.* sweepings. 9. the taking or winning of all; complete victory or success, as in a series of contests. 10. a long oar. 11. a long pole mounted on a pivot, with a bucket at one end: used for raising water, as from a well. 12. a sweepstakes. 13. in *physics,* the irreversible process by which a substance tends to settle into thermal equilibrium.
sweep·back (swēp′bak′), *n.* the angle formed by the line of declination of an airplane wing and the lateral axis of the airplane.
sweep·er (swēp′ẽr), *n.* 1. a person who sweeps. 2. a device for sweeping: as, a carpet *sweeper.*
sweep·ing (swēp′iŋ), *adj.* [ppr. of *sweep*], 1. that sweeps; cleansing or carrying away with or as with a broom. 2. extending over the whole range or a great space. 3. extensive; complete; comprehensive; thoroughgoing. *n.* 1. *pl.* things swept up; dirt, etc. swept from a floor. 2. the act, work, etc. of a person or thing that sweeps.
sweep·stake (swēp′stāk′), *n.* a sweepstakes.
sweepstakes (swēp′stāks′), *n.* [*pl.* SWEEPSTAKES], [so named because the winner "sweeps" in all of the stakes], 1. a lottery in which each person taking part puts up a stake of money in a common fund which is given as the prize to the winner or in shares to several winners. 2. a contest, especially a horse race, the result of which determines the winner or winners of such a lottery. 3. the prize or prizes won in such a lottery.
sweep ticket, a chance or ticket in a sweepstakes.
sweet (swēt), *adj.* [ME. *swete, swote;* AS. *swete* < *swot,* sweetness; akin to G. *süss* (OHG. *suozi*); IE. base **swad-,* pleasing to taste, as also in L. *suavis* (< **swadwis*), sweet (cf. SUAVE)], 1. *a)* having a taste of, or like that of, sugar. *b)* containing sugar in some form: as, *sweet* wines. 2. *a)* having a generally agreeable taste, smell, sound, appearance, etc.; pleasant. *b)* agreeable to the mind; gratifying: as, *sweet* praise. *c)* having a friendly, pleasing disposition; characterized by kindliness and gentleness: as, a *sweet* girl: formerly used as a polite form of address, as, *sweet* sir, *sweet* knight. *d)* [Slang], good, delightful, etc.: a generalized epithet of approval. 3. not salty or salted: as, *sweet* water. 4. not rancid or spoiled; fresh. 5. good for growing crops: said of soil. 6. in *chemistry,* free from excessive acid, sulfur, etc. 7. in *jazz music, a)* designating or of playing characterized by more or less strict adherence to melody, blandness, and a relatively moderate tempo: distinguished from *hot. b)* designating or of music played in this way. *n.* 1. the quality of being sweet; sweetness. 2. something sweet; specifically, *a) usually in pl.* a candy; sweetmeat. *b)* [British], a sweet dish served as dessert. *c) often in pl.* pleasure or a pleasurable experience. *d)* [Colloq.], a sweet potato. 3. a sweet, or beloved, person; darling. *adv.* sweetly.
be sweet on, [Colloq.], to be in love with.
Sweet, Henry (swēt), 1845–1912; English linguist and phonetician.
sweet alyssum, a short plant with small spikes of tiny, fragrant, white flowers.
sweet basil, a plant with bluish-white flowers and fragrant leaves used in cooking.
sweet bay, 1. any of a number of related laurel trees. 2. a variety of magnolia.
sweet·bread (swēt′bred′), *n.* [Early Mod. Eng.; *sweet* + *bread* in the AS. sense "morsel"], the pancreas (*stomach sweetbread*) or the thymus (*neck,* or *throat, sweetbread*) of a calf or other animal, when used as food.
sweet·bri·er, sweet·bri·ar (swēt′brī′ẽr), *n.* a semiclimbing rose with fragrant leaves, pink flowers, and tall, prickly stems; eglantine.
sweet cicely, a plant of the parsley family, with small, white flowers and finely cut, fragrant leaves used in cooking; myrrh.
sweet cider, cider that has not fermented.
sweet clover, any of various plants of the pea family, with butterfly-shaped, white or yellow flowers, and leaves in groups of three, grown for fodder; melilot.
sweet corn, a variety of Indian corn, rich in sugar and eaten as a table vegetable in its unripe, or milky, stage.
sweet·en (swē′t'n), *v.t.* 1. to make sweet with or as with sugar. 2. to make pleasant or agreeable. 3. to mollify; alleviate; appease. 4. [Colloq.], in *finance,* to increase the value of (collateral for a loan) by adding valuable securities. 5. [Slang], in *poker,* to add further stakes to (the pot) before opening.
sweet·en·ing (swē′t'n-iŋ, swēt′niŋ), *n.* 1. the process of making sweet. 2. something that sweetens.
sweet fern, a sweet-smelling plant with finely cut, fernlike leaves, and spikes of flowers.
sweet flag, a marsh plant with long, grasslike leaves and sweet, edible roots.
sweet gale, a fragrant marsh shrub with spikes of flowers and bitter leaves.
sweet gum, a tall tree with shining, maplelike leaves, spiny balls of fruit, and fragrant juice.
sweet·heart (swēt′härt′), *n.* a lover; especially, a woman with reference to her lover: sometimes used as a term of endearment.
sweet·ie (swē′ti), *n.* [Colloq.], a sweetheart.
sweet·ing (swē′tiŋ), *n.* 1. a variety of sweet apple. 2. [Archaic], a sweetheart.
sweet·ish (swē′tish), *adj.* rather sweet.
sweet marjoram, a fragrant herb whose leaves are used in cooking.
sweet·meat (swēt′mēt′), *n.* [cf. AS. *swetmettas,* delicacies; *meat* is used in the orig. sense "food"], any sweet food or delicacy prepared with sugar or honey, as a cake, confection, preserve, etc.; specifically, a candy, candied fruit, etc.
sweet oil, olive oil.
sweet pea, a climbing plant with large, variously colored, fragrant flowers.
sweet pepper, 1. a kind of pepper plant producing a mild fruit. 2. its fruit.
sweet potato, 1. a tropical, trailing plant with purplish flowers and a fleshy, orange or yellow root used as a vegetable. 2. its root. 3. [Colloq.] an ocarina.
sweet-scent·ed (swēt′sent′id), *adj.* having a pleasant scent or fragrance.
sweet·sop (swēt′sop′), *n.* 1. a tropical American tree having green, scaly, egg-shaped fruit with a sweet pulp and black seeds. 2. its fruit.
sweet spirit of niter, a solution of nitrous ether, $C_2H_5NO_2$, in alcohol, used in medicine as a sedative, to induce sweating, etc.
sweet-tem·pered (swēt′tem′pẽrd), *adj.* having a gentle, amiable disposition; good-natured.
sweet tooth, [Colloq.], a fondness or craving for sweets.
sweet William, sweet william, a plant of the pink family, with dense, round clusters of small, variously colored flowers.
swell (swel), *v.i.* [SWELLED (sweld), SWELLED or SWOLLEN (swōl′'n), SWELLING], [ME. *swellen;* AS. *swellan;* akin to G. *schwellen;* IE. base **swel-*], 1. to increase in volume or become larger as a result of pressure from within; expand; dilate. 2. to become larger at a given point; curve out; bulge; protrude. 3. to extend beyond or above the normal or surrounding level: as, clouds that *swell* above the horizon. 4. to be or become filled (*with* pride, indignation, a sense of importance, etc.); puff up. 5. to increase within one: said of an emotion,

etc., as, anger *swelled* in him. 6. to increase in size, force, intensity, degree, etc.: as, our ranks *swelled* to over a hundred. 7. to increase in volume or loudness: said of sound, musical instruments, etc. *v.t.* to cause to swell; specifically, *a*) to cause to increase in size, volume, extent, degree, etc. *b*) to cause to bulge or protrude. *c*) to fill with pride, indignation, etc.; inflate; puff. *d*) to cause (a tone, chord, etc.) to increase in loudness. *n.* 1. a part that swells; bulge; curve; protuberance; specifically, *a*) a swollen part or area of the body. *b*) a large wave that moves steadily without breaking. *c*) a piece of rising ground; rounded hill or slope. 2. a swelling or being swollen. 3. an increase in size, amount, extent, degree, etc. 4. [Colloq.], a person who is strikingly stylish or fashionable, especially in dress. 5. in *music, a*) a gradual increase in volume (*crescendo*), usually followed by a gradual decrease (*diminuendo*). *b*) a sign (<>) indicating this. *c*) a device for controlling the loudness of tones in an organ, harpsichord, etc. *adj.* [ME. *swelle*, tumid, proud], 1. [Colloq.], stylish; very fashionable. 2. [Slang], first-rate; excellent: a generalized epithet of approval. —*SYN.* see **expand.**

swell box, a chamber enclosing one or more sets of organ pipes or reeds and fitted with movable shutters that regulate the loudness of tone.

swelled head, [Colloq.], undue self-esteem; conceit.

swell·fish (swel′fish′), *n.* [*pl.* SWELLFISH, SWELLFISHES (-iz); see FISH], a fish capable of inflating its body with air; puffer.

swell·ing (swel′iŋ), *n.* 1. an increasing or being increased in size, volume, etc. 2. something swollen; especially, an abnormally swollen part of the body. *adj.* that swells, or curves outward.

swel·ter (swel′tẽr), *v.i.* [freq. of ME. *swelten*, to die, swoon away, faint; AS. *sweltan*, to die; IE. base **swel-*, to burn; cf. SULTRY], to perspire, be faint, or feel oppressed with great heat. *v.t.* 1. to cause to swelter. 2. [Archaic], to exude (venom or poison). *n.* 1. the condition of sweltering. 2. oppressive heat.

swel·ter·ing (swel′tẽr-iŋ), *adj.* 1. that swelters or suffers with the heat. 2. very hot; sultry.

swel·try (swel′tri), *adj.* [SWELTRIER (-tri-ẽr), SWELTRIEST (-tri-ist)], [cf. SULTRY], sweltering.

swept (swept), past tense and past participle of **sweep.**

swerve (swũrv), *v.i. & v.t.* [SWERVED (swũrvd), SWERVING], [ME. *swerven;* AS. *sweorfan*, to file away, scour], to turn aside or cause to turn aside from a straight line, course, etc. *n.* 1. the act or degree of swerving. 2. something that swerves. —*SYN.* see **deviate.**

S.W.G., standard wire gauge.

swift (swift), *adj.* [ME.; AS.; IE. base **sweip-* < **swei-*, to bend, swing], 1. moving or capable of moving with great speed; rapid; fast. 2. coming, happening, or done quickly or suddenly; undelayed. 3. acting or responding quickly; prompt; ready. *adv.* swiftly. *n.* 1. a cylinder in a carding machine. 2. an expanding reel used to hold skeins of silk, etc. that are being wound off. 3. a sooty-brown, swift-flying bird resembling the swallow, as the chimney swift. 4. any of several swift-moving newts or lizards. —*SYN.* see **fast.**

Swift, Jonathan (swift), 1667–1745; English satirist, born in Ireland.

swift·er (swif′tẽr), *n.* [< obs. *swift*, to tighten, fasten with a taut rope], in *nautical usage*, 1. [Obs.], a rope run lengthwise about the hull of a boat to strengthen it or protect its sides. 2. a rope fastened to the extreme ends of the capstan bars to keep them in their sockets while the capstan is being turned. 3. any of the foremost shrouds of a lower mast.

swift-foot·ed (swift′foot′id), *adj.* that can run swiftly.

swig (swig), *v.t. & v.i.* [SWIGGED (swigd), SWIGGING], [< Early Mod. Eng. slang], [Colloq.], to drink, especially in great gulps or large quantities. *n.* [Colloq.], an instance of swigging; deep draft, especially of liquor.

swig·ger (swig′ẽr), *n.* a person or animal that swigs.

swill (swil), *v.t.* [ME. *swilen;* AS. *swilian;* IE. base **swel-*, to devour; cf. SWALLOW], 1. to flood with water so as to wash or rinse. 2. to drink greedily or in large quantity. 3. to fill with drink: used reflexively. *v.i.* to drink, especially liquor, in large quantities. *n.* 1. garbage, table scraps, etc. mixed with liquid and used for feeding animals, especially pigs; wash. 2. garbage. 3. the act of swilling. 4. a swig; deep drink of liquor.

swim (swim), *v.i.* [SWAM (swam) or *archaic* or *dial.* SWUM (swum), SWUM, SWIMMING], [ME. *swimmen;* AS. *swimman;* akin to G. *schwimmen;* IE. base **swem-*, to move vigorously, be in motion, as also in W. *chwyfio*, to move], 1. to move through water by movements of the arms, legs, fins, tail, etc. 2. to move with a smooth, gliding motion, as though swimming. 3. to float on the surface of a liquid. 4. to be covered or saturated with or as with a liquid. 5. to overflow; be flooded: as, eyes *swimming* with tears. *v.t.* 1. to move in or across (a body of water) by swimming. 2. to cause to swim or float. *n.* 1. the act or motion of swimming. 2. a period of swimming for sport: as, I had a *swim.* 3. a distance swum or to be swum. 4. a swimming bladder.

in the swim, conforming to the currently fashionable in style, opinions, etc., or active in current society, business affairs, or the like.

swim (swim), *n.* [ME. *swime;* AS. *swima;* akin to D. *zwijmen*, to faint; IE. base **swei-*, to bend, turn], the condition of being dizzy: as, her head was in a *swim.* *v.i.* [SWAM (swam), SWUM (swum), SWIMMING], 1. to be dizzy. 2. to have a hazy, reeling, or whirling appearance: as, the room *swam* before his eyes.

swim·mer (swim′ẽr), *n.* a person or animal that swims.

swim·mer·et (swim′ẽr-et′), *n.* any of a series of small, abdominal legs or appendages in certain crustaceans, used primarily in swimming and for carrying eggs.

swim·ming (swim′iŋ), *n.* the action of a person or animal that swims, especially for sport. *adj.* 1. that swims. 2. used in swimming. 3. flooded or overflowing with or as with water: as, *swimming* eyes.

swim·ming (swim′iŋ), *n.* [cf. SWIM (dizziness)], dizziness. *adj.* affected with a dizzy, whirling sensation.

swimming bladder, the air bladder of a fish.

swimming hole, a pool or a deep place in a river, creek, etc. used for swimming.

swim·ming·ly (swim′iŋ-li), *adv.* [ppr. of *swim* + *-ly*], easily and with success: as, the entertainment went over *swimmingly.*

swimming pool, a pool of water used for swimming; especially, an artificially created pool, or tank, either indoors or outdoors.

swim suit, a garment designed for swimming; bathing suit.

Swin·burne, Algernon Charles (swin′bẽrn), 1837–1909; English poet and critic.

swin·dle (swin′d'l), *v.t.* [SWINDLED (-d'ld), SWINDLING], [back-formation < *swindler*], 1. to get money or property from (another) under false pretenses; cheat; defraud. 2. to get by false pretenses or fraud. *v.i.* to engage in swindling others. *n.* an act of swindling; trick; cheat; fraud. —*SYN.* see **cheat.**

swin·dler (swin′dlẽr), *n.* [G. *schwindler* < *schwindeln*, to be dizzy, defraud, cheat], a person who swindles; cheat.

swine (swin), *n.* [*pl.* SWINE], [ME. & AS. *swin;* akin to G. *schwein;* IE. base **su-*, pig, sow, as also in L. *sus, suinus*, etc.; cf. SOW], 1. a pig or hog: usually used collectively. 2. a vicious, contemptible person.

swine·herd (swin′hũrd′), *n.* a person who tends swine.

swine pox, [Archaic], a variety of chicken pox.

swing (swiŋ), *v.i.* [SWUNG (swuŋ) or *archaic* or *dial.* SWANG (swaŋ), SWUNG, SWINGING], [ME. *swingen;* AS. *swingan;* akin to G. *schwingen*, to brandish, etc.; IE. base **sweng-*, to curve, swing; cf. SWANK], 1. to sway backward and forward with regular movement, as a freely hanging object; oscillate. 2. to walk, trot, etc. with freely swaying, relaxed movements of the limbs: as, we watched the regiment *swing* down the road. 3. to turn or pivot, as on a hinge or swivel: as, the door *swung* open. 4. to hang; be suspended; specifically, to be hanged in execution. 5. to move backward and forward on a swing (*n.* 10). *v.t.* 1. *a*) to move or wave (a weapon, tool, bat, etc.) with a sweeping motion; flourish; brandish. *b*) to lift or hoist with a sweeping motion: as, he *swung* the bag onto his back. 2. to cause (a hanging object) to sway backward and forward; specifically, to cause (a person on a swing) to move backward and forward by pushing or pulling. 3. to cause to turn or pivot, as on a hinge or swivel: as, he *swung* the door open. 4. to cause to hang freely, so as to be capable of easy movement: as, the sailors *swung* their hammocks below decks. 5. to cause to come about successfully; manage or handle with the desired results: as, I think we can *swing* the election. 6. to play or arrange (a piece of music) in the style of swing. *n.* 1. the act or process of swinging. 2. the arc, or the length of the arc, through which something swings: as, what is the *swing* of that pendulum? 3. the manner of swinging; specifically, the manner of striking with a golf club, baseball bat, etc. 4. freedom to do as one wishes or is naturally inclined: as, he gave us full *swing* in the matter. 5. a free, relaxed motion, as in walking. 6. a sweeping blow or stroke. 7. the course, development, or movement of some activity, business, etc. 8. the power, or force, behind something swung or thrown; impetus. 9. rhythm, as of poetry or music. 10. a device consisting of a seat hanging from two or more ropes or chains, on which one can sit and swing backward and forward as a form of recreation. 11. *a*) jazz music, especially in its development after about 1935, characterized by the use of larger bands, contrapuntal improvisation, and written arrangements for ensemble playing. *b*) the characteristic rhythmic element of such music. 12. [Colloq.], in *commerce*, regular upward and downward change in the price of stocks or in some other business activity. *adj.* of, in, or playing swing (music).

in full swing, in complete and active operation; going on without reserve or restraint.

swing round the circle, a political campaign tour.

SYN.—**swing** suggests the to-and-fro motion of something that is suspended, hinged, pivoted, etc. so that it is free to turn or swivel at the point or points of attachment (a *swinging* door); **sway** describes the swinging motion of something flexible or self-balancing, whether attached or unattached, in yielding to pressure, weight, etc. (branches *swaying* in the wind); to **oscillate** is to swing back and forth, within certain limits, in the manner of a pendulum; **vibrate** suggests the rapid, regular back-and-forth motion of a plucked, taut string and is applied in physics to a similar movement of the particles of a fluid or elastic medium (sound *vibrations*); **fluctuate** implies continual, irregular alternating movements and is now most common in its extended sense (*fluctuating* prices); **undulate** implies a gentle wavelike motion or form (*undulating* land).

swing bridge, a bridge that can be swung back in a horizontal plane to allow tall vessels, etc. to pass.

swinge (swinj), *v.t.* [SWINGED (swinjd), SWINGEING], [ME. *swengen;* AS. *swengan*, caus. of *swingan*, to swing], [Archaic], to punish with blows; beat; whip.

swinge·ing (swin′jiŋ), *adj.* [ppr. of *swinge;* cf. STRAPPING], [Colloq.], 1. huge; very large. 2. extremely good; first-rate.

swinging door, a door hung so that it can be opened in either direction and swings shut of itself.

swin·gle (swiŋ′g'l), *v.t.* [SWINGLED (-g'ld), SWINGLING], [ME. *swinglen;* MD. *swinghelen* < *swinghel*, a swingle], to clean (flax or hemp) by beating or scraping with a swingle. *n.* [ME. < AS. *swingele* & MD. *swinghel* < base of *swing*], 1. a wooden, swordlike tool used to clean flax or hemp by beating or scraping. 2. the swiple, or striking part, of a flail.

swin·gle·bar (swiŋ′g'l-bär′), *n.* a swingletree.

swin·gle·tree (swiŋ′g'l-trē′), *n.* a whippletree or singletree.

swing shift, [Colloq.], in those factories operating on a 24-hour basis, the evening work shift, from about midafternoon to about midnight.

swing·tree (swiŋ′trē′), *n.* a swingletree.

swin·ish (swin′ish), *adj.* [ME. *swinisch*], of, like, fit for, or characteristic of swine; beastly; piggish; coarse.

swink (swiŋk), *v.i.* [SWANK (swaŋk) or SWONK (swoŋk), SWONKEN (swoŋ′k'n), SWINKING], [ME. *swinken;* AS. *swincan* < the base seen in *swing*], [Archaic], to labor; toil; drudge. *n.* [Archaic], labor; toil; drudgery.

Swin·ner·ton, Frank (swin′ẽr-tən), 1884– ; English novelist and critic.

swipe (swīp), *n.* [ME. *swipe;* ON. *svipr*, a stroke; prob. < the base of *sweep*], 1. a lever or handle, as on a pump. 2. [Colloq.], a hard, sweeping blow. *v.t.* [SWIPED (swīpt), SWIPING], 1. [Colloq.], to hit with a hard, sweeping blow. 2. [Slang], to steal; pilfer. *v.i.* [Colloq.], to make a sweeping blow or stroke. —*SYN.* see **steal.**

swipes (swīps), *n.pl.* [< *swipe*, in obs. sense of "gulp down"], [British Slang], beer, especially weak or inferior beer.

swi·ple, swip·ple (swip′'l), *n.* [prob. < or akin to *swipe*], the part of a flail that strikes the grain in threshing.

swirl (swũrl), *v.i.* [prob. < ON. *svirla*, to whirl], 1. to move with a twisting, whirling motion; eddy. 2. to swim, or be dizzy, as the head. *v.t.* to cause to swirl; whirl. *n.* 1. a swirling motion; whirl; eddy. 2. something swirled or swirling; twist; curl; whirl; whorl.

swirl·y (swũr′li), *adj.* 1. full of swirls. 2. [Scot.], knotted; tangled.

swish (swish), *v.i.* [echoic], 1. to move with a sharp, hissing sound, as a cane swung through the air. 2. to rustle, as skirts in walking. *v.t.* 1. to cause to swish. 2. to whip or flog. *n.* 1. a hissing or rustling sound. 2. a movement, etc. that makes this sound. 3. *a*) a rod or cane for flogging. *b*) a stroke with this.

Swiss (swis), *adj.* [Fr. *suisse*], of Switzerland, its people, or culture. *n.* [*pl.* SWISS], a native or inhabitant of Switzerland.

the Swiss, the Swiss people.

Swiss chard, a chard (sense 2).

Swiss cheese, [orig. made in Switzerland], a white or pale-yellow hard cheese with many large holes.

Swiss·er (swis′ẽr), *n.* a Switzer.

Swiss Guards, a corps of Swiss mercenary soldiers, especially those hired as bodyguards to the Pope in the Vatican.

Swiss steak, a thick cut of round or shoulder steak pounded with flour and cooked, usually with a sauce of tomato and onion.

Swit., Switzerland.

switch (swich), *n.* [Early Mod. Eng.; prob. < a LG. source; cf. LG. *zwuske*, long, thin rod, MD. *swick*, a whip, etc.], 1. a thin, flexible twig, rod, stick, etc., especially one used for whipping. 2. the bushy part of the tail in some animals, as the cow. 3. a tress of detached, sometimes false, hair bound at one end and used by women as part of a coiffure. 4. an abrupt, sharp, lashing movement, as with a switch. 5. a device used to open, close, or divert an electric circuit. 6. a movable section of railroad track used in transferring a train from one set of tracks to another. 7. the act or process of changing the position of a switch. 8. a shift or transference; change; turn. *v.t.* 1. to whip or beat with or as with a switch. 2. to jerk or swing sharply; lash: as, the cat *switched* its tail in anger. 3. to shift; transfer; change; turn aside; divert. 4. *a*) to operate the switch of (an electric circuit) so as to connect, disconnect, or divert; hence, *b*) to turn (an electric light or appliance) *on* or *off* in this way. 5. to transfer (a train or car) from one set of tracks to another by use of a switch. 6. [Colloq.], to change or exchange: as, we *switched* places. *v.i.* 1. to move from or as from one set of tracks to another. 2. to shift; transfer; change.

switch·back (swich′bak′), *n.* 1. a road or railroad following a winding or zigzag course up a steep grade. 2. [British], a roller coaster.

switch-blade knife (swich′blād′), a large jackknife having a blade that opens rapidly when a button or other device on the handle is pressed.

switch·board (swich′bôrd′, swich′bōrd′), *n.* a board or panel equipped with apparatus for controlling the operation of a system of electric circuits, as in a telephone exchange: abbreviated **swbd.**

switch box, a box containing a switch or switches, usually mounted on a wall or panel.

switch·man (swich′mən), *n.* [*pl.* SWITCHMEN (-mən)], a railroad employee who operates switches.

switch·yard (swich′yärd′), *n.* a railroad yard where cars are shifted from one track to another by means of a system of switches, as in making up trains.

Swith·in or **Swith·un,** Saint (swith′ən, swith′ən), ?–862 A.D.; English prelate: his day is July 15.

Switz·er (swit′sẽr), *n.* [MHG. (G. *Schweizer*) < *Switz*, *Swiz*, Switzerland], 1. a Swiss. 2. a Swiss mercenary soldier. Also **Swisser.**

Switz·er·land (swit′sẽr-lənd), *n.* a country in west central Europe, in the Alps: area, 15,940 sq. mi.; pop., 5,318,000; capital, Bern; Latin name, *Helvetia;* German name, *Schweiz;* French name, *Suisse.*

swiv·el (swiv′'l), *n.* [ME. *swiuel* < base of AS. *swifan*, to revolve], 1. a part or fastening that allows free turning of the parts attached to it; specifically, *a*) a chain link made in two parts, one piece fitting like a collar below the bolthead of the other and turning freely about it. *b*) the platform support for a swivel chair or swivel gun. 2. a swivel gun. *v.t.* [SWIVELED or SWIVELLED (-'ld), SWIVELING or SWIVELLING], 1. to cause to turn or rotate on or as on a swivel. 2. to fit, fasten, or support with a swivel. *v.i.* to turn on or as on a swivel.

SWIVEL
C, chain; S, swivel; H, hook

swivel chair, a chair whose seat turns horizontally on a pivot in the base.

swivel gun, an artillery piece mounted on a platform in such a way that it can be turned horizontally or vertically for aiming.

swiz·zle (swiz′'l), *n.* [var. of *switchel;* prob. < *switch*, *v.* with reference to the mixing], any of several alcoholic drinks containing liquor, ice, sugar, bitters, etc.

swizzle stick, a stick or rod for stirring mixed drinks.

swob (swob), *n.* & *v.t.* [SWOBBED (swobd), SWOBBING], swab.

swol·len (swō′lən), alternative past participle of **swell.** *adj.* increased in volume or size, as from inner pressure; blown up; distended; bulging.

swonk (swoŋk), alternative past tense of **swink.**

swonk·en (swoŋ′k'n), past participle of **swink.**

swoon (swōōn), *v.i.* [ME. *swounen* < *swoweninge*, swooning < AS. *geswogen*, unconscious, pp. of a lost v.], to faint. *n.* a fainting fit; syncope.

swoop (swōōp), *v.t.* [ME. *swopen, swapen;* AS. *swapan*, to sweep along, rush; akin to G. *schweifen;* for IE. base see SWIFT], to snatch or seize suddenly, with a sweeping movement: often with *up*, etc. *v.i.* to descend suddenly and swiftly, as a bird in hunting; pounce or sweep (*down* or *upon*). *n.* the act of swooping or pouncing; sudden, violent descent.

swop (swop, swôp), *n.*, *v.t.* & *v.i.* [SWOPPED (swopt, swôpt), SWOPPING], swap.

sword (sôrd, sōrd), *n.* [ME.; AS. *sweord, swurd, sword;* akin to G. *schwert;* thought by some to be < IE. *swertom*, that hangs, with reference to method of carrying the weapon], 1. a hand weapon having typically a long, sharp-pointed blade, a hilt, and, usually, a sharp edge on one or both sides: the term includes the broadsword, rapier, saber, scimitar, etc. 2. *a*) the sword regarded as an instrument of death, destruction, etc.; hence, *b*) power; especially, military power. *c*) the military class or profession. *d*) war; warfare.

at swords' points, ready to quarrel or fight.

cross swords, 1. to fight. 2. to argue violently.

put to the sword, 1. to kill with a sword or swords. 2. to slaughter, especially in war.

sword bayonet, a short sword that can be mounted on a rifle for use as a bayonet.

sword belt, a belt from which a sword is hung.

sword·bill (sôrd′bil′, sōrd′bil′), *n.* a variety of South American hummingbird with a very long bill.

sword-billed hummingbird (sôrd′bild′, sōrd′bild′), a swordbill.
sword cane, a weapon consisting of a sword concealed in a scabbard made to resemble a walking stick.
sword·craft (sôrd′kraft′, sōrd′kräft′), *n.* 1. swordsmanship. 2. the use of military force; tactics of warfare.
sword dance, any dance involving the use of swords, especially one performed around bare swords laid on the ground.
sword·fish (sôrd′fish′, sōrd′fish′), *n.* [*pl.* SWORDFISH, SWORDFISHES (-iz); see FISH], a large marine food fish with the upper jawbone extending in a long swordlike point.

SWORDFISH (7 ft. long)

sword grass, any of a number of sedges or grasses with toothed or sword-shaped leaves.
sword knot, a loop of leather, ribbon, etc. attached to a sword hilt as an ornament or, originally, for support around the wrist during swordplay.
sword lily, the gladiolus.
sword·man (sôrd′mən, sōrd′mən), *n.* [*pl.* SWORDMEN (-mən)], a swordsman.
sword·play (sôrd′plā′, sōrd′plā′), *n.* the act or art of using a sword; fencing.
swords·man (sôrdz′mən, sōrdz′mən), *n.* [*pl.* SWORDSMEN (-mən)], 1. a person who uses a sword in fencing or fighting. 2. a person skilled in using a sword.
swords·man·ship (sôrdz′mən-ship′, sōrdz′mən-ship′), *n.* [see -SHIP], skill in using a sword; art or skill of a swordsman.
sword·tail (sôrd′tāl′, sōrd′tāl′), *n.* a small, vividly colored fresh-water fish of Mexico and Central America, often kept in aquariums.
swore (swôr, swōr), alternative past tense of **swear.**
sworn (swôrn, swōrn), past participle of **swear.** *adj.* bound, pledged, promised, etc. by or as by an oath.
swot (swot), *n. & v.t.* [SWOTTED (-id), SWOTTING], swat.
swound (swound, swōōnd), *n. & v.i.* [ME. *swounde, swounden* < form of *swounen* (cf. SWOON) with unhistoric *-d*], [Archaic], swoon; faint.
'swounds (zwoundz, zoundz), *interj.* [Archaic], God's wounds: a euphemistic contraction used as an oath: also **zounds.**
swum (swum), past participle and archaic or dialectal past tense of **swim** (to move through water).
swum (swum), past participle of **swim** (to be dizzy).
swung (swuŋ), past participle and alternative past tense of **swing.**
Syb·a·ris (sib′ə-ris), *n.* an ancient Greek city in southern Italy, famed as a center of luxury: destroyed in 510 B.C.
Syb·a·rite (sib′ə-rīt′), *n.* [L. *Sybarita;* Gr. *Sybaritēs*], 1. any of the people of ancient Sybaris; hence, 2. [s-], anyone very fond of luxury and pleasure; voluptuary.
Syb·a·rit·ic (sib′ə-rit′ik), *adj.* [L. *Sybariticus;* Gr. *Sybaritikos*], 1. of or characterisitc of Sybaris or the Sybarites. 2. [s-], luxurious; voluptuous.
syb·a·rit·i·cal (sib′ə-rit′i-k′l), *adj.* sybaritic.
syb·a·rit·ism (sib′ə-rīt-iz′m), *n.* the habits, practices, etc. of a sybarite; voluptuousness.
Syb·il (sib′′l), a feminine name: see **Sibyl.**
syc·a·mine (sik′ə-min, sik′ə-mīn′), *n.* [L. *sycaminus;* Gr. *sykaminos*], a tree mentioned in Luke 17:6, believed to be the black mulberry.
syc·a·more (sik′ə-môr′, sik′ə-mōr′), *n.* [ME. *sicomore;* OFr. *sicamor, sichamor;* L. *sycomorus;* Gr. *sykomoros;* prob. < Heb. *shiqmāh,* sycamore, but altered after Gr. *sykon,* fig + *moron,* black mulberry], 1. a shade tree of Egypt and Asia Minor, with figlike fruit. 2. a maple shade tree with yellow flowers and coarse-toothed leaves, found in Europe and Asia. 3. any of a number of related American plane trees; especially, the buttonwood.
syce (sīs), *n.* [Ar. *sa'is* < *sus,* to tend a horse], in India, a groom (for horses).
sy·cee (sī-sē′), *n.* [< dial. (Canton) form of Chin. *hsi ssŭ,* fine silk: so called because if pure it may, when heated, be spun into fine threads], silver in the form of ingots, usually stamped, used in China as money.
sy·co·ni·um (sī-kō′ni-əm), *n.* [Mod. L. < Gr. *sykon,* fig], a fleshy, hollow fruit composed of two or more pistils growing together, as a fig.
syc·o·phan·cy (sik′ə-fən-si), *n.* [*pl.* SYCOPHANCIES (-siz)], [L. *sycophantia;* Gr. *sykophantia*], the behavior or character of a sycophant; servile flattery.
syc·o·phant (sik′ə-fənt), *n.* [L. *sycophanta;* Gr. *sykophantēs,* informer, lit., fig shower < *sykon,* a fig + *phainein,* to show], a person who seeks favor by flattering people of wealth or influence; parasite; toady. —*SYN.* see **parasite.**
syc·o·phan·tic (sik′ə-fan′tik), *adj.* [Gr. *sykophantikos*], of, or having the nature of, a sycophant.
syc·o·phan·ti·cal (sik′ə-fan′ti-k′l), *adj.* sycophantic.
sy·co·sis (sī-kō′sis), *n.* [Mod. L.; Gr. *sykōsis* < *sykon,* fig], a chronic disease of the hair follicles, especially of the beard, caused by certain staphylococci and characterized by the formation of papules and pustules.
Syd·ney (sid′ni), *n.* seaport and capital of New South Wales, Australia: pop., 1,484,000 (1947).
Syd·ney (sid′ni), a masculine name: see **Sidney.**
Sy·e·ne (sī-ē′nē), *n.* Aswan, city in Egypt: ancient name.
sy·e·nite (sī′ə-nīt′), *n.* [Fr. *syénite* < L. *Syenites* (*lapis*), Syenite (stone) < *Syene* < Gr. *Syēnē,* Syene], a kind of gray, igneous rock containing feldspar, hornblende, and some silicates.
sy·e·nit·ic (sī′ə-nit′ik), *adj.* of or like syenite.
syl- (sil), see **syn-.**
syl·la·bar·y (sil′ə-ber′i), *n.* [*pl.* SYLLABARIES (-iz)], [Mod. L. *syllabarium* < L. *syllaba;* see SYLLABLE], 1. a set or table of syllables. 2. a system of written characters representing spoken syllables rather than individual sounds.
syl·la·bi (sil′ə-bī′), *n.* alternative plural of **syllabus.**
syl·lab·ic (si-lab′ik), *adj.* [Mod. L. *syllabicus;* Gr. *syllabikos*], 1. of a syllable or syllables. 2. designating a consonant that in itself forms a syllable with no appreciable vowel sound, as the *l* in *tattle* (tat′l). 3. pronounced distinctly, syllable by syllable. 4. designating a form of verse arranged according to the number of syllables per line rather than by rhythm or accent. *n.* a syllabic sound; sonant.
syl·lab·i·cal·ly (si-lab′i-k′l-i, si-lab′ik-li), *adv.* syllable by syllable; by syllables.
syl·lab·i·cate (si-lab′i-kāt′), *v.t.* [SYLLABICATED (-id), SYLLABICATING], [< *syllabication*], to syllabify.
syl·lab·i·ca·tion (si-lab′i-kā′shən), *n.* [ML. *syllabicatio*], syllabification.
syl·lab·i·fi·ca·tion (si-lab′ə-fi-kā′shən), *n.* [< *syllabify*], formation of or division into syllables.
syl·lab·i·fy (si-lab′ə-fī′), *v.t.* [SYLLABIFIED (-fīd′), SYLLABIFYING], [ML. *syllabificare* < L. *syllaba,* a syllable + *facere,* to make], to form or divide into syllables; syllabicate.
syl·la·bism (sil′ə-biz′m), *n.* [< L. *syllaba* (see SYLLABLE); + *-ism*], 1. the use of syllabic characters, rather than letters, in writing. 2. division into syllables.
syl·la·bize (sil′ə-bīz′), *v.t.* [SYLLABIZED (-bīzd′), SYLLABIZING], [ML. *syllabizare;* Gr. *syllabizein* < *syllabē;* see SYLLABLE], to syllabify.
syl·la·ble (sil′ə-b′l), *n.* [ME. *sillable;* OFr. *sillabe;* L. *syllaba;* Gr. *syllabē,* a syllable, lit., that which holds together < *syn-,* together + *lambanein,* to hold], 1. a word or part of a word pronounced with a single, uninterrupted sounding of the voice; unit of pronunciation, consisting of a single sound of great sonority (usually a vowel) and generally one or more sounds of lesser sonority (usually consonants). 2. one or more letters or symbols written to represent, more or less, a spoken syllable. In this dictionary, the syllables of entry words are separated by centered dots and do not always correspond to the syllables in speaking. 3. the least bit of expression; slightest detail: as, don't mention a *syllable* of this. *v.t. & v.i.* [SYLLABLED (-b′ld), SYLLABLING], to pronounce in or as in syllables.
syl·la·bub (sil′ə-bub′), *n.* a sillabub.
syl·la·bus (sil′ə-bəs), *n.* [*pl.* SYLLABUSES (-iz), SYLLABI (-bī′)], [Mod. L. < *syllabas* in a 15th-c. edition of Cicero, a misprint for *sittybas,* pl. of *sittyba,* a list < Gr. *syttyba,* piece of parchment used as a label], 1. a summary or outline containing the main points, especially of a course of study. 2. in *law,* notes preceding and explaining the decision in the written report of a trial.
syl·lep·sis (si-lep′sis), *n.* [*pl.* SYLLEPSES (-sēz)], [L.; Gr. *syllēpsis,* a putting together < *syllambanein,* to take together, lay hold of], a grammatical construction in which a single word is used to modify or govern syntactically two or more words in the same sentence, though it can grammatically agree with only one of them. Example: Either they or I am wrong.
syl·lep·tic (si-lep′tik), *adj.* [Gr. *syllēptikos*], of, having the nature of, or involving syllepsis.
syl·lo·gism (sil′ə-jiz′m), *n.* [ME. *silogime;* OFr. *silogime, sillogisme;* L. *syllogismus;* Gr. *syllogismos,* a reckoning together < *syllogizesthai,* to reckon together, sum up < *syn-* together + *logizesthai,* to reason < *logos,* a word], 1. an argument or form of reasoning in which two statements or premises are made and a logical conclusion drawn from them. Example: All mammals are warm-blooded (*major premise*); whales are mammals (*minor premise*); therefore, whales are warm-blooded (*conclusion*). 2. reasoning from the general to the particular; deductive logic. 3. subtle, tricky, or specious reasoning.
syl·lo·gis·tic (sil′ə-jis′tik), *adj.* of, like, using, or consisting of syllogisms. *n.* reasoning by syllogisms.
syl·lo·gis·ti·cal (sil′ə-jis′ti-k′l), *adj.* syllogistic.
syl·lo·gize (sil′ə-jīz′), *v.i. & v.t.* [SYLLOGIZED (-jīzd′), SYLLOGIZING], [ME. *sylogysen;* OFr. *silogiser;* ML. *syllogizare*], to reason or infer by use of syllogisms.
sylph (silf), *n.* [< Mod. L. *sylphes,* pl.; ? coined (by Paracelsus) < L. *sylvestris,* of a forest + *nympha,* nymph], 1. in Paracelsus' system, any of a class of mortal, but soulless, beings supposed to inhabit the air. 2. a slender, graceful woman or girl.
sylph·id (sil′fid), *n.* [Fr. *sylphide;* see SYLPH & -ID], a small or young sylph.

sylph·id·ine (sil′fi-din, sil′fi-dīn′), *adj.* of or like a sylphid.
sylph·like (silf′līk′), *adj.* like a sylph; slender; graceful.
syl·va (sil′və), *n.* [*pl.* SYLVAS (-vəz), SYLVAE (-vē)], silva.
Syl·van (sil′vən), a masculine name: also spelled **Silvan**: see **Sylvanus.**
syl·van (sil′vən), *adj.* [< Fr. or L.; Fr. *sylvain;* L. *silvanus* < *silva, sylva,* a wood], 1. of or characteristic of the woods or forest. 2. living, found, or carried on in the woods or forest. 3. wooded. *n.* 1. one who lives in the woods. 2. a deity or spirit of the woods. Also spelled **silvan.**
syl·van·ite (sil′vən-īt′), *n.* [< Tran*sylvan*ia (where first found) + *-ite*], a gray or silvery crystalline telluride of gold and silver, $AgAuTe_4$.
Syl·va·nus (sil-vā′nəs), [L. *Silvanus, Sylvanus;* see SYLVAN (woody)], a masculine name: variant, *Sylvan;* feminine, *Sylvia:* also spelled **Silvanus.**
Syl·ves·ter (sil-ves′tẽr), [L. *Silvester* < *silvester, silvestris,* of a wood or forest < *silva,* a wood], a masculine name: also spelled **Silvester.**
Syl·vi·a (sil′vi-ə), [L. *Silvia* < *silva,* a wood], a feminine name: diminutives, *Syl, Sylvie:* also spelled **Silvia.**
syl·vi·cul·ture (sil′vi-kul′chẽr), *n.* silviculture.
syl·vin, syl·vine (sil′vin), *n.* sylvite.
syl·vite (sil′vīt), *n.* [< Mod. L. *sal digestivus sylvii,* old name of the salt (prob. after Franz de la Boë *Sylvius,* 1614–1672, physician and professor of medicine at Leyden); + *-ite*], native potassium chloride, KCl, occurring in crystalline masses and used as a fertilizer.
sym- (sim), see **syn-.**
sym., 1. symbol. 2. symphony.
sym·bi·ont (sim′bī-ont′, sim′bi-ont′), *n.* [< Gr. *symbiountos,* ppr. of *symbioun;* see SYMBIOSIS], an organism living in a state of symbiosis.
sym·bi·o·sis (sim′bī-ō′sis, sim′bi-ō′sis), *n.* [Mod. L.; Gr. *symbiōsis* < *symbioun,* to live together < *syn-,* together + *bioun,* to live], in *biology,* the living together of two dissimilar organisms in close association or union, especially where this is advantageous to both, as distinguished from parasitism.
sym·bi·ot·ic (sim′bī-ot′ik, sim′bi-ot′ik), *adj.* [Gr. *symbiōtikos*], of or characterized by symbiosis.
sym·bi·ot·i·cal (sim′bī-ot′i-k′l, sim′bi-ot′i-k′l), *adj.* symbiotic.
sym·bol (sim′b′l), *n.* [< Fr. & L.; Fr. *symbole;* L. *symbolus, symbolum;* Gr. *symbolon,* token, pledge, sign by which one infers a thing < *symballein,* to throw together, compare < *syn-,* together + *ballein,* to throw], 1. something that stands for or represents another thing; especially, an object used to represent something abstract; emblem: as, the dove is a *symbol* of peace, the cross is the *symbol* of Christianity. 2. a written or printed mark, letter, abbreviation, etc. standing for an object, quality, process, quantity, etc., as in music, mathematics, or chemistry. 3. in *psychoanalysis,* an act or object representing an unconscious desire that has been repressed. *v.t.* to symbolize. Abbreviated **sym.**
ym·bol·ic (sim-bol′ik), *adj.* [LL. *symbolicus;* Gr. *symbolikos*], 1. of or expressed in a symbol or symbols. 2. that serves as a symbol (*of* something). 3. using symbols; characterized by symbolism.
ym·bol·i·cal (sim-bol′i-k′l), *adj.* symbolic.
ym·bol·i·cal·ly (sim-bol′i-k′l-i, sim-bol′ik-li), *adv.* in a symbolic manner; by means of a symbol or symbols.
ym·bol·ism (sim′b′l-iz′m), *n.* 1. the representation of things by use of symbols, especially in fine art or literature. 2. a system of symbols. 3. symbolic meaning. 4. a group of symbolists, as in art or literature. 5. the theories or practices of such a group.
ym·bol·ist (sim′b′l-ist), *n.* 1. a person who uses symbols. 2. a person who practices symbolism in representing ideas, etc., especially in fine art or literature; specifically, any of a group of French and Belgian writers and artists of the late 19th century who rejected realism and tried to express ideas, emotions, and attitudes by the use of symbolic words, figures, objects, etc. 3. a person who studies or is expert in interpreting symbols or symbolism. 4. in *theology,* a person who regards the Eucharist as merely symbolical and denies the doctrine of transubstantiation.
ym·bol·is·tic (sim′b′l-is′tik), *adj.* of or characteristic of symbolism or symbolists.
ym·bol·i·za·tion (sim′b′l-i-zā′shən, sim′b′l-ī-zā′shən), *n.* a symbolizing or being symbolized.
ym·bol·ize (sim′b′l-īz′), *v.t.* [SYMBOLIZED (-īzd′), SYMBOLIZING], [Fr. *symboliser;* Mod. L. *symbolizare*], 1. to be a symbol of; typify; stand for. 2. to represent by a symbol or symbols. 3. to make into a symbol; treat as a symbol. *v.i.* to use symbols.
ym·bol·o·gy (sim-bol′ə-ji), *n.* [< *symbol* + *-logy*], 1. the study or interpretation of symbols. 2. representation or expression by means of symbols; symbolism.
ym·met·al·lism (sim-met″l-iz′m), *n.* [< *sym-* + *metal* + *-ism*], a system of coinage based on a unit of two or more metals in combination, each of a specified minimum weight.
sym·met·ric (si-met′rik), *adj.* symmetrical.
sym·met·ri·cal (si-met′ri-k′l), *adj.* [< *symmetry*], having or showing symmetry, or correspondence in form, size, or arrangement of parts; specifically, *a)* in *botany,* that can be divided into similar parts by a plane passing through the center; also, having the same number of parts in each whorl of leaves: said of a flower. *b)* in *chemistry,* exhibiting a regular repeated pattern of atoms in the structural formula; specifically, designating a compound (benzene derivative) in which substitution takes place at the alternate carbon atoms. *c)* in *mathematics & logic,* designating an equation, relation, etc. whose terms can be interchanged without affecting its validity. *d)* in *medicine,* affecting corresponding parts of the body simultaneously in the same way: said of a disease, etc.
sym·met·ri·cal·ly (si-met′ri-k′l-i, si-met′rik-li), *adv.* in a symmetrical manner.
sym·me·tri·za·tion (sim′ə-tri-zā′shən, sim′ə-trī-zā′shən), *n.* a symmetrizing or being symmetrized.
sym·me·trize (sim′ə-trīz′), *v.t.* [SYMMETRIZED (-trīzd′), SYMMETRIZING], to make symmetrical.
sym·me·try (sim′ə-tri), *n.* [*pl.* SYMMETRIES (-triz)], [< Fr. or L.; obs. Fr. *symmetrie* (now *symétrie*); L. *symmetria;* Gr. *symmetria* < *symmetros,* measured together < *syn-,* together + *metron,* a measure], 1. similarity of form or arrangement on either side of a dividing line or plane; correspondence of opposite parts in size, shape, and position; condition of being symmetrical: an attribute of the whole or of the parts of which it is composed. 2. excellence or beauty of form or proportion as a result of such correspondence.
SYN.—**symmetry,** with reference to the interrelation of parts to form an aesthetically pleasing whole, strictly implies correspondence in the form, size, arrangement, etc. of parts on either side of a median line or plane; **proportion** implies a gracefulness that results from the measured fitness in size or arrangement of parts to each other or to the whole; **harmony** implies such agreement or proportionate arrangement of parts in size, color, form, etc. as to make a pleasing impression; **balance** suggests the offsetting or contrasting of parts so as to produce an aesthetic equilibrium in the whole.
Sym·onds, John Ad·ding·ton (ad′iŋ-tən sim′ənz, sim′əndz), 1840–1893; English poet and writer.
Sy·mons, Arthur (sī′mənz), 1865–1945; English poet and critic, born in Wales.
sym·pa·thet·ic (sim′pə-thet′ik), *adj.* [Mod. L. *sympatheticus;* Gr. *sympathētikos* < *sympatheia;* see SYMPATHY], 1. of, expressing, resulting from, feeling, or showing sympathy; sympathizing. 2. in agreement with one's tastes, mood, feelings, disposition, etc.; congenial. 3. [Colloq.], showing favor, approval, or agreement: as, he was *sympathetic* to our plan. 4. in *anatomy & physiology,* designating or of that part of the autonomic nervous system whose nerves originate in the lumbar and thoracic regions of the spinal cord and whose functions include the innervation of smooth muscles, heart muscle, and glands: cf. **parasympathetic.** 5. in *physics & acoustics,* caused by vibrations transmitted from a neighboring vibrating body: said of vibrations, sound, etc. —*SYN.* see **tender.**
sym·pa·thet·i·cal·ly (sim′pə-thet′i-k′l-i, sim′pə-thet′ik-li), *adv.* in a sympathetic manner.
sympathetic ink, invisible ink.
sym·pa·thize (sim′pə-thīz′), *v.i.* [SYMPATHIZED (-thīzd′), SYMPATHIZING], [Fr. *sympathiser*], 1. to share or understand the feelings or ideas of another; be in sympathy. 2. to feel or express sympathy, especially in pity or compassion; commiserate (*with* someone or something). 3. to be in harmony or accord.
sym·pa·thy (sim′pə-thi), *n.* [*pl.* SYMPATHIES (-thiz)], [L. *sympathia;* Gr. *sympatheia* < *syn-,* together + *pathos,* feeling], 1. sameness of feeling; affinity between persons or of one person for another. 2. an action or response arising from this. 3. agreement in qualities; harmony; accord. 4. a mutual liking or understanding arising from sameness of feeling. 5. the entering into or ability to enter into another person's mental state, feelings, emotions, etc.; especially, pity or compassion for another's trouble, suffering, etc. 6. in *physics,* a relation or harmony between bodies of such a nature that vibrations in one cause sympathetic vibrations in the other or others. 7. in *physiology,* a relation between parts of the body of such a nature that a disorder, pain, etc. in one induces a similar effect in another. —*SYN.* see **pity.**
sympathy (or **sympathetic**) **strike,** a strike by a group of workers in support of another group of workers who are on strike.
sym·pet·al·ous (sim-pet′'l-əs), *adj.* [*sym-* + *petalous*], having the petals united; gamopetalous.
sym·phon·ic (sim-fon′ik), *adj.* [< *symphony* + *-ic*], 1. of, or having the nature of, a symphony. 2. of or

having to do with harmony of sound. 3. having a similar sound or sounds.

symphonic poem, an extended musical composition for full symphony orchestra, usually in one movement, programmatic in nature, and freer in form than the symphony: also called *tone poem.*

sym·pho·ni·ous (sim-fō′ni-əs), *adj.* [< L. *symphonia,* harmony (see SYMPHONY); + *-ous*], harmonious.

sym·pho·nize (sim′fə-nīz′), *v.t. & v.i.* [SYMPHONIZED (-nīzd′), SYMPHONIZING], [see SYMPHONY], to harmonize.

sym·pho·ny (sim′fə-ni), *n.* [*pl.* SYMPHONIES (-niz)], [ME. *symfonye;* OFr. *simphonie;* L. *symphonia;* Gr. *symphōnia* < *syn-,* together + *phōnē,* a sound], 1. harmony of sounds especially of instruments. 2. harmony of any kind, especially of color. 3. anything, as a picture, characterized by harmonious composition. 4. in *music,* *a)* an extended composition in sonata form for full orchestra, having several (usually four) movements related in subject, but varying in form and execution. *b)* an instrumental passage in a composition that is largely vocal or choral. *c)* a symphony orchestra. *d)* [Colloq.], a symphony concert. Abbreviated **sym.**

symphony orchestra, a large orchestra for playing symphonic works, composed of string, wind, and percussion sections: distinguished from *band.*

sym·phy·sis (sim′fə-sis), *n.* [*pl.* SYMPHYSES (-sēz′)], [Mod. L.; Gr. *symphysis,* a growing together < *syn-,* with + *phyein,* to grow], a growing together; fusing; specifically, 1. in *anatomy & zoology, a)* the growing together of bones originally separate, as of the two halves of the lower jaw or the two pubic bones. *b)* the line of junction of such bones. 2. in *botany,* the growing together of similar parts of a plant; coalescence.

sym·po·di·um (sim-pō′di-əm), *n.* [*pl.* SYMPODIA (-ə)], [Mod. L.; see SYM- & -PODIUM], in *botany,* a stem made up of a series of branches growing on each other, giving the effect of a simple stem.

sym·po·si·ac (sim-pō′zi-ak′), *adj.* [L. *symposiaca,* neut. pl. of *symposiacus,* belonging to a banquet, convivial; Gr. *symposiakos*], of, having the nature of, or appropriate to a symposium. *n.* a symposium.

sym·po·si·arch (sim-pō′zi-ärk′), *n.* [Gr. *symposiarchos,* master of a feast; see SYMPOSIUM & -ARCH], 1. the master or director of an ancient Greek symposium; hence, 2. a toastmaster.

sym·po·si·um (sim-pō′zi-əm), *n.* [*pl.* SYMPOSIUMS (-əmz), SYMPOSIA (-ə)], [L.; Gr. *symposion* < *syn-,* together + *posis,* a drinking], 1. in ancient Greece, an entertainment characterized by drinking, music, and intellectual discussion; hence, 2. any meeting or social gathering at which ideas are freely exchanged. 3. a conference organized for the discussion of some particular subject. 4. a collection of opinions or essays on a given subject.

symp·tom (simp′təm), *n.* [ME. *symthoma* < Gr. *symptōma,* anything that has befallen one, casualty < *sympiptein,* to fall together, happen < *syn-,* together + *piptein,* to fall; Mod. Eng. modified after Fr. *symptôme*], any circumstance, event, or condition that accompanies something and indicates its existence or occurrence; sign; indication; specifically, in *medicine,* any condition accompanying or resulting from a disease and serving as an aid in diagnosis. —***SYN.*** see **sign.**

symp·to·mat·ic (simp′tə-mat′ik), *adj.* [Fr. *symptomatique;* Gr. *symptōmatikos*], 1. of or having to do with symptoms. 2. that constitutes a symptom (*of* something, especially disease). 3. in accordance with symptoms: as, a *symptomatic* treatment.

symp·to·mat·i·cal (simp′tə-mat′i-k′l), *adj.* symptomatic.

symp·to·mat·i·cal·ly (simp′tə-mat′i-k′l-i, simp′tə-mat′ik-li), *adv.* with regard to symptoms.

symp·tom·a·tol·o·gy (simp′təm-ə-tol′ə-ji), *n.* [Mod. L. *symptomatologia* < Gr. *symptōma,* a symptom + *-logia,* -logy], the branch of medicine dealing with the symptoms of diseases; semeiology.

syn- (sin), [< Gr. *syn,* with], a prefix meaning *with, together with, at the same time, by means of,* as in *synagogue, synapse*: *syn-* assimilates to *syl-* before *l,* as in *syllogism; sym-* before *m, p, b,* as in *symbiosis; sys-* before *s* and before an aspirate *h,* as in *systole, system.*

syn., 1. synonym. 2. synonymous. 3. synonymy.

syn·aer·e·sis (si-ner′ə-sis), *n.* syneresis.

syn·aes·the·si·a (sin′əs-thē′zhə, sin′əs-thē′zhi-ə), *n.* synesthesia.

syn·a·gog·i·cal (sin′ə-goj′i-k′l), *adj.* of a synagogue.

syn·a·gogue (sin′ə-gôg′, sin′ə-gog′), *n.* [ME. & OFr. *sinagoge;* LL. *synagoga;* Gr. *synagōgē,* a bringing together, assembly < *synagein,* to bring together < *syn-* together + *agein,* to bring, drive], 1. an assembly of Jews for worship and religious study. 2. a building or place used by Jews for worship and religious study. 3. the Jewish religion as organized in such local congregations.

syn·a·loe·pha, syn·a·le·pha (sin′ə-lē′fə), *n.* [L. *synaloepha;* Gr. *synaloiphē,* lit., a melting together < *syn-,* together + *aleiphein,* to smear, anoint], the contraction into one syllable of two adjacent vowels, usually by elision. Example: *th' eagle* for *the eagle.*

syn·apse (si-naps′), *n.* [Mod. L. *synapsis;* Gr. *synapsis,* a union, joining], the point of contact between adjacent neurons, where nerve impulses are transmitted from one to the other.

syn·ap·sis (si-nap′sis), *n.* [*pl.* SYNAPSES (-sēz)], [Mod. L.; Gr. *synapsis,* a junction, connection; *syn-,* together + *apsis,* a joining < *aptein,* to join], 1. in *genetics,* the conjugation of homologous maternal and paternal paired chromosomes in the early stages of meiosis. 2. in *physiology,* a synapse.

syn·ap·tic (si-nap′tik), *adj.* of synapsis.

syn·ar·thro·di·a (sin′är-thrō′di-ə), *n.* [*pl.* SYNARTHRODIAE (-ē′)], synarthrosis.

syn·ar·thro·sis (sin′är-thrō′sis), *n.* [*pl.* SYNARTHROSES (-sēz)], [Mod. L.; Gr. *synarthrōsis,* a being jointed together < *synarthroun,* to link together < *syn-,* with + *arthron,* a joint], in *anatomy,* any of various immovable articulations, or joints.

syn·carp (sin′kärp), *n.* [Mod. L. *syncarpium;* see SYN- & -CARP], a fruit composed of the ripened pistils of one or more flowers, as a blackberry; collective fruit.

syn·car·pous (sin-kär′pəs), *adj.* 1. composed of two or more pistils growing together. 2. of a syncarp.

syn·chro·mesh (siŋ′krə-mesh′), *adj.* [*synchr*onized + *mesh*], in motor vehicles, designating or employing a device by which synchronized shifting can be effected. *n.* 1. a synchromesh gear system. 2. any gear in such a system.

syn·chro·nal (siŋ′krə-nəl), *adj.* [< LL. *synchronus* (see SYNCHRONOUS); + *-al*], synchronous.

syn·chron·ic (sin-kron′ik, siŋ-kron′ik), *adj.* synchronous.

syn·chron·i·cal (sin-kron′i-k′l, siŋ-kron′i-k′l), *adj.* synchronic.

syn·chro·nism (siŋ′krə-niz′m), *n.* [Mod. L. *synchronismus;* Gr. *synchronismos* < *synchronos,* contemporaneous; *syn-,* together + *chronos,* time], 1. the fact or state of being synchronous; simultaneous occurrence. 2. a chronological listing of persons or events in history.

syn·chro·nis·tic (siŋ′krə-nis′tik), *adj.* synchronous.

syn·chro·nis·ti·cal (siŋ′krə-nis′ti-k′l), *adj.* synchronistic.

syn·chro·ni·za·tion (siŋ′krə-ni-zā′shən, siŋ′krə-nī-zā′shən), *n.* a synchronizing or being synchronized.

syn·chro·nize (siŋ′krə-nīz′), *v.i.* [SYNCHRONIZED (-nīzd′), SYNCHRONIZING], [Gr. *synchronizein* < *synchronos,* contemporary; *syn-,* together + *chronos,* time], to move or occur at the same time or rate; be synchronous. *v.t.* 1. to cause to agree in rate or speed; regulate (clocks, a flashgun and camera shutter, etc.) so as to make synchronous. 2. to assign (events, etc.) to the same date or period; represent as or show to be coincident or simultaneous. 3. in *motion pictures, a)* to add or adjust (sound effects or dialogue) so as to coincide with the action of a picture. *b)* to add or adjust such sound effects or dialogue to (a picture).

synchronized shifting, a type of gear shifting in motor vehicles, in which the gears to be meshed are automatically brought to the same speed of rotation before the shift is completed.

syn·chron·o·scope (sin-kron′ə-skōp′, siŋ-kron′ə-skōp′), *n.* a synchroscope.

syn·chro·nous (siŋ′krə-nəs), *adj.* [LL. *synchronus;* Gr. *synchronos;* see SYNCHRONIZE], 1. happening at the same time; occurring together; simultaneous. 2. having the same period between movements, occurrences, etc. having the same rate and phase, as vibrations. —***SYN.*** see **contemporary.**

synchronous machine, an alternating-current motor, generator, or converter whose normal operating speed is exactly proportional to the frequency of the current by which it is supplied.

synchronous speed, a fixed speed for an alternating-current machine, determined by the frequency of the current by which it is supplied.

syn·chro·scope (siŋ′krə-skōp′), *n.* [*synchro*nism + *-scope*], a device for indicating the degree of synchronism, as between two or more airplane engines also **synchronoscope.**

syn·chro·tron (siŋ′krə-tron′), *n.* [*synchr*onize + *elec*tron], a type of cyclotron for accelerating the velocities of charged particles, especially of electrons, through the use of a low-frequency magnetic field in combination with a high-frequency electrostatic field.

syn·clas·tic (sin-klas′tik, siŋ-klas′tik), *adj.* [*syn-* + Gr. *klastos,* broken], in *mathematics & physics,* having the same curvature in all directions at any given point said of a surface, as of a sphere: opposed to *anticlastic*

syn·cli·nal (sin-klī′n′l, siŋ′kli-n′l), *adj.* [< Gr. *synklinein,* to incline together; *syn-,* together + *klinein,* to incline], 1. sloping downward in opposite directions so as to meet. 2. of, formed by, or forming a syncline. *n.* a syncline.

syn·cline (siŋ′klīn), *n.* [see SYNCLINAL], in *geology,* a fold of stratified rock inclining upward in opposite directions from both sides of its axis: opposed to *anticline.*

syn·co·pate (siŋ′kə-pāt′), *v.t.* [SYNCOPATED (-id), SYNCOPATING], [< LL. *syncopatus,* pp. of *syncopare,* to swoon < *syncope;* see SYNCOPE], 1. to shorten (a word) by syncope. 2. in *music, a)* to begin (a tone) on an unaccented beat and continue it through the next accented beat, or to begin (a tone) on the last half of a beat and continue it through the first half of the following beat. *b)* to use such shifted accents in (a musical composition, passage, etc.).

syn·co·pa·tion (siŋ'kə-pā'shən), *n.* 1. a syncopating or being syncopated. 2. syncopated music. 3. in *grammar,* syncope.

SYNCOPATION

syn·co·pa·tor (siŋ'kə-pā'-tẽr), *n.* a person who syncopates.

syn·co·pe (siŋ'kə-pi, sin'-kə-pē'), *n.* [LL.; Gr. *synkopē* < *syn-,* together + *koptein,* to cut; ME. had *syncopis, syncopin,* via OFr. *sincopin*], 1. the dropping of sounds or letters from the middle of a word, as in *Wooster* for *Worcester.* 2. a fainting, or loss of consciousness, caused by a temporary deficiency of blood supply to the brain. 3. syncopation.

syn·cret·ic (sin-kret'ik, siŋ-kret'ik), *adj.* syncretistic.

syn·cre·tism (siŋ'krə-tiz'm), *n.* [Fr. *syncrétisme;* Mod.L. *syncretismus;* Gr. *synkrētismos,* union of two parties against a third < *synkrētizein,* to combine], 1. the combination or reconciliation of differing beliefs in religion, philosophy, etc., or an attempt to effect such compromise. 2. in *philology,* the merging into one of two or more differently inflected grammatical categories.

syn·cre·tis·tic (siŋ'krə-tis'tik), *adj.* of or characterized by syncretism.

syn·cre·tize (siŋ'krə-tīz'), *v.t. & v.i.* [SYNCRETIZED (-tīzd'), SYNCRETIZING], [Mod. L. *syncretizare;* Gr. *synkrētizein;* see SYNCRETISM], to combine or reconcile.

syn·cri·sis (siŋ'kri-sis), *n.* [Mod. L.; Gr. *synkrisis; syn-,* together + *krisis,* a choosing < *krinein,* to decide, judge], in *rhetoric,* a figure of speech in which opposite things are compared; contrast.

syn·dac·tyl, syn·dac·tyle (sin-dak'til), *adj.* [< *syn-* + Gr. *-daktylos,* fingered < *daktylos,* finger, toe], having two or more digits united, as by webbing. *n.* a syndactyl animal or bird, or, abnormally, person.

syn·dac·tyl·ism (sin-dak'til-iz'm), *n.* the condition of being syndactyl.

syn·des·mo·sis (sin'des-mō'sis), *n.* [*pl.* SYNDESMOSES (-sēz)], [Mod. L. < Gr. *syndesmos,* ligament; + *-osis*], the joining of bones by ligaments or membranes.

syn·des·mot·ic (sin'des-mot'ik), *adj.* of, or having the nature of, syndesmosis.

syn·det·ic (sin-det'ik), *adj.* [Gr. *syndetikos* < *syndein,* to tie up; *syn-,* together + *dein,* to bind], connecting or connected by means of conjunctions; connective.

syn·det·i·cal (sin-det'i-k'l), *adj.* syndetic.

syn·dic (sin'dik), *n.* [Fr.; LL. *syndicus,* representative of a corporation; Gr. *syndikos,* helping in a court of justice; hence, defendant's advocate, judge < *syn-,* together + *dikē,* justice], 1. the business agent or manager of a corporation, especially of a university. 2. variously, any of certain government officials; especially, a civil magistrate or the like.

syn·di·cal (sin'di-k'l), *adj.* of a syndic.

syn·di·cal·ism (sin'di-k'l-iz'm), *n.* [Fr. *syndicalisme* < *syndical,* of a syndic or labor union (*chambre syndicale*) < *syndic;* see SYNDIC], a theory and movement of trade unionism, originating in France, in which all means of production and distribution would be brought under the control of federations of labor unions by the use of direct action, such as general strikes.

syn·di·cal·is·tic (sin'di-k'l-is'tik), *adj.* of, like, or characteristic of syndicalism.

syn·di·cate (sin'di-kit; *for v.,* sin'di-kāt'), *n.* [Fr. *syndicat;* ML. *syndicatus* < *syndicus;* see SYNDIC], 1. a group or council of syndics. 2. an association of bankers, corporations, etc. formed to carry out some financial project requiring much capital, especially to gain control of the market in a particular commodity. 3. an organization that sells special articles or features to a number of different newspapers for simultaneous publication. *v.t.* [SYNDICATED (-id), SYNDICATING], [< ML. *syndicatus,* pp. of *syndicare* < LL. *syndicus;* see SYNDIC], 1. to manage as or form into a syndicate. 2. to sell (an article, feature, etc.) through a syndicate for simultaneous publication in a number of newspapers. *v.i.* to form a syndicate. —*SYN.* see **monopoly.**

syn·di·ca·tion (sin'di-kā'shən), *n.* a syndicating or being syndicated.

syn·dro·me (sin'drōm, sin'drə-mē'), *n.* [Mod. L.; Gr. *syndromē* < *syn-,* with + *dramein,* to run], a number of symptoms occurring together and characterizing a specific disease.

syne (sīn), *adv., conj., prep.* [Scot. < ME. *sithen;* see SINCE], [Scot.], since; ago.

syn·ec·do·che (si-nek'də-ki), *n.* [ME. *synodoche;* L. < Gr. *synekdochē,* lit., a receiving together < *synekdechesthai,* to receive together; *syn-,* together + *ekdechesthai,* to receive], a figure of speech in which a part or individual is used for a whole or class, or the reverse of this. Example: *bread* for *food,* or *the army* for *a soldier.*

syn·e·cious (si-nē'shəs), *adj.* synoecious.

syn·er·e·sis (si-ner'ə-sis), *n.* [Mod. L.; Gr. *synairesis,* a taking or drawing together < *syn-,* together + *hairein,* to take], 1. the contraction of two consecutive vowels or syllables into one syllable, especially so as to form a diphthong: opposed to *dieresis.* 2. synizesis. Also spelled **synaeresis.**

syn·er·get·ic (sin'ẽr-jet'ik), *adj.* [Gr. *synergētikos* < *synergein,* to work together < *syn-,* together + *ergon,* work], working together; co-operating: as, *synergetic* muscles.

syn·er·gic (si-nũr'jik), *adj.* of or characterized by synergy.

syn·er·gism (sin'ẽr-jiz'm), *n.* [Mod. L. *synergismus* < Gr. *synergos,* working together], 1. the simultaneous action of separate agencies which, together, have greater total effect than the sum of their individual effects: said especially of drugs. 2. in *theology,* the doctrine that the human will co-operates with divine grace in effecting regeneration.

syn·er·gist (sin'ẽr-jist), *n.* 1. a synergetic organ, muscle, drug, etc. 2. in *theology,* a believer in synergism.

syn·er·gis·tic (sin'ẽr-jis'tik), *adj.* synergetic.

syn·er·gy (sin'ẽr-ji), *n.* [Gr. *synergia,* joint work < *synergein,* to work together < *syn-,* together + *ergon,* work], combined or cooperative action or force; specifically, in *medicine, a)* the combined or correlated action of different organs or parts of the body, as in performing complex movements. *b)* the combined or correlated action of two or more drugs.

syn·e·sis (sin'ə-sis), *n.* [Gr. *synesis,* sagacity, quick perception], grammatical construction which conforms to the meaning rather than to strict syntactical agreement or reference. Example: *Most* of the team *are* invalided.

syn·es·the·si·a (sin'əs-thē'zhə, sin'əs-thē'zhi-ə), *n.* [Mod. L. *synaesthesia* < Gr. *syn-,* together + *aisthēsis,* sensation], 1. in *physiology,* sensation felt in one part of the body when another part is stimulated. 2. in *psychology,* a process in which one type of stimulus produces a secondary, subjective sensation, as when a specific color evokes a specific smell sensation. Also spelled **synaesthesia.**

syn·gam·ic (sin-gam'ik, siŋ-gam'ik), *adj.* of or characteristic of syngamy.

syn·ga·mous (siŋ'gə-məs), *adj.* syngamic.

syn·ga·my (siŋ'gə-mi), *n.* [*syn-* + *-gamy*], 1. sexual reproduction; union of male and female gametes to form a fertilized ovum. 2. conjugation.

Synge, John Mil·ling·ton (mil'iŋ-tən siŋ), 1871–1909; Irish dramatist and poet.

syn·gen·e·sis (sin-jen'ə-sis), *n.* [Mod. L.; see SYN- & -GENESIS], sexual reproduction.

syn·ge·net·ic (sin'jə-net'ik), *adj.* of or characteristic of syngenesis; reproduced sexually.

syn·i·ze·sis (sin'ə-zē'sis), *n.* [L.; Gr. *synizēsis* < *synizanein,* to sink in, collapse < *syn-,* with + *hizein,* to sit], 1. the contraction of two adjacent vowels into a single syllable, as in Latin, without forming a diphthong. 2. in *biology,* the massing of the chromatin in meiosis just before the maturation division.

syn·od (sin'əd), *n.* [ME. *sinod* (altered after Late OFr. *synode*) < ME. *sinoth;* AS. *synoth;* L. *synodus;* Gr. *synodos,* lit., a coming together < *syn-,* together + *hodos,* way], 1. a council of churches or church officials; ecclesiastical council. 2. any assembly or council.

syn·od·al (sin'əd-'l), *adj.* [LL. *synodalis*], of a synod.

syn·od·ic (si-nod'ik), *adj.* synodical.

syn·od·i·cal (si-nod'i-k'l), *adj.* [LL. *synodicus;* Gr. *synodikos* < *synodos;* see SYNOD], 1. synodal. 2. in *astronomy,* of or having to do with conjunction, especially with the interval between two successive conjunctions of the same bodies, as of a planet with the sun.

syn·od·i·cal·ly (si-nod'i-k'l-i, si-nod'ik-li), *adv.* in the manner of or by means of a synod.

syn·oe·cious (si-nē'shəs), *adj.* [< *syn-* + Gr. *oikos,* house; + *-ous*], in *botany,* having male and female organs in the same flower, as some composite plants, or in the same receptacle, as certain mosses.

syn·o·nym (sin'ə-nim), *n.* [Fr. *synonyme;* LL. *synonyma,* pl. of *synonymum* < Gr. *synōnymon,* of like meaning or like name < *syn-,* together + *onyma,* a name], 1. a word having the same or nearly the same meaning in one or more senses as another in the same language: opposed to *antonym.* 2. a metonym. 3. in *biology,* an incorrect or outmoded systemic name. Abbreviated **syn.**

syn·o·nym·ic (sin'ə-nim'ik), *adj.* of, using, or constituting a synonym or synonyms.

syn·o·nym·i·cal (sin'ə-nim'i-k'l), *adj.* synonymic.

syn·on·y·mies (si-non'ə-miz), *n.* plural of **synonymy.**

syn·o·nym·i·ty (sin'ə-nim'ə-ti), *n.* the state or fact of being synonymous; identity of nature or meaning.

syn·on·y·mize (si-non′ə-mīz′), *v.t.* [SYNONYMIZED (-mīzd′), SYNONYMIZING], to furnish a synonym or synonyms for (a word).

syn·on·y·mous (si-non′ə-məs), *adj.* [ML. *synonymus;* Gr. *synōnymos* < *syn-*, together + *onyma*, a name], of the same or nearly the same meaning: abbreviated **syn.**

syn·on·y·my (si-non′ə-mi), *n.* [*pl.* SYNONYMIES (-miz)], [LL. *synonymia;* Gr. *synōnymia*], 1. the study of synonyms. 2. a list or listing of synonyms. 3. *a)* the scientific names used in different nomenclature systems to designate the same species, etc. *b)* a list of such names. 4. the quality of being synonymous; identity or near identity of meaning. Abbreviated **syn.**

syn·op·sis (si-nop′sis), *n.* [*pl.* SYNOPSES (-sēz)], [LL.; Gr. *synopsis; syn-*, together + *opsis*, a sight], a statement giving a brief, general review or condensation; summary, as of a story. —***SYN.*** see **abridgment.**

syn·op·tic (si-nop′tik), *adj.* [Mod. L. *synopticus;* Gr. *synoptikos*], 1. of or constituting a synopsis; presenting a general view or summary. 2. giving an account from the same point of view: said especially [often S-] of the first three Gospels.

syn·op·ti·cal (si-nop′ti-k'l), *adj.* synoptic.

synoptic chart, a chart showing meteorological conditions over a region at a given time; weather map.

syn·o·vi·a (si-nō′vi-ə), *n.* [Mod. L.; coined by Paracelsus prob. < *syn-*, with + L. *ovum*, egg], the clear, albuminous lubricating fluid secreted by the membranes of joint cavities, tendon sheaths, etc.

syn·o·vi·al (si-nō′vi-əl), *adj.* of or secreting synovia.

syn·o·vi·tis (sin′ə-vī′tis), *n.* [see -ITIS], inflammation of a synovial membrane.

syn·sep·al·ous (sin-sep′'l-əs), *adj.* [*syn-* + *sepal* + *-ous*], having the sepals united; gamosepalous.

syn·tac·tic (sin-tak′tik), *adj.* syntactical.

syn·tac·ti·cal (sin-tak′ti-k'l), *adj.* [< Mod. L. *syntacticus* (Gr. *syntaktikos* < *syntaxis*); + *-al;* see SYNTAX], of or in accordance with the rules of syntax.

syn·tac·ti·cal·ly (sin-tak′ti-k'l-i, sin-tak′tik-li), *adv.* according to the rules of syntax.

syn·tax (sin′taks), *n.* [Fr. *syntaxe;* LL. *syntaxis;* Gr. *syntaxis* < *syntassein*, to join, put together; *syn-*, together + *tassein*, to arrange], 1. [Obs.], orderly or systematic arrangement. 2. *a)* in *grammar*, the arrangement of words as elements in a sentence to show their relationship; sentence structure. *b)* the branch of grammar dealing with this.

syn·the·sis (sin′thə-sis), *n.* [*pl.* SYNTHESES (-sēz′)], [L.; Gr. *synthesis* < *syn-*, together + *tithenai*, to place], 1. the putting together of parts or elements so as to form a whole: opposed to *analysis.* 2. a whole made up of parts or elements put together. 3. the formation of a complex chemical compound by the combining of two or more simpler compounds, elements, or radicals. 4. in *philosophy*, deductive reasoning, from the simple elements of thought into the complex whole, from cause to effect, from a principle to its application, etc.

syn·the·sist (sin′thə-sist), *n.* a person who uses synthesis or follows a synthetic method.

syn·the·size (sin′thə-sīz′), *v.t.* [SYNTHESIZED (-sīzd′), SYNTHESIZING], 1. to bring together into a whole by synthesis. 2. to form by bringing together separate parts. 3. to treat synthetically.

syn·thet·ic (sin-thet′ik), *adj.* [Fr. *synthétique;* Gr. *synthetikos*], 1. of, involving, or using synthesis: opposed to *analytic.* 2. produced by synthesis; specifically, produced by chemical synthesis, rather than of natural origin; hence, 3. artificial; not real or genuine: as, *synthetic* enthusiasm. 4. characterized by the use of inflectional adjuncts, or affixes, to express syntactical relationships: opposed to *analytical.* *n.* something synthetic; specifically, a substance produced by chemical synthesis. —***SYN.*** see **artificial.**

syn·thet·i·cal (sin-thet′i-k'l), *adj.* synthetic.

syn·thet·i·cal·ly (sin-thet′i-k'l-i, sin-thet′ik-li), *adv.* in a synthetic manner; through synthesis.

synthetic rubber, any of several substances resembling natural rubber, prepared by polymerization of butadiene, chloroprene, and other hydrocarbons.

syn·the·tize (sin′thə-tīz′), *v.t.* [SYNTHETIZED (-tīzd′), SYNTHETIZING], to synthesize.

syn·ton·ic (sin-ton′ik), *adj.* [< *syn-* + Gr. *tonos*, a tone; + *-ic*], in *radio*, of or having to do with resonance.

syn·to·ni·za·tion (sin′tə-ni-zā′shən, sin′tə-nī-zā′shən), *n.* the act or process of syntonizing.

syn·to·nize (sin′tə-nīz′), *v.t.* [SYNTONIZED (-nīzd′), SYNTONIZING], [see SYNTONIC & -IZE], to adjust (radio transmitters and receivers) in resonance with each other.

syn·to·ny (sin′tə-ni), *n.* [< *syntonic*], in *radio*, resonance.

sy·pher (sī′fẽr), *v.t.* [var. of *cipher*], to overlap the chamfered edges of (planks, etc.) so as to form a smooth joint.

syph·i·lis (sif′ə-lis), *n.* [Mod. L. < *Syphilis sive Morbus Gallicus*, title of a poem (1530) by Girolamo Fracastoro: so named after the hero *Syphilus*, a shepherd], an infectious venereal disease, caused by a spirochete and usually transmitted by sexual intercourse or acquired congenitally: if untreated, it usually passes through three stages, the first (*primary syphilis*) characterized by a hard chancre on the genitals or other point of inoculation, the second (*secondary syphilis*) by variable lesions of the skin and mucous membranes, and the third (*tertiary syphilis*) by the infection and disablement of bones, muscles, nerve tissue, etc.

syph·i·lit·ic (sif′ə-lit′ik), *adj.* [Mod. L. *syphiliticus*], of, caused by, or having syphilis. *n.* a syphilitic person.

syph·i·loid (sif′ə-loid′), *adj.* resembling syphilis.

syph·i·lol·o·gy (sif′ə-lol′ə-ji), *n.* the study and treatment of syphilis.

syph·i·lous (sif′ə-ləs), *adj.* syphilitic.

sy·phon (sī′fən), *n., v.i. & v.t.* siphon.

Syr., 1. Syria. 2. Syriac. 3. Syrian.

Syr·a·cuse (sêr′ə-kūs′, sêr′ə-kūz′), *n.* 1. a city in central New York: pop., 216,000. 2. *a)* an ancient city on the east coast of Sicily. *b)* a modern city on the same site: pop., 68,000: Italian name, *Siracusa.*

Syr Dar·ya (sêr där′yä), a river in the Soviet Union, in central Asia, flowing into Lake Aral: length, 1,300 mi.: ancient name, *Jaxartes.*

syr·ette (si-ret′), *n.* [*syringe* + *-ette*], an injection unit consisting of a small, collapsible tube fitted with a hypodermic needle and filled with a single dose of medication: a trade-mark (**Syrette**).

Syr·i·a (sêr′i-ə), *n.* 1. an ancient country in Asia, along the eastern coast of the Mediterranean. 2. a former territory comprising modern Syria and Lebanon: French mandate (1922–1941): also called *Levant States.* 3. a country in southwestern Asia, south of Turkey: a region of the United Arab Republic (1958–1961): area, 72,000 sq. mi.; pop., 4,421,000; capital, Damascus.

Syr·i·ac (sêr′i-ak′), *adj.* of Syria or its language. *n.* the ancient Aramaic language of Syria, spoken from the 3d century A.D. to the 13th.

Syr·i·an (sêr′i-ən), *adj.* of Syria, its people, their language, culture, etc. *n.* 1. a member of the Semitic people of Syria. 2. the modern Arabic dialect of the Syrians.

sy·rin·ga (sə-riŋ′gə), *n.* [Mod. L. < Gr. *syrinx, syringos*, a pipe, tube: said to be so called from the use of the plants for making pipes or pipestems], 1. any of a number of related plants of the olive family, with large, fragrant clusters of white, pink, red, purplish, or bluish flowers; lilac. 2. any of a group of ornamental shrubs of the saxifrage family, with white or creamy flowers; mock orange.

syr·inge (sə-rinj′, sir′inj), *n.* [ME. *siringe;* ML. *sirynga;* Gr. *syrinx, syringos*, a reed, pipe, tube], a device consisting of a narrow tube fitted at one end with a rubber bulb or piston by means of which a liquid can be drawn in and then ejected in a stream: used to inject fluids into the body, cleanse wounds, etc. *v.t.* [SYRINGED (-rinjd′, -injd), SYRINGING], to cleanse or inject by using a syringe.

sy·rin·ge·al (sə-rin′ji-əl), *adj.* of the syrinx.

sy·rin·go·my·e·li·a (sə-riŋ′gō-mī-ē′li-ə), *n.* [Mod. L. < Gr. *syrinx, syringos*, a pipe, tube + *myelos*, marrow], a chronic, progressive disease of the spinal cord, characterized by the formation of cavities filled with liquid in the spinal substance and occurring most frequently in young adults.

syr·inx (sir′iŋks), *n.* [*pl.* SYRINGES (sə-rin′jēz), SYRINXES (sir′iŋks-iz)], [Mod. L.; Gr. *syrinx*, a pipe], 1. the vocal organ of songbirds, located at the base of the trachea, the branching of the bronchi, or both. 2. a Panpipe. 3. the Eustachian tube.

syr·phi·an (sũr′fi-ən), *adj.* of the syrphus fly or its family. *n.* a syrphus fly.

syr·phid (sũr′fid), *adj. & n.* syrphian.

syr·phus fly (sũr′fəs), [Mod. L. *Syrphus*, name of the genus < Gr. *syrphos*, a gnat], any of a family of two winged flies resembling the hive bee: the larvae of some species feed on plant lice.

syr·up (sir′əp, sũr′əp), *n.* sirup.

sy·rup·y (sir′əp-i, sũr′əp-i), *adj.* sirupy.

sys·sar·co·sis (sis′är-kō′sis), *n.* [Mod. L.; Gr. *syssarkōsis*, a being overgrown with flesh < *syn-*, with + *sarx, sarkos*, flesh], the connection of two or more bones by means of muscle.

syst., system.

sys·tal·tic (sis-tal′tik), *adj.* [LL. *systalticus;* Gr. *systaltikos*, drawing together < *systellein*, to draw together < *syn-*, together + *stellein*, to send], characterized by, or capable of, alternate contraction and dilatation, as the action of the heart.

sys·tem (sis′təm), *n.* [LL. *systema;* Gr. *systēma, systēmatos* < *synistanai*, to place together < *syn-*, together + *histanai*, to set; cf. Fr. *système*], 1. a set or arrangement of things so related or connected as to form a unity or organic whole: as, a solar *system*, irrigation *system*, supply *system.* 2. the world or universe. 3. the body considered as a functioning organism: as, my *system* needs toning up. 4. a set of facts, principles, rules, etc. classified or arranged in a regular, orderly form so as to show a logical plan linking the various parts. 5. a method or plan of classification. 6. a regular, orderly way of doing something; order; method; regularity. 7. a number of bodily organs acting together to perform one of the main bodily functions: as, the circulatory *system*, di gestive *system.* 8. an arrangement of rocks showing evidence, as through fossils, of having been formed during a given geological period: as, the Devonian *system.* 9. a group of transportation lines under a common owner. 10. in *chemistry*, a group of substances in or approaching equilibrium: a system with two components is called binary, one with three, ternary, etc. —*SYN.* see **method.**

ys·tem·at·ic (sis'tə-mat'ik), *adj.* [Gr. *systēmatikos*], 1. forming or constituting a system. 2. based on or involving a system. 3. made or arranged according to a system, method, or plan; regular; orderly. 4. characterized by the use of method or orderly planning; methodical. 5. of or having to do with classification, especially in biology. —*SYN.* see **orderly.**

ys·tem·at·i·cal (sis'tə-mat'i-k'l), *adj.* systematic.

ys·tem·at·i·cal·ly (sis'tə-mat'i-k'l-i, sis'tə-mat'ik-li), *adv.* in a systematic manner; according to a system.

ys·tem·at·ics (sis'tə-mat'iks), *n.pl.* [construed as sing.], [see SYSTEMATIC & -ICS], the science or a method of classification.

ys·tem·a·tism (sis'təm-ə-tiz'm), *n.* the practice or process of systematizing.

ys·tem·a·tist (sis'təm-ə-tist), *n.* 1. a person who works according to a system. 2. a taxonomist.

ys·tem·a·ti·za·tion (sis'təm-ə-ti-zā'shən, sis'təm-ə-tī-zā'shən), *n.* a systematizing or being systematized.

ys·tem·a·tize (sis'tem-ə-tīz'), *v.t.* [SYSTEMATIZED (-tīzd'), SYSTEMATIZING], to make into a system; arrange according to a system; make systematic.

ys·tem·ic (sis-tem'ik), *adj.* of a system; specifically, in *physiology*, of or affecting the entire bodily system.

sys·tem·i·za·tion (sis'təm-i-zā'shən, sis'təm-ī-zā'shən), *n.* a systemizing or being systemized.

sys·tem·ize (sis'təm-īz'), *v.t.* [SYSTEMIZED (-īzd'), SYSTEMIZING], to systematize.

sys·to·le (sis'tə-lē'), *n.* [Mod. L.; Gr. *systolē* < *systellein*, to contract, shorten < *syn-*, together + *stellein*, to draw, put], 1. the usual rhythmic contraction of the heart, especially of the ventricles, following each dilatation (*diastole*), during which the blood is driven onward from the chambers. 2. in *Greek & Latin prosody*, the shortening of a naturally long syllable: opposed to *diastole.*

sys·tol·ic (sis-tol'ik), *adj.* of or characterized by systole.

syz·y·gy (siz'ə-ji), *n.* [*pl.* SYZYGIES (-jiz)], [LL. *syzygia;* Gr. *syzygia* < *syn-*, together + *zygon*, a yoke], 1. in *astronomy*, either of two opposing points in the orbit of a heavenly body, especially of the moon, at which it is in conjunction with or in opposition to the sun. 2. in *ancient prosody*, a group of two feet, as a dipody: sometimes restricted to a combination of different feet.

Sza·bad·ka (sä'bät-kä), *n.* Subotica: Hungarian name.

Szcze·cin (shche-tsēn'), *n.* Stettin: the Polish name.

Sze·chwan (se'chwän'; Chin. su'chwän'), *n.* a province of central China: area, 156,675 sq. mi.; pop., 47,108,000 (est. 1947); capital, Chengtu; chief city, Chungking.

Sze·ged (se'ged), *n.* a city in southern Hungary: pop., 137,000: German name, *Szegedin.*

Sze·ge·din (se'gə-din), *n.* Szeged: the German name.

Szom·bat·hely (sôm'bät-hā'), *n.* a city in western Hungary: pop., 38,000: German name, *Steinamanger.*

T

, t (tē), *n.* [*pl.* T's, t's, Ts, ts (tēz)], 1. the twentieth letter of the English alphabet: from the Greek *tau*, derived from the Hebrew *taw:* see **alphabet,** table. 2. the sound of T or t, usually a voiceless tongue-apex stop, IPA [t]. 3. a type or impression for T or t. 4. *a symbol for* the twentieth in a sequence or group (or the nineteenth if J is omitted). *adj.* 1. of T or t. 2. twentieth (or nineteenth if J is omitted) in a sequence or group.

(tē), *n.* 1. an object shaped like T. 2. a medieval Roman numeral for 160; with a superior bar (T̄), 160,000. *adj.* shaped like T.

to a T, to perfection; exactly.

, it: a contraction used with a verb initially, as in *twas*, or finally, as in *do't.*

-, in *chemistry*, triple bond.

, a suffix used to form past participles and adjectives derived from participles, as in *slept, gilt:* variant of *-ed.*

., 1. tablespoon; tablespoons. 2. Testament. 3. Tuesday. 4. Turkish.

., **t.,** 1. tenor. 2. territorial. 3. territory. 4. *tomus*, L.], volume. 5. ton; tons.

, 1. tare. 2. target. 3. teaspoon; teaspoons. 4. telephone. 5. temperature. 6. tempo. 7. *tempore*, L.], in the time (of). 8. tense. 9. time. 10. tome. 1. town(ship). 12. transit. 13. transitive. 14. troy.

a, in *chemistry*, tantalum.

aal (täl), *n.* [D., language, speech; akin to Eng. *tale*], the Dutch dialect spoken in South Africa; Afrikaans.

.b (tab) *n.* [earlier also *tabb* < Eng. dial.; in some senses contr. of *tablet;* in others, associated or merged with *tag*], 1. a small, flat loop or strap fastened to something for pulling it, hanging it up, etc. 2. a small, usually ornamental, flap or piece fastened to the edge or surface of something, as a dress, coat, etc. 3. an attached or projecting piece of a card or paper, useful in filing. 4. [Colloq.], a record; reckoning. 5. in *aeronautics*, a small auxiliary airfoil set into the trailing edge of an aileron, etc.

keep tab (or **tabs**) **on,** [Colloq.], to keep a check on.

b., tables.

b·a·nid (tab'ə-nid), *n.* any of a family of large blood-sucking flies; horsefly or gadfly.

b·ard (tab'ẽrd), *n.* [ME. *tabard;* OFr. *tabart;* L. *tapete*, tapestry], 1. originally, a loose, sleeved or sleeveless jacket worn out of doors. 2. a short-sleeved, blazoned cloak worn by knights over their armor. 3. a herald's official coat, blazoned with his king's or lord's arms.

tab·a·ret (tab'ẽr-it), *n.* [trade name, prob. < *tabby* after *taboret*], a silk cloth with satin stripes, used in upholstering.

Ta·bas·co (tə-bas'kō; *also, for 1*, Sp. tä-bäs'kô), *n.* 1. a state of southeastern Mexico, on the Gulf of Campeche: area, 9,782 sq. mi.; pop., 286,000; capital, Villahermosa. 2. a very hot sauce made from a kind of pepper: a trade-mark.

tab·by (tab'i), *n.* [*pl.* TABBIES (-iz)], [Fr. *tabis*, earlier *atabis;* ML. *attabi;* Ar. *'attābi* < *'Attābi*, quarter of Bagdad where it was manufactured: so named after a prince called *'Attāb*], 1. a silk taffeta with stripes or wavy markings; watered silk. 2. a gray or brown cat with dark stripes. 3. any domestic cat, especially a female. 4. an old maid. 5. a female gossip. *adj.* 1. having wavy markings; made of, or like, tabby. 2. having dark stripes over gray or brown; brindled. *v.t.* [TABBIED (-id), TABBYING], to make wavy markings in (silk, etc.).

tab·er·nac·le (tab'ẽr-nak''l), *n.* [ME.; OFr.; L. *tabernaculum*, a tent, dim. of *taberna*, a hut, shed, tavern], 1. *a)* a temporary shelter, as a tent. *b)* a dwelling place. 2. the human body considered as the dwelling place of the soul. 3. [T-], *a)* the portable sanctuary carried by the Jews in their wanderings from Egypt to Palestine: Ex. 25, 26, 27. *b)* later, the Jewish temple. 4. a shrine, niche, etc. with a canopy. 5. a place of worship; especially, a church with a large seating capacity. 6. in *ecclesiastical usage*, an ornamental container for the consecrated host: now usually placed on the middle of the altar. *v.i.* [TABERNACLED (-'ld), TABERNACLING], 1. to live in a tabernacle, or temporary shelter; hence, 2. to dwell temporarily: as, the soul is said to *tabernacle* in the body. *v.t.* to place in or as in a tabernacle.

tab·er·nac·u·lar (tab'ẽr-nak'yoo-lẽr), *adj.* of, like, or characteristic of a tabernacle.

ta·bes (tā'bēz), *n.* [L., a wasting away < *tabere*, to waste away], in *medicine*, 1. formerly, any wasting disease or progressive emaciation; consumption. 2. tabes dorsalis.

ta·bes·cence (tə-bes''ns), *n.* the quality or condition of being tabescent.

T U

, āpe, bâre, cär; ten, ēven, hêre, ovẽr; is, bīte; lot, gō, hôrn, tōōl, look; oil, out; up, ūse, fũr; get; joy; yet; chin; she; thin, en; zh, leisure; ŋ, ring; ə for *a* in *ago*, *e* in *agent*, *i* in *sanity*, *o* in *comply*, *u* in *focus;* ' as in *able* (ā'b'l); Fr. bål; ë, Fr. eur; ö, Fr. feu; Fr. mo*n*; ô, Fr. coq; ü, Fr. duc; H, G. ich; kh, G. doch. See pp. x–xii. ‡ foreign; * hypothetical; < derived from.

ta·bes·cent (tə-bes''nt), *adj.* [L. *tabescens,* ppr. of *tabescere,* to dwindle away < *tabere,* to waste away], wasting or withering away.
tabes dor·sa·lis (dôr-sā'lis), [Mod. L., tabes of the back; see TABES & DORSAL], locomotor ataxia.
ta·bet·ic (tə-bet'ik, tə-bē'tik), *adj.* of or having tabes. *n.* a tabetic person.
tab·id (tab'id), *adj.* tabetic.
Tab·i·tha (tab'ə-thə), [LL.; Gr. *Tabitha, Tabeitha;* Aram. *ṭabhīthā,* lit., roe, gazelle], a feminine name.
tab·la·ture (tab'lə-chẽr), *n.* [Fr. < L. *tabula,* a table, board], 1. an obsolete form of musical notation; specifically, a form used for the lute and other stringed instruments, in which the lines of the staff represented the strings and the letters or figures on them indicated the finger stops. 2. [Archaic], a flat surface or tablet with an inscription, painting, or design on it.
ta·ble (tā'b'l), *n.* [ME.; OFr.; L. *tabula,* a board, painting, tablet], 1. originally, a thin, flat tablet or slab of metal, stone, or wood, used for inscriptions. 2. a piece of furniture consisting of a flat top set horizontally on legs. 3. such a table set with food for a meal. 4. food served at table; feasting as entertainment: as, the host's *table* was sumptuous. 5. the people seated at a table to eat, talk, etc. 6. a compact, systematic list of details, contents, etc.; hence, 7. a compact arrangement of related facts, figures, values, etc. in orderly sequence, and usually in rows and columns, for convenience of reference: as, the multiplication *table.* 8. a tableland. 9. any flat, horizontal surface, as for holding the work in a machine tool. 10. in *anatomy,* the hard inner or outer layer of the bony tissue of the skull. 11. in *architecture, a)* any horizontal, projecting piece, as a molding or cornice; stringcourse. *b)* a plain or decorated rectangular piece set into or raised on a wall; panel. 12. in *backgammon, a)* either of the two folding leaves of a backgammon board. *b) pl.* [Obs.], backgammon. 13. in *geology,* a horizontal stratum. 14. in *jewelry, a)* the upper, flat surface cut in a precious stone. *b)* a diamond or other stone cut with such a surface. 15. in *palmistry,* part of the palm of the hand. *v.t.* [TABLED (-b'ld), TABLING], 1. [Rare], to make a list or compact arrangement of; tabulate. 2. to put on a table. 3. to postpone indefinitely the discussion or consideration of, as a legislative bill, motion, etc., by referring it to the table of the presiding officer.
on the table, postponed or shelved: said of a bill, etc. referred to the table of the presiding officer.
the tables, laws, as the Ten Commandments or ancient Roman codes, inscribed on flat stone slabs.
turn the tables, to reverse completely a situation existing between oneself and another person or between two opposing groups.
tab·leau (tab'lō, tab-lō'), *n.* [*pl.* TABLEAUX (-lōz, -lōz'; *occas.* -lō'), TABLEAUS], [Fr., dim. of *table;* see TABLE], 1. a graphic scene; picture. 2. a tableau vivant.
‡tab·leau vi·vant (tȧ'blō' vē'vän'), [*pl.* TABLEAUX VIVANTS (-blō' -vän')], [Fr., lit., living tableau], a representation of a scene, picture, etc. by a person or group of persons appropriately costumed and posing silently without moving.
table board, meals without rental of a room: distinguished from *room and board.*
ta·ble·cloth (tā'b'l-klôth'), *n.* a cloth for covering a table, especially at meals.
ta·ble d'hôte (tä'b'l dōt'; Fr. tȧ'bl' dōt'), [*pl.* TABLES D'HÔTE (-b'lz; Fr. -bl')], [Fr., lit., table of the host], 1. a common table for guests at a hotel or restaurant. 2. a complete meal with courses as specified on the menu, served at a restaurant or hotel for a set price: distinguished from *à la carte.*
ta·ble·land (tā'b'l-land'), *n.* a high, broad, generally level region; plateau.
table linen, tablecloths, napkins, etc.
Table Mountain, a mountain in Cape Province, South Africa: height, 3,550 ft.
ta·ble·spoon (tā'b'l-spōōn', tā'b'l-spoon'), *n.* 1. a large spoon used for eating soup, for serving at the table, and as a measuring unit in cookery. 2. a tablespoonful. Abbreviated **tbs., tbsp., T.** (*sing. & pl.*).
ta·ble·spoon·ful (tā'b'l-spōōn'fool, tā'b'l-spoon-fool'), *n.* [*pl.* TABLESPOONFULS (-foolz, -foolz')], as much as a tablespoon will hold; 3 teaspoonfuls or 1/2 fluid ounce.
tab·let (tab'lit), *n.* [ME. *tablette;* OFr. *tablete,* dim. of *table;* see TABLE], 1. a flat, thin piece of stone, wood, metal, etc. shaped for a specific purpose. 2. such a piece with an inscription, used as a memorial wall panel. 3. a smooth, flat leaf made of wood, ivory, metal, etc. and used to write on. 4. a set of such leaves fastened together; hence, 5. a writing pad containing sheets of paper fastened together at one edge. 6. a small, flat piece of solid or compressed material, as medicine, soap, etc.
table talk, conversation at meals.
table tennis, a game somewhat like tennis in miniature, played on a large, rectangular table, usually indoors, with a small, hollow celluloid ball and small, racket-shaped paddles: cf. **ping-pong.**
ta·ble·ware (tā'b'l-wâr'), *n.* dishes, knives, forks, spoons, etc., used at the table for meals.
tab·loid (tab'loid), *n.* [< *tablet* + *-oid*], 1. a small tablet of medicine, a drug, etc. in compressed or concentrated form: a trade-mark (**Tabloid**). 2. a newspaper, usually half the ordinary size, with many pictures and short news stories. *adj.* condensed; short.
ta·boo (tə-bōō', ta-bōō'), *n.* [Tongan *tabu*], 1. among primitive tribes, a sacred prohibition put upon certain people, things, or acts which makes them untouchable, unmentionable, etc. 2. the highly developed system or practice of such prohibitions. 3. any social prohibition or restriction that results from convention or tradition. 4. in *linguistics,* the substitution of one term for another because of taboo. *adj.* 1. sacred and prohibited by taboo. 2. restricted by taboo: said of people. 3. prohibited or forbidden by tradition, convention, etc. *v.t.* 1. to put under taboo. 2. to prohibit or forbid because of tradition, convention, etc. Also spelled **tabu.**
ta·bor (tā'bẽr), *n.* [ME. & OFr. *tabur, tabour* < Per. *tabīrah,* a drum; cf. TAMBOUR], a small drum, formerly often played to accompany a fife or pipe. *v.i.* to beat or drum on or as on a tabor. Also spelled **tabour.**
tab·o·ret (tab'ə-rit, tab'ə-ret'), *n.* [OFr., a stool, lit., little drum; dim. of *tabour,* a drum; see TABOR], 1. a small tabor. 2. a stool. 3. a low ornamental stand. 4. a frame for embroidery. Also spelled **tabouret.**
tab·o·rin, tab·o·rine (tab'ə-rēn', tab'ə-rēn'), *n.* [OFr. *tabourin,* dim. of *tabour;* see TABOR], a small tabor played with only one stick: also spelled **tabourine.**
ta·bour (tā'bẽr), *n. & v.i.* tabor.
tab·ou·ret (tab'ə-ret', tab'ẽr-it), *n.* a taboret.
tab·ou·rine (tab'ə-rēn', tab'ə-rēn'), *n.* a taborin.
tab·ret (tab'rit), *n.* 1. a small tabor; taboret. 2. [Obs.], a person who plays a tabret.
Ta·briz (tȧ-brēz'), *n.* a city in northwestern Iran: pop., 214,000.
ta·bu (tə-bōō', ta-bōō'), *n., adj., v.t.* taboo.
tab·u·lar (tab'yoo-lẽr), *adj.* [L. *tabularis* < *tabula,* a table, board], 1. having a tablelike surface; flat: as, *tabular* rock. 2. *a)* of or arranged in a table or tabulated scheme. *b)* computed from or calculated by such a table or tables.
‡ta·bu·la ra·sa (tab'ū-lə rā'sə), [L.], 1. a blank tablet; clean slate; hence, 2. the mind before impressions are recorded upon it by experience.
tab·u·lar·ly (tab'yoo-lẽr-li), *adv.* in or by means of a table.
tab·u·late (tab'yoo-lāt'; *for adj.,* tab'yoo-lit), *v.t.* [TABULATED (-id), TABULATING], [< L. *tabula,* a table + *-ate*], 1. to put (facts, statistics, etc.) in a table or tables (senses 6 & 7); list or arrange systematically. 2. to give a flat, tablelike surface to. *adj.* 1. having a flat surface. 2. having or made of thin, horizontal plates, as some corals.
tab·u·la·tion (tab'yoo-lā'shən), *n.* a tabulating or being tabulated; orderly arrangement, as in a table.
tab·u·la·tor (tab'yoo-lā'tẽr), *n.* 1. a person or machine that tabulates. 2. a typewriter device used to put figures into columns.
tac·a·ma·hac (tak'ə-mə-hak'), *n.* [Sp. *tacamahaca,* earlier *tecomahaca* < Nahuatl *tecomahca,* lit., stinking copal], 1. a strong-smelling gum resin used in ointments and incenses. 2. any of several trees, as the balsam poplar, yielding this resin. Also **tacmahack.**
tac·a·ma·hac·a (tak'ə-mə-hak'ə), *n.* tacamahac.
‡ta·cet (tā'set), *v.imp.* [L., 3d pers. sing., pres. indic. of *tacere,* to be silent; see TACIT], in *music,* it is silent: a direction to be silent for the indicated time.
tache, tach (tach), *n.* [ME.; OFr., a nail, hook; see TACK (small nail)], [Archaic], a device, as a buckle, hook and eye, etc., for fastening two parts together.
tach·i·na fly (tak'i-nə), [Mod. L. *tachina* < Gr. *tachinos* swift, for *tachys,* swift], any of a large group of gray and black, two-winged flies whose larvae are parasitic on and destructive to caterpillars, grubs, etc.
Ta Ch'ing (dä chiŋ), the Manchu dynasty of China overthrown in 1911.
tach·i·ol (tak'i-ōl', tak'i-ol), *n.* [< *tachy-* + *-ol*], silver fluoride, AgF·H_2O, used as an antiseptic.
ta·chis·to·scope (tə-kis'tə-skōp'), *n.* [< Gr. *tachistos* superl. of *tachys,* swift; + *-scope*], in *psychology,* an apparatus for testing attention, memory, etc. by throwing images of objects on a screen for a brief measured period, a fraction of a second.
tach·o·graph (tak'ə-graf', tak'ə-gräf'), *n.* [< Gr. *tachos,* speed; + *-graph*], 1. a tachometer that records or registers its measurements. 2. its record.
ta·chom·e·ter (tə-kom'ə-tẽr), *n.* [< Gr. *tachos,* speed + *-meter*], 1. a device that indicates or measures the revolutions per minute of a revolving shaft or the velocity of a machine. 2. a device for measuring the speed of the current in a river, the blood stream, etc.
ta·chom·e·try (tə-kom'ə-tri), *n.* the use of a tachometer.
tach·y- (tak'i), [< Gr. *tachys,* swift], a combining form meaning *rapid, swift, fast,* as in *tachymeter.*
tach·y·car·di·a (tak'i-kär'di-ə), *n.* [< *tachy-* + Gr. *kardia,* heart], an abnormally fast heartbeat.

tach·y·graph (tak′i-graf′, tak′i-gräf′), *n.* [Fr. *tachygraphe* < Gr. *tachygraphos*, swift writer < *tachys*, swift + *graphein*, to write], 1. something written in tachygraphy. 2. a tachygrapher.

ta·chyg·ra·pher (ta-kig′rə-fẽr), *n.* a person skilled in tachygraphy.

tach·y·graph·ic (tak′i-graf′ik), *adj.* of or written in tachygraphy.

tach·y·graph·i·cal (tak′i-graf′i-k'l), *adj.* tachygraphic.

ta·chyg·ra·phy (ta-kig′rə-fi), *n.* [*tachy-* + *-graphy*], the art or use of rapid writing; especially, ancient Greek and Roman shorthand or the medieval cursive writing, with abbreviations, etc., in these languages.

tach·y·lyte, tach·y·lite (tak′i-līt′), *n.* [G. *tachylit* < Gr. *tachys*, swift + *lytos*, soluble < *lyein*, to dissolve: so called because of its rapid decomposition in acids], a kind of basaltic glass once considered a mineral.

tach·y·lyt·ic (tak′i-lit′ik), *adj.* of, like, or consisting of tachylyte.

ta·chym·e·ter (ta-kim′ə-tẽr, tə-kim′ə-tẽr), *n.* [*tachy-* + *-meter*], a surveying instrument for rapid determination of distances, elevations, etc.

ta·chym·e·try (ta-kim′ə-tri, tə-kim′ə-tri), *n.* the use of a tachymeter.

ta·chys·ter·ol (tə-kis′tə-rōl), *n.* [*tachy-* + *sterol*], an isomer of ergosterol formed during the production of calciferol by the irradiation of ergosterol.

tac·it (tas′it), *adj.* [< Fr. or L.; Fr. *tacite*; L. *tacitus*, pp. of *tacere*, to be silent; akin to Goth. *thahan*, ON. *thegja*, to be silent], 1. making no sound; saying nothing; still. 2. unspoken; silent. 3. not expressed or declared openly, but implied. 4. in *law*, happening without contract but by operation of law.

tac·i·turn (tas′ə-tũrn′), *adj.* [< Fr. or L.; Fr. *taciturne*; L. *taciturnus* < *tacere*; see TACIT], almost always silent; not liking to talk; uncommunicative. —*SYN.* see **silent.**

tac·i·tur·ni·ty (tas′ə-tũr′nə-ti), *n.* the quality or state of being taciturn; habitual disinclination to talk.

Tac·i·tus (tas′i-təs), *n.* (*Publius Cornelius Tacitus*), Roman historian; 55?–117? A.D.

tack (tak), *n.* [ME. *takke*; ONorm.Fr. *taque*; OFr. *tache*, a nail, fibula < Gmc. base seen in MLG. *tacke*, point; cf. TAG, ATTACH], 1. a short nail or pin with a sharp point and a relatively large, flat head. 2. *a)* a stitch; especially, a long stitch used for temporary sewing. *b)* a fastening, especially in a slight or temporary way. 3. a zigzag course, or movement in such a course. 4. a course of action or policy, especially one differing from another or preceding course. 5. food; foodstuff: as, hard*tack*. 6. in *nautical usage*, *a)* a rope for holding securely the forward lower corner of some sails. *b)* the corner thus held. *c)* the direction a ship goes in relation to the position of the sails. *d)* a change of direction made by changing the position of the sails. *e)* a course against the wind. *f)* one of a series of zigzag movements in such a course. *v.t.* 1. to fasten or attach with tacks. 2. to attach temporarily, as by sewing with long stitches. 3. to attach as a supplement; add: as, *tack* an amendment to the bill. 4. in *nautical usage*, *a)* to change the course of (a ship) by turning her with her head to the wind. *b)* to maneuver (a ship) against the wind by a series of tacks. *v.i.* 1. to go in a zigzag course. 2. to change suddenly one's policy or course of action. 3. in *nautical usage*, *a)* to tack a ship. *b)* to change its course by being tacked, or sail against the wind by a series of tacks: said of a ship.

ack·i·ness (tak′i-nis), *n.* a tacky quality or state.

ack·le (tak′'l), *n.* [ME. *takel*; prob. < LG.; cf. D., LG. *takel*, pulley, rope, MLG. *takel*, equipment in general; < MLG. *taken*, to take], 1. apparatus; equipment; gear: as, fishing *tackle*. 2. a rope and pulley block, or a system of ropes and pulleys, used to lower, raise, or move weights: see **pulley**, illus. 3. the act of tackling, as in football. 4. in *football*, either of the two players (*right tackle* and *left tackle*) between the guard and the end on either side of the line of scrimmage. 5. in *nautical usage*, *a)* originally, a ship's rigging. *b)* later, the running rigging and pulleys to operate the sails. *v.t.* [TACKLED (-'ld), TACKLING], 1. to fasten by means of tackle. 2. to harness (a horse). 3. to take hold of; seize. 4. to try to do or solve, as something difficult; begin dealing with; undertake: as, he *tackled* the job. 5. in *football*, to stop or throw (an opponent carrying the ball). *v.i.* in *football*, to stop or throw an opponent.

ack·ling (tak′liŋ), *n.* [Rare], gear; tackle.

ack·y (tak′i), *adj.* [TACKIER (-i-ẽr), TACKIEST (-i-ist)], [*tack*, in sense of "slight fastening" + *-y*], sticky, as varnish, glue, etc. before completely dry.

ack·y (tak′i), *adj.* [TACKIER (-i-ẽr), TACKIEST (-i-ist)], [prob. specialized use of *tacky* (sticky); but cf. G. dial. *taklig*, *takelig*, untidy], [Colloq.], dowdy; shabby.

ac·ma·hack (tak′mə-hak′), *n.* tacamahac.

'ac·na (täk′nä; Eng. tak′nə), *n.* a department of southern Peru: pop., 52,000.

Tac·na-A·ri·ca (täk′nä-ä-rē′kä; Eng. tak′nə-ə-rē′kə), *n.* a disputed region in western South America: divided (1929) into two departments, Tacna, Peru and Arica, Chile.

Ta·co·ma (tə-kō′mə), *n.* a seaport in western Washington, on Puget Sound: pop., 148,000.

Tacoma, Mount, Mount Rainier: the Indian name.

tac·on·ite (tak′ə-nīt′), *n.* [? < *Taconic*, old name for a rock series in the Lake Superior region; + *-ite*], a dull-colored quartz containing from 25 to 35 per cent hematite and magnetite: it is a low-grade iron ore.

tact (takt), *n.* [Fr.; L. *tactus*, pp. of *tangere*, to touch], 1. originally, the sense of touch. 2. delicate perception of the right thing to say or do without offending.

SYN.—**tact** implies the skill in dealing with persons or difficult situations of one who has a quick and delicate sense of what is fitting and thus avoids giving offense (it will require *tact* to get his consent); **poise** implies composure in the face of disturbing or embarrassing situations (despite the social blunder, she maintained her *poise*); **diplomacy** implies a smoothness and adroitness in dealing with others, sometimes in such a way as to gain one's own ends (his lack of *diplomacy* lost him the contract); **savoir-faire** implies a ready knowledge of the right thing to do or say in any situation.

tact·ful (takt′fəl), *adj.* having or showing tact.

tac·tic (tak′tik), *adj.* [Mod. L. *tacticus*; Gr. *taktikos*; see TACTICS], in *biology*, of, showing, or characteristic of taxis.

tac·tic (tak′tik), *n.* 1. tactics. 2. a detail or branch of tactics. *adj.* of arrangement or system.

tac·ti·cal (tak′ti-k'l), *adj.* 1. of tactics, especially in military or naval maneuvers. 2. characterized by or showing cleverness and skill in tactics.

tac·ti·cal·ly (tak′ti-k'l-i, tak′tik-li), *adv.* by or in regard to tactics.

tac·ti·cian (tak-tish′ən), *n.* 1. an expert in tactics; hence, 2. a clever, skillful manager.

tac·tics (tak′tiks), *n.pl.* [Gr. (*ta*) *taktika*, lit., (the) matters of arrangement < *taktikos*, fit for arranging < *tassein*, *tattein*, to arrange, put in order], 1. [construed as sing.], the science of arranging and maneuvering military and naval forces in action or before the enemy. 2. actions in accord with this science; hence, 3. any skillful methods used to gain an end.

tac·tile (tak′t'l, tak′til), *adj.* [Fr.; L. *tactilis* < *tangere*, to touch], 1. that can be perceived by the touch; tangible. 2. of or having the sense of touch.

tac·til·i·ty (tak-til′ə-ti), *n.* tactile quality or state.

tac·tion (tak′shən), *n.* [L. *tactio* < *tactus*; see TACT], a touching or being touched; contact.

tact·less (takt′lis), *adj.* not having or showing tact.

tac·tu·al (tak′choo-əl), *adj.* [< L. *tactus* (see TACT); + *-al*], 1. of the sense or organs of touch. 2. causing a sensation of touch; caused by touch.

tac·tu·al·ly (tak′choo-əl-i), *adv.* by means of touch.

Ta·cu·ba·ya (tä′koo-bä′yä), *n.* a district of Mexico City, in the southwestern part: formerly, a city: site of the national observatory.

tad (tad), *n.* [prob. short for *tadpole*], a little child.

Tadema, Sir **Lawrence Alma-,** see **Alma-Tadema.**

Tad·mor (täd′môr), *n.* Palmyra: the Biblical name.

tad·pole (tad′pōl′), *n.* [ME. *taddepol* < *tade*, *tadde*, toad + *poll*, head; hence, the toad that seems all head], the larva of certain amphibians, as frogs and toads, having gills and a tail and living in water: as it matures, the gills and tail are lost and legs develop.

Ta·dzhik (tä′jik), *n.* [*pl.* TADZHIK], one of a people of Iranian descent living in the region of the Tadzhik S.S.R.: also spelled **Tadjik, Tajik.**

Ta·dzhik·i·stan (tȧ-jēk′i-stän′), *n.* the Tadzhik S.S.R.

Ta·dzhik Soviet Socialist Republic (tȧ-jēk′), a republic of the U.S.S.R. in Central Asia: area, 55,584 sq. mi.; pop., 1,982,000; capital, Stalinabad.

tael (tāl), *n.* [Port.; Malay *tahil*, a weight], 1. any of various units of weight of eastern Asia; especially, a Chinese unit equal to 1/16 catty. 2. a Chinese unit of money equal in value to a tael of silver.

ta'en (tān), [Poetic], taken.

tae·ni·a (tē′ni-ə), *n.* [*pl.* TAENIAE (-ē)], [L.; Gr. *tainia*, ribbon, tape], 1. an ancient Greek headband or fillet. 2. in *anatomy*, a ribbonlike part or structure, as of muscle or nerve tissue. 3. in *architecture*, a band between the frieze and the architrave of a Doric entablature. 4. in *zoology*, a tapeworm. Also spelled **tenia.**

tae·ni·a·cide (tē′ni-ə-sīd′), *n.* [*taenia* + *-cide*], a drug, etc. that destroys tapeworms: also spelled **teniacide.**

tae·ni·a·fuge (tē′ni-ə-fūj′), *n.* [< *taenia* + L. *fugare*, to drive away], a drug, etc. that expels tapeworms from the body: also spelled **teniafuge.**

tae·ni·a·sis (ti-nī′ə-sis), *n.* [Mod. L.; see TAENIA & -IASIS], infestation with tapeworms: also spelled **teniasis.**

taf·fa·rel, taf·fer·el (taf′ə-rel′, taf′ẽr-əl), *n.* [D. *tafereel*, a panel, picture; dim. of *tafel*, table < L. *tabula*, a table], 1. formerly, the upper, flat part of a ship's stern: so called from its carved panels. 2. a taffrail.

taf·fe·ta (taf′i-tə), *n.* [ME. *taffata;* OFr. *taffetas;* ult. < Per. *tāftah* < *tāftan*, to weave, spin, twist], 1. a fine, rather stiff, silk cloth with a sheen. 2. loosely, a similar cloth of cotton, linen, etc. *adj.* 1. like or made of taffeta. 2. gaudy; florid. 3. dainty; delicate.

taf·fi·a (taf′i-ə), *n.* tafia.

taff·rail (taf′rāl′), *n.* [altered (by confusion of *-rel* with *rail*) < *tafferel;* see TAFFEREL], the rail around the stern of a ship.

TAFFRAIL

taf·fy (taf′i), *n.* [early form of *toffee*], 1. a chewy candy made of sugar or molasses boiled down and pulled: cf. **toffee.** 2. [Colloq.], flattery.

taf·i·a (taf′i-ə), *n.* [Creole Fr.; cf. Malay *tāfia*, spirit distilled from molasses], a low-grade rum made in the West Indies from cheap molasses or refuse sugar.

Ta·fi·lelt (tȧ′fi-lelt′), *n.* a region in southeastern Morocco: area, c. 500 sq. mi.; pop., 188,000.

Taft, Lo·ra·do (lə-rā′dō taft), 1860–1936; American sculptor.

Taft, William Howard, 1857–1930; twenty-seventh president of the United States (1909–1913); chief justice, United States Supreme Court (1921–1930).

tag (tag), *n.* [ME. *tagge;* prob. < ON.; cf. Sw. *tagg*, a point, prickle, spike, Norw. *tagg*, a point; akin to G. *zacke*, a point, jag; for IE. base see TAIL], 1. originally, a hanging end or rag, as on a torn skirt. 2. any small part or piece hanging from or loosely attached to the main piece. 3. a hard-tipped end, as of metal, on a string or lace, to give stiffness for drawing through holes. 4. a bright piece of material next to the fly on a fishhook. 5. a card, paper, etc. tied or attached to something as a label. 6. an ornamental or instructive ending for a speech, story, etc. 7. a short, familiar quotation used as such an ending. 8. the last words of an actor's speech, a song, etc. 9. the last part of any proceeding. 10. a loop on a garment for hanging it up, or on a boot for pulling it on. 11. a flourish or decorative stroke in writing. 12. *a*) a lock of hair. *b*) a matted lock of wool. 13. [Obs.], the rabble: now only in combination with *rag*, as "*rag, tag,* and *bobtail*." 14. a children's game in which one player, called "it," chases the others with the object of touching, or tagging, one of them and making him "it" in turn. *v.t.* [TAGGED (tagd), TAGGING], 1. to provide with a tag; fasten a tag to. 2. to end (a speech, story, etc.) with a tag. 3. to overtake and touch in or as in the game of tag. 4. [Colloq.], to follow close behind. *v.i.* [Colloq.], to follow close behind a person or thing (usually with *along, after,* etc.).

Ta·gal (tä-gäl′), *n.* Tagalog.

Ta·ga·log (tä-gä′log; Eng. tag′ə-log′, tag′ə-lôg′), *n.* 1. a member of a Malayan people of the Philippine Islands. 2. their Indonesian language, the chief native language of the Philippine Islands: abbreviated **Tag.**

Ta·gan·rog (tä′gän-rôk′), *n.* a seaport in the southern European U.S.S.R., on the Sea of Azov: pop., 189,000.

tag day, a day set aside for public soliciting of contributions to a stated fund: a tag is given to each person who contributes.

tag end, 1. any loosely attached or hanging end. 2. the last part of something; remnant.

Tag·gard, Genevieve (tag′ẽrd), 1894–1948; American poet.

tag·ger (tag′ẽr), *n.* 1. a person or thing that tags. 2. *pl.* thin sheets of metal, usually coated with tin.

Ta·gore, Sir **Ra·bin·dra·nath** (rə-bēn′drə-nät′ tä′gôr; Eng. tə-gôr′, tə-gōr′), 1861–1941; Hindu poet; received Nobel prize in literature, 1913.

Ta·gus (tā′gəs), *n.* a river flowing through central Spain and Portugal into the Atlantic: length, 565 mi.: Spanish name, *Tajo;* Portuguese name, *Tejo.*

Ta·hi·ti (tä-hē′ti, tī′tē), *n.* one of the Society Islands of French Oceania, in the South Pacific: area, 600 sq. mi.; pop., 23,000: in French, *Taïti:* former name, *Otaheite.*

Ta·hi·ti·an (tä-hē′ti-ən, tə-hē′shən), *adj.* of Tahiti, its people, their language, etc. *n.* 1. a native or inhabitant of Tahiti; especially, a member of the native Polynesian people of Tahiti. 2. the Polynesian language of the Tahitians.

Ta·hoe, Lake (tä′hō, tā′hō), a lake between California and Nevada: length, 22 mi.: a summer resort.

tah·sil·dar (tə-sēl′där′), *n.* [Ar. & Per. *taḥṣīl*, collection + *dār*, holder], in India, a local revenue officer or tax collector.

Ta·i (tä′ē, tī), *n.* & *adj.* Thai.

tai·ga (tī′gə), *n.* [Russ.], the coniferous forests in the far northern regions of Eurasia and North America.

Tai·ho·ku (tī-hō′kōō; Chin. tī′hu′kōō′), *n.* Taipeh: Japanese name.

tail (tāl), *n.* [ME.; AS. *tægel;* akin to G. dial. *zagel;* IE. base **dek̂-*, to tear, tear off, as also in Sans. *daçā*, fringe; cf. TAG], 1. the rear end of an animal's body, especially when extending from the trunk as a distinct flexible appendage. 2. a horsetail as a former Turkish standard borne before a pasha. 3. anything like an animal's tail in form or position: as, the *tail* of a shirt. 4. a luminous train behind a comet or meteor. 5. the hind, bottom, last, or inferior part of anything. 6. *usually pl.* the reverse side of a coin from the side with the head, date, etc. 7. a long braid or tress of hair; switch. 8. *a*) a line of people waiting their turn; cue. *b*) a retinue. 9. *pl.* [Colloq.], *a*) a swallow-tailed coat. *b*) full dress attire for men. 10. the lower end of a stream or pool. 11. in *aeronautics*, the rear part of an airship; especially, a set of stabilizing planes at the rear of an airplane. 12. in *printing*, the bottom of a page. 13. in *prosody*, the short line or lines ending certain stanzas or verse forms. *v.t.* 1. to provide with a tail. 2. to cut or detach the tail or taillike part from. 3. to form the tail or end of, as a group or procession; be at the rear or end of. 4. to fasten or connect at or by the tail. 5. [Slang], to follow stealthily; shadow. 6. in *architecture*, to fasten one end of (a brick, board, etc.) into a wall, etc. (with *in* or *on*). *v.i.* 1. to become scattered in a line; straggle. 2. to become gradually smaller or fainter; almost disappear: as, the noise *tailed* away. 3. to form, or become part of, a line or tail. 4. [Colloq.], to follow close behind. 5. in *architecture*, to be fastened into a wall, etc. by one end: said of a brick or board. 6. in *nautical usage*, to go aground or be anchored stern foremost. *adj.* 1. at the rear or rear end. 2. from the rear: as, a *tail* wind.
turn tail, to run from danger, difficulty, hardship, etc.
with the tail between the legs, in defeat or in escape from expected defeat; with fear or dejection.

tail (tāl), *n.* [ME. *taile, talie;* OFr. *taille*, a cutting < *taillier;* see TAILOR], a limitation on the inheritance of an estate. *adj.* limited in a specified manner as to inheritance: as, fee *tail.*

tail·board (tāl′bôrd′, tāl′bōrd′), *n.* the board that forms the back of a wagon, cart, etc.: it is completely removed or swung down on hinges for loading or unloading.

tail coat, a man's coat with long tails in the back, usually worn on formal occasions.

tail dive, a tail-forward, downward plunge of an airplane.

tailed (tāld), *adj.* having a (specified kind of) tail: usually in combination, as *bobtailed.*

tail end, 1. the rear or bottom end of anything. 2. the concluding or last part of anything.

tail·gate (tāl′gāt′), *n.* a tailboard.

tail·ing (tāl′iŋ), *n.* [*tail, v.* + *-ing*], 1. *pl.* waste or refuse left in various processes of milling, mining, distilling, etc. 2. in *architecture*, the part of a projecting brick, stone, etc. embedded in a wall.

tail lamp, a taillight.

taille (tāl; Fr. tä′y′), *n.* [OFr. < *taillier*, to cut; see TAILOR], 1. a French feudal tax imposed by the king or a lord. 2. form or shape, especially of the bust. 3. the waist of a dress or its fit, cut, etc.

tail·light (tāl′līt′), *n.* a light at the back of a vehicle to warn approaching vehicles of its presence at night: also **tail lamp.**

tai·lor (tā′lẽr), *n.* [ME. *tailour;* OFr. *tailleor* < *taillier*, to cut, decide, fix; LL. *taliare*, to split, cut], a person who makes, repairs, or alters clothes, especially suits, coats, etc. *v.i.* to work as a tailor. *v.t.* 1. to make (clothes) by tailor's work. 2. to fit or provide (a person) with clothes made by a tailor. 3. to cut, form, produce, alter, etc. so as to meet requirements or particular conditions: as, her novel is *tailored* to popular tastes. 4. to fashion (women's garments, etc.) with trim, simple lines like those of men's clothes.

tai·lor·bird (tā′lẽr-bũrd′), *n.* any of several small Asiatic and African birds that stitch leaves together to make a camouflaged holder for their nests.

tai·lor·ing (tā′lẽr-iŋ), *n.* 1. the occupation of a tailor. 2. the workmanship or skill of a tailor.

tai·lor-made (tā′lẽr-mād′), *adj.* made by or as by a tailor or according to his methods; specifically, *a*) made with trim, simple lines: said of a woman's garment. *b*) made to order or to meet particular conditions: as, furniture *tailor-made* for the small apartment.

tail·piece (tāl′pēs′), *n.* 1. a piece or part added to or forming the end of something. 2. the small triangular piece of wood at the lower end of a violin, cello, etc., to which the strings are attached: see **violin,** illus. 3. a short beam or rafter with one end tailed in a wall and the other supported by a header. 4. in *printing*, an ornamental design, engraving, etc. put at the end of a chapter or at the bottom of a page.

tail plane, a horizontal supporting surface at the rear of an aircraft; stabilizer.

tail·race (tāl′rās′), *n.* 1. the lower part of a millrace. 2. the channel through which water flows after going over a water wheel. 3. a water channel to carry away tailings from a mine.

tail·spin (tāl′spin′), *n.* the descent of an airplane

with nose down and tail spinning in circles overhead: often used figuratively: also **(tail) spin.**

tail·stock (tāl'stok'), *n.* in *mechanics*, the adjustable part of a lathe, containing the dead center which holds the work.

tail wind, a wind blowing from behind an airplane, ship, etc. in motion.

Tai·myr Peninsula (tī-mêr'), a large peninsula in northern Siberia, between the Yenisei and Khatanga Rivers: also spelled **Taimir.**

tain (tān), *n.* [Fr., tin foil; altered form of *étain*, tin], 1. tin plate in thin sheets. 2. tin foil used for mirrors.

Tai·nan (tī'nän'), *n.* a seaport in Taiwan; pop., 230,000.

Taine, Hip·po·lyte A·dolphe (ē'pô'lēt' à'dôlf' ten; Eng. tān), 1828–1893; French critic and historian.

Tai·no (tī'nō), *n.* 1. [*pl.* TAINOS (-nōz)], a member of an extinct, aboriginal Indian tribe of the West Indies. 2. its Arawakan language.

taint (tānt), *v.t.* [contr. < *attaint;* meaning influenced by Fr. *teint*, pp. of *teindre* < L. *tingere*, to wet, moisten], 1. to affect with something physically injurious, unpleasant, etc.; infect; spoil. 2. to make morally corrupt or depraved: as, greed *tainted* his mind. 3. [Obs.], to dye; color. 4. [Obs.], to sully or stain (a person's honor). ***v.i.*** to become tainted. ***n.*** 1. a trace of corruption, disgrace, evil, etc. 2. an infectious or contaminating trace; infection; contamination. 3. [Obs.], a tinge or tint. —***SYN.*** see **contaminate.**

Tai·pei, Tai·peh (tī'pe'), *n.* the capital of Taiwan; pop., 759,000: Japanese name, *Taihoku.*

Tai·ping (tī'piŋ'), *adj.* [Chin. *t'ai-p'ing*, great peace: designation of the dynasty that was to be established], designating or of a rebellion (1850–1864) against the Manchu dynasty, led by Hung Siu-tsuan.

Tai·sho (tī'shō'), *n.* the Japanese designation of the reign (1912–1926) of Yoshihito.

Tai·wan (tī'wän'), *n.* an island province off southeastern China: seat of the Kuomintang government: area, 13,890 sq. mi.; pop., 9,410,000; capital, Taipei: also called *Formosa.* See also **China.**

Taiwan Strait, Formosa Strait: the Chinese name.

Tai·yü·an (tī'yü-än'), *n.* the capital of Shansi province, northern China: pop., 305,000.

Ta·jik (tä'jik), *n.* [*pl.* TAJIK], Tadzhik.

Ta·jik Soviet Socialist Republic (tà-jēk'), Tadzhik Soviet Socialist Republic.

Taj Ma·hal (täj' mà-häl', täzh' mə-häl'), [Per., best of buildings], the famous mausoleum at Agra, India, built (1632–1645) by Shah Jahan for his favorite wife.

Ta·jo (tä'hô), *n.* Tagus: the Spanish name.

take (tāk), *v.t.* [TOOK (took), TAKEN (tā'k'n), TAKING], [ME. *taken;* (late) AS. *tacan* < ON. *taka;* IE. base **dēg-*, to lay hold of], I. *to get possession of by force or skill; seize, grasp, catch, capture, win, or the like* 1. to get by conquering; capture; seize. 2. to trap or snare (a bird, animal, or fish). 3. *a*) to win, as a game, a part of a game, or a trick at cards. *b*) to remove (an opponent's piece) from play by capturing. 4. to get hold of; grasp. 5. to hit (a person) *in* or *on* some part. 6. to affect; attack: as, he was *taken* by violent shaking. 7. to catch (a person) in some act, especially a fault. 8. to capture the fancy of; charm. II. *to get by action not involving force or skill; obtain, acquire, assume, etc.* 1. to get into one's hand or hold; transfer to oneself. 2. to eat, drink, swallow, etc. for bodily nourishment. 3. [Rare], to get benefit from by exposure to: as, she *took* the air. 4. to enter into a special relationship with: as, she *took* students to add to her income, he *took* a wife. 5. to buy: as, he *took* the first suit that the clerk offered. 6. to rent or lease: as, we *took* a cottage for the summer. 7. to get regularly by paying for: as, we *take* two daily newspapers. 8. to assume as a responsibility, task, etc.: as, he *took* the job. 9. to assume or adopt (a badge or symbol of duty, office, etc.): as, the president *took* the chair. 10. to obligate oneself by: as, he *took* a vow. 11. to become a member of; join, as a party or side in a contest, disagreement, etc. 12. to assume (something) as if granted or due one: as, he *took* the blame, she *took* her leave. 13. [Slang], to cheat; trick. 14. in *grammar*, to have or admit of according to usage, nature, etc.; be used with in construction: as, a transitive verb *takes* an object. III. *to get, adopt, use, etc. by selection or choice* 1. to choose; select. 2. to use or employ; resort to: as, he *took* a whip to his son. 3. to travel by; get in or on as a means of traveling: as, she *took* a train. 4. to go to (a place) for shelter, safety, etc.: as, the birds *took* cover. 5. to deal with; consider: as, he *took* the matter gravely. 6. to occupy: as, *take* a chair. 7. [Colloq.], to require; demand; need: used impersonally, as, it *takes* money to make money. IV. *to get from a source* 1. to derive or draw, as a name, quality, etc., from. 2. to extract, as for quotation; excerpt: as, he *took* a verse from the Bible. 3. to obtain by observation, experiment, study, etc.: as, he *took* a poll. 4. to write down; copy: as, *take* notes. 5. to draw, photograph, etc. a likeness of: as, let me *take* your picture. V. *to get as offered or due; receive, accept, suffer, etc.* 1. to win, as a prize, reward, etc. 2. to be the object of; undergo: as, *take* punishment. 3. to occupy oneself in; enjoy: as, *take* a nap. 4. to accept (something offered): as, *take* a bet, *take* advice. 5. to have a specified reaction to: as, he *took* the joke in earnest. 6. to confront and get over, through, etc.: as, the horse *took* the jump. 7. to be affected by (a disease, etc.): as, he *took* cold. 8. to absorb; become impregnated with, as a dye, polish, etc. VI. *to receive mentally* 1. *a*) to understand the remarks of (a person). *b*) to comprehend the meaning of (words, remarks, etc.). *c*) to understand or interpret in a specified way. 2. to suppose; presume: as, I *take* him to be an intelligent person. 3. to have or feel, as an emotion, mental state, etc.: as, *take* pity, *take* notice. 4. to hold and act upon, as an idea, resolution, etc. VII. *to make or complete by action* 1. to do; perform (an act): as, *take* a walk. 2. to make or put forth as the result of thought, as a resolution or objection. 3. [Colloq.], to aim and execute (a specified action) at an object: as, he *took* a short jab at his opponent. VIII. *to move, remove, etc.* 1. to conduct; lead: as, this path *takes* you to the river. 2. to carry: as, *take* your skates with you. 3. to remove from a person or thing; extract: as, the thief *took* the silver. 4. to remove by death. 5. to subtract: as, the storekeeper *took* a dollar from the price. 6. to direct (oneself); go. ***v.i.*** 1. to get possession. 2. to hook or engage with another part: said of a mechanical device. 3. to take root; begin growing: said of a plant. 4. to lay hold; catch: as, the fire *took* rapidly. 5. to gain public favor; be popular: as, the play *took* from its first performance. 6. to be effective in action, operation, etc.: as, the smallpox vaccination *took*, the dye *takes* well. 7. to remove a part; detract (with *from*): as, nothing *took* from the scene's beauty. 8. to be made or adapted to be taken in a specified way. 9. to go; proceed: as, the horse *took* to the roadside. 10. [Colloq. or Dial.], to become (ill or sick). 11. [Colloq.], to be photographed in a specified way: as, she *takes* well. 12. in *law*, to take possession of property. ***n.*** 1. the act or process of taking. 2. something that has been taken. 3. the amount or quantity of something taken: as, the day's *take* of fish. 4. [Slang], the money received; receipts or profit. 5. in *motion pictures*, *a*) a scene photographed or to be photographed with an uninterrupted run of the camera. *b*) the process of photographing such a scene.

take after, to be, act, or look like.

take amiss, 1. originally, to be wrong concerning; mistake. 2. to misunderstand the reason behind (an act); become offended at.

take at one's word, to accept as true, correct, etc.

take back, 1. to regain use or possession of. 2. to retract (something said, promised, etc.).

take down, 1. to remove from a higher place and put in a lower one; pull down. 2. to unfasten; take apart. 3. to make less conceited; humble (a person). 4. to put in writing; record.

take for, 1. to consider to be; regard as. 2. to mistake for. 3. [Slang], to cheat (a person) of.

take in, 1. to admit; receive. 2. to shorten (a sail) by reefing or furling. 3. to make smaller or more compact. 4. to include; comprise. 5. to understand; comprehend. 6. to cheat; trick; deceive. 7. to visit: as, we *took in* all the sights. 8. to receive into one's home for pay, as roomers, work, etc.

take it, 1. to suppose; believe. 2. [Slang], to withstand difficulty, criticism, hardship, ridicule, etc.

take it lying down, [Colloq.], to submit without protest to oppression, etc.; offer no resistance; be meek.

take it on the chin, [Slang], to be defeated; undergo punishment, pain, difficulties, etc.

take it out of, [Colloq.], 1. to exhaust; tire. 2. to obtain payment or satisfaction from.

take it out on, [Colloq.], to make (another) suffer for one's own anger, irritation, bad temper, etc.

take off, 1. to remove, as a garment. 2. to draw or conduct away. 3. to go away; depart (used reflexively). 4. to deduct; subtract. 5. to kill, as an assassin, disease, etc. 6. to make a copy or likeness of. 7. to leave the ground or water in flight, as an airplane; hence, 8. [Colloq.], to start. 9. [Colloq.], to imitate in a burlesque manner; mimic.

take on, 1. to acquire; assume, as form, quality, etc. 2. to employ; hire. 3. to begin to do, as a task, etc.; undertake. 4. to play against; oppose. 5. [Colloq.], to show violent emotion, especially anger or sorrow.

take (one's) time, to be slow or unhurried; delay.

take out, 1. to remove; extract. 2. to obtain by application to the proper authority. 3. [Colloq.], to escort. 4. in *bridge*, to bid higher than (one's partner) but in a different suit.

take over, to begin controlling, managing, etc.

take to, 1. to develop a habit or practice of doing, using, etc. 2. to go to, as for hiding, rest, etc. 3. to become fond of; care for; be attracted to.

take up, 1. to raise; lift. 2. to make tighter or shorter. 3. to pay off; recover by buying, as a mortgage, note, etc. 4. to absorb (a liquid). 5. to accept, as a challenge, bet, etc. 6. to assume protection, custody, etc. of (a person). 7. to interrupt (a person) in disapproval, rebuke, etc. 8. to resume (something interrupted). 9. to become interested in or devoted to, as an occupation, study, belief, etc.; adopt (an idea). 10. to occupy or fill (place or time).

take upon (or **on**) **oneself,** 1. to take the responsibility for; accept as a charge or duty. 2. to begin (to do anything); undertake. Also **take upon** (or **on**) **one.**

take up with, [Colloq.], to become an associate or companion of; be friendly with.

SYN.—**take** is the general word meaning to get hold of by or as by the hands (to *take* a book, the opportunity, etc.); to **seize** is to take suddenly and forcibly (he *seized* the gun from the robber, to *seize* power); **grasp** implies a seizing and holding firmly (to *grasp* a rope, an idea, etc.); **clutch** implies a tight or convulsive grasping of that which one is eager to take or keep hold of (she *clutched* his hand in terror); **grab** implies a roughness or unscrupulousness in seizing (the child *grabbed* all the candy, to *grab* credit); **snatch** stresses an abrupt quickness and, sometimes, a surreptitiousness in seizing (she *snatched* the letter from my hand, to *snatch* a purse). See also **bring, receive.**

take·down (tāk'doun'), *n.* 1. the act or process of taking down, especially of disassembling mechanically. 2. [Colloq.], humiliation; mortification. *adj.* made to be easily taken apart: as, a *takedown* firearm.

take-home pay (tāk'hōm'), wages or salary after deductions for income tax, social security, etc. have been made.

take-in (tāk'in'), *n.* [Colloq.], a taking in; specifically, cheating; trickery.

tak·en (tā'k'n), past participle of **take.**

taken aback, suddenly confused or startled; dumbfounded.

take-off (tāk'ôf'), *n.* 1. the act of leaving the ground, as in jumping or flight. 2. the place from which one leaves the ground. 3. [Colloq.], an amusing or mocking imitation; caricature; burlesque.

tak·er (tāk'ẽr), *n.* a person who takes something, as a bet, tickets, another's property, etc.

take-up (tāk'up'), *n.* 1. the act or process of taking up, making tight, etc. 2. a mechanical device to tighten something.

tak·ing (tāk'iŋ), *adj.* 1. that captures interest; attractive; winning. 2. [Colloq.], contagious; infectious: said of disease. *n.* 1. the act of a person or thing that takes. 2. something taken; catch. 3. [Colloq.], a state of agitation or excitement. 4. *pl.* earnings; profits; receipts.

tal·a·poin (tal'ə-poin'), *n.* [Port. *talapões*, pl. of *talapão* < Burmese *tala poi*, my lord], 1. a Buddhist monk. 2. a small, long-tailed monkey of West Africa.

ta·la·ri·a (tə-lâr'i-ə), *n.pl.* [L. < *talaris*, of the ankles < *talus*, an ankle], winged sandals or wings on the ankles, represented as an attribute of Hermes, or Mercury, and other gods.

talc (talk), *n.* [Fr.; ML. *talcum;* Ar. *ṭalq;* Per. *talk*], a very soft mineral, magnesium silicate, $H_2Mg_3(SiO_3)_4$, used to make talcum powder, lubricants, etc. *v.t.* [TALCKED or TALCED (talkt), TALCKING or TALCING], to use talc on.

talc·ose (tal'kōs), *adj.* of or containing talc.

talc·ous (tal'kəs), *adj.* talcose.

tal·cum (tal'kəm), *n.* [ML.; see TALC], 1. talc. 2. talcum powder.

talcum powder, a powder for the body and face made of powdered talc that has been purified and, usually, perfumed.

tale (tāl), *n.* [ME.; AS. *talu*, speech, number; akin to G. *zahl*, number, D. *taal*, speech; IE. base **del-*, to aim, reckon, figure on, etc., seen also in L. *dolus*, artifice, evil intent], 1. something told or related; relation or recital of happenings; hence, 2. *a*) a story or account of true, legendary, or fictitious events; narrative. *b*) a literary composition in narrative form. 3. idle or malicious gossip. 4. a fiction; falsehood; lie. 5. [Archaic or Poetic], a tally; count; enumeration. 6. a complete tally; total: as, the flood's *tale* of dead. 7. [Obs.], the act of telling; talk. —*SYN.* see **story.**

tale·bear·er (tāl'bâr'ẽr), *n.* a person who gossips or tells secrets, scandal, etc.

tale·bear·ing (tāl'bâr'iŋ), *adj.* telling secrets or scandal; gossiping. *n.* the act of a talebearer.

tale·car·ri·er (tāl'kar'i-ẽr), *n.* a talebearer.

tale·mon·ger (tāl'muŋ'gẽr), *n.* a talebearer.

tal·ent (tal'ənt), *n.* [ME.; AS.; OFr.; LL.; L. *talentum*, a talent (sense 1); Gr. *talanton*, a balance, thing weighed, weighed amount of money, weight; sense 2, etc. < basic notion "weight of inclination"], 1. a unit of weight or of money (the value of a talent weight in gold, silver, etc.) used in ancient Greece, Rome, the Middle East, etc.: it varied widely in value at different times and in different places but was usually large, the lowest estimated weight being about 58 pounds avoirdupois. 2. any natural ability or power; natural endowment. 3. a special, superior ability in an art, mechanics, learning, etc. 4. people who have talent: used collectively, as, he encouraged young *talent*. 5. [Slang], habitual betters or gamblers.

SYN.—**talent** implies a native ability for a specific pursuit and connotes either that it is or can be cultivated by the one possessing it (a *talent* for drawing); **gift** suggests of a special ability that it is bestowed upon one, as by nature, and not acquired through effort (a *gift* for making plants grow); **aptitude** implies a natural inclination for a particular work, specifically as pointing to special fitness for, or probable success in, it (*aptitude* tests); **faculty** implies a special ability that is either inherent or acquired, as well as a ready ease in its exercise (the *faculty* of judgment); **knack** implies an acquired faculty for doing something cleverly and skillfully (the *knack* of rhyming); **genius** implies an inborn mental endowment, specifically of a creative or inventive kind in the arts or sciences, that is exceptional or phenomenal (the *genius* of Leonardo da Vinci).

tal·ent·ed (tal'ən-tid), *adj.* having talent; gifted.

ta·ler (tä'lẽr), *n.* [*pl.* TALER], [G.; see DOLLAR], a former German silver coin: also spelled **thaler.**

ta·les (tā'lēz), *n.pl.* [L., pl. of *talis*, such; from use in *tales de circumstantibus*, such of those standing about, phr. in writ summoning them], in *law*, 1. people summoned to fill jury vacancies when the regular panel has become deficient in number by challenge, etc. 2. [construed as sing.], the writ that summons them.

ta·les·man (tālz'mən, tā'liz-mən), *n.* [*pl.* TALESMEN (-mən)], in *law*, a person summoned as one of the tales.

tale·tell·er (tāl'tel'ẽr), *n.* 1. a storyteller. 2. a talebearer.

Ta·li·en·wan (dä'lyen'wän'), *n.* Dairen, a city in Manchuria: the Chinese name: also **Talien.**

tal·i·on (tal'i-ən), *n.* [Fr.; L. *talio* < *talis*, such], punishment that exacts a penalty just like the crime; retaliation, as the principle of an eye for an eye, a tooth for a tooth.

tal·i·ped (tal'ə-ped'), *adj.* having talipes; clubfooted. *n.* a person with a clubfoot.

tal·i·pes (tal'ə-pēz'), *n.* [Mod. L. < L. *talus*, an ankle + *pes, pedis*, a foot], clubfoot.

tal·i·pot (tal'i-pot'), *n.* [Bengali *tālipāt*, palm leaf < Sans. *tāli*, fan palm + *pattra*, leaf], a palm tree of the East Indies, with fan-shaped leaves used for fans, umbrellas, writing paper, etc.: also **talipot palm.**

tal·is·man (tal'is-mən, tal'iz-mən), *n.* [*pl.* TALISMANS (-mənz)], [Fr.; Sp.; Ar. *ṭilasm*, colloq. *tilsam*, magic figure, horoscope < Gr. *telesma*, payment (later, religious rite) < *telein*, to complete, initiate], 1. something, as a ring or stone, bearing engraved figures or symbols supposed to bring good luck, keep away evil, etc.; hence, 2. anything supposed to have magic power; a charm.

tal·is·man·ic (tal'is-man'ik, tal'iz-man'ik), *adj.* of, like, or used as a talisman.

tal·is·man·i·cal (tal'is-man'i-k'l, tal'iz-man'i-k'l), *adj.* talismanic.

talk (tôk), *v.i.* [Early ME. *talken, talkien* (akin to Fris. *talken*, to chatter); prob. freq. based on AS. *talian*, to reckon (base as in *tell, tale*); for the *-k-* freq. suffix, cf. *walk, stalk, lurk*, etc.], 1. to put ideas into, or exchange ideas by, spoken words; speak; converse. 2. to express ideas by speech substitutes: as, *talk* by signs. 3. to speak emptily or trivially; chatter. 4. to gossip. 5. to confer; consult. 6. to make noises suggestive of speech. *v.t.* 1. to put into spoken words; utter. 2. to make use of in speaking: as, to *talk* Spanish, to *talk* slang. 3. to speak at length about; discuss. 4. to put (oneself or another) into a specified condition, state of mind, etc. by talking: as, *talk* oneself hoarse, *talk* him into agreement. *n.* 1. *a*) the act of talking; speech. *b*) conversation, especially of an informal nature. 2. a speech or lecture. 3. a formal discussion; conference. 4. rumor; gossip. 5. the subject of conversation, gossip, etc. 6. empty, frivolous discussion or conversation: as, it's just *talk*. 7. [Colloq.], a particular kind of speech; dialect; lingo. —*SYN.* see **speak, speech.**

big talk, [Slang], a bragging, or boasting.

make talk, 1. to talk in an idle, forced manner in an effort to pass time. 2. to cause gossip.

talk around, to talk (a person) over; persuade.

talk at, to make comments intended for (a person) without directly speaking to him.

talk away, 1. to pass (a specified length of time) by talking. 2. to talk continuously; chatter.

talk back, to answer impertinently, brazenly, or rudely.

talk big, [Slang], to boast; brag.

talk down, to talk louder, longer, or more effectively than (a person); silence (an argument or person).

talk down to, to talk to (people of less or supposedly less intelligence than oneself) so that they will understand; patronize by pointedly simple speech.

talk of, 1. to speak about; discuss. 2. to express the possibility or intention of (doing something).

talk one's head (or **arm**) **off,** [Slang], to talk without pause or for a long time: also **talk to death.**

talk out, 1. to exhaust (a subject) by discussing it. 2. [Colloq.], to speak loudly and clearly. 3. [British], to discuss (a proposed parliamentary bill) so long that adjournment prevents a vote on it.
talk over, 1. to have a conversation about; discuss. 2. to win (a person) over to one's opinion, belief, etc. by talking; persuade.
talk up, 1. to discuss in order to create interest; praise. 2. [Colloq.], to speak loudly and clearly. 3. [Colloq.], to speak boldly, impertinently, etc.
talk with, 1. to speak or discuss with. 2. to try to persuade, convince, etc.

talk·a·tive (tôk′ə-tiv), *adj.* talking, or fond of talking, a great deal; loquacious.
SYN.—**talkative,** implying a fondness for talking frequently or at length, is perhaps the least derogatory of these words (a gay, *talkative* girl); **loquacious** usually implies a disposition to talk incessantly or to keep up a constant flow of chatter (a *loquacious* mood); **garrulous** implies a wearisome loquacity about trivial matters (a *garrulous* old man); **voluble** suggests a continuous flow of glib talk (a *voluble* oration).

talk·ie (tôk′i), *n.* [Colloq.], a talking picture.

talk·ing (tôk′iŋ), *n.* the act of a person who talks; discussion; conversation. *adj.* that talks; talkative.

talking machine, a phonograph.

talking picture, a motion picture with a synchronized sound track for reproducing dialogue, music, etc. to accompany the action.

talk·ing-to (tôk′iŋ-too̅′), *n.* [Colloq.], a rebuke; scolding.

talk·y (tôk′i), *adj.* 1. talkative. 2. containing too much talk, or dialogue: as a *talky* novel.

tall (tôl), *adj.* [ME. *tal*, dexterous, seemly; AS. (*ge*)*tæl*, swift, prompt; akin to OHG. *gizal*, swift], 1. high in stature; higher than the average. 2. having a stated height: as, five feet *tall*. 3. [Obs.], *a*) fine; handsome. *b*) bold; brave. 4. [Colloq.], exaggerated; hard to believe: as, a *tall* tale. 5. [Colloq.], large; huge: as, a *tall* drink. 6. [Colloq.], high-flown; pompously eloquent: as, *tall* talk. —*SYN.* see **high.**

tal·lage (tal′ij), *n.* [ME. *taillage, talliage*; OFr. *taillage*; see TAIL (a tax) & -AGE], originally, in feudalism, 1. a tax levied by kings upon towns and crown lands; hence, 2. a tax levied by a feudal lord upon his tenants. *v.t.* [TALLAGED (-ijd), TALLAGING], to levy a tallage upon; tax.

Tal·la·has·see (tal′ə-has′i), *n.* a city in northern Florida: its capital: pop., 48,000.

tall·boy (tôl′boi′), *n.* 1. [British], a tall chest of drawers; highboy. 2. a kind of tall chimney pot.

Tal·ley·rand-Pé·ri·gord, Charles Mau·rice de (shärl′ mô′rēs′ də tȧ′lā′rän′pā′rē′gôr′), Prince de Bénévent, 1754–1838; French statesman and diplomat: often shortened to **Talleyrand** (Eng. tal′i-rand′).

tal·li·er (tal′i-ēr), *n.* a person who keeps a tally, as a scorekeeper or a dealer in some card games.

Tal·linn (tȧl′lin), *n.* the capital of the Estonian S.S.R., on the Gulf of Finland: pop., 280,000: Russian name, *Revel;* German name, *Reval.*

tall·ish (tôl′ish), *adj.* somewhat tall.

tal·lith (tal′ith, tä′lis), *n.* [Late Heb. *tallēth*, a sheet, cover, cloak < *tālal*, to cover], in *Judaism*, 1. a shawl or scarf with fringes (*zizith*) on each corner, worn over the shoulders or head during morning prayer: Deut. 22:12. 2. a similarly fringed undergarment covering the chest and back, worn by orthodox Jews.

tall oil (täl), *n.* [Sw. *tallöl*, pine beer], a resinous liquid obtained as a by-product in the manufacture of chemical wood pulp: it is used in the manufacture of soap, varnishes, etc.

tal·low (tal′ō), *n.* [ME. *talgh*; prob. < MLG. *talg, talch;* akin to AS. *tælg*, a color, *telgan*, to color: supposedly so called from the use of this substance for coloring the hair among ancient Gmc. tribes], the hard, coarse fat in cows, sheep, etc.: it is melted and used to make candles, soap, etc. *v.t.* 1. to cover or smear with tallow. 2. to fatten (animals) so as to form tallow.

tal·low·y (tal′ə-wi), *adj.* 1. like tallow in consistency; oily; greasy. 2. like tallow in color; pale yellow. 3. full of tallow; fat: said of an animal.

tal·ly (tal′i), *n.* [*pl.* TALLIES (-iz)], [ME. *talie, talye;* Anglo-Fr. *tallie;* Anglo-Lat. *talia;* L. *talea*, a stick, cutting], 1. originally, a stick with cross notches representing the amount of a debt owing or paid: usually the stick was split lengthwise, half for the debtor and half for the creditor. 2. anything used as a record for an account. 3. an account; reckoning; score. 4. either of two corresponding parts of something; counterpart. 5. agreement; correspondence. 6. a notch or mark made on a tally. 7. a mark representing a certain number of objects in a tally; hence, 8. any number of objects used as a unit in counting. 9. an identifying tag or label. *v.t.* [TALLIED (-id), TALLYING], 1. to put on or as on a tally; record. 2. to count (usually with *up*). 3. to put a label or tag on. 4. to make (two things) agree or correspond. *v.i.* 1. to record something, as a score. 2. to agree; correspond. —*SYN.* see **agree.**

tal·ly·ho (tal′i-hō′; *for n. & v.*, tal′i-hō′), *interj.* [altered < Fr. *taiaut, tayaut*], the cry of a hunter on sighting the fox. *n.* 1. a cry of "tallyho." 2. a coach drawn by four horses. *v.t.* to announce sight of (the fox) by the cry of "tallyho." *v.i.* to cry "tallyho."

tal·ly·man (tal′i-mən), *n.* [*pl.* TALLYMEN (-mən)], 1. a person who sells goods to be paid for in installments. 2. a person who tallies something.

Tal·mud (tal′mud, täl′mood), *n.* [Heb. *talmūdh*, instruction < *lāmadh*, to learn], the collection of writings constituting the Jewish civil and religious law: it consists of two parts, the Mishnah (text) and the Gemara (commentary), but the term is sometimes restricted to the Gemara; cf. **Halakah** and **Haggada.**

Tal·mud·ic (tal-mud′ik), *adj.* of or in the Talmud.

Tal·mud·i·cal (tal-mud′i-k′l), *adj.* Talmudic.

Tal·mud·ist (tal′məd-ist), *n.* 1. any of the compilers of the Talmud. 2. a student of or expert in the Talmud. 3. a person who accepts the authority of the Talmud.

tal·on (tal′ən), *n.* [ME., a talon, claw; OFr., a heel, spur; LL. **talo* < L. *talus*, an ankle], 1. *usually in pl.* the claw of an animal or bird of prey, as the hawk, vulture, etc.; hence, 2. *pl.* human fingers or hands like claws in appearance or grasp. 3. in a lock, the part of the bolt upon which the key presses as it is turned. 4. in *architecture*, an ogee molding. 5. in *card games*, the cards remaining after the hands are dealt; the stock.

tal·oned (tal′ənd), *adj.* having talons.

Ta·los (tā′los), *n.* [Gr. *Talōs*], 1. in *Greek mythology*, *a*) an inventor killed because of jealousy by Daedalus, his uncle. *b*) a man of brass given by Zeus to Minos, King of Crete, as a watchman. 2. a long-range guided missile of the United States Navy and Air Force, launched either from the ground or from a ship.

tal·pa·ta·te (täl′pä-tä′tā), *n.* [Sp. *tepetate* < Nahuatl *tepetatl* < *tetl*, a stone + *petlatl*, a mat], in *geology*, 1. a Central and South American rock containing volcanic ash. 2. a Central American volcanic soil of low grade.

tal·pe·ta·te (täl′pi-tä′tā), *n.* talpatate.

tal. qual., *talis qualis*, [L.], of ordinary sort; average.

ta·luk (tä′look, tä-look′), *n.* [Ar. *ta'alluq* < *alaqa*, to adhere], in India, 1. an estate inherited by the native owner. 2. a part of a district subdivided for tax collection.

ta·lus (tā′ləs), *n.* [*pl.* TALUSES (-iz), TALI (-lī)], [L., an ankle], 1. the anklebone; astragalus. 2. the entire ankle.

ta·lus (tā′ləs), *n.* [Fr.; OFr. *talu;* said to be < L. *talus*, an ankle, in special sense], 1. a slope. 2. the sloping face of a wall, narrow at the top and wide at the base, in a fortification. 3. in *geology*, a sloping pile of rock fragments at the foot of a cliff.

tam (tam), *n.* a tam-o'-shanter.

tam·a·ble (tām′ə-b′l), *adj.* that can be tamed: also spelled **tameable.**

ta·ma·le (tə-mä′li), *n.* [Mex. Sp. *tamal*, pl. *tamales;* Nahuatl *tamalli*], a native Mexican food of minced meat and red peppers rolled in corn meal, wrapped in corn husks, and cooked by baking, steaming, etc.

tam·an·du (tam′ən-do̅o̅′), *n.* a tamandua.

ta·man·dua (tä′män-dwä′), *n.* [Port. *tamanduá* < Braz. (Tupi) *tamanduá* < *taixi*, ant + *mondê*, to catch], a small, tree-dwelling anteater of tropical America.

tam·a·rack (tam′ə-rak′), *n.* [< Am. Ind. (Algonquian)], 1. any of a number of related larch trees usually found in swamps. 2. the wood of any of these trees.

ta·ma·rau (tä′mə-rou′), *n.* a small, wild buffalo native to the island of Mindoro in the Philippines.

tam·a·rin (tam′ə-rin), *n.* [Fr. < the native (Carib) name in Guiana], any of several South American marmosets like squirrels, having long, silky fur.

tam·a·rind (tam′ə-rind′), *n.* [Sp. *tamarindo;* Ar. *tamr hindī*, date of India], 1. a tropical tree with red-streaked yellow flowers and brown pods with an acid pulp. 2. its fruit, used in foods, medicine, etc.

tam·a·risk (tam′ə-risk′), *n.* [LL. *tamariscus*, var. of *tamarix* < Ar. *tamr*, a date; cf. TAMARIND], any of a number of related trees or shrubs with slender branches and feathery clusters of pinkish flowers.

ta·ma·sha (tə-mä′shə), *n.* [Ar. *tamāsha*, a walking around], in India, a spectacle; show; entertainment.

Ta·ma·tave (tä′mȧ-täv′), *n.* a seaport in Malagasy: pop., 49,000.

Ta·ma·u·li·pas (tä-mä′oo-lē′päs), *n.* a state of northeastern Mexico, on the Gulf of Mexico: area, 30,731 sq. mi.; pop., 978,000; capital, Ciudad Victoria.

Tam·bo·ra (täm′bô-rä′), *n.* a volcano on Sumbara Island, Indonesia: height, 9,042 ft.

tam·bour (tam′boor), *n.* [Fr., a drum; It. *tamburo;* Ar. *ṭanbūr*, colloq. *ṭanbur*, stringed instrument < Per.; meaning altered by association with OFr. *tabour* (see

TABOR)], 1. a drum. 2. an embroidery frame of two closely fitting hoops that hold the cloth stretched between them. 3. embroidery worked on such a frame. *v.t. & v.i.* to embroider on a tambour.

tam·bou·rin (tam′boo-rin; Fr. tän′bōō′ran′), *n.* [Fr., dim. of *tambour;* see TAMBOUR], 1. a kind of long drum used in Provence. 2. *a*) a quick, sprightly dance of Provence, originally accompanied by such a drum. *b*) the music for this dance.

tam·bou·rine (tam′bə-rēn′), *n.* [< Fr. *tambourin;* see TAMBOURIN], a shallow hand drum having one head with jingling metal disks around it: it is played by shaking, hitting with the knuckles, etc.

TAMBOURINE

Tam·bov (täm-bôf′), *n.* 1. a region of central European R.S.F.S.R.: pop., 1,547,000. 2. its capital: pop., 170,000.

tame (tām), *adj.* [ME.; AS. *tam;* akin to G. *zahm;* IE. base *domā-, etc., to tame, subdue, seen also in L. *domare,* Gr. *damāein,* to tame; cf. DOME, DOMESTIC, etc.], 1. changed from a wild to a domesticated state, as animals trained for man's use. 2. like a domesticated animal in nature; gentle; docile. 3. crushed by or as by domestication; submissive; servile. 4. without spirit or force; dull: as, *tame* talk. 5. in *agriculture,* cultivated: said of plants or land. *v.t.* [TAMED (tāmd), TAMING], 1. to make tame, or domestic. 2. to overcome the wildness or fierceness of; make gentle, docile, or spiritless; subdue. 3. to make less intense; soften; dull.

tame·a·ble (tām′ə-b'l), *adj.* tamable.

tame·less (tām′lis), *adj.* 1. not tamed. 2. not tamable.

tam·er (tām′ēr), *n.* a person or thing that tames: as, a lion *tamer.*

Tam·er·lane (tam′ēr-lān′), *n.* (*Timur Lenk*), Mongol warrior whose conquests extended from the Volga River to the Persian Gulf; 1336?–1405.

Tam·il (tam′il, tum′il), *n.* [Tamil *Tamir, Tamiḷ,* native name of the people and their language], 1. any of a Dravidian people of southern India and northern Ceylon. 2. the Dravidian language of the Tamils, ancient or modern, spoken over a wide area of southern India and in northern Ceylon.

Taming of the Shrew, a comedy (c. 1594) by Shakespeare.

Tam·ma·ny (tam′ə-ni), *n.* [altered < *Tamanend,* lit., the affable, name of a 17th-c. chief of the Delaware Indians celebrated for his wisdom and friendliness toward white men, and hence, as *Saint Tammany,* humorously regarded as patron saint of the U.S.], a powerful Democratic political organization of New York City, founded in 1789: also **Tammany Society.** *adj.* of Tammany's theories, practices, members, etc.

Tammany Hall, 1. Tammany. 2. the headquarters of Tammany: now called *Chatham Hall.*

Tam·mer·fors (täm′ēr-fôrs′), *n.* Tampere.

Tam·muz (tä′mooz), *n.* [Heb. *tammūz;* Assyr.-Bab. *Du'uzu;* Sumerian *dummuzi,* lit., ? son of life, son who rises], 1. a Babylonian and Assyrian god whose supposed annual death and resurrection symbolized the winter and spring cycle. 2. the tenth month of the Jewish year: see **Jewish calendar.** Also spelled **Thammuz.**

tam-o'-shan·ter (tam′ə-shan′tēr), *n.* [< the name of the main character of Burns's poem "Tam o' Shanter"], a Scottish cap with a round, flat top and, often, a center tassel: also **tam.**

TAM-O'-SHANTER

tamp (tamp), *v.t.* [? back-formation < *tampin,* var. of *tampion*], 1. in blasting, to pack clay, sand, etc. around the charge in (the drill hole). 2. to pack or pound down by a series of blows or taps.

Tam·pa (tam′pə), *n.* a seaport in west central Florida: pop., 275,000.

tamp·er (tamp′ēr), *n.* 1. a person or thing that tamps. 2. a heavy bar or timber with a flat, metal tip, for tamping.

tam·per (tam′pēr), *v.i.* [var. of *temper*], to contrive something secretly; plot; scheme.

tamper with, 1. to make secret, illegal arrangements with; bribe. 2. to interfere with; meddle. 3. to change by meddling; make corrupt, illegal, etc.

Tam·pe·re (täm′pe-re), *n.* a city in southwestern Finland: pop., 122,000: Swedish name, *Tammerfors.*

Tam·pi·co (tam-pē′kō; Sp. täm-pē′kô), *n.* a seaport in east central Mexico, in Tamaulipas state: pop., 106,000.

tam·pi·on (tam′pi-ən), *n.* [Fr. *tampon,* nasalized form < *tapon, tape,* a bung < Gmc. base of Eng. *tap,* G. *zapfen,* a bung], 1. a plug or stopper put in the muzzle of a gun when it is not in use. 2. a similar plug for the end of an organ pipe. Also **tompion.**

tam·pon (tam′pon), *n.* [Fr.; see TAMPION], a plug of cotton or other absorbent material put into a wound, cavity, etc. to stop bleeding or absorb secretions. *v.t.* to put a tampon into.

tam-tam (tum′tum′), *n.* [Hind.; of echoic origin], 1. a large, slightly convex, disk-shaped gong, struck with a felt-covered drumstick. 2. a tom-tom.

tan (tan), *n.* [Fr.; ML. *tannum*], 1. the bark of oak and certain other trees, crushed to make tannin. 2. bark from which tannin has been extracted, used to cover racecourses, etc. 3. tannin or a solution made from it, used to tan leather. 4. a yellowish-brown color. 5. such a color given to the skin by exposure to the sun. *adj.* [TANNER (-ēr), TANNEST (-ist)], 1. of or for tanning. 2. yellowish-brown. *v.t.* [TANNED (tand), TANNING], [Late AS. *tannian* & ME. *tannen,* ML. *tannare* < the *n.*], 1. to change (hide) into leather by soaking in tannin. 2. to produce a tan color in, as by exposure to the sun. 3. [Colloq.], to whip severely; flog. *v.i.* to become tanned.

tan one's hide, [Colloq.], to whip one severely; flog.

tan, tan., tangent.

Ta·na (tä′nä), *n.* 1. a river in northern Norway, forming part of the boundary with Finland and flowing into the Arctic Ocean. 2. a river in Kenya colony, eastern Africa, flowing into the Indian Ocean: length, 500 mi. 3. a lake in northern Ethiopia: area, 1,10[illegible] sq. mi.

tan·a·ger (tan′ə-jēr), *n.* [Mod. L. *tanagra;* Port. *tângara* < Braz. (Tupi) *tangara*], any of several small America[n] songbirds: the males usually are brilliantly colored.

Tan·a·gra (tan′ə-grə), *n.* an ancient Greek town in Boeotia, known for the figurines found there.

Ta·na·na (tan′ə-nä′, tä-nä-nä′), *n.* a river in eastern Alaska, flowing into the Yukon River.

Ta·na·na·rive (tä′nä′nä′rēv′), *n.* a city in central Malagasy republic: its capital: pop., 206,000: formerly called *Antananarivo.*

tan·bark (tan′bärk′), *n.* any bark containing tannin, used to tan hides and, after the tannin has been ex[-]tracted, to cover race tracks, circus rings, etc.

Tan·cred (taŋ′krid), *n.* Norman leader of the firs[t] crusade; 1078?–1112.

tan·dem (tan′dəm), *adv.* [orig. punning use of L. *tandem,* at length (of time)], one behind another; in single file. *n.* 1. a two-wheeled carriage drawn by horses harnessed tandem. 2. a team, as of horses, harnessed tandem. 3. a bicycle with two seats and two sets of pedals placed tandem. *adj.* having two parts or things placed tandem.

Ta·ney, Roger Brooke (brook tô′ni), 1777–1864, American jurist; chief justice, United States Supreme Court (1836–1864).

tang (taŋ), *n.* [ME. *tange;* ON. *tangi,* a sting, point, dagger; cf. TONGS], 1. a projecting point or prong on a chisel, file, knife, etc. to fit into the handle. 2. a strong and penetrating taste or odor. 3. a touch or trace (with *of*). 4. a special or characteristic flavor, quality, etc. *v.t.* to provide (a knife, etc.) with a tang.

tang (taŋ), *n.* [echoic], a loud, ringing sound; twang. *v.t. & v.i.* to sound with a loud ringing.

Tan·gan·yi·ka (taŋ′gan-yē′kə), *n.* a country in eastern Africa, on the Indian Ocean, a member of the British Commonwealth of Nations: until 1961, a British trust territory: area, 361,800 sq. mi.; pop., 9,238,000; capital, Dar es Salaam.

Tanganyika, Lake, a lake between the Congo (sense 2) and Tanganyika: area, 12,700 sq. mi.

Tang Dynasty (täŋ), a Chinese dynasty (618–90[7] A.D.) under which printing was developed and art and literature flourished.

tan·ge·lo (tan′jə-lō′), *n.* [*pl.* TANGELOS (-lōz′)], [*tangerin*[*e*] + *pomelo*], a fruit produced by crossing a tangerine with a grapefruit, or pomelo.

tan·gen·cy (tan′jən-si), *n.* the state of being tangent.

tan·gent (tan′jənt), *adj.* [L. *tangens,* ppr. of *tangere,* to touch; see TACT], 1. touching. 2. in *geometry,* meeting a curved line or surface at one point but ordinarily not intersecting it: said of a line or surface. *n.* 1. a tangent curve, line, or surface. 2. in *trigonometry,* the ratio of the side opposite the given acute angle in a right-angled triangle to the side opposite the other acute angle: the tangent of an obtuse angle is numerically equal to that of its supplement, but is of opposite sign. Abbreviated **tan, tan.** —*SYN.* see **adjacent.**

go (or **fly**) **off at** (or **on**) **a tangent,** to break off suddenly from a line of action or train of thought and pursue another course.

tan·gen·tial (tan-jen′shəl), *adj.* 1. of, like, or in the direction of, a tangent. 2. drawn as a tangent. 3. turned aside from a straight course; digressing. 4. merely touching a subject, not dealing with it at length.

tan·ge·rine (tan′jə-rēn′, tan′jə-rēn′), *n.* [< Fr. *Tanger,* Tangier, Morocco], 1. a small, loose-skinned orang[e] with a deep, reddish-yellow color and segments that are easily separated. 2. a deep, reddish-yellow color.

tan·gi·bil·i·ty (tan'jə-bil'ə-ti), *n.* the quality or state of being tangible.

tan·gi·ble (tan'jə-b'l), *adj.* [LL. *tangibilis* < L. *tangere*, to touch; see TACT], 1. that can be touched; that can be felt by touch; having actual form and substance. 2. that can be appraised for value: as, *tangible* assets. 3. that can be understood; definite; objective. ***n.pl.*** property that can be appraised for value; assets having real substance; material things. —***SYN.*** see **perceptible.**

tan·gi·bly (tan'jə-bli), *adv.* in a tangible manner.

Tan·gier (tan-jêr'), *n.* 1. a province in the sultanate of Morocco: it was an international zone until 1956: area, 135 sq. mi.; pop., 183,000. 2. its capital on the Strait of Gibraltar: pop., 60,000.

tan·gle (taŋ'g'l), *v.t.* [TANGLED (-g'ld), TANGLING], [nasalized (Anglo-N.) var. of obs. *tagle;* ME. *taglen* < ON.; prob. confused with following word], 1. to hinder, obstruct, or confuse by covering, circling, entwining, etc. 2. to catch in or as in a net or snare; trap. 3. to make a knot or snarl of; intertwine. *v.i.* to become tangled. *n.* 1. an intertwined, confused mass of things, as string, branches, etc.; snarl. 2. a jumbled, confused condition; muddle. 3. a perplexed state.
to tangle with, to come to grips or blows with.

tan·gle (taŋ'g'l), *n.* [< Scand.; cf. Norw. *tongul,* ON. *thöngull*], either of two kinds of large, edible seaweed.

tan·gle·ber·ry (taŋ'g'l-ber'i), *n.* [*pl.* TANGLEBERRIES (-iz)], [*tangle* (intertwine) + *berry*], a kind of huckleberry found especially in the eastern United States.

tan·gly (taŋ'gli), *adj.* full of tangles; snarled; confusing.

tan·go (taŋ'gō), *n.* [*pl.* TANGOS (-gōz)], [Am. Sp., a dance; Sp., a Negro dance from Cuba], 1. a South American dance with long gliding steps and intricate movements and poses. 2. music for this dance in 2/4 or 4/4 time. *v.i.* to dance the tango.

tan·gram (taŋ'grəm), *n.* [prob. arbitrary coinage on analogy of *anagram, cryptogram,* etc.], a Chinese puzzle made by cutting a square into five triangles, a square, and a rhomboid, and using these pieces to form different figures and designs.

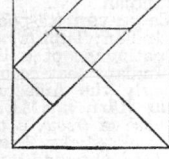

TANGRAM

tang·y (taŋ'i), *adj.* [TANGIER (-i-ẽr), TANGIEST (-i-ist)], having a tang, or flavor.

Ta·nis (tā'nis), *n.* an ancient city in Egypt, in the Nile delta: Biblical name, *Zoan.*

tan·ist (tan'ist, thôn'ist), *n.* [Ir. & Gael. *tānaiste,* next heir, hence lord of a country, lit., second, parallel < OIr. *tān,* estate], the elected heir of a Celtic chief.

tan·ist·ry (tan'is-tri, thôn'is-tri), *n.* in ancient Ireland, the system of electing a tanist from among the chief's relatives during his lifetime.

Tan·jore (tan-jôr', tan-jōr'), *n.* a city in Madras state, India: pop., 67,000.

tank (taŋk), *n.* [in sense 1 < Gujarati *tānkh;* in other senses < or influenced by Port. *tanque,* a tank, pond, pool < L. *stagnum,* a pond, standing water; cf. STAGNANT], 1. originally, in India, a natural or artificial pool or pond used for water storage. 2. any large container for liquid or gas: as, a gasoline *tank,* a swimming *tank.* 3. [name orig. used for purpose of secrecy during manufacture], an armored, self-propelled vehicle moving on caterpillar treads: valuable in modern warfare for its fire power, rapid movement, and ability to operate over most kinds of terrain. *v.t.* to put, store, or process in a tank.

TANK

tank·age (taŋk'ij), *n.* [see -AGE], 1. the capacity of a tank or a number of tanks collectively. 2. the storage of fluids, gases, etc. in tanks. 3. the charge for such storage. 4. slaughterhouse waste from which the fat has been rendered in tanks: it is dried and ground for use as fertilizer or feed.

tank·ard (taŋk'ẽrd), *n.* [ME.; OFr. *tanquart;* akin to D. *tanckaert,* ML. *tancardus*], a large drinking cup with a handle and, often, a hinged lid.

tank car, 1. a large tank on wheels, for carrying liquids and gases by rail. 2. a tank truck.

tank destroyer, a highly mobile, armored half-track on which antitank guns are mounted.

tank·er (taŋk'ẽr), *n.* 1. a ship especially equipped to carry large quantities of oil or other liquids. 2. a tank car. 3. a tank truck.

tank farming, the growing of plants in nutrient solutions instead of in soil; hydroponics.

tank·ful (taŋk'fool), *n.* as much as a tank will hold.

tank town, 1. a railroad stop for locomotives to fill their boilers with water: it usually became the site of a small town. 2. any small or unimportant town.

tank truck, a motor truck built to transport gasoline, oil, or other liquids.

tan·nage (tan'ij), *n.* [see -AGE], 1. the act or process of tanning. 2. something that has been tanned.

tan·nate (tan'āt), *adj.* a salt of tannic acid.

Tan·nen·berg (tan'ən-bũrg'; G. tän'ən-berkh'), *n.* a town in northern Poland, formerly in East Prussia: scene of a battle (1914) of World War I, in which the Germans overwhelmingly defeated the Russians.

tan·ner (tan'ẽr), *n.* a person whose work is making leather by tanning hides.

tan·ner·y (tan'ẽr-i), *n.* [*pl.* TANNERIES (-iz)], a place where leather is made by tanning hides.

Tann·häu·ser (tän'hoi-zẽr; Eng. *also* tan'hoi-zẽr), *n.* [G.], 1. a German knight and minnesinger of the 13th century, identified with a legendary knight who seeks absolution after giving himself up to revelry in the Venusberg. 2. an opera by Wagner (1845) based on this legend.

tan·nic (tan'ik), *adj.* of, like, or obtained from tan (sense 1) or tannin.

tannic acid, [< *tan, n.* + *-ic*], 1. a yellowish, astringent substance, $C_{14}H_{10}O_9$, derived from oak bark, gallnuts, etc. and used in tanning, dyeing, medicine, etc. 2. any of a number of similar substances.

tan·nin (tan'in), *n.* [Fr. *tanin* < *tan,* tan], tannic acid.

tan·ning (tan'iŋ), *n.* [*tan* + *-ing*], 1. the art or process of making leather from hides. 2. the act of making the skin brown by exposure to the sun or weather. 3. [Colloq.], a severe whipping; flogging.

Tan·nu Tu·va (tä'noo too-vä'), the Tuva Autonomous Region: the former name.

tan·sy (tan'zi), *n.* [*pl.* TANSIES (-ziz)], [ME.; OFr. *tanesie;* ML. *athanasia;* Gr. *athanasia,* immortality: from the medicinal properties of some varieties or because the dried flowers retain their appearance], any of a number of related, strong-smelling plants with clusters of small, yellow flowers, used in medicine.

Tan·ta (tän'tä), *n.* a city in northern Egypt, in the center of the Nile delta: pop., 95,000.

tan·ta·late (tan'tə-lāt'), *n.* a salt of tantalic acid.

tan·tal·ic (tan-tal'ik), *adj.* 1. of, derived from, or containing tantalum, especially with a valence of five. 2. designating a colorless crystalline acid, $HTaO_3$, that forms complex salts.

tan·ta·lite (tan'tə-līt'), *n.* [G.; see TANTALUM & -ITE], a heavy, black, crystalline mineral, $Fe(TaO_3)_2$, a tantalate of iron.

tan·ta·li·za·tion (tan'tə-li-zā'shən, tan'tə-lī-zā'shən), *n.* a tantalizing or being tantalized.

tan·ta·lize (tan'tə-līz'), *v.t.* [TANTALIZED (-līzd'), TANTALIZING], [< *Tantalus*], to promise or show something desirable to (a person) and then remove or withhold it; arouse hope and then disappointment in; tease.

tan·ta·liz·ing (tan'tə-līz'iŋ), *adj.* [ppr. of *tantalize*], that tantalizes; teasing.

tan·ta·lous (tan'tə-ləs), *adj.* of, derived from, or containing tantalum, especially with a valence of three.

tan·ta·lum (tan'tə-ləm), *n.* [Mod. L. < *Tantalus:* so named because its insolubility in most acids made extraction from the mineral difficult], a rare, steel-blue, corrosion-resisting, metallic chemical element found in various minerals and used for electric light filaments, grids and plates in radio tubes, surgical instruments, etc.: symbol, Ta; at. wt., 180.88; at. no., 73.

Tan·ta·lus (tan'tə-ləs), *n.* [ME. *Tantale;* L.; Gr. *Tantalos*], 1. in *Greek mythology,* a king, son of Zeus, whose punishment in the lower world was eternal hunger and thirst: he was doomed to stand in water that always receded when he tried to drink it and under branches of fruit he could never reach; hence, 2. [t-], a stand with decanters that, although plainly visible, cannot be removed until the bar that locks them in place is raised.

tan·ta·mount (tan'tə-mount'), *adj.* [< Anglo-Fr. *tant amunter,* to amount to as much < L. *tantus,* so much + OFr. *amonter* (see AMOUNT)], having equal force, value, effect, etc.; equivalent.

tan·ta·ra (tan'tə-rə, tan-tar'ə, tan-tä'rə), *n.* [echoic], 1. a trumpet blast or fanfare. 2. a sound like this.

tan·tiv·y (tan-tiv'i), *adv.* [prob. echoic of sound of a horse galloping], at full gallop; headlong. *adj.* swift; fast. *n.* [*pl.* TANTIVIES (-iz)], 1. a gallop; rapid movement. 2. a hunting cry to signal a faster chase.

‡tant mieux (tän' myö'), [Fr.], so much the better.

‡tan·to (tän'tô), *adv.* [It.; L. *tantum,* so much], in *music,* too much; so much: a direction to the performer, as, allegro non *tanto.*

‡tant pis (tän' pē'), [Fr.], so much the worse.

tan·trum (tan'trəm), *n.* [earlier form *tantarum* suggests pseudo-L. coinage on *tantara*], a violent, willful outburst of annoyance, rage, etc.; fit of bad temper.

Tao·ism (tou'iz'm, dou'iz'm), *n.* [Chinese *tao,* the

way; + *-ism*], a Chinese religion and philosophy based on the doctrines of Lao-tse (6th century B.C.) and advocating simplicity, selflessness, etc.

Tao·ist (tou'ist, dou'ist), ***n.*** a person who believes in or practices Taoism. ***adj.*** of Taoism or Taoists.

Tao·is·tic (tou-is'tik, dou-is'tik), ***adj.*** Taoist.

Taos (tous), ***n.*** a resort town in northern New Mexico.

tap (tap), ***v.t.*** [TAPPED (tapt), TAPPING], [ME. *tappen;* OFr. *taper;* of echoic origin], 1. to strike lightly and rapidly. 2. to strike something lightly with: as, he *tapped* a stick against the window. 3. to make or do by tapping: as, he *tapped* a message with his fingers. 4. to repair (a shoe) by adding a thickness of leather to the heel or sole. ***v.i.*** to strike a light, rapid blow. ***n.*** 1. a light, rapid blow, or the sound made by it. 2. the leather added in tapping a shoe.

tap (tap), ***n.*** [ME. *tappe;* AS. *tæppe;* akin to G. *zapfen,* ON. *tappi;* IE. base **dāp-, *dəp- < *dā(i)-,* to cut out, tear out], 1. a device for starting or stopping the flow of liquid in a pipe, barrel, etc.; faucet. 2. a plug, cork, etc. for stopping or opening a hole in a container holding a liquid. 3. liquor of a certain kind or quality, as drawn from a certain tap. 4. a tool used to cut threads in internal screws. 5. [Colloq.], a place that serves liquor; bar; taproom. 6. in *electricity,* a place in a circuit where a connection can be made. ***v.t.*** [TAPPED (tapt), TAPPING], [AS. *tæppian* < the *n.*], 1. to put a tap or spigot on. 2. to put a hole in for drawing off liquid: as, the farmer *tapped* a sugar maple tree. 3. to pull out the tap or plug from. 4. to draw (liquid) from a container, etc. 5. to drain liquid from (a cavity, abscess, etc.) by surgical operation. 6. to make an opening in or connection with: as, they *tapped* the water main to supply the new building. 7. to cut threads on the inner surface of (a nut, etc.). 8. to make a connection with secretly: as, the detective *tapped* the telephone wires to overhear what was said.
on tap, 1. in a tapped or open cask (of liquor) and ready to be drawn; on draft. 2. [Colloq.], ready for consideration or action.

ta·pa (tä'pä), ***n.*** [< native Polynesian name], an unwoven cloth made by people in the Pacific islands from the treated inner bark of a kind of mulberry tree.

Ta·pa·józ (tä'pə-zhôs'), ***n.*** a river in central Brazil, flowing northward into the Amazon: length, 1,100 mi.

tap-dance (tap'dans', tap'däns'), ***v.i.*** to perform or dance a tap dance.

tap dance, a dance performed with sharp, loud taps of the foot, toe, or heel at each step.

tape (tāp), ***n.*** [ME. *tappe, tape;* AS. *tæppe,* a fillet; prob. < base of *tæppa;* see TAP (faucet)], 1. a strong, narrow, woven strip of cotton, linen, etc. used to bind seams in garments, tie bundles, etc. 2. a narrow strip or band of steel, paper, etc. 3. a strip of cloth stretched between posts as the finishing line of a race track. 4. a tapeline. See also **adhesive tape, friction tape,** etc. ***v.t.*** [TAPED (tāpt), TAPING], 1. to put tape on or around, as for binding, tying, etc. 2. to measure by using a tapeline. 3. [Colloq.], to tape-record.

tape·line (tāp'lin'), ***n.*** a tape with marks in inches, feet, etc. for measuring.

tape measure, a tapeline.

ta·per (tā'pẽr), ***n.*** [ME.; AS. *tapur;* prob. by dissimilation < L. *papyrus;* see PAPER], 1. *a)* originally, a wax candle used in religious services. *b)* a very slender candle. 2. a long wick coated with wax, used for lighting candles, lamps, etc. 3. any feeble light. 4. *a)* a gradual decrease in width or thickness: as, the *taper* of a pyramid. *b)* a gradual decrease in action, power, etc. 5. something that tapers. ***adj.*** gradually decreased in size to a point. ***v.t. & v.i.*** 1. to decrease gradually in width or thickness. 2. to lessen; diminish.
taper off, 1. to become smaller gradually toward one end. 2. to stop gradually.

tape-re·cord (tāp'ri-kôrd'), ***v.t.*** to record on a tape recorder.

tape recorder, a recording device similar to a wire recorder, but using a magnetic tape instead of a wire.

tap·es·try (tap'is-tri), ***n.*** [*pl.* TAPESTRIES (-triz)], [Late ME. *tapsterie,* earlier *tapicerie;* OFr. *tapisserie* < *tapis, tapiz,* a carpet; LL. **tapitium;* Gr. *tapētion,* dim. of *tapēs,* a carpet], a heavy cloth woven by hand or machinery with decorative designs and pictures and used as a wall hanging, furniture covering, etc. ***v.t.*** [TAPESTRIED (-trid), TAPESTRYING], 1. to decorate as with a tapestry. 2. to depict by weaving in a tapestry.

ta·pe·tum (tə-pē'təm), ***n.*** [*pl.* TAPETA (-tə)], [LL. < L. *tapete,* a carpet], 1. in *anatomy & zoology,* any of various membranous layers; especially, the iridescent choroid membrane in the eyes of certain animals, as the cat. 2. in *botany,* a layer of cells lining the inner wall of a sporangium or anther.

tape·worm (tāp'wũrm'), ***n.*** any of several kinds of ribbonlike worms that live as parasites in the intestines of man and other animals.

tap·house (tap'hous'), ***n.*** [*tap* (faucet) + *house*], a tavern, inn, or bar: also **tap house.**

tap·i·o·ca (tap'i-ō'kə), ***n.*** [Port. & Sp. < Braz. (Tupi) *tipyoca* < *ty,* juice + *pya,* heart + *oc, og,* to squeeze out], a starchy granular substance prepared from the root of the cassava plant, used to make puddings, thicken soups, etc.

ta·pir (tā'pẽr), ***n.*** [*pl.* TAPIRS (-pẽrz), TAPIR; see PLURAL, II, D, 1], [Sp.; Braz. (Tupi) *tapyra,* large mammal, tapir], any of several large, hoglike mammals of tropical America and the Malayan peninsula: tapirs have flexible snouts, feed on plants, and move about at night.

SOUTH AMERICAN TAPIR (3 ft. high at shoulder)

tap·is (tap'ē, tap'is; Fr. tȧ'pē'), ***n.*** [Fr.; see TAPESTRY], tapestry used as a curtain, tablecloth, carpet, or the like.
on (or upon) the tapis, under consideration or deliberation.

tap·per (tap'ẽr), ***n.*** a person or thing that taps; specifically, a telegraph key.

tap·pet (tap'it), ***n.*** [< *tap* (to strike)], in a machine, a projection or lever that moves or is moved by intermittent contact with another part.

tap·ping (tap'iŋ), ***n.*** 1. the act of a person or thing that taps. 2. *pl.* that which runs from a tap or is drawn by tapping.

tap·room (tap'rōōm', tap'room'), ***n.*** [cf. TAPHOUSE], a barroom.

tap·root (tap'rōōt', tap'root'), ***n.*** [*tap* (faucet) + *root*], a main root, growing almost vertically downward, from which small branch roots spread out.

taps (taps), ***n.pl.*** [< *tap* (to strike), because originally a drum signal], a bugle call or drum signal to put out lights in retiring for the night, as in an army camp: also sounded at the burial of a soldier, sailor, etc.

tap·ster (tap'stẽr), ***n.*** [ME. *tappestere;* AS. *tæppestre,* barmaid < *tæppe;* see TAP (faucet)], 1. originally, a barmaid. 2. a bartender.

Ta·pu·ya (tä-pōō'yä), ***n.*** [*pl.* TAPUYA], a Tapuyan Indian.

Ta·pu·yan (tä-pōō'yən), ***adj.*** [Port. *Tapuya,* Tapuyan Indian; Tupi *tapuya,* a savage, enemy; + *-an*], designating or of a linguistic group of South American Indians that occupied a large part of Brazil, particularly the Amazon Valley.

tar (tär), ***n.*** [ME. *tere, terre;* AS. *teru, tero;* prob. < base of *treow,* a tree, in sense "product of trees"], a thick, sticky, brown to black liquid with a pungent odor, obtained by the destructive distillation of wood, coal, peat, shale, etc.: tars are composed of hydrocarbons and their derivatives, and are used for protecting and preserving surfaces, in making various organic compounds, etc. ***v.t.*** [TARRED (tärd), TARRING], to cover or smear with or as with tar. ***adj.*** 1. of or like tar. 2. tarred.
tar and feather, to cover (a person) with tar and feathers as a punishment: it is a practice of mob law.
tarred with the same brush (or **stick**), having similar characteristics or traits, especially obnoxious ones.

tar (tär), ***n.*** [abbrev. of *tarpaulin*], [Colloq.], a sailor.

ta·ran·tass, ta·ran·tas (tä'rän-täs'), ***n.*** [Russ. *tarantas*], a large, low, four-wheeled carriage without springs, used in Russia.

tar·an·tel·la (tar'ən-tel'ə), ***n.*** [It., dim. of *Taranto,* Italy; popularly associated with the *tarantula* because said to be a cure for *tarantism*], 1. a fast, whirling, southern Italian dance for couples, in 6/8 time. 2. music for this.

tar·ant·ism (tar'ən-tiz'm), ***n.*** [It. *tarantismo* < *Taranto,* Italy: so called because formerly epidemic in the vicinity of Taranto; popularly associated with the tarantula, by whose bite it was said to be caused; cf. TARANTULA, TARANTELLA], a nervous disease characterized by hysteria and a mania for dancing, especially as prevalent in southern Italy during the 16th and 17th centuries: also spelled **tarentism.**

tar·ant·ist (tar'ən-tist), ***n.*** a person who has tarantism.

Ta·ran·to (tə-ran'tō; It. tä'rän-tô'), ***n.*** 1. a gulf of the Mediterranean. 2. a city in southeastern Italy, on the Gulf of Taranto: pop., 179,000 (est. 1947): ancient name, *Tarentum.*

ta·ran·tu·la (tə-ran'choo-lə), ***n.*** [ML. < *Taranto,* Italy (L. *Tarentum*): so called because the spider was found near by], any of a number of large, hairy, somewhat poisonous spiders of southern Europe, the southern United States, and tropical America; specifically, an Italian species whose bite was popularly but wrongly supposed to cause tarantism.

Ta·ra·wa (tä-rä'wä, tä'rä-wä), ***n.*** one of the Gilbert Islands in the Pacific, near the equator: site of a battle (1943) in World War II.

TARANTULA (1–3 in. long)

ta·rax·a·cum (tə-rak'sə-kəm),

n. [Mod. L.; Ar. *tarakhshaqūn*, wild chicory < Per.], a drug made from the dried rhizome and roots of the dandelion, used as a tonic.

tar·boosh (tär-bōōsh′), *n.* [Ar. *ṭarbūsh*], a brimless cap of cloth or felt shaped like a truncated cone, worn by Moslem men, sometimes as the inner part of a turban.

Tar·dieu, An·dré Pierre Ga·bri·el A·mé·dée (äṅ′drā′ pyâr gȧ′brē′el′ ȧ′mā′dā′ tȧr′dyö′), 1876–1945; French statesman; premier of France (1929–1930; 1932).

tar·di·grade (tär′di-grād′), *adj.* [Fr.; L. *tardigradus*; see TARDY & GRADE], 1. moving slowly; slow-paced; sluggish. 2. designating or of any of a class of minute water animals with segmented bodies and four pairs of legs, usually considered as belonging to the arthropods. *n.* a tardigrade animal.

tar·di·ly (tär′di-li), *adv.* in a tardy manner; late.

tar·di·ness (tär′di-nis), *n.* the quality or condition of being tardy.

‡tar·do (tär′dô), *adj.* & *adv.* [It.; see TARDY], in *music*, slow: a direction to the performer.

tar·dy (tär′di), *adj.* [TARDIER (-di-ẽr), TARDIEST (-di-ist)], [Fr. *tardif*; LL. **tardivus* < L. *tardus*, slow], 1. slow; slow-moving. 2. late; behind time; delayed; dilatory.

SYN.—**tardy** applies to that which comes or occurs after the proper or appointed time, either from a lack of punctuality or because of inadvertent delay (two of the pupils were *tardy* this morning); **late** applies to that which fails to occur at the usual or proper time, as because of slowness of movement, development, etc. (summer came *late* that year); **overdue** is applied to something delayed, unpaid, etc. beyond the scheduled time, as because of someone's tardiness, procrastination, etc. (an *overdue* ship, rent, etc.). —*ANT.* prompt.

tare (târ), *n.* [ME., orig., small seed; present sense < Biblical transl.; prob. < MD. *tarwe*, *terwe*, wheat; IE. base **derwā-*, kind of grain, seen also in Sans. *dūrvā*, millet grass; sense extension by transl. confusion or metonymy], 1. any of a number of related trailing or climbing plants with many small leaflets, grown for fodder; vetch. 2. the seed of any of these plants. 3. in the *Bible*, a noxious weed.

tare (târ), *n.* [Fr.; It. & Sp. *tara*; Ar. *ṭarḥah* < *ṭaraḥa*, to reject], 1. the weight of a container, wrapper, box, truck, etc. deducted from the total weight to determine the weight of the contents or load. 2. the deduction of this. *v.t.* [TARED (târd), TARING], to find out, allow for, or mark the tare of. Abbreviated **t.**

tare (târ), archaic or dialectal past tense and past participle of **tear** (to pull apart).

tar·ent·ism (târ′ən-tiz′m), *n.* tarantism.

Ta·ren·tum (tə-ren′təm), *n.* Taranto: the ancient name.

targe (tärj), *n.* [ME.; Late AS.; ON. (prob. via OFr.); akin to OHG. *zarga*, a rim, frame; IE. base **dergh-*, to grip, seize, seen also in Gr. *drakhmē*, lit., handful (see DRACHMA)], [Archaic], a shield or buckler.

tar·get (tär′git), *n.* [ME.; OFr. *targette*, dim. of *targe*, a shield; see TARGE], 1. originally, a small shield, especially a round one. 2. a round, flat board, straw coil, etc., usually marked with concentric circles, set up to be aimed at, as in archery or rifle practice. 3. any object that is shot at. 4. a ship, building, site, etc. that is the object of a military attack. 5. an object of verbal attack, criticism, or ridicule. 6. something resembling a target in shape or use, as the sliding sight on a surveyor's leveling rod, a disk-shaped signal on a railroad switch, the metallic surface (in an X-ray tube) upon which the stream of cathode rays impinge and from which X rays emanate, etc. Abbreviated **t.**

tar·get·eer (tär′gi-têr′), *n.* formerly, a soldier armed with a target (shield).

Tar·gum (tär′gəm; Heb. tär-gōōm′), [*pl.* TARGUMS (-gəmz); Heb. TARGUMIM (tär′goo-mēm′)], [Heb.; Aram. *targūm*, lit., interpretation], any of several translations or paraphrases of parts of the Old Testament, written in the vernacular (Aramaic) of Judea.

Tar·heel (tär′hēl′), *n.* [Colloq.], a native or inhabitant of North Carolina (the *Tarheel State*).

tar·iff (tar′if), *n.* [It. *tariffa*; Ar. *ta'rīf*, information, explanation < *'arafa*, to know, inform], 1. a list or system of taxes placed by a government upon exports or, especially, imports. 2. a tax of this kind, or its rate. 3. any list or scale of prices, charges, etc. *v.t.* 1. to make a schedule of tariffs on; set a tariff on. 2. to fix the price of according to a tariff.

Ta·rim (tä-rēm′), *n.* a river in northwestern China: length, 1,250 mi.

Tar·king·ton, Booth (tär′kiŋ-tən), (*Newton Booth Tarkington*), 1869–1946; American novelist.

tar·la·tan, tar·le·tan (tär′lə-t′n), *n.* [Fr. *tarlatane*, earlier *tarnatane*; ? of East Indian origin], a thin, stiff, open-weave muslin.

tarn (tärn), *n.* [ME. *terne*; ON. *tjörn*, a tarn, lit., hole filled with water; for IE. base see TEAR (to pull apart)], a small mountain lake.

'tar·nal (tär′n'l), *adj.* [Dial.], 1. eternal; hence, 2. confounded; damned: as, he's a *'tarnal* liar. *adv.* [Dial.], confoundedly; damned; very.

tar·na·tion (tär-nā′shən), *interj.* & *n.* [blend of *'tarnal* & *damnation*], [Dial.], damnation. *adv.* [Dial.], damned; very.

tar·nish (tär′nish), *v.t.* [< an inflectional stem of Fr. *ternir*, to make dim < *terne*, dull; Gmc. base seen in AS. *derne*, obscure], 1. to dull the luster of, as a metallic surface by oxidation. 2. to besmirch or sully (a reputation, etc.). *v.i.* 1. to lose luster; grow dull; discolor, as from oxidation. 2. to become sullied or soiled. *n.* 1. the condition of being tarnished; dullness. 2. a stain; blemish. 3. a tarnished surface.

Tar·no·pol (tȧr-nô′pôl), *n.* a city in the western Ukrainian S.S.R., formerly in Poland: pop., 52,000: Russian name, *Ternopol*.

Tar·nów (tär′noof), *n.* a city in southern Poland: pop., 33,000.

ta·ro (tä′rō), *n.* [*pl.* TAROS (-rōz)], [Tahitian], 1. a tropical plant of the arum family, with a starchy, tuberous root that is edible. 2. the root of this plant.

tar·pau·lin (tär-pô′lin, tär′pə-lin), *n.* [*tar* + *-paulin* (said to be < *palling* < *pall*, a covering, but at least influenced by ME. *palyoun*, a canopy, esp. in early form *tarpaulian*, etc.; orig. sense, "canopy, awning")], 1. canvas waterproofed with tar, paint, etc., or a sheet of this used to spread over anything to protect it from getting wet. 2. a hat or coat of tarpaulin. 3. [Archaic or Rare], a sailor; tar.

Tar·pe·ia (tär-pē′ə), *n.* [L., fem. of *Tarpeius*, Roman proper name], in *Roman legend*, a girl who treacherously opened the Capitoline citadel to the invading Sabines on their promise of giving her what they wore on their arms: instead of the gold bracelets she meant, they threw their shields on her and crushed her to death.

Tar·pe·ian (tär-pē′ən), *adj.* [L. *Tarpeianus* < *Tarpeius*; see TARPEIA], designating or of a cliff on the Capitoline hill in Rome from which traitors to the state were hurled to death.

tar·pon (tär′pon), *n.* [*pl.* TARPONS (-ponz), TARPON; see PLURAL, II, D, 1], [same word as D. *tarpoen*; prob. < W.Ind. native name], a large, silvery game fish of the herring group, found in the warmer parts of the western Atlantic: tarpons measure up to seven feet in length and weigh up to three hundred pounds.

Tar·quin (tär′kwin), *n.* (*Lucius Tarquinius Superbus*), last king of early Rome (534–510 B.C.): called *the Proud*.

tar·ra·gon (tar′ə-gon′), *n.* [Sp. *taragona*; Ar. *ṭarkhun* < Gr. *drakōn*, dragon], 1. a plant of the aster family, whose fragrant leaves are used for seasoning. 2. the leaves of this plant.

tar·ri·er (tar′i-ẽr), *n.* a person who tarries.

tar·ry (tar′i), *v.i.* [TARRIED (-id), TARRYING], [ME. *tarien*, to delay, vex, hinder < AS. *tergan*, to vex, provoke, merged with OFr. *targer*, to delay < LL. *tardicare* < L. *tardare*, to delay < *tardus*, slow (cf. TARDY)], 1. to delay; linger; loiter; be tardy. 2. to stay, as in a town, etc., especially longer than originally intended; remain temporarily. 3. to wait. *v.t.* [Archaic], to wait for. *n.* a sojourn; stay. —*SYN.* see **stay**.

tar·ry (tär′i), *adj.* [TARRIER (-i-ẽr), TARRIEST (-i-ist)], 1. of or like tar. 2. covered or smeared with tar.

Tar·ry·town (tar′i-toun′), *n.* a town near New York City, on the Hudson River: pop., 11,000.

tar·sal (tär′s'l), *adj.* [< Mod. L. *tarsus* (see TARSUS); + *-al*], of the tarsus of the foot or the tarsi of the eyelids. *n.* a tarsal bone or plate.

Tar·shish (tär′shish), *n.* an ancient region mentioned in the Bible and believed to have been on the southern coast of Spain: I Kings 10:22.

tar·si·er (tär′si-ẽr), *n.* [Fr. < *tarse*, tarsus: from the foot structure], any of several small animals of the East Indies and the Philippines, with large, gogglelike eyes, large ears, a long, tufted tail, and unusually long tarsal bones: tarsiers are related to the lemurs, live in trees, are active at night, and feed on insects.

tar·so- (tär′sō), [< Mod. L. *tarsus*], a combining form meaning *tarsus* or *tarsal*: also, before a vowel, **tars-**.

tar·so·met·a·tar·sus (tär′sō-met′ə-tär′səs), *n.* [see TARSUS & METATARSUS], the large bone in the lower part of a bird's leg, connecting with the tibia and the toes.

Tar·sus (tär′səs), *n.* an ancient city, now in southern Turkey: pop., 34,000: birthplace of St. Paul.

tar·sus (tär′səs), *n.* [*pl.* TARSI (-sī)], [Mod. L.; Gr. *tarsos*, flat of the foot, any broad flat surface], 1. in *anatomy*, *a*) the ankle. *b*) the seven bones forming the ankle: see **skeleton**, illus. *c*) the small plate of connective tissue stiffening the eyelid. 2. in *zoology*, *a*) the tarsometatarsus. *b*) the terminal segment of the leg in insects and certain other arthropods.

tart (tärt), *adj.* [ME.; AS. *teart*; Gmc. **trat-*; for IE. base see TEAR (to pull apart)], 1. sharp in taste; sour; acid; acidulous. 2. sharp in meaning or implication; cutting: as, a *tart* answer. —*SYN.* see **sour.**

tart (tärt), *n.* [ME. & OFr. *tarte*], 1. a small shell of pastry filled with jam, jelly, etc. 2. in England, a fruit pie, with a top crust.

tart (tärt), *n.* [orig., slang term of endearment, for *sweetheart*], a prostitute or any woman of loose morals.

tar·tan (tär′t'n), *n.* [prob. merging of ME. *tirtaine* (< OFr. *tiretaine*), mixed fabric & ME. *tartarin, tartayne* (< OFr. *tartarin*, lit., cloth of Tartary), a rich material from China], 1. woolen cloth with a woven pattern of straight lines of different colors and widths crossing at right angles, worn especially in the Scottish Highlands, where each clan had its own pattern. 2. any plaid cloth like this. 3. any tartan pattern. *adj.* of or like tartan.

tar·tan (tär′t'n), *n.* [Fr. *tartane;* It. *tartana;* Ar. *ṭarīdah*, freighter, cattleboat], a small, single-masted Mediterranean ship with a large lateen sail and a jib.

Tar·tar (tär′tẽr), *n.* [ML. *Tartarus*, a Tartar; altered (after *Tartarus*, hell) < Per. *Tatar*], 1. a Tatar. 2. [usually t-], an irritable, violent, intractable person. *adj.* of Tatary or the Tatars.

catch a tartar, to attack or oppose someone too strong for one; get more than one bargained for.

tar·tar (tär′tẽr), *n.* [ME. & OFr. *tartre;* ML. *tartarum;* MGr. *tartaron;* said to be < Ar.], 1. potassium bitartrate, $KHC_4H_4O_6$, present in grape juice, and forming a reddish, crustlike deposit in wine casks: its purified form is cream of tartar: see also **cream of tartar.** 2. a hard deposit on the teeth, consisting of saliva proteins and calcium phosphate.

Tar·tar·e·an (tär-târ′i-ən), *adj.* of Tartarus; infernal.

tartar emetic, potassium antimonyl tartrate, $KSbOC_4H_4O_6 \cdot \frac{1}{2}H_2O$, a poisonous white salt used in medicine to cause expectoration, vomiting, and perspiring, and in dyeing as a mordant.

tar·tare sauce (tär′tẽr), [Fr. *sauce tartare;* see TARTAR], a sauce, as for fried fish, consisting of mayonnaise with chopped pickles, olives, chives, capers, etc.

Tar·tar·i·an (tär-târ′i-ən), *adj.* of Tatary or the Tatars.

tar·tar·ic (tär-tar′ik, tär-tär′ik), *adj.* of, containing, or derived from tartar or tartaric acid.

tartaric acid, a clear, colorless crystalline acid, $(CHOH \cdot COOH)_2$, found in vegetable tissues and fruit juices and obtained commercially from tartar: it is used in dyeing, photography, medicine, etc.

tar·tar·i·za·tion (tär′tẽr-i-zā′shən, tär′tẽr-ī-zā′shən), *n.* 1. a tartarizing or being tartarized. 2. the forming of tartar.

tar·tar·ize (tär′tẽr-iz′), *v.t.* [TARTARIZED (-izd′), TARTARIZING], 1. to treat, impregnate, or combine with tartar. 2. to rectify with cream of tartar.

tar·tar·ous (tär′tẽr-əs), *adj.* of, like, or containing tartar.

Tar·ta·rus (tär′tə-rəs), *n.* [L.; Gr. *Tartaros*], in *Greek mythology*, 1. the infernal abyss below Hades, where Zeus hurled the rebel Titans. 2. Hades; hell.

Tar·ta·ry (tär′tə-ri), *n.* Tatary.

Tar·ti·ni, Giu·sep·pe (jōō-zep′pe tär-tē′nē), 1692–1770; Italian violinist, composer, and musical theorist.

tart·let (tärt′lit), *n.* [see -LET], a small tart (pastry).

tar·trate (tär′trāt), *n.* [Fr.; see TARTAR (potassium bitartrate) & -ATE], a salt or ester of tartaric acid.

tar·trat·ed (tär′trā-tid), *adj.* 1. derived from or containing tartar. 2. combined with tartaric acid.

Tar·tu (tär′tōō), *n.* a city in the eastern Estonian S.S.R.: pop., 60,000: Russian name, *Yurev;* German name, *Dorpat.*

Tar·tufe (tär-toof′; Fr. tȧr′tüf′), *n.* [Fr.; It. *tartufo*, lit., a truffle], 1. the titular hero of Molière's satirical comedy, a religious hypocrite. 2. [t-], a hypocrite.

Tar·tuffe (tär-toof′), *n.* Tartufe.

Tash·kent, Tash·kend, (täsh-kent′), *n.* the capital of the Uzbek S.S.R., central Asia: pop., 585,000.

ta·sim·e·ter (tə-sim′ə-tẽr), *n.* [< Gr. *tasis*, a stretching < *teinein*, to stretch; + *-meter*], an electric instrument for measuring minute expansions or motions of solids and the variations in temperature that cause these.

tas·i·met·ric (tas′i-met′rik), *adj.* having to do with a tasimeter or tasimetry.

ta·sim·e·try (tə-sim′ə-tri), *n.* the use of or measurement by a tasimeter.

task (task, täsk), *n.* [ME. *taske;* ONorm.Fr. *tasque* (OFr. *tasche*); LL. **tasca*, for **taxa*, a tax < L. *taxare*, to rate, value], 1. originally, a tax. 2. a piece of work assigned to or demanded of a person. 3. any undertaking or piece of work. 4. an undertaking involving labor or difficulty. *v.t.* 1. originally, to tax. 2. to assign a task to; require or demand a piece of work of. 3. to burden; strain; overtax.

take to task, to call to account; scold; reprove.

***SYN.*—task** refers to a piece of work assigned to or demanded of someone, as by another person, by duty, etc., and usually implies that this is difficult or arduous work (he has the *task* of answering letters); **chore** applies to any of the routine domestic activities for which one is responsible (his *chore* is washing the dishes); **stint** refers to a task that is one's share of the work done by a group and usually connotes a minimum to be completed in the allotted time (we've all done our daily *stint*); **assignment** applies to a specific, prescribed task allotted by someone in authority (classroom *assignments*); **job**, in this connection, refers to a specific piece of work, as in one's trade or as voluntarily undertaken for pay (the *job* of painting our house).

task force, a specially trained, self-contained military unit assigned a specific mission or task, as the raiding of enemy shore installations.

task·mas·ter (task′mas′tẽr, täsk′mäs′tẽr), *n.* a person who assigns tasks to others, especially when exacting or severe; overseer.

task·work (task′wũrk′, täsk′wũrk′), *n.* 1. work assigned as a task. 2. distasteful work. 3. piecework.

Tas·man, A·bel Jans·zoon (ä′bəl yän′sōn täs′män; Eng. taz′mən), 1603–1659; Dutch navigator who discovered Tasmania and New Zealand.

Tas·ma·ni·a (taz-mā′ni-ə, taz-mān′yə), *n.* an island off southeastern Australia: a state of the Commonwealth of Australia: area, 26,215 sq. mi.; pop., 257,000 (est. 1947); capital, Hobart: former name, *Van Diemen's Land*: abbreviated **Tasm.**

Tas·ma·ni·an (taz-mā′ni-ən, taz-mān′yən), *adj.* of Tasmania or its people. *n.* a native or inhabitant of Tasmania.

Tasmanian devil, a flesh-eating marsupial of Tasmania, having a black coat with a white band across the chest: it attacks sheep.

Tasmanian wolf (or **tiger**), the thylacine.

Tas·man Sea (taz′mən), a part of the Pacific, between Australia and New Zealand.

Tass (täs), *n.* [Russ. *T*elegraphnoye *A*genstvo *S*ovyetskovo *S*oyuza, Telegraph Agency of the Soviet Union], a Soviet agency for gathering and distributing news.

tass (tas, täs), *n.* [OFr. *tasse;* Ar. *ṭass, ṭassah* < Per. *tast*, a cup], [Obs. or Scot.], 1. a drinking cup; small goblet. 2. its contents; a small draft.

tasse (tas), *n.* [OFr., purse, pouch], *usually in pl.* any of a series of jointed metal plates forming a skirtlike protection of armor for the lower trunk and thighs: see **armor,** illus.

tas·sel (tas′'l), *n.* [ME.; OFr., a knob, knot, button; prob. < LL. *tessella*, small cube, piece of mosaic], 1. originally, a clasp or fibula. 2. an ornamental tuft of threads, cords, etc. of equal length, hanging loosely from a knob or from the knot by which they are tied together. 3. something resembling this; specifically, the tassellike inflorescence of some plants, as corn. *v.t.* [TASSELED or TASSELLED (-'ld), TASSELING or TASSELLING], 1. to make into tassels. 2. to ornament with tassels. 3. to remove tassels from (corn, etc.) to strengthen the plants. *v.i.* to grow tassels, as corn.

tas·sel (tas′'l), *n.* a tercel: in *tassel-gentle.*

Tas·so, Tor·qua·to (tôr-kwä′tô täs′sô; Eng. tas′ō), 1544–1595; Italian epic poet.

taste (tāst), *v.t.* [TASTED (-id), TASTING], [ME. *tasten;* OFr. *taster*, to handle, touch, taste; LL. **tastare;* prob. < **taxitare*, freq. of L. *taxare*, to feel, touch sharply, judge of], 1. originally, to test by touching. 2. to test the flavor of by putting a little in one's mouth. 3. to detect or distinguish the flavor of by the sense of taste: as, I *taste* sage in the dressing. 4. to eat or drink a small amount of. 5. to eat or drink: as, he hasn't *tasted* a thing. 6. to receive the sensation of, as for the first time; experience; have: as, at last they *tasted* freedom. 7. to have limited experience of: as, I have merely *tasted* manhood. 8. [Archaic or Rare], to like the taste of; like. *v.i.* 1. to tell flavors by the sense of taste; have the sense of taste. 2. to eat or drink a small amount (often with *of*). 3. to have a specific flavor: as, the salad *tastes* of garlic. 4. to have a sensation, limited experience, or anticipating sense (*of* something). *n.* [ME. *taste;* OFr. *tast* < the *v.*], 1. originally, *a*) a test; trial. *b*) a tasting. 2. that one of the five senses that is stimulated by contact of a substance with the taste buds on the surface of the tongue and is capable of distinguishing between sweet, sour, salt, and bitter: the flavor of any specific substance is usually recognized by its combined taste, smell, and texture. 3. the quality of a thing that is perceived through the sense of taste; flavor; savor. 4. a small amount put into the mouth to test the flavor. 5. the distinguishing flavor of a substance: as, a chocolate *taste.* 6. a slight experience of something; sample: as, he got a *taste* of her anger. 7. a bit; trace; suggestion; touch. 8. the ability to notice, appreciate, and judge what is beautiful, appropriate, or harmonious, or what is excellent in art, music, decoration, clothing, etc. 9. a specific preference; partiality; predilection: as, a *taste* for red ties. 10. a liking; inclination; fondness; bent: as, he has no *taste* for business.

in bad (poor, etc.) **taste,** in a form, style, or manner showing lack or impairment of a sense of beauty, excellence, fitness, propriety, etc.

in good (excellent, etc.) **taste,** in a form or manner showing a sense of beauty, excellence, fitness, etc.

in taste, in good taste.

to one's taste, 1. pleasing or satisfying to one. 2. so as to please or satisfy one.

taste bud, any of the clusters of cells at the base of

the papillae of the tongue, functioning as the sense organs of taste.

taste·ful (tāst′fəl), *adj.* 1. [Rare], tasty. 2. having or showing good taste (sense 8).

taste·less (tāst′lis), *adj.* 1. *a)* without taste or flavor; flat; insipid. *b)* dull; uninteresting. 2. lacking good taste; showing poor taste. 3. [Rare], unable to taste.

tast·er (tās′tẽr), *n.* [ME. & Anglo.Fr. *tastour*], 1. a person who tastes; specifically, *a)* a person employed to test the quality of (wines, teas, etc.) by tasting. *b)* a servant, as of a royal house, who tastes his master's food and drink to detect poisoning. 2. any of several devices used for tasting, sampling, or testing.

tast·i·ly (tās′t′l-i), *adv.* in a tasty manner.

tast·i·ness (tās′ti-nis), *n.* the quality of being tasty.

tast·y (tās′ti), *adj.* [TASTIER (-ti-ẽr), TASTIEST (-ti-ist)], 1. that tastes good; flavorful; savory. 2. [Colloq.], showing good taste; tasteful: now seldom used.

tat (tat), *v.t.* [TATTED (-id), TATTING], [prob. back-formation < *tatting*], to make by tatting. *v.i.* to do tatting.

tat (tat), *n.* [? < *tap*, a blow], a tap or blow: now only in *tit for tat.*

tit for tat, 1. blow for blow. 2. retaliation in kind.

Ta·tar (tä′tẽr), *n.* [Per.], 1. a member of any of the Mongolian and Turkic tribes who took part in the invasion of central and western Asia and eastern Europe in the Middle Ages. 2. any of a Turkic people who live in the Tatar A.S.S.R., the Crimea, and parts of Asia. 3. any of their Turkic languages. *adj.* of the Tatars or their languages. Also **Tartar.**

Tatar Autonomous Soviet Socialist Republic, a division of the R.S.F.S.R. in east European Russia: area, 26,200 sq. mi.; pop., 2,847,000; capital, Kazan.

Ta·tar·i·an (tä-târ′i-ən), *adj.* Tatar.

Ta·tar·ic (tä-tar′ik), *adj.* Tatar.

Ta·ta·ry (tä′tə-ri), *n.* in *European history*, a vast region of central and western Siberia and southern Russia, invaded and inhabited by Tatar tribes: also **Tartary.**

'ta·ter (tā′tẽr), *n.* [Dial.], a potato.

Tat·ler, the (tat′lẽr), a tri-weekly English periodical composed of short essays, published and chiefly written by Richard Steele with contributions by Joseph Addison: 271 issues appeared from 1709 to 1711: see also **Spectator, the.**

tat·ou·ay (tat′ōō-ā′, tä′tōō-ī′), *n.* [Sp. *tatuay* < Braz. (Guarani) < *tatu-ai* < *tatu*, armadillo + *ai*, worthless: so named because its flesh is not edible], a large South American armadillo.

Tat·ra Mountains (tä′trä), a part of the Carpathian Mountains in northern Czechoslovakia and southern Poland: also **High Tatra Mountains.**

tat·ter (tat′ẽr), *n.* [ME., also *totter;* ON. *töturr*, rags, tatters; IE. base **də-t-* < **dā(i)-*, to cut out, tear out], 1. a torn and hanging shred or piece, as of a garment. 2. a separate shred or scrap; rag. 3. *pl.* torn, ragged clothes. *v.t.* to reduce to tatters; make ragged. *v.i.* to become ragged.

tat·ter·de·mal·ion (tat′ẽr-di-māl′yən, tat′ẽr-di-mal′i-ən), *n.* [*tatter* + extension of *demon;* cf. RAGAMUFFIN], a person in torn, ragged clothes; ragamuffin.

tat·tered (tat′ẽrd), *adj.* [ME. *tatered*], 1. in tatters; torn and ragged. 2. wearing torn and ragged clothes.

tat·ter·sall (tat′ẽr-sôl′), *adj.* [< *Tattersall's*, a London horse market and gamblers' rendezvous], having a bright checkered pattern: as, a *tattersall* vest.

tat·ting (tat′iŋ), *n.* [prob. < Brit. dial. *tat*, to tangle], 1. a kind of lace made by looping and knotting heavy thread that is wound on a hand shuttle. 2. the act or process of making this.

tat·tle (tat′′l), *v.i.* [TATTLED (-′ld), TATTLING], [ME.; MD. *tatelen;* of echoic origin], 1. to talk idly; chatter; gossip. 2. to reveal other people's secrets; tell tales. *v.t.* to reveal (a secret) through gossiping; say in tattling. *n.* idle talk; chatter; tattling.

tat·tler (tat′′l-ẽr, tat′lẽr), *n.* 1. a person who tattles; gossip. 2. a type of sandpiper known for its loud cry.

tat·tle·tale (tat′′l-tāl′), *n.* a telltale; talebearer; tattler.

tat·too (ta-tōō′), *v.t.* [TATTOOED (-tōōd′), TATTOOING], [Tahitian *tatu* < *ta*, a mark], 1. to make permanent marks or designs on (the skin) by puncturing it and inserting indelible colors. 2. to make (marks or designs) on the skin in this way. *n.* [*pl.* TATTOOS (-tōōz′)], a tattooed mark or design.

tat·too (ta-tōō′), *n.* [*pl.* TATTOOS (-tōōz′)], [earlier *taptoo;* D. *tap toe*, shut the tap: a signal for closing barrooms], 1. a signal on a drum, bugle, etc. summoning soldiers, etc. to their quarters at night. 2. any continuous drumming, rapping, etc.

tau (tô, tou), *n.* [ME. *taw, tau* (esp. with ref. to the tau cross); ML. & L. *tau;* Gr. *tau* < Sem.; cf. Heb. *tāw*], the nineteenth letter of the Greek alphabet (Τ, τ), corresponding to English *T, t:* see **alphabet,** table.

tau cross, a cross shaped like a capital tau.

taught (tôt), past tense and past participle of **teach.**

taunt (tônt, tänt), *adj.* [< earlier *al ataunt, ataunto*, fully rigged; prob. < Fr. *autant*, as much (as possible); OFr. *al*, again + *tant* (< L. *tantus*), so much], very tall: said of a ship's mast.

taunt (tônt, tänt), *v.t.* [? < Fr. *tant pour tant*, tit for tat], 1. to reproach in scornful or sarcastic language; jeer at; mock. 2. to drive or provoke (a person) by taunting. *n.* 1. a scornful or jeering remark; gibe. 2. [Obs.], a taunted person. —*SYN.* see **ridicule.**

Taun·ton (tôn′tən, tän′t′n), *n.* 1. a city in southeastern Massachusetts: pop., 41,000. 2. a city in southwestern England, the county seat of Somersetshire: pop., 34,000.

taupe (tōp), *n.* [Fr. < L. *talpa*, a mole], a dark, brownish gray, the color of moleskin.

tau·ri·form (tô′ri-fôrm′), *adj.* [see TAURUS & -FORM], having the shape of a bull.

tau·rin (tôr′in), *n.* taurine.

tau·rine (tôr′īn, tôr′in), *adj.* [L. *taurinus* < *taurus*, a bull], 1. of or like a bull. 2. of Taurus, the sign of the zodiac.

tau·rine (tôr′ēn, tôr′īn, tôr′in), *n.* [< L. *taurus*, bull, ox; + *-ine:* so named because first obtained (by Gmelin, in 1826) from ox bile], a colorless, neutral, crystalline compound, $C_2H_7O_3NS$, found in bile and formed by the hydrolysis of taurocholic acid.

tau·ro·cho·lic acid (tôr′ə-kō′lik, tôr′ə-kol′ik), [< *taur*ine + *cholic*], a colorless, crystalline acid, $C_{26}H_{45}O_7NS$, found as the sodium salt in bile.

Tau·rus (tôr′əs), *n.* [ME.; L., a bull], 1. a northern constellation, containing the Pleiades, supposedly resembling the forequarters of a bull in shape: see **constellation,** chart. 2. the second sign of the zodiac (♉), entered by the sun on or about April 20: see **zodiac,** illus.

Taurus Mountains, a mountain range in southern Asia Minor, Turkey: highest peak, c. 11,500 ft.

Taus·sig, Frank William (tou′sig), 1859–1940; American political economist.

taut (tôt), *adj.* [ME. *toght*, tight, firm; prob. < pp. of *togen* (AS. *togian*), to pull; cf. TOW, *v.*], 1. tightly stretched, as a rope; hence, 2. tense: as, a *taut* smile. 3. neat; trim; tidy; snug. —*SYN.* see **tight.**

taut·en (tôt′′n), *v.t.* & *v.i.* to make or become taut.

tau·to- (tô′tō, tô′tə), [Gr. *tauto-* < *to auto*, the same], a combining form meaning *the same*, as in *tautology.*

tau·tog (tô-tog′), *n.* [Am. Ind. (Algonquian) *tautauog*, pl. of *tautau*, kind of blackfish], any of a group of black or greenish food fishes found off the Atlantic coast of the United States: also called *blackfish.*

tau·to·log·i·cal (tô′tə-loj′i-k′l), *adj.* of, involving, or using tautology.

tau·tol·o·gism (tô-tol′ə-jiz′m), *n.* 1. the use of tautology. 2. an example of tautology.

tau·tol·o·gist (tô-tol′ə-jist), *n.* a person who habitually uses tautology.

tau·tol·o·gize (tô-tol′ə-jīz′), *v.i.* [TAUTOLOGIZED (-jīzd′), TAUTOLOGIZING], to use tautology; be repetitious.

tau·tol·o·gy (tô-tol′ə-ji), *n.* [*pl.* TAUTOLOGIES (-jiz)], [LL. *tautologia;* Gr. *tautologia; tauto*, the same + *-logia*, -logy], 1. needless repetition of an idea in a different word, phrase, or sentence; redundancy; pleonasm. Example: necessary essentials. 2. an example of this.

tau·to·mer·ic (tô′tə-mer′ik), *adj.* of or having tautomerism.

tau·tom·er·ism (tô-tom′ẽr-iz′m), *n.* [< *tauto-* + Gr. *meros*, a part; + *-ism*], in *chemistry*, the property of some substances of being in a condition of equilibrium between two isomeric forms and of reacting to form either.

tau·to·nym (tô′tə-nim), *n.* [*tauto-* + Gr. *onyma*, a name], in *botany* & *zoology*, a name consisting of two terms, in which the generic and specific names are the same: this kind of name is no longer approved by the International Code of Botanical Nomenclature.

tau·to·nym·ic (tô′tə-nim′ik), *adj.* of or comprising a tautonym.

tav (täv; Heb. tôf), *n.* [Heb.], the twenty-third letter of the Hebrew alphabet (ת), corresponding to English *T, t:* also **tau, taw:** see **alphabet,** table.

tav·ern (tav′ẽrn), *n.* [ME. & OFr. *taverne;* L. *taberna*, a tavern, booth, stall made of boards], 1. a place where liquors, beer, etc. are sold to be drunk on the premises; saloon; bar. 2. an inn.

tav·ern·er (tav′ẽr-nẽr), *n.* [ME. *tauerner;* akin to OFr. *tavernier*], [Archaic], 1. the proprietor of a tavern. 2. a frequenter of taverns.

taw (tô), *n.* [also *tor, alley-tor;* ? an abbrev. or < *tau*, the Gr. letter with reference to method of indicating a mark as the juncture of two straight lines (T)], 1. a marble used to shoot with: it is usually large and fancy. 2. a game of marbles. 3. the line or mark from which players at marbles shoot.

taw (tô), *v.t.* [ME. *tawen;* AS. *tawian*, to prepare; akin to Goth. *taujan*, to do, make; prob. IE. base *dew(a)-, to put forward, move forward, as also in *tool*], 1. to prepare (a natural product) for further treatment or use. 2. to make (skins) into leather by treating with alum, salt, etc. 3. [Obs. or Dial.], to whip; flog.

taw·dri·ly (tô'dri-li), *adv.* in a tawdry manner.

taw·dri·ness (tô'dri-nis), *n.* the condition or quality of being tawdry.

taw·dry (tô'dri), *adj.* [TAWDRIER (-dri-ẽr), TAWDRIEST (-dri-ist)], [by syllabic merging of *St. Audrey*, esp. in *St. Audrey lace* or *St. Audrey's laces*, women's neckpieces sold at St. Audrey's fair, Norwich, England], gaudy and cheap; sleazy; showy. —*SYN.* see **gaudy.**

taw·ni·ness (tô'ni-nis), *n.* the quality of being tawny.

taw·ny (tô'ni), *adj.* [TAWNIER (-ni-ẽr), TAWNIEST (-ni-ist)], [ME. *tauni, tauny;* OFr. *tanné*, pp. of *tanner*, to tan], brownish-yellow; tan. *n.* tawny color. Also spelled **tawney.** —*SYN.* see **dusky.**

tax (taks), *v.t.* [ME. *taxen;* OFr. *taxer*, to tax < L. *taxare*, to appraise, tax, censure < base of *tangere*, to touch: used interchangeably with *tasken* (cf. TASK) in ME.], 1. originally, to determine the value of; assess. 2. *a*) to require (a person) to pay a percentage of his income, property value, etc. for the support of the government. *b*) to require (a person) to pay a special assessment, as in a society, labor union, etc. 3. to assess a tax on (income, property, purchases, etc.). 4. to impose a burden on; put a strain on: as, the work *taxed* his strength. 5. to accuse; charge: as, he was *taxed* with negligence. *n.* [ME. & OFr. *taxe* < the *v.*], 1. *a*) a compulsory payment of a percentage of income, property value, sales price, etc. for the support of a government. *b*) a special assessment, as in a society, labor union, etc. 2. a heavy demand; burden; strain. 3. [Colloq.], a charge, as in a restaurant, etc.

tax·a·bil·i·ty (tak'sə-bil'ə-ti), *n.* the state or quality of being taxable.

tax·a·ble (tak'sə-b'l), *adj.* [Fr.], that can be taxed; liable or subject to taxation.

tax·a·ceous (tak-sā'shəs), *adj.* [< Mod. L. *Taxaceae*, the yew family (< L. *taxus*, yew); + *-ous*], of the yew family, a group of trees and shrubs with needle- or scalelike leaves, berrylike fruit, and stamens and pistils in separate flowers on the same plants.

tax·a·tion (tak-sā'shən), *n.* [ME. *taxacion;* OFr. *taxation;* L. *taxatio* < pp. of *taxare;* see TAX], 1. a taxing or being taxed. 2. the principle of levying taxes. 3. a tax or tax levy. 4. revenue from taxes.

tax·eme (taks'ēm), *n.* [Gr. *taxis;* + phon*eme*], in *linguistics*, a feature in grammatical construction; specifically, selection of words, order of words or morphemes, modulation in stress and pitch, or phonetic modification.

tax-ex·empt (taks'ig-zempt'), *adj.* exempt from taxation; that may not be taxed.

tax·i (tak'si), *n.* [*pl.* TAXIS (-siz)], [short for *taxicab*], a taxicab. *v.i.* [TAXIED (-sid), TAXIING or TAXYING], 1. to ride in a taxi; travel by taxi. 2. to move along the ground or on the water under its own power: said of an airplane. *v.t.* to cause (an airplane) to taxi.

tax·i·cab (tak'si-kab'), *n.* [short for *taximeter cab*], an automobile in which passengers are carried for a fare at a rate usually recorded by a taximeter.

taxi dancer, [so called (after *taxicab*) because hired to dance], a girl or woman who may be hired at a dance hall or cabaret as a dance partner at a fixed charge for each dance.

tax·i·der·mal (tak'si-dũr'm'l), *adj.* having to do with taxidermy.

tax·i·der·mic (tak'si-dũr'mik), *adj.* taxidermal.

tax·i·der·mist (tak'si-dũr'mist), *n.* a person whose profession is taxidermy.

tax·i·der·my (tak'si-dũr'mi), *n.* [< Gr. *taxis* (see TAXIS) + *derma*, a skin], the art of preparing, stuffing, and mounting the skins of animals so as to appear lifelike.

tax·i·me·ter (tak'si-mē'tẽr), *n.* [Fr. *taximètre* < *taxe*, a tax, tariff + *mètre*, a meter], an automatic device installed in taxicabs, that computes and registers the fare due.

tax·is (tak'sis), *n.* [Gr. *taxis*, arrangement, division < *tassein*, to arrange], 1. in ancient Greece, a unit of troops, varying in size from the modern company to the regiment. 2. [Mod. L. < Gr.], in *biology*, the movement of an organism in response to some external stimulus. 3. in *surgery*, the replacement by hand of some displaced part, as a hernial protrusion, without cutting any tissue.

-tax·is (tak'sis), [Mod. L.; Gr. *-taxis* < *taxis*], a combining form meaning *arrangement, order, taxis*, as in *parataxis, thermotaxis:* also **-taxy.**

tax·ite (tak'sīt), *n.* [< Gr. *taxis* (see TAXIS); + *-ite*], volcanic rock that appears to be a combination of two or more minerals or kinds of rock fragments.

tax·it·ic (tak-sit'ik), *adj.* that is or resembles taxite.

tax·o·nom·ic (tak'sə-nom'ik), *adj.* having to do with taxonomy.

tax·o·nom·i·cal (tak'sə-nom'i-k'l), *adj.* taxonomic.

tax·o·nom·i·cal·ly (tak'sə-nom'i-k'l-i, tak'sə-nom'ik-li), *adv.* according to the principles of taxonomy.

tax·on·o·my (tak-son'ə-mi), *n.* [Fr. *taxonomie* < Gr. *taxis* (see TAXIS) + *nomos*, a law], 1. the science of classification; laws and principles covering the classifying of objects. 2. classification, especially of animals and plants into phyla, species, etc.

tax·pay·er (taks'pā'ẽr), *n.* any person who pays a tax; person subject to taxation.

tax rate, the percentage of income, property value, etc. assessed as tax.

tax title, the title conveyed to the purchaser of property sold for nonpayment of taxes.

-tax·y (tak'si), -taxis.

Tay (tā), *n.* a river in eastern Scotland, flowing into the North Sea: length, 125 mi.

Tay, Firth of, an estuary of the Tay: length, 25 mi.

Ta·yg·e·ta (tā-ij'i-tə), *n.* [L. *Taygete;* Gr. *Taugetē*], in *Greek mythology*, one of the Pleiades.

Tay·lor, Bay·ard (bī'ẽrd *or* bā'ärd, tā'lẽr), 1825–1878; American poet, writer, and translator.

Taylor, Brook (brook), 1685–1731; English mathematician.

Taylor, Deems (dēmz), (*Joseph Deems Taylor*), 1885– ; American music critic and composer.

Taylor, Jeremy, 1613–1667; English bishop and writer.

Taylor, Zachary, 1784–1850; American general; twelfth president of the United States (1849–1850); commanded American forces in Mexican War.

‡taz·za (tät'sä), *n.* [It.], a shallow, ornamental cup or vase, usually with a pedestal.

Tb, in *chemistry*, terbium.

TB, T.B., tb., t.b., 1. tubercle bacillus. 2. tuberculosis.

t.b., trial balance.

Tbi·li·si (tbi-lē-sē'), *n.* the capital of the Georgian S.S.R.: pop., 519,000: official Georgian name of *Tiflis.*

T-bone steak (tē'bōn'), any steak with a T-shaped bone, as a club steak or porterhouse.

tbs., tbsp., tablespoon; tablespoons.

Tc, in *chemistry*, technetium.

tc., tierce; tierces.

Tchad (chad, chäd), *n.* Chad, a French colony and lake in central Africa: the French spelling.

Tchai·kov·sky, Pëtr Il·ich (pyô'tr' il-yēch' chi-kôf'ski), 1840–1893; Russian composer: also spelled **Tschaikowsky, Chaikovsky.**

Tchekhov, Anton Pavlovich, see **Chekhov.**

tcher·vo·netz (cher-vô'nits), *n.* [*pl.* TCHERVONTSI (-vôn'tsi)], a chervonetz.

T/D, time deposit.

T.D., 1. Traffic Director. 2. Treasury Department.

te (tā), *n.* in *music*, ti.

Te, in *chemistry*, tellurium.

tea (tē), *n.* [see PLURAL, II, D, 3], [D. *thee;* Malay *teh;* Chin. dial. *t'e*, for Mandarin *ch'a*, tea], 1. a white-flowered evergreen plant grown in China, India, Japan, etc. 2. its dried and prepared leaves, used to make a beverage. 3. the beverage made by soaking tea leaves in boiling water. 4. any of several plants resembling or used as tea. 5. a tealike beverage made from such a plant or from a meat extract: as, camomile *tea*, beef *tea*. 6. [Chiefly British], a light meal in the late afternoon or the evening, at which tea is the usual beverage. 7. a reception or other social gathering in the afternoon, at which tea, coffee, etc. are served.

TEA SHOOT

TEA LEAVES AND FLOWERS

tea ball, 1. a hollow, perforated metal ball used to hold tea leaves in making tea. 2. a small, porous bag of cloth or paper, containing tea leaves and used in making an individual cup of tea: also **tea bag.**

tea·ber·ry (tē'ber'i), *n.* [*pl.* TEABERRIES (-iz)], 1. a creeping plant with shiny leaves, bell-shaped white flowers, and red fruit; checkerberry; wintergreen. 2. its berrylike fruit.

tea biscuit, any of a variety of cookies often served with tea.

teach (tēch), *v.t.* [TAUGHT (tôt), TEACHING], [ME. *techen;* AS. *tæcan* < base of *tacn*, a sign, symbol (see TOKEN); basic sense "to show, demonstrate," as in cognate G. *zeigen*], 1. to show how to do something; give instructions to; train: as, he *taught* his child how to write. 2. to give lessons to (a student or pupil); guide the study of; instruct. 3. to give lessons in (a subject); hold classes in. 4. to provide with knowledge, insight, etc.: as, experience will *teach* him common sense. *v.i.* to give lessons or instruction; be a teacher.

SYN.—**teach** is the basic, inclusive word for the imparting of knowledge or skills and usually connotes some individual attention to the learner (he *taught* her how to skate); **instruct** implies systematized teaching, usually in some particular subject (she *instructs* in chemistry); **educate** stresses the development of latent faculties and powers by formal, systematic teaching, especially in institutions of higher learning (he was *educated* in European universities); **train** implies the development of a particular faculty or skill, or instruction toward a particular occupation, as by methodical discipline, exercise, etc. (he was *trained* as a mechanic); **school**, often equivalent to any of the preceding, sometimes specifically connotes a disciplining to endure something difficult (he had to *school* himself to obedience).

Teach, Edward (tēch), see **Blackbeard.**

teach·a·bil·i·ty (tēch'ə-bil'ə-ti), *n.* the condition or quality of being teachable.

teach·a·ble (tēch'ə-b'l), *adj.* that can be taught.

teach·er (tēch'ẽr), *n.* a person who teaches, especially as a profession; instructor.

teacher bird, 1. an ovenbird (American warbler). 2. a red-eyed vireo: see **vireo.**

teach·ing (tēch'iŋ), *n.* 1. the action of a person who teaches; profession of a teacher. 2. *often pl.* something taught; precept, doctrine, or instruction.

tea·cup (tē'kup'), *n.* 1. a cup for drinking tea, etc. 2. a teacupful.

tea·cup·ful (tē'kup-fool'), *n.* as much as a teacup will hold, about four fluid ounces.

tea dance, 1. a dance at which afternoon tea is served; hence, 2. a dance held in the afternoon.

tea·house (tē'hous'), *n.* in the Orient, a place where tea and other refreshments are served.

teak (tēk), *n.* [Port. *teca;* Malayalam *tēkka*], 1. a large East Indian tree with white flowers and hard, yellowish-brown wood used for shipbuilding, carved work, etc. 2. its wood.

tea·ket·tle (tē'ket''l), *n.* a covered kettle with a spout and handle, for heating water to make tea, etc.

teak·wood (tēk'wood'), *n.* teak.

teal (tēl), *n.* [ME. *tele;* prob. < AS. via dial.; akin to D. *taling*], 1. [*pl.* TEALS (tēlz), TEAL; see PLURAL, II, D, 1], any of a large group of small, short-necked, fresh-water ducks. 2. a dark grayish blue: also **teal blue.**

team (tēm), *n.* [ME.; AS., offspring, succession, long row (akin to G. *zaum*, a bridle, rein); prob. < base of *tēon*, to draw, *togian*, to pull, etc. (cf. TOW, TUG); ? merged with sense of AS. *tieman*, to bring forth, which is actually < *team*], 1. *a*) [Obs.], progeny, race, or lineage. *b*) [Dial.], a brood of young animals, especially of ducks or pigs. 2. two or more horses, oxen, etc. harnessed to the same vehicle or plow. 3. *a*) two or more draft animals and their vehicle. *b*) one draft animal and its vehicle. 4. a group of people working or playing together, especially as one side in a contest. *v.t.* 1. to harness or yoke together in a team. 2. to haul with a team. *v.i.* 1. to drive a team. 2. to join in co-operative activity (often with *up*): as, the boys *teamed* up on the paper route.

team·mate (tēm'māt'), *n.* a person on the same team.

team·ster (tēm'stẽr), *n.* a person who drives a team (now, often, a truck) for hauling loads.

team·work (tēm'wūrk'), *n.* 1. joint action by a group of people, in which each person subordinates his individual interests and opinions to the unity and efficiency of the group; co-ordinated effort, as of an athletic team. 2. work done by or with a team.

tea party, a social gathering at which tea is served.

tea·pot (tē'pot'), *n.* a pot with a spout, handle, and lid, for making and pouring tea.

tea·poy (tē'poi), *n.* [Hind. *tipāī* < *tīn*, three + Per. *pāē*, foot; sp. affected by association with *tea*], 1. a small, three-legged stand. 2. a small table used in serving tea.

tear (târ), *v.t.* [TORE (tôr, tōr), TORN (tôrn, tōrn), TEARING; *archaic* or *dial.* p.t. & pp. TARE (târ)], [ME. *teren;* AS. *teran*, to rend; akin to G. *zehren*, to destroy, consume; IE. base *der-, to flay, split, split off, etc., seen also in Sans. *dar-*, to make burst], 1. to pull apart or separate into pieces by force; rip; rend, as cloth or paper. 2. to make or cause by tearing or puncturing: as, the nail *tore* a hole in her dress. 3. to wound by tearing; lacerate: as, the saw *tore* his skin. 4. to force apart or divide into factions; disrupt; split: as, their ranks were *torn* by dissension. 5. to divide with doubt, uncertainty, etc.; agitate; torment: as, his mind was *torn* between duty and desire. 6. to remove by or as by tearing, pulling, etc. (with *up, out, away, off*, etc.): as, he *tore* the plant up by its roots, he *tore* himself away. *v.i.* 1. to be torn. 2. to move violently or with speed. *n.* 1. the act of tearing. 2. the result of a tearing; torn place; rent. 3. a violent outburst; rage. 4. [Slang], a carousal; spree.

tear at, to make violent, pulling motions at in an attempt to tear or remove.

tear down, 1. to dismantle; wreck; demolish, as a building. 2. to controvert or disprove (an argument, etc.) point by point.

tear into, [Colloq.], to attack impetuously and, often, devastatingly.

SYN.—**tear** implies a pulling apart by force, so as to lacerate or leave ragged edges (to *tear* paper wrappings); **rip** suggests a forcible tearing, especially along a seam or in a straight line (to *rip* a hem); **rend**, a somewhat literary term, implies a tearing with violence (the tree was *rent* by a bolt of lightning).

tear (têr), *n.* [ME. *tere, ter;* AS. *tear, teagor;* akin to G. *zähre;* IE. **dakru*, tears, seen also in L. *lacrima*, tear (see LACHRYMAL) < OL. *dacruma*], 1. a drop of the salty fluid secreted by the lachrymal gland, which serves normally to lubricate the eyeball and in weeping flows from the eye. 2. anything resembling this, as a drop of transparent gum; tearlike mass. 3. *pl.* sorrow; grief. *v.i.* to shed, or fill with, tears.

in tears, crying; weeping.

tear bomb (têr), a bomb that releases tear gas upon explosion.

tear·drop (têr'drop'), *n.* a tear. *adj.* shaped like a tear.

tear·ful (têr'fəl), *adj.* 1. in tears; weeping. 2. causing tears; sad.

tear gas (têr), a gas that causes irritation of the eyes, excessive flow of tears, and temporary blindness.

tear·ing (târ'iŋ), *adj.* violent; impetuous; hasty.

tear-jerk·er (têr'jũr'kẽr), *n.* [Slang], a play, motion picture, etc. with a very sad or sentimental theme.

tear·less (têr'lis), *adj.* 1. without tears; not weeping. 2. unable to weep.

tea·room (tē'rōōm', tē'room'), *n.* a restaurant that serves tea, coffee, light lunches, etc.

tea rose, 1. a kind of rose having an odor supposedly resembling that of tea. 2. its yellowish-pink color.

tear sheet, a sheet torn, or taken in unbound form, from a publication for special distribution by the publisher.

tear-stained (têr'stānd'), *adj.* stained with tears.

tear·y (têr'i), *adj.* [TEARIER (-i-ẽr), TEARIEST (-i-ist)], 1. tearful; crying. 2. of or like tears.

Teas·dale, Sara (tēz'dāl), 1884–1933; American poet.

tease (tēz), *v.t.* [TEASED (tēzd), TEASING], [ME. *tesen;* AS. *tæsan*, to pull about, pluck, tease; akin to D. *teezen;* IE. **di-s* < base **dā(i)-*, to part, cut apart, tear out (cf. TATTER)], 1. to separate the fibers of; card or comb (flax, wool, etc.). 2. to raise a nap on (cloth) by brushing with teasels; teasel. 3. to annoy or harass by persistent, irritating actions or remarks, or by poking fun at. 4. to urge persistently; beg; importune. *v.i.* to indulge in teasing. *n.* 1. a teasing or being teased. 2. a person who teases. —*SYN.* see **annoy.**

tea·sel (tē'z'l), *n.* [ME. *tesel;* AS. *tæsel* < base of *tæsan*, to tease; cf. TEASE, -EL, -LE], 1. any of a number of related thistlelike plants with bristly, yellowish or purplish flowers. 2. the flower of the species *fuller's teasel*, used when dried for raising a nap on cloth. 3. any device for raising a nap on cloth. *v.t.* [TEASELED or TEASELLED (-'ld), TEASELING or TEASELLING], to raise a nap on (cloth) by means of teasels. Also spelled **teazel, teazle.**

tea·sel·er, tea·sel·ler (tē'z'l-ẽr), *n.* 1. a person who teasels. 2. a machine for teaseling.

teas·er (tēz'ẽr), *n.* 1. a person or thing that teases. 2. an annoying or puzzling problem.

tea·spoon (tē'spōōn', tē'spoon'), *n.* 1. a spoon for stirring tea, coffee, etc. and eating some soft foods. 2. a teaspoonful. Abbreviated **t., tsp.** (*sing. & pl.*).

tea·spoon·ful (tē'spōōn-fool', tē'spoon-fool'), *n.* [*pl.* TEASPOONFULS (-foolz')], as much as a teaspoon will hold; 1/3 tablespoonful (1 1/3 fluid drams).

teat (tēt), *n.* [ME. & OFr. *tete* < Gmc. base of AS. *tit;* see TIT], the small protuberance on a breast or udder, through which the milk passes in suckling the young; nipple; pap.

tea-ta·ble (tē'tā'b'l), *adj.* supposedly characteristic of people at a tea: as, *tea-table* talk.

tea table, a small table from which tea, etc. is served.

tea·tast·er (tē'tās'tẽr), *n.* a person whose business is tasting tea for grading.

tea tray, a tray for carrying cups, plates, spoons, etc. in serving tea or other light refreshment.

tea wagon, a small table on wheels for holding a tea service, extra dishes at a dinner, etc.

tea·zel, tea·zle (tē'z'l), *n. & v.t.* teasel.

Te·bet, Te·beth (tā-vāth', tā'vis), *n.* [Heb.], the fourth month of the Jewish year: see **Jewish calendar.**

tech., 1. technical. 2. technically. 3. technology.

tech·ne·ti·um (tek-nē'shi-əm), *n.* [Mod. L. < Gr.

technētos, artificial; + *-ium*], a metallic chemical element obtained by the irradiation of molybdenum with deuterons and in the fission of uranium: symbol, Tc; at. wt., 99 (?); at. no., 43 (formerly designated as *masurium*).

tech·nic (tek'nik), *adj.* [Gr. *technikos* < *technē*, an art, artifice; IE. base **tekth-*, to build (of wood), cut, seen also in Gr. *tektōn*, a carpenter, L. *texere*, to weave, build], [Now Rare], technical. *n.* 1. [Now Rare], technique. 2. technics (sense 1).

tech·ni·cal (tek'ni-k'l), *adj.* [*technic* + *-al*], 1. having to do with the practical, industrial, or mechanical arts or the applied sciences: as, *technical* schools offer courses in welding, engineering, etc. 2. of, used in, or peculiar to a specific science, art, profession, craft, etc.; specialized: as, *technical* vocabulary. 3. of, in, or showing technique: as, *technical* skill. 4. in terms of some science, art, etc.; according to principles or rules: as, a *technical* difference. 5. in *finance*, designating or of a market in which prices are sharply affected by manipulation and speculation. Abbreviated **tech.**

tech·ni·cal·i·ty (tek'ni-kal'ə-ti), *n.* [*pl.* TECHNICALITIES (-tiz)], 1. the state or quality of being technical. 2. the use of technical terms, methods, etc. 3. a point, detail, term, method, etc. of or peculiar to an art, science, code, or skill; rule, etc. that only a technical expert would be aware of. 4. a minute formal point, detail, etc. brought to bear upon a main issue: as, convicted on a *technicality*.

technical knockout, in *boxing*, a victory won when the opponent, though not knocked out, is so badly beaten that the referee stops the match: abbreviated **T.K.O., TKO** (no period).

tech·ni·cal·ly (tek'ni-k'l-i, tek'nik-li), *adv.* 1. in a technical manner; according to technical principles. 2. in a technical sense; in technical terms.

technical sergeant, 1. in the *United States Army*, formerly, the second grade of enlisted man (now *sergeant first class*). 2. in the *United States Marine Corps & Air Force*, the second grade of enlisted man, ranking just below master sergeant.

tech·ni·cian (tek-nish'ən), *n.* 1. a person skilled in the technicalities of some subject; specifically, an artist, writer, musician, etc. who has great technical skill or knowledge. 2. in the *United States Army*, formerly, any of several alternative ranks of enlisted man, of the third, fourth, and fifth grades.

tech·ni·col·or (tek'ni-kul'ẽr), *n.* the process of reproducing colors on a motion-picture film by combining several separate, synchronized films each of which is sensitive to a single color: a trade-mark (**Technicolor**).

tech·nics (tek'niks), *n.pl.* [construed as sing.], [see TECHNIC], 1. the study or principles of an art or of the arts, especially the practical arts. 2. technique.

tech·nique (tek-nēk'), *n.* [Fr. < Gr. *technikos;* see TECHNIC], 1. the method of procedure (with reference to practical or formal details) in rendering an artistic work or carrying out a scientific or mechanical operation. 2. the degree of expertness in following this: as, the pianist had good phrasing but poor *technique*.

tech·no- (tek'nō, tek'nə), [< Gr. *technē;* see TECHNIC], a combining form meaning: 1. *art, science, skill*, as in *technocracy*. 2. *technical, technological*, as in *technochemistry*.

tech·no·chem·is·try (tek'nə-kem'is-tri), *n.* industrial chemistry.

tech·noc·ra·cy (tek-nok'rə-si), *n.* [*techno-* + *-cracy*], government by technicians; specifically, the theory or doctrine of a proposed system of government, regarded by its proponents as suitable for a technological age, in which all economic resources, and hence the entire social system, would be controlled by scientists and engineers.

tech·no·crat (tek'nə-krat'), *n.* an advocate of technocracy.

tech·no·crat·ic (tek'nə-krat'ik), *adj.* of technocracy or technocrats.

tech·nog·ra·phy (tek-nog'rə-fi), *n.* [*techno-* + *-graphy*], the description of arts and techniques.

tech·no·log·ic (tek'nə-loj'ik), *adj.* technological.

tech·no·log·i·cal (tek'nə-loj'i-k'l), *adj.* 1. of or having to do with technology. 2. due to developments in technology; resulting from technical progress in the use of machinery in industry, agriculture, etc.: as, *technological* productivity, *technological* unemployment.

tech·no·log·i·cal·ly (tek'nə-loj'i-k'l-i, tek'nə-loj'ik-li), *adv.* 1. by means of technology. 2. according to, or from the viewpoint of, technology.

tech·nol·o·gy (tek-nol'ə-ji), *n.* [Gr. *technologia*, systematic treatment; see TECHNIC & -LOGY], 1. the science or study of the practical or industrial arts. 2. the terms used in a science, art, etc.; technical terminology. 3. applied science. Abbreviated **tech., technol.**

tech·y (tech'i), *adj.* [TECHIER (-i-ẽr), TECHIEST (-i-ist)], [< ME. *teche, tecche, tache*, manners, quality; OFr. *tache*, a quality, mark, orig., a spot, blemish], touchy; irritable; peevish: also spelled **tetchy.**

tec·ton·ic (tek-ton'ik), *adj.* [LL. *tectonicus;* Gr. *tektonikos* < *tektōn*, a carpenter, builder; see TECHNIC], 1. of or having to do with building; constructional; hence, 2. architectural. 3. of or resulting from changes in the structure of the earth's crust.

tec·ton·ics (tek-ton'iks), *n.pl.* [construed as sing.], [see prec.], 1. the constructive arts in general; especially, the art of making things that have both beauty and usefulness. 2. geology that deals with land structure.

Te·cum·seh (ti-kum'sə), *n.* American Shawnee chief; 1768?–1813; fought with the British in the War of 1812.

Te·cum·tha (ti-kum'thə), *n.* Tecumseh.

ted (ted), *v.t.* [TEDDED (-id), TEDDING], [ME. *tedden;* prob. < ON. *tethja*, to manure], to spread or scatter (newly cut grass) for drying.

ted·der (ted'ẽr), *n.* 1 a person who teds. 2. a machine for tedding.

ted·dy (ted'i), *n.* [*pl.* TEDDIES (-iz)], [prob. < the nickname *Teddy*], *usually pl.* a woman's one-piece undergarment consisting of a top combined with loose-fitting drawers.

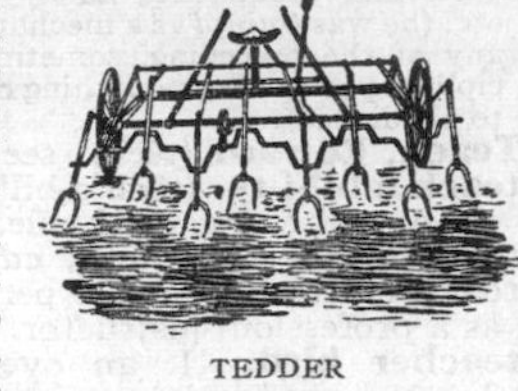
TEDDER

teddy bear, [c. 1907; after *Teddy*, nickname for *Theodore*, with reference to Theodore Roosevelt], a child's toy somewhat resembling a small stuffed bear.

‡Te De·um (tē dē'əm), [L.], 1. an old Christian hymn beginning *Te Deum laudamus* (We praise thee, O God). 2. the music of this hymn. 3. a religious service of which this hymn is a main feature.

te·di·ous (tē'di-əs, tē'jəs), *adj.* [ME.; LL. *taediosus*], full of tedium; long and wearisome; tiresome; boring.

te·di·um (tē'di-əm), *n.* [L. *taedium* < *taedet*, it disgusts, offends], the condition or quality of being tiresome, wearisome, or monotonous; tediousness.

tee (tē), *n.* [*pl.* TEES (tēz)], 1. the letter T, t. 2. anything shaped like a T. *adj.* shaped like a T.
to a tee, exactly; precisely.

tee (tē), *n.* [< *tee* (T): the mark was orig. T-shaped], a mark aimed at in quoits, curling, etc.

tee (tē), *n.* [prob. contr. < earlier *teaz*, Scot. dial. word, but now associated with prec. in form and sense], in *golf*, 1. a small, cone-shaped mound of sand, earth, etc. on which the ball is placed when a player drives. 2. a small, pointed, wooden or plastic holder now generally substituted for this. 3. the place from which a player makes the first stroke on each hole. *v.t. & v.i.* [TEED (tēd), TEEING], to place (a golf ball) on a tee.
tee off, to play (a golf ball) from a tee.

teem (tēm), *v.i.* [ME. *temen;* AS. *tieman*, to produce, bear < base of *team*, progeny; see TEAM], 1. originally, to produce offspring; bear. 2. to be full, as though ready to bring forth young; be prolific; abound; swarm: as, the river *teems* with fish.

teem (tēm), *v.t.* [ME. *temen;* ON. *tæma*, to empty], to empty; pour out. *v.i.* to pour: said of rain, water, etc

teen (tēn), *n.* [ME. *tene;* AS. *teona* (akin to OFris *tiona*, injury), basic sense "accusation" < base of AS. *teon;* IE. base as in *diction*], [Archaic or Dial.], 1 injury. 2. anger. 3. grief.

-teen (tēn), [ME. *-tene;* AS. *-tene, -tyne* (akin to G *-zehn*), inflected form of *tien*, ten; see TEN], a suffix meaning *ten and*, used to form the cardinal numbers from *thirteen* to *nineteen*.

teen-age (tēn'āj'), *adj.* 1. in one's teens. 2. of characteristic of, or for persons in their teens.

teen-ag·er (tēn'āj'ẽr), *n.* a person in his teens.

teens (tēnz), *n.pl.* the numbers, or years of one's age between thirteen and nineteen inclusive.

tee·ny (tē'ni), *adj.* [TEENIER (-ni-ẽr), TEENIEST (-ni ist)], [var. of *tiny*], [Colloq.], tiny.

tee·pee (tē'pē), *n.* a tepee.

Tees (tēz), *n.* a river in northern England, flowing into the North Sea: length, 70 mi.

tee·ter (tē'tẽr), *n., v.i. & v.t.* [dial. *titter*, to move unsteadily, teeter; ME. *titeren;* ON. *titra*, to tremble quiver; IE. base **drā-*, to step, trip], seesaw; waver.

tee·ter-tot·ter (tē'tẽr-tot'ẽr, tē'tẽr-tô'tẽr), *n. & v.i.* seesaw.

teeth (tēth), *n.* plural of **tooth.** For phrases see **tooth**

teethe (tēth), *v.i.* [TEETHED (tēthd), TEETHING], [ME *tethen* < *tethe*, teeth], to grow teeth; cut one's teeth.

teeth·ing ring (tēth'iŋ), a ring of ivory, plastic, etc for teething babies to bite on.

teeth·ridge (tēth'rij'), *n.* 1. the ridge of the jaw where the teeth sockets are located. 2. in *phonetics*, the upper front teethridge.

tee·to·tal (tē-tō't'l), *adj.* [formed by redupl., for emphasis, of initial letter of *total*], 1. [Colloq.], entire complete. 2. of or advocating teetotalism.

tee·to·tal·er (tē-tō't'l-ẽr, tē-tōt'lẽr), *n.* [see TEETOTAL] a person who never drinks any alcoholic liquor.

tee·to·tal·ism (tē-tō't'l-iz'm), *n.* [see TEETOTAL], the principle or practice of never drinking any alcoholic liquor; total abstinence.

tee·to·tum (tē-tō'təm), *n.* [earlier *T totum* < the

(for *totum*) marked on one side + *totum*, the name of the toy < L. *totum*, neut. of *totus;* see TOTAL: the four sides were orig. marked *T* (*totum*, all), *A* (*aufer*, take), *D* (*depone*, put), *N* (*nihil*, nothing)], a kind of top spun with the fingers, especially one with four lettered sides used in a game of chance.

teg·men (teg′men), *n.* [*pl.* TEGMINA (-mi-nə)], [L. < *tegere*, to cover], 1. a covering; tegument. 2. in *botany*, the inner coat of a seed.

teg·mi·nal (teg′mi-n′l), *adj.* of or serving as a tegmen.

Te·gu·ci·gal·pa (te-gōō′sē-gäl′pä), *n.* the capital of Honduras: pop., 47,200.

teg·u·lar (teg′yoo-lẽr), *adj.* [< L. *tegula*, a tile < *tegere*, to cover], 1. of or like a tile or tiles. 2. arranged like tiles.

teg·u·ment (teg′yoo-mənt), *n.* [L. *tegumentum* < *tegere*, to cover], the natural covering of the body, or of some organ, of an animal or plant; integument.

teg·u·men·tal (teg′yoo-men′t'l), *adj.* of or serving as a tegument.

teg·u·men·ta·ry (teg′yoo-men′tẽr-i), *adj.* of, in, or serving as a tegument.

te-hee (tē-hē′), *interj. & n.* [ME.; echoic], the sound of a titter or light, derisive laugh. *v.i.* [TE-HEED (-hēd′), TE-HEEING], to titter; giggle; snicker.

Te·her·an, Te·hran (te′ə-rän′, tē′ə-ran′; Per. te-hrän′), *n.* the capital of Iran: pop., 540,000: scene of a conference (November, 1943) of Roosevelt, Churchill, and Stalin: see **Iran and Iraq**, map.

Te·huan·te·pec, Gulf of (te-wän′tə-pek′, te-wän′tə-pek′), an arm of the Pacific, off southern Mexico.

Tehuantepec, Isthmus of, a part of Mexico, between the Gulf of Tehuantepec and the Gulf of Campeche: width, 130 mi.

Te·huel·che (te-wel′che), *n.* [native word in Patagonia, lit., southeast, but said of northern Patagonian natives], the dominant aboriginal tribe of Patagonia, known for their tallness.

Tei·de, Mount (tā′the), Mount Teyde.

te ig·i·tur (tē ij′ə-tẽr), [L., thee therefore], in the *Roman Catholic Church*, the opening words of the Canon of the Mass.

teil (tēl), *n.* [OFr.; L. *tilia*, lime tree], the linden tree: also **teil tree.**

Te·jo (te′zhoo), *n.* Tagus: the Portuguese name.

tel- (tel), 1. tele-. 2. telo- (end).

tel., 1. telegram. 2. telegraph(ic). 3. telephone.

tel·aes·the·si·a (tel′es-thē′zhə, tel′es-thē′zhi-ə), *n.* telesthesia.

tel·a·mon (tel′ə-mon′), *n.* [*pl.* TELAMONES (tel′ə-mō′nēz)], [L.; Gr. *telamōn*, bearer], a supporting column in the form of a man's figure: see also **atlantes, caryatid.**

tel·an·gi·ec·ta·sis (tel-an′ji-ek′tə-sis), *n.* [*pl.* TELANGIECTASES (-sēz′)], [Mod. L. < Gr. *telos*, an end + *angeion*, receptacle + *ektasis*, extension, dilatation], in *medicine*, chronic dilatation of capillaries and small arterial branches, producing small, reddish tumors in the skin, as of the face.

tel·an·gi·ec·tat·ic (tel-an′ji-ek-tat′ik), *adj.* of or having telangiectasis.

tel·au·to·gram (tel-ô′tə-gram′), *n.* a message, picture, etc. transmitted by telautograph.

tel·au·to·graph (tel-ô′tə-graf′, tel-ô′tə-gräf′), *n.* [*tel-* (tele-) + *autograph*], a telegraphic apparatus for transmitting writing, pictures, etc.: it produces facsimiles at the receiving end by means of an electrically controlled pen that makes the same motions as the transmitting pen.

Tel A·viv (tel′ ä-vēv′, tel′ ə-viv′), a city in Israel, on the Mediterranean Sea: pop., with Jaffa, 354,000.

tel·e- (tel′ə), [Gr. *tēle-* < *tēle*, far off; use in Eng. chiefly after *telescope*], a combining form meaning: 1. *operating at a distance*, as in *telegraph*. 2. *of, in,* or *by television*, as in *telecast*. Also, before a vowel, **tel-**.

tel·e·cast (tel′ə-kast′, tel′ə-käst′), *v.t. & v.i.* [TELECAST OR TELECASTED (-id), TELECASTING], [*tele*vision + broad*cast*], to broadcast by television. *n.* a television broadcast.

tel·e·course (tel′ə-kôrs′, tel′ə-kōrs′), *n.* [*tele*vision + *course*], a course of televised lectures offered for credit by a college or other school.

tel·e·du (tel′ə-dōō′), *n.* [Malay *teledu*], a small, flesh-eating, burrowing animal resembling a skunk, native to Java, Borneo, and Sumatra.

tel·e·fo·to (tel′ə-fō′tō), *n., v.i. & v.t.* telephotograph: a trade-mark (**Telefoto**).

teleg., 1. telegram. 2. telegraph. 3. telegraphy.

te·le·ga (te-leg′ä), *n.* [Russ. *teljēga*], a four-wheeled Russian cart or wagon without springs.

tel·e·gen·ic (tel′ə-jen′ik), *adj.* [*tele-* + *-genic*], artistically suited for being televised, as a person.

tel·e·gon·ic (tel′ə-gon′ik), *adj.* of or affected by telegony.

te·leg·o·ny (tə-leg′ə-ni), *n.* [*tele-* + *-gony*], the supposed transmission of characteristics of one sire to offspring subsequently borne to other sires by the same female.

tel·e·gram (tel′ə-gram′), *n.* [*tele-* + *-gram*], a message transmitted by telegraph: abbreviated **tel., teleg.**

tel·e·graph (tel′ə-graf′, tel′ə-gräf′), *n.* [Fr. *télégraphe:* see TELE- & -GRAPH: orig. used of a semaphore], 1. originally, any signaling apparatus. 2. an apparatus or system for transmitting messages by electric impulses sent through a wire or converted into radio waves: basically it involves the use of a code of short and long signals, called *dots* and *dashes*, produced by the closing and opening of an electric circuit by means of a lever, or key: see also **telautograph, teletypewriter.** 3. a telegram. *v.t.* 1. to send (a message) by telegraph. 2. to send a telegram to. *v.i.* to send a telegram or telegrams. Abbreviated **tel., teleg.**

TELEGRAPH KEY

te·leg·ra·pher (tə-leg′rə-fẽr), *n.* a telegraph operator.

tel·e·graph·ese (tel′ə-gra-fēz′), *n.* the shortened, sometimes cryptic, language typical of telegrams.

tel·e·graph·ic (tel′ə-graf′ik), *adj.* 1. of or transmitted by telegraph. 2. in the concise style of a telegram.

tel·e·graph·i·cal·ly (tel′ə-graf′i-k'l-i, tel′ə-graf′ik-li), *adv.* 1. by telegraph. 2. in the manner or style of a telegram; concisely; briefly.

te·leg·ra·phist (tə-leg′rə-fist), *n.* a telegraph operator.

tel·e·graph·o·scope (tel′ə-graf′ə-skōp′), *n.* [< *tele-* + *-graph* + *-scope*], an apparatus for transmitting pictures by telegraph.

te·leg·ra·phy (tə-leg′rə-fi), *n.* 1. the operation of telegraph apparatus or the study of this. 2. transmission of messages by telegraph. 3. the making of telegraph instruments. Abbreviated **teleg.**

Tel·e·gu (tel′ə-gōō′), *n.* Telugu.

tel·e·lec·tric (tel′i-lek′trik), *adj.* [*tel-* (tele-) + *electric*], designating or of the transmission of music, etc. to a distance by electricity.

Te·lem·a·chus (tə-lem′ə-kəs), *n.* [L.; Gr. *Tēlemachos*], in *Greek legend*, the son of Odysseus and Penelope, who helped his father slay his mother's suitors.

tel·e·me·chan·ics (tel′ə-mə-kan′iks), *n.pl.* [construed as sing.] [*tele-* + *mechanics*], the science of operating mechanisms from a distance by radio waves.

te·lem·e·ter (tə-lem′ə-tẽr), *n.* [*tele-* + *-meter*], 1. an instrument for determining the distance of an object remote from the observer; range finder. 2. any electronic device for measuring pressure, temperature, radiation, etc. and transmitting the information to a distant receiver: now used in the study of outer space. *v.t. & v.i.* to measure or transmit by telemeter.

tel·e·met·ric (tel′ə-met′rik), *adj.* of or determined by a telemeter or telemetry.

te·lem·e·try (tə-lem′ə-tri), *n.* the use of a telemeter.

tel·e·mo·tor (tel′ə-mō′tẽr), *n.* a hydraulic or electrical device controlling the action of mechanical apparatus at a distance; specifically, such a device controlling the steering gear of a ship.

tel·en·ce·phal·ic (tel′en-sə-fal′ik), *adj.* of the telencephalon.

tel·en·ceph·a·lon (tel′en-sef′ə-lon′), *n.* [Mod. L.; *tel-* + *encephalon*], the anterior end of the embryonic brain structure of a vertebrate, from which the cerebral hemispheres are developed.

tel·e·o·log·i·cal (tel′i-ə-loj′i-k'l, tē′li-ə-loj′i-k'l), *adj.* having to do with teleology; relating to final causes; concerned with design or purpose in nature.

tel·e·ol·o·gist (tel′i-ol′ə-jist, tē′li-ol′ə-jist), *n.* a student of or believer in teleology.

tel·e·ol·o·gy (tel′i-ol′ə-ji, tē′li-ol′ə-ji), *n.* [Mod. L. *teleologia* < Gr. *telos, teleos*, an end; + *-logia* (see -LOGY)], 1. the study of final causes. 2. the fact or quality of being directed toward a definite end or of having an ultimate purpose, especially as attributed to natural processes. 3. a belief, as that of vitalism, that natural phenomena are determined not only by mechanical causes but by an over-all design or purpose in nature: opposed to *mechanism.* 4. the study of evidence for this belief.

tel·e·ost (tel′i-ost′, tē′li-ost′), *n.* [< Gr. *teleos*, complete + *osteon*, bone], any of a subclass of fishes, including most of those extant, characterized by a bony skeleton. *adj.* of or belonging to the teleosts.

tel·e·os·te·an (tel′i-os′ti-ən, tē′li-os′ti-ən), *adj. & n.* teleost.

tel·e·path·ic (tel′ə-path′ik), *adj.* of or acting through telepathy.

tel·e·path·i·cal·ly (tel′ə-path′i-k'l-i, tel′ə-path′ik-li), *adv.* by telepathy.

te·lep·a·thist (tə-lep′ə-thist), *n.* 1. a believer in or student of telepathy. 2. a person supposedly possessing telepathic power.

te·lep·a·thy (tə-lep′ə-thi), *n.* [*tele-* + *-pathy;* coined

(1882) by F. W. Myers (1843-1901), Eng. writer], supposed communication between minds by some means other than the normal sensory channels; transference of thought.

tel·e·phone (tel′ə-fōn′), *n.* [*tele-* + *-phone;* adopted by Bell (1876) after use for other sound instruments], an instrument or system for conveying speech over distances by converting sound into electric impulses sent through a wire: it consists of a transmitter and receiver, often with a dialing mechanism for connecting lines. *v.i.* [TELEPHONED (-fōnd′), TELEPHONING], to talk over a telephone; convey a message by telephone. *v.t.* 1. to convey (a message) by telephone. 2. to speak to or reach (a person) by telephone; call. Abbreviated **tel., t., teleph.** Often shortened to **phone.**

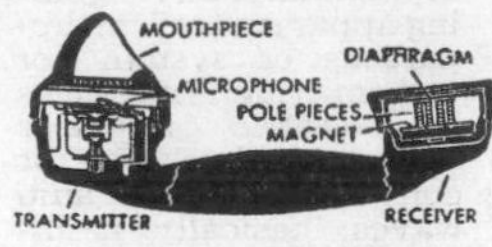

DIAGRAM OF TELEPHONE

telephone receiver, that part of a telephone which is held to the ear and converts the varying electrical impulses into sound: it is either a separate unit or a part of a handset.

tel·e·phon·ic (tel′ə-fon′ik), *adj.* 1. of or having to do with telephones. 2. transmitted by a telephone.

tel·e·phon·i·cal·ly (tel′ə-fon′i-k′l-i, tel′ə-fon′ik-li), *adv.* by telephone.

tel·e·pho·no·graph (tel′ə-fō′nə-graf′, tel′ə-fō′nə-gräf′), *n.* a device for recording telephone messages.

te·leph·o·ny (tə-lef′ə-ni), *n.* 1. the science of telephonic transmission. 2. the making or operation of telephones.

tel·e·phote (tel′ə-fōt′), *n.* [*tele-* + Gr. *phōs, phōtos,* light], any of various devices for reproducing photographs at a distance.

tel·e·pho·to (tel′ə-fō′tō), *adj.* 1. telephotographic. 2. designating or of a compound lens that produces a large image of a distant object in a camera of ordinary focal length. *n.* a telephotograph.

tel·e·pho·to·graph (tel′ə-fō′tə-graf′, tel′ə-fō′tə-gräf′), *n.* 1. a photograph taken with a telephoto lens. 2. a photograph transmitted by telephotography. *v.t. & v.i.* 1. to take (photographs) with a telephoto lens. 2. to transmit (photographs) by telephotography.

tel·e·pho·to·graph·ic (tel′ə-fō′tə-graf′ik), *adj.* of, having to do with, or used in telephotography.

tel·e·pho·tog·ra·phy (tel′ə-fə-tog′rə-fi), *n.* 1. the art or process of photographing distant objects by using a telephoto lens or a telescope with the camera. 2. the science or process of transmitting photographs over distances by converting light rays into electric signals which are sent over wire or radio channels: the receiver converts the electric signals back into light rays to which a photographic film is exposed.

tel·e·print·er (tel′ə-prin′tẽr), *n.* [Chiefly British], a teletypewriter.

Tel·e·promp·ter (tel′ə-promp′tẽr), *n.* an electronic device that, unseen by the audience, unrolls a prepared speech, script, etc. line by line, as a prompting aid to a speaker or actor: a trade-mark.

tel·e·ran (tel′ə-ran′), *n.* [< *tele*vision *r*adar *a*ir *n*avigation], an electronic aid to aerial navigation by which data received by radar, maps of the terrain, etc. are transmitted to aircraft by television.

tel·e·scope (tel′ə-skōp′), *n.* [It. *telescopio* (Galileo, 1611); Mod. L. *telescopium* < Gr. *tēleskopos,* seeing from a distance < *tēle,* far off + *skopein,* to view], an instrument for making distant objects, as the stars, appear nearer and consequently larger: it consists of a tube or series of tubes containing lenses and is of two types, *refracting,* in which the image is focused on a lens, and *reflecting,* in which the image is focused on a mirror. *adj.* having parts that slide one inside another. *v.i.* [TELESCOPED (-skōpt′), TELESCOPING], to slide or be forced one into another like the concentric tubes of a small, collapsible telescope. *v.t.* 1. to cause to telescope; hence, 2. to condense; shorten.

HAND TELESCOPE

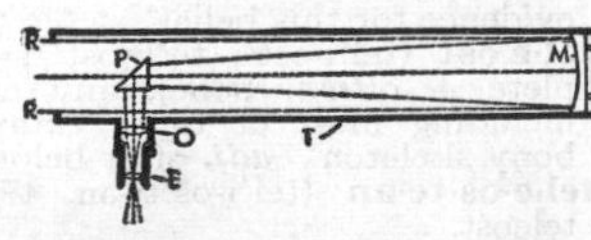
DIAGRAM OF REFLECTING TELESCOPE

T, tube; R, rays reflected from M, mirror to P, prism to O, objective lens to E, eyepiece

tel·e·scop·ic (tel′ə-skop′ik), *adj.* 1. of a telescope or telescopes. 2. seen or obtained by a telescope. 3. visible only with the aid of a telescope. 4. having distant vision; farseeing. 5. having sections that slide one inside another: as, a *telescopic* drinking tumbler.

tel·e·scop·i·cal·ly (tel′ə-skop′i-k′l-i, tel′ə-skop′ik-li), *adv.* 1. by means of a telescope. 2. in a telescopic manner.

te·les·co·pist (tə-les′kə-pist), *n.* a person skilled in using a telescope and in making telescopic observations.

Tel·e·sco·pi·um (tel′ə-skō′pi-əm), *n.* [Mod. L.], a southern constellation: see **constellation,** chart.

te·les·co·py (tə-les′kə-pi), *n.* 1. the art or practice of using a telescope. 2. the science of making telescopes.

tel·e·sis (tel′ə-sis), *n.* [Mod. L. < Gr. *telein,* to fulfill, complete < *telos,* an end], the purposeful use of natural and social forces; planned progress.

tel·e·spec·tro·scope (tel′ə-spek′trə-skōp′), *n.* an instrument combining a telescope and a spectroscope, for producing the spectra of stars, etc.

tel·e·ster·e·o·scope (tel′ə-ster′i-ə-skōp′, tel′ə-stêr′i-ə-skōp′), *n.* a binocular telescope which provides a stereoscopic view of distant objects.

tel·es·the·si·a (tel′əs-thē′zhə, tel′əs-thē′zhi-ə), *n.* [Mod. L. < *tele-* + *esthesia*], extrasensory perception of distant objects, events, etc.

te·les·tich, tel·es·tic (tə-les′tik, tel′ə-stik′), *n.* [< Gr. *telos,* an end + *stichos,* a line], a short poem, etc. in which the last letters of the lines spell a word or words when taken in order: cf. **acrostic.**

tel·e·ther·mom·e·ter (tel′ə-thẽr-mom′ə-tẽr), *n.* a thermometer that records its reading electrically at a distance.

Tel·e·type (tel′ə-tīp′), *n.* [often t-], 1. a form of teletypewriter: a trade-mark. 2. communication by means of Teletype. *v.t. & v.i.* [TELETYPED (-tīpt′), TELETYPING], [often t-], to send (messages) by Teletype.

tel·e·type·writ·er (tel′ə-tīp′rīt′ẽr), *n.* a form of telegraph in which the receiver prints messages typed on the keyboard of the transmitter: the striking of the keys produces electrical impulses that cause the corresponding keys on the receiver to register.

tel·e·view (tel′ə-vū′), *v.t. & v.i.* to view or watch (a performance, event, etc.) by television.

tel·e·vise (tel′ə-vīz′), *v.t.* [TELEVISED (-vīzd′), TELEVISING], to transmit or receive by television.

tel·e·vi·sion (tel′ə-vizh′ən), *n.* [*tele-* + *vision*], 1. the process of transmitting scenes or views by radio or, rarely, by direct wire: the transmitting televisor, by means of an electronic tube (either an *iconoscope* or *Orthicon*), converts light rays into electronic impulses for further conversion into radio waves; the receiving televisor reconverts the corresponding impulses into electron beams that are projected against the luminescent screen of the *kinescope,* reproducing the original image. 2. the science of making or operating television apparatus. 3. the field of radio broadcasting that employs television.

tel·fer (tel′fẽr), *n. & v.t.* telpher.

tel·fer·age (tel′fẽr-ij), *n.* telpherage.

tel·ford (tel′fẽrd), *adj.* [after T. *Telford* (1757–1834), Scot. civil engineer], designating or of a road pavement made of stones and gravel rolled smooth.

tel·har·mo·ni·um (tel′här-mō′ni-əm), *n.* [*tel-* (tele-) + *harmonium*], an instrument consisting of a keyboard that controls alternating currents of electricity for producing music at a distant point.

te·li·al (tē′li-əl, tel′i-əl), *adj.* 1. of a telium. 2. designating or of the final and teliospore-bearing stage in the life cycle of the rust fungi.

tel·ic (tel′ik), *adj.* [Gr. *telikos* < *telos,* an end], directed toward an end; purposeful.

te·li·o·spore (tē′li-ə-spôr′, tel′i-ə-spōr′), *n.* [< *telium* + *spore*], a resting spore that develops in the telial stage of the rust fungi and germinates at the end of the winter.

te·li·o·stage (tē′li-ə-stāj′, tel′i-ə-stāj′), *n.* [< Mod. L. *telium,* the spore fruit < Gr. *telos, teleos,* completion, end; + *stage*], the last stage in the life cycle of rust fungi, in which they develop two-celled resting spores.

te·li·um (tē′li-əm, tel′i-əm), *n.* [*pl.* TELIA (-ə)], [Gr. *telos,* an end], the teliospore-bearing sorus of the rust fungi.

tell (tel), *v.t.* [TOLD (tōld), TELLING], [ME. *tellen;* AS. *tellan,* lit., to calculate, reckon < base of *tæl,* number, *talu,* series, calculation, list (see TALE); Gmc. **taljan,* akin to G. *zählen,* to reckon, count (cf. *erzählen,* to narrate)], 1. to enumerate; count; reckon: as, *tell* one's beads. 2. to relate in order; narrate; recount: as, he *told* a story. 3. to express in spoken or written words; utter; say: as, *tell* the facts, *tell* the truth. 4. to report; announce; publish. 5. to reveal; disclose; make known: as, her face *told* her joy. 6. to recognize; distinguish; discriminate: as, I can *tell* the difference. 7. to decide; know: as, I can't *tell* what to do. 8. to let know; inform; acquaint: as, *tell* me the truth. 9. to request; direct; order; command: as, I *told* him to be here. 10. to state emphatically; assure: as, I disagree, I *tell* you. *v.i.* 1. to give an account or description (of something). 2. to give evidence or be an indication (of something). 3. to carry tales; reveal secrets: as, kiss and *tell.* 4. to produce a result; be effective; have a marked effect: as, every hammer blow *told.*

tell off, 1. to count (persons, etc.) and separate from

the total number. 2. [Colloq.], to rebuke severely.
tell on, 1. to tire; wear out. 2. [Colloq.], to carry tales about; inform against.

SYN.—**tell,** in this connection, is the simple, general word meaning to convey the facts or details of some circumstance or occurrence (*tell* me what happened); **relate** suggests the orderly telling of something that one has personally experienced or witnessed (*relate* your dream to us); **recount** implies the telling of events in consecutive order and in elaborate detail and, hence, often takes a plural object (to *recount* one's adventures); **narrate** suggests the use of the techniques of fiction, such as plot development, building up to a climax, etc. (to *narrate* the story of one's life); **report** suggests the recounting for others' information of something that one has investigated or witnessed (he will *report* the convention proceedings). See also **reveal.**

Tell, William (tel), in *Swiss legend,* a hero in the fight for independence from Austria: at the command of the Austrian governor on pain of death, he is supposed to have shot an apple off his son's head with bow and arrow: German name, *Wilhelm* (vil'helm) *Tell.*

tell·a·ble (tel'ə-b'l), *adj.* 1. that can be told. 2. worth being told.

tell·er (tel'ẽr), *n.* 1. a person who tells (a story, etc.); narrator; recounter. 2. a person who counts; specifically, *a)* one who counts votes, as in a legislative body. *b)* a bank clerk who pays out or receives money.

tell·er·ship (tel'ẽr-ship'), *n.* [see -SHIP], the position of a teller.

Té·llez, Ga·bri·el (gä'bri-el' te'lyeth), (pseudonym *Tirso de Molina*), 1571?–1648; Spanish dramatist.

tell·ing (tel'iŋ), *adj.* [ME.; see TELL], having an effect; forceful; striking: as, a *telling* retort. —*SYN.* see **valid.**

tell·tale (tel'tāl'), *n.* 1. a person who carries tales; talebearer; tattler. 2. an outward indication of something secret. 3. any of various devices for indicating or recording information; an indicator; specifically, *a)* a row of strips hung over a railroad track to warn of an approaching low bridge. *b)* a device indicating the position of a ship's rudder. *c)* a time clock. *d)* in *music,* a gauge on an organ showing the air pressure. *adj.* being or serving as a telltale.

tel·lu·rate (tel'yoo-rāt'), *n.* a salt of telluric acid.

tel·lu·ret (tel'yoo-ret'), *n.* [Obs.], a telluride.

tel·lu·ri·an (te-loor'i-ən, tel-yoor'i-ən), *adj.* [< L. *tellus, telluris,* the earth; + *-an*], of the earth. *n.* 1. an inhabitant of the earth. 2. an apparatus for demonstrating how the earth's position and movement (diurnal rotation, annual revolution, etc.) causes day and night and the cycle of the seasons.

tel·lu·ric (te-loor'ik, tel-yoor'ik), *adj.* of, derived from, or containing tellurium, especially in a higher valence than in the corresponding tellurous compounds.

tel·lu·ric (te-loor'ik, tel-yoor'ik), *adj.* 1. tellurian. 2. of or arising from the earth, or soil.

tel·lu·rid (tel'yoo-rid), *n.* telluride.

tel·lu·ride (tel'yoo-rīd', tel'yoo-rid), *n.* a compound of tellurium combined with an electropositive element or with a radical.

tel·lu·ri·on (te-loor'i-on', tel-yoor'i-on'), *n.* a tellurian (sense 2).

tel·lu·rite (tel'yoo-rīt'), *n.* 1. a salt of tellurous acid, containing tetravalent tellurium. 2. native tellurium dioxide, TeO_2.

tel·lu·ri·um (te-loor'i-əm, tel-yoor'i-əm), *n.* [Mod. L. < L. *tellus, telluris,* the earth], a rare, tin-white, brittle, nonmetallic chemical element, belonging to the same family of elements as sulfur and selenium and occurring naturally in mineral tellurite and tellurides: symbol, Te; at. wt., 127.61; at. no., 52.

tel·lu·rize (tel'yoo-rīz'), *v.t.* [TELLURIZED (-rīzd'), TELLURIZING], to combine or treat with tellurium: used chiefly in the past participle.

tel·lu·rous (tel'yoo-rəs, te-loor'əs, tel-yoor'əs), *adj.* of, derived from, or containing tellurium, especially in a lower valence than in the corresponding telluric compounds.

Tel·lus (tel'əs), *n.* [L.], in *Roman mythology,* the goddess of the earth.

tel·o- (tel'ə), tele-.

tel·o- (tel'ə), [< Gr. *telos,* an end, completion], a combining form meaning *end,* as in *telophase:* also, before a vowel, **tel-.**

tel·o·dy·nam·ic (tel'ə-dī-nam'ik), *adj.* [*telo-* (tele-) + *dynamic*], of or for the transmission of mechanical power to a distance by cables and pulleys.

tel·o·phase (tel'ə-fāz'), *n.* [*telo-* (end) + *phase*], in *biology,* the final stage of mitosis, in which the parent cell becomes completely divided into two cells, each having a nucleus.

tel·pher (tel'fẽr), *n.* [< *tel-* (tele-) + Gr. *pherein,* to bear], an electrically driven car suspended from overhead cables. *v.t.* to transport by telpher. Also spelled **telfer.**

tel·pher·age (tel'fẽr-ij), *n.* [see -AGE], a transportation system using telphers: also spelled **telferage.**

tel·son (tel'sən), *n.* [Mod. L.; Gr. *telson,* a limit, boundary], the last segment of the body of a segmented animal, as of a crustacean, etc.

Tel·u·gu (tel'oo-gōō'), *n.* [< the Telugu name], 1. a Dravidian language spoken in eastern India. 2. [*pl.* TELUGU, TELUGUS (-gōōz')], a member of a Dravidian people living in Hyderabad, India, who speak this language. *adj.* of Telugu or the Telugu. Also **Telegu.**

tem·blor (tem-blôr'), *n.* [*pl.* TEMBLORS (-blôrz'), TEMBLORES (-blô'rās)], [Sp. < *temblar,* to tremble; LL. **tremulare;* see TREMBLE], an earthquake.

tem·er·ar·i·ous (tem'ə-râr'i-əs), *adj.* [L. *temerarius* < *temere,* rashly], reckless; rash.

te·mer·i·ty (tə-mer'ə-ti), *n.* [ME. *temeryte;* L. *temeritas* < *temere,* rashly], foolish boldness; foolhardiness; recklessness; rashness.

SYN.—**temerity** refers to a rashness or foolish boldness that results from underrating the dangers or failing to evaluate the consequences (he had the *temerity* to criticize his employer); **audacity** suggests either great presumption or defiance of social conventions, morals, etc. (shocked at the *audacity* of his proposal); **effrontery,** always derogatory in usage, connotes shamelessness or insolence in defying the rules of propriety, courtesy, etc. (the *effrontery* of her refusal to help); **nerve, cheek,** and **gall** are colloquial equivalents of effrontery, but **nerve** and **cheek** usually suggest mere impudence or sauciness and **gall,** unmitigated insolence.

Tem·es·vár (tem'esh-vär'), *n.* Timișoara: the Hungarian name.

temp., 1. temperance. 2. temperature. 3. temporary. 4. *tempore,* [L.], in the time of.

Tem·pe, Vale of (tem'pi), a beautiful valley between Mounts Olympus and Ossa in Thessaly, Greece, anciently regarded as sacred to Apollo.

tem·per (tem'pẽr), *v.t.* [ME. *tempren* < AS. *temprian* & OFr. *temprer,* both < L. *temperare,* to regulate, temper, mix properly], 1. to make suitable, desirable, or free from excess by mingling with something else; reduce in intensity, especially by the admixture of some other quality; moderate; assuage; mollify: as, *temper* your criticism with reason. 2. to bring to the proper texture, consistency, hardness, etc. by mixing with something or treating in some way: as, some paints are *tempered* with oil; steel or glass is *tempered* by heating and sudden cooling; clay is *tempered* by moistening and kneading. 3. [Rare], to fit; adapt. 4. [Archaic], to mix in proper proportions. 5. in *music,* to adjust the pitch of (a note, instrument, etc.) by temperament; tune. *v.i.* to be or become tempered. *n.* 1. the state of being tempered; specifically, *a)* [Archaic], properly proportioned mixture. *b)* the state of a metal with regard to the degree of hardness and resiliency. 2. frame of mind; disposition; mood: as, in a bad *temper.* 3. calmness of mind; composure: now used only in the phrases *lose one's temper, keep one's temper.* 4. a tendency to become angry readily: as, she has a *temper.* 5. anger; rage: as, he went into a *temper.* 6. something used to temper a mixture, etc. 7. [Archaic], mean; middle course. 8. [Obs.], *a)* character; quality. *b)* bodily constitution. —*SYN.* see **disposition, mood.**

tem·per·a (tem'pẽr-ə), *n.* [It. < *temperare;* see TEMPER], 1. a process of painting in which pigments are mixed with size, casein, or egg, especially egg yolk, to produce a dull finish. 2. the paint used in this process.

tem·per·a·ment (tem'prə-mənt, tem'pẽr-ə-mənt), *n.* [ME.; L. *temperamentum,* proper mixing < *temperare,* to mingle, qualify, temper], 1. originally, a tempering; proportionate mixture or balance of ingredients. 2. in medieval physiology, any one of the four conditions of body and mind, the *sanguine, phlegmatic, choleric* (or *bilious*), and *melancholic temperaments,* attributed to an excess of one of the four corresponding humors: see **humor.** 3. frame of mind; disposition; nature: as, he has an excitable *temperament.* 4. a disposition that rebels at restraints and is often moody or capricious: as, many artists have *temperament.* 5. [Obs.], *a)* climate. *b)* temperature. 6. in *music,* a system of adjustment of the intervals between the tones of an instrument of fixed intonation: it may be *pure temperament,* in which the intervals are set exactly according to theory, or *equal temperament* (as in a piano), in which the pitch of the tones is slightly adjusted to make them suitable for all keys. —*SYN.* see **disposition.**

tem·per·a·men·tal (tem'prə-men't'l, tem'pẽr-ə-men't'l), *adj.* 1. of or caused by temperament. 2. having an excitable temperament; easily upset; moody.

tem·per·a·men·tal·ly (tem'prə-men't'l-i, tem'pẽr-ə-men't'l-i), *adv.* by temperament: as, *temperamentally* unsuited for office work.

tem·per·ance (tem'pẽr-əns, tem'prəns), *n.* [ME.; OFr.; L. *temperantia,* moderation, sobriety < ppr. of *temperare,* to mix in due proportions], 1. the state or quality of being temperate; self-restraint in conduct, expression, indulgence of the appetites, etc.; moderation, originally as one of the four cardinal virtues. 2.

moderation in eating and drinking, especially in drinking alcoholic liquors. 3. total abstinence from alcoholic liquors. Abbreviated **temp.**

tem·per·ate (tem'pẽr-it, tem'prit), *adj.* [ME. *temperat;* L. *temperatus,* pp. of *temperare,* to mix in due proportions], 1. moderate in indulging the appetites; not self-indulgent; abstemious, especially in the use of alcoholic liquors. 2. moderate in one's actions, speech, etc.; self-restrained. 3. characterized by moderation or restraint, as things, actions, etc. 4. neither very hot nor very cold: said of climate, etc. 5. in *music,* tempered: said of a scale or interval. —*SYN.* see **moderate.**

Temperate Zone, either of two zones of the earth (*North Temperate Zone* and *South Temperate Zone*) between the tropics and the polar circles: also called *Variable Zone*: see **zone,** illus.

tem·per·a·ture (tem'prə-chẽr, tem'pẽr-ə-chẽr), *n.* [L. *temperatura* < *temperatus,* temperate], 1. the degree of hotness or coldness of anything, usually as measured on a thermometer. 2. *a*) the degree of heat of a living body. *b*) the excess of this over the normal (about 98.6°F. or 37°C. in man). Abbreviated **temp., t.** 3. [Obs.], *a*) temperateness, as of climate. *b*) temperament.

temperature gradient, the rate of temperature change with increase in altitude.

tem·pered (tem'pẽrd), *adj.* 1. having been given the desired temper, consistency, hardness, etc.: as, *tempered* steel. 2. modified by addition of or mixture with other qualities, ingredients, etc.: as, *tempered* boldness. 3. having a (specified kind of) temper: as, *bad-tempered.* 4. in *music,* adjusted to a temperament, especially equal temperament.

tem·pest (tem'pist), *n.* [ME. & OFr. *tempeste;* L. *tempestas,* portion of time, weather, a calamity, storm, tempest < *tempus,* time], 1. a violent and extensive wind, especially one accompanied by rain, hail, or snow. 2. any violent commotion or tumult. *v.t.* to affect as a tempest does; agitate violently.

tem·pes·tu·ous (tem-pes'choo-əs), *adj.* [OFr. *tempestueux;* LL. *tempestuosus* < L. *tempestas*], 1. of, involving, or like a tempest. 2. violent; turbulent.

tem·pi (tem'pi), *n.* alternative plural of **tempo.**

Tem·plar (tem'plẽr), *n.* [ME. *templer;* OFr. *templier;* ML. *templarius* < L. *templum* (see TEMPLE); so named from occupying quarters near the site of Solomon's Temple in Jerusalem], 1. a member of a religious military order established by the Crusaders at Jerusalem in 1118 to protect pilgrims and the Holy Sepulcher. 2. [t-], a barrister or law student of the Temple in London. 3. a member of the Masonic order of Knights Templar: also **Knight Templar.**

tem·plate (tem'plit), *n.* [Fr. *templet, templette,* dim. of *temple* < L. *templum,* small timber, purlin], 1. in *architecture, a*) a short stone or timber placed under a beam to help distribute the pressure. *b*) a beam for supporting joists over an open space, as a doorway. 2. a pattern, usually in the form of a thin plate, for testing accuracy of form in woodworking, etc.

tem·ple (tem'p'l), *n.* [ME. < AS. *tempel, templ* & OFr. *temple,* both < L. *templum,* a temple, sanctuary, orig., space marked out], 1. a building for the worship of a god or gods. 2. [T-], any of three buildings for worshiping Jehovah, successively built in Jerusalem. 3. the place of worship of a reformed Jewish congregation: distinguished from *synagogue.* 4. a Christian church. 5. [T-], either of two (*Inner* and *Middle Temple*) of four sets of London buildings housing England's principal law societies: their site was formerly occupied by the London branch of Knights Templars. 6. a building, usually of imposing size, etc., serving the public or an organization in some special way: as, a *temple* of art, a Masonic *temple.*

tem·ple (tem'p'l), *n.* [OFr. *temple, tempe;* LL. **tempula,* dim. of L. *tempora,* the temples, pl. of *tempus,* the right place, fatal spot], 1. either of the flat surfaces behind the forehead and in front of the ear. 2. either of the sidepieces of a pair of glasses that fit against the temples and over the ears.

tem·ple (tem'p'l), *n.* [Fr.; see TEMPLATE], a device for keeping the cloth in a loom stretched to its correct width during weaving.

Tem·ple, Sir **William** (tem'p'l), 1628–1699; English statesman and writer.

Temple Bar, a former London gateway before the Temple buildings: the heads of traitors and criminals were exhibited on it.

tem·pled (tem'p'ld), *adj.* 1. having many temples (places of worship). 2. enshrined in or as in a temple.

tem·plet (tem'plit), *n.* a template.

tem·po (tem'pō), *n.* [*pl.* TEMPOS (-pōz), TEMPI (-pi)], [It.; L. *tempus,* time], 1. the rate of speed at which a musical composition is, or is supposed to be, played: it is indicated by such notations as *allegro, andante,* etc. or by reference to metronome timing. 2. rate of activity: as, the *tempo* of modern living. Abbreviated **t.**

tem·po·ral (tem'pẽr-əl), *adj.* [ME.; OFr. *temporel;* L. *temporalis* < *tempus, temporis,* time], 1. lasting only for a time; transitory; temporary: distinguished from *eternal.* 2. of this world; worldly: distinguished from *spiritual.* 3. civil; secular: distinguished from *ecclesiastical.* 4. of or limited by time: distinguished from *spatial.* 5. in *grammar,* that expresses time. *n.* 1. *usually pl.* anything temporal. 2. *pl.* temporalities.

tem·po·ral (tem'pẽr-əl), *adj.* [LL. *temporalis* < L. *tempora,* the temples (of the head)], of or near the temple or temples (of the head).

temporal bone, either of a pair of compound bones forming the sides of the skull: see **skull,** illus.

tem·po·ral·i·ty (tem'pə-ral'ə-ti), *n.* [*pl.* TEMPORALITIES (-tiz)], [ME. *temporalite;* L. *temporalitas;* for earlier *temporalte*], 1. the quality or state of being temporal or temporary: distinguished from *perpetuity.* 2. *usually pl.* secular properties of a church, especially church revenues. 3. the laity.

tem·po·rar·i·ly (tem'pə-rer'ə-li, tem'pə-rer'ə-li), *adv.* for a time only; for the time being.

tem·po·rar·i·ness (tem'pə-rer'i-nis), *n.* the quality or state of being temporary.

tem·po·rar·y (tem'pə-rer'i), *adj.* [L. *temporarius* < *tempus, temporis,* time], lasting, enjoyed, used, etc. for a time only; not permanent: abbreviated **temp.**

SYN.—**temporary** applies to a post held (or to the person holding such a post) for a limited time, subject to dismissal by those having the power of appointment (a *temporary* mail carrier); **provisional** is specifically applied to a government established for the time being in a new state until a permanent government can be formed; **ad interim** refers to an appointment for an intervening period, as between the death of an official and the election of his successor; **acting** is applied to one who temporarily takes over the powers of a regular official during the latter's absence (a vice-president often serves as *acting* president). —*ANT.* permanent.

tem·po·ri·za·tion (tem'pẽr-i-zā'shən, tem'pẽr-ī-zā'shən), *n.* a temporizing; procrastination; gaining of time.

tem·po·rize (tem'pə-rīz'), *v.i.* [TEMPORIZED (-rīzd'), TEMPORIZING], [Fr. *temporiser* < L. *tempus, temporis,* time], 1. to suit one's actions to the time or occasion; conform to the circumstances. 2. *a*) to give temporary compliance or agreement, evade immediate decision, etc., so as to gain time or avoid argument. *b*) to parley or deal (*with* a person, etc.) so as to gain time. 3. to effect a compromise (*with* a person, etc., or *between* persons or parties).

tem·po·ro- (tem'pẽr-ō, tem'pẽr-ə), [< L. *tempora;* see TEMPORAL], a combining form, used in anatomical terms, meaning *temporal and,* as in *temporomaxillary.*

tempt (tempt), *v.t.* [ME. *tempten, tenten;* OFr. *tempter;* LL. *temptare* < L. *tentare,* to try the strength of, urge, intens. of *tendere,* to stretch], 1. originally, to test; try. 2. to try to persuade (a person); induce; entice; allure, especially to something sensually pleasurable or immoral. 3. to rouse desire in; be inviting to; attract: as, that pie *tempts* me. 4. to provoke or run the risk of provoking (fate, etc.). 5. to dispose or incline strongly: as, I am *tempted* to accept. —*SYN.* see **lure.**

temp·ta·tion (temp-tā'shən), *n.* [re-Latinized ME. *tentaciun;* OFr. *tentation;* L. *tentatio,* a trial, temptation < pp. of *tentare;* see TEMPT], 1. a tempting or being tempted. 2. something that tempts; enticement.

tempt·er (temp'tẽr), *n.* [ME. *temptour;* Late OFr. *tempteur*], a person who tempts.

the Tempter, the Devil; Satan.

tempt·ing (temp'tiŋ), *adj.* [ppr. of *tempt*], that tempts; alluring; attractive; seductive.

tempt·ress (temp'tris), *n.* a woman who tempts, especially sexually.

‡**tem·pus fu·git** (tem'pəs fū'jit), [L.], time flies.

ten (ten), *adj.* [ME.; AS. *ten, tȳn, tene;* akin to G. *zehn;* IE. **dekm̥,* ten, seen also in Sans. *dáça,* Gr. *dĕka,* L. *decem,* etc.; cf. DECIMAL], totaling one more than nine. *n.* 1. the cardinal number between nine and eleven; 10; X. 2. any group of ten persons or things. 3. the tenth in a series. 4. a playing card marked with the number 10 and ten spots of its suit. 5. [Colloq.], a ten-dollar bill.

ten- (ten), teno-.

ten., 1. tenor. 2. in *music,* tenuto.

ten·a·bil·i·ty (ten'ə-bil'ə-ti), *n.* the state or quality of being tenable.

ten·a·ble (ten'ə-b'l), *adj.* [Fr. < *tenir;* L. *tenere,* to hold], that can be held, defended, or maintained.

ten·ace (ten'ās), *n.* [< Sp. *tenaza,* lit., tongs, pincers < L. *tenaces,* things that hold fast < *tenax;* see TENACIOUS], in *bridge,* etc., a combination in one hand of the ace and queen or the king and jack of the same suit.

te·na·cious (ti-nā'shəs), *adj.* [L. *tenax, tenacis* < *tenere,* to hold], 1. holding firmly: as, a *tenacious* grip. 2. that retains well; retentive: as, a *tenacious* memory. 3. that holds together strongly; cohesive; tough: as, *tenacious* wood. 4. that clings; adhesive; sticky. 5. persistent; stubborn: as, *tenacious* courage.

te·nac·i·ty (ti-nas'ə-ti), *n.* the quality or state of being tenacious; firmness of hold, retentiveness, cohesiveness, adhesiveness, or persistence. —*SYN.* see **perseverance.**

te·nac·u·lum (ti-nak'yoo-ləm), *n.* [*pl.* TENACULA (-lə)], [LL., instrument for holding < L. *tenere,* to hold], in *surgery,* a pointed, hooked instrument for lifting and holding parts, as blood vessels.

te·naille, te·nail (te-nāl′), *n.* [Fr. *tenaille*, lit., pincers, tongs; L. *tenacula*, pl. of *tenaculum*, holder, dim. < base of *tenax;* see TENACIOUS], in *fortifications*, an outwork before the curtain between two bastions.

ten·an·cy (ten′ən-si), *n.* [*pl.* TENANCIES (-siz)], 1. the condition of being a tenant; renting of land, a building, etc. 2. property occupied by a tenant. 3. the duration of such an occupancy. 4. possession of lands, etc. by any kind of title.

ten·ant (ten′ənt), *n.* [ME. *tenaunt;* OFr. *tenant*, orig. ppr. of *tenir*, to hold; L. *tenere*, to hold], 1. a person who pays rent to occupy or use land, a building, etc.: distinguished from *landlord*. 2. an occupant; inhabitant. 3. a person who possesses lands, etc. by any kind of title. *v.t.* to hold as a tenant; occupy.

ten·ant·a·ble (ten′ənt-ə-b'l), *adj.* fit to be lived in by a tenant.

tenant farmer, a person who farms land owned by another and pays rent in cash or in a share of the crops.

ten·ant·ry (ten′ənt-ri), *n.* [*pl.* TENANTRIES (-riz)], [ME.; also *tenandrie*], 1. tenants collectively. 2. the condition of being a tenant.

ten-cent store (ten′sent′), a five-and-ten-cent store.

tench (tench), *n.* [*pl.* TENCHES (-iz), TENCH; see PLURAL, II, D, 1], [ME. & OFr. *tenche* < LL. *tinca*], a European fresh-water fish of the carp family.

Ten Commandments, in the *Bible*, the ten rules of living and religious observance given to Moses by God on Mount Sinai; the Decalogue: Ex. 20:2–17; Deut. 5:6–22.

tend (tend), *v.t.* [ME. *tenden;* contr. of *attenden;* see ATTEND], 1. to take care of; minister to; watch over; cultivate: as, he *tends* his plants. 2. to be in charge of; manage; operate: as, they *tend* the store. 3. in *nautical usage*, to be on the alert to keep (a rope, etc.) from fouling. *v.i.* [Colloq.], to pay attention; attend.
tend on, to wait upon; serve.

tend (tend), *v.i.* [ME. *tenden;* OFr. *tendre;* L. *tendere*, to stretch, extend, tend], 1. to proceed; be directed: as, the road *tends* south. 2. to have an inclination, disposition, bias, etc. to do something; be apt; incline: as, he *tends* to exaggerate, she *tends* toward selfishness. 3. to lead or be directed (*to* or *toward* a specified result).

tend·ance (ten′dəns), *n.* 1. attendance; attention; care. 2. [Obs.], attendants collectively.

ten·den·cious (ten-den′shəs), *adj.* tendentious.

tend·en·cy (ten′dən-si), *n.* [*pl.* TENDENCIES (-siz)], [ML. *tendentia* < L. *tendens*, ppr. of *tendere*, to stretch, extend, tend], 1. an inclination to move or act in a particular direction or way; constant disposition to some action or state; leaning; bias; propensity; bent. 2. a course toward some purpose, object, or result; drift. 3. a definite purpose or point of view in a literary work: usually used attributively, as *tendency* drama.
SYN.—**tendency** refers to an inclination or disposition to move in a particular direction or act in a certain way, especially as a result of some inherent quality or habit (he has a *tendency* toward exaggeration); **trend** suggests a general direction, with neither a definite course nor goal, subject to change or fluctuation by some external force (a recent *trend* in literature); **current** differs from **trend** in connoting a clearly defined course, also subject, however, to change (the *current* of one's life); **drift** refers either to the course along which something is being carried or driven (the *drift* toward absolute conformity) or to a course taken by something that has unstated implications (what is the *drift* of this argument?); **tenor**, equivalent to **drift** in its second sense, connotes more strongly the clarity or purport of the unstated purpose or objective (the general *tenor* of the Bill of Rights).

ten·den·tious (ten-den′shəs), *adj.* [G. *tendenziös* < *tendenz* (< ML. *tendentia*), tendency], characterized by a deliberate tendency or aim; especially, advancing a definite point of view or doctrine: as, *tendentious* writings.

ten·der (ten′dẽr), *adj.* [ME. & OFr. *tendre* < L. *tener*, soft, delicate, tender], 1. easily chewed, broken, cut, etc.; delicate in texture; soft, fragile, succulent, etc. 2. weak of constitution or physique; unable to endure severe weather, hardship, etc.; feeble; frail. 3. having weakness due to youth; immature; young: as, the *tender* years. 4. of soft quality or delicate tone; subdued: as, *tender* colors. 5. that requires careful handling; ticklish; delicate: as, a *tender* question. 6. mild; light; not rough or heavy: as, a *tender* touch. 7. that has or expresses affection, love, consideration, etc.; gentle; affectionate: as, a *tender* smile. 8. careful; considerate: as, *tender* of another's feelings. 9. sparing; chary: as, *tender* of one's praise. 10. acutely sensitive, especially to pain. 11. sensitive to impressions, emotions, moral influences, etc.; impressionable: as, *tender* conscience. 12. sensitive to others' feelings; sympathetic; compassionate: as, a *tender* heart. 13. in *nautical usage*, leaning over too easily under sail; crank. *v.t.* 1. to make tender. 2. [Archaic], to treat with tenderness.
SYN.—**tender**, in this connection, implies a softness or gentleness in one's relations with others that is expressive of warm affection, concern, etc. (a *tender* caress); **compassionate** is applied to one who is easily affected by another's troubles or pains and is quick to show pity or mercy (a *compassionate* judge); **sympathetic** implies the ability or disposition to enter into another's mental state or emotions and thus to share his sorrows, joys, desires, etc. (he took a *sympathetic* interest in her career); **warm** and **warmhearted** suggest a sympathetic interest or affection characterized by cordiality, generosity, etc. (*warm*, or *warmhearted*, hospitality).

ten·der (ten′dẽr), *v.t.* [Fr. *tendre;* L. *tendere*, to stretch, extend, tend], 1. to offer in payment of an obligation. 2. to present for acceptance; offer: as, he *tendered* his resignation. *n.* 1. an offer of money, services, etc. made to satisfy an obligation in order to avoid prosecution. 2. a formal offer, as of marriage, contractual terms, etc. 3. something offered in payment, especially money: as, the currency of any country is legal *tender* in that country. —***SYN.*** see **offer.**

tend·er (ten′dẽr), *n.* 1. a person who tends, or has charge of, something. 2. a small ship for supplying a large one. 3. a boat for carrying passengers, etc. to or from a large ship close to shore. 4. a railroad car carrying coal and water for a steam locomotive, to the rear of which it is attached.

ten·der·foot (ten′dẽr-foot′), *n.* [*pl.* TENDERFOOTS (-foots′); *rarely*, TENDERFEET (-fēt′)], 1. a newcomer to the ranching and mining country of the West, unused to the hardships of the life. 2. any newcomer, novice, or inexperienced person. 3. a beginner in the Boy Scouts.

ten·der·heart·ed (ten′dẽr-här′tid), *adj.* having a tender heart; easily moved to pity; sympathetic.

ten·der·ize (ten′dẽr-īz′), *v.t.* [TENDERIZED (-īzd′), TENDERIZING], to make tender, as meat.

ten·der·loin (ten′dẽr-loin′), *n.* 1. the tenderest part of a loin of beef, pork, etc., located under the short ribs and consisting of the psoas muscle. 2. [usually T-], *a*) formerly, a district in New York City, below 42d Street west of Broadway, in which there was much vice and corruption: so called because regarded as a choice assignment for police grafters; hence, *b*) any similar district in another city.

ten·di·nous (ten′di-nəs), *adj.* [Fr. *tendineux* < ML. *tendo*], 1. of or like a tendon or tendons. 2. consisting of tendons.

ten·don (ten′dən), *n.* [Fr.; ML. *tendo* < Gr. *tenōn*, a sinew < *teinein*, to stretch; form influenced by L. *tendere*, to stretch], any of the inelastic cords of tough, fibrous connective tissue in which muscle fibers end and by which muscles are attached to bones or other parts; a sinew.

ten·drac (ten′drak), *n.* a tenrec.

ten·dril (ten′dril), *n.* [Fr. *tendrillon;* prob. < *tendre*, to stretch out, but associated with *tendre*, tender, soft, etc.], a threadlike part of a climbing plant, serving to support it by clinging to or coiling around an object.

Ten·e·brae (ten′ə-brē′), *n.pl.* [L., pl., shadows, darkness], in the *Roman Catholic Church*, the matins and lauds sung for the following day in the afternoon or evening of Wednesday, Thursday, and Friday of Holy Week, at which the Crucifixion is commemorated by the extinguishing of candles.

ten·e·brif·ic (ten′ə-brif′ik), *adj.* [< L. *tenebrae* (see TENEBRAE); + *-fic*], making dark; obscuring.

ten·e·brous (ten′ə-brəs), *adj.* [ME. & OFr. *tenebrus;* L. *tenebrosus* < *tenebrae;* see TENEBRAE], dark; gloomy.

Ten·e·dos (ten′ə-dos′), *n.* a Turkish island in the Aegean, near the Dardanelles.

ten·e·ment (ten′ə-mənt), *n.* [ME.; OFr., a holding; ML. *tenementum* < L. *tenere*, to hold], 1. in *law*, land, buildings, offices, franchises, etc. held of another by tenure. 2. a dwelling house. 3. a room or set of rooms tenanted as a separate dwelling. 4. a tenement house. 5. [Poetic], a dwelling place; abode.

ten·e·men·tal (ten′ə-men′t'l), *adj.* 1. having to do with tenements. 2. held by a tenant or tenants.

ten·e·men·ta·ry (ten′ə-men′tẽr-i), *adj.* 1. tenemental. 2. for lease to tenants.

tenement house, a building divided into tenements, or apartments, especially one that is in the poorer section of a city and is overcrowded, dirty, or deteriorated.

Ten·er·ife, Ten·er·iffe (ten′ə-rif′; Sp. te′ne-rē′fe), *n.* the largest of the Canary Islands, off northwestern Africa: area, 782 sq. mi.; pop., 219,000.

Tenerife, Peak of, see **Teyde, Mount.**

te·nes·mus (ti-nez′məs, ti-nes′məs), *n.* [ML.; L. *tenesmos;* Gr. *teinesmos* < *teinein*, to stretch], in *medicine*, a feeling of urgent need to defecate or urinate, with a straining but unsuccessful effort to do so.

ten·et (ten′it, tē′nit), *n.* [L., he holds], a principle, doctrine, or opinion maintained, as by an organization or school of thought. —***SYN.*** see **doctrine.**

ten·fold (ten′fōld′), *adj.* [see -FOLD], 1. having ten parts. 2. having ten times as much or as many. *adv.* ten times as much or as many.
ten-gal·lon hat (ten′gal′ən), a very tall, wide-brimmed felt hat, originally worn by American cowboys.
Ten·gri Khan (teŋ′gri khän), the highest mountain of the Tien Shan range, in the eastern Khirgiz S.S.R., central Asia: height, 23,622 ft.
Ten·gri Nor (teŋ′gri nôr, nōr), a salt lake in eastern Tibet, 15,186 ft. above sea level: area, c. 700 sq. mi.
te·ni·a (tē′ni-ə), *n.* [*pl.* TENIAE (-ē′)], taenia.
te·ni·a·cide (tē′ni-ə-sīd′), *n.* taeniacide.
te·ni·a·fuge (tē′ni-ə-fūj′), *n.* a taeniafuge.
te·ni·a·sis (ti-nī′ə-sis), *n.* taeniasis.
Ten·iers, David (ten′yẽrz; Fl. tə-nêrs′), 1. 1582–1649; Flemish painter: called *the Elder*. 2. 1610–1690; son of the above; Flemish painter: called *the Younger*.
Tenn., Tennessee.
Ten·nes·se·an (ten′ə-sē′ən), *adj.* of Tennessee. *n.* a native or inhabitant of Tennessee.
Ten·nes·see (ten′ə-sē′), *n.* 1. a south central State of the United States: area, 42,246 sq. mi.; pop., 3,567,000; capital, Nashville: abbreviated **Tenn.** 2. a river flowing through Tennessee, Alabama, and Kentucky into the Ohio River: length, 652 mi.
Tennessee Valley Authority, a Federal corporation organized in 1933 to provide cheap electrical power, flood control, improved navigation, irrigation, etc. by developing the potentialities of the Tennessee River and its tributaries: work was first begun at Wilson Dam in Muscle Shoals: abbreviated **TVA, T.V.A.**
Ten·niel, Sir **John** (ten′yəl), 1820–1914; English illustrator and cartoonist.
ten·nis (ten′is), *n.* [ME. *tenetz;* prob. < Anglo-Fr. *tenetz*, receive, hold (imperative for OFr. *tenez*) < OFr. *tenir*, to hold: a cry before play by the server], any of various games played by batting a ball back and forth with rackets or paddles; specifically, *a)* a game, usually played outdoors, in which players bat a fabric-covered, hollow rubber ball back and forth over a net stretched across a specially prepared court of turf, clay, asphalt, etc.: officially called *lawn tennis*. *b)* an old indoor game (*court tennis*), in which players batted a ball back and forth over an embankment or against a wall, originally with the palms of their hands, later with paddles: modern modifications of this game are rackets, squash, handball, etc.
tennis court, a place for playing tennis, with a surface of grass, clay, asphalt, boards, etc., divided by a net and marked with lines.
tennis shoe, 1. a light, rubber-soled, heelless shoe of canvas or leather, worn in playing tennis, etc. 2. a similar leather shoe with short spikes, sometimes worn in playing tennis on a grass court.
Ten·ny·son, Alfred (ten′ə-s'n), first Baron Tennyson (*Alfred, Lord Tennyson*), 1809–1892; English poet; poet laureate (1850–1892).
Ten·ny·so·ni·an (ten′ə-sō′ni-ən), *adj.* of, like, or characteristic of Tennyson or his poetry.
ten·o- (ten′ō, ten′ə), [< Gr. *tenōn*, tendon], a combining form meaning *tendon*, as in *tenotomy:* also, before a vowel, **ten-**.
ten·on (ten′ən), *n.* [ME. *tenon, tenown;* (early) Fr. *tenon* < *tenir* (L. *tenere*), to hold], a projecting part cut on the end of a piece of wood for insertion into a corresponding hole (*mortise*) in another piece to make a joint: see **mortise**, illus. *v.t. & v.i.* 1. to make a tenon (on). 2. to joint by mortise and tenon.
ten·o·ni·tis (ten′ə-nī′tis), *n.* [Mod. L.; see TENDON & -ITIS], inflammation of a tendon.
ten·or (ten′ẽr), *n.* [ME. & OFr. *tenour;* L. *tenor* < *tenere*, to hold], 1. general course or tendency: as, the even *tenor* of his life. 2. general meaning; drift; purport. 3. general character or nature. 4. the exact wording or an exact copy of a legal document. 5. [OFr. *tenour;* It. *tenore;* L. *tenor*: so called because the tenor voice "held" the melody (*canto fermo*)], the highest adult male voice, usually ranging from about an octave below middle C to an octave above: see also **falsetto.** 6. the part written for or sung by this voice. 7. a person or instrument having this range or performing this part. 8. that bell of a peal or set having the lowest tone. *adj.* of, in, for, or having the range of the tenor: as, a *tenor* saxophone. Abbreviated **ten., T., t.** (in music). —***SYN.*** see **tendency.**
tenor clef, the C clef on the fourth line, used in notation for the tenor trombone, the upper range of the cello and bassoon, etc.
te·nor·rha·phy (tə-nôr′ə-fi, tə-nor′ə-fi), *n.* [*pl.* TENORRHAPHIES (-fiz)], [*teno-* + Gr. *-rrhaphy* < *rhaphe*, suture], in *surgery*, suture of a tendon.
te·not·o·my (tə-not′ə-mi), *n.* [*teno-* + *-tomy*], in *surgery*, the cutting or dividing of a tendon.
ten·pen·ny (ten′pen′i; *also, for 1,* ten′pən-i), *adj.* 1. in England, worth ten pence. 2. designating a nail of large size (three inches in length).
ten·pins (ten′pinz′), *n.pl.* 1. [construed as sing.], a game in which ten wooden pins are set up in a triangle at one end of an alley and bowled at. 2. these pins.
ten·rec (ten′rek), *n.* [Fr. *tanrac, tenrec* < Malagasy *tàndraka*], any of a number of insect-eating animals of Madagascar: also **tendrac.**
tense (tens), *adj.* [L. *tensus*, pp. of *tendere*, to stretch], 1. stretched tight; strained; taut. 2. undergoing or showing mental or nervous strain. 3. in *phonetics*, spoken with tensed muscles, especially of the tongue: opposed to *lax, flaccid*. *v.t. & v.i.* [TENSED (tenst), TENSING], to make or become tense. —***SYN.*** see **tight.**
tense (tens), *n.* [ME. & OFr. *tens* < L. *tempus*, time], 1. any of the forms of a verb that show the time of its action or state of being: the English tenses are usually listed as *present, past, future, perfect, past perfect* (*pluperfect*), and *future perfect*, in accordance with Latin models; but the use of English verbal forms is determined more by the manner of action (aspect, mode) than by the time of action. 2. a set of such inflectional forms for any given time: as, conjugate the present *tense* of *be*. Abbreviated **t.**
ten·si·bil·i·ty (ten′sə-bil′ə-ti), *n.* the quality or state of being tensible.
ten·si·ble (ten′sə-b'l), *adj.* [ML. *tensibilis* < L. *tensus;* see TENSE, *adj.*], that can be stretched; tensile.
ten·si·bly (ten′sə-bli), *adv.* by means of tension.
ten·sile (ten′s'l, ten′sil), *adj.* [Mod. L. *tensilis* < L. *tensus;* see TENSE, *adj.*], 1. of, undergoing, or exerting tension. 2. capable of being stretched.
tensile strength, resistance to lengthwise stress, measured by the greatest load in weight per unit area pulling in the direction of length that a given substance can bear without tearing apart.
ten·sil·i·ty (ten-sil′ə-ti), *n.* a tensile quality or state.
ten·sim·e·ter (ten-sim′ə-tẽr), *n.* [*tension* + *-meter*], an instrument for measuring the tension, or pressure, of gases or vapors; manometer.
ten·si·om·e·ter (ten′si-om′ə-tẽr), *n.* [*tension* + *-meter*], an instrument for measuring the tautness of a stretched wire, rope, etc.
ten·sion (ten′shən), *n.* [< Fr. or L.; Fr. *tension;* L. *tensio* < *tensus;* see TENSE, *adj.*], 1. a tensing or being tensed. 2. mental or nervous strain, often accompanied by muscular tautness. 3. a state of strained relations; uneasiness due to mutual hostility. 4. a device for making something tense or taut, as thread in a sewing machine. 5. electromotive force; electric potential or potential difference. 6. the expansive force, or pressure, of a gas or vapor. 7. *a)* stress on a material produced by the pull of forces tending to cause extension. *b)* a force or combination of forces exerting such a pull against the resistance of the material.
ten·sion·al (ten′shən-'l), *adj.* having to do with tension.
ten·si·ty (ten′sə-ti), *n.* a tense state or quality.
ten·sive (ten′siv), *adj.* [Fr. *tensif*], causing tension.
ten·sor (ten′sẽr, ten′sôr), *n.* [Mod. L. < L. *tensus*, pp. of *tendere*, to stretch], any muscle that stretches, or tenses, some part of the body.
ten-strike (ten′strīk′), *n.* 1. in *tenpins*, a strike. 2. [Colloq.], any entirely successful action.
tent (tent), *n.* [ME. & OFr. *tente;* LL. *tenta* < L. *tentus*, alternative pp. of *tendere*, to stretch; cf. L. *tentorium*, awning], 1. a portable shelter consisting of a covering of canvas, or formerly skins, stretched over poles and attached to stakes. 2. anything more or less like this, as an airtight shelter (*oxygen tent*) placed over the bed of a patient receiving oxygen. *v.i.* to live in a tent; encamp. *v.t.* [Rare], to lodge in tents.
tent (tent), *n.* [ME. *tente;* OFr. *tente*, a probe < *tenter*, to try, test; L. *tentare*], in *surgery*, a plug of gauze, lint, etc. placed into an opening or wound to dilate it or keep it open. *v.t.* to insert a tent in.
ten·ta·cle (ten′tə-k'l), *n.* [Mod. L. *tentaculum* < L. *tentare*, to touch, handle, try], 1. any of various kinds of long, slender, flexible growths about the head or mouth of some invertebrate animals, used variously to feel, grasp food, propel, or cling. 2. in *botany*, a sensitive hair, as on some leaves.
ten·ta·cled (ten′tə-k'ld), *adj.* having tentacles.
ten·tac·u·lar (ten-tak′yoo-lẽr), *adj.* of, like, or serving as a tentacle or tentacles.
ten·ta·tive (ten′tə-tiv), *adj.* [ML. *tentativus* < pp. of L. *tentare*, to touch, handle, try], having the nature of an experiment or trial made or done provisionally; experimental; provisional.
tent caterpillar, a kind of caterpillar that lives in colonies in large, tentlike webs which it spins on trees.
tent·ed (ten′tid), *adj.* covered by or living in a tent or tents.
ten·ter (ten′tẽr), *n.* [ME. *tentoure* < L. *tentus;* see TENT (a shelter)], 1. a frame on which cloth is stretched after having been milled, so as to dry evenly without shrinking. 2. a tenterhook. *v.t. & v.i.* [ME. *tenteren*], to stretch on a tenter or tenters.
ten·ter·hook (ten′tẽr-hook′), *n.* any of the hooked nails that hold cloth stretched on a tenter.
on tenterhooks, in suspense; filled with anxiety.
tent fly, an outer sheet of canvas, etc. stretched over a tent roof to provide double protection.
tenth (tenth), *adj.* [Early ME. *tenthe*, replacing AS.

teogotha, teotha, etc.; see TEN & -TH], 1. preceded by nine others in a series; 10th. 2. designating any of the ten equal parts of something. *n.* 1. the one following the ninth. 2. any of the ten equal parts of something; 1/10.

tenth·ly (tenth′li), *adv.* in the tenth place.

tent show, a show, as a circus, given in a tent.

tent stitch, [prob. < *tent* (a shelter)], an embroidery stitch that forms a series of parallel slanting lines.

ten·u·is (ten′ū-is), *n.* [*pl.* TENUES (-ēz′)], [L. (see TENUOUS): used as transl. of Gr. *psilos*, bare, unaspirated (so applied by Aristotle)], in *phonetics*, formerly, a voiceless stop (*p, t, k*).

ten·u·i·ty (ten-ū′ə-ti, ti-nōō′ə-ti), *n.* [*pl.* TENUITIES (-tiz)], [Fr. *tenuité*; L. *tenuitas*], the quality or state of being tenuous; specifically, *a*) thinness; slenderness; fineness. *b*) lack of substance; rarity, as of air. *c*) faintness, as of light or voice. *d*) meagerness; slightness.

ten·u·ous (ten′ū-əs), *adj.* [L. *tenuis*, thin; for IE. base see THIN], 1. physically thin, slender, or fine. 2. rare; not dense, as air at high altitudes. 3. unsubstantial; slight; flimsy: as, a *tenuous* plot. —*SYN.* see **thin.**

ten·ure (ten′yẽr), *n.* [ME. *tenur;* OFr. < *tenir;* L. *tenere*, to hold], 1. a holding, as of property, office, etc. 2. the right to hold or possess something. 3. the length of time something is held: as, *tenure* of office. 4. conditions of possession. 5. permanent possession, as of an office or position.

ten·u·ri·al (ten-yoor′i-əl), *adj.* of or dependent on tenure.

‡te·nu·to (te-nōō′tô), *adj.* [It., pp. of *tenere* (< L. *tenere*), to hold], in *music*, held for its full value: said of a tone or chord: abbreviated **ten.** or indicated by a short line over the note, as ꜧ.

te·o·cal·li (tē′ə-kal′i, tā′ə-käl′yi; Sp. te′ô-kä′yē), *n.* [*pl.* TEOCALLIS (-iz, -yiz; Sp. -yēs)], [Sp.; Nahuatl *teocalli* < *teotl*, god + *calli*, house], an ancient Mexican or Central American temple, usually a building on a truncated pyramid.

te·o·sin·te (tē′ə-sin′ti), *n.* [Sp.; Nahuatl *teocentli*, lit., divine maize < *teotl*, god + *centli*, maize], a tall fodder grass of Mexico and Central America, resembling Indian corn in its broad leaves and tassels of flowers.

te·pee (tē′pē), *n.* [Am. Ind. (Siouan) *tīpi* < *ti*, to dwell + *pi*, used for], a cone-shaped tent used by the American Indians: also spelled **teepee.**

tep·e·fac·tion (tep′ə-fak′shən), *n.* a tepefying or being tepefied.

tep·e·fy (tep′ə-fī′), *v.t. & v.i.* [TEPEFIED (-fīd′), TEPEFYING], [L. *tepefacere* < *tepere*, to be slightly warm + *facere*, to make], to make or become tepid.

teph·rite (tef′rīt), *n.* [< Gr. *tephra*, ashes; + *-ite*], a volcanic rock consisting of plagioclase, nephelite, etc.

teph·rit·ic (tef-rit′ik), *adj.* of or like tephrite.

tep·id (tep′id), *adj.* [ME. *teped;* L. *tepidus* < *tepere*, to be slightly warm], moderately warm; lukewarm.

tep·i·dar·i·um (tep′ə-dâr′i-əm), *n.* [*pl.* TEPIDARIA (-ə)], [L., orig. neut. of *tepidarius*, of a tepid bath < *tepidus;* see TEPID], in an ancient Roman bath, the warm room, intermediate between the hot and the cold rooms.

te·pid·i·ty (ti-pid′ə-ti), *n.* a tepid quality or state.

te·qui·la (ti-kē′lä), *n.* [< *Tequila*, a district in Mexico], 1. a century plant growing in Mexico. 2. an alcoholic liquor distilled from the juice of the stem of this plant.

ter., 1. terrace. 2. territory.

ter·a·phim (ter′ə-fim), *n.pl.* [*sing.* TERAPH (ter′əf), TERAPHIM], [Heb. *tĕrāphim*], small idols representing household gods, used in divination among the ancient Hebrews and other Semitic peoples.

ter·a·tism (ter′ə-tiz′m), *n.* [*terat-* + *-ism*], a monstrosity; malformed fetus.

ter·a·to- (ter′ə-tō, ter′ə-tə), [< Gr. *teras, teratos*, a wonder, monster], a combining form meaning *monster, monstrosity*, as in *teratology:* also, before a vowel, **terat-.**

ter·a·toid (ter′ə-toid′), *adj.* [*terat-* + *-oid*], in *biology*, resembling a monster; monstrous.

ter·a·tol·o·gy (ter′ə-tol′ə-ji), *n.* [*terato-* + *-logy*], the scientific study of biological monstrosities and malformations: abbreviated **teratol.**

ter·bi·a (tũr′bi-ə), *n.* [Mod. L.; see TERBIUM], terbium oxide, Tb_2O_3, a white powder soluble in dilute acids.

ter·bi·um (tũr′bi-əm), *n.* [Mod. L. < *Ytterby*, Sweden], a metallic chemical element of the rare-earth group, found in gadolinite and other minerals: symbol, Tb; at. wt., 159.2; at. no., 65.

Ter Borch, Ge·rard (gā′rärt tẽr bôrkh′), 1617–1681; Dutch painter: also **Terborch.**

Ter·cei·ra (ter-sā′rə), *n.* a Portuguese island in the Azores: area, 223 sq. mi; pop., 48,000.

ter·cel (tũr′s′l), *n.* [ME.; OFr.; ML. *tertiolus* < L. *tertius*, third: said to be so named because a third smaller than the female], a male hawk, especially the male peregrine: see **tassel** (a hawk).

terce·let (tũrs′lit), *n.* a tercel.

ter·cen·te·nar·y (tẽr-sen′tə-ner′i, tũr′sen-ten′ə-ri), *n.* [*pl.* TERCENTENARIES (-iz, -riz)], [L. *ter*, three times; + *centenary*], 1. a period of 300 years. 2. a 300th anniversary or a celebration of this. *adj.* of a period of 300 years.

ter·cet (tũr′sit, tẽr-set′), *n.* [Fr.; It. *terzetto*, dim. of *terzo* (< L. *tertius*), a third], 1. a group of three lines that rhyme with one another or are connected by rhyme with an adjacent triplet or triplets. 2. in *music*, a triplet.

ter·e·bene (ter′ə-bēn′), *n.* [*tereb*inth + *terp*ene], a mixture of terpenes obtained by the action of sulfuric acid on turpentine.

te·reb·ic acid (te-reb′ik, te-rē′bik), [*tereb*inth + *-ic*], a white, crystalline acid, $C_7H_{10}O_4$, a product of the oxidation of turpentine.

ter·e·binth (ter′ə-binth′), *n.* [ME. *terebint, therebinth;* OFr. *therebint(he);* L. *terebinthus;* Gr. *terebinthos*], a small European tree of the sumac family, yielding turpentine.

ter·e·bin·thic (ter′ə-bin′thik), *adj.* terebinthine.

ter·e·bin·thine (ter′ə-bin′thin), *adj.* [L. *terebinthinus;* Gr. *terebinthinos*], 1. of the terebinth tree. 2. of or like turpentine.

te·re·do (te-rē′dō), *n.* [*pl.* TEREDOS (-dōz), TEREDINES (-di-nēz′)], [ME. *terredo;* L.; Gr. *terēdōn*, borer], a small mollusk that bores into and destroys submerged wood, as in ship bottoms; shipworm.

Ter·ence (ter′əns), [L. *Terentius*, name of a Roman gens], a masculine name: diminutive, *Terry.* *n.* (*Publius Terentius Afer*), Roman writer of comedies; 190?–159? B.C.

Te·re·sa (tə-rē′sə, tə-rē′zə), a feminine name: see **Theresa.**

te·rete (tə-rēt′, ter′ēt), *adj.* [L. *teres, teretis*, round, smooth], cylindrical or slightly conical in form and circular in cross section.

Te·reus (têr′ūs, têr′i-əs), *n.* [L.; Gr. *Tēreus*], in *Greek mythology*, a king of Thrace: see **Philomela.**

ter·gal (tũr′g′l), *adj.* [< L. *tergum*, the back; + *-al*], of the tergum, or back; dorsal.

ter·gem·i·nate (tẽr-jem′ə-nit), *adj.* [< L. *tergeminus*, triple < *ter*, thrice + *geminus*, twin-born; + *-ate*], having a pair of leaflets on each of three stalks growing from a common point.

ter·gi·ver·sate (tũr′ji-vẽr-sāt′), *v.i.* [TERGIVERSATED (-id), TERGIVERSATING], [< L. *tergiversatus*, pp. of *tergiversari*, to turn one's back, decline, shift < *tergum*, the back + *versari*, to turn], 1. to desert a cause, party, etc.; become a renegade; apostatize. 2. to use evasions or subterfuge; equivocate.

ter·gi·ver·sa·tion (tũr′ji-vẽr-sā′shən), *n.* [L. *tergiversatio* < *tergiversatus;* see TERGIVERSATE], 1. desertion of a cause, etc.; apostasy. 2. evasion; subterfuge.

ter·gum (tũr′gəm), *n.* [*pl.* TERGA (-gə)], [L.], in *zoology*, the back.

term (tũrm), *n.* [ME. & OFr. *terme;* L. *terminus*, a limit, boundary, end], 1. originally, a point of time designating the beginning or end of a period; set date. 2. a date set for payment, termination of tenancy, etc. 3. a period of time having definite limits; time during which anything lasts; duration; specifically, *a*) a regularly set period of time during which courses of study are taken and completed. *b*) a stipulated length of time that a person may hold office. 4. *pl.* conditions of a contract, agreement, sale, etc. that limit or define its scope or the action involved: as, *terms* of payment, the *terms* of a treaty. 5. *pl. a*) mutual relationship between or among persons; footing: as, on speaking *terms. b*) good or equal footing. 6. a word or phrase having a limiting and definite meaning in some science, art, etc.: as, *tergum* is a zoological *term.* 7. any word or phrase used in a definite or precise sense; expression: as, patriot is the *term* he deserves. 8. *pl.* words that express ideas in a limited or special form: as, he spoke in derogatory *terms.* 9. [Archaic or Rare], a limit; boundary; extremity. 10. *pl.* [Obs.], condition; circumstances. 11. in *architecture*, a boundary post, especially one consisting of a pedestal topped by a bust, as of the god Terminus. 12. in *law, a*) the time a court is in session. *b*) the length of time for which an estate is granted. *c*) the estate itself. *d*) time allowed a debtor to pay. 13. in *logic, a*) either of two concepts that have a stated relation, as the subject and predicate of a proposition. *b*) any one of the three parts of a syllogism. 14. in *mathematics, a*) either of the two quantities of a fraction or a ratio. *b*) each of the quantities in a series. *c*) each of the quantities connected by plus or minus signs in an algebraic expression. *v.t.* to call by a term; name.

bring to terms, to reduce to submission; force to agree.

come to terms, to arrive at an agreement.

make terms, to come to an agreement.

term., 1. terminal. 2. termination.

ter·ma·gan·cy (tũr′mə-gən-si), *n.* the state or quality of being a termagant; shrewishness.

ter·ma·gant (tũr′mə-gənt), *n.* [ME. & OFr. *Tervagant*, idol, imaginary Moslem deity; prob. name of eastern origin brought over by the Crusaders], 1. [T-], an imaginary deity supposed by medieval Christians to be worshiped by Moslems and represented as a boisterous, overbearing figure; hence, 2. a boisterous, quarrelsome, scolding woman; shrew; virago. *adj.* of the nature of a termagant; quarrelsome; scolding.

term day, the day set for payment of rent due, etc.

term·er (tũr′mẽr), *n.* 1. a person serving a term, especially in prison: usually in hyphenated compounds, as, *third-termer*. 2. [Obs.], a termor.

ter·mi·na·bil·i·ty (tũr′mi-nə-bil′ə-ti), *n.* the quality or state of being terminable.

ter·mi·na·ble (tũr′mi-nə-b'l), *adj.* 1. that can be terminated. 2. that terminates after a specified time, as a contract.

ter·mi·na·bly (tũr′mi-nə-bli), *adv.* so as to be terminable.

ter·mi·nal (tũr′mə-n'l), *adj.* [L. *terminalis*], 1. of, at, or forming the end, extremity, or terminus of something. 2. occurring at the end of a series; concluding; closing; final. 3. having to do with a term or established period of time; occurring regularly in terms. 4. connected with, charged at, etc. the end of a railroad line: as, *terminal* rates. 5. in *botany*, growing at the end of a stem or branch: as, a *terminal* leaflet. *n.* 1. a terminating part; end; extremity; limit. 2. either end of an electric circuit or a connection at either end. 3. either end of a transportation line, as a railroad, including station, yards, etc. 4. *a*) a station or city at such a terminus. *b*) a station at an important point or junction of a transportation line. 5. in *architecture*, *a*) a term (sense 11). *b*) an ornamental carving at the end of a structural element. —*SYN.* see **last.**

terminal leave, the final leave granted to a member of the armed forces immediately before his discharge, equal in duration to his accumulated unused leave.

ter·mi·nal·ly (tũr′mə-n'l-i), *adv.* 1. at the end. 2. as concerns termination. 3. every term.

ter·mi·nate (tũr′mə-nāt′), *v.t.* [TERMINATED (-id), TERMINATING], [< L. *terminatus*, pp. of *terminare*, to end, limit < *terminus;* see TERM], 1. to bring to an end in space or time; form the end or conclusion of; limit, bound, finish, or conclude. 2. to put an end to; stop; cease. *v.i.* 1. to come to an end in space or time; stop; end. 2. to have its end (*in* something): as, the road *terminates* in woods. —*SYN.* see **close.**

ter·mi·na·tion (tũr′mə-nā′shən), *n.* [L. *terminatio*], 1. a terminating or being terminated. 2. the end of something in space or time; limit, bound, conclusion, or finish. 3. the end of a word; final sound, morpheme, or syllable. 4. a thing's outcome or result: as, a friendly *termination* of dispute.

ter·mi·na·tion·al (tũr′mə-nā′shən-'l), *adj.* 1. of or forming a termination or terminations. 2. in *grammar*, formed by inflectional endings.

ter·mi·na·tive (tũr′mə-nā′tiv), *adj.* terminating or tending to terminate. *n.* in *linguistics*, a suffix.

ter·mi·na·tor (tũr′mə-nā′tẽr), *n.* [LL.], 1. a person or thing that terminates. 2. the line dividing the illuminated and dark parts of the disk of the moon or a planet.

ter·mi·na·to·ry (tũr′mi-nə-tôr′i, tũr′mi-nə-tō′ri), *adj.* 1. terminative. 2. terminal.

ter·mi·no·log·i·cal (tũr′mi-nə-loj′i-k'l), *adj.* having to do with terminology.

ter·mi·nol·o·gy (tũr′mə-nol′ə-ji), *n.* [*pl.* TERMINOLOGIES (-jiz)], [< L. *terminus* (see TERM); + *-logy*], 1. the system of terms used in a specific field of art, science, etc.; nomenclature. 2. [Rare], the science or study of terms in specific branches of knowledge.

ter·mi·nus (tũr′mə-nəs), *n.* [*pl.* TERMINI (-nī′), TERMINUSES (-nəs-iz)], [L.; see TERM], 1. [Rare], a boundary or limit. 2. a boundary stone or marker. 3. [T-], in *Roman mythology*, the deity presiding over boundaries and landmarks. 4. an end; extremity or goal. 5. either end of a railroad, bus, or air line. 6. [Chiefly British], the station or city at the end of such a line.

‡ter·mi·nus ad quem (tũr′mi-nəs ad kwem), [L., lit., end toward which], a destination; conclusion.

‡ter·mi·nus a quo (tũr′mi-nəs ā kwō), [L., lit., end from which], a starting point.

ter·mite (tũr′mīt), *n.* [L. *termes*, *termitis*, wood-boring worm < base of *terere*, to rub, bore; cf. TERETE], any of various pale-colored social insects that are very destructive to wooden structures and are found in the Temperate Zones and in the tropics: also called *white ant.*

term·less (tũrm′lis), *adj.* 1. limitless; boundless. 2. unconditional.

term·or (tũr′mẽr), *n.* [ME.; Anglo-Fr. *termer* < *terme;* see TERM & -ER], in *law*, a person holding an estate for a certain period or for life.

tern (tũrn), *n.* [< ON. *therna*, via East Anglian dial.; ? akin to ON. *therna*, female slave or servant (akin to G. *dirne*) < IE. base **teq-*, to run], any of several sea birds related to the gulls, but smaller, with a more slender body and beak, and a deeply forked tail: they are found on both sides of the Atlantic.

tern (tũrn), *n.* [Fr. *terne* < L. *terni*, three each < *tres*, three], 1. a lottery prize won by drawing a combination of three numbers. 2. the three numbers.

ter·na·ry (tũr′nẽr-i), *adj.* [ME.; L. *ternarius* < *terni;* see prec.], 1. made up of three parts; threefold; triple. 2. third. 3. in *chemistry*, of or containing three different elements, radicals, etc. 4. in *mathematics*, *a*) having three as a base. *b*) involving three variables. 5. in *metallurgy*, of an alloy of three metals. *n.* [*pl.* TERNARIES (-iz)], [Rare], a group or set of three.

Ter·na·te (ter-nä′te), *n.* one of the Molucca Islands, in Indonesia: area, 53 sq. mi.; pop., 19,000.

ter·nate (tũr′nāt), *adj.* [Mod. L. *ternatus* < L. *terni;* see TERN (lottery prize)], 1. consisting of three. 2. arranged in threes. 3. in *botany*, growing in groups of three, as some leaves.

terne·plate (tũrn′plāt′), *n.* [Fr. *terne*, dull (cf. TARNISH); + *plate*], sheet iron or steel coated with an alloy of tin and lead: it has a dull finish and is considered inferior to standard tin plate.

ter·ni·on (tũr′ni-ən), *n.* [L. *ternio*, a triad < *terni;* see TERN (lottery prize)], a set of three, especially of three folded sheets of paper.

Ter·no·pol (tyer-nô′pôl-y′), *n.* Tarnopol: Russian name.

ter·pene (tũr′pēn), *n.* [*terp*entine (obs. form of *turpentine*) + *-ene*], any of a series of isomeric hydrocarbons of the general formula $C_{10}H_{16}$, found in resins, essential oils, etc.

ter·pin·e·ol (tẽr-pin′i-ōl′, tẽr-pin′i-ol), *n.* [*terpin* (see TERPENE & -IN) + *-ol*], any of three isomeric alcohols, $C_{10}H_{17}OH$, with a lilac odor, found in certain volatile oils and used in perfumes.

Terp·sich·o·re (tũrp-sik′ə-rē′), *n.* [Gr. *Terpsichorē* < *terpsichoros*, delighting in the dance < *terpein*, to delight in + *choros*, a dance], in *Greek mythology*, the Muse of dancing.

terp·si·cho·re·an (tũrp′si-kə-rē′ən), *adj.* 1. [T-], of Terpsichore. 2. having to do with dancing. *n.* a dancer: literary or humorous usage.

terr., 1. terrace. 2. territory.

‡ter·ra (ter′ə), *n.* [L.], (the) earth.

terra al·ba (al′bə), [L., lit., white earth], any of several white earths, as gypsum, magnesia, kaolin, etc.

ter·race (ter′is), *n.* [Fr. *terrasse;* LL. **terracea* < L. *terra*, earth], 1. a raised, flat mound of earth with sloping sides. 2. any of a series of flat platforms of earth with sloping sides, rising one above the other, as on a hillside. 3. a geological formation of this nature. 4. an unroofed, paved area immediately adjacent to a house and overlooking a lawn or garden. 5. a flat roof, especially of a house of Spanish or Oriental architecture. 6. a row of houses on ground raised from the street. 7. a street in front of such houses: often used in street names. 8. a parklike strip in the middle of a boulevard, etc. *v.t.* [TERRACED (-ist), TERRACING], to form into, lay out in, or surround with a terrace or terraces. Abbreviated **ter., terr.**

ter·ra-cot·ta (ter′ə-kot′ə), *adj.* 1. of terra cotta. 2. brownish-red.

terra cotta, [It., lit., baked earth < L.; cf. TERRA & COOK], 1. a hard, brown-red, usually unglazed earthenware used for pottery, statuettes, ornamental facing, etc. 2. its brown-red color.

terra fir·ma (fũr′mə), [L.], firm earth; solid ground.

ter·rain (tə-rān′, te-rān′, ter′ān), *n.* [Fr.; LL. **terranum*, for L. *terrenum* < *terrenus*, of earth, earthen < *terra*, earth], 1. ground or a tract of ground, especially considered with regard to its natural features or fitness for some use. 2. in *geology*, a terrane.

ter·ra in·cog·ni·ta (ter′ə in-kog′ni-tə), [*pl.* TERRAE INCOGNITAE (-ē -tē′)], [L.], 1. an unknown land; unexplored territory; hence, 2. an unknown or unexplored field of knowledge.

ter·ra·my·cin (ter′ə-mī′sin), *n.* [< L. *terra*, earth + Gr. *mykēs*, fungus; + *-in*], an antibiotic drug derived from an earth, effective against certain viruses, rickettsiae, and protozoa, as well as against bacteria.

ter·rane (tə-rān′, te-rān′, ter′ān), *n.* [Fr. *terrain;* see TERRAIN], a geological formation or series of continuously related formations.

ter·ra·pin (ter′ə-pin), *n.* [of Am. Ind. (Algonquian) origin; earlier *torope*, tortoise], 1. any of several North American fresh-water or tidewater turtles, especially the diamondback terrapin found along the Atlantic and Gulf Coasts. 2. its flesh used as food.

ter·ra·que·ous (ter-ā′kwi-əs), *adj.* [< L. *terra*, earth; + *aqueous*], consisting of both land and water.

ter·rar·i·um (te-râr′i-əm), *n.* [*pl.* TERRARIUMS (-əmz), TERRARIA (-ə)], [< L. *terra*, earth + *-arium* as in *aquarium*], 1. an enclosure for keeping small animals. 2. a bottle, bowl, or other container enclosing a garden of small plants.

ter·raz·zo (ter-rät′sô), *n.* [It.; LL. **terracea;* see TERRACE], flooring of small chips of marble set in cement and polished.

Ter·re Haute (ter′ə hōt′), a city in western Indiana, on the Wabash River: pop., 73,000.

ter·rene (te-rēn′, ter′ēn), *adj.* [L. *terrenus;* see TERRAIN], 1. of earth; earthy. 2. worldly; mundane. *n.* 1. the earth. 2. a land or territory.

terre·plein (ter′plān′), *n.* [Fr. < *terre* (< L. *terra*), earth + *plein*, level; OFr. *plain;* see PLAIN], a level platform behind a parapet, rampart, etc., where guns are mounted.

ter·res·tri·al (tə-res′tri-əl), *adj.* [ME. *terrestrialle* < L. *terrestris* < *terra*, earth], 1. of this world; worldly; earthly; mundane: opposed to *celestial*. 2. of, constituting, or representing the earth: as, a *terrestrial* globe. 3. consisting of land as distinguished from water. 4. living on land: distinguished from *aquatic, arboreal, aerial*. 5. growing on land or in the ground: distinguished from *aquatic, marine, parasitic, epiphytic*. *n.* an inhabitant of the earth. —*SYN.* see **earthly.**

ter·ret (ter′it), *n.* [ME. *teret, toret;* OFr. *toret*, dim. of *tour*, a turn], 1. a ring for attaching a leash, as on a dog collar. 2. any of the rings on a harness, through which the reins pass.

terre-verte (ter′vert′), *n.* [Fr. < *terre* (< L. *terra*), earth + *vert, verte*, green], any of several greenish earths used as a green pigment; especially, a kind of glauconite.

ter·ri·ble (ter′ə-b'l), *adj.* [ME.; (late) OFr.; L. *terribilis* < *terrere*, to frighten], 1. causing terror; fearful; frightful; dreadful. 2. extreme; intense; severe. 3. [Colloq.], very bad, unpleasant, or disagreeable.

ter·ri·bly (ter′ə-bli), *adv.* 1. in a terrible manner. 2. [Colloq.], extremely; exceedingly; very.

ter·ric·o·lous (te-rik′ə-ləs), *adj.* [< L. *terricola*, earth dweller < *terra*, earth + *colere*, to dwell; + *-ous*], in *botany & zoology*, living in or on the ground.

ter·ri·er (ter′i-ēr), *n.* [ME. *terrere, terryare;* (early) Fr. (*chien*) *terrier*, hunting (dog) < *terrier*, hillock, burrow < ML. *terrarius*, of earth < L. *terra*, earth], any of several breeds of active, intelligent, typically small dog, formerly used to burrow after small game: they include the Airedale, schnauzer, bull terrier, fox terrier, Bedlington terrier, Boston terrier, Clydesdale terrier, Dandie Dinmont terrier, Irish terrier, Scottish (or Scotch) terrier, Sealyham terrier, etc.

ter·ri·er (ter′i-ēr), *n.* [OFr.; ML. *terrarius* (*liber*), (book) concerning the land (or landed estates) < L. *terra*, earth], a book in which are recorded the landholdings of persons and corporations, with details on site, boundaries, acreage, etc.

ter·rif·ic (tə-rif′ik), *adj.* [L. *terrificus* < base of *terrere*, to frighten + *facere*, to make, do], 1. causing great fear; terrifying; dreadful; appalling. 2. [Colloq.], unusually great, intense, excellent, etc.; extraordinary.

ter·rif·i·cal·ly (tə-rif′i-k'l-i, tə-rif′ik-li), *adv.* 1. in a terrific manner. 2. to a terrific degree.

ter·rif·ic·ly (tə-rif′ik-li), *adv.* terrifically.

ter·ri·fy (ter′ə-fī′), *v.t.* [TERRIFIED (-fīd′), TERRIFYING], [L. *terrificare* < base of *terrere*, to frighten + *facere*, to make, do], to fill with terror; frighten greatly; alarm. —*SYN.* see **frighten.**

ter·rig·e·nous (te-rij′i-nəs), *adj.* [L. *terrigenus* < *terra*, earth + *gignere*, to be born], 1. earthborn. 2. designating or of sediments, etc. on the sea bottom that are derived from land that has washed away.

ter·rine (te-rēn′), *n.* [Fr.; see TUREEN], 1. a small earthenware jar in which table delicacies are sold. 2. a kind of stew.

ter·ri·to·ri·al (ter′ə-tôr′i-əl, ter′ə-tō′ri-əl), *adj.* [LL. *territorialis*], 1. of territory or land. 2. of, belonging to, or limited to a specific territory or district: as, a *territorial* industry, waters, etc. 3. [T-], of the territory of a state; of a Territory or Territories. 4. [often T-], organized primarily for home defense: as, the *Territorial* Army of Great Britain. *n.* a member of a territorial force; specifically, [T-], a member of the Territorial Army of Great Britain. Abbreviated **T., t.**

ter·ri·to·ri·al·ism (ter′ə-tôr′i-əl-iz′m, ter′ə-tō′ri-əl-iz′m), *n.* 1. a system giving the landowning class predominance in a state; landlordism. 2. a system of church government under which the supreme authority is placed in the civil power: also **territorial system.**

ter·ri·to·ri·al·i·ty (ter′ə-tôr′i-al′ə-ti, ter′ə-tō′ri-al′ə-ti), *n.* the state or quality of being territorial.

ter·ri·to·ri·al·i·za·tion (ter′ə-tôr′i-əl-i-zā′shən, ter′ə-tō′ri-əl-i-zā′shən), *n.* a territorializing or being territorialized.

ter·ri·to·ri·al·ize (ter′ə-tôr′i-ə-līz′, ter′ə-tō′ri-ə-līz′), *v.t.* [TERRITORIALIZED (-līzd′), TERRITORIALIZING], 1. to add territory to. 2. to reduce to the status of a territory. 3. to distribute among territories; establish on a territorial basis.

ter·ri·to·ri·al·ly (ter′ə-tôr′i-əl-i, ter′ə-tō′ri-əl-i), *adv.* as regards territory or territories.

territorial system, territorialism (sense 2).

ter·ri·to·ry (ter′ə-tôr′i, ter′ə-tō′ri), *n.* [*pl.* TERRITORIES (-iz, -riz)], [ME.; L. *territorium* < *terra*, earth], 1. the land and waters under the jurisdiction of a nation, state, ruler, etc. 2. a part of a country or empire that does not have the full status of a principal division; specifically, *a*) [T-], formerly, a part of the United States having its own legislature but without the status of a State and under the administration of an appointed governor: Hawaii was the last remaining territory of the United States. *b*) [T-], a similar region in Canada or Australia without the status of a Province or State. 3. any large tract of land; region; district. 4. an assigned area, as of a traveling salesman. 5. a sphere or province of action, existence, thought, etc. 6. in *football, hockey*, etc., either half of the field with regard to its possession by a team: as, deep in Notre Dame's *territory*. Abbreviated **T., t., ter., terr., Ty.**

ter·ror (ter′ēr), *n.* [ME. *terrour;* OFr. *terreur;* L. *terror* < *terrere*, to frighten], 1. intense fear. 2. *a*) a person or thing that causes intense fear. *b*) the quality of causing dread; terribleness. 3. [T-], a period characterized by political executions, as during revolution, especially such a period (also called the *Reign of Terror*) during the French Revolution, from 1793 to 1794. 4. a program of terrorism or a party, group, etc. resorting to terrorism. 5. [Colloq.], a very annoying or unmanageable person; nuisance; pest. —*SYN.* see **fear.**

ter·ror·ism (ter′ēr-iz′m), *n.* [Fr. *terrorisme*], 1. a terrorizing; use of terror and violence to intimidate, subjugate, etc., especially as a political weapon or policy. 2. intimidation and subjugation produced in this way.

ter·ror·ist (ter′ēr-ist), *n.* [Fr. *terroriste*], a person who practices or favors terrorism; specifically, *a*) an agent or supporter of the revolutionary tribunal during the French Reign of Terror. *b*) a member of any of certain extreme revolutionary societies in czarist Russia.

ter·ror·is·tic (ter′ə-ris′tik), *adj.* characterized by or practicing terrorism.

ter·ror·i·za·tion (ter′ēr-i-zā′shən, ter′ēr-ī-zā′shən), *n.* a terrorizing or being terrorized.

ter·ror·ize (ter′ə-rīz′), *v.t.* [TERRORIZED (-rīzd′), TERRORIZING], 1. to fill with terror; terrify. 2. to coerce, maintain power, etc. by inducing terror; practice terrorism. —*SYN.* see **frighten.**

ter·ror-strick·en (ter′ēr-strik″n), *adj.* stricken with terror; terrified.

ter·ry (ter′i), *n.* [*pl.* TERRIES (-iz)], [prob. < Fr. *tiré*, pp. of *tirer*, to draw], 1. any of the loops forming the pile of a fabric, when left uncut. 2. a cloth having a pile in which the loops are left uncut: also **terry cloth.**

Ter·ry, Ellen Alicia (ter′i), (*Mrs. James Carew*), 1847–1928; English actress.

terse (tũrs), *adj.* [L. *tersus*, wiped off, clean, pp. of *tergere*, to wipe], free of superfluous words; concise; succinct; to the point. —*SYN.* see **concise.**

ter·tial (tũr′shəl), *adj.* [< L. *tertius*, third; + *-al*], designating or of the third row of flight feathers on a bird's wing, along the humerus. *n.* a tertial feather.

ter·tian (tũr′shən), *adj.* [ME. *tercian;* L. (*febris*) *tertiana*, tertian (fever) < *tertius*, third], occurring every other day (i.e., every third day, counting both days of occurrence). *n.* a tertian fever, etc.

ter·ti·ar·y (tũr′shi-er′i, tũr′shə-ri), *adj.* [L. *tertiarius* < *tertius*, third], 1. of the third rank, order, formation, etc.; third. 2. of the third order in a monastic system. 3. in *chemistry*, *a*) third in order or type; involving the substitution of three atoms or radicals. *b*) characterized by or designating a carbon atom attached to three other carbon atoms in a chain or ring. 4. [T-], in *geology*, designating or of the first period of the Cenozoic Era or its system of rocks. 5. in *zoology*, tertial. *n.* [*pl.* TERTIARIES (-iz, -riz)], 1. a member of the third order of a monastic system. 2. a tertial feather.

the Tertiary, the Tertiary Period or its rocks: see **geology,** chart.

‡ter·ti·um quid (tũr′shi-əm kwid), [L., lit., third something], something related to but distinct from two other things; intermediate person or thing.

Ter·tul·li·an (tēr-tul′i-ən, tēr-tul′yən), *n.* (*Quintus Septimius Florens Tertullianus*), Latin church father; 160?–230? A.D.

ter·va·lent (tēr-vā′lənt), *adj.* [L. *ter*, thrice; + *-valent*], 1. having three valences. 2. having a valence of three. Also, esp. for 2, **trivalent.**

‡ter·za ri·ma (ter′tsä rē′mä; Eng. tũrt′sə rē′mə), [It., lit., third rhyme < L. *tertia*, third + Fr. *rime;* see RHYME], a verse form of Italian origin, consisting of a continuous series of tercets in which the second line of each tercet rhymes with the first and third lines of the following one (*aba, bcb, cdc*, etc.): it was used by Dante in the *Divine Comedy*.

Ter·zin (ter′zin), *n.* a fortress in Czechoslovakia, used as a Nazi concentration camp and extermination center.

Tes·la, Ni·ko·la (nik′ə-lə tes′lə), 1856–1943; American inventor born in Austria-Hungary.

Tess (tes), a feminine name: see **Theresa.**

tes·sel·late (tes′ə-lāt′), *v.t.* [TESSELLATED (-id), TES-

SELLATING], [< L. *tessellatus* < *tessella*, little square stone], to lay out, inlay, or pave in a mosaic pattern of small, square blocks. *adj.* (tes'ə-lit), tessellated.

tes·sel·la·tion (tes'ə-lā'shən), *n.* 1. a tessellating or being tessellated. 2. tessellated work; mosaic.

tes·ser·a (tes'ẽr-ə), *n.* [*pl.* TESSERAE (-ə-rē')], [L., square piece, cube; Gr. dial. *tessera*, four (for Gr. *tessara*)], 1. in ancient Rome, a small tablet of wood, ivory, etc. used as a token, ticket, or label. 2. a small, square piece of marble, glass, etc. used in mosaic work.

Tes·sin (te-sēn'), *n.* Ticino: the German name.

test (test), *n.* [ME., a cupel; OFr., a pot, cupel < L. *testum*, earthen vessel < *testa*, piece of burned clay, shell, skull; akin to Sans. *tashta*, a cup; ? < same IE. base as Gr. *technē* (see TECHNIC); the mod. meaning derives from use of the cupel in treating or examining metals], 1. a cupel, a cuplike porous vessel used in the assaying or refining of precious metals. 2. an examination or assaying of metal by means of the cupel; hence, 3. an examination or trial, as to prove the value or ascertain the nature of something. 4. *a*) a method, process, or means used in making such an examination or trial. *b*) a standard or criterion by which the qualities of a thing are tried. 5. an event, set of circumstances, etc. that proves or tries a person's qualities: as, the delay was a *test* of his patience. 6. a set of questions, problems, or exercises for determining a person's knowledge, abilities, aptitude, or qualifications; examination. 7. in *chemistry*, *a*) a trial or reaction for identifying a substance or ingredient. *b*) the reagent used in the procedure. *c*) a positive indication obtained by it. *v.t.* 1. to refine (metal), as in a cupel. 2. to subject to a test; try. 3. in *chemistry*, to examine by means of a reagent or reagents. —*SYN.* see **trial.**

test (test), *n.* [L. *testa;* see prec.], the hard outer covering, or shell, of certain invertebrate animals, as crabs, clams, etc.

Test., Testament.

tes·ta (tes'tə), *n.* [*pl.* TESTAE (-tē)], [L.; see TEST (cupel)], 1. in *botany*, the hard outer covering or integument of a seed. 2. in *zoology*, a test (shell).

tes·ta·cean (tes-tā'shən), *adj.* [< Mod. L. *Testacea*, name of the order < L. *testaceum*, shellfish < *testaceus;* see TESTACEOUS], of or belonging to an order of shell-covered rhizopods.

tes·ta·ceous (tes-tā'shəs), *adj.* [L. *testaceus*, consisting of brick, tile, or shell < *testa;* see TEST (cupel)], 1. of, or of the nature of, a shell or shells. 2. having a hard shell. 3. in *botany & zoology*, of the color of unglazed earthenware; reddish-brown or brownish-yellow.

tes·ta·cy (tes'tə-si), *n.* in *law*, the condition of being testate.

tes·ta·ment (tes'tə-mənt), *n.* [ME.; Fr.; L. *testamentum* < *testari*, to testify, make a will < *testis*, a witness], 1. in the *Bible*, a covenant; hence, 2. [T-], either of the two parts of the Bible, the *Old Testament* and the *New Testament:* so called because considered covenants between God and man. 3. [T-], [Colloq.], the New Testament. 4. in *law*, a will: now rare except in the phrase *last will and testament*. Abbreviated **T., Test.**

tes·ta·men·ta·ry (tes'tə-men'tə-ri), *adj.* [L. *testamentarius*], 1. of a testament, or will, or its administration. 2. bequeathed by will; contained in a will. 3. done in accordance with a will.

tes·tate (tes'tāt), *adj.* [L. *testatus*, pp. of *testari;* see TESTAMENT], having made and left a legally valid will. *n.* a person who has died testate.

tes·ta·tor (tes'tā-tẽr, tes-tā'tẽr), *n.* [L. < pp. of *testari;* see TESTAMENT], a person who has made a will or has died leaving a legally valid will.

tes·ta·trix (tes-tā'triks), *n.* [*pl.* TESTATRICES (-tri-sēz')], [LL.], a female testator.

test·er (tes'tẽr), *n.* a person or thing that tests.

tes·ter (tes'tẽr), *n.* [ME. *testere;* OFr. *testiere*, headpiece, crown of a hat < *teste*, the head; L. *testa;* see TEST (cupel)], a canopy, as over a bed.

tes·tes (tes'tēz), *n.* plural of **testis.**

tes·ti·cle (tes'ti-k'l), *n.* [L. *testiculus*, dim. of *testis*, testicle], the sex gland of the male; either of two oval structures that are suspended in the scrotum and secrete spermatozoa; testis.

tes·tic·u·late (tes-tik'yoo-lit), *adj.* [< L. *testiculus* (see TESTICLE); + *-ate*], in *botany*, 1. shaped like a testicle. 2. having two testicle-shaped tubers, as certain orchids.

tes·ti·fi·ca·tion (tes'tə-fi-kā'shən), *n.* [MFr. *testification;* L. *testificatio* < pp. of *testificari;* see TESTIFY], 1. a testifying. 2. testimony.

tes·ti·fi·er (tes'tə-fī'ẽr), *n.* a person who testifies.

tes·ti·fy (tes'tə-fī'), *v.i.* [TESTIFIED (-fīd'), TESTIFYING], [ME. *testifien;* OFr. *testifier;* L. *testificari* < *testis*, a witness + *facere*, to make], 1. to make a serious declaration to substantiate a fact; bear witness; give evidence, especially under oath in court. 2. to be evidence; serve as an indication: as, his words *testify* to his impatience. *v.t.* 1. to bear witness to; affirm; give as evidence, especially under oath in court. 2. to be evidence of; indicate; manifest. 3. to profess or proclaim publicly, as one's belief.

tes·ti·ly (tes't'l-i), *adv.* in a testy manner.

tes·ti·mo·ni·al (tes'tə-mō'ni-əl), *n.* [ME. & OFr.; LL. *testimonialis* < L. *testimonium;* see TESTIMONY], 1. a written statement testifying as to a person's qualifications, abilities, and character or to the value of some product, service, etc.; letter or statement of recommendation. 2. something given as an expression of gratitude for a person's services, of esteem for his achievements, or as a tribute to his memory.

tes·ti·mo·ny (tes'tə-mō'ni), *n.* [*pl.* TESTIMONIES (-niz)], [ME.; L. *testimonium* < *testis*, a witness], 1. a declaration or statement made to establish a fact, especially one made under oath by a witness in court. 2. any affirmation or declaration. 3. any form of evidence, indication, etc.; proof: as, his smile was *testimony* of his disbelief. 4. in the *Bible*, *a*) the tables of the law: Ex. 25:16. *b*) *pl.* the precepts of God. 5. public avowal, as of faith; profession. —*SYN.* see **proof.**

tes·ti·ness (tes'ti-nis), *n.* the quality or condition of being testy.

tes·tis (tes'tis), *n.* [*pl.* TESTES (-tēz)], [L.], a testicle.

tes·ton (tes't'n), *n.* [Fr.; It. *testone* < *testa*, the head; L. *testa;* see TEST (cupel)], formerly, any of several coins with the image of a head on one side; especially, *a*) a silver French coin of the 16th century. *b*) an English coin with the head of Henry VIII, originally worth a shilling, later, sixpence.

tes·toon (tes-to͞on'), *n.* a teston.

tes·tos·ter·one (tes-tos'tə-rōn'), *n.* [< *testes* + *sterol* + *-one*], a male sex hormone, $C_{19}H_{28}O_2$, produced as a white, crystalline substance by isolation from animal testes, or synthesized.

test paper, 1. a paper on which a test has been written. 2. paper prepared with a reagent for making chemical tests: see also **litmus paper.**

test pilot, a pilot who tests new or newly designed airplanes in flight, subjecting them to various strains to prove their fitness for use.

test tube, a tube of thin, transparent glass closed at one end, used in chemical experiments, etc.

tes·tu·di·nal (tes-to͞o'də-n'l, tes-tū'də-n'l), *adj.* [< L. *testudineus* < *testudo* (see TESTUDO); + *-al*], of or like a tortoise or its shell.

tes·tu·di·nar·i·ous (tes-to͞o'də-nâr'i-əs, tes-tū'də-nâr'i-əs), *adj.* [< L. *testudo, testudinis* (see TESTUDO); + *-arious*], testudinal.

tes·tu·di·nate (tes-to͞o'də-nāt', tes-tū'də-nit), *adj.* [LL. *testudinatus*], 1. arched or vaulted like a tortoise shell. 2. of a tortoise or tortoises. *n.* a tortoise.

tes·tu·do (tes-to͞o'dō, tes-tū'dō), *n.* [*pl.* TESTUDINES (-də-nēz')], [L., tortoise, tortoise shell, hence protective covering, shed], 1. any of a number of land tortoises. 2. *a*) a movable shelter or screen with a strong arched roof, used as a protection by ancient Roman soldiers. *b*) a protective covering formed by a body of ancient Roman soldiers by interweaving their shields above their heads.

tes·ty (tes'ti), *adj.* [TESTIER (-ti-ẽr), TESTIEST (-ti-ist)], [ME. *testif;* Anglo-Fr. *testif* < OFr. *teste*, the head; L. *testa;* see TEST (cupel)], irritable; touchy; peevish.

te·tan·ic (ti-tan'ik), *adj.* [L. *tetanicus;* Gr. *tetanikos* < *tetanos*, spasm], of, like, characterized by, or producing tetanus. *n.* any drug, as strychnine, which in overdoses can cause tetanic spasms of the muscles, often resulting in death.

tet·a·nize (tet'ə-nīz'), *v.t.* [TETANIZED (-nīzd'), TETANIZING], to produce tetanus in.

tet·a·nus (tet'ə-nəs), *n.* [L.; Gr. *tetanos*, spasm (of muscles), lit., stretched], 1. in *medicine*, an acute infectious disease, often fatal, caused by the toxins of a specific bacillus which usually enters the body through wounds: it is characterized by spasmodic contractions and rigidity of some or all of the voluntary muscles: cf. **lockjaw.** 2. in *physiology*, the state of continuous contraction of a muscle undergoing a series of rapidly repeated stimuli.

tet·a·ny (tet'ə-ni), *n.* [< Mod. L. *tetania;* see TETANUS], an abnormal condition characterized by tetanic spasms of the arm and leg muscles, resulting usually from the faulty metabolism of calcium salts.

te·tar·to- (ti-tär'tō, ti-tär'tə), [< Gr. *tetartos*, fourth], a combining form meaning *(a)fourth*, as in *tetartohedral*.

te·tar·to·he·dral (ti-tär'tə-hē'drəl), *adj.* [*tetarto-* + *-hedral*], having one fourth of the planes needed for crystallographic symmetry.

tetched (techt), *adj.* [Dial. or Humorous], touched; slightly demented.

tetch·y (tech'i), *adj.* [TETCHIER (-i-ẽr), TETCHIEST (-i-ist)], [see TECHY], touchy; irritable; peevish: also spelled **techy.**

tête-à-tête (tāt'ə-tāt'; Fr. te'tà'tet'), *n.* [Fr., lit., head-to-head], 1. a private or intimate conversation between two people. 2. an S-shaped seat on which two people can sit facing each other. *adj.* for or of two people in private; face to face. *adv.* together privately: said of two people: as, they spoke *tête-à-tête.*

tête-bêche (tet'besh'), *adj.* [Fr., *tête*, head + *bêche* < *bechevet*, double bed head], printed so that one is inverted in relation to the other: said of a pair of postage stamps.

‡tête-de-pont (tet'də-pōn'), *n.* [*pl.* TETES-DE-PONT (tet'-)], [Fr.], a bridgehead.

teth (teth, tes), *n.* [Heb. *ṭeth*], the ninth letter of the Hebrew alphabet (ט), corresponding to English *T, t*: see **alphabet**, table.

teth·er (teth'ẽr), *n.* [ME.; ON. *tiōthr;* akin to MD. *tudder;* IE. base **deu-*, to draw, pull, seen also in L. *ducere*, to draw, lead, *dux*, leader (cf. DUKE, DUCE)], 1. a rope or chain fastened to an animal so as to keep it within certain bounds. 2. the range of one's abilities, resources, etc. *v.t.* to fasten or confine with a tether. **at the end of one's tether**, at the end of one's endurance, resources, etc.

Te·thys (tē'this), *n.* [L.; Gr. *Tēthys*], in *Greek mythology*, a Titaness, daughter of Uranus and wife of Oceanus.

tet·ra- (tet'rə), [Gr. *tetra-* < base of *tettares, tessares*, four; for IE. base see FOUR], a combining form meaning *four*, as in *tetrachord:* also, before a vowel, **tetr-**.

tet·ra·bas·ic (tet'rə-bā'sik), *adj.* [*tetra-* + *basic*], designating or of an acid having four replaceable hydrogen atoms per molecule.

tet·ra·brach (tet'rə-brak), *n.* [Gr. *tetrabrachys*, consisting of four short syllables], in *Greek & Latin prosody*, a word or foot containing four short syllables.

tet·ra·bran·chi·ate (tet'rə-braŋ'ki-āt'), *adj.* [< *tetra-* + Gr. *branchia*, gills; + *-ate*], of or belonging to an order of cephalopods with four gills, including the nautilus and many extinct forms.

tet·ra·chlo·ride (tet'rə-klôr'īd, tet'rə-klō'rid), *n.* any chemical compound with four chlorine atoms to the molecule.

tet·ra·chord (tet'rə-kôrd'), *n.* [Gr. *tetrachordon*, musical instrument < *tetrachordos*, four-stringed; see TETRA- & CHORD], in *music*, a series of four consecutive full tones comprising a total interval of a fourth; half an octave.

tet·ra·chor·dal (tet'rə-kôr'd'l), *adj.* of a tetrachord.

te·trac·id (te-tras'id), *n.* [*tetr-* + *acid*], 1. a base that can react with four molecules of a monobasic acid to form a salt. 2. an alcohol having four OH groups per molecule.

tet·rad (tet'rad), *n.* [Gr. *tetras, tetrados*, four], 1. the number four. 2. a group or set of four. 3. a group of four chromosomes formed by the division of a pair during meiosis. 4. an atom, radical, or element having a valence of four.

te·trad·y·mite (te-trad'ə-mīt'), *n.* [G. *tetradymit* < Gr. *tetradymos*, fourfold: so named because it occurs in compound twin crystals], a native bismuth telluride, Bi_2Te_3, a pale, steel-gray mineral in foliated form.

tet·ra·eth·yl lead (tet'rə-eth'əl), a heavy, colorless, poisonous compound of lead, $Pb(C_2H_5)_4$, added to gasoline to increase power and prevent engine knock.

tet·ra·gon (tet'rə-gon'), *n.* [LL. *tetragonum;* Gr. *tetragōnon* < *tetra-*, four + *gōnia*, a corner, angle], a plane figure with four angles and four sides; quadrangle.

te·trag·o·nal (tet-rag'ə-n'l), *adj.* 1. of, or having the form of, a tetragon; quadrangular. 2. designating or of a system of crystallization in which the three axes are at right angles and the two lateral axes are equal.

tet·ra·gram (tet'rə-gram'), *n.* [Gr. *tetragrammon;* see TETRA- & -GRAM], 1. a word of four letters. 2. [also T-], the Tetragrammaton.

Tet·ra·gram·ma·ton (tet'rə-gram'ə-ton'), *n.* [Mod. L.; Gr. *tetragrammaton* < *tetra-*, four + *gramma*, a letter], the four consonants of the ancient Hebrew name for God (variously written JHVH, IHVH, JHWH, YHVH, YHWH), considered too sacred to pronounce: the word *Adonai* (Lord) is substituted for this name in utterance, and the vowels of *Adonai* or *Elohim* (God) are inserted in Hebrew texts, so that the modern reconstructions are *Yahweh, Jehovah*, etc.

tet·ra·he·dral (tet'rə-hē'drəl), *adj.* of, or having the form of, a tetrahedron.

tet·ra·he·drite (tet'rə-hē'drīt), *n.* [G. *tetraëdrit;* see TETRAHEDRON & -ITE], a gray to blackish mineral occurring in tetrahedral crystals, essentially a sulfide of copper and antimony, $3Cu_2S \cdot Sb_2S_3$: in many forms the copper is partly replaced by iron, lead, silver, etc.

tet·ra·he·dron (tet'rə-hē'drən), *n.* [*pl.* TETRAHEDRONS (-drənz), TETRAHEDRA (-drə)], [Mod. L. < LGr. *tetraedros*, four-sided; see TETRA- & -HEDRON], a solid figure with four triangular surfaces.

TETRAHEDRON

te·tral·o·gy (te-tral'ə-ji), *n.* [*pl.* TETRALOGIES (-jiz)], [Gr. *tetralogia;* see TETRA- & -LOGY], 1. a series of four dramas, three tragic and one satiric, performed together at ancient Athens at the festival of Dionysus; hence, 2. any series of four related dramatic, operatic, or literary compositions.

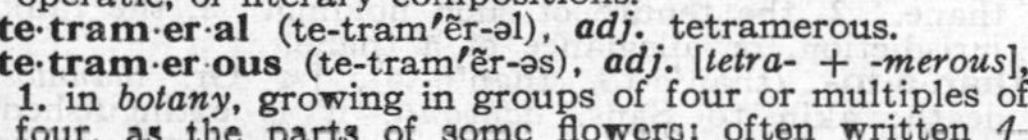

te·tram·er·al (te-tram'ẽr-əl), *adj.* tetramerous.

te·tram·er·ous (te-tram'ẽr-əs), *adj.* [*tetra-* + *-merous*], 1. in *botany*, growing in groups of four or multiples of four, as the parts of some flowers: often written *4-merous*. 2. in *zoology*, having or seeming to have four joints in the tarsi.

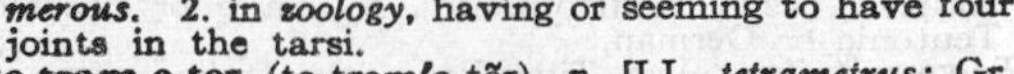

te·tram·e·ter (te-tram'ə-tẽr), *n.* [LL. *tetrametrus;* Gr. *tetrametros;* see TETRA- & METER (rhythm)], 1. a line of verse containing four metrical feet or measures. Example: "Térĕnce, | thís ĭs | stúpĭd | stúff." 2. verse consisting of tetrameters. *adj.* having four metrical feet or measures.

tet·ra·pet·al·ous (tet'rə-pet''l-əs), *adj.* four-petaled.

te·trap·ter·ous (te-trap'tẽr-əs), *adj.* [Gr. *tetrapteros;* see TETRA- & -PTEROUS], 1. in *biology*, having four wings. 2. in *botany*, having four winglike parts, as certain fruits.

te·trarch (tet'rärk, tē'trärk), *n.* [ME. *tetrarche;* LL. *tetrarcha;* L. *tetrarches;* Gr. *tetrarchēs* < *tetra-*, four + *archos*, ruler], 1. in the ancient Roman Empire, the ruler of part (originally a fourth part) of a province. 2. a subordinate prince, governor, etc.

te·trarch·ate (tet'rär-kāt', tē'trär-kit), *n.* 1. a quarter of a province of the ancient Roman Empire. 2. the territory ruled by a tetrarch.

te·trarch·y (tet'rär-ki, tē'trär-ki), *n.* [*pl.* TETRARCHIES (-kiz)], 1. the rule or territory of a tetrarch. 2. government by four persons. 3. a group of four rulers. 4. a country divided into four subordinate governments.

tet·ra·spore (tet'rə-spôr', tet'rə-spōr'), *n.* any of the asexual algae spores produced in groups of four.

tet·ra·stich (tet'rə-stik'), *n.* [L. *tetrastichon;* Gr. *tetrastichon* < *tetra-*, four + *stichos*, a row, verse], a poem or stanza of four lines.

tet·ra·stich·ic (tet'rə-stik'ik), *adj.* 1. of a tetrastich. 2. in tetrastichs. 3. having four lines.

te·tras·ti·chous (te-tras'ti-kəs), *adj.* [Gr. *tetrastichos*, in four rows; see TETRASTICH], in *botany*, in four vertical rows, as the flowers on some spikes.

tet·ra·syl·lab·ic (tet'rə-si-lab'ik), *adj.* having four syllables.

tet·ra·syl·la·ble (tet'rə-sil'ə-b'l), *n.* a word of four syllables.

tet·ra·tom·ic (tet'rə-tom'ik), *adj.* 1. designating or of a molecule consisting of four atoms. 2. having four replaceable atoms or groups. 3. [Rare], tetravalent.

tet·ra·va·lent (tet'rə-vā'lənt, te-trav'ə-lənt), *adj.* 1. having a valence of four. 2. having four valences. Also, esp. for 2, **quadrivalent**.

Te·traz·zi·ni, Lu·i·sa (lōō-ē'zä te'trä-tsē'ni; Eng. tet'rə-zē'ni), 1874–1940; Italian operatic soprano.

tet·rode (tet'rōd), *n.* [*tetr-* + *-ode*], an electron tube containing four elements (usually, a cathode, a plate, and two grids).

te·trox·id (te-trok'sid), *n.* tetroxide.

te·trox·ide (te-trok'sīd, te-trok'sid), *n.* any oxide with four atoms of oxygen in each molecule.

tet·ryl (tet'ril), *n.* [*tetra*nitromethy*l*aniline], a yellow powder, $C_7H_5N_5O_8$, used as an explosive, especially in detonators.

tet·ter (tet'ẽr), *n.* [ME.; AS. *teter;* cf. Sans. *dadru*, skin disease], any of various skin diseases, as eczema, characterized by itching.

Te·tuán (te-twän'), *n.* a seaport in Spanish Morocco, on the Mediterranean: its capital: pop., 73,000.

Tet·zel, Jo·hann (yō'hän tet'səl), 1465?–1519; German Dominican monk castigated by Luther for his misuse of absolution and indulgences.

Teu·cri·an (tōō'kri-ən, tū'kri-ən), *adj. & n.* [< *Teucer* (Gr. *Teukros*), first king of Troy], Trojan.

Teut., 1. Teuton. 2. Teutonic.

Teu·to·bur·ger Wald (toi'tô-boor'gẽr vält), a mountain range in eastern Westphalia, Germany: scene of a disastrous Roman defeat by the Germans (9 A.D.).

Teu·ton (tōō't'n, tū't'n), *n.* [< L. *Teutones*], 1. a member of the Teutones. 2. a member of any Teutonic people; especially, a German.

Teu·to·nes (tōō'tə-nēz', tū'tə-nēz'), *n.pl.* [L.; prob. < Gmc. base seen also in G. *deutsch;* see DEUTSCHLAND], an ancient tribe, variously considered as Teutonic or Celtic, that lived north of the Elbe in Jutland.

Teu·ton·ic (tōō-ton'ik, tū-ton'ik), *adj.* 1. of the ancient Teutons. 2. German. 3. designating or of a group of north European peoples including the German, Scandinavian, Dutch, English, etc. 4. in *ethnology*, Nordic: term now seldom used. 5. in *linguistics*, Germanic: term now seldom used.

Teu·ton·i·cism (tōō-ton'ə-siz'm, tū-ton'ə-siz'm), *n.* 1. a Teutonic or German idiom, expression, or manner of speech. 2. Teutonic or German spirit, custom, etc.

Teutonic Order, a military and religious order of German knights (*Teutonic Knights*) originally organized in 1191 for service in the Holy Land and later active in the military conquests by medieval Germany of Baltic and Slavic lands.

Teu·ton·ism (tōō't'n-iz'm, tū't'n-iz'm), *n.* 1. belief in the supposed racial superiority of the Teutons, especially of the Germans. 2. Teutonic culture.

Teu·ton·ize (tōō't'n-īz', tū't'n-īz'), *v.t. & v.i.* [TEU-

TONIZED (-īzd′), TEUTONIZING], to make or become Teutonic or German.

Te·ve·re (te′ve-re), ***n.*** Tiber River: the Italian name.

Tewkes·bur·y (to͞oks′ber′i, tūks′bə-ri), ***n.*** a town in Gloucestershire, England: site of defeat of the Lancastrians (1471), ending the Wars of the Roses.

Tex., 1. Texan. 2. Texas.

Tex·an (tek′s′n), ***adj.*** of Texas. ***n.*** a native or inhabitant of Texas.

Tex·ar·kan·a (tek′sär-kan′ə), ***n.*** a city in Texas and Arkansas: the part in each State is administered separately: pop., 50,000.

Tex·as (tek′səs), ***n.*** [Sp. < Am. Ind. (Caddo) *techas,* allies (against the Apaches)], 1. [*pl.* TEXAS], a member of a Caddoan tribe of American Indians. 2. a Southern State of the United States, on the Gulf of Mexico and the Mexican border: area, 267,339 sq. mi.; pop., 9,580,000; capital, Austin: abbreviated **Tex.**: nicknamed *Lone Star State.* 3. [t-], [name given to the officers' quarters on Mississippi steamboats because they were the largest of the staterooms, which were named after States], a structure on the hurricane deck of a steamboat, containing the officers' quarters, etc. and having the pilothouse on top or in front.

Texas City, a seaport in southeastern Texas, near Galveston: pop., 32,000.

Texas fever, an infectious disease of cattle, carried by ticks.

Texas leaguer, [< the *Texas* (baseball) *League*], [Slang], in *baseball,* a fly ball that falls between the infield and outfield and is a safe hit.

Texas Ranger, a member of the mounted State police of Texas.

Texas sparrow, an olive-green finch of southeastern Texas and eastern Mexico.

text (tekst), ***n.*** [ME. & OFr. *texte;* L. *textus,* fabric, structure, text; pp. of *texere,* to weave], 1. the actual structure of words in a piece of writing or printing; wording; hence, 2. the actual or original words of an author, as distinguished from notes, commentary, paraphrase, translation, etc. 3. *a)* the wording set forth by an editor as most nearly representing the author's original work, or an edition containing this: as, the Caxton *text* of Chaucer. *b)* any form in which a writing exists: as, a corrupt *text.* 4. the principal matter on a printed or written page, as distinguished from notes, headings, etc. 5. letterpress, as distinguished from illustrations, etc. 6. a Biblical passage quoted as authority for a belief or as the topic of a sermon; hence, 7. a topic; subject. 8. large handwriting; text hand. 9. any of several bold-faced styles of type. 10. a textbook. 11. any of various versions or recensions of all or part of the Scriptures, taken to represent the authentic reading. —***SYN.*** see **subject.**

text·book (tekst′book′), ***n.*** a book giving instructions in the principles of a subject of study; any book used as the basis or partial basis of a course of study.

text hand, large handwriting: so called from its former use to distinguish the text of manuscripts from notes.

tex·tile (teks′t'l, teks′til, teks′tīl), ***adj.*** [L. *textilis* < *textus;* see TEXT], 1. having to do with weaving or woven fabrics. 2. woven. 3. that can be woven: as, *textile* material. ***n.*** 1. a woven fabric; cloth. 2. raw material suitable for weaving, as cotton, flax, wool, etc.

tex·tu·al (teks′cho͞o-əl), ***adj.*** [ME.; OFr. *textuel* < L. *textus;* see TEXT], 1. of or contained in a text. 2. based on or conforming to a text; hence, 3. literal; word for word.

tex·tu·al·ism (teks′cho͞o-əl-iz'm), ***n.*** 1. strict adherence to the text, especially of the Scriptures. 2. the art of textual criticism.

tex·tu·al·ist (teks′cho͞o-əl-ist), ***n.*** a person who is versed in, or adheres strictly to, the text, especially of the Scriptures.

tex·tu·al·ly (teks′cho͞o-əl-i), ***adv.*** as regards the text.

tex·tu·ar·y (teks′cho͞o-er′i), ***adj.*** textual. ***n.*** [*pl.* TEXTUARIES (-iz)], a textualist.

tex·tur·al (teks′chẽr-əl), ***adj.*** having to do with texture.

tex·ture (teks′chẽr), ***n.*** [L. *textura* < *texere,* to weave], 1. originally, a woven fabric; textile. 2. the character of a woven fabric resulting from the arrangement, size, quality, etc. of the fabric's threads: as, a fine or coarse *texture,* a ribbed or twilled *texture.* 3. the arrangement of the particles or constituent parts of any material, as wood, metal, etc.; structure; composition. 4. the structural quality of a work of art, resulting from the artist's method of using his medium. 5. basic structure: as, the *texture* of society.

Tey·de, Mount (tā′*th*e), a volcanic mountain of Tenerife in the Canary Islands: height, 12,192 ft.: also spelled **Teide**: also called *Peak of Tenerife.*

-th, [ME. *-th, -the;* AS. *-thu, -tho, -th;* akin to Goth. *-itha* (IE. **-itā,* etc.); in words such as *height, sleight,* the *-th* has become *-t*], a suffix, used in forming nouns from verbs and adjectives, meaning: 1. *the action of —ing,* as in *stealth.* 2. *the state or quality of being or having,* as in *wealth.*

-th, [ME. *-the;* AS. *-tha, -the, -otha, -othe;* akin to Gr. *-tos,* L. *-tus;* in *fifth, sixth, eleventh, twelfth,* it replaced the orig. AS. *-ta, -te*], a suffix used in forming ordinal numerals, as *fourth, ninth:* also, after a vowel, **-eth.**

-th, [ME. & AS. *-th;* see -ETH], contracted form of *-eth,* archaic ending of the third person singular, present indicative, of verbs, as in *hath, doth.*

Th, in *chemistry,* thorium.

Th., Thursday.

T.H., (former) Territory of Hawaii.

Thack·er·ay, William Make·peace (māk′pēs′ thak′ẽr-i), 1811–1863; English novelist.

Thad·de·us, Thad·e·us (thad′i-əs), [LL. *Thaddaeus;* Gr. *Thaddaios*], a masculine name: diminutive, *Tad.*

Tha·i (tä′ē, tī), ***n.*** 1. a branch of the Sino-Tibetan languages, including Siamese and Shan. 2. a member of a group of Thai-speaking peoples in Indochina. 3. a native of Thailand. ***adj.*** 1. of these people or their language. 2. of Thailand. Also spelled **Tai.**

Thai·land (tī′lənd), ***n.*** a country in southeastern Asia, on the Gulf of Siam and Bay of Bengal: area, 200,234 sq. mi.; pop., 25,520,000; capital, Bangkok: former name, *Siam*: abbreviated **Thai.**

Tha·is (thā′is), ***n.*** 1. Greek courtesan who accompanied Alexander the Great on his Asiatic campaign; 4th century B.C. 2. (tä-ēs′), the heroine of a French opera (1894) by Jules Massenet, after a novel (1890) by Anatole France: she is an Alexandrian courtesan converted by a monk who, however, in the end succumbs to her charms: also spelled **Thaïs.**

thal·a·men·ceph·a·lon (thal′ə-men-sef′ə-lon′), ***n.*** [Mod. L.; see THALAMUS & ENCEPHALON], the posterior part of the embryonic forebrain, from which the thalamus develops: also called *diencephalon.*

tha·lam·ic (thə-lam′ik), ***adj.*** of the thalamus, especially the optic thalamus.

thal·a·mus (thal′ə-məs), ***n.*** [*pl.* THALAMI (-mī′)], [L.; Gr. *thalamos,* inner chamber], 1. in *anatomy,* a large, ovoid mass of gray matter situated at the base of the brain and involved in the transmission and integration of certain sensations: also **optic thalamus.** 2. in *botany,* the receptacle of a flower; torus.

tha·las·sic (thə-las′ik), ***adj.*** [Fr. *thalassique* < Gr. *thalassa,* sea], 1. of the sea or ocean; marine. 2. of bays, gulfs, etc. and smaller or inland seas: distinguished from *oceanic.*

tha·ler (tä′lẽr), ***n.*** [*pl.* THALER], a taler.

Tha·les (thā′lēz), ***n.*** Greek philosopher; 640?–546 B.C.

Tha·li·a (thā′li-ə, thāl′yə), [L.; Gr. *Thaleia* < *thallein,* to flourish, bloom], a feminine name. ***n.*** (thə-lī′ə), in *Greek mythology,* 1. the Muse of comedy and pastoral poetry. 2. one of the three Graces.

thal·lic (thal′ik), ***adj.*** designating or of a chemical compound containing thallium with a valence of three.

thal·li·ous (thal′i-əs), ***adj.*** thallous.

thal·li·um (thal′i-əm), ***n.*** [Mod. L. < Gr. *thallos,* young, green shoot: from the green line that it gives in the spectrum, which led to its discovery], a rare, bluish-white, soft, metallic chemical element, the lightest of the elements having naturally radioactive isotopes: used in making antiknock compound, rat poisons, etc.: symbol, Tl; at. wt., 204.39; at. no. 81.

thal·loid (thal′oid), ***adj.*** of or like a thallus.

thal·lo·phyte (thal′ə-fīt′), ***n.*** [< Gr. *thallos* (see THALLUS); + *-phyte*], any of a primary division of plants showing no clear distinction of roots, stem, or leaves, including the bacteria, algae, fungi, and lichens.

thal·lous (thal′əs), ***adj.*** designating or of a chemical compound containing thallium with a valence of one.

thal·lus (thal′əs), ***n.*** [*pl.* THALLI (-ī), THALLUSES (-iz)], [Mod. L.; Gr. *thallos,* young shoot, sprout, frond], the plant body of a thallophyte, showing no clear distinction of roots, stem, or leaves.

Thames (temz; *for 2, usually* thāmz, *also* tāmz), ***n.*** 1. a river in southern England, flowing eastward through London to the North Sea: length, 210 mi. 2. an estuary in southeastern Connecticut, flowing into Long Island Sound: length, 15 mi. 3. a river in southeastern Ontario, Canada, flowing into Lake St. Clair: length, 135 mi.

Tham·muz (tä′mooz), ***n.*** Tammuz.

than (*th*an, *th*en; *unstressed th*ən, *th*'n), ***conj.*** [ME. *than, thene, thonne;* AS. *thenne, thanne, thonne,* orig., then; IE. base as in *that, the, then, there*], a particle used *a)* to introduce the second element in a comparison, following an adjective or adverb in the comparative degree: as, I am taller *than* Bruce, we arrived earlier *than* they did. *b)* to express exception, following an adjective or adverb: as, it was none other *than* Sam. ***prep.*** compared to: used only in the phrases *than whom, than which*: as, a writer *than whom* there is none finer.

than·age (thān′ij), ***n.*** [ME.; Anglo-Fr. *thaynage, thanage;* see THANE & -AGE], 1. the land held by a thane. 2. the tenure of such holding. 3. the rank, jurisdiction, or allegiance of a thane.

than·a·to- (than′ə-tō, than′ə-tə), [< Gr. *thanatos,* death; akin to Sans. *adhvanīt,* it is extinguished, vanishes], a combining form meaning *death,* as in *thanatophobia:* also, before a vowel, **thanat-.**

than·a·to·pho·bi·a (than′ə-tə-fō′bi-ə), ***n.*** [*thanato-* + *-phobia*], an abnormally great fear of death.

than·a·top·sis (than′ə-top′sis), ***n.*** [Mod. L.; *thanat-* + *-opsis*], a view of or musing upon death.

Than·a·tos (than′ə-tos), ***n.*** [Gr.], in *Greek mythology*, death personified.

thane (thān), ***n.*** [ME. *thein, theign;* AS. *thegen, thegn;* akin to ON. *thegn;* IE. base **teq-*, to engender, beget, seen also in Sans. *takman-*, child; basic sense "freeborn man"], 1. among the Anglo-Saxons and Scandinavians in early England, a member of a class of freemen who held land of the king or a lord in return for military services, and who corresponded to the later knights and barons. 2. in early Scotland, a person of rank who held land of the king; any chief of a clan who became a baron under the king. Also spelled **thegn.**

thank (thaŋk), ***v.t.*** [ME. *thankien;* AS. *thancian;* akin to G. *danken;* IE. base **tong-*, to think, seen also in L. *tongere*, to know, Eng. *think*], 1. to give one's thanks to; express appreciation or gratitude to. 2. to hold responsible; blame: an ironic use, as, he can be *thanked* for our failure.
 have oneself to thank, to be oneself the cause or agent of (something unpleasant).

thank·ful (thaŋk′fəl), ***adj.*** feeling or expressing thanks.

thank·less (thaŋk′lis), ***adj.*** 1. not feeling or expressing thanks; ungrateful. 2. that receives or deserves no thanks; unappreciated.

thanks (thaŋks), ***n.pl.*** [pl. of ME. *thank, thanc;* AS. *thanc, thonc*, thanks; for IE. base see THANK, *v.*], an expression of gratitude; grateful acknowledgment of something received by or done for one. ***interj.*** I thank you.
 thanks to, 1. thanks be given to. 2. on account of.

thanks·giv·ing (thaŋks′giv′iŋ, thaŋks′giv′iŋ), ***n.*** 1. a giving of thanks. 2. an expression of this. 3. a formal, often public, expression of thanks to God in the form of a prayer, etc. 4. [T-], an annual United States holiday, usually the fourth Thursday of November, instituted by the Pilgrims to give thanks to God for their survival: in full, **Thanksgiving Day.**

thank·wor·thy (thaŋk′wũr′*th*i), ***adj.*** worthy of thanks.

Thant, U (ōō thônt), 1909– ; Burmese statesman; secretary-general of the United Nations (1961–).

Thap·sus (thap′səs), ***n.*** an ancient town in northern Africa, on the eastern coast of present Tunisia: site of a battle (46 B.C.), in which Caesar defeated Pompey.

Thar Desert (tũr, tär), Indian Desert.

Tha·sos (thä′sôs), ***n.*** a Greek island in the northern Aegean: area, 150 sq. mi.; pop., 13,800.

that (*th*at; *unstressed th*ət), ***pron.*** [*pl.* THOSE (*th*ōz)], [ME. *that, thet;* AS. *thæt*, nom. & acc. neut. of the def. article (nom. masc. *se*, nom. fem. *seo;* cf. THE); akin to G. neut. nom. & acc. *dass;* IE. demonstrative base **-to-, *-tā-*, seen also in L. *istum, istam, istud*, that, Eng. *there, thither*, etc.], I. as a demonstrative pronoun: 1. the person or thing mentioned or understood: as, *that* is John, *that* tastes good. 2. the thing farther away: distinguished from *this*, as, I can see this more clearly than *that*. 3. one of two things which are compared or contrasted, as contradistinguished from *this:* as, of the two possibilities, this is more likely than *that*. II. as a relative pronoun: 1. who, whom, or which: used generally in restrictive clauses (e.g., the road *that* we took) and often omitted (e.g., the road we took). 2. where; at which; on which: as, the place *that* I saw him. 3. when; in which; on which: as, the year *that* he was born. ***adj.*** 1. designating the person or thing mentioned or understood: as, *that* man is John, *that* pie tastes good. 2. designating the thing farther away: distinguished from *this*, as, I can see this house more clearly than *that* one across the street. 3. designating one of two things that are compared or contrasted, as contradistinguished from *this:* as, of the two, this possibility is more likely than *that* one. 4. designating something or someone that is not described but that is well known or easily recognizable: sometimes with implications of disparagement, as, *that* certain feeling, there comes *that* smile!, *that* George! ***conj.*** as a conjunction, *that* is used 1. to introduce a noun clause: as, *that* he's gone is obvious, the truth was *that* we never saw him. 2. to introduce a clause expressing purpose: as, they died *that* we might live. 3. to introduce a clause expressing result: as, he ran so fast *that* I couldn't catch up. 4. to introduce a clause expressing cause: as, I'm sorry *that* I caused you such annoyance. 5. to introduce an elliptical sentence expressing surprise, indignation, or desire: as, *that* he should say such a thing!, oh, *that* this day were over! ***adv.*** to that extent; so: as, I can't see *that* far ahead: also used colloquially before an adjective modified by a clause of result, as, I'm *that* tired I could drop.
 at that, [Colloq.], 1. at that point; with no further discussion, etc. 2. all things considered; even so.
 in that, because.
 that's that! that is done (or settled or decided, etc.)!

thatch (thach), ***n.*** [altered (after the *v.*) < older *thack;* ME. *thac;* AS. *thæc*, a thatch, roof], 1. a roof or roofing of straw, rushes, palm leaves, etc. 2. material for such a roof. 3. any of a number of palms whose leaves are used for thatch: also **thatch palm.** 4. the hair growing on the head. ***v.t.*** [ME. *thecchen;* AS. *thecc(e)an;* akin to G. *decken*, to cover; IE. base **(s)teg-*, to cover, seen also in *integument, tile, protect*, etc.], to cover with or as with thatch.

thatch·ing (thach′iŋ), ***n.*** 1. the act of a person who thatches. 2. thatch (sense 2).

thatch·y (thach′i), ***adj.*** [THATCHIER (-i-ẽr), THATCHIEST (-i-ist)], of or like thatch.

thau·ma·tol·o·gy (thô′mə-tol′ə-ji), ***n.*** [< Gr. *thauma, thaumatos*, a miracle, wonder; + *-logy*], the study or lore of miracles.

thau·ma·trope (thô′mə-trōp′), ***n.*** [Gr. *thauma*, a wonder; + *-trope*], a device consisting of a card with different designs on either side, which, when the card is twirled, appear to blend into one: it demonstrates the persistence of vision.

thau·ma·turge (thô′mə-tũrj′), ***n.*** [Fr.; ML. *thaumaturgus* < Gr. *thaumaturgos*, working wonders < *thauma*, a wonder + *-ergos*, working], a person who supposedly works miracles.

thau·ma·tur·gic (thô′mə-tũr′jik), ***adj.*** of or involving thaumaturgy.

thau·ma·tur·gi·cal (thô′mə-tũr′ji-k′l), ***adj.*** thaumaturgic.

thau·ma·tur·gy (thô′mə-tũr′ji), ***n.*** [Gr. *thaumatourgia* < *thauma*, a wonder + *ergon*, work], the supposed working of miracles; magic.

thaw (thô), ***v.i.*** [ME. *thawen;* AS. *thawian;* akin to D. *dooien*, G. *(ver)dauen*, to digest; IE. base **tā-, *tu-*, etc., to melt, dissolve, vanish, seen also in L. *tabere, tabescere*, to melt, vanish], 1. to melt; become liquid or semiliquid, as ice, snow, etc. 2. to have its contents melt: as, our water pipe hasn't *thawed*. 3. to rise above freezing, so that snow, etc. melts: with the impersonal *it*, in reference to the weather, as, it will *thaw* tomorrow. 4. to lose one's coldness or reserve of manner. ***v.t.*** to cause to thaw. ***n.*** 1. a thawing. 2. a spell of weather warm enough to allow thawing. 3. a becoming less reserved in manner. —***SYN.*** see **melt.**

Th.B., *Theologiae Baccalaureus*, [L.], Bachelor of Theology.

Th.D., *Theologiae Doctor*, [L.], Doctor of Theology.

the (*th*ə; *before vowels*, *th*i), ***adj., definite article*** [ME. indeclinable article < AS. *se* (nom. masc. article) with *th-* < other AS. case & gender forms (*thone, thæs, thære, thæm, thy*); for base & cognates, cf. THAT; the meaning is controlled by the basic notion "a previously recognized, noticed, or encountered" in distinction to A, AN], I. *the* (as opposed to *a, an*) is used to refer to a particular person, thing, or group, as: 1. that (one) being spoken of or already mentioned: as, *the* story ended. 2. that (one) which is present, close, nearby, etc., as distinguished from all others, which are considered remote: as, *the* day just started, *the* heat is oppressive. 3. that (one) designated or identified, as by a title: as, *the* President (of the United States), *the* Mississippi (River). 4. that (one) considered outstanding, most fashionable, etc.: as, that's *the* restaurant in town: usually given special emphasis when spoken and italicized when printed. 5. that (one) belonging to a person previously mentioned: as, take me by *the* hand, rub into *the* face: equivalent to *your, his, her, my, our, one's*, etc. 6. that (one) considered as a unit of purchase, etc.: as, at five dollars *the* half ton: equivalent to *a, per, each*, etc. 7. [Colloq.], that (one) who has a specific family relationship to one: as, *the* wife, *the* kid sister. II. *the* is used to refer to that one of a number of persons or things which is identified by a modifier, as by: 1. an attributive adjective: as, *the* front door. 2. a relative clause: as, "ask *the* man who owns one." 3. a prepositional phrase: as, *the* hit of the week. 4. an infinitive phrase: as, *the* right to strike. 5. a participle: as, follow *the* directions given. III. *the* is used to refer to a person or thing considered generically or universally, as: 1. one taken as the representative of the entire genus or type: as, he learned to use *the* typewriter, *the* cow is a domestic animal. 2. an adjective used substantively: as, *the* good, *the* beautiful, *the* true. ***adv.*** 1. that much; to that extent: as, *the* better to see you with. 2. by how much. . .by that much; to what extent. . .to that extent: used in a correlative construction expressing comparison, as, *the* sooner *the* better.

the·a·ceous (thi-ā′shəs), ***adj.*** [< Mod. L. *Theaceae*, name of the family < *Thea*, generic name (adopted by Linnaeus), after Gr. *thea*, goddess (as being a divine herb), but < source of Eng. *tea;* see TEA], of the tea family of trees and shrubs, having five-petaled flowers with many stamens, and dry or fleshy fruit.

the·an·throp·ic (thē′an-throp′ik), ***adj.*** having or of a nature both human and divine.

the·an·thro·pism (thi-an′thrə-piz'm), ***n.*** [< Gr. *theanthrōpos* < *theos*, god + *anthrōpos*, man; + *-ism*], 1. *a*) the attributing of human characteristics to God (or gods; anthropomorphism. *b*) belief in a theanthropic being or beings. 2. the theological doctrine of the union of divine and human natures in Jesus Christ.

the·ar·chy (thē′är-ki), ***n.*** [*pl.* THEARCHIES (-kiz)], [< Gr. *theos*, god; + *-archy*], 1. government by God or gods; theocracy. 2. a class or order of ruling deities.

theat., theatrical.

the·a·ter, the·a·tre (thē′ə-tẽr; *also formerly, now dial. or humorous,* thē-ā′tẽr), ***n.*** [OFr. *theatre* (Fr. *théâtre*); L. *theatrum;* Gr. *theatron* < base of *theasthai*, to see, view], 1. a place where plays, operas, motion pictures, etc. are presented; especially, a building expressly designed for such presentations. 2. any place resembling a theater, especially one having ascending rows of seats, as a lecture hall, surgical clinic, etc. 3. any place where events take place; scene of operations: as, the Pacific *theater* of war. 4. *a*) the dramatic art; drama. *b*) the theatrical world; people engaged in theatrical activity. 5. theatrical technique, production, etc. with reference to its effectiveness: as, the play was good *theater*.

the·a·ter·go·er, the·a·tre·go·er (thē′ə-tẽr-gō′ẽr), ***n.*** a person who goes to the theater, especially one who goes habitually.

the·at·ric (thi-at′rik), ***adj.*** theatrical.

the·at·ri·cal (thi-at′ri-k'l), ***adj.*** [LL. *theatricus;* Gr. *theatrikos*], 1. having to do with the theater, the drama, a play, actors, etc. 2. characteristic of the theater; dramatic; histrionic; especially (in disparagement), melodramatic; pompous; affected.

the·at·ri·cal·ism (thi-at′ri-k'l-iz'm), ***n.*** theatrical style, manner, etc.; especially, affectation, show, pomp, etc.

the·at·ri·cal·i·ty (thi-at′ri-kal′ə-ti), ***n.*** the quality of being theatrical; theatricalism.

the·at·ri·cals (thi-at′ri-k'lz), ***n.pl.*** performances of stage plays, especially by amateurs.

the·at·rics (thi-at′riks), ***n.pl.*** [construed as sing.], the art of the theater.

The·ba·id (thē′bə-id), ***n.*** [L. *Thebais, Thebaidis* < *Thebae,* Thebes], 1. the district around Egyptian Thebes or Boeotian Thebes. 2. a poem about the siege of Boeotian Thebes, especially an epic by the Latin poet Statius (1st century A.D.).

the·ba·in (thē′bə-in, thi-bā′in), ***n.*** thebaine.

the·ba·ine (thē′bə-ēn′, thi-bā′in), ***n.*** [< L. *Thebae* (Gr. *Thēbai*), Thebes; + *-ine:* named after an Egyptian opium produced at Thebes], a colorless, poisonous alkaloid, $C_{19}H_{21}NO_3$, obtained from opium and used in medicine.

The·ban (thē′bən), ***adj.*** [L. *Thebanus* < *Thebae,* Thebes], of Thebes in Greece or Thebes in Egypt. ***n.*** a native or inhabitant of either of these cities.

Thebes (thēbz), ***n.*** 1. an ancient city in Egypt on the Nile, near modern Luxor: site of the Temple of Karnak: see **Ancient Egypt**, map. 2. an ancient city of Greece in Boeotia.

the·ca (thē′kə), ***n.*** [*pl.* THECAE (-sē)], [L.; Gr. *thēkē*, a case], 1. in ***botany***, a spore case, sac, or capsule. 2. in ***zoology & anatomy***, any sac enclosing an organ or a whole organism, as the covering of an insect pupa.

the·cal (thē′k'l), ***adj.*** of or resembling a theca.

the·cate (thē′kit), ***adj.*** having a theca; sheathed.

‡thé dan·sant (tā′ dän′sän′), [*pl.* THÉS DANSANTS (tā′ dän′sän′)], [Fr. < *thé*, tea + *dansant*, ppr. of *danser*, to dance], a tea dance.

thee (thē), ***pron.*** [ME. & AS. *the*, dat. & acc. of *thu*, thou; see THOU], the objective case of **thou**: also used in place of *thou* by Friends (Quakers) with the verb in the third person singular: as, *thee* speaks harshly.

thee·lin (thē′lin), ***n.*** [< Gr. *thēlys*, female; + *-in*], estrone, a female sex hormone.

thee·lol (thē′lōl, thē′lol), ***n.*** [< Gr. *thēlys*, female; + *-ol*], estriol, a female sex hormone.

theft (theft), ***n.*** [ME. *thefte, thiefthe;* AS. *thiefth;* see THIEF & 1st -TH], 1. the act or an instance of stealing; larceny. 2. [Obs.], something stolen.

SYN.—**theft** is the general term and **larceny** the legal term for the unlawful or felonious taking away of another's property without his consent and with the intention of depriving him of it; **robbery** in its strict legal sense implies the felonious taking of another's property from his person or in his immediate presence by the use of violence or intimidation; **burglary** in legal use implies a breaking into a house with intent to commit theft or other felony and is often restricted to such an act accomplished at night.

thegn (thān), ***n.*** a thane.

the·in (thē′in), ***n.*** theine.

the·ine (thē′in, thē′ēn), ***n.*** [Fr. *théine* < *thé*, tea; Mod. L. *thea;* see THEACEOUS], caffeine, especially as found in tea.

their (thâr), ***pron.*** [ME. *their, theyr* < ON. *theirra*, genit. pl. of the demonstrative pron. replacing ME. *here*, AS. *hira;* see THEY], possessive form of **they.** ***possessive pronominal adj.*** of, belonging to, or done by them.

theirs (thârz), ***pron.*** [*their* + *-s* by analogy with *his*], that or those belonging to them: the absolute form of *their*, used without a following noun, often after *of*, as, a friend of *theirs*, that book is *theirs*, *theirs* are better.

the·ism (thē′iz'm), ***n.*** [< Gr. *theos*, god; + *-ism*], 1. belief in a god or gods. 2. belief in one God; monotheism: opposed to ***pantheism, polytheism.*** 3. belief in one God who is creator and ruler of the universe and known by revelation: distinguished from ***deism.***

Theiss (tīs), ***n.*** Tisza.

the·ist (thē′ist), ***n.*** an adherent of theism. ***adj.*** theistic.

the·is·tic (thē-is′tik), ***adj.*** of theism or theists.

the·is·ti·cal (thē-is′ti-k'l), ***adj.*** theistic.

the·is·ti·cal·ly (thē-is′ti-k'l-i, thē-is′tik-li), ***adv.*** according to theistic doctrine.

the·li·tis (thi-lī′tis), ***n.*** [Mod. L. < Gr. *thēlē*, nipple; + *-itis*], inflammation of the nipple.

Thel·ma (thel′mə), [said to be Gr., nurseling, but often a var. of *Selma*], a feminine name.

them (*th*em; *unstressed th*əm, *th*'m), ***pron.*** [ME. *theim;* ON. *theim*, dat. of the demonstrative pron.; see THEY], the objective case of **they:** also used colloquially as a predicate complement with a linking verb (e.g., that's *them*).

the·mat·ic (thē-mat′ik), ***adj.*** of or constituting a theme or themes.

the·mat·i·cal·ly (thē-mat′i-k'l-i, thē-mat′ik-li), ***adv.*** 1. in or by means of a theme or themes. 2. by the nature of its theme or themes.

theme (thēm), ***n.*** [ME. & OFr. *teme;* L. *thema;* Gr. *thema*, what is laid down < base of *tithenai*, to put, place], 1. a topic or subject, as of a lecture, sermon, essay, etc. 2. a short essay, especially one written as an assignment in a school course. 3. a short, melodic series of notes constituting the subject of a musical composition or a phrase upon which variations are developed. 4. the part of a word to which inflectional endings are added; stem. 5. in *radio*, etc., a theme song, or signature. —***SYN.*** see **subject.**

theme song, 1. a song repeated several times during a musical play or motion picture and popularly associated with it: it is often intended to set the mood of the dramatic theme. 2. in *radio*, etc., a song or tune used to identify a program, performer, etc.; signature.

The·mis (thē′mis), ***n.*** in *Greek mythology*, a goddess of law and justice, daughter of Uranus and Gaea: represented as holding aloft a scale for weighing opposing claims.

The·mis·to·cles (thə-mis′tə-klēz′), ***n.*** Athenian general and statesman; 527?–460? B.C.

them·selves (*th*əm-selvz′), ***pron.*** [Late (Northern) ME. *thaim selfe* for ME. *hemselve(n)* (cf. THEY) + *-s* pl. suffix], a form of the third person plural pronoun, used: *a*) as an intensive: as, they went *themselves.* *b*) as a reflexive: as, they hurt *themselves.*

then (*th*en), ***adv.*** [ME.; see THAN], 1. at that time: as, we were young *then*, *then* I shall go. 2. soon afterward; next in time: as, he got up, took his hat, and *then* left. 3. next in order: as, first there is Fred's desk, *then* there is David's. 4. in that case; therefore; accordingly: as, if he read it, *then* he knows; do it your own way, *then.* 5. besides; moreover: as, but I like to walk, and *then* it's cheaper. 6. at another time: used as a correlative with *now, sometimes*, etc., as, now she's sullen, *then* gay. ***adj.*** of that time; being such at that time: as, the *then* director. ***n.*** that time: as, by *then*, they were gone.

but then, but on the other hand; but at the same time.

then and there, at that time and in that place; at once.

what then? what would happen in that case?

the·nar (thē′när), ***n.*** [Mod. L.; Gr. *thenar*], 1. the palm of the hand or, sometimes, the sole of the foot. 2. the fleshy bulge at the base of the thumb. ***adj.*** of a thenar.

thence (*th*ens, thens), ***adv.*** [ME. *thens, thennes, thannes* (with adv. genit. suffix *-es*) < AS. *thanan, thonon*, thence; for base see THAT], 1. from that place; therefrom. 2. from that time; thenceforth. 3. on that account; therefore.

thence·forth (*th*ens′fôrth′, thens′fōrth′), ***adv.*** from that time onward; thereafter.

thence·for·ward (*th*ens′fôr′wẽrd, thens′fôr′wẽrd), ***adv.*** thenceforth.

thence·for·wards (*th*ens′fôr′wẽrdz, thens′fôr′wẽrdz), ***adv.*** thenceforward.

the·o- (thē′ō, thē′ə), [< Gr. *theos*, god], a combining form meaning *a god* or *God*, as in *theocentric*: also, before a vowel, **the-.**

The·o·bald (thē′ə-bôld′), [prob. via L. **Theobaldus*, altered after names beginning with *Theo-* (< Gr. *theos*, God, a god) < OG. *Theudobald, Theodbald* (akin to AS. *Theodbeald*) < *theuda*, folk, people + *bald*, brave, bold], a masculine name.

the·o·bro·min (thē′ə-brō′min), ***n.*** theobromine.

the·o·bro·mine (thē′ə-brō′mēn, thē′ə-brō′min), ***n.*** [< Mod. L. *Theobroma*, name of a genus of trees of the chocolate family (< Gr. *theos*, god + *brōma*, food); + *-ine*], a bitter, crystalline alkaloid, $C_7H_8O_2N_4$, extracted from the leaves and seeds of the cacao plant, used in medicine as a diuretic and nerve stimulant: it is related to theophylline and caffeine.

the·o·cen·tric (thē'ə-sen'trik), *adj.* [*theo-* + *centric*], assuming God as its center or center of interest.

the·oc·ra·cy (thē-ok'rə-si), *n.* [*pl.* THEOCRACIES (-siz)], [Gr. *theokratia* < *theos*, god + *kratein*, to rule], 1. literally, the rule of a state by God or a god; hence, 2. government by priests claiming to rule with divine authority. 3. a country governed in this way. 4. a group of clerics with political power.

the·oc·ra·sy (thē-ok'rə-si), *n.* [Gr. *theocrasia* < *theos*, god + *krasis*, mixture], 1. a mixture of several deities in one. 2. a mixture of the worship of several deities. 3. mystic union of the soul with God.

the·o·crat (thē'ə-krat'), *n.* 1. the ruler or one of the rulers in a theocracy. 2. a person who believes in or advocates theocracy.

the·o·crat·ic (thē'ə-krat'ik), *adj.* of or under a theocracy.

the·o·crat·i·cal (thē'ə-krat'i-k'l), *adj.* theocratic.

The·oc·ri·tus (thē-ok'ri-təs), *n.* Greek pastoral poet; lived 3d century B.C.

the·od·i·cy (thē-od'ə-si), *n.* [*pl.* THEODICIES (-siz)], [Fr. *théodicée* < Gr. *theos*, god + *dikē*, justice], a vindication of divine justice in allowing evil to exist.

the·od·o·lite (thē-od'ə-lit'), *n.* [Mod. L. & Early Mod. Eng. *theodelitus;* prob. invented (c. 1571) by Eng. mathematician Leonard Digges], a surveying instrument used to measure vertical and horizontal angles.

The·o·dor·a (thē'ə-dôr'ə, thē'ə-dō'rə), [Gr. *Theodōra;* see THEODORE], a feminine name: diminutive, *Dora.*

The·o·dore (thē'ə-dôr', thē'ə-dōr'), [L. *Theodorus;* Gr. *Theodōros* < *theos*, god + *dōron*, gift], a masculine name: diminutives, *Ted, Teddy;* feminine, *Theodora.*

The·od·o·ric (thē-od'ēr-ik), [LL. *Theodoricus*, altered (after *Theodorus*, Theodore) < Goth. **Thiudoreiks* < *thiuda*, folk, people + *reiks*, ruler, leader], a masculine name. *n.* Ostrogothic general; 454?–526 A.D.; king of the Ostrogoths (474–526 A.D.): called *the Great.*

The·o·do·si·a (thē'ə-dō'shi-ə), [Gr. *Theodosia;* see THEODOSIUS], a feminine name.

The·o·do·si·us (thē'ə-dō'shi-əs), [LL.; Gr. *Theodosios* < *theos*, god + *dosis*, a giving, gift], a masculine name: feminine, *Theodosia.*

Theodosius I, (*Flavius Theodosius*), 346?–395 A.D.; Roman general; emperor of Rome (379–395 A.D.): called *the Great.*

the·o·gon·ic (thē'ə-gon'ik), *adj.* of theogony.

the·og·o·ny (thē-og'ə-ni), *n.* [*pl.* THEOGONIES (-niz)], [Gr. *theogonia* < *theos*, god + *gonos*, generation], the origin or genealogy of the gods, as told in myths.

theol., 1. theologian. 2. theological. 3. theology.

the·o·lo·gi·an (thē'ə-lō'jən, thē'ə-lō'ji-ən), *n.* [Fr. *théologien*], a person who is a student of or authority on theology or a theology: abbreviated **theolog.**

the·o·log·ic (thē'ə-loj'ik), *adj.* theological.

the·o·log·i·cal (thē'ə-loj'i-k'l), *adj.* 1. of the word of God; of divine revelation; scriptural; specifically, designating the three virtues faith, hope, and charity. 2. of theology. Abbreviated **theol.**

the·o·log·i·cal·ly (thē'ə-loj'i-k'l-i, thē'ə-loj'ik-li), *adv.* according to theology.

the·ol·o·gize (thē-ol'ə-jīz'), *v.t.* [THEOLOGIZED (-jīzd'), THEOLOGIZING], to put into theological terms; fit into a theology. *v.i.* to speculate theologically.

the·ol·o·gy (thē-ol'ə-ji), *n.* [*pl.* THEOLOGIES (-jiz)], [ME. *theologie, teologie;* OFr. *theologie;* L. *theologia;* Gr. *theologia* < *theos*, god + *logos*, discourse], 1. the study of God and the relations between God and the universe; study of religious doctrines and matters of divinity. 2. a specific form or system of this study, as expounded by a particular religion or denomination.

the·om·a·chy (thē-om'ə-ki), *n.* [*pl.* THEOMACHIES (-kiz)], [Gr. *theomachia* < *theos*, god + *machē*, combat], 1. battle against the gods. 2. strife among the gods.

the·o·mor·phic (thē'ə-môr'fik), *adj.* [Gr. *theomorphos;* see THEO- & -MORPHIC], having the form, likeness, or aspect of God or a god.

the·op·a·thy (thē-op'ə-thi), *n.* [*pl.* THEOPATHIES (-thiz)], [*theo-* + *-pathy*], religious emotion; mystical ecstasy.

the·oph·a·ny (thē-of'ə-ni), *n.* [*pl.* THEOPHANIES (-niz)], [LL. *theophania;* Gr. *theophaneia* < *theos*, god + base of *phainesthai*, to appear], a supposed visible appearance of God or a god to man.

The·oph·i·lus (thē-of'ə-ləs), [L. Gr. *Theophilos* < *theos*, god + *philos*, loving], a masculine name.

The·o·phras·tus (thē'ə-fras'təs), *n.* Greek Aristotelian philosopher and natural scientist; ?–287? B.C.

the·o·phyl·lin (thē'ə-fil'in), *n.* theophylline.

the·o·phyl·line (thē'ə-fil'ēn, thē'ə-fil'in), *n.* [< Mod. L. *thea*, tea + Gr. *phyllon*, leaf; + *-ine*], a colorless, crystalline alkaloid, $C_7H_8O_2N_4 \cdot H_2O$, extracted from tea leaves: an isomer of, and used like, theobromine.

theor., theorem.

the·or·bo (thē-ôr'bō), *n.* [Fr. *théorbe, téorbe;* It. *tiorba;* ? < name of inventor], an obsolete type of lute with a double neck and two sets of strings.

the·o·rem (thē'ə-rəm), *n.* [< Fr. or L.; Fr. *théorème;* L. *theorema;* Gr. *theōrēma* < *theōrein*, to look at, view], 1. a proposition that is not self-evident but that can be proved from accepted premises and so is established as a law or principle. 2. an expression of relations in an equation or formula. 3. in *mathematics & physics*, a proposition embodying something to be proved.

the·o·re·mat·ic (thē'ə-rə-mat'ik), *adj.* of, or having the nature of, a theorem or theorems.

the·o·ret·ic (thē'ə-ret'ik), *adj.* theoretical.

the·o·ret·i·cal (thē'ə-ret'i-k'l), *adj.* [LL. *theoreticus;* Gr. *theōrētikos*], 1. of or constituting theory. 2. limited to or based on theory; hypothetical; ideal: opposed to *practical* or *applied.* 3. tending to theorize; speculative.

the·o·ret·i·cal·ly (thē'ə-ret'i-k'l-i, thē'ə-ret'ik-li), *adv.* in theory; by means of theory; according to a theory.

the·o·re·ti·cian (thē'ə-rə-tish'ən), *n.* a person who is a student of or authority on the theory of some art, science, etc.

the·o·ret·ics (thē'ə-ret'iks), *n.pl.* [construed as sing.], the theoretical part of a field of knowledge.

the·o·rist (thē'ə-rist), *n.* a person who theorizes; especially, one who specializes in the theory of some art, science, etc.

the·o·ri·za·tion (thē'ə-ri-zā'shən, thē'ə-rī-zā'shən), *n.* a theorizing.

the·o·rize (thē'ə-rīz'), *v.i.* [THEORIZED (-rīzd'), THEORIZING], to form a theory or theories; speculate.

the·o·ry (thē'ə-ri), *n.* [*pl.* THEORIES (-riz)], [< Fr. or LL.; Fr. *théorie;* LL. *theoria;* Gr. *theōria*, a looking at, contemplation, speculation, theory < *theōrein*, to look at], 1. originally, a mental viewing; contemplation. 2. an idea or mental plan of the way to do something; hence, 3. a systematic statement of principles involved: as, the *theory* of equations in mathematics. 4. a formulation of apparent relationships or underlying principles of certain observed phenomena which has been verified to some degree: distinguished from *hypothesis.* 5. that branch of an art or science consisting in a knowledge of its principles and methods rather than in its practice; pure, as opposed to applied, science, etc. 6. popularly, a mere hypothesis, conjecture, or guess: as, my *theory* is that he's lying.

SYN.—**theory,** as compared here, implies considerable evidence in support of a formulated general principle explaining the operation of certain phenomena (the *theory* of evolution); **hypothesis** implies an inadequacy of evidence in support of an explanation that is tentatively inferred, often as a basis for further experimentation (the nebular *hypothesis*); **law** implies an exact formulation of the principle operating in a sequence of events in nature observed to occur with unvarying uniformity under the same conditions (the *law* of the conservation of energy).

theos., 1. theosophical. 2. theosophist. 3. theosophy.

the·o·soph·ic (thē'ə-sof'ik), *adj.* of theosophy or theosophists.

the·o·soph·i·cal (thē'ə-sof'i-k'l), *adj.* theosophic.

the·os·o·phist (thē-os'ə-fist), *n.* a believer in theosophy.

the·os·o·phy (thē-os'ə-fi), *n.* [ML. *theosophia;* LGr. *theosophia*, knowledge of divine things < *theosophos*, wise in divine matters < *theos*, god + *sophos*, wise], 1. any of various philosophies or religious systems that propose to establish direct contact with divine principle through contemplation, revelation, etc. and to gain thereby a spiritual insight superior to empirical knowledge. 2. [often T-], the doctrines and beliefs of a modern sect of this nature that incorporates elements of Buddhism and Brahmanism. Abbreviated **theos.**

ther·a·peu·tic (ther'ə-pū'tik), *adj.* [Mod. L. *therapeuticus;* Gr. *therapeutikos* < *therapeutēs*, attendant, servant, one who treats medically < *therapeuein*, to nurse, serve, treat medically], 1. serving to cure or heal; curative. 2. of therapeutics.

ther·a·peu·ti·cal (ther'ə-pū'ti-k'l), *adj.* therapeutic.

ther·a·peu·tics (ther'ə-pū'tiks), *n.pl.* [construed as sing.], the branch of medicine that deals with the treatment and cure of diseases; therapy: abbreviated **therap.**

ther·a·pist (ther'ə-pist), *n.* a person skilled in a particular branch of therapeutics: as, a hydro*therapist.*

ther·a·py (ther'ə-pi), *n.* [*pl.* THERAPIES (-piz)], [Mod. L. *therapia;* Gr. *therapeia* < *therapeuein*, to nurse, cure], 1. therapeutics: often used in compounds, as *hydrotherapy.* 2. therapeutic nature or power.

there (*th*âr), *adv.* [ME. *ther*, there, where; AS. *ther, thær*, there, where; IE. base **tor-*, **ter-*, there < **to-*, **tā-*, demonstrative base, seen in *that, then*, etc.], 1. at or in that place: often used as an intensive, as, John *there* is a good ball player. 2. toward, to, or into that place; thither: as, go *there.* 3. at that point in action, speech, etc.; then. 4. in that matter, respect, etc.; as to that: as, *there* you are wrong. 5. at the moment; right now: as, *there* goes the whistle. *There* is also used *a)* in interjectional phrases of approval, encouragement, etc. (e.g., *there's* a fine fellow!). *b)* with pronominal force in impersonal constructions in which the real subject follows the verb (e.g., *there* is very little time, *there* are three men here). ***n.*** that place: as, we left *there* at six. ***interj.*** *there* is used as an exclamation expressing: 1. defiance, dismay, satisfaction, etc. (e.g., *there*, that's done!). 2. sympathy, concern, etc. (e.g., *there, there!* don't worry.).

there·a·bout (*thâr'*ə-bout'), ***adv.*** thereabouts.

there·a·bouts (*thâr'*ə-bouts'), ***adv.*** 1. near that place. 2. near that time or point in action, speech, etc. 3. near that number, amount, degree, etc.

there·aft·er (*thâr*-af'tẽr, *thâr*-äf'tẽr), ***adv.*** 1. after that in time or sequence; following that; subsequently. 2. [Archaic or Rare], accordingly.

there·a·gainst (*thâr'*ə-genst'), ***adv.*** against or contrary to that; in opposition.

there·at (*thâr*-at'), ***adv.*** 1. at that place; there. 2. at that time; when that occurred. 3. at that; for that reason.

there·by (*thâr*-bī', *thâr'*bī'), ***adv.*** 1. by or through that; by that means. 2. connected with that: used chiefly in expressions such as ***thereby hangs a tale.*** 3. thereabouts.

come thereby, come into possession of it.

there·for (*thâr*-fôr'), ***adv.*** for this; for that; for it.

there·fore (*thâr'*fôr', *thâr'*fōr'), ***adv. & conj.*** [Early ME. *ther fore;* see THERE & FORE], as a result of this or that; for this or that reason; consequently; hence.

there·from (*thâr*-frum', *thâr*-from'), ***adv.*** from this; from that; from it.

there·in (*thâr*-in'), ***adv.*** 1. in there; in or into that place or thing. 2. in that writing, speech, etc. 3. in that matter, detail, etc.

there·in·aft·er (*thâr'*in-af'tẽr, *thâr'*in-äf'tẽr), ***adv.*** in the following part (of that document, speech, etc.).

there·in·to (*thâr*-in'tōō, *thâr'*in-tōō'), ***adv.*** 1. into that place or thing. 2. into that matter, condition, etc.

ther·e·min (ther'ə-min), ***n.*** [after Leo *Theremin* (1896–), Russ. inventor], an electronic musical instrument whose tone and pitch are controlled by moving the hands through the air varying distances from two projecting antennas: a trade-mark (**Theremin**).

there·of (*thâr*-uv', *thâr*-ov'), ***adv.*** 1. of that; of it; concerning that or it. 2. from that as a cause, reason, etc.; therefrom.

there·on (*thâr*-on', *thâr*-ôn'), ***adv.*** 1. on that; concerning that subject, etc. 2. immediately following that; thereupon.

there's (*thâ*rz), there is.

The·re·sa (tə-rē'sə, tə-rē'zə), [< Fr. *Thérèse* or Port. *Theresa;* L. *Therasia;* ? < Gr. *therizein*, to reap], a feminine name: variant, *Teresa;* diminutives, *Terry, Tess.*

Theresa, Saint, 1515–1582; Spanish mystic; founder of the reformed order of Carmelites: her day is October 15: also spelled **Teresa.**

there·to (*thâr*-tōō'), ***adv.*** 1. to that place, thing, etc.; thereunto. 2. [Archaic or Poetic], in addition to that; moreover; besides.

there·to·fore (*thâr'*tə-fôr', *thâr'*tə-fōr'), ***adv.*** up to that time; until then; before that.

there·un·der (*thâr*-un'dẽr), ***adv.*** 1. under that; under it. 2. under that in number; fewer than that. 3. under that title, etc.; by that authority.

there·un·to (*thâr'*ən-tōō', *thâr*-un'tōō), ***adv.*** thereto (sense 1).

there·up·on (*thâr'*ə-pon', *thâr'*ə-pôn'), ***adv.*** 1. immediately following that; at once. 2. as a consequence of that. 3. upon that; concerning that subject, etc.

there·with (*thâr*-with', *thâr*-with'), ***adv.*** 1. with that or this; with it. 2. in addition to that; withal. 3. immediately thereafter; thereupon.

there·with·al (*thâr'*with-ôl'), ***adv.*** 1. with all that or this; in addition; besides. 2. [Obs.], therewith; with that or this.

The·re·zi·na (te're-zē'nə), ***n.*** a city in northeastern Brazil, on the Parnahyba River: pop., 64,000.

the·ri·an·throp·ic (thêr'i-an-throp'ik), ***adj.*** [< Gr. *thērion*, beast + *anthrōpos*, man], 1. that combines human and animal form, as the centaur. 2. of religions having therianthropic gods.

ther·i·o·mor·phic (thêr'i-ə-môr'fik), ***adj.*** [< Gr. *thēriomorphos* < *thērion*, beast + *morphē*, form; + *-ic*], conceived of as having the form of an animal: said of gods.

ther·i·o·mor·phous (thêr'i-ə-môr'fəs), ***adj.*** theriomorphic.

therm (thũrm), ***n.*** [< Gr. *thermē*, heat; for IE. base see WARM], in *physics*, 1. a great calorie or, occasionally, a small calorie. 2. a unit of heat equal to 1,000 great calories. 3. a unit of heat equal to 100,000 B.T.U.'s. Also spelled **therme.**

therm-, thermo-.

therm., thermometer.

Ther·ma (thũr'mə), ***n.*** Salonika, a city in Greece: an ancient name.

ther·mae (thũr'mē), ***n.pl.*** [L.; Gr. *thermai*, pl. of *thermē*, heat], hot or warm springs or baths; specifically, the public baths or bathhouses of the ancient Romans.

ther·mal (thũr'm'l), ***adj.*** [Fr. < Gr. *thermē*, heat], 1. having to do with heat, hot springs, etc. 2. warm or hot.

ther·mal·ly (thũr'm'l-i), ***adv.*** by means of heat.

therm·an·es·the·si·a, therm·an·aes·the·si·a (thũrm'-an-əs-thē'zhə, thũrm'an-əs-thē'zhi-ə), ***n.*** thermoanesthesia.

therm·es·the·si·a, therm·aes·the·si·a (thũrm'es-thē'-zhə, thũrm'es-thē'zhi-ə), ***n.*** [Mod. L.; see THERMO- & AESTHESIA], in *physiology*, the sense by which heat and cold are perceived; temperature sense.

ther·mic (thũr'mik) ***adj.*** [< Gr. *thermē*, heat; + *-ic*], of or caused by heat.

‡Ther·mi·dor (târ'mē'dôr'; Eng. thũr'mi-dôr'), ***n.*** [Fr. < Gr. *thermē*, heat + *dōron*, gift], the eleventh month (July 19–August 17) of the French Revolutionary Calendar, adopted by the First Republic in 1793.

therm·i·on (thũrm'ī'ən, thũr'mi-ən), ***n.*** [*therm-* + *ion*], an electrically charged particle emitted by an incandescent material: positively charged thermions are called *ions*, and negatively charged, *electrons.*

therm·i·on·ic (thũrm'ī-on'ik, thũr'mi-on'ik), ***adj.*** of or operating by means of thermions.

thermionic current, an electric current caused by directed thermionic emission.

therm·i·on·ics (thũrm'ī-on'iks, thũr'mi-on'iks), ***n.pl.*** [construed as sing.], the study and science of thermionic activity.

thermionic valve, [British], an electron tube.

ther·mit (thũr'mit), ***n.*** [G. < Gr. *thermē*, heat], a mixture of finely granulated aluminum with an oxide of iron or other metal, which produces great heat and is used in welding and in incendiary bombs: a trade-mark (**Thermit**).

ther·mite (thũr'mīt), ***n.*** thermit.

ther·mo- (thũr'mō, thũr'mə), [< Gr. *thermē*, heat], a combining form meaning: 1. *heat*, as in *thermodynamics*. 2. *thermoelectric*, as in *thermocouple*. Also, before a vowel, **therm-.**

ther·mo·an·es·the·si·a, ther·mo·an·aes·the·si·a (thũr'-mō-an'əs-thē'zhə, thũr'mō-an'əs-thē'zhi-ə), ***n.*** [Mod. L.], the lack or loss of the ability to perceive heat and cold: also **thermanesthesia, thermanaesthesia.**

ther·mo·bar·o·graph (thũr'mō-bar'ə-graf', thũr'mō-bar'ə-gräf'), ***n.*** an instrument consisting of a thermograph combined with a barograph.

ther·mo·ba·rom·e·ter (thũr'mō-bə-rom'ə-tẽr), ***n.*** 1. a barometric instrument for measuring atmospheric pressure and, hence, altitudes, by the boiling point of water. 2. a siphon barometer that can be adapted for use as a thermometer.

ther·mo·chem·is·try (thũr'mō-kem'is-tri), ***n.*** the branch of chemistry that deals with the relationship of heat to chemical change: abbreviated **thermochem.**

ther·mo·cou·ple (thũr'mō-kup''l), ***n.*** a thermoelectric couple for measuring differences in temperature.

ther·mo·dy·nam·ic (thũr'mō-dī-nam'ik), ***adj.*** 1. having to do with thermodynamics. 2. operated by heat converted into motive power.

ther·mo·dy·nam·ics (thũr'mō-dī-nam'iks), ***n.pl.*** [construed as sing.], [*thermo-* + *dynamics*], the science that deals with the relationship of heat and mechanical energy and the conversion of one into the other: abbreviated **thermodyn.**

ther·mo·e·lec·tric (thũr'mō-i-lek'trik), ***adj.*** having to do with thermoelectricity.

ther·mo·e·lec·tri·cal (thũr'mō-i-lek'tri-k'l), ***adj.*** thermoelectric.

thermoelectric couple, a junction of two bars, wires, etc. of dissimilar metals which produces thermoelectric current when heated: it is used in temperature measurements, etc.: also **thermoelectric pair.**

ther·mo·e·lec·tric·i·ty (thũr'mō-i-lek'tris'ə-ti), ***n.*** electricity produced by heat, as by means of a thermoelectric couple.

ther·mo·e·lec·trom·e·ter (thũr'mō-i-lek'trom'ə-tẽr), ***n.*** [*thermo-* + *electrometer*], an instrument for measuring the power of an electric current by the amount of heat it produces, or for measuring the heating power of an electric current.

ther·mo·e·lec·tro·mo·tive (thũr'mō-i-lek'trə-mō'tiv), ***adj.*** designating or of the electromotive force produced as by a thermoelectric couple.

ther·mo·gen·e·sis (thũr'mō-jen'ə-sis), ***n.*** [Mod. L.; see THERMO- & -GENESIS], the production of heat, especially by physiological action in an animal body.

ther·mo·ge·net·ic (thũr'mō-jə-net'ik), ***adj.*** of thermogenesis.

ther·mo·gen·ic (thũr'mə-jen'ik), ***adj.*** [*thermo-* + *-genic*], having to do with the production of heat.

ther·mog·e·nous (thẽr-moj'ə-nəs), ***adj.*** [*thermo-* + *-genous*], producing heat.

ther·mo·graph (thũr'mə-graf', thũr'mə-gräf'), ***n.*** [*thermo-* + *-graph*], a thermometer for recording variations in temperature automatically.

ther·mo·kin·e·mat·ics (thũr'mō-kin'ə-mat'iks), ***n.pl.***

[construed as sing.], [*thermo-* + *kinematics*], the science of the relationship of heat and motive power.

ther·mo·la·bile (thũr′mō-lā′b'l, thũr′mō-lā′bil), *adj.* [*thermo-* + *labile*], designating or of substances, as some toxins, enzymes, etc., that are destroyed or lose their special properties when heated to 55° C. or above: opposed to *thermostable*.

ther·mol·y·sis (thẽr-mol′ə-sis), *n.* [Mod. L.; see THERMO- & -LYSIS], 1. in *chemistry*, dissociation of a compound by heat. 2. in *physiology*, the loss or dispersion of heat from the body.

ther·mom·e·ter (thẽr-mom′ə-tẽr), *n.* [*thermo-* + *-meter*], 1. an instrument for measuring temperatures, consisting of a graduated glass tube with a sealed, capillary bore in which mercury, colored alcohol, etc. rises or falls as it expands or contracts from changes in temperature. 2. any similar instrument, as one operating by means of a thermocouple. The three principal types of thermometers are: *Fahrenheit*, in which the freezing point of water is 32° and the boiling point 212°; *centigrade*, in which the freezing point is 0° and the boiling point 100°; and *Reaumur*, in which the freezing point is 0° and the boiling point 80°.

ther·mo·met·ric (thũr′mə-met′rik), *adj.* of or measured by a thermometer.

ther·mo·met·ri·cal (thũr′mə-met′ri-k'l), *adj.* thermometric.

ther·mom·e·try (thẽr-mom′ə-tri), *n.* 1. measurement of temperature. 2. the science of making or using thermometers.

ther·mo·mo·tor (thũr′mə-mō′tẽr), *n.* [*thermo-* + *motor*], an engine operated by heat, especially by the expansion of heated air.

ther·mo·nu·cle·ar (thũr′mō-nōō′kli-ẽr, thũr′mō-nū′kli-ẽr), *adj.* [*thermo-* + *nuclear*], designating, of, or employing the heat energy released in nuclear fission.

ther·mo·pile (thũr′mə-pīl′), *n.* [*thermo-* + *pile* (a heap)], an instrument consisting of a series of thermocouples, used for measuring minute changes in temperature or for generating thermoelectric current.

ther·mo·plas·tic (thũr′mə-plas′tik), *adj.* becoming or remaining soft and moldable when subjected to heat: said of certain plastics: cf. **thermosetting.** *n.* a thermoplastic substance.

Ther·mop·y·lae (thẽr-mop′ə-li), *n.* a mountain pass in eastern Greece: scene of a battle (480 B.C.) in which the Spartans under Leonidas were overcome after holding off the Persian army under Xerxes.

ther·mos bottle (or **flask, jug**), (thũr′məs), [Gr. *thermos*, hot], a bottle, flask, or jug for keeping liquids at almost their original temperature for several hours: it has two walls enclosing a vacuum and is fitted in a metal outer case: a trade-mark (**Thermos**).

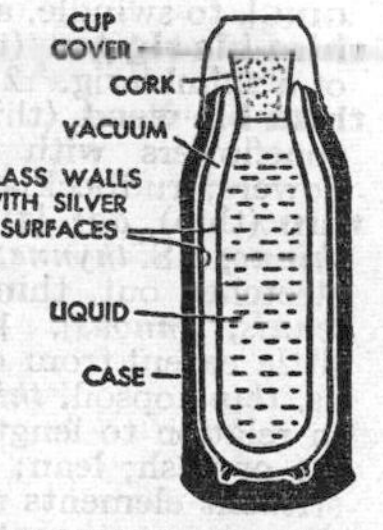

THERMOS BOTTLE

ther·mo·scope (thũr′mə-skōp′), *n.* [*thermo-* + *-scope*], an instrument for indicating changes in temperature without accurately measuring them.

ther·mo·scop·ic (thũr′mə-skop′ik), *adj.* of or indicated by a thermoscope.

ther·mo·scop·i·cal (thũr′mə-skop′i-k'l), *adj.* thermoscopic.

ther·mo·set·ting (thũr′mō-set′iŋ), *adj.* becoming permanently hard and unmoldable when once subjected to heat: said of certain plastics: cf. **thermoplastic.**

ther·mo·si·phon (thũr′mə-sī′fən), *n.* an apparatus consisting of an arrangement of siphon tubes for inducing the circulation of a liquid, as in the water-cooling system of an internal-combustion engine.

ther·mo·sta·ble (thũr′mō-stā′b'l), *adj.* [*thermo-* + *stable, adj.*], designating or of substances, as some toxins, enzymes, etc., that can be heated to moderately high temperatures without losing their special properties: opposed to *thermolabile*.

ther·mo·stat (thũr′mə-stat′), *n.* [*thermo-* + *-stat*], 1. an apparatus for regulating temperature, especially one that automatically controls a heating unit. 2. a device that sets off a sprinkler, etc. at a certain heat.

ther·mo·stat·ic (thũr′mə-stat′ik), *adj.* of or operated by a thermostat.

ther·mo·stat·i·cal·ly (thũr′mə-stat′i-k'l-i, thũr′mə-stat′ik-li), *adv.* by means of a thermostat.

ther·mo·stat·ics (thũr′mə-stat′iks), *n.pl.* [construed as sing.], [*thermo-* + *statics*], the science that deals with the equilibrium of heat.

ther·mo·tank (thũr′mə-taŋk′), *n.* a tank for heating or cooling air passing through it, by means of a series of pipes through which water, steam, air, etc. circulates.

ther·mo·tax·ic (thũr′mə-tak′sik), *adj.* 1. of thermotaxis. 2. regulating body temperature.

ther·mo·tax·is (thũr′mə-tak′sis), *n.* [Mod. L.; see THERMO- & -TAXIS], 1. in *biology*, movement of an organism toward or from a source of heat. 2. in *physiology*, the normal regulation of body temperature.

ther·mo·ten·sile (thũr′mō-ten′s'l, thũr′mō-ten′sil), *adj.* having to do with variations in tensile strength caused by changes in temperature.

ther·mo·trop·ic (thũr′mə-trop′ik), *adj.* of or having thermotropism.

ther·mot·ro·pism (thẽr-mot′rə-piz'm), *n.* [*thermo-* + *-tropism*], the tendency of a plant to grow toward or away from a source of heat.

-ther·my (thũr′mi), [< Gr. *thermē*, heat], a combining form meaning *heat* or *the production of heat*, as in *diathermy*.

the·roid (thêr′oid), *adj.* [Gr. *thēr*, a wild beast; + *-oid*], like or characteristic of an animal; beastlike.

Ther·si·tes (thẽr-sī′tēz), *n.* [L.; Gr. *Thersitēs*], in *Greek legend*, an ugly, loud, abusive Greek soldier in the Trojan War, killed by Achilles.

ther·sit·i·cal (thẽr-sit′i-k'l), *adj.* characteristic of Thersites; loud and abusive; scurrilous.

the·sau·rus (thi-sô′rəs), *n.* [*pl.* THESAURI (-rī), THESAURUSES (-iz)], [L. < Gr. *thēsauros*, a treasure], 1. a treasury or storehouse; hence, 2. a book containing a store of words, as a dictionary or, especially, a book of classified synonyms and antonyms.

these (*th*ēz), *pron. & adj.* plural of **this.**

The·se·an (thi-sē′ẽn), *adj.* of or like Theseus.

The·seus (thē′sōōs, thē′sūs, thē′si-əs), *n.* [L.; Gr. *Thēseus*], in *Greek legend*, the principal hero of Attica, son of Aegeus and king of Athens: he is famed for many exploits, especially for his killing of the Minotaur.

the·sis (thē′sis), *n.* [*pl.* THESES (-sēz)], [L.; Gr. *thesis*, a placing, position, proposition < the base of *tithenai*, to put, place], 1. in classical poetry, the accented syllable of a foot. 2. the unaccented syllable of a foot in poetry: usage due to misinterpretation of the classical Greek word. 3. an accented note in music, indicated by a downward stroke in conducting. 4. a proposition to be maintained or defended in argument, formerly one publicly disputed by a candidate for a degree in a medieval university; hence, 5. an essay or dissertation presented by a candidate for an academic degree as evidence of his knowledge of and individual research in a subject. 6. in *logic*, an unproved statement assumed as a premise; postulate: distinguished from *hypothesis*. Opposed to *arsis* (in senses 1, 2, 3).

Thes·pi·an (thes′pi-ən), *adj.* 1. of Thespis; hence, 2. having to do with the drama, especially with tragedy. *n.* an actor; especially, a tragedian: a somewhat humorous or pretentious usage.

Thes·pis (thes′pis), *n.* Greek poet; 6th century B.C.; traditionally the originator of Greek tragedy.

Thes·sa·li·an (the-sā′li-ən), *adj.* of Thessaly, its people, etc. *n.* 1. a native or inhabitant of ancient Thessaly. 2. the ancient Greek dialect spoken in Thessaly.

Thes·sa·lo·ni·an (thes′ə-lō′ni-ən), *adj.* of Thessalonica or its people. *n.* a native or inhabitant of Thessalonica.

Thes·sa·lo·ni·ans (thes′ə-lō′ni-ənz), *n.pl.* [construed as sing.], either of the Epistles to the Thessalonians, two books of the New Testament which were messages from the Apostle Paul to the Christians of Thessalonica: abbreviated **Thess.**

Thes·sa·lon·ic·a (thes′ə-lon′i-kə), *n.* Salonika, a city in Greece: an ancient name: also **Thes·sa·lo·ni·ke** (thes′á-lô-nē′kē), the Greek name.

Thes·sa·ly (thes′ə-li), *n.* an ancient region in northeastern Greece.

the·ta (thā′tə, thē′tə), *n.* [Gr. *thēta;* of Sem. origin], the eighth letter of the Greek alphabet (Θ, θ, ϑ), corresponding to English *th*: see **alphabet**, table.

thet·ic (thet′ik), *adj.* [Gr. *thetikos*, fit for placing < *thetos*, placed < base of *tithenai;* see THESIS], 1. set forth dogmatically; prescribed. 2. in *Greek & Latin poetry*, beginning with, or constituting, the thesis.

The·tis (thē′tis), *n.* [L.; Gr. *Thetis*], in *Greek mythology*, Achilles' mother, one of the Nereids.

the·ur·gic (thē-ũr′jik), *adj.* of theurgy; magic.

the·ur·gi·cal (thē-ũr′ji-k'l), *adj.* theurgic.

the·ur·gist (thē′ẽr-jist), *n.* a person who practices theurgy; magician.

the·ur·gy (thē′ẽr-ji), *n.* [*pl.* THEURGIES (-jiz)], [LL. *theurgia;* Gr. *theourgia* < *theourgos*, divine worker < *theos*, god + *ergon*, work], 1. supposed divine or supernatural intervention in human affairs. 2. magic; sorcery, especially that practiced by certain Neoplatonists who professed to work miracles by the intervention of beneficent, divine spirits.

thew·less (thū′lis, thōō′lis), *adj.* [Chiefly Scot.], lacking thews, or bodily strength; without vigor or spirit.

thews (thūz, thōōz), *n.pl.* [*sing.* THEW (thū, thōō)], [ME. *theawes*, good qualities, hence, later, good physical qualities, strength < AS. *theaw*, custom, habit, hence characteristic quality; akin to OS. *thau*, custom; IE. base **teu-*, to pay friendly attention to, notice, seen also in L. *tueri*, to keep in sight, observe, look after (cf. TUTOR, TUITION)], 1. muscular power; bodily strength. 2. *rarely in sing.* muscles or sinews.

thew·y (thū′i, thōō′i), ***adj.*** [THEWIER (-i-ẽr), THEWIEST (-i-ist)], having thews; muscular.

they (thā), ***pron.*** [for *sing.* see HE, SHE, IT], [ME. *thei* < ON. *thei-r*, nom. masc. pl. of the demonstrative pron.; like *their* & *them* (ME. *theim*), also < the ON. demonstrative forms, *thei* replaced earlier ME. *he* (*hi*) because the native pronouns were phonetically confused with the forms of the pers. pron. (ME. *he, hire, hem, him,* etc.); cf. THEIR, THEM, SHE], 1. the persons, animals, or things previously mentioned: *they* is the nominative case form, *them* the objective, *their* and *theirs* the possessive, and *themselves* the intensive and reflexive, of the third personal plural pronoun. 2. people (or a person) generally or indefinitely: as, *they* say it's so.

they'd (*th*ād), 1. they had. 2. they would.

they'll (*th*āl), 1. they will. 2. they shall.

they're (*th*âr), they are.

they've (*th*āv), they have.

thi- (thī), thio-.

thi·a·min (thī′ə-min), ***n.*** thiamine.

thi·a·mine (thī′ə-mēn′, thī′ə-min), ***n.*** [*thi-* + *amine*], a complex white, crystalline compound, $C_{12}H_{17}ON_4SCl \cdot HCl$, found in the outer coating of cereal grains, green peas, beans, egg yolk, liver, etc., and also prepared synthetically; vitamin B_1: a deficiency of this vitamin results in beriberi and certain nervous disorders: also **thiamine chloride, thiamine hydrochloride.**

thi·a·zin (thī′ə-zin), ***n.*** thiazine.

thi·a·zine (thī′ə-zēn′, thī′ə-zin), ***n.*** [*thi-* + *azine*], any of a group of heterocyclic compounds whose molecules contain one atom of nitrogen, one atom of sulfur, and four atoms of carbon, arranged in a ring.

thi·a·zol (thī′ə-zōl′, thī′ə-zol), ***n.*** thiazole.

thi·a·zole (thī′ə-zōl′), ***n.*** [*thi-* + *azole*], 1. a colorless liquid, C_3H_3NS, with a five-membered ring. 2. any of its various derivatives, used in dyes and drugs.

Thi·bet (ti-bet′), ***n.*** Tibet.

Thi·bet·an (ti-bet′ən), ***adj. & n.*** Tibetan.

thick (thik), ***adj.*** [ME. *thikke, thicke;* AS. *thicce*, thick, dense; akin to G. *dick;* IE. base **tegu-*, thick, fat, seen also in Sans. *tiug*], 1. having relatively great depth; of considerable extent from one surface or side to the opposite: as, a *thick* layer of stones, a *thick* board. 2. having relatively large diameter in relation to length: as, a *thick* rod, *thick* pipe. 3. measured in the third dimension or between opposite surfaces: as, three inches *thick:* distinguished from *long, wide.* 4. having the constituent elements arranged close together; dense; compact; abundant; specifically, *a*) filled or covered completely; dense; luxuriant: as, a *thick* head of hair, *thick* woods. *b*) great in number; abundant; crowded: as, a *thick* crowd. *c*) of great density or consistency; not very fluid; viscous; heavy: as, *thick* soup, *thick* smoke. *d*) not clear; turbid; muddy; foggy; close: as, the air was *thick* with fumes. 5. not clear; husky; hoarse: as, a *thick* voice. 6. not clear in understanding; stupid; dull. 7. [Colloq.], very friendly; intimate. 8. [British Colloq.], too much to be tolerated; excessive. Opposed to *thin* (in senses 1, 2, 4*a*, 4*b*, 4*c*. ***adv.*** thickly. ***n.*** the thickest part or the period of greatest activity: as, in the *thick* of the argument. —***SYN.*** see **close.**

lay it on thick, [Colloq.], to give exaggerated blame or praise.

through thick and thin, in good times and hard times; without wavering in loyalty.

thick·en (thik′ən), ***v.t. & v.i.*** 1. to make or become thick or thicker. 2. to make or become more complex or involved: as, the plot *thickened.*

thick·en·ing (thik′ən-iŋ), ***n.*** 1. the action of a person or thing that thickens. 2. a material used to thicken soup, etc. 3. something thickened or the thickened part.

thick·et (thik′it), ***n.*** [ME.; AS. *thiccet* < *thicce* (see THICK) + *-et*, denominating suffix], a thick growth of shrubs, underbrush, or small trees; copse.

thick·head (thik′hed′), ***n.*** a stupid person; blockhead.

thick·head·ed (thik′hed′id), ***adj.*** stupid.

thick·ish (thik′ish), ***adj.*** somewhat thick.

thick·ness (thik′nis), ***n.*** 1. the quality or condition of being thick. 2. dimension from surface to opposite surface: distinguished from *length, width.* 3. a layer, stratum, etc.: as, three *thicknesses* of cloth. 4. the thickest place or part.

thick·set (thik′set′), ***adj.*** 1. planted thickly or closely. 2. thick in body; stout; stocky. ***n.*** a thicket.

thick-skinned (thik′skind′), ***adj.*** 1. having a thick skin. 2. insensitive to criticism, insult, etc.; callous.

thick-skulled (thik′skuld′), ***adj.*** thickheaded.

thick-wit·ted (thik′wit′id), ***adj.*** thickheaded.

thief (thēf), ***n.*** [*pl.* THIEVES (thēvz)], [ME. *thief, theof;* AS. *theof, thiof, thef;* akin to G. *dieb;* IE. base **teup-*, to cower, lurk], a person who steals, especially secretly; one guilty of theft, or larceny.

Thiers, Lou·is A·dolphe (lwē′ å′dôlf′ tyâr′), 1797–1877; French statesman and historian.

thieve (thēv), ***v.t. & v.i.*** [THIEVED (thēvd), THIEVING], [< AS. *theofian* < *theof* (see THIEF)], to steal.

thiev·er·y (thēv′ẽr-i), ***n.*** [*pl.* THIEVERIES (-iz)], 1. the act or practice of stealing or an instance of this; theft. 2. [Rare], something stolen.

thieves (thēvz), ***n.*** plural of **thief.**

thiev·ish (thēv′ish), ***adj.*** 1. addicted to thieving, or stealing. 2. of, like, or characteristic of a thief; stealthy; furtive.

thigh (thī), ***n.*** [ME. *thi, thih;* AS. *theoh;* cf. D. *dij*, MHG. *diech*, etc.], 1. the part of the human leg between the knee and the hip. 2. a corresponding part in other vertebrates; region of the femur or, as in birds, the next lower segment of the leg. 3. the third segment (from the base) of an insect's leg; femur.

thigh·bone (thī′bōn′), ***n.*** the bone of the thigh, articulating with the tibia and the pelvis; femur: also **thigh bone.**

thig·mo·tac·tic (thig′mə-tak′tik), ***adj.*** of thigmotaxis.

thig·mo·tax·is (thig′mə-tak′sis), ***n.*** [Mod. L. < Gr. *thigma*, touch; + *-taxis*], in *biology*, involuntary reaction to simple contact with some outside object or body, as in motile cells.

thig·mot·ro·pism (thig-mot′rə-piz′m), ***n.*** [Mod. L. < Gr. *thigma*, touch; + *-tropism*], stereotropism.

thill (thil), ***n.*** [ME. & AS. *thille*, a stake, pole, plank; base as in *deal* (wood)], either of the two long pieces between which a horse is hitched to a wagon; shaft.

thim·ble (thim′b'l), ***n.*** [ME. *thimbel* (with unhistoric *-b-*), *thymel;* AS. *thymel*, thumbstall < *thuma*, a thumb, with *-el*, dim. suffix (cf. -LE)], 1. a small, pitted cap of metal, plastic, etc. worn on the finger in sewing to protect it in pushing the needle through the fabric, etc. 2. something resembling this; especially, a grooved, metal ring inserted in a loop of rope or in a sail's rope hole to prevent wear.

thim·ble·ber·ry (thim′b'l-ber′i), ***n.*** [*pl.* THIMBLEBERRIES (-iz)], any of various raspberries or blackberries with fruit shaped like a thimble.

thim·ble·ful (thim′b'l-fool′), ***n.*** [*pl.* THIMBLEFULS (-foolz′)], 1. as much as a thimble will hold; hence, 2. a very small quantity.

thim·ble·rig (thim′b'l-rig′), ***n.*** [cf. RIG], 1. a swindling game in which spectators are challenged to bet on the location of a small object ostensibly concealed under one of three cups or nutshells manipulated by a sleight-of-hand operator: also called *shell game.* 2. a thimblerigger. ***v.t.*** [THIMBLERIGGED (-rigd′), THIMBLERIGGING], to swindle, as by this game.

thim·ble·rig·ger (thim′b'l-rig′ẽr), ***n.*** 1. an operator of a thimblerig. 2. a swindler.

thim·ble·weed (thim′b'l-wēd′), ***n.*** 1. any of various coneflowers with cone-shaped disks and daisylike flowers; rudbeckia. 2. a variety of wood anemone.

thin (thin), ***adj.*** [THINNER (-ẽr), THINNEST (-ist)], [ME. *thinne;* AS. *thynne;* akin to G. *dünn;* IE. base **t(ə)nu-s*, stretched out, thin (< **ten-*, to stretch), seen also in *tenuis, tenuous*], 1. having relatively little depth; of little extent from one surface or side to the opposite: as, *thin* topsoil, *thin* paper. 2. having small diameter in relation to length: as, *thin* thread. 3. having little fat or flesh; lean; gaunt; slender. 4. having the constituent elements arranged loosely or at intervals; not dense or compact; sparse; specifically, *a*) scant in number; scattered: as, the audience was *thin. b*) of little density or consistency; very fluid; rare; tenuous: as, *thin* milk, *thin* air. *c*) of little body, richness, strength, etc.: as, a *thin* soup. 5. of little intensity; dim; faint; pale: as, *thin* colors. 6. of little volume or resonance; high-pitched and weak: as, a *thin* voice. 7. of little opacity; transparent; flimsy: as, a *thin* fabric; hence, 8. easily seen through; slight: as, a *thin* excuse. 9. of little substance or content; unsubstantial; inadequate; scanty: as, a *thin* plot, *thin* argument. 10. in *photography*, lacking contrast of light and shade: said of a negative or print. Opposed to *thick* (in senses 1, 2, 4*a*, 4*b*). ***adv.*** thinly. ***v.t. & v.i.*** [THINNED (thind), THINNING], [ME. *thinnen;* AS. (*ge*)*thynnian* < the *adj.*], to make or become thin or thinner: with *out, down,* etc.

SYN.—**thin** implies relatively little extent from one surface or side of a thing to the opposite and connotes lack of fleshiness, fullness, substance, etc.; **slender** and **slim** suggest a physical spareness that is more or less pleasing in proportion, but in extended senses, the words carry connotations of meagerness scantiness, etc. (a *slender* income, a *slim* possibility); **lean,** implying an absence of fat, figuratively connotes a lack of richness, productiveness, etc. (*lean* years); **slight** implies smallness and lightness or fragility in form or build and, in extended senses, suggests inconsiderableness in amount, extent, significance, etc. (a *slight* figure, difference, etc.); **tenuous** implies extreme physical thinness or fineness and, in extended senses, suggests insubstantiality, flimsiness, extreme subtlety, etc. (a *tenuous* film, plot, etc.). —***ANT.*** thick, substantial.

thine (*th*īn), ***pron.*** [ME. *thin;* AS. *thin*, genit. of *thu*, thou; ME. loss of *-n* before a consonant gives Mod. Eng. *thy*], the possessive case of **thou.** ***adj.*** thy: used especially before a word beginning with a vowel or unaspirated *h.*

thing (thiŋ), *n.* [ME.; AS. *thing*, a council, court, controversy; akin to G. *ding*, ON. *thing;* basic sense, "public assembly"; hence development "affairs—matters—things"; IE. base **teng-*, to draw, extend, in sense "span of time," whence Gmc. sense "specified time (for a meeting)"], 1. any matter, circumstance, affair, or concern. 2. that which is done, has been done, or is to be done; a happening, act, deed, incident, event, etc.: as, what a *thing* to do, he'll accomplish great *things*. 3. that which constitutes an end to be achieved, a step in a process, etc.: as, the next *thing* is to mix thoroughly. 4. that which is conceived, spoken of, or referred to as existing as an individual, distinguishable entity; specifically, *a*) any single entity distinguished from all others: as, every *thing* in the universe. *b*) a tangible object, as distinguished from a concept, quality, etc.: as, the book is a *thing;* its color is a quality. *c*) an inanimate object. *d*) an item, detail, etc.: as, not a *thing* has been overlooked. *e*) that which is represented, as distinguished from the word or symbol that represents it. 5. *pl. a*) personal belongings. *b*) clothes or clothing. 6. [Colloq.], a person: used in expressions of contempt, affection, pity, etc., as, poor *thing*!, a dear little *thing*. 7. [Colloq.], something mentioned but unnamed, as in contempt, or because the name is not known or remembered: as, it's that other *thing* I want. 8. in *law*, that which may be owned; a property: distinguished from *person*.

make a good thing of, [Colloq.], to profit by (some enterprise or experience).

see things, [Colloq.], to have hallucinations.

the thing, 1. that which is wise, advisable, essential, etc. 2. that which is the height of fashion or style.

‡thing (thiŋ, tiŋ), *n.* [ON., assembly; see prec.], a Scandinavian legislative body: also **ting**.

thing-in-it·self (thiŋ'in-it-self'), *n.* [transl. of G. *ding an sich*], in *Kantian philosophy*, that aspect of a thing which has reality beyond human perception and knowledge and, hence, can never be known.

thing·um·a·jig (thiŋ'əm-ə-jig'), *n.* [Colloq.], a thingumbob.

thing·um·bob (thiŋ'əm-bob'), *n.* [extension of older *thingum* < *thing*], [Colloq.], any device; contrivance; gadget: humorous substitute for a name not known or temporarily forgotten.

think (thiŋk), *v.t.* [THOUGHT (thôt), THINKING], [< ME. *thenchen*, to think, confused with *thinchen*, to seem; AS. *thencan*, to think, caus. of *thyncan*, to seem; for IE. base see THANK, *v.*], 1. to form or have in the mind; conceive: as, I am *thinking* black thoughts. 2. to hold in one's opinion; judge; consider: as, I *think* her charming. 3. to believe; surmise; expect: as, they *think* they can come, I did not *think* to see you. 4. to determine, resolve, work out, etc. by reasoning: as, he *thought* his way out of the dilemma. 5. to have in intent; purpose; intend: as, he *thinks* to deceive me. 6. to put, throw, etc. (into a specified condition) by mental concentration: as, she *thought* herself into this dilemma. 7. to bring to mind, or recollect: as, *think* how we were once friends. 8. to keep continually in the mind; be obsessed with: as, he *thinks* model airplanes all day long. *v.i.* 1. to use the mind for arriving at conclusions, making decisions, drawing inferences, etc.; reflect; reason: as, you must learn to *think*. 2. to have an opinion, belief, expectation, etc.: as, I just *think* so. 3. to weigh something mentally; reflect: as, *think* before you act.

think aloud, to speak one's thoughts as they occur: also **think out loud**.

think better of, 1. to form a new, more favorable opinion of. 2. to make a more sensible or practical decision after reconsidering.

think nothing of, 1. to attach no importance to. 2. to regard as easy to do.

think of, 1. to call to mind; recall; remember. 2. to have an opinion, judgment, etc. of. 3. to discover; invent; conceive of. 4. to allow oneself to consider. 5. to have regard for; consider the welfare of.

think out, 1. to think about completely or to the end. 2. to work out, solve, discover, or plan by thinking.

think over, to give thought to; ponder well, as for reconsideration.

think through, to think about until one reaches a conclusion or resolution.

think twice, to reconsider; pause to think about again.

think up, to invent, contrive, plan, etc. by thinking.

SYN.—**think** is the general word meaning to exercise the mental faculties so as to form ideas, arrive at conclusions, etc. (learn to *think* clearly); **reason** implies a logical sequence of thought, starting with what is known or assumed and advancing through the inferences drawn to a definite conclusion (he *reasoned* that she would come); **cogitate** is used, sometimes humorously, of a person who is, or appears to be, thinking hard (I was not daydreaming but rather *cogitating*); **reflect** implies a turning of one's thoughts on or back on a subject and connotes deep or quiet continued thought (he *reflected* on the day's events); **speculate** implies a reasoning on the basis of incomplete or uncertain evidence and therefore stresses the conjectural character of the opinions formed (to *speculate* on the possibility of life on Mars); **deliberate** implies careful and thorough consideration of a matter in order to arrive at a conclusion (the jury *deliberated* on the case).

think (thiŋk), *v.i.* [THOUGHT (thôt), THINKING], [< ME. *thinchen*, to seem, confused with *thenchen*, to think; AS. *thyncan;* cf. prec. THINK], to seem; appear: used impersonally with an indirect object, now only in the compounds *methinks* and *methought*.

think·a·ble (thiŋk'ə-b'l), *adj.* that can be thought; conceivable.

think·ing (thiŋk'iŋ), *adj.* [pp. of *think*], 1. that thinks or can think; rational. 2. thoughtful or reflective by nature. *n.* the action of one who thinks or the result of such action; thought.

thin·ner (thin'ẽr), *n.* a person or thing that thins; especially, a substance or liquid added, as turpentine to paint, for thinning.

thin·nish (thin'ish), *adj.* somewhat thin.

thin-skinned (thin'skind'), *adj.* 1. having a thin skin. 2. sensitive to criticism, insult, etc.; easily hurt.

thi·o- (thī'ō, thī'ə), [< Gr. *theion*, brimstone], a combining form meaning *sulfur*, used in chemical terms to indicate the replacement of oxygen in an acid radical by negatively divalent sulfur: also, before a vowel, **thi-**.

thi·o·al·de·hyde (thī'ō-al'də-hīd'), *n.* [*thio-* + *aldehyde*], any of a group of organic chemical compounds containing the monovalent radical -CHS; an aldehyde in which sulfur has replaced the oxygen.

thi·o·an·ti·mo·nate (thī'ō-an'ti-mə-nāt'), *n.* any of a group of chemical compounds considered salts of thioantimonic acid.

thi·o·an·ti·mo·ni·ate (thī'ō-an'ti-mō'ni-āt'), *n.* thioantimonate.

thi·o·an·ti·mon·ic acid (thī'ō-an'ti-mon'ik), [*thio-* + *antimonic*], a hypothetical acid, H_3SbS_4, known only in the form of its salts.

thi·o·an·ti·mo·ni·ous acid (thī'ō-an'ti-mō'ni-əs), [*thio-* + *antimonious*], any of a group of hypothetical acids, H_3SbS_3, $HSbS_2$, $H_4Sb_2S_5$, and $H_2Sb_4S_7$, known only in the forms of their salts in solution.

thi·o·an·ti·mo·nite (thī'ō-an'ti-mə-nīt'), *n.* any of a group of chemical compounds known only in solution and considered salts of the thioantimonious acids.

thi·o·ar·se·nate (thī'ō-är'sə-nāt'), *n.* any of a group of chemical compounds considered salts of the thioarsenic acids.

thi·o·ar·sen·ic acid (thī'ō-är-sen'ik), [*thio-* + *arsenic*], any of three hypothetical acids, H_3AsS_4, $HAsS_3$, and $H_4As_2S_7$, known only in the forms of their salts.

thi·o·ar·se·ni·ous acid (thī'ō-är-sē'ni-əs), [*thio-* + *arsenious*], any of a group of hypothetical acids, H_3AsS_3, $HAsS_2$, $H_4As_2S_5$, known only in the forms of their salts.

thi·o·ar·se·nite (thī'ō-är'sə-nīt'), *n.* any of a group of chemical compounds considered salts of the thioarsenious acids.

thi·o·cy·a·nate (thī'ō-sī'ə-nāt'), *n.* a salt or ester of thiocyanic acid, containing the monovalent radical -SCN.

thi·o·cy·an·ic acid (thī'ō-si-an'ik), [*thio-* + *cyanic*], a colorless, unstable acid, HSCN, with a penetrating odor, known chiefly in the form of its salts.

thi·ol (thī'ōl, thī'ol), *n.* [< *thio-* + *-ol*], any of a class of chemical compounds analogous to the alcohols and characterized by the substitution of sulfur for oxygen in the OH radical; mercaptan.

thi·on·ic (thī-on'ik), *adj.* [< Gr. *theion*, brimstone, sulfur; + *-ic*], of, containing, or derived from sulfur.

thionic acid, 1. any organic chemical compound containing the monovalent CS·OH radical. 2. any of a group of acids with the general formula $H_2S_nO_6$, in which n varies from 2 to 5.

thi·o·nine (thī'ə-nēn', thī'ə-nin), *n.* [< Gr. *theion*, brimstone, sulfur; + *-ine*], a dark-green crystalline thiazine base, $C_{12}H_9N_3S$, producing a violet dye in solution, used especially as a stain in microscopy.

thi·o·nyl (thī'ə-nil), *n.* [< Gr. *theion*, brimstone, sulfur; + *-yl*], the divalent radical SO.

thi·o·phen (thī'ə-fen), *n.* thiophene.

thi·o·phene (thī'ə-fēn'), *n.* [*thio-* + *phenyl* + *-ene*], a heterocyclic chemical compound, C_4H_4S, a colorless liquid resembling benzene and found in coal tar.

thi·o·sin·am·in (thī'ō-sin-am'in), *n.* thiosinamine.

thi·o·sin·am·ine (thī'ō-sin-am'in, thī'ə-sin'ə-mēn'), *n.* [*thio-* + *sinamine* (< L. *sinapis*, mustard; + *amine*)], a colorless, crystalline chemical compound, $C_4H_8N_2S$, produced by the reaction of ammonia on mustard oil and used in medicine for resolving scar tissue.

thi·o·sul·fate (thī'ə-sul'fāt), *n.* a salt of thiosulfuric acid; especially, sodium thiosulfate: see **hypo**.

thi·o·sul·fu·ric acid (thī'ō-sul-fyoor'ik), [*thio-* + *sul-*

furic], an unstable acid, $H_2S_2O_3$, whose salts are used in photography, as an antichlor in bleaching, etc.

thi·o·u·re·a (thī'ō-yoo-rē'ə, thī'ō-yoor'i-ə), *n.* [Mod. L.; see THIO- & UREA], a colorless, crystalline chemical compound, $CS(NH_2)_2$, used in organic synthesis and as a reagent for bismuth.

third (thūrd), *adj.* [ME. *thirde, thridde;* AS. *thridda, thrydda* < base of *thrie,* three + suffix (IE. **-tjos*); akin to G. *dritte,* L. *tertius* (cf. TERTIARY); altered in ME. by metathesis], 1. preceded by two others in a series; 3(r)d. 2. designating any of the three equal parts of something. *n.* 1. the one following the second. 2. any of the three equal parts of something; 1/3. 3. one sixtieth of a second, as of time or of the arc of an angle. 4. the third forward gear ratio of an automotive vehicle: in most automobiles it is the highest. 5. *pl.* in *law,* *a*) the third part of a deceased man's estate, which, under certain conditions, goes unrestrictedly to his widow. *b*) loosely, a widow's dower. 6. in *music,* *a*) an interval of three degrees in a diatonic scale. *b*) a tone three degrees above or below a given tone. *c*) the combination of two notes separated by this interval. *d*) the third tone of a diatonic scale.

third base, in *baseball,* the base between second base and home plate, located on the pitcher's right.

third-class (thūrd'klas', thūrd'kläs'), *adj.* of the class, rank, excellence, etc. next below the second; specifically, *a*) designating or of accommodations next below the second: as, a *third-class* railway carriage. *b*) designating or of a class of mail consisting of books, circulars, etc. *adv.* 1. with accommodations next below the second: as, they traveled to Berlin *third-class.* 2. as or by third-class mail.

third-de·gree (thūrd'di-grē'), *adj.* of the third degree.

third degree, 1. in *Freemasonry,* the degree of master mason. 2. [prob. < ritual of Freemasons in conferring the preceding], severe treatment or torture by police, etc. to force a confession or information.

third estate, see **estate** (sense 2).

third eyelid, the nictitating membrane.

Third International, the international organization of Communist parties, founded in Moscow in 1919 and dissolved in 1943: also called *Communist International, Comintern.*

third·ly (thūrd'li), *adv.* in the third place; third: used chiefly in enumerating topics.

third person, that form of a pronoun or verb which refers to the person or thing spoken of: in *he does, he* and *does* are in the third person.

third rail, an extra rail used in some electric railroads, instead of an overhead wire, for supplying power.

third-rate (thūrd'rāt'), *adj.* 1. third in quality or other rating; third-class. 2. definitely inferior; very poor.

Third Republic, the republic established in France in 1870, after the fall of Napoleon III, lasting until the German occupation of France in World War II.

thirl (thūrl), *n.* thirlage. *v.t. & v.i.* [AS. *thyrlian* < *thyrel,* a hole]. [Dial.], 1. to pierce. 2. to thrill.

thirl·age (thūrl'ij), *n.* [< ME. *thrillen, thirlen,* to hold in bondage, hold to a condition of servitude], 1. a form of feudal servitude, by which tenants were required to grind their grain at a specified mill and pay a specified fee for this. 2. the fee paid.

thirst (thūrst), *n.* [ME. *thirst, thurst;* AS. *thurst;* akin to G. *durst;* Gmc. **thur-stus;* IE. base **ters-,* to dry, seen also in *torrid, torrent*], 1. the uncomfortable or distressful feeling caused by a desire or need for water or other drink and characterized generally by a sensation of dryness in the mouth and throat. 2. [Colloq.], a craving for alcoholic liquor. 3. a strong desire; craving; longing. *v.i.* 1. to want to drink; be thirsty. 2. to have a strong desire or craving.

thirst·i·ly (thūrs't'l-i), *adv.* in a thirsty manner.

thirst·i·ness (thūrs'ti-nis), *n.* the state of being thirsty.

thirst·y (thūrs'ti), *adj.* [THIRSTIER (-ti-ēr), THIRSTIEST (-ti-ist)], [ME. *thyrsti;* AS. *thurstig*], 1. feeling thirst; wanting to drink. 2. lacking water or moisture; dry; parched: as, *thirsty* fields. 3. [Colloq.], causing thirst: as, *thirsty* work. 4. having strong desire; craving.

thir·teen (thūr'tēn'), *adj.* [ME. *thrittene;* AS. *threotyne;* see THREE & -TEEN], three more than ten. *n.* the cardinal number between twelve and fourteen; 13; XIII.

thir·teenth (thūr'tēnth'), *adj.* [ME. *thirtenth;* see THIRTEEN & -TH], 1. preceded by twelve others in a series; 13th. 2. designating any of the thirteen equal parts of something. *n.* 1. the one following the twelfth. 2. any of the thirteen equal parts of something; 1/13.

thir·ti·eth (thūr'ti-ith), *adj.* [< ME. *thrittythe,* with form changed after *thirty;* AS. *thritigotha;* see -TH], 1. preceded by twenty-nine others in a series; 30th. 2. designating any of the thirty equal parts of something. *n.* 1. the one following the twenty-ninth. 2. any of the thirty equal parts of something; 1/30.

thir·ty (thūr'ti), *adj.* [ME. *thirti* (late form), *thritti;* AS. *thritig, thrittig* < *thri, threo,* three; see THREE & -TY (tens)], three times ten. *n.* [*pl.* THIRTIES (-tiz)], the cardinal number between twenty-nine and thirty-one; 30; XXX.

the thirties, the years from thirty through thirty-nine (of a century or a person's age).

Thir·ty-nine Articles (thūr'ti-nīn'), the thirty-nine points of doctrine of the Church of England and the Episcopal Church.

thir·ty-sec·ond note (thūr'ti-sek'ənd), in *music,* a note (𝅘𝅥𝅰) having 1/32 the duration of a whole note: also called *demisemiquaver.*

thir·ty-two·mo (thūr'ti-tōō'mō'), *n.* [see -MO], 1. the page size of a book made up of printer's sheets folded into 32 leaves, each leaf approximately 3 1/2 by 5 1/2 inches. 2. a book consisting of pages of this size: written *32mo* (no period). *adj.* consisting of pages of this size.

Thirty Years' War, a series of European wars (1618–1648) on political and religious issues, fought originally between German Catholics and German Protestants, but later involving the Swedish, French, and Spanish.

this (*th*is), *pron.* [*pl.* THESE (*th*ēz)], [ME. *this, thes;* AS. *thes,* masc., *this,* neut. < the base of the demonstrative pron.; see THAT], 1. the person or thing mentioned or understood: as, *this* is John, *this* tastes good. 2. the thing that is nearer: distinguished from *that,* as, I can see *this* more clearly than that. 3. one of two things that are compared or contrasted: distinguished from *that,* as, of the two possibilities, *this* is more likely than that. 4. the fact, idea, etc. that is about to be stated: as, "*this* above all: to thine ownself be true." 5. the fact, idea, etc. that has just been mentioned: as, *this* leads us to the following conclusion. *adj.* 1. designating the person or thing mentioned or understood: as, *this* man was John, *this* pie tastes good. 2. designating the thing that is nearer: distinguished from *that,* as, I can see *this* house more clearly than that one across the street. 3. designating one of two things that are compared or contrasted, as contradistinguished from *that*: as, of the two, *this* possibility is more likely than that one. 4. designating something about to be stated: as, *this* claim I make: I was his friend. 5. designating something that has just been mentioned: as, *this* evidence leads us to the following conclusion. 6. these: used of things considered collectively or as a unit: as, by *this* means. *adv.* to this extent; so: as, it was *this* big.

Thisbe, see **Pyramus and Thisbe.**

this·tle (this''l), *n.* [ME. & AS. *thistel;* akin to G. *distel;* IE. base **(s)teig-,* a point, seen also in Sans. *tig-má-h,* pointed, sharp], any of various related plants with prickly leaves and heads of white, purple, pink, or yellow flowers.

THISTLE

this·tle·down (this''l-doun'), *n.* the down attached to the flower head of a thistle.

this·tly (this'li), *adj.* [THISTLIER (-li-ēr), THISTLIEST (-li-ist)], 1. like a thistle or thistles; prickly. 2. full of or overgrown with thistles.

thith·er (thi*th*'ēr, *th*i*th*'ēr), *adv.* [ME. *thider;* AS. *thider, thyder* < demonstrative stem seen in *the, that, there, this,* etc.], to or toward that place or direction: opposed to *hither.* *adj.* on that (more distant) side.

thith·er·to (thi*th*'ēr-tōō', *th*i*th*'ēr-tōō'), *adv.* until that time; up to then.

thith·er·ward (thi*th*'ēr-wērd, *th*i*th*'ēr-wērd), *adv.* thither.

thith·er·wards (thi*th*'ēr-wērdz, *th*i*th*'ēr-wērdz), *adv.* thitherward.

tho, tho' (*th*ō), *conj. & adv.* though.

thole (thōl), *n.* [ME. & AS. *thol;* akin to D. *dol;* IE. **tu-el* < base **tēu-,* to swell, rise, increase, seen also in *tumor, tumult*], a pin or either of a pair of pins, made of metal or wood and set vertically in the gunwale of a boat to serve as a fulcrum for an oar.

thole (thōl), *v.t.* [THOLED (thōld), THOLING], [ME. *tholien, tholen;* AS. *tholian;* IE. base **tel-, *tol-,* to bear, seen also in *tolerate*], [Archaic or British Dial.], to suffer; endure; undergo; tolerate.

thole·pin (thōl'pin'), *n.* a thole.

Thom·as (tom'əs), [LL.; Gr. *Thōmas;* Ar. *tě'ōma,* lit., a twin], a masculine name: diminutives, *Tom, Tommy.* *n.* one of the twelve apostles, who doubted at first the resurrection of Jesus: John 20:24–29.

Tho·mas, Am·broise (än'brwàz' tô'mä'), 1811–1896; French composer.

Thom·as, George Henry (tom'əs), 1816–1870; Union general in the Civil War.

Thomas, Norman Mat·toon (mə-tōōn'), 1884– ; American Socialist leader.

Thomas, Theodore, 1835–1905; American orchestral conductor born in Germany.

Thomas à Beck·et, Saint (ə bek'it), 1118?–1170; archbishop of Canterbury; opposed Henry II and was murdered: his day is December 29.

Thomas à Kem·pis (ə kem′pis), (*Thomas Hamerken von Kempen* or *Thomas Hämmerlein*), 1380–1471; German monk and scholar; regarded as author of *Imitation of Christ.*

Thomas Aquinas, Saint, see **Aquinas.**

Tho·mism (tō′miz'm, thō′miz'm), *n.* the theological and philosophical doctrines of Thomas Aquinas and his followers: it formed the basis of 13th-century scholasticism.

Tho·mist (tō′mist, thō′mist), *adj.* having to do with Thomas Aquinas, his doctrines, or his followers. *n.* a follower of Thomas Aquinas; adherent of Thomism.

Thomp·son, Francis (tomp′s'n, tom′s'n), 1859–1907; English poet.

Thompson submachine gun, a type of submachine gun: a trade-mark: see **submachine gun.**

Thom·son, James (tom′s'n, tomp′s'n), 1700–1748; Scottish poet.

Thomson, J. Arthur, (*John Arthur Thomson*), 1861–1933; Scottish naturalist and author.

Thomson, Sir **Joseph John,** 1856–1940; English physicist; received Nobel prize in physics, 1906.

Thomson, William, see **Kelvin, William Thomson.**

thong (thôŋ), *n.* [ME. *thong, thwang;* AS. *thwang,* a twisted string, thong; for IE. base see TWINGE], 1. a narrow strip of leather, etc. used as a lace, strap, etc. 2. a whiplash, as of plaited strips of hide.

Thor (thôr), *n.* [ON. *Thorr* < base seen in *thunder;* cf. THURSDAY], in *Norse mythology,* the god of thunder, war, and strength, and the son of Odin: he had a magic hammer with which he destroyed the foes of the gods.

tho·rac·ic (thô-ras′ik, thō-ras′ik), *adj.* [Mod. L. *thoracicus;* Gr. *thōrakikos*], of, in, or near the thorax.

thoracic duct, the main canal of the lymphatic system, passing along the front of the spinal column and serving to collect lymph from various parts of the body, conveying it into the left subclavian vein.

tho·ra·ci·co- (thô-ras′i-kō, thō-ras′i-kō), thoraco- (sense 2).

tho·rac·i·co·lum·bar (thô-ras′i-kō-lum′bẽr, thō-ras′i-kō-lum′bẽr), *adj.* thoracolumbar.

tho·ra·co- (thôr′ə-kō, thō-rā′kō), [Gr. *thōrako-*], a combining form meaning: 1. *the thorax,* as in *thoracoplasty.* 2. *the thorax and,* as in *thoracolumbar.* Also, before a vowel, **thorac-.**

tho·ra·co·lum·bar (thôr′ə-kō-lum′bẽr, thō-rā′kō-lum′bẽr), *adj.* of the thoracic and lumbar regions.

tho·ra·co·plas·ty (thôr′ə-kō-plas′ti, thō-rā′kō-plas′ti), *n.* [*thoraco-* + *-plasty*], plastic surgery of the thorax.

tho·rax (thôr′aks, thō′raks), *n.* [*pl.* THORAXES (-iz), THORACES (-ə-sēz′, -rə-sēz′)], [L.; Gr. *thōrax,* the chest, breastplate], 1. in man and the higher vertebrates, the part of the body between the neck and the abdomen, containing the heart, lungs, etc.; chest. 2. the middle one of the three main segments of an insect's body.

Thor·eau, Henry David (thôr′ō, thə-rō′, thō′rō), 1817–1862; American naturalist, philosopher, and writer.

tho·ri·a (thôr′i-ə, thō′ri-ə), *n.* [Mod. L.; see THORIUM], thorium oxide, ThO_2, a white, earthy powder.

tho·ri·a·nite (thôr′i-ə-nīt′, thō′ri-ə-nīt′), *n.* [< *thorium* + *-ite*], a black, crystalline, radioactive mineral, consisting chiefly of the oxides of thorium and uranium.

thor·ic (thôr′ik, thō′rik), *adj.* of or containing thorium.

tho·rite (thôr′īt, thō′rīt), *n.* [Sw. *thorit;* see THOR & -ITE], a dark-brown or black mineral, $ThSiO_4$, a native silicate of thorium.

tho·ri·um (thôr′i-əm, thō′ri-əm), *n.* [Mod. L. < *Thor*], a rare, grayish, radioactive chemical element occurring in monazite and thorite: symbol, Th; at. wt., 232.12; at. no., 90.

Thorn (tôrn), *n.* Toruń.

thorn (thôrn), *n.* [ME.; AS.; akin to G. *dorn;* IE. base *(*s*)*ter-*, prickly plant, prob. < **ster-*, to be stiff, be rigid], 1. a very short, hard, leafless branch or stem with a sharp point. 2. any small tree or shrub bearing thorns. 3. the wood of any of these plants. 4. a sharp, pointed protuberance on an animal; spine. 5. any tenacious cause of hurt, irritation, annoyance, or worry: from the manner in which thorns prick. 6. in Old English & Old Norse, the runic character (þ), corresponding to either sound of English *th,* as in *this* or *thick:* so called because it was the first letter of the word *thorn:* cf. **ye** (the).

thorn in the flesh (or **side**), a cause of annoyance, irritation, etc., especially a persistent one.

thorn apple, 1. a hawthorn or its applelike fruit; haw. 2. a Jimson weed or any other related plant.

thorn·back (thôrn′bak′), *n.* 1. a European ray with many tubercles on its back and a double row of spines on its tail. 2. a large spider crab with a spiny back.

Thorn·dike, Edward Lee (thôrn′dīk′), 1874–1949; American psychologist, educator, and lexicographer.

thorn·i·ness (thôr′ni-nis), *n.* the state or quality of being thorny.

thorn letter, a thorn (sense 6).

thorn·y (thôr′ni), *adj.* [THORNIER (-ni-ẽr), THORNIEST (-ni-ist)], 1. full of thorns; brambly; prickly. 2. having thorns or spines: said of some animals. 3. like a thorn; sharp. 4. full of obstacles, vexations, pain, etc.: as, the *thorny* road to peace. 5. full of controversial points; difficult; contentious: as, a *thorny* problem.

thor·o (thũr′ō, thũr′ə), *adj., prep., adv.* thorough.

tho·ron (thôr′on, thō′ron), *n.* [Mod. L. < *thorium* + *-on* as in *argon*], a radioactive isotope of radon, resulting from the disintegration of thorium: symbol, Tn; at. wt., 220; at. no., 86.

thor·ough (thũr′ō; *also, esp. in compounding,* thũr′ə), *prep. & adv.* [ME. *thoruh, thuruh:* an emphatic var. of *through* (see THROUGH)], [Obs.], through. *adj.* 1. originally, passing through: now chiefly in combination, as in *thoroughfare.* 2. done or proceeding through to the end; thoroughgoing; complete; finished. 3. that is completely (as described); out-and-out; absolute: as, a *thorough* rascal. 4. very exact, accurate, or painstaking, especially with regard to details: as, a *thorough* person. *n.* [T-], in *English history,* the thorough, ruthless administrative policies under Charles I, as carried out by William Laud and the Earl of Strafford.

thorough bass (bās), in *music,* 1. formerly, a system of indicating accompanying chords by placing figures representing complete chords under the notes of the bass. 2. the figures so used. 3. loosely, the theory of harmony.

thorough brace, either of a pair of leather straps supporting the body of a coach or other horse-drawn vehicle and often serving as springs.

thor·ough·bred (thũr′ə-bred′), *adj.* 1. of pure stock; bred of parents of official pedigree: said of horses, dogs, etc. 2. thoroughly trained, educated, cultured, etc.; well-bred. *n.* 1. a thoroughbred animal; specifically, [T-], any of a breed of race horses developed originally by crossing English with Turkish and Arabic horses. 2. a cultured, well-bred person.

thor·ough·fare (thũr′ə-fâr′), *n.* [ME. *thurghfare, thorough fare* < *thurgh* (see THROUGH) + *fare* (see FARE); cf. AS. *thurhfaran, v.*], 1. a way or passage through. 2. a public, unobstructed street open at both ends, especially one through which there is much traffic; highway; main road.

thor·ough·go·ing (thũr′ə-gō′iŋ), *adj.* very thorough (senses 2, 3, 4).

thor·ough·paced (thũr′ə-pāst′), *adj.* 1. thoroughly trained in all paces or gaits: said of horses; hence, 2. thoroughgoing; out-and-out.

thor·ough·wort (thũr′ə-wũrt′), *n.* a short plant with flat clusters of grayish-white flowers and a stem passing through the leaf blade; boneset.

thorp, thorpe (thôrp), *n.* [ME. *thorp, thrope;* AS. *throp, thorp;* akin to G. *dorf,* village], a little group of houses in the country; village; hamlet: now mainly in place names.

those (thōz), *adj. & pron.* [ME. *thas, thos;* AS. *thas, thæs,* pl. of *thes,* this; cf. THIS, THAT], plural of **that.**

Thoth (thōth, tōt), *n.* [L.; Gr. *Thōth;* Egypt. *Ṭeḥuti*], the ancient Egyptian god of learning and magic, the measurer of time and inventor of numbers, represented as having a human body and the head of a dog or of an ibis.

thou (*th*ou), *pron.* [*pl. nom. & obj.* YOU (yōō), YE (yē, yi), *poss.* YOUR (yoor, yũr), YOURS (yoorz, yũrz)], [ME. *thu, thou;* AS. *thu;* akin to G. *du;* IE. **tu,* seen also in L. *tu,* Sans. *tu,* etc.], the nominative second person singular of the personal pronoun: formerly used in familiar address but now replaced by *you* except in poetic or religious use, the speech of Friends, or Quakers (cf. **thee**), and some British dialects: *thee* is the objective case form, *thy* or *thine* the possessive, and *thyself* the intensive and reflexive.

though (*th*ō), *conj.* [ME. *thah, theah, thogh* < AS. *theah* but influenced by ON. *tho;* akin to G. *doch,* yet, still, however], 1. in spite of the fact that; notwithstanding that; although: as, *though* the car was repaired, it still rattled. 2. all the same; yet; still: as, they finally made it, *though* I never thought they would. 3. even if; supposing that: as, *though* he may fail, he will have tried. *adv.* however; nevertheless: used as a conjunctive adverb. Also spelled **tho, tho'.**

as though, as it (or I, you, he, etc.) would if; as if.

thought (thôt), *n.* [ME. *thouht;* AS. *thoht* < **thanxt* < base of *thencan* (see THINK); akin to *-dacht-* in G. *gedachtnis,* memory], 1. the act or process of thinking; reflection; meditation; cogitation. 2. the power of reasoning or of conceiving ideas; capacity for thinking; intellect; imagination. 3. a result of thinking; idea, concept, opinion, etc. 4. the ideas, principles, opinions, etc. prevalent at a given time, among a given people, or in a given place: as, modern *thought* in child education. 5. attention; consideration; heed: as, don't give it a moment's *thought.* 6. mental engrossment; preoccupation; concentration: as, deep in *thought.* 7.

intention or expectation: as, I had no *thought* of seeing her. 8. a little; trifle; as, please be a *thought* more careful. —*SYN.* see **idea.**

thought (thôt), past tense and past participle of **think.**

thought·ful (thôt′fəl), *adj.* 1. full of thought; meditative; thinking: as, John was quiet and *thoughtful* for a while. 2. showing or characterized by thought; serious: as, a *thoughtful* essay. 3. heedful, careful, attentive, etc.; especially, considerate of others; kind.

SYN.—**thoughtful,** as compared here, implies the showing of thought for the comfort or well-being of others, as by anticipating their needs or wishes (it was *thoughtful* of you to call); **considerate** implies a thoughtful or sympathetic regard for the feelings or circumstances of others, as in sparing them pain, distress, or discomfort (*considerate* enough to extend the time for payment); **attentive** implies a constant thoughtfulness as shown by repeated acts of consideration, courtesy, or devotion (an *attentive* suitor). —*ANT.* thoughtless.

thought·less (thôt′lis), *adj.* 1. not stopping to think; careless; heedless; reckless. 2. not given thought; ill-considered; rash. 3. not considerate of others; inconsiderate; remiss. 4. stupid; dull-witted.

thou·sand (thou′z′nd), *adj. & n.* [ME. & AS. *thusend;* akin to G. *tausend;* IE. base ***tēu-**, to swell, increase, prob. with 2d element < or influenced by the base of *hund-* in *hundred*], ten hundred; 1,000 or M.

thou·sand·fold (thou′z′nd-fōld′), *adj.* [see -FOLD], 1. having a thousand parts. 2. having a thousand times as much or as many. *adv.* a thousand times as much or as many: with *a.* *n.* a number or amount a thousand times as great.

Thousand Island dressing, mayonnaise with minced capers or pickles, catsup, etc., used as a salad dressing.

Thousand Islands, a group of islands in the upper St. Lawrence River, belonging to New York State and Ontario, Canada.

thou·sandth (thou′z′ndth), *adj.* [*thousand* + *-th*], 1. coming last in a series of a thousand. 2. designating any of the thousand equal parts of something. *n.* 1. the thousandth one of a series. 2. any of the thousand equal parts of something.

thow·less (thou′lis), *adj.* [Scot.], thewless.

Thrace (thrās), *n.* an ancient region in the eastern Balkan Peninsula: see **Roman Empire,** map.

Thra·cian (thrā′shən), *adj.* of Thrace, its people, or culture. *n.* a native or inhabitant of Thrace.

thrall (thrôl), *n.* [ME. *thral;* AS. *thræl* < ON. *thræll;* prob. < Gmc. ***thranhilaz**, lit., the constrained one < IE. base ***trenq-**, to shove, press hard, seen also in G. *drängen*, to press], 1. originally, a slave or bondman. 2. a person in moral or psychological bondage. 3. thralldom. *v.t.* [Archaic], to put in thralldom; enslave. *adj.* [Rare], enslaved.

thrall·dom, thral·dom (thrôl′dəm), *n.* the condition of being a thrall; servitude; slavery.

thrash (thrash), *v.t.* [ME. *threschen;* AS. *threscan, therscan;* akin to G. *dreschen*, to thresh; ? < IE. base ***ter-**, to rub, rub away], 1. to thresh. 2. to beat or flog, as with a flail; hence, 3. to defeat completely or mercilessly. *v.i.* 1. to thresh. 2. to move violently, especially swinging one's arms about like threshing flails; toss about; lash. 3. in *nautical usage*, to force one's way against opposing wind, tide, etc. *n.* the act of thrashing; specifically, in *swimming*, a kick used in the crawl and backstroke.—*SYN.* see **beat.**

thrash out, to discuss thoroughly and conclusively.

thrash·er (thrash′ẽr), *n.* 1. a person or thing that thrashes. 2. a thresher (sense 3).

thrash·er (thrash′ẽr), *n.* [Eng. dial. *thresher*, ult. < same source as *thrush*], any of a group of American songbirds resembling the thrush but having a long, stiff tail and a long bill.

thrash·ing (thrash′iŋ), *n.* a beating; flogging.

thra·son·i·cal (thrə-son′i-k′l), *adj.* [< L. *Thraso* (< Gr. *Thrason* < *thrasus*, too bold, rash), braggart in Terence's *Eunuch;* + *-ical*], boastful.

thrawn (thrôn), *adj.* [< *thraw*, dial. form of *throw*], [Scot.], 1. crooked; twisted. 2. perverse.

thread (thred), *n.* [ME. *threde;* AS. *thræd* (akin to G. *draht*) < base of *thrawan*, to twist; see THROW], 1. a very fine cord composed of a strand or strands of spun silk, flax, cotton, etc., used in sewing: used without the article to mean such cords collectively, as, use black *thread.* 2. any of the yarns of which a fabric is woven. 3. a fine, threadlike filament, as of organic tissue, metal, glass, plastic, etc. 4. a thin line, stratum, vein, stream, ray, etc. of something. 5. an element suggestive of a thread in its continuousness, length, sequence, etc.: as, the *thread* of a story, the *thread* of life. 6. the spiral or helical ridge of a screw, bolt, nut, etc. *v.t.* 1. to put a thread through the eye of (a needle, etc.). 2. to string (beads, etc.) on or as on a thread. 3. *a*) to pass through like a thread; weave in and out of: as, he *threaded* the streets. *b*) to pervade: as, a note of hope *threaded* the story. *c*) to follow or proceed on in a threadlike fashion: as, *thread* one's way. 4. to fashion a thread (sense 6) on or in (a screw, pipe, etc.). *v.i.* 1. to go along or proceed in a threadlike fashion; wind one's way or its way. 2. to form a thread when dropped from a spoon: said of boiling sirup, etc. that has reached a certain consistency.

thread·bare (thred′bâr′), *adj.* 1. worn down so that the threads show; having the nap or surface fibers worn off: as, *threadbare* carpets. 2. wearing old, worn clothes; shabby. 3. that has lost freshness or novelty; stale; trite: as, a *threadbare* argument.

thread·fin (thred′fin′), *n.* any of a group of fish whose pectoral fin ends in threadlike rays.

thread mark, a marking of paper currency by incorporating colored silk fibers in the paper pulp to make counterfeiting difficult.

thread·worm (thred′wûrm′), *n.* any of a group of threadlike, parasitic worms; especially, the pinworm.

thread·y (thred′i), *adj.* [THREADIER (-i-ẽr), THREADIEST (-i-ist)], 1. of or like a thread; stringy; fibrous; filamentous. 2. forming threads; viscid: said of liquids. 3. of or covered with threads or threadlike parts; fibrous. 4. resembling a thread in thinness or feebleness: as, a *thready* voice.

threap (thrēp), *v.t.* [ME. *threpen;* AS. *threapian*, to rebuke], [Scot. or British Dial.], 1. to scold; chide. 2. to maintain or assert obstinately.

threat (thret), *n.* [ME. *threte;* AS. *threat*, a throng, painful pressure; akin to G. (*ver*)*driessen*, to grieve, annoy; IE. base ***treud-**, to push, press, seen also in *intrude, protrude;* cf. THRUST], 1. a statement or expression of intention to hurt, destroy, punish, etc., as in retaliation or intimidation. 2. an indication of imminent danger, harm, evil, etc.: as, the *threat* of war. *v.t. & v.i.* [Obs.], to threaten.

threat·en (thret′′n), *v.t.* [ME. *thretnen;* AS. *threatnian*], 1. to make threats against; express one's intention of hurting, punishing, etc. 2. to be a menacing indication of (something dangerous, evil, etc.): as, those clouds *threaten* snow. 3. to be a source of danger, harm, etc. to. 4. to express intention to inflict (injury, retaliation, etc.). *v.i.* 1. to make threats. 2. to give an indication of danger or distress; be menacing.

SYN.—**threaten** implies a warning of impending punishment, danger, evil, etc. by words, actions, events, conditions, signs, etc. (he *threatened* to retaliate, the clouds *threaten* rain); **menace** stresses the frightening or hostile character of that which threatens (he *menaced* me with a revolver).

three (thrē), *adj.* [ME. *thri, thre;* AS. *threo, thrie;* akin to G. *drei;* IE. base ***trei-**, seen also in L. *tres, tria, tri-*, etc.; cf. TRI-], totaling one more than two. *n.* 1. the cardinal number between two and four; 3; III. 2. a domino, die, card, etc. with three spots.

three-bag·ger (thrē′bag′ẽr), *n.* [Slang], a three-base hit.

three-base hit (thrē′bās′), in *baseball*, a hit by which the batter can reach third base without benefit of an error: also called *triple.*

three-col·or process (thrē′kul′ẽr), a process of printing, lithographing, etc. in full color by making superimposed impressions from three separate plates, each reproducing one primary color.

three-cor·nered (thrē′kôr′nẽrd), *adj.* having three corners or angles.

3-D (thrē′dē′), three dimensions or three-dimensional: used of a motion-picture system in which a stereoscopic picture is projected on a flat screen and viewed through polaroid glasses: cf. **wide-angle.**

three-deck·er (thrē′dek′ẽr), *n.* 1. a ship with three decks; especially, a former type of warship with three decks of cannon. 2. a structure with three levels. 3. a sandwich made with three slices of bread.

three·fold (thrē′fōld′), *adj.* [see -FOLD], 1. having three parts. 2. having three times as much or as many. *adv.* three times as much or as many. *n.*

three-mast·er (thrē′mas′tẽr, thrē′mäs′tẽr), *n.* a sailing ship with three masts.

three-mile limit (thrē′mīl′), the outer limit of a zone of water extending three miles offshore, regarded under international law as the extent of the territorial jurisdiction of the adjacent country.

three·pence (thrip′′ns, threp′′ns), *n.* 1. the sum of three pence. 2. a British silver coin of this value, equal to about six cents. Also **thrippence.**

three·pen·ny (thrē′pen′i, thrip′ə-ni), *adj.* 1. worth three pence. 2. of little value; cheap; paltry.

three-phase (thrē′fāz′), *adj.* in *electricity*, designating or of a system of alternating-current circuits, each of which differs in phase by 120 degrees.

three-piece (thrē′pēs′), *adj.* designating a garment or costume composed of three separate pieces, as of a skirt, jacket, and topcoat.

three-ply (thrē′plī′), *adj.* having three layers, strands, etc.

three-point landing (thrē′point′), 1. a perfect airplane landing in which both main wheels and the tail wheel or skid touch the ground at the same time. 2. [Colloq.], a successful conclusion to any venture.

three-quar·ter (thrē′kwôr′tẽr), *adj.* 1. of or involving three fourths of something. 2. showing the face intermediate between profile and full face: as, a *three-quarter* portrait.

three-quarter binding, a type of bookbinding in which the material of the back, usually leather, is extended onto the covers for one third of their width: usually the outer corners are tipped with triangles of the same material.

three-ring circus (thrē′riŋ′), 1. a circus having three rings for simultaneous performances; hence, 2. any event or occasion characterized by a variety of simultaneous occurrences.

Three Rivers, Trois-Rivières.

three·score (thrē′skôr′, thrē′skōr′), ***adj.*** [see SCORE], three times twenty; sixty.

three·some (thrē′səm), ***adj.*** [ME. *thresum;* see -SOME], of or engaged in by three. ***n.*** 1. a group of three persons. 2. a game played by three persons; specifically, in *golf*, a match in which one participant plays against two others, who alternate strokes on a single ball.

three-square (thrē′skwâr′), ***adj.*** forming an equilateral triangle in cross section: said of a type of file with three surfaces.

threm·ma·tol·o·gy (threm′ə-tol′ə-ji), ***n.*** [< Gr. *thremma, thremmatos,* a nursling; + *-logy*], the branch of biology that deals with the propagation of domestic animals and plants.

thre·node (thrē′nōd, thren′ōd), ***n.*** a threnody.

thre·no·di·al (thri-nō′di-əl), ***adj.*** threnodic.

thre·nod·ic (thri-nod′ik), ***adj.*** of or like a threnody.

thren·o·dist (thren′ə-dist), ***n.*** a person who sings or composes threnodies.

thren·o·dy (thren′ə-di), ***n.*** [*pl.* THRENODIES (-diz)], [Gr. *thrēnōdia* < *thrēnos,* lamentation + *ōdē,* song], a song of lamentation; funeral song; dirge.

thresh (thresh), ***v.t.*** [ME. *threshen;* AS. *threscan, therscan;* earlier form of *thrash,* with etym. meaning], 1. to beat out (grain) from its husk, as with a flail. 2. to beat grain out of (husks). 3. [Rare], to flog; thrash. ***v.i.*** 1. to thresh grain. 2. to toss about; thrash.
  thresh out, to discuss thoroughly and conclusively.

thresh·er (thresh′ẽr), ***n.*** 1. a person who threshes. 2. a threshing machine. 3. a large shark of temperate and tropical seas, having a long tail with which it is said to thresh the water and drive its prey together.

threshing machine, a large, power-driven farm machine for threshing.

thresh·old (thresh′ōld, thresh′hōld), ***n.*** [ME. *threschwold;* AS. *therscwold, therscold* (akin to G. dial. *drischaufel*) < base of *therscan* (see THRESH) in sense "to trample, tread down"], 1. a piece of wood, stone, metal, etc. placed beneath a door; doorsill. 2. the entrance or beginning point of something. 3. in *physiology & psychology,* the point at which a stimulus is just strong enough to be perceived or produce a response: as, the *threshold* of pain.

threw (thrōō), past tense of **throw.**

thrice (thrīs), ***adv.*** [ME. *thries* < *thri, thre,* three + -*(e)s,* adv. genit. suffix, after *ones* (see ONCE)], 1. three times. 2. three times as much or as many; threefold; hence, 3. very; greatly; highly.

thrift (thrift), ***n.*** [ME.; ON. < *thrifa* (see THRIVE) + noun suffix *-t*], 1. originally, the condition of thriving; prosperity. 2. economical management; economy; frugality. 3. [Rare], physical thriving; vigorous growth. 4. any of a number of short plants with narrow leaves and small white, pink, red, or purplish flowers. 5. [Scot.], a means of thriving; work; labor.

thrift·i·ly (thrif′tə-li), ***adv.*** in a thrifty manner.

thrift·i·ness (thrif′ti-nis), ***n.*** the quality or state of being thrifty.

thrift·less (thrift′lis), ***adj.*** without thrift; wasteful.

thrift·y (thrif′ti), ***adj.*** [THRIFTIER (-ti-ẽr), THRIFTIEST (-ti-ist)], 1. practicing thrift; provident; economical. 2. thriving; flourishing; prospering. 3. growing vigorously, as a plant.
SYN.—**thrifty** implies industry and clever management of one's money or resources, usually so as to result in some savings (the *thrifty* housewife watched for sales); **frugal** stresses the idea of saving and suggests spending which excludes any luxury or lavishness and provides only the simplest fare, dress, etc. (the Amish are a *frugal* people); **sparing** implies such restraint in spending as restricts itself to the bare minimum or involves deprivation (*sparing* to the point of niggardliness); **economical** implies prudent management of one's money or resources so as to avoid any waste in expenditure or use (it is often *economical* to buy in large quantities); **provident** implies management with the foresight to provide for future needs (never *provident,* he quickly spent his inheritance). —*ANT.* lavish, prodigal, wasteful.

thrill (thril), ***v.t.*** [ME. *thrillen, thyrlen;* AS. *thyr(e)lian,* to pierce < *thyrel,* perforation, hole < base of *thurh,* through (see THROUGH); cf. NOSTRIL], 1. to cause emotional excitement in, as though by piercing; make shiver or tingle with excitement. 2. to produce vibrations or quivering in; cause to tremble. ***v.i.*** 1. to feel emotional excitement; shiver or tingle with excitement. 2. to tremble; vibrate; quiver. ***n.*** [new formation < the *v.*], 1. a thrilling or being thrilled; tremor of excitement. 2. the quality of thrilling: as, this movie lacks *thrill.* 3. a vibration; tremor; quiver; specifically, in *medicine,* an abnormal tremor, as of the circulatory system, that can be felt on palpation.

thrill·er (thril′ẽr), ***n.*** a person or thing that thrills; specifically, a thrilling story, motion picture, etc.

thrip·pence (thrip′′ns), ***n.*** threepence.

thrips (thrips), ***n.*** [L.; Gr. *thrips,* woodworm], any of a group of very small, destructive insects that live by sucking the juices of plants, as of tobacco.

thrive (thrīv), ***v.i.*** [THROVE (thrōv) or THRIVED (thrīvd), THRIVED or THRIVEN (thriv′′n), THRIVING], [ME. *thrifen;* ON. *thrīfask,* to have oneself in hand, reflex. < *thrifa,* to grasp], 1. to prosper; flourish; be successful, especially as the result of economical management. 2. to grow vigorously or luxuriantly; improve physically. —*SYN.* see **succeed.**

thro′, thro (thrōō), ***prep., adv., adj.*** through.

throat (thrōt), ***n.*** [ME. & AS. *throte;* akin to G. *dross(el),* throat; IE. base **tru-d-,* stretched or swollen (as in L. *struma,* thick neck, etc.) < *(s)ter-,* stiff, erect, etc.; cf. STRETCH], 1. the front part of the neck. 2. the upper part of the passage leading from the mouth and nose to the stomach and lungs, including the pharynx and the upper larynx, trachea, and esophagus. 3. any narrow, throatlike passage, especially one serving as an entrance: as, the *throat* of a chimney. ***v.t.*** 1. to provide with a throat; make a throat in. 2. to pronounce or sing in the throat, i.e., with a harsh, guttural quality.
  cut one another's throats, [Colloq.], to ruin one another, as by underselling in business.
  cut one's own throat, [Colloq.], to be the means of one's own destruction or ruin.
  jump down one's throat, [Colloq.], to attack or criticize one suddenly and violently.
  lump in the throat, a feeling of constriction in the throat, as from restrained emotion.
  ram (something) down one's throat, to force one to accept, hear, etc. something.
  stick in one's throat, to be hard to say, as from reluctance.

-throat·ed (thrōt′id), a combining form used in hyphenated compounds, meaning *having a* (specified kind of) *throat,* as in *ruby-throated.*

throat·i·ly (thrōt′′l-i), ***adv.*** in a throaty manner.

throat·i·ness (thrōt′i-nis), ***n.*** a throaty quality.

throat·latch (thrōt′lach′), ***n.*** a strap that passes under a horse's throat, for holding a bridle or halter in place.

throat·y (thrōt′i), ***adj.*** [THROATIER (-i-ẽr), THROATIEST (-i-ist)], produced in the throat, as some speech sounds or tones, or characterized by such sounds, as the voice; guttural; hoarse.

throb (throb), ***v.i.*** [THROBBED (throbd), THROBBING], [ME. *throbben;* var. *frob* suggests echoic origin], 1. to beat, pulsate, vibrate, etc. 2. to beat strongly or fast; palpitate, as the heart under exertion. 3. to feel or show emotional excitement, as by quivering, shivering, etc. ***n.*** the act of throbbing; beat or pulsation, especially a strong one, as of the heart.

throb·ber (throb′ẽr), ***n.*** a person or thing that throbs.

throe (thrō), ***n.*** [ME. *throwe;* prob. < AS. *thrawu,* pain, affliction, influenced by *thrawen,* to twist (see THROW); for mod. sp. cf. HOE, ROE (of fish)], 1. a spasm or pang of pain. 2. *pl.* pangs of childbirth; labor pains. 3. *pl.* desperate or agonizing struggle; agony, as the pangs of death. ***v.i.*** [THROED (thrōd), THROEING], to suffer throes.

throm·bin (throm′bin), ***n.*** [*thrombus* + *-in*], the enzyme of the blood that causes clotting by forming fibrin.

throm·bo·gen (throm′bə-jen′), ***n.*** [< Gr. *thrombos,* a lump, clot; + *-gen*], prothrombin.

throm·bo·sis (throm-bō′sis), ***n.*** [Mod. L.; Gr. *thrombōsis,* coagulation < *thrombos,* a clot, lump], coagulation of the blood in some part of the circulatory system, forming a clot that obstructs circulation in that part.

throm·bot·ic (throm-bot′ik), ***adj.*** of or having thrombosis.

throm·bus (throm′bəs), ***n.*** [*pl.* THROMBI (-bī)], [Mod. L.; Gr. *thrombos,* a clot, lump], the fibrinous clot formed in thrombosis.

throne (thrōn), ***n.*** [ME. & OFr. *trone;* L. *thronus;* Gr. *thronos,* a seat], 1. the chair on which a king, cardinal, etc. sits on formal occasions: it usually is on a dais, covered with a canopy, and highly decorated. 2. the power or rank of a king, etc.; sovereignty. 3. a sovereign, ruler, etc.: as, orders from the *throne.* 4. in *theology,* an order in the hierarchy of angels. ***v.t.*** [THRONED (thrōnd), THRONING], to enthrone.

throng (thrôŋ), ***n.*** [ME. *throng, thrang;* AS. *(ge)thrang* (akin to G. *drang;* cf. STURM UND DRANG) < the base of *thringan,* to press, crowd (akin to G. *dringen,* to press, crowd); for IE. base cf. THRALL], 1. a great number of people gathered together; crowd. 2. a crowding together of people; crowded condition. 3. any great number of things considered together; multitude. *v.i.* to gather together, move, or press in a throng; crowd. *v.t.* 1. to crowd or press upon in large numbers. 2. to crowd into; fill with a multitude. 3. to gather together into a throng. —*SYN.* see **crowd.**

thros·tle (thros″'l), *n.* [ME.; AS.; akin to G. *drossel;* IE. base **troz-*, thrush, as also in AS. *thrysce* (Gmc. **thruskjon*); see THRUSH], 1. [Scot.], a thrush, as the European song thrush. 2. [from the humming sound it makes], a machine for spinning wool, etc.

throt·tle (throt″'l), *n.* [dim. of *throat;* see -LE], 1. [Rare], the throat or windpipe. 2. the valve in an internal-combustion engine that regulates the amount of fuel vapor entering the cylinders. 3. the hand lever or foot pedal that controls this valve. *v.t.* [THROTTLED (-'ld), THROTTLING], [ME. *throtlen* < *throte*, throat], 1. to choke; strangle. 2. to stop the utterance of; suppress; silence. 3. to reduce the flow of (fuel vapor) by means of a throttle; hence, 4. to slow (*down*) by this or similar means. *v.i.* to choke or suffocate.

throttle valve, a throttle (sense 2).

through (thrōō), *prep.* [ME. *thurgh, thrugh, thuruh;* AS. *thurh;* akin to G. *durch;* IE. base **ter-*, away through, seen also in L. *terminus, trans* (cf. TERMINAL, TRANSIT, etc.)], 1. in one side and out the other side of; from end to end of; between the parts of. 2. in the midst of; among. 3. by way of. 4. over the entire extent or surface of. 5. to various places in; around: as, he toured *through* France. 6. from beginning to end of; throughout; during the time of. 7. by means of: as, *through* her help. 8. as a result of; because of: as, done *through* error. *adv.* 1. in one side and out the other; from end to end; between the parts. 2. from the beginning to the end. 3. completely to the end; to a conclusion: as, he saw it *through.* 4. thoroughly; completely: as, soaked *through* (often reduplicatively, *through and through*). *adj.* 1. extending from one place to another; allowing free passage: as, a *through* street. 2. traveling to the destination without stops: as, a *through* train. 3. not necessitating changes; good for traveling without intermediate transfer: as, a *through* ticket. 4. arrived at the end; finished: as, I'm *through* with this assignment. 5. at the end of one's usefulness, resources, etc.: as, he's *through* in politics. 6. having no further dealings, connections, etc.: as, I'm *through* with that crowd. *Through* is also used in various idiomatic expressions (e.g., get *through,* see *through*), many of which are entered in this dictionary under the key words. Also spelled **thro', thro, thru.**

through·ly (thrōō′li), *adv.* [Archaic], thoroughly.

through·out (thrōō-out′), *prep.* all the way through; in or during every part of. *adv.* in or during every part; everywhere; the whole time; in every respect.

throve (thrōv), alternative past tense of **thrive.**

throw (thrō), *v.t.* [THREW (thrōō), THROWN (thrōn), THROWING], [ME. *throwen, threowen, thrawen;* AS. *thrawan,* to throw, twist; akin to G. *drehen,* to twist, turn; IE. base **ter-*, to rub, hence, to rub by turning, turn, etc., seen also in L. *terere,* to rub (cf. TERMITE, TRITE, etc.)], 1. to twist strands of (silk, etc.) into thread. 2. to cause to fly through the air by releasing from the hand at the end of a rapid motion of the arm; cast; hurl. 3. to discharge through the air from a catapult, pump, etc. 4. to hurl violently, as in anger, etc.; dash: as, she *threw* the vase on the ground. 5. to cause to fall; upset; overthrow; dislodge: as, he *threw* the other wrestler, she was *thrown* by her horse. 6. to move or send rapidly; advance: as, they *threw* reinforcements into the battle. 7. to put suddenly and forcibly into or onto a specified object or place: as, she *threw* the clothes into the suitcase. 8. to put suddenly and forcibly into a specified condition or situation: as, he was *thrown* into prison, the meeting was *thrown* into confusion. 9. to cast or roll (dice). 10. to make (a specified cast) at dice: as, he *threw* a five. 11. to cast off; shed: as, snakes *throw* their skins, the horse *threw* its shoe. 12. to bring forth (young); give birth to: said of domesticated animals. 13. to move (the lever of a switch, clutch, etc.) or connect, disconnect, engage, etc. by so doing. 14. to direct, cast, turn, project, etc. (variously with *at, on, upon, over, towards,* etc.): as, she *threw* a glance at me, his shadow was *thrown* on the ground, the window *threw* an eerie light. 15. to put (blame *on,* influence *into,* obstacles *before,* etc.). 16. [Colloq.], to lose (a game, race, etc.) deliberately, as by prearrangement. 17. [Slang], to give (a party, dance, etc.). 18. in *card games,* to play or discard (a card) from the hand. 19. in *ceramics,* to shape on a potter's wheel. *v.i.* to cast or hurl something. *n.* 1. the action of a person who throws; a cast. 2. a cast of dice, or the numbers cast; hence, 3. a venture; risk. 4. the distance something is or can be thrown: as, a stone's *throw.* 5. *a*) a spread or coverlet for draping over a bed, etc. *b*) a scarf or the like for throwing around the shoulders. 6. *a*) the motion of a moving part, as a cam, eccentric, etc. *b*) the extent of such a motion. 7. in *geology,* the amount of displacement at a fault. 8. in *wrestling, a*) the act of throwing an opponent. *b*) a particular way of doing this.

throw away, 1. to rid oneself of; discard. 2. to be wasteful of; waste. 3. to fail to make use of.

throw a (monkey) wrench into, to stop or obstruct by direct interference; sabotage.

throw back, to revert to the type of an ancestor.

throw cold water on, to discourage by one's indifference or disparagement.

throw in, 1. to engage (a clutch) or cause (gears) to mesh. 2. to add extra or free. 3. to add to others.

throw off, 1. to rid oneself of; cast off. 2. to evade (a pursuer). 3. to expel, emit, etc. 4. [Colloq.], to write or utter quickly, in an offhand manner.

throw on, to put on (a garment) carelessly or hastily.

throw oneself at, to try very hard to win the friendship, affection, or love of.

throw oneself into, to engage in with great vigor.

throw oneself upon (or **on**), rely on for support.

throw open, 1. to open completely and suddenly. 2. to remove all restrictions from.

throw out, 1. to discard. 2. to reject. 3. to put forth or utter, as a hint or suggestion. 4. to disengage (a clutch). 5. in *baseball,* to throw the ball to a baseman so as to put out (a runner).

throw over, 1. to give up; abandon. 2. to jilt.

throw the bull, [Slang], to talk glibly, especially untruthfully or insincerely.

throw together, to make or assemble hurriedly and carelessly.

throw up, 1. to give up or abandon. 2. to vomit. 3. to construct rapidly. 4. to mention (something) repeatedly (*to* someone), as in reproach or criticism.

SYN.—**throw** is the general word meaning to cause to move through the air by a rapid propulsive motion of the arm, etc.; **cast,** the preferred word in certain connections (to *cast* a fishing line), generally has a more archaic or lofty quality than throw (they *cast* stones at him); to **toss** is to throw lightly or carelessly and, usually, with an upward or sidewise motion (to *toss* a coin); **hurl** and **fling** both imply a throwing with force or violence, but **hurl** suggests that the object thrown moves swiftly for some distance (to *hurl* a javelin) and **fling,** that it is thrust sharply or vehemently so that it strikes a surface with considerable impact (she *flung* the plate to the floor); **pitch** implies a throwing with a definite aim or in a definite direction (to *pitch* a baseball).

throw·a·way (thrō′ə-wā′), *n.* a leaflet, handbill, etc. distributed as in the streets or from house to house.

throw·back (thrō′bak′), *n.* 1. a throwing back; check. 2. reversion to an ancestral type or characteristic, or an instance of this.

thrown (thrōn), past participle of **throw.** *adj.* 1. pitched; hurled. 2. unseated from a horse. 3. cast to the ground, as in wrestling.

throw·ster (thrō′stẽr), *n.* [see THROW, *v.t.* 1], a person whose work is making threads of silk.

thru (thrōō), *prep., adv., adj.* through.

thrum (thrum), *n.* [ME. & AS. *thrum* (in comp.), ligament; akin to G. *trumm;* IE. base as in *through*], 1. *pl.* the row of warp thread ends left on a loom when the web is cut off. 2. any of these ends. 3. any short end thread or fringe. 4. *pl.* in *nautical usage,* short pieces of woolen or hempen yarn for thrumming canvas. *v.t.* [THRUMMED (thrumd), THRUMMING], 1. to provide with or make of thrums; fringe. 2. in *nautical usage,* to insert thrums in (canvas) to make a rough surface for preventing chafing, stopping leaks, etc.

thrum (thrum), *v.t.* [THRUMMED (thrumd), THRUMMING], [echoic], 1. to play on (a stringed instrument) monotonously, idly, or unskillfully; strum. 2. to tell in a monotonous, tiresome way. 3. to drum on with the fingers. *v.i.* 1. to thrum a stringed instrument. 2. to sound when so played: said of a guitar, etc. 3. to drum with the fingers. *n.* a thrumming or the sound of this.

thrum·my (thrum′i), *adj.* [THRUMMIER (-i-ẽr), THRUMMIEST (-i-ist)], of or covered with thrums; shaggy.

thrush (thrush), *n.* [ME. *thrusch;* AS. *thrysce;* Gmc. **thurskjon;* IE. base **troz-*, thrush; cf. THROSTLE], any of a large group of songbirds, most of which have plain plumage, including the robin, wood thrush, bluebird, hermit thrush, etc. of North America and the common thrush, blackbird, ouzel, etc. of Europe.

thrush (thrush), *n.* [cf. Dan. *troske,* Sw. *trosk*], 1. a disease, especially of children, caused by a fungus and characterized by the formation of milky-white lesions on the membranes of the mouth, lips, and throat. 2. a disease of a horse's foot, characterized by the formation of pus.

thrust (thrust), *v.t.* [THRUST, THRUSTING], [ME. *thrusten, thristen;* ON. *thrysta;* prob. < IE. base seen in *threat*], 1. to push with sudden force; shove; drive. 2. to pierce; stab. 3. to put (a person) in some position or situation against his wishes or the wishes of others: often used reflexively, as, she *thrust* herself upon us two months ago. 4. to interject or interpose: as, he *thrust* a question in occasionally. 5. to extend, as in growth: as, the tree *thrusts* its branches high. *v.i.* 1. to push or shove against something. 2. to make a thrust, or stab. 3. to force one's way: with *into,* *through*, etc. 4. to extend, as in growth. *n.* 1. the act of thrusting; specifically, *a*) a sudden, forceful push or shove. *b*) a lunge or stab, as with a weapon. 2. continuous pressure of one part against another, as of a rafter against a wall. 3. *a*) the driving force of a propeller in the line of its shaft. *b*) the forward force produced in reaction by the escaping gases in jet propulsion. 4. in *geology*, an almost horizontal fault. —*SYN.* see **push.**

Thu·cyd·i·des (thoo-sid'ə-dēz', thū-sid'ə-dēz'), *n.* Athenian historian; 471?–400? B.C.

thud (thud), *n.* [prob. < dial. var. of ME. *thidden* (AS. *thyddan*), to strike, thrust, influenced by echoism], 1. a blow. 2. a dull sound, as that of a heavy, solid object dropping on a soft but solid surface. *v.i.* [THUDDED (-id), THUDDING], to hit or fall with a thud.

thug (thug), *n.* [Hind. *ṭhag*, swindler (euphemism); Prakrit *ṭhaga;* Sans. *sthaga*, a cheat, rogue], 1. [also T-], a member of a former religious organization of India who murdered and robbed in the service of Kali, a god of destruction; hence, 2. any assassin, cutthroat, or ruffian.

thug·gee (thug'ē), *n.* [Hind. *ṭhagī;* see THUG], murder and robbery as formerly practiced by the thugs of India.

thu·ja (thū'jə), *n.* [Mod. L. < Gr. *thyia*, African tree with aromatic wood], any of various related trees of the pine family, with fragrant, soft, waxy, scalelike leaves; arborvitae.

Thu·le (thoo'li, thū'lē), *n.* [L.; Gr. *Thoulē, Thylē*], in *ancient geography*, the northernmost region of the world, possibly Norway, Iceland, or Mainland (the largest of the Shetland Islands): often in *ultima Thule* (farthest Thule).

thu·li·a (thoo'li-ə, thū'li-ə), *n.* thulium oxide, Tm_2O_3.

thu·li·um (thoo'li-əm, thū'li-əm), *n.* [Mod. L.; see THULE], a metallic chemical element of the rare-earth group: symbol, Tm; at. wt., 169.4; at. no., 69.

thumb (thum), *n.* [ME. *thoume, thoumbe* (with unhistoric *-b-*); AS. *thuma;* akin to G. *daume(n);* IE. base **tēu-*, to swell, increase, seen also in *tumor, tumult;* basic sense, "enlarged finger"], 1. the short, thick inner digit of the human hand, apposable to the other fingers; pollex. 2. a corresponding part in other animals. 3. that part of a glove or mitten which covers the thumb. 4. in *architecture*, an ovolo. *v.t.* 1. to handle, turn, soil, or wear with or as with the thumb: as, the page was badly *thumbed.* 2. [Colloq.], *a*) to solicit (a ride) in a passing automobile by extending a thumb in the direction one wishes to travel. *b*) to make (one's way) in this manner.

all thumbs, clumsy; fumbling.

thumb one's nose, to raise one's thumb to the nose with the fingers extended, as a coarse gesture of defiance or insult.

thumbs down, a signal of rejection or disapproval.

thumbs up, a signal of acceptance or approval.

thumb through, to glance rapidly through (a book), as by releasing pages along their edge with the thumb.

under one's thumb, under one's influence or sway.

thumb-in·dex (thum'in'deks), *v.t.* to furnish (a book) with a thumb index.

thumb index, a reference index for books, consisting of a series of rounded notches cut in the front edge of a book with a tab at the base of each notch bearing a letter or title: the desired section can be turned to quickly by placing a finger on the proper notch.

thumb·kin (thum'kin), *n.* a thumbscrew (sense 2).

thumb·nail (thum'nāl'), *n.* 1. the nail of the thumb. 2. something as small as a thumbnail. *adj.* of the size of a thumbnail; very small, brief, or concise: as, a *thumbnail* sketch.

thumb·screw (thum'skroo'), *n.* 1. a screw with a head flattened in such a way that it may be turned with the thumb and fingers. 2. a former instrument of torture for squeezing the thumbs.

thumb·stall (thum'stôl'), *n.* a kind of thimble or protective sheath for the thumb, made of leather.

thumb·tack (thum'tak'), *n.* a kind of tack with a wide, flat head, that can be pressed into a board, etc. with the thumb.

Thum·mim (thum'im; Heb. toom'im), *n.pl.* [Heb. *tummīm, thummīm*, pl. of *tōm*, perfection, completeness], see **Urim and Thummim.**

thump (thump), *n.* [echoic; parallel with similar formations in North & West Gmc. languages], 1. a blow with something heavy and blunt, as with a cudgel. 2. the dull sound made by such a blow. *v.t.* 1. to strike with a thump or thumps. 2. to thrash; beat severely. *v.i.* 1. to hit or fall with a thump. 2. to make a dull, heavy sound; pound; throb.

thump·er (thum'pẽr), *n.* 1. a person or thing that thumps. 2. a heavy blow.

thump·ing (thum'piŋ), *adj.* 1. that thumps. 2. [Colloq.], very large; whopping.

Thun (toon), *n.* a city in central Switzerland, near the Lake of Thun: pop., 24,000.

Thun, Lake of, a lake in central Switzerland, formed by the widening of the Aar River: length, 10 mi.

thun·der (thun'dẽr), *n.* [ME. *thuner, thunder* (with unhistoric *-d-*); AS. *thunor;* akin to G. *donner;* IE. base **(s)ten-*, loud rustling, deep noise, as also in L. *tonare*, to thunder; cf. THURSDAY, ASTOUND], 1. the sound that follows a flash of lightning, caused by the sudden disturbance of air by electrical discharge. 2. any sound resembling this. 3. a threatening, menacing, or extremely vehement utterance. 4. [Obs. or Poetic], a thunderbolt. *v.i.* 1. to produce thunder: usually in the impersonal construction, as, it is *thundering.* 2. to make a sound like thunder. 3. to make vehement speeches, denunciations, etc. *v.t.* 1. to say in a thundering voice. 2. to strike, drive, attack, etc. with the sound or violence of thunder.

steal one's thunder, to use one's ideas or methods without permission and without giving credit; especially, to lessen the effectiveness of another's statement or action by anticipating him in this.

thun·der·bird (thun'dẽr-bũrd'), *n.* in the mythology of certain North American Indians, an enormous bird supposed to produce thunder, lightning, and rain.

thun·der·bolt (thun'dẽr-bōlt'), *n.* 1. a flash of lightning and the accompanying thunder. 2. a bolt or missile imagined as hurled to earth by a stroke of lightning. 3. something that stuns with the speed and force of a thunderbolt: as, the news was a *thunderbolt.* 4. a person acting with sudden violence or force.

thun·der·clap (thun'dẽr-klap'), *n.* 1. a clap, or loud crash, of thunder. 2. anything resembling this in being sudden, startling, violent, etc.

thun·der·cloud (thun'dẽr-kloud'), *n.* a storm cloud charged with electricity and producing lightning and thunder.

thun·der·er (thun'dẽr-ẽr), *n.* 1. a person who thunders. 2. [T-], Zeus; Jupiter.

thun·der·head (thun'dẽr-hed'), *n.* a round mass of cumulus clouds appearing before a thunderstorm.

thun·der·ing (thun'dẽr-iŋ), *adj.* 1. that thunders. 2. [Colloq.], very large; thumping; whopping.

thun·der·ous (thun'dẽr-əs), *adj.* 1. full of or making thunder. 2. making a noise like thunder.

thun·der·peal (thun'dẽr-pēl'), *n.* a peal, or loud crash, of thunder; thunderclap.

thun·der·show·er (thun'dẽr-shou'ẽr), *n.* a shower accompanied by thunder and lightning.

thun·der·squall (thun'dẽr-skwôl'), *n.* a squall accompanied by thunder and lightning.

thun·der·stone (thun'dẽr-stōn'), *n.* a rounded stone, fossil, prehistoric implement, etc. formerly thought to have been hurled to earth by lightning and thunder.

thun·der·storm (thun'dẽr-stôrm'), *n.* a storm accompanied by thunder and lightning.

thun·der·strick·en (thun'dẽr-strik''n), *adj.* thunderstruck.

thun·der·struck (thun'dẽr-struk'), *adj.* struck with amazement, terror, etc., as if by a thunderbolt.

thun·der·y (thun'dẽr-i), *adj.* 1. that sounds like thunder. 2. accompanied with or betokening thunder.

Thur., Thursday.

Thur·ber, James (thũr'bẽr), (*James Grover Thurber*), 1894–1961; American writer, humorist, and cartoonist.

Thur·gau (toor'gou), *n.* a canton of northeastern Switzerland: pop., 150,000.

thu·ri·ble (thoor'ə-b'l, thyoor'ə-b'l), *n.* [L. *thuribulum* < *thus, thuris*, frankincense < Gr. *thyos*, incense, sacrifice], a censer.

thu·ri·fer (thoor'i-fẽr, thyoor'i-fẽr), *n.* [Mod. L. < L. *thus, thuris*, frankincense + *ferre*, to bear], an acolyte or altar boy who carries a thurible.

Thü·ring·en (tü'riŋ-ən), *n.* Thuringia.

Thu·rin·gi·a (thoo-rin'ji-ə, thyoo-rin'ji-ə), *n.* a former region of central Germany, including duchies and principalities: later, a division of East Germany: German name, *Thüringen.*

Thu·rin·gi·an (thoo-rin'ji-ən, thyoo-rin'ji-ən), *adj.* of Thuringia, its people, or culture. *n.* 1. a member of an ancient Germanic tribe of central Germany. 2. a native or inhabitant of Thuringia.

Thurs·day (thũrz'di), *n.* [ME. *Thoresdai, Thunres dai* < AS. *Thunres dæg*, ON. *Thorsdagr*, Thor's day, rendering LL. *Jovis deis;* cf. Fr. *jeudi*, G. *Donnerstag*], the fifth day of the week: abbreviated **Th., Thur., Thurs.**

Thursday Island, an Australian island in the Torres Strait: pop., 1,600.

thus (*th*us), *adv.* [ME.; AS.; for the IE. base see THAT], 1. in this or that manner; in the way just stated or in the following manner. 2. to this or that degree or extent; so. 3. according to this or that; consequently; therefore; hence.

thwack (thwak), *v.t.* [prob. < ME. *thakken;* AS. *thaccian*, to clap, with *-w-* after *whack*, etc.; basically echoic], to strike with something flat; whack. *n.* a heavy blow as with something flat; whack.

thwart (thwôrt), *adj.* [ME. *thwert;* ON. *thvert*, neut. of *thverr*, transverse; IE. base **terek-*, to turn, as also in L. *torquere*, to twist, turn (cf. TORQUE, TORSION)], 1. lying or extending across something else; transverse; oblique. 2. [Obs.], perverse. *adv. & prep.* [Archaic], athwart. *n.* 1. a rower's seat extending across a boat. 2. a brace extending across a canoe. *v.t.* 1. originally, to extend or place over or across. 2. to hinder, obstruct, frustrate, or defeat (a person, plans, wishes, etc.). —*SYN.* see **frustrate.**

thy (*th*ī), *possessive pronominal adj.* [ME. *thi*, contr. < *thin*, thy, orig. before consonants], of, belonging to, or done by thee: archaic or dialectal variant of *your:* see also **thine.**

Thy·es·te·an banquet (or **feast**), (thī-es'ti-ən, thī'es-tē'ən), [see THYESTES], a banquet at which human flesh is served.

Thy·es·tes (thī-es'tēz), *n.* [L.; Gr. *Thyestēs*], in *Greek legend*, a brother of Atreus and son of Pelops: see **Atreus.**

thy·la·cine (thī'lə-sīn', thī'lə-sin), *n.* [Fr. < Gr. *thylax*, a pouch], a fierce, flesh-eating marsupial of Tasmania, somewhat like a dog but with dark stripes on the back: it is almost extinct: also called *Tasmanian tiger, Tasmanian wolf.*

thyme (tīm), *n.* [ME. *time;* OFr. *tim;* L. *thymum;* Gr. *thymon* < *thyein*, to offer sacrifice], any of various related plants of the mint family, with white, pink, or red flowers and fragrant leaves used for seasoning.

thym·e·lae·a·ceous (thim'ə-li-ā'shəs), *adj.* [< L. *thymelaea*, kind of plant, flax-leaved daphne (< Gr. *thymelaia*); + *-aceous*], of the mezereon family of trees, shrubs, and herbs, having very tough bark.

thy·mic (thī'mik), *adj.* of the thymus.

thym·ic (tīm'ik), *adj.* of or derived from thyme.

thy·mol (thī'mōl, thī'mol), *n.* [< *thyme* + *-ol*], an aromatic, colorless, crystalline compound, $C_{10}H_{14}O$, extracted from the volatile oil of thyme or made synthetically, and used as an antiseptic.

thy·mus (thī'məs), *n.* [Mod. L.; Gr. *thymos*], a ductless, glandlike body, of undetermined function, situated in the upper thorax near the throat: it is most prominent at puberty, after which it disappears or becomes vestigial: the thymus of an animal, when used as food, is called *sweetbread*: also **thymus gland.**

thy·my (tīm'i), *adj.* 1. overgrown with thyme. 2. having the scent of thyme.

thy·re·o- (thī'ri-ō, thī'ri-ə), a combining form meaning *thyroid*, as in *thyreotomy:* also **thyro-, thyre-.**

thy·re·oid (thī'ri-oid'), *adj. & n.* thyroid.

thy·roid (thī'roid), *adj.* [Gr. *thyreoeidēs*, shield-shaped < *thyreos*, large shield + *-eidēs*, form], 1. designating or of a large ductless gland lying in front and on either side of the trachea and secreting the hormone thyroxine, which regulates the growth of the body: the malfunctioning or congenital absence of this gland can cause goiter, cretinism, etc. 2. designating or of the principal cartilage of the larynx, forming the Adam's apple. *n.* 1. the thyroid gland. 2. the thyroid cartilage. 3. a preparation of the thyroid gland of certain domesticated animals, used in treating goiter, myxedema, etc.: also **thyroid extract.**

thy·roid·ec·to·my (thī'roid-ek'tə-mi), *n.* [see -ECTOMY], the surgical removal of all or part of the thyroid gland.

thy·roid·i·tis (thī'roid-ī'tis), *n.* [Mod. L.; see -ITIS], inflammation of the thyroid gland.

thy·rox·in (thī-rok'sin), *n.* thyroxine.

thy·rox·ine (thī-rok'sēn, thī-rok'sin), *n.* [< *thyroid* + *oxy-* + *-ine*], a colorless, crystalline compound, $C_{15}H_{11}O_4NI_4$, the active hormone of the thyroid gland, often prepared synthetically and used in treating goiter, cretinism, and myxedema.

thyrse (thūrs), *n.* a thyrsus.

thyr·soid (thūr'soid), *adj.* [Gr. *thyrsoeidēs* < *thyrsos*, thyrsus + *eidos*, form], in *botany*, resembling a thyrsus.

thyr·soi·dal (thūr-soi'd'l), *adj.* thyrsoid.

thyr·sus (thūr'səs), *n.* [*pl.* THYRSI (-sī)], [L.; Gr. *thyrsos*], 1. a staff tipped with a pine cone and sometimes entwined with ivy or vine leaves, which Dionysus, the satyrs, etc. were represented as carrying. 2. in *botany*, a flower cluster in which the main stem is racemose and the secondary stems are cymose, as in the lilac.

THYRSUS
(of horse chestnut)

thy·sa·nu·ran (thī'sə-nyoor'ən, this'ə-nyoor'ən), *adj.* [< Mod. L. *thysanura* (< Gr. *thysanos*, a tassel + *oura*, a tail); + *-an*], designating or of an order of wingless insects that have bristlelike appendages at their rear ends. *n.* a thysanuran insect; bristletail.

thy·sa·nu·rous (thī'sə-nyoor'əs, this'ə-nyoor'əs), *adj.* of or like a thysanuran or thysanurans.

thy·self (*th*ī-self'), *pron.* [ME. *thi self*, superseding earlier *the self*, lit., thee self; AS. *the self;* in ME., *self*, orig. adj., was regarded as n.], the reflexive or emphatic form of **thou**: an archaic or dialectal variant of *yourself.*

ti (tē), *n.* [altered < *si;* see GAMUT], in *music*, a syllable representing the seventh tone of the diatonic scale: also **te:** see **solfeggio.**

ti (tē), *n.* [Maori & Samoan], any of various related Asiatic and Polynesian trees, some of which are valued for their roots and leaves: also **ti palm.**

Ti, in *chemistry*, titanium.

Tian Shan (tyän'shän'), Tien Shan.

ti·ar·a (tī-âr'ə, ti-âr'ə, ti-ä'rə), *n.* [L.; Gr. *tiara;* prob. of Oriental origin], 1. an ancient Persian headdress. 2. *a*) the Pope's triple crown. *b*) the position or authority of the Pope. 3. a woman's crownlike headdress of jewels, flowers, etc.; coronet.

Ti·ber (tī'bēr), *n.* a river in central Italy, flowing southward through Rome to the Mediterranean: length, 244 mi.: Italian name, *Tevere.*

Ti·ber·i·as, Sea of (tī-bêr'i-əs), the Sea of Galilee, in northeastern Palestine.

Ti·ber·i·us (tī-bêr'i-əs), *n.* (*Tiberius Claudius Nero Caesar*), Roman general and emperor (14 A.D.–37 A.D.); lived 42 B.C.–37 A.D.

Ti·bet (ti-bet'), *n.* a nominal Chinese dependency in south central Asia: area, 469,194 sq. mi.; pop., 1,000,000 (est. 1947); capital, Lhasa: also spelled **Thibet**: Chinese name, *Sitsang*: see also **Nearer Tibet.**

Ti·bet·an (ti-bet''n), *adj.* of Tibet, its people, their language, etc. *n.* 1. a member of the Mongolic people of Tibet. 2. the Sino-Tibetan language of Tibet. Abbreviated **Tibet.** Also spelled **Thibetan.**

Ti·bet·o-Bur·man (ti-bet'ō-būr'mən), *adj.* designating or of a subdivision of the Sino-Tibetan family of languages, including Tibetan and Burmese.

tib·i·a (tib'i-ə), *n.* [*pl.* TIBIAE (-ē'), TIBIAS (-əz)], [L.], 1. the inner and thicker of the two bones of the human leg between the knee and the ankle; shinbone: see **skeleton**, illus. 2. a corresponding bone in the leg of other vertebrates. 3. the fourth segment (from the base) of an insect's leg. 4. an ancient type of flute, originally made from an animal's tibia.

tib·i·al (tib'i-əl), *adj.* [L. *tibialis*], of the tibia.

Ti·bul·lus, Al·bi·us (al'bi-əs ti-bul'əs), 54?–18? B.C.; Roman elegiac poet.

Ti·bur (tī'bēr), *n.* Tivoli.

tic (tik), *n.* [Fr.; It. *ticchis;* of Gmc. origin], any involuntary, regularly repeated, spasmodic contraction of a muscle, generally of neurotic origin; especially, tic douloureux.

ti·cal (ti-käl', ti-kôl', tē'kəl), *n.* [Malay *tikal*], 1. the former monetary unit of Siam, replaced by the baht. 2. a former Siamese unit of weight equivalent to about half an ounce.

tic dou·lou·reux (tik' do͞o'lo͞o-ro͞o'; Fr. tēk' do͞o'lo͞o'-rö'), [Fr., lit., painful tic], a tic of the facial muscles, accompanied by severe neuralgic pains; trigeminal neuralgia.

Ti·ci·no (tē-chē'nô), *n.* 1. a canton of southern Switzerland: pop., 162,000. 2. a river flowing through Switzerland and Italy, into the Po River: length, 150 mi.: German name, *Tessin.*

tick (tik), *n.* [ME. *tek, tekk;* prob. < Gmc. echoic base seen in D. *tikk*, MHG. *zicken*, to tick, etc.], 1. originally, a light touch; pat. 2. a light clicking or tapping sound, as that made by the escapement of a watch or clock. 3. a mark made to check off items; check mark (√, /, etc.). 4. [Colloq.], the time between two ticks of a clock; moment; instant. *v.i.* to make a tick or series of ticks. *v.t.* 1. to indicate, record, or count by a tick or ticks. 2. to mark or check off (an item in a list, etc.) with a tick.

tick (tik), *n.* [ME. *tike, teke;* AS. *ticia* (? for *tiica*, or *ticca*); Gmc. **tīkan* or **tikkan*, as also in MD. *teke*, G. *zecke;* IE. base **deiĝh-*, to prickle, itch, seen also in Arm. *tiz*, tick, MIr. *dega*, stag bettle], 1. any of a large group of wingless, blood-sucking insects or mites that infest man, cattle, sheep, and other animals. 2. any of various degenerate, two-winged, parasitic insects.

tick (tik), *n.* [ML. *teca;* L. *theca;* Gr. *thēkē*, a case], 1. the cloth case or covering that is filled with cotton, feathers, hair, etc. to form a mattress or pillow. 2. [Colloq.], ticking.

tick (tik), *n.* [contr. of *ticket*], [Chiefly British Colloq.], credit; trust: as, I bought it on *tick.*

tick·er (tik'ēr), *n.* 1. a person or thing that ticks. 2. a telegraphic device that records stock market quotations, etc. on a paper tape. 3. [Slang], a watch or clock. 4. [Slang], the heart.

ticker tape, paper tape used in a ticker for recording telegraphed stock market quotations, etc.

tick·et (tik'it), *n.* [Fr. *étiquette;* OFr. *estiquete* < *estiquer*, to stick; cf. ETIQUETTE], 1. [Now Rare], a note or memorandum, or a slip of paper containing this. 2.

a printed card or piece of paper that gives a person a specified right, as to attend a theater, ride on a train, claim a purchase, etc. 3. a license or certificate, as of a ship's captain or of an airplane pilot. 4. a card, piece of paper, or piece of cloth fastened to goods to tell the size, color, price, quantity, etc.; label; tag. 5. a slip recording a transaction or a sum paid or due, to be entered in a permanent account book. 6. the list of candidates nominated by a political party in an election; ballot. 7. [Colloq.], a summons to court for a traffic violation. ***v.t.*** 1. to put a ticket on; label; tag. 2. to provide a ticket or tickets for.

that's the ticket! [Slang], that's the correct or proper thing! that's right!

ticket agent, a person or agency that sells theater tickets, railroad tickets, etc.

ticket office, an office, as in railroad stations, where tickets are sold.

tick·et-of-leave (tik′it-əv-lēv′), ***adj.*** [British], having a ticket of leave.

ticket of leave, [British], formerly, a permit allowing a convict to be at liberty, with certain restrictions, before his sentence had expired: equivalent to *parole*.

tick fever, any infectious disease transmitted by the bite of a tick, as Rocky Mountain spotted fever.

tick·ing (tik′iŋ), ***n.*** strong, heavy cotton or linen cloth, often striped, of which bed ticks, etc. are made.

tick·le (tik′′l), ***v.t.*** [TICKLED (-′ld), TICKLING], [ME. *tikelen;* akin to G. dial. *zickeln;* for the base see TICK (insect)], 1. to please; gratify: as, this dessert will *tickle* the palate. 2. to amuse; delight: as, the story *tickled* him. 3. to excite the surface nerves of by touching or stroking lightly with the finger, a feather, etc. so as to cause involuntary twitching, laughter, etc. 4. to rouse, stir, move, get, etc. by or as by touching lightly. ***v.i.*** 1. to have an itching or tingling sensation: as, my palm *tickles*. 2. to be affected by excitation of the surface nerves; be ticklish. ***n.*** 1. a tickling or being tickled. 2. a tickling sensation.

tickle one pink, [Slang], to please one greatly.

tick·ler (tik′lẽr), ***n.*** 1. a person or thing that tickles. 2. a memorandum pad, file, or other device for aiding the memory. 3. an irritating problem; puzzle. 4. an account book showing notes due and the dates of these.

tick·lish (tik′lish), ***adj.*** 1. sensitive to tickling. 2. easily upset; unstable; unsteady; touchy; fickle. 3. needing careful handling; precarious; delicate.

tick·seed (tik′sēd′), ***n.*** [*tick* (insect) + *seed:* from the appearance], 1. any of various related plants of the daisy family, having yellow, red, orange, or purplish flowers with toothed petals and wiry stems; coreopsis. 2. a tick trefoil.

tickseed sunflower, a variety of bur marigold with large petals.

tick·tack (tik′tak′), ***n.*** [echoic redupl. of *tick*], 1. a recurring sound like the ticking of a clock. 2. a device for making a tapping sound on a window pane or door as a prank: it consists typically of a weight hung next to the window, etc. and manipulated from a distance by a string.

tick-tack-toe (tik′tak-tō′, ti′ta-tō′), ***n.*** a game in which two players take turns marking either crosses or circles in a block of nine squares, the object being to complete a straight or diagonal line of one's mark before the other player does: also **tit-tat-toe.**

tick·tock (tik′tok′), ***n.*** the sound made by a clock or watch. ***v.i.*** to make this sound.

tick trefoil, any of various related plants of the pea family, with clusters of small purple flowers, leaves in groups of three, and jointed prickly pods.

Ti·con·der·o·ga, Fort (tī′kon-də-rō′gə, tī-kon′də-rō′gə), an old fort in New York State, on Lake Champlain: captured from the French by the British in 1759 and from the British by Ethan Allen in 1775.

tid·al (tī′d′l), ***adj.*** of, having, caused by, determined by, or dependent on a tide or tides.

tidal wave, 1. an unusually great, destructive wave sent inshore by an earthquake or a very strong wind. 2. any great or widespread movement, expression of prevalent feeling, etc.

tid·bit (tid′bit′), ***n.*** [dial. *tid,* small object + *bit*], a pleasing or choice bit of food, gossip, etc.: also **titbit.**

tid·dle·dy·winks (tid′′l-di-wiŋks′), ***n.*** tiddlywinks.

tid·dly·winks (tid′′l-i-wiŋks′, tid′li-wiŋks′), ***n.*** [prob. < *tiddly,* child's form of *little;* the word first occurs in sense "illicit grogshop"], a game in which the players try to snap little colored disks from a table, etc. into a cup by pressing their edges with larger disks.

tide (tīd), ***n.*** [ME. *tide, tid,* tide, time, season; AS. *tid,* time; akin to G. *zeit;* IE. base *$*d\bar{a}(i)$-, to part, divide up, seen also in *time*], 1. originally, a period of time: now only in combination, as in *Eastertide, eventide,* or in the proverb "Time and tide wait for no man." 2. [prob. influenced by MLG. or MD.], the alternate rise and fall of the surface of oceans, seas, and the bays, rivers, etc. connected with them, caused by the attraction of the moon and sun. The tide occurs twice in each period of 24 hours and 51 minutes (*lunar day*). During its rise, tide is called *flood tide,* and during its fall, *ebb tide.* When the moon is new or full, the tide is unusually high and is called *spring tide;* when the moon is at first or third quarter, the tide is unusually low and is called *neap tide.* 3. something that rises and falls like the tide. 4. a stream, current, tendency, etc.: as, the *tide* of public opinion. 5. the period during which something is at its highest or fullest point. 6. [Archaic], an opportune time or occasion. ***adj.*** tidal. ***v.i.*** [TIDED (-id), TIDING], 1. to flow or surge like a tide. 2. in *nautical usage,* to drift with the tide, especially so as to work its way into or out of a harbor, etc. ***v.t.*** to carry with or as with the tide.

tide over, 1. to help along temporarily, as through a period of difficulty. 2. to overcome; survive; endure.

turn the tide, to reverse a condition or conditions.

tide (tīd), ***v.i.*** [TIDED (-id), TIDING], [ME. *tiden;* AS. *tidan* < *tid* (see TIDE); cf. BETIDE], [Archaic], to betide; happen.

tide·land (tīd′land′), ***n.*** land covered by flood tide.

tide·mark (tīd′märk′), ***n.*** a mark indicating the highest point of flood tide or, sometimes, the lowest point of ebb tide.

tide·rip (tīd′rip′), ***n.*** water made rough by currents or tides flowing in opposing directions: also **rip.**

tide·wait·er (tīd′wāt′ẽr), ***n.*** formerly, a customs official who boarded incoming ships and checked unloading to prevent customs evasion.

tide·wa·ter (tīd′wô′tẽr, tīd′wä′tẽr), ***n.*** 1. water brought into an area by the action of the rising tide. 2. water, as of a certain area or in certain streams, that is affected by the tide; hence, 3. an area in which water is affected by the tide; specifically, [T-], the eastern part of Virginia. 4. [T-], the English dialect of eastern Virginia. ***adj.*** 1. of or along a tidewater. 2. [T-], of (the) Tidewater.

tide·way (tīd′wā′), ***n.*** 1. a channel through which a tide runs. 2. the tidal part of a river. 3. a tidal current.

ti·di·ly (tī′d′l-i), ***adv.*** in a tidy manner.

ti·di·ness (tī′di-nis), ***n.*** a tidy condition or quality.

ti·dings (tī′diŋz), ***n.pl.*** [sometimes construed as sing.], [ME. *tidinge* < AS. *tidung* but influenced by ON. *tithindi,* news, message; akin to G. *zeitung,* newspaper], news; information.

ti·dy (tī′di), ***adj.*** [TIDIER (-di-ẽr), TIDIEST (-di-ist)], [ME. *tidi,* seasonable, honest, hence in good condition < *tide;* see TIDE], 1. neat in personal appearance, ways, etc.; orderly. 2. neat in arrangement; in order; trim. 3. [Colloq.], fairly good; satisfactory. 4. [Colloq.], rather large; considerable: as, a *tidy* sum of money. ***v.t. & v.i.*** [TIDIED (-did), TIDYING], to make (things) tidy: often with *up*. ***n.*** [*pl.* TIDIES (-diz)], a small cover of lace, embroidery, etc. used on the arms and backs of chairs and sofas to prevent soiling; antimacassar. —***SYN.*** see **neat.**

ti·dy·tips (tī′di-tips′), ***n.*** [*pl.* TIDYTIPS], any of a group of plants of the aster family, with yellow, daisylike flowers, often tipped with white.

tie (tī), ***v.t.*** [TIED (tīd), TYING], [ME. *tien;* AS. *tigan, tegan* < base of *teag, teah,* a rope; for IE. base see TOW], 1. to fasten, attach, or bind (one thing to another or two or more things together) by entwining with a piece of string, cord, rope, etc., which is then knotted. 2. to draw together or join the parts, ends, or sides of by tightening and knotting laces, strings, etc.: as, he *tied* his shoes, she *tied* her apron. 3. to make (a knot). 4. to make a knot in: as, he *tied* his bow tie. 5. to fasten, connect, or join in any way. 6. to confine; restrain; restrict. 7. *a*) to equal the score of (an opponent) in a contest. *b*) to equal (the score of an opponent). 8. [Colloq.], to join in marriage. 9. in *music,* to connect with a tie. ***v.i.*** 1. to be capable of being tied; make a tie. 2. to make the same score in a contest. ***n.*** [ME. *tege, teige;* AS. *teag, teah,* a rope], 1. a string, lace, cord, etc. used to tie things. 2. something that connects, binds, or joins; bond; link: as, a business *tie, ties* of affection. 3. something that confines, limits, or restricts: as, legal *ties.* 4. a necktie, or cravat. 5. a beam, rod, etc. that holds together parts of a building and strengthens against stress. 6. any of the parallel crossbeams to which the rails of a railroad are fastened; sleeper. 7. an equality of scores in a contest; hence, 8. a contest or match in which there is such an equality; draw; stalemate. 9. in *music,* a curved line above or below two notes of the same pitch, indicating that the tone is to be held unbroken for the duration of their combined values.

tie down, to confine; restrain; restrict.

ties, low, laced shoes; oxfords.

tie up, 1. to tie firmly or securely. 2. to wrap up and tie with string, etc. 3. to moor to a dock. 4.

to obstruct; hinder; stop. 5. to cause to be already in use, retained, committed, or otherwise rendered unavailable.

SYN.—**tie** and **bind** are often interchangeable, but in discriminative use, **tie** specifically implies the connection of one thing with another by means of a rope, string, etc. which can be knotted (to *tie* a horse to a hitching post), and **bind** suggests the use of an encircling band which holds two or more things firmly together (to *bind* someone's legs); **fasten**, a somewhat more general word, implies a joining of one thing to another, as by tying, binding, gluing, nailing, pinning, etc.; **attach** emphasizes the joining of two or more things in order to keep them together as a unit (*attach* your references to the application form). —*ANT.* separate, part.

tie·back (tī′bak′), *n.* a sash, ribbon, tape, etc. used to tie curtains or draperies to one side.

tie beam, a beam serving as a tie in a roof, etc.

tie-in (tī′in′), *adj.* designating or of a sale in which two or more articles are offered together, often at a reduced price, or something scarce, desirable, etc. can be bought only in combination with some other, generally undesired item. *n.* 1. such a sale. 2. an article sold in this way.

tie·mann·ite (tē′mən-īt′), *n.* [after its discoverer, W. *Tiemann*, mineralogist], a grayish mineral with a metallic luster, a compound of mercury and selenium, HgSe.

Tien Shan (tyen′ shän′), a mountain range in the Kirghiz S.S.R. and northern Sinkiang province, China: highest peak, Tengri Khan, 23,622 ft.: also **Tian Shan.**

Tien·tsin (tin′tsin′; Chin. tyen′jin′), *n.* a city and port in Hopeh province, northeastern China: pop., 1,686,000 (est. 1947).

tie·pin (tī′pin′), *n.* a decorative pin for fastening a necktie.

Tie·po·lo, Gio·van·ni Bat·tis·ta (jô-vän′nē bät-tēs′tä tye′pô-lô′), 1696–1770; Venetian painter.

tier (têr), *n.* [< OFr. *tire*, order, rank, row; or < Fr. *tir*, a shooting (cf. It. *tiro*, tier of guns); first used of ordnance], 1. a row, or rank, of seats. 2. any of a series of rows, or ranks, arranged one above or behind another. *v.t. & v.i.* to arrange or be arranged in tiers.

ti·er (tī′ẽr), *n.* 1. a person or thing that ties. 2. a type of pinafore worn by children.

tierce (têrs), *n.* [OFr. *tierce, terce;* L. *tertia*, fem. of *tertius*, (a) third < base of *tres*, three], 1. originally, a third. 2. the third canonical hour (9 A.M.) or its office. 3. an old liquid measure, equal to 1/3 pipe (42 gallons). 4. a cask of this capacity, between a barrel and a hogshead in size. 5. in *card games*, a sequence of three cards in the same suit. 6. in *fencing*, the third position, from which a lunge or parry can be made. Abbreviated **tc.** (*sing. & pl.*).

Tier·ra del Fue·go (tyer′rä del fwe′gô; Eng. ti-er′ə del′ fū-ā′gō), 1. a group of islands belonging to Chile and Argentina, south of the Strait of Magellan: area, 27,600 sq. mi. 2. the chief island in the group: area, 18,530 sq. mi.

‡tiers é·tat (tyâr′ zā′tȧ′), [Fr.], the third estate; the common people, as distinguished from the nobility and the clergy.

tie-up (tī′up′), *n.* 1. a temporary stoppage or interruption of production, traffic, etc. 2. [Colloq.], connection; relation.

tiff (tif), *n.* [also early & dial. *tift;* ? echoic or same word as *tiff* (drink)], 1. a slight fit of anger or bad humor; huff; pet. 2. a slight quarrel; spat. *v.i.* to be in or have a tiff.

tiff (tif), *n.* [also early & dial. *tift;* ? < ON. *thēfr*, a smell (cf. Norw. *teft*, a scent); cf. SNIFTER, TIFFIN], [Rare or Obs.], 1. liquor; especially, weak liquor. 2. a sip or little drink of diluted liquor or punch.

tif·fa·ny (tif′ə-ni), *n.* [*pl.* TIFFANIES (-niz)], [OFr. *tiphanie*, Epiphany; LL. *theophania;* Gr. *theophania*, lit., manifestation of God: ? so called because worn on Epiphany], a thin gauze of silk or muslin.

tif·fin (tif′in), *n., v.i. & v.t.* [Anglo-Ind. for *tiffing*, drinking, hence, by extension, eating < *tiff* (to drink)], [British], lunch.

Ti·flis (tif′lis; Russ. tif-lēs′), *n.* Tbilisi: former name.

ti·ger (tī′gẽr), *n.* [*pl.* TIGERS (-gẽrz), TIGER; see PLURAL, II, D, 1], [ME. & OFr. *tigre;* L. *tigris;* Gr. *tigris* < Iranian base meaning "sharp, pointed"], 1. a large, fierce, flesh-eating animal of the cat family, about the size of a lion, having a tawny coat striped with black: it is native to most of Asia. 2. any of several similar animals; especially, *a)* the South American jaguar. *b)* the South African leopard. *c)* the Tasmanian tiger or wolf. 3. a cruel, bloodthirsty person. 4. a loud yell (often the word "tiger") at the end of a round of cheers.

tiger beetle, any of various beetles with larvae that burrow in soil and feed on other insects.

tiger cat, 1. any of various wildcats smaller than, but somewhat resembling, the tiger, as the serval, ocelot, margay, etc. 2. a domestic cat with tigerlike markings.

ti·ger·eye (tī′gẽr-ī′), *n.* a semiprecious, yellow-brown stone, usually oxidized crocidolite, used for ornament.

ti·ger·ish (tī′gẽr-ish), *adj.* 1. like or characteristic of a tiger. 2. cruel; ferocious.

tiger lily, 1. a variety of lily having orange flowers with purplish-black spots. 2. any of several kinds of lilies resembling this flower.

tiger moth, any of a group of stout-bodied moths with brightly striped or spotted wings.

ti·ger's-eye (tī′gẽrz-ī′), *n.* a tigereye.

tight (tīt), *adj.* [ME. *tight, thight;* AS. *thiht* (in comp.), strong; akin to MHG. *dichte*, tight; the immediate etymon may be Anglo-N. **thēht-* (ON. *thēttr*), tight, watertight; IE. base **teuq-*, to draw together, be thick], 1. originally, dense. 2. so close or compact in structure that water, air, etc. cannot pass through: as, the boat is *tight*. 3. drawn, packed, etc. closely together: as, a *tight* weave; hence, 4. [Dial.], snug; trim; neat. 5. fixed securely; held firmly; firm: as, a *tight* joint. 6. fully stretched; taut: opposed to *slack, loose*. 7. fitting closely, especially so as to be uncomfortable. 8. strict; restraining; severe: as, she kept *tight* control over her children. 9. difficult to manage: especially in *a tight corner, squeeze*, etc., a difficult situation. 10. showing tension or strain: as, a *tight* smile. 11. almost even or tied; close: as, a *tight* race. 12. *a)* difficult to get; scarce in relation to demand: said of commodities on a market. *b)* characterized by such scarcity: as, a *tight* market. 13. concise; condensed: said of language. 14. [Archaic or Dial.], well-proportioned; shapely. 15. [Dial.], competent; capable. 16. [Colloq.], stingy; parsimonious. 17. [Slang], drunk. *adv.* tightly.

sit tight, 1. to maintain one's opinion; remain firm. 2. to maintain one's position; refrain from action.

SYN.—**tight**, in this connection, implies a constricting or binding encirclement (a *tight* collar) or such closeness or compactness of parts as to be impenetrable (air*tight*); **taut** (and, loosely, also **tight**) is applied to a rope, cord, cloth, etc. that is pulled or stretched to the point where there is no slackness (*taut* sails); **tense** suggests a tightness or tautness that results in great strain (*tense* muscles). —*ANT.* loose, slack, lax.

-tight (tīt), [< *tight*], a combining form meaning *impervious to*, as in *watertight, airtight*.

tight·en (tīt′'n), *v.t. & v.i.* to make or become tight or tighter.

tight·fist·ed (tīt′fis′tid), *adj.* stingy; closefisted.

tight-lipped (tīt′lipt′), *adj.* 1. having the lips closed tightly. 2. not saying much; secretive.

tight·rope (tīt′rōp′), *n.* a tightly stretched rope or cable on which acrobats walk or do balancing acts.

tights (tīts), *n.pl.* a tightly fitting garment for the lower half of the body and legs, worn by acrobats, dancers, etc.

tight·wad (tīt′wäd′, tīt′wôd′), *n.* [*tight* + *wad* (roll of money)], [Slang], a stingy person; miser.

Tig·lath-pi·le·ser III (tig′lath-pi-lē′zẽr), ?– 727 B.C.; king of Assyria (745–727 B.C.).

tig·lic acid (tig′lik), [< Mod. L. *tiglium*, croton-oil plant < Gr. *tilos*, thin feces: the seeds have a cathartic effect], an unsaturated, monobasic acid, C_4H_7COOH, occurring as a glyceride in croton oil and camomile oil.

Ti·gré (tē-grā′), *n.* a province of Ethiopia: formerly a kingdom of eastern Africa.

ti·gress (tī′gris), *n.* 1. a female tiger. 2. a cruel, ferocious woman.

Ti·gris (tī′gris), *n.* a river in southeastern Turkey and Iraq, joining with the Euphrates to flow into the Persian Gulf: length, 1,150 mi.: see **Chaldea**, map.

ti·grish (tī′grish), *adj.* tigerish.

Ti·hwa (dē′hwä′), *n.* the capital of Sinkiang province, northwestern China: pop., 20,000: also called *Urumchi*.

tike (tīk), *n.* a tyke.

til (til, tēl), *n.* [Hind.; Sans. *tila*], sesame, a plant with small, edible seeds.

til·bu·ry (til′bẽr-i), *n.* [*pl.* TILBURIES (-iz)], [after the inventor, *Tilbury*, a London coach builder], a light, two-wheeled carriage for two persons.

til·de (til′də), *n.* [Sp. < L. *titulus;* see TITLE], a diacritical mark (~) used: *a)* in Spanish, over an *n* to indicate a palatal nasal sound (ny), as in *señor*. *b)* in Portuguese, over a vowel or the first vowel of a diphthong to indicate nasalization, as in *lã, pão:* the same mark is also used in some phonetic systems to indicate any of various other sounds.

Til·den, Samuel Jones (til′dən), 1814–1886; American lawyer and statesman; Democratic candidate for president (1876).

tile (tīl), *n.* [ME. *tile, tegele;* AS. *tigele;* L. *tegula*, a tile < *tegere*, to cover; for the IE. base see THATCH], 1. a thin, usually rectangular piece of unglazed, fired clay, stone, or concrete, used for roofing, flooring, etc. 2. a thin, usually rectangular piece of glazed, fired clay, often decorated, used for fireplace borders, bathroom walls, etc. 3. a similar piece of other material, as of metal or plastic, used in the same way. 4. tiles collectively; tiling. 5. a drain of tiles or earthenware pipe. 6. any of the pieces, or counters, in mah-jongg. 7. [Colloq.], a high, stiff hat. *v.t.* [TILED (tīld), TILING], to cover with tiles.

tile·fish (tīl′fish′), *n.* [*pl.* TILEFISH, TILEFISHES (-iz); see FISH], [contr. < the generic name Lophalo*tilus*], a large, deep-sea food fish with a golden-spotted blue or purple body, yellow-spotted fins, and a fleshy crest on its head.

til·er (tīl′ẽr), *n.* a person who makes or lays tiles.

til·er·y (tīl′ẽr-i), *n.* [*pl.* TILERIES (-iz)], a place where tiles are made.

til·i·a·ceous (til′i-ā′shəs), *adj.* [LL. *tiliaceus* < L. *tilia*, linden tree], of the linden family of plants, having fibrous bark and gummy sap.

til·ing (tīl′iŋ), *n.* 1. the action of a person who tiles. 2. tiles collectively. 3. a covering or structure of tiles.

till (til), *prep.* [ME. & AS. *til;* ON.; akin to G. *ziel*, point aimed at, goal, end; for the IE. base see TILL, *v.*], 1. up to the time of; until. 2. [Obs. or Scot.], up to the place of; as far as. 3. [Scot.], to, concerning, for, by, etc. *conj.* until.

till (til), *v.t. & v.i.* [ME. *tilien;* AS. *tilian*, lit., to strive for, work for; akin to G. *zielen*, to aim, strive, *ziel*, point aimed at (cf. TILL, *prep.*); prob. IE. base **del-*, to aim at, reckon, etc. (cf. TELL)], to prepare (land) for raising crops, as by plowing, fertilizing, etc.; cultivate.

till (til), *n.* [earlier *tille;* prob. < ME. *tyllen, tillen*, to draw (AS. **-tillan*) < base of *till, v.*], 1. a drawer or tray, as in a store counter, etc., for keeping money; hence, 2. ready cash.

till (til), *n.* [var. of ME. *thill*, in same sense; ? < AS. *thille*, a board, flooring, etc.], unstratified, glacial drift of clay, sand, and gravel, forming poor subsoil impervious to water.

till·age (til′ij), *n.* [*till, v.* + *-age*], 1. the tilling of land. 2. the state of being tilled; cultivation. 3. land that is tilled. 4. the crops on such land.

til·land·si·a (ti-land′zi-ə), *n.* [Mod. L., after Elias *Tillands*, Swed. botanist], a mosslike plant having slender, gray stems covered with tiny leaves, found hanging in strands from many trees in the South; Spanish moss.

till·er (til′ẽr), *n.* [OFr. *telier;* ML. *telarium*, weaver's beam < *tela*, a web; nautical sense prob. influenced by ME. *tillen*, to pull, draw; cf. TILL (drawer)], a bar or handle for turning a boat's rudder.

till·er (til′ẽr), *n.* a person who tills; farmer; cultivator.

till·er (til′ẽr), *n.* [< AS. *telgor* (extension of *telga*, a branch, bough, shoot) via dial.], a shoot growing from the root or base of the stem. *v.i.* to send forth tillers: said of plants.

Til·sit (til′zit), *n.* 1. a city in the western U.S.S.R., on the Memel River: formerly in East Prussia: pop., 57,000.

tilt (tilt), *v.t.* [ME. *tilten*, to be overthrown, totter < AS. *tealt*, shaky, unstable (prob. via. AS. **tieltan*); akin to Sw. *tulta*, to totter], 1. to cause to slope; slant; tip. 2. to poise or thrust (a lance) in a tilt. 3. to rush at (one's opponent) in a tilt. 4. to forge or hammer with a tilt hammer. *v.i.* 1. to slope; incline; slant; tip. 2. to poise or thrust one's lance, or to charge (*at* one's opponent), in a tilt. 3. to take part in a tilt or joust; hence, 4. to dispute; argue. *n.* 1. a medieval contest in which two armed horsemen thrust with lances in an attempt to unseat each other; joust. 2. any spirited contest between two persons, as a debate. 3. a thrust or parry, as with a lance. 4. a tilting or being tilted (sense 1). 5. a slope. 6. a seesaw. 7. a tilt hammer.

(at) full tilt, at full speed; with the greatest force.

tilt at windmills, [from Don Quixote's encounter with windmills, which he took for giants], to attack imaginary opponents.

tilt (tilt), *n.* [ME. *tilde, teld* (< AS. *teld*, a tent, akin to G. *zelt*), prob. merged with *tillette* (< OFr. *telete*), wrapper of cloth], a cloth covering or canopy of a boat, stall, cart, etc. *v.t.* to furnish or cover with a tilt.

tilth (tilth), *n.* [ME. *tilthe;* AS. *tilth, tilthe* < base of *tilian* (see TILL, *v.*) + *-th;* akin to OFris. *tilath*, cultivation], 1. a tilling or being tilled; cultivation of land. 2. tilled land.

tilt hammer, a heavy drop hammer used in forging.

tilt·yard (tilt′yärd′), *n.* a place where tilts were held.

Tim., Timothy.

ti·ma·rau (tē′mə-rou′), *n.* [< the native name in Mindoro], a small, stocky Philippine buffalo with brownish-black hide and short, thick horns.

tim·bal (tim′b′l), *n.* [Fr. *timbale*, altered (after *cymbale*, cymbal) < earlier *attabale;* Sp. *atabal;* see ATABAL], 1. a kettledrum. 2. a cicada's vibrating membrane.

tim·bale (tim′b′l; Fr. tan′bȧl′), *n.* [Fr., lit., kettledrum; see TIMBAL], 1. a custardlike, highly flavored dish made of chicken, lobster, fish, etc. baked in a small, drum-shaped mold. 2. a type of fried pastry shell, filled with a cooked food: also **timbal case.**

tim·ber (tim′bẽr), *n.* [ME. & AS.; akin to G. *zimmer*, room (OHG. *zimbar*, wooden structure); IE. base **dem-, *demā-*, to join together, build, seen also in L. *domus*, house (cf. DOME, DOMICILE), Eng. *tame*], 1. originally, *a)* a building. *b)* building material. 2. wood suitable for building houses, ships, etc., whether cut or in the form of trees. 3. a large, heavy, dressed piece of wood used in building; beam. 4. [British], lumber. 5. trees collectively. 6. timberland. 7. personal quality or character: as, a man of his *timber*. 8. in *shipbuilding*, a wooden rib. *v.t.* to provide, build, shore, or prop up with timbers. *adj.* of or for timber. *interj.* a warning shout by a lumberman that a cut tree is about to fall.

tim·bered (tim′bẽrd), *adj.* 1. made or provided with timbers. 2. covered with timber trees; wooded.

timber hitch, in *nautical usage*, a knot used for tying a rope to a spar: see **knot**, illus.

tim·ber·ing (tim′bẽr-iŋ), *n.* 1. timbers collectively. 2. work made of timber.

tim·ber·land (tim′bẽr-land′), *n.* land with trees suitable for timber; wooded land.

tim·ber-line (tim′bẽr-līn′), *adj.* of a timber line.

timber line, the imaginary line on mountains and in polar regions beyond which trees do not grow.

timber wolf, a large, gray or brindled wolf of North America.

tim·ber·work (tim′bẽr-wũrk′), *n.* work made of timber; timbering.

tim·bre (tim′bẽr, tam′bẽr; Fr. tan′br′), *n.* [Fr.; OFr.; see TIMBREL], 1. the characteristic quality of sound that distinguishes one voice or musical instrument from another: it is determined by the harmonics of the sound and is distinguished from the *intensity* and *pitch*. 2. in *phonetics*, the degree of resonance of a voiced sound, especially of a vowel.

tim·brel (tim′brəl), *n.* [dim. of ME. *timbre;* OFr. *timbre*, small bell < L. *tympanum;* see TYMPANUM], an ancient type of tambourine.

Tim·buk·tu (tim-buk′tōō, tim′buk-tōō′), *n.* a town in the French Sudan, on the Niger River: pop., 7,000: French name, *Tombouctou*.

time (tīm), *n.* [ME.; AS. *tima;* IE. **dī-men* < base **dā(i)-*, to part, divide up, etc., seen also in *tide*], I. *a period or interval* 1. the period between two events or during which something exists, happens, or acts; measured or measurable interval. 2. *usually pl.* a period of history, characterized by a given social structure, set of customs, etc.: as, medieval *times*.

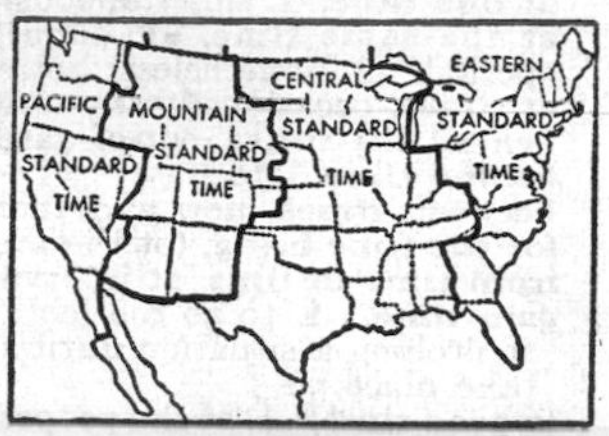

UNITED STATES TIME ZONES

3. *often pl.* a period of history or of the history of a region, with reference to a famous person living then: as, in Lincoln's *time*. 4. *usually pl.* prevailing conditions, past, present, or future: as, *times* are bad. 5. a period characterized by a prevailing condition: as, a *time* of sorrow. 6. a period or occasion with reference to one's personal reaction to it: as, I had a good *time*. 7. a period of duration set or thought of as set; specifically, *a)* a period of existence; lifetime: as, my *time* is almost over. *b)* the period of pregnancy. *c)* a term of apprenticeship. *d)* a term of imprisonment. 8. a period or periods necessary, sufficient, or available for something: as, I don't have *time* for reading. 9. the usual, shortest, or allotted period during which something is done: as, the runner's *time* was 1.47 minutes, baking *time*, 20 minutes. 10. *a)* the period worked or to be worked by an employee. *b)* the pay due for this. 11. rate of speed in marching, driving, working, etc.: as, go at double *time*. 12. in *drama*, one of the three unities. 13. in *music*, *a)* the grouping of rhythmic beats into measures of equal length. *b)* the characteristic rhythm of a composition or passage in terms of this grouping, indicated by the time signature: also called *meter, rhythm:* see also **common time, duple, quadruple time, triple time, two-part time.** *c)* the rate of speed at which a composition or passage is played; tempo; hence, *d)* loosely, the rhythm and tempo characteristic of a kind of composition: as, waltz *time*, march *time*. *e)* the duration of a note or rest. 14. in *prosody*, *a)* a unit of quantitative meter; especially, *b)* a mora, or short syllable. II. *a point in duration; moment; instant; occasion* 1. a precise instant, second, minute, hour, day, week, month, or year, determined by clock or calendar: as, the *time* of the accident was 5:46 P.M., March 12, 1949. 2. the point at which something has happened, is happening, or will happen; occasion: as, at the *time* they arrived, I was away. 3. the usual, natural, traditional, or appointed moment for something to happen, begin, or end: as, *time* to get up; specifically, *a)* the moment of death: as, my *time* is close at hand. *b)* the moment of childbirth: said of a pregnant woman,

as, she is near her *time*. 4. the suitable, proper, favorable, or convenient moment: as, now is the *time* to act. 5. any one of a series of moments at which the same or nearly the same thing recurs; a repeated occasion: as, this is the fifth *time* I've told you, *time* and *time* again. III. *duration; continuance* 1. indefinite, unlimited duration in which things are considered as happening in the past, present, or future; every moment there has ever been or ever will be. 2. *a*) the entire period of existence of the known universe; finite duration, as distinguished from infinity. *b*) the entire period of existence of the world or of humanity; earthly duration, as distinguished from eternity. 3. a system of measuring duration: as, solar *time*, standard *time*, etc. 4. [T-], Father Time. ***interj.*** in *sports*, etc., a signal that a period of play or activity is ended or that play is temporarily suspended. ***v.t.*** 1. to arrange or set the time of so as to be acceptable, suitable, opportune, etc.: as, the director *timed* the play, he *timed* his visit to find her in. 2. to adjust, set, play, etc. so as to coincide in time with something else: as, *time* your watch with mine. 3. to regulate (a mechanism) for a given speed or length of operation. 4. to set the duration of (a syllable or musical note) as a unit of rhythm. 5. to calculate or record the pace, speed, finishing time, etc. of; clock: as, the winning horse was *timed* at 3.02. ***v.i.*** [Rare], to move in time; keep time. ***adj.*** 1. having to do with time. 2. set or regulated so as to explode, open, etc. at a given time: as, a *time* bomb. 3. payable later or on a specified future date: as, a *time* loan. 4. having to do with purchases in which payment is made over a period of time: as, a *time* payment. Abbreviated **t.**

abreast of the times, 1. up-to-date; modern in ideas, dress, etc. 2. informed about current matters.

against time, trying to finish in a given time; as fast as possible.

ahead of time, sooner than due; early.

at one time, 1. simultaneously. 2. formerly.

at the same time, 1. simultaneously; in the same period. 2. nonetheless; however.

at times, occasionally; sometimes.

behind the times, out-of-date; old-fashioned.

behind time, late.

between times, now and then; occasionally.

for the time being, for the present; temporarily.

from time to time, at intervals; now and then.

gain time, 1. to go too fast: said of a timepiece. 2. to prolong a situation until a desired occurrence can take place.

in good time, 1. at the proper time. 2. in a creditably short time; quickly.

in no time, almost instantly; very quickly.

in time, 1. in the course of time; eventually. 2. before it is too late. 3. keeping the set rhythm, tempo, pace, etc.

lose time, 1. to go too slow: said of a timepiece. 2. to let time go by without advancing one's objective.

make time, 1. to compensate for lost time by going faster, as a train. 2. to travel, work, etc. at a specified, especially fast, rate of speed: as, we *made* (good) *time* between Boston and Albany.

many a time, often; frequently.

on one's own time, during time for which one is not paid; during other than working hours.

on time, 1. at the appointed time; punctual or punctually. 2. to be paid for in installments over a period of time.

out of time, 1. not at the usual time; unseasonable. 2. not keeping the set rhythm, tempo, pace, etc.

pass the time of day, to exchange a few words of greeting, etc.

time after time, again and again; continually: also **time and again.**

time of life, age (of a person).

time of one's life, [Colloq.], an experience of unusual pleasure for one.

times, multiplied by: symbol, ×.

time·card (tīm′kärd′), ***n.*** a card for showing the number of hours an employee has worked.

time clock, a clock with a mechanism for recording on a timecard the time an employee begins and ends a work period.

time deposit, a bank deposit payable at a specified future date or upon advance notice: abbreviated **T/D.**

time discount, in *commerce*, a discount in price for payment made before the bill is due.

time draft, a draft payable at a future date specified on the draft.

time exposure, 1. an exposure of photographic film for a relatively long period, generally longer than half a second. 2. a photograph taken in this way.

time-hon·ored (tīm′on′ẽrd), ***adj.*** honored or observed because in existence or usage for a long time.

time immemorial, 1. time so long past as to be forgotten or vague. 2. in *English law*, time beyond legal memory, fixed by statute as prior to 1189, the beginning of the reign of Richard I.

time·keep·er (tīm′kēp′ẽr), ***n.*** 1. a timepiece. 2. a person who keeps time; specifically, *a*) a person employed to keep account of the hours worked by employees. *b*) a person who beats time for a band, etc. *c*) a person who keeps account of the elapsed time in the periods of play in certain sports.

time·less (tīm′lis), ***adj.*** 1. that cannot be measured by time; unending; eternal. 2. referred or restricted to no specific time; always valid or true; dateless. 3. [Obs.], untimely.

time limit, a fixed period of time during which something must be done or ended.

time·li·ness (tīm′li-nis), ***n.*** the state or quality of being timely.

time loan, a loan to be paid by a specified time.

time lock, a lock with a mechanism that prevents opening before the time set.

time·ly (tīm′li), ***adj.*** [TIMELIER (-li-ẽr), TIMELIEST (-li-ist)], [ME. *tymeli, timlich;* AS. *timlice;* see **TIME & -LY**], 1. happening, done, said, etc. at a suitable time; well-timed; opportune. 2. [Obs. or Rare], appearing in good time; early. ***adv.*** [Archaic or Poetic], early; soon.

SYN.—**timely** applies to that which happens or is done at an appropriate time, especially at such a time as to be of help or service (a *timely* interruption); **opportune** refers to that which is so timed, often as if by accident, as to meet exactly the needs of the occasion (the *opportune* arrival of a supply train); **seasonable** applies literally to that which is suited to the season of the year or, figuratively, to the moment or occasion (*seasonable* weather).

time·ous (tīm′əs), ***adj.*** [Scot.], timely.

time out, 1. any time not counted toward a work record, score, etc. 2. in *football, basketball*, etc., any time requested during play to make substitutions, discuss strategy, etc. and not counted in the playing time.

time·piece (tīm′pēs′), ***n.*** any apparatus for measuring and recording time; especially, a clock or watch.

tim·er (tīm′ẽr), ***n.*** 1. a timekeeper. 2. a timepiece; especially, a stop watch. 3. in internal-combustion engines, a mechanism for causing the spark to be produced in the cylinder at the required instant.

time·sav·ing (tīm′sāv′iŋ), ***adj.*** that saves time because of greater efficiency, etc.

time·serv·er (tīm′sũr′vẽr), ***n.*** a person who for his own advantage deliberately surrenders his principles and acts in conformity with the patterns of behavior prevailing at the time or sanctioned by those in authority.

time·serv·ing (tīm′sũr′viŋ), ***n.*** the action or behavior of a timeserver. ***adj.*** of, or having the nature of, a timeserver.

time signature, in *music*, a sign, after the key signature, indicating the time, or tempo.

Times Square, a square in New York City, at Broadway and 42d Street: it marks the lower limit of the main theater and entertainment section.

time study, study of operational or production procedures and the time consumed by them, for the purpose of devising methods of increasing efficiency or productivity of workers.

time·ta·ble (tīm′tā′b'l), ***n.*** a schedule of the times certain things are to happen, especially of the times of arrival and departure of trains, busses, ships, etc.

time-test·ed (tīm′tes′tid), ***adj.*** having value proved by long use or experience.

time·work (tīm′wũrk′), ***n.*** work paid for by the hour or day: distinguished from *piecework.*

time·worn (tīm′wôrn′), ***adj.*** worn or deteriorated by long use or existence.

time zone, see **standard time.**

tim·id (tim′id), ***adj.*** [L. *timidus* < *timere*, to fear], 1. easily frightened; lacking self-confidence; shy; timorous. 2. showing fear or lack of self-confidence; hesitant: as, a *timid* reply. —***SYN.*** see **afraid.**

ti·mid·i·ty (ti-mid′ə-ti), ***n.*** [L. *timiditas*], the condition or quality of being timid; fearfulness; shyness.

tim·ing (tīm′iŋ), ***n.*** the regulation of the speed with which something is performed so as to produce the most effective results: as, the *timing* of a play, of an engine, of a golfer's swing, etc.

Ti·miş·oa·ra (tē′mē-shwä′rȧ), ***n.*** a city in western Romania: pop., 90,000: Hungarian name, *Temesvár.*

ti·moc·ra·cy (tī-mok′rə-si), ***n.*** [OFr. *tymocracie;* ML. *timocratia;* Gr. *timokratia* < *timē*, honor, worth + *-kratia* (see -CRACY)], 1. in Plato's politics, a state in which love of honor and glory is the guiding principle of the rulers. 2. in Aristotle's politics, a state in which political power is in direct proportion to property ownership.

ti·mo·crat·ic (tī′mə-krat′ik), ***adj.*** of or characteristic of a timocracy.

Ti·mor (tē′môr, ti-môr′), ***n.*** an Indonesian and Portuguese island of the East Indies, north of Australia: area, 13,700 sq. mi.: see also **Timor Archipelago, Portuguese Timor.**

Timor Archipelago, a province of the United States of Indonesia, including western Timor, Sumbawa, Sumba, Flores, and smaller adjacent islands: area, 24,449 sq. mi.; pop., 1,657,000; capital, Kupang, Timor.

tim·or·ous (tim′ẽr-əs), ***adj.*** [OFr. *timoreus, temeros;*

ML. *timorosus* < L. *timor*, fear], 1. full of or subject to fear; timid. 2. showing or caused by timidity. —***SYN.*** see **afraid.**

Timor Sea, an arm of the Indian Ocean, between Timor and Australia.

Ti·mo·shen·ko, Sem·yon Kon·stan·ti·no·vich (si-myôn' kôn'stan-tē'nô-vich tē'mô-sheŋ'kô; Eng. tim'ə-sheŋ'kō), 1895– ; Soviet marshal in World War II.

Tim·o·thy (tim'ə-thi), [Fr. *Timothée;* L. *Timotheus;* Gr. *Timotheos* < *timē*, honor + *theos*, God], a masculine name: diminutive, *Tim.* ***n.*** in the *Bible*, 1. a disciple of the Apostle Paul. 2. either of the Epistles to Timothy, two books of the New Testament which were messages from the Apostle Paul: abbreviated **Tim.**

tim·o·thy (tim'ə-thi), ***n.*** [after *Timothy* Hanson, who took the seed from New York to the Carolinas, c. 1720], a grass with long, narrow leaves and bearded spikes of flowers, used for fodder: also **timothy grass.**

tim·pa·ni (tim'pə-ni), ***n.pl.*** [*sing.* TIMPANO (-nō')], [It., pl. of *timpano;* see TYMPANUM], kettledrums; especially, a set of kettledrums of different pitches played by one performer in an orchestra: also spelled **tympani.**

tim·pa·nist (tim'pə-nist), ***n.*** a person who plays kettledrums.

tin (tin), ***n.*** [ME.; AS.; akin to G. *zinn;* only in Gmc. languages], 1. a soft, silver-white, metallic chemical element, malleable at ordinary temperatures, capable of a high polish, and used as an alloy in tin foils, solders, utensils, type metals, etc. and in making tin plate: symbol, Sn; at. wt., 118.70; at. no., 50. 2. tin plate. 3. *a)* a can, pot, pan, box, etc. made of tin plate. *b)* [British], a can in which foodstuffs are preserved. 4. [Obs. Slang], money. ***v.t.*** [TINNED (tind), TINNING], 1. to cover or plate with tin. 2. [British], to preserve in tins; can.

tin·a·mou (tin'ə-mōō'), ***n.*** [Fr. < the native (Carib) name, *tinamu*], any of a number of South and Central American birds resembling the partridge and quail, but belonging to the ostrich group.

tin·cal (tiŋ'kəl, tiŋ'käl, tiŋ'kôl), ***n.*** [Malay *tiṅkal;* Per. *tinkāl, tinkar* < Sans. *ṭaṅkaṇa*], crude borax.

tinct (tiŋkt), ***adj.*** [L. *tinctus*, pp. of *tingere;* see TINGE], [Poetic], tinged; tinted. ***n.*** [Poetic], a color; tint. ***v.t.*** [Obs.], to tincture.

tinc·to·ri·al (tiŋk-tôr'i-əl, tiŋk-tō'ri-əl), ***adj.*** [< L. *tinctorius* < *tinctor*, dyer < pp. of *tingere*, to tinge, dye], having to do with color, dyeing, or staining.

tinc·ture (tiŋk'chẽr), ***n.*** [ME.; L. *tinctura* < *tinctus*, pp. of *tingere*, to dye], 1. originally, a dye. 2. a light color; tint; tinge. 3. a slight trace, smattering, shade, vestige, taste, etc. 4. a medicinal substance in solution, especially in an alcoholic solvent: as, *tincture* of iodine: distinguished from *spirit.* 5. in *heraldry*, any color, metal, or fur. ***v.t.*** [TINCTURED (-chẽrd), TINCTURING], 1. to color lightly; tint; tinge. 2. to imbue or permeate slightly with a trace, taste, odor, etc. 3. to affect slightly with a quality: as, a message *tinctured* with hope. Abbreviated **tinct.**

Tin·dal (or **Tin·dale**), **William** (tin'd'l), see **Tyndale, William.**

tin·der (tin'dẽr), ***n.*** [ME. & AS. *tynder* (akin to G. *zunder*) < base of AS. *-tendan*, to kindle], any dry, easily inflammable material, especially that formerly used for starting a fire by catching a spark from flint and steel struck together.

tin·der·box (tin'dẽr-boks'), ***n.*** 1. formerly, a metal box for holding tinder, flint, and steel for starting a fire. 2. any highly inflammable object or structure, excitable person, etc.

tine (tīn), ***n.*** [ME. & AS. *tind*], a sharp, projecting point; spike; prong: as, the *tines* of a fork.

tin·e·a (tin'i-ə), ***n.*** [L., a gnawing worm, moth], any of various skin diseases caused by a fungus; especially, ringworm.

tin·e·id (tin'i-id), ***n.*** [< L. *tinea*, gnawing worm, moth; + *-id*], any of a group of small moths, including the common clothes moth. ***adj.*** designating or of these moths.

tin-foil (tin'foil'), ***adj.*** made of tin foil.

tin foil, a very thin sheet or sheets of tin or an alloy of tin and lead, used to wrap candy, cigarettes, etc.

ting (tiŋ), ***n.*** [echoic], a single, light, ringing sound, as of a small bell being struck. ***v.t. & v.i.*** to make or cause to make a ting.

‡**ting** (tiŋ), ***n.*** a thing (assembly).

ting-a-ling (tiŋ'ə-liŋ'), ***n.*** the sound of a small bell ringing.

tinge (tinj), ***v.t.*** [TINGED (tinjd), TINGEING or TINGING], [L. *tingere*, to dye, stain], 1. to color slightly; give a tint to. 2. to give a trace, slight flavor or odor, shade, etc. to: as, his memory was *tinged* with sorrow. ***n.*** 1. a slight coloring; tint. 2. a slight trace, flavor, odor, etc.; smack; touch. —***SYN.*** see **color.**

tin·gle (tiŋ'g'l), ***v.i.*** [TINGLED (-g'ld), TINGLING], [var. of *tinkle*], 1. to have a prickling, slightly stinging feeling, as from cold, a sharp slap, etc. 2. to cause this feeling. ***v.t.*** to cause to have this feeling. ***n.*** this feeling.

tin·gly (tiŋ'gli), ***adj.*** [TINGLIER (-gli-ẽr), TINGLIEST (-gli-ist)], having or characterized by a tingling.

tin hat, [Slang], a soldier's steel helmet (especially in World War I).

tin·horn (tin'hôrn'), ***adj.*** [from the flashy appearance and cheap quality of *tin horns*], [Slang], pretending to have money, influence, ability, etc., though actually lacking in these; cheap and showy: as, a *tinhorn* sport.

tink·er (tiŋ'kẽr), ***n.*** [ME. *tinkere;* ? < *tinken*, to make a tinkling sound; of echoic origin: tinkers are said to have struck pots and pans to announce their coming], 1. a person who mends pots, pans, etc., usually traveling at his trade. 2. a person who can make all kinds of minor repairs; jack-of-all-trades. 3. a clumsy or unskillful worker; bungler; botcher. 4. the action of such a person; bungling attempt. 5. a young mackerel. 6. a silversides. ***v.i.*** 1. to work as a tinker. 2. to make clumsy, unsuccessful attempts to mend or repair something. 3. to fuss or putter aimlessly or uselessly. ***v.t.*** to mend as a tinker; patch up.

tinker's damn (or **dam**), [< *tinker* + *damn:* with reference to the lowly status and profane speech of tinkers], something of no value: especially in *not worth a tinker's damn.*

tin·kle (tiŋ'k'l), ***v.i.*** [TINKLED (-k'ld), TINKLING], [freq. of ME. *tinken*, to make a tinkling sound; echoic word, prob. unconnected with AS. *tinclian*, to tickle], to make a series of small, short, light, clinking sounds like those of a very small bell. ***v.t.*** 1. to cause to tinkle. 2. to indicate, signal, etc. by tinkling. ***n.*** 1. the act of tinkling. 2. a tinkling sound.

tin·kling (tiŋ'kliŋ), ***n.*** 1. a tinkle or tinkles. 2. a Jamaican grackle with a tinkling voice.

tin·kly (tiŋ'kli), ***adj.*** [TINKLIER (-kli-ẽr), TINKLIEST (-kli-ist)], characterized by tinkling.

tin·man (tin'mən), ***n.*** [*pl.* TINMEN (-mən)], a tinsmith.

tinned (tind), ***adj.*** 1. plated with tin. 2. [British], preserved in tins; canned.

tin·ner (tin'ẽr), ***n.*** 1. a tin miner. 2. a tinsmith. 3. [British], a canner.

tin·ni·ly (tin'ə-li), ***adv.*** in a tinny manner.

tin·ni·ness (tin'i-nis), ***n.*** a tinny quality or state.

tin·ni·tus (ti-nī'təs, tin'i-təs), ***n.*** [L. < *tinnire*, to tinkle], a sound as of ringing or whistling in the ear, not resulting from an external stimulus.

tin·ny (tin'i), ***adj.*** [TINNIER (-i-ẽr), TINNIEST (-i-ist)], 1. of, containing, or yielding tin. 2. like tin in appearance or strength; bright but cheap; not durable. 3. of or like the sound made in striking a tin object. 4. tasting of tin.

tin-pan alley (tin'pan'), 1. a street or part of a city, especially of New York, where there are many musicians, publishers of popular music, etc.; hence, 2. the publishers, writers, and promoters of popular music.

tin-plate (tin'plāt'), ***v.t.*** to plate with tin.

tin plate, thin sheets of iron or steel plated with tin.

tin·sel (tin's'l), ***n.*** [Fr. *étincelle*, a spark; OFr. *estincelle;* L. *scintilla*, a spark, flash], 1. formerly, a cloth of wool, etc. interwoven with glittering threads of gold, silver, or other metal. 2. thin sheets, strips, or threads of tin, metal foil, etc., used for inexpensive decoration. 3. something that glitters like precious metal but has little worth; empty show; sham splendor. ***adj.*** 1. made of or decorated with tinsel. 2. having sham splendor; showy; gaudy. ***v.t.*** [TINSELED or TINSELLED (-s'ld), TINSELING or TINSELLING], 1. to make glitter with or as with tinsel. 2. to give a false appearance of splendor to.

tins·man (tinz'mən), ***n.*** [*pl.* TINSMEN (-mən)], a tinsmith.

tin·smith (tin'smith'), ***n.*** a person who works in tin or tin plate; maker of tinware.

tin·stone (tin'stōn'), ***n.*** cassiterite, native tin dioxide.

tint (tint), ***n.*** [for earlier *tinct* < L. *tinctus*, a dyeing, dipping; pp. of *tingere*, to dye; cf. TINGE], 1. a delicate color or hue; tinge. 2. a color; especially, a gradation of a color with reference to its mixture with white. 3. in *engraving*, an even shading produced by fine parallel lines. 4. in *printing*, a light colored background, as for an illustration. ***v.t.*** to give a tint to. —***SYN.*** see **color.**

Tin·tag·el Head (tin-taj'əl), a cape of western Cornwall, England: legendary birthplace of King Arthur.

tin·tin·nab·u·lar (tin'ti-nab'yoo-lẽr), ***adj.*** tintinnabulary.

tin·tin·nab·u·lar·y (tin'ti-nab'yoo-ler'i), ***adj.*** [< L. *tintinnabulum*, little bell, dim. < *tintinnare*, to jingle, ring < *tinnire*, to jingle; + *-ary*], of bells or the ringing of bells.

tin·tin·nab·u·la·tion (tin'ti-nab'yoo-lā'shən), ***n.*** [see TINTINNABULARY & -TION], the ringing sound of bells.

tin·tin·nab·u·lous (tin'ti-nab'yoo-ləs), *adj.* tintinnabulary.

Tin·to·ret·to, Il (ēl tēn'tô-ret'tô; Eng. tin'tə-ret'ō), (*Jacopo Robusti*), 1518–1594; Venetian painter.

tin·type (tin'tīp'), *n.* a positive photograph taken directly on a sensitized plate of enameled tin or iron; ferrotype.

tin·ware (tin'wâr'), *n.* pots, pans, etc. made of tin plate.

tin·work (tin'wũrk'), *n.* 1. work done in tin. 2. *pl.* [construed as sing.], a place where tin is smelted, rolled, etc.

ti·ny (tī'ni), *adj.* [TINIER (-ni-ẽr), TINIEST (-ni-ist)], [< ME. *tine*, *n.*, a little (something), always preceded by *litel*, little], very small; diminutive; minute. —*SYN.* see **small.**

-tion (shən), [< Fr., OFr., or L.; Fr. *-tion;* OFr. *-cion;* L. *-tio, -tionis* < *-t-* of pp. stem + *-io, -ionis*, suffix], a suffix used to form nouns from verbs, meaning: 1. *a ——ing* or *being ——ed*, as in *relation*. 2. *something ——ed*, as in *creation*.

-tious (shəs), [< Fr. or L.; Fr. *-tieux;* L. *-tiosus* < *-t-* of pp. stem + *-iosus*, -ous], a suffix used in forming adjectives corresponding to nouns in *-tion*, as *cautious*.

tip (tip), *n.* [ME. *tippe;* prob. < MD. or MLG. *tip*, point, top; akin to G. *zipf-* in *zipfel*, an end, tip; prob. IE. base **dā(i)-*, to part, divide up (cf. TIDE, TIME)], 1. the pointed, tapering, or rounded end or top of something long and slim. 2. something attached to the end, as a cap, ferrule, etc. 3. a top or apex, as of a mountain. *v.t.* [TIPPED (tipt), TIPPING], 1. to make a tip on. 2. to cover the tip or tips of (*with* something). 3. to serve as the tip of.

tip (tip), *v.t.* [TIPPED (tipt), TIPPING], [prob. < ME. *tippe*, a tip, or its base], 1. to strike lightly and sharply; tap. 2. to give a small present of money to (a waiter, porter, etc.) for some service. 3. [Colloq.], to give secret information to in an attempt to be helpful: often with *off*. 4. in *baseball*, etc., to hit (the ball) a glancing blow. *v.i.* to give a tip or tips. *n.* 1. a light, sharp blow; tap. 2. a piece of information given secretly or confidentially in an attempt to be helpful: as, he gave me a *tip* on the race. 3. a suggestion, hint, warning, etc. 4. a small present of money given to a waiter, porter, etc. for services; gratuity.

tip (tip), *v.t.* [TIPPED (tipt), TIPPING], [ME. *tipen* (short vowel prob. < p.t. *tipte*); Northern word, prob. < ON.], 1. to overturn or upset: often with *over*. 2. to cause to tilt or slant. 3. to raise slightly or touch the brim of (one's hat) in salutation. *v.i.* 1. to tilt or slant. 2. to overturn or topple: often with *over*. *n.* a tipping or being tipped; tilt; slant.

ti palm, a ti (tree).

tip cart, a cart with a body that can be tipped for dumping its contents.

tip·cat (tip'kat'), *n.* [*tip* (to overturn) + *cat*], 1. a game in which a small piece of wood, usually tapered at both ends, is struck on one end with a bat or stick so that it is sprung into the air where it can be batted for distance. 2. the small piece of wood used in this game. Also called *cat, catty*.

tip-off (tip'ôf'), *n.* 1. the act of tipping off. 2. a tip; confidential disclosure, hint, or warning.

Tip·pe·ca·noe (tip'i-kə-nōō'), *n.* 1. a river of northern Indiana, flowing into the Wabash: length, 200 mi. 2. nickname of William Henry Harrison: from his leadership of American troops in a battle (1811) with Tecumseh's Indians, fought near the Tippecanoe.

tip·per (tip'ẽr), *n.* a person who gives tips, or gratuities.

Tip·per·ar·y (tip'ə-râr'i), *n.* 1. a county of Munster province in south central Ireland: pop., 138,000. 2. a town in this county: pop., 5,500.

tip·pet (tip'it), *n.* [ME. *tipet;* prob. dim. of *tip*, a point; cf. G. *zipfel*, lappet, with same sense development], 1. formerly, a long, hanging part of a hood, cape, or sleeve. 2. a scarflike garment of fur, wool, etc. for the neck and shoulders, hanging down in front. 3. in the *Anglican Church*, a long, black scarf worn by the clergy.

tip·ple (tip''l), *v.i. & v.t.* [TIPPLED (-'ld), TIPPLING], [prob. freq. of *tip* (to overturn)], to drink (alcoholic liquor) often and habitually. *n.* alcoholic liquor.

tip·ple (tip''l), *n.* [see prec.], 1. an apparatus for emptying freight cars by tipping them. 2. a place where this is done.

tip·pler (tip'lẽr), *n.* a person who tipples; habitual drinker.

tip·si·ly (tip'sə-li), *adv.* in a tipsy manner.

tip·si·ness (tip'si-nis), *n.* a tipsy quality or state.

tip·staff (tip'staf', tip'stäf'), *n.* [*pl.* TIPSTAFFS (-stafs', -stäfs'), TIPSTAVES (-stāvz', -stävz')], 1. a staff with a metal tip, formerly carried as an emblem by certain officials; hence, 2. an official who carried such a staff, especially, in England, a bailiff or constable.

tip·ster (tip'stẽr), *n.* [Colloq.], a person who sells tips, as on horse races, for stock speculation, etc.

tip·sy (tip'si), *adj.* [TIPSIER (-si-ẽr), TIPSIEST (-si-ist)], 1. that tips easily; not steady; shaky. 2. crooked; awry. 3. somewhat drunk; intoxicated enough to be somewhat unsteady, fuddled, etc.

tip·toe (tip'tō'), *n.* the tip of a toe or the tips of the toes. *v.i.* [TIPTOED (-tōd'), TIPTOEING], to walk stealthily or cautiously on one's tiptoes. *adj.* 1. standing on one's tiptoes; hence, 2. *a)* lifted up; exalted. *b)* eager; excited; alert. *c)* stealthy; cautious. *adv.* on tiptoe.
  on tiptoe, 1. on one's tiptoes; hence, 2. eager or eagerly. 3. silently; stealthily.

tip·top (tip'top'), *n.* [*tip* (end) + *top*], 1. the highest point; very top; hence, 2. [Colloq.], the highest in quality or excellence; best. *adj. & adv.* 1. at the highest point, or top. 2. [Colloq.], at the highest point of excellence, health, etc.

Ti·rach Mir (tē'rəch mêr'), the highest mountain of the Hindu Kush range, in northwestern Pakistan: height, 25,263 ft.

ti·rade (tī'rād, ti-rād'), *n.* [Fr.; It. *tirata*, a volley < pp. of *tirare*, to draw, fire], a long, vehement speech, especially one of denunciation; harangue.

‡ti·rail·leur (tē'rä'yẽr'), *n.* [Fr. < *tirailler*, to tease, skirmish < *tirer*, to draw, fire], a sharpshooter or skirmisher in the French army.

Ti·ra·na, Ti·ra·në (tē-rä'nə), *n.* the capital of Albania: pop., 31,000.

tire (tīr), *v.i.* [TIRED (tīrd), TIRING], [ME. *tiren* < AS. *tiorian, teorian*, to fail, be tired, via northern dial.; prob. < Gmc. **tiuzōn*, to stay behind; IE. base **deus-*, to fail, be wanting], 1. to become weary or fatigued; lose physical strength by exertion. 2. to lose interest or patience; become bored or impatient. *v.t.* 1. to diminish the physical strength of by exertion, etc.; fatigue; weary. 2. to diminish the patience or interest of, as by persistent or dull talk, etc.; make weary.
  tire of, to lose patience with or interest in.
  tire out, to tire completely; exhaust.

tire (tīr), *n.* [ME. *tyre*, short for *attire*, in sense "equipment"], 1. a hoop of iron or rubber around the wheel of a vehicle, forming the tread. 2. *a)* a rubber tube filled with air, fixed about the wheel of a vehicle to reduce shock: one type of automobile tire consists of a rubber inner tube filled with air at a specified pressure and enclosed in a heavy, treaded, rubber casing: see also **tubeless tire.** *b)* the casing alone, as distinguished from the inner tube. *v.t.* [TIRED (tīrd), TIRING], to furnish with a tire or tires.

tire (tīr), *v.t.* [TIRED (tīrd), TIRING], [ME. *tiren*], [Archaic], attire; dress. *n.* [Archaic], 1. attire. 2. a woman's headdress.

tire (tīr), *v.t. & v.i.* [TIRED (tīrd), TIRING], [ME. *tyren;* OFr. *tirer*, to draw, pull; cf. TIER], [Obs.], 1. to seize or tear at (something). 2. to be mentally absorbed (in).

tired (tīrd), *adj.* [ME. (Northern) *tyrit* < *tiren;* see TIRE (to be fatigued)], fatigued; weary.
SYN.—**tired** is applied to one who has been drained of much of his strength and energy through exertion, boredom, impatience, etc. (*tired* by years of hard toil); **weary** (or **wearied**) suggests such depletion of energy or interest as to make one unable or unwilling to continue (*weary* of study); **exhausted** implies a total draining of strength and energy, as after a long, hard climb; **fatigued** refers to one who has lost so much energy through prolonged exertion that rest and sleep are essential (*fatigued* at the end of the day); **fagged**, an informal word, suggests great exhaustion or fatigue from hard, unremitting work or exertion (completely *fagged* after a set of tennis).

tire·less (tīr'lis), *adj.* that does not become tired.

Ti·re·si·as (tə-res'i-əs, tī-rē'si-əs, tī-rē'shi-əs), *n.* [L.; Gr. *Teiresias*], in *Greek legend*, a blind soothsayer of Thebes.

tire·some (tīr'səm), *adj.* [see -SOME], tiring; boring; wearisome; tedious.

tire·wom·an (tīr'woom'ən), *n.* [*pl.* TIREWOMEN (-wim'-in)], [see TIRE (attire)], [Archaic], a lady's maid.

tir·ing room (tīr'iŋ), [for *attiring room*], [Archaic], a dressing room, especially in a theater.

tirl (tũrl), *v.t. & v.i.* [var. of *trill* (to turn)], [Scot.], to cause (a string) to make a vibrating sound by plucking or striking. *n.* [Scot.], such a sound.

ti·ro (tī'rō), *n.* [*pl.* TIROS (-rōz)], a tyro.

Tir·ol (tir'ol, tē-rōl'), *n.* Tyrol.

Tir·o·lese (tir'ə-lēz'), *adj. & n.* Tyrolese.

Tir·pitz, Al·fred von (äl'frāt fôn tir'pits), 1849–1930; German admiral.

Tir·so de Mo·li·na (têr'sô *the* mô-lē'nä), see **Téllez, Gabriel.**

'tis (tiz), it is.

ti·sane (ti-zan'; Fr. tē'zán'), *n.* [Fr.; see PTISAN], in *pharmacy*, a decoction, as of herbs.

Tish·ah b'Ab (tish'ä bôv'), [Heb. *tishāh b'āb*, ninth (day) of Ab], a Jewish fast day commemorating the destruction of the Temple: see **Jewish holidays.**

Tish·ri (tish'ri), *n.* [Heb.], the first month of the Jewish year: see **Jewish calendar.**

Ti·siph·o·ne (ti-sif'ə-nē'), *n.* in *Greek & Roman mythology*, one of the three Furies.

tis·sue (tish'ōō, tish'oo), *n.* [ME. *tissu, tissewe;* OFr. *tissu*, pp. of *tistre*, to weave < L. *texere*, to weave; cf. TEXTILE], 1. cloth; especially, light, thin cloth, as gauze. 2. an interwoven or intricate mass or series; mesh; network; web: as, his excuse was a *tissue* of lies. 3. tissue paper. 4. in *biology*, *a)* the substance of an organic body or organ, consisting of cells and intercellular material. *b*) any of the distinct structural materials of an organism, having a particular function: as, epithelial *tissue*.

tissue culture, in *biology*, the process or science of growing tissue artificially in a special medium.

tissue paper, very thin, unsized, nearly transparent paper for wrapping fine articles, for toilet use, etc.

Ti·sza (tē′sä), *n.* a river flowing through Hungary and Yugoslavia, into the Danube: length, 800 mi.: German name, *Theiss*.

tit (tit), *n.* [< *titmouse*], a titmouse, titlark, or other small bird.

tit (tit), *n.* [ME. *titte;* AS. *titt;* var. of *teat*], 1. a teat; nipple; hence, 2. a breast: in this sense now vulgar.

tit (tit), *n.* [ME. *tit-* in *titmose* (cf. TITMOUSE), *titling*, etc.; prob. children's term for "little", seen also in ON. *titlingr*, little bird, Norw. *titta*, little girl, etc.], 1. a small, worn-out, inferior horse; nag; jade. 2. [Slang], a girl or woman: usually in depreciation.

tit (tit), *n.* [var. of *tip* (to strike) in earlier *tip for tap* (Fr. *tant pour tant*), tit for tat], a blow; tap: now only in *tit for tat*, blow for blow; retaliation in kind.

Tit., Titus.

tit., title.

Ti·tan (tī′t'n), *n.* [ME.; L.; Gr. *Titan*], 1. in *Greek mythology, a*) any of a race of giant deities whose rule was overthrown and succeeded by the Olympian gods. *b*) any of their descendants. 2. the personification of the sun; Helios, the sun god: so called by certain Latin poets. 3. [t-], any person or thing of great size or power. *adj.* [also t-], Titanic.

ti·tan·ate (tī′tə-nāt′), *n.* any salt of titanic acid.

Ti·tan·esque (tī′t'n-esk′), *adj.* Titanic.

Ti·tan·ess (tī′t'n-is), *n.* a female Titan.

Ti·ta·ni·a (ti-tā′ni-ə, tī-tā′ni-ə), *n.* the queen of fairyland and wife of Oberon in Shakespeare's *Midsummer Night's Dream*.

Ti·tan·ic (tī-tan′ik), *adj.* [Gr. *Titanikos*], 1. of or like the Titans. 2. [t-], of great size, strength, or power.

ti·tan·ic (tī-tan′ik, ti-tan′ik), *adj.* designating or of a chemical compound containing titanium with a valence of four.

titanic acid, either of two weak acids, H_2TiO_3 or H_4TiO_4, derived from titanic oxide.

titanic oxide, a crystalline compound, TiO_2, used as a pigment, ceramic glaze, etc.: also **titanic dioxide**.

ti·tan·if·er·ous (tī′tə-nif′ēr-əs), *adj.* [< *titanium* + *-ferous*], containing titanium.

Ti·tan·ism (tī′t'n-iz'm), *n.* [also t-], the characteristic quality or spirit of the Titans, who overthrew Uranus; spirit of revolt or defiance, as against the established order or social conventions.

ti·tan·ite (tī′tə-nīt′), *n.* [G. *titanit;* see TITANIUM & -ITE], sphene, a mineral.

ti·ta·ni·um (tī-tā′ni-əm, ti-tā′ni-əm), *n.* [Mod. L. < L. *Titani* or *Titanes;* Gr. *Titanes*, pl. of *Titan*, a Titan], a dark-gray, lustrous, metallic chemical element found in rutile and other minerals and used as a cleaning and deoxidizing agent in molten steel, etc.: symbol, Ti; at. wt., 47.90; at. no., 22.

Ti·tan·om·a·chy (tī′tə-nom′ə-ki), *n.* [Gr. *Titanomachia;* see TITAN & -MACHY], in *Greek mythology*, the war between the Titans and the Olympian gods.

ti·tan·ous (tī-tan′əs, ti-tan′əs), *adj.* designating or of a chemical compound containing titanium with a valence of three.

tit·bit (tit′bit′), *n.* a tidbit.

ti·ter (tī′tēr, tē′tēr), *n.* [Fr. *titre*, standard, title], in *chemistry, physiology, & immunology*, 1. a standard strength or degree of concentration of a solution as established through titration. 2. the minimum weight or volume of a substance necessary to cause a given result in titration. Also spelled **titre**.

tith·a·ble (tīth′ə-b'l), *adj.* subject to tithes.

tithe (tīth), *n.* [ME. *tithe, tethe;* AS. *teothe, teogotha*, a tenth; see TENTH], 1. one tenth of the annual produce of one's land, etc., or its equivalent in money, paid as a tax to support the church or the clergy. 2. a tenth part or any small part. 3. any tax or levy. *v.t.* [TITHED (tīthd), TITHING], [ME. *tithen, tethien;* AS. *teothian* < the *n.*], 1. to pay a tithe of (one's produce, etc.). 2. to levy or collect a tithe from (someone).

tith·ing (tīth′iŋ), *n.* 1. a levying or paying of tithes. 2. a tithe. 3. formerly, in England, a unit of civil administration originally consisting of ten families.

Ti·tho·nus (ti-thō′nəs), *n.* [L.; Gr. *Tithōnos*], in *Greek mythology*, the son of Laomedon, loved by Eos, who got for him immortality but not eternal youth, so that he shriveled up and was turned into a grasshopper.

ti·ti (tē′ti), *n.* [Sp. < Aymara Indian name], 1. a small evergreen tree or shrub with fragrant, white or pinkish flowers, found in swamps in the southern United States. 2. any of a number of related trees, as the white titi.

ti·ti (ti-tē′), *n.* [Sp. *tití;* Guarani *titi*], any of several small South American monkeys.

Ti·tian (tish′ən), *n.* (*Tiziano Vecellio*), Venetian painter; 1477–1576.

ti·tian (tish′ən, tish′i-ən), *n.* reddish yellow; auburn: so called because Titian often painted hair this shade in his portraits.

Ti·ti·ca·ca, Lake (tit′i-kä′kə; Sp. tē′tē-kä′kä), a lake between Peru and Bolivia: area, 3,200 sq. mi.; altitude, 12,600 ft.

tit·il·late (tit″l-āt′), *v.t.* [TITILLATED (-id), TITILLATING], [< L. *titillatus*, pp. of *titillare*, to tickle], 1. to tickle. 2. to excite or stimulate pleasurably.

tit·il·la·tion (tit″l-ā′shən), *n.* [ME. *titillacione;* L. *titillatio*], a titillating or being titillated.

tit·il·la·tive (tit″l-ā′tiv), *adj.* titillating or tending to titillate.

tit·i·vate (tit′ə-vāt′), *v.t. & v.i.* [TITIVATED (-id), TITIVATING], [earlier *tidivate, tiddivate;* prob. < *tidy*, with quasi-Latin suffix], [Colloq.], to dress up; spruce up: also spelled **tittivate**.

tit·i·va·tion (tit′ə-vā′shən), *n.* a titivating or being titivated: also spelled **tittivation**.

tit·lark (tit′lärk′), *n.* [*tit* (small horse, bird, etc.) + *lark*], a pipit, a larklike bird.

ti·tle (tī′t'l), *n.* [ME.; OFr.; L. *titulus*, inscription, label, title, sign], 1. a division of a law book, statute, etc., usually larger than a section or article. 2. the name of a poem, essay, chapter, book, picture, statue, piece of music, etc. 3. a title page. 4. a descriptive name or appellation; epithet. 5. an appellation given to a person or family as a sign of privilege, distinction, or profession: as, the title of *lord*. 6. a claim or right. 7. *a*) in the *Church of England*, etc., a source of income or field of work required of a candidate for ordination. *b*) in the *Roman Catholic Church*, any of the parish churches in Rome having a cardinal for its head. 8. in *law, a*) the name of a statute or act. *b*) the heading designating a proceeding. *c*) a right to ownership, especially of real estate. *d*) evidence of such right of ownership. *e*) a document stating such a right; deed. 9. in *sports*, etc., a championship. *v.t.* [TITLED (-t'ld), TITLING], to give a title to; designate by a specified name, or title; entitle. Abbreviated **tit.**

ti·tled (tī′t'ld), *adj.* having a title, especially of nobility.

title deed, a document that establishes title to property.

title page, the page in the front of a book that gives the title, author, publisher, etc.: abbreviated **t.p.**

title role (or **part**), the character in a play, motion picture, etc. whose name is used as the title.

tit·mouse (tit′mous′), *n.* [*pl.* TITMICE (-mis′)], [altered, after *mouse* < ME. *titemose;* prob. < *tit-*, little + AS. *mase*, titmouse], any of a number of small birds with dull-colored feathers, including the chickadee.

Ti·to (tē′tō), Marshal (*Josip Broz*), 1891– ; Communist leader of Yugoslavia: premier (1945–).

ti·trate (tī′trāt, tit′rāt), *v.t. & v.i.* [TITRATED (-id), TITRATING], [< Fr. *titrer* (< *titre*, a standard, title); + *-ate*], to test by or be subjected to titration.

ti·tra·tion (tī-trā′shən, ti-trā′shən), *n.* [< *titrate* + *-ion*], in *chemistry, physiology, & immunology*, the process of finding out how much of a certain substance is contained in a solution by measuring how much of another substance it is necessary to add to the solution in order to produce a given reaction.

ti·tre (tī′tēr, tē′tēr), *n.* titer.

tit-tat-toe (ti′ta-tō′), *n.* tick-tack-toe.

tit·ter (tit′ēr), *v.i.* [of Gmc. echoic origin], to laugh in a half-suppressed way, suggestive of foolishness, nervousness, etc.; giggle. *n.* the act or an instance of tittering. —*SYN.* see **laugh.**

tit·tie (tit′i), *n.* [Scot.], a sister: also spelled **titty**.

tit·ti·vate (tit′ə-vāt′), *v.t. & v.i.* [TITTIVATED (-id), TITTIVATING], to titivate.

tit·tle (tit″l), *n.* [ME. *titel, title*, orig. same word as *title*], 1. a dot or other small mark used as a diacritic. 2. a very small particle; iota; jot; whit.

tit·tle-tat·tle (tit″l-tat″l), *n. & v.i.* [TITTLE-TATTLED (-'ld), TITTLE-TATTLING], [redupl. of *tattle*], gossip; chatter.

tit·tup (tit′əp), *n.* [prob. echoic of hoof beats], a lively movement; frolicsome behavior; frisk; caper. *v.i.* [TITTUPED or TITTUPPED (-əpt), TITTUPING or TITTUPPING], to behave in a frolicsome manner; caper.

tit·ty (tit′i), *n.* a teat: a childish diminutive, now regarded as vulgar.

tit·u·ba·tion (tich′oo-bā′shən), *n.* [L. *titubatio*, a staggering or stammering], a stumbling or staggering gait characteristic of certain nervous disorders.

tit·u·lar (tich′oo-lēr, tit′yoo-lēr), *adj.* [L. *titulus* (see TITLE); + *-ar*], 1. of, or having the nature of, a title. 2. having a title. 3. existing only in title; in name only; nominal: as, a *titular* sovereign. 4. from whose name the title is taken: as, the *titular* character of a novel. 5. designating a bishop holding the title of a defunct see. *n.* a person who holds a title, especially without any obligations of office.

tit·u·lar·y (tich′oo-ler′i, tit′yoo-ler′i), *adj. & n.* [*pl.* TITULARIES (-iz)], titular.

Ti·tus (tī′təs), [L.; Gr. *Titos*], a masculine name. *n.* 1. (*Titus Flavius Sabinus Vespasianus*), Roman general and emperor (79–81 A.D.); lived 40?–81 A.D. 2. *a*) a disciple of the Apostle Paul. *b*) an Epistle to Titus, a book of the New Testament, which was a message from Paul: abbreviated **Tit.**

Ti·u (tē′o͞o), *n.* in *Germanic mythology*, a god of war and of the sky: identified with the Norse god Tyr.

Tiv·o·li (tiv′ə-li; It. tē′vô-lē′), *n.* a town in Italy, near Rome: pop., 25,800: ancient name, *Tibur.*

tiz·zy (tiz′i), *n.* [< ?], [Slang], a state of frenzied excitement or distraction, especially over some trivial matter.

T.K.O., TKO, in *boxing*, a technical knockout.

Tl, in *chemistry*, thallium.

T/L, time loan.

T.L., trade-last.

Tlin·git (tliŋ′git), *n.pl.* [< Am. Ind. (Tlingit); cf. *lingit*, people], 1. the members of several tribes of seafaring American Indians of the coastal areas of southern Alaska and northern British Columbia. 2. [construed as sing.], their language, consisting of several dialects.

Tlin·kit (tliŋ′kit), *n.pl.* Tlingit.

Tm, in *chemistry*, thulium.

tme·sis (tmē′sis, mē′sis), *n.* [L.; Gr. *tmēsis*, a cutting], in *rhetoric & prosody*, separation of the parts of a compound word by an intervening word or words. Example: *what person soever* for *whatsoever person.*

Tn, in *chemistry*, thoron.

tn., ton; tons.

Tng., Training.

TNT, T.N.T., trinitrotoluene, or trinitrotoluol.

to (to͞o; *unstressed* too, tə), *prep.* [ME.; AS.; akin to G. *zu;* IE. ***-dō-**, up towards, seen also in L. *quan-do*, when, then, *donec, donique*, so long as, until], 1. *a*) in the direction of; toward: as, turn *to* the left, he was traveling *to* Pittsburgh. *b*) in the direction of and reaching; as far as: as, he went *to* Boston, it dropped *to* the ground. 2. as far as: as, wet *to* the skin, honest *to* a fault. 3. toward or into a condition of: as, he grew *to* manhood, her rise *to* fame. 4. on, onto, against, at, next, etc.: used to indicate nearness or contact, as, apply the lotion *to* the skin, a house *to* the right. 5. [Dial.], at or in (a specified place): as, he's *to* home. 6. until: as, no parking from four *to* six. 7. for the purpose of; for: as, they came *to* our aid. 8. as concerns; in respect of; involving: as, that's all there is *to* it, open *to* attack. 9. producing, causing, or resulting in: as, *to* my amazement nothing happened, torn *to* pieces. 10. with; along with; accompanied by; as an accompaniment for: as, add this *to* the others, dance *to* the music. 11. being the proper appurtenance, possession, or attribute of; of: as, the key *to* the house. 12. compared with; as against: as, the score was 7 *to* 0. 13. in agreement, correspondence, or conformity with: as, not *to* my taste. 14. comprising; constituting; in: as, twenty *to* the bushel. 15. with (a specified person or thing) as the recipient, or indirect object, of the action: as, they listened *to* me, give the book *to* her. 16. in honor of: as, a toast *to* your success. 17. [Colloq.], with: as, a field planted *to* corn. *To* is also used before a verb as a sign of the infinitive (e.g., I came *to* listen, it was easy *to* read, *to* live is sweet) or, elliptically, to denote the infinitive (e.g., tell him if you want *to*). *adv.* 1. forward: as, his hat is on wrong side *to*. 2. in the normal or desired direction, position, or condition; especially, shut or closed: as, the door was blown *to*. 3. to the matter at hand: as, they took off their coats and fell *to*. 4. at hand: as, we were close *to* when it happened. 5. in *nautical usage*, close to the wind: said of a sailing vessel. *To* is used in many idiomatic phrases entered in this dictionary under their key words (e.g., *come to, go to*).

to and fro, first in one direction and then in the opposite; back and forth.

to- (too, tə), [ME. & AS.; akin to G. *zer-*, L. *dis-*], an obsolete prefix, formerly used as an intensive with verbs, meaning *to pieces, asunder*, as in *to-broken*, broken to pieces.

t.o., 1. turnover. 2. turn over.

toad (tōd), *n.* [ME. *tode;* AS. *tade*, earlier *tadige* (cf. TADPOLE); there are no known cognates in other languages], 1. any of a group of small, froglike animals that eat insects and live on land rather than in water, except during breeding: also applied to other tailless amphibians, including frogs. 2. a person regarded as loathsome, contemptible, etc.

toad·eat·er (tōd′ēt′ẽr), *n.* [see TOADY], a flattering parasite; sycophant; toady.

toad·fish (tōd′fish′), *n.* [*pl.* TOADFISH, TOADFISHES (-iz); see FISH], any of a group of scaleless fishes with broad, froglike heads, found in shallows off the Atlantic coast of America.

toad·flax (tōd′flaks′), *n.* [so named from the spotted and flaxlike appearance of the parts], 1. a common weed having yellow flowers spotted with orange: also called *butter and eggs.* 2. any other related plant.

toad spit (or **spittle**), cuckoo spit.

toad·stone (tōd′stōn′), *n.* [*toad* + *stone*, after L., Gr. *batrachites*, or ML. *crapodines*, 13th-c. OFr. *crapaudine*, etc.; cf. G. *krötenstein*], any stone or similar object formerly thought to have been formed inside a toad's head or body and often worn as a charm.

toad·stool (tōd′sto͞ol′), *n.* [ME. *todestole;* cf. similar D. *paddestoel*], any of a number of fleshy, umbrella-shaped fungi; mushroom; especially, in popular usage, any poisonous mushroom.

toad·y (tōd′i), *n.* [*pl.* TOADIES (-iz)], [short for *toadeater*, quack doctor's assistant who pretended to eat toads (thought to be poisonous) to show the efficacy of quack medicines], a servile flatterer; sycophant. *v.t. & v.i.* [TOADIED (-id), TOADYING], to be a toady (to); flatter. —*SYN.* see **parasite.**

toad·y·ism (tōd′i-iz′m), *n.* the behavior of a toady; servile flattery; sycophancy.

to-and-fro (to͞o′ən-frō′, to͞o′ənd-frō′), *adj.* [ME.], moving forward and backward; back-and-forth.

toast (tōst), *v.t.* [ME. *tosten;* OFr. *toster* < L. *tostus*, pp. of *torrere*, to parch, roast; cf. TORRID], 1. to brown the surface of (bread, cheese, etc.) by heating in a toaster, over or near a fire, or in an oven. 2. to warm thoroughly: as, *toast* yourself by the campfire. *v.i.* to become toasted. *n.* sliced bread browned by heat.

toast (tōst), *n.* [from the use of toasted spiced bread to give flavor to the wine, and the notion that the person, etc. honored also added flavor], 1. a person, institution, sentiment, etc. in honor of which a person or persons raise their glasses and drink. 2. a proposal to drink to some person, etc. 3. a drink in honor of a person, etc. *v.t.* to propose or drink a toast to. *v.i.* to drink a toast or toasts.

toast·er (tōs′tẽr), *n.* any of various utensils or appliances for toasting bread.

toast·er (tōs′tẽr), *n.* a person who proposes or drinks a toast.

toasting fork, a long-handled fork for toasting bread, marshmallows, etc. over a fire.

toast·mas·ter (tōst′mas′tẽr, tōst′mäs′tẽr), *n.* the person at a banquet who proposes toasts, introduces after-dinner speakers, etc.

Tob., Tobit.

to·bac·co (tə-bak′ō), *n.* [*pl.* TOBACCOS (-ōz)], [Sp. *tabaco* < W. Ind. (Carib) *tabaco*, pipe or tube in which the Indians smoked the plant: name transferred by the Spaniards to the plant itself], 1. any of a number of related plants of the nightshade family, with white or pink flowers and large, lance-shaped leaves. 2. the leaves of any of these plants, prepared for smoking, chewing, or snuffing. 3. products prepared from these leaves; cigars, cigarettes, snuff, etc. 4. the use of tobacco for smoking, etc.

TOBACCO PLANT (4–6 ft. high)

tobacco heart, a functional disorder of the heart, characterized by irregular action and caused by the excessive use of tobacco.

to·bac·co·nist (tə-bak′ə-nist), *n.* [< *tobacco;* orig. applied to a user of tobacco], [Chiefly British], a dealer in tobacco and other smoking supplies.

tobacco worm, either of two large, green caterpillars, with slanting white markings, which feed on tobacco plants.

To·ba·go (tō-bā′gō), *n.* an island in the West Indies, northeast of Trinidad: part of the country of Trinidad and Tobago: area, 116 sq. mi.; pop., 35,000.

To·bi·ah (tō-bī′ə, tə-bī′ə), [LL. *Tobias;* Gr. *Tōbias;* Heb. *ṭōbhīyāh*, lit., the lord is good], a masculine name: diminutive, *Toby.*

To·bi·as (tō-bī′əs, tə-bī′əs), a masculine name: see **Tobiah.** *n.* in the *Bible*, Tobit.

To·bit (tō′bit), *n.* a book of the Old Testament Apocrypha: abbreviated **Tob.**

to·bog·gan (tə-bog′ən), *n.* [Canad. Fr. *tabagan* < Am. Ind. (Algonquian); cf. Abnaki *udâbâgân*], 1. a long, narrow, flat sled without runners, made of thin boards curved back at the front end and often having side rails: now used for the sport of coasting down a prepared slope or chute. 2. a similar sled with very low runners. *v.i.* 1. to coast, travel,

TOBOGGAN

etc. on a toboggan; hence, 2. to decline rapidly: as, prices *tobogganed.*

to·bog·gan·ist (tə-bog′ən-ist), *n.* a person who toboggans.

To·bol (tô-bôl′y′), *n.* a river in western Siberia, flowing into the Irtish River: length, 800 mi.

To·bolsk (tô-bôl′y′sk), *n.* a town in western Siberia, at the junction of the Tobol and Irtish Rivers: pop., 23,500.

To·by (tō′bi), *n.* [*pl.* TOBIES (-biz)], [< *Toby*, dim. or familiar form of *Tobias*], 1. a jug or mug for ale or beer, shaped like a stout man with a three-cornered hat: also **Toby jug.** 2. [Slang], a type of long, slender, inferior cigar.

To·can·tins (tô′kän-tēns′), *n.* a river flowing northward from central Brazil to the Pará River: length, 1,700 mi.

toc·ca·ta (tə-kä′tə), *n.* [It., orig. fem. of pp. of *toccare*, to touch; see TOUCH], a composition in free style for the organ, piano, etc., generally characterized by the use of full chords and running passages and often used as the prelude of a fugue: it was originally designed to display the technique of the performer.

To·char·i·an (tō-kâr′i-ən, tō-kä′ri-ən), *n.* [< *Tochri*, word used to designate the language in certain accompanying (Uigur) writings; identified with Gr. *Tocharoi*, Oriental people mentioned by Strabo], 1. a member of a people living in central Asia until about 1000 A.D. 2. their Indo-European language, comprising two dialects: the earliest record known is from the 7th century A.D. *adj.* of the Tocharians or their language. Also **Tokharian, Tokharic.**

to·col·o·gy (tō-kol′ə-ji), *n.* [< Gr. *tokos*, childbirth; + *-logy*], obstetrics or midwifery: also spelled **tokology.**

to·coph·er·ol (tō-kof′ẽr-ōl′, tō-kof′ẽr-ol), *n.* [< Gr. *tokos*, childbirth + *pherein*, to carry, bear; + *-ol*], any of a group of alcohols having the properties of vitamin E, the antisterility vitamin, and occurring chiefly in wheat-germ oil, cottonseed oil, lettuce, etc.

Tocque·ville, A·lex·is de (å′lek′sē′ də tôk′vēl′), (*Alexis Charles Henri Maurice Clérel de Tocqueville*), 1805–1859; French author and statesman.

toc·sin (tok′sin), *n.* [Fr.; Pr. *tocasenh* < *toc*, a stroke (of echoic origin) + *senh*, a bell < LL. *signum*, a signal, bell (L., a sign, token)], 1. an alarm bell. 2. its sound. 3. any alarm, or sound of warning.

tod (tod), *n.* [ME. *todde;* prob. < LG. source; cf. E.Fris. *todde, tod*, a bundle, pack, load, etc.; akin to G. *zotte*, tuft of hair; IE. base ***de-s-, *də-s-** (< **dā* [*i*], to part, divide up, pluck out), seen also in *tease*], 1. a former English weight for wool, about 28 pounds. 2. a bushy clump of ivy, etc.

tod (tod), *n.* [? < *tod* (bushy clump), with reference to the fox's tail], [Scot.], a fox.

to·day, to-day (tə-dā′, too-dā′), *adv.* [ME. *to-daye;* AS. *to dæg;* see TO, *prep.* & DAY], 1. on or during the present day. 2. in the present time or age; nowadays. *n.* 1. the present day; this day. 2. the present time, period, or age.

tod·dle (tod′′l), *v.i.* [TODDLED (-′ld), TODDLING], [? freq. of *totter*, via northern dial. *doddle;* cf. DODDER], to walk with short, uncertain steps, as a child. *n.* a toddling.

tod·dy (tod′i), *n.* [*pl.* TODDIES (-iz)], [Anglo-Ind. < Hind. *tāṛī*, fermented sap of palmyra tree < *tāṛ*, palm tree; Sans. *tāla*, palmyra], 1. the sweet sap of various East Indian palms, used as a beverage. 2. an intoxicating liquor made by fermenting this sap. 3. a drink of brandy, whisky, etc. mixed with hot water, sugar, and, usually, spices.

toddy palm, any of several palms yielding toddy.

to-do (tə-dōō′, too-dōō′), *n.* [Colloq.], a commotion; stir; fuss.

to·dy (tō′di), *n.* [*pl.* TODIES (-diz)], [Fr. *todier* < L. *todus*, small bird], any of several small, insect-eating birds of the West Indies related to the kingfisher, especially the Jamaican species that is green with a red throat.

toe (tō), *n.* [ME. *to;* AS. *ta*, earlier *tahe;* akin to G. *zehe, zeh;* IE. base ***deik-**, to point, show, seen also in L. *digitus* (< **dicitus;* cf. DIGIT), *dicere*, to say (cf. DICTION), Eng. *token, teach*, etc.; basic sense "the pointer"], 1. any of the five digits of the human foot. 2. any of the digits of an animal's foot. 3. the fore part of the human foot: distinguished from *heel*. 4. that part of a shoe, sock, etc. which covers the toes. 5. anything suggesting a toe in location, shape, or function; specifically, *a*) a pivot or journal extending vertically in a bearing. *b*) a projecting arm raised or moved by a cam. *v.t.* [TOED (tōd), TOEING], 1. to provide with a toe or toes: as, she *toed* the stockings. 2. to touch, follow, or kick with the toes: as, they *toed* the starting line. 3. *a*) to drive (a nail) slantingly. *b*) to fasten with nails driven slantingly; toenail. *v.i.* to stand, walk, or be formed so that the toes are in a specified position: as, he *toes* in, she *toes* out.

on one's toes, [Colloq.], mentally or physically alert.

toe the line (or **mark**), 1. to stand or crouch with the toes touching the starting line of a race, etc. 2. to follow orders, rules, doctrines, etc. strictly.

toe·cap (tō′kap′), *n.* that part of a shoe or boot which covers the toes.

toe crack, a lesion (*sand crack*) in the front part of a horse's hoof.

toed (tōd), *adj.* 1. having (a specified kind or number of) toes: usually in hyphenated compounds, as *pigeon-toed.* 2. *a*) driven obliquely: said of a nail. *b*) fastened by obliquely driven nails.

toe-dance (tō′dans′, tō′däns′), *v.i.* to do a toe dance.

toe dance, a dance performed on the tips of the toes, as in ballet.

toe hold, 1. a small space or ledge for supporting the toe of the foot in climbing, etc.; hence, 2. any means of surmounting obstacles, gaining entry, etc. 3. a slight footing or advantage. 4. in *wrestling*, a hold in which one wrestler twists the other's foot.

toe-in (tō′in′), *n.* an adjustment of the front wheels of an automobile or other motor vehicle so that they are not perfectly parallel but tend to converge slightly toward the front.

toe·less (tō′lis), *adj.* 1. having no toe or toes. 2. having the toe open or uncovered: as, a *toeless* shoe.

toe·nail (tō′nāl′), *n.* 1. the nail of a toe. 2. in *carpentry*, a nail driven obliquely, as through the side of a vertical plank to fasten it to the horizontal plank on which it is based. *v.t.* in *carpentry*, to fasten with a toenail.

tof·fee, tof·fy (tôf′i, tof′i), *n.* [later Brit. form of *taffy;* ? connected with *tafia*], a hard, chewy candy made with brown sugar or molasses, often coated with nuts; kind of taffy.

toft (tôft), *n.* [ME.; Late AS.; ON. *topt*, a homestead, ground marked out for building, knoll; for IE. base see TIMBER, DOME], [British Dial.], 1. originally, a house site or homestead. 2. a homestead with its arable land; messuage. 3. a knoll; hillock.

tog (tog, tôg), *n.* [prob. < cant *togeman(s)*, *togman*, a cloak, coat; ult. < L. *toga*, toga], 1. [Old Slang], a coat; hence, 2. *pl.* [Colloq.], clothes: as, tennis *togs*. *v.t. & v.i.* [TOGGED (togd, tôgd), TOGGING], [Colloq.], to put clothes on; dress (often with *up* or *out*).

to·ga (tō′gə), *n.* [*pl.* TOGAS (-gəz), TOGAE (-jē)], [L. < *tegere*, to cover], 1. in ancient Rome, a loose, one-piece outer garment worn in public by citizens. 2. a robe of office; characteristic gown of a profession.

ROMAN TOGA

to·gaed (tō′gəd), *adj.* wearing a toga.

to·gat·ed (tō′gā-tid), *adj.* 1. togaed. 2. dignified.

‡to·ga vi·ri·lis (tō′gə vi-rī′lis), [L., lit., toga of a man], the toga of manhood, put on by boys of ancient Rome in their fourteenth year.

to·geth·er (tə-geth′ẽr, too-geth′ẽr), *adv.* [ME. *togeder;* AS. *togædre, togadere;* *to* (see TO) + *gædre*, together < base of *gaderian* (see GATHER)], 1. in or into one gathering, group, mass, or place: as, the employees were called *together*. 2. in or into contact, collision, companionship, union, etc. with each other: as, the cars skidded *together*, they live *together* in the same house. 3. considered collectively; added up: as, he's lost more than all of us *together*. 4. with one another; in association: as, the books were compared *together*. 5. at the same time; simultaneously: as, the shots were fired *together*. 6. in succession; continuously: as, he worked for eight hours *together*. 7. in or into agreement, cooperation, etc.: as, get *together* on this. *Together* is also used colloquially as an intensive after *add, join*, etc.

tog·ger·y (tog′ẽr-i, tôg′ẽr-i), *n.* [< *tog* + *-ery*], [Colloq.], 1. clothes; togs. 2. [*pl.* TOGGERIES (-iz)], a clothing store; especially, a haberdashery.

tog·gle (tog′′l), *n.* [prob. naut. var. of dial. *tuggle*, freq. of *tug*], 1. a rod, pin, or bolt for inserting between the strands or through a loop of a rope, through a link of a chain, etc. to make an attachment, prevent slipping, or tighten by twisting. 2. a toggle joint or a device having one. *v.t.* [TOGGLED (-′ld), TOGGLING], to provide or fasten with a toggle or toggles.

toggle joint, a knee-shaped joint consisting of two bars pivoted together at one end: when pressure is put on the joint to straighten it, opposite, outward pressures are transmitted to the open ends.

toggle switch, a switch consisting of a projecting lever moved back or forth through a small arc to open or close an electric circuit.

To·go (tō′gō), *n.* a country in western Africa, on the Gulf of Guinea, east of Ghana; formerly, a French mandate (1922–1946) and trust territory (1946–1960): area, 22,000 sq. mi.; pop., 1,642,000; capital, Lomé: former name, *Togoland*.

To·go, Count (later, Marquis) **Hei·ha·chi·ro** (hā'hä-che'rō tō'gō), 1847–1934; Japanese admiral.
To·go·land (tō'gō-land'), *n.* 1. a former British mandate (1922–1946) and trust territory (1946–1957) in northwestern Africa; merged with the Gold Coast (1957) to form Ghana: area, 13,041 sq. mi. 2. Togo: the former name.
toil (toil), *v.i.* [ME. *toilen;* Anglo-Fr. *toiler,* to strive, dispute; OFr. *toeillier,* to pull about, begrime; L. *tudiculare,* to stir about < *tudicula,* small machine for bruising olives < *tudes,* mallet], 1. to work hard and continuously; labor untiringly. 2. to proceed laboriously; advance with painful effort: as, they *toiled* up the mountain. *v.t.* to make or accomplish with great effort: as, they *toiled* their way. *n.* [ME.; Anglo-Fr., turmoil, struggle < the *v.*], 1. originally, contention; struggle; strife. 2. hard, exhausting work or effort; tiring labor. 3. a task performed by such effort. —*SYN.* see **work.**
toil (toil), *n.* [OFr. *toile, teile,* a net, web, cloth; L. *tela,* a web, woven material], 1. [Archaic], a net for trapping. 2. *pl.* any snares or traps suggestive of a net.
toile (twäl), *n.* [Fr.; see TOIL (net)], 1. a variety of sheer linen cloth. 2. a variety of fine cretonne.
toi·let (toi'lit), *n.* [Fr. *toilette,* orig., cloth covering used in shaving or hairdressing < *toile,* cloth; L. *tela;* see TOIL (net)], 1. a dressing table. 2. the process of dressing or grooming oneself, especially, formerly, of dressing one's hair. 3. toilette; dress; attire; costume. 4. *a)* a room or booth equipped with a washbowl, water closet, etc. *b)* a water closet. *adj.* of or for the toilet: as, *toilet* articles, *toilet* paper.
make one's toilet, to bathe and dress, arrange one's hair, etc.
toi·let·ry (toi'lit-ri), *n.* [*pl.* TOILETRIES (-riz)], soap, powder, cologne, etc. used in making one's toilet.
toi·lette (toi-let', twä-let'), *n.* [Fr.; see TOILET], 1. the process of grooming oneself, including bathing, hairdressing, putting on cosmetics, and dressing: said of women. 2. dress or manner of dress; attire; costume.
toilet water, a perfumed, slightly alcoholic liquid, as cologne, applied to the skin in making one's toilet.
toil·ful (toil'fəl), *adj.* full of toil; laborious.
toil·some (toil'səm), *adj.* [see -SOME], requiring or involving toil; laborious; wearisome.
toil·worn (toil'wôrn'), *adj.* worn by or showing the effects of toil.
To·jo, Hi·de·ki (hi'de-ki tō'jō), 1885–1948; Japanese general; minister of war (1940–1941); premier of Japan (1941–1944); executed for war crimes.
To·kay (tō-kā'), *n.* 1. a sweet, rich wine made in Tokay, Hungary. 2. any wine like this. 3. a large, sweet, whitish or purplish grape used for the wine.
to·ken (tō'kən), *n.* [ME.; AS. *tacn;* akin to G. *zeichen;* IE. base ***deik-,** to point, show; cf. TOE, DIGIT, etc.], 1. a sign, indication, or symbol: as, this gift is a *token* of my affection. 2. something serving as a sign of authority, identity, genuineness, etc. 3. a distinguishing mark or feature. 4. a keepsake. 5. a piece of stamped metal with a face value higher than its real value, issued as a substitute for currency. 6. any of various similar devices of metal, paper, etc. used as for transportation fares or the payment of a sales tax. *v.t.* to be a token of; betoken or symbolize. *adj.* 1. by way of a token, symbol, indication, etc.: as, a *token* gesture; hence, 2. merely simulated; slight or of no real account: as, *token* resistance. —*SYN.* see **pledge, sign.**
by this (or **the same**) **token,** following from this.
in token of, as evidence of.
token payment, a partial payment made as a token of intention to pay the remainder of the debt later.
To·khar·i·an (tō-kâr'i-ən, tō-kä'ri-ən), *n. & adj.* Tocharian.
To·khar·ic (tō-kâr'ik, tō-kä'rik), *n. & adj.* Tocharian.
to·kol·o·gy (tō-kol'ə-ji), *n.* tocology.
To·ku·shi·ma (tô'koo-shē'mä), *n.* a seaport in eastern Shikoku, Japan: pop., 171,000.
To·ky·o (tō'ki-ō'; Japan. tô'kyô'), *n.* the capital of Japan, on Tokyo Bay: pop., 6,969,000 (with suburbs, 8,034,000): also spelled **Tokio:** former names, *Edo, Yedo.*
Tokyo Bay, an arm of the Pacific, extending into Honshu Island, Japan.
to·la (tō'lä), *n.* [Hind. < Sans. *tulā,* a balance], in India, a unit of weight equal to 180 grains (the weight of one silver rupee).
to·lan (tō'lan), *n.* tolane.
to·lane (tō'lān), *n.* [*tol*uene + *-ane*], a colorless, crystalline hydrocarbon, $C_{14}H_{10}$.
tol·booth (tōl'bōōth', tōl'bōōth'), *n.* [ME. *tolbothe,* orig., booth at which toll is collected], [Scot.], a jail or prison: also spelled **tollbooth.**
told (tōld), past tense and past participle of **tell.**
all told, all (being) counted; in all: as, there were forty *all told.*
tole (tōl), *v.t.* [TOLED (tōld), TOLING], [var. of *toll* (to allure)], [Archaic or Dial.], to allure; entice.
tole, tôle (tōl), *n.* [Fr. *tôle,* sheet iron, plate; dial. var. of *table;* see TABLE], a type of lacquered or enameled metalware popular in the 18th century and reproduced today in the form of trays, lamps, etc.: it is commonly dark-green or black with gilt decoration.
To·le·do (tə-lē'dō; *also, for 2,* Sp. tô-lā'thô), *n.* 1. a port in northwestern Ohio, on Lake Erie: pop., 318,000. 2. a city in central Spain, on the Tagus River: pop., 35,000. 3. [*pl.* TOLEDOS (-dōz)], a fine-tempered sword or sword blade made in Toledo, Spain.
tol·er·a·ble (tol'ẽr-ə-b'l), *adj.* [ME. *tollerabill* < (late) OFr. or L.; OFr. *tolérable;* L. *tolerabilis*], 1. that can be tolerated; endurable; bearable. 2. fairly good; passable. 3. [Colloq.], in reasonably good health.
tol·er·a·bly (tol'ẽr-ə-bli), *adv.* 1. in a tolerable manner. 2. to a tolerable degree; moderately; fairly.
tol·er·ance (tol'ẽr-əns), *n.* [ME. *tolleraunce;* Late OFr. *tolerance;* L. *tolerantia*], 1. a tolerating or being tolerant, especially of others' views, beliefs, practices, etc.; freedom from bigotry or prejudice. 2. the amount of variation allowed from a standard, accuracy, etc.; specifically, *a)* the amount that coins are legally allowed to vary from a standard of weight, fineness, etc. *b)* the difference between the allowable maximum and minimum sizes of some mechanical part, as a basis for determining the accuracy of a fitting. 3. [Rare], an enduring or the ability to endure. 4. in *medicine,* the natural or developed ability to endure, or resist the harmful effects of, the continued or increasing use of a drug, etc.
tol·er·ant (tol'ẽr-ənt), *adj.* 1. inclined to tolerate others' beliefs, practices, etc., or favoring tolerance. 2. in *medicine,* of or having tolerance.
tol·er·ate (tol'ə-rāt'), *v.t.* [TOLERATED (-id), TOLERATING], [< L. *toleratus,* pp. of *tolerare,* to bear, sustain, tolerate; IE. base ***tel-,** to lift up, bear, seen also in L. *tollere,* to lift up, Eng. *thole*], 1. to allow; permit; not interfere with. 2. to recognize and respect (others' beliefs, practices, etc.) without necessarily agreeing or sympathizing. 3. to put up with; bear: as, he *tolerates* his brother-in-law. 4. in *medicine,* to have tolerance for (a specific drug, etc.). —*SYN.* see **bear.**
tol·er·a·tion (tol'ə-rā'shən), *n.* [Fr. *tolération;* L. *toleratio*], tolerance; especially, freedom of religious worship; freedom to hold religious views that differ from the established ones.
tol·er·a·tion·ist (tol'ə-rā'shən-ist), *n.* a person who advocates toleration, especially in religious matters.
tol·er·a·tive (tol'ə-rā'tiv), *adj.* tolerating or tending to tolerate.
tol·er·a·tor (tol'ə-rā'tẽr), *n.* a person who tolerates.
tol·i·din (tol'ə-din), *n.* tolidine.
tol·i·dine (tol'ə-dēn', tol'ə-din), *n.* [*tol*uol + benz*idine*], any of a group of isomeric dimethyl derivatives of benzidine, $C_{14}H_{16}N_2$.
To·li·ma, Mount (tô-lē'mä), *n.* a volcanic mountain of the Andes in west central Colombia: height, 18,438 ft.
toll (tōl), *n.* [ME. *tol;* AS. *toll;* akin to G. *zoll;* said to be < LL. *toloneum,* L. *teloneum,* tollhouse < Gr. *telōnion* < *telōnēs,* tax collector < *telos,* tax], 1. a tax or charge for a privilege, especially for permission to pass over a bridge, along a highway, etc. 2. the right to demand toll. 3. a charge for service or extra service, as for transportation, for a long-distance telephone call, or, formerly, for milling one's grain. 4. the number lost, taken, exacted, etc.; exaction: as, the accident took a heavy *toll* of lives.
toll (tōl), *v.t.* [ME. *tollen,* to pull; prob. var. < AS. *-tillan,* to touch, influenced by echoism], 1. [Dial. or Rare], to allure or entice; especially, to decoy (game, etc.). 2. to ring (a church bell, etc.) slowly with regularly repeated strokes, especially for announcing a death. 3. to announce, summon, etc. by this. 4. to announce the death of (someone) in this way. *v.i.* to sound or ring slowly in regularly repeated strokes: said of a bell. *n.* 1. the act or sound of tolling a bell. 2. a single stroke of the bell.
toll·age (tōl'ij), *n.* [see -AGE], 1. toll (tax). 2. payment or demand of toll.
toll bar, a bar, gate, etc. for stopping travel at a point where toll is taken.
toll booth (tōl'bōōth', tōl'bōōth'), *n.* a tolbooth.
toll bridge, a bridge at which toll is paid for passage.
toll call, a long-distance telephone call, for which there is a charge beyond the local rate.
toll·er (tōl'ẽr), *n.* a person or thing that tolls; specifically, *a)* a dog trained to toll, or decoy, ducks. *b)* a person who tolls a bell. *c)* a bell for tolling.
Tol·ler, Ernst (ernst tō'lẽr), 1893–1939; German anti-Nazi dramatist and poet.
toll·gate (tōl'gāt'), *n.* a gate for stopping travel at a point where toll is taken.
toll·house (tōl'hous'), *n.* 1. a house at a tollgate, in which the tollkeeper lives. 2. a booth, etc. where toll is taken.
tollhouse cooky, [made according to a recipe used at the *Toll House* in Whitman, Massachusetts], a kind of cooky containing bits of solid chocolate.
toll·keep·er (tōl'kēp'ẽr), *n.* a person who takes toll at a tollgate.
toll line, a long-distance telephone line.

toll road, a road for travel on which toll must be paid.
Tolstoy, Count **Lev** (Eng. **Leo**) **Nikolayevich** (lyev nē'kô-lä'ye-vich tôl-stoi'; Eng. tol'stoi), 1828–1910; Russian novelist and social reformer: also spelled **Tolstoi.**
Tol·tec (tol'tek), *n.* [Nahuatl *Tolteca*], a member of an ancient group of Nahuatl Indians who lived in Mexico before the Aztecs: their culture shows Mayan influence. *adj.* of the Toltecs or their culture.
Tol·tec·an (tol'tek-ən), *adj.* Toltec.
to·lu (tō-lōō'), *n.* [Sp. *tolú* < Santiago de *Tolú*, seaport in Colombia], the balsam yielded by the tolu tree: also **tolu balsam.**
tol·u·ate (tol'ū-āt'), *n.* a salt or ester of toluic acid.
To·lu·ca (tô-lōō'kä; Eng. tə-lōō'kə), *n.* 1. the capital of Mexico state, Mexico: pop., 43,000. 2. a volcanic mountain of Mexico state: height, 15,448 ft.
tol·u·ene (tol'ū-ēn'), *n.* [*tolu* + *benzene*], a colorless liquid hydrocarbon, $C_6H_5CH_3$, obtained originally from tolu balsam but now generally from coal tar and used in making dye explosives, etc. and as a solvent.
to·lu·ic acid (tol-ū'ik, tol'ū-ik), any of four isomeric acids, $C_8H_8O_2$, carboxyl derivatives of toluene.
tol·u·id (tol'ū-id), *n.* a toluide.
tol·u·ide (tol'ū-id', tol'ū-id), *n.* any of a class of chemical compounds having the general formula $RCONHC_6H_4CH_3$, derived from the toluidines by the substitution of an acid radical for one of the amino H atoms.
to·lu·i·din (tol-ū'ə-din), *n.* a toluidine.
to·lu·i·dine (tol-ū'ə-dēn', tol-ū'ə-din), *n.* any of three isomeric amino derivatives, C_7H_9N, of toluene, used in the synthesis of dyes and medicines.
tol·u·ol (tol'ū-ōl', tol'ū-ol), *n.* [*tolu* + *-ol*], toluene; especially, crude commercial toluene.
tol·u·ole (tol'ū-ōl'), *n.* toluol.
tolu tree, a large South American tree with rough, thick bark, yielding a fragrant balsam used in perfume, medicine, etc.
tol·u·yl (tol'ū-il), *n.* [*toluic* + *-yl*], the monovalent acid radical C_7H_7CO.
tol·yl (tol'il), *n.* [*toluic* + *-yl*], the monovalent radical $CH_3C_6H_4$, derived from toluene.
tom (tom), *n.* [< *Tom*, dim. of *Thomas;* esp. after *tomcat*, earlier *Tom the Cat* (c. 1760); cf. similar use of *jack*], the male of some animals, especially of the cat. *adj.* male: as, a *tom* turkey. Sometimes used in compounds, occasionally with derived senses, as *tomcod.*
tom·a·hawk (tom'ə-hôk', tom'i-hôk'), *n.* [of Am. Ind. (Algonquian) origin], a light ax, originally having a stone or bone head, used by North American Indians as a tool and a weapon. *v.t.* to hit, cut, or kill with a tomahawk.
bury the tomahawk, to stop fighting; make peace.
tom·al·ley (tom'al'i), *n.* [prob. < Carib name], the liver of the lobster, which turns green when boiled and is considered a delicacy.
Tom and Jerry, [from name of two chief characters in Egan's *Life in London* (1821)], a hot drink made of rum, beaten eggs, sugar, water or milk, and nutmeg.
to·ma·to (tə-mā'tō, tə-mä'tō), *n.* [*pl.* TOMATOES (-tōz)], [Sp. *tomate;* Nahuatl *tomatl*], 1. a red or yellowish fruit, more or less round, with a juicy pulp, used as a vegetable: botanically it is a berry. 2. the plant that it grows on. 3. [Slang], a woman or girl.
tomb (tōōm), *n.* [ME. *toumbe;* Anglo-Fr. *tumbe* (OFr. *tombe*); LL. *tumba;* Gr. *tymbos*, a tomb, funeral mound], 1. a vault or grave for the dead. 2. a tombstone or burial monument. *v.t.* [Rare], to entomb.
the tomb, death.
the Tombs, New York City prison.
tom·bac, tom·back, tom·bak (tom'bak), *n.* [Fr. & Port. *tombac;* Malay *tĕmbaga*, copper; Sans. *tāmraka*], an alloy of copper and zinc, used in making cheap jewelry.
Tom·big·bee (tom-big'bē), *n.* a river in Mississippi and Alabama, flowing into the Alabama River near Mobile Bay: length, 409 mi.
Tom·bouc·tou (tōn'bōōk'tōō'), *n.* Timbuktu.
tom·boy (tom'boi'), *n.* [see TOM], a girl who behaves like a boisterous boy; hoyden.
tom·boy·ish (tom'boi'ish), *adj.* of or like a tomboy.
tomb·stone (tōōm'stōn'), *n.* a stone or monument, usually with an engraved inscription, marking a tomb or grave; gravestone.
tom·cat (tom'kat'), *n.* [see TOM], a male cat.
tom·cod (tom'kod'), *n.* [see TOM], a small, salt-water food fish resembling the cod.
Tom Collins, see **Collins.**
Tom, Dick, and Harry, everyone; anyone; people taken at random: usually preceded by *every* and used in a disparaging sense.
tome (tōm), *n.* [Fr.; L. *tomus;* Gr. *tomos*, piece cut off, hence part of a book, volume < *temnein*, to cut], 1. originally, any volume of a work of several volumes. 2. a book, especially a large, heavy one. Abbreviated **t.**
-tome (tōm), [Gr. *-tomon* < *tomos;* see TOME], a combining form meaning *cutter*, used in forming names of surgical instruments, as *microtome, osteotome.*
to·men·tose (tō-men'tōs), *adj.* [Mod. L. *tomentosus* < L. *tomentum;* see TOMENTUM], in *botany, entomology,* etc., covered with short, matted, woolly hairs.
to·men·tum (tō-men'təm), *n.* [*pl.* TOMENTA (-tə)], [L., a stuffing (of hair, wool, etc.); for IE. base see TUMOR], 1. a growth of short, matted, woolly hairs, as on the stems or leaves of some plants. 2. a network of very small blood vessels in the pia mater and the cortex of the cerebrum.
tom·fool (tom'fōōl'), *n.* [cf. *Tom o'Bedlam, poor Tom,* etc., names formerly applied to the demented, imbeciles, etc.], a foolish, stupid, or silly person. *adj.* foolish, stupid, or silly.
tom·fool·er·y (tom'fōōl'ẽr-i), *n.* [*pl.* TOMFOOLERIES (-iz)], [see prec.], foolish behavior; silliness; nonsense.
-tom·ic (tom'ik), a combining form used to form adjectives corresponding to nouns ending in *-tome.*
Tom·my, tom·my (tom'i), *n.* [*pl.* TOMMIES (-iz)], a Tommy Atkins; British soldier: a nickname.
Tommy At·kins (at'kinz), [from the use of the fictitious name *Thomas Atkins* in sample forms used in the British Army], a British (noncolonial) soldier: a nickname.
Tommy gun, [Colloq.], 1. a Thompson submachine gun. 2. loosely, any submachine gun.
tom·my·rot (tom'i-rot'), *n.* [< the nickname *Tommy*, in dial. sense of "fool" (cf. TOMFOOL) + *rot*], [Slang], nonsense; foolishness; rubbish.
to·mog·ra·phy (tə-mog'rə-fi), *n.* [< Gr. *tomos*, a piece cut off, section; + *-graphy*], in *medicine*, a technique of X-ray photography by which a single selected plane is photographed, with the outline of structures in other planes eliminated.
to·mor·row, to-mor·row (tə-mor'ō, too-môr'ō), *adv.* [ME. *to morwe* < *to morwen;* AS. *to morgen;* see TO & MORROW], on or for the day after today. *n.* 1. the day after today. 2. an indefinite time in the near future.
tom·pi·on (tom'pi-ən), *n.* a tampion.
Tomsk (tômsk), *n.* a city in the Novosibirsk territory, Siberian U.S.S.R.: pop., 141,000.
Tom Thumb, 1. a tiny hero of many English folk tales. 2. any dwarf or small person; specifically, (*General Tom Thumb*), an American midget, Charles S. Stratton (1838–1883), exhibited by P. T. Barnum.
tom·tit (tom'tit', tom'tit'), *n.* [see TOM], 1. [British], a titmouse; tit. 2. a wren, chickadee, or any of various other small birds.
tom-tom (tom'tom'), *n.* [Hind. *tam-tam*, of echoic origin], 1. any of various drums of primitive origin, played with the hands or with sticks. 2. a tam-tam. *v.i.* to play on or beat a tom-tom.
-to·my (tə-mi), [Gr. *-tomia* < *tomē*, a cutting < *temnein*, to cut], a combining form meaning: 1. *a cutting, dividing*, as in *dichotomy.* 2. *a surgical operation*, as in *appendectomy.*
ton (tun), *n.* [ME. *tonne, tunne;* AS. *tunne;* 17th-c. differentiated var. of *tun*], 1. a unit of weight equal to 2,240 pounds avoirdupois (or 1,016.06 kilograms), commonly used in Great Britain: in full **long ton, shipping ton.** 2. a unit of weight equal to 2,000 pounds avoirdupois (or 907.20 kilograms), commonly used in the United States, Canada, South Africa, etc.: in full **short ton.** 3. a metric ton. 4. a unit of internal capacity of ships, equal to 100 cubic feet (or 2.8317 cubic meters). 5. a unit of carrying capacity of ships, usually equal to 40 cubic feet: in full **measurement ton, freight ton.** 6. a unit for measuring displacement of ships, equal to 35 cubic feet: it is approximately equal to the volume of a long ton of sea water: in full **displacement ton.** 7. [Colloq.], a very large amount or number. Abbreviated **T., t., tn.** (*sing. & pl.*).
‡**ton** (tōn), *n.* [Fr.; see TONE], style; vogue.
ton·al (tō'n'l), *adj.* [ML. *tonalis*], of a tone or tones.
to·nal·i·ty (tō-nal'ə-ti), *n.* [*pl.* TONALITIES (-tiz)], 1. quality of tone. 2. in *art*, the arrangement of tones, or color scheme, in a painting. 3. in *music, a*) a key. *b*) the tonal character of (a) composition, as determined by the relationship of the tones to the tonic, or keynote.
ton·al·ly (tō'n'l-i), *adv.* as regards tone.
tone (tōn), *n.* [ME. *ton, tone;* OFr. *ton;* L. *tonus*, a sound < Gr. *tonos*, a stretching, tone < *teinein*, to stretch], 1. *a*) a vocal or musical sound. *b*) its quality. 2. an intonation, pitch, modulation, etc. of the voice that expresses a particular meaning or feeling of the speaker: as, a *tone* of contempt. 3. a manner of speaking or writing that shows a certain attitude on the part of the speaker or writer, consisting in choice of words, phrasing, etc.: as, the letter had a friendly *tone.* 4. normal resiliency or elasticity: as, this wood has lost its *tone.* 5. *a*) the prevailing or predominant style,

character, spirit, trend, morale, or state of morals of a place or period: as, her house has a conservative *tone.* *b)* distinctive style; elegance. 6. *a)* a quality or value of color; tint; shade. *b)* any of the slight modifications of a particular color; hue: as, it has three *tones* of green. 7. in *linguistics, a)* the musical pitch of a sound, word, etc. *b)* a rising, falling, or other inflection by which words otherwise pronounced the same are distinguished, as in ancient Greek or Pekingese Chinese. 8. in *music & acoustics, a)* a sound that is distinct and identifiable by its regularity of vibration, or constant pitch, and that may be put into harmonic relation with other such sounds: distinguished from *noise. b)* the simple or fundamental tone of a musical sound as distinguished from its overtones. *c)* any one of the full intervals of a diatonic scale; step: also called *whole tone. d)* any of the nine psalm tunes in plainsong: also called *Gregorian tone.* 9. in *painting,* the effect produced by the combination of light, shade, and color. 10. in *phonetics, a)* sound produced by vibration of the vocal cords; voice. *b)* a pitch of voice. *c)* syllabic stress. 11. in *physiology, a)* the condition of an organism, organ, or part with reference to its normal, healthy functioning. *b)* the normal tension, or resistance to stretch, of a healthy muscle, independent of that caused by voluntary innervation. *v.t.* [TONED (tōnd), TONING], 1. [Rare], to intone. 2. to give a tone to; specifically, to give the proper or desired tone to (a musical instrument, a painting, etc.). 3. to change the tone of. *v.i.* to assume a tone. —*SYN.* see **sound.**

tone down, 1. to give a lower or less intense tone to. 2. to become softened.

tone in with, to harmonize with.

tone up, 1. to give a higher or more intense tone to. 2. to become strengthened or heightened.

tone arm, a pickup (sense 7*b*).

tone color, timbre.

tone control, a device in a radio or electric phonograph by which the intensity of tones of varying frequencies is regulated.

tone-deaf (tōn′def′), ***adj.*** not able to distinguish accurately differences in musical pitch.

‡to·ne·la·da (tô′ne-lä′thä), ***n.*** [Sp. & Port. < *tonel,* an old measure < Catalan *tonell* < *tona,* a tub; Pr. *tona* < Celt. base], 1. in Spain, a unit of weight equal to 2,028.7 pounds. 2. (Port. too′ne-lä′thə), in Brazil, a unit of weight equal to 1,748.79 pounds.

tone·less (tōn′lis), ***adj.*** without tone.

tone poem, an elaborate, orchestral composition, usually in one movement, having no fixed form and based upon some nonmusical poetic or descriptive theme: also called *symphonic poem.*

to·net·ic (tō-net′ik), ***adj.*** [< *tone,* after *phonetic*], in *linguistics,* designating tones (sense 7) or languages which distinguish word meanings by tone variations.

to·net·ics (tō-net′iks), ***n.pl.*** [construed as sing.], the science of speech tones.

tong (tôŋ, toŋ), ***v.t.*** to seize, collect, handle, or hold with tongs. *v.i.* to use tongs.

tong (tôŋ, toŋ), ***n.*** [Chin. *t'ang,* a hall, meeting place, hence society], 1. a Chinese association or political party. 2. in the United States, a private or secret society of Chinese.

Ton·ga (toŋ′gə), ***n.*** a group of islands in the South Pacific, east of the Fiji Islands: a native kingdom and British protectorate: area, 256 sq. mi.; pop., 66,000; capital, Nukualofa: also called the *Friendly Islands.*

ton·ga (toŋ′gə), ***n.*** [Hind. *tāṅgā*], a light, two-wheeled carriage used in India.

Ton·gan (toŋ′gən), ***n.*** 1. a native of Tonga. 2. the Polynesian language of the Tongans.

tongs (tôŋz, toŋz), ***n.pl.*** [sometimes construed as sing.], [ME. *tonge, tonges;* AS. *tange, tangan;* akin to G. *zange;* IE. base **denk-,* to bite; basic sense "those that bite together"], a device for seizing or lifting objects, generally having two long arms pivoted or hinged together.

tongue (tuŋ), ***n.*** [ME. & AS. *tunge;* akin to G. *zunge;* IE. base **dṇghū-,* tongue, seen also in L. ***lingua*** (cf. LINGUAL, etc.) < OL. *dingua*], 1. the movable muscular structure attached to the floor of the mouth: it is an important organ in the ingestion of food, the perception of taste, and, in man, the articulation of speech sounds. 2. an animal's tongue used as food. 3. the human tongue as the organ of speech. 4. ideas expressed by speaking; talk; speech. 5. the act or power of speaking. 6. a manner or style of speaking in regard to tone, meaning, intention, etc. 7. a language or dialect. 8. the cry of a hunting dog, etc. in sight of game. 9. something resembling a tongue in shape, position, movement, or use; specifically, *a)* the flap under the laces or strap of a shoe. *b)* the clapper of a bell. *c)* the pin of a buckle. *d)* the pole of a wagon, etc. *e)* the projecting tenon of a tongue-and-groove joint. *f)* in machines, a projecting flange, rib, etc. *g)* the vibrating end of the reed in a wind instrument. *h)* a narrow strip of land extending into a sea, river, etc. *i)* a narrow inlet of water. *j)* the movable rail in a railroad switch. *k)* a long, narrow flame. *l)* the pointer of a scale, etc. *v.t.* [TONGUED (tuŋd), TONGUING], 1. to reproach or scold. 2. [Archaic], to speak or say. 3. to touch, etc. with the tongue. 4. *a)* to cut a tongue (sense 9*e*) on or in. *b)* to join by means of a tongue-and-groove joint. 5. in *music,* to play by tonguing: see **tonguing.** *v.i.* 1. [Rare], to talk or talk much. 2. to project like a tongue. 3. in *music,* to use tonguing: see **tonguing.**

find one's tongue, to recover the ability to talk after shock or embarrassment.

give tongue, to start to bark: said of hounds.

hold one's tongue, to refrain from speaking.

on everyone's tongue, prevailing as common gossip.

on the tip of one's (or **the**) **tongue,** 1. almost said by one. 2. about to be said: especially of something forgotten that is almost but not quite recalled.

tongue-and-groove joint (tuŋ′'n-gro͞ov′), a kind of joint in which a tongue or rib on one board fits exactly into a groove in another.

tongued (tuŋd), ***adj.*** having a tongue: usually in hyphenated compounds, meaning *having a* (specified kind of) *tongue,* as in *loose-tongued.*

tongue-lash·ing (tuŋ′lash′iŋ), ***n.*** [Colloq.], a sharp reprimand; severe reproof.

tongue·less (tuŋ′lis), ***adj.*** 1. having no tongue; hence, 2. speechless; mute; dumb.

tongue-tie (tuŋ′tī′), ***n.*** the limited motion of the tongue, caused, usually, by an abnormally short frenum and resulting in indistinct articulation. *v.t.* to make tongue-tied.

tongue-tied (tuŋ′tīd′), ***adj.*** 1. having a condition of tongue-tie; hence, 2. speechless from amazement, embarrassment, etc.

tongue twister, a phrase or sentence hard to speak fast, usually because of alliteration or a sequence of nearly similar sounds. Example: She sells sea shells by the seashore.

tongu·ing (tuŋ′iŋ), ***n.*** the use of the tongue to produce a rapidly staccato effect on a musical wind instrument or to modify the intonation.

ton·ic (ton′ik), ***adj.*** [Gr. *tonikos* < *tonos;* see TONE], 1. of, producing, or tending to produce good muscular tone, or tension; hence, 2. mentally or morally invigorating; stimulating. 3. having to do with tones; specifically, *a)* in *music,* designating or based on the first tone (*keynote*) of a diatonic scale: as, a *tonic* chord. *b)* in *painting,* having to do with the tone or tones of a picture. *c)* in *phonetics,* designating or of sounds characterized by resonance in the head cavities: in this sense, no longer used; also, accented. 4. in *linguistics,* tonetic: as, Chinese is a *tonic* language. 5. in *medicine & physiology, a)* of or characterized by tone, or tonus. *b)* of or characterized by continuous muscular contraction: as, a *tonic* spasm. *n.* 1. anything that invigorates or stimulates; specifically, a tonic medicine. 2. a carbonated beverage flavored with a little quinine and served in a mixed drink with gin, vodka, etc.: also called *quinine water.* 3. in *music,* the first, or basic, tone of a diatonic scale; keynote. 4. in *phonetics, a)* a sound characterized by resonance in the head cavities: in this sense, no longer used. *b)* an accented syllable.

tonic accent, 1. a vocal accent, or stress, as distinguished from a written, or graphic, accent: term no longer so used. 2. in *phonetics,* emphasis given to a syllable by changing, especially by raising, the pitch.

to·nic·i·ty (tō-nis′ə-ti), ***n.*** the quality or condition of being tonic; especially, in *physiology,* the normal tension of a muscle at rest; tonus.

tonic sol-fa, a system of musical notation based on the relationship between the tones of a key, using the syllables of solmization (*do, re, mi,* etc.), instead of the usual staff symbols: used especially in elementary singing instruction.

to·night, to-night (tə-nīt′, too-nīt′), ***adv.*** [ME. & AS. *to niht;* see TO, *prep.* & NIGHT], 1. on or during the present or coming night. 2. [Obs. or Dial.], last night. *n.* 1. the present night. 2. the night coming after the present day.

ton·ka bean (toŋ′kə), [< the native name in Guiana], 1. the fragrant, almond-shaped seed of a tall South American tree of the bean family, used for perfuming and flavoring. 2. the tree that it grows on.

Ton·kin (ton′kin′), ***n.*** a former state of French Indo-China, on the Gulf of Tonkin: it is now part of North Viet-Nam: area, 44,670 sq. mi.; pop., 11,000,000; capital, Hanoi: also called *Tongking:* see **Viet-Nam.**

ton·kin (ton′kin′), ***n.*** [after *Tonkin*], a kind of bamboo, used for fishing poles, etc.

Tonkin, Gulf of, an arm of the South China Sea.

Ton·le Sap (ton′lā säp′), a lake in central Cambodia: area in flood season, c. 9,500 sq. mi.

ton·nage (tun′ij), ***n.*** [ME. *tonage;* OFr. *tonnage;* see TON & -AGE], 1. a duty or tax on ships, based on tons carried. 2. a charge per ton on cargo or freight on a canal, at a port, etc. 3. the total amount of shipping of a country or port, calculated in tons. 4. the carrying capacity of a ship, calculated in tons. 5. weight in tons. Also spelled **tunnage.** Abbreviated **tonn.**

ton·neau (tu-nō′, tə-nō′), ***n.*** [*pl.* TONNEAUS, TONNEAUX (-nōz′)], [Fr., lit., a cask; see TUN], 1. an enclosed rear compartment for passengers in an early type of automobile. 2. the whole body of such an automobile.

to·nom·e·ter (tō-nom'ə-tẽr), *n.* [< Gr. *tonos*, tone; + *-meter*], 1. an instrument for determining the pitch of a tone; especially, a tuning fork or set of tuning forks. 2. an instrument for measuring vapor pressure. 3. in *medicine & physiology*, any of various instruments for measuring tension, as of the eyeball, or pressure, as of the blood.

ton·o·met·ric (ton'ə-met'rik, tō'nə-met'rik), *adj.* 1. of or determined by a tonometer. 2. having to do with tonometry.

to·nom·e·try (tō-nom'ə-tri), *n.* the science of using a tonometer.

ton·sil (ton's'l, ton'sil), *n.* [L. *tonsillae*, *pl.*], either of a pair of oval masses of lymphoid tissue, one on each side of the back of the mouth, leading to the pharynx.

ton·sil·lar, ton·sil·ar (ton's'l-ẽr, ton'si-lẽr), *adj.* of the tonsils.

ton·sil·lec·to·my (ton's'l-ek'tə-mi, ton'si-lek'tə-mi), *n.* [*pl.* TONSILLECTOMIES (-miz)], [< L. *tonsillae*, tonsils; + *-ectomy*], the surgical removal of the tonsils.

ton·sil·lit·ic (ton's'l-it'ik, ton'si-lit'ik), *adj.* of or having tonsillitis.

ton·sil·li·tis (ton's'l-ī'tis, ton'si-lī'tis), *n.* [Mod. L. < L. *tonsillae*, tonsils; + *-itis*], inflammation of the tonsils.

ton·sil·lot·o·my (ton's'l-ot'ə-mi, ton'si-lot'ə-mi), *n.* [< L. *tonsillae*, tonsils; + *-tomy*], the surgical incision of a tonsil; especially, a tonsillectomy.

ton·so·ri·al (ton-sôr'i-əl, ton-sō'ri-əl), *adj.* [L. *tonsorius*, of clipping < *tonsor*, clipper < *tonsus*, pp. of *tondere*, to clip, shear], of a barber or his work: often used humorously, as, a *tonsorial* artist.

ton·sure (ton'shẽr), *n.* [ME.; Late OFr.; L. *tonsura* < *tonsus;* see TONSORIAL], 1. the act of shaving the head or, especially, the crown of a person entering the priesthood or a monastic order. 2. the state of being so shaven. 3. the part of the head left bare by so shaving. *v.t.* [TONSURED (-shẽrd), TONSURING], to shave the head or crown of.

ton·tine (ton'tēn, ton-tēn'), *n.* [Fr.; It. *tontina* < Lorenzo *Tonti*, Neapolitan banker who introduced the system into France in the 17th c.], 1. an annuity shared among a group of persons, or a loan based on a group of annuities, with the provision that as each beneficiary dies, his share is divided among the survivors until the entire amount accrues to the last or last two or three survivors. 2. the subscribers to such an annuity, collectively. 3. the total annuity or the share of each subscriber. 4. any similar insurance system.

to·nus (tō'nəs), *n.* [Mod. L.; L. < Gr.; see TONE], tone, or tonicity; especially, muscular tone.

To·ny (tō'ni), a masculine name: see **Anthony.**

ton·y (tō'ni), *adj.* [TONIER (-ni-ẽr), TONIEST (-ni-ist)], [Slang], high-toned; luxurious; stylish: often ironic.

too (to͞o), *adv.* [stressed form of *to, prep.*, with differentiated sp.], 1. in addition; as well; besides; also. 2. more than enough; superfluously; overly: as, the hat is *too* big. 3. to a regrettable extent: as, that's *too* bad! 4. extremely; very: as, it was just *too* delicious! *too* is often used as a mere emphatic, as, I will *too* go!

took (took), past tense of **take.**

tool (to͞ol), *n.* [ME. *tol, tole;* AS. *tol;* akin to ON. *tōl;* for the base see TAW, *v.*], 1. any implement, instrument, or utensil held in the hand and used for cutting, hitting, digging, rubbing, etc.: knives, saws, hammers, shovels, rakes, etc. are tools. 2. *a*) any similar instrument that is the working part of a power-driven machine, as a drill, band-saw blade, etc. *b*) the whole machine; machine tool. 3. anything that serves in the manner of a tool; a means: as, books are a scholar's *tools.* 4. a person used by another to accomplish his purposes, especially when these are illegal or unethical; dupe; stooge. 5. in *law*, any instrument or device necessary to one's profession or occupation. *v.t.* 1. to form, shape, or work with a tool. 2. to provide tools or machinery for (a factory, industry, etc.). 3. [British Colloq.], to drive (a vehicle) or convey (a person in a vehicle). 4. in *bookbinding*, to impress letters or designs on (a book cover) with special tools. *v.i.* 1. to use a tool or tools. 2. [British Colloq.], to ride or drive in a vehicle. —*SYN.* see **implement.**

tool·ing (to͞ol'iŋ), *n.* 1. work or decoration done with tools. 2. the process of fitting out a factory with machine tools in readiness for going into production.

tool·mak·er (to͞ol'māk'ẽr), *n.* a maker of tools; especially, a machinist who makes, maintains, and repairs machine tools.

toon (to͞on), *n.* [Hind. *tun, tūn;* Sans. *tunna*], 1. a large Australian and East Indian tree with soft, close-grained, reddish wood used in furniture and with flowers that yield a dye. 2. its wood.

toot (to͞ot), *v.i.* [< D. or LG. *tuten* < a Gmc. echoic base], 1. to blow a horn, whistle, etc., especially in short blasts. 2. to sound in short blasts: said of a horn, whistle, etc. 3. to make a sound like a horn or whistle. *v.t.* 1. to cause to sound in short blasts. 2. to sound (tones, blasts, etc.), as on a horn. *n* a. short blast of a horn, whistle, etc.

tooth (to͞oth), *n.* [*pl.* TEETH (tēth)], [ME. *tothe;* AS. *toth* (< *tanth); akin to G. *zahn;* IE. base **edont-* (< **ed-*, to eat), seen also in L. *dens* (see DENTAL), Gr. *odontos* (see ODONT-)], 1. *a*) any of a set of hard, bonelike structures (normally 32 in the human adult) set in the jaws of most vertebrates and used for biting, tearing, and chewing: a tooth consists typically of a sensitive, vascular pulp surrounded by dentine and coated on the crown with enamel and on the root with cement. *b*) any of various analogous processes in invertebrates. 2. something resembling a tooth; a toothlike part, as on a saw, fork, rake, gear, etc.; tine; prong; cog. 3. appetite or taste for something: as, a sweet *tooth.* 4. something that bites, pierces, or gnaws like a tooth: as, the *teeth* of the storm. 5. in *botany*, any small, sharp lobe, as of a leaf or of the fringe surrounding the opening of a capsule in mosses. *v.t.* 1. to provide with teeth. 2. to make jagged; indent. *v.i.* to mesh, or become interlocked, as gears.

armed to the teeth, fully armed.

in the teeth of, 1. directly against; in the face of. 2. in opposition to; defying.

put teeth in (a law, etc.), to enforce or facilitate the enforcement of (a law, etc.).

set one's teeth, to prepare to meet firmly something difficult or unpleasant.

show one's teeth, to show hostility; threaten angrily.

throw (something) in one's teeth, 1. to reproach one for (something). 2. to hurl (a challenge, taunt, etc.) at one.

tooth and nail, with all one's strength or resources.

SYN.—**tooth** is the general, inclusive word (see the definition above); **tusk** refers to a long, pointed, enlarged tooth projecting outside the mouth in certain animals, as the elephant, wild boar, and walrus, and used for digging or as a weapon; **fang** refers either to one of the long, sharp teeth with which meat-eating animals tear their prey or to the long, hollow tooth through which poisonous snakes inject their venom.

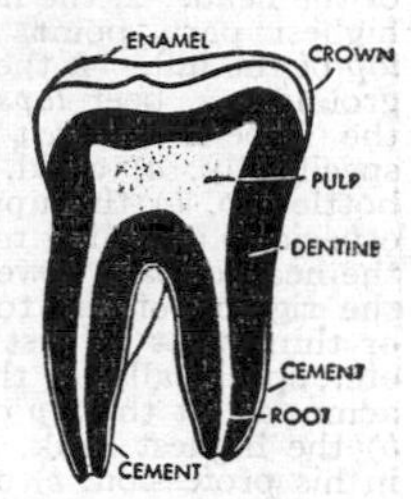

DIAGRAM OF TOOTH

PERMANENT TEETH OF RIGHT SIDE

Upper Jaw: A, central incisor; B, lateral incisor; C, canine; D, first premolar; E, second premolar; F, first molar; G, second molar; H, third molar. Lower Jaw: I, central incisor; J, lateral incisor; K, canine; L, first premolar; M, second premolar; N, first molar; O, second molar; P, third molar

tooth·ache (to͞oth'āk'), *n.* an ache in a tooth or the teeth.

tooth·brush (to͞oth'brush'), *n.* a small brush for cleaning the teeth.

toothed (to͞otht, to͞o*th*d), *adj.* 1. having teeth. 2. notched; indented.

-toothed (to͞otht, to͞o*th*d), a combining form used in hyphenated compounds, meaning *having* (a specified number or kind of) *teeth*, as in *big-toothed.*

tooth paste, a paste for brushing the teeth.

tooth·pick (to͞oth'pik'), *n.* a slender, pointed instrument, as a sliver of wood, etc., for dislodging food particles from between the teeth.

tooth powder, a powder for brushing the teeth.

tooth·some (to͞oth'səm), *adj.* [*tooth* + *-some*], pleasing to the taste; palatable.

tooth·wort (to͞oth'wûrt'), *n.* 1. any of a number of related plants with white, toothlike roots and clusters of white, purplish, or rose flowers. 2. any of a number of related parasitic plants having roots covered with tooth-shaped scales.

too·tle (to͞o't'l), *v.i.* [TOOTLED (-t'ld), TOOTLING], [freq. of *toot*], to toot softly and usually more or less continuously on a horn, whistle, flute, etc. *n.* the act or sound of tootling.

toots (toots), *n.* [< *tootsy*], [Slang], darling; dear: affectionate or playful term of address.

toot·sy (toot'si), *n.* [*pl.* TOOTSIES (-siz)], [child's term of endearment], [Slang], 1. a child's or woman's small foot. 2. toots.

top (top), *n.* [ME.; AS. *top;* akin to G. *zopf,* tuft of hair, summit; IE. base **də-p* < **dā(i),* to part, divide up, tear out (cf. TIDE, TIME); prob. sense development "what can be plucked out—hair tuft—hair—highest point"], 1. originally, *a)* a tuft of hair. *b)* the hair of the head. 2. the head, or crown of the head. 3. the highest part, point, or surface of anything: as, the *top* of the hill. 4. the part of a plant that grows above ground: as, beet *tops.* 5. something that constitutes the uppermost part or covering of something else; specifically, *a)* a lid, cover, cap, etc.: as, a box *top,* bottle *top.* *b)* the upper part of an automobile body, especially a folding roof or cover. *c)* a platform around the head of each lower mast of a sailing ship, to which the rigging of the topmast is attached. 6. a person or thing that is first in order, excellence, importance, etc.; specifically, *a)* the highest degree or pitch; zenith; acme: as, at the *top* of his voice, the *top* of her career. *b)* the highest rank, position, etc.: as, he's at the *top* in his profession. *c)* a person in this rank, etc. *d)* the choicest part; pick; cream: as, the *top* of the crop. 7. the beginning, or earliest part: as, the *top* of the year. 8. in *card games,* the card or (in *pl.*) cards that will win the first or second round of a suit. 9. in *chemistry,* the most volatile part of a mixture. 10. in *sports & games,* *a)* a stroke that hits the ball above center or near its top. *b)* the forward spin given the ball by such a stroke. *adj.* of, situated at, or being the top; uppermost; highest: as, the *top* drawer, *top* honors. *v.t.* [TOPPED (topt), TOPPING], 1. to take off the top of (a plant, etc.). 2. to provide or cover with a top. 3. to be a top for. 4. to reach the top of; be on a level with. 5. to equal or exceed in amount, height, etc.: as, the fish *topped* 75 pounds. 6. to surpass; outdo: as, he *tops* them all at tennis. 7. to go over the top of (a rise of ground, etc.). 8. to be at the top of; head; lead. 9. in *chemistry,* to remove the volatile parts from, by distillation. 10. in *dyeing,* to finish with a certain dye. 11. in *sports & games,* *a)* to hit (the ball) above center or near its top, giving it a forward spin. *b)* to make (a stroke) by hitting the ball in this way. *v.i.* to top someone or something (in any sense).

blow one's top, [Slang], 1. to lose one's temper. 2. to become insane.

on top, at the top; successful.

on top of, 1. on or at the top of. 2. resting upon. 3. in addition to; besides. 4. following immediately after.

on top of the world, [Colloq.], in a position of great success, prosperity, happiness, etc.

over the top, 1. over the front of the trench, as in attacking. 2. exceeding the assigned quota or goal.

(the) tops, [Slang], pre-eminent in quality, ability, popularity, etc.; the very best: used predicatively.

top off, to complete by adding a finishing touch.

top (top), *n.* [ME.; Late AS.; akin to D. dial. *top;* prob. IE. base **dheubh* < **dheu-,* to fly, whirl, etc.], a child's toy shaped somewhat like an inverted cone, with a point at its apex upon which it is spun, usually by unwinding a string.

sleep like a top, to sleep soundly.

to·paz (tō′paz), *n.* [ME. *topace;* OFr. *topace, topase;* L. *topazus;* Gr. *topazos*], 1. a native aluminum silicate, $Al_2SiO_4F_2$, occurring in white, yellow, pale-blue, or pale-green crystals: the yellow variety is used as a gem. 2. any of various similarly colored gems or semiprecious stones, as a yellow variety of sapphire and a yellow variety of quartz. 3. either of two large, brightly colored hummingbirds of South America.

to·paz·o·lite (tō-paz′ə-līt′), *n.* [< Gr. *topazos,* topaz; + *-lite*], a yellow variety of garnet.

top boot, any of several high boots reaching to just below the knee and usually having its upper part of a different material.

top·coat (top′kōt′), *n.* an overcoat; especially, a lightweight overcoat.

top-drawer (top′drôr′), *adj.* of first importance, rank, privilege, etc.

top-dress (top′dres′), *v.t.* to put top-dressing on.

top-dress·ing (top′dres′iŋ), *n.* 1. material applied to a surface, as fertilizer on land or crops, or stones on a road. 2. the applying of such material.

tope (tōp), *v.t. & v.i.* [TOPED (tōpt), TOPING], [Fr. *toper,* to accept the stakes in gambling; present Eng. meaning prob. from the custom of drinking to the conclusion of the wager], [Archaic], to drink (alcoholic liquor) in large amounts and often.

tope (tōp), *n.* [Hind. *ṭop;* ult. < Sans. *stūpa,* a mound, tope], a Buddhist shrine in the form of a dome with a cupola.

tope (tōp), *n.* [said to be (1686) < Cornish], a small European shark, about five feet long.

to·pee (tō-pē′, tō′pē), *n.* [Hind. *ṭopī*], in India, a hat or cap, especially a pith sun helmet: also **topi.**

To·pe·ka (tə-pē′kə), *n.* the capital of Kansas, on the Kansas River: pop., 119,000.

top·er (tōp′ẽr), *n.* a person who topes; drunkard.

top-flight (top′flīt′), *adj.* [Colloq.], best; first-rate.

top·gal·lant (tə-gal′ənt, top′gal′ənt), *adj.* 1. situated above the topmast and below the royal mast on a sailing ship. 2. higher than the adjoining parts of the ship: said of a rail, deck, etc. *n.* 1. a topgallant mast, sail, spar, etc. 2. [Rare], summit; zenith.

toph (tōf), *n.* tufa.

top-ham·per (top′ham′pẽr), *n.* 1. the upper masts, spars, and rigging of a sailing ship, usually kept aloft. 2. rigging, spars, etc. not needed immediately and an encumbrance aloft or on deck. Also **top hamper.**

top hat, a tall, black, cylindrical hat, usually of silk, worn by men in formal dress.

tophe (tōf), *n.* tufa.

top-heav·i·ness (top′hev′i-nis), *n.* the quality or state of being top-heavy.

top-heav·y (top′hev′i), *adj.* heavier at the top than below, so as to be likely to fall over or collapse; overweighted at the top with stacked objects: also used figuratively, as of an overcapitalized financial structure.

To·phet, To·pheth (tō′fit, tō′fet), *n.* [ME.; Heb. *tōpheth,* ? altar; ? < Aram.], 1. in the Old Testament, apparently a place where human sacrifices by fire were made to Moloch, possibly in the Valley of Hinnom; hence, 2. hell.

top-hole (top′hōl′), *adj.* [British Slang], first-rate.

to·phus (tō′fəs), *n.* [*pl.* TOPHI (-fī)], [L., tufa], in *medicine,* an abnormal mineral deposit, as of calcium carbonate, about the joints, on the roots of the teeth, etc., in a person who has the gout.

to·pi (tō-pē′, tō′pē), *n.* a topee.

to·pi·ar·y (tō′pi-er′i), *adj.* [L. *topiarius,* concerning an ornamental garden < *topia* (*opera*), ornamental gardening < Gr. *topos,* place], designating or of the art of trimming and training shrubs or trees into unnatural, ornamental shapes. *n.* [*pl.* TOPIARIES (-iz)], 1. topiary art or work. 2. a topiary garden.

top·ic (top′ik), *n.* [L. *topica* < Gr. *ta topika,* title of a work by Aristotle < *topikos,* local, concerning *topoi,* commonplaces < *topos,* a place], 1. formerly, a kind of consideration suitable for rhetorical discourse. 2. the subject of a paragraph, essay, speech, etc. 3. a subject for discussion. 4. a heading or item in an outline. —*SYN.* see **subject.**

top·i·cal (top′i-k'l), *adj.* 1. of a particular place; local. 2. of or using a topic or topics. 3. having to do with topics of the day; of current or local interest: as, *topical* allusions in literature. 4. in *medicine,* of or for a particular part of the body: as, a *topical* remedy.

top kick, [Military Slang], a first sergeant.

top·knot (top′not′), *n.* 1. a knot of feathers, ribbons, etc. worn as a headdress. 2. *a)* a tuft of hair on the crown of the head of a person or animal. *b)* a tuft of feathers on a bird's head.

top·loft·i·ness (top′lôf′ti-nis), *n.* [Colloq.], the quality of being toplofty.

top·loft·y (top′lôf′ti), *adj.* [Colloq.], lofty in manner; haughty; pompous; supercilious.

top·mast (top′məst, top′mast′, top′mäst′), *n.* the second mast above the deck of a sailing ship, supported by the lower mast and often supporting a topgallant mast in turn.

top minnow, any of a group of small, surface-feeding fish that produce their young fully formed.

top·most (top′mōst′, top′məst), *adj.* at the very top; uppermost; highest.

top-notch (top′noch′), *adj.* [Colloq.], first-rate; best.

to·pog·ra·pher (tə-pog′rə-fẽr, tō-pog′rə-fẽr), *n.* 1. an expert or specialist in topography. 2. a person who describes or maps the topography of a place or region.

top·o·graph·ic (top′ə-graf′ik), *adj.* topographical: abbreviated **topog.**

top·o·graph·i·cal (top′ə-graf′i-k'l), *adj.* of or done by topography: abbreviated **topog.**

top·o·graph·i·cal·ly (top′ə-graf′i-k'l-i, top′ə-graf′ik-li), *adv.* as regards topography.

to·pog·ra·phy (tə-pog′rə-fi, tō-pog′rə-fi), *n.* [*pl.* TOPOGRAPHIES (-fiz)], [ME. *topographye;* LL. *topographia;* Gr. *topographia* < *topos,* a place + *graphein,* to write], 1. originally, the accurate and detailed description of a place. 2. the science of drawing on maps and charts or otherwise representing the surface features of a region, including hills, valleys, rivers, lakes, canals, bridges, roads, cities, etc. 3. these surface features. 4. topographic surveying. Abbreviated **topog.**

top·o·nym (top′ə-nim′), *n.* [< *toponymy*], 1. a name of a place. 2. a name that indicates origin, natural locale, etc., as in zoological nomenclature.

top·o·nym·ic (top′ə-nim′ik), *adj.* 1. of a toponym or toponyms. 2. having to do with toponymy.

top·o·nym·i·cal (top′ə-nim′i-k'l), *adj.* toponymic.

to·pon·y·my (tə-pon′ə-mi), *n.* [< Gr. *topos,* a place + *-onymia,* a naming < *onoma, onyma,* a name], 1. the place names of a country, district, etc. or the study of these. 2. in *anatomy,* the nomenclature of the regions (as distinguished from the organs) of the body.

top·per (top′ẽr), *n.* 1. a device for removing tops, as of vegetables. 2. [Slang], a top-notch person or thing. 3. [Slang], *a)* a top hat. *b)* a topcoat; especially, a woman's short, loose-fitting topcoat.

top·ping (top′iŋ), *n.* 1. the action of a person or thing

that tops. 2. something that forms the top of something else. *adj.* 1. that tops in height, degree, rank, etc. 2. [British Colloq.], superior; excellent; first-rate.
top·ple (top'′l), *v.i.* [TOPPLED (-′ld), TOPPLING], [< *top, v.* + *-le*], 1. to fall top forward; fall over from top-heaviness, etc. (often with *over*). 2. to lean forward as if on the point of falling; overbalance; overhang; totter. *v.t.* to cause to topple; overturn.
top·sail (top′s'l, top′sāl′), *n.* 1. in a square-rigged vessel, the square sail next above the lowest sail on a mast. 2. in a fore-and-aft-rigged vessel, the small sail set above the gaff of a fore-and-aft sail.
top-se·cret (top′sē′krit), *adj.* designating or of military or government information of the greatest secrecy.
top sergeant, [Colloq.], in the United States Army, a first sergeant.
top·side (top′sīd′), *n.* *usually in pl.* the part of a ship's side above the water line. *adv.* on or to the upper side of a ship; on deck.
top·soil (top′soil′), *n.* the upper layer of soil, usually darker and richer than the subsoil; surface soil. *v.t.* to remove the topsoil from (land).
top·sy-tur·vi·ly (top′si-tũr′və-li), *adv.* in a topsy-turvy manner.
top·sy-tur·vi·ness (top′si-tũr′vi-nis), *n.* the quality or state of being topsy-turvy.
top·sy-tur·vy (top′si-tũr′vi), *adv. & adj.* [earlier *topsy-tervy;* prob. < *top*, highest part + ME. *terven*, to roll], 1. upside down; in a reversed condition. 2. in confusion or disorder. *n.* 1. a topsy-turvy condition; inverted state. 2. a state of confusion.
toque (tōk), *n.* [Fr., a cap; Sp. *toca* < Basque *tauka*, kind of cap], a woman's small, round, close-fitting hat, with or without a brim: a modification of a 16th-century, small, plumed hat, worn by men and women.
tor (tôr), *n.* [ME.; AS. *torr* (? via OW. *turr* < L.), a tower, rock; L. *turris*, a tower], a high, rocky hill.
to·rah, to·ra (tō′rə, tō′rō), *n.* [*pl.* TOROTH (-rōth, -rōs)], [Heb. *tōrāh*, a law], in *Judaism*, 1. *a)* learning, law, instruction, etc. *b)* the whole body of Jewish religious literature, including the Scripture, the Talmud, etc. 2. [usually T-], *a)* the Pentateuch. *b)* a parchment scroll containing the Pentateuch.
torch (tôrch), *n.* [ME. & OFr. *torche;* LL. **torca*, lit., twisted object < *torquere*, to twist], 1. a portable light consisting of a long piece of resinous wood, or twisted tow dipped in tallow, etc., flaming at one end; link; flambeau. 2. anything considered as a source of enlightenment, illumination, inspiration, etc.: as, the *torch* of science. 3. any of various portable devices for producing a very hot flame, used in welding, burning off paint, etc. 4. [British], a flashlight.
carry a (or the) torch for, [Slang], to be in love with.
torch·bear·er (tôrch′bâr′ẽr), *n.* 1. a person who carries a torch; hence, 2. a person who brings enlightenment, inspiration, truth, etc.
torch·ier, torch·iere (tôr-chêr′, tôr-shêr′), *n.* [< Fr. *torchère*, small, high candlestand < OFr. *torche;* see TORCH], a floor lamp with a reflector bowl and no shade, for casting light upward so as to give indirect illumination.
torch·light (tôrch′līt′), *n.* the light of a torch or torches. *adj.* done or carried on by torchlight.
tor·chon lace (tôr′shon; Fr. tôr′shōn′), [Fr. *torchon*, dishcloth, duster < *torche;* see TORCH], 1. a strong, bobbin lace made of coarse linen thread in simple, open, geometric patterns. 2. an imitation of this made by machine.
torch singer, a person who sings torch songs.
torch song, [< phrase *carry a torch for*], a sentimental popular song, especially of unrequited love.
torch·wood (tôrch′wood′), *n.* 1. any of a number of related trees with resinous wood from which torches can be made. 2. the wood.
Tor·de·sil·las (tôr′*th*e-sē′lyäs), *n.* a town in northern Spain, where a treaty defining claims of discovery in the New World was signed in 1494 by Spain and Portugal.
tore (tôr, tōr), alternative past tense of **tear** (to pull apart).
tore (tôr, tōr), *n.* in *architecture & geometry*, a torus.
tor·e·a·dor (tôr′i-ə-dôr′; Sp. tō′re-ä-*th*ôr′), *n.* [Sp. < *torear*, to fight bulls < *toro*, a bull; L. *taurus*, a bull], a bullfighter, especially one on horseback: term no longer used in bullfighting.
‡to·re·ro (tô-re′rô), *n.* [*pl.* TOREROS (-rôs)], [Sp. < *torear;* see TOREADOR], a bullfighter on foot.
to·reu·tic (tə-rōō′tik), *adj.* [Gr. *toreutikos* < *toreuein*, to work in relief, bore], designating or of embossed or chased work, especially in metal.
to·reu·tics (tə-rōō′tiks), *n.pl.* [construed as sing.], the art of making toreutic work.
to·ri (tôr′ī, tō′rī), *n.* plural of **torus.**
tor·ic (tôr′ik, tor′ik), *adj.* of or shaped like a torus.
toric lens, a lens of which one surface is a segment of the surface of a torus: used especially in eyeglasses.
to·ri·i (tō′ri-ē′), *n.* [*pl.* TORII], [Japan.], a gateway at the entrance to a Japanese Shinto temple, consisting of two uprights supporting a curved lintel, with a straight crosspiece below.

TORII

To·ri·no (tô-rē′nô), *n.* Turin.
tor·ment (tôr′ment; *for v.*, tôr-ment′), *n.* [ME.; OFr. *torment*, *tourment;* L. *tormentum*, a rack, instrument of torture, torture, pain, orig., machine for hurling missiles < *torquere*, to twist], 1. originally, *a)* an instrument of torture. *b)* torture. 2. great pain or anguish, physical or mental; suffering; agony. 3. a source of pain, anxiety, or annoyance. *v.t.* [ME. *tormenten;* OFr. *tourmenter* < the *n.*], 1. [Rare], to torture. 2. to cause great physical pain or mental anguish in. 3. to annoy; harass; tease. 4. [Obs.], to stir up; agitate.
SYN.—**torment** implies harassment or persecution by the continued or repeated infliction of suffering or annoyance (*tormented* by the mosquitoes); **torture** implies the infliction of acute physical or mental pain, such as to cause agony (*tortured* by his memories); **rack** suggests the excruciating pain suffered on the rack, an ancient instrument of torture on which the limbs were pulled out of place (*racked* by the pain of arthritis). See also **bait.** —*ANT.* comfort
tor·ment·er (tôr-men′tẽr), *n.* a tormentor.
tor·men·til (tôr′men-til′), *n.* [Fr. *tormentille;* ML. *tormentilla* < L. *tormentum* (see TORMENT) from belief in the pain-killing power of the plant], a yellow-flowered, trailing plant whose root is used in medicine, dyeing, and tanning.
tor·men·tor (tôr-men′tẽr), *n.* [ME. *tormentour;* OFr. *tormenteor*], 1. a person or thing that torments. 2. [so called because it obstructs a full view of the stage by those sitting at the sides], in the *theater*, either of the wings or curtains projecting out onto each side of the stage, directly behind the proscenium. 3. in *motion pictures*, a covered screen for absorbing echoes on a set.
torn (tôrn, tōrn), alternative past participle of **tear** (to pull apart).
tor·nad·ic (tôr-nad′ik), *adj.* of or like a tornado.
tor·na·do (tôr-nā′dō), *n.* [*pl.* TORNADOES, TORNADOS (-dōz)], [Sp. *tronada*, thunder, thunderstorm < *tronar*, to thunder; L. *tonare*, to thunder; prob. merged with Sp. *tornar*, to turn], 1. a violent whirling wind, especially in the central United States, accompanied by a rapidly rotating, funnel-shaped cloud that usually destroys everything along its narrow path. 2. any whirlwind or hurricane.
to·roid (tō′roid), *n.* [< *tore* + *-oid*], in *geometry*, a surface, or its enclosed solid, generated by any closed plane curve rotating about a straight line in its own plane: a *torus* is a specialized form of *toroid.*
To·ron·to (tə-ron′tō), *n.* the capital of Ontario, Canada, on Lake Ontario: pop., 676,000 (with suburbs, 1,117,-000).
to·rose (tō′rōs, tō-rōs′), *adj.* [L. *torosus*, full of muscle, brawny < *torus*, muscle], 1. bulging, knobbed, protuberant, swollen, etc. 2. in *botany*, cylindrical, with swellings at intervals.
to·rous (tō′rəs), *adj.* torose.
tor·pe·do (tôr-pē′dō), *n.* [*pl.* TORPEDOES (-dōz)], [L., numbness, crampfish < *torpere*, to be stiff, numb, or torpid], 1. an electric ray (kind of fish); numbfish; crampfish. 2. a large, cigar-shaped, self-propelled, under-water projectile for launching against enemy ships from a submarine, airplane, etc.: it explodes on contact by means of a timing mechanism or by radio control. 3. a metal case containing explosives, especially one used as an underwater mine. 4. a small firework consisting of a percussion cap and gravel wrapped in tissue paper, which explodes with a loud report when thrown against a hard surface. 5. an explosive cartridge placed on a railroad track and detonated by a train wheel as a signal to the crew. 6. an explosive cartridge lowered into oil wells, where it is detonated to clear the bore or break through into the oil pocket. 7. [Slang], a gangster or gunman serving as a bodyguard, ready to shoot or attack with no warning. *v.t.* to attack, destroy, damage, or ruin with or as with a torpedo.

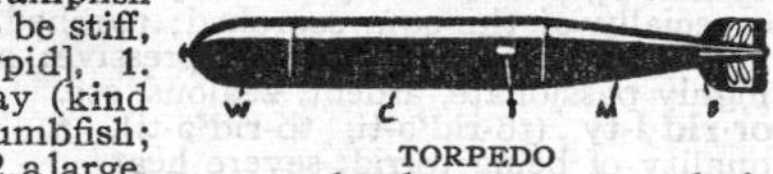

TORPEDO
W, war head; C, compressed air chamber; T, trigger; M, motor; F, fins, propellers, and rudder

torpedo boat, a small, fast, maneuverable warship for attacking with torpedoes, armed with only light guns.
tor·pe·do-boat destroyer (tôr-pē′dō-bōt′), a warship like a torpedo boat but larger and more heavily armed,

originally designed to destroy enemy torpedo boats but later used offensively as a torpedo boat.

torpedo body, a design of automobile body somewhat like that of a submarine torpedo, with flush sides for reducing wind resistance.

torpedo tube, a tube for launching torpedoes, located in surface vessels below or close to the water line.

tor·pid (tôr'pid), *adj.* [L. *torpidus* < *torpere,* to be numb or torpid], 1. having lost temporarily all or part of the power of sensation or motion, as a hibernating animal; dormant. 2. dull; sluggish; apathetic.

tor·pid·i·ty (tôr-pid'ə-ti), *n.* the condition or quality of being torpid.

tor·por (tôr'pẽr), *n.* [L. < *torpere;* see TORPID], 1. a state of being dormant or inactive; temporary loss of all or part of the power of sensation or motion; stupor. 2. dullness; sluggishness; apathy. —*SYN.* see **lethargy.**

tor·por·if·ic (tôr'pə-rif'ik), *adj.* causing torpor.

tor·quate (tôr'kwāt), *adj.* [L. *torquatus*], having a torques; collared.

Tor·quay (tôr-kē'), *n.* a city in southern Devonshire, England: pop., 53,000.

torque (tôrk), *n.* [< L. *torques;* directly influenced (in senses 2 & 3) by *torquere;* see TORQUES], 1. a twisted metal collar or necklace worn by ancient Teutons, Gauls, Britons, etc. 2. in *physics, a)* a force or combination of forces that produces or tends to produce a twisting or rotating motion (called *torsion*). *b)* the tendency to produce torsion. 3. in *optics,* a rotary effect produced by some crystals and liquids on the plane of polarization of light passing through them.

Tor·que·ma·da, To·más de (tô-mäs' *the* tôr'ke-mä'*thä;* Eng. tôr'ki-mä'də), 1420–1498; Dominican monk and first inquisitor general of Spain: often regarded as a type of fanatical, cruel intolerance.

tor·ques (tôr'kwēz), *n.* [L. *torques, torquis,* a twisted necklace < *torquere,* to twist], a ring of hair, feathers, or modified skin around the neck of an animal or bird, of a distinctive color or form.

Tor·rance (tôr'əns, tor'əns), *n.* a city in southwestern California: suburb of Los Angeles: pop., 101,000.

tor·re·fac·tion (tôr'ə-fak'shən, tor'ə-fak'shən), *n.* a torrefying or being torrefied.

tor·re·fy (tôr'ə-fī', tor'ə-fī'), *v.t.* [TORREFIED (-fīd'), TORREFYING], [Fr. *torréfier;* L. *torrefacere* < *torrere,* to dry or roast by heat + *facere,* to make], to dry or parch with heat, as some drugs. Also spelled **torrify.**

Tor·rens, Lake (tôr'ənz, tor'ənz), a salt lake in eastern South Australia: length, 130 mi.

tor·rent (tôr'ənt, tor'ənt), *n.* [Fr.; L. *torrens,* burning, roaring, rushing, impetuous; ppr. of *torrere,* to parch, dry, roast, consume; cf. TORRID, THIRST], 1. a swift, violent stream, especially of water. 2. a rapid, profuse, or violent flow of words, mail, etc.; flood; rush. 3. a heavy fall of rain. *adj.* [Rare], of or like a torrent.

tor·ren·tial (tô-ren'shəl, to-ren'shəl), *adj.* 1. of, or having the nature of, a torrent. 2. like a torrent, as in violence, swiftness, copiousness, etc.; overwhelming; outpouring. 3. resulting from the action of a torrent.

tor·ren·tial·ly (tô-ren'shəl-i, to-ren'shəl-i), *adv.* in the manner of a torrent; overwhelmingly.

Tor·res Strait (tôr'iz, tor'iz), a strait between New Guinea and northeastern Australia: width, 90 mi.

Tor·ri·cel·li, E·van·ge·lis·ta (e'vän-je-lēs'tä tôr'rē-chel'lē; Eng. tôr'i-chel'i), 1608–1647; Italian physicist; discovered principle of the barometer.

tor·rid (tôr'id, tor'id), *adj.* [L. *torridus* < *torrere;* see TORRENT], 1. dried by or subjected to intense heat, especially of the sun; scorched; parched; arid. 2. so hot as to be parching or oppressive; scorching. 3. highly passionate, ardent, zealous, etc.

tor·rid·i·ty (tô-rid'ə-ti, to-rid'ə-ti), *n.* the state or quality of being torrid; severe heat.

Torrid Zone, the area of the earth between the Tropic of Cancer and the Tropic of Capricorn and divided by the equator: see **zone,** illus.

tor·ri·fy (tôr'ə-fī', tor'ə-fī'), *v.t.* [TORRIFIED (-fīd'), TORRIFYING], to torrefy.

Tor·ring·ton (tôr'iŋ-tən, tor'iŋ-tən), *n.* a city in northwestern Connecticut: pop., 30,000.

tor·sade (tôr-sād'), *n.* [Fr. < ML. *torsus,* for L. *tortus,* pp. of *torquere,* to twist], 1. a twisted cord used in drapery, etc. 2. a molded or worked ornament resembling this.

tor·si (tôr'sē), *n.* alternative plural of **torso.**

tor·si·bil·i·ty (tôr'sə-bil'ə-ti), *n.* ability to undergo, or resistance to, torsion.

tor·sion (tôr'shən), *n.* [ME. *torcion;* Late OFr.; LL. *torsio, tortio* < pp. of L. *torquere,* to twist], 1. a twisting or being twisted; specifically, the twisting of a body by holding one end firm and turning the other along the longitudinal axis. 2. in *mechanics,* the tendency of a twisted wire, bar, etc. to return to its untwisted condition.

tor·sion·al (tôr'shən-'l), *adj.* of or caused by torsion.

torsion balance, an instrument for measuring minute electric impulses, etc. by the torsion caused in a fine wire.

torsk (tôrsk), *n.* [*pl.* TORSK, TORSKS (tôrsks); see PLURAL, II, D, 2], [< Norw. *torsk* (ON. *thorskr*); base as in *thirst*], 1. a cusk, a kind of fish. 2. a codfish.

tor·so (tôr'sō), *n.* [*pl.* TORSOS (-sōz), TORSI (-sē)], [It., a stump, trunk of a statue; L. *thyrsus,* a stalk, stem; Gr. *thyrsos,* a stem, wand], 1. the trunk of a statue of the nude human figure, especially of such a statue lacking the head and limbs. 2. the trunk of the human body. 3. any unfinished or fragmentary piece of work.

torso murder, a murder in which the victim's body is dismembered.

tort (tôrt), *n.* [ME.; OFr. < L. *tortus,* pp. of *torquere,* to twist], in *law,* a wrongful act, injury, or damage (not involving a breach of contract), for which a civil action can be brought.

torte (tôrt; G. tôr'tə), *n.* [*pl.* TORTES (tôrts); G. TORTEN (-tən)], [G.] a rich cake, variously made, as of eggs, finely chopped nuts, and crumbs or a little flour.

tor·ti·col·lis (tôr'ti-kol'is), *n.* [Mod. L. < L. *tortus,* twisted + *collum,* the neck], in *medicine,* a condition of persistent involuntary contraction of the neck muscles causing the head to be twisted to an abnormal position; wryneck.

tor·tile (tôr't'l, tôr'til), *adj.* [L. *tortilis* < *tortus;* see TORT], twisted or coiled.

tor·til·la (tôr-tē'yä), *n.* [Sp., dim. of *torta,* a cake; LL. *torta,* twisted loaf < pp. of *torquere,* to twist], a flat, unleavened corn cake baked on an iron plate or flat stone: used throughout Mexico as the equivalent of bread.

tor·tious (tôr'shəs), *adj.* [ME. *torcious* < Anglo-Fr.], in *law,* of or involving a tort.

tor·toise (tôr'təs), *n.* [*pl.* TORTOISES (-iz), TORTOISE; see PLURAL, II, D, 1], [ME. *tortuce;* ML. *tortuca;* prob. < It. *tortuca,* altered (prob. by association with L. *tortus,* twisted) < *tartaruca* < Gr. *tartaruchos,* evil demon: so called because in Greek belief the tortoise was a demon; cf. Fr. *tortue*], a turtle, especially one that lives on land: see **turtle.**

tortoise beetle, any of a group of small beetles shaped somewhat like a tortoise.

tor·toise-shell (tôr'təs-shel'), *adj.* 1. made of tortoise shell or of a synthetic substance like it. 2. having the coloring or appearance of tortoise shell.

tortoise shell, 1. the hard, mottled, yellow-and-brown shells of some turtles and tortoises, used in inlaying and in making combs, spectacle frames, etc. 2. a tortoise-shell butterfly.

tortoise-shell butterfly, any of a group of common, black and yellow-brown butterflies with markings resembling those of tortoise shell.

tor·tri·cid (tôr'tri-sid), *adj.* [< Mod. L. *Tortricidae,* name of the family < *Tortrix,* type genus < L. *tortus,* pp. of *torquere,* to twist], designating or of any of a group of small, broad-bodied moths.

Tor·tue (tôr'tü'), *n.* Tortuga.

Tor·tu·ga (tôr-too͞'gə), *n.* an island of Haiti in the West Indies: area, 117 sq. mi.: French name, *Tortue.*

tor·tu·os·i·ty (tôr'choo͞-os'ə-ti), *n.* [L. *tortuositas*], 1. the quality or condition of being tortuous. 2. [*pl.* TORTUOSITIES (-tiz)], a twist, turn, winding, etc.

tor·tu·ous (tôr'choo͞-əs), *adj.* [ME.; Anglo-Fr.; L. *tortuosus* < *tortus,* pp. of *torquere,* to twist], 1. full of twists, turns, curves, or windings; winding; crooked; hence, 2. not straightforward; devious; specifically, deceitful; immoral.

tor·ture (tôr'chẽr), *n.* [Fr.; LL. *tortura,* a twisting, torture < pp. of L. *torquere,* to twist], 1. the inflicting of severe pain to force information or confession, get revenge, etc. 2. any method by which such pain is inflicted. 3. any severe physical or mental pain; agony; anguish. 4. a cause of such pain or agony. 5. [Rare], a violent twisting, distortion, perversion, etc. *v.t.* [TORTURED (-chẽrd), TORTURING], 1. to subject to torture. 2. to cause (a person) extreme physical or mental pain; agonize. 3. to twist or distort (meaning, etc.). —*SYN.* see **torment.**

tor·tur·ous (tôr'chẽr-əs), *adj.* [OFr. *tortureus*], full of, involving, or causing torture.

To·ruń (tô'roon-y'), *n.* a city in Poland, on the Vistula River: pop., 80,000: German name, *Thorn.*

to·rus (tôr'əs, tō'rəs), *n.* [*pl.* TORI (-ī, -rī)], [L., a bulge, protuberance], 1. a large, convex molding used at the base of columns, etc., just above the plinth: also **tore.** 2. in *anatomy,* any rounded projection or swelling. 3. in *botany,* that part of a plant on which the floral leaves grow; receptacle. 4. in *geometry,* a surface, or its enclosed solid, generated by the revolution of a conic section, especially a circle, about any axis in its plane other than its diameter: also **tore.**

To·ry (tôr'i, tō'ri), *n.* [*pl.* TORIES (-iz, -riz)], [Ir. *tōruidhe,* robber, pursuer (later applied to outlaws and armed Irish Papists) < *tōir,* to pursue; akin to Gael. *tōir,* pursuit], 1. [sometimes t-], *a)* in the 17th century, any of the dispossessed Irish who became outlaws, killed English settlers and soldiers, and lived by plundering. *b)* later, any armed Irish Papist or Royalist. 2. in 1679–1680, a person who opposed the exclusion of James, Duke of York, from succession to the English throne; hence, 3. after 1689, a member of one of the two major political parties of England: opposed to *Whig*, and later, to *Liberal*, *Radical*, *Laborite;* changed officially c. 1830 to *Conservative*. 4. in the American Revolution, a person who advocated or actively supported continued allegiance to Great Britain. 5. [often t-], any extreme conservative; reactionary. *adj.* [also t-], of, being, or having the conservative principles of a Tory.

To·ry·ism (tôr'i-iz'm, tō'ri-iz'm), *n.* the principles or behavior of a Tory.

Tos·ca·na (tôs-kä'nä), *n.* Tuscany.

Tos·ca·ni·ni, Ar·tu·ro (är-too'rô tôs'kä-nē'nē; Eng. tos'kə-nē'ni), 1867–1957; Italian orchestral conductor in America.

toss (tôs, tos), *v.t.* [TOSSED or *obs.* or *poetic* TOST (tôst, tost), TOSSING], [prob. < ON. via dial.; cf. Norw. dial. *tossa*, to spread, strew; akin to MLG. *tōsen*, to tear, ME. *(to)tusen*, to pull to pieces; basic sense "to tear up" < IE. base **dā(i)*, to part, tear; cf. TOP], 1. to throw about; fling about; pitch about; buffet: as, the waves *tossed* the boat. 2. to disturb; agitate; disquiet. 3. to throw, especially upward, lightly, and easily, from the hand. 4. to lift quickly; jerk upward: as, the horse *tossed* its head. 5. to toss up with (someone *for* something): see phrase below. *v.i.* 1. to be flung to and fro; be thrown about or pitched about. 2. to fling oneself about in sleep, etc.; be restless in bed: as, I *tossed* all night long. 3. to move or go impatiently, angrily, or disdainfully, as with a toss of the head. 4. to toss up: see phrase below. *n.* 1. a tossing or being tossed; fling: as, a *toss* of the head. 2. a tossup. 3. the distance that something is or can be tossed. —*SYN.* see **throw**.

toss off, 1. to make, do, write, etc. quickly, casually, and without effort. 2. to drink up in one draft.

toss up, to toss a coin for deciding something according to which side lands uppermost.

toss·pot (tôs'pot', tos'pot'), *n.* [*toss, v.* + *pot*], a heavy drinker; drunkard; toper.

toss·up (tôs'up', tos'up'), *n.* 1. the act of tossing or flipping a coin, etc. to decide something according to which side lands uppermost; hence, 2. an even chance.

tost (tôst, tost), obsolete or poetic past tense and past participle of **toss**.

tot (tot), *n.* [prob. (via dial.) < ON. *tuttr*, dwarf], 1. a very small amount or thing. 2. a young child. 3. [British Dial.], a small drink of alcoholic liquor.

tot (tot), *v.t.* [TOTTED (-id), TOTTING], [contr. of *total*], [British Colloq.], to add up; total (with *up*).

to·tal (tō't'l), *adj.* [ME.; Late OFr.; LL. *totalis* < L. *totus*, all, whole], 1. constituting the (or a) whole; entire; whole. 2. complete; utter: as, a *total* loss. *n.* the whole amount or number; sum; aggregate. *v.t.* [TOTALED or TOTALLED (-t'ld), TOTALING or TOTALLING], 1. to find the total of; add. 2. to equal a total of; add up to. *v.i.* to amount (*to*) as a whole. —*SYN.* see **complete, sum**.

total depravity, in *Calvinist theology*, the utter depravity, or sinfulness, of man, due to original sin and persisting until regeneration through the Spirit of God.

to·tal·i·sa·tor (tō't'l-ə-zā'tẽr), *n.* a totalizator.

to·tal·i·tar·i·an (tō-tal'ə-târ'i-ən, tō'tal-ə-târ'i-ən), *adj.* [< *totality* + *-arian*], designating, of, or characteristic of a government or state in which one political party or group maintains complete control and illegalizes all others. *n.* a person who favors or participates in such a government or state.

to·tal·i·tar·i·an·ism (tō-tal'ə-târ'i-ən-iz'm, tō'tal-ə-târ'-i-ən-iz'm), *n.* totalitarian government, doctrines, etc.

to·tal·i·ty (tō-tal'ə-ti), *n.* 1. the fact or condition of being total; entirety. 2. the total amount or sum.

in totality, as a whole; altogether.

to·tal·i·za·tor (tō't'l-ə-zā'tẽr), *n.* [Fr. *totalisateur*], any machine for computing and showing totals of measurements, etc.; especially, a machine for computing and showing the total number and amount of bets, as at a horse race; pari-mutuel: also **totalisator, totalizer**.

to·tal·ize (tō't'l-iz'), *v.t.* [TOTALIZED (-izd'), TOTALIZING], to make a total of; combine into a total.

to·tal·iz·er (tō't'l-iz'ẽr), *n.* 1. a totalizator. 2. an adding machine.

to·tal·ly (tō't'l-i), *adv.* wholly; completely; altogether.

total war, warfare that uses all possible means of attack, military, scientific, and psychological, against both enemy troops and civilians.

tote (tōt), *v.t.* [TOTED (-id), TOTING], [earlier *toat; ?* < early Fr. *tauter*, to remove on rollers], [Colloq.], 1. to carry or haul, especially in the arms or on the back. 2. to be armed with (a gun, etc.). *n.* [Colloq.], 1. a toting. 2. something toted; load; haul.

tote board (tōt), [Colloq.], a totalizator.

to·tem (tō'təm), *n.* [of Am. Ind. (Algonquian) origin; cf. Ojibway *ototeman*, Cree *ototema*, his relations], 1. among primitive peoples, an animal or natural object considered as being related by blood to a given family or clan and taken as its symbol. 2. an image of this.

to·tem·ic (tō-tem'ik), *adj.* of a totem or totems.

to·tem·ism (tō'təm-iz'm), *n.* 1. belief in totems and totemic relationships. 2. the use of totems to distinguish families. 3. social customs based on this.

to·tem·ist (tō'təm-ist), *n.* a member of a family or clan having a totem.

to·tem·is·tic (tō'təm-is'tik), *adj.* of totemism or totemists.

totem pole, a pole or post carved and painted with totems, often erected in front of their dwellings by Indian tribes of the northwest coast of North America.

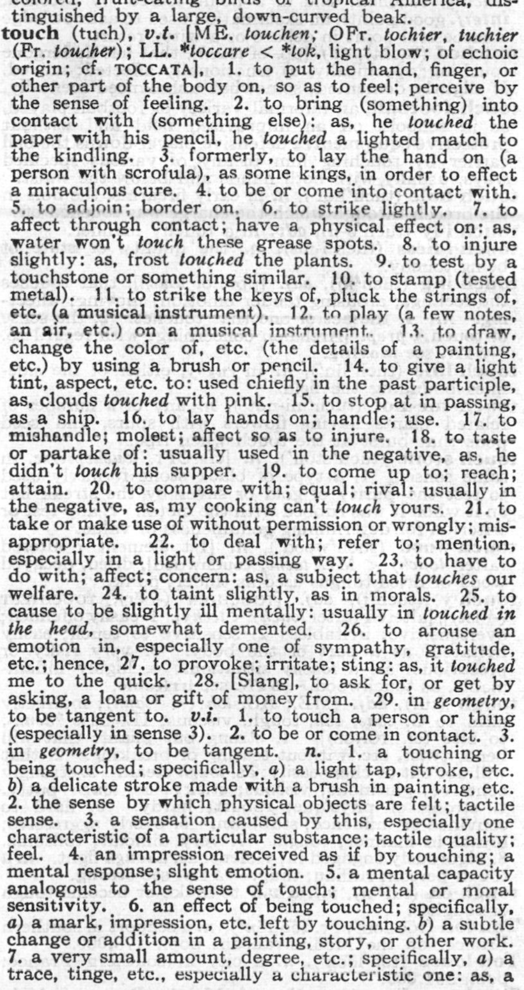

TOTEM POLE

toth·er, t'oth·er, 'toth·er (tuth'ẽr), *adj.* & *pron.* [ME. *the tother*, earlier *thet other, that other*], [Chiefly Dial.], that (or the) other.

to·ti- (tō'ti), [< L. *totus*, whole], a combining form meaning *whole, entire, wholly, entirely*, as in *totipalmate*.

‡to·ti·dem ver·bis (tot'i-dem vũr'bis), [L.], in so many words.

to·ti·pal·mate (tō'ti-pal'māt), *adj.* [*toti-* + *palmate*], having all four toes completely united by a web, as ducks, geese, cormorants, pelicans, etc. *n.* a totipalmate bird.

to·ti·pal·ma·tion (tō'ti-pal-mā'shən), *n.* the condition of being totipalmate.

Tot·ten·ham (tot''n-əm), *n.* a city in Middlesex, England, near London: pop., 129,000 (est. 1946).

tot·ter (tot'ẽr), *v.i.* [ME. *toteren;* prob. < ON.; cf. Norw. dial. *totra*, to quiver, shake; base as in *dodder*], 1. to rock or shake as if about to fall; be unsteady. 2. to be unsteady on one's feet; stagger; toddle. *n.* a tottering. —*SYN.* see **stagger**.

tot·ter·y (tot'ẽr-i), *adj.* tottering; unsteady; shaky.

tou·can (too'kan, too-kän', too'kən), *n.* [Fr.; Port. *tucano;* Tupi *tucano, tucana*], any of a group of brightly colored, fruit-eating birds of tropical America, distinguished by a large, down-curved beak.

touch (tuch), *v.t.* [ME. *touchen;* OFr. *tochier, tuchier* (Fr. *toucher*); LL. **toccare* < **tok*, light blow; of echoic origin; cf. TOCCATA], 1. to put the hand, finger, or other part of the body on, so as to feel; perceive by the sense of feeling. 2. to bring (something) into contact with (something else): as, he *touched* the paper with his pencil, he *touched* a lighted match to the kindling. 3. formerly, to lay the hand on (a person with scrofula), as some kings, in order to effect a miraculous cure. 4. to be or come into contact with. 5. to adjoin; border on. 6. to strike lightly. 7. to affect through contact; have a physical effect on: as, water won't *touch* these grease spots. 8. to injure slightly: as, frost *touched* the plants. 9. to test by a touchstone or something similar. 10. to stamp (tested metal). 11. to strike the keys of, pluck the strings of, etc. (a musical instrument). 12. to play (a few notes, an air, etc.) on a musical instrument. 13. to draw, change the color of, etc. (the details of a painting, etc.) by using a brush or pencil. 14. to give a light tint, aspect, etc. to: used chiefly in the past participle, as, clouds *touched* with pink. 15. to stop at in passing, as a ship. 16. to lay hands on; handle; use. 17. to mishandle; molest; affect so as to injure. 18. to taste or partake of: usually used in the negative, as, he didn't *touch* his supper. 19. to come up to; reach; attain. 20. to compare with; equal; rival: usually in the negative, as, my cooking can't *touch* yours. 21. to take or make use of without permission or wrongly; misappropriate. 22. to deal with; refer to; mention, especially in a light or passing way. 23. to have to do with; affect; concern: as, a subject that *touches* our welfare. 24. to taint slightly, as in morals. 25. to cause to be slightly ill mentally: usually in *touched in the head*, somewhat demented. 26. to arouse an emotion in, especially one of sympathy, gratitude, etc.; hence, 27. to provoke; irritate; sting: as, it *touched* me to the quick. 28. [Slang], to ask for, or get by asking, a loan or gift of money from. 29. in *geometry*, to be tangent to. *v.i.* 1. to touch a person or thing (especially in sense 3). 2. to be or come in contact. 3. in *geometry*, to be tangent. *n.* 1. a touching or being touched; specifically, *a)* a light tap, stroke, etc. *b)* a delicate stroke made with a brush in painting, etc. 2. the sense by which physical objects are felt; tactile sense. 3. a sensation caused by this, especially one characteristic of a particular substance; tactile quality; feel. 4. an impression received as if by touching; a mental response; slight emotion. 5. a mental capacity analogous to the sense of touch; mental or moral sensitivity. 6. an effect of being touched; specifically, *a)* a mark, impression, etc. left by touching. *b)* a subtle change or addition in a painting, story, or other work. 7. a very small amount, degree, etc.; specifically, *a)* a trace, tinge, etc., especially a characteristic one: as, a

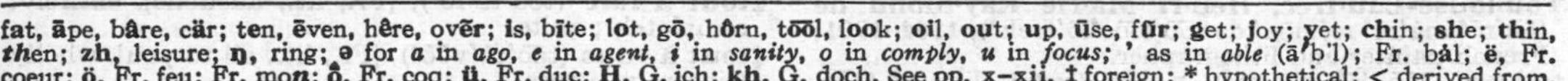

touch of humor. *b*) a slight attack: as, a *touch* of the flu. 8. *a*) touchstone. *b*) the quality of gold, silver, etc. as determined by touchstone. *c*) an official stamp indicating this. 9. any test or criterion. 10. [Slang], *a*) the act of asking for, or getting in this way, a gift or loan of money. *b*) money so acquired. 11. in *music*, *a*) the manner in which a performer strikes the keys of a keyboard instrument: as, a delicate *touch*. *b*) the manner in which the action of a piano, etc. responds to the fingers: as, a piano with a heavy *touch*. *c*) in bell ringing, a set of changes less than a peal. 12. in *rugby*, the area outside the sidelines. —*SYN.* see **affect.**

in touch with, 1. in communication or contact with. 2. responsive or sensitive to.

out of touch with, no longer well-informed on or in close communication with.

touch at, to stop briefly at (a port, etc.): said of ships and travelers.

touch off, 1. to represent accurately or aptly. 2. to make explode; fire. 3. to motivate or initiate.

touch on (or **upon**), 1. to come near to; come close to; verge on. 2. to pertain to. 3. to treat (a topic) slightly or in passing; merely mention.

touch up, 1. to stimulate or rouse, as by touching. 2. to improve or finish (a painting, literary work, etc.) by minor changes or additions.

touch-and-go (tuch′ən-gō′), *adj.* 1. hasty, rapid, casual, etc. 2. uncertain; risky; precarious.

touch and go, 1. a hasty or casual act. 2. an uncertain or dangerous situation.

touch·back (tuch′bak′), *n.* in *football*, a play in which a player grounds the ball behind his own goal line when the ball was caused to pass the goal line by an opponent: distinguished from *safety*.

touch·down (tuch′doun′), *n.* in *football*, 1. a play in which a player grounds the ball on or past the opponent's goal line. 2. a score (6 points) so made.

‡tou·ché (tōō′shā′), *adj.* [Fr., pp.; see TOUCH], in *fencing*, touched: said of a point scored by a touch. *interj.* good point!: an exclamation used to acknowledge a successful point in debate or a witty retort.

touched (tucht), *adj.* [pp. of *touch*], that has undergone touching; specifically, *a*) emotionally affected; moved. *b*) slightly demented; somewhat unbalanced mentally.

touch football, an informal variety of football played, as in schools, on an improvised field and without protective equipment: a defensive player downs the ball carrier by touching him in any of various specified ways, usually with both hands and below the waist.

touch·hole (tuch′hōl′), *n.* in early firearms, the hole in the breech through which the charge was touched off.

touch·i·ly (tuch′ə-li), *adv.* in a touchy manner.

touch·i·ness (tuch′i-nis), *n.* the quality or state of being touchy.

touch·ing (tuch′iŋ), *adj.* [ppr. of *touch*], that touches the feelings; arousing tender emotion; moving; affecting. *n.* 1. the act of one that touches. 2. the sense of touch. *prep.* [Archaic], concerning; with regard to. —*SYN.* see **moving.**

touch·line (tuch′līn′), *n.* in *rugby*, either of the sidelines bounding the field.

touch-me-not (tuch′mi-not′), *n.* any of a number of related plants having flowers with spurs, and seed pods that burst at the touch when ripe.

touch·stone (tuch′stōn′), *n.* [cf. OFr. *touchepierre*, in same sense], 1. a type of black stone formerly used to test the purity of gold or silver by the streak left on it when it was rubbed with the metal. 2. any test or criterion for determining genuineness or value.

touch·wood (tuch′wood′), *n.* [1st element ? altered (after *touch*) < ME. *tache*, touchwood], dried, decayed wood or dried fungus used as tinder; punk.

touch·y (tuch′i), *adj.* [TOUCHIER (-i-ẽr), TOUCHIEST (-i-ist)], [altered (after *touch*) < *techy*], 1. easily offended; oversensitive; irritable. 2. sensitive to touch; easily irritated, as a part of the body. 3. very risky or precarious: as, a *touchy* situation. 4. highly inflammable, as touchwood. —*SYN.* see **irritable.**

tough (tuf), *adj.* [ME.; AS. *toh* (< **tanh*); indirectly akin to G. *zähe, zäh*, tough, viscous; IE. base **denk-*, to bite (cf. TONGS)], 1. strong but pliant; that will bend, twist, etc. without tearing or breaking. 2. that will not cut or chew easily: as, *tough* steak. 3. strongly cohesive; glutinous; viscous; sticky: as, *tough* putty. 4. strong of physique; robust; hardy. 5. hard to convince or influence; stubborn. 6. overly aggressive; brutal in manner; rough. 7. very difficult; toilsome. 8. vigorously engaged in; violent: as, a *tough* fight. *n.* a tough person; ruffian; thug. —*SYN.* see **strong.**

tough·en (tuf′'n), *v.t. & v.i.* to make or become tough or tougher.

Tou·lon (tōō-lon′; Fr. tōō′lōn′), *n.* a seaport in southern France, on the Mediterranean: pop., 173,000.

Tou·louse (tōō′lōōz′), *n.* a city in southern France: pop., 331,000.

Tou·louse-Lau·trec, Hen·ri Ma·rie Ray·mond de (äṅ′rē′ mà′rē′ re′mōṅ′ də tōō′lōōz′lō′trek′), 1864–1901; French painter and lithographer.

tou·pee (tōō-pā′, tōō-pē′), *n.* [Fr. *toupet*, dim. of OFr. *toup, top*, tuft of hair; cf. TOP], 1. formerly, a curl or lock of hair worn on top of the head, sometimes as part of a wig. 2. a small wig for covering a bald spot.

tour (toor, tōōr), *n.* [ME.; Late OFr. < *torner, tourner*, to turn], 1. a turn, spell, or shift, as of work; especially, in *military usage*, a period of duty at a single place. 2. a long trip, as for sightseeing: cf. **grand tour.** 3. any trip, as for inspection; round; circuit; specifically, a trip by a theatrical company to give performances at a number of cities. *v.i.* to go on a tour. *v.t.* 1. to take a tour through or around. 2. to take (a play, theatrical company, etc.) on a tour.

on tour, touring.

tou·ra·co (tōō′rä-kō′), *n.* [Fr. < W. Afr. native name], any of a group of brightly colored tropical birds related to the cuckoo.

Tou·raine (tōō-rān′; Fr. tōō′ren′), *n* a former province of western France.

tour·bil·lion (toor-bil′yən), *n.* [Fr. *tourbillon*, whirlwind < L. *turbo;* see TURBINE], 1. originally, a whirlwind. 2. a firework that rises with a spiral motion.

Tour·coing (tōōr′kwaṅ′), *n.* a city in France, on the Belgian border: pop., 90,000.

tour de force (toor′ də fôrs′, tōōr′ də fôrs′; Fr. tōōr′ də fôrs′), [Fr.], a feat of strength, skill, or ingenuity, often one that is merely clever or spectacular.

touring car, an early type of open automobile, often with a folding top, seating five or more passengers.

tour·ism (toor′iz'm, tōōr′iz'm), *n.* tourist travel, especially when regarded as a source of income for a country, business, etc.

tour·ist (toor′ist, tōōr′ist), *n.* a person who makes a tour, especially for pleasure. *adj.* 1. of or for tourists. 2. designating the lowest-priced class of accommodations, as on a passenger ship.

tour·ma·line (toor′mə-lin, toor′mə-lēn′), *n.* [Fr.; ult. < Singhalese *tōramalli*, a carnelian], a red, pink, green, blue, yellow, brown, black, or colorless semiprecious mineral, any of a group of complex silicates, used as a gem and in optical instruments: also **turmaline.**

Tour·nai (tōōr′nā′), *n.* a city in western Belgium: pop., 33,000: also spelled **Tournay.**

tour·na·ment (toor′nə-mənt, tũr′nə-mənt), *n.* [ME. *tournement, torneiment;* OFr. *torneiement, tornoiement* < *torneier;* see TOURNEY], 1. in the Middle Ages, *a*) a sport consisting of an encounter between knights on horseback, in which the opponents tried to unseat one another with lances, the winner receiving a prize; jousting contest. *b*) a series of such encounters presented as an entertainment. 2. a series of contests in some sport, usually a competition for championship. 3. any similar series of contests, as in chess or bridge.

tour·ney (toor′ni, tũr′ni), *n.* [*pl.* TOURNEYS (-niz)], [ME. *turnai, tournei;* OFr. *tornei, tornoi* < *tornoier, torneier* < base of *tourner;* see TURN], a tournament. *v.i.* to take part in a tournament; joust.

tour·ni·quet (toor′ni-ket′, tũr′ni-kā′), *n.* [Fr. < *tourner*, to turn], any device for compressing a blood vessel to stop bleeding or control the circulation of blood to some part, as a bandage twisted about a limb or a pad pressed down by a screw.

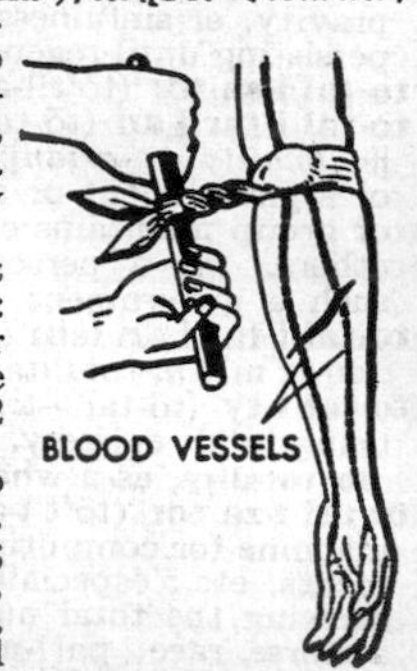

TOURNIQUET

Tours (tōōr), *n.* a city in west central France, on the Loire: pop., 96,000: the Franks under Charles Martel defeated the Saracens in a decisive battle (732 A.D.) fought near here.

tou·sle (tou′z'l), *v.t.* [TOUSLED (-z'ld), TOUSLING], [freq. of ME. *tusen* (in comp.), to pull, tear; cf. TOSS], to disorder, dishevel, muss, etc. *n.* a tousled condition, mass of hair, etc. Also spelled **touzle.**

‡tous-les-mois (tōō′lā′mwȧ′), *n.* [Fr., lit., all the months; prob. altered (because edible in all seasons) < *toloman*, name in the Fr. Antilles], an edible starch made from the fleshy roots of the canna.

Tous·saint L'Ou·ver·ture, Pierre Do·mi·nique (pyâr dô′mē′nēk′ tōō′saṅ′ lōō′vâr′tür′), 1743–1803; Haitian Negro liberator and general.

tout (tout), *v.i.* [ME. *toten;* AS. *totian*, to peep, look out after], 1. [Colloq.], to solicit customers, patrons, votes, etc. 2. [Slang], *a*) especially in England, to spy on race horses in training, etc. in order to secure tips for betting. *b*) to provide betting tips on horse races. *v.t.* 1. [Colloq.], to solicit or importune. 2. [Colloq.], to praise or recommend highly; puff. 3. [Slang], *a*) to spy out or otherwise get information on (race horses). *b*) to give a tip on (a race horse) for a price. *n.* a person who touts; especially, a person who makes a business of selling tips on race horses.

‡tout à fait (tōō′tȧ′fe′), [Fr., lit., all done], entirely; completely; quite.

‡tout à vous (tōō′tȧ′vōō′), [Fr., lit., all to you], wholly (sincerely) yours.

‡**tout de suite** (to͞ot' swēt'), [Fr., lit., all in succession], immediately; right away.
‡**tout en·sem·ble** (to͞o'tän'sän'bl'), [Fr., lit., all (taken) together], the general effect; total impression, as of a work of art or a costume.
‡**tout le monde** (to͞o' lə mōnd'), [Fr., lit., all the world], everyone.
tou·zle (tou'z'l), *n.* & *v.t.* [TOUZLED (-z'ld), TOUZLING], tousle.
to·va·risch (tō-vär'ish; Russ. tô-vär'ishch), *n.* [Russ. *tovarishch*], comrade: a title used among Communists in the Soviet Union.
tow (tō), *v.t.* [ME. *towen, toghen;* AS. *togian;* akin to OHG. *zōgen*, to draw, tug; for the IE. base see TUG], 1. to pull by a rope or chain: as, one ship or automobile is sometimes *towed* by another. 2. to pull or drag behind. *n.* 1. a towing or being towed. 2. something towed. 3. towline. —*SYN.* see **pull.**
in tow, 1. being towed. 2. in one's company or retinue. 3. under one's influence or charge.
tow (tō), *n.* [ME.; AS. *tow-*, for spinning or weaving; prob. < base seen in *taw, v.* & *tool*], the coarse and broken fibers of hemp, flax, etc. before spinning. *adj.* of or resembling tow.
tow·age (tō'ij), *n.* [Anglo-L. *towagium;* see -AGE], 1. a towing or being towed. 2. the charge for this.
to·ward (tôrd, tō'ẽrd; *also, for prep., occas.* tə-wôrd'), *prep.* [ME.; AS. *toweard;* see TO & -WARD], 1. in the direction of. 2. facing. 3. in a manner designed to achieve or along a course likely to result in: as, efforts *toward* a peaceful settlement, steps *toward* war. 4. concerning; regarding; about: as, his attitude *toward* me. 5. close to or just before (in time): as, they left *toward* four o'clock. 6. in anticipation of; for: as, they're saving *toward* a new car. Also **towards.** *adj.* [Archaic or Rare], 1. favorable; propitious. 2. ready to learn; promising; apt. 3. docile; compliant; tractable. 4. at hand; imminent. 5. being done; in progress: used predicatively.
to·ward·ly (tôrd'li, tō'ẽrd-li), *adj.* [*toward* + *-ly*], [Archaic or Rare], 1. favorable; propitious. 2. tractable; docile.
to·wards (tôrdz, tō'ẽrdz; *occas.* tə-wôrdz'), *prep.* [ME. *towardes* (AS. *toweardes*), with adv. genit. (*-e*)*s*], toward.
tow·boat (tō'bōt'), *n.* a small, sturdy boat for towing ships, barges, etc.; tugboat.
tow·el (tou''l, toul), *n.* [ME. *towaille;* OFr. *toaille* (Fr. *touaille*) < Gmc. word seen in OHG. *dwahila*, towel < *dwahan* (AS. *thwean*), to wash], a piece of cloth or absorbent paper for wiping or drying things, especially for drying oneself after washing or bathing. *v.t.* [TOWELED or TOWELLED (-'ld, tould), TOWELING or TOWELLING], to wipe or dry with a towel.
tow·el·ing, tow·el·ling (toul'iŋ, tou''l-iŋ), *n.* material for making towels.
tow·er (tou'ẽr), *n.* [ME. *tour, tur;* OFr. *tur;* L. *turris*, a tower; cf. TOR], 1. a structure that is relatively high for its length and width, either a separate building or part of another. 2. such a structure used as a fortress or prison. 3. a person or thing that resembles a tower in height, strength, dominance, etc. *v.i.* to rise high or stand high like a tower.
tow·er (tō'ẽr), *n.* a person or thing that tows.
tow·ered (tou'ẽrd), *adj.* 1. having a tower or towers. 2. rising into the air like a tower.
tow·er·ing (tou'ẽr-iŋ), *adj.* 1. that towers; very high. 2. very violent or intense. —*SYN.* see **high.**
Tower of London, a series of buildings on the north bank of the Thames in London, forming a palace and fortress surrounding the original tower (*White Tower*): it was built in the 11th century and served as a royal residence and, for many years, as a jail for political prisoners.
tow·er·y (tou'ẽr-i), *adj.* 1. having towers; towered. 2. towering; high; lofty.
tow·head (tō'hed'), *n.* 1. a head of pale-yellow hair or, rarely, tousled hair. 2. a person having such hair.
tow·head·ed (tō'hed'id), *adj.* having pale-yellow hair or, rarely, tousled hair.
tow·hee (tou'hē, tō'hē), *n.* [echoic of the note], any of various small North American finches related to the sparrows and buntings; especially, the chewink: also **towhee bunting.**
tow·line (tō'lin'), *n.* a rope, chain, etc. used for towing.
town (toun), *n.* [ME. *tun, toun;* AS. *tun*, enclosed space, group of houses, village, town; akin to G. *zaun*, fence, hedge < base also seen in OIr. *dūn*, fortified camp], 1. [Dial.], a group of houses; hamlet; village. 2. a more or less concentrated group of houses and private and public buildings, larger than a village but smaller than a city; especially, *a*) in most of the United States, a township. *b*) in New England, a rural or urban unit of local government smaller than a city, a political subdivision of a State, having its sovereignty vested in a town meeting. 3. in England, *a*) a village that holds a market periodically. *b*) a large, thickly populated place, as a borough, city, etc. 4. the business center of a city: as, I'm going into *town.* 5. the town or city being spoken of or understood: as, they just got into *town.* 6. the inhabitants, voters, etc. of a town. 7. [Colloq.], any populated place spoken of familiarly: as, New York's an exciting *town. adj.* of, for, or characteristic of a town. Abbreviated **t.**
go to town, [Slang], 1. to go on a spree. 2. to work or act fast and efficiently. 3. to be eminently successful.
on the town, 1. dependent on the public charity of the town or city. 2. [Slang], out for a good time at the theater, night clubs, etc.
paint the town red, [Slang], to go on a boisterous spree; carouse.
town car, an automobile with an enclosed rear seat separated by a glass partition from the open or partially enclosed driver's seat.
town clerk, an official in charge of the records, legal business, etc. of a town.
town crier, a person who formerly cried public announcements through the streets of a village or town.
town hall, a building in a town, containing the offices of public officials, the council chamber, and often a hall for public assembly.
town·house (toun'hous'), *n.* a town hall.
town house, a city residence, especially as distinguished from a country residence of the same owner.
town meeting, 1. a meeting of the people of a town. 2. especially in New England, a meeting of the qualified voters of a town to act upon town business.
towns·folk (tounz'fōk'), *n.* townspeople.
town·ship (toun'ship), *n.* [ME. *tunscipe;* AS. *tunscipe*, people living in a *tun;* see TOWN & -SHIP], 1. originally, in England, a parish or division of a parish, as a unit of territory and administration. 2. in most of the United States, a division of a county, constituting a unit of local government with administrative control of local schools, roads, etc. 3. in New England, a town. 4. a unit of territory in the United States land survey, generally six miles square, containing thirty-six mile-square sections, and sometimes, but not necessarily, coextensive with a governmental township. 5. in Canada, a subdivision of a province. Abbreviated **twp., tp., t.**
towns·man (tounz'mən), *n.* [*pl.* TOWNSMEN (-mən)], 1. a person who lives in, or has been reared in, a town. 2. a person who lives in one's own or the same town. 3. in New England, a selectman.
towns·peo·ple (tounz'pē'p'l), *n.pl.* 1. people of a town. 2. people brought up in a town or city, as distinguished from those brought up in the country.
tow·path (tō'path', tō'päth'), *n.* a path alongside a canal, used by men or animals towing canalboats.
tow·rope (tō'rōp'), *n.* a rope used in towing.
tox·ae·mi·a (tok-sē'mi-ə), *n.* toxemia.
tox·ae·mic (tok-sē'mik), *adj.* toxemic.
tox·al·bu·min (toks'al-bū'min), *n.* [< *toxic* + *albumin*], any poisonous albumin.
tox·e·mi·a (tok-sē'mi-ə), *n.* [Mod. L. < L. *toxicum* (see TOXIC) + Gr. *haima*, blood], any condition of blood poisoning, especially that caused by bacterial toxins transported through the blood stream from a focus of infection.
tox·e·mic (tok-sē'mik, tok-sem'ik), *adj.* 1. of, having the nature of, or caused by toxemia. 2. having toxemia.
tox·ic (tok'sik), *adj.* [ML. *toxicus* < L. *toxicum*, a poison; Gr. *toxikon*, a poison, orig., poison in which arrows were dipped < *toxikos*, of or for a bow < *toxon*, a bow], 1. of, affected by, or caused by a toxin, or poison. 2. poisonous.
tox·i·cant (tok'si-kənt), *adj.* [LL. *toxicans*, ppr.; see TOXICATION], poisonous; toxic. *n.* a poison.
tox·i·ca·tion (tok'si-kā'shən), *n.* [< pp. of LL. *toxicare*, to smear with poison < L. *toxicum;* see TOXIC], poisoning.
tox·ic·i·ty (tok-sis'ə-ti), *n.* [*pl.* TOXICITIES (-tiz)], the state, quality, or degree of being toxic, or poisonous.
tox·i·co- (tok'si-kō, tok'si-kə), [< Gr. *toxikon;* see TOXIC], a combining form meaning *poison*, as in *toxicogenic:* also, before a vowel, **toxic-.**
tox·i·co·gen·ic (tok'si-kō-jen'ik), *adj.* [*toxico-* + *-genic*], 1. produced by a toxic substance. 2. producing a toxic substance.
tox·i·co·log·i·cal (tok'si-kə-loj'i-k'l), *adj.* having to do with toxicology.
tox·i·col·o·gy (tok'si-kol'ə-ji), *n.* [Fr. *toxicologie;* see TOXIC & -LOGY], the science of poisons, their effects, antidotes, etc.: abbreviated **tox., toxicol.**
tox·i·co·sis (tok'si-kō'sis), *n.* [Mod. L.; see TOXIC & -OSIS], any diseased condition caused by a poison.
tox·in (tok'sin), *n.* [< *toxic* + *-in*], 1. any of various unstable poisonous compounds produced by some

microorganisms and causing certain diseases. 2. any of various similar poisons, related to proteins, secreted by plants and animals, as snake venom.

tox·in-an·ti·tox·in (tok′sin-an′ti-tok′sin), *n.* a mixture of toxin and antitoxin for producing active immunity against a specific disease, especially diphtheria: now largely superseded by toxoids.

tox·ine (tok′sin, tok′sēn), *n.* a toxin.

tox·i·pho·bi·a (tok′si-fō′bi-ə), *n.* [Mod. L.; see TOXICO- & -PHOBIA], an abnormal fear of being poisoned.

tox·oid (tok′soid), *n.* a toxin that has been treated, as with chemical agents, so as to eliminate the toxic qualities while retaining the antigenic properties.

tox·oph·i·lite (tok-sof′ə-līt′), *n.* [< *Toxophilus*, title of a book by Ascham (1545) < Gr. *toxon*, a bow + *philos*, lover; + *-ite*], a person who is especially fond of archery; archer.

tox·oph·i·lit·ic (tok-sof′ə-lit′ik), *adj.* [< *toxophilite* + *-ic*], of archers or archery.

tox·o·plas·mo·sis (tok′sō-plaz-mō′sis), *n.* [Mod. L.; see TOXIC, -PLASM, -OSIS], a disease of man, dogs, cats, and certain other mammals, caused by a parasitic microorganism and affecting especially the nervous system.

toy (toi), *n.* [ME. *toye* in sense 1 (? a distinct word); normal mod. senses < D. *tuig*, tools, implements (akin to G. *zeug*, stuff, gear) < base seen in *tow, tug;* cf. D. *speeltuig*, G. *spielzeug*, plaything], 1. originally, *a*) amorous behavior; flirtation. *b*) pastime; sport. 2. a thing of little value or importance; trifle. 3. a little ornament; bauble; trinket. 4. a plaything, especially one for children. 5. any small thing, person, or animal; specifically, a small breed of dog, etc.: as, a *toy* terrier. 6. [Obs. or Rare], in Scotland, a woman's headdress of linen or wool, with flaps that hang over the shoulders. *adj.* 1. like a toy, or plaything, in size, use, etc. 2. made as a toy; especially, being a miniature imitation: as, a *toy* stove. *v.i.* to play or trifle (*with* a piece of food, another's affection, an idea, etc.). —*SYN.* see **trifle.**

To·ya·ma (tô′yä-mä′), *n.* a seaport on Honshu Island, Japan: pop., 138,000 (est. 1947).

To·yo·ha·shi (tô′yô-hä′shē), *n.* a city on the southern coast of Honshu, Japan: pop., 129,000 (est. 1947).

to·yon (tō′yən), *n.* [Sp., also *tollon;* prob. < Mex. Ind. name], an evergreen shrub with shining, toothed leaves, clusters of white flowers, and bright-red berries.

toy·shop (toi′shop′), *n.* a shop where toys are sold.

tp., township.

t.p., title page.

Tr, in *chemistry*, terbium.

tr., 1. trace. 2. transitive. 3. translated. 4. translation. 5. translator. 6. transpose. 7. treasurer.

T.R., 1. *tempore regis*, [L.], in the time of the king. 2. tons registered (of a ship).

tra·be·at·ed (trā′bi-ā′tid), *adj.* [< L. *trabem*, acc. of *trabs*, a beam], 1. built with horizontal beams or lintels, instead of arches. 2. of such construction.

tra·be·a·tion (trā′bi-ā′shən), *n.* trabeated construction or structure.

tra·bec·u·la (trə-bek′yoo-lə), *n.* [*pl.* TRABECULAE (-lē′)], [L., dim. of *trabs*, a beam], 1. in *anatomy & zoology*, a small septum of fibers forming, with others of its kind, an essential part of the framework of an organ or part. 2. in *botany*, a row or bridge of cells extending across the cavity of the sporangium of a moss.

tra·bec·u·lar (trə-bek′yoo-lẽr), *adj.* of a trabecula or trabeculae.

Trab·zon (tråb′zôn′), *n.* Trebizond.

trace (trās), *n.* [ME.; OFr. < *tracier* (Fr. *tracer*); LL. **tractiare* < L. *tractus*, a drawing along, track; pp. of *trahere*, to draw], 1. originally, a way followed or path taken. 2. a mark, footprint, etc. left by the passage of a person, animal, or thing. 3. a beaten path or trail left by the passage of persons, vehicles, etc.: as, the Natchez *Trace*. 4. a visible mark left by a past person, thing, or event; sign; evidence; vestige: as, the war left its *traces*. 5. a barely observable amount; very small quantity: as, a *trace* of anger, *trace* of salt. 6. a drawn or traced mark. 7. the traced record of a recording instrument. 8. in *psychology*, an engram. 9. in *chemistry*, a very small amount, usually one quantitatively immeasurable. *v.t.* [TRACED (trāst), TRACING], [ME. *tracen;* OFr. *tracier;* see the *n.*], 1. to move along, follow, or traverse (a path, route, etc.). 2. to follow the trail or footprints of; track. 3. to follow the development, process, or history of, especially by proceeding from the latest to the earliest evidence, etc. 4. to find or determine (an origin, source, date, etc.) by this procedure. 5. to discover or ascertain by investigating traces or vestiges of (something prehistoric, etc.). 6. to draw with lines; delineate. 7. *a*) to make a drawing, diagram, etc. of. *b*) to mark the course of on a map, plan, etc. 8. to ornament with tracery: used chiefly in the past participle. 9. to copy (a drawing, etc.) by following its lines on a superimposed, transparent sheet; make a tracing of. 10. to form (letters, etc.) carefully or laboriously. 11. to make or copy with a tracer. 12. to record by means of a curved, broken, or wavy line, as in a seismograph. *v.i.* to follow a path, route, development, etc.; make one's way. Abbreviated **tr.**

SYN.—**trace,** literally applying to a mark, footprint, etc. left by the passage of an animal or vehicle, commonly refers to any mark showing that something has existed or occurred (a faint *trace* of egg on his vest); **vestige** applies to some slight remains of something that is no longer in actual existence (the *vestiges* of an ancient civilization); **track,** equivalent to **trace** in its literal sense, suggests a continuous mark or series of marks that can be followed for some distance (automobile *tracks* in the sand).

trace (trās), *n.* [ME. *traice, trais;* OFr. *traiz, trais*, pl. of *trait;* see TRAIT], 1. either of two straps, chains, etc. connecting a draft animal's harness to the vehicle drawn. 2. a rod, pivoted at each end, that transmits motion from one moving part of a machine to another.
kick over the traces, to shake off control; show insubordination or independence.

trac·er (trās′ẽr), *n.* 1. a person or thing that traces; specifically, *a*) a person whose work is tracing lost or missing articles. *b*) an instrument for tracing designs on cloth, etc. 2. an inquiry sent out for a letter, package, etc. that is missing in transport. 3. *a*) the chemical added to a tracer bullet or shell to leave a trail of smoke or fire. *b*) a tracer bullet or shell.

tracer bullet (or **shell**), a bullet or shell that traces its own course in the air with a trail of smoke or fire, so as to facilitate adjustment of the aim.

trac·er·y (trās′ẽr-i), *n.* [*pl.* TRACERIES (-iz)], [< *trace*, *v.* + *-ery*], ornamental work of interlacing or branching lines, as in a Gothic window, some embroidery, etc.

tra·che- (trā′ki), tracheo-.

tra·che·a (trā′ki-ə, trə-kē′ə), *n.* [*pl.* TRACHEAE (-ē′)], [ML.; LL. *trachia*, windpipe; Gr. *tracheia* (*arteria*), rough (windpipe) < *trachys*, rough], 1. in the respiratory tract of vertebrates, that part which conveys air from the larynx to the bronchi; windpipe: see **lung,** illus. 2. in the respiratory system of insects and other invertebrates, any of the small tubules for conveying air. 3. in *botany*, a tubelike duct in plants, formed by a row of cells whose partitioning cell walls have disappeared.

tra·che·al (trā′ki-əl, trə-kē′əl), *adj.* 1. of, like, or having a trachea or tracheae. 2. of or composed of tracheal tissue.

tracheal tissue, in *botany*, a woody tissue composed of tracheae or tracheids, or both; tissue of xylem.

tra·che·id (trā′ki-id), *n.* [*trache-* + *-id*], in *botany*, any of the large, thick-walled, water-conducting, tubelike cells found in woody tissue, as of the conifers.

tra·che·i·dal (trə-kē′i-d'l, trā′ki-ī′d'l), *adj.* of or like a tracheid.

tra·che·i·tis (trā′ki-ī′tis), *n.* [Mod. L.; see -ITIS], inflammation of the trachea.

tra·che·o- (trā′ki-ō, trə-kē′ə), [< *trachea*], a combining form meaning: 1. *of the trachea*, as in *tracheotomy*. 2. *the trachea and*, as in *tracheobronchial*: also, before a vowel, **trache-.**

tra·che·o·bron·chi·al (trā′ki-ō-broŋ′ki-əl), *adj.* tracheal and bronchial.

tra·che·os·co·py (trā′ki-os′kə-pi), *n.* [*tracheo-* + *-scopy*], examination of the interior of the trachea by means of a laryngoscope, etc.

tra·che·ot·o·my (trā′ki-ot′ə-mi), *n.* [see -TOMY], surgical incision of the trachea, as for making an artificial breathing hole.

tra·cho·ma (trə-kō′mə), *n.* [Mod. L.; Gr. *trachōma*, roughness < *trachys*, rough], a contagious form of conjunctivitis, characterized by the formation of inflammatory granulations on the inner eyelid.

tra·chom·a·tous (trə-kom′ə-təs, trə-kō′mə-təs), *adj.* of or having trachoma.

tra·chy- (trā′ki, trak′i), [< Gr. *trachys*, rough], a combining form meaning *rough*, as in *trachycarpous*.

tra·chy·car·pous (trā′ki-kär′pəs, trak′i-kär′pəs), *adj.* [*trachy-* + *-carpous*], bearing rough fruit.

tra·chyte (trā′kīt, trak′īt), *n.* [Fr. < Gr. *trachys* rough], a light-colored volcanic rock, consisting largely of feldspar and having a rough surface when broken.

tra·chyt·ic (trə-kit′ik), *adj.* of, characteristic of, or occurring in trachyte: trachytic rock contains long feldspar crystals in nearly parallel lines.

trac·ing (trās′iŋ), *n.* 1. the action of one that traces. 2. something made by tracing; specifically, *a*) a copy of a drawing, etc. made by tracing the lines on a superimposed, transparent sheet. *b*) the record of a recording instrument, in the form of a traced line.

tracing paper, thin, strong, transparent paper on which tracings may be made.

track (trak), *n.* [Late ME. *trak;* OFr. *trac*, a track, tract, trace; prob. Gmc. < IE. **dreg-*, to pluck], 1. a mark or series of marks left by a person, animal, or thing that has passed, as a footprint, wheel rut, wake of a boat, etc. 2. a trace or vestige. 3. a beaten path or trail left by the passage of persons, animals, or vehicles. 4. a course or line of motion or action; route; way. 5. a sequence of ideas, events, etc.; succession. 6. a path or circuit laid out for running horse racing, etc. 7. a pair of parallel metal rails with their crossties and roadbed, on which trains, streetcars, etc. run. 8. the distance in inches between parallel wheels, as of an automobile. 9. *a)* athletic sports performed on a track, as running, hurdling, etc.: distinguished from *field sports*. *b)* track and field sports together. *v.t.* 1. *a)* to follow the track of: as, they *track* game. *b)* to follow (a track, etc.). 2. to trace by means of vestiges, evidence, etc. 3. to tread or travel. 4. to leave tracks or footprints on (often with *up*). 5. to leave in the form of tracks: as, he *tracked* dirt over the floor. 6. to provide with tracks or rails. *v.i.* 1. to run in the same (width) track. 2. to be in alignment, as wheels or gears. 3. to have a (specified) width between the wheels: as, a narrow-gauge car *tracks* less than 56 inches. *adj.* 1. having to do with a railroad track. 2. of or performed on an athletic track. —*SYN.* see **trace.**

in one's tracks, where one is at the moment.

keep track of, to keep an account of; stay informed about.

lose track of, to fail to keep informed about; lose sight or knowledge of.

make tracks, [Colloq.], to proceed or depart hurriedly.

off the track, straying from the subject, objective, or goal; in error.

on the track, keeping to the subject, objective, or goal; correct.

track down, 1. to pursue until caught, as by following tracks. 2. to investigate or search for until found, by examining evidence, etc.

track·age (trak′ij), *n.* [see -AGE], 1. all the tracks of a railroad. 2. permission for a railroad to use the tracks of another. 3. a charge for this.

track·less (trak′lis), *adj.* without a track, trail, or path; specifically, not running on tracks: as, a *trackless* trolley: cf. **trolley bus.**

track·man (trak′mən), *n.* [*pl.* TRACKMEN (-mən)], a trackwalker.

track man, an athlete who competes in track events.

track·walk·er (trak′wô′kẽr), *n.* a person whose work is walking along, and inspecting, sections of railroad track.

tract (trakt), *n.* [L. *tractus*, a drawing out, extent; pp. of *trahere*, to draw], 1. [Poetic], *a)* duration or lapse of time. *b)* a period of time. 2. a continuous expanse of land, etc.; stretch; extent; area. 3. in *anatomy & zoology*, *a)* a system of parts or organs having some special function: as, the genito-urinary *tract*. *b)* a bundle of nerve fibers having the same origin, termination, and function. 4. [ML. *tractus*], in the *Roman Catholic Church*, a penitential chant of Lent, etc., consisting either of a complete psalm or of a few verses of Scripture, often from the Psalms: it is sung straight through without interruption.

tract (trakt), *n.* [ME. *tracte;* L. *tractatus;* see TRACTATE], 1. formerly, a short treatise. 2. a pamphlet or leaflet, especially one on a religious subject.

trac·ta·bil·i·ty (trak′tə-bil′ə-ti), *n.* [L. *tractabilitas*], the quality or state of being tractable.

trac·ta·ble (trak′tə-b′l), *adj.* [L. *tractabilis* < *tractare*, to drag, haul, freq. of *trahere*, to draw], 1. easily managed, taught, or controlled; docile; compliant. 2. easily worked; malleable. —*SYN.* see **obedient.**

trac·ta·bly (trak′tə-bli), *adv.* in a tractable manner.

Trac·tar·i·an (trak-târ′i-ən), *n.* a founder of or believer in Tractarianism. *adj.* of Tractarians or Tractarianism.

Trac·tar·i·an·ism (trak-târ′i-ən-iz′m), *n.* the principles of the Oxford Movement, opposed to the tendency toward evangelical Protestantism in the Church of England and favoring a return to early Catholic doctrines and practices: so called from the ninety "Tracts for the Times," a series of pamphlets issued at Oxford from 1833 to 1841: also called *Puseyism.*

trac·tate (trak′tāt), *n.* [L. *tractatus*, a handling, treatise; pp. of *tractare;* see TRACTABLE], a treatise; tract.

trac·tile (trak′t′l, trak′til), *adj.* [< L. *tractus* (see TRACTION); + *-ile*], that can be drawn out in length; ductile; tensile.

trac·tion (trak′shən), *n.* [ML. *tractio* < L. *tractus*, pp. of *trahere*, to draw], 1. *a)* a pulling or drawing, especially of a load over a road, track, or other surface. *b)* the state of being pulled or drawn. 2. a pulling, as of the muscles of the leg, arm, etc., in order to bring a fractured or dislocated bone into place. 3. the pulling power of a locomotive, etc.: as, steam *traction*. 4. adhesive friction, as of a wheel on a rail: as, the train got little *traction* on the hill.

trac·tion·al (trak′shən-′l), *adj.* having to do with traction.

traction engine, a steam locomotive for pulling heavy wagons, plows, etc. on roads or in fields.

trac·tive (trak′tiv), *adj.* [< L. *tractus* (see TRACTION); + *-ive*], used for pulling or drawing.

trac·tor (trak′tẽr), *n.* [Mod. L. < L. *tractus;* see TRACTION], 1. a small, powerful vehicle with a gasoline or Diesel engine and, sometimes, caterpillar treads, for pulling farm machinery, hauling loads, etc. 2. a kind of truck with a driver's cab and no body, designed for hauling one or more large vans, or trailers. 3. an airplane with a tractor propeller or propellers.

TRACTOR

tractor propeller, an airplane propeller mounted in front of the wings.

trade (trād), *n.* [MLG., a track; OS. *trada*, a trace, trail; akin to ME. *trede*, tread; see TREAD], 1. originally, *a)* a track; path. *b)* a course; regular procedure. 2. a means of earning one's living; occupation; work; especially, skilled work, as distinguished from unskilled work or from a profession or business; craft. 3. buying and selling; barter; commerce. 4. all the persons in a particular line of business. 5. customers; clientele. 6. a purchase or sale; deal; bargain. 7. an exchange; swap. 8. *pl.* the trade winds. *v.i.* [TRADED (-id), TRADING], 1. to carry on a trade or business. 2. to have business dealings (*with* someone). 3. to make an exchange (*with* someone). 4. [Colloq.], to be a customer (*at* a specified store or shop). *v.t.* to exchange; barter; swap. —*SYN.* see **business, sell.**

trade in, to give (one's used automobile, etc.) as part of the purchase price of a new one.

trade on (or **upon**), to take advantage of; presume or impose upon.

trade acceptance, a bill of exchange or draft drawn upon the purchaser by the seller and accepted by the purchaser for payment at a specified time.

trade association, an association of merchants or business firms for the unified promotion of their common interests.

trade discount, a deduction from the list price allowed a retailer by a manufacturer, wholesaler, or distributor, or allowed one firm by another in the same trade.

trade edition, that edition of a book sold through regular channels to the general public, as distinguished from a school edition, etc. of the same book.

trade-in (trād′in′), *n.* 1. something given or taken as payment or, especially, part payment for something else. 2. an exchange involving a trade-in. 3. the valuation allowed by the seller on a trade-in.

trade journal, a magazine devoted to the interests of a specific trade, business, or industry.

trade-last (trād′last′, trād′läst′), *n.* [Colloq.], a flattering remark that one has overheard and offers to report to the person so complimented if he will report a similar compliment about oneself: abbreviated **T.L.**

trade-mark, trade·mark (trād′märk′), *n.* a symbol, design, word, letter, etc. used by a manufacturer or dealer to distinguish his products from those of competitors, and usually registered and protected by law. *v.t.* 1. to put a trade-mark on (a product). 2. to register (a symbol, etc.) as a trade-mark.

trade name, 1. the name by which a commodity is commonly known in trade. 2. a name used as a trade-mark, especially one registered and protected by law. 3. the name under which a company carries on business.

trad·er (trād′ẽr), *n.* 1. a person who trades; merchant. 2. a ship used in trade. 3. a member of a stock exchange who trades for himself and not as an agent for customers.

trade route, any route customarily taken by trading ships, caravans, etc.

trad·es·can·ti·a (trad′es-kan′shi-ə), *n.* [Mod. L., after John *Tradescant*, 17th-c. Eng. naturalist & traveler], any of a number of related plants of the spiderwort family, with showy, white, red, or blue flowers.

trade school, a school where a trade or trades are taught.

trades·folk (trādz′fōk′), *n.pl.* tradespeople.

trades·man (trādz′mən), *n.* [*pl.* TRADESMEN (-mən)], 1. [Dial.], a craftsman or artisan. 2. a person engaged in trade, especially a storekeeper.

trades·peo·ple (trādz′pē′p′l), *n.pl.* people engaged in trade, especially storekeepers and their families.

trades union, [Chiefly British], a trade union.

trades·wom·an (trādz′woom′ən), *n.* [*pl.* TRADESWOMEN (-wim′in)], a girl or woman storekeeper.

trade-un·ion (trād′ūn′yən), *adj.* of a trade union or trade unions. *n.* a trade union.

trade union, an association of workers to promote and protect the welfare, interests, and rights of its members, primarily by collective bargaining; labor union: abbreviated **T.U.**

trade unionism, 1. the principle or practice of organizing into trade unions. 2. the policies and activities of trade unions. Also **trade-unionism.**
trade unionist, 1. a member of a trade union. 2. a person who believes in or supports trade unionism. Also **trade-unionist.**
trade wind, [earlier *trade, adv.*, steadily, in phr. *to blow trade*], a wind that blows toward the equator from the northeast on the north side of the equator and from the southeast on the south side.
trad·ing (trād′iŋ), *adj.* [ppr. of *trade*], that trades; engaged in trade; commercial. *n.* the action of a person who trades; buying and selling; commerce.
trading post, a store or station in an outpost, settlement, etc., where trading is done, as with natives.
trading stamp, a stamp given by some merchants as a premium to customers, redeemable in a specified quantity for merchandise from those dealers.
tra·di·tion (trə-dish′ən), *n.* [ME. *tradycion;* OFr. *tradicion;* L. *traditio*, a surrender, delivery, tradition < *traditus*, pp. of *tradere*, to deliver], 1. originally, a surrender; betrayal. 2. the handing down orally of stories, beliefs, customs, etc. from generation to generation. 3. a story, belief, custom, proverb, etc. handed down this way. 4. a long-established custom or practice that has the effect of an unwritten law; specifically, any of the usages of a school of art or literature handed down through the generations, and generally observed. 5. in *theology, a)* among Jews, the unwritten religious code and doctrine regarded as handed down from Moses. *b)* among Christians, the unwritten teachings regarded as handed down from Jesus and the Apostles. *c)* among Moslems, the sayings and acts attributed to Mohammed, not in the Koran, but orally transmitted.
tra·di·tion·al (trə-dish′ən-'l), *adj.* of, handed down by, or conforming to tradition; conventional; customary.
tra·di·tion·al·ism (trə-dish′ən-'l-iz'm), *n.* 1. adherence to or excessive respect for tradition. 2. the doctrine that the only valid religious belief is that handed down from an original divine revelation.
tra·di·tion·al·ist (trə-dish′ən-'l-ist), *n.* 1. a person who upholds traditions. 2. a believer in traditionalism.
tra·di·tion·al·is·tic (trə-dish′ən-'l-is′tik), *adj.* of or characterized by traditionalism.
tra·di·tion·al·ly (trə-dish′ən-'l-i), *adv.* according to tradition.
tra·di·tion·ar·y (trə-dish′ən-er′i), *adj.* traditional.
tra·di·tion·ist (trə-dish′ən-ist), *n.* 1. a traditionalist. 2. a specialist in or recorder of traditions.
trad·i·tive (trad′ə-tiv), *adj.* [< obs. Fr. *traditif, traditive* < L. *traditus;* see TRADITION], traditionary; traditional.
trad·i·tor (trad′ə-tẽr), *n.* [*pl.* TRADITORES (trad′ə-tôr′-ēz)], [L. < *traditus;* see TRADITION], among the early Christians, a traitor during the Roman persecution.
tra·duce (trə-dōōs′, trə-dūs′), *v.t.* [TRADUCED (-dōōst′, -dūst′), TRADUCING], [L. *traducere*, to lead along, exhibit as a spectacle, disgrace, transfer < *trans*, across, over + *ducere*, to lead], to defame; slander; vilify.
tra·du·cian·ism (trə-dōō′shən-iz'm, trə-dū′shən-iz'm), *n.* [< LL. *traducianus*, believer in this doctrine < *tradux*, a shoot, vine branch, lit., that which is brought over < *traducere;* see TRADUCE], the theological doctrine that the soul is inherited, along with the body, from the parents: opposed to **creationism.**
Tra·fal·gar (trə-fal′gẽr; Sp. trä′fäl-gär′), *n.* a cape at the entrance of the Strait of Gibraltar, southwestern Spain: site of a naval battle (1805) in which Lord Nelson's English fleet defeated Napoleon's fleet.
traf·fic (traf′ik), *n.* [Fr. *trafic, trafique;* It. *traffico* < *trafficare*, to trade < L. *trans*, across + It. *ficcare*, to thrust in, bring; LL. **figicare*, intens. for L. *figere;* see FIX], 1. originally, *a)* transportation of goods for trading. *b)* trading over great distances; commerce. 2. buying and selling; barter; trade. 3. corrupt or illegal trade. 4. dealings, business, or intercourse (*with* someone). 5. *a)* the movement or number of automobiles along a street, pedestrians along a sidewalk, ships in a port, etc. *b)* the automobiles, pedestrians, ships, etc. 6. the business done by a transportation company, measured by the number of passengers, quantity of freight, etc. carried during a given period. 7. the business done by a communications company, measured by the telegrams, calls, etc. transmitted during a given period. 8. the passengers, freight, communications, etc. thus measured. *adj.* of, for, or regulating traffic: as, a *traffic* policeman. *v.i.* [TRAFFICKED (-ikt), TRAFFICKING], 1. to carry on traffic, especially illegal trade (*in* a commodity). 2. to have traffic, trade, or dealings (*with* someone).
traf·fick·er (traf′ik-ẽr), *n.* a person who traffics; trader; dealer; merchant.
traffic light, a set of signal lights placed at intersections of streets to regulate traffic.
trag·a·canth (trag′ə-kanth′), *n.* [Fr. *tragacanthe;* L. *tragacantha;* Gr. *tragakantha* < *tragos*, goat + *akantha*, thorn], 1. a white or reddish, tasteless and odorless gum used in pharmacy, calico printing, etc. 2. any plant yielding this substance.
tra·ge·di·an (trə-jē′di-ən), *n.* [ME. & OFr. *tragedien*], 1. a writer of tragedies. 2. an actor of tragedy.
tra·ge·di·enne, tra·gé·di·enne (trə-jē′di-en′), *n.* [Fr. *tragédienne*], an actress of tragedy.
trag·e·dy (traj′ə-di), *n.* [*pl.* TRAGEDIES (-diz)], [ME. *tragedye;* OFr. *tragedie;* L. *tragoedia;* Gr. *tragōdia*, tragedy, lit., the song of the goat < *tragos*, he-goat + *ōidē*, song; variously explained as referring to a goat offered as a prize or to the goatskin dress of the performers in early plays of this sort], 1. a serious play having an unhappy or disastrous ending brought about by the characters or central character impelled, in ancient drama, by fate or, more recently, by moral weakness, psychological maladjustment, or social pressures. 2. the branch of drama consisting of plays of this type. 3. the writing, acting, or theoretical principles of this kind of drama. 4. a novel or other literary work with similar characteristics. 5. the tragic element of such a literary work, or of a real event. 6. a very sad or tragic event or events; disaster. Abbreviated **trag.**
trag·ic (traj′ik), *adj.* [Fr. *tragique;* L. *tragicus;* Gr. *tragikos*], 1. of, or having the nature of, tragedy. 2. like or characteristic of tragedy; very sad, pathetic, calamitous, disastrous, fatal, etc. 3. appropriate to the acting of tragedy: as, in a *tragic* voice. 4. writing or acting in tragedy. Abbreviated **trag.**
the tragic, the tragic elements of art and literature, or of life.
trag·i·cal (traj′i-k'l), *adj.* tragic.
trag·i·com·e·dy (traj′i-kom′ə-di), *n.* [*pl.* TRAGICOMEDIES (-diz)], [Fr. *tragicomédie;* LL. *tragicomedia*, contr. of L. *tragicocomoedia;* Gr. *tragikokomōdia*], 1. a play or other literary work combining tragic and comic elements. 2. a real situation or incident like this.
trag·i·com·ic (traj′i-kom′ik), *adj.* of, or having the nature of, tragicomedy; having both tragic and comic elements.
trag·i·com·i·cal (traj′i-kom′i-k'l), *adj.* tragicomic.
trag·o·pan (trag′ə-pan′), *n.* [Mod. L.; L., fabulous bird; Gr. *tragopan*, lit., goat-Pan < *tragos*, goat + *Pan*, Pan], any of several brightly colored Asiatic pheasants with eyelike markings.
tra·gus (trā′gəs), *n.* [*pl.* TRAGI (-jī)], [LL.; Gr. *tragos*, hairy part of the ear, lit., goat], the fleshy, cartilaginous protrusion at the front of the external ear, partly extending over the opening of the ear and, in men, often bearing a tuft of hair.
trail (trāl), *v.t.* [ME. *trailen;* OFr. *trailler;* LL. **tragulare* < *tragula*, small drag, sledge < L. *trahere*, to drag], 1. *a)* to drag or let drag behind one, especially on the ground, etc. *b)* to bring along behind: as, he *trailed* dirt into the house. 2. *a)* to make or mark (a path, track, etc.), as by treading down. *b)* to make a path in (grass, etc.). 3. to follow the tracks of; track. 4. to hunt by tracking. 5. to follow behind, especially in a lagging manner. 6. in *military usage*, to carry (a rifle, etc.) in the right hand with the arm extended downward so that the muzzle is slightly forward and the butt near the ground. *v.i.* 1. to hang down, especially behind, so as to drag on the ground, etc. 2. to grow so long as to extend along the ground, over rocks, etc.: said of some plants. 3. to extend in an irregular line; straggle. 4. to flow behind in a long, thin stream, wisp, etc.: as, smoke *trailed* from the chimney. 5. to move, walk, go along, etc. wearily, heavily, or slowly; crawl; drag. 6. to follow or lag behind. 7. to track game: said of hounds. *n.* [ME. *traile;* Fr. *traille* < the *v.*], 1. something that trails or is trailed behind. 2. a mark, footprint, scent, etc. left by a person, animal or thing that has passed. 3. a path or track made by continual passing or deliberately blazed. 4. in *military usage, a)* the position of trailing a rifle. *b)* a beamlike part of a gun carriage, which may be lowered to the ground to form a rear brace.
trail blazer, 1. a person who blazes a trail; hence, 2. a pioneer in any field.
trail·er (trāl′ẽr), *n.* 1. a person, animal, or thing that trails another. 2. a cart, wagon, or large van for hauling furniture, produce, etc., designed to be pulled by an automobile, truck, or tractor. 3. a closed vehicle designed to be pulled by an automobile and equipped as a place to live in, usually with a bed or beds, cooking facilities, etc. 4. in *motion pictures*, a short film containing scenes from a feature picture to be shown later, used for advertising: so called because originally attached to the end of a reel of film.
trailer camp, a number of parked trailers serving as a temporary housing project for workers, tourists, etc.
trail·ing arbutus (trāl′iŋ), a trailing, evergreen plant with pink flowers; Mayflower.
trailing edge, in *aeronautics*, the rear edge of a plane propeller, etc.
trail rope, a rope used in trailing.
train (trān), *n.* [ME. *traine;* OFr. *traïn, trahin* (masc.) *traïne, trahine* (fem.) < *traïner, trahiner*, to draw on LL. **traginare* < L. *trahere*, to pull, drag], 1. something that hangs down and drags behind; specifically, *a)* a part of a dress, skirt, etc. that trails. *b)* the tail-feathers of a bird: as, the *train* of a peacock. *c)* a stream

of something trailing behind. 2. a group of persons that follow after another as attendants in a procession; retinue; suite. 3. a group of persons, animals, vehicles, etc. that follow one another in a line; procession; caravan; cortege. 4. the persons, animals, and vehicles accompanying an army to carry its supplies, ammunition, food, etc. 5. a series of events or circumstances that follow some happening: as, the war brought famine and disease in its *train*. 6. any connected order or arrangement; series; sequence: as, a *train* of thought. 7. a series of connected mechanical parts for transmitting motion: as, a *train* of gears. 8. a line of connected railroad cars pulled or pushed by a locomotive or locomotives. 9. a line of gunpowder that serves as a fuse for an explosive charge. *v.t.* [ME. *trainen;* OFr. *trahiner*], 1. [Rare], to trail or drag. 2. to guide the growth of (a plant), as by tying, pruning, etc. 3. to guide the mental, moral, etc. development of; bring up; rear. 4. to instruct so as to make proficient or qualified: as, nurses are *trained* at this hospital. 5. to discipline or condition (animals) to perform tricks. 6. to prepare or make fit for an athletic contest, etc. 7. to aim (a gun, binoculars, etc.) at something; bring to bear (usually with *on*). 8. [Colloq.], to condition (a child, puppy, etc.) to defecate and urinate in the proper place. *v.i.* to administer or undergo training. —*SYN.* see **teach.**

train·band (trān′band′), *n.* [contr. of *trained band*], in *English History*, a band of citizens trained as soldiers to supplement the regular army.

train·ee (trān-ē′), *n.* a person or animal undergoing training; especially, a military recruit.

train·er (trān′ẽr), *n.* 1. a person who trains; specifically, *a)* a person who trains animals to do tricks. *b)* a person who trains athletes for sports contests. 2. an apparatus used in training.

train·ing (trān′iŋ), *n.* 1. the action of one that trains. 2. a being trained or undergoing training. *adj.* of or used in training. Abbreviated **Tng.**

training school, a school that gives training in a specific field or profession, as nursing, acting, etc.

training ship, a ship on which persons are trained in seamanship, especially in a navy.

train·man (trān′mən), *n.* [*pl.* TRAINMEN (-mən)], a person who works on a railroad train, usually as a conductor's assistant; especially, a brakeman.

train·mas·ter (trān′mas′tẽr, trān′mäs′tẽr), *n.* a railroad official in charge of some division of a line.

train oil, [earlier *train, trane;* D. *traan;* akin to G. *träne*, a tear; basic sense "exuded oil"], oil obtained from blubber or from seals, codfish, etc.

traipse (trāps), *v.i.* [TRAIPSED (trāpst), TRAIPSING], [earlier *trapass;* prob. < OFr. *trapasser*, to pass beyond; hence a var. of *trespass*], [Dial. or Colloq.], 1. to walk or wander idly; gad; trudge. 2. to trail untidily. *v.t.* [Dial.], to tramp; trample.

trait (trāt), *n.* [Fr., a draft, line, stroke < L. *tractus*, pp. of *trahere*, to draw], 1. [Rare], a trace; touch; stroke; flash. 2. a distinguishing quality or characteristic, especially of personality. —*SYN.* see **quality.**

trai·tor (trā′tẽr), *n.* [ME. *traitour;* OFr. *traitor, traiteur*, a traitor; L. *traditor*, one who betrays < *traditus*, pp. of *tradere*, to hand over, betray], a person who betrays his country, cause, friends, etc.; one guilty of treason.

trai·tor·ous (trā′tẽr-əs), *adj.* 1. of, or having the nature of, a traitor; treacherous; faithless. 2. of or involving treason; treasonable. —*SYN.* see **faithless.**

trai·tress (trā′tris), *n.* a woman who is a traitor.

Tra·jan (trā′jən), *n.* (*Marcus Ulpius Trajanus*), Roman statesman and general, born in Spain; lived 52?–117 A.D.; Roman emperor (98–117 A.D.).

tra·ject (trə-jekt′), *v.t.* [< L. *trajectus*, pp. of *trajicere*, to throw, cast, or fling over or across < *trans*, across + *jacere*, to throw], [Rare], to throw, cast, or transmit through space or some other medium.

tra·jec·to·ry (trə-jek′tẽr-i), *n.* [*pl.* TRAJECTORIES (-iz)], [ML. *trajectorius* < L. *trajectus;* see TRAJECT], 1. the curved path of something hurtling through space, especially that of a projectile from the time it leaves the muzzle of the gun. 2. in *mathematics*, a curve or surface that passes through all the curves of a given system at the same angle.

Tra·lee (trə-lē′), *n.* the county seat of Kerry, Ireland: pop., 10,000.

tram (tram), *n.* [Fr. *trame;* L. *trama*, the woof], a double, twisted silk thread used as the weft in fine silks and velvets.

tram (tram), *n.* [Eng. dial. *tram*, shaft, wooden frame for carrying, rail, coal wagon; prob. < LG. *traam*, a beam; current senses < *tramroad*], 1. an open railway car for carrying loads in mines. 2. [British], a tramcar; streetcar. 3. the basket or car of an overhead conveyor. 4. [British], a tramline. 5. a tramway.

tram (tram), *n.* [shortened < *trammel*], 1. a trammel (sense 6). 2. correct adjustment. *v.t.* & *v.i.* [TRAMMED (tramd), TRAMMING], to adjust, align, or measure with a trammel (sense 6).

tram·car (tram′kär′), *n.* [< earlier *tramway car*], 1. a tram (mine car). 2. [British], a streetcar.

tram·line (tram′līn′), *n.* [British], a streetcar line.

tram·mel (tram′'l), *n.* [ME. *tramaile;* Late OFr. *tramail* (Fr. *trêmail*), a net; LL. *tramacula, tremaculum*, kind of fishing net < L. *tres*, three + *macula*, a mesh], 1. a fishing net consisting of two outer layers of coarse mesh and a loosely hung middle layer of fine mesh: also **trammel net.** 2. a kind of shackle for a horse, especially one to teach ambling. 3. *often pl.* something that confines, restrains, or shackles. 4. a pothook. 5. an instrument for drawing ellipses. 6. any of several devices for adjusting or aligning parts of a machine. *v.t.* [TRAMMELED or TRAMMELLED (-'ld), TRAMMELING or TRAMMELLING], 1. to entangle, as in a trammel (also with *up*). 2. to confine, restrain, or shackle.

tram·mel·er, tram·mel·ler (tram′'l-ẽr), *n.* a person or thing that trammels.

tra·mon·tane (trə-mon′tān), *adj.* [ME. *tramountayne*, north wind; It. *tramontano;* L. *transmontanus*, beyond the mountains < *trans*, beyond + *mons, montis*, mountain], located beyond or coming from beyond the mountains, especially the Alps (from an Italian viewpoint): also **transmontane.** *n.* 1. originally, a tramontane person; hence, 2. a foreigner; stranger.

tramp (tramp), *v.i.* [ME. *trampen* < LG. source; cf. LG. *trampen*, to trample < nasalized form of the base in *trap* (IE. base *dreb-)], 1. to step or walk firmly and heavily. 2. to travel about on foot, especially doing odd jobs or begging for a living. *v.t.* 1. to step on firmly and heavily; trample. 2. to walk or ramble through. *n.* 1. a person who travels about on foot, especially one doing odd jobs or begging for a living; hobo; vagrant. 2. the sound of heavy steps, as of people marching. 3. the act of tramping; especially, a journey on foot; hike; trudge. 4. a freight ship that has no regular schedule, but picks up cargo and passengers wherever it may be. 5. an iron plate on the sole of a shoe to protect it in spading, etc. 6. [Slang], a prostitute, or tart. —*SYN.* see **vagrant.**

tram·ple (tram′p'l), *v.i.* [TRAMPLED (-p'ld), TRAMPLING], [ME. *trampelen*, freq. of *trampen;* see TRAMP], to tread heavily; tramp. *v.t.* to crush, destroy, hurt, violate, etc. by or as by treading heavily on. *n.* the sound of trampling.

trample under foot, 1. to crush or hurt by trampling. 2. to treat harshly or ruthlessly; domineer over. Also **trample on, trample upon.**

tram·po·line, tram·po·lin (tram′pə-lin), *n.* [< It. *trampoli*, stilts], 1. originally, a performance by an acrobat on stilts. 2. a net of strong canvas stretched tightly on a frame, used by acrobats, as in a circus, for performing various feats of tumbling.

tram·road (tram′rōd′), *n.* [< dial. *tram*, wooden rail + *-road*], a road for trams, having tracks of wood, stone, or metal; especially, such a road in a mine.

tram·way (tram′wā′), *n.* [cf. TRAMROAD], 1. a tramroad. 2. [British], a streetcar line; tramline.

trance (trans, träns), *n.* [ME. & OFr. *transe*, great anxiety, fear < *transir*, to perish; L. *transire*, to die, lit., go across; *trans*, across + *ire*, to go], 1. a state resembling sleep, in which consciousness may remain although voluntary movement is lost, as in catalepsy or hypnosis. 2. a stunned condition; daze; stupor. 3. a condition of great mental concentration or abstraction, especially one induced by religious fervor or mysticism. 4. a condition in which a spiritualist medium allegedly loses consciousness and passes under the control of some external force, as for the supposed transmission of communications from the dead. *v.t.* [TRANCED (transt, tränst), TRANCING], to entrance.

tran·quil (traŋ′kwil, tran′kwil), *adj.* [TRANQUILER or TRANQUILLER (-ẽr), TRANQUILEST or TRANQUILLEST (-ist)], [Fr. *tranquille;* L. *tranquillus*, calm, quiet, still < *trans-*, beyond + base akin to *quies*, rest, calm, quiet; cf. QUIET], 1. free from emotional disturbance or agitation; calm; serene; placid. 2. quiet or motionless; even; steady: as, *tranquil* waters. —*SYN.* see **calm.**

tran·quil·i·ty (traŋ-kwil′ə-ti, tran-kwil′ə-ti), *n.* tranquillity.

tran·quil·i·za·tion (traŋ′kwil-i-zā′shən, tran′kwil-ī-zā′shən), *n.* a tranquilizing or being tranquilized.

tran·quil·ize (traŋ′kwə-līz′, tran′kwə-līz′), *v.t.* & *v.i.* [TRANQUILIZED (-līzd′), TRANQUILIZING], to make or become tranquil. Also spelled **tranquillize.**

tran·quil·iz·er (traŋ′kwə-līz′ẽr, tran′kwə-līz′ẽr), *n.* a person or thing that tranquilizes; specifically, any of certain drugs, as chlorpromazine, reserpine, etc., used as a depressant in relieving and controlling various emotional disturbances, anxiety and tension neuroses, certain psychoses, etc.: also spelled **tranquillizer.**

tran·quil·li·ty (traŋ-kwil′ə-ti, tran-kwil′ə-ti), *n.* [OFr *tranquillité;* L. *tranquillitas*], the quality or state of being tranquil; calmness; peacefulness; serenity; quiet.

trans- (trans, tranz), [L. < *trans*, across, over, orig., prob. ppr. of **trare*, to pass, seen in *intrare, extrare* < IE. base **ter-*, over, beyond, seen also in Sans. *tiras*, over, through, OIr. *tri, tre*, through], a prefix meaning: 1. *on the other side of, to the other side of, over, across*, as in *transatlantic:* opposed to *cis-*. 2. *so as to change thoroughly*, as in *transliterate*. 3. *above and beyond, transcending*, as in *trans-sonic*.

trans., 1. transactions. 2. transitive. 3. translated. 4. translation. 5. translator. 6. transportation. 7. transpose.

trans·act (tran-sakt′, tran-zakt′), ***v.t.*** [< L. *transactus*, pp. of *transigere*, to drive or thrust through, settle < *trans-* + *agere*, to drive], to carry on, perform, conduct, or complete (business, etc.). ***v.i.*** [Rare], to do business or a piece of business; negotiate.

trans·ac·tion (tran-sak′shən, tran-zak′shən), ***n.*** [L. *transactio*], 1. a transacting or being transacted. 2. something transacted; specifically, *a)* a piece of business; deal. *b) pl.* a record of the proceedings of a society, convention, etc., especially a published one.

trans·ac·tion·al (trans-sak′shən-'l, tran-zak′shən-'l), ***adj.*** having to do with transacting or a transaction.

trans·ac·tor (tran-sak′tẽr, tran-zak′tẽr), ***n.*** a person who transacts.

trans·al·pine (trans-al′pin, tranz-al′pīn), ***adj.*** [L. *transalpinus*], on that (the northern) side of the Alps: from the viewpoint of Rome.

trans·at·lan·tic (trans′ət-lan′tik, tranz′ət-lan′tik), ***adj.*** 1. crossing or spanning the Atlantic. 2. on the other side of the Atlantic.

trans·ca·len·cy (trans-kā′lən-si), ***n.*** the quality of being transcalent.

trans·ca·lent (trans-kā′lənt), ***adj.*** [< *trans-* + L. *calens*, ppr. of *calere*, to be hot], conducting heat readily; pervious to heat.

Trans·cau·ca·sia (trans′kô-kā′zhə, trans′kô-kā′shə), ***n.*** the region south of the Caucasus Mountains, U.S.S.R., containing the republics of Georgia, Armenia, and Azerbaijan: former name, *Transcaucasian Socialist Federated Soviet Republic.*

Trans·cau·ca·sian (trans′kô-kā′zhən, trans′kô-kā′shən), ***adj.*** of Transcaucasia or its people. ***n.*** a native or inhabitant of Transcaucasia.

tran·scend (tran-send′), ***v.t.*** [ME. *transcenden;* L. *transcendere*, to climb over < *trans*, over + *scandere*, to climb], 1. to go beyond the limits of; overstep; exceed: as, the story *transcends* belief. 2. to be superior to; surpass; excel. 3. in *philosophy & theology*, to be separate from or beyond (experience, the material universe, etc.): said of God or a god. ***v.i.*** [Archaic], to be transcendent; excel. —***SYN.*** see **excel.**

tran·scend·ence (tran-sen′dəns), ***n.*** [ML. *transcendentia*], the fact or state of being transcendent.

tran·scend·en·cy (tran-sen′dən-si), ***n.*** transcendence.

tran·scend·ent (tran-sen′dənt), ***adj.*** [L. *transcendens*, ppr. of *transcendere*], 1. transcending; surpassing; excelling; extraordinary. 2. in *philosophy*, beyond the limits of possible experience and, hence (in Kantianism), beyond human knowledge. 3. in *theology*, that exists apart from the material universe: said of God, divine spirit, etc.: distinguished from *immanent*.

tran·scen·den·tal (tran′sen-den′t'l), ***adj.*** [ML. *transcendentalis*], 1. transcendent. 2. supernatural. 3. abstract; metaphysical. 4. in *Kantian philosophy*, not derived from experience but based on the a priori elements of experience, which are the necessary conditions of human knowledge; transcending human experience but not knowledge.

tran·scen·den·tal·ism (tran′sen-den′t'l-iz'm), ***n.*** [G. *transcendentalismus;* see TRANSCENDENTAL & -ISM], 1. any of various philosophies that propose to discover the nature of reality by investigating the process of thought rather than the objects of sense experience: the philosophies of Kant, Hegel, and Fichte are types of transcendentalism. 2. by extension, the philosophical ideas of Ralph Waldo Emerson and some other 19th-century New Englanders, based on a search for reality through spiritual intuition. 3. popularly, any obscure, visionary, or idealistic thought.

trans·con·ti·nen·tal (trans′kon-tə-nen′t'l), ***adj.*** 1. that crosses a (or the) continent. 2. on the other side of a (or the) continent.

tran·scribe (tran-skrīb′), ***v.t.*** [TRANSCRIBED (-skrībd′), TRANSCRIBING], [L. *transcribere* < *trans-*, over, across + *scribere*, to write], 1. to make a written or typewritten copy of (shorthand notes, a speech, etc.). 2. to arrange or adapt (a piece of music) for an instrument, voice, or ensemble other than that for which it was originally written. 3. in *radio*, to record (a program, commercial, etc.) for broadcast at some later time.

tran·script (tran′skript′), ***n.*** [ME. *transcripte, transcrit;* L. *transcriptus*, pp. of *transcribere;* see TRANSCRIBE], 1. something made by transcribing; a written or typewritten copy. 2. any copy or reproduction.

tran·scrip·tion (tran-skrip′shən), ***n.*** [Fr.; L. *transcriptio* < *transcriptus;* see TRANSCRIPT], 1. the act or process of transcribing. 2. something transcribed; specifically, *a)* a transcript; copy. *b)* an arrangement of a piece of music for an instrument, voice, or combination of instruments or voices other than that for which it was originally written. *c)* a recording made for radio broadcasting; also, the act or practice of using such recordings: as, a program brought you by *transcription*.

trans·cur·rent (trans-kũr′ənt), ***adj.*** [L. *transcurrens*, ppr. of *transcurrere*, to run across; *trans-*, over, across + *currere*, to run], extending or passing across.

trans·duc·er (trans-dōōs′ẽr, trans-dūs′ẽr), ***n.*** [< L. *transducere*, to lead across (*trans-*, over + *ducere*, to lead); + *-er*], in *physics*, a device that transmits power from one system to another system.

tran·sect (tran-sekt′), ***v.t.*** [*trans-* + L. *sectus*, pp. of *secare*, to cut], to cut across or divide by cutting.

tran·sec·tion (tran-sek′shən), ***n.*** 1. a transecting or being transected. 2. a transverse section.

tran·sept (tran′sept), ***n.*** [ML. *transseptum* for L. *transversum septum* < *transversus*, transverse + *septum*, enclosure], 1. the part of a cross-shaped church at right angles to the long, main section, or nave. 2. either arm of this part, outside the nave.

tran·sep·tal (tran-sep′t'l), ***adj.*** having to do with a transept.

trans·e·unt (tran′si-ənt), ***adj.*** [< L. *transiens, transeuntis*, ppr. of *transire;* see TRANSIENT], operating outside itself; having an outside effect: opposed to *immanent*.

transf., transfd., transferred.

trans·fer (trans-fũr′; *also, and for n. always*, trans′fẽr), ***v.t.*** [TRANSFERRED (-fũrd′, -fẽrd), TRANSFERRING], [ME. *transferren;* L. *transferre; trans-*, across + *ferre*, to bear], 1. to convey, carry, remove, or send from one person, place, or position to another. 2. to make over the legal title, right, or ownership of to another. 3. to convey (a picture, design, etc.) from one surface to another by any of several processes. ***v.i.*** 1. to transfer oneself: as, he *transferred* to the New York office. 2. to be transferred. 3. to change from one bus, streetcar, etc. to another, usually by presenting a transfer (sense 3). ***n.*** 1. *a)* a transferring or being transferred. *b)* a means of transferring. 2. a thing or person that is transferred; specifically, a picture or design transferred or to be transferred from one surface to another. 3. a ticket, provided free or at a small extra charge, entitling the bearer to change from one bus, streetcar, etc. to another at a specified place and within a specified period. 4. a place for transferring. 5. a form or document effecting a transfer, as of a student. 6. in *law*, *a)* the transferring of a title, right, or property from one person to another. *b)* the document effecting this. Abbreviated **tfr.** —***SYN.*** see **move.**

trans·fer·ee (trans′fẽr-ē′), ***n.*** 1. a person to whom something is transferred, especially legally. 2. a person who is transferred.

trans·fer·ence (trans-fũr′əns, trans′fẽr-əns), ***n.*** 1. a transferring or being transferred. 2. in *psychoanalysis*, a reproduction of emotions relating to repressed experiences, especially of childhood, and a replacement of another person, as the psychoanalyst, for the original object of the repressed impulses.

trans·fer·en·tial (trans′fẽr-en′shəl), ***adj.*** of or involving a transfer or transference.

trans·fer·or (trans-fũr′ẽr), ***n.*** a person who legally transfers a right, property, etc.

trans·fer·rer (trans-fũr′ẽr), ***n.*** a person or thing that transfers.

trans·fig·u·ra·tion (trans-fig′yoo-rā′shən, trans′fig-yoo-rā′shən), ***n.*** 1. a transfiguring or being transfigured. 2. [T-], the change in the appearance of Jesus on the mountain: Matt. 17; Mark 9. 3. [T-], a church festival commemorating this, held on August 6.

trans·fig·ure (trans-fig′yoor), ***v.t.*** [ME. *transfiguren;* OFr. *transfigurer;* L. *transfigurare; trans-*, across + *figurare;* see FIGURE, *v.*], 1. to change the figure, form, or outward appearance of; transform. 2. to transform so as to exalt or glorify. —***SYN.*** see **transform.**

trans·fix (trans-fiks′), ***v.t.*** [< L. *transfixus*, pp. of *transfigere*, to transfix; *trans-*, through + *figere*, to fix, fasten], 1. to pierce through with or as with something pointed. 2. to fasten in this manner; impale. 3. to make motionless, as if pierced through: as, *transfixed* with horror.

trans·fix·ion (trans-fik′shən), ***n.*** a transfixing or being transfixed.

trans·flu·ent (trans′flōō-ənt), ***adj.*** [L. *transfluens*, ppr. of *transfluere;* see TRANS- & FLUENT], flowing across or through.

trans·form (trans-fôrm′), ***v.t.*** [ME. *transformen;* OFr. *transformer;* L. *transformare;* see TRANS- & FORM, *v.*], 1. to change the form or outward appearance of. 2. to change the condition, nature, or function of; convert. 3. to change the personality or character of. 4. in *electricity*, to change in potential or type: said of currents. 5. in *mathematics*, to change (an expression, figure, etc.) in form but not in value. 6. in *physics*, to change (one form of energy) into another. ***v.i.*** [Rare], to be or become transformed.

***SYN.*—transform**, the broadest in scope of these terms,

implies a change either in external form or in inner nature, in function, etc. (she was *transformed* into a happy girl); **transmute**, from its earlier use in alchemy, suggests a change in basic nature that seems almost miraculous (*transmuted* from a shy youth into a gay man about town); **convert** implies a change in details so as to be suitable for a new use (to *convert* an attic into an apartment); **metamorphose** suggests a startling change produced as if by magic (a tadpole is *metamorphosed* into a frog); **transfigure** implies a change in outward appearance which seems to exalt or glorify (his whole being *transfigured* by an illuminating love). See also **change**.

trans·for·ma·ble (trans-fôr′mə-b'l), *adj.* that can be transformed; alterable.

trans·for·ma·tion (trans′fẽr-mā′shən), *n.* 1. a transforming or being transformed. 2. a woman's wig.

trans·form·a·tive (trans-fôr′mə-tiv), *adj.* [ML. *transformativus*], transforming or tending to transform.

trans·form·er (trans-fôr′mẽr), *n.* 1. a person or thing that transforms. 2. an apparatus for transforming the voltage of an electric current: there are two types, a *step-down transformer*, which changes high voltage into low voltage, and a *step-up transformer*, which changes low voltage into high voltage.

trans·fuse (trans-fūz′), *v.t.* [TRANSFUSED (-fūzd′), TRANSFUSING], [ME. *transfusen;* L. *transfusus*, pp. of *transfundere*, to pour from one container into another; *trans-*, across + *fundere*, to pour], 1. to transfer (liquid) by pouring from one container into another. 2. to make permeate; instill; imbue; infuse. 3. in *medicine*, *a*) to transfer (blood) from one individual into a blood vessel, usually a vein, of another. *b*) to inject (a saline solution, etc.), directly into a blood vessel. *c*) to give a transfusion to.

trans·fus·i·ble (trans-fūz′ə-b'l), *adj.* that can be transfused.

trans·fu·sion (trans-fū′zhən), *n.* a transfusing, especially of blood from one individual into another.

trans·fu·sive (trans-fū′siv), *adj.* tending or serving to transfuse.

trans·gress (trans-gres′, tranz-gres′), *v.t.* [Fr. *transgresser* < L. *transgressus*, pp. of *transgredi*, to step over, pass over < *trans-*, over, across + *gradi*, to step, walk], 1. to overstep or break (a law, commandment, etc.). 2. to go beyond (a limit, boundary, etc.). *v.i.* to break a law, commandment, etc.; sin.

trans·gres·sion (trans-gresh′ən, tranz-gresh′ən), *n.* a transgressing; violation; sin.

trans·gres·sive (trans-gres′iv, tranz-gres′iv), *adj.* transgressing or tending to transgress.

trans·gres·sor (trans-gres′ẽr, tranz-gres′ẽr), *n.* a person who transgresses; offender; sinner.

tran·ship (tran-ship′), *v.t.* to transship.

tran·sience (tran′shəns), *n.* the quality or state of being transient.

tran·sien·cy (tran′shən-si), *n.* transience.

tran·sient (tran′shənt), *adj.* [L. *transiens*, ppr. of *transire;* see TRANSIT], 1. *a*) passing away with time; not permanent; temporary; transitory. *b*) passing quickly or soon; fleeting; ephemeral. 2. transeunt. 3. staying only for a short time: as, a *transient* lodger. 4. in *music*, designating or of a temporary modulation. *n.* a transient person or thing, as a temporary lodger.

SYN.—**transient** applies to that which lasts or stays but a short time (a *transient* guest, feeling, etc.); **transitory** refers to that which by its inherent nature must sooner or later pass or end (life is *transitory*); **ephemeral** literally means existing only one day and, by extension, applies to that which is markedly short-lived (*ephemeral* glory); **momentary** implies duration for a moment or an extremely short time (a *momentary* lull in the conversation); **evanescent** applies to that which appears momentarily and fades quickly away (*evanescent* mental images); **fleeting** implies of a thing that it passes swiftly and cannot be held (a *fleeting* thought).—*ANT.* lasting, permanent.

tran·sil·i·ence (tran-sil′i-əns), *n.* the quality or state of being transilient.

tran·sil·i·ent (tran-sil′i-ənt), *adj.* [L. *transiliens*, ppr. of *transilire*, to leap across < *trans-*, over, across + *salire*, to leap], passing abruptly or leaping from one thing, condition, form, etc. to another.

trans·il·lu·mi·nate (trans′i-lōō′mə-nāt′, trans′i-lū′mə-nāt′), *v.t.* [TRANSILLUMINATED (-id), TRANSILLUMINATING], [*trans-* + *illuminate*], in *medicine*, to pass a strong light through (an organ or part) in examination.

tran·sis·tor (tran-zis′tẽr, tran-sis′tẽr), *n.* [< *transfer* + *resistor*], a minute electronic device, similar in function to the electronic tube, but which controls current flow, without employing a vacuum, through the peculiar conductive properties of germanium: because of its very small size, the transistor can be used wherever compactness is desired, as in hearing aids and in very small radios.

trans·it (tran′sit, tran′zit), *n.* [ME. *transite* < L. *transitus*, pp. of *transire; trans-*, over, across + *ire*, to go], 1. *a*) passage through or across. *b*) a transition; change. 2. a carrying or being carried through or across; conveyance: as, goods in *transit*. 3. a surveying instrument for measuring horizontal angles, a kind of theodolite: called in full *transit theodolite*. 4. in *astronomy*, *a*) the apparent passage of a heavenly body across a given meridian or through the field of a telescope. *b*) the apparent passage of a smaller heavenly body across the disk of a larger one, as of Mercury across the sun. *v.t.* 1. to make a transit through or across, especially in astronomical senses. 2. to revolve (the telescope of a transit) around its horizontal transverse axis. *v.i.* to make a transit (senses 1 & 4). Abbreviated **t.**

transit instrument, 1. a telescope mounted at right angles to a horizontal east-west axis so that it can be rotated only in the vertical plane of the meridian at its site, for observing the transit of heavenly bodies across the meridian. 2. a transit (sense 3).

tran·si·tion (tran-zish′ən, tran-sish′ən), *n.* [L. *transitio* < *transitus;* see TRANSIT], 1. a passing from one condition, form, stage, activity, place, etc. to another. 2. the period when this occurs. 3. a word, phrase, sentence, or group of sentences that relates a preceding topic with a succeeding one. 4. in *music*, *a*) a modulation; especially, a brief or passing modulation. *b*) an abrupt change into a remote key.

tran·si·tion·al (tran-zish′ən-'l, tran-sish′ən-'l), *adj.* of, showing, or characterized by transition.

tran·si·tive (tran′sə-tiv), *adj.* [LL. *transitivus* < L. *transitus;* see TRANSIT], 1. [Rare], transitional. 2. transeunt. 3. expressing an action that is thought of as passing over to and taking effect on some person or thing; taking a direct object to complete the meaning: said of certain verbs. *n.* a transitive verb or construction. Abbreviated **t., trans., tr.**

tran·si·to·ri·ly (tran′sə-tôr′ə-li, tran′zə-tō′rə-li), *adv.* in a transitory manner.

tran·si·to·ri·ness (tran′sə-tôr′i-nis, tran′zə-tō′ri-nis), *n.* the quality or condition of being transitory.

tran·si·to·ry (tran′sə-tôr′i, tran′zə-tō′ri), *adj.* [ME. *transitorye;* OFr. *transitoire;* L. *transitorius* < *transitus;* see TRANSIT], of a passing nature; not enduring or permanent; temporary, fleeting, or ephemeral; transient.—*SYN.* see **transient.**

Trans-Jor·dan (trans-jôr′d'n, tranz-jôr′d'n), *n.* Jordan: a former name.

Trans·jor·da·ni·a (trans′jôr-dā′ni-ə, tranz′jôr-dān′yə), *n.* Jordan: a former name.

Trans-Jor·da·ni·an (trans′jôr-dā′ni-ən, tranz′jôr-dān′yən), *adj.* of Trans-Jordan or its people. *n.* a native or inhabitant of Trans-Jordan.

transl., 1. translated. 2. translation.

trans·lat·a·ble (trans-lāt′ə-b'l, tranz-lāt′ə-b'l), *adj.* capable of being translated.

trans·late (trans-lāt′, tranz′lāt), *v.t.* [TRANSLATED (-id), TRANSLATING], [ME. *translaten* < L. *translatus*, transferred, used as pp. of *transferre;* see TRANSFER], 1. to change from one place, position, or condition to another; transfer; specifically, *a*) to convey to heaven, originally without death. *b*) to transfer (a bishop) from one see to another. *c*) to move (a saint's body, relics, etc.) from one place of interment to another. 2. to change from one language into another; hence, 3. to change into another medium or form: as, *translate* ideas into action. 4. to put into different words; interpret. 5. to repeat or retransmit (a telegraphic message) by means of an automatic relay. 6. [Archaic or Rare], to enrapture; entrance. 7. in *mechanics*, to impart translation to. *v.i.* 1. to make translations (into other languages). 2. to be capable of being translated: as, this poetry does not *translate* easily.

trans·la·tion (trans-lā′shən, tranz-lā′shən), *n.* [ME. *translacioun;* OFr. *translation;* L. *translatio*], 1. a translating or being translated. 2. the result of a translating, especially a translated version of a literary work. 3. in *mechanics*, motion in which every point of the moving object has simultaneously the same velocity and direction of motion: distinguished from *rotation*. Abbreviated **transl., trans., tr.**

SYN.—**translation** implies the rendering from one language into another of something written or spoken (a German *translation* of Shakespeare); **version** is applied to a particular translation of a given work, specifically of the Bible (the King James *Version*); **paraphrase**, in this connection, is applied to a free translation of a passage or work from another language; **transliteration** implies the writing of words with characters of another alphabet that represent the same sound or sounds (in this dictionary Greek is *transliterated* with letters of the English alphabet).

trans·la·tion·al (trans-lā′shən-'l, tranz-lā′shən-'l), *adj.* having to do with translation.

trans·la·tor (trans-lā′tẽr, tranz′lā′tẽr), *n.* 1. a person who translates; specifically, *a*) a person who translates books, articles, etc. *b*) a person who translates speech; interpreter. 2. an automatic repeater in a long-distance telegraph relay. Abbreviated **trans., tr.**

trans·lit·er·ate (trans-lit′ə-rāt′, tranz-lit′ə-rāt′), *v.t.*

[TRANSLITERATED (-id), TRANSLITERATING], [< *trans-* + L. *litera, littera,* letter], to write or spell (words, etc.) in the characters of another alphabet that represent the same sound or sounds.

trans·lit·er·a·tion (trans-lit'ə-rā'shən, tranz'lit-ə-rā'-shən), ***n.*** 1. a transliterating or being transliterated. 2. a transliterated word, text, etc. Abbreviated **translit.** —***SYN.*** see **translation.**

trans·lo·cate (trans-lō'kāt), ***v.t.*** [TRANSLOCATED (-id), TRANSLOCATING], to cause to change location or position; dislocate; displace.

trans·lo·ca·tion (trans'lō-kā'shən), ***n.*** 1. a translocating; dislocation. 2. in *botany,* the transference of food materials from one part of a plant to another.

trans·lu·cence (trans-lōō's'ns, tranz-lū's'ns), ***n.*** the quality or condition of being translucent.

trans·lu·cen·cy (trans-lōō's'n-si, tranz-lū's'n-si), ***n.*** translucence.

trans·lu·cent (trans-lōō's'nt, tranz-lū's'nt), ***adj.*** [L. *translucens,* ppr. of *translucere,* to shine through; *trans-,* over, across, through + *lucere,* to shine], 1. originally, shining through. 2. [Rare], transparent. 3. letting light pass but diffusing it so that objects on the other side cannot be distinguished; partially transparent, as frosted glass. —***SYN.*** see **clear.**

trans·lu·cid (trans-lōō'sid, tranz-lū'sid), ***adj.*** translucent.

trans·ma·rine (trans'mə-rēn', tranz'mə-rēn'), ***adj.*** [L. *transmarinus;* see TRANS- & MARINE], 1. crossing the sea. 2. on the other side of the sea.

trans·mi·grant (trans-mī'grənt, tranz-mī'grənt), ***adj.*** [L. *transmigrans,* ppr. of *transmigrare*], transmigrating. ***n.*** a person or thing that transmigrates; specifically, an emigrant passing through a country or place on his way to the country in which he will be an immigrant.

trans·mi·grate (trans-mī'grāt, tranz-mī'grāt), ***v.i.*** [TRANSMIGRATED (-id), TRANSMIGRATING], [ME. *transmigraten, v.t.* < L. *transmigratus,* pp. of *transmigrare;* see TRANS- & MIGRATE], 1. to move from one habitation, country, etc. to another. 2. in some religions, to pass into another body at death: said of the soul.

trans·mi·gra·tion (trans'mī-grā'shən, tranz'mī-grā'-shen), ***n.*** the act or process of transmigrating; specifically, the supposed passing of the soul at death into another body.

trans·mi·gra·tor (trans-mī'grā-tēr, tranz-mī'grā-tēr), ***n.*** a person or thing that transmigrates.

trans·mi·gra·to·ry (trans-mī'grə-tôr'i, tranz-mī'grə-tō'ri), ***adj.*** 1. of transmigration. 2. accustomed or likely to transmigrate.

trans·mis·si·bil·i·ty (trans-mis'ə-bil'ə-ti, tranz'mis-ə-bil'ə-ti), ***n.*** the quality or state of being transmissible.

trans·mis·si·ble (trans-mis'ə-b'l, tranz-mis'ə-b'l), ***adj.*** [< L. *transmissus,* pp. of *transmittere*], capable of being transmitted.

trans·mis·sion (trans-mish'ən, tranz-mish'ən), ***n.*** [L. *transmissio* < *transmissus,* pp. of *transmittere*], 1. a transmitting or being transmitted. 2. something transmitted. 3. the part of an automobile, truck, etc. that transmits motive force from the engine to the wheels, usually by means of gears or hydraulic cylinders. 4. the passage of radio waves through space between the transmitting station and the receiving station.

trans·mis·sive (trans-mis'iv, tranz-mis'iv), ***adj.*** [< L. *transmissus,* pp. of *transmittere*], 1. having the quality of transmitting or being transmitted. 2. transmitting or capable of transmitting.

trans·mit (trans-mit', tranz-mit'), ***v.t.*** [TRANSMITTED (-id), TRANSMITTING], [ME. *transmitten;* L. *transmittere; trans-,* over, across + *mittere,* to send], 1. to send or cause to go from one person or place to another, especially across intervening space or distance; transfer; convey. 2. to hand down to others by heredity, inheritance, etc. 3. to communicate. 4. to cause (light, heat, sound, etc.) to pass through air or some other medium. 5. to allow the passage of; conduct: as, water will *transmit* sound. 6. to convey (force, movement, etc.) from one mechanical part to another. 7. to send out (radio or television signals) by electromagnetic waves. —***SYN.*** see **carry.**

trans·mit·tal (trans-mit''l, tranz-mit''l), ***n.*** a transmitting; transmission.

trans·mit·ter (trans-mit'ēr, tranz-mit'ēr), ***n.*** 1. a person who transmits. 2. a thing that transmits; specifically, *a*) the part of a telegraphic instrument by which messages are sent. *b*) the part of a telephone, behind or including the mouthpiece, that converts speech sound into electric impulses for transmission: see **telephone,** illus. *c*) the apparatus that generates radio waves, modulates their amplitude or frequency, and sends them through space by means of an antenna: also **transmitting set.**

trans·mit·ti·ble (trans-mit'ə-b'l, tranz-mit'ə-b'l), ***adj.*** that can be transmitted; transmissible.

trans·mog·ri·fi·ca·tion (trans-mog'rə-fi-kā'shən, tranz-mog'rə-fi-kā'shən), ***n.*** a transmogrifying or being transmogrified.

trans·mog·ri·fy (trans-mog'rə-fī', tranz-mog'rə-fī'), ***v.t.*** [TRANSMOGRIFIED (-fīd'), TRANSMOGRIFYING], [humorous pseudo-L. formation], to change completely; transform, especially in a grotesque or strange manner.

trans·mon·tane (trans-mon'tān, tranz'mon-tān'), ***adj.*** [L. *transmontanus*], tramontane.

trans·mun·dane (trans-mun'dān, tranz-mun'dān), ***adj.*** beyond the world; beyond worldly matters.

trans·mut·a·bil·i·ty (trans-mūt'ə-bil'ə-ti, tranz'mū-tə-bil'ə-ti), ***n.*** the quality or state of being transmutable.

trans·mut·a·ble (trans-mūt'ə-b'l, tranz-mūt'ə-b'l), ***adj.*** [ML. *transmutabilis*], capable of being transmuted.

trans·mut·a·bly (trans-mūt'ə-bli, tranz-mūt'ə-bli), ***adv.*** so as to be transmutable.

trans·mu·ta·tion (trans'mū-tā'shən, tranz'mū-tā'shən), ***n.*** [ME. *transmutacioun* < (? via Late OFr.) L. *transmutatio* < pp. of *transmutare*], 1. a transmuting or being transmuted; change of one thing into another. 2. [Rare], a fluctuation. 3. in the Middle Ages, the supposedly possible conversion of base metals into gold and silver by alchemy. 4. the conversion of one element into another, as in radioactive disintegration or by nuclear bombardment.

trans·mut·a·tive (trans-mū'tə-tiv, tranz-mū'tə-tiv), ***adj.*** [ML. *transmutativus*], 1. tending to transmute. 2. having to do with transmutation.

trans·mute (trans-mūt', tranz-mūt'), ***v.t.*** [TRANSMUTED (-id), TRANSMUTING], [ME. *transmuten* (earlier *transmuwen*); L. *transmutare; trans-,* over, across + *mutare,* to change], to change from one form, species, condition, nature, or substance into another; transform; convert. —***SYN.*** see **transform.**

trans·o·ce·an·ic (trans'ō-shi-an'ik, tranz'ō-shi-an'ik), ***adj.*** 1. crossing or spanning the ocean. 2. on the other side of the ocean.

tran·som (tran'səm), ***n.*** [Late ME. *traunsom;* prob. < L. *transtrum,* crossbeam, lit., that which is across; see TRANS-], 1. a crosspiece in a structure; specifically, *a*) a lintel. *b*) a horizontal crossbar across the top or middle of a window or the top of a door. 2. a small window or shutterlike panel directly over a door or window, usually hinged to the transom (sense 1*b*). 3. any crosspiece; specifically, ***a***) the horizontal beam of a cross or gallows. *b*) the seat of a throne, boat's cabin, etc. *c*) any of the transverse beams attached to the sternpost of a wooden ship.

tran·son·ic (tran-son'ik), ***adj.*** transsonic.

trans·pa·cif·ic (trans'pə-sif'ik), ***adj.*** 1. crossing or spanning the Pacific. 2. on the other side of the Pacific.

trans·pa·dane (trans'pə-dān', trans-pā'dān), ***adj.*** [L. *transpadanus* < *trans-,* over, across + *Padus,* the Po], on the other (or northern) side of the river Po: from the viewpoint of Rome.

trans·par·ence (trans-pâr'əns), ***n.*** the quality or state of being transparent.

trans·par·en·cy (trans-pâr'ən-si), ***n.*** 1. the quality or state of being transparent. 2. [*pl.* TRANSPARENCIES (-siz)], something transparent; specifically, a piece of transparent or translucent material having a picture or design that is visible when light shines through it.

trans·par·ent (trans-pâr'ənt), ***adj.*** [ME. *transparaunt* after Fr. *transparent;* ML. *transparens,* ppr. of *transparere,* to be transparent; L. *trans-,* over, across, through + *parens,* ppr. of *parere,* to appear], 1. transmitting light rays so that objects on the other side may be distinctly seen; capable of being seen through: as, window glass is *transparent:* opposed to ***opaque*** and distinguished from *translucent.* 2. so fine in texture or open in mesh that objects on the other side may be seen relatively clearly; sheer; gauzy; diaphanous. 3. easily understood; very clear. 4. easily recognized or detected; obvious. 5. open; frank; candid. 6. [Obs. or Poetic], luminous; penetrating. —***SYN.*** see **clear.**

trans·pierce (trans-pêrs'), ***v.t.*** [Fr. *transpercer;* see TRANS- & PIERCE], 1. to pierce through completely. 2. to pierce; penetrate.

tran·spi·ra·tion (tran'spə-rā'shən), ***n.*** [Fr.], the act or process of transpiring; specifically, the giving off of moisture, etc. through the pores of the skin or through the surface of leaves and other parts of plants.

tran·spir·a·to·ry (tran-spir'ə-tôr'i, tran-spir'ə-tō'ri), ***adj.*** 1. of transpiration. 2. that can be transpired.

tran·spire (tran-spir'), ***v.t.*** [TRANSPIRED (-spird'), TRANSPIRING], [Fr. *transpirer* < L. *trans,* over, across, through + *spirare,* to breathe], to cause (vapor, moisture, etc.) to pass through tissue or other permeable substances, especially through the pores of the skin or the surface of leaves and other parts of plants. ***v.i.*** 1. to give off vapor, moisture, etc., as through the pores of the skin. 2. to be given off, passed through pores, exhaled, etc. 3. to leak out; become known. 4. to come to pass; happen: in this sense, regarded by some grammarians as a loose usage. —***SYN.*** see **happen.**

trans·plant (trans-plant', trans-plänt'; *for n.,* trans'-plant', trans'plänt'), ***v.t.*** [LL. *transplantare;* see TRANS- & PLANT], 1. to remove from one place and plant in another. 2. to remove (people) from one place and resettle in another. 3. in *surgery,* to transfer (tissue or an organ) from one individual or part of the body to another; graft. ***v.i.*** 1. to do transplanting.

2. to be capable of enduring transplantation. *n.* 1. a transplanting. 2. something transplanted, as a seedling or body tissue.

trans·plan·ta·tion (trans′plan-tā′shən), *n.* 1. a transplanting. 2. something transplanted.

trans·po·ni·ble (trans-pō′nə-b'l), *adj.* [< L. *transponere*, to transpose; + *-ible*], capable of being transposed.

trans·pon·tine (trans-pon′tin, trans-pon′tīn), *adj.* [< *trans-*, over, across + L. *pons, pontis*, a bridge], 1. on the other side of a bridge. 2. south of the Thames (and its bridges) in London.

trans·port (trans-pôrt′, trans-pōrt′; *for n.*, trans′pôrt, trans′pōrt), *v.t.* [ME. *transporten;* OFr. *transporter;* L. *transportare*, to carry across; *trans-*, over, across + *portare*, to carry], 1. to carry from one place to another, especially over long distances. 2. to carry away with emotion; enrapture; entrance. 3. to carry off to a penal colony, etc.; banish; deport. 4. [Obs.], to carry off by death; kill. *n.* 1. the act or process of transporting; transportation; conveyance. 2. the condition of being carried away with emotion; rapture. 3. a ship used for transporting soldiers, military supplies, etc. 4. a large commercial airplane for carrying passengers, freight, etc. 5. a convict sentenced to transportation. —*SYN.* see **banish, carry, ecstasy.**

trans·por·ta·tion (trans′pēr-tā′shən), *n.* [Fr.; L. *transportatio* < pp. of *transportare*], 1. a transporting or being transported. 2. a means of conveyance: as, our *transportation* was camel. 3. cost of being transported; fare. 4. a ticket for transport. 5. banishment for crime, as to a penal colony; deportation.

trans·pos·al (trans-pōz′'l), *n.* [Rare], transposition.

trans·pose (trans-pōz′), *v.t.* [TRANSPOSED (-pōzd′), TRANSPOSING], [ME. *transposen;* OFr. *transposer* (for L. *transponere*); see TRANS- & POSE (to put)], 1. [Rare], to transfer. 2. to change the usual, normal, relative, or respective order or position of; interchange: as, one may *transpose* "he went down" to "down went he." 3. to transfer (an algebraic term) from one side of an equation to the other, reversing the plus or minus value. 4. to write or play (a musical composition) in a different key. 5. [Obs.], to transform. *v.i.* 1. to write or play music in a different key. 2. to be capable of being transposed. Abbreviated **tr., trans.** —*SYN.* see **reverse.**

trans·po·si·tion (trans′pə-zish′ən), *n.* [Fr.; ML. *transpositio* < L. *transpositus*, pp. of *transponere*; see TRANSPOSE], 1. a transposing or being transposed. 2. the result of this; something transposed.

trans·pos·i·tive (trans-poz′ə-tiv), *adj.* involving transposition.

trans·ship (trans-ship′, tran-ship′), *v.t.* [TRANSSHIPPED (-shipt′), TRANSSHIPPING], to transfer from one ship, train, etc. to another for reshipment: also **tranship.**

trans·ship·ment (trans-ship′mənt, tran-ship′mənt), *n.* 1. a transshipping. 2. something transshipped.

Trans-Si·be·ri·an Railroad (trans′sī-bêr′i-ən), a railroad in the U.S.S.R., extending across Siberia from the Ural Mountains to Vladivostok: length, c. 4,000 mi.

trans·son·ic (trans-son′ik, tran-son′ik), *adj.* [< *trans-* + L. *sonus*, sound; + *-ic*], of, designating, or traveling at speeds approximating the speed of sound in air (which is about 738 miles per hour): the limits are variously set from as low as 550 miles per hour to as high as 900 miles per hour.

tran·sub·stan·ti·ate (tran′səb-stan′shi-āt′), *v.t.* [< ML. *transubstantiatus*, pp. of *transubstantiare*, to transubstantiate < L. *trans-*, over, across + *substantia*, substance], 1. to change one substance into another; transmute; transform. 2. in the *Roman Catholic & Orthodox Eastern Churches*, to bring about transubstantiation in (bread and wine).

tran·sub·stan·ti·a·tion (tran′səb-stan′shi-ā′shən), *n.* 1. a transubstantiating; changing of one substance into another. 2. in the *Roman Catholic & Orthodox Eastern Churches*, the doctrine that, in the Eucharist, the whole substances of the bread and of the wine are changed into the body and blood of Christ, only the accidents of bread and wine remaining.

tran·su·date (tran′soo-dāt′, tran′syoo-dāt′), *n.* [< *transudation*], something transuded.

tran·su·da·tion (tran′soo-dā′shən, tran′syoo-dā′shən), *n.* [Fr. *transsudation*], 1. a transuding. 2. a transudate.

tran·sude (tran-sōōd′, tran-sūd′), *v.i.* [TRANSUDED (-id), TRANSUDING], [Fr. *transsuder* < L. *trans*, over, across, through + *sudare*, to sweat], to ooze or exude through pores, interstices, etc. as or like sweat.

trans·u·ran·ic (trans′yoo-ran′ik), *adj.* designating or of the elements having atomic numbers higher than that of uranium, as neptunium, plutonium, etc.

Trans·vaal (trans-väl′, tranz-väl′), *n.* a province of the Union of South Africa, in the northeastern part: area, 110,450 sq. mi.; pop., 3,624,000; capital, Pretoria.

trans·val·ue (trans-val′ū), *v.t.* [TRANSVALUED (-ūd), TRANSVALUING], to evaluate by a new principle, especially one rejecting conventional or accepted standards.

trans·ver·sal (trans-vũr′s'l, tranz-vũr′s'l), *adj.* [ML. *transversalis*], transverse. *n.* a line that intersects two or more other lines.

trans·verse (trans-vũrs′, tranz-vũrs′), *adj.* [L. *transversus*, pp. of *transvertere;* see TRAVERSE], 1. lying, situated, placed, etc. across; crossing from side to side; crosswise. 2. in *geometry*, designating the axis that passes through the foci of a conic section (in an ellipse, the longer axis). *n.* 1. a transverse part, beam, etc. 2. in *geometry*, a transverse axis.

transverse process, a process projecting laterally from a vertebra.

trans·ves·tite (trans-ves′tīt), *n.* [< *trans-*, across + L. *vestire*, to clothe], a person who derives sexual pleasure from dressing in the clothes of the opposite sex.

Trans-Vol·ta Togoland (trans-vol′tə), a region in Ghana made up of Togoland and the Volta River basin: area, 16,534 sq. mi.; pop., 436,000.

Tran·syl·va·ni·a (tran′sil-vā′ni-ə, tran′s'l-vān′yə), *n.* a province in central Romania, north of the Transylvanian Alps: area, 24,020 sq. mi.

Tran·syl·va·ni·an (tran′sil-vā′ni-ən, tran′s'l-vān′yən), *adj.* of Transylvania, its people, their language, etc. *n.* a native or inhabitant of Transylvania.

Transylvanian Alps, a mountain range in central Romania, an extension of the Carpathian Mountains.

trap (trap), *n.* [ME. *trappe;* AS. *træppe;* akin to G. *treppe*, stairway; IE. base **dreb-*, to run, tread; basic sense prob. "what one runs or steps into"; cf. TRAMP], 1. any device for catching animals, as one that snaps shut tightly when stepped on or jiggled; gin, snare, or pitfall. 2. any stratagem, ambush, etc. designed to catch or trick unsuspecting persons. 3. any of various devices for preventing the escape of gas, offensive odors, etc.; especially, a U-shaped or S-shaped part of a drainpipe, in which water seals off sewer gas. 4. an apparatus for throwing balls, disks, etc. into the air to be struck or shot at, as in trapball or trapshooting; hence, 5. *a)* trapball. *b)* *pl.* [Slang], trapshooting. 6. a light, two-wheeled carriage with springs. 7. a rattletrap. 8. a trap door. 9. *pl.* the drums, cymbals, bells, etc. in an orchestra or band. 10. [Slang], the mouth. 11. in *golf*, any of various hazards: as, a sand *trap*. *v.t.* [TRAPPED or *occas.* TRAPT (trapt), TRAPPING], 1. to catch in a trap; entrap. 2. to hold back or seal off by a trap (also with *out*). 3. to furnish with a trap or traps. *v.i.* 1. to set traps for game. 2. to trap animals, especially for their furs.

SYN.—**trap**, as applied to a device for capturing animals, specifically suggests a snapping device worked by a spring; **pitfall**, a concealed pit with a collapsible cover; **snare**, a noose which jerks tight upon the release of a trigger. In extended senses, these words apply to any danger into which unsuspecting or unwary persons may fall, **trap** specifically suggesting a deliberate stratagem or ambush (a speed *trap*), **pitfall**, a concealed danger, source of error, etc. (the *pitfalls* of the law), and **snare**, enticement and entanglement (the *snares* of love). See also **catch.**

trap (trap), *n.* [Sw. *trapp* < *trappa*, stair], any of several kinds of dark-colored igneous rock found in other rock in steplike formations: also **traprock.**

trap (trap), *v.t.* [TRAPPED (trapt), TRAPPING], [ME. *trappen* < *trappe*, trappings; prob. < OFr. *drap*, cloth; cf. *drapure*, covering for a horse], to cover with trappings; caparison. *n.* 1. [Obs.], trappings, as for a horse. 2. *pl.* [Colloq.], personal belongings; luggage.

tra·pan (trə-pan′), *n.* & *v.t.* [TRAPANNED (-pand′), TRAPANNING], trepan (trick).

Tra·pa·ni (trä′pä-nē′), *n.* a city in Sicily, on the northwestern coast: pop., 73,000 (est. 1947).

trap·ball (trap′bôl′), *n.* 1. an old game in which the batter strikes a trap with his bat so that a ball is thrown into the air and then hits the ball to a distance. 2. the ball used in this game. Also **trap ball.**

trap door, a hinged or sliding door in a roof, ceiling, or floor.

trap-door spider (trap′dôr′, trap′dōr′), any of a number of large spiders that dig a burrow and cover the entrance with a hinged lid like a trap door.

tra·peze (trə-pēz′, tra-pēz′), *n.* [Fr. *trapèze;* L. *trapezium:* from its shape], 1. a short horizontal bar, hung at a height by two ropes, on which gymnasts, circus performers, etc. swing. 2. a trapezium (senses 1 & 2).

tra·pe·zi·form (trə-pē′zə-fôrm′), *adj.* shaped like a trapezium.

tra·pe·zi·um (trə-pē′zi-əm), *n.* [*pl.* TRAPEZIUMS (-əmz), TRAPEZIA (-ə)], [Mod. L.; Gr. *trapezion*, trapezium, lit., small table or counter, dim. of *trapeza*, table, lit., four-footed bench; *tra-* for *tetra*, four + *peza*, a foot, akin to *pous*, a foot], 1. a plane figure with four sides no two of which are parallel. 2. [British], a trapezoid. 3. in *anatomy*, *a)* a small bone of the

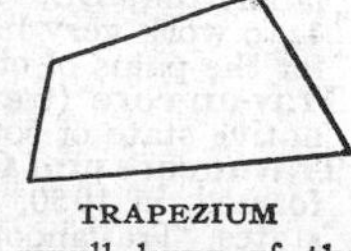
TRAPEZIUM

wrist near the base of the thumb. *b*) the trapezoid body.
trap·e·zo·he·dron (trap'i-zə-hē'drən, trə-pē'zə-hē'drən), *n.* [Mod. L. < *trapezium* + Gr. *hedra*, a seat, base], a solid figure all of whose faces are trapeziums.
trap·e·zoid (trap'ə-zoid'), *n.* [Mod. L. *trapezoides* < Gr. *trapezoeides*, shaped like a trapezoid; see TRAPEZIUM & -OID], 1. a plane figure with four sides two of which are parallel. 2. [British], a trapezium (sense 1). 3. in *anatomy*, a small bone of the wrist near the base of the index finger. *adj.* 1. shaped like a trapezoid. 2. in *anatomy*, designating or of a bundle of transverse fibers (*trapezoid body*) in the pons of the brain.

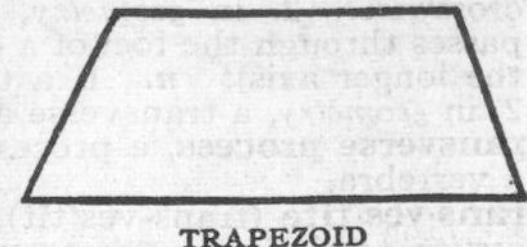
TRAPEZOID

trap·e·zoi·dal (trap'ə-zoi'd'l), *adj.* trapezoid.
trap·pe·an (trap'i-ən, trə-pē'ən), *adj.* of or like trap (rock).
trap·per (trap'ẽr), *n.* a person who traps; especially, one who traps fur-bearing animals for their skins.
trap·pings (trap'iŋz), *n.pl.* [< ME. *trappe;* see TRAP (to caparison)], 1. an ornamental covering for a horse. 2. dress, especially of an ornamental kind; adornments; embellishments.
Trap·pist (trap'ist), *n.* [Fr. *trappiste* < La *Trappe*, abbey in Normandy where the rule was established in 1664], a monk of a branch of the Cistercian order, known for austerity of living and perpetual silence. *adj.* of or having to do with the Trappists.
trap·rock (trap'rok'), *n.* trap (rock).
trap·shoot·er (trap'shōōt'ẽr), *n.* a person who does trapshooting.
trap·shoot·ing (trap'shōōt'iŋ), *n.* the sport of shooting at clay pigeons, glass balls, etc. sprung into the air from traps.
trapt (trapt), occasional past tense of **trap.**
trash (trash), *n.* [prob. < Anglo-N. etymon of Norw. dial. *trask*, lumber, trash; akin to ON. *tros*, broken twigs, etc.; IE. base **der-*, to tear, split off], 1. parts that have been broken off, stripped off, etc., especially leaves, twigs, husks, and other plant trimmings. 2. broken, discarded, or worthless things; rubbish; refuse. 3. worthless ideas, talk, or writing; nonsense. 4. a worthless or disreputable person or people. 5. the refuse of sugar cane after the juice has been pressed out. *v.t.* 1. to trim (trees or plants) of trash. 2. to regard or treat as trash; discard as worthless.
trash (trash), *v.t.* [OFr. *trachier*, var. of *tracier;* see TRACE (track)], 1. to restrain by a leash; hence, 2. to restrain; retard. *n.* 1. a collar, halter, or leash for trashing a dog. 2. any restraint or hindrance.
trash·i·ly (trash'ə-li), *adv.* in a trashy manner.
trash·i·ness (trash'i-nis), *n.* the quality or state of being trashy.
trash·y (trash'i), *adj.* [TRASHIER (-i-ẽr), TRASHIEST (-i-ist)], containing, consisting of, or like trash; worthless.
Tra·si·me·no (trä'se-me'nô), *n.* a lake in central Italy: scene of a victory by Hannibal over the Romans (217 B.C.).
trass (tras), *n.* [G.; D. *tras* < earlier *terras*; OFr. *terrace;* see TERRACE], a volcanic earth used in hydraulic cement.
trau·ma (trô'mə, trou'mə), *n.* [*pl.* TRAUMATA (-mə-tə), TRAUMAS (-məz)], [Mod. L.; Gr. *trauma*], 1. in *medicine, a*) an injury or wound violently produced. *b*) the condition or neurosis resulting from this. 2. in *psychiatry*, an emotional experience, or shock, which has a lasting psychic effect.
trau·mat·ic (trô-mat'ik), *adj.* [LL. *traumaticus;* Gr. *traumatikos*], 1. of, having the nature of, or resulting from a trauma. 2. used in the treatment of wounds.
trau·ma·tism (trô'mə-tiz'm), *n.* [< Gr. *trauma, traumatos*, a wound; + *-ism*], 1. the abnormal condition caused by a trauma. 2. a trauma.
trau·ma·tize (trô'mə-tīz'), *v.t.* [TRAUMATIZED (-tīzd'), TRAUMATIZING], 1. to injure or wound (tissues). 2. in *psychiatry*, to subject to a trauma.
trav., 1. traveler. 2. travels.
trav·ail (trav'āl, trav''l), *n.* [ME.; OFr.; LL. **tripalium*, instrument of torture composed of three stakes < *tria*, three + *palus*, a stake], 1. very hard work; toil. 2. labor pains; pains of childbirth. 3. intense pain; agony. *v.i.* [ME. *travaillen;* OFr. *travaillier*, to labor, toil; LL. **tripaliare*, to torment < **tripalium*], 1. to work very hard; toil. 2. to have labor pains; suffer the pains of childbirth. —*SYN.* see **work.**
Trav·an·core (trav'ən-kôr', trav'ən-kōr'), *n.* a former native state of southwestern India.
Travancore and Cochin, a state of southwestern India, formed, in 1950, by the merging of two former native states, Travancore and Cochin: area, 9,115 sq. mi.; pop., 7,493,000 (est. 1950); capital, Trivandrum.
trave (trāv), *n.* [ME.; OFr.; L. *trabs, trabis*, a beam], 1. *a*) a crossbeam. *b*) a division made by crossbeams, as in a ceiling. 2. a wooden frame for enclosing a restive horse, etc. while being shod.
trav·el (trav''l), *v.i.* [TRAVELED or TRAVELLED (-'ld), TRAVELING or TRAVELLING], [var. of *travail*, with stress-changed form & differentiated sense], 1. to go from one place to another; make a journey or journeys. 2. to go from place to place as a traveling salesman. 3. to walk or run. 4. to move, pass, or be transmitted; pass from one point or place to another. 5. to move or be capable of moving in a given path or for a given distance: said of mechanical parts, etc. 6. [Colloq.], to move or advance with speed. *v.t.* to make a journey over or through; traverse. *n.* 1. the act or process of traveling. 2. *pl. a*) the trips, journeys, tours, etc. taken by a person or persons. *b*) a written account of these. 3. passage or movement of any kind. 4. the number of persons, vehicles, or ships traveling on a route, through a given place, etc.; traffic. 5. *a*) mechanical motion, especially reciprocating motion. *b*) the distance of a mechanical stroke, etc.
trav·eled (trav''ld), *adj.* 1. that has traveled much. 2. much used by travelers: as, a *traveled* road.
trav·el·er (trav''l-ẽr, trav'lẽr), *n.* 1. a person who travels. 2. [Chiefly British], a traveling salesman; commercial traveler. 3. a thing that travels; specifically, *a*) any mechanical part or apparatus, as a traveling crane, that moves or slides along a support. *b*) in *nautical usage*, a metal ring that slides on a rope, rod, or spar; also, the rope, rod, or spar it slides on. 4. a slip on which a customer's various purchases are noted so that they may all be paid for at once.
traveler's check, a check or draft, usually one of a set, issued by a bank, etc. in any of several denominations and sold to a traveler who signs it at issuance and can cash it by having the payer witness and verify his signature of endorsement.
traveling salesman, a salesman who travels from place to place soliciting orders for the business firm he represents.
trav·elled (trav''ld), *adj.* traveled.
trav·el·ler (trav''l-ẽr, trav'lẽr), *n.* a traveler.
trav·e·logue, trav·e·log (trav'ə-lôg', trav'ə-log'), *n.* [< *travel* + *-logue*], 1. a lecture describing travels, usually accompanied by the showing of pictures. 2. a motion picture of travels.
trav·ers·a·ble (trav'ẽr-sə-b'l), *adj.* that can be traversed.
trav·ers·al (trav'ẽr-s'l), *n.* a traversing or being traversed.
trav·erse (trav'ẽrs, trə-vũrs'), *v.t.* [TRAVERSED (-ẽrst, -vũrst'), TRAVERSING], [ME. *traversen;* OFr. *traverser;* LL. **transversare* < L. *transversus*, pp. of *transvertere*, to turn across; *trans-*, over, across + *vertere*, to turn], 1. *a*) to pass over, across, or through; cross. *b*) to go back and forth over or along; cross and recross. 2. to go counter to; oppose; thwart. 3. to survey or examine carefully. 4. to turn (a gun, lathe, etc.) laterally; swivel. 5. in *law, a*) to deny or contradict formally (something alleged by the opposing party in a lawsuit). *b*) to take issue upon (an indictment) or upon the validity of (an inquest of office). 6. in *nautical usage*, to brace (a yard) fore and aft. *v.i.* 1. to move across; cross over. 2. to move back and forth over a place, etc.; cross and recross. 3. to swivel or pivot. 4. in *fencing*, to move one's blade toward the opponent's hilt while pressing one's foil hard against his. *n.* 1. something that traverses or crosses; specifically, *a*) a line that intersects others. *b*) a crossbar, crossbeam, transom, etc. *c*) a screen, curtain, etc. placed crosswise. *d*) a parapet or wall of earth, etc. across a rampart or trench. *e*) a gallery, loft, etc. crossing a building. *f*) a straight line surveyed across a plot, region, etc. 2. something that opposes or thwarts; obstacle. 3. a traversing; specifically, *a*) a passing across or through; crossing. *b*) a lateral, pivoting, oblique, or zigzagging movement. 4. a part, device, etc. that causes a traversing movement. 5. a passage by which one may cross; way across. 6. *a*) a zigzagging course or route taken by a vessel, as in sailing against the wind. *b*) a single leg of such a course. 7. a formal denial in a lawsuit. *adj.* [OFr. *travers;* L. *transversus;* see the *v.*], 1. passing or extending across; transverse. 2. designating or of drapes (and the rods and hooks for them) hung in pairs that can be drawn together or apart by pulling cords at the side. *adv.* [Obs.], across; crosswise.
trav·er·tin (trav'ẽr-tin), *n.* travertine.
trav·er·tine (trav'ẽr-tin, trav'ẽr-tēn'), *n.* [It. *travertino, tibertino, tiburtino;* L. *lapis Tiburtinus*, stone of Tibur: so called because formed by the waters of Anio at Tibur (now Tivoli)], a light-colored limestone formed as a deposit of limy springs, etc.: it is quarried in Italy.
trav·es·ty (trav'is-ti), *n.* [*pl.* TRAVESTIES (-tiz)], [orig. an adj. < Fr. *travesti*, pp. of *travestir*, to disguise, travesty; It. *travestire* < L. *trans*, over, across + *vestire*, to dress, attire], 1. a grotesque or farcical imitation for purposes of ridicule; burlesque. 2. a crude and ridiculous representation; ludicrous distortion. *v.t.* [TRAVESTIED (-tid), TRAVESTYING], to make a travesty of; burlesque. —*SYN.* see **caricature.**
tra·vois (trə-voi'), *n.* [*pl.* TRAVOIS (-voiz'), TRAVOISES (-voi'ziz)], [Canad. Fr. < *travail*, a brake], a crude

sledge of the North American Plains Indians, consisting of a net or platform dragged along the ground on the two poles that support it and serve as shafts for the draft animal.

tra·voise (trə-voiz′), *n.* a travois.

trawl (trôl), *n.* [doubtful Late ME. *trawelle;* prob. var. of *trail* (for the vowel cf. BRAWL & early form *trawl* for *trail* (of a gun)], 1. a large, baglike net dragged by a boat along the bottom of a fishing bank. 2. a long line supported by buoys, from which many short fishing lines are hung. *v.t. & v.i.* to fish or catch with a trawl.

trawl·er (trôl′ẽr), *n.* 1. a person who trawls. 2. a boat used in trawling.

tray (trā), *n.* [ME. *treie;* AS. *treg, trig,* wooden board; IE. base **derew-*, tree, seen also in *tree, trough*], 1. a flat receptacle made of wood, metal, glass, plastic, etc. with slightly raised edges or low sides, used for holding or carrying articles. 2. a tray with its contents: as, a *tray* of food. 3. a shallow, boxlike, removable compartment of a trunk, cabinet, etc.

tray agriculture, hydroponics.

treach·er·ous (trech′ẽr-əs), *adj.* [ME. *trecherous;* OFr. *trecheros*], 1. characterized by treachery; traitorous; disloyal; perfidious. 2. giving a false appearance of safety, honesty, etc.; untrustworthy, unreliable, or insecure: as, *treacherous* rocks. —*SYN.* see **faithless.**

treach·er·y (trech′ẽr-i), *n.* [*pl.* TREACHERIES (-iz)], [ME. *trecherie;* OFr. *tricherie,* trickery < *trichier,* to trick, cheat], 1. betrayal of trust or faith; deceit; perfidy. 2. treason. 3. an act of perfidy or treason.

trea·cle (trē′k'l), *n.* [ME. & OFr. *triacle;* L. *theriaca,* antidote for poison; Gr. *thēriakē,* remedy for bites of venomous beasts < *thērion,* wild beast, dim. of *thēr,* animal; cf. DEER], 1. originally, *a*) a remedy for poison. *b*) any effective remedy. 2. [British], molasses.

trea·cly (trē′kli), *adj.* [TREACLIER (-kli-ẽr), TREACLIEST (-kli-ist)], like or covered with treacle; sticky.

tread (tred), *v.t.* [TROD (trod) or *archaic* TRODE (trōd), TRODDEN (trod′'n) or TROD, TREADING], [ME. *treden;* AS. *tredan;* akin to G. *treten;* IE. base **dreu-* (< **der-*, **drā-*, etc., to run, step), seen also in *trade*], 1. to walk on, in, along, across, over, etc. 2. to do or follow by walking, dancing, stepping, etc.: as, they *tread* the measures gaily. 3. to press or beat with the feet so as to crush or injure; trample. 4. to oppress or subdue, as if by stepping on. 5. to copulate with: said of male birds. 6. [TREADED (-id), TREADING], to put a tread on (a pneumatic tire). *v.i.* 1. to move on foot; step; walk. 2. to set one's foot (with *on,* etc.); make a step; step. 3. to trample (with *on* or *upon*). 4. to copulate: said of birds. *n.* 1. [Rare], a mark made by treading; footprint. 2. a treading. 3. manner or sound of treading. 4. something on which a person or thing treads or moves, as the part of a shoe sole, wheel, etc. that makes contact, the part of a rail on which a car wheel runs, the horizontal upper surface of a stair, or the outer, grooved rim of a pneumatic tire. 5. the distance between the points of contact (with the ground) of paired wheels, as of an automobile. 6. the cicatricle or chalaza of a bird's egg.

tread on air, 1. to walk gaily. 2. to be gay or happy.

tread on one's toes, to hurt or offend one.

tread the boards, to play parts on the stage.

tread water, [*p.t.* now usually TREADED (tred′id)], in *swimming,* to keep the body upright and the head above water by moving the legs up and down in a treading motion.

trea·dle (tred′'l), *n.* [ME. *tredil;* AS. *tredel* < *tredan;* see TREAD], a lever or pedal moved by the foot to operate a sewing machine, etc. *v.i.* [TREADLED (-'ld), TREADLING], to work a treadle.

tread·mill (tred′mil′), *n.* 1. a kind of mill wheel turned by the weight of persons treading steps arranged around its circumference: it was formerly used as an instrument of prison discipline. 2. a mill driven by an animal treading a sloping, endless belt. 3. any monotonous round of duties, work, etc. in which one seems to get nowhere.

treas., 1. treasurer. 2. treasury.

trea·son (trē′z'n), *n.* [ME. *treison, tresun, traison;* OFr. *traïson;* L. *traditio* < pp. of *tradere,* to give or deliver over or up < *trans-*, over + *dare,* to give], 1. [Rare], betrayal of trust or faith; treachery. 2. violation of the allegiance owed to one's sovereign or state; betrayal of one's country: the Constitution of the United States (Article III, Section 3) declares, "Treason against the United States shall consist only in levying war against them, or in adhering to their enemies, giving them aid and comfort." —*SYN.* see **sedition.**

trea·son·a·ble (trē′z'n-ə-b'l), *adj.* of, having the nature of, or involving treason; traitorous.

trea·son·a·bly (trē′z'n-ə-bli), *adv.* 1. in a treasonable manner. 2. by an act of treason.

trea·son·ous (trē′z'n-əs), *adj.* treasonable; traitorous.

treasr., treasurer.

treas·ure (trezh′ẽr), *n.* [ME. *tresoure;* OFr. *tresor;* L. *thesaurus;* Gr. *thēsauros,* a store, treasure; cf. THESAURUS], 1. accumulated or stored wealth in the form of money, precious metals, jewels, etc. 2. any person or thing that is considered very valuable. *v.t.* [TREASURED (-ẽrd), TREASURING], 1. to store away or save up (money, valuables, etc.) as for future use; hoard. 2. to value greatly; cherish. —*SYN.* see **appreciate.**

treasure house, a building or room where treasure is stored.

treas·ur·er (trezh′ẽr-ẽr), *n.* [ME. *tresorer;* Anglo-Fr. *tresorer;* OFr. *tresorier* < *tresor;* see TREASURE], a person in charge of a treasure or treasury; specifically, an officer in charge of the funds or finances of a government, corporation, society, etc.: abbreviated **treas., treasr., tr.**

treas·ure-trove (trezh′ẽr-trōv′), *n.* [Anglo-Fr. *tresor trové* < *tresor* (see TREASURE) + OFr. *trové,* pp. of *trover,* to find], 1. treasure found hidden, the original owner of which is unknown. 2. any valuable discovery.

treas·ur·y (trezh′ẽr-i), *n.* [*pl.* TREASURIES (-iz)], [ME. & OFr. *tresorie*], 1. a place where treasure is kept; room or building where valuable objects are preserved. 2. a place where public or private funds are kept, received, disbursed, and recorded. 3. the funds or revenues of a state, corporation, society, etc. 4. [T-], the department of a state or nation that is in charge of revenue, taxation, and public finances. 5. a collection of treasures in art, literature, etc.: as, a *treasury* of verse. Abbreviated **treas.**

treasury note, a note or bill issued by the United States Treasury Department, serving as legal tender for all debts.

treat (trēt), *v.i.* [ME. *treten;* OFr. *traitier,* to handle, meddle, treat < L. *tractare,* freq. of *trahere,* to draw], 1. to carry on business or discuss terms (*with* a person); negotiate; bargain. 2. to stand the cost of another's entertainment. *v.t.* 1. to deal with (a subject) in writing, music, painting, etc., especially in a certain manner or style. 2. to act or behave toward (a person, animal, etc.) in a specified manner. 3. to have a specified opinion or view of and behave accordingly in regard to: as, he *treated* the mistake as a joke. 4. to pay for the food, drink, entertainment, etc. of (another): as, he *treated* her to a soda. 5. to subject to some process, usually for a definite purpose; specifically, *a*) to give medical or surgical care to. *b*) to subject to chemical action. *c*) to cover or coat with some preparation for protection, appearance, etc. *n.* 1. a meal, drink, entertainment, etc. given or paid for by someone else. 2. anything that gives great or unusual pleasure; a delight. 3. *a*) the act of treating or entertaining. *b*) one's turn to treat.

treat of, to deal with in speaking or writing; make the subject of a discourse.

trea·tise (trē′tis), *n.* [ME. *tretis;* Anglo-Fr. *tretiz;* OFr. **treiteiz* < *traitier;* see TREAT], 1. a formal, systematic essay or book on some subject, especially a discussion of facts, evidence, or principles and the conclusions based on these. 2. [Obs.], a narrative.

treat·ment (trēt′mənt), *n.* 1. act, manner, method, etc. of treating, as a person, a substance in processing, or a subject in art or literature. 2. medical or surgical care, especially a systematic course of this.

trea·ty (trē′ti), *n.* [*pl.* TREATIES (-tiz)], [ME. *trete;* Anglo-Fr. *treté;* OFr. *traité;* L. *tractatus,* consultation < pp. of *tractare,* to handle, manage, treat], 1. formerly, *a*) treatment. *b*) negotiation. *c*) entreaty. *d*) any agreement or contract. 2. *a*) a formal agreement between two or more nations, relating to peace, alliance, trade, etc. *b*) the document embodying such an agreement.

treaty port, a port that must be kept open for foreign trade according to the terms of a treaty, as, formerly, any of certain ports in China.

Treb·bia (treb′byä), *n.* a river in northwestern Italy, flowing into the Po: length, 71 mi.: scene of a victory by Hannibal over the Romans (218 B.C.).

Treb·i·zond (treb′i-zond′), *n.* 1. a medieval empire around the Black Sea and in the Caucasus. 2. a seaport of Turkey on the Black Sea: pop., 33,000: now called *Trabzon.*

tre·ble (treb′'l), *adj.* [ME.; OFr.; L. *triplus,* threefold < *tres,* three + *plexus,* fold], 1. threefold; triple. 2. *a*) of or for the highest part in musical harmony. *b*) playing or singing this part. 3. high-pitched; shrill. *n.* 1. the highest part in musical harmony; soprano. 2. a singer or instrument that takes this part. 3. a high-pitched or shrill voice or sound. *v.t. & v.i.* [TREBLED (-'ld), TREBLING], to make or become threefold.

treble clef, in *music,* 1. a sign on a staff (𝄞), indicating that the notes on the staff are above middle C. 2. the range so indicated. Also called *G clef,* and distinguished from *F,* or *bass, clef.*

Treb·link·a (treb-lēŋ′kä), *n.* a Nazi concentration camp and extermination center northeast of Warsaw, Poland.

tre·bly (treb′li), *adv.* [TREBLIER (-li-ẽr), TREBLIEST (-li-ist)], three times; triply.

treb·u·chet (treb′yoo-shet′), *n.* [ME. & OFr. < *trebucher*, to stumble < *tre-*, *tra-* (< L. *trans*, over) + *buc*, trunk, body < OS. *buk*, trunk], a medieval engine of war for hurling large stones.

tre·buck·et (trē′buk-it), *n.* a trebuchet.

‡**tre·cen·to** (tre-chen′tô), *n.* [It., lit., three hundred, short for *mil trecento*, thirteen hundred], the period of the 14th century in Italian art, literature, etc.

tree (trē), *n.* [ME. *tre*, *trew;* AS. *treow;* akin to Goth. *triu;* IE. base **derew-*, a tree; cf. DRYAD, TRAY, TROUGH], 1. a woody perennial plant with one main stem or trunk which develops many branches: most trees are over ten feet tall. 2. a treelike bush or shrub: as, a rose *tree.* 3. a wooden beam, bar, pole, post, stake, etc. 4. a gallows. 5. anything resembling a tree, as in having a stem and branches; specifically, *a*) a diagram of family descent (*family* or *genealogical tree*). *b*) in *chemistry*, a treelike formation of crystals. 6. shortened form of **boot tree, saddletree, crosstree, Christmas tree,** etc. 7. [Archaic], the cross on which Jesus was crucified. 8. [Obs.], wood. *v.t.* [TREED (trēd), TREEING], 1. to chase up a tree. 2. to place or stretch on a boot tree. 3. [Colloq.], to corner, as if chased up a tree; place in a difficult position.

up a tree, [Colloq.], in a situation without escape; in a difficult position; cornered.

Tree, Sir **Herbert Beerbohm** (trē), (born *Herbert Beerbohm*), 1853–1917; English actor and theatrical manager.

tree fern, any large, treelike fern with a woody trunk.

tree frog, 1. any of various frogs that live in trees. 2. a tree toad.

tree heath, a short European shrub with globe-shaped flowers.

tree kangaroo, any of a number of tree-dwelling kangaroos of New Guinea and northern Australia.

tree lawn, the unpaved strip of ground between a city street and its parallel sidewalk: lawns and trees are often planted here.

tree·nail (trē′nāl′, tren′'l), *n.* [ME. *trenayle* < *tre* (see TREE) in early sense "wood"], a wooden peg used to join timbers: it swells from moisture and is therefore used in shipbuilding, etc.: also **trenail, trunnel.**

tree of heaven, a fast-growing tree with smooth, brown bark, pinnate leaves, and greenish flowers; ailanthus: the stamen-bearing flowers smell bad.

tree of knowledge, in the *Bible*, the tree whose fruit Adam and Eve tasted in disobedience to God: Gen. 2, 3: also **tree of knowledge of good and evil.**

tree of life, 1. the arborvitae. 2. in the *Bible, a*) a tree in the Garden of Eden bearing fruit which, if eaten, gave everlasting life: Gen. 2:9; 3:22. *b*) a tree in the heavenly Jerusalem whose leaves are for healing the nations: Rev. 22:2.

tree surgeon, a person skilled in tree surgery.

tree surgery, treatment of damaged trees as by filling cavities, removing parts, treating fresh wounds, etc.

tree toad, any of many tree-dwelling, toadlike amphibians with small, adhesive pads on the toes: they change coloration so as to blend with their surroundings.

tree·top (trē′top′), *n.* the topmost branches of a tree.

tre·foil (trē′foil), *n.* [ME. *trifolie*, *treyfoyle*, etc.; Anglo-Fr. *trifoil;* L. *trifolium*, three-leaved plant; *tri-*, three + *folium*, a leaf], 1. any of a number of plants with leaves divided into three leaflets, as the clover. 2. any ornamental figure resembling a threefold leaf.

trefoil knot, a kind of knot: see **knot,** illus.

tre·ha·lose (trē′hə-lōs′), *n.* [< Mod. L. *trehala*, material composing the cocoons of the beetle *Larinus maculatus* (< Turk. *tīghāheh;* Per. *tīghāl*) + *-ose*: orig. obtained from *trehala*], a crystalline sugar, $C_{12}H_{22}O_{11}$, extracted from yeast, mushrooms and other fungi.

Treitsch·ke, Hein·rich von (hīn′riH fôn trich′kə), 1834–1896; German historian and writer.

trek (trek), *v.i.* [TREKKED (trekt), TREKKING], [S. Afr. D. < D. *trekken*, to draw], 1. in South Africa, to travel by ox wagon; hence, 2. to travel slowly or laboriously. *v.t.* in South Africa, to draw (a wagon): said of an ox. *n.* 1. in South Africa, a journey made by ox wagon, or one leg of it. 2. a journey or leg of a journey. 3. a migration.

trek·ker (trek′ẽr), *n.* a person who treks.

trel·lis (trel′is), *n.* [ME. *trelis;* OFr. *treliz;* LL. **trilicius* < L. *trilix*, triple-twilled < *tri-*, three + *licium*, a thread; influenced by OFr. *treille*, arbor < L. *trichila*, bower, arbor], 1. a structure of thin wooden or metal strips crossing each other in an open pattern of squares, diamonds, etc., on which vines or other creeping plants are trained; lattice. 2. a bower, archway, etc. of this. *v.t.* 1. to furnish with a trellis or trellises. 2. to train on a trellis. 3. to cross or interweave like a trellis.

trel·lis·work (trel′is-wũrk′), *n.* open network of wooden or metal strips; latticework.

trem·a·tode (trem′ə-tōd′, trē′mə-tōd′), *n.* [< Mod. L. *Trematoda*, name of the class < Gr. *trēmatōdēs*, perforated < *trēma*, *trēmatos*, a hole + *eidos*, form], any of a large group of parasitic flatworms, including the flukes. *adj.* of a trematode.

trem·ble (trem′b'l), *v.i.* [TREMBLED (-b'ld), TREMBLING], [ME. *tremlen*, *trenblen;* OFr. *trembler;* LL. *tremulare* < L. *tremulus*, trembling < *tremere*, to tremble], 1. to shake involuntarily from cold, fear, excitement, fatigue, etc.; shiver; hence, 2. to feel great fear or anxiety: as, I *tremble* for your safety. 3. to quiver, quake, totter, vibrate, etc. *n.* 1. *a*) a trembling. *b*) *sometimes pl.* a fit or state of trembling. 2. *pl.* a disease of cattle and sheep caused by eating any of various poisonous weeds and characterized by muscular tremors and a stumbling gait: communicated to man as milk sickness: cf. **milk sickness.** —*SYN.* see **shake.**

trem·bly (trem′bli), *adj.* [TREMBLIER (-bli-ẽr), TREMBLIEST (-bli-ist)], trembling; tremulous.

tre·men·dous (tri-men′dəs), *adj.* [L. *tremendus* < *tremere*, to tremble], 1. such as to make one tremble; terrifying; dreadful. 2. [Colloq.], *a*) very large; great; enormous. *b*) wonderful, amazing, extraordinary, etc. —*SYN.* see **enormous.**

trem·o·lite (trem′ə-līt′), *n.* [after *Tremola*, Switzerland, where it was found], a white or green variety of amphibole, $CaMg_3(SiO_3)_4$, a silicate of calcium and magnesium.

trem·o·lo (trem′ə-lō′), *n.* [*pl.* TREMOLOS (-lōz′)], [It. < L. *tremulus;* see TREMULOUS], in *music*, 1. a tremulous effect produced by the rapid reiteration of the same tone, as by the rapid up-and-down movement of the bow or plectrum: in singing, sometimes interchangeable with *vibrato.* 2. a device, as in an organ, for producing such a tone.

trem·or (trem′ẽr, trē′mẽr), *n.* [ME. & OFr. *tremour;* L. *tremor* < *tremere*, to tremble], 1. a trembling, shaking, or shivering. 2. a vibratory or quivering motion. 3. a nervous thrill; trembling sensation. 4. a trembling sound. 5. a state of tremulous excitement: as, she was in a *tremor* of delight all afternoon.

trem·u·lant, trem·u·lent (trem′yoo-lənt), *adj.* [L. *tremulans*, ppr. of *tremulare;* see TREMBLE], tremulous.

trem·u·lous (trem′yoo-ləs), *adj.* [L. *tremulus* < *tremere*, to tremble], 1. trembling; quivering; palpitating. 2. fearful; timid; timorous. 3. marked by or showing trembling or quivering: as, *tremulous* excitement.

tre·nail (trē′nāl′, tren′'l), *n.* a treenail.

trench (trench), *v.t.* [OFr. *trencher* (Fr. *trancher*), to cut, hack < L. *truncare*, to cut off], 1. to cut or make by cutting. 2. to cut into, cut off, cut to pieces, etc.; slice; slash; gash. 3. *a*) to cut a deep furrow or furrows in. *b*) to dig a ditch or ditches in. 4. to surround or fortify with trenches. *v.i.* 1. to cut or make a cutting; cut its way. 2. to dig a ditch or ditches, as for fortification. *n.* [ME. & OFr. *trenche* (Fr. *tranche*, a slice) < *trencher*], 1. a deep furrow. 2. a long, narrow ditch from which the earth is thrown up in front as a parapet, used in battle for cover and concealment.

trench on (or **upon**), 1. to infringe upon (another's land, rights, time, etc.). 2. to come close to in meaning, relationship, etc.

trench·an·cy (tren′chən-si), *n.* a trenchant quality.

trench·ant (tren′chənt), *adj.* [ME. *trenchaunt;* OFr. *trenchant*, ppr. of *trencher;* see TRENCH], 1. originally, cutting; sharp. 2. keen; penetrating; incisive: as, *trenchant* words. 3. forceful; vigorous; energetic: as, a *trenchant* argument. 4. clear-cut; distinct: as, a *trenchant* pattern. —*SYN.* see **incisive.**

trench coat, a heavy, belted raincoat in a military style.

trench·er (tren′chẽr), *n.* [ME. *trenchere;* OFr. *trencheor* < *trencher;* see TRENCH], 1. *a*) a wooden board or platter on which meat was formerly carved or served. *b*) any platter. 2. [Archaic], *a*) food served on a trencher. *b*) a supply of food. 3. [Obs.], a slice of bread used as a plate or platter. 4. [Obs.], a knife.

trench·er (tren′chẽr), *n.* a person who trenches; specifically, *a*) a person who digs trenches or ditches. *b*) [Obs.], a person who carves at table.

trench·er·man (tren′chẽr-mən), *n.* [*pl.* TRENCHERMEN (-mən)], 1. an eater; especially, a heavy eater; person with a hearty appetite. 2. a person who frequents a patron's table; sponger; parasite; hanger-on.

trench fever, an infectious, probably rickettsial, disease transmitted by body lice and characterized by a remittent fever, muscular pains, etc.: it affected troops in the trenches in World War I.

trench foot, a diseased condition of the feet resulting from prolonged exposure to wet and cold and the circulatory disorders caused by inaction, as of soldiers in trenches.

trench knife, a double-edged military knife or dagger, for hand-to-hand combat.

trench mortar (or **gun**), any of various portable mortars or guns for shooting projectiles at a high trajectory, used especially in trench warfare: abbreviated **T.M.:** see **mortar.**

trench mouth, an infectious disease of the mucous membranes of the mouth and throat, caused by a spirochete and commonly affecting troops in trenches: also called *Vincent's angina.*

trend (trend), *v.i.* [ME. *trenden*, to roll; AS. *trendan*, to turn, roll; akin to AS. *trinde*, round lump; IE. base **der-*, to split off (cf. TEAR); basic sense "to split off a piece of a tree trunk as a disk or wheel"], 1. to extend, turn, incline, bend, etc. in a specific direction; tend; run: as, the river *trends* northward. 2. to have a general tendency: said of events, discussions, opinions, etc. *n.* 1. the general direction of a coast, river, road, etc. 2. the general tendency or course, as of events, a discussion, etc.; drift. —*SYN.* see **tendency.**

Treng·ga·nu (treŋ-gä′no͞o), *n.* a state of the Federation of Malaya: area, 5,050 sq. mi.; pop., 278,000; capital, Kuala Trengganu.

Trent (trent), *n.* 1. a city in northern Italy: pop., 75,000: ancient name, *Tridentum;* Italian name, *Trento.* 2. a river in central England, flowing northward to the River Humber: length, 170 mi.

Trent, Council of, the council of the Roman Catholic Church held intermittently at Trent, Italy, 1545–1563: it condemned the Reformation, undertook Catholic reform, and defined Catholic doctrines.

‡trente et qua·rante (trän′tā′kȧ′ränt′), [Fr., lit., thirty and forty], a gambling game in which cards are dealt and added up for each of the two colors, red and black, on which bets have been laid: the winners are those who have bet on that color for which the total of points is closest to thirty but not more than forty: also called *rouge et noir.*

Tren·ti·no-Al·to A·di·ge (tren-tē′nô-äl′tô ä′dē-je), a region of northern Italy, a part of the Tyrol.

Tren·to (tren′tô), *n.* Trent: the Italian name.

Tren·ton (tren′tən), *n.* the capital of New Jersey, on the Delaware River: pop., 114,000.

tre·pan (tri-pan′), *n.* [ME. *trepane;* ML. *trepanum* < Gr. *trypanon*, carpenters' tool, auger, trepan < *trypan*, to bore], 1. an obsolete form of the trephine. 2. a heavy boring tool for sinking shafts, quarrying, etc. *v.t.* [TREPANNED (-pand′), TREPANNING], 1. to trephine. 2. to cut a disk out of (a metal plate, ingot, etc.).

tre·pan (tri-pan′), *n.* [older *trapan;* prob. < *trap*, but influenced by fig. use of prec.], 1. a person or thing that tricks, traps, or ensnares. 2. a trick; stratagem; trap. *v.t.* [TREPANNED (-pand′), TREPANNING], to trick; trap; ensnare; lure. Also **trapan.**

trep·a·na·tion (trep′ə-nā′shən), *n.* [Fr. *trépanation*], a trepanning or being trepanned.

tre·pang (tri-paŋ′), *n.* [Malay *trīpang*], any of a number of sea cucumbers found near Australia and in the Malay Archipelago: they are boiled, dried, and smoked, and used in China for making soup.

tre·pan·ner (tri-pan′ẽr), *n.* a person who trepans.

tre·phine (tri-fīn′, tri-fēn′), *n.* [earlier *trafine*, formed after *trepan* < L. *tres*, three + *fines*, ends], a type of small crown saw used in surgery to remove circular discs of bone from the skull. *v.t.* [TREPHINED (-fīnd′, -fēnd′), TREPHINING], to operate on with a trephine.

trep·i·da·tion (trep′ə-dā′shən), *n.* [L. *trepidatio* < *trepidatus*, pp. of *trepidare*, to tremble < *trepidus*, disturbed, alarmed], 1. tremulous or trembling movement; quaking; tremor. 2. fear; alarm; dread.

trep·o·ne·ma (trep′ə-nē′mə), *n.* [Mod. L. < Gr. *trepein*, to turn + *nēma*, a thread], any of a group of spirochetes, including the causative agent of syphilis.

tres·pass (tres′pəs, tres′pas′), *v.i.* [ME. *trespassen;* OFr. *trespasser;* ML. *transpassare*, to pass across; L. *trans-*, over, across + *passare*, to pass; cf. TRAIPSE], 1. to go beyond the limits of what is considered right or moral; commit a transgression; transgress; offend; sin. 2. to go on another's land or property unlawfully. 3. to intrude; encroach: as, he is always *trespassing* on my time. 4. in *law*, to commit a trespass. *n.* [ME. & OFr. *trespas* < the *v.*], a trespassing; specifically, *a)* an offense; sin; transgression. *b)* an encroachment; intrusion. *c)* in *law*, an illegal act done with violence against another's person, rights, or property; also, legal action for damages resulting from this.

SYN.—**trespass** implies an unlawful or unwarranted entrance upon the property, rights, etc. of another (to *trespass* on a private beach); to **encroach** is to make such inroads by stealth or gradual advances (squatters *encroaching* on his lands); **infringe** implies an encroachment that breaks a law or agreement or violates the rights of others (to *infringe* on a patent); **intrude** implies a thrusting oneself into company, situations, etc. without being asked or wanted (to *intrude* on one's privacy); **invade** implies a forcible or hostile entrance into the territory or rights of others (to *invade* a neighboring state).

tres·pass·er (tres′pəs-ẽr, tres′pas′ẽr), *n.* a person who trespasses, especially by going upon another's land.

tress (tres), *n.* [ME. *tresse;* OFr. *tresce* (Fr. *tresse*); LL. *tricia;* prob. < Frank. **thrēhja*, twisted object; IE. base **trek-*, to twist], 1. originally, a braid or plait of hair, etc. 2. a lock or curl of human hair. 3. *pl.* a woman's or girl's hair, especially when long and hanging loosely.

-tress (tris), see **-ess.**

tressed (trest), *adj.* arranged in or having tresses.

tres·sure (tresh′ẽr), *n.* [OFr. *tressure, tresseor* < *tresce;* see TRESS], a narrow band following the contour of and somewhat inside the edge of a coat of arms, often ornamented with fleurs-de-lis.

tres·sy (tres′i), *adj.* [TRESSIER (-i-ẽr), TRESSIEST (-i-ist)], like or adorned with tresses.

tres·tle (tres″l), *n.* [ME. & OFr. *trestel;* LL. **transtellum*, dim. of L. *transtrum*, a beam; cf. TRANSOM], 1. a frame consisting of a horizontal beam fastened to two pairs of spreading legs, used to support planks to form a table, etc. 2. a framework of vertical or slanting uprights and crosspieces, supporting a bridge, etc.

TRESTLE (bridge)

TRESTLE (frame)

tres·tle·tree (tres′'l-trē′), *n.* either of two horizontal fore-and-aft beams, one on each side of a mast, that support the crosstrees, top, and fid of the mast above.

tres·tle·work (tres″l-wũrk′), *n.* 1. a trestle or system of trestles for supporting a bridge, etc. 2. a bridge or other structure supported by trestles.

tret (tret), *n.* [Anglo-Fr. (Fr. *trait*), a pull (of the scale) < OFr. *traire* (< L. *trahere*), to draw], an allowance formerly made to buyers of certain goods for waste, damage, or deterioration during transit; specifically, an allowance of 4 lbs. in every 104 lbs. by weight after the deduction for tare.

Tre·vel·yan, George Macaulay (tri-vel′yən), 1876–1962; son of *George Otto;* English historian.

Trevelyan, Sir **George Otto,** 1838–1928; English historian, biographer, and statesman.

Trèves, Treves (trev; Eng. trēvz), *n.* Trier.

trews (tro͞oz), *n.pl.* [Ir. *trius* < Ir. & Gael. *triubhas*], [Scot.], close-fitting tartan trousers.

trey (trā), *n.* [ME. *treie;* OFr. *trei, treis;* L. *tres*, three], 1. a throw or play of three at dice, dominoes, or cards. 2. a die, domino, or playing card with three spots.

tri- (trī, tri), [< Fr., L., or Gr.; Fr. *tri-* < L. *tri-* (< *tres*, three) or Gr. *tri-* (< *treis*, three, *tris*, thrice); cf. THREE], a combining form meaning: 1. *of three, having three parts*, etc., as in *triplane.* 2. *three times, into three*, as in *trisect.* 3. *every three, every third*, as in *triannual.* 4. in *chemistry, having three atoms, groups, or equivalents of* (the thing specified), as in *tribasic.*

tri·a·ble (trī′ə-b'l), *adj.* 1. that can be tried or tested. 2. subject to trial in a law court.

tri·ac·id (trī-as′id), *adj.* 1. capable of reacting with three molecules of a monobasic acid: said of a base. 2. containing three replaceable hydrogen atoms: said of an acid or acid salt.

tri·ad (trī′ad), *n.* [Fr. *triade;* L. *trias, triadis;* Gr. *trias, triados* < *treis;* see TRI-], 1. a group of three persons, things, ideas, etc.; trinity. 2. a musical chord of three tones, especially one consisting of a root tone and its third and fifth: a triad with a major third and perfect fifth is called a *major triad;* a triad with a minor third and perfect fifth is called a *minor triad.*

tri·al (trī′əl, trīl), *n.* [Anglo-Fr. < *trier;* see TRY], 1. *a)* the act or process of trying, testing, or putting to the proof; test. *b)* a testing of qualifications, attainments, or progress; probation. *c)* experimental treatment or operation; an experiment. 2. a being tried by suffering, temptation, etc.; hence, 3. a hardship, pain, etc. that tries one's endurance. 4. a source of annoyance or irritation: as, his son is a great *trial.* 5. a formal examination of the facts of a case by a court of law to decide the validity of a charge or claim. 6. an attempt; endeavor; effort. *adj.* 1. of a trial or trials. 2. made, done, or used for the purpose of trying, testing, or putting to the proof.

SYN.—**trial** implies the trying of a person or thing in order to establish his or its worth in actual performance (hired on *trial*); **experiment** implies a showing by trial whether a thing will be effective (the honor system was instituted as an *experiment*) and, in addition, is used of any action or process undertaken to discover something not yet known or to demonstrate something known (*experiments* in nuclear physics); **test** implies a putting of a thing to decisive proof by thorough examination or trial under controlled conditions and with fixed standards in mind (a *test* of a new jet plane). See also **affliction.**

trial and error, the process of making repeated trials, experiments, tests, etc. to find a desired result or solution.

trial balance, a statement of the debit and credit

balances of all open accounts in a double-entry bookkeeping ledger to test their equality: abbreviated **t.b.**

trial balloon, 1. a balloon equipped with instruments for testing air currents, wind velocities, etc.; hence, 2. any action, statement, etc. intended to test public opinion on an issue or pending project.

trial jury, a jury of twelve persons impaneled to decide a court case; petit jury: distinguished from *grand jury.*

tri·an·gle (trī'aŋ'g'l), *n.* [ME.; OFr.; L. *triangulum;* see TRI- & ANGLE], 1. a geometrical figure having three angles and three sides. 2. any three-sided or three-cornered figure, area, object, part, etc. 3. a right-angled, flat, triangular instrument used in drafting. 4. *a*) a group of three involved in some situation, as one in which two men are in love with the same woman. *b*) such a situation. 5. a musical percussion instrument consisting of a steel rod bent in a triangle with one angle open: it produces a high-pitched, tinkling sound.

tri·an·gu·lar (trī-aŋ'gyoo-lẽr), *adj.* [LL. *triangularis*], 1. of or shaped like a triangle; three-cornered. 2. of or involving three persons, factions, things, or parts. 3. having bases that are triangles, as a prism.

tri·an·gu·lar·i·ty (trī'aŋ-gyoo-lar'ə-ti, trī-aŋ'gyoo-lar'ə-ti), *n.* the quality or state of being triangular.

tri·an·gu·lar·ly (trī-aŋ'gyoo-lẽr-li), *adv.* in the shape of a triangle.

tri·an·gu·late (trī-aŋ'gyoo-lāt'; *for adj., usually* trī-aŋ'gyoo-lit), *v.t.* [TRIANGULATED (-id), TRIANGULATING], [< L. *triangulum* (see TRIANGLE); + *-ate*], 1. to divide into triangles. 2. to survey or map (a region) by dividing into triangles and measuring their angles. 3. to make triangular. 4. to measure by trigonometry. *adj.* 1. of triangles; triangular. 2. marked with triangles.

tri·an·gu·la·tion (trī-aŋ'gyoo-lā'shən), *n.* 1. the act or process of triangulating, especially in surveying. 2. the triangles marked out in this process.

Tri·an·gu·lum (trī-aŋ'gyoo-ləm), *n.* [L., triangle], a small northern constellation: see **constellation,** chart: also **Triangulum Minor.**

Triangulum Aus·tra·le (ôs-trā'lē), [L., southern triangle], a southern constellation: see **constellation,** chart.

tri·arch·y (trī'är-ki), *n.* [*pl.* TRIARCHIES (-kiz)], [Gr. *triarchia;* see TRI- & -ARCHY], 1. government by three rulers; a triumvirate. 2. a country governed by three rulers.

Tri·as (trī'əs), *n.* [LL.; see TRIAD: so called because divisible into three groups], the series of geological strata lying immediately below the Jurassic.

Tri·as·sic (trī-as'ik), *adj.* designating or of the first period of the Mesozoic Era, characterized by the dominance of reptiles and the appearance of cycadaceous trees.

the Triassic, the Triassic Period or its rocks: see **geology,** chart.

tri·at·ic stay (trī-at'ik), in *nautical usage,* a rope, secured to the heads of the foremast and mainmast, to which hoisting tackles can be attached.

tri·a·tom·ic (trī'ə-tom'ik), *adj.* designating or of: *a*) a molecule consisting of three atoms. *b*) a molecule containing three replaceable atoms or groups.

tri·ax·i·al (trī-ak'si-əl), *adj.* having three axes.

tri·a·zin (trī'ə-zin, trī-az'in), *n.* triazine.

tri·a·zine (trī'ə-zēn', trī'ə-zin, trī-az'ēn, trī-az'in), *n.* [*tri-* + *azine*], 1. any of three isomeric heterocyclic compounds having the formula $C_3H_3N_3$. 2. any derivative of these.

tri·a·zo·ic (trī'ə-zō'ik), *adj.* hydrazoic.

tri·a·zole (trī'ə-zōl', trī-az'ōl), *n.* [*tri-* + *azole*], any of four isomeric heterocyclic compounds having the formula $C_2H_3N_3$.

trib·al (trī'b'l), *adj.* of or characteristic of a tribe or tribes.

trib·al·ism (trī'b'l-iz'm), *n.* tribal organization, culture, loyalty, etc.

trib·al·ly (trī'b'l-i), *adv.* by or in a tribe or tribes.

tri·bas·ic (trī-bā'sik), *adj.* [*tri-* + *basic*], 1. containing in its molecule three atoms of hydrogen that are replaceable by basic atoms or radicals. 2. producing three hydrogen ions per molecule in solution. Said of an acid.

tribe (trīb), *n.* [ME. *trybe, tribu;* L. *tribus,* one of the three groups into which the Romans were originally divided, tribe < *tres, tria,* three + orig. form of base in L. *fu-,* to become (cf. FUTURE)], 1. a group of persons, families, or clans descended from a common ancestor and forming, together with their slaves, adopted strangers, etc., a community. 2. a group of this kind having recognized ancestry; specifically, *a*) any of the three divisions of the ancient Romans, traditionally of Latin, Sabine, and Etruscan origin. *b*) any of the later political and territorial divisions of the ancient Romans, originally thirty and subsequently thirty-five in number. *c*) any of the phylae of ancient Greece. *d*) any of the twelve divisions of the ancient Israelites. 3. any primitive or nomadic group of people of generally common ancestry, possessing common leadership. 4. any group of people having the same occupation, habits, ideas, etc.: chiefly in a derogatory sense, as, the *tribe* of daubers. 5. a subdivision of an order or suborder of animals or plants; hence, 6. any group, class, or kind of animals, plants, etc. 7. in stock breeding, the animals descended from the same female through the female line. 8. a number or company of persons or animals. 9. a family: a humorous or derogatory usage.

tribes·man (trībz'mən), *n.* [*pl.* TRIBESMEN (-mən)], a member of a tribe.

tri·brach (trī'brak, trib'rak), *n.* [L. *tribrachys;* Gr. *tribrachys; tri-* (see TRI-) + *brachys,* short], a metrical foot consisting of three short syllables, two belonging to the thesis and one to the arsis.

tri·bro·mo·eth·a·nol (trī-brō'mō-eth'ə-nōl', trī-brō'mō-eth'ə-nol), *n.* [< *tri-* + *bromine* + *ethanol*], a colorless, crystalline bromine derivative of ethyl alcohol, CBr_3CH_2OH, used as a general anesthetic.

trib·u·la·tion (trib'yoo-lā'shən), *n.* [ME. & OFr. *tribulacion;* LL. *tribulatio* < pp. of L. *tribulare,* to thrash, beat < *tribulum,* threshing sledge], 1. great misery or distress, as from oppression; deep sorrow. 2. something that causes suffering or distress; an affliction; trial. —*SYN.* see **affliction.**

tri·bu·nal (tri-bū'n'l, trī-bū'n'l), *n.* [L. < *tribunus;* see TRIBUNE], 1. a seat or bench upon which a judge or judges sit in a court. 2. a court of justice; hence, 3. any real or imagined seat of judgment: as, the *tribunal* of popular sentiment.

trib·u·nate (trib'yoo-nit, trib'yoo-nāt'), *n.* [Fr. *tribunat;* L. *tribunatus*], 1. the rank, office, or authority of a tribune. 2. a group of tribunes.

trib·une (trib'ūn; *in names of newspapers, often* tri-būn'), *n.* [L. *tribunus,* a tribune, magistrate, lit., chief of a tribe < *tribus,* Roman tribal division; see TRIBE], 1. any of several ancient Roman magistrates, especially one appointed to protect the interests and rights of plebeians against violation by patricians; hence, 2. a champion of the people. 3. any of the six officers of an ancient Roman legion who rotated command over a period of a year.

trib·une (trib'ūn), *n.* [Fr.; It. *tribuna* < L. *tribunal;* see TRIBUNAL], a raised platform or dais for speakers.

trib·une·ship (trib'ūn-ship'), *n.* [see -SHIP], the rank, office, or term of office of a tribune.

trib·u·ni·tial, trib·u·ni·cial (trib'yoo-nish'əl), *adj.* of or suitable to a tribune.

trib·u·tar·i·ly (trib'yoo-ter'ə-li), *adv.* as a tributary or tributaries.

trib·u·tar·y (trib'yoo-ter'i), *adj.* [Late ME. *tributori;* L. *tributarius*], 1. paying tribute; hence, 2. subject: as, a *tributary* nation. 3. in the nature of tribute; owed or paid as tribute. 4. making additions or furnishing supplies; subsidiary; contributory: as, *tributary* streams. *n.* [*pl.* TRIBUTARIES (-iz)], 1. a tributary nation. 2. a stream or river that flows into a larger one. Abbreviated **trib.**

trib·ute (trib'ūt), *n.* [ME. & OFr. *tribut;* L. *tributum,* neut. of *tributus,* pp. of *tribuere,* to assign, allot, pay < *tribus,* Roman tribal division; see TRIBE], 1. money paid regularly by one ruler or nation to another as acknowledgment of subjugation, for protection from invasion, etc. 2. a tax levied for this. 3. under feudalism, a tax paid by a vassal to his overlord. 4. the obligation to make such a payment. 5. any forced payment, as through bribery. 6. a gift, statement, testimonial, etc. that shows gratitude, respect, or honor; hence, 7. praise; laudation.

SYN.—**tribute,** the broadest in scope of these words, is used of praise manifested by any act, situation, etc. as well as that expressed in speech or writing (their success was a *tribute* to his leadership); **encomium** suggests an enthusiastic, sometimes high-flown expression of praise (*encomiums* lavished on party leaders at a convention); **eulogy** generally applies to a formal speech or writing in exalting praise, especially of a person who has just died; **panegyric** suggests superlative or elaborate praise expressed in poetic or lofty language (Cicero's *panegyric* upon Cato).

trice (trīs), *v.t.* [TRICED (trīst), TRICING], [ME. *trisen* < MD. *trisen,* to pull, hoist < *trise,* windlass, roller], to haul up (a sail, etc.) and secure with a small line (usually with *up*). *n.* [< the *v.*], 1. originally, one pull or effort: in *at a trice;* hence, 2. a very short time; instant; moment: now only in *in a trice.*

tri·cen·ten·ni·al (trī'sen-ten'i-əl), *adj.* & *n.* tercentenary.

tri·ceps (trī'seps), *n.* [*pl.* TRICEPSES (-sep-siz)], [Mod. L. < L., triple-headed < *tri-,* three + *caput,* a head], a muscle having three heads, or points of origin; especially, the large muscle at the back of the upper arm that extends the forearm when contracted.

tri·chi·a·sis (tri-kī'ə-sis), *n.* [Mod. L.; Gr. *trichiasis* < *thrix, trichos,* hair], in *medicine,* 1. an abnormal condition in which hairs, especially the eyelashes, grow inward. 2. the appearance of hairlike structures in the urine.

tri·chi·na (tri-kī'nə), *n.* [*pl.* TRICHINAE (-nē)], [Mod. L. < Gr. *trichinos,* hairy < *thrix, trichos,* hair], a very small worm whose larvae infest the intestines and voluntary muscles of man, causing trichinosis.

trich·i·nized (trik'ə-nīzd'), *adj.* infected with trichinae.

Trich·i·nop·o·ly (trich'i-nop'ə-li), *n.* a city in Madras state, India: pop., 159,000.

trich·i·nosed (trik'ə-nōzd'), *adj.* trichinous.

trich·i·no·sis (trik'ə-nō'sis), *n.* [Mod. L.; see TRICHINA & -OSIS], a disease caused by the presence of trichinae in the intestines and muscle tissues and usually acquired by eating insufficiently cooked pork from an infected hog: it is characterized by fever, nausea, diarrhea, and muscular pains.

trich·i·nous (trik'ə-nəs), *adj.* 1. infected with trichinae; trichinized. 2. of or having trichinosis.

trich·ite (trik'īt), *n.* [< Gr. *thrix, trichos,* hair; + *-ite*], a hairlike crystallite found in vitreous igneous rocks.

tri·chlor·id (trī-klôr'id, trī-klō'rid), *n.* trichloride.

tri·chlo·ride (trī-klôr'īd, trī-klō'rid), *n.* a chloride having three chlorine atoms to the molecule.

tri·chlo·ro·phe·nox·y·a·ce·tic acid (trī-klôr'ə-fi-nok'-si-ə-sē'tik), [*tri-* + *chloro-* + *phenoxy* + *acetic*], a trichloride derivative of phenoxy acetic acid, $Cl_3C_6H_2O$-CH_2·COOH, used as a weed killer.

trich·o- (trik'ō, trī'kə), [Gr. *tricho-* < *thrix, trichos,* hair], a combining form meaning *hair,* as in *trichosis.*

trich·o·cyst (trik'ə-sist'), *n.* [*tricho-* + *-cyst*], any of many tiny stinging organs on the body of some infusorians.

trich·o·gyne (trik'ə-jin, trik'ə-jīn'), *n.* [*tricho-* + Gr. *gynē,* woman, female], the long, hairlike part of a procarp in red algae, acting as a receptor for the male fertilizing bodies.

tri·choid (trik'oid), *adj.* hairlike.

tri·cho·ma (tri-kō'mə), *n.* [Gr. *trichōma,* growth of hair < *trichoun,* to cover with hair < *thrix, trichos,* hair], 1. introversion of the edge of the eyelid or of any similar structure. 2. a matted and crusted condition of the hair. 3. any of the threadlike structures, or filaments, of certain algae.

tri·chome (trī'kōm, trik'ōm), *n.* [see TRICHOMA], 1. any hairlike outgrowth on a plant, as a bristle, prickle, root hair, etc. 2. a trichoma (sense 3).

tri·chom·ic (tri-kom'ik), *adj.* having the nature of a trichome or trichoma.

trich·o·mon·ad (trik'ō-mon'ad), *n.* [*tricho-* + *monad*], any flagellated protozoan of a group parasitic in man and lower animals.

tri·chord (trī'kôrd'), *n.* [< Gr. *trichordos,* of three strings < *tri-,* three + *chordē,* a string], a musical instrument having three strings, as some lyres.

tri·cho·sis (tri-kō'sis), *n.* [Mod. L.; *trich-* + *-osis*], any disease of the hair.

trich·o·tom·ic (trik'ə-tom'ik), *adj.* involving trichotomy; divided into three parts.

tri·chot·o·mous (trī-kot'ə-məs), *adj.* of or involving trichotomy; trichotomic.

tri·chot·o·my (trī-kot'ə-mi), *n.* [Gr. *tricha,* threefold; + *-tomy*], division into three parts; specifically, the theological division of human nature into body, soul, and spirit.

tri·chro·ic (trī-krō'ik), *adj.* 1. having or showing three colors. 2. exhibiting trichroism.

tri·chro·ism (trī'krō-iz'm), *n.* [< Gr. *trichroos,* of three colors < *tri-,* three + *chroia,* color], the property that some crystals have of transmitting light of three different colors in three different directions.

tri·chro·mat·ic (trī'krō-mat'ik), *adj.* [*tri-* + *chromatic*], of, having, or using three colors, as in the three-color process in printing and photography.

tri·chro·ma·tism (trī-krō'mə-tiz'm), *n.* 1. the condition of being trichromatic. 2. the use or combination of three colors. 3. trichroism.

tri·chro·mic (trī-krō'mik), *adj.* trichromatic.

trick (trik), *n.* [ONorm.Fr. *trique* < *trikier;* OFr. *trichier,* to trick, cheat (cf. TREACHERY); some senses influenced by D. *trek,* a pull, *trekken,* to draw, pull (cf. TREK)], 1. an action or device designed to deceive, swindle, etc.; artifice; dodge; ruse; stratagem; deception. 2. a practical joke; mischievous or playful act; prank. 3. a freakish, foolish, mean, or stupid act. 4. *a)* a clever or difficult act intended to amuse; especially, an act of jugglery or sleight of hand; also, an illusion of the kind created by legerdemain. *b)* any feat requiring skill. 5. the art, method, or process of doing something successfully or of getting a result quickly; knack: as, the *trick* of making good pastry. 6. an expedient or convention of an art, craft, or trade: as, he learned the *tricks* of the trade: often used in an unfavorable sense. 7. a personal mannerism: as, a *trick* of stroking his nose. 8. a turn or round of duty. 9. [Colloq.], any child, girl, etc. regarded playfully. 10. in *card games,* the cards played and won in a single round. *v.t.* to deceive, swindle, or cheat. *adj.* 1. having to do with a trick or tricks. 2. that tricks.

do (or **turn**) **the trick,** to bring about the desired result.

trick out (or **up**), to dress up; deck; adorn; array.

SYN.—**trick** is the common word for an action or device in which ingenuity and cunning are used to outwit others and implies deception either for fraudulent purposes or as a prank, etc.; **ruse** applies to that which is contrived as a blind for one's real intentions or for the truth (her apparent illness was merely a *ruse*); a **stratagem** is a more or less complicated ruse, by means of which one attempts to outwit or entrap an enemy or antagonist (military *stratagems*); **maneuver,** specifically applicable to military tactics, in general use suggests the shrewd manipulation of persons or situations to suit one's purposes (a political *maneuver*); **artifice** stresses inventiveness or ingenuity in the contrivance of an expedient, trick, etc. (*artifices* employed to circumvent the tax laws); **wile** implies the use of allurements or beguilement to ensnare (womanly *wiles*). See also **cheat.**

trick·er·y (trik'ēr-i), *n.* [*pl.* TRICKERIES (-iz)], the act or practice of tricking; use of tricks; deception; fraud. —*SYN.* see **deception.**

trick·i·ly (trik''l-i), *adv.* in a tricky manner.

trick·i·ness (trik'i-nis), *n.* the quality or condition of being tricky.

trick·ish (trik'ish), *adj.* 1. given to trickery; deceitful. 2. characterized by or full of tricks.

trick·le (trik''l), *v.i.* [TRICKLED (-'ld), TRICKLING], [ME. *triklen;* prob. < *striklen,* freq. of *striken,* to strike; see STRIKE], 1. to flow slowly in a thin stream or fall in drops. 2. to move, enter, etc. slowly or little by little: as, the crowd began to *trickle* away. *v.t.* to cause to trickle. *n.* 1. a trickling. 2. a slow flow or thin stream; drip.

trick·si·ness (trik'si-nis), *n.* the condition or quality of being tricksy.

trick·ster (trik'stēr), *n.* a person who tricks; cheat.

trick·sy (trik'si), *adj.* [TRICKSIER (-si-ēr), TRICKSIEST (-si-ist)], 1. tricked out; spruce; smart. 2. full of tricks; playful; mischievous. 3. tricky.

trick·track (trik'trak'), *n.* [Fr. *trictrac*], backgammon, especially a variety using both pegs and pieces.

trick·y (trik'i), *adj.* [TRICKIER (-i-ēr), TRICKIEST (-i-ist)], 1. given to or characterized by trickery; deceitful. 2. like a trick in deceptiveness; intricate; catchy. —*SYN.* see **sly.**

tri·clin·ic (trī-klin'ik), *adj.* [< *tri-* + Gr. *klinein,* to incline; + *-ic*], having three unequal axes intersecting at oblique angles: said of some crystals.

tri·clin·i·um (trī-klin'i-əm), *n.* [*pl.* TRICLINIA (-ə)], [L. < Gr. *triklinion,* dim. of *triklinos* < *tri-,* three (see TRI-) + *klinē,* a couch], 1. a couch extending around three sides of an ancient Roman dining table, for reclining at meals. 2. an ancient Roman dining room, especially one containing such a couch.

tri·col·or (trī'kul'ēr), *n.* [Fr. *tricolore;* LL. *tricolor;* see TRI- & COLOR], a flag having three colors in large areas; especially, the flag of France, which has three broad, vertical stripes of blue, white, and red, respectively, from the hoist out. *adj.* having three colors.

tri·corn (trī'kôrn), *adj.* [Fr. *tricorne;* L. *tricornis* < *tri-* + *cornu,* horn], having three horns or corners, as a hat with the brim folded up against the crown so as to form three sides. *n.* a tricorn hat.

tri·cos·tate (trī-kos'tāt), *adj.* [< *tri-* + L. *costa,* a rib; + *-ate*], in *botany* & *zoology,* having three ribs or riblike parts.

tri·cot (trē'kō; Fr. trē'kō'), *n.* [Fr. < *tricoter,* to knit; OFr. **estricoter* < LG. *striken,* to make movements; akin to Eng. *strike*], 1. a woolen, silk, cotton, rayon, or nylon cloth, knitted, or woven so as to resemble knitting. 2. a type of ribbed cloth for dresses.

tric·o·tine (trik'ə-tēn'), *n.* [Fr.; see TRICOT & -INE], a woolen cloth resembling twill.

tri·crot·ic (trī-krot'ik), *adj.* [< *tri-* + Gr. *krotein,* to beat; + *-ic*], designating or of a pulse having three separate rhythmic waves to each beat.

tri·cro·tism (trī'krə-tiz'm, trik'rə-tiz'm), *n.* the quality or condition of being tricrotic.

tric·trac, tric-trac (trik'trak'), *n.* tricktrack.

tri·cus·pid (trī-kus'pid), *adj.* [L. *tricuspis, tricuspidis*], 1. having three cusps, or points: as, a *tricuspid* tooth. 2. designating or of a valve with three flaps, between the right auricle and right ventricle of the heart. *n.* the tricuspid valve.

tri·cus·pi·date (trī-kus'pi-dāt'), *adj.* having three cusps; three-pointed.

tri·cy·cle (trī'si-k'l), *n.* [Fr.; see TRI- & CYCLE], 1. a light, three-wheeled vehicle operated by pedals or, rarely, hand levers; especially, such a vehicle for children. 2. a three-wheeled motorcycle.

tri·cy·clic (trī-sī'klik, trī-sik'lik), *adj.* of or having three cycles.

tri·dent (trī'd'nt), *n.* [L. *tridens, tridentis; tri-,* three + *dens, dentis,* a tooth], 1. a three-pronged spear used by the retiarius in ancient Roman gladiatorial combats. 2. a three-pronged fish spear. 3. in *Greek & Roman mythology,* a three-pronged spear borne as a scepter by the sea god Poseidon, or Neptune. *adj.* three-pronged.

tri·den·tate (trī-den′tāt), *adj.* [Mod. L. *tridentatus;* see TRIDENT], having three teeth, prongs or points.
tri·den·tat·ed (trī-den′tā-tid), *adj.* tridentate.
Tri·den·tine (trī-den′tin, tri-den′tīn), *adj.* [ML. *Tridentinus* < *Tridentum,* Trent], 1. of Trent, Italy. 2. of the Council of Trent, or in accord with its decrees.
Tri·den·tum (trī-den′təm), *n.* Trent, Italy: the ancient name.
tri·di·men·sion·al (trī′də-men′shən-′l), *adj.* of or having three dimensions; having depth or thickness as well as length and width.
tri·e·cious (trī-ē′shəs), *adj.* trioecious.
tried (trīd), past tense and past participle of **try.** *adj.* 1. tested; proved; hence, 2. trustworthy; faithful.
tri·en·ni·al (trī-en′i-əl), *adj.* [< L. *triennium,* three years < *tri-,* three + *annus,* a year], 1. happening every three years. 2. lasting three years. *n.* 1. an event that takes place every three years. 2. a third anniversary.
tri·en·ni·al·ly (trī-en′i-əl-i), *adv.* every three years.
Trier (trêr), *n.* a city in the Rhineland, Germany, on the Moselle River: pop., 64,000 (est. 1947): French name, *Trèves.*
tri·er (trī′ẽr), *n.* a person or thing that tries.
tri·er·arch (trī′ẽr-ärk′), *n.* [L. *trierarchus;* Gr. *triērarchos* < *triērēs,* a trireme + *archos,* leader, chief], in ancient Greece, 1. the commander of a trireme. 2. at Athens, a person who built, outfitted, and maintained a trireme for the service of the state.
tri·er·arch·y (trī′ẽr-är′ki), *n.* [*pl.* TRIERARCHIES (-kiz)], [Gr. *triērarchia*], 1. the rank, authority, or duties of a trierarch. 2. trierarchs collectively. 3. in ancient Athens, the system by which citizens built, outfitted, and maintained triremes for the service of the state.
Tri·est (tri-est′), *n.* Trieste: the German name.
Tri·este (tri-est′; It. trē-es′te), *n.* a city on the Adriatic Sea, in northeastern Italy: pop., 271,000: an area, part of Italy (1919–1947), including this city was administered as the Free Territory of Trieste by the United Nations from 1947 to 1954, when it was divided between Italy and Yugoslavia.
tri·fa·cial (trī-fā′shəl), *adj.* & *n.* trigeminal.
tri·fid (trī′fid), *adj.* [L. *trifidus* < *tri-,* three + the base of *findere,* to divide], divided into three lobes or parts by clefts, as some leaves; tridentate.
tri·fle (trī′f′l), *n.* [ME. *trifle, trufle;* OFr. *trufle, truffle,* mockery, dim. of *truffe,* mockery, deception], 1. something of little value or importance; trivial thing, idea, etc.; paltry matter. 2. a small amount of money. 3. a small amount; a little. 4. a dessert consisting of spongecake soaked in wine and covered with macaroons, almonds, whipped cream, etc. 5. *a*) a kind of pewter. *b*) *pl.* utensils made of this. *v.i.* [TRIFLED (-f′ld), TRIFLING], 1. to talk or act jokingly, mockingly, or lightly: as, he *trifled* with my plan. 2. to play or toy (*with* something). 3. to dally; play fast and loose (*with* a person's affections, etc.). *v.t.* to spend idly; waste (usually with *away*): as, he *trifles* the hours away.
SYN.—**trifle** is the general term meaning to treat without earnestness, full attention, definite purpose, etc. (to *trifle* with a person, an idea, etc.); **flirt** implies a light, transient interest or attention that quickly moves on to another person or thing (she's always *flirting* with men); **dally** implies a playing with a subject or thing that one has little or no intention of taking seriously (to *dally* with painting); **coquet** suggests the behavior of a flirtatious woman who promiscuously seeks attention or admiration without serious intent; **toy** implies a trifling or dallying with no purpose beyond that of amusement or idling away time (to *toy* with one's food).
tri·fling (trī′fliŋ), *adj.* [ppr. of *trifle*], 1. that trifles; frivolous; shallow; fickle. 2. having little value or importance; trivial. —*SYN.* see **petty.**
tri·fo·cal (trī-fō′k′l; *also, esp. for the n.,* trī′fō′k′l), *adj.* adjusted or ground to three different focal lengths. *n.* a lens like a bifocal but with an additional narrow area ground to adjust the eye for intermediate focus (about 30 inches).
tri·fo·li·ate (trī-fō′li-it, trī-fō′li-āt′), *adj.* [*tri-* + L. *foliatus* < *folium,* a leaf], 1. having three leaves. 2. loosely, trifoliolate.
tri·fo·li·at·ed (trī-fō′li-ā′tid), *adj.* trifoliate.
tri·fo·li·o·late (trī-fō′li-ə-lāt′), *adj.* [< *tri-* + Mod. L. *foliolum,* dim. of L. *folium,* a leaf; + *-ate*], divided into three leaflets, as the leaf of a clover.
tri·fo·li·um (trī-fō′li-əm), *n.* [L., trefoil], any of a number of related plants of the pea family, the clovers, having leaflets in groups of three and small, rounded flowers of white, yellow, red, or purple.
tri·fo·ri·um (trī-fôr′i-əm, trī-fō′ri-əm), *n.* [*pl.* TRIFORIA (-ə)], [ML. < L. *tri-,* three + *foris,* door], a gallery or arcade in the wall above the arches of the nave, choir, or transept of a church.
tri·form (trī′fôrm), *adj.* [L. *triformis* < *tri-,* three + *forma,* form], having three parts, forms, natures, etc.
tri·formed (trī′fôrmd), *adj.* triform.
tri·fur·cate (trī-fũr′kit, trī-fũr′kāt), *adj.* [< L. *trifurcus* < *tri-,* three + *furca,* a fork], having three forks or branches.
tri·fur·cat·ed (trī-fũr′kā-tid), *adj.* trifurcate.
trig (trig), *adj.* [ME. *trigg;* ON. *tryggr,* trusty, firm, true; base as in *true*], 1. trim; neat; spruce. 2. in good condition; strong; sound. 3. [Rare], prim; precise. *v.t.* [TRIGGED (trigd), TRIGGING], [Dial.], to make trig (often with *out* or *up*).
trig (trig), *v.t.* [TRIGGED (trigd), TRIGGING], [prob. back-formation < dial. *trigger,* brake], 1. to prevent (a wheel, etc.) from rolling by placing a wedge, stone, etc. under it. 2. to prop or support. *n.* a stone, wedge, etc. used in trigging.
trig., 1. trigonometric. 2. trigonometry.
tri·gem·i·nal (trī-jem′ə-n′l), *adj.* [< L. *trigeminus,* born three together (*tri-,* three + *geminus,* twin); + *-al*], designating or of either of the fifth pair of cranial nerves, each of which divides into three branches supplying the head and face. *n.* a trigeminal nerve. Also called *trifacial.*
trig·ger (trig′ẽr), *n.* [earlier *tricker;* D. *trekker* < *trekken,* to draw, pull; cf. TREK, TRICK], 1. a small lever or part which when pulled or pressed releases a catch, spring, etc. 2. in firearms, a small lever which when pressed back by the finger releases the firing hammer. *v.t.* [Colloq.], to initiate (an action); set off: as, the fights *triggered* a riot.
quick on the trigger, [Colloq.], 1. quick to fire a gun; hence, 2. quick to act, understand, etc.; alert.
trig·ger·fish (trig′ẽr-fish′), *n.* [*pl.* TRIGGERFISH, TRIGGERFISHES (-iz); see FISH], [so called because depression of the second spine of the fin causes the first to snap down], any of a group of brightly colored tropical fishes having an anterior dorsal fin with two or three spines.
tri·glyph (trī′glif), *n.* [L. *triglyphus;* Gr. *triglyphos* < *tri-,* three + *glyphē,* sculpture], in a Doric frieze, a slightly projecting, rectangular block occurring at regular intervals and having two vertical grooves (*glyphs*) and two chamfers or half grooves at the sides.
tri·glyph·ic (trī-glif′ik), *adj.* of or having triglyphs.
‡**tri·go** (trē′gō), *n.* [Sp.], wheat.
tri·gon (trī′gon), *n.* [L. *trigonum;* Gr. *trigōnon,* triangle, lyre < *tri-,* three + *gōnia,* an angle], 1. a triangle. 2. an ancient, triangular lyre or harp. 3. in *astrology,* *a*) any of the four sets of three signs into which the zodiac is divided. *b*) trine.
trigon., 1. trigonometric. 2. trigonometry.
trig·o·nal (trig′ə-nəl), *adj.* [L. *trigonalis*], 1. of a triangle; triangular. 2. of a trigon.
trig·o·nom·e·ter (trig′ə-nom′ə-tẽr), *n.* an instrument for rapid solving of plane right-angled triangles.
trig·o·no·met·ric (trig′ə-nə-met′rik), *adj.* of, having to do with, or performed by trigonometry: abbreviated **trig., trigon.**
trig·o·no·met·ri·cal (trig′ə-nə-met′ri-k′l), *adj.* trigonometric.
trig·o·no·met·ri·cal·ly (trig′ə-nə-met′ri-k′l-i, trig′ə-nə-met′rik-li), *adv.* by means of or according to trigonometry.
trig·o·nom·e·try (trig′ə-nom′ə-tri), *n.* [*pl.* TRIGONOMETRIES (-triz)], [Mod. L. *trigonometria* < Gr. *trigōnon,* triangle + *-metria,* measurement], 1. the branch of mathematics that deals with the ratios between the sides of a right triangle with reference to either acute angle (*trigonometric functions*), the relations between these ratios, and the application of these facts in finding the unknown sides or angles of any triangle, as in surveying, navigation, engineering, etc. 2. a textbook on this subject. Abbreviated **trig., trigon.**
trig·o·nous (trig′ə-nəs), *adj.* [L. *trigonus;* Gr. *trigōnos* < *trigōnon;* see TRIGON], 1. having three angles; triangular. 2. three-cornered.
tri·graph (trī′graf′, trī′gräf′), *n.* [*tri-* + *-graph*], three letters representing one sound, as *eau* in *bureau.*
tri·he·dral (trī-hē′drəl), *adj.* of, or having the form of, a trihedron.
tri·he·dron (trī-hē′drən), *n.* [*pl.* TRIHEDRONS (-drənz), TRIHEDRA (-drə)], [Mod. L.; see TRI- & -HEDRON], a solid figure with three plane surfaces meeting in a point.
tri·hy·drox·y (trī′hī-drok′si), *adj.* containing three hydroxyl groups.
tri·ju·gate (trī′joo-gāt′, trī-jōō′git), *adj.* [< L. *trijugus,* threefold < *tri-,* three + *jugum,* a yoke], having three pairs of leaflets on a common stem.
tri·ju·gous (trī′joo-gəs, trī-jōō′gəs), *adj.* trijugate.
tri·lat·er·al (trī-lat′ẽr-əl), *adj.* [< L. *trilaterus,* three-sided < *tri-,* three + *latus, lateris,* a side], three-sided.
tri·lat·er·al·ly (trī-lat′ẽr-əl-i), *adv.* with three sides.
tri·lin·e·ar (trī-lin′i-ẽr), *adj.* [*tri-* + *linear*], of, enclosed by, or involving three lines.
tri·lin·gual (trī-liŋ′gwəl), *adj.* [< L. *trilinguis* < *tri-,* three + *lingua,* a tongue, language], of, using, written in, or spoken in three languages.
tri·lit·er·al (trī-lit′ẽr-əl), *adj.* [< *tri-* + L. *litera,* a letter; + *-al*], consisting of three letters. *n.* a three-letter word or base.
tri·lit·er·al·ism (trī-lit′ẽr-əl-iz′m), *n.* the quality of being triliteral; specifically, the characteristic quality of Semitic languages of containing many bases having three consonants, on which words are formed by the addition of various vowel sounds.

trill (tril), *n.* [Fr. *trille;* It. *trilla, trillo* < *trillare,* to trill; echoic], 1. *a)* a rapid alternation of two musical tones a degree or half degree apart. *b)* musical vibrato. 2. a similar sound, as of birds; warble. 3. a rapid vibration of the tongue or uvula, as in pronouncing *r* in some languages. 4. a consonant pronounced with such a vibration. ***v.t. & v.i.*** [It. *trillare*], to sound, speak, sing, or play with a trill or trills.

tril·lion (tril'yən), *n.* [Fr.; *tri-* + *million*], 1. in the United States and France, a thousand billions (1,000,000,000,000). 2. in Great Britain and Germany, a million billions (1,000,000,000,000,000,000). ***adj.*** amounting to one trillion in number.

tril·lionth (tril'yənth), ***adj.*** 1. coming last in a series of a trillion. 2. designating any of the trillion equal parts of something. ***n.*** 1. the last in a series of a trillion. 2. any of the trillion equal parts of something.

tril·li·um (tril'i-əm), *n.* [Mod. L. < L. *tri-,* three], any of a number of related plants with white, violet, pinkish, or greenish flowers and leaves in groups of three.

tri·lo·bal (trī-lō'b'l), ***adj.*** trilobate.

tri·lo·bate (trī-lō'bāt), ***adj.*** having three lobes, as some leaves.

tri·lo·bat·ed (trī-lō'bā-tid), ***adj.*** trilobate.

tri·lobed (trī'lōbd), ***adj.*** trilobate.

tri·lo·bite (trī'lə-bīt'), *n.* [Mod. L. *Trilobites, Trilobita;* see TRI- & LOBE], any of a large group of extinct arthropods having the body divided into three lobes, found as fossils in Paleozoic rocks.

tri·lo·bit·ic (trī'lə-bit'ik), ***adj.*** of, like, or containing trilobites.

tri·loc·u·lar (trī-lok'yoo-lẽr), ***adj.*** [*tri-* + *locular*], having three chambers, cells, or cavities.

tril·o·gy (tril'ə-ji), *n.* [*pl.* TRILOGIES (-jiz)], [Gr. *trilogia;* see TRI- & -LOGY], a set of three related plays, novels, etc. which, though each has its own unity, form together a larger work.

trim (trim), *v.t.* [TRIMMED (trimd), TRIMMING], [AS. *trymian, trymman,* to make firm, set in order, array < *trum,* strong, firm; for IE. base see TREE], 1. originally, to prepare; fit out; dress. 2. to put in proper order; make neat or tidy, especially by clipping, lopping, etc.: as, he *trimmed* his mustache. 3. to clip, lop, cut, etc. (often with *off*): as, he *trimmed* dead branches off the tree. 4. to smooth or dress (lumber). 5. to decorate: as, she *trimmed* the Christmas tree. 6. *a)* to balance (a ship) by shifting cargo, etc. *b)* to put (sails) in order for sailing. 7. to balance (an airplane) in flight by regulating the surface controls and tabs. 8. to modify according to expediency; adjust; adapt. 9. [Colloq.], *a)* to scold; chide; rebuke. *b)* to beat, punish, thrash, etc. *c)* to defeat. *d)* to cheat. ***v.i.*** 1. to change one's opinions or viewpoint so as to satisfy opposing factions, etc.; keep a middle-of-the-road policy; compromise. 2. *a)* to keep in balance: said of a ship. *b)* to keep a ship in balance; adjust the sails or yards in managing a vessel. ***n.*** 1. order; arrangement; condition: as, in proper *trim.* 2. good condition or order: as, he got into *trim.* 3. equipment; gear; dress. 4. a trimming by clipping, cutting, etc. 5. window dressing. 6. the lighter interior or exterior woodwork of a building, especially around windows and doors. 7. the interior furnishings of an automobile body. 8. any ornamental trimming. 9. *a)* the condition of being trimmed or ready to sail: said of ships. *b)* the position of a boat or ship in the water. *c)* the balance of a ship. *d)* the difference between the draft forward and the draft aft. *e)* the adjustment of the sails or yards in managing a vessel. 10. the degree of buoyancy of a submarine. 11. the position of an airplane in relation to a fore-and-aft horizontal axis. 12. something that is trimmed, as sections of motion-picture film cut out in editing. 13. [Obs.], character (of a person). ***adj.*** [TRIMMER (-ẽr), TRIMMEST (-ist)], 1. orderly; neat; tidy. 2. well-proportioned; smartly designed. 3. in good condition. 4. [Obs.], fine; nice. ***adv.*** in a trim manner. —***SYN.*** see **neat.**

trim·er·ous (trim'ẽr-əs), ***adj.*** [*tri-* + *-merous*], 1. in *botany,* having the parts in sets of three: said of a flower: often written *3-merous.* 2. in *entomology, a)* consisting of three segments or joints. *b)* having three joints in each tarsus.

tri·mes·ter (trī-mes'tẽr), *n.* [Fr. *trimestre* < L. *trimestris,* of three months < *tri-,* three + *mensis,* month], a period or term of three months.

trim·e·ter (trim'ə-tẽr), *n.* [L. *trimetrus;* Gr. *trimetros;* see TRI- & METER (rhythm)], 1. a line of verse containing three metrical feet or measures. 2. verse consisting of trimeters. ***adj.*** having three metrical feet.

tri·met·ric (trī-met'rik), ***adj.*** 1. having three metrical feet. 2. orthorhombic.

tri·met·ri·cal (trī-met'ri-k'l), ***adj.*** trimetric.

trimetric projection, a type of geometric projection in which the three dimensions are measured by different scales according to arbitrarily chosen angles.

tri·met·ro·gon (trī-met'rə-gon'), *n.* [< *tri-* + Gr. *metron,* a measure + *gōnia,* an angle], a system of aerial photography in which three high-speed, wide-angle cameras are so placed in an airplane as to take photographs of the earth from horizon to horizon.

trim·mer (trim'ẽr), *n.* 1. a person who trims a ship during loading or unloading, by distributing the cargo. 2. a machine for trimming lumber, etc. 3. a beam in a floor frame that receives the ends of headers, as around a stair well. 4. a person who changes his opinions, policies, etc. to suit the occasion; timeserver. 5. a person or thing that trims (in any sense).

trim·ming (trim'iŋ), *n.* 1. the action of a person who trims; specifically, [Colloq.], *a)* a scolding. *b)* a beating; thrashing. *c)* a defeat. *d)* a cheating. 2. something used to trim; specifically, *a)* decoration; ornament. *b) pl.* the side dishes or garnishings of a meal: as, turkey with all the *trimmings.* 3. *pl.* parts trimmed off.

tri·mo·lec·u·lar (trī'mə-lek'yoo-lẽr), ***adj.*** of or formed from three molecules.

tri·month·ly (trī-munth'li), ***adj.*** happening or appearing every three months.

tri·morph (trī'môrf), *n.* [*tri-* + *-morph;* cf. TRIMORPHISM], 1. a substance that crystallizes in three distinct forms. 2. any of these forms.

tri·mor·phism (trī-môr'fiz'm), *n.* [< Gr. *trimorphos,* of three forms < *tri-,* three + *morphē,* form; + *-ism*], 1. in *zoology,* the existence of three distinct forms in the same species. 2. in *botany,* the existence of three distinct forms of flowers, leaves, or other organs on the same plant or on different plants of the same species. 3. in *crystallography,* the property of crystallizing in three distinct forms.

Tri·mur·ti (tri-moor'ti), *n.* [Sans. *trimūrti* < *tri,* three + *mūrti,* body, shape], the trinity of Hindu gods (Brahma, the Creator; Vishnu, the Preserver; and Siva, the Destroyer).

Tri·na·cri·an (tri-nā'kri-ən, trī-nā'kri-ən), ***adj.*** [< L. *Trinacria,* Sicily], Sicilian.

tri·nal (trī'n'l), ***adj.*** [LL. *trinalis* < L. *trinus;* see TRINE], having three parts; threefold; triple.

tri·na·ry (trī'nẽr-i), ***adj.*** [LL. *trinarius,* of three kinds, for L. *ternarius;* see TERNARY], threefold; ternary.

trine (trīn), ***adj.*** [ME.; OFr.; L. *trinus,* triple < *tres,* three], 1. threefold; triple. 2. in *astrology, a)* in trine; hence, *b)* favorable. ***n.*** 1. a group of three; triad. 2. [T-], the Trinity. 3. in *astrology,* the aspect of two planets 120 degrees apart, considered favorable.

Trin·i·dad (trin'ə-dad'; Sp. trē'nē-*thäth'*), *n.* an island in the West Indies, off the coast of Venezuela: part of the country of Trinidad and Tobago: area, 1,864 sq. mi.; pop., 824,000; capital, Port of Spain.

Trinidad and Tobago, a country on the islands of Trinidad and Tobago, in the West Indies, north of Venezuela: formerly a British colony, since 1962 a member of the British Commonwealth of Nations: area, 1,976 sq. mi.; pop., 859,000; capital, Port of Spain, on Trinidad.

Trin·i·tar·i·an (trin'ə-târ'i-ən), ***adj.*** [Mod. L. *trinitarius* < L. *trinitas*], 1. [also t-], *a)* having to do with the Trinity or the doctrine of the Trinity. *b)* believing in this doctrine. 2. [t-], forming a trinity; threefold. ***n.*** one who believes in the doctrine of the Trinity.

Trin·i·tar·i·an·ism (trin'ə-târ'i-ən-iz'm), *n.* 1. the doctrine of the Trinity. 2. belief in this.

tri·ni·tro·cre·sol (trī-nī'trō-krē'sōl, trī-nī'trō-krē'sol), *n.* [*tri-* + *nitro-* + *cresol*], a yellow, crystalline chemical compound, $C_7H_5O(NO_2)_3$, used as an antiseptic and in explosives.

tri·ni·tro·tol·u·ene (trī-nī'trō-tol'ū-ēn'), *n.* [*tri-* + *nitro-* + *toluene*], a high explosive, any of several isomeric derivatives, $CH_3C_6H_2(NO_2)_3$, of toluene, used for blasting, in artillery shells, etc.: abbreviated **TNT, T.N.T.**

tri·ni·tro·tol·u·ol (trī-nī'trō-tol'ū-ōl, trī-nī'trō-tol'ū-ol), *n.* trinitrotoluene: abbreviated **TNT, T.N.T.**

trin·i·ty (trin'ə-ti), *n.* [*pl.* TRINITIES (-tiz)], [ME. *trinite;* OFr. *trinité;* L. *trinitas,* triad (in LL., Trinity) < *trinus;* see TRINE & -ITY], 1. the condition of being three or threefold. 2. a set of three persons or things that form a unit. 3. [T-], Trinity Sunday. 4. [T-], [after Gr. *trias*], in *Christian theology,* the union of the three divine persons (Father, Son, and Holy Spirit, or Holy Ghost) in one Godhead.

Trinity Sunday, the Sunday next after Whitsunday or Pentecost, dedicated to the Trinity.

trink·et (triŋ'kit), *n.* [ME. *trenket,* shoemakers' knife, toy knife carried by ladies, ornament; ONorm. Fr. *trenquet;* OFr. *trenchet, tranchet* < *trenchier, tranchier,* to cut; cf. TRENCH, TRENCHER], 1. a small ornament, piece of jewelry, etc. 2. a trifle or toy.

tri·nod·al (trī-nō'd'l), ***adj.*** having three nodes or nodal points.

tri·no·mi·al (trī-nō'mi-əl), ***adj.*** [*tri-* + *binomial*], consisting of three terms. ***n.*** 1. a mathematical expression consisting of three terms connected by plus or minus signs. 2. the scientific name of a plant or animal, consisting of three words designating in order the genus, species, and subspecies or variety.

tri·o (trē'ō; *for 4, occas.* trī'ō), *n.* [*pl.* TRIOS (-ōz)], [Fr.; It. < L. *tres, tria,* three], 1. a musical composition for three voices or three instruments. 2. the three performers of such a composition. 3. the middle section of a minuet, scherzo, etc., originally written in three voices, or parts. 4. a set of three persons or things.

tri·ode (trī'ōd), *n.* [*tri-* + electr*ode*], an electron tube having three electrodes, a cathode, anode, and control grid, and used to produce, detect, or amplify radio waves.

tri·oe·cious (trī-ē'shəs), *adj.* [< *tri-* + Gr. *oikos,* a house; + *-ous*], having male, female, and two-sexed flowers on separate plants: also spelled **triecious.**

tri·oi·cous (trī-oi'kəs), *adj.* trioecious.

tri·o·let (trī'ə-lit, trē'ə-let'), *n.* [Fr., dim. of *trio,* three], a poem or stanza having eight lines and two rhymes, the first line being repeated as the fourth and seventh, and the second as the eighth: the rhyme scheme is *abaaabab.*

tri·ox·id (trī-ok'sid), *n.* trioxide.

tri·ox·ide (trī-ok'sīd, trī-ok'sid), *n.* an oxide having three oxygen atoms to the molecule.

trip (trip), *v.i.* [TRIPPED or *occas.* TRIPT (tript), TRIPPING], [ME. *trippen;* OFr. *triper, treper;* prob. < MD. *trippen,* to tread, trip; for the IE. base see TRAP (snare)], 1. to walk, run, or dance with light, rapid steps; skip; caper. 2. to stumble. 3. to make a false step, inaccuracy, or mistake; err. 4. to falter in speaking. 5. to run past the pallet of the escapement: said of a tooth of the escapement wheel of a watch, etc. 6. [Rare], to take a trip; journey. 7. to tilt; tip. *v.t.* 1. to perform (a dance) lightly and nimbly. 2. to make stumble, as by catching the foot (often with *up*). 3. *a*) to cause to make a false step or mistake. *b*) to cause to fail or stop; obstruct. 4. to catch (a person) in a lie, error, etc. (also with *up*). 5. *a*) to release (a spring, wheel, or other mechanical part), as by the action of a detent. *b*) to start or operate by this. 6. to tilt; tip up. 7. in *nautical usage, a*) to raise (an anchor) clear of the bottom. *b*) to tilt (a yard) into position for lowering. *c*) to raise (an upper mast) so that the fid may be removed before lowering. *n.* 1. a light, quick tread. 2. a going from one place to another, or a going to a place and returning; journey, especially a short one; excursion, voyage, jaunt, etc. 3. a stumble; hence, 4. a mistake; blunder. 5. a faltering; slip; lapse. 6. a maneuver for causing someone to stumble or fall, as by catching his foot. 7. *a*) any mechanical contrivance for tripping a part, as a pawl. *b*) its action.

SYN.—**trip** strictly implies a relatively short course of travel, although it is also commonly used as an equivalent for **journey** (a vacation *trip*); **journey**, a more formal word, generally implies travel of some length, usually over land, and does not necessarily suggest the idea of return (the *journey* was filled with hardships); **voyage**, in current use, implies a relatively long journey by water (a *voyage* across the Atlantic); **jaunt** is applied to a short, casual trip taken for pleasure or recreation (a *jaunt* to the city); **expedition** is applied to a journey, march, etc. taken by an organized group for some definite purpose (a military *expedition,* a zoological *expedition* to Africa).

tri·par·tite (trī-pär'tīt; *rarely,* trip'ẽr-tīt'), *adj.* [L. *tripartitus; tri-,* three + *partitus,* pp. of *partiri,* to divide], 1. divided into three parts; threefold. 2. having three corresponding parts or copies. 3. made or existing between three parties, as an agreement.

tri·par·ti·tion (trī'pär-tish'ən), *n.* division into three parts or among three parties.

tripe (trīp), *n.* [ME.; OFr. *tripe, trippe* < Ar. *tharb,* entrails, a net], 1. part of the stomach of an ox or similar animal, used as food. 2. [Slang], anything worthless, offensive, etc.; rubbish; trash.

tri·pe·dal (trī'pi-d'l, trī-pē'd'l, trip'i-d'l), *adj.* [L. *tripedalis* < *tri-,* three + *pes, pedis,* a foot], having three feet.

tri·per·son·al (trī-pũr's'n-əl), *adj.* in *theology,* consisting of or existing in three persons: said of the Godhead.

tri·pet·al·ous (trī-pet''l-əs), *adj.* having three petals.

trip ham·mer (trip'ham'ẽr), *n.* a heavy, power-driven hammer, alternately raised and allowed to fall by a tripping device: also **trip hammer.**

tri·phen·yl·meth·ane (trī-fen'il-meth'ān, trī-fē'nil-meth'ān), *n.* [*tri-* + *phenyl* + *methane*], a colorless, crystalline hydrocarbon, $CH(C_6H_5)_3$, used in organic synthesis and in making dyes.

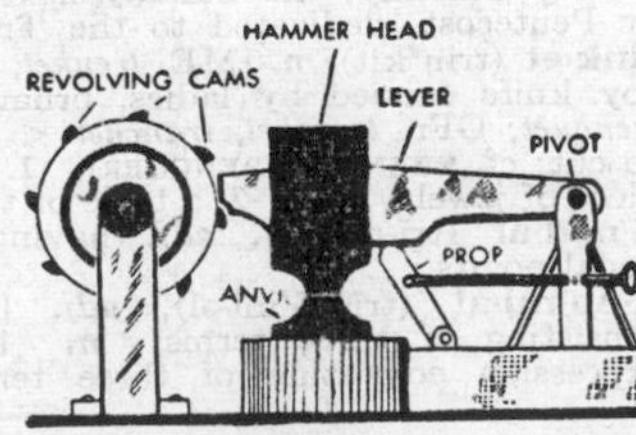

TRIPHAMMER

triph·thong (trif'thôŋ), *n.* [*tri-* + di*phthong*], 1. a combination of three vowel sounds in one syllable. Example: *fire* (in the British pronunciation, IPA [faɪə]). 2. loosely, a trigraph.

triph·y·line (trif'ə-lin, trif'ə-lēn'), *n.* triphylite.

triph·y·lite (trif'ə-līt'), *n.* [< *tri-* + Gr. *phylē,* a class, family; + *-ite:* so named because of its three bases], a greenish-blue, crystalline mineral, $LiFePO_4$, a native phosphate of lithium and iron.

tri·pin·nate (trī-pin'āt), *adj.* in *botany,* pinnate three times over; bipinnate with each division pinnate, as the leaves of some ferns.

tri·pin·nat·ed (trī-pin'ā-tid), *adj.* tripinnate.

tri·plane (trī'plān'), *n.* an early type of airplane with three wings arranged one above another.

tri·ple (trip''l), *adj.* [ME.; OFr.; L. *triplus; tri-,* three + *-plus,* -fold, as in *duplus,* twofold, double], 1. consisting of or including three; threefold. 2. repeated three times; treble. 3. three times as much or as many. *n.* 1. an amount three times as much or as many. 2. a group of three; triad. 3. in *baseball,* a three-base hit. *v.t.* [TRIPLED (-'ld), TRIPLING], to make three times as much or as many. *v.i.* 1. to become three times as much or as many. 2. in *baseball,* to hit a triple.

Triple Alliance, 1. an alliance of England, Sweden, and the Netherlands against France in 1668. 2. an alliance of Great Britain, France, and the Netherlands against Spain in 1717. 3. an alliance of Great Britain, Austria, and Russia against France in 1795. 4. the Dreibund, an alliance of Germany, Austria, and Italy in 1882.

Triple Entente, 1. the military understanding reached by Great Britain, France, and Russia before World War I as a counterbalance to the Dreibund. 2. these three countries as parties to the understanding.

tri·ple-ex·pan·sion engine (trip''l-ik-span'shən), a steam engine with three cylinders or sets of cylinders, in which the steam is successively expanded.

triple measure, triple time.

tri·ple-nerved (trip''l-nũrvd'), *adj.* in *botany,* having three nerves, or veins; specifically, having three nerves arising from or near the base, as some leaves.

triple play, in *baseball,* a play by which three players are put out.

tri·plet (trip'lit), *n.* [< *triple*], 1. a collection or group of three, usually of one kind; specifically, *a*) a group of three successive lines of poetry, usually rhyming. *b*) a group of three musical notes to be played in the time of two of the same value. 2. *a*) one of three offspring born at a single birth. *b*) *pl.* three offspring born at a single birth.

tri·ple·tail (trip''l-tāl'), *n.* any of a group of large food fishes of warm seas, characterized by long hind fins that extend back along the caudal fin so as to give the effect of a three-lobed tail.

triple time, musical time or rhythm having three beats to the measure, with the first beat accented.

tri·plex (trī'leks, trī'pleks), *adj.* [L.; *tri-* + *-plex,* -fold < base of *plaga,* surface, region; see DUPLEX], triple; threefold. *n.* 1. a thing that is triplex. 2. triple time.

trip·li·cate (trip'lə-kit; *also, and for the v. always,* trip'lə-kāt'), *adj.* [ME.; L. *triplicatus,* pp. of *triplicare,* to treble < *triplex;* see TRIPLEX], 1. made in or forming three identical copies. 2. threefold; triple. *n.* one of three identical copies or things. *v.t.* [TRIPLICATED (-id), TRIPLICATING], 1. to make three copies of. 2. to increase threefold; treble.

in triplicate, in three identical copies.

trip·li·ca·tion (trip'lə-kā'shən), *n.* 1. a triplicating or being triplicated. 2. something triplicated.

tri·plic·i·ty (tri-plis'ə-ti), *n.* [*pl.* TRIPLICITIES (-tiz)], [ME. *triplicite;* Early Fr. *triplicité* < L. *triplex;* see TRIPLEX], 1. the quality or condition of being triple. 2. a group of three. 3. in *astrology,* a trigon.

trip·lite (trip'līt), *n.* [G. *triplit* < Gr. *triplous,* threefold; cf. TRIPLE], a dark-brown, greasy mineral, a fluophosphate of iron and manganese, $(Fe,Mn)_2FPO_4$.

trip·loid (trip'loid), *adj.* in *biology,* having three times the haploid number of chromosomes.

tri·ply (trip'li), *adv.* in a triple amount or degree.

tri·pod (trī'pod), *n.* [L. *tripus, tripodis;* Gr. *tripous; tri-,* three + *pous, podos,* a foot], 1. a three-legged caldron, stool, table, etc. 2. a three-legged support for a camera, etc., usually adjustable for height.

trip·o·dal (trip'ə-d'l), *adj.* [*tripod* + *-al*], having three legs or feet, as a stool.

tri·pod·ic (trī-pod'ik), *adj.* [*tripod* + *-ic*], having or using three feet.

trip·o·dy (trip'ə-di), *n.* [*pl.* TRIPODIES (-diz)], [*tri-* + di*pody*], a verse or phrase of three metrical feet.

Trip·o·li (trip'ə-li; It. trē'pô-lē'), *n.* 1. a former Barbary State, now a part of Libya. 2. the capital of Libya, on the Mediterranean Sea: pop., 108,000. 3. a seaport in northwestern Lebanon: pop., 72,000 (est. 1943).

trip·o·li (trip'ə-li), *n.* [< *Tripoli,* Africa], a light, porous rock, white, gray, pink, red, buff, or yellow in color, consisting of weathered chert and siliceous limestones: it is used as a polishing powder and abrasive: also called *rottenstone, tripoli powder* (or *stone*).

Tri·pol·i·tan (tri-pol′ə-t'n), *adj.* of Tripoli, its people, or culture. *n.* a native or inhabitant of Tripoli.

Tri·pol·i·ta·ni·a (trip′ol-i-tā′ni-ə; It. trē′pô-lē-tä′nyä), *n.* a province of northwestern Libya: area, 350,000 sq. mi.; pop., 352,000; capital, Tripoli.

tri·pos (trī′pos), *n.* [*pl.* TRIPOSES (-iz)], [L. *tripus;* see TRIPOD], 1. originally, a tripod. 2. at Cambridge University, *a)* formerly, a scholar who sat on a three-legged stool at commencement and disputed humorously with candidates for a degree; hence, *b)* any of the examinations for the B.A. degree with honors, originally for honors in mathematics.

trip·per (trip′ẽr), *n.* a person or thing that trips; specifically, *a)* a mechanical part for tripping, or releasing a catch, as a cam, pawl, etc.; also, a tripping device that operates a signal on a railroad. *b)* [British Colloq.], a person who takes a trip; traveler; tourist.

trip·pet (trip′it), *n.* [< *trip*], a cam or other mechanical part designed to strike another part at regular intervals.

trip·ping (trip′iŋ), *adj.* [ppr. of *trip*], stepping lightly and quickly; nimble. *n.* 1. the action of a person or thing that trips. 2. a light, graceful dance.

trip·tane (trip′tān), *n.* [contr. < *tripentane;* see TRI- & PENTANE], a high antiknock fuel for use in internal-combustion engines, especially in airplanes.

trip·ter·ous (trip′tẽr-əs), *adj.* [< *tri-* + Gr. *pteron,* wing; + *-ous*], having three winglike parts, as some fruits or seeds.

Trip·tol·e·mus, Trip·tol·e·mos (trip-tol′i-məs), *n.* in *Greek mythology,* a legendary hero who was supposed to have given man the secret of cultivating grain.

trip·tych (trip′tik), *n.* [< Gr. *triptychos,* threefold < *tri-,* three + *ptyx, ptychos,* a fold], 1. an ancient writing tablet of three leaves hinged or tied together. 2. a set of three panels with pictures, designs, or carvings, often hinged so that the two side panels may be folded over the central one: it is used as an altarpiece, etc.

Tri·pu·ra (tri′poo-rä′), *n.* a state of northeastern India: area, 4,116 sq. mi.; pop., 513,000 (est. 1950).

tri·que·trous (trī-kwē′trəs, trī-kwet′rəs), *adj.* [L. *triquetrus* < *tri-,* three + base akin to AS. *hwæt,* sharp, bold; hence orig., three-pointed], 1. triangular. 2. having a triangular cross section. 3. trihedral.

tri·ra·di·ate (trī-rā′di-āt′), *adj.* having three rays or raylike projections.

tri·reme (trī′rēm), *n.* [Fr. *trirème* < L. *triremis,* having three banks of oars < *tri-,* three + *remus,* an oar], an ancient Greek or Roman galley, usually a warship, with three banks of oars on each side.

tri·sac·cha·ride (trī-sak′ə-rīd′, trī-sak′ẽr-id), *n.* a carbohydrate yielding three monosaccharides upon hydrolysis.

tri·sect (trī-sekt′), *v.t.* [< *tri-* + L. *sectus,* pp. of *secare,* to cut], 1. to cut or divide into three parts. 2. in *geometry,* to divide into three equal parts.

tri·sec·tion (trī-sek′shən), *n.* a trisecting; division into three (equal) parts.

tri·sec·tor (trī-sek′tẽr), *n.* a line, plane, etc. that trisects.

tri·sep·al·ous (trī-sep′'l-əs), *adj.* having three sepals.

tri·sep·tate (trī-sep′tāt), *adj.* [*tri-* + *septate*], in *botany* & *zoology,* having three septa, or dividing walls.

tri·se·ri·al (trī-sêr′i-əl), *adj.* 1. arranged in three rows or series. 2. in *botany,* having only three verticils.

tris·kele (tris′kēl), *n.* a triskelion.

tris·kel·i·on (tris-kel′i-on), *n.* [< Gr. *triskelēs,* three-legged < *tri-,* three + *skelos,* a leg], a design, usually symbolic, consisting of three curved branches or three bent legs or arms radiating from a center.

BRONZE FROM IRELAND

SHELL DISK FROM TENNESSEE

GREEK SHIELD

TRISKELIONS

Tris·me·gis·tus (tris′mə-jis′təs), see **Hermes Trismegistus.**

tris·mic (triz′mik, tris′mik), *adj.* of, or having the nature of, trismus.

tris·mus (triz′məs, tris′məs), *n.* [Mod. L.; Gr. *trismos,* gnashing of the teeth, a grinding], lockjaw.

tris·oc·ta·he·dral (tris-ok′tə-hē′drəl), *adj.* of, or having the form of, a trisoctahedron.

tris·oc·ta·he·dron (tris-ok′tə-hē′drən), *n.* [Gr. *tris,* thrice; + *octahedron*], a solid figure or crystal with twenty-four plane surfaces, every three of which correspond to a single surface of an octahedron imagined as underlying them: trisoctahedrons are of two kinds, the *trigonal trisoctahedron,* having triangular surfaces, and the *tetragonal trisoctahedron,* or *trapezohedron,* having quadrilateral surfaces.

TRISOCTAHEDRONS A, tetragonal; B, trigonal

tri·sper·mous (trī-spũr′məs), *adj.* [< *tri-* + Gr. *sperma,* a seed; + *-ous*], three-seeded.

tri·spor·ic (trī-spôr′ik, trī-spor′ik), *adj.* having three spores.

tri·spor·ous (trī-spôr′əs, trī-spō′rəs), *adj.* trisporic.

Tris·tam (tris′təm), a masculine name: see **Tristram.**

Tris·tan (tris′tən), a masculine name: see **Tristram.**

Tris·tan da Cu·nha (tris′tan də kōōn′yə), a group of British islands in the South Atlantic.

‡triste (trēst), *adj.* [Fr.], sad; sorrowful.

‡tris·tesse (trēs′tes′), *n.* [Fr.], sadness; melancholy.

trist·ful (trist′fool), *adj.* [obs. *trist,* sad (< OFr. *triste;* L. *tristis*); + *-ful*], sad; sorrowful; melancholy.

tris·tich (tris′tik), *n.* [< *tri-,* after *distich*], a group or stanza of three lines of verse; triplet.

tris·tich·ous (tris′ti-kəs), *adj.* [Gr. *tristichos,* in three rows; *tri-,* three + *stichos,* a row], having parts, leaves, etc. arranged in three rows.

Tris·tram (tris′trəm), [OFr. *Tristran, Tristan,* altered (after L. *tristis,* sad) < Celt. *Drystan* < *drest, drust,* tumult, din], a masculine name: diminutive, *Tris;* variants, *Tristam, Tristan.* *n.* in *medieval legend,* a knight sent to Ireland by King Mark of Cornwall to bring back the princess Isolde to be the king's bride: Isolde (called *the Fair*) and Tristram unwittingly drink a magic potion, fall in love, and ultimately die together; in some versions, Tristram is married to another Isolde (called *Isolde of the White Hand*); the story is the subject of a number of poems and an opera by Wagner (*Tristan und Isolde*).

tri·sty·lous (trī-stī′ləs), *adj.* [< *tri-* + *style* + *-ous*], in *botany,* having three styles.

tri·sul·fide (trī-sul′fīd, trī-sul′fid), *n.* a sulfide having three sulfur atoms to the molecule.

tri·syl·lab·ic (trī′si-lab′ik, tris′i-lab′ik), *adj.* having three syllables. *n.* a metrical foot of three syllables.

tri·syl·lab·i·cal·ly (trī′si-lab′i-k'l-i, tris′i-lab′ik-li), *adv.* in or as three syllables.

tri·syl·la·ble (trī-sil′ə-b'l, tri-sil′ə-b'l), *n.* a word of three syllables.

trit., triturate.

trite (trīt), *adj.* [TRITER (-ẽr), TRITEST (-ist)], [L. *tritus,* pp. of *terere,* to rub, wear out], worn out by constant use; no longer having freshness, originality, or novelty; hackneyed; stale: as, "busy as a bee" is a *trite* expression.

SYN.—**trite** is applied to something, especially an expression or idea, which through repeated use or application has lost its original freshness and impressive force (e.g., "like a bolt from the blue"); **hackneyed** refers to such expressions which through constant use have become virtually meaningless (e.g., "last but not least"); **stereotyped** applies to those fixed expressions which seem invariably to be called up in certain situations (e.g. "I point with pride" in a political oration); **commonplace** is used of any obvious or conventional remark or idea (e.g., "it isn't the heat, it's the humidity"). —*ANT.* original, fresh.

tri·the·ism (trī′thē-iz'm), *n.* [< *tri-* + Gr. *theos,* god; + *-ism*], the doctrine of the existence of three distinct gods; specifically, in *Christian theology,* the doctrine that the Father, Son, and Holy Spirit are separate and distinct Gods.

trit·i·um (trit′i-əm, trish′i-əm), *n.* [Mod. L. < Gr. *tritos,* third + L. *-ium,* n. suffix], an isotope of hydrogen having an atomic weight of 3: symbol, T or H^3.

Tri·ton (trī′t'n), *n.* [L.; Gr. *Tritōn*], 1. in *Greek mythology, a)* a sea god, son of Poseidon and Amphitrite, pictured as having the head and upper body of a man and the tail of a fish and as carrying a conch-shell trumpet. *b)* later, one of many attendants of the sea gods. 2. [t-], *a)* a kind of sea snail with a long, spiral shell, often brightly colored. *b)* its shell.

tri·tone (trī′tōn′), *n.* [ML. *tritonus;* Gr. *tritonos,* of three tones], in *music,* an interval of three whole tones.

trit·u·ra·ble (trich′ẽr-ə-b'l), *adj.* that can be triturated.

trit·u·rate (trich′ə-rāt′), *v.t.* [TRITURATED (-id), TRITURATING], [< LL. *trituratus,* pp. of *triturare,* to grind < L. *tritura,* a rubbing < *terere,* to rub], to rub, crush, or grind into very fine particles or powder; pulverize. *n.* 1. something triturated. 2. a trituration (sense 2).

trit·u·ra·tion (trich′ə-rā′shən), *n.* 1. a triturating or being triturated. 2. in *pharmacy,* a triturated preparation, especially one containing a pulverized mixture of a medicinal substance with lactose.

trit·u·ra·tor (trich'ə-rā'tẽr), *n.* a person or thing that triturates.

tri·umph (trī'əmf), *n.* [ME. & OFr. *triumphe, triomphe;* L. *triumphus* < Gr. *thriambos,* hymn to Bacchus sung in festal processions (AS. has *triumpha* directly < L.)], 1. in ancient Rome, a procession celebrating the return of a victorious general and his army. 2. the act or fact of being victorious; victory; success; achievement. 3. exultation or joy for a victory, achievement, etc. 4. [Obs.], any public spectacle or celebration. *v.i.* [OFr. *triumpher;* L. *triumphare* < the *n.*], 1. to gain victory or success; be victorious or successful; win mastery. 2. to rejoice or exult over victory, achievement, etc. 3. to celebrate a Roman triumph. *v.t.* [Obs.], to conquer. —*SYN.* see **victory.**

tri·um·phal (trī-um'f'l), *adj.* 1. of, or having the nature of, a triumph. 2. celebrating or commemorating a triumph.

tri·um·phant (trī-um'fənt), *adj.* [L. *triumphans;* ppr. of *triumphare;* see TRIUMPH], 1. successful; victorious. 2. rejoicing for victory; exulting in success; elated. 3. [Now Rare], triumphal. 4. [Obs.], magnificent.

tri·um·vir (trī-um'vẽr), *n.* [*pl.* TRIUMVIRS (-vẽrz), TRIUMVIRI (-vi-rī')], [L. back-formation < *trium virorum,* of three men; *trium,* genit. of *tres,* three + *virorum,* genit. pl. of *vir,* a man], 1. in ancient Rome, any of a group of three administrators sharing authority equally. 2. any of three persons associated in office or authority.

tri·um·vi·ral (trī-um'vẽr-əl), *adj.* of a triumvir or triumvirate.

tri·um·vi·rate (trī-um'vẽr-it), *n.* [L. *triumviratus*], 1. the office, functions or term of a triumvir. 2. government by three men or by a coalition of three parties; hence, 3. any association of three in authority. 4. any group or set of three persons or, rarely, things.

tri·une (trī'ūn, trī-ūn'), *adj.* [< *tri-* + L. *unus,* one], being three in one: as, a *triune* God. *n.* 1. a triad. 2. [T-], the Trinity.

tri·u·ni·tar·i·an (trī-ū'nə-târ'i-ən), *n.* a Trinitarian.

tri·u·ni·ty (trī-ū'nə-ti), *n.* the quality or condition of being triune; trinity.

tri·va·lence (trī-vā'ləns, triv'ə-ləns), *n.* the condition or quality of being trivalent.

tri·va·len·cy (trī-vā'lən-si, triv'ə-lən-si), *n.* trivalence.

tri·va·lent (trī-vā'lənt, triv'ə-lənt), *adj.* [*tri-* + *-valent*], 1. having a valence of three. 2. having three valences. Also, esp. for 2, **tervalent.**

tri·valve (trī'valv), *adj.* having three valves, as a shell.

Tri·van·drum (tri-van'drəm), *n.* seaport and capital of Travancore and Cochin, near the southern tip of India: pop., 128,000.

triv·et (triv'it), *n.* [ME. *trevet;* AS. *trefet* < L. *tripes,* tripod; see TRIPOD], 1. a three-legged stand for holding pots, kettles, etc. over or near a fire. 2. a short-legged metal plate for holding hot dishes on a table.

triv·i·a (triv'i-ə), *n.pl.* [Mod. L., pl.; see TRIVIAL], unimportant matters; trivialities; trifles.

triv·i·al (triv'i-əl, triv'yəl), *adj.* [ME. *trivialle;* L. *trivialis,* of the crossroads, hence commonplace < *trivium,* place where three roads meet < *tri-,* three + *via,* a road], 1. unimportant; insignificant; trifling. 2. [Archaic], commonplace. —*SYN.* see **petty.**

triv·i·al·ism (triv'i-əl-iz'm), *n.* 1. trivial character. 2. a triviality.

triv·i·al·i·ty (triv'i-al'ə-ti), *n.* [Fr. *trivialité*], 1. the quality or state of being trivial. 2. [*pl.* TRIVIALITIES (-tiz)], a trivial thing, matter, idea, etc.; trifle.

triv·i·um (triv'i-əm), *n.* [*pl.* TRIVIA (-ə)], [ML. < L.; see TRIVIAL], in the Middle Ages, the lower division of the seven liberal arts, consisting of the three arts, grammar, logic, and rhetoric: the other four were called the *quadrivium.*

tri·week·ly (trī-wēk'li), *adj. & adv.* 1. (occurring or appearing) every three weeks. 2. (occurring or appearing) three times a week. *n.* [*pl.* TRIWEEKLIES (-liz)], a publication that appears triweekly.

-trix (triks), [*pl.* -TRIXES (-iz), -TRICES (tri-sēz', trī'sēz)], [L.], an ending of some feminine nouns of agent, corresponding to the masculine form *-(t)or,* as in *aviatrix:* cf. **-(tr)ess.**

Tro·ad, the (trō'ad), Troas.

Tro·as (trō'as, trō'əs), *n.* the ancient region in Asia Minor in which Troy was located: also called *the Troad.*

tro·car (trō'kär), *n.* [Fr. *trocart, trois-quarts* < *trois,* three + *carre,* a side, face: so called from the shape of the point], a surgical instrument consisting of a sharp stylet enclosed in a tube (*cannula*) and inserted through the containing wall of a body cavity: the stylet is withdrawn permitting fluid to drain off through the tube.

tro·cha·ic (trō-kā'ik), *adj.* [< Fr. *trochaïque* or L. *trochaicus;* Gr. *trochaikos*], of or made up of trochees. *n.* 1. a trochaic verse. 2. a trochee.

tro·chal (trō'k'l), *adj.* [< Gr. *trochos* (see TROCHE); + *-al*], in *zoology,* resembling a wheel.

tro·chan·ter (trō-kan'tẽr), *n.* [Mod. L.; Gr. *trochantēr* < *trechein,* to run], any of several jutting processes (in man, two) at the upper end of the femur of many vertebrates.

tro·char (trō'kär), *n.* a trocar.

tro·che (trō'ki), *n.* [shortened < *trochisk;* Fr. *trochisque;* L. *trochiscus,* a pill, small ball; Gr. *trochiskos,* a small wheel, lozenge < *trochos,* a wheel < *trechein,* to run], a small, usually round, medicinal lozenge.

tro·chee (trō'kē), *n.* [L. *trochaeus;* Gr. *trochaios,* running < *trechein,* to run], a metrical foot consisting of a long syllable followed by a short one, or an accented syllable followed by an unaccented one. Example: "Pétĕr, | Pétĕr, | púmpkĭn | éatĕr."

troch·i·lus (trok'i-ləs), *n.* [*pl.* TROCHILI (-lī')], [L.; Gr. *trochilos,* lit., a runner < *trechein,* to run], 1. a small Egyptian bird thought by the ancients to accompany the crocodile and pick its teeth; crocodile bird. 2. a kind of hummingbird. 3. any of several European warblers.

troch·le·a (trok'li-ə), *n.* [*pl.* TROCHLEAE (-li-ē')], [L.; Gr. *trochilia* < *trochos,* a wheel, *trechein,* to run], in *anatomy,* a pulley-shaped part or structure, as the lower part of the humerus, which articulates with a corresponding part of the ulna.

troch·le·ar (trok'li-ẽr), *adj.* 1. in *anatomy,* of, having the nature of, or forming a trochlea. 2. in *botany,* shaped like a pulley; round and contracted in the middle.

tro·choid (trō'koid), *n.* [< Gr. *trochos* (see TROCHE); + *-oid*], a curve produced by a point on or connected with a circle rolling along a straight line. *adj.* having a wheellike rotary motion, as a joint.

tro·choi·dal (trō-koi'd'l), *adj.* of, or having the nature of, a trochoid.

troch·o·phore (trok'ə-fôr', trok'ə-fōr'), *n.* [Gr. *trochos,* a wheel; + *-phore*], a free-swimming ciliated larva of marine annelid worms and certain other aquatic invertebrates.

trod (trod), past tense and alternative past participle of **tread.**

trod·den (trod''n), alternative past participle of **tread.**

trode (trōd), archaic past tense of **tread.**

trog·lo·dyte (trog'lə-dīt'), *n.* [L. *troglodyta;* Gr. *trōglodytēs,* one who creeps into holes, cave dweller < *trōglē,* a hole, cave (< *trōgein,* to gnaw) + *dyein,* to creep in, enter], 1. a member of an ancient or prehistoric people that lived in caves; cave man; hence, 2. *a)* a hermit; recluse. *b)* anyone who lives in a primitive, low, or degenerate fashion. 3. an anthropoid ape, as a chimpanzee or gorilla.

trog·lo·dyt·ic (trog'lə-dit'ik), *adj.* [L. *troglodyticus;* Gr. *trōglodytikos*], of a troglodyte or troglodytes.

trog·lo·dyt·i·cal (trog'lə-dit'i-k'l), *adj.* troglodytic.

tro·gon (trō'gon), *n.* [Mod. L. < Gr. *trōgōn,* gnawing, ppr. of *trōgein,* to gnaw], any of a large group of bright-colored tropical birds.

troi·ka (troi'kə), *n.* [Russ.], in Russia, 1. a vehicle drawn by a team of three horses abreast. 2. the team of horses.

Tro·i·lus (trō'i-ləs, troi'ləs), *n.* [L.; Gr. *Trōilos*], in *Greek legend,* a son of King Priam, killed by Achilles: in medieval romance and in works by Boccaccio, Chaucer, and Shakespeare, Troilus was the lover of Cressida.

troilus butterfly, a large, black, American butterfly with yellow spots on the edge of the front wings and blue on the rear.

Trois Ri·vières (trwä' rē'vyâr'), a city in Quebec, Canada, on the St. Lawrence River: pop., 42,000: English name, *Three Rivers.*

Tro·jan (trō'jən), *adj.* [L. *Trojanus* < *Troja,* Troy], of ancient Troy, its people, or culture. *n.* 1. a native or inhabitant of ancient Troy. 2. a person of energy and determination: as, he worked like a *Trojan.*

Trojan horse, 1. in *classical legend,* a huge, hollow wooden horse filled with Greek soldiers and left at the gates of Troy: when it was brought into the city, the soldiers came out at night and opened the gates to the Greek army, which destroyed the city: also called *wooden horse;* hence, 2. the infiltration of troops or agents (or those so infiltrated) into enemy territory for disrupting or weakening the defense; fifth column.

Trojan War, in *Greek legend,* the war waged against Troy by the Greeks in order to get back Helen, the wife of King Menelaus, who had been abducted by Paris, son of King Priam of Troy.

troke (trōk), *n., v.t. & v.i.* [Scot.], trade; barter.

troll (trōl), *v.t.* [ME. *trollen,* to roll, troll, wander; OFr. *troller* < MHG. *trollen,* to walk or run with short steps; for IE. base see TREND], 1. to roll; revolve. 2. [Now Rare], to pass (a vessel) around in drinking. 3. to sing the parts of (a round, catch, etc.) in succession. 4. to sing lustily or in a full, rolling voice; chant merrily. 5. to fish for with a moving line, especially one with a revolving lure. 6. to fish in (a lake, etc.) by this method. *v.i.* 1. [Now Rare], *a)* to speak fast *b)* to wag: said of the tongue. 2. to sing in a round catch, etc. 3. *a)* to sing lustily or in a full, rolling voice. *b)* to be uttered in such a voice. 4. to fish with a moving line, especially one with a revolving lure, as from a boat. 5. to roll, spin, or whirl. *n.* 1. a trolling; a going or moving round. 2. a song having parts sung in succession; round. 3. *a*) the method of trolling in fishing. *b*) a lure or lure and line used in trolling.

troll (trōl), *n.* [ON. & Sw., lit., wanderer < base of *troll, v.*: adopted by 19th-c. antiquaries], in *Scandinavian folklore*, any of a race of supernatural beings, variously conceived of as giants, dwarfs, or imps, living underground or in caves.

trol·ley (trol'i), *n.* [*pl.* TROLLEYS (-iz)], [< East Anglian dial. < *troll, v.*], 1. [British], any of various low carts or trucks. 2. a wheeled carriage, basket, etc. that runs suspended from an overhead track. 3. an apparatus for collecting electric current from an overhead wire and transmitting it to a motor of a streetcar, etc.: it is of two types, the *bow trolley*, having a bow-shaped contact on a flexible frame, and the *wheel trolley*, having a wheel contact at the end of a pole. 4. a trolley car; streetcar. *v.t. & v.i.* to carry or ride on a trolley car. Also spelled **trolly.**

trolley bus, an electric bus that gets its motive power from an overhead wire by means of a trolley, but does not run on tracks; trackless trolley.

trolley car, an electric streetcar that gets its motive power from an overhead wire by means of a trolley.

trolley line, an electric streetcar system or route.

trol·lop (trol'əp), *n.* [Scot. < ME. *trollen* (see TROLL, *v.*); prob. influenced by *trull*], 1. an untidy or dirty woman; slattern. 2. a prostitute.

Trol·lope, Anthony (trol'əp), 1815–1882; English novelist.

trol·ly (trol'i), *n.* [*pl.* TROLLIES (-iz)], a trolley. *v.t. & v.i.* [TROLLIED (-id), TROLLYING], to trolley.

trom·bi·di·a·sis (trom'bi-dī'ə-sis), *n.* [Mod. L. < *Trombidium*, a genus of mites; + *-iasis*], the state of being infested with chiggers.

trom·bone (trom'bōn, trom-bōn'), *n.* [It. < *tromba*, a trumpet < Gmc.], a large, brass-wind instrument consisting of a long tube bent parallel to itself twice and ending in a bell mouth: it is of two types, the *slide trombone*, in which different tones are produced by moving the slide, or movable section of the tube, in or out, and the *valve trombone*, played, like the trumpet, with valves.

TROMBONE

trom·bon·ist (trom'bōn-ist, trom-bōn'ist), *n.* a person who plays the trombone.

trom·mel (trom''l), *n.* [G., a drum], a sieve, usually a revolving cylindrical one, used in screening ore, coal, etc.

tro·mom·e·ter (trə-mom'ə-tẽr), *n.* [< Gr. *tromos*, trembling; + *-meter*], an instrument for detecting or measuring very slight earth tremors.

trompe (tromp), *n.* [Fr., lit., trumpet; see TRUMPET], an apparatus for producing a blast in a forge, blast furnace, etc. by means of a stream of water falling through a tube and sucking in air which is diverted to the furnace.

tro·na (trō'nə), *n.* [Sw. < Ar. *trōn*, contr. < *natrūn*; see NATRON], a monoclinic hydrous sodium carbonate, $Na_2CO_3 \cdot NaHCO_3 \cdot 2H_2O$, gray or yellowish-white.

Trond·heim (trôn'hām), *n.* a seaport on Trondheim Fjord, in central Norway: pop., 56,000 (est. 1946): also called *Trondhjem*: former name, *Nidaros*.

Trond·hjem (trôn'yem), *n.* Trondheim.

trone (trōn), *n.* [Scot. *tron;* OFr. *trone;* L. *trutina;* Gr. *trytanē*, a balance], [Scot.], a machine for weighing heavy articles.

troop (trōōp), *n.* [Fr. *troupe*, back-formation < *troupeau* < LL. *troppus*, a flock < Frank. **throp*, a crowd; akin to AS. *throp, thorp*, village; cf. THORP], 1. a group of persons, animals, or, formerly, things; herd, flock, band, etc. 2. loosely, a great number; lot. 3. *usually pl.* a body of soldiers. 4. a subdivision of a cavalry regiment, commanded by a captain: it corresponds to a company of infantry. 5. a group of sixteen or thirty-two boy scouts. 6. [Archaic], a group of actors; troupe. *v.i.* 1. to gather or go in or as in troops: as, the crowd *trooped* out of the stadium. 2. to walk, go, etc.: as, the children *trooped* along the sidewalk. 3. [Archaic], to associate or consort. *v.t.* to form into a troop or troops. Abbreviated **Tr.**

SYN.—**troop** is applied to a group of people organized as a unit (a cavalry *troop*), or working or acting together in close co-operation (*troops* of sightseers); **troupe** is the preferred form with reference to a group of performers, as in the theater, a circus, etc.; **company** is the general word for any group of people associated in any of various ways; **band** suggests a relatively small group of people closely united for some common purpose (a *band* of thieves, a brass *band*).

troop·er (trōōp'ẽr), *n.* [*troop* + *-er*], 1. a cavalryman. 2. a cavalry horse. 3. [Chiefly British], a troopship. 4. a mounted policeman. 5. [Colloq.], a State policeman.

troop·ship (trōōp'ship'), *n.* a ship used for carrying troops; transport.

troost·ite (trōōst'īt), *n.* [after G. *Troost* (1776–1850), Am. metallurgist], a kind of willemite, occurring in large, reddish crystals, in which zinc is partially replaced by manganese.

‡**trop** (trō), *adv.* [Fr.], too; too much; too many.

trop., 1. tropic. 2. tropical.

tro·pae·o·lin, tro·pae·o·line (trə-pē'ə-lin), *n.* [< *tropaeolum* + *-ine*: from resembling the hues of the flowers], any of a group of orange or orange-yellow azo dyes: also spelled **tropeolin, tropeoline.**

tro·pae·o·lum (trə-pē'ə-ləm), *n.* [Mod. L., dim. < Gr. *tropaion* (see TROPHY): from the shieldlike leaves and helmetlike flowers], any of a number of related plants having shield-shaped, finely cut or lobed leaves, and trumpet-shaped, red, yellow, or orange flowers with spurs; nasturtium.

-tropal, [< Gr. *tropos*, turning (see TROPE); + *-al*], a combining form meaning *turning.*

trope (trōp), *n.* [< Fr. or L.; Fr. *trope;* L. *tropus;* Gr. *tropos*, a turning, turn, figure of speech (akin to *tropē*, a turn) < *trepein*, to turn < IE. base **trap-*, to turn], 1. *a*) the use of a word in a figurative sense. *b*) a figure of speech. *c*) figurative language in general. 2. any of various short, formulistic phrases used in Gregorian chants. 3. in the medieval church, *a*) the interpolation of a phrase or passage into the authorized service: such passages were later developed into semi-dramatic dialogues. *b*) any such passage. 4. a heading of subject matter.

-trope (trōp), [Gr. *-tropos;* see TROPE], a combining form meaning *turning*: see **-tropic.**

troph·ic (trof'ik), *adj.* [Gr. *trophikos* < *trophē*, food < *trephein*, to feed], of nutrition; having to do with the processes of nutrition.

troph·i·cal (trof'i-k'l), *adj.* trophic.

tro·phied (trō'fid), *adj.* decorated with trophies.

troph·o- (trof'ō, trof'ə), [< Gr. *trophē*, nourishment; see TROPHIC], a combining form meaning *of nutrition*, as in *trophoplasm*: also, before a vowel, **troph-.**

troph·o·blast (trof'ə-blast'), *n.* [*tropho-* + *blast*], a layer of ectoderm outside the blastoderm, by which the fertilized ovum is attached to the uterine wall and the developing embryo receives its nourishment.

troph·o·plasm (trof'ə-plaz'm), *n.* [*tropho-* + *-plasm*], 1. the nutritive or vegetative substance of an organic cell: distinguished from *idioplasm*. 2. formerly, a cytoplasmic substance distinguished from archoplasm.

tro·phy (trō'fi), *n.* [*pl.* TROPHIES (-fiz)], [Fr. *trophée;* L. *trophaeum, tropaium*, sign of victory < Gr. *tropaion*, a token of an enemy's defeat (e.g., helmet, shield); neut. adj. < *tropē*, a turning, defeat < *trepein;* see TROPE], 1. in ancient Greece and Rome, a memorial of victory erected on the battlefield or in some public place, consisting originally of a display of captured arms or other spoils. 2. a representation of this on a medal. 3. an architectural ornament representing a group of weapons. 4. something taken from the enemy and kept as a memorial of victory, as captured arms. 5. a lion's skin, deer's head, etc. displayed as evidence of hunting prowess. 6. a prize, usually a silver cup, awarded in an athletic or sports contest. 7. any memorial or memento.

-trophy, [Gr. *-trophia* < *trophein*, to nourish], a combining form meaning *nutrition, nourishment*, as in *hypertrophy.*

trop·ic (trop'ik), *n.* [ME. *tropik;* LL. *tropicus;* Gr. *tropikos*, belonging to a turn (of the sun at the solstices) < *tropē;* see TROPE], 1. either of two circles of the celestial sphere parallel to the equator, one, the *Tropic of Cancer*, 23°27′ north, and the other, the *Tropic of Capricorn*, 23°27′ south: they are the limits of the apparent north-and-south journey of the sun. 2. either of two lines of latitude on the earth that correspond to these and mark the boundaries of the Torrid Zone. 3. [also T-], *pl.* the region of the earth lying between these latitudes; Torrid Zone. *adj.* of the tropics; tropical. Abbreviated **trop.**

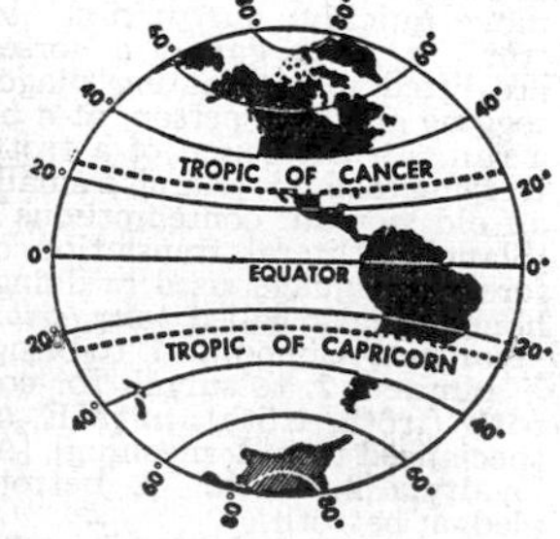

THE TROPICS

-trop·ic (trop′ik), [< Gr. *-tropos*, turning < *trepein;* see TROPE], a combining form meaning *turning, changing, tending to turn, tending to change, responding to a* (specified kind of) *stimulus*, as in *phototropic*.
trop·i·cal (trop′i-k′l), *adj.* 1. of, in, or characteristic of the tropics; hence, 2. very hot; sultry; torrid. 3. [L. *tropicus;* Gr. *tropikos*], of, or having the nature of, a trope; figurative. Abbreviated **trop.**
tropic bird, any of a number of tropical sea birds characterized by white plumage with black markings, a pair of long tail feathers, and webbed toes.
Tropic of Cancer, the parallel of latitude that is the northern boundary of the Torrid Zone: it is 23°27′ north of the equator: see **tropic**, map.
Tropic of Capricorn, the parallel of latitude that is the southern boundary of the Torrid Zone: it is 23°27′ south of the equator: see **tropic**, map.
tro·pin (trō′pin), *n.* tropine.
tro·pine (trō′pēn, trō′pin), *n.* [< *atropine*], a poisonous, colorless heterocyclic alkaloid, $C_8H_{15}ON$, produced by the hydrolysis of atropine or hyoscyamine.
tro·pism (trō′piz′m), *n.* [< Gr. *tropē*, a turn (see TROPE); + *-ism*], the tendency of a plant, animal, or part to move or turn in response to an external stimulus, either by attraction or repulsion, as a sunflower turns toward light.
-tropism, a combining form meaning *tropism, tendency to turn toward* or *away from* (something specified), as in *thermotropism, heliotropism.*
tro·pis·tic (trō-pis′tik), *adj.* of a tropism.
trop·o·log·i·cal (trop′ə-loj′i-k′l), *adj.* of or involving tropology; figurative.
tro·pol·o·gy (trō-pol′ə-ji), *n.* [LL. *tropologia;* Late Gr. *tropologia* < *tropos* (see TROPE) + *logos*, speech, discourse], 1. the use of tropes or figurative language. 2. a method of considering or interpreting Scripture in a figurative as well as a literal sense. 3. [*pl.* TROPOLOGIES (-jiz)], a treatise on figurative language.
trop·o·pause (trop′ə-pôz′), *n.* [< *tropo-*, as in *troposphere* + Gr. *pausis* (see PAUSE)], a transition zone between the troposphere and the stratosphere, at which the drop in temperature with increasing height ceases.
tro·poph·i·lous (trō-pof′ə-ləs), *adj.* [< Gr. *tropos*, a turning (see TROPE); + *-philous*], in *botany*, able to adjust to conditions of heat or cold, dryness or moisture, etc., as in seasonal changes: said of plants.
trop·o·phyte (trop′ə-fīt′), *n.* [< Gr. *tropos*, a turning (see TROPE); + *-phyte*], any tropophilous plant, as the deciduous trees of temperate zones.
trop·o·phyt·ic (trop′ə-fit′ik), *adj.* of, or having the nature of, a tropophyte.
trop·o·sphere (trop′ə-sfêr′), *n.* [Fr. *troposphère* < Gr. *tropos*, a turning (see TROPE) + Fr. *sphère* (see SPHERE)], the atmosphere below the stratosphere: in this stratum clouds form, convective disturbances occur, and the temperature decreases with the altitude.
-tropous, [< Gr. *tropos*, a turning (see TROPE); + *-ous*], a combining form meaning *turning* or *turned* (in some specified way or in response to some specified stimulus): used in forming botanical terms, as *phototropous.*
‡trop·po (trôp′pô; Eng. trop′ō), *adv.* [It.; LL. **troppus;* prob. < Frank. **throp*, a crowd; see TROOP], too; too much so: used in musical directions (e.g., *adagio ma non troppo*, slowly but not too much so).
-tropy, [< Gr. *tropē;* see TROPE], a combining form meaning *turning*, equivalent to: 1. -tropism. 2. -tropous.
Tros·sachs (tros′əks), *n.* a valley in Perth county, central Scotland: scene of Scott's *Lady of the Lake.*
trot (trot), *v.i.* [TROTTED (-id), TROTTING], [ME. *trotten;* OFr. *troter;* OHG. *trottōn*, to tread; for base see TREAD], 1. to move, ride, drive, run, or go at a trot. 2. to move quickly; hurry; run. *v.t.* to cause to go at a trot. *n.* 1. a gait of a horse, etc. in which the legs are lifted in alternating diagonal pairs; hence, 2. a jogging gait of a person, at a pace between a walk and a run. 3. the sound of a trotting horse. 4. [Rare], a trotting race. 5. [Rare], a small child; tot. 6. [Archaic], an old woman: contemptuous term. 7. a trotline. 8. [Slang], a literal translation of a literary work in a foreign language, used in doing school work, often dishonestly: also called *pony, crib.*
trot out, [Colloq.], 1. to bring out for others to see or admire. 2. to submit for consideration or approval.
troth (trôth, trōth), *n.* [ME. *trouthe* (see TRUTH) with specialized form & meaning], [Archaic], 1. faithfulness; loyalty. 2. truth. 3. betrothal. *v.t.* [Archaic], to pledge; betroth.
troth·plight (trôth′plīt′, trōth′plīt′), *n.* [Archaic], betrothal. *adj.* [Archaic], betrothed. *v.t.* [Archaic], to betroth.
trot·line (trot′līn′), *n.* [*trot, v.* + *line*], a strong fishing line suspended over the water, with short, baited lines hung from it at intervals; trawl line.
Trot·sky, Leon (trot′ski; Russ. trôt′ski), (born *Lev Davidovich Bronstein*), 1877–1940; Russian revolutionist and writer; Soviet commissar of war (1918–1925); exiled (1929).
Trot·sky·ism (trot′ski-iz′m), *n.* the doctrines, methods, and practices of Leon Trotsky and his followers.
Trot·sky·ist (trot′ski-ist), *n.* a Trotskyite.
Trot·sky·ite (trot′ski-īt′), *n.* an adherent of Trotskyism.
trot·ter (trot′ẽr), *n.* 1. an animal that trots; especially, a horse bred and trained for trotting races. 2. a person who moves about energetically and constantly. 3. the foot of a sheep or pig used as food.
tro·tyl (trō′til, trō′tēl), *n.* [trini*trotol*uene + *-yl*], trinitrotoluene.
trou·ba·dour (trōō′bə-dôr′, trōō′bə-dōr′, trōō′bə-door′), *n.* [Fr.; Pr. *trobador* < *trobar*, to find, compose in verse (LL. **tropare*); cf. It. *trovatore*], 1. any of a class of lyric poets and poet-musicians who lived in Provence, Catalonia, southern France, and northern Italy in the 11th, 12th, and 13th centuries and wrote poems of love and chivalry, usually with intricate stanza form and rhyme scheme; hence, 2. loosely, any minstrel or ballad singer.
trou·ble (trub′'l), *v.t.* [TROUBLED (-'ld), TROUBLING], [ME. *trublen;* OFr. *trubler, troubler;* LL. **turbulare* < L. *turbula*, disorderly group, dim. of *turba*, crowd], 1. to disturb or agitate: now used chiefly in the passive, as, the waters were *troubled.* 2. to cause (a person) mental agitation; worry; harass; perturb; vex. 3. to cause pain or discomfort to; afflict: as, his wound *troubles* him. 4. to cause (a person) difficulty or inconvenience; incommode: as, may I *trouble* you to change seats with him? 5. to pester, annoy, tease, bother, etc. *v.i.* 1. to make an effort; take pains; bother: as, do not *trouble* about a reply. 2. to be distressed; worry. *n.* 1. a state of mental distress; worry. 2. *a)* a misfortune; calamity; mishap. *b)* a distressing or difficult situation. 3. a person, circumstance, or event that causes annoyance, distress, difficulty, etc. 4. public disturbance; civil disorder. 5. effort; bother; pains: as, he took the *trouble* to shake hands with everyone present. 6. an illness; ailment.
trou·ble·mak·er (trub′'l-māk′ẽr), *n.* a person who habitually makes trouble for others.
trou·ble-shoot·er (trub′'l-shōōt′ẽr), *n.* a person who locates and repairs mechanical breakdowns; person charged with locating and eliminating the source of trouble in any flow of work: also **trouble shooter.**
trou·ble·some (trub′'l-səm), *adj.* [see -SOME], characterized by or causing trouble.
trou·blous (trub′ləs), *adj.* [OFr. *troubleus*], 1. troubled; agitated; disturbed; unsettled. 2. that causes trouble; troublesome. Now chiefly a literary usage.
‡trou-de-loup (trōō′də-lōō′), *n.* [*pl.* TROUS-DE-LOUP (trōō′də-lōō′)], [Fr., wolf hole], in *military usage*, any of the conical pits with a vertical pointed stake in the center of each, formerly built in rows as an obstacle to the enemy, especially to enemy cavalry.
trough (trôf; *occas.* trôth), *n.* [ME. *trogh, trough;* AS. *trog, troh;* akin to G. *trog;* IE. base **dru-k* < **derew-*, a tree (cf. TREE, TRAY); basic sense "wooden object"], 1. a long, narrow, open container of wood, stone, etc. for holding water or food for animals. 2. any similarly shaped vessel, as one for kneading or washing something. 3. a gutter under the eaves of a building, for carrying off rain water. 4. a long, narrow hollow or depression, as between waves.
trounce (trouns), *v.t.* [TROUNCED (trounst), TROUNCING], [orig. sense ("to trouble, distress") & var. *trounce* for *trance* suggest deriv. < ME. *traunse* (see TRANCE) in early sense, "extreme fear"], 1. to beat; thrash; flog. 2. [Colloq.], to defeat.
troupe (trōōp), *n.* [Fr., a troop; see TROOP], a troop; company; band; group, especially of actors, singers, etc. *v.i.* to travel as a member of a company of actors or entertainers. —*SYN.* see **troop.**
troup·er (trōōp′ẽr), *n.* 1. a member of a troupe; hence, 2. any actor of long experience.
troup·i·al (trōōp′i-əl), *n.* [Fr. *troupiale* < *troupe;* see TROOP: from their gregarious habit], any bird of a group including the North American orioles, meadow larks, cowbirds, grackles, and blackbirds, and the Central American caciques.
trou·sers (trou′zẽrz), *n.pl.* [lengthened (prob. after *drawers*) < obs. *trouse;* Ir. *triubhas;* cf. TREWS], an outer garment, especially for men and boys, covering the lower half of the body from the waist to the ankles (or, sometimes, as in boy's trousers, to the knees) and divided into separate coverings for the legs: also called *pants.*
trous·seau (trōō-sō′, trōō′sō), *n.* [*pl.* TROUSSEAUX, TROUSSEAUS (-sōz′, -sōz)], [< Fr., small bundle, dim. of *trousse*, a bundle, truss; see TRUSS; also early ME. *trusseau* (< Late OFr.) in sense 1], 1. originally, a bundle. 2. a bride's outfit of clothes, linen, jewelry, etc.
trout (trout), *n.* [*pl.* TROUT, TROUTS (trouts); see PLURAL, II, D, 2], [ME. *troute;* AS. *truht;* LL. *tructus, tructa* < Gr. *trōktēs*, kind of fish < *trōgein*, to gnaw], 1. any of various kinds of food and game fishes of the salmon family, usually spotted, found chiefly in fresh water: the most common types in North America are the brook (or speckled) trout, rainbow trout,

Great Lakes trout, and steelhead. 2. any of several unrelated troutlike fishes.

trou·vère (tro͞o-vâr′), *n.* [Fr.; OFr. *trovere* < *trover*, to find, compose (Pr. *trobar;* see TROUBADOUR)], any of a class of narrative poets in northern France from the 11th to the 14th century.

trou·veur (tro͞o-vũr′), *n.* a trouvère.

Trou·ville-sur-Mer (tro͞o′vēl′sür′mâr′), *n.* a seaport in northwestern France, on the English Channel: pop., 7,000.

tro·ver (trō′vẽr), *n.* [substantive use of OFr. *trover*, to find], in *law*, 1. originally, an action against a person who found another's goods and refused to return them. 2. an action to recover damages for goods withheld or used by another illegally.

trow (trō, trou), *v.i. & v.t.* [ME. *trowen, treowen;* AS. *treowian, truwian*, to have trust in (akin to G. *trauen*) < *treowe*, faith, belief; see TRUE], 1. [Obs.], to believe. 2. [Archaic], to think; suppose; imagine.

trow·el (trou′əl), *n.* [ME. *truel;* OFr. *troele, truelle;* LL. *truella* for L. *trulla*, small ladle, scoop, trowel < *trua*, stirring spoon, ladle], any of several small hand tools for spreading, smoothing, scooping, etc.; specifically, *a*) a thin, flat, rectangular tool of wood or metal, used for smoothing plaster. *b*) a thin, flat, pointed metal tool for applying and shaping mortar, as in bricklaying. *c*) a pointed, scooplike metal tool for loosening soil, digging holes, etc., as in transplanting. *v.t.* [TROWELED or TROWELLED (-əld), TROWELING or TROWELLING], to spread, smooth, shape, dig, etc. with a trowel.

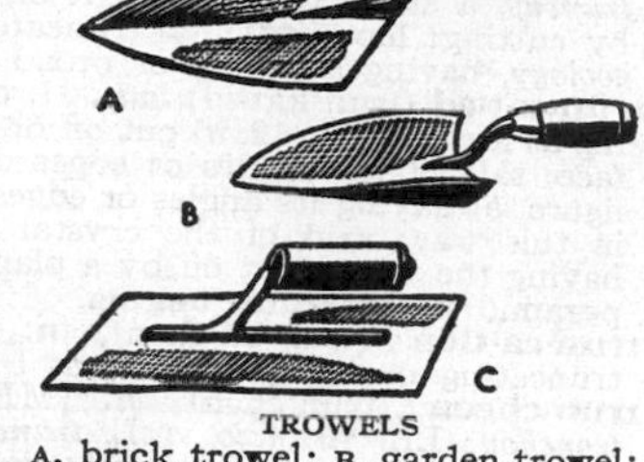

TROWELS
A, brick trowel; B, garden trowel; C, cement trowel

Troy (troi), *n.* 1. an ancient city in northwestern Asia Minor: scene of the Trojan War: also called *Ilium, Ilion.* 2. a city in east central New York, on the Hudson River: pop., 67,000.

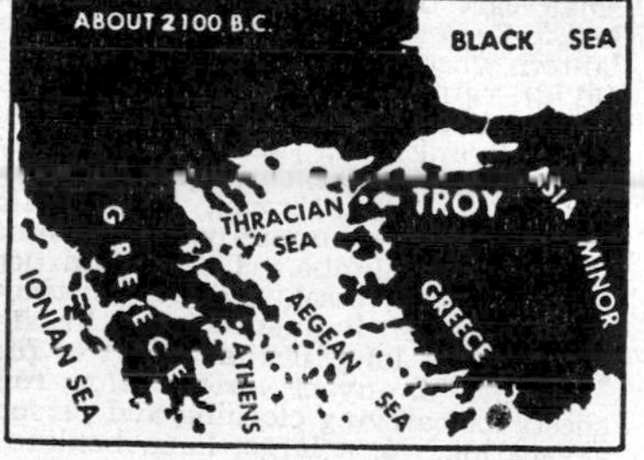

TROY

troy (troi), *adj.* by or in troy weight. *n.* troy weight. Abbreviated **t.**

Troyes (trwȧ), *n.* a city in northeastern France, on the Seine: pop., 59,000.

troy weight, [after *Troyes*, France, where it was first used], a system of weights for gold, silver, precious stones, etc., based on a pound containing 5,760 grains (0.82286 lb. avoirdupois), in which 24 grains = 1 pennyweight, 20 pennyweights = 1 ounce, and 12 ounces = 1 pound.

tru·an·cy (tro͞o′ən-si), *n.* 1. [*pl.* TRUANCIES (-siz)], the act or an instance of playing truant. 2. the state of being truant; truant behavior.

tru·ant (tro͞o′ənt), *n.* [ME.; OFr., a beggar, vagabond; of Celt. origin], 1. formerly, a lazy, idle person; hence, 2. a pupil who stays away from school without permission. 3. a person who shirks or neglects his work or duties. *adj.* 1. that is a truant; that plays truant. 2. idle; shiftless. 3. characteristic of a truant; errant; straying. *v.i.* to play truant.

truant officer, a school official who deals with cases of truancy.

truce (tro͞os), *n.* [ME. *triwes, treowes, trewes*, pl. of *trewe*, a pledge; AS. *treowa, truwa*, compact, faith; akin to *treowe*, true; see TRUE], 1. a temporary cessation of warfare by agreement between the belligerents; armistice. 2. any pause or respite, especially from trouble, pain, etc.

Tru·cial O·man (tro͞o′shəl ō-män′), a group of seven British-protected sheikdoms in eastern Arabia, on the Persian Gulf: pop., 86,000: also *Trucial States.*

truck (truk), *n.* [prob. < L. *trochus*, a hoop < Gr. *trochos*, a wheel, disk < *trechein*, to run], 1. a small, solid wheel or roller, especially one for a gun carriage. 2. a small wooden block or disk with holes for halyards, especially one at the top of a flagpole or mast. 3. a kind of barrow, consisting of an open frame with a pair of wheels at one end, used to carry trunks, crates, etc. 4. any of various low frames or platforms on wheels, sometimes motor-driven, for carrying heavy articles, as in a warehouse. 5. an automotive vehicle for hauling loads along highways, streets, etc.: also **motor truck.** 6. [British], an open railroad freight car. 7. a swiveling frame with two, three, or four pairs of wheels, usually provided with brakes and springs, forming the wheel unit under each end of a railroad car, streetcar, etc. *v.t.* to carry on a truck or trucks. *v.i.* 1. to do trucking. 2. to drive a truck.

truck (truk), *v.t. & v.i.* [Fr. *troquer*, to exchange, barter; origin obscure], 1. to exchange; barter. 2. [Rare], to peddle. *n.* [Anglo-Fr. *truke;* OFr. *troque* (Fr. *troc*) < the *v.*], 1. barter. 2. payment of wages in goods produced instead of money. 3. small commercial articles. 4. small articles of little value. 5. vegetables raised for sale in markets. 6. [Colloq.], dealings. 7. [Colloq.], trash; rubbish.

truck·age (truk′ij), *n.* [see -AGE], 1. transportation of goods by truck. 2. the charge for this.

truck·er (truk′ẽr), *n.* 1. a person who drives a truck; truck driver. 2. a person or company engaged in trucking.

truck·er (truk′ẽr), *n.* 1. a truck farmer. 2. a person who sells commodities or engages in barter.

truck farm, a farm where vegetables are grown to be marketed.

truck·ing (truk′iŋ), *n.* the business or process of carrying goods by truck.

truck·le (truk′'l), *n.* [ME. & OFr. *trocle;* L. *trochlea*, a pulley, roller; Gr. *trochilea* < *trochos*, a wheel; see TRUCK (vehicle)], 1. originally, a small wheel or caster. 2. a truckle bed. *v.i.* [TRUCKLED (-'ld), TRUCKLING], [< *truckle* in *truckle bed*], 1. to move on small wheels or casters. 2. to be servile; cringe, submit, toady, etc. (with *to*). *v.t.* to move (something) on small wheels or casters.

truckle bed, a low bed on small wheels or casters, that can be rolled under another bed when not in use; trundle bed.

truck·man (truk′mən), *n.* [*pl.* TRUCKMEN (-mən)], a trucker.

truc·u·lence (truk′yoo-ləns, tro͞o′kyoo-ləns), *n.* [L. *truculentia*], the quality or state of being truculent.

truc·u·len·cy (truk′yoo-lən-si, tro͞o′kyoo-lən-si), *n.* truculence.

truc·u·lent (truk′yoo-lənt, tro͞o′kyoo-lənt), *adj.* [< L. *truculentus* < *trux, trucis*, fierce, savage], 1. fierce; cruel; savage; ferocious; hence, 2. rude, harsh, mean, scathing, etc.: said especially of speech or writing.

trudge (truj), *v.i.* [TRUDGED (trujd), TRUDGING], [earlier *tredge, tridge* beside *trudge* suggest AS. **trycgan* (via dial., akin to AS. *trucian*, to fail, run short, MLG. *trüggelen*, to beg) < IE. base **dreu-g;* cf. Eng. dial. *truck*, to fail], to walk, especially wearily or laboriously. *n.* a walk or tramp, especially a wearying, tedious one.

trudg·en stroke (truj′ən), [after John *Trudgen*, Eng. amateur who introduced it (1873) from Argentina], a swimming stroke in which a double overarm motion and a scissors kick are used: also **trudgen.**

true (tro͞o), *adj.* [TRUER (-ẽr), TRUEST (-ist)], [ME. *treue, trewe;* AS. *treowe, trywe;* akin to G. *treu;* IE. base **derew-*, a tree (see TREE); basic sense "firm (as a tree)", as also in *trim*], 1. faithful; loyal; constant. 2. reliable; certain: as, a *true* indication. 3. in accordance with fact; that agrees with reality; not false. 4. truthful. 5. conforming to an original, pattern, rule, standard, etc.; exact; accurate; right; correct. 6. rightful; lawful; legitimate: as, the *true* heirs. 7. accurately fitted, placed, or shaped: as, the board is not *true.* 8. *a*) real; genuine; authentic: as, a *true* diamond. *b*) conforming to the ideal character of such; rightly so called: as, a *true* scholar. 9. [Archaic], honest; virtuous. 10. in *biology*, conforming to the essential characteristics of a genus, class, etc. 11. in *navigation, surveying*, etc., determined by the poles of the earth's axis, not by the earth's Magnetic Poles: as, *true* north. *adv.* 1. truly. 2. in *biology*, in accordance with the parental type; without variation: in phrase *breed true.* *v.t.* [TRUED (tro͞od), TRUING or TRUEING], to make true; especially, to fit, place, or shape accurately. *n.* that which is true (with *the*).

come true, to happen according to prediction or expectation; become a realized fact.

in true, properly set, adjusted, etc.; exact.

out of true, not properly set, adjusted, etc.; inexact.

true up, to fit, place, or shape accurately.

***SYN.*—true, actual,** and **real** are often used interchangeably to imply correspondence with fact, but in discriminating use, **true** implies conformity with a standard or model (he is not a *true* democrat) or with what actually exists (a *true* story), **actual** stresses existence or occurrence and is, hence, strictly applied to concrete things (*actual* and hypothetical examples), and **real** implies conformity between what something is and what it seems or pretends to be (*real* rubber, *real* courage).

true bill, a bill of indictment endorsed by a grand jury as supported by evidence sufficient to warrant a hearing of the case.

true-blue (trōō′blōō′), ***adj.*** very loyal; stanch.

true blue, 1. originally, a fast blue dye or color. 2. a 17th-century Scottish Presbyterian, or Covenanter: so called from the blue worn by the Covenanters in contradistinction to the red of the Royalists. 3. great loyalty. 4. a very loyal person.

true·born (trōō′bôrn′), ***adj.*** being a (specified) type of person from the nature of birth or early environment: as, a *trueborn* New Yorker.

true·bred (trōō′bred′), ***adj.*** 1. well-bred. 2. purebred.

true·heart·ed (trōō′här′tid), ***adj.*** loyal, faithful, honest, or sincere.

true level, an imaginary surface that is perpendicular at every point to the plumb line; specifically, the mean sea level thought of as extending throughout the globe; the geoid.

true·love (trōō′luv′), ***n.*** 1. a sweetheart; loved one. 2. the herb Paris, a plant having a whorl of four leaves which, with the flower or berry in the center, suggests a truelove knot. 3. [Obs.], a truelove knot.

truelove knot, a kind of bowknot that is hard to untie, a symbol of lasting love.

true-lov·er's knot (trōō′luv′ẽrz), a truelove knot.

true·pen·ny (trōō′pen′i), ***n.*** [Archaic], an honest or trusty person.

true ribs, see **rib.**

truf·fle (truf′′l, trōō′f′l), ***n.*** [< Fr. *truffe;* OIt. *truffa* < Oscan-Umbrian *tufera* < L. *tuber,* a knob, mushroom, truffle], any of a number of related fleshy, edible, potato-shaped fungi that grow underground.

tru·ism (trōō′iz′m), ***n.*** a statement the truth of which is obvious and well known; platitude; commonplace. —***SYN.*** see **platitude.**

Truk Islands (trōōk, trook; Eng. truk), a group of islands in the Caroline Islands: Japanese naval base during World War II: area, c. 50 sq. mi.

trull (trul), ***n.*** [G. *trolle, trulle* (via thieves' slang) < base seen in *troll, n. & v.;* cf. TROLLOP], a prostitute.

tru·ly (trōō′li), ***adv.*** 1. in a true manner; accurately, genuinely, faithfully, etc. 2. in fact; really; indeed.

Tru·man, Harry S. (trōō′mən), 1884– ; United States senator (1935–1944); thirty-third president of the United States (1945–1953).

Trum·bull, John (trum′b′l), 1. 1750–1831; American poet and satirist. 2. 1756–1843; son of *Jonathan;* American painter.

Trumbull, Jonathan, 1710–1785; American statesman.

trump (trump), ***n.*** [altered < *triumph;* cf. Fr. *triomphe,* It. *trionfo,* a trump], 1. any playing card of a suit that for the duration of a particular hand is ranked higher than any other suit, as through a winning bid: a trump can take any card of a suit other than its own, regardless of its denomination. 2. *sometimes pl.* a suit of trumps. 3. [Colloq.], a nice person, good fellow, etc. ***v.t.*** 1. to take (a trick, another card, etc.) by playing a trump. 2. to surpass; outdo. ***v.i.*** to play a trump.

trump up, to devise or concoct deceitfully or fraudulently, as a charge against a person.

trump (trump), ***n., v.t. & v.i.*** [ME. *trumpe;* OFr. *trompe;* prob. < Frank. **trumpa,* a tube; akin to ON. *trumba,* a tube], [Archaic or Poetic], trumpet.

trump·er·y (trum′pẽr-i), ***n.*** [*pl.* TRUMPERIES (-iz)], [Late MScot. *trompery;* Fr. *tromperie* < *tromper,* to deceive, cheat; origin obscure], 1. something showy but worthless; hence, 2. rubbish; nonsense. ***adj.*** showy but worthless; trashy; paltry.

trum·pet (trum′pit), ***n.*** [ME. *trumpete;* OFr. *trompette,* dim. of *trompe;* see TRUMP (trumpet)], 1. a brass-wind instrument with a powerful tone, consisting of a tube in an oblong loop, with a flared bell at one end, a cupped mouthpiece at the other, three valves for producing changes in tone, and small, secondary, looped tubes. 2. a person who plays this instrument in an orchestra, etc. 3. something shaped like a trumpet; especially, an ear trumpet. 4. *pl.* any of several plants with trumpet-shaped leaves. 5. a sound like that of a trumpet, especially one made by an elephant. 6. a trumpet-toned organ stop. ***v.i.*** 1. to blow a trumpet. 2. to make a sound like a trumpet. ***v.t.*** 1. to sound on a trumpet. 2. to sound or utter with a trumpetlike tone. 3. to proclaim loudly; noise abroad.

TRUMPET

trumpet creeper, any of a number of related woody vines with red, trumpet-shaped flowers.

trum·pet·er (trum′pit-ẽr), ***n.*** 1. a person who plays a trumpet. 2. a soldier, herald, etc. who signals on a trumpet; hence, 3. a person who proclaims or heralds something. 4. a long-legged, long-necked South American bird having a loud cry. 5. a trumpeter swan. 6. a crested pigeon with feathered feet.

trumpeter swan, a North American wild swan with a loud, resonant cry.

trumpet flower, 1. any of a number of plants with trumpet-shaped flowers, as the trumpet creeper and the trumpet honeysuckle. 2. the flower of any of these.

trumpet honeysuckle, an American honeysuckle with trumpet-shaped flowers that are scarlet on the outside and yellow on the inside.

trumpet vine, a trumpet creeper.

trum·pet·weed (trum′pit-wēd′), ***n.*** 1. a shrubby plant with flat clusters of grayish-white or purple flowers; boneset. 2. a tall plant with large clusters of rose or purplish flowers; joe-pye weed.

trum·pet·wood (trum′pit-wood′), ***n.*** a tree whose hollow stems are used for wind instruments.

trun·cate (truŋ′kāt), ***v.t.*** [TRUNCATED (-id), TRUNCATING], [< L. *truncatus,* pp. of *truncare,* to cut off < *truncus,* a stem, trunk], to cut off a part of; shorten by cutting; lop. ***adj.*** 1. truncated. 2. in *botany* & *zoology,* having a square or broad end: see **leaf,** illus.

trun·cat·ed (truŋ′kāt-id), ***adj.*** 1. cut short or appearing as if cut short. 2. *a*) cut off or replaced by a plane face: said of the angles or edges of a crystal or solid figure. *b*) having its angles or edges cut off or replaced in this way: said of the crystal or solid figure. 3. having the vertex cut off by a plane: said of a cone or pyramid: cf. **frustum, ungula.**

trun·ca·tion (truŋ-kā′shən), ***n.*** [LL. *truncatio*], a truncating or being truncated.

trun·cheon (trun′chən), ***n.*** [ME. *tronchoun;* OFr. *tronchon;* LL. **truncio* < L. *truncus,* a stem, trunk], 1. a short, thick staff; cudgel; club: now used chiefly of a policeman's baton. 2. any staff or baton of authority. 3. [Archaic], the shaft of a spear. 4. [Obs.], a trunk or stem, especially one with the branches lopped off. ***v.t.*** to beat with a truncheon.

trun·dle (trun′d′l), ***n.*** [altered (after the *v.*) < earlier *trendle, trindle;* AS. *trendel,* a ring, circle < *trendan,* to roll; see TREND], 1. a small wheel or caster. 2. a small cart or truck with low wheels. 3. a trundle bed. 4. *a*) a rolling motion. *b*) its sound. 5. *a*) a lantern wheel. *b*) any of its bars. ***v.t. & v.i.*** [TRUNDLED (-d′ld), TRUNDLING], 1. to roll along. 2. to rotate.

trundle bed, a low bed on casters; truckle bed.

trunk (truŋk), ***n.*** [ME.; OFr. *tronc;* L. *truncus,* a stem, trunk < *truncus,* maimed, mutilated; prob. < base akin to Eng. *throng*], 1. the main stem of a tree. 2. the body of a human being or animal, not including the head and limbs. 3. the main body or stem of a nerve, blood vessel, etc., as distinguished from its branches. 4. [influenced by Fr. *trompe,* trumpet, proboscis], a long, flexible snout or proboscis, as of an elephant. 5. any of various large, reinforced boxes or chests for carrying clothing and personal effects, as for a vacation. 6. a large, long, boxlike pipe, shaft, etc. for conveying air, water, etc. 7. *pl.* trunk hose; hence, 8. *pl.* tight-fitting, very short breeches worn by men for athletics, etc. 9. a trunk engine. 10. a trunk line. 11. the thorax of an insect. 12. a compartment in an automobile, usually in the rear, for holding a spare tire, luggage, etc. 13. in *architecture,* the shaft of a column. 14. in *nautical usage, a*) the part of a cabin above the upper deck. *b*) a boxlike or funnel-like casing, as for a centerboard, for connecting upper and lower hatches, etc. ***adj.*** designating or of a main line, as of a railroad or telephone system.

trunk engine, a steam or internal-combustion engine in which the connecting rod is pivoted to the piston.

trunk·fish (truŋk′fish′), ***n.*** [*pl.* TRUNKFISH, TRUNKFISHES (-iz); see FISH], any of a group of tropical fishes whose bodies are encased in fused, bony plates, with only the mouth, eyes, fins, and tail projecting through.

trunk hose, full, baglike breeches reaching about halfway to the knee, worn by men in the 16th and 17th centuries.

trunk line, a main line of a railroad, canal, telephone system, etc.

trun·nel (trun′′l), ***n.*** a treenail.

trun·nion (trun′yən), ***n.*** [Fr. *trognon,* a stump, trunk], either of two projecting journals or gudgeons on each side of a cannon, etc., on which it pivots.

truss (trus), ***v.t.*** [ME. *trussen;* OFr. *trousser,* to bundl together, pack; cf. TROUSSEAU], 1. originally, to ti into a bundle; bundle. 2. [Now Rare], *a*) to enclose c gird (the body) with a garment. *b*) to tie, fasten, c tighten (a garment, etc.). 3. to skewer or bind th wings, etc. of (a fowl) before cooking. 4. to support c strengthen with a constructional truss. ***n.*** [ME *trusse;* OFr. *trousse* < *trousser*], 1. a bundle or pacl 2. a bundle of hay, especially one of a certain weigh (usually 56–60 lbs.), or of straw (usually 36 lbs. 3. an iron band around a mast, having a goosenec for securing a yard. 4. an architectural bracket c modillion. 5. a flower cluster growing at the top a stem. 6. a framework of wood, metal, or both, for supporting a roof, bridge, etc. 7. an appliance for giving support in cases of rupture or hernia, usually consisting of a pad on a special belt.

truss bridge, a bridge supported largely by trusses.

truss·ing (trus'iŋ), *n.* 1. the act of a person who trusses. 2. the beams, rods, etc. forming a truss. 3. constructional trusses collectively. 4. bracing by or as by trusses.

TRUSS BRIDGE

trust (trust), *n.* [ME. *trust, tryst;* ON. *traust,* trust, lit., firmness < base seen in *true*], 1. firm belief or confidence in the honesty, integrity, reliability, justice, etc. of another person or thing; faith; reliance. 2. the person or thing trusted. 3. confident expectation, anticipation, or hope: as, have *trust* in the future. 4. [Rare], trustworthiness; loyalty. 5. *a)* the fact of having confidence placed in one. *b)* responsibility or obligation resulting from this. 6. keeping; care; custody. 7. something entrusted to a person; a charge, duty, etc. 8. confidence in a purchaser's intention or future ability to pay for goods, etc. delivered; credit: as, he sells on *trust.* 9. *a)* a combination of corporations in the same industry or allied industries, usually the largest producers, in which the stockholders turn over their stock to a board of trustees, who issue trust certificates to them and pay them dividends: the purposes of trusts are to reduce costs of production, control prices, and eliminate competition, thereby establishing a monopoly and increasing profits; they have been declared illegal in the United States. *b)* any association of industrialists, business firms, etc. for establishing a national or international monopoly by price fixing, ownership of controlling stock, etc.; cartel: see also **monopoly.** 10. in *law, a)* the confidence reposed in a person by giving him nominal ownership of property, which he is to keep, use, or administer for another's benefit. *b)* an estate or property under the charge of a trustee or trustees. *c)* a trustee or group of trustees. *d)* a person's right to property held in trust for him. *v.i.* [ME. *trusten,* altered (after the *n.*) < ON. *treysta,* to trust, confide < base of *traust*], 1. to have trust or faith; place reliance; be confident. 2. to hope (with *for*). 3. to give business credit. *v.t.* 1. to believe in the honesty, integrity, justice, etc. of; have confidence in; rely on. 2. to commit (*to* a person's care); entrust (*to* a person). 3. to put something confidently in the charge of (a person): as, I *trusted* him with my car. 4. to allow to do something without fear of the outcome: as, I *trust* my child to cross the street by himself. 5. to believe; suppose. 6. to hope; expect. 7. to give business credit to. *adj.* 1. relating to a trust or trusts. 2. held in trust. 3. managing for an owner; acting as trustee. —***SYN.*** see **belief, monopoly, rely.**

in trust, in the condition of being entrusted to another's care.

trust to, to rely on.

trust buster, a government official who seeks to dissolve trusts (sense 9) through the vigorous enforcement of antitrust laws.

trust company, 1. a company formed to act as trustee. 2. a bank organized to handle trusts and carry on all banking operations except the issuance of bank notes.

trus·tee (trus-tē'), *n.* 1. a person to whom another's property or the management of another's property is entrusted. 2. any of a group or board of persons appointed to manage the affairs of a college, hospital, etc. 3. a person in whose hands the property of a debtor is attached by the trustee process; garnishee. *v.t.* [TRUSTEED (-tēd'), TRUSTEEING], 1. to commit (property or management) to a trustee or trustees. 2. to attach by the trustee process; garnish.

trustee process, garnishment.

trus·tee·ship (trus-tē'ship), *n.* [see -SHIP], 1. the position or function of a trustee. 2. *a)* a commission from the United Nations to a country to administer some region, colony, etc. (called the *trust territory*). *b)* the condition or fact of being a trust territory.

trust·ful (trust'fəl), *adj.* full of trust; ready to confide or believe; trusting.

trust fund, money, stock, etc. held in trust.

trust·i·ly (trus't'l-i), *adv.* in a trusty manner.

trust·i·ness (trus'ti-nis), *n.* the quality of being trusty.

trust·ing (trus'tiŋ), *adj.* that trusts; trustful.

trust·less (trust'lis), *adj.* 1. not to be trusted; unreliable; treacherous. 2. distrustful.

trust territory, a region, colony, etc. placed under the administrative authority of a country by the United Nations: such territories include former mandates held under the League of Nations and colonies, etc. taken from Axis countries following World War II.

trust·wor·thi·ly (trust'wũr'*th*ə-li), *adv.* in a trustworthy manner.

trust·wor·thi·ness (trust'wũr'*th*i-nis), *n.* the quality of being trustworthy.

trust·wor·thy (trust'wũr'*th*i), *adj.* worthy of trust; dependable; reliable. —***SYN.*** see **reliable.**

trust·y (trus'ti), *adj.* [TRUSTIER (-ti-ẽr), TRUSTIEST (-ti-ist)], 1. [Now Rare], trustful. 2. that can be relied upon; dependable; trustworthy. *n.* [*pl.* TRUSTIES (-tiz)], 1. a trusted person. 2. a convict granted special privileges because of good behavior. —***SYN.*** see **reliable.**

truth (trōōth), *n.* [*pl.* TRUTHS (trōō*th*z, trōōths)], [ME. *treuthe;* AS. *treowth, triuwth;* see TRUE & -TH], 1. the quality or state of being true; specifically, *a)* formerly, loyalty; trustworthiness. *b)* sincerity; genuineness; honesty. *c)* the quality of being in accordance with experience, facts, or reality; conformity with fact. *d)* reality; actual existence. *e)* agreement with a standard, rule, etc.; correctness; accuracy. 2. that which is true; statement, etc. which accords with fact or reality. 3. an established or verified fact, principle, etc.

in truth, truly; in fact.

of a truth, certainly.

SYN.—**truth** suggests conformity with the facts or with reality, either as an idealized abstraction ("What is *truth?*" said jesting Pilate) or in actual application to statements, ideas, act, etc. (there is no *truth* in that rumor); **veracity,** as applied to persons or to their utterances, connotes habitual adherence to the truth (I cannot doubt his *veracity*); **verity,** as applied to things, connotes correspondence with fact or with reality (the *verity* of his thesis); **verisimilitude,** as applied to literary or artistic representations, connotes correspondence with actual, especially universal, truths (the *verisimilitude* of the characterizations in a novel). —***ANT.*** falseness, falsity.

truth·ful (trōōth'fəl), *adj.* 1. telling the truth; presenting the facts; veracious; honest. 2. corresponding with fact or reality, as an artistic representation.

try (trī), *v.t.* [TRIED (trīd), TRYING], [ME. *trien;* OFr. *trier;* ? < LL. **tritare,* to cull out, grind < L. *tritus,* pp. of *terere,* to rub, thresh grain; cf. TRITE], 1. originally, to separate; set apart; hence, 2. *a)* to melt out or render, as fat. *b)* to extract or refine by heating, as metal. Usually with *out.* 3. [Now Rare], to settle (a matter, quarrel, etc.) by a test or contest; fight out: as, the knights *tried* the dispute in a joust. 4. *a)* to examine and decide (a case) in a law court. *b)* to determine legally the guilt or innocence of (a person). *c)* to preside as judge at the trial of (a case or person). 5. to put to the proof; test. 6. to make smooth or even with a trying plane. 7. to subject to trials, annoyance, etc.; afflict: as, he was sorely *tried.* 8. to subject to a severe test or strain: as, rigors that *try* one's stamina. 9. to test the operation or effect of; experiment with; make a trial of: as, *try* this new recipe. 10. to attempt to find out by experiment or effort: as, he left the farm to *try* his fortune in the city. 11. to make an effort to do; attempt; endeavor. 12. [Obs.], to find to be so by test or experience; prove. *v.i.* 1. to make an effort, attempt, or endeavor: colloquially, *try* in this sense is often followed by *and* and a co-ordinate verb, as, please *try* and behave. 2. to make an experiment. *n.* 1. a trying; attempt; effort; trial. 2. in *Rugby football,* a grounding of the ball on or behind the opponent's goal line: this play counts 3 points and entitles the scoring team to try to kick a goal for 2 additional points.

try on, to test the fit or appearance of (a garment) by putting it on.

try out, 1. to test or find out the quality, result, value, etc. of; experiment with. 2. to test one's ability to qualify in a competition, for a job, etc.

SYN.—**try** is commonly the simple direct word for putting forth effort to do something (*try* to come), but specifically it connotes experimentation in testing or proving something (I'll *try* your recipe); **attempt,** somewhat more formal, suggests a setting out to accomplish something but often connotes failure (he had *attempted* to take his life); **endeavor** suggests exertion and determined effort in the face of difficulties (we shall *endeavor* to recover your loss); **essay** connotes a tentative experimenting to test the feasibility of something difficult (he will not *essay* the high jump); **strive** suggests great, earnest exertion to accomplish something (*strive* to win); **struggle** suggests a violent striving to overcome obstacles or to free oneself from an impediment (he *struggled* to reach the top).

try·ing (trī'iŋ), *adj.* [ppr. of *try*], that tries; annoying; exasperating; irksome; painful.

trying plane, a long finishing plane for use on edges, etc. that must be accurate.

try·ma (trī'mə), *n.* [Mod. L. < Gr. *tryma, trymē,* a hole < *tryein,* to rub down, wear away], a nut having a fleshy or fibrous epicarp that bursts upon ripening, as the walnut and hickory.

try·out (trī'out'), *n.* [Colloq.], an opportunity to prove, or a test to determine, fitness or qualifications, as for competition in sports, a role in a play, etc.

tryp·a·no·so·ma (trip′ə-nə-sō′mə), *n.* a trypanosome.

tryp·a·no·some (trip′ə-nə-sōm′), *n.* [< Gr. *trypanon*, borer; + *-some* (body)], any of a group of flagellate protozoans that live as parasites in the blood of man and other vertebrates and often cause serious diseases, as sleeping sickness.

tryp·a·no·so·mi·a·sis (trip′ə-nō′sō-mī′ə-sis), *n.* [see -IASIS], any disease caused by a trypanosome.

tryp·sin (trip′sin), *n.* [G. < Gr. *tripsis*, a rubbing < *tribein*, to rub; + pep*sin*], 1. a digestive enzyme in the pancreatic juice: it changes proteins into peptones. 2. any of several similar enzymes.

tryp·tic (trip′tik), *adj.* of, or having the nature of, a trypsin.

tryp·to·phan (trip′tə-fan′), *n.* [< *tryptic* + *-phane*], an aromatic, crystalline amino acid, $C_{11}H_{12}O_2N_2$, produced in digestion by the action of trypsin on proteins.

tryp·to·phane (trip′tə-fān′), *n.* tryptophan.

try·sail (trī′s'l, trī′sāl′), *n.* [< naut. phr. *a try*, the position of lying to in a storm], a small, stout, fore-and-aft sail hoisted when other canvas has been lowered, to keep a vessel's head to the wind in a storm.

try square, an instrument consisting of two pieces set at right angles, used for testing the accuracy of square work and for marking off right angles.

tryst (trist, trīst), *n.* [ME. *trist, tristre;* OFr. *tristre*, hunting station, hence hunting rendezvous; prob. < ON. base], 1. an appointment to meet at a specified time and place, as one made by lovers. 2. a meeting held by appointment. 3. a trysting place. 4. [Scot.], a market; fair. *v.t. & v.i.* [Scot.], to agree to meet.

trysting place, an appointed meeting place, as of lovers; rendezvous.

tsa·di (tsä′di), *n.* the eighteenth letter of the Hebrew alphabet (צ, ץ), corresponding phonetically to English *ts*: see **alphabet**, table: also **sadhe.**

tsar (tsär), *n.* a czar.

tsar·dom (tsär′dəm), *n.* czardom.

tsar·e·vitch (tsär′ə-vich′), *n.* a czarevitch.

tsa·rev·na (tsä-rev′nə), *n.* a czarevna.

tsa·ri·na (tsä-rē′nə), *n.* a czarina.

tsar·ism (tsär′iz'm), *n.* czarism.

tsar·ist (tsär′ist), *adj. & n.* czarist.

Tsa·ri·tsyn (tsä-rit′sin), *n.* Stalingrad: former name.

tsa·rit·za (tsä-rēt′sä), *n.* a czarina.

Tschaikowsky, Pëtr Ilich, see **Tchaikovsky.**

tset·se (tset′si), *n.* [S.Afr. D. < the Bantu (Bechuana) name], any of several small flies of central and southern Africa, one of which is a carrier of nagana and another a carrier of sleeping sickness: also **tsetse fly.**

TSETSE FLY (1/4 in. long)

T.Sgt., Technical Sergeant.

Tshi (chwē, chē), *n.* [Tshi], a group of Sudanic languages of the Gold Coast, Africa. *adj.* designating or of these languages or their speakers.

T-shirt (tē′shûrt′), *n.* [so named because T-shaped], a collarless, cotton, pull-over shirt with very short sleeves.

Tsi·nan (tsē′nän′; Chin. jē′nän′), *n.* a city in northeastern China, on the Hwang Ho River: capital of Shantung province: pop., 472,000.

Tsing·ta·o (tsiŋ′tou′; Chin. chiŋ′dou′), *n.* a seaport in Shantung province, China, on the Yellow Sea: pop., 788,000 (est. 1947).

Tsin·ling Shan (tsin′liŋ′ shän; Chin. jē′liŋ′ shän), a mountain range in central China.

Tsi·tsi·har (tsē′tsē′här′; Chin. chē′chē′här′), *n.* Lungkiang, a city in Manchuria: the Japanese name.

tsp., teaspoon; teaspoons.

T square, a T-shaped ruler for drawing parallel lines.

Tsu·shi·ma (tsoo͞′shē-mä′), *n.* a Japanese island between Korea and Japan: area, 271 sq. mi.

Tsushima Strait, a strait between the islands of Tsushima and Kyushu, Japan: scene of a Japanese naval victory over the Russians (1905).

T SQUARE

Tu, in *chemistry*, thulium.

Tu., Tuesday.

T.U., 1. Trade Union. 2. Training Unit.

Tu·a·mo·tu Archipelago (too͞′ä-mô′-too͞), a group of French islands in Polynesia, South Pacific: area, 330 sq. mi.; pop., 4,800: also called *Paumoto Archipelago, Low Archipelago.*

Tua·reg (twä′reg), *n.* [Berber pronun. of Ar. *Tawāriq*, pl. of *Tāriq* < *tereq*, to give up: reason for name obscure], 1. a member of a group of Berber tribes of the western and central Sahara. 2. their Hamitic language.

tub (tub), *n.* [ME. *tubbe;* MD. *tubbe;* IE. base (**dəp-*) < **dā(i)-*, to part, divide, cut up (cf. TAP, TIP, TOP)], 1. a round, broad, open, wooden container, usually formed of staves and hoops fastened around a flat bottom. 2. any similarly large, open container of metal, stone, etc., as for washing. 3. the contents of a tub, or a tub and its contents. 4. a small cask holding about four gallons. 5. *a*) a bucket or tram for carrying coal, ore, etc. in a mine. *b*) the lining of a mining shaft. 6. a bathtub. 7. [British Colloq.], a bath in a tub. 8. [Colloq.], a slow-moving, clumsy ship or boat. *v.t. & v.i.* [TUBBED (tubd), TUBBING], 1. [Colloq.], to wash in a tub. 2. [British Colloq.], to bathe (oneself).

tu·ba (too͞′bə, tū′bə), *n.* [*pl.* TUBAS (-bəz), TUBAE (-bē)], [L., a trumpet], 1. in ancient Rome, a straight war trumpet. 2. a large brass-wind instrument of the saxhorn group. 3. a powerful reed organ stop of 8-foot pitch.

tub·al (too͞′b'l, tū′b'l), *adj.* of a tube; especially, of a Fallopian tube. *n.* a Fallopian tube.

Tu·bal-cain (too͞′bəl-kān′, tū′bəl-kān′), *n.* in the *Bible*, a worker in brass and iron: Gen. 4:22.

tu·bate (too͞′bāt, tū′bāt), *adj.* having or forming a tube or tubes.

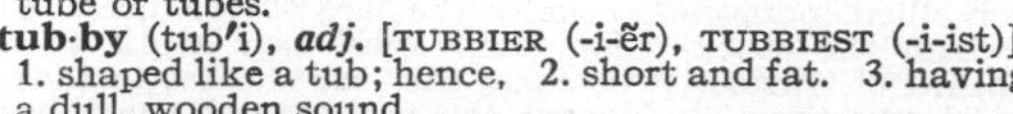

TUBA

tub·by (tub′i), *adj.* [TUBBIER (-i-ẽr), TUBBIEST (-i-ist)], 1. shaped like a tub; hence, 2. short and fat. 3. having a dull, wooden sound.

tube (too͞b, tūb), *n.* [Fr.; L. *tubus*, a pipe], 1. a hollow cylinder or pipe of metal, glass, rubber, etc., usually long in proportion to its diameter, used for conveying fluids, etc. 2. an enclosed, hollow cylinder of thin, soft metal, fitted at one end with a screw cap and used for holding toothpaste, artist's paints, etc. 3. an instrument, part, organ, etc. resembling a tube: as, a bronchial *tube.* 4. an electron tube. 5. *a*) an underground tunnel for an electric railroad. *b*) [Colloq.], the electric railroad itself. 6. [Archaic], a telescope. 7. in *botany*, the lower, united part of a gamopetalous corolla or a gamosepalous calyx. 8. in *electricity*, a tubular space bounded by lines of force or induction: also **tube of force, tube of induction.** *v.t.* [TUBED (too͞bd, tūbd), TUBING], 1. to provide with, place in, or pass through a tube or tubes. 2. to make tubular.

tube·less tire (too͞b′lis, tūb′lis), a kind of tire for a vehicle, consisting of a single air-filled unit instead of an outer casing and inner tube.

tu·ber (too͞′bẽr, tū′bẽr), *n.* [L., lit., a swelling, knob, truffle], 1. a short, thickened, fleshy part of an underground stem, as a potato: new plants develop from the buds, or eyes, that grow in the axils of the minute scale leaves of a tuber. 2. a tubercle; swelling.

tu·ber·cle (too͞′bẽr-k'l, tū′bẽr-k'l), *n.* [L. *tuberculum*, dim. of *tuber;* see TUBER], any small, rounded projection or process; specifically, *a*) in *botany*, any of the wartlike growths on the roots of some plants. *b*) in *anatomy*, a knoblike elevation, as on a bone. *c*) in *medicine*, any abnormal hard nodule or swelling; especially, the typical nodular lesion of tuberculosis.

tubercle bacillus, the bacillus causing tuberculosis: abbreviated **TB, T.B., tb., t.b.**

tu·ber·cu·lar (too͞-bũr′kyoo-lẽr, tū-bũr′kyoo-lẽr, tə-bũr′kyoo-lẽr), *adj.* [< L. *tuberculum* (see TUBERCLE); + *-ar*], 1. of, like, or having a tubercle or tubercles. 2. tuberculous. *n.* a tuberculous person.

tu·ber·cu·late (too͞-bũr′kyoo-lit, tū-bũr′kyoo-lāt′, tə-bũr′kyoo-lit), *adj.* [Mod. L. *tuberculatus* < L. *tuberculum;* see TUBERCLE], 1. tuberculated. 2. tubercular.

tu·ber·cu·lat·ed (too͞-bũr′kyoo-lā′tid, tū-bũr′kyoo-lā′-tid, tə-bũr′kyoo-lā′tid), *adj.* having, characterized by, or shaped like a tubercle or tubercles.

tu·ber·cu·la·tion (too͞-bũr′kyoo-lā′shən, tū-bũr′kyoo-lā′shən, tə-bũr′kyoo-lā′shən), *n.* the development of tubercles.

tu·ber·cu·lin (too͞-bũr′kyoo-lin, tū-bũr′kyoo-lin, tə-bũr′kyoo-lin), *n.* [< L. *tuberculum* (see TUBERCLE); + *-in*], a sterile liquid preparation made from the growth products or extracts of a tubercle bacillus culture and injected into the skin as a test for tuberculosis.

tu·ber·cu·line (too͞-bũr′kyoo-lin, tū-bũr′kyoo-lēn′, tə-bũr′kyoo-lin), *n.* tuberculin.

tu·ber·cu·lo- (too͞-bũr′kyoo-lō, tū-bũr′kyoo-lə, tə-bũr′-kyoo-lō), [< L. *tuberculum;* see TUBERCLE], a combining form meaning: 1. *tuberculous.* 2. *tubercle bacillus.* 3. *tuberculosis.* Also, before a vowel, **tubercul-.**

tu·ber·cu·loid (too͞-bũr′kyoo-loid′, tū-bũr′kyoo-loid′, tə-bũr′kyoo-loid′), *adj.* resembling a tubercle.

tu·ber·cu·lo·sis (too͞-bũr′kyoo-lō′sis, tū-bũr′kyoo-lō′sis, tə-bũr′kyoo-lō′sis), *n.* [Mod. L. < L. *tuberculum;* see TUBERCLE & -OSIS], an infectious disease caused by the tubercle bacillus and characterized by the formation of tubercles in various tissues of the body; especially, tuberculosis of the lungs; pulmonary phthisis; consumption: abbreviated **TB, T.B., tb., t.b.**

tu·ber·cu·lous (to͞o-bũr′kyoo-ləs, tū-bũr′kyoo-ləs, tə-bũr′kyoo-ləs), *adj.* 1. having tuberculosis. 2. tubercular.

tube·rose (to͞ob′rōz′, tūb′rōz′), *n.* [Mod. L. *tuberosa* < L. *tuberosus*, knobby < *tuber;* see TUBER], a plant with a bulblike root, short, grasslike leaves, and sweet, white, funnel-shaped flowers.

tu·ber·ose (to͞o′bẽr-ōs′, tū′bẽr-ōs′), *adj.* tuberous.

tu·ber·os·i·ty (to͞o′bə-ros′ə-ti, tū′bə-ros′ə-ti), *n.* [*pl.* TUBEROSITIES (-tiz)], [Fr. *tubérosité*], 1. the quality or condition of being tuberous. 2. a rounded swelling or projection, as on a bone for the attachment of a muscle or tendon.

tu·ber·ous (to͞o′bẽr-əs, tū′bẽr-əs), *adj.* [Fr. *tubéreux;* L. *tuberosus;* see TUBEROSE, *n.*], 1. covered with rounded, wartlike swellings; knobby. 2. in *botany*, of, like, or having a tuber or tubers.

tuberous root, a tuberlike root without buds or scale leaves, as of the dahlia.

tub·ing (to͞ob′iŋ, tūb′iŋ), *n.* 1. the process of making tubes. 2. a series or system of tubes. 3. tubes collectively. 4. material in the form of a tube. 5. a piece of a tube.

tu·bu·lar (to͞o′byoo-lẽr, tū′byoo-lẽr), *adj.* [< L. *tubulus*, dim. of *tubus*, a tube, pipe], 1. of or shaped like a tube or tubes. 2. made or furnished with tubes. 3. sounding as if produced by blowing through a tube.

tu·bu·late (to͞o′byoo-lāt, tū′byoo-lāt; *also, for adj.,* to͞o′byoo-lit), *adj.* [L. *tubulatus*], 1. tubular (senses 1 & 2). 2. of, shaped like, or provided with a tubulure. *v.t.* [TUBULATED (-id), TUBULATING], to shape into or provide with a tube or tubulure.

tu·bu·la·tion (to͞o′byoo-lā′shən, tū′byoo-lā′shən), *n.* a tubulating or being tubulated.

tu·bule (to͞o′būl, tū′būl), *n.* [< L. *tubulus;* see TUBULAR], a small tube; minute tubular structure in an animal or plant.

tu·bu·li- (to͞o′byoo-li, tū′byoo-lə), [< L. *tubulus;* see TUBULAR], a combining form meaning *tubule.*

tu·bu·li·flo·rous (to͞o′byoo-lə-flôr′əs, tū′byoo-lə-flôr′əs), *adj.* having flowers all of whose corollas are tubular: said of certain composite plants.

tu·bu·lous (to͞o′byoo-ləs, tū′byoo-ləs), *adj.* [< *tubule* + *-ous*], 1. tubular. 2. having small, tubelike flowers.

tu·bu·lure (to͞o′byoo-lyoor, tū′byoo-lyoor), *n.* [Fr. < L. *tubulus;* see TUBULAR], a short tube or tubular opening at the top of a retort, etc.

Tu·ca·na (to͞o-kā′nə, tū-kā′nə), *n.* [Mod. L.], a southern constellation: see **constellation,** chart.

tuck (tuk), *v.t.* [ME. *touken, tuken* < MD. *tucken*, to tuck & cognate AS. *tucian*, to ill-treat, lit., to tug; for the base see TOW, TUG], 1. to pull up or gather up in a fold or folds; draw together, as to make shorter (usually with *up*). 2. *a)* to thrust the edges of (a sheet, napkin, etc.) under or in, in order to make secure (usually with *up, in,* etc.). *b)* to cover or wrap snugly in or as in this way: as, she *tucked* the baby in bed. 3. to put or press snugly into a small space; cram; fit: as, she managed to *tuck* her shoes in the suitcase. 4. to make a sewed fold or folds in (a garment). *v.i.* 1. to draw together; pucker. 2. to make tucks. *n.* 1. a sewed fold in a garment, for shortening or decoration. 2. the part of a ship under the stern where the ends of the bottom planks meet. 3. [British Slang], food.
tuck away (or **in**), [British Slang], to eat or drink heartily.

tuck (tuk), *n.* [Fr. *estoc* < OFr. *estoquier* < D. *stocken*, to stick, pierce], [Archaic], a thin sword or rapier.

tuck (tuk, to͝ok), *v.t. & n.* [ME. *tukken;* OFr. (Northern) *toker, toquer*, var. of *toucher*, to touch; cf. TOCSIN, TUCKET], [Scot.], beat; tap.

Tuck, Friar (tuk), a jovial friar who was a member of Robin Hood's band.

tuck·a·hoe (tuk′ə-hō′), *n.* [< Am. Ind. (Algonquian); cf. Virginian *tockawhoughe*], a brown, underground fungus, producing an edible, weblike substance: also called *Indian bread, Virginia truffle.*

tuck·er (tuk′ẽr), *n.* [ME. *toukere*, person who dresses cloth stretched on tenterhooks (whence personal name TUCKER) < *touken;* see TUCK (to pull up)], 1. a person who makes tucks. 2. a sewing machine attachment for making tucks. 3. a neck and shoulder covering worn with a low-cut bodice by women in the 17th and 18th centuries. 4. a detachable collar or chemisette of thin muslin, etc.

tuck·er (tuk′ẽr), *v.t.* [prob. related to *tuck* (to pull up) in sense "to finish (cloth)"], [Colloq.], to tire; weary (usually with *out*).

tuck·et (tuk′it), *n.* [< *tuck* (to beat a drum); cf. TOCCATA], [Archaic], a flourish on a trumpet.

Tuc·son (to͞o′son, to͞o-son′), *n.* a city in southern Arizona: pop., 213,000.

Tu·cu·mán (to͞o′ko͞o-män′), *n.* a city in northern Argentina: pop., 245,000.

-tude (to͞od, tūd), [Fr.; L. *-tudo, -tudinis*], a noun-forming suffix corresponding to *-ness*, as in *certitude.*

Tu·dor (to͞o′dẽr, tū′dẽr), *adj.* 1. of or belonging to a ruling family of England (1485–1603), descended from Owen Tudor, a Welsh nobleman who married the widow of Henry V: it included Henry VII, Henry VIII, Edward VI, Mary I, and Elizabeth I. 2. of the period of their reigns. 3. designating or of a style of architecture that prevailed during the reign of the Tudors: it is characterized by flat arches, shallow moldings, profuse paneling, etc. *n.* 1. a sovereign of the Tudor line. 2. a poet, artist, etc. of the time of the Tudors.

Tues·day (to͞oz′di, tūz′di), *n.* [ME. *Tuesdai, Twisdai;* AS. *Tiwes dæg*, Tiw's day, rendering L. *Martis dies;* AS. *Tiw*, god of war, is cognate with Gr. *Zeus*, L. *deus* (cf. JUPITER)], the third day of the week: abbreviated **T., Tu., Tues.**

tu·fa (to͞o′fə, tū′fə), *n.* [It. *tufo, tufa*, kind of porous stone < L. *tofus*, tuff, tufa], 1. a porous limestone formed by deposits from springs and streams. 2. tuff. Also **toph, tophe.**

tu·fa·ceous (to͞o-fā′shəs, tyoo-fā′shəs), *adj.* of or like tufa.

tuff (tuf), *n.* [Fr. *tuf*, earlier *tufe, tuffe;* It. *tufo;* see TUFA], a porous rock, usually stratified, formed by consolidation of volcanic ashes, dust, etc.

tuff·a·ceous (tuf-ā′shəs), *adj.* of or like tuff.

tuft (tuft), *n.* [ME.; OFr. *tuffe;* prob. < Gmc. (cf. TOP); the *-t* is unhistoric (cf. GRAFT)], 1. a bunch of hairs, feathers, grass, etc. growing closely together or attached at the base. 2. any similar cluster; specifically, *a)* a clump of plants or trees. *b)* any of the clusters of threads drawn tightly through a mattress, quilt, etc. to hold the padding in place; also, a button to which such a tuft is fastened. *v.t.* 1. to provide or decorate with a tuft or tufts. 2. to secure the padding of (a quilt, mattress, etc.) by means of regularly spaced tufts. *v.i.* to grow in or form into tufts.

tuft·ed (tuf′tid), *adj.* 1. having, provided with, or decorated with a tuft or tufts. 2. formed into or growing in a tuft or tufts.

tuft·hunt·er (tuft′hun′tẽr), *n.* [*tuft* (in Eng. university slang sense of "titled undergraduate": from the tuft or tassel formerly worn by titled undergraduates at Oxford and Cambridge) + *hunter*], a person who tries to get acquainted with distinguished or wealthy people; social climber; sycophant; toady; snob.

tuft·y (tuf′ti), *adj.* 1. full of or covered with tufts. 2. growing in or forming a tuft or tufts.

tug (tug), *v.i.* [TUGGED (tugd), TUGGING], [ME. *tuggen, toggen;* prob. < ON. *toga*, to draw, pull, but taken as intens. < pp. base of AS. *teon*, to pull; IE. base **deuk-*, to draw, pull, as also in L. *ducere* (cf. DUKE, EDUCATE, etc.), Eng. *tow*], 1. to labor; toil; struggle. 2. to exert great effort in pulling; pull hard; drag; haul (often with *at*). *v.t.* 1. to pull at with great force; strain at. 2. to drag; haul. 3. to tow with a tugboat. *n.* 1. a tugging; a hard pull. 2. a great effort or strenuous contest. 3. a rope, chain, etc. used for tugging or pulling; especially, a trace of a harness: see **harness,** illus. 4. a tugboat. —*SYN.* see **pull.**

tug·boat (tug′bōt′), *n.* a small, sturdily built, powerful boat designed for towing or pushing ships, barges, etc.

tug·ger (tug′ẽr), *n.* a person or thing that tugs.

tug of war, 1. a contest in which two teams pull at opposite ends of a rope, each trying to drag the other across a central line. 2. any hard struggle between two parties.

Tui·ler·ies (twē′lẽr-iz; Fr. twēl′rē′), *n.* a former royal palace in Paris, burned in 1871.

tuille (twēl), *n.* [Fr. *tuile*, lit., tile; L. *tegula;* see TILE], in medieval plate armor, one of the plates protecting the thigh.

tu·i·tion (to͞o-ish′ən, tū-ish′ən), *n.* [ME. *tuicione;* Anglo-Fr. *tuycioun;* L. *tuitio*, protection < *tuitus*, pp. of *tueri*, to watch, protect], 1. originally, guardianship. 2. teaching; instruction. 3. the charge for instruction, especially for class instruction.

tu·i·tion·al (to͞o-ish′ən-'l, tū-ish′ən-'l), *adj.* having to do with tuition.

tu·i·tion·ar·y (to͞o-ish′ən-er′i, tū-ish′ən-er′i), *adj.* tuitional.

Tu·la (to͞o′lä), *n.* 1. a region of the R.S.F.S.R., in central European Russia: pop., 1,192,000. 2. its capital: pop., 345,000.

tu·la·re·mi·a, tu·la·rae·mi·a (to͞o′lə-rē′mi-ə), *n.* [Mod. L. < *Tulare* County, California + *-emia* < Gr. *-aimia*, designating a blood condition < *haima*, blood], an infectious disease of rodents, especially rabbits, caused by a bacterium and transmitted to man in handling the flesh of infected animals or by the bite of certain insects: it is characterized by an irregular fever, aching, inflammation of the lymph glands, etc.: also called *rabbit fever.*

tu·le (to͞o′le), *n.* [Sp.; Nahuatl *tollin*, bulrush], a large bulrush found in lakes and marshes of the Southwest.

tu·lip (tōō′lip, tū′ləp), ***n.*** [Fr. *tulipe* (obs. *tulipan*); It. *tulipano;* Turk. *tülbend* for *dülbend,* turban (see TURBAN): so called because the flower somewhat resembles a turban], 1. any of a number of related bulb plants, mostly spring-blooming, with long, broad, pointed leaves and, usually, a single large, cup-shaped, variously colored flower. 2. the flower. 3. the bulb.

tulip tree, 1. a tree of the magnolia family, with bluish-green leaves, tulip-shaped, greenish-yellow flowers, and long, conelike fruit. 2. any of a number of trees with tuliplike flowers.

tu·lip·wood (tōō′lip-wood′, tū′ləp-wood′), ***n.*** 1. the light, soft wood of the tulip tree, used in cabinetwork, etc. 2. any of several cabinet woods with stripes or streaks of color. 3. any tree having such wood.

tulle (tōōl; Fr. töl), ***n.*** [after *Tulle,* city in France], a thin, fine netting of silk, rayon, or nylon, used for veils, scarfs, etc.

tul·li·bee (tul′ə-bē′), ***n.*** [Canad. Fr. *toulibi;* Cree *otonabi,* mouth water], a kind of whitefish found in the Great Lakes, etc.

Tul·ly (tul′i), ***n.*** [Englishing of Marcus *Tullius* Cicero], Cicero.

Tul·sa (tul′sə), ***n.*** a city in Oklahoma, on the Arkansas River: pop., 262,000: oil-producing center.

tum·ble (tum′b'l), ***v.i.*** [TUMBLED (-b'ld), TUMBLING], [ME. *tombelen,* freq. of *tumben, tomben;* AS. *tumbian,* to fall, jump, dance; akin to G. *tummeln;* Gmc. base borrowed in Fr. *tomber,* to fall], 1. to do somersaults, handsprings, or other acrobatic feats. 2. to fall suddenly, clumsily, or helplessly. 3. to stumble; trip. 4. to toss about or roll around. 5. to move, go, etc. in a hasty, awkward, or disorderly manner: as, she *tumbled* out of bed half awake. 6. [Slang], to understand something suddenly (with *to*). ***v.t.*** 1. to cause to tumble; make fall, throw down, toss about, roll over, etc. 2. to put into disorder by or as by tossing here and there; disarrange. 3. to whirl in a tumbling box or barrel. ***n.*** 1. a tumbling; specifically, *a*) a somersault, handspring, etc. *b*) a fall. *c*) a stumble. 2. disorder; confusion. 3. a confused heap.

tum·ble·bug (tum′b'l-bug′), ***n.*** any of several beetles that roll balls of dung, in which they deposit their larvae.

tum·ble-down (tum′b'l-doun′), ***adj.*** ready to tumble down; dilapidated.

tum·ble·dung (tum′b'l-duŋ′), ***n.*** a tumblebug.

tum·bler (tum′blẽr), ***n.*** 1. a person who does somersaults, handsprings, etc.; acrobat. 2. a kind of dog formerly used to catch rabbits: so called from the manner in which it caught its prey. 3. a kind of pigeon that does somersaults during flight. 4. an ordinary drinking glass, having no foot or stem: so called because originally it had a rounded or pointed bottom and could not be set down until emptied. 5. its contents. 6. [British Dial. or Scot.], a tumbrel. 7. the part of a gunlock through which the mainspring acts upon the hammer. 8. a part of a lock whose position must be changed by a key in order to release the bolt. 9. on a revolving or rocking part, a projecting piece that strikes and moves another part. 10. a part moving a gear into place in an automobile transmission. 11. an easily tipped, self-righting toy. 12. a tumbling box or barrel.

tum·ble·weed (tum′b'l-wēd′), ***n.*** any of a number of plants, as the pigweed, Russian thistle, etc., which break off near the ground in autumn and are blown about by the wind.

tumbling box (or **barrel**), a device consisting of a box or cylindrical container pivoted at the ends or at two corners so that it can be revolved: used for mixing materials, polishing metal objects by letting them tumble about together with an abrasive, etc.: also called *rumble, rumbler.*

tum·brel, tum·bril (tum′brəl), ***n.*** [ME. *tomberel, tomerel;* OFr. *tumbrel, tumberel,* tip cart < *tomber,* to fall, totter, stumble, dance, leap < LL. **tumbare,* to descend into a tomb (< *tumba;* see TOMB) & Frank. *tumon,* to turn, reel < LG. or D. cognate of Eng. *tumble*], 1. formerly, an instrument of punishment, as the cucking stool. 2. a farmer's cart or wagon, especially one that may be tilted for emptying. 3. any of the carts used to carry the condemned to the guillotine during the French Revolution. 4. a two-wheeled military cart for carrying ammunition, etc.

tu·me·fa·cient (tōō′mə-fā′shənt, tū′mə-fā′shənt), ***adj.*** [L. *tumefaciens,* ppr. of *tumefacere;* see TUMEFY], causing or tending to cause swelling.

tu·me·fac·tion (tōō′mə-fak′shən, tū′mə-fak′shən), ***n.*** [Fr. *tuméfaction*], 1. a tumefying or being tumefied. 2. a swollen part.

tu·me·fy (tōō′mə-fī′, tū′mə-fī′), ***v.t. & v.i.*** [TUMEFIED (-fīd′), TUMEFYING], [Fr. *tuméfier;* L. *tumefacere,* to cause to swell < *tumere,* to swell + *facere,* to make], to swell.

tu·mes·cence (tōō-mes′'ns, tū-mes′'ns), ***n.*** [< *tumescent*], 1. a swelling. 2. a swollen part.

tu·mes·cent (tōō-mes′'nt, tū-mes′'nt), ***adj.*** [L. *tumescens,* ppr. of *tumescere,* to swell up, inceptive of *tumere,* to swell], swelling; becoming tumid or swollen.

tu·mid (tōō′mid, tū′mid), ***adj.*** [L. *tumidus* < *tumere,* to swell], 1. swollen; bulging; distended. 2. inflated; pompous; bombastic. 3. [Rare], teeming; bursting.

tu·mid·i·ty (tōō-mid′ə-ti, tū-mid′ə-ti), ***n.*** [LL. *tumiditas*], the condition or quality of being tumid.

tum·my (tum′i), ***n.*** stomach: a child's word.

tu·mor (tōō′mẽr, tū′mẽr), ***n.*** [L., a swelling < *tumere,* to swell], 1. a swelling on some part of the body; especially, a mass of new tissue growth independent of its surrounding structures, having no physiological function; neoplasm: tumors are classified as benign or malignant. 2. [Obs.], high-flown language; bombast.

tu·mor·ous (tōō′mẽr-əs, tū′mẽr-əs), ***adj.*** 1. of, or having the nature of, a tumor. 2. having a tumor or tumors.

tu·mour (tōō′mẽr, tū′mẽr), ***n.*** tumor: British spelling.

tu·mu·lar (tōō′myoo-lẽr, tū′myoo-lẽr), ***adj.*** of or like a tumulus.

tu·mu·lose (tōō′myoo-lōs′, tū′myoo-lōs′), ***adj.*** [L. *tumulosus*], full of tumuli, or mounds.

tu·mult (tōō′mult, tū′mult), ***n.*** [ME. & OFr. *tumulte;* L. *tumultus,* a swelling or surging up, tumult < *tumere,* to swell], 1. noisy commotion, as of a crowd; uproar. 2. confusion; agitation; disturbance. 3. great emotional disturbance; agitation of mind or feeling.

tu·mul·tu·ar·y (tōō-mul′chōō-er′i, tū-mul′chōō-er′i), ***adj.*** [L. *tumultuarius*], 1. irregular; disorderly; unsystematic; confused. 2. tumultuous.

tu·mul·tu·ous (tōō-mul′chōō-əs, tū-mul′chōō-əs), ***adj.*** [OFr.; L. *tumultuosus*], 1. full of or characterized by tumult; noisy and violent; riotous. 2. making a tumult; turbulent. 3. greatly disturbed or agitated.

tu·mu·lus (tōō′myoo-ləs, tū′myoo-ləs), ***n.*** [*pl.* TUMULUSES (-iz), TUMULI (-lī′)], [L., a mound, hillock], an artificial mound; especially, an ancient burial mound.

tun (tun), ***n.*** [ME. & AS. *tunne,* large cask; akin to G. *tonne;* cf. TON], 1. a large cask, especially for wine, beer, or ale; hence, 2. a varying measure of capacity for liquids, formerly 252 wine gallons. ***v.t.*** [TUNNED (tund), TUNNING], to put into or store in a tun or tuns.

Tun., Tunisia.

tu·na (tōō′nə), ***n.*** [*pl.* TUNA, TUNAS (-nəz); see PLURAL, II, D, 2], [Am. Sp.; ult. < same source as *tunny*], a tunny, a large food fish of the mackerel group; specifically, *a*) the variety caught off the Pacific coast. *b*) the variety caught off the coast of Florida, Central America, and the West Indies. Also **tuna fish.**

tu·na (tōō′nə), ***n.*** [Sp.; of W. Ind. origin], 1. any of a number of related plants of the cactus family, the prickly pears; opuntia. 2. the edible fruit of any of these plants.

tun·a·ble (tōō′nə-b'l, tū′nə-b'l), ***adj.*** 1. capable of being tuned. 2. in tune. 3. tuneful. Also spelled **tuneable.**

tun·a·bly (tōōn′ə-bli, tūn′ə-bli), ***adv.*** in a tunable manner; tunefully.

Tun·bridge Wells (tun′brij welz′), a city in southeastern Kent, England: pop., 38,000.

tun·dra (tun′drə, toon′drə), ***n.*** [Russ.], any of the vast, nearly level, treeless plains of the arctic regions.

tune (tōōn, tūn), ***n.*** [ME. & Anglo-Fr. < OFr. *ton;* see TONE], 1. originally, a tone. 2. a rhythmical succession of musical tones; melody; air. 3. a musical setting of a hymn or psalm, for use in public worship. 4. *a*) the condition of being in proper musical pitch or of agreeing in pitch; hence, *b*) harmony; agreement; concord; adjustment. Now used chiefly in phrases *in tune, out of tune,* as, the violin is *in tune,* he's *out of tune* with the times. ***v.t.*** [TUNED (tōōnd, tūnd), TUNING], 1. to adjust (a musical instrument) to some standard of pitch; put in tune. 2. to adapt (music, the voice, etc.) to some pitch, tone, or mood. 3. to adapt to some condition, mood, etc.; bring into harmony or agreement. 4. to utter or express musically. ***v.i.*** to be in tune; harmonize. —***SYN.*** see **melody.**

change one's tune, to change one's attitude or manner, as from scorn to respect.

sing a different tune, to talk or act differently; change one's tune.

to the tune of, [Colloq.], to the sum of; at the price of.

tune in (on), to adjust a radio receiver to a given frequency so as to receive (a station, program, etc.).

tune out, to adjust a radio receiver so as to eliminate (interference, etc.).

tune up, 1. to adjust (musical instruments) to the same pitch, as in an orchestra. 2. to adjust to the proper or required condition, as a motor.

tune·ful (tōōn′fəl, tūn′fəl), ***adj.*** 1. full of music or melody; melodious; harmonious. 2. producing musical sounds.

tune·less (tōōn′lis, tūn′lis), ***adj.*** 1. not musical or melodious; untuneful. 2. not producing music; silent.

tun·er (tōōn′ẽr, tūn′ẽr), ***n.*** a person or thing that tunes; specifically, *a*) a person who tunes musical instruments: as, a piano *tuner. b*) the part of a radio receiver that detects signals; especially, such a part in the form of a separate unit.

tune-up (tōōn′up′), ***n.*** an adjusting, as of a motor, to the proper or required condition.

tung oil (tuŋ), [< Chin. *yu-t'ung* < *yu*, oil + *t'ung*, name of the tree], a yellow, poisonous oil from the nuts of a tree grown in China, Japan, and Florida, used instead of linseed oil in paints, varnishes, etc. for a higher gloss and more water-resistant finish.
tung·state (tuŋ'stāt), *n.* a salt of tungstic acid.
tung·sten (tuŋ'stən), *n.* [Sw., lit., heavy stone; *tung*, heavy + *sten*, stone], a hard, heavy, gray-white, metallic chemical element, found in wolframite, scheelite, and tungstite, and used in steel for high-speed tools, in electric lamp filaments, etc.: symbol, W; at. wt., 183.92; at. no., 74: also called *wolfram*.
tung·sten·ic (tuŋ-sten'ik), *adj.* of or containing tungsten.
tungsten lamp, an electric lamp having filaments of tungsten and a very low wattage.
tungsten steel, a very hard, heat-resistant, tenacious steel made with tungsten.
tung·stic (tuŋ'stik), *adj.* designating or of a chemical compound containing tungsten, especially with a valence of five or six.
tungstic acid, any of a group of acids produced by the combination of tungstic trioxide, WO_3, with water; specifically, the monohydrate acid, H_2WO_4.
tung·stite (tuŋ'stīt), *n.* a yellow or yellow-green mineral, WO_3, native tungstic trioxide.
Tung·ting (to͝oŋ'tiŋ'; Chin. do͝oŋ'tiŋ'), *n.* a lake in northern Hunan province, China: area, 1,900 sq. mi.
Tun·gus (to͝on-go͞oz'), *n.* 1. [*pl.* TUNGUSES (-iz), TUNGUS], a member of a group of Tungusic-speaking tribes (*Tunguses*) of Mongolian descent, including the Manchu, living in Siberia east of the Yenisei in the Amur basin, and, formerly, in Manchuria. 2. their Tungusic language. *adj.* of the Tunguses or their language; Tungusic. Also spelled **Tunguz**.
Tun·gus·ic (to͝on-go͞oz'ik), *n.* a family of languages spoken in central and eastern Siberia and Manchuria: it includes Tungus and Manchu, and may be related to the Mongolian and Turkic language families. *adj.* 1. of the Tunguses. 2. of Tungusic.
Tun·gus·ka (to͝on-go͞os'kȧ), *n.* any of three rivers (the *Upper*, *Stony*, and *Lower Tunguska* rivers) in central Siberia, flowing westward to the Yenisei River.
tu·nic (to͞o'nik, tū'nik), *n.* [Early ME. *tunice*, *tuneke*; AS. *tunece*; L. *tunica*], 1. a loose, gownlike garment worn by men and women in ancient Greece and Rome. 2. a blouselike garment extending to the hips or lower, usually gathered at the waist, often with a belt. 3. [Chiefly British], a short coat forming part of the uniform of soldiers, policemen, etc. 4. a tunicle. 5. a natural covering of a plant, animal, organ, etc.
tu·ni·ca (to͞o'ni-kə, tū'ni-kə), *n.* [*pl.* TUNICAE (-sē')], [Mod. L.; see TUNIC], in *anatomy* & *zoology*, an enclosing or covering layer of tissue or membrane, as of the ovaries.
tu·ni·cate (to͞o'ni-kāt', tū'ni-kāt'), *adj.* [L. *tunicatus*, pp. of *tunicare*, to put on a tunic < *tunica*, a tunic], 1. in *botany*, of or covered with concentric layers or tunics, as an onion. 2. in *zoology*, having a tunic or mantle. *n.* any of several primitive sea chordates enclosed by a thick tunic, as a sea squirt.
tu·ni·cat·ed (to͞o'ni-kā'tid, tū'ni-kā'tid), *adj.* tunicate.
tu·ni·cle (to͞o'ni-k'l, tū'ni-k'l), *n.* [ME.; L. *tunicula*, dim. of *tunica*, a tunic], in the *Roman Catholic Church*, a vestment worn by a subdeacon over the alb or by a bishop under the dalmatic.
tuning fork, a small steel instrument with two prongs, which when struck sounds a certain fixed tone in perfect pitch: it is used as a guide in tuning instruments.

TUNING FORK

Tu·nis (to͞o'nis, tū'nis), *n.* 1. the capital of Tunisia, on the Mediterranean, near the site of ancient Carthage: pop., 220,000. 2. a former Barbary State in northern Africa, now Tunisia.
Tu·ni·si·a (to͞o-nish'i-ə, tū-nish'ə, to͞o-nē'zhə), *n.* a country in northern Africa, on the Mediterranean: French protectorate (1881–1946): an associated state of the French Union (1946–1956): area, 48,300 sq. mi.; pop., 3,782,000; capital, Tunis.
Tu·ni·si·an (to͞o-nish'i-ən, tū-nish'ən, to͞o-nē'zhən), *adj.* of Tunis or Tunisia, their people, or culture. *n.* a native or inhabitant of Tunis or Tunisia.
tun·nage (tun'ij), *n.* tonnage.
tun·nel (tun''l), *n.* [< Fr. *tonnelle*, arbor, semicircular vault & OFr. *tonnel*, dim. of *tonne*, a tun; cf. TUN], 1. originally, *a*) a flue. *b*) a funnel. 2. an underground or underwater passageway, as for motor traffic, a railroad, etc. 3. an animal's burrow. 4. any tunnellike passage, as one in a mine. *v.t.* [TUNNELED or TUNNELLED (-'ld), TUNNELING or TUNNELLING], 1. to dig (a passage) in the form of a tunnel. 2. to make a tunnel through or under. 3. to make (one's way or a way) by digging a tunnel. *v.i.* to make a tunnel.
tunnel disease, decompression sickness.
tun·nel·er, tun·nel·ler (tun''l-ēr), *n.* a person or thing that tunnels.
tun·ny (tun'i), *n.* [*pl.* TUNNIES (-iz), TUNNY; see PLURAL, II, D, 1], [Fr. *thon*; Pr. *ton*; L. *thynnus*, *thunnos*; Gr. *thynnos*], 1. any of several large, edible sea fishes of the mackerel group, with coarse, somewhat oily flesh, weighing up to 1,000 pounds; a tuna. 2. any of certain related fishes, as the albacore.
tup (tup), *n.* [ME. (Scot. & Northern) *tupe*, *tope*; prob. < ON.], 1. a male sheep; ram. 2. the striking part of a pile driver or power hammer. *v.t.* [TUPPED (tupt), TUPPING], to copulate with (a ewe): said of a ram.
tu·pe·lo (to͞o'pi-lō'), *n.* [*pl.* TUPELOS (-lōz')], [of Am. Ind. (Muskhogean) origin], 1. any of a number of related trees with small, greenish flowers and blue or purple fruit; black, sour, or cotton gum tree. 2. the tough wood of any of these trees. Also **tupelo gum**.
Tu·pi (to͞o-pē'), *n.* [Tupi, comrade], 1. [*pl.* TUPIS (-pēz'), TUPI], a member of a group of South American Indian tribes living in parts of Brazil, chiefly along the coast and along the lower Amazon, and in part of Paraguay. 2. their language, especially the northern dialect, used as a lingua franca in the Amazon region.
Tu·pi·an (to͞o-pē'ən), *adj.* 1. of the Tupis or their language. 2. designating or of a large linguistic stock of South American Indians, comprising the Tupis and the Guaranis.
tup·pence (tup''ns), *n.* twopence.
Tu·pun·ga·to, Mount (to͞o'po͞oŋ-gä'tô), a mountain of the Andes on the central Argentina-Chile border: height, 21,810 ft.
tuque (to͞ok, tūk), *n.* [Canad. Fr. < Fr. *toque*, a cap], a winter cap consisting of a knitted bag tapered and closed at both ends, worn with one end tucked into the other.
‡tu quo·que (to͞o kwō'kwi, tū kwō'kwi), [L.], thou also; you too: a retort accusing an accuser of the same charge.
Tu·ra·ni·an (too-rā'ni-ən, tyoo-rā'ni-ən), *n.* [Per. *Tūrān*, the area north of the Oxus River; + *-ian*], 1. the Ural-Altaic family of languages. 2. a member of any of the peoples who speak them. *adj.* designating or of these languages or peoples.
tur·ban (tũr'bən), *n.* [Fr. (earlier *turbant*, *tulban*); Port. *turbante*; Turk. *tülbend*, dial. form of *dülbend* < Ar. & Per. *dulband*, turban, sash; *dul*, a turn, round + *band*, a band], 1. a headdress of Moslem origin, consisting of a cap with a scarf wound round it. 2. a similar headdress consisting of a scarf or cloth wound round the head. 3. a kind of hat worn by women, with no brim or a very short brim turned up closely.
tur·baned (tũr'bənd), *adj.* wearing a turban.
tur·ba·ry (tũr'bẽr-i), *n.* [*pl.* TURBARIES (-iz)], [ME. *turbarye*; OFr. *turberie* < *tourbe*, turf; of Gmc. origin; cf. TURF], in *English law*, 1. the right to dig turf or peat on another's land. 2. land where turf or peat is dug.
tur·bel·lar·i·an (tũr'bə-lâr'i-ən), *adj.* [Mod. L. *Turbellaria*, name of the class (< L. *turbellae*, a bustle, stir, dim. of *turba*, a crowd, disturbance: so called from water currents caused by the cilia); + *-an*], designating or of a group of flatworms, mostly aquatic and nonparasitic, characterized by leaf-shaped bodies covered with many cilia. *n.* a flatworm of this group.
tur·bid (tũr'bid), *adj.* [L. *turbidus* < *turbare*, to trouble < *turba*, a crowd], 1. having the sediment stirred up; muddy; cloudy. 2. thick, dense, or dark, as clouds or smoke. 3. confused; perplexed; muddled.
tur·bi·dim·e·ter (tũr'bi-dim'ə-tẽr), *n.* [<*turbidity*+ *-meter*], a device for measuring the turbidity of a liquid, as in a water-purification plant.
tur·bid·i·ty (tũr-bid'ə-ti), *n.* turbid quality or state.
tur·bi·nal (tũr'bi-n'l), *adj.* [< L. *turbo*, *turbinis*, a whirl, rotation; + *-al*], turbinate. *n.* a turbinate bone.
tur·bi·nate (tũr'bi-nit, tũr'bi-nāt'), *adj.* [L. *turbinatus* < *turbo*, a whirl, rotation, top], 1. shaped like a cone resting on its apex; top-shaped. 2. shaped like a scroll or spiral; specifically, in *anatomy* & *zoology*, designating or of any of certain spiral spongy bones in the nasal passages. *n.* 1. a turbinate shell. 2. a turbinate bone.
tur·bi·na·tion (tũr'bi-nā'shən), *n.* a turbinate formation.
tur·bine (tũr'bin, tũr'bīn), *n.* [Fr. < L. *turbo*, *turbinis*, whirl, whirlwind, top], an engine or motor driven by the pressure of steam, water, or air against the curved vanes of a wheel or set of wheels.
tur·bit (tũr'bit), *n.* [? < L. *turbo*, a top: from the shape], any of a variety of domestic pigeons distinguished by a short head and beak and a ruffled breast.
tur·bo- (tũr'bō), [< L. *turbo*, thing that spins], a combining form meaning: 1. *consisting of a turbine*. 2. *driven by and directly coupled to a turbine*.

tur·bo·gen·er·a·tor (tũr′bō-jen′ẽr-ā′tẽr), *n.* a generator driven by and directly coupled to a turbine.

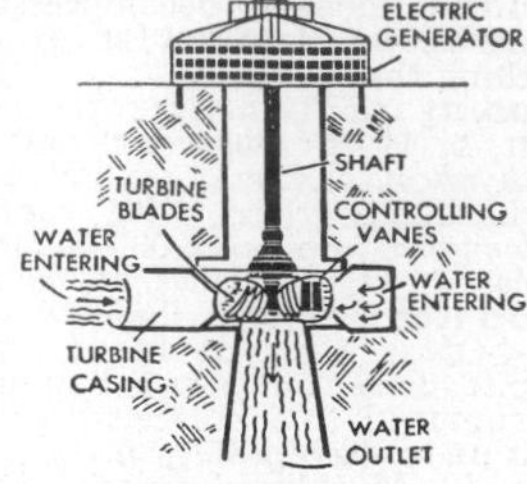

TURBOGENERATOR

tur·bo·jet (engine) (tũr′-bō-jet′), in *aeronautics,* a jet engine in which the energy of the jet operates a turbine which in turn operates the air compressor.

tur·bo·prop (engine) (tũr′bō-prop′), [*turbo-* + *prop*eller], in *aeronautics,* a jet engine in which the energy of the jet operates a turbine which drives the propeller.

tur·bot (tur′bət), *n.* [*pl.* TURBOT, TURBOTS (-bəts); see PLURAL, II, D, 2], [ME. *turbut;* OFr. *tourbout;* prob. < OSw. *törnbut; törn,* a thorn + *but,* butt], 1. a large European flatfish, highly regarded as food. 2. any of a number of other flatfishes resembling the turbot.

tur·bu·lence (tũr′byoo-ləns), *n.* the condition or quality of being turbulent; disorder; commotion.

tur·bu·len·cy (tũr′byoo-lən-si), *n.* turbulence.

tur·bu·lent (tũr′byoo-lənt), *adj.* [Fr.; L. *turbulentus* < *turbare;* see TURBID], 1. causing disturbance; disorderly; unruly; boisterous. 2. characterized by disturbance; disturbed; agitated; tumultuous.

Tur·co (tũr′kō), *n.* [*pl.* TURCOS (-kōz)], [Fr. < Sp., Port., or It. *turco,* lit., a Turk: the Turks ruled Algeria from 1518 to 1830], a member of the body of native Algerian infantry in the French army.

Tur·co- (tũr′kō, tũr′kə), Turko-.

Tur·co·man (tũr′kə-mən), *n.* [*pl.* TURCOMANS (-mənz)], a Turkoman.

tur·di·form (tũr′di-fôrm′), *adj.* [< L. *turdus,* a thrush; + *-form*], having the form or appearance of a thrush.

tur·dine (tũr′dīn, tũr′din), *adj.* [< L. *turdus,* a thrush; + *-ine*], of or belonging to a large and widely distributed group of songbirds comprising the true thrushes and allied groups.

tu·reen (too-rēn′), *n.* [earlier *terreen;* Fr. *terrine,* earthen vessel < L. *terrenus,* earthy < *terra,* earth], a large, deep dish with a lid, for serving soup, etc.

Tu·renne, Vicomte de (də tü′ren′), (*Henri de La Tour d'Aubergne*), 1611–1675; French marshal.

turf (tũrf), *n.* [*pl.* TURFS (tũrfs), *archaic* TURVES (tũrvz)], [ME.; AS.; akin to ON. *torf;* IE. **dorbh-os,* sod, lit., twisted together < base **derbh-,* to twist together], 1. a surface layer of earth containing grass plants with their matted roots; sod; sward. 2. a piece of this layer. 3. peat, or a piece of it for use as fuel. 4. *a*) a track for horse racing; hence, *b*) horse racing. Usually with *the* (in sense 4). *v.t.* to cover with turf.

turf·man (tũrf′mən), *n.* [*pl.* TURFMEN (-mən)], a person interested in horse racing.

turf·y (tũr′fi), *adj.* [TURFIER (-fi-ẽr), TURFIEST (-fi-ist)], 1. of or covered with turf; grassy. 2. of the nature of or resembling turf. 3. having to do with horse racing.

Tur·ge·nev, I·van Ser·ge·ye·vich (ē-vän′ syer-gyā′ye-vich toor-gā′nyef; Eng. toor-gen′yif, tẽr-gen′if), 1818–1883; Russian novelist: also spelled **Turgenieff, Turgeniev.**

tur·gent (tũr′jənt), *adj.* [L. *turgens,* ppr. of *turgere,* to swell], [Now Rare], swelling or swollen.

tur·ges·cence (tũr-jes′′ns), *n.* [< *turgescent*], 1. a swelling. 2. swollen condition.

tur·ges·cent (tũr-jes′′nt), *adj.* [L. *turgescens,* ppr. of *turgescere,* to swell up], becoming turgid or swollen.

tur·gid (tũr′jid), *adj.* [L. *turgidus* < *turgere,* to swell], 1. swollen; distended; bloated; inflated. 2. bombastic; pompous; grandiloquent. —*SYN.* see **bombastic.**

tur·gid·i·ty (tẽr-jid′ə-ti), *n.* a turgid quality or state.

tur·gite (tũr′jīt), *n.* [< *Turginsk,* copper mine in the Ural Mountains + *-ite*], a crimson iron ore, probably a solid solution of goethite with hematite.

tur·gor (tũr′gẽr), *n.* [LL. < *turgere,* to swell], 1. turgescence or turgidity. 2. the normal distention and resiliency of living animal and plant cells.

Tur·got, Anne Ro·bert Jacques (än′ rô′bâr′ zhäk′ tür′gō′), Baron de l'Aulne, 1727–1781; French statesman and economist.

Tu·rin (toor′in, tyoor′in, tyoo-rin′), *n.* a city in northwestern Italy, on the Po river: pop., 722,000: Italian name, *Torino.*

Turk (tũrk), *n.* [ME. *Turke;* OFr. *Turc;* ML. *Turcus;* Ar. *Turk*], 1. a native or inhabitant of Turkey; especially, a member of the Moslem people of Turkey or, formerly, of the Ottoman Empire. 2. a member of any of the Turki peoples. 3. [Now Rare], a fierce, cruel person: in allusion to the conquering Turks of the Ottoman Empire. 4. a Turkish horse.

Turk., 1. Turkey. 2. Turkish.

Tur·ke·stan (tũr′ki-stan′, tũr′ki-stän′), *n.* a region in central Asia, including parts of the U.S.S.R., Sinkiang, and Afghanistan.

Tur·key (tũr′ki), *n.* a republic occupying Asia Minor and a part of the Balkan Peninsula: area, 296,380 sq. mi.; pop., 26,881,000; capital, Ankara.

tur·key (tũr′ki), *n.* [*pl.* TURKEYS (-kiz), TURKEY; see PLURAL, II, D, 1], [earlier *Turkey-cock,* term orig. applied to the guinea fowl, sometimes imported through Turkey and for a time identified with the Am. fowl], 1. either of two varieties of large, wild or domesticated, North American birds with a small, naked head and spreading tail, bred as poultry in many parts of the world. 2. its flesh, prized as food. 3. [Slang], a failure: said of a play, musical comedy, etc.
talk turkey, to talk candidly and bluntly.

turkey buzzard, a dark-colored vulture of South and Central America and the southern United States, resembling a turkey in having a naked, reddish head.

turkey cock, 1. a male turkey. 2. a strutting or pompous person.

Turkey red, 1. a bright red produced on cotton cloth by alizarin. 2. cotton cloth of this color.

tur·key-trot (tũr′ki-trot′), *v.i.* to dance the turkey trot.

turkey trot, [cf. FOXTROT], a ballroom dance to ragtime music, popular in the early 20th century.

Tur·ki (toor′kē), *adj.* [Per.; see TURK], 1. designating or of the Southern Turkic languages, including Turkish, Osmanli, Turkoman, etc. 2. designating or of the peoples who speak them. *n.* 1. the Turki languages. 2. a member of any Turki people.

Tur·kic (tũr′kik), *adj.* 1. designating or of a subfamily of Altaic languages divided into Southern, or Turki, and Eastern, Western, and Central branches. 2. designating or of the peoples who speak any of these languages. 3. loosely, Turkish. *n.* the Turkic subfamily of languages.

Turk·ish (tũr′kish), *adj.* of Turkey, the Turks, their language, etc. *n.* Osmanli, the Turkic language of Turkey.

Turkish bath, 1. a kind of bath in which the bather, after a period of heavy perspiration in a room of hot air or steam, is washed, massaged, and cooled. 2. a place where such a bath is given.

Turkish delight (or **paste**), a kind of candy consisting of cubes of a sweetened and flavored jellylike substance covered with powdered sugar.

Turkish Empire, the Ottoman Empire.

Turkish pound, the Turkish lira: symbol £T (no period).

Turkish towel, turkish towel, a thick cotton towel with a rough nap of uncut loops.

Turk·ism (tũr′kiz′m), *n.* Turkish culture, beliefs, customs, principles, etc.

Turk·man (tũrk′mən), *n.* [*pl.* TURKMEN (-mən)], a native or inhabitant of the Turkmen S.S.R.

Turk·men (tũrk′men), *n.* the East Turkic language of the Turkomans: also **Turkoman.**

Turk·me·ni·an (tũrk-mē′ni-ən), *adj.* of the Turkmen S.S.R., its people (*Turkmen*), etc.

Turk·men·i·stan (tũrk′men-i-stan′, tũrk′men-i-stän′; Russ. toork-men′i-stän′), *n.* the Turkmen S.S.R.

Turkmen Soviet Socialist Republic (tũrk′men; Russ. toork-men′), a republic of the U.S.S.R., in central Asia, north of Iran: area, 189,370 sq. mi.; pop., 1,520,000; capital, Ashkhabad: also **Turkomen, Turkmenistan.**

Tur·ko- (tũr′kō, tũr′kə), a combining form meaning: 1. *of Turkey, of the Turks.* 2. *Turkey and, the Turks and.* Also **Turco-.**

Tur·ko·man (tũr′kə-mən), *n.* [Per. *Turkumān,* one like a Turk], 1. [*pl.* TURKOMANS (-mənz)], a member of a group of seminomadic tribes living in the Turkmen, Uzbek, and Kazakh Soviet Socialist Republics and in parts of Iran and Afghanistan. 2. the language of the Turkomans; Turkmen. Also spelled **Turcoman.**

Tur·ko·men (tũrk′ə-men′), *n.* the Turkmen S.S.R.

Turks and Cai·cos Islands (tũrks, kī′kōs), a group of islands in the Bahamas, belonging to Jamaica: area, 166 sq. mi.; pop., 7,000; capital, Grand Turk.

Turk's-cap lily (tũrks′kap′), 1. a lily having purplish-red to violet-rose flowers with rolled-back petals; martagon. 2. a lily resembling the martagon, having orange-red flowers spotted with purple.

Turk's-head (tũrks′hed′), *n.* in *nautical usage,* a turbanlike knot made on a rope by means of a small line.

Tur·ku (toor′koo), *n.* a city on the southwestern coast of Finland: pop., 120,000: Swedish name, *Abo.*

tur·ma·line (tũr′mə-lin, tũr′mə-lēn′), *n.* tourmaline.

tur·mer·ic (tũr′mẽr-ik), *n.* [earlier also *tormerik, tarmaret;* Fr. *terre-mérite;* ML. *terra merita,* lit., deserved (or deserving) earth; prob. altered < Ar. *karkam, kurkum,* saffron], 1. an East Indian plant whose root in powdered form is used as a yellow dye, seasoning, and medicine. 2. its root.

turmeric paper, paper impregnated with turmeric, used as a test for alkali, which turns it brown, or for boric acid, which turns it red-brown.

tur·moil (tũr′moil), *n.* [prob. a merged word, based on OFr. *trumel,* tumult, noisy quarreling, but influenced by *moil*], tumult; commotion; uproar; confusion.

turn (tũrn), *v.t.* [ME. *turnen, tornen* < AS. *turnian* &

OFr. *turner*, *tourner*, both < L. *tornare*, to turn in a lathe, turn < *tornus*, a lathe; Gr. *tornos*, a lathe, carpenter's compasses], I. *to cause to revolve or rotate* 1. to rotate (a wheel, etc.). 2. to give circular motion to; move around or partly around: as, *turn* the key. 3. to do by a revolving motion: as, he *turned* a somersault. II. *to form by revolving, etc.* 1. to give circular shape to by rotating against a tool, as in a lathe. 2. to give rounded shape or form to in any way. 3. to give a well-rounded or graceful form to: as, he can *turn* fine phrases. III. *to change the position of* 1. to change the position of, as by a rotating motion: as, *turn* your chair around. 2. to revolve in the mind; ponder (often with *over*): as, she *turned* the plan over in her mind. 3. to bend, fold, twist, etc.: as, *turn* the sheet back. 4. to bend back (the cutting edge of a knife, etc.); blunt. 5. to reverse the position or sides of; invert; specifically, *a*) to change so that the undersurface is on top and vice versa: as, he *turned* the pages. *b*) to spade, plow, etc. so that the undersoil comes to the surface. *c*) to alter (a collar, coat, etc.) so that the inner surface becomes the outer and vice versa. 6. to cause to become upside down, topsy-turvy, etc. 7. to upset (the stomach). IV. *to change the movement or course of* 1. to bend the course of; deflect; divert; avert: as, he *turned* the blow. 2. to cause to change one's intentions, actions, etc.: as, I *turned* him from his purpose; specifically, *a*) to convert or persuade: as, I *turned* her to progressive views. *b*) to prejudice: as, they *turned* his family against him. 3. to go around (a corner, an army's flank, etc.). 4. to reach or pass (a certain age, amount, etc.). 5. to reverse the course of; specifically, *a*) to cause to move back or retreat; repel: as, we *turned* the attack. *b*) to cause to recoil, rebound, etc.: as, his own criticism was *turned* against him. 6. to drive, set, let go, etc. in some way: as, they *turned* him adrift. 7. to keep (money, goods, etc.) circulating or moving. V. *to change the direction, trend, etc. of* 1. to change the direction of (one's eyes, face, etc.). 2. to direct, point, aim, etc.: as, he *turned* his gun on me. 3. to change the trend, focus, etc. of: as, *turn* your thoughts to practical matters. 4. to put to (a specified) use or result; employ; apply: as, he *turned* his knowledge to good account, he *turned* his hand to writing. VI. *to change the nature or condition of* 1. to change; convert; transmute: as, it *turns* cream into butter. 2. to exchange for: as, she *turns* her eggs into hard cash. 3. to subject: as, she *turned* his remarks to ridicule. 4. to translate or paraphrase. 5. to derange, dement, distract, or infatuate. 6. to make sour. 7. to affect (a person) in some way: as, it *turns* her nauseous. 8. to change the color of. *v.i.* I. *to revolve, rotate, etc.* 1. to move in a circle or around an axis; rotate; revolve; pivot. 2. to move in a circular manner; move around or partly around: as, the key won't *turn*. 3. to reel; be in a whirl: as, my head is *turning*. II. *to form something by revolving* 1. to run a lathe. 2. to be shaped on a lathe. III. *to change position* 1. *a*) to move in a rotary manner so as to change position. *b*) to shift or twist the body as if on an axis. 2. to become curved or bent. 3. to reverse position so that bottom becomes top and top becomes bottom, etc.; become inverted. 4. to become upset: said of the stomach. IV. *to change course or movement* 1. to change one's or its course so as to be moving, going, etc. in a different direction; deviate. 2. to reverse one's or its course; start to move, go, etc. in the opposite direction: as, the tide has *turned*. V. *to change in direction, trend, etc.* 1. to change one's or its direction; face about; shift. 2. to direct or shift one's attention, abilities, thoughts, etc. to: as, he *turned* back to his work, she *turned* to music. 3. to reverse one's feelings, attitude, allegiance, etc., especially in relation to a specific person or thing: as, he *turned* against his former friends. 4. [Obs.], to vacillate. VI. *to become changed in nature or condition* 1. to enter into a specified condition; become: as, the milk *turned* sour. 2. to change into another form: as, the rain *turned* to sleet. 3. to become rancid, putrid, sour, etc. 4. to change color: as, the leaves are *turning*. *n.* I. *rotation; circular motion, etc.* 1. a turning around; complete or partial rotation, as of a wheel, handle, etc.; revolution. 2. *a*) a winding of one thing around another. *b*) a single twist, coil, winding, etc.; convolution. 3. the condition of being twisted, bent, etc. in a circular form. 4. the direction of this. 5. a musical figure consisting of four tones the second and fourth of which are the same, or principal, tone, the first, normally, being a degree above, and the third a degree below: if the first is a degree below and the third a degree above, it is called an *inverted turn*. II. *change of movement, direction, etc.* 1. a changing of position or posture, as by a rotating motion. 2. a change or reversal of course or direction: as, the *turn* of the tide, a *turn* to the right. 3. *a*) a walk taken about a building, area, etc., as for inspection; tour. *b*) a short walk or ride, returning to the starting place, as for exercise. 4. the place where a change in direction occurs; bend; curve. III. *change of nature, condition, etc.* 1. a change in trend, circumstances, events, policy, health, etc., often for better or for worse, sometimes occurring at a crisis. 2. the time of a chronological change: as, at the *turn* of the century. 3. a turning point. 4. [Colloq.], a momentary shock, as from fright. IV. *an occasional or repeated action, performance, etc.* 1. an action that harms or, more usually, benefits another: as, he did me a good *turn*. 2. a bout; spell; try: as, a *turn* at gardening. 3. an attack of illness, dizziness, rage, etc.; fit. 4. the right, duty, or opportunity to do something, usually in regular order, coming to each of a number of people: as, it's my *turn* to go. 5. [British], a shift of work. 6. *a*) a short performance given as part of a variety show; act. *b*) its performer or performers. 7. a transaction on the stock exchange involving both purchase and sale of particular securities. V. *trend, form, style, character, etc.* 1. a distinctive form, manner, cast, detail, etc.: as, a quaint *turn* to her speech, dress, etc. 2. natural inclination or aptitude; flair: as, an inquisitive *turn* of mind. 3. a tendency; drift; trend: as, the discussion took a new *turn*. 4. a variation or interpretation of the original: as, she gave the sonata a lively *turn*.

at every turn, in every instance; constantly.
by turns, one after another; alternately; in succession: also **turn and turn about**.
in turn, in proper sequence or succession.
on the turn, [Colloq.], about to turn or change.
out of turn, 1. not in proper sequence or order. 2. at the wrong time. 3. [Colloq.], rashly; imprudently.
take turns, to speak, do, etc. one after another in regular order.
to a turn, to just the right degree; perfectly.
turn and turn about, one after another in regular order: also **turn about**.
turn down, 1. to reject (a request, advice, etc.). 2. to reject the request, advice, etc. of (someone).
turn in, 1. to make a turn into; enter. 2. to point (toes) inward. 3. to deliver; hand in. 4. to give back; return. 5. to fold over; double. 6. [Colloq.], to go to bed.
turn off, 1. to leave (a road) and enter another road branching off. 2. to branch off: said of a road. 3. to shut off. 4. to put out (a light). 5. to deflect; divert. 6. [British], to discharge (employees).
turn on, 1. to start the flow of. 2. to open; release. 3. to attack or oppose suddenly. 4. to be contingent on; hinge on; depend on. 5. to put on (a light).
turn out, 1. to put out (a light, etc.). 2. to shut off. 3. to put outside. 4. to drive out; dismiss or discharge. 5. to come or go out, as to assemble somewhere. 6. to produce as the result of labor. 7. to result; eventuate. 8. to prove to be; be found. 9. to come to be; become. 10. to equip, dress, etc. 11. [Colloq.], to get out of bed.
turn over, 1. to change the position of, as by rolling. 2. to reverse the position of; turn upside down; invert. 3. to shift one's position, as from one side to the other; roll over. 4. to think about carefully; ponder. 5. to hand over; transfer. 6. to relinquish; delegate. 7. to put to a different use; convert. 8. to sell and replenish (a stock of goods). 9. to buy and sell, or do business, to the amount of.
turn to, 1. to refer to; consult. 2. to go to for assistance; apply to; rely on. 3. to get to work; get busy.
turn up, 1. to fold or bend back or over upon itself. 2. to shorten (a dress, etc.) by folding back the bottom edge and making a new hem. 3. to lift up or turn face upwards, as to see the other side. 4. to bring to light by digging, etc. 5. to increase the flow, speed, intensity, loudness, etc. of, as by turning a handle or knob. 6. *a*) to make a turn onto and ascend (a street on a hill, etc.). *b*) to make a turn into any street or road. 7. to have an upward direction. 8. to come about; happen. 9. to make an appearance; arrive. 10. to be found.
turn upon, to turn on (senses 3 & 4).

SYN.—**turn**, the general word in this connection, implies motion around, or partly around, a center or axis (a wheel *turns*, he *turned* on his heel); **rotate** implies movement of a body around its own center or axis (the earth *rotates* on its axis); **revolve** is sometimes interchangeable with **rotate**, but in strict discrimination, it suggests movement in an orbit around a center (the earth *revolves* around the sun); **gyrate** implies movement in a circular or spiral course, as by a tornado; **spin** and **whirl** suggest very fast and continuous rotation or revolution (a top *spins*, the leaves *whirled* about the yard). See also **curve**.

turn·a·bout (tũrn'ə-bout'), *n.* 1. the act of turning about, as to face the other way. 2. a shift or reversal of allegiance, opinion, etc.; about-face. 3. a merry-go-round. 4. [Obs. or Rare], one who favors change.

turn-a·bout-face (tũrn'ə-bout'fās'), *n.* a turnabout (sense 2).

turn-and-bank indicator (tũrn'ən-baŋk'), an airplane instrument that indicates the rate of turn and degree of bank at the same time, so that the pilot can judge whether the airplane is properly banked for a particular turn.

turn·buck·le (tũrn'buk''l), *n.* 1. originally, a catch for shutters or casement windows, consisting of a flat bar that drops into a slot. 2. a kind of coupling for use between lengths of rod or wire, consisting of a metal loop or sleeve with opposite internal threads at each end or with an internal thread at one end and a swivel at the other: the effective length of the rod or wire can be increased or decreased by turning the metal loop.

TURNBUCKLE

turn·coat (tũrn'kōt'), *n.* [from the notion of a coat worn right side out or inside out, according to circumstances], a person who goes over to the opposite side or party; renegade; apostate.

turn·down (tũrn'doun'), *adj.* 1. that can be turned down. 2. having the upper part folded down: as, a *turndown* collar.

turned comma, an inverted comma (').

turn·er (tũr'nẽr), *n.* a person or thing that turns; specifically, a person who operates a lathe.

turn·er (tũr'nẽr), *n.* [G. < *turnen*, to engage in gymnastics < Fr. *tourner*, to turn; see TURN], 1. a member of a Turnverein; hence, 2. a gymnast; tumbler.

Tur·ner, Frederick Jackson (tũr'nẽr), 1861–1932; American historian.

Turner, Joseph Mal·lord William (mal'ẽrd), 1775–1851; English painter.

turn·er·y (tũr'nẽr-i), *n.* [*pl.* TURNERIES (-iz)], [*turner* + *-y;* cf. Fr. *tournerie*], the work, technique, product, or workshop of a person who operates a lathe.

turn·ing (tũr'niŋ), *n.* 1. the action of a person or thing that turns; a revolving, winding, twisting, inverting, etc. 2. the art or process of shaping things on a lathe; turnery. 3. a shaping or fashioning (of literary work). 4. a place where a road, etc. turns or turns off.

turning point, 1. a point at which something turns or changes direction. 2. a point in time at which a decisive change occurs; crisis.

tur·nip (tũr'nip), *n.* [earlier *turnep;* prob. < Fr. *tour* or Eng. *turn,* in the sense of "turned, round" + ME. *nepe* < AS. *næp,* a turnip < L. *napus*], 1. either of two plants of the mustard family (the *white turnip* and the *Swedish turnip,* or *rutabaga*) with hairy leaves and a roundish, light-colored, fleshy root used as a vegetable. 2. the root of either of these plants.

tur·nix (tũr'niks), *n.* [Mod. L., contr. < L. *coturnix,* quail < **quocturnix;* of echoic origin], any of a group of small, three-toed game birds resembling the plovers, found in southern Europe, northern Africa, and Asia.

turn·key (tũrn'kē'), *n.* [*pl.* TURNKEYS (-kēz')], a person in charge of the keys of a prison; warder; jailer.

turn-out (tũrn'out'), *n.* 1. a turning out. 2. a gathering of people, as at a meeting. 3. [British], a labor strike or striker. 4. things produced; output. 5. a wider part of a narrow road, or a short side road, enabling vehicles to pass one another. 6. a railroad siding. 7. a carriage with its horse or horses; equipage. 8. equipment; outfit; array.

turn·o·ver (tũrn'ō'vẽr), *n.* 1. a turning over; specifically, *a*) an upset. *b*) a change from one use, side, opinion, etc. to another. 2. a tart or a small pie made by folding one half of a circular crust back over the filling and other half. 3. *a*) the number of times a stock of goods is sold and replenished in a given period of time. *b*) the amount of business done during a given period of time in terms of the money used in buying and selling. *c*) the number of shares sold in a stock market during a given period of time. *d*) the amount of money loaned on call during a given period of time. 4. *a*) the number of workers hired to replace those who have left during a given period of time. *b*) the ratio of this to the average number of workers employed. Abbreviated **t.o.** *adj.* that turns over or is turned over: as, a *turnover* collar.

turn·pike (tũrn'pīk'), *n.* [ME. *turnpyke,* a spiked barrier across a road, used in war; see TURN & PIKE], 1. formerly, a turnstile. 2. a tollgate. 3. a road having tollgates; toll road. 4. loosely, any highway.

turn·plate (tũrn'plāt'), *n.* a turntable.

turn·sole (tũrn'sōl'), *n.* [ME. *turnesole;* Early Fr. *tournesol* < It. *tornasole* or Sp. *tornasol* < *tornar*(*e*), to turn + *sol*(*e*), sun], 1. any of a number of plants whose flowers turn toward the sun, as the sunflower, heliotrope, and sun spurge. 2. a Mediterranean plant yielding a purple dye. 3. this dye.

turn·spit (tũrn'spit'), *n.* 1. a person who turns a spit. 2. formerly, a breed of small dog trained to turn a spit by means of a treadmill.

turn·stile (tũrn'stīl'), *n.* 1. a post supporting two revolving horizontal crossed bars, placed in an entrance to allow the passage of persons but not of horses, cattle, etc. 2. a similar mechanical apparatus, used at entrances to subways, theaters, etc. to admit persons one at a time: it is often coin-operated.

TURNSTILE

turn·stone (tũrn'stōn'), *n.* any of several small, ploverlike, migratory shore birds related to the sandpipers: so called because they turn over pebbles in search of food.

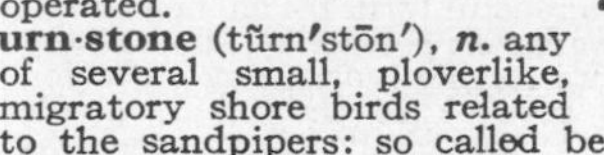

turn·ta·ble (tũrn'tā'b'l), *n.* 1. a circular revolving platform with a track, used for turning locomotives, as in a roundhouse. 2. any of various horizontal revolving platforms: as, a phonograph *turntable.*

turn·up (tũrn'up'), *n.* something turned up; a turned-up part. *adj.* that turns up or is turned up.

‡**Turn·ver·ein** (toorn'fer-īn'), *n.* [G. < *turnen,* to exercise + *verein,* a union, association, club], a club of turners, or gymnasts.

tur·pen·tine (tũr'pən-tīn'), *n.* [ME. *turpentyne, terbentyne;* OFr. *turbentine;* L. *terebinthinus,* of the turpentine tree < *terebinthus,* turpentine tree; Gr. *terebinthos*], 1. the brownish-yellow, sticky, semifluid oleoresin (*Chian turpentine*) exuding from the terebinth. 2. any of the various oleoresins obtained from pines and other coniferous trees. 3. a light-colored, volatile oil distilled from such oleoresins, used in paints, varnishes, etc., and in medicine: in full, **oil** (or **spirits**) **of turpentine.** *v.t.* [TURPENTINED (-tīnd'), TURPENTINING], 1. to apply turpentine to. 2. to extract turpentine from (trees).

tur·peth (tũr'peth, tũr'pith), *n.* [ML. *turpethum,* ult. < Ar. (colloq.) & Per. *tirbid*], 1. an emetic made from the root of an Australasian plant. 2. this plant. 3. basic mercuric sulfate, $HgSO_4 \cdot 2HgO$, a heavy, lemon-yellow powder, used as a purgative.

Tur·pin, Dick (tũr'pin), 1706–1739; English highwayman; hanged.

tur·pi·tude (tũr'pə-tōōd', tũr'pə-tūd'), *n.* [Fr.; L. *turpitudo* < *turpis,* base, vile], 1. baseness; vileness; depravity. 2. an instance of this.

tur·quoise (tũr'koiz, tũr'kwoiz), *n.* [ME. *turkeis;* OFr. *turqueise,* fem. of OFr. *turqueis,* Turkish (see TURK): so named because brought to western Europe through Turkey], 1. a sky-blue, greenish-blue, or greenish-gray semiprecious stone, a hydrous phosphate of aluminum containing a small amount of copper. 2. the color of turquoise; greenish-blue: also **turquoise blue.** *adj.* greenish-blue.

tur·ret (tũr'it), *n.* [ME. *turet, toret;* OFr. *tourete,* dim. of *tour;* see TOWER], 1. a small tower projecting from a building, usually at a corner: it is often only ornamental. 2. a wooden, usually square tower on wheels, carrying soldiers, battering-rams, catapults, etc., used in ancient warfare for attacking fortresses and walled cities. 3. *a*) a low, armored, usually revolving, tower-like structure for a gun and gunner or guns and their crew, as on a warship, tank, or fortress. *b*) a transparent hemisphere of plexiglass, etc., for a gun and gunner, as on a bomber. 4. an attachment for a lathe, drill, etc., consisting of a block holding several cutting tools, which may be rotated to present any of the tools to the work: also **turrethead.**

tur·ret·ed (tũr'it-id), *adj.* 1. having a turret or turrets. 2. shaped like a turret. 3. having whorls forming a high, conical spiral, as some shells.

tur·ret·head (tũr'it-hed'), *n.* a turret (sense 4).

turret lathe, a lathe with a turret (sense 4).

tur·ric·u·late (tə-rik'yoo-lit, tə-rik'yoo-lāt'), *adj.* [< L. *turricula,* dim. of *turris,* a tower; + *-ate*], 1. having or resembling a small turret or turrets. 2. turreted (sense 3).

tur·ric·u·lat·ed (tə-rik'yoo-lā'tid), *adj.* turriculate.

tur·ri·lite (tũr'ə-līt'), *n.* [< Mod. L. *Turrilites,* name of the genus < L. *turris,* a tower + Gr. *lithos,* stone], an extinct Cretaceous cephalopod with a turreted shell.

tur·tle (tũr't'l), *n.* [*pl.* TURTLES (-t'lz), TURTLE; see PLURAL, II, D, 1], [altered after *turtledove* (see TURTLEDOVE) < Fr. *tortue* or Sp. *tortuga,* tortoise; see TORTOISE], 1. any of a large and widely distributed group of land, fresh-water, and salt-water reptiles having a toothless beak and a soft body encased in a hard shell into which, in most species, the head, tail, and four legs may be withdrawn: although fresh-water and, particularly, sea species are usually called *turtle,* and land species are usually called *tortoise,* the terms are properly interchangeable for all species. 2. the flesh of some turtles, used as food. 3. [Archaic], a turtledove. *v.i.* [TURTLED (-t'ld), TURTLING], to hunt for or catch turtles.

turn turtle, to turn upside down; capsize.

tur·tle·back (tũr't'l-bak'), *n.* 1. an arched structure built over the bow and, sometimes, the stern of a ship as a protection against heavy seas: also **turtle deck.**

2. a similar structure protecting the decks of early gunboats from enemy fire.

tur·tle·dove (tũr'tʼl-duv'), *n.* [ME. *turtle, tortle;* AS. *turtle, turtla;* L. *turtur;* of echoic origin; cf. TURTLE], any of several wild doves noted for their plaintive cooing and the affection that the mates show toward each other.

tur·tle·head (tũr'tʼl-hed'), *n.* any of several hardy American herbs of the figwort group, with large white or purple flowers.

tur·tle-neck (tũr'tʼl-nek'), *adj.* designating a sweater, etc. with a turtle neck.

turtle neck, a high, turned-down collar that fits snugly about the neck, as on some pull-over sweaters.

turves (tũrvz), *n.* archaic plural of **turf.**

Tus·ca·loo·sa (tus'kə-lōō'sə), *n.* a city in west central Alabama: pop., 63,000.

Tus·can (tus'kən), *adj.* [L. *Tuscanus* < *Tuscus,* a Tuscan, Etruscan], 1. of Tuscany, its people, etc. 2. designating or of a classical (Roman) order of architecture characterized by unfluted columns with a ringlike capital and a frieze like the Doric. *n.* 1. a native or inhabitant of Tuscany. 2. any of the Italian dialects of Tuscany, especially that one accepted as standard literary Italian.

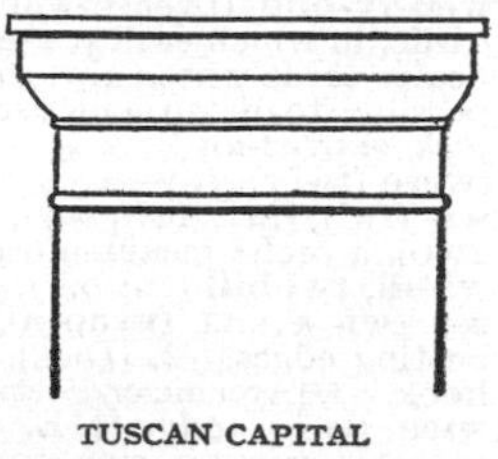

TUSCAN CAPITAL

Tus·ca·ny (tus'kə-ni), *n.* formerly a grand duchy, later a region, of western Italy: area, 8,861 sq. mi.; pop., 3,159,000; chief city, Florence: Italian name, *Toscana.*

Tus·ca·ror·a (tus'kə-rôr'ə, tus'kə-rō'rə), *n.* [*pl.* TUSCARORA, TUSCARORAS (-əz, -rəz)], a member of a tribe of Iroquoian Indians at one time living in North Carolina but later, after joining the Iroquois Confederacy in 1722, living in New York and Ontario.

tush (tush), *interj.* an exclamation expressing impatience, reproof, contempt, etc.

tush (tush), *n.* [ME. *tusch;* AS. *tucs, tux;* var. of *tusk*], 1. a tusk. 2. a canine tooth of a horse.

tusk (tusk), *n.* [ME. *tusk;* by metathesis < AS. *tucs, tux;* akin to OFris. *tusk;* Gmc. **tunth-ska* < **tunth-* < IE. base **edont-,* tooth < **ed-,* to eat (cf. TOOTH)], 1. a very long, pointed tooth, usually one of a pair, projecting outside the mouth and used for defense, digging up food, etc., as in elephants, wild boars, or walruses. 2. any long, protruding tooth. 3. a projecting, tusklike part. *v.t.* to dig, gore, etc. with a tusk or tusks. —***SYN.*** see **tooth.**

tusked (tuskt), *adj.* having tusks.

Tus·ke·gee (tus-kē'gi), *n.* a city in eastern Alabama, near Montgomery: pop., 1,800.

tusk·er (tus'kẽr), *n.* an animal with large tusks, as an elephant, wild boar, etc.

tus·sah (tus'ə), *n.* [Hind. *tasar;* Sans. *tasara, trasara,* lit., a shuttle, kind of silkworm], 1. an undomesticated Asiatic silkworm that produces a coarse, tough silk. 2. this silk: also **tussah silk.** Also **tusseh, tussa, tussar, tusser, tussor, tussore, tussur.**

tus·sal (tus'əl), *adj.* [< L. *tussis,* a cough; + *-al*], of, or having the nature of, a cough.

tus·sis (tus'is), *n.* [L.], in *medicine,* a cough.

tus·sive (tus'iv), *adj.* [< L. *tussis,* a cough; + *-ive*], of or caused by a cough.

tus·sle (tus''l), *v.i.* [TUSSLED (-'ld), TUSSLING], [freq. of obs. *touse,* to tease, pull; ME. *tusen* (in comp.), to pull; cf. TOUSLE], to fight, struggle, contend, etc. vigorously or vehemently; wrestle; scuffle. *n.* a vigorous or vehement struggle, contest, or contention; scuffle.

tus·sock (tus'ək), *n.* [prob. extension of earlier *tusk,* tuft of hair, after words in *-ock;* ? < specialized use of *tusk*], 1. a thick tuft or clump of grass, sedge, twigs, etc. 2. [Now Rare], a tuft or bunch of hair.

tussock moth, any of a large group of moths whose caterpillars are covered with long tufts of hair.

tus·sock·y (tus'ək-i), *adj.* 1. forming or like a tussock or tussocks. 2. covered with tussocks; tufty.

tut (tut: *conventionalized pronun.*), *interj.* an exclamation of impatience, annoyance, contempt, etc.

Tut·ankh·a·men (tōōt'äŋk-ä'mən), *n.* Egyptian king of the 18th dynasty; 14th century B.C.; tomb discovered in 1922.

tu·te·lage (tōō'tʼl-ij, tū'tʼl-ij), *n.* [< L. *tutela,* protection; + *-age*], 1. the function of a guardian; guardianship; care, protection, etc. 2. teaching; instruction. 3. the condition of being under a guardian or tutor.

tu·te·lar (tōō'tʼl-ẽr, tū'tʼl-ẽr), *adj. & n.* tutelary.

tu·te·lar·y (tōō'tʼl-er'i, tū'tʼl-er'i), *adj.* [L. *tutelarius* < *tutela,* protection], 1. protecting; watching over; guardian. 2. of or serving as a guardian. *n.* [*pl.* TUTELARIES (-iz)], a tutelary god, spirit, saint, etc.

tu·tor (tōō'tẽr, tū'tẽr), *n.* [ME. *tutour;* OFr. *tutor, tutour;* L. *tutor* < *tutus* for *tuitus,* pp. of *tueri,* to look after, guard; cf. TUITION, TUTELARY], 1. a private teacher. 2. a legal guardian of a minor and his property. 3. in English universities, a college official in charge of the studies of an undergraduate. 4. in some American universities and colleges, a teacher ranking below an instructor; teaching assistant. *v.t.* 1. to act as a tutor to. 2. to teach; instruct. 3. to train under discipline; discipline; admonish. *v.i.* 1. to act as a tutor, or instructor. 2. [Colloq.], to be tutored, or instructed, especially by a private teacher.

tu·tor·age (tōō'tẽr-ij, tū'tẽr-ij), *n.* [see -AGE], 1. the position, duties, or authority of a tutor; tutorship. 2. a charge for tutoring.

tu·to·ri·al (tōō-tôr'i-əl, tū-tō'ri-əl), *adj.* [< L. *tutorius;* + *-al*], of a tutor or tutors.

tutorial system, a system of instruction, as in some universities, in which a tutor directs the studies of and has general supervision over each of the small group of students assigned to him.

tu·tor·ship (tōō'tẽr-ship', tū'tẽr-ship'), *n.* [see -SHIP], the position, duties, or authority of a tutor.

tut·ti (tōō'ti; It. tōōt'tē), *adj.* [It. (pl. of *tutto*), lit., all < LL. **tottus* for L. *totus,* all, whole; cf. TOTAL], for all instruments or voices: a musical direction to the performers. *n.* [*pl.* TUTTIS (-tiz)], 1. a passage played or sung by all performers. 2. a tonal effect produced by the concerted playing or singing of all performers.

tut·ti-frut·ti (tōō'ti-frōō'ti), *n.* [It., lit., all fruits; cf. prec.], a preserve, candy, or ice cream made with a mixture of fruits or fruit flavorings. *adj.* made or flavored with a mixture of fruits.

‡**tut·to** (tōōt'tô), *adj.* [It.], all; entire: a musical direction.

tut·ty (tut'i), *n.* [ME. & Late OFr. *tutie;* Ar. *tūtiyā,* zinc oxide; prob. of Per. or Indic origin; cf. Sans. *tuttha,* blue vitriol], crude zinc oxide in the form of a waste product from the flues of smelting furnaces.

tu·tu (tōō'tōō; Fr. tü'tü'), *n.* [Fr.], a very short, full, projecting skirt worn by ballet dancers.

Tu·tu·i·la (tōō'tōō-ē'lä), *n.* an island of American Samoa, in the South Pacific: area, 52 sq. mi.; pop., 17,000; chief city, Pago Pago.

Tu·va Autonomous Region (tōō'vä), an autonomous region of the R.S.F.S.R., northwest of the Mongolian People's Republic: area, 64,000 sq. mi.; pop., 172,000; capital, Kyzyl: formerly called Tannu Tuva.

tu-whit tu-whoo (tōō-hwit' tōō-hwōō'), a representation of the characteristic vocal sound made by an owl: sometimes also used as a verb.

tux (tuks), *n.* [Colloq.], a tuxedo.

tux·e·do (tuk-sē'dō), *n.* [*pl.* TUXEDOS (-dōz)], [< the name of a country club at *Tuxedo* Park, near *Tuxedo* Lake, N.Y.], 1. a man's tailless jacket for evening wear, usually black with satin lapels, considered less formal than a swallowtail coat; dinner jacket. 2. a suit with such a jacket.

tu·yère (twē'yâr', twêr; Fr. tü'yâr'), *n.* [Fr. *tuyère,* nozzle < *tuyau,* a pipe], the pipe or nozzle through which air is forced into a blast furnace, forge, etc.

TV, television.

TVA, T.V.A., Tennessee Valley Authority.

Tver (tver), *n.* Kalinin, city in U.S.S.R.: former name.

twa (twä), *adj. & n.* [ME. (Northern & Scot.); AS.], [Scot.], two.

twad·dle (twäd''l), *n.* [earlier *twattle;* prob. collateral form of *tattle,* in *twiddle-twaddle* for *tittle-tattle*], foolish, empty talk or writing; nonsense. *v.t. & v.i.* [TWADDLED (-'ld), TWADDLING], to talk or write in a foolish or senseless manner; prattle.

twain (twān), *n. & adj.* [ME. *twene, tweyne,* etc.; AS. *twegen,* nom. & acc. masc. form of *two;* in ME., this became a mere secondary form of *two,* of which the main form came < AS. (fem.) *twa;* cf. TWA, TWO], [Archaic or Poetic], two.

Twain, Mark (twān), (pseudonym of *Samuel Langhorne Clemens*), 1835–1910; American novelist and humorist.

twang (twaŋ), *n.* [echoic], 1. a quick, sharp, vibrating sound, as of a taut string suddenly plucked or released. 2. a sharp, vibrant, nasal speech sound; nasal intonation. 3. a way of speaking, especially a dialect, characterized by such sounds. 4. [Dial.], a twinge. *v.i.* 1. to make a twang, as a bowstring, banjo, etc. 2. to speak with a twang. 3. to be released with a twang: said of an arrow. *v.t.* 1. to cause to twang. 2. to say with a twang. 3. to shoot (an arrow), release (a bowstring), etc., with a twang.

twan·gle (twaŋ'g'l), *n., v.i. & v.t.* [TWANGLED (-g'ld), TWANGLING], [*twang* + *-le,* freq. suffix], [Rare], twang.

twang·y (twaŋ'i), *adj.* [TWANGIER (-i-ẽr), TWANGIEST (-i-ist)], having a twang.

'twas (twuz, twäz; *unstressed* twəz), it was.

twat·tle (twät''l), *n., v.i. & v.t.* [TWATTLED (-'ld),

TWATTLING], [< *tattle;* cf. TWADDLE], twaddle.

tway·blade (twā'blād'), *n.* [archaic *tway*, two (ME. *twei;* see TWAIN); + *blade*], 1. a variety of orchid with two broad leaves and small, red-veined, yellow flowers. 2. any of several orchids having two leaves springing from the roots.

tweak (twēk), *v.t.* [var. of dial. *twick* < ME. *twikken;* AS. *twiccan*, to twitch; cf. TWITCH], to seize and pull (the nose, ear, etc.) with a sudden jerk and, usually, twist. *n.* a sudden, sharp, twisting pinch or pluck.

Tweed (twēd), *n.* a river in southern Scotland and England, flowing into the North Sea: length, 95 mi.

tweed (twēd), *n.* [< misreading of *tweel*, Scot. form of *twill;* later associated with the *Tweed*, river flowing through the region where the cloth is woven], 1. a wool fabric with a rough surface, in a plain, twill, or herringbone twill weave of two or more colors or shades of the same color. 2. a jacket, suit, etc. of this. 3. *pl.* clothes of tweed.

Tweed, William Mar·cy (mär'si twēd), 1823–1878; American politician: called *Boss Tweed.*

Tweed·dale (twēd'dāl', twē'd'l), *n.* Peebles, Scotland.

twee·dle (twē'd'l), *v.i.* [TWEEDLED (-d'ld), TWEEDLING], [echoic of a reed pipe], to play a series of shrill tones: said of a musical instrument or its player. *v.t.* 1. to play carelessly or casually on (a musical instrument). 2. [influenced by *wheedle*], to cajole or wheedle, as by music. *n.* a sound produced by tweedling.

twee·dle·dum and twee·dle·dee (twē'd'l-dum''n-twē'd'l-dē'), [< *tweedle*, echoic word for a shrill note: first used of rival musicians], 1. two persons or things so much alike as to be almost indistinguishable. 2. [T- T-], two almost identical characters in *Alice's Adventures in Wonderland*, by Lewis Carroll.

Tweed Ring, a group of Tammany politicians, headed by W. M. Tweed, who misappropriated millions of dollars while in control of New York City (1868–1871).

Tweeds·muir, Baron (twēdz'myoor), see **Buchan, John.**

'tween (twēn), *prep.* [ME. *twene*, aphetic for *atwene*, between], [Poetic], between.

tweet (twēt), *n. & interj.* [echoic], a thin, chirping sound characteristic of small birds. *v.i.* to utter this sound.

tweet·er (twēt'ẽr), *n.* in radio, sound reproduction, etc., a small loud-speaker that reproduces high audio-frequency sound waves: distinguished from *woofer.*

tweeze (twēz), *n.* [for *twees, etweese;* Fr. *étuis*, pl. of *étui;* see ETUI], [Obs.], a case or set of small instruments, especially surgical instruments: also spelled **tweese.** *v.t.* [back-formation < *tweezers*], [Colloq.], to pluck, remove, handle, etc. with or as with tweezers.

tweez·er (twēz'ẽr), *n.* [< *tweeze;* in mod. use a back-formation < *tweezers*], tweezers.

tweez·ers (twēz'ẽrz), *n.pl.* [altered (after *pincers, scissors*, etc.) < *tweeze*], 1. small pincers for plucking out hairs, handling little objects, etc.: often **pair of tweezers.** 2. [Obs.], a tweeze.

TWEEZERS

twelfth (twelfth), *adj.* [ME. *twelfthe, twelfte;* AS. *twelfta;* see TWELVE & -TH], 1. preceded by eleven others in a series; 12th. 2. designating any of the twelve equal parts of something. *n.* 1. the one following the eleventh. 2. any of the twelve equal parts of something; 1/12. 3. in *music, a)* an interval of twelve degrees in a diatonic scale. *b)* a tone twelve degrees above or below a given tone. *c)* the combination of two tones separated by this interval.

Twelfth-day (twelfth'dā'), *n.* January 6, the twelfth day after Christmas, on which the Epiphany is celebrated: formerly observed as the official end of the Christmas season.

Twelfth-night (twelfth'nīt'), *n.* the evening preceding Twelfth-day, formerly celebrated with games and feasting.

Twelfth-tide (twelfth'tīd'), *n.* the season of Twelfth-night and Twelfth-day.

twelve (twelv), *adj.* [ME. *twelue, twelfe;* AS. *twelf;* akin to G. *zwölf* (Goth. *twalif*); comp. < bases of *two* & *leave;* basic sense "two left" (i.e., after ten); cf. ELEVEN], two more than ten. *n.* 1. the cardinal number between eleven and thirteen; 12; XII. 2. a group of twelve persons or things; dozen.
  the Twelve, the Twelve Apostles.

Twelve Apostles, the twelve disciples chosen by Jesus to go forth to teach the gospel: see **apostle.**

twelve·fold (twelv'fōld'), *adj.* [see -FOLD], 1. having twelve parts. 2. having twelve times as much or as many. *adv.* twelve times as much or as many.

twelve·mo (twelv'mō), *adj. & n.* [*pl.* TWELVEMOS (-mōz)], duodecimo.

twelve·month (twelv'munth'), *n.* a year.

Twelve Tables, the early code of Roman law, written 451–450 B.C.

twelve-tone (twelv'tōn'), *adj.* in *music*, designating or of a system or technique of composition, developed by Arnold Schönberg, in which the twelve tones of the chromatic scale are used without reference to a specific tonal center, or key, but in an arbitrary, fixed order.

twen·ti·eth (twen'ti-ith), *adj.* [ME. *twentithe;* new formation for AS. *twentigotha, twentogotha;* see TWENTY & -TH], 1. preceded by nineteen others in a series; 20th. 2. designating any of the twenty equal parts of something. *n.* 1. the one following the nineteenth. 2. any of the twenty equal parts of something; 1/20.

twen·ty (twen'ti), *adj.* [ME. *twenti;* AS. *twentig, twegentig*, lit., two tens; see TWAIN & -TY (tens); akin to G. *zwanzig*, Goth. *twai tigjus*], two times ten. *n.* [*pl.* TWENTIES (-tiz)], the cardinal number between nineteen and twenty-one; 20; XX.
  the twenties, the years from twenty through twenty-nine (of a century or person's age).

twen·ty·fold (twen'ti-fōld'), *adj.* [see -FOLD], 1. having twenty parts. 2. having twenty times as much or as many. *adv.* twenty times as much or as many.

twen·ty-one (twen'ti-wun'), *n.* a gambling game at cards, in which each player's aim is to obtain from the dealer cards whose pips total twenty-one or as near as possible to it without exceeding it: also called *black-jack, vingt-et-un.*

'twere (twûr), it were.

twi- (twī), [ME. *twi-, twy-;* AS. *twi-;* for the IE. base see TWO], a prefix meaning *two, double, twice.*

twi·bil, twi·bill (twī'bil'), *n.* [ME. *twibil;* AS. *twibil(e);* see TWI- & BILL (weapon)], 1. [Obs.], an ax with two cutting edges. 2. [Dial.], *a)* a mattock. *b)* a reaping hook. 3. [Archaic or Poetic], a double-bladed battle-ax.

twice (twīs), *adv.* [ME. *twies;* AS. *twiges* < *twiga*, twice + *-es*, genit. sing. ending], 1. on two occasions or in two instances. 2. two times. 3. in twofold amount or degree; doubly: as, *twice* the money.

twice-laid (twīs'lād'), *adj.* 1. made from the yarns of old rope. 2. made from remnants or used material.

twice-told (twīs'tōld'), *adj.* 1. told twice. 2. told many times; hackneyed; trite.

Twick·en·ham (twik'ən-əm), *n.* a city on the Thames, near London, England: pop., 99,000.

twid·dle (twid''l), *v.t.* [TWIDDLED (-'ld), TWIDDLING], [prob. via dial. < ON. *tvidla*, to stir; influenced by echoism], to twirl or play with lightly. *v.i.* 1. to toy or trifle with some object. 2. to be busy about trifles. 3. to move in a twirling manner. *n.* a light twirling motion, as with the fingers.
  twiddle one's thumbs, 1. to twirl one's thumbs idly around one another. 2. to do nothing; be idle.

twig (twig), *n.* [ME. & AS. *twigge;* indirectly akin to G. *zweig;* IE. **dwi-gho* < base **dwōu-*, two (cf. TWO): prob. with reference to the forking of the twig], a small branch or shoot of a tree or shrub.

twig (twig), *v.t. & v.i.* [TWIGGED (twigd), TWIGGING], [via thieves' slang < Ir. *tuigim*, I understand], [British Slang], 1. to observe; notice. 2. to understand.

twig·gy (twig'i), *adj.* 1. like a twig; slender, delicate, etc. 2. full of or covered with twigs.

twi·light (twī'līt'), *n.* [ME. < *twi-* + *light;* akin to G. *zwielicht;* basic sense prob. "the light between"], 1. the subdued light just after sunset or, sometimes, just before sunrise. 2. the period from sunset to dark. 3. any faint light. 4. any condition or period preceding or, more commonly, following full development, victory, etc. *adj.* of or characteristic of twilight.

Twilight of the Gods, [see RAGNAROK], in *Norse mythology*, Ragnarok, the destruction of the gods and of the world in a final conflict with the powers of evil.

twilight sleep, a state of partial anesthesia and semi-consciousness induced by the injection of morphine and scopolamine, as to lessen the pains of childbirth.

twill (twil), *n.* [ME. *twyll, twile;* AS. *twili* < *twi-;* see TWI-; cf. DRILL, DIMITY], 1. a cloth woven so as to have parallel diagonal lines or ribs. 2. the pattern of this weave or its appearance. *v.t.* to weave so as to produce a twill.

'twill (twil), it will.

twilled (twild), *adj.* [see TWILL], woven in parallel diagonal lines or ribs.

twin (twin), *adj.* [ME.; AS. *twinn* & ON. *tvinnr*, double; both < base of *twi-*], 1. *a)* consisting of or being two separate but similar or closely related things; forming a pair; double; paired. *b)* being one of a pair of such things; being a counterpart. 2. *a)* being two that have been born at the same birth: as, *twin* girls. *b)* being either one of two born at the same birth: as, a *twin* sister. *n.* 1. either one of two born at the same birth: twins are either *identical* (produced from the same ovum) or *fraternal* (produced from separate ova). 2. either one of two persons or things very much alike in appearance, shape, structure, etc. 3. [T-], *pl.* Gemini, a constellation and sign of the zodiac. 4. a compound crystal of two crystals or parts in reversed positions with respect to each other. *v.i.* [TWINNED (twind), TWINNING], 1. to give birth to twins. 2. [Rare], to be born at the same birth. 3. to be paired or coupled (with another). *v.t.* 1. to give birth to as twins. 2. to be or provide a counterpart to. 3. to pair or couple.

twin·ber·ry (twin'ber'i), *n.* [*pl.* TWINBERRIES (-iz)],

1. a variety of honeysuckle with purple flowers. 2. a trailing vine with red berries; partridgeberry.
twin·born (twin'bôrn'), *adj.* born as a twin or twins.
Twin Cities, St. Paul and Minneapolis.
twine (twīn), *n.* [ME. & AS. *twin*, twisted thread < base of *twi-*], 1. strong thread, string, or cord of two or more strands twisted together. 2. a twining or being twined. 3. a twined thing or part; twist; convolution. 4. a tangle; snarl. 5. a twining branch or spray of a plant. *v.t.* [TWINED (twīnd), TWINING], [ME. *twinen;* prob. < D. *twijnen*, to twine, twist, lit. to double & < the *n.*], 1. *a)* to twist together; intertwine; interlace. *b)* to form by twisting, intertwining, or interlacing. 2. to encircle or wreathe (one thing) with another. 3. to wind (something) around something else. 4. to enfold, embrace, etc.: as, the wreath *twined* his brow. *v.i.* 1. to twist, interlace, wreathe, etc. 2. to twist and turn; wind about.
Twin Falls, a waterfall of the Snake River, southern Idaho: height, 180 ft.
twin·flow·er (twin'flou'ẽr), *n.* a trailing plant of the honeysuckle family, with glossy leaves and small, fragrant, pink, bell-shaped flowers growing in pairs.
twinge (twinj), *v.t.* [TWINGED (twinjd), TWINGING], [ME. *twengen;* AS. *twengan*, to squeeze, press, pinch; ? for **thwengan*, caus. < base **thwing-* (IE. **twengh-*), seen in G. *zwingen*, to oppress, compel], to cause to have a sudden, sharp pain, pang, or qualm. *v.i.* to have a sudden, sharp pain. *n.* 1. a sudden, sharp pain; pang. 2. a qualm, as of conscience.
twi-night, twi·night (twī'nīt'), *adj.* [< *twi*light + *night*], in *baseball*, designating a double-header which starts in the late afternoon and continues into the evening.
twin·kle (twiŋ'k'l), *v.i.* [TWINKLED (-k'ld), TWINKLING], [ME. *twinklen;* AS. *twinclian*, freq. < base seen in G. *zwinken*, to wink], 1. to shine in rapid, intermittent gleams, as some stars; sparkle; glimmer; scintillate. 2. to light up, as with amusement: said of the eyes. 3. to move rapidly to and fro in a sparkling manner, as dancers' feet; flutter; flicker. 4. [Archaic], to wink or blink. *v.t.* 1. to cause to twinkle. 2. to emit (light) in rapid, intermittent gleams. *n.* 1. a flicker or wink of the eye. 2. a glint, as of amusement, in the eye. 3. an intermittent gleam; sparkle. 4. the time occupied by a wink; a twinkling.
twin·kling (twiŋ'kliŋ), *n.* 1. the action of a thing that twinkles. 2. a rapid gleam or little flash; twinkle. 3. the time occupied by a wink; instant.
twinned (twind), *adj.* 1. born as a twin or twins. 2. paired or coupled. 3. consisting of two crystals united so as to form a twin.
twin·ning (twin'iŋ), *n.* 1. the bearing of twins. 2. a pairing or coupling. 3. the formation of a twin crystal or crystals.
twin-screw (twin'skrōō'), *adj.* having two screw propellers, rotating in opposite directions, as some ships.
twirl (twũrl), *v.t. & v.i.* [altered (with emphatic *tw-*) < ME. *tirlen;* by metathesis < *trillen*, to turn], 1. to rotate rapidly; spin. 2. to turn in a circle; whirl around. 3. in *baseball*, to pitch. *n.* 1. a twirling or being twirled. 2. something twirled; specifically, *a)* a twist, coil, etc. *b)* a twisting line; flourish.
twist (twist), *v.t.* [ME. *twisten* < AS. *twist*, a rope (in *mæst-twist*, a stay, rope to stay a mast)| < base of *twi-;* cf. TWIN, TWINE], I. *to wind, entwine, etc.* 1. *a)* to wind (two or more threads or strands) around one another, as by spinning. *b)* to wind two or more threads or strands of (cotton, silk, etc.) around one another so as to produce thread or cord. *c)* to produce (thread, cord, etc.) by winding two or more threads or strands around one another. 2. to wreathe; twine. 3. to wind or coil (thread, rope, etc.) around something. 4. to encircle with a coil of. 5. to entwine or interweave in something else. II. *to make spiral, wrench, contort, etc.* 1. to give spiral shape to by turning the ends in opposite directions; hence, 2. to subject to torsion. 3. to put out of shape in this manner; wrench; sprain: as, he *twisted* his arm painfully. 4. to contort or distort (the face, etc.). 5. to wring; torment; harass. 6. to confuse: as, I'm all *twisted.* 7. to break off, snap off, etc. by turning the end (with *off*). 8. to wrest, distort, or pervert the meaning of. III. *to revolve, etc.* 1. to cause to turn around or rotate. 2. to make (a ball) go in a curve by throwing or striking it so as to give it a spinning motion. *v.i.* 1. to undergo twisting: as, the wire *twists* easily. 2. to spiral, coil, twine, etc. (*around* or *about* something). 3. to revolve or rotate. 4. to turn to one side; change direction. 5. to turn one way and then another, as a path; wind; meander. 6. to twist something. 7. to squirm; writhe. 8. to move in a curved path, as a ball that has been thrown or struck so as to have a spinning motion. *n.* I. *something twisted* 1. a thread or cord of two or more twisted strands of hemp, cotton, silk, wool, etc.; specifically, *a)* closely twisted cotton yarn used as warp thread. *b)* strong, closely twisted silk thread used for making buttonholes, etc. 2. tobacco in the form of a twisted roll. 3. a loaf of bread or roll made of one or more twisted pieces of dough. 4. a knot, etc. made by twisting. II. *a twisting or being twisted* 1. rotation; spin, turn, twirl, etc. 2. a spin given to a ball in throwing or striking it. 3. spiral movement along and around an axis. 4. the condition of being twisted in a spiral; torsional stress. 5. the degree of this; angle of torsion. 6. a contortion, as of the face. 7. a wrench or sprain. 8. a turning aside; turn; bend. 9. a personal tendency, especially an eccentric one; bias. **10. a distorting or perverting of meaning.** —***SYN.*** see **curve.**
twist drill, a kind of drill with deep spiral grooves for carrying out chips.
twist·er (twis'tẽr), *n.* 1. a person who twists. 2. a thing that twists; specifically, *a)* a machine for twisting threads, etc. *b)* a thrown or batted ball that has been given a twist. 3. a tornado or cyclone.
twit (twit), *v.t.* [TWITTED (-id), TWITTING], [by loss of initial *a* < ME. *atwiten*, to twit; AS. *ætwitan; æt*, at + *witan*, to accuse; base as in *wit*], to reproach, upbraid, taunt, etc., especially by reminding of a fault or mistake. *n.* 1. act of twitting. 2. a reproach or taunt.
twitch (twich), *v.t. & v.i.* [ME. *twicchen;* AS. *twiccian*, to pluck, catch hold of; akin to G. *zwicken;* prob. < base of *twi-;* basic sense "to pinch off"; cf. TWEAK], 1. to pull (at) with a sudden jerk; pluck; snatch. 2. to move with a quick, sudden motion or convulsively. *n.* 1. a sudden, quick jerk. 2. a sudden, quick motion, especially a convulsive one: as, a facial *twitch.*
twitch grass, couch grass, a weedy kind of grass.
twit·ter (twit'ẽr), *v.i.* [ME. *twiteren;* cf. G. *zwitschern* & Eng. *tweet*], 1. to make a series of light, sharp, intermittent vocal sounds; chirp continuously or tremulously: said of birds. 2. to talk in a rapid, tremulous manner expressive of agitation, timidity, etc.; chatter. 3. to tremble with excitement, eagerness, etc. 4. to titter. *v.t.* to express or say in a twittering manner. *n.* 1. a light, sharp, intermittent vocal sound of a bird; chirping. 2. any similar sound. 3. a condition of tremulous excitement; flutter.
twit·ter (twit'ẽr), *n.* a person who twits.
'twixt (twikst), ***prep.*** [Poetic or Dial.], betwixt.
two (tōō), *adj.* [ME. *two, tu;* AS. *twa*, fem. & neut., *tu*, neut. (cf. TWAIN); akin to G. *zwei;* IE. base **dwōu-*, two, seen also in L. *duo*, two (cf. DUAL), Gr. *duo*, etc.; cf. TWI-, TWIN, TWINE, TWIG, TWITCH, etc.], totaling one more than one. *n.* 1. the cardinal number between one and three; 2; II. 2. something that has two of anything as its outstanding characteristic, as a playing card or domino marked with two spots.
in two, in two parts; asunder.
put two and two together, to reach an obvious conclusion by considering several facts together.
two-bag·ger (tōō'bag'ẽr), *n.* [Slang], a two-base hit.
two-base hit (tōō'bās'), in *baseball*, a hit by which the batter can reach second base without benefit of an error: also called *double.*
two-bit (tōō'bit'), *adj.* [see BIT (small piece), sense 3], [Slang], 1. worth or costing twenty-five cents; hence, 2. cheap; worthless.
two bits, [see prec.], [Slang], twenty-five cents.
two-by-four (tōō'bə-fôr', tōō'bī-fôr'), *adj.* 1. that measures two inches by four inches, two feet by four feet, etc.; hence, 2. [Colloq.], small, narrow, cramped, etc. *n.* (tōō'bə-fôr', tōō'bī-fôr'), any length of lumber two inches thick and four inches wide.
two-col·or (tōō'kul'ẽr), *adj.* of, in, or using two colors.
two-cy·cle (tōō'sī'k'l), *n.* a two-stroke cycle in an internal-combustion engine. *adj.* having a two-stroke cycle.
two-edged (tōō'ejd'), *adj.* 1. that has two edges, usually on opposite sides; hence, 2. that can have two different meanings; especially, that can be taken either as a compliment or insult.
two-faced (tōō'fāst'), *adj.* 1. having two faces, surfaces, etc.; hence, 2. deceitful; hypocritical; treacherous.
two-fac·ed·ly (tōō'fās'id-li, tōō'fāst'li), *adv.* in a two-faced manner; deceitfully.
two-fist·ed (tōō'fis'tid), *adj.* [Colloq.], 1. having, and able to use, both fists; hence, 2. vigorous; virile.
two·fold (tōō'fōld'), *adj.* [see -FOLD], 1. having two parts. 2. having twice as much or as many. *adv.* twice as much or as many.
two-four (tōō'fôr', tōō'fōr'), *adj.* designating or of a musical rhythm with two quarter notes to a measure.
two-hand·ed (tōō'han'did), *adj.* 1. that needs to be used or wielded with both hands. 2. needing two people to operate: as, a *two-handed* saw. 3. for two people: as, a *two-handed* game. 4. having two hands. 5. able to use both hands equally well; ambidextrous.
two-leg·ged (tōō'leg'id, tōō'legd'), *adj.* having two legs.

two-mast·er (tōō′mas′tẽr, tōō′mäs′tẽr), *n.* a sailing ship with two masts.
two-name (tōō′nām′), *adj.* designating or of commercial paper bearing the names of two parties, the maker and the endorser, as liable.
two-part time (tōō′pärt′), musical time that has two beats or multiples of two beats to a measure.
two·pence (tup′′ns), *n.* 1. the sum of two pence; two British pennies. 2. a former British silver coin of this value, since 1662 coined only as alms money for Maundy Thursday. 3. a British copper coin of this value, current in the reign of George III.
two·pen·ny (tup′ən-i; *also, esp. of nails,* tōō′pen′i), *adj.* 1. worth or costing twopence (cf. **-penny**); hence, 2. cheap; worthless.
two-phase (tōō′fāz′), *adj.* in *electricity,* diphase.
two-piece (tōō′pēs′), *adj.* consisting of two separate parts: as, a *two-piece* bathing suit.
two-ply (tōō′plī′), *adj.* 1. having two thicknesses, layers, strands, etc. 2. woven double.
Two Sic·i·lies (sis′′l-iz), a former kingdom including Naples (with lower Italy) and Sicily: united with the Kingdom of Italy in 1860.
two-sid·ed (tōō′sīd′id), *adj.* 1. having two sides. 2. having two aspects: as, a *two-sided* question.
two·some (tōō′səm), *n.* 1. two people together; a couple. 2. a game, etc. for or played by two people. 3. these people. *adj.* consisting of or engaged in by two.
two-spot (tōō′spot′), *n.* 1. a playing card, domino, etc. with two spots, or pips; deuce. 2. [Colloq.], *a*) a two-dollar bill; hence, *b*) two dollars.
two-step (tōō′step′), *n.* 1. a ballroom dance in 2/4 time. 2. a piece of music for this dance.
two-thirds rule (tōō′thũrdz′), formerly, a rule in Democratic presidential conventions requiring a vote of at least two-thirds of the delegates to nominate a candidate.
two-time (tōō′tīm′), *v.t.* [Slang], to deceive in love; be unfaithful to (one's lover, wife, or husband).
'twould (twood), it would.
two-way (tōō′wā′), *adj.* 1. having two ways, lanes, etc.; allowing passage in either direction: as, a *two-way* street. 2. that connects a pipe, wire, etc. to two others. 3. in *mathematics, a*) that extends in two directions or dimensions. *b*) that has two modes of variation. 4. that is used for both transmission and reception: as, a *two-way* radio outfit.
twp., township.
T.W.U.A., 1. Textile Workers Union of America: an AFL-CIO labor union. 2. Transport Workers Union of America: an AFL-CIO labor union.
-ty (ti), [ME. *-tee, -tie, -te;* OFr. *-té;* L. *-tas, -tatis*], a suffix meaning *quality of, condition of,* found in some abstract nouns of Latin origin, as *paucity.*
-ty (ti), [ME. *-ti, -tie;* AS. *-tig;* akin to G. *-zig,* Goth. *tigus* (pl. *tigjus*), ten; IE. **dekm̥t-mi(s)*, dat. pl. < **dekm̥-*, ten; cf. TEN], a suffix meaning *tens, times ten,* as in *twenty, thirty,* etc.
Ty., Territory.
Ty·burn (tī′bẽrn), *n.* a former place of public execution in London, England.
Ty·che (tī′ki), *n.* in *Greek mythology,* the goddess of chance, identified with the Roman Fortuna.
ty·coon (tī-kōōn′), *n.* [Japan. *taikun,* mighty lord < Chin. *ta,* great + *kiun,* prince], 1. a title applied by foreigners to the former shogun of Japan. 2. [Colloq.], a wealthy and powerful industrialist, financier, etc.
Ty·deus (tī′dūs, tid′i-əs), *n.* [L.; Gr. *Tydeus*], in *Greek legend,* the father of Diomedes, and one of the Seven against Thebes: see **Seven against Thebes.**
ty·ing (tī′iŋ), present participle of **tie.**
tyke (tīk), *n.* [ME. *tike;* ON. *tik,* a bitch], 1. a dog; especially, a mongrel or cur. 2. [Scot.], a boor. 3. [Colloq.], a small child: term of endearment, especially for a lively or mischievous child. Also spelled **tike.**
Ty·ler (tī′lẽr), *n.* a city in northeastern Texas: pop., 51,000.
Ty·ler, John (tī′lẽr), 1790–1862; tenth president of the United States (1841–1845).
Tyler, Wat (wät), (*Walter Tyler*), ?–1381; English rebel; leader of the Peasants' Revolt.
tym·pan (tim′pən), *n.* [ME. *timpane;* OFr. *tympan;* L. *tympanum;* Gr. *tympanon,* a drum, area of a pediment, panel of a door < *typtein,* to strike, beat], 1. formerly, a drum. 2. a piece of paper, parchment, etc. stretched over the platen or impression cylinder of a printing press to serve as a cushion behind the paper being printed and equalize type pressure: in some kinds of printing, packing is also used beneath the tympan. 3. any membranelike part of an apparatus. 4. in *architecture,* a tympanum.
tym·pa·ni (tim′pə-ni), *n.pl.* [*sing.* TYMPANO (-nō′)], timpani.
tym·pan·ic (tim-pan′ik), *adj.* 1. of or like a drum or drumhead. 2. in *anatomy & zoology,* of the tympanum or eardrum.
tympanic bone, a bone in the skull of mammals, supporting the eardrum and partly enclosing the tympanum.
tympanic membrane, the eardrum: see **ear,** illus.
tym·pa·nist (tim′pə-nist), *n.* [Fr. *tympaniste;* L. *tympanista;* Gr. *tympanistēs* < *tympanon,* a drum; see TYMPAN], a member of an orchestra who plays drums and other percussion instruments.
tym·pa·ni·tes (tim′pə-nī′tēz), *n.* a distention of the abdomen by the accumulation of gas or air in the intestines or peritoneal cavity.
tym·pa·nit·ic (tim′pə-nit′ik), *adj.* of or having tympanites.
tym·pa·ni·tis (tim′pə-nī′tis), *n.* inflammation of the membrane lining the tympanum.
tym·pa·num (tim′pə-nəm), *n.* [*pl.* TYMPANUMS (-nəmz), TYMPANA (-nə)], [L.; see TYMPAN], 1. the middle ear or, sometimes, the eardrum: see **ear.** 2. *a*) a drum or drumlike instrument. *b*) a drumhead. 3. in *architecture, a*) the recessed space, usually triangular, enclosed by the slanting cornices of a pediment, often ornamented with sculpture. *b*) a corresponding semicircular space enclosed by an arch and the top of the door or window below it. 4. in *electricity,* the diaphragm of a telephone.
tym·pa·ny (tim′pə-ni), *n.* [*pl.* TYMPANIES (-niz)], [ML. *tympanias;* Gr. *tympanias* < *tympanon,* drum; see TYMPAN], 1. inflated or distended condition; hence, 2. inflated behavior or style; bombast; conceit.
Tyn·dale, William (tin′d′l), 1492?–1536; English theologian; translator of the Bible; executed: also spelled **Tindal, Tindale.**
Tyn·dall, John (tin′d′l), 1820–1893; British physicist.
Tyn·da·re·us (tin-dâr′i-əs), *n.* [L.; Gr. *Tyndareos*], a legendary Spartan king: see **Leda.**
Tyne (tīn), *n.* a river in Northumberland, England, flowing into the North Sea: length, 80 mi.
Tyne·mouth (tīn′məth, tin′məth), *n.* a city in northeastern England, at the mouth of the Tyne: pop., 69,000.
typ., 1. typographer. 2. typographical. 3. typography.
typ·al (tīp′′l), *adj.* 1. of or serving as a type or types; typical. 2. [Rare], typographical.
type (tīp), *n.* [Fr.; L. *typus;* Gr. *typos,* a blow, mark of the blow, figure, outline < *typtein,* to beat, strike], 1. a person, thing, or event that represents or symbolizes another, especially another that is to come; symbol; emblem; token; sign. 2. [Rare], a distinguishing mark, sign, or impress. 3. the general form, structure, plan, style, etc. characterizing or distinguishing the members of a class or group. 4. a kind, class, or group having distinguishing characteristics in common: as, a new *type* of airplane, an animal of the dog *type:* in colloquial usage, often used elliptically immediately preceding the noun, as, a new *type* airplane. 5. a person, animal, or thing that is representative of, or has the distinctive characteristics of, a class or group; typical individual or instance. 6. *a*) a perfect example; model; pattern; archetype: as, John is the very *type* of an honest leader. *b*) in *biology,* a genus or species that best exemplifies the characters of a larger group and often gives its name to it. 7. *a*) a rectangular piece of metal or, sometimes, wood with a raised letter, figure, etc. in reverse on its upper end, which when inked and pressed against a piece of paper or other material, as in a printing press, leaves an ink impression of its face. *b*) such pieces collectively. Types are classified according to class, style, size, width, or weight (heaviness of tone): as, roman *type,* Bodoni *type,* 6-point *type,* condensed *type,* boldface *type:* see also **roman, italic, boldface, condensed, pica, point system,** etc. 8. a printed character or characters: as, small *type* is hard on the eyes. 9. in *agriculture,* the combination of characters of an animal or breed that make it most suitable for a particular use: as, beef *type,* dairy *type.* 10. in *mathematics,* the simplest of a set of equivalent forms. *v.t.* [TYPED (tīpt), TYPING], 1. to prefigure. 2. to typify; represent. 3. to classify according to type: as, he is *typed* as a villain in the theater. 4. to typewrite. 5. in *medicine,* to determine the type of (a blood sample). *v.i.* to typewrite.

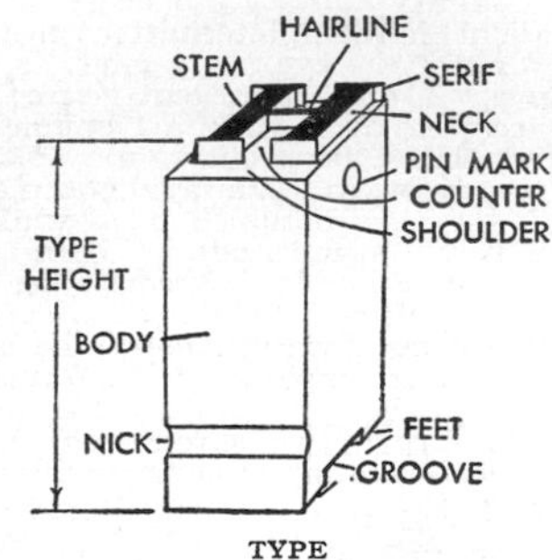

TYPE

SYN.—**type** is used of a group or category of persons or things whose distinguishing characteristics held in common clearly set it apart from related groups or categories (a new *type* of shock absorber); **kind** basically refers to a natural group or division (the rodent *kind*), but it is sometimes interchangeable with **sort** when used in vague reference to a less explicit group (all *sorts,* or *kinds,* of games); **nature,** in precise use, implies that the distinguishing characteristics are inherent or innate (earthquakes and other phenomena of that *nature*).

-type (tīp), [Gr. *-typon* < *typos;* see TYPE], a combining form meaning: 1. *type, representative form, example,* as in *prototype.* 2. *stamp, print, printing type,* etc., as in *daguerreotype, monotype.*
type founder, a person who casts metal type.
type foundry, a place where metal type is cast.
type genus, in *biology,* the genus that is theoretically most typical of a family or group and gives it its name: abbreviated **t.g.**
type-high (tīp'hī'), *adj.* exactly as high as type of standard height (0.9186 inch).
type metal, an alloy of tin, lead, and antimony used for making type, etc.
type·script (tīp'skript'), *n.* typewritten matter or copy.
type·set·ter (tīp'set'ẽr), *n.* 1. a person who sets type; compositor. 2. a machine for setting type.
type·set·ting (tīp'set'iŋ), *n.* the act or process of setting type. *adj.* of or used for setting type.
type species, in *biology,* the species that is theoretically most typical of a genus and gives it its name.
type specimen, the individual animal or plant used as the basis of the scientific description of a species, etc.
type·write (tīp'rīt'), *v.t. & v.i.* [TYPEWROTE (-rōt'), TYPEWRITTEN (-rit''n), TYPEWRITING], to write with a typewriter: now usually shortened to *type.*
type·writ·er (tīp'rīt'ẽr), *n.* 1. a writing machine with a keyboard for reproducing letters, figures, etc. that resemble printed ones: when the keys are struck, raised letters on bars are pressed against an inked ribbon, making the impression on an inserted piece of paper. 2. a typist. 3. a kind of printer's type made to appear like typewriter print.
type·writ·ing (tīp'rīt'iŋ), *n.* 1. the art, act, or process of using a typewriter. 2. work done by typewriting.
type·writ·ten (tīp'rit''n), past participle of **typewrite.** *adj.* written with a typewriter.
type·wrote (tīp'rōt'), past tense of **typewrite.**
typh- (tif), typho-.
typh·lit·ic (tif-lit'ik), *adj.* of or having typhlitis.
typh·li·tis (tif-lī'tis), *n.* [Mod. L. < Gr. *typhlos,* blind, closed; + *-itis*], inflammation of the caecum.
typh·lol·o·gy (tif-lol'ə-ji), *n.* [< Gr. *typhlos,* blind; + *-logy*], the branch of medicine that deals with blindness.
typh·lo·sis (tif-lō'sis), *n.* [Mod. L.; Gr. *typhlōsis* < *typhlos,* blind], in *medicine,* blindness.
ty·pho- (tī'fō, tī'fə), [< Gr. *typhos;* see TYPHUS], a combining form meaning *typhus, typhoid,* as in *typhogenic.*
Ty·pho·eus (tī-fō'ūs), *n.* in *Greek mythology,* a monster with a hundred heads, killed by Zeus.
ty·pho·gen·ic (tī'fə-jen'ik), *adj.* [*typho-* + *-genic*], causing typhus or typhoid fever.
ty·phoid (tī'foid), *adj.* [< Gr. *typhos,* a vapor, fever, stupor; + *-oid*], 1. originally, of or like typhus; hence, 2. designating or of an acute infectious disease (*typhoid fever*) caused by a bacillus and acquired through drinking infected milk, water, etc.: it was formerly considered a form of typhus and is characterized by fever, intestinal disorders, etc. *n.* typhoid fever.
ty·phoi·dal (tī-foi'd'l), *adj.* of or like typhoid fever.
typhoid bacillus, the bacillus that causes typhoid fever.
ty·phoi·din (tī-foi'din), *n.* [*typhoid* + *-in*], a preparation from a culture of the typhoid bacillus, injected in the skin for determining the presence of a typhoid infection.
ty·pho·ma·lar·i·al (tī'fō-mə-lâr'i-əl), *adj.* designating a fever having the symptoms of typhoid, but believed to be of malarial origin.
Ty·phon (tī'fon), *n.* in *Greek & Roman mythology,* a monster, variously regarded as a son of Typhoeus or as Typhoeus himself.
ty·phon·ic (tī-fon'ik), *adj.* of or like a typhoon.
ty·phoon (tī-fōōn'), *n.* [< Chin. dial. *tai-fung,* lit., great wind (or ? < *Tai,* Formosa; hence, Formosa wind); influenced by earlier *tuphan, tufan;* Port. *tufão;* Ar. *ṭūfān* < Gr. *typhōn,* hurricane], a violent cyclonic storm, especially one in the China Sea and adjacent regions; hurricane.
ty·phous (tī'fəs), *adj.* of, or having the nature of, typhus.
ty·phus (tī'fəs), *n.* [Mod. L. < Gr. *typhos,* a vapor, fever, stupor], an acute infectious disease caused by a rickettsia transmitted to man by the bite of fleas, lice, etc., and characterized by fever, nervous disorders, weakness, and an eruption of red spots on the skin: also **typhus fever.**
typ·ic (tip'ik), *adj.* typical.
typ·i·cal (tip'i-k'l), *adj.* [ML. *typicalis* < L. *typicus;* Gr. *typikos*], 1. serving as a type; symbolic. 2. having or showing the characteristics, qualities, etc. of a kind, class, or group so fully as to be a representative example. 3. of or belonging to a type or representative example; characteristic. —*SYN.* see **normal.**
typ·i·fi·ca·tion (tip'ə-fi-kā'shən), *n.* a typifying or being typified.
typ·i·fi·er (tip'ə-fī'ẽr), *n.* a person or thing that typifies.
typ·i·fy (tip'ə-fī'), *v.t.* [TYPIFIED (-fīd'), TYPIFYING], [< L. *typus,* a type; + *-fy*], 1. to be a type or emblem of; symbolize; prefigure. 2. to have or show the distinctive characteristics of; be typical of; exemplify.
typ·ist (tīp'ist), *n.* a person who operates a typewriter, especially one hired to do so.
ty·po- (tī'pō, tī'pə), [< Gr. *typos;* see TYPE], a combining form meaning *type,* as in *typography.*
typo., typog., 1. typographer. 2. typographic. 3. typographical. 4. typography.
ty·pog·ra·pher (tī-pog'rə-fẽr), *n.* [< *typography*], a person skilled in typography; printer: abbreviated **typ., typo., typog.**
ty·po·graph·ic (tī'pə-graf'ik), *adj.* typographical.
ty·po·graph·i·cal (tī'pə-graf'i-k'l), *adj.* 1. of typography; having to do with printing. 2. in print; printed. Abbreviated **typ., typo., typog.**
ty·po·graph·i·cal·ly (tī'pə-graf'i-k'l-i, tī'pə-graf'ik-li), *adv.* in a typographical manner; as regards printing.
ty·pog·ra·phy (tī-pog'rə-fi), *n.* [Fr. *typographie;* ML. *typographia;* see TYPO- & -GRAPHY], 1. the art of printing with type. 2. the setting and arranging of types and printing from them. 3. the arrangement, style, or general appearance of matter printed from type. Abbreviated **typ., typo., typog.**
ty·pol·o·gy (tī-pol'ə-ji), *n.* [*typo-* + *-logy*], 1. the study of types, symbols, or symbolism. 2. symbolic meaning or representation; symbolism.
ty·poth·e·tae (tī-poth'ə-tē', tī'pə-thē'tē), *n.pl.* [Mod. L. < Gr. *typos* (see TYPE) + *tithenai,* to place, set], 1. an association of master printers; hence, 2. printers: used in the names of organizations of printers.
Tyr (têr), *n.* [ON.; cf. TUESDAY], in *Norse mythology,* the god of war and son of Odin.
ty·ran·nic (ti-ran'ik, tī-ran'ik), *adj.* tyrannical.
ty·ran·ni·cal (ti-ran'i-k'l, tī-ran'i-k'l), *adj.* [L. *tyrannicus;* Gr. *tyrannikos*], 1. of or suited to a tyrant; arbitrary; despotic; hence, 2. harsh, cruel, unjust, oppressive, etc.
ty·ran·ni·cal·ly (ti-ran'i-k'l-i, tī-ran'ik-li), *adv.* in a tyrannical manner.
ty·ran·ni·cide (ti-ran'ə-sīd', tī-ran'ə-sīd'), *n.* [in sense 1 < L. *tyrannicidium;* in sense 2 < L. *tyrannicida;* see TYRANT & -CIDE], 1. the act of killing a tyrant. 2. a person who kills a tyrant.
tyr·an·nize (tir'ə-nīz'), *v.i.* [TYRANNIZED (-nīzd'), TYRANNIZING], [Fr. *tyranniser*], 1. to govern as a tyrant; rule with absolute power; hence, 2. to govern tyrannically; rule with cruelty, injustice, etc. 3. to use power or authority harshly; be oppressive. *v.t.* to treat tyrannically; oppress.
ty·ran·no·saur (ti-ran'ə-sôr', tī-ran'ə-sôr'), *n.* [< Gr. *tyrannos,* tyrant + *sauros,* lizard], a huge, two-footed, flesh-eating dinosaur of the Upper Cretaceous Period in North America.
ty·ran·no·sau·rus (ti-ran'ə-sôr'əs, tī-ran'ə-sôr'əs), *n.* a tyrannosaur.
tyr·an·nous (tir'ə-nəs), *adj.* 1. tyrannical; despotic. 2. involving tyranny; cruel, oppressive, unjust, etc.
tyr·an·ny (tir'ə-ni), *n.* [*pl.* TYRANNIES (-niz)], [ME. *tirannie, tyrannie;* OFr. *tirannie;* L. *tyrannia;* Gr. *tyrannia*], 1. the office, authority, government, or jurisdiction of a tyrant or absolute ruler. 2. oppressive and unjust government; despotism. 3. very cruel and unjust use of power or authority; hence, 4. harshness; rigor; severity. 5. a tyrannical act.
ty·rant (tī'rənt), *n.* [ME. *tirant, tiraunt;* OFr. *tiran, tyran;* L. *tyrannus;* Gr. *tyrannos,* lord, absolute sovereign, usurper], 1. an absolute ruler; specifically, in ancient Greece, etc., one who seized sovereignty illegally; usurper. 2. a cruel, oppressive ruler; despot. 3. any person who exercises his authority in an oppressive manner; cruel master. 4. a tyrannical influence.
Tyre (tīr), *n.* an important seaport in ancient Phoenicia, now in Lebanon: see **Israel,** map.
tyre (tīr), *n.* a tire: British spelling.
Tyr·i·an (tir'i-ən), *adj.* [< L. *Tyrius,* of Tyre < *Tyrus* (Gr. *Tyros*), Tyre], 1. of ancient Tyre, its people, culture, etc. 2. of Tyrian purple. *n.* a native of Tyre.
Tyr·i·an-pur·ple (tir'i-ən-pũr'p'l), *adj.* of the color of Tyrian purple; bluish-red.
Tyrian purple (or **dye**), 1. a purple or crimson dye used by the ancient Romans and Greeks: it was made from certain mollusks, originally at Tyre. 2. bluish red.
ty·ro (tī'rō), *n.* [*pl.* TYROS (-rōz)], [ML.; L. *tiro,* young soldier, beginner], a beginner in learning something; novice: also spelled **tiro.** —*SYN.* see **amateur.**
ty·ro·ci·din (tī'rə-sī'din), *n.* tyrocidine.
ty·ro·ci·dine (tī'rə-sī'dēn, tī'rə-sī'din), *n.* [*tyro*sine + *-cide* + *-ine*], an antibiotic drug, similar to penicillin, obtained from a soil bacillus.
Tyr·ol (tir'ol, tē-rōl'), *n.* a region in the Alps of western Austria and northern Italy: also spelled **Tirol.**
Ty·ro·le·an (ti-rō'li-ən), *adj. & n.* Tyrolese.

Tyr·o·lese (tir'ə-lēz'), *adj.* of the Tyrol or its people. *n.* [*pl.* TYROLESE], a native of the Tyrol. Also spelled **Tirolese.**

‡**Ty·ro·lienne** (tē'rô'lyen'), *n.* [Fr., fem. of *Tyrolien*, Tyrolese], 1. a Tyrolese folk dance. 2. music for this.

Ty·rone (ti-rōn'), *n.* a county of Northern Ireland: pop., 132,000; capital, Omagh.

ty·ro·sin (tī'rə-sin, tir'ə-sin), *n.* tyrosine.

ty·ro·sine (tī'rə-sēn', tir'ə-sin), *n.* [Gr. *tyros*, cheese; + *-ine*], a white, crystalline amino acid, $C_9H_{11}O_3N$, formed by the decomposition of proteins, as in the putrefaction of cheese.

ty·ro·thri·cin (tī'rə-thrī'sin, tī'rə-thris'in), *n.* [< *tyrosine;* + Gr. *thrix*, a hair; + *-in*], an antibiotic drug, similar to penicillin, obtained from a soil bacillus and used in localized infections.

Tyr·rhe·ni·an Sea (ti-rē'ni-ən), a part of the Mediterranean Sea, surrounded by western Italy, Sicily, Sardinia, and Corsica: see **Capri**, map.

Tyr·tae·us (tũr-tē'əs), *n.* a Greek poet of the 7th century B.C.

tzar (tsär), *n.* a czar.

tzar·dom (tsär'dəm), *n.* czardom.

tzar·e·vitch (tsär'ə-vich), *n.* a czarevitch.

tza·rev·na (tsä-rev'nə), *n.* a czarevna.

tza·ri·na (tsä-rē'nə), *n.* a czarina.

tzar·ism (tsär'is'm), *n.* czarism.

tzar·ist (tsär'ist), *adj.* & *n.* czarist.

tza·rit·za (tsä-rēt'sä), *n.* a czaritza.

tzet·ze (tset'si), *n.* a tsetse.

‡**tzi·gane** (tsē'gån'), *n.* [Fr.; Hung. *czigány;* cf. ZINGARO & G. *zigeuner*], a gypsy; especially, a Hungarian gypsy.

U

U, u (ū), *n.* [*pl.* U's, u's, Us, us (ūz)], 1. the twenty-first letter of the English alphabet: formerly a variant of *V, v;* not until the 18th century was it established as a vowel symbol only: see **alphabet**, table. 2. a sound of U or **u**: in Anglo-Saxon there were two vowel values for *u*, one long and one short, but both with the quality of the high back rounded (ōō) in Modern English *brute;* in Middle English the Anglo-Saxon short *u* remained unchanged in sound and spelling, but the long *u* was spelled *ou* to distinguish it from the high front rounded French *u;* in Modern English *u* represents several distinct sounds: (u), as in *hut, cut;* (ū), as in *use, unit;* (oo), as in *bush, pull;* (ōō), as in *crude, brute;* (w), as in *queen, language;* it is also often silent after *g*, as in *guide, guilt.* 3. a type or impression for U or u. 4. *a symbol for* the twenty-first in a sequence or group (or the twentieth if J is omitted). *adj.* 1. of U or u. 2. twenty-first (or twentieth if J is omitted) in a sequence or group.

U (ū), *n.* 1. an object shaped like U. 2. in *chemistry, the symbol for* uranium. *adj.* shaped like U.

U., 1. Uncle. 2. Union. 3. University.

U., u., upper.

U.A.W., UAW, United Automobile, Aircraft, and Agricultural Implement Workers of America: an AFL-CIO labor union.

U.B., United Brethren (in Christ).

U·ban·gi (ōō-bäŋ'gi), *n.* a river between the Central African Republic and the Congo (sense 2), flowing into the Congo River: length, 700 mi.: French spelling, **Oubangui.**

U·ban·gi-Sha·ri (ōō-bäŋ'gi-shä'ri), *n.* a former French colony in central Africa: since 1960, the independent Central African Republic: French spelling **Oubangui-Chari.**

‡**Ü·ber·mensch** (ü'bẽr-mensh'), *n.* [G.], superman; overman: term used by Nietzsche.

u·bi·e·ty (ū-bī'ə-ti), *n.* [Mod. L. *ubietas* < L. *ubi*, where], the condition or quality of being located in space; local relationship.

‡**u·bi·que** (ū-bī'kwi), *adv.* [L.], everywhere.

u·biq·ui·tous (ū-bik'wə-təs), *adj.* [see UBIQUITY & -OUS], present, or seeming to be present, everywhere at the same time; omnipresent.—*SYN.* see **omnipresent.**

u·biq·ui·ty (ū-bik'wə-ti), *n.* [Fr. *ubiquité* < L. *ubique*, everywhere], the state, fact, or capacity of being everywhere at the same time; omnipresence.

‡**u·bi su·pra** (ū'bi sōō'prə, sū'prə), [L.], where (mentioned) above: abbreviated **u.s.**

U-boat (ū'bōt'), *n.* [< G. *U-boot*, abbrev. of *Unterseeboot*, undersea boat], a German submarine or, sometimes, any submarine.

U bolt, a U-shaped bolt with threads and a nut at each end.

U.C., Upper Canada.

u.c., 1. *una corda*, [It.], in *music*, lit., one string; soft pedal. 2. in *printing*, upper case.

U·ca·ya·li (ōō'kä-yä'li), *n.* a river in Peru, joining the Marañón to form the Amazon: length, 1,220 mi.

U·dall, Nicholas (ū'd'l), 1505–1556; English schoolmaster, translator, and playwright; wrote the first English comedy: also **Uvedale.**

ud·der (ud'ẽr), *n.* [ME. *uddre;* AS. (rare) *udr;* akin to G. *euter;* IE. base **ēudh-*, **oudh-*, **ūdh-*, udder, as also in Sans. *ūdhar*, L. *uber*, udder], a mammary gland, especially one that is relatively large and pendulous, with two or more teats, as in cows.

U·di·ne (ōō'dē-ne), *n.* a city in northeastern Italy: pop., 85,000.

Ud·murt Autonomous Soviet Socialist Republic (ōōd-mōōrt'), a division of the R.S.F.S.R. in east central European Russia: area, 16,250 sq. mi.; pop., 1,372,000; capital, Izhevsk: also called *Votyak A.S.S.R.*

u·do (ōō'dō), *n.* [Japan.], a Japanese plant with blanched, edible shoots resembling celery.

u·dom·e·ter (ū-dom'ə-tẽr), *n.* [Fr. *udomètre* < L. *udus*, moist + Fr. *-mètre*, -meter], a rain gauge.

u·do·met·ric (ū'də-met'rik), *adj.* of a udometer or udometry.

u·dom·e·try (ū-dom'ə-tri), *n.* the measurement of rainfall by means of a udometer.

Ue·le (wā'lə), *n.* a river that flows through the northern Congo (sense 2) and joins the Bomu to form the Ubangi River: length, 700 mi.

U.E.W., UEW, United Electrical, Radio, and Machine Workers of America: a labor union: in full, **U.E.R.M.W.A.**

U·fa (ōō-fä'), *n.* the capital of the Bashkir A.S.S.R., in the eastern European part of the U.S.S.R.: pop., 610,000.

UFO, unidentified flying object.

U·gan·da (ū-gan'də, ōō-gän'dä), *n.* a country in east central Africa, west of Kenya: formerly a British protectorate, since 1962 a member of the British Commonwealth of Nations: area, 93,981 sq. mi.; pop., 6,845,000; capital, Kampala.

ugh (ookh, uH, oo, *etc.;* ug *is a conventionalized pronun.*), *interj.* [echoic], an exclamation of annoyance, disgust, horror, etc.

ug·li·fi·ca·tion (ug'lə-fi-kā'shən), *n.* an uglifying or being uglified.

ug·li·fy (ug'lə-fī'), *v.t.* [UGLIFIED (-fīd'), UGLIFYING], to make ugly; disfigure.

ug·li·ly (ug'lə-li), *adv.* in an ugly manner.

ug·li·ness (ug'li-nis), *n.* 1. the state or quality of being ugly. 2. an ugly thing. 3. disgusting wickedness; moral offensiveness.

ug·ly (ug'li), *adj.* [UGLIER (-li-ẽr), UGLIEST (-li-ist)], [ME. *ugli, uglike;* ON. *uggligr*, fearful, dreadful < *uggr*, fear; for base see AWE], 1. very unpleasant to the sight; aesthetically offensive; unsightly. 2. bad; vile; disagreeable; repulsive; offensive; objectionable. 3. threatening; ominous; dangerous. 4. [Colloq.], ill-tempered; cross; quarrelsome.

ugly duckling, [from a story by H. C. Andersen about a supposed ugly duckling that turns out to be a swan], one whose lack of personal beauty, charm, etc. in childhood or youth turns out to be only temporary.

U·gri·an (ōō'gri-ən, ū'gri-ən), *adj.* [< Russ. *Ugri*, an Asiatic people living east of the Urals; + *-an*], 1. designating or of a group of Finno-Ugric peoples of western Siberia and Hungary, including the Magyars. 2. Ugric. *n.* 1. a member of any of the Ugrian peoples. 2. Ugric.

U·gric (ōō'grik, ū'grik), *adj.* 1. designating or of a branch of the Finno-Ugric family of languages comprising Hungarian (Magyar), Vogul, and Ostyak. 2. Ugrian. *n.* the Ugric languages.

UHF, ultrahigh frequency.

uh·lan (ōō'län, ū'lən, ōō-län'), *n.* [G.; Pol. *ulan*, a lancer < Turk. *oghlān*, a youth], 1. a mounted soldier of a type formerly prominent in Poland, armed usually with a lance. 2. a cavalryman in the former German Army, similarly equipped.

Uh·land, Jo·hann Lud·wig (yō′hän lo͞ot′viH o͞o′länt), 1787–1862; German poet and historical writer.

u.i., *ut infra*, [L.], as below.

Ui·gur (wē′goor), *n.* [E. Turki *uighur* < *ui*, to follow + *-gur*, adj. suffix], 1. a member of a Turkic people ruling in Mongolia and Turkestan from the 8th to the 12th century A.D. 2. their East Turki language.

u·in·ta·ite, u·in·tah·ite (ū-in′tə-īt′), *n.* [after the *Uinta* Mountains, Utah], a black kind of asphalt found in an almost pure state in parts of Utah and western Colorado: also called *gilsonite.*

U·in·ta Mountains (ū-in′tə), a mountain range in northeastern Utah, part of the Rocky Mountains.

‡uit·land·er (üt′län′dẽr; Eng. īt′lan′dẽr), *n.* [S.Afr.D. < *uit*, out + *land*, land], [sometimes U-], in South Africa, a foreigner; outlander.

U·ji·ji (o͞o-jē′ji), *n.* a town in Tanganyika Territory, Africa, on Lake Tanganyika: pop., 25,000.

Uj·pest (o͞o′i-pesht′), *n.* a city on the Danube in Hungary, near Budapest: pop., 73,000: German name, *Neupest.*

U.K., United Kingdom (of Great Britain and Northern Ireland).

u·kase (ū′kās, ū-kāz′), *n.* [Russ. *ukaz*, edict], 1. in Czarist Russia, an imperial order or decree, having the force of law. 2. any official decree or proclamation.

U·kra·i·na (o͞o′krä-ē′nä), *n.* the Ukraine.

U·kraine (ū′krān, ū-krān′, ū-krīn′), *n.* a region in the southwestern U.S.S.R.: now the Ukrainian S.S.R.: Russian name, *Ukraina:* abbreviated **Ukr.**

U·krain·i·an (ū-krā′ni-ən, ū-krī′ni-ən), *adj.* of the Ukraine, its people, their language, etc. *n.* 1. a native or inhabitant of the Ukraine. 2. the East Slavic language of the Ukrainians, very closely related to (Great) Russian; Little Russian.

Ukrainian Soviet Socialist Republic, a republic of the U.S.S.R., in the southwestern European part, on the Black Sea: area, 202,540 sq. mi.; pop., 42,273,000; capital, Kiev.

u·ku·le·le (ū′kə-lā′li; Haw. o͞o′koo-lā′lā), *n.* [Haw., lit., flea < *uku*, insect + *lele*, to jump: from the finger movements], a small, four-stringed musical instrument resembling and played like a guitar: colloquially shortened to **uke.**

UKULELE

u·lan (o͞o′län, ū′-lən), *n.* an uhlan.

U·lan Ba·tor Kho·to (o͞o′län bä′tôr khō′tō), the capital of the Mongolian People's Republic: pop., 70,000: formerly called *Urga;* Chinese name, *Kulun.*

ul·cer (ul′sẽr), *n.* [L. *ulcus, ulceris;* akin to Gr. *helkos*, abscess, wound], 1. an open sore (other than a wound) on the skin or some mucous membrane, as the lining of the stomach (*peptic ulcer*), characterized by the disintegration of the tissue and, often, the discharge of pus; hence, 2. any corrupting or festering condition or influence.

ul·cer·ate (ul′sə-rāt′), *v.t. & v.i.* [ULCERATED (-id), ULCERATING], [< L. *ulceratus*, pp. of *ulcerare*], to make or become ulcerous.

ul·cer·a·tion (ul′sə-rā′shən), *n.* [L. *ulceratio*], 1. an ulcerating. 2. an ulcer or group of ulcers.

ul·cer·a·tive (ul′sə-rā′tiv), *adj.* 1. of, having the nature of, or causing an ulcer or ulcers. 2. ulcerous.

ul·cer·ous (ul′sẽr-əs), *adj.* [L. *ulcerosus*], 1. having an ulcer or ulcers. 2. ulcerative.

-ule (ūl), [Fr. or L.; Fr. *-ule* < L. *-ulus, -ula, -ulum*], a suffix added to nouns to form diminutives, as in *sporule, umbellule.*

u·le·ma (o͞o′lə-mä′), *n.pl.* [Turk. *'ulema;* Ar. *'ulamā*, pl. of *'alim*, wise < *'alama*, to know], 1. Moslem scholars or men of authority in religion and law, especially in Turkey. 2. [construed as sing.], a council or college of such men.

-u·lent (yoo-lənt), [< Fr. or L.; Fr. *-ulent;* L. *-ulentus*], a suffix meaning *full of, abounding in*, as in *fraudulent.*

Ul·fi·la (ul′fi-lə), *n.* Ulfilas.

Ul·fi·las (ul′fi-ləs), *n.* Christian bishop of the Goths; translated the Bible into Gothic; lived 311?–382? A.D.

ull·age (ul′ij), *n.* [Anglo-Fr. *ulliage;* OFr. *ouillage, eullage*, a filling up to the brim or the bunghole < *ouiller*, to fill (a cask) to the bunghole < *ueil*, an eye, fig. bunghole < L. *oculus*, an eye], 1. the amount by which a container of liquor falls short of being full. 2. the amount of grain, etc. lost through spilling or sifting through a bag. 3. the loss of liquor from a container through evaporation or leakage, or of grain, etc. through spilling or sifting.

Ulm (oolm), *n.* a city in southern Germany, on the Danube: pop., 62,000.

ul·ma·ceous (ul-mā′shəs), *adj.* [< L. *ulmus*, elm; + *-aceous*], of the elm family of trees and shrubs, characterized by alternate leaves, one- or two-sexed flowers without petals, and upright anthers.

ul·na (ul′nə), *n.* [*pl.* ULNAE (-nē), ULNAS (-nəz)], [L., the elbow], 1. the larger of the two bones of the forearm, on the side opposite the thumb. 2. a corresponding bone in the forelimb of other vertebrates.

ul·nar (ul′nẽr), *adj.* of or near the ulna.

ul·no- (ul′nō, ul′nə), a combining form meaning *the ulna and.*

-u·lose (yoo-lōs′), [L. *-ulosus;* see -ULE & -OSE], a suffix meaning *characterized by, marked by*, as in *granulose.*

U·lot·ri·chi (ū-lot′ri-kī′), *n.pl.* [Mod. L. < Gr. *oulothrix*, woolly-haired < *oulos*, crisp, woolly + *thrix, trichos*, hair], the woolly-haired peoples: term used in T. H. Huxley's system of anthropological classification.

u·lot·ri·chous (ū-lot′ri-kəs), *adj.* of the Ulotrichi; woolly-haired.

-u·lous (yoo-ləs), [< L. *-ulosus;* see -ULOSE], a suffix meaning *tending to, full of*, or *characterized by*, as in *tremulous, populous.*

Ul·pi·an (ul′pi-ən), *n.* (*Domitius Ulpianus*), Roman jurist; lived 170?–228 A.D.

Ul·ri·ca (ul′ri-kə), [G., Latinized fem. of *Ulrich;* OHG. *Uolrich*, contr. < *Uodalrich* < *uodal, udal*, home (akin to *adal;* see ALBERT) + *rikhi*, rich], a feminine name.

Ul·ster (ul′stẽr), *n.* 1. a former province of northern Ireland, now divided between Northern Ireland and Ireland. 2. a province of northern Ireland: area, 3,093 sq. mile.; pop., 266,000 (1943). 3. [Colloq.], Northern Ireland.

ul·ster (ul′stẽr), *n.* [< *Ulster*, Ireland, where orig. made and worn], a long, loose, heavy overcoat, especially one with a belt, originally made of Irish frieze.

ult., 1. ultimate. 2. ultimately. 3. ultimo.

ul·te·ri·or (ul-têr′i-ẽr), *adj.* [L., compar. of *ulter*, beyond, farther], 1. lying beyond or on the farther side. 2. later, subsequent, or future. 3. further; more remote; especially, beyond what is expressed, implied, or evident; undisclosed: as, her true purpose was *ulterior* but praiseworthy.

ul·ti·ma (ul′tə-mə), *n.* [L., fem. of *ultimus*, last], the last syllable of a word.

ul·ti·mate (ul′tə-mit), *adj.* [LL. *ultimatus*, pp. of *ultimare*, to come to an end < L. *ultimus*, last], 1. beyond which it is impossible to go; farthest; most remote or distant. 2. in which a process or series comes to an end; final. 3. beyond which further analysis, division, etc. cannot be made; elemental; fundamental; primary. 4. greatest possible; maximum. *n.* something ultimate; final point or result, fundamental principle, etc. Abbreviated **ult.** —*SYN.* see **last.**

ul·ti·mate·ly (ul′tə-mit-li), *adv.* finally; at last; in the end: abbreviated **ult.**

ul·ti·ma Thu·le (ul′tə-mə tho͞o′li, thū′li), [L.], 1. farthest Thule: to the ancients, the northernmost region; hence, 2. any far-off, unknown region. 3. *a)* the farthest possible point or limit. *b)* the uttermost degree or goal attainable.

ul·ti·ma·tum (ul′tə-mā′təm), *n.* [*pl.* ULTIMATUMS (-təmz), ULTIMATA (-tə)], [Mod. L.; LL., neut. of *ultimatus;* see ULTIMATE], a final offer or proposal; especially, the final statement of terms or conditions by one of the parties in diplomatic negotiations, the rejection of which by the other party or parties usually leads to a break in friendly relations and may result in war.

ul·ti·mo (ul′tə-mō′), *adv.* [L. *ultimo (mense)*, (in the) last (month), abl. sing. of *ultimus;* see ULTIMATE], in the last (month); in the preceding month: abbreviated **ult., ulto.**

ul·ti·mo·gen·i·ture (ul′tə-mō-jen′ə-chẽr), *n.* [< L. *ultimus*, last + *-geniture* as in *primogeniture*], inheritance or succession by the youngest son of the family: opposed to *primogeniture.*

ul·tra (ul′trə), *adj.* [L., beyond, on the other side of], going beyond the usual limit; excessive; extravagant; extreme, especially in opinions. *n.* a person having extreme opinions, favoring extreme policies, etc.; extremist.

ul·tra- (ul′trə), [< L. *ultra;* see ULTRA], a prefix meaning: 1. *beyond, on the further side of*, as in *ultraviolet.* 2. (something) *excessive, to an extreme degree*, as in *ultra-*

modern, ultraism. 3. *beyond the range of,* as in *ultramicroscopic.*
ul·tra·con·serv·a·tive (ul′trə-kən-sũr′və-tiv), *adj.* conservative to an extreme degree.
ul·tra·high frequency (ul′trə-hī′), in *radio & television,* any frequency of 300 megacycles or higher: abbreviated **UHF:** cf. **very high frequency.**
ul·tra·ism (ul′trə-iz'm), *n.* [*ultra-* + *-ism*], 1. the opinions, principles, etc. of those who are extreme; extremism. 2. an instance of this; extreme act, etc.
ul·tra·ist (ul′trə-ist), *n. & adj.* extremist.
ul·tra·ma·rine (ul′trə-mə-rēn′), *adj.* [< ML. *ultramarinus;* see ULTRA- & MARINE: lapis lazuli was brought from beyond the sea, from Asia], 1. beyond the sea. 2. deep-blue. *n.* 1. a blue pigment made from powdered lapis lazuli. 2. a blue pigment prepared artificially from other substances. 3. any of certain other pigments: as, yellow *ultramarine.* 4. deep blue.
ul·tra·mi·crom·e·ter (ul′trə-mī-krom′ə-tẽr), *n.* a very sensitive micrometer, calibrated to a fine scale.
ul·tra·mi·cro·scope (ul′trə-mī′krə-skōp′), *n.* an instrument equipped to pick up the reflections of light rays dispersed by ultramicroscopic objects lighted from the side and against a dark background, thus making them visible.
ul·tra·mi·cro·scop·ic (ul′trə-mī′krə-skop′ik), *adj.* 1. too small to be seen with an ordinary microscope. 2. of an ultramicroscope.
ul·tra·mi·cro·scop·i·cal (ul′trə-mī′krə-skop′i-k'l), *adj.* ultramicroscopic.
ul·tra·mi·cros·co·py (ul′trə-mī-kros′kə-pi, ul′trə-mī′-krə-skō′pi), *n.* the act or practice of using an ultramicroscope.
ul·tra·mod·ern (ul′trə-mod′ẽrn), *adj.* modern to an extreme degree.
ul·tra·mon·tane (ul′trə-mon′tān), *adj.* [ML. *ultramontanus* < L. *ultra,* beyond + *mons, montis,* mountain], 1. beyond the mountains; especially, beyond the Alps: applied to the Italians by peoples to the north. 2. of the Italian party in the Roman Catholic Church; hence, 3. of or favoring the doctrine of papal supremacy. *n.* 1. a person living beyond the mountains, especially south of the Alps. 2. a member or adherent of the ultramontane party in the Roman Catholic Church.
ul·tra·mon·ta·nism (ul′trə-mon′tə-niz'm), *n.* [Fr. *ultramontainisme*], the principles and practices of the ultramontane party in the Roman Catholic Church.
ul·tra·mun·dane (ul′trə-mun′dān), *adj.* [< L.; see ULTRA- & MUNDANE], 1. being beyond the world or the limits of our solar system. 2. beyond life.
ul·tra·na·tion·al·ism (ul′trə-nash′ən-'l-iz'm), *n.* nationalism that is excessive or extreme.
ul·tra·red (ul′trə-red′), *adj.* infrared.
ul·tra·some (ul′trə-sōm′), *n.* [*ultra-* + *-some* (body)], an intracellular particle too small to be seen by usual microscopic methods.
ul·tra·trop·i·cal (ul′trə-trop′i-k'l), *adj.* 1. outside the tropics. 2. hotter than is usual in the tropics.
ul·tra·vi·o·let (ul′trə-vī′ə-lit), *adj.* lying just beyond the violet end of the visible spectrum: said of certain light rays of extremely short wave length: cf. **infrared.**
‡**ul·tra vi·res** (ul′trə vī′rēz), [L.], beyond (legal) power; beyond authority (of a court, corporation, etc.).
ul·tra·vi·rus (ul′trə-vī′rəs), *n.* [Mod. L.; *ultra-* + *virus*], an ultramicroscopic virus, so small as to pass through the pores of the finest filter; filtrable virus.
u·lu (ōō′lōō), *n.* [Esk.], a type of knife used by Eskimo women.
ul·u·lant (ūl′yoo-lənt, ul′yoo-lənt), *adj.* [L. *ululans,* ppr. of *ululare*], ululating; howling.
ul·u·late (ūl′yoo-lāt′, ul′yoo-lāt′), *v.i.* [ULULATED (-id), ULULATING], [< L. *ululatus,* pp. of *ululare,* to howl; echoic], 1. to howl or hoot. 2. to wail or lament loudly.
ul·u·la·tion (ūl′yoo-lā′shən, ul′yoo-lā′shən), *n.* [LL. *ululatio*], the act or sound of ululating; howling, hooting, or wailing.
U·lys·ses (yoo-lis′ēz), [L., var. of *Ulixes* (for Gr. *Odysseus,* but prob. < Etruscan *Uluxe*)], a masculine name. *n.* 1. Odysseus, king of Ithaca and one of the Greek chiefs in the Trojan War. 2. a celebrated psychological novel (1922) by James Joyce, divided into episodes paralleling those of Homer's *Odyssey.*
um·bel (um′b'l), *n.* [L. *umbella,* a parasol, dim. of *umbra,* a shadow; cf. UMBRELLA], a cluster of flowers with stalks of nearly equal length which spring from about the same point, like the ribs of an umbrella.

UMBEL
(of wild carrot)

um·bel·lar (um′b'l-ẽr), *adj.* umbellate.
um·bel·late (um′b'l-it, um′b'l-āt′), *adj.* [Mod. L. *umbellatus*], having, consisting of, resembling, or forming an umbel or umbels.
um·bel·lat·ed (um′b'l-ā′tid), *adj.* umbellate.
um·bel·let (um′b'l-it), *n.* an umbellule.
um·bel·lif·er·ous (um′bə-lif′ẽr-əs), *adj.* [< *umbel* + *-ferous*], having an umbel or umbels, as the large family of plants that includes carrots and parsley.
um·bel·lu·late (um-bel′yoo-lit, um-bel′yoo-lāt′), *adj.* characterized by umbellules.
um·bel·lule (um′b'l-ūl′, um-bel′ūl), *n.* [Mod. L. *umbellula,* dim.], one of the secondary umbels in a primary, or compound, umbel.
um·ber (um′bẽr), *n.* [Fr. (*terre d'*)*ombre;* It. (*terra d'*)*ombra,* lit., (earth of) shade; prob. < L. *umbra,* a shade, shadow; but ? < *Umbria,* Italian province], 1. a kind of earth containing oxides of manganese and iron, used as a pigment: raw umber is yellowish-brown; burnt, or calcined, umber is reddish-brown. 2. a yellowish-brown or reddish-brown color. *adj.* of the color of raw umber or burnt umber. *v.t.* to make umber-colored; color with or as with umber.
um·ber (um′bẽr), *n.* [ME. & OFr. *umbre* (Fr. *ombre*); L. *umbra;* see prec.], 1. [Dial.], shade; shadow. 2. the grayling. 3. the umbrette: also **umber bird.**
um·bil·i·cal (um-bil′i-k'l), *adj.* [ML. *umbilicalis*], 1. of or like an umbilicus, or navel. 2. designating or of a cordlike structure (*umbilical cord*) connecting a fetus with the placenta of the mother and serving to convey food to, and remove waste from, the fetus. 3. [Rare], descended through the female line.
um·bil·i·cate (um-bil′ə-kit, um-bil′ə-kāt′), *adj.* [L. *umbilicatus*], 1. having an umbilicus, or navel. 2. shaped or depressed like an umbilicus, or navel.
um·bil·i·ca·tion (um-bil′ə-kā′shən), *n.* 1. the condition of being umbilicate. 2. a navellike pit or depression, as in a pustule.
um·bil·i·cus (um-bil′i-kəs, um′bi-lī′kəs), *n.* [*pl.* UMBILICI (-sī′, -sī)], [L.], 1. the navel. 2. a navellike depression, as the hilum of a seed.
um·bil·i·form (um-bil′ə-fôrm′), *adj.* [< *umbilicus* + *-form*], shaped like an umbilicus, or navel.
um·ble pie (um′b'l), [see HUMBLE PIE], a meat pie made of umbles; humble pie.
um·bles (um′b'lz), *n.pl.* [var. of *numbles*], [Obs.], numbles; entrails, especially of a deer.
um·bo (um′bō), *n.* [*pl.* UMBONES (um-bō′nēz), UMBOS (-bōz)], [L.; akin to Eng. *navel,* G. *nabel;* orig., any convex elevation], 1. the boss or knob at the center of a shield. 2. something resembling this; specifically, *a*) the elevation beside the hinge on each half of a bivalve shell. *b*) the prominence on the eardrum at the point of attachment of the malleus.
um·bo·nal (um′bə-n'l), *adj.* 1. of, forming, or near an umbo. 2. umbonate.
um·bo·nate (um′bə-nit, um′bə-nāt′), *adj.* [Mod. L. *umbonatus*], 1. having the rounded or conical shape of an umbo. 2. having an umbo.
um·bon·ic (um-bon′ik), *adj.* 1. umbonate. 2. umbonal.
um·bra (um′brə), *n.* [*pl.* UMBRAE (-brē)], [L., a shade, shadow], 1. shade; shadow. 2. the dark cone of shadow projecting from a planet or satellite on the side opposite the sun. 3. the dark central part of a sunspot. 4. in *physics,* a perfect or complete shadow, in which no direct light is received from the source of illumination. Cf. **penumbra.**
um·brage (um′brij), *n.* [ME.; OFr. < L. *umbraticus,* of shade < *umbra,* a shade, shadow], 1. [Obs. or Poetic], shade; shadow. 2. foliage, considered as shade-giving. 3. offense; resentment and displeasure. 4. [Archaic], a semblance or shadowy appearance. —*SYN.* see **offense.**
um·bra·geous (um-brā′jəs), *adj.* [Fr. *ombrageux,* shy, suspicious, orig. shady < *ombrage;* OFr. *umbrage;* see UMBRAGE], 1. giving shade; shady; shaded. 2. easily offended or aroused to suspicion; feeling, taking, or inclined to take, umbrage.
um·brel·la (um-brel′ə), *n.* [It. *ombrella* (altered after *ombre,* shade < L. *umbra*) < LL. *umbrella* (altered after L. *umbra,* shade) < L. *umbella,* umbrella, parasol, dim. of *umbra,* shade], 1. a shade or screen, usually of cloth on a folding radial frame, carried for protection against the rain or sun. 2. something shaped like or suggestive of this, as the disk or body of a jellyfish, or a force of military aircraft sent up to screen and protect ground or naval forces.
umbrella bird, any of several large, black South and Central American birds with a large, umbrellalike, erectile crest and a feathered wattle hanging from the neck.
umbrella leaf, a plant with one large, lobed, shield-shaped leaf, two smaller leaves, white flowers, and blue berries.
umbrella palm, a tall palm with a dense crown of broad leaves: it is native to Lord Howe's Island, in the Solomon Islands.
umbrella tree, 1. a variety of magnolia with clusters of long leaves at the ends of the branches, bad-smelling white flowers, and reddish fruit. 2. any of a number of other trees or shrubs whose leaves are umbrella-shaped or grow with an umbrellalike effect.
um·brette (um-bret′), *n.* [< Fr. or Mod. L.; Fr. *ombrette,* dim. of *ombre,* shade; or Mod. L. *umbretta,* dim.; both < L. *umbra,* a shade, shadow], a dark-brown

African wading bird related to the storks and herons: also **umber, umber bird.**

Um·bri·a (um'bri-ə; It. o͞om'brē-ä'), *n.* an ancient region of central Italy: now a department.

Um·bri·an (um'bri-ən), *adj.* of Umbria, its people, etc. *n.* 1. a native or inhabitant of (ancient or modern) Umbria. 2. the Italic language of ancient Umbria, extinct since ancient times.

um·brif·er·ous (um-brif'ẽr-əs), *adj.* [L. *umbrifer*, shade-bringing < *umbra*, a shade, shadow + *ferre*, to bear; + *-ous*], casting shade.

u·mi·ak, u·mi·ack (o͞o'mi-ak'), *n.* [Esk. (Eastern dial.)], a large open boat made of skins stretched on a wooden frame, used by Eskimos, especially Eskimo women: also spelled **oomiac, oomiak.**

um·laut (oom'lout), *n.* [G., change of sound; *um*, about + *laut*, a sound: term invented by Jacob Grimm], in *linguistics*, 1. a change in sound of a vowel, caused by its assimilation to another vowel or semivowel originally occurring in the next syllable but now generally lost; mutation: in English, the differences of vowel in certain singulars and plurals (e.g., *foot—feet, mouse—mice*) or causative verbs and the words from which they are derived (e.g., *gold—gild*) are due to the effects of umlaut on the second word of each pair. 2. a vowel resulting from such assimilation. 3. the diacritical mark (¨) placed over a vowel, especially in German, to indicate umlaut: cf. **dieresis.** *v.t.* to modify, sound, or write with an umlaut.

um·pir·age (um'pīr-ij, um'pi-rij), *n.* [see -AGE], 1. the position or authority of an umpire. 2. an action, ruling, etc. of an umpire; arbitrament.

um·pire (um'pīr), *n.* [loss of initial *n* through faulty separation of *a numpire* < ME. *noumpere* (cf. ADDER, APRON, etc.); OFr. *nomper, nonper*, uneven, hence an uneven number, third person; *non*, not + *per*, even], 1. a person chosen to render a decision in a dispute; judge; arbiter: used especially of the officials who administer the rules in team sports, as baseball. 2. something that decides a matter. *v.t.* [UMPIRED (-pīrd), UMPIRING], to act as umpire in or of. *v.i.* to act as umpire. —*SYN.* see **judge.**

ump·steen (ump'stēn), *adj.* [*umps-*, indefinite sound for an uncertain number + *-teen* as in *thirteen*], [Slang], a great number of; very many.

ump·teen (ump'tēn), *adj.* [Slang], umpsteen.

UMT, Universal Military Training.

UMW, U.M.W., United Mine Workers of America: a labor union.

un- (un), either of two prefixes, meaning: 1. [ME. *un-*; AS. *un-*; akin to Gr. *an-, a-* (cf. A-, AN-), L. *in-* (cf. IN-), and to the negative elements in *no, not, nor*], *not, lack of, the opposite of*, as in *unhappy, untruth, unemployment*; cf. **non-.** 2. [ME. *un-, on-*; AS. *un-, on-, and-*, back; akin to G. *ent-*, D. *ont-*, etc.; cf. ANSWER], *back*: it is added to verbs to indicate a reversal of the action of the verb, as in *unfasten* or *unchain*, and to nouns to indicate a removal or release from the state expressed by the noun, as in *unbosom;* sometimes it has a mere intensive force, as in *unloosen.* The list at the bottom of the following pages includes the more common compounds formed with *un-* (either prefix) that do not have special meanings.

UN, U.N., United Nations.

U·na (ū'nə), [Ir. *Una, Oonagh;* also < L. *una*, one], a feminine name.

un·ac·com·mo·dat·ed (un'ə-kom'ə-dāt'id), *adj.* 1. not accommodated or adapted. 2. having no accommodations.

un·ac·com·pa·nied (un'ə-kum'pə-nid), *adj.* 1. not accompanied. 2. in *music*, without accompaniment.

un·ac·com·plished (un'ə-kom'plisht), *adj.* 1. not accomplished, completed, or achieved. 2. having no accomplishments or skills.

un·ac·count·a·ble (un'ə-koun'tə-b'l), *adj.* 1. that cannot be explained or accounted for; strange; mysterious. 2. not accountable; not responsible.

un·ac·count·a·bly (un'ə-koun'tə-bli), *adv.* so as to be unaccountable; mysteriously; inexplicably.

un·ac·count·ed-for (un'ə-koun'tid-fôr'), *adj.* not explained or accounted for.

un·ac·cus·tomed (un'ə-kus'təmd), *adj.* 1. not accustomed or habituated; not used (*to*): as, *unaccustomed* to such kindness. 2. uncommon; strange.

un·ad·dressed (un'ə-drest'), *adj.* lacking an address: said of a letter, etc.

un·ad·vised (un'əd-vīzd'), *adj.* 1. without counsel or advice. 2. indiscreet; rash; thoughtlessly hasty.

un·ad·vis·ed·ly (un'əd-vīz'id-li), *adv.* in an unadvised, rash, or indiscreet manner.

un·ad·vis·ed·ness (un'əd-vīz'id-nis), *n.* the quality or state of being unadvised; rashness; indiscretion.

un·af·fect·ed (un'ə-fek'tid), *adj.* 1. not changed, affected, or influenced. 2. without affectation; simple; sincere; natural. —*SYN.* see **sincere.**

U·na·las·ka (o͞o'nə-las'kə, un'ə-las'kə), *n.* an Alaskan island in the eastern Aleutians: c. 75 mi. long: site of Dutch Harbor, a United States naval base.

un-A·mer·i·can (un'ə-mer'ə-kən), *adj.* not American; regarded as not characteristically or properly American; especially, regarded as opposed or dangerous to the United States, its institutions, etc.

U·na·mu·no, Mi·guel de (mē-gel' *thā* o͞o'nä-mo͞o'nô), 1864–1936; Spanish scholar, philosopher, and writer.

un·a·neled (un'ə-nēld'), *adj.* [Archaic], not aneled; not having received extreme unction.

u·na·nim·i·ty (ū'nə-nim'ə-ti), *n.* [ME. & OFr. *unanimite;* L. *unanimitas*], the state or quality of being unanimous.

u·nan·i·mous (yoo-nan'ə-məs), *adj.* [L. *unanimus, unanimis* < *unus*, one + *animus*, the mind], 1. agreeing completely; united in opinion. 2. showing, or based on, complete agreement.

un·ap·proach·a·ble (un'ə-prōch'ə-b'l), *adj.* 1. not to be approached; inaccessible; distant; aloof. 2. having no rival or equal; unmatched.

un·ap·pro·pri·at·ed (un'ə-prō'pri-āt'id), *adj.* not appropriated; specifically, *a*) not owned by or assigned to any particular person or agent. *b*) not granted or set aside for any particular use or purpose: said of sums of money, etc.

un·apt (un-apt'), *adj.* 1. not fitting or suitable. 2. not likely or inclined. 3. not quick or skillful; dull.

un·ar·gued (un-är'gūd), *adj.* 1. not argued or debated. 2. accepted without dispute.

un·arm (un-ärm'), *v.t.* 1. [Archaic], to strip of armor. 2. to disarm.

un·armed (un-ärmd'), *adj.* 1. having no weapons, especially firearms, or armor; defenseless. 2. lacking scales, claws, or the like: said of plants or animals.

un·as·sail·a·ble (un'ə-sāl'ə-b'l), *adj.* not assailable; specifically, *a*) that cannot be successfully attacked or assaulted. *b*) that cannot be successfully denied or contested.

un·as·sum·ing (un'ə-so͞om'iŋ, un'ə-sūm'iŋ), *adj.* not assuming, pretending, or forward; modest; retiring.

un·at·tached (un'ə-tacht'), *adj.* 1. not attached or fastened. 2. not connected with any particular group, institution, etc.; independent. 3. not engaged or married.

u·nau (yoo-nô', o͞o-nou'), *n.* [Fr. < native Braz. (Tupi) name], the two-toed sloth of South America.

un·a·vail·ing (un'ə-vāl'iŋ), *adj.* not availing; futile.

un·a·void·a·ble (un'ə-void'ə-b'l), *adj.* 1. that cannot be avoided; inevitable. 2. that cannot be voided or nullified.

un·a·void·a·bly (un'ə-void'ə-bli), *adv.* in a way that cannot or could not be avoided; inevitably.

---

unabashed
unabated
unabbreviated
unabetted
unable
unabridged
unabsolved
unacademic
unaccented
unacceptable
unaccepted
unacclimated
unaccommodating
unaccounted
unaccredited
unacknowledged
unacquainted
unadaptable
unadjustable
unadorned
unadulterated
unadvisable
unaesthetic
unaffiliated
unafraid
unaggressive
unaided
unaimed
unalleviated
unallied
unallowable
unalloyed
unalterable
unaltered
unambiguous
unambitious
unamusing
unanalytic
unanalyzable
unannealed
unannounced
unanswerable
unanswered
unappalled
unapparent
unappealable
unappeasable
unappeased
unappetizing
unappreciated
unappreciative
unapproached
unarmored
unarrested
unartistic
unashamed
unasked
unaspirated
unaspiring
unassailed
unassignable
unassigned
unassisted
unassumed
unattainable
unattained
unattempted
unattended
unattested
unattired
unattracted
unattractive
unauspicious
unauthentic
unauthenticated
unauthorized
unavailable
unavenged
unavowed
unawakened

---

un·a·ware (un'ə-wâr'), *adj.* 1. not aware or conscious: as, *unaware* of danger. 2. unwary; heedless; thoughtless. *adv.* unawares.

un·a·wares (un'ə-wârz'), *adv.* 1. without knowing or being aware; unintentionally. 2. unexpectedly; suddenly; by surprise: as, we took him *unawares*.

un·backed (un-bakt'), *adj.* 1. not broken to riding: said of a horse. 2. not backed, helped, supported, or endorsed. 3. having no money bet in favor of it.

un·baked (un-bākt'), *adj.* 1. not baked. 2. undeveloped; immature.

un·bal·ance (un-bal'əns), *v.t.* [UNBALANCED (-ənst), UNBALANCING], 1. to disturb the balance or equilibrium of. 2. to disturb the functioning of; derange (the mind). *n.* the condition of being unbalanced; lack of balance.

un·bal·anced (un-bal'ənst), *adj.* 1. not in balance or equilibrium. 2. not equal as to debit and credit. 3. not functioning properly; deranged: said of the mind. 4. *a)* mentally deranged. *b)* not stable, steady, or sound in character or judgment.

un·bat·ed (un-bāt'id), *adj.* 1. [Poetic], not abated or diminished. 2. [Archaic], not dulled or blunted, as a fencing foil.

un·bear (un-bâr'), *v.t.* to remove or loosen the bearing rein of (a horse).

un·be·com·ing (un'bi-kum'iŋ), *adj.* 1. not becoming; not appropriate or suited. 2. not proper or decent.

un·be·known (un'bi-nōn'), *adj.* not known; unknown; unperceived: often used in an adverbial sense.
unbeknown to, without the knowledge of, or unperceived by (a specified person): also **unbeknownst to.**

un·be·knownst (un'bi-nōnst'), *adj.* [Dial.], unbeknown.

un·be·lief (un'bə-lēf'), *n.* a withholding or lack of belief, especially in religion or in the doctrines of a given religion.
SYN.—**unbelief** implies merely a lack of belief, as because of insufficient evidence, especially in matters of religion or faith; **disbelief** suggests a positive refusal to believe an assertion, theory, etc. because one is convinced of its falseness or unreliability (a *disbelief* in superstition); **incredulity** implies a general skepticism or unwillingness to believe. —*ANT.* belief, credulity.

un·be·liev·er (un'bə-lēv'ẽr), *n.* 1. a person who does not believe; doubter. 2. a person who does not accept the doctrines of a given religion, or who has no religious belief. —*SYN.* see **atheist.**

un·be·liev·ing (un'bə-lēv'iŋ), *adj.* not believing; doubting; skeptical; incredulous; characterized by unbelief.

un·belt (un-belt'), *v.t.* 1. to loosen or remove the belt of. 2. to take off (a sword, etc.) by removing a belt.

un·bend (un-bend'), *v.t.* [UNBENT (-bent') or UNBENDED (-id), UNBENDING], [ME. *unbenden;* see UN- (not) & BEND], 1. to release, as a bow, from strain or tension. 2. to relax, as from mental strain or effort. 3. to make straight (something bent or crooked). 4. in *nautical usage, a)* to loosen or unfasten (a rope, sail, etc.). *b)* to untie (a rope). *v.i.* 1. to become straight or less bent. 2. to become free from constraint, stiffness, or severity; relax and be less formal, more genial, etc.

un·bend·ing (un-ben'diŋ), *adj.* 1. not bending; rigid; stiff; inflexible. 2. firm; unyielding; resolute. *n.* relaxation of restraint, severity, etc.

un·bid·den (un-bid''n), *adj.* [ME. *unbiden;* see UN- (not) & BID, *v.*], 1. not commanded. 2. uninvited.

un·bind (un-bīnd'), *v.t.* [UNBOUND (-bound'), UNBINDING], [ME. *unbinden;* AS. *unbindan;* see UN- (back) & BIND], 1. to untie; unfasten. 2. to free from bonds or restraints; release.

un·bit·ted (un-bit'id), *adj.* 1. having no bit or bridle on; hence, 2. unrestrained; uncontrolled; ungoverned.

un·blessed, un·blest (un-blest'), *adj.* 1. not hallowed or consecrated. 2. not blessed or given benediction. 3. accursed; wicked. 4. wretched; unhappy.

un·blood·y (un-blud'i), *adj.* 1. not marked with blood. 2. without bloodshed. 3. not bloodthirsty.

un·blush·ing (un-blush'iŋ), *adj.* 1. not blushing. 2. shameless.

un·bod·ied (un-bod'id), *adj.* 1. having no body or form; incorporeal. 2. disembodied.

un·bolt (un-bōlt'), *v.t. & v.i.* to withdraw the bolt or bolts of (a door, etc.); unbar; open.

un·bolt·ed (un-bōl'tid), *adj.* not fastened with a bolt, as a door.

un·bolt·ed (un-bōl'tid), *adj.* not bolted; not sifted.

un·boned (un-bōnd'), *adj.* 1. having no bones; boneless. 2. not having the bones removed.

un·bon·net (un-bon'it), *v.t. & v.i.* to take the bonnet or head covering off; uncover.

un·bon·net·ed (un-bon'it-id), *adj.* having no bonnet or other headdress; bareheaded.

un·born (un-bôrn'), *adj.* 1. not born or brought into being. 2. not yet born; yet to come or be; future.

un·bos·om (un-booz'əm, un-bōō'zəm), *v.t.* [*un-* (back) + *bosom*], to let out; tell; reveal; give vent to (feelings, secrets, etc.). *v.i.* to reveal what one feels, knows, etc.
unbosom oneself, to tell or reveal one's feelings, secrets, etc.

un·bound (un-bound'), past tense and past participle of **unbind.** *adj.* 1. released from bonds, ties, or shackles. 2. without a binding, as a book.

un·bowed (un-boud'), *adj.* 1. not bowed or bent. 2. not yielding or giving in; unsubdued.

un·box (un-boks'), *v.t.* to take out of a box.

un·brace (un-brās'), *v.t.* [UNBRACED (-brāst'), UNBRACING], 1. to free from braces or bands. 2. to loosen; relax. 3. to make slack or feeble.

un·braid (un-brād'), *v.t.* to separate the braids or strands of.

un·bred (un-bred'), *adj.* 1. ill-bred; unmannerly. 2. untrained or uninstructed.

un·bri·dled (un-brī'd'ld), *adj.* 1. having no bridle on: said of a horse, etc.; hence, 2. unrestrained; uncontrolled; ungoverned.

un·bro·ken (un-brō'k'n), *adj.* 1. not broken; whole; intact. 2. not tamed or subdued. 3. continuous; uninterrupted. 4. not disordered, impaired, or disorganized.

un·buck·le (un-buk''l), *v.t.* [UNBUCKLED (-'ld), UNBUCKLING], to unfasten the buckle or buckles of.

un·build (un-bild'), *v.t.* [for prin. pts. see BUILD], to tear down (something built); demolish; raze.

un·bur·den (un-bũr'd'n), *v.t.* 1. to free from a burden. 2. to relieve, as oneself or one's soul, mind, etc., by revealing or disclosing something hard to bear, as guilt. 3. to get rid of the burden of (anything heavy or hard to bear, as guilt, etc.), often by disclosure.

un·called-for (un-kôld'fôr'), *adj.* 1. not called for or required. 2. unnecessary and out of place; impertinent.

un·can·ni·ly (un-kan''l-i), *adv.* in an uncanny manner.

un·can·ni·ness (un-kan'i-nis), *n.* the quality of being uncanny.

un·can·ny (un-kan'i), *adj.* [see UN- (not) & CANNY], 1. mysterious or unfamiliar, especially in such a way as to frighten or make uneasy; preternaturally strange; eerie; weird. 2. so good, acute, etc. as to seem preternatural: as, *uncanny* shrewdness. 3. [Scot. & North Eng. Dial.], *a)* dangerous. *b)* hard. —*SYN.* see **weird.**

un·cap (un-kap'), *v.t.* [UNCAPPED (-kapt'), UNCAPPING], 1. to remove the cap from the head of (a person). 2. to remove the cap, or cover, from (a bottle, etc.). *v.i.* to remove one's cap from the head, as in respect.

un·ca·pa·ble (un-kā'pə-b'l), *adj.* [Obs.], incapable.

un·caused (un-kôzd'), *adj.* not caused or created; self-existent.

un·cer·e·mo·ni·ous (un'ser-ə-mō'ni-əs), *adj.* 1. less formal and ceremonious than is usual or expected; informal; familiar. 2. curt; abrupt; lacking courtesy.

un·cer·tain (un-sũr't'n), *adj.* [ME. *uncertayn*], 1. not surely or certainly known; questionable; problematical. 2. not sure or certain in knowledge; doubtful. 3. vague; not definite or determined. 4. liable to vary or change; not dependable or reliable. 5. not steady or constant; varying. Abbreviated **uncert.**

un·cer·tain·ty (un-sũr't'n-ti), *n.* 1. lack of certainty; doubt. 2. [*pl.* UNCERTAINTIES (-tiz)], something uncertain.
SYN.—**uncertainty** ranges in implication from a mere lack of absolute sureness (*uncertainty* about a date of birth) to such vagueness as to preclude anything more than guesswork (the *uncertainty* of the future); **doubt** implies such a lack of conviction, as through absence of sufficient evidence, that there can be no certain opinion or decision (there is *doubt* about his guilt); **dubiety** suggests uncertainty characterized by wavering between conclusions; **dubiosity** connotes uncertainty charac-

unballasted
unbaptized
unbar
unbearable
unbeaten
unbefitting
unbelievable
unbeloved
unbeseeming
unbesought
unbetrayed
unbetrothed
unbewailed
unbiased
unbiassed
unblamable
unblamably
unblamed
unbleached
unblemished
unbookish
unborrowed
unbought
unbounded
unbraced
unbranched
unbranded
unbreakable
unbreathable
unbreeched
unbribable
unbridgeable
unbridged
unbridle
unbrotherly
unbruised
unbrushed
unburied
unburned
unburnt
unbusinesslike
unbutton
uncage
uncalculated
uncalculating
uncanceled
uncancelled
uncandid
uncanonical
uncarburetor
uncared-for
uncarpeted
uncaught
unceasing
uncelebrated
uncensored
uncensured
uncertified
unchain
unchallenged

terized by vagueness or confusion; **skepticism** implies an unwillingness to believe, often a habitual disposition to doubt, in the absence of absolute certainty or proof. —*ANT.* conviction, assurance, certitude.

un·chanc·y (un-chan′si, un-chän′si), *adj.* [*un-* (not) + *chancy*], [Scot.], 1. unlucky; ill-fated. 2. dangerous. 3. poorly-timed; inopportune.

un·charge (un-chärj′), *v.t.* [ME. *unchargen;* see UN- (back) & CHARGE], 1. [Rare], to free from a load. 2. [Obs.], to acquit of blame, guilt, etc.

un·char·i·ta·ble (un-char′ə-tə-b'l), *adj.* harsh or severe, as in opinion; unforgiving, ungenerous, or censorious.

un·char·i·ta·bly (un-char′ə-tə-bli), *adv.* in an uncharitable manner.

un·chris·tian (un-kris′chən), *adj.* 1. not having or practicing a Christian religion. 2. not in accord with the principles of Christianity. 3. not characteristic of people practicing a Christian religion. 4. unbefitting or unworthy of a Christian or any decent, civilized person.

un·church (un-chũrch′), *v.t.* 1. to deprive (a person) of membership in a given church. 2. to deprive (an entire congregation) of its rights as a church.

un·ci·al (un′shi-əl, un′shəl), *adj.* [L. *uncialis,* of an inch, inch-high < *uncia,* an inch], designating or of a kind of large, rounded letters used in the script of manuscripts between 300 and 900 A.D. *n.* 1. an uncial letter. 2. uncial script.

Bellum
caveat
emptor
caesar

LATIN UNCIALS

un·ci·form (un′si-fôrm′), *adj.* [< L. *uncus,* a hook; + *-form*], 1. hook-shaped. 2. in *anatomy, a)* designating or of a bone in the distal row of the wrist, on the same side as the ulna. *b)* designating a hooked process on the unciform bone, or a similar process on the ethmoid bone. *n.* an unciform bone.

un·ci·nal (un′si-n'l), *adj.* [< L. *uncinus*], uncinate.

un·ci·na·ri·a·sis (un′si-nə-rī′ə-sis), *n.* [Mod. L. < *Uncinaria,* name of a genus including the hookworm (< L. *uncinus,* a hook); + *-iasis*], infestation by hookworms; ancylostomiasis.

un·ci·nate (un′si-nit, un′si-nāt′), *adj.* [L. *uncinatus* < *uncinus,* a hook < *uncus,* a hook], hooklike; hooked.

un·cir·cum·cised (un-sũr′kəm-sīzd′), *adj.* 1. not circumcised. 2. Gentile. 3. heathen.

un·cir·cum·ci·sion (un′sẽr-kəm-sizh′ən), *n.* 1. the condition of being uncircumcised. 2. in the *Bible,* the Gentiles.

un·civ·il (un-siv″l), *adj.* 1. not civilized; barbarous. 2. not civil or courteous; ill-mannered. —*SYN.* see **rude.**

un·civ·i·lized (un-siv″l-īzd′), *adj.* not civilized; barbarous; savage; unenlightened.

un·clad (un-klad′), alternative past tense and past participle of **unclothe.** *adj.* not clad; wearing no clothes; naked.

un·clasp (un-klasp′, un-kläsp′), *v.t.* 1. to open or loosen the clasp of. 2. to release from a clasp or grasp. *v.i.* 1. to become unfastened; open. 2. to relax the clasp or grasp.

un·cle (uŋ′k'l), *n.* [ME.; Anglo-Fr.; OFr. *uncle, oncle* < L. *avunculus,* one's mother's brother, lit. little grandfather, double dim. of *avus,* grandfather], 1. the brother of one's father or mother. 2. the husband of one's aunt. 3. [Colloq.], elderly man: a term of address. 4. [Slang], a pawnbroker.

un·clean (un-klēn′), *adj.* 1. dirty; filthy; foul. 2. ceremonially impure. 3. morally impure; unchaste, obscene, or vile.

un·clean·li·ness (un-klen′li-nis), *n.* the quality or condition of being uncleanly.

un·clean·ly (un-klen′li), *adj.* not cleanly; unclean; dirty.

un·clean·ly (un-klēn′li), *adv.* in an unclean manner.

un·clench (un-klench′), *v.t.* & *v.i.* to open: said of something clenched, or clinched.

Uncle Sam, [extended < abbrev. U.S.; ? after Samuel Wilson, meat inspector during the War of 1812, who stamped barrels of meat with the initials U.S.—E.A., for *U*nited *S*tates—*E. A*nderson (the food contractor)], [Colloq.], the United States (government or people), personified as a tall, spare man with chin whiskers, dressed in a red, white, and blue costume of swallowtail coat, striped trousers, and tall hat: abbreviated **U. S.**

Uncle Tom, the main character in Harriet Beecher Stowe's antislavery novel, *Uncle Tom's Cabin* (1852), an elderly Negro slave devoted to his kind master but mistreated by the cruel Simon Legree after the master's death: sometimes applied contemptuously to Negroes whose behavior toward whites is regarded as fawning or abjectly servile.

un·clinch (un-klinch′), *v.t.* & *v.i.* to unclench.

un·cloak (un-klōk′), *v.t.* & *v.i.* 1. to remove a cloak or other covering (from). 2. to reveal; expose.

un·close (un-klōz′), *v.t.* & *v.i.* [UNCLOSED (-klōzd′), UNCLOSING], [ME. *unclosen;* see UN- (back) & CLOSE, *v.*], 1. to open. 2. to disclose or reveal.

un·clothe (un-klōth′), *v.t.* [UNCLOTHED (-klōthd′) or UNCLAD (-klad′), UNCLOTHING], [ME. *unclothen*], to strip of or as of clothes; undress, uncover, or divest.

un·co (uŋ′kō), *adj.* [contr. < *uncouth;* ME. *unkow*], [Scot. & N.Eng. Dial.], 1. unknown; strange. 2. weird; uncanny. 3. notable; great; remarkable. *adv.* [Scot. & N.Eng. Dial.], remarkably; extremely; exceedingly; very. *n.* [*pl.* UNCOS (-kōz)], [Scot. & N.Eng. Dial.], 1. a strange person or thing. 2. *pl.* news.

un·coil (un-koil′), *v.t.* & *v.i.* [*un-* (back) + *coil*], to unwind.

un·com·fort·a·ble (un-kum′fẽr-tə-b'l, un-kumf′tẽr-b'l), *adj.* 1. not comfortable; feeling discomfort. 2. not pleasant or agreeable; causing discomfort. 3. ill at ease.

un·com·fort·a·bly (un-kum′fẽr-tə-bli, un-kumf′tẽr-bli), *adv.* so as to be uncomfortable.

un·com·mer·cial (un′kə-mũr′shəl), *adj.* 1. of or concerned with things other than trade or commerce. 2. not in accordance with the principles or methods of commerce.

un·com·mit·ted (un′kə-mit′id), *adj.* 1. not committed or carried out, as a crime. 2. not bound or pledged, as to doing a certain thing. 3. not jailed or imprisoned.

un·com·mon (un-kom′ən), *adj.* 1. rare; not common or usual. 2. strange; remarkable; extraordinary. —*SYN.* see **rare.**

un·com·mon·ly (un-kom′ən-li), *adv.* 1. rarely; not commonly or usually. 2. strangely; remarkably.

un·com·mu·ni·ca·tive (un′kə-mū′nə-kā′tiv), *adj.* not communicative; tending to withhold information, expression of opinions, feelings, etc.; reserved; silent.

un·com·pro·mis·ing (un-kom′prə-mīz′iŋ), *adj.* not compromising or yielding; firm; inflexible; determined.

un·con·cern (un′kən-sũrn′), *n.* 1. lack of interest; apathy; indifference. 2. lack of concern; state or fact of being free from solicitude or anxiety.

un·con·cerned (un′kən-sũrnd′), *adj.* not concerned; not solicitous or anxious; disinterested or indifferent. —*SYN.* see **indifferent.**

un·con·cern·ed·ly (un′kən-sũr′nid-li), *adv.* in an unconcerned manner; indifferently; disinterestedly.

un·con·di·tion·al (un′kən-dish′ən-'l), *adj.* without conditions or reservations; absolute.

un·con·di·tion·al·ly (un′kən-dish′ən-'l-i), *adv.* without conditions or reservations; absolutely.

un·con·di·tioned (un′kən-dish′ənd), *adj.* 1. unconditional. 2. in *philosophy,* infinite; absolute. 3. in *psychology,* not conditioned; natural; not learned: as, an *unconditioned* reflex.

unchangeable
unchanged
unchanging
unchaperoned
uncharted
unchartered
unchary
unchaste
unchastened
unchastised
unchecked
uncherished
unchewed
unchilled
unchivalrous
uncholeric
unchosen
unchristened

unclaimed
unclarified
unclassed
unclassifiable
unclassified
uncleaned
uncleansed
uncleared
unclipped
unclog
unclothed
unclouded
uncloyed
uncoagulated
uncoated
uncocked
uncoerced
uncollectable

uncollected
uncollectible
uncolonized
uncolored
uncombed
uncombinable
uncombined
uncomely
uncomforted
uncomforting
uncommanded
uncommissioned
uncompanionable
uncomplaining
uncomplaisant
uncompleted
uncompliable
uncomplicated

uncomplimentary
uncomplying
uncompounded
uncomprehending
uncomprehensible
uncompressed
uncompromised
uncomputed
unconcealable
unconcealed
unconceded
unconcerted
unconciliated
unconcluded
uncondemned
uncondensed
unconfined
unconfirmed

un·con·form·a·ble (un'kən-fôr'mə-b'l), *adj.* 1. not conforming or conforming. 2. in *geology*, showing unconformity.

un·con·form·i·ty (un'kən-fôr'mə-ti), *n.* [*pl.* UNCONFORMITIES (-tiz)], 1. a lack of conformity; inconsistency; incongruity. 2. in *geology*, a break in the continuity of strata lying next to each other, resulting from an interruption in formation.

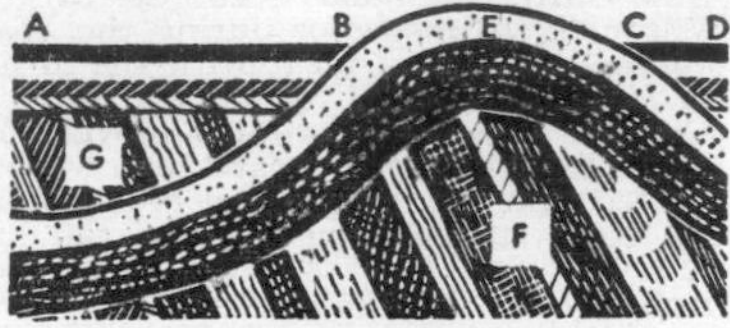

UNCONFORMITY
E, stratum unconformable to strata AB, CD, G, and F

un·con·scion·a·ble (un-kon'shən-ə-b'l), *adj.* 1. not guided or restrained by conscience; unscrupulous. 2. unreasonable, excessive, or immoderate.

un·con·scion·a·bly (un-kon'shən-ə-bli), *adv.* 1. in an unconscionable manner. 2. to an unconscionable degree.

un·con·scious (un-kon'shəs), *adj.* 1. *a*) not endowed with consciousness; mindless. *b*) temporarily deprived of consciousness. 2. not aware (*of*): as, he was *unconscious* of his mistake. 3. not known, realized, or intended by the person himself: as, an *unconscious* act, an *unconscious* insult. 4. not aware of one's own existence; not conscious of self. 5. having to do with those of one's mental processes that one is unable to bring into his consciousness.

the unconscious, in *psychoanalysis*, the sum of all thoughts, impulses, desires, feelings, etc. of which the individual is not conscious but which influence his behavior; that part of one's psyche which comprises repressed desires and other matter excluded from, but often tending to affect, the consciousness.

un·con·scious·ness (un-kon'shəs-nis), *n.* the quality or condition of being unconscious; lack of consciousness.

un·con·sti·tu·tion·al (un'kon-stə-tōō'shən-'l, un'kon-stə-tū'shən-'l), *adj.* not in accordance with the principles of the constitution; not constitutional.

un·con·sti·tu·tion·al·i·ty (un'kon-stə-tōō'shən-al'ə-ti, un'kon-stə-tū'shən-al'ə-ti), *n.* condition, fact, quality, or instance of being unconstitutional.

un·con·ven·tion·al (un'kən-ven'shən-'l), *adj.* that violates the rules or customs established by society, as in dress, speech, or behavior; free from conventionality.

un·con·ven·tion·al·i·ty (un'kən-ven'shən-al'ə-ti), *n.* 1. the quality or condition of being unconventional; freedom from the restraints of custom and convention. 2. [*pl.* UNCONVENTIONALITIES (-tiz)], an unconventional act, remark, etc.

un·cork (un-kôrk'), *v.t.* to pull the cork out of.

un·count·ed (un-koun'tid), *adj.* 1. not counted. 2. inconceivably numerous; innumerable.

un·cou·ple (un-kup''l), *v.t.* [UNCOUPLED (-'ld), UNCOUPLING], 1. to loose (dogs, etc.) from a leash or couple. 2. to disconnect; unfasten (something coupled).

un·couth (un-kōōth'), *adj.* [ME.; AS. *uncuth*, unknown; *un-*, not + *cuth*, pp. of *cunnan*, to know; cf. UNCO], 1. [Rare], not known or familiar; strange. 2. awkward; clumsy; ungainly. 3. uncultured; crude; boorish.

un·cov·e·nant·ed (un-kuv'ə-nən-tid), *adj.* 1. not promised, secured, or sanctioned by a covenant. 2. not bound by or committed to the terms of a covenant.

un·cov·er (un-kuv'ẽr), *v.t.* 1. to make known; disclose; reveal. 2. to lay bare or open by removing a covering. 3. to remove the cover or protection from. 4. to remove the hat, cap, etc. from (the head), as in respect or reverence. *v.i.* 1. to bare the head, as in respect or reverence. 2. to remove a cover or coverings.

un·cov·ered (un-kuv'ẽrd), *adj.* 1. having no covering; exposed. 2. not covered or protected by insurance, collateral, etc. 3. wearing no hat, cap, etc.; bareheaded.

un·crowned (un-kround'), *adj.* 1. not crowned; not officially installed as ruler by a coronation ceremony: as, Edward VIII was an *uncrowned* king. 2. ruling without the title or position of king, queen, etc.

unc·tion (uŋk'shən), *n.* [ME. *unccioun;* L. *unctio* < *ungere*, to anoint], 1. the act of anointing, as in medical treatment or a religious ceremony. 2. the oil, ointment, etc. used for this. 3. anything that soothes or comforts. 4. a quality or manner of utterance, especially in dealing with religious themes, that is fervent and earnest, or meant to express or arouse deep spiritual feeling; hence, 5. a quality or manner of utterance characterized by a mere pretense or affectation of fervor, etc., or by unctuosity.

unc·tu·os·i·ty (uŋk'chōō-os'ə-ti), *n.* [ME. & OFr. *unctuosite;* ML. *unctuositas*], an unctuous quality.

unc·tu·ous (uŋk'chōō-əs), *adj.* [ME.; ML. *unctuosus*, greasy < L. *unctum*, ointment < *ungere*, to anoint], 1. *a*) having the nature or quality of, or characteristic of, an ointment or unguent; oily or greasy. *b*) made up of or containing fat or oil. 2. like oil, soap, or grease to the touch, as certain minerals. 3. soft and rich: said of soil. 4. plastic. 5. characterized by a smug, smooth pretense of spiritual feeling, fervor, or earnestness, especially in an attempt to influence or persuade; too suave, bland, or oily, as in speech or manner.

un·cut (un-kut'), *adj.* not cut; specifically, *a*) not trimmed. *b*) having untrimmed margins: said of the pages of a book. *c*) not ground to shape: said of a gem.

un·damped (un-dampt'), *adj.* [*un-* (not) + *damped*], 1. not disheartened or discouraged. 2. in *electricity*, not decreasing in amplitude.

un·daunt·ed (un-dôn'tid, un-dän'tid), *adj.* not daunted; not faltering or hesitating because of fear or discouragement; undismayed; intrepid.

un·dé (un'dā), *adj.* [OFr. *unde* (Fr. *ondé*) < L. *unda*, a wave], in *heraldry*, wavy: also spelled **undée.**

un·dec·a·gon (un-dek'ə-gon'), *n.* [< L. *undecim*, eleven + Gr. *gōnia*, a corner, angle], a plane figure with eleven angles and eleven sides.

un·de·ceive (un'di-sēv'), *v.t.* [UNDECEIVED (-sēvd'), UNDECEIVING], [*un-* (back) + *deceive*], to free from deception, mistake, error, or illusion.

un·de·cid·ed (un'di-sīd'id), *adj.* 1. that is not decided or settled. 2. not having come to a decision; irresolute.

un·de·mon·stra·tive (un'di-mon'strə-tiv), *adj.* not demonstrative; giving little outward expression of the feelings; restrained; reserved.

un·de·ni·a·ble (un'di-nī'ə-b'l), *adj.* 1. that cannot be denied. 2. unquestionably good or excellent.

un·de·ni·a·bly (un'di-nī'ə-bli), *adv.* so as to be undeniable; indisputably; incontestably.

un·der (un'dẽr), *prep.* [ME. & AS.; akin to G. *unter;* IE. **n̥dhos, *n̥dheri*, under, seen also in L. *infra* (< **infera*), below; cf. INFRA], 1. in, at, or to a position down from; lower than; below: as, his shoes are *under* the bed. 2. covered, surmounted, enveloped, or con-

unconfused
unconfuted
uncongeal
uncongealable
uncongenial
uncongeniality
unconnected
unconquerable
unconquered
unconscientious
unconsecrated
unconsenting
unconsidered
unconsoled
unconsolidated
unconsonant
unconstant
unconstituted
unconstrained
unconstricted
unconsumed
uncontaminated
uncontemplated
uncontested
uncontradictable
uncontradicted
uncontrite
uncontrollable
uncontrolled
uncontroverted
uncontrovertible
unconversant
unconverted
unconvinced
unconvincing
uncooked
un-co-operative
un-co-ordinated
uncorked
uncorrected
uncorroborated
uncorrupt
uncorrupted
uncorruptly
uncountable
uncourteous
uncourtly
uncredited
uncrippled
uncritical
uncriticizable
uncross
uncrossed
uncrowded
uncrown
uncrystalline
uncrystallizable
uncrystallized
uncultivable
uncultivated
uncultured
uncumbered
uncurable
uncurbed
uncurdled
uncured
uncurious
uncurl
uncurled
uncursed
uncurtained
uncushioned
uncustomary
undamaged
undangered
undated
undaughterly
undazzled
undebatable
undecayed
undecaying
undecipherable
undecipherably
undeciphered
undeclared
undeclinable
undeclined
undecomposable
undecomposed
undecorated
undefaceable
undefaced
undefeatable
undefeated
undefended
undefensible
undefiled
undefinable
undefined
undeformed
undelayable
undelayed
undelineated
undeliverable
undelivered
undemocratic
undemocratically
undemonstrable
undemonstrably
undenied
undenominational
undependable
undeplored
undeposed
undepraved
undepreciated

cealed by: as, he's wearing a jacket *under* his raincoat. 3. beneath the surface of: as, twenty thousand leagues *under* the sea. 4. *a*) lower in authority, position, power, etc. than. *b*) lower in value, amount, etc. than; less than. *c*) lower than the required or standard degree of: as, *under* age. 5. below and to the other side of: as, we drove *under* the bridge. 6. in a position or condition regarded as lower or inferior; specifically, *a*) subject to the control, government, direction, instruction, or influence of: as, he studied the violin *under* Auer. *b*) in a state of liability or limitation with respect to; bound by: as, he is *under* oath. *c*) burdened, oppressed, or distressed by. *d*) subjected to; undergoing: as, *under* an anesthetic, *under* repair. 7. with the character, pretext, disguise, or cover of: as, he goes *under* an alias. 8. in or included in (the designated category, division, class, etc.): as, spiders are classified *under* arachnids. 9. in the time of: as, literature flourished *under* Elizabeth. 10. being the subject of: as, the question *under* discussion. 11. having regard for; because of: as, *under* the circumstances. 12. with the authorization or sanction of; attested by: as, *under* her signature. 13. planted with; sowed with: as, an acre *under* corn. ***adv.*** 1. in or to a position below something; beneath; underneath. 2. in or to a condition that is inferior or subordinate. 3. so as to be covered, surmounted, enveloped, or concealed. 4. less than the required or assigned amount, etc. ***adj.*** 1. located or moving below something else or on the lower surface. 2. lower in authority, position, power, etc.; subordinate. 3. held in control or restraint: used predicatively. 4. lower in amount, degree, etc.: used predicatively.

go under, to fail, as in business.

un·der- (un′dẽr), [ME. *under-*, *onder-*; AS. *under-*; see UNDER], a prefix meaning: 1. *in, on, to,* or *from a lower place* or *side; beneath* or *below,* as in *undershirt.* 2. *in an inferior* or *subordinate position* or *rank,* as in *undergraduate.* 3. *to a degree, extent,* or *amount that is below standard* or *inadequate,* as in *underdevelop.*

un·der·act (un′dẽr-akt′), ***v.t. & v.i.*** to act (a theatrical role) with too great restraint and subtlety; underplay.

un·der·age (un′dẽr-āj′), ***adj.*** 1. not of full or mature age. 2. below the usual or required age.

un·der·arm (un′dẽr-ärm′), ***adj.*** 1. under the arm; in the armpit. 2. in *cricket,* etc., performed with the hand below the level of the shoulder, as a bowl, or characterized by such a method of delivery; underhand. ***adv.*** with an underarm delivery or motion.

un·der·armed (un′dẽr-ärmd′), ***adj.*** not sufficiently armed; not provided with enough weapons.

un·der·bid (un′dẽr-bid′), ***v.t.*** [UNDERBID, UNDERBIDDING], to offer a lower price than; bid lower than.

un·der·bid·der (un′dẽr-bid′ẽr), ***n.*** one who underbids.

un·der·bred (un′dẽr-bred′), ***adj.*** 1. lacking good manners; ill-bred. 2. not of pure breed.

un·der·brush (un′dẽr-brush′), ***n.*** small trees, shrubs, etc. that grow beneath large trees in woods or forests; undergrowth.

un·der·buy (un′dẽr-bī′), ***v.t.*** [UNDERBOUGHT (-bôt′), UNDERBUYING], 1. to buy at less than the real value or asking price. 2. to buy more cheaply than (another or others).

un·der·car·riage (un′dẽr-kar′ij), ***n.*** 1. a supporting frame or structure, as of an automobile. 2. the landing gear of an airplane.

un·der·charge (un′dẽr-chärj′; *for n.,* un′dẽr-chärj′), ***v.t.*** 1. to charge less than is usual or correct (for): as, the grocer has *undercharged* us. 2. to load with an insufficient charge, as a gun. ***n.*** 1. an insufficient charge. 2. the act of undercharging.

un·der·class·man (un′dẽr-klas′mən, un′dẽr-kläs′mən), ***n.*** [*pl.* UNDERCLASSMEN (-mən)], a freshman or sophomore.

un·der·clothes (un′dẽr-klōz′, un′dẽr-klōthz′), ***n.pl.*** clothes worn next to the skin, or under a suit, dress, etc.

un·der·cloth·ing (un′dẽr-klōth′iŋ), ***n.*** underclothes.

un·der·coat (un′dẽr-kōt′), ***n.*** 1. a coat worn under another. 2. an under layer of short hair in an animal's coat. 3. a coating of tarlike material applied to the exposed undersurface of an automobile to prevent rust, etc. ***v.t.*** to apply an undercoat (sense 3) to.

un·der·cov·er (un′dẽr-kuv′ẽr), ***adj.*** acting or carried out in secret.

un·der·croft (un′dẽr-krôft′, un′dẽr-kroft′), ***n.*** [*under* + obs. *croft,* a vault (ult. < L. *crypta;* see CRYPT)], an underground room or vault, especially in a church.

un·der·cur·rent (un′dẽr-kũr′ənt), ***n.*** 1. a current flowing below another or beneath the surface. 2. a hidden or underlying tendency, influence, opinion, etc., usually one at variance with another that is more obvious.

un·der·cut (un′dẽr-kut′; *for v.,* un′dẽr-kut′), ***n.*** 1. a cut made below or underneath another so as to leave an overhang or concave profile. 2. a part cut in this way. 3. a notch cut in a tree below the level of the major cut and on the side to which the tree is to fall. 4. [Chiefly British], a tenderloin or fillet of beef. 5. in *sports, a*) backspin, as in golf. *b*) a cut, slice, or chop made with an underhand motion, as in tennis. ***adj.*** that is undercut. ***v.t.*** [UNDERCUT, UNDERCUTTING], 1. to make a cut below or under. 2. to make an undercut in. 3. to undersell or work for lower wages than. 4. in *sports, a*) to impart backspin to (a ball), as in golf. *b*) to cut, slice, or chop (a ball) with an underhand motion, as in tennis. ***v.i.*** to undercut something or someone (in various senses).

un·der·de·vel·op (un′dẽr-di-vel′əp), ***v.t. & v.i.*** to develop to a point below what is usual or needed.

un·der·do (un′dẽr-doo′), ***v.i. & v.t.*** [UNDERDID (-did′), UNDERDONE (-dun′), UNDERDOING], to do less than is usual, advisable, needed, or called for.

un·der·dog (un′dẽr-dôg′), ***n.*** 1. the losing or defeated dog in a dog fight; hence, 2. a person or group that is losing, as in a contest or struggle; one that is handicapped or underprivileged, as in the struggle of life.

un·der·done (un′dẽr-dun′), ***adj.*** not thoroughly cooked: said of food, especially beef: cf. **rare.**

un·der·drain·age (un′dẽr-drān′ij), ***n.*** drainage by an underground system of drains, as in agriculture.

un·der·dress (un′dẽr-dres′), ***v.i.*** to dress more plainly or informally than is indicated by the occasion.

un·der·es·ti·mate (un′dẽr-es′tə-māt′; *for n., usually* un′dẽr-es′tə-mit), ***v.t. & v.i.*** to estimate below the actual value, amount, etc. ***n.*** an estimate that is too low.

un·der·es·ti·ma·tion (un′dẽr-es′tə-mā′shən), ***n.*** an underestimating or underestimate.

un·der·ex·pose (un′dẽr-ik-spōz′), ***v.t.*** to expose (a photographic plate or film, etc.) for too short a time.

un·der·ex·po·sure (un′dẽr-ik-spō′zhẽr), ***n.*** 1. the act of underexposing. 2. an underexposed film or plate.

un·der·feed (un′dẽr-fēd′), ***v.t.*** [UNDERFED (-fed′), UNDERFEEDING], 1. to feed less than is needed. 2. to stoke (a fire) from below.

un·der·fired (un′dẽr-fīrd′), ***adj.*** fired, or heated, from beneath.

un·der·foot (un′dẽr-foot′), ***adv. & adj.*** 1. under the foot or feet; on the ground or floor at one's feet; hence, 2. in the way.

un·der·fur (un′dẽr-fũr′), ***n.*** the softer, finer fur under the outer coat of some animals, as beavers and seals.

un·der·gar·ment (un′dẽr-gär′mənt), ***n.*** a garment worn beneath a suit, dress, etc., especially next to the skin.

un·der·gird (un′dẽr-gũrd′), ***v.t.*** to gird, strengthen, or brace from the bottom side.

un·der·glaze (un′dẽr-glāz′), ***adj.*** in *ceramics,* designating colors, designs, etc. applied before the glaze is put on, as in the process of painting porcelain.

un·der·go (un′dẽr-gō′), ***v.t.*** [UNDERWENT (-went′), UNDERGONE (-gôn′), UNDERGOING], to experience; endure; go through; be subjected to.

un·der·grad·u·ate (un′dẽr-graj′oo-it), ***n.*** a student at a university or college who has not yet received the first, or bachelor's, degree. ***adj.*** 1. of, consisting of, or characteristic of undergraduates. 2. having the status of an undergraduate.

un·der·ground (un′dẽr-ground′; *also, for adj. & adv.,* un′dẽr-ground′), ***adj.*** 1. occurring, working, placed, used, etc. beneath the surface of the earth. 2. secret; hidden; undercover. ***adv.*** 1. beneath the surface of the earth. 2. in or into secrecy or hiding; so as to be undercover; surreptitiously. ***n.*** 1. the entire region beneath the surface of the earth. 2. an underground space or passage. 3. a secret movement organized in a country to oppose or overthrow the government in power or enemy forces of occupation: as, the *underground* of France in World War II. 4. [British], a subway: short for **underground railway.**

underground railroad, 1. a railroad running through tunnels under the ground; especially, a subway: also **underground railway.** 2. in the United States before 1861, a system set up by certain opponents of slavery to help fugitive slaves from the South escape to free States and Canada.

un·der·grown (un′dẽr-grōn′), ***adj.*** not grown to full or normal size or development.

un·der·growth (un′dẽr-grōth′), ***n.*** 1. small trees, shrubs, etc. that grow beneath large trees in woods or forests; underbrush. 2. an undercoat (sense 2). 3. the state of being undergrown.

un·der·hand (un′dẽr-hand′), ***adj.*** 1. done with the hand below the level of the elbow or shoulder. 2. secret; sly; deceitful; not open or straightforward. ***adv.*** 1. with an underhand motion. 2. slyly; secretly; unfairly. —***SYN.*** see **secret.**

un·der·hand·ed (un′dẽr-han′did), ***adj.*** 1. underhand; secret, sly, etc. 2. lacking the required number of hands, or workers, players, etc.; shorthanded.

un·der·hung (un'dẽr-huŋ'), *adj.* 1. projecting beyond the upper jaw: said of the lower jaw. 2. having such a lower jaw. 3. underslung. 4. resting or moving on a track or rail beneath, as some sliding doors.
un·der·laid (un'dẽr-lād'), *adj.* 1. laid or placed underneath. 2. raised or supported by something lying underneath; having an underlay.
un·der·lap (un'dẽr-lap'), *v.t.* [UNDERLAPPED (-lapt'), UNDERLAPPING], to lie or extend partly under.
un·der·lay (un'dẽr-lā'; *for v.*, un'dẽr-lā'), *n.* 1. something laid underneath, especially a thickness of paper, etc. laid under type to raise the level of the face. 2. in *mining*, an inclination or dip of a vein from the vertical. *v.t.* [UNDERLAID (-lād'), UNDERLAYING], [ME. *underlein;* AS. *underlecgan; under* + *lecgan*, to lay], 1. to cover or extend over the bottom of. 2. to lay (something) under something else, especially as a support, wedge, etc. 3. to raise or support with something laid underneath; provide with an underlay. *v.i.* in *mining*, to incline from the vertical: said of a vein.
un·der·lay (un'dẽr-lā'), past tense of **underlie.**
un·der·let (un'dẽr-let'), *v.t.* [for prin. pts. see LET], 1. to let at a price below the real value. 2. to sublet.
un·der·lie (un'dẽr-lī'), *v.t.* [UNDERLAY (-lā'), UNDERLAIN (-lān'), UNDERLYING], [ME. *underlien, underliggen;* AS. *underlicgan; under* + *licgan*, to lie], 1. to lie or be placed under; be beneath. 2. to support; form the basis or foundation of. 3. [Obs.], to be subordinate to. 4. in *finance*, to be prior to (another): said of a right, security, etc., as, this claim *underlies* that.
un·der·line (un'dẽr-līn'), *v.t.* [UNDERLINED (-līnd'), UNDERLINING], 1. to draw a line beneath; underscore; hence, 2. to stress or emphasize. *n.* (un'dẽr-līn'), a line underneath, as an underscore.
un·der·ling (un'dẽr-liŋ), *n.* [ME.; AS.; see UNDER & -LING, dim. suffix], a person who has little rank or authority in comparison with another whom he serves; subordinate: usually contemptuous or disparaging.
un·der·lip (un'dẽr-lip'), *n.* the lower lip.
un·der·ly·ing (un'dẽr-lī'iŋ), *adj.* 1. lying under; placed beneath. 2. fundamental; basic. 3. obscure; not clearly evident. 4. in *finance*, prior, as a claim.
un·der·mine (un'dẽr-mīn'), *v.t.* [UNDERMINED (-mīnd'), UNDERMINING], 1. to dig beneath; excavate ground from under, so as to form a tunnel or mine. 2. to wear away at the base or foundation. 3. to injure, weaken, or impair, especially by subtle or stealthy means. —*SYN.* see **weaken.**
un·der·most (un'dẽr-mōst'), *adj.* & *adv.* lowest in place, position, rank, etc.
un·der·neath (un'dẽr-nēth', un'dẽr-nēth'), *adv.* [ME. *undernethe;* AS. *underneothan, under neothan*, downward], 1. under; below; beneath. 2. on the underside; at a lower level. *prep.* 1. under; below; beneath. 2. under the form, guise, or authority of. *adj.* under; lower. *n.* the under part.
un·der·nour·ish (un'dẽr-nũr'ish), *v.t.* to give insufficient nourishment to; provide with less than the least amount of food needed for health and growth.
un·der·pass (un'dẽr-pas', un'dẽr-päs'), *n.* a passage, road, etc. passing under something; especially, a passageway for automobiles, pedestrians, etc. that runs under a railway or highway, from one side to the other.
un·der·pay (un'dẽr-pā'), *v.t.* [UNDERPAID (-pād'), UNDERPAYING], to pay less than is right.
un·der·pin (un'dẽr-pin'), *v.t.* [UNDERPINNED (-pind'), UNDERPINNING], 1. to support or strengthen from beneath, as with props. 2. to support; corroborate.
un·der·pin·ning (un'dẽr-pin'iŋ), *n.* 1. a supporting structure or foundation, especially one placed beneath a wall. 2. a support. 3. *pl.* [Colloq.], the legs.
un·der·play (un'dẽr-plā'), *v.t.* & *v.i.* 1. to play, or act, with less than the usual emphasis, in an intentionally restrained manner: as, he likes to *underplay* Hamlet's scene with Gertrude. 2. to act (a role, etc.) with insufficient emphasis, in a bare or casual manner. 3. to play (one's hand at cards, etc.) without fully realizing, or taking advantage of, the potentialities.
un·der·plot (un'dẽr-plot'), *n.* a secondary or subordinate plot in a story, play, etc.
un·der·priv·i·leged (un'dẽr-priv'ə-lijd), *adj.* deprived of fundamental social rights, or privileges, and security through poverty, discrimination, etc.
the underprivileged, those who are underprivileged.
un·der·pro·duc·tion (un'dẽr-prə-duk'shən), *n.* the production of less than is usual or needed, or of less than the quantity required to meet the economic demand.
un·der·proof (un'dẽr-prōōf'), *adj.* containing less alcohol than proof spirit does: abbreviated **up., u.p.**
un·der·prop (un'dẽr-prop'), *v.t.* [UNDERPROPPED (-propt'), UNDERPROPPING], to prop underneath; support.
un·der·quote (un'dẽr-kwōt'), *v.t.* 1. to quote (goods) at a lower price than another price or than the market price. 2. to quote a lower price than (another or others).
un·der·rate (un'dẽr-rāt'), *v.t.* to rate too low; undervalue; underestimate.
un·der·run (un'dẽr-run'), *v.t.* [for prin. pts. see RUN], to run, go, or pass under. *n.* something running or passing underneath, as a stream.
un·der·score (un'dẽr-skôr', un'dẽr-skōr'), *v.t.* [UNDERSCORED (-skôrd', -skōrd'), UNDERSCORING], to underline. *n.* a line drawn beneath a printed or written word, passage, etc., as for emphasis.
un·der·sea (un'dẽr-sē'), *adj.* & *adv.* beneath the surface of the sea.
un·der·seas (un'dẽr-sēz'), *adv.* undersea.
un·der·sec·re·tar·y (un'dẽr-sek'rə-ter'i), *n.* [*pl.* UNDERSECRETARIES (-iz)], an assistant secretary.
un·der·sell (un'dẽr-sel'), *v.t.* [UNDERSOLD (-sōld'), UNDERSELLING], 1. to sell at a lower price than. 2. to sell at a price lower than the actual value.
un·der·serv·ant (un'dẽr-sũr'vənt), *n.* a servant under the authority of another servant; subordinate servant.
un·der·set (un'dẽr-set'), *n.* an ocean undercurrent.
un·der·sher·iff (un'dẽr-sher'if), *n.* a deputy sheriff.
un·der·shirt (un'dẽr-shũrt'), *n.* a piece of underclothing worn under an outer shirt, next to the skin.
un·der·shot (un'dẽr-shot'), *adj.* 1. having the lower front teeth protruding beyond the upper front teeth when the mouth is closed. 2. having a protruding lower jaw. 3. turned by water passing beneath: said of a water wheel.

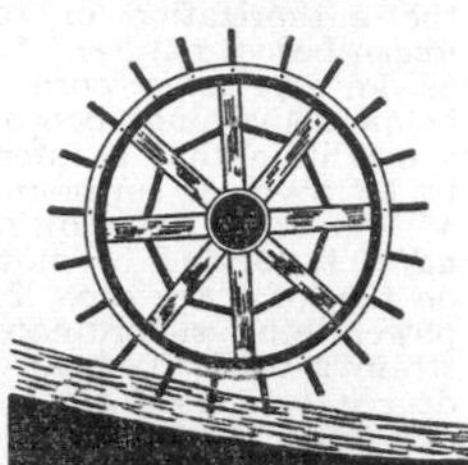
UNDERSHOT WHEEL

un·der·shrub (un'dẽr-shrub'), *n.* any low-growing, woody, bushy plant.
un·der·side (un'dẽr-sīd'), *n.* the side or surface that is underneath.
un·der·sign (un'dẽr-sīn'), *v.t.* to sign one's name at the end of (a letter, document, etc.).
un·der·signed (un'dẽr-sīnd'), *adj.* 1. signed at the end. 2. whose name is signed at the end.
the undersigned, the person or persons having signed at the end.
un·der·size (un'dẽr-sīz'), *adj.* undersized.
un·der·sized (un'dẽr-sīzd'), *adj.* smaller in size than is usual, average, or proper.
un·der·skirt (un'dẽr-skũrt'), *n.* a skirt worn under another.
un·der·sleeve (un'dẽr-slēv'), *n.* a sleeve worn under another.
un·der·slung (un'dẽr-sluŋ'), *adj.* 1. attached to the underside of the axles: said of an automobile frame. 2. having an underslung frame.
un·der·soil (un'dẽr-soil'), *n.* subsoil.
un·der·song (un'dẽr-sôŋ'), *n.* 1. a song or refrain sung as accompaniment to another song. 2. a hidden or underlying meaning.
un·der·staffed (un'dẽr-staft', un'dẽr-stäft'), *adj.* having too small a staff; having insufficient personnel.
un·der·stand (un'dẽr-stand'), *v.t.* [UNDERSTOOD (-stood'), UNDERSTANDING], [ME. *understanden;* AS. *understandan*, lit., to stand under or among; akin to G. *unterstehen*], 1. to get or perceive the meaning of; know or grasp what is meant by. 2. to take or interpret as the meaning or implication; infer; assume. 3. to take as meant or meaning; interpret. 4. to take as a fact; accept as a condition. 5. to supply mentally (an idea, word, answer, etc.). 6. to get as information; learn. 7. to know thoroughly; grasp or perceive clearly and fully the nature, character, functioning, etc. of. *v.i.* 1. to have understanding, comprehension, or discernment, either in general or with reference to some specific statement, situation, etc. 2. to be informed; believe; assume (usually parenthetical): as, he is, I *understand*, no longer here.
SYN.—**understand** and **comprehend** are used interchangeably to imply clear perception of the meaning of something, but, more precisely, **understand** stresses the full awareness or knowledge arrived at, and **comprehend**, the process of grasping something mentally (a foreigner may *comprehend* the words in an American idiom without *understanding* at all what is meant); **appreciate** implies sensitive, discriminating perception of the exact worth or value of something (to *appreciate* the difficulties of a situation).
un·der·stand·a·ble (un'dẽr-stan'də-b'l), *adj.* that can be understood.
un·der·stand·a·bly (un'dẽr-stan'də-bli), *adv.* so as to be understandable; in an understandable manner.
un·der·stand·ing (un'dẽr-stan'diŋ), *n.* 1. the mental quality, act, or state of a person who understands; comprehension; knowledge; discernment. 2. the power or ability to think and learn; intelligence; judgment; sense. 3. a specific interpretation: as, this is my *understanding* of the matter. 4. mutual agreement, especially one that settles differences or is informal and not made public. 5. mutual comprehension, as of ideas, intentions, etc. *adj.* that understands; having or characterized by comprehension, discernment, sympathy, etc.
un·der·state (un'dẽr-stāt'), *v.t.* & *v.i.* [UNDERSTATED (-id), UNDERSTATING], to make a weaker statement (of)

than is warranted by truth, accuracy, or importance; state (something) too weakly or moderately.

un·der·state·ment (un'dẽr-stāt'mənt), *n.* 1. the act of understating. 2. a statement that is too weak or moderate.

un·der·stock (un'dẽr-stok'), *n.* a plant or part of a plant upon which a graft is made.

un·der·stock (un'dẽr-stok'), *v.t.* to supply inadequately with stock, or goods.

un·der·stood (un'dẽr-stood'), past tense and past participle of **understand.** *adj.* 1. agreed upon. 2. implied but not expressed; assumed.

un·der·strap·per (un'dẽr-strap'ẽr), *n.* [< *under-* + *strap* + *-er*], a person having low rank or position; subordinate; underling.

un·der·stra·tum (un'dẽr-strā'təm, un'dẽr-strat'əm), *n.* [*pl.* UNDERSTRATA (-tə, -ə), UNDERSTRATUMS (-təmz, -əmz)], a substratum.

un·der·stud·y (un'dẽr-stud'i), *n.* [*pl.* UNDERSTUDIES (-iz)], 1. an actor who studies the part of another actor so that he can serve as a substitute when necessary. 2. any person who learns the duties of another so that he can serve as a substitute. *v.t. & v.i.* [UNDERSTUDIED (-id), UNDERSTUDYING], 1. to act as an understudy (to). 2. to learn (a part) as an understudy.

un·der·sur·face (un'dẽr-sũr'fis), *n.* the underside.

un·der·take (un'dẽr-tāk'), *v.t.* [UNDERTOOK (-took'), UNDERTAKEN (-tāk''n), UNDERTAKING], 1. to take upon oneself; agree to do; enter into or upon (a task, journey, etc.). 2. to give a promise or pledge that; contract: as, he *undertook* to be our guide. 3. to promise; guarantee. 4. to make oneself responsible for; take over as a charge. 5. [Obs.], to respond to the challenge of; take on in or as in combat. *v.i.* 1. [Archaic], to take on responsibility, pledge oneself, guarantee, or be surety (*for*). 2. [Colloq.], to act as an undertaker (sense 2).

un·der·tak·er (un'dẽr-tāk'ẽr; *for 2,* un'dẽr-tāk'ẽr), *n.* 1. a person who undertakes something. 2. a person whose business is to prepare the dead for burial and manage funerals.

un·der·tak·ing (un'dẽr-tāk'iŋ; *for 3,* un'dẽr-tāk'iŋ), *n.* 1. something undertaken; task; charge; enterprise. 2. a promise; guarantee. 3. the business of an undertaker (sense 2). 4. the act of one who undertakes some task, responsibility, etc.

un·der·ten·ant (un'dẽr-ten'ənt), *n.* a subtenant.

un·der·tint (un'dẽr-tint'), *n.* a faint or subdued tint.

un·der·tone (un'dẽr-tōn'), *n.* 1. a low tone of sound or voice. 2. something said in an undertone. 3. a faint or subdued color, especially one seen through other colors, as in some glazes. 4. anything that exists in or as in the background; underlying quality, factor, element, etc.: as, an *undertone* of horror.

un·der·took (un'dẽr-took'), past tense of **undertake.**

un·der·tow (un'dẽr-tō'), *n.* [*under-* + *tow* (to pull)], a current of water moving beneath and in a different direction from that of the surface water: said especially of a seaward current beneath breaking surf.

un·der·trump (un'dẽr-trump'), *v.t.* 1. to trump with a trump of lower denomination than has previously been played. 2. to play a lower trump than (one's partner).

un·der·val·u·a·tion (un'dẽr-val'ū-ā'shən), *n.* 1. an undervaluing. 2. an estimate or valuation that is too low.

un·der·val·ue (un'dẽr-val'ū), *v.t.* 1. to value too low, or below the real worth. 2. to regard or esteem too lightly. 3. to lower the value of.

un·der·vest (un'dẽr-vest'), *n.* [British], an undershirt.

un·der·waist (un'dẽr-wāst'), *n.* a waist worn under another.

un·der·wa·ter (un'dẽr-wô'tẽr, un'dẽr-wä'tẽr), *adj.* 1. being, placed, done, etc. beneath the surface of the water. 2. used or for use under water. 3. below the water line of a ship.

un·der·wear (un'dẽr-wâr'), *n.* clothes worn next to the skin beneath outer clothing; underclothes.

un·der·weight (un'dẽr-wāt'), *adj.* weighing too little; deficient in weight. *n.* weight below what is normal, required, etc.

un·der·went (un'dẽr-went'), past tense of **undergo.**

un·der·wing (un'dẽr-wiŋ'), *n.* a wing growing under and to the rear of another, as in some moths.

un·der·wood (un'dẽr-wood'), *n.* small trees, shrubs, etc. that grow beneath large trees in woods or forests; undergrowth; underbrush.

un·der·world (un'dẽr-wũrld'), *n.* 1. the earth. 2. the world of the dead; Hades. 3. the opposite side of the earth; antipodes. 4. the criminal members of society; people living by vice or crime.

un·der·write (un'dẽr-rīt'), *v.t.* [for prin. pts. see WRITE], [ME. *underwriten;* used as transl. of L. *subscribere;* see SUBSCRIBE], 1. to write under something, especially under something written; subscribe. 2. to sign one's name to. 3. to agree to pay or give (a specified sum of money) by signing one's name to a document, etc. 4. to agree to buy (an issue of stocks, bonds, etc.) on a given date and at a fixed price, or to guarantee the purchase of (stocks or bonds to be made available to the public for subscription). 5. to subscribe or agree to, especially by signature. 6. to agree to pay for or finance (an undertaking, etc.). 7. in *insurance, a)* to write one's signature at the end of (an insurance policy), thus assuming liability in the event of specified loss or damage. *b)* to insure. *c)* to assume liability to the amount of (a specified sum). *v.i.* 1. to underwrite something. 2. to be in business as an underwriter.

un·der·writ·er (un'dẽr-rīt'ẽr), *n.* 1. a person or agent who underwrites insurance. 2. a person who underwrites issues of stocks, bonds, etc.

un·de·sign·ing (un'di-zīn'iŋ), *adj.* not designing; straightforward; honest; not crafty or underhanded.

un·de·sir·a·ble (un'di-zīr'ə-b'l), *adj.* not desirable; objectionable. *n.* an undesirable person.

un·did (un-did'), past tense of **undo.**

un·dies (un'diz), *n.pl.* [dim. euphemistic abbrev.; prob. after *frillies,* frilly things], [Colloq.], (women's or children's) underwear.

un·dine (un-dēn', un'dēn, un'dīn), *n.* [G.; Mod. L. *Undina* < L. *unda,* a wave], in *folklore,* a female water spirit who could acquire a soul by marrying, and having a child by, a mortal.

un·di·rect·ed (un'də-rek'tid, un'dī-rek'tid), *adj.* 1. not directed; not guided. 2. not addressed, as a letter.

un·dis·posed (un'dis-pōzd'), *adj.* not disposed (of).

un·do (un-dōō'), *v.t.* [UNDID (-did'), UNDONE (-dun'), UNDOING], [ME. *undon;* AS. *undon; un-* (back) + *don,* to do], 1. to open, release, or untie (a fastening). 2. to open (a parcel, door, etc.) by this means. 3. to reverse the doing of (something accomplished); do away with; cancel; annul. 4. to put an end to; bring to ruin or downfall. 5. [Obs.], to solve; explain.

un·do·ing (un-dōō'iŋ), *n.* 1. a reversal of the doing of something done or accomplished; canceling or annulling. 2. the act of bringing to ruin or destruction. 3. the cause or source of ruin or destruction.

un·done (un-dun'), past participle of **undo.** *adj.* ruined; destroyed.

un·done (un-dun'), *adj.* not done; not performed, accomplished, completed, etc.

un·dou·ble (un-dub''l), *v.t.* [UNDOUBLED (-'ld), UNDOUBLING], to cause to be no longer doubled or double; unfold or make single.

undescribable
undescribed
undescried
undeserved
undeserving
undesignated
undesigned
undesirability
undesired
undesirous
undesisting
undespairing
undestroyed
undetachable
undetached
undetected
undeterminable
undetermined
undeterred
undeveloped
undeviating
undevoured
undevout
undifferentiated
undiffused
undigested
undigestible
undignified
undilated
undiluted
undiminishable
undiminished
undimmed
undiplomatic
undiscerned
undiscernible
undiscernibly
undiscerning
undischarged
undisciplined
undisclosed
undisconcerted
undiscordant
undiscouraged
undiscoverable
undiscovered
undiscredited
undiscriminating
undiscussed
undisguised
undisheartened
undishonored
undisillusioned
undismantled
undismayed
undismembered
undismissed
undispatched
undispelled
undispensed
undisputable
undisputed
undissected
undissembling
undisseminated
undissolved
undissolving
undistilled
undistinguishable
undistinguished
undistinguishing
undistracted
undistraught
undistressed
undistributed
undisturbed
undiversified
undiverted
undivested
undivided
undivorced
undivulged
undomestic
undomesticated

un·doubt·ed (un-dout'id), *adj.* not doubted or called in question; accepted; indubitable.
un·doubt·ed·ly (un-dout'id-li), *adv.* without or beyond doubt; admittedly; certainly.
un·draw (un-drô'), *v.t. & v.i.* [UNDREW (-drōō'), UNDRAWN (-drôn'), UNDRAWING], to draw back, away, or aside: as, *undraw* the curtain.
un·dress (un-dres'; *for n., usually* un'dres'), *v.t.* 1. to take off the clothing of; strip. 2. to divest of ornament. 3. to remove the dressing from (a wound). *v.i.* to take off one's clothes; strip. *n.* 1. loose, informal dress. 2. ordinary clothing, as opposed to uniform, full dress, etc. *adj.* of undress, or ordinary clothing.
Und·set, Si·grid (si'grid oon'set), 1882–1949; Norwegian novelist; received Nobel prize in literature, 1928.
‡**und so wei·ter** (oont zō vī'tẽr), [G.], and so forth; et cetera: abbreviated **usw, u.s.w.**
un·due (un-dōō', un-dū'), *adj.* 1. not yet owing or payable, as a debt. 2. improper; not appropriate or suitable. 3. not just, legal, or equitable. 4. excessive; unreasonable; immoderate.
un·du·lant (un'joo-lənt, un'doo-lənt), *adj.* undulating.
undulant fever, a persistent infectious disease caused by a bacterium transmitted to man in the milk of infected cows and goats, and characterized by an undulating, or recurrent, fever, an enlarged spleen, sweating, and pains in the joints: also called *Malta* (or *Mediterranean*) *fever.*
un·du·late (un'joo-lāt', un'doo-lāt'; *for adj., usually* un'joo-lit, un'doo-lit), *v.t.* [UNDULATED (-id), UNDULATING], [< L. *undulatus*, undulated < *unda*, a wave], 1. to cause to move in waves; move up and down or to and fro in undulations. 2. to give a wavy form, margin, or surface to. *v.i.* 1. to move in or as in waves. 2. to have a wavy form, margin, or surface. *adj.* having a wavy form, margin, or surface; undulating. —*SYN.* see **swing.**
un·du·lat·ed (un'joo-lāt'id, un'doo-lāt'id), *adj.* undulate.
un·du·la·tion (un'joo-lā'shən, un'doo-lā'shən), *n.* 1. an undulating or undulating motion, as of a snake. 2. a wavy, curving form or outline, especially one of a series. 3. pulsation. 4. in *physics*, wave motion, as of light or sound, or a wave or vibration.
un·du·la·tive (un'joo-lā'tiv, un'doo-lā'tiv), *adj.* of or characterized by undulations; undulatory.
un·du·la·to·ry (un'joo-lə-tôr'i, un'doo-lə-tō'ri), *adj.* 1. of, caused by, or characterized by undulations. 2. wavelike. 3. undulating.
un·du·ly (un-dōō'li, un-dū'li), *adv.* 1. improperly; unjustly. 2. beyond a due degree; excessively.
un·dy·ing (un-dī'iŋ), *adj.* not dying or ending; immortal or eternal.
un·earned (un-ũrnd'), *adj.* 1. not earned by work or service. 2. not deserved.
unearned increment, an increase in the value of land or other property coming about through no effort or expenditure on the part of the owner, as through an increase in area population.
un·earth (un-ũrth'), *v.t.* 1. to dig up from out of the earth. 2. to bring to light; discover; disclose. —*SYN.* see **learn.**
un·earth·li·ness (un-ũrth'li-nis), *n.* the state or quality of being unearthly.
un·earth·ly (un-ũrth'li), *adj.* 1. not earthly; not of this world; supernatural; ghostly. 2. weird; mysterious. 3. [Colloq.], fantastic; outlandish. —*SYN.* see **weird.**
un·eas·i·ly (un-ē'z'l-i, un-ē'zi-li), *adv.* in an uneasy manner.
un·eas·i·ness (un-ē'zi-nis), *n.* the quality or state of being uneasy.
un·eas·y (un-ē'zi), *adj.* [UNEASIER (-zi-ẽr), UNEASIEST (-zi-ist)], 1. having, showing, or allowing no ease of body or mind; uncomfortable. 2. awkward; constrained. 3. disturbed by anxiety or apprehension; restless; unsettled; perturbed.
un·em·ploy·a·ble (un'im-ploi'ə-b'l), *adj.* not employable; specifically, that cannot be employed, as in industry, because of age, physical or mental deficiency, or the like. *n.* an unemployable person.
un·em·ployed (un'im-ploid'), *adj.* 1. not employed; without work. 2. not being used; idle. *n.* an unemployed person.
the unemployed, people who are out of work.
un·em·ploy·ment (un'im-ploi'mənt), *n.* the state of being unemployed; lack of employment.
unemployment compensation, payment, as by a State government, of a certain amount of money to the unemployed, usually at regular intervals during a fixed period of time.
un·e·qual (un-ē'kwəl), *adj.* 1. not of the same size, strength, ability, value, rank, number, amount, etc. 2. not balanced or symmetrical: as, an *unequal* pattern. 3. not even, regular, or uniform; variable; fluctuating. 4. not equal or adequate (with *to*): as, she proved *unequal* to the job. 5. not equitable; unjust; unfair. *n.* an unequal person or thing.
un·e·qualed, un·e·qualled (un-ē'kwəld), *adj.* not equaled; unmatched; unrivaled; supreme.
un·e·quiv·o·cal (un'i-kwiv'ə-k'l), *adj.* not equivocal; plain; straightforward; clear; not ambiguous.
un·err·ing (un-ũr'iŋ, un-er'iŋ), *adj.* 1. free from error. 2. not missing or failing; certain; sure; exact.
UNESCO (yoo-nes'kō), *n.* the United Nations Educational, Scientific, and Cultural Organization.
un·es·sen·tial (un'i-sen'shəl), *adj.* not essential; not of great importance. *n.* an unessential thing.
un·e·ven (un-ē'vən), *adj.* [ME.; AS. *unefen*], 1. not even; not level, smooth, or flat; rough; irregular. 2. not straight or parallel. 3. unequal, as in length, thickness, etc. 4. not uniform; varying; fluctuating. 5. [Rare], not equitable; unfair. 6. in *mathematics*, odd; not evenly divisible by two. —*SYN.* see **rough.**
un·ex·am·pled (un'ig-zam'p'ld, un'ig-zäm'p'ld), *adj.* having no precedent, parallel, or similar case; without example; unprecedented.
un·ex·cep·tion·a·ble (un'ik-sep'shən-ə-b'l), *adj.* not exceptionable; without flaw or fault; not warranting even the slightest criticism or objection; irreproachable.
un·ex·cep·tion·a·bly (un'ik-sep'shən-ə-bli), *adv.* so as to be unexceptionable; in an unexceptionable manner.
un·ex·cep·tion·al (un'ik-sep'shən-'l), *adj.* 1. not exceptional; not uncommon or unusual; ordinary. 2. not admitting of any exception. 3. unexceptionable.
un·ex·pect·ed (un'ik-spek'tid), *adj.* not expected; unforeseen; sudden.
un·ex·press·ive (un'ik-spres'iv), *adj.* 1. inexpressive. 2. [Obs.], that cannot be expressed; inexpressible.
un·fail·ing (un-fāl'iŋ), *adj.* 1. not failing. 2. never ceasing or falling short; inexhaustible. 3. always reliable; certain; sure.
un·fair (un-fâr'), *adj.* [ME.; AS. *unfæger*, unfair, frightful; *un-*, not + *fæger*, fair], 1. not just or impartial; biased; inequitable. 2. dishonest, dishonorable, or unethical in business dealings involving relations with employees, customers, or competitors.
un·faith·ful (un-fāth'fəl), *adj.* 1. failing to observe the terms of a vow, promise, understanding, etc., or false to allegiance or duty; faithless; disloyal. 2. lacking

undoubting
undrained
undramatic
undramatically
undramatized
undrape
undreamed
undried
undrilled
undrinkable
undutiful
undyed
uneatable
uneaten
unecclesiastic
uneclipsed
uneconomic
uneconomical
unedible
unedifying
uneducable
uneducated
uneffaced
uneliminated
unemancipated
unembarrassed
unembellished
unemotional
unemphatic
unemphatically
unemptied
unenclosed
unencumbered
unendangered
unendeared
unended
unending
unendorsed
unendowed
unendurable
unenduring
unenforceable
unenforced
unenfranchised
unengaged
unengaging
un-English
unenjoyable
unenjoyed
unenlightened
unenlivened
unenriched
unenrolled
unenslaved
unentangled
unentered
unenterprising
unentertaining
unenthralled
unenthusiastic
unentitled
unenviable
unenvied
unenvious
unenvying
unequipped
unerased
unescapable
unessayed
unestablished
unesthetic
unestimated
unethical
uneventful
unexacting
unexaggerated
unexalted
unexamined
unexcavated
unexcelled
unexchangeable
unexcited
unexciting
unexcluded
unexcused
unexecuted
unexercised
unexhausted
unexpanded
unexpectant
unexpended
unexpendible
unexperienced
unexpert
unexpiated
unexpired
unexplainable
unexplained
unexplicit
unexploded
unexploited
unexplored
unexported
unexposed
unexpressed
unexpunged
unexpurgated
unextended
unexterminated
unextinguishable
unextinguished
unfadable
unfaded
unfading
unfallen
unfaltering

good faith; dishonest. 3. not true, accurate, or reliable; untrustworthy. 4. adulterous; guilty of adultery. 5. [Obs.], infidel.

un·fa·mil·iar (un'fə-mil'yẽr), *adj.* 1. not familiar or well known; strange. 2. having no experience (*with*); not conversant: as, he was *unfamiliar* with tools.

un·fa·mil·i·ar·i·ty (un'fə-mil'i-ar'ə-ti), *n.* lack of familiarity; state or quality of being unfamiliar.

un·fa·thered (un-fä'*th*ẽrd), *adj.* 1. having no father; fatherless. 2. of unknown paternity; illegitimate; bastard. 3. of unknown authorship or unestablished authenticity.

un·fa·vor·a·ble (un-fā'vẽr-ə-b'l), *adj.* not favorable; not propitious; adverse, contrary, or disadvantageous.

Unfederated Malay States, a former division of the Malay Peninsula, including the native states of Kelantan, Kedah, Johore, Perlis, and Trengganu: area, 22,070 sq. mi.: since 1948, a part of the Federation of Malaya.

un·feel·ing (un-fēl'iŋ), *adj.* 1. incapable of feeling or sensation; insensate or insensible. 2. incapable of sympathy or mercy; hardhearted; callous; cruel.

un·feigned (un-fānd'), *adj.* not feigned; genuine; real; sincere. —*SYN.* see **sincere.**

un·fet·ter (un-fet'ẽr), *v.t.* to free from fetters; free from restraint of any kind; liberate.

un·fin·ished (un-fin'isht), *adj.* 1. not finished; not completed or perfected; incomplete. 2. having no finish, or final coat, as of paint. 3. not sheared or processed after looming, as woolen cloth.

un·fit (un-fit'), *adj.* 1. incapable of meeting requirements or qualifications; not suitable. 2. not physically fit or sound. 3. not adapted or fitted for a given purpose. *v.t.* [UNFITTED (-id), UNFITTING], to make unfit; disqualify or incapacitate.

un·fix (un-fiks'), *v.t.* [*un-* (back) + *fix*], 1. to unfasten; loosen; detach. 2. to unsettle.

un·fledged (un-flejd'), *adj.* 1. not fully fledged; unfeathered, as a young bird. 2. immature; undeveloped.

un·flesh·ly (un-flesh'li), *adj.* not fleshly or carnal; spiritual.

un·flinch·ing (un-flin'chiŋ), *adj.* not flinching, yielding, or shrinking; steadfast; resolute; firm.

un·fold (un-fōld'), *v.t.* [ME. *unfolden;* AS. *unfealdan; un-*, back + *fealdan*, to fold], 1. to open the folds of; open and spread out. 2. to make known or lay open to view; reveal, disclose, display, or explain. 3. to develop. 4. to unwrap. *v.i.* to become unfolded.

un·formed (un-fôrmd'), *adj.* 1. having no regular form or shape; shapeless. 2. not organized or developed. 3. not made; uncreated.

un·for·tu·nate (un-fôr'chə-nit), *adj.* not fortunate; characterized by bad fortune; unsuccessful, unhappy, inauspicious, or unlucky. *n.* an unfortunate person.

un·found·ed (un-foun'did), *adj.* 1. not founded on fact or truth; baseless. 2. not established.

un·friend·ed (un-fren'did), *adj.* having no friends; friendless.

un·friend·li·ness (un-frend'li-nis), *n.* an unfriendly state or quality; unfriendly manner or behavior.

un·friend·ly (un-frend'li), *adj.* 1. not friendly or kind; hostile. 2. not favorable or propitious. *adv.* in an unfriendly manner.

un·frock (un-frok'), *v.t.* 1. to remove a frock from. 2. to deprive of the rank of priest or minister.

un·fruit·ful (un-frōōt'fəl), *adj.* 1. not reproducing; barren; unproductive. 2. yielding no worthwhile result; fruitless; unprofitable. —*SYN.* see **sterile.**

un·furl (un-fũrl'), *v.t. & v.i.* to open or spread out from a furled state; unfold.

un·gain·li·ness (un-gān'li-nis), *n.* the quality or condition of being ungainly.

un·gain·ly (un-gān'li), *adj.* [ME. *ungeinliche* < *ungein*, perilous < *un-*, not + ON. *gegn*, ready, serviceable], awkward; clumsy. *adv.* in an ungainly manner.

Un·ga·va (un-gä'və, un-gä'və), *n.* a former region in northeastern Canada, including most of Labrador: now a part of Quebec.

un·gen·er·ous (un-jen'ẽr-əs), *adj.* 1. not generous; stingy; mean. 2. not liberal or charitable; harsh.

un·gird (un-gũrd'), *v.t.* [ME. *ungirden;* AS. *ongyrdan* < *un-*, back + *gyrdan*, to gird], 1. to remove the belt or girdle of. 2. to remove by unfastening a belt or girdle.

un·girt (un-gũrt'), *adj.* [ME. *ungyrt* < *ungirden*], 1. having the girdle off or slackened; not girded. 2. loose; not braced or drawn tight; slack.

un·glued (un-glōōd'), *adj.* broken open; separated: said of things glued together.

un·god·li·ness (un-god'li-nis), *n.* the state or quality of being ungodly.

un·god·ly (un-god'li), *adj.* 1. not godly or religious; impious. 2. sinful; wicked. 3. [Colloq.], outrageous; dreadful. *adv.* 1. [Archaic], in an impious, sinful, or wicked manner. 2. [Colloq.], outrageously; dreadfully: as, it's *ungodly* early.

un·gov·ern·a·ble (un-guv'ẽrn-ə-b'l), *adj.* that cannot be governed or restrained; unruly; wild; rebellious. —*SYN.* see **unruly.**

un·gra·cious (un-grā'shəs), *adj.* 1. unacceptable; unpleasant; unattractive. 2. rude; discourteous; impolite; not gracious or affable.

un·gram·mat·i·cal (un'grə-mat'i-k'l), *adj.* 1. not in accordance with the principles or rules of grammar. 2. using ungrammatical language.

un·gual (uŋ'gwəl), *adj.* [< L. *unguis*, a claw, nail], of, like, or having a nail, claw, or hoof.

un·guard·ed (un-gärd'id), *adj.* 1. having no guard; unprotected. 2. careless; thoughtless; imprudent.

un·guent (uŋ'gwənt), *n.* [L. *unguentum* < *unguere*, to anoint], a salve or ointment.

un·guen·tar·y (uŋ'gwən-ter'i), *adj.* of, having the nature of, like, or used in an unguent.

un·guic·u·late (uŋ-gwik'yoo-lit, uŋ-gwik'yoo-lāt'), *adj.* [< L. *unguiculus*, fingernail, dim. of *unguis*, fingernail, claw, talon; + *-ate*], 1. having nails, claws, or talons instead of hoofs. 2. in *botany*, having an unguis. *n.* a mammal having claws or nails.

un·gui·nous (uŋ'gwi-nəs), *adj.* [L. *unguinosus* < *unguen*, fat, ointment], of or like fat or oil.

un·guis (uŋ'gwis), *n.* [*pl.* UNGUES (-gwēz)], [L.], 1. a nail, claw, or hoof. 2. in *botany*, the claw-shaped base of a petal.

un·gu·la (uŋ'gyoo-lə), *n.* [*pl.* UNGULAE (-lē')], [L., a hoof < *unguis*, a hoof, claw, talon], 1. a hoof. 2. a nail or claw. 3. an unguis. 4. a part or segment of a solid, especially of a cone or cylinder, remaining after the top has been cut off in a plane oblique to the base.

un·gu·lar (uŋ'gyoo-lẽr), *adj.* of, having the nature of, or like an ungula; ungual.

un·gu·late (uŋ'gyoo-lit, uŋ'gyoo-lāt'), *adj.* [LL. *ungulatus* < L. *ungula*, a hoof], 1. having hoofs; of or belonging to the group of mammals having hoofs. 2. shaped like a hoof. *n.* a mammal having hoofs.

un·hair (un-hâr'), *v.t. & v.i.* to make or become free from hair, as hides before tanning.

unfashionable
unfasten
unfatherly
unfathomable
unfathomed
unfavored
unfeared
unfearing
unfeasible
unfed
unfederated
unfeigningly
unfelt
unfeminine
unfenced
unfermented
unfertile
unfertilized
unfettered
unfilial
unfilled
unfilmed
unfiltered
unfired
unfitted
unfitting
unfixed
unflagging
unflattering
unflavored
unflickering
unfoiled
unfoldment
unforbearing
unforbidden
unforced
unfordable
unforeboding
unforeknown
unforeseeable
unforeseeing
unforeseen
unforested
unforetold
unforfeited
unforged
unforgetful
unforgettable
unforgetting
unforgivable
unforgiven
unforgiving
unforgotten
unformulated
unforsaken
unfortified
unfought
unfound
unframed
unfranchised
unfraternal
unfraught
unfree
unfreezable
unfreeze
un-French
unfrequent
unfrequented
unfrozen
unfulfilled
unfunded
unfurnished
unfurrowed
ungallant
ungarnished
ungartered
ungathered
ungenial
ungenteel
ungentle
ungentlemanly
ungently
ungifted
ungladdened
unglazed
unglossed
ungloved
unglue
ungot
ungotten
ungoverned
ungowned
ungraced
ungraceful
ungraded
ungrafted
ungrained
ungrateful
ungratified
ungrounded
ungrudging
unguided
unhackneyed
unhailed

un·hal·low (un-hal′ō), *v.t.* to desecrate; profane.
un·hal·lowed (un-hal′ōd), *adj.* 1. not hallowed or consecrated; unholy. 2. wicked; profane; impious.
un·hand (un-hand′), *v.t.* to loose or release from the hand or hands; let go of.
un·hand·some (un-han′səm), *adj.* 1. not handsome; plain; homely; not attractive. 2. rude; unbecoming; not gracious or courteous. 3. stingy; mean.
un·hap·py (un-hap′i), *adj.* [UNHAPPIER (-i-ẽr), UNHAPPIEST (-i-ist)], 1. unlucky; unfortunate. 2. sad; miserable; wretched; sorrowful. 3. not suitable or appropriate; ill-chosen. 4. [Obs.], evil; reprehensible.
un·har·ness (un-här′nis), *v.t.* 1. to free from harness or gear. 2. to strip or divest of armor.
un·health·y (un-hel′thi), *adj.* [UNHEALTHIER (-thi-ẽr), UNHEALTHIEST (-thi-ist)], 1. having or showing poor health; sickly; not well. 2. harmful to health; unwholesome. 3. harmful to morals or character.
un·heard (un-hũrd′), *adj.* 1. not heard; not perceived by the ear: as, the cry went *unheard*. 2. not given a hearing. 3. not heard of before; unknown.
un·heard-of (un-hũrd′uv′, un-hũrd′ov′), *adj.* not heard of before; unprecedented or unknown.
un·helm (un-helm′), *v.t. & v.i.* [Archaic], to remove the helm or helmet (of).
un·hinge (un-hinj′), *v.t.* [UNHINGED (-hinjd′), UNHINGING], 1. to remove from the hinges. 2. to remove the hinges from. 3. to dislodge or detach. 4. to throw (the mind, etc.) into confusion; unbalance or upset.
un·hitch (un-hich′), *v.t.* 1. to free from a hitch. 2. to unfasten; release; detach.
un·ho·li·ly (un-hō′lə-li), *adv.* in an unholy manner.
un·ho·ly (un-hō′li), *adj.* [UNHOLIER (-li-ẽr), UNHOLIEST (-li-ist)], [ME.; AS. *unhalig; un-*, not + *halig*, holy], 1. not sacred, hallowed, or consecrated. 2. wicked; profane; impious. 3. [Colloq.], frightful; dreadful.
un·hook (un-hook′), *v.t.* 1. to remove or loosen from a hook. 2. to undo or unfasten the hook or hooks of. *v.i.* to become unhooked.
un·hoped (un-hōpt′), *adj.* not hoped for; not expected: usually with *for*, as, an *unhoped-for* advantage.
un·horse (un-hôrs′), *v.t.* [UNHORSED (-hôrst′), UNHORSING], 1. to throw (a rider) from a horse. 2. to overthrow; upset. 3. to take a horse or horses from.
un·hu·man (un-hū′mən), *adj.* 1. [Rare], inhuman. 2. superhuman. 3. not human in kind, quality, etc.
u·ni- (ū′nə, ū′ni), [< L. *unus*, one], a combining form meaning *having* or *consisting of one only*, as in *unicellular*.
U·ni·at (ū′ni-at′), *n.* [Russ. *uniyat* < *uniya*, a union < L. *unus*, one: so named from "union" with the Roman Church], a member of any Eastern Christian Church that recognizes the Pope as primate but keeps to its own liturgy, rites, etc. *adj.* of such a church.
U·ni·ate (ū′ni-it, ū′ni-āt′), *n. & adj.* Uniat.
u·ni·ax·i·al (ū′ni-ak′si-əl), *adj.* having a single axis.
u·ni·cam·er·al (ū′ni-kam′ẽr-əl), *adj.* [< *uni-* + LL. *camera*, a vault, chamber; + *-al*], of or having a single legislative chamber.
u·ni·cel·lu·lar (ū′ni-sel′yoo-lẽr), *adj.* [*uni-* + *cellular*], having or consisting of a single cell.
unicellular animal, a protozoan.
u·ni·col·or (ū′ni-kul′ẽr), *adj.* of only one color.
u·ni·corn (ū′nə-kôrn′), *n.* [ME. & OFr. *unicorne* < L. *unicornis*, one-horned < *unus*, one + *cornu*, a horn], 1. a mythical horselike animal having a single horn growing from the center of its forehead. 2. in the *Bible*, a two-horned, ox-like animal called *rĕ'ēm* in Hebrew: Deut. 33:17.

UNICORN

u·ni·cos·tate (ū′ni-kos′tāt, ū′ni-kôs′tāt), *adj.* 1. having only one costa, rib, or riblike part. 2. in *botany*, having only one main rib: said of a leaf.
u·ni·cus·pid (ū′ni-kus′pid), *adj.* having a single cusp.
u·ni·cy·cle (ū′ni-si′k'l), *n.* [see CYCLE], any vehicle having a single wheel.
un·i·de·aed (un′ī-dē′əd), *adj.* having no ideas; stupid.
u·ni·di·rec·tion·al (ū′ni-di-rek′shən-'l, ū′ni-dī-rek′shən-'l), *adj.* having, or moving in, only one direction.
u·ni·fi·a·ble (ū′nə-fī′ə-b'l), *adj.* that can be unified.
u·ni·fi·ca·tion (ū′nə-fi-kā′shən), *n.* the act of unifying or the state of being unified.
u·ni·fi·er (ū′nə-fī′ẽr), *n.* a person or thing that unifies.
u·ni·fi·lar (ū′ni-fī′lẽr), *adj.* [*uni-* + *filar*], of or having only one thread, wire, etc.
u·ni·flo·rous (ū′ni-flôr′əs, ū′ni-flō′rəs), *adj.* bearing a single flower.
u·ni·fo·li·ate (ū′ni-fō′li-it, ū′ni-fō′li-āt′), *adj.* [see FOLIATE], in *botany*, 1. bearing only one leaf. 2. loosely, unifoliolate.
u·ni·fo·li·o·late (ū′ni-fō′li-ə-lāt′), *adj.* [see FOLIOLATE], in *botany*, 1. bearing only one leaflet although compound in structure, as a leaf of the orange. 2. having leaves of this sort.

UNIFOLIOLATE LEAF (of orange)

u·ni·form (ū′nə-fôrm′), *adj.* [Fr. *uniforme;* L. *uniformis* < *unus*, one + *forma*, a form], 1. always the same; not varying or changing in form, rate, degree, manner, etc. 2. having the same form, appearance, manner, etc.; not varying among themselves; conforming to a given standard; always alike. 3. having a consistent action, effect, etc.; being identical throughout a state, country, etc.: as, a *uniform* minimum wage. *n.* 1. the official or distinctive clothes worn by the members of a particular group, as policemen or soldiers, especially when on duty. 2. a suit or outfit of such clothes. *v.t.* 1. to clothe or supply with a uniform. 2. to make uniform. —*SYN.* see **steady.**
uniform with, having the same form, appearance, etc. as.
Uniform Code of Military Justice, the body of laws governing members of the armed forces of the United States: superseded the Articles of War in 1951.
u·ni·formed (ū′nə-fôrmd′), *adj.* wearing a uniform.
u·ni·form·i·tar·i·an (ū′nə-fôr′mə-târ′i-ən), *adj.* 1. of or holding the doctrine that all geological phenomena may be explained as resulting from observable processes that have operated in a uniform way. 2. of or adhering to uniformity in something. *n.* a person who adheres to some doctrine of uniformity.
u·ni·form·i·ty (ū′nə-fôr′mə-ti), *n.* [*pl.* UNIFORMITIES (-tiz)], [Late ME. & Late OFr. *uniformite;* L. *uniformitas*], state, quality, or instance of being uniform.
u·ni·fy (ū′nə-fī′), *v.t.* [UNIFIED (-fīd′), UNIFYING], [< Fr. or ML.; Fr. *unifier;* ML. *unificare* < L. *unus*, one + *facere*, to make], to make into a unit; cause to become one; consolidate; unite.
u·nij·u·gate (yoo-nij′oo-gāt′, ū′ni-jōō′git, ū′ni-jōō′gāt), *adj.* [< *uni-* + L. *jugatus;* see JUGATE], in *botany*, having only one pair of leaflets: said of a pinnate leaf.
u·ni·lat·er·al (ū′ni-lat′ẽr-əl), *adj.* [Mod. L. *unilateralis;* see UNI- & LATERAL], 1. of, occurring on, or affecting one side only. 2. involving or obligating one only of several persons or parties; done or undertaken by one only; not reciprocal: as, a *unilateral* contract. 3. taking into account one side only of an issue, matter, etc.; one-sided. 4. showing descent through only one line of the family. 5. turned to one side. 6. in *biology*, arranged, disposed, or produced on one side of an axis. 7. in *phonetics*, formed on one side of the tongue.
u·ni·lobed (ū′ni-lōbd′), *adj.* having only one lobe.
u·ni·loc·u·lar (ū′ni-lok′yoo-lẽr), *adj.* having, or made up of, only one loculus, compartment, cell, or chamber.
un·im·peach·a·ble (un′im-pēch′ə-b'l), *adj.* not impeachable; that cannot be doubted, questioned, or discredited; blameless; irreproachable.
un·im·proved (un′im-prōōvd′), *adj.* 1. not bettered or improved, as by planting, building, etc.: as, *un-*

unhammered
unhampered
unhandicapped
unhandily
unhandled
unhandy
unhanged
unhappily
unhappiness
unharassed
unhardened
unharmed
unharmful
unharmonious
unharnessed
unharrowed
unharvested
unhasty
unhat
unhatched
unhealed
unhealthful
unhealthily
unhealthiness
unheated
unheeded
unheedful
unheeding
unhelped
unhelpful
unheralded
unheroic
unheroically
unhesitating
unhewn
unhindered
unhired
unhistoric
unhomogeneous
unhonored
unhostile
unhouse
unhoused
unhumanize
unhung
unhurried
unhurt
unhusk
unhygienically
unhyphenated
unhyphened
unideal
unidentified
unidiomatic
unidiomatically
unilluminated
unillumined
unillustrated
unimaginable
unimaginably
unimaginative
unimagined
unimbued
unimitated
unimpaired
unimpassioned
unimpeached
unimpeded
unimplored
unimportance
unimportant
unimposing
unimpressed
unimpressible
unimpressionable
unimpressive

improved land. 2. not made use of; not turned to advantage. 3. not improved in health.

un·in·tel·li·gent (un'in-tel'ə-jənt), *adj.* having or showing a lack or deficiency of intelligence.

un·in·ter·est·ed (un-in'tẽr-is-tid, un-in'tris-tid), *adj.* 1. having no interest (with *in*). 2. paying no attention.

un·ion (ūn'yən), *n.* [ME.; Late OFr.; L. *unio*, oneness < *unus*, one], 1. a uniting or being united; combination; junction; fusion. 2. an agreeing or leaguing together for mutual benefit. 3. the unity or solidarity produced by this. 4. a combining or grouping together of nations, states, political groups, etc. for some specific purpose. 5. marriage. 6. in England, *a)* a combination of parishes for the joint administration of relief for the poor. *b)* a workhouse kept up by such a union. 7. something united or unified; a whole made up of united parts. 8. a device symbolizing political union, used in a flag or ensign: it may cover the entire field, as the three crosses in the British national flag, or it may be placed in the upper inner corner, as the white stars on a blue field in the flag of the United States. 9. a trade union; labor union. 10. a device for joining together parts, as of a machine; especially, a coupling for linking the ends of pipes. 11. a fabric made of two or more different kinds of material, as cotton and linen. Abbreviated U. —*SYN.* see **alliance, unity.**

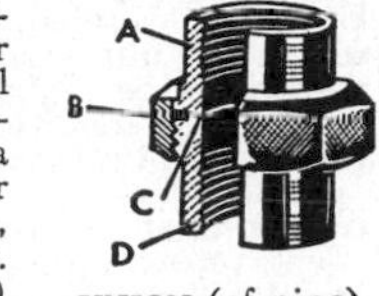

UNION (of pipe) A, D, sections of pipe; B, nut; C, fitted seat

the Union, the United States of America.

union card, a card serving to identify one as a member in good standing of a specified labor union.

Union City, a city in New Jersey, near Jersey City: pop., 52,000.

un·ion·ism (ūn'yən-iz'm), *n.* 1. the principle of union. 2. support of this principle or of a specified union. 3. the system or principles of labor unions. 4. [U-], loyalty to the federal union of the United States, especially during the Civil War.

un·ion·ist (ūn'yən-ist), *n.* 1. a person who believes in unionism. 2. a member of a labor union. 3. [U-], a supporter of the federal union of the United States, especially during the Civil War. 4. [U-], a person who believed in keeping all of Ireland within the United Kingdom, as opposed to a person advocating home rule; hence, 5. [U-], a member of the British Conservative party.

un·ion·i·za·tion (ūn'yən-i-zā'shən, ūn'yən-ī-zā'shən), *n.* a unionizing or being unionized.

un·ion·ize (ūn'yən-īz'), *v.t.* [UNIONIZED (-īzd'), UNIONIZING], 1. to form into a union. 2. to organize (a group of workers in a shop, industry, etc.) into a labor union. 3. to bring into conformity with the rules, standards, etc. of a labor union. *v.i.* to join or organize a union, especially a labor union.

union jack, 1. a jack or flag consisting only of a union, especially of the union of a national flag. 2. [U- J-], the national flag of the United Kingdom.

Union of South Africa, South Africa: the former name.

Union of Soviet Socialist Republics, a federation of fifteen republics of eastern Europe and northern Asia, extending from the Arctic Ocean to the Black Sea and east to the Pacific, including most of the former Russian Empire: area, 8,600,000 sq. mi.; pop., 218,000,000; capital, Moscow: also called *Soviet Union*; *Soviet Russia;* former name (still loosely used), *Russia:* abbreviated **USSR, U.S.S.R.**

union shop, 1. a shop, business establishment, etc. in which a contract between the employer and a labor union permits the hiring of nonunion workers but requires that all new employees join the union within a specified period, often thirty days, and remain members of the union throughout their employment. 2. a shop, business establishment, or part thereof in which wages, hours, and working conditions of all employees are fixed by contract between the employer and a labor union. Cf. **closed shop, open shop.**

union suit, a suit of men's underwear uniting shirt and drawers in a single garment.

Un·ion·town (ūn'yən-toun'), *n.* a city in southwestern Pennsylvania: pop., 18,000.

u·nip·a·rous (yoo-nip'ə-rəs), *adj.* [Mod. L. *uniparus* < L. *unus*, one + *parere*, to bear], 1. producing only one egg or offspring at a time. 2. in *botany*, producing only one axis at each branching, as certain flower clusters.

u·ni·per·son·al (ū'ni-pũr's'n-'l), *adj.* 1. existing as or in, consisting of, or manifested in the form of, only one person. 2. in *grammar*, used in only one person (specifically, the third person singular): said of certain verbs, as *methinks*.

u·ni·pet·al·ous (ū'ni-pet''l-əs), *adj.* in *botany*, having only one petal.

u·ni·pla·nar (ū'ni-plā'nẽr), *adj.* occurring in one plane.

u·ni·pod (ū'ni-pod'), *n.* [*uni-* + *-pod*, after *tripod*], a one-legged prop or support. *adj.* having only one leg.

u·ni·po·lar (ū'ni-pō'lẽr), *adj.* 1. of or having only one pole or one kind of polarity. 2. designating a nerve cell, as in spinal ganglia, having only one process.

u·nique (ū-nēk'), *adj.* [Fr. < L. *unicus*, single; akin to *unus*, one], 1. one and only; single; sole. 2. different from all others; having no like or equal. 3. singular; unusual; extraordinary; rare: still regarded by some as an objectionable usage. —*SYN.* see **single.**

u·ni·sex·u·al (ū'ni-sek'shoo-əl), *adj.* [Mod.L. *unisexualis;* see UNI- & SEXUAL], of only one sex; specifically, *a)* in *botany*, diclinous. *b)* in *zoology*, either male or female; not hermaphroditic.

u·ni·son (ū'nə-s'n, ū'nə-z'n), *n.* [OFr.; ML. *unisonus*, having the same sound < L. *unus*, one + *sonus*, a sound], 1. identity of musical pitch, as of two or more voices or tones, or the interval of a perfect prime. 2. agreement; concord; harmony.

in unison, 1. sounding the same note at the same time. 2. sounding together in octaves. 3. with all the voices or instruments performing the same part: said of a musical composition or passage.

u·nis·o·nal (yoo-nis'ə-n'l), *adj.* unisonous.

u·nis·o·nant (yoo-nis'ə-nənt), *adj.* unisonous.

u·nis·o·nous (yoo-nis'ə-nəs), *adj.* [ML. *unisonus*], characterized by or being in unison.

u·nit (ū'nit), *n.* [abbrev. < *unity*], 1. the smallest whole number; one. 2. any fixed quantity, amount, distance, measure, etc. used as a standard; specifically, *a)* in *education*, a fixed amount of work used as a basis in awarding scholastic credits, usually determined by the number of hours spent in class. *b)* in *medicine*, etc., the amount of a drug, vaccine, serum, or antigen needed to produce a given result, as on a certain animal or on animal tissues. 3. a single person or group of individuals, especially as distinguished from others or as part of a whole. 4. a single, distinct part or object, especially one used for a specific purpose: as, the power *unit* of a jet plane, the lens *unit* of a camera, etc. 5. in *mathematics*, a magnitude or number regarded as an undivided whole. 6. in *military usage*, any organized body of troops that is a subdivision of a larger body.

u·nit·age (ū'nit-ij), *n.* [see -AGE], a designation of the amount or quantity of a unit of measure.

U·ni·tar·i·an (ū'nə-târ'i-ən), *n.* [< Mod. L. *unitarius*, unitary + *-an;* also in part < *unity* + *-arian*], 1. a person who denies the doctrine of the Trinity, believing in the teachings, but rejecting the divinity, of Jesus, and holding that God is a single being. 2. a member of a Protestant denomination based on this doctrine and characterized by congregational autonomy, emphasis on the importance of character, and tolerance of differing religious views. *adj.* 1. of Unitarians or their doctrines, or adhering to Unitarianism. 2. [u-], unitary. Abbreviated **Unit.**

U·ni·tar·i·an·ism (ū'nə-târ'i-ən-iz'm), *n.* the doctrines or beliefs of Unitarians or the Unitarian Church.

u·ni·tar·y (ū'nə-ter'i), *adj.* 1. of a unit or units. 2. of, based on, or characterized by unity. 3. having the nature of or used as a unit.

unit character, a character, or trait, transmitted as a unit in heredity according to Mendelian principles.

u·nite (yoo-nīt'), *v.t.* [UNITED (-id), UNITING], [ME. *unyten* < L. *unitus*, pp. of *unire*, to unite < *unus*,

uninaugurated
uninclosed
unincorporated
unincubated
unincumbered
unindemnified
unindicated
unindorsed
uninfected
uninfested
uninflammable
uninflected
uninfluenced
uninfluential
uninformed
uninfringed
uninhabitable
uninhabited
uninhibited
uninitiated
uninjured
uninspired
uninspiring
uninstructed
uninstructive
uninsurable
uninsured
unintellectual
unintelligibility
unintelligible
unintelligibly
unintended
unintentional
uninteresting
unintermitted
unintermittent
unintermitting
uninterpolated
uninterpreted
uninterrupted
unintimidated
unintoxicated
uninvaded
uninvented
uninventive
uninverted
uninvested
uninvited
uninviting
uninvoked
uninvolved
unissued

one], 1. to put or bring together so as to make one; combine or join into a whole. 2. to bring together in common cause, interest, opinion, etc.; join, as in action, through fellowship, agreement, legal bonds, etc. 3. to have or show (qualities, characteristics, etc.) in combination. 4. to join in marriage. 5. to cause to adhere. *v.i.* 1. to become combined or joined together; become one or as one, by adhering, associating, etc. 2. to join together in action.—*SYN.* see **join.**

u·nite (ū'nīt, yoo-nīt'), *n.* [< *unite, v.*, with reference to the union of England and Scotland], a former English gold coin of James I, equal to 20 shillings.

u·nit·ed (yoo-nīt'id), *adj.* [pp. of *unite*], 1. combined; joined; made one. 2. of or resulting from joint action or association. 3. in agreement or harmony.

United Arab Republic, a republic in the Middle East consisting of Egypt and (from 1958 to 1961) Syria.

United Kingdom, 1. Great Britain and Northern Ireland: area, 94,279 sq. mi.; pop., 52,157,000; capital, London: official name, **United Kingdom of Great Britain and Northern Ireland.** 2. formerly (1801–1922), Great Britain and Ireland. Abbreviated **U.K.**

United Nations, an international organization formed January 2, 1942, by the nations opposed to the fascist coalition of Germany, Japan, Italy, and their satellites. The 26 nations that met to form the organization were: the United States, the United Kingdom of Great Britain and Northern Ireland, the Union of Soviet Socialist Republics, China, Australia, Belgium, Canada, Luxembourg, the Netherlands, New Zealand, Nicaragua, Norway, Panama, Poland, Costa Rica, Cuba, Czechoslovakia, the Dominican Republic, El Salvador, Greece, Guatemala, Haiti, Honduras, India, the Union of South Africa, and Yugoslavia; by 1963 additional members were Afghanistan, Albania, Algeria, Argentina, Austria, Bolivia, Brazil, Bulgaria, Burma, Burundi, the Byelorussian S.S.R., Cambodia, Cameroun, Central African Republic, Ceylon, Chad, Chile, Colombia, Congo (Brazzaville), Congo (Léopoldville), Cyprus, Dahomey, Denmark, Ecuador, Ethiopia, Finland, France, Gabon, Ghana, Guinea, Hungary, Iceland, Indonesia, Iran, Iraq, Ireland, Israel, Italy, Ivory Coast, Jamaica, Japan, Jordan, Kuwait, Laos, Lebanon, Liberia, Libya, Malagasy, Malaya, Mali, Mauritania, Mexico, Mongolian People's Republic, Morocco, Nepal, Niger, Nigeria, Pakistan, Paraguay, Peru, the Philippines, Portugal, Romania, Rwanda, Saudi Arabia, Senegal, Sierra Leone, Somali, Spain, Sudan, Sweden, Syria, Tanganyika, Thailand, Togo, Trinidad and Tobago, Tunisia, Turkey, Uganda, the Ukrainian S.S.R., the United Arab Republic, Upper Volta, Uruguay, Venezuela, and Yemen. The members were organized to promote world peace and security under a permanent charter at San Francisco in 1945, and since 1946 have had their headquarters in New York City: abbreviated **UN. U.N.**

United Press International, a large, privately owned agency for gathering and distributing news, formed (1958) by a merger of **United Press** and **International News Service:** abbreviated **UPI** (no period).

United Provinces, Uttar Pradesh: the former name.

United States Army, the Regular Army, or permanent military force, of the United States: abbreviated **U.S.A., USA:** cf. **Army of the United States.**

United States of America, a country mostly in North America, made up of fifty States and the District of Columbia: possessions include the Panama Canal Zone, Virgin Islands, etc.: (of the United States proper) area, 3,615,211 sq. mi.; pop., 179,323,000; (of possessions) area, 4,455 sq. mi.; pop., 2,517,000; capital, Washington, D.C.: also called *United States, America:* abbreviated **U.S.A., U.S., US** (no period).

unit factor, a gene involved in the inheritance of a given unit character.

u·ni·tive (ū'nə-tiv), *adj.* [ML. *unitivus*], 1. having unity. 2. tending to unite.

unit rule, a rule, as in some political conventions, that the entire vote of a delegation shall be cast as a unit in accordance with the vote of the majority of its members.

u·ni·ty (ū'nə-ti), *n.* [*pl.* UNITIES (-tiz)], [ME. *unite;* OFr. *unité;* L. *unitas*, oneness < *unus*, one], 1. the state of being one; oneness; singleness; being united. 2. something considered complete in itself; single, separate thing. 3. the quality of being one in spirit, sentiment, purpose, etc. harmony; agreement; concord; uniformity. 4. unification. 5. a group or body formed by this. 6. the quality or fact of being a totality or whole, especially a complex that is a union of related parts. 7. an arrangement of parts or material that will produce a single, harmonious design or effect in an artistic or literary production. 8. a design or effect so produced. 9. constancy, continuity, or fixity of purpose, action, etc. 10. in *mathematics, a*) any quantity, magnitude, etc. considered or identified as a unit or 1. *b*) the numeral or unit 1.

the unities, the three principles of dramatic construction (the *unities of action, time, and place*) derived by French neoclassicists from Aristotle's *Poetics*, holding that a play should have one unified plot, that all the action should occur within one day, and that the setting should be confined to one locale.

SYN.—**unity** implies the oneness, as in spirit, aims, interests, feelings, etc. of that which is made up of diverse elements or individuals (national *unity*); **union** implies the state of being united into a single organization for a common purpose (a labor *union*); **solidarity** implies such firm and complete unity in an organization, group, class, etc. as to make for the greatest possible strength in influence, action, etc.

Univ., 1. Universalist. 2. University.

univ., 1. universal. 2. universally.

u·ni·va·lence (ū'nə-vā'ləns, yoo-niv'ə-ləns), *n.* the quality or condition of being univalent.

u·ni·va·len·cy (ū'nə-vā'lən-si, yoo-niv'ə-lən-si), *n.* univalence.

u·ni·va·lent (ū'nə-vā'lənt, yoo-niv'ə-lənt), *adj.* [< *uni-* + L. *valens*, ppr. of *valere*, to be worth], 1. in *biology*, single; unpaired: said of a chromosome. 2. in *chemistry, a*) having one valence. *b*) having a valence of one. Also, esp. for *b*, **monovalent.**

u·ni·valve (ū'nə-valv'), *n.* [*uni-* + *valve*], 1. a mollusk having a one-piece shell, as a snail. 2. such a one-piece shell. *adj.* 1. designating or having a one-piece shell. 2. having one valve only.

u·ni·valved (ū'nə-valvd'), *adj.* univalve.

u·ni·val·vu·lar (ū'ni-val'vyoo-lẽr), *adj.* univalve.

u·ni·ver·sal (ū'nə-vũr's'l), *adj.* [ME. & OFr. *universel;* L. *universalis* < *universus;* see UNIVERSE], 1. of, for, or including all or the whole of something specified; not limited or restricted. 2. of the universe; present or occurring everywhere or in all things. 3. being, or regarded as, a complete whole; entire; whole. 4. broad in knowledge, interests, ability, etc. 5. that can be used for all kinds, forms, sizes, etc.; adaptable to any use: as, a *universal* voltage regulator, calculator, etc. 6. used, intended to be used, or understood by all. 7. in *logic*, not restricted or particular in application; predicating something of every member of a class; generic. *n.* 1. in *logic, a*) a universal proposition. *b*) any of the five predicables (genus, species, difference, property, accident). *c*) a general term or concept. *d*) that which such a term or concept covers. 2. in *philosophy*, a metaphysical entity characterized by repeatability and unchanging nature through a series of changing relations, as the ego. Abbreviated **univ.**

SYN.—**universal** implies applicability to every case or individual, without exception, in the class, category, etc. concerned (a *universal* practice among primitive peoples); **general** implies applicability to all, nearly all, or most of a group or class (a *general* election); **generic**, implies applicability to every member of a class or, specifically in biology, of a genus (a *generic* name).

U·ni·ver·sal·ism (ū'nə-vũr's'l-iz'm), *n.* 1. the theological doctrine that all souls will eventually find salvation in the grace of God. 2. [u-], universality.

U·ni·ver·sal·ist (ū'nə-vũr's'l-ist), *n.* 1. a believer in Universalism. 2. [u-], a person characterized by universality, as of interests or activities.

u·ni·ver·sal·i·ty (ū'nə-vẽr-sal'ə-ti), *n.* [*pl.* UNIVERSALITIES (-tiz)], 1. quality, state, or instance of being universal. 2. complete versatility; universal range, as of knowledge, interests, abilities, etc.

u·ni·ver·sal·ize (ū'nə-vũr's'l-īz'), *v.t.* [UNIVERSALIZED (-īzd'), UNIVERSALIZING], to make universal.

universal joint (or **coupling**), a joint or coupling, as the ball-and-socket, that permits a swing of limited angle in any direction, especially one used to transmit rotary motion from one shaft to another not in line with it, as in the drive shaft of an automobile.

A

B

UNIVERSAL JOINTS
A, single; B, double

u·ni·ver·sal·ly (ū'nə-vũr's'l-i), *adv.* in a universal manner; specifically, *a*) in every instance. *b*) in every part or place. Abbreviated **univ.**

universal suffrage, suffrage for all adult citizens.

u·ni·verse (ū'nə-vũrs'), *n.* [Fr. *univers;* L. *universum*, the universe, neut. of *universus*, all together < *unus*, one + *versus*, pp. of *vertere*, to turn], 1. the totality of all the things that exist; creation; the cosmos. 2. the world. 3. an area, province, or sphere, as of thought or activity, regarded as a distinct, comprehensive system or world. —*SYN.* see **earth.**

universe of discourse, in *logic*, the totality of facts, things, or ideas implied or assumed in a given discussion, argument, or discourse.

u·ni·ver·si·ty (ū'nə-vũr'sə-ti), *n.* [*pl.* UNIVERSITIES (-tiz)], [ME. *universite;* OFr. *université;* L. *universitas*, the whole, universe, society, guild < *universus;* see UNIVERSE], 1. an educational institution of the highest level, typically with one or more undergraduate schools, or colleges, together with a program of graduate studies and a number of professional schools, and authorized to confer various degrees, as the bachelor's, master's, and doctor's: European universities generally comprise only graduate or professional schools, or both. 2. the grounds, buildings, etc. of a university. 3. the faculty and student body of a university. Abbreviated **U., Univ.**

University City, a city in Missouri, near St. Louis: pop., 51,000.

university extension, see **extension** (sense 4).

un·joint (un-joint′), ***v.t.*** 1. to separate (a joint). 2. to separate the joints of.

un·just (un-just′), ***adj.*** 1. not just or right; unfair; contrary to justice. 2. [Obs.], dishonest or unfaithful.

un·kempt (un-kempt′), ***adj.*** [*un-* + *kempt*, pp. of dial. *kemben*, to comb; ME. *kemben;* AS. *cemban* < *camb*, a comb], 1. not combed. 2. untidy; messy. 3. not polished or refined; crude; rough. —***SYN.*** see **slovenly.**

un·kenned (un-kend′; Scot. un-kent′), ***adj.*** [Obs. or Dial.], unknown; strange.

un·ken·nel (un-ken′'l), ***v.t.*** [UNKENNELED or UNKENNELLED (-'ld), UNKENNELING or UNKENNELLING], 1. to drive or release from a kennel or hole. 2. to uncover; bring to light. ***v.i.*** to come out of a kennel or hole.

un·kind (un-kīnd′), ***adj.*** not kind, sympathetic, or considerate of the feelings of others; harsh; cruel.

un·knit (un-nit′), ***v.t. & v.i.*** [UNKNITTED (-id) or UNKNIT, UNKNITTING], [ME. *unknytten;* AS. *uncnyttan*], to untie, undo, or unravel, as something knitted or knotted, or smooth out, as something wrinkled.

un·know·a·ble (un-nō′ə-b'l), ***adj.*** not knowable; that cannot be known; specifically, beyond the range of human comprehension or experience. ***n.*** something unknowable, or that which is unknowable.

the Unknowable, in *philosophy*, absolute reality, postulated as lying beyond the range of human comprehension or experience.

un·known (un-nōn′), ***adj.*** 1. not known; not in one's knowledge, understanding, or acquaintance; unfamiliar; strange. 2. not discovered, identified, or brought to knowledge: as, an *unknown* island. ***n.*** an unknown person or thing; specifically, in *mathematics*, an unknown quantity; also, a symbol for such a quantity.

Unknown Soldier, [also u- s-], an unidentified soldier who died in World War I, chosen and enshrined as representative of a nation's war dead.

un·lace (un-lās′), ***v.t.*** [UNLACED (-lāst′), UNLACING], 1. to undo the laces of; unfasten (something laced). 2. to loosen or remove the clothing of by or as by unfastening laces.

un·lade (un-lād′), ***v.t. & v.i.*** [for prin. pts. see LADE], 1. to unload (a ship, etc.). 2. to discharge (a cargo, etc.).

un·latch (un-lach′), ***v.t.*** to open or unfasten by releasing a latch. ***v.i.*** to come open or unfastened at the latch; become unlatched.

un·law·ful (un-lô′fəl), ***adj.*** 1. against the law; illegal. 2. illegitimate; bastard.

un·lay (un-lā′), ***v.t. & v.i.*** [UNLAID (-lād′), UNLAYING], [*un-* (back) + *lay, v.t.*, 14], in *nautical usage*, to untwist: said of a rope.

un·lead·ed (un-led′id), ***adj.*** 1. not covered or weighted with lead. 2. in *printing*, not having the lines separated by leads; not spaced with leads, as lines of type.

un·learn (un-lũrn′), ***v.t.*** [for prin. pts. see LEARN], [ME. *unlernen; un-* (back) + *learn*], 1. to forget (something learned). 2. to teach the contrary of (something learned, especially erroneously).

un·learn·ed (un-lũr′nid; *for 3*, un-lũrnd′), ***adj.*** 1. not learned or educated; ignorant. 2. showing a lack of learning or education. 3. *a*) not learned or mastered: as, *unlearned* lessons. *b*) known or possessed, as knowledge, without being learned. —***SYN.*** see **ignorant.**

un·leash (un-lēsh′), ***v.t.*** to release or let go from or as from a leash.

un·less (ən-les′), ***conj.*** [for *on less*, earlier *on lesse that, in lesse that*, in less that, at less than, for less], if not; in any case other than; except that; except when. ***prep.*** except; save (with a verb implied): as, *unless* disaster, nothing will result.

un·let·tered (un-let′ẽrd), ***adj.*** 1. not lettered; ignorant; uneducated. 2. illiterate. —***SYN.*** see **ignorant.**

un·like (un-līk′), ***adj.*** [ME. *unliche;* see UN- (not) & LIKE], 1. having little or no resemblance; not alike; different; dissimilar. 2. [Archaic or Dial.], unlikely. ***prep.*** different from; not like: as, this action is *unlike* him, she is *unlike* anyone I've known: see **like,** ***prep.***

un·like·li·hood (un-līk′li-hood′), ***n.*** [see -HOOD], the state or quality of being unlikely; improbability.

un·like·li·ness (un-līk′li-nis), ***n.*** unlikelihood.

un·like·ly (un-līk′li), ***adj.*** [ME. *unlikly;* prob. after ON. *ūlīkligr*], 1. not likely; improbable. 2. not likely to succeed; unpromising. ***adv.*** improbably.

un·lim·ber (un-lim′bẽr), ***v.t. & v.i.*** [*un-* (back) + *limber*], 1. to prepare (a field gun) for use by detaching the limber, or front part of the gun carriage. 2. to get ready for use or action.

un·lim·it·ed (un-lim′it-id), ***adj.*** 1. without limits or restrictions. 2. vast; illimitable. 3. not defined; indefinite.

un·link (un-liŋk′), ***v.t.*** to separate or unfasten the links of (a chain, etc.).

un·list·ed (un-lis′tid), ***adj.*** 1. not listed; not constituting an entry in a list. 2. not listed among those admitted for the purpose of trading on the stock exchange: said of securities.

un·live (un-liv′), ***v.t.*** 1. to live so as to wipe out the consequences or results of; live down. 2. to annul or wipe out (past experience, etc.).

un·load (un-lōd′), ***v.t.*** 1. to remove or take off (a load, cargo, etc.). 2. to relieve of something that troubles, burdens, etc. 3. to take a load or cargo from. 4. to remove the charge from (a gun). 5. to get rid of: as, the grocer is *unloading* his supply of sugar. ***v.i.*** to discharge or get rid of something, especially a cargo.

un·lock (un-lok′), ***v.t.*** 1. to open or unfasten (something locked). 2. to open, release, or unfasten by or as by undoing a lock. 3. to bring to light; reveal; disclose. ***v.i.*** to become unlocked.

un·looked-for (un-lookt′fôr′), ***adj.*** not looked for; not expected or foreseen.

un·loose (un-lōōs′), ***v.t.*** to loose; set free, release, undo, or unfasten.

un·loos·en (un-lōōs′'n), ***v.t.*** to loosen; unloose.

un·love·ly (un-luv′li), ***adj.*** not lovely, pleasing, or attractive; unpleasant; disagreeable; ugly.

un·luck·i·ly (un-luk′'l-i), ***adv.*** so as to be unlucky; unfortunately.

un·luck·i·ness (un-luk′i-nis), ***n.*** the quality or state of being unlucky.

un·luck·y (un-luk′i), ***adj.*** [UNLUCKIER (-i-ẽr), UNLUCKIEST (-i-ist)], not lucky; having, attended with, bringing, or involving bad luck; unfortunate, ill-fated, or ill-omened.

un·make (un-māk′), ***v.t.*** [UNMADE (-mād′), UNMAKING], 1. to cause to be as before being made; cause to revert to the original form, elements, or condition. 2. to ruin; destroy. 3. to depose from a position, rank, or authority.

un·man (un-man′), ***v.t.*** [UNMANNED (-mand′), UNMANNING], 1. to deprive of the qualities considered characteristic of a man; make weak, nervous, timid, etc.; unnerve. 2. to emasculate; castrate. 3. to deprive of men. —***SYN.*** see **unnerve.**

un·manned (un-mand′), ***adj.*** [pp. of *unman*], 1. deprived of manly qualities. 2. emasculated. 3. deprived of or lacking men. 4. uninhabited. 5. [Obs.], not tamed or broken: said of an animal, especially a hawk.

un·man·ner·li·ness (un-man′ẽr-li-nis), ***n.*** the state or quality of being unmannerly.

un·man·ner·ly (un-man′ẽr-li), ***adj.*** [ME. *unmanerli*], having or showing poor manners; rude; discourteous. ***adv.*** in an unmannerly way; rudely.

unjaded
unjoined
unjointed
unjudged
unjudicial
unjustifiable
unjustifiably
unkept
unkindled
unkindly
unkingly
unkissed
unknightly
unknot
unknotted
unknowing
unlabeled
unlabelled
unlabored
unlaboured
unlaced
unladen
unladylike
unlaid
unlamented
unlash
unlaundered
unleased
unleavened
unlessened
unlessoned
unlevel
unlevied
unlibidinous
unlicensed
unlifelike
unlighted
unlikable
unlikeable
unlined
unliquefiable
unliquefied
unlit
unlived
unliveliness
unlively
unlocated
unlocked
unlovable
unloved
unloveliness
unloving
unlubricated
unmagnified
unmaidenly
unmailable
unmalleable
unmanageable
unmanful
unmangled
unmanifested
unmanly
unmannered
unmannish
unmanufacturable
unmanufactured
unmarked
unmarketable
unmarketed
unmarred
unmarriageable
unmarried

un·mask (un-mask′, un-mäsk′), ***v.t.*** 1. to remove a mask or disguise from. 2. to disclose the true nature of; expose; reveal. ***v.i.*** 1. to take off a mask or disguise. 2. to appear in true character.

un·mean·ing (un-mēn′iŋ), ***adj.*** 1. lacking in meaning, sense, or significance. 2. showing no sense or intelligence; empty; expressionless.

un·meet (un-mēt′), ***adj.*** [ME. *unmete;* AS. *unmæte*], not meet, fit, or proper; unsuitable; unseemly.

un·men·tion·a·ble (un-men′shən-ə-b'l), ***adj.*** considered improper for polite conversation; not fit to be mentioned.

un·men·tion·a·bles (un-men′shən-ə-b'lz), ***n.pl.*** things regarded as improper to be mentioned or talked about; specifically, and humorously, undergarments or (formerly) trousers.

un·mer·ci·ful (un-mũr′si-fəl), ***adj.*** having or showing no mercy; cruel; relentless; pitiless.

un·mind·ful (un-mīnd′fəl), ***adj.*** forgetful; heedless; careless; not mindful or attentive.

un·mis·tak·a·ble (un′mis-tāk′ə-b'l), ***adj.*** that cannot be mistaken or misinterpreted; leaving room for no misunderstanding; clear; obvious.

un·mis·tak·a·bly (un′mis-tāk′ə-bli), ***adv.*** so as to be unmistakable.

un·mit·i·gat·ed (un-mit′ə-gāt′id), ***adj.*** [*un-* (not) + *mitigated*], 1. not lessened or eased: as, *unmitigated* suffering. 2. unmodified; clear-cut; absolute: as, he's an *unmitigated* villain.

un·moor (un-moor′), ***v.t.*** 1. to free (a ship, etc.) from moorings. 2. to cast off from all but one anchor. ***v.i.*** to become unmoored.

un·mor·al (un-môr′əl, un-mor′əl), ***adj.*** 1. having no morality; neither moral nor immoral; nonmoral. 2. unable to distinguish right from wrong.

un·mo·ral·i·ty (un′mô-ral′ə-ti, un′mə-ral′ə-ti), ***n.*** the state or quality of being unmoral.

un·muf·fle (un-muf′'l), ***v.t.*** [UNMUFFLED (-'ld), UNMUFFLING], 1. to remove the covering from, as the face, head, etc. 2. to remove the muffling from (oars, a drum, etc.). ***v.i.*** to take off something that muffles.

un·muz·zle (un-muz′'l), ***v.t.*** 1. to free (a dog, etc.) from a muzzle. 2. to free from restraint or censorship of what is written or spoken.

un·nat·u·ral (un-nach′ẽr-əl), ***adj.*** 1. contrary to, or at variance with, nature or what is considered normal; abnormal; strange. 2. artificial, affected, or strained. 3. characterized by a lack of emotions, attitudes, or behavior regarded as natural, normal, or right. 4. abnormally evil or cruel. —***SYN.*** see **irregular.**

un·nec·es·sar·y (un-nes′ə-ser′i), ***adj.*** not necessary or required; beyond what is needed; needless.

un·nerve (un-nũrv′), ***v.t.*** [UNNERVED (-nũrvd′), UNNERVING], to cause to feel weak, nervous, or incapable; deprive of nerve, courage, self-confidence, etc.; unman.
SYN.—**unnerve** implies a causing to lose courage or self-control as by shocking, dismaying, etc. (the screams *unnerved* her); **enervate** implies a gradual loss of strength or vitality, as because of climate, indolence, etc. (*enervating* heat); **unman** implies a loss of manly courage, fortitude, or spirit (he was so *unmanned* by the news that he broke into tears).

un·num·bered (un-num′bẽrd), ***adj.*** 1. countless; innumerable. 2. having no identifying number or numbers. 3. not counted.

un·oc·cu·pied (un-ok′yoo-pīd′), ***adj.*** 1. vacant; empty; having no occupant. 2. at leisure; idle.

un·or·gan·ized (un-ôr′gə-nīzd′), ***adj.*** 1. having no organic structure. 2. having no regular order, system, or organization. 3. not being a member of a labor union. 4. not being a member of a fraternity or sorority, as at a college.

unorganized ferment, an enzyme.

un·owned (un-ōnd′), ***adj.*** 1. having no owner. 2. not admitted or acknowledged.

un·pack (un-pak′), ***v.t.*** 1. to open and remove the contents of. 2. to take out of a package, trunk, etc. 3. to remove a pack from (a horse, etc.) or a load from (a truck, etc.). ***v.i.*** 1. to unpack a packed trunk, bag, etc. 2. to admit of being unpacked.

un·paged (un-pājd′), ***adj.*** having the pages not numbered: said of a book, etc.

un·par·al·leled (un-par′ə-leld′), ***adj.*** that has no parallel, equal, or counterpart; unmatched.

un·par·lia·men·ta·ry (un′pär-lə-men′tə-ri, un′pär-lə-men′tri), ***adj.*** contrary to parliamentary law or usage.

un·peg (un-peg′), ***v.t.*** [UNPEGGED (-pegd′), UNPEGGING], 1. to remove a peg or pegs from. 2. to unfasten or detach in this way.

un·peo·ple (un-pē′p'l), ***v.t.*** [UNPEOPLED (-p'ld), UNPEOPLING], to remove people from; remove the occupants or inhabitants from; depopulate.

un·pin (un-pin′), ***v.t.*** [UNPINNED (-pind′), UNPINNING], 1. to remove a pin or pins from. 2. to unfasten or detach in this way.

un·plait (un-plāt′), ***v.t.*** [*un-* (back) + *plait*], to unbraid.

un·pleas·ant (un-plez′'nt), ***adj.*** not pleasant; offensive; disagreeable.

un·pleas·ant·ness (un-plez′'nt-nis), ***n.*** 1. an unpleasant quality or condition. 2. an unpleasant situation, relationship, etc. 3. a quarrel or disagreement.

un·plumbed (un-plumd′), ***adj.*** 1. not plumbed, fathomed, or measured; unknown. 2. having no plumbing. 3. not sealed with lead.

un·polled (un-pōld′), ***adj.*** [*un-* (not) + *polled,* pp. of *poll, v.*], 1. not having voted. 2. not cast or entered: said of a vote.

un·pop·u·lar (un-pop′yoo-lẽr), ***adj.*** not popular; not liked or approved of by the public or by the majority.

unmastered
unmatched
unmated
unmaternal
unmatted
unmatured
unmeant
unmeasurable
unmeasured
unmechanical
unmedicated
unmeditated
unmelodious
unmelted
unmenaced
unmendable
unmended
unmensurable
unmentioned
unmercenary
unmerchantable
unmerited
unmeriting
unmethodical
unmilitary
unmilled
unmingled
unmirthful
unmistaken
unmiter
unmitigable
unmitre
unmixed
unmodified
unmodish
unmoistened
unmold
unmolested
unmollified
unmolten
unmortgaged
unmortise
unmotivated
unmounted
unmourned
unmovable
unmoved
unmoving
unmown
unmurmuring
unmusical
unmystified
unnail
unnamable
unnameable
unnamed
unnaturalized
unnavigable
unnavigated
unnecessarily
unneeded
unneedful
unnegotiable
unneighborly
unnoted
unnoticeable
unnoticed
unnurtured
unobjectionable
unobliged
unobliging
unobnoxious
unobscured
unobservant
unobserved
unobserving
unobstructed
unobtainable
unobtained
unobtruding
unobtrusive
unoccasioned
unoffended
unoffending
unoffensive
unoffered
unofficial
unofficious
unoiled
unopen
unopened
unopposed
unoppressed
unordained
unoriginal
unornamental
unornate
unorthodox
unorthodoxy
unostentatious
unowned
unoxidized
unpacified
unpaid
unpaid-for
unpainful
unpaired
unpalatable
unpardonable
unpardonably
unpardoned
unparental
unparted
unpartisan
unpasteurized
unpatched
unpatented
unpatriotic
unpatriotically
unpaved
unpeaceable
unpeaceful
unpedigreed
unpen
unpenetrated
unpensioned
unperceivable
unperceived
unperceiving
unperfected
unperformed
unperplexed
unpersuadable
unpersuaded
unpersuasive
unperturbed
unperused
unphilanthropic
unphilological
unphilosophic
unphilosophical
unphonetic
unpicked
unpicturesque
unpierced
unpile
unpitied
unpitying
unplaced
unplagued
unplanned
unplanted
unplayed
unpleasing
unpledged
unpliable
unpliant
unplighted
unploughed
unplowed
unplucked
unplug
unpoetic
unpoetical
unpointed
unpoised
unpolarized
unpolished
unpolitic
unpolitical
unpolluted
unpondered
unpopularity
unpopulated
unposted
unpractical

un·prac·ticed, un·prac·tised (un-prak′tist), ***adj.*** 1. not practiced; not habitually or repeatedly done, performed, etc. 2. not skilled or experienced; inexpert.

un·prec·e·dent·ed (un-pres′ə-den′tid), ***adj.*** having no precedent or parallel; unheard-of; novel; unexampled.

un·prej·u·diced (un-prej′oo-dist), ***adj.*** 1. without prejudice or bias; impartial. 2. not impaired.

un·pre·med·i·tat·ed (un′pri-med′ə-tāt′id), ***adj.*** done without plan or forethought; not premeditated.

un·priced (un-prīst′), ***adj.*** 1. having no fixed price. 2. priceless.

un·prin·ci·pled (un-prin′sə-p'ld), ***adj.*** characterized by lack of moral principles; unscrupulous.
 unprincipled in, uninstructed in the principles of.

un·print·a·ble (un-print′ə-b'l), ***adj.*** not printable; not fit to be printed, as because of obscenity.

un·pro·fes·sion·al (un′prə-fesh′ən-'l), ***adj.*** 1. violating the rules or ethical code of a given profession. 2. not of, characteristic of, belonging to, or connected with a profession; nonprofessional.

un·pub·lished (un-pub′lisht), ***adj.*** 1. not published. 2. in *copyright law*, designating a literary work that has neither been given public distribution nor been made available for sale in reproduced form, as of the time of registration.

un·qual·i·fied (un-kwäl′ə-fīd′), ***adj.*** 1. lacking the usual or necessary qualifications. 2. not modified, limited, or restricted: as, an *unqualified* endorsement. 3. absolute; downright: as, an *unqualified* success.

un·ques·tion·a·ble (un-kwes′chən-ə-b'l), ***adj.*** 1. not to be questioned, doubted, or disputed; certain. 2. unexceptionable.

un·ques·tion·a·bly (un-kwes′chən-ə-bli), ***adv.*** beyond any question or doubt; indisputably; certainly.

un·ques·tioned (un-kwes′chənd), ***adj.*** not questioned; specifically, *a*) not interrogated. *b*) not disputed. *c*) not subjected to inquiry.

un·qui·et (un-kwī′ət), ***adj.*** 1. not quiet; restless; disturbed; agitated. 2. anxious; uneasy. 3. disturbing.

un·quote (un-kwōt′), ***v.t. & v.i.*** [UNQUOTED (-id), UNQUOTING], to end (a quotation): generally used absolutely.

un·rav·el (un-rav″'l), ***v.t.*** [UNRAVELED or UNRAVELLED (-'ld), UNRAVELING or UNRAVELLING], 1. to undo (something woven, tangled, or raveled up); untangle or separate the threads of. 2. to make clear of confusion or involvement; solve. ***v.i.*** to become unraveled.

un·read (un-red′), ***adj.*** 1. not read: as, the book remained *unread*. 2. having read little or nothing.

un·read·a·ble (un-rēd′ə-b'l), ***adj.*** not readable; specifically, *a*) illegible. *b*) uninteresting to read. *c*) unsuitable for reading.

un·read·i·ly (un-red″'l-i), ***adv.*** in an unready manner.

un·read·i·ness (un-red′i-nis), ***n.*** the quality or state of being unready.

un·read·y (un-red′i), ***adj.*** 1. not ready; not prepared, as for action. 2. not prompt or alert; slow; hesitant. 3. [Obs. or Dial.], undressed; not fully clothed.

un·re·al (un-rē′əl, un-rēl′), ***adj.*** not real or actual; fantastic; imaginary; fanciful; visionary; insubstantial.

un·re·al·i·ty (un′ri-al′ə-ti), ***n.*** [*pl.* UNREALITIES (-tiz)], 1. the state or quality of being unreal. 2. something unreal. 3. a tendency to be visionary or fanciful.

un·rea·son (un-rē′z'n), ***n.*** lack of reason; irrationality; stupidity; absurdity.

un·rea·son·a·ble (un-rē′z'n-ə-b'l), ***adj.*** 1. not reasonable or rational; having or showing little sense or judgment. 2. excessive; immoderate; exorbitant. —***SYN.*** see **irrational.**

un·rea·son·a·bly (un-rē′z'n-ə-bli), ***adv.*** so as to be unreasonable; in an unreasonable manner.

un·rea·son·ing (un-rē′z'n-iŋ), ***adj.*** not reasoning; without reason; blind; thoughtless; irrational.

un·re·con·struc·ted (un′rē-kən-struk′tid), ***adj.*** that had not yet undergone, or was not reconciled to, the Reconstruction.

un·reel (un-rēl′), ***v.t. & v.i.*** to unwind as from a reel.

un·reeve (un-rēv′), ***v.t.*** [UNROVE (-rōv′) or UNREEVED (-rēvd′), UNREEVING], to withdraw (a rope, etc.) from a block, deadeye, or the like. ***v.i.*** 1. to become unreeved, as a rope. 2. to unreeve a rope.

un·re·gen·er·ate (un′ri-jen′ẽr-it), ***adj.*** 1. not regenerate; not spiritually reborn or converted. 2. loosely, wicked; sinful.

un·re·gen·er·at·ed (un′ri-jen′ẽr-āt′id), ***adj.*** unregenerate.

un·re·lent·ing (un′ri-len′tiŋ), ***adj.*** 1. refusing to yield or relent; inflexible; relentless. 2. without mercy or compassion; cruel; merciless. 3. not relaxing or slackening, as in effort, speed, etc.

un·re·li·gious (un′ri-lij′əs), ***adj.*** 1. irreligious. 2. not connected with or involving religion; neither religious nor irreligious; nonreligious.

un·re·mit·ting (un′ri-mit′iŋ), ***adj.*** [*un-* (not) + *remitting*], not stopping, relaxing, or slackening; incessant; persistent.

un·re·pair (un′ri-pâr′), ***n.*** disrepair.

un·re·serve (un′ri-zũrv′), ***n.*** lack of reserve or restraint; frankness; candor.

un·re·served (un′ri-zũrvd′), ***adj.*** 1. not reserved in speech or behavior; frank; candid. 2. not restricted or qualified; unlimited.

un·re·serv·ed·ly (un′ri-zũr′vid-li), ***adv.*** in an unreserved manner; without reservation.

---

unpredictable
unpreoccupied
unprepared
unprepossessing
unprescribed
unpresentable
unpreserved
unpressed
unpresumptuous
unpretending
unpretentious
unprevailing
unpreventable
unprevented
unprimed
unprincely
unprinted
unprivileged
unprizable
unprized
unprobed
unprocessed
unprocurable
unproductive
unprofaned
unprofitable
unprogressive
unprohibited
unpromising
unprompted
unpronounceable
unpronounced
unpropitiable
unpropitiated
unpropitious
unproportionate
unproportioned
unproposed
unprosperous
unprotected
unproved
unproven
unprovided
unprovoked
unprovoking
unpruned
unpunctual
unpunishable
unpunished
unpurchasable
unpure
unpurged
unpurified
unpurposed
unpursuing
unpuzzle
unquailing
unquaking
unqualifying
unquelled
unquenchable
unquenched
unquestioning
unquotable
unquoted
unraised
unransomed
unrated
unratified
unravaged
unravelment
unrazored
unreachable
unreached
unrealizable
unrealized
unreasoned
unreasoningly
unrebukable
unrebuked
unreceipted
unreceivable
unreceived
unreceptive
unreciprocated
unreclaimable
unreclaimed
unrecognizable
unrecognized
unrecommended
unrecompensed
unreconcilable
unreconciled
unrecorded
unrecounted
unrecoverable
unrecruited
unrectified
unredeemed
unredressed
unrefined
unreflected
unreflecting
unreformable
unreformed
unrefreshed
unrefreshing
unregarded
unregeneracy
unregistered
unregretted
unregulated
unrehearsed
unrelated
unrelaxed
unrelaxing
unreliability
unreliable
unreliably
unrelievable
unrelieved
unrelished
unremarked
unremedied
unremembered
unremittable
unremitted
unremorseful
unremovable
unremoved
unremunerated
unremunerative
unrendered
unrenewed
unrenounced
unrenowned
unrented
unrepaid
unrepairable
unrepaired
unrepealed
unrepentant
unrepented
unrepenting
unrepining
unreplaced
unreplenished
unreported
unrepresentative
unrepresented
unrepressed
unreprievable
unreprieved
unreprovable
unreproved
unrequested
unrequited
unresented
unresentful
unresigned
unresistant
unresisted
unresisting
unresolved
unrespectable
unrespectful
unrespited
unresponsive

---

un·rest (un-rest′), *n.* a troubled or disturbed state; restlessness; disquiet; uneasiness: sometimes applied euphemistically to a condition of angry discontent verging on revolt.
un·rid·dle (un-rid′'l), *v.t.* [UNRIDDLED (-'ld), UNRIDDLING], to solve or explain (a riddle, mystery, etc.).
un·rig (un-rig′), *v.t.* [UNRIGGED (-rigd′), UNRIGGING], to strip of rigging or of equipment, gear, etc.
un·right·eous (un-rī′chəs), *adj.* 1. not righteous; wicked; sinful. 2. not right; unjust; unfair.
un·rip (un-rip′), *v.t.* [UNRIPPED (-ript′), UNRIPPING], to rip open; take apart or detach by ripping.
un·ripe (un-rīp′), *adj.* 1. not ripe or mature; green: said of fruit, etc. 2. [Obs.], premature: said especially of death.
un·ri·valed, un·ri·valled (un-rī′v'ld), *adj.* having no rival, equal, or competitor; matchless; peerless.
un·roll (un-rōl′), *v.t.* 1. to open or extend (something rolled up). 2. to present to view; display. 3. [Rare], to remove from a roll or list. *v.i.* to become unrolled.
un·roof (un-rōōf′, un-roof′), *v.t.* to take off the roof or covering of.
un·root (un-rōōt′, un-root′), *v.t.* to uproot.
un·round (un-round′), *v.t.* in *phonetics,* 1. to pronounce without rounding the lips, as a vowel usually rounded. 2. to make (the lips) not rounded, as in pronouncing the vowel in *she.*
un·rove (un-rōv′), alternative past tense and past participle of **unreeve.** *adj.* withdrawn from a block, deadeye, or the like, as a rope.
UNRRA, U.N.R.R.A., United Nations Relief and Rehabilitation Administration.
un·ruf·fled (un-ruf′'ld), *adj.* not ruffled, disturbed, or agitated; calm; smooth; serene. —*SYN.* see **cool.**
un·rul·i·ness (un-rōō′li-nis), *n.* quality, state, or instance of being unruly.
un·rul·y (un-rōō′li), *adj.* [UNRULIER (-li-ẽr), UNRULIEST (-li-ist)], hard to control, restrain, or keep in order; disobedient; unmanageable; disorderly; refractory; not submitting or conforming to rule or discipline.
***SYN.*—unruly** implies a lack of submissiveness or obedience to rule or restraint (an *unruly* child); **unmanageable** and **ungovernable** both imply incapability of being controlled or directed (a delirious, *unmanageable* patient, an *ungovernable* temper); **intractable** and **refractory** both imply stubborn resistance to or a balking at direction, control, manipulation, etc. (an *intractable,* or *refractory,* will); **recalcitrant** implies defiant resistance to authority or control (a *recalcitrant* prisoner). —*ANT.* tractable, manageable, docile.
un·sad·dle (un-sad′'l), *v.t.* [UNSADDLED (-'ld), UNSADDLING], 1. to take the saddle off (a horse, etc.). 2. to throw from the saddle; unhorse. *v.i.* to take the saddle off a horse, etc.
un·sat·u·rat·ed (un-sach′oo-rāt′id), *adj.* 1. not saturated. 2. in *chemistry, a)* designating or of a compound in which some element possesses the capacity of combining further with other elements. *b)* designating or of a solution that is not in equilibrium with the undissolved solute. *c)* designating an organic radical with a double or triple bond that links two atoms of carbon.
un·sa·vor·y, un·sa·vour·y (un-sā′vẽr-i), *adj.* 1. without flavor; tasteless. 2. unpleasant to taste or smell. 3. offensive, disagreeable, or unpleasant, especially morally.
un·say (un-sā′), *v.t.* [UNSAID (-sed′), UNSAYING], to take back or retract (what has been said).
un·scathed (un-skāthd′), *adj.* not scathed; uninjured.
un·scram·ble (un-skram′b'l), *v.t.* [UNSCRAMBLED (-b'ld), UNSCRAMBLING], [Colloq.], to cause to be no longer scrambled, disordered, or mixed up: as, he *unscrambled* the coded message.
un·screw (un-skrōō′), *v.t.* 1. to remove a screw or screws from. 2. to remove, detach, or loosen by removing a screw or screws, or by turning. *v.i.* to become unscrewed or admit of being unscrewed.
un·scru·pu·lous (un-skrōō′pyoo-ləs), *adj.* not restrained by ideas of right and wrong; having no moral principles; not scrupulous; unprincipled.
un·seal (un-sēl′), *v.t.* 1. to break or remove the seal of. 2. to open (something sealed or closed as if sealed).
un·seam (un-sēm′), *v.t.* to open or undo the seam or seams of; rip.
un·search·a·ble (un-sũrch′ə-b'l), *adj.* that cannot be searched into or explored; mysterious; inscrutable.
un·search·a·bly (un-sũrch′ə-bli), *adv.* so as to be unsearchable.
un·sea·son·a·ble (un-sē′z'n-ə-b'l), *adj.* 1. not usual for or appropriate to the season: as, *unseasonable* heat. 2. coming, said, etc. at the wrong time; untimely; inopportune.
un·sea·son·a·bly (un-sē′z'n-ə-bli), *adv.* so as to be unseasonable; in an unseasonable manner.
un·sea·soned (un-sē′z'nd), *adj.* not seasoned; specifically, *a)* not ripened, dried, etc. by enough seasoning: as, *unseasoned* wood. *b)* not matured by experience; inexperienced. *c)* not flavored with seasoning: said of food.
un·seat (un-sēt′), *v.t.* 1. to throw or dislodge from a seat. 2. to remove from office, deprive of rank, etc. 3. to unhorse.
un·seem·ly (un-sēm′li), *adj.* not seemly, decent, or becoming; improper; indecorous. *adv.* in an unseemly manner. —*SYN.* see **improper.**
un·seen (un-sēn′), *adj.* 1. not seen; unperceived, unobserved, unnoticed, or undiscovered. 2. invisible.
un·set·tle (un-set′'l), *v.t.* [UNSETTLED (-'ld), UNSETTLING], to make unsettled, insecure, or unstable; disturb, displace, disarrange, or disorder. *v.i.* to become unsettled.
un·set·tled (un-set′'ld), *adj.* 1. not settled or orderly; disordered. 2. not stable or fixed; changeable; uncertain. 3. not decided or determined. 4. not paid, allotted, or otherwise disposed of: as, an *unsettled* debt, estate, etc. 5. having no settlers; unpopulated. 6. not established in a place or abode.
un·sex (un-seks′), *v.t.* to deprive of the qualities considered characteristic of one's sex; especially, to make unwomanly.
un·shack·le (un-shak′'l), *v.t.* [UNSHACKLED (-'ld), UNSHACKLING], 1. to loosen or remove the shackles from. 2. to free.
un·shaped (un-shāpt′), *adj.* not shaped; shapeless; unformed; unshapen.
un·shap·en (un-shā′pən), *adj.* 1. unshaped; shapeless. 2. badly shaped; misshapen, malformed, or deformed.
un·sheathe (un-shēth′), *v.t.* [UNSHEATHED (-shēthd′), UNSHEATHING], to remove (a sword, knife, etc.) from or as from a sheath or scabbard.
un·ship (un-ship′), *v.t.* [UNSHIPPED (-shipt′), UNSHIPPING], 1. to take (cargo, etc.) out of or off from a ship. 2. to remove (an oar, mast, etc.) from the proper position for use. 3. to disembark (passengers). 4. [Colloq.], to unload; get rid of.

---

unrested
unrestrainable
unrestraint
unrestricted
unretarded
unretentive
unretracted
unretrieved
unreturned
unrevealed
unrevenged
unreversed
unrevised
unrevoked
unrewarded
unrhetorical
unrhymed
unrhythmic
unrhythmical
unriddled
unrighted
unrightful
unripened
unroasted
unrobe
unromantic
unromantically
unrough
unrounded
unruled
unsaddled
unsafe
unsafety
unsaintly
unsalability
unsalable
unsalaried
unsaleability
unsaleable
unsalted
unsanctified
unsanctioned
unsanitary
unsated
unsatiable
unsatiated
unsatiating
unsatisfactorily
unsatisfactory
unsatisfied
unsatisfying
unsaved
unsavorily
unsavoriness
unsawn
unsayable
unscaled
unscanned
unscarified
unscarred
unscented
unsceptical
unscheduled
unscholarlike
unscholarly
unschooled
unscientific
unscientifically
unscorched
unscorned
unscoured
unscourged
unscraped
unscratched
unscreened
unscriptural
unsculptured
unsealed
unseated
unseaworthy
unseconded
unsectarian
unsecured
unseeded
unseeing
unseemliness
unsegmented
unseized
unselected
unselective
unselfish
unsent
unsentimental
unserved
unserviceable
unset
unsevered
unsew
unsexual
unshaded
unshadowed
unshakable
unshakeable
unshaken
unshamed
unshapely
unshared
unshaved
unshaven
unshed
unshell
unshelled
unsheltered
unshod
unshorn
unshrinkable
unshrinking
unshriven
unshroud
unshrouded
unshrunk
unshunned
unshut
unsifted

un·sight (un-sīt′), *adj.* not examined or inspected: only in *unsight, unseen,* as, he bought a car *unsight, unseen* (i.e., without having seen or examined it).
un·sight·ly (un-sīt′li), *adj.* not sightly; not pleasant to look at; ugly.
un·skilled (un-skild′), *adj.* 1. having no special skill or training. 2. requiring or using no special skill or training: as, *unskilled* labor.
un·skill·ful, un·skil·ful (un-skil′fəl), *adj.* having little or no skill or dexterity; awkward; clumsy.
un·sling (un-sliŋ′), *v.t.* [UNSLUNG (-sluŋ′), UNSLINGING], 1. to take (a rifle, etc.) from a slung position. 2. in *nautical usage,* to release from slings.
un·snap (un-snap′), *v.t.* [UNSNAPPED (-snapt′), UNSNAPPING], 1. to undo the snap or snaps of. 2. to loosen or detach by so doing.
un·snarl (un-snärl′), *v.t.* to untangle; free of snarls or entanglement.
un·so·cia·bil·i·ty (un′sō-shə-bil′ə-ti), *n.* 1. the quality or state of being unsociable. 2. unsociable behavior or character.
un·so·cia·ble (un-sō′shə-b'l), *adj.* 1. avoiding association with others; not sociable or friendly. 2. not conducive to sociability.
un·so·cia·bly (un-sō′shə-bli), *adv.* in an unsociable manner.
un·so·cial (un-sō′shəl), *adj.* having or showing a dislike for the society of others.
SYN.*—unsocial** implies an aversion for the society or company of others (an *unsocial* neighbor); **asocial** implies complete indifference to the interests, welfare, etc. of society and connotes abnormal or irresponsible self-centeredness (the *asocial* behavior of a psychopath); **antisocial** applies to that which is believed to be detrimental to or destructive of the social order, social institutions, etc. (*antisocial* racism); **nonsocial** simply expresses a negation of *social* in any of its senses (*nonsocial* fields of interest). —ANT.*** social.
un·sol·der (un-sod′ẽr), *v.t.* 1. to take apart (things soldered together). 2. to disunite; separate; sunder.
un·son·sy (un-son′si), *adj.* [*un-* + *sonsy*], [Scot. & British Dial.], bringing or indicating bad luck; ominous.
un·so·phis·ti·cat·ed (un′sə-fis′tə-kāt′id), *adj.* 1. not sophisticated; artless; simple; ingenuous; lacking worldly experience. 2. not adulterated; genuine or pure. —***SYN.*** see **naive.**
un·sound (un-sound′), *adj.* 1. not sound, whole, or perfect; not in perfect health or condition. 2. at variance with fact, truth, or reason; false; ill-founded. 3. not safe, firm, or solid; insecure. 4. not deep; light: said of sleep.
un·spar·ing (un-spâr′iŋ), *adj.* 1. not sparing or stinting; lavish; liberal; profuse. 2. not merciful or forgiving; severe.
un·speak (un-spēk′), *v.t.* [UNSPOKE (-spōk′), UNSPOKEN (-spō′kən), UNSPEAKING], to take back (something spoken); retract; unsay.
un·speak·a·ble (un-spēk′ə-b'l), *adj.* 1. that cannot be spoken. 2. unutterable; ineffable; inexpressible. 3. inexpressibly bad, evil, or objectionable.
un·speak·a·bly (un-spēk′ə-bli), *adv.* so as to be unspeakable; in an unspeakable manner.
un·sphere (un-sfêr′), *v.t.* [UNSPHERED (-sfẽrd′), UNSPHERING], to remove from its sphere or from one's sphere.
un·sta·ble (un-stā′b'l), *adj.* 1. not stable; not fixed, firm, or steady; easily upset, shifted, or unbalanced. 2. changeable; inconstant; variable; fluctuating; hence, 3. unreliable; fickle. 4. emotionally unsettled or variable. 5. in *chemistry,* tending to decompose or change into other compounds. —***SYN.*** see **inconstant.**
un·stead·y (un-sted′i), *adj.* 1. not steady, firm, or stable; shaky. 2. changeable; inconstant; wavering. 3. erratic in habits, purpose, or behavior.
un·steel (un-stēl′), *v.t.* to make no longer steeled; soften.
un·step (un-step′), *v.t.* [UNSTEPPED (-stept′), UNSTEPPING], in *nautical usage,* to remove (a mast) from its step or socket.
un·stick (un-stik′), *v.t.* [UNSTUCK (-stuk′), UNSTICKING], to cause to stick, or adhere, no longer; loosen or free, as something stuck.
un·stop (un-stop′), *v.t.* [UNSTOPPED (-stopt′), UNSTOPPING], 1. to remove the stopper from. 2. to clear (a pipe, etc.) of a stoppage or obstruction; open. 3. to open the stops of (an organ).
un·strap (un-strap′), *v.t.* [UNSTRAPPED (-strapt′), UNSTRAPPING], to loosen or remove the strap or straps of.
un·string (un-striŋ′), *v.t.* [UNSTRUNG (-struŋ′), UNSTRINGING], 1. to loosen or remove the string or strings of. 2. to remove from a string. 3. to loosen; relax. 4. to weaken or disorder; make unstrung (usually in the passive).
un·strung (un-struŋ′), past tense and past participle of **unstring.** ***adj.*** 1. weak; nervous; upset. 2. having the string or strings loosened or detached, as a bow.
un·stud·ied (un-stud′id), *adj.* 1. not got by study or conscious effort. 2. spontaneous; natural; unforced; unaffected. 3. not having studied; unlearned or unversed.
un·sub·stan·tial (un′səb-stan′shəl), *adj.* 1. not substantial; having no material substance. 2. not solid or heavy; flimsy; light. 3. unreal; visionary.
un·suit·a·bil·i·ty (un-sōōt′ə-bil′ə-ti, un-sūt′ə-bil′ə-ti), *n.* the state or quality of being unsuitable.
un·suit·a·ble (un-sōōt′ə-b'l, un-sūt′ə-b'l), *adj.* not suitable or fitting; unbecoming; inappropriate.
un·suit·a·bly (un-sōōt′ə-bli, un-sūt′ə-bli), *adv.* in an unsuitable manner.
un·sung (un-suŋ′), *adj.* 1. not sung. 2. not honored or celebrated in song or poetry.
un·sus·pect·ed (un′sə-spek′tid), *adj.* 1. not suspected; not under suspicion. 2. not imagined to be existent, probable, etc.
un·swathe (un-swāth′), *v.t.* [UNSWATHED (-swāthd′), UNSWATHING], to remove a swathe or wrappings from.
un·swear (un-swâr′), *v.t.* & *v.i.* [for prin. pts. see SWEAR], to recant or take back (something sworn to), as by another oath; abjure.
un·tan·gle (un-taŋ′g'l), *v.t.* [UNTANGLED (-g'ld), UNTANGLING], 1. to free from a snarl or tangle; disentangle. 2. to clear up; put in order; straighten out.
un·taught (un-tôt′), past tense and past participle of **unteach.** ***adj.*** 1. not taught or instructed; uneducated; ignorant. 2. got without teaching; natural.

unsighted
unsightliness
unsigned
unsilenced
unsimilar
unsingable
unsinkable
unsisterly
unsized
unslacked
unslaked
unsleeping
unsmiling
unsmirched
unsmoked
unsoaked
unsoftened
unsoiled
unsold
unsoldierly
unsolicited
unsolicitous
unsolid
unsoluble
unsolvable
unsolved
unsoothed
unsophistication
unsorted
unsought
unsounded
unsoured
unsowed
unsown
unspecified
unspeculative
unspelled
unspent
unspilled
unspilt
unspiritual
unspirituality
unspoiled
unspoilt
unspoken
unsportsmanlike
unsprung
unsquandered
unsquared
unstably
unstack
unstainable
unstained
unstalked
unstamped
unstandardized
unstarched
unstarred
unstated
unstatesmanlike
unsteadfast
unsteadily
unsteadiness
unstemmed
unsterilized
unstigmatized
unstinted
unstitched
unstrained
unstratified
unstressed
unstriated
unstripped
unstuffed
unstung
unsubdued
unsubmissive
unsubscribed
unsubsidized
unsubstantiality
unsubstantiated
unsuccess
unsuccessful
unsuggestive
unsuited
unsullied
unsunk
unsupportable
unsupported
unsuppressed
unsure
unsurmountable
unsurpassable
unsurpassed
unsusceptible
unsuspecting
unsuspicious
unsustainable
unsustained
unswayed
unsweetened
unswept
unswerving
unsworn
unsymmetrical
unsymmetry
unsympathetic
unsympathetically
unsympathizing
unsystematic
unsystematically
unsystematized
untack
untactful
untainted
untaken
untalented
untalked-of
untamable
untame
untameable
untamed
untanned
untapped
untarnished
untasted
untaxable
untaxed

un·teach (un-tēch′), *v.t.* [UNTAUGHT (-tôt′), UNTEACHING], 1. to cause to forget something learned. 2. to teach, or cause to believe, the opposite of something previously taught. 3. to teach the opposite of.
Un·ter den Lin·den (oon′tẽr den lin′dən), [G., lit., under the lindens], a famous avenue in Berlin.
Un·ter·mey·er, Louis (un′tẽr-mī′ẽr), 1885– ; American poet, journalist, anthologist, and critic.
‡**Un·ter·see·boot** (oon′tẽr-zā′bōt′), *n.* [G.], undersea boat; submarine: often shortened to **U-boat.**
Un·ter·wal·den (oon′tẽr-väl′dən), *n.* a canton of central Switzerland: pop., **34,000.**
un·thank·ful (un-thaŋk′fəl), *adj.* 1. not thankful; ungrateful. 2. thankless.
un·think (un-thiŋk′), *v.t.* [UNTHOUGHT (-thôt′), UNTHINKING], to retract mentally, rid one's mind of, or change one's mind about.
un·think·a·ble (un-thiŋk′ə-b'l), *adj.* not thinkable; that cannot be thought, conceived, or considered.
un·think·ing (un-thiŋk′iŋ), *adj.* 1. thoughtless; heedless; inconsiderate. 2. lacking the ability to think. 3. showing lack of thought.
un·thread (un-thred′), *v.t.* 1. to remove the thread or threads from. 2. to disentangle; unravel. 3. to find one's way through.
un·ti·di·ly (un-tī′d'l-i), *adv.* in an untidy manner.
un·ti·di·ness (un-tī′di-nis), *n.* the quality or state of being untidy.
un·ti·dy (un-tī′di), *adj.* [UNTIDIER (-di-ẽr), UNTIDIEST (-di-ist)], not tidy; not neat or in good order; disarranged; slovenly; careless. —*SYN.* see **slovenly.**
un·tie (un-tī′), *v.t.* [UNTIED (-tīd′), UNTYING or UNTIEING], 1. to loosen, undo, or unfasten (something tied or knotted). 2. to free or make clear, as from difficulty, restraint, etc. 3. to resolve (perplexities, etc.). *v.i.* to become untied.
un·til (un-til′, ən-til′), *prep.* [ME. *untill, ontil* < *un-* (see UNTO) + *till, til,* till, to], 1. up to the time of; till (a time or occurrence specified): as, *until* your departure. 2. before (a time specified): used with a negative, as, the show doesn't begin *until* nine o'clock. 3. [Scot. & N. Eng. Dial.], unto; to. *conj.* 1. up to the time when or that. 2. to the point, degree, or place that: as, he walked slowly *until* he was out of sight. 3. before: used with a negative, as, he didn't arrive *until* the concert was over.
un·time·li·ness (un-tīm′li-nis), *n.* the state or quality of being untimely.
un·time·ly (un-tīm′li), *adj.* 1. coming, said, done, etc. before the usual or proper time; premature: as, his was an *untimely* end. 2. coming, said, done, etc. at the wrong time; poorly timed; inopportune; unseasonable. *adv.* 1. inopportunely. 2. prematurely.
un·time·ous (un-tīm′əs), *adj.* [Scot.], untimely.
un·ti·tled (un-tī′t'ld), *adj.* 1. not having a title: as, an *untitled* book, *untitled* noblemen. 2. having no right or claim.
un·to (un′too, un′too), *prep.* [ME.; *un-* (< ON. *und,* unto, up to) + *to,* to], [Archaic or Poetic], 1. to (except as the sign of an infinitive). 2. until; till.
un·told (un-tōld′), *adj.* 1. not told, related, or revealed. 2. too great or numerous to be counted or measured; incalculable. 3. not counted or enumerated.
un·touch·a·bil·i·ty (un′tuch-ə-bil′ə-ti), *n.* 1. the state or quality of being untouchable. 2. the defiling character attributed by Hindus of high caste, especially Brahmans, to those of low caste or to non-Hindus: the doctrine of untouchability was abolished, and its practice forbidden, by constitutional law in 1949.
un·touch·a·ble (un-tuch′ə-b'l), *adj.* 1. being beyond reach of touch; out of reach. 2. not to be touched or handled, as because of fear of defilement. 3. intangible or impalpable. *n.* in India, formerly, a member of the lowest caste, whose touch was regarded as defiling to Hindus of high caste, especially to Brahmans.
un·to·ward (un-tôrd′, un-tō′ẽrd), *adj.* [*un-* (not) + *toward*], 1. hard to manage or deal with; perverse; stubborn; unruly. 2. inconvenient; unfortunate; unfavorable. 3. unseemly. 4. [Obs.], awkward.
un·trav·eled, un·trav·elled (un-trav′'ld), *adj.* 1. not used or frequented by travelers: said of a road, etc. 2. not having done much traveling, as to relatively far places.
un·tread (un-tred′), *v.t.* [for prin. pts. see TREAD], to retrace.
un·tried (un-trīd′), *adj.* 1. not tried; not attempted, tested, or proved. 2. not tried in court.
un·true (un-trōō′), *adj.* [ME. *untrewe;* AS. *untreowe; un-,* not + *treowe,* true], 1. contrary to fact or truth; false; incorrect. 2. not agreeing with or conforming to a standard, rule, or measure. 3. not faithful or loyal.
un·tru·ly (un-trōō′li), *adv.* in an untrue manner.
un·truss (un-trus′), *v.t.* 1. to undo. 2. to undress.
un·truth (un-trōōth′), *n.* [ME. *untrouthe;* AS. *untreowth; un-,* not + *treowth,* truth], 1. the quality or state of being untrue; falsity; lack of veracity. 2. an untrue statement; falsehood; lie. 3. [Obs.], unfaithfulness or disloyalty.
un·truth·ful (un-trōōth′fəl), *adj.* 1. not in accordance with the truth; untrue. 2. given to telling untruths; likely to tell lies. —*SYN.* see **dishonest.**
un·tuck (un-tuk′), *v.t.* to undo a tuck or tucks in; free from a tuck or fold.
un·tu·tored (un-tōō′tẽrd, un-tū′tẽrd), *adj.* 1. not tutored; untaught. 2. simple; naive; unsophisticated. —*SYN.* see **ignorant.**
un·twine (un-twīn′), *v.t.* [UNTWINED (-twīnd′), UNTWINING], to undo (something twined or twisted); disentangle. *v.i.* to become untwined.
un·twist (un-twist′), *v.t. & v.i.* [*un-* (back) + *twist*], to turn in the opposite direction so as to loosen or separate; untwine; unravel; disentangle.
un·used (un-ūzd′), *adj.* 1. not used; not in use. 2. unaccustomed. 3. that has never been used.
un·u·su·al (un-ū′zhōō-əl), *adj.* not usual or common; strange; rare; exceptional. —*SYN.* see **rare.**
un·ut·ter·a·ble (un-ut′ẽr-ə-b'l), *adj.* [*un-* (not) + *utterable*], 1. that cannot be pronounced. 2. that cannot be expressed or described.
un·ut·ter·a·bly (un-ut′ẽr-ə-bli), *adv.* so as to be unutterable.
un·var·nished (un-vär′nisht), *adj.* 1. not varnished. 2. plain; simple; unadorned; not embellished.
un·veil (un-vāl′), *v.t.* to remove a veil or covering from; make visible; disclose; reveal. *v.i.* to take off a veil or covering; reveal oneself.
un·voice (un-vois′), *v.t.* [UNVOICED (-voist′), UNVOICING], in *phonetics,* to utter or pronounce without voice; render surd in pronouncing: as, one normally *unvoices* the *s* in *has* when saying "has to."
un·voiced (un-voist′), *adj.* 1. not expressed; not spoken or uttered. 2. in *phonetics,* voiceless; surd.
un·war·i·ly (un-wâr′ə-li), *adv.* in an unwary manner.
un·war·i·ness (un-wâr′i-nis), *n.* the quality or state of being unwary.
un·war·y (un-wâr′i), *adj.* not wary; not watchful or cautious; careless of danger; rash; unguarded.
un·wea·ried (un-wêr′id), *adj.* 1. not weary or tired. 2. never wearying; tireless; indefatigable.
un·well (un-wel′), *adj.* not well; ailing; ill; sick.
un·wept (un-wept′), *adj.* 1. not shed: said of tears. 2. not wept for; unmourned.
un·whole·some (un-hōl′səm), *adj.* not wholesome; specifically, *a*) harmful to body or mind; unhealthful. *b*) of unsound health, or of unhealthy appearance. *c*) morally harmful or corrupt.

---

unteachable
untechnical
untempered
untenable
untenanted
untended
unterrified
untested
untether
unthanked
unthatched
untheatrical
unthought
unthoughtful
unthought-of
unthriftiness
unthrifty
unthrone
untillable
untilled
untinged
untired
untiring
untouched
untraceable
untraced
untracked
untractable
untrained
untrammeled
untrammelled
untransferable
untransferred
untranslatable
untranslated
untransmitted
untrapped
untraversable
untraversed
untreasured
untrimmed
untroubled
untrustworthy
untufted
untunable
untuned
untuneful
unturned
untwilled
untwisted
untypical
unurged
unusable
unutilizable
unuttered
unvaccinated
unvacillating
unvalidated
unvalued
unvanquished
unvaried
unvarying
unveiled
unventilated
unverifiable
unverified
unversed
unvexed
unvisited
unvitrified
unvocal
unvolatilized
unvulcanized
unwakened
unwalled
unwanted
unwarlike
unwarmed
unwarned
unwarranted
unwashed
unwasted
unwasting
unwatched
unwavering
unweakened
unweaned
unwearable
unweary
unwearying
unweathered
unweave
unwed
unwedded
unweeded
unwelded
unwetted
unwhetted
unwhipped
unwhipt

un·wield·i·ly (un-wēl′d'l-i), *adv.* in an unwieldy manner; so as to be unwieldy.
un·wield·i·ness (un-wēl′di-nis), *n.* the quality or state of being unwieldy.
un·wield·y (un-wēl′di), *adj.* 1. hard to wield, manage, handle, or deal with, as because of large size or weight, or awkward form. 2. awkward; clumsy.
un·will·ing (un-wil′iŋ), *adj.* 1. not willing or inclined; reluctant; loath; averse. 2. done, said, given, etc. reluctantly.
un·wind (un-wīnd′), *v.t.* [for prin. pts. see WIND (to turn)], 1. to wind off or undo (something wound). 2. to uncoil. 3. to straighten out or untangle (something confused or involved). *v.i.* to become unwound.
un·wise (un-wīz′), *adj.* having or showing a lack of wisdom or sound judgment; foolish; imprudent.
un·wish (un-wish′), *v.t.* 1. to cease wishing (something). 2. [Obs.], to do away with by wishing.
un·wit·ting (un-wit′iŋ), *adj.* 1. not knowing or aware; unconscious. 2. unintentional.
un·wont·ed (un-wun′tid), *adj.* [*un-* (not) + *wonted*], 1. not accustomed, familiar, or used (usually with *to*). 2. uncommon; unusual; infrequent; rare.
un·world·li·ness (un-wũrld′li-nis), *n.* 1. the quality or state of being unworldly. 2. unworldly behavior.
un·world·ly (un-wũrld′li), *adj.* 1. not concerned with worldly things. 2. not of this world; spiritual or unearthly.
un·wor·thi·ly (un-wũr′*th*ə-li), *adv.* so as to be unworthy; in an unworthy manner.
un·wor·thi·ness (un-wũr′*th*i-nis), *n.* the quality or state of being unworthy.
un·wor·thy (un-wũr′*th*i), *adj.* [UNWORTHIER (-*th*i-ẽr), UNWORTHIEST (-*th*i-ist)], 1. without merit or value; worthless. 2. not deserving (usually with *of*). 3. not fit, becoming, or suitable (usually with *of*). 4. shameful; despicable.
un·wound (un-wound′), past tense and past participle of **unwind.**
un·wrap (un-rap′), *v.t.* [UNWRAPPED (-rapt′), UNWRAPPING], to take off the wrapping of; open or undo (something wrapped). *v.i.* to become unwrapped.
un·writ·ten (un-rit′'n), *adj.* 1. not in writing; not written. 2. operating only through custom or tradition: said of laws, etc. 3. not written on; blank.
unwritten law, 1. law originating in custom, usage, court decisions, etc., rather than in the action of any law-making body: also called **common law.** 2. any rule or principle rigidly observed notwithstanding the fact that it is not law and may be contrary to law. 3. the assumed right of a person to avenge his honor or that of his family, especially in cases of seduction, adultery, or rape, as by criminally harming the person regarded as guilty.
un·yoke (un-yōk′), *v.t.* [UNYOKED (-yōkt′), UNYOKING], 1. to release from a yoke. 2. to separate or disconnect. *v.i.* 1. to become unyoked. 2. to remove a yoke.
U. of S. Afr., U. of S. A., Union of South Africa.
up (up), *adv.* [ME.; AS. *up, uppe;* akin to G. *auf* (OHG. *ūf*); IE. **upo,* from below up, as also in L. *sub* (< **eks-up-* or **ads-up-*) & L. *summus* (< **supmos*); cf. SUMMIT], 1. from a lower to a higher place; away from the ground. 2. in or on a higher position or level; off the ground. 3. in a direction or place thought of as higher or above. 4. above the horizon. 5. from an earlier to a later period or person: as, from his childhood *up.* 6. from a lower to a higher or better condition or station. 7. to a higher amount, degree, etc.: as, prices are going *up.* 8. *a*) in or into a standing position. *b*) out of bed. 9. in or into existence, action, view, evidence, consideration, etc.: as, bring *up* the matter at the next meeting. 10. into an excited or troubled state: as, she was wrought *up* by the news. 11. aside; away; by: as, we must lay *up* grain for the winter. 12. so as to be even with in space, time, degree, etc.: as, keep *up* with the times. 13. in or into a close space: as, tie *up* the package. 14. completely; entirely; thoroughly. 15. in *baseball,* to one's turn at batting. 16. in *nautical usage,* to the windward point: as, put *up* the helm. 17. in *sports,* ahead of an opponent with reference to the number of points, goals, strokes, etc. The adverb *up* is used idiomatically *a*) to form a verb-adverb combination which changes the meaning of the verb (e.g., look *up* this word, he didn't turn *up*). *b*) as an intensive with verbs (e.g., dress *up,* eat *up,* clean *up*). *c*) as a virtually meaningless element colloquially added to almost any verb (e.g., light *up* a cigarette, write *up* a story). *prep.* 1. to, toward, or at a higher place on or in. 2. to, toward, or at a higher condition or station on or in: as, *up* the social ladder. 3. to, toward, or at a point farther along: as, *up* the road. 4. toward the source of (a river, etc.); in a direction contrary to that of the movement of. 5. in or toward the interior, often the more elevated part, of (a country, territory, etc.). *adj.* 1. tending or directed toward a position that is higher or is regarded as being higher. 2. in a higher position, condition, or station. 3. *a*) above the ground. *b*) above the horizon. 4. advanced in amount, degree, etc.: as, rents are *up.* 5. *a*) in a standing position. *b*) out of bed. 6. in an active, excited, or agitated state: as, the wind is *up,* her anger was *up.* 7. even with in space, time, degree, etc. 8. living or located in the inner or elevated part of a country, territory, etc. 9. at an end; over: as, the jig is *up.* 10. at stake in gambling: as, he has two dollars *up* on the horse. 11. [Colloq.], going on; happening: as, what's *up?* 12. in *baseball,* at bat. 13. in *golf,* on the green: said of the ball. 14. in *sports, a*) ahead of an opponent with reference to the number of points, goals, strokes, etc. *b*) needed for winning or ending the game: said of the specified number of points, etc. As an adjective, *up* is usually predicative. *n. usually pl.* a person or thing that is up; specifically, *a*) an upward slope. *b*) an upward movement or course. *c*) an upbound train, bus, etc. Usually distinguished from, and used in combination with, *down.* *v.i.* [UPPED (upt), UPPING], [Colloq.], to get up; rise. *v.t.* [Colloq.], 1. to put up, lift up, or take up. 2. to increase, or cause to rise: as, *up* prices. 3. to raise, or bet more than (a preceding bet or bettor).
it's all up with, there is no further hope for; the end is near for.
on the up and up, [Slang], open and aboveboard; honest.
up against, [Colloq.], face to face with; confronted with: as he's *up against* trouble now.
up against it, [Colloq.], in difficulty; especially, in financial difficulty.
up and doing, busy; active.
up for, 1. presented or considered for (an elective office, an election, etc.). 2. before a court for (trial).
up on (or **in**), [Colloq.], well informed concerning or well versed in.
ups and downs, changes in fortune.
up to, [Colloq.], 1. occupied with; doing; scheming; devising. 2. equal to; capable of (doing, undertaking, etc.). 3. dependent upon the decision or action of. 4. incumbent upon.
up (up), *adv.* [phonetic respelling of *ap*iece, influenced by prec. *up*], apiece; each: as, the score is seven *up.*
up- (up), [ME. & AS. *up-,* identical with *up, adv.*], a combining form meaning *up,* as in *upgrade, uphill.*
UP, U.P., United Press: see **United Press International.**
up., 1. upper. 2. under proof (of alcohol): also **u.p.**
up-and-com·ing (up′'n-kum′iŋ), *adj.* [Colloq.], enterprising, alert, and promising.
up-and-down (up′'n-doun′), *adj.* 1. going alternately up and down, to and fro, etc. 2. variable; fluctuating.
U·pan·i·shad (o͞o-pan′i-shad′, o͞o-pän′i-shäd′), *n.* [Sans. *upaniṣad*], one of a group of late Vedic metaphysical treatises dealing with man in his relation to the universe and emphasizing the pantheism of the ancient Hindu religion.
u·pas (ū′pəs), *n.* [short for Malay *pohon upas,* tree of poison], 1. a tall Javanese tree whose whitish bark yields a poisonous milky juice used as an arrow poison. 2. the juice of this tree. 3. something harmful or deadly in its influence.
up·bear (up-bâr′), *v.t.* [for prin. pts. see BEAR], to hold, raise, or carry aloft; bear up; support.
up·beat (up′bēt′), *n.* in *music,* an unaccented beat, especially when on the last note of a bar.
up·borne (up-bôrn′, up-bōrn′), past participle of **upbear.** *adj.* borne up; lifted or carried aloft; elevated.
up-bow (up′bō′), *n.* a stroke on a violin, etc. in which the bow is drawn across the strings from the tip to the handle: symbol (V).
up·braid (up-brād′), *v.t.* [ME. *upbreiden;* AS. *up-bregdan; up-,* up + *bregdan,* to pull, shake, weave; cf. BRAID], 1. to scold or chide for some wrongdoing, offense, or error; take to task; reprove; reproach. 2.

unwifelike
unwifely
unwilled
unwincing
unwinking
unwisdom
unwished
unwished-for
unwithered
unwithering
unwitnessed
unwomanlike
unwomanly
unwon
unwooded
unwooed
unworkable
unworked
unworkmanlike
unworn
unworshiped
unworshipped
unwounded
unwoven
unwreathe
unwrinkle
unwrinkled
unwrought
unwrung
unyielding
unyouthful
unzealous

to serve as a reproach to. *v.i.* to speak with reproach. —*SYN.* see **scold.**
up·braid·ing (up-brād′iŋ), *n.* the act or utterance of a person who upbraids; reproof. *adj.* reproachful.
up·bring·ing (up′briŋ′iŋ), *n.* [obs. *upbring,* to rear, train + *-ing*], the training and education received during childhood; rearing; bringing up; nurture.
up·build (up-bild′), *v.t.* [for prin. pts. see BUILD], to build up (in various senses).
up·burst (up′būrst′), *n.* an upward burst.
up·cast (up′kast′, up′käst′), *n.* 1. a casting upward or being cast upward. 2. something cast or thrown up. 3. in *mining,* a ventilating shaft. *adj.* 1. thrown upward. 2. turned or directed upward.
up·coun·try (up′kun′tri), *adj.* 1. of or located in the interior of a country; inland; hence, 2. rustic; unsophisticated: used derogatorily. *n.* the interior of a country. *adv.* in or toward the interior of a country.
up·date (up-dāt′), *v.t.* [for prin. pts. see DATE], to bring up to date; make conform to the most recent facts, methods, ideas, etc.
up·end (up-end′), *v.t. & v.i.* to set, turn, or stand on end.
up·grade (up′grād′), *n.* an upward slope or incline. *adj. & adv.* uphill. *v.t.* [for prin. pts. see GRADE], to raise to a higher grade, higher rate of pay, etc.
on the upgrade, 1. rising. 2. progressing; improving.
up·growth (up′grōth′), *n.* 1. the process of growing up; development. 2. something that grows up.
up·heav·al (up-hē′v′l), *n.* 1. a heaving up or being heaved up, as by volcanic eruption. 2. a sudden, violent change or disturbance in affairs.
up·heave (up-hēv′), *v.t.* [for prin. pts. see HEAVE], to heave or lift up; raise from beneath. *v.i.* to rise as if forced up; be raised from beneath.
up·held (up-held′), past tense and past participle of **uphold.**
up·hill (up′hil′), *adj.* 1. passing to a higher level; going or sloping up; rising. 2. calling for prolonged effort; tiring; difficult. 3. located on high ground. *n.* a sloping rise or ascent. *adv.* to or toward a higher level on or as if on an incline; upward at an angle.
up·hold (up-hōld′), *v.t.* [for prin. pts. see HOLD], 1. to hold up; raise. 2. to keep from falling; support. 3. to give moral or spiritual support or encouragement to. 4. to decide in favor of; agree with and support against opposition; confirm; sustain. —*SYN.* see **support.**
up·hol·ster (up-hōl′stēr), *v.t.* [back-formation < *upholsterer*], 1. to fit out (furniture) with coverings, springs, cushions, padding, etc. 2. to furnish (a room) with curtains, carpets, etc.
up·hol·ster·er (up-hōl′stēr-ēr), *n.* [altered < earlier *upholdster;* altered < ME. *upholder,* auctioneer, tradesman], a person whose business is upholstering furniture.
up·hol·ster·y (up-hōl′stēr-i, up-hōl′stri), *n.* [*pl.* UPHOLSTERIES (-iz, -striz)], [< *upholster*], 1. the fittings and material used in upholstering. 2. the business or work of an upholsterer.
u·phroe (ū′frō, ū′vrō), *n.* a euphroe.
UPI, United Press International.
up·keep (up′kēp′), *n.* 1. the act of keeping up buildings, equipment, etc.; maintenance. 2. the condition of being kept up; repair. 3. the cost of maintenance.
up·land (up′lənd, up′land′), *n.* land elevated above other land, as of a region. *adj.* of or situated in upland.
upland plover, a large, short-billed sandpiper found in the fields and uplands of eastern North America.
up·lift (up-lift′; *for n.,* up′lift′), *v.t.* 1. to raise aloft; lift up; elevate. 2. to raise to a higher moral, social, or spiritual level or condition. *n.* 1. the act or process of lifting up; elevation; raising. 2. the act or process of raising to a higher moral, social, or spiritual level. 3. any influence, movement, etc. that tends or attempts to raise morally, spiritually, etc. 4. a type of brassiere designed to lift and support the breasts: in full, **uplift brassiere.** 5. in *geology,* an upheaval.
up·most (up′mōst′), *adj.* uppermost.
U·po·lu (ōō-pō′lōō), *n.* an island of Western Samoa, in the South Pacific: area, 430 sq. mi.; pop. (with Savaii), 97,000; chief town, Apia.
up·on (ə-pon′, ə-pôn′), *prep.* [ME. < ON. *upp* (akin to Eng. *up*) + *on,* on], on (in various senses), or up and on: used generally as an equivalent of *on,* without much distinction except for reasons of rhythm, etc. *adv.* 1. on: used only to complete the idea of a verb, as the canvas has not been painted *upon.* 2. [Obs.], on it; on one's person. 3. [Obs.], thereupon; thereafter.
up·per (up′ēr), *adj.* [ME.; orig., compar. of *up*], 1. higher in place or physical position. 2. farther inland. 3. higher in rank, authority, dignity, etc.; superior. 4. worn outside others; outer: said of clothes. 5. [U-], in *geology,* more recent; later: used of a division of a period, as, *Upper* Cambrian. *n.* 1. the part of a shoe or boot above the sole. 2. *pl.* cloth gaiters. 3. [Colloq.], an upper berth. Abbreviated **U., u., up.**
on one's uppers, [Colloq.], 1. wearing worn-out shoes. 2. in need or want; poor; shabby.
Upper Austria, a province in northern Austria: area, 4,626 sq. mi.; pop., 1,109,000; capital, Linz.
Upper Canada, a former province of Canada: now a part of the province of Ontario: abbreviated **U.C.**
up·per-case (up′ēr-kās′), *adj.* 1. capital: said of a letter, as distinguished from *small,* or *lower-case.* 2. in *printing,* of the upper case.
upper case, capital letters: abbreviated **u.c.**
up·per-class (up′ēr-klas′, up′ēr-kläs′), *adj.* 1. of or characteristic of the upper class, or social class above the middle class. 2. of or characteristic of the junior and senior classes in a high school, college, etc.
up·per·class·man (up′ēr-klas′mən, up′ēr-kläs′mən), *n.* [*pl.* UPPERCLASSMEN (-mən)], a student in the junior or senior class of a high school, college, etc.
upper crust, 1. the top crust, as of a loaf of bread. 2. [Colloq.], people having wealth and high social position.
up·per·cut (up′ēr-kut′), *n.* in *boxing,* a short, swinging blow directed upward, as to the chin. *v.t. & v.i.* [UPPERCUT, UPPERCUTTING], to hit with an uppercut.
upper hand, the position of advantage or control.
Upper House, [often u- h-], in a legislature having two branches, that branch which is usually smaller and less representative, as the British House of Lords.
up·per·most (up′ēr-mōst′), *adj.* highest in place, position, power, authority, influence, etc.; topmost; predominant; foremost. *adv.* in the highest place, position, rank, etc.; at the top; first.
Upper Silesia, a former province of Prussia (part of Silesia) divided between Germany and Poland after World War I and again after World War II.
Upper Volta, a country in western Africa, north of Ghana: a former French colony, it is now a member of the French Community: area, 105,800 sq. mi.; pop., 3,567,000; capital, Ouagadougou.
upper works, in *nautical usage,* those parts of a loaded ship that project above the surface of the water.
up·pish (up′ish), *adj.* [< *up, adv.* + *-ish*], [Colloq.], inclined to be haughty, arrogant, snobbish, etc.
up·pi·ty (up′ə-ti), *adj.* [Colloq.], uppish.
Upp·sa·la (oop′sä′lä; Eng. up′sä′lə), *n.* a city in eastern Sweden: pop., 75,000: also spelled **Upsala.**
up·raise (up-rāz′), *v.t.* to raise up; lift; elevate.
up·rear (up-rêr′), *v.t.* 1. to rear up; raise. 2. to exalt. 3. to bring up. *v.i.* to rise up.
up·right (up′rīt′; *also, for adv.,* up-rīt′), *adj.* [ME.; AS. *upriht;* see UP & RIGHT], 1. standing, pointing, or directed straight up; in a vertical or perpendicular position; erect. 2. honest; just; honorable. *adv.* in an upright position or direction. *n.* 1. the state of being upright or vertical. 2. something having an upright position; vertical part or member. 3. an upright piano. 4. *pl.* in *football,* the goal posts.
SYN.—**upright** implies an unbending moral straightness and integrity; **honest** implies complete fairness and openness in one's dealings with others and stresses freedom from deceit or fraud; **just,** of things, stresses fairness or equitableness and, of persons, high moral rectitude; **honorable** implies a keen sense of, and strict adherence to, what is considered morally or ethically right, especially in one's social class, profession, position, etc.; **scrupulous** implies a meticulous conscientiousness with regard to the morality of one's actions, aims, etc. —*ANT.* dishonest, unjust.
upright piano, a piano with a rectangular body mounted vertically.
up·rise (up-rīz′; *for n.,* up′rīz′), *v.i.* [UPROSE (-rōz′), UPRISEN (-riz′′n), UPRISING], 1. to get up; rise. 2. to move or slope upward; ascend. 3. to rise into view, being, or activity. 4. to be or become erect or upright. 5. to increase in size, volume, etc.; swell, as sound. 6. to rise in revolt. *n.* 1. the act or process of rising up. 2. an upward slope or ascent.
up·ris·ing (up′rīz′iŋ, up-rīz′iŋ), *n.* 1. the action of rising up. 2. an upward slope or ascent. 3. a revolt. —*SYN.* see **rebellion.**
up·roar (up′rôr′, up′rōr′), *n.* [D. *oproer,* a stirring up], 1. violent disturbance or commotion, especially one accompanied by loud, confused noise, as of shouting; tumult. 2. loud, confused noise; din. —*SYN.* see **noise.**
up·roar·i·ous (up-rôr′i-əs, up-rō′ri-əs), *adj.* 1. making, or characterized by, an uproar. 2. loud and boisterous, as laughter; noisy and confused, as sounds.
up·root (up-rōōt′, up-root′), *v.t.* 1. to tear up by the roots. 2. to destroy or remove utterly; eradicate.
up·rose (up-rōz′), past tense of **uprise.**
up·rouse (up-rouz′), *v.t.* to rouse; stir up; awaken.
Up·sa·la (oop′sä′lä; Eng. up′sä′lə), *n.* Uppsala.
up·set (up-set′; *for n., and occas. adj.,* up′set′), *v.t.* [UPSET, UPSETTING], [ME. *upsetten;* see UP & SET], 1. to tip over; overturn; capsize. 2. to disturb or disorder the functioning or course of: as, the accident *upset* the railroad's schedule. 3. to defeat or overthrow, especially unexpectedly. 4. to perturb; discompose; distress: as, his death *upset* us all. 5. in *mechanics, a*) to shorten and thicken (a red-hot iron) by beating on the end; swage. *b*) to shorten (a tire) in the process of resetting it. *v.i.* to become overturned or upset. *n.* 1. an upsetting or being upset; overturn. 2. a disturbance; disorder; derangement. 3. an overthrow or defeat, specifically one that is

unexpected. 4. in *mechanics, a)* a swage used for upsetting. *b)* an upset piece or part. ***adj.*** 1. [Rare], set up; erected. 2. established; fixed: as, an *upset* price. 3. tipped over; overturned. 4. disturbed; disordered. 5. perturbed; distressed.

SYN.—**upset** is the ordinary word implying a toppling, disorganization, etc. as a result of a loss of balance or stability (to *upset* a glass, one's plans, etc., emotionally *upset*); **overturn** implies a turning of a thing upside down or flat on its side and, in extended use, connotes the destruction of something established (to *overturn* a chair, a government, etc.); **capsize** specifically implies the overturning or upsetting of a boat.

upset price, the price fixed as the minimum at which something will be sold, as at an auction.

up·shot (up'shot'), ***n.*** [orig., the final shot in an archery match], the conclusion; result; outcome.

up·side (up'sīd'), ***n.*** the upper side or part.

up·side-down (up'sīd'doun'), ***adj.*** that is upside down: used attributively, as, *upside-down* logic.

upside down, [ME. *up so doun,* lit., up as if down: altered through popular etym.], 1. with the upper part underneath or turned over. 2. in disorder or confusion; topsy-turvy.

up·si·lon (ūp'sə-lon', ūp'sə-lən; Brit. ūp-sī'lən), ***n.*** [Gr. *ypsilon,* lit., simple *u*: so called in contrast with the spelling *oi,* which represented the sound in Late Gr.], the twentieth letter of the Greek alphabet (Υ, υ), corresponding to English *U, u,* or *Y, y:* see **alphabet,** table.

up·spring (up-spriŋ'; *for n.,* up'spriŋ'), ***v.i.*** [for prin. pts. see SPRING], to spring up (in various senses). ***n.*** a spring upward.

up·stage (up'stāj'), ***adv.*** toward or at the rear of the stage. ***adj.*** 1. of or having to do with the rear of the stage. 2. [Colloq.], haughtily or disdainfully aloof, conceited, or supercilious. ***v.t.*** 1. to place oneself on stage so as to hinder the audience's view of (a fellow actor). 2. [Colloq.], to treat in a haughty or disdainful manner.

up·stairs (up'stârz'), ***adv.*** 1. up the stairs; so as to climb a flight of stairs. 2. in, on, or toward an upper floor. ***adj.*** of or on an upper floor. ***n.*** an upper story or stories, especially the one next above the first floor.

kick upstairs, [Colloq.], to promote so as to get rid of.

up·stand·ing (up-stan'diŋ), ***adj.*** 1. erect. 2. having a well-formed figure and good posture. 3. honorable; straightforward; upright.

up·start (up'stärt'), ***n.*** a person who has recently come into wealth, power, importance, etc.; especially, such a person who is pushing, presumptuous, etc.; parvenu. ***adj.*** 1. newly rich or powerful. 2. of or characteristic of an upstart.

up·start (up-stärt'), ***v.i. & v.t.*** to start up or cause to start up.

up·state (up'stāt'), ***adj.*** designating, of, or from the more northerly part of a State, or that part of a State lying away from the coast: used especially of New York. ***n.*** such a part of a State; especially, the northern part of New York. ***adv.*** in or toward such a part of a State.

up·stat·er (up'stāt'ẽr), ***n.*** an upstate inhabitant.

up·stream (up'strēm'), ***adv.*** in or toward the source or upper part of a stream or current; against the stream or current. ***adj.*** 1. of or situated at the upper part of a stream. 2. moving or directed against the stream or current.

up·stroke (up'strōk'), ***n.*** 1. an upward stroke or movement. 2. a line, brushmark, etc. made with an upward stroke.

up·surge (up-sũrj'; *for n.,* up'sũrj'), ***v.i.*** to surge up. ***n.*** a surge upward.

up·sweep (up'swēp'; *for v.,* up-swēp'), ***n.*** 1. a sweep or curve upward, as of the underjaw of the bulldog. 2. an upswept hair-do. ***v.t. & v.i.*** [UPSWEPT (-swept'), UPSWEEPING], to sweep or curve upward.

up·swell (up-swel'), ***v.i.*** [for prin. pts. see SWELL], to swell up.

up·swept (up'swept'), ***adj.*** 1. curved or sloped upward; having an upsweep. 2. designating or of a style of hair-do in which the hair is combed up smoothly in the back and piled on the top of the head.

up·swing (up'swiŋ'; *for v.,* up-swiŋ'), ***n.*** 1. a swing, trend, or movement upward. 2. an advance or improvement. ***v.i.*** [for prin. pts. see SWING], 1. to swing or move upward. 2. to advance or improve.

up·take (up'tāk'), ***n.*** 1. the act of lifting or taking up. 2. the act of or capacity for understanding or comprehending. 3. a pipe carrying smoke and gases from a furnace to its chimney. 4. a ventilating shaft or pipe.

up·throw (up'thrō'), ***n.*** a throwing up; upheaval.

up·thrust (up'thrust'), ***n.*** 1. an upward push or thrust. 2. an upheaval of a part of the earth's crust.

up·tilt (up-tilt'), ***v.t.*** to tilt up.

up-to-date (up'tə-dāt'), ***adj.*** 1. extending to the present time; using or including the latest facts, methods, ideas, data, etc. 2. keeping up with or conforming to what is most recent or modern in style, taste, manners, methods, information, etc.

up·town (up'toun'), ***adj.*** of, going toward, or in the upper part of a city or town, or the part away from the main business district. ***adv.*** in or toward the upper part of a city or town. ***n.*** the upper part of a city or town. Cf. **downtown.**

up·turn (up-tũrn'; *for n.,* up'tũrn'), ***v.t. & v.i.*** to turn up or over. ***n.*** an upward turn, curve, or trend.

up·turned (up-tũrnd', up'tũrnd'), ***adj.*** 1. turned upward. 2. turned over, or upside down. 3. having the end or tip turned upward: as, an *upturned* nose.

U.P.W.A., 1. United Packinghouse Workers of America: a C.I.O. labor union. 2. United Public Workers of America: a labor union.

up·ward (up'wẽrd), ***adv.*** [ME.; AS. *upweard;* see UP & -WARD], 1. to or toward a higher place or position. 2. to or toward the source, center, interior, etc. 3. toward the body, head, or upper parts: as, the swelling spread from his legs *upward.* 4. toward a higher degree, amount, price, rank, etc. 5. on into future years or later life. 6. in a higher or the highest place or position. 7. more; above; over. ***adj.*** directed or moving toward, or situated in, a higher position.

upward of, more than.

up·wards (up'wẽrdz), ***adv.*** [ME. *upwardes;* AS. *upweardes; upweard,* upward + adv. genit. -*(e)s*], upward.

Ur (ũr), ***n.*** 1. an ancient city of the Sumerians, on the Euphrates River. 2. the district surrounding this city.

ur-, uro-.

ur- (o͞or), [G.], a prefix meaning *original, primitive.*

Ur, in *chemistry,* uranium.

u·rae·mi·a (yoo-rē'mi-ə, yoo-rēm'yə), ***n.*** uremia.

u·rae·mic (yoo-rē'mik), ***adj.*** uremic.

u·rae·us (yoo-rē'əs), ***n.*** [Mod. L. < Gr. *ouraios,* of a tail < *oura,* a tail], the figure of the sacred asp or cobra on the headdress of ancient Egyptian rulers.

HEADDRESS WITH URAEUS

U·ral (yoor'əl), ***n.*** 1. ***pl.*** a mountain range in the U.S.S.R., between Europe and Asia: divided into North Urals, Middle Urals, and South Urals: highest peak, Tel-pos-iz, 5,535 ft. 2. a river flowing from the South Urals into the Caspian: length, 1,400 mi. ***adj.*** designating or of these mountains or this river.

U·ral-Al·ta·ic (yoor'əl-al-tā'ik), ***adj.*** 1. of the region of the Ural and Altai Mountains. 2. designating or of a postulated group of languages which includes, among others, the Uralic and Altaic families. 3. of the peoples using these languages. ***n.*** this group of languages.

U·ra·li·an (yoo-rā'li-ən), ***adj. & n.*** Uralic.

U·ra·lic (yoo-rā'lik), ***adj.*** designating or of a family of languages including the Finno-Ugric and Samoyed subfamilies. ***n.*** this family of languages.

u·ral·ite (yoor'əl-īt'), ***n.*** [G. *uralit;* see URAL & -ITE], amphibole, altered from pyroxene, found originally in the Ural Mountains.

u·ral·it·ic (yoor'ə-lit'ik), ***adj.*** of or like uralite.

u·ra·nal·y·sis (yoor'ə-nal'ə-sis), ***n.*** urinalysis.

U·ra·ni·a (yoo-rā'ni-ə), ***n.*** [L.; Gr. *Ourania,* lit., the heavenly one], 1. in *Greek mythology,* the Muse of astronomy. 2. an epithet applied to Aphrodite.

U·ra·ni·an (yoo-rā'ni-ən), ***adj.*** of Uranus.

u·ran·ic (yoo-ran'ik), ***adj.*** [< Gr. *ouranos,* heaven, sky; + *-ic*], of or having to do with the heavens; celestial; astronomical.

u·ran·ic (yoo-ran'ik), ***adj.*** [< *uranium* + *-ic*], of or containing uranium, especially in its higher valence.

u·ran·i·nite (yoo-ran'ə-nīt'), ***n.*** [< *uranium*], a black, opaque mineral containing uranium, radium, thorium, lead, and, sometimes, the gases helium and argon: its massive variety is called *pitchblende.*

u·ra·nite (yoor'ə-nīt'), ***n.*** [G. *uranit;* see URANIUM & -ITE], any of a group of native phosphates of uranium with calcium and copper.

u·ra·nit·ic (yoor'ə-nit'ik), ***adj.*** of or containing uranite or uranium.

u·ra·ni·um (yoo-rā'ni-əm), ***n.*** [Mod. L. < *Uranus,* the planet], a very hard, heavy, moderately malleable, radioactive metallic chemical element: it is found only in combination, chiefly in pitchblende, and is important in work on atomic energy, especially in the isotope of mass number 235 (**U-235**), which can undergo continuous fission, and in the more plentiful U-238, from which plutonium is produced: symbol, U; at. wt., 238.07; at. no., 92.

uranium metals, the actinide series: a former name.

u·ra·nog·ra·phy (yoor'ə-nog'rə-fi), ***n.*** [Gr. *ouranographia* < *ouranos*, heaven + *graphein*, to write], the branch of astronomy dealing with the description of the heavens and celestial bodies, as by the construction of maps, charts, etc., especially of the fixed stars.

u·ra·nol·o·gy (yoor'ə-nol'ə-ji), ***n.*** [< Gr. *ouranos*, heaven; + *-logy*], 1. a written description of the heavens and celestial bodies. 2. uranography.

u·ra·nom·e·try (yoor'ə-nom'ə-tri), ***n.*** [< Gr. *ouranos*, heaven; + *-metry*], 1. the measurement of the heavens. 2. a map, chart, or listing of celestial bodies, especially of visible fixed stars.

u·ra·nous (yoor'ə-nəs), ***adj.*** [< *uranium* + *-ous*], of or containing uranium, especially in its lower valence.

U·ra·nus (yoor'ə-nəs), ***n.*** [LL.; Gr. *Ouranos* < *ouranos*, heaven], 1. in *Greek mythology*, a god who was the personification of Heaven, regarded as the husband or son of Gaea (Earth) and father of the Titans, Furies, and Cyclopes: he was overthrown by his son Cronus (Saturn). 2. a planet of the solar system, seventh in distance from the sun: diameter, c. 31,000 mi.; diurnal rotation, apparently 10 hrs., 45 min.; period of revolution, c. 84 yrs.; symbol, ♅.

u·ra·nyl (yoor'ə-nil), ***n.*** [< *uranium* + *-yl*], the divalent radical UO_2, present in many compounds of uranium.

u·ra·nyl·ic (yoor'ə-nil'ik), ***adj.*** of, like, or containing uranyl.

u·rase (yoor'ās, yoor'āz), ***n.*** urease.

u·rate (yoor'āt), ***n.*** a salt of uric acid.

ur·ban (ũr'bən), ***adj.*** [L. *urbanus* < *urbs*, a city], 1. of, in, constituting, or comprising a city or town. 2. characteristic of the city as distinguished from the country; citified. Opposed to *rural*.

Ur·ban II (ũr'bən), 1042?–1099; Pope (1088–1099); excommunicated Henry IV and Philip I of France.

Ur·ban·a (ũr-ban'ə), ***n.*** a city in east central Illinois: pop., 27,000.

urban district, in the British Isles, a densely populated community, like a borough but lacking a borough charter.

ur·bane (ũr-bān'), ***adj.*** [Fr. *urbain;* L. *urbanus;* see URBAN], polite and suave; smooth and polished in manner; courteous and affable. —***SYN.*** see **suave.**

ur·ban·i·ty (ũr-ban'ə-ti), ***n.*** [*pl.* URBANITIES (-tiz)], [Fr. *urbanité;* L. *urbanitas*], 1. the quality of being urbane. 2. *pl.* civilities, courtesies, or amenities.

ur·ban·i·za·tion (ũr'bən-i-zā'shən, ũr'bən-ī-zā'shən), ***n.*** an urbanizing or being urbanized.

ur·ban·ize (ũr'bən-īz'), ***v.t.*** [URBANIZED (-īzd'), URBANIZING], 1. to change from rural to urban in character; make like or characteristic of a city. 2. [Rare], to make urbane; polish; refine.

ur·ce·o·late (ũr'si-ə-lit, ũr'si-ə-lāt'), ***adj.*** [< L. *urceolus*, dim. of *urceus*, a pitcher], shaped like a pitcher or urn.

ur·chin (ũr'chin), ***n.*** [ME. *urchone, irchoun;* OFr. *ireçon, irechon* < L. *ericius*, a hedgehog < *er*, hedgehog, for earlier **her* (akin to Gr. *chēr*) < IE. base **ĝher-*, to bristle, be stiff, seen also in L. *horrere* (cf. HORROR), etc.], 1. [Archaic or Dial.], a hedgehog. 2. a sea urchin. 3. a small boy, or any youngster, especially one who is roguish or mischievous. 4. [Obs.], an elf.

Ur·du (oor'dōō, oor-dōō', ũr-dōō'), ***n.*** [Hind. *urdū*, short for *zaban-i-urdū*, language of the camp; Per. *urdu*, camp; Turk. *ordu;* cf. HORDE], 1. a language used by Moslems in India: it developed from Hindustani but with Arabic characters. 2. Hindustani.

-ure (ẽr), [Fr.; L. *-ura*], a suffix meaning *act* or *result of an action, agent* or *instrument of action, state of being*, etc., as in *exposure, composure.*

u·re·a (yoo-rē'ə, yoor'i-ə), ***n.*** [Mod. L.; Fr. *urée;* Gr. *ouron*, urine], a very soluble, crystalline solid, $CO(NH_2)_2$, found in the urine of mammals and produced synthetically: used in making plastics, adhesives, etc.

u·re·al (yoo-rē'əl, yoor'i-əl), ***adj.*** of or containing urea.

urea resins, a group of resins produced by the interaction of urea and formaldehyde.

u·re·ase (yoor'i-ās', yoor'i-āz'), ***n.*** [< *urea* + *-ase*], an enzyme that promotes the hydrolysis of urea into ammonium carbonate: also **urase.**

u·re·do (yoo-rē'dō), ***n.*** [L., a blight, blast, burning itch < *urere*, to burn], hives; urticaria.

u·re·do·stage (yoo-rē'dō-stāj'), ***n.*** [*uredo* + *stage*], in *botany*, the stage in which rust fungi develop one-celled summer spores with reddish or yellowish spots.

u·re·id (yoor'i-id), ***n.*** a ureide.

u·re·ide (yoor'i-īd', yoor'i-id), ***n.*** any of several compounds derived by the elimination of water in the reaction of urea with an acid or aldehyde.

u·re·mi·a (yoo-rē'mi-ə, yoo-rēm'yə), ***n.*** [Mod. L. < Gr. *ouron*, urine + *haima*, blood], a toxic condition caused by the presence in the blood of waste products normally eliminated in the urine: it results from an inadequate secretion of urine: also spelled **uraemia.**

u·re·mic (yoo-rē'mik), ***adj.*** of or having uremia: also spelled **uraemic.**

-u·ret (yoo-ret), [Mod. L. *-uretum;* replacing earlier *-ure* < Fr.], a suffix equivalent to *-ide*, formerly used to form chemical terms.

u·re·ter (yoo-rē'tẽr), ***n.*** [Mod. L.; Gr. *ourētēr* < *ourein*, to urinate], a duct or tube that carries urine from a kidney to the bladder or cloaca.

u·re·ter·al (yoo-rē'tẽr-əl), ***adj.*** of or having to do with the ureter.

u·re·ter·ic (yoor'ə-ter'ik), ***adj.*** ureteral.

u·re·ter·o- (yoo-rē'tẽr-ō, yoo-rē'tẽr-ə), [< *ureter*], a combining form meaning *the ureter* or *the ureter and*, as in *ureterostomy*: also, before a vowel, **ureter-.**

u·re·ter·os·to·my (yoo-rē'tẽr-os'tə-mi), ***n.*** [*uretero-* + *-stomy*], the surgical creation of an artificial opening for the direct discharge of urine from the ureter.

u·re·than (yoor'ə-thăn', yoo-reth'ən), ***n.*** urethane.

u·re·thane (yoor'ə-thăn', yoo-reth'ăn), ***n.*** [Fr. *uréthane;* see UREA, ETHER, -ANE], 1. a white, crystalline compound, $C_3H_7O_2N$, produced by the action of ammonia on ethyl carbonate or by heating urea nitrate and ethyl alcohol: it is used as a hypnotic and sedative. 2. any ester of carbamic acid.

u·re·thra (yoo-rē'thrə), ***n.*** [*pl.* URETHRAE (-thrē), URETHRAS (-thrəz)], [LL.; Gr. *ourēthra* < *ouron*, urine], the membranous canal through which urine is discharged from the bladder in most mammals: in the male, sperm is also discharged through the urethra.

u·re·thral (yoo-rē'thrəl), ***adj.*** of the urethra.

u·re·thrit·ic (yoor'i-thrit'ik), ***adj.*** of or having urethritis.

u·re·thri·tis (yoor'i-thrī'tis), ***n.*** [Mod. L.; see URETHRA & -ITIS], inflammation of the urethra.

u·re·thro- (yoo-rē'thrō, yoo-rē'thrə), [< *urethra*], a combining form meaning *the urethra* or *the urethra and*, as in *urethroscope*: also, before a vowel, **urethr-.**

u·re·thro·scope (yoo-rē'thrə-skōp'), ***n.*** [*urethro-* + *-scope*], an instrument for examining the interior of the urethra.

u·re·thros·co·py (yoor'i-thros'kə-pi), ***n.*** examination of the urethra with a urethroscope.

u·ret·ic (yoo-ret'ik), ***adj.*** [LL. *ureticus;* Gr. *ourētikos*], of the urine; urinary; diuretic.

U·rey, Harold Clay·ton (klā'tən yoor'i), 1893– ; American chemist; discoverer of heavy hydrogen; received Nobel prize in chemistry, 1934.

Ur·fa (oor-fä'), ***n.*** a city in southeastern Turkey: pop., 37,000: ancient name, *Edessa.*

Ur·ga (oor'gä), ***n.*** Ulan Bator Khoto: the former name.

urge (ũrj), ***v.t.*** [URGED (ũrjd), URGING], [L. *urgere*, to press hard], 1. to press upon the attention; present or speak of earnestly and repeatedly; plead, allege, or advocate strongly. 2. to drive or force onward; press forward vigorously. 3. to entreat or plead with; ask, persuade, or solicit earnestly; press; exhort. 4. to force; incite; impel; drive. 5. to ply vigorously, as oars. ***v.i.*** 1. to make an earnest presentation of arguments, claims, charges, entreaties, solicitations, etc. 2. to exert a force that drives or impels, as to action. ***n.*** 1. the act of urging. 2. an impulse to do a certain thing; an impelling influence or force of an involuntary nature.

***SYN.*—urge** implies a strong effort to persuade one to do something, as by entreaty, argument, or forceful recommendation (he *urged* us to accept the offer); **exhort** implies an earnest urging or admonishing to action or conduct considered proper or right (the minister *exhorted* his flock to forsake Mammon); **press** suggests a continuous, insistent urging that is difficult to resist (we *pressed* him to stay); **importune** implies persistent efforts to break down resistance against a demand or request, often to the point of being annoying or wearisome (not too proud to *importune* for help).

ur·gen·cy (ũr'jən-si), ***n.*** [*pl.* URGENCIES (-siz)], [< *urgent;* cf. Fr. *urgence*], 1. the quality or state of being urgent; need for action, haste, etc.; stress; pressure, as of necessity. 2. insistence; importunity. 3. something urgent.

ur·gent (ũr'jənt), ***adj.*** [Fr.; L. *urgens*, ppr. of *urgere*, to press hard, urge], 1. calling for haste, immediate action, etc.; grave; pressing. 2. insistent; importunate.

-ur·gy (ũr'ji), [Gr. *-ourgia* < *-ourgos*, worker], a combining form meaning *a fabricating* or *working of* (a specified material), as in *crystallurgy, zymurgy.*

U·ri (ōō'rē), ***n.*** a canton of eastern Switzerland: pop., 29,000.

-u·ri·a (yoor'i-ə), [Mod. L.; Gr. *-ouria* < *ouron*, urine], a combining form meaning *a (diseased) condition of the urine resulting from the presence of* (a specified substance), as in *glycosuria, albuminuria.*

U·ri·ah (yoo-rī'ə), [Heb. *ūriyāh*, lit., God is light], a masculine name. ***n.*** in the *Bible*, a Hittite captain whose beautiful wife, Bathsheba, aroused David's lust: David arranged for Uriah to die in battle and then married Bathsheba: II Sam. 11:15.

U·ri·as (yoo-rī'əs), a masculine name: see **Uriah.**

u·ric (yoor'ik), ***adj.*** [Fr. *urique* < *urine* + *-ique*, -ic], of, contained in, or derived from urine.

uric acid, a white, odorless, crystalline substance, $C_5H_4N_4O_3$, found in urine, slightly soluble in water.

u·ri·co- (yoor'i-kō, yoor'i-kə), [< *uric*], a combining form meaning *uric acid*, as in *uricometer:* also **uric-**.

U·ri·el (yoor′i-əl), *n.* [Heb. *ūrī'ēl*, lit., light of God], one of the archangels: in Milton's *Paradise Lost* he is called "regent of the sun."

U·rim and Thum·mim (yoor′im; thum′im), [Heb. *ūrīm; tummīm*], certain unidentified objects mentioned in the Old Testament as being worn in the breastplate of the high priest and apparently serving as a device for determining the will of God: Ex. 28:30.

u·ri·nal (yoor′ə-n'l), *n.* [ME. *urynale, orynal;* OFr.; LL. < L. *urinalis*, of urine < *urina*, urine], 1. a container or receptacle for urine, especially one used by the sick or bedridden. 2. a place for urinating; especially, a fixture for use by men in urinating.

u·ri·nal·y·sis (yoor′ə-nal′ə-sis), *n.* [*pl.* URINALYSES (-sēz′)], [Mod. L.], chemical analysis of the urine: also spelled **uranalysis**.

u·ri·nar·y (yoor′ə-ner′i), *adj.* [< L. *urina*, urine; + *-ary*], 1. of urine. 2. of the organs concerned in the secretion and discharge of urine. *n.* [*pl.* URINARIES (-iz)], 1. a urinal. 2. a reservoir to hold urine and dung for use as manure.

urinary calculus, a concretion of urinary constituents occurring in the urinary tract.

u·ri·nate (yoor′ə-nāt′), *v.i.* [URINATED (-id), URINATING], [< ML. *urinatus*, pp. of *urinare*], to discharge urine from the body; micturate.

u·ri·na·tion (yoor′ə-nā′shən), *n.* the act or process of urinating.

u·rine (yoor′in), *n.* [ME.; OFr.; L. *urina*, urine], in mammals, the yellowish fluid containing urea and other waste products, secreted from the blood by the kidneys, passed down the ureters to the bladder, where it is stored, and periodically discharged from the body through the urethra.

urine analysis, the analysis of urine; urinalysis.

u·ri·nif·er·ous (yoor′ə-nif′ẽr-əs), *adj.* conveying urine.

u·ri·no- (yoor′ə-nō, yoor′ə-nə), [< L. *urina*, urine], a combining form meaning *urine, urinary tract*, as in *urinogenital:* also, before a vowel, **urin-**.

u·ri·no·gen·i·tal (yoor′ə-nō-jen′ə-t'l), *adj.* designating or of the urinary and genital organs; genitourinary.

u·ri·nose (yoor′ə-nōs′), *adj.* urinous.

u·ri·nous (yoor′ə-nəs), *adj.* [Mod. L. *urinosus*], 1. of, like, or containing urine. 2. having the odor of urine.

Ur·mi·a, Lake (o͞or′mi-ə), a lake in northwestern Iran: area, 1,750 sq. mi.: also called *Urumiyeh*.

urn (ũrn), *n.* [ME.; L. *urna*, urn < base of *urere*, to burn; so called because made of burnt clay], 1. a vase in any of various forms and materials, usually with a foot or pedestal. 2. such a vase used to hold the ashes of the dead after cremation. 3. figuratively, the grave. 4. a metal container with a faucet, used for making or serving coffee, etc. at the table. 5. in *botany*, the part of a moss capsule that bears the spores.

u·ro- (yoor′ō, yoor′ə), [< Gr. *ouron*, urine], a combining form meaning *urine, urination, urinary tract*, as in *urolith*: also, before a vowel, **ur-**.

u·ro- (yoor′ō, yoor′ə), [< Gr. *oura*, tail], a combining form meaning *tail*, as in *uropod, urochord*.

u·ro·chord (yoor′ə-kôrd′), *n.* [*uro-* (tail) + *chord*], in *zoology*, the notochord of ascidians and tunicates, mainly or more noticeably present in the larva, and restricted chiefly to the caudal region.

u·ro·chor·dal (yoor′ə-kôr′d'l), *adj.* of, having, or having the nature of, a urochord.

u·ro·chrome (yoor′ə-krōm′), *n.* [*uro-* (urine) + *chrome*], the pigment responsible for the characteristic yellow color of urine.

u·ro·gen·i·tal (yoor′ō-jen′ə-t'l), *adj.* urinogenital.

u·rog·e·nous (yoo-roj′ə-nəs), *adj.* [*uro-* + *-genous*], 1. producing urine. 2. contained in or obtained from urine.

u·ro·lith (yoor′ə-lith), *n.* [*uro-* + *-lith*], a urinary calculus.

u·ro·lith·ic (yoor′ə-lith′ik), *adj.* of a urolith or uroliths.

u·ro·log·ic (yoor′ə-loj′ik), *adj.* urological.

u·ro·log·i·cal (yoor′ə-loj′i-k'l), *adj.* of urology.

u·rol·o·gist (yoo-rol′ə-jist), *n.* a specialist in urology.

u·rol·o·gy (yoo-rol′ə-ji), *n.* [*uro-* + *-logy*], the branch of medicine dealing with the urinogenital system and its diseases.

u·ro·pod (yoor′ə-pod′), *n.* [*uro-* (tail) + *-pod*], any appendage along the abdomen of an arthropod, as in the lobster, shrimp, etc.

u·ro·pyg·i·al (yoor′ə-pij′i-əl), *adj.* of the uropygium.

uropygial gland, an oil-secreting gland located at the base of the tail in most birds.

u·ro·pyg·i·um (yoor′ə-pij′i-əm), *n.* [Mod. L.; Gr. *ouropygion*, after *oura*, tail, for *orrhopygion* < *orrhos*, end of the os sacrum + *pygē*, rump], the hump at the rear extremity of a bird's body, from which the tail feathers grow.

u·ro·scop·ic (yoor′ə-skop′ik), *adj.* of uroscopy.

u·ros·co·py (yoo-ros′kə-pi), *n.* [*uro-* + *-scopy*], examination of the urine, as for the diagnosis of disease.

u·ro·xan·thin (yoor′ə-zan′thin), *n.* [*uro-* (urine) + *xanthin*], indican, as found in urine.

Ur·quhart, Sir **Thomas** (ũr′kẽrt, ũr′kärt), 1611–1660; Scottish writer and translator.

Ur·sa (ũr′sə), *n.* [L., she-bear], 1. Ursa Major. 2. Ursa Minor.

Ursa Major, [L., lit., Great Bear], the most conspicuous of the constellations in the northern sky. It is near the pole and contains fifty-three visible stars, seven of which form the Big Dipper: also called *Great Bear:* see **constellation**, chart.

Ursa Minor, [L., lit., Little Bear], the northernmost constellation. It contains twenty-three visible stars, including those forming the Little Dipper: the most important of these is Polaris, the North Star: also called *Little Bear*: see **constellation**, chart.

ur·si·form (ũr′sə-fôrm′), *adj.* [< L. *ursus*, a bear; + *-form*], having the form or appearance of a bear.

ur·sine (ũr′sīn, ũr′sin), *adj.* [L. *ursinus* < *ursus*, a bear], 1. of, like, or characteristic of a bear or the bear family. 2. covered with bristles, as certain caterpillars.

ursine howler, the red howling monkey native to the northern part of South America.

‡Ur·spra·che (o͞or′shprä′khə), *n.* [G.; *ur-*, original + *sprache*, language], a (hypothetical) parent language: as, the Indo-European *Ursprache* has been reconstructed by the methods of comparative linguistics.

Ur·su·la (ũr′syoo-lə, ũr′sə-lə), [ML., dim. of L. *ursa*, she-bear], a feminine name.

Ursula, Saint, ? c. 300 A.D.; a legendary British princess of Christian faith who was supposedly killed, together with 11,000 virgins, by the Huns at Cologne.

Ur·su·line (ũr′syoo-lin, ũr′sə-līn′), *n.* [Mod. L. *Ursulina*: so called after Saint *Ursula* of Cologne, patron of the order], in the *Roman Catholic Church*, a member of an order of nuns founded c. 1537 to carry on the work of teaching and nursing. *adj.* of this order.

ur·ti·ca·ceous (ũr tə-kā′shəs), *adj.* [< L. *urtica*, nettle; + *-aceous*], in *botany*, of the nettle family, a group of herbs, trees, and shrubs having clusters of small flowers and leaves often covered with stinging hairs.

ur·ti·ca·ri·a (ũr′tə-kâr′i-ə), *n.* [Mod. L. < L. *urtica*, a nettle], an allergic skin condition characterized by the eruption of smooth, itching patches, or wheals; hives.

ur·ti·car·i·al (ũr′tə-kâr′i-əl), *adj.* of, or having the nature of, urticaria.

ur·ti·cate (ũr′tə-kāt′), *v.t. & v.i.* [URTICATED (-id), URTICATING], [< ML. *urticatus*, pp. of *urticare*, to sting < L. *urtica*, a nettle], to sting with or as with nettles.

ur·ti·ca·tion (ũr′tə-kā′shən), *n.* [ML. *urticatio*], in *medicine*, 1. formerly, the flogging of a paralyzed limb, etc. with nettles for the stimulating effect produced. 2. any sensation of stinging or itching. 3. the formation of urticaria.

U·ru·guay (yoor′ə-gwā′, yoor′ə-gwī′; Sp. o͞o′ro͞o-gwī′), *n.* 1. a country in southern South America, on the Atlantic: area, 72,153 sq. mi.; pop., 2,803,000; capital, Montevideo. 2. a river in southern South America, flowing into the Plata River: length, 1,000 mi. Abbreviated **Uru.**

U·ru·guay·an (yoor′ə-gwā′ən, yoor′ə-gwī′ən), *adj.* of Uruguay, its people, or culture. *n.* a native or inhabitant of Uruguay.

U·rum·chi (o͞o-ro͞om′chi), *n.* Tihwa, city in China.

U·ru·mi·yeh (oo-ro͞om′i-ye), *n.* Urmia.

U·run·di (oo-roon′di), *n.* formerly, a district of German East Africa: now a part of Ruandi-Urundi.

u·rus (yoor′əs), *n.* [L. < Gmc. name; cf. AS. & OHG. *ur;* see AUROCHS], a shaggy, long-horned wild ox, now extinct, common in Europe at the beginning of the Christian Era.

u·ru·shi·ol (o͞o′ro͞o-shi-ōl′, o͞o′ro͞o-shi-ol′), *n.* [Japan. *urushi*, lacquer; + *-ol*], a poisonous, irritant liquid, $C_{21}H_{32}O_2$, present in poison ivy and the Japanese lac tree.

U.R.W.A., United Rubber Workers of America: an AFL-CIO labor union.

us (us), *pron.* [ME. *us, ous*, acc. & dat. of *we* (cf. WE); AS. *us*, dat., but also used, beside *usic*, as acc.; akin to G. *uns* (for the loss of *-n-*, cf. TOOTH, SOFT, etc.); IE. base **ns-* < **nes-*, **nos-*, pl. of **ne-*, **no-*, we; cf. L. *nos*, we, of the same ult. origin], the objective case of **we**: also used colloquially as a predicate complement with a linking verb (e.g., that's *us*).

U.S., 1. Uncle Sam. 2. United Service.

U.S., US, United States.

u.s., [L.], 1. *ubi supra*. 2. *ut supra*.

U.S.A., Union of South Africa.

U.S.A., USA, 1. United States of America. 2. United States Army.

us·a·bil·i·ty (ūz′ə-bil′ə-ti), *n.* the state or quality of being usable: also spelled **useability**.

us·a·ble (ūz'ə-b'l), *adj.* that can be used; fit, convenient, or available for use: also spelled **useable.**
U.S.A.F., USAF, United States Air Force.
us·age (ūs'ij, ūz'ij), *n.* [ME.; OFr.; ML. *usagium, usaticum*], 1. the act or way of using or treating; treatment; use. 2. long-continued or established custom or practice; habitual or customary use or way of acting; custom; habit. 3. the way in which a word, phrase, etc. is used to express a particular idea; customary manner of using a given language in speaking or writing, or an instance of this. —*SYN.* see **habit.**
us·ance (ūz'ns), *n.* [ME. *usaunce;* OFr. *usance;* ML. *usancia*], 1. income or other benefits derived from wealth or the use of wealth. 2. the time allowed for the payment of a foreign bill of exchange, as established by custom and excluding any period of grace. 3. [Obs.], *a)* use. *b)* usage; custom. *c)* interest paid for the use of money.
Us·beg (us'beg), *n.* & *adj.* Uzbek.
Us·bek (us'bek), *n.* & *adj.* Uzbek.
U.S.C., United States of Colombia.
U.S.C. & G.S., United States Coast and Geodetic Survey.
U.S.C.G., United States Coast Guard.
use (ūz; *for n.,* ūs), *v.t.* [USED (ūzd), USING], [ME. *usen;* OFr. *user;* LL. **usare* < L. *usus,* pp. of *uti,* to use], 1. to put or bring into action or service; employ for or apply to a given purpose. 2. to practice; exercise: as, you must *use* your judgment. 3. to act or behave toward; treat: as, she *used* her friends badly. 4. to consume, expend, or exhaust by use (often with *up*): as, he has *used* up all his energy. 5. to smoke or chew (tobacco). 6. to make familiar; accustom (used in the passive with *to*): as, they were *used* to the old ways. 7. [Colloq.], to exploit, as a person; treat as a means to some selfish end. *v.i.* 1. to be accustomed; be wont (now only in the past tense, with an infinitive expressed or implied): as, he *used* to enter every contest. 2. [Archaic or Dial.], to frequent; resort. *n.* [ME. & OFr. *us* < L. *usus,* use < *uti,* to use], 1. the act of using or the state of being used; usage. 2. the power or ability to use: as, he has regained the *use* of his hand. 3. the right or permission to use: as, he granted them the *use* of his name. 4. the need, opportunity, or occasion to use: as, we will have no further *use* for his services. 5. way of using. 6. the quality that makes a thing useful or suitable for a given purpose; advantage; usefulness; worth; utility. 7. the object, end, or purpose for which something is used. 8. function; service. 9. constant, continued, customary, or habitual employment, practice, or exercise, or an instance of this; custom; habit; practice; wont. 10. in *law, a)* the enjoyment of property, as from occupying, employing, or exercising it. *b)* [influenced by OFr. *ues,* gain < L. *opus,* a work], profit, benefit, or advantage, especially that of lands and tenements held in trust by another. 11. in *liturgy,* the particular form of ritual or liturgy practiced in a given church, diocese, etc.: as, the Lutheran *use.*
have no use for, 1. to have no need of. 2. to have no wish to deal with; be impatient with. 3. to have no affection or respect for; dislike strongly.
in use, in the process of being used.
make use of, to use; have occasion to use.
put to use, to use; find a use for.
SYN.—**use** implies the putting of a thing (or, usually in an opprobrious sense, a person regarded as a passive thing) to a given purpose so as to accomplish an end (to *use* a pencil, a suggestion, etc., he *used* his brother to advance himself); **employ,** a somewhat more elevated term, implies the putting to useful work of something not in use at that moment (to *employ* a vacant lot as a playground) and, with reference to persons, suggests a providing of work and pay (he *employs* five mechanics); **utilize** implies the putting of something to a practical or profitable use (to *utilize* by-products).
use·a·bil·i·ty (ūz'ə-bil'ə-ti), *n.* usability.
use·a·ble (ūz'ə-b'l), *adj.* usable.
use·ful (ūs'fəl), *adj.* that can be used to advantage; serviceable; helpful; beneficial; advantageous; often, having practical utility.
use·less (ūs'lis), *adj.* having or of no use; unserviceable; worthless; ineffectual; of no avail. —*SYN.* see **futile.**
us·er (ūz'ẽr), *n.* [sense 1 < *use, v.;* in sense 2 a substantive use of OFr. *user,* to use], 1. a person or thing that uses. 2. in *law, a)* the exercise of a right of use (see **use,** *n.,* 10*a*). *b)* a right of use, based on long use.
USES, U.S.E.S., United States Employment Service.
U-shaped (ū'shāpt'), *adj.* having the shape of a U.
U·shas (oo'shəs, oo-shäs'), *n.* [Sans. *Uṣas,* dawn], the Hindu, or Vedic, goddess of the dawn.
ush·er (ush'ẽr), *n.* [ME. *uscher;* OFr. *ussier, huissier* < *huis,* door; L. *ostium,* door], 1. an official doorkeeper. 2. a person whose duty it is to show people to their seats in a church, theater, etc. 3. a person whose official duty is to precede someone of rank, as in a procession, or to make introductions between those unacquainted with one another. 4. [Obs.], in Great Britain, an assistant teacher. *v.t.* 1. to act as an usher to; escort or conduct (others) to seats, etc. 2. to precede and introduce, or be a forerunner of.
ush·er·ette (ush'ẽr-et'), *n.* a woman or girl usher, as in a theater.
USIS, U.S.I.S., United States Information Service.
Usk (usk), *n.* a river in Wales and southwestern England, flowing into the estuary of the Severn River; length, 60 mi.
Üs·küb, Üs·küp (üs-küp'), *n.* Skoplje, a city in Yugoslavia: the Turkish name.
Üs·kü·dar (üs-kü'där, üs'kü-där'), *n.* a section of Istanbul, on the Asiatic side of the Bosporus: pop., 155,000: also called *Scutari.*
U.S.M., 1. United States Mail. 2. United States Marines. 3. United States Mint.
U.S.M.A., United States Military Academy.
USMC, U.S.M.C., 1. United States Marine Corps. 2. United States Maritime Commission.
U.S.N., USN, United States Navy.
U.S.N.A., 1. United States National Army. 2. United States Naval Academy.
U.S.N.G., United States National Guard.
U.S.N.R., USNR, United States Naval Reserve.
U.S.N.R.F., United States Naval Reserve Force.
USO, U.S.O., United Service Organizations.
U.S.P., U.S.Pharm., United States Pharmacopoeia.
Us·pal·la·ta Pass (o͞os'pä-yä'tä), a mountain pass in the Andes, between Chile and Argentina: height, 12,870 ft.: also called *La Cumbre.*
U.S.P.H.S., United States Public Health Service.
U.S.P.O., United States Post Office.
us·que·baugh (us'kwi-bô', us'kwi-bä'), *n.* [Ir. & Gael. *uisgebeatha; uisge,* water + *beatha,* life], whisky (in Scotland or Ireland).
U.S.R., United States Reserves.
U.S.R.C., United States Reserve Corps.
U.S.S., 1. United States Senate. 2. United States Service. 3. United States Ship. 4. United States Steamer. 5. United States Steamship.
U.S.S.B., United States Shipping Board.
U.S.S.Ct., United States Supreme Court.
U.S.S.R., USSR, Union of Soviet Socialist Republics.
U.S.S.S., United States Steamship.
Us·su·ri (o͞o-so͞o'ri), *n.* a river in the U.S.S.R., flowing into the Amur River and forming part of the eastern boundary of Manchuria: length, c. 450 mi.
us·tu·late (us'choo-lit, us'choo-lāt'), *adj.* [L. *ustulatus,* pp. of *ustulare;* see USTULATION], discolored or blackened, as if burned or scorched.
us·tu·la·tion (us'choo-lā'shən), *n.* [ML. *ustulatio* < L. *ustulare,* to scorch < base of *urere,* to burn], 1. in *pharmacy,* the drying or roasting of moist substances in preparation for pulverization. 2. the burning of wine. 3. the act of burning, scorching, or searing.
u·su·al (ū'zho͞o-əl, ū'zhool), *adj.* [ME.; OFr.; LL. *usualis* < L. *usus;* see USE], such as is in common or ordinary use; such as ordinarily happens or occurs; common; customary; habitual: abbreviated **usu.**
as usual, as is or was customary; in the usual way.
SYN.—**usual** applies to that which past experience has shown to be the normal, common, hence expected thing (the *usual* results, price, answer, etc.); **customary** refers to that which accords with the usual practices of some individual or with the prevailing customs of some group (his *customary* mid-morning coffee, it was *customary* to dress for dinner); **habitual** implies a fixed practice as the result of habit (her *habitual* tardiness); **wonted** is a somewhat literary equivalent for **customary** or **habitual** (according to their *wonted* manner); **accustomed** is equivalent to **customary** but suggests less strongly a settled custom (he sat in his *accustomed* place). See also **normal.** —*ANT.* extraordinary, unusual.
u·su·al·ly (ū'zho͞o-əl-i, ū'zhoo-li), *adv.* according to what is usual or customary; generally; commonly; ordinarily: abbreviated **usu.**
u·su·fruct (ū'zyoo-frukt', ū'syoo-frukt'), *n.* [LL. *usufructus* < L. *usus,* a use + *fructus,* a fruit], in *Roman & Civil Law,* the right of using and enjoying all the advantages and profits of the property of another without altering or damaging the substance.
u·su·fruc·tu·ar·y (ū'zyoo-fruk'cho͞o-er'i, ū'syoo-fruk'cho͞o-er'i), *n.* [*pl.* USUFRUCTUARIES (-iz)], [LL. *usufructuarius*], a person or agent having the usufruct of property. *adj.* of, or having the nature of, a usufruct.
u·su·rer (ū'zhoo-rẽr), *n.* [ME.; OFr. *usurier;* ML. *usurarius,* usurer < L. *usura;* see USURY], 1. a person who lends money at a rate of interest that is excessive or unlawfully high. 2. [Obs.], a person who lends money at interest; moneylender.
u·su·ri·ous (ū-zhoor'i-əs), *adj.* 1. practicing usury; lending money at an excessive or unlawfully high rate of interest. 2. of or constituting usury.
u·surp (ū-zũrp', ū-sũrp'), *v.t.* [ME. & OFr. *usurper;* L. *usurpare* < *usus,* a use + *rapere,* to seize], to take or assume and hold in possession by force or without right: said of seizures of power, position, rights, functions, etc. *v.i.* to practice or commit usurpation.
u·sur·pa·tion (ū'zẽr-pā'shən, ū'sẽr-pā'shən), *n.* [ME. & OFr. *usurpacion;* L. *usurpatio*], the act of usurping; unlawful or violent seizure of a throne, power, rights, etc.

u·su·ry (ū′zhoo-ri), *n.* [*pl.* USURIES (-riz)], [ME. *usurie* < *usure;* OFr. *usure;* L. *usura* < *usus;* see USE], 1. the act or practice of lending money at a rate of interest that is excessive or unlawfully high. 2. an excessive or unlawfully high rate or amount of interest. 3. [Obs.], interest paid on a loan.

U.S.V., United States Volunteers.

usw, u.s.w., *und so weiter,* [G.], and so forth.

U.S.W.A., 1. United Shoe Workers of America: an AFL-CIO labor union. 2. United Steelworkers of America: an AFL-CIO labor union.

ut (ut, ōōt), *n.* [ME.; L.; see GAMUT], in *music,* a syllable formerly used in solmization: now replaced by *do.*

U.T., u.t., in *astronomy,* universal time.

U·tah (ū′tô, ū′tä), *n.* a Western State of the United States: area, 84,916 sq. mi.; pop., 891,000; capital, Salt Lake City: abbreviated **Ut.**

U·tah·an (ū′tô-ən, ū′tä-ən), *adj.* of Utah. *n.* a native or inhabitant of Utah.

ut dict., *ut dictum,* [L.], as directed.

Ute (ūt, ū′ti), *n.* [*pl.* UTE, UTES (ūts, -tiz)], 1. a member of a tribe of nomadic Shoshonean Indians that lived in Colorado and Utah, ranging down into New Mexico and Arizona. 2. their Uto-Aztecan language.

u·ten·sil (ū-ten′s'l), *n.* [ME. *utensele;* OFr. *utensile;* L. *utensilis,* fit for use < *uti,* to use], 1. any implement or container ordinarily used in a kitchen, dairy, or the like: as, cooking *utensils.* 2. any implement or tool, as for use in farming, etc. —*SYN.* see **implement.**

u·ter·ine (ū′tẽr-in, ū′tẽr-īn′), *adj.* [LL. *uterinus*], 1. of the uterus. 2. having the same mother but a different father: as, *uterine* sisters.

u·ter·o- (ū′tẽr-ō, ū′tẽr-ə), [< *uterus*], a combining form meaning *the uterus* or *the uterus and,* as in *utero-abdominal:* also **uter-.**

u·ter·us (ū′tẽr-əs), *n.* [*pl.* UTERI (-ī′)], [L.], a hollow, muscular organ of female mammals in which the ovum is deposited and the embryo and fetus are developed and protected; womb.

U·ther (ū′thẽr), *n.* a legendary king of Britain, father of King Arthur.

U·ti·ca (ū′ti-kə), *n.* a city in central New York: pop., 100,000.

u·tile (ū′til), *adj.* [L. *utilis* < *uti,* to use], [Obs.], useful; practical; advantageous.

u·ti·lise (ū′t'l-īz′), *v.t.* [UTILISED (-īzd′), UTILISING], to utilize: the British spelling.

u·til·i·tar·i·an (ū-til′ə-târ′i-ən), *adj.* [< *utility* + *-arian:* coined by Bentham], 1. of or having to do with utility. 2. stressing the importance of utility over beauty or other considerations. 3. made for or aiming at utility. 4. of, or having belief in, utilitarianism. *n.* a person who believes in utilitarianism.

u·til·i·tar·i·an·ism (ū-til′ə-târ′i-ən-iz′m), *n.* 1. the doctrine that the worth or value of anything is determined solely by its utility. 2. the doctrine that the purpose of all action should be to bring about the greatest happiness of the greatest number.

u·til·i·ty (ū-til′ə-ti), *n.* [*pl.* UTILITIES (-tiz)], [Fr. *utilité;* L. *utilitas* < *utilis,* useful < *uti,* to use], 1. the quality or property of being useful; usefulness. 2. the greatest happiness of the greatest number. 3. something useful. 4. something useful to the public, especially the service of electric power, gas, water, telephone, etc. 5. a company providing such a service. 6. *pl.* shares of stock in such a company. 7. in *economics,* the power to satisfy the needs or wants of humanity.

u·ti·liz·a·ble (ū′t'l-īz′ə-b'l), *adj.* that can be utilized.

u·ti·li·za·tion (ū′t'l-i-zā′shən, ū′t'l-ī-zā′shən), *n.* a utilizing or being utilized.

u·ti·lize (ū′t'l-īz′), *v.t.* [UTILIZED (-īzd′), UTILIZING], [Fr. *utiliser* < *utile,* useful; L. *utilis* < *uti,* to use], to put to use; make use of; get profit or benefit from by using. —*SYN.* see **use.**

‡**ut in·fra** (ut in′frə), [L.], as below: abbreviated **u.i.**

u·ti pos·si·de·tis (ū′tī pos′ə-dē′tis), [L., lit., as you possess], in *international law,* the principle that at the end of a war either belligerent is entitled to absolute possession of such territory as is actually occupied and controlled by it.

ut·most (ut′mōst′, ut′məst), *adj.* [ME. *utemest;* AS. *utemest, ytemest,* double superl. of *ut,* out], 1. situated at the farthest point or limit; most extreme or distant; farthest. 2. of or to the greatest or highest degree, amount, number, etc.; greatest. *n.* the most or the greatest that is possible; extreme limit or degree. Also **uttermost.**

U·to-Az·tec·an (ū′tō-az′tek-ən), *adj.* designating or of a large American Indian linguistic family of the western United States, Mexico, and Central America. *n.* the Uto-Aztecan languages, comprising the Shoshonean, Nahuatl, Piman, Hopi, Ute, etc.

U·to·pi·a (ū-tō′pi-ə), *n.* [Mod. L. < Gr. *ou,* not + *topos,* a place], 1. an imaginary island described as having a perfect political and social system: subject and title of a book written by Sir Thomas More in 1516. 2. [often u-], any place, state, or situation of ideal perfection. 3. [often u-], any visionary scheme or system for an ideally perfect social order.

U·to·pi·an (ū-tō′pi-ən), *adj.* [Mod. L. *Utopianus*], 1. of or like Utopia. 2. [often u-], having the nature of, or inclined to draw up schemes for, a utopia; idealistic; visionary. *n.* 1. an inhabitant of Utopia. 2. [often u-], a person who believes in a utopia, especially of a social or political nature; visionary; idealist.

u·to·pi·an·ism (ū-tō′pi-ən-iz′m), *n.* the ideas, doctrines, aims, etc. of a utopian; visionary schemes for producing perfection in social or political conditions.

U·trecht (ū′trekt; D. ü′treHt), *n.* 1. a province of the Netherlands, in the central part: pop., 663,000. 2. its capital: pop., 252,000: a series of treaties were made there in 1713 at the end of the War of the Spanish Succession.

u·tri·cle (ū′tri-k'l), *n.* [< Fr. or L.; Fr. *utricule;* L. *utriculus,* little bag or bottle, dim. of *uter,* leather bag, wineskin], 1. a small sac, vesicle, or baglike part; specifically, in *anatomy,* the larger of the two saclike cavities (the other being the *saccule*) in the membranous labyrinth of the inner ear. 2. in *botany,* a small, one-celled seed vessel with a thin, membranous wall and one or several seeds.

u·tric·u·lar (ū-tri′kyoo-lẽr), *adj.* in *botany,* 1. of, or having the nature of, a utricle. 2. having one or more utricles.

u·tric·u·late (ū-trik′yoo-lit, ū-trik′yoo-lāt′), *adj.* utricular.

u·tric·u·li·tis (ū-trik′yoo-lī′tis), *n.* [Mod. L.; see UTRICLE & -ITIS], inflammation of the utricle of the inner ear.

u·tric·u·lus (ū-trik′yoo-ləs), *n.* [*pl.* UTRICULI (-lī′)], [L.; see UTRICLE], a utricle, especially of the inner ear.

‡**ut su·pra** (ut sōō′prə, sū′prə), [L.], as above: abbreviated **u.s.**

Ut·tar Pra·desh (ut′ẽr prä′desh), a state of northern India: area, 113,409 sq. mi.; pop., 63,216,000; capital, Lucknow: former name, *United Provinces.*

ut·ter (ut′ẽr), *adj.* [ME. *uttre, utter;* AS. *utor, uttor,* compar. of *ut,* out], 1. complete; total. 2. unqualified; absolute; unconditional.

ut·ter (ut′ẽr), *v.t.* [ME. *uttren, outren* < *utter,* outward < *ut, out,* out], 1. originally, to give out; put forth: obsolete except when used of the passing of counterfeit money or forgeries, or the publication of libel. 2. to pronounce, speak, or express audibly, as words, thoughts, vocal sounds, etc. 3. to express in any way. 4. to emit (nonvocal sounds), as if speaking. 5. to make known; divulge; reveal. 6. [Obs.], to publish (a book, etc.). 7. [Obs.], to sell.

SYN.—**utter** implies the communication of an idea or feeling by means of vocal sounds, such as words, exclamations, etc. (he *uttered* a sigh of relief); **express,** the broadest of these terms, suggests a revealing of ideas, feelings, one's personality, etc. by means of speech, action, or creative work (to *express* oneself in music); **voice** suggests expression through words, either spoken or written (he *voiced* his opinions in letters to the editor); **broach** suggests the utterance or mention of an idea to someone for the first time (I'll *broach* the subject to him at dinner); **enunciate** suggests the announcement or open attestation of some idea (to *enunciate* a theory, doctrine, etc.).

ut·ter·ance (ut′ẽr-əns, ut′rəns), *n.* 1. the act of uttering, or expressing by voice. 2. the power or style of speaking. 3. that which is uttered; especially, a word or words uttered, whether written or spoken. 4. [Rare], the act of uttering, or circulating (counterfeit money, etc.).

ut·ter·ance (ut′ẽr-əns, ut′rəns), *n.* [ME.; OFr. *oultrance;* L. *ultra,* beyond], [Obs.], the last, or utmost, extremity; i.e., death.

ut·ter·ly (ut′ẽr-li), *adv.* in an utter manner; entirely; completely; absolutely.

ut·ter·most (ut′ẽr-mōst′, ut′ẽr-məst), *adj. & n.* utmost.

U.T.W.A., United Textile Workers of America: an AFL-CIO labor union.

u·va·rov·ite (ōō-vä′rôf-īt′), *n.* [after S.S. *Uvarov* (1786–1855), Russ. statesman and author], an emerald-green variety of garnet containing chromium.

u·ve·a (ū′vi-ə), *n.* [ML. < L. *uva,* a grape, bunch of grapes], 1. [Obs.], the posterior, pigmentary layer of the iris. 2. the iris, ciliary body, and choroid, together forming the entire pigmentary layer of the eye.

u·ve·al (ū′vi-əl), *adj.* of the uvea.

Uve·dale, Nicholas (ūv′dāl), see **Udall, Nicholas.**

u·ve·it·ic (ū′vi-it′ik), *adj.* of, or having the nature of, uveitis.

u·ve·i·tis (ū′vi-ī′tis), *n.* [Mod. L. < *uvea* + *-itis*], inflammation of the uvea.

u·ve·ous (ū′vi-əs), *adj.* uveal.

u·vu·la (ū′vyoo-lə), *n.* [*pl.* UVULAS (-ləz), UVULAE (-lē′)], [ML.; dim. of L. *uva,* a grape], the small, fleshy process hanging down from the middle of the soft palate above the back of the tongue.

u·vu·lar (ū′vyoo-lẽr), *adj.* [Mod. L. *uvularis*], 1. of or having to do with the uvula. 2. in *phonetics*, pronounced with a vibration of the uvula, or with the back of the tongue near or in contact with the uvula. *n.* in *phonetics*, a uvular sound.

u·vu·li·tis (ū′vyoo-lī′tis), *n.* [Mod. L. < *uvula* + *-itis*], inflammation of the uvula.

ux., *uxor*, [L.], wife.

Ux·mal (ōōz-mäl′), *n.* a ruined Mayan city in Yucatan state, Mexico.

ux·o·ri·al (uk-sôr′i-əl, ug-zō′ri-əl), *adj.* [< L. *uxorius* (see UXORIOUS); + *-al*], of, befitting, or characteristic of a wife.

ux·or·i·cide (uk-sôr′ə-sīd′, ug-zō′rə-sīd′), *n.* [< L. *uxor*, wife; + *-cide*], 1. the murder of a wife by her husband. 2. a man who murders his wife.

ux·o·ri·ous (uk-sôr′i-əs, ug-zō′ri-əs), *adj.* [L. *uxorius* < *uxor*, wife], dotingly or irrationally fond of or submissive to one's wife.

Uz·beg (uz′beg), *n. & adj.* Uzbek.

Uz·bek (uz′bek; Russ. ooz′bek), *n.* 1. a member of a Turkic people living in the region of the Uzbek S.S.R. 2. the Central Turkic language of the Uzbeks. *adj.* of the Uzbek S.S.R., its people, their language, etc. Also **Usbek, Uzbeg, Usbeg.**

Uz·bek·i·stan (ooz′bek-i-stän′), *n.* the Uzbek S.S.R.

Uz·bek Soviet Socialist Republic (ooz-bek′), a republic of the U.S.S.R., in central Asia: area, 146,000 sq. mi.; pop., 6,282,000; capital, Tashkent: also called *Uzbekistan.*

V

V, v (vē), *n.* [*pl.* V's, v's, Vs, vs (vēz)], 1. the twenty-second letter of the English alphabet: from the Latin *V*, derived from one form of the Greek *Y* (upsilon): formerly used interchangeably in English with U both as a vowel and as a consonant, now only as a consonant: see **alphabet**, table. 2. the sound of V or v: in English, a voiced fricative formed by pressing the lower lips against the upper teeth, as also for (voiceless) *f*. 3. a type or impression for V or v. 4. *a symbol for* the twenty-second in a sequence or group (or the twenty-first if J is omitted). *adj.* 1. of V or v. 2. twenty-second (or twenty-first if J is omitted) in a sequence or group.

V (vē), *n.* 1. an object shaped like V. 2. a Roman numeral for 5; with a superior bar ($\overline{V}$), 5,000. 3. *a symbol for* victory of the nations allied against the Axis powers in World War II. 4. [Colloq.], a five-dollar bill. 5. in *chemistry*, *a symbol for* vanadium. *adj.* shaped like V.

V, v, 1. velocity. 2. volt; volts. 3. in *mathematics*, vector.

V., 1. Venerable. 2. Vicar. 3. Viscount.

v., 1. valve. 2. ventral. 3. verb. 4. [*pl.* vv.], verse. 5. version. 6. verso. 7. versus. 8. *vide*, [L.], see. 9. village. 10. [*pl.* vv.], violin. 11. vise. 12. vocative. 13. voice. 14. voltage. 15. volume. 16. *von*, [G.], of.

V-1, [< G. *vergeltungswaffe, eins*, vengeance weapon 1], a German jet-propelled bomb resembling a pilotless airplane, used against England in World War II; robot bomb.

V-2, [< G. *vergeltungswaffe, zwei*, vengeance weapon 2], a German rocket-propelled bomb, used against England in World War II: at the height of its trajectory it reached the stratosphere and attained a speed said to be greater than that of sound.

VA, V.A., Veterans' Administration.

Va., Virginia.

V.A., 1. Vicar Apostolic. 2. Vice Admiral.

v.a., 1. verb active. 2. verbal adjective.

Vaal (väl), *n.* a river flowing between the Transvaal and Orange Free State, into the Orange River: length, 700 mi.

va·ca (vä′kə), *n.* [Sp.], in the Southwest, a cow.

va·can·cy (vā′kən-si), *n.* [*pl.* VACANCIES (-siz)], [ML. *vacantia* < L. *vacans*], 1. the state of being vacant, or empty; emptiness. 2. *a*) empty space. *b*) a vacant space; gap, blank, break, or opening, as in a row or series. 3. the state of being empty in mind; lack of intelligence, interest, or thought; vacuity. 4. [Now Rare], the state of being free from work, activity, etc.; inactivity; idleness. 5. *a*) a vacating or being vacant, or unoccupied: of a position or office. *b*) the time such position or office is unoccupied. *c*) an unoccupied position or office; unfilled post, situation, or job. 6. untenanted quarters, as in an apartment house.

va·cant (vā′kənt), *adj.* [ME. *vacaunt*; OFr. *vacant*; L. *vacans*, ppr. of *vacare*, to be empty], 1. having nothing in it, as a space; devoid of contents; empty; void. 2. not held, filled, or occupied, as a position or office. 3. having no occupant: as, a *vacant* seat. 4. untenanted; not in use, as a room or house. 5. not filled with activity or work; free; leisure. 6. *a*) having or showing emptiness of mind or lack of intelligence, interest, thought, etc. *b*) empty of thought: said of the mind. 7. in *law*, *a*) unoccupied or unused, as land. *b*) having no claimant, as an estate or succession. *c*) not yet granted, as public lands. —*SYN.* see **empty.**

va·cate (vā′kāt), *v.t.* [VACATED (-id), VACATING], [< L. *vacatus*, pp. of *vacare*; see VACANT], 1. to make vacant; specifically, *a*) to cause (an office, position, etc.) to be unfilled or unoccupied, as by resignation. *b*) to leave (a house, room, etc.) uninhabited or untenanted; give up the occupancy of. 2. in *law*, to make void; annul. *v.i.* 1. to make an office, position, place, etc. vacant. 2. [Colloq.], to go away; leave.

va·ca·tion (və-kā′shən, vā-kā′shən), *n.* [ME. *vacacioun*; OFr.; L. *vacatio*], 1. freedom from any activity; rest; respite; intermission. 2. a period of rest and freedom from work, study, etc.; time of recreation, usually a specific interval in a year: as, two weeks' *vacation*. 3. [Rare], the act of vacating, or making vacant. 4. in *law*, a formal recess between terms of a court. *v.i.* 1. to take a vacation. 2. to pass one's vacation: as, he *vacationed* in Maine last summer.

va·ca·tion·er (və-kā′shən-ẽr, vā-kā′shən-ẽr), *n.* a vacationist.

va·ca·tion·ist (və-kā′shən-ist, vā-kā′shən-ist), *n.* a person taking a vacation, especially one who is traveling or at a resort.

vac·ci·nal (vak′sə-n′l), *adj.* of vaccine or vaccination.

vac·ci·nate (vak′sə-nāt′), *v.t.* [VACCINATED (-id), VACCINATING], [< *vaccine, adj.*], to inoculate with a specific vaccine in order to prevent or lessen the effect of some disease; specifically, to inoculate with cowpox vaccine in order to immunize against smallpox. *v.i.* to perform vaccination.

vac·ci·na·tion (vak′sə-nā′shən), *n.* 1. the act or practice of vaccinating. 2. the scar on the skin where the vaccine has been applied.

vac·ci·na·tor (vak′sə-nā′tẽr), *n.* a person or thing that vaccinates; especially, an instrument used for scarifying the skin where the vaccine is to be applied.

vac·cine (vak′sēn, vak′sin), *adj.* [L. *vacinnus* < *vacca* a cow], 1. [Rare], of or obtained from a cow. 2. of vaccinia or vaccination. *n.* 1. lymph, or a preparation of this, from a cowpox vesicle, containing the causative virus and used in vaccination against cowpox or smallpox. 2. any preparation of dead bacteria introduced into the body to produce immunity to a specific disease by causing the formation of antibodies.

vac·cin·i·a (vak-sin′i-ə), *n.* [Mod. L. < *vaccinus*; see VACCINE], cowpox.

vac·cin·i·a·ceous (vak-sin′i-ā′shəs), *adj.* [< Mod. L. *Vaccineaceae*, name of the family (< L. *vaccinium* blueberry); + *-ous*], of a family of shrubs including the blueberries, cranberries, huckleberries, etc.

vac·ci·ni·za·tion (vak′sə-ni-zā′shən, vak′sə-nī-zā′shən), *n.* repeated vaccination with the same vaccine until the virus has no further effect.

vac·il·late (vas′ə-lāt′), *v.i.* [VACILLATED (-id), VACILLATING], [< L. *vacillatus*, pp. of *vacillare*, to sway to and fro, waver], 1. to sway to and fro; waver; totter; stagger. 2. to fluctuate. 3. to waver in mind; show indecision; be irresolute. —*SYN.* see **hesitate.**

vac·il·lat·ing (vas′ə-lāt′iŋ), *adj.* tending to vacillate; wavering or tending to waver in motion, opinion, etc.

vac·il·la·tion (vas′ə-lā′shən), *n.* 1. the act, fact, or condition of vacillating; a swaying to and fro; unsteady movement. 2. the act, fact, or condition of wavering in mind, opinion, or course of action; irresolution.

vac·il·la·to·ry (vas'ə-lə-tôr'i, vas'ə-lə-tō'ri), *adj.* inclined to vacillate; vacillating.

vac·u·a (vak'ū-ə), *n.* alternative plural of **vacuum.**

va·cu·i·ty (va-kū'ə-ti), *n.* [*pl.* VACUITIES (-tiz)], [L. *vacuitas* < *vacuus*, empty], 1. the quality or state of being empty; emptiness. 2. an empty space; void; vacuum. 3. the quality or state of being empty in mind; lack of intelligence, interest, or thought. 4. anything pointless or inane; something foolish. 5. inanity.

vac·u·o·late (vak'ū-ə-lāt'), *adj.* vacuolated.

vac·u·o·lat·ed (vak'ū-ə-lāt'id), *adj.* having one or more vacuoles; containing vacuoles.

vac·u·o·la·tion (vak'ū-ə-lā'shən), *n.* the formation or arrangement of vacuoles.

vac·u·ole (vak'ū-ōl'), *n.* [Fr. < L. *vacuus*, empty], in *biology*, 1. a relatively clear, bubblelike space or cavity in the protoplasm of a cell, containing air, water, or partially digested fluid, and believed to have the function of discharging wastes. 2. a small cavity or vesicle in the tissues of an organism.

vac·u·ous (vak'ū-əs), *adj.* [L. *vacuus*], 1. empty. 2. having or showing lack of intelligence, interest, or thought; stupid; senseless; inane. 3. characterized by lack of purpose, of profitable employment, etc.; idle; purposeless. —***SYN.*** see **empty.**

vac·u·um (vak'ū-əm; *also, esp. as attrib.*, vak'yoom), *n.* [*pl.* VACUUMS (-əmz), VACUA (-ə)], [L., neut. sing. of *vacuus*, empty], 1. a space with nothing at all in it; completely empty space. 2. *a*) a space, as that inside a vacuum tube, out of which most of the air or gas has been taken, as by pumping; space containing air or gas at a pressure below that of the atmosphere. *b*) the degree to which pressure has been brought below atmospheric pressure. 3. a space left empty by the removal or absence of something usually found in it; void: often figurative. *adj.* 1. of a vacuum. 2. used to make a vacuum. 3. having a vacuum; partially or completely exhausted of air or gas. 4. working by suction or the creation of a partial vacuum. *v.t.* [Colloq.], to clean with a vacuum cleaner.

vacuum bottle, a bottlelike container used to keep liquids hot or cold by means of a vacuum between its inner and outer wall.

vacuum cleaner, a machine for cleaning carpets, floors, upholstery, etc. by suction.

vacuum gauge, an instrument for measuring the pressure of the air or gas in a partial vacuum.

vacuum pump, 1. a pump used to draw air or gas out of sealed space. 2. a pump for water, worked by the sucking effect of condensing steam.

vacuum tube, 1. a sealed glass or metal tube containing highly rarefied air or gas and a cathode (or filament), an anode (or plate), and a grid for controlling the flow of electrons from one to the other: it is used in radio, television, etc. as a rectifier, detector, amplifier, etc.; electron tube. 2. a sealed tube having the air or gas in it exhausted to a high degree and containing metallic electrodes between which electric discharges may be passed.

VACUUM TUBE

vacuum valve, [British], a vacuum tube.

va·de me·cum (vā'di mē'kəm), [L., lit., go with me], something carried about by a person for constant use, reference, etc.; specifically, a handbook or manual.

Va·duz (vä'doots), *n.* the capital of Liechtenstein, on the Rhine: pop., 1,700.

‡**vae vic·tis** (vē vik'tis), [L.], woe to the conquered.

vag·a·bond (vag'ə-bond'), *adj.* [ME. *vagabound;* OFr.; L. *vagabundus, adj.*, strolling about < *vagari*, to wander], 1. moving from place to place, with no fixed abode; wandering. 2. living an unsettled, drifting, or irresponsible life; vagrant; hence, 3. shiftless; worthless; good-for-nothing. 4. of or characteristic of a wandering, shiftless, or irresponsible way of life. 5. aimlessly following an irregular course or path; drifting. *n.* 1. a person who wanders from place to place, having no fixed abode. 2. a tramp; wandering beggar. 3. an idle, disreputable, or shiftless person; ne'er-do-well; rascal. *v.i.* to wander. —***SYN.*** see **vagrant.**

vag·a·bond·age (vag'ə-bon'dij), *n.* [Fr.; see -AGE], 1. the state or condition of being a vagabond; wandering or vagrant way of life. 2. vagabonds collectively; vagrants.

vag·a·bond·ism (vag'ə-bon-diz'm), *n.* vagabond way of life; vagabondage.

va·gar·i·ous (və-gâr'i-əs), *adj.* 1. full of vagaries; characterized by vagaries; erratic; unpredictable. 2. wandering; roaming.

va·gar·y (və-gâr'i), *n.* [*pl.* VAGARIES (-iz)], [earlier used as *v.*, to wander < L. *vagari*, to wander], 1. an odd, eccentric, or unexpected action or bit of conduct. 2. an odd, whimsical, or freakish idea or notion; oddity; caprice. —***SYN.*** see **caprice.**

va·gi·na (və-jī'nə), *n.* [*pl.* VAGINAS (-nəz), VAGINAE (-nē)], [L., a sheath], 1. in *anatomy & zoology*, a sheath or sheathlike structure; specifically, in female mammals, the canal leading from the vulva to the uterus. 2. in *botany*, the sheath formed by the base of certain leaves where it envelops a stem.

vag·i·nal (vaj'ə-n'l, və-jī'n'l), *adj.* in *anatomy & zoology*, 1. of or like a sheath. 2. of or for the vagina of a female mammal.

vag·i·nate (vaj'ə-nit, vaj'ə-nāt'), *adj.* [Mod. L. *vaginatus*], 1. having a vagina or sheath; sheathed. 2. in the form of a sheath; like a sheath.

vag·i·ni·tis (vaj'ə-nī'tis), *n.* [Mod. L.; see VAGINA & -ITIS], inflammation of the vagina.

vag·i·no- (vaj'ə-nō, vaj'ə-nə), [< L. *vagina*], a combining form meaning: 1. *vagina*, as in *vaginitis*. 2. *vagina and*. Also, before a vowel, **vagin-.**

va·gran·cy (vā'grən-si), *n.* [*pl.* VAGRANCIES (-siz)], [< *vagrant*], 1. a wandering in thought or talk; digression. 2. a wandering from place to place; vagabondage. 3. shiftless or idle wandering without money or work, as of tramps, beggars, etc.; conduct or way of life of a vagrant (sense 3).

va·grant (vā'grənt), *n.* [ME. *vagarant;* prob. < OFr. *wa(u)crant*, ppr. of *wa(u)crer*, to wander about, walk; influenced in form by *vagabond* or L. *vagari*, to wander], 1. a person who wanders from place to place or lives a wandering life; rover. 2. a person who wanders from place to place without a regular job, supporting himself by begging, etc.; idle wanderer; vagabond; tramp. 3. in *law*, a tramp, beggar, prostitute, or similar idle or disorderly person whose way of living makes him liable to be arrested and jailed. *adj.* 1. wandering from place to place or living a wandering life; roaming; nomadic. 2. living the life of a vagabond or tramp. 3. of or characteristic of a vagrant. 4. characterized by straggling growth: said of plants. 5. following no fixed direction or course; moving at random; wayward: said of things.

***SYN.*—vagrant** refers to a person without a fixed home who wanders about from place to place, supporting himself by begging, etc., and in legal usage, implies such a person regarded as a public nuisance, subject to arrest; **vagabond,** originally the more derogatory term, implying shiftlessness, thievery, etc., now often connotes no more than a carefree, roaming existence; **bum, tramp,** and **hobo** are informal equivalents for the preceding, variously discriminated, but **bum** always connotes an idle, dissolute, often alcoholic person who never works, **tramp** connotes a vagrant, whether he lives by begging or by doing odd jobs, and **hobo** is now most commonly restricted to a migratory laborer who follows such seasonal work as crop picking or works on construction jobs, etc. See also **itinerant.**

va·grom (vā'grəm), *adj.* [Archaic], vagrant.

vague (vāg), *adj.* [Fr.; L. *vagus*, wandering], 1. not clearly, precisely, or definitely expressed or stated. 2. not clearly outlined; indefinite in shape or form; hazily, obscurely, or indistinctly seen or sensed. 3. not sharp, certain, or precise in thought or expression: said of persons, the mind, etc. 4. not precisely determined or known; uncertain. —***SYN.*** see **obscure.**

va·gus (vā'gəs), *n.* [*pl.* VAGI (-jī)], [L., wandering], either of the tenth pair of cranial nerves, arising in the medulla oblongata and innervating the larynx, lungs, heart, esophagus, and most of the abdominal organs; pneumogastric nerve: also **vagus nerve.**

vail (vāl), *v.i.* [ME. *vailen* < OFr. *vaill*, 1st pers. sing., pres. indic., of *valoir*, to be of worth; cf. AVAIL], [Archaic], to be of use, service, or profit; avail. *n.* [Archaic], a tip; gratuity.

vail (vāl), *v.t.* [ME. *valen* < OFr. *valer* or aphetic < *avaler*, to descend < *à val*, down < L. *ad vallum*, lit., to the valley], [Archaic], 1. to lower; let sink or fall down. 2. to take off (a hat, etc.) as a sign of respect or submission.

vail (vāl), *n. & v.t.* [Obs.], veil.

vain (vān), *adj.* [ME. *vain, veyn;* OFr. *vain, vein;* L. *vanus*, empty, vain; akin to Goth. *wans*, lacking, Eng. *wan, want*], 1. having no real value or significance; worthless, empty, idle, hollow, etc.: as, *vain* pomp. 2. without force or effect; futile, fruitless, unprofitable, unavailing, etc.: as, a *vain* endeavor. 3. having or showing an excessively high regard for one's self, looks, possessions, ability, etc.; indulging in or resulting from personal vanity; conceited. 4. [Archaic], lacking in sense; foolish.

in vain, 1. fruitlessly; vainly. 2. lightly; profanely.

***SYN.*—vain,** in this connection, applies to that which has little or no real value, worth, or meaning (*vain* studies); **idle** refers to that which is baseless or worthless because it can never be realized or have a real effect (*idle* hopes, *idle* talk); **empty** and **hollow** are used of that which lacks real substance and only appears to be genuine, sincere, worthwhile, etc. (*empty threats, hollow* pleasures); **otiose** applies to that which has no real purpose or function and is therefore useless or superfluous (this *otiose* name-calling). See also **futile.**

vain·glo·ri·ous (vān'glôr'i-əs, vān'glō'ri-əs), *adj.* [< *vainglory* + *-ous*], 1. boastfully vain and proud of oneself. 2. showing or characterized by boastful vanity.

vain·glo·ry (vān'glôr'i, vān'glō'ri), *n.* [ME. *vainglorie;* OFr. *vaine gloire;* ML. *vana gloria;* see VAIN & GLORY], extreme self-pride and boastfulness; excessive and ostentatious vanity. —*SYN.* see **pride.**

vain·ly (vān'li), *adv.* 1. in vain; uselessly; fruitlessly; without success. 2. conceitedly.

vair (vâr), *n.* [ME. & OFr. *vair, veir;* L. *varium* < *varius;* see MINIVER, VARIOUS], 1. a fur, usually from a gray and white squirrel, used for trimming and lining clothes in the 13th and 14th centuries. 2. in *heraldry,* a fur, represented by rows of small bells, one row upright, the next turned down.

Val., Valenciennes (lace).

val., 1. valuation. 2. value.

Va·lais (và'le'), *n.* a canton of southwestern Switzerland: pop., 148,000.

val·ance (val'əns), *n.* [prob. < OFr. **avalance* < *avalant,* ppr. of *avaler,* to hang, descend; but ? < *Valence,* France], 1. a short drapery or curtain hanging from the edge of a bed, shelf, table, etc., often to the floor. 2. a short drapery across the top of a window. 3. a facing of wood or metal imitating this.

val·anced (val'ənst), *adj.* fitted with a valance.

Val·dai Hills (väl-dī'), a region of hills in the southern Leningrad and northern Kalinin regions, R.S.F.S.R.: highest point, c. 1,000 ft.: source of the Volga, Dvina, and Dnepr Rivers.

Val·de·mar I (väl'də-mär'), see **Waldemar I.**

vale (vāl), *n.* [ME. & OFr. *val;* L. *vallis*], [Chiefly Poetic], a valley.

‡**va·le** (vā'li), *interj. & n.* [L.], farewell.

val·e·dic·tion (val'ə-dik'shən), *n.* [< L. *valedictus,* pp. of *valedicere,* to say farewell; *vale,* farewell (imperative of *valere,* to be strong or well) + *dicere,* to say], 1. a farewell; a bidding or saying farewell. 2. something said in parting; farewell utterance.

val·e·dic·to·ri·an (val'ə-dik-tôr'i-ən, val'ə-dik-tō'ri-ən), *n.* in schools and colleges, the student, usually the one ranking highest in scholarship, who delivers the valedictory at graduation.

val·e·dic·to·ry (val'ə-dik'tə-ri), *adj.* [< L. *valedictus* (see VALEDICTION); + *-ory*], said or done at parting, by way of farewell; uttered as a valediction. *n.* [*pl.* VALEDICTORIES (-riz)], a farewell speech, especially one delivered at graduation from school or college.

va·lence (vā'ləns), *n.* [ML. *valentia,* worth, value < L. *valens,* ppr. of *valere,* to be strong], 1. in *biology,* the ability of chromosomes, serums, vaccines, etc. to combine with definite organisms, allergens, and allied matter, or produce a specific effect upon them. 2. in *chemistry,* the capacity of an element or radical to combine with another, as measured by the number of hydrogen atoms which one radical or one atom of the element will combine with or replace: as, oxygen has a *valence* of two (i.e., one atom of oxygen combines with two hydrogen atoms). 3. a unit of valence.

Va·len·ci·a (və-len'shi-ə, və-len'shə; Sp. vä-len'thyä), *n.* 1. a region in eastern Spain: formerly a kingdom: area, 4,239 sq. mi.; pop., 1,393,000 (est. 1946). 2. a city in eastern Spain, on the Mediterranean: pop., 544,000 (est. 1946). 3. a city in north central Venezuela: pop., 49,000.

Va·len·ci·ennes (və-len'si-enz'; Fr. và'län'syen'), *n.* 1. a city in northern France, near Belgium: pop., 39,000 (1946). 2. [< *Valenciennes,* France], a flat bobbin lace having a simple floral pattern on a background of fine, diamond-shaped mesh: abbreviated **Val.**: also **Valenciennes lace, Val lace.**

va·len·cy (vā'lən-si), *n.* [*pl.* VALENCIES (-siz)], [L. *valentia*], in *chemistry,* valence.

-va·lent (vā'lənt), in *chemistry,* a suffix meaning: 1. *having a specified valence.* 2. *having a specified number of valences.* Although both the Greek set of prefixes (*mono-, di-, tri-, tetra-,* etc.) and the Latin (*uni-, bi-, ter-, quadri-,* etc.) are used with *-valent,* the latter set is preferred when designating the number of valences an element exhibits and the former when designating the specific valence of some atom or radical.

Val·en·tine (val'ən-tīn'), [L. *Valentinus* < *Valens,* a masculine name < *valens,* ppr. of *valere,* to be strong or healthy], a masculine name.

val·en·tine (val'ən-tīn'), *n.* [ME.; OFr.; after Saint *Valentine;* L. *Valentinus*], 1. *a*) a sweetheart chosen or complimented on Saint Valentine's day. *b*) one's sweetheart. 2. *a*) a greeting card or note sent to a real or pretended sweetheart on this day, and containing lines of sentimental love. *b*) a burlesque of this, often sent anonymously. 3. a gift presented on Saint Valentine's day.

Valentine, Saint, 3d century A.D.; Christian martyr of Rome.

Val·en·tin·i·an (val'ən-tin'i-ən), *n.* (*Valentinianus*), name of three Roman emperors: I, 364–375 A.D. (lived c. 321–375 A.D.); II, 375–392 A.D. (lived c. 372–392 A.D.); III, 425–455 A.D. (lived c. 419–455 A.D.).

Valera, Eamon De, see **De Valera, Eamon.**

Va·le·ra y Al·ca·lá Ga·lia·no, Juan (hwän vä-le'rä ē äl'kä-lä' gä-lyä'nô), 1824–1905; Spanish author and statesman.

Va·ler·i·a (və-lêr'i-ə), [L., fem. of *Valerius,* name of a Roman gens; prob. < *valere,* to be strong], a feminine name: equivalent, Fr. *Valérie:* also **Valerie.**

Va·ler·i·an (və-lêr'i-ən), *n.* (*Publius Licinius Valerianus*), Roman emperor (253–260 A.D.); lived ?–269? A.D.

va·le·ri·an (və-lêr'i-ən), *n.* [Fr. *valériane;* ML. *valeriana,* valerian; as if < the personal name *Valerius*], 1. any of a number of related plants with clusters or spikes of white, pink, red, or purplish flowers. 2. a drug made from the roots of some of these plants and used as a sedative and antispasmodic.

va·le·ri·a·na·ceous (və-lêr'i-ə-nā'shəs), *adj.* [< Mod. L. *Valerianaceae,* name of the family; + *-ous*], of a family of herbs with opposite leaves and small flowers, as the spikenard, valerian, etc.

va·le·ri·an·ic (və-lêr'i-an'ik), *adj.* valeric.

va·ler·ic (və-ler'ik, və-lêr'ik), *adj.* designating or of any of four isomeric acids, C_4H_9COOH, some originally found in valerian root, but all now made synthetically.

Val·er·ie (val'ẽr-i), a feminine name: see **Valeria.**

Va·lé·ry, Paul Am·broise (pôl än'brwàz' và'lā'rē'), 1871–1945; French poet, essayist, and philosopher.

val·et (val'it, val'ā; Fr. và'lā'), *n.* [Fr., a groom, yeoman; OFr. *valet, vaslet, varlet;* see VARLET], 1. a personal manservant who takes care of one's clothes, helps one in dressing, etc. 2. a hotel employee who cleans or presses clothes or performs other personal services. *v.t. & v.i.* to serve (a person) as a valet.

‡**va·let de cham·bre** (và'lā' də shän'br'), [*pl.* VALETS DE CHAMBRE (và'lā' də shän'br')], [Fr., chamber servant], a valet (sense 1).

val·e·tu·di·nar·i·an (val'ə-tōō'də-nâr'i-ən, val'ə-tū'də-nâr'i-ən), *n.* [< L. *valetudinarius,* sickly, infirm, an invalid < *valetudo, valetudinis,* state of health, sickness, infirmity < *valere,* to be strong, hearty], 1. a person in poor health; invalid. 2. a person who thinks constantly and anxiously about his health. *adj.* 1. in poor health; sickly; invalid. 2. anxiously concerned about one's health. 3. characterized by poor health.

val·e·tu·di·nar·i·an·ism (val'ə-tōō'də-nâr'i-ən-iz'm, val'ə-tū'də-nâr'i-ən-iz'm), *n.* a valetudinarian condition; state of being or feeling in poor health.

val·e·tu·di·nar·y (val'ə-tōō'də-ner'i, val'ə-tū'də-ner'i), *adj.* valetudinarian. *n.* [*pl.* VALETUDINARIES (-iz)], [Rare], a valetudinarian.

val·gus (val'gəs), *n.* [L., bowlegged], 1. an abnormal turning outward of the foot so as to produce knock-knee. 2. [Obs.], varus. *adj.* knock-kneed.

Val·hall (val-hal'), *n.* Valhalla.

Val·hal·la (val-hal'ə), *n.* [Mod. L. < ON. *valhöll,* genit. *valhallar,* hall of the slain (cf. VALKYRIE) < *valr,* slaughter, the slain + *höll,* hall], in *Norse mythology,* the great hall where Odin receives and feasts the souls of heroes who have fallen bravely in battle: also **Walhalla, Valhall.**

val·iance (val'yəns), *n.* [OFr. *vaillance* < *vaillant,* valiant; see VALIANT], [Archaic], valiancy.

val·ian·cy (val'yən-si), *n.* [< *valiant*], 1. bravery; courage. 2. [*pl.* VALIANCIES (-siz)], a brave deed.

val·iant (val'yənt), *adj.* [ME. *valliant;* OFr. *valiant, vaillant,* ppr. of *valoir* < L. *valere,* to be strong; for IE base see WIELD], brave; courageous: said of persons or their acts. —*SYN.* see **brave.**

val·id (val'id), *adj.* [Fr. *valide;* L. *validus,* strong, powerful < *valere,* to be strong, have power], 1. having legal force; properly executed and binding under the law. 2. sound; well grounded on principles or evidence; able to withstand criticism or objection, as an argument: opposed to *invalid.* 3. effective, effectual, cogent, etc. 4. [Rare], robust; strong; healthy.

SYN.—**valid** applies to that which can not be objected to because it conforms to law, logic, the facts, etc. (a *valid* criticism); **sound** refers to that which is firmly grounded on facts, evidence, logic, etc. and is therefore free from error or superficiality (a *sound* method); **cogent** implies such a powerful appeal to the mind, as because of validity, as to appear conclusive (*cogent* reasoning); **convincing** implies such validity as to persuade or overcome doubts, opposition, etc. (a *convincing* argument); **telling** suggests the power to have the required effect by being forcible, striking, relevant, etc. (a *telling* rejoinder). —*ANT.* fallacious.

val·i·date (val'ə-dāt'), *v.t.* [VALIDATED (-id), VALIDATING], [< ML. *validatus,* pp. of *validare,* to validate], 1. to make binding under the law; give legal force to; declare legally valid. 2. to prove to be valid; confirm the validity of. —*SYN.* see **confirm.**

val·i·da·tion (val'ə-dā'shən), *n.* a making or declaring valid; proof; confirmation.

va·lid·i·ty (və-lid′ə-ti), *n.* [*pl.* VALIDITIES (-tiz)], [Fr. *validité;* L. *validitas*], the state, quality, or fact of being valid in law or in argument, proof, authority, etc.; (legal) soundness.
va·lise (və-lēs′), *n.* [Fr.; It. *valigia;* ? < Ar.], a suitcase.
Val·kyr (val′kẽr), *n.* a Valkyrie.
Val·kyr·i·an (val-kẽr′i-ən), *adj.* of, like, or characteristic of a Valkyrie.
Val·kyr·ie (val-kẽr′i, val-kī′ri, val′ki-ri), *n.* [ON. *valkyrja,* lit., chooser of the slain < *valr,* those slain (cf. VALHALLA) + *kjōsa,* to choose (akin to AS. *ceosan*)], in *Norse mythology,* any of the maidens of Odin who conduct the souls of heroes slain in battle to Valhalla and wait on them there: also **Walkyrie, Valkyr.**
Val·la·do·lid (val′ə-dō′lid; Sp. vä′lyä-*th*ō-lēth′), *n.* a city in north central Spain: pop., 137,000.
val·la·tion (va-lā′shən), *n.* [LL. *vallatio* < L. *vallatus,* pp. of *vallare,* to protect with a rampart < *vallum,* a rampart], 1. a wall or earthwork used for military defense; rampart. 2. the art or process of building such military defenses.
val·lec·u·la (və-lek′yoo-lə), *n.* [*pl.* VALLECULAE (-lē′)], [Mod. L.; dim. < L. *vallis, valles,* valley], in *anatomy* & *botany,* a groove or furrow, as the depression between the epiglottis and the base of the tongue, or any of the grooves on a stalk of celery.
val·lec·u·lar (və-lek′yoo-lẽr), *adj.* of, or having the nature of, a vallecula.
val·lec·u·late (və-lek′yoo-lāt′), *adj.* having a vallecula or valleculae.
Val·le·jo (va-lā′hō), *n.* a city in California, just north of Oakland: pop., 61,000.
Val·let·ta (vä-let′å), *n.* seaport and capital of Malta: pop., 18,000.
val·ley (val′i), *n.* [*pl.* VALLEYS (-iz)], [ME. *vale;* OFr. *valee* < *val;* L. *vallis,* a vale], 1. a stretch of low land lying between hills or mountains and usually having a river or stream flowing through it. 2. the land drained or watered by a great river system: as, the Nile *valley,* Mississippi *valley.* 3. any dip or hollow like a valley, as the trough of a wave. 4. in *architecture,* the trough formed where two slopes of a roof meet, or where the roof meets a wall; gutter.
Valley Forge, a village in southeastern Pennsylvania, where Washington and his troops encamped in the winter of 1777–1778.
Valley of Ten Thousand Smokes, a volcanic region in Katmai National Monument, southwestern Alaska.
Val·lom·bro·sa (väl′lôm-brô′sä; Eng. val′əm-brō′sə), *n.* a resort in Tuscany, Italy, near Florence.
Val·ois (vål′wä′), *n.* 1. a duchy of northern France in the Middle Ages. 2. the ruling family of France (1328–1589).
Va·lo·na (vä-lô′nä), *n.* a seaport in Albania, on the Adriatic: pop., 15,000: also **Avlona.**
va·lo·ni·a (və-lō′ni-ə), *n.* [It. *vallonia, vallonea;* Mod. Gr. *balania, belania,* evergreen oak < Gr. *balanos,* acorn], the acorn cups of an oak of Europe and Asia (*valonia oak*), used in dyeing, tanning, etc.
val·or (val′ẽr), *n.* [ME. & OFr. *valour;* LL. *valor,* worth, hence courage < L. *valere,* to be strong, to be worth], courage; fearlessness; bravery, especially in battle.
val·or·i·za·tion (val′ẽr-i-zā′shən, val′ẽr-ī-zā′shən), *n.* [Port. *valorização* < *valor,* a price, worth; L. *valor;* see VALOR], a fixing of prices, usually by government action, as by buying up a commodity at the fixed price or lending money to producers so that they can keep their goods off the market.
val·or·ize (val′ẽr-īz′), *v.t.* & *v.i.* [VALORIZED (-īzd′), VALORIZING], to fix or control the price of (a commodity) by valorization.
val·or·ous (val′ẽr-əs), *adj.* [OFr. *valeureux;* ML. *valorosus*], having or showing valor; fearless; brave.
val·our (val′ẽr), *n.* valor: British spelling.
Val·pa·rai·so, Val·pa·ra·í·so (val′pə-rā′zō, val′pə-rī′sō; Sp. väl′pä-rä-ē′sô), *n.* a seaport in central Chile: pop., 222,000.
‡**valse** (våls), *n.* [Fr.], a waltz.
val·u·a·ble (val′yoo-b′l, val′ū-ə-b′l), *adj.* 1. having material value; being worth money. 2. having great value in terms of money: as, a *valuable* diamond. 3. being highly thought of; being prized highly; being of great worth in some way, usually nonmaterial. *n. usually in pl.* an article of value, especially one of small size, as a piece of jewelry. —*SYN.* see **costly.**
val·u·a·bly (val′yoo-bli, val′ū-ə-bli), *adv.* so as to be of great value; usefully.
val·u·a·tion (val′ū-ā′shən), *n.* [OFr. *valuacion*], 1. the act of determining the value or price of anything; evaluation; appraisal. 2. determined or estimated value or price. 3. estimation of the worth, merit, etc. of anything: as, his *valuation* of our work was not high. Abbreviated **val.**
val·u·a·tor (val′ū-ā′tẽr), *n.* a person who estimates value; appraiser.
val·ue (val′ū), *n.* [ME.; OFr., fem. of *valu,* pp. of *valoir* (L. *valere*), to be strong, be worth], 1. a fair or proper equivalent in money, commodities, etc. for something sold or exchanged; fair price. 2. the worth of a thing in money or goods at a certain time; market price. 3. the equivalent (of something) in money: as, she lost jewels to the *value* of four thousand dollars. 4. estimated or appraised worth or price; valuation. 5. purchasing power: as, the *value* of a dollar fluctuates. 6. that quality of a thing according to which it is thought of as being more or less desirable, useful, estimable, important, etc.; worth or the degree of worth. 7. that which is desirable or worthy of esteem for its own sake; thing or quality having intrinsic worth. 8. precise meaning, as of a word. 9. in *art, a*) relative lightness or darkness of a color. *b*) proportioned effect, as of light and shade, in an artistic work. 10. in *mathematics,* the quantity or amount for which a symbol stands: as, 27 is the *value* of x in this equation. 11. in *music,* the relative duration of a note, tone, or rest. 12. in *phonetics,* the quality of sound of a letter or diphthong: as, each of the vowels has several *values* in English. 13. *pl.* in *sociology,* acts, customs, institutions, etc. regarded in a particular, especially favorable, way by a people, ethnic group, etc. *v.t.* [VALUED (-ūd), VALUING], 1. to estimate the value of; set a price for; determine the worth of; appraise. 2. to place a certain estimate of worth on in a scale of values: as, I *value* health above wealth. 3. to think highly of; esteem; prize: as, I *value* your friendship. Abbreviated **val.** —*SYN.* see **appreciate, worth.**
val·ued (val′ūd), *adj.* [pp. of *value*], 1. estimated; appraised: as, a hat *valued* at ten dollars. 2. highly thought of; esteemed: as, a *valued* friend.
valued policy, an insurance policy in which the insurer agrees to pay the full amount of the policy in case of total loss of the property, regardless of its actual value at the time of the loss.
val·ue·less (val′ū-lis), *adj.* of no value or use; worthless.
val·u·er (val′ū-ẽr), *n.* 1. a person who values. 2. [British], an appraiser.
‡**va·lu·ta** (vä-loo′tä), *n.* [It., value], the value of a currency; specifically, the exchange value of the currency of any of certain European countries with reference to the currency of a specified country.
valv·ar (val′vẽr), *adj.* valvular.
val·vate (val′vāt), *adj.* [L. *valvatus,* having folding doors < *valva;* see VALVE], in *botany,* 1. meeting without overlapping, as the petals of some flower buds. 2. opening by valves, as a pea pod. 3. having a valve or valves.
valve (valv), *n.* [ME., a door leaf < L. *valva,* leaf of a folding door], 1. [Now Rare], either of the halves of a double door or any of the leaves of a folding door. 2. a gate regulating the flow of water in a sluice, channel, etc. 3. in *anatomy,* a membranous fold or structure which permits body fluids to flow in one direction only, or opens and closes a tube or opening. 4. in *botany, a*) one of the segments into which a pod or capsule separates when it bursts open. *b*) a lidlike part in some anthers, through which pollen is discharged. 5. in *electricity, a*) an electrolytic cell or other device that permits a flow of current in one direction only. *b*) [British], an electron tube. 6. in *mechanics, a*) any device in a pipe or tube that permits a flow in one direction only, or regulates the flow of whatever is in the pipe, by means of a flap, lid, plug, etc. acting to open or block passage. *b*) the flap, lid, plug, etc. in such a device. 7. in *music,* a device in certain wind instruments, as the trumpet, that opens an auxiliary to the main tube, lengthening the air column and lowering the pitch. 8. in *zoology, a*) one of the parts making up the shell of a mollusk, barnacle, clam, etc. *b*) a part forming the sheath of an ovipositor in certain insects. Abbreviated **v.** *v.t.* & *v.i.* [VALVED (valvd), VALVING], 1. to fit with or make use of a valve or valves. 2. to regulate the flow of (a fluid) by means of a valve or valves.

VALVE

GLOBE VALVE

valve-in-head engine (valv′in-hed′), an internal-combustion engine, as in some automobiles, having the intake and exhaust valves in the cylinder head instead of the block.
valve·let (valv′lit), *n.* a small valve; valvule.
val·vu·lar (val′vyoo-lẽr), *adj.* 1. having the form or function of a valve. 2. having a valve or valves. 3. of a valve or valves; especially, of the valves of the heart: as, a *valvular* disorder.
val·vule (val′vūl), *n.* [Fr., dim. < L. *valva*], a small valve; valvelet.

val·vu·li·tis (val'vyoo-lī'tis), *n.* [Mod. L. < *valvula* (dim. of L. *valva;* see VALVE); + *-itis*], inflammation of a valve, especially a valve of the heart.

va·moose (va-mōōs'), *v.i. & v.t.* [VAMOOSED (-mōōst'), VAMOOSING], [Sp. *vamos,* let us go], [Slang], to leave quickly; go away or depart (from) hurriedly.

va·mose (va-mōs'), *v.i. & v.t.* [VAMOSED (-mōst'), VAMOSING], [Slang], to vamoose.

vamp (vamp), *n.* [ME. *vampe;* OFr. *avampié* < *avant,* before + *pié, pied,* a foot], 1. the part of a boot or shoe covering the instep and toe. 2. [< the *v.*], *a*) something patched up; something fixed up to seem new; patchwork. *b*) something patched on. 3. in *music,* a simple accompaniment improvised to fit a song. *v.t.* 1. to put a vamp on; provide or mend with a new vamp; hence, 2. to patch (*up*); repair. 3. to make over (something old) by addition or alteration. 4. in *music,* to improvise (a simple accompaniment, variation of a tune, etc.). *v.i.* in *music,* to improvise a simple accompaniment, variation of a tune, etc.

vamp (vamp), *n.* [Slang], a vampire (sense 3) or unscrupulous flirt. *v.t.* [Slang], to seduce or beguile (a man) by the use of one's feminine charms and wiles. *v.i.* [Slang], to act the part of a vamp.

vam·pire (vam'pīr), *n.* [Fr.; G. *vampir;* of Slav. origin], 1. in folklore and popular superstition, a corpse that becomes reanimated and leaves its grave at night to suck the blood of sleeping persons; hence, 2. an unscrupulous person who preys ruthlessly on others, as a blackmailer or usurer. 3. *a*) a beautiful but unscrupulous woman who seduces men and leads them to their ruin. *b*) an actress who plays the part of such a woman. 4. a vampire bat.

vampire bat, 1. any of several species of tropical American bats which live on the blood of animals. 2. any of various bats mistakenly believed to be bloodsuckers.

vam·pir·ic (vam-pir'ik), *adj.* of or like a vampire.

vam·pir·ism (vam'pīr-iz'm, vam'pi-riz'm), *n.* 1. superstitious belief in vampires. 2. the habits or practices of vampires. 3. a wicked preying on other people.

Van (vän), *n.* 1. a salt lake in eastern Turkey: area, 1,425 sq. mi. 2. a town on this lake: pop., 22,000.

van (van), *n.* [abbrev. < *vanguard*], 1. the front of an army or fleet when advancing or in battle array. 2. the foremost position in a line, movement, field of endeavor, etc., or those in the foremost position.

van (van), *n.* [< L. *vannus,* a van, fan; or South Brit. var. of *fan, n.*], 1. [Archaic or British Dial.], a winnowing fan or machine, or a shovel for washing ore. 2. [Poetic], a wing.

van (van), *n.* [abbrev. < *caravan*], 1. a large closed truck or wagon for carrying furniture, freight, etc. 2. [British], a closed railway car for baggage, etc.

van (van; D. vän), *prep.* [D.], of; from: in Dutch family names it originally indicated place of origin: in American and British usage, it is often capitalized as part of a personal name.

van·a·date (van'ə-dāt'), *n.* in *chemistry,* a salt or ester of vanadic acid.

va·na·di·ate (və-nā'di-āt'), *n.* a vanadate.

va·nad·ic (və-nad'ik, və-nā'dik), *adj.* designating or of chemical compounds containing trivalent or pentavalent vanadium.

vanadic acid, any of several acids containing vanadium.

va·nad·i·nite (və-nad'ə-nīt'), *n.* a mineral, lead vanadate and lead chloride, occurring in bright crystals, usually yellow, brown, or red.

va·na·di·ous (və-nā'di-əs), *adj.* vanadous.

va·na·di·um (və-nā'di-əm), *n.* [Mod. L. < ON. *Vanadis,* one of the names of the goddess Freya], a rare, malleable, ductile, silver-white metallic chemical element: it is alloyed with steel, to which it adds tensile strength: symbol, V; at. wt., 50.95; at. no., 23.

vanadium steel, a steel alloy containing 0.10 to 0.15 per cent vanadium to harden and toughen it: used in the manufacture of machinery and tools.

van·a·dous (van'ə-dəs), *adj.* designating or of chemical compounds containing divalent or trivalent vanadium: also **vanadious.**

Van Al·len (radiation) belt (van al'ən), [after James A. *Van Allen* (1914–), Am. physicist], either of two broad zones (inner and outer) of intense, natural radiation encircling the earth at varying levels in the upper atmosphere.

Van·brugh, Sir **John** (van-brōō'; Brit. van'brə), 1664–1726; English playwright and architect.

Van Bu·ren, Martin (van byoor'ən), 1782–1862; eighth president of the United States (1837–1841).

Van·cou·ver (van-kōō'vẽr), *n.* 1. a seaport in southwestern British Columbia, Canada: pop., 385,000 (with suburbs, 790,000). 2. an island of British Columbia, off the southwestern coast: area, 12,408 sq. mi.; pop., 291,000; chief city, Victoria. 3. a city in southern Washington: pop., 32,000.

Vancouver, Mount, a mountain in the St. Elias Range, on the border between Alaska and Canada: height, 15,696 ft.

Van·dal (van'd'l), *n.* [L. *Vandalus* < Gmc. base seen also in AS. *Wendil,* ON. *Vendill*], 1. a member of an East Germanic tribe that ravaged Gaul, Spain, and northern Africa and sacked Rome (455 A.D.). 2. [v-], a person who, out of malice or ignorance, destroys or spoils, especially that which is beautiful or artistic. *adj.* 1. of the Vandals. 2. [v-], like or characteristic of a vandal; ruthlessly destructive.

Van·dal·ic (van-dal'ik), *adj.* 1. of or characteristic of the Vandals. 2. [v-], ignorantly and willfully destructive; barbarous. *n.* the East Germanic language of the Vandals, known only through proper names and scattered loan words in the Romance languages.

van·dal·ism (van'd'l-iz'm), *n.* the conduct, attitudes, or an act of the Vandals or vandals; malicious or ignorant destruction, especially of that which is beautiful or artistic.

Van·der·bilt, Cornelius (van'dẽr-bilt'), 1794–1877; American capitalist and railroad industrialist.

Van Die·men's Land (van dē'mənz), Tasmania, an island off southeastern Australia: the former name.

Van Do·ren, Carl (van dôr'ən, dō'rən), 1885–1950; American editor, literary critic, and author.

Van Doren, Mark, 1894– ; brother of *Carl;* American poet, novelist, and critic.

Van Dru·ten, John William (van drōō't'n), 1901–1957; English playwright in America.

Van Dyck, Sir **Anthony** (van dīk'), 1599–1641; Flemish portrait painter in England: also spelled **Vandyke.**

Van·dyke (van-dīk'), *n.* 1. a portrait or painting by Anthony Van Dyck (or Vandyke). 2. a Vandyke beard. 3. a Vandyke collar. *adj.* 1. of, or in the style of, Van Dyck. 2. of or imitating the dress, fashions, etc. depicted in portraits by Van Dyck.

Vandyke beard, a closely trimmed, pointed beard.

Vandyke brown, 1. a deep-brown pigment used by Van Dyck; hence, 2. any of several brown pigments or colors.

Vandyke collar (or **cape**), a broad linen or lace collar with a deeply indented edge.

VANDYKE BEARD

vane (vān), *n.* [South Brit. var. of *fane,* small flag or pennon < AS. *fana,* a flag], 1. a flat piece of metal, strip of cloth, etc. set up high to swing with the wind and show which way it is blowing; weathercock; weather vane. 2. any of several flat or curved pieces set around an axle, forming a wheel to be rotated by moving air, water, etc., or, if mechanically rotated, to move the air or water: as, the *vane* of a windmill, propeller, etc. 3. a target set to slide on a leveling rod, for use in surveying. 4. one of the sights on a compass, quadrant, etc. 5. the web or flat part of a feather, containing the barbs.

Vane, Sir **Henry** (vān), 1613–1662; English statesman: also called *Sir Harry Vane.*

Vä·ner, Lake (ve'nẽr), a lake in southern Sweden: area, 2,149 sq. mi.: also spelled **Vener.**

vang (vaŋ), *n.* [D. *vang,* a catch < *vangen,* to catch; cf. FANG], in *nautical usage,* one of two ropes running from a gaff to the deck, used to steady the gaff.

van Gogh, Vincent, see **Gogh, Vincent van.**

van·guard (van'gärd'), *n.* [ME. *vant-guard;* OFr. *avant-garde; avant,* before + *garde* (see GUARD)], 1. the part of an army which goes ahead of the main body in an advance; the van. 2. the leading position in a movement. 3. those leading a movement.

va·nil·la (və-nil'ə), *n.* [Mod. L.; Sp. *vainilla,* small pod, husk, dim. of *vaina,* a pod; L. *vagina,* a case, pod, sheath], 1. any of a number of related climbing orchids with fragrant, greenish-yellow flowers. 2. the podlike capsule (*vanilla bean*) of some of these plants. 3. a flavoring made from these capsules, used in cooking, etc.

va·nil·lic (və-nil'ik), *adj.* of or derived from vanilla or vanillin.

van·il·lin (van'ə-lin, və-nil'in), *n.* a fragrant, white, crystalline substance, $C_8H_8O_3$, produced from the vanilla bean or made synthetically, and used for flavoring.

VANILLA (branch with fruit 6–10 in. long)

Va·nir (vä'nir), *n.pl.* in *Norse mythology,* a race of gods who preceded the Aesir.

van·ish (van'ish), *v.i.* [ME. *vanissen* < ppr. stem of OFr. *esvanir;* LL. **exvanire,* for L. *evanescere;* see EVANESCE], 1. to disappear; pass suddenly from sight. 2. to decay or fade to nothing; pass gradually out of existence. 3. to cease to exist; come to an end. 4. in *mathematics,* to become zero. *n.* in *phonetics,* the faint last part of certain vowel sounds, as the faint *i* ending the vowel sound of *pay.*

SYN.—**vanish** implies a sudden, complete, often mysterious passing from sight or existence (the stain had *vanished* overnight); **disappear,** a more general term, implies either a sudden or gradual passing from sight or existence (customs that have long since *disappeared*): **fade** suggests a gradual, complete or partial disappearance, as by losing color or brilliance (the design on this fabric won't *fade*, his fame has *faded*). —*ANT.* appear, emerge.

van·ish·ing point (van'ish-iŋ), in *perspective*, the point where parallel lines receding from the observer seem to come together.

van·i·ty (van'ə-ti), *n.* [*pl.* VANITIES (-tiz)], [ME. *vanite;* OFr. *vanité;* L. *vanitas*, emptiness, worthlessness < *vanus*, vain], 1. any thing or act that is vain, futile, idle, or worthless. 2. the quality or fact of being vain, or worthless; futility. 3. the quality or fact of being vain, or excessively proud of oneself or one's qualities or possessions; self-satisfaction. 4. a thing about which one is vain; source of self-satisfaction. 5. a vanity case. 6. a dressing table. —*SYN.* see **pride.**

vanity case (or **box**), a small case containing powder, rouge, a mirror, etc., carried by women.

Vanity Fair, 1. in Bunyan's *Pilgrim's Progress*, a fair always going on in the town of Vanity, symbolic of worldly folly, frivolity, and show; hence, 2. the world, especially the social world, or a city, society, etc., regarded as dominated by folly, frivolity, and show. 3. a novel (1847–1848) by Thackeray.

van Leyden, Lucas, see **Leyden, Lucas van.**

van Loon, Hen·drik Wil·lem (hen'drik vil'əm van lōn'), 1882–1944; American author, born in the Netherlands.

van·quish (vaŋ'kwish), *v.t.* [ME. *vencusen, venquissen* < ppr. stem of OFr. *veinquir;* L. *vincere*, to conquer], 1. to conquer or defeat in battle; force into submission; hence, 2. *a)* to defeat in any conflict, as in argument or competition. *b)* to overcome or subdue (a feeling, condition, etc.); suppress: as, his success *vanquished* fear. —*SYN.* see **conquer.**

Van Rens·se·laer, Stephen (van ren'sə-lẽr, ren'sə-lêr'), 1764–1839; American general and statesman.

Van·sit·tart, Robert Gilbert (van-sit'ẽrt), first Baron Vansittart of Denham; 1881–1957; British diplomat.

van·tage (van'tij), *n.* [contr. < ME. *avantage;* see ADVANTAGE], 1. advantage; superiority; favorable or advantageous position or chance against one's opponent: as, point of *vantage*. 2. in *tennis*, the first point scored after deuce; advantage.

vantage ground, a favorable or advantageous situation; good position for defense or attack.

Va·nu·a Le·vu (vä-nōō'ä le'vōō), one of the Fiji Islands: area, 2,130 sq. mi.; pop., 30,000.

van·ward (van'wẽrd), *adj.* in or toward the van, or front, as of an army.

Van·zet·ti, Bar·to·lo·me·o (bär'tō-lō-mā'ō van-zet'i; It. vän-dzet'te), 1888–1927: see **Sacco, Nicola.**

vap·id (vap'id), *adj.* [L. *vapidus*, stale, insipid], 1. tasteless; flavorless; flat. 2. uninteresting; lifeless; dull; unexciting: as, *vapid* talk. —*SYN.* see **insipid.**

va·pid·i·ty (va-pid'ə-ti), *n.* the state or quality of being vapid; flatness; dullness; insipidity.

va·por (vā'pẽr), *n.* [Anglo-Fr. *vapour;* OFr. *vapeur;* L. *vapor* < IE. base **qwap-*, **qwep-*, to smoke, fume, cloud, seen also in Gr. *kapnos*, smoke, Goth. *afhwapjan*, to suffocate], 1. *a)* a steamlike mist which rises into the air from water or damp objects subjected to heat; visible particles of moisture floating in the air; fog; mist; steam. *b)* any cloudy or imperceptible exhalation, as smoke, noxious fumes, etc. 2. the gaseous form of any substance which is usually a liquid or a solid. 3. *a)* any substance vaporized for use in machinery, medical therapy, etc. *b)* a mixture of such a vaporized substance with air, as the explosive mixture in an automobile cylinder. 4. anything insubstantial. 5. *pl.* [Archaic], hypochondria or depressed spirits (often with *the*). *v.i.* 1. to rise or pass off in the form of vapor; become vapor; evaporate. 2. to give off vapor. 3. to indulge in idle talk or boasting; brag or bluster. *v.t.* 1. to vaporize. 2. [Archaic], to affect with the vapors.

va·por·es·cence (vā'pẽr-es''ns), *n.* formation of vapor.

va·por·es·cent (vā'pẽr-es''nt), *adj.* forming, or tending to form, vapor.

va·por·if·ic (vā'pẽr-if'ik), *adj.* [see VAPOR & -FIC], 1. forming vapor. 2. vaporous.

va·por·im·e·ter (vā'pẽr-im'ə-tẽr), *n.* an instrument with which vapor pressure and volume are measured.

va·por·ing (vā'pẽr-iŋ), *adj.* 1. that vapors. 2. boastful, bombastic, ostentatious, vaunting, etc. *n.* vaporing talk or behavior.

va·por·ish (vā'pẽr-ish), *adj.* 1. like vapor. 2. full of vapor or vapors. 3. having, or inclined to have, the vapors; in low spirits or easily depressed.

va·por·iz·a·ble (vā'pẽr-īz'ə-b'l), *adj.* that can be vaporized.

va·por·i·za·tion (vā'pẽr-i-zā'shən, vā'pẽr-ī-zā'shən), *n.* 1. a vaporizing or being vaporized; specifically, the turning of water into steam, as in a boiler. 2. medical treatment with vapor.

va·por·ize (vā'pẽr-īz'), *v.t.* [VAPORIZED (-īzd'), VAPORIZING], to change into vapor, as by heating or spraying. *v.i.* to be changed into vapor.

va·por·iz·er (vā'pẽr-īz'ẽr), *n.* a device for vaporizing liquids, as an atomizer, or a jet in a carburetor.

va·por·os·i·ty (vā'pẽr-os'ə-ti), *n.* the state or quality of being vaporous.

va·por·ous (vā'pẽr-əs), *adj.* [LL. *vaporosus*], 1. giving off or forming vapor. 2. full of vapor; foggy; misty. 3. like, having the nature of, or characteristic of vapor. 4. *a)* fleeting, unsubstantial, fanciful, etc.: said of things, ideas, etc. *b)* given to such ideas or talk.

vapor pressure (or **tension**), the pressure of a confined vapor that has accumulated above its liquid: it is determined by the nature of the liquid and the temperature.

va·por·y (vā'pẽr-i), *adj.* vaporous.

va·pour (vā'pẽr), *n., v.i. & v.t.* vapor: British spelling.

va·que·ro (vä-kâr'ō; Sp. vä-ke'rô), *n.* [*pl.* VAQUEROS (-ōz; Sp. -rôs)], [Sp. < *vaca* (L. *vacca*), a cow; cf. BUCKAROO], in Spanish America and the southwestern United States, a person who herds cattle; cowboy.

var., 1. [*pl.* VARS.], variant. 2. variation. 3. variety. 4. various.

va·ra (vä'rä), *n.* [Sp. & Port., lit., a rod, stick; L., a forked pole < *varus*, bent], a Spanish, Portuguese, and Latin American unit of linear measure, varying in different countries from 32 to 43 inches: a square vara, as a unit of area, is sometimes called a *vara*.

Va·ran·gi·an (və-ran'ji-ən), *n.* [< ML. *Varangus;* MGr. *Barangos;* via Slav. < ON. *Væringi*, lit., an ally, confederate < *vārar*, pl., pledges], any of a Scandinavian people who settled in Russia in the 9th century and founded the first Russian dynasty, under Rurik.

Var·dar (vär'där), *n.* a river in southern Yugoslavia and northern Greece, flowing into the Gulf of Salonika: length, 200 mi.

Var·gas, Ge·tu·lio Dor·nel·les (zhə-tōō'lyōō dōōr-ne'-lis vár'gəs), 1883–1954; Brazilian statesman; president of Brazil (1934–1945; 1951–1954).

var·i·a·bil·i·ty (vâr'i-ə-bil'ə-ti), *n.* [< *variable* + *-ity;* cf. Fr. *variabilité*], 1. the state or quality of being variable. 2. a tendency to vary.

var·i·a·ble (vâr'i-ə-b'l), *adj.* [ME.; OFr.; LL. *variabilis*], 1. apt or likely to change or vary; changeable, inconstant, fickle, fluctuating, etc. 2. that can be changed or varied. 3. in *astronomy*, changing in brightness or apparent magnitude: said of certain stars. 4. in *biology*, tending to deviate in some way from the type; aberrant. 5. in *mathematics*, having no fixed value. *n.* 1. anything changeable; thing that varies or may vary. 2. in *astronomy*, a variable star. 3. in *mathematics*, *a)* a quantity that may have a number of different values. *b)* a symbol for such a quantity. 4. in *nautical usage*, a shifting wind, or one which blows stronger or weaker at intervals: distinguished from *trade wind*.

the variables, a region of shifting winds lying between the belts of the steady northeast and southeast trade winds.

Variable Zone, Temperate Zone.

var·i·a·bly (vâr'i-ə-bli), *adv.* in a variable manner.

var·i·ance (vâr'i-əns), *n.* [ME.; OFr.; LL. *variantia;* L. *varians*, ppr. of *variare*, to change], 1. the quality, state, or fact of varying or being variant; a changing or being changeable; tendency to change. 2. degree of change or difference; divergence; discrepancy. 3. an active disagreement; quarrel; dispute. 4. in *law*, a lack of agreement between two parts of a legal proceeding which should agree, as between a statement and the evidence offered in support of it.

at variance, 1. disagreeing; quarreling; not in accord: said of persons. 2. not in agreement with each other; differing; conflicting: said of things.

var·i·ant (vâr'i-ənt), *adj.* [ME.; OFr.; L. *varians*], 1. varying; different; especially, different in some way from others of the same kind or class, or from some standard or type. 2. variable; changeable. *n.* anything that is variant, as a different spelling of the same word, a different version of a tale, myth, or literary passage, etc.; variant form. Abbreviated **var.**

var·i·ate (vâr'i-it), *n.* in *statistics*, 1. loosely, a variable (sense 3). 2. a particular value of such a variable.

var·i·a·tion (vâr'i-ā'shən), *n.* [ME. *variacioun;* OFr.; L. *variatio*], 1. the act, fact, or process of varying; modification; change or deviation in form, condition, appearance, extent, etc. from a former or usual state, or from an assumed standard. 2. the degree or extent of such change: as, a *variation* of ten feet in height. 3. a thing which is somewhat different from another of the same kind. 4. in *astronomy*, a change in or deviation from the mean motion or orbit of a planet, satellite, etc. 5. in *biology*, *a)* a deviation from the usual or parental type in structure or form. *b*) an organism showing such deviation. 6. in *magnetism*, the deviation of a compass needle from true north and south; declination. 7. in *mathematics*, a relation between two quantities so that one changes with the other in the same ratio. 8. in *music*, the repetition of a melody or theme with changes or embellishments in harmony, rhythm, key, etc., especially one of a series of such repetitions. Abbreviated **var.**

var·i·a·tion·al (vâr′i-ā′shən-'l), ***adj.*** 1. of variation. 2. showing or characteristic of variation. 3. involving variation.

var·i·cel·la (var′ə-sel′ə), ***n.*** [Mod. L., dim. of *variola;* see VARIOLA], chicken pox.

var·i·cel·late (var′ə-sel′it, var′ə-sel′āt), ***adj.*** [< *varicella*, dim. of *varix* + *-ate*], in *zoology*, marked with small ridges: said of shells.

var·i·cel·loid (var′ə-sel′oid), ***adj.*** resembling varicella, or chicken pox.

var·i·ces (vâr′ə-sēz′), ***n.*** plural of **varix.**

var·i·co- (var′ə-kō, var′ə-kə), [< L. *varix;* see VARIX], a combining form meaning *an enlarged vein*, as in *varicocele*: also, before a vowel, **varic-.**

var·i·co·cele (var′ə-kō-sēl′), ***n.*** [*varico-* + *-cele*], a varicose condition of the veins of the spermatic cord in the scrotum.

var·i·col·ored (vâr′i-kul′ẽrd), ***adj.*** [< L. *varius*, varied; + *colored*], 1. of several or many colors. 2. varied; diversified.

var·i·cose (var′ə-kōs′), ***adj.*** [L. *varicosus* < *varix*, *varicis*, enlarged vein], 1. abnormally and irregularly swollen or dilated: as, *varicose* veins. 2. of or having varicose veins.

var·i·co·sis (var′ə-kō′sis), ***n.*** [Mod. L.; see VARICO- & -OSIS], 1. the formation of varicose veins. 2. varicosity.

var·i·cos·i·ty (var′ə-kos′ə-ti), ***n.*** 1. the condition of being varicose. 2. [*pl.* VARICOSITIES (-tiz)], a varix.

var·i·cot·o·my (var′ə-kot′ə-mi), ***n.*** [*varico-* + *-tomy*], the surgical excision of a varix, especially of a varicose vein.

var·ied (vâr′id), ***adj.*** 1. of different kinds; various. 2. showing different colors; variegated. 3. changed; altered.

var·i·e·gate (vâr′i-ə-gāt′, vâr′i-gāt′), ***v.t.*** [VARIEGATED (-id), VARIEGATING], [< LL. *variegatus*, pp. of *variegare*, to variegate < L. *varius*, various], 1. to make varied in appearance by differences, as in colors; diversify. 2. to make varied; give variety to; diversify.

var·i·e·gat·ed (vâr′i-ə-gāt′id, vâr′i-gāt′id), ***adj.*** [pp. of *variegate*], 1. of different colors in spots, streaks, etc.; parti-colored. 2. varied; having variety in character, form, appearance, etc.; diversified.

var·i·e·ga·tion (vâr′i-ə-gā′shən, vâr′i-gā′shən), ***n.*** 1. a variegating or being variegated. 2. diversity or variety in character or appearance; specifically, varied coloration.

var·i·er (vâr′i-ẽr), ***n.*** a person who varies.

va·ri·e·tal (və-rī′ə-t'l), ***adj.*** 1. of, connected with, or characterizing a variety. 2. constituting a variety.

va·ri·e·ty (və-rī′ə-ti), ***n.*** [*pl.* VARIETIES (-tiz)], [Fr. *variété;* L. *varietas*], 1. the state or quality of being various or varied; absence of monotony or sameness. 2. a different form of some thing, condition, or quality; sort; kind: as, *varieties* of cloth. 3. a number of different things thought of together; collection of varied things: as, there is a *variety* of items in the basement. 4. difference; variation. 5. in *biology*, a group having characteristics of its own within a species; subdivision of a species; subspecies. 6. [Chiefly British], entertainment of the kind given in a variety show. ***adj.*** of or in a variety show, or vaudeville. Abbreviated **var.**

variety show, a stage show made up of different kinds of acts, as comic skits, songs, dances, etc.; vaudeville show.

var·i·form (vâr′ə-fôrm′), ***adj.*** varied in form; having various forms.

var·i·o·coup·ler (vâr′i-ō-kup′lẽr), ***n.*** [*vario-* < L. *varius*, various; + *coupler*], in *electricity*, a coupler with a movable coil for changing the mutual inductance.

va·ri·o·la (və-rī′ə-lə), ***n.*** [ML. < L. *varius*, various], smallpox.

va·ri·o·lar (və-rī′ə-lẽr), ***adj.*** variolous.

var·i·o·late (vâr′i-ə-lāt′), ***v.t.*** [VARIOLATED (-id), VARIOLATING], [< *variola* + *-ate*], to inoculate with the virus of smallpox.

var·i·ole (vâr′i-ōl′), ***n.*** [Fr.; ML. *variola*, smallpox < L. *varius*, various, spotted], 1. a tiny pit or depression in the skin; foveola. 2. any of the whitish spherules in variolite.

var·i·o·lite (vâr′i-ə-līt′), ***n.*** [G. *variolit* < ML. *variola* (see VARIOLE): from its pitted surface], a rock, especially diorite, in which whitish spherules of other rock are embedded, making a pitted or specked surface.

var·i·o·lit·ic (vâr′i-ə-lit′ik), ***adj.*** 1. having a specked or pitted surface; pock-marked in appearance. 2. of or like variolite.

var·i·o·loid (vâr′i-ə-loid′), ***adj.*** 1. resembling variola, or smallpox. 2. of varioloid. ***n.*** a mild form of variola occurring in a person who has had a previous attack or who has been vaccinated.

va·ri·o·lous (və-rī′ə-ləs), ***adj.*** [ML. *variolosus*], 1. of or having variola, or smallpox. 2. having pitted scars, as pockmarks.

var·i·om·e·ter (vâr′i-om′ə-tẽr), ***n.*** [< L. *varius*, various; + *-meter*], in *electricity*, 1. an instrument for comparing magnetic forces or determining variations of magnetic force, especially at different places on the earth. 2. an instrument for varying inductance in an electric circuit, consisting of a movable coil within a fixed coil, the two connected in series: used in radio tuning.

var·i·o·rum (vâr′i-ôr′əm, vā′ri-ō′rəm), ***n.*** [L., of various (scholars)], an edition or text, as of a literary work, containing variant readings or notes by various editors, scholars, etc. ***adj.*** of such an edition or text.

var·i·ous (vâr′i-əs), ***adj.*** [L. *varius*, diverse, parti-colored], 1. differing one from another; of several kinds. 2. several; many: as, *various* sections of the country. 3. many-sided; versatile. 4. characterized by variety; varied in nature or appearance. 5. [Rare], changeable. Abbreviated **var.** —***SYN.*** see **different.**

var·ix (vâr′iks), ***n.*** [*pl.* VARICES (-ə-sēz′)], [L.; see VARICOSE], in *medicine*, a permanently and irregularly swollen or dilated blood or lymph vessel, especially a vein; varicose vein.

var·let (vär′lit), ***n.*** [ME.; OFr., a servant, valet, page; var. of *vaslet* (cf. VALET) as if < **vasalet* < base of *vasal* (cf. VASSAL); for sense development cf. KNAVE], [Archaic], 1. an attendant. 2. a boy or youth serving as a knight's page. 3. a rascal; scoundrel; knave.

var·let·ry (vär′lit-ri), ***n.*** [Archaic], 1. varlets collectively. 2. the rabble; mob.

var·mint, var·ment (vär′mənt), ***n.*** [var. of dial. *vermin*, with unhistoric *-t*], [Dial. or Colloq.], vermin; especially, a person or animal regarded as troublesome or objectionable: also used as a generalized epithet of disparagement.

Var·na (vär′nä), ***n.*** a seaport in northeastern Bulgaria, on the Black Sea: pop., 70,000.

var·nish (vär′nish), ***n.*** [ME. *vernisch;* OFr. *vernis*, varnish; ML. *veronix*, *veronice*, a resin; ? ult. < Gr. *Berenikē*, ancient city], 1. *a*) a preparation made of resinous substances dissolved in oil (*oil varnish*) or in a liquid like alcohol which evaporates quickly (*spirit varnish*), and used to give a glossy surface to wood, metal, etc. *b*) any of various natural or prepared products used for the same purpose. 2. the smooth, hard, glossy surface of this after it has dried. 3. a surface gloss or smoothness, as of manner; outward attractiveness, often deceptive. ***v.t.*** 1. to cover with varnish; brush varnish on. 2. to impart a smooth surface to, as with varnish; give a varnished appearance to. 3. to make attractive on the surface; embellish, often deceptively. 4. to polish up; brighten.

varnish tree, any of a number of trees whose sap or juice can be made into a lacquer or varnish.

Var·ro (var′ō), ***n.*** (*Marcus Terentius Varro*), Roman scholar and writer; 116–27 B.C.

var·si·ty (vär′sə-ti), ***n.*** [*pl.* VARSITIES (-tiz)], [contr. < *university* in 18th-c. pronun.], a team, usually athletic, that represents a university, college, or school in any competition. ***adj.*** designating or of a university, college, or school team or competition.

Var·u·na (var′oo-nə, vur′oo-nə), ***n.*** [Sans.], the Hindu god of the cosmos.

var·us (vâr′əs), ***n.*** [Mod. L. < L., bent, grown inward], an abnormal turning inward of the foot so as to produce bowleg. ***adj.*** bowlegged. Cf. **valgus.**

varve (värv), ***n.*** [Sw. *varv*, a layer], in *geology*, a layer in a deposit of sedimentary material, showing seasonal variation caused by differences in summer and winter deposition: characteristic of certain recent deposits in glaciated regions, and used to estimate the length of glacial and interglacial periods.

var·y (vâr′i), ***v.t.*** [VARIED (-id), VARYING], [ME. *varien;* OFr. *varier;* L. *variare*, to vary, change < *varius*, various], 1. to change in form, appearance, nature, substance, etc.; alter; modify. 2. to make different from one another. 3. to give variety to; diversify: as, *vary* your reading. 4. in *music*, to repeat (a melody or theme) with changes in harmony, rhythm, key, etc. ***v.i.*** 1. to undergo change in any way; become different. 2. to be different or diverse; differ: as, the second edition *varied* little from the first. 3. to deviate, diverge, or depart (*from*). 4. to alter in succession; alternate. 5. in *biology*, to show variation. 6. in *mathematics*, to change (directly or inversely) in the same ratio. —***SYN.*** see **change.**

‡vas (vas), ***n.*** [*pl.* VASA (vā′sə)], [L., a vessel, dish], in *anatomy* & *biology*, a vessel or duct.

Va·sa·ri, Gior·gio (jôr′jô vä-zä′rē), 1511–1574; Italian painter, architect, and biographer of artists.

Vasco da Gama, see **Gama, Vasco da.**

vas·cu·lar (vas′kyoo-lẽr), ***adj.*** [Mod. L. *vascularis* < L. *vasculum*, small vessel, dim. of *vas*, a vessel, dish], of or having vessels or ducts; specifically, *a*) in *anatomy* & *zoology*, designating or of the vessels, or system of vessels, for conveying blood or lymph. *b*) in *botany*, designating or of the ducts for conveying sap.

vascular bundle, in *botany*, a cluster of fibers and vessels.

vas·cu·lar·i·ty (vas′kyoo-lar′ə-ti), ***n.*** vascular form or condition.

vascular system, in *botany*, the arrangement of all the vascular tissue in a plant.

vascular tissue, in *botany*, tissue composed of the ducts that carry sap through any of the higher plants.

vas·cu·lose (vas′kyoo-lōs′), ***adj.*** of, full of, or supplied by or with ducts or vessels; vascular.

vas·cu·lous (vas′kyoo-ləs), ***adj.*** vasculose.

vas·cu·lum (vas′kyoo-ləm), ***n.*** [*pl.* VASCULA (-lə)], [L.; see VASCULAR], 1. a metal case used by botanists to carry specimen plants. 2. in *botany*, an ascidium.

‡vas de·fe·rens (def′ə-renz′), [*pl.* VASA DEFERENTIA (def′ə-ren′shi-ə)], [Mod. L. < L. *vas*, a vessel + *deferens*, carrying down (see DEFERENCE)], the convoluted duct that conveys sperm from the testicle to the ejaculatory duct of the penis.

vase (vās, vāz; Brit. väz), ***n.*** [Fr.; L. *vasum*, *vas*, a vessel, dish], an open container of metal, glass, pottery, etc., of any size and almost any shape, but usually rounded and of greater height than width, used for decoration, displaying flowers, etc.

vas·ec·to·my (vas-ek′tə-mi), ***n.*** [*vas* + *-ectomy*], the surgical removal of all or part of the vas deferens.

vas·e·line (vas′ə-lēn′, vas′'l-in), ***n.*** [irregular formation < G. *wasser*, water + Gr. *elaion*, oil; + *-ine* (suffix used to form commercial names)], a petroleum jelly, light yellow or white, used as a lubricant or ointment; petrolatum: a trade-mark (**Vaseline**).

Vash·ti (vash′tī), ***n.*** [Heb. *washtī*], in the *Bible*, the queen of Ahasuerus of Persia: because she refused to present herself at his command to his guests at a feast, he repudiated her: Esth. 1.

vas·o- (vas′ō, vas′ə), [< L. *vas*, a vessel], a combining form meaning: 1. *the blood vessels*, as in *vasomotor*. 2. *the vas deferens*, as in *vasectomy*. 3. *vasomotor*. Also, before a vowel, **vas-**.

vas·o·con·stric·tor (vas′ō-kən-strik′tẽr), ***adj.*** [*vaso-* + *constrictor*], in *physiology*, causing constriction of the blood vessels. ***n.*** a nerve or drug causing such constriction.

vas·o·di·la·tor (vas′ō-dī-lā′tẽr, vas′ō-di-lā′tẽr), ***adj.*** [*vaso-* + *dilator*], in *physiology*, causing dilatation of the blood vessels. ***n.*** a nerve or drug causing such dilatation.

vas·o·mo·tor (vas′ō-mō′tẽr), ***adj.*** [*vaso-* + *motor*], in *physiology*, regulating the size (i.e., caliber) of blood vessels by causing contraction or dilatation: said of a nerve, nerve center, or drug.

vas·sal (vas′'l), ***n.*** [ME. *vassale;* OFr.; ML. *vassalus*, manservant, extension of *vassus*, servant < Celt.; cf. W. *gwas*, youth; the form suggests direct borrowing < Gaulish; cf. VARLET, VALET], 1. in the Middle Ages, a person who held land under the feudal system, doing homage and pledging fealty to an overlord, and performing military or other duties in return for his protection; feudal tenant. 2. a subordinate, dependent, subject, etc. 3. *a*) a servant. *b*) a slave. ***adj.*** 1. of or like a vassal; dependent, subject, servile, subservient, etc. 2. being a vassal or vassals.

vas·sal·age (vas′'l-ij), ***n.*** [ME.; OFr.; ML. *vassallagium*], 1. the state of being a vassal. 2. the homage, loyalty, and service required of a vassal. 3. dependence; subordinate position; servitude. 4. lands held by a vassal; fief. 5. a body of vassals.

vast (vast, väst), ***adj.*** [L. *vastus*], 1. of very great size; huge; enormous; immense. 2. of very great extent; extensive; far-reaching. 3. very great in number, amount, or quantity. 4. very great in degree, intensity, etc.: as, *vast* knowledge. ***n.*** [Poetic], a vast space.

vas·ti·tude (vas′tə-tōōd′, väs′tə-tūd′), ***n.*** 1. the quality or condition of being vast; vastness. 2. a vast extent or space.

vast·ly (vast′li, väst′li), ***adv.*** to a vast extent; very.

vast·y (vas′ti, väs′ti), ***adj.*** [VASTIER (-ti-ẽr), VASTIEST (-ti-ist)], vast; immense; huge.

vat (vat), ***n.*** [ME. *vat*, *vet*, Southern dial. var. of *fat* < AS. *fæt*, a cask, vessel; akin to G. *fass*, container; IE. base **pēd-*, **pōd-*, to seize, hold, as also in G. *fassen*, to hold, grasp; basic sense "a container"], 1. a large tank, tub, or cask for holding liquids to be used in a manufacturing process or to be stored for fermenting or ripening. 2. a liquid containing a dye that does not color materials dipped in it until they are exposed to air. ***v.t.*** [VATTED (-id), VATTING], 1. to place or store in a vat. 2. to dip into a vat (dyeing solution).

vat dye, a dye used in a vat (sense 2).

vat·ic (vat′ik), ***adj.*** [< L. *vates*, a prophet], of or characteristic of a prophet; prophetic.

vat·i·cal (vat′i-kəl), ***adj.*** vatic.

Vat·i·can (vat′i-kən), ***n.*** [L. *Vaticanus* (*mons*), Vatican (hill)], 1. the papal palace, consisting of a group of buildings in Vatican City. 2. the papal government, as distinguished from the Quirinal, or Italian civil government. Abbreviated **Vat.**

Vatican City, the papal state within Rome, established in 1929: it includes the Vatican and St. Peter's Church: area, 1/6 sq. mi.; pop., 1,000: Italian name, *Città del Vaticano*.

Vat·i·can·ism (vat′i-kən-iz′m), ***n.*** the doctrine of papal infallibility, and the system of theology and church government based upon it, beginning with the Vatican Council of 1869–1870: an opprobrious term.

va·tic·i·nal (və-tis′ə-n'l), ***adj.*** [< L. *vaticinus* (see VATICINATE); + *-al*], having the nature of or characterized by prophecy; prophetic.

va·tic·i·nate (və-tis′ə-nāt′), ***v.t. & v.i.*** [VATICINATED (-id), VATICINATING], [< L. *vaticinatus*, pp. of *vaticinari*, to foretell, prophesy < *vaticinus*, prophetic < *vates*, a seer, prophet], to prophesy; foretell.

vat·i·ci·na·tion (vat′ə-si-nā′shən), ***n.*** [L. *vaticinatio* < *vaticinatus;* see VATICINATE], 1. a prophecy; inspired prediction. 2. a prophesying; foretelling.

va·tic·i·na·tor (və-tis′ə-nā′tẽr), ***n.*** [L.; see VATICINATE], a prophet; seer.

Vät·ter, Lake (vet′tẽr), a lake in southern Sweden: area, 735 sq. mi.: also spelled **Vetter.**

Vau·ban, Marquis **de** (də vō′bän′), (*Sébastien Le Prestre*), 1633–1707; French soldier and military engineer; marshal of France.

Vaud (vō), ***n.*** a canton of western Switzerland: area, 1,239 sq. mi.; pop., 343,000; capital, Lausanne: German name, *Waadt*.

vaude·ville (vōd′vil, vô′də-vil), ***n.*** [Fr., earlier *vau-de-vire* < *Vau-de-Vire*, the valley of the Vire (in Normandy), famous for light, convivial songs], 1. *a*) a stage show consisting of mixed specialty acts, including songs, dances, skits, acrobatic performances, etc.; variety show. *b*) such entertainment generally. 2. [Now Rare], a comic theatrical piece interspersed with songs and dances. 3. [Obs.], a light popular song, usually satirical or topical, often with pantomime.

Vau·dois (vō-dwä′), ***n.*** 1. [*pl.* VAUDOIS], a native or inhabitant of Vaud. 2. the dialect spoken there.

Vau·dois (vō-dwä′), ***n.pl.*** [Fr.; ML. *Valdenses;* see WALDENSES], the Waldenses.

Vaughan, Henry (vôn), 1622–1695; English poet and metaphysician: called *the Silurist*.

Vaughan Williams, Ralph, 1872–1958; English composer.

vault (vôlt), ***n.*** [ME. *voute;* OFr. *vaulte*, *voulte*, etc.; LL. **volta*, **voluta*, a vault < L. *volutus*, pp. of *volvere*, to turn around, roll: from the rounded or arched top of vaults], 1. an arched roof, ceiling, or covering of masonry. 2. an arched chamber or space, especially when underground; hence, 3. a cellar room used for storage, as of wine. 4. a burial chamber for the dead. 5. a room for the safekeeping of valuables or money, as in a bank. 6. an underground cave with a naturally arched roof. 7. the sky as a vault-like canopy. 8. in *anatomy*, any arched cavity or structure: as, the cranial *vault*. ***v.t.*** 1. to make a vault over; cover with a vault. 2. to build in the form of a vault. ***v.i.*** to curve like a vault.

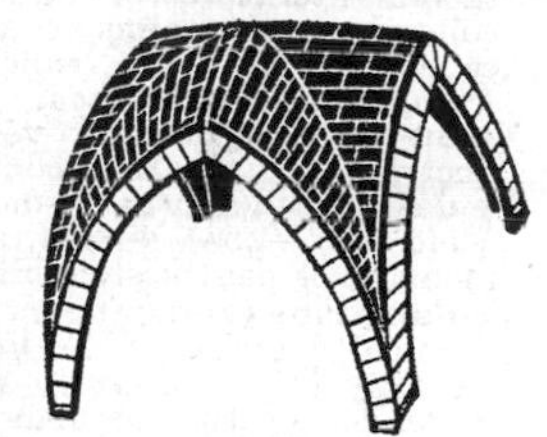

GROINED VAULT

vault (vôlt), ***v.i.*** [OFr. *volter*, *vouter* < source of *vault* (arched roof); influenced in form by *vaulte*, *voulte*, etc., an arch], to jump, leap, or spring, as over a barrier or from one position to another, especially with the help of the hands supported on the barrier, etc., or holding a long pole. ***v.t.*** 1. to vault over: as, he *vaulted* the fence. 2. to mount (a horse, etc.) by leaping. ***n.*** [sense 1 < the *v.*; sense 2 < Fr. *volte*, a turn, bound, leap; It. *volta;* LL. **volta;* see VAULT (arched roof)], 1. a vaulting. 2. a leap or bound made by a horse; curvet.

vault·ed (vôl′tid), ***adj.*** 1. having the form of a vault; arched. 2. built with an arched roof; having a vault.

vault·ing (vôl′tiŋ), ***n.*** 1. the building of a vault or vaults. 2. the arched work forming a vault. 3. a vault, or vaults collectively.

vault·ing (vôl′tiŋ), ***adj.*** [ppr. of *vault* (to leap)], 1. leaping; leaping over; hence, 2. overreaching; unduly confident: as, *vaulting* ambition. 3. used in vaulting.

vaunt (vônt, vänt), ***v.i.*** [ME. *vaunten*, *vanten;* OFr. *vanter;* LL. *vanitare* < L. *vanus*, vain; cf. VAIN], [Now Rare], to boast; brag. ***v.t.*** to boast about (something); brag of. ***n.*** a boast; brag. —***SYN.*** see **boast.**

fat, āpe, bâre, cär; ten, ēven, hêre, ovẽr; is, bīte; lot, gō, hôrn, tōōl, look; oil, out; up, ūse, fũr; get; joy; yet; chin; she; thin, *th*en; zh, leisure; ŋ, ring; ə for *a* in *ago*, *e* in *agent*, *i* in *sanity*, *o* in *comply*, *u* in *focus;* ′ as in *able* (ā′b'l); Fr. bål; ë, Fr. coeur; ö, Fr. feu; Fr. mo*n*; ô, Fr. coq; ü, Fr. duc; H, G. ich; kh, G. doch. See pp. x–xii. ‡ foreign; * hypothetical; < derived from.

vaunt-cour·i·er (vänt′koor′i-ēr, vônt′koor′i-ēr), *n.* [Fr. *avant-courrier*], 1. [Obs.], a soldier sent out in advance of an army. 2. a forerunner; precursor.
vaunt·y (vôn′ti), *adj.* [Scot.], boastful; vain.
v. aux., auxiliary verb.
vav (väv, vôv), *n.* [Heb. *vāv*, lit., a hook], the sixth letter of the Hebrew alphabet (ו), corresponding to English *V*, *v*: with diacritical marks, it often serves as a neutral vowel: cf. **aleph**: see **alphabet**, table.
vav·a·sor (vav′ə-sôr′, vav′ə-sōr′), *n.* [ME.; OFr. *vavasour*; ML. *vavassor*; prob. < *vassus vassorum*, vassal of vassals; cf. VASSAL, VARLET, VALET], in the Middle Ages, a feudal vassal holding lands from a superior lord and having vassals under himself.
vav·a·sour (vav′ə-soor′), *n.* a vavasor.
vb., 1. verb. 2. verbal.
V.C., 1. Veterinary Corps. 2. Vice-Chairman. 3. Vice-Chancellor. 4. Vice-Consul. 5. Victoria Cross.
Vd, in *chemistry*, vanadium.
V.D., venereal disease.
V-Day (vē′dā′), *n.* Victory Day: see **V-E Day, V-J Day.**
've, have: a contraction.
Ve·a·dar (vē′ə-där′, vā-ô′där), *n.* [Heb. *wĕ-adhār*, lit., and Adar, hence second Adar], an extra month of the Jewish year, occurring about once every three years between Adar and Nisan: see **Jewish calendar.**
veal (vēl), *n.* [ME. *vele*, *veel*; OFr. *veël*; L. *vitellus*, little calf, dim. of *vitulus*, a calf], 1. the flesh of a calf used as food. 2. [Now Rare], a calf, especially as intended for food.
Veb·len, Thor·stein (thôr′stīn veb′lən), 1857–1929; American political economist, author, and educator.
vec·tion (vek′shən), *n.* [L. *vectio* < pp. of *vehere*, to carry], in *medicine*, passage of disease germs from an infected to a healthy person.
vec·tor (vek′tēr), *n.* [L., a bearer, carrier < *vectus*, pp. of *vehere*, to carry], 1. in *astronomy*, an imaginary line joining the center of an attracting body, as the sun, with the center of a body revolving around it: also called *radius vector*. 2. in *biology*, any organism that is the carrier of a disease-producing virus, as one of the many insect hosts of microorganisms parasitic to man. 3. in *mathematics*, *a*) a quantity, such as a force or velocity, having direction and magnitude. *b*) a line representing such a quantity, drawn from its point of origin to its final position. *c*) a radius vector.
vec·to·ri·al (vek-tôr′i-əl, vek-tō′ri-əl), *adj.* of a vector or vectors.
Ve·da (vā′də, vē′də), *n.* [Sans. *veda*, knowledge; IE. base **weid-*, **woid-*, **wid-*, to know, seen also in L. *videre*, to see, Eng. *wit*, *wise*], *often in pl.* the ancient sacred literature of Hinduism, consisting of four collections of psalms, chants, sacred formulas, etc., called the *Rig-Veda* (which see), *Yajur-Veda*, *Sama-Veda*, and *Atharva-Veda*.
Ve·da·ism (vā′də-iz′m, vē′də-iz′m), *n.* the religious doctrine and practices contained in the Vedas.
Ve·dan·ta (vi-dän′tə, vi-dan′tə), *n.* [Sans. *Vedānta* < *Veda* (see VEDA) + *anta*, an end], a system of Hindu monistic or pantheistic philosophy based on the Vedas.
Ve·dan·tism (vi-dän′tiz′m, vi-dan′tiz′m), *n.* the philosophical doctrine of the Vedanta.
V-E Day (vē′ē′), May 8, 1945, the day on which the surrender of the German forces in Europe was announced, officially ending the European phase of World War II.
Ved·da, Ved·dah (ved′ə), *n.* [Singh., a hunter], any of the aboriginal people of Ceylon.
ve·dette (vi-det′), *n.* [Fr. *vedette*; It. *vedetta*; altered after *vedere*, to see < *veletta*, sentry box; Sp. *vela*, a watch, watching, vigil < L. *vigilare*, to watch], 1. in *military usage*, a mounted sentinel posted in advance of the outposts of an army. 2. in *naval usage*, a small scout boat, used to watch the enemy: also **vedette boat.** Also spelled **vidette.**
Ved·ic (vā′dik, vē′dik), *adj.* of the Vedas. *n.* the language in which the Vedas are written, an early form of Sanskrit.
vee (vē), *n.* 1. the letter V, v, or anything shaped like it. 2. [Colloq.], a five-dollar bill. *adj.* shaped like V.
veer (vêr), *v.i.* [altered, after *veer* (to let out) < Fr. *virer*, to turn around; cf. ENVIRON], 1. to change direction; shift; turn or swing around. 2. to change sides; shift, as from one opinion or attitude to another. 3. in *meteorology*, to shift; especially, to shift clockwise: said of the wind: opposed to *back*. 4. in *nautical usage*, *a*) to change the direction of a ship by swinging its stern to the wind; wear ship. *b*) to be so turned: said of a ship. *v.t.* 1. to turn or swing; change the course of. 2. in *nautical usage*, to change the direction or course of (a ship) by swinging its stern to the wind; wear. *n.* a change of direction. —*SYN.* see **deviate.**
veer (vêr), *v.t.* & *v.i.* [ME. *veren*; MD. *vieren*, to let out], in *nautical usage*, to let out (a line, chain, anchor, etc.): often with *out*.
veer·y (vêr′i), *n.* [*pl.* VEERIES (-iz)], [prob. echoic], a brown thrush native to the eastern United States: also called *Wilson's thrush*.
Ve·ga (vē′gə), *n.* [ML. < Ar. (*al nasr*) *al waqi'*, the falling (vulture)], a blue-white star of the first magnitude in the constellation Lyra: see **constellation**, chart.
Ve·ga, Lo·pe de (lô′pe *the* ve′gä), (*Lope Félix de Vega Carpio*), 1562–1635; Spanish dramatist and poet.
veg·e·ta·ble (vej′tə-b'l, vej′i-tə-b'l), *n.* [Fr. *végétable*; LL. *vegetabilis*, animating, hence full of life < L. *vegetare*; see VEGETATE], 1. broadly, any plant, as distinguished from animal or inorganic matter. 2. *a*) specifically, any plant that is eaten whole or in part, raw or cooked, generally with an entree or in a salad but not as a dessert, as the tomato, potato, lettuce, cucumber, cabbage, etc. *b*) the edible part of such a plant, as the root of the carrot or seed of the pea. *adj.* 1. of, having the nature of, made from, or produced by edible vegetables. 2. of, or having the nature of, plants in general: as, the *vegetable* kingdom.
vegetable butter, an edible, fatty substance, solid at ordinary temperatures, yielded by some plants.
vegetable ivory, 1. the ivorylike seed of a South American palm, used to make buttons, ornaments, etc.; ivory nut. 2. the shell of the coquilla nut.
vegetable kingdom, the division of nature including all plant life.
vegetable marrow, 1. a large, smooth-skinned, meaty variety of squash. 2. its flesh.
vegetable oyster, 1. a plant with a long, tapering, edible white root, grasslike leaves, and heads of purple flowers; salsify. 2. the root, used for food.
vegetable silk, a cottony, fibrous material got from the seeds of a prickly-stemmed Brazilian tree, used in pillows, etc.
vegetable tallow, a fatty, tallowlike substance got from various plants, used in candles, soap, etc.
vegetable wax, a white, waxy substance found on the leaves or fruit of some plants and in the stems of others.
veg·e·tal (vej′ə-t'l), *adj.* [ME. *vegytalle*; ML. **vegetalis* < L. *vegetus*, showing life], 1. of, or having the nature of, plants or vegetables. 2. of or having the characteristics common to both plants and animals, as absorption, nutrition, growth, etc. (as distinguished from rationality, sensibility, and volition). 3. vegetative (sense 3).
veg·e·tant (vej′ə-tənt), *adj.* [L. *vegetans*, *vegetantis*, ppr. of *vegetare*; see VEGETABLE], 1. stimulating growth and vigor; invigorating; animating. 2. of, or having the nature of, vegetation; vegetal.
veg·e·tar·i·an (vej′ə-târ′i-ən), *n.* [*vegetable* + *-arian*], a person who eats no meat, and sometimes no animal products (as milk, eggs, etc.); one who advocates a strict vegetable diet as the proper one for all people for reasons of health or because of principles opposing the killing of animals. *adj.* 1. of vegetarians or vegetarianism. 2. advocating vegetarianism. 3. consisting only of vegetables.
veg·e·tar·i·an·ism (vej′ə-târ′i-ən-iz′m), *n.* the principles or practices of vegetarians.
veg·e·tate (vej′ə-tāt′), *v.i.* [VEGETATED (-id), VEGETATING], [< L. *vegetatus*, pp. of *vegetare*, to enliven < *vegetus*, lively < *vegere*, to quicken; present meaning influenced by Eng. *vegetable*], 1. to grow as plants. 2. to exist with little mental and physical activity; lead a very inactive life. 3. in *medicine*, to grow or increase in size, as a wart or other abnormal outgrowth.
veg·e·ta·tion (vej′ə-tā′shən), *n.* [ML. *vegetatio*], 1. the act or process of vegetating. 2. plant life in general. 3. dull, passive existence. 4. in *medicine*, any abnormal outgrowth on a part of the body.
veg·e·ta·tion·al (vej′ə-tā′shən-'l), *adj.* of or like vegetation.
veg·e·ta·tive (vej′ə-tā′tiv), *adj.* [ME. *vegetatyf*; ML. *vegetativus* < L. *vegetatus*, pp. of *vegetare*, to quicken], 1. *a*) of vegetation, or plants. *b*) of or concerned with vegetation, or plant growth. 2. growing, or capable of growing, as plants. 3. designating or of those functions or parts of plants concerned with growth and nutrition as distinguished from reproduction. 4. capable of causing growth in plants: as, *vegetative* soil. 5. involuntary or passive like the growth of plants; showing little mental activity: as, a *vegetative* existence.
veg·e·tive (vej′ə-tiv), *adj.* vegetative.
ve·he·mence (vē′ə-məns; *occas.* vē′hi-məns), *n.* [Fr. *véhémence*; L. *vehementia*], the quality or state of being vehement; specifically, *a*) great force; violence; impetuousness. *b*) great fervor; passion; intense feeling.
ve·he·men·cy (vē′ə-mən-si; *occas.* vē′hi-mən-si), *n.* vehemence.
ve·he·ment (vē′ə-mənt; *occas.* vē′hi-mənt), *adj.* [Fr. *véhément*; L. *vehemens*, eager, vehement < base of *vehere*, to carry], 1. acting or moving with great force; violent; impetuous. 2. fervent; passionate; intense, as feelings or thoughts. 3. characterized by intense feeling or passionate expression.
ve·hi·cle (vē′ə-k'l; *occas.* vē′hi-k'l), *n.* [Fr. *véhicule*; L. *vehiculum*, carriage < *vehere*, to carry], 1. any device on wheels or runners for conveying persons or objects, as a cart, sled, automobile, etc. 2. any means of carrying, conveying, or communicating. 3. a means

by which ideas are expressed or made known: as, music can be a *vehicle* for ideas. 4. in *painting*, a liquid, as water or oil, with which pigments are mixed for use. 5. in *pharmacy*, a substance, as sweet sirup, in which medicines are given. 6. in the *theater*, a play thought of as a means of communication or as a means of presenting a specified actor or company.

ve·hic·u·lar (vē-hik′yoo-lẽr), *adj.* [LL. *vehicularis*], 1. of or for vehicles: as, a *vehicular* tunnel. 2. serving as a vehicle.

‡**Vehm·ge·richt** (fām′gə-riHt′), *n.* [*pl.* VEHMGERICHTE (-riH′tə)], [G., older form of *Fehmgericht* < *vehm*, judgment; ? < D. *veem*, a society, guild (? especially one for avenging misdeeds) + G. *gericht*, court, tribunal], in medieval Germany, especially in Westphalia, a kind of irregular tribunal that met secretly and exercised great power, often meting out death.

Ve·ii (vē′yī), *n.* an ancient Etruscan town, destroyed by the Romans.

veil (vāl), *n.* [ME. & ONorm. Fr. *veile*, veil, sail, curtain < L. *vela*, pl. of *velum*, a sail, cloth, curtain; IE. base **weg-*, to weave, attach, a textile, seen also in OIr. *figim*, I weave, AS. *wice*, wick], 1. a piece of light fabric, as of net or gauze, worn, especially by women, over the face or head or draped from a hat to conceal, protect, or enhance the face. 2. any piece of cloth used as a concealing or separating screen or curtain. 3. anything like a veil in that it covers or conceals: as, a *veil* of mist, a *veil* of silence. 4. a part of a nun's headdress, draped along the sides of the face and over the shoulders. 5. the state or life of a woman who has taken the vows of a nun or novice: used especially in *take the veil*, to become a nun. 6. [Dial.], a caul. 7. in *botany* & *zoology*, a velum. *v.t.* 1. to cover with or as with a veil; hence, 2. to conceal; hide or disguise.

veiled (vāld), *adj.* 1. wearing a veil. 2. covered with a veil. 3. concealed; hidden; disguised. 4. not openly expressing or expressed: as, a *veiled* threat.

veil·ing (vāl′iŋ), *n.* 1. the act of covering with or as with a veil. 2. a veil; curtain. 3. thin, transparent fabric used for veils.

vein (vān), *n.* [ME. & OFr. *veine*; L. *vena*; ? < base of *vehere*, to carry], 1. *a*) any blood vessel that carries blood from some part of the body back to the heart. *b*) loosely, any blood vessel. 2. any of the riblike supports strengthening the membranous wings of an insect. 3. any of the bundles of vascular tissue forming the framework of a leaf blade. 4. *a*) a fissure, crack, or seam in rock, filled with a mineral deposited by the flow of underground water. *b*) a deposit of such mineral: when metallic, usually called *lode*. 5. a stratum or bed of coal, etc. lying parallel with the fault of the rock: see **mine**, illus. 6. a streak or marking of a different color or substance from the surrounding material, as in marble or wood. 7. any distinctive quality or strain regarded as running through one's character, speech, writing, etc.: as, there was a *vein* of humor in his essay. 8. a temporary state of mind; mood: as, let me speak in a serious *vein*. *v.t.* 1. to streak or mark with or as with veins. 2. to branch out through in the manner of veins. 3. to furnish with veins. —*SYN.* see **mood**.

veined (vānd), *adj.* [pp. of *vein*], having or showing veins or veinlike markings.

vein·ing (vān′iŋ), *n.* the formation or arrangement of veins or veinlike markings.

vein·let (vān′lit), *n.* a small vein.

vein·stone (vān′stōn′), *n.* in *mining*, worthless rocky material in an ore-bearing vein; gangue.

vein·ule (vān′ūl), *n.* [*vein* + *-ule*], a veinlet; venule.

vein·y (vān′i), *adj.* [VEINIER (-i-ẽr), VEINIEST (-i-ist)], 1. having or showing veins. 2. full of veins, as marble.

vel., vellum.

Ve·la (vē′lə), *n.* [L., a veil], a subdivision of the constellation Argo: see **constellation**, chart.

ve·la (vē′lə), *n.* plural of **velum**.

ve·la·men (və-lā′mən), *n.* [*pl.* VELAMINA (-lam′ə-nə)], [L., a covering < *velare*, to cover], 1. in *anatomy*, a membrane or velum. 2. in *botany*, the corky outer layer of the aerial roots of certain orchids.

ve·lar (vē′lẽr), *adj.* [L. *velaris*, belonging to a veil or curtain < *velum*, a veil], 1. of a velum; especially, of the soft palate in the mouth. 2. in *phonetics*, pronounced with the back of the tongue touching or near the soft palate, as the sound of *k* when followed by a back vowel such as *o͞o* or *ô*.

ve·lar·i·um (və-lâr′i-əm), *n.* [*pl.* VELARIA (-ə)], [L. < *velum*, a covering, veil], in ancient Rome, a large awning over an amphitheater or theater.

ve·lar·ize (vē′lẽr-īz′), *v.t.* [VELARIZED (-īzd′), VELARIZING], in *phonetics*, to change the pronunciation of (a sound) by bringing the back of the tongue up to or near the soft palate.

Ve·lás·quez (ve-läs′keth), see **Velázquez**.

ve·late (vē′lāt, vē′lit), *adj.* [L. *velatus*, pp. of *velare*, to cover, veil], having a velum.

Ve·láz·quez, Die·go Ro·drí·guez de Sil·va y (dye′gô rô-*thr*ē′geth *th*e sēl′vä ē ve-läth′keth; Eng. və-las′kwiz), 1599–1660; Spanish painter: also **Velásquez**.

veld, veldt (velt, felt), *n.* [D. *veld*, a field], in South Africa, open grassy country, with few bushes and almost no trees; grassland.

‡**ve·li·tes** (vē′lə-tēz′), *n.pl.* [L., pl. of *veles*, *velitis*; akin to *velox*, swift], in ancient Rome, lightly armed foot soldiers.

vel·le·i·ty (və-lē′ə-ti), *n.* [*pl.* VELLEITIES (-tiz)], [< Fr. or ML.; Fr. *velléité*; ML. *velleitas* < *velle*, to wish], 1. the weakest kind of desire or volition. 2. a mere wish that does not lead to the slightest action.

vel·li·cate (vel′ə-kāt′), *v.t.* & *v.i.* [VELLICATED (-id), VELLICATING], [L. *vellicatus*, pp. of *vellicare*, to twitch, pinch < *vellere*, to pluck], to twitch or pluck.

vel·li·ca·tion (vel′ə-kā′shən), *n.* [L. *vellicatio*; see VELLICATE], 1. a twitching or plucking. 2. a twitch, especially of a muscle or muscles.

vel·lum (vel′əm), *n.* [ME. *velim*, *velum*; OFr. *velin*, vellum, prepared calfskin < *vel*; see VEAL], 1. a fine kind of parchment prepared from calfskin, lambskin, or kidskin, used as writing parchment or for binding books. 2. a manuscript written on vellum. 3. paper made to resemble vellum. *adj.* of or like vellum. Abbreviated **vel.**

ve·loc·i·pede (və-los′ə-pēd′), *n.* [Fr. *vélocipède* < L. *velox*, *velocis*, swift, speedy + *pes*, *pedis*, a foot], 1. originally, any of various early bicycles or tricycles. 2. now, a child's tricycle. 3. a type of handcar for use on railroad tracks.

VELOCIPEDE

ve·loc·i·ty (və-los′ə-ti), *n.* [*pl.* VELOCITIES (-tiz)], [Fr. *vélocité*; L. *velocitas* < *velox*, speedy, swift], 1. quickness or rapidity of motion or action; swiftness; speed. 2. *a*) rate of change of position, in relation to time. *b*) rate of motion in a particular direction, as of the rotation of a sphere, in relation to time.

ve·lours (və-loor′), *n.* [*pl.* VELOURS], [Fr.; see VELURE], a fabric with a nap like velvet, made of wool, silk, linen, or cotton, and used for upholstery, draperies, hats, clothing, etc.: also spelled **velour**.

‡**ve·lou·té** (və-lo͞o′tā′), *n.* [Fr., velvety, soft and smooth], a rich white sauce made from meat stock thickened with flour and butter: also **velouté sauce**.

ve·lum (vē′ləm), *n.* [*pl.* VELA (-lə)], [L., a veil, sail], in *biology*, any of various veillike membranous partitions or coverings; specifically, the soft palate.

ve·lure (və-loor′), *n.* [Fr. *velours*; OFr. *velous*; LL. *villosus*, shaggy < *villus*, shaggy hair], 1. velvet or a fabric like velvet, used for draperies, upholstery, etc. 2. a silk or plush pad used for brushing silk hats. *v.t.* [VELURED (-loord′), VELURING], to brush with a velure.

ve·lu·ti·nous (və-lo͞o′t'n-əs), *adj.* [< It. *velluto*, velvet (ult. < L. *villus*; see VELVET); + *-ous*], in *botany* & *zoology*, covered with short, dense, silky, upright hairs; soft and velvety.

vel·vet (vel′vit), *n.* [ME. *velvet*, *velwet*; ML. *velvetum*; ult. < L. *villus*, shaggy hair], 1. a rich fabric of silk, silk and cotton back, rayon, etc. with a soft, thick pile: *pile velvet* has the pile uncut, standing in loops; *cut velvet* has the loops cut apart. 2. anything with a surface like that of velvet. 3. a soft, furry skin on a deer's growing antlers. 4. [Slang], clear profit; winnings; gain. *adj.* 1. made of or covered with velvet. 2. smooth or soft like velvet.

vel·vet·een (vel′və-tēn′), *n.* [< *velvet*], 1. a cotton cloth with a short, thick pile, resembling velvet. 2. *pl.* clothes, especially trousers, made of velveteen.

vel·vet·y (vel′vi-ti), *adj.* 1. smooth or soft like velvet. 2. smooth-tasting; mellow; not harsh: said of liquors.

Ven., 1. Venerable. 2. Venice.

‡**ve·na** (vē′nə), *n.* [*pl.* VENAE (-nē)], [L.], a vein.

vena ca·va (kā′və), *n.* [*pl.* VENAE CAVAE (-vē)], [Mod. L. < L. *vena*, vein + *cava*, fem. of *cavus*, hollow], in *anatomy*, either of two large veins conveying blood to the right atrium of the heart.

ve·nal (vē′n'l), *adj.* [L. *venalis*, salable, for sale < *venum*, *venus*, sale; akin to Sans. *vasnam*, a reward, Gr. *onos*, a price], 1. that can readily be bribed or corrupted; mercenary: as, a *venal* judge. 2. capable of being obtained for a price: as, *venal* services. 3. characterized by corruption or bribery: as, a *venal* bargain.

ve·nal·i·ty (vē-nal′ə-ti), *n.* [*pl.* VENALITIES (-tiz)], [< Fr. or LL.; Fr. *venalité*; LL. *venalitas*], state, quality, or instance of being venal; willingness to be bribed or bought off, or to sell one's services to the highest bidder; prostitution of talents or services for mercenary considerations.

ve·nat·ic (vē-nat′ik), *adj.* [L. *venaticus*, of hunting < *venatus*, hunting < *venari*, to hunt], 1. of or used in hunting. 2. fond of hunting. 3. living by hunting.

ve·nat·i·cal (vē-nat′i-k'l), *adj.* venatic.

ve·nat·i·cal·ly (vē-nat′i-k'l-i, vē-nat′ik-li), *adv.* in a venatic manner; by hunting.

ve·na·tion (vē-nā′shən), *n.* [< L. *vena*, a vein], 1. the arrangement of veins, as in an insect's wing or a leaf: see **leaf**, illus. 2. such veins collectively.

vend (vend), *v.t.* [Fr. *vendre;* L. *vendere*, contr. < *venum dare*, to offer for sale; *venum*, sale + *dare*, to give], 1. to sell. 2. to give public expression to (opinions); publish. *v.i.* 1. to sell goods. 2. to be purchased; find a market. —*SYN.* see **sell.**

ven·dace (ven′dās), *n.* [*pl.* VENDACE, VENDACES (-iz); see PLURAL, II, D, 2], [OFr. *vandoise*, dace], a fresh-water whitefish native to England and Scotland.

Ven·de·an (ven-dē′ən), *adj.* of the Vendée or its people. *n.* 1. a native of the Vendée. 2. a member of the royalist revolt against the French Republic that broke out in the Vendée in 1793.

Ven·dée (vän′dā′), *n.* a department in western France.

vend·ee (ven-dē′), *n.* [*vend* + *-ee*], the person to whom a thing is sold; buyer.

‡Ven·dé·miaire (vän′dā′myâr′), *n.* [Fr. < *vindemia*, vintage], the first month (September 22–October 21) of the French Revolutionary Calendar, adopted by the First Republic in 1793.

vend·er (ven′dẽr), *n.* a vendor.

ven·det·ta (ven-det′ə), *n.* [*pl.* VENDETTAS (-əz)], [It.; L. *vindicta*, vengeance], a blood feud in which the relatives of a murdered person try to kill the murderer or members of his family, as formerly in Corsica and parts of Italy.

vend·i·bil·i·ty (ven′də-bil′ə-ti), *n.* the state or quality of being vendible, or salable.

vend·i·ble (ven′də-b'l), *adj.* [ME.; L. *vendibilis* < *vendere;* see VEND], 1. capable of being sold. 2. venal. *n.* something vendible.

vend·i·bly (ven′də-bli), *adv.* so as to be vendible, or salable; salably.

vending machine, a coin slot machine for selling merchandise.

ven·di·tion (ven-dish′ən), *n.* [L. *venditio*], the act of vending, or selling; sale.

Ven·dôme, Lou·is Jo·seph de (lwē zhô′zef′ də vän′dōm′), Duc, 1654–1712; French general; marshal of France.

ven·dor (ven′dẽr), *n.* [Anglo-Fr. < Fr. *vendre*], 1. one who vends, or sells; seller. 2. a vending machine.

ven·due (ven-dōō′, ven-dū′), *n.* [D. *vendu;* obs. Fr. *vendue*, sale < *vendu*, pp. of *vendre;* see VEND], a public auction.

ve·neer (və-nêr′), *v.t.* [G. *furniren, furnieren*, to veneer < Fr. *fournir*, to furnish; cf. FURNISH], 1. to cover with a thin layer of fine material; especially, to cover (wood) with wood of finer quality, as in furniture. 2. to cover (anything common or coarse) with a material having an attractive or superior surface. 3. to cement (thin layers of wood) into plywood. *n.* 1. a thin surface layer, usually of wood, laid over a base of common material. 2. any of the thin layers glued together in plywood. 3. any attractive but superficial appearance or display: as, a *veneer* of culture.

ve·neer·ing (və-nêr′iŋ), *n.* [earlier *faneering;* G. *furnierung;* see VENEER], 1. the act of one who veneers. 2. veneer (senses 1 & 2).

ven·e·punc·ture (ven′i-puŋk′chẽr, vē′ni-puŋk′chẽr), *n.* [< L. *vena*, vein; + *puncture*], the surgical puncture of a vein, as with a hypodermic needle: also spelled **venipuncture.**

Vener, Lake (ven′ẽr), Lake Väner.

ven·er·a·bil·i·ty (ven′ẽr-ə-bil′ə-ti), *n.* the state or quality of being venerable.

ven·er·a·ble (ven′ẽr-ə-b'l, ven′rə-b'l), *adj.* [Fr. *vénérable;* L. *venerabilis*, to be reverenced < *venerari;* see VENERATE], 1. worthy of respect or reverence by reason of age and dignity, character, position, etc. 2. impressive on account of age or historic or religious associations: as, a *venerable* monument. In the *Anglican Church*, it is a title given to an archdeacon; in the *Roman Catholic Church*, it is a title given to persons who have attained the lowest of the three degrees of sanctity, the others being beatification and canonization.

ven·er·a·bly (ven′ẽr-ə-bli, ven′rə-bli), *adv.* in a venerable manner.

ven·er·ate (ven′ə-rāt′), *v.t.* [VENERATED (-id), VENERATING], [< L. *veneratus*, pp. of *venerari*, to worship, reverence < *venus, veneris*, love], to look upon with feelings of deep respect; regard as venerable; revere. —*SYN.* see **revere.**

ven·er·a·tion (ven′ə-rā′shən), *n.* 1. a venerating or being venerated. 2. a feeling of deep respect and reverence. 3. an act of showing this. —*SYN.* see **awe.**

ven·er·a·tor (ven′ə-rā′tẽr), *n.* [L.], a person who venerates.

ve·ne·re·al (və-nêr′i-əl), *adj.* [< L. *venereus* < *Venus, Veneris*, Venus, love], 1. having to do with sexual love or intercourse. 2. transmitted by sexual intercourse with an infected person: as, syphilis and gonorrhea are *venereal* diseases. 3. infected with a venereal disease. 4. for the cure of such a disease: as, a *venereal* remedy.

ven·er·y (ven′ẽr-i), *n.* [< L. *Venus, Veneris*, Venus, love], [Archaic], sexual intercourse; indulgence of sexual desire.

ven·er·y (ven′ẽr-i), *n.* [ME. & OFr. *venerie* < *vener* (L. *venari*), to hunt], hunting, as an art or sport; the chase.

ven·e·sec·tion (ven′ə-sek′shən, vē′nə-sek′shən), *n.* [< L. *vena*, a vein + *sectio*, a cutting], in *medicine*, phlebotomy.

Ve·ne·ti·a (və-nē′shi-ə, və-nē′shə), *n.* 1. an ancient Roman province in what is now northeastern Italy and northwestern Yugoslavia. 2. Veneto. 3. Venezia (sense 3).

Ve·ne·tian (və-nē′shən; *occas.* və-nish′ən), *adj.* of Venice, its people, culture, etc. *n.* 1. a native or inhabitant of Venice. 2. [often v-], [Colloq.], *a)* a Venetian blind. *b) pl.* a tape or braid used on Venetian blinds.

Venetian blind, a window blind made of a number of thin wooden or metal slats that can be set together at any angle to regulate the light and air passing through.

Venetian glass, a fine glassware made in or near Venice.

Venetian red, 1. a red pigment formerly made from native ferric oxides but now prepared synthetically. 2. a brownish-red color.

Venetian school, painting by artists in and near Venice in the 15th and 16th centuries, notably Giorgione, Tintoretto, Titian, and Veronese.

Ve·ne·to (ve′ne-tô′), *n.* a region in northeastern Italy: area, 9,856 sq. mi.; pop., 3,918,000.

Ve·ne·zia (ve-ne′tsyä), *n.* 1. Venice: the Italian name. 2. a province in Veneto, Italy. 3. a former region in Italy, generally corresponding to ancient Venetia.

Venezia Giu·lia (jōō′lyä), a former region in northeastern Italy, most of which was ceded to Yugoslavia in 1947: the part remaining in Italy is the region called *Friuli-Venezia Giulia.*

Venezia Tri·den·ti·na (trē′den-tē′nä), Trentino-Alto Adige: the former name.

Ven·e·zue·la (ven′ə-zwē′lə, ven′i-zwā′lə; Am. Sp. ve′ne-swe′lä), *n.* a country in northern South America, on the Caribbean: area, 352,143 sq. mi.; pop., 6,709,000; capital, Caracas: abbreviated **Venez.**

Ven·e·zue·lan (ven′ə-zwē′lən, ven′i-zwā′lən), *adj.* of Venezuela, its people, or culture. *n.* a native or inhabitant of Venezuela.

venge·ance (ven′jəns), *n.* [ME.; OFr. < *venger* (L. *vindicare*), to avenge; see VINDICATE], the return of an injury for an injury, in punishment or retribution; the avenging of an injury or offense; revenge.

with a vengeance, 1. with great force or fury. 2. extremely; very. 3. excessively; to an unusual extent.

venge·ful (venj′fəl), *adj.* [*venge* < OFr. *venger* (see VENGEANCE); + *-ful*], 1. desiring revenge; seeking vengeance; vindictive. 2. arising from or showing a desire for vengeance: said of actions or feelings. 3. inflicting or serving to inflict vengeance. —*SYN.* see **vindictive.**

ve·ni·al (vē′ni-əl, vēn′yəl), *adj.* [ME.; OFr.; LL. *venialis*, pardonable < L. *venia*, a grace, favor], 1. that may be forgiven; pardonable: as, a *venial* sin: in theology, opposed to *mortal.* 2. that may be excused or overlooked, as an error or fault; excusable.

ve·ni·al·i·ty (vē′ni-al′ə-ti), *n.* the quality or fact of being venial.

venial sin, in the *Roman Catholic Church*, an offense against the law of God, as one committed without awareness of its seriousness or without full consent, that can be remitted by prayer or other good works and does not deprive the soul of sanctifying grace.

Ven·ice (ven′is), *n.* a seaport in northeastern Italy, built on more than a hundred small islands in the Lagoon of Venice: pop., 322,000: it was a city-state under the doges and a maritime power from the 10th to the 16th century: abbreviated **Ven.**: Italian name, *Venezia.*

Venice, Gulf of, the northern end of the Adriatic.

Venice, Lagoon of, an inlet of the Gulf of Venice, in northeastern Italy.

ven·i·punc·ture (ven′i-puŋk′chẽr, vē′ni-puŋk′chẽr), *n.* venepuncture.

ve·ni·re fa·ci·as (vi-nī′rē fā′shi-as′), [L., cause to come], in *law*, a writ or order issued by a judge to a sheriff or coroner, instructing him to summon persons to serve as jurors: also **venire.**

ve·ni·re·man (vi-nī′ri-mən), *n.* [*pl.* VENIREMEN (-mən)], a person called to jury service on a writ of venire.

ven·i·son (ven′i-z'n, ven′i-s'n; *Brit.* ven′z'n), *n.* [ME. *veneison;* OFr. *veneisun, veneson* < L. *venatio*, the chase < *venatus*, pp. of *venari*, to hunt], the flesh of a game animal, now especially the deer, used as food.

Ve·ni·te (vi-nī'tē), *n.* [L., come, 2d pers. pl., imperative, of *venire,* to come: from the opening word in the Latin version], 1. the 95th Psalm in the King James Version (94th in the Vulgate), used as a canticle at matins or morning prayer. 2. music for this.

‡**ve·ni, vi·di, vi·ci** (vē'nī vī'dī vī'sī, wā'nē wē'dē wē'kē), [L.], I came, I saw, I conquered: Julius Caesar's report to the Roman Senate of a victory.

Ve·ni·ze·los, E·leu·the·rios (e'lyef-the'ryôs ve'nyi-ze'lôs; Eng. ven'i-zā'los), 1864–1936; Greek statesman.

ven·om (ven'əm), *n.* [ME. & OFr. *venim, venin;* L. *venenum,* a poison], 1. the poison secreted by some snakes, spiders, insects, etc., introduced into the body of the victim by bite or sting. 2. [Rare], poison of any kind. 3. malignancy; spite; malice.

ven·om·ous (ven'əm-əs), *adj.* [ME. *venimous;* OFr. *venimeux*], 1. containing or full of venom; poisonous. 2. malignant; spiteful; malicious. 3. in *zoology,* having a poison gland or glands; able to inflict a poisonous wound by biting or stinging.

ve·nose (vē'nōs), *adj.* in *botany,* venous.

ve·nos·i·ty (vi-nos'ə-ti), *n.* the state or quality of being venose or venous.

ve·nous (vē'nəs), *adj.* [L. *venosus*], 1. of a vein or veins. 2. in *botany,* having veins; veiny; full of veins: also **venose.** 3. in *physiology,* designating blood being carried in the veins back to the heart and lungs: venous blood has given up oxygen and taken up carbon dioxide, and is characterized by a dark-red color.

vent (vent), *n.* [altered (after Fr. *vent,* a wind) < ME. *fent, fente;* OFr. *fente,* a cleft, rift, chink, slit < *fendre;* L. *findere,* to cleave] 1. the action of escaping or passing out, or the means or opportunity to do this; issue; outlet; passage; escape; hence, 2. expression; release: as, giving *vent* to emotion. 3. a small hole or opening to permit passage or escape, as of a gas. 4. in old guns, the small hole at the breech through which a spark passes to set off the charge. 5. the crusted opening in a volcano from which gas and molten rock erupt. 6. in *tailoring,* a slit in a garment, especially the one at the back of a coat. 7. in *zoology,* the excretory opening of animals; especially, the external opening of the cloaca in birds, reptiles, amphibians, and fishes. *v.t.* 1. to make a vent in. 2. to let out at an opening; allow to escape through a hole. 3. to give release or expression to, as feelings. 4. to relieve or unburden by giving vent to feelings: as, he *vented* himself in an outburst of profanity. 5. to publish or utter as opinions.

vent·age (ven'tij), *n.* [see -AGE], 1. a small hole or opening; vent. 2. in *music,* a finger hole in a wind instrument.

ven·tail (ven'tāl), *n.* [ME. *ventaylle;* OFr. *ventaille* < *vent* (L. *ventus*), a wind], the movable piece of armor forming the lower front part of a metal helmet.

ven·ter (ven'tẽr), *n.* [Anglo-Fr. *ventre, venter;* L. *venter*], 1. in *anatomy & zoology, a)* the belly, or abdomen. *b)* a protuberance like a belly, as on a muscle. *c)* a cavity or hollowed surface, as in a bone. 2. in *law,* the womb; hence, a mother in relation to her children.

ven·ti·duct (ven'ti-dukt'), *n.* [< L. *ventus,* a wind + *ductus,* pp. of *ducere,* to lead], an air pipe; ventilating duct or passage.

ven·ti·late (ven't'l-āt'), *v.t.* [VENTILATED (-id), VENTILATING], [< L. *ventilatus,* pp. of *ventilare,* to fan, ventilate < *ventus,* a wind], 1. to circulate fresh air in (a room, etc.), driving out foul air. 2. to circulate in (a room, etc.) so as to freshen: said of air. 3. to provide with an opening for the escape of air, gas, etc.; furnish a means for airing. 4. to expose (a substance) to fresh air so as to keep in good condition. 5. to examine and discuss in public; bring out into the open, as a grievance, problem, etc. 6. to aerate (blood); oxygenate. 7. [Obs.], to winnow, as grain; fan.

ven·ti·la·tion (ven't'l-ā'shən), *n.* [L. *ventilatio*], 1. the act or process of ventilating. 2. means of doing this; ventilating equipment.

ven·ti·la·tive (ven't'l-ā'tiv), *adj.* 1. of ventilation. 2. serving to ventilate.

ven·ti·la·tor (ven't'l-ā'tẽr), *n.* a thing that ventilates; especially, any opening or device used to bring in fresh air and drive out foul air.

ven·tral (ven'trəl), *adj.* [< Fr. or L.; Fr. *ventral;* L. *ventralis* < *venter,* belly], 1. in *anatomy & zoology,* of, near, on, or toward the belly or the side of the body where the belly is located; in man, anterior (or front), in most other animals, inferior (or lower): opposed to *dorsal.* 2. in *botany,* of or belonging to the inner or lower surface. Abbreviated **v.**

ven·tral·ly (ven'trəl-i), *adv.* in a ventral position or direction; toward the belly, or abdomen.

ven·tri·cle (ven'tri-k'l), *n.* [< Fr. or L.; Fr. *ventricule;* L. *ventriculus,* a stomach, ventricle, dim. of *venter,* belly], in *anatomy & zoology,* any of various cavities or hollow organs; specifically, *a)* either of the two lower chambers of the heart which receive blood from the auricles and pump it into the arteries: see **heart,** illus. *b)* any of the four small continuous cavities within the brain.

ven·tri·cose (ven'tri-kōs'), *adj.* [Mod. L. *ventricosus* < L. *venter,* belly], 1. large-bellied. 2. in *botany & zoology,* swelling out on one side.

ven·tri·cos·i·ty (ven'tri-kos'ə-ti), *n.* a ventricose condition.

ven·tri·cous (ven'tri-kəs), *adj.* ventricose.

ven·tric·u·lar (ven-trik'yoo-lẽr), *adj.* [< L. *ventriculus* (see VENTRICLE); + *-ar*], 1. of, or having the nature of, a ventricle. 2. having a bulge or belly.

ven·tric·u·lose (ven-trik'yoo-lōs'), *adj.* [L. *ventriculosus* < *ventriculus;* see VENTRICLE], somewhat ventricose.

ven·tric·u·lus (ven-trik'yoo-ləs), *n.* [*pl.* VENTRICULI (-lī')], [L.; see VENTRICLE], in *zoology,* 1. that part of the alimentary tract of an insect, analogous to the stomach, where digestion takes place. 2. the gizzard of a bird.

ven·tril·o·qual (ven-tril'ə-kwəl), *adj.* ventriloquial.

ven·tri·lo·qui·al (ven'tri-lō'kwi-əl), *adj.* of, belonging to, or using ventriloquism.

ven·tri·lo·qui·al·ly (ven'tri-lō'kwi-əl-i), *adv.* in a ventriloquial manner.

ven·tril·o·quism (ven-tril'ə-kwiz'm), *n.* [< L. *ventriloquus,* lit., one who speaks from the belly < *venter,* belly + *loquor,* to speak; + *-ism*], the art or practice of speaking in such a way that the voice seems to come from some source other than the speaker.

ven·tril·o·quist (ven-tril'ə-kwist), *n.* a person who practices ventriloquism; specifically, an entertainer who uses ventriloquism to carry on a pretended conversation with a puppet or dummy.

ven·tril·o·quis·tic (ven-tril'ə-kwis'tik), *adj.* of ventriloquism or ventriloquists.

ven·tril·o·quize (ven-tril'ə-kwīz'), *v.i. & v.t.* [VENTRILOQUIZED (-kwīzd'), VENTRILOQUIZING], to utter (words or sounds) as a ventriloquist.

ven·tril·o·quy (ven-tril'ə-kwi), *n.* [Fr. *ventriloquie*], ventriloquism.

ven·tro- (ven'trō, ven'trə), [< L. *venter,* belly], a combining form meaning: 1. *abdomen, belly.* 2. *ventral and,* as in *ventrodorsal.*

ven·tro·dor·sal (ven'trə-dôr's'l), *adj.* [*ventro-* + *dorsal*], of or involving both the ventral and dorsal surfaces.

ven·ture (ven'chẽr), *n.* [abbrev. < ME. *aventure;* see ADVENTURE], 1. a risky or dangerous undertaking; especially, a business enterprise in which there is danger of loss as well as chance for profit. 2. something on which a risk is taken, as the merchandise in a commercial enterprise or a stake in gambling. 3. chance; fortune: now only in *at a venture,* by mere chance, without consideration, at random. *v.t.* [VENTURED (-chẽrd), VENTURING], 1. to expose to danger or risk: as, he *ventured* his life. 2. to expose to chance of loss, as money or merchandise. 3. to take the risk of; brave. 4. to express at the risk of criticism, objection, denial, etc.: as, may I *venture* an opinion? *v.i.* to do or go at some risk; dare.

ven·ture·some (ven'chẽr-səm), *adj.* 1. inclined to venture; daring. 2. venturous; risky; hazardous.

ven·tu·ri (tube) (ven-toor'i), [after G. B. *Venturi* (1746–1822), It. physicist], a short tube with a constricted, throatlike passage that increases the velocity and lowers the pressure of a fluid conveyed through it: used to measure the flow of a fluid or operate certain instruments, as in aircraft, to regulate gasoline and air mixture in a carburetor, etc.

ven·tur·ous (ven'chẽr-əs), *adj.* 1. inclined to venture, or take chances; bold and enterprising; not timid. 2. involving danger or risk; risky; hazardous.

ven·ue (ven'ū, ven'ōō), *n.* [ME. *veneu;* OFr. *venue,* coming, arrival, approach < *venir,* to come], in *law,* 1. the county or locality in which a cause of action occurs or a crime is committed. 2. the county or locality in which a jury is drawn and a case tried. 3. that part of a declaration in an action that designates the county in which the trial is to occur. 4. [Rare], the clause in an affidavit designating the place where it was sworn to.

change of venue, in *law,* the substitution of another place of trial, as when the jury or court is likely to be prejudiced.

ven·u·lar (ven'yoo-lẽr), *adj.* of a venule or venules.

ven·ule (ven'ūl), *n.* [L. *venula,* dim. of *vena,* vein], 1. in *anatomy,* a small vein; veinlet. 2. in *zoology,* any of the small branches of a vein in the wing of an insect. Also **veinule.**

ven·u·lose (ven'yoo-lōs'), *adj.* full of venules.

ven·u·lous (ven'yoo-ləs), *adj.* venulose.

Ve·nus (vē'nəs), *n.* [ME.; Late AS. *Uenus;* L.], 1. in *Roman mythology,* an ancient Italian goddess of spring, bloom, and beauty, later identified with the Greek Aphrodite as goddess of love. 2. a statue or image of Venus. 3. a very beautiful woman. 4. the most brilliant planet in the solar system, second in distance from the sun, anciently or poetically called Lucifer as the morning star and Hesperus as the evening star: diameter, 7,600 mi.; year, 225 days; symbol, ♀. 5. in *alchemy*, copper.

Ve·nus·berg (vē'nəs-bũrg'; G. vā'noos-berkh'), *n.* [G., Venus mountain], in *medieval legend*, a mountain in Germany between Eisenach and Gotha, where it was believed Venus held court in a cavern, enticing travelers who became loath to leave: in Wagner's opera, Tannhäuser struggles to free himself from her spell.

Venus of Me·los (mē'los), Venus of Milo.

Venus of Mi·lo (mē'lō; *popularly* mī'lō), a famous marble statue of Venus found on the island of Melos in 1820 and later placed in the Louvre in Paris.

VENUS OF MILO

Ve·nus's-fly·trap (vē'nəs-iz-flī'trap'), *n.* a white-flowered plant of the North and South Carolina swamps, having leaves with two hinged blades which close upon insects.

Ve·nus's-hair (vē'nəs-iz-hâr'), *n.* a kind of maidenhair fern.

Ver., 1. Veracruz. 2. Version.

ver., verse; verses.

Ver·a (vêr'ə), [Russ. *Vjera*, faith; also < L. *vera*, fem. of *verus*, true], a feminine name.

ver·a (ver'ə, var'ə), *adj. & adv.* [Scot.], very.

ve·ra·cious (və-rā'shəs), *adj.* [< L. *verax*, speaking truly < *verus*, true], 1. habitually truthful; honest. 2. true; accurate.

ve·rac·i·ty (və-ras'ə-ti), *n.* [*pl.* VERACITIES (-tiz)], [Fr. *véracité;* ML. *veracitas*, truthfulness < L. *verus*, true], 1. habitual truthfulness; honesty. 2. accuracy of statement; accordance with truth. 3. accuracy or precision, as of perception, measurement, etc. 4. that which is true; truth. —*SYN.* see **honesty, truth.**

Ver·a·cruz (ver'ə-krōōz'; Am. Sp. ve'rä-krōōs'), *n.* 1. a state of Mexico, on the eastern coast: area, 27,736 sq. mi.; pop., 1,615,000; capital, Jalapa. 2. a city in this state: pop., 71,000. Formerly *Vera Cruz.*

ve·ran·da, ve·ran·dah (və-ran'də), *n.* [Port. *varanda*, a balcony; of Hind. origin], an open porch or portico, usually roofed, extending along the outside of a building; porch; piazza.

ve·ra·tri·a (və-rā'tri-ə, və-rat'ri-ə), *n.* veratrine.

ve·rat·ric (və-rat'rik), *adj.* [< L. *veratrum*, hellebore; + *-ic*], designating or of a white, crystalline acid, $(CH_3O)_2C_6H_3\cdot COOH$, found in sabadilla seeds and also produced synthetically.

ve·rat·ri·din (və-rat'rə-din), *n.* veratridine.

ve·rat·ri·dine (və-rat'rə-dēn', və-rat'rə-din), *n.* [< L. *veratrum*, hellebore; + *-ide* + *-ine*], an amorphous alkaloid, $C_{36}H_{51}O_{11}N$, found in sabadilla seeds.

ver·a·trin (ver'ə-trin), *n.* veratrine.

ver·a·tri·na (ver'ə-trī'nə), *n.* veratrine.

ver·a·trine (ver'ə-trēn', ver'ə-trin), *n.* [Fr. *vératrine* < L. *veratrum*, hellebore; see -INE], 1. a mixture of alkaloids obtained from sabadilla seeds and used in treating neuralgia, arthritis, etc. 2. veratridine.

verb (vũrb), *n.* [ME.; OFr. *verbe;* L. *verbum*, a word; cf. WORD], in *grammar*, 1. any of a class of words expressing action, existence, or occurrence: as, *take, be*, and *appear* are *verbs*. 2. any phrase or construction used as a verb. *adj.* of, or having the nature or function of, a verb. Abbreviated **v., vb.**

ver·bal (vũr'b'l), *adj.* [Fr.; LL. *verbalis*, of a word < *verbum;* see VERB], 1. of, in, or by means of words: as, a *verbal* image. 2. concerned merely with words, as distinguished from facts or ideas. 3. in speech; oral rather than written: as, a *verbal* contract. 4. word for word; literal: as, a *verbal* translation. 5. in *grammar*, *a*) of, having the nature of, or derived from a verb: as, a *verbal* noun. *b*) used to form verbs: as, *-ate* is a *verbal* suffix. *n.* a verbal noun or other word derived from a verb: in English, gerunds, infinitives, and participles are verbals. Abbreviated **vb.** —*SYN.* see **oral.**

ver·bal·ism (vũr'b'l-iz'm), *n.* 1. a verbal expression; expression in words; a word or phrase. 2. words only, without any real meaning; mere verbiage. 3. any virtually meaningless phrase or form of words.

ver·bal·ist (vũr'b'l-ist), *n.* 1. a person who is skilled in verbal expression; one who uses words well. 2. a person who fixes his attention or emphasis on mere words, rather than on facts or ideas.

ver·bal·i·za·tion (vũr'b'l-i-zā'shən, vũr'b'l-ī-zā'shən), *n.* a verbalizing or being verbalized.

ver·bal·ize (vũr'b'l-īz'), *v.i.* [VERBALIZED (-īzd'), VERBALIZING], [< Fr. *verbaliser* (see VERBAL) or < *verbal* + *-ize*], to be wordy, or verbose. *v.t.* 1. to express in words. 2. to change (a noun, etc.) into a verb.

ver·bal·ly (vũr'b'l-i), *adv.* [*verbal* + *-ly*], 1. word for word. 2. in or with words only, often without real meaning or understanding. 3. in words; in writing or speech. 4. in spoken words; orally.

verbal noun, in *grammar*, a noun derived from a verb and acting in some respects like a verb: in English, it is either a noun ending in *-ing* (a gerund) or an infinitive, as, *walking* is healthful, *to err* is human.

ver·ba·tim (vẽr-bā'tim), *adv.* [ML. < L. *verbum*, a word], word for word; in exactly the same words. *adj.* following the original word for word: as, a *verbatim* account.

‡**ver·ba·tim et li·te·ra·tim** (vẽr-bā'tim et lit'ẽr-ā'tim), [L.], word for word and letter for letter; precisely as written or printed.

ver·be·na (vẽr-bē'nə), *n.* [L., foliage, branches, vervain], any of a number of related plants with spikes or clusters of red, white, or purplish flowers.

ver·be·na·ceous (vũr'bə-nā'shəs), *adj.* in *botany*, of the verbena family, a group of plants with opposite leaves and usually irregular flowers, including the verbena, vervain, lantana, and some trees, as the teak.

ver·bi·age (vũr'bi-ij), *n.* [Fr. < OFr. *verbier*, to speak < L. *verbum*, a word], an excess of words beyond those needed to express concisely what is meant; wordiness.

ver·bid (vũr'bid), *n.* in *grammar*, a gerund, infinitive, or participle that functions in part as a verb, as in taking an object (*watching* television can be tiring).

verb·i·fy (vũr'bə-fī'), *v.t.* [VERBIFIED (-fīd'), VERBIFYING], to change (a noun, etc.) into a verb; verbalize.

ver·bose (vẽr-bōs'), *adj.* [L. *verbosus*, full of words < *verbum*, a word], using or containing too many words; wordy; long-winded; prolix. —*SYN.* see **wordy.**

ver·bos·i·ty (vẽr-bos'ə-ti), *n.* [Fr. *verbosité;* LL. *verbositas*], the quality of being verbose; wordiness.

‡**ver·bo·ten** (fer-bō'tən), *adj.* [G.], forbidden.

‡**ver·bum sat sa·pi·en·ti (est)** (vũr'bəm sat' sap'i-en'tī est'), [L.], a word to the wise (is) enough: abbreviated **verb. sap., verbum sap., verbum sat.**

Ver·cin·get·o·rix (vũr'sin-jet'ə-riks, vũr'sin-get'ə-riks), *n.* Gallic chieftain defeated by Julius Caesar; died c. 45 B.C.

ver·dan·cy (vũr'd'n-si), *n.* 1. a verdant condition or appearance; greenness. 2. immaturity; inexperience.

ver·dant (vũr'd'nt), *adj.* [prob. < *verdure* + *-ant*], 1. green. 2. covered with green vegetation. 3. inexperienced; immature; innocent: as, *verdant* youth.

verd antique (vũrd), [older form of Fr. *vert antique;* OFr. *verd*, green + *antique*, ancient], 1. a green mottled or veined marble, used for interior decoration. 2. any of various green porphyritic rocks. 3. a green surface formed on bronze or brass by long exposure; patina; verdigris.

Verde, Cape (vũrd), the westernmost point of Africa, at Dakar, French West Africa.

ver·der·er, ver·der·or (vũr'dẽr-ẽr), *n.* [Anglo-Fr. *verderer;* extended < *verder;* OFr. *verdier* < *verd, vert;* L. *viridis*, green], in medieval England, a judicial officer appointed to handle all matters of trespass, etc. on the king's forests.

Ver·di, Giu·sep·pe (jōō-zep'pe ver'dē), 1813–1901; Italian operatic composer.

ver·dict (vũr'dikt), *n.* [ME. *verdit;* Anglo-Fr. *verdit* (OFr. *veirdit*); ML. *veredictum*, true saying, verdict < L. *vere*, truly + *dictum*, a thing said < *dicere*, to say], 1. in *law*, the formal and unanimous finding of a jury on the matter submitted to them in a trial; hence, 2. a decision; judgment.

ver·di·gris (vũr'di-grēs', vũr'di-gris), *n.* [ME. *verte grece;* OFr. *verd de gris, vert de Grece*, lit., green of Greece; *verd*, green + *de*, of + *Grece*, Greece], 1. a green or greenish-blue poisonous compound prepared by treating copper with acetic acid, used as a medicine, pigment, and dye. 2. a green or greenish-blue coating that forms like rust on brass, bronze, or copper.

ver·din (vũr'din), *n.* [Fr., yellowhammer], a very small bird of the titmouse family, with a bright-yellow head, found in the Southwest and in Mexico.

ver·di·ter (vũr'di-tẽr), *n.* [OFr. *verd de terre*, lit., green of the earth, earth green], either of two basic copper carbonate pigments, the one (*blue verditer*) usually consisting of ground azurite, the other (*green verditer*) usually of ground malachite; bice.

Ver·dun (vẽr-dun'; Fr. vâr'dön'), *n.* 1. a city in northeastern France, on the Meuse River: scene of a long, bloody battle (1916) in World War I: pop., 15,000 (1946). 2. a city in Quebec, Canada, near Montreal: pop., 77,000.

ver·dure (vũr'jẽr), *n.* [ME.; OFr. < *verd* (L. *viridis*), green], 1. the fresh green color of growing things; greenness. 2. green growing plants and trees; green vegetation. 3. vigorous or flourishing condition.

ver·dur·ous (vũr'jẽr-əs), *adj.* 1. flourishing and richly green: said of vegetation. 2. covered with or consisting of verdure, or rich green vegetation. 3. of or characteristic of verdure.

ver·e·cund (ver'i-kund'), *adj.* [L. *verecundus*], [Rare], bashful, shy, or modest.

‡**Ver·ein** (fer-īn'), *n.* [G.], a society; association.

verge (vũrj), *n.* [ME.; OFr., a rod, wand, stick, yard, hoop; L. *virga*, a twig, rod, wand; the semantic flow is from sense 5 through 6, 2, and 1], 1. the edge, brink, or margin (*of* something): as, the *verge* of the forest: also used figuratively, as, on the *verge* of hysteria. 2. *a*) an enclosing line or border; boundary, especially of something more or less circular. *b*) the area so enclosed. 3. the shaft of a column. 4. the edge of the tiling that projects over a gable. 5. a rod or staff symbolic of an office, as that carried before a church official in processions. 6. in *English feudal law*, *a*) a rod held in the hand by a feudal tenant as he swore fealty to his lord. *b*) the area over which an official had special jurisdiction, as the land surrounding the royal palace, under the jurisdiction of the king's marshal. 7. in *watchmaking*, the spindle of a balance wheel in a clock with a vertical escapement. *v.i.* [VERGED (vũrjd), VERGING], to be on the verge, edge, brink, or border (usually with *on* or *upon*): as, streets *verging* on the slum area: also used figuratively, as, such talk *verges* on the ridiculous.

verge (vũrj), *v.i.* [VERGED (vũrjd), VERGING], [L. *vergere*, to bend, turn], 1. to tend; incline (with *to* or *toward*). 2. to be in the process of change or transition into something else; come close to in gradation; approach (with *into* or *on*): as, broad humor *verging* on slapstick.

verg·er (vũr'jẽr), *n.* [Fr.], 1. a person who carries a verge before a bishop, dean, etc. in a procession. 2. a person who takes care of the interior of a church.

Ver·gil (vũr'jil), a masculine name: see **Virgil.**

Ver·gil·i·an (vũr-jil'i-ən), *adj.* Virgilian.

ve·rid·i·cal (və-rid'i-k'l), *adj.* [< L. *veridicus*, speaking the truth < *verus*, truth + *dicere*, to speak; + *-al*], telling the truth; truthful; veracious.

ve·rid·i·cal·i·ty (və-rid'i-kal'ə-ti), *n.* [*veridical* + *-ity*], the condition or quality of being veridical.

ver·i·est (ver'i-ist), *adj.* [superl. of *very*, *adj.*], utmost; greatest: as, the *veriest* nonsense.

ver·i·fi·a·ble (ver'ə-fī'ə-b'l), *adj.* capable of verification; that can be proved to be true by examination or investigation.

ver·i·fi·ca·tion (ver'ə-fi-kā'shən), *n.* [OFr. *verificacion*], 1. a verifying or being verified. 2. the establishment or confirmation of the truth of a fact, theory, etc. 3. in *law*, a statement at the end of a pleading to the effect that the pleader is ready to prove his allegations.

ver·i·fi·ca·tive (ver'ə-fi-kā'tiv), *adj.* [ML. *verificatus*], serving or tending to verify.

ver·i·fy (ver'ə-fī'), *v.t.* [VERIFIED (-fīd'), VERIFYING], [ME. *verifien*; OFr. *verifier*; ML. *verificare*, to make true < L. *verus*, true + *facere*, to make], 1. to prove to be true by demonstration, evidence, or testimony; confirm or substantiate. 2. to test or check the accuracy or correctness of, as by investigation, comparison with a standard, or reference to the facts. 3. in *law*, *a*) to affirm formally or upon oath. *b*) to add a verification to (a pleading). —***SYN.*** see **confirm.**

ver·i·ly (ver'ə-li), *adv.* [ME. *verrayly*, *verali*, etc.; see VERY & -LY], [Archaic], in very truth; in fact; really.

ver·i·sim·i·lar (ver'ə-sim'ə-lẽr), *adj.* [< L. *verisimilis* < *verus*, true + *similis*, like], seeming to be true or real; probable.

ver·i·si·mil·i·tude (ver'ə-si-mil'ə-tōōd', ver'ə-si-mil'ə-tūd'), *n.* [L. *verisimilitudo* < *verisimilis*; see VERISIMILAR], 1. the appearance of being true or real. 2. something that has the mere appearance of being true or real. —***SYN.*** see **truth.**

ver·ism (vêr'iz'm), *n.* [< L. *verus*, true; + *-ism*], the theory that art and literature should adhere closely to reality, even in representing the ugly and distasteful aspects of life.

ver·i·ta·ble (ver'i-tə-b'l), *adj.* [OFr. < *verite*; see VERITY], 1. true; real; actual. 2. having all the distinctive qualities of the person or thing specified: as, he is a *veritable* tyrant. —***SYN.*** see **authentic.**

ver·i·ta·bly (ver'i-tə-bli), *adv.* 1. truly; really; actually. 2. in a veritable manner.

ver·i·ty (ver'i-ti), *n.* [*pl.* VERITIES (-tiz)], [ME. *verite*; OFr. *verite(t)*; L. *veritas*, truth < *verus*, true], 1. conformity to truth or fact; truth; reality. 2. a principle, belief, etc. taken to be fundamentally and permanently true; a truth; a reality. —***SYN.*** see **truth.**

ver·juice (vũr'jōōs'), *n.* [ME. *vergeous*; OFr. *verjus* < *vert*, green + *jus*, juice], 1. the sour, acid juice of green or unripe fruit, as crab apples, grapes, etc., formerly used in cooking. 2. sourness of temper, looks, etc.

Ver·laine, Paul (pôl vâr'len'), 1844–1896; French symbolist poet.

Ver·meer, Jan (yän vẽr-mâr'; Eng. vẽr-mêr'), 1632–1675; Dutch painter: also called *Jan van der Meer van Delft*.

ver·meil (vũr'mil), *n.* [ME. *vermayle*; OFr.; L. *vermiculus*, dim. of *vermis*, a worm], 1. [Obs. or Poetic], *a*) vermilion. *b*) the bright-red color of vermilion. 2. gilded copper, bronze, or silver. *adj.* vermilion.

ver·mi- (vũr'mə), [< L. *vermis*, a worm], a combining form meaning *worm*, as in *vermicide*.

ver·mi·cel·li (vũr'mə-sel'i, vũr'mə-chel'i; It. ver'mē-chel'lē), *n.* [It., lit., little worms; L. *vermiculus*, dim. of *vermis*, a worm], a food made of a wheat flour paste dried in long threads, thinner than spaghetti.

ver·mi·cide (vũr'mə-sīd'), *n.* [*vermi-* + *-cide*], in *medicine*, a drug used to kill worms, especially intestinal worms.

ver·mic·u·lar (vẽr-mik'yoo-lẽr), *adj.* [< L. *vermiculus*, dim. of *vermis*, a worm; + *-ar*], 1. shaped like a worm. 2. moving like a worm. 3. having wavy or winding marks or outlines, like worms or worm tracks. 4. made, done, or caused by worms; worm-eaten.

ver·mic·u·late (vẽr-mik'yoo-lāt'; *for adj.*, *usually* vẽr-mik'yoo-lit), *v.t.* [VERMICULATED (-id), VERMICULATING], [< L. *vermiculatus*, pp. of *vermiculari*, to be full of worms < *vermiculus*, dim. of *vermis*, a worm], 1. to make worm-eaten. 2. to form, as by inlaying, with wavy or winding lines or marks like worm tracks. *adj.* 1. having wavy or winding markings like worms or worm tracks. 2. moving like a worm; twisting or wriggling; hence, 3. insinuating; sinuous. 4. worm-eaten.

VERMICULATED WORK

ver·mic·u·lat·ed (vẽr-mik'yoo-lāt'id), *adj.* vermiculate.

ver·mic·u·la·tion (vẽr-mik'yoo-lā'shən), *n.* [L. *vermiculatio*; see VERMICULATE], 1. motion like that of a worm; especially, the wavelike contractions of the intestines; peristalsis. 2. a worm-eaten condition. 3. vermicular markings or ornamentation.

ver·mic·u·lite (vẽr-mik'yoo-līt'), *n.* [< L. *vermiculus*, dim. of *vermis*, worm; + *-ite*], any of a number of hydrous silicates resulting usually from alterations of mica and occurring in tiny leafy scales.

ver·mi·form (vũr'mə-fôrm'), *adj.* [*vermi-* + *-form*], shaped like a worm.

vermiform appendix, an appendix (sense 2).

vermiform process, in *anatomy*, 1. the median lobe of the cerebellum, or either surface of this lobe. 2. the vermiform appendix.

ver·mi·fuge (vũr'mə-fūj'), *adj.* [< L. *vermis*, a worm + *fugare*, to expel], serving to expel worms and other parasites from the intestinal tract. *n.* a vermifuge drug.

ver·mil·ion (vẽr-mil'yən), *n.* [ME. *vermilion*; OFr. *vermillon* < *vermeil*, bright-red; see VERMEIL], 1. bright-red mercuric sulfide, used as a pigment. 2. any of several other red earths resembling this. 3. bright yellowish red. *adj.* of the color vermilion.

ver·min (vũr'min), *n.* [*pl.* VERMIN], [ME. & OFr. *vermine*; L. *vermis*, a worm; cf. VARMINT], 1. any of a number of small animals with filthy, destructive, troublesome habits, as flies, lice, bedbugs, mice, rats, and weasels. 2. [British], any bird or animal that kills game. 3. *a*) a person who is vile, worthless, or objectionable. *b*) such persons collectively.

ver·mi·na·tion (vũr'mə-nā'shən), *n.* [L. *verminatio*], 1. the fact or condition of being infested with vermin or worms. 2. in *zoology*, rapid growth and breeding of vermin under favorable conditions.

ver·min·ous (vũr'min-əs), *adj.* [L. *verminosus*], 1. of, having the nature of, or resembling vermin. 2. infested with vermin. 3. caused or produced by vermin.

Ver·mont (vẽr-mont'), *n.* a New England State of the United States: area, 9,609 sq. mi.; pop., 390,000; capital, Montpelier: nicknamed *Green Mountain State*: abbreviated **Vt.**

Ver·mont·er (vẽr-mon'tẽr), *n.* a native or inhabitant of Vermont.

ver·mouth (vẽr-mōōth', vũr'mōōth; Fr. vâr'mōōt'), *n.* [Fr.; G. *wermuth*, *wermut*, wormwood], a fortified white wine flavored with aromatic herbs: it may be sweet or dry, and is used chiefly in cocktails.

ver·nac·u·lar (vẽr-nak'yoo-lẽr), *adj.* [< L. *vernaculus*, belonging to homeborn slaves, domestic, native, indigenous < *verna*, a homeborn slave], 1. using the native language of a country or place, as a writer. 2. commonly spoken by the people of a particular country or place: said of a language or dialect: often distinguished from *literary*. 3. of or in the native language. 4. native to a country: as, the *vernacular* arts of Brittany. 5. peculiar to a particular locality: as, a *vernacular* disease. 6. designating or of the common name of an animal or plant, as distinguished from the scientific term for it in Latin nomenclature. *n.* 1. the native speech, language, or dialect of a country or place. 2. the common everyday language of ordinary people in a particular locality. 3. the shop talk or idiom of a profession or trade. 4. *a*) a vernacular word or term. *b*) the vernacular name of an animal or plant. —***SYN.*** see **dialect.**

ver·nac·u·lar·ism (vẽr-nak'yoo-lẽr-iz'm), *n.* 1. a vernacular word, phrase, or usage. 2. the use of vernacular language.

ver·nac·u·lar·ly (vẽr-nak'yoo-lẽr-li), *adv.* 1. in a vernacular manner. 2. in vernacular phrasing or usage.

ver·nal (vũr'n'l), *adj.* [L. *vernalis* < *vernus*, belonging to spring < *ver*, spring], 1. of, or appearing or occurring in, the spring. 2. springlike; fresh, warm, and mild. 3. fresh and young; youthful.

vernal equinox, the equinox that is reached about March 21: see **equinox**: also **vernal point.**

ver·nal·i·za·tion (vũr'n'l-i-zā'shən, vũr'n'l-ī-zā'shən), *n.* the act or process of vernalizing.

ver·nal·ize (vũr'n'l-īz'), *v.t.* [VERNALIZED (-īzd'), VERNALIZING], [*vernal* + *-ize*], to stimulate the growth of (a plant) by artificially hastening the dormant period, as by subjecting the seed to low temperatures away from light.

ver·na·tion (vẽr-nā'shən), *n.* [Mod. L. *vernatio* < L. *vernare*, to be verdant, flourish < *ver*, spring], in *botany*, the arrangement of leaves in a leaf bud.

Verne, Jules (jōōlz vũrn; Fr. zhül vârn), 1828–1905; French novelist.

Ver·ner's law (or **phenomenon**), (vũr'nẽrz), in *linguistics*, Karl Verner's explanation, published in 1876, of the apparent exceptions to Grimm's table of consonant correspondences between Indo-European and Germanic (see **Grimm's law**): the phenomenon is illustrated in *luxurious* (as compared with *luxury*), in which the cluster [ks] becomes voiced [gz] when the accent shifts to the following syllable.

ver·ni·er (vũr'ni-ẽr, vũr'nêr), *n.* [after Pierre *Vernier*], 1. a short graduated scale that slides along a longer graduated instrument and is used to indicate fractional parts of divisions, as in a micrometer: see **sextant**, illus.: also **vernier scale.** 2. any device that makes possible a finer setting of a tool or measuring instrument. *adj.* of or fitted with a vernier: as, *vernier* calipers.

Ver·nier, Pierre (pyâr vâr'nyā'; Eng. vũr'ni-ẽr), 1580–1637; French mathematician; inventor of the vernier.

Ver·no·le·ninsk (ver'nô-lye-nēnsk'), *n.* Nikolaev, a city in the Ukrainian S.S.R.: the former name.

Ver·non (vũr'nən), [< the surname *Vernon;* prob. < *Vernon*, a town in France], a masculine name.

Ver·non, Edward (vũr'nən), 1684–1757; English admiral: called *Old Grog.*

Ve·ro·na (və-rō'nə; It. ve-rô'nä), *n.* a city in northeastern Italy: pop., 166,000.

ver·o·nal (ver'ə-n'l), *n.* [G. < L. *ver*, spring], barbital: a trade-mark (**Veronal**).

Ver·o·nese (ver'ə-nēz'), *adj.* of Verona, its people, or culture. *n.* [*pl.* VERONESE], a native or inhabitant of Verona.

Ve·ro·ne·se, Pa·o·lo (pä'ô-lô' ve'rô-ne'se; Eng. ver'ə-nēz'), (born *Paolo Cagliari*), 1528–1588; Venetian painter born in Verona.

Ve·ron·i·ca (və-ron'i-kə), [see VERONICA, *n.*], a feminine name.

ve·ron·i·ca (və-ron'i-kə), *n.* [ML. < LL. *veraiconica* < L. *verus*, true + *iconicus*, of an image (see ICON): later taken as the name of the saint], 1. *a*) the image or representation of the face of Jesus as it was miraculously supposed to have appeared on the handkerchief used by Saint Veronica to wipe the bleeding face of Jesus on the road to Calvary. *b*) [often V-], the handkerchief itself. *c*) a similar representation of the face of Jesus on a cloth or garment. 2. [Mod. L.; prob. after Saint *Veronica*], any of a group of plants and shrubs of the figwort family, with blue, pink, purple, or white flowers in spikes; especially, the speedwell.

Veronica, Saint, a woman of Jerusalem, said to have wiped the bleeding face of Jesus on the way to Calvary.

Ver·ra·za·no, Gio·van·ni da (jô-vän'nē dä ver'rä-tsä'nô), 1485?–1528?; Italian navigator in the service of France.

Ver·roc·chio, An·dre·a del (än-dre'ä del ve-rôk'kyô), (born *Andrea di Michele Cione*), 1435–1488; Florentine sculptor, silversmith, and painter.

ver·ru·ca (ve-rōō'kə), *n.* [*pl.* VERRUCAE (-sē)], [L., wart, orig. a steep place, height], 1. a wart. 2. a wartlike elevation, as on the back of a toad.

ver·ru·cose (ver'oo-kōs'), *adj.* [L. *verrucosus* < *verruca*, wart], covered with warts or wartlike growths.

ver·ru·cos·i·ty (ver'oo-kos'ə-ti), *n.* the condition of being verrucose.

ver·ru·cous (ver'oo-kəs), *adj.* verrucose.

vers., in *trigonometry*, versed sine.

Ver·sailles (vẽr-sālz', vẽr-sī'; Fr. vâr'sä'y'), *n.* a city in France, near Paris: pop., 70,000 (1946): site of a palace built by Louis XIV: scene of the signing of a treaty (1919) between the Allies and Germany following World War I.

ver·sant (vũr'sənt), *n.* [Fr.; L. *versans*, ppr. of *versare*, to turn often, freq. of *vertere*, to turn], 1. the slope of a mountain or mountain chain; hence, 2. the general slope, or declination, of a region.

ver·sa·tile (vũr'sə-til), *adj.* [Fr.; L. *versatilis*, that turns around, movable, versatile < *versatus*, pp. of *versare*, to turn often, freq. of *vertere*, to turn], 1. competent in many things; able to turn easily from one subject or occupation to another; many-sided. 2. that can be turned or moved around, as on a hinge or pivot. 3. [Rare], fickle; inconstant. 4. in *botany*, turning about freely on the filament to which it is attached, as an anther of the passionflower. 5. in *zoology*, *a*) moving forward or backward, as the toes of a bird. *b*) movable in any direction, as the antenna of an insect or mollusk.

ver·sa·til·i·ty (vũr'sə-til'ə-ti), *n.* [Fr. *versatilité*], the quality or state of being versatile; specifically, *a*) competence in many things. *b*) ability to move freely, as on an axis, or in any direction.

‡**vers de so·cié·té** (vâr' də sô'syā'tā'), [Fr., verse of society], light, witty, polished poetry.

verse (vũrs), *n.* [ME. *vers* < AS. *fers* & OFr. *vers*, both < L. *versus*, a turning, verse, line, row, pp. of *vertere*, to turn], 1. a sequence of words arranged metrically in accordance with some rule or design; single line of poetry. 2. *a*) metrical writing or speaking; poetry in general, especially when light or trivial or merely metered and rhymed, but without much serious content or artistic merit. *b*) a particular form of metrical composition: as, blank *verse*, trochaic *verse.* 3. a single metrical composition; poem. 4. a stanza or similar short subdivision of a metrical composition: sometimes distinguished from *chorus*, or *refrain.* 5. in the *Bible*, any of the single, usually numbered, short divisions of a chapter, generally a sentence or part of a sentence. *v.t. & v.i.* [VERSED (vũrst), VERSING], [Now Rare], to versify. Abbreviated **ver.** (*sing.* & *pl.*), **v.**

versed (vũrst), *adj.* [< L. *versatus*, pp. of *versari*, to occupy oneself, be busy or engaged (in something); in form as if pp. of *verse*, to instruct, make conversant < OFr. *verser;* L. *versare*, freq. of *vertere*, to turn], acquainted by experience and study; skilled; learned.

versed (vũrst), *adj.* [< L. *versus*, pp. of *vertere*, to turn; + *-ed*], in *mathematics*, turned: as, a *versed* sine.

ver·si·cle (vũr'si-k'l), *n.* [ME.; L. *versiculus*, dim. of *versus*], a short or little verse; especially, one of the short sentences said or sung in a church service by a minister and followed by the response of the congregation.

ver·si·col·or (vũr'si-kul'ẽr), *adj.* [L. < *versare*, to change + *color*, a color], 1. having many colors; variegated. 2. changing in color; iridescent.

ver·sic·u·lar (vẽr-sik'yoo-lẽr), *adj.* of, characterized by, or consisting of versicles or verses.

ver·si·fi·ca·tion (vũr'sə-fi-kā'shən), *n.* [L. *versificatio*], 1. the act of versifying. 2. the art, practice, or theory of poetic composition. 3. the form or style of a poem; metrical structure. 4. a metrical version (*of* something).

ver·si·fi·er (vũr'sə-fī'ẽr), *n.* 1. a person who versifies; poet. 2. a person who writes light, cheap, or inferior verses; poetaster. —***SYN.*** see **poet.**

ver·si·fy (vũr'sə-fī'), *v.i.* [VERSIFIED (-fīd'), VERSIFYING], [ME. *versifien;* OFr. *versifier;* L. *versificare* < *versus*, a verse + *facere*, to make], to compose verses. *v.t.* 1. to tell or treat in verse; make a poem about. 2. to rewrite (prose) in verse form.

ver·sion (vũr'zhən, vũr'shən), *n.* [Fr.; ML. *versio*, a turning < L. *versus;* see VERSE], 1. *a*) a translation. *b*) [often V-], a translation of the Bible, in whole or part: as, the Douay and King James *versions.* 2. an account showing one point of view; particular description or report given by one person or group: as, his *version* agreed with ours. 3. a particular form or variation of something. 4. in *medicine*, *a*) displacement of the uterus in which it is deflected but not bent upon itself. *b*) the operation of turning the fetus during childbirth to make delivery easier. Abbreviated **v., Ver.** —***SYN.*** see **translation.**

ver·sion·al (vũr'zhən-'l, vũr'shən-'l), *adj.* of a version or versions.

vers li·bre (vâr' lē'br'), [Fr.], free verse.

vers li·brist (vâr' lē'brist), [Fr.], a writer of free verse.

ver·so (vũr'sō), *n.* [*pl.* VERSOS (-sōz)], [L., abl. of *versus;* see VERSE], 1. in *printing*, any left-hand page of a book; back of a leaf: opposed to *recto.* 2. the back of a coin or medal: opposed to *obverse.* Abbreviated **v., vo.**

verst (vũrst, verst), *n.* [Russ. *versta;* partly via Fr. *verste* & G. *werst*], a Russian unit of linear measure, equal to c. 3,500 feet, or about 2/3 mile.

ver·sus (vũr'səs), *prep.* [L., toward, turned in the direction of < *vertere*, to turn], 1. in *law & sports*, against: as, plaintiff *versus* defendant, Detroit *versus* Cleveland at baseball: abbreviated **vs., v.** 2. considered as an alternative to; contrasted with: as, they debated the open shop *versus* the closed shop.

vert (vũrt), *n.* [ME. *verte;* OFr.; L. *viridis*, green], 1. in *English forest law*, *a*) the green growth of a forest, as cover for deer. *b)* the right to cut green wood in a forest. 2. in *heraldry,* the color green, represented by diagonal lines from dexter (right) to sinister (left).

vert., vertical.

ver·te·bra (vũr'tə-brə), *n.* [*pl.* VERTEBRAE (-brē'), VERTEBRAS (-brəz)], [L., a joint, vertebra < *vertere,* to turn], any of the single bones or segments of the spinal column, articulating in the higher vertebrates with those adjacent to it by means of elastic fibrous discs.

VERTEBRA
A, four vertebrae joined together; B, top view of vertebra

ver·te·bral (vũr'tə-brəl), *adj.* [Mod. L. *vertebralis*], 1. of, or having the nature of, a vertebra or vertebrae. 2. having or composed of vertebrae.

ver·te·brate (vũr'tə-brāt', vũr'tə-brit), *adj.* [L. *vertebratus* < *vertebra;* see VERTEBRA], 1. having a backbone, or spinal column. 2. of or belonging to the vertebrates. *n.* any of a large division of animals that have a spinal column, or backbone, of bone or cartilage.

ver·te·brat·ed (vũr'tə-brā'tid), *adj.* 1. having a backbone; vertebrate. 2. consisting of vertebrae.

ver·te·bra·tion (vũr'tə-brā'shən), *n.* vertebral formation; segmentation into vertebrae.

ver·te·bro- (vũr'tə-brō, vũr'tə-brə), [< *vertebra*], a combining form meaning: 1. *vertebrae.* 2. *vertebral and.* Also, before a vowel, **vertebr-.**

ver·tex (vũr'teks), *n.* [*pl.* VERTEXES (-iz), VERTICES (-tə-sēz')], [L., the top, properly the turning point < *vertere,* to turn], 1. the highest point; top; summit; apex. 2. in *anatomy,* the top or crown of the head. 3. in *astronomy,* the point in the sky directly overhead; zenith. 4. in *geometry, a)* the point of intersection of two lines of a figure, opposite to the base and furthest from it. *b)* the point in a curve at which the axis meets it. *c)* the point of any angle of a triangle or polygon. 5. in *optics,* the point at which the axis cuts the curve of a lens.

ver·ti·cal (vũr'ti-k'l), *adj.* [Fr.; ML. *verticalis* < L. *vertex, verticis;* see VERTEX], 1. of the vertex, or highest point; at or in the vertex, or zenith; directly overhead. 2. perpendicular, or at a right angle to the plane of the horizon; upright; straight up and down. 3. in *anatomy & zoology,* of the vertex of the head. 4. in *botany, a)* at a right angle to the horizon or to the supporting surface. *b)* in the direction in which the axis lies; lengthwise. 5. in *economics,* of or controlling businesses concerned with all the processes in the manufacture and sale of a particular product: as, a *vertical* trust. *n.* 1. a vertical line, plane, circle, etc.: see **horizontal,** illus. 2. upright position. 3. a vertical or upright member in a truss. Abbreviated **vert.**

SYN.—**vertical** is specifically applied to that which rises in a straight line so as to form a right angle with the plane of the horizon (the *vertical* studs in a wall); **perpendicular,** the preferred term in geometry, refers to a straight line forming a right angle with any other line or plane (a line *perpendicular* to the hypotenuse of a triangle); **plumb** is a term used by carpenters, masons, etc. with reference to the perpendicularity or, especially, verticality of something, as determined by dropping a weight at the end of a line (this door is now *plumb*). —*ANT.* horizontal.

vertical circle, in *astronomy,* any great circle in the celestial sphere passing through the zenith and the nadir, its plane cutting the plane of the horizon at a right angle at the point of observation.

ver·ti·cal·i·ty (vũr'ti-kal'ə-ti), *n.* 1. the condition of the sun at the zenith, when it is directly overhead. 2. vertical position; perpendicularity.

ver·ti·cal·ly (vũr'ti-k'l-i, vũr'tik-li), *adv.* 1. in a vertical manner. 2. straight overhead or straight up and down.

vertical union, a labor union whose members all work in the same industry but not necessarily at the same trade; industrial union: opposed to *horizontal union.*

ver·ti·ces (vũr'tə-sēz'), *n.* alternative plural of **vertex.**

ver·ti·cil (vũr'ti-sil), *n.* [L. *verticillus,* a whirl, dim. of *vertex;* see VERTEX], in *botany,* a circular arrangement of leaves or flowers around a stem; whorl.

ver·ti·cil·las·ter (vũr'tə-si-las'tẽr), *n.* [Mod. L. < L. *verticillus* (see VERTICIL); + *-aster*], in *botany,* an almost circular flower arrangement formed by a pair of clusters facing each other on the stem, as in some mints.

ver·tic·il·late (vẽr-tis''l-it, vẽr-tis''l-āt', vũr'tə-sil'āt), *adj.* [Mod. L. *verticillatus* < L. *verticillus*], in *botany,* 1. arranged in verticils, or whorls. 2. having leaves, flowers, etc. arranged in this way.

ver·tic·il·lat·ed (vẽr-tis''l-ā'tid), *adj.* verticillate.

ver·tic·il·la·tion (vẽr-tis''l-ā'shən), *n.* in *botany,* arrangement of flowers, leaves, etc. in verticils, or whorls.

ver·tig·i·nous (vũr-tij'ə-nəs), *adj.* [L. *vertiginosus*], 1. rotating; revolving; whirling. 2. of or having vertigo; dizzy. 3. tending to cause vertigo. 4. characterized by rapid change; unstable; inconstant.

ver·ti·go (vũr'ti-gō'), *n.* [*pl.* VERTIGOES (-gōz'), VERTIGINES (vẽr-tij'ə-nēz')], [L., dizziness < *vertere,* to turn], in *medicine,* a sensation of dizziness or giddiness.

ver·tu (vẽr-tōō', vũr'tōō), *n.* virtu.

Ver·tum·nus (vẽr-tum'nəs), *n.* [L. < *vertere,* to turn], in *Roman mythology,* the god of the changing seasons and of growing flowers and fruits, husband of Pomona: also **Vortumnus.**

Ver·u·la·mi·um (ver'oo-lā'mi-əm, ver'yoo-lā'mi-əm), *n.* St. Albans, a city in England: the ancient name.

ver·vain (vũr'vān), *n.* [ME. & OFr. *verveine;* L. *verbena,* a shoot, green branch], any of a number of related plants of the verbena family, with spikes or clusters of red, white, or purplish flowers.

verve (vũrv), *n.* [Fr.; prob. < L. *verba,* pl. of *verbum,* a word], 1. vigor and energy in ideas or expression of them. 2. vigor; enthusiasm. 3. [Rare], aptitude.

ver·vet (vũr'vit), *n.* [Fr.; prob. < *vert,* green + *grivet*], a small monkey found in East and South Africa, related to the grivet and green monkey, but with black hands, feet, and chin.

ver·y (ver'i), *adj.* [VERIER (-i-ẽr), VERIEST (-i-ist)], [ME. & OFr. *verai,* true; LL. **veraius* < L. *verus,* true], 1. in the fullest sense; complete; absolute: as, the *very* reverse of the truth. 2. the same; identical: as, that is the *very* hat I lost. 3. even; even the: used as an intensive, as, the *very* rafters shook. 4. actual: as, caught in the *very* act. 5. [Archaic], *a)* real; true; genuine. *b)* legitimate; lawful; rightful. *adv.* 1. in a high degree; to a great extent; extremely; exceedingly. 2. truly; really: used as an intensive, as, the *very* same man. —*SYN.* see **same.**

very high frequency, in *radio & television,* any frequency of between 30 and 300 megacycles: abbreviated **VHF:** cf. **ultrahigh frequency.**

Ver·y signal (or **light**), (ver'i, vêr'i), a colored flare fired from a special pistol (the *Very pistol*) at night and used for signaling: invented in 1877 by E. W. Very.

Ve·sa·li·us, An·dre·as (an'dri-əs vi-sā'li-əs), 1514–1564; Flemish anatomist in Italy.

‡**ve·si·ca** (vi-sī'kə), *n.* [*pl.* VESICAE (-sē)], [L.], a bladder.

ves·i·cal (ves'i-k'l), *adj.* [Mod. L. *vesicalis* < L. *vesica,* bladder], of a bladder, especially the urinary bladder.

ves·i·cant (ves'i-kənt), *adj.* [< L. *vesica,* a blister], causing blisters; vesicatory. *n.* 1. a vesicant agent. 2. any agent, as mustard gas, used in chemical warfare to blister and burn body tissues by contact with the skin or inhalation.

ves·i·cate (ves'i-kāt'), *v.t. & v.i.* [VESICATED (-id), VESICATING], [< L. *vesica,* a bladder, blister], to blister.

ves·i·ca·to·ry (ves'i-kə-tôr'i, və-sik'ə-tō'ri), *adj.* [< *vesicate* + *-ory*], causing or tending to cause blisters. *n.* [*pl.* VESICATORIES (-iz, -riz)], a vesicatory agent.

ves·i·cle (ves'i-k'l), *n.* [< Fr. or L.; Fr. *vésicule;* L. *vesicula,* little bladder, dim. of *vesica,* bladder], a small membranous cavity, sac, or cyst; specifically, *a)* in *anatomy & zoology,* a small, round elevation of the skin containing a serous fluid; blister. *b)* in *botany,* a small, bladderlike sac filled with air. *c)* in *geology,* a small, spherical cavity in volcanic rock, produced by bubbles of air or gas in the molten rock.

ves·i·co- (ves'i-kō, ves'i-kə), [< L. *vesica,* the bladder], a combining form meaning *bladder* or *bladder and.*

ves·i·cot·o·my (ves'i-kot'ə-mi), *n.* [*vesico-* + *-tomy*], a surgical incision into the urinary bladder.

ve·sic·u·lar (və-sik'yoo-lẽr), *adj.* [Mod. L. *vesicularis*], 1. of, composed of, or having vesicles. 2. having the form or structure of a vesicle.

ve·sic·u·late (və-sik'yoo-lit), *adj.* vesicular. *v.t. & v.i.* (və-sik'yoo-lāt'), [VESICULATED (-id), VESICULATING], to make or become vesicular.

ve·sic·u·la·tion (və-sik'yoo-lā'shən), *n.* the formation of vesicles.

Ves·pa·si·an (ves-pā'zhi-ən, ves-pā'zhən), *n.* (*Titus Flavius Sabinus Vespasianus*), Roman emperor (69–79 A.D.); lived 9–79 A.D.

ves·per (ves'pẽr), *n.* [ME., evening star; L. *vesper,* masc., also *vespera,* fem., evening; akin to Gr. *hesperos*], 1. evening; eventide. 2. *a)* an evening prayer, service, etc. *b)* a vesper bell. 3. [V-], the evening star, Hesperus; the planet Venus seen as the evening star. *adj.* 1. of evening. 2. of vespers. See **vespers.**

ves·per·al (ves'pẽr-əl), *adj.* [LL. *vesperalis* < L. *vespera*], [Rare], of evening or vespers. *n.* in *ecclesiastical usage,* 1. a book containing the chants, psalms, etc. used at vespers. 2. a cloth cover for protecting the altar cloth.

ves·pers (ves'pẽrz), *n.pl.* [OFr. *vespres;* ML. *vesperae* < L. *vespera;* see VESPER], 1. *a)* a church service held in the late afternoon or evening, as in the Anglican Church. *b)* a prayer or song for this service. 2. in the *Roman Catholic Church, a)* the sixth of the seven canonical hours. *b*) the service for this hour. *c*) a public ceremony in which part of this service is chanted on Sundays or holy days. Also **Vespers.**

vesper sparrow, an American sparrow with white markings on its outer tail feathers: so called from its practice of singing in the evening.

ves·per·til·i·o·nid (ves'pẽr-til'i-ə-nid), ***adj.*** vespertilionine. ***n.*** a vespertilionine bat.

ves·per·til·i·o·nine (ves'pẽr-til'i-ə-nīn', ves'pẽr-til'i-ə-nin), ***adj.*** [L. *vespertilio, vespertilionis*, a bat (< *vesper*, evening); + *-ine*], designating or of the family of long-tailed bats found throughout the Temperate Zones.

ves·per·ti·nal (ves'pẽr-tī'n'l), ***adj.*** vespertine.

ves·per·tine (ves'pẽr-tin, ves'pẽr-tīn'), ***adj.*** [L. *vespertinus* < *vesper;* see VESPER], 1. of evening. 2. appearing or occurring in the evening. 3. in *botany*, opening or blossoming in the evening. 4. in *zoology*, becoming active or flying in the early evening.

ves·pi·ar·y (ves'pi-er'i), ***n.*** [*pl.* VESPIARIES (-iz)], [< L. *vespa*, a wasp, after Eng. *apiary*], 1. a nest of any of the social wasps, made of paperlike material and hung, as from a tree, or buried underground. 2. the colony in the nest.

ves·pid (ves'pid), ***n.*** [< Mod. L. *Vespidae*, name of the family < L. *vespa*, a wasp], any of a world-wide group of social wasps, as the hornet and yellow jacket, which live in colonies consisting of a queen, males, and workers. ***adj.*** of these wasps.

ves·pine (ves'pīn, ves'pin), ***adj.*** [< L. *vespa*, a wasp; + *-ine*], of or like a wasp.

Ves·puc·ci, A·me·ri·go (ä'me-rē'gô ves-po͞ot'chē), (L. name *Americus Vespucius*), 1451–1512; Italian navigator after whom America is named.

ves·sel (ves''l), ***n.*** [ME.; OFr.; L. *vascellum*, dim. of *vas*, a vessel], 1. a utensil for holding something, as a vase, bowl, pitcher, kettle, etc. 2. [Chiefly Biblical], a person thought of as being the receiver or repository of some spirit, influence, etc.: as, a *vessel* of wrath. 3. a craft for traveling on water; ship or boat, especially one larger than a rowboat. 4. an airship. 5. in *anatomy & zoology*, a tube or duct containing or circulating a body fluid: as, a blood *vessel*. 6. in *botany*, a tube or canal serving to conduct water. Abbreviated **ves.**

vest (vest), ***n.*** [Fr. & It. *veste;* L. *vestis*, a garment, vesture], 1. a short, tight-fitting, sleeveless garment worn under a suit coat by men; waistcoat. 2. an undervest, or undershirt. 3. an insert or trimming worn under the bodice by women, simulating the front of a man's vest. 4. [Archaic], robe; garment; clothing. 5. [Obs.], a long, cassocklike garment worn by men in the time of Charles II. ***v.t.*** 1. to clothe; dress, as in church vestments. 2. to place (authority, power, property rights, etc.) in the control of a person or group (with ***in***). 3. to put (a person) in possession or control of, as power or authority; invest (***with*** something). ***v.i.*** 1. to put on garments or vestments; clothe oneself. 2. to pass to a person; become fixed upon or vested in a person, as property (with ***in***).

Ves·ta (ves'tə), ***n.*** [L.], 1. in *Roman mythology*, the goddess of the hearth and the hearth fire, identified with the Greek Hestia: she was worshiped in a temple in which a sacred fire on the altar was tended by the vestal virgins. 2. [v-], *a*) originally, a short wax friction match. *b*) later, a short wooden match.

ves·tal (ves't'l), ***adj.*** 1. of or sacred to Vesta. 2. of the vestal virgins; hence, 3. chaste; pure. ***n.*** 1. a vestal virgin. 2. a chaste woman; virgin. 3. a nun.

vestal virgin, in ancient Rome, any of six virgins, priestesses of Vesta, who, sworn to remain chaste, tended the sacred fire in her temple.

vest·ed (ves'tid), ***adj.*** [pp. of *vest*], 1. clothed; robed, especially in church vestments. 2. in *law*, fixed; settled; absolute; not contingent upon anything: as, a *vested* interest.

vest·ee (ves-tē'), ***n.*** [dim. of *vest*], a vest (sense 3).

ves·ti·ar·y (ves'ti-er'i), ***adj.*** [ME. *vestiare;* OFr. *vestiairie;* ML. *vestiarium;* see VESTRY], of clothes or vestments. ***n.*** [Obs.], a vestry or cloakroom.

ves·tib·u·lar (ves-tib'yoo-lẽr), ***adj.*** of, like, or having the nature of, a vestibule.

ves·ti·bule (ves'tə-būl'), ***n.*** [L. *vestibulum*, entrance hall], 1. a small entrance hall or room, either to a building or to a room within a building. 2. the enclosed passage between passenger cars of a train, having doors for entrance or exit. 3. in *anatomy & zoology*, any cavity or space serving as an entrance to another cavity or space: as, the *vestibule* of the inner ear leading into the cochlea. ***v.t.*** [VESTIBULED (-būld'), VESTIBULING], to furnish with a vestibule.

ves·tige (ves'tij), ***n.*** [Fr.; L. *vestigium*, a footprint], 1. a trace, mark, or sign of something which has once existed but has passed away or disappeared: as, there was no *vestige* of the town. 2. a trace; bit: as, there was no *vestige* of woodland. 3. in *biology*, a degenerate, atrophied, or rudimentary organ or part, more fully developed or functional in an earlier stage of development of the individual or species. —***SYN.*** see **trace.**

ves·tig·i·al (ves-tij'i-əl), ***adj.*** of, or having the nature of, a vestige.

ves·tig·i·um (ves-tij'i-əm), ***n.*** [*pl.* VESTIGIA (-ə)], in *biology*, a vestige; vestigial organ or part.

vest·ing (ves'tiŋ), ***n.*** cloth for vests; especially, a rich, heavy fabric used in vests for evening dress.

vest·ment (vest'mənt), ***n.*** [ME. *vestiment;* OFr. *vestement;* L. *vestimentum* < *vestire*, to clothe], 1. a garment; robe; gown; especially, an official robe or gown. 2. in *ecclesiastical usage*, any of the garments worn by officiants and their assistants during certain services and rites.

vest-pock·et (vest'pok'it), ***adj.*** 1. made to fit into a vest pocket; hence, 2. relatively small: as, a *vest-pocket* edition of a book.

ves·try (ves'tri), ***n.*** [*pl.* VESTRIES (-triz)], [ME. *vestrie;* OFr. *vestiarie;* ML. *vestiarium*, a wardrobe < L. *vestis*, a garment], 1. a room in a church, where the clergy put on their vestments and the sacred vessels are kept; sacristy. 2. a room in a church or church building where prayer meetings, Sunday Schools, etc. are held. 3. in the *Anglican & Episcopal churches*, a group of church members who manage the temporal affairs of the church. 4. in the *Anglican Church*, *a*) a meeting of such a group or of the parishioners in general. *b*) the place where this is held.

ves·try·man (ves'tri-mən), ***n.*** [*pl.* VESTRYMEN (-mən)], a member of a vestry.

ves·ture (ves'chẽr), ***n.*** [ME.; OFr.; LL. *vestitura* < L. *vestire*, to clothe], 1. [Rare or Archaic], clothing; garments; apparel. 2. [Rare or Archaic], a covering; wrapper. 3. in *law*, everything growing on land except trees, as grass or grain. ***v.t.*** [VESTURED (-chẽrd), VESTURING], [Rare or Archaic], to cover; clothe; dress.

Ve·su·vi·an (və-so͞o'vi-ən, və-sū'vi-ən), ***adj.*** of or like Mount Vesuvius; volcanic. ***n.*** [v-], 1. vesuvianite. 2. an early type of match for lighting cigars, etc.; fusee.

ve·su·vi·an·ite (və-so͞o'vi-ən-īt', və-sū'vi-ən-īt'), ***n.*** [< L. *Vesuvius;* + *-an* + *-ite*], a glassy mineral, brown to green in color, a basic silicate of calcium and aluminum, first found at Mt. Vesuvius; idocrase.

Ve·su·vi·us (və-so͞o'vi-əs, və-sū'vi-əs), ***n.*** an active volcano near Naples, Italy: height, 3,858 ft.: severe eruptions occurred in 79 A.D. (destroying Pompeii) and in 1906.

vet (vet), ***n.*** [Colloq.], a veterinarian. ***v.t.*** [VETTED (-id), VETTING], [Colloq.], to examine or treat as a veterinarian does. ***v.i.*** [Colloq.], to be a veterinarian.

vet (vet), ***n.*** [Colloq.], a veteran.

vet., 1. veteran. 2. veterinarian. 3. veterinary.

vetch (vech), ***n.*** [ME. *feche, veche;* OFr. *veche* (Fr. *vesche*); L. *vicia*, vetch], any of a number of related short, leafy, climbing or trailing plants of the pea family, grown chiefly for fodder and as a soil restorer.

vetch·ling (vech'liŋ), ***n.*** [*vetch* + *-ling*], any of a group of small plants of the pea family.

vet·er·an (vet'ẽr-ən, vet'rən), ***adj.*** [L. *veteranus* < *vetus, veteris*, old], 1. old and experienced; long practiced, especially in war or military service. 2. of a veteran or veterans. ***n.*** 1. a person of long experience in some service or position, especially in military service. 2. a person who has served in the armed forces of a country, especially in time of war. Abbreviated **vet.**

Veterans' Administration, a Federal agency, created in 1930, in which all agencies concerned with veterans' affairs were consolidated for administering all laws dealing with relief or benefits for veterans of the army, navy, etc.: abbreviated **V.A., VA** (no period).

Veterans' Day, see **Armistice Day.**

Veterans of Foreign Wars, an organization of United States veterans founded in 1899: abbreviated **V.F.W., VFW** (no period).

vet·er·i·nar·i·an (vet'ẽr-ə-nâr'i-ən, vet'rə-nâr'i-ən), ***n.*** [< L. *veterinarius*], a person who practices veterinary medicine or surgery: abbreviated **vet.**

vet·er·i·nar·y (vet'ẽr-ə-ner'i, vet'rə-ner'i), ***adj.*** [L. *veterinarius*, of beasts of burden < *veterina*, beasts of burden; as if < *vetus, veteris*, old, in the sense "beasts of a certain age"], designating or of the branch of medicine dealing with the investigation, treatment, and prevention of diseases in animals, especially domestic animals. ***n.*** [*pl.* VETERINARIES (-iz)], a veterinarian. Abbreviated **vet., veter.**

vet·i·ver (vet'ə-vẽr), ***n.*** [Fr. *vétiver* < Tamil *veṭṭivēru*, lit., root that is dug up < *vēr*, root], 1. an East Indian grass whose roots yield a fragrant oil used in perfumes. 2. its fibrous roots, also used for making screens, mats, etc.

ve·to (vē'tō), ***n.*** [*pl.* VETOES (-tōz)], [L., I forbid < *vetare*, to forbid], 1. an order prohibiting some proposed or intended act; prohibition, especially by a person in authority. 2. the power to prevent action by such prohibition. 3. the constitutional right or power of a ruler or legislature to reject bills passed by another branch of the government; specifically, in the United States, *a*) the power of the President to refuse to sign a bill passed by Congress, preventing it from becoming law unless it is passed again (with a two-thirds majority) by both houses. *b*) a similar power held by the governors of States. *c*) the exercise of this power. 4. a document or message giving the reasons of the executive for rejecting a bill: also **veto message.** *v.t.* [VETOED (-tōd), VETOING], 1. to prevent (a bill) from becoming law by a veto. 2. to forbid; prohibit; refuse consent to.

Vet·ter, Lake (vet′ẽr), Lake Vätter.

vex (veks), *v.t.* [ME. *vexen;* OFr. *vexer,* to vex, torment; L. *vexare,* to shake, agitate < *vehere,* to carry], 1. to make trouble for; disturb; annoy; irritate, especially in little things. 2. [Rare], to afflict (a person): said of disease. 3. to trouble seriously; torment. 4. to discuss at length; bring up again and again for discussion: as, a *vexed* point. 5. [Obs.], to shake up; toss about; agitate. —*SYN.* see **annoy.**

vex·a·tion (vek-sā′shən), *n.* [ME. *vexacioun;* OFr.; L. *vexatio*], 1. a vexing or being vexed. 2. something that vexes; cause of annoyance or distress.

vex·a·tious (vek-sā-′shəs), *adj.* 1. causing vexation; annoying. 2. characterized by vexation; disturbed. 3. in *law,* instituted without real grounds, chiefly to cause annoyance to the defendant: said of legal actions.

vexed (vekst), *adj.* [pp. of *vex*], 1. troubled; annoyed; irritated; disturbed. 2. much debated or discussed; brought up again and again: as, a *vexed* question.

vex·ed·ly (vek′sid-li), *adv.* with vexation; in a vexed manner.

vex·il (vek′sil), *n.* a vexillum (sense 2).

vex·il·lar (vek′sə-lẽr), *adj.* vexillary.

vex·il·lar·y (vek′sə-ler′i), *adj.* [L. *vexillarius* < *vexillum;* see VEXILLUM], 1. of an ensign or standard. 2. in *botany,* of a vexillum. *n.* in ancient Rome, 1. any of a class of veteran soldiers serving under a special standard. 2. a standard-bearer.

vex·il·late (vek′sə-lit, vek′sə-lāt′), *adj.* having a vexillum or vexilla.

vex·il·lum (vek-sil′əm), *n.* [*pl.* VEXILLA (-ə)], [L., a standard, flag, dim. < base of *velum;* see VEIL], 1. in ancient Rome, *a)* a square flag, or standard, carried by troops. *b)* a company of soldiers serving under one standard. 2. in *botany,* the large, erect upper petal of a flower of the pea family. 3. in *zoology,* the web or vane of a feather.

V.F.W., VFW, Veterans of Foreign Wars.

V.G., Vicar General.

VHF, very high frequency.

Vi, in *chemistry,* virginium.

V.I., Virgin Islands.

v.i., 1. intransitive verb. 2. *vide infra,* [L.], see below.

vi·a (vī′ə; *occas.* vē′ə), *prep.* [L., abl. sing. of *via,* a way], by way of; passing through: as, to Baltimore *via* Washington.

vi·a·bil·i·ty (vī′ə-bil′ə-ti), *n.* [Fr. *viabilité*], the state or quality of being viable.

vi·a·ble (vī′ə-b′l), *adj.* [Fr., likely to live < *vie* (L. *vita*), life], able to live; specifically, *a)* at that stage of development that will permit it to live and develop under normal conditions, outside of the uterus: said of a fetus or newborn, especially premature, infant. *b)* able to take root and grow: as, *viable* seeds.

vi·a·duct (vī′ə-dukt′), *n.* [(after *aqueduct*) < L. *via,* a way], 1. a long bridge consisting of a series of short concrete or masonry spans supported on piers or towers, usually to carry a road or railroad over a valley, gorge, etc. 2. a similar structure of steel girders and towers.

VIADUCT

vi·al (vī′əl), *n.* [ME. & OFr. *viole;* L. *phiala,* saucer < Gr. *phialē,* shallow cup; cf. PHIAL], a small vessel or bottle, usually of glass, for containing medicines or other liquids; phial. *v.t.* [VIALED or VIALLED (-əld), VIALING or VIALLING], to put or keep in or as in a vial.

‡**vi·a me·di·a** (vī′ə mē′di-ə), [L.], a middle way; course between two extremes.

vi·and (vī′ənd), *n.* [ME. *vyaunde;* OFr. *viande;* LL. **vivanda,* for L. *vivenda,* neut. pl. gerundive of *vivere,* to live], 1. an article of food. 2. *pl.* food; victuals; especially, choice dishes.

vi·at·ic (vī-at′ik), *adj.* [L. *viaticus,* of a way or road < *via,* a way], of a road, a journey, or travel.

vi·at·i·cal (vī-at′i-k′l), *adj.* viatic.

vi·at·i·cum (vī-at′i-kəm), *n.* [*pl.* VIATICA (-kə), VIATICUMS (-kəmz)], [L., provision for a journey < *viaticus;* see VIATIC], 1. in ancient Rome, money or supplies provided as traveling expenses to an officer on an official mission; hence, 2. money or supplies for any journey. 3. the Eucharist as given to a dying person or to one in danger of death.

vi·a·tor (vī-ā′tôr), *n.* [*pl.* VIATORES (vī′ə-tō′rēz)], [L. < *viare,* to travel < *via,* a way], a traveler; wayfarer.

Vi·borg (vē′bôr-y′), *n.* Viipuri: the Swedish name.

vi·brac·u·lar (vī-brak′yoo-lẽr), *adj.* 1. of, or having the nature of, vibracula. 2. having vibracula.

vi·brac·u·loid (vī-brak′yoo-loid′), *adj.* like a vibraculum or vibracula.

vi·brac·u·lum (vī-brak′yoo-ləm), *n.* [*pl.* VIBRACULA (-lə)], [Mod. L., dim. < L. *vibrare,* to shake, vibrate], in *zoology,* any of the freely movable, spinelike or whiplike defensive organs of certain bryozoans.

vi·bran·cy (vī′brən-si), *n.* the state or quality of being vibrant; resonance.

vi·brant (vī′brənt), *adj.* [L. *vibrans,* ppr. of *vibrare,* to vibrate, shake], 1. quivering; vibrating; especially, vibrating in such a way as to produce sound. 2. produced by vibration; resonant: said of sound. 3. giving the impression of much energetic activity; pulsing: as, *vibrant* streets. 4. vigorous; energetic: as, a *vibrant* woman. 5. in *phonetics,* voiced. *n.* a voiced sound.

vi·bra·phone (vī′brə-fōn′), *n.* [< *vibrate* + *-phone*], a musical instrument resembling the marimba, but with electrically operated valves in the resonators, that produce a gentle vibrato.

vi·brate (vī′brāt), *v.t.* [VIBRATED (-id), VIBRATING], [< L. *vibratus,* pp. of *vibrare,* to vibrate, shake], 1. to give off (light or sound) by vibration. 2. to set in to-and-fro motion; cause to quiver. *v.i.* 1. to swing back and forth; oscillate, as a pendulum. 2. to move rapidly back and forth; quiver, as a plucked string. 3. to resound: said of sounds. 4. to be emotionally stirred; thrill: as, she *vibrated* with joy. 5. to waver or vacillate, as between two choices. —*SYN.* see **swing.**

vi·bra·tile (vī′brə-til, vī′brə-til′), *adj.* [< L. *vibratus;* see VIBRATE], 1. of, characterized by, or having the nature of, vibration. 2. capable of vibrating or of being vibrated. 3. having a vibratory motion.

vi·bra·til·i·ty (vī′brə-til′ə-ti), *n.* the state or property of being vibratile.

vi·bra·tion (vī-brā′shən), *n.* 1. a vibrating; specifically, *a)* motion back and forth, as of a pendulum; oscillation. *b)* rapid rhythmic motion back and forth; quiver. 2. vacillation; wavering, as between two choices or opinions. 3. a stirring; thrill, as of the emotions. 4. in *physics, a)* rapid rhythmic motion back and forth across a position of equilibrium of the particles of a fluid or an elastic solid when its equilibrium has been disturbed, as in transmitting sound. *b)* the vibrating motion of a string, etc. in producing sound. *c)* a single, complete vibrating motion; quiver.

vi·bra·tion·al (vī-brā′shən-′l), *adj.* of, or having the nature of, vibration.

vi·bra·tive (vī′brə-tiv), *adj.* vibratory; vibrating.

vi·bra·to (vi-brä′tō; It. vē-brä′tô), *n.* [It., pp. of *vibrare;* see VIBRATE], in *music,* a tremulous effect obtained by rapidly alternating the original tone with a slightly perceptible variation in the pitch, as by the rapid pulsation of the finger on the string of a violin: in singing, sometimes interchangeable with *tremolo.*

vi·bra·tor (vī′brā-tẽr), *n.* something that vibrates or causes vibration; specifically, *a)* the hammer of an electric bell. *b)* an electrical instrument with a vibrating rubber head or pad, used in massage, etc. *c)* in *electricity,* an oscillator.

vi·bra·to·ry (vī′brə-tôr′i, vī′brə-tō′ri), *adj.* 1. of, having the nature of, or consisting of vibration. 2. causing vibration. 3. vibrating or capable of vibration. 4. vibrant, as the voice.

vib·ri·o (vib′ri-ō′), *n.* [Mod. L. < L. *vibrare,* to shake, vibrate], any of a group of short, flagellate, Gram-negative bacteria shaped like a comma or the letter S: one species is the causative agent of cholera.

vib·ri·oid (vib′ri-oid′), *adj.* in *botany,* of or like a vibrio. *n.* a vibrioid body.

vibrioid body, in *botany,* any of the cylindrical, threadlike bodies in the cells of some algae and fungi.

vi·bris·sa (vī-bris′ə), *n.* [*pl.* VIBRISSAE (-ē)], [L. *vibrissae,* pl. < *vibrare,* to vibrate], in *anatomy & zoology,* 1. any of the stiff hairs growing in or near the nostrils of certain animals and often serving as organs of touch, as a cat's whiskers. 2. any of the bristlelike feathers growing near the mouth of certain insect-eating birds, as the whippoorwill.

vi·bro·scope (vī′brə-skōp′), *n.* [< L. *vibrare;* + *-scope*], an instrument for observing and recording vibrations.

vi·bur·num (vī-bũr′nəm), *n.* [L., the wayfaring tree], 1. any of a large group of shrubs or small trees of the honeysuckle family, with white flowers and black, green, or red berries. 2. the bark of several species of this plant, used in medicine to relieve spasm.

Vic., 1. Vicar. 2. Vicarage. 3. Victoria.

vic·ar (vik′ẽr), *n.* [ME. *vicar, vicair;* OFr. *vicaire;* L. *vicarius* < *vicis,* a change, alteration], 1. a person who acts in place of another; deputy; hence, 2. in the *Anglican Church,* the priest of a parish who is not a rector; priest of a parish in which the tithes go to a layman or a religious corporation, the priest himself receiving only a salary. 3. in the *Episcopal Church,* a minister in charge of one chapel in a parish, as deputy of another minister. 4. in the *Roman Catholic Church, a)* a priest or other church officer acting as deputy of a bishop. *b)* [V-], the Pope, regarded as earthly representative of Christ: in full, *Vicar of (Jesus) Christ.* Abbreviated **V., Vic.**

vic·ar·age (vik'ẽr-ij), *n.* [ME. *vicerege;* see -AGE], 1. the residence of a vicar. 2. the benefice or salary of a vicar. 3. [Rare], the position or duties of a vicar. Abbreviated **Vic.**

vicar apostolic, in the *Roman Catholic Church,* 1. formerly, a bishop or archbishop to whom the Pope delegated part of his jurisdiction. 2. a titular bishop administering a vacant diocese, etc., or a missionary bishop acting as a delegate of the Holy See in a region where no regular see has yet been organized. Abbreviated **V.A.**

vic·ar·ate (vik'ẽr-it, vik'ə-rāt'), *n.* a vicariate.

vicar fo·rane (fô-rān', fō-rān'), [< *vicar* + ML. *foraneus,* outside of the episcopal city, rural; see FOREIGN], in the *Roman Catholic Church,* a priest appointed by a bishop to a limited jurisdiction in a particular town or district in his diocese.

vic·ar-gen·er·al (vik'ẽr-jen'ẽr-əl), *n.* [*pl.* VICARS-GENERAL], 1. in the *Anglican Church,* a layman serving as deputy to an archbishop or bishop in certain legal or administrative matters. 2. in the *Roman Catholic Church,* a priest or higher official acting as deputy to a bishop in administering his diocese. 3. in English history, the title given to Thomas Cromwell as vicegerent of Henry VIII. Abbreviated **V.G.**

vi·car·i·al (vī-kâr'i-əl, vi-kâr'i-əl), *adj.* 1. of a vicar or vicars. 2. acting as a vicar. 3. delegated; handed over to a deputy; vicarious: as, *vicarial* powers.

vi·car·i·ate (vī-kâr'i-it, vi-kâr'i-āt'), *n.* [ML. *vicariatus* < L. *vicarius*], 1. the office or authority of a vicar. 2. the district administered by a vicar.

vi·car·i·ous (vī-kâr'i-əs, vi-kâr'i-əs), *adj.* [L. *vicarius,* substituted < *vicis,* a change, alteration], 1. taking the place of another thing or person; substitute; deputy. 2. endured, suffered, or performed by one person in place of another: as, *vicarious* punishment. 3. held or handled by one person as the deputy of another; delegated: as, *vicarious* authority or power. 4. enjoyed or experienced by someone through his imagined participation in another's experience: as, a *vicarious* thrill. 5. in *physiology,* designating or of a function abnormally performed by other than the usual organ or part: as, *vicarious* menstruation.

vic·ar·ly (vik'ẽr-li), *adj.* of, like, or suggesting a vicar, as in manner or dress.

vic·ar·ship (vik'ẽr-ship'), *n.* [*vicar* + *-ship*], the office or position of a vicar.

vice (vīs), *n.* [ME.; OFr.; L. *vitium,* vice, fault], 1. a serious fault of character; grave moral failing. 2. evil or wicked conduct; corruption; depravity. 3. a particular immoral, depraved, or degrading habit. 4. [V-], in old English morality plays, a character, often a buffoon, representing a vice or vice in general. 5. a fault, defect, or blemish. 6. a physical defect or imperfection. 7. a bad or harmful trick or habit in a domestic animal, as in a horse or dog. —*SYN.* see **fault.**

vi·ce (vī'si), *prep.* [L.; see VICE-], in the place of; instead of.

vice (vīs), *n. & v.t.* vise.

vice- (vīs), [< L. *vice,* in the place of another, abl. of *vicis,* a change], a prefix meaning *one who acts in the place of, subordinate, deputy,* as in *vice-president.*

vice-ad·mi·ral (vīs'ad'mə-rəl), *n.* a naval officer next in rank above a rear admiral and below an admiral: abbreviated **V.A.**

vice-ad·mi·ral·ty (vīs'ad'mə-rəl-ti), *n.* the rank, office, or command of a vice-admiral.

vice-chan·cel·lor (vīs'chan'sə-lẽr, vīs'chän'slẽr), *n.* 1. an official next in rank below a chancellor, as of a university, and authorized to act as his deputy. 2. in *law,* a judge serving as assistant to a chancellor. Abbreviated **V.C.**

vice-con·sul (vīs'kon's'l), *n.* an officer who is subordinate to or a substitute for a consul: abbreviated **V.C.**

vice-con·su·late (vīs'kon's'l-it), *n.* a consular office of subordinate rank.

vice·ge·ral (vīs'jêr'əl), *adj.* of a vicegerent.

vice·ge·ren·cy (vīs'jêr'ən-si), *n.* 1. the office, function, or authority of a vicegerent. 2. a district ruled by a vicegerent.

vice·ge·rent (vīs'jêr'ənt), *n.* [ML. *vicegerens;* L. *vicem gerens,* acting in another's place < *vicis,* a change + *gerere,* to direct], a person appointed by another, especially by a ruler, to exercise the latter's power and authority; deputy; vicar. *adj.* 1. wielding the power of another. 2. characterized by delegated power.

vic·e·nar·y (vis'ə-ner'i), *adj.* [L. *vicenarius* < *viceni,* twenty each], 1. of or consisting of twenty. 2. using twenty as the basic unit of notation.

vi·cen·ni·al (vī-sen'i-əl), *adj.* [< L. *vicennium,* period of twenty years < *vicies,* twenty times + *annus,* year], 1. happening every twenty years. 2. lasting or existing for twenty years.

Vi·cen·za (vē-chen'tsä), *n.* a city in northeastern Italy: pop., 77,000 (est. 1947).

vice-pres·i·den·cy (vīs'prez'ə-dən-si), *n.* the office or term of office of a vice-president.

vice-pres·i·dent (vīs'prez'ə-dənt), *n.* 1. an officer next in rank below a president, acting in his place during his absence or incapacity. 2. [V- P-], the elected officer of this rank in the government of the United States, acting as president of the Senate, but not as executive assistant to the President: he succeeds to the Presidency in the event that the President dies or otherwise leaves office. 3. in some corporations, any of several officers, each in charge of a separate department. Also **vice president.** Abbreviated **Vice-Pres., V.P.**

vice-pres·i·den·tial (vīs'prez'ə-den'shəl), *adj.* of a vice-president.

vice·re·gal (vīs'rē'g'l), *adj.* [*vice-* + *regal*], of a viceroy.

vice-re·gent (vīs'rē'jənt), *n.* a person who acts in place of a regent; deputy regent. *adj.* of, or holding the office of, vice-regent.

vice·reine (vīs'rān), *n.* [Fr. *vice-reine; vice-* (see VICE-) + *reine* (L. *regina*), queen], the wife of a viceroy.

vice·roy (vīs'roi), *n.* [Fr. *viceroi; vice-* (see VICE-) + *roi* (L. *rex*), a king], 1. a person ruling a country, province, or colony as the deputy of a sovereign. 2. an American butterfly of striking red and black coloring, much like the monarch butterfly, but smaller.

vice·roy·al·ty (vīs'roi'əl-ti), *n.* [*pl.* VICEROYALTIES (-tiz)], [< Fr. *vice-royauté;* see VICE- & ROYALTY], 1. the office, dignity, or authority of a viceroy. 2. his term of office. 3. a district ruled by a viceroy.

vice·roy·ship (vīs'roi-ship'), *n.* [see -SHIP], viceroyalty.

vice squad, that division of a police force charged with the suppression or control of prostitution, gambling, and other vices.

vi·ce ver·sa (vī'si vũr'sə; *now often* vīs' vũr'sə), [L.], the order or relation being reversed; conversely: abbreviated **v.v.**

Vi·chy (vish'i, vē'shi; Fr. vē'shē'), *n.* a city in central France: pop., 29,000 (1946): capital of unoccupied France (1940–1944).

Vi·chy·ssoise (vē'shē'swȧz'), *n.* [Fr.], a thick cream soup of potatoes, onions, etc., usually served cold: sometimes also **Vichysoisse.**

Vichy water, 1. a sparkling mineral water found at Vichy. 2. a natural or manufactured water like this.

vic·i·nage (vis''n-ij), *n.* [ME.; OFr. *visenage, voisenage* < L. *vicinus;* see VICINITY], 1. the region or area surrounding a particular place; neighborhood; vicinity. 2. the people living in a particular neighborhood. 3. the fact of being a neighbor; proximity.

vic·i·nal (vis''n-əl), *adj.* [L. *vicinalis* < *vicinus;* see VICINITY], 1. neighboring; near-by. 2. designating a road that is local and not a highway. 3. in *mineralogy,* designating faces on a crystal which approximate or take the place of fundamental planes.

vi·cin·i·ty (və-sin'ə-ti), *n.* [*pl.* VICINITIES (-tiz)], [L. *vicinitas* < *vicinus,* near], 1. a being near or close by; nearness; proximity: as, two theaters in close *vicinity.* 2. a near-by or surrounding region; neighborhood.

vi·cious (vish'əs), *adj.* [ME.; OFr. *vicieus;* L. *vitiosus,* full of faults, corrupt, vicious < *vitium,* a fault, vice], 1. given to or characterized by vice or evil; wicked; depraved; immoral: as, a *vicious* person. 2. having a vice, flaw, fault, or defect; faulty: as, a *vicious* argument. 3. having bad habits; unruly; dangerous: as, a *vicious* horse. 4. malicious; spiteful; mean: as, a *vicious* rumor. 5. debasing; corrupting: as, the experience had a *vicious* effect on her. 6. [Obs.], impure, foul, or noxious, as air or water.

SYN.—**vicious** suggests such reprehensible qualities as wickedness, depravity, cruelty, etc. (a *vicious* bigot, remark, etc.); **villainous,** more or less synonymous with **vicious,** suggests the evil or criminality of a villain (a *villainous* attack); **iniquitous** implies the absence of all righteousness or justice and indifference to moral principles (the *iniquitous* practices of colonialism); **nefarious** implies unspeakable wickedness and total disregard of morality and ethics (a *nefarious* scheme for robbing the poor); **infamous** suggests scandalous or notorious wickedness (an *infamous* crime). —*ANT.* virtuous, righteous.

vicious circle, 1. a situation in which the solution of one problem gives rise to another, but the solution of this, or of other problems rising out of it, brings back the first, often with greater involvement. 2. in *logic,* *a*) an argument which is invalid because its conclusion rests on a premise which itself depends on the conclusion. *b*) the definition of a word by another which is in turn defined by the first. 3. in *medicine,* a situation in which one disease or disorder results in another which in turn aggravates the first.

vi·cis·si·tude (vi-sis'ə-tōōd', vi-sis'ə-tūd'), *n.* [Fr.; L. *vicissitudo* < *vicis,* a turn, change], 1. *usually pl.* changes or variations occurring irregularly in the course of something; especially, change of circumstances in life; ups and downs of fortune. 2. regular succession or alternation, as of night and day. 3. change or alternation, as a natural process of life. —*SYN.* see **difficulty.**

vi·cis·si·tu·di·nar·y (vi-sis'ə-tōō'd'n-er'i, vi-sis'ə-tū'd'n-er'i), *adj.* involving or subject to vicissitude, or alternation; changing in succession.

vi·cis·si·tu·di·nous (vi-sis'ə-tōō'd'n-əs, vi-sis'ə-tū'd'n-əs), *adj.* vicissitudinary.

Vicks·burg (viks'bũrg), *n.* a city in Mississippi, on the

Mississippi River: pop., 29,000: besieged (1863) in the Civil War by Grant: battleground now a national military park.

vi·con·ti·el (vī-kon′ti-əl), *adj.* [Anglo-Fr. < *viconte*, viscount, sheriff], of a viscount (sheriff).

Vict., 1. Victoria. 2. Victorian.

vic·tim (vik′tim), *n.* [L. *victima*, victim, beast for sacrifice], 1. a person or animal killed as a sacrifice to some god in a religious rite. 2. someone or something killed, destroyed, injured, or otherwise harmed by, or suffering from, some act, condition, agency, or circumstance: as, *victims* of war. 3. a person who suffers some loss, especially by being swindled; dupe.

vic·tim·i·za·tion (vik′tim-i-zā′shən, vik′tim-ī-zā′shən), *n.* a victimizing or being victimized.

vic·tim·ize (vik′tim-īz′), *v.t.* [VICTIMIZED (-īzd′), VICTIMIZING], to make a victim of; specifically, *a*) to kill, destroy, etc. as or like a sacrificial victim. *b*) to cheat; swindle; dupe.

Vic·tor (vik′tẽr), [L.; see VICTOR (winner)], a masculine name: diminutive, *Vic;* feminine, *Victoria.*

vic·tor (vik′tẽr), *n.* [ME.; L. < *vincere*, to conquer], the winner in a battle, struggle, or contest; conqueror. *adj.* of, or having the nature of, a victor; victorious.

Victor Emmanuel I, 1759–1824; Italian king of Sardinia (1802–1821); abdicated.

Victor Emmanuel II, 1820–1878; first king of Italy (1861–1878).

Victor Emmanuel III, 1869–1947; son of Humbert I; king of Italy (1900–1946): monarchy dissolved (1946).

Vic·to·ri·a (vik-tôr′i-ə, vik-tōr′yə), [L.; see VICTORY], a feminine name: diminutive, *Vicky;* equivalents, Fr. *Victoire*, It. *Vittoria*, Sp. *Vitoria.* *n.* 1. granddaughter of George III; 1819–1901; queen of Great Britain (1837–1901) and empress of India (1876–1901). 2. a state of the Commonwealth of Australia: area, 87,884 sq. mi.; pop., 2,815,000; capital, Melbourne: abbreviated **Vic., Vict.** 3. seaport and capital of Hong Kong colony: pop., c. 1,000,000: also called *Hong Kong.* 4. the capital of British Columbia, Canada, on Vancouver Island: pop., 55,000. 5. a city in southeastern Texas: pop., 33,000.

vic·to·ri·a (vik-tôr′i-ə, vik-tōr′yə), *n.* [after Queen *Victoria*], 1. a low four-wheeled carriage for two passengers, with a folding top and a high seat in front for the coachman. 2. an early touring automobile with a folding top over the rear seat. 3. [Mod. L. *Victoria regia*, lit., royal Victoria], any of a number of related South American water lilies with platterlike leaves up to seven feet in diameter and large, night-blooming, pineapple-scented flowers which turn from white to pink.

VICTORIA

Victoria, Lake, a lake in east central Africa: area, 26,200 sq. mi.: also called *Victoria Nyanza.*

Victoria Cross, the highest British military decoration, given for deeds of exceptional valor: abbreviated **V.C.**

Victoria Falls, a waterfall of the Zambezi River, between Northern and Southern Rhodesia, Africa: height 343 ft.

Victoria Island, an island of Northwest Territories, Canada, north of the mainland: area, 74,000 sq. mi.

Victoria Land, a region in Antarctica, west of the Ross Sea.

Vic·to·ri·an (vik-tôr′i-ən, vik-tōr′yən), *adj.* 1. of or characteristic of the time when Victoria was queen of England (1837–1901); hence, 2. showing the middle-class respectability, prudery, bigotry, etc. generally attributed to the Victorians. 3. designating or of a style of furniture of the 19th century, characterized by ornate, flowery carving and patterned upholstery. *n.* a person, especially a writer, of the time of Queen Victoria. Abbreviated **Vict.**

Victoria Nile, the part of the Nile flowing from Lake Victoria to Lake Albert: length, 300 mi.

Vic·to·ri·an·ism (vik-tôr′i-ən-iz′m, vik-tōr′yən-iz′m), *n.* the quality or an instance of being Victorian in conduct, thought, style, etc.

Victoria Nyan·za (ni-an′zə, nyän′zä), Lake Victoria.

vic·to·ri·ous (vik-tôr′i-əs, vik-tōr′yəs), *adj.* [ME. *victoriouse;* L. *victoriosus*], 1. having won a victory in any battle or contest; winning; conquering. 2. of, belonging to, or bringing about victory.

vic·to·ry (vik′tə-ri, vik′tri), *n.* [*pl.* VICTORIES (-riz, -triz)], [ME. & OFr. *victorie;* L. *victoria* < *victor*, a victor < *vincere*, to conquer], 1. final and complete supremacy or superiority in battle or war. 2. an instance of this; military engagement ending in triumph. 3. success in any contest or struggle involving the defeat of an opponent or the overcoming of obstacles. *SYN.*—**victory** implies the winning of a contest or struggle of any kind (a *victory* in battle, in sports, etc.); **conquest** implies a victory in which one subjugates others and brings them under complete control (the *conquests* of Napoleon); **triumph** implies a victory in which one exults because of its outstanding and decisive character (the *triumphs* of modern medicine). —*ANT.* defeat.

vic·tress (vik′tris), *n.* a female victor.

Vic·tro·la (vik-trō′lə), *n.* a phonograph: a trade-mark.

vict·ual (vit′'l), *n.* [ME. & OFr. *vitaille*, provisions; LL. *victualia*, provisions < L. *victualis*, of food < *victus*, food], 1. [Archaic or Dial.], food or other provisions. 2. *pl.* [Dial. or Colloq.], articles of food, especially when prepared for use. *v.t.* [VICTUALED or VICTUALLED (-'ld), VICTUALING or VICTUALLING], to supply with victuals. *v.i.* 1. [Rare or Archaic], to eat or feed. 2. to lay in or take on a supply of food.

vict·ual·er, vict·ual·ler (vit′'l-ẽr, vit′lẽr), *n.* [ME. *vittailler, vittaler;* OFr. *vitailleur* < *vitaillier*], 1. a person who supplies victuals, as to an army or a ship; sutler. 2. [British], an innkeeper. 3. a supply ship.

vi·cu·ña (vi-kōōn′yə, vi-kū′nə), *n.* [*pl.* VICUÑAS (-yəz, -nəz), VICUÑA; see PLURAL, II, D, 1], [Sp.; of Quechuan origin], 1. a cud-chewing animal found wild in the mountains of South America, related to the llama and alpaca of the camel family, and domesticated for its soft, shaggy wool. 2. a soft fabric made from this wool or from a substitute for it: also **vicuña cloth.**

Vi·da (vē′də, vī′də), [W., dim. of *Davida*, fem. of *David*], a feminine name.

‡vi·de (vī′di), [L., imperative sing. of *videre*, to see], see; refer to: used to direct attention to a particular page, book, etc.: abbreviated **v., vid.**

‡vi·de an·te (vī′di an′ti), [L.], see before (in the book, etc.): abbreviated **v.a.**

‡vi·de in·fra (vī′di in′frə), [L.], see below; see further on (in the book, etc.): abbreviated **v.i.**

‡vi·de·li·cet (vi-del′ə-sit), *adv.* [L. < *videre licet*, it is permitted to see], that is; namely: abbreviated **viz.**

vid·e·o (vid′i-ō′), *adj.* [L., I see: used by analogy with *audio*], 1. of or used in television. 2. designating or of the picture phase of a television broadcast, as distinguished from the *audio* (or sound) portion. *n.* television.

video tape, a magnetic tape on which the electronic impulses of the video and audio portions of a television program can be recorded for later broadcasting.

‡vi·de post (vī′di pōst), [L.], see after; see further on (in the book, etc.).

‡vi·de su·pra (vī′di sōō′prə, sū′prə), [L.], see above (in the book, etc.): abbreviated **v.s.**

vi·dette (vi-det′), *n.* a vedette.

‡vi·de ut su·pra (vī′di ut sōō′prə, sū′prə), [L.], see what is stated above.

vie (vī), *v.i.* [VIED (vīd), VYING], [ME. *vien*, short for *envien;* OFr. *envier*, to invite, vie in games; L. *invitare*, to invite], to struggle for superiority (*with* someone) or enter into competition (*for* something); compete. *v.t.* 1. [Obs.], to bet; wager; hazard. 2. [Rare or Archaic], to do, offer, display, or match in competition or rivalry: as, they *vied* stories with each other.

Vi·en·na (vi-en′ə), *n.* the capital of Austria, on the Danube: pop., 1,616,000: German name, *Wien.*

Vienna International, an international Socialist organization formed at Vienna in 1921, merged in 1923 with the Second International to form the Labor and Socialist International.

Vienne (vyen), *n.* a city in southeastern France, on the Rhone River: pop., 25,000.

Vi·en·nese (vē′ə-nēz′), *adj.* of Vienna, its people, culture, etc. *n.* [*pl.* VIENNESE], a native or inhabitant of Vienna.

Vien·tiane (vyan′tyȧn′), *n.* the capital of Laos, on the Mekong River: pop., 80,000.

‡vi et ar·mis (vī′ et är′mis), [L.], with force and arms; with actual violence: used in law with reference to a trespass which is the direct cause of damage.

Vi·et·nam, Vi·et-Nam (vē′ət-näm′, vēt′näm′), *n.* a country in southeastern Asia, on the Indochinese Peninsula: formerly a part of French Indochina: since 1954 divided into two republics: *a*) South Vietnam, area, 65,958 sq. mi.; pop., 13,960,000; capital, Saigon, and *b*) North Vietnam, area, 60,156 sq. mi.; pop., 15,170,000; capital, Hanoi. Also **Viet Nam.**

Viet·nam·ese, Viet-Nam·ese (vēt′nə-mēz′), *adj.* of Vietnam, its people, etc. *n.* [*pl.* VIETNAMESE, VIET-NAMESE], a native or inhabitant of Vietnam.

view (vū), *n.* [ME. *vewe;* OFr. *veue* < *veoir*, to see; L. *videre*, to see], 1. a seeing or looking, as in inspection or examination. 2. sight or vision; especially, range of vision: as, not a person in *view.* 3. mental examination or survey; critical contemplation: as, he takes a correct *view* of the situation. 4. that which is seen; scene or prospect, as of a landscape: as, a beautiful *view* from the window. 5. a picture, sketch, or photograph of a scene, especially of a landscape. 6. visual appearance or aspect of something. 7. manner of regarding or considering something; judgment; opinion: as, may I have your *views* on the matter? 8. that which is worked toward or sought; object; aim; goal: as, he had a *view* to bettering his condition. 9. expectation; prospect: as, we had no *view* of failure. 10. a general survey or summary: as, the author gave a brief *view* of his book. 11. in *law*, a formal inspection by the jury of the scene of the alleged crime. *v.t.* 1. to inspect; scrutinize. 2. to see; behold. 3. to survey mentally; consider.

in view, 1. in sight. 2. under consideration. 3. in mind or memory. 4. as an end or object aimed at. 5. in expectation; as a hope or wish.
in view of, in consideration of; because of.
on view, displayed or exhibited publicly.
point of view, viewpoint.
with a view to, 1. with the purpose of; intending. 2. with a hope or anticipation of; looking forward to.

SYN.—**view** is the general word for that which is exposed to the sight or lies within the range of vision (the *view* is cut off by the next building); **prospect** suggests an extensive view as afforded by a position from which one can look out to a distance (a commanding *prospect* of the countryside); **scene** has aesthetic or dramatic connotations with reference to a view or a representation of a view (a rustic *scene*); **vista** suggests a view seen through a long narrow passage, as between rows of trees. See also **opinion, see.**

view finder, a finder (sense 2).

view halloo, a shout given by a huntsman when he sees the fox break into the open: also **view hallo, view halloa.**

view·less (vū′lis), *adj.* 1. offering no view, or prospect. 2. that cannot be seen; invisible. 3. having or expressing no views, or opinions.

view·point (vū′point′), *n.* 1. place of observation. 2. mental attitude or standpoint. Also **point of view.**

view·y (vū′i), *adj.* [VIEWIER (-i-ẽr), VIEWIEST (-i-ist)], [Colloq.], 1. having odd or fantastic views or opinions; visionary. 2. showy; ostentatious.

vi·ges·i·mal (vī-jes′ə-m′l), *adj.* [< L. *vigesimus*, var. of *vicesimus* < *viceni*, twenty each < *viginti*, twenty], 1. twentieth. 2. of or based on twenty. 3. proceeding by twenties: as, *vigesimal* counting.

vig·il (vij′əl), *n.* [ME. & OFr. *vigile;* L. *vigilia*, a watch < *vigil*, awake < *vigere*, to be vigorous or lively], 1. a purposeful or watchful staying awake during the usual hours of sleep. 2. a watch kept, or the period of this. 3. in *ecclesiastical usage, a*) the eve of a festival, especially when the eve is a fast. *b*) a devotional watch kept on such an eve. *c*) *pl.* devotional services held on such an eve.

vig·i·lance (vij′ə-ləns), *n.* [Fr.; L. *vigilantia*], 1. the quality or state of being vigilant; watchfulness. 2. in *medicine*, sleeplessness; insomnia.

vigilance committee, 1. a group of persons organized without legal authorization professedly to keep order and punish crime when ordinary law enforcement agencies apparently fail to do so. 2. especially formerly in the South, such a group organized to terrorize and control Negroes and Abolitionists and, during the Civil War, to suppress support of the Union.

vig·i·lant (vij′ə-lənt), *adj.* [Fr.; L. *vigilans*, ppr. of *vigilare*, to watch < *vigil*, awake], characterized by vigilance, or wakefulness; especially, alert to danger; watchful. —***SYN.*** see **watchful.**

vig·i·lan·te (vij′ə-lan′ti), *n.* [Sp., vigilant], a member of a vigilance committee.

vi·gin·ti- (vī-jin′ti), [< L. *viginti*, twenty], a combining form meaning *twenty*, as in *vigintiangular*.

vi·gin·ti·an·gu·lar (vī-jin′ti-aŋ′gyoo-lẽr), *adj.* having twenty angles.

vi·gnette (vin-yet′), *n.* [Fr., dim. < *vigne*, a vine], 1. an ornamental design of vine leaves, tendrils, and grapes, used as a border, inset, headpiece, or tailpiece on a page. 2. any ornamental design or illustration used as an inset, headpiece, or tailpiece on a page. 3. a picture or illustration with no definite border, shading off gradually at the edges; especially, a photographic portrait showing only the head, or the head and shoulders, and shading off at the edges into the background. 4. a short literary composition characterized by compactness, subtlety, and delicacy. *v.t.* [VIGNETTED (-id), VIGNETTING], to make a vignette of; specifically, to finish (a photograph) in the manner of a vignette.

vi·gnett·er (vin-yet′ẽr), *n.* in *photography*, a device used in printing vignettes.

vi·gnett·ist (vin-yet′ist), *n.* a maker of vignettes, as a painter, photographer, or writer.

Vi·gny, Comte **Al·fred Vic·tor de** (äl′fred′ vēk′tôr′ də vē′nyē′), 1797–1863; French poet, novelist, and playwright.

Vi·go (vē′gō), *n.* a seaport in northern Spain, on the Atlantic: pop., 162,000.

vig·or (vig′ẽr), *n.* [ME. & OFr. *vigour;* L. *vigor* < *vigere*, to be strong], 1. active physical or mental force or strength; vitality. 2. active or healthy growth: as, the *vigor* of a plant. 3. intensity, force, or energy: as, the *vigor* of her denial. 4. effective legal or binding force; validity: as, the *vigor* of a law.

‡**vi·go·ro·so** (vē′gō-rô′sō), *adj.* [It.], in *music*, vigorous; energetic: a direction to the performer.

vig·or·ous (vig′ẽr-əs), *adj.* [ME. *vigerous*, etc.; OFr.; ML. *vigorosus*], 1. living or growing with full vital strength; strong; robust. 2. of, characterized by, or requiring vigor or strength. 3. forceful; powerful; strong; energetic. 4. acting, or ready to act, with energy and force. —***SYN.*** see **active.**

vig·our (vig′ẽr), *n.* vigor: British spelling.

Vii·pu·ri (vē′poo-rē′), *n.* a city in the northwestern R.S.F.S.R., on the Gulf of Finland: pop., 51,000: Swedish name, *Viborg*.

vik·ing (vī′kiŋ), *n.* [ON. *vikingr;* cf. AS. *wicing*], any of the Scandinavian sea rovers and pirates who ravaged the coasts of Europe during the 8th, 9th, and 10th centuries.

vil., village.

vi·la·yet (vē′lä-yet′), *n.* [Turk.; Ar. *wilāyat* < *wāli*, a ruler, governor], any of the main administrative districts into which Turkey is divided.

vile (vīl), *adj.* [ME. & OFr. *vil;* L. *vilis*, cheap, base], 1. morally base or evil; wicked; depraved; sinful. 2. offensive to the senses or sensibilities; repulsive; disgusting. 3. cheap; worthless. 4. degrading; lowly; mean: said of conditions, situations, etc. 5. of poor quality; very inferior: often a generalized counterword for anything objectionable, as, *vile* weather. —***SYN.*** see **base.**

vil·i·fi·ca·tion (vil′ə-fi-kā′shən), *n.* a vilifying or being vilified.

vil·i·fy (vil′ə-fī′), *v.t.* [VILIFIED (-fīd′), VILIFYING], [LL. *vilificare* < L. *vilis*, cheap, base + *facere*, to make], 1. to use abusive or slanderous language about or of; calumniate; revile; defame. 2. [Rare], to degrade.

vil·i·pend (vil′ə-pend′), *v.t.* [Fr. *vilipender;* L. *vilipendere* < *vilis*, vile + *pendere*, to weigh, consider], 1. to treat or regard contemptuously or slightingly; disparage; belittle. 2. to vilify; revile.

vil·la (vil′ə), *n.* [It.; L., a country seat, farm], 1. originally, a country house, with its outbuildings and grounds. 2. a rural or suburban residence, especially one that is large and pretentious.

Vil·la, Fran·cis·co (frän-sēs′kô vē′yä), (born *Doroteo Arango*), 1877–1923; Mexican revolutionary leader: called *Pancho Villa*.

vil·la·dom (vil′ə-dəm), *n.* [*villa* + *-dom*], [Chiefly British], villas and their occupants, collectively; suburban society, regarded as smug, dull, and well-to-do.

vil·lage (vil′ij), *n.* [ME.; OFr.; L. *villaticus*, belonging to a country house < *villa*, a country house, farm], 1. a group of houses in the country, larger than a hamlet and smaller than a city or town. 2. such a community incorporated as a municipality. 3. the people of a village, collectively; villagers. 4. a group or cluster of the habitations of animals or birds: as, a prairie-dog *village*. *adj.* of or characteristic of a village. Abbreviated **v., vil.**

village community, a primitive type of organized farming community, regarded as the basic self-governing political unit from which the modern state developed, and characterized by communal ownership of land, part of which was apportioned among householders for cultivation, the nonarable part being left as common land.

vil·lag·er (vil′ij-ẽr), *n.* a person who lives in a village.

vil·lain (vil′ən), *n.* [ME. *vilein;* OFr. *vilain;* LL. *villanus*, a farm servant < *villa*, a country seat, farm], 1. a person guilty or capable of committing great crimes; wicked person; scoundrel. 2. a wicked or unprincipled character in a novel, play, etc. who opposes the protagonist or hero. 3. in the *theater* & *motion pictures*, an actor regularly cast in the role of such a character. 4. a villein. 5. [Obs.], a boorish or clownish rustic person.

vil·lain·ous (vil′ən-əs), *adj.* 1. of, like, or characteristic of a villain; depraved; evil; criminal. 2. very bad; disagreeable; objectionable. —***SYN.*** see **vicious.**

vil·lain·y (vil′ən-i), *n.* [*pl.* VILLAINIES (-iz)], [ME. *vileinie;* Anglo-Fr. & OFr. *vilainie* < *vilain*], 1. the fact or state of being villainous. 2. villainous conduct. 3. a villainous act; crime. 4. [Obs.], villeinage.

Vil·la-Lo·bos, Hei·tor (ā′toor vēl′lä-lô′boosh), 1881–1959; Brazilian composer.

vil·lan·age (vil′ən-ij), *n.* villeinage.

vil·la·nel·la (vil′ə-nel′ə; It. vēl′lä-nel′lä), *n.* [*pl.* VILLANELLE (-i; It. -lē)], [It., fem. dim. of *villano* < LL. *villanus;* see VILLAIN], 1. an old rustic Italian song and accompanying dance. 2. a type of 16th-century part song for unaccompanied voices, like the madrigal, originating in Naples.

vil·la·nelle (vil′ə-nel′), *n.* [Fr. < It. *villanella;* see VILLANELLA], a short poem of fixed form, French in origin, consisting of several stanzas (usually five) of three lines each and a final stanza of four lines: it has only two rhymes throughout.

Vil·lard, Oswald Garrison (vi-lärd′), 1872–1949; American journalist and author.

Vil·lars, Claude Lou·is Hec·tor de (klōd lwē ek'tôr' də vē'lär'), Duc de Villars, 1653–1734; French general; marshal of France.

vil·lat·ic (vi-lat'ik), *adj.* [L. *villaticus*], of a villa, country house, or farm; rustic; rural.

vil·lein (vil'ən), *n.* [ME.; see VILLAIN], in feudal England, any member of a class of serfs, or peasants, who by the 13th century had become freemen in their legal relations to all others except their lord, to whom they remained entirely subject as slaves.

vil·lein·age, vil·len·age (vil'ən-ij), *n.* [Anglo-Fr. & OFr. *villenage* < *villein, vilain;* see VILLAIN], in *feudal law*, 1. the status or condition of a villein. 2. the conditions of tenure by which a villein held his land. Also spelled **villanage.**

vil·li (vil'ī), *n.* plural of **villus.**

Vil·liers, Frederic (vil'ẽrz, vil'yẽrz), 1852–1922; English artist and war correspondent.

Villiers, George, 1. first Duke of Buckingham, 1592–1628; English statesman: lord high admiral; assassinated. 2. second Duke of Buckingham, 1628–1687; son of the above; English statesman.

vil·li·form (vil'ə-fôrm'), *adj.* [< *villus* + *-form*], like villi in form or appearance; like the pile or nap of velvet, as the small, closely set teeth of certain fishes.

Vil·lon, Fran·çois (frän'swȧ' vē'yōn'), (born *François de Montcorbier*), 1431– ?; French lyric poet; banished from Paris (1463).

vil·lose (vil'ōs), *adj.* villous.

vil·los·i·ty (vi-los'ə-ti), *n.* [*pl.* VILLOSITIES (-tiz)], 1. the condition of being villous. 2. a villus. 3. a coating or surface of villi.

vil·lous (vil'əs), *adj.* [ME.; L. *villosus*], of, having the nature of, or covered with villi.

vil·lus (vil'əs), *n.* [*pl.* VILLI (-ī)], [L., shaggy hair, tuft of hair, var. of *vellus*, a fleece, wool], 1. in *anatomy*, any of numerous hairlike or fingerlike vascular processes on certain mucous membranes of the body, as of the small intestine, serving to secrete mucus and absorb fats, etc. 2. in *botany*, any of the long, soft, fine hairs on certain plants.

Vil·na (vil'nə; Russ. vēl'nȧ), *n.* Vilnius.

Vil·ni·us (vil'ni-oos'), *n.* the capital of the Lithuanian S.S.R.: pop., 235,000: Russian name, *Vilna;* Polish name, *Wilno.*

vim (vim), *n.* [L., acc. of *vis*, strength], energy; vigor.

vi·men (vī'men), *n.* [*pl.* VIMINA (vim'ə-nə)], [L., a twig < base of *viere*, to bend, twist], in *botany*, a long, flexible shoot.

Vim·i·nal (vim'ə-n'l), *n.* one of the seven hills on which ancient Rome was built.

vim·i·nal (vim'ə-n'l), *adj.* [L. *viminalis* < *vimen;* see VIMEN], [Rare], of, consisting of, or having twigs.

vi·min·e·ous (vi-min'i-əs), *adj.* [L. *vimineus* < *vimen*, a twig], 1. made or woven of twigs. 2. in *botany*, of or having long, flexible twigs.

v. imp., impersonal verb.

Vi·my (vē'mē'), *n.* a town in northern France: a battle (1917) of World War I took place on a near-by ridge.

‡vin (van), *n.* [Fr.], wine.

vi·na (vē'nä), *n.* [Sans. *vīṇā*], a Hindu musical instrument of the zither family: it has seven strings on a long, fretted fingerboard, which is attached to two gourds serving as resonators.

vi·na·ceous (vī-nā'shəs), *adj.* [L. *vinaceus* < *vinum*, wine], 1. of or like wine or grapes. 2. wine-colored; red.

vin·ai·grette (vin'i-gret'), *n.* [Fr. < *vinaigre*, vinegar], 1. a small ornamental box or bottle with a perforated lid, used for holding aromatic vinegar, smelling salts, etc. 2. vinaigrette sauce.

vinaigrette sauce, a savory sauce made of vinegar, oil, herbs, etc., and used on cold meats.

‡vin blanc (van' blänk'), [Fr.], white wine.

Vin·cennes (vin-senz'; *for 2*, Fr. van'sen'), *n.* 1. a city in Indiana on the Wabash River: pop., 18,000: first settlement in Indiana. 2. a city in northern France, east of Paris: pop., 50,000.

Vin·cent (vin's'nt), [LL. *Vincentius* < *vincens*, ppr. of *vincere*, to conquer], a masculine name: equivalents, G. *Vincenz*, It. *Vincenzo*, Sp. *Vicente.*

Vincent, Saint, ?–304 A.D.; Spanish martyr; patron saint of winegrowers: his day is January 22.

Vincent de Paul, Saint, 1581?–1660; French priest who founded the Lazarists and the Sisters of Charity.

Vin·cent's angina (or **infection**) (vin's'nts), [after J. H. *Vincent* (1862–1950), Fr. physician], trench mouth.

Vin·ci, Le·o·nar·do da (le'ô-när'dô dä vēn'chē; Eng. də vin'chi), 1452–1519; Italian painter, sculptor, architect, scientist, musician, and natural philosopher.

vin·ci·bil·i·ty (vin'sə-bil'ə-ti), *n.* the state or quality of being vincible, or conquerable.

vin·ci·ble (vin'sə-b'l), *adj.* [L. *vincibilis*, easily overcome < *vincere*, to overcome], that can be overcome or defeated; conquerable.

‡vin·cit om·ni·a ve·ri·tas (vin'sit om'ni-ə ver'i-tas'), [L.], truth conquers all things.

vin·cu·lum (viŋ'kyoo-ləm), *n.* [*pl.* VINCULA (-lə)], [L. < *vincere*, to bind], 1. that which binds; bond; tie. 2. in *anatomy*, a band, connecting fold, or ligament; frenum. 3. in *mathematics*, a line drawn over two or more terms of a compound quantity to show that they are to be treated together (e.g., $a-\overline{x+y}$).

‡vin·cu·lum ma·tri·mo·ni·i (viŋ'kyoo-ləm mat'ri-mō'ni-ī'), [L.], the bond of matrimony; marriage tie.

Vind·hya Hills (vind'yä), a range of hills in central India, north of the Narbada River.

Vind·hya Pra·desh (vind'yä prä'desh), a former state of central India: now part of Madhya Pradesh.

vin·di·ca·bil·i·ty (vin'di-kə-bil'ə-ti), *n.* the state or quality of being vindicable.

vin·di·ca·ble (vin'di-kə-b'l), *adj.* [< L. *vindicare;* + *-able*], that can be vindicated; justifiable; defensible.

vin·di·cate (vin'də-kāt'), *v.t.* [VINDICATED (-id), VINDICATING], [< L. *vindicatus*, pp. of *vindicare*, to claim, avenge < *vim*, acc. sing. of *vis*, force + *dicere*, to say], 1. to clear from criticism, censure, suspicion, etc.; uphold by evidence or argument. 2. to defend or maintain (a cause, claim, etc.) against opposition. 3. to serve as justification for; justify: as, his success *vindicated* their belief in him. 4. to claim or establish possession of (*for* oneself or another). 5. [Obs.], *a*) to avenge; revenge. *b*) to punish. —*SYN.* see **absolve.**

vin·di·ca·tion (vin'də-kā'shən), *n.* [L. *vindicatio*, a claiming < *vindicare;* see VINDICATE], 1. a vindicating or being vindicated; justification. 2. a fact or circumstance that vindicates, or justifies. 3. assertion or maintenance, as of a claim.

vin·dic·a·tive (vin'də-kā'tiv, vin-dik'ə-tiv), *adj.* [ML. *vindicativus*], serving to vindicate; justifying.

vin·di·ca·tor (vin'də-kā'tẽr), *n.* [LL.], a person who vindicates.

vin·di·ca·to·ry (vin'di-kə-tôr'i, vin'di-kə-tō'ri), *adj.* 1. serving to vindicate; vindicative. 2. punishing; avenging; bringing retribution.

vin·dic·tive (vin-dik'tiv), *adj.* [abbrev. < *vindicative* (by association with L. *vindicta*, a revenge) < *vindicatus;* see VINDICATE], 1. revengeful in spirit; inclined to vengeance. 2. said or done in revenge; characterized by vengeance: as, *vindictive* punishment.

SYN.—**vindictive** stresses the unforgiving nature of one who is animated by a desire to get even with another for a wrong, injury, etc. (*vindictive* feelings); **vengeful** and **revengeful** more directly stress the strong impulsion to action and the actual seeking of vengeance (a *vengeful*, or *revengeful*, foe); **spiteful** implies a mean or malicious vindictiveness (*spiteful* gossip).

vine (vīn), *n.* [ME.; OFr. *vine, vigne;* L. *vinea*, a vine < *vinum*, wine; akin to Gr. *oinē*, vine (cf. WINE); the word is prob. a loan word from a pre-IE. language of the Pontus region], 1. any plant with a long, thin stem that grows along the ground or climbs a wall or other support by means of tendrils, etc. 2. the stem of such a plant. 3. a grapevine.

vine·dress·er (vīn'dres'ẽr), *n.* a person who cultivates or prunes grapevines.

vin·e·gar (vin'i-gẽr), *n.* [ME. *vinegre;* OFr. *vinaigre* < *vin*, wine + *aigre* (L. *acer*), sour], 1. a sour liquid containing acetic acid, made by fermenting dilute alcoholic liquids, as cider, wine, malt, etc.: it is used as a condiment and preservative. 2. sour or ill-tempered speech, character, etc.

vinegar eel (or **worm**), a small nematode worm found in vinegar and other fermenting liquids.

vin·e·gar·ette (vin'ə-gẽr-et'), *n.* a vinaigrette.

vin·e·gar·ish (vin'i-gẽr-ish), *adj.* vinegary.

vin·e·gar·roon (vin'i-gə-rōōn'), *n.* [< Sp. *vinagre*, vinegar: so called from its odor when disturbed], a large scorpion found in the Southwest and in Mexico.

vin·e·gar·y (vin'i-gẽr-i), *adj.* 1. of, or having the nature of, vinegar; hence, 2. sour in speech or disposition; ill-tempered.

Vine·land (vīn'lənd), *n.* a city in southern New Jersey: pop., 38,000.

vin·er·y (vīn'ẽr-i), *n.* [*pl.* VINERIES (-iz)], [ME. *vinary;* OFr. *vignerie;* ML. *vinarium* < L. *vinea*, a vine, vineyard], 1. a greenhouse in which grapevines are grown. 2. vines collectively. 3. [Obs.], a vineyard.

vine·yard (vin'yẽrd), *n.* [*vine* + *yard*, after AS. *wingeard*], 1. land devoted to cultivating grapevines. 2. a field of activity, especially of spiritual labor.

‡vingt et un (van' tā' ẽn'), [Fr., lit., twenty and one, twenty-one], blackjack, a card game.

vin·i- (vin'i), [< L. *vinum*, wine], a combining form meaning *wine grapes* or *wine*, as in *viniculture.*

vi·nic (vī'nik, vin'ik), *adj.* [< L. *vinum*, wine; + *-ic*], of, found in, or derived from wine.

vin·i·cul·tur·al (vin'i-kul'chẽr-əl), *adj.* of viniculture.

vin·i·cul·ture (vin'i-kul'chẽr), *n.* [*vini-* + *culture*], the cultivation of wine grapes.

vin·i·fi·ca·tor (vin′ə-fi-kā′tẽr), *n.* [< *vini-* + L. *-ficatus*, pp. of *-ficare* (in comp. for *facere*), to make; + *-or*], an apparatus for collecting and condensing the alcohol vapors which rise from fermenting wine.

vin·om·e·ter (vin-om′ə-tẽr, vī-nom′ə-tẽr), *n.* [< L. *vinum*, wine; + *-meter*], a hydrometer for determining the percentage of alcohol in a wine.

‡**vin or·di·naire** (van′ ôr′dē′nâr′), [Fr., lit., ordinary wine], any cheap red wine customarily served with meals in France.

vi·nos·i·ty (vī-nos′ə-ti), *n.* [LL. *vinositas*], 1. the state or quality of being vinous. 2. addiction to wine.

vi·nous (vī′nəs), *adj.* [L. *vinosus*, full of wine < L. *vinum*, wine], 1. of, having the nature of, or characteristic of wine. 2. *a*) addicted to drinking wine. *b*) resulting from such addiction: as, in a *vinous* state. 3. of the color of red wine; vinaceous.

Vin·son, Frederick Moore (vin′sən), 1890–1953; chief justice of the United States (1946–1953).

vin·tage (vin′tij), *n.* [altered (after *vintner*) < ME. *vindage, vendage;* OFr. *vendange* < L. *vindemia*, vintage < *vinum*, wine + *demere*, to remove < *de-*, off + *emere*, to take], 1. the crop or yield of a particular vineyard or grape-growing region in a single season, with reference either to the grapes or the resultant wine. 2. wine; especially, the wine of a particular region in a specified year. 3. the region or year of a particular wine. 4. the act or season of gathering grapes or of making wine. 5. the type or model of a particular, especially earlier, time: as, an automobile of ancient *vintage*. *adj.* of a good vintage; choice: as, *vintage* wine.

vin·tag·er (vin′tij-ẽr), *n.* [< *vintage* + *-er*], a person who harvests wine grapes.

vint·ner (vint′nẽr), *n.* [altered < ME. *viniter*, a vintner; OFr. *vinetier, vinotier* < *vinot*, dim. of *vin* (L. *vinum*), wine], [Chiefly British], a person who sells wine, especially at wholesale; wine merchant.

vin·y (vīn′i), *adj.* [VINIER (-i-ẽr), VINIEST (-i-ist)], 1. of, or having the nature of, vines. 2. abounding in vines; covered with vines.

vi·nyl (vī′nil, vin′il), *n.* [< L. *vinum*, wine; + *-yl*], the monovalent radical CH_2CH, characteristic of many derivatives of ethylene, its hydride: various vinyl compounds are polymerized to form resins and plastics, used as for high-fidelity, unbreakable phonograph records.

vi·ol (vī′əl), *n.* [altered (after Fr. *viole*) < earlier *vielle;* OFr. *vielle;* ML. *vitula;* cf. FIDDLE], 1. any of an early family of stringed instruments, forerunner of the violin family, characterized generally by six strings, frets, a flat back, and C-shaped sound holes. 2. any instrument of the violin family: as, the bass *viol*.

Vi·o·la (vī-ō′lə, vī-ō′lə; *esp. for n.*, vī′ə-lə), [< L. *viola*, a violet], a feminine name: diminutive, *Vi.* *n.* the heroine of Shakespeare's *Twelfth Night*.

vi·o·la (vi-ō′lə, vī-ō′lə; It. vyô′lä), *n.* [It. < same source as *viol*], 1. a stringed instrument of the violin family, slightly larger than a violin and tuned a fifth lower. 2. an organ stop, generally of 8-foot pitch, producing a tone somewhat like that of a viola.

vi·o·la (vī′ə-lə, vī-ō′lə), *n.* [ME.; L., a violet], any of a large group of plants including the violet, pansy, etc.

vi·o·la·bil·i·ty (vī′ə-lə-bil′ə-ti), *n.* the state or condition of being violable.

vi·o·la·ble (vī′ə-lə-b'l), *adj.* [L. *violabilis* < *violare;* see VIOLATE], that can be violated; easily violated.

vi·o·la·bly (vī′ə-lə-bli), *adv.* so as to be violable.

vi·o·la·ceous (vī′ə-lā′shəs), *adj.* [L. *violaceus*, violet-colored < *viola*, a violet], 1. violet in color. 2. in *botany*, of the violet family.

viola clef, the C clef on the third line; alto clef.

‡**vio·la da brac·cio** (vyô′lä dä brät′chô), [It., lit., viol for the arm], an early stringed instrument of the viol family, forerunner of the viola.

‡**vi·o·la da gam·ba** (vyô′lä dä gäm′bä), [It., lit., viol for the leg], 1. an early stringed instrument of the viol family, held between the knees like the violoncello of which it is the forerunner. 2. an organ stop of 8-foot pitch producing a stringlike tone.

‡**vio·la d'a·mo·re** (vyô′lä dä-mô′re), [It., lit., viol of love], an early stringed instrument of the viol family having sympathetic strings of wire stretched behind the bowed strings, producing soft, clear, ringing tones.

vi·o·late (vī′ə-lāt′), *v.t.* [VIOLATED (-id), VIOLATING], [ME. *violaten* < L. *violatus*, pp. of *violare*, to use force or violence], 1. to break (a law, rule, promise, etc.); fail to keep or observe; infringe on. 2. to rape (a girl or woman); ravish. 3. to treat without reverence; desecrate or profane, as a sacred place. 4. to break in upon; interrupt; disturb: as, I shall not *violate* his privacy. 5. to offend, insult, or outrage: as, his callousness *violates* my sense of decency. 6. [Obs.], to treat (someone) roughly or abusively; mistreat.

vi·o·la·tion (vī′ə-lā′shən), *n.* [ME. *vyolacion;* L. *violatio*], a violating or being violated; specifically, *a*) infringement or breach, as of a law, right, etc. *b*) rape; ravishment. *c*) desecration of something sacred, as a church. *d*) interruption; disturbance.

vi·o·la·tive (vī′ə-lā′tiv), *adj.* serving or tending to violate.

vi·o·la·tor (vī′ə-lā′tẽr), *n.* a person who violates.

vi·o·lence (vī′ə-ləns), *n.* [ME.; OFr.; L. *violentia* < *violentus*, violent], 1. physical force used so as to injure or damage; roughness in action. 2. a use of force so as to injure or damage; rough, injurious act. 3. natural or physical energy or force in action; intensity; severity: as, the *violence* of the storm. 4. unjust use of force or power, as in deprivation of rights. 5. great force or strength of feeling, conduct, or language; passion; fury. 6. distortion of meaning, phrasing, etc.: as, to do *violence* to a text. 7. desecration; profanation.

vi·o·lent (vī′ə-lənt), *adj.* [ME.; OFr.; L. *violentus*, violent], 1. acting with or characterized by great physical force, so as to injure or damage; rough. 2. acting or characterized by force unlawfully used. 3. caused by violence: as, a *violent* death. 4. showing, or resulting from, strong feeling or emotion; passionate; immoderate; furious: as, *violent* language. 5. extreme; intense; very strong: as, a *violent* storm. 6. tending to distort the meaning: as, a *violent* construction of a text.

vi·o·les·cent (vī′ə-les′'nt), *adj.* [< L. *viola*, a violet; + *-escent*], shading off toward a violet color.

Vi·o·let (vī′ə-lit), [< *violet*, the flower], a feminine name: diminutive, *Vi.*

vi·o·let (vī′ə-lit), *n.* [ME.; OFr. *violette*, dim. of *viole;* L. *viola*, a violet; cf. VIOLA], 1. any of a number of related short plants with fragrant white, blue, purple, or yellow flowers. 2. the flower of any of these plants. 3. any of various similar but unrelated plants, or their flowers. 4. a bluish-purple color. *adj.* of a violet color.

violet ray, 1. the shortest ray of the visible spectrum, producing the color violet. 2. loosely, the ultraviolet ray.

vi·o·lin (vī′ə-lin′), *n.* [It. *violino*, dim. of *viola*, a viol], 1. any instrument of the modern family of string instruments played with a bow, developed from the viol and characterized by four strings, a lack of frets, a somewhat rounded back, and *f*-shaped sound holes; specifically, the smallest and highest pitched instrument of this family, held horizontally under the chin, resting against the collarbone; fiddle. 2. a violinist, especially as a member of an orchestra. Abbreviated **v.**

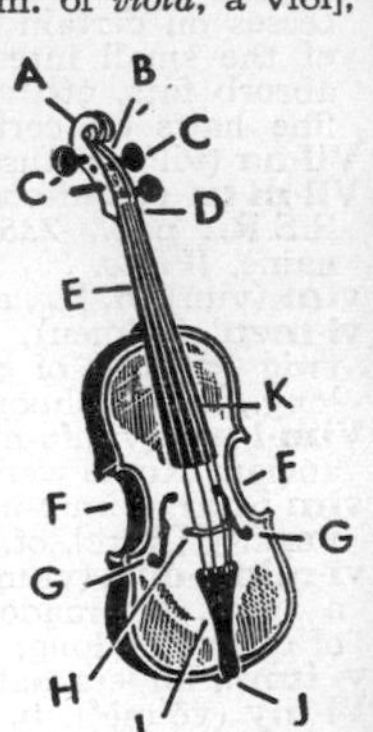

VIOLIN
A, scroll; B, pegbox; C, pegs; D, nut; E, neck; F, waist; G, sound holes; H, bridge; I, tailpiece; J, button; K, finger board

vi·o·lin·ist (vī′ə-lin′ist), *n.* [It. *violinista*], a player on the violin.

vi·ol·ist (vī′əl-ist; *for 2*, vi-ō′list), *n.* 1. a player on the viol. 2. a player on the viola.

vi·o·lon·cel·list (vē′ə-lon-chel′ist, vī′ə-lən-chel′ist), *n.* a cellist.

vi·o·lon·cel·lo (vē′ə-lon-chel′ō, vī′ə-lən-chel′ō), *n.* [*pl.* VIOLONCELLOS (-ōz)], [It., dim. of *violone*, bass viol < *viola*, viol], a cello.

‡**vio·lo·ne** (vyô-lô′ne), *n.* [It., augmentative of *viola*, a viol], 1. the contrabass; double bass. 2. an organ stop of 16-foot pitch producing a stringlike tone.

vi·os·ter·ol (vī-os′tẽr-ōl′, vī-os′tẽr-ol′), *n.* [ultra*vi*olet + ergo*sterol*], a preparation of ergosterol, irradiated with ultraviolet rays and dissolved in oil, used in medicine to supply a vitamin D deficiency.

V.I.P., VIP, [Slang], very important person.

vi·per (vī′pẽr), *n.* [OFr.; L. *vipera*, short for *vivipara*, producing live young; prob. < *vivus*, living + *parere*, to bear], 1. a snake belonging to either of two worldwide groups of venomous snakes: the *true vipers*, found in Europe, Africa, and Asia, include the common, horned, or long-nosed vipers, puff adders, etc., and the *pit vipers*, found in Asia and America, include the water viper, copperhead, fer-de-lance, bushmaster, rattlesnake, etc. 2. any of various other venomous or supposedly venomous snakes. 3. a malicious or spiteful person. 4. a treacherous person.

vi·per·ine (vī′pẽr-in, vī′pẽr-in′), *adj.* [L. *viperinus*], of, having the nature of, or like that of a viper; venomous.

vi·per·ish (vī′pẽr-ish), *adj.* viperous; venomous; especially, spiteful or malicious.

vi·per·ous (vī′pẽr-əs), *adj.* of, having the nature of, or like a viper; especially, spiteful or venomous.

viper's bugloss, blueweed.

vi·ra·go (vi-rā′gō, vī-rā′gō), *n.* [*pl.* VIRAGOES, VIRAGOS (-gōz)], [ME.; AS.; L., a manlike maiden < *vir*, a man], 1. a bold, quarrelsome, shrewish woman; scold. 2. [Archaic], a strong, large, manlike woman; amazon.

Vir·chow, Ru·dolf (rōō′dôlf fir′khō), 1821–1902; German pathologist, anthropologist, and statesman.

‡**vire·lai** (vêr′lā′), *n.* [Fr.], a virelay.

vir·e·lay (vir′ə-lā′), *n.* [ME. *vyrelaye;* OFr. *virelai;*

prob. altered after *lai* (cf. LAY, kind of poem) < OFr. *virli, vireli,* jingle used as the refrain of a song], 1. an old French form of short poem, consisting of short lines with two rhymes and having two opening lines repeated at intervals. 2. any of several other more or less similar verse forms, especially one consisting of stanzas that have some shorter lines and some longer lines, the lines of each sort rhyming together in each stanza and the rhyme of the longer lines of one stanza being a repetition of that of the shorter lines of the preceding stanza.

vir·e·o (vir'i-ō'), *n.* [*pl.* VIREOS (-ōz')], [L., greenfinch], any of a number of small, insect-eating North American songbirds, with olive-green or gray plumage.

vir·e·o·nine (vir'i-ə-nīn', vir'i-ə-nin), *adj.* of or like a vireo; of the vireo family. *n.* a bird of this family.

vi·res·cence (vī-res''ns), *n.* [< *virescent*], the condition of becoming green; specifically, in *botany*, the turning green of petals or other parts that are not normally so, due to the abnormal presence of chlorophyll.

vi·res·cent (vī-res''nt), *adj.* [L. *virescens*, ppr. of *virescere*, to grow green < *virere*, to be green], 1. turning or becoming green. 2. greenish.

Virg., Virginia.

vir·gate (vũr'git, vũr'gāt), *n.* [ML. *virgata* (*terrae*) < L. *virga*, a rod, twig: used as transl. of AS. *gierdland*, yardland], an old English measure of land varying greatly in size, but most commonly equal to a quarter of a hide, or about thirty acres.

vir·gate (vũr'git, vũr'gāt), *adj.* [L. *virgatus*, made of twigs < *virga*, a twig], in *botany*, 1. shaped like a rod or wand. 2. having many small twigs.

Vir·gil (vũr'jil), [< L. *Vergilius*, name of the Roman gens to which the poet belonged], a masculine name. *n.* (*Publius Vergilius Maro*), Roman poet; 70–19 B.C.; author of *The Aeneid*, etc. Also spelled **Vergil.**

Vir·gil·i·an (vũr-jil'i-ən), *adj.* [L. *Vergilianus*], of or like the poetry of Virgil: also spelled **Vergilian.**

vir·gin (vũr'jin), *n.* [ME. & OFr. *virgine;* L. *virgo, virginis*, a maiden; ? akin to *virga*, slender branch, twig, shoot], 1. *a*) a woman, especially a young woman, who has not had sexual intercourse; hence, *b*) a girl or unmarried woman. 2. less commonly, a man, especially a youth, who has not had sexual intercourse. 3. a female animal that has not copulated. 4. [V-], in *astronomy*, the constellation Virgo. 5. in *ecclesiastical usage*, *a*) a member of a religious order of women, as a nun, who has taken a vow of chastity. *b*) [V-], Mary, the mother of Jesus: usually with *the.* 6. in *entomology*, a female insect that lays eggs without impregnation by the male. *adj.* 1. being a virgin. 2. composed of virgins. 3. characteristic of or proper to a virgin; chaste; modest. 4. like or suggesting a virgin because untouched, unmarked, pure, clean, etc.: as, *virgin* snow. 5. up to this time unused, untrod, uncultivated, undiscovered, etc. by man: as, *virgin* forest. 6. never having had contact with or experience (*of*): as, a forest *virgin* of hunters. 7. occurring uncombined in its native form: as, *virgin* silver. 8. being the first; initial: as, a *virgin* voyage. 9. *a*) obtained from the first pressing, without the use of heat: said of an oil, as of olives. *b*) obtained directly from an ore or from the first smelting: said of a metal.

vir·gin·al (vũr'ji-n'l), *adj.* [ME.; OFr.; L. *virginalis*], 1. of, characteristic of, or proper to a virgin; maidenly. 2. remaining in a state of virginity. 3. pure; fresh; untouched; unsullied. 4. in *zoology*, not fertilized.

vir·gin·al (vũr'ji-n'l), *n.* [Fr. *virginale;* ? < the prec. *adj.* (i.e., played by virgins, or young girls); ? < L. *virga*, a rod, jack (sense 8)], a harpsichord; especially, a small, rectangular harpsichord of the 16th century, placed on a table or held in the lap to be played: sometimes called *pair of virginals.*

VIRGINAL

virgin birth, 1. in *Christian theology*, the doctrine that Jesus was born to Mary without prejudice to her virginity and that she was his only human parent: cf. **Immaculate Conception.** 2. in *zoology*, parthenogenesis.

virgin gold, pure, unalloyed gold.

Vir·gin·i·a (vẽr-jin'yə, vẽr-jin'i-ə), [L., fem. of *Virginius, Verginius*, name of a Roman gens], a feminine name: equivalent, Fr. *Virginie.*

Vir·gin·ia (vẽr-jin'yə), *n.* a Southern State of the United States: area, 40,815 sq. mi.; pop., 3,967,000; capital, Richmond: abbreviated **Va., Virg.**

Virginia City, a town in western Nevada, formerly a center of gold and silver mining: site of the discovery (1859) of the Comstock Lode: pop., 500.

Virginia cowslip (or **bluebell**), a plant with clusters of blue or purple bell-shaped flowers that develop from pink buds.

Virginia creeper, a climbing vine having leaflets in groups of five, greenish flowers, and bluish-black berries: also called *American ivy, woodbine.*

Virginia deer, any of a large group of American white-tailed deer having a white-spotted red coat in summer and a diffuse gray-brown coat in winter: found from Canada to Peru.

Virginia fence, a zigzag fence made of rails laid across each other at the ends; worm fence: also **Virginia rail fence.**

Vir·gin·ian (vẽr-jin'yən), *adj.* of Virginia. *n.* a native or inhabitant of Virginia.

Virginia reel, 1. a country dance, the American variety of the reel, performed by a number of couples facing each other in two parallel lines. 2. music for this dance.

Virginia trumpet flower, any of a number of related climbing plants with clusters of orange-red, trumpet-shaped flowers; trumpet creeper.

‡vir·gi·ni·bus pu·e·ris·que (vẽr-jin'ə-bəs pū'ẽr-is'kwi), [L.], for girls and boys.

Virgin Islands, a group of islands in the West Indies, east of Puerto Rico: some belong to the United States and some to Great Britain: abbreviated **V.I.**

British Virgin Islands, those of the Virgin Islands that are a part of the Leeward Islands and constitute a colony of Great Britain: area, 58 sq. mi.; pop., 8,000; capital, Road Town.

Virgin Islands of the United States, those of the Virgin Islands that the United States bought from Denmark in 1917: area, 132 sq. mi.; pop., 32,000; capital, Charlotte Amalie: formerly called *Danish West Indies.*

vir·gin·i·ty (vẽr-jin'ə-ti), *n.* [ME. *virginite;* OFr. *virginité;* L. *virginitas*], 1. the state or fact of being a virgin; maidenhood, chastity, spinsterhood, etc. 2. the state of being virgin, pure, clean, untouched, etc.

vir·gin·i·um (vẽr-jin'i-əm), *n.* [Mod. L. < *Virginia* (the State)], a name given to chemical element 87, supposedly discovered in 1930: symbol, Vi: cf. **francium.**

Virgin Mary, Mary, the mother of Jesus.

Virgin Queen, Queen Elizabeth I of England.

vir·gin's-bow·er (vũr'jinz-bou'ẽr), *n.* a white-flowered, rambling variety of clematis.

virgin wool, wool that has never before been processed.

Vir·go (vũr'gō), *n.* [ME.; L., lit., virgin], 1. an equatorial constellation between Leo and Libra, supposedly outlining a woman, and containing 39 visible stars of which Spica is the brightest; the Virgin: see **constellation,** chart. 2. the sixth sign of the zodiac (♍), which the sun enters about August 22: see **zodiac,** illus.

vir·gu·late (vũr'gyoo-lit, vũr'gyoo-lāt'), *adj.* [< L. *virgula* (see VIRGULE); + *-ate*], rod-shaped.

vir·gule (vũr'gūl), *n.* [Fr.; L. *virgula*, a small rod, twig, dim. of *virga*, a slender branch, twig, shoot], a short diagonal line (/) placed between two words to indicate that either word can be used in interpreting the statement. Example: and/or; i.e., either "and" or "or".

vir·i·des·cence (vir'ə-des''ns), *n.* the quality or state of being viridescent; greenishness.

vir·i·des·cent (vir'ə-des''nt), *adj.* [LL. *viridescens*, ppr. of *viridescere*, to become green < *viridis*, green], greenish; somewhat green.

vi·rid·i·an (və-rid'i-ən), *n.* [< L. *viridis*, green], a bluish-green pigment, hydrated chromic oxide, Cr_2O_3, used in paints or dyes.

vi·rid·i·ty (və-rid'ə-ti), *n.* [OFr. *viridité;* L. *viriditas* < *viridis*, green], 1. greenness, as of young leaves or grass; verdancy; hence, 2. freshness; liveliness.

vir·ile (vir'əl; *rarely*, vī'rəl), *adj.* [Fr. *viril;* L. *virilis*, < *vir*, a man; for IE. base see WEREWOLF], 1. of, belonging to, or characteristic of an adult man; manly; masculine; male. 2. having manly strength or vigor; forceful. 3. of or capable of procreation. —***SYN.*** see **male.**

vir·i·lism (vir'əl-iz'm), *n.* [< *virile* + *-ism*], the abnormal appearance of secondary male sexual characteristics in a woman, as the growth of facial hair.

vi·ril·i·ty (vi-ril'ə-ti), *n.* [Fr. *virilité;* L. *virilitas*], the state or quality of being virile.

vi·ro·sis (vī-rō'sis), *n.* [*pl.* VIROSES (-sēz)], [Mod. L.; *virus* + *-osis*], any disease caused by a virus, especially a filtrable virus.

v. irr., irregular verb.

vir·tu (vẽr-tōō', vũr'tōō), *n.* [It., excellence, virtue; L. *virtus*, strength, virtue], 1. a knowledge or love of, or taste for, artistic objects or curios. 2. the quality of being artistic, beautiful, rare, or otherwise such as to interest a collector. 3. such art objects and curios, collectively. Also spelled **vertu.**

vir·tu·al (vũr'choo-əl), *adj.* [ME. *vertual;* ML. *virtualis;* L. *virtus,* strength, virtue], 1. being so in effect or essence, although not in actual fact or name: as, he is a *virtual* stranger, although we've met. 2. [Rare or Archaic], effective because of certain inherent virtues, or powers.

vir·tu·al·i·ty (vũr'choo-al'ə-ti), *n.* the state or quality of being virtual.

vir·tu·al·ly (vũr'choo-əl-i), *adv.* in effect although not in fact; for all practical purposes: as, *virtually* identical.

vir·tue (vũr'choo), *n.* [ME. & OFr. *vertu,* virtue, goodness, power; L. *virtus,* manliness, worth], 1. general moral excellence; right action and thinking; goodness of character. 2. a specific moral quality regarded as good or meritorious: as, generosity is a great *virtue;* specifically, in *philosophy* & *theology,* any of the cardinal virtues or the theological virtues. 3. chastity, especially in a woman. 4. *a)* excellence in general; merit; value: as, there is some *virtue* in what you say. *b)* a specific excellence; good quality or feature: as, the *virtues* of teaching as a profession. 5. effective power or force; efficacy; potency; especially, the ability to heal or strengthen: as, the *virtue* of a medicine. 6. [Obs.], manly quality; strength, courage, etc. 7. *pl.* in *theology,* one of the orders of angels.
by (or **in**) **virtue of,** because of; on the grounds of.
make a virtue of necessity, to do what one has to do as if from inclination or a sense of duty.

vir·tu·os·i·ty (vũr'choo-os'ə-ti), *n.* [*pl.* VIRTUOSITIES (-tiz)], [< *virtuoso*], 1. interest in or taste for the fine arts; especially, a sensitive but amateur or trifling interest. 2. great technical skill in some fine art, especially in the performance of music; sometimes, mere technical skill. 3. virtuosos (sense 1) collectively.

vir·tu·o·so (vũr'choo-ō'sō), *n.* [*pl.* VIRTUOSOS (-sōz), VIRTUOSI (-si)], [It., skilled, learned; LL. *virtuosus;* see VIRTUOUS], 1. a person with great interest and sensitive taste in the fine arts; collector or connoisseur of art objects or curios. 2. a person having great technical skill in some fine art, especially in the performance of music. 3. [Obs.], a person learned in the arts and sciences; scholar; savant. —*SYN.* see **aesthete.**

vir·tu·ous (vũr'choo-əs), *adj.* [ME. & OFr. *vertuous;* LL. *virtuosus* < L. *virtus,* worth, virtue], 1. having, or characterized by, moral virtue; righteous. 2. chaste: said of a woman. 3. [Archaic], having effective virtue, or potency; efficacious. —*SYN.* see **chaste, moral.**

vir·u·lence (vir'yoo-ləns, vir'oo-ləns), *n.* [LL. *virulentia*], 1. the quality of being virulent or poisonous; deadliness, as of poison. 2. the relative infectiousness of a microorganism causing disease. 3. violent or bitter animosity.

vir·u·len·cy (vir'yoo-lən-si, vir'oo-lən-si), *n.* virulence.

vir·u·lent (vir'yoo-lənt, vir'oo-lənt), *adj.* [ME. *verelent;* L. *virulentus,* full of poison < *virus,* a poison], 1. poisonous; venomous; extremely injurious; deadly. 2. bitterly hostile; violently antagonistic or spiteful; full of hate and enmity. 3. in *medicine, a)* violent and rapid in its course; highly malignant: said of a disease. *b)* able to overcome the natural defenses of the host; highly infectious: said of a microorganism.

vi·rus (vī'rəs), *n.* [L., a slimy liquid, poison; cf. FITCHEW], 1. venom, as of a snake. 2. *a)* any of a group of ultramicroscopic or submicroscopic infective agents that cause various diseases, as smallpox: viruses are capable of multiplying in connection with living cells and are variously regarded as living organisms and as complex proteins. *b)* specifically, a filtrable virus. *c)* the exudation from the vesicles of cowpox, used as a vaccine for smallpox. 3. anything that corrupts or poisons the mind or character; evil or harmful influence.

‡**vis** (vis), *n.* [*pl.* VIRES (vī'rēz)], [L.], force; strength.

Vis., 1. Viscount. 2. Viscountess.

vi·sa (vē'zə), *n.* [Fr.; L. fem. of *visus,* pp. of *videre,* to see], an endorsement stamped or written on a passport, showing that it has been examined by the proper officials of a country and granting entry into that country. *v.t.* [VISAED (-zəd), VISAING], 1. to put a visa on (a passport). 2. to give a visa to (someone).

vis·age (viz'ij), *n.* [ME.; OFr. < *vis,* a face; L. *visus,* a look, a seeing < pp. of *videre,* to see], 1. the face, with reference to the form and proportions of the features or to the expression; countenance. 2. appearance; aspect. —*SYN.* see **face.**

-vis·aged (viz'ijd), a combining form meaning *having a (specified) kind of visage,* as in *round-visaged.*

vis·ard (viz'ẽrd), *n.* a vizard.

vis-à-vis (vē'zə-vē'; Fr. vē'zà'vē'), *adj. & adv.* [Fr.], face to face; opposite. *prep.* 1. face to face with; opposite to. 2. in comparison with; in relation to. *n.* 1. a person who is face to face with another, as in fencing. 2. a carriage with facing seats. 3. an S-shaped seat or sofa on which two people can sit facing each other.

Vi·sa·yan (vē-sä'yən), *n.* 1. a member of a large racial group of the Visayan Islands and northern Mindanao. 2. the Malay language of the Visayans. Also **Bisayan.**

Visayan Islands, a group of islands in the central Philippines: also **Bisayas.**

Vis·by (viz'bi; Sw. vēs'bü), *n.* a seaport on Gotland, a Swedish island in the Baltic: member of the former Hanseatic League: pop., 14,000: German name, *Wisby.*

Visc., 1. Viscount. 2. Viscountess.

vis·ca·cha (vis-kä'chə), *n.* [Sp. < Quechua *uiscacha, huiscacha*], any of a group of large burrowing rodents of South America, related to the chinchilla.

vis·cer·a (vis'ẽr-ə), *n.pl.* [*sing.* (rare) VISCUS (-kəs)], [L., pl. of *viscus,* inner parts of the body], 1. the internal organs of the body, especially of the thorax and abdomen, as the heart, lungs, liver, kidneys, intestines, etc. 2. popularly, the intestines.

vis·cer·al (vis'ẽr-əl), *adj.* [ML. *visceralis*], of, having the nature of, situated in, or affecting the viscera.

vis·cid (vis'id), *adj.* [LL. *viscidus,* sticky < L. *viscum, viscus,* birdlime], 1. thick, sirupy, and sticky; viscous. 2. covered with a viscid substance: said of leaves.

vis·cid·i·ty (vi-sid'ə-ti), *n.* 1. the quality or condition of being viscid. 2. something viscid.

vis·coid (vis'koid), *adj.* [see -OID], somewhat viscous.

vis·coi·dal (vis-koi'd'l), *adj.* viscoid.

vis·com·e·ter (vis-kom'ə-tẽr), *n.* a viscosimeter.

vis·cose (vis'kōs), *adj.* [LL. *viscosus;* see VISCOUS], 1. viscous. 2. of, containing, or made of viscose. *n.* an amber-colored, siruplike solution made by treating cellulose with potassium hydroxide and carbon disulfide: used in making rayon thread and fabrics, and cellophane.

vis·co·sim·e·ter (vis'kō-sim'ə-tẽr), *n.* [*viscosity* + *-meter*], any of various devices for measuring the viscosity of a liquid, as by determining the rate of flow through a small opening.

vis·cos·i·ty (vis-kos'ə-ti), *n.* [*pl.* VISCOSITIES (-tiz)], [ME. *viscosite;* ML. *viscositas*], 1. the state or quality of being viscous. 2. in *physics, a)* the internal fluid resistance of a substance, caused by molecular attraction, which makes it resist a tendency to flow. *b)* the property of a solid of yielding steadily before a constant stress.

vis·count (vī'kount), *n.* [ME.; OFr. *visconte, viscomte;* ML. *vice comes;* L. *vice,* in place of + *comes,* a companion, later, count], 1. formerly, *a)* a deputy of a count or earl; specifically, *b)* a sheriff. 2. a nobleman next below an earl or count and above a baron: abbreviated **V., Vis., Visc., Visct.**

vis·count·cy (vī'kount-si), *n.* [*pl.* VISCOUNTCIES (-siz)], the title, rank, etc. of a viscount.

vis·count·ess (vī'koun-tis), *n.* 1. the wife of a viscount. 2. a woman holding a corresponding rank in her own right. Abbreviated **Vis., Visc., Visct.**

vis·count·ship (vī'kount-ship'), *n.* [*viscount* + *-ship*], a viscountcy.

vis·count·y (vī'koun-ti), *n.* [*pl.* VISCOUNTIES (-tiz)], 1. a viscountcy. 2. formerly, the territory under the jurisdiction of a viscount (sense 1).

vis·cous (vis'kəs), *adj.* [ME. *viscouse;* LL. *viscosus* < L. *viscum, viscus,* birdlime made from mistletoe berries < *viscum,* mistletoe], 1. thick, sirupy, and sticky; viscid. 2. in *botany,* covered with a sticky substance, as leaves. 3. in *physics,* having viscosity.

Visct., 1. Viscount. 2. Viscountess.

vis·cus (vis'kəs), *n.* [Rare], singular of **viscera.**

vise (vīs), *n.* [ME. & OFr. *vis,* a screw; L. *vitis,* a vine, lit., that which winds], a device, usually fastened to a workbench, consisting of two jaws opened and closed by a screw, lever, etc. and used for holding firmly an object being worked on. *v.t.* [VISED (vīst), VISING], to hold or squeeze with or as with a vise. Also spelled **vice.** Abbreviated **v.**

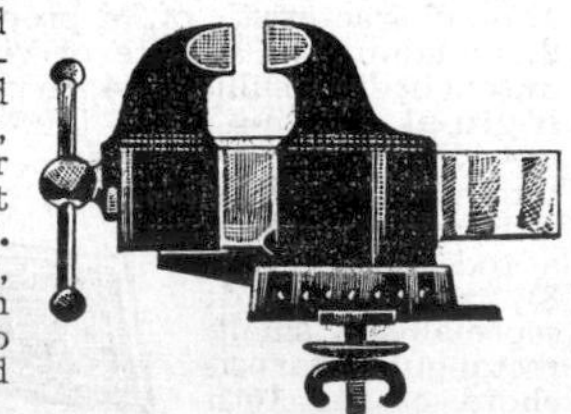
VISE

vi·sé (vē'zā, vē-zā'), *n.* & *v.t.* [VISÉED (-zād, -zād'), VISÉING], [Fr., pp. of *viser,* to view, inspect; L. *visus,* pp. of *videre,* to see], visa.

Vish·in·sky, An·drei Yan·u·ar·e·vich (än-dryā' yän'oo-är'ye-vich vish-in'ski), 1883–1954; Soviet jurist and statesman.

Vish·nu (vish'noo), *n.* [Sans. *Viṣṇu,* lit., prob. all-pervader], in *Hindu theology,* the second member of the trinity (Brahma, Vishnu, and Siva), called "the Preserver": he is popularly believed to have had several human incarnations, most important of which is Krishna.

vis·i·bil·i·ty (viz'ə-bil'ə-ti), *n.* [*pl.* VISIBILITIES (-tiz)], [LL. *visibilitas*], 1. the fact or condition of being visible. 2. *a)* the relative possibility of being seen under the conditions of distance, light, and atmosphere prevailing at a particular time: as, high *visibility. b)* the relative distance at which an object can be seen under the prevailing conditions; range of vision: as, *visibility* is 300 yards. 3. a visible object.

vis·i·ble (viz'ə-b'l), *adj.* [ME. *visible;* L. *visibilis* < *visus,* pp. of *videre,* to see], 1. that can be seen; perceptible by the eye. 2. that can be perceived or observed with the mind; evident; manifest. 3. on hand or available: as, *visible* supply. 4. so constructed as to bring to view parts or elements that are normally not perceptible.

vis·i·bly (viz'ə-bli), ***adv.*** so as to be visible or evident; manifestly; clearly; observably: as, he was *visibly* tired.

Vis·i·goth (viz'i-goth', viz'i-gôth'), ***n.*** [LL. *Visigothi*, pl.; *visi-* (< Gmc. base prob. meaning "west") + *Gothi*, Goths], any of the West Goths, a Teutonic people who invaded the Roman Empire late in the 4th century A.D., overran it, and set up a kingdom in France and Spain which lasted until about 700 A.D.

Vis·i·goth·ic (viz'i-goth'ik), ***adj.*** of or characteristic of the Visigoths.

vi·sion (vizh'ən), ***n.*** [ME. *visioun;* OFr.; L. *visio* < *visus*, pp. of *videre*, to see], 1. the act or power of seeing with the eye; sense of sight. 2. something supposedly seen by other than normal sight; something perceived in a dream, trance, etc. or supernaturally revealed, as to a prophet. 3. a mental image; especially, an imaginative contemplation: as, he has *visions* of power. 4. the ability to perceive something not actually visible, as through mental acuteness or keen foresight: as, his breadth of *vision* made this project possible. 5. force or power of the imagination: as, a dramatist of great *vision*. 6. something seen, especially something such as might be seen in a dream or trance. 7. something or someone, especially a woman, of extraordinary beauty. ***v.t.*** to see in or as in a vision.

vi·sion·al (vizh'ən-əl), ***adj.*** 1. of, or having the nature of, a vision or visions. 2. seen, or as if seen, in a vision; unreal.

vi·sion·ar·y (vizh'ən-er'i), ***adj.*** 1. seeing a vision; especially, habitually seeing visions; hence, 2. characterized by impractical ideas or schemes. 3. of, having the nature of, or seen in a vision; hence, 4. *a*) not real; imaginary. *b*) not capable of being carried out; merely speculative and impractical: said of an idea or scheme. ***n.*** [*pl.* VISIONARIES (-iz)], 1. a person who sees visions; hence, 2. a person who has impractical or fantastic ideas or schemes. —***SYN.*** see **imaginary.**

vis·it (viz'it), ***v.t.*** [ME. *visiten;* OFr. *visiter;* L. *visitare*, freq. < *visere*, to go to see < *visus*, pp. of *videre*, to see], 1. to go or come to see (someone) out of friendship or for social purposes. 2. to stay with as a guest for a more or less extended sojourn. 3. to go or come to see in a business or professional capacity; attend, as a doctor. 4. to go or come to (a place) in order to inspect or investigate. 5. to go or come to (in a general sense): as, I *visited* the library last night. 6. to go or come to in order to comfort or help. 7. to come upon or afflict; assail: as, a drouth *visited* the valley. 8. *a*) to inflict (punishment, suffering, etc.) upon someone. *b*) to afflict (*with* punishment, suffering, etc.). *c*) to inflict punishment for (wrongdoing); avenge: as, *visiting* the sins of the fathers upon the children. ***v.i.*** to visit someone or something; specifically, *a*) to inflict punishment or revenge. *b*) to make a social call or calls: often followed by *with*, as, I'll *visit* with mother tomorrow. *c*) [Colloq.], to converse or chat, as during a visit. ***n.*** a visiting; specifically, *a*) a social call. *b*) a stay as a guest; sojourn. *c*) an official or professional call, as of a doctor. *d*) an official call as for inspection or investigation; especially, in *marine law*, the boarding of a ship of a neutral nation by an officer of a nation at war to search it for contraband, etc. *e*) [Colloq.], a friendly conversation or chat.

vis·it·a·ble (viz'it-ə-b'l), ***adj.*** 1. that can be visited. 2. suitable for or worth visiting. 3. subject to visitation, or inspection.

vis·it·ant (viz'ə-tənt), ***n.*** [< Fr. or L.; Fr. *visitant* < L. *visitans*, ppr. of *visitare;* see VISIT], 1. a visitor, especially one from a strange or foreign place. 2. a supernatural being, as revealed to a human being. 3. in *zoology*, a migratory bird in any of its temporary resting places. —***SYN.*** see **visitor.**

vis·it·a·tion (viz'ə-tā'shən), ***n.*** [ME. & Anglo-Fr. *visitacioun;* L. *visitatio*], 1. the act or an instance of visiting; especially, an official visit to inspect or examine, as that made by a bishop, etc. to a church in his diocese. 2. a visiting of reward or, especially, punishment, as by God; hence, 3. any affliction or disaster thought of as an act of God. 4. [V-], in the *Roman Catholic Church*, *a*) the visit of the Virgin Mary to Elisabeth: Luke 1:39–56. *b*) a church feast (July 2) in commemoration of this. 5. in *zoology*, migration of animals or birds to a particular place at an unusual time or in unusual numbers.

vis·it·a·tion·al (viz'ə-tā'shən-'l), ***adj.*** of or characteristic of a visitation or visitations.

vis·it·a·to·ri·al (viz'i-tə-tôr'i-əl, viz'i-tə-tō'ri-əl), ***adj.*** 1. of or for visitation. 2. having the power of visitation, or inspection.

vis·it·ing card (viz'it-iŋ), a calling card.

visiting nurse, a graduate nurse employed by a community agency, originally one who visited the sick in their homes to give nursing care.

visiting teacher, an elementary school teacher who gives instruction to bedridden students through regular visits to their homes.

vis·i·tor (viz'ə-tẽr), ***n.*** a person making a visit.
SYN.—**visitor** is the general term for one who comes to see a person or spend some time in a place, whether for social, business, or professional reasons, for sightseeing, etc.; **visitant** now generally suggests a supernatural rather than a human visitor and, in biology, is applied to a migratory bird in any of its temporary resting places; **guest** applies to one who is hospitably entertained at the home or table of another or, by extension, to one who pays for his lodgings, meals, etc. at a hotel; **caller** applies to one who makes a brief, often formal visit, as for business or social reasons.

vis·i·to·ri·al (viz'ə-tôr'i-əl, viz'ə-tō'ri-əl), ***adj.*** visitatorial.

‡vis ma·jor (vis mā'jẽr), [L., greater force], force majeure.

vis·or (vī'zẽr; *rarely*, viz'ẽr), ***n.*** [ME. *visere;* Anglo-Fr. *viser;* OFr. *visiere* < *vis*, a face; see VISAGE], 1. in ancient armor, the movable part of a helmet, covering the face, especially a section that came down over and protected the eyes. 2. a mask, as for disguise; vizard. 3. the projecting front brim of a cap, for shading the eyes. 4. a fixed or movable shade fastened to the windshield of a car, for shading the eyes. ***v.t.*** to hide, protect, or shade with a visor. Also spelled **vizor.**

vis·ta (vis'tə), ***n.*** [It., sight; L. < *visus*, pp. of *videre*, to see], 1. a view or outlook, especially one seen through a long passage, as between rows of houses or trees. 2. a long row of trees, etc., framing such a view. 3. a comprehensive mental view of a series of remembered or anticipated events. —***SYN.*** see **view.**

Vis·tu·la (vis'choo-lə), ***n.*** a river in Poland, flowing into the Baltic Sea: length, 630 mi.: Polish name, *Wisla;* German name, *Weichsel*.

vis·u·al (vizh'ōō-əl), ***adj.*** [ME.; LL. *visualis* < L. *visus*, a sight < *videre*, to see], 1. of, connected with, or used in seeing. 2. that is or can be seen; visible. 3. of, having the nature of, or occurring as a mental image, or vision. 4. in *optics*, optical.

visual aids, motion pictures, lantern slides, charts, and other devices involving the sense of sight (other than books), used in teaching, illustrating lectures, etc.

vis·u·al·i·za·tion (vizh'ōō-əl-i-zā'shən, vizh'ōō-əl-ī-zā'shən), ***n.*** 1. a visualizing or being visualized. 2. anything visualized; mental picture.

vis·u·al·ize (vizh'ōō-əl-īz'), ***v.t.*** [VISUALIZED (-īzd'), VISUALIZING], [*visual* + *-ize*], to form a mental image, or vision, of (something not visible, as an abstraction). ***v.i.*** to form a mental image or images.

vis·u·al·i·zer (vizh'ōō-əl-īz'ẽr), ***n.*** a person who visualizes; especially, one whose mental imagery is largely visual, rather than auditory, olfactory, etc.

vis·u·al·ly (vizh'ōō-əl-i), ***adv.*** in a visual manner; by sight.

visual purple, a purplish pigment in the rods of the retina, bleached to visual yellow by the action of light and considered a factor in transforming light rays into the sensory impulses of vision: also called *rhodopsin*.

visual yellow, the yellowish pigment into which visual purple is bleached by the action of light: also called *retinene*.

vi·ta·ceous (vī-tā'shəs), ***adj.*** [< Mod. L. *Vitaceae*, name of the family (< L. *vitis*, a vine); + *-ous*], in *botany*, of the grape family, a group of climbing woody vines with tendrils, clusters of small, greenish flowers, and berrylike fruit.

vi·tal (vī't'l), ***adj.*** [ME.; OFr.; L. *vitalis*, vital < *vita*, life], 1. of, concerned with, or manifesting life: as, *vital* energy. 2. necessary or essential to life; being a source or support of life: as, *vital* organs. 3. destroying life; fatal; deadly: as, a *vital* wound. 4. *a*) essential to the existence or continuance of something; indispensable; hence, *b*) of greatest importance: as, this matter is *vital*. 5. affecting the validity, truth, etc. of something: as, a *vital* error. 6. full of life and vigor; energetic: as, a *vital* personality. ***n.pl.*** 1. the vital organs, as the heart, brain, lungs, etc. 2. the essential parts of anything, that are indispensable for its existence, continuance, etc. —***SYN.*** see **living.**

vital force, vital principle.

vi·tal·ism (vī't'l-iz'm), ***n.*** [*vital* + *-ism;* cf. Fr. *vitalisme*], the doctrine that the life in living organisms is caused and sustained by a vital principle that is distinct from all physical and chemical forces and that life is, in part, self-determining and self-evolving: opposed to *mechanism*.

vi·tal·is·tic (vī't'l-is'tik), ***adj.*** of, or having the nature of, vitalism.

vi·tal·i·ty (vī-tal'ə-ti), ***n.*** [*pl.* VITALITIES (-tiz)], [L.

vitalitas], 1. vital principle or force. 2. power to live or go on living. 3. power to endure or survive, as of an institution. 4. mental or physical vigor; energy.

vi·tal·i·za·tion (vī't'l-i-zā'shən, vī't'l-ī-zā'shən), *n.* a vitalizing or being vitalized.

vi·tal·ize (vī't'l-īz'), *v.t.* [VITALIZED (-īzd'), VITALIZING], 1. to make vital; give life to. 2. to give vigor or animation to: as, *vitalize* a dull report. —*SYN.* see **animate.**

vi·tal·li·um (vī-tal'i-əm), *n.* an alloy of cobalt, chromium, and molybdenum, used in bone surgery, etc.: a trade-mark (**Vitallium.**).

vital principle, the basic force or principle regarded as the source and cause of life in living organisms: see **vitalism**: also **vital force.**

vital statistics, data concerning births, deaths, marriages, etc.

vi·ta·min (vī'tə-min), *n.* [< L. *vita*, life; + *amine*], any of a number of unrelated, complex organic substances found variously in most foods and essential, in small amounts, for the normal functioning of the body: the principal known vitamins include:

vitamin A, a fat-soluble aliphatic alcohol, $C_{20}H_{29}OH$, found in fish-liver oil, egg yolk, butter, etc., and (as carotene) in carrots and other vegetables: a deficiency of this vitamin results in night blindness and degeneration of epithelial tissue: it occurs in two forms, **vitamin A_1** and **vitamin A_2.**

vitamin B (complex), a group of unrelated water-soluble substances including: *a*) **vitamin B_1** (see **thiamine**). *b*) **vitamin B_2** (see **riboflavin**). *c*) **vitamin B_6** (see **pyridoxine**). *d*) nicotinic acid. *e*) pantothenic acid. *f*) biotin: also called *vitamin H*. *g*) inositol. *h*) para-aminobenzoic acid. *i*) choline. *j*) folic acid.

vitamin C, an organic compound, $C_6H_8O_6$, occurring in citrus fruits, tomatoes, and various vegetables: a deficiency of this vitamin tends to produce scurvy: also called *ascorbic acid*, *cevitamic acid*.

vitamin D, any of several related vitamins occurring in fish-liver oils, milk, egg yolks, etc.: a deficiency of this vitamin tends to produce rickets; specifically, *a*) **vitamin D_1,** a mixture of calciferol with another sterol prepared by the ultraviolet irradiation of ergosterol. *b*) **vitamin D_2** (see **calciferol**). *c*) **vitamin D_3,** a substance similar to vitamin D_2, found chiefly in fish-liver oils.

vitamin E, a substance consisting of a mixture of tocopherols, believed to restore fertility to sterile mammals: formerly called *vitamin X*: see **tocopherol.**

vitamin G, vitamin B_2 (see **riboflavin**).

vitamin H, see **biotin.**

vitamin K, a vitamin occurring in certain green vegetables, fish meal, hempseed, etc. and used to promote blood clotting, and thus prevent hemorrhage, by aiding in the synthesis of prothrombin by the liver: the two varieties are **vitamin K_1,** found chiefly in alfalfa leaves, and **vitamin K_2,** found chiefly in fish meal.

vitamin P, a mixture of flavones occurring especially in citrus juice and paprika: a deficiency of this vitamin results in the increased permeability of capillary walls and, hence, greater susceptibility to hemorrhage: also called *citrin*.

vitamin X, a former name for *vitamin E*.

vi·ta·mine (vī'tə-mēn', vī'tə-min', vī'tə-min), *n.* [Rare], a vitamin.

vi·ta·min·ic (vī'tə-min'ik), *adj.* of vitamins.

vi·ta·scope (vī'tə-skōp'), *n.* [L. *vita*, life; + *-scope*], an early type of motion-picture projector.

Vi·tebsk (vē'tepsk), *n.* a city in the Byelorussian S.S.R., on the Dvina River: pop., 167,000.

vi·tel·lin (vi-tel'in, vī-tel'in), *n.* [< L. *vitellus*, the yolk of an egg, orig., dim. of *vitulus*, a calf; + *-in*], in *chemistry*, a protein occurring in the yolk of eggs.

vi·tel·line (vi-tel'in, vī-tel'in), *adj.* [ME. *vitellyn* < L. *vitellus* (see VITELLIN); + *-ine*], 1. of the yolk of an egg, as the *vitelline* membrane, which surrounds it. 2. of the yellow color of an egg yolk. *n.* an egg yolk.

vi·tel·lus (vi-tel'əs, vī-tel'əs), *n.* [L., dim. of *vitulus*, a calf], the yolk of an egg.

vi·ti·a·ble (vish'i-ə-b'l), *adj.* that can be vitiated.

vi·ti·ate (vish'i-āt'), *v.t.* [VITIATED (-id), VITIATING], [< L. *vitiatus*, pp. of *vitiare*, to vitiate < *vitium*, a vice], 1. to make imperfect, faulty, or impure; spoil; corrupt. 2. to weaken morally; debase; pervert. 3. to make legally ineffective; invalidate, as a contract.

vi·ti·at·ed (vish'i-āt'id), *adj.* [pp. of *vitiate*], 1. made defective; spoiled. 2. debased; corrupted, as taste. 3. invalidated, as a contract.

vi·ti·a·tion (vish'i-ā'shən), *n.* [L. *vitiatio*], a vitiating or being vitiated.

vi·ti·a·tor (vish'i-ā'tēr), *n.* a person or thing that vitiates.

vit·i·cul·tur·al (vit'i-kul'chēr-əl), *adj.* of viticulture.

vit·i·cul·ture (vit'i-kul'chēr), *n.* [< L. *vitis*, a vine; + *culture*], the cultivation of the grapevine; grape-growing or the science of this.

vit·i·cul·tur·ist (vit'i-kul'chēr-ist), *n.* an expert in viticulture.

Vi·ti Le·vu (vē'tē le'vōō), one of the Fiji Islands: area, 4,053 sq. mi.; pop., 111,000: chief town, Suva.

vit·i·li·go (vit'i-lī'gō), *n.* [L., a kind of cutaneous eruption, tetter], a skin disease characterized by the formation of smooth, white, pigmentless patches on various parts of the body.

Vi·to·ri·a (vē-tô'ryä), *n.* a city in northern Spain: pop., 56,000 (est. 1946): site of a French defeat (1813).

vit·re·ous (vit'ri-əs), *adj.* [L. *vitreus*, glassy < *vitrum*, glass], 1. of, having the nature of, or like glass; glassy. 2. derived from or made of glass. 3. of the vitreous humor.

vitreous electricity, positive electricity, as that produced by rubbing glass with silk.

vitreous humor (or **body**), the transparent, colorless, jellylike substance that fills the eyeball between the retina and lens: see **eye**, illus.

vi·tres·cence (vi-tres''ns), *n.* [< *vitrescent*], the state of becoming vitreous, or glassy.

vi·tres·cent (vi-tres''nt), *adj.* [< L. *vitrum*, glass; + *-escent*], 1. that can be formed into glass. 2. becoming, or tending to become, glass.

vit·ric (vit'rik), *adj.* [< L. *vitrum*, glass; + *-ic*], of, having the nature of, or like glass: cf. *ceramic*.

vit·rics (vit'riks), *n.pl.* [see VITRIC & -ICS], 1. [construed as sing.], the art or study of making and decorating articles of glass. 2. articles of glassware.

vit·ri·fac·tion (vit'rə-fak'shən), *n.* [< L. *vitrum*, glass + *facere*, to make], vitrification.

vit·ri·fi·a·ble (vit'rə-fī'ə-b'l), *adj.* capable of being vitrified; that can be made into glass by heat.

vit·ri·fi·ca·tion (vit'rə-fi-kā'shən), *n.* [Fr. *vitrification*; see VITRIFY], 1. a vitrifying or being vitrified. 2. something vitrified.

vit·ri·form (vit'rə-fôrm'), *adj.* [< L. *vitrum*, glass; + *-form*], having the form or appearance of glass.

vit·ri·fy (vit'rə-fī'), *v.t. & v.i.* [VITRIFIED (-fīd'), VITRIFYING], [Fr. *vitrifier* < L. *vitrum*, glass + *facere*, to make], to change into glass or a glasslike substance by fusion due to heat; make or become vitreous.

vit·ri·ol (vit'ri-əl), *n.* [ME.; OFr.; ML. *vitriolum*, vitriol < L. *vitreus*, glassy: so called from the glassy appearance], 1. any of several sulfates of metals, as copper sulfate (blue vitriol), iron sulfate (green vitriol), zinc sulfate (white vitriol), etc. 2. sulfuric acid: also **oil of vitriol.** 3. anything sharp or caustic: as, his language was pure *vitriol*. *v.t.* [VITRIOLED or VITRIOLLED (-əld), VITRIOLING or VITRIOLLING], to apply sulfuric acid to.

vit·ri·ol·ic (vit'ri-ol'ik), *adj.* [Fr. *vitriolique*], 1. of, like, or derived from a vitriol. 2. extremely biting or caustic; sarcastic; sharp and bitter: as, *vitriolic* talk.

vit·ri·ol·i·za·tion (vit'ri-əl-i-zā'shən, vit'ri-əl-ī-zā'shən), *n.* a vitriolizing or being vitriolized.

vit·ri·ol·ize (vit'ri-əl-īz'), *v.t.* [VITRIOLIZED (-īzd'), VITRIOLIZING], 1. to convert into vitriol. 2. to subject to the action of vitriol. 3. to injure or try to injure (a person) as by throwing vitriol on the face.

Vi·tru·vi·us Pol·li·o, Marcus (vi-trōō'vi-əs pol'i-ō'), 1st century B.C.; Roman architect and engineer.

vit·ta (vit'ə), *n.* [*pl.* VITTAE (-ē)], [L.], 1. in ancient Rome, a headband or ribbon. 2. in *botany*, an oil tube in the fruit of most plants of the carrot family. 3. in *botany & zoology*, a band or streak of color.

vit·tate (vit'āt), *adj.* [L. *vittatus*, bound with a fillet; see VITTA], 1. in *botany*, having a vitta or vittae. 2. in *botany & zoology*, striped lengthwise.

vit·tle (vit''l) *n.* [Dial.], victual.

vit·u·line (vich'oo-līn', vich'oo-lin), *adj.* [L. *vitulinus* < *vitulus*, a calf], of or like a calf, calves, or veal.

vi·tu·per·ate (vī-tōō'pə-rāt', vi-tū'pə-rāt'), *v.t.* [VITUPERATED (-id), VITUPERATING], [< L. *vituperatus*, pp. of *vituperare*, to blame < *vitium*, a fault, vice + *parare*, to make ready], to speak abusively to or about; berate; revile. —*SYN.* see **scold.**

vi·tu·per·a·tion (vī-tōō'pə-rā'shən, vi-tū'pə-rā'shən), *n.* 1. the act of vituperating. 2. bitter, abusive language.

vi·tu·per·a·tive (vī-tōō'pə-rā'tiv, vi-tū'pə-rā'tiv), *adj.* having the nature of or characterized by vituperation; abusive.

vi·tu·per·a·tor (vī-tōō'pə-rā'tēr, vi-tū'pə-rā'tēr), *n.* [L.], a person who vituperates.

‡**vi·va** (vē'vä), *interj.* [It.], literally, (long) live (someone specified)!: an exclamation of acclaim. *n.* a shout of "viva."

‡**vi·va·ce** (vē-vä'che), *adj.* [It. < L. *vivax*; see VIVACIOUS], in *music*, lively; rapid; spirited: a direction to the performer: abbreviated **viv.**

vi·va·cious (vi-vā'shəs, vī-vā'shəs), *adj.* [< L. *vivax*, *vivacis*, vigorous < *vivere*, to live], 1. full of life and animation; spirited; lively. 2. [Archaic], long-lived; hard to kill or destroy. —*SYN.* see **lively.**

vi·vac·i·ty (vi-vas'ə-ti, vī-vas'ə-ti), *n.* [ME. *vivacite*; L. *vivacitas*], 1. the quality or state of being vivacious. 2. liveliness of spirit; animation. 3. [*pl.* VIVACITIES (-tiz)], a vivacious act or expression.

Vi·val·di, An·to·nio (än-tô'nyô vē-väl'dē; Eng. vi-väl'di), 1680?–1743; Italian composer.

‡**vi·van·dière** (vē'vän'dyâr'), *n.* [Fr., fem. of *vivandier*;

see VIAND], formerly, especially in France, a woman who accompanied troops and sold them wines, refreshments, and supplies.

vi·var·i·um (vī-vâr′i-əm), *n.* [*pl.* VIVARIUMS (-əmz), VIVARIA (-ə)], [L. < *vivarius*, concerning living creatures < *vivere*, to live], an enclosed place for raising plants or animals under conditions closely resembling those of their natural environment.

vi·va-vo·ce (vī′və-vō′si), *adj.* expressed orally.

vi·va vo·ce (vī′və vō′si), [L., with living voice, abl. fem. of *vivus*, living + abl. of *vox*, voice], by word of mouth; orally.

‡vive (vēv), *interj.* [Fr.], (long) live (someone specified)!: an exclamation of acclaim.

‡vive la ré·pu·blique (vēv′ lä′ rā′pü′blēk′), [Fr.], (long) live the republic!

‡vive le roi (vēv′ lə rwä′), [Fr.], (long) live the king!

vi·ver·rine (vī-ver′īn, vi-ver′in), *adj.* [< L. *viverra*, a ferret; + *-ine*], of or belonging to the civet family. *n.* an animal of the civet family.

vives (vīvz), *n.* [Fr.; contr. of OFr. *avives*; Sp. *avivas*, *adivas* < Ar. *addhība*, she-wolf], chronic inflammation of the submaxillary glands of a horse.

Viv·i·an (viv′i-ən, viv′yən), [L. *Vivianus* < *vivus*, alive], 1. a masculine name: equivalent, Fr. *Vivien*. 2. a feminine name: equivalent, Fr. *Vivienne*. *n.* in *Arthurian legend*, an enchantress, mistress of Merlin: also called *Lady of the Lake*.

viv·id (viv′id), *adj.* [L. *vividus*, lively < *vivere*, to live], 1. full of life; vigorous; lively; striking: as, a *vivid* personality. 2. *a*) bright; intense; brilliant: said of colors, light, etc. *b*) brightly colored: as, a *vivid* painting. 3. forming clear or striking mental images; strong; active; daring: as, a *vivid* imagination. 4. clearly perceived by the mind, as a recollection. 5. bringing strikingly real or lifelike images to the mind: as, *vivid* description. —*SYN.* see **graphic**.

viv·i·fi·ca·tion (viv′ə-fi-kā′shən), *n.* [LL. *vivificatio*], a vivifying or being vivified.

viv·i·fy (viv′ə-fī′), *v.t.* [VIVIFIED (-fīd′), VIVIFYING], [Fr. *vivifier*; LL. *vivificare* < L. *vivus*, alive + *facere*, to make], 1. to give life to; make come to life; animate. 2. to make more lively, active, striking, etc.

viv·i·par·i·ty (viv′ə-par′ə-ti), *n.* the quality or state of being viviparous.

vi·vip·a·rous (vī-vip′ə-rəs), *adj.* [L. *viviparus* < *vivus*, alive + *parere*, to produce], 1. bearing or bringing forth living young (as most mammals and some other animals) instead of laying eggs: opposed to *oviparous*. 2. in *botany*, germinating while still on the parent plant, as certain seeds or bulbs. 3. producing such seeds or bulbs; proliferous.

viv·i·sect (viv′ə-sekt′, viv′ə-sekt′), *v.t.* [back-formation < *vivisection*, after *dissect*], to perform vivisection on. *v.i.* to practice vivisection.

viv·i·sec·tion (viv′ə-sek′shən), *n.* [< L. *vivus*, alive + *sectio*, a cutting < *secare*, to cut], 1. a surgical operation performed on a living animal to study the structure and function of living organs and parts, and to investigate the effects of diseases and therapy. 2. experimental research involving such surgical operation.

viv·i·sec·tion·al (viv′ə-sek′shən-′l), *adj.* 1. of, or having the nature of, vivisection. 2. performing vivisection.

viv·i·sec·tion·ist (viv′ə-sek′shən-ist), *n.* 1. a person who practices vivisection. 2. a person who advocates or defends vivisection as essential to scientific progress.

viv·i·sec·tor (viv′ə-sek′tẽr), *n.* a person who practices vivisection.

vix·en (vik′s′n), *n.* [Southern dial. form of ME. *fixen* < AS. **fyxen* < base of *fox*, **fuhs-* + fem. suffix **-in*; cf. G. *füchsin*], 1. a female fox. 2. an ill-tempered, shrewish, or malicious woman.

vix·en·ish (vik′s′n-ish), *adj.* of, like, or characteristic of a vixen; ill-tempered, quarrelsome, or malicious.

viz. (viz; *often read* "namely"), [ML., altered (because abbrev. for L. *et* resembled a *z*) < earlier *viet.*, contr. for L. *videlicet*], videlicet; that is; namely.

viz·ard (viz′ẽrd), *n.* [altered < earlier *visar*, var. of *visor*], 1. a visor. 2. a mask. Also spelled **visard**.

vi·zier (vi-zêr′, viz′yẽr), *n.* [Turk. *vezīr*; Ar. *wazīr*, a vizier, lit., bearer of burdens, porter < *wazara*, to bear a burden: so named because the vizier bears the duties actually incumbent upon the ruler], in Moslem countries, a high officer in the government; especially, a minister of state: also **vizir**.

vi·zier·ate (vi-zêr′it, viz′yẽr-āt′), *n.* [Fr. *vizirat*; Ar. *wizārat*], the office, authority, dignity, or term of office of a vizier.

vi·zier·i·al (vi-zêr′i-əl, viz′yẽr-əl), *adj.* of a vizier.

vi·zier·ship (vi-zêr′ship, viz′yẽr-ship′), *n.* [*vizier* + *-ship*], the office or term of office of a vizier.

vi·zir (vi-zêr′), *n.* a vizier.

viz·or (vī′zẽr; *rarely*, viz′ẽr), *n.* a visor.

V-J Day (vē′jā′), the day on which the fighting with Japan officially ended in World War II (August 14, 1945) or the day on which the surrender was formally signed (September 2, 1945).

VL, Vulgar Latin.

Vla·di·kav·kaz (vlä′di-käf-käs′), *n.* Ordzhonikidze, a city in the Caucasus, U.S.S.R.: the former name.

Vlad·i·mir I (vlad′ə-mir; Russ. vlä-dē′mür), 956?–1015; czar of Russia (980–1015); converted to Christianity: called *the Great* and *Saint Vladimir*.

Vla·di·vos·tok (vlad′i-vos′tok; Russ. vlä′di-vôs-tôk′), *n.* a seaport in Siberia, U.S.S.R., on the Sea of Japan: it is the eastern terminus of the Trans-Siberian Railroad: pop., 206,000.

Vl·ta·va (vul′tä-vä), *n.* Moldau River: Czech name.

V-mail (vē′māl′), *n.* a mail service of World War II, by which letters to or from the armed forces were reduced to microfilm to conserve shipping space, and enlarged and printed for delivery.

V.M.D., *Veterinariae Medicinae Doctor*, [L.], Doctor of Veterinary Medicine.

v.n., neuter verb.

vo., verso.

voc., vocative.

vo·ca·ble (vō′kə-b′l), *n.* [Fr.; L. *vocabulum*, a name, title, word < *vocare*, to call], a word or term; especially, a word regarded as a unit of sounds or letters rather than as a unit of meaning.

vo·cab·u·lar·y (vō-kab′yoo-ler′i, və-kab′yoo-ler′i), *n.* [*pl.* VOCABULARIES (-iz)], [ML. *vocabularium* < L. *vocabulum*, a word; see VOCABLE], 1. a list of words and, sometimes, phrases, usually arranged in alphabetical order and defined; dictionary, glossary, or lexicon. 2. all the words of a language. 3. all the words used by a particular person, class, profession, etc.: sometimes, all the words recognized and understood by a particular person, although not necessarily used by him (in full, *passive vocabulary*). Abbreviated **vocab.**

vo·cal (vō′k′l), *adj.* [ME.; L. *vocalis* < *vox*, *vocis*, a voice], 1. uttered, produced, or performed by the voice; spoken or sung; oral: as, *vocal* music. 2. having a voice; capable of speaking or making oral sounds. 3. of, used in, connected with, or belonging to the voice: as, *vocal* organs. 4. full of voice or voices. 5. inclined to express oneself in speech; speaking freely or vociferously. 6. in *phonetics*, *a*) vocalic. *b*) voiced.

vocal cords, either of two pairs of membranous cords or folds in the larynx, consisting of a thicker upper pair (*false vocal cords*) and a lower pair (*true vocal cords*): voice is produced when air from the lungs causes the lower (true) cords to vibrate: pitch is controlled by varying the tension on the cords, and volume, by regulating the air passing through the larynx.

vo·cal·ic (vō-kal′ik), *adj.* 1. having many vowels; composed mainly or entirely of vowels. 2. of, consisting of, having the nature of, or affecting a vowel or vowels.

vo·cal·ism (vō′k′l-iz′m), *n.* 1. the use of the voice, as in speaking or singing. 2. the act or art of singing. 3. a vocalic sound; vowel. 4. a system of vowels, as of a particular language.

vo·cal·ist (vō′k′l-ist), *n.* [*vocal* + *-ist*], a singer.

vo·cal·i·ty (vō-kal′ə-ti), *n.* 1. the quality of having vocal powers, or voice. 2. the quality of being vocal or vocalic.

vo·cal·ize (vō′k′l-īz′), *v.t.* [VOCALIZED (-īzd′), VOCALIZING], 1. to make vocal; utter with the voice; speak or sing. 2. to give a voice to; make vocal, or articulate. 3. to add the diacritical marks of vowel sounds to (the characters of Hebrew, Arabic, or other languages lacking alphabetical letters for the vowels). 4. in *phonetics*, *a*) to change into or use as a vowel: as, *w* is often *vocalized* at the end of a syllable. *b*) to voice. *v.i.* 1. to utter sounds; speak or sing; specifically, in *singing*, to practice tones sung on vowels. 2. to be changed into a vowel.

vo·cal·ly (vō′k′l-i), *adv.* 1. in a vocal manner; orally. 2. by singing. 3. in regard to vowels.

vo·ca·tion (vō-kā′shən), *n.* [ME. *vocacioun*; L. *vocatio* < *vocare*, to call], 1. a call, summons, or impulsion to perform a certain function or enter a certain career, especially a religious one; hence, 2. the function or career toward which one believes himself to be called. 3. any trade, profession, or occupation.

vo·ca·tion·al (vō-kā′shən-′l), *adj.* of a vocation, trade, profession, occupation, etc.

vocational guidance, the work of testing and interviewing persons in order to guide them toward the choice of a vocation suitable to their abilities or toward training for such vocation.

vo·ca·tion·al·ly (vō-kā′shən-′l-i), *adv.* in regard to a vocation.

voc·a·tive (vok′ə-tiv), *adj.* [< OFr. or L.; OFr. *vocatif*; L. *vocativus* (*casus*) < *vocare*, to call < *vox*, the voice], 1. of, characteristic of, or used in calling. 2. in *grammar*, in certain inflected languages, designating or of the case of nouns, adjectives, etc., used in direct address to indicate the person or thing addressed. *n.* 1. the vocative case. 2. a word in this case. Abbreviated **V.**, **voc.**

‡vo·ces (vō′sēz), *n.* plural of **vox.**

vo·cif·er·ance (vō-sif′ēr-əns), *n.* [< *vociferant*], a shouting or the noise of shouting; clamor.

vo·cif·er·ant (vō-sif′ēr-ənt), *adj.* [L. *vociferans*, ppr. of *vociferari*], vociferating; shouting; clamorous. *n.* a person who is vociferant.

vo·cif·er·ate (vō-sif′ə-rāt′), *v.t. & v.i.* [VOCIFERATED (-id), VOCIFERATING], [< L. *vociferatus*, pp. of *vociferari*, to cry out < *vox*, *vocis*, voice + *ferre*, to bear], to cry out loudly; shout; bawl; assert noisily.

vo·cif·er·a·tion (vō-sif′ə-rā′shən), *n.* [ME. *vocyferacion;* L. *vociferatio*], a vociferating; loud outcry; clamor.

vo·cif·er·a·tor (vō-sif′ə-rā′tēr), *n.* [LL.], a person who shouts or vociferates.

vo·cif·er·ous (vō-sif′ēr-əs), *adj.* [L. *vociferari* (see VOCIFERATE); + *-ous*], 1. making a loud outcry; shouting noisily; clamorous. 2. characterized by such outcry or clamor: as, a *vociferous* demand.

***SYN.*—vociferous** suggests loud and unrestrained shouting or crying out (a *vociferous* crowd, *vociferous* cheers); **clamorous** suggests an urgent or insistent vociferousness, as in demand or complaint (*clamorous* protests); **blatant** implies a bellowing loudness and, hence, suggests vulgar or offensive noisiness, clamor, etc. (*blatant*, insolent heckling); **strident** suggests a harsh, grating loudness (a *strident* voice); **boisterous** implies roughness or turbulence and, hence, suggests unrestrained exuberance in noisemaking (*boisterous* revels); **obstreperous** implies an unruliness that is noisy or boisterous in resisting control (an *obstreperous* child).

vod·ka (vod′kə; Russ. vôd′kä), *n.* [Russ., brandy, dim. of *voda*, water], a Russian alcoholic liquor distilled from wheat, rye, potatoes, etc.

vogue (vōg), *n.* [Fr., a fashion, reputation, lit., rowing of a ship < *voguer* (It. *vogare*), to row, sail < MHG. *wogen*, to sail < *woge*, a wave], 1. the current accepted fashion or style; mode: often with *the.* 2. popularity: general favor or acceptance: as, ballad singers have acquired a great *vogue.* —***SYN.*** see **fashion.**

Vo·gul (vō′gool), *n.* 1. a member of a Finno-Ugric people living in western Siberia. 2. the Ugric language of the Voguls.

voice (vois), *n.* [ME. *vois, voce;* OFr. *vois;* L. *vox, vocis*, a voice], 1. sound made through the mouth, especially by human beings, as in talking, singing, etc. 2. the ability to make sounds through the mouth: as, he lost his *voice.* 3. *a*) any sound regarded as like vocal utterance: as, the *voice* of the sea. *b*) anything regarded as like vocal utterance in communicating to the mind: as, the *voice* of his conscience. 4. a specified condition or quality of vocal sound: as, an angry *voice.* 5. the characteristic speech sounds normally made by a particular person: as, I recognized John's *voice.* 6. expressed wish, choice, opinion, etc. 7. the right to express one's wish, choice, opinion, etc., or to make it prevail; vote: as, we have a *voice* in our government. 8. expression: as, give *voice* to your opinion. 9. the person or other agency by which something is expressed or made known: as, this newspaper is the *voice* of the administration. 10. [Obs.], *a*) rumor; report. *b*) fame; reputation. 11. in *grammar*, *a*) one of the forms of a verb showing the connection between the subject and the verb, either as performing (*active voice*) or receiving (*passive voice*) the action. *b*) such forms or categories, collectively. 12. in *music*, *a*) musical sound made with the mouth; singing. *b*) the quality of a particular person's singing: as, a good *voice.* *c*) a singer. *d*) any of the parts of a musical phrase or composition in harmony: as, a song for three *voices.* *e*) ability to sing: as, he really has no *voice.* 13. in *phonetics*, sound made by vibrating the vocal cords with air forced from the lungs, as in pronouncing all vowels and such consonants as *b, d, g, m*, etc. *v.t.* [VOICED (voist), VOICING], 1. to give utterance or expression to (an opinion, desire, hope, etc.). 2. in *music*, to regulate the tone of (organ pipes, etc.). 3. in *phonetics*, to utter with voice. Abbreviated **v.** —***SYN.*** see **utter.**

in voice, with the voice in good condition, as for singing.

with one voice, unanimously.

voiced (voist), *adj.* [pp. of *voice*], 1. having a voice. 2. having or using (a specified kind or tone of) voice: often in hyphenated compounds, as *deep-voiced.* 3. expressed by the voice. 4. in *phonetics*, made with voice; sonant: said of certain consonants.

voice·ful (vois′fəl), *adj.* having, or as if having, voice or a voice, especially a loud voice; vocal; sounding.

voice·less (vois′lis), *adj.* 1. having no voice; dumb; mute. 2. not speaking; silent. 3. not spoken; not uttered: as, a *voiceless* wish. 4. lacking a musical voice or the ability to sing. 5. having no voice, or vote; lacking suffrage. 6. in *phonetics*, uttered without voice; surd: as, *k, p, t*, etc. are *voiceless* consonants.

SYN.*—voiceless** is applied to one who has no voice, either from birth or through deprivation (the throat operation left him *voiceless*); **speechless** usually implies temporary or momentary deprivation of the ability to speak (*speechless* with horror); **dumb** implies a lack of the power of speech and is now more often applied to brute animals and inanimate objects than to persons with impaired speech organs (a *dumb* beast); **mute** is applied to persons incapable of speech, specifically as because of congenital deafness and not through absence or impairment of the speech organs. —ANT.*** articulate.

voice part, in *music*, the melody or part for a particular voice or instrument in a polyphonic composition.

void (void), *adj.* [ME. *voide;* OFr. *voide, voit, vuit;* LL. **vocitus*, pp. of **vocitare*, to make empty < LL. *vocuus*, for L. *vacuus*, empty], 1. not occupied; vacant: said of benefices, offices, etc. 2. containing nothing; empty. 3. being without; lacking: as, *void* of judgment. 4. having no effect or result; ineffective; useless. 5. in *law*, *a*) of no legal force; not binding; invalid; null. *b*) loosely, voidable. *n.* 1. that which is void; an empty space; vacuum. 2. a feeling of emptiness or loss: as, his sudden death left a *void.* 3. a break or open space, as in a surface; gap; opening. *v.t.* 1. [Now Rare], *a*) to make empty or vacant; clear. *b*) to leave; vacate. 2. to empty (the contents of something); evacuate; discharge. 3. to make void, or of no effect; nullify; annul. —***SYN.*** see **empty, nullify.**

void·a·ble (void′ə-b'l), *adj.* that can be made or adjudged void, or of no effect.

void·ance (void′'ns), *n.* [ME. *voydaunce;* Anglo-Fr. *voidaunce;* OFr. *vuidance*], a voiding; specifically, *a*) annulment, as of a contract. *b*) vacancy, as of a benefice.

void·ed (void′id), *adj.* 1. made void. 2. having an opening or hole cut. 3. in *heraldry*, having the central part cut out, leaving a narrow border: said of a charge or ordinary.

‡voi·là (vwȧ′lȧ′), [Fr., see there], behold; there it is: often used as an interjection.

voile (voil; Fr. vwȧl), *n.* [Fr., a veil; see VEIL], a thin, sheer fabric of cotton, silk, rayon, or wool, used for dresses, curtains, etc.

‡voir dire (vwȧr′ dêr′), [Fr.; *voir(e)*, truly + *dire*, to say], in *law*, 1. an oath administered to a person by which he swears to answer truthfully in an examination to determine his competence as a witness or juror. 2. the examination itself.

‡voi·ture (vwȧ′tür′), *n.* [Fr.], a carriage or wagon.

‡voix cé·leste (vwȧ′ sā′lest′), [Fr., lit., heavenly voice], an organ stop consisting of two soft-toned pipes for each tone, one of which is pitched slightly sharp so as to produce a wavering, tremulous effect.

Vol., Volunteer.

vol., 1. volcanic. 2. volcano. 3. [*pl.* VOLS.], volume.

Vo·lans (vō′lanz), *n.* [L. (*Piscis*) *Volans*, flying (fish)], a small southern constellation: see **constellation**, chart.

vo·lant (vō′lənt), *adj.* [< Fr. or L.; Fr. *volant;* L. *volans*], 1. flying or capable of flying. 2. nimble; agile; quick. 3. in *heraldry*, represented as flying.

Vo·la·pük (vō′lä-pük′), *n.* [< Volapük *vol*, world + *pük*, language], an artificial language invented about 1879 by J. M. Schleyer of Baden, Germany, for proposed international use as an auxiliary language.

Vol·a·puk (vol′ə-pook′), *n.* Volapük.

vo·lar (vō′lēr), *adj.* [< L. *vola*, palm of the hand, sole of the foot; + *-ar*], in *anatomy*, of the palm of the hand or sole of the foot.

vol·a·tile (vol′ə-t'l), *adj.* [ME. & OFr. *volatil;* L. *volatilis* < *volare*, to fly], 1. changing readily to vapor; quickly evaporating. 2. changeable; fickle; transient. 3. [Obs.], flying or able to fly; volant.

volatile oil, any of a number of highly volatile, nonsaponifying oils distilled from the tissues of plants; essential oil: distinguished from *fixed oil.*

vol·a·til·i·ty (vol′ə-til′ə-ti), *n.* a volatile quality.

vol·a·til·iz·a·ble (vol′ə-t'l-īz′ə-b'l), *adj.* that can be volatilized.

vol·a·til·i·za·tion (vol′ə-t'l-i-zā′shən, vol′ə-t'l-ī-zā′shən), *n.* a volatilizing or being volatilized.

vol·a·til·ize (vol′ə-t'l-īz′), *v.t.* [VOLATILIZED (-īzd′), VOLATILIZING], to make volatile; cause to pass off as vapor. *v.i.* to become volatile, or pass off as vapor.

‡vol-au-vent (vô′lō′vän′), *n.* [Fr., lit., flight in the wind], a baked pastry shell of puff paste, filled with a stew of chicken, game, fish, etc.

vol·can·ic (vol-kan′ik), *adj.* [Fr. *volcanique;* It. *volcanico*], 1. of, thrown from, caused by, or characteristic of a volcano. 2. having, or composed of, volcanoes. 3. like a volcano; violently and powerfully explosive or capable of explosion. Abbreviated **vol.**

vol·can·i·cal·ly (vol-kan′i-k'l-i, vol-kan′ik-li), *adv.* in the manner of a volcano; by volcanic action.

volcanic glass, natural glass, as obsidian, formed by the very rapid cooling of molten lava.

vol·can·ic·i·ty (vol′kə-nis′ə-ti), *n.* [Fr. *volcanicité*], the quality or state of being volcanic; volcanic activity.

vol·can·ism (vol′kə-niz'm), *n.* [Fr. *volcanisme*], volcanic action or phenomena.

vol·can·ist (vol′kə-nist), *n.* [Fr. *volcaniste*], a student of or specialist in volcanoes and their phenomena.

vol·can·ize (vol′kə-nīz′), *v.t.* [VOLCANIZED (-nīzd′), VOLCANIZING], to subject to, or change by, volcanic heat.

vol·ca·no (vol-kā′nō), *n.* [*pl.* VOLCANOES, VOLCANOS (-nōz)], [It. < L. *Volcanus*, Vulcan, the god of fire], 1. a vent in the earth's crust through which rocks, dust, and ash, or molten rock in the form of liquid magma are ejected: a volcano is *active* while erupting, *dormant* during a long period of inactivity, or *extinct* when all activity has finally ceased. 2. a cone-shaped hill or mountain, wholly or chiefly of volcanic materials, built up around the vent. Abbreviated **vol.**

Volcano Islands, three Japanese islands in the western Pacific, including Iwo Jima.

vol·can·o·log·i·cal (vol′kə-nə-loj′i-k'l), *adj.* of or having to do with volcanology.

vol·can·ol·o·gy (vol′kə-nol′ə-ji), *n.* [*volcano* + *-logy*], the science dealing with volcanoes and volcanic phenomena: also **vulcanology.**

vole (vōl), *n.* [abbrev. < *vole mouse; vole* (Norw. *vold, voll*), a field < ON. *vǫllr;* akin to Eng. *weald, wold*, G. *wald*, etc.], any of several burrowing rodents of the mouse and rat family, including the European field mouse and the North American meadow mouse.

vole (vōl), *n.* [Fr.; prob. < *voler* (L. *volare*), to fly], in *card games*, the winning of all the tricks in a deal; slam. *v.i.* [VOLED (vōld), VOLING], to win all the tricks in a deal.

go the vole, to risk everything for great gain.

vol·er·y (vol′ẽr-i), *n.* [*pl.* VOLERIES (-iz)], [Fr. *volerie*, a flying < *voler*, to fly; L. *volare*], 1. a place where birds are raised or kept; aviary. 2. [Rare], the birds in an aviary.

Vol·ga (vol′gə; Russ. vôl′gä), *n.* a river in the European U.S.S.R., flowing into the Caspian: length, 2,300 mi.

vol·i·tant (vol′ə-tənt), *adj.* [L. *volitans*, ppr. of *volitare*, to fly to and fro, freq. of *volare*, to fly], 1. flying, flitting, or constantly in motion. 2. capable of flight.

vol·i·ta·tion (vol′ə-tā′shən), *n.* [ML. *volitatio* < L. *volitare;* see VOLITANT], 1. the act of flying; flight. 2. ability to fly.

vo·li·tion (vō-lish′ən), *n.* [Fr.; ML. *volitio* < L. *volo*, pres. indic.. of *velle*, to be willing, to will], 1. act of willing; exercise of the will. 2. settlement of vacillation or deliberation by a decision or choice; determination by the will. 3. the power of willing. —*SYN.* see **will.**

vo·li·tion·al (vō-lish′ən-'l), *adj.* 1. of, belonging to, or proceeding from volition. 2. having or exercising the power of volition.

vo·li·tion·al·ly (vō-lish′ən-'l-i), *adv.* by volition; by the will.

vol·i·tive (vol′ə-tiv), *adj.* [ML. *volitivus* < L. *volo;* see VOLITION], 1. of or arising from the will. 2. in *grammar*, expressing a wish, as a verb, mood, etc.

‡**Volk** (fôlk), *n.* [G.], a folk; people; nation.

‡**Volks·lied** (fôlks′lēt′), *n.* [*pl.* VOLKSLIEDER (-lē′dẽr)], [G.], a folk song.

‡**Volks·sturm** (fôlks′shtoorm′), *n.* [G.], in *Nazi Germany*, a home guard army formed toward the end of World War II of men and boys unfit for regular military service.

vol·ley (vol′i), *n.* [*pl.* VOLLEYS (-iz)], [Fr. *volée* < *voler* (L. *volare*), to fly], 1. the simultaneous discharge of a number of firearms or other weapons. 2. the bullets, arrows, stones, etc. so discharged. 3. a burst or shooting forth of a number of things simultaneously or in quick succession: as, a *volley* of curses. 4. in *cricket*, a ball bowled so as to hit the wicket before touching the ground. 5. in *soccer*, a kick at a ball in play before it touches the ground. 6. in *tennis*, *a*) the flight of a ball in play before it touches the ground. *b*) a return of the ball before it touches the ground. *v.t. & v.i.* [VOLLEYED (-id), VOLLEYING], 1. to discharge or be discharged in or as in a volley. 2. in *sports*, to return (a ball) before it touches the ground.

vol·ley·ball (vol′i-bôl′), *n.* 1. a game played on a court by two teams who hit a large, light, inflated ball back and forth over a high net with the hands, each team trying to return the ball before it touches the ground. 2. the ball used in this game.

Vo·log·da (vô′lôg-dä), *n.* 1. a region in the R.S.F.S.R., in north central European Russia: pop., 1,662,000. 2. its capital: pop., 95,000.

vo·lost (vō′lost), *n.* [Russ. *volost'*], 1. formerly, a small administrative district of peasants in czarist Russia. 2. a rural soviet in the Soviet Union.

vol·plane (vol′plān′), *v.i.* [VOLPLANED (-plānd′), VOLPLANING], [Fr. *vol plané; vol*, flight < *voler* (L. *volare*), to fly + *plané*, pp. of *planer*, to glide < *plan*, a level surface; L. *planus*], to glide down with the engine cut off: said of an airplane or the pilot maneuvering it. *n.* such a glide.

Vol·sci (vol′sī), *n.pl.* [L.], an ancient people of Latium who were conquered by the Romans in the 4th century B.C.

Vol·scian (vol′shən), *adj.* of the Volsci. *n.* any of the Volsci.

Vol·stead·ism (vol′sted-iz'm), *n.* [after Rep. Andrew J. *Volstead* (1860–1947), who introduced the act], the policy of prohibiting the sale of intoxicating liquors or the enforcement of this policy by an act of Congress passed in 1919 and repealed in 1933.

Vol·sun·ga Saga (vol′sooŋ-gə), [ON. *Völsunga saga*, lit., saga of the Volsungs, the descendants of **Volsi*, a legendary king], an Icelandic saga relating the legend of Sigurd and the Nibelungs: it is also told, with variations, in a Germanic version, the Nibelungenlied.

volt (vōlt), *n.* [Fr. *volte;* It. *volta*, a turn < L. *volta*, fem. pp. of *volvere*, to roll, turn about or around], 1. a turning movement or gait of a horse, in which it moves sideways around a center. 2. in *fencing*, a leap to avoid a thrust.

volt (vōlt), *n.* [after Alessandro *Volta*], the unit of electromotive force, being that electromotive force, or potential difference, which will cause a current of one ampere to flow through a conductor whose resistance is one ohm: abbreviated **V, v** (no period).

Vol·ta (vol′tə), *n.* a river in the Gold Coast, western Africa, flowing into the Bight of Benin: length, 250 mi.: it is formed by the confluence of the *Black Volta* (c. 540 mi. long) and the *White Volta*.

vol·ta (vol′tə; It. vôl′tä), *n.* [*pl.* VOLTE (-tā)], [It., a turn, fem. pp. of *volvere*, to turn], in *music*, a turn; time: used in directions, as, *una volta*, once.

vol·ta- (vol′tə), [cf. VOLTAIC], in *electricity*, a combining form meaning *voltaic*, as in *voltaelectric*.

Vol·ta, Count **A·les·san·dro** (ä′le-sän′drô vôl′tä), 1745–1827; Italian physicist.

vol·ta·e·lec·tric (vol′tə-i-lek′trik), *adj.* of voltaic electricity.

volt·age (vōl′tij), *n.* [see -AGE], in *electricity*, electromotive force, or difference in electrical potential, expressed in volts.

vol·ta·ic (vol-tā′ik), *adj.* [< Alessandro *Volta* + *-ic;* cf. VOLT (unit)], 1. *a*) designating or of electricity produced by chemical action. *b*) used in producing electricity by chemical action. 2. designating or of electricity that moves in a current, as distinguished from static electricity. 3. [V-], of or relating to Alessandro Volta.

voltaic battery, in *electricity*, 1. a battery composed of voltaic cells. 2. a voltaic cell.

voltaic cell, in *electricity*, a device for producing an electric current by the action of two plates of different metals in an electrolyte.

voltaic couple, two dissimilar metallic plates acting in an electrolyte to produce an electric current.

Vol·taire (vol-târ′; Fr. vôl′târ′), *n.* (born *François Marie Arouet*), French satirist, philosopher, dramatist, and historian: lived 1694–1778.

vol·ta·ism (vol′tə-iz'm), *n.* [< *Volta* (cf. VOLTAIC) + *-ism*], voltaic electricity or the branch of electrical science dealing with this.

vol·tam·e·ter (vol-tam′ə-tẽr), *n.* [< *voltaic* + *-meter*], in *physics*, an instrument used to measure the amount of electricity passing through a conductor by the amount of electrolysis produced.

vol·ta·met·ric (vol′tə-met′rik), *adj.* in *physics*, of a voltameter or its use in the measurement of electricity.

volt·am·me·ter (vōlt′am′mē′tẽr), *n.* in *physics*, an instrument for measuring voltage and amperage; wattmeter.

volt-am·pere (vōlt′am′pêr), *n.* a unit of electrical measurement equal to the product of one volt and one ampere: in a direct current it is equal to one watt.

‡**volte-face** (vôlt′fās′; Eng. volt′fās′, vol′tə-fās′), *n.* [Fr.; It. *volta faccia; volta*, a turn + *faccia*, a face], 1. a turn so as to face the opposite way; about-face. 2. a complete reversal of opinion, attitude, etc.

vol·ti (vôl′tē), *v. imperative* [It.], in *music*, turn (the page): a direction to the performer.

volt·me·ter (vōlt′mē′tẽr), *n.* [*volt* (unit) + *-meter*], in *electricity*, an instrument for measuring an electromotive force, or a difference in electrical potential, by volts.

Vol·tur·no (vôl-tōōr′nô), *n.* a river in central Italy, flowing from the Apennines into the Tyrrhenian Sea: length, 110 mi.

vol·u·bil·i·ty (vol′yoo-bil′ə-ti), *n.* [< Fr. or L.; Fr. *volubilité;* L. *volubilitas*], a voluble quality or state.

vol·u·ble (vol′yoo-b'l), *adj.* [Fr.; L. *volubilis*, easily turned about < *volutus*, pp. of *volvere*, to roll, turn about or around], 1. characterized by a great flow of words or fluency of speech; talkative, glib, garrulous, etc. 2. [Rare], rolling easily on an axis; rotating. 3. in *botany*, twining or twisting, as a vine. —*SYN.* see **talkative.**

vol·u·bly (vol′yoo-bli), *adv.* in a voluble manner; glibly; garrulously.

vol·ume (vol′yoom), *n.* [ME.; OFr.; L. *volumen*, a roll, scroll, hence a book written on a parchment < *volutus*, pp. of *volvere*, to roll], 1. originally, a roll of parchment, a scroll, etc. 2. *a*) a collection of written, typewritten, or printed sheets bound together; book. *b*) one of the books in a set or a complete work. 3. the amount of space occupied in three dimensions; cubic contents or cubic magnitude. 4. a quantity, bulk, mass, or amount. 5. a large quantity; bulk, amount, etc. 6. the quantity, strength, or loudness of sound; hence, 7. in *music*, fullness of tone. Abbreviated **v.**, **vol.** —*SYN.* see **bulk**.

speak volumes, to be very expressive or meaningful.

vo·lu·me·ter (və-lo͞o′mə-tẽr, və-lū′mə-tẽr), *n.* [< *volume* + *-meter*], in *physics*, an instrument used to measure the volume of liquids and gases directly, and of solids by the amount of liquid they displace.

vol·u·met·ric (vol′yoo-met′rik), *adj.* [< *volume* + *metric*], of or based on the measurement of volume.

vol·u·met·ri·cal (vol′yoo-met′ri-k'l), *adj.* volumetric.

vol·u·met·ri·cal·ly (vol′yoo-met′ri-k'l-i, vol′yoo-met′-rik-li), *adv.* in a volumetric manner; by volumetric means.

volumetric analysis, the quantitative analysis of a chemical solution by determining the amount of reagent necessary to effect a reaction in a known volume of the solution.

vo·lu·me·try (və-lo͞o′mə-tri, və-lū′mə-tri), *n.* 1. the measurement of volumes. 2. volumetric analysis.

vo·lu·mi·nos·i·ty (və-lo͞o′mə-nos′ə-ti, və-lū′mə-nos′ə-ti), *n.* the state or quality of being voluminous.

vo·lu·mi·nous (və-lo͞o′mə-nəs, və-lū′mə-nəs), *adj.* [LL. *voluminosus*, full of rolls or folds < *volumen*; see VOLUME], 1. writing, producing, consisting of, or forming such a mass of material as to fill volumes. 2. of great volume; large; bulky; full. 3. [Rare or Archaic], characterized by many coils or windings.

vol·un·tar·i·ly (vol′ən-ter′ə-li, vol′ən-târ′ə-li), *adv.* in a voluntary manner; of one's own free will; freely.

vol·un·tar·i·ness (vol′ən-ter′i-nis), *n.* the quality or state of being voluntary.

vol·un·ta·rism (vol′ən-tə-riz'm), *n.* in *philosophy*, any theory which holds that reality is ultimately of the nature of will or that the will is the primary factor in experience.

vol·un·ta·ris·tic (vol′ən-tə-ris′tik), *adj.* of, having the nature of, or adhering to voluntarism.

vol·un·tar·y (vol′ən-ter′i), *adj.* [ME. *voluntarie;* L. *voluntarius*, voluntary < *voluntas*, free will < *volo*, I wish, pres. indic., of *velle*, to be willing, to will], 1. brought about by one's own free choice; given or done of one's own free will; freely chosen or undertaken. 2. acting in a specified capacity willingly or of one's own accord. 3. intentional; not accidental: as, *voluntary* manslaughter. 4. controlled by the will: as, *voluntary* muscles. 5. able to will; having the power of free decision: as, man is a *voluntary* agent. 6. supported by contributions or freewill offerings; not supported or maintained by the state: as, *voluntary* churches. 7. arising in the mind without external constraint; spontaneous. 8. in *law*, *a*) acting or done without compulsion or persuasion. *b*) done without profit, payment, or any valuable consideration. *n.* [*pl.* VOLUNTARIES (-iz)], 1. a voluntary act or piece of work. 2. in *music*, a piece or solo, often an improvisation, played on the organ before, during, or after a church service.

SYN.—**voluntary** implies the exercise of one's own free choice or will in an action, whether or not external influences are at work (*voluntary* services); **intentional** applies to that which is done on purpose for a definite reason and is in no way accidental (an *intentional* slight); **deliberate** implies full realization of the significance of what one intends to do and of its effects (a *deliberate* lie); **willful** implies obstinate and perverse determination to follow one's own will despite influences, arguments, advice, etc. in opposition (a *willful* refusal).

vol·un·tar·y·ism (vol′ən-ter′i-iz'm), *n.* 1. the doctrine that churches, schools, etc. should be supported by voluntary contributions and not by the state. 2. a system based on this principle.

vol·un·teer (vol′ən-têr′), *n.* [Fr. *volontaire*, a voluntary], 1. a person who enters or offers to enter into any service of his own free will. 2. a person who enters naval or military service of his own free will, without being compelled to do so by law: opposed to *conscript*, *draftee*. 3. in *law*, *a*) a person who enters into any transaction of his own free will. *b*) a person to whom property is transferred without valuable consideration. *adj.* 1. composed of volunteers, as an army. 2. serving as a volunteer. 3. of a volunteer or volunteers. 4. voluntary. 5. in *botany*, growing from self-sown or naturally fallen seed. *v.t.* to offer or give of one's own free will. *v.i.* to enter or offer to enter into any service of one's own free will; enlist. Abbreviated **Vol.**

Volunteers of America, an organization, somewhat like the Salvation Army, established in 1896 to bring religious and material help to those who need it.

vo·lup·tu·ar·y (və-lup′cho͞o-er′i), *n.* [*pl.* VOLUPTUARIES (-iz)], [L. *voluptuarius* < *voluptas*, pleasure], a person devoted to luxurious living and sensual pleasures; sensualist; sybarite. *adj.* of or characterized by luxury and sensual pleasures.

vo·lup·tu·ous (və-lup′cho͞o-əs), *adj.* [ME. *voluptuouse;* OFr. *voluptueux;* L. *voluptuosus*, full of pleasure < *voluptas*, pleasure], 1. full of, producing, or characterized by sensual delights and pleasures; sensual. 2. fond of or directed toward luxury, elegance, and the pleasures of the senses. 3. suggesting or expressing sensual pleasure or gratification. 4. arising from sensual gratification. —*SYN.* see **sensuous.**

vo·lute (və-lo͞ot′, və-lūt′), *n.* [Fr.; It. *voluta;* L. *voluta*, orig., fem. of *volutus*, pp. of *volvere*, to roll], 1. in *architecture*, a spiral scroll forming one of the chief features of Ionic and Corinthian capitals. 2. a spiral or twisting form; turn; whorl. 3. in *zoology*, any of the turns or whorls of a spiral shell. *adj.* 1. rolled up; spiraled. 2. in *machinery*, *a*) having a spirally shaped part. *b*) having a combined circular and lateral motion.

vo·lut·ed (və-lo͞ot′id, və-lūt′id), *adj.* 1. grooved or twisted in spirals. 2. in *architecture*, having a volute.

vo·lu·tion (və-lo͞o′shən, və-lū′shən), *n.* [< L. *volutus;* see VOLUTE], 1. a revolving; rolling. 2. a spiral turn or twist; coil; convolution. 3. a whorl of a spiral shell.

vol·va (vol′və), *n.* [L.], the membranous covering enclosing some mushrooms in the early stage of growth.

vol·vu·lus (vol′vyoo-ləs), *n.* [Mod. L. < L. *volvere*, to roll, turn], intestinal obstruction caused by a twisting or displacement of the intestines.

vo·mer (vō′mẽr), *n.* [L., plowshare], in *anatomy*, a thin, flat bone forming part of the nasal septum separating the nasal passages.

vo·mer·ine (vō′mẽr-in, vom′ẽr-in), *adj.* of the vomer.

vom·i·ca (vom′i-kə), *n.* [L., ulcer, abscess < *vomere*, to vomit], 1. a pus-filled cavity in some organ, especially the lungs. 2. the pus in such a cavity. 3. the coughing up of such pus in profuse quantities.

vom·it (vom′it), *n.* [ME.; L. *vomitus*, a discharging, vomiting < *vomitus*, pp. of *vomere*, to discharge, vomit], 1. the act or process of ejecting the contents of the stomach through the mouth. 2. matter ejected in this way. 3. a drug which causes vomiting; emetic. *v.i.* 1. to eject the contents of the stomach through the mouth; throw up. 2. to be thrown up or out with force or violence; rush out. *v.t.* 1. to throw up, as food. 2. to discharge or throw out with force or in copious quantities; belch forth.

vom·i·tive (vom′i-tiv), *adj.* of or causing vomiting; emetic. *n.* an emetic.

vom·i·to (vom′i-tō′; Sp. vô′mē-tô′), *n.* [Sp.; L. *vomitus*], 1. the black vomit of yellow fever. 2. yellow fever.

vom·i·to·ry (vom′i-tôr′i, vom′i-tō′ri), *adj.* [L. *vomitorius*], vomitive; emetic. *n.* [*pl.* VOMITORIES (-iz, -riz)], 1. an emetic. 2. any opening, funnel, etc. through which matter is to be discharged. 3. in Roman amphitheaters, etc., any of the entrances leading to the tiers of seats.

vom·i·tu·ri·tion (vom′i-choo-rish′ən), *n.* 1. repeated but unsuccessful attempts to vomit; retching. 2. vomiting that brings up but little matter.

‡**von** (fôn; Eng. von), *prep.* [G.], of; from: a prefix occurring in many names of German and Austrian families, especially of the nobility: abbreviated **v.**

voo·doo (vo͞o′do͞o), *n.* [*pl.* VOODOOS (-do͞oz)], [Creole Fr. < a W.Afr. word], 1. a body of primitive rites and practices, based on a belief in sorcery and in the power of charms, fetishes, etc., found among natives of the West Indies and in the southern United States, and ultimately of African origin. 2. a person who practices these rites. 3. a voodoo charm, fetish, etc. *adj.* of voodoos or voodooism. *v.t.* to affect by voodoo magic. Cf. **hoodoo.**

voo·doo·ism (vo͞o′do͞o-iz'm), *n.* the system of voodoo beliefs and practices.

voo·doo·is·tic (vo͞o′do͞o-is′tik), *adj.* of or like voodoo.

vo·ra·cious (vô-rā′shəs, vō-rā′shəs), *adj.* < [L. *vorax*, *voracis*, greedy to devour < *vorare*, to devour], 1. greedy in eating; devouring or eager to devour large quantities of food; ravenous; gluttonous. 2. very greedy or eager in some desire or pursuit; insatiable: as, a *voracious* reader.

vo·rac·i·ty (vô-ras′ə-ti, vō-ras′ə-ti), *n.* [Fr. *voracité;* L. *voracitas*, hungriness < *vorax, voracis;* see VORACIOUS], the quality or condition of being voracious.

Vo·ro·nezh (vô-rô′nesh), *n.* 1. a region in the R.S.F.S.R., in south central European Russia: pop., 3,363,000. 2. its capital, on the Don River: pop., 454,000.

Vo·ro·shi·lov, Kle·ment E·fre·mo·vich (klĕ′myent ye-fryem′ô-vich vô-rô-shē′lôf; Eng. vor′ə-shē′lov), 1881- ; Soviet Russian general; president of the U.S.S.R. (1953–1960).

Vo·ro·shi·lov·grad (vô′rô-shē′lôf-grät′), *n.* a city in the eastern Ukrainian S.S.R.: pop., 274,000: former name, *Lugansk*.

-vo·rous (vẽr-əs), [L. *-vorus* < *vorare*, to devour], a combining form meaning *feeding on*, *eating*, as in *omnivorous*, *carnivorous*.

vor·tex (vôr′teks), *n.* [*pl.* VORTEXES (-iz), VORTICES (-tə-sēz′)], [L. *vortex*, *vertex* < *vertere*, to turn, whirl], 1. a whirling mass of water forming a vacuum at its center, into which anything caught in the motion is drawn; whirlpool. 2. a whirl or powerful eddy of air;

whirlwind. 3. any activity, situation, or state of affairs that resembles a whirl or eddy in its rush, absorbing effect, irresistible and catastrophic power, etc.

vor·ti·cal (vôr′ti-k'l), *adj.* 1. of, characteristic of, or like a vortex. 2. moving in a vortex; whirling.

vor·ti·cel·la (vôr′tə-sel′ə), *n.* [*pl.* VORTICELLAE (-ē)], [Mod. L., dim. < L. *vortex;* see VORTEX], in *zoology,* a one-celled animal living in water, with a bell-shaped body on a thin stem by which it attaches itself to other objects.

vor·ti·cose (vôr′tə-kōs′), *adj.* [L. *vorticosus* < *vortex;* see VORTEX], whirling; vortical.

vor·tig·i·nous (vôr-tij′ə-nəs), *adj.* [L. *vertiginosus* < *vertigo;* see VERTIGO], 1. whirling: said of motion. 2. moving in or like a vortex.

Vor·tum·nus (vôr-tum′nəs), *n.* Vertumnus.

Vosges Mountains (vōzh), a range in northeastern France, west of the Rhine: highest peak, c. 4,700 ft.

vot·a·ble (vōt′ə-b'l), *adj.* that can be submitted to a vote; subject to a vote: also spelled **voteable.**

vo·ta·ress (vō′tə-ris), *n.* a girl or woman votary: also **votress.**

vo·ta·rist (vō′tə-rist), *n.* a votary.

vo·ta·ry (vō′tə-ri), *n.* [*pl.* VOTARIES (-riz)], [< L. *votus,* pp. of *vovere,* to vow], 1. a person bound by a vow or promise, especially one bound to religious vows, as a monk or nun. 2. a person devoted to a particular religion or a certain form of religious worship. 3. a devoted or ardent supporter, as of a cause, ideal, etc. 4. a person who is devoted to any game, study, pursuit, etc. *adj.* 1. consecrated by a vow. 2. of, or having the nature of, a vow.

vote (vōt), *n.* [L. *votum,* a wish, vow < *votum,* neut. of *votus,* pp. of *vovere,* to vow < IE. base **ewegwh-,* to speak solemnly, vow, seen also in Sans. *vāghát,* one who vows], 1. a decision by one or more persons on a proposal, resolution, bill, etc., or a choice between candidates for office, expressed by written ballot, voice, show of hands, etc. 2. *a)* the expression or indication of such a decision or choice. *b)* the ticket, ballot, voice, or any other means by which it is expressed. 3. the right to exercise such a decision or choice, as in a meeting, election, etc.; suffrage. 4. *a)* the total number of ballots cast: as, the *vote* was light. *b)* votes collectively: as, get out the *vote.* 5. [Obs.], a voter. 6. [Obs.], a vow. 7. [Obs.], a prayer. *v.i.* [VOTED (-id), VOTING], to express the will or preference in a matter by ballot, voice, etc.; give or cast a vote. *v.t.* 1. *a)* to decide, enact, or authorize by vote. *b)* to grant or confer by vote. *c)* to support (a specified party ticket) in voting. 2. to declare by general opinion: as, they *voted* the party a success. 3. [Colloq.], to suggest.

vote down, to defeat by voting; decide against.

vote in, to elect.

vote out, to defeat an incumbent in an election.

vot·er (vōt′ẽr), *n.* 1. a person who has a right to vote; elector. 2. a person who votes.

voting machine, a machine working on the principle of an adding machine, on which the votes in an election are cast, registered, and counted.

vo·tive (vō′tiv), *adj.* [L. *votivus* < *votum;* see VOTE], 1. given, dedicated, consecrated, done, etc., in fulfillment of a vow or pledge: as, *votive* offerings. 2. in the *Roman Catholic Church,* designating or of a special or extraordinary Mass said at the option of the priest.

vo·tress (vō′tris), *n.* a votaress.

Vo·tyak Autonomous Soviet Socialist Republic (vô-tyäk′), Udmurt Autonomous Soviet Socialist Republic, a division of the R.S.F.S.R.: former name.

vouch (vouch), *v.t.* [ME. *vouchen;* OFr. *voucher* < L. *vocare,* to call < *vox, vocis,* a voice], 1. to attest; give evidence for; affirm or guarantee: as, *vouch* a statement. 2. to cite or appeal to (authority, example, books, authors, etc.) in support of one's views or actions. 3. to uphold by demonstration. 4. [Archaic], to call as witness. 5. in *law,* to call (a person) into court to give warranty of title. *v.i.* 1. to give assurance, affirmation, or a guarantee (with *for*): as, his friends *vouched* for his honesty. 2. to serve as evidence or assurance (with *for*): as, his references *vouch* for his ability. *n.* [Rare or Archaic], a vouching; assertion or attestation.

vouch·er (vouch′ẽr), *n.* [substantive use of Anglo-Fr. *voucher,* to vouch], 1. a person who vouches, as for the truth of a statement. 2. a paper attesting or serving as evidence; specifically, a receipt or statement serving as evidence of payment of a debt or of the accuracy of an account. 3. in *old English law,* the summoning of a person into court to warrant another's title to a property.

vouch·safe (vouch-sāf′), *v.t.* [VOUCHSAFED (-sāft′), VOUCHSAFING], [contr. of ME. *vouchen safe,* to vouch as safe], to be gracious enough or condescend to grant: as, *vouchsafe* a reply. *v.i.* to condescend; deign.

vouch·safe·ment (vouch-sāf′mənt), *n.* 1. the act or fact of vouchsafing. 2. that which is vouchsafed.

vous·soir (vōō-swär′), *n.* [ME. *vousore;* OFr. *volsoir,* curvature of a vault; LL. **volsorium* < **volsus,* for L. *volutus,* pp. of *volvere,* to roll], in *architecture,* any of the wedge-shaped stones of which an arch or vault is built.

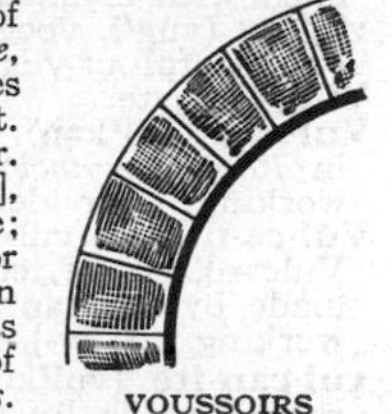

VOUSSOIRS

vow (vou), *n.* [ME. *vow, vou;* OFr. *vou, vo, veu;* L. *votum;* see VOTE], 1. a solemn promise or pledge; especially, one made to God or a god, dedicating oneself to an act, service, or way of life, such as that of a nun. 2. a promise of love and fidelity: as, marriage *vows.* 3. a solemn affirmation or assertion. *v.t.* 1. to promise solemnly. 2. to make a solemn resolution to do, get, etc. 3. to declare emphatically, earnestly, or solemnly. *v.i.* to make a vow.

take vows, to enter a religious order.

vow·el (vou′əl), *n.* [ME. *vowelle;* OFr. *vouele;* L. *vocalis* (*littera*), vocal (letter), vowel < *vox, vocis,* a voice, sound], 1. a voiced speech sound characterized by generalized friction of the air passing in a continuous stream through the pharynx and opened mouth, with relatively no narrowing or other obstruction of the speech organs. 2. a letter, as *a, e, i, o,* and *u,* representing such a sound. Distinguished from *consonant. adj.* of a vowel or vowels.

vow·el·i·za·tion (vou′əl-i-zā′shən, vou′əl-ī-zā′shən), *n.* 1. the act of vowelizing. 2. the state of being vowelized.

vow·el·ize (vou′əl-iz′), *v.t.* [VOWELIZED (-izd′), VOWELIZING], to add vowel signs or points to, as a Hebrew or Arabic text.

vowel point, in certain languages whose written form normally consists only of consonants, as Hebrew, a diacritical mark inserted above or below a consonant to indicate the following vowel sound.

‡vox (voks), *n.* [*pl.* VOCES (vō′sēz)], [L.], voice.

‡vox an·ge·li·ca (voks an-jel′i-kə), [L., lit., angelic voice], an organ stop consisting of two ranks of pipes, one tuned slightly sharper than the other so as to produce beats resulting in a wavy, tremulous tone: also called *vox caelestis, voix céleste.*

‡vox cae·les·tis (voks si-les′tis), [L., lit., heavenly voice], vox angelica.

‡vox hu·ma·na (voks hyoo-mā′nə), [L., human voice], in *music,* an organ stop producing tones like those of the human voice.

‡vox po·pu·li (voks pop′yoo-lī′), [L.], the voice of the people: abbreviated **vox pop.**

‡vox populi, vox De·i (dē′ī), [L.], the voice of the people (is) the voice of God.

voy·age (voi′ij), *n.* [ME. *viage, veage;* OFr. *veiage, voiage,* a voyage; L. *viaticum,* provision for a journey < *viaticus,* of a journey < *via,* way, journey], 1. a relatively long journey or passage by sea or other large body of water, or, formerly, by land. 2. a journey by aircraft. 3. a written account of a voyage. 4. [Obs.], a project; enterprise. *v.i.* [VOYAGED (-ijd), VOYAGING], to travel by sea, water, or air. *v.t.* to sail or travel over or on. —*SYN.* see **trip.**

voy·ag·er (voi′ij-ẽr), *n.* 1. a person who makes a voyage. 2. a person who makes a journey; traveler.

‡vo·ya·geur (vwȧ′yȧ′zhẽr′), *n.* [*pl.* VOYAGEURS (-zhẽr′)], [Fr.], 1. a traveler. 2. in Canada, *a)* a person who transports goods and men by rivers and lakes to trading posts for the fur companies. *b)* any woodsman or boatman of the Canadian wilds.

vo·yeur (vwä-yũr′), *n.* [Fr. < *voir,* to see], a person given to voyeurism; a Peeping Tom.

vo·yeur·ism (vwä-yũr′iz'm), *n.* a perversion in which sexual gratification is obtained by looking at sexual objects or scenes.

V.P., Vice-President.

v.p., passive verb.

V.R., *Victoria Regina,* [L.], Queen Victoria.

v.r., reflexive verb.

‡vrai·sem·blance (vre′sän′bläns′), *n.* [Fr.], the appearance or semblance of truth; verisimilitude.

V. Rev., Very Reverend.

Vries, Hu·go de (hü′gō də vrēs′), 1848–1935; Dutch botanist.

‡vrouw (vrou; S.Afr.D. frou), *n.* [D.], a woman; housewife: a title corresponding to *Mrs.*

vs., versus.

V.S., Veterinary Surgeon.

v.s., *vide supra,* [L.], see above.

V-shaped (vē′shāpt′), *adj.* shaped like the letter V.

Vt., Vermont.

v.t., transitive verb.

V-type engine (vē′tīp′), an engine, as a gasoline engine, in which the cylinders are set at an angle, or in two banks forming a V.

Vuel·ta A·ba·jo (vwel′tô ä-bä′hô), a region in western Cuba: famous for its tobacco production.

vug, vugg, vugh (vug, voog), *n.* [Corn. *vooga*, a cave], in *mining*, a cavity or hollow in a rock or lode, often lined with crystals.
vug·gy (vug'i, voog'i), *adj.* [VUGGIER (-i-ẽr), VUGGIEST (-i-ist)], full of vugs, or cavities: said of rock.
Vul., Vulgate.
Vul·can (vul'kən), *n.* [L. *Vulcanus, Volcanus*, Vulcan], in *Roman mythology*, the god of fire and of metalworking: later identified with the Greek Hephaestus.
Vul·ca·ni·an (vul-kā'ni-ən), *adj.* [L. *Vulcanius*, of Vulcan], 1. of, characteristic of, associated with, or made by, Vulcan. 2. [v-], having to do with metalworking. 3. [v-], in *geology, a)* volcanic. *b)* Plutonic.
vul·can·ite (vul'kən-īt'), *n.* [*Vulcan* + *-ite*], a hard rubber made by treating crude rubber with a large amount of sulfur and subjecting it to intense heat; ebonite: used in combs, electrical insulation, etc.
vul·can·i·za·tion (vul'kən-i-zā'shən, vul'kən-ī-zā'shən), *n.* [< *vulcanize* + *-ation*], the process of treating crude rubber with sulfur or its compounds and subjecting it to heat in order to make it nonplastic and increase its strength and elasticity: the degree of hardness of vulcanized rubber varies directly with the amount of sulfur used and the intensity of the heat applied.
vul·can·ize (vul'kən-īz'), *v.t.* [VULCANIZED (-īzd'), VULCANIZING], to subject to vulcanization. *v.i.* to undergo vulcanization.
vul·can·ol·o·gy (vul'kən-ol'ə-ji), *n.* volcanology.
Vulg., Vulgate.
vulg., 1. vulgar. 2. vulgarly.
vul·gar (vul'gẽr), *adj.* [ME. *vulgare;* L. *vulgaris* < *vulgus* or *volgus*, the common people], 1. of, belonging to, or common to the great mass of people in general; common; popular: as, a *vulgar* superstition. 2. designating, of, or in the popular, or vernacular, speech. 3. characterized by a lack of culture, refinement, taste, sensitivity, etc.; coarse; crude; boorish. *n.* 1. [Archaic], the common people (with *the*). 2. [Obs.], the vernacular. —***SYN.*** see **coarse, common.**
vulgar fraction, a common fraction.
vul·gar·i·an (vul-gâr'i-ən), *n.* a vulgar person; especially, a rich or well-to-do person with coarse, showy manners or tastes.
vul·gar·ism (vul'gẽr-iz'm), *n.* 1. a word, phrase, or expression occurring only in common colloquial usage or, especially, in coarse speech. 2. vulgar behavior, quality, etc.; vulgarity.
vul·gar·i·ty (vul-gar'ə-ti), *n.* [L. *vulgaritas*], 1. the state or quality of being vulgar, crude, coarse, unrefined, etc. 2. [*pl.* VULGARITIES (-tiz)], a vulgar act, habit, usage in speech or writing, etc.
vul·gar·i·za·tion (vul'gẽr-i-zā'shən, vul'gẽr-ī-zā'shən), *n.* a vulgarizing or being vulgarized.
vul·gar·ize (vul'gẽr-īz'), *v.t.* [VULGARIZED (-īzd'), VULGARIZING], to make vulgar.
Vulgar Latin, the everyday speech of the Roman people, from which the Romance languages developed; popular Latin as distinguished from standard or literary Latin.
vul·gar·ly (vul'gẽr-li), *adv.* 1. commonly; generally; popularly. 2. in a vulgar manner; in bad taste.
Vul·gate (vul'gāt, vul'git), *n.* [ML. *vulgata* (*editio*), popular (edition) < L. *vulgatus*, common, usual, orig. pp. of *vulgare*, to make common < *vulgus*, a crowd], 1. a Latin version of the Bible prepared by St. Jerome in the 4th century, serving as the authorized version of the Roman Catholic Church. 2. [v-], any text or version in common acceptance. *adj.* 1. of or in the Vulgate. 2. [v-], commonly accepted; popular. Abbreviated **Vul., Vulg.**
vul·ner·a·bil·i·ty (vul'nẽr-ə-bil'ə-ti) *n.* the quality or condition of being vulnerable.
vul·ner·a·ble (vul'nẽr-ə-b'l), *adj.* [LL. *vulnerabilis*, wounding, likely to injure; also, in pass. sense, vulnerable < L. *vulnerare*, to wound < *vulnus, vulneris*, a wound], 1. that can be wounded or physically injured. 2. open to criticism or attack: as, a *vulnerable* reputation. 3. open to attack or assault by armed forces: as, the Maginot line proved to be *vulnerable*. 4. in *contract bridge*, liable to an increased penalty if defeated or to an increased bonus if successful: said of a team which has won one game.
vul·ner·a·bly (vul'nẽr-ə-bli), *adv.* so as to be vulnerable.
vul·ner·ar·y (vul'nẽr-er'i), *adj.* [L. *vulnerarius* < *vulnus, vulneris*, a wound], used for healing wounds. *n.* [*pl.* VULNERARIES (-iz)], any vulnerary drug, plant, etc.
Vul·pec·u·la (vul-pek'yoo-lə), *n.* [L., dim. of *vulpes*, a fox], in *astronomy*, the Little Fox, a small northern constellation between Cygnus and Aquila: see **constellation**, chart.
Vulpecula cum An·ser·e (kum an'sə-rē'), [L.; *vulpecula*, dim. of *vulpes*, a fox + *cum*, with + *ansere*, abl. of *anser*, a goose], in *astronomy*, the Little Fox with the Goose: a name sometimes used for the constellation Vulpecula.
vul·pec·u·lar (vul-pek'yoo-lẽr), *adj.* [< L. *vulpecula*, dim. of *vulpes*, a fox; + *-ar*], of a fox, especially a young one; vulpine.
vul·pi·cide (vul'pə-sīd'), *n.* [< L. *vulpes*, a fox + *caedere*, to kill], [British], 1. the killing of a fox by some means other than hunting it with hounds. 2. a person who does this.
vul·pine (vul'pīn, vul'pin), *adj.* [L. *vulpinus*, foxlike < *vulpes*, a fox], 1. of a fox or foxes. 2. like a fox; foxy; clever; cunning; tricky.
vul·ture (vul'chẽr), *n.* [ME. *voutur, volture, vultur;* OFr. *voutour, voltour;* L. *vultur*], 1. any of a number of large birds of prey related to the eagles and hawks, with naked and usually brightly colored heads and dark plumage: vultures live on carrion and are found in tropical and temperate regions. 2. any greedy and ruthless person who preys on others.

VULTURE
(2 1/2 ft. long)

vul·tur·ine (vul'chẽr-īn', vul'chẽr-in), *adj.* [L. *vulturinus* < *vultur*, a vulture], 1. of the vulture family. 2. of, characteristic of, or like a vulture or vultures.
vul·tur·ous (vul'chẽr-əs), *adj.* like a vulture; preying; ravenous.
vul·va (vul'və), *n.* [L. *vulva, volva*, wrapper, covering, womb < *volvere*, to roll or turn about], the external genital organs of the female, including the labia majora, labia minora, clitoris, and the entrance to the vagina.
vul·val (vul'v'l), *adj.* of the vulva.
vul·vi·form (vul'və-fôrm'), *adj.* like a vulva in form or appearance.
vul·vo- (vul'vō, vul'və), [< L. *vulva*, a covering, womb], a combining form meaning: 1. *vulva.* 2. *vulva and.* Also, **vulv-.**
vv., 1. verses. 2. violins.
v.v., vice versa.
vv. ll., *variae lectiones*, [L.], variant readings.
Vyat·ka (vyät'kä), *n.* 1. a river in east central European R.S.F.S.R., flowing into the Kama River: length, 875 mi. 2. Kirov, a city on this river: former name.
Vyer·nyi (vyer'ni), *n.* Alma-Ata: the former name.
vy·ing (vī'iŋ), *adj.* [ppr. of *vie*], that vies; that competes.

W, w (dub''l-yoo), *n.* [*pl.* W's, w's, Ws, ws], 1. the twenty-third letter of the English alphabet: its sound was represented in Anglo-Saxon manuscripts by uu or u until about 900 A.D., then by ƿ (*wen*) borrowed from the runic alphabet, or sometimes by wu, v, wo, vo, uo, or o. In the 11th century a ligatured VV or vv was introduced by Norman scribes to replace the *wen.* 2. the sound of W or w: in English, it is a lip-rounded tongue-back semivowel like a quickly cut-off o͞o at the beginning of words; concluding a diphthong it is a *u*-glide. Before r, as in *wrist*, and in some words, as *answer, sword, two*, it is silent. 3. a type or impression of W or w. 4. *a symbol for* the twenty-third in a sequence or group (or the twenty-second if J is omitted).

adj. 1. of W or w. 2. twenty-third (or twenty-second if J is omitted) in a sequence or group.
W, 1. watt; watts. 2. west. 3. in *chemistry, the symbol for* tungsten (wolfram).
w, watt; watts.
W., 1. Wales. 2. Washington. 3. Wednesday. 4. Welsh. 5. Western.
W., w., 1. warden. 2. warehouse. 3. watt; watts. 4. weight. 5. west. 6. western. 7. width. 8. in *physics,* work.
w., 1. week; weeks. 2. wide. 3. wife. 4. with. 5. won.
wa' (wô, wä), *n.* [Scot.], wall.
W.A., 1. West Africa. 2. Western Australia.
WAAC, W.A.A.C., 1. Women's Auxiliary Army Corps: replaced by WAC. 2. [British], Women's Army Auxiliary Corps.
Waadt (vät), *n.* Vaud, Switzerland: the German name.
Waaf (waf), *n.* in Great Britain, a member of the Women's Auxiliary Air Force: also written **WAAF, W.A.A.F.**
Waal (wäl), *n.* a branch of the Rhine River, flowing through the Netherlands.
Waals, Jo·han·nes Di·de·rik van der (yô-hä'nəs dē'də-rik vän dẽr våls'), 1837–1923; Dutch physicist; received Nobel prize in physics, 1910.
Wa·bash (wô'bash), *n.* a river in Ohio, Indiana, and Illinois flowing into the Ohio River: length, 475 mi.
wab·ble (wäb''l), *n., v.i. & v.t.* [WABBLED (-'ld), WABBLING], wobble.
wab·ble (wäb''l), *n.* [var. of *warble* (tumor)], the larva of a botfly which is parasitic on squirrels.
wab·bly (wäb'li), *adj.* [WABBLIER (-li-ẽr), WABBLIEST (-li-ist)], wobbly.
Wac (wak), *n.* a member of the Women's Army Corps.
WAC, W.A.C., the Women's Army Corps.
Wace, Robert (wās, wäs), 12th century; Anglo-Norman chronicler and poet.
wack (wak), *n.* [see WACKY], [Slang], a person whose behavior is eccentric, erratic, or so irrational as to seem crazy.
wack·e (wak'ə), *n.* [G.; OHG. *wacko,* earlier *waggo,* gravel, stone], a rock like sandstone in texture, resulting from the disintegration of volcanic rock.
wack·y (wak'i), *adj.* [WACKIER (-i-ẽr), WACKIEST (-i-ist)], [? < *whack* (a blow) + *-y;* cf. SLAP-HAPPY], [Slang], erratic, eccentric, or irrational: also **whacky.**
Wa·co (wā'kō), *n.* a city in central Texas: pop., 98,000.
wad (wäd, wôd), *n.* [in sense 1, akin to D., G. *watte,* Sw. *vadd;* the Eng. word is formally akin to the Sw.; ult. origin prob. non-IE.], 1. *a)* a small, soft mass, as a handful of cotton, crumpled paper, etc. *b)* [British Dial.], a bundle, especially a small one, as of straw or hay. 2. a lump or small, compact mass of something: as, a *wad* of chewing tobacco. 3. a mass of soft or fibrous material used for padding, packing, stuffing, etc. 4. a plug of hemp, tow, paper, etc., stuffed against a charge to keep it firmly in the breech of a muzzle-loading gun or in a cartridge. 5. [Colloq.], a roll of paper money; hence, 6. [Slang], a stock of wealth or money. *v.t.* [WADDED (-id), WADDING], 1. to compress into a wad. 2. to roll up into a wad, as paper. 3. to plug or stuff with a wad. 4. to line or pad with or as with wadding. 5. to hold (a charge) in place by a wad, as in a gun or cartridge.
wad (wäd; *unstressed* wəd), *v.* [Scot.], would.
Wa·dai (wä-dī'), *n.* a former independent sultanate of the Sudan: now the eastern part of Chad, on the southeastern border of the Sahara.
wad·der (wäd'ẽr, wôd'ẽr), *n.* a person or thing that wads.
wad·ding (wäd'iŋ, wôd'iŋ), *n.* 1. any soft or fibrous material for use in padding, packing, stuffing, etc.; especially, cotton made up into loose, fluffy sheets, or batting. 2. any soft material for making wads, as for guns or cartridges. 3. *a)* wads collectively. *b)* a wad.
wad·dle (wäd''l, wôd''l), *v.i.* [WADDLED (-'ld), WADDLING], [freq. of *wade*], 1. to walk with short steps and a swaying motion from side to side, as a duck. 2. to move clumsily with a motion like this; toddle, as a baby. *n.* 1. the act of waddling. 2. a waddling gait or movement.
wad·dy (wäd'i, wôd'i), *adj.* like a wad.
wad·dy (wäd'i), *n.* [*pl.* WADDIES (-iz)], [< the native name in Australia], in Australia, 1. a short, thick club used by aborigines as a weapon. 2. a walking stick; cane. *v.t.* [WADDIED (-id), WADDYING], to strike or beat with a waddy.
wade (wād), *v.i.* [WADED (-id), WADING], [ME. *waden;* AS. *waden,* to go; akin to G. *waten,* to wade; IE. base **wādh-,* to go, stride forward, as also in L. *vadere,* to go (cf. VADE MECUM), *vadare,* to wade], 1. to walk through any substance, as water, mud, snow, sand, tall grass, etc., that offers resistance. 2. to go forward with effort or difficulty: as, *wade* through a dull book. 3. [Obs.], to go; proceed; pass. *v.t.* to go across or through by wading: as, *wade* the brook. *n.* 1. an act of wading. 2. a place to be waded; ford.
wade in (or **into**), [Colloq.], to begin energetically; attack with vigor.
wad·er (wād'ẽr), *n.* 1. a person or thing that wades. 2. any of several long-legged shore birds that wade the shallows and marshes for food, as the crane, heron, rail, coot, sandpiper, and snipe. 3. *pl.* high waterproof boots; hip boats.
wa·di (wä'di), *n.* [*pl.* WADIS, WADIES (-diz)], [Ar. *wādī,* channel of a river, a river, ravine, valley], in Arabia, northern Africa, etc., 1. a valley, ravine, or watercourse that is dry except during the rainy season. 2. the stream or rush of water that flows through it. 3. an oasis. Also spelled **wady.**
Wa·di Hal·fa (wä'di häl'fə), a city in the northern Sudan: pop., 11,000.
wad·na (wäd'nə), [Scot.], would not.
wad·set (wäd'set'), *n.* [Scot. (MScot. *wedsett*); *wad,* a pledge + *set,* to place], in *Scots law,* the pledge of land, etc. as security for a debt; mortgage. *v.t.* [WADSETTED (-id), WADSETTING], to put in pledge; mortgage.
wad·set·ter (wäd'set'ẽr), *n.* in *Scots law,* the receiver of a wadset.
wa·dy (wä'di), *n.* [*pl.* WADIES (-diz)], a wadi.
wae (wā), *n.* [Scot. & N. Eng. Dial.], woe; sorrow.
wae·sucks (wā'suks), *interj.* [Scot. *wae,* woe + *sucks,* sakes; see SAKE, *n.*], [Scot. & N. Eng. Dial.], alas!
Waf (waf), *n.* a member of the WAF.
waf (waf, wäf), *adj. & n.* [Scot.], waff (worthless, etc.).
WAF, Women in the Air Force.
Wafd (wäft), *n.* [Ar., a deputation], in Egypt, an extreme Nationalist party formed by Saad Zaghlul Pasha in 1919.
wa·fer (wā'fẽr), *n.* [ME. *wafre;* OFr. *waufre;* D. *wafel,* a wafer, waffle (cf. WAFFLE); for IE. base see WEAVE], 1. a thin, flat, crisp cracker or cake; hence, 2. anything resembling this. 3. a thin cake of unleavened bread used in the Eucharist, as in the Roman Catholic Church. 4. a small adhesive disk, as of dried paste, gelatin, or the like, used as a seal on letters, documents, etc. 5. a thin, flat disk or piece of candy. *v.t.* to seal, close, attach, or fasten with a wafer or wafers (sense 4).
waff (waf, wäf), *n.* [var. of *wave*], [Scot. & N. Eng. Dial.], 1. a wave, or waving motion, as in signaling. 2. a puff, whiff, or gust, as of air. 3. a glimpse. 4. a ghost; wraith. *v.t. & v.i.* [Scot.], to wave.
waff (waf, wäf), *adj.* [var. of *waif*], [Scot.], 1. worthless. 2. solitary. *n.* [Scot.], a vagabond. Also spelled **waf.**
waf·fle (wäf''l, wôf''l), *n.* [D. *wafel*], a batter cake cooked in a waffle iron: it is crisper than a pancake.
waffle iron, a utensil for cooking waffles, having two flat, studded plates, now usually of aluminum, pressed together so that the waffle bakes between them.
W. Afr., 1. West Africa. 2. West African.
WAFS, W.A.F.S., Women's Auxiliary Ferrying Squadron.
waft (waft, wäft), *v.t.* [back-formation < obs. *wafter,* a convoy; D. *wachter,* lit., a watcher], 1. to carry or propel lightly over water or through the air, as objects, sounds, odors, etc. 2. to transport as if in this manner. 3. [altered < dial. *waff,* to wave], [Obs.], to beckon or signal to, as by a wave of the hand. 4. [Obs.], to turn (the eyes). *v.i.* 1. to float, as on the wind. 2. to blow gently: said of breezes. *n.* 1. the act or fact of floating or being carried lightly along. 2. an odor, sound, etc. carried through the air. 3. a breath or gust of wind. 4. a wave, waving, or wafting movement. 5. in *nautical usage,* a waif (sense 5).
waft (waft, wäft), *n.* [Scot.], weft.
waft·age (waf'tij, wäf'tij), *n.* [see -AGE], [Archaic], a wafting or being wafted; conveyance by wafting.
waft·er (waf'tẽr, wäf'tẽr), *n.* a person or thing that wafts; especially, a revolving fan in a blower.
waf·ture (waf'chẽr, wäf'chẽr), *n.* 1. the act of waving or wafting. 2. something wafted, as on or by a breeze.
wag (wag), *v.t.* [WAGGED (wagd), WAGGING], [ME. *waggen;* prob. < ON.; cf. ON. *vagga,* a cradle, Sw. *vagga,* to rock], 1. to cause (something fastened at one end) to move rapidly and repeatedly back and forth, from side to side, or up and down: as, the dog *wagged* his tail. 2. to move (the tongue) in talking, especially in idle or malicious gossip. *v.i.* 1. to move rapidly and repeatedly back and forth, from side to side, or up and down, as a part of the body. 2. to keep moving in talk, especially in idle or malicious gossip: said of the tongue. 3. to continue at a regular pace; move along; proceed: as, that's the way the world *wags.* 4. to walk or move with a swaying motion; waddle. 5. [British Colloq.], to leave; depart; go off. 6. [British Slang], to play truant, as from school. *n.* the act or an instance of wagging: as, the *wag* of a dog's tail.
wag (wag), *n.* [< *wag, v.;* prob. as shortening of *waghalter* as applied to a joker, rogue, etc.], a comical or humorous person; joker; wit.

wage (wāj), *v.t.* [WAGED (wājd), WAGING], [ME. *wagen;* ONorm.Fr. *wagier* (OFr. *gagier*) < *wage* (OFr. *gage*), a stake, pledge; ML. *wadium;* Goth. *wadi*, a pledge], 1. to engage in; carry on: as, *wage* war. 2. [Obs.], to pledge. 3. [Obs.], to wager; bet. 4. [Obs. or British Dial.], to hire. *v.i.* [Obs.], to do battle; fight. *n.* 1. *usually pl.* money paid to an employee for work done, and usually figured on an hourly, daily, or piecework basis: often distinguished from *salary*. 2. *usually pl.* what is given in return; reward; recompense: formerly the plural form was often construed as singular, as, "The *wages* of sin is death." 3. [Obs.], *a*) a pledge. *b*) the state of being pledged; pawn. 4. *pl.* in *economics*, the share of the total product of industry that goes to labor, as distinguished from the share taken by capital.
SYN.—**wages** (less commonly **wage**) applies to money paid an employee at relatively short intervals, often daily, or weekly, especially for manual or physical labor; **salary** applies to fixed compensation usually paid at longer intervals, often monthly or semi-monthly, especially to clerical or professional workers; **stipend** is a somewhat lofty substitute for **salary**, or it is applied to a pension or similar fixed payment; **fee** applies to the payment requested or given for professional services, as of a doctor, lawyer, artist, etc.; **pay** is a general term equivalent to any of the preceding, but it is specifically used of compensation to members of the armed forces; **emolument** is an elevated, now somewhat jocular, substitute for **salary** or **wages**.

wage earner, a person who works for wages.

wag·er (wā'jẽr), *n.* [ME. *wageoure;* ONorm. Fr. *wageure* < *wagier;* see WAGE], 1. a bet (senses 1, 2, 3). 2. formerly, a pledge to do something or abide by an outcome: especially in *wager of battle*, a challenge by a defendant to prove his innocence by personal combat. *v.t. & v.i.* to bet (all senses).

wage scale, 1. a schedule of wages paid for the performance of related jobs or tasks in a given industry, plant, etc. 2. the schedule of wages paid by a given employer.

wage·work·er (wāj'wũr'kẽr), *n.* one who works for wages.

wage·work·ing (wāj'wũr'kiŋ), *adj.* doing work for wages.

wag·ger·y (wag'ẽr-i), *n.* [*pl.* WAGGERIES (-iz)], [< *wag* (joker) + *-ery*], 1. the action, spirit, or manner of a wag; roguish jocularity or merriment. 2. a joke or jest; especially, a practical joke.

wag·gish (wag'ish), *adj.* [< *wag* (joker) + *-ish*], 1. like, characteristic of, or befitting a wag; roguishly jocular or merry. 2. done, said, or made in waggery; playful; sportive.

wag·gle (wag''l), *v.t.* [WAGGLED (-'ld), WAGGLING], [freq. of *wag*, *v.*], to wag, especially with short, abrupt movements. *v.i.* to move in a shaky or wobbly manner; totter. *n.* the act or an instance of waggling.

wag·gly (wag'li), *adj.* waggling or tending to waggle.

wag·gon (wag'ən), *n. & v.t.* wagon: British spelling.

Wag·ner, Rich·ard (riH'ärt väg'nẽr), (*Wilhelm Richard Wagner*), 1813–1883; German composer.

Wag·ne·ri·an (väg-nêr'i-ən), *adj.* 1. of or like Richard Wagner or his music, theories, methods, etc. 2. designating or of an operatic singer specializing in Wagner's operas: as, a *Wagnerian* soprano. *n.* an admirer or follower of Wagner's music, theories, etc.

Wag·ner·ism (väg'nẽr-iz'm), *n.* 1. Richard Wagner's theory, practice, and method of composing music dramas, characterized by emphasis on the co-ordination of all the components (vocal and instrumental music, text, action, setting, etc.), by constant use of the leitmotif, and by a general departure from the conventions of previous, especially Italian, opera. 2. the influence of Wagner's theories on other composers and musicians, or the tendency to imitate Wagner.

wag·on (wag'ən), *n.* [< D. *wagen* (G. *wagen*), wheeled vehicle; cf. WAIN, *n.*], 1. any of various types of four-wheeled vehicles, either open or covered, especially one for hauling heavy loads, as of freight. 2. [British], a railroad freight car. 3. [Colloq.], an enclosed vehicle used by the police for carrying arrested people to the police station or jail: usually **the wagon;** in full **police** (or **patrol**) **wagon.** 4. [Obs.], a chariot. 5. [W-], in *astronomy*, Charles's Wain. Cf. also **station wagon, battle wagon, tea wagon,** etc. *v.t.* to carry or transport in a wagon.
hitch one's wagon to a star, to set oneself an ambitious goal.
on the (water) wagon, [Slang], no longer drinking alcoholic liquors.

wag·on·age (wag'ən-ij), *n.* [see -AGE], 1. transport by wagon. 2. money paid for this. 3. a collection of wagons; wagons collectively.

wag·on·er (wag'ən-ẽr), *n.* [? after D. *waghenaer*], 1. a person who drives a wagon. 2. [Obs.], a charioteer. 3. [W-], in *astronomy*, *a*) the northern constellation Auriga. *b*) Charles's Wain.

wag·on·ette (wag'ən-et'), *n.* [dim. of *wagon*], a light, open, four-wheeled carriage with two seats set lengthwise facing each other behind the driver's seat.

wag·on-head·ed (wag'ən-hed'id), *adj.* in *architecture*, shaped like the top of a covered wagon; curved like the top half of a cylinder: said of a ceiling, roof, etc.

‡**wag·on-lit** (vȧ'gōn'lē'), *n.* [Fr.; *wagon*, a car, railway coach (< Eng. *wagon*); + *lit*, a bed], in Europe, a railroad sleeping car.

wag·on·load (wag'ən-lōd'), *n.* the load that a wagon carries or will carry.

wagon train, a line or convoy of wagons traveling together, especially one carrying military supplies.

Wa·gram (vä'gräm), *n.* a village in Austria, near Vienna: scene of a battle (1809) of the Napoleonic Wars, in which the French defeated the Austrians.

wag·tail (wag'tāl'), *n.* 1. any of numerous small birds related to the pipits, mostly native to Europe, characterized by long wing feathers and a very long tail that wags up and down. 2. any of various similar birds, as an American water thrush of the wood warbler family.

Wa·ha·bi, Wa·ha·bee (wä-hä'bē), *n.* [Ar. *wahhābī*], a member of a strict Moslem sect which adheres closely to the Koran: it was founded by Abdul-Wahhab (1691–1787) and now flourishes in Arabia: also spelled **Wahhabi.**

Wa·ha·bi·ism (wä-hä'bi-iz'm), *n.* the doctrines and practices of the Wahabis.

Wa·ha·bism (wä-hä'biz'm), *n.* Wahabiism.

Wa·ha·bit (wä-hä'bit), *n.* a Wahabi.

Wa·ha·bite (wä-hä'bīt), *adj.* of or belonging to the Wahabis. *n.* a Wahabi.

wa·hoo (wä-hōō', wä'hōō), *n.* [Am. Ind. (Dakota) *wanhu*, lit., arrow wood], a large shrub or tree having small, purple flowers and purple fruit with red seeds; burning bush.

wa·hoo (wä-hōō', wä'hōō), *n.* [Am. Ind. (Creek) *ûhawhu*, cork elm], 1. a variety of elm with corky bark. 2. the basswood tree. 3. any of various other American trees or shrubs, as the cascara buckthorn.

Wai·chow (wī'chou'; Chin. wī'jō'), *n.* a city in Kwangtung province, southeastern China: pop., 400,000.

waif (wāf), *n.* [ME.; ONorm.Fr. (OFr. *gaif*); ? < ON. *veif*, anything flapping about < *veifa*, to wave, swing], 1. anything found by chance that is without an owner. 2. a person without home or friends; especially, a homeless child. 3. a strayed animal. 4. in *law*, goods stolen and thrown away by the thief in his flight. 5. in *nautical usage*, a signal flag or pennant, or a signal made with a flag or pennant; waft.

Wai·ki·ki (wī'kē-kē', wī'kē-kē'), *n.* a famous bathing resort in Honolulu, Hawaii.

wail (wāl), *v.i.* [ME. *weilen, wailen;* ON. *væla, vala, to* lament < *væ*, woe; cf. WOE], 1. to express grief or pain by long, loud cries. 2. to make a plaintive, sad, crying sound: as, the wind *wails*. *v.t.* 1. to lament; mourn: as, they *wailed* his death. 2. to cry out in mourning or lamentation. *n.* 1. a long, pitiful cry of grief and pain. 2. a sound like this. 3. a wailing. —***SYN.*** see **cry.**

wail·ful (wāl'fəl), *adj.* 1. wailing; sorrowful; expressive of sorrow. 2. like, or giving forth, a wail or cry of sorrow.

Wail·ing Place (or **Wall**) **of the Jews** (wāl'iŋ), a courtyard in Jerusalem bordered by a high wall believed to contain stones from Solomon's temple: Jews gather there weekly for prayer and lamentation: also **Wailing Wall.**

wail·some (wāl'səm), *adj.* 1. wailing; lamenting. 2. causing lamentation; lamentable.

wain (wān), *n.* [ME.; AS. *wægn*, wheeled vehicle; akin to D. *wagen* (cf. WAGON); IE. base as in *weigh*], [Archaic], a wagon or cart.
the Wain, Charles's Wain, the seven bright stars in the Big Dipper.

wain·scot (wān'skət, wān'skot'), *n.* [ME. *waynescote* < MLG. or MD.; cf. D. *wagenschot*, wainscot; prob. < *wagen*, a carriage + *schot*, an enclosure or partition of boards; exact origin disputed], 1. a wood lining or paneling on the walls of a room. 2. such a paneling on the lower part of a room only; hence, 3. *a*) the lower part of a room when it has a finish different from that of the upper. *b*) any applied finish, as tile, linoleum, etc., laid on a wall. 4. [British], a fine imported oak used for interior paneling. *v.t.* [WAINSCOTED or WAINSCOTTED (-id), WAINSCOTING or WAINSCOTTING], to line (a wall or room) with wood or other material.

wain·scot·ing, wain·scot·ting (wān'skət-iŋ, wān'skot'-iŋ), *n.* 1. paneling of wood or other material laid on like wood; wainscot. 2. material used for this.

wain·wright (wān'rīt'), *n.* [*wain* (a wagon) + *wright*], a person who builds or repairs wagons.

Wain·wright, Jonathan May·hew (mā'hū wān'rīt'), 1883–1953; American general.

waist (wāst), *n.* [ME. *waste* < the base of AS. *weaxan*, to grow (cf. WAX, *v.*); the sense developed < the notion, "size of the body," hence "thickness"], 1. the part of the body between the ribs and the hips. 2. *a*) the part of a garment that covers the waist. *b*) the narrow part of a woman's dress, etc., worn at the waist or above or below it as the styles change; waistline. *c*) the part of a garment covering the body from the shoulders to a line above the hips. *d*) the upper part of a woman's dress; bodice. *e*) a blouse. *f*) a child's undershirt. 3. the narrow part of any object which is wider at the ends: as, the *waist* of a violin, shoe, etc.: see **violin,** illus. 4. in *nautical usage*, the middle part of the upper deck of a ship, or that part between the forecastle and the quarter-deck. 5. in *zoology*, the narrow part of the front of the abdomen of certain insects, as ants, wasps, etc.

waist·band (wāst′band′), *n.* a band encircling the waist; especially, the band at the top of a skirt, trousers, or other garment.

waist·cloth (wāst′klôth′), *n.* a garment consisting of a cloth drawn around the hips and sometimes through the crotch, and fastened at the waist; loincloth.

waist·coat (wāst′kōt′, wes′kət), *n.* 1. [British], a short, sleeveless jacket worn under a suit coat; vest. 2. a similar garment worn by women. 3. a somewhat longer, heavily ornamented sleeveless jacket formerly worn under a doublet.

waist-high (wāst′hī′), *adj.* reaching up to the waist.

waist·line (wāst′līn′), *n.* 1. the line of the waist, between the ribs and the hips. 2. *a*) the narrow part of a woman's dress, etc., worn at the waist or above or below it as styles change. *b*) the line where the waist and skirt of a dress join.

wait (wāt), *v.i.* [ME. *waiten;* ONorm.Fr. *waitier;* OHG. *wahtēn* < *wahta*, a guard, watch], 1. to stay in a place or remain inactive or in anticipation until something expected takes place (often with *for, until,* etc.): as, *wait* until we call, *wait* for us. 2. to be ready or at hand: as, dinner is *waiting* for us. 3. to remain temporarily undone or neglected: as, that work will have to *wait.* 4. to serve food at a meal (with *at* or *on*): as, she will *wait* at table. *v.t.* 1. to be, remain, or delay in expectation or anticipation of; await: as, *wait* orders, *wait* your turn. 2. to serve food at: as, he *waits* table. 3. [Colloq.], to put off serving; delay (a meal) until someone comes: as, *wait* dinner. 4. [Obs.], to attend upon or escort, especially as a token of respect or honor. 5. [Obs.], to attend as a consequence. *n.* 1. the act or fact of waiting: as, we had a long *wait.* 2. a time of waiting: as, a four-hour *wait.* 3. an ambush; trap: usually in *lie in wait.* 4. in England, any of a group of singers and musicians who go through the streets at Christmas time playing and singing songs and carols for small gifts of money. 5. [Obs.], a member of a band of musicians formerly employed by a city or town in England to play at entertainments. 6. [Obs.], a watchman. —*SYN.* see **stay.**

wait on (or **upon**), 1. to act as a servant to. 2. to call on or visit (someone, especially a superior) in order to pay one's respects, ask a favor, etc. 3. to result from; be a consequence of. 4. to supply the needs or requirements of (a person at table, a customer in a store, etc.), as a waiter, clerk, etc.

wait up, [Colloq.], to put off going to bed until some one expected arrives (often with *for*).

wait-a-bit (wāt′ə-bit′), *n.* [*transl.* of S.Afr.D. *wacht-en-beetje*: so named for their clinging thorns], any of a number of plants having sharp or hooked thorns.

Waite, Mor·ri·son Rem·ick (mor′i-s'n rem′ik wāt), 1816–1888; American jurist; chief justice, United States Supreme Court (1874–1888).

wait·er (wāt′ẽr), *n.* [ME. *waitere*, watchman], 1. a person who waits or awaits. 2. a man who waits on table, as in a restaurant. 3. a tray for carrying dishes; salver. 4. [Obs.], a watchman or attendant.

wait·ing (wāt′iŋ), *adj.* 1. that waits. 2. of or for a wait. 3. that serves or is in attendance. *n.* 1. the act of one that waits. 2. a period of waiting.

in waiting, 1. in attendance (on a king or other person of royalty). 2. in *British military & naval usage*, next in turn for some duty, privilege, etc.

waiting room, a room in which people wait, as in a railroad station, a dentist's office, etc.

wait·ress (wāt′ris), *n.* a woman or girl who waits on table, as in a restaurant or hotel.

waive (wāv), *v.t.* [WAIVED (wāvd), WAIVING], [ME. *waiven, weiven;* Anglo-Fr. *waiver* (OFr. *gaiver*), to renounce; prob. < ON. *veifa*, to fluctuate; cf. WAIF], 1. to give up or forgo, as a right, claim, privilege, etc. 2. to refrain from insisting on or taking advantage of. 3. to put off until later; postpone; defer. 4. in *law*, to forgo or relinquish voluntarily, as a right which one is legally entitled to enforce. 5. [Obs.], to leave, reject, or abandon. —*SYN.* see **relinquish.**

waiv·er (wāv′ẽr), *n.* [substantive use of Anglo-Fr. inf. *waiver*, to waive], in *law*, 1. the action or an act of waiving, or relinquishing voluntarily a right, claim, privilege, etc. 2. a formal written statement of such relinquishment: as, we signed a *waiver* of our claim.

Wa·ka·ya·ma (wä′kä-yä′mä), *n.* a city on the coast of southern Honshu, Japan: pop., 172,000 (est. 1947).

wake (wāk), *v.i.* [WAKED (wākt) or WOKE (wōk), WAKED or, *rarely*, WOKEN (wōk′'n), WAKING], [ME. *wakien, waken* < AS. *wacian*, to be awake & *wacan*, to arise; akin to G. *wachen;* IE. base **weĝ-*, to be active, seen also in L. *vigil* (cf. VIGIL), *vegetus* (cf. VEGETABLE), *vigere* (cf. VIGOR, etc.); cf. WAKEN], 1. to come out of sleep or a state like or suggestive of sleep, as a stupor, trance, etc.; awake (often with *up*). 2. to be or stay awake. 3. to become active or animated after inactivity or dormance (often with *up*). 4. to become alert (*to* a realization, possibility, etc.). 5. [Dial. or Archaic], to keep watch or vigil; especially, to hold a wake (sense 2). *v.t.* 1. to cause to wake (senses 1, 3, 4): often with *up.* 2. to arouse, excite, or stir up, as passions, or evoke, as a sound or echo. 3. [Dial. or Archaic], to keep watch or vigil over; especially, to hold a wake over (a corpse). *n.* 1. [Poetic], the state of being awake. 2. a watch kept at night, or a vigil, as for some ritual purpose; especially, an all-night vigil over a corpse before burial, formerly often with festivities (common among the Irish). 3. in the *Anglican Church*, *a*) an annual festival in honor of the dedication of a parish church. *b*) a vigil held the night before this.

wake (wāk), *n.* [D. *wak;* prob. < ON. *vök*, a hole, opening in the ice], 1. the track left in the water by a moving ship or boat; hence, 2. the track or course of anything that has gone before or passed by.

in the wake of, 1. in *nautical usage*, following directly behind (a ship or boat); hence, 2. following close behind. 3. following as a consequence.

Wake·field (wāk′fēld′), *n.* a city in Yorkshire, England: pop., 58,000 (est. 1946).

wake·ful (wāk′fəl), *adj.* 1. keeping awake; not sleeping; hence, 2. alert; watchful; vigilant. 3. unable to sleep. 4. sleepless: as, a *wakeful* night.

Wake Island (wāk), a small island in the northern Pacific between Midway and Guam, belonging to the United States: area, 4 sq. mi.: naval air base.

wake·less (wāk′lis), *adj.* unbroken; deep: said of sleep.

wak·en (wāk′'n), *v.i.* [ME. *waknen;* AS. *wacnian, wæcnan*, to become awake < base of *wacan* + *-n*, inchoative suffix], 1. to become awake; come to one's senses after sleep or a state like sleep. 2. to become active, animated, or alive after inactivity or dormance. *v.t.* 1. to awake. 2. to urge or stir into action or activity; arouse; excite. 3. [Scot.], to guard. —*SYN.* see **stir.**

wake·rife (wāk′rīf′), *adj.* [see WAKE, *v.* & RIFE, *adj.*], [Scot. & N. Eng. Dial.], wakeful.

wake-rob·in (wāk′rob′in), *n.* 1. any of a number of related plants with leaves in groups of three and white, pink, purple, or greenish three-part flowers; trillium. 2. [British], any of a number of related plants with variously colored, hoodlike leaves arching over flower spikes; any of several arums, especially the cuckoopint. 3. the jack-in-the-pulpit.

wake-up (wāk′up′), *n.* [Colloq.], the flicker.

Waks·man, Sel·man Abraham (sel′mən waks′mən), 1888–; American biologist born in Russia; discovered streptomycin; received Nobel prize in medicine, 1952.

Wal., 1. Walachian. 2. Walloon.

Wa·la·chi·a (wä-lā′ki-ə, wä-lāk′yə), *n.* a former principality in southeastern Europe: now a part of Romania: also spelled **Wallachia.**

Wa·la·chi·an (wä-lā′ki-ən, wä-lāk′yən), *adj.* of Walachia, its people, or their language. *n.* 1. a native or inhabitant of Walachia. 2. the language of the Walachians. Also spelled **Wallachian.** Abbreviated **Wal., Walach.**

Wal·che·ren (väl′khə-rən), *n.* an island of the Netherlands, in Zeeland province, off the southwestern coast.

Wal·de·mar I (väl′də-mär′), 1131–1182; king of Denmark (1157–1182): also **Valdemar I**: called *the Great.*

Wal·den·ses (wäl-den′sēz), *n.pl.* [ML., after Peter *Waldo*, 12th-c. Fr. merchant and founder of the sect], a sect of puritan dissenters from the Roman Catholic Church which arose about 1170 in southern France through the preaching of Peter Waldo: they were excommunicated in 1184 and persecuted, but still survive in the Alps of France and Italy: also called *Vaudois.*

Wal·den·si·an (wäl-den′si-ən, wäl-den′shən), *adj.* of the Waldenses.

wald·grave (wôld′grāv′), *n.* [G. *waldgraf; wald*, a forest + *graf*, a ruler], in the old German empire, 1. the head keeper of a royal forest. 2. in the Rhine districts, a nobleman of a certain rank.

Wal·do (wôl′dō, wäl′dō), [Frank. or OHG. < *Waldan*, to rule; also G., contr. for names beginning with *Walde-* (e.g. *Waldemar*), of same origin], a masculine name.

Wal·dorf salad (wôl′dôrf), [after the old *Waldorf-Astoria* hotel in New York City], a salad made of diced raw apples, celery, and walnuts, with mayonnaise.

Wald·stein (vält′shtīn′), see **Wallenstein.**

wale (wāl), *n.* [ME.; AS. *walu*, a rod, hence a blow, mark left by a blow, ridge raised by a blow, weal; cf. GUNWALE], 1. a raised line or streak made on the skin by the slash of a stick or whip; wheal; welt. 2. *a*) a ridge on the surface of cloth, as corduroy; hence, *b*) texture of cloth. 3. a timber fastened to a row of piles in a dam, to strengthen and brace them. 4. in *basketmaking*, a band or ridge woven around the body of a basket to brace it. 5. in *nautical usage*, *a*) the gunwale. *b*) *usually in pl.* any of several strakes or heavy planks fastened to the outside of the hull of a wooden ship. ***v.t.*** [WALED (wāld), WALING], 1. to mark (the skin) with a wale or wales. 2. to fasten, protect, or brace with a wale or wales. 3. to make, as cloth, or weave, as wickerwork, with a wale or wales.

wale (wāl), ***n.*** [ME. *wal;* ON. *val;* akin to G. *wahl,* choice, a choosing; IE. base as in WILL, *v.*], [Scot. & N. Eng. Dial.], 1. a choosing; choice. 2. that chosen as best. ***v.t.*** [WALED (wāld), WALING], [Scot. & N. Eng. Dial.], to choose; pick out; select.

Wal·er (wāl′ẽr), ***n.*** [Anglo-Ind. < New South *Wales*], [Colloq.], 1. a cavalry horse bred in New South Wales, Australia. 2. any Australian horse. Term first and chiefly used in India, where many Australian horses are imported.

Wales (wālz), ***n.*** a division of Great Britain, bounded on the east by England: area, 7,466 sq. mi.; pop., 2,158,000; chief cities, Cardiff and Swansea: abbreviated **W.**

Wal·fish Bay (wôl′fish), Walvis Bay.

Wal·hal·la (wal-hal′ə, wäl-hä′lə), ***n.*** Valhalla.

walk (wôk), ***v.i.*** [ME. *walken;* AS. *wealcan,* to roll, journey; akin to G. *walken,* to full (cloth), cudgel; IE. base **walg-* < **wel-,* to turn, twist, etc., seen also in L. *volvere,* to roll, etc. (cf. REVOLVE, INVOLVE)], 1. to go along or move about on foot at a moderate pace; specifically, *a*) to move by placing one foot firmly on the ground before lifting the other, as two-legged creatures do, or by placing two feet firmly on the ground before lifting either of the others, as four-legged creatures do: distinguished from *run, gallop, trot,* etc. *b*) to go about on foot for exercise or pleasure; hike. 2. to return after death and appear on earth as a ghost. 3. to advance or move in a manner suggestive of walking: said of inanimate objects. 4. to follow a certain course of life; conduct oneself in a certain way: as, let us *walk* in peace. 5. [Obs.], to be active or in motion, or to keep moving. 6. in *baseball,* to be advanced to first base as a result of being pitched four balls. 7. in *basketball,* to commit the foul of advancing more than two steps with the ball without either passing or dribbling it. ***v.t.*** 1. to go through, over, or along at a moderate pace on foot: as, he is *walking* the deck. 2. to traverse on foot in order to survey, inspect, or repair, as a boundary, fence, tracks, etc. 3. *a*) to cause (a horse, dog, etc.) to move at a walk; lead, ride, or drive at a walk. *b*) to train and exercise (a horse, dog, etc.) by walking. 4. to accompany (a person) on a walk or stroll: as, I'll *walk* you to the corner. 5. *a*) to force (a person) to move at a walk, as by grasping the shoulders and pushing. *b*) to help (a disabled person) to walk. 6. to bring (a person or animal) to a specified state by walking: as, they *walked* me to exhaustion. 7. to cause to move in a manner suggestive of walking. 8. in *baseball,* to advance (a batter) to first base by pitching four balls. 9. in *basketball,* to commit the foul of advancing more than two steps with (the ball) without passing or dribbling. ***n.*** 1. the act of walking. 2. a period or course of walking for pleasure or exercise; stroll; hike. 3. a route traversed by walking: as, his usual *walk* was along the bluff. 4. a distance walked, often in terms of the time required: as, the town was an hour's *walk* from us. 5. the pace of one who walks: as, the horse came home at a *walk.* 6. a manner of walking: as, I knew her by her *walk.* 7. a particular station in life, sphere of activity, occupation, etc.: as, people from all *walks* of life. 8. mode of living; general conduct or behavior. 9. a path or avenue specially prepared or set apart for walking. 10. a ropewalk. 11. *a*) a plantation of trees in rows with a space between. *b*) the space between any two such rows. 12. a place or enclosure for grazing or exercising animals; specifically, a sheepwalk. 13. [British], the route covered by a vendor, hawker, etc. 14. in England, a part of a forest under the care of a keeper. 15. [Obs.], a resort or haunt. 16. in *athletics,* a walking race. 17. in *baseball,* an advancing to first base as the result of four balls pitched to the batter.

walk off, 1. to go away, especially without warning. 2. to get rid of by walking, as excess energy or fat.

walk off with, 1. to steal. 2. to win or gain.

walk out, [Colloq.], to go on strike.

walk out on, [Colloq.], to leave; desert; abandon.

walk the plank, 1. to be executed by being forced to walk off the end of a plank thrust over the side of a ship, as by pirates; hence, 2. to be forced to resign from an office or a position.

walk·a·way (wôk′ə-wā′), ***n.*** an easily won victory.

walk·ie-talk·ie (wôk′i-tôk′i), ***n.*** a compact radio transmitter and receiver that can be carried by one person: also spelled **walky-talky.**

walk·ing (wôk′iŋ), ***adj.*** that walks; specifically, *a*) that is drawn by an animal and guided by a person walking: as, a *walking* plow. *b*) that moves back and forth; oscillating: as, a *walking* beam. *c*) that moves forward in a manner suggestive of walking: as, a *walking* crane. ***n.*** 1. the act of a person or thing that walks. 2. manner of walking; gait. 3. the condition of the ground, a path, etc. with reference to its suitability for walking on: as, easy *walking* along this road.

walking bass, a repeated figure, commonly in eighth notes, much used as the bass part in boogie-woogie music.

walking beam, in a vertical steam engine, a beam pivoted in the middle and connected to a piston rod at one end and a flywheel at the other, used to transmit power from a piston to a drive shaft: it has a characteristic see-saw motion.

walking delegate, a labor-union official who goes from place to place inspecting working conditions, representing the union to its locals, negotiating with employers, etc.: term now seldom used.

walking fern, a walking leaf (sense 2).

walking leaf, 1. any of a group of insects with wings and limbs resembling leaves. 2. an evergreen fern having fronds that bend backward and often take root at the tip.

walking papers, [Colloq.], dismissal from a position or job.

walking stick, 1. a stick carried when walking; cane. 2. an insect resembling a twig; stick insect.

walk-on (wôk′on′), ***n.*** a minor role in which the actor has no speaking lines.

walk·out (wôk′out′), ***n.*** [Colloq.], a strike of workers.

walk·o·ver (wôk′ō′vẽr), ***n.*** 1. a race in which the one horse entered has merely to walk over the course to win; hence, 2. [Colloq.], an easily won victory.

walk-up (wôk′up′), ***n.*** [Colloq.], an apartment house without an elevator. ***adj.*** [Colloq.], of or in such a building: as, a *walk-up* apartment.

‡**Wal·kü·re, Die** (dē väl-kü′rə), [G.; cf. VALKYRIE], the second in a tetralogy of music dramas by Richard Wagner: see **Ring of the Nibelung.**

Wal·kyr·ie (wal-kẽr′i, väl-kẽr′i), ***n.*** a Valkyrie.

walk·y-talk·y (wôk′i-tôk′i), ***n.*** a walkie-talkie.

wall (wôl), ***n.*** [ME. *wal;* AS. *weall* (akin to G. *wall*) < L. *vallum,* a rampart < *vallus,* a stake, palisade; for IE. base see WALK], 1. an upright structure of wood, stone, brick, etc., serving to enclose, divide, support, or protect; specifically, *a*) such a structure forming a side or inner partition of a building. *b*) such a continuous structure serving to enclose an area, separate fields, etc. *c*) *usually in pl.* such a structure used as a military defense; fortification. *d*) such a structure used to hold back water; levee; dike. 2. something resembling a wall in appearance or function, as the side or inside surface of a container, body cavity, etc. 3. something suggestive of a wall in that it holds back, divides, hides, etc.: as, a *wall* of secrecy. ***adj.*** 1. of a wall. 2. placed or growing on or against a wall. ***v.t.*** 1. to furnish, line, enclose, divide, protect, etc. with or as with a wall or walls (often with *off*). 2. to close up (an opening) with a wall (usually with *up*).

drive (or push) to the wall, to place in a desperate or extreme position.

go to the wall, 1. to be forced to retreat or yield in a conflict; suffer defeat. 2. to fail in business; become bankrupt.

wal·la (wä′lä), ***n.*** a wallah.

wal·la·by (wäl′ə-bi), ***n.*** [*pl.* WALLABIES (-biz), WALLABY; see PLURAL, II, D, 1], [< Australian native name *wolabā*], any of various small and medium-sized kangaroos, some about the size of a rabbit.

Wal·lace (wôl′is, wäl′is), [< the surname *Wallace;* prob. < ME. *Walisc,* Welsh, foreign], a masculine name: diminutive, *Wally.*

Wallace, Alfred Russel, 1823–1913; English naturalist.

Wallace, Henry A·gard (ā′gärd), 1888– ; American statesman; secretary of agriculture (1933–1941), vice-president of the United States (1941–1945); secretary of commerce (1945–1946).

Wallace, Lew (lo͞o, lū), (*Lewis Wallace*), 1827–1905; American general and novelist.

Wallace, Sir **William,** 1272?–1305; Scottish national hero; leader in struggle against Edward I of England.

Wal·la·chi·a (wä-lā′ki-ə, wä-lāk′yə), ***n.*** Walachia.

Wal·la·chi·an (wä-lā′ki-ən, wä-lāk′yən), ***adj.* & *n.*** Walachian.

wal·lah (wä′lä), ***n.*** [Anglo-Ind. < Hind. *-vālā,* a suffix of agency], in ***Anglo-Indian use,*** 1. a person, or sometimes a thing, connected with a particular thing or function. 2. [Colloq.], a person. Also spelled **walla.**

wal·la·roo (wäl′ə-ro͞o′), ***n.*** [< Australian native name *wolarū*], any of a group of kangaroos characterized by their great size, long narrow hind feet, and thick gray fur.

Wal·la·sey (wäl′ə-si), ***n.*** a seaport in Cheshire, western England, near Liverpool: pop., 98,000 (est. 1946).

wall·board (wôl′bôrd′, wôl′bōrd′), ***n.*** fibrous material made up into thin slabs for use in making or covering walls, partitions, and ceilings, in place of plaster, paneling, etc.

wall creeper, any of several small birds related to the tree creepers and living in cliffs and town walls, mainly in Europe, Asia, and North Africa.

walled (wôld), ***adj.*** 1. having a wall or walls; enclosed by a wall. 2. fortified: as, a *walled* town. 3. enclosed or hedged in as if by a wall.

Wal·len·stein, Al·brecht Eu·se·bi·us Wen·zel von (äl′breHt oi-zā′bi-oos ven′tsəl fôn väl′ən-shtīn′; Eng.

wôl′ən-stīn′), Duke of Friedland, 1583–1634; Austrian general in the Thirty Years' War; assassinated: also **Waldstein.**

Wal·ler, Edmund (wôl′ẽr, wäl′ẽr), 1606–1687; English poet.

wal·let (wäl′it, wôl′it), *n.* [ME. *walet;* prob. altered < *watel,* a hurdle, basket, hence bag; cf. WATTLE], 1. [Now Rare], a bag for carrying provisions, clothing, food, etc. on a journey on foot; knapsack. 2. a pocketbook, usually of leather, for carrying cards, unfolded paper money, etc.; billfold.

wall·eye (wôl′ī′), *n.* [back-formation < *walleyed*], 1. an eye, as of a horse, with a whitish iris or white, opaque cornea. 2. *a)* an eye that turns outward, showing more white than is normal. *b)* divergent strabismus. Opposed to *cross-eye.* 3. leucoma of the cornea. 4. a large, staring eye, as of some fishes. 5. any of several fishes with large, staring eyes; specifically, *a)* the walleyed pike. *b)* the walleyed pollack. *c)* the walleyed surf fish. *d)* the alewife.

wall·eyed (wôl′īd′), *adj.* [ME. *waldeyed, wawileyed;* ON. *valdeygthr;* altered < *vagl eygr; vagl,* a film on the eye + *eygr,* having eyes], 1. having one or both eyes with a whitish iris or white, opaque cornea. 2. having eyes that turn outward, showing more white than is normal, because of divergent strabismus. 3. having leucoma of the cornea. 4. having large, staring eyes, as some fishes. 5. glary-eyed; fierce-eyed. 6. [Slang], drunk.

walleyed pike (or **perch**), any of several North American fresh-water food fishes of the perch family, with large, staring eyes.

walleyed pollack, any of a group of large, black ocean food fishes common off the west coast of North America.

walleyed surf fish, any of a group of common black salt-water fishes found off the coast of California, which bear live young.

wall fern, a small, hardy fern with densely matted, creeping stems, found on cliffs and walls.

wall·flow·er (wôl′flou′ẽr), *n.* 1. any of a number of related plants with lance-shaped leaves and clusters of fragrant yellow, red, orange, or purple flowers. 2. [Colloq.], a person, especially a girl or woman, who sits by the wall, or only looks on, at a dance, sometimes from shyness but ordinarily from not having been sought as a partner.

Wal·lo·ni·an (wä-lō′ni-ən), *adj. & n.* Walloon.

Wal·loon (wä-lo͞on′), *n.* [Fr. *Wallon;* ML. *Wallo;* of Gmc. origin; cf. OHG. *walh,* foreigner, AS. *Wealh,* Briton, foreigner], 1. a member of a people living chiefly in southern and southeastern Belgium and near by parts of France. 2. the French dialect of the Walloons. Abbreviated **Wal.** *adj.* of the Walloons or Walloon.

wal·lop (wäl′əp, wôl′əp), *v.i.* [ME. *walopen,* to gallop; ONorm.Fr. *waloper* (OFr. *galoper*); see GALLOP], [Dial. or Colloq.], 1. to move heavily and clumsily; flounder. 2. to gallop. *v.t.* [Colloq.], 1. to beat soundly; thrash. 2. to strike with a very hard blow. 3. to defeat convincingly or crushingly. *n.* 1. [Dial. or Colloq.], *a)* a heavy, clumsy movement of the body. *b)* a gallop. 2. [Colloq.], *a)* a hard blow. *b)* the power to strike a hard blow.

wal·lop·er (wäl′əp-ẽr, wôl′əp-ẽr), *n.* [Colloq.], 1. a person or thing that wallops. 2. something huge, enormous, or greatly exaggerated; whopper.

wal·lop·ing (wäl′əp-iŋ, wôl′əp-iŋ), *adj.* [ppr. of *wallop*], [Colloq.], enormous; very large: as, a *walloping* big boy. *n.* [Colloq.], 1. a thrashing. 2. a crushing defeat.

wal·low (wäl′ō, wôl′ō), *v.i.* [ME. *walwen;* AS. *wealwian,* to roll around; for IE. base see WALK], 1. to roll about or flounder, as in mud, dust, water, slime, etc.: as, pigs *wallow* in filth. 2. to move heavily and clumsily; roll and pitch, as a ship. 3. to live or indulge oneself fully with animal pleasure or luxurious enjoyment (*in* a specified thing, condition, etc.): as, *wallow* in riches, *wallow* in vice. 4. to surge up or billow forth, as smoke, flame, etc. *n.* 1. an act of wallowing. 2. a muddy or dusty place in which animals wallow. 3. a pit or depression produced by animals' wallowing.

wall·pa·per (wôl′pā′pẽr), *n.* paper, usually with colored patterns printed on it, for covering the walls or ceiling of a room. *v.t.* to hang or apply wallpaper on or in.

wall pellitory, a tufted, weedlike European herb found on old walls.

wall plate, 1. a timber laid horizontally along a wall to support the ends of joists, girders, etc. and distribute their weight. 2. a metal plate fastened to a wall for attaching a bearing, bracket, etc.

wall rock, in *geology & mining,* the rock mass on either side of a fault or vein.

wall rocket, a yellow-flowered plant of the mustard family, found in quarries and on old walls.

wall rue, a small, delicate, light-green fern, usually growing on cliffs or walls.

Walls·end (wôlz′end′), *n.* [after *Wallsend* on the Tyne, where it was mined], [British], a size or grade of coal.

Wall Street, 1. a street in lower Manhattan, New York City: the main financial center of the United States; hence, 2. American financiers and their power, influence, policies, etc., or the American money market.

wal·ly (wā′li), *adj.* [cf. WALE (choicest part)], [Scot.], 1. fine; first-rate. 2. ample, large, strong, or robust. 3. pleasing; agreeable. *n.* [*pl.* WALLIES (-liz)], [Scot.], 1. a toy, gimcrack, or bauble. 2. *pl.* finery.

wal·ly·drag (wā′li-drag′, wäl′i-dräg′), *n.* [Scot.], a weak, underdeveloped creature, as the last-born of a litter.

wal·ly·drai·gle (wā′li-drā′g'l, wäl′i-drā′g'l), *n.* [Scot.], a wallydrag.

wal·nut (wôl′nut′, wôl′nət), *n.* [ME. *walnote, walnot;* AS. *wealh hnutu; wealh,* foreign (cf. WELSH) + *hnutu,* a nut], 1. a roundish, edible nut with a two-lobed seed. 2. any of a number of related trees bearing such a nut, as the *English walnut,* the *black walnut,* etc. 3. the wood of any of these trees, used in furniture, woodwork, etc. 4. a shagbark tree or its nut. 5. a shade of brown characteristic of the heartwood of the black walnut.

Wal·pole, Horace (wôl′pōl′, wäl′pōl′), fourth Earl of Orford, 1717–1797; son of *Robert;* English writer.

Walpole, Hugh, (*Sir Hugh Seymour Walpole*), 1884–1941; English novelist, born in New Zealand.

Walpole, Robert, first earl of Orford, 1676–1745; English statesman; prime minister (1715–1717; 1721–1742).

‡Wal·pur·gis·nacht (väl-poor′gis-näkht′), *n.* [G.], Walpurgis Night.

Wal·pur·gis Night (väl-poor′gis), [G. < *Walburga, Walpurgis,* St. Walpurgis, English missionary in Germany in the 8th century; her feast day is April 30], 1. April 30, the eve of May Day, when witches were supposed to gather and revel on Brocken peak in the Harz Mountains of Germany; hence, 2. a witches' sabbath; diabolical revelry.

wal·rus (wôl′rəs, wäl′rəs), *n.* [*pl.* WALRUSES (-iz), WALRUS; see PLURAL, II, D, 1], [Dan. *hvalros;* prob. by metathesis of ON. *hrosshvalr,* lit., horse whale; *hross,* a horse + *hvalr,* a whale; AS. has *horshwæl,* lit., horse whale, rendering ON., but the name orig. applied to some kind of small whale], either of two massive sea animals of the seal family, one native to the North Pacific, the other to the North Atlantic, having two tusks projecting from the upper jaw, a thick mustache, a very thick hide, and a heavy layer of blubber. *adj.* of, characteristic of, or suggestive of a walrus; specifically, designating a mustache with long, drooping ends.

WALRUS (10–11 ft. long)

Wal·sall (wôl′sôl), *n.* a city in Staffordshire, England, north of Birmingham: pop., 120,000.

Wal·sing·ham, Sir Francis (wôl′siŋ-əm), 1530?–1590; English statesman.

Wal·ter (wôl′tẽr), [ONorm.Fr. *Waltier;* Frank. *Waldheri* < *waldan,* to rule + *heri, hari,* army, host; also < G. *Walter, Walther* < OHG. form of same name], a masculine name: diminutives, *Walt, Wat.*

Wal·ter, Bru·no (bro͞o′nō väl′tẽr), (born *Bruno Schlesinger*), 1876–1962; German orchestra conductor in America.

Wal·tham (wôl′thəm, wôl′tham), *n.* a city in Massachusetts, west of Boston: pop., 55,000.

Wal·tham·stow (wôl′thəm-stō′, wôl′təm-stō′), *n.* a city in Essex, England, near London: pop., 108,000.

Wal·ther von der Vo·gel·wei·de (väl′tẽr fôn dẽr fō′gəl-vī′də), 1170?–1230?; German minnesinger.

Wal·ton, I·zaak (ī′zək wôl′t'n), 1593–1683; English writer and celebrated fisherman.

waltz (wôlts; *esp.* Brit. wôls), *n.* [abbrev. < G. *walzer* < *walzen,* to roll, dance about, waltz; for IE. base see WALK, WALLOW], 1. a ballroom dance for couples, in moderate 3/4 time with marked accent on the first beat of the measure. 2. music for this dance or in its characteristic rhythm. *adj.* of, for, or characteristic of a waltz. *v.i.* 1. to dance a waltz. 2. to move lightly and nimbly; whirl. *v.t.* to cause to waltz.

Wal·vis Bay (wôl′vis), 1. a bay off the coast of South West Africa. 2. a small region around this bay surrounded by South West Africa, but declared by the Union of South Africa to be an integral part of Cape Province: area, 274 sq. mi. Also called *Walfish.*

wal·y (wāl′i, wôl′i), *interj.* [Scot.], an exclamation of sorrow or grief.

wam·ble (wäm′'l, wam′'l), *v.i.* [WAMBLED (-'ld), WAMBLING], [ME. *wamlen;* cf. Norw. *vamla,* to stagger, Dan. *vamle,* to feel nausea], [Chiefly Dial.], 1. to turn, twist, writhe, roll, or wriggle about. 2. to move unsteadily; stagger or reel. 3. *a)* [Obs.], to be nauseated.

b) to give the sensation of nausea, as if turning about: said of the stomach or its contents. ***n.*** [Chiefly Dial.], 1. *a*) a wambling, twisting, writhing, etc. *b*) an unsteady movement; a staggering. 2. a sensation of nausea.

wam·bly (wäm′li, wam′li), ***adj.*** [see WAMBLE], [Chiefly Dial.], 1. unsteady, shaky, staggering, or reeling. 2. feeling nausea; nauseated.

wame (wām), ***n.*** [var. of *womb*], [Scot. & N. Eng. Dial.], 1. the belly. 2. the womb.

wam·mus (wäm′əs), ***n.*** a wamus.

Wam·pa·no·ag (wäm′pə-nō′ag), ***n.*** [*pl.* WAMPANOAG, WAMPANOAGS (-agz)], a member of a tribe of Algonquian Indians that lived in the region of Cape Cod: these were the first Indians met by the Pilgrims after the landing at Plymouth. ***adj.*** of this tribe.

wam·pum (wäm′pəm, wôm′pəm), ***n.*** [short for *wampumpeag*], 1. small beads made of shells and used by North American Indians as money, for ornament, etc.: they were of two varieties, white and black (or dark purple), the latter being worth twice the former. 2. [Slang], money.

wam·pum·peag (wäm′pəm-pēg′, wôm′pəm-pēg′), ***n.*** [< Am. Ind. (Algonquian) *wampumpeage*, lit., white string of beads; cf. Massachusett *wanpanpiag* < *wap*, white + *umpe*, string + *-ag*, pl. suffix], 1. white shell beads used by North American Indians as money; hence, 2. shell money; wampum.

wam·pus (wäm′pəs), ***n.*** a wamus.

wa·mus (wô′məs, wäm′əs), ***n.*** [D. *wammes*, earlier *wambuis;* OFr. *wambois*, *wambais*, leather doublet < OHG. *wamba*, the belly; see WOMB], 1. a kind of cardigan. 2. an outer jacket made of tough, long-wearing fabric. Also **wammus, wampus.**

wan (wän, wôn), ***adj.*** [WANNER (-ẽr), WANNEST (-ist)], [ME.; AS. *wann*, dark; ? akin to *wane;* sense development: dark—unhealthy in color—livid, pale (aided by astrological sense "obscured")], 1. sickly pale; pallid; colorless: as, a *wan* complexion. 2. indicative or suggestive of a sickly condition or great weariness, grief, etc.; faint or feeble: as, a *wan* smile. 3. [Obs.], *a*) dark; gloomy. *b*) sad. ***v.t. & v.i.*** [WANNED (wänd, wônd), WANNING], to make or become sickly pale. —***SYN.*** see **pale.**

wan (wan), obsolete past tense of **win.**

Wan·a·ma·ker, John (wän′ə-mā′kẽr, wôn′ə-mā′kẽr), 1838–1922; American merchant; postmaster-general (1889–1893).

wand (wänd, wônd), ***n.*** [ME. < Anglo-N.; cf. ON. *vöndr*, a wand < base seen in Eng. *wind;* basic sense "flexible"], 1. a slender, supple switch or shoot, as of a young tree, especially a willow. 2. a slender rod, as a musician's baton. 3. a rod or staff carried as a symbol of authority; scepter. 4. *a*) a magic rod, as used by a fairy. *b*) the slender, batonlike rod of a magician or conjuror. *c*) any rod of supposed magic power, as a divining rod. 5. in *archery* (in the United States), a slat used as a mark, 6 feet long and 2 inches wide: placed at a distance of 100 yards for men and 60 yards for women.

wan·der (wän′dẽr, wôn′dẽr), ***v.i.*** [ME. *wandren*, *wandrien;* AS. *wandrian;* akin to G. *wandern;* for IE. base see WIND, *v.*, WEND, *v.*], 1. to move or go aimlessly about, without plan or fixed destination; ramble; roam. 2. to go to a place by any way or at any pace that suits the fancy; idle; stroll. 3. *a*) to turn aside or astray (*from* a path, course, etc.); lose one's way. *b*) to stray from home, friends, familiar places, etc. (often with *off*). 4. to go astray in mind or purpose; specifically, *a*) to drift away from a subject, as in discussion. *b*) to turn away from accepted thought or morals; go wrong morally or intellectually. *c*) to be disjointed, disordered, incoherent, etc. 5. to pass or extend in an irregular course; meander, as a river. 6. to move idly from one object to another: said of the eyes, a glance, the hands, etc. ***v.t.*** [Poetic], to roam through, in, or over without plan or destination: as, he *wandered* the forests.

wan·der·ing (wän′dẽr-iŋ, wôn′dẽr-iŋ), ***adj.*** 1. that wanders; moving from place to place; roaming, roving, straying, etc. 2. nomadic: said of tribes. 3. winding: said of rivers and roads. ***n.*** 1. an aimless going about. 2. *pl.* travels; especially, extended and apparently purposeless travels. 3. *pl.* incoherent or disordered thoughts or utterances, as in delirium.

wandering albatross, a large white sea bird with black wings, native to southern seas.

Wandering Jew, 1. a legendary Jew who, according to medieval folklore, was condemned to wander the earth until the second coming of Christ because of his scornful behavior just before the Crucifixion. 2. [w- J-], any of several trailing plants having smooth stems and leaves, and white, red, or blue flowers.

‡**Wan·der·jahr** (vän′dẽr-yär′), ***n.*** [G., lit., wander-year], a year of travel before settling down to work: an old custom of European journeymen.

wan·der·lust (wän′dẽr-lust′, wôn′dẽr-lust′; G. vän′dẽr-loost′), ***n.*** [G. < *wandern*, to travel, wander + *lust*, joy], an impulse, longing, or urge to wander or travel.

wan·der·oo (wän′də-rōō′), ***n.*** [Singh. *vanduru*, pl. of *vandurā* < Sans. *vānara*, a monkey], 1. any of a rare species of monkey of the macaque family, native to south India, with a black coat, a thick ruff of gray hair about the face, and a short, tufted tail. 2. any of a group of purple-faced langur monkeys of Ceylon.

wan·dle (wän′d'l, wän′'l), ***adj.*** [back-formation < AS. *wandlung*, changeableness], [Scot.], supple; agile.

Wands·worth (wändz′wũrth′), ***n.*** a borough of London.

wane (wān), ***v.i.*** [WANED (wānd), WANING], [ME. *wanien;* AS. *wanian*, *wonian*, to decrease, grow less < base of *wana*, lacking; for IE. base see WANT], 1. to grow gradually less in extent: said of the visible face of the moon during the period after it has become full. 2. to become less intense, bright, etc.; grow dim or faint: said of light, etc. 3. to decline in power, importance, prosperity, influence, etc. 4. to approach the end: said of a period of time, as, the day *wanes.* Opposed to *wax.* ***n.*** 1. *a*) the gradual decrease in the visible face of the moon after it has become full. *b*) the time when this takes place. 2. a gradual decrease in power, importance, prosperity, intensity, etc., especially after a gradual climb to a peak. 3. a period of decline. 4. the slanting or beveled defective edge of a board or plank cut from an unsquared log or block of wood.

on the wane, waning; declining, decreasing, etc.

SYN.—**wane** implies a fading or weakening of that which has reached a peak of force, excellence, etc. (his fame *waned* rapidly); **abate** suggests a progressive lessening in degree, intensity, etc. (the fever is *abating*); **ebb**, applied specifically to a fluctuating force, refers to one of the periods of recession or decline (their *ebbing* fortunes); **subside** suggests a quieting or slackening of violent activity or turbulence (her temper had *subsided*). —***ANT.*** wax, increase, revive.

wan·gle (waŋ′g'l), ***v.t.*** [WANGLED (-g'ld), WANGLING], [prob. a slang formation on *angle*], [Colloq.], 1. to get, make, or bring about by persuasion, influence, adroit manipulation, contrivance, etc. 2. to manipulate or change for a selfish or dishonest purpose, as statistics, etc.; falsify; juggle. 3. to wiggle or wriggle. ***v.i.*** [Colloq.], 1. to make use of contrivance, adroit manipulation, or tricky and indirect methods in order to achieve one's aims. 2. to wriggle, as out of a difficult situation. ***n.*** [Colloq.], an act of wangling.

Wan·hsien (wän′shyen′), ***n.*** a city in Szechwan province, China, on the Yangtze River: pop., 211,000.

wan·ion (wôn′yən), ***n.*** [altered < ME. *waneand*, Northern dial. ppr. of *wanien*, to wane; sense < notion of the waning of the moon as unlucky time], [Archaic], bad luck; curse; plague; vengeance: in *with* (or *in*) *a wanion.*

wan·nish (wän′ish, wôn′ish), ***adj.*** somewhat wan.

want (wänt, wônt), ***v.t.*** [ME. *wanten;* ON. *vanta*, to be lacking, want; see the ***n.***], 1. to lack; have too little of; be deficient in. 2. to be short by (a specified amount) of a certain total or result: as, it *wants* twelve minutes of midnight. 3. to feel the need of; crave; long for: as, he *wants* adventure. 4. to desire; wish (followed by the infinitive): as, she *wants* to go with us. 5. *a*) to wish to see or speak with (someone): as, your mother *wants* you. *b*) to wish to apprehend, as for questioning or arrest: usually in the passive voice, as, *wanted* by the police. 6. [Chiefly British], to require; need: as, this *wants* attending to. *Want* is also used colloquially as an auxiliary meaning *ought* or *should:* as, you *want* to eat before you go. ***v.i.*** 1. to have a need or lack (usually with *for*): as, we shall not *want* for money. 2. to lack the necessaries of life; be destitute or impoverished. 3. [Rare or Archaic], to be lacking or missing for completeness or a certain result: as, there *wants* but his approval. ***n.*** [ME.; ON. *vant*, neut. of *vanr*, deficient (cf. WANE); IE. base ***ewā-**, to lack, etc., seen also in L. *vanus*, empty, vacant, etc. (cf. VAIN)], 1. the state or fact of lacking, or having too little of, something needed or desired; scarcity; shortage; lack: as, there is a *want* of confidence in him. 2. a lack of the necessaries of life; poverty; destitution. 3. a wish or desire for something; craving. 4. something needed or desired but lacking; need. —***SYN.*** see **desire, lack, poverty.**

want in (or **out, off,** etc.), [Colloq. or Dial.], to want to get, go, or come in (or out, off, etc.).

want ad, [Colloq.], an advertisement, as in the classified advertising section of a newspaper, announcing that one wants a job, an apartment to rent, a specified type of employee, etc., or that one has something specified to sell or trade.

want·age (wän′tij, wôn′tij), ***n.*** [see -AGE], an amount lacking; shortage.

want·ing (wän′tiŋ, wôn′tiŋ), ***adj.*** 1. absent; lacking; missing: as, a coat with some buttons *wanting.* 2. not up to some standard; inadequate in some essential: as, weighed and found *wanting.* ***prep.*** 1. lacking (something); without. 2. minus; less: as, a full payment, *wanting* ten dollars.

wanting in, deficient in (some quality, part, etc.).

wan·ton (wän′tən, wôn′tən), ***adj.*** [ME. *wantowen*, var. of *wantogen*, wanton, irregular; AS. *wan-*, used as negative prefix < *wan*, lacking, deficient + *togen*, pp. of *teon*, to draw, educate, bring up], 1. originally, undisciplined; unmanageable: as, *wanton* boys. 2. unchaste; lewd; immoral. 3. [Poetic], *a*) frisky; playful; frolicsome: as, a *wanton* child. *b*) unrestrained in play: as, *wanton* winds. 4. senseless, unprovoked, unjustifiable, or deliberately malicious: as, *wanton* cruelty, a *wanton* insult. 5. recklessly or arrogantly disregardful of justice, decency, people's rights or feelings, etc. 6. *a*) [Poetic], luxuriant: said of vegetation, etc. *b*) lavish, luxurious, or extravagant: said of speech, dress, etc. ***n.*** a wanton person or thing; especially, an immoral or unchaste woman. ***v.i.*** 1. to indulge in playful, indiscriminate, or excessive lovemaking. 2. to be playful; frolic heedlessly. 3. to indulge in excesses of conduct, language, etc. 4. to grow luxuriantly; run riot. ***v.t.*** to waste carelessly or in luxurious pleasures.

wan·y (wān′i), ***adj.*** [WANIER (-i-ẽr), WANIEST (-i-ist)], 1. waning. 2. having an edge or edges slanting or beveled: said of planks, etc. cut from an unsquared log or block. Also spelled **waney.**

wap (wäp, wap), ***v.t. & v.i.*** [WAPPED (wäpt, wapt), WAPPING], ***n.*** [Dial. or Archaic], whop.

wap·en·take (wäp′ən-tāk′, wap′ən-tāk′), ***n.*** [AS. *wæpengetæc;* ON. *vapnatak,* lit., a weapon-taking or weapon-touching; prob. used territorially from brandishing of weapons as symbol of an assent vote; cf. WAPPENSCHAWING], in England, formerly, 1. a subdivision of certain northern counties originally under Norse domination, corresponding to the hundred in other counties. 2. a law court in such a subdivision.

wap·i·ti (wäp′ə-ti), ***n.*** [*pl.* WAPITIS (-tiz), WAPITI; see PLURAL, II, D, 1], [< Am. Ind. (Algonquian) name; cf. Shawnee *wapiti,* pale, white], a North American deer or elk related to the European red deer, but larger, with long, branching antlers.

wap·pen·schaw (wäp′ən-shô′, wap′ən-shô′), ***n.*** a wappenschawing: also spelled **wappenshaw, wapinschaw.**

wap·pen·schaw·ing (wäp′ən-shô′iŋ, wap′ən-shô′iŋ), ***n.*** [< *wapen,* weapon (see WEAPON) + *schawing,* a showing (see SHOW)], in *Scottish history,* a review or mustering of men under arms, held at periodic intervals in each district: also spelled **wappenshawing.**

wap·per·jaw (wäp′ẽr-jô′), ***n.*** [Colloq.], an underjaw that projects or is crooked.

wap·per·jawed (wäp′ẽr-jôd′), ***adj.*** [Colloq.], having a wapperjaw.

war (wôr), ***n.*** [ME. & ONorm.Fr. *werre;* OHG. *werra,* confusion, strife; prob. IE. base **wers-,* to sweep, drag, etc.; exact sense development unknown], 1. open armed conflict between countries or between factions within the same country. 2. any active hostility or contention; conflict; strife: as, the *war* between the sexes. 3. military operations as a science, art, or profession, or as a department of activity. 4. [Obs. or Poetic], a battle. ***adj.*** of, used in, or resulting from war. ***v.i.*** [WARRED (wôrd), WARRING], 1. to carry on war; engage in military operations. 2. to be in a state of hostility or contention; contend; strive.

at war, in a state of active armed conflict.

declare war (on), 1. to make a formal declaration of being at war (with). 2. to announce one's hostility or open opposition (to).

go to war, 1. to enter into a war. 2. to become a member of the armed forces during a war.

war (wär), ***adj. & adv.*** [ME.; ON. *verre, adj., verr, adv.;* see WORSE], [Scot. & N. Eng. Dial.], worse: also **waur.**

War between the States, the American Civil War (1861–1865): so called generally in the South.

war·ble (wôr′b'l), ***v.t.*** [WARBLED (-b'ld), WARBLING], [ME. *werblen;* ONorm.Fr. *werbler* < the Gmc. base seen in G. *wirbeln,* to whirl, warble; cf. WHIRL], 1. to sing melodiously, with trills, quavers, runs, etc., as a bird. 2. to tell in song or verse. ***v.i.*** 1. to sing melodiously, with trills, etc. 2. to make a musical sound; babble, as a stream. 3. to yodel. ***n.*** 1. a song or carol. 2. an act of warbling. 3. a warbling sound; trill.

war·ble (wôr′b'l), ***n.*** [Early Mod. Eng.; prob. for a ME. dial. **warbuld, warbled;* akin to obs. Sw. *varbulde,* boil; *var,* pus + *bulde,* tumor], 1. a small, hard tumor on the back of a horse, caused by the rubbing and pressing of a saddle. 2. a lump or swelling under the hide of an animal, especially on the back, caused by the presence of a larva of the warble fly or botfly. 3. the larva of the warble fly. 4. the warble fly.

warble fly, any of a number of two-winged flies whose larvae burrow beneath the hides of cattle, horses, and other animals, producing warbles.

war·bler (wôr′blẽr), ***n.*** 1. a bird or person that warbles; singer; songster. 2. any of a large family of small, insect-eating New World birds (*wood warblers*), many of which are brightly colored, as the yellow warbler, the golden warbler, the American redstart, etc. 3. any of a family of small songbirds, as the whitethroat, the **reed** warbler, etc., found chiefly in the Old World.

war bonnet, a ceremonial headdress worn by some tribes of North American Indians, consisting of a headband and trailing part studded with feathers.

war cry, 1. a name, phrase, slogan, etc. shouted in a charge or battle. 2. a phrase or slogan adopted by a party in any conflict, contest, election, etc.

ward (wôrd), ***v.t.*** [ME. *wardien;* AS. *weardian,* to keep, watch; akin to G. *warten,* affected by OFr. *warder* < Gmc.; IE. base **wer-,* to guard, keep safe, seen also in L. *vereri,* to observe anxiously (cf. REVERE, GUARD, WARE)], 1. to turn aside; fend off; parry (usually with *off*). 2. to place (a person) in a ward, as in a hospital. 3. [Archaic], to keep watch over; guard; protect. ***n.*** 1. a guarding: now only in *watch and ward.* 2. the state of being under guard. 3. *a*) guardianship, as of a child or person not capable of handling his own affairs. *b*) the condition of being under the control of a guardian; wardship. *c*) a child or incompetent person placed by law under the care of a guardian or court. *d*) a person under another's protection or care. 4. each of the parts or divisions of a jail or prison; hence, 5. a room or division of a hospital, asylum, etc., set apart for a specific class or group of patients: as, a maternity *ward.* 6. a district or division of a city or town, for purposes of administration, representation, voting, etc. 7. one of the administrative districts into which some counties in northern England and Scotland are divided, corresponding to the hundred and wapentake. 8. a means of defense or protection. 9. a defensive posture, position, or motion, as in fencing. 10. an open space enclosed by the walls of a castle or fortification. 11. [Archaic], a garrison; the guard or watch. 12. in *lockmaking, a*) a projecting ridge in a keyhole or lock face that allows only the right key to enter. *b*) the notch in a key that matches this ridge.

-ward (wẽrd), [ME. *-werd, ward;* AS. *-weard, weardes* < base of *weorthan,* to become (cf. WORTH)], a suffix meaning *in a* (specified) *direction* or *course,* as in *backward, eastward:* also, in adverbial variants, **-wards.**

Ward, Ar·te·mas (är′ti-məs wôrd), 1727–1800; American statesman and general in the Revolutionary War.

Ward, Ar·te·mus (är′ti-məs), (pseudonym of *Charles Farrar Browne*), 1834–1867; American humorous writer.

Ward, Mrs. **Humphrey,** (born *Mary Augusta Arnold*), 1851–1920; British novelist.

war dance, a ceremonial dance performed by primitive tribes before battle or after victory.

ward·ed (wôr′did), ***adj.*** having wards, or notches, etc., as a lock or key.

Ward·en (wôr′d'n), ***n.*** [ME. *wardon;* prob. < ONorm. Fr. *warder,* to keep < Gmc.; cf. WARD, *v.*], a medium-sized winter pear used chiefly for cooking: also **warden.**

ward·en (wôr′d'n), ***n.*** [ME. & ONorm.Fr. *wardein;* OFr. *gardein,* warden; see GUARDIAN, WARD], 1. a person who guards, or has charge of, something; keeper, custodian, or special supervisory official: as, air-raid *warden,* game *warden.* 2. the head keeper or top administrative official of a prison. 3. in England, a high government officer: now obsolete except in titles; specifically, *a*) a governor. *b*) an officer in charge of a certain department of the government. *c*) the superintendent of a port or market. 4. in England, a governing officer in certain colleges, guilds, hospitals, etc.; trustee. 5. in Connecticut, the chief executive of a borough. 6. in the *Episcopal Church,* etc., a churchwarden. 7. [Rare], a gatekeeper or watchman. Abbreviated **W., w.**

ward·en·ry (wôr′d'n-ri), ***n.*** [*pl.* WARDENRIES (-riz)], 1. the office or position of a warden. 2. the district or jurisdiction of a warden.

ward·en·ship (wôr′d'n-ship′), ***n.*** [see **-SHIP**], the office, jurisdiction, or term of office of a warden.

ward·er (wôr′dẽr), ***n.*** [ME. *wardere;* Anglo-Fr. *wardour;* OFr. *guarder;* see GUARD, WARD], 1. a person who guards; watchman. 2. a person who guards an entrance. 3. [Chiefly British], a warden, custodian, or jail official in charge of prisoners.

ward·er (wôr′dẽr), ***n.*** [Late ME.; < ?], formerly, a staff or rod carried by a king, commander, etc. as a mark of authority, and used to signal his wishes.

ward heeler, a hanger-on of a ward committee or politician; ward worker who solicits votes for his party and performs various small tasks for his political bosses: a contemptuous term.

ward·ress (wôrd′ris), ***n.*** [Chiefly British], a woman warder.

ward·robe (wôrd′rōb′), ***n.*** [ME. & ONorm.Fr. *warderobe;* see WARD & ROBE], 1. a closet or movable cabinet, usually relatively tall and provided with hooks, etc., for holding clothes. 2. a room where clothes are kept; especially, a room in a theater where costumes are kept. 3. a collection of clothes; especially, *a*) the complete supply of clothes of a person. *b*) a supply of clothes for a particular season or purpose: as, a spring *wardrobe.* *c*) the clothes and costumes of a theater or theatrical company. 4. in a royal or similar household, the department in charge of clothes.

ward·room (wôrd′ro͞om′, wôrd′room′), ***n.*** [*ward, n.* + *room*], 1. in a warship, living or eating quarters for all officers above an ensign in rank, except the captain. 2. these officers collectively.

-wards (wẽrdz), -ward.

ward·ship (wôrd′ship′), *n.* [see -SHIP], 1. the office of a guardian; guardianship; custody, as of a minor. 2. the condition of being a ward, or in the care of a guardian.

ware (wâr), *n.* [ME. *ware;* AS. *waru,* merchandise; specialized use of *waru,* watchful care, in the sense "what is kept safe"; for IE. base see WARD], 1. anything made to sell; anything that a store, merchant, peddler, etc. has to sell. 2. things, usually of the same general kind, which are for sale; a (specified) kind of merchandise, collectively: generally in compounds, as *hardware, earthenware, glassware.* 3. dishes made of baked and glazed clay; pottery, or a specified kind or make of pottery. 4. *pl.* things for sale, collectively.

ware (wâr), *adj.* [ME. *war;* AS. *wær* < base of *waru;* cf. WARE, *n.*, WARD], [Archaic], 1. aware; conscious (of). 2. on one's guard; ready; wary. 3. prudent; cautious; wise. *v.t.* [WARED (wârd), WARING], [ME. *waren;* AS. *warian*], to beware of; look out for: usually in the imperative, especially in hunting, as, *ware* hounds.

ware (wâr), *v.t.* [WARED (wârd), WARING], [ME. < Scand.; cf. ON. *verja,* AS. *werian* (see WEAR)], [Scot. & N. Eng. Dial.], to spend, as money, time, etc.

ware·house (wâr′hous′; *for v., usually* wâr′houz′), *n.* [ME.; see WARE, *n.* & HOUSE], 1. a building where wares, or goods, are stored, as before being distributed to retailers; storehouse. 2. [Chiefly British], a wholesale store or, sometimes, a large retail store. Abbreviated **W., w.** *v.t.* to place or store in a warehouse; especially, to store in a bonded or government warehouse until the duties are paid.

ware·house·man (wâr′hous′mən), *n.* [*pl.* WAREHOUSEMEN (-mən)], a man who owns, manages, or works in a warehouse.

warehouse receipt, a receipt issued by a warehouse for goods stored there: it is usually negotiable.

ware·room (wâr′ro͞om′, wâr′room′), *n.* a room used for storing or displaying things for sale.

war·fare (wôr′fâr′), *n.* 1. the action of waging war; armed conflict. 2. conflict of any kind; struggle.

War·field, David (wôr′fēld), 1866–1951; American actor.

war game, 1. military tactical exercises carried out as training by officers using maps, pins, and tokens to represent terrain, troops, guns, etc. 2. *pl.* practice maneuvers.

war head, the head, or forward section, of a self-propelled torpedo or of a rocket- or jet-propelled projectile, containing the explosive charge.

war horse, 1. a horse used in battle; charger. 2. [Colloq.], a person who has been through many battles or struggles; veteran.

war·i·ly (wâr′ə-li), *adv.* in a wary manner; cautiously.

war·i·ness (wâr′i-nis), *n.* a wary quality or state.

war·i·son (war′ə-s′n), *n.* [ME.; OFr.; see GARRISON], 1. [Obs.], a reward or gift given by a superior. 2. [Pseudoarchaic], a note sounded to signal an attack: erroneously so used by Scott.

wark (wärk), *n.* & *v.i.* [var. of *work*], [Scot. & Eng. Dial.], ache; pain.

war·like (wôr′līk′), *adj.* 1. fit for, fond of, or ready for war; bellicose; martial. 2. of or belonging to war. 3. threatening war; indicative of war. —*SYN.* see **martial.**

war·lock (wôr′lok′), *n.* [ME. *warlawe, warloghe;* AS. *wærloga,* a traitor, liar < *wær,* faith + *leogan,* to lie (cf. LIE)], [Scot. & Archaic], 1. a person who supposedly cast magic spells, etc. by means of a pact with the Devil; sorcerer. 2. a conjurer or the like.

war lord, 1. a high military officer in a warlike nation. 2. an aggressive tyrant. 3. in China, a local ruler or bandit leader with some sort of military following in a district where the established government is weak.

warm (wôrm), *adj.* [ME.; AS. *wearm;* akin to G. *warm;* IE. base **gwher-,* hot, seen also in Gr. *thermos,* warm (cf. THERM, THERMO-), L. *fornax* (cf. FURNACE), etc.], 1. *a*) having or giving off a moderate degree of heat: as, *warm* iron, *warm* weather, *warm* coffee. *b*) giving off heat: as, a *warm* fire. 2. having the natural heat of living beings: said of the body, blood, etc. 3. *a*) heated or overheated, as with exercise or hard work. *b*) such as to make one heated or overheated: as, *warm* exercise, work, etc. 4. made of a cloth or material which keeps body heat in: as, *warm* clothing. 5. characterized by lively disagreement: said of argument or controversy. 6. fervent; ardent; enthusiastic: as, *warm* encouragement. 7. lively, vigorous, brisk, or animated. 8. fiery; quick to anger; irascible; heated. 9. *a*) genial; cordial: as, a *warm* welcome. *b*) sincere; grateful: as, *warm* thanks. *c*) sympathetic, affectionate, or loving. *d*) passionate; amorous. 10. suggesting warmth; having yellow, orange, or red hue: said of colors: opposed to *cool.* 11. newly made; fresh; strong: said of a scent or trail; hence, 12. [Colloq.], close to discovering something; on the verge of guessing or finding, as in games. 13. [Colloq.], disagreeable; uncomfortable; hot: as, we made things *warm* for him. 14. [Colloq.], well-to-do; well off. *adv.* so as to be warm; warmly. *v.t.* [ME; *warmen;* AS. *wearmian,* to warm], 1. to make warm; raise the temperature of to a moderate extent. 2. to make excited, animated, ardent, enthusiastic, lively, etc. 3. to fill with pleasant or kindly emotions: as, the sight of the children *warms* my heart. *v.i.* 1. to become warm. 2. to become friendly, kindly, affectionate, or sympathetic (often with *to* or *toward*). 3. to become excited, ardent, enthusiastic, lively, etc. *n.* [Colloq.], a warming or being warmed. —*SYN.* see **tender.**

warm up, 1. to heat or be heated; make or become warm. 2. to heat again, after cooling: said of food: also **warm over.** 3. to make or become more animated, excited, ardent, enthusiastic, lively, etc. 4. in *sports,* to practice or exercise a while before going into a game, test of skill, race, etc.

warm-blood·ed (wôrm′blud′id), *adj.* 1. having warm blood and a constant natural body heat, specific for each species: said of mammals and birds. 2. having or characterized by an eager, lively, or passionate temperament; ardent; fervent; impetuous.

warm·heart·ed (wôrm′här′tid), *adj.* 1. kind; sympathetic; friendly. 2. loving; ardent. —*SYN.* see **tender.**

warming pan, a long-handled, covered pan for holding live coals: formerly used to warm beds.

warm·ish (wôrm′ish), *adj.* somewhat warm.

war·mon·ger (wôr′muŋ′gẽr), *n.* a person or agency that advocates war or tries to bring about war.

Warm Springs, a town in western Georgia: site of a foundation for treatment of poliomyelitis.

warmth (wôrmth), *n.* [ME. *wermthe;* prob. < AS. **wiermthu;* see WARM & -TH], 1. the state or quality of having or giving off a moderate degree of heat. 2. the natural heat of a living body. 3. the degree of heat in a substance, especially when it is moderate; mild heat. 4. excitement, strength, or vigor of feeling; enthusiasm; ardor; zeal. 5. slight anger. 6. a glowing or intense effect obtained by using red, yellow, or orange.

warm-up (wôrm′up′), *n.* the act of practicing or exercising before going into a game, contest, race, etc.

warn (wôrn), *v.t.* [ME. *warnien, warnen;* AS. *wearnian;* akin to G. *warnen;* for IE. base see WARD], 1. to tell (a person) of a danger, coming evil, misfortune, etc.; put on guard against a person or thing. 2. to advise to be wary or cautious. 3. to caution about certain acts; admonish: as, you have been *warned* against smoking here. 4. to notify in advance; inform. 5. to give notice to (a person), as that he must appear at a specified place and time, or that he must stay or keep (*off, out,* etc.). *v.i.* to give warning: as, a rattlesnake *warns* before it strikes. —*SYN.* see **advise.**

War·ner (wôr′nẽr), [ONorm.Fr. *Warnier;* OHG. **warnhari* < Gmc. *warn-,* to warn, protect + *hari-,* army, host], a masculine name.

warn·ing (wôr′niŋ), *n.* 1. the act of one that warns, or the state of being warned. 2. something that serves to warn. *adj.* that warns; serving to warn.

war nose, 1. the nose, or tip, of a shell, containing the primer and firing mechanism, and sometimes the explosive charge. 2. the explosive tip of a torpedo or other projectile.

War of 1812, a war (1812–1815) between the United States and Great Britain.

War of American Independence, [British], the American Revolution.

War of Independence, the American Revolution; Revolutionary War.

War of Secession, (1861–1865), the American Civil War: also called *War between the States.*

warp (wôrp), *n.* [ME.; AS. *wearp* < the base of *weorpan,* to throw; akin to G. *werfen*], 1. *a*) a distortion, as a twist or bend, in wood or in an object made of wood, caused by contraction in drying; hence, *b*) any like distortion. *c*) the state or fact of being so distorted. 2. a mental twist, quirk, aberration, or bias. 3. *a*) silt, sediment, or mud dropped by water, as by a stream. *b*) a deposit of this. 4. in *nautical usage,* a rope or line run from a ship to a pile, buoy, anchor, etc., and used to move or haul the ship into position. 5. in *weaving,* the threads running lengthwise in the loom and crossed by the weft or woof: see **weaving,** illus. *v.t.* [ME. *warpen,* to throw, bend; AS. *weorpan,* to throw], 1. to bend, curve, or twist out of shape; distort. 2. *a*) to turn from the true, natural, or right course. *b*) to turn from a healthy, sane, or normal condition; pervert; bias: said of the mind, character, judgment, etc. *c*) to twist; distort in telling; misinterpret: as, a *warped* account. 3. to fasten by binding with rope, string, twine, etc.: as, *warp* two sticks together. 4. in *aeronautics,* to bend or twist (a wing) at one or both ends, as to keep or regain lateral balance. 5. in *nautical usage,* to move, as a ship, by hauling on a line fastened to a pile, dock, anchor, etc. 6. in *weaving,* to arrange (threads or yarns) so as to form a warp. *v.i.* 1. to become bent or twisted out of shape, as wood in drying. 2. to turn aside from the true, natural, or right course. 3. in *nautical usage,* to move by warping or being warped, as a ship. —*SYN.* see **deform.**

war paint, 1. a pigment applied to the face and body by primitive tribes in preparation for war. 2. [Slang], ceremonial dress; regalia. 3. [Slang], cosmetics; powder, rouge, and lipstick, as used by women.

war·path (wôr′path′, wôr′päth′), *n.* the path or course taken by American Indians on a warlike expedition.
on the warpath, 1. at war, ready for war, or looking for war. 2. actively angry; ready to fight.
warp beam, in *weaving*, the roller on which the warp is wound in a loom: see **weaving,** illus.
warp·ing (wôrp′iŋ), *n.* in *geology*, the gradual distortion of rock strata by general crustal disturbance.
war·plane (wôr′plān′), *n.* any airplane for use in war.
war·rant (wôr′ənt, wär′ənt), *n.* [ME. & ONorm.Fr. *warant;* OFr. *garant*, a warrant; OHG. *weren*, a warranty; cf. GUARANTY], 1. *a)* authorization or sanction, as by a superior or the law. *b)* justification or reasonable grounds for some act, course, statement, or belief. 2. something that serves as an assurance, or guarantee, of some event or result. 3. a writing serving as authorization or certification for something; specifically, *a)* authorization in writing for the payment or receipt of money; voucher. *b)* [British], a receipt for goods stored in a warehouse. *c)* in *law*, a writ or order authorizing an officer to make an arrest, seizure, or search, or perform some other designated act. *d)* in *military usage*, the certificate of appointment to the grade of warrant officer: cf. **warrant officer.** *v.t.* 1. *a)* to give (someone) authorization or sanction to do something. *b)* to authorize (the doing of something). 2. to serve as justification or reasonable grounds for (an act, belief, etc.): as, my remarks did not *warrant* her tears. 3. to give formal assurance, or guarantee, to (someone) or for (something); specifically, *a)* to guarantee the quality, quantity, condition, etc. of (goods) to the purchaser. *b)* to guarantee to (the purchaser) that goods sold are as represented. *c)* to guarantee to (the purchaser) the title of goods purchased; assure of indemnification against loss. *d)* in *law*, to guarantee the title of granted property to (the grantee). 4. [Colloq.], to state with confidence; affirm emphatically: as, I *warrant* he'll be late. —*SYN.* see **assert.**
war·rant·a·ble (wôr′ən-tə-b'l, wär′ən-tə-b'l), *adj.* that can be warranted.
war·rant·a·bly (wôr′ən-tə-bli, wär′ən-tə-bli), *adv.* so as to be warrantable.
war·ran·tee (wôr′ən-tē′, wär′ən-tē′), *n.* in *law*, a person to whom a warranty is given.
war·rant·er (wôr′ən-tẽr, wär′ən-tẽr), *n.* a person who warrants: cf. **warrantor.**
warrant officer, in the *United States armed forces*, an officer of either of two grades ranking above an enlisted man but below a second lieutenant or ensign, generally holding his office on a warrant instead of a commission: abbreviated **W.O.**
war·ran·tor (wôr′ən-tôr′, wär′ən-tôr′), *n.* in *law*, a person who warrants, or gives warranty.
war·ran·ty (wôr′ən-ti, wär′ən-ti), *n.* [*pl.* WARRANTIES (-tiz)], [ME. & ONorm.Fr. *warantie;* OFr. *garantie* < *garant;* see WARRANT], 1. official authorization or sanction. 2. justification; reasonable grounds, as for an opinion or action. 3. in *law*, a guarantee; specifically, *a)* a guarantee or an assurance, explicit or implied, of something having to do with a contract, as of sale; especially, the seller's assurance to the purchaser that the goods or property is or shall be as represented. *b)* a guarantee by the insured that the facts are as stated in regard to an insurance risk, or that specified conditions shall be fulfilled: it constitutes a part of the contract and must be fulfilled to keep the contract in force. *c)* a covenant by which the seller of real estate gives assurance of, and binds himself to defend, the security of the title: also called *covenant of warranty*. *d)* a warrant or writ.
warranty deed, in *law*, a deed to real estate containing a covenant of warranty (see **warranty,** 3*c*): distinguished from *quitclaim deed*.
War·ren (wôr′ən, wär′ən), [ONorm.Fr. *Warin;* prob. < OG. *Warin*, the Varini, a people mentioned by Tacitus], a masculine name. *n.* 1. a city in northeastern Ohio: pop., 60,000. 2. a city in southeastern Michigan: suburb of Detroit: pop., 89,000.
war·ren (wôr′ən, wär′ən), *n.* [ME. *wareine;* ONorm.Fr. *warenne* < OFr. *warir*, to preserve; of Gmc. origin; cf. WARD, GUARD], 1. originally, a piece of land enclosed for the breeding of game. 2. a space or limited area in which rabbits breed or are numerous. 3. any building or group of buildings crowded like a rabbit warren.
Warren, Earl, 1891– ; chief justice of the United States (1953–).
Warren, Robert Penn, 1905– ; American writer.
war·ren·er (wôr′ən-ẽr, wär′ən-ẽr), *n.* the owner or keeper of a warren.
War·ring·ton (wôr′iŋ-t'n, wär′iŋ-t'n), *n.* a city in Lancashire, England; pop., 79,000.
war·ri·or (wôr′i-ẽr, wär′yẽr), *n.* [ME. *werreour;* ONorm.Fr. *werreiur* < *werrier*, to make war < *werre;* see WAR], a man experienced in war or battle; fighting man.
war risk insurance, United States government insurance carried in time of war by members of the armed forces.
War·saw (wôr′sô), *n.* the capital of Poland, on the Vistula River: pop., 1,095,000: Polish name, *Warszawa*.
war·saw (wôr′sô), *n.* [altered < Sp. *guasa*], a very large grouper found in the warm waters about the West Indies and Florida.
war·ship (wôr′ship′), *n.* any ship constructed or armed for combat use, as a battleship, destroyer, etc.
war·sle (wär′s'l), *v.i. & v.t.* [WARSLED (-s'ld), WARSLING], *n.* [Scot., Irish, & N. Eng. Dial.], wrestle: also spelled **warstle.**
Wars of the Roses, the English civil war (1455–1485) fought between the House of York, whose emblem was a white rose, and the House of Lancaster, whose emblem was a red rose: the war ended with the establishment of the House of Tudor on the English throne.
War·sza·wa (vär-shä′vȧ), *n.* Warsaw.
wart (wôrt), *n.* [ME. *werte, warte;* AS. *wearte*, a wart; akin to G. *warze;* IE. base **wer-*, a raised place, seen also in L. *verruca*, wart (cf. VERRUCA)], 1. a small, usually hard, tumorous growth on the skin. 2. a small protuberance, as a glandular protuberance on a plant.
War·ta (vär′tȧ), *n.* Warthe: the Polish name.
Wart·burg (värt′boorkh), *n.* a medieval castle in Thuringia, Germany, where Luther translated the New Testament.
War·the (vär′tə), *n.* a river in western Poland, flowing into the Oder River: length, 445 mi.
wart hog, any of a group of wild African hogs having a broad flat face, very large incurved tusks, and a number of conical warts between the eyes and tusks.

WART HOG
(3 ft. high at shoulder)

war·time (wôr′tīm′), *n.* any time or period of war.
wart·y (wôr′ti), *adj.* [WARTIER (-ti-ẽr), WARTIEST (-ti-ist)], 1. having warts; full of warts. 2. having lumps like warts. 3. having the nature of a wart or warts; like a wart.
war whoop, a loud shout or yell uttered, as by North American Indians, on going into battle, etc.
War·wick (wôr′ik, wär′ik; *for 3, usually* wôr′wik), *n.* 1. Warwickshire. 2. the county seat of Warwickshire, England: pop., 15,000. 3. a city in eastern Rhode Island: pop., 69,000.
War·wick (wôr′ik, wär′ik), Earl of, (*Richard Neville*), 1428–1471; English soldier and statesman: called *the Kingmaker*.
War·wick·shire (wôr′ik-shir′, wär′ik-shir′), *n.* a county in central England: pop., 1,862,000; county seat, Warwick: also **Warwick.**
war·y (wâr′i), *adj.* [WARIER (-i-ẽr), WARIEST (-i-ist)], [< *ware, adj.* + *-y*], 1. cautious; on one's guard. 2. characterized by caution: as, a *wary* look. —*SYN.* see **careful.**
wary of, careful of; suspicious of.
was (wuz, wäz; *unstressed* wəz), [ME.; AS. *wæs*, 1st & 3d pers. sing. of *wesan*, to be; IE. base **wes-*, to dwell, stay, seen also in Sans. *vastū*, house; not orig. connected with *be;* cf. WERE], the first and third person singular, past tense, of **be.**
Wa·satch Range (wô′sach), a mountain range in northern Utah and southeastern Idaho: highest peak, Mt. Timpanogos, 11,957 ft.
wase (wāz), *n.* [ME.; cf. Sw. *vase*, MLG. *wase*], [Obs. or Dial.], a bundle, wisp, or pad of straw, hay, etc.
wash (wôsh, wäsh), *v.t.* [ME. *wasshen;* AS. *wæscan;* akin to G. *waschen;* IE. base **wed-*, to moisten, make wet, seen also in *water, wet*], 1. to clean by means of water or other liquid, as by dipping, tumbling, or scrubbing, often with soap, etc. 2. to make clean in a religious or moral sense; purify. 3. to make wet; moisten; drench or flush with water or other liquid. 4. to flow over, past, or against: said of a sea, river, lake, waves, etc. 5. *a)* to soak out or flush off and carry away, as dirt, a dye, etc., by or as by the use or action of water, or like water (with *off, out,* or *away*). *b)* to pick up and carry along or away: as, the waves *washed* the stick away. 6. *a)* to make by flowing over and wearing away substance: as, the rain *washed* gullies in the bank. *b)* to cut into or erode; wear away by flowing over (with *out* or *away*): as, the flood *washed* out the road. 7. to act as a suitable cleaning agent for: as, that soap will *wash* silks. 8. to cover with a thin or watery coating of paint, especially of water color. 9. to cover with a thin layer of metal. 10. in *chemistry*, *a)* to pass distilled water through (a precipitate in a filter). *b)* to pass (a gas) over or through a liquid in order to remove soluble matter. 11. in *mining*, *a)* to pass water through or over (earth, gravel, etc.) in order to separate ore, metal, precious stones, etc. *b)* to separate (the ore, etc.) in this way. *v.i.* 1. to

wash oneself or one's hands, face, etc.: often with *up.* 2. *a*) to wash clothes. *b*) to clean anything in, or by means of, water, etc. 3. to undergo washing, especially without fading or other damage. 4. to be removed by washing (usually with *out*): as, the stain *washed* out. 5. to sweep, beat, or flow (*over, against, along*, etc.) with a characteristic sound, as, in, or as in waves. 6. to be cut, worn, or carried by the action of water (with *out* or *away*): as, the bridge had *washed* out. 7. to be eroded, as by the action of rain or a river. 8. [British Colloq.], to withstand a test or examination: as, his story won't *wash.* ***n.*** 1. the act or process of washing. 2. a quantity of clothes, etc. washed, or to be washed, in one batch. 3. waste liquid; refuse liquid food, as from cooking; swill; hogwash. 4. *a*) the rush, sweep, or surge of water or waves. *b*) the sound of this. *c*) water rushing, sweeping, or surging in waves. *d*) the surge or eddy of water caused by a propeller, oars, paddle wheel, etc.; hence, *e*) a disturbed eddy of air left behind a moving airplane, propeller, etc. 5. wear or erosion caused by a flow or falling of water, or by the action of waves. 6. silt, mud, debris, etc. carried and dropped by running water, as of a stream. 7. soil or earth from which metals, ores, precious stones, etc. may be washed. 8. *a*) low ground which is flooded part of the time, and partly dry the rest, with water standing in pools. *b*) a bog; marsh. *c*) a shallow pool or pond, or a small stream. *d*) a shallow arm of the sea or part of a river. 9. a channel made by running water. 10. in the western United States, the dry bed of a stream which flows only occasionally, usually in a ravine or canyon. 11. a thin, watery layer of paint, especially of water color, applied with even, continuous movement of the brush. 12. a thin coating of metal applied to a surface in liquid form. 13. any of various liquids for cosmetic, medicinal, or toilet use: as, a hair *wash*, mouth *wash.* 14. fermented liquor ready for distillation. 15. a liquid for washing, tinting, etc. 16. weak liquor or liquid food. 17. [Colloq.], water, carbonated water, beer, etc. drunk after a drink of undiluted whisky or other strong liquor; chaser. ***adj.*** that can be washed without damage; washable: as, a *wash* dress.

come out in the wash, [Slang], to be revealed or explained sooner or later.

wash down, 1. to clean by washing, especially with a stream of water. 2. to follow (a bite of food, a meal, a drink of whisky, etc.) with a drink, as of water.

wash one's hands of, to disclaim any further responsibility for or interest in.

wash out, [Slang], to drop or be dropped from a course, especially in military aviation, because of failure.

SYN.—**wash,** the most general of these words, refers to any earthy material carried and deposited by running water; **drift,** the more precise term as used in geology, is usually qualified by a word descriptive of the manner in which the material is transported (glacial or fluvial *drift*); **alluvium** usually refers to a deposit of relatively fine particles, such as soil, left by a flood, etc.; **silt** applies to material composed of very fine particles, such as that deposited on river beds or suspended in standing water.

Wash, The (wôsh, wäsh), a shallow bay off east central England: length, c. 22 mi.; width, c. 15 mi.

Wash., Washington (State).

wash·a·ble (wôsh'ə-b'l, wäsh'ə-b'l), ***adj.*** that can be washed without damage: said of fabric, dyes, etc.

wash and wear, designating or made of a fabric that needs little or no ironing after washing.

wash·ba·sin (wôsh'bā's'n, wäsh'bā's'n), ***n.*** [Chiefly British], a washbowl.

wash·board (wôsh'bôrd', wäsh'bōrd'), ***n.*** 1. a board or frame with a ridged surface of metal, glass, etc., used for scrubbing dirt out of clothes. 2. a board fastened along the base of a wall at the floor; baseboard. 3. in *nautical usage*, a thin, broad plank fastened along the gunwale of a boat or on the sill of a lower deck port to keep out the sea and spray.

wash·bowl (wôsh'bōl', wäsh'bōl'), ***n.*** a bowl or basin for use in washing one's hands and face, etc.

wash·cloth (wôsh'klôth', wäsh'klôth'), ***n.*** a small cloth used in washing the body.

wash·day (wôsh'dā', wäsh'dā'), ***n.*** a day, often the same day every week, when the clothes of a household are washed.

washed-out (wôsht'out', wäsht'out'), ***adj.*** 1. faded; having little color. 2. [Colloq.], tired; spiritless. 3. [Colloq.], tired-looking; pale and wan.

washed-up (wôsht'up', wäsht'up'), ***adj.*** 1. cleaned up. 2. [Colloq.], tired; exhausted. 3. [Slang], finished; done for; discarded or dismissed as a failure.

wash·er (wôsh'ẽr, wäsh'ẽr), ***n.*** 1. a person who washes. 2. a flat disk or ring of metal, leather, rubber, etc., used to make a seat for the head of a bolt or for a nut, to lock a nut in place, to provide a bearing surface for anything that pivots, to provide packing, etc. 3. a machine for washing something, as clothes, dishes, etc. 4. a device for washing gases.

wash·er·man (wôsh'ẽr-mən, wäsh'ẽr-mən), ***n.*** [*pl.* WASHERMEN (-mən)], a man whose work is washing clothes, etc., especially for hire.

wash·er·wom·an (wôsh'ẽr-woo'mən, wäsh'ẽr-woo'mən), ***n.*** [*pl.* WASHERWOMEN (-wim'in)], a woman whose work is washing clothes, etc., especially for hire.

wash goods, fabrics or garments that can be washed without injury to fibers or finish.

wash-in (wôsh'in', wäsh'in'), ***n.*** [*wash, v.* + *in*], a warp of an airplane wing, giving an increase of the angle of attack toward the tip.

wash·i·ness (wôsh'i-nis, wäsh'i-nis), ***n.*** the quality or condition of being washy.

wash·ing (wôsh'iŋ, wäsh'iŋ), ***n.*** 1. the act or process of a person or thing that washes; especially, the act of cleaning with water, soap and water, or other liquid. 2. the act or process of drenching, flushing, or coating with a liquid, or of dipping into a liquid, etc. 3. *a*) *also pl.* liquid which has been used to wash something. *b*) matter, especially waste matter, removed by washing. 4. *a*) the process of carrying away matter by the flow of running water. *b*) matter carried away by this action. *c*) metal, ore, gems, etc. obtained by washing. *d*) a placer or similar deposit where metal, etc. may be obtained by washing. 5. a thin coating or covering, as of metal, put on in liquid form. 6. clothes or other things washed or to be washed, especially in one batch or at one time. 7. the act of making a wash sale. ***adj.*** of, for, or used in washing.

washing machine, a machine for washing clothes, etc., especially one operated by electricity.

washing soda, a crystalline form of sodium carbonate, used in washing.

Wash·ing·ton (wôsh'iŋ-tən, wäsh'iŋ-tən), ***n.*** 1. a Western State of the United States: area, 68,192 sq. mi.; pop., 2,853,000; capital, Olympia: abbreviated **Wash., W.** 2. a city in southwestern Pennsylvania: pop., 24,000. 3. the capital of the United States, coextensive with the District of Columbia: pop., 764,000 (metropolitan area, 2,002,000).

Washington, Book·er Tal·ia·ferro (book'ẽr täl'ə-vẽr), 1856–1915; American Negro educator and author.

Washington, George, 1732–1799; first president of the United States (1789–1797); commander in chief of the colonial armies in the American Revolution: called *Father of his Country.*

Washington, Lake, a lake in western Washington, near Seattle: length, 20 mi.

Washington, Mount, the highest peak in New England, in the White Mountains of New Hampshire: height, 6,288 ft.

Wash·ing·to·ni·an (wôsh'iŋ-tō'ni-ən, wäsh'iŋ-tō'ni-ən), ***adj.*** 1. of Washington, D.C. 2. of Washington (State). ***n.*** a native or inhabitant of either of these places.

Washington National Monument, a white marble obelisk, 555 ft. high, in Potomac Park, Washington, D.C., in memory of George Washington.

Washington palm, a tall, slender palm crowned with large, fan-shaped leaves, native to southern California.

Washington pie, a layer cake with a filling of cream, custard, chocolate, fruit jelly, or the like.

Wash·i·ta (wôsh'i-tô', wäsh'i-tô'), ***n.*** Ouachita River.

wash·out (wôsh'out', wäsh'out'), ***n.*** 1. the washing away of soil, earth, rocks, etc. by a sudden, strong flow of water. 2. a hole or gap made by such washing away, as in a railroad bed. 3. [Slang], a complete failure.

wash·rag (wôsh'rag', wäsh'rag'), ***n.*** a washcloth.

wash·room (wôsh'rōōm', wäsh'room'), ***n.*** 1. a room for washing. 2. a rest-room.

wash sale, in the stock exchange, the illegal and pretended sale of a security, to make it seem that the market is active.

wash·stand (wôsh'stand', wäsh'stand'), ***n.*** 1. a table holding a bowl and pitcher, etc., for washing the face and hands. 2. a plumbing fixture consisting essentially of a bowl or basin fitted with water faucets and a drain, used for washing the face and hands, etc.

wash·tub (wôsh'tub', wäsh'tub'), ***n.*** a tub for washing clothes, etc.; often, a stationary metal tub fitted with water faucets and a drain.

wash·wom·an (wôsh'woom'ən, wäsh'woom'ən), ***n.*** [*pl.* WASHWOMEN (-wim'in)], a washerwoman.

wash·y (wôsh'i, wäsh'i), ***adj.*** [WASHIER (-i-ẽr), WASHIEST (-i-ist)], [*wash* + *-y*], 1. watery; diluted; weak. 2. without force or substance; insipid; feeble. 3. [Rare], bringing rain or moisture: said of wind or weather.

was·n't (wuz''nt, wäz''nt), was not.

wasp (wäsp, wôsp), ***n.*** [ME. *waspe;* AS. *wæsp;* akin to G. *wespe;* Gmc. base **waps-;* IE. **whobhesa* < base **webh-*, to weave (cf. WEAVE), with reference to the cocoonlike nest], 1. any of a large, world-wide family of winged insects characterized by a slender body with the abdomen attached by a narrow stalk, biting mouth parts, and, in the females and workers, a vicious sting: some wasps, as the hornet, are characterized by a colonial or social organization. 2. a waspish person.

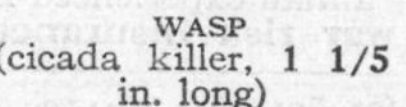

WASP (cicada killer, 1 1/5 in. long)

wasp·ish (wäsp′ish, wôsp′ish), ***adj.*** 1. of or like a wasp. 2. having a slender waist, like a wasp. 3. bad-tempered; easily irritated and made spiteful; snappish.

wasp waist, a very slender or pinched-in waist.

wasp-waist·ed (wäsp′wās′tid, wôsp′wās′tid), ***adj.*** 1. having a slender waist. 2. having the waist pinched in; tightly corseted.

wasp·y (wäsp′i, wôsp′i), ***adj.*** [WASPIER (-i-ẽr), WASPIEST (-i-ist)], of, like, or characteristic of a wasp.

was·sail (wäs′'l, was′'l, wäs′āl), ***n.*** [ME. *wassail, weseil* < ON. *ves heill,* lit., be hale, be hearty; replacing AS. *wes hal,* lit., be whole], 1. a salutation formerly given in drinking the health of a person, as at a festivity. 2. the spiced ale or other liquor with which such healths were drunk. 3. a celebration or festivity with much drinking; drinking bout. 4. [Obs. or British Dial.], a drinking song. ***v.i.*** to drink wassails; carouse. ***v.t.*** to drink to the health or prospering of.

was·sail·er (wäs′'l-ẽr, was′'l-ẽr), ***n.*** a person who takes part in a wassail; merrymaker; reveler.

Was·ser·mann, Au·gust von (ou′goost fôn väs′ẽr-män′; Eng. wäs′ẽr-mən), 1866–1925; German physician.

Wassermann, Ja·kob (yä′kôp), 1873–1934; German novelist.

Wassermann test (or **reaction**), a test for the diagnosis of syphilis by determining the presence of syphilitic antibodies in the blood serum: devised by August von Wassermann.

wast (wäst; *unstressed* wəst), archaic second person singular, past indicative of **be**: used with *thou.*

wast·age (wās′tij), ***n.*** [see -AGE], 1. loss by use, decay, deterioration, etc. 2. the process of wasting. 3. what is wasted; waste. 4. in *geology,* the process by which snow and ice masses eventually become water or vapor.

waste (wāst), ***v.t.*** [WASTED (-id), WASTING], [ME. *wasten;* Anglo-Fr. & ONorm.Fr. *waster* (OFr. *gaster, guaster*) < L. *vastare,* to lay waste, devastate (< *vastus;* see VAST); influenced by Gmc. **wostjan;* cf. OHG. *wuostēn*], 1. to destroy; devastate; ruin, as land. 2. to wear away; consume gradually; use up. 3. to make weak, feeble, or emaciated; wear away the strength, vigor, or life of: said especially of disease, decay, age, etc. 4. to use up or spend without need, profit, or proper return; squander. 5. to fail to take proper advantage of: as, you *wasted* a good opportunity. ***v.i.*** 1. to lose strength, health, vigor, flesh, etc., as by disease; become weak or enfeebled (often with *away*). 2. to be used up or worn down gradually; become smaller or fewer by gradual loss. 3. [Now Rare], to pass or be spent: said of time. 4. to be wasted, or not put to full or proper use. ***adj.*** [ME. & Anglo-Fr. *wast* (OFr. *gast, guast*); L. *vastus;* see VAST], 1. uncultivated or uninhabited, as a desert; wild; barren; desolate. 2. left over, superfluous, refuse, or no longer of use: as, a *waste* product, *waste* paper. 3. produced in excess of what is or can be used: as, *waste* energy. 4. excreted from the body as useless or superfluous material, as feces or urine. 5. *a*) used to carry off waste: as, a *waste* pipe. *b*) used to hold discarded waste: as, a *waste* basket. ***n.*** [ME.; Anglo-Fr. *wast;* ONorm.Fr. *waste* < the *adj.;* also in part < L. *vastum,* neut. of *vastus*], 1. uncultivated or uninhabited land, as a desert or wilderness. 2. a desolate, uncultivated, or devastated stretch, tract, or area: as, Berlin was a *waste* of tumbled walls. 3. a wasting or being wasted; specifically, *a*) a useless or profitless spending or consuming; squandering, as of money, time, etc. *b*) a failure to take advantage (*of* something). *c*) a gradual loss, decrease, or destruction by use, wear, decay, deterioration, etc. 4. useless, unneeded, or superfluous matter; discarded or excess material, as ashes, garbage, by-products, etc. 5. superfluous matter excreted from the body, as feces or urine. 6. cotton fiber or yarn left over from the process of milling, used for wiping machinery, packing bearings, etc. 7. [Archaic], ruin or devastation, as by war, etc. 8. in *physical geography,* material derived by erosion or disintegration of rock, such as is carried to the sea by rivers, etc.

go to waste, to be or become wasted.

lay waste, to destroy; devastate; make desolate.

SYN.—**waste,** in this connection, is the general word for any stretch of uncultivable, hence uninhabitable, land; a **desert** is a barren, arid, usually sandy tract of land; **badlands** is applied to a barren, hilly waste where rapid erosion has cut the soft rocks into fantastic shapes; **wilderness** refers to an uninhabited waste where a lack of paths or trails makes it difficult to find one's way, specifically, to such a region thickly covered with trees and underbrush.

waste·bas·ket (wāst′bas′kit, wāst′bäs′kit), ***n.*** a basket or open-topped box for waste paper or other useless material: also **wastepaper basket.**

waste·ful (wāst′fəl), ***adj.*** 1. in the habit of wasting; characterized by waste. 2. using more than is needed; squandering; extravagant.

waste·land (wāst′land′), ***n.*** land that is uncultivated, barren, or without vegetation: also **waste land.**

waste·pa·per (wāst′pā′pẽr), ***n.*** paper thrown away after use or as useless: also **waste paper.**

wastepaper basket, a wastebasket.

waste pipe, a pipe for carrying off waste water, sink drainage, excess steam, etc.: distinguished from *soil pipe.*

wast·er (wās′tẽr), ***n.*** a person or thing that wastes; especially, a spendthrift or prodigal; wastrel.

wast·ing (wās′tiŋ), ***adj.*** 1. desolating; destructive; ruinous: as, *wasting* war. 2. causing waste. 3. destructive to health or vigor, as a disease.

wast·rel (wās′trəl), ***n.*** [dim. of *waster*], 1. a person who wastes; especially, one who squanders money; spendthrift. 2. a good-for-nothing.

watch (wäch, wôch), ***n.*** [ME. *wacche;* AS. *wæcce* < the base of *wacian;* cf. WAKE], 1. the act or fact of keeping awake, especially of keeping awake and alert, in order to look after, protect, or guard. 2. *a*) any of the several periods into which the night was divided in ancient times; hence, *b*) a part of the night: as, the still *watches* of the night. 3. *a*) close observation for a time, in order to see or find out something. *b*) vigilant, careful guarding: as, keep a close *watch* over the baby. 4. a person or group on duty, especially at night, to protect or guard; lookout or guard. 5. *a*) the period of duty of a guard. *b*) the post of a guard. 6. a small spring-driven timepiece carried in the pocket, worn on the wrist, etc. 7. [Obs.], *a*) a vigil; wake. *b*) vigilance. 8. [Obs.], a candle marked off into sections, used for keeping time: each section burned for a known period. 9. [Obs.], a watchman's cry. 10. in *nautical usage, a*) any of the periods of duty (five of four hours, and two of two hours), into which the day is divided on shipboard, to split the labor of working the ship between alternating parts of the crew. *b*) the part of the crew, usually half of all personnel, on duty during such periods. *c*) a ship's chronometer. ***v.i.*** 1. to stay awake at night in devotion; keep religious vigil. 2. to stay awake and alert at night; care for or guard something at night. 3. to be on the alert; be on the lookout; be on guard; keep guard. 4. to look; observe: as, most people just *watched.* 5. to be looking or waiting attentively (with *for*): as, *watch* for your chance. ***v.t.*** 1. to guard. 2. to keep looking at; keep a close eye on; observe carefully and constantly. 3. to view mentally; keep informed about. 4. to be on the alert or lookout for; wait for and look for: as, *watch* your chance. 5. to keep watch over; tend, as a flock.

on the watch, watching; on the lookout, as for some thing or person expected.

watch out, to be alert and on one's guard; be careful.

watch·case (wäch′kās′, wôch′kās′), ***n.*** the metal case, or outer covering, of a watch.

watch chain, a chain by which a watch is attached to the clothing, worn usually as an ornament draped across the vest.

watch·dog (wäch′dôg′, wôch′dôg′), ***n.*** 1. a dog kept to guard property, as by barking or by attacking intruders. 2. any watchful guardian.

watch fire, a fire kept burning at night as a signal or for the use of those staying awake to watch, or guard.

watch·ful (wäch′fəl, wôch′fəl), ***adj.*** 1. vigilant; alert; attentive; closely observant. 2. characterized by vigilance. 3. [Archaic], wakeful; unsleeping.

SYN.—**watchful** is the general word implying a being observant and prepared, as to ward off danger or seize an opportunity (under the *watchful* eye of her guardian); **vigilant** implies an active, keen watchfulness and connotes the immediate necessity for this (a *vigilant* sentry); **alert** implies a quick intelligence and a readiness to take prompt action (*alert* to the danger that confronted them); **wide-awake** more often implies an alertness to opportunities than to dangers and connotes an awareness of all the surrounding circumstances (a *wide-awake* young salesman).

watch guard, a chain, cord, or strap used to fasten a watch to clothing.

watch·mak·er (wäch′māk′ẽr, wôch′māk′ẽr), ***n.*** a person who makes or repairs watches.

watch·mak·ing (wäch′māk′iŋ, wôch′māk′iŋ), ***n.*** the business of making or repairing watches.

watch·man (wäch′mən, wôch′mən), ***n.*** [*pl.* WATCHMEN (-mən)], a person hired to watch or guard, especially at night; specifically, *a*) one who guards a factory, warehouse, estate, etc., as against thieves or trespassers. *b*) formerly, one whose duty was to guard or police the streets at night.

watch meeting, a religious service held on New Year's Eve.

watch night, 1. New Year's Eve. 2. a watch meeting.

watch pocket, a small pocket, usually in a vest or trousers, for carrying a watch.

watch·tow·er (wäch′tou′ẽr, wôch′tou′ẽr), ***n.*** a high tower from which watch is kept, as for enemies, forest fires, etc.

watch·word (wäch′wũrd′, wôch′wũrd′), ***n.*** 1. a word

known to only a few, and used for identification, as on challenge by a watch, or sentry; password. 2. a word or phrase embodying a principle or precept, especially as the slogan or cry of a group or party; motto.

wa·ter (wô′tēr, wät′ēr), *n.* [ME.; AS. *wæter;* akin to G. *wasser;* IE. **wodōr* < base **wed-*, to wet; cf. WET, WASH], 1. the colorless, transparent liquid occurring on earth as rivers, lakes, oceans, etc., and falling from the clouds as rain: it is chemically a compound of hydrogen and oxygen, H_2O, and under laboratory conditions it freezes hard, forming ice, at 32° F. (0° C.) and boils, forming steam, at 212° F. (100° C.). 2. water in any of its forms, or in any amount, or occurring or distributed in any specified way, or for any use, as drinking, washing, etc. 3. *often pl.* a large body of water, as a river, lake, sea, etc. 4. *a*) water with reference to its depth: as, ten feet of *water* at the dam. *b*) water with reference to the depth of displacement of anything in it: as, the boat draws six feet of *water*. *c*) water with reference to its surface: as, above *water*, under *water*. *d*) water with reference to its level in a sea, river, etc.: as, high *water*, low *water*. 5. a leaking, breaking, or slopping of water into a boat, etc.: as, the ship is making *water*. 6. each of the applications of water in any process: as, diapers must be rinsed in three *waters*. 7. *pl.* the water of a mineral spring or group of such springs, used in therapy, etc.: as, take the *waters* at Saratoga. 8. any body fluid or secretion; specifically, *a*) urine, saliva, tears, gastric and pancreatic juices, etc. *b*) the fluid surrounding the fetus in pregnancy; amniotic fluid. 9. a solution of any substance, often a gas, in water: as, mineral *water*, ammonia *water*. 10. *a*) the degree of transparence and luster of a precious stone, as a measure of its quality: as, a diamond of the first *water;* hence, *b*) degree of quality or conformity to type: as, an artist of the first or purest *water*. 11. a wavy, lustrous finish given to linen, silk, rayon, etc., or to a metal surface. 12. a water-color painting: opposed to *oil* (painting). 13. in *finance*, *a*) a valuation given to the assets of a business in excess of their real value. *b*) an issue of capital stock which brings the face value of all the stock issued by a business to a figure higher than the actual value of its assets. *v.t.* [ME. *wateren;* AS. *wæterian* < the *n.*], 1. to give (an animal) water to drink. 2. to supply with water: as, large tanks were there to *water* the troops. 3. to give water to (soil, crops, etc.) by sprinkling, pouring, or irrigating. 4. to bring water to (land): said of a river, canal, etc. 5. to put water on (a pavement, etc.), by sprinkling, hosing, etc.; soak or moisten with water (often with *down*). 6. to add water to so as to weaken; dilute: as, she *waters* the milk. 7. to give a wavy luster to the surface of (silk, etc.). 8. in *finance*, to add to the total face value of (stock) without increasing assets to justify this valuation (often with *down*). *v.i.* 1. to fill with tears: said of the eyes. 2. to secrete or fill with saliva: as, his mouth *watered* at the sight of food. 3. to take on a supply of water. 4. to drink water: said of animals. *adj.* 1. of or for water. 2. in or on water: as, *water* sports. 3. growing in or living on or near water: as, *water* plants, *water* birds. 4. *a*) operated by water: as, a *water* wheel. *b*) derived from running water: as, *water* power. 5. containing water or fluid: as, a *water* blister. 6. prepared with water, as for thinning or hardening. 7. ruling, or having dominion, over water: as, *water* gods.

above water, out of difficulty or trouble; free from debt, worry, etc.

by water, by ship or boat.

hold water, 1. to contain water without leaking; hence, 2. to remain sound, consistent, or logical, with no breaks or weaknesses: as, the argument should *hold water*. 3. to keep a boat at a standstill by holding the oars steady in the water.

like water, lavishly; freely: said of money spent, etc.

make one's mouth water, to create a desire or appetite in one; be or seem tasty.

make (or **pass**) **water**, to urinate.

water adder, 1. a water moccasin. 2. a water snake.

wa·ter·age (wô′tēr-ij, wät′ēr-ij), *n.* [see -AGE], in England, 1. the movement of goods by water. 2. the fee for this.

water back, a tank or coil behind the fire pot of a stove, for heating water.

Water Bearer, in *astronomy*, Aquarius.

water beetle, any of many beetles that live in freshwater ponds and streams, having the last pair of legs fringed and functioning as oars.

water bird, any bird that swims in, or lives on or near, the water; aquatic bird; waterfowl.

water biscuit, a cracker made of water, flour, and shortening.

water blister, a blister containing a clear, watery fluid without pus or blood.

wa·ter-borne (wô′tēr-bôrn′, wät′ēr-bôrn′), *adj.* 1. floating on water. 2. floated on water; launched. 3. carried by water, as in a ship.

wa·ter·brain (wô′tēr-brān′, wät′ēr-brān′), *n.* gid (in sheep).

water brash, pyrosis; heartburn.

wa·ter·buck (wô′tēr-buk′, wät′ēr-buk′), *n.* [*pl.* WATERBUCK, WATERBUCKS (-buks′); see PLURAL, II, D, 2], [D. *waterbok*], any of a number of African antelopes that frequent streams or rivers; specifically, either of two species of large, reddish or grayish antelopes of eastern and southern Africa, having lyre-shaped horns.

water buffalo, any of several slow, powerful, oxlike animals native to Asia, Malaya, Africa, and the Philippine Islands, having a pair of large, strong horns growing from the sides of the head: it likes to wallow in mud and water and is used as a draft animal: also called *water ox* and (in the Philippine Islands) *carabao*.

water bug, 1. a cockroach; croton bug. 2. any of a large group of true beetles that live in water.

Wa·ter·bur·y (wô′tēr-ber′i, wät′ēr-ber′i), *n.* a city in Connecticut: pop., 107,000.

water chestnut (or **caltrop**), 1. any of a number of related water plants with floating leaves, small white flowers, and nutlike fruit. 2. the fruit of any of these.

water chinquapin, 1. a water plant with blue-green leaves, large yellow flowers, and nutlike seeds; American lotus. 2. its seed.

water clock, a mechanism for measuring time by the fall or flow of water; clepsydra.

water closet, 1. a small room with a bowl-shaped fixture in which to defecate or urinate, fitted with a device for flushing with water. 2. the bowl-shaped fixture. Abbreviated **w.c.**

wa·ter-col·or (wô′tēr-kul′ēr, wät′ēr-kul′ēr), *adj.* painted with water colors.

water color, 1. a paint composed of a pigment mixed with water instead of oil. 2. a painting done with such paints. 3. the art of painting with water colors.

wa·ter-col·or·ist (wô′tēr-kul′ēr-ist, wät′ēr-kul′ēr-ist), *n.* a person who paints pictures with water colors.

wa·ter-cool (wô′tēr-kōōl′, wät′ēr-kōōl′), *v.t.* to keep (an engine, etc.) from overheating by circulating water around or through it, as in pipes or a jacket.

wa·ter-cooled (wô′tēr-kōōld′, wät′ēr-kōōld′), *adj.* kept from overheating by circulating water: as, a *water-cooled* engine: distinguished from *air-cooled*.

water cooler, a device for cooling water, as for drinking, by passing it in a coil through ice or other refrigerant.

wa·ter·course (wô′tēr-kôrs′, wät′ēr-kôrs′), *n.* 1. a stream of water; river, brook, etc. 2. a channel for water, as a canal or stream bed.

wa·ter·craft (wô′tēr-kraft′, wät′ēr-kräft′), *n.* 1. skill in handling boats or ships. 2. skill in a water sport, as swimming. 3. a boat, ship, raft, etc. 4. ships or boats, collectively. Also **water craft** (in senses 3 & 4).

water crake, 1. the water ouzel. 2. the spotted crake.

wa·ter-cress (wô′tēr-kres′, wät′ēr-kres′), *adj.* of water cress.

water cress, [ME. *watercresse;* cf. CRESS], a white-flowered plant of the mustard family, whose leaves are used in salads, soups, etc.: it grows in water or wet soil.

water cure, 1. hydropathy or hydrotherapy. 2. [Colloq.], a form of torture in which the victim is forced to swallow large quantities of water.

water dog, 1. any of various dogs especially fond of the water, as the water spaniel. 2. any of several hunting dogs trained to retrieve waterfowl. 3. any of various salamanders; mud puppy. 4. [Colloq.], a person who is at home in or on the water; especially, an old sailor.

wa·tered (wô′tērd, wät′ērd), *adj.* [pp. of *water*], 1. sprinkled with water. 2. supplied with water; having streams: said of land. 3. having a wavy, lustrous pattern: said of cloth, metal surfaces, etc. 4. treated, prepared, or diluted with water. 5. in *finance*, inflated above its real value: said of stock, etc.

Wa·ter·ee (wô′tə-rē′), *n.* a river in North and South Carolina, joining the Congaree to form the Santee River: length, 300 mi.: in North Carolina called the *Catawba*.

wa·ter·fall (wô′tēr-fôl′, wät′ēr-fôl′), *n.* 1. a steep fall of water, as of a stream, from a height; cascade. 2. a roll of hair worn low on the neck; chignon.

wa·ter·find·er (wô′tēr-fin′dēr, wät′ēr-fin′dēr), *n.* a person who seeks out underground water and determines where to sink wells, by means of a divining rod; dowser.

water flea, any of many minute fresh-water or salt-water crustaceans which swim with spasmodic leaps.

Wa·ter·ford (wô′tēr-fērd, wät′ēr-fērd), *n.* 1. a county of Munster province, Ireland: pop., 74,000. 2. its county seat: pop., 29,000.

wa·ter·fowl (wô′tēr-foul′, wät′ēr-foul′), *n.* [*pl.* WATERFOWLS (-foulz′), WATERFOWL; see PLURAL, II, D, 1], a water bird, especially one that swims: the collective plural is used of swimming game birds especially.

wa·ter-front (wô′tēr-frunt′, wät′ēr-frunt′), *adj.* of a water front.

water front, 1. land at the edge of a stream, harbor, etc. 2. the part of a city or town on such land; wharf or dock area. Also **waterfront**, *n.*

water gap, a break in a mountain ridge, with a stream flowing through it.

water gas, a poisonous mixture of hydrogen and carbon monoxide, made by forcing steam over incandescent carbon fuel, as coke, and used as a fuel gas, etc.

water gate, a gate controlling the flow of water; floodgate.
water gauge, 1. a gauge for measuring the level or flow of water in a stream or channel. 2. a device, as a glass tube, that shows the water level in a tank, boiler, etc.
wa·ter·glass (wô′tẽr-glas′, wät′ẽr-gläs′), *n.* water glass.
water glass, 1. *a*) a drinking glass or goblet. *b*) a glass container for water, etc. 2. a glass water gauge. 3. a glass-bottomed tube or box for looking at things under water. 4. sodium silicate or, sometimes, potassium silicate, occurring as a stony powder, usually dissolved in water to form a colorless, sirupy liquid used as an adhesive, as a protective or waterproofing coat, as a preservative for eggs, etc. 5. a water clock; clepsydra. Also **waterglass.**
water gum, a tree with small, greenish-white flowers and purplish fruit; sour gum; tupelo.
wa·ter-ham·mer (wô′tẽr-ham′ẽr, wät′ẽr-ham′ẽr), *v.i.* to thump, as a steam pipe.
water hammer, 1. a sealed glass tube containing water and no air: when it is shaken, the water strikes against the ends with a hammerlike sound, demonstrating that solids and liquids fall at the same rate in a vacuum. 2. *a*) the sound caused in a pipe containing water when live steam is passed through it. *b*) the thump of water in a pipe when a faucet is suddenly closed.
water hemlock, a plant with strong-smelling leaves, clusters of small white flowers, and a poisonous root.
water hen, 1. the American coot. 2. any of various birds of the rail family, as the gallinule, moor hen, etc.
water hole, a dip or hole in the surface of the ground, in which water collects; pond; pool, especially one left in the dry bed of a stream.
water ice, 1. ice formed directly by the freezing of fresh water or salt water, as in a lake, bay, etc., rather than by the packing down of snow. 2. [British], sherbet.
wa·ter-inch (wô′tẽr-inch′, wät′ẽr-inch′), *n.* a former unit of hydraulic measure, calculated as the discharge of water through a circular opening one inch in diameter from a reservoir in which the water level stays just high enough to cover the mouth of the opening, equal to about fourteen pints per minute, or about 500 cubic feet per 24 hours.
wa·ter·i·ness (wô′tẽr-i-nis, wät′ẽr-i-nis), *n.* the state or quality of being watery.
wa·ter·ing (wô′tẽr-iŋ, wät′ẽr-iŋ), *n.* 1. the act of a person or thing that waters. 2. a wavy, lustrous appearance on silk fabric, etc. *adj.* 1. that waters. 2. having water, as for animals. 3. [Chiefly British], of or having mineral **springs** or resort facilities for bathing, boating, etc.: as, a *watering* place.
watering pot, a container, especially a can with a spout having a perforated nozzle, for watering plants, etc.; sprinkling can.
wa·ter·ish (wô′tẽr-ish, wät′ẽr-ish), *adj.* watery.
wa·ter-jack·et (wô′tẽr-jak′it, wät′ẽr-jak′it), *v.t.* to encase or equip with a water jacket.
water jacket, a casing holding water, placed around something to be cooled or kept at a constant temperature, as by the circulation of the water; especially, such a casing around the cylinder or cylinders of an internal-combustion engine.
water jump, a pond, ditch, or other small body of water that a horse has to jump over, as in a steeplechase.
wa·ter·less (wô′tẽr-lis, wät′ẽr-lis), *adj.* without water; dry.
water level, 1. *a*) the surface of still water. *b*) the height of this. 2. the upper limit of ground water; water table. 3. a leveling instrument containing water in a glass tube. 4. the line to which the surface of the water comes on the side of a ship or boat; water line.
water lily, 1. any of various related water plants having large, flat, floating leaves and showy flowers in a wide range of color. 2. the flower of such a plant.
wa·ter·line (wô′tẽr-līn′, wät′ẽr-līn′), *n.* a water line.
water line, 1. the line to which the surface of the water comes on the side of a ship or boat; water level. 2. any of several lines parallel with this, marked at various heights on the hull of a ship, indicating the various degrees of submergence when the ship is fully or partly loaded, or unloaded, and on an even keel.
wa·ter-logged (wô′tẽr-lôgd′, wät′ẽr-logd′), *adj.* 1. soaked or filled with water so as to be almost awash, and heavy and sluggish in movement: said of boats or floating objects. 2. soaked with water; swampy.
Wa·ter·loo (wô′tẽr-lo͞o′; *now often* wô′tẽr-lo͞o′), *n.* 1. a village in Belgium, just south of Brussels: pop., 7,700: scene of Napoleon's final defeat (June 18, 1815) by the Allies under Wellington; hence, 2. any disastrous or decisive defeat. 3. a city in eastern Iowa: pop., 72,000.
water main, a main pipe in a system of pipes which carry water.
wa·ter·man (wô′tẽr-mən, wät′ẽr-mən), *n.* [*pl.* WATERMEN (-mən)], 1. a person who works on or handles boats; ferryman. 2. a person skilled in rowing, etc.; oarsman.
wa·ter·man·ship (wô′tẽr-mən-ship′, wät′ẽr-mən-ship′), *n.* [see -SHIP], 1. the work, business, or skill of a waterman (sense 1). 2. skill in rowing, etc.; oarsmanship.
water marigold, a yellow-flowered water plant with finely cut leaves.
wa·ter·mark (wô′tẽr-märk′, wät′ẽr-märk′), *n.* 1. a mark showing the limit to which water has risen. 2. in *papermaking*, *a*) a mark in paper, produced by pressure of a projecting design, as in the mold, during manufacture: it can be seen when the paper is held up to the light. *b*) the projecting design that produces this. Abbreviated **wmk.** *v.t.* 1. to mark (paper) with a watermark. 2. to impress (a design)| as a watermark.
wa·ter·mel·on (wô′tẽr-mel′ən, wät′ẽr-mel′ən), *n.* [*water* + *melon*: from its abundant watery juice], 1. a large, round or oblong fruit with a hard, green rind and juicy, pink or red pulp containing many seeds. 2. the vine on which it grows.
water meter, an instrument which measures and records the amount of water flowing through a pipe, etc.
water milfoil, any of a number of related graceful, feathery plants growing under water.
water mill, a mill whose machinery is driven by water.
water moccasin, 1. a large, poisonous, olive-brown viper with dark cross-bars, related to the copperhead and found along river banks and swamps of the southern United States: also called *cottonmouth.* 2. any of several harmless water snakes resembling this.
water nymph, in *Greek & Roman mythology*, a goddess having the form of a lovely young girl, supposed to dwell in a stream, pool, lake, etc.; naiad, Nereid, Oceanid, etc.
water oak, 1. any of several American oaks. 2. an oak of the southeastern United States, found mainly along rivers, streams, etc.
water of crystallization, water that occurs as a constituent of crystalline substances and can be removed from them by the application of heat: the loss of water usually results in the loss of crystalline structure.
water of hydration, water which is chemically combined with a substance to form a hydrate.
water ouzel, any of a group of water birds with thick plumage, related to the thrushes and found in Europe, Asia, and America; dipper.
water ox, the water buffalo.
water parting, a watershed; divide.
water pepper, the smartweed or any of various other related plants that grow in wet places.
water pimpernel, 1. a small plant with oblong leaves and white, pink, or blue flowers, generally found along the edge of brooks; brooklime; brookweed. 2. the common pimpernel.
water pipe, 1. a pipe for carrying water. 2. a kind of smoking pipe in which the smoke is drawn through water; narghile; hookah.
water plant, 1. any plant living entirely below water or sending up stems and leaves to or above the surface. 2. any plant able to grow either on land or in water.
water plantain, any of a number of related water plants with large, heart-shaped leaves and small, usually white, flowers.
water polo, a water game played with a round, partly inflated ball by two teams of swimmers, the object of the game being to pass or take the ball over the opponent's goal line.
water power, 1. the power of running or falling water, used to drive machinery, etc., or capable of being so used. 2. a fall of water that can be so used. 3. a water right or privilege owned by a mill.
water pox, a kind of chicken pox.
wa·ter·proof (wô′tẽr-pro͞of′, wät′ẽr-pro͞of′), *adj.* that keeps out water; especially, treated with rubber, plastic, etc., so that water will not penetrate: said of fabric, a garment, etc. *n.* 1. waterproof cloth or other material. 2. [Chiefly British], a raincoat or other outer garment of waterproof material. *v.t.* to make waterproof.
water purslane, a red-stemmed trailing plant found in watery or muddy places.
water rat, 1. any of several European voles that live on the banks of streams and ponds. 2. an American muskrat. 3. [Slang], a waterfront thief or tramp.
water sapphire, [transl. of Fr. *saphir d'eau*], a deep-blue, transparent variety of iolite, sometimes used as a gem.
wa·ter·scape (wô′tẽr-skāp′, wät′ẽr-skāp′), *n.* [< *water*, after *landscape*], a view of a body of water; especially, a picture containing such a view; seascape.
water scorpion, any of a number of four-winged insects of the family of water beetles, distinguished by a long breathing tube at the end of the abdomen.
wa·ter·shed (wô′tẽr-shed′, wät′ẽr-shed′), *n.* 1. a ridge or stretch of high land dividing the areas drained by

different rivers or river systems. 2. the area drained by a river or river system.

water shield, 1. a purple-flowered water plant having floating leaves coated underneath with a jellylike substance. 2. any of a number of related water plants with roundish leaves on the water and finely cut leaves below.

wa·ter-sick (wô′tẽr-sik′, wät′ẽr-sik′), ***adj.*** not fertile or cultivable because of too much water: said of land which is irrigated to excess.

wa·ter·side (wô′tẽr-sīd′, wät′ẽr-sīd′), ***n.*** land at the edge of a body of water; shore. ***adj.*** 1. of or located on the waterside. 2. living or working along the shore.

wa·ter-ski (wô′tẽr-skē′, wät′ẽr-skē′), ***v.i.*** [for prin. pts. see SKI], in water sports, to be towed on ski-like boards by a line attached to a speedboat.

water snake, any of various nonpoisonous snakes living in fresh-water streams and rivers, and feeding on water animals.

wa·ter-soak (wô′tẽr-sōk′, wät′ẽr-sōk′), ***v.t.*** to soak with water; saturate.

wa·ter-sol·u·ble (wô′tẽr-sol′yoo-b'l, wät′ẽr-sol′yoo-b'l), ***adj.*** that can be dissolved in water: said especially of certain vitamins, and opposed to *fat-soluble.*

water spaniel, either of two breeds of spaniel especially suited to retrieving game shot over water, and characterized by a curly, reddish-brown coat.

water speedwell, a common garden herb having blue flowers and growing in wet places.

wa·ter·spout (wô′tẽr-spout′, wät′ẽr-spout′), ***n.*** 1. a hole, pipe, or spout from which water runs. 2. a fast-moving, rapidly rotating, funnel-shaped or tubelike column of air full of mist and moisture, extending downward from a storm cloud to the surface of a body of water.

water sprite, a spirit, nymph, etc. dwelling in or haunting the water; water nymph.

water starwort, any of various related small water or mud plants with smooth-edged leaves and tiny flowers.

water strider, any of several fresh-water insects with a slender body and very long legs, swimming about on the surface of the water.

water supply, 1. the water available for use of a community or in an area. 2. the system for storing and supplying such water, as the reservoirs, mains, etc.

water system, 1. a river with all its tributaries. 2. a water supply; plumbing system.

water table, 1. the level below which the ground is saturated with water. 2. in *architecture,* a projecting ledge or molding which throws off rainwater.

water thrush, 1. any of several North American warblers, usually found near streams. 2. the European water ouzel.

wa·ter·tight (wô′tẽr-tīt′, wät′ẽr-tīt′), ***adj.*** 1. so snugly put together that no water can get in or through. 2. so carefully stated that it cannot be misconstrued or misunderstood. 3. that cannot be defeated, nullified, etc.: as, a *watertight* plan.

Wa·ter·ton Lakes National Park (wô′tẽr-tən), a park in southwestern Alberta, Canada: with Glacier National Park of Montana, it forms International Peace Park.

water tower, 1. an elevated tank used for water storage and for maintaining equalized pressure on a water system. 2. a firefighting apparatus that can be used to lift high pressure hose and nozzles to great heights.

Wa·ter·town (wô′tẽr-toun′), ***n.*** 1. a town in Massachusetts, near Boston: pop., 39,000. 2. a city in north central New York: pop., 33,000.

water vapor, water in the form of mist or tiny diffused particles, especially when below the boiling point, as in the air: distinguished from *steam.*

wa·ter-wave (wô′tẽr-wāv′, wät′ẽr-wāv′), ***v.t.*** [WATER-WAVED (-wāvd′), WATER-WAVING], to make water waves in (hair).

water wave, 1. a wave made in hair by moistening and setting it with a comb, and drying it with heat, usually from a drier. 2. a wave of water; billow.

wa·ter·way (wô′tẽr-wā′, wät′ẽr-wā′), ***n.*** 1. a channel or runnel through or along which water runs. 2. any body of water wide enough and deep enough for boats, ships, etc., as a stream, canal, or channel; water route.

wa·ter·weed (wô′tẽr-wēd′, wät′ẽr-wēd′), ***n.*** any water plant having inconspicuous flowers, as pondweed, etc.

water wheel, 1. a wheel turned by running or falling water, usually for power. 2. a wheel with buckets on its rim, used for lifting water.

water wings, a device, inflated with air, used to keep one afloat while learning to swim: it is shaped somewhat like a pair of wings and is worn under the arms.

water witch, 1. a person who professes to have the power to find underground water with a divining rod, etc. 2. any of various diving birds, as the horned grebe.

water witching, the supposed finding of underground water by the use of a divining rod.

wa·ter·works (wô′tẽr-wũrks′, wät′ẽr-wũrks′), ***n.pl.*** [often construed as sing. in senses 1 & 2], 1. a system of reservoirs, pumps, pipes, etc., used to bring a water supply to a town or city; water system. 2. a pumping station in such a system, with its machinery, sediment basins, filters, etc. 3. [Slang], *a)* the source of tears. *b)* tears: usually in *turn on the waterworks,* to shed tears, weep.

wa·ter·worn (wô′tẽr-wôrn′, wät′ẽr-wōrn′), ***adj.*** worn, smoothed, or polished by the action of running water.

wa·ter·y (wô′tẽr-i, wät′ẽr-i), ***adj.*** 1. of or connected with water. 2. containing or full of water; moist. 3. bringing rain, as clouds. 4. like water. 5. thin; diluted: as, *watery* tea. 6. tearful; weeping. 7. sweaty. 8. in or consisting of water: as, a *watery* grave. 9. weak; insipid; without force. 10. soft, soggy, or flabby. 11. full of, secreting, or giving off a morbid discharge resembling water.

Wat·ling (wät′liŋ), ***n.*** San Salvador, one of the Bahama Islands.

Wat·son, John Broa·dus (brô′dəs wät′s'n, wôt′s'n), 1878–1958; American psychologist.

Watson, Sir **William,** 1858–1935; English poet.

watt (wät, wôt), ***n.*** [after James *Watt,* Scot. inventor], in *electricity,* a unit of electric power, equal to a current of one ampere under one volt of pressure, or one joule per second, or about 1/746 of one horsepower: abbreviated **W, w, W., w.** (*sing. & pl.*).

Watt, James (wät, wôt), 1736–1819; Scottish inventor.

watt·age (wät′ij, wôt′ij), ***n.*** [see -AGE], in *electricity,* 1. amount of electric power, expressed in watts, and arrived at by multiplying amperage by voltage. 2. the total number of watts needed to operate a given appliance or device.

Wat·teau, Jean An·toine (zhän än′twȧn′ vȧ′tō′; Eng. wä-tō′), 1684–1721; French painter.

watt-hour (wät′our′, wôt′our′), ***n.*** in *electricity,* a unit of electrical energy or work, equal to one watt acting for one hour: abbreviated **watt-hr.** (*sing. & pl.*), **wh., whr.**

wat·tle (wät′'l, wôt′'l), ***n.*** [ME. *watel;* AS. *watel, watol,* a hurdle, woven twigs (cf. WALLET); prob. IE. base **wedh-,* to knit, bind], 1. a sort of woven work made of sticks intertwined with twigs or branches, used for walls, fences, and roofs. 2. [British Dial.], *a)* a stick, rod, twig, or wand. *b)* a hurdle or framework made of sticks, rods, etc. 3. *pl.* rods or poles used as the framework of a thatched roof. 4. in Australia, any of various acacias: so called because the flexible branches were much used by early settlers for making wattles. 5. a fleshy, wrinkled, often brightly colored piece of skin which hangs from the chin or throat of certain birds and reptiles, as cocks and turkeys. 6. a barbel of a fish. ***adj.*** made of or roofed with wattle or wattles. ***v.t.*** [WATTLED (-'ld), WATTLING], 1. to twist or intertwine (sticks, twigs, branches, etc.) so as to form an interwoven structure or fabric. 2. to construct, as a fence, by intertwining sticks, twigs, etc. 3. to build of, or roof, fence, bind, etc. with, wattle or wattles.

wat·tle·bird (wät′'l-bũrd′, wôt′'l-bũrd′), ***n.*** any of a number of Australian birds of the honey eater family, with wattles hanging from the ears.

wat·tled (wät′'ld, wôt′'ld), ***adj.*** 1. built with wattles. 2. having wattles, as a bird.

watt·less (wät′lis, wôt′lis), ***adj.*** in *electricity,* having no watts; wholly without power: said of an alternating current that differs in phase by 90 degrees from the electromotive force producing it, or of an electromotive force that differs in phase by 90 degrees from the current which it produces.

watt·me·ter (wät′mē′tẽr, wôt′mē′tẽr), ***n.*** [*watt* + *-meter*], an instrument for measuring in watts the power in an electric circuit.

Watts, George Frederic (wäts, wôts), 1817–1904; English painter and sculptor.

Watts, Isaac, 1674–1748; English theologian and writer of hymns.

Waugh, Evelyn (wô), (*Evelyn Arthur St. John Waugh*), 1903– ; English novelist.

Waugh, Frederick Judd (jud), 1861–1940; American painter and illustrator.

Wau·ke·gan (wô-kē′gən), ***n.*** a city in northeastern Illinois, on Lake Michigan: pop., 56,000.

waul (wôl), ***v.i. & n.*** [cf. CATERWAUL], wail, squall, or howl: also spelled **wawl.**

waur (wôr, wär), ***adj. & adv.*** [see WAR (worse)], [Scot. & N. Eng. Dial.], worse: also **war.**

Wau·sau (wô′sô), ***n.*** a city in central Wisconsin: pop., 32,000.

Wau·wa·to·sa (wô′wə-tō′sə), ***n.*** a city in Wisconsin, near Milwaukee: pop., 57,000.

Wave, WAVE (wāv), ***n.*** a member of the Women's Reserve of the United States Naval Reserve (WAVES).

wave (wāv), ***v.i.*** [WAVED (wāvd), WAVING], [ME. *waven;* AS. *wafian,* to wave, fluctuate; akin to G. *waben,* to fluctuate; IE. base **webh-,* to move to and fro, later associated with **webh-,* to weave (cf. WEAVE); see WAVER], 1. to move up and down or back and forth in a curving or undulating motion; swing, sway, or flutter to and fro: said of flexible things free at one end, as, the *flag* waves. 2. to signal by moving a hand, arm, light, etc. to and fro. 3. to have the form of a series of curves or undulations: as, her hair *waves* naturally. ***v.t.*** 1. to cause to wave, undulate, or sway to and fro, as a flag. 2. to swing; brandish, as a weapon.

3. *a*) to move or swing (something) as a signal. *b*) to signal (something) by doing this: as, we *waved* farewell. *c*) to signal or signify something to (someone) by doing this: as, he *waved* us on. 4. to give an undulating form to; make sinuous: as, she *waves* her hair. 5. to give a wavy, or watered, appearance to (silk, etc.). ***n.*** [altered (after the *v.*) < ME. *wawe*, a wave], 1. a curving ridge or swell moving along the surface of a liquid, running in a more or less straight line at a right angle to the movement. 2. [Poetic], water; especially, the sea or other body of water. 3. *a*) an undulation or series of undulations in or on a surface, such as that caused by wind over a field of grain. *b*) a curve or series of curves or curls, as in the hair. *c*) a wavy or undulating line on a watered fabric. 4. a motion to and fro or up and down, such as that made by the hand in signaling. 5. something like a wave in action or effect; specifically, *a*) an upsurge or rise, as to a crest, or a progressively swelling manifestation: as, a crime *wave*, heat *wave*, *wave* of emotion, etc. *b*) a movement of people, etc., in groups or masses, which recedes or grows smaller before subsiding or being followed by another: as, a *wave* of immigrants. 6. in *electricity*, a periodic variation of an electric current or voltage. 7. in *physics*, any of the series of advancing impulses set up by a vibration, pulsation, or disturbance in air or some other medium, as in the transmission of heat, light, sound, etc.

SYN.—**wave** is the general word for a curving ridge or swell in the surface of the ocean or other body of water; **ripple** is used of the smallest kind of wave, such as that caused by a breeze ruffling the surface of water; **roller** is applied to any of the large, heavy, swelling waves that roll in to the shore, as during a storm; **breaker** is applied to such a wave when it breaks, or is about to break, into foam upon the shore or upon rocks; **billow** is a somewhat poetic or rhetorical term for a great, heaving ocean wave.

wave front, in *physics*, an imaginary surface composed of all the points reached at any given instant by a wave or vibration in its advance.

wave guide, an electric conductor consisting of a metal tubing, usually circular or rectangular in cross section, used for the conduction or directional transmission of microwaves or ultra-high-frequency waves.

wave length, 1. the distance between corresponding points on two successive waves. 2. in *physics*, the distance, measured in the direction of progression of a wave, from any given point to the next point characterized by the same phase. Abbreviated **w.l.**

wave·let (wāv′lit), ***n.*** a little wave; ripple.

Wa·vell, Archibald Percival (wā′v'l), Earl Wavell, 1883–1950; British field marshal; commander in chief of British armies in the Middle East (1939–1941); viceroy of India (1943–1947).

wa·vell·ite (wā′v'l-īt′), ***n.*** [after William *Wavell*, Eng. discoverer], a hydrous phosphate of aluminum, vitreous, translucent, and white, greenish-yellow, or brown.

wa·ver (wā′vẽr), ***v.i.*** [ME. *waveren*, freq. of *waven*, to wave], 1. to swing or sway to and fro; flutter. 2. to show doubt or indecision; find it hard, or be unable, to decide; vacillate. 3. to become unsteady; begin to give way; falter. 4. to tremble; quaver: said of the voice, etc. 5. to flicker; vary in brightness: said of light. 6. to fluctuate. 7. to totter. ***n.*** a wavering. —***SYN.*** see **hesitate.**

WAVES, W.A.V.E.S. (wāvz), [< *W*omen *A*ppointed for *V*oluntary *E*mergency *S*ervice], the Women's Reserve of the United States Naval Reserve.

wave train, in *physics*, a group of waves sent out on the same course and at regular intervals, as by a vibrating body.

wav·i·ly (wāv′ə-li), ***adv.*** in a wavy manner.

wav·i·ness (wāv′i-nis), ***n.*** a wavy quality or state.

wav·y (wāv′i), ***adj.*** [WAVIER (-i-ẽr), WAVIEST (-i-ist)], 1. having waves. 2. moving in a wavelike motion. 3. having undulating curves; forming waves and hollows; sinuous. 4. like, characteristic of, or suggestive of waves. 5. wavering; fluctuating; unsteady.

wawl (wôl), ***v.i.*** & ***n.*** waul.

wax (waks), ***n.*** [ME.; AS. *weax*; akin to G. *wachs*; IE. base ***wokso-** < ***weg-**, to weave; cf. G. *wabe*, wax < *weben*, to weave: so called from appearance of the honeycomb], 1. a plastic, dull-yellow substance secreted by bees for building cells; beeswax: it is hard when cold, easily molded when warm, melts at about 148° F., cannot be dissolved in water, and is used for candles, modeling, etc. 2. any plastic substance like this; specifically, *a*) paraffin. *b*) a waxlike substance exuded by the ears; earwax; cerumen. *c*) a waxy substance produced by scale insects. *d*) any waxlike substance yielded by plants or animals. *e*) a resinous substance used by shoemakers to rub on thread. *f*) sealing wax. 3. any of a group of substances made up of esters, fatty acids, free alcohols, and hydrocarbons, as spermaceti. ***v.t.*** to rub, polish, cover, smear, or treat with wax. ***adj.*** made of wax.

wax (waks), ***v.i.*** [WAXED (wakst), WAXED or *poetic* WAXEN (wak′s'n), WAXING], [ME. *waxen*; AS. *weaxan*, to grow (cf. WAIST); akin to G. *wachsen*; IE. base ***aweg-**, ***aug-**, seen also in L. *augere* (cf. AUGMENT), *auctor* (cf. AUTHOR), etc.], 1. to grow gradually larger, more numerous, etc.; increase in strength, intensity, volume, etc. 2. to increase in the size of its lighted portion; become gradually full: said of the moon: opposed to *wane*. 3. to become; grow: as, *wax* old.

wax (waks), ***n.*** [? < phr. *wax angry*, etc.], [Chiefly British Colloq.], a fit of anger or temper; a rage.

wax bean, 1. a variety of the string-bean plant with long, narrow, yellow pods. 2. the seed pod of this, used for food. Also called *butter bean.*

wax·ber·ry (waks′ber′i), ***n.*** [*pl.* WAXBERRIES (-iz)], 1. a shrub with showy white berries lasting into winter; snowberry. 2. the wax myrtle or its grayish-white fruit; bayberry.

wax·bill (waks′bil′), ***n.*** any of a group of Old World birds belonging to the weaverbird family, with waxy pink, scarlet, or white bills, often kept as cage birds, as the Java sparrow.

wax·en (wak′s'n), ***adj.*** 1. made of wax. 2. like wax, as in being white, soft, smooth, lustrous, pale, plastic, pliable, impressionable, etc. 3. covered with wax.

wax·en (wak′s'n), poetic past participle of **wax** (to increase).

wax·i·ness (wak′si-nis), ***n.*** a waxy state or quality.

wax insect, any of various homopterous insects that secrete a waxy substance, as a certain Chinese scale insect.

wax myrtle, any of a number of related shrubs or trees having grayish berries coated with a waxy substance used for candles; bayberry.

wax palm, either of two South American palm trees yielding a waxy substance used in making candles.

wax paper, a kind of paper made moistureproof by a wax, or paraffin, coating: also **waxed paper.**

wax·weed (waks′wēd′), ***n.*** a small plant with sticky, hairy stems and purple flowers.

wax·wing (waks′wiŋ′), ***n.*** any of a group of related birds found in many parts of the Northern Hemisphere, with silky-brown plumage, a showy crest, and distinctive scarlet spines, suggesting sealing wax, at the ends of the secondary quill feathers.

wax·work (waks′wũrk′), ***n.*** work, or objects, figures, etc., made of wax; often, a single figure made of wax.

wax·works (waks′wũrks′), ***n.pl.*** [construed as sing.], an exhibition of wax figures, usually representations of well-known persons.

wax·y (wak′si), ***adj.*** [WAXIER (-si-ẽr), WAXIEST (-si-ist)], 1. full of, covered with, or made of wax. 2. like wax in nature or appearance. 3. in *medicine*, designating, of, or characterized by a degeneration resulting from the deposit of an insoluble, waxlike substance in an organ.

way (wā), ***n.*** [ME. *wei*, *way*; AS. *weg*; akin to G. *weg*; IE. base ***wegh-**, to go, seen also in L. *vehere* (cf. VEHICLE), *vehemens* (cf. VEHEMENT), etc.], 1. a means of passing from one place to another, as a road, street, path, etc.: as, the *way* was rough; hence, 2. *a*) room or space for passing; free area; an opening, as in a crowd: as, the police made *way* for him. *b*) freedom of action or opportunity. 3. a route or course that is or may be used to go from one place to another. 4. travel or movement along a certain route or in a certain direction: as, on the *way* to town. 5. a path in life; course or habits of life or conduct: as, fall into evil *ways*. 6. a course of action; method or manner of doing something: as, do it this *way*. 7. a usual or customary manner of living, acting, or being: as, the *way* of the world. 8. a characteristic manner of acting or doing: as, that's just his *way*, you must learn their *ways*. 9. manner; style: as, he had a pleasant *way*. 10. progress; advance; movement, as of a boat: as, under *way*: also spelled **weigh.** 11. distance: as, a long *way* off: also [Colloq.], **ways.** 12. direction of movement or action: as, go this *way*, look this *way*. 13. respect; point; particular; feature: as, in some *ways* you are right. 14. wish; desire; will: as, have one's *way*. 15. range or scope, as of experience: as, that never came my *way*. 16. [Colloq.], a (good, bad, etc.) state or condition: as, he is in a bad *way*, the business is in a fair *way*. 17. [Colloq.], line of work, occupation, or calling. 18. [Colloq.], a district; locality; area: as, out our *way*. 19. in *law*, the privilege that a person or group of persons, as residents in a village, have to go over certain ground; right of way. 20. in *mechanics*, a surface or slide on which the carriage of a lathe, etc. moves along its bed. 21. *pl.* in *shipbuilding*, a timber framework on which a ship is built and from which it slides in launching. ***adv.*** [Colloq.], away; far; at some distance: as, *way* behind. —***SYN.*** see **method.**

by the way, 1. incidentally. 2. on or beside the way.

by way of, 1. passing through; through; via. 2. as a way, method, mode, or means of. 3. [Chiefly

British], in the condition or position of: as, she is *by way of* being a fine pianist.
come one's way, 1. to come within one's scope or range; come to one. 2. [Slang], to turn out successfully for one.
give way, 1. to withdraw; yield. 2. to break down.
give way to, to step aside for; yield to.
go out of the (or **one's**) **way,** to inconvenience oneself; do something that one would not ordinarily do, or that requires extra effort or trouble.
in the way, in such a position or of such a nature as to obstruct, hinder, impede, or prevent.
make one's way, 1. to advance or proceed. 2. to advance in life, as by one's own efforts.
make way, to make room; clear a passage.
out of the way, 1. in a position so as not to hinder or interfere; hence, 2. disposed of. 3. out of existence; (put) to death. 4. not on the right or usual route or course; hence, 5. *a*) improper; wrong; amiss. *b*) unusual; uncommon. *c*) lost.
pave the way for, to make things easier for in advance; prepare for.
see one's way (clear), 1. to be willing (to do something). 2. to find it convenient or possible.
take one's way, to go.
under way, 1. moving; advancing; making progress. 2. in *nautical usage,* making headway: said of a boat: also **under weigh.**

way·bill (wā'bil'), *n.* a paper giving a list of goods and shipping instructions, sent with or fastened to goods in transit: abbreviated **W.B., W/B** (no period).

way·far·er (wā'fâr'ẽr), *n.* a person who travels by road, especially on foot; traveler.

way·far·ing (wā'fâr'iŋ), *adj. & n.* traveling, especially on foot.

wayfaring tree, 1. a tall, wild, white-flowered European shrub; viburnum. 2. a similar shrub found in America; hobblebush.

way·go·ing (wā'gō'iŋ), *adj.* 1. going away; departing. 2. of someone departing. 3. in *law,* designating a crop that will not ripen until after a tenant's term of occupancy has expired, and in which he has an interest.

way·laid (wā'lād'), past tense and past participle of **waylay.**

Way·land (wā'lənd), *n.* [AS. *Weland;* akin to ON. *Vīlnudr;* cf. Jiriczek, *Die Deutsche Heldensage,* pp. 1–54], in *Germanic & English folklore,* an invisible smith: also **Wayland (the) Smith.**

way·lay (wā'lā'), *v.t.* [WAYLAID (-lād'), WAYLAYING], [*way* + *lay,* after MLG. *wegelagen,* to waylay < *wegelage,* an ambush], 1. to lie in wait for and attack; ambush, as in order to rob, etc. 2. to wait for and accost by surprise.

Wayne (wān), [< surname *Wayne*], a masculine name.

Wayne, Anthony (wān), 1745–1796; American general in the Revolutionary War: called *Mad Anthony Wayne.*

ways (wāz), *n.pl.* [construed as sing.], [Colloq.], way (sense 11).

-ways (wāz), [*way* + adv. genit. *-s*], a suffix used to form adverbs from adjectives and nouns, meaning *in a* (specified) *direction, position,* or *manner,* as in *endways:* it is usually equivalent to the adverbial suffix *-wise.*

ways and means, 1. methods and resources at the disposal of a person, company, etc. 2. methods of raising money, as for government.

way·side (wā'sīd'), *n.* the edge of a road; the area close to the side of a road. *adj.* on, near, or along the side of a road.

way station, a small railroad station between more important ones, where through trains stop only on signal.

way train, a train that stops at all stations on the line; local.

way·ward (wā'wẽrd), *adj.* [ME. *weiward,* short for *aweiward;* see AWAY & -WARD], 1. insistent upon having one's own way contrary to others' advice, wishes, or commands; headstrong, willful, disobedient, etc. 2. conforming to no fixed rule or pattern; unpredictable; irregular; capricious; erratic. 3. [Archaic], not expected or wanted: as, his *wayward* fate.

way·worn (wā'wôrn', wā'wōrn'), *adj.* tired from traveling.

Wa·zir·i·stan (wä-zêr'i-stän'), *n.* a mountainous region in Pakistan.

W.B., W/B, waybill.

w.b., 1. warehouse book. 2. westbound. 3. in *nautical usage,* water ballast.

WbN, west by north.

WbS, west by south.

W.C., West Central (postal district in London).

w.c., 1. water closet. 2. without charge.

W.C.T.U., Woman's Christian Temperance Union.

wd., 1. ward. 2. word.

W.D., War Department.

we (wē; *unstressed* wi), *pron.* [for *sing.* see I], [ME.; AS.; akin to G. *wir,* Goth. *weis;* IE. base **we-,* we, seen also in Sans. *vayám*], the persons speaking or writing: sometimes used by a person in referring to several persons including himself, or by a king, author, editor, judge, etc. in referring to himself. *We* is the nominative case form, *us* the objective, *our* and *ours* the possessive, and *ourselves* (or, by a king, etc., *ourself*) the intensive and reflexive, of the first personal plural pronoun.

weak (wēk), *adj.* [ME. *weik;* ON. *veikr;* akin to AS. *wac,* feeble, which the ON. word replaced; IE. base **weig-,* to bend, yield, as also in G. *weich,* tender, L. *vicis,* change, etc. (cf. VICISSITUDE)], 1. lacking in strength of body or muscle; not physically strong. 2. lacking in fighting strength or skill; not strong in combat or competition: as, a *weak* team. 3. lacking in moral strength or firmness of character; lacking will power. 4. lacking in mental power, or intelligence; deficient in the ability to think, judge, decide, etc. 5. lacking ruling power, or authority; incapable of issuing orders and seeing that they are carried out: as, a *weak* monarch. 6. lacking in force or effectiveness: as, *weak* authority. 7. lacking in strength of material; unable to resist strain, pressure, etc.; easily torn, broken, bent, etc.: as, a *weak* rail, a *weak* spot in a fabric. 8. not sound or secure; unable to stand up to an attack, etc.: as, a *weak* fortification. 9. lacking physical vitality; feeble by reason of age, illness, etc.; infirm. 10. not performing well or in a normal manner: said of a body organ or part, as, *weak* eyes, *weak* ears. 11. indicating or suggesting moral or physical weakness: as, *weak* features. 12. lacking in volume, intensity, etc.; faint: as, a *weak* voice, a *weak* current. 13. lacking in the full or proper strength of some ingredient; diluted: as, *weak* tea. 14. lacking, poor, or deficient in something specified: as, *weak* in grammar, a baseball team *weak* in pitchers. 15. *a*) ineffective; unconvincing: as, a *weak* argument. *b*) faulty: as, *weak* logic. 16. having a relatively low gluten content: said of a flour or wheat. 17. in *finance,* tending toward lower prices: said of a stock or stock market. 18. in *grammar, a*) inflected by the addition of a suffix such as *-ed* or *-d* rather than by an internal vowel change: said of verbs popularly called *regular. b*) inflected by the addition of a suffix originally belonging to a stem ending in *-n:* said of Germanic adjectives and nouns. 19. in *phonetics,* unstressed or lightly stressed. 20. in *photography,* lacking contrast; thin: said of a negative. 21. in *prosody,* designating or of a verse ending in which the stress falls on a word or syllable that is normally unstressed, often a preposition whose object occurs in the following line.

SYN.—**weak,** the broadest in application of these words, basically implies a lack or inferiority of physical, mental, or moral strength (a *weak* muscle, mind, character, foundation, excuse, etc.); **feeble** suggests a pitiable weakness or ineffectiveness (a *feeble* old man, a *feeble* joke); **frail** suggests an inherent or constitutional delicacy or weakness, so as to be easily broken or shattered (her *frail* body, conscience, etc.); **infirm** suggests a loss of strength or soundness, as through illness or age (his *infirm,* old grandfather); **decrepit** implies a being broken down, worn out, or decayed, as by old age or long use (a *decrepit* old pensioner, a *decrepit* sofa). —*ANT.* strong, sturdy, robust.

weak·en (wē'kən), *v.t. & v.i.* to make or become weak or weaker.

SYN.—**weaken,** the most general of these words, implies a lessening of strength, power, soundness, etc. (*weakened* by disease, to *weaken* an argument); **debilitate** suggests a partial or temporary weakening, as by disease or dissipation (*debilitated* by alcoholic excesses); **enervate** implies a lessening of force, vigor, energy, etc., as through indulgence in luxury (*enervated* by idleness); **undermine** and **sap** both suggest a weakening or impairing by subtle or stealthy means (his authority had been *undermined* by the rumors, her strength had been *sapped* by disease). —*ANT.* strengthen, energize.

weak·fish (wēk'fish'), *n.* [*pl.* WEAKFISH, WEAKFISHES (-iz); see FISH], [< obs. D. *weekvisch; week,* soft + *visch,* a fish], any of several ocean fishes used for food, especially a species common off the Atlantic coast of the United States.

weak-kneed (wēk'nēd'), *adj.* 1. having weak knees. 2. lacking in courage, determination, etc.; timid.

weak·li·ness (wēk'li-nis), *n.* the state or quality of being weakly.

weak·ling (wēk'liŋ), *n.* 1. a person or animal low in physical strength or vitality. 2. a person of weak character or intellect. *adj.* weak; feeble.

weak·ly (wēk'li), *adj.* [WEAKLIER (-li-ẽr), WEAKLIEST (-li-ist)], sickly; feeble; weak. *adv.* in a weak manner.

weak-mind·ed (wēk'mīn'did), *adj.* 1. not firm of mind; indecisive; unable to refuse or deny. 2. having a weak mind; feeble-minded.

weak·ness (wēk'nis), *n.* 1. the state or quality of being weak. 2. a weak point; fault; defect, as in one's character. 3. a liking; especially, an unreasonable fondness (*for* something). 4. something of which one is unreasonably fond: as, candy is a *weakness* of mine. —*SYN.* see **fault.**

weal (wēl), *n.* [form of *wale* (a ridge)], a mark, line, or ridge raised on the skin, as by a blow; welt; wale.

weal (wēl), *n.* [ME. *wele;* AS. *wela, weola,* wealth, well-being; akin to OS. *wela;* for IE. base see WILL, *v.*], 1. [Archaic], a sound or prosperous state; well-being; welfare: as, the common *weal.* 2. [Obs.], wealth; riches.

weald (wēld), *n.* [readoption of AS. (W.S.) *weald* (ME. *weeld*), forest, wold, wilderness; var. of *wold* & akin to

G. *wald*, forest; cf. WOLD (plain)], [Poetic], 1. a wooded area; forest. 2. wild open country.

The Weald, a (former) woodland district in southeastern England, now mainly agricultural.

wealth (welth), *n.* [ME. *welthe*, wealth, happiness; cf. WEAL (welfare) & -TH], 1. much money or property; great worldly possessions; riches. 2. a large amount (of something); abundance: as, a *wealth* of ideas. 3. valuable products, contents, or derivatives: as, the *wealth* of the oceans. 4. [Obs.], weal; well-being. 5. in *economics*, *a)* everything having economic value measurable in price. *b)* any useful material thing capable of being bought, sold, or stocked for future disposition.

wealth·i·ly (wel′thə-li), *adv.* in a wealthy manner.

wealth·i·ness (wel′thi-nis), *n.* the quality or state of being wealthy.

Wealth·y (wel′thi), *n.* a red, medium-sized variety of fall apple.

wealth·y (wel′thi), *adj.* [WEALTHIER (-thi-ẽr), WEALTHIEST (-thi-ist)], 1. having wealth; rich; prosperous. 2. of, characterized by, or suggestive of wealth. 3. rich (*in* something specified); abundant: as, a language *wealthy* in nuances. —*SYN.* see **rich.**

wean (wēn), *v.t.* [ME. *wenen;* AS. *wenian*, to accustom, wean, with sense affected by *awenian*, to wean (cf. G. *entwöhnen*, to wean); IE. base **wen-*, in the sense "to be satisfied, be wont," seen also in L. *venus*, love, satisfaction in love (cf. VENUS, VENEREAL, VENERY, etc.)], 1. to cause (a child or young animal) to become accustomed gradually to food other than its mother's milk; stop suckling. 2. to withdraw (a person) by degrees (*from* a habit, object of affection, occupation, etc.), as by substituting some other interest.

wean (wēn), *n.* [contr. of Scot. *wee ane*, little one], [Scot.], a child or baby.

wean·ling (wēn′liŋ), *n.* a child or young animal that has just been weaned. *adj.* recently weaned.

weap·on (wep′ən), *n.* [ME. *wepen;* AS. *wæpen;* akin to G. *waffe* (cf. LUFTWAFFE), ON. *vāpn*, (cf. WAPENTAKE); IE. base **wēb-*, weapon, but found only in Gmc.], 1. an instrument of any kind used for fighting. 2. any organ (of an animal or plant) so used. 3. any means of attack or defense: as, his best *weapon* was silence.

wear (wâr), *v.t.* [WORE (wôr, wōr), WORN (wôrn, wōrn), WEARING], [ME. *weren;* AS. *werian;* akin to ON. *verja*, Goth. *wasjan*, to clothe; IE. base **wes-*, to clothe, seen also in L. *vestis*, clothing, *vestire*, to clothe (cf. DIVEST, VEST, VESTMENT, VESTIBULE, etc.)], 1. to have on the body or carry on the person for covering, protection, ornament, defense, etc., as a hat, a ring, a pistol, etc. 2. to have or show in one's expression or appearance: as, she *wore* a smile, *wearing* an air of expectancy. 3. to have on the person habitually or as a general practice: as, does he *wear* glasses? 4. to have or bear as a characteristic or attribute: as, he *wears* a famous name. 5. to hold, keep, or arrange (a part of the body) in a specified way: as, she *wears* her hair curled, he *wore* his head high. 6. to fly or show (its flag): said of a ship. 7. to impair, consume, or diminish by constant use, handling, friction, etc. (often with *away*). 8. to bring by use to a specified state: as, he *wore* his coat to rags. 9. to make, cause, or produce by the friction of rubbing, scraping, flowing, etc.: as, it will *wear* a hole in the floor. 10. to tire or exhaust (a person). 11. to pass (time) slowly or tediously (often with *away* or *out*). *v.i.* 1. to become impaired, consumed, or diminished by constant use, friction, etc.: as, that cloth will *wear* soon. 2. to hold up in use; bear continued use or handling; last: as, that suit *wears* well. 3. to become in time; gradually reach a specified state: as, my courage *wore* thin. 4. to pass away gradually (often with *away* or *on*): said of time, as, the year *wore* on. 5. [Obs.], to be commonly worn or used; be in style. *n.* 1. the act of wearing or the state of being worn, as on the person. 2. things, especially clothes, worn, or for wearing, on the body: as, men's *wear*. 3. the fashion or proper style of dress or the like. 4. *a)* the gradual impairment, loss, or diminution from use, friction, etc. *b)* the amount of such loss. 5. the ability to resist impairment or loss from use, friction, etc.: as, there's much *wear* left in my coat.

wear down, 1. to make or become worn; lose or cause to lose thickness or height by use, friction, etc. 2. to tire out; weary; exhaust (a person). 3. to overcome the resistance of by persistence.

wear off, to pass away or diminish by degrees.

wear out, 1. to make or become useless from continued wear or use. 2. to waste or consume by degrees. 3. to tire out; exhaust.

wear (wâr), *v.t.* [WORE (wôr, wōr), WORN (wôrn, wōrn), WEARING], [altered form of *veer* (to let out)], to turn or bring (a ship) about by swinging its bow away from the wind; veer: opposed to *tack*. *v.i.* to turn or come about by having the bow swung away from the wind.

wear·a·ble (wâr′ə-b'l), *adj.* that can be worn; suitable for wear. *n. pl.* wearable things; garments; clothing.

wear and tear, loss and damage resulting from use.

wea·ri·ful (wêr′i-fəl), *adj.* that makes weary; tiresome.

wea·ri·less (wêr′i-lis), *adj.* unwearying; tireless.

wea·ri·ly (wêr′ə-li), *adv.* in a weary manner.

wea·ri·ness (wêr′i-nis), *n.* 1. the condition or quality of being weary; fatigue. 2. something that wearies.

wear·ing (wâr′iŋ), *adj.* 1. of or intended for wear: as, *wearing* apparel. 2. causing wear, or gradual impairment or diminution. 3. wearying; tiring.

wearing apparel, garments; clothing.

wea·ri·some (wêr′i-səm), *adj.* causing weariness; tiring, tiresome, or tedious.

wea·ry (wêr′i), *adj.* [WEARIER (-i-ẽr), WEARIEST (-i-ist)], [ME. *weri;* AS. *werig;* akin to OHG. *wuorag*, drunk; IE. base **wōr-*, giddiness, faintness, seen also in Gr. *hōrakian*, to be giddy], 1. tired; worn out. 2. without further liking, patience, tolerance, zeal, etc.; bored (with *of*): as, *weary* of singing. 3. tiring: as, *weary* work. 4. irksome; tedious; tiresome. *v.t. & v.i.* [WEARIED (-id), WEARYING], to make or become weary. —*SYN.* see **tired.**

wea·sand (wē′z'nd), *n.* [ME. *wesand;* AS. *wæsend*, the windpipe; akin to OHG. *weisant, weisunt;* ppr. form prob. < IE. base **weis-*, to flow out, with basic sense "the flowing"; cf. WEASEL], [Archaic], 1. the trachea, or windpipe. 2. the esophagus, or the throat generally.

wea·sel (wē′z'l), *n.* [*pl.* WEASELS (-z'lz), WEASEL; see PLURAL, II, D, 1], [ME. *wesel;* AS. *wesle;* akin to G. *wiesel;* prob. IE. base **weis-*, to flow out, with reference to the rank odor emitted from the animal; cf. L. *vis(s)io*, a stink], 1. any of a worldwide group of cunning, agile, flesh-eating mammals related to the stoats and martens, with a long, slender body, short legs, and a long, bushy tail: they feed on rats, mice, birds, eggs, etc. 2. a person likened to this animal, as in cunning or slyness.

WEASEL (15 in. long including tail)

weasel words, words or remarks that are equivocal or deliberately ambiguous.

weather (weth′ẽr), *n.* [ME. & AS. *weder;* akin to G. *wetter;* IE. base **we-, *awe-*, to blow, seen also in OSlav. *vedro*, good weather, etc.], 1. the general condition of the atmosphere at a particular time and place, with regard to the temperature, moisture, cloudiness, etc.: distinguished from *climate*. 2. disagreeable or harmful atmospheric conditions; storm, rain, etc.: as, for protection against the *weather*. *v.t.* 1. to expose to the action of weather or atmosphere, as for airing, drying, seasoning, etc. 2. to wear away, discolor, disintegrate, or otherwise change for the worse by exposure to the atmosphere. 3. to pass through safely or survive: as, they *weathered* the storm. 4. to slope (a roof, shingles, etc.) so as to throw off rain, etc. 5. in *nautical usage*, to pass to the windward of (a cape, reef, etc.). *v.i.* 1. to become discolored, disintegrated, etc. by exposure to the weather or atmosphere. 2. to endure such exposure in a specified manner: as, this canvas will *weather* well. *adj.* designating or of the side of a ship, etc. facing the wind; windward.

keep one's weather eye open, [Colloq.], to be on the alert; stay on guard.

under the weather, [Colloq.], 1. not feeling well; somewhat sick; ailing. 2. somewhat drunk.

weather through, to pass or go safely through a storm, peril, difficulty, etc.

weather beam, in *nautical usage*, the side of a ship facing the wind.

weath·er-beat·en (weth′ẽr-bē′t'n), *adj.* showing the effect of exposure to weather, as, *a)* stained, damaged, or worn down. *b)* sunburned, roughened, hardened, etc.: said of a person, his face, etc.

weath·er·board (weth′ẽr-bôrd′, weth′ẽr-bōrd′), *n.* 1. a board so shaped that its thin upper edge is overlapped by the board above, and its thick lower edge covers the top edge of the one below, in order to shed water; clapboard. 2. in *nautical usage*, the windward side of a ship. *v.t.* to nail weatherboards on (a roof or wall).

weath·er·board·ing (weth′ẽr-bôr′diŋ, weth′ẽr-bōr′diŋ), *n.* 1. the act of covering a roof or wall with weatherboards. 2. weatherboards collectively.

weath·er-bound (weth′ẽr-bound′), *adj.* delayed or halted by bad weather, as a ship, airplane, etc.

Weather Bureau, a division of the Department of Commerce that gathers and compiles data on weather conditions over the United States, on the basis of which weather forecasts are made: abbreviated **W.B.**

weath·er·cock (weth′ẽr-kok′), *n.* 1. a vane in the form of a cock, which swings to point the direction of the wind; weather vane. 2. a fickle or changeable person or thing.

weath·ered (weth'ẽrd), *adj.* 1. seasoned by the weather; stained, worn, or beaten by the weather. 2. given a stained or discolored finish intended to resemble that produced by exposure to the weather. 3. in *architecture*, made sloping, so as to shed water.

weather gauge, 1. a position of advantage to the windward: said of one ship in relation to another. 2. any position of advantage.

weath·er·glass (weth'ẽr-glas', weth'ẽr-gläs'), *n.* an instrument used to forecast the weather by showing changes in the pressure of the atmosphere; barometer or similar device.

weath·er·ing (weth'ẽr-iŋ), *n.* 1. in *architecture*, a slope built to shed water. 2. in *geology*, the erosive effects of the forces of weather on the surface of the earth, forming soil, sand, etc.

weath·er·li·ness (weth'ẽr-li-nis), *n.* the state or quality of being weatherly.

weath·er·ly (weth'ẽr-li), *adj.* in *nautical usage*, that can sail close to the wind with very little drift to leeward.

weath·er·man (weth'ẽr-man'), *n.* [*pl.* WEATHERMEN (-men')], [Colloq.], a person who forecasts the weather, especially one employed by the Weather Bureau.

weather map, a map or chart showing the condition of the weather in a certain area at a given time by indicating barometric pressures, temperatures, wind velocity and direction, etc.

weath·er·proof (weth'ẽr-prōōf'), *adj.* that can withstand exposure to wind, rain, snow, etc. without being damaged. *v.t.* to make weatherproof.

weather station, a post or office where weather conditions are recorded and studied and forecasts are made.

weath·er-strip (weth'ẽr-strip'), *v.t.* to fit or provide with weather strips.

weather strip, a thin strip of metal, felt, wood, etc., used to cover the joint between a door or window sash and the jamb, casing, or sill, so as to keep out drafts, rain, etc.

weather stripping, 1. a weather strip. 2. weather strips collectively.

weather vane, a vane for showing in what direction the wind is blowing; weathercock.

weath·er-wise (weth'ẽr-wīz'), *adj.* 1. skilled in predicting the weather; hence, 2. skilled in predicting shifts of opinion, feeling, etc.

weath·er·worn (weth'ẽr-wôrn', weth'ẽr-wōrn'), *adj.* weather-beaten.

weave (wēv), *v.t.* [WOVE (wōv) or *rarely* WEAVED (wēvd), WOVEN (wōv''n) or WOVE, WEAVING], [ME. *weven;* AS. *wefan;* akin to G. *weben;* IE. base **webh-*, to weave, plait, etc., seen also in Eng. *web*], 1. *a)* to make (a fabric) by interlacing threads or yarns; make on a loom. *b)* to form (threads) into a fabric. 2. *a)* to construct in the mind or imagination. *b)* to form (details, incidents, etc.) into a story, poem, etc. 3. *a)* to make by interlacing twigs, flowers, reeds, etc.: as, *weave* a basket. *b)* to twist or interlace (twigs, flowers, etc.) so as to form something. 4. to twist or interlace (something) into, through, or among: as, *weave* flowers into one's hair. 5. to make or spin (a web): said of spiders, etc. *v.i.* 1. to do weaving; make cloth. 2. to become interlaced or intertwined. 3. to move from side to side or in and out. *n.* a method, manner, or pattern of weaving: as, a cloth of English *weave*.

weave one's way, to go by turning, twisting, and moving from side to side.

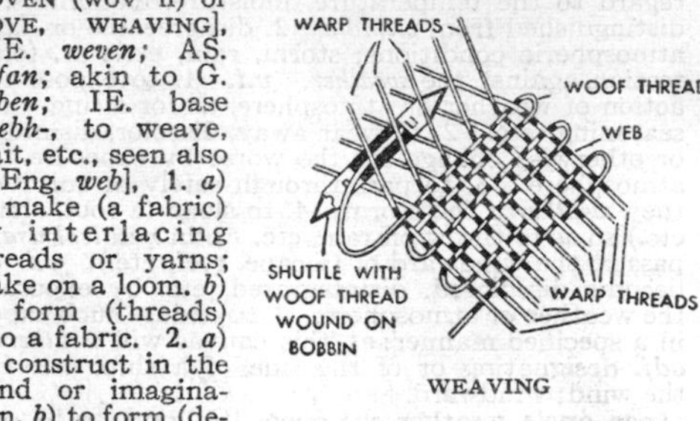

WEAVING

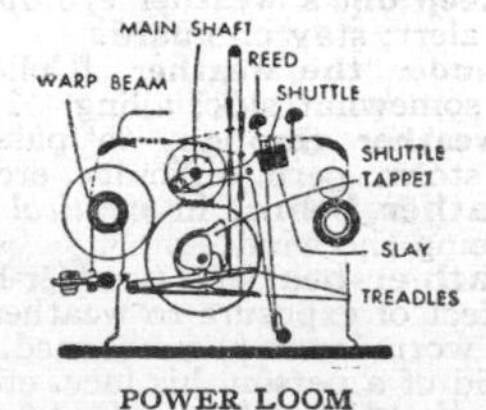

POWER LOOM

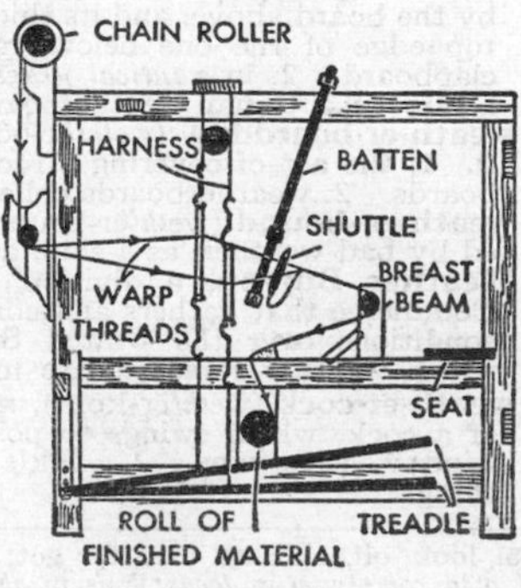

HAND LOOM

weav·er (wēv'ẽr), *n.* 1. a person who weaves; especially, one whose work is weaving. 2. a weaverbird.

weav·er·bird (wēv'ẽr-bũrd'), *n.* any of a number of related birds resembling the finches and found mainly in Africa and Asia, which weave elaborate nests of sticks, grass, etc.

weaver's hitch (or **knot**), a sheet bend, a type of knot: see **knot**, illus.

web (web), *n.* [ME. *web, webbe;* AS. *webb;* akin to D. *webbe, web;* IE. base **webh-*, to weave; cf. WEAVE], 1. any woven fabric; especially, a length of cloth being woven on a loom or just taken off. 2. *a)* the woven or spun network of a spider; cobweb. *b)* a similar network spun by the larvae of certain insects. 3. a carefully woven trap or snare. 4. a complicated work of the mind, imagination, etc.: as, a *web* of lies. 5. anything like a web; network. 6. in *anatomy*, *a)* a tissue or membrane. *b)* an abnormal membrane joining the fingers and toes at the base. 7. in *architecture*, the portion of a ribbed vault between the ribs. 8. in *mechanics*, *a)* a thin plate between stiffeners, ribs, or other heavy structures. *b)* the blade of a saw, key, etc. 9. in *printing*, a large roll of paper, especially newsprint. 10. in *zoology*, *a)* the vane of a feather. *b)* a membrane partly or completely joining the toes of various water birds, water animals, etc. *v.t.* [WEBBED (webd), WEBBING], 1. to join by a web. 2. to cover with or as with a web. 3. to catch or snare in or as in a web.

Webb, Beatrice Potter (web), 1858–1943; wife of *Sidney James;* English sociologist, economist, and author.

Webb, Sidney James, first Baron Passfield, 1859–1947; English statesman, economist, sociologist, and author.

webbed (webd), *adj.* 1. formed like a web or made of webbing. 2. joined by a web: as, *webbed* toes. 3. having the digits joined by a web: as, a *webbed* foot.

web·bing (web'iŋ), *n.* [see WEB], 1. a strong, tough fabric woven in strips and used for belts, in upholstery, etc. 2. a strong edging strip woven into a piece of fabric, as in rugs. 3. a membrane uniting the fingers or toes, as of a duck, goose, frog, etc.

web·by (web'i), *adj.* [WEBBIER (-i-ẽr), WEBBIEST (-i-ist)], 1. of, having the nature of, or like a web. 2. webbed or palmated.

we·ber (vā'bẽr, wē'bẽr), *n.* [after Wilhelm *Weber*, G. physicist], 1. the practical unit of magnetic flux, equal to 10^8 maxwells. 2. formerly, a coulomb or ampere; later, a maxwell.

We·ber, Ernst Hein·rich (ernst hīn'riH vā'bẽr), 1795–1878; German physiologist.

We·ber, Karl Ma·ri·a von (kärl mä-rē'ä fôn vā'bẽr), Baron, 1786–1826; German composer.

We·ber, Wil·helm E·du·ard (vil'helm ā'dōō-ärt vā'bẽr), 1804–1891; brother of *Ernst Heinrich;* German physicist.

web·foot (web'foot'), *n.* [*pl.* WEBFEET (-fēt')], 1. a foot with two or more toes webbed. 2. a person, animal, or bird with webbed feet.

web-foot·ed (web'foot'id), *adj.* having webfeet.

web·ster (web'stẽr), *n.* [AS. *webbestre*, fem. of *webba*, weaver; see WEB & -STER], [Obs.], a weaver.

Web·ster, Daniel (web'stẽr), 1782–1852; American statesman and orator; United States senator (1827–1841; 1845–1850); secretary of state (1841–1843; 1850–1852).

Webster, John, 1580?–1625?; English dramatist.

Webster, Noah, 1758–1843; American lexicographer, editor, and author.

Web·ste·ri·an (web-stêr'i-ən), *adj.* of Daniel or Noah Webster.

web-toed (web'tōd'), *adj.* web-footed.

web·worm (web'wũrm'), *n.* any of various caterpillars, generally gregarious, which spin large webs.

wed (wed), *v.t.* [WEDDED (-id), WEDDED or WED, WEDDING], [ME. *wedden;* AS. *weddian*, lit., to pledge, engage < *wed*, a pledge; akin to G. *wetten*, to pledge, wager; IE. base **wadh-*, a pledge, to redeem a pledge, as also in L. *vas, vadis*, a pledge; cf. WAGER, GAGE], 1. to marry; specifically, *a)* to take for one's husband or wife. *b)* to conduct the marriage ceremony for; join in wedlock. 2. to unite or join closely: as, the project *weds* science and art. *v.i.* to become married; take a husband or wife.

we'd (wēd), 1. we had. 2. we should. 3. we would.

Wed., Wednesday.

wed·ded (wed'id), *adj.* 1. married: as, the *wedded* pair. 2. of or arising from marriage: as, *wedded* bliss. 3. devoted: as, *wedded* to one's work. 4. joined: as, *wedded* by common interests.

Wed·dell Sea (wed''l, wə-del'), an arm of the Atlantic between the Falkland Islands and Antarctica.

wed·ding (wed'iŋ), *n.* [ME.; AS. *weddung* < *weddian;* see WED], 1. *a)* the act or ceremony of becoming married; marriage. *b)* the marriage ceremony with its attendant festivities. 2. an anniversary of a marriage or the celebration of this: as, a golden *wedding*. —*SYN.* see **marriage**.

We·de·kind, Frank (fräŋk vā'də-kint), 1864–1918; German dramatist and poet.

wedge (wej), *n.* [ME. *wegge;* AS. *wecg;* akin to G. dial. *weck;* thought by some to be < IE. **wogʷhni-s*, ploughshare, as in L. *vomis*, OHG. *waganso*, etc.], 1. a piece of hard material, as wood or metal, tapering from a thick back to a thin edge that can be driven or forced into a narrow opening: used to split wood, lift weights, reinforce structures, etc. 2. anything shaped like a wedge: as, a *wedge* of pie; specifically, *a)* a wedge-shaped stroke in cuneiform writing. *b)* a wedge-shaped tactical formation, as of troops or football players, used to penetrate a narrow front to a great depth. 3. any action or procedure that serves to open the way for a gradual change, disruption, intrusion, etc. *v.t.* [WEDGED (wejd), WEDGING], 1. to split or force apart with or as with a wedge. 2. to fix solidly in place by driving a wedge or wedges under, beside, etc. 3. to force or pack in (often with *in*). 4. to force or crowd together in a narrow space. *v.i.* to push or be forced as or like a wedge.

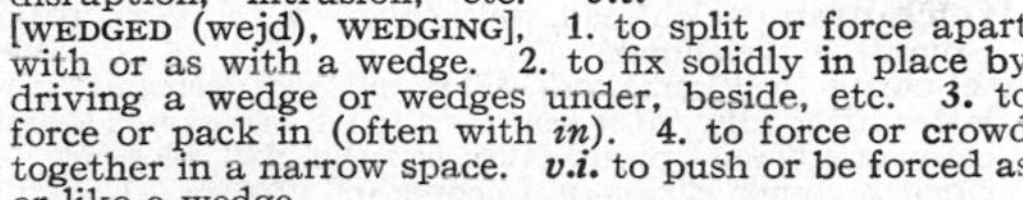

WEDGE

wedg·ie (wej'i), *n.* [Colloq.], a style of women's shoe having a wedge-shaped piece under the heel and forming a solid sole, flat from heel to toe.

Wedg·wood, Josiah (wej'wood'), 1730–1795; English potter.

Wedgwood (ware), [after Josiah *Wedgwood*], a fine English pottery, with delicately designed neoclassical figures which are applied in a white, cameolike relief on a tinted background, before the firing.

wedg·y (wej'i), *adj.* [WEDGIER (-i-ẽr), WEDGIEST (-i-ist)], shaped or used like a wedge.

wed·lock (wed'lok), *n.* [ME. *wedlok;* AS. *wedlac; wed*, a compact, pledge + *-lac* < the Gmc. base in Goth. *laiks*, a dance], the state of being married; matrimony. —*SYN.* see **marriage.**

Wednes·day (wenz'di), *n.* [ME. *Wednes dei;* AS. *Wodnes dæg*, Woden's day < *Woden*, chief of the Gmc. deities (cf. WODEN, ODIN); used as AS. transl. of L. *dies Mercurii*, Mercury's day, fourth day of the week], the fourth day of the week: abbreviated **Wed., W.**

wee (wē), *adj.* [WEER (wē'ẽr), WEEST (wē'ist)], [ME. *we, wei*, small quantity (only in north Eng & Scot. dial.); AS. (Anglian) *wege, weg* < base of *weigh*], very small; tiny. *n.* [Scot. & Eng. Dial.], a little bit; especially, a short time: as, bide a *wee*.

weed (wēd), *n.* [ME. *weede;* AS. *weod;* akin to LG. *wēd;* not known outside W.Gmc.], 1. any undesired, uncultivated plant that grows in profusion so as to crowd out a desired crop, disfigure a lawn, etc. 2. [Colloq.], *a)* tobacco: with *the*. *b)* a cigar. 3. something useless; specifically, a horse that is unfit for racing or breeding. 4. [Archaic], wild, luxuriant growth, as of underbrush. *v.t.* 1. to remove the weeds from, as a garden. 2. to remove (a weed): often with *out*. 3. to remove or eliminate as useless, harmful, etc.: often with *out*. 4. to rid of elements regarded as useless or harmful. *v.i.* to remove weeds, etc.

weed (wēd), *n.* [ME. *wede;* AS. *wæde, wæd*, a garment; akin to OHG. *wāt* (G. *-wand*, in *leinwand*, linen); IE. base **awē-*, to weave], 1. [Archaic], a garment or clothing. 2. *pl.* black mourning clothes, especially those worn by a widow. 3. a black mourning band, as of crape, worn on a man's hat or sleeve.

weed·er (wēd'ẽr), *n.* 1. a person who weeds. 2. a device for removing weeds.

weed·i·ness (wēd'i-nis), *n.* the state of being weedy.

weed·y (wēd'i), *adj.* [WEEDIER (-i-ẽr), WEEDIEST (-i-ist)], 1. having weeds; full of weeds. 2. of or like a weed or weeds, as in rapid, rank growth. 3. lean, lanky, ungainly, etc.: said of persons or animals.

week (wēk), *n.* [ME. *weke* < AS. *wicu* with lengthened & lowered vowel; akin to G. *woche* (OHG. *wehha, wohha*); IE. base **weig-*, to bend, yield, etc. (cf. WEAK), seen also in L. *vicis*, change (cf. VICISSITUDE), G. *wechsel*, exchange; basic sense "period of change, or which changes"], 1. a period of seven days, especially one beginning with Sunday and ending with Saturday. 2. the hours or days of work in a seven-day period: as, he works a 40-hour *week*. Abbreviated **w., wk.**

Sunday (or **Monday, Tuesday,** etc.) **week,** [Chiefly British], a week (counting backward or forward) from Sunday (or Monday, Tuesday, etc.).

this day (or **yesterday,** etc.) **week,** [Chiefly British], a week (counting backward or forward) from today (or yesterday, etc.).

week after week, every week.

week by week, each week.

week in, week out, every week.

week·day (wēk'dā'), *n.* 1. any day of the week except Sunday (or, as in *Judaism*, Saturday). 2. any day not in the weekend.

week·end, week-end (wēk'end'), *n.* 1. the period from Friday night or Saturday to Monday morning; end of the week. 2. a house party held over this period. Also **week end.** *adj.* of or on a weekend. *v.i.* to spend the weekend (*at* or *in* a specified place).

long weekend, a weekend plus one or two days before or after.

Week·ley, Ernest (wēk'li), 1865–1954; English linguist, etymologist, and lexicographer.

week·ly (wēk'li), *adj.* 1. continuing or lasting for a week. 2. done, happening, appearing, payable, etc. once a week, or every week: as, a *weekly* visit. 3. of a week, or each week: as, a *weekly* wage. *adv.* once a week; every week. *n.* [*pl.* WEEKLIES (-liz)], a periodical published once a week.

Weems, Ma·son Locke (mā'sən wēmz), 1759–1825; American preacher and writer: called *Parson Weems*.

ween (wēn), *v.i. & v.t.* [ME. *wenen;* AS. *wenan;* akin to G. *wähnen;* IE. base **wen-*, to be satisfied (with special sense in Gmc.), seen also in L. *venus*, love (cf. VENUS); see WEAN], [Archaic], to think; suppose; imagine.

wee·nie, wee·ny (wē'ni), *n.* [*pl.* WEENIES (-niz)], [Colloq.], a wiener.

weep (wēp), *v.i.* [WEPT (wept), WEEPING], [ME. *wepen;* AS. *wepan* < **wopjan* < *wop*, outcry; akin to OS. *wōpian;* IE. base **wab-*, to cry, complain], 1. to manifest or give expression to a strong emotion, usually grief or sorrow, by crying, wailing, or, especially, shedding tears. 2. to lament or mourn (with *for*). 3. to let fall drops of water or other liquid; especially, to drip moisture condensed from the air: as, cold pipes *weep* in hot weather. 4. to exude water or other liquid, as a wound, the stem of a plant, etc. *v.t.* 1. to weep for; lament; bewail; mourn: as, she *wept* her misfortune. 2. to shed (tears or other drops of liquid). 3. to bring to a specified condition by weeping: as, she *wept* herself to sleep. *n.* 1. *often pl.* a fit of weeping. 2. an exudation or dripping of moisture. —*SYN.* see **cry.**

weep (wēp), *n.* [so called from its characteristic cry], the lapwing.

weep·er (wēp'ẽr), *n.* 1. a person who weeps; especially, one who weeps habitually. 2. a hired mourner at a funeral. 3. a conventional badge of mourning, as, formerly, a white cuff band or, now, a black band of crape.

weep·ing (wēp'iŋ), *n.* the act of one who or that which weeps. *adj.* 1. that weeps; tearful. 2. having graceful, drooping branches: as, a *weeping* willow.

wee·ver (wē'vẽr), *n.* [ONorm.Fr. *wivre* (OFr. *guivre*), orig., serpent, dragon; L. *vipera*, viper], any of a number of ocean fishes found at the bottom of temperate seas near shrimp beds, and distinguished by long, soft, dorsal and anal fins, eyes near the top of the head, and several sharp spines.

wee·vil (wē'v'l), *n.* [ME. *wevel;* AS. *wifel;* akin to MLG. *wevel;* IE. base **webh-*, to move to and fro, as also in Eng. *wave, waver*], any of a large number of beetles with the head ending in a projecting snout: the larvae are very destructive to many crops, the various species attacking cotton, fruits, grain, and nuts, and destroying plants and trees by boring.

wee·vil·y, wee·vil·ly (wē'v'l-i), *adj.* infested with weevils.

weft (weft), *n.* [ME. *weft*, warp; AS. *weft, wefta* < base of *wefan*, to weave (cf. WEAVE) + *-t* (cf. -T)], 1. the yarns carried by the shuttle back and forth across the warp in weaving; woof; filling. 2. something woven.

‡Wehr·macht (vār'mäkht'), *n.* [G., lit., defense force], the armed forces of Germany.

Weich·sel (vik'səl), *n.* Vistula River: German name.

wei·ge·la (wi-jē'lə, wi-gē'lə), *n.* [Mod. L., after C. E. *Weigel* (1748–1831), G. physician], any of a number of related shrubs of the honeysuckle family, with clusters of pink, red, or white bell-shaped flowers on drooping branches.

weigh (wā), *v.t.* [ME. *weien, wegen*, to weigh, bear; AS. *wegan*, to carry, bear; akin to G. *wiegen, wägen;* IE. base **weĝh-*, to move, draw, etc., seen also in L. *vehere*, to carry, bring (cf. VEHICLE); cf. WAIN], 1. to determine the weight of by means of a scale or balance. 2. to lift or balance (an object) in the hand or hands, in order to estimate its heaviness or weight. 3. to measure out, dole out, or apportion, by or as by weight (often with *out*). 4. *a)* to consider and choose carefully: as, *weigh* one's words. *b)* to balance or ponder in the mind; consider in order to make a choice: as, *weigh* one plan against another. 5. to burden; bear or press down upon, as with heaviness or oppression (with *down*). 6. [Obs.], to hold in high regard; esteem; value. 7. in *nautical usage*, to hoist, or lift (an anchor). *v.i.* 1. to have weight; be heavy; especially, to have a specified weight: as, it *weighs* ten pounds. 2. to have significance, importance, or influence: as, his word *weighs* heavily with me. 3. to be a burden; press or bear down (with *on* or *upon*): as, the theft *weighs* on his mind. 4. in *nautical usage, a)* to hoist anchor; hence, *b)* to start to sail. —*SYN.* see **consider.**

weigh in, 1. to weigh (a boxer, jockey, etc.) before or after a contest in order to verify his declared weight. 2. to be so weighed.

weigh (wā), ***n.*** [var. of *way,* in phr. *under way,* modified by the notion of "weighing anchor"], way: a popular variant in *under weigh,* progressing, advancing.

weigh·bridge (wā'brij'), ***n.*** a large platform scale set flush with a road, for weighing cars, wagons, cattle, etc.

weight (wāt), ***n.*** [ME. *weiht,* new formation < *weien, weihen,* to weigh; AS. had *(ge)wiht* < *wegan;* see WEIGH], 1. a portion or quantity weighing a definite or specified amount: as, we had ten pounds *weight* of lead. 2. heaviness as a quality of things; attraction of a material body by gravitational pull toward the center of the earth: in physics, distinguished from *mass.* 3. quantity or amount of heaviness; how much a thing weighs: as, the *weight* of an egg. 4. *a)* any unit of heaviness or mass. *b)* any system of such units: as, troy *weight,* avoirdupois *weight. c)* a piece of metal, wood, etc. of a specific standard heaviness, used on a balance or scale in weighing. 5. any block or mass of material used for its heaviness; specifically, *a)* one used to hold light things down: as, a paper *weight. b)* one used to drive a mechanism: as, the *weights* in a clock. *c)* one used to maintain balance: as, *weights* placed on an automobile wheel. *d)* one of a particular heaviness, lifted as an athletic exercise. 6. a burden or oppressiveness, as of responsibility or sorrow. 7. importance or consequence: as, a matter of great *weight.* 8. influence, power, or authority: as, he threw his *weight* to the losing side. 9. the relative thickness or heaviness of an article of clothing as proper to a particular season: as, a suit of summer *weight.* 10. any of the several classifications into which boxers and wrestlers are placed according to how much they weigh. 11. in *statistics, a)* the frequency, hence relative importance, of a single item in a frequency list of related items. *b)* the value or number used to express such frequency. Abbreviated **wt., W, W.** ***v.t.*** 1. to add weight to; make heavy or heavier. 2. to burden; load down; oppress. 3. to treat (thread or fabric) with a solution of metallic salts, in order to increase its weight. 4. in *statistics,* to give a weight, or value, to (an item in a frequency list). —*SYN.* see **important, influence.**

by weight, as determined by weighing.

carry weight, to be important, influential, etc.

pull one's weight, to do one's share.

weight·i·ly (wāt'ə-li), ***adv.*** in a weighty manner.

weight·i·ness (wāt'i-nis), ***n.*** the state or quality of being weighty.

weight·lift·ing (wāt'lif'tiŋ), ***n.*** the athletic exercise or competitive sport of lifting disk-shaped metal weights balanced on either end of a long bar: also **weight-lifting, weight lifting.**

weight·y (wāt'i), ***adj.*** [WEIGHTIER (-i-ẽr), WEIGHTIEST (-i-ist)], 1. having much weight; very heavy; ponderous. 2. burdensome; oppressive: as, *weighty* responsibilities. 3. of great significance or moment; serious: as, *weighty* matters of state. 4. of great influence or importance: as, a *weighty* personage. —*SYN.* see **heavy.**

Wei·hai·wei (wā'hī'wā'), ***n.*** a city in Shantung province, China, on the Yellow Sea: pop., 154,000.

Wei·mar (vī'mär), ***n.*** a city in central Germany: capital of Thuringia: pop., 49,000.

Weimar Republic, the German republic (1919–1933): its constitutional assembly met in Weimar in 1919.

Wein·gart·ner, Fe·lix von (fā'liks fôn vīn'gärt'nẽr), 1863–1942; Swiss conductor and composer.

weir (wêr), ***n.*** [ME. & AS. *wer,* a weir, dam (akin to G. *wehr)* < base of *werian,* to defend, hence dam up; IE. base **wer-,* to shut up, cover, as also in Eng. *warn,* etc.], 1. a low dam built in a river to back up or divert water, as for a mill; milldam. 2. a brushwood or stake fence built in a stream, channel, arm of the sea, etc., for catching or penning fish. 3. an obstruction placed in a stream or channel, diverting the water through a prepared aperture for measuring the rate of flow.

weird (wêrd), ***adj.*** [< Scot. *weird,* fate; ME. *wirde, werde;* AS. *wyrd,* fate < the base of *weorthan,* to become; basic sense "what is to come"], 1. suggestive of ghosts, evil spirits, or other supernatural things; mysterious; eerie. 2. [Colloq.], queer; unusual; startingly odd: as, he wore a *weird* costume. 3. [Archaic], of fate or destiny. ***n.*** [Scot. or Archaic], 1. fate or destiny. 2. any of the Fates. 3. a prophecy. 4. a spell.

SYN.—**weird** applies to that which is supernaturally mysterious or fantastically strange (a *weird* experience); **eerie** applies to that which inspires a vague, superstitious uneasiness or dread (the *eerie* howling of a dog); **uncanny** applies to that which is unnaturally strange or remarkable (*uncanny* insight); **unearthly** applies to that which is so strange or extraordinary as to seem to belong to another world (an *unearthly* light).

Weird Sisters, 1. the three Fates. 2. in Shakespeare's *Macbeth,* the three prophetic witches whom Macbeth consults.

Weis·mann, Au·gust (ou'goost vīs'män), 1834–1914; German biologist.

Weis·mann·ism (vīs'män-iz'm), ***n.*** [after August *Weismann*], a theory of heredity in which the germ plasm is regarded as the vehicle of inheritance from generation to generation, no acquired characteristics being transmitted from parent to offspring except those that affect the germ plasm.

weiss beer (vīs), [< G. *weissbier,* white beer], an effervescent, light-colored beer, brewed especially from wheat.

Weiss·horn (vīs'hôrn'), ***n.*** a mountain of the Alps, in southern Switzerland: height, 14,804 ft.

Weiz·mann, Cha·im (khī'yim vīts'män; Eng. wīts'mən), 1874–1952; Israeli chemist and Zionist leader, born in Russia; president of Israel (1948–1952).

we·jack (wē'jak), ***n.*** [< Am. Ind. (Algonquian) name; cf. Cree *otchek*], a pekan.

we·ka (wā'kä, wē'kə), ***n.*** [Maori: from its cry], any of several large, tawny-colored, flightless birds of the rail family, native to New Zealand.

Welch (welch, welsh), ***adj.*** & ***n.*** Welsh.

welch (welch, welsh), ***v.t.*** & ***v.i.*** [Slang], to welsh.

Welch·man (welch'mən, welsh'mən), ***n.*** [*pl.* WELCHMEN (-mən)], a Welshman.

wel·come (wel'kəm), ***adj.*** [ME. *wilcome, welcume,* (the latter after OFr. *bien venu,* etc.); AS. *wilcuma,* a welcome guest; *wil-,* prefix (akin to *willa,* will, pleasure) + *cuma,* a comer < *cuman,* to come (cf. COME)], 1. gladly and cordially received: as, a *welcome* guest. 2. agreeable or gratifying: as, *welcome* news. 3. freely and willingly permitted or invited (to use): as, you are *welcome* to (use) my car: also used in a conventional response to thanks ("you're welcome"), meaning *under no obligation for the favor given.* ***n.*** an act or expression of welcoming: as, a hearty (or cold) *welcome.* ***interj.*** you are welcome: an expression of cordial greeting. ***v.t.*** [WELCOMED (-kəmd), WELCOMING], 1. to greet with pleasure and hospitality. 2. to receive or accept with pleasure or satisfaction: as, he always *welcomes* criticism.

bid welcome, to receive with cordial greetings.

wear out one's welcome, to come so often or stay so long that one is no longer welcome.

weld (weld), ***v.t.*** [altered with unhistoric *-d* < *well* (to boil)], 1. to unite (pieces of metal) by heating until molten and fused or until soft enough to hammer or press together. 2. to bring into close or intimate union; unite in a single, compact whole. ***v.i.*** to be welded or capable of being welded: as, these alloys *weld* at different heats. ***n.*** 1. the act of welding. 2. the joint formed by welding: as, it broke at the *weld.*

weld (weld), ***n.*** [ME. *welde,* corresponding to AS. **wealde;* prob. < base of *weald,* forest (cf. WEALD)], 1. a European mignonette that yields a yellow dye. 2. the dye. Also **woald, wold, would.**

wel·fare (wel'fâr'), ***n.*** [ME. *wel,* well + *fare* < AS. *faru,* lit., a journey < *faran,* to fare, go; cf. FARE], 1. the state of being or doing well; condition of health, happiness, and prosperity; well-being. 2. welfare work.

Welfare Island, an island in the East River, in New York City: site of city hospitals and prison: formerly called *Blackwells Island.*

welfare state, a state in which the welfare of its citizens is promoted largely by the organized efforts of the government rather than by private institutions.

welfare work, the organized effort of a community or organization to improve the living conditions and standards of its members.

wel·kin (wel'kin), ***n.*** [ME. *welkne, wolkne;* AS. *wolcen;* akin to G. *wolke;* orig. meaning, cloud, with sense development as in *sky;* IE. base **welg-,* wet], [Archaic or Poetic], the curved vault of the sky, or the upper air: now chiefly in *make the welkin ring,* to make a very loud sound.

well (wel), ***n.*** [ME. *welle;* AS. *wella* < the base *weallan, wiellan,* to boil up (cf. the *v.*); akin to G. *welle,* wave; IE. base **wel-,* to turn, roll, etc., seen also in L. *volvere,* to roll; see WELD], 1. a flow of water from the earth; natural spring and pool. 2. a deep hole or shaft sunk into the earth to tap an underground supply of water, gas, oil, etc. 3. a source of abundant supply; fount: as, he was a *well* of information. 4. any of various shafts or deep enclosed spaces resembling a well; especially, *a)* an open shaft in a building for a staircase; stairwell. *b)* a shaft in a building or between buildings, open to the sky for light and air; airshaft. *c)* an elevator shaft. *d)* in English law courts, an open space before the bench, for solicitors. *e)* in *nautical usage,* an enclosure in the hold of a ship for containing the pumps and protecting them from damage. 5. any of various vessels, containers, etc. for holding liquid, as an inkwell. ***v.i.*** [ME. *wellen,* to well up, bubble, boil, weld; AS. *wellan, wyllan,* to bubble, well up], to flow or spring from or as from a well; gush (often with *up, forth, down,* etc.). ***v.t.*** to pour forth; gush: as, her eyes *welled* tears.

well (wel), ***adv.*** [BETTER (bet'ẽr), BEST (best)], [ME. *wel;* AS. *wel, well;* akin to G. *wohl;* for IE. base see WILL, *v.;* basic sense "according to desire"], 1. in a pleasing or desirable manner; satisfactorily: as, the affair ended *well.* 2. in a proper, friendly, or attentive manner: as, treat him *well.* 3. skillfully; expertly: as, she sings *well.* 4. in an appropriate manner; fittingly: as, spoken *well.* 5. prosperously; in comfort and plenty: as, they lived *well* in Paris. 6. with good reason; in justice: as, you may *well* ask. 7. satisfactorily in regard to health or physical condition: as, the patient is doing *well.* 8. to a considerable extent or degree: as, *well* advanced. 9. thoroughly: as, stir *well* before cooking. 10. with certainty; definitely: as, you know perfectly *well* that he was there. 11. intimately; familiarly; closely: as, I know him *well.* 12. in good spirit; with good grace: as, he took the news *well. Well* is sometimes used in hyphenated compounds meaning *properly, satisfactorily, thoroughly,* etc., as in *well-defined, well-able, well-worn.* ***adj.*** 1. suitable; proper; advisable: as, it is *well* that you came. 2. in good health: as, she is quite *well.* 3. in a good or satisfactory condition; favorable; comfortable: as, things are *well* with us these days. ***interj.*** an exclamation used to express surprise, acquiescence, agreement, resignation, expostulation, etc., or merely to preface or resume one's remarks. —***SYN.*** see **healthy.**

as well, 1. besides; in addition. 2. with equal justification or propriety; equally.

as well as, 1. equally with; just as much or as good as. 2. in addition to.

we'll (wēl), 1. we shall. 2. we will.

well·a·day (wel'ə-dā'), ***interj.*** [Archaic], wellaway.

Wel·land Canal (wel'ənd), a canal in Ontario, Canada, between Lake Erie and Lake Ontario: length, 27 1/2 mi.

well-ap·point·ed (wel'ə-poin'tid), ***adj.*** excellently furnished or equipped: as, a *well-appointed* office.

well·a·way (wel'ə-wā'), ***interj.*** [ME. *wei la wei,* lit., woe! lo! woe!; *wei* < ON. *vei,* woe + *la* < AS. *la,* lo; cf. WOE, LO], [Archaic], alas!: an exclamation of sorrow, regret, etc.

well-bal·anced (wel'bal'ənst), ***adj.*** 1. nicely or exactly balanced, adjusted, or regulated; evenly proportioned: as, a *well-balanced* formula. 2. of a steady, judicious temper; sane, sensible, and reliable.

well-be·haved (wel'bi-hāvd'), ***adj.*** behaving well; conducting oneself properly; displaying good manners.

well-be·ing (wel'bē'iŋ), ***n.*** the state of being well, happy, or prosperous; welfare.

well·born (wel'bôrn'), ***adj.*** born of good family.

well-bred (wel'bred'), ***adj.*** 1. showing good breeding; courteous and considerate in manner or actions. 2. of good stock: said of animals.

well-chos·en (wel'chō'z'n), ***adj.*** chosen with care and judgment; proper; appropriate.

well-con·tent (wel'kən-tent'), ***adj.*** thoroughly pleased or satisfied.

well-dis·posed (wel'dis-pōzd'), ***adj.*** 1. suitably or properly placed or arranged. 2. inclined to be friendly, kindly, or favorable (*toward* a person) or receptive (*to* an idea, etc.).

well-do·er (wel'dōō'ẽr), ***n.*** a person who does well; especially, one who does good deeds.

well·do·ing (wel'dōō'iŋ), ***n.*** good or benevolent action or conduct.

well-done (wel'dun'), ***adj.*** 1. performed with skill and efficiency. 2. thoroughly cooked: said of meat: opposed to *rare.* ***interj.*** an exclamation of approval of another's action.

Welles·ley (welz'li), ***n.*** a town in eastern Massachusetts: pop., 26,000.

well-fa·vored (wel'fā'vẽrd), ***adj.*** handsome; pretty.

well-fed (wel'fed'), ***adj.*** showing the effect of much good food; plump; fat.

well-found (wel'found'), ***adj.*** properly and adequately equipped: as, a *well-found* ship.

well-found·ed (wel'foun'did), ***adj.*** based on facts, good evidence, or sound judgment: as, a *well-founded* suspicion.

well-groomed (wel'grōōmd'), ***adj.*** 1. carefully cared for: as, a *well-groomed* horse. 2. clean and neat; carefully washed, combed, dressed, etc.

well-ground·ed (wel'groun'did), ***adj.*** 1. having a thorough basic knowledge of a subject. 2. based on good reasons; well-founded.

well-han·dled (wel'han'd'ld), ***adj.*** capably and efficiently managed.

well·head (wel'hed'), ***n.*** 1. the source of a spring of water; spring. 2. a source; fountainhead.

well-heeled (wel'hēld'), ***adj.*** [*well, adv.* + pp. of *heel*], [Slang], having considerable money; rich; prosperous.

well-in·formed (wel'in-fôrmd'), ***adj.*** 1. having thorough knowledge of a subject. 2. having considerable knowledge of many subjects, especially those of current interest.

Wel·ling·ton (wel'iŋ-tən), ***n.*** seaport and capital of New Zealand, on North Island: pop., 145,000.

Wel·ling·ton (wel'iŋ-tən), first Duke of, (*Arthur Wellesley*), 1769–1852; British general and statesman; defeated Napoleon at Waterloo (1815); prime minister (1828–1830).

well-in·ten·tioned (wel'in-ten'shənd), ***adj.*** having or showing good, kindly, or benevolent intentions: usually connoting failure or miscarriage of intention.

well-knit (wel'nit'), ***adj.*** strong; sturdy; close-knit.

well-known (wel'nōn'), ***adj.*** 1. widely or generally known; famous or notorious. 2. thoroughly known.

well-made (wel'mād'), ***adj.*** 1. well-proportioned; strongly built; skillfully and soundly put together. 2. in *literature & drama, a*) skillfully constructed or contrived, as a plot. *b*) having a skillfully contrived plot: as, a *well-made* play or novel.

well-man·nered (wel'man'ẽrd), ***adj.*** having or showing good manners; polite; courteous.

well-mean·ing (wel'mēn'iŋ), ***adj.*** having or showing good or kindly intentions: see **well-intentioned.**

well-meant (wel'ment'), ***adj.*** said or done with good intention.

well-nigh (wel'nī'), ***adv.*** very nearly; almost.

well-off (wel'ôf'), ***adj.*** 1. in a favorable or fortunate condition or circumstance. 2. prosperous; well-to-do. Also **well off.**

well-or·dered (wel'ôr'dẽrd), ***adj.*** properly or carefully arranged or organized.

well-pre·served (wel'pri-zũrvd'), ***adj.*** in good condition or of good appearance, in spite of age.

well-read (wel'red'), ***adj.*** 1. having read much (*in* a particular subject). 2. having a wide knowledge of books through having read much.

Wells, H. G. (welz), (*Herbert George Wells*), 1866–1946; English novelist, historian, and sociologist.

wells·ite (welz'īt), ***n.*** [after H. L. *Wells* (1855–1924), Am. chemist], a colorless or white, crystalline silicate of aluminum, barium, calcium, and potassium, $(Ba,Ca,K_2)Al_2Si_3O_{10}\cdot 3H_2O$.

well-spo·ken (wel'spō'kən), ***adj.*** 1. speaking easily or fluently. 2. speaking in a courteous or gracious manner. 3. properly or aptly spoken.

well·spring (wel'spriŋ'), ***n.*** 1. the source of a stream, spring, etc.; fountainhead. 2. a source of abundant and continual supply: as, a *wellspring* of knowledge.

well sweep, a sweep (sense 11).

well-thought-of (wel'thôt'uv'), ***adj.*** having a good reputation; of good repute.

well-timed (wel'tīmd'), ***adj.*** said or done at exactly the right moment; timely.

well-to-do (wel'tə-dōō'), ***adj.*** prosperous; well-off; wealthy: also **well to do.** —***SYN.*** see **rich.**

well-wish·er (wel'wish'ẽr), ***n.*** a person who wishes well to another, or to a cause, movement, etc.

well-wish·ing (wel'wish'iŋ), ***adj.*** that wishes well to others; kindly disposed. ***n.*** the act, or an expression, of wishing well to others.

well-worn (wel'wôrn', wel'wōrn'), ***adj.*** 1. much worn; much used; hence, 2. overused; trite; hackneyed: as, a *well-worn* joke. 3. worn or carried becomingly.

Wels·bach burner (welz'bak; G. vels'bäkh), [after Carl Auer von *Welsbach* (1858–1929), Austrian chemist, its inventor], a gas burner with a gauze mantle impregnated with thorium oxide and about one per cent of cerium oxide: when lighted, the gauze becomes incandescent and gives off a bright, greenish light.

Welsh (welsh, welch), ***adj.*** [ME. *Wel(i)sch;* AS. *Welisc* < *Wealh,* Briton, foreigner], of Wales, its people, their language, etc. ***n.*** the (Brythonic) Celtic language spoken in Wales. Abbreviated **W.** Also **Welch.**

the Welsh, the people of Wales: also called *the Cymry.*

welsh (welsh), ***v.t. & v.i.*** [19th-c. slang; ? back-formation < *welsher*], [Slang], 1. to cheat or swindle by failing to pay a bet or other debt. 2. to evade or fail to fulfill (an obligation). Often with *on.* Also **welch.**

Welsh cor·gi (kôr'gi), [W. corgi < *corr,* dwarf + *ci,* dog], either of two breeds of short-legged dog with a foxlike head, originally from Wales.

welsh·er (wel'shẽr), ***n.*** [prob. for *Welsher,* Welshman, with opprobrious reference to supposed propensities], [Slang], a person who welshes; cheat; swindler.

Welsh·man (welsh'mən, welch'mən), ***n.*** [*pl.* WELSHMEN (-mən)], a native of Wales: also **Welchman.**

Welsh rabbit, [prob., orig., a humorous usage], a dish of melted cheese, often mixed with ale or beer, served on crackers or toast: also, through faulty etymologizing, **Welsh rarebit.**

Welsh terrier, any of a breed of lean wire-haired terrier closely resembling the Airedale, but smaller: believed to have originated in Wales.

welt (welt), ***n.*** [ME. *welte, walt;* prob. < an AS. **wealt* either < base of *wealtan,* to roll or < base of Eng. *wale* (ridge)], 1. a strip of leather stitched into the seam between the sole and upper of a shoe to strengthen the joining. 2. a strip of material, often folded over a cord, placed at the edge or seam of a garment to reinforce or trim it. 3. *a*) a raised ridge left on the skin by a slash or blow; wale; weal. *b*) such a slash or blow. ***v.t.*** 1. to furnish with a welt or welts. 2. [Colloq.], to beat severely; thrash.

‡Welt·an·schau·ung (velt'än'shou'ooŋ), ***n.*** [G., lit.,

fat, āpe, bâre, cär; ten, ēven, hêre, ovẽr; is, bīte; lot, gō, hôrn, tōōl, look; oil, out; up, ūse, fũr; get; joy; yet; chin; she; thin, *th*en; zh, leisure; ŋ, ring; ə for *a* in *ago, e* in *agent, i* in *sanity, o* in *comply, u* in *focus;* ' as in *able* (ā'b'l); Fr. bál; ë, Fr. coeur; ö, Fr. feu; Fr. mo*n*; ô, Fr. coq; ü, Fr. duc; H, G. ich; kh, G. doch. See pp. x–xii. ‡ foreign; * hypothetical; < derived from.

world view], one's philosophy or conception of the universe and of life.

‡**Welt·an·sicht** (velt'än'ziHt), *n.* [G.], a world view; a particular attitude toward life and reality.

welt·er (wel'tẽr), *v.i.* [ME. *weltren;* MD. *welteren*, freq. formation < base of AS. *wealtan*, to roll; for IE. base see WELL (a spring)], 1. to roll about or wallow, as a pig in mud: sometimes used figuratively, as, they *weltered* in sin. 2. to be soaked, stained, or bathed: as, the corpses *weltered* in their blood. 3. to rise and fall; tumble; toss about, as the sea. *n.* 1. a tossing and tumbling, as of waves. 2. a confusion; turmoil.

welt·er·weight (wel'tẽr-wāt'), *n.* [prob. < *welt*, to thrash + *-er*], 1. a weight of twenty-eight pounds carried by a horse in a race as a handicap. 2. a boxer or wrestler who weighs between 136 and 147 pounds. *adj.* of welterweights.

‡**Welt·po·li·tik** (velt'pô-li-tēk'), *n.* [G.], world politics; international politics.

‡**Welt·schmerz** (velt'shmerts'), *n.* [G., world pain], a melancholy weariness of life; sentimental pessimism over the state of the world.

Wem·bley (wem'bli), *n.* a city in southeastern England: suburb of London: pop., 131,000.

Wemyss (wēmz), *n.* a parish in Fife county, Scotland: site of Wemyss castle: pop., 27,000.

wen (wen), *n.* [ME. *wenne;* AS. *wenn*], a benign skin tumor, especially of the scalp, consisting of a cyst containing sebaceous matter.

wen (wen), *n.* [ME. & AS.; var. of AS. *win, wyn*, joy, bliss], an Old English rune (ƿ), replaced in the 11th century by the letter *w*.

Wen·ces·laus (wen'səs-lôs'), *n.* Holy Roman emperor (1378–1400); lived 1361–1419; as, Wenceslaus IV, king of Bohemia (1378–1419): German name, *Wenzel.*

Wenceslaus, Saint, 903–935 A.D.; Christian martyr; patron saint of Bohemia: his day is September 28.

wench (wench), *n.* [ME. *wenche;* shortened < *wenchel*, child, boy, girl, young woman; AS. *wencel*, a child; prob. < base of AS. *wancol*, unsteady, with reference to an infant's gait], 1. a girl or young woman: derogatory or facetious term. 2. [Archaic], *a)* a country girl. *b)* a female servant. *c)* a prostitute or loose woman. *v.i.* [Archaic], to associate with prostitutes or loose women.

Wen·chow (wen'chou'; Chin. wun'jō'), *n.* a city in Chekiang province, southeastern China: pop., 157,000.

Wend (wend), *n.* [G. *wende*], one of a Slavic people of eastern Germany, descendants of the Sorbs.

wend (wend), *v.i.* [ME. *wenden;* AS. *wendan*, to turn; akin to G. *wenden;* caus. formation < the base of AS. *windan*, to wind (cf. WIND, to turn)], [Archaic], to go; journey; travel. *v.t.* [Now Chiefly Poetic], to direct one's steps on; proceed on; go: as, *wend* one's way.

Wen·dell (wen'd'l), [< the surname *Wendell*], a masculine name.

Wen·dic (wen'dik), *adj. & n.* Wendish.

Wend·ish (wen'dish), *adj.* of the Wends or their language. *n.* the West Slavic language of the Wends; Sorbian.

wen·nish (wen'ish), *adj.* of, like, or having a wen.

wen·ny (wen'i), *adj.* wennish.

went (went), [old p.t. of *wend*, now used to replace missing form of *go*], past tense of **go.**

wen·tle·trap (wen't'l-trap'), *n.* [D. *wenteltrap*, lit., a winding staircase; *wentel*, a winding + *trap*, stair], any of a group of sea mollusks enclosed in a single, usually white, spiral shell crossed by numerous ridges.

Wen·zel (ven'tsəl), see **Wenceslaus.**

wept (wept), past tense and past participle of **weep.**

were (wũr; *unstressed* wẽr), [ME. *weren;* AS. *wæron;* akin to G. *waren;* Gmc. base **wæz-* < IE. base **wes-* (cf. WAS)], the plural and second person singular, past indicative, and the past subjunctive, of **be.**

we're (wêr), we are.

were·gild (wũr'gild', wer'gild'), *n.* wergild.

were·n't (wũrnt), were not.

were·wolf (wêr'woolf', wũr'woolf'), *n.* [*pl.* WEREWOLVES (-woolvz')], [ME. *werwolf;* AS. *werwulf; wer*, a man + *wulf*, a wolf], in *folklore*, a person changed into a wolf, or one capable of assuming the form of a wolf at will: also spelled **werwolf.**

Wer·fel, Franz (fränts ver'fəl), 1890–1945; German poet, novelist, and dramatist, born in Prague.

wer·gild (wũr'gild', wer'gild'), *n.* [AS. *wergild; wer*, a man + *gild, geld*, payment, recompense, compensation; cf. YIELD], in early Germanic and Anglo-Saxon law, a price paid by the family of a manslayer to the family of the person killed, to atone for the killing and avoid reprisals: also spelled **weregild.**

wer·ner·ite (wũr'nẽr-īt'), *n.* [< A. G. *Werner* (1750–1817), G. geologist and mineralogist; + *-ite*], a mineral, a silicate of aluminum and calcium; scapolite.

wert (wũrt; *unstressed* wẽrt), archaic second person singular, past indicative and subjunctive, of **be**: used with *thou.*

wer·wolf (wêr'woolf', wũr'woolf'), *n.* [*pl.* WERWOLVES (-woolvz')], a werewolf.

We·ser (vā'zẽr), *n.* a river in western Germany, flowing into the North Sea: length, 280 mi.

We·ser·mün·de (vā'zẽr-mün'də), *n.* Bremerhaven: a former name.

Wes·ley (wes'li, wez'li), [< the surname *Wesley*], a masculine name.

Wesley, Charles, 1707–1788; brother of *John;* English Methodist clergyman and hymn writer.

Wesley, John, 1703–1791; English clergyman; founder of Methodism.

Wes·ley·an (wes'li-ən, wez'li-ən), *adj.* of John Wesley or the Methodist Church. *n.* a follower of John Wesley; Methodist.

Wes·ley·an·ism (wes'li-ən-iz'm, wez'li-ən-iz'm), *n.* the religious doctrines and method taught by John Wesley; Methodism.

Wes·sex (wes'iks), *n.* 1. a former Anglo-Saxon kingdom in southern England. 2. a corresponding section in modern England, chiefly in Dorsetshire, referred to as the locale of Thomas Hardy's novels.

west (west), *n.* [ME.; AS.; akin to G. *west;* IE. base **we-*, down from, away from, as prob. seen also in L. *vesper*, evening (cf. VESPER, VESPERUS)], 1. the direction to the left of a person facing north; direction in which sunset occurs: it is properly the point on the horizon at which the center of the sun sets at the equinox. 2. the point on a compass at 90°, directly opposite east. 3. a region or district in or toward this direction. 4. [W-], the western part of the earth, especially the Western Hemisphere or the Western Hemisphere and Europe; Occident. 5. [W-], the Western Roman Empire. *adj.* 1. in, of, to, toward, or facing the west. 2. from the west: as, a *west* wind. 3. [W-], designating the western part of a continent, country, etc.: as, *West* Africa, *West* Ohio. 4. designating or in that part of a church directly opposite the altar: from the conventional location of the altar at the eastern end. *adv.* in or toward the west; in a westerly direction. Abbreviated **W, W., w, w.**

the West, the western part of the United States; specifically, *a)* formerly, the region west of the Allegheny Mountains. *b)* the region west of the Mississippi, especially the northwestern part of this region.

West, Benjamin (west), 1738–1820; American painter in England.

West, Rebecca, (pseudonym of *Cecily Isabel Fairfield*), 1892– ; English novelist and critic.

West., west., western.

West Al·lis (al'is), a city in Wisconsin, near Milwaukee: pop., 68,000.

West Bengal, a state of northeastern India: until 1948, a part of Bengal, British India: area, 34,945 sq. mi.; pop., 26,302,000; capital, Calcutta.

west·bound (west'bound'), *adj.* bound west; going westward: abbreviated **w.b.**

West Brom·wich (brum'ich, brum'ij, brom'ich), a city in Staffordshire, England, near Birmingham: pop., 94,000.

west by north, the direction, or the point on a mariner's compass, halfway between due west and west-northwest; 11° 15' north of due west: abbreviated **WbN** (no period).

west by south, the direction, or the point on a mariner's compass, halfway between due west and west-southwest; 11°15' south of due west: abbreviated **WbS**(no period).

West End, the west part of London, essentially an upper-class residential section.

west·er (wes'tẽr), *v.i.* to move, turn, or shift to the west.

west·er·ly (wes'tẽr-li), *adj.* 1. in, of, or toward the west. 2. from the west: as, a *westerly* wind. *n.* [*pl.* WESTERLIES (-liz)], a wind blowing from the west. *adv.* 1. toward the west. 2. from the west: as, the wind blew *westerly.*

Wes·ter·marck, Edward Alexander (wes'tẽr-märk'; Finn. ves'tẽr-märk'), 1862–1939; Finnish anthropologist.

west·ern (wes'tẽrn), *adj.* [ME.; AS. *westerne*], 1. in, of, toward, or facing the west. 2. from the west: as, a *western* wind. 3. [W-], of or characteristic of the West. 4. [W-], of the Western Church. *n.* 1. a westerner. 2. a story, motion picture, etc. on the life of cowboys or frontiersmen in the western United States. Abbreviated **W., w., West., west.**

Western Australia, a state of Australia: area, 975,920 sq. mi.; pop., 719,000; capital, Perth: abbreviated **W.A.**

Western Church, 1. that part of the Catholic Church which recognizes the Pope as patriarch as well as pontiff and which follows the Latin Rite: it now comprises most of the Roman Catholic Church, excepting only certain Eastern churches. 2. broadly, all the Christian churches of Western Europe and America.

west·ern·er (wes'tẽr-nẽr), *n.* 1. a native or inhabitant of the west. 2. [W-], a native or inhabitant of the western part of the United States.

Western Hemisphere, that half of the earth which includes North and South America.

Western India States, a former agency of British India including a number of native states in western

India: since 1956, part of the state of Bombay.
Western Islands, 1. the Azores, a group of Portuguese islands in the Atlantic. 2. the Hebrides, a group of islands west of Scotland.
west·ern·ism (west'ẽrn-iz'm), ***n.*** a word, expression, or practice peculiar to the west, especially one peculiar to the western United States.
west·ern·ize (wes'tẽrn-īz'), ***v.t.*** [WESTERNIZED (-īzd'), WESTERNIZING], to make western in habits, ideas, etc.
west·ern·most (wes'tẽrn-mōst'), ***adj.*** farthest west.
Western Ocean, the Atlantic: the ancient name.
Western Reserve, a section of land in northeastern Ohio, on Lake Erie, which Connecticut reserved for settlers when its western lands were ceded to the Federal Government in 1786.

WESTERN RESERVE

Western (Roman) Empire, the western part of the Roman Empire after it was divided in 395 A.D. by Theodosius.
Western Samoa, a country in the South Pacific, consisting of two large islands and several small ones: it was formerly a New Zealand trust territory: area, 1,130 sq. mi.; pop., 115,000; capital, Apia.

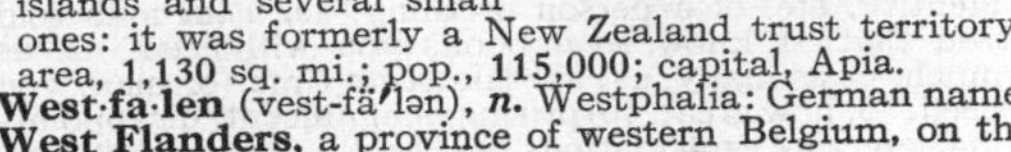

West·fa·len (vest-fä'lən), ***n.*** Westphalia: German name.
West Flanders, a province of western Belgium, on the North Sea: pop., 1,073,000; capital, Bruges.
West Ham (ham), a city in England, east of London: pop., 157,000.
West Hartford, a town in Connecticut, near Hartford: pop., 62,000.
West Har·tle·pool (här't'l-po͞ol'), a seaport in northeastern England: pop., 78,000.
West Haven, a town in Connecticut, near New Haven: pop., 43,000.
West Indian, 1. of the West Indies. 2. a native or inhabitant of the West Indies. Abbreviated **W. Ind., W.I.**
West Indies, 1. a large group of islands between the United States and South America: divided into the Bahamas, Greater Antilles, and Lesser Antilles. 2. a federation (1958–1962) of nine British colonies in the West Indies. Abbreviated **W.I.**

WEST INDIES

west·ing (wes'tiŋ), ***n.*** in *nautical usage,* the distance due west covered by a ship sailing in any westerly direction.
West·ing·house, George (wes'tiŋ-hous'), 1846–1914; American inventor and manufacturer.
West Ir·i·an (ir'i-ən), the western half of New Guinea: a former territory (*Netherlands New Guinea*) of the Netherlands, since 1963 a province of Indonesia: area, 160,000 sq. mi.; pop., c. 700,000; capital, Kotabaru.
West Lo·thi·an (lō'*th*i-ən), a county of Scotland, on the Firth of Forth: pop., 93,000; county seat, Linlithgow: formerly called *Linlithgow.*
West·min·ster (west'min'stẽr), ***n.*** a borough (officially, a city) of London: site of the Houses of Parliament, etc.: abbreviated **Westm.**
Westminster Abbey, a Gothic church in Westminster where English monarchs are crowned: it is also the burial place of English monarchs, famous writers, etc.: see TYPES OF ARCHITECTURE, p. 77.
Westminster Assembly, an assembly of clergymen that met at Westminster, London (1643–1649), and formulated certain articles of faith now generally accepted as authoritative by Presbyterian churches.
West·mor·land (west'mẽr-lənd), ***n.*** a county of northwestern England: pop., 67,000; county seat, Appleby.
West New York, a city in New Jersey, across the Hudson from New York City: pop., 36,000.
west-north·west (west'nôrth'west'; *in nautical usage,* west'nôr-west'), ***n.*** the direction, or the point on a mariner's compass, halfway between due west and northwest; 22°30' north of due west. ***adj. & adv.*** 1. in or toward this direction. 2. from this direction: as, a *west-northwest* wind. Abbreviated **WNW, W.N.W., w.n.w.**
West Orange, a city in northeastern New Jersey: pop., 40,000.
West Palm Beach, a resort town on the southeastern coast of Florida: pop., 56,000.
West·pha·li·a (west-fā'li-ə, west-fāl'yə), ***n.*** a region of Western Germany that was a former province of Prussia: a treaty was signed there by France, Sweden, and the Holy Roman Empire in 1648, at the end of the Thirty Years' War: German name, *Westfalen.*
West·pha·li·an (west-fā'li-ən, west-fāl'yən), ***adj.*** of Westphalia, its people, culture, etc. ***n.*** a native or inhabitant of Westphalia.
West Point, a military post in southeastern New York, on the Hudson: site of the United States Military Academy.
West Prussia, a former province of Prussia: since 1945, a part of Poland.
West Riding, a division of Yorkshire, England: pop., 3,641,000.
west-south·west (west'south'west'), ***n.*** the direction, or the point on a mariner's compass, halfway between due west and southwest; 22°30' south of due west. ***adj. & adv.*** 1. in or toward this direction. 2. from this direction: as, a *west-southwest* wind. Abbreviated **WSW, W.S.W., w.s.w.**
West Virginia, an Eastern State of the United States: area, 24,181 sq. mi.; pop., 1,860,000; capital, Charleston: nicknamed *Panhandle State*: abbreviated **W.Va.**
West Virginian, 1. of West Virginia. 2. a native or inhabitant of West Virginia.
west·ward (west'wẽrd), ***adj. & adv.*** [see -WARD], toward the west. ***n.*** a westward direction, point, or region.
west·ward·ly (west'wẽrd-li), ***adj. & adv.*** 1. toward the west. 2. from the west: as, a *westwardly* wind.
west·wards (west'wẽrdz), ***adv.*** westward.
wet (wet), ***adj.*** [WETTER (-ẽr), WETTEST (-ist)], [ME. *wet, wete;* AS. *wæt;* for IE. base see WATER, WASH], 1. moistened, covered, or saturated with water or other liquid. 2. rainy; foggy; misty: as, a *wet* day. 3. not yet dry: as, *wet* paint. 4. preserved or bottled in a liquid. 5. using water; done with or in water or other liquid: as, *wet* sanding. 6. permitting or favoring the manufacture or sale of alcoholic liquor; opposing, or not enforcing, prohibition: as, a *wet* candidate, *wet* town. ***n.*** 1. that which moistens or makes wet; water or other liquid; moisture. 2. rain or rainy weather: as, come in out of the *wet.* 3. a person who favors the manufacture or sale of alcoholic liquor; one opposed to prohibition. ***v.t. & v.i.*** [WET or WETTED (-id), WETTING], to make or become wet (often with *through* or *down*); specifically, to make (a bed, oneself, etc.) wet by urination.
all wet, [Slang], wrong; mistaken; in error.
wet one's whistle, [Colloq.], to take a drink.
SYN.—**wet** is applied to something covered or soaked with water or other liquid (*wet* streets, clothes, etc.) or to something not yet dry (*wet* paint); **damp** implies slight, usually undesirable or unpleasant wetness (a *damp* room); **dank** suggests a disagreeable, chilling, unwholesome dampness (a *dank* fog); **moist** implies slight wetness but, unlike **damp,** often suggests that the absence of dryness is desirable (*moist* air); **humid** implies such permeation of the air with moisture as to make for discomfort(a hot, *humid* day). —*ANT.* dry.
wet·back (wet'bak'), ***n.*** [from the fact that many cross the border by swimming or wading the Rio Grande], [Colloq.], a Mexican agricultural laborer who illegally enters or is brought into the United States to work.
wet blanket, a person or thing that dampens, or discourages, activity, enthusiasm, or pleasure.
wet bulb, in a psychrometer, that bulb of one of the two thermometers which is kept moistened in measuring humidity.
weth·er (weth'ẽr), ***n.*** [ME.; AS.; akin to G. *widder;* IE. base **wet-*, a year, seen also in L. *vetus,* old, *vitulus,* calf, etc.; basic sense "a year-old animal"], a castrated male sheep.
wet-nurse (wet'nũrs'), ***v.t.*** [WET-NURSED (-nũrst'), WET-NURSING], to act as wet nurse to.
wet nurse, a woman hired to suckle another's child.
wet pack, in *medicine,* a type of bath, as for reducing a fever, in which the patient is wrapped in wet sheets or blankets.
wet·ter (wet'ẽr), ***n.*** a person or thing that wets.
Wet·ter·horn (vet'ẽr-hôrn'), ***n.*** a mountain of the Bernese Alps in south central Switzerland: height, 12,149 ft.
wet·tish (wet'ish), ***adj.*** somewhat wet.
we've (wēv), we have.
Wex·ford (weks'fẽrd), ***n.*** 1. a county of Leinster province, Ireland: pop., 87,000. 2. its county seat: pop., 12,000.
Wey·gand, Max·ime (mȧk'sēm' vā'gän'), 1867– ; French general; commander in chief at the time of French capitulation to Germany in World War II.
w.f., wf, in *printing,* wrong font.
WFTU, W.F.T.U., World Federation of Trade Unions.
W.G., w.g., wire gauge.
W. Gmc., West Germanic.
wh., watt-hour.

whack (hwak), ***v.t. & v.i.*** [echoic], 1. [Colloq.], to strike or slap with a sharp, resounding blow. 2. [Slang], to share; divide (often with *up*). ***n.*** 1. [Colloq.], *a*) a sharp, resounding blow. *b*) the sound of this. 2. [Slang], a share; portion. 3. [Slang], an attempt; trial; chance: as, I had a *whack* at the problem. 4. [Slang], proper condition or adjustment: as, the motor is out of *whack*.

whack·ing (hwak'iŋ), ***adj.*** [ppr. of *whack*], [Chiefly British Colloq.], very large; tremendous.

whack·y (hwak'i), ***adj.*** [WHACKIER (-i-ẽr), WHACKIEST (-i-ist)], [Slang], wacky.

whale (hwāl), ***n.*** [*pl.* WHALES (hwālz), WHALE; see PLURAL, II, D, 1], [ME. *whal;* AS. *hwæl;* akin to G. *wal-* in *walfisch*, lit., whalefish; IE. **(s)qwa-lo-s*, huge fish, seen also in L. *squalus*, big sea fish], any of various large, warm-blooded, fishlike mammals that breathe air, bear live young, and are found in all seas; specifically, any of the larger, toothless species (as distinguished from dolphins and porpoises) having sheets of baleen, or whalebone, suspended from the upper jaw. ***v.i.*** [WHALED (hwāld), WHALING], to engage in the work of hunting whale.

SPERM WHALE (63 ft. long)

a whale of a, [Colloq.], an exceptionally large, fine, impressive, etc. example of a (class of things).

whale (hwāl), ***v.t.*** [WHALED (hwāld), WHALING], [var. of *wale* (to ridge)], [Colloq.], to beat; whip; thrash.

whale·back (hwāl'bak'), ***n.*** something rounded on top like the back of a whale; specifically, a freight steamer with the bow and upper deck rounded so that heavy seas will wash right over: formerly used on the Great Lakes for bulk cargoes as grain, ore, coal, etc.

whale·boat (hwāl'bōt'), ***n.*** a large, long rowboat, pointed at both ends to increase maneuverability: used by whalers, coastguards, etc., or as a ship's lifeboat.

whale·bone (hwāl'bōn'), ***n.*** 1. the horny elastic material that hangs in fringed sheets from the upper jaw or palate of certain whales, and serves to strain the minute sea animals on which they feed; baleen. 2. something made of whalebone; especially, a strip of this used as a corset stay, etc.

whale·man (hwāl'mən), ***n.*** [*pl.* WHALEMEN (-mən)], a man whose work is whaling; whaler.

whal·er (hwāl'ẽr), ***n.*** 1. a whaling ship. 2. a man whose work is whaling; whaleman.

Whales, Bay of, an arm of the Ross Sea, indenting the Ross Shelf Ice near Little America.

whal·ing (hwāl'iŋ), ***n.*** the trade or occupation of hunting and killing whales for their blubber, whalebone, etc.

whal·ing (hwāl'iŋ), ***n.*** [< *whale* (to beat) + *-ing*], [Colloq.], a sound thrashing; whipping.

wham·my (hwam'i), ***n.*** [*pl.* WHAMMIES (-iz)], [Slang], a jinx or the evil eye: usually in *put a* (or *the*) *whammy on.*

whang (hwaŋ), ***v.t.*** [of echoic origin], 1. to strike with a resounding blow; whack. 2. [Dial.], to beat or thrash. ***v.i.*** to make a whanging noise. ***n.*** a whack.

whang·doo·dle (hwaŋ'do͞o'd'l), ***n.*** [fanciful coinage], a mythical creature with undefined characteristics: a humorous usage.

whang·ee (hwaŋ-ē'), ***n.*** [prob. < Chin. *huang-li; huang*, yellow + *li*, bamboo cane], 1. any of a number of related Chinese and Japanese bamboos. 2. a walking stick made from any of these bamboos.

whap (hwop), ***v.i.*** [WHAPPED (hwopt), WHAPPING], [Dial. or Archaic], to whop.

whap·per (hwop'ẽr), ***n.*** [Colloq.], a whopper.

wharf (hwôrf), ***n.*** [*pl.* WHARVES (hwôrvz), WHARFS (hwôrfs)], [ME. & AS. *hwerf*, a dam or bank to keep out water, lit., a turning < base of *hweorfan*, to turn; akin to G. *werf*], 1. a structure of wood or stone, sometimes roofed over, built at the shore of a harbor, river, etc. for ships to lie alongside, as during loading or unloading; pier; dock. 2. [Obs.], a band at the water's edge; shore. Abbreviated **whf.** ***v.t.*** 1. to bring to a wharf; moor at a wharf. 2. to unload or store on a wharf. 3. to furnish with a wharf or wharves.

wharf·age (hwôr'fij), ***n.*** [see -AGE], 1. the use of a wharf for mooring, loading, or unloading a ship, or for storing goods. 2. a fee charged for this. 3. wharves collectively; port facilities.

wharf·in·ger (hwôr'fin-jẽr), ***n.*** [altered < earlier *wharfager* < *wharfage;* cf. PASSENGER], a person who owns or manages a wharf.

wharf rat, 1. a large brown rat found around wharves. 2. a vagrant or petty criminal who haunts wharves.

Whar·ton, Edith (hwôr't'n), (born *Edith Newbold Jones*), 1862–1937; American novelist.

wharve (hwôrv), ***n.*** [ME. *wherve;* AS. *hweorfa* < base of *hweorfan*, to turn], in *spinning*, 1. originally, a small flywheel on the lower end of the spindle of a spinning wheel, for giving momentum to the wheel. 2. a small drive pulley on a spindle of a modern spinning machine.

wharves (hwôrvz), ***n.*** alternative plural of **wharf.**

what (hwut, hwät; *unstressed* hwət), ***pron.*** [ME. *hwat, hwet;* AS. *hwæt*, neut. of *hwa*, who; cf. WHO], 1. which thing, event, circumstance, etc.: used interrogatively in asking for the specification of an identity, quantity, quality, etc.; specifically, *a*) in asking about the nature or class of a thing: as, *what* is that object? *b*) in asking for an explanation or repetition of something previously said: as, you told him *what?* *c*) in asking about the value, importance, or effect of something: as, *what* is life without Shirley? *What* is often used elliptically with the sense of 1 *b*, or, especially as a British colloquialism, to end a sentence with a general or rhetorical interrogative force: as, you're rather late, *what?* 2. that which or those which: as, I know *what* you want: used as a compound relative pronoun with the specific senses of *a*) anything that: as, do *what* you will. *b*) the exact person or thing that: as, as a swimmer, I am not *what* I was ten years ago. *c*) that or who: now regarded as substandard (the man *what* gave it to me) except in *but what*, but that or but who, as, there is no one *but what* would approve this act: also used elliptically for *what it is, what to do*, etc. (I'll tell you *what*) and with an intensive force in exclamations (*what* I know about you!). ***adj.*** 1. which or which kind of: used interrogatively or relatively in asking for or specifying the nature, identity, etc. of a person or thing: as, *what* man told you that? I know *what* books you will need. 2. as much, or as many, as: as, take *what* time (or men) you need. 3. how great, surprising, magnificent, disappointing, etc.: in exclamations, as *what* a man! *what* nonsense! ***adv.*** 1. in what respect? to what degree? how?: as, *what* does it help to complain? 2. in some manner or degree; in part; partly (usually followed by *with*): as, *what* with singing and joking, the time passed quickly. 3. how greatly, surprisingly, etc.: in exclamations, as, *what* tragic news! 4. [Obs.], why? ***conj.*** 1. that: in *but what*, but that, as, never doubt *but what* he loves you. 2. [Dial.], so far as; as much as: as, we warned them *what* we could. ***interj.*** an exclamation of surprise, anger, confusion, etc.: as, *what!* no dinner?

and what not, and other things of all sorts.

what for, 1. for what purpose? why? 2. [Slang], punishment; especially, a whipping: as, I'll give him *what for!*

what have you, [Colloq.], anything else of a similar sort: as, he sells games, toys, or *what have you.*

what if, what would happen if; suppose; supposing.

what it takes, [Colloq.], whatever is necessary for success or popularity, as wealth, beauty, or intelligence.

what's what, [Colloq.], the true state of affairs.

what·e'er (hwət-er'), ***pron. & adj.*** [Poetic], whatever.

what·ev·er (hwət-ev'ẽr), ***pron.*** what: an emphatic variant; specifically, *a*) which thing, event, circumstance, etc.: used as an interrogative expressing perplexity or wonder, as, *whatever* can he mean by that? *b*) anything that: as, tell her *whatever* you like. *c*) no matter what: as, *whatever* you may think, he's innocent. ***adj.*** 1. of no matter what type, degree, quality, etc.: as, Don can make *whatever* repairs are needed. 2. being who it may be: as, *whatever* man told you that, it is not true. *Whatever* is sometimes used following the word that it modifies: as, I have no plans *whatever.*

what·not (hwut'not', hwät'not'), ***n.*** 1. a nondescript or indescribable thing or, sometimes, person. 2. a set of open shelves used for bric-a-brac, books, etc.

what's (hwuts, hwäts; *unstressed* hwəts), what is.

what·so·e'er (hwut'sō-er', hwät'sō-er'), ***pron. & adj.*** [Poetic], whatsoever.

what·so·ev·er (hwut'sō-ev'ẽr, hwät'sō-ev'ẽr), ***pron. & adj.*** whatever: an emphatic form.

whaup (hwäp, hwôp), ***n.*** [prob. of echoic origin], [Scot. or Eng. Dial.], the curlew.

wheal (hwēl), ***n.*** [ME. *whele;* akin to AS. *hwelian*, to suppurate], 1. a pustule; pimple. 2. a small, itching elevation of the skin, as from the bite of an insect.

wheal (hwēl), ***n.*** [altered from *weal*, a wale, by association with ME. *whele*, a pustule; cf. prec.], a raised stripe or ridge on the skin, as from a lash of a whip; wale.

wheat (hwēt), ***n.*** [see PLURAL, II, D, 3], [ME. *whete;* AS. *hwæte;* akin to G. *weizen;* IE. base **kweit-*, to gleam, bright, white, as also in Eng. *white;* the grain is named from the white seed], 1. any of a number of related cereal grasses having spikes filled with seeds: the spikes in some species have awns (*bearded wheat*) and in others are bare (*beardless*, or *bald, wheat*). 2. the seed of any of these grasses, used for making flour, cereals, etc: next to rice, the most widely used grain.

wheat·ear (hwēt'ēr'), ***n.*** [earlier *white ears* < *white* + *eeres, ers*, var. of *arse*: so named in reference to its white rump], any of a group of small, long-legged, migrating birds of Northern Europe, Asia, and America, belonging to the family of chats: it is grayish-brown above, white below, with the wings and tip of the tail black.

wheat·en (hwēt''n), ***adj.*** 1. made of wheat or wheat flour. 2. of the pale-yellow color of wheat.

Wheat·ley, Phillis (hwēt′li), 1753?–1784; American poet, born in Africa and brought to America as a slave.

Wheat·stone's bridge (hwēt′stənz, hwēt′stōnz′), [after Sir Charles *Wheatstone* (1802–1875), Eng. physicist who designed it], in *electricity*, a device for measuring resistances: also **Wheatstone bridge.**

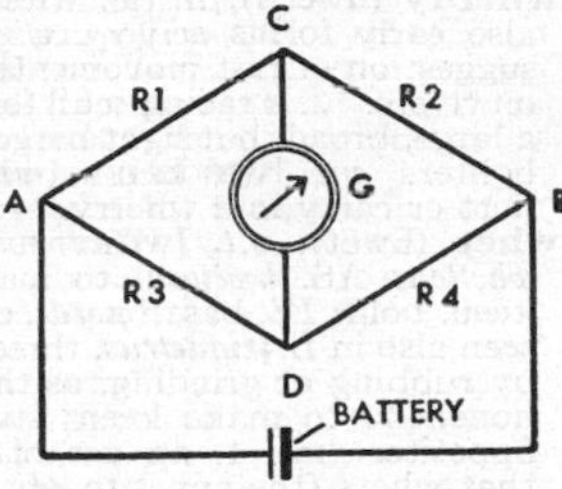

WHEATSTONE'S BRIDGE
G, galvanometer; R1, R2, arms of known resistance; R3, resistance to be measured; R4, arm of variable resistance; when no current is shown on galvanometer $\frac{\text{R1}}{\text{R2}} = \frac{\text{R3}}{\text{R4}}$

wheat·worm (hwēt′wûrm′), *n.* a small roundworm that destroys wheat.

whee·dle (hwē′d'l), *v.t. & v.i.* [WHEEDLED (-d'ld), WHEEDLING], [17th-c. cant; prob. < G. *wedeln*, to wag the tail, fan, hence to flatter < *wedel*, a fan, tail], 1. to influence or persuade by flattery, soft words, begging, etc.; coax. 2. to obtain by coaxing or flattery: as, *wheedle* a gift from him. —***SYN.*** see **coax.**

wheel (hwēl), *n.* [ME. *whele;* AS. *hweol*, earlier *hweogol;* akin to D. *wiel;* IE. base **qwel-*, to turn, seen also in L. *colere*, to engage in, be occupied with (cf. COLONY), *columna*, pillar (cf. COLUMN)], 1. a solid disk, or a circular frame connected by spokes to a central hub, capable of turning on a central axis and used to move vehicles or transmit power in machinery. 2. anything like a wheel in shape, movement, action, etc., as a firework that revolves in a circular orbit while burning. 3. a device or apparatus of which the principal element is a wheel or wheels; specifically, *a)* in the Middle Ages, an instrument of torture consisting of a circular frame on which the victim's limbs were broken. *b)* a wheel with projecting handles for controlling the rudder of a ship. *c)* the steering wheel of a motor vehicle. *d)* [Colloq.], a bicycle or, rarely, a tricycle. *e)* a spinning wheel. *f)* a potter's wheel. 4. *usually pl.* the moving, propelling, or controlling forces or agencies: as, the *wheels* of progress. 5. a turning about; rotation or revolution; specifically, in *military usage*, a turning movement of troops or ships in line, in which the line is maintained while one end makes a circular movement about the other as pivot. 6. the refrain of a song. ***v.t.*** 1. *a)* to move or roll on wheels: as, he *wheeled* the cart into the yard. *b)* to transport in a wheeled vehicle. 2. to cause to turn, revolve, or rotate. 3. to perform in a circular movement. 4. to furnish with a wheel or wheels. ***v.i.*** 1. to turn on or as on an axis; pivot; rotate; revolve. 2. to reverse one's course of action, opinion, attitude, etc.: often with *about.* 3. to turn in a swooping circular motion: said of birds. 4. to move or roll along on or as on wheels.

at the wheel, 1. steering or directing a ship or motor vehicle; at the steering wheel; hence, 2. in charge; directing activities.

wheel of fortune, 1. the wheel which the goddess of fortune was believed to rotate to bring about the alternations or reverses in human affairs; hence, 2. the changes or vicissitudes of life.

wheels within wheels, a series of involved circumstances, motives, etc., reacting upon one another.

wheel and axle, a pulley fixed solidly to a shaft or drum, and used for lifting weights: the turning of the pulley by a rope or chain in the groove winds a rope on the shaft or drum: it is one of the simple machines.

wheel·bar·row (hwēl′bar′ō), *n.* [ME. *wilberwe;* cf. WHEEL & BARROW], a shallow, open box for moving small loads, having a single wheel in front forming a tripod with the two legs in back, and two shafts with handles for raising the vehicle off its legs and pushing or pulling it. ***v.t.*** to move or transport in a wheelbarrow.

wheel·base (hwēl′bās′), *n.* in a motor vehicle, the distance in inches from the center of the hub of a front wheel to the center of the hub of the corresponding back wheel: also **wheel base.**

wheel bug, any of a group of large North American insects distinguished by a high, saw-toothed crest on the prothorax and a piercing proboscis for sucking the blood of other insects.

wheel chair, a mobile chair for invalids, mounted on large wheels.

wheeled (hwēld), *adj.* having a wheel or wheels: often in hyphenated compounds, meaning *having a* (specified kind or number of) *wheels*, as in *four-wheeled.*

wheel·er (hwēl′ẽr), *n.* 1. a person or thing that wheels. 2. a wheel horse (sense 1). 3. something having a wheel or wheels: usually in hyphenated compounds, meaning *something having a* (specified kind or number of) *wheels*, as in *side-wheeler, two-wheeler.*

Whee·ler, Joseph (hwē′lẽr), 1836–1906; American Confederate general in the Civil War and United States major general in the Spanish-American War.

wheel horse, 1. the horse, or one of the horses, nearest the front wheels of the vehicle, as distinguished from a *leader* (sense 2). 2. a person who works especially hard and steadily in any enterprise.

wheel·house (hwēl′hous′), *n.* a shelter built around the steering wheel of a ship; pilothouse.

Wheel·ing (hwēl′iŋ), *n.* a port in northern West Virginia, on the Ohio River: pop., 53,000.

wheel·ing (hwēl′iŋ), *n.* 1. the act or fact of traveling on wheels; especially, cycling. 2. a turning movement; circle; revolution. 3. the condition of a road, etc. with reference to traveling it on wheels: as, good *wheeling.*

wheel lock, a firing mechanism on certain obsolete firearms, consisting of a rough wheel which spun on a flint when the trigger was pulled, throwing sparks into the pan and setting off the charge.

wheel·man (hwēl′mən), *n.* [*pl.* WHEELMEN (-mən)], 1. a cyclist. 2. a wheelsman.

wheels·man (hwēlz′mən), *n.* [*pl.* WHEELSMEN (-mən)], a person who steers a ship; helmsman.

wheel·work (hwēl′wûrk′), *n.* an arrangement of wheels or gears in a machine, or mechanical contrivance.

wheel·wright (hwēl′rīt′), *n.* [ME. *whelwryht;* see WRIGHT], a person who makes and repairs wheels and wheeled vehicles.

wheen (hwēn), *n.* [ME. *qwheyn(e);* AS. *whēne, whǣne,* instrumental case of *whōn*, (a) few], [Scot. & Eng. Dial.], a few.

wheeze (hwēz), *v.i.* [WHEEZED (hwēzd), WHEEZING], [ME. *whesen;* ON. *hvaesa*, to hiss], 1. to breathe hard with a whistling, breathy sound, as in asthma. 2. to make a similar sound: as, the old organ *wheezed.* ***v.t.*** to utter with a sound of wheezing. ***n.*** 1. an act or sound of wheezing. 2. [Slang], an overworked or trite remark, joke, or gag.

wheez·i·ly (hwēz′ə-li), *adv.* in a wheezy manner; with a whistling sound.

wheez·i·ness (hwēz′i-nis), *n.* the state or condition of being wheezy.

wheez·y (hwēz′i), *adj.* [WHEEZIER (-i-ẽr), WHEEZIEST (-i-ist)], wheezing or characterized by wheezing.

whelk (hwelk), *n.* [ME. *wilke, welke;* AS. *wiloc, wioluc;* prob. < IE. base **wel-*, to turn, with reference to the spiral shell], any of various large marine snails with spiral shells, especially those used in Europe for food.

whelk (hwelk), *n.* [ME. *whelke;* AS. *hwylca*, a pustule < base of *hwelian*, to exude pus], a pimple or pustule.

whelked (hwelkt), *adj.* twisted or ridged like the shell of a whelk.

whelm (hwelm), *v.t.* [ME. *welmen, whelmen;* prob. a merging of AS. *-hwelfan*, to overwhelm, with *helmian*, to cover (cf. HELM) and other words of like form], 1. to submerge, cover, or engulf; hence, 2. to overpower or crush; overwhelm.

whelp (hwelp), *n.* [ME.; AS. *hwelp;* akin to G. *welf*, puppy; prob. IE. base **wl̥p-, *lup-*, in names of voracious animals, seen also in L. *volpes*, a fox], 1. a young dog; puppy. 2. the young of any of various flesh-eating animals, as of a lion, tiger, leopard, bear, wolf, etc. 3. a youth or child: a contemptuous usage. 4. any of the teeth on a sprocket wheel. 5. *usually in pl.* in *nautical usage*, any of the ribs or ridges along the barrel of a capstan or the drum of a windlass. ***v.t. & v.i.*** to bring forth (young); give birth to: said of animals, and contemptuously of a woman, as, she has *whelped* thieves.

when (hwen; *unstressed, often* hwən), *adv.* [ME. *whenne, whanne;* AS. *hwænne;* akin to G. *wann*, when, *wenn*, if; a derivative of the base seen in AS. *hwa*, who (cf. WHO), *hwæt*, what (cf. WHAT)], at what time? on what occasion?: used interrogatively and in indirect questions, as, *when* did that happen? he asked *when* he should go. ***conj.*** 1. at what time: as, he told us *when* to eat. 2. at which time: as, he came at six, *when* the sun was setting. 3. at which: as, now is the time *when* we must fight. 4. at the time that: as, *when* we were college freshmen. 5. as soon as: as, we will eat *when* father comes. 6. at whatever time; whenever: as, she cries *when* you criticize her. 7. although; whereas; while on the contrary: as, he's reading a book *when* he might be out playing. 8. if; considering the fact that: as, how can we finish, *when* you won't help? ***pron.*** what or which time: as, until *when* will you remain? we came a week ago since *when* we've had no rest. ***n.*** the time or moment (*of* an event): as, I know the *when* and where of his arrest.

when·as (hwen-az′), *conj.* [*when* + *as*], [Archaic], 1. when. 2. inasmuch as. 3. whereas.

whence (hwens), *adv.* [ME. *whennes*, with adv. genit. ending *-es*, replacing AS. *hwanan, hwanon*, etc.], 1. from what place; from where: as, *whence* do you come? I know *whence* he comes. 2. from what source or cause: as, *whence* does he get his strength? 3. to the place from which: as, return *whence* you came.

whence·so·ev·er (hwens'sō-ev'ẽr), *adv. & conj.* from whatever place, source, or cause.

when·e'er (hwen-er', hwən-er'), *adv. & conj.* [Poetic], whenever.

when·ev·er (hwen-ev'ẽr, hwən-ev'ẽr), *adv.* [Colloq.], when: an emphatic form expressing surprise or bewilderment, as, *whenever* will you learn? *conj.* 1. at whatever time: as, I'll be here *whenever* he arrives. 2. on whatever occasion: as, visit us *whenever* you can.

when·so·ev·er (hwen'sō-ev'ẽr), *adv. & conj.* whenever: an emphatic form.

where (hwâr), *adv.* [ME. *wher;* AS. *hwær;* akin to G. *wo* & to *war-* in *warum;* an extension of the interrogative base in AS. *hwa* (see WHO)], 1. in or at what place?: as, *where* is my hat? 2. to or toward what place or point?: as, *where* did he go? 3. in what situation or position?: as, *where* will we be if we lose? 4. in what respect?: as, *where* do I come into the matter? 5. from what place or source?: as, *where* did you get your information? *conj.* 1. in or at what place: as, I know *where* they are. 2. in or at which place: as, we came home, *where* we had dinner. 3. in or at the place or situation in which: as, I am *where* I should be. 4. in whatever place, situation, or respect in which: as, there is never peace *where* men are greedy. 5. *a*) to or toward the place to which: as, I will take you *where* you're going. *b*) to a place in which: as, I never go *where* I'm not wanted. 6. to or toward whatever place: as, I don't care *where* you go. *pron.* 1. the place or situation in, at, or to which: as, I live just two miles from *where* I was born. 2. what or which place: as, *where* do you come from? *n.* the place (*of* an event): as, I don't know the when and *where* of his arrest.

where·a·bout (hwâr'ə-bout'), *adv. & n.* [Rare], whereabouts.

where·a·bouts (hwâr'ə-bouts'), *adv.* 1. near or at what place?; where? 2. [Obs.], about or concerning which. *n.* the place where a person or thing is: as, do you know the *whereabouts* of that person?

where·as (hwâr-az'), *conj.* 1. it being the case that; in view of the fact that: used in the preamble to a formal document, as, *whereas* the following incidents have occurred. 2. while on the contrary; when in fact: as, she is slender, *whereas* he is stout. *n.* [*pl.* WHEREASES (-iz)], a statement beginning with "whereas".

where·at (hwâr-at'), *adv.* [Rare or Archaic], at what?: as, *whereat* was he offended? *conj.* at which; upon which: as, he turned to leave, *whereat* she began to weep.

where·by (hwâr-bī'), *adv.* 1. by which; by means of which: as, a device *whereby* to make money. 2. by what? how?: as, *whereby* did you expect to profit?

wher·e'er (hwâr-er'), *adv. & conj.* [Poetic], wherever.

where·fore (hwâr'fôr', hwâr'fōr'), *adv.* 1. for what reason or purpose? why?: as, *wherefore* did you go? 2. for which: as, the reason *wherefore* we have met. *conj.* on account of which; because of which; therefore; as, we ran out of water, *wherefore* we surrendered. *n.* the reason; cause: as, never mind the why and *wherefore*.

where·from (hwâr-frum', hwâr-from'), *adv.* from which; whence.

where·in (hwâr-in'), *adv.* 1. in what?: as, *wherein* was I wrong? 2. in which: as, the room *wherein* he lay.

where·in·to (hwâr-in'too, hwâr'in-too'), *adv.* into which.

where·of (hwâr-uv', hwâr-ov'), *adv.* of what, which, or whom.

where·on (hwâr-on'), *adv.* 1. on what?: as, *whereon* do you rely? 2. on which: as, the hill *whereon* we stand.

where·so·e'er (hwâr'sō-er'), *adv. & conj.* [Poetic], wheresoever.

where·so·ev·er (hwâr'sō-ev'ẽr), *adv. & conj.* at, in, or to whatever place; wherever: an emphatic form.

where·through (hwâr-thro͞o'), *adv.* through which.

where·to (hwâr-to͞o'), *adv.* 1. to what? toward what place, direction, or end? 2. to which.

where·un·to (hwâr-un'too, hwâr'ən-to͞o'), *adv.* [Archaic], whereto.

where·up·on (hwâr'ə-pon'), *adv.* upon what or upon which? whereon? *conj.* at which; upon which; as a consequence of which: as, I explained the matter, *whereupon* he laughed heartily.

wher·ev·er (hwâr-ev'ẽr), *adv.* [Colloq.], where: an emphatic form expressing surprise or bewilderment, as, *wherever* did you hear that? *conj.* in, at, or to whatever place or situation: as, he thinks of us, *wherever* he is.

where·with (hwâr-with', hwâr-with'), *adv.* 1. [Archaic], with what?: as, *wherewith* shall I save him? 2. with which: as, I have not the money *wherewith* to pay them. *pron.* that with which: as, they shall have *wherewith* to stock their larder. *n.* [Rare], wherewithal.

where·with·al (hwâr'with-ôl'; *for adv. & conj.*, hwâr'with-ôl'), *n.* that with which something can be done; necessary means or resources, especially money (usually with *the*): as, I haven't the *wherewithal* to continue my education. *adv. & conj.* [Archaic], wherewith.

wher·ry (hwer'i), *n.* [*pl.* WHERRIES (-iz)], [ME. *whery;* also early forms *whyrry, wirrie,* etc.; ? < *whir,* with suggestion of fast movement], 1. a light rowboat used on rivers. 2. a racing scull for one person. 3. [British], a large, broad, but light barge, used for moving freight; lighter. *v.t.* [WHERRIED (-id), WHERRYING], to transport or carry in a wherry.

whet (hwet), *v.t.* [WHETTED (-id), WHETTING], [ME. *whetten;* AS. *hwettan,* to make keen < *hwæt,* sharp, keen, bold; IE. base **qwēd-*, etc., to stick, pierce; prob. seen also in L. *triquetrus,* three-cornered], 1. to sharpen by rubbing or grinding, as the edge of a knife or tool; hone. 2. to make keen; stimulate: as, it'll *whet* the appetite. *n.* 1. an act of whetting. 2. something that whets (the appetite, etc.).

wheth·er (hweth'ẽr), *conj.* [ME. *whether, wether;* AS. *hwæther* (akin to G. *weder,* neither) < base of *who* + compar. suffix, in sense "which of two"; cf. EITHER], 1. if it be the case or fact that: used to introduce an indirect question. Example: He asked *whether* I would help. 2. in case; in either case that: used to introduce alternatives, the second of which is introduced by *or* or by *or whether.* Example: *Whether* he drives *or* (*whether* he) takes the train, he'll be on time. The second alternative is sometimes merely implied or understood. Example: I don't know *whether* he'll improve (or not). 3. either: as, he was completely ignored, *whether* by accident or design. *pron.* [Archaic], which (especially of two): used interrogatively and relatively.

whether or no, in any case; no matter what the circumstances.

whet·stone (hwet'stōn'), *n.* [ME. *whetston;* AS. *hwetstan* < *hwettan* (see WHET) + *stan,* a stone], an abrasive stone for sharpening knives or other edged tools.

whet·ter (hwet'ẽr), *n* a thing used for whetting.

whew (hwū; *conventionalized pronun., but often unvoiced*), *interj.* [echoic], an exclamation of surprise, disgust, dismay, relief, etc.

whey (hwā), *n.* [ME. *whei;* AS. *hwæg;* akin to D. *wei;* IE. base **kwei-*, slime, mud, seen also in L. *obscenus,* dirty, filthy (see OBSCENE)], the thin, watery part of milk which separates from the thicker part (curds) after coagulation, as in cheesemaking.

whey·ey (hwā'i), *adj.* of, like, consisting of, or containing whey.

whey·face (hwā'fās'), *n.* [*whey* + *face*], 1. a pale or pallid face. 2. a person having such a face.

whey·faced (hwā'fāst'), *adj.* pale or pallid, as from fear, sickness, etc.

whf., wharf.

which (hwich), *pron.* [ME. *whiche;* AS. *hwylc, hwelc,* etc., for **hwa-lic,* lit., who like (Goth. *hwileiks,* OHG. *hwelīh,* G. *welch*); see WHO, LIKE, -LY], 1. what one (or ones) of the number of persons, things, or events mentioned or implied?: as, *which* of the men answered? *which* do you want? 2. the one (or ones) that: as, I know *which* you want. 3. who, whom, or that: used as a relative in a restrictive or nonrestrictive clause referring to the thing or event (or, archaically, person) specified in the antecedent word, phrase, or clause: as, my hat, *which* is on the table; the war *which* had just ended. 4. either, or any, of the persons, things, or events previously mentioned or implied; whichever: as, you may take *which* you prefer. 5. a thing or fact that: as, you are late—*which* reminds me, where were you yesterday? *adj.* 1. what one or ones (of the number mentioned or implied): as, *which* man (or men) answered?, *which* books shall I choose? 2. whatever; no matter what: as, try *which* method you please, you cannot succeed. 3. being the one just mentioned: as, he is very old, *which* fact is important. Abbreviated **wh.**

which·ev·er (hwich-ev'ẽr), *pron. & adj.* 1. any one (of two or more): as, he may choose *whichever* (desk) he wishes. 2. no matter which: as, *whichever* (desk) he chooses, they won't be pleased.

which·so·ev·er (hwich'sō-ev'ẽr), *pron. & adj.* whichever: an emphatic form.

whid (hwid, hwud), *v.i.* [WHIDDED (-id), WHIDDING], [? < ON. *hvitha,* a squall], [Scot.], to move nimbly.

whid·ah bird (hwid'ə), [altered < *widow bird,* by association with *Whidah,* seaport in Dahomey, Africa], any of several black West African weaverbirds, the male of which has long drooping tail-feathers growing to twice the length of its body during the breeding season; widow bird: also **whidah, whidah finch, whydah.**

whiff (hwif), *n.* [echoic], 1. a light puff or gust of air or wind; breath. 2. a slight wave or gust of odor; faint momentary smell: as, a *whiff* of garlic. 3. a puff of smoke or vapor; especially, an exhaling of tobacco smoke. 4. an inhaling of tobacco smoke. *v.t.* 1. to blow or propel with a puff or gust; waft. 2. to blow out (tobacco smoke) in puffs. 3. to smoke (a pipe, etc.). *v.i.* 1. to blow or move in puffs: as, the wind *whiffed* through the trees. 2. to inhale or exhale whiffs, as in smoking.

whif·fet (hwif'it), *n.* [dim. of *whiff*], 1. a little whiff, or puff. 2. a small dog. 3. [Colloq.], an insignificant person: a term of contempt.

whif·fle (hwif''l), *v.i.* [WHIFFLED (-'ld), WHIFFLING], [freq. of *whiff*], 1. to blow fitfully; blow in puffs or gusts: said of the wind. 2. to shift; veer; vacillate. *v.t.* to blow or scatter with or as with a puff of wind.

whif·fler (hwif'lẽr), *n.* [< *whiffle* + *-er*], a person who vacillates or shifts position frequently in argument.

whif·fle·tree (hwif''l-trē'), *n.* a whippletree.

Whig (hwig), *n.* [shortened form of *whiggamore*, applied to Scot. Covenanters who marched on Edinburgh in 1648; this is itself an erratic form of W. Scot. *whiggamaire* < *whig*, a cry to urge on horses + *mare*, a horse], 1. in England, a political party (1697–c. 1832) which championed popular rights and change in the direction of democracy: it later became the Liberal Party: opposed to *Tory*. 2. in the American Revolution, a person who opposed continued allegiance to Great Britain and supported the Revolution. 3. an American political party (c. 1836–1856) opposing the Democratic Party and advocating protection of industry and limitation of the power of the executive branch of government. *adj.* 1. that is a Whig. 2. composed of Whigs. 3. adhering to, or characteristic of, Whiggism.

Whig·ger·y (hwig'ẽr-i), *n.* the principles or practices of Whigs.

Whig·gish (hwig'ish), *adj.* of or like Whigs or their doctrines.

Whig·gism (hwig'iz'm), *n.* the doctrines and principles of Whigs, especially of English Whigs.

while (hwīl), *n.* [ME. *while, hwile*; AS. *hwil*; akin to G. *weile*; IE. base **qweje-*, to rest, seen also in L. *tranquil-us*, lit., very quiet (cf. TRANQUIL), *quies*, rest (cf. QUIET)], a period or space of time: as, a short *while*. *conj.* 1. during or throughout the time that: as, we waited *while* he dined. 2. *a*) at the same time that; although on the one hand: as, *while* he was not poor, he had no ready cash. *b*) [Colloq.], whereas; and: as, the walls are green, *while* the ceiling is white. 3. [Dial.], until. *v.t.* [WHILED (hwīld), WHILING], [< the *n.*, but prob. influenced in meaning by *wile*], to spend (time) in a pleasant way; occupy; cause to pass idly (often with *away*): as, we *whiled* away the afternoon.

between whiles, now and then; at intervals.

the while, at the same time; during this very time.

worth one's while, worth one's time, consideration, etc.; profitable (in any way).

whiles (hwīlz), *adv.* [ME. < *-whiles* in *otherwhiles*, etc.; formed < *while* + adv. genit. *-s*], [Archaic or Dial.], sometimes. *conj.* [Archaic], while.

whi·lom (hwī'ləm), *adv.* [ME. *whilum, hwilum*, etc.; AS. *hwilum*, dat. pl. of *hwil*, while], [Archaic], at one time; formerly. *adj.* [Archaic], formerly such; former: as, their *whilom* friends.

whilst (hwīlst), *conj.* [ME. *whilest*; extended < *whiles*, adv. genit. of *while*], [Chiefly British], while.

whim (hwim), *n.* [short for *whim-wham*, a whim, trinket; a redupl. ? based on ON. *hvima*, to wander with the eyes], 1. a sudden fancy; idle and passing notion; freakish idea; caprice. 2. a kind of winch or capstan, consisting of a vertical drum with extended arms to which one or more horses may be hitched: used in mines to raise ore or water. —*SYN.* see **caprice.**

whim·brel (hwim'brəl), *n.* [earlier *whimrel*; prob. echoic of its cry], any of a group of European shore birds closely resembling the curlew, but smaller, with a pale stripe along the crown: they breed on the islands north of England.

whim·per (hwim'pẽr), *v.i.* [? freq. < base of *whine*], to cry with low, whining, broken sounds: as, the child *whimpers*. *v.t.* to utter or say with a whimper. *n.* a whimpering sound or cry. —*SYN.* see **cry.**

whim·sey (hwim'zi), *n.* [*pl.* WHIMSEYS (-ziz)], whimsy.

whim·si·cal (hwim'zi-k'l), *adj.* 1. full of or characterized by whims or whimsy. 2. oddly out of the ordinary; fantastic; freakish.

whim·si·cal·i·ty (hwim'zi-kal'ə-ti), *n.* 1. the quality of being whimsical. 2. [*pl.* WHIMSICALITIES (-tiz)], a whimsical speech, notion, or action; caprice.

whim·sy (hwim'zi), *n.* [*pl.* WHIMSIES (-ziz)], [prob. < *whim*], 1. an odd fancy; idle notion; whim. 2. curious, quaint, or fanciful humor: as, poems full of *whimsy*. Also spelled **whimsey.** —*SYN.* see **caprice.**

whin (hwin), *n.* [ME. *whin, whinne*; prob. < ON.; cf. obs. Dan. *hvine*, Sw. *hven*, applied to coarse grasses; the IE. base is **kwei-*, slime, dirt, as also in Eng. *whey*], a low, spiny evergreen shrub with yellow flowers, common on wastelands in Europe; furze; gorse.

whin (hwin), *n.* [ME. (Northern) *quin*; prob. < same base as prec. *whin*], any of several very hard, usually basaltic rocks; greenstone; trap; whinstone.

whin·chat (hwin'chat'), *n.* [*whin* (shrub) + *chat*, a warbler (< *chat*, to chatter): so named from frequenting whins (furze)], any of a group of migrating songbirds which frequent the heaths and meadows of Europe and western Asia, with brown and buff plumage and white over each eye and on each side of the base of the tail.

whine (hwīn), *v.i.* [WHINED (hwīnd), WHINING], [ME. *whinen*; AS. *hwinan*; akin to ON. *hvina*; IE. echoic base **kwei-*, to whizz, hiss, etc., seen also in Eng. *whistle*, *whisper*, L. *quiritare*, to cry loudly], 1. to utter a low, protracted, peevish, somewhat nasal sound, as in complaint, distress, fear, etc. 2. to complain in a childish, undignified way. *v.t.* to utter with a whine. *n.* 1. an act of whining. 2. the sound of whining. 3. a complaint uttered in a whining tone.

whin·ny (hwin'i), *adj.* [WHINNIER (-i-ẽr), WHINNIEST (-i-ist)], covered with whin, or furze.

whin·ny (hwin'i), *v.i.* [WHINNIED (-id), WHINNYING], [< *whine*], to neigh in a low and gentle way: said of a horse. *v.t.* to express with a whinny. *n.* [*pl.* WHINNIES (-iz)], the low and gentle neighing of a horse, or a similar sound.

whin·stone (hwin'stōn'), *n.* [*whin* (rock) + *stone*], any of various very hard, dark, especially basaltic rocks.

whin·y (hwīn'i), *adj.* [WHINIER (-i-ẽr), WHINIEST (-i-ist)], of, addicted to, or characterized by whining: as, a *whiny* child.

whip (hwip), *v.t.* [WHIPPED or WHIPT (hwipt), WHIPPING], [ME. *whippen*; MD. *wippen*, to swing, move up and down; IE. base **weib-*, **weip-*, to turn, swing, seen also in L. *vibrare*, to set in rapid motion (cf. VIBRATE), Eng. *wipe*], 1. to move, pull, jerk, snatch, throw, etc. suddenly and quickly (usually with *out*, *off*, *up*, etc.): as, he *whipped* out a knife. 2. *a*) to strike, as with a strap, rod, etc.; lash; beat. *b*) to punish in this manner. 3. to force, drive, compel, urge, etc. by or as by whipping. 4. to strike as a whip does: as, the rain *whipped* her face. 5. to attack with stinging words; flay. 6. to cover (a cord, rope, etc.) with cord or thread wound round and round, so as to prevent fraying. 7. to wind or bind (cord, etc.) around something. 8. to fish (a stream, etc.) by making repeated casts with a rod and line. 9. to beat (eggs, cream, etc.) into a froth with a fork, egg beater, mixer, etc. 10. to sew (a seam, etc.) with a loose overcasting or overhand stitch. 11. [Colloq.], to defeat or outdo, as in a contest. 12. in *nautical usage*, to hoist by means of a rope passing through an overhead pulley. *v.i.* 1. to move, go, pass, etc. quickly and suddenly: as, he *whipped* down the stairs. 2. to flap or thrash about in a whiplike manner: as, flags *whip* in high wind. 3. to cast with a fishing rod, using a quick, whiplike motion. *n.* [ME. *whippe*; MD. *wippe*], 1. an instrument for striking or flogging, consisting of a stiff rod with a long lash attached to one end or a long, flexible rod with a short lash attached to the tip. 2. a blow, cut, etc. made with or as with a whip. 3. a person who uses a whip, as a coachman, a huntsman who whips on the hounds, etc.; hence, 4. *a*) an officer of a political party in Congress, Parliament, etc. who maintains discipline, enforces attendance, etc.: also **party whip.** *b*) a call issued to party members in a lawmaking body to be in attendance at a certain time. 5. a whipping motion. 6. a dessert made of fruit, sugar, and whipped cream or stiffly beaten egg whites. 7. something resembling a whip in its action, as a windmill vane, mechanical part, etc. 8. a hoisting apparatus consisting of a single rope passing through an overhead pulley. —*SYN.* see **beat.**

whip in, to bring together or assemble, as a party whip does.

whip up, 1. to rouse; excite. 2. [Colloq.], to cook or prepare quickly and easily.

whip·cord (hwip'kôrd'), *n.* 1. a hard, twisted or braided cord used for whiplashes, etc. 2. a strong worsted cloth with a hard, diagonally ribbed surface. 3. a kind of catgut.

whip·graft (hwip'graft', hwip'gräft'), *v.t.* to graft by means of whip graftage.

whip graftage, a type of grafting in which the scion and stock, both cut on a long slant with a slit in each cut surface, are fitted together by inserting the tongue of one into the slot of the other: also **whip grafting, whip graft.**

whip hand, 1. the hand in which a driver holds his whip; hence, 2. the position of advantage or control: as, he has the *whip hand* in this situation.

whip·lash (hwip'lash'), *n.* the lash of a whip.

whip·per (hwip'ẽr), *n.* a person or thing that whips.

whip·per-in (hwip'ẽr-in'), *n.* [*pl.* WHIPPERS-IN], 1. [Chiefly British], a huntsman's assistant who keeps the hounds together in the pack. 2. a party whip.

whip·per·snap·per (hwip'ẽr-snap'ẽr), *n.* [extended < *whip-snapper*, one who snaps whips], an insignificant, especially young, person who appears impertinent or presumptuous.

whip·pet (hwip′it), *n.* [dim. < *whip*], a swift dog resembling a small greyhound, used in coursing and racing.

WHIPPET
(18 in. high at shoulder)

whip·ping (hwip′iŋ), *n.* 1. the action of a person or thing that whips; especially, a flogging or beating, as in punishment. 2. cord, twine, etc. used to whip, or bind.

whipping boy, 1. originally, a boy who was brought up and educated together with a young prince and was required to take the punishment for the misdeeds of the latter; hence, 2. a scapegoat (sense 2).

whipping post, a post to which offenders are tied to be publicly whipped as a legal punishment.

whip·ple·tree (hwip″'l-trē′), *n.* [< *whip*], the pivoted crossbar at the front of a wagon or carriage, to which the traces of the harness are attached: also **whiffletree.**

whip·poor·will (hwip′ẽr-wil′), *n.* [*pl.* WHIPPOORWILLS (-wilz′), WHIPPOORWILL; see PLURAL, II, D, 1], [echoic of its cry], a bird of eastern North America related to the goatsucker or nightjar and active at night.

whip·saw (hwip′sô′), *n.* a narrow, tapering ripsaw from 5 to 7 1/2 feet long with its ends held in a wooden frame: it is used by one or two persons. *v.t.* 1. to cut with a whipsaw; hence, 2. to defeat or get the best of (a person) two ways at once, as, in *faro*, by winning two different bets in a single play.

whip scorpion, any of a group of arachnids resembling the scorpion but having a long, whiplike tail at the end of the abdomen and no sting.

whip snake, any of several nonpoisonous snakes of Asia and South America that live largely in trees.

whip·stitch (hwip′stich′), *v.t. & v.i.* in *sewing*, to overcast or whip. *n.* a stitch made in this way.

whip·stock (hwip′stok′), *n.* the handle of a whip.

whip·worm (hwip′wũrm′), *n.* [*whip* + *worm*: so named from its shape], a roundworm, about two inches in length, found parasitic in the human intestine.

whir (hwũr), *v.i. & v.t.* [WHIRRED (hwũrd), WHIRRING], [? back-formation of *whirl*], to fly, revolve, vibrate, or otherwise move quickly with a whizzing or buzzing sound. *n.* 1. a whizzing or buzzing sound, as that made by the rapid motion of a bird's wings, a revolving propeller, etc. 2. hurry; bustle. Also spelled **whirr.**

whirl (hwũrl), *v.i.* [ME. *whirlen;* ON. *hvirfla;* IE. base **kwerp-*, to rotate, seen also in Eng. *wharf*], 1. to move rapidly in a circular manner or as in an orbit; circle swiftly: as, they *whirled* round the dance floor. 2. to rotate or spin fast; gyrate. 3. to move, go, drive, etc. swiftly. 4. to seem to spin; reel: as, my head is *whirling*. *v.t.* 1. to cause to rotate, revolve, or spin rapidly. 2. to move, carry, drive, etc. with a rotating motion: as, the wind *whirled* the leaves. 3. [Obs.], to hurl. *n.* [G. *wirbel;* Dan. *hvirvel*], 1. the act of whirling. 2. a whirling motion. 3. something whirling or being whirled: as, a *whirl* of dust. 4. a fast round of parties, etc. 5. a tumult; uproar; stir. 6. a confused or giddy condition: as, my head is in a *whirl*. —***SYN.*** see **turn.**

whirl·a·bout (hwũrl′ə-bout′), *n.* 1. a whirling about. 2. a whirligig.

whirl·er (hwũr′lẽr), *n.* 1. anything that whirls. 2. a rotating hook used in making rope.

whirl·i·gig (hwũr′li-gig′), *n.* [ME. *whirlgigge;* see WHIRL & GIG (whirling object)], 1. any of various child's toys that whirl or spin. 2. a merry-go-round. 3. something that seems to whirl, or revolve in a cycle. 4. a whirling motion. 5. a whirligig beetle.

whirligig beetle, a water beetle that moves swiftly about in circles on the surface of water.

whirl·pool (hwũrl′pōōl′), *n.* 1. water in rapid, violent, whirling motion caused by two meeting currents, by winds meeting tides, etc. and tending to form a vacuum at the center of the circle toward and into which floating objects are drawn; a vortex or eddy of water. 2. anything resembling a whirlpool, as in violent motion.

whirl·wind (hwũrl′wind′), *n.* [ME. *whirlwynd;* prob. after ON. *hvirfilvindr*], 1. a current of air whirling violently in spiral form around a more or less vertical axis that has a forward motion. 2. anything resembling a whirlwind, as in violent or destructive action, etc.

reap the whirlwind, to suffer the consequences of evil or folly: Hos. 8:7.

whirl·y·bird (hwũr′li-bũrd′), *n.* [Slang], a helicopter.

whirr (hwũr), *v.i. & v.t., n.* whir.

whir·ry (hwũr′i), *v.t. & v.i.* [WHIRRIED (-id), WHIRRYING], [Scot.], to whirl.

whish (hwish), *v.i.* [echoic], to move with a soft rushing or whizzing sound; whiz; swish. *n.* a sound so made, as by a whiplash.

whisht (hwisht; Scot. hwusht), *interj.* hush!: an exclamation ordering silence. *adj.* still; silent; hushed. *v.t.* to silence. *v.i.* to be silent. *n.* 1. silence. 2. a faint sound; whisper. Now dial., chiefly Scot.

whisk (hwisk), *v.t.* [< MScot. & prob. < ON.; cf. Dan. *viske*, to wipe, Sw. *viska*], 1. to move, remove, carry, brush, etc. with a quick, sweeping motion (usually with *away, off, out*, etc.): as, she *whisked* out a handkerchief, *whisked* off the crumbs. 2. [Chiefly British], to beat (eggs, cream, etc.) into a froth; whip. *v.i.* to move quickly, nimbly, or briskly: as, the cat *whisked* around the corner. *n.* [ME. *wisk* < the *v.*, but also < ON. *visk*, a wisp], 1. the act of whisking. 2. a quick, light, sweeping motion. 3. a small bunch of straw, twigs, hair, etc. used for brushing; hence, 4. a whisk broom. 5. [Chiefly British], a kitchen utensil consisting of several loops of wire fixed in a handle, for whipping eggs, cream, etc.

whisk broom, a small, short-handled broom for brushing clothes, etc.

whisk·er (hwis′kẽr), *n.* [ME. *wisker*, something used for whisking; see WHISK & -ER], 1. originally, anything that whisks. 2. *pl.* *a)* formerly, a mustache. *b)* the hair growing on a man's face; especially, the beard on the cheeks. 3. *a)* a hair of a man's beard. *b)* any of the long bristly hairs growing on the upper lip of a cat, rat, etc. at each side. 4. in *nautical usage*, either of two spars extending laterally one on each side of the bowsprit, for spreading the jib and flying jib guys: also **whisker boom.**

whisk·ered (hwis′kẽrd), *adj.* having whiskers.

whis·key (hwis′ki), *n.* [*pl.* WHISKEYS (-kiz)] *& adj.* whisky.

whis·ky (hwis′ki), *n.* [*pl.* WHISKIES (-kiz)], [short for *usquebaugh;* Ir. *uisgebeatha; uisge*, water + *beatha*, life, lit., water of life], 1. a strong alcoholic liquor distilled from the fermented mash of various grains, especially of rye, wheat, corn, or barley. 2. a drink of whisky. *adj.* of, for, or made with whisky.

whis·ky-jay (hwis′ki-jā′), *n.* [altered < *whiskey john*, itself altered (after *whiskey* + *John*) < the Am. Ind. (Algonquian) name; cf. Cree *wiskatjân*], the common gray jay of Canada.

whisky sour, a mixed drink of lemon juice, sugar, soda water, and whisky, shaken with cracked ice.

whis·per (hwis′pẽr), *v.i.* [ME. *whisperen;* AS. *hwisprian;* akin to G. *wispern;* IE. base **kwei-*, to whizz, hiss, seen also in Eng. *whine, whistle*], 1. to speak very softly, especially without the resonance produced by the vibration of the vocal chords. 2. to talk quietly or furtively, as in gossiping, maligning, or plotting. 3. to make a soft, rustling sound like a whisper, as the leaves of a tree. *v.t.* 1. to say very softly, especially without the resonance produced by the vibration of the vocal chords. 2. to tell privately or as a secret. 3. [Rare], to tell or speak to (someone) in or as in a whisper. *n.* 1. a whispering; soft, low speech produced with breath but, usually, without voice. 2. *a)* something whispered; hence, *b)* a secret, confidence, hint, rumor, etc. 3. a soft rustling sound suggestive of a whisper.

whis·per·ing (hwis′pẽr-iŋ), *adj.* that whispers or is like a whisper. *n.* 1. the act of one who whispers. 2. something whispered; whispered sound, speech, etc.

whispering campaign, a campaign to defame a person, organization, etc. by spreading rumors to be passed around privately from person to person.

whis·per·ous (hwis′pẽr-əs), *adj.* characterized by or full of whispers; like a whisper.

whis·per·y (hwis′pẽr-i), *adj.* whisperous.

whist (hwist), *interj.* [ME.; echoic], hush!: an exclamation ordering silence. *adj.* still; silent. *v.t.* to silence. *v.i.* to be silent. *n.* silence. Now archaic or dial.

whist (hwist), *n.* [altered < earlier *whisk;* prob. so named from the habit of whisking the tricks from the table as soon as played], a card game played with a full pack of 52 cards, usually by two pairs of players, and similar to bridge, of which it is the forerunner.

whis·tle (hwis″'l), *v.i.* [WHISTLED (-'ld), WHISTLING], [ME. *whistlen;* AS. *hwistlian;* for IE. base see WHINE, WHISPER], 1. to make a clear, shrill sound or note, or a series of these, by forcing breath between the teeth or through a narrow opening made by contracting the lips. 2. to make a clear, shrill cry: said of some birds and animals. 3. to move through the air with a high, shrill sound: as, the wind *whistled* past. 4. *a)* to blow a whistle: as, the policeman *whistled*. *b)* to have its whistle blown: as, the train *whistled*. *v.t.* 1. to produce (a tune, etc.) by whistling. 2. to summon, signal, direct, etc. by whistling. 3. to cause to move with a whistling sound. *n.* 1. an instrument for making whistling sounds, as by forcing the breath or steam into a cavity or against a thin edge. 2. a clear, shrill sound made by whistling or blowing a whistle. 3. the act of whistling. 4. a signal, summons, etc. made by whistling. 5. a whistling sound, as of the wind.

wet one's whistle, to take a drink.

whistle for, to seek or expect in vain; fail to get.

whis·tler (hwis′lẽr), *n.* 1. a person or thing that whistles. 2. any of various birds having a whistling call or making a whistling sound in flight, as the goldeneye. 3. a broken-winded horse. 4. a large marmot found in the mountains of northwestern North America.

Whis·tler, James Abbott McNeill (mək-nēl′ hwis′lẽr), 1834–1903; American painter and etcher in England.

Whis·tle·ri·an (hwis-lêr′i-ən), *adj.* of or characteristic of Whistler or his style of painting.

whistle stop, a small town, originally one at which a train stopped only upon signal, to which the engineer responded by tooting his whistle.

whis·tling (hwis′liŋ), *n.* [ME. *whistlinge;* AS. *hwistlung*], 1. the act or sound of a person, animal, or thing that whistles. 2. a disease of horses, similar to roaring.

whit (hwit), *n.* [Early Mod. Eng. resp. of *wiht,* a wight (see WIGHT) as used in *any wight, no wight*], the smallest particle; least bit; jot; iota: usually used in negative constructions, as he doesn't seem a *whit* concerned.

Whit·by (hwit′bi), *n.* a seaport in Yorkshire, England: pop., 12,000.

white (hwīt), *adj.* [ME. *whit, white;* AS. *hwit;* akin to G. *weiss;* IE. base **kweit-,* to gleam, pale, etc., seen also in Eng. *wheat*], 1. having the color of pure snow or milk; of the color of radiated, transmitted, or reflected light containing all of the visible rays of the spectrum: opposite to black: see **color.** 2. of a light or pale color; specifically, *a)* gray; silvery; hoary. *b)* very blond. *c)* pale; wan; pallid; ashen: as, a face *white* with terror. *d)* light-yellow or amber: as, *white* wines. *e)* blank: said of a space unmarked by printing, writing, etc. *f)* of a light-gray color and lustrous appearance; unburnished: said of silver and other metals. *g)* made of silver. *h)* snowy: as, a *white* Christmas. 3. clothed in white; wearing a white habit: as, the *White* Friars. 4. morally or spiritually pure; spotless; innocent. 5. free from evil intent; harmless: as, *white* magic, a *white* lie. 6. [Rare], happy; fortunate; auspicious: said of times and seasons. 7. *a)* having a light-colored skin; Caucasian. *b)* of or controlled by the white race: as, *white* supremacy. *c)* [< notions of racial superiority], [Slang], honest; honorable; fair; dependable. 8. being at white heat. 9. reactionary, counterrevolutionary, or royalist, as opposed to *red* (radical or revolutionary). *n.* 1. the color of pure snow or milk; color of radiated, transmitted, or reflected light containing all of the visible rays of the spectrum; achromatic color opposite to black. 2. whiteness; specifically, *a)* fairness of complexion. *b)* purity; innocence. 3. a white or light-colored part; specifically, *a)* the albumen of an egg. *b)* the white part of the eyeball. *c)* a blank space in printing, writing, etc. *d)* the white or light-colored part of meat, wood, etc. 4. something white or nearly white in color; specifically, *a)* white cloth. *b) pl.* white garments or vestments; white uniform. *c)* white wine. *d)* white pigment: as, Chinese *white. e)* a white breed, especially of pig. *f)* a fine flour made from the whitest part of the wheat. 5. a person with a light-colored skin; member of the Caucasian division of mankind. 6. a member of a reactionary or counterrevolutionary faction, party, etc. in certain European countries. 7. *pl.* leucorrhea. 8. in *archery, a)* [Archaic], a white target. *b)* the outermost ring of a target. *c)* a hit on this ring. 9. in *checkers & chess, a)* the white or light-colored pieces. *b)* the player who has them. *v.t.* [WHITED (-id), WHITING], [ME. *whiten;* AS. *hwitian* < the *adj.*], 1. to make white; whiten. 2. to leave blank spaces in (printed or written matter): as, *white* out this line.

bleed white, to drain (a person) completely of money, resources, etc.

White, Edward Douglass (hwīt), 1845–1921; chief justice of the United States (1910–1921).

White, Gilbert, 1720–1793; English naturalist and clergyman.

White, Stan·ford (stan′fẽrd), 1853–1906; American architect.

White, William Allen, 1868–1944; American newspaper editor.

white admiral, a butterfly of the northeastern United States, with showy, white bands on its wings.

white alkali, 1. refined soda ash. 2. the white crust formed on some alkali soils, consisting of a mixture of sodium and magnesium sulfates and sodium chloride.

white ant, a termite.

white·bait (hwīt′bāt′), *n.* 1. the young of the herring and sprat, eaten as a delicacy. 2. any of various other very small fishes resembling these and used as food.

white bear, a polar bear.

white·beard (hwīt′bêrd′), *n.* an old man with a white or gray beard.

white birch, 1. the North American birch with white or ash-colored paperlike bark. 2. the European birch with white or ash-colored bark.

white book, a publication issued by the government of Germany, Czechoslovakia, Japan, or certain other countries, containing an official report on certain political affairs: so called from the binding.

white bread, bread of a light color made from finely sifted wheat flour.

white bryony, a variety of bryony with white fleshy roots, five-lobed leaves, clusters of greenish-white flowers, and red or black berries.

white·cap (hwīt′kap′), *n.* 1. a wave with its crest broken into white foam. 2. [W-], formerly, in the United States, a member of a lawless, secret organization that, under the pretext of protecting the community, committed crimes of terrorism and violence, especially against Negroes: they wore white hoods.

white cedar, 1. a variety of cedar growing in swampy land. 2. its soft, light-colored wood, used for shingles, woodenware, etc. 3. American arborvitae.

White·chap·el (hwīt′chap′'l), *n.* a district in eastern London, England.

white clover, a creeping variety of clover with small, round, white flowers.

white coal, water as a source of power.

white-col·lar (hwīt′kol′ẽr), *adj.* [from the customary business dress], designating or of clerical or professional workers or the like: white-collar workers are usually salaried employees in work not essentially manual.

white damp, carbon monoxide, occurring as a poisonous gas in coal mines.

whited sepulcher, a hypocrite: Matt. 23:27.

white elephant, 1. a rare, pale-gray variety of elephant, regarded as sacred by the Burmese, Siamese, etc. 2. something from which little profit or use is derived; especially, such a possession acquired and maintained at much expense.

white-eye (hwīt′ī′), *n.* any of various small songbirds of India, Australia, etc. having rings of white feathers around the eyes.

white-faced (hwīt′fāst′), *adj.* 1. having a pale face; pallid. 2. having a white mark on the front of the head: as, a *white-faced* horse.

white feather, [from the belief that a white feather in the tail of a gamecock indicates bad breeding, hence cowardice], a symbol of cowardice.

show the white feather, to behave like a coward.

White·field, George (hwīt′fēld′), 1714–1770; English Methodist clergyman and evangelist.

white·fish (hwīt′fish′), *n.* [*pl.* WHITEFISH, WHITEFISHES (-iz); see FISH], 1. any of various white or silvery freshwater food fishes of the salmon family, found in the lakes of the northeastern United States. 2. any of various other similarly colored fishes, as the menhaden. 3. the white whale; beluga.

white flag, a white banner or cloth hoisted as a signal of truce or surrender.

White Friar, a Carmelite friar: so called from the white habit of the order.

White·fri·ars (hwīt′frī′ẽrz), *n.* a district in Fleet Street, London, about the site of a former monastery.

white gold, gold alloyed with about 20 per cent of platinum, palladium, nickel, etc. to give it a white, platinumlike appearance for use in jewelry.

white gum, 1. a variety of eucalyptus tree with light-colored bark. 2. a sweet gum tree.

White·hall (hwīt′hôl′), *n.* 1. a former royal palace near Westminster Abbey: also **Whitehall Palace.** 2. a street in Westminster where several government offices are located; hence, 3. the British government.

White·head, Alfred North (hwīt′hed′), 1861–1947; English mathematician and philosopher in America.

white-head·ed (hwīt′hed′id), *adj.* 1. having white hair, feathers, etc. on the head. 2. having flaxen or very blond hair; fair-haired. 3. [Irish], favorite: as, the *white-headed* boy.

white heat, 1. the degree of intense heat (beyond red heat) at which metal, etc. becomes glowing white. 2. a state of intense emotion, excitement, etc.

White·horse (hwīt′hôrs′), *n.* the capital of the Yukon Territory, Canada, in the southern part: pop., 3,000.

white-hot (hwīt′hot′), *adj.* 1. glowing white with heat. 2. extremely angry, excited, enthusiastic, etc.

White House, the, 1. the official residence of the President of the United States in Washington, D.C.: a white building in colonial style: officially called *Executive Mansion;* hence, 2. the executive branch of the United States Government.

white lead, 1. a poisonous, heavy, white powder, basic lead carbonate, $2PbCO_3 \cdot Pb(OH)_2$, used in making paint. 2. native lead carbonate; cerussite.

white leather, leather treated with alum and salt: also **whitleather.**

white lie, a lie regarded as excusable because it concerns a trivial matter and is told out of politeness, etc. and without harmful intent.

white-liv·ered (hwīt′liv′ẽrd), *adj.* 1. pale and sickly. 2. cowardly.

white lupine, a plant with deeply cut leaves and spikes of white flowers, grown for fodder.
white·ly (hwīt′li), *adv.* so as to be white; with a white or pale appearance.
white man's burden, the alleged duty of the white, or Caucasian, peoples to bring their civilization to other peoples regarded as backward: phrase popularized by Kipling and other apologists for imperialism.
white matter, whitish nerve tissue of the brain and spinal cord, consisting chiefly of medullated nerve fibers: distinguished from *gray matter.*
white meat, [ME. *whyt-mete;* in sense 2, *meat* is in its orig. sense "food in general"], 1. any light-colored meat, as the breast of chicken or turkey, veal, etc. 2. [Obs. or Dial.]. cheese, butter, or other dairy product.
white metal, any of various alloys containing large proportions of lead or tin, as pewter, plumber's solder, type metal, etc.
White Mountains, a mountain range of the Appalachian system, in northern New Hampshire.
whit·en (hwīt′'n), *v.t. & v.i.* [ME. *whitnen;* cf. WHITE & -EN], to make or become white or whiter.
white·ness (hwīt′nis), *n.* 1. the quality or condition of being white; specifically, *a*) white color or appearance. *b*) paleness; pallor. *c*) freedom from stain. *d*) moral pureness; innocence. 2. a white substance or part.
White Nile, a branch of the Nile, flowing northward through the Sudan to join the Blue Nile.
whit·en·ing (hwīt′'n-iŋ), *n.* 1. the act or process of making white. 2. the act, fact, or process of becoming white. 3. a preparation used for making something white; whiting.
white oak, 1. any of a number of oaks having long leaves that are usually seven-lobed, whitish or grayish bark, and hard wood. 2. the wood of any of these trees, used in furniture, woodwork, etc.
white paper, an official government report on some subject of less importance or less complete than that treated in a white book or blue book: so called from the white paper used as binding.
White Pass, a mountain pass in southeastern Alaska, near Skagway: height, 2,800 ft.
white pepper, pepper ground from the husked dried seeds of the pepper berry.
white perch, a small, silvery food fish found in coastal waters and streams of the eastern United States.
white pine, 1. a pine of eastern North America, with bluish-green or grayish-green needles in clusters of five, hanging brown cones, and soft, light wood. 2. the wood of this tree. 3. any of various closely related pines.
white plague, tuberculosis, especially of the lungs.
White Plains, a city in New York, near New York City: pop., 50,000: scene of a battle (1776) of the Revolutionary War, in which the British defeated the Americans.
white poplar, 1. any of a number of poplar trees having lobed leaves with white or gray down on the undersides. 2. the wood of the tulip tree.
white potato, the common potato; Irish potato: see **potato** (sense 2).
white primary, in some southern States of the United States, a direct primary election from which Negroes are excluded from voting.
white race, loosely, the Caucasian division of mankind: see **Caucasian.**
white rat, an albino rat; especially, one of a breed of albino Norway rats used in biological experiments.
White River, a river in Arkansas, flowing into the Mississippi: length, 690 mi.
White Russia, Byelorussia.
White Russian, 1. Byelorussian. 2. a Russian member of, or sympathizer with, a faction which fought the Bolsheviks (Reds) in the Russian civil war.
White Russian Soviet Socialist Republic, the Byelorussian Soviet Socialist Republic.
white sapphire, a precious stone of clear, colorless corundum.
white sauce, a sauce for vegetables, meat, fish, etc., made of fat or butter, flour, milk, and seasoning cooked together.
White Sea, an arm of the Arctic Ocean extending into the European U.S.S.R.: area, 36,000 sq. mi.
white-slave (hwīt′slāv′), *adj.* 1. of white slaves; in white slavery: as, *white-slave* traffic. 2. against white slavery: as, *White-slave Act* (see **Mann Act**).
white slave, a woman unwillingly forced into or held in prostitution for the profit of others.
white slaver, a person engaged in white-slave traffic.
white slavery, 1. the business or practice of prostitution with white slaves. 2. the condition of white slaves.
white·smith (hwīt′smith′), *n.* 1. a worker in white metals; especially, a tinsmith. 2. a worker in iron who does finishing, polishing, or galvanizing.
white squall, a sudden squall at sea in the tropics, with no accompanying cloud formation.
white·tail (hwīt′tāl′), *n.* 1. the white-tailed deer. 2. [Dial.], the wheatear.
white-tailed deer (hwīt′tāld′), the most widely distributed deer of the United States, having a tail that is white on the undersurface: also called *Virginia deer.*
white·thorn (hwīt′thôrn′), *n.* the common hawthorn.
white·throat (hwīt′thrōt′), *n.* 1. any of several species of European warbler, with a whitish throat and belly. 2. the white-throated sparrow.
white-throat·ed sparrow (hwīt′thrōt′id), a common North American sparrow having a square white patch on the throat.
white tie, 1. a white bow tie, properly worn with a swallow-tailed coat; hence, 2. a swallow-tailed coat and the proper accessories. Distinguished from *black tie.*
white vitriol, hydrated zinc sulfate, $ZnSO_4 \cdot 7H_2O$, used as an antiseptic and emetic in medicine, as a mordant in dyeing, etc.
white·wash (hwīt′wôsh′, hwīt′wäsh′), *n.* 1. a mixture of lime, whiting, size, water, etc., for whitening walls, etc. 2. a toilet preparation for making the skin fair. 3. *a*) a glossing over or concealing of faults or defects in an effort to exonerate or give the appearance of soundness. *b*) something said or done for this purpose. 4. [Colloq.], in *sports,* a defeat in which the loser scores no points at all. *v.t.* 1. to cover with whitewash. 2. to gloss over or conceal the faults or defects of; give a favorable interpretation of or a falsely virtuous appearance to. 3. [Colloq.], in *sports,* to defeat (an opponent) without permitting him to score.
white whale, the beluga.
white·wing (hwīt′wiŋ′), *n.* a street cleaner wearing a white uniform.
white·wood (hwīt′wood′), *n.* 1. any of a number of trees with white or light-colored wood, as the tulip tree, linden, cottonwood, etc. 2. the wood of any of these trees.
whith·er (hwi*th*′ẽr), *adv.* [ME. *whider, hwider;* AS. *hwider, hwyder;* same base as in *which*], 1. to what place, point, condition, result, etc.? where?: used to introduce questions, as, *whither* are we drifting? 2. to which place, point, condition, result, etc.: used relatively, as, the island *whither* we drifted. 3. to whatever place, point, condition, result, etc.; wherever: as, let them go *whither* they will. *Whither* is now largely replaced by *where* except in poetical or rhetorical usage.
whith·er·so·ev·er (hwi*th*′ẽr-sō-ev′ẽr), *adv.* to whatever place; wherever: an emphatic usage.
whith·er·ward (hwi*th*′ẽr-wẽrd), *adv.* in what or which direction; where: used relatively or interrogatively.
whit·ing (hwīt′iŋ), *n.* [*pl.* WHITINGS (-iŋz), WHITING; see PLURAL, II, D, 1], [ME.; MD. *wijting* < *wit,* white], any of various fishes; specifically, *a*) a European sea fish of the cod family. *b*) any of a group of spiny-finned North American fishes, as the drumfish and weakfish. *c*) the silver hake. *d*) the menhaden.
whit·ing (hwīt′iŋ), *n.* [< *white, v.* + *-ing*], powdered chalk used in making whitewash, silver polish, etc.
whit·ish (hwīt′ish), *adj.* somewhat white.
whit·leath·er (hwit′le*th*′ẽr), *n.* white leather.
whit·low (hwit′lō), *n.* [ME. *whitflowe, whitflawe;* of disputed origin; cf. WHITE & FLAW (defect)], a painful, pus-producing inflammation at the end of a finger or toe, near or under the nail; felon.
Whit·man, Walt (wôlt hwit′mən), (*Walter Whitman*), 1819–1892; American poet.
Whit·mon·day (hwit′mun′di), *n.* [after *Whitsunday*], the Monday immediately following Whitsunday: in England, a bank holiday.
Whit·ney, Eli (hwit′ni), 1765–1825; American inventor of the cotton gin.
Whit·ney, Mount (hwit′ni), a mountain of the Sierra Nevada Range, in eastern California: height, 14,501 ft.: second highest peak in the United States.
Whit·sun (hwit′s'n), *adj.* [ME. *whitsone* < *whitsondei* analyzed as *Whitsun Day;* cf. WHITSUNDAY], of or observed on Whitsunday or at Whitsuntide.
Whit·sun·day (hwit′sun′di, hwit′s'n-dā′), *n.* [ME. *whitsondei;* AS. *Hwita Sunnandæg,* lit., white Sunday: so named from the white garments of candidates for baptism], the seventh Sunday (fiftieth day) after Easter, observed in certain Christian churches to commemorate the descent of the Holy Spirit upon the apostles: also called *Pentecost.*
Whit·sun·tide (hwit′s'n-tīd′), *n.* [ME. *whitsunetide;* see WHITSUN & TIDE (time)], the week beginning with Whitsunday, especially the first three days of that week: also **Whitsun Tide.**
Whit·ti·er (hwit′i-ẽr), *n.* a city in southwestern California: suburb of Los Angeles: pop., 34,000.
Whit·ti·er, John Green·leaf (grēn′lēf hwit′i-ẽr), 1807–1892; American poet.
Whit·ting·ton, Dick (hwit′iŋ-tən), (*Richard Whittington*), 1358?–1423; English merchant; lord mayor of London: the subject of several English legends.
whit·tle (hwit′'l), *v.t.* [WHITTLED (-'ld), WHITTLING], [< obs. *whittle,* a knife; ME. *thwitel,* dim. < AS. *thwitan,* to cut], 1. *a*) to cut or pare thin shavings from (wood) with a knife. *b*) to make or fashion (an object) in this

manner: as, he *whittled* a small dog for his grandson. 2. to reduce, destroy, or get rid of gradually, as if by whittling away with a knife: usually with *down, away,* etc., as, he *whittled* down the cost of the project. ***v.i.*** to whittle wood; especially, to cut away aimlessly at a stick, etc. ***n.*** [Obs.], a knife.

whit·y (hwīt'i), ***adj.*** [WHITIER (-i-ẽr), WHITIEST (-i-ist)], whitish: often used [W-], as a nickname for a person with light blond hair.

whiz, whizz (hwiz), ***v.i.*** [WHIZZED (hwizd), WHIZZING], [echoic], 1. to make the whirring or hissing sound of something rushing through the air. 2. to speed by with this sound: as, the bullet *whizzed* past him. ***v.t.*** to cause to whiz, especially by rotating rapidly. ***n.*** 1. the whirring or hissing sound of something rushing through the air. 2. [cf. WIZ], [Slang], *a*) a person who is very quick, adroit, or skilled at something: as, he's a *whiz* at football. *b*) a person or thing regarded as excellent, attractive, etc.: as, a *whiz* of an automobile. *c*) an agreement; bargain. *d*) a celebration.

whiz-bang, whizz-bang (hwiz'baŋ'), ***n.*** [Slang], 1. a high-explosive shell of great speed whose sound of explosion occurs immediately after its sound of flight. 2. a firework having an effect somewhat like this.

who (ho͞o), ***pron.*** [*obj.* WHOM (ho͞om), *poss.* WHOSE (ho͞oz)], [ME. *who, ho, hwo;* AS. *hwa,* masc. & fem., *hwæt,* neut., who? what?; cf. WHAT], 1. what person or persons: used to introduce a question, as, *who* came? 2. which person or persons: as, I don't know *who* came. 3. *a*) (the, or a, person or persons) that: used to introduce a relative clause, as, the man *who* came to dinner. *b*) any person or persons that; whoever: used as an indefinite relative with an implied antecedent, as, "*who* steals my purse steals trash."

as who should say, as if one should say.

who's who, 1. who the important people are. 2. [often W- W-], a book or list containing the names and short biographies of the prominent contemporary persons of a country, city, profession, etc.

whoa (hwō), ***interj.*** [for *ho, interj.*], stop!: used especially in directing a horse to stand still.

who·dun·it (ho͞o-dun'it), ***n.*** [< *who* + *done* + *it*: coined in 1930 by D. Gordon in *American News of Books*], [Slang], a mystery novel, play, etc. in which a crime is solved at the end by the principal character, usually a detective, using clues scattered throughout the story.

who·ev·er (ho͞o-ev'ẽr), ***pron.*** 1. any person at all that; whatever person. 2. no matter what person: as, *whoever* did it, I didn't. 3. what person? who?: an emphatic usage, as, *whoever* told you that?

whole (hōl), ***adj.*** [ME. *hol, hal;* AS. *hal,* healthy, whole, hale; the sp. with *wh-* < Late ME. pronun. (o͞oəl); akin to G. *heil,* ON. *heill* (cf. HALE); IE. base **qailo-,* sound, uninjured, as also in W. *coel,* omen], 1. *a*) in sound health; not diseased or injured. *b*) [Archaic], healed: said of a wound. 2. not broken, damaged, injured, defective, etc.; intact. 3. containing all of its elements or parts; entire, complete: as, a *whole* set of Dickens. 4. not divided up; in a single unit. 5. constituting the entire amount, extent, number, etc.: as, he slept through the *whole* night. 6. having both parents in common: as, a *whole* brother: distinguished from *half.* 7. in *arithmetic,* not a fraction: as, 28 is a *whole* number. ***n.*** 1. the entire amount, quantity, extent, or sum of something; totality: as, the *whole* is equal to the sum of its parts. 2. a complete organization of parts; unity, entirety, or system. —***SYN.*** see **complete.**

as a whole, as a complete unit; altogether.

made out of whole cloth, completely fictitious or false; made up.

on the whole, all things considered; in general.

whole blood, blood for transfusion from which none of the elements has been removed: cf. **plasma.**

whole·heart·ed (hōl'här'tid), ***adj.*** doing or done with all one's energy, enthusiasm, etc.; sincere; earnest.

whole milk, milk from which none of the elements has been removed: distinguished from *skim milk.*

whole·ness (hōl'nis), ***n.*** the quality or condition of being whole; completeness.

whole note, in *music,* a note (𝅝) having four times the duration of a quarter note: also called *semibreve.*

whole number, a number that is not a fraction or a mixed number; integer: as, 28 is a *whole number.*

whole·sale (hōl'sāl'), ***n.*** [ME. *holesale* < phr. *by hole sale,* by wholesale], the selling of goods in relatively large quantities; especially, the sale of such goods to retailers who then sell them to the consumer: opposed to *retail.* ***adj.*** 1. of or engaged in selling at wholesale. 2. sold in relatively large quantities, usually at a lower cost per item: as, what is the *wholesale* price of these notebooks? 3. extensive and general; without singling out: as, modern warfare involves the *wholesale* destruction of peoples. ***adv.*** in relatively large quantities; by wholesale: as, he bought (or sold) them *wholesale.* ***v.i.*** [WHOLESALED (-sāld'), WHOLESALING], 1. to be engaged in wholesale selling. 2. to be sold in relatively large quantities: as, these pencils *wholesale* at $3.00 per gross. ***v.t.*** to sell (goods) at wholesale.

by wholesale, 1. in large quantities and, usually, at a reduced price; hence, 2. extensively and generally, without singling out.

whole·some (hōl'səm), ***adj.*** [ME. *holsom; hol* (see WHOLE) & *-som* (see -SOME), after ON. *heilsamr,* wholesome], 1. promoting or conducive to good health or well-being; healthful: as, a *wholesome* climate. 2. tending to improve the mind or morals; as, a *wholesome* moving picture for children. 3. characterized by health and vigor; sound: as, a *wholesome* girl. 4. tending to suggest health, or soundness of body and mind: as, there was something *wholesome* about his smile.

whole-souled (hōl'sōld'), ***adj.*** doing or done with one's whole soul; noble; generous; wholehearted.

whole step, in *music,* an interval consisting of two adjacent half steps; whole tone.

whole-wheat (hōl'hwēt'), ***adj.*** 1. made of the entire grain of wheat, including a large part of the bran: as, *whole-wheat* flour. 2. made of whole-wheat flour: as, *whole-wheat* bread.

who'll (ho͞ol), 1. who shall. 2. who will.

whol·ly (hō'li), ***adv.*** [ME. *hooli, holi,* etc.; cf. -Y], to the whole quantity or extent; completely, entirely, etc.

whom (ho͞om), ***pron.*** [ME. *whom, hwom;* AS. *hwam,* dat. of *hwa;* see WHO], the objective case of **who:** in colloquial usage, now often replaced by *who.*

whom·ev·er (ho͞om-ev'ẽr), ***pron.*** the objective case of **whoever.**

whom·so·ev·er (ho͞om'sō-ev'ẽr), ***pron.*** the objective case of **whosoever.**

whoop (ho͞op, hwo͞op), ***n.*** [ME. *houpen,* to call, shout; OFr. *houper,* to call afar off, cry out], a loud shout, cry, or noise; specifically, *a*) a shrill and prolonged cry, as of excitement, intense joy, ferocity, exultation, etc. *b*) a hoot, as of an owl. *c*) the deep-sounding, convulsive intake of air immediately following a fit of coughing in whooping cough. ***v.i.*** to utter a whoop or whoops. ***v.t.*** 1. to utter with a whoop or whoops. 2. to drive, urge on, chase, etc. with whoops. ***interj.*** an exclamation of excitement, joy, exultation, etc.

not worth a whoop, [Colloq.], worth nothing at all.

whoop it (or **things**) **up,** [Slang], 1. to create a noisy disturbance, as in celebrating. 2. to create enthusiasm (*for* something or someone).

whoop·ee (hwo͞o'pē, hwoop'ē), ***interj.*** [< *whoop*], an exclamation used to express great enjoyment, gay abandonment, etc. ***n.*** a shout of "whoopee!"

make whoopee, [Slang], to have a gay, noisy time.

whoop·er (ho͞o'pẽr, hwo͞o'pẽr), ***n.*** a person or thing that whoops; specifically, an Old World swan with a characteristic whooping cry.

whooping cough, an acute infectious disease, usually affecting children, caused by a bacillus and characterized by catarrh of the respiratory tract and repeated attacks of coughing that end in a forced inspiration, or whoop; pertussis.

whoops (hwo͞ops, hwoops), ***interj.*** an exclamation uttered as in regaining one's balance after stumbling or one's composure after a slip of the tongue.

whop (hwop), ***v.t. & v.i.*** [WHOPPED (hwopt), WHOPPING], [< ME. *whappen;* prob. echoic], [Dial. or Archaic], 1. to beat, thrash, or strike. 2. to throw (oneself) down suddenly; flop. ***n.*** [Dial. or Archaic], 1. a blow, stroke, fall, bump, etc. 2. the noise made by any of these. Also spelled **whap.**

whop·per (hwop'ẽr), ***n.*** [< *whop, v.*], [Colloq.], anything extraordinarily large; especially, a great lie: also spelled **whapper.**

whop·ping (hwop'iŋ), ***adj.*** [< *whop, v.*], [Colloq.], extraordinarily large or great.

whore (hôr, hōr), ***n.*** [ME. & AS. *hore;* ON. *hora;* for the *wh-* sp., cf. WHOLE; akin to G. *hure;* IE. base **qa-,* to like, be fond of, desire, seen also in L. *carus,* dear, precious (cf. CARESS); orig., prob. a euphemism], a woman who engages in illegal sexual intercourse, especially one who engages in promiscuous sexual intercourse for pay; prostitute; harlot. ***v.i.*** [WHORED (hôrd, hōrd), WHORING], 1. to be a whore. 2. to fornicate with whores. ***v.t.*** [Archaic], to make a whore of.

who're (ho͞o'ẽr), who are.

whore·dom (hôr'dəm, hōr'dəm), ***n.*** [ME. *hordom;* ON. *hordomr*], 1. prostitution or fornication. 2. the fact of being false to God; idolatry: so used in the Bible.

whore·house (hôr'hous', hōr'hous'), ***n.*** a place where prostitutes are for hire; brothel.

whore·mas·ter (hôr'mas'tẽr, hōr'mäs'tẽr), ***n.*** 1. a man who fornicates with whores; lecher. 2. a pimp; pander.

whore·mon·ger (hôr'muŋ'gẽr, hōr'muŋ'gẽr), ***n.*** a whoremaster.

whore·son (hôr's'n, hōr's'n), ***n.*** [ME. *hores son,* lit., son of a whore, bastard, after OFr. *fiz a putain*], [Archaic], 1. a bastard. 2. a scoundrel; knave: a general epithet of abuse. *adj.* [Archaic], vile, detestable, knavish, etc.

whor·ish (hôr′ish, hōr′ish), *adj.* having the nature of a whore; lewd.

whorl (hwũrl, hwôrl), *n.* [ME. *whorwyl*, dial. var. of *whirl*], 1. a small flywheel on a spindle, as for regulating the speed of a spinning wheel. 2. anything that whirls or appears to whirl like the whorl on a spindle; specifically, *a*) *usually in pl.* any of the circular ridges that form the design of a fingerprint. *b*) in *botany*, an arrangement of leaves, petals, etc. about the same point on a stem. *c*) in *zoology*, any of the turns in a spiral shell.

whorled (hwũrld, hwôrld), *adj.* having, or arranged in, a whorl or whorls.

whort (hwũrt), *n.* [< AS. *horta*, a bilberry, via SW. Brit. dial.], the European whortleberry.

whor·tle (hwũr′t'l), *n.* the whort.

whor·tle·ber·ry (hwũr′t'l-ber′i), *n.* [*pl.* WHORTLEBERRIES (-iz)], [< SW. Brit. dial. form of earlier *hurtleberry* < AS. *horta*, a bilberry; cf. WHORT], 1. *a*) a small European shrub of the blueberry family, with pink flowers and blue or blackish edible berries. *b*) any of these berries. 2. the huckleberry.

who's (ho͞oz), who is.

whose (ho͞oz), *pron.* [ME. *whos, hwas;* AS. *hwæs*, genit. of *hwa;* see WHO], the possessive case of **who**, and now, usually, of **which**.

whose·so·ev·er (ho͞oz′sō-ev′ẽr), *pron.* of whomsoever.

whos·ev·er (ho͞oz-ev′ẽr), *pron.* of whomever.

who·so (ho͞o′sō), *pron.* [ME. *who se, whose* < AS. *hwa swa* (cf. WHO)], [Archaic], whoever; whosoever.

who·so·ev·er (ho͞o′sō-ev′ẽr), *pron.* whoever: an emphatic form.

whr., watt-hour.

why (hwī), *adv.* [ME. *hwi;* AS. *hwi*, instrumental case of *hwa;* see WHO], 1. for what reason, cause, or purpose; with what motive: used interrogatively and relatively, as, *why* did he go? I'll tell you *why* he went. 2. because of which; on account of which: used relatively, often after *reason*, as, I can think of no reason *why* you shouldn't go. 3. the reason for which: as, this is *why* he went. *n.* [*pl.* WHYS (hwīz)], the reason, cause, motive, purpose, etc.: as, never mind the *why* and wherefore. *interj.* an exclamation used to express surprise, impatience, indignation, hesitation, etc.

whyd·ah (hwid′ə), *n.* a whidah bird.

W.I., 1. West Indies. 2. West Indian.

Wich·i·ta (wich′ə-tô′), *n.* a city in southern Kansas, on the Arkansas River: pop., 255,000.

Wichita Falls, a city in north central Texas: pop., 102,000.

wick (wik), *n.* [ME. *wicke, weke;* AS. *weoca;* akin to G. *wieche*, wick yarn; IE. base **weg-*, to spin, knit together, seen also in L. *velum*, sail, cloth, etc.], a piece of cord or tape, or a thin bundle of threads, in a candle, oil lamp, cigarette lighter, etc., that absorbs the fuel by capillary attraction and, when lighted, burns with a small steady flame.

wick (wik), *n.* [ME. *wik;* AS. *wic;* akin to G. *weich-* in *weichbild*, town precinct; prob. < L. *vicus*, row of dwellings, quarter of a city, etc. (cf. VICINITY)], a village, town, or hamlet: now archaic except as compounded (often in the form *-wich*) in certain place names, etc., as in *Warwick, Greenwich, bailiwick*.

wick·ed (wik′id), *adj.* [ME. < *wikke*, evil; akin to AS. *wicca*, a witch; cf. WITCH], 1. having or resulting from bad moral character; evil; depraved. 2. generally bad, painful, etc., but without any moral considerations involved: as, it was a *wicked* blow on the head. 3. naughty in a playful way; mischievous. —*SYN.* see **bad**.

wick·ed·ness (wik′id-nis), *n.* 1. the quality or condition of being wicked. 2. wicked action or a wicked act.

wick·er (wik′ẽr), *n.* [ME. *wiker, wikir;* prob. < ON.; cf. Sw. dial. *viker*, Dan. dial. *vigger*, willow, Sw. *vika*, to bend; for IE. base see WEAK], 1. a thin, flexible twig; withe. 2. *a*) such twigs woven together, as in baskets or furniture; wickerwork. *b*) something made of such twigs. *adj.* made of or covered with wicker.

wick·er·work (wik′ẽr-wũrk′), *n.* 1. thin, flexible twigs woven together; wicker. 2. things made of wicker.

wick·et (wik′it), *n.* [ME. & Anglo-Fr. *wiket* (Fr. *guichet*); prob. < the IE. base of *wicker, weak*, etc.], 1. a small door or gate, especially one set in or near a larger door or gate. 2. a small window or opening, as for a bank teller or in a box office. 3. a small gate for regulating the flow of water to a water wheel or for emptying a canal lock. 4. [from orig. resemblance to a gate], in *cricket*, *a*) either of two sets of three vertical sticks (*stumps*) each, with two small pieces (*bails*) resting on top of them. *b*) the playing space between the two wickets. *c*) an unplayed or unfinished inning. *d*) a player's turn at bat. 5. in *croquet*, any of the small wire arches through which the balls must be hit; hoop.

wick·et·keep·er (wik′it-kēp′ẽr), *n.* in *cricket*, the fielder stationed immediately behind the wicket.

wick·ing (wik′iŋ), *n.* cord, yarn, etc. for wicks.

wick·i·up (wik′i-up′), *n.* [< Am. Ind. (Algonquian) name; cf. Sac & Fox *wikiyap;* akin to *wigwam*], a kind of hut built by the nomadic Indians of the southwestern United States, consisting of an oval-shaped frame covered with grass, brush, etc.: also spelled **wikiup**.

Wickliffe, or **Wiclif, John**, see **Wycliffe, John.**

Wick·low (wik′lō), *n.* 1. a county of Leinster province, Ireland: pop., 60,000. 2. its county seat: pop., 3,000.

wic·o·py (wik′ə-pi), *n.* [< Am. Ind. (Algonquian) name; cf. Cree *wikupiy*], any of various trees with strong, flexible shoots and tough bark, as the leatherwood, basswood, etc.

wide (wīd), *adj.* [ME.; AS. *wid;* akin to G. *weit;* IE. **wi-tos*, lit., gone apart < base **ei-*, to go, seen also in L. *itare* (cf. ITINERARY); an exact L. cognate is seen in L. *vitare*, lit., to go away from, hence avoid], 1. extending over a large area; especially, extending over a larger area from side to side than is usual or normal: as, a *wide* bed: distinguished from *long* and opposed to *narrow*. 2. of a specified extent from side to side: as, three miles *wide*. 3. of great extent, range, or inclusiveness: as, a *wide* variety, *wide* reading. 4. roomy; ample; loose; full: as, a *wide* blouse. 5. open or extended to full width: as, her eyes grew *wide* with fear. 6. landing, striking, or ending far from the point, issue, etc. aimed at: usually with *of*, as, *wide* of the target. 7. in *phonetics*, pronounced with the tongue and other vocal organs in a more or less relaxed position; lax, as the *i* in *bit* or the *e* in *bed*. *adv.* 1. over a relatively large area; widely: as, he traveled far and *wide*. 2. to a large or full extent; fully: as, the door was *wide* open. 3. so as to miss the point, issue, etc. aimed at; astray: as, his blow went *wide*. *n.* 1. [Rare or Poetic], a wide area or extent. 2. in *cricket*, a ball that is bowled out of the batsman's reach, counted as a run for the team at bat. —*SYN.* see **broad**.

wide-an·gle (wīd′aŋ′g'l), *adj.* 1. designating or of a kind of camera lens that covers a wider angle of view than the ordinary lens. 2. designating or of any of several motion-picture systems (variously trademarked, as **Cinerama, CinemaScope**, etc.) employing one or more cameras (and projectors) and an especially wide, curved screen to simulate normal panoramic vision: cf. **3-D** (following the entry for **three**).

wide-a·wake (wīd′ə-wāk′), *adj.* 1. completely awake. 2. alert. *n.* an obsolete kind of soft felt hat with a broad brim: also **wide-awake hat.** —*SYN.* see **watchful.**

wide-eyed (wīd′īd′), *adj.* with the eyes opened widely.

wide·ly (wīd′li), *adv.* 1. over a wide area: as, he's traveled *widely*. 2. to a wide extent: as, *widely* different.

wid·en (wīd′'n), *v.t. & v.i.* to make or become wide or wider.

wide-o·pen (wīd′ō′p'n), *adj.* 1. opened wide. 2. not enforcing, or careless in enforcing, laws prohibiting or regulating prostitution, gambling, the sale of liquor, etc.: as, a *wide-open* city.

wide·spread (wīd′spred′), *adj.* spread widely; especially, spread or occurring over a wide area or extent.

widg·eon (wij′ən), *n.* [*pl.* WIDGEONS (-ənz), WIDGEON; see PLURAL, II, D, 1], [OFr. *vigeon;* prob. < L. *vipio*, small crane], any of various kinds of wild, fresh-water ducks, found in Europe, northern Africa, and northern Asia: also spelled **wigeon**.

wid·ow (wid′ō), *n.* [ME. *widwe;* AS. *widewe;* akin to G. *wittwe;* IE. base **weidh-, *widh-*, to separate, seen also in L. *vidua*, a widow, (*di*)*videre*, to divide (cf. DIVIDE)], 1. a woman who has outlived the man to whom she was married at the time of his death; especially, such a woman who has not remarried. 2. in certain card games, an extra hand dealt to the table. 3. in *printing*, an incomplete line, as that ending a paragraph, carried over to the top of a new page or column: it is generally avoided by rewriting copy to eliminate the line or fill it out. *v.t.* 1. to cause to become a widow: usually in the past participle, as, she was *widowed* by the war. 2. to deprive of something valued; bereave. 3. [Rare], to survive as the widow of. 4. [Rare], to endow with the rights of a widow.

widow bird, [after Port. *viuva*, widow bird, lit., widow (L. *vidua*): so named from the resemblance of its dark plumage and long black tail feathers to a widow's clothing and veil], the whidah bird.

wid·ow·er (wid′ō-ẽr), *n.* [ME. *widuare, widuer* < *widwe*, a widow], a man who has outlived the woman to whom he was married at the time of her death; especially, such a man who has not remarried.

wid·ow·hood (wid′ō-hood′), *n.* [see -HOOD], the condition or period of being a widow.

widow's cruse, a supply that is apparently inexhaustible: I Kings 17:10–17; II Kings 4:1–8.

widow's mite, a small gift or contribution freely given by one who can scarcely afford it: Mark 12:41–44.

widow's peak, a point often formed by hair growing down in the middle of a forehead: formerly believed to be a foretelling of early widowhood.

width (width), *n.* [< *wide*, by analogy with *length, breadth*], 1. the fact, quality, or condition of being wide; wideness. 2. the size of something in terms of how wide it is; distance from side to side. 3. a piece of something having a specified distance from side to side: as, sew two *widths* of cloth together. Abbreviated **W., w.**

Wi·du·kind (vē'do͞o-kint), see **Wittekind.**

‡**wie geht's?** (vē gāts'), [G.], how goes it? how are you?

Wie·land, Chris·toph Mar·tin (kris'tôf mär'tēn vē'-länt), 1733–1813; German writer and translator.

wield (wēld), *v.t.* [ME. *welden*, a blend of AS. *wealdan* & *wyldan*, with the form < the latter; partly akin to G. *walten;* IE. base **wal-*, to be strong, seen also in L. *valere*, to be strong (cf. VALIANT, etc.)], 1. to handle and use (a tool or weapon), especially with skill and control. 2. to exercise (power, control, influence, etc.). 3. [Obs.], to govern, rule, or direct. —*SYN.* see **handle.**

wield·y (wēl'di), *adj.* [WIELDIER (-di-ẽr), WIELDIEST (-di-ist)], that can be wielded easily; manageable.

Wien (vēn), *n.* Vienna, Austria: the German name.

wie·ner (wē'nẽr), *n.* [short for G. *Wiener wurst*, Vienna sausage], a smoked sausage of beef or beef and pork, usually enclosed in a membranous casing and made in links a few inches long; frankfurter: also **weenie, weeny.**

Wie·ner schnit·zel (vē'nẽr shnit's'l), [G.; *Wiener*, of Vienna + *schnitzel*, dim. of *schnitz*, a little piece, cutlet < *schneiden*, to cut], a breaded veal cutlet served with various garnishings, as anchovy fillets, fried eggs, etc.

wie·ner·wurst (wē'nẽr-wũrst'), *n.* [G.; *Wiener*, of Vienna + *wurst*, a sausage], a wiener.

Wies·ba·den (vēs'bä'dən), *n.* a city in western Germany: resort: pop., 172,000.

wife (wīf), *n.* [*pl.* WIVES (wīvz)], [ME.; AS. *wif*, a woman; akin to G. *weib;* ascribed to both IE. base **weik-*, a dwelling & **weip-*, to twist, turn, in the basic sense "the hidden or veiled person"], 1. [Archaic or Rare], a woman: still so used in certain compounds, as *housewife*. 2. a married woman; specifically, a woman in her relationship to her husband. Abbreviated **w.**

take to wife, to marry (a specified woman).

wife·hood (wīf'hood), *n.* [ME. *wifhod;* AS. *wifhad; wif*, a wife + *-had* (cf. -HOOD)], the condition of being a wife.

wife·less (wīf'lis), *adj.* having no wife.

wife·like (wīf'līk'), *adj.* like, characteristic of, or suitable to a wife.

wife·ly (wīf'li), *adj.* [WIFELIER (-li-ẽr), WIFELIEST (-li-ist)], [ME. *wyfely;* AS. *wiflic*], of, like, or suitable to a wife.

wig (wig), *n.* [shortened < *periwig*], an artificial covering of hair for the head, worn as part of a costume, to conceal baldness, etc. *v.t.* [WIGGED (wigd), WIGGING], 1. to furnish with a wig or wigs. 2. [British Colloq.], to scold, censure, rebuke, etc.

Wig·an (wig'ən), *n.* a city in Lancashire, western England: pop., 84,000 (est. 1946).

wig·an (wig'ən), *n.* [so called after *Wigan*], a canvaslike cotton cloth used to stiffen hems, lapels, and other parts of garments.

wi·geon (wij'ən), *n.* [*pl.* WIGEONS (-ənz), WIGEON; see PLURAL, II, D, 1], a widgeon.

wigged (wigd), *adj.* wearing a wig.

wig·ger·y (wig'ẽr-i), *n.* 1. *a)* a wig. *b)* wigs collectively. 2. the practice of wearing a wig.

Wig·gin, Kate Douglas (wig'in), (née *Kate Smith*), 1856–1923; American educator and writer of children's novels.

wig·ging (wig'iŋ), *n.* [British Colloq.], a scolding or reprimand.

wig·gle (wig''l), *v.t. & v.i.* [WIGGLED (-'ld), WIGGLING], [ME. *wigelen;* prob. < MD. & MLG. *wiggelen*, freq. of *wiggen*, to move from side to side], to move or cause to move with short, jerky motions from side to side; wriggle shakily or sinuously. *n.* the act or an instance of wiggling.

wig·gler (wig'lẽr), *n.* 1. a person or thing that wiggles. 2. the larva of a mosquito; wriggler.

wig·gly (wig'li), *adj.* [WIGGLIER (-li-ẽr), WIGGLIEST (-li-ist)], 1. that wiggles; wiggling. 2. having a form that suggests wiggling; wavy: as, a *wiggly* line.

wight (wīt), *n.* [ME. & AS. *wiht;* akin to G. *wicht*, creature; IE. base **weqti-*, thing], [Archaic], a human being; person: now sometimes used humorously.

wight (wīt), *adj.* [ME. *wihte;* ON. *vigt*, neut. of *vigr*, skilled in arms], [Archaic], strong, brisk, active, brave, etc.

Wight, Isle of (wīt), an island in the English Channel, off the coast of England: area, 147 sq. mi.; pop., 86,000; capital, Newport: abbreviated **I.W.**

WIGGLER (of mosquito)

Wig·town (wig'tən), *n.* 1. a county on the southwestern coast of Scotland: pop., 31,000 (est. 1946): also **Wigtownshire.** 2. its county seat: pop., 1,300.

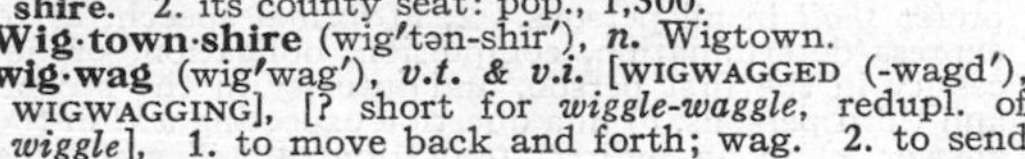

Wig·town·shire (wig'tən-shir'), *n.* Wigtown.

wig·wag (wig'wag'), *v.t. & v.i.* [WIGWAGGED (-wagd'), WIGWAGGING], [? short for *wiggle-waggle*, redupl. of *wiggle*], 1. to move back and forth; wag. 2. to send (a message) by waving flags, lights, etc. back and forth in accordance with a code. *n.* 1. the act or practice of sending messages in this way. 2. a message so sent.

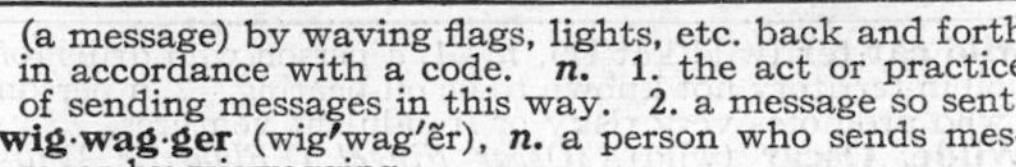

wig·wag·ger (wig'wag'ẽr), *n.* a person who sends messages by wigwagging.

wig·wam (wig'wäm, wig'wôm), *n.* [< Am. Ind. (Algonquian) name; cf. Ojibway *wigiwam*, lodge, lit., their dwelling, akin to Chippewa *wigiw*, he dwells], 1. a more or less conical shelter made by Indians of eastern and central North America, consisting of a framework of poles covered with bark, hides, etc. 2. [Colloq.], a building used by a political group; especially, a large, temporary structure for a political convention.

the Wigwam, [Colloq.], Tammany Hall.

WIGWAM

wik·i·up (wik'i-up'), *n.* a wickiup.

Wil·ber·force, William (wil'bẽr-fôrs', wil'bẽr-fōrs'), 1759–1833; English philanthropist and vigorous opponent of the slave trade.

Wil·bert (wil'bẽrt), [G. *Willebert, Willibert* < OHG. *willeo, willio*, a will, wish + *beraht, berht*, bright], a masculine name.

Wil·bur (wil'bẽr), [AS. *Wilburh;* prob. a place name < **Wiligburh*, lit., willow town], a masculine name.

wild (wīld), *adj.* [ME. & AS. *wilde;* akin to G. *wild;* IE. base **wel-* in the sense "unkempt"; cf. WOOL], 1. living or growing in its original, natural state; not domesticated or cultivated: as, *wild* flowers or *wild* animals. 2. not lived in or cultivated; desolate; waste: as, *wild* land. 3. not civilized; savage; primitive: as, a *wild* tribe. 4. not easily restrained or regulated; not submitting to control: as, *wild* children. 5. *a)* dissipated, licentious, etc.: as, *wild* youth. *b)* characterized by a lack of moral restraint; immoral; unbridled; orgiastic: as, a *wild* party. 6. violently disturbed; turbulent; stormy: as, a *wild* seacoast. 7. in a state of mental excitement; specifically, *a)* eager or enthusiastic, as with desire or anticipation: as, *wild* with delight. *b)* angered, vexed, crazed, etc.: as, he was *wild* with desperation. 8. in a state of disorder, disarrangement, confusion, etc.: as, *wild* hair. 9. fantastically impractical; visionary: as, a *wild* scheme. 10. showing a lack of sound judgment; reckless; imprudent: as, a *wild* wager. 11. going wide of the mark aimed at; missing the target: as, a *wild* pitch in baseball. 12. in certain card games, having any value desired by the holder: said of a card, as, when deuces are *wild* in poker, they may be counted as aces, kings, etc. *adv.* in a wild manner; wildly; without aim or control: as, he fired *wild*. *n. usually pl.* a wilderness, waste, desert, etc.

run wild, to grow or exist without control or regulation.

the wild, the wilderness, nature, the out-of-doors, etc.: as, the call of *the wild*.

wild allspice, a shrub with small, fragrant, yellowish flowers and red berries; spicebush.

wild boar, a variety of hog living wild in Europe and Asia, from which the domesticated hog was developed.

wild brier, any kind of wild rose, especially the sweetbrier or dog rose.

wild carrot, a weed with white, lacelike flowers, from which the cultivated carrot originated; Queen Anne's lace.

wild·cat (wīld'kat'), *n.* [*pl.* WILDCATS (-kats'), WILDCAT; see PLURAL, II, D, 1], 1. *a)* any of a large group of fierce, medium-sized, undomesticated animals of the cat family, found throughout North America, as the bobcat, or lynx. *b)* any of a group of undomesticated cats of Europe, similar to but slightly larger than the domestic cat. 2. any person considered like a wildcat in being fierce, aggressive, quick-tempered, etc. 3. an unsound or risky business scheme. 4. a productive oil well drilled in an area not previously known to have oil. 5. in *railroading*, a locomotive and tender without cars sent out on special tasks, as to help haul a train. Also **wild cat.** *adj.* 1. unsound or financially risky: as, a *wildcat* venture. 2. designating a business, etc. that is illegal or unethical. 3. in *railroading*, running without authorization or on an irregular schedule: said of a train or locomotive. *v.t.* [WILDCATTED (-id), WILDCATTING], to drill for oil in (an area previously considered unproductive).

wildcat bank, in the period before the National Bank Act of 1863–1864, any bank that issued notes without sufficient capital to redeem them.

wildcat strike, a labor strike without the authorization of the union representing the strikers.

wild·cat·ter (wīld′kat′ẽr), *n.* 1. a person who drills for oil in territory not known to be oil-bearing. 2. a person who promotes very risky or fraudulent ventures.
Wilde, Oscar (wīld), (*Oscar Fingal O'Flahertie Wills Wilde*), 1854–1900; British poet, novelist, and dramatist, born in Ireland.
wil·de·beest (wil′də-bēst′; D. vil′də-bāst′), *n.* [*pl.* WILDEBEESTS (-bēsts′; D. -bāsts′), WILDEBEEST; see PLURAL, II, D, 1], [S.Afr.D. < D. *wild*, wild + *beeste*, beast], a gnu.
wil·der (wil′dẽr), *v.i. & v.t.* [either aphetic < *bewilder* or formed < *wilderness*], [Archaic or Poetic], 1. to lose or cause to lose one's way. 2. to bewilder or become bewildered.
Wil·der, Thorn·ton (thôrn′tən wīl′dẽr), (*Thornton Niven Wilder*), 1897– ; American novelist and playwright.
Wil·der·ness (wil′dẽr-nis), *n.* a region in northeastern Virginia, south of the Rapidan River: several battles of the Civil War were fought there (1864) between the armies of Grant and Lee.
wil·der·ness (wil′dẽr-nis), *n.* [ME. *wildernesse* < *wilderne*, wild place, wilderness + *-ness;* AS. *wilder*, *wilddeor*, wild animal < *wilde*, wild + *deor*, animal, deer], 1. an uncultivated, uninhabited region; waste; wild. 2. any barren, empty, or open area, as of ocean. 3. a large, confused mass or tangle of persons or things. 4. [Obs.], a wild condition or quality. —***SYN.*** see **waste**.
wild-eyed (wīld′īd), *adj.* staring in a wild or distracted manner, as from fear.
wild·fire (wīld′fīr′), *n.* 1. originally, *a*) a highly destructive fire. *b*) a highly inflammable substance, difficult to extinguish, formerly used in warfare; Greek fire: now mainly in *spread like wildfire*, to be disseminated widely and rapidly, as a rumor. 2. lightning without thunder; heat lightning. 3. the will-o'-the-wisp. 4. [Obs.], *a*) erysipelas. *b*) a disease of sheep characterized by inflammation of the skin.
wild·flow·er (wīld′flou′ẽr), *n.* a wild flower.
wild flower, 1. any plant growing without cultivation in fields, woods, etc. 2. its flower.
wild·fowl (wīld′foul′), *n.* wild fowl.
wild fowl, wild birds; especially, game birds, as wild ducks, wild geese, partridges, pheasants, quail, etc.
wild goose, any undomesticated goose; especially, in America, the Canada goose.
wild-goose chase (wīld′gōōs′), 1. a useless search or pursuit: so called because of the futility of trying to catch a wild goose by chasing it; hence, 2. any futile attempt or enterprise.
Wild Hunt, in *European folklore*, a nighttime ride of spectral huntsmen across the countryside or the sky.
Wild Huntsman, in *European folklore*, the leader of the Wild Hunt, originally probably Odin.
wild hyacinth, a variety of hyacinth with blue, bell-shaped flowers; wood hyacinth; bluebell.
wild indigo, any of a number of related plants with triangle-shaped leaflets, clusters of blue, yellow, or white flowers, and short pods.
wild·ing (wīl′diŋ), *n.* 1. a wild plant; especially, a wild apple tree. 2. its fruit. 3. a plant originally cultivated, but growing wild. 4. a person or thing that does not conform to type. *adj.* not cultivated or domesticated; wild.
wild lettuce, any species of uncultivated lettuce growing as a weed; especially, a species having prickly leaves, small yellow flowers, and milky juice.
wild·ling (wīld′liŋ), *n.* [*wild* + *-ling*, dim. suffix], an uncultivated plant or undomesticated animal.
wild madder, 1. madder (senses 1 & 2*a*). 2. either of two species of bedstraw.
wild mandrake, the May apple, a plant with shield-shaped leaves, white flowers, and lemon-shaped fruit.
wild mustard, a yellow-flowered, rapid-spreading weed whose seeds are sometimes used to flavor food; charlock.
wild oat (or **oats**), a tall, oatlike grass used for fodder.
sow one's wild oats, to be promiscuous or dissolute in youth before settling down: usually said of a man.
wild olive, 1. a spiny tree with small, inedible, olive-like fruit; oleaster. 2. any tree resembling the olive.
wild pansy, an uncultivated pansy with small flowers in combinations of white, yellow, and purple.
wild parsley, 1. any of several perennial herbs of the carrot group, especially a nine-leaf variety used as forage. 2. lovage.
wild parsnip, the wild, original form of the cultivated parsnip, used as forage.
wild pink, any of a number of related plants with lance-shaped leaves and flat clusters of pink or white flowers.
wild rose, any of many roses growing wild, as the sweet-brier.
wild rubber, rubber obtained from uncultivated trees.
wild rye, any of various tall related grasses like rye.
wild turkey, the wild, original form of the North American domesticated turkey, now rare.
wild vanilla, a purple-flowered shrub whose leaves when bruised give off a vanilla scent.
Wild West, wild West, the western United States in its early frontier period of lawlessness.
Wild West show, a circuslike spectacle featuring horsemanship and other feats by cowboys, Indians, etc.
wild·wood (wīld′wood′), *n.* a natural woodland or forest, especially when unfrequented.
wild yam, an uncultivated species of yam of eastern North America.
wile (wīl), *n.* [ME.; AS. *wil;* prob. < the Anglo-N. form **vihl* of ON. *vēl*, a trick, stratagem], 1. a sly trick; deceitful artifice; stratagem. 2. a beguiling or coquettish trick. 3. trickery; deceit. *v.t.* [WILED (wīld), WILING], to beguile; lure. —***SYN.*** see **trick.**
wile away, to while away (time, etc.): by confusion with *while*.
Wil·fred, Wil·frid (wil′frid), [AS. *Wilfrith* < *will*, a will, wish + *frith*, peace], a masculine name.
wil·ful (wil′fəl), *adj.* willful.
Wil·helm I (vil′helm), William I (sense 3): German name.
Wilhelm II, William II (sense 2): German name.
Wil·hel·mi·na (wil′hel-mē′nə; D. vil′hel-mē′nä), [G. *Wilhelmine*, fem. of *Wilhelm;* see WILLIAM], a feminine name. *n.* 1880–1962; queen of the Netherlands (1890–1948); ruled in exile (1940–1945).
Wilhelmina, Mount, a mountain of the Orange range, in Netherlands New Guinea: height, 15,580 ft.
Wil·helms·ha·ven (vil′helms-hä′fən), *n.* a seaport in northern Germany, on the North Sea: pop., 101,000.
Wil·helm·stras·se (vil′helm-shträ′sə), *n.* 1. an avenue in Berlin, former location of the German foreign office and other government buildings; hence, 2. formerly, the German foreign ministry or its policies.
wil·i·ly (wīl′ə-li), *adv.* in a wily manner.
wil·i·ness (wīl′i-nis), *n.* a wily quality or condition.
Wilkes, Charles (wilks), 1798–1877; American naval officer and explorer.
Wilkes, John, 1727–1797; English political agitator and reformer.
Wilkes-Bar·re (wilks′bar′i), *n.* a city in northeastern Pennsylvania: pop., 64,000.
Wil·kins, Sir **George Hubert** (wil′kinz), 1888–1958; Australian explorer of the Arctic and Antarctic.
Wil·kins·burg (wil′kinz-bũrg′), *n.* a city in Pennsylvania, near Pittsburgh: pop., 30,000.
will (wil), *n.* [ME. *wille;* AS. *willa;* akin to G. *wille*, *willen;* IE. base **wel-*, to wish, choose; cf. next entry], 1. the act or process of volition; specifically, *a*) wish; desire; longing. *b*) inclination; disposition; pleasure. *c*) [Obs.], appetite; lust. 2. something wished by a person, especially by one with power or authority; specifically, *a*) a request: as, it is his *will* that you appear. *b*) a command; decree: as, His *will* be done. 3. strong purpose, intention, or determination: as, where there's a *will* there's a way. 4. energy or enthusiasm: as, he works with a *will*. 5. the power of self-direction or self-control: as, he has no strong *will*. 6. the power of conscious and deliberate action or choice: as, freedom of the *will*. 7. disposition or attitude toward others: as, I bear her no ill *will*. 8. *a*) the legal statement of a person's wishes concerning the disposal of his property after death. *b*) the document containing this. *v.t.* [ME. *willien;* AS. *willian* < *willan*, to desire], 1. formerly, to long for; desire. 2. to decide upon; make a choice of; hence, 3. to resolve firmly; determine: as, he *willed* to survive. 4. to decree; ordain. 5. to influence or control as by hypnotic power: as, he *willed* her to die. 6. to bequeath by a will. 7. [Obs.], to command; order. *v.i.* [Archaic], to wish, prefer, or choose.
at will, when one wishes; at one's discretion.
do the will of, to obey the wish or command of.
SYN.—**will,** the more inclusive term here, basically denotes the power of choice and deliberate action or the intention resulting from the exercise of this power (freedom of the *will*, "Thy *will* be done"); **volition** stresses the exercise of the will in making a choice or decision (he came of his own *volition*).
will (wil), *v.* [p.t. WOULD (wood); *archaic* 2d pers. sing., pres. indic., WILT (wilt); *archaic* 2d pers. sing., p.t., WOULDEST (wood′ist), WOULDST (woodst); *obs.* pp. WOLD (wôld), WOULD; no other forms now in use], [ME. *willen;* AS. *willan;* akin to G. *wollen*, will; IE. base **wel-*, to wish, choose, seen also in L. *volo* (for **velo*), *vult* (for **velt*), *velle*, etc. (cf. VOLITION, VOLUNTARY), *voluptas* (cf. VOLUPTUOUS)], an auxiliary used: 1. to express futurity, usually with implications of intention, determination, compulsion, obligation, or necessity: in this sense *will* is generally used instead of *shall* except in questions in the first person, singular or plural (e.g., Shall we go tomorrow?); *shall* and *will* are used interchangeably to express determination, compulsion, obligation, and necessity, but there is some tendency to prefer *shall* in all persons. 2. in formal speech, *a*) to express determination, compulsion, obligation, or necessity in the first person, and futurity in the second and third persons. *b*) in a question expecting *will* in the answer. *c*) in an indirect quotation, if *will* would be used in the direct form of the quotation. These formal conventions, however, do not reflect and have not reflected prevailing usage. See also **shall, should, would.** 3. to express willingness: as, *will* you go? 4. to express

ability, capability, or capacity: as, it *will* hold another quart. 5. to express habit or customary practice: as, she *will* talk for hours on end. 6. colloquially, to express expectation, surmise, etc.: as, that *will* be his wife with him, I suppose. ***v.t. & v.i.*** to wish; desire: as, what *will* you, master? do as you *will*.

will·a·ble (wil′ə-b'l), ***adj.*** that can be willed, wished, determined, etc.

Wil·lam·ette (wi-lam′it), ***n.*** a river in western Oregon, flowing northward into the Columbia River near Portland: length, 190 mi.

Wil·lard (wil′ẽrd), [< the surname *Willard*], a masculine name.

Wil·lard, Frances Elizabeth Caroline (wil′ẽrd), 1839–1898; American temperance leader.

Willard, Jess (jes), 1883– ; American prize fighter; world's heavyweight champion (1915–1919).

will-call (wil′kôl′), ***adj.*** designating or of that department in a large store at which a deposit may be made on a purchase to be called for when paid in full.

willed (wild), ***adj.*** having a will: used especially in hyphenated compounds, meaning *having a* (specified kind of) *will*, as in ***strong-willed***.

wil·lem·ite (wil′əm-īt′), ***n.*** [D. *willemit*, after *Willem* I, king of the Netherlands], native silicate of zinc, Zn_2SiO_4, found in massive or crystalline form in various colors from pale yellow-green to red.

Wil·lem·stad (wil′əm-stät′), ***n.*** the capital of the Netherlands Antilles, on Curaçao Island in the West Indies: pop., 47,000.

Willes·den (wilz′dən), ***n.*** a city in Middlesex, England, near London: pop., 174,000.

wil·let (wil′it), ***n.*** [*pl.* WILLETS (-its), WILLET; see PLURAL, II, D, 1], [echoic of its cry], any of a group of long-legged, snipelike wading birds of central North America.

will·ful (wil′fəl), ***adj.*** 1. said or done deliberately or intentionally. 2. following one's own will unreasoningly; obstinate; stubborn. Also spelled **wilful**. —***SYN.*** see **voluntary**.

Wil·liam (wil′yəm), [ONorm.Fr. *Willaume, Willame* (OFr. *Guillaume, Guilielm*); OHG. *Willehelm, Willahelm* (G. *Wilhelm*) < *willeo, willio*, will, what is desired + *helm, helmut*, protection], a masculine name: diminutives, *Bill, Billy, Will, Willy*; equivalents, It. *Guglielmo*, D. *Willem*, Fr. *Guillaume*, G. *Wilhelm*, Sp. *Guillermo*.

William I, 1. (*William the Conqueror*), 1027–1087; Norman duke who invaded England and defeated Harold at Battle of Hastings (1066); king of England (1066–1087). 2. Prince of Orange (*William of Nassau*), 1533–1584; leader in Dutch war of independence; assassinated: called *the Silent*. 3. (*Wilhelm Friedrich Ludwig*), 1797–1888; son of *Frederick William III;* king of Prussia (1861–1888); emperor of Germany (1871–1888).

William II, 1. (*William Rufus*), 1056–1100; son of *William the Conqueror;* king of England (1087–1100). 2. (*Friedrich Wilhelm Viktor Albert*), 1859–1941; last German emperor (1888–1918); abdicated.

William III, Prince of Orange, (*William of Nassau*), 1650–1702; king of England (1689–1702); reigned jointly with his wife, Mary II, until 1694.

William IV, 1765–1837; son of George III; king of England (1830–1837): called the *Sailor-King*.

William of Malmesbury, see **Malmesbury, William of.**

Williams, Ralph Vaughan, see **Vaughan Williams, Ralph.**

Williams, Roger, 1603?–1683; English colonist in America; founder of Rhode Island.

Williams, William, 1731–1811; American statesman; signer of the Declaration of Independence.

Williams, William Car·los (kär′lōs), 1883–1963; American writer and physician.

Wil·liams·burg (wil′yəmz-bũrg′), ***n.*** a town in southeastern Virginia: pop., 7,000: the early capital of Virginia, restored to its colonial appearance.

Wil·liams·port (wil′yəmz-pôrt′, wil′yəmz-pōrt′), ***n.*** a city in central Pennsylvania, on the Susquehanna: pop., 42,000.

Wil·liams·town (wil′yəmz-toun′), ***n.*** a town in northwestern Massachusetts: pop., 5,000.

William Tell, see **Tell, William.**

William the Conqueror, see **William I.**

wil·lies (wil′iz), ***n.pl.*** [? < *willy-nilly* as orig. referring to a state of nervous indecision], [Slang], nervousness; jitters (with *the*).

will·ing (wil′iŋ), ***adj.*** [ME.; AS. *willung* < *willian*, to will], 1. favorably disposed or consenting (to do something specified or implied); not objecting. 2. acting, giving, etc. readily and cheerfully: as, a *willing* assistant. 3. done, given, offered, etc. readily or gladly; voluntary. 4. of the power of choice; volitional.

Wil·lis (wil′is), [< the surname *Willis;* prob. < *Willson, Wilson* (< *Will's son*)], a masculine name.

Will·kie, Wendell Lewis (wil′ki), 1892–1944; American lawyer and political leader.

will-o'-the-wisp (wil′ə-*th*ə-wisp′), ***n.*** [earlier *Will with the wisp* < *Will* (personal name) + *wisp*], 1. ignis fatuus. 2. anything deceptive, elusive, or misleading.

wil·low (wil′ō), ***n.*** [ME. *wilowe, wilwe;* AS. *wilig, welig;* akin to D. *wilg;* IE. base **wel-*, to turn, twist, bend, akin to Gr. *helikē* (for **welikē*), willow (cf. HELIX); named for its pliancy], 1. any of a number of related trees with narrow leaves, tassellike spikes of flowers, and, usually, flexible twigs used in weaving baskets, etc. 2. the wood of any of these trees. 3. [Colloq.], something made of willow wood, as a baseball bat. 4. a machine with revolving spikes for cleaning cotton or wool. ***adj.*** 1. of or covered with willows. 2. made of willow wood. ***v.t.*** to clean (cotton, etc.) with a willow.

wil·low·er (wil′ō-ẽr), ***n.*** a person or machine that willows (cotton, etc.).

willow herb, any of a number of related plants with small, purplish, white, or yellow flowers, willowlike leaves, and long pods.

wil·low·ish (wil′ō-ish), ***adj.*** resembling a willow.

willow pattern, a decorative design for china, originated in England (1780) by Thomas Turner, and picturing a river, pagodas, willow trees, etc., usually in blue on a white background.

wil·low·ware (wil′ō-wâr′), ***n.*** articles of china decorated with the willow pattern.

wil·low·y (wil′ō-i, wil′ə-wi), ***adj.*** 1. covered or shaded with willows. 2. like a willow; slender, graceful, etc.

will power, strength of will, mind, or determination; self-control.

will·yard (wil′yẽrd, wul′yẽrd), ***adj.*** [Scot.], 1. willful. 2. bewildered; shy.

will·yart (wil′yẽrt, wul′yẽrt), ***adj.*** [Scot.], willyard.

wil·ly-nil·ly (wil′i-nil′i), ***adv.*** [contr. < *will I, nill I;* see WILL (wish) & NILL], whether one wishes it or not; willingly or unwillingly. ***adj.*** 1. that is or happens whether one wishes it or not. 2. loosely, indecisive; vacillating; irresolute.

Wil·ma (wil′mə), [G., var. of *Wilmot*, contr. < *Wilhelmina;* see WILLIAM], a feminine name.

Wil·ming·ton (wil′miŋ-tən), ***n.*** 1. a port in northern Delaware, on the Delaware River: pop., 96,000. 2. a city in southeastern North Carolina: pop., 44,000.

Wil·no (vil′nō; Pol. vēl′nô), ***n.*** Vilna: Polish name.

Wil·son, Mount (wil′s'n), a mountain in southwestern California: height, 5,710 ft.: site of a famous observatory.

Wilson, Woodrow, (*Thomas Woodrow Wilson*), 1856–1924; twenty-eighth president of the United States (1913–1921); received Nobel peace prize, 1919.

Wilson Dam, a dam at Muscle Shoals on the Tennessee River, in northwestern Alabama: height, 137 ft.

Wilson's thrush, a veery.

Wilson's warbler, any of a group of small, yellow, North American warblers with black crowns.

wilt (wilt), ***v.i.*** [var. of obs. *welk*, to wither; ME. *welken*, to fade, wither, dry up], 1. to become limp, as from heat or lack of water; wither; droop: said of plants. 2. to become weak or faint; lose strength; languish; hence, 3. to lose courage; quail. ***v.t.*** to cause to wilt. ***n.*** 1. a wilting or becoming wilted. 2. a state of weakness or faintness; languor. 3. *a*) a highly infectious disease of some caterpillars, in which the carcasses liquefy. *b*) any of several plant diseases caused by certain bacteria or fungi and characterized chiefly by wilting of the leaves. Also **wilt disease.**

wilt (wilt), archaic second person singular, present indicative, of **will.**

Wil·ton (wil′t'n), ***n.*** [after *Wilton*, England, where it was first made], a kind of carpet with a velvety pile of cut loops: also **Wilton carpet, Wilton rug.**

Wilts (wilts), ***n.*** Wiltshire.

Wilt·shire (wilt′shir; *for 2, also* wilt′shẽr), ***n.*** 1. a county of southern England: pop., 423,000; county seat, Salisbury: also **Wilts.** 2. any of an old breed of pure-white sheep originating in England and characterized by a long head and long curved horns.

wi·ly (wī′li), ***adj.*** [WILIER (-li-ẽr), WILIEST (-li-ist)], full of wiles; crafty; sly. —***SYN.*** see **sly.**

wim·ble (wim′b'l), ***n.*** [ME. *wimbel;* OFr. *wimble;* MD. *wimmel*, an auger, whence also OFr. *guimbel;* cf. GIMLET], 1. any of various tools for boring, as a gimlet, auger, etc. 2. a device for removing the rubble from a hole bored in mining. ***v.t.*** [WIMBLED (-b'ld), WIMBLING], to bore with a wimble.

Wim·ble·don (wim′b'l-dən), ***n.*** a city in Surrey, England, near London: pop., 58,000: scene of international tennis matches.

wim·ple (wim′p'l), ***n.*** [ME. & AS. *wimpel;* akin to G. *wimpel*, pennon; IE. base **weip-, *weib*, to turn, swing, as also in Eng. *wipe, whip*], 1. a woman's head covering for outdoor protection, consisting of a cloth arranged about the head, cheeks, chin, and neck, leaving only the face exposed: it is now worn only by certain orders of nuns. 2. [Scot.], *a*) a fold or plait. *b*) a winding;

turn; curve. *c*) a ripple. ***v.t.*** [WIMPLED (-p'ld), WIMPLING], 1. to cover or clothe with or as with a wimple. 2. to lay in folds. 3. to cause to ripple or undulate, as the surface of a lake ***v.i.*** 1. to lie in folds. 2. to ripple 3. [Scot.], to meander, as a brook.

win (wn), ***v.i.*** [WON (wun) or *obs.* WAN (wan), WON, WINNING], ME. *winnen;* AS. *winnan,* to fight, endure, struggle; akin to G. *winnen,* to struggle, contend; IE. base **wen-*, to strive, strive for, as also in L. *venus,* love, Eng. *wish;* cf. WEEN], 1. to gain a victory; be victorious; triumph; succeed (sometimes with *out*). 2. to reach or come into a specified state or condition; get (with *across, away, back, down, off, over, through,* etc., or with certain adverbs): as, he *won* loose from the crowd. ***v.t.*** 1. to get by effort, labor, struggle, etc.; specifically, *a*) to gain; acquire: as, he *won* distinctions. *b*) to make, achieve, or cause to prevail: as, you've *won* your point. *c*) to gain in competition, as a prize or award. *d*) to obtain or earn (a livelihood, security, etc.). 2. to be successful or victorious in (a contest, game, dispute, etc.). 3. to get to, usually with effort; reach: as, they *won* the camp by noon. 4. to prevail upon; influence; persuade (also with *over*): as, I *won* him over to my side. 5. *a*) to gain the sympathy, favor, affection, or love of: as, he *won* a supporter, friend, etc. *b*) to gain (one's sympathy, affection, love, etc.). 6. to persuade to marry one. 7. *a*) to extract (metal, minerals, etc.) from ore. *b*) to obtain (coal, ore, etc.) by mining. *c*) to prepare (a vein, shaft, etc.) for mining. ***n.*** [Colloq.], 1. an act of winning; victory, as in a contest. 2. winnings or profit.

wince (wins), ***v.i.*** [WINCED (winst), WINCING], [ME. *wincen, winchen, wenchen;* MHG. *wenken,* to flinch; OHG. **wankjan* < *wankon,* to totter, turn; cf. WENCH], to shrink or draw back suddenly, as in pain; flinch. ***n.*** the act or an instance of wincing. —***SYN.*** see **recoil.**

wince (wins), ***n.*** [var. of *winch*], a reel or roller used between dyeing vats, etc. to facilitate the transfer of long pieces of cloth.

winch (winch), ***n.*** [ME. *winche;* AS. *wince;* IE. **we-n-g*, to be curved, bowed, as also in Eng. *wink*], 1. a crank with a handle for transmitting motion, as to a grindstone. 2. any of various devices operated by turning a crank; specifically, a type of windlass for hoisting or hauling, having a crank connected by gears to a horizontal drum around which the rope or chain is wound. ***v.t.*** to hoist or haul with or as with a winch.

WINCH

winch (winch), ***v.i. & n.*** [Obs. or Dial.], wince (flinch).

Win·ches·ter (win'ches'tẽr, win'chis-tẽr), ***n.*** a city in southern England: pop., 24,000: capital of ancient Wessex and of Anglo-Saxon England.

Win·ches·ter (rifle) (win'ches'tẽr, win'chis-tẽr), [after Oliver F. *Winchester,* the manufacturer], a type of repeating rifle with a tubular magazine set horizontally under the barrel: a trade-mark.

Winck·el·mann, Jo·hann Jo·a·chim (yō'hän yō'ä-khim viŋ'kəl-män'), 1717–1768; German archaeologist and scholar in classic art.

wind (wīnd), ***v.t.*** [WOUND (wound) or *rarely* WINDED (-id), WINDING], [ME. *winden;* AS. *windan;* akin to G. *winden;* IE. base **wendh-*, to turn, wind, twist, as also in Arm. *gind,* a ring; cf. WEND, WANDER], 1. to turn; make revolve: as, *wind* the crank. 2. to turn or coil (something) into a ball or around something else so as to encircle it closely; twine; wreathe: as, *wind* the bandage around your finger. 3. to wrap or cover by encircling with something turned in the manner of a coil; entwine: as, *wind* the spool with thread. 4. to make (one's way) in a winding or twisting course. 5. to cause to move in a winding or twisting course. 6. to introduce deviously; insinuate: as, he *wound* his criticism into his argument. 7. to hoist or haul by or as by winding rope on a winch (often with *up*). 8. to tighten the operating spring of (a clock, etc.) by turning a stem or the like (often with *up*). ***v.i.*** 1. to move, go, or extend in a curving, zigzagging, or sinuous manner; meander. 2. to double on one's track, so as to throw off pursuers. 3. to take a circuitous, devious, or subtle course in behavior, argument, etc. 4. to insinuate oneself. 5. to coil, twine, or spiral (*about* or *around* something). 6. to warp or twist: said of wood. 7. to walk with a defective gait in which one leg tends to twist around the other: said of a horse. 8. to undergo winding: as, this clock *winds* easily. ***n.*** [ME. *winde* (in comp.) < the *v.*], 1. a winding. 2. a single turn of something wound. 3. a turn; twist; bend; curve.

wind off, to unwind or remove by unwinding.

wind up, 1. to wind or roll into a ball, etc. 2. to conclude; end; finish; settle. 3. to bring into a condition of high tension; excite greatly. 4. in *baseball,* to swing the arm preparatory to pitching.

wind (wind; *for n., also poetic* wīnd), ***n.*** [ME.; AS.; akin to G. *wind;* IE. **wē-ntos,* as seen also in L. *ventus,* wind < base **we-*, to blow; cf. VENTILATE, WEATHER], 1. air in motion; especially, any noticeable natural movement of air parallel to the earth's surface. 2. a strong, fast-moving, or destructive natural current of air; gale; storm. 3. the direction from which a wind blows: now chiefly in *the four winds,* with reference to the cardinal points of the compass. 4. a natural current of air regarded as a bearer of odors or scents, as in hunting: as, the dogs are keeping the *wind;* hence, 5. figuratively, air regarded as bearing information, indicating trends, etc.; intimation; hint: as, get *wind* of something, what's in the *wind?* 6. air artificially put in motion, as by an air pump or fan. 7. breath or the power of breathing: as, he got the *wind* knocked out of him. 8. *a*) idle or empty talk; nonsense. *b*) bragging; pomposity; conceit. 9. gas in the stomach or intestines; flatulence. 10. *pl.* the wind instruments of an orchestra. 11. [Boxing Slang], the solar plexus, where a blow may stop the breath temporarily by paralyzing the diaphragm. ***v.t.*** 1. to expose to the wind or air, as for drying; air. 2. to get or follow the scent of; scent. 3. to cause to be out of breath: as, the run *winded* him. 4. to rest (a horse, etc.) so as to allow recovery of breath.

between wind and water, 1. close to the water line of a ship. 2. in a dangerous spot.

break wind, to expel gas from the bowels.

down the wind, in the same direction as the wind.

get (or **have**) **wind of,** to receive (or have) information concerning; hear (or know) of.

how the wind blows (or **lies**), what the trend of affairs, public opinion, etc. is.

in the teeth of the wind, straight against the wind: also **in the wind's eye.**

in the wind, happening or about to happen.

into the wind, in the direction from which the wind is blowing.

off the wind, with the wind coming from behind.

on the wind, approximately in the direction from which the wind is blowing.

sail close to the wind, 1. to sail as nearly as possible straight against the wind. 2. to be economical in one's affairs. 3. to border on indecency, foolhardiness, etc.

take the wind out of one's sails, to remove one's advantage, nullify one's argument, etc. suddenly or unexpectedly.

up the wind, in a direction opposite to that of the wind.

SYN.—**wind** is the general term for any natural movement of air, whether of high or low velocity or great or little force; **breeze** is popularly applied to a light, fresh wind and meteorologically, to a wind having a velocity of from 4 to 31 miles an hour; **gale** is popularly applied to strong, somewhat violent wind and meteorologically, to a wind having a velocity of from 32 to 63 miles an hour; **gust** and **blast** apply to sudden, brief winds, **gust** suggesting a light puff, and **blast** a driving rush, of air; **zephyr** is a poetic term for a soft, gentle breeze.

wind (wīnd, wind), ***v.t.*** [WOUND (wound) or *rarely* WINDED (-id), WINDING], [Early Mod. Eng. < *wind, n.*], 1. to blow (a horn, etc.). 2. to sound (a signal, etc.), as on a horn.

wind·age (win'dij), ***n.*** [see -AGE], 1. the disturbance of air around a moving projectile. 2. deflection of a projectile caused by the wind, or the degree of this. 3. the degree of deflection of the wind gauge necessary in firing a gun to compensate for displacement by the wind. 4. the space between the inside wall of the barrel of a firearm and its projectile, to allow for the expansion of gas in firing: it is measured by the difference in diameters of the bore and projectile. 5. the part of a ship's surface exposed to the wind.

wind·bag (wind'bag'), ***n.*** [Colloq.], a person who talks much and pretentiously but says little of importance.

wind-blown (wind'blōn'), ***adj.*** 1. blown by the wind. 2. twisted in growth by the prevailing wind: said of a tree. 3. designating or of a woman's coiffure in which the hair is bobbed and brushed forward.

wind-borne (wind'bôrn', wind'bōrn'), ***adj.*** transported by the wind, as certain pollen.

wind·break (wind'brāk'), ***n.*** a hedge, fence, or row of trees that serves as a protection from wind.

wind·break·er (wind'brāk'ẽr), ***n.*** a warm sports jacket of leather, wool, etc., having a closefitting elastic waistband and cuffs: a trade-mark (**Windbreaker**).

wind-bro·ken (wind'brō'k'n), ***adj.*** having the heaves, a disease characterized by difficulty in breathing: said of a horse.

wind cone, a wind sock.

wind·ed (win'did), ***adj.*** out of breath.

wind·er (win'dẽr), ***n.*** 1. a person who winds material or operates a winding machine in textile and other industries. 2. an apparatus for winding or on which winding is done. 3. a key, knob, etc. for winding a spring-operated mechanism. 4. any of the steps in a winding staircase. 5. a plant that winds or twines.

Win·der·mere, Lake (win'dẽr-mêr'), a lake in northwestern England, the largest lake in England: length, 10 1/2 mi.

wind·fall (wind'fôl'), ***n.*** 1. something blown down by

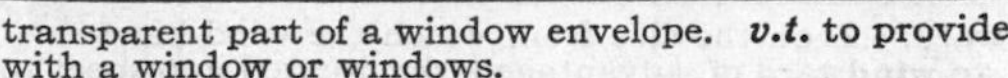

the wind, as fruit from a tree. 2. any unexpected financial gain or stroke of luck.

wind·flaw (wind'flô'), *n.* a gust of wind; flaw.

wind·flow·er (wind'flou'ẽr), *n.* any of a number of related plants with white, pink, red, or purplish, cup-shaped flowers; anemone.

wind·gall (wind'gôl'), *n.* [*wind* + *gall*: from the earlier notion that it contained wind], a soft swelling on the fetlock joint of a horse.

wind gap, a notch in a mountain ridge, not deep enough to serve as the bed of a stream.

wind gauge, 1. an instrument for measuring wind velocity; anemometer. 2. a graduated attachment on a gunsight for indicating the degree of deflection necessary to counteract windage.

Wind·hoek (vint'hook), *n.* the capital of South West Africa: pop., 10,600.

wind·hov·er (wind'huv'ẽr), *n.* a kestrel: so called from its ability to hover in the air.

wind·i·ly (win'd'l-i), *adv.* in a windy manner.

wind·i·ness (win'di-nis), *n.* the quality or condition of being windy.

wind·ing (win'diŋ), *n.* 1. the action or effect of a person or thing that winds; specifically, *a)* a sinuous path or course. *b)* devious methods, actions, etc. *c)* a coiling, spiraling, or twining. *d)* a single turn. 2. something that winds; specifically, *a)* wire, thread, etc. wound around something: as, the *winding* on an electric coil. *b)* a single turn of this. *c)* the manner in which this is wound: as, a shunt *winding.* 3. the condition or fact of being warped or twisted: as, a board in *winding.* 4. a defective gait of horses in which one leg tends to twist around the other. *adj.* that winds, turns, coils, etc.

winding sheet, a cloth in which the body of a dead person is wrapped for burial; shroud.

wind instrument (wind), a musical instrument played by blowing air through it, especially a portable one played with the breath, as a *wood wind* (flute, oboe, bassoon, clarinet, etc.) or a *brass wind* (trumpet, trombone, horn, tuba, etc.).

wind·jam·mer (wind'jam'ẽr), *n.* 1. in *nautical usage, a)* a sailing ship: so called originally in contempt by seamen on early steamships. *b)* a crew member of such a ship. 2. [Slang], a talkative person.

wind·lass (wind'ləs), *n.* [altered, after obs. *windle,* a wheel, winder (ME. *windel,* in comp. < *winden,* to wind) < ME. *windas,* windlass; ON. *vindass* < *vinda,* to wind + *ass,* a beam], an apparatus operated by hand or machine, for hauling or hoisting, consisting of a drum or cylinder upon which is wound the rope, cable, or chain which is attached to the object to be lifted. *v.t. & v.i.* to hoist or haul with a windlass.

WINDLASS

win·dle·straw (win'd'l-strô'), *n.* [< AS. *windelstreaw* (via Scot. dial.); *windel,* a bundle (< *windan,* to wind; cf. WIND) + *streaw,* straw], [Scot. or Dial.], 1. a dried stalk of grass, used in plaiting, etc. 2. a slender or weak person or thing.

wind·mill (wind'mil'), *n.* 1. a mill operated by the wind's rotation of large, oblique sails or vanes radiating from a shaft: it is used as a cheap source of power for grinding grain, pumping water, etc. 2. anything like a windmill, as a propellerlike toy revolved by wind. **fight** (**or tilt at**) **windmills,** to fight imaginary evils or opponents: from Don Quixote's tilting at windmills under the delusion that they were giants.

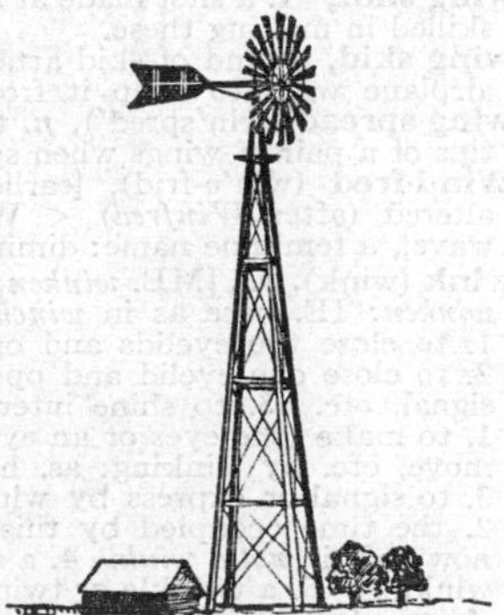

WINDMILL

win·dow (win'dō), *n.* [ME. *windoge;* ON. *vindauga,* a window, lit., wind eye < *vindr,* wind + *auga,* an eye; cf. WIND, *n.* & EYE], 1. an opening in a building, vehicle, ship, etc. for admitting light and air, usually having a pane or panes of glass, etc. set in a frame or sash that is generally movable for opening or shutting it. 2. a windowpane: as, he broke the *window.* 3. a window with its sash and casement. 4. any opening resembling a window in shape, position, or use, as the transparent part of a window envelope. *v.t.* to provide with a window or windows.

window box, 1. a long, narrow box on or outside a window ledge, for growing plants. 2. any of the grooves along the sides of a window frame for containing the weights that counterbalance the sash.

window dressing, 1. the arrangement or display of goods and trimmings in a store window to attract customers; hence, 2. statements or actions intended to give a misleadingly favorable impression.

window envelope, an envelope having a transparent part through which the address on the enclosed matter can be seen.

win·dow·pane (win'dō-pān'), *n.* a pane of glass in a window.

window seat, a long seat built in beneath a window or windows and usually containing storage space.

window shade, a shade for a window, especially one consisting of a piece of stiffened cloth or heavy paper on a spring roller, with a pull to lower and raise it.

win·dow-shop (win'dō-shop'), *v.i.* [WINDOW-SHOPPED (-shopt'), WINDOW-SHOPPING], to look at displays of goods in store windows without entering the stores to buy.

wind·pipe (wind'pīp'), *n.* the trachea.

wind-pol·li·nat·ed (wind'pol'ə-nāt'id), *adj.* in *botany,* fertilized by pollen carried by the wind.

Wind River Range, a mountain range in western Wyoming: highest point, Gannett Peak, 13,785 ft.

wind rose, a diagram that shows for a particular place the frequency and intensity of wind from different directions.

wind·row (wind'rō', win'rō'), *n.* 1. a row of hay raked together to dry before being made into heaps or cocks. 2. any similar row, as of grain. 3. a row of dry leaves, dust, etc. that has been swept together by the wind. 4. a deep furrow for planting cuttings of sugar cane. *v.t.* 1. to rake, sweep, etc. into a windrow or windrows. 2. to plant (sugar-cane cuttings) in windrows.

wind scale, a scale used in meteorology to designate relative wind intensities, as the Beaufort scale in which wind velocities are graded from 0 to 12.

wind shake, a condition of timber in which there is separation of the concentric rings, supposedly due to strain from strong winds during growth.

wind-shak·en (wind'shāk'ən), *adj.* 1. shaken by the wind. 2. affected by wind shake.

wind·shield (wind'shēld'), *n.* in automobiles, trucks, speedboats, motorcycles, etc., a transparent screen in front, as of glass, that protects the occupant or occupants from wind, etc. while riding.

wind sleeve, a wind sock.

wind sock, a long, cone-shaped cloth bag attached to the top of a mast, as at an airfield, to show the direction of the wind: also called *wind cone, wind sleeve.*

Wind·sor (win'zẽr), *n.* 1. a city in Berkshire, England, on the Thames: pop., 29,000: site of Windsor Castle: officially called *New Windsor.* 2. a city in Ontario, Canada, across the Detroit River from Detroit: pop., 120,000.

Wind·sor (win'zẽr), *n.* the ruling family of England since 1917, when the name was officially changed from *Saxe-Coburg and Gotha.*

Windsor, Duke of, (*Edward Albert*), 1894– ; son of George V; as Edward VIII, king of England (1936); abdicated.

Windsor Castle, a residence of English sovereigns since the time of William the Conqueror.

Windsor chair, a style of wooden chair, especially popular in 18th-century England and America, with spreading legs, spindle back, and usually a saddle seat.

Windsor tie, a wide necktie of silk cut on the bias, tied in a double bow.

wind·storm (wind'stôrm'), *n.* a storm with a strong wind but little or no rain.

wind·suck·er (wind'suk'ẽr), *n.* a horse given to wind sucking.

wind sucking, the habit that some horses have of swallowing air, as in crib biting.

WINDSOR CHAIR

wind-swept (wind'swept'), *adj.* swept by or exposed to winds.

wind·tight (wind'tīt'), *adj.* airtight.

wind tunnel, a tunnellike chamber through which air is forced and in which scale models of airplanes, etc. are tested to determine the effects of wind pressure.

wind·up (wind'up'), *n.* 1. a winding up; conclusion; close; end. 2. in *baseball,* the loosening movements of the arm preparatory to pitching the ball.

wind·ward (wind'wẽrd; *in nautical usage,* win'dẽrd), *n.* the direction or side from which the wind blows: opposed to *leeward.* *adv.* in the direction from which the wind blows; toward the wind. *adj.* 1. moving wind-

ward. 2. on the side from which the wind blows.
to windward of, advantageously situated in respect to.
Windward Islands, 1. the southern group of islands in the Lesser Antilles, in the West Indies: all except Martinique belong to Great Britain: see **West Indies,** map. 2. a British possession in the West Indies, comprising the colonies of St. Lucia, St. Vincent, and Grenada in the Windward Islands and Dominica in the Leeward Islands: area, 821 sq. mi.; pop., 260,000; capital, St. George's.
Windward Passage, the strait between Cuba and Hispaniola, in the West Indies.
wind·y (win′di), ***adj.*** [WINDIER (-di-ẽr), WINDIEST (-di-ist)], 1. characterized or accompanied by wind: as, a *windy* day. 2. exposed to wind: as, a *windy* city. 3. like wind; stormy, changeable, gusty, etc.: as, *windy* anger. 4. produced by wind or compressed air: as, a *windy* tone. 5. airy; intangible. 6. that talks much and says little; verbose. 7. boastful; pompous. 8. *a)* causing or apt to cause gas in the stomach or intestines. *b)* caused by or troubled with flatulence; flatulent.
wine (wīn), ***n.*** [ME. & AS. *win;* L. *vinum,* wine; cf. VINE], 1. the fermented juice of grapes, used as an alcoholic beverage and in cooking, religious ceremonies, etc.: wines vary as to color (red or white) and sugar content (sweet or dry), may be effervescent (sparkling) or non-effervescent (still), and are sometimes strengthened with additional alcohol (fortified). 2. the fermented juice of other fruits or plants, used as a beverage: as, dandelion *wine.* 3. intoxication, as from wine. 4. [British], a wine party. 5. a dark, purplish red resembling the color of red wines. 6. in *pharmacy,* a medicinal solution in which wine is the solvent. ***v.t.*** [WINED (wīnd), WINING], to entertain with wine. ***v.i.*** to drink wine.
new wine in old bottles, something new that is too potent to be confined in old forms: Matt. 9:17.
wine·bib·ber (wīn′bib′ẽr), ***n.*** a person who drinks a great deal of wine; drunkard.
wine·bib·bing (wīn′bib′iŋ), ***adj.*** that drinks much wine. ***n.*** the drinking of much wine.
wine cellar, 1. a cellar where wine is stored; hence, 2. a stock of wine.
wine-col·ored (wīn′kul′ẽrd), ***adj.*** having the color of red wine; dark purplish-red.
wine gallon, an old English gallon of 231 cu. in., now the standard gallon in the United States: see **gallon.**
wine·glass (wīn′glas′, wīn′gläs′), ***n.*** a small glass for drinking wine.
wine·glass·ful (wīn′glas-fool′, wīn′gläs-fool′), ***n.*** [*pl.* WINEGLASSFULS (-foolz′)], as much as a wineglass will hold, ordinarily two fluid ounces.
wine·grow·er (wīn′grō′ẽr), ***n.*** a person who grows grapes and makes wine from them.
wine·grow·ing (wīn′grō′iŋ), ***n.*** the art or process of cultivating grapes and making wine from them.
wine measure, a former English system of measure for wine, etc., in which the gallon equaled 231 cu. in.
wine palm, a palm from the sap of which wine is made.
wine press, a vat in which grapes are trodden, or a machine for pressing them, in order to extract the juice for making wine.
win·er·y (wīn′ẽr-i), ***n.*** [*pl.* WINERIES (-iz)], an establishment where wine is made.
Wine·sap (wīn′sap′), ***n.*** a dark-red, medium-sized variety of winter apple grown in the United States.
wine·skin (wīn′skin′), ***n.*** in Eastern countries, a large bag for holding wine, made of the skin of an animal.
Win·fred (win′frid), [AS. *Winfrith* < *wine,* friend + *frithu,* peace], a masculine name.
wing (wiŋ), ***n.*** [ME. *winge, weng* < ON. *vaengir,* pl. of *vaengr;* the word replaced AS. *fethra,* wings, pl. of *fether* (cf. FEATHER)], 1. either of the two forelimbs of a bird, developed for flying, the lifting surface being formed by overlapping feathers. 2. *a)* either of the two forelimbs of a domesticated fowl, not sufficiently developed for use in flying. *b)* such a forelimb used as food: as, a chicken *wing.* 3. either of the paired organs of flight of a bat, the lifting surface of which is formed of membranous skin connecting the long, modified digits of the forelimbs. 4. either of the paired organs of flight of insects, similar in appearance and use but structurally unrelated to the wings of vertebrates. 5. either of a pair of similar structures attributed to angels, demons, etc. 6. any of various winglike structures of certain animals, as of the flying fish, flying squirrel, etc. 7. something used as a wing or in the manner of a wing; specifically, *a)* one of the main supporting structures of an airplane; a plane: see **airplane,** illus. *b)* a float or other device attached to the shoulder: as, water *wings.* 8. something resembling a wing in position or in relation to the main part; specifically, *a)* a part or extension of a building architecturally subordinate to the main part; hence, *b)* a part of a large building of any shape, regarded as a separate section according to its use or to its location with relation to a central point: as, a surgical *wing,* east *wing.* *c)* an outlying area, as of an estate. *d)* either of two side extensions of the back of a wing chair. *e)* either part of a double door, screen, etc. *f)* in *anatomy,* an ala. *g)* in *botany,* either lateral petal of a papilionaceous flower; also, a winglike extension on some stems and leafstalks. *h)* in the *theater,* any of the sidepieces in scenery; also, either side of the stage out of sight of the audience. 9. a group of persons or things having a winglike relation to another; specifically, *a)* the right or left section of an army, fleet, etc. *b)* a group of political party members, legislators, etc. representing some specified shade of opinion or political doctrine: as, a right *wing,* agrarian *wing.* *c)* an organization affiliated with or subsidiary to a parent organization. *d)* a position or player on a team to the right or left of the center position or player. 10. *a)* a unit of military aircraft and their personnel, larger than a group and smaller than a command. *b)* *pl.* the insignia worn by pilots and crew members of military aircraft. 11. *a)* a means of flying or traveling. *b)* a flying or manner of flying; flight. 12. anything represented as flying or soaring, or as carrying one to soaring heights: as, on *wings* of song. 13. something that beats the air, as a vane. 14. either of the longer sides of an outwork in a fortification, extending back to the main work. 15. [Colloq.], an arm of a human being: a humorous usage. ***v.t.*** 1. to fly across, over, through, etc. 2. to provide with wings; hence, 3. to enable to fly or hasten; send flying; speed: as, he *winged* his words. 4. to feather (an arrow). 5. to do, make, etc. by or as by means of wings. 6. to transport by or as by flight. 7. to furnish with side parts, as a building. 8. to wound (a bird) in the wing or (a person) in the arm, shoulder, etc. ***v.i.*** to fly.
on the wing, in flight; continually moving about.
take wing, to take flight; fly away.
under the wing of, under the protection, patronage, etc. of.
wing and wing, in *nautical usage,* with sails extended on either side by booms.
wing back formation, in *football,* either of two offensive formations, the *single wing back formation,* in which one of the backs is placed behind and usually slightly beyond the end on his side, or the *double wing back formation,* in which both backs are so placed.
wing bow (bō), a mark of color on the bend of the wing of a domesticated fowl.
wing chair, an upholstered armchair with a high back from each side of which extend high sides, or wings, to give additional head rest and protection from drafts.
wing cover (or **case**), an elytron.
wing covert, any of the small feathers covering the bases of the wing quills.
winged (wiŋd; *for 2 & 3, often poetic* wiŋ′id), ***adj.*** 1. having wings or winglike parts. 2. moving on or as if on wings; hence, 3. *a)* lofty; sublime. *b)* swift; rapid. 4. *a)* wounded in the wing. *b)* [Colloq.], wounded in an arm or, sometimes, in any nonvital part. 5. swarming with flying creatures.
wing-foot·ed (wiŋ′foot′id), ***adj.*** 1. having winged feet; hence, 2. swift.
wing·less (wiŋ′lis), ***adj.*** having no wings or very rudimentary ones.
wing·let (wiŋ′lit), ***n.*** 1. a small wing. 2. the bastard wing of a bird; alula.
wing loading, the total weight of a loaded airplane, divided by the area of the supporting surfaces, exclusive of stabilizer and elevators: also **wing load.**
wing shot, 1. a shot made at a flying bird. 2. a person skilled in making these.
wing skid, a kind of skid attached under the tip of an airplane wing to keep it from touching the ground.
wing·spread (wiŋ′spred′), ***n.*** the distance between the tips of a pair of wings when spread.
Win·i·fred (win′ə-frid), [earlier *Winefred, Wynifreed,* altered (after *Winfred*) < W. *Gwenfrewi,* lit., white wave], a feminine name: diminutive, *Winnie.*
wink (wiŋk), ***v.i.*** [ME. *winken;* AS. *wincian;* akin to G. *winken;* IE. base as in *winch;* basic sense "to nod"], 1. to close the eyelids and open them again quickly. 2. to close one eyelid and open it again quickly, as a signal, etc. 3. to shine intermittently; twinkle. ***v.t.*** 1. to make (the eyes or an eye) wink. 2. to move, remove, etc. by winking: as, he *winked* back his tears. 3. to signal or express by winking. ***n.*** 1. a winking. 2. the time occupied by this; an instant. 3. a nap: now only in *not a wink.* 4. a signal, hint, etc. given by winking. 5. a twinkle or twinkling.
forty winks, [Colloq.], a short nap.
wink at, to pretend not to see, as in connivance.
***SYN.*—wink** usually implies a deliberate movement in the quick closing and opening of one or both eyelids one or more times (he *winked* at her knowingly); **blink** implies a rapid series of such movements, usually performed involuntarily and with the eyes half-shut (to *blink* in the harsh sunlight).
Win·kel·ried, Arnold von (ar′nôlt fôn viŋ′kəl-rēt′), died c. 1386; Swiss patriot.
wink·er (wiŋk′ẽr), ***n.*** 1. a person or thing that winks. 2. a blinder for a horse. 3. [Colloq.], an eyelash or eye.
win·kle (wiŋ′k'l), ***n.*** [shortened < *periwinkle*], any of various edible sea snails; a periwinkle.
Win·ne·ba·go (win′ə-bā′gō), ***n.*** [*pl.* WINNEBAGOS, WIN-

NEBAGOES (-gōz)], a member of a tribe of Siouan Indians that lived in eastern Wisconsin, where some still survive: others now live in Nebraska.

Winnebago, Lake, a lake in eastern Wisconsin: length, 30 mi.

Win·ne·pe·sau·kee, Lake (win'ə-pə-sô'ki), a lake in central New Hampshire: length, 25 mi.

win·ner (win'ẽr), ***n.*** a person or thing that wins.

win·ning (win'iŋ), ***adj.*** 1. that wins; victorious. 2. attractive; charming. ***n.*** 1. the action of a person that wins; a victory. 2. ***pl.*** something won, especially money. 3. a shaft, bed, etc. in a coal mine, opened or ready for mining.

winning gallery, in *court tennis*, a netted opening opposite the spectator's gallery: a ball played into it is considered winning.

winning opening, in *court tennis*, any of various openings, as the spectator's gallery, winning gallery, etc.: a ball played into any of these is considered winning.

winning post, the post marking the end of a racecourse.

Win·ni·peg (win'ə-peg'), ***n.*** 1. the capital of Manitoba, Canada, on the Red River: pop., 255,000 (with suburbs, 409,000). 2. a large lake in southern Manitoba: area, 8,555 sq. mi. 3. a river in southern Canada, flowing from the Lake of the Woods to Lake Winnipeg: length, 140 mi.

Win·ni·pe·go·sis, Lake (win'i-pə-gō'sis), a lake in southwestern Manitoba, Canada: area, 2,000 sq. mi.

win·now (win'ō), ***v.t.*** [ME. *winewen, windewen;* AS. *windwian, wyndwian,* to winnow < *wind,* wind], 1. to blow the chaff from (grain) by wind or a forced current of air. 2. to blow off (chaff) in this manner; hence, 3. to blow away; scatter: as, the wind *winnowed* the leaves. 4. to analyze or examine carefully in order to separate the various elements; sift; hence, 5. *a)* to separate out or eliminate (the worthless part or parts of something). *b)* to extract or select (the good part or parts of something). 6. *a)* to fan with or as with the wings. *b)* to flap (the wings). *c)* to make (one's or its way) by or as by flying. ***v.i.*** 1. to winnow grain. 2. to fly with or as with wings. ***n.*** 1. a winnowing. 2. an apparatus for winnowing.

win·now·er (win'ō-ẽr, win'ə-wẽr), ***n.*** 1. a person who winnows. 2. a machine for winnowing grain.

Wi·no·na (wi-nō'nə), ***n.*** a city in southeastern Minnesota, on the Mississippi River: pop., 25,000.

Wins·low, Edward (winz'lō), 1595–1655; one of the founders and a governor of Plymouth colony.

win·some (win'səm), ***adj.*** [ME. *winsum;* AS. *wynsum,* pleasant, delightful < *wynn,* delight, joy + *-sum* (cf. -SOME)], attractive in appearance, character, manner, etc.; charming; engaging.

Win·ston-Sa·lem (win'st'n-sā'ləm), ***n.*** a city in north central North Carolina: tobacco center: pop., 111,000.

win·ter (win'tẽr), ***n.*** [ME.; AS.; akin to G.; prob. IE. base **wed-*, to make wet, as also in Eng. *water, wet,* etc.], 1. the coldest season of the year, regarded in the North Temperate Zone as including the months of December, January, and February: in the astronomical year, that period between the winter solstice and the vernal equinox. 2. a year as reckoned by this season: as, a man of eighty *winters.* 3. any period regarded, like winter, as a time of decline, dreariness, adversity, etc. ***adj.*** 1. of or characteristic of the winter. 2. done, used, played, etc. during the winter: as, *winter* sports. 3. that will keep during the winter: as, *winter* apples. 4. planted in the fall to be harvested in the spring: as, *winter* wheat. ***v.i.*** to pass the winter: as, we *winter* in Florida. ***v.t.*** to keep or maintain during the winter.

winter aconite, a small perennial herb having bright-yellow flowers that blossom early in spring.

win·ter·ber·ry (win'tẽr-ber'i), ***n.*** [*pl.* WINTERBERRIES (-iz)], any of a number of related evergreen trees or shrubs with glossy leaves and bright-red berries; holly.

win·ter·bourne (win'tẽr-bôrn', win'tẽr-bōrn', win'tẽr-boorn'), ***n.*** [AS. *winter burna;* cf. WINTER & BURN, ***n.***], a stream that flows only or principally in winter.

win·ter·feed (win'tẽr-fēd'), ***v.t.*** [WINTERFED (-fed'), WINTERFEEDING], to feed (animals) during the winter.

win·ter·green (win'tẽr-grēn'), ***n.*** [after G. *wintergrün,* D. *wintergroen:* so named because evergreen], 1. a plant with egg-shaped leaves, white bell-shaped flowers, and red berries; checkerberry. 2. an oil (*oil of wintergreen*) made from the leaves of this plant and used as a flavor and in medicine. 3. its flavor or anything flavored with it. 4. any of a number of related plants with white, greenish, or purple flowers on slender stalks; shinleaf.

win·ter·ize (win'tẽr-īz'), ***v.t.*** [WINTERIZED (-īzd'), WINTERIZING], to put into condition for or equip for winter, as an automotive vehicle.

win·ter·kill (win'tẽr-kil'), ***v.t. & v.i.*** to kill or die by exposure to winter cold: said of plants.

win·ter·ly (win'tẽr-li), ***adj.*** wintry.

winter melon, 1. a large, mildly scented muskmelon that keeps through the cold season. 2. the plant it grows on.

winter solstice, the time in the Northern Hemisphere when the sun is farthest south of the equator; December 21 or 22.

win·ter·tide (win'tẽr-tīd'), ***n.*** [ME. *wintertid*], [Archaic or Poetic], wintertime.

win·ter·time (win'tẽr-tīm'), ***n.*** the season of winter.

win·ter·y (win'tẽr-i, win'tri), ***adj.*** wintry.

Win·throp, John (win'thrəp), 1. 1588–1649; English colonist in America; first governor of Massachusetts Bay colony. 2. 1606–1676; son of the above; governor of Connecticut colony (1635; 1657; 1659–1676).

win·tri·ly (win'trə-li), ***adv.*** in a wintry manner.

win·tri·ness (win'tri-nis), ***n.*** the quality of being wintry.

win·try (win'tri), ***adj.*** [WINTRIER (-tri-ẽr), WINTRIEST (-tri-ist)], of or like winter; cold, snowy, etc.: also used figuratively.

win·y (wīn'i), ***adj.*** like wine in taste, smell, color, etc.

winze (winz), ***n.*** [prob. < ***winds,*** pl. of ***wind,*** winder, windlass], a shaft or inclined passage from one level to another in a mine.

wipe (wīp), ***v.t.*** [WIPED (wīpt), WIPING], [ME. ***wipen;*** AS. ***wipian;*** akin to OHG. ***wīfan,*** to wind around; IE. base **weip-*, **weib-*, to turn, twist, etc., turning motion, seen also in L. *vibrare* (cf. VIBRATE); cf. WIMPLE], 1. to rub or pass over with a cloth, mop, etc., as for cleaning or drying. 2. to clean or dry in this manner: as, ***wipe*** the dishes. 3. to rub or pass (a cloth, etc.) over something. 4. to apply by wiping: as, ***wipe*** the oil into the surface. 5. to remove by or as by wiping (with ***away, off, up, out***). 6. to form (a joint in lead pipe) by applying liquid solder and rubbing with a leather pad, greased cloth, etc. ***n.*** 1. a wiping. 2. a blow; swipe. 3. a wiper (sense 4). 4. [Dial. or Colloq.], a gibe; jeer. 5. [Slang], a handkerchief.

wipe out, 1. to remove; erase; hence, 2. to kill off.

wip·er (wīp'ẽr), ***n.*** 1. a person or thing that wipes. 2. something used for wiping, as a towel. 3. a moving electrical contact, as in a rheostat. 4. a projecting piece on a rotating or rocking part, which raises and lowers or trips another, usually reciprocating, part; cam; eccentric. 5. [Slang], a handkerchief.

wire (wīr), ***n.*** [ME. & AS. ***wir;*** akin to LG. ***wīr;*** IE. base **wei-*, to bend, turn, as also in L. *vitilis,* braided], 1. metal that has been drawn into a very long, thin thread or rod, usually circular in cross section. 2. a length of this, used for various purposes such as conducting electric current, stringing musical instruments, etc. 3. wire netting or other wirework. 4. anything made of wire or wirework, as a telephone cable, barbed wire fence, a snare, etc. 5. telegraph: as, reply by ***wire.*** 6. [Colloq.], a telegram. 7. in *horse racing,* a wire above the finish line of a race. ***adj.*** made of wire or wirework. ***v.t.*** [WIRED (wīrd), WIRING], 1. to furnish, connect, bind, attach, string, etc. with a wire or wires. 2. to snare with a wire or wires. 3. to supply with a system of wires for electric current. 4. [Colloq.], to telegraph. 5. in *croquet,* to block (a ball) by placing it behind the wire of a wicket. ***v.i.*** [Colloq.], to telegraph.

get under the wire, to manage to enter or achieve barely on time.

pull wires, [from the wires used to operate puppets], to use private influence to achieve a purpose.

wire cloth, a type of fine wire netting for strainers, etc.

wire cutter, a scissorlike tool for cutting wire.

wire·danc·er (wīr'dan'sẽr, wīr'dän'sẽr), ***n.*** a person who performs acrobatic feats on a taut, high wire.

wire·draw (wīr'drô'), ***v.t.*** [WIREDREW (-drōō'), WIREDRAWN (-drôn'), WIREDRAWING], [back-formation < ***wire-drawer; wire + drawer*** (one who draws)], 1. to draw (metal) into wire; hence, 2. to draw out; spin out; protract; prolong. 3. to reduce to the finest subtleties, as a point in argument; overrefine; strain.

wire entanglement, a military defense consisting of rows of barbed wire twisted back and forth around stakes set in the ground.

wire gauge, an instrument for measuring the diameter of wire, thickness of sheet metal, etc.: it usually consists of a disk with notches of graduated sizes along its edge: abbreviated **W.G., w.g.**

wire gauze, very fine, gauzelike wire netting.

wire glass, sheet glass containing wire netting.

wire grass, any of several grasses with wiry stems, flat leaves, and umbrella-shaped groups of flower spikes.

wire·hair (wīr'hâr'), ***n.*** a fox terrier with a wiry coat: also **wire-haired terrier.**

wire-haired (wīr'hârd'), ***adj.*** having stiff and coarse, or wiry, hair.

wire·less (wīr'lis), ***adj.*** 1. without wire or wires; specifically, operating with electromagnetic waves and not with conducting wire. 2. [Chiefly British], radio. ***n.*** 1. wireless telegraphy. 2. wireless telephony. 3. [Chiefly British], radio. ***v.t. & v.i.*** to communicate (with) by wireless.

wireless telegraphy (or **telegraph**), telegraphy by radio-transmitted signals.
wireless telephone, a telephone operating by radio-transmitted signals.
wireless telephony, telephony by radio-transmitted signals.
wire·man (wīr′mən), *n.* [*pl.* WIREMEN (-mən)], a person who installs and repairs telegraph, telephone, and electric power wires; lineman.
wire netting, netting of woven wire, used in various sizes for fences, guards, etc.
wire·pho·to (wīr′fō′tō), *n.* 1. a system of reproducing photographs at a distance by means of electric impulses transmitted by wire. 2. an apparatus for sending or receiving such electric impulses. 3. a photograph so reproduced. A trade-mark (**Wirephoto**).
wire·pull·er (wīr′pool′ẽr), *n.* 1. a person who pulls wires, as in working puppets. 2. a person who uses private influence to gain his ends.
wire·pull·ing (wīr′pool′iŋ), *n.* the action or practice of a wirepuller.
wir·er (wīr′ẽr), *n.* 1. a person who wires; wireman. 2. a person who uses wire to snare game.
wire recorder, a machine for recording sound electromagnetically on a thin wire running between two spools and for playing it back: a wire may have its sound erased by demagnetization and be used for new recordings any number of times.
wire rope, rope made of twisted wires.
wire·spun (wīr′spun′), *adj.* 1. drawn out in the form of wire. 2. figuratively, drawn out too fine; over-subtle; overrefined.
wire-stitched (wīr′sticht′), *adj.* stitched with wire, as some bindings.
wire tapper, 1. a person who taps telephone wires, etc. to get information secretly. 2. [Colloq.], a person who gives tips for betting on the strength of information supposedly got by wire tapping or interception.
wire tapping, the act or practice of tapping telephone wires, etc. to get information secretly.
wire·work (wīr′wũrk′), *n.* netting, grilled work, etc. made of wire.
wire·works (wīr′wũrks′), *n.pl.* [also construed as sing.], a factory where wire or wire articles are made.
wire·worm (wīr′wũrm′), *n.* 1. a slender, hard-bodied larva of any of the click beetles, which often attacks the roots of crops. 2. a millepede.
wire-wove (wīr′wōv′), *adj.* 1. designating or of a very fine grade of paper with a smooth surface, made in a frame of wire gauze. 2. made of woven wire.
wir·i·ly (wīr′ə-li), *adv.* in a wiry manner.
wir·i·ness (wīr′i-nis), *n.* a wiry quality or condition.
wir·ing (wīr′iŋ), *n.* 1. the action of a person or thing that wires. 2. a system of wires, as to provide a house with electricity. *adj.* 1. that wires. 2. used in wiring.
wir·y (wīr′i), *adj.* [WIRIER (-i-ẽr), WIRIEST (-i-ist)], 1. of wire. 2. like wire in shape and substance; stiff: as, *wiry* hair. 3. lean, sinewy, and strong: said of persons and animals. 4. produced by or as if by a vibrating wire: as, a *wiry* sound.
wis (wis), *v.t.* [< *iwis*, erroneously understood as "I know"; cf. YWIS], [Archaic], to suppose; imagine; deem.
Wis·by (wiz′bi; G. vis′bi), *n.* Visby: German name.
Wis·con·sin (wis-kon′s'n), *n.* 1. a Middle Western State of the United States: area, 56,154 sq. mi.; pop., 3,952,000; capital, Madison: nicknamed *Badger State*: abbreviated **Wis., Wisc.** 2. a river in Wisconsin, flowing into the Mississippi: length, 430 mi.
Wis·con·sin·ite (wis-kon′s'n-īt′), *n.* a native or inhabitant of Wisconsin.
wis·dom (wiz′dəm), *n.* [ME.; AS.; *wis*, wise + *-dom* (see -DOM)], 1. the quality of being wise; the power of judging rightly and following the soundest course of action, based on knowledge, experience, understanding, etc.; good judgment; discretion; sagacity. 2. learning; knowledge; erudition: as, the *wisdom* of the ages. 3. wise discourse or teaching. 4. [Rare], a wise saying, action, etc. —*SYN.* see **information.**
Wisdom of Jesus, Son of Si·rach (sī′rak), Ecclesiasticus.
Wisdom of Solomon, one of the books of the Old Testament Apocrypha: called *Wisdom* in the Douay Bible: abbreviated **Wisd.**
wisdom tooth, [after Gr. *sōphronistēres*: so named from late appearance], the back tooth on each side of each jaw in human beings, the third molar, appearing usually between the ages of 17 and 25.
cut one's wisdom teeth, to arrive at the age of discretion.
wise (wīz), *adj.* [ME. & AS. *wis;* IE. base **weid-*, to see, know; seen also in L. *videre*, to see (cf. VISION), *visere*, to visit (cf. VISIT), etc.], 1. having or showing good judgment; sagacious; prudent; discreet. 2. prompted by wisdom; judicious; sound: as, a *wise* saying, *wise* action. 3. informed: as, none the *wiser*. 4. learned; erudite. 5. shrewd; crafty; cunning. 6. [Obs. or Dial.], having knowledge of black magic, etc. 7. [Slang], *a)* annoyingly self-assured, knowing, conceited, etc.: as, a *wise* guy. *b)* impudent; fresh.
be (or **get**) **wise to,** [Slang], to be (or become) aware of; have (or attain) a proper understanding of.
get wise, [Slang], to become aware of the true facts or circumstances.
put wise (to), [Slang], to give (a person) information, explanation, etc. (about); enlighten (concerning).
wise up, [Slang], to make or become informed.
SYN.—**wise** implies the ability to judge and deal with persons, situations, etc. rightly, based on a broad range of knowledge, experience, and understanding (a *wise* parent); **sage** suggests the venerable wisdom of age, experience, and philosophical reflection (*sage* counsel); **sapient**, a literary term now sometimes used ironically, implies sageness or learnedness (a *sapient* assembly); **judicious** implies the ability to make wise decisions, based on the possession and use of sound judgment (a *judicious* approach to a problem); **prudent**, as compared here, suggests the wisdom of one who is able to discern the most suitable or politic course of action in practical matters (a *prudent* policy). —*ANT.* foolish, stupid.
wise (wīz), *n.* [ME.; AS.; akin to G. *weise;* for IE. base see WISE, *adj.*], way; manner; fashion: used chiefly in the phrases *in no wise, in this wise*, etc.
-wise (wīz), [< *wise, n.*], a suffix used to form adverbs, meaning: 1. *in a* (specified) *direction, position*, or *manner*, as in *sidewise, anywise*: in this sense, equivalent to *-ways*. 2. *in a manner characteristic of*, as in *clockwise*. 3. *with regard to; in connection with:* although regarded by some as a loose usage, now freely used in compounds, as *weatherwise, budgetwise*.
Wise, Stephen Samuel (wīz), 1874–1949; American rabbi and Jewish leader, born in Hungary.
wise·a·cre (wīz′ā′kẽr), *n.* [D. *wijssegger*, altered (after *wijs*, wise + *zeggen*, to say) < OHG. *wizzago*, a prophet], a person who thinks he knows everything.
wise·crack (wīz′krak′), *n.* [Slang], a flippant or facetious remark, often a gibe or retort. *v.i.* [Slang], to make a wisecrack or wisecracks: also **crack wise.** *v.t.* [Slang], to say as a wisecrack. —*SYN.* see **joke.**
wise·ly (wīz′li), *adv.* 1. in a wise manner; with wisdom or good judgment. 2. knowingly.
wish (wish), *v.t.* [ME. *wisshen, wischen;* AS. *wyscan;* akin to G. *wünschen;* IE. base **wen-*, to strive (for), as also in L. *Venus* (cf. VENEREAL)], 1. to have a longing for; want; desire; crave. 2. to have or express a desire concerning: as, I *wish* the week were over. 3. to have or express a desire concerning the fortune, circumstances, etc. of: as, I *wish* you good luck. 4. to give a (specified) greeting to; bid: as, she *wished* me good morning. 5. to request or order: as, I *wish* you to leave. 6. to impose (with *on*): as, another duty *wished on* him. *v.i.* 1. to have a desire; long; yearn. 2. to make a wish. *n.* 1. a wishing; felt or expressed desire for something. 2. something wished for: as, he got his *wish*. 3. a behest; request: as, it is her *wish* that you enter. 4. *pl.* expressed desire for a person's health, good fortune, etc.: as, they send their *wishes*. —*SYN.* see **desire.**
wish·bone (wish′bōn′), *n.* the forked bone in front of the breastbone of most birds: so called from the custom whereby two persons make wishes and snap a dried wishbone in two, the longer fragment being a token of fulfillment of the holder's wish.
wish·ful (wish′fəl), *adj.* having or showing a wish; desirous; longing.
wishful thinking, thinking in which one consciously or unconsciously interprets facts in terms of what he would like to believe.
wish-wash (wish′wôsh′, wish′wäsh′), *n.* [redupl. of *wash*], a weak or insipid drink.
wish·y-wash·y (wish′i-wôsh′i, wish′i-wäsh′i), *adj.* [redupl. of *washy*], 1. watery; insipid; thin; hence, 2. weak; feeble; unsubstantial.
Wis·la (vē′slä), *n.* the Vistula River: the Polish name.
Wis·mar (vis′mär), *n.* a seaport in northern Germany, on the Baltic Sea: pop., 26,000.
wisp (wisp), *n.* [ME. *wisp, wips;* prob. < ON.; same base as in WHISK], 1. a small bundle or bunch, as of straw. 2. a slender, twisted piece: as, use a *wisp* of paper to light the fire. 3. a thin, slight, or filmy piece, portion, mass, etc.; shred: as, a *wisp* of smoke. 4. a will-o'-the-wisp. 5. a whisk broom. *v.t.* to roll into a wisp.
wisp·y (wisp′i), *adj.* [WISPIER (-pi-ẽr), WISPIEST (-pi-ist)], like a wisp; slender, slight, filmy, etc.
Wiss·ler, Clark (wis′lẽr), 1870–1947; American anthropologist.
wist (wist), past tense and past participle of **wit.**
wis·ta·ri·a (wis-târ′i-ə), *n.* wisteria.
Wis·ter, Owen (wis′tẽr), 1860–1938; American novelist.
wis·te·ri·a (wis-têr′i-ə), *n.* [Mod. L., after Casper *Wistar* (1761–1818), Am. anatomist], any of a number of related twining shrubs of the pea family, with showy clusters of bluish, white, pink, or purplish flowers.
wist·ful (wist′fəl), *adj.* [altered (after *wishful*) < earlier *wistly*, closely attentive; prob. < *whist, interj.*], showing or expressing vague yearnings; longing pensively.
wit (wit), *n.* [ME. *witte;* AS.; akin to G. *witz;* for IE. base see WISE, *adj.*], 1. originally, the mind. 2. *pl. a)* powers of thinking and reasoning; intellectual and perceptive powers. *b)* mental faculties with respect to their state of balance, especially in their normal con-

dition of sanity. 3. [Rare], good sense; wisdom. 4. the ability to make clever, ironic, or satirical remarks, usually by perceiving the incongruous and expressing it in a surprising or epigrammatic manner. 5. a person having this ability. 6. any clever disparagement or raillery. 7. [Archaic], intellect; reason.

at one's wits' end, at a point where one's mental resources are exhausted; at a loss as to what to do.

keep (or **have**) **one's wits about one,** to remain mentally alert; function with undiminished keenness of mental powers, as in an emergency.

live by one's wits, to live by trickery or craftiness.

***SYN.*—wit** refers to the ability to perceive the incongruous and to express it in quick, sharp, spontaneous, often sarcastic remarks that delight or entertain; **humor** is applied to the ability to perceive and express that which is comical, ludicrous, or ridiculous, but connotes kindliness, geniality, sometimes even pathos, in the expression and a reaction of sympathetic amusement from the audience; **irony** refers to the humor implicit in the contradiction between literal expression and intended meaning or in the discrepancy between appearance and reality in life; **satire** applies to the use, especially in literature, of ridicule, sarcasm, irony, etc. in exposing and attacking vices or follies; **repartee** refers to the ability to reply or retort with quick, skillful wit or humor.

wit (wit), ***v.t.* & *v.i.*** [WIST or WISTE (wist), WIST, WITING or WITTING], [ME. ***witen;*** AS. ***witan,*** to know < the IE. base seen in WISE, *adj.*], [Archaic], to know or learn. *Wit* was conjugated, in the present indicative: (I) *wot,* (thou) *wost* or *wot(t)est,* (he, she, it) *wot* or *wot(t)eth,* (we, ye, they) *wite,* or *witen.*

to wit, that is to say; namely.

wit·an (wit'ən), ***n.pl.*** [AS., pl. of ***wita,*** one who knows < wise man, councilor < ***witan,*** to know; cf. WIT, *n.*], in the Anglo-Saxon period of English history, the members of the king's council, or the council itself.

witch (wich), ***n.*** [ME. ***wicche;*** AS. ***wicce,*** fem. of ***wicca,*** sorcerer; prob. < ***wiccian,*** to use sorcery; IE. base ****weiq-,*** violent strength, as also in L. ***vincere,*** to conquer (cf. VICTOR, VICTIM); see WICKED], 1. a woman supposedly having supernatural power by a compact with evil spirits; sorceress: the term formerly was also applied to men. 2. an ugly and ill-tempered old woman; hag; crone. 3. [Colloq.], a bewitching or fascinating woman or girl. ***v.t.*** 1. to put a magic spell on; bewitch. 2. to cause, bring, effect, etc. by witchcraft. 3. to charm; fascinate.

witch broom, a witches'-broom.

witch·craft (wich'kraft', wich'kräft'), ***n.*** [ME. ***wicche-crafte;*** AS. ***wiccecræft***], 1. the power or practices of witches; black magic; sorcery. 2. an instance of this. 3. bewitching attraction or charm. —***SYN.*** see **magic.**

witch doctor, among primitive tribes, a person who professes to detect and counteract the effects of witchcraft; medicine man.

witch-elm (wich'elm'), ***n.*** wych-elm.

witch·er·y (wich'ẽr-i), ***n.*** [*pl.* WITCHERIES (-iz)], 1. witchcraft; sorcery. 2. bewitching charm; fascination.

witch·es'-be·som (wich'iz-bē'zəm), ***n.*** a witches'-broom.

witch·es'-broom (wich'iz-bro͞om', wich'iz-broom'), ***n.*** an abnormal growth of shoots at the ends of branches, usually caused by certain fungi; hexenbesen.

witches' Sabbath, a midnight meeting of witches, sorcerers, and demons, supposed in medieval times to have been held annually as a demonic orgy.

witch grass, [altered < ***quitch grass***], a hairy grass with loosely flowered spikes.

witch hazel, [< ME. ***wyche;*** AS. ***wice,*** applied to trees with pliant branches < base of ***weak***], 1. a shrub with yellow, wavy-petaled flowers and woody fruit. 2. a lotion consisting of an alcoholic solution of an extract from the leaves and bark of this plant.

witch hunt, [so named in allusion to persecutions of persons alleged to be witches], an investigation usually conducted with much publicity, supposedly to uncover subversive political activity, disloyalty, etc., but really to harass and weaken the entire political opposition.

witch·ing (wich'iŋ), ***n.*** the action or practice of a person who witches; witchcraft or enchantment. ***adj.*** that witches; bewitching or enchanting.

witch moth, any of several noctuid moths of the southern United States and the West Indies, having brightly colored wings marbled with dark markings.

wite (wīt), ***n.* & *v.t.*** [WITED (-id), WITING], [ME. ***witen;*** AS. ***witan;*** cf. TWIT], [Obs. or Scot.], blame; censure.

wit·e·na·ge·mot, wit·e·na·ge·mote (wit'ə-nə-gə-mōt'), ***n.*** [AS. ***witena-gemot; witena,*** genit. pl. of ***wita*** (see WITAN) + ***(ge)mot,*** a meeting; lit., assembly of the wise men], the national council of the Anglo-Saxons.

with (with, with), ***prep.*** [ME.; AS., orig., against, in opposition to; prob. shortened < AS. ***wither,*** against; IE. base ****wi-,*** asunder, separate, of which AS. ***wither*** (G. ***wider***) would represent the compar. (dual) form], 1. in opposition to; against: as, he argued ***with*** his wife. 2. *a*) alongside of; close to; near to. *b*) in the company of. *c*) into; among: as, mix blue ***with*** yellow. 3. as an associate, or companion, of, in conversation, games, war, etc.: as, he talked, played, saw service ***with*** me. 4. as a member of: as, he plays ***with*** a string quartet. 5. concerning; specifically, *a*) in terms of relationship to: as, friendly ***with*** strangers. *b*) in regard to: as, pleased ***with*** her gift. 6. in the same terms as; compared to; contrasted to: as, having equal standing ***with*** the others. 7. as well, completely, etc. as: as, he can jump ***with*** the best. 8. of the same opinions, belief, etc. as: as, I'm ***with*** you there; hence, 9. in support of; on the side of: as, he voted ***with*** the Tories. 10. *a*) in the region, sphere, circumstances, etc. of. *b*) in the opinion or estimation of: as, whatever you decide is all right ***with*** me. 11. as the result of; because of: as, faint ***with*** hunger. 12. *a*) by means of: as, stir ***with*** a spoon. *b*) by the use, presence, etc. of; by: as, filled ***with*** air. 13. *a*) accompanied by, attended by, circumstanced by, etc.: as, he entered ***with*** confidence; hence, *b*) having received: as, ***with*** your permission, I'll go. 14. having as a possession, attribute, accoutrement, etc.: as, the man ***with*** brown hair. 15. exhibiting: as, he plays ***with*** skill. 16. in the keeping, care, etc. of: as, leave the children ***with*** grandmother. 17. added to; and: as, the woman, ***with*** her two daughters, arrived. 18. in spite of; notwithstanding: as, ***with*** all his boasting, he is a coward. 19. *a*) at the same time as: as, to rise ***with*** the chickens. *b*) in the same direction as: as, travel ***with*** the sun. *c*) in the same degree as; in proportion to: as, grow wise ***with*** age. 20. to; onto: as, join this end ***with*** that one. 21. from: as, to part ***with*** one's gains. Abbreviated **w.**

in with, associated with; in league with.

with that, after that; whereupon.

with- (with, with), [AS. ***with-;*** see WITH], a combining form meaning: 1. *away, back,* as in ***withdraw.*** 2. *against, from,* as in ***withhold.***

with·al (with-ôl', with-ôl'), ***adv.*** [ME. ***with alle***], [Archaic], 1. besides. 2. thereby. 3. thereupon. 4. still. ***prep.*** [Archaic], with: used at the end of a clause or sentence, as, a staff to support himself ***withal.***

with·draw (with-drô', with-drô'), ***v.t.*** [WITHDREW (-dro͞o'), WITHDRAWN (-drôn'), WITHDRAWING], [ME. ***withdrawen;*** see WITH- & DRAW], 1. to take back; draw back; remove. 2. to retract or recall (a statement, etc.). ***v.i.*** 1. to move back; go away; retire; retreat. 2. in parliamentary procedure, to retract a motion, statement, etc. —***SYN.*** see **go.**

with·draw·al (with-drô'əl, with-drô'əl), ***n.*** a withdrawing, as of money from the bank, a person or thing from its place or position, etc.

withdrawing room, [Archaic], a drawing room.

with·draw·ment (with-drô'mənt, with-drô'mənt), ***n.*** [Rare], withdrawal.

with·drawn (with-drôn', with-drôn'), ***adj.*** withdrawing within oneself; shy, reserved, abstracted, etc.

withe (with, with, wīth), ***n.*** [ME. ***wythe, witthe, wythth;*** AS. ***withthe, withig,*** willow, twig of willow; IE. base ****wei-,*** to bend, twist, as also in Eng. ***wire***], a tough, flexible twig of willow, osier, etc., used for binding things; withy. ***v.t.*** to bind with a withe or withes.

with·er (with'ẽr), ***v.i.*** [ME. ***widren,*** var. of ***wederen,*** lit., to weather, expose to the weather < ***weder,*** weather; cf. WEATHER, *v.*], 1. to dry up, as from great heat; shrivel; wilt: said of plants; hence, 2. to lose vigor or freshness; become wasted or decayed. 3. to weaken; languish: as, her affections ***withered.*** ***v.t.*** 1. to cause to wither. 2. to cause to quail or feel abashed, as by a scornful glance.

SYN.*—wither** implies a drying up, decaying, wilting, fading, etc., as from a loss of natural juices (apples ***withering on the bough); **shrivel** implies a shrinking, wrinkling, or curling, as from exposure to intense heat (blossoms ***shriveling*** in the hot sun); **wizen,** now usually in the past participle, implies a shrinking and wrinkling, as from advanced age, malnourishment, etc. (the ***wizened*** face of the old beggar).

with·er·ite (with'ẽr-īt'), ***n.*** [after its discoverer, W. *Withering* (1741–1799), Eng. scientist], native barium carbonate, $BaCO_3$, occurring in white, yellowish, or grayish crystals, often in columnar or granular masses.

withe rod, a shrub with osierlike shoots, having clusters of white flowers in June, and heavy clusters of blue-black, pink, or yellowish-green berries in fall.

with·ers (with'ẽrz), ***n.pl.*** [< ME. ***wither,*** resistance, lit., things that resist; that which the horse opposes to his load; AS. ***withre,*** resistance < ***wither,*** against; cf. WITH], the highest part of the back of a horse or other animal, located between the shoulder blades.

With·er(s), George (with'ẽr, with'ẽrz), 1588–1667; English poet.

with·er·shins (with'ẽr-shinz'), ***adv.*** [< MLG. ***wedder-sinnes*** < MHG. ***widdersinnes*** < ***wider,*** against (cf. WITH) + ***sinnes,*** genit. of ***sin(d),*** way, direction], [Scot.], in a direction contrary to the apparent course of the sun.

With·er·spoon, John (with'ẽr-spo͞on'), 1723–1794; American clergyman and educator; signer of the Declaration of Independence.

with·hold (with-hōld′, *with*-hōld′), *v.t.* [WITHHELD (-held′), WITHHOLDING], [ME. *withholden;* see WITH- & HOLD, *v.*], 1. to hold back; keep back; restrain. 2. to refrain from granting, permitting, etc.; refuse. *v.i.* to refrain; forbear. —*SYN.* see **keep.**

withholding tax, the amount of income tax paid by employees through the employer's withholding of part of their wages or salaries.

with·in (*with*-in′, with-in′), *adv.* [ME. *withinne;* AS. *withinnan;* see WITH & IN], 1. in or into the interior; on the inside; internally. 2. indoors. 3. inside the body, mind, heart, etc.; inwardly. *prep.* 1. in the inner part of; inside. 2. not beyond in distance, time, degree, etc.: as, *within* a mile, *within* one's experience. 3. inside the limits of: as, *within* the law.

with·in·doors (*with*-in′dôrz′, with-in′dōrz′), *adv.* [Archaic], indoors.

with·out (*with*-out′, with-out′), *adv.* [ME. *withoute, withuten, withouten;* AS. *withutan;* see WITH & OUT], 1. on the outside; externally. 2. out of doors. *prep.* 1. at, on, to, or toward the outside of: opposed to *within.* 2. beyond: as, *without* his reach: opposed to *within.* 3. not with; lacking. 4. free from: as, *without* fear. 5. with avoidance of: as, he passed *without* speaking. 6. lacking or in the absence of (something previously mentioned): used with the object understood, as, we went *without.* 7. [Obs.], besides. *conj.* [Dial.], unless: often followed by *that,* as, I can't go, *without* (that) I get some money.

with·out·doors (*with*-out′dôrz′, with-out′dōrz′), *adv.* [Archaic], out of doors.

with·stand (with-stand′, *with*-stand′), *v.t. & v.i.* [WITHSTOOD (-stood′), WITHSTANDING], [see WITH- & STAND], to oppose, resist, or endure. —*SYN.* see **oppose.**

with·y (*with*′i, with′i), *n.* [*pl.* WITHIES (-iz)], [ME. *wythe, withe, withi;* AS. *withig,* a willow, twig of willow; cf. WITHE], 1. a tough, flexible twig of willow, osier, etc., used for binding things; withe. 2. a rope or leash made of withes. *adj.* 1. tough and flexible, as a withy. 2. wiry: said of people.

wit·less (wit′lis), *adj.* lacking wit or intelligence; foolish.

wit·ling (wit′liŋ), *n.* one who fancies himself a wit.

wit·ness (wit′nis), *n.* [ME. *witnesse;* AS. *gewitnes, witness,* knowledge, testimony < *witan,* to know; cf. WIT, *n.*], 1. an attesting of a fact, statement, etc.; evidence; testimony. 2. a person who saw, or can give a firsthand account of, something. 3. a person who testifies in court. 4. a person called upon to observe a transaction, signing, etc. in order to testify concerning it if it is later held in question. 5. something providing or serving as evidence. *v.t.* 1. to testify to. 2. to serve as evidence of. 3. to act as witness of, often by signing a statement to that effect. 4. to be present at; see personally. 5. to be the scene or setting of: as, this field has *witnessed* many battles. *v.i.* to give, or serve as, evidence; testify.
bear witness, to be or give evidence; testify.

witness stand, the place from which a witness gives his testimony in a law court.

Wit·te, Ser·ge·i Yul·ie·vich (syer-gyā′ yōōl′yə-vich vēt′yə), Count, 1849–1915; Russian statesman.

wit·ted (wit′id), *adj.* having wit: usually in hyphenated compounds, meaning *having* (a specified kind of) *wit,* as in *slow-witted.*

Wit·te·kind (vit′ə-kint), *n.* Saxon leader and warrior; ?–807? A.D.; also called *Widukind.*

Wit·ten·berg (wit′'n-bũrg′; G. vit′ən-berH′), *n.* a city in eastern Germany, on the Elbe: the Protestant Reformation (1517) originated here: pop., 41,000.

wit·ti·cism (wit′ə-siz'm), *n.* [< *witty,* after *Anglicism, criticism,* etc.], a witty remark. —*SYN.* see **joke.**

wit·ti·ly (wit′'l-i), *adv.* in a witty manner.

wit·ti·ness (wit′i-nis), *n.* the quality of being witty.

wit·ting (wit′iŋ), *adj.* [ME. *wytting;* chiefly < *witte* (cf. WIT) + *-ing*], done or acting knowingly; deliberate.

wit·ting·ly (wit′iŋ-li), *adv.* consciously; intentionally.

wit·tol (wit′'l), *n.* [Late ME. *wetewold,* formed, after *cokewold* (cf. CUCKOLD) < *weten, witen,* to know; cf. WIT], [Archaic], a man who knows and is tolerant of his wife's adultery.

wit·ty (wit′i), *adj.* [WITTIER (-i-ẽr), WITTIEST (-i-ist)], [ME. *witti, witie;* AS. *witig, wittig* < *wit,* knowledge], 1. having, showing, or characterized by wit; cleverly amusing. 2. [Obs. or Dial.], intelligent; clever.
SYN.—**witty** implies sharp cleverness and spontaneity in perceiving and expressing, sometimes sarcastically, the incongruous, especially as evidenced in quick repartee; **humorous** connotes more geniality, gentleness, or whimsicality in saying or doing something that is deliberately comical or amusing; **facetious** is now usually derogatory in suggesting an attempt to be witty or humorous that is unsuccessful because it is inappropriate or in bad taste; **jocular** implies a happy or playful disposition characterized by the desire to amuse others; **jocose** suggests a mildly mischievous quality in joking or jesting, sometimes to the point of facetiousness. —*ANT.* serious, solemn, sober.

Wit·wa·ters·rand (wit-wô′tẽrz-rand′, wit-wä′tẽrz-ränt′), *n.* a ridge in the Union of South Africa, near Johannesburg: a site of rich gold fields: popularly also called *the Rand.*

wive (wīv), *v.i.* [WIVED (wīvd), WIVING], [ME. *wiven;* AS. *wifian,* to take a wife < *wif,* a woman, wife], to marry a woman; take a wife. *v.t.* 1. to marry (a woman); take for a wife. 2. to provide with a wife.

wi·vern (wī′vẽrn), *n.* [ME. *wivere;* ONorm.Fr. *wivre* (OFr. *guivre*), dragon, serpent; L. *vipera;* see VIPER], a two-legged dragon with wings and a barbed tail, represented on some coats of arms: also spelled **wyvern.**

wives (wīvz), *n.* plural of **wife.**

wiz (wiz), *n.* [< *wizard;* but cf. WHIZ], [Slang], a person regarded as exceptionally clever or gifted at studies, etc.: as, he's a *wiz* at chemistry.

wiz·ard (wiz′ẽrd), *n.* [ME. *wisard;* OFr. *guischart, guisart* < ON. *viskr,* clever, knowing; but understood as *wise* + *-ard*], 1. originally, a sage. 2. a magician; conjurer; sorcerer. 3. [Colloq.], a very skillful or clever person. *adj.* 1. of wizards or wizardry. 2. magic.

wiz·ard·ly (wiz′ẽrd-li), *adj.* of or like a wizard or wizardry.

wiz·ard·ry (wiz′ẽrd-ri), *n.* the art or practice of a wizard; witchcraft; magic; sorcery. —*SYN.* see **magic.**

wiz·en (wiz′'n; *dial.* wē′z'n), *v.t. & v.i.* [ME. *wisenen;* AS. *wisnian,* to become dry], to dry up; wither; shrivel. *adj.* wizened. —*SYN.* see **wither.**

wiz·ened (wiz′'nd; *dial.* wē′z'nd), *adj.* [pp. of *wizen*], dried up; shriveled; withered; shrunken.

wk., [*pl.* WKS.], 1. week. 2. work.

wkly., weekly.

w.l., wave length.

WLB, War Labor Board.

WMC, War Manpower Commission.

wmk., watermark.

WNW, W.N.W., w.n.w., west-northwest.

wo (wō), *n. & interj.* woe.

W.O., 1. War Office. 2. Warrant Officer.

woad (wōd), *n.* [ME. *wod;* AS. *wad;* akin to G. *waid*], 1. a plant of the mustard family, with small, yellow flowers. 2. a blue dye extracted from its leaves.

woad·wax·en (wōd′wak′s'n), *n.* woodwaxen.

woald (wōld), *n.* a weld (flower).

wob·ble (wob′'l), *v.i.* [WOBBLED (-'ld), WOBBLING], [? < LG. *wabbeln,* to wobble; for IE. base see WAVE; cf. WAVER], 1. to move unsteadily from side to side, as in walking. 2. to rotate unevenly so as to move from side to side. 3. to shake; tremble: as, jelly *wobbles.* 4. to waver in one's opinions, etc.; vacillate. *v.t.* [Colloq.], to cause to wobble. *n.* wobbling motion. Also **wabble.** —*SYN.* see **shake.**

wob·bling (wob′liŋ), *adj.* that wobbles: also **wabbling.**

wob·bly (wob′li), *adj.* [WOBBLIER (-li-ẽr), WOBBLIEST (-li-ist)], inclined to wobble; shaky: also **wabbly.**

wob·bly (wob′li), *n.* [*pl.* WOBBLIES (-liz)], [said to be < Chin. mispronunciation of *I.W.W.* as *I. wobbly wobbly*], [also W-], [Slang], a member of the Industrial Workers of the World (I.W.W.).

wo·be·gone (wō′bi-gôn′, wō′bi-gon′), *adj.* woebegone.

Wo·burn (wō′bẽrn, wōō′bẽrn), *n.* a city in northeastern Massachusetts, near Boston: pop., 31,000.

Wo·den, Wo·dan (wō′d'n), *n.* [AS. *Woden;* akin to G. *Wotan* & ON. *Odinn;* see EDDA; cf. WEDNESDAY], the chief Germanic god, identified with the Norse Odin.

woe (wō), *n.* [ME. *wo;* AS. *wa,* woe < an IE. interj. seen in Goth. *wai,* W. *gwae,* L. *vae,* etc.], 1. great sorrow; grief; misery. 2. a cause of sorrow; affliction; trouble. *interj.* alas! Also spelled **wo.**—*SYN.* see **sorrow.**

woe·be·gone (wō′bi-gôn′, wō′bi-gon′), *adj.* [ME. *wo begon; wo,* woe + *begon,* pp. of *begon,* to go around; AS. *began, begangan*], 1. [Archaic], woeful. 2. of woeful appearance; showing woe; looking sorrowful, mournful, or wretched. Also spelled **wobegone.**

woe·ful (wō′fəl), *adj.* 1. full of woe; sad; mournful. 2. of, causing, or involving woe. 3. pitiful; wretched; miserable. Also spelled **woful.**

Wof·fing·ton, Peg (peg wof′iŋ-t'n), (*Margaret Woffington*), 1714?–1760; Irish actress in England.

woke (wōk), alternative past tense of **wake.**

wok·en (wō′kən), rare past participle of **wake.**

wold (wōld), *n.* [ME. *wold;* AS. (Anglian) *wald,* corresponding to W.S. *weald;* cf. WEALD], a treeless, rolling plain, especially a high one.

wold (wōld), *n.* a weld (flower).

wold (wôld), alternative obsolete past participle of **will.**

wolf (woolf), *n.* [*pl.* WOLVES (woolvz)], [ME.; AS. *wulf;* akin to G. *wolf;* IE. base **wlp-*, **lup-*, name of animals of prey, as also in L. *lupus* (cf. LUPINE), Gr. *lykos* (cf. LYCANTHROPY)], 1. any of a large group of flesh-eating, doglike mammals widely distributed throughout the Northern Hemisphere. 2. *a*) a fierce, cruel, or greedy person. *b*) [Slang], a man who flirts aggressively with many women; philanderer. 3. a larva of various small beetles or moths that infests grain. 4. *a*) the dissonance of some chords on an organ,

TIMBER WOLF
(2 ft. high at shoulder)

piano, etc. that has been tuned in a system of unequal temperament; also, a chord in which such dissonance is heard. *b*) harshness of tone in instruments of the violin group, due to faulty vibration in some tones. *v.t.* to eat ravenously, as a wolf does.

cry wolf, to give a false alarm.

keep the wolf from the door, to provide the necessities of life in sufficient quantity to prevent privation.

Wolf, Hu·go (hōō′gō vôlf), 1860–1903; Austrian composer.

wolf·ber·ry (woolf′ber′i), *n.* [*pl.* WOLFBERRIES (-iz)], a shrub with spikelike clusters of white berries.

wolf dog, 1. any of several breeds of large Irish dogs formerly trained to hunt wolves. 2. a hybrid of a wolf and a dog.

Wolfe, James (woolf), 1727–1759; British general; defeated Montcalm at the battle of Quebec (1759).

Wolfe, Thomas Clay·ton (klā′t'n), 1900–1938; American novelist.

Wolff·i·an body (wool′fi-ən, vôl′fi-ən), [after K. F. *Wolff* (1733–1794), G. embryologist], the mesonephros.

wolf fish, any of several large, savage sea fishes of the blenny group.

wolf·hound (woolf′hound′), *n.* a large dog of any of several breeds formerly used for hunting wolves: see **Irish wolfhound, Russian wolfhound.**

wolf·ish (wool′fish), *adj.* of or like a wolf; rapacious.

wolf·ram (wool′frəm), *n.* [G., apparently < *wolf* + MHG. *ram*, dirt, soot: so named prob. because wolfram was considered of little value in comparison to tin, and caused a loss of tin in the smelting process], 1. tungsten: symbol W (no period). 2. wolframite.

wolf·ram·ite (wool′frəm-īt′), *n.* [G. *wolframit* < *wolfram;* see WOLFRAM], a brownish or blackish mineral, $(Fe,Mn)WO_4$, a tungstate of iron and manganese.

wolf·ra·mi·um (wool-frā′mi-əm), *n.* tungsten.

Wol·fram von Esch·en·bach (vôl′främ fôn esh′ən-bäkh′), 1170?–1220?; medieval German poet.

wolfs·bane (woolfs′bān′), *n.* [transl. of L. *lycoctonum* < Gr. *lykotonon* < *lykos*, a wolf + base of *kteinein*, to kill], any of a number of related poisonous plants having large, showy, blue, white, or yellow flowers with hooded sepals; aconite; monkshood: also **wolf's-bane.**

wol·las·ton·ite (wool′əs-t'n-īt′), *n.* [after William H. *Wollaston* (1766–1828), Eng. physicist], a white mineral, $CaSiO_3$, native calcium silicate.

Wol·sey, Thomas (wool′zi), Cardinal, 1475?–1530; English statesman and prelate.

wol·ver (wool′vẽr), *n.* a person who hunts wolves.

Wol·ver·hamp·ton (wool′vẽr-hamp′tən), *n.* a city in Staffordshire, west central England: pop., 155,000 (est. 1946).

wol·ver·ine (wool′və-rēn′, wool′və-rēn′), *n.* [*pl.* WOLVERINES (-rēnz′, -rēnz′), WOLVERINE; see PLURAL, II, D, 1], [dim. formed < *wolf*, because of its supposed fierce, bloodthirsty disposition], 1. a stocky, flesh-eating mammal with thick fur, found in the northern United States and Canada and closely related to the European glutton. 2. [W-], [Colloq.], a native or inhabitant of Michigan, called the *Wolverine State.* Also spelled **wolverene.**

WOLVERINE (3 ft. long)

wolves (woolvz), *n.* plural of **wolf.**

wom·an (woom′ən), *n.* [*pl.* WOMEN (wim′in)], [ME. *wumman, wimmon, wifmon;* AS. *wifmann*, later *wimmann* < *wif*, a female + *mann*, a human being, man; change of vowel due to influence of the initial *w*-], 1. the female human being, or women collectively, as distinguished from man. 2. an adult female human being. 3. a female servant. 4. *a*) a wife. *b*) a sweetheart or a mistress. 5. a man with qualities conventionally regarded as feminine, such as weakness, timidity, etc. 6. womanly qualities or characteristics; femininity: as, it's the *woman* in her. *adj.* 1. of or characteristic of a woman or women; feminine. 2. female: as, a *woman* scientist.

***SYN.*—woman** is the standard general term for the adult human being of the sex distinguished from *man*; **female,** referring specifically to sex, is applied to plants and animals, but is now regarded as a contemptuous equivalent for **woman** (that strong-minded *female* is here again), except in scientific or statistical use, as in population tables; **lady,** once restricted to a woman of the upper classes or high social position, is now used in polite or genteel reference to any woman (there's a *lady* to see you, the *ladies*' room) or, in the plural, in addressing a group of women (*ladies* and gentlemen).

wom·an-hat·er (woom′ən-hāt′ẽr), *n.* a man who dislikes women; misogynist.

wom·an·hood (woom′ən-hood′), *n.* [see -HOOD], 1. the condition of being a woman. 2. womanly qualities; womanliness. 3. women; womankind.

wom·an·ish (woom′ən-ish), *adj.* like, characteristic of, or suitable to a woman; feminine or effeminate. —***SYN.*** see **female.**

wom·an·ize (woom′ən-īz′), *v.t.* [WOMANIZED (-īzd′), WOMANIZING], 1. to make effeminate. 2. [Colloq.], to practice adultery with women.

wom·an·kind (woom′ən-kīnd′), *n.* women in general.

wom·an·like (woom′ən-līk′), *adj.* like a woman; womanly.

wom·an·li·ness (woom′ən-li-nis), *n.* the quality of being womanly.

wom·an·ly (woom′ən-li), *adj.* 1. like a woman; womanish. 2. characteristic of a woman; womanlike. 3. suitable to a woman. —***SYN.*** see **female.**

wom·an-suf·frage (woom′ən-suf′rij), *adj.* of woman suffrage.

woman suffrage, the right of women to vote in governmental elections.

wom·an-suf·fra·gist (woom′ən-suf′rə-jist), *n.* a person who believes in or advocates woman suffrage.

womb (wōōm), *n.* [ME. *wombe;* AS. *wamb;* akin to G. *wamme;* prob. IE. base **wenəbh-* < base in **wĕdero*, belly; cf. L. *venter*, belly < **wend-ri*, of same ult. origin], 1. originally, the belly. 2. the uterus; hence, 3. any place or part that holds, envelops, generates, etc.: as, the *womb* of time.

wom·bat (wom′bat), *n.* [altered < Australian native name *womback, vombach*], any of a group of burrowing marsupials resembling small bears, found in Australia, Tasmania, and several Pacific islands.

wom·en (wim′in), *n.* plural of **woman.**

wom·en·folk (wim′in-fōk′), *n.pl.* women; womankind.

wom·en·folks (wim′in-fōks′), *n.pl.* womenfolk.

women's rights, the rights claimed by and for women of equal privileges and opportunities with men: also **woman's rights.**

wom·er·a (wom′ẽr-ə), *n.* [Australian native name], a spear-throwing device used by Australian aborigines: also **woomera.**

won (wun), past tense and past participle of **win.**

won (wun, woon, wōn), *v.i.* [WONNED (wund, woond, wōnd), WONNING], [Archaic or Dial.], to dwell; abide.

won·der (wun′dẽr), *n.* [ME. *wunder, wonder;* AS. *wundor;* akin to G. *wunder;* only in Gmc.], 1. a person, thing, or event that causes astonishment and admiration; prodigy; marvel. 2. the feeling of surprise, admiration, and awe aroused by something strange, unexpected, incredible, etc. 3. a miracle. *v.i.* [AS. *wundrian*, to wonder], 1. to be seized or filled with wonder; feel amazement; marvel. 2. to have doubt mingled with curiosity. *v.t.* to have doubt and curiosity about; want to know: as, I *wonder* why he came.

for a wonder, surprisingly.

won·der·ful (wun′dẽr-fəl), *adj.* [ME.; AS. *wundorfull*], 1. that causes wonder; marvelous; amazing. 2. [Colloq.], very good; excellent; fine: generalized term of approval.

won·der·ing (wun′dẽr-iŋ), *adj.* [ppr. of *wonder*], feeling or showing wonder.

won·der·land (wun′dẽr-land′), *n.* [cf. G. *wunderland*], 1. an imaginary land full of wonders; hence, 2. any place of great beauty, etc.

won·der·ment (wun′dẽr-mənt), *n.* 1. a state or expression of wonder; amazement; astonishment. 2. something causing wonder; a marvel.

won·der-strick·en (wun′dẽr-strik″'n), *adj.* struck with wonder; feeling surprise, admiration, etc.

won·der-struck (wun′dẽr-struk′), *adj.* wonder-stricken.

won·der·work (wun′dẽr-wũrk′), *n.* [ME. *wonder werk;* AS. *wundorweorc*], 1. a wonderful work; wonder. 2. a miraculous act; miracle.

won·der-work·er (wun′dẽr-wũr′kẽr), *n.* a worker of wonders; person who performs miracles.

won·der-work·ing (wun′dẽr-wũr′kiŋ), *adj.* working wonders; performing miracles.

won·drous (wun′drəs), *adj.* [altered (after *-ous*) < ME. *wundres*, adv. genit. of *wunder*, wonder], wonderful. *adv.* extraordinarily; surprisingly. Now only literary or rhetorical.

won·ky (woŋ′ki), *adj.* [WONKIER (-ki-ẽr), WONKIEST (-ki-ist)], [prob. < or suggested by dial. words based on AS. *wancol*, shaky, tottering], [British Slang], shaky; tottery; feeble.

won·na (wun′nə), [Scot.], will not.

won·ner (wun′ẽr), *n., v.i. & v.t.* [Dial.], wonder.

Won·san (wŏn′sän′), *n.* Gensan, a city in Korea: the Japanese name.

wont (wunt, wōnt, wônt), *adj.* [ME. *wunt, woned*, pp. of *wunien*, to be accustomed, dwell; AS. *wunian*, to dwell; cf. WEAN], accustomed: used predicatively, as, he was *wont* to rise early. *n.* usual practice; habit. *v.t.* [WONT, WONT or WONTED (-id), WONTING], [altered (after the *adj.*) < ME. *wune*, custom, habit; AS. (*ge*)*wuna*], to accustom. *v.i.* to be accustomed. —***SYN.*** see **habit.**

won't (wōnt), [contr. < ME. *wol not*, will not], will not.

wont·ed (wun′tid, wōn′tid, wôn′tid), ***adj.*** [ME.; see WONT, *n.* & -ED], 1. customary; habitual. 2. accustomed; habituated. —***SYN.*** see **usual.**
woo (wōō), ***v.t.*** [ME. *wowen;* AS. *wogian* < base of *woh,* bent, crooked; basic sense "to incline toward, bend toward"], 1. to make love to, usually with the intention of proposing marriage; court. 2. to try to get; seek: as, she *wooed* fame. 3. to entreat solicitously; coax; urge. *v.i.* 1. to make love; court. 2. to make entreaty.
wood (wood), ***n.*** [ME. *wode;* AS. *wudu,* earlier *widu;* akin to OHG. *wito;* IE. base **widhu-,* tree, seen also in OIr. *fid,* tree, forest], 1. *often pl.* a thick growth of trees; forest; grove. 2. the hard, fibrous substance beneath the bark in the stems and branches of trees and shrubs; xylem. 3. trees cut and dressed for use in making things; lumber or timber. 4. firewood. 5. something made of wood; specifically, *a*) the cask as a container for liquor, as opposed to the bottle: as, whisky aged in *wood.* *b*) a wood block (sense 2). *c*) a wooden wind instrument, or wood winds collectively. ***adj.*** 1. made of wood; wooden. 2. for cutting, shaping, or holding wood. 3. growing or living in woods. ***v.t.*** 1. to plant trees thickly over. 2. to furnish with wood, especially firewood. ***v.i.*** to get or take on a supply of wood.
out of the woods, [Colloq.], out of difficulty, danger, etc.
wood (wood), ***adj.*** [AS. *wōd*], [Archaic or Dial.], 1. out of one's mind; insane. 2. violently angry; enraged.
Wood, Grant (wood), 1892–1942; American painter.
Wood, Leonard, 1860–1927; American general and statesman; governor general of the Philippine Islands (1921–1927).
wood alcohol, methyl alcohol.
wood anemone, any of a number of related anemones with airy, white flowers.
wood betony, 1. the betony. 2. a variety of lousewort of eastern North America, with hairy, fernlike leaves and yellowish or reddish flowers.
wood·bin (wood′bin′), ***n.*** a bin for firewood.
wood·bind (wood′bīnd′), ***n.*** woodbine.
wood·bine (wood′bīn′), ***n.*** [ME. *wodebinde;* AS. *wudubinde; wudu,* wood + *binde* < *bindan,* to bind], 1. a European variety of climbing honeysuckle with fragrant, yellowish-white flowers. 2. the Virginia creeper, a woody vine with greenish flowers and dark-blue berries; American ivy.
wood-block (wood′blok′), ***adj.*** made or printed from wood blocks.
wood block, 1. a block of wood. 2. a printing die cut on fine-grained wood. 3. a woodcut.
wood·chat (wood′chat′), ***n.*** [prob. < *wood* + *chat* (see WHINCHAT); but cf. G. *waldkatze,* lit., wood cat], 1. any of several small Asiatic birds of the thrush group. 2. a European shrike.
wood·chuck (wood′chuk′), ***n.*** [folk-etymologized form of Am. Ind. (Algonquian) name formerly spelled *wejack;* cf. Cree & Chippewa *otchek*], any of a group of common American burrowing and hibernating marmots with coarse, red-brown fur: also called *ground hog.*

WOODCHUCK (20 in. long)

wood coal, 1. charcoal. 2. lignite.
wood·cock (wood′kok′), ***n.*** [*pl.* WOODCOCKS (-koks′), WOODCOCK; see PLURAL, II, D, 1], [ME. *wodekoc;* AS. *wuducoc; wudu,* wood + *coc,* a cock], 1. a small, European, migratory game bird with short legs and a long bill, related to the snipe and sandpiper. 2. a similar, related North American bird. 3. [Obs.], a fool; dupe.
wood·craft (wood′kraft′, wood′kräft′), ***n.*** 1. matters relating to the woods, as camping, hunting, trapping, etc. 2. woodworking. 3. skill in either of these.
wood·crafts·man (wood′krafts′mən, wood′kräfts′mən), ***n.*** [*pl.* WOODCRAFTSMEN (-mən)], a person who practices, or has skill in, woodcraft.
wood·cut (wood′kut′), ***n.*** 1. a wooden block engraved with a picture, etc. 2. a print made from this.
wood·cut·ter (wood′kut′ẽr), ***n.*** a person who fells trees, cuts wood, etc.
wood·cut·ting (wood′kut′iŋ), ***n.*** the work of a woodcutter.
wood·ed (wood′id), ***adj.*** covered with trees or woods.
wood·en (wood′′n), ***adj.*** 1. made of or consisting of wood. 2. stiff, lifeless, expressionless, etc., as if made of wood. 3. dull; insensitive; stupid.
wood engraver, a person who makes wood engravings.
wood engraving, 1. the art or process of engraving on wood. 2. a woodcut.
wood·en·head (wood′′n-hed′), ***n.*** [Colloq.], a stupid person; blockhead.
wood·en·head·ed (wood′′n-hed′id), ***adj.*** [Colloq.], stupid; blockish.
wooden horse, Trojan horse (sense 1).
wooden Indian, 1. a wooden image of an American Indian in a standing position, formerly placed in front of cigar stores as an advertisement; hence, 2. [Colloq.], a person who is dull, spiritless, or inarticulate.
wood·en·ware (wood′′n-wâr′), ***n.*** bowls, tubs, dishes, etc. made of wood.
wood hyacinth, the wild hyacinth; bluebell.
wood ibis, any of several large wading birds resembling storks, found in the wooded swamps of the southern United States and of Central and South America.
wood·i·ness (wood′i-nis), ***n.*** the condition or quality of being woody.
wood·land (wood′land′; *also, and for adj. always,* wood′lənd), ***n.*** land covered with woods or trees; a woods or forest. ***adj.*** of, in, or relating to the woods.
wood·land·er (wood′lən-dẽr), ***n.*** a person who lives in the woods.
wood lark, a European lark similar to but smaller than a skylark.
wood lot, a piece of land on which trees are cultivated and cut.
wood louse, any of a large number of crustaceans with flattened, oval, segmented bodies, found in damp soil, under decaying wood, etc.
wood·man (wood′mən), ***n.*** [*pl.* WOODMEN (-mən)], 1. [Chiefly British], a forester. 2. a woodcutter. 3. a person who lives in the woods.
wood-note (wood′nōt′), ***n.*** a sound of a forest bird or animal.
wood nymph, 1. a nymph that lives in the woods; dryad. 2. any of several South American hummingbirds. 3. any of several moths with brightly colored larvae. 4. any of a group of brown and gray butterflies with eyespots on the wings.
wood·peck·er (wood′pek′ẽr), ***n.*** any of various climbing birds distinguished by a strong, pointed bill used to peck holes in bark to get insects.

RED-HEADED WOODPECKER (9 in. long)

wood pigeon, 1. a European ringdove or any of several related pigeons. 2. a wild pigeon of western North America.
wood·pile (wood′pīl′), ***n.*** a pile of wood, especially of firewood.
wood pulp, pulp made from wood fiber, used in paper manufacture.
wood rat, a pack rat.
Wood·row (wood′rō), [< the surname *Woodrow;* popularized < the name of Thomas *Woodrow* Wilson], a masculine name: diminutive, *Woody.*
wood·ruff (wood′ruf′), ***n.*** [ME. *woderove;* AS. *wudurofe; wudu,* wood + *-rofe,* an element prob. < same base as *(a)rafian,* to untwine; name prob. means "tree twiner"], any of various related European plants with small, white, pink, or blue, lily-shaped flowers, and leaves arranged in circles around the stem.
Woods, Lake of the, see **Lake of the Woods.**
wood·shed (wood′shed′), ***n.*** a shed for storing firewood.
wood·si·a (wood′zi-ə), ***n.*** [Mod. L., after Joseph *Woods* (1776–1864), Eng. botanist], any of a number of small related ferns with wiry leafstalks, found chiefly on rock ledges.
woods·man (woodz′mən), ***n.*** [*pl.* WOODSMEN (-mən)], 1. a person who lives or works in the woods, as a hunter, trapper, woodcutter, etc. 2. a person accustomed to the woods or skilled in woodcraft.
wood sorrel, [transl. of MFr. *sorrel de boys*], any of a number of related plants having white, pink, red, yellow, or purplish flowers made up of five petals on a cone-shaped tube; oxalis.
wood spirit, methyl alcohol.
wood·sy (wood′zi), ***adj.*** [WOODSIER (-zi-ẽr), WOODSIEST (-zi-ist)], of, characteristic of, or like the woods.
wood tar, a dark, sticky, siruplike substance obtained by the dry distillation of wood and used in the preservation of wood, etc.
wood thrush, 1. a large thrush of eastern North America, having a rusty-brown mantle and a strong, clear song. 2. the European missel thrush.
wood turner, a person who turns wood on a lathe.
wood-turn·ing (wood′tũr′niŋ), ***adj.*** of or for wood turning.
wood turning, the art or process of turning, or shaping, wood on a lathe.
wood vinegar, pyroligneous acid or crude acetic acid obtained by the distillation of wood.
wood·wax (wood′waks′), ***n.*** [Obs. or Dial.], woodwaxen.
wood·wax·en (wood′wak′s′n), ***n.*** [ME. *wodewexen;* AS. *wuduweaxe* < *wudu,* wood + *weaxe* < base of *weaxan,* to grow (cf. WAX, *v.*)], a plant of the pea family, with clusters of showy, yellow flowers and striped branches: also **woadwaxen.**

wood-wind (wood′wind′), *adj.* of the wood winds.

wood wind, 1. *pl.* the wind instruments of an orchestra made, especially originally, of wood: the principal modern wood winds are the clarinet, oboe, bassoon, flute, and English horn. 2. any of these instruments.

wood·work (wood′wŭrk′), *n.* 1. work done in wood. 2. things made of wood, especially the interior moldings, doors, stairs, etc. of a house.

wood·work·er (wood′wŭr′kẽr), *n.* a person who makes things out of wood.

wood·work·ing (wood′wŭr′kiŋ), *n.* the art or process of making things out of wood. *adj.* of woodworking.

wood·worm (wood′wŭrm′), *n.* any of a number of insect larvae that live on and burrow in wood.

wood·y (wood′i), *adj.* [WOODIER (-i-ẽr), WOODIEST (-i-ist)], 1. covered with trees; wooded. 2. consisting of or forming wood; ligneous: as, a *woody* plant. 3. [Rare], of a wood or woods. 4. like wood.

woo·er (wōō′ẽr), *n.* a person who woos; suitor.

woof (wōōf), *n.* [altered, by influence of *weave* < ME. *oof;* AS. *owef; o-*, prefix + *-wef* < base of *wefan* to weave (cf. WEAVE)], 1. the threads woven back and forth across the fixed threads of the warp in a loom; weft: see **weaving,** illus. 2. cloth; texture; fabric.

woof·er (woof′ẽr), *n.* in radio, sound reproduction, etc., a large loud-speaker that reproduces low audio-frequency sound waves: distinguished from *tweeter.*

wool (wool), *n.* [see PLURAL, II, D, 3], [ME. *wolle;* AS. *wull;* akin to G. *wolle;* IE. base **wel-*, hair, wool, grass, etc., seen also in L. *lana*, Gr. *lēnos*, wool (cf. LANOLIN)], 1. the soft, curly or crisped hair of sheep. 2. the hair of some other animals, as the goat, llama, or alpaca, having a similar texture. 3. woolen yarn used for knitting, etc. 4. cloth, clothing, etc. made of wool. 5. short, curly human hair: a humorous usage. 6. any material with a texture like wool: as, rock *wool.* *adj.* of wool or woolen goods.

all wool and a yard wide, genuine or admirable.

pull the wool over one's eyes, to deceive or trick one.

wool clip, annual production of wool.

wool·en (wool′ən), *adj.* [ME. & AS. *wullen*], 1. made of wool. 2. of or relating to wool or woolen cloth. *n. pl.* woolen goods or clothing. Also spelled **woollen.**

Woolf, Virginia (woolf), (born *Adeline Virginia Stephen*), 1882–1941; English novelist and critic.

wool fat, lanolin, a fatty oil found on sheep's wool: also **wool grease.**

wool fell (wool′fel′), *n.* [*wool* + *fell* (a hide)], the pelt of a wool-bearing animal with the wool still on it.

wool·gath·er·ing (wool′ga*th*′ẽr-iŋ), *n.* [used in reference to gathering tufts of wool caught on thorns and hedges], absent-mindedness or daydreaming. *adj.* absent-minded or indulging in fancies.

wool·grow·er (wool′grō′ẽr), *n.* a person who raises sheep for wool.

wool·i·ness (wool′i-nis), *n.* woolliness.

Wooll·cott, Alexander (wool′kət), 1887–1943; American writer and critic.

wool·len (wool′ən), *adj.* & *n.* woolen.

wool·li·ness (wool′i-nis), *n.* the condition or quality of being woolly: also spelled **wooliness.**

wool·ly (wool′i), *adj.* [WOOLLIER (-i-ẽr), WOOLLIEST (-i-ist)], 1. of or like wool. 2. bearing wool. 3. covered with wool or something resembling wool in texture. 4. having a soft, clinging consistency: said of some foods. 5. having characteristics of the early frontier life of the western United States; rough and uncivilized: used chiefly in *wild and woolly.* *n.* [*pl.* WOOLLIES (-iz)], 1. in the western United States, a sheep. 2. a woolen garment, especially one with a fleecelike surface. Also spelled **wooly.**

woolly bear, any of a group of caterpillars covered with long fine hairs.

wool·pack (wool′pak′), *n.* 1. a large bag of canvas, cotton, etc. into which wool or fleece is packed for carrying or sale. 2. a bale of wool so packed, usually weighing 240 pounds. 3. a fleecy cumulus cloud.

wool·sack (wool′sak′), *n.* 1. a sack of wool. 2. a cushion stuffed with wool, on which the British Lord Chancellor sits in the House of Lords.

wool·sort·ers' disease (wool′sôr′tẽrz), pulmonary anthrax, an occupational disease of workers in unprocessed wool, contracted by inhaling the spores of the anthrax bacillus.

wool stapler, 1. a person who sells wool. 2. a person who sorts wool according to its staple, or fiber.

Wool·wich (wool′ij, wool′ich), *n.* a borough in the eastern part of London, on the Thames: pop., 148,000.

Wool·worth, Frank Win·field (win′fēld wool′wẽrth), 1852–1919; American merchant; originator of the five-and-ten-cent store.

wool·y (wool′i), *adj.* [WOOLIER (-i-ẽr), WOOLIEST (-i-ist)], & *n.* [*pl.* WOOLIES (-iz)], woolly.

woo·mer·a (wōō′mẽr-ə), *n.* a womera.

Woon·sock·et (wōōn-sok′it), *n.* a city in northern Rhode Island, on the Blackstone River: pop., 47,000.

woo·ra·li (wōō-rä′li), *n.* [var. of *curare*], curare.

Woo·sung (wōō′sooŋ′), *n.* a seaport in eastern China, near Shanghai.

wooz·y (wōō′zi, wooz′i), *adj.* [WOOZIER (-zi-ẽr, -i-ẽr), WOOZIEST (-zi-ist, -i-ist)], [prob. coined after *wooze*, var. of *ooze*], [Slang], befuddled, as with liquor; muddled.

wop (wop), *n.* [? < It. dial. *guappo*, braggart, fop < L. *vappa*, worthless fellow, good-for-nothing; see H. L. Mencken, *Am. Lang., Suppl. I*, pp. 604–607], [Slang], a dark-skinned person of Latin, especially Italian, descent: vulgar term of prejudice and contempt.

Worces·ter (woos′tẽr), *n.* 1. a city in central Massachusetts: pop., 187,000. 2. Worcestershire. 3. the county seat of Worcestershire, England: pop., 64,000.

Worces·ter, Joseph Emerson (woos′tẽr), 1784–1865; American lexicographer.

Worcester china, a fine china or porcelain made at Worcester, England, from 1751: also **Worcester porcelain** and, by royal warrant, **Royal Worcester.**

Worces·ter·shire (woos′tẽr-shir′), *n.* a county of west central England: pop., 523,000; county seat, Worcester.

Worcestershire sauce, a spicy sauce for meats, poultry, etc., containing soy, vinegar, and other ingredients: originally made in Worcester, England.

word (wŭrd), *n.* [ME.; AS.; akin to G. *wort;* IE. base **wer-*, to say, speak; in the extended form **wer-bh*, seen also in L. *verbum*, a word (cf. VERB, VERBAL)], 1. a brief expression; remark: as, a *word* of advice. 2. a promise; affirmation; assurance: as, he gave his *word.* 3. news; information; tidings: as, no *word* from home. 4. *a)* a password; signal: as, they gave the *word.* *b)* a command; order. 5. *usually pl.* *a)* talk; speech. *b)* lyrics; text; libretto. 6. *pl.* a quarrel; dispute. 7. a speech sound or series of them, having meaning and used as a unit of language: words may consist of a single morpheme or of combinations of morphemes. 8. a letter or group of letters, written or printed, representing such a unit of language. 9. [Archaic], a saying; proverb. *v.t.* to express in words; phrase.

at a word, in quick response to a request or command; immediately.

be as good as one's word, to live up to one's promises.

break one's word, to fail to keep one's promise.

by word of mouth, by speech, not by writing; orally.

eat one's words, to retract a statement.

give one's word, to promise.

hang on one's words, to listen to one eagerly.

have a word with, to have a brief conversation with.

have no words for, to be incapable of describing.

have words with, to argue angrily with.

in a word, in short; briefly.

in so many words, precisely; succinctly.

man of his word, a person who keeps his promises.

of few words, untalkative; laconic.

of many words, wordy; talkative; garrulous.

take one at one's word, to take one's words literally or seriously and, often, act accordingly.

take the words out of one's mouth, to say what one was about to say oneself.

the Word, 1. the Logos. 2. the Bible; Scriptures.

(upon) my word, indeed! really!: an exclamation of surprise, irritation, etc.

word for word, in precisely the same words; exactly.

word·age (wŭr′dij), *n.* words collectively, or the number of words (*of* a story, novel, etc.).

word-blind (wŭrd′blīnd′), *adj.* having word blindness.

word blindness, a cerebral disorder characterized by loss of ability to read; alexia.

word·book (wŭrd′book′), *n.* [after G. *wörterbuch; wörter*, pl. of *wort*, word + *buch*, book], 1. a dictionary or vocabulary. 2. a libretto. 3. a book of song lyrics.

word deafness, a cerebral disorder characterized by loss of ability to understand spoken words; auditory aphasia.

word·i·ly (wŭr′də-li), *adv.* in a wordy manner or style.

word·i·ness (wŭr′di-nis), *n.* wordy quality or condition.

word·ing (wŭr′diŋ), *n.* choice and arrangement of words; phrasing.

word·less (wŭrd′lis), *adj.* 1. without words; speechless. 2. unexpressed. 3. inexpressible.

Word of God, the Bible.

word of honor, pledged word; solemn promise.

word order, the arrangement of words in a phrase, clause, or sentence.

word·play (wŭrd′plā′), *n.* 1. subtle or clever exchange of words; repartee. 2. punning or a pun.

word square, a square made of letters so arranged that they spell the same words in the same order horizontally and vertically.

Words·worth, William (wŭrdz′wẽrth), 1770–1850; English poet; poet laureate (1843–1850).

word·y (wŭr′di), *adj.* [WORDIER (-di-ẽr),

WORDIEST (-di-ist)], 1. of words; verbal. 2. containing or using many or too many words; verbose.

SYN.—**wordy** is the general word implying the use of more words in speaking or writing than are necessary for communication (a *wordy* document); **verbose** suggests a wordiness that results in obscurity, tediousness, bombast, etc. (a *verbose* acceptance speech); **prolix** implies such a tiresome elaboration of trivial details as to be boring or dull (his *prolix* sermons); **diffuse** suggests such verbosity and loose construction as to lose all force and sharpness (a rambling, *diffuse* harangue); **redundant,** in this connection, implies the use of unnecessary or repetitious words or phrases (a *redundant* literary style). —*ANT.* concise, terse, pithy.

wore (wôr, wōr), past tense of **wear.**

work (wũrk), *n.* [ME. *werk;* AS. *werc, weorc;* akin to G. *werk;* IE. base **werĝ-*, to do, act, seen also in Gr. *ergon* (for **wergon*), action, work (cf. ERG), *organon,* tool, instrument (cf. ORGAN)], 1. bodily or mental effort exerted to do or make something; purposeful activity; labor; toil. 2. employment: as, out of *work.* 3. occupation; business; trade; craft; profession: as, his *work* is selling. 4. *a*) something one is making, doing, or acting upon, especially as one's occupation or duty; task; undertaking: as, he laid out his *work.* *b*) the amount of this: as, a day's *work.* 5. something that has been made or done; result of effort or activity; specifically, *a*) *usually pl.* an act; deed: as, a person of good *works.* *b*) *pl.* collected writings: as, the *works* of Whitman. *c*) *pl.* engineering structures, as bridges, dams, docks, etc. *d*) a fortification. *e*) needlework; embroidery. *f*) a work of art. 6. material that is being or is to be processed, as in a machine tool, in some stage of manufacture. 7. *pl.* [construed as sing.], a place where work is done, as a factory, public utility plant, etc. 8. *pl.* the working parts of a watch, etc.; mechanism. 9. manner, style, quality, rate, etc. of working; workmanship. 10. foam due to fermentation, as in cider. 11. in *mechanics,* transference of force from one body or system to another, measured by the product of the force and the amount of displacement in the line of force. 12. *pl.* in *theology,* moral acts: distinguished from *faith.* Abbreviated **W., w.** *adj.* of, for, or used in work. *v.i.* [WORKED (wũrkt) or WROUGHT (rôt), WORKING], [AS. *wyrcan, wircan, wercan*], 1. to exert oneself in order to do or make something; do work; labor; toil. 2. to be employed. 3. to perform its function; operate; act. 4. to ferment. 5. to operate effectively; be effectual: as, the makeshift *works.* 6. to produce results or exert an influence: as, let it *work* in their minds. 7. to be manipulated, kneaded, etc.: as, this putty *works* easily. 8. to move, proceed, etc. slowly and with or as with difficulty. 9. to move, twitch, etc. as from agitation: as, his face *worked* with emotion. 10. to change into a specified condition, as by repeated movement: as, the door *worked* loose. 11. to make a passage: as, her elbow had *worked* through her sleeve. 12. in *nautical usage,* to strain so, as in a storm, that the fastenings become slack: said of a ship. *v.t.* 1. to cause; bring about; effect: as, his idea *worked* harm. 2. to mold; shape; form: as, she *works* silver. 3. to weave, knit, embroider, etc.: as, she *worked* the sweater. 4. to solve (a mathematical problem). 5. to draw, paint, carve, etc. (a portrait or likeness). 6. to manipulate; knead: as, *work* the butter well. 7. to bring into a specified condition, as by repeated movement: as, they *worked* it loose. 8. to cultivate (soil). 9. to cause to function; operate; manage; use. 10. to cause to ferment. 11. to cause to work: as, he *works* his men hard. 12. to influence; persuade; induce: as, *work* him to your way of thinking. 13. to make (one's way, passage, etc.) by work or effort. 14. to provoke; rouse: as, she *worked* herself into a rage. 15. to carry on activity in; operate in; cover: as, the salesman who *works* this region. 16. [Colloq.], to make use of, especially by artful contriving: as, *work* your connections. 17. [Colloq.], to use artifice with (a person) to gain some profit or advantage.

at work, working.

get the works, [Slang], to be the victim of extreme measures.

give one the works, [Slang], 1. to murder one. 2. to subject one to an ordeal, either maliciously or jokingly.

make short (or **quick**) **work of,** to do or dispose of quickly.

out of work, without a job; unemployed.

shoot the works, [Slang], 1. to risk everything on one chance or play. 2. to make a supreme effort or attempt.

work in, 1. to introduce or insert. 2. to be introduced or inserted.

work off, to get rid of or dissipate, as by exertion.

work on (or **upon**), 1. to influence. 2. to try to persuade.

work out, 1. to make its way out, as from being embedded. 2. to exhaust (a mine, etc.). 3. to pay off (an obligation) by work instead of in money. 4. to bring about by work; accomplish. 5. to solve. 6. to calculate. 7. to result in some way. 8. to add up to a total (*at* a specified amount). 9. to develop; elaborate. 10. to put into practice.

work up, 1. to make one's (or its) way up; advance; rise. 2. to manipulate, mix, etc. into a specified object or shape. 3. to develop; elaborate. 4. to acquire knowledge of or skill at. 5. to arouse; excite.

SYN.—**work,** in this connection, is the general word for effort put forth in doing or making something, whether physical or mental, easy or difficult, pleasant or unpleasant, etc.; **labor** more often implies strenuous physical work (sentenced to three years at hard *labor*); **travail,** now a somewhat literary word, suggests painful exertion or oppressive labor (wearied by long *travail*); **toil** implies long, exhausting work, whether physical or mental (the irksome *toil* of cataloguing); **grind** suggests prolonged, tedious, uninspiring work (the *grind* of routine tasks). —*ANT.* rest, play.

work·a·bil·i·ty (wũr'kə-bil'ə-ti), *n.* the condition or quality of being workable.

work·a·ble (wũr'kə-b'l), *adj.* 1. that can be worked. 2. practicable, as a plan, method, etc.; feasible.

work·a·day (wũr'kə-dā'), *adj.* [ME. *werkedai;* ON. *virkr dagr,* working day], 1. of or suitable for working days; everyday; hence, 2. commonplace; ordinary.

work·bag (wũrk'bag'), *n.* a bag for holding implements and materials for work, especially needlework.

work·bench (wũrk'bench'), *n.* a table at which work is done, as by a mechanic.

work·book (wũrk'book'), *n.* 1. a book for the use of students, containing questions and exercises based on a textbook or course of study. 2. a book containing instructions on the method of operation. 3. a book in which one keeps a record of work planned or done.

work·box (wũrk'boks'), *n.* a box for holding implements and materials for work, especially needlework.

work·day (wũrk'dā'), *n.* [ME. *werkdai;* prob. < *werk* + *dai;* AS. had *weorcdæg*], 1. a day on which work is done; working day. 2. the part of a day during which work is done: as, a 7-hour *workday.* *adj.* workaday.

work·er (wũr'kẽr), *n.* 1. a person, animal, or thing that works; specifically, *a*) a person who works for a living, either with hand or brain; especially, one who does industrial or manual work for wages. *b*) any of a class of sterile or sexually imperfect female ants, bees, wasps, etc. that do general or specialized work for the colony. 2. in *printing,* an electrotype used to print from, as distinguished from one used as a mold for making duplicate electrotypes.

work·folk (wũrk'fōk'), *n.pl.* working people.

work·folks (wũrk'fōks'), *n.pl.* workfolk.

work·house (wũrk'hous'), *n.* 1. originally, a workshop. 2. in England, a poorhouse. 3. a kind of prison, where petty offenders are confined and made to work.

work·ing (wũr'kiŋ), *adj.* 1. that works. 2. of, for, used in, or taken up by work: as, a *working* day, *working* clothes. 3. sufficient to get work done: as, a *working* majority. 4. on which further work is or may be based: as, a *working* hypothesis. 5. moving or jerking convulsively, as from emotion: said of the face or facial features. *n.* 1. the act or process of a person or thing that works (in various senses). 2. convulsive movement or jerking, as of the face. 3. slow or gradual progress involving great effort or exertion. 4. *usually pl.* a part of a mine, quarry, etc. where work is or has been done.

working capital, 1. in *accounting,* excess of readily convertible assets over current liabilities. 2. in *finance,* the part of a company's capital that remains readily convertible into cash.

work·ing-class (wũr'kiŋ-klas', wũr'kiŋ-kläs'), *adj.* of or characteristic of the working class.

working class, workers as a class; especially, industrial workers as a class; proletariat.

work·ing-day (wũr'kiŋ-dā'), *adj.* of or suitable for working days; workaday.

working day, 1. a day on which work is ordinarily done, as distinguished from a Sunday, holiday, etc.; workday. 2. the part of a day during which work is done; specifically, the number of hours constituting the required day's work for the regular wage or salary.

working drawing, a drawing made to scale, for the guidance of those doing the work illustrated by it.

work·ing·man (wũr'kiŋ-man'), *n.* [*pl.* WORKINGMEN (-men')], a worker; especially, an industrial or manual worker; laborer.

working papers, any official papers that legalize the employment of a minor.

working substance, the air, gas, or liquid that works the pistons, vanes, etc. of an engine.

work·ing·wom·an (wũr'kiŋ-woom'ən), *n.* [*pl.* WORKINGWOMEN (-wim'in)], a woman worker; especially, a woman industrial or manual worker.

work·man (wũrk'mən), *n.* [*pl.* WORKMEN (-mən)], 1. a worker; laborer. 2. a person who does his work in some specified way: as, a careful *workman.*

work·man·like (wũrk'mən-līk'), *adj.* characteristic of a good workman; skillful. *adv.* in a workmanlike manner.

work·man·ly (wũrk'mən-li), *adv.* workmanlike.

work·man·ship (wũrk'mən-ship'), *n.* [see -SHIP], 1. skill as a workman; craftsmanship; artistry. 2. evidence of this skill in something produced; execution: as, the vase has the highest *workmanship*. 3. something produced: as, the bookcases are my *workmanship*.

workmen's compensation, the compensation to an employee for injury or occupational disease suffered in connection with his employment, paid under a government-supervised insurance system contributed to by employers.

work of art, 1. something produced in one of the fine arts, especially in one of the plastic or graphic arts, as a painting, sculpture, carving, etc. 2. anything beautifully made, played, sung, acted, etc.

work·out (wũrk′out′), *n.* [Colloq.], 1. a test, practice, etc. to develop, keep, or acquire proficiency, as for a competition. 2. any strenuous exercise, work, etc.

work·peo·ple (wũrk′pē′p'l), *n.pl.* workers; especially, industrial or manual workers.

work·room (wũrk′rōōm′, wũrk′room′), *n.* a room in which work is done.

works council, a committee of workers in a factory, business, etc., organized by an employer to discuss industrial relations.

work sheet, any sheet of paper on which a record of work, working time, etc. is kept.

work·shop (wũrk′shop′), *n.* 1. a room or building where work is done. 2. a group of people who meet for a period of intensive study, work, etc. in some field.

work·ta·ble (wũrk′tā′b'l), *n.* a table at which work is done, as a small table with drawers, for needlework.

work-up (wũrk′up′), *n.* in *printing*, a mark on a printed page caused by the rising of spacing material.

work·week (wũrk′wēk′), *n.* the total number of hours worked in a week.

work·wom·an (wũrk′woom′ən), *n.* [*pl.* WORKWOMEN (-wim′in)], a woman who works; especially, a woman industrial or manual worker.

world (wũrld), *n.* [ME. *werld, world, worlde;* AS. *weoruld, weorold,* etc., world, lit., age of man < *wer*, a man (cf. WEREWOLF) + base of *old;* basic sense "the age of man"], 1. the earth. 2. the universe. 3. the earth and its inhabitants. 4. *a)* the human race; mankind. *b)* the public: as, the discovery startled the *world*. 5. *a)* [also W-], some part of the earth: as, the Old *World*. *b)* some period of history, its society, etc.: as, the ancient *world*. *c)* any sphere or domain: as, the dog *world*, the animal, vegetable, or mineral *world*. *d)* any sphere of human activity: as, the *world* of music. *e)* any sphere or state of existence. 6. individual experience, outlook, etc.: as, his *world* is narrow. 7. *a)* secular life and interests, as distinguished from the religious or spiritual; social life and its concerns. *b)* people primarily concerned with the affairs and pursuits of the present life. 8. *often pl.* a large amount; great deal: as, the rest did him a *world* (or *worlds*) of good. 9. a star or planet. —*SYN.* see **earth.**

bring into the world, to give birth to.

come into the world, to be born.

for all the world, 1. for any reason or consideration at all. 2. in every respect; exactly.

in the world, 1. on earth or in the universe; anywhere. 2. at all; ever.

on top of the world, [Slang], lifted up with joy, pride, success, etc.; elated; exultant.

out of this (or **the**) **world,** [Slang], exceptionally fine; extraordinary; remarkable.

world without end, forever.

World Court, a court (*Permanent Court of International Justice*) set up by the League of Nations to settle disputes between nations.

world·li·ness (wũrld′li-nis), *n.* the condition or quality of being worldly.

world·ling (wũrld′liŋ), *n.* a worldly person.

world·ly (wũrld′li), *adj.* [WORLDLIER (-li-ẽr), WORLDLIEST (-li-ist)], 1. of this world; temporal or secular: opposed to ***heavenly, spiritual, ecclesiastical,*** etc. 2. devoted to or concerned with the affairs, pleasures, etc. of this world. 3. worldly-wise. —*SYN.* see **earthly.**

world·ly-mind·ed (wũrld′li-mīn′did), *adj.* worldly (sense 2).

world·ly-wise (wũrld′li-wīz′), *adj.* wise in the ways or affairs of the world; sophisticated.

world power, [transl. of G. *weltmacht*], a nation or organization large or powerful enough to have a worldwide influence.

world series, an annual series of games between the winning teams of the two major American baseball leagues to decide the championship: also **world's series.**

world's fair (wũrldz), an exhibition of the arts, crafts, industrial and agricultural products, scientific advances, etc. of various countries of the world.

world soul, the soul of the world, a universal animating principle analogous to the soul of the individual.

World War I, the war between the Allies (Great Britain, France, Russia, the United States, Italy, Japan, etc.) and the Central Powers (Germany, Austria-Hungary, etc.), fought from 1914 to 1918.

World War II, the war between the United Nations (Great Britain, France, the Soviet Union, the United States, etc.) and the Axis (Germany, Italy, Japan, etc.), fought from 1939 to 1945.

world-wea·ry (wũrld′wêr′i), *adj.* weary of the world or of living.

world-wide (wũrld′wīd′), *adj.* extending throughout the world.

worm (wũrm), *n.* [ME. *werm, worm, wurm;* AS. *wyrm*, serpent, dragon; akin to G. *wurm;* IE. base ***wer-**, to twist, curve, seen also in L. *vermis* (for **vormis*), a worm; cf. VERMI-], 1. any of many long, slender, soft-bodied, creeping animals, some segmented, that live by burrowing underground or as parasites, as the earthworm, tapeworm, etc. 2. popularly, an insect larva, as a caterpillar, grub, or maggot. 3. an abject, wretched, or contemptible person. 4. something thought of as being wormlike because of its spiral shape, etc., as the thread of a screw or the coil of a still. 5. something that gnaws or distresses one inwardly, suggesting a parasitic worm: as, the *worm* of conscience. 6. a mechanical device thought of as resembling a worm; specifically, *a)* an Archimedean screw or similar apparatus. *b)* a short, rotating screw that meshes with the teeth of a worm wheel or a rack. 7. in *anatomy*, any organ or part resembling a worm, as the vermiform process. 8. *pl.* in *medicine*, any disease or disorder caused by the presence of parasitic worms in the intestines, etc. 9. in *zoology*, a lytta. *v.i.* to move, proceed, etc. like a worm, in a winding, creeping, or devious manner. *v.t.* 1. to bring about, make, etc. in a winding, creeping, or devious manner: as, he *wormed* his way in. 2. to insinuate (oneself) into a situation, conversation, etc. 3. to extract (information, secrets, etc.) by insinuation, cajolery, or subtle questioning. 4. to purge of intestinal worms. 5. to extract the lytta from the tongue of (a dog, etc.). 6. in *nautical usage*, to wind yarn or small rope in and around the strands of (a rope or cable) in order to smooth the surface.

worm-eat·en (wũrm′ēt′'n), *adj.* 1. eaten into by worms, termites, etc.; hence, 2. worn-out, ragged, decrepit, out-of-date, etc.

worm fence, a zigzag fence of rails; snake fence.

worm gear, 1. a worm wheel. 2. a gear consisting of a worm and worm wheel.

worm·hole (wũrm′hōl′), *n.* a hole made by a worm, termite, etc.

worm·root (wũrm′rōōt′, wũrm′root′), *n.* an herb used in treating intestinal worms.

Worms (vôrmz; Eng. wũrmz), *n.* a city in Hesse, western Germany, on the Rhine: pop., 50,000: at a meeting (*Diet of Worms*) held there in 1521, Martin Luther was condemned as a heretic.

WORM GEAR

worm·seed (wũrm′sēd′), *n.* 1. any of a number of plants whose seeds are used in medicine as a remedy for worms, as santonica, American wormseed, etc. 2. the seed of any of these plants.

worm wheel, a toothed wheel designed to gear with the thread of a worm.

worm·wood (wũrm′wood′), *n.* [altered by folk etym. < ME. & AS. *wermod;* akin to G. *wermut* (whence Fr. *vermout;* cf. VERMOUTH); Weekley suggests deriv. < AS. *wer*, a man (cf. WEREWOLF); + base of *mood* in the sense "courage" from use of the plant as an aphrodisiac], 1. any of a number of related strong-smelling plants with white or yellow flowers; specifically, a species that yields a bitter-tasting, dark-green oil used in making absinthe. 2. any bitter, unpleasant, or mortifying experience; bitterness.

worm·y (wũr′mi), *adj.* [WORMIER (-mi-ẽr), WORMIEST (-mi-ist)], 1. containing a worm or worms; worm-eaten: as, a *wormy* apple. 2. infested with worms. 3. like a worm; hence, 4. mean; debased; groveling.

worn (wôrn, wōrn), past participle of **wear.** *adj.* 1. showing the effects of use, wear, etc. 2. damaged by use or wear. 3. showing the effects of worry or anxiety. 4. exhausted; enfeebled; spent.

worn-out (wôrn′out′, wōrn′out′), *adj.* 1. used or worn until no longer effective, usable, or serviceable. 2. exhausted; tired out.

wor·ri·ment (wũr′i-mənt), *n.* 1. a worrying or being worried; mental disturbance; anxiety. 2. a cause of worry.

wor·ri·some (wũr′i-səm), *adj.* 1. causing worry or anxiety. 2. having a tendency to worry.

wor·ry (wũr′i), *v.t.* [WORRIED (-id), WORRYING], [ME. *wirwen, worien*, etc.; AS. *wyrgan*, to strangle, injure; akin to G. *würgen;* IE. ***wer-ĝh** < base ***wer-**, to twist, bend, seen also in Eng. *worm*], 1. to harass or treat roughly with or as with continual biting or tearing with the teeth: as, the dog was *worrying* an old shoe. 2.

to annoy; pester; bother. 3. to cause to feel troubled or uneasy; make anxious; distress. *v.i.* 1. to bite, pull, or tear (*at* an object) with the teeth. 2. to feel distressed in the mind; be anxious, troubled, or uneasy. 3. to manage to get (*along* or *through*) in the face of trials and difficulties. *n.* [*pl.* WORRIES (-iz)], 1. an act of worrying. 2. a troubled state of mind; anxiety; distress; care; uneasiness. 3. something that causes anxiety or mental distress. —*SYN.* see **care.**

worse (wũrs), *adj.* [comparative of *bad* & *ill*], [ME. *werse;* AS. *wiersa,* used as compar. of *yfel,* bad, evil (cf. EVIL); akin to OHG. *wirsiro* < the base seen in OHG. *werran,* to confuse; prob. basic sense "the higher" < the IE. base **wer-*, a raised place, seen also in Eng. *wart*], 1. bad, evil, harmful, unpleasant, etc. in a greater degree; less good. 2. in poorer health or physical condition; more ill; less well. 3. in a less favorable condition; in a more unsatisfactory situation. *adv.* [comparative of *badly* & *ill*], in a worse manner or way; to a worse extent or degree. *n.* that which is worse.

wors·en (wũr's'n), *v.t.* & *v.i.* [orig., a dial. word < *worse* + *-en,* introduced into literature by Romantic writers], to make or become worse.

wors·er (wũrs'ẽr), *adj.* & *adv.* worse: a redundant form now considered a vulgarism.

wor·ship (wũr'ship), *n.* [ME. *worschip;* AS. *weorthscipe, wyrthscipe,* honor, dignity, worship < *weorth, wurth,* worthy, honorable (cf. WORTH) + *-scipe* (cf. -SHIP)], 1. a prayer, church service, or other rite showing reverence or devotion for a deity; religious homage or veneration. 2. extreme devotion; intense love or admiration of any kind. 3. something worshiped. 4. [Chiefly British], a title of honor used in addressing magistrates and certain others holding high rank. 5. [Obs. or Archaic], greatness of character; honor; dignity; worthiness. *v.t.* [WORSHIPED or WORSHIPPED (-shipt), WORSHIPING or WORSHIPPING], 1. to show religious devotion or reverence for; adore or venerate as a deity. 2. to have intense love or admiration for; idolize. *v.i.* to engage in worship; specifically, to perform any act of religious devotion; offer prayers, attend church services, etc. —*SYN.* see **revere.**

wor·ship·er (wũr'ship'ẽr), *n.* a person who worships.

wor·ship·ful (wũr'ship-fəl), *adj.* 1. worthy of being worshiped; honorable; respected: used as a title of respect for magistrates, certain lodge officials, etc. 2. feeling or offering great devotion or respect; worshiping.

wor·ship·per (wũr'ship-ẽr), *n.* a worshiper.

worst (wũrst), *adj.* [superlative of *bad* & *ill*], [ME. *worste, werste;* AS. *wyrsta, wersta* < the base of *wiersa* with *-st,* superl. suffix], bad, evil, harmful, unpleasant, etc. in the highest degree; least good. *adv.* [superlative of *badly* & *ill*], in the worst manner; to a degree that is most bad, evil, unpleasant, etc. *n.* that which is worst. *v.t.* to get the better of; defeat.

at worst, under the worst circumstances; at the greatest disadvantage.

give one the worst of it, to defeat or get the better of one.

if worst comes to worst, if the worst possible thing happens.

(in) the worst way, [Slang], very much; greatly; intensely.

make the worst of, to be pessimistic about; consider only the least favorable aspects of.

wor·sted (woos'tid; woor'stid *is a sp. pronun.*), *n.* [ME. *wurstede,* after *Worsted,* now *Worstead,* England, where first made], 1. a smooth, hard-twisted thread or yarn made from long-staple wool. 2. fabric made from this, with a smooth, hard surface. *adj.* made of worsted.

wort (wũrt), *n.* [ME. *wort, worte;* AS. *wyrt-* (in compounds); akin to G. *wurze,* a spice; IE. base **wrād-*, etc., twig, root, seen also in L. *radix,* a root (cf. RADICAL, ERADICATE, etc.)], a liquid prepared with malt which, after fermenting, becomes beer, ale, etc.

wort (wũrt), *n.* [ME.; AS. *wyrt,* a root, herb, plant < same base as prec.], a plant or herb: now usually in compounds, as *spleenwort, liverwort.*

worth (wũrth), *n.* [ME.; AS. *weorth;* akin to G. *wert;* IE. base **wert-* < **wer-*, to turn; prob. basic sense "price given for something"], 1. material value, especially as expressed in terms of money or some other medium of exchange. 2. the esteem in which a person or thing is held; importance, value, merit, excellence, etc. 3. the amount or quantity of something that may be had for a given sum: as, a dollar's *worth* of nickels, fifty cents' *worth* of sugar. 4. wealth; possessions; riches. *adj.* 1. deserving or worthy of; meriting. 2. equal in worth or value to something specified. 3. having wealth or possessions amounting to.

for all one is worth, to the extent of one's powers or ability; to the utmost.

put in one's two cents worth, to give one's own opinion, as in a discussion; speak up.

SYN.—**worth** and **value** are used interchangeably when applied to the desirability of something material as measured by its equivalence in money, goods, etc. (the *worth* or *value* of a used car), but, in discrimination, **worth** implies an intrinsic excellence resulting as from superior moral, cultural, or spiritual qualities, and **value** suggests the excellence attributed to something with reference to its usability, importance, etc. (the true *worth* of Shakespeare's plays cannot be measured by their *value* to the commercial theater).

worth (wũrth), *v.i.* [ME. *worthen;* AS. *weorthan,* to become, used as auxiliary of the passive voice; akin to G. *werden;* for IE. base see prec.], [Archaic], to betide; befall; become: as, woe *worth* the day.

wor·thi·ly (wũr'thə-li), *adv.* in a worthy manner.

wor·thi·ness (wũr'thi-nis), *n.* the fact of being worthy.

worth·less (wũrth'lis), *adj.* without worth or merit; useless, valueless, good-for-nothing, etc.

worth-while (wũrth'hwīl'), *adj.* important or valuable enough to repay time or effort spent; of true value, merit, or importance.

wor·thy (wũr'thi), *adj.* [WORTHIER (-thi-ẽr), WORTHIEST (-thi-ist)], [ME. *worthi, wurdi*], 1. having worth, value, or merit. 2. having enough worth or merit; deserving; meriting (often with *of* or an infinitive): as, a candidate *worthy* of support. 3. [Obs.], merited; well-deserved. *n.* [*pl.* WORTHIES (-thiz)], a person of outstanding worth or importance: often used humorously.

wot (wot), [Archaic], first and third person singular, present indicative, of **wit** (to know).

Wouk, Herman (wōk), 1915– ; American writer.

would (wood), [ME. & AS. *wolde,* p.t. of *willan,* to will, wish; cf. WILL], past tense and alternative obsolete past participle of **will.** *Would* is also used: 1. to express condition, as, he *would* write if you *would* answer. 2. in indirect discourse to express futurity, as, he said he *would* bring it. 3. to express a wish, as, *would* that he were still living. 4. to soften somewhat the force of a statement or request, as, *would* you do this for me? Cf. **should.**

would (wōld), *n.* a weld (flower).

would-be (wood'bē'), *adj.* [ME. (northern) *walde be*], 1. that would be; wishing or pretending to be. 2. intended to be.

would·est (wood'ist), alternative archaic second person singular of **would:** used with *thou.*

would·n't (wood''nt), would not.

wouldst (woodst), alternative archaic second person singular of **would:** used with *thou.*

wound (wōōnd), *n.* [ME.; AS. *wund;* akin to G. *wunde;* IE. base **wen-*, to hit, as also in AS. *wenn* (cf. WEN); the older pronun. (wound) is still heard among surgeons], 1. an injury to the body in which the skin or other tissue is broken, cut, pierced, torn, etc. 2. a mark or scar resulting from this. 3. an injury to a plant caused by cutting, scraping, or other external force. 4. any hurt or injury to the feelings, honor, etc. *v.t.* & *v.i.* [ME. *wundien;* AS. *wundian* < the *n.*], to inflict a wound or wounds (on or upon); hurt; injure.

wound (wound), 1. past tense and past participle of **wind** (to twist). 2. past tense and past participle of **wind** (to blow).

wove (wōv), past tense and alternative past participle of **weave.**

wo·ven (wōv''n), alternative past participle of **weave.**

wove paper, paper made on a mold in which the wires are so closely woven together that the finished sheets do not show wire marks as on laid paper.

wow (wou), *interj.* an expression of surprise, wonder, pleasure, pain, etc. *n.* [Slang], 1. something very amusing. 2. a great success. *v.t.* [Slang], to be a great success with.

wow·ser (wou'zẽr), *n.* in Australia, a person who is rigorously puritanical, as in his objections to Sunday amusements or sports.

WPA, W.P.A., Work Projects Administration.

WPB, W.P.B., War Production Board.

wrack (rak), *n.* [ME. & MD. *wrak,* something damaged, wreck; cf. WRECK], 1. ruin; destruction: now chiefly in the phrase *wrack and ruin.* 2. a wrecked ship. 3. wreckage. 4. seaweed or other marine plant life cast up on shore. 5. [Scot. & Dial.], weeds. *v.t.* & *v.i.* [Archaic], to wreck or be wrecked.

wrack (rak), *n.* a rack of clouds or other vapor.

WRAF, W.R.A.F., Women's Royal Air Force.

wraith (rāth), *n.* [Scot., earlier *warth,* guardian angel; ON. *vörthr,* guardian < *vartha,* to ward, guard; cf. WARD], a ghost; specifically, the spectral figure of a person supposedly seen just before or after his death.

Wran·gel Island (raŋ'g'l; Russ. vrän'gel'y'), an island of the U.S.S.R. in the Arctic Ocean, off the northeastern coast of Siberia: area, 1,800 sq. mi.

Wran·gell (raŋ'g'l), *n.* 1. a mountain range in southeastern Alaska: highest peak, Mt. Bona, 16,420 ft. 2. a mountain in this range: height, 14,005 ft.

wran·gle (raŋ'g'l), *v.i.* [WRANGLED (-g'ld), WRANGLING], [ME. *wranglen,* freq. of *wringen,* prob. < a LG. source; see WRING], 1. to dispute or quarrel angrily and noisily. 2. to argue; dispute. *v.t.* 1. to argue (with *into, out of,* etc.). 2. to herd or round up (livestock). *n.* an angry, noisy dispute or quarrel. —*SYN.* see **quarrel.**

wran·gler (raŋ'glẽr), *n.* 1. a person who wrangles; specifically, *a)* one who argues. *b)* a cowboy who rounds up livestock. 2. a student in the highest class of honors in mathematics at Cambridge University.

wrap (rap), ***v.t.*** [WRAPPED or WRAPT (rapt), WRAPPING], [ME. *wrappen* (also *wlappen*), a word merging *lappen* (cf. LAP, *v.*) with some word or words with initial *wr-*], 1. to wind or fold (a covering) around something. 2. to cover by this means. 3. to conceal; cover; envelop; hide: as, the housetops were *wrapped* in smoke. 4. to enclose and fasten in a wrapper of paper, etc.; do up in a package or wrapping. 5. to wind or fold: as, she *wrapped* her arms around him. ***v.i.*** to twine, extend, coil, etc. (usually with *over, around*, etc.). ***n.*** 1. an outer covering, especially a garment worn by being wrapped around the body. 2. a blanket. 3. *pl.* secrecy; censorship; concealment: as, plans kept under *wraps*. **wrapped up in,** 1. devoted to; absorbed in (work, etc.). 2. involved or implicated in.

wrap·per (rap'ẽr), ***n.*** 1. a person or thing that wraps. 2. that in which something is wrapped; covering; cover; specifically, *a*) the outer leaf of tobacco covering a cigar. *b*) [Chiefly British], the dust jacket of a book. *c*) the paper wrapping in which a newspaper, magazine, etc. is enclosed for mailing. 3. a woman's dressing gown.

wrap·ping (rap'iŋ), ***n.*** *usually pl.* the material, as paper, in which something is wrapped.

wrapping paper, heavy paper made for wrapping parcels, etc.

wrapt (rapt), alternative past tense and past participle of **wrap.**

wrasse (ras), ***n.*** [Corn. *wrach*], any of a number of sea food fishes having thick lips, spiny fins, strong teeth, and bright coloring.

wrath (rath, räth; Brit. rôth), ***n.*** [ME. *wraththe, wraeththe;* AS. *wrætho* < *wrath*, wroth; cf. WROTH], 1. intense anger; rage; fury. 2. any action carried out in great anger, especially for punishment or vengeance. ***adj.*** [Rare or Archaic], wrathful. —***SYN.*** see **anger.**

wrath·ful (rath'fəl, räth'fəl), ***adj.*** 1. full of wrath; intensely angry. 2. resulting from, characterized by, or expressing wrath.

wrath·i·ly (rath'ə-li, räth'ə-li), ***adv.*** [Colloq.], in a wrathful manner.

wrath·i·ness (rath'i-nis, räth'i-nis), ***n.*** [Colloq.], the state of being wrathful.

wrath·y (rath'i, räth'i), ***adj.*** [Colloq.], wrathful.

wreak (rēk), ***v.t.*** [ME. *wreken;* AS. *wrecan*, to revenge, punish; akin to G. *rächen;* IE. base **werg-* to shove, press, seen also in L. *urgere*, to press (cf. URGE); cf. WRECK], 1. to give vent or free play to (anger, malice, rage, etc.): as, he *wreaked* his anger on the students. 2. to inflict (vengeance, etc.). 3. [Archaic], to avenge.

wreath (rēth), ***n.*** [*pl.* WREATHS (rēthz)], [ME. *wrethe;* AS. *wræth*, a twisted band, bandage < p.t. stem of *writhan*, to twist; cf. WRITHE], 1. a twisted band or ring of leaves, flowers, etc.; a chaplet worn as a mark of honor or victory, or a garland laid upon a grave, hung on a door, window, etc. 2. something suggesting or resembling this in shape; twisted or circular band: as, *wreaths* of smoke. 3. Corona Australis, a constellation.

wreathe (rēth), ***v.t.*** [WREATHED (rēthd), WREATHED or *archaic* WREATHEN (-'n), WREATHING], [< *wreath* & also < ME. *wrethen*, pp. of *writhen;* see WRITHE], 1. to coil, twist, or entwine, especially so as to form a wreath. 2. to coil, twist, or entwine around; encircle: as, clouds *wreathed* the mountains. 3. to decorate with wreaths. 4. to cover or envelop: as, a face *wreathed* in wrinkles, smiles, etc. ***v.i.*** 1. to have a twisting or coiling movement. 2. to have or take the form of a wreath.

wreck (rek), ***n.*** [ME. *wrek, wrecke;* Anglo-Fr. *wrec, wrech* < Anglo-N. *wrek* (Norw., Ice. *rek*) < the base of *wreak*], 1. goods or wreckage cast ashore after a shipwreck. 2. *a*) the disabling or destruction of a ship by any disaster of navigation; shipwreck. *b*) a ship that has been broken or destroyed by any disaster of navigation. 3. the remains of anything that has been destroyed or badly damaged. 4. a person in very poor health. 5. a wrecking or being wrecked; destruction; ruin. ***v.t.*** 1. to cause the wreck of; destroy or damage badly. 2. to tear down; dismantle (a building, etc.). 3. to bring to ruin or disaster; overthrow; thwart; defeat. 4. to destroy the health or physical soundness of. ***v.i.*** 1. to be wrecked; suffer damage, destruction, or ruin. 2. to be a wrecker.

wreck·age (rek'ij), ***n.*** [see -AGE], 1. a wrecking or being wrecked. 2. the remains of something that has been wrecked.

wreck·er (rek'ẽr), ***n.*** 1. a person or thing that wrecks. 2. a person who causes ruin, obstruction, or disruption of any kind. 3. a person, car, train, boat, etc. that salvages or clears away wrecks. 4. a person who tears down and salvages old buildings, etc.

wreck·ing (rek'iŋ), ***n.*** the act or work of a wrecker. ***adj.*** engaged or used in dismantling, clearing, or salvaging wrecks: as, a *wrecking* crew.

Wren (ren), ***n.*** [British Colloq.], a member of the Women's Royal Naval Service.

wren (ren), ***n.*** [ME. *wrenne;* AS. *wrenna;* akin to OHG. *wrendo* & prob. < same base as AS. *wræne*, lecherous; IE. base **wrei-*, to grimace, seen also in L. *ridere*, to laugh; the name may be due to the bird's habits or its cry], any of a large number of small songbirds having a long bill, rounded wings, and a stubby, erect tail.

Wren, Sir **Christopher** (ren), 1632–1723; English architect.

wrench (rench), ***n.*** [ME.; AS. *wrenc*, a trick, deceit; akin to G. *ränke*, a bend, twist; IE. base **wreng-* (cf. WRING) < **wer-*, to twist, turn; cf. WORM], 1. a sudden, violent twist or pull. 2. an injury caused by a twist or jerk, as to the back, a joint, etc. 3. a sudden feeling of anguish, grief, etc., as from separation: as, the *wrench* of saying good-by. 4. any of a number of tools used for holding and turning nuts, bolts, pipes, etc. 5. a false or strained interpretation of an original meaning. ***v.t.*** 1. to twist, pull, or jerk suddenly and violently. 2. to injure (a part of the body) with a twist or wrench. 3. to distort, strain, or give a false interpretation of (a meaning, statement, etc.).

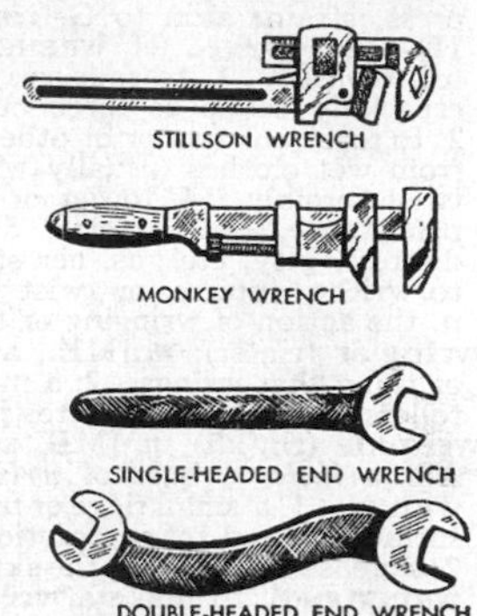

WRENCHES

wrest (rest), ***v.t.*** [ME. *wresten;* AS. *wræstan*, to twist violently; akin to ON. *reista;* IE. base **wer-*, to turn, bend, twist, as also in Eng. *wrist*], 1. to turn or twist; especially, to pull or force away violently with a twisting motion. 2. to take or extract by force; usurp; extort; wring. 3. to distort or change the true meaning, purpose, use, etc. of; pervert; twist. ***n.*** 1. the act of wresting; a twist; wrench. 2. a wrenchlike key used for tuning pianos, harps, etc. by turning the pins around which the strings are coiled.

wres·tle (res''l), ***v.i.*** [WRESTLED (-'ld), WRESTLING], [ME. *wrestlen, wrastlen;* AS. *wræstlian*, freq. of *wræstan*, to twist, wrestle (cf. WREST)], 1. to struggle hand to hand with an opponent in an attempt to throw or force him to the ground without striking blows. 2. to struggle in opposition; strive; contend. ***v.t.*** 1. to struggle or fight with by wrestling; wrestle with. 2. in the western United States, to throw (a calf, etc.) for branding. ***n.*** 1. the action of wrestling; wrestling bout. 2. a struggle or contest.

wres·tler (res'lẽr), ***n.*** a person who wrestles, especially one who takes part in regular wrestling bouts.

wres·tling (res'liŋ), ***n.*** a form of sport in which the opponents wrestle, or struggle hand to hand attempting to throw or force each other to the ground without striking blows.

wrest pin, either of two metal pins between which a single string of a piano, harp, etc. is stretched: the pins are turned to tune the instrument.

wretch (rech), ***n.*** [ME. *wrecche;* AS. *wrecca*, an outcast, lit., one driven out < *wrecan*, to drive out, wreak, avenge; cf. WREAK], 1. a miserable or unhappy person; person in deep distress or misfortune. 2. a person who is despised or looked upon with contempt.

wretch·ed (rech'id), ***adj.*** [ME. *wrecched* < *wrecche;* AS. *wræcc*, wretched < *wrecan;* see WREAK, WRETCH], 1. deeply distressed or unhappy; miserable; unfortunate. 2. characterized by or causing distress or misery; woeful; depressing; dismal. 3. poor in quality; very inferior; unsatisfactory: as, he has done a *wretched* job. 4. contemptible; despicable; mean.

wrick (rik), ***n.*** [via S.W. dial. < ME. *wrikken*, to move jerkily; MLG. *-wricken* (whence G. *wricken*)], a wrench or sprain. ***v.t.*** to wrench, twist, or sprain.

wrig·gle (rig''l), ***v.i.*** [WRIGGLED (-'ld), WRIGGLING], [MLG. *wriggeln;* akin to Eng. *wry*], 1. to move to and fro with a twisting, writhing motion; twist and turn; squirm. 2. to move along with a wriggling motion. 3. to make one's way by subtle or shifty means; dodge; equivocate. ***v.t.*** 1. to cause to wriggle. 2. to bring into a specified condition, form, etc. by wriggling. ***n.*** a wriggling movement or action.

wrig·gler (rig'lẽr), ***n.*** 1. a person or thing that wriggles. 2. the larva of a mosquito.

wrig·gly (rig'li), ***adj.*** [WRIGGLIER (-li-ẽr), WRIGGLIEST (-li-ist)], wriggling; twisting; squirming.

wright (rīt), ***n.*** [ME. *wrighte, wrihte;* AS. *wyrhta*, a worker, workman, maker, creator < *wyrcan*, to work; cf. WORK], a person who makes or constructs: used chiefly in compounds, as, *wheelwright, shipwright.*

Wright, Frank Lloyd (rīt), 1869–1959; American architect.

Wright, Joseph, 1855–1930; British philologist and lexicographer.
Wright, Orville, 1871–1948; American airplane inventor in collaboration with his brother *Wilbur.*
Wright, Wilbur, 1867–1912; American airplane inventor in collaboration with his brother *Orville.*
wring (riŋ), *v.t.* [WRUNG (ruŋ) or *rare* WRINGED (riŋd), WRINGING], [ME. *wringen;* AS. *wringan,* to press, compress, strain; akin to G. *ringen,* to struggle, wrestle; IE. base **wreng-,* (cf. WRENCH) < **wer-,* to turn, bend (cf. WORM)], 1. to squeeze, press, twist, or compress, especially so as to force out water or other liquid. 2. to force out (water or other liquid) by this means, as from wet clothes (usually with *out*). 3. to wrench or twist forcibly. 4. to get or extract by force, threats, persistence, etc.; extort. 5. to afflict with anguish, distress, pity, etc.: as, her story *wrung* his heart. *v.i.* to writhe, squirm, or twist with force or great effort. *n.* the action of wringing or twisting.
wring·er (riŋ′ẽr), *n.* [ME., an oppressor], 1. a person or thing that wrings. 2. a machine fitted with opposed rollers which squeeze water from wet clothes.
wrin·kle (riŋ′k'l), *n.* [ME. *wrinkel, wrinkil,* a wrinkle; AS. *wrincle* < base of *wringan,* to press, wring; cf. WRING], 1. a small ridge or furrow in a normally smooth surface, caused by contraction, crumpling, folding, etc. 2. a crease or pucker in the skin. *v.t.* [WRINKLED (-k'ld), WRINKLING], to make a wrinkle or wrinkles in, as by contracting; pucker; crease. *v.i.* to be or become wrinkled; form wrinkles, as by contracting.
wrin·kle (riŋ′k'l), *n.* [prob. dim. ult. < AS. *wrenc,* a trick, guile; cf. WRENCH], [Colloq.], a clever trick, idea, or device; novelty.
wrin·kly (riŋ′kli), *adj.* [WRINKLIER (-kli-ẽr), WRINKLIEST (-kli-ist)], having wrinkles; wrinkled.
wrist (rist), *n.* [ME. *wriste, wrist;* AS. < the base of *wræstan,* to twist (cf. WREST)], 1. the joint or part of the arm between the hand and the forearm; carpus. 2. the corresponding part in an animal. 3. the part of a sleeve, glove, etc. covering the wrist. 4. a wrist pin.
wrist·band (rist′band′, riz′bənd), *n.* the band at the end of a full-length sleeve, that fits at the wrist; cuff, especially of a shirt.
wrist-drop (rist′drop′), *n.* paralysis of the extensor muscles of the hand, due to injury or, especially, lead poisoning: also **wrist drop.**
wrist·let (rist′lit), *n.* 1. a band or strap worn around the wrist for warmth, to secure a watch, etc. 2. a bracelet. 3. [Slang], a handcuff.
wrist·lock (rist′lok′), *n.* a wrestling hold in which one wrestler twists his opponent's arm from a hold at the wrist.
wrist pin, the stud or pin by which a connecting rod is attached to a wheel, crank, etc.
wrist watch, a watch worn on a strap or band that fits around the wrist.
writ (rit), *n.* [ME.; AS., a writing, writ < *writan,* to write], 1. [Rare or Archaic], something written; writing; document. 2. a formal legal document ordering or prohibiting the performance of some action.
  Holy Writ, the Bible.
write (rīt), *v.t.* [WROTE (rōt), WRITTEN (rit′'n), WRITING; *archaic* p.t. & pp. WRIT (rit)], [ME. *writen;* AS. *writan,* to scratch, score, engrave, hence to write; akin to G. *reizen,* to tear; IE. base **wer-,* to tear off, scratch, as also in Sans. *vraṇá-h,* wound, tear], 1. to form or inscribe (words, letters, symbols, etc.) on a surface, as by cutting, carving, or, especially, marking with a pen or pencil. 2. to form the words, letters, or symbols of with pencil, chalk, typewriter, etc.; put down in writing: as, *write* your name, he *wrote* the formula on the blackboard. 3. to produce (a literary or musical composition); compose. 4. to draw up or compose in legal form. 5. to fill in (a check, printed form, etc.) with necessary writing. 6. to cover with writing: as, he stopped after *writing* three pages. 7. to communicate in writing: as, he *wrote* that he would be late. 8. to communicate with in writing; write a letter or note to: as, *write* me before you go. 9. to call, entitle, or designate in writing: as, he *writes* himself "Judge." 10. to underwrite. 11. to leave marks, signs, or evidence of; show clearly: as, greed was *written* on his face. *v.i.* 1. to form or inscribe words, letters, symbols, etc. on a surface, especially by making marks with a pen or pencil. 2. to write books or other literary matter; be an author or writer. 3. to write a letter or letters. 4. to be employed at written work, as a clerk, copyist, etc. 5. to produce writing of a specified kind: as, he *writes* very legibly, the pen *writes* scratchily.
  write down, 1. to put into written form; write a record of. 2. to disparage or depreciate by writing.
  write off, 1. to cancel or remove from accounts: said of bad debts, claims, etc., as in accounting or bookkeeping. 2. to drop from consideration.
  write out, 1. to put into writing. 2. to write in full.
  write up, 1. to write a record or account of. 2. to complete or bring up to date in writing. 3. to praise or make much of in writing. 4. in *accounting,* to set down an excessive value for (an asset).
write-in (rīt′in′), *n.* 1. the act of voting for some person whose name is not on the ballot by writing the name in. 2. a name so written in.
writ·er (rīt′ẽr), *n.* 1. a person who writes. 2. a person whose business or occupation is writing; specifically, *a*) a copyist, amanuensis, or clerk. *b*) an author, journalist, or the like. 3. [Scot.], a solicitor or lawyer.
writ·er's cramp (rīt′ẽrz), painful spasmodic contraction of the muscles of the hand and fingers, resulting from excessive use in writing.
write-up (rīt′up′), *n.* 1. [Colloq.], a written report or description, especially one that praises or is favorable to the subject written about, as in a newspaper, magazine, etc. 2. in *finance,* a statement of the alleged assets of a corporation in excess of the true value.
writhe (rīth), *v.t.* [WRITHED (rīthd), WRITHED or *archaic* or *poetic* WRITHEN (rith′n), WRITHING], [ME. *writhen;* AS. *writhan,* to twist, wind about; akin to ON. *rītha;* IE. base **wer-,* to bend, twist; cf. WREATH], to cause to twist or turn; contort. *v.i.* 1. to make twisting or turning movements; contort the body, as in agony; squirm. 2. to suffer great emotional distress, as from embarrassment, revulsion, etc. *n.* an act of writhing; writhing movement; contortion.
writh·en (rith′'n), *adj.* [ME. *wrythen,* pp. of *writhen,* to writhe], [Archaic or Poetic], writhed; twisted; contorted.
writ·ing (rīt′iŋ), *n.* 1. the act of a person who writes. 2. something written, as a letter, document, inscription, etc. 3. written form. 4. handwriting. 5. a book, poem, article, or other literary work. 6. the profession or occupation of a writer. 7. the art, practice, style, or form of literary composition. *adj.* 1. that writes. 2. used in writing.
writing paper, 1. paper for writing on. 2. stationery.
writ of prohibition, an order from a higher court to a lower one directing it to cease operating in some matter outside its jurisdiction.
writ of right, a legal writ protecting or restoring title rights in freehold real estate.
writ·ten (rit′'n), past participle of **write.**
W.R.N.S., Women's Royal Naval Service (Wrens).
wrnt., warrant.
Wroc·law (vrôts′läf), *n.* Breslau, Poland: Polish name.
wrong (rôŋ), *adj.* [ME. *wrong, wrang,* crooked, twisted, wrong; AS. *wrang;* ON. *rangr, wrangr,* wrong, twisted < the same base as AS. *wringan,* to twist (cf. WRING, WRENCH)], 1. not morally right or just; sinful; wicked; immoral. 2. not in accordance with an established standard, previous arrangement, given intention, etc.: as, this is the *wrong* method, he came on the *wrong* day. 3. not suitable or appropriate: as, that was the *wrong* thing to say. 4. *a*) contrary to truth, fact, etc.; incorrect; inaccurate. *b*) acting, judging, believing, etc. incorrectly; mistaken. 5. unsatisfactory; in a bad state or condition. 6. not functioning properly; out of order: as, something is *wrong* with my eyes. 7. designed to be worn or placed inward or under and not displayed: as, the *wrong* side of a fabric. *adv.* in a wrong manner, direction, etc.; so as to be wrong; incorrectly; amiss. *n.* 1. something that is wrong, especially a wicked or unjust act. 2. in *law,* a violation of a legal right; tort. *v.t.* 1. to treat badly or unjustly; do wrong to; injure. 2. to think badly of without real justification; hence, 3. to malign; dishonor. 4. to seduce (a woman).
  get (someone) in wrong, [Colloq.], to bring (someone) into disfavor.
  go wrong, 1. to turn out badly. 2. to change from good behavior to bad; go astray.
  in the wrong, wrong.
  SYN.—**wrong** implies the inflicting of unmerited injury or harm upon another (he was *wronged* by false charges); **oppress** implies a burdening with harsh, rigorous impositions or the cruel or unjust use of power (*oppressed* by heavy taxation); **persecute** suggests constant harassment or the relentless infliction of cruelty and suffering (the *persecuted* minorities of Nazi Germany); **aggrieve** suggests the inflicting of such wrongs or injuries as seem a just cause for complaint or resentment (*aggrieved* by her ill-treatment of him); **abuse** suggests improper or hurtful treatment, as by the use of insulting or coarse language (her much *abused* husband). See also **injustice.**
wrong·do·er (rôŋ′dōō′ẽr), *n.* a person who does wrong.
wrong·do·ing (rôŋ′dōō′iŋ), *n.* any act or behavior that is wrong; the doing of wrong; transgression.
wrong font, in *printing,* the incorrect font: used to designate a type face of the wrong size or style: abbreviated, **wf, w.f.**
wrong·ful (rôŋ′fəl), *adj.* 1. full of wrong; unjust, unfair, or injurious. 2. unlawful.
wrong·head·ed (rôŋ′hed′id), *adj.* stubbornly refusing to yield, agree, etc. even when wrong; perverse.
wrote (rōt), past tense of **write.**
wroth (rôth; Brit. rōth), *adj.* [ME. *wroth, wrath;* AS. *wrath,* bad, wroth < the p.t. stem of *writhan,* to twist (cf. WRITHE); cf. WRATH], angry; wrathful; incensed.
wrought (rôt), alternative past tense and past participle of **work.** *adj.* 1. formed; fashioned; made. 2. shaped by hammering or beating: said of metals. 3. made with great care; elaborated. 4. decorated; ornamented.
wrought-i·ron (rôt′ī′ẽrn), *adj.* made of wrought iron.

wrought iron, a kind of iron that contains some slag and very little carbon: it is tough and hard to break yet soft enough to be pounded into shape and is used for fences, grating, etc.
wrought-iron casting, 1. the process of casting with mitis metal. 2. a casting made by this process.
wrought-up (rôt′up′), *adj.* disturbed; excited.
W.R.S.S.R., White Russian Soviet Socialist Republic.
wrung (ruŋ), past tense and past participle of **wring.**
wry (rī), *v.t. & v.i.* [WRIED (rīd), WRYING], [ME. *wrien,* to twist, bend; AS. *wrigian,* to turn, twist; akin to OFris. *wrigia,* to bend, stoop; IE. base **wreik-* (as also in L. *rica,* head veil) < **wer-,* to turn, bend], to writhe or twist. *adj.* [WRIER (rī′ẽr), WRIEST (rī′ist)], [ME. *wrie* < the *v.*], 1. turned or bent to one side; twisted; distorted. 2. made by twisting or distorting the features: as, a *wry* face. 3. perverse; contrary. 4. distorted in meaning, interpretation, etc.
wry·neck (rī′nek′), *n.* 1. a condition in which the neck is twisted by a muscle spasm; torticollis. 2. [Colloq.], a person afflicted with this. 3. a kind of bird related to the woodpecker, distinguished by its habit of stretching and twisting its neck.
W.S., West Saxon.
WSW, W.S.W., w.s.w., west-southwest.
wt., weight.
Wu·chang (wōō′chäŋ′), *n.* a city in Hupeh province, eastern China: see **Wuhan.**
Wu·han (wōō′hän′), *n.* three cities, Hankow, Hanyang, and Wuchang, in eastern China, forming one metropolitan area; capital of Hupeh province: pop., 1,800,000: also called *Han Cities.*
Wu·hu (wōō′hōō′), *n.* a city in Anhwei province, China, on the Yangtze River: pop., 204,000.
wul·fen·ite (wool′fən-īt′), *n.* [G. *wulfenit,* after F. X. von *Wulfen* (1728–1805), Austrian mineralogist], a mineral, lead molybdate, $PbMoO_4$, having a high luster and occurring in various colors.
Wundt, Wil·helm (vil′helm voont), 1832–1920; German physiologist and psychologist.
Wup·per·tal (voop′ẽr-täl′), *n.* a city in the Ruhr district, Germany: pop., 416,000.
Würt·tem·berg (wũr′təm-bẽrg; G. vür′təm-berkh′), *n.* a former division of southwestern Germany; earlier, a kingdom.
Würz·burg (wũrts′bẽrg; G. vürts′boorkh), *n.* a city in northwestern Bavaria, Germany, on the Main River: pop., 111,000.
Wu·sih (wōō′sē′), *n.* a city in Kiangsu province, eastern China: pop., 273,000.
W. Va., West Virginia.
Wy·an·dot (wī′ən-dot′), *n.* 1. a member of the former Huron tribe or confederacy of North American Indians. 2. an Iroquoian language. Also spelled **Wyandotte.**
Wy·an·dotte (wī′ən-dot′), *n.* 1. Wyandot. 2. a city in Michigan, on the Detroit River: pop., 44,000. 3. [< sense 1], any of a breed of American domestic fowls, a cross between the Brahma and the Hamburg.
Wy·att, Sir **Thomas** (wī′ət), 1503?–1542; English poet, statesman, and courtier.
wych-elm (wich′elm′), *n.* [< *witch,* as in *witch hazel*: so called because of the pliant branches], 1. a small variety of elm found in Europe and northern Asia. 2. its wood. Also spelled **witch-elm.**
Wych·er·ley, William (wich′ẽr-li), 1640?–1716; English dramatist.
wych-ha·zel (wich′hā′z'l), *n.* 1. witch hazel. 2. a wych-elm.
Wyc·liffe or **Wyc·lif, John** (wik′lif), 1320?–1384; English religious reformer; first translator of the Bible into English: also spelled **Wiclif, Wickliffe.**
Wyc·lif·fite, Wyc·lif·ite (wik′lif-īt′), *n.* [ML. *Wiclefita* < L. form of name *Wyclif*], a follower of John Wycliffe; a Lollard. *adj.* of or having to do with John Wycliffe or his followers.
Wye (wī), *n.* a river in eastern Wales and western England flowing into the Severn estuary: length, 130 mi.
wye (wī), *n.* [*pl.* WYES (wīz)], 1. the letter Y. 2. something shaped like Y.
Wyld, Henry Cecil Kennedy (wīld), 1870–1945; English linguist and lexicographer.
Wy·lie, Elinor (wī′li), (*Mrs. William Rose Benét*), 1885–1928; American poet and novelist.
wynd (wīnd), *n.* [MScot. *wynde* < ME. *winden,* to wind], [Scot.], a narrow lane or alley.
Wy·o·ming (wī-ō′miŋ), *n.* 1. a Western State of the United States: area, 97,914 sq. mi.; pop., 330,000; capital, Cheyenne: abbreviated **Wyo., Wy.** 2. a city in southwestern Michigan: suburb of Grand Rapids: pop., 46,000.
Wy·o·ming·ite (wī-ō′miŋ-īt′), *n.* a native or inhabitant of Wyoming.
Wyoming Valley, a valley of the Susquehanna River, in eastern Pennsylvania: site of a massacre, 1778.
Wythe, George (with), 1726–1806; American lawyer; signer of the Declaration of Independence.
wy·vern (wī′vẽrn), *n.* a wivern.

X

X, x (eks), *n.* [*pl.* X's, x's, Xs, xs (-iz)], 1. the twenty-fourth letter of the English alphabet: from a western Greek alphabet: see **alphabet,** table. 2. the sound of X or x, phonetically equal to (ks) normally: in English, it also has the sound of (gz), IPA [gz], as in *exact;* (ksh), IPA [kʃ], as in *anxious;* (gzh), IPA [gʒ,] as in *luxurious;* and (z), as in *xylophone.* 3. a type or impression for X or x. 4. *a symbol for* the twenty-fourth in a sequence or group (or the twenty-third if J is omitted, or the twenty-first if V and W are also omitted). *adj.* 1. of X or x. 2. twenty-fourth (or twenty-third if J is omitted, or twenty-first if V and W are also omitted) in a sequence or group.
X (eks), *n.* 1. an object shaped like X. 2. a mark shaped like an X used: *a*) to represent the signature of a person who cannot write. *b*) to indicate a particular point on a map, diagram, etc. *c*) as a symbol for a kiss in letters, etc. 3. the Roman numeral 10: with a superior bar ($\overline{X}$), 10,000: XX equals 20, XXX equals 30, and X before another Roman numeral expresses a number 10 less than that numeral. 4. a person or thing unknown or unrevealed. 5. Christ: used also in combination, as in *Xmas.* 6. in *chemistry, a symbol for* xenon. *adj.* shaped like X.
x, in *mathematics,* 1. an unknown quantity. 2. a sign of multiplication: as, $3 \times 3 = 9$. 3. an abscissa.
xanth-, xantho-.
xan·thate (zan′thāt), *n.* a salt or ester of xanthic acid.
xan·the·in (zan′thi-in), *n.* [< *xanth-* + *-in*], the water-soluble part of the yellow pigment of yellow flowers.
Xan·thi·an (zan′thi-ən), *adj.* of or having to do with Xanthus, an ancient city of Asia Minor.
xan·thic (zan′thik), *adj.* [Fr. *xanthique;* see XANTHO- & -IC], 1. yellow or yellowish in color. 2. of or having to do with xanthin or xanthine. 3. designating or of an unstable colorless acid, $C_3H_6OS_2$, that decomposes into ethyl alcohol and carbon disulfide at 24° C.
xan·thin (zan′thin), *n.* [*xanth-* + *-in*], the insoluble part of the yellow pigment of yellow flowers.
xan·thin (zan′thin), *n.* xanthine.
xan·thine (zan′thēn, zan′thin), *n.* [*xanth-* + *-ine*], a white crystalline nitrogenous compound, $C_5H_4N_4O_2$, resembling uric acid: it is present in blood, urine, and certain plants.
Xan·thip·pe (zan-tip′i), *n.* wife of Socrates; 5th century B.C.: the prototype of the quarrelsome, nagging wife.
xan·tho- (zan′thō, zan′thə), [< Gr. *xanthos,* yellow], a combining form meaning *yellow,* as in *xanthochroid*: also, before a vowel, **xanth-.**
xan·tho·chroid (zan′thə-kroid′), *adj.* [< *xantho-* + Gr. *chroa;* + *-oid*], having light-colored hair and complexion. *n.* a xanthochroid person.
xan·tho·phyll, xan·tho·phyl (zan′thə-fil), *n.* [*xantho-* + *-phyll*], a yellow crystalline pigment, $C_{40}H_{56}O_2$, found in plants: it is related to carotene and is the basis of the yellow seen in autumn leaves.

xan·thous (zan′thəs), *adj.* [Gr. *xanthos*, yellow], 1. yellow. 2. of or having to do with the yellow-skinned, especially Mongolian, peoples. 3. of or having to do with the branches of mankind having yellowish, brown, or red hair.

Xan·thus (zan′thəs), *n.* an ancient city in Lycia, southwestern Asia Minor.

Xa·vi·er, Saint **Francis** (zā′vi-ēr, zav′i-ēr), (born *Francisco Javier*), 1506–1552; Spanish Jesuit missionary: called the ***Apostle of the Indies.***

X.C., x.c., x-cp., ex coupon.

X chromosome, a sex chromosome.

X.D., x.d., X-div., x-div., ex dividend.

Xe, in *chemistry,* xenon.

xe·bec (zē′bek), *n.* [altered < earlier *chebec* (after the older Sp. form) < Fr. *chébec;* Sp. *jabeque,* earlier *xabeque;* Ar. *shabbak*], a small, three-masted ship having an overhanging bow and stern and both square and lateen sails: once common in the Mediterranean, especially as used by corsairs.

xe·ni·a (zē′ni-ə), *n.* [Mod. L. < Gr. *xenia,* hospitality < *xenos,* a guest], in *botany,* the immediate influence of pollen from one strain of a plant upon the seed of another strain, resulting in hybrid characteristics in the form, color, etc. of the resulting growth.

xen·o- (zen′ō, zen′ə), [< Gr. *xenos,* strange, foreign, a stranger], a combining form meaning: 1. *stranger, foreigner,* as in *xenophobia.* 2. *strange, foreign, extraneous,* as in *xenolith.* Also, before a vowel, **xen-.**

Xe·noc·ra·tes (zi-nok′rə-tēz′), *n.* Greek philosopher; lived 396–314 B.C.

xe·nog·a·mous (zi-nog′ə-məs), *adj.* of or having to do with xenogamy.

xe·nog·a·my (zi-nog′ə-mi), *n.* [*xeno-* + *-gamy*], in *botany,* cross-fertilization.

xen·o·gen·e·sis (zen′ə-jen′ə-sis), *n.* [Mod. L.; see XENO- & -GENESIS], 1. spontaneous generation; abiogenesis. 2. alternation of generations; metagenesis. 3. the supposed production of an individual completely different from either of its parents.

xen·o·ge·net·ic (zen′ə-jə-net′ik), *adj.* of or having to do with xenogenesis.

xen·o·gen·ic (zen′ə-jen′ik), *adj.* xenogenetic.

xen·o·lith (zen′ə-lith), *n.* [*xeno-* + *-lith*], a rock fragment embedded in the mass of another rock.

xen·o·mor·phic (zen′ə-môr′fik), *adj.* [*xeno-* + *-morphic*], having a form not characteristic of its kind, but determined by the pressure of surrounding constituents: said of the granular constituents of crystalline rock.

xe·non (zē′non, zen′on), *n.* [Gr., neut. of *xenos,* strange], a heavy, colorless, inert, gaseous chemical element present in the air in minute quantities: symbols, Xe, X; at. no., 54; at. wt., 131.3.

Xe·noph·a·nes (zi-nof′ə-nēz′), *n.* Greek Eleatic philosopher; lived 6th century B.C.

xen·o·pho·bi·a (zen′ə-fō′bi-ə), *n.* [Mod. L.; see XENO- & -PHOBIA], fear or hatred of strangers or foreigners.

Xen·o·phon (zen′ə-fən), *n.* Greek general and historian; lived 434?–355? B.C.

Xe·res (she′res), *n.* Jerez, city in Spain: former name.

xe·ro- (zêr′ō, zêr′ə), [< Gr. *xēros,* dry], a combining form meaning *dry,* as in *xerophyte*: also, before a vowel, **xer-.**

xe·ro·der·ma (zêr′ə-dũr′mə), *n.* [*xero-* + Gr. *derma,* the skin], a skin disease characterized by roughness and dryness and, often, the formation of scales.

xe·roph·i·lous (zi-rof′ə-ləs), *adj.* [*xero-* + *-philous*], capable of thriving in a hot, dry climate, as certain plants and animals.

xe·roph·thal·mi·a (zêr′of-thal′mi-ə), *n.* [LL.; Gr. *xērophthalmia* < *xēros,* dry + *ophthalmia,* disease of the eyes < *ophthalmos,* the eye], a form of conjunctivitis characterized by a dry and lusterless condition of the eyeball and caused by a deficiency of vitamin A.

xe·ro·phyte (zêr′ə-fīt′), *n.* [*xero-* + *-phyte*], a xerophilous plant.

xe·ro·phyt·ic (zêr′ə-fit′ik), *adj.* of, or having the nature of, a xerophyte; xerophilous.

xe·ro·sis (zi-rō′sis), *n.* [Gr. *xērosis* < *xēros,* dry], in *medicine,* an abnormal dryness, as of the skin or eyeball.

Xer·xes I (zũrk′sēz), 519?–465 B.C.; son of *Darius the Great;* king of Persia (486–465 B.C.): called *the Great.*

xi (zī, sī; Gr. ksē), *n.* [Gr.], the fourteenth letter of the Greek alphabet (Ξ, ξ), corresponding to English *X, x*: see **alphabet,** table.

X.i., x-i., x-int., ex interest.

Xin·gú (shiŋ-gōō′), *n.* a river in central Brazil, flowing northward into the Amazon: length, 1,250 mi.

-xion, (c)tion: British spelling, as in *connexion* (connection).

xiph·i·ster·num (zif′i-stũr′nəm), *n.* [*pl.* XIPHISTERNA (-nə)], [Mod. L. < Gr. *xiphos,* sword; + *sternum*], the xiphoid process.

xiph·oid (zif′oid), *adj.* [Gr. *xiphoeides,* sword-shaped < *xiphos,* a sword + *eidos,* a form], 1. shaped like a sword; ensiform. 2. designating or of a cartilaginous process at the lower end of the sternum, or breastbone. *n.* the xiphoid process.

xiph·o·su·ran (zif′ə-soor′ən, zif′ə-syoor′ən), *adj.* [< Gr. *xiphos,* a sword + *oura,* a tail; + *-an*], designating or of an order of primitive arachnids made up of the king crabs. *n.* any member of this order.

Xmas (kris′məs; *popularly* eks′məs), *n.* [see X (sense 5)], Christmas.

Xn., Christian.

Xnty., Christianity.

X particle, a mesotron.

X-ray (eks′rā′), *adj.* of, by, or having to do with X rays. *v.t.* to examine, treat, or photograph with X rays.

X ray, [so called by the discoverer because of its unknown character], 1. a non-luminous electromagnetic ray or radiation of extremely short wave length, generally less than 2 angstroms, produced by the bombardment of a substance (usually one of the heavy metals) by a stream of electrons moving at great velocity, as in a vacuum tube. X rays are capable of penetrating opaque or solid substances, ionizing gases and tissues through which they pass, and affecting photographic plates and fluorescent screens. They are widely used in medicine for study, diagnosis, and treatment of certain organic disorders, especially of internal structures of the body. 2. a photograph made by means of X rays.

Xtian., Christian.

Xty., Christianity.

xy·lan (zī′lan), *n.* [< Gr. *xylon,* wood; + *-an*], a yellow, gummy pentosan that is found in woody tissues and yields xylose upon hydrolysis.

xy·lem (zī′lem), *n.* [G. < Gr. *xylon,* wood], the woody tissue of a plant, especially, in higher forms, the part of the vascular bundle, consisting of tracheal tissue, parenchyma, etc., that gives firmness and conducts moisture.

xy·lene (zī′lēn), *n.* [*xyl(o)-* + *-ene*], any of three isomeric, colorless hydrocarbons, $C_6H_4(CH_3)_2$, having the characteristics of benzene and derived from coal tar and wood tar: used as solvents, antiseptics, etc.

xy·lic acid (zī′lik, zil′ik), any of six isomeric crystalline acids, $C_6H_3(CH_3)_2COOH$, carboxyl derivatives of xylene.

xy·li·din (zī′lə-din, zil′ə-din), *n.* xylidine.

xy·li·dine (zī′lə-dēn, zil′ə-din), *n.* [< *xyl*ene + *-ide* + *-ine*], 1. any of the isomeric compounds having the formula $C_6H_3(CH_3)_2NH_2$, resembling aniline and derived from xylene. 2. a mixture of these isomeric compounds, used in making certain dyes.

xy·lo- (zī′lō, zī′lə), [< Gr. *xylon,* wood], a combining form meaning *wood,* as in *xylograph*: also, before a vowel, **xyl-.**

xy·lo·graph (zī′lə-graf′, zī′lə-gräf′), *n.* [*xylo-* + *-graph*], a wood engraving or an impression from this.

xy·log·ra·pher (zī-log′rə-fēr), *n.* [*xylo-* + *-grapher*], a wood engraver.

xy·lo·graph·ic (zī′lə-graf′ik), *adj.* of or made by xylography.

xy·lo·graph·i·cal (zī′lə-graf′i-k'l), *adj.* xylographic.

xy·log·ra·phy (zī-log′rə-fi), *n.* [*xylo-* + *-graphy*], the art of engraving on wood or of taking printed impressions from such engravings.

xy·loid (zī′loid), *adj.* [*xyl-* + *-oid*], of or like wood; woody.

xy·lol (zī′lōl, zī′lol), *n.* [*xyl-* + *-ol*], xylene.

xy·loph·a·gous (zī-lof′ə-gəs), *adj.* [Gr. *xylophagos* < *xylon,* wood + *phagein,* to eat], eating or boring into wood, as the larvae of certain insects.

xy·lo·phone (zī′lə-fōn′, zil′ə-fōn′), *n.* [*xylo-* + Gr. *phōnē,* a voice], a musical percussion instrument consisting of a series of wooden bars graduated in length so as to sound the notes of the scale when struck with small wooden hammers.

xy·loph·o·nist (zī-lof′ə-nist, zi-lof′ə-nist, zī′lə-fō′nist), *n.* a person who plays the xylophone.

XYLOPHONE

xy·lose (zī′lōs), *n.* [< *xylan* + *-ose*], a colorless, crystalline pentose, $C_5H_{10}O_5$, formed by the hydrolysis of xylan.

xy·lot·o·mous (zī-lot′ə-məs), *adj.* [< *xylo-* + base of Gr. *temnein,* to cut], that can bore into or cut wood: said of certain insects.

xy·lot·o·my (zī-lot′ə-mi), *n.* [*xylo-* + *-tomy*], the preparation of sections of wood for microscopic inspection.

xys·ter (zis′tēr), *n.* [Mod. L.; Gr. *xystēr* < *xyein,* to scrape], a surgical instrument for scraping bones.

Y

Y, y (wī), *n.* [*pl.* Y's, y's, Ys, ys (wīz)], 1. the twenty-fifth letter of the English alphabet: from the Greek *upsilon*: see **alphabet**, table. 2. the sound of Y or y, phonetically, a front-tongue semivowel glide when occurring at the beginning of a syllable, as in *yield* or *vineyard*: within a syllable, it is the lowered high front unrounded vowel (i), as in *myth*, or the diphthong (ī), IPA [aɪ], as in *psychology*. 3. a type or impression for Y or y. 4. *a symbol for* the twenty-fifth in a sequence or group (or the twenty-fourth if J is omitted, or the twenty-second if V and W are also omitted). *adj.* 1. of Y or y. 2. twenty-fifth (or twenty-fourth if J is omitted, or twenty-second if V and W are also omitted) in a sequence or group.

Y (wī), *n.* 1. an object shaped like Y, as a branched piece of piping, a forked support for a telescope, etc. 2. a medieval Roman numeral for 150: with a superior bar ($\overline{Y}$), 150,000. 3. in *chemistry, the symbol for* yttrium. *adj.* shaped like Y.

y, in *mathematics,* 1. the second of a set of unknown quantities, *x* usually being the first. 2. an ordinate.

y- (i), [ME. *y-, i-;* AS. *ge-*, perfective prefix; basic sense "together"], an obsolete or archaic prefix formerly used regularly with the past participles of verbs: its use, as a poetic archaism, survived until the end of the 16th century, as in *yclept.*

-y (i; *occas.* ē), [ME. *-y, -i, -ie;* prob. after OFr. *-i, -e,* in such familiar names as *Davi* (for *David*), *Mathe* (for *Matheu*), etc.], a suffix used in forming diminutives, nicknames, and terms of endearment or familiarity, as in *kitty, Billy, daddy*: often spelled **-ie**, as in *lassie.*

-y (i; *occas.* ē), [ME. *-y, -ie;* AS. *-ig;* akin to L. *-ic-*], an adjective-forming suffix meaning: 1. *having, full of,* or *characterized by,* as in *dirty, healthy.* 2. *rather, somewhat,* as in *yellowy, chilly, dusky.* 3. *inclined* or *tending to,* as in *drowsy, sticky.* 4. *suggestive of, somewhat like,* as in *wavy, horsy.* Sometimes used with a slight intensive force that does not change the meaning of the root adjective, as in *stilly.*

-y (i; *occas.* ē), [Fr. *-ie;* L. *-ia* < or akin to Gr. *-ia, -eia*], a suffix used to form abstract nouns, often corresponding to adjectives ending in *-ous* and *-ic,* meaning in general *quality* or *condition of* (*being*), as in *allergy, jealousy.*

-y (i; *occas.* ē), [Anglo-Fr. *-ie;* L. *-ium*], a noun-forming suffix meaning *action of,* as in *inquiry, entreaty.*

Y., Young Men's Christian Association.

y., 1. yard; yards. 2. year; years.

yab·ber (yab'ẽr), *v.i. & n.* [< native Australian *yabba*], [Australian Colloq.], talk; jabber.

Ya·blo·noi Mountains (yä'blô-noi'), the southern range of the Stanovoi Mountains, in eastern Siberia.

Ya·blo·no·voi Mountains (yä'blô-nô-voi'), Yablonoi Mountains.

yacht (yät), *n.* [D. *jacht,* earlier *jaghte,* short for *jaght-schip,* pursuit ship., lit. hunting ship (i.e., against pirates) < *jaght,* a hunt < *jagen,* to chase + *schip,* a ship], any of various relatively small ships for pleasure cruises, racing, etc. *v.i.* to sail in a yacht.

yacht·ing (yät'iŋ), *n.* the action or sport of sailing in a yacht.

yachts·man (yäts'mən), *n.* [*pl.* YACHTSMEN (-mən)], a person who owns or sails a yacht.

yachts·man·ship (yäts'mən-ship'), *n.* the practice or skill of sailing a yacht.

yachts·wom·an (yäts'woom'ən), *n.* [*pl.* YACHTSWOMEN (-wim'ən)], a woman who owns or sails a yacht.

Yad·kin (yad'kin), *n.* Pee Dee, a river in North and South Carolina: so called in North Carolina.

ya·ger (yā'gẽr), *n.* a jäger.

yah (yä, ya, *etc.*), *interj.* an exclamation of derision, defiance, or disgust.

Ya·hoo (yä'hoo, yā'hoo, ya-hoo'), *n.* 1. in Swift's *Gulliver's Travels,* any of a race of brutish, degraded creatures having the form and all the vices of man: see **Houyhnhnm.** 2. [y-], a vicious, bestial person. 3. [y-], a crude or ill-mannered person; bumpkin.

Yah·ve, Yah·veh (yä've), *n.* Yahweh.

Yah·weh, Yah·we (yä'we), *n.* God: a modern form of the Hebrew name in the Old Testament commonly transliterated Jehovah.

Yah·wism (yä'wiz'm), *n.* 1. the worship of Yahweh (Jehovah). 2. the use of *Yahweh* as a name for God.

Yah·wist (yä'wist), *n.* the unidentified writer or writers of certain Old Testament passages in which *Yahweh* (Jehovah) instead of *Elohim* is used as the name for God: cf. **Elohist.**

Yah·wis·tic (yä-wis'tik), *adj.* 1. of or written by the Yahwist(s). 2. using *Yahweh* (Jehovah) instead of *Elohim* as the name for God: said of certain Old Testament passages.

yak (yak), *n.* [*pl.* YAKS (yaks), YAK; see PLURAL, II, D, 1], [Tibet. *gyak*], the long-haired wild ox of Tibet and central Asia, often domesticated as a beast of burden.

YAK (5 ft. high at shoulder)

Yak·i·ma (yak'ə-mə), *n.* a city in south central Washington: pop., 43,000.

Ya·kut (yä-koot'), *n.* 1. any of a people living in the Yakutsk A.S.S.R. 2. their Altaic language: linguists are undecided whether it should be classified as Turkic or Mongolian.

Yakut Autonomous Soviet Socialist Republic, Yakutsk Autonomous Soviet Socialist Republic.

Ya·kutsk (yä-kootsk'), *n.* the capital of the Yakutsk A.S.S.R., on the Lena River: pop., 74,000.

Yakutsk Autonomous Soviet Socialist Republic, a division of the R.S.F.S.R. in northeastern Siberia: area, 1,169,927 sq. mi.; pop., 489,000; capital, Yakutsk.

Yal·ta (yäl'tə; Russ. yäl'tä), *n.* a town in the Crimea, U.S.S.R., on the Black Sea: see **Crimea**, map.

Yalta Conference, a conference of Roosevelt, Churchill, and Stalin at Yalta in February, 1945: also called *Crimea Conference.*

Ya·lu (yä'lü'), *n.* a river flowing between Manchuria and Korea into the Yellow Sea: length, 300 mi.

yam (yam), *n.* [Port. *inhame* < Senegal *nyami,* to eat], 1. the edible, starchy, tuberous root of any of several tropical climbing plants. 2. any of these plants. 3. [Scot.], the common (or Irish) potato. 4. [Dial.], the sweet potato.

Ya·ma (yum'ə), *n.* [Sans.], a Hindu god, judge of the dead and king of the underworld.

Ya·ma·shi·ta, To·mo·yu·ki (tô'mô-ū'kē yä'mä-shē'-tä), 1885–1946; Japanese general; executed for war crimes: called *the Tiger of Malaya.*

ya·men (yä'mən), *n.* [Chin.], formerly in China, the office or residence of a mandarin or public official.

yam·mer (yam'ẽr), *v.i.* [ME. *yameren* < AS. *geomerian,* to lament, groan < *geomor,* sad, mournful, wretched; influenced by the cognate MD. & MLG. *jammeren*], [Colloq. or Dial.], 1. to whine, whimper, or complain. 2. to shout, yell, clamor, etc. *v.t.* to say in a complaining tone. *n.* the act of yammering.

Yang·tze (yaŋ'sē'; Chin. yäŋ'tse'), *n.* a river in China flowing from Tibet to the East China Sea: length, 3,000 mi.

Yang·tze Kiang (yaŋ'sē' kyaŋ'; Chin. yäŋ'tse' jyäŋ'), the Yangtze River.

Ya·ni·na (yä'nē-nä'), *n.* Janina.

Yank (yaŋk), *n.* [Slang], a Yankee; especially, an American soldier in World Wars I and II. *adj.* of or like a Yank or Yanks.

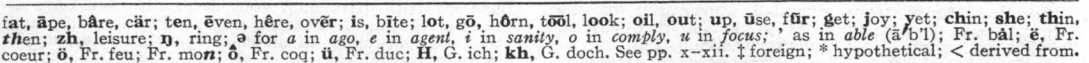

yank (yaŋk), *n.* [< New England Dial.], [Colloq.], a jerk. *v.t. & v.i.* [Colloq.], to jerk.

Yan·kee (yaŋ′ki), *n.* [prob. < D. *Jan Kees* (taken as pl.); *Jan*, John + *Kees*, dial. form of *kaas*, cheese; orig. (*Jan Kaas*) used as disparaging nickname for a Hollander, later for Dutch freebooter; applied by colonial Dutch in New York to English settlers in Connecticut. For discussion of this and other hypotheses see H. L. Mencken, *Am. Lang. Suppl. I*, pp. 192–197], 1. a native or inhabitant of New England. 2. *a)* a native or inhabitant of a Northern State; Northerner. *b)* a Union soldier in the Civil War. 3. a native or inhabitant of the United States. *adj.* of, like, or characteristic of the Yankees.

Yan·kee·dom (yaŋ′ki-dəm), *n.* 1. Yankees collectively. 2. the northern United States, especially New England. 3. the United States.

Yankee Doo·dle (do͞o′d'l), [< *Yankee* + ? *tootle*, the sound made in tonguing a flute or fife, for which the tune was apparently first written], an early American song with several versions of humorous verses, popular during the Revolutionary War.

Yan·kee·ism (yaŋ′ki-iz'm), *n.* 1. Yankee character or characteristics. 2. a particular Yankee mannerism, idiom, etc.

Ya·oun·dé (yȧ′o͞on′dā′), *n.* the capital of the French mandate of Cameroun, Africa: pop., 20,000.

Yap (yäp, yap), *n.* one of the Caroline Islands in the western Pacific: area, 80 sq. mi.; pop., 6,500.

yap (yap), *v.i.* [YAPPED (yapt), YAPPING], [echoic], 1. to make a sharp, shrill bark or yelp. 2. [Slang], to talk noisily and stupidly; jabber. *n.* 1. a sharp, shrill bark or yelp. 2. [Slang], noisy, stupid talk; jabber. 3. [Slang], a crude, noisy person. 4. [Slang], a rowdy; hoodlum. 5. [Slang], the mouth.

ya·pok, ya·pock (yə-pok′), *n.* [< *Oyapok*, a river in Guiana], a small, water-dwelling opossum of Central and South America, having the hind feet webbed.

Ya·qui (yä′kē), *n.* [*pl.* YAQUI, YAQUIS (-kēz)], [after the *Yaqui* River in northwestern Mexico, where they formerly lived], a member of a tribe of Uto-Aztecan Indians now settled in Sonora, Mexico.

Yar·bor·ough (yär′bũr′ō, yär′bẽr-ə), *n.* [said to be so named after an Earl of *Yarborough* who would bet 1,000 to 1 against its occurring], a bridge or whist hand containing no card higher than a nine.

yard (yärd), *n.* [ME. *yerde, gerde;* AS. *gyrd, gierd*, a rod, staff, yard measure; akin to obs. G. *gerte*, a rod; IE. base **ghasto-, *ghazdho-*, a rod, pole, as also in L. *hasta*, a pole, spear], 1. a measure of length, equal to 3 feet, or 36 inches: one yard is equivalent to .914 meter: abbreviated **yd., y.** (*sing. & pl.*). 2. in *nautical usage*, a slender rod or spar, tapering toward the ends, fastened at right angles across a mast to support a sail.

yard (yärd), *n.* [ME. *yerd;* AS. *geard*, enclosure; akin to ON. *garthr* (cf. GARTH); IE. base **gherdh-*, prob. to surround, seen also in Russ. *górod*, town, Eng. *girdle*], 1. the space or grounds surrounding or surrounded by a building or group of buildings: often in combination, as, *churchyard, farmyard*, etc. 2. an enclosed place used for a particular purpose or business: as, a lumber *yard*, ship*yard*. 3. a place where wild deer, moose, etc. herd together for feeding during the winter. 4. a railroad center where trains are made up, serviced, switched from track to track, etc. *v.t.* to put, keep, or enclose in a yard (often with *up*).

yard·age (yär′dij), *n.* [see -AGE], 1. measurement in yards. 2. the extent or amount of something so measured.

yard·age (yär′dij), *n.* [see -AGE], 1. the use of a yard for storage, etc. 2. the charge for this.

yard·arm (yärd′ärm′), *n.* in *nautical usage*, either end of a yard supporting a square sail.

yard grass, a tough, coarse annual grass topped with long spikes.

yard·man (yärd′mən), *n.* [*pl.* YARDMEN (-mən)], a man who works in a yard, especially a railroad yard.

yard·mas·ter (yärd′mas′tẽr, yärd′mäs′tẽr), *n.* a man in charge of a railroad yard.

yard·stick (yärd′stik′), *n.* 1. a graduated stick or rod one yard in length, used in measuring. 2. any test or standard used in measuring, judging, or comparing. —*SYN.* see **standard**.

yard·wand (yärd′wänd′, yärd′wônd′), *n.* a yardstick.

yare (yâr), *adj.* [ME. *yare, yarwe;* AS. *gearo* (akin to OS. *garu*); prob. < *ge-* (cf. Y-) + *earu*, ready], [Archaic or Dial.], 1. ready; prepared. 2. brisk; active; quick. 3. responding quickly and truly to the helm: said of a ship. *adv.* [Obs.], quickly; promptly.

Yar·kand (yär′känd′), *n.* Soche, a city in China.

Yar·mouth (yär′məth), *n.* Great Yarmouth, a city in England.

yarn (yärn), *n.* [ME.; AS. *gearn*, yarn; akin to G. *garn;* IE. base **gher-*, intestine, as also in L. *haru-spex*, soothsayer, lit., intestine-seer, Gr. *chordē* (cf. CHORD); the Eng. sense from stranded appearance of the intestines], 1. any fiber, as wool, silk, flax, cotton, nylon, etc., spun into strands for weaving, knitting, or making thread. 2. [Colloq.], a tale or story, especially one that seems exaggerated or hard to believe. *v.i.* [Colloq.], to tell yarns; spin a yarn.

spin a yarn, [Colloq.], to tell a yarn or yarns.

yarn-dyed (yärn′dīd′), *adj.* woven of yarn that was dyed before weaving.

Ya·ro·slavl (yä′rô-släv′'l), *n.* 1. a region of the R.S.F.S.R., in north central European Russia: pop., 2,271,000. 2. its capital: pop., 298,000.

yar·o·vize (yär′ə-vīz′), *v.t.* [YAROVIZED (-vīzd′), YAROVIZING], to jarovize.

yar·row (yar′ō), *n.* [ME. *yarowe, yarwe;* AS. *gæruwe, gearuwe;* akin to G. *garbe*], a common herb having a strong smell and taste, finely divided leaves, and clusters of small, pink or white flowers.

yash·mak, yash·mac (yäsh-mäk′, yash′mak), *n.* [Ar. *yashmaq*], the double veil worn by Moslem women in public.

Yas·sy (yä′si), *n.* Jassy, a city in the Moldavian S.S.R.

yat·a·ghan, yat·a·gan (yat′ə-gan, yat′ə-gən), *n.* [Turk. *yātāghan*], a type of Turkish short saber with a double-curved blade and a handle without a guard.

yaud (yôd, yäd), *n.* [Scot.], an old, worn-out mare; jade.

yauld (yôd, yäd, yäld), *adj.* [Scot.], active, nimble, vigorous, etc.

yaup (yôp, yäp), *v.i. & n.* yawp.

yau·pon (yô′pən), *n.* [Am. Ind. (Catawba) *yopún*, dim. of *yop*, a shrub], an evergreen of the holly family, native to the southern United States: its leaves are sometimes used as a substitute for tea.

yaw (yô), *v.i.* [ON. *jaga*, to sway (like a door on its hinges) < MHG. *jagen*, to hunt; cf. YACHT], 1. to turn or deviate unintentionally from the intended course or heading: said of a ship or boat. 2. to swing on the vertical axis to the right or left so that the longitudinal axis forms an angle with the line of flight: said of a projectile, aircraft, etc. *v.t.* to cause to yaw. *n.* 1. an act of yawing. 2. the angle formed by a yawing aircraft, etc.

yawl (yôl), *n.* [< MLG. *jolle* or D. *jol*: said to be applied orig. to Jutland boats, whence also Dan. *jolle*, etc.; cf. JOLLY-BOAT], 1. a ship's boat; jolly-boat. 2. a small sailboat rigged fore-and-aft, with a short mizzenmast astern of the rudder post: distinguished from *ketch*.

YAWL

yawl (yôl), *n. & v.i.* [Dial.], yowl.

yawn (yôn), *v.i.* [ME. *yanen, yonen;* merging AS. *ginian* (*geonian*) & the synonymous *ganian*, to gape; akin to G. *gähnen;* IE. base **ĝhei-*, to gape, prob. echoic of the yawning sound, seen also in L. *hiare* (cf. HIATUS)], 1. to open the mouth wide, especially involuntarily, and with a deep inhalation, as a result of fatigue, drowsiness, or boredom. 2. to be or become wide open; gape: as, a *yawning* chasm. *v.t.* to express or utter with a yawn. *n.* 1. an act of yawning or opening wide. 2. a wide opening; chasm.

yawp (yôp, yäp), *v.i.* [ME. *yolpen*, prob. an echoic var. of *yelpen;* cf. YELP], 1. to utter a loud, harsh call or cry. 2. [Slang], to talk noisily and stupidly; yap. 3. [Colloq.], to yawn aloud; gape. *n.* the act or sound of yawping. Also spelled **yaup**.

yaws (yôz), *n.pl.* [prob. of W.Ind. origin], a tropical infectious disease caused by a spirochete and characterized by raspberrylike skin eruptions followed by destructive lesions of the skin and bones (with *the*); frambesia.

Yaz·oo (yaz′o͞o), *n.* a river in western Mississippi, flowing into the Mississippi River: length, 300 mi.

Yb, in *chemistry*, ytterbium.

Y.B., Yearbook.

Y chromosome, a sex chromosome.

y·clept, y·clept (i-klept′), *pp.* [ME. *ycleped;* AS. *geclypod*, pp. of *clipian*, to call; popularized by Spenser & Milton], [Archaic], called; named; known as: as, a giant *yclept* Barbarossa: also spelled **ycleped, y-cleped.**

yd., yard; yards.

ye (*thē, thə, thi;* yē *is incorrect*), *adj.* [Archaic], the: *Y* was substituted by early printers for the thorn (þ), the Old and Middle English character representing the sound *th*: sometimes written y^e, as though a contraction.

ye (yē; *unstressed* yi), *pron.* [ME. *yhe, ge;* AS. *ge*, ye, nom. pl. corresponding to *thu*, thou; akin to Goth. *jus*, but with vowel modified after *we* (cf. WE); for IE. base see YOU], [Archaic], you: originally used only as nominative plural, later as nominative singular, and still later, especially in dialectal speech, as accusative singular and plural.

yea (yā), *adv.* [ME. *ye;* AS. *gea;* akin to G. *ja;* ult. < the pronominal *ei-, seen also in Eng. *it;* cf. YEAH], 1. yes: used to express affirmation. 2. indeed; truly; verily: used to introduce a question or statement. 3. [Archaic], not only that, but more; moreover: as, he was a good, *yea*, a fine man. *n.* 1. an affirmative statement or vote. 2. a person voting in the affirmative.

yeah (ye, ya, *etc.*), *adv.* [prob. after D. & G. *ja*, merged with the cognate Eng. *yea*], [Colloq.], yes.

yean (yēn), *v.t. & v.i.* [ME. *genen;* AS. **ge-eanian* (cf. *geean*, pregnant); *ge-* (cf. Y-) + *eanian*, to bring forth lambs; akin to D. *oonen;* IE. base **agwh-nos*, lamb, seen also in L. *agnus*, lamb, etc.], to bring forth (young): said of a sheep or goat.

yean·ling (yēn′liŋ), *n.* [*yean* + *-ling*], a lamb or kid. *adj.* newborn.

year (yêr), *n.* [ME. *yere;* AS. *gear;* akin to G. *jahr;* IE. base **jē-* (< **ei*, to go, as also in L. *Janus*, orig., god of the speeding sun, *janua*, door); basic sense "that goes, passes"], 1. *a*) a period of 365 days (in leap year, 366 days) divided into 12 months and regarded as beginning January 1 and ending the following December 31. *b*) a period of more or less the same length in other calendars. 2. the period of time, 365 days, 5 hours, 48 minutes, and 46 seconds, spent by the sun in making its apparent passage from vernal equinox to vernal equinox: also **astronomical, natural, equinoctial, solar,** or **tropical year.** 3. the period of time, 365 days, 6 hours, 9 minutes, and 9 seconds, spent by the sun in its apparent passage from a fixed star and back to the same position again: the difference in time between this and the astronomical year is due to the precession of the equinoxes: also **sidereal year.** 4. a period of 12 lunar months: also **lunar year.** 5. the period of time occupied by any planet in making one complete revolution around the sun. 6. a period of 12 calendar months reckoned from any date: as, we shall return one *year* from today. 7. a particular annual period of less than 365 days: as, a fisherman's work *year*, a short school *year*, etc. 8. *pl.* *a*) age: as, he seems old for his *years*. *b*) time; especially, a long time: as, he died *years* ago. Abbreviated **y.** (*sing. & pl.*), **yr.**

year after year, every year.

year by year, each year.

year in, year out, every year.

year·book (yêr′book′), *n.* a book published yearly, especially one giving statistics and data of the preceding year; annual: abbreviated **Y.B.**

year·ling (yêr′liŋ, yũr′liŋ), *n.* 1. an animal one year old or in its second year. 2. in *racing*, a horse one year old, reckoned from January 1 of the year of its foaling.

year·long (yêr′lôŋ), *adj.* lasting or continuing for a full year.

year·ly (yêr′li), *adj.* 1. continuing or lasting for a year. 2. done, happening, appearing, payable, etc. once a year, or every year: as, a *yearly* event. 3. of a year, or each year. *adv.* annually; every year.

yearn (yũrn), *v.i.* [ME. *yernen;* AS. *gyrnan* < *georn*, eager], 1. to be filled with longing or desire. 2. to be deeply moved, especially with pity or sympathy.

yearn·ing (yũr′niŋ), *n.* [*yearn* + *-ing*], deep or anxious longing, desire, etc.

yeast (yēst), *n.* [ME. *yest;* AS. *gist;* akin to G. *gischt*, spray, froth & OHG. *jesan*, to ferment; IE. base **jes-*, to foam, boil up, seen also in Gr. *zeein*, to boil (cf. ECZEMA, ENZYME)], 1. a yellow, frothy substance consisting of a mass of minute fungi which germinate and multiply in the presence of starch or sugar and form alcohol and carbon dioxide during a process of fermentation induced by an enzyme: used in making beer and as a leavening agent in baking. 2. any of the family of fungi that form yeast; yeast plant. 3. yeast mixed with flour or meal, usually made up in small cakes. 4. foam; froth. 5. *a*) something that agitates or causes ferment; leaven. *b*) ferment; agitation. *v.i.* [Rare], to froth or ferment.

yeast cake, a small cake made by mixing yeast with flour or meal: sold commercially for use in baking, etc.

yeast plant, yeast (sense 2).

yeast·y (yēs′ti), *adj.* [YEASTIER (-ti-ẽr), YEASTIEST (-ti-ist)], 1. of, like, or containing yeast. 2. frothy; foamy. 3. light; superficial; frivolous. 4. in a ferment; unsettled; restless.

Yeats, William Butler (yāts), 1865–1939; Irish essayist, poet, and dramatist; received Nobel prize in literature, 1923.

Yed·o, Yed·do (ye′dô′), *n.* Tokyo: a former name.

yegg (yeg), *n.* [said to be from name of famous safecracker], [Slang], a criminal; especially, a safecracker or burglar.

yegg·man (yeg′mən), *n.* [*pl.* YEGGMEN (-mən)], [Slang], a yegg.

yeld (yeld), *adj.* [ME.; AS. *gelde;* cf. ON. *geldr;* see GELD], [Scot.], 1. barren. 2. not giving milk.

yelk (yelk), *n.* [Archaic or Dial.], a yolk.

yell (yel), *v.i.* [ME. *yellen;* AS. *gellan, giellan, gyllan*, to yell, cry out, resound; IE. base **ghel-*, to cry out; cf. YELP], to cry out loudly; shriek; scream. *v.t.* to utter by yelling. *n.* 1. a loud outcry or shout; shriek; scream. 2. a rhythmic cheer given in unison, as by college students at a football game.

yel·low (yel′ō), *adj.* [ME. *yelwe;* AS. *geolo, geolu;* akin to G. *gelb;* IE. base **ĝhel-*, to gleam, seen also in L. *helvus*, tawny], 1. of the color of gold, butter, or ripe lemons. 2. changed to a yellowish color as by age or illness, as old paper, jaundiced skin, etc. 3. having a yellowlike pigmentation of the skin, as that characteristic of the Mongolians. 4. jealous or melancholy. 5. [Colloq.], cowardly or untrustworthy. 6. cheaply sensational to an offensive degree: said of certain newspapers. *n.* 1. a yellow color; any color lying between red and green in the color spectrum. 2. a pigment or dye that is yellow or capable of producing yellow. 3. the yolk of an egg. 4. *pl.* any of several fungus or virus diseases of plants, causing yellowing of the leaves, stunting of growth, etc. 5. *pl.* jaundice, especially in farm animals. 6. *pl.* [Obs.], a bad humor; jealousy. *v.t. & v.i.* to make or become yellow.

yel·low·bird (yel′ō-bũrd′), *n.* 1. the American goldfinch. 2. the yellow warbler.

yellow daisy, the black-eyed Susan or any of several similar flowers.

yel·low-dog contract (yel′ō-dôg′), an employer-employee contract, now illegal, by which a person being hired is first made to agree that he will join no labor union while employed.

yellow fever, an acute infectious tropical disease caused by a virus transmitted by the bite of certain mosquitoes, and characterized by fever, jaundice, vomiting, etc.

yel·low-green (yel′ō-grēn′), *n.* a color between yellow and green in the spectrum. *adj.* of this color.

yel·low·ham·mer (yel′ō-ham′ẽr), *n.* [earlier *yellowammer* < *yellow* + AS. *amore*, kind of bird], 1. a small European finch having a yellow head, neck, and breast. 2. the golden-winged woodpecker, or flicker, of North America.

yel·low·ish (yel′ō-ish, yel′ə-wish), *adj.* rather yellow.

yellow jack, 1. yellow fever. 2. a yellow flag used as a signal of quarantine. 3. a West Indian carangoid food fish having a gold and silver coloring.

yellow jacket, any of several social wasps and hornets having bright-yellow markings.

yellow jasmine, the jasmine, a flowering plant: also **yellow jessamine.**

yellow journalism, [< the use of yellow ink, to attract readers, in printing the "Yellow Kid," a cartoon strip, in the *New York World* (1895)], the use of cheaply sensational or unscrupulous methods in newspapers, etc. to attract or influence the readers.

yellow lead ore, wulfenite.

yel·low·legs (yel′ō-legz′), *n.* [*pl.* YELLOWLEGS], either of two sandpipers having long, yellow legs and brown and white markings.

yellow metal, 1. gold. 2. brass that is 60 parts copper and 40 parts zinc.

yellow peril, the alleged danger to the world supremacy of the white, or Caucasian, peoples created by the vast numbers and potential political power of the yellow, or Mongolian, peoples.

yellow pine, 1. any of several American pines having yellowish wood. 2. the wood of any of these.

yellow race, loosely, the Mongolian division of mankind: see **Mongolian.**

Yellow River, Hwang Ho, a river in China.

Yellow Sea, an arm of the Pacific, between China and Korea: Chinese name, *Hwang Hai.*

yellow spot, the small, yellowish area in the retina where vision is most acute.

Yel·low·stone (yel′ō-stōn′), *n.* a river in Wyoming and Montana, flowing into the Missouri: length, 671 mi.

Yellowstone Falls, waterfalls of the Yellowstone River in Yellowstone National Park: upper falls, 109 ft. high; lower falls, 308 ft. high.

Yellowstone Lake, a lake in Yellowstone National Park: area, 140 sq. mi.

Yellowstone National Park, a national park in northwestern Wyoming, extending over into Idaho and Montana, containing geysers, boiling springs, petrified forests, the Grand Canyon of the Yellowstone, etc.: area, 3,472 sq. mi.

yellow streak, a tendency to be cowardly, craven, etc.

yel·low·tail (yel′ō-tāl′), *n.* [*pl.* YELLOWTAILS (-tālz′), YELLOWTAIL; see PLURAL, II, D, 1], any of several fishes having a yellowish tail; specifically, *a*) the California rockfish. *b*) the menhaden. *c*) a carangoid fish found along the California coast.

yel·low·throat (yel′ō-thrōt′), *n.* any of various American warblers.

yellow warbler, a small, bright-yellow North American warbler.

yel·low·weed (yel′ō-wēd′), *n.* 1. any of several kinds of goldenrod. 2. the European ragwort. 3. the bulbous crowfoot. 4. sneezeweed.

yel·low·wood (yel′ō-wood′), *n.* 1. any of several trees yielding yellow wood; especially, *a*) a smooth-barked, white-flowering tree of the southern United States, source of a yellow dye. *b*) Osage orange. *c*) the smoke tree. 2. the wood of any of these.

yel·low·y (yel′ō-i, yel′ə-wi), *adj.* somewhat yellow.

yelp (yelp), *v.i.* [ME. *yelpen,* to boast; AS. *gilpan, gielpan, gylpan,* to boast noisily < **galpjan;* akin to MHG. *gelfen;* IE. base **ghel-,* to cry out; cf. YELL], 1. to utter a short, sharp cry or bark, as a dog. 2. to cry out sharply, as in pain. *v.t.* to utter or express by yelping. *n.* a short, sharp cry or bark.

Yem·en (yem′ən, yā′mən), *n.* an Arab kingdom in southwestern Arabia, on the Red Sea: area, 75,000 sq. mi.; pop., 5,000,000; capital, San'a.

Yem·en·i (yem′ə-ni, yā′mə-ni), *adj. & n.* Yemenite.

Yem·en·ite (yem′ən-īt′, yā′mən-īt′), *adj.* of Yemen or its people. *n.* a native or inhabitant of Yemen.

yen (yen), *n.* [*pl.* YEN], [Japan. < Chin. *yüan,* round, dollar], the monetary unit of Japan, equal to 100 sen: valued, in 1963, at .28 cent.

yen (yen), *n.* [Chin., opium, smoke], [Colloq.], a deep longing or desire. *v.i.* [YENNED (yend), YENNING], [Colloq.], to have a yen (*for*); long; yearn.

Yen·an (yen′än′), *n.* a city in northern Shensi province, China: pop., c. 50,000.

Ye·ni·sei (ye′ni-sā′), *n.* a river in central Siberia, flowing into the Arctic Ocean: length, c. 2,800 mi.

yeo·man (yō′mən), *n.* [*pl.* YEOMEN (-mən)], [ME. *yeman, yoman;* not in AS; prob. contr. < *yengman, yung man,* young man], 1. originally, *a*) an attendant or manservant in a royal or noble household. *b*) an assistant or subordinate, as to a sheriff. *c*) a freeholder of a class below the gentry, who worked his own land. 2. [British], *a*) a yeoman of the guard. *b*) a member of the yeomanry (sense 2). 3. in the *United States Navy,* a petty officer assigned to clerical duty.

yeo·man·ly (yō′mən-li), *adj.* 1. of, characteristic of, or befitting a yeoman; hence, 2. brave; sturdy; faithful. *adv.* in a yeomanly manner; bravely.

yeoman of the (royal) guard, any of the 100 men forming a ceremonial guard for the English royal family: the guard was instituted in 1485 by Henry VII and still wears a traditional 15th-century uniform.

yeo·man·ry (yō′mən-ri), *n.* 1. yeomen collectively. 2. a British volunteer cavalry force organized in 1761 as a home guard, but since 1907, a part of the Territorial Army. Abbreviated **yeo.**

yeoman's service, exceptionally good or loyal service or assistance: also **yeoman service.**

yep (yep), *adv.* [Slang], yes: an affirmative reply.

-yer (yẽr), -ier: usually after *w,* as in *lawyer.*

Yer·ba Bue·na (yâr′bə bwā′nə), an island in San Francisco Bay, between San Francisco and Oakland: tunnel across this island connects two spans of the San Francisco-Oakland bridge.

yes (yes), *adv.* [ME. *yis, yus;* AS. *gese, gise,* yes; prob. < *gea,* yea + *si, sy,* be it so, 3d pers. sing., pres. subj., of *beon,* to be (cf. BE)], 1. aye; yea; it is so: the opposite of *no,* and used to express agreement, consent, affirmation, or confirmation. 2. not only that, but more; moreover: as, I shall be ready, *yes,* eager to help you. *Yes* is sometimes used alone in inquiry to signify "What is it?", "Do you wish to say (or add) something?" or as a mere expression of interest equivalent to "Is it so?" *n.* [*pl.* YESES (-iz)], 1. the act of saying *yes;* affirmative reply; agreement. 2. an affirmative vote or a person voting this way: usually *aye. v.t. & v.i.* [YESSED (yest), YESSING], to say *yes* (to).

ye·shi·va (yə-shē′və), *n.* [*pl.* YESHIVAS, YESHIVOTH (ye′shē-vōt′)], [< Heb. *yeshīvāh,* lit., a sitting], 1. a seminary for the training of orthodox rabbis. 2. a Jewish school for religious and secular studies.

yes man, [Slang], a person who indicates indiscriminating approval of every suggestion or opinion offered by his superior; servile sycophant.

yes·ter (yes′tẽr), *adj.* [1st element of *yesterday* used as a combining form], 1. of yesterday. 2. previous to this. Usually in combination: as, *yestereve, yesteryear.*

yes·ter·day (yes′tẽr-di, yes′tẽr-dā′), *n.* [ME. *yistredai, gisterdai;* AS. *geostrandæg; geostran, giestran,* yesterday + *dæg,* day; *geostran* (akin to G. *gestern,* yesterday) < IE. base **ĝhjes-,* yesterday, seen also in L. *heri,* yesterday, *hesternus,* of yesterday, etc.], 1. the day before today; day just past. 2. a recent day or time. *adv.* 1. on the day before today. 2. recently. *adj.* of yesterday: as, *yesterday* morning.

yes·ter·eve (yes′tẽr-ēv′), *n. & adv.* [Archaic or Poetic], yesterevening

yes·ter·eve·ning (yes′tẽr-ēv′niŋ), *n. & adv.* [Archaic or Poetic], (on) the evening of yesterday.

yes·ter·morn (yes′tẽr-môrn′), *n. & adv.* [Archaic or Poetic], yestermorning.

yes·ter·morn·ing (yes′tẽr-môr′niŋ), *n. & adv.* [Archaic or Poetic], (on) the morning of yesterday.

yes·tern (yes′tẽrn), *adj.* [Archaic], yester.

yes·ter·night (yes′tẽr-nīt′), *n. & adv.* [Archaic or Poetic], (on) the night before today; last night.

yes·ter·year (yes′tẽr-yêr′), *n. & adv.* [used by Dante Gabriel Rossetti to translate Fr. *antan*], [Archaic or Poetic], last year.

yes·treen (yes-trēn′), *n. & adv.* [MScot. *yystrewin* (*yester* + *even*); contr. to *yistrene* in 16th c.], [Scot. or Poetic], yesterevening.

yet (yet), *adv.* [ME. *yit, yete;* AS. *giet, gieta;* akin to OFris. *ieta* & prob. to G. *jetzt,* now < Gmc. **hiu-to* < IE. **k̑o-,* **kjo-,* etc., this], 1. up to now or to the time specified; thus far: as, they had not *yet* finished eating. 2. at the present time; now: as, we can't leave just *yet.* 3. still; even now; in the time still remaining: as, there is *yet* a chance for peace. 4. now or at a particular time, as continuing from a preceding time: as, I could hear him *yet.* 5. in addition; further; still; even (usually with a comparative): as, he was *yet* more kind. 6. as much as; even: as, he did not come, nor *yet* write. 7. now, after all the time that has elapsed: as, hasn't he finished *yet?* 8. nevertheless: as, she was lovely, *yet* stupid. *conj.* nevertheless; however: as, she seems happy, *yet* she is troubled.
as yet, up to now.

yew (ū), *n.* [ME. *ew;* AS. *iw, eow;* akin to G. *eibe* (OHG. *īuui*); IE. base **əiwa-,* etc., berry, hence berry-bearing tree, seen also in L. *uva* (< **oiwa*), bunch of grapes], 1. a cone-bearing evergreen tree of Europe and Asia, having fine-grained, elastic wood, dark-green leaves, and red berries. 2. its wood, used especially for making archers' bows. 3. [Archaic], a bow of yew.

Yezd (yezd), *n.* a city in central Iran: pop., 64,000.

Ye·zo (ye′zō), *n.* Hokkaido, Japan: the former name.

Ygg·dra·sill (ig′drə-sil′), *n.* [ON. *Yggdra Syll* < *Yggr,* a name of Odin], in *Norse mythology,* the great ash tree whose roots and branches hold together the universe.

YHVH, YHWH, Yahweh: see **Jehovah, Tetragrammaton.**

Yid·dish (yid′ish), *n.* [G. *jüdisch,* short for *jüdischdeutsch,* Jewish-German; *jüdisch,* Jewish < *Jude,* a Jew; L. *Judaeus*], a language spoken by many European Jews and their descendants on other continents: it is a dialect of High German written in characters of the Hebrew alphabet and containing elements of Hebrew, Russian, Polish, etc.: abbreviated **Yid.** *adj.* 1. of or in this language. 2. [Slang], Jewish.

yield (yēld), *v.t.* [ME. *yelden;* AS. *gieldan, geldan,* to pay, give; akin to G. *gelten,* to be worth; IE. **ghel-tō,* (I) give, pay], 1. to produce; specifically, *a*) to give or furnish as a natural process or as the result of cultivation: as, our orchard *yielded* a good crop this year. *b*) to give in return; produce as a result, profit, etc.: as, their advice to us *yielded* many benefits. 2. to give up under pressure; surrender: sometimes used reflexively (with *up*), as, he *yielded* himself up to pleasure. 3. to give; concede; grant: as, he *yielded* his consent, they must *yield* the point. 4. [Archaic], to pay; recompense. *v.i.* 1. to produce or bear: as, the mine has *yielded* poorly. 2. to give up; surrender; submit. 3. to give way to physical force: as, the gate would not *yield* to their blows. 4. to give place; lose precedence, leadership, etc. (often with *to*). *n.* 1. the act of yielding, or producing. 2. the amount yielded or produced; return on labor, investment, etc.; product.

SYN.*—yield** implies a giving way under the pressure or compulsion of force, entreaty, persuasion, etc. (to *yield* to demands); **capitulate** implies surrender to a force that one has neither the strength nor will to resist further (to *capitulate* to the will of the majority); **succumb** stresses the weakness of the one who gives way or the power and irresistibility of that which makes one yield (she *succumbed* to his charms); **relent** suggests the yielding or softening of one in a dominant position who has been harsh, stern, or stubborn (he *relented* at the sight of her grief); **defer** implies a yielding to another because of respect for his dignity, authority, knowledge, etc. (to *defer* to another's judgment). See also **surrender.** —ANT.*** resist.

yield·ing (yēl′diŋ), *adj.* that yields; submissive; obedient.

yill (yil), *n.* [Scot.], ale.

yin (yin), *adj., pron., n.* [Scot.], one.

Ying·kow (yiŋ′kou′), *n.* a city in southern Manchuria, on the Gulf of Liaotung: pop., 181,000: also called *Newchwang.*

yip (yip), *n.* [echoic], [Colloq.], a yelp. *v.i.* [YIPPED (yipt), YIPPING], [Colloq.], to yelp, as a young dog.

yipe (yīp), *interj.* an exclamation of pain, dismay, alarm, etc.

yird (yũrd), *n.* [Scot.], earth.

-yl (il; *now rarely* ēl), [< Gr. *hylē,* wood, substance], a combining form used in chemistry to form the names of radicals, as in *amyl, ethyl.*

y·lang-y·lang (ē′läŋ-ē′läŋ), *n.* ilang-ilang.

Y.M.C.A., Young Men's Christian Association.

Y.M.Cath.A., Young Men's Catholic Association.

Y.M.H.A., Young Men's Hebrew Association.

Y·mir (ē′mir), *n.* [ON.], in *Norse mythology,* the giant from whose body the gods created the world.

yod, yodh (yōd; Heb. yood), *n.* [Heb., lit., hand], the tenth letter of the Hebrew alphabet (ʼ), corresponding to English initial *Y, y*: see **alphabet**, table.

yo·del (yō′d'l), *v.t. & v.i.* [YODELED or YODELLED (-d'ld), YODELING or YODELLING], [G. *jodeln*], to sing with abrupt alternating changes between the normal chest voice and the falsetto. *n.* 1. the act or sound of yodeling. 2. a song or refrain sung in this way to meaningless syllables: popular among the mountain people of Switzerland and the Austrian Tyrol.

yo·del·er, yo·del·ler (yō′d'l-ẽr, yō′dlẽr), *n.* a person who yodels.

yo·dle (yō′d'l), *n., v.t. & v.i.* [YODLED (-d'ld), YODLING], yodel.

yo·dler (yō′dlẽr), *n.* a yodeler.

yo·ga (yō′gə), *n.* [Sans., union], in *Hindu philosophy*, a practice involving intense and complete concentration upon something, especially the deity, in order to establish identity of consciousness with the object of concentration: it is a mystic and ascetic practice, usually involving the discipline of prescribed postures, controlled breathing, etc.

yogh (yōkh), *n.* [ME.], the name of the Middle English character ȝ, representing: *a)* a voiceless fricative, or guttural, similar to Modern German *ch*, as in *doch*: it is now written *gh* and is usually silent, as in *though*, or pronounced (f), as in *cough*. *b)* a voiced palatal fricative, now represented by the *y* of *yes*.

yo·gi (yō′gi), *n.* [*pl.* YOGIS (-giz)], [Hind. *yogī;* Sans. *yogin*], 1. one who practices yoga. 2. loosely, yoga.

yo·gin (yō′gin), *n.* a yogi.

yo·gurt, yo·ghurt (yō′goort), *n.* [Turk. *yōghurt*], a thick, semisolid food made from milk fermented by a bacterium, originating in Turkey, Bulgaria, etc.: it is believed to have a beneficial effect on the intestines and is now sometimes prescribed dietetically: also **yohourt**.

yo-heave-ho (yō′hēv′hō′), *interj.* a chant formerly used by sailors while pulling or lifting together in rhythm.

yoh·ourt (yō′oort), *n.* yogurt.

yoicks (yoiks), *interj.* [earlier *hoik, hike,* also *yoaks;* prob. echoic], [British], a cry used for urging on the hounds in fox hunting.

yoke (yōk), *n.* [ME. *yok;* AS. *geoc, gioc;* akin to G. *joch;* IE. base **jeug-*, to yoke together, bind together, as also in L. *jugum*, yoke (cf. JUGATE, CONJUGAL)], 1. a wooden frame or bar with loops or bows at either end, used for harnessing together a pair of oxen, etc. 2. a pair of animals harnessed together: as, a *yoke* of oxen. 3. an ox yoke, arch of spears, etc. held over the shoulders of the conquered in ancient times. 4. any mark or symbol of bondage or servitude. 5. subjection; bondage; servitude. 6. something that binds, unites, or connects: as, the *yoke* of brotherhood. 7. something like a yoke in shape or function; specifically, *a)* a frame fitting over the shoulders for carrying pails, etc., one on either end. *b)* a clamp, coupling, slotted piece, etc. used to hold a part in place, guide or control its movement, etc. *c)* the crosspiece to which the steering cables are attached on a ship's rudder. *d)* the bar used in double harnessing to connect the horse's collar to the tongue of the wagon or carriage. 8. a part of a garment fitted closely to the shoulders or hips as a support for the gathered parts of the skirt, etc. 9. [Obs.], the usual amount of land plowed by a yoke of oxen in one day. 10. [Scot.], the time during which a yoke of oxen and the plowman work at a single, continuous stretch; hence, 11. [Scot.], a part of the working day. *v.t.* [YOKED (yōkt), YOKING], 1. to put a yoke on. 2. *a)* to harness an animal to (a plow, etc.). *b)* to harness (an animal) to a plow, etc. 3. to join together; link; couple. 4. to marry. 5. [Rare], to bring into bondage; enslave. *v.i.* to be joined together or closely united. —***SYN.*** see **pair**.

YOKE
(on pair of oxen)

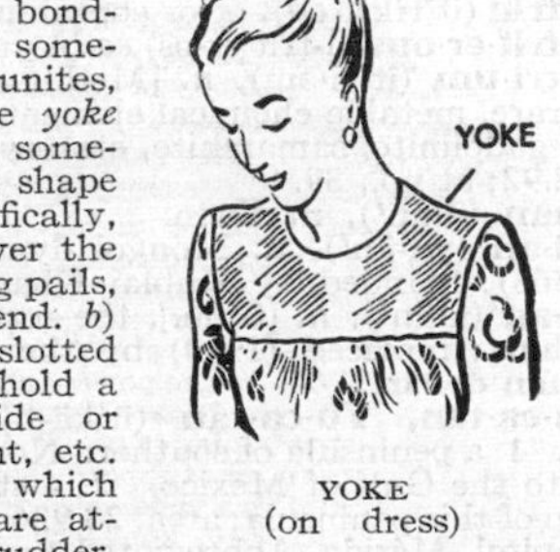

YOKE
(on dress)

yoke·fel·low (yōk′fel′ō), *n.* 1. a companion, partner, or associate. 2. a husband or wife.

yo·kel (yō′k'l), *n.* [prob. < *yokel, youkell*, dial. forms of *hickwall*, green woodpecker], a person living in a rural area; rustic; country bumpkin: used contemptuously.

Yo·ko·ha·ma (yō′kə-hä′mə; Jap. yô′kô-hä′mä), *n.* a seaport in Honshu, Japan, near Tokyo: pop., 1,144,000.

Yo·ko·su·ka (yō′kə-sōō′kə; Jap. yô′kô-sōō′kä), *n.* a seaport in Honshu, Japan, near Yokohama: pop., 279,000.

yolk (yōk; *now rarely* yōlk), *n.* [ME. *yolke, yelke;* AS. *geolca, gioleca*, yolk, lit., yellow part < the base of *geolu* (cf. YELLOW)], 1. the yellow, principal substance of an egg, as distinguished from the albumen, or white. 2. in *biology*, the contents of the ovum, including the protoplasm from which the embryo itself develops and, especially, the protoplasm that serves as nourishment for the growing embryo. 3. the oily secretion present in sheep's wool.

yolk·y (yōk′i; *now rarely* yōlk′i), *adj.* [YOLKIER (-i-ẽr), YOLKIEST (-i-ist)], of, like, or full of yolk.

yom (yom; Heb. yōm), *n.* [*pl.* YOMIM (yô′mim)], [Heb. *yōm*], day: used in names of various Jewish holidays.

Yom Kip·pur (yom′ kip′ẽr; Heb. yōm′ ki-pōōr′, kip′oor), [Heb. *yōm kipūr*, day of atonement], a Jewish holiday and day of fasting, the Day of Atonement: Lev. 16:29–34: see **Jewish holidays.**

yon (yon), *adj. & adv.* [ME. *yone;* AS. *geon;* akin to G. *jener*, that; for IE. base see IT; now regarded as shortened < *yonder*], [Archaic or Dial.], yonder. *pron.* [Archaic or Dial.], that or those at a distance.

yond (yond), *adv. & adj.* [ME. *yond;* AS. *geond* < *geon* (cf. YON)], [Archaic or Dial.], yonder.

yon·der (yon′dẽr), *adj.* [ME. *yonder, yender*, extension of *yone;* cf. YON & -THER], 1. farther; more distant (with *the*). 2. being at a distance, but within, or as within, sight; that or those over there. *adv.* at or in that (specified or relatively distant) place; over there.

Yon·kers (yoŋ′kẽrz), *n.* a city in southeastern New York, on the Hudson: pop., 191,000.

yore (yôr, yōr), *adv.* [ME. *yore, yare;* AS. *geara*, adv. formation < *gear*, year (cf. YEAR)], [Obs.], long ago; in times long past. *n.* time long past: now only in *of yore*, formerly.

York (yôrk), *n.* 1. Yorkshire, England. 2. the county seat of Yorkshire: pop., 105,000: ancient name, *Eboracum*. 3. a city in southeastern Pennsylvania: pop., 55,000.

York (yôrk), *n.* the ruling family of England (1461–1485).

York, Cape, a cape of northeastern Australia, on Torres Strait.

york·er (yôr′kẽr), *n.* [orig. *Yorker* < the county of York, England; prob. a favorite bowl of Yorkshire teams], in *cricket*, a bowled ball that hits the ground directly under or in front of the bat.

York·ist (yôr′kist), *n.* a member or supporter of the English royal house of York. *adj.* of or supporting the house of York, especially as opposed to the house of Lancaster in the Wars of the Roses.

York·shire (yôrk′shir), *n.* the largest county of England, on the northeastern coast: divided into North Riding, East Riding, and West Riding: pop., 4,623,000; county seat, York: also called *York*.

Yorkshire pudding, [after prec. entry], a batter pudding baked in the drippings of roasting meat.

Yorkshire terrier, a small, long-haired terrier of a breed originating in Yorkshire, England.

York·town (yôrk′toun′), *n.* a town in southeastern Virginia: scene of a battle (1781) of the American Revolution, in which Washington forced the surrender of Cornwallis.

Yo·ru·ba (yō′roo-bä′), *n.* [*pl.* YORUBA, YORUBAS (-bäz′)], 1. a member of a numerous Negro people and linguistic family along the coast of West Africa, chiefly between the Niger River and the Dahomey River. 2. the Sudanic language of the Yoruba.

Yor·u·ba·land (yō′roo-bä-land′), *n.* a region of Nigeria, Africa: formerly a kingdom.

Yo·sem·i·te (yō-sem′ə-ti), *n.* a valley in central California: part of Yosemite National Park.

Yosemite Falls, a series of waterfalls in Yosemite National Park: upper falls, 1,430 ft. high; central falls, 620 ft. high; lower falls, 320 ft. high; total height (with rapids), 2,525 ft.

Yosemite National Park, a national park in east central California, containing high waterfalls, cliffs, and redwood trees: area, 1,189 sq. mi.

Yo·shi·hi·to (yô′shē-hē′tô), *n.* 1879–1926; father of *Hirohito*; emperor of Japan (1912–1926).

you (ū; *unstressed* yoo, yə), *pron.* [ME. *you, ou, eow;* AS. *eow*, dat. & acc. pl. of *ge*, ye; akin to D. *u;* IE. base **iw-*, you, seen also in Sans. *yuvám*, you; cf. YE], 1. the person or persons to whom one is speaking or writing: *you* is the nominative and objective form (sing. & pl.), *your* and *yours* the possessive (sing. & pl.), and *yourself* (sing.) and *yourselves* (pl.) the intensive and reflexive, of the second personal pronoun. 2. a person or people generally: equivalent in sense to indefinite *one*, as, *you* can never tell!

fat, āpe, bâre, cär; ten, ēven, hêre, ovẽr; is, bīte; lot, gō, hôrn, tōōl, look; oil, out; up, ūse, fũr; get; joy; yet; chin; she; thin, *th*en; zh, leisure; ŋ, ring; ə for *a* in *ago*, *e* in *agent*, *i* in *sanity*, *o* in *comply*, *u* in *focus;* ' as in *able* (ā′b'l); Fr. bål; ë, Fr. coeur; ö, Fr. feu; Fr. mo*n*; ô, Fr. coq; ü, Fr. duc; H, G. ich; kh, G. doch. See pp. x–xii. ‡ foreign; * hypothetical; < derived from.

you'd (ūd; *unstressed* yood, yəd), 1. you had. 2. you would.
you'll (ūl; *unstressed* yool, yəl), 1. you will. 2. you shall.
young (yuŋ), *adj.* [ME. *yonge;* AS. *geong;* akin to G. *jung;* IE. base **juwen-*, seen also in L. *juvenis*, young (cf. JUVENILE)], 1. being in an early period of life or growth; not old. 2. characteristic of youth in quality, appearance, or behavior; fresh; vigorous; strong; active. 3. representing or embodying a new tendency, social movement, progressivism, etc.: as, the *Young* Turks. 4. of or having to do with youth or early life. 5. lately begun; not advanced or developed; in an early stage; hence, 6. lacking experience or practice; immature; raw; ignorant; green. 7. younger than another of the same name or family: as, they say *young* Jones is ill. 8. in *geology*, youthful. *n.* offspring, especially young offspring, collectively: as, a bear and her *young*.
the young, young people.
with young, pregnant.
SYN.—**young** is the general word for one in an early period of life and variously connotes the vigor, strength, immaturity, etc. of this period (a *young* child, man, etc., *young* blood); **youthful** applies to one who is, or appears to be, in the period between childhood and maturity or to that which is appropriate to such a person (a *youthful* executive, *youthful* hopes); **juvenile** applies to that which relates to, is suited to, or is intended for young persons (*juvenile* delinquency, behavior, books, etc.); **puerile** implies reference to adults who unbecomingly display the immature qualities of a child (*puerile* petulance); **adolescent** applies to one in the period between puberty and maturity and especially suggests the awkwardness, emotional instability, etc. of this period (*adolescent* yearnings). —*ANT.* old, mature.
Young, Art (ärt yuŋ), (*Arthur Henry Young*), 1866–1943; American cartoonist.
Young, Brig·ham (brig'əm), 1801–1877; American head of the Mormon Church (1847–1877).
Young, Edward, 1683–1765; English poet.
Young, Owen D., 1874–1962; American lawyer, financier, and statesman.
young·ber·ry (yuŋ'ber'i), *n.* [*pl.* YOUNGBERRIES (-iz)], [after B. M. *Young*, Am. horticulturist], a large, sweet, dark-red berry, a cross between a blackberry and a dewberry.
young blood, 1. young people; youth. 2. youthful strength, vigor, ideas, etc.
young-eyed (yuŋ'īd'), *adj.* 1. having the bright, clear, keen eyes associated with youth; hence, 2. having a youthful or fresh outlook; enthusiastic, optimistic, etc.
young·ish (yuŋ'ish), *adj.* rather young.
young·ling (yuŋ'liŋ), *n.* [ME. *yongling;* AS *geongling*, dim. of *geong*, young], 1. a young person; youth. 2. a young animal or plant. 3. an inexperienced person; novice. *adj.* young.
Young Pretender, Charles Edward Stuart.
young·ster (yuŋ'stẽr), *n.* 1. a child. 2. a youth. 3. a young animal. 4. in the United States Naval Academy, a member of the second-year class.
Youngs·town (yuŋz'toun'), *n.* a city in northeastern Ohio: pop., 167,000.
youn·ker (yuŋ'kẽr), *n.* [D. *jonker, jonkheer*, younker < *jong*, young + *heer*, lord, gentleman; cf. JUNKER], 1. originally, a young nobleman or gentleman. 2. [Now Rare], a youngster.
your (yoor; *unstressed* yẽr), *pron.* [ME. *your, eower;* AS. *eower*, genit. of *ge*, ye with base as in *eow* (cf. YOU)], possessive form of **you** (sing. & pl.). ***possessive pronominal adj.*** of, belonging to, or done by you: also used before some formal titles, as, *your* Honor, *your* Majesty. Abbreviated **yr.**
you're (yoor, ūr; *unstressed* yẽr), you are.
yours (yoorz), *pron.* [ME. *youres; your* + genit. *-es;* hence, in form, a double possessive], that or those belonging to you: the absolute form of **your,** used without a following noun, often after *of*, as, a friend of *yours*, that book is *yours*, *yours* are better. Abbreviated **yrs.**
your·self (yoor-self', yẽr-self'), *pron.* [*pl.* YOURSELVES (-selvz')], a form of the second person singular pronoun, used: *a*) as an intensive: as, you *yourself* went. *b*) as a reflexive: as, you hurt *yourself*. *c*) as a quasi-noun meaning "your real, true, or actual self" (e.g., you are not *yourself* when you rage like that): in this construction *you* may be considered a possessive pronominal adjective and *self* a noun, and they may be separated: as, *your* own sweet *self*.
yours truly, 1. a phrase or formula used before the signature in ending a letter. 2. [Colloq.], I or me: used in humorous allusion to oneself.
youth (ūth), *n.* [*pl.* YOUTHS (ūths, ūthz)], [ME. *youthe;* AS. *geoguthe* < **juguнthi* < **juwunthi* with *g* for *w* after **dugunthi-* (*dugoth*, the doughty ones, veterans); IE. base as in YOUNG; formation exactly parallel to L. *juvencus*, youth], 1. the state or quality of being young. 2. the period of life coming between childhood and maturity; adolescence. 3. an early stage of growth or existence. 4. young people collectively. 5. a young person; especially, a young man.
youth·ful (ūth'fəl), *adj.* 1. young; possessing youth; not yet old or mature. 2. of, characteristic of, or suitable for youth. 3. fresh; vigorous; active. 4. new; early; in an early stage. 5. in *geology*, having only begun to cause or undergo erosion. —*SYN.* see **young.**
youth hostel, any of a system of supervised shelters providing cheap lodging on a co-operative basis for young people on bicycle tours, hikes, etc.
you've (ūv; *unstressed* yoov, yəv), you have.
yow (you), *interj.* an exclamation of pain, surprise, alarm, etc.
yowl (youl), *v.i.* [ME. *goulen, youlen;* ON. *gaula*, to howl, yell], to utter a long, mournful cry; howl; wail. *n.* a long, mournful cry; howl; wail.
yo-yo (yō'yō'), *n.* [arbitrary formation; ? influenced by Tagalog], a spoollike toy attached to a string upon which it may be made to spin up and down by manipulating the string: a trade-mark (**Yo-Yo**).
y·per·ite (ē'pẽr-īt), *n.* [Fr. *ypérite*, after *Ypres*, Belgium], mustard gas.
Y-po·ten·tial (wī'pə-ten'shəl), *n.* Y potential.
Y potential, in *electricity*, the difference in potential between a terminal and the neutral point of an armature wound in three phases.
Y·pres (ē'pr'; *sometimes Anglicized to* wī'pẽrz), *n.* a town in northwestern Belgium, near the French border: pop., 17,000: center of hostilities, World War I: Flemish name, *Ieperen*.
Y.P.S.C.E., Young People's Society of Christian Endeavor.
Yp·si·lan·ti (ip'sə-lan'ti), *n.* a town in southeastern Michigan: pop., 21,000.
Yp·si·lan·ti, Alexander (ip'sə-lan'ti; Gr. ēp'sē-län'tē), 1792–1828; Greek revolutionary leader.
Ypsilanti, De·me·tri·os (dē-me'trē-ôs'), 1793–1832; brother of *Alexander;* Greek revolutionary leader.
Y·quem (ē'kem'), *n.* [< the Château *Yquem*, an estate in southwestern France], a fine variety of sauterne wine.
yr., 1. [*pl.* YRS.], year. 2. younger. 3. your.
yrs., 1. years. 2. yours.
Y·sa·ye, Eu·gène (ö'zhen' ē'zȧ'ē'), 1858–1931; Belgian violinist, teacher, and composer.
Y·ser (ē'zâr'; Eng. ī'zẽr), *n.* a river in France and Belgium, flowing into the North Sea: length, 55 mi.
Y·seult (i-sōōlt'), *n.* Iseult (Isolde).
Yt, in *chemistry*, yttrium.
Y.T., Yukon Territory.
yt·ter·bi·a (i-tũr'bi-ə), *n.* [Mod. L. < *ytterbium*], white ytterbium oxide, Yb_2O_3.
yt·ter·bic (i-tũr'bik), *adj.* of or containing ytterbium.
yt·ter·bi·um (i-tũr'bi-əm), *n.* [Mod. L. < *Ytterby*, Sweden], a rare, metallic chemical element of the rare-earth group, resembling and found with yttrium in gadolinite and certain other minerals: symbol, Yb; at. wt., 173.04; at. no., 70.
ytterbium metals, a group of rare-earth elements including dysprosium, erbium, lutecium, holmium, thulium, and ytterbium.
yt·tri·a (it'ri-ə), *n.* [Mod. L.; see YTTRIUM], yttrium oxide, Y_2O_3, a heavy, white, insoluble powder.
yt·tric (it'rik), *adj.* of or containing yttrium.
yt·trif·er·ous (i-trif'ẽr-əs), *adj.* yielding yttrium.
yt·tri·um (it'ri-əm), *n.* [Mod. L. < *Ytterby*, Sweden], a rare, metallic chemical element found in combination in gadolinite, samarskite, etc.: symbols, Y, Yt; at. wt., 88.92; at no., 39.
Yuan (ū-än'), *n.* Yuen.
Yü·an (yü-än'), *n.* Mongol dynasty of China (1260–1368): founded by Kublai Khan.
yu·an (ū-än'), *n.* [Chin.], the former monetary unit of China: replaced (1949) by the People's Dollar: also **yuan dollar.**
Yu·ca·tan, Yu·ca·tán (ū'kä-tän'; Eng. ū'kə-tan'), *n.* 1. a peninsula of southern North America extending into the Gulf of Mexico. 2. a state of Mexico on the tip of this peninsula: area, 23,926 sq. mi.; pop., 614,000; capital, Mérida. Abbreviated **Yuc.**
yuc·ca (yuk'ə), *n.* [Mod. L.; Sp. *yuca* < W.Ind. (prob. Taino) native name], 1. a plant of the lily family having stiff, sword-shaped leaves and white flowers in a single cluster, found in the southwestern United States and Latin America. 2. the flower of this plant.
Yuen (ū-en'), *n.* a river in central China, flowing northeastward into Tungting Lake: length, 1,000 mi.: also **Yuan, Yuen-kiang.**
Yu·ga (yoo'gə), *n.* [Sans. *yuga*, an age, yoke; cf. YOKE, JUGATE], any of the four ages or eras of the world according to Hindu religious writings, each period being shorter, darker, and less righteous than the preceding: the first is the golden age (*Krita Yuga*), 1,728,000 years; the second (*Treta Yuga*), 1,296,000 years; the third (*Dvapara Yuga*), 864,000 years; the last, the present age (*Kali Yuga*), 432,000 years. The whole period is called *Maha Yuga*.
Yu·go·slav (ū'gō-släv', ū'gə-slav'), *adj.* of Yugoslavia or its people. *n.* a member of a Slavic people, including Serbs, Croats, and Slovenes, that live in Yugoslavia. Also spelled **Jugoslav.**
Yu·go·sla·vi·a (ū'gō-slä'vi-ə, ū'gə-släv'yə), *n.* a republic on the Balkan Peninsula, bordering the Adriatic,

established as a nation in 1918: area, 95,576 sq. mi.; pop., 18,704,000; capital, Belgrade: former name (1918–1929), **Kingdom of the Serbs, Croats, and Slovenes**: also spelled **Jugoslavia**.

Yu·go·sla·vi·an (ū'gō-slä'vi-ən, ū'gə-släv'yən), *adj.* & *n.* Yugoslav: also spelled **Jugoslavian**.

Yu·go·slav·ic (ū'gō-slä'vik, ū'gə-slav'ik), *adj.* Yugoslav; Yugoslavian: also spelled **Jugoslavic**.

Yu·kon (ū'kon), *n.* 1. a territory of northwest Canada, east of Alaska: area, 207,076 sq. mi.; pop., 12,000; capital, Whitehorse: abbreviated **Yuk.** 2. a river flowing through Yukon Territory and Alaska into the Bering Sea: length, 2,300 mi.

yule (ūl), *n.* [ME.; AS. *geol, giul, iul, geohol,* Christmas, the feast of the nativity, orig., name of a heathen festival at the winter solstice; IE. base **jek-,* to speak, speak jokingly, seen also in L. *jocus* (cf. JOKE, JOCUND); primary sense (in Gmc. **jewlā*), "time of happy talking"], Christmas or the Christmas season.

yule log, a large log formerly used as the foundation for the ceremonial Christmas-Eve fire.

yule·tide (ūl'tīd'), *n.* Christmas time.

Yu·ma (ū'mə), *n.* [*pl.* YUMA, YUMAS (-məz)], 1. a Yuman Indian. 2. a city in southwestern Arizona: pop., 24,000.

Yu·man (ū'mən), *adj.* 1. of the Yumas or their language. 2. designating or of a North American Indian linguistic stock of the southwestern United States and northwestern Mexico, including Yuma and Mohave. *n.* this linguistic stock.

Yün·nan (yoo'nan'; Chin. yün'nän'), *n.* 1. a province of southern China: area, 147,849 sq. mi.; pop., 17,473,000; capital, Kunming. 2. Kunming: the former name.

Yur·ev (yoor'yef), *n.* Tartu, Estonia: Russian name.

Yu·zov·ka (yoo'zôf-kä), *n.* Stalino: the former name.

Y.W.C.A., Young Women's Christian Association.

Y.W.H.A., Young Women's Hebrew Association.

y·wis (i-wis'), *adv.* [Obs.], iwis.

Z

Z, z (zē; Brit. zed), *n.* [*pl.* Z's, z's, Zs, zs], 1. the twenty-sixth and last letter of the English alphabet: via Latin from the Greek *zeta*: see **alphabet**, table. 2. the sound of Z or z, phonetically, a voiced tongue-apex fricative, corresponding to the unvoiced *s*. 3. a type or impression for Z or z. 4. *a symbol for* the twenty-sixth in a sequence or group (or the twenty-fifth if J is omitted, or the twenty-third if V and W are also omitted). *adj.* 1. of Z or z. 2. twenty-sixth (or twenty-fifth if J is omitted, or twenty-third if V and W are also omitted) in a sequence or group.

Z (zē; Brit. zed), *n.* 1. an object shaped like Z. 2. a medieval Roman numeral for 2,000: with a superior bar ($\bar{Z}$), 2,000,000. *adj.* shaped like Z.

Z., 1. in *astronomy*, zenith distance. 2. in *chemistry*, atomic number.

Z., z., zone.

z, in *mathematics*, an unknown quantity.

Zab·rze (zäb'zhe), *n.* a city in southwestern Poland, formerly in Germany: pop., 181,000: German name, *Hindenburg*.

Za·ca·te·cas (sä'kä-te'käs), *n.* 1. a state of central Mexico: area, 24,471 sq. mi.; pop., 745,000. 2. its capital: pop., 27,000.

za·ca·tón (sä'kä-tōn'; Sp. thä'kä-tôn'), *n.* [Sp.; see SACATON], a tough, wiry grass found in the southwestern United States and Mexico: it is used in making brushes, brooms, etc.

Zach·a·ri·ah (zak'ə-rī'ə), [LL. *Zacharias;* Gr. *Zacharias;* Heb. *zĕharyah*, lit., God remembers], a masculine name: diminutive, *Zach;* variants, *Zacharias, Zachary, Zechariah. n.* in the *Bible*, 1. the father of John the Baptist. 2. a man named as a martyr by Jesus: Matt. 23:35.

Zach·a·ri·as (zak'ə-rī'əs), a masculine name: see **Zachariah.** *n.* Zachariah.

Zach·a·ry (zak'ẽr-i), a masculine name: see **Zachariah.** *n.* Zachariah.

zaf·fer, zaf·fre (zaf'ẽr), *n.* [< Fr. *zafre* or It. *zaffera;* prob. < Ar. *ṣufr*, yellow copper, brass], unrefined oxide of cobalt, used in making smalt and as a blue pigment in ceramic glazes, glassmaking, etc.

Zagh·lul Pa·sha, Saad (säd zäg-lo͞ol' pä'shä), 1860?–1927; premier of Egypt (1924).

Za·greb (zä'greb), *n.* a city in northwestern Yugoslavia: pop., 351,000: German name, *Agram*.

zai·ba·tsu (zī'bät-so͞o'), *n.* [*pl.* ZAIBATSU], [Japan. *zai,* property + *batsu,* family], the few families that own and control most of the industry in Japan.

Za·kyn·thos (zä'kēn-thôs'), *n.* Zante: the Greek name.

Za·ma (zā'mə, zä'mä), *n.* an ancient town in Numidia, Africa: scene of a battle (202 B.C.) of the Second Punic War between Carthage and Rome.

Zam·be·zi (zam-bē'zi, zȧm-bā'zi), *n.* a river in southern Africa, flowing from Northern Rhodesia into the Indian Ocean: length, 1,600 mi.

Zam·bo·an·ga (säm'bō-äŋ'gä), *n.* a city on the western coast of Mindanao, in the Philippines: pop., 131,000.

za·mi·a (zā'mi-ə), *n.* [Mod. L.; L. *zamiae* (pl.), false reading in Pliny for (*nuces*) *azaniae*, pine (nuts)], a palmlike shrub or tree having a thick trunk, a crown of feather-shaped leaves, and oblong cones.

za·min·dar (zə-mēn'där'), *n.* [Hind. & Per. *zamīndār,* an occupant of land, landholder; *zamīn*, land, earth + *-dār*, holding, possessing], in India, 1. formerly, a collector of the revenue for land. 2. a landowner, especially one paying revenue. Also **zemindar.**

Za·mo·ra y Tor·res, Ni·ce·to Al·ca·lá (ni-the'tô al'kä-lä' thä-mô'rä ē tôr'res), 1877–1949; Spanish statesman; first president of Spanish republic (1931–1936).

Zanes·ville (zānz'vil), *n.* a city in east central Ohio: pop., 39,000.

Zan·gwill, Israel (zaŋ'gwil), 1864–1926; English writer of novels, plays, etc., especially about Jewish life.

Zan·te (zän'te), *n.* one of the Ionian Islands: area, 156 sq. mi.; pop., 38,000: Greek name, *Zakynthos*.

za·ny (zā'ni), *n.* [*pl.* ZANIES (-niz)], [Fr. *zani;* It. *zanni,* a zany, clown, orig. a familiar abbrev. pronun. of *Giovanni,* John], 1. a clown or buffoon; specifically, a former stock character in comedies who clownishly aped the principal actors. 2. a fool; dolt; simpleton. *adj.* [ZANIER (-ni-ẽr), ZANIEST (-ni-ist)], of or characteristic of a zany; specifically, comical in an extravagantly ludicrous or slapstick manner.

Zan·zi·bar (zan'zə-bär', zan'zə-bär'), *n.* 1. an island off the east coast of Africa: area, 640 sq. mi.; pop., 165,000. 2. a British protectorate, including the islands of Zanzibar and Pemba: area, 1,020 sq. mi.; pop., 299,000: a strip of land on the eastern African coast, belonging to Zanzibar, is leased and administered by Kenya. 3. the capital of the protectorate, a seaport on Zanzibar island: pop., 58,000.

Za·po·rozh·e (zä'pô-rôzh'ye), *n.* a city in the southern Ukrainian S.S.R., on the Dnepr: pop., 435,000: formerly called *Aleksandrovsk*.

zap·ti·ah (zup-tē'ä), *n.* [Turk. *ḍabṭīyah;* Ar. *ḍābiṭīyah* < *ḍabṭ*, government], a Turkish policeman.

zap·ti·eh (zup-tē'e), *n.* a zaptiah.

Za·ra (zä'rä; It. dzä'rä), *n.* a seaport in western Yugoslavia, formerly belonging to Italy: pop., 20,000.

Za·ra·go·za (thä'rä-gô'thä, sä'rä-gô'sä), *n.* Saragossa, a city in Spain: the Spanish name.

Zar·a·thus·tra (zar'ə-tho͞os'trə), *n.* Zoroaster.

za·ra·tite (zä'rə-tīt'), *n.* [Sp. *zaratita*, after a Señor *Zarate*], a hydrated, basic carbonate of nickel, $NiCO_3 \cdot 2Ni(OH)_2 \cdot 4H_2O$, found in emerald-green incrustations.

za·re·ba, za·ree·ba (zə-rē'bə), *n.* [Ar. *zarība*, a pen], in the Sudan and surrounding territory, a camping place or enclosure formed by a palisade or thorn hedge.

zarf (zärf), *n.* [Ar. *ẓarf*, a sheath], a small, metal, cuplike stand, usually ornamented, used in the Levant for holding hot coffee cups.

zax (zaks), *n.* [var. of *sax;* AS. *seax,* a knife], a tool used for trimming roofing slates; slate ax.

za·yin (zä′yin), *n.* [Heb. *zāyin*], the seventh letter of the Hebrew alphabet (ז), corresponding to English *Z, z:* see **alphabet**, table.

z.B., *zum Beispiel,* [G.], for example.

Ze·a (zē′ä), *n.* Keos, one of the Cyclades Islands.

zeal (zēl), *n.* [< OFr. or LL.; OFr. *zele;* LL. *zelus,* zeal < Gr. *zēlos,* zeal, ardor, fervor; ? akin to OSlav. *jaru,* furious], eager interest and enthusiasm; ardent endeavor or devotion; ardor; fervor. —***SYN.*** see **passion.**

Zea·land (zē′lənd), *n.* an island of Denmark, between Jutland and Sweden: area, 2,710 sq. mi.; pop., 1,145,-000; chief city, Copenhagen: Danish name, *Sjælland:* also **Seeland.**

zeal·ot (zel′ət), *n.* [LL. *zelotes;* Gr. *zēlōtēs* < *zēlos,* zeal], 1. a person who is zealous, especially to an extreme or excessive degree; fanatic. 2. [Z-], among the ancient Jews, a member of a sect of religious zealots who openly resisted Roman rule in Palestine.

SYN.—**zealot** implies extreme or excessive devotion to a cause and vehement activity in its support (*zealots* of reform); **fanatic** suggests the unreasonable overzealousness of one who goes to any length to maintain or carry out his beliefs (a temperance *fanatic*); an **enthusiast** is one who is animated by an intense and eager interest in an activity, cause, etc. (a sports *enthusiast*); **bigot** implies blind and intolerant devotion to a creed, opinion, etc. (a religious *bigot*).

zeal·ot·ry (zel′ət-ri), *n.* extreme zeal; fanaticism.

zeal·ous (zel′əs), *adj.* [ML. *zelosus;* LL. *zelus;* see ZEAL], full of, characterized by, or showing zeal; ardently devoted to a purpose; fervent; enthusiastic.

ze·bec, ze·beck (zē′bek), *n.* a xebec.

Zeb·e·dee (zeb′ə-dē′), *n.* [LL. *Zebedaeus;* Gr. *Zebedaios;* prob. < Heb. *zĕbhadyāh,* lit., God has bestowed], in the *Bible,* father of the disciples James and John.

ze·bra (zē′brə), *n.* [*pl.* ZEBRAS (-brəz), ZEBRA; see PLURAL, II, D, 1], [Port. < the native name in the Congo], an African animal related to and resembling the horse and the ass: it has dark stripes on a white or tawny body.

ZEBRA (4 1/2 ft. high at shoulder)

ze·brass (zē′bras′), *n.* [< *zebra* + *ass*], the offspring of a male zebra and a female ass.

ze·bra·wood (zē′brə-wood′), *n.* 1. the hard, striped wood of a tree native to Guiana, used in cabinetmaking. 2. the striped wood of various other trees. 3. any of these trees.

ze·brine (zē′brīn, zē′brin), *adj.* of or like the zebra.

ze·bru·la (zē′broo-lə), *n.* the offspring of a male zebra and a female horse.

ze·brule (zē′brōōl), *n.* a zebrula.

ze·bu (zē′bū), *n.* [*pl.* ZEBUS (-būz), ZEBU; see PLURAL, II, D, 1], [Fr. *zébu;* of Tibet. origin], an oxlike domestic animal native to Asia and parts of Africa: it has a large hump over the shoulders, short, curving horns, and a large dewlap.

ZEBU (4 1/2 ft. at shoulder)

zec·chi·no (tsek-kē′nô), *n.* [*pl.* ZECCHINI (-nē)], [It.], a sequin (gold coin).

Zech·a·ri·ah (zek′ə-rī′ə), a masculine name: see **Zachariah.** *n.* in the *Bible,* 1. a Hebrew prophet of the 6th century B.C. who urged the rebuilding of the Temple. 2. a book of the Old Testament containing his prophecies: abbreviated **Zech.**

zech·in (zek′in), *n.* [It. *zecchino*], a sequin (gold coin).

zed (zed), *n.* [ME. *zedde;* Late OFr. *zede;* L. *zeta;* Gr. *zēta,* zed], the British name for the letter Z, z.

zed·o·a·ry (zed′ō-ēr′i), *n.* [OFr. *zedoaire;* ML. *zedoaria;* Ar. *jadwār;* Per. *zadwār*], an aromatic substance obtained from the root of an East Indian turmeric and used in perfumes and medicines.

zee (zē), *n.* [*pl.* ZEES (zēz)], [D.], the letter Z, z.

Zee·brug·ge (zā′brükh′ə; Eng. zē′broog′ə), *n.* a seaport in northwestern Belgium.

Zee·land (zē′lənd; D. zā′länt), *n.* a province of the southwestern Netherlands: area, 1,040 sq. mi.; pop., 262,000 (est. 1947); capital, Middelburg.

‡**Zeit·geist** (tsīt′gīst′), *n.* [G., time spirit], the spirit of the age; trend of thought and feeling in a period.

ze·min·dar (zi-mēn′där′), *n.* a zamindar.

zem·stvo (zemst′vō), *n.* [*pl.* ZEMSTVOS (-vōz)], [Russ. < *zemlya,* earth, land], a local administrative body in Czarist Russia.

Zen (zen), *n.* [Jap. < Chin. *ch'an;* ult. < Sans. *dhyāna*], 1. an anti-rational Buddhist sect developed in India and now widespread in Japan: it differs from other Buddhist sects in seeking the truth through introspection and intuition rather than in Pali scripture. 2. the doctrines of this sect.

ze·na·na (ze-nä′nə), *n.* [Hind. *zenāna, zanāna;* Per. *zanāna* < *zan,* woman; akin to Gr. *gynē,* woman; for IE. base see QUEEN], in India and Persia, the part of the house reserved for women.

Zend (zend), *n.* [Per., interpretation], 1. the Middle Persian translation of and commentary on the Zoroastrian Avesta. 2. the original language of the Avesta, an ancient form of Persian or Iranian.

Zend-Av·es·ta (zen′də-ves′tə), *n.* [altered < *Avesta-va-Zend,* lit., (sacred) text and interpretation], the sacred writings of the Zoroastrians.

Zend·ic (zen′dik), *adj.* of or having to do with Zend or the Zend.

ze·nith (zē′nith; Brit. zen′ith), *n.* [ME. *senyth;* OFr. *cenith, cenit;* ML. *cenith, cenit* < Ar. *semt,* road, path (as in *semt-ar-ras,* zenith, lit., way of the head) < L. *semita,* path, way], 1. the point in the sky directly overhead: opposed to *nadir.* 2. the highest point; culmination; peak; summit. —***SYN.*** see **summit.**

zenith distance, the angular distance of a heavenly body from the zenith.

Ze·no (zē′nō), *n.* 1. Greek Eleatic philosopher; 5th century B.C. 2. Greek philosopher; 336?–264? B.C.; founder of Stoicism.

Ze·no·bi·a (zə-nō′bi-ə, zə-nōb′yə), [L.; Gr. *Zēnobia*], a feminine name. *n.* queen of Palmyra (267–272 A.D.).

ze·o·lite (zē′ə-līt′), *n.* [Sw. *zeolit* < Gr. *zeein,* to boil: so named by A. F. Cronstedt (1702?–1765), Sw. mineralogist, from its swelling up when heated], any of a number of hydrous silicates of aluminum, sodium, or calcium found in the cavities of igneous rocks.

Zeph·a·ni·ah (zef′ə-nī′ə), *n.* [Heb. *tsĕphanyāh,* lit., the Lord has hidden], 1. a Hebrew prophet of the 7th century B.C. 2. the book in the Old Testament containing his prophecies: abbreviated **Zeph.**

zeph·yr (zef′ēr), *n.* [ME. *zeferus, zephirus;* L. *zephyrus* < Gr. *zephyros,* the west wind], 1. the west wind. 2. a soft, gentle breeze. 3. a fine, soft, lightweight yarn, cloth, or garment. 4. something light, airy, or unsubstantial. —***SYN.*** see **wind.**

Zeph·y·rus (zef′ēr-əs), *n.* [L.; see ZEPHYR], the personification of the west wind, considered by the Greeks the most mild and gentle of all sylvan deities.

zep·pe·lin (zep′ə-lin, zep′lin; G. tsep′ə-lēn′), *n.* [after Count Ferdinand von *Zeppelin* (1838–1917), G. general and inventor], [often Z-], a type of dirigible airship designed around 1900.

ze·ro (zêr′ō), *n.* [*pl.* ZEROS, ZEROES (-ōz)], [Fr. *zéro;* It. < Ar. *sifr,* a cipher], 1. the symbol or numeral 0; cipher; naught. 2. the point, marked 0, from which positive or negative quantities are reckoned on a graduated scale, as on thermometers; specifically, *a)* on a centigrade thermometer, the freezing point of water. *b)* on a Fahrenheit thermometer, a point 32° below the freezing point of water. 3. a temperature that causes a thermometer to register zero. 4. the point intermediate between positive and negative quantities. 5. nothing. 6. the lowest point: as, his chances of success sank to *zero.* 7. in *gunnery,* a sight setting for a range, allowing for both elevation and windage. Abbreviated **z.** *v.t.* to adjust (an instrument, etc.) to a zero point or to an arbitrary point from which all positive and negative readings are to be measured.

zero in, to adjust the sight settings of (a rifle) by calibrated firing on a standard range when there is no deflection due to wind.

zero hour, 1. the time set for the beginning of an attack or other military operation. 2. any crucial or decisive moment; critical point.

zest (zest), *n.* [Fr. *zeste,* partition membrane in a nut, hence piece of orange or orange peel used to give piquancy (give *zest* to)], 1. something that gives flavor, relish, or piquancy. 2. stimulating or exciting quality; flavor; relish; piquancy. 3. keen enjoyment or inclination; gusto (often with *for*): as, a *zest* for life. 4. [Rare], peel of orange or lemon used as flavoring. *v.t.* to give zest or relish to.

zest·ful (zest′fəl), *adj.* full of or characterized by zest.

ze·ta (zā′tə, zē′tə), *n.* [Gr. *zēta*], the sixth letter (Z, ζ) of the Greek alphabet, corresponding to English *Z,* z: see **alphabet,** table.

Zet·land (zet′lənd), *n.* the Shetland Islands.

zeug·ma (zōōg′mə, zūg′mə), *n.* [L.; Gr. *zeugma* < *zeugnynai,* to join], a figure of speech in which a single modifier, usually a verb or adjective, applies to two or more words, with only one of which it seems logically connected (e.g., The room was not light, but his fingers were).

Zeus (zōōs, zūs), *n.* [Gr.], the supreme deity of the ancient Greeks, son of Cronus and Rhea and husband

of Hera: identified by the Romans with Jupiter.
Zeux·is (zook′sis, zūk′sis), *n.* Greek painter; lived 5th century B.C.
Zhi·to·mir (zhi-tô′mir), *n.* a city in the western Ukrainian S.S.R.: pop., 117,000.
Zhu·kov, Gri·go·ri Kon·stan·ti·no·vich (gri-gô′ri kôn′stän-tē′nô-vich zhōō′kôf), 1895?– ; Russian marshal.
zib·el·ine, zib·el·line (zib′ə-lin′, zib′ə-lin), *adj.* [Fr. *zibeline;* It. *zibellino* < Slav. base; see SABLE], of or having to do with sables. *n.* 1. the fur of the sable. 2. a soft woolen dress material with a furlike nap.
zib·et, zib·eth (zib′it), *n.* [< ML. or It.; ML. *zibethum;* It. *zibetto;* Ar. *zabād*], the Asiatic or Indian civet.
Zieg·feld, Flor·enz (flôr′ənz zig′feld), 1867–1932; American theatrical producer.
Zif (zif), *n.* [Heb.], Iyar: the early Hebrew name: see **Jewish calendar.**
zig·gu·rat (zig′oo-rat), *n.* [Assyr. *ziqquratu,* height, pinnacle], a temple tower of the ancient Assyrians and Babylonians, in the form of a terraced pyramid with each story smaller than the one below it.
zig·zag (zig′zag′), *n.* [Fr.; G. *zickzack;* prob. redupl. < *zacke,* a tooth, sharp prong or point], 1. any of a series of short, sharp angles or turns in alternate directions, as in a line or course. 2. something characterized by such a series, as a design, path, etc. *adj.* having the form of or characterized by a zigzag. *adv.* so as to form a zigzag; in a zigzag course. *v.t.* & *v.i.* [ZIGZAGGED (-zagd′), ZIGZAGGING], to move or form in a zigzag.
zik·ku·rat, zik·u·rat (zik′oo-rat), *n.* a ziggurat.
zil·lion (zil′yən), *n.* [arbitrary coinage, after *million, billion,* etc.], [Colloq.], an indefinitely large number.
Zil·pah (zil′pə), *n.* in the *Bible,* the mother of Gad: Gen. 30:10.
Zim·ba·list, Ef·rem (ef′rəm zim′bə-list), 1889– ; Russian violinist in America.
zinc (ziŋk), *n.* [G. *zink,* zinc], a bluish-white, metallic chemical element, usually found in combination, used as a protective coating for iron, as a constituent in various alloys, as an electrode in electric batteries, and, in the form of salts, in medicines: symbol, Zn; at. no., 30; at. wt., 65.38. *v.t.* [ZINCKED or ZINCED (ziŋkt), ZINCKING or ZINCING], to coat or treat with zinc.
zinc·ate (ziŋk′āt), *n.* a salt produced by the reaction of amphoteric zinc hydroxide as an acid.
zinc blende, sphalerite.
zinc·ic (ziŋk′ik), *adj.* of or containing zinc.
zinc·if·er·ous (ziŋk-if′ẽr-əs, zin-sif′ẽr-əs), *adj.* [< *zinc* + *-ferous*], yielding or containing zinc.
zinc·i·fy (ziŋk′ə-fī′), *v.t.* [ZINCIFIED (-fīd′), ZINCIFYING], to coat or impregnate with zinc.
zinc·ite (ziŋk′īt), *n.* native oxide of zinc, ZnO, a deep-red to yellowish mineral.
zinck·y (ziŋk′i), *adj.* zincic: also spelled **zinky.**
zin·co·graph (ziŋ′kə-graf′, ziŋ′kə-gräf′), *n.* 1. a zinc plate prepared by zincography. 2. a print made from such a plate.
zin·cog·ra·pher (ziŋ-kog′rə-fẽr), *n.* a person who works in zincography.
zin·co·graph·ic (ziŋ′kə-graf′ik), *adj.* of, or having the nature of, a zincograph.
zin·co·graph·i·cal (ziŋ′kə-graf′i-k'l), *adj.* zincographic.
zin·cog·ra·phy (ziŋ-kog′rə-fi), *n.* [< *zinc* + *-graphy*], the art or process of engraving or etching on zinc plates for printing.
zinc ointment, an ointment containing zinc oxide.
zin·cous (ziŋk′əs), *adj.* 1. zincic. 2. of or having to do with the zinc element in an electric battery.
zinc oxide, a white powder, ZnO, used as a pigment and in the manufacture of rubber articles, glass, cosmetics, ointments, etc.
zinc white, zinc oxide used as a white pigment.
zing (ziŋ), *n.* [echoic], [Slang], 1. vitality; zest. 2. a shrill, high-pitched sound, as of something moving at high speed. *v.i.* [Slang], to make such a sound.
‡zin·ga·ra (tsēŋ′gä-rä′), *n.* [*pl.* ZINGARE (-re′)], [It.], a gypsy woman or girl.
‡zin·ga·ro (tsēŋ′gä-rô′), *n.* [*pl.* ZINGARI (-rē′)], [It.], a gypsy.
zin·gi·ber·a·ceous (zin′ji-bə-rā′shəs), *adj.* [< Mod. L. *Zingiberaceae,* name of the family (< L. *zingiber,* ginger); + *-ous*], of or having to do with a family of tropical monocotyledonous plants including the ginger, turmeric, etc., characterized by large leaves and highly aromatic rootstocks.
Zin·jan·thro·pus (zin-jan′thrə-pəs), *n.* [Mod. L. < Ar. *Zinj,* East Africa + Gr. *anthrōpos,* man], a type of prehistoric man who lived about 1,750,000 years ago and whose remains were found in Tanganyika in 1959.
zin·ken·ite (ziŋ′kə-nīt′), *n.* [G. *zinkenit,* after J. K. L. *Zinken,* director of mines in Anhalt, Germany], a steel-gray metallic mineral, $PbSb_2S_4$: also spelled **zinckenite.**
zink·y (ziŋk′i), *adj.* zincky; zincic.
zin·ni·a (zin′i-ə, zin′yə), *n.* [Mod. L.; after J. G. *Zinn,* a G. botanist], any of several plants of the aster family, having colorful, composite flowers.
Zins·ser, Hans (zin′sẽr), 1878–1940; American bacteriologist.
zin·zi·ber·a·ceous (zin′zi-bə-rā′shəs), *adj.* zingiberaceous.
Zi·on (zī′ən), *n.* [ME. *Syon;* AS. *Sion;* LL. *Sion;* Heb. *Tsiyon,* a hill], 1. a hill in Jerusalem, site of the Temple and of the royal palace of David and his successors: regarded by Jews as a symbol of the center of Jewish national life. 2. the Jewish people. 3. heaven; the heavenly city. 4. the theocracy of God. Also **Sion.**
Zi·on·ism (zī′ən-iz'm), *n.* a movement formerly for re-establishing, now for advancing, the Jewish national state in Palestine.
Zi·on·ist (zī′ən-ist), *n.* a person supporting the principles of Zionism. *adj.* of, supporting, or having to do with Zionism.
Zi·on·is·tic (zī′ən-is′tik), *adj.* Zionist.
Zion National Park, a national park in southwestern Utah: area, 206 sq. mi.
zip (zip), *n.* [echoic], 1. a short, sharp hissing or whizzing sound, as of a passing bullet. 2. [Colloq.], energy; vim. *v.i.* [ZIPPED (zipt), ZIPPING], 1. to make, or move with, a zip. 2. [Colloq.], to act or move with speed or energy. *v.t.* to fasten with a slide fastener.
Zi·pan·gu (zi-paŋ′gōō), *n.* Japan: the name used by Marco Polo.
ZIP code, [*z*one *i*mprovement *p*lan], a system devised to speed mail deliveries, under which the post office assigns a code number to individual areas and places.
zip gun, a crude, improvised pistol made from a piece of pipe with a firing pin actuated by a rubber band.
zip·per (zip′ẽr), *n.* 1. a boot or overshoe fitted with a slide fastener: a trade-mark (**Zipper**). 2. popularly, a slide fastener.
zip·py (zip′i), *adj.* [ZIPPIER (-i-ẽr), ZIPPIEST (-i-ist)], [< *zip* + *-y*], [Colloq.], full of vim and energy; brisk.
zir·con (zũr′kon), *n.* [Fr. < Ar. *zarqūn,* cinnabar < Per. *zargūn,* gold-colored < *zar,* gold], a silicate of zirconium, $ZrSiO_4$, a mineral occurring in tetragonal crystals colored yellow, brown, red, etc.: transparent varieties are used as gems.
zir·con·ate (zũr′kə-nāt′), *n.* a salt produced by the reaction of zirconium hydroxide as an acid.
zir·co·ni·a (zẽr-kō′ni-ə), *n.* [Mod. L.; see ZIRCON], zirconium dioxide, ZrO_2, a white, infusible powder used in making crucibles, furnace linings, and, because of its luminosity, in incandescent burners.
zir·con·ic (zẽr-kon′ik), *adj.* of or derived from zirconium.
zir·co·ni·um (zẽr-kō′ni-əm), *n.* [Mod. L.; see ZIRCON], a gray or black metallic chemical element found combined in zircon, etc., and used in alloys, ceramics, etc.: symbol, Zr; at. wt., 91.22; at. no., 40.
Zis·ka, Jo·hann (yō′hän tsis′kä), Jan Žižka: German name.
zith·er (zith′ẽr), *n.* [G.; L. *cithara;* Gr. *kithara,* a lute], a musical instrument having from thirty to forty strings stretched across a flat soundboard and played with a plectrum.
zith·ern (zith′ẽrn), *n.* a zither.
zit·tern (zit′ẽrn), *n.* a cittern.
‡zi·zith (tsē′tzith, tsi′tsis), *n.pl.* [Heb. *tsītsīth*], the fringes or tassels worn by orthodox Jews, formerly on the corners of the outer garment, now on the tallith: Deut. 22:12.
Žiž·ka, Jan (yän zhish′kä), 1360?–1424; Bohemian general and leader of the Hussites: also **Johann Ziska.**

ZITHER

zlo·ty (zlô′ti), *n.* [*pl.* ZLOTYS (-tiz)], [Pol. *złoty,* lit., golden], the monetary unit of Poland.
Zn, in *chemistry,* zinc.
zo- (zō), zoo-.
zo·a (zō′ə), *n.* plural of **zoon.**
-zo·a (zō′ə), [Mod. L. < Gr. *zōion,* an animal], a combining form used in zoology to form the names of groups, as in *Hydrozoa, Protozoa.*
Zo·an (zō′an), *n.* Tanis, Egypt: the Biblical name.
zo·an·thro·py (zō-an′thrə-pi), *n.* [< *zo-* + Gr. *anthrōpos,* man], a form of mental disorder in which the patient imagines himself to be a beast.

zo·di·ac (zō′di-ak′), *n.* [ME. *zodiak;* OFr. *zodiaque;* L. *zodiacus,* zodiac < Gr. *zōdiakos* (*kyklos*), zodiac (circle), lit., circle of animals < *zōdion,* dim. of *zōion,* animal], 1. an imaginary belt in the heavens extending for eight degrees on either side of the apparent path of the sun and including the paths of the moon and the principal planets: it is divided into twelve equal parts, or signs, each named for a different constellation. 2. a figure or diagram representing the zodiac and its signs: used in astrology. 3. [Rare], a circle or circuit. 4. [Rare], a girdle. Abbreviated **zod.**

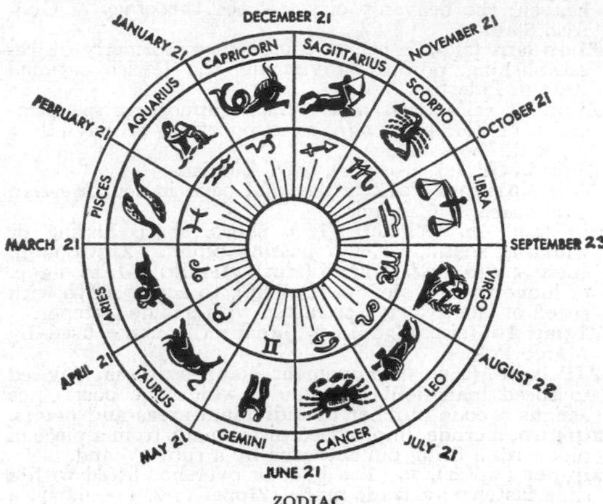

ZODIAC

zo·di·a·cal (zō-dī′ə-k'l), *adj.* of or in the zodiac.

zodiacal light, a faint, elliptical disk of light around the sun, sometimes visible in the west during or after twilight and in the east before daybreak.

Zo·e (zō′ē), [Gr. *Zōē,* lit., life], a feminine name.

zois·ite (zois′īt), *n.* [after Baron *Zois* von Edelstein (1747–1819), its discoverer], a vitreous silicate of calcium and aluminum, $HCa_2Al_3Si_3O_{13}$, in which the aluminum is often replaced by iron.

Zo·la, É·mile (ā′mēl′ zô′lä′; Eng. zō′lə), 1840–1902; French novelist and critic.

‡Zoll·ver·ein (tsôl′fer-īn′), *n.* [G. *zoll,* toll, custom, duty + *verein,* union, association], 1. a union formed by the states of the German Empire during the 19th century to establish uniform tariff rates among themselves and between themselves and other countries. 2. any customs or tariff union among states.

zom·bi, zom·bie (zom′bi), *n.* [*pl.* ZOMBIS, ZOMBIES (-biz)], [of Afr. origin; cf. Congo *zumbi,* fetish], 1. in West African voodoo cults, the python deity. 2. any voodoo snake deity, as in Haiti and parts of southern United States. 3. in West Indian superstition, a supernatural power through which a corpse may be brought to a state of trancelike animation and made to obey the commands of the person exercising the power. 4. a corpse so animated; hence, 5. [Slang], a dull, stupid, unattractive person. 6. a cocktail containing a mixture of rums, fruit juices, and soda.

zom·bi·ism (zom′bi-iz'm), *n.* belief in or the practice of zombi worship.

zon·al (zōn′'l), *adj.* 1. of or having to do with a zone or zones. 2. formed or divided in zones; zoned.

zon·a·ry (zōn′ə-ri), *adj.* [L. *zonarius*], 1. zonal. 2. like a zone, or girdle; beltlike.

zon·ate (zōn′āt), *adj.* 1. marked with zones or bands; belted; striped. 2. in *botany,* arranged in one row, as the tetraspores of certain algae.

zo·nat·ed (zōn′ā-tid), *adj.* zonate.

zo·na·tion (zō-nā′shən), *n.* 1. the state of being zonal or arranged in zones. 2. arrangement in zones, or bands, as of color.

zone (zōn), *n.* [Fr.; L. *zona* < Gr. *zōnē,* a belt < *zōnnynai,* to gird], 1. [Now Poetic], a belt or girdle. 2. an encircling band, stripe, course, etc. distinct in color, texture, structure, etc. from the surrounding medium. 3. any of the five great latitudinal divisions of the earth's surface, named according to the prevailing climate; specifically, the *torrid zone,* bounded by the Tropic of Cancer and the Tropic of Capricorn, two *temperate* (or *variable*) *zones* bounded by the Tropics and the polar circles, and two

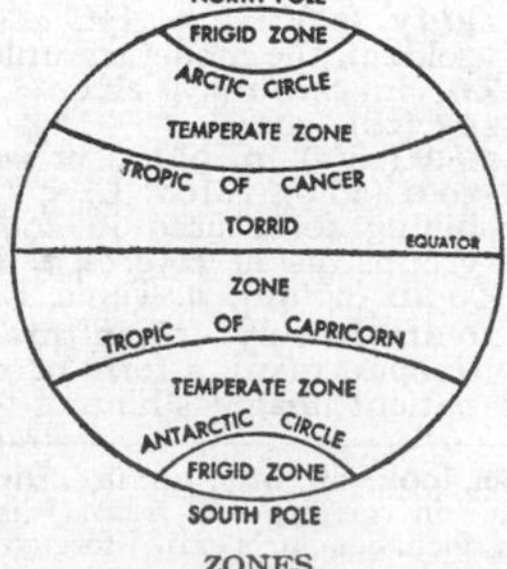

ZONES

frigid zones lying between the polar circles and the poles. 4. any area or region considered as separate or distinct from others because of its particular use, crops, plant or animal life, status in time of war, geological features, etc.: as, a canal *zone,* cotton *zone,* demilitarized *zone.* 5. any section or district in a city restricted by law for a particular use, as for homes, parks, businesses, etc. 6. *a*) any of the sections into which a large metropolitan area is divided, each assigned a number to be added to the address on all postal matter to facilitate its delivery. *b*) any of a series of ring-shaped areas concentric upon a given point, each having a different postage rate for goods shipped from that point. 7. any similar area used by railroads, telephone companies, etc. in determining the fare or tariff charged from one point to another. 8. the total number of railroad stations available in a given circumference about a particular shipping point. 9. in *mathematics,* a part of the surface of a sphere lying between two parallel planes that intersect the figure. ***v.t.*** [ZONED (zōnd), ZONING], 1. to mark off or divide into zones; specifically, to divide (a city, etc.) into areas determined by specific restrictions on types of construction, as into residential and business areas. 2. to surround with or as with a belt or girdle; encircle. 3. to mark with bands or stripes. ***v.i.*** to be or become zoned. Abbreviated **Z., z.**

zon·ule (zōn′ūl), *n.* [L. *zonula,* dim. of *zona,* a zone], a small zone, or belt.

zoo (zōō), *n.* [< *zoological garden*], a place where wild animals are kept for public showing; menagerie.

zo·o- (zō′ō, zō′ə), [< Gr. *zōion,* an animal], a combining form meaning: 1. *animal, animals,* as in *zoology.* 2. *zoology and,* as in *zoogeography.* Words beginning with *zoo-* are also written **zoö-**; also, before a vowel, **zo-.**

zo·o·chem·is·try (zō′ə-kem′is-tri), *n.* [*zoo-* + *chemistry*], the chemistry of the solids and fluids in the animal body: abbreviated **zoochem.**

zo·o·ge·og·ra·pher (zō′ə-ji-og′rə-fẽr), *n.* a student of or expert in zoogeography.

zo·o·ge·o·graph·ic (zō′ə-jē′ə-graf′ik), *adj.* of or having to do with zoogeography.

zo·o·ge·o·graph·i·cal (zō′ə-jē′ə-graf′i-k'l), *adj.* zoogeographic.

zo·o·ge·og·ra·phy (zō′ə-ji-og′rə-fi), *n.* [*zoo-* + *geography*], the science dealing with the geographical distribution of animals; specifically, the study of the relationship between specific animal forms and species and the regions in which they live: abbreviated **zoogeog.**

zo·o·gloe·a (zō′ə-glē′ə), *n.* [Mod. L. < *zoo-* + Gr. *gloios,* glutinous substance, gum], a colony of bacteria forming a jellylike mass as the result of the swelling of the cell walls through the absorption of water.

zo·o·graph·ic (zō′ə-graf′ik), *adj.* of or having to do with zoography.

zo·o·graph·i·cal (zō′ə-graf′i-k'l), *adj.* zoographic.

zo·og·ra·phy (zō-og′rə-fi), *n.* [*zoo-* + *-graphy*], the branch of zoology concerned with the description of animals, their habits, etc.

zo·oid (zō′oid), *adj.* [*zo-* + *-oid*], in *biology,* of, or having the nature of, an animal. ***n.*** in *biology,* 1. an independent animal organism produced by other than sexual methods, as by fission, gemination, etc. 2. any of the distinct individuals of a colonial or compound organism, as the coral. 3. any organic body or cell having independent locomotion, as a spermatozoon.

zo·oi·dal (zō-oi′d'l), *adj.* zooid.

zo·ol·a·try (zō-ol′ə-tri), *n.* [< *zoo-* + Gr. *latreia,* worship], worship of animals.

zo·o·log·ic (zō′ə-loj′ik), *adj.* zoological.

zo·o·log·i·cal (zō′ə-loj′i-k'l), *adj.* of or having to do with zoology or with animals: abbreviated **zool.**

zoological garden, a place where a collection of wild animals is kept for public showing; zoo.

zo·ol·o·gist (zō-ol′ə-jist), *n.* a student of or specialist in zoology.

zo·ol·o·gy (zō-ol′ə-ji), *n.* [*zoo-* + *-logy*], 1. the science that deals with the classification of animals and the study of animal life: a division of biology, distinguished from *botany.* 2. the animals collectively (*of* a particular region). 3. a treatise on zoology. Abbreviated **zool.**

zoom (zōōm), *v.i.* [echoic], 1. to make a loud, low-pitched, buzzing or humming sound. 2. to climb in an airplane suddenly and sharply at an angle greater than normal, using the energy of momentum. ***v.t.*** to cause to zoom. ***n.*** the act of zooming.

Zoom·ar (zōō′mär), *n.* a system of lenses, as in a motion-picture or television camera, that can be rapidly adjusted for close-up shots or distance views while keeping the image in focus: a trade-mark.

zo·o·met·ric (zō′ə-met′rik), *adj.* of or having to do with zoometry.

zo·om·e·try (zō-om′ə-tri), *n.* [*zoo-* + *-metry*], the measurement and comparison of the relative sizes of the different parts of animals.

zo·o·mor·phic (zō′ə-môr′fik), *adj.* [*zoo-* + *-morphic*], of or having animal form: as, a *zoomorphic* deity.

zo·o·mor·phism (zō′ə-môr′fiz'm), *n.* [< *zoo-* + Gr. *morphē,* a form, shape; + *-ism*], 1. the attributing of

animal form or characteristics to God or the gods: cf. **anthropomorphism.** 2. the representation of animal forms in decorative art or symbolism.
zo·on (zō′on), *n.* [*pl.* ZOA (-ə)], [Mod. L.; Gr. *zōion*, an animal], any of the fully developed individual members of a compound animal.
zo·on·al (zō-on′'l), *adj.* of or having to do with a zoon.
zo·oph·i·lous (zō-of′ə-ləs), *adj.* [*zoo-* + *-philous*], 1. loving animals. 2. adapted to pollination by animals: said of plants.
zo·o·pho·bi·a (zō′ə-fō′bi-ə), *n.* [*zoo-* + *-phobia*], an abnormal fear of animals.
zo·o·phyte (zō′ə-fīt′), *n.* [Mod. L. *zoophyton;* Gr. *zōophyton* < Gr. *zōion* + *phyton*, a plant], any animal, as a coral, sponge, etc., having somewhat the appearance and character of a plant.
zo·o·phyt·ic (zō′ə-fit′ik), *adj.* of, or having the nature of, zoophytes.
zo·o·phyt·i·cal (zō′ə-fit′i-k'l), *adj.* zoophytic.
zo·o·plas·tic (zō′ə-plas′tik), *adj.* of or having to do with zooplasty.
zo·o·plas·ty (zō′ə-plas′ti), *n.* [*zoo-* + *-plasty*], the surgical operation of grafting living tissue from a lower animal onto the human body.
zo·o·sperm (zō′ə-spūrm′), *n.* [*zoo-* + *sperm*], 1. a spermatozoon. 2. [Obs.], a zoospore (sense 1).
zo·o·sper·mat·ic (zō′ə-spēr-mat′ik), *adj.* of or having to do with a zoosperm.
zo·o·spo·ran·gi·al (zō′ə-spə-ran′ji-əl), *adj.* of or having to do with a zoosporangium.
zo·o·spo·ran·gi·um (zō′ə-spə-ran′ji-əm), *n.* [*pl.* ZOOSPORANGIA (-ə)], [Mod. L.; see ZOO- & SPORANGIUM], a sporangium producing zoospores.
zo·o·spore (zō′ə-spôr′, zō′ə-spōr′), *n.* [*zoo-* + *spore*], 1. an asexual spore, especially of certain fungi or algae, capable of independent motion usually by means of cilia. 2. a motile flagellate or amoeboid cell or body in certain protozoa.
zo·o·spor·ic (zō′ə-spôr′ik, zō′ə-spō′rik), *adj.* of or having to do with a zoospore.
zo·os·po·rous (zō-os′pə-rəs, zō′ə-spôr′əs, zō′ə-spō′rəs), *adj.* zoosporic.
zo·o·tom·ic (zō′ə-tom′ik), *adj.* of or having to do with zootomy.
zo·o·tom·i·cal (zō′ə-tom′i-k'l), *adj.* zootomic.
zo·ot·o·my (zō-ot′ə-mi), *n.* [Mod. L. *zootomia;* see ZOO- & -TOMY], the anatomy or dissection of animals, especially of those other than man.
zoot suit (zōōt), [redupl.], a former, exaggerated style of man's suit with baggy trousers narrowing at the cuffs and a long, draped coat.
zor·il (zôr′il, zor′il), *n.* [Fr. *zorille;* Sp. *zorilla, zorillo*, dim. of *zorra, zorro*, a fox], a small, South African animal of the weasel family, resembling the skunk.
zo·ril·a (zō-ril′ə), *n.* a zoril.
Zorn, An·ders Le·o·nhard (ȧn′dērs lā′ô-nȧrd′ sôrn), 1860–1920; Swedish painter and etcher.
Zo·ro·as·ter (zō′rō-as′tēr), *n.* founder of the ancient Persian religion, Zoroastrianism; fl. in the 6th or 7th century B.C.: also called *Zarathustra.*
Zo·ro·as·tri·an (zō′rō-as′tri-ən), *adj.* of or having to do with Zoroaster or his religious system. *n.* a follower of Zoroaster.
Zo·ro·as·tri·an·ism (zō′rō-as′tri-ən-iz'm), *n.* the religious system of the Persians before their conversion to Islam: according to tradition, it was founded by Zoroaster, and its principles, contained in the Zend-Avesta, include belief in an afterlife and in the continuous struggle of the universal spirit of good (Ormazd) with the spirit of evil (Ahriman), the good ultimately to prevail.
Zor·ril·la, Jo·sé (hô-se′ thô-rē′lyä), 1817–1893; Spanish poet and dramatist.
zos·ter (zos′tēr), *n.* [L.; Gr. *zōstēr*], 1. in ancient Greece, a belt or girdle. 2. in *medicine*, herpes zoster.
Zou·ave (zōō-äv′, zwäv), *n.* [Fr., Ar. *Zouaoua*, a Kabyle tribe living in the Jurjura Mountains of Algeria, from whom the Zouaves were originally recruited], 1. a member of an infantry unit in the French army, originally recruited from Algerians, noted for their hardiness and courage and wearing a colorful oriental uniform. 2. a member of any military group having a similar uniform; specifically, a member of any of various volunteer regiments in the American Civil War.
zounds (zoundz), *interj.* [altered < the oath *God's-wounds*], [Archaic], a mild oath used as an exclamation of surprise or anger.
Zr, in *chemistry*, zirconium.
zuc·chet·to (tsōō-ket′ō), *n.* [erroneous var. of It. *zucchetta*, a cap, orig., dim. of *zucca*, a gourd], a skullcap worn by ecclesiastics of the Roman Catholic Church: a priest's is black, a bishop's purple, a cardinal's red, and the Pope's white.
zuc·chi·ni (zōō-kē′ni), *n.* [It., pl. of *zucchino*, dim. of *zucca*, a squash], a variety of green-skinned summer squash, shaped somewhat like a cucumber.
Zug (tsookh), *n.* 1. a canton of central Switzerland: pop., 37,000. 2. its capital: pop., 12,000.
Zui·der Zee (zī′dēr zē′; D. zöi′dēr zā′), an arm of the North Sea extending into the Netherlands: it was shut off from the sea by dikes and part of the land was reclaimed: also called *Ijesselmeer, Zuyder Zee.*
Zu·lo·a·ga, Ig·na·cio (ēg-nä′thyô thōō′lô-ä′gä), 1870–1945; Spanish painter.
Zu·lu (zōō′lōō), *n.* [*pl.* ZULUS (-lōōz), ZULU], 1. a member of a great Bantu nation of southeastern Africa. 2. their agglutinative Bantu language. *adj.* of the Zulus, their culture, or their language.
Zu·lu·land (zōō′lōō-land′), *n.* a region in Natal province, Union of South Africa: area, 10,427 sq. mi.; pop., 255,000.
‡zum Bei·spiel (tsoom bī′shpēl′), [G.], for example: abbreviated **z.B.**
Zu·ñi (zōō′nyi, sōō′nyi), *n.* [*pl.* ZUÑI, ZUÑIS (-nyiz)], [Sp. < Am. Ind.], a member of a pueblo-dwelling tribe of North American Indians living in New Mexico and constituting a linguistic family.
Zu·ñi·an (zōō′nyi-ən, sōō′nyi-ən), *n.* Zuñi.
Zur·ba·rán, Fran·cis·co de (frän-thēs′kô *the* thōōr′bä-rän′), 1598?–1664; Spanish painter.
Zur·ich, Zür·ich (zoor′ik; G. tsü′riH), *n.* 1. a canton in northern Switzerland: area, 668 sq. mi.; pop., 674,000. 2. its capital, on the Lake of Zurich: pop., 336,000.
Zurich, Lake of, a lake in northern Switzerland: area, 34 sq. mi.
Zuy·der Zee (zī′dēr zē′; D. zöi′dēr zā′), the Zuider Zee.
Zweig, Ar·nold (är′nôlt tsvīH; Eng. tswīg), 1887– ; German novelist, essayist, and dramatist in Israel.
Zweig, Stef·an (shte′fän), 1881–1942; Austrian novelist, dramatist, poet, and biographer; exiled.
Zwick·au (tsvik′ou), *n.* a city in the state of Saxony, central Germany: pop., 85,000.
zwie·back (tswē′bäk′, zwē′bäk, swī′bak; G. tsvē′bäk′), *n.* [G. < *zwie-*, two, twice, var. of *zwei*, two + *backen*, to bake], a kind of rusk or biscuit that is sliced and toasted after baking.
Zwing·li, Ul·rich (ool′riH tsviŋ′lē; Eng. zwiŋ′gli), 1484–1531; Swiss patriot and Protestant reformer.
Zwing·li·an (zwiŋ′gli-ən, tsviŋ′li-ən), *adj.* of Zwingli or his doctrines, especially the doctrine that the body of Christ is not actually present in the Eucharist and that the ceremony is merely a commemorative one. *n.* a follower of Zwingli.
zwit·ter·i·on (tsvit′ēr-ī′ən), *n.* a zwitter ion.
zwit·ter ion (tsvit′ēr), in *physical chemistry*, an ion carrying both a positive and a negative charge, as in certain protein molecules.
zwit·ter·i·on·ic (tsvit′ēr-ī-on′ik), *adj.* of or having to do with a zwitter ion.
zyg·ap·o·phys·e·al, zyg·ap·o·phys·i·al (zig′ap-ə-fiz′i-əl), *adj.* of a zygapophysis.
zyg·a·poph·y·sis (zig′ə-pof′ə-sis, zī′gə-pof′ə-sis), *n.* [Mod. L. < Gr. *zygon*, yoke; + *apophysis*], any of the processes of the neural arch of a vertebra by which it articulates with the adjoining vertebrae.
zy·go- (zī′gō, zig′ə), [< Gr. *zygon*, a yoke], a combining form meaning *yoke, articulation, pair*, as in *zygodactyl*: also, before a vowel, **zyg-.**
zy·go·dac·tyl (zī′gə-dak′til, zig′ə-dak′til), *adj.* [*zygo-* + *dactyl*], having the toes arranged in two opposed pairs, two in front and two in the rear. *n.* a zygodactyl bird, as the parrot.
zy·go·ma (zī-gō′mə, zi-gō′mə), *n.* [*pl.* ZYGOMATA (-mə-tə)], [Mod. L.; Gr. *zygōma* < *zygoun*, to yoke < *zygon*, a yoke], 1. the zygomatic arch. 2. the zygomatic bone. 3. the zygomatic process.
zy·go·mat·ic (zī′gə-mat′ik, zig′ə-mat′ik), *adj.* [< Mod. L. *zygoma* (see ZYGOMA); + *-ic*], in *anatomy* & *zoology*, 1. designating or of a bony arch on either side of the face just below the eye, consisting of the zygomatic bone and process. 2. designating either of a pair of quadrangular bones of the zygomatic arch forming the prominence of each cheek. 3. designating a process of the temporal bone forming part of the zygomatic arch.
zy·go·mor·phic (zī′gə-môr′fik, zig′ə-môr′fik), *adj.* [*zygo-* + *-morphic*], in *biology*, bilaterally symmetrical; that can be divided in two identical halves by a single plane passing through the axis: said of organisms, organs, or parts.
zy·go·mor·phism (zī′gə-môr′fiz'm, zig′ə-môr′fiz'm), *n.* the condition of being zygomorphic.
zy·go·mor·phous (zī′gə-môr′fəs, zig′ə-môr′fəs), *adj.* zygomorphic.
zy·go·phyl·la·ceous (zī′gō-fi-lā′shəs, zig′ō-fi-lā′shəs), *adj.* [< Mod. L. *Zygophyllaceae*, name of the family (< *zygo-* + Gr. *phyllon*, leaf); + *-ous*], designating or of a number of herbs and shrubs of the caltrop or bean

caper family, having jointed branches, stipulate leaves, and axillary flowers.

zy·go·phyte (zī'gə-fīt', zig'ə-fīt'), ***n.*** [*zygo-* + *-phyte*], a plant that reproduces by means of zygospores.

zy·gose (zī'gōs, zig'ōs), ***adj.*** of zygosis.

zy·go·sis (zī-gō'sis, zi-gō'sis), ***n.*** [Mod. L.; Gr. *zygosis*, a balancing, joining < *zygon*, a yoke], in *biology*, conjugation; union of cells or gametes.

zy·go·spore (zī'gə-spôr', zig'ə-spōr'), ***n.*** [*zygo-* + *spore*], a spore formed by conjugation of two similar gametes.

zy·gote (zī'gōt, zig'ōt), ***n.*** [< Gr. *zygōtos*, yoked < *zygon*, a yoke], any cell formed by the union of two gametes.

zy·mase (zī'mās), ***n.*** [Fr. *zymase;* see ZYME & -ASE], an enzyme, present in yeast, which causes fermentation by breaking down glucose and some other carbohydrates into alcohol and carbon dioxide or into lactic acid.

zyme (zīm), ***n.*** [Gr. *zymē*, a leaven], 1. a ferment or enzyme. 2. the principle regarded as the specific cause of a zymotic disease.

zy·mo- (zī'mō, zī'mə), [< Gr. *zymē*, a leaven], a combining form meaning *fermentation*, as in *zymology*: also, before a vowel, **zym-**.

zy·mo·gen (zī'mə-jən), ***n.*** [Fr. *zymogène;* see ZYMO- & -GEN], 1. a substance capable of becoming an enzyme. 2. any bacteria capable of producing an enzyme.

zy·mo·gene (zī'mə-jēn'), ***n.*** a zymogen.

zy·mo·gen·e·sis (zī'mə-jen'ə-sis), ***n.*** [Mod. L.; see ZYMO- & -GENESIS], the process by which a zymogen becomes an enzyme.

zy·mo·gen·ic (zī'mə-jen'ik), ***adj.*** 1. of or having to do with a zymogen. 2. that can produce a ferment.

zymogenic organism, a yeast or other microorganism which causes fermentation.

zy·mo·log·ic (zī'mə-loj'ik), ***adj.*** of or having to do with zymology.

zy·mol·o·gy (zī-mol'ə-ji), ***n.*** [*zymo-* + *-logy*], 1. the science dealing with fermentation. 2. [*pl.* ZYMOLOGIES (-jiz)], a treatise on fermentation.

zy·mol·y·sis (zī-mol'ə-sis), ***n.*** [Mod. L.; *zymo-* + *-lysis*], 1. the fermentative action of enzymes. 2. fermentation or other changes resulting from this.

zy·mo·lyt·ic (zī'mə-lit'ik), ***adj.*** of or having to do with zymolysis.

zy·mom·e·ter (zī-mom'ə-tẽr), ***n.*** [*zymo-* + *-meter*], an instrument used to measure the degree of fermentation.

zy·mo·sis (zī-mō'sis), ***n.*** [Mod. L.; Gr. *zymōsis*, fermentation < *zymē*, a leaven, ferment], 1. fermentation. 2. a process like fermentation by which infectious diseases were formerly believed to be developed; hence, 3. [Rare], a zymotic disease.

zy·mot·ic (zī-mot'ik), ***adj.*** [Gr. *zymōtikos*, causing to ferment < *zymoun*, to ferment < *zymē*, a ferment], 1. of, causing, or caused by or as by, fermentation. 2. designating or of any infectious disease, as smallpox, formerly believed to be caused by a fermentative process.

zy·mur·gy (zī'mẽr-ji), ***n.*** [*zym-* + *-urgy*], the chemistry of fermentation, as applied in wine making, brewing, etc.

COLLEGES AND UNIVERSITIES OF THE UNITED STATES

This list, compiled according to the latest available information, includes those colleges and universities of the United States and its possessions that offer nothing less than a bachelor's degree. After the official name of the institution the following information is given: its location; its date of founding; the nature of its enrollment (for men, for women, or coeducational); the type of control (state, county, private, etc.) or its affiliation with another institution; the nature of its curriculum (undergraduate, graduate, professional). The key at the bottom of every right-hand page explains the symbols and abbreviations for this information.

Abilene Christian C., Abilene, Tex.; 1906; coed.; P.; ‡
Adams State C. of Colorado, Alamosa, Colo.; 1921; coed.; S.; ‡
Adelphi U., Garden City, N.Y.; 1896; coed.; P.; ‡ #
Adrian C., Adrian, Mich.; 1845; coed.; P.; †
Agnes Scott C., Decatur, Ga.; 1889; women; P.; †
***Agricultural and Mechanical C. of Texas**, College Station, Tex.; 1876; coed.; S.; ‡ #
Agricultural and Technical C. of North Carolina, Greensboro, N.C.; 1891; coed.; S.; ‡
Agricultural, Mechanical and Normal C., Pine Bluff, Ark.; 1873; coed.; S.; †
***Akron, U. of**, Akron, O.; 1870; coed.; Mun.; ‡
Alabama C., Montevallo, Ala.; 1896; women; S.; †
Alabama State Agriculture and Mechanical Institute, Normal, Ala.; 1875; coed.; S.; †
Alabama State C., Montgomery, Ala.; 1874; coed.; S.; ‡
***Alabama, U. of**, University, Ala.; 1831; coed.; S.; ‡ #
Alaska, U. of, College, Alas.; 1917; coed.; S.; ‡
Albany State C., Albany, Ga.; 1903; coed.; S.; †
Albertus Magnus C., New Haven, Conn.; 1925; women; P.; †
Albion C., Albion, Mich.; 1835; coed.; P.; ‡
Albright C., Reading, Pa.; 1856; coed.; P.; †
Alcorn Agricultural and Mechanical C., Alcorn, Miss.; 1871; coed.; S.; †
Alderson-Broaddus C., Philippi, W. Va.; 1871; coed.; P.; †
Alfred U., Alfred, N.Y.; 1836; coed.; P. & S.; ‡
Allegheny C., Meadville, Pa.; 1815; coed.; P.; ‡
Allen U., Columbia, S.C.; 1870; coed.; P.; † #
Alliance C., Cambridge Springs, Pa.; 1912; coed.; P.; †
Alma C., Alma, Mich.; 1886; coed.; P.; †
Alma White C., Zarephath, N.J.; 1917; coed.; P.; ‡
Alverno C., Milwaukee, Wis.; 1887; women; P.; †
American Institute for Foreign Trade, Phoenix, Ariz.; 1946; coed.; P.; ⸸
American International C., Springfield, Mass.; 1885; coed.; P.; ‡
***American U.**, Washington, D.C.; 1893; coed.; P.; ‡
Amherst C., Amherst, Mass.; 1821; men; P.; ‡
Anderson C. and Theological Seminary, Anderson, Ind.; 1917; coed.; P.; † #
Anna Maria C. for Women, Paxton, Mass.; 1946; women; P.; †
Annhurst C., South Woodstock, Conn.; 1941; women; P.; †
Antioch C., Yellow Springs, O.; 1853; coed.; P.; †
Appalachian State Teachers C., Boone, N.C.; 1903; coed.; S.; ‡
Aquinas C., Grand Rapids, Mich.; 1923; coed.; P.; †
Arizona State C., Flagstaff, Ariz.; 1899; coed.; S.; ‡
***Arizona State C. at Tempe**, Tempe, Ariz.; 1885; coed.; S.; ‡
***Arizona, U. of**, Tucson, Ariz.; 1885; coed.; S.; ‡ #
Arkansas Agricultural and Mechanical C., College Heights, Ark.; 1909; coed.; S.; †
Arkansas Baptist C., Little Rock, Ark.; 1884; coed.; P.; †
Arkansas C., Batesville, Ark.; 1872; coed.; P.; †
Arkansas Polytechnic C., Russelville, Ark.; 1909; coed.; S.; †
Arkansas State C., State College, Ark.; 1910; coed.; S.; ‡
Arkansas State Teachers C., Conway, Ark.; 1908; coed.; S.; †
***Arkansas, U. of**, Fayetteville, Ark.; 1871; coed.; S.; ‡ #
Armstrong C., Berkeley, Calif.; 1918; coed.; P.; ‡
Aroostook State Teachers C., Presque Isle, Me.; 1903; coed.; S.; †
Art Center School, Los Angeles, Calif.; 1930; coed.; P.; ‡
Art Institute of Chicago, School of the, Chicago, Ill.; 1866; coed.; P.; ‡
Asbury C., Wilmore, Ky.; 1890; coed.; P.; †
Ashland C., Ashland, O.; 1878; coed.; P.; †
Assumption C., Worcester, Mass.; 1904; men; P.; ‡
Athens C., Athens, Ala.; 1842; coed.; P.; †
Atlanta U., Atlanta, Ga.; 1867; coed.; P.; ‡ #
Atlantic Christian C., Wilson, N.C.; 1902; coed.; P.; †
Atlantic Union C., South Lancaster, Mass.; 1882; coed.; P.; †
Auburn U., Auburn, Ala.; 1872; coed.; S.; ‡ #
Augsburg C. and Theological Seminary, Minneapolis, Minn.; 1869; coed.; P.; † #
Augustana C., Rock Island, Ill.; 1860; coed.; P.; †
Augustana C., Sioux Falls, S.Dak.; 1860; coed.; P.; †
Aurora C., Aurora, Ill.; 1893; coed.; P.; †
Austin C., Sherman, Tex.; 1849; coed.; P.; ‡
Austin Peay State C., Clarksville, Tenn.; 1929; coed.; S.; ‡

Babson Institute, Babson Park, Mass.; 1919; men; P.; ‡
Baker U., Baldwin, Kan.; 1858; coed.; P.; †
Baldwin-Wallace C., Berea, O.; 1845; coed.; P.; †
***Ball State Teachers C.**, Muncie, Ind.; 1918; coed.; S.; ‡
Baltimore, U. of, Baltimore, Md.; 1925; coed.; P.; ‡
Barat C. of the Sacred Heart, Lake Forest, Ill.; 1918; women; P.; †
Barber-Scotia C., Concord, N.C.; 1867; women; P.; †
Bard C., Annandale-on-Hudson, N.Y.; 1860; coed.; P.; †
Barnard C., New York City, N.Y.; 1889; women's college of Columbia U.; †
Barry C., Miami, Fla.; 1940; women; P.; ‡
Bates C., Lewiston, Me.; 1864; coed.; P.; †
***Baylor U.**, Waco, Dallas & Houston, Tex.; 1846; coed.; P.; ‡ #
Beaver C., Jenkintown, Pa.; 1853; women; P.; †
Belhaven C., Jackson, Miss.; 1894; women; P.; †
Bellarmine C., Louisville, Ky.; 1950; men; P.; †
Belmont Abbey C., Belmont, N.C.; 1878; men; P.; †
Belmont C., Nashville, Tenn.; 1951; coed.; P.; †
Beloit C., Beloit, Wis.; 1846; coed.; P.; ‡
Bemidji State C., Bemidji, Minn.; 1919; coed.; S.; ‡
Benedict C., Columbia, S.C.; 1870; coed.; P.; † #
Benedictine Heights C., Guthrie, Okla.; 1917; women; P.; †
Bennett C., Greensboro, N.C.; 1873; women; P.; †
Bennington C., Bennington, Vt.; 1932; women; P.; †
Berea C., Berea, Ky.; 1855; coed.; P.; †
Berkeley Baptist Divinity School, Berkeley, Calif.; 1889; coed.; P.; ⸸ #
Berry C., Mount Berry, Ga.; 1902; coed.; P.; †
Bethany C., Lindsborg, Kan.; 1881; coed.; P.; †
Bethany C., Bethany, W. Va.; 1840; coed.; P.; †
Bethany Nazarene C., Bethany, Okla.; 1899; coed.; P.; † #
Bethel C., North Newton, Kan.; 1888; coed.; P.; †
Bethel C., McKenzie, Tenn.; 1842; coed.; P.; †
Bethune-Cookman C., Daytona Beach, Fla.; 1904; coed.; P.; †
Birmingham-Southern C., Birmingham, Ala.; 1856; coed.; P.; ‡
Bishop C., Marshall, Tex.; 1880; coed.; P.; ‡
Blackburn C., Carlinville, Ill.; 1857; coed.; P.; †
Black Hills Teachers C., Spearfish, S.Dak.; 1883; coed.; S.; †
Bloomfield C. and Seminary, Bloomfield, N.J.; 1878; coed.; P.; †
Bluefield State C., Bluefield, W.Va.; 1895; coed.; S.; †
Blue Mountain C., Blue Mountain, Miss.; 1873; women; P.; †
Bluffton C., Bluffton, O.; 1900; coed.; P.; †
Bob Jones U., Greenville, S.C.; 1927; coed.; P.; ‡ #
***Boston C.**, Chestnut Hill, Mass.; 1863; men; P.; ‡ #
***Boston U.**, Boston, Mass.; 1869; coed.; P.; ‡ #
Bowdoin C., Brunswick, Me.; 1794; men; P.; †
Bowling Green C. of Commerce, Bowling Green, Ky.; 1922; coed.; P.; †
***Bowling Green State U.**, Bowling Green, O.; 1914; coed.; S.; ‡
Bradley U., Peoria, Ill.; 1897; coed.; P.; ‡
Brandeis U., Waltham, Mass.; 1947; coed.; P.; ‡
Brenau C., Gainesville, Ga.; 1878; women; P.; †
Brescia C., Owensboro, Ky.; 1925; coed.; P.; †
Briar Cliff C., Sioux City, Ia.; 1930; women; P.; †
Bridgeport, U. of, Bridgeport, Conn.; 1927; coed.; P.; ‡
Bridgewater C., Bridgewater, Va.; 1880; coed.; P.; †
***Brigham Young U.**, Provo, Ut.; 1875; coed.; P.; ‡
***Brooklyn C.**, see **New York, C. of the City of.**
Brooklyn Law School, Brooklyn, N.Y.; 1901; coed.; P.; #
***Brooklyn, Polytechnic Institute of**, Brooklyn, N.Y.; 1854; men; P.; ‡
***Brown U.**, Providence, R.I.; 1764; men; P.; ‡
Bryant C. of Business Administration, Providence, R.I.; 1863; coed.; P.; †
Bryn Mawr C., Bryn Mawr, Pa.; 1885; women; P.; ‡ #
Bucknell U., Lewisburg, Pa.; 1846; coed.; P.; ‡
Buena Vista C., Storm Lake, Ia.; 1886; coed.; P.; †
***Buffalo, U. of**, Buffalo, N.Y.; 1846; coed.; P.; ‡ #
***Butler U.**, Indianapolis, Ind.; 1854; coed.; P.; ‡ #

Caldwell C. for Women, Caldwell, N.J.; 1939; women; P.; †
California C. of Arts and Crafts, Oakland, Calif.; 1907; coed.; P.; ‡
California C. of Medicine, Los Angeles, Calif.; 1914; coed.; P.; #
California Institute of Technology, Pasadena, Calif.; 1891; men; P.; ‡
California Maritime Academy, Vallejo, Calif.; 1929; men; S.; ‡
California School of Fine Arts, San Francisco, Calif.; 1874; coed.; P.; †
***California State Polytechnic C.**, San Luis Obispo, Calif.; 1901; coed.; S.; ‡
***California, U. of**, Berkeley, Calif.; 1868; coed.; S.; ‡ #; seven affiliated colleges and universities including
- ***California, U. of, at Los Angeles**, Los Angeles; 1881; coed.; ‡ #
- **California, U. of, Medical Center at San Francisco**, San Francisco; 1873; coed.; ⸸ #
- **California, U. of, Santa Barbara C.**, Santa Barbara; 1944; coed.; ‡

Others are at Riverside, Davis, La Jolla and Mt. Hamilton.

C., College; U., University; J.C., Junior College; P., Private; S., State; Mun., Municipal; Ter., Territorial; Fed., Federal; Dist., District; Co., County; † undergraduate; ‡ undergraduate & graduate; ⸸ graduate; # professional; * enrollment of 3,000 or more.

California Western U., San Diego, Calif.; 1924; coed.; P.; †
Calvin C., Grand Rapids, Mich.; 1876; coed.; P.; †
Canisius C., Buffalo, N.Y.; 1870; men; P.; ‡
Capital U., Columbus, O.; 1850; coed.; P.; † #
Cardinal Stritch C., Milwaukee, Wis.; 1933; women; P.; †
Carleton C., Northfield, Minn.; 1866; coed.; P.; †
***Carnegie Institute of Technology**, Pittsburgh, Pa.; 1900; coed.; P.; ‡
Carroll C., Helena, Mont.; 1910; coed.; P.; †
Carroll C., Waukesha, Wis.; 1846; coed.; P.; †
Carson-Newman C., Jefferson City, Tenn.; 1851; coed.; P.; †
Carthage C., Carthage, Ill.; 1870; coed.; P.; †
Cascade C., Portland, Oreg.; 1918; coed.; P.; † #
Case Institute of Technology, Cleveland, O.; 1880; men; P.; ‡
Castleton Teachers C., Castleton, Vt.; 1787; coed.; S.; †
Catawba C., Salisbury, N.C.; 1851; coed.; P.; †
***Catholic U. of America**, Washington, D.C.; 1887; coed.; P.; ‡ #
Catholic U. of Puerto Rico, Ponce, P.R.; 1948; coed.; P.; †
Cedar Crest C., Allentown, Pa.; 1867; women; P.; †
Cedarville Baptist C., Cedarville, O.; 1894; coed.; P.; † #
Centenary C. of Louisiana, Shreveport, La.; 1825; coed.; P.; †
Central Bible Institute and Seminary, Springfield, Mo.; 1922; coed.; P.; †#
Central C., Pella, Ia.; 1853; coed.; P.; †
Central C., Fayette, Mo.; 1854; coed.; P.; †
Central Connecticut State C., New Britain, Conn.; 1849; coed.; S.; ‡
Central Michigan C., Mount Pleasant, Mich.; 1892; coed.; S.; ‡
Central Missouri State C., Warrensburg, Mo.; 1871; coed.; S.; ‡
Central State C., Wilberforce, O.; 1887; coed.; S.; †
Central State C., Edmond, Okla.; 1890; coed.; S.; †
Central Washington C. of Education, Ellensburg, Wash.; 1891; coed.; S.; ‡
Centre C. of Kentucky, Danville, Ky.; 1819; coed.; P.; †
Chapman C., Orange, Calif.; 1861; coed.; P.; †
Charleston, C. of, Charleston, S.C.; 1770; coed.; P.; †
Chatham C., Pittsburgh, Pa.; 1869; women; P.; †
Chattanooga, U. of, Chattanooga, Tenn.; 1886; coed.; P.; ‡
Chestnut Hill C., Chestnut Hill, Pa.; 1871; women; P.; †
Chicago C. of Osteopathy, Chicago, Ill.; 1900; coed.; P.; #
Chicago Conservatory C., Chicago, Ill.; 1857; coed.; P.; ‡
Chicago-Kent C. of Law, Chicago, Ill.; 1887; coed.; P.; #
Chicago Medical School, Chicago, Ill.; 1912; coed.; P.; #
Chicago Musical C., Chicago, Ill.; 1867; coed.; P.; a division of Roosevelt U.; ‡
***Chicago Teachers C.**, Chicago, Ill.; 1869; coed.; Mun.; ‡
Chicago Technical C., Chicago, Ill.; 1904; men; P.; †
***Chicago, U. of**, Chicago, Ill.; 1890; coed.; P.; ‡ #
Chico State C., Chico, Calif.; 1887; coed.; S.; ‡
Christian Brothers C., Memphis, Tenn.; 1871; men; P.; †
Cincinnati, College-Conservatory of Music of, Cincinnati, O.; 1867; coed.; P.; ‡
***Cincinnati, U. of**, Cincinnati, O.; 1819; coed.; Mun.; ‡ #
Citadel, The, Charleston, S.C.; 1842; men; S.; †
***City C.**, see **New York, C. of the City of.**
Claflin U., Orangeburg, S.C.; 1869; coed.; P.; †
Claremont Men's C., Claremont, Calif.; 1947; men; P.; affiliated with Pomona C. and Scripps C.; †
Clark C., Atlanta, Ga.; 1869; coed.; P.; †
Clarke C., Dubuque, Ia.; 1843; women; P.; †
Clarkson C. of Technology, Potsdam, N.Y.; 1896; men; P.; ‡
Clark U., Worcester, Mass.; 1887; coed.; P.; ‡
Clemson Agricultural C., Clemson, S.C.; 1889; men; S.; ‡
Coe C., Cedar Rapids, Ia.; 1851; coed.; P.; †
Coker C., Hartsville, S.C.; 1908; women; P.; †
Colby C., Waterville, Me.; 1813; coed.; P.; †
Colgate U., Hamilton, N.Y.; 1819; men; P.; ‡
Colorado C., Colorado Springs, Colo.; 1874; coed.; P.; ‡
Colorado School of Mines, Golden, Colo.; 1874; coed.; ‡
Colorado State C., Greeley, Colo.; 1890; coed.; S.; ‡
***Colorado State U.**, Fort Collins, Colo.; 1870; coed.; S.; ‡ #
***Colorado, U. of**, Boulder, Colo.; 1871; coed.; S.; ‡ #
Columbia Bible C., Columbia, S.C.; 1923; coed.; P.; ‡ #
Columbia C., Chicago, Ill. & Los Angeles, Calif.; 1890; coed.; P.; ‡
Columbia C., Columbia, S.C.; 1854; women; P.; †
Columbia Theological Seminary, Decatur, Ga.; 1828; men; P.; ‡ #
***Columbia U.**, New York City, N.Y.; 1754; coed.; P.; ‡ #
Concord C., Athens, W.Va.; 1872; coed.; S.; †
Concordia C., Moorhead, Minn.; 1891; coed.; P.; †
Concordia Senior C., Fort Wayne, Ind.; 1839; men; P.; †
Concordia Teachers C., River Forest, Ill.; 1864; coed.; P.; †
Concordia Teachers C., Seward, Neb.; 1894; coed.; P.; †
Connecticut C., New London, Conn.; 1911; women; P.; ‡
***Connecticut, U. of**, Storrs, Conn.; 1881; coed.; S.; ‡ #
Converse C., Spartanburg, S.C.; 1890; women; P.; ‡
Cooper Union, New York City, N.Y.; 1859; coed.; P.; †
Cornell C., Mount Vernon, Ia.; 1853; coed.; P.; †
***Cornell U.**, Ithaca & New York City, N.Y.; 1865; coed.; P. & S.; ‡ #
Creighton U., Omaha, Neb.; 1878; coed.; P.; ‡ #
Culver-Stockton C., Canton, Mo.; 1852; coed.; P.; †
Cumberland U., Lebanon, Tenn.; 1842; coed.; P.; #
Curry C., Milton, Mass.; 1879; coed.; P.; ‡
Curtis Institute of Music, Philadelphia, Pa.; 1924; coed.; P.; †

Dakota Wesleyan U., Mitchell, S.Dak.; 1885; coed.; P.; †
Dana C., Blair, Neb.; 1884; coed.; P.; †
Danbury State C., Danbury, Conn.; 1904; coed.; S.; †
Dartmouth C., Hanover, N.H.; 1769; men; P.; ‡
David Lipscomb C., Nashville, Tenn.; 1891; coed.; P.; †
Davidson C., Davidson, N.C.; 1837; men; P.; †
Davis and Elkins C., Elkins, W.Va.; 1904; coed.; P.; †
***Dayton, U. of**, Dayton, O.; 1850; coed.; P.; ‡
Defiance C., Defiance, O.; 1850; coed.; P.; †
Delaware State C., Dover, Del.; 1891; coed.; S.; †
***Delaware, U. of**, Newark, Del.; 1833; coed.; S.; ‡
Delta State C., Cleveland, Miss.; 1924; coed.; S.; †
Denison U., Granville, O.; 1831; coed.; P.; †
***Denver, U. of**, Denver, Colo.; 1864; coed.; P.; ‡ #
***De Paul U.**, Chicago, Ill.; 1898; coed.; P.; ‡ #
DePauw U., Greencastle, Ind.; 1837; coed.; P.; ‡
Detroit C. of Law, Detroit, Mich.; 1891; coed.; P.; #
Detroit Institute of Technology, Detroit, Mich.; 1891; coed.; P.; † #
***Detroit, U. of**, Detroit, Mich.; 1877; coed.; P.; ‡ #
Dickinson C., Carlisle, Pa.; 1773; coed.; P.; †
Dickinson School of Law, Carlisle, Pa.; 1834; coed.; P.; #
Dillard U., New Orleans, La.; 1935; coed.; P.; †
District of Columbia Teachers C., Washington, D.C.; 1955; coed.; Mun.; ‡
Doane C., Crete, Neb.; 1872; coed.; P.; †
Dominican C. of San Rafael, San Rafael, Calif.; 1890; women; P.; ‡
Douglass C., New Brunswick, N.J.; 1918; women's college of Rutgers U.; †
***Drake U.**, Des Moines, Ia.; 1881; coed.; P.; ‡ #
Drew U., Madison, N.J.; 1867; coed.; P.; ‡ #
***Drexel Institute of Technology**, Philadelphia, Pa.; 1891; coed.; P.; ‡
Dropsie C. for Hebrew and Cognate Learning, Philadelphia, Pa.; 1907; coed.; P.; ‡
Drury C., Springfield, Mo.; 1873; coed.; P.; ‡
Dubuque, U. of, Dubuque, Ia.; 1852; coed.; P.; † #
Duchesne C., Omaha, Neb.; 1881; women; P.; †
***Duke U.**, Durham, N.C.; 1838; coed.; P.; ‡ #
Dunbarton C. of Holy Cross, Washington, D.C.; 1935; women; P.; †
***Duquesne U.**, Pittsburgh, Pa.; 1878; coed.; P.; ‡ #
D'Youville C., Buffalo, N.Y.; 1908; women; P.; †

Earlham C., Richmond, Ind.; 1847; coed.; P.; †
East Carolina C., Greenville, N.C.; 1909; coed.; S.; ‡
East Central State C., Ada, Okla.; 1909; coed.; S.; ‡
Eastern Baptist C., St. Davids, Pa.; 1952; coed.; P.; †
Eastern Baptist Theological Seminary, Philadelphia, Pa.; 1925; coed.; P.; #
Eastern Illinois State C., Charleston, Ill.; 1895; coed.; S.; ‡
Eastern Kentucky State C., Richmond, Ky.; 1906; coed; S.; ‡
Eastern Michigan C., Ypsilanti, Mich.; 1849; coed.; S.; ‡
Eastern Montana C. of Education, Billings, Mont.; 1927; coed.; S.; ‡
Eastern Nazarene C., Wollaston Park, Mass.; 1918; coed.; P.; † #
Eastern New Mexico U., Portales, N. Mex.; 1934; coed.; S.; ‡
Eastern Oregon C. of Education, La Grande, Oreg.; 1929; coed.; S.; ‡
Eastern Pilgrim C., Allentown, Pa.; 1921; coed.; P.; †
Eastern Washington C. of Education, Cheney, Wash.; 1890; coed.; S.; ‡
East Tennessee State C., Johnson City, Tenn.; 1911; coed.; S.; ‡
East Texas Baptist C., Marshall, Tex.; 1917; coed.; P.; ‡
East Texas State C., Commerce, Tex.; 1894; coed.; S.; ‡
Edgewood C. of the Sacred Heart, Madison, Wis.; 1927; women; P.; †
Elizabeth City State Teachers C., Elizabeth City, N.C.; 1891; coed.; S.; †
Elizabethtown C., Elizabethtown, Pa.; 1899; coed.; P.; †
Elmhurst C., Elmhurst, Ill.; 1871; coed.; P.; †
Elmira C., Elmira, N.Y.; 1855; women; P.; †
Elon C., Elon College, N.C.; 1889; coed.; P.; †
Emerson C., Boston, Mass.; 1880; coed.; P.; ‡
Emmanuel C., Boston, Mass.; 1919; women; P.; †
Emmanuel Missionary C., Berrien Springs, Mich.; 1874; coed.; P.; †
Emory and Henry C., Emory, Va.; 1839; coed.; P.; †
***Emory U.**, Atlanta, Ga.; 1836; coed.; P.; ‡ #
Emporia, C. of, Emporia, Kan.; 1882; coed.; P.; †
Erskine C., Due West, S.C.; 1839; coed.; P.; †
Eureka C., Eureka, Ill.; 1855; coed.; P.; †
Evansville C., Evansville, Ind.; 1854; coed.; P.; †

Fairfield U., Fairfield, Conn.; 1942; men; P.; ‡
***Fairleigh Dickinson U.**, Rutherford & Teaneck, N.J.; 1941; coed.; P.; ‡ #
Fairmont State C., Fairmont, W.Va.; 1867; coed.; S.; †
Farmington State Teachers C., Farmington, Me.; 1864; coed.; S.; †
Fayetteville State Teachers C., Fayetteville, N.C.; 1877; coed.; S.; †
***Fenn C.**, Cleveland, O.; 1923; coed.; P.; †
Ferris Institute, Big Rapids, Mich.; 1884; coed.; S.; †
Finch C., New York City, N.Y.; 1900; women; P.; †
Findlay C., Findlay, O.; 1882; coed.; P.; †
Fisk U., Nashville, Tenn.; 1866; coed.; P.; ‡
Flora Macdonald C., Red Springs, N.C.; 1896; women; P.; †
Florence State Teachers C., Florence, Ala.; 1873; coed.; S.; †
Florida Agricultural and Mechanical C., Tallahassee, Fla.; 1887; coed.; S.; ‡
Florida Normal and Industrial Memorial C., St. Augustine, Fla.; 1892; coed.; P.; †

Florida Southern C., Lakeland, Fla.; 1885; coed.; P.; †
***Florida State U.**, Tallahassee, Fla.; 1857; coed.; S.; ‡ #
***Florida, U. of**, Gainesville, Fla.; 1853; coed.; S.; ‡ #
Fontbonne C., St. Louis, Mo.; 1923; a women's college of St. Louis U.; †
***Fordham U.**, New York City, N.Y.; 1841; men; P.; ‡ #
Fort Hays Kansas State C., Hays, Kan.; 1902; coed.; S.; ‡
Fort Valley State C., Fort Valley, Ga.; 1895; coed.; S.; †
Fort Wayne Bible C., Fort Wayne, Ind.; 1904; coed.; P.; †
Franklin and Marshall C., Lancaster, Pa.; 1787; men; P.; ‡
Franklin C. of Indiana, Franklin, Ind.; 1834; coed.; P.; †
***Fresno State C.**, Fresno, Calif.; 1910; coed.; S.; ‡
Friends U., Wichita, Kan.; 1898; coed.; P.; ‡ #
Furman U., Greenville, S.C.; 1826; coed.; P.; ‡

Gallaudet C., Washington, D.C.; 1864; coed.; P.; †
Gannon C., Erie, Pa.; 1941; men; P.; †
Garrett Biblical Institute, Evanston, Ill.; 1855; coed.; P.; ↓ #
General Beadle State Teachers C., Madison, S. Dak.; 1883; coed.; S.; †
***General Motors Institute**, Flint, Mich.; 1919; men; P.; †
General Theological Seminary, New York, N.Y.; 1822; men; P.; #
Geneva C., Beaver Falls, Pa.; 1848; coed.; P.; †
George Fox C., Newberg, Oreg.; 1891; coed.; P.; † #
George Peabody C. for Teachers, Nashville, Tenn.; 1875; coed.; P.; ‡ #
George Pepperdine C., Los Angeles, Calif.; 1937; coed.; P.; ‡
Georgetown C., Georgetown, Ky.; 1829; coed.; P.; †
***Georgetown U.**, Washington, D.C.; 1789; men; P.; ‡ #
***George Washington U.**, Washington, D.C.; 1821; coed.; P.; ‡ #
George Williams C., Chicago, Ill.; 1890; coed.; P.; ‡
***Georgia Institute of Technology**, Atlanta, Ga.; 1885; men; S.; ‡
Georgia, Medical C. of, Augusta, Ga.; 1828; coed.; S.; ↓ #
Georgian Court C., Lakewood, N.J.; 1908; women; P.; †
Georgia Southern C., Collegeboro, Ga.; 1908; coed.; S.; ‡
Georgia State C. for Women, Milledgeville, Ga.; 1889; women; S.; †
***Georgia, U. of**, Athens, Ga.; 1785; coed.; S.; ‡ #
Gettysburg C., Gettysburg, Pa.; 1832; coed.; P.; †
Glassboro State C., Glassboro, N.J.; 1923; coed.; S.; ‡
Glenville State C., Glenville, W. Va.; 1872; coed.; S.; †
Goddard C., Plainfield, Vt.; 1863; coed.; P.; †
Golden Gate C., San Francisco, Calif.; 1901; coed.; P.; ‡ #
Gonzaga U., Spokane, Wash.; 1887; coed.; P.; ‡ #
Good Counsel C., White Plains, N.Y.; 1923; women; P.; †
Gordon C. and Gordon Divinity School, Beverly Farms, Mass.; 1889; coed.; P.; † #
Gorham State Teachers C., Gorham, Me.; 1878; coed.; S.; †
Goshen C., Goshen, Ind.; 1894; coed.; P.; † #
Goucher C., Towson, Md.; 1888; women; P.; ‡
Grace Bible Institute, Omaha, Neb.; 1943; coed.; P.; †
Grace Theological Seminary and Grace C., Winona Lake, Ind.; 1937; coed.; P.; †
Grambling C., Grambling, La.; 1901; coed.; S.; †
Grand Canyon C., Phoenix, Ariz.; 1949; coed.; P.; †
Great Falls, C. of, Great Falls, Mont.; 1932; coed.; P.; †
Greensboro C., Greensboro, N.C.; 1838; coed.; P.; †
Greenville C., Greenville, Ill.; 1892; coed.; P.; † #
Grinnell C., Grinnell, Ia.; 1846; coed.; P.; †
Grove City C., Grove City, Pa.; 1876; coed.; P.; †
Guilford C., Guilford College, N.C.; 1837; coed.; P.; †
Gustavus Adolphus C., St. Peter, Minn.; 1862; coed.; P.; †

Hahnemann Medical C. and Hospital, Philadelphia, Pa.; 1848; coed.; P.; ‡ #
Hamilton C., Clinton, N.Y.; 1812; men; P.; †
Hamline U., St. Paul, Minn.; 1854; coed.; P.; ‡
Hampden-Sydney C., Hampden-Sydney, Va.; 1776; men; P.; †
Hampton Institute, Hampton, Va.; 1868; coed.; P.; †
Hanover C., Hanover, Ind.; 1827; coed.; P.; †
Harding C., Searcy, Ark.; 1919; coed.; P.; †
Hardin-Simmons U., Abilene, Tex.; 1891; coed.; P.; ‡
Harpur C., see **New York, State U. of.**
Harris Teachers C., St. Louis, Mo.; 1857; coed.; Mun.; †
Hartford C., West Hartford, Conn.; 1939; women; P.; †
Hartwick C., Oneonta, N.Y.; 1928; coed.; P.; †
***Harvard U.**, Cambridge, Mass.; 1636; men; P.; ‡ #
Harvey Mudd C., Claremont, Calif.; 1955; coed.; P.; †
Hastings C., Hastings, Neb.; 1882; coed.; P.; †
Haverford C., Haverford, Pa.; 1833; men; P.; ‡
***Hawaii, U. of**, Honolulu, Hawaii; 1907; coed.; S.; ‡
Hebrew Teachers C., Brookline, Mass.; 1921; coed.; P.; ‡ #
Hebrew Union C.-Jewish Institute of Religion, Cincinnati, O.; 1875; men; P.; ‡ #; branches in Los Angeles & New York.
Heidelberg C., Tiffin, O.; 1850; coed.; P.; †
Henderson State Teachers C., Arkadelphia, Ark.; 1929; coed.; S.; †
Hendrix C., Conway, Ark.; 1884; coed.; P.; †
High Point C., High Point, N.C.; 1924; coed.; P.; †
Hillsdale C., Hillsdale, Mich.; 1844; coed.; P.; †
Hillyer C., Hartford, Conn.; 1879; coed.; P.; †
Hiram C., Hiram, O.; 1850; coed.; P.; †
Hobart and William Smith Colleges, Geneva, N.Y.; 1822; coed.; P.; consists of Hobart C. and William Smith C.; ‡
***Hofstra C.**, Hempstead, N.Y.; 1935; coed.; P.; ‡
Hollins C., Hollins College, Va.; 1842; women; P.; †
Holy Cross, C. of the, Worcester, Mass.; 1843; men; P.; ‡
Holy Names C., Spokane, Wash.; 1907; women; P.; †
Holy Names, C. of the, Oakland, Calif.; 1880; women; P.; †
Hood C., Frederick, Md.; 1893; women; P.; †
Hope C., Holland, Mich.; 1852; coed.; P.; †
Houghton C., Houghton, N.Y.; 1883; coed.; P.; †
Houston Baptist C., Houston, Tex.; 1960; coed.; P.; †
***Houston, U. of**, Houston, Tex.; 1934; coed.; Mun.; ‡
Howard C., Birmingham, Ala.; 1842; coed.; P.; †
Howard Payne C., Brownwood, Tex.; 1889; coed.; P.; ‡
***Howard U.**, Washington, D.C.; 1867; coed.; P.; ‡ #
H. Sophie Newcomb Memorial C., New Orleans, La.; 1886; women's college of Tulane U.; †
Humboldt State C., Arcata, Calif.; 1914; coed.; S.; †
***Hunter C.**, see **New York, C. of the City of.**
Huntingdon C., Montgomery, Ala.; 1854; coed.; P.; †
Huntington C., Huntington, Ind.; 1897; coed.; P.; † #
Huron C., Huron, S. Dak.; 1883; coed.; P.; †
Huston-Tillotson C., Austin, Tex.; 1952; coed.; P.; †

Idaho, C. of, Caldwell, Ida.; 1891; coed.; P.; ‡
Idaho State C., Pocatello, Ida.; 1902; coed.; S.; †
***Idaho, U. of**, Moscow, Ida.; 1889; coed.; S.; ‡ #
Iliff School of Theology, Denver, Colo.; 1892; coed.; P.; † #
Illinois C., Jacksonville, Ill.; 1829; coed.; P.; †
Illinois C. of Optometry, Chicago, Ill.; 1872; coed.; P.; † #
***Illinois Institute of Technology**, Chicago, Ill.; 1940; men; P.; ‡
Illinois State Normal U., Normal, Ill.; 1857; coed.; S.; ‡
***Illinois, U. of**, Urbana & Chicago, Ill.; 1868; coed.; S.; ‡ #
Illinois Wesleyan U., Bloomington, Ill.; 1850; coed.; P.; ‡
Immaculata C., Immaculata, Pa.; 1920; women; P.; †
Immaculate Heart C., Los Angeles, Calif.; 1916; women; P.; ‡
Incarnate Word C., San Antonio, Tex.; 1881; women; P.; ‡
Indiana Central C., Indianapolis, Ind.; 1902; coed.; P.; †
***Indiana State Teachers C.**, Terre Haute, Ind.; 1870; coed.; S.; ‡
***Indiana U.**, Bloomington & Indianapolis, Ind.; 1820; coed.; S.; ‡ #
Inter American University of Puerto Rico, San Germán, P.R.; 1912; coed.; P.; †
Iona C., New Rochelle, N.Y.; 1940; men; P.; †
Iowa State Teachers C., Cedar Falls, Ia.; 1876; coed.; S.; ‡
***Iowa, State U. of**, Iowa City, Ia.; 1847; coed.; S.; ‡ #
***Iowa State U. of Science and Technology**, Ames, Ia.; 1858; coed.; S.; ‡ #
Iowa Wesleyan C., Mt. Pleasant, Ia.; 1842; coed.; P.; †
Ithaca C., Ithaca, N.Y.; 1892; coed.; P.; ‡

Jackson C., Honolulu, Hawaii; 1948; coed.; P.; ‡ #
Jackson State C., Jackson, Miss.; 1877; coed.; S.; †
Jamestown C., Jamestown, N. Dak.; 1883; coed.; P.; †
Jarvis Christian C., Hawkins, Tex.; 1912; coed.; P.; †
Jefferson Medical C. of Philadelphia, Philadelphia, Pa. 1825; men; P.; ↓ #
Jersey City State C., Jersey City, N.J.; 1929; coed.; S.; †
Jewish Theological Seminary of America, New York City, N.Y.; 1887; coed.; P.; ‡ #
John Brown U., Siloam Springs, Ark.; 1919; coed.; P.; †
John Carroll U., University Heights, O.; 1886; men; P.; ‡
John Marshall Law School, Chicago, Ill.; 1899; coed.; P.; #
***Johns Hopkins U.**, Baltimore, Md.; 1876; men; P.; ‡ #
Johnson Bible C., Kimberlin Heights, Tenn.; 1893; coed.; P.; †
Johnson C. Smith U., Charlotte, N.C.; 1867; coed.; P.; † #
Johnson Teachers C., Johnson, Vt.; 1867; coed.; S.; †
Judson C., Marion, Ala.; 1838; women; P.; †
Juilliard School of Music, New York City, N.Y.; 1905; coed.; P.; ‡
Juniata C., Huntingdon, Pa.; 1876; coed.; P.; †

Kalamazoo C., Kalamazoo, Mich.; 1833; coed.; P.; ‡
Kansas City C. of Osteopathy and Surgery, Kansas City, Mo.; 1916; coed.; P.; #
Kansas City, U. of, Kansas City, Mo. 1933; coed.; P.; ‡ #
***Kansas State C. of Agriculture and Applied Science**, Manhattan, Kan.; 1863; coed.; S.; ‡ #
Kansas State Teachers C., Emporia, Kan.; 1863; coed.; S.; ‡
Kansas State Teachers C., Pittsburg, Kan.; 1903; coed.; S.; ‡
***Kansas, U. of**, Lawrence, Kan.; 1866; coed.; S.; ‡ #
Kansas Wesleyan U., Salina, Kan.; 1886; coed.; P.; †
Keene Teachers C., Keene, N.H.; 1909; coed.; S.; ‡
***Kent State U.**, Kent, O.; 1910; coed.; S.; ‡
Kentucky State C., Frankfort, Ky.; 1886; coed.; S.; †
***Kentucky, U. of**, Lexington, Ky.; 1865; coed.; S.; ‡ #
Kentucky Wesleyan C., Owensboro, Ky.; 1860; coed.; P.; †
Kenyon C., Gambier, O.; 1824; men; P.; † #
Keuka C., Keuka Park, N.Y.; 1890; women; P.; †
King C., Bristol, Tenn.; 1866; coed.; P.; †
King's C., Wilkes-Barre, Pa.; 1946; men; P.; †
Kirksville C. of Osteopathy and Surgery, Kirksville, Mo. 1892; coed.; P.; #
Knox C., Galesburg, Ill.; 1837; coed.; P.; †
Knoxville C., Knoxville, Tenn.; 1875; coed.; P.; †

Ladycliff C., Highland Falls, N.Y.; 1933; women; P.; †
Lafayette C., Easton, Pa.; 1826; men; P.; †
La Grange C., La Grange, Ga.; 1831; coed.; P.; †
Lake Erie C., Painesville, O.; 1859; women; P.; †
Lake Forest C., Lake Forest, Ill.; 1857; coed.; P.; †
Lakeland C., Sheboygan, Wis.; 1862; coed.; P.; †

C., College; U., University; J.C., Junior College; P., Private; S., State; Mun., Municipal; Ter., Territorial; Fed., Federal; Dist., District; Co., County; † undergraduate; ‡ undergraduate & graduate; ↓ graduate; # professional; * enrollment of 3,000 or more.

Lamar State C. of Technology, Beaumont, Tex.; 1923; coed.; S.; ‡

Lambuth C., Jackson, Tenn.; 1924; coed.; P.; †

La Mennais C., Alfred, Me.; 1951; men; P.; †

Lander C., Greenwood, S.C.; 1872; coed.; S.; †

Lane C., Jackson, Tenn.; 1882; coed.; P.; †

Langston U., Langston, Okla.; 1897; coed.; S.; †

La Salle C., Philadelphia, Pa.; 1863; men; P.; ‡

La Sierra C., Arlington, Calif.; 1922; coed.; P.; †

La Verne C., La Verne, Calif.; 1891; coed.; P.; †

Lawrence C., Appleton, Wis.; 1847; coed.; P.; ‡

Lawrence Institute of Technology, Detroit, Mich.; 1932; men; P.; †

Lebanon Valley C., Annville, Pa.; 1866; coed.; P.; †

Lehigh U., Bethlehem, Pa.; 1865; men; P.; ‡

Le Moyne C., Syracuse, N.Y.; 1946; coed.; P.; †

LeMoyne C., Memphis, Tenn.; 1870; coed.; P.; †

Lenoir Rhyne C., Hickory, N.C.; 1891; coed.; P.; †

Lesley C., Cambridge, Mass.; 1909; women; P.; †

Lewis and Clark C., Portland, Oreg.; 1867; coed.; P.; ‡

Limestone C., Gaffney, S.C.; 1845; women; P.; †

Lincoln Bible Institute, Lincoln, Ill.; 1944; coed.; P.; ‡

Lincoln Memorial U., Harrogate, Tenn.; 1897; coed.; P.; †

Lincoln U., Jefferson City, Mo.; 1866; coed.; S.; †

Lincoln U., Lincoln University, Pa.; 1854; men; P.; † #

Lindenwood C., St. Charles, Mo.; 1827; women; P.; †

Linfield C., McMinnville, Oreg.; 1857; coed.; P.; ‡

Little Rock U., Little Rock, Ark.; 1927; coed.; P.; †

Livingstone C., Salisbury, N.C.; 1879; coed.; P.; † #

Long Beach State C., Long Beach, Calif.; 1949; coed.; S.; ‡

***Long Island U.,** Brooklyn, N.Y.; 1926; coed.; P.; ‡

Longwood C., Farmville, Va.; 1884; women; S.; †

Loras C., Dubuque, Ia.; 1839; men; P.; †

Loretto Heights C., Loretto, Colo.; 1918; women; P.; †

Los Angeles C. of Optometry, Los Angeles, Calif.; 1904; coed.; P.; #

Los Angeles Conservatory of Music and Arts, Los Angeles, Calif.; 1883; coed.; P.; ‡

Los Angeles Pacific C., Los Angeles, Calif.; 1903; coed.; P.; †

***Los Angeles State C. of Applied Arts and Sciences,** Los Angeles, Calif.; 1947; coed.; S.; ‡

Louisiana C., Pineville, La.; 1906; coed.; P.; †

Louisiana Polytechnic Institute, Ruston, La.; 1894; coed.; S.; †

***Louisiana State U. and Agricultural and Mechanical C.,** Baton Rouge & New Orleans, La.; 1860; coed.; S.; ‡ #

***Louisville, U. of,** Louisville, Ky.; 1798; coed.; Mun.; ‡ #

Lowell Technological Institute, Lowell, Mass.; 1897; coed.; S.; ‡

Loyola C., Baltimore, Md.; 1852; men; P.; ‡

***Loyola U.,** Chicago, Ill.; 1870; coed.; P.; ‡ #

Loyola U., New Orleans, La.; 1912; men; P.; ‡ #

Loyola U. of Los Angeles, Los Angeles, Calif.; 1911; men; P.; ‡ #

Lutheran Theological Seminary, Philadelphia, Pa.; 1864; men; P.; ⸸ #

Luther C., Decorah, Ia.; 1861; coed.; P.; †

Luther Theological Seminary, St. Paul, Minn.; 1879; men; P.; ⸸ #

Lycoming C., Williamsport, Pa.; 1812; coed.; P.; †

Lynchburg C., Lynchburg, Va.; 1903; coed.; P.; †

Lyndon Teachers C., Lyndon Center, Vt.; 1912; coed.; S.; †

Macalester C., St. Paul, Minn.; 1885; coed.; P.; ‡

MacMurray C., Jacksonville, Ill.; 1846; women; P.; ‡

Madison C., Madison College, Tenn.; 1904; coed.; P.; †

Madison C., Harrisonburg, Va.; 1908; women; S.; ‡

Maine Maritime Academy, Castine, Me.; 1941; men; S.; †

***Maine, U. of,** Orono, Me.; 1865; coed.; S.; ‡

Malone C., Canton, O.; 1892; coed.; P.; † #

Manchester C., North Manchester, Ind.; 1895; coed.; P.; †

Manhattan C., New York City, N.Y.; 1849; men; P.; ‡

Manhattan School of Music, New York City, N.Y.; 1917; coed.; P.; ‡

Manhattanville C. of the Sacred Heart, New York City, N.Y.; 1841; women; P.; ‡

Mankato State C., Mankato, Minn.; 1867; coed.; S.; ‡

Mansfield State C., Mansfield, Pa.; 1857; coed.; S.; †

Marian C., Indianapolis, Ind.; 1937; coed.; P.; †

Marietta C., Marietta, O.; 1835; coed.; P.; ‡

Marion C., Marion, Ind.; 1920; coed.; P.; †

Marist C., Poughkeepsie, N.Y.; 1946; men; P.; †

Marlboro C., Marlboro, Vt.; 1947; coed.; P.; ‡

***Marquette U.,** Milwaukee, Wis.; 1886; coed.; P.; ‡ #

***Marshall C.,** Huntington, W. Va.; 1837; coed.; S.; ‡

Mary Baldwin C., Staunton, Va.; 1842; women; P.; †

Marycrest C., Davenport, Ia.; 1939; women; P.; †

Marygrove C., Detroit, Mich.; 1910; women; P.; †

Mary Hardin-Baylor C., Belton, Tex.; 1845; women; P.; †

Maryknoll Seminary, Glen Ellyn, Ill.; 1949; men; P.; †

Maryknoll Teachers C., Maryknoll, N.Y.; 1942; women; P.; †

Maryland State Teachers C., Bowie, Md.; 1867; coed.; S.; †

Maryland State Teachers C., Frostburg, Md.; 1902; coed.; S.; †

Maryland State Teachers C., Salisbury, Md.; 1925; coed.; S.; †

Maryland State Teachers C., Towson, Md.; 1866; coed.; S.; †

***Maryland, U. of,** College Park, Md.; 1807; coed.; S.; ‡ #

Marylhurst C., Marylhurst, Oreg.; 1930; women; P.; †

Mary Manse C., Toledo, O.; 1922; women; P.; †

Marymount C., Palos Verdes Estates, Calif.; 1932; women; P.; †

Marymount C., Salina, Kan.; 1922; women; P.; †

Marymount C., Tarrytown, N.Y.; 1918; women; P.; †

Maryville C., St. Louis, Mo.; 1872; a women's college of St. Louis U.; †

Maryville C., Maryville, Tenn.; 1819; coed.; P.; †

Mary Washington C., Fredericksburg, Va.; 1908; women's college of U. of Virginia; †

Marywood C., Scranton, Pa.; 1915; women; P.; ‡

Massachusetts C. of Optometry, Boston, Mass.; 1894; coed.; P.; † #

Massachusetts C. of Pharmacy, Boston, Mass.; 1823; coed.; P.; #

***Massachusetts Institute of Technology,** Cambridge, Mass.; 1861; coed.; P.; ‡

Massachusetts School of Art, Boston, Mass.; 1873; coed.; S.; †

***Massachusetts, U. of,** Amherst, Mass.; 1867; coed.; S.; ‡

McCormick Theological Seminary, Chicago, Ill.; 1829; coed.; P.; ⸸ #

McKendree C., Lebanon, Ill.; 1828; coed.; P.; †

McMurry C., Abilene, Tex.; 1923; coed.; P.; ‡

McNeese State C., Lake Charles, La.; 1939; coed.; S.; †

McPherson C., McPherson, Kan.; 1887; coed.; P.; †

Medical C. of South Carolina, Charleston, S.C.; 1823; coed.; S.; ‡ #

Medical Evangelists, C. of, Loma Linda & Los Angeles, Calif.; 1910; coed.; P.; #

Meharry Medical C., Nashville, Tenn.; 1876; coed.; P.; #

Memphis State C., Memphis, Tenn.; 1912; coed.; S.; ‡

Menlo C., Menlo Park, Calif.; 1927; men; P.; †

Mercer U., Macon, Ga.; 1833; coed.; P.; ‡ #

Mercy C., Detroit, Mich.; 1941; women; P.; †

Mercyhurst C., Erie, Pa.; 1926; women; P.; †

Meredith C., Raleigh, N.C.; 1899; women; P.; †

Merrimack C., Andover, Mass.; 1947; men; P.; †

***Miami U.,** Oxford, O.; 1809; coed.; S.; ‡

***Miami, U. of,** Coral Gables, Fla.; 1926; coed.; P.; ‡ #

Michigan C. of Mining and Technology, Houghton & Sault Ste. Marie, Mich.; 1885; coed.; S.; ‡

***Michigan State U.,** East Lansing, Mich.; 1857; coed.; S.; ‡ #

***Michigan, U. of,** Ann Arbor, Mich.; 1817; coed.; S.; ‡ #

Middlebury C., Middlebury, Vt.; 1800; coed.; P.; ‡

Middle Tennessee State C., Murfreesboro, Tenn.; 1911; coed.; S.; ‡

Midland C., Fremont, Neb.; 1887; coed.; P.; †

Midwestern U., Wichita Falls, Tex.; 1922; coed.; Mun.; ‡

Miles C., Birmingham, Ala.; 1907; coed.; P.; †

Milligan C., Milligan College, Tenn.; 1882; coed.; P.; †

Millikin U., Decatur, Ill.; 1901; coed.; P.; ‡

Millsaps C., Jackson, Miss.; 1892; coed.; P.; †

Mills College, Oakland, Calif.; 1852; women; P.; ‡

Milton C., Milton, Wis.; 1844; coed.; P.; †

Milwaukee-Downer C., Milwaukee, Wis.; 1851; women; P.; †

Milwaukee School of Engineering, Milwaukee, Wis.; 1903; men; P.; †

***Minnesota, U. of,** Minneapolis, St. Paul & Duluth, Minn.; 1851; coed.; S.; ‡ #

Misericordia, C., Dallas, Pa.; 1923; women; P.; †

Mississippi C., Clinton, Miss.; 1826; coed.; P.; ‡

Mississippi Industrial C., Holly Springs, Miss.; 1905; coed.; P.; †

Mississippi Southern C., Hattiesburg, Miss.; 1912; coed.; S.; ‡

***Mississippi State C.,** State College, Miss.; 1878; coed.; S.; ‡

Mississippi State C. for Women, Columbus, Miss.; 1884; women; S.; †

Mississippi, U. of, University, Miss.; 1848; coed.; S.; ‡ #

Missouri School of Mines and Metallurgy, Rolla, Mo.; 1870; part of U. of Missouri; ‡ #

***Missouri, U. of,** Columbia, Mo.; 1839; coed.; S.; ‡ #

Missouri Valley C., Marshall, Mo.; 1888; coed.; P.; †

Monmouth C., Monmouth, Ill.; 1853; coed.; P.; †

Montana School of Mines, Butte, Mont.; 1893; men; S.; ‡

Montana State C., Bozeman, Mont.; 1893; coed.; S.; ‡

Montana State U., Missoula, Mont.; 1893; coed.; S.; ‡ #

Montclair State C., Upper Montclair, N.J.; 1908; coed.; S.; ‡

Moorhead State C., Moorhead, Minn.; 1887; coed.; S.; ‡

Moravian C., Bethlehem, Pa.; 1807; coed.; P.; † #

Morehead State C., Morehead, Ky.; 1923; coed.; S.; ‡

Morehouse C., Atlanta, Ga.; 1867; men; P.; † #

Morgan State C., Baltimore, Md.; 1867; coed.; S.; †

Morningside C., Sioux City, Ia.; 1894; coed.; P.; †

Morris Brown C., Atlanta, Ga.; 1881; coed.; P.; †

Morris Harvey C., Charleston, W. Va.; 1888; coed.; P.; †

Mt. Angel Seminary, St. Benedict, Oreg.; 1889; men; P.; †

Mt. Angel Women's C., Mt. Angel, Oreg.; 1887; women; P.; †

Mt. Holyoke C., South Hadley, Mass.; 1837; women; P.; ‡

Mt. Mary C., Milwaukee, Wis.; 1913; women; P.; †

Mt. Mercy C., Pittsburgh, Pa.; 1929; women; P.; †

Mt. St. Agnes C., Baltimore, Md.; 1890; women; P.; †

Mt. St. Joseph-on-the-Ohio, C. of, Mount Saint Joseph, O.; 1920; women; P.; †

Mt. St. Joseph Teachers C., Buffalo, N.Y.; 1937; women; P.; ‡

Mt. St. Mary C., Hookset, N.H.; 1934; women; P.; †

Mt. St. Mary's C., Los Angeles, Calif.; 1925; women; P.; †

Mt. St. Mary's C., Emmitsburg, Md.; 1808; men; P.; †

Mt. St. Scholastica C., Atchison, Kan.; 1863; women; P.; †

Mt. St. Vincent, C. of, New York City, N.Y.; 1910; women; P.; †

Mt. Union C., Alliance, O.; 1846; coed.; P.; †

Muhlenberg C., Allentown, Pa.; 1848; men; P.; †

Multnomah School of the Bible, Portland, Oreg.; 1936; coed.; P.; † #

Mundelein C., Chicago, Ill.; 1930; women; P.; †

Murray State C., Murray, Ky.; 1923; coed.; S.; ‡

Muskingum C., New Concord, O.; 1837; coed.; P.; †

Nasson C., Springvale, Me.; 1912; coed.; P.; †

National C. of Education, Evanston, Ill.; 1886; coed.; P.; †

National U., Washington, D.C.; 1869; coed.; P.; ‡

Nazareth C., Louisville, Ky.; 1920; women; P.; ‡ #
Nazareth C., Nazareth, Mich.; 1897; women; P.; †
Nazareth C., Rochester, N.Y.; 1924; women; P.; ‡
Nebraska Central C., Central City, Neb.; 1899; coed.; P.; †
Nebraska State Teachers C., Chadron, Neb.; 1911; coed.; S.; †
Nebraska State Teachers C., Kearney, Neb.; 1905; coed.; S.; †
Nebraska State Teachers C., Peru, Neb.; 1867; coed.; S.; †
Nebraska State Teachers C., Wayne, Neb.; 1910; coed.; S.; †
*__Nebraska, U. of__, Lincoln, Neb.; 1869; coed.; S.; ‡ #
Nebraska Wesleyan U., Lincoln, Neb.; 1887; coed.; P.; †
Nevada, U. of, Reno, Nev.; 1874; coed.; S.; ‡
*__Newark C. of Engineering__, Newark, N.J.; 1881; men; S. & Mun.; ‡
Newark State C., Newark, N.J.; 1855; coed.; S.; ‡
Newberry C., Newberry, S.C.; 1856; coed.; P.; †
New Church, Academy of the, Bryn Athyn, Pa.; 1877; coed.; P.; †
New England C., Henniker, N.H.; 1946; coed.; P.; † #
New England Conservatory of Music, Boston, Mass.; 1865; coed.; P.; ‡
*__New Hampshire, U. of__, Durham, N.H.; 1866; coed.; S.; ‡
New Haven State Teachers C., New Haven, Conn.; 1893; coed.; S.; †
New Mexico Highlands U., Las Vegas, N. Mex.; 1893; coed.; S.; ‡
New Mexico Institute of Mining and Technology, Socorro, N.Mex.; 1889; coed.; S.; ‡
New Mexico State U. of Agriculture, Engineering, and Science, University Park, N. Mex.; 1889; coed.; S.; ‡
*__New Mexico, U. of__, Albuquerque, N. Mex.; 1889; coed.; S.; ‡ #
New Mexico Western C., Silver City, N.Mex.; 1893; coed.; S.; ‡
New Rochelle, C. of, New Rochelle, N.Y.; 1904; women; P.; †
New School for Social Research, New York City, N.Y.; 1918; coed.; P.; ‡
Newton C. of the Sacred Heart, Newton, Mass.; 1946; women; P.; †
*__New York, C. of the City of__, New York City, N.Y.; 1847; Mun.; the corporate title of
  *__Brooklyn C.__, Brooklyn; 1930; coed.; ‡
  *__City C.__, New York City; 1847; coed.; ‡
  *__Hunter C. of the City of New York__, New York City; 1870; coed.; ‡
  *__Queens C.__, Flushing; 1937; coed.; ‡
New York Law School, New York City, N.Y.; 1891; coed.; P.; #
New York Medical C., New York City, N.Y.; 1860; coed.; P.; † #
New York School of Social Work, New York City, N.Y.; 1898; coed.; part of Columbia U.; ↓ #
New York, State U. of, Albany, N.Y.; 1948; S.; comprised of 33 colleges, schools, and institutes including
  Harpur C., Endicott; 1946; coed.; †
  New York State Maritime Academy, Bronx; 1874; men; †
  New York State C. for Teachers, Albany; 1844; coed.; ‡
  New York State Teachers C., Brockport; 1867; coed.; ‡
  New York State Teachers C., Buffalo; 1867; coed.; ‡
  New York State Teachers C., Cortland; 1867; coed.; †
  New York State Teachers C., Fredonia; 1866; coed.; ‡
  New York State Teachers C., Geneseo; 1871; coed.; ‡
  New York State Teachers C., New Paltz; 1886; coed.; †
  New York State Teachers C., Oneonta; 1889; coed.; ‡
  New York State Teachers C., Oswego; 1861; coed.; ‡
  New York State Teachers C., Plattsburg; 1889; coed.; ‡
  New York State Teachers C., Potsdam; 1869; coed.; †
*__New York U.__, New York City, N.Y.; 1831; coed.; P.; ‡ #
Niagara U., Niagara University, N.Y.; 1856; coed.; P.; ‡
North Carolina C. at Durham, Durham, N.C.; 1910; coed.; S.; ‡ #
North Carolina State of the U. of North Carolina at Raleigh, Raleigh, N.C.; 1887; men; ‡
*__North Carolina, U. of__, Chapel Hill, N.C.; 1795; coed.; S.; ‡ #
North Carolina, Woman's C. of the U. of, Greensboro, N.C.; 1891; women; S.; ‡
North Central C., Naperville, Ill.; 1861; coed.; P.; †
North Dakota Agricultural C., Fargo, N.Dak.; 1889; coed.; S.; ‡
North Dakota, U. of, Grand Forks, N.Dak.; 1883; coed.; S.; ‡ #
Northeastern State C., Tahlequah, Okla.; 1909; coed.; S.; †
*__Northeastern U.__, Boston, Mass.; 1898; coed.; P.; ‡ #
Northeast Louisiana State C., Monroe, La.; 1950; coed.; S.; †
Northeast Missouri State Teachers C., Kirksville, Mo.; 1867; coed.; S.; ‡
Northern Baptist Theological Seminary, Chicago, Ill.; 1913; coed.; P.; ‡ #
Northern Illinois State Teachers C., De Kalb, Ill.; 1899; coed.; S.; ‡
Northern Michigan C., Marquette, Mich.; 1899; coed.; S.; †
Northern Montana C., Havre, Mont.; 1929; coed.; S.; †
Northern State Teachers C., Aberdeen, S.Dak.; 1901; coed.; S.; †
North Georgia C., Dahlonega, Ga.; 1873; coed.; S.; †
Northland C., Ashland, Wis.; 1892; coed.; P.; †
North Park C. and Theological Seminary, Chicago, Ill.; 1891; coed.; P.; †
*__North Texas State C.__, Denton, Tex.; 1899; coed.; S.; ‡
Northwestern C., Watertown, Wis.; 1865; men; P.; †
Northwestern State C., Natchitoches, La.; 1885; coed.; S.; †
Northwestern State C., Alva, Okla.; 1897; coed.; S.; †
*__Northwestern U.__, Evanston & Chicago, Ill.; 1851; coed.; P.; ‡ #
Northwest Missouri State C., Maryville, Mo.; 1905; coed.; S.; †
Northwest Nazarene C., Nampa, Ida.; 1913; coed.; P.; †
Norwich U., Northfield, Vt.; 1819; men; P.; †
Notre Dame C., St. Louis, Mo.; 1925; a women's college of St. Louis U.; †
Notre Dame C., Manchester, N.H.; 1950; coed.; P.; †
Notre Dame C., South Euclid, O.; 1922; women; P.; †
Notre Dame, C. of, Belmont, Calif.; 1868; women; P.; †
Notre Dame C. of Staten Island, Grymes Hill, N.Y.; 1931; women; P.; †
Notre Dame of Maryland, C. of, Baltimore, Md.; 1873; women; P.; †
Notre Dame Seminary, New Orleans, La.; 1923; men; P.; ‡
*__Notre Dame, U. of__, Notre Dame, Ind.; 1842; men; P.; ‡ #
Nyack Missionary C., Nyack, N.Y.; 1882; coed.; P.; † #

Oakland City C., Oakland City, Ind.; 1885; coed.; P.; †
Oakwood C., Huntsville, Ala.; 1896; coed.; P.; †
Oberlin C., Oberlin, O.; 1833; coed. P.; ‡
Occidental C., Los Angeles, Calif.; 1887; coed.; P.; ‡
Oglethorpe U., Oglethorpe University, Ga.; 1835; coed.; P.; †
Ohio Northern U., Ada, O.; 1871; coed.; P.; † #
*__Ohio State U.__, Columbus, O.; 1873; coed.; S.; ‡ #
*__Ohio U.__, Athens, O.; 1804; coed.; S.; ‡
Ohio Wesleyan U., Delaware, O.; 1842; coed.; P.; ‡
Oklahoma Baptist U., Shawnee, Okla.; 1911; coed.; P.; †
Oklahoma C. for Women, Chickasha, Okla.; 1908; women; S.; †
Oklahoma City U., Oklahoma City, Okla.; 1904; coed.; P.; ‡
*__Oklahoma State U.__, Stillwater, Okla.; 1891; coed.; S.; ‡
*__Oklahoma, U. of__, Norman, Okla.; 1892; coed.; S.; ‡ #
Olivet C., Olivet, Mich.; 1844; coed.; P.; †
Olivet Nazarene C., Kankakee, Ill.; 1909; coed.; P.; †
*__Omaha, Municipal U. of__, Omaha, Neb.; 1908; coed.; Mun.; ‡
Oregon C. of Education, Monmouth, Oreg.; 1856; coed.; S.; ‡
*__Oregon State U.__, Corvallis, Oreg.; 1868; coed.; S.; ‡
*__Oregon, U. of__, Eugene & Portland, Oreg.; 1876; coed.; S.; ‡ #
Osteopathic Physicians and Surgeons, C. of, Los Angeles, Calif.; 1914; coed.; P.; #
Ottawa U., Ottawa, Kan.; 1865; coed.; P.; †
Otterbein C., Westerville, O.; 1847; coed.; P.; †
Ouachita Baptist C., Arkadelphia, Ark.; 1886; coed.; P.; †
Our Lady of Cincinnati C., Cincinnati, O.; 1935; women; P.; †
Our Lady of the Elms, C. of, Chicopee, Mass.; 1928; women; P.; †
Our Lady of the Lake C., San Antonio, Tex.; 1896; women; P.; ‡ #
Owosso C., Owosso, Mich.; 1909; coed.; P.; †
Ozarks, C. of the, Clarksville, Ark.; 1834; coed.; P.; †

*__Pace C.__, New York City, N.Y.; 1906; coed.; P.; †
Pacific Bible C. of Azusa, Azusa, Calif.; 1899; coed.; P.; ‡
Pacific, C. of the, Stockton, Calif.; 1851; coed.; P.; ‡
Pacific Lutheran C., Parkland, Wash.; 1894; coed.; P.; ‡
Pacific School of Religion, Berkeley, Calif.; 1866; coed.; P.; †#
Pacific U., Forest Grove, Oreg.; 1849; coed.; P.; ‡
Pacific Union C., Angwin, Calif.; 1882; coed.; P.; ‡
Paine C., Augusta, Ga.; 1883; coed.; P.; †
Pan American C., Edinburg, Tex.; 1952; coed.; S. & Co.; †
Pan Handle Agricultural and Mechanical C., Goodwell, Okla.; 1909; coed.; S.; †
Park C., Parkville, Mo.; 1879; coed.; P.; †
Parsons C., Fairfield, Ia.; 1875; coed.; P.; †
Pasadena C., Pasadena, Calif.; 1902; coed.; P.; ‡
Paterson State C., Wayne, N.J.; 1855; coed.; S.; †
Peabody Institute of the City of Baltimore, Baltimore, Md.; 1857; coed.; P.; ‡
Pembroke C., Providence, R.I.; 1891; women's college of Brown U.; †
Pembroke State C., Pembroke, N.C.; 1887; coed.; S.; †
Pennsylvania Military C., Chester, Pa.; 1821; men; P.; †
Pennsylvania State C. of Optometry, Philadelphia, Pa.; 1919; coed.; P.; #
*__Pennsylvania State U.__, University Park, Pa.; 1855; coed.; S.; ‡ #
*__Pennsylvania, U. of__, Philadelphia, Pa.; 1740; coed.; P.; ‡ #
Pestalozzi Froebel Teachers C., Chicago, Ill.; 1896; coed.; P.; †
Pfeiffer C., Misenheimer, N.C.; 1935; coed.; P.; †
Philadelphia C. of Osteopathy, Philadelphia, Pa.; 1899; coed.; P.; #
Philadelphia C. of Pharmacy and Science, Philadelphia, Pa.; 1821; coed.; P.; ‡ #
Philadelphia Textile Institute, Philadelphia, Pa.; 1884; coed.; P.; †
Philander Smith C., Little Rock, Ark.; 1868; coed.; P.; †
Phillips U., Enid, Okla.; 1907; coed.; P.; ‡
Physicians and Surgeons of San Francisco, C. of, San Francisco, Calif.; 1896; coed.; P.; #
Piedmont C., Demorest, Ga.; 1897; coed.; P.; †
Pikeville C., Pikeville, Ky.; 1889; coed.; P.; †
*__Pittsburgh, U. of__, Pittsburgh, Pa.; 1787; coed.; P.; ‡ #
Plymouth Teachers C., Plymouth, N.H.; 1871; coed.; S.; ‡
Pomona C., Claremont, Calif.; 1887; coed.; P.; †
Portia Law School and Calvin Coolidge C. of Liberal Arts, Boston, Mass.; 1908; coed.; P.; ‡

C., College; U., University; J.C., Junior College; P., Private; S., State; Mun., Municipal; Ter., Territorial; Fed., Federal; Dist., District; Co., County; † undergraduate; ‡ undergraduate & graduate; ↓ graduate; # professional; * enrollment of 3,000 or more.

***Portland State C.**, Portland, Oreg.; 1955; coed.; S.; †
Portland U., Portland, Me.; 1921; coed.; P.; † #
Portland, U. of, Portland, Oreg.; 1901; coed.; P.; ‡
Prairie View Agricultural and Mechanical C. of Texas, Prairie View, Tex.; 1876; coed.; part of Agricultural and Mechanical C. of Texas; ‡
Pratt Institute, Brooklyn, N.Y.; 1887; coed.; P.; ‡ #
Presbyterian C., Clinton, S.C.; 1880; coed.; P.; †
Princeton Theological Seminary, Princeton, N.J.; 1812; men; P.; ‡ #
***Princeton U.**, Princeton, N.J.; 1746; men; P.; ‡
Principia C., Elsah, Ill.; 1910; coed.; P.; †
Providence C., Providence, R.I.; 1917; men; P.; †
***Puerto Rico, U. of**, Rio Piedras, Mayaguez & San Juan, P.R.; 1903; coed.; Ter.; ‡ #
Puget Sound, U. of, Tacoma, Wash.; 1888; coed.; P.; ‡
***Purdue U.**, Lafayette, Ind.; 1869; coed.; S.; ‡ #

Queens C., see **New York, C. of the City of.**
Queens C., Charlotte, N.C.; 1857; women; P.; †
Quincy C., Quincy, Ill.; 1860; coed.; P.; †
Quinnipiac C., Hamden, Conn.; 1929; coed.; P.; †

Radcliffe C., Cambridge, Mass.; 1879; women's college of Harvard U.; ‡
Radford C., Radford, Va.; 1913; women's college of Virginia Polytechnic Institute; †
Randolph-Macon C., Ashland, Va.; 1830; men; P.; †
Randolph-Macon Woman's C., Lynchburg, Va.; 1891; women; P.; †
Redlands, U. of, Redlands, Calif.; 1909; coed.; P.; ‡
Reed C., Portland, Oreg.; 1911; coed.; P.; ‡
Regis C., Denver, Colo.; 1887; men; P.; †
Regis C. for Women, Weston, Mass.; 1927; women; P.; †
***Rensselaer Polytechnic Institute**, Troy, N.Y.; 1824; men; P.; ‡
Rhode Island C., Providence, R.I.; 1854; coed.; S.; ‡
Rhode Island School of Design, Providence, R.I.; 1877, coed.; P.; †
Rhode Island, U. of, Kingston, R.I.; 1892; coed.; S.; ‡
Rice U., Houston, Tex.; 1912; coed.; P.; ‡
Richmond, U. of, Richmond, Va.; 1832; coed.; P.; ‡ #
Ricker C., Houlton, Me.; 1926; coed.; P.; †
Ricks C., Rexburg, Ida.; 1888; coed.; P.; †
Rider C., Trenton, N.J.; 1865; coed.; P.; †
Rio Grande C., Rio Grande, O.; 1876: coed.; P.; †
Ripon C., Ripon, Wis.; 1851; coed.; P.; †
Rivier C., Nashua, N.H.; 1933; women; P.; ‡
Roanoke C., Salem, Va.; 1842; coed.; P.; †
Roberts Wesleyan C., North Chili, N.Y.; 1866; coed.; P.; †
***Rochester Institute of Technology**, Rochester, N.Y.; 1829; coed.; P.; †
***Rochester, U. of**, Rochester, N.Y.; 1850; coed.; P.; ‡ #
Rockford C., Rockford, Ill.; 1847; coed.; P.; ‡
Rockhurst C., Kansas City, Mo.; 1910; men; P.; †
Rocky Mountain C., Billings, Mont.; 1883; coed.; P.; †
Rollins C., Winter Park, Fla.; 1885; coed.; P.; †
***Roosevelt U.**, Chicago, Ill.; 1945; coed.; P.; ‡
Rosary C., River Forest, Ill.; 1901; women; P.; ‡
Rosary Hill C., Buffalo, N.Y.; 1948; women; P.; †
Rosemont C., Rosemont, Pa.; 1921; women; P.; †
Rose Polytechnic Institute, Terre Haute, Ind.; 1874; men; P.; ‡
Russell Sage C., Troy, N.Y.; 1916; women; P.; ‡
Rust C., Holly Springs, Miss.; 1866; coed.; P.; †
***Rutgers U.**, New Brunswick, N.J.; 1766; coed.; S.; ‡
***Rutgers U., Newark Colleges of**, Newark, N.J.; 1908; coed.; part of Rutgers U.; ‡ #

***Sacramento State C.**, Sacramento, Calif.; 1947; coed.; S.; ‡
Sacred Heart C., Wichita, Kan.; 1933; women; P.; †
Sacred Heart, C. of the, Santurce, P.R.; 1881; women; P.; †
Salem C., Winston-Salem, N.C.; 1772; women; P.; †
Salem C., Salem, W. Va.; 1888; coed.; P.; †
Salmon P. Chase C., Cincinnati, O.; 1885; coed.; P.; † #
Salve Regina C., Newport, R.I.; 1934; women; P.; †
Sam Houston State Teachers C., Huntsville, Tex.; 1879; coed.; S.; ‡
***San Diego State C.**, San Diego, Calif.; 1897; coed.; S.; ‡
San Diego, U. of, San Diego, Calif.; 1949; coed.; P.; ‡
San Francisco C. for Women, San Francisco, Calif.; 1921; women; P.; ‡
***San Francisco State C.**, San Francisco, Calif.; 1899; coed.; S.; ‡
San Francisco Theological Seminary, San Anselmo, Calif.; 1871; coed.; P.; ↓ #
San Francisco, U. of, San Francisco, Calif.; 1855; men; P.; ‡
***San Jose State C.**, San Jose, Calif.; 1862; coed.; S.; ‡
Santa Clara, U. of, Santa Clara, Calif.; 1851; men; P.; †
Sarah Lawrence C., Bronxville, N.Y.; 1928; women; P.; †
Savannah State C., State College Branch, Ga.; 1890; coed.; S.; †
Scarritt C. for Christian Workers, Nashville, Tenn.; 1924; coed.; P.; ‡
Scranton, U. of, Scranton, Pa.; 1888; men; P.; † #
Scripps C., Claremont, Calif.; 1926; women; P.; †
Seattle Pacific C., Seattle, Wash.; 1891; coed.; P.; ‡
Seattle U. Seattle, Wash.; 1891; coed.; P.; ‡
***Seton Hall C.**, South Orange, Newark & Jersey City, N.J.; 1856; coed.; P.; ‡ #
Seton Hill C., Greensburg, Pa.; 1883; women; P.; †
Shaw U., Raleigh, N.C.; 1865; coed.; P.; †
Shepherd C., Shepherdstown, W.Va.; 1872; coed.; S.; †
Sherwood Music School, Chicago, Ill.; 1895; coed.; P.; ‡
Shimer C., Mount Carroll, Ill.; 1853; coed.; P.; †
Shorter C., Rome, Ga.; 1873; women; P.; †
Siena Heights C., Adrian, Mich.; 1919; women; P.; †
Simmons C., Boston, Mass.; 1899; women; P.; ‡ #
Simpson C., Indianola, Ia.; 1860; coed.; P.; †
Sioux Falls C., Sioux Falls, S.Dak.; 1883; coed.; P.; †
Skidmore C., Saratoga Springs, N.Y.; 1922; women; P.; †
Smith C., Northampton, Mass.; 1871; women; P.; ‡ #
South Carolina State C., Orangeburg, S.C.; 1896; coed.; S.; ‡
***South Carolina, U. of**, Columbia, S.C.; 1801; coed.; S.; ‡ #
South Dakota School of Mines and Technology, Rapid City, S.Dak.; 1876; coed; S.; ‡
South Dakota State C. of Agriculture and Mechanic Arts, Brookings, S.Dak.; 1881; coed.; S.; ‡
South Dakota, U. of, Vermillion, S.Dak.; 1882; coed.; S.; ‡
South-Eastern Bible C., Lakeland, Fla.; 1935; coed.; P.; †
Southeastern Louisiana C., Hammond, La.; 1925; coed.; S.; †
Southeastern State C., Durant, Okla.; 1909; coed.; S.; †
Southeastern U., Washington, D.C.; 1907; coed.; P.; ‡
Southeast Missouri State C., Cape Girardeau, Mo.; 1873; coed.; S.; †
Southern Baptist Theological Seminary, Louisville, Ky.; 1859; coed.; P.; ↓ #
Southern California Bible C., Costa Mesa, Calif.; 1920; coed.; P.; † #
***Southern California, U. of**, Los Angeles, Calif.; 1880; coed.; P.; ‡ #
Southern C. of Optometry, Memphis, Tenn.; 1932; coed.; P.; #
***Southern Illinois U.**, Carbondale, Ill.; 1869; coed.; S.; ‡
***Southern Methodist U.**, Dallas, Tex.; 1916; coed.; P.; ‡ #
Southern Missionary C., Collegedale, Tenn.; 1893; coed.; P.; †
Southern Oregon C. of Education, Ashland, Oreg.; 1926; coed.; S.; ‡
Southern State C., Magnolia, Ark.; 1909; coed.; S.; †
Southern State Teachers C., Springfield, S.Dak.; 1897; coed.; S.; †
Southern U. and Agricultural and Mechanical C., Baton Rouge, La.; 1880; coed.; S.; †
Southern Utah, C. of, Cedar City, Ut.; 1897; coed.; branch of Utah State U.; †
South Jersey, C. of, Camden, N.J.; 1926; coed.; part of Rutgers U.; † #
South Texas C., Houston, Tex.; 1923; coed.; P.; #
South, U. of the, Sewanee, Tenn.; 1857; men; P.; ‡ #
Southwestern at Memphis, Memphis, Tenn.; 1848; coed.; P.; †
Southwestern Bible Institute, Waxahachie, Tex.; 1927; coed.; P.; †
Southwestern C., Winfield, Kan.; 1885; coed.; P.; †
Southwestern Louisiana, U. of, Lafayette, La.; 1898; coed.; S.; †
Southwestern State C., Weatherford, Okla.; 1901; coed.; S.; †
Southwestern U., Georgetown, Tex.; 1840; coed.; P.; ‡
Southwest Missouri State C., Springfield, Mo.; 1906; coed.; S.; †
Southwest Texas State Teachers C., San Marcos, Tex.; 1899; coed.; S.; ‡
Spelman C., Atlanta, Ga.; 1881; women; P.; †
Springfield C., Springfield, Mass.; 1885; men; P.; ‡
Spring Hill C., Spring Hill, Ala.; 1830; coed.; P.; †
St. Ambrose C., Davenport, Ia.; 1881; men; P.; †
St. Anselm's C., Manchester, N.H.; 1889; men; P.; †
St. Augustine's C., Raleigh, N.C.; 1867; coed.; P.; †
St. Benedict, C. of, St. Joseph, Minn.; 1913; women; P.; †
St. Benedict's C., Atchison, Kan.; 1859; men; P.; †
St. Bernard C., St. Bernard, Ala.; 1892; men; P.; †
St. Bernardine of Siena C., Loudonville, N.Y.; 1937; men; P.; ‡
St. Bonaventure C., St. Bonaventure, N.Y.; 1856; men; P.; ‡
St. Catherine, C. of, St. Paul, Minn.; 1905; women; P.; ‡
St. Cloud State C., St. Cloud, Minn.; 1869; coed.; S.; ‡
St. Edward's Seminary, Kenmore, Wash.; 1931; men; P.; †
St. Edward's U., Austin, Tex.; 1876; men; P.; †
St. Elizabeth, C. of, Convent Station, N.J.; 1899; women; P.; †
St. Francis C., Brooklyn, N.Y.; 1884; men; P.; †
St. Francis C., Loretto, Pa.; 1847; coed.; P.; †
St. Francis, C. of, Joliet, Ill.; 1925; women; P.; †
St. John C. of Cleveland, Cleveland, O.; 1928; women; P.; ‡
St. John Fisher C., Rochester, N.Y.; 1947; men; P.; †
St. John's C., Camarillo & Los Angeles, Calif.; 1939; men; P.; †
St. John's C., Annapolis, Md.; 1696; coed.; P.; ‡
St. John's U., Collegeville, Minn.; 1857; men; P.; †
***St. John's U.**, Brooklyn, N.Y.; 1870; men; P.; ‡
St. Joseph C., West Hartford, Conn.; 1932; women; P.; †
St. Joseph on the Rio Grande, C. of, Albuquerque, N. Mex.; 1940; coed.; P.; †
St. Joseph's C., Rensselaer, Ind.; 1889; men; P.; †
St. Joseph's C., North Windham, Me.; 1915; women; P.; †
St. Joseph's C., Emmitsburg, Md.; 1809; women; P.; †
St. Joseph's C., Philadelphia, Pa.; 1851; men; P.; †
St. Joseph's C. for Women, Brooklyn, N.Y.; 1916; women; P.; †
St. Lawrence U., Canton, N.Y.; 1856; coed.; P.; ‡ #
St. Louis C. of Pharmacy and Allied Sciences, St. Louis, Mo.; 1864; coed.; P.; † #
***St. Louis U.**, St. Louis, Mo.; 1818; coed.; P.; ‡ #
St. Martin's C., Olympia, Wash.; 1895; men; P.; †
St. Mary C., Xavier, Kan.; 1923; women; P.; ‡
St. Mary, C. of, Omaha, Neb.; 1923; women; P.; †
St. Mary of the Springs, C. of, Columbus, O.; 1911; women; P.; †
St. Mary-of-the-Wasatch, Salt Lake City, Ut.; 1926; women; P.; †

St. Mary-of-the-Woods C., Saint Mary-of-the-Woods, Ind.; 1840; women; P.; †
St. Mary's C., Notre Dame, Ind.; 1844; women; P.; ‡
St. Mary's C., Orchard Lake, Mich.; 1885; men; P.; †
St. Mary's C., Winona, Minn.; 1912; men; P.; †
St. Mary's C. of California, St. Mary's College, Calif.; 1863; men; P.; †
St. Mary's Dominican C., New Orleans, La.; 1910; women; P.; †
St. Mary's Seminary and U., Baltimore, Md.; 1791; men; P.; ‡ #
St. Mary's U. of San Antonio, San Antonio, Tex.; 1852; men; P.; † #
St. Michael's C., Santa Fe, N. Mex.; 1947; men; P.; †
St. Michael's C., Winooski Park, Vt.; 1904; men; P.; ‡
St. Norbert C., West De Pere, Wis.; 1898; coed.; P.; †
St. Olaf C., Northfield, Minn.; 1874; coed.; P.; †
St. Patrick's Seminary, Menlo Park, Calif.; 1898; men; P.; †
St. Paul Bible Institute, St. Paul, Minn.; 1916; coed.; P.; ‡
St. Paul Seminary, St. Paul, Minn.; 1885; men; P.; ‡
St. Paul's Polytechnic Institute, Lawrenceville, Va.; 1888; coed.; P.; †
St. Peter's C., Jersey City, N.J.; 1872; men; P.; †
St. Procopius C., Lisle, Ill., 1887; men; P.; †
St. Rose, C. of, Albany, N.Y.; 1920; women; P.; ‡
St. Scholastica, C. of, Duluth, Minn.; 1912; women; P.; †
St. Teresa, C. of, Winona, Minn.; 1909; women; P.; †
St. Teresa, C. of, Kansas City, Mo.; 1917; women; P.; †
St. Thomas, C. of, St. Paul, Minn.; 1885; men; P.; ‡
St. Thomas, U. of, Houston, Tex.; 1947; coed.; P.; †
St. Vincent C., Latrobe, Pa.; 1846; men; P.; †
St. Xavier C., Chicago, Ill.; 1847; women; P.; †
Staley C. of the Spoken Word, Brookline, Mass.; 1900; coed.; P.; ‡
*__Stanford U.__, Stanford, Calif.; 1885; coed.; P.; ‡ #
State Normal and Industrial C., Ellendale, N.Dak.; 1899; coed.; S.; †
State Teachers C., Jacksonville, Ala.; 1883; coed.; S.; †
State Teachers C., Livingston, Ala.; 1840; coed.; S.; †
State Teachers C., Troy, Ala.; 1877; coed.; S.; †
State Teachers C., Bridgewater, Mass.; 1840; coed.; S.; ‡
State Teachers C., Fitchburg, Mass.; 1895; coed.; S.; ‡
State Teachers C., Framingham Center, Mass.; 1839; women; S.; †
State Teachers C., Lowell, Mass.; 1894; coed.; S.; †
State Teachers C., North Adams, Mass.; 1894; coed.; S.; ‡
State Teachers C., Salem, Mass.; 1854; coed.; S.; †
State Teachers C., Westfield, Mass.; 1839; coed.; S.; †
State Teachers C., Worcester, Mass.; 1871; coed.; S.; ‡
State Teachers C., Dickinson, N.Dak.; 1918; coed.; S.; †
State Teachers C., Mayville, N.Dak.; 1889; coed.; S.; †
State Teachers C., Minot, N.Dak.; 1913; coed.; S.; †
State Teachers C., Valley City, N.Dak.; 1889; coed.; S.; †
State Teachers C., Bloomsburg, Pa.; 1839; coed.; S.; †
State Teachers C., California, Pa.; 1852; coed.; S.; †
State Teachers C., Cheyney, Pa.; 1837; coed.; S.; †
State Teachers C., Clarion, Pa.; 1867; coed.; S.; †
State Teachers C., East Stroudsburg, Pa.; 1893; coed.; S.; †
State Teachers C., Edinboro, Pa.; 1861; coed.; S.; †
State Teachers C., Indiana, Pa.; 1875; coed.; S.; †
State Teachers C., Kutztown, Pa.; 1866; coed.; S.; †
State Teachers C., Lock Haven, Pa.; 1870; coed.; S.; †
State Teachers C., Mansfield, Pa.; 1857; coed.; S.; †
State Teachers C., Millersville, Pa.; 1855; coed.; S.; †
State Teachers C., Shippensburg, Pa.; 1873; coed.; S.; †
State Teachers C., Slippery Rock, Pa.; 1889; coed.; S.; †
State Teachers C., West Chester, Pa.; 1871; coed.; S.; †
State Teachers C. at Boston, Boston, Mass.; 1852; coed.; S.; ‡
Stephen F. Austin State C., Nacogdoches, Tex.; 1923; coed.; S.; ‡
Sterling C., Sterling, Kan.; 1887; coed.; P.; †
Stetson U., De Land, Fla.; 1883; coed.; P.; ‡ #
Stevens Institute of Technology, Hoboken, N.J.; 1870; men; P.; ‡
Stillman C., Tuscaloosa, Ala.; 1876; coed.; P.; †
Stonehill C., North Easton, Mass.; 1948; coed.; P.; †
Stout State C., Menomonie, Wis.; 1903; coed.; S.; ‡
Stowe Teachers C., St. Louis, Mo.; 1890; coed.; Mun.; †
Suffolk U., Boston, Mass.; 1906; coed.; P.; ‡ #
Sul Ross State C., Alpine, Tex.; 1920; coed.; S.; ‡
Susquehanna U., Selingsgrove, Pa.; 1858; coed.; P.; †
Swarthmore C., Swarthmore, Pa.; 1864; coed.; P.; ‡
Sweet Briar C., Sweet Briar, Va.; 1901; women; P.; †
*__Syracuse U.__, Syracuse & Utica, N.Y.; 1870; coed.; P.; ‡ #

Talladega C., Talladega, Ala.; 1867; coed.; P.; †
Tampa, U. of, Tampa, Fla.; 1931; coed.; P.; †
Tarkio C., Tarkio, Mo.; 1883; coed.; P.; †
Taylor U., Upland, Ind.; 1846; coed.; P.; †
Teachers C., New York City, N.Y.; 1888; coed.; part of Columbia U.; ‡
*__Temple U.__, Philadelphia, Pa.; 1884; coed.; P.; ‡ #
Tennessee Agricultural and Industrial State U., Nashville, Tenn.; 1912; coed.; S.; ‡
Tennessee Polytechnic Institute, Cookeville, Tenn.; 1915; coed.; S.; †
*__Tennessee, U. of__, Knoxville & Memphis, Tenn.; 1794; coed.; S.; ‡ #
Tennessee Wesleyan C., Athens, Tenn.; 1857; coed.; P.; †
Texas C., Tyler, Tex.; 1895; coed.; P.; †
*__Texas Christian U.__, Fort Worth, Tex.; 1873; coed.; P.; ‡ #
Texas C. of Arts and Industries, Kingsville, Tex.; 1925; coed.; S.; ‡
Texas Lutheran C., Seguin, Tex.; 1891; coed.; P.; †
*__Texas Southern U.__, Houston, Tex.; 1947; coed.; S.; ‡
*__Texas Woman's U.__, Denton, Tex.; 1903; women; S.; ‡ #
*__Texas Technological C.__, Lubbock, Tex.; 1923; coed.; S.; ‡
*__Texas, U. of__, Austin, El Paso, Galveston & Houston, Tex.; 1881; coed.; S.; ‡ #
Texas Wesleyan C., Fort Worth, Tex.; 1891; coed.; P.; ‡
*__Texas Western C.__, El Paso, Tex.; 1913; coed.; part of U. of Texas; ‡
Thiel C., Greenville, Pa.; 1870; coed.; P.; †
Tift C., Forsyth, Ga.; 1849; women; P.; †
*__Toledo, U. of__, Toledo, O.; 1872; coed.; Mun.; ‡ #
Tougaloo C., Tougaloo, Miss.; 1869; coed.; P.; †
Transylvania C., Lexington, Ky.; 1780; coed.; P.; †
Trenton State C., Trenton, N.J.; 1855; coed.; S.; ‡
Trinity C., Hartford, Conn.; 1823; men; P.; ‡
Trinity C., Washington, D.C.; 1897; women; P.; †
Trinity C., Burlington, Vt.; 1925; women; P.; †
Trinity U., San Antonio, Tex.; 1869; coed.; P.; ‡
Tri-State C., Angola, Ind.; 1884; coed.; P.; †
*__Tufts U.__, Medford, Mass.; 1852; coed.; P.; ‡ #
*__Tulane U. of Louisiana__, New Orleans, La.; 1834; coed.; P.; ‡ #
Tulsa, U. of, Tulsa, Okla.; 1894; coed.; P.; ‡
Tusculum C., Greeneville, Tenn.; 1794; coed.; P.; †
Tuskegee Institute, Tuskegee Institute, Ala.; 1881; coed.; P.; ‡

Union C., Barbourville, Ky.; 1879; coed.; P.; †
Union C., Lincoln, Neb.; 1891; coed.; P.; †
Union Theological Seminary in New York, New York City, N.Y.; 1836; coed.; P.; ↓ #
Union Theological Seminary in Virginia, Richmond, Va.; 1812; coed.; P.; ‡ #
Union U., Schenectady & Albany, N.Y.; 1795; coed.; P.; ‡ #
Union U., Jackson, Tenn.; 1834; coed.; P.; †
United States Air Force Academy, Colorado Springs, Colo.; 1954; men.; Fed.; †
United States Coast Guard Academy, New London, Conn.; 1876; men; Fed.; †
United States Merchant Marine Academy, Kings Point, N.Y.; 1942; men; Fed.; †
United States Military Academy, West Point, N.Y.; 1802; men; Fed.; †
*__United States Naval Academy__, Annapolis, Md.; 1845; men; Fed.; †
United States Naval Postgraduate School, Monterey, Calif.; 1909; men; Fed.; ↓
United Theological Seminary, Dayton, O.; 1871; coed.; P.; †
Upper Iowa U., Fayette, Ia.; 1857; coed.; P.; †
Upsala C., East Orange, N.J.; 1893; coed.; P.; †
Ursinus C., Collegeville, Pa.; 1869; coed.; P.; ‡
Ursuline C., Louisville, Ky.; 1938; women; P.; †
Ursuline C. for Women, Cleveland, O.; 1871; women; P.; †
*__Utah State U.__, Logan & Cedar City, Ut.; 1888; coed.; S.; †
*__Utah, U. of__, Salt Lake City, Ut.; 1850; coed.; S.; ‡ #

Valdosta State C., Valdosta, Ga.; 1906; coed.; S.; †
Valparaiso U., Valparaiso, Ind.; 1859; coed.; P.; †
*__Vanderbilt U.__, Nashville, Tenn.; 1873; coed.; P.; ‡ #
Vassar C., Poughkeepsie, N.Y.; 1861; women; P.; ‡
*__Vermont, U. of, and State Agricultural C.__, Burlington, Vt.; 1791; coed.; S. & P.; ‡ #
Villa Madonna C., Covington, Ky.; 1921; coed.; P.; †
Villa Maria C., Erie, Pa.; 1925; women; P.; †
Villanova U., Villanova, Pa.; 1842; men; P.; †
Virginia, Medical C. of, Richmond, Va.; 1838; coed.; S.; ‡ #
Virginia Military Institute, Lexington, Va.; 1839; men; S.; †
*__Virginia Polytechnic Institute__, Blacksburg & Radford, Va.; 1872; coed.; S.; ‡
*__Virginia State C.__, Petersburg, Va.; 1882; coed.; S.; ‡
Virginia Theological Seminary and C., Lynchburg, Va.; 1887; coed.; P.; †
Virginia Union U., Richmond, Va.; 1899; coed.; P.; † #
*__Virginia, U. of__, Charlottesville, Va.; 1819; men; S.; ‡ #
Viterbo C., La Crosse, Wis.; 1931; women; P.; †

Wabash C., Crawfordsville, Ind.; 1832; men; P.; †
Wagner C., Grymes Hill, N.Y.; 1883; coed.; P.; ‡
Wake Forest C., Winston-Salem, N.C.; 1834; coed.; P.; ‡ #
Walla Walla C., College Place, Wash.; 1892; coed.; P.; ‡
Wartburg C., Waverly, Ia.; 1852; coed.; P.; †
Washburn U. of Topeka, Topeka, Kan.; 1865; coed.; Mun.; † #
Washington and Jefferson C., Washington, Pa.; 1781; men; P.; ‡
Washington and Lee U., Lexington, Va.; 1749; men; P.; † #
Washington C., Chestertown, Md.; 1782; coed.; P.; †
Washington Missionary C., Takoma Park, D.C.; 1904; coed.; P.; †
*__Washington, State C. of__, Pullman, Wash.; 1892; coed.; S.; ‡ #
Washington State Teachers C., Machias, Me.; 1909; coed.; S.; †
*__Washington U.__, St. Louis, Mo.; 1853; coed.; P.; ‡ #
*__Washington, U. of__, Seattle, Wash.; 1861; coed.; S.; ‡ #
Wayland Baptist C., Plainview, Tex.; 1908; coed.; P.; †
Waynesburg C., Waynesburg, Pa.; 1850; coed.; P.; †
*__Wayne State U.__, Detroit, Mich.; 1933; coed.; S.; ‡ #

C., College; U., University; J.C., Junior College; P., Private; S., State; Mun., Municipal; Ter., Territorial; Fed., Federal; Dist., District; Co., County; † undergraduate; ‡ undergraduate & graduate; ↓ graduate; # professional; * enrollment of 3,000 or more.

Webb Institute of Naval Architecture, Glen Cove, N.Y.; 1889; men; P.; ‡
Webster C., Webster Groves, Mo.; 1915; a women's college of St. Louis U.; †
Wellesley C., Wellesley, Mass.; 1870; women; P.; ‡
Wells C., Aurora, N.Y.; 1868; women; P.; ‡
Wesleyan C., Macon, Ga.; 1836; women; P.; †
Wesleyan U., Middletown, Conn.; 1831; men; P.; ‡
Western Carolina C., Cullowhee, N.C.; 1889; coed.; S.; ‡
Western C. for Women, Oxford, O.; 1853; women; P.; †
Western Illinois State C., Macomb, Ill.; 1899; coed.; S.; ‡
Western Kentucky State C., Bowling Green, Ky.; 1906; coed.; S.; ‡
Western Maryland C., Westminster, Md.; 1867; coed.; P.; ‡
***Western Michigan C.,** Kalamazoo, Mich.; 1903; coed.; S.; ‡
Western Montana C. of Education, Dillon, Mont.; 1897; coed.; S.; †
Western New England C., Springfield, Mass.; 1919; coed.; P.; † #
***Western Reserve U.,** Cleveland, O.; 1826; coed.; P.; ‡ #
Western State C. of Colorado, Gunnison, Colo.; 1901; coed.; S.; ‡
Western Washington C. of Education, Bellingham, Wash.; 1899; coed.; S.; ‡
Westhampton C., Richmond, Va.; 1914; women's college of U. of Richmond; †
West Liberty State C., West Liberty, W.Va.; 1838; coed.; S.; †
Westmar C., Le Mars, Ia.; 1900; coed.; P.; †
Westminster C., Fulton, Mo.; 1851; men; P.; †
Westminster C., New Wilmington, Pa.; 1852; coed.; P.; ‡
Westminster C., Salt Lake City, Ut.; 1875; coed.; P.; †
Westminster Choir C., Princeton, N.J.; 1926; coed.; P.; ‡
Westmont C., Santa Barbara, Calif.; 1940; coed.; P.; †
West Texas State C., Canyon, Tex.; 1910; coed.; S.; ‡
West Virginia Institute of Technology, Montgomery, W.Va.; 1895; coed.; S.; †
West Virginia State C., Institute, W.Va.; 1891; coed.; S.; †
***West Virginia U.,** Morgantown, W.Va.; 1867; coed.; S.; ‡ #
West Virginia Wesleyan C., Buckhannon, W.Va.; 1890; coed.; P.; †
Wheaton C., Wheaton, Ill.; 1860; coed.; P.; ‡ #
Wheaton C., Norton, Mass.; 1834; women; P.; †
Wheeling C., Wheeling, W.Va.; 1954; coed.; P.; †
Wheelock C., Boston, Mass.; 1889; women; P.; ‡
Whitman C., Walla Walla, Wash.; 1859; coed.; P.; †
Whittier C., Whittier, Calif.; 1901; coed.; P.; ‡
Whitworth C., Spokane, Wash.; 1890; coed.; P.; ‡
***Wichita, U. of,** Wichita, Kan.; 1895; coed.; Mun.; ‡
Wilberforce U., Wilberforce, O.; 1856; coed.; P.; †
Wiley C., Marshall, Tex.; 1873; coed.; P.; †
Wilkes C., Wilkes-Barre, Pa.; 1933; coed.; P.; †
Willamette U., Salem, Oreg.; 1842; coed.; P.; ‡ #
William and Mary, C. of, Williamsburg, Norfolk & Richmond, Va.; 1693; coed.; S.; ‡
William Carey C., Hattiesburg, Miss.; 1906; coed.; P.; †
William Jennings Bryan U., Dayton, Tenn.; 1903; coed.; P.; †
William Jewell C., Liberty, Mo.; 1849; coed.; P.; †
William Mitchell C. of Law, St. Paul, Minn.; 1900; coed.; P.; #
William Penn C., Oskaloosa, Ia.; 1873; coed.; P.; †
Williams C., Williamstown, Mass.; 1793; men; P.; ‡
William Smith C., Geneva, N.Y.; 1908; women's college of Hobart & William Smith Colleges; ‡
Willimantic State C., Willimantic, Conn.; 1889; coed.; S.; †
Wilmington C., Wilmington, O.; 1871; coed.; P.; †
Wilson C., Chambersburg, Pa.; 1869; women; P.; †
Windham C., Putney, Vt.; 1951; coed.; P.; †
Winona State C., Winona, Minn.; 1858; coed.; S.; ‡
Winston-Salem Teachers C., Winston-Salem, N.C.; 1892; coed.; S.; †
Winthrop C., Rock Hill, S.C.; 1886; women; S.; ‡
Wisconsin State C., Eau Claire, Wis.; 1915; coed.; S.; †
Wisconsin State C., La Crosse, Wis.; 1909; coed.; S.; †
Wisconsin State C., Oshkosh, Wis.; 1871; coed.; S.; †
Wisconsin State C., Platteville, Wis.; 1866; coed.; S.; †
Wisconsin State C., River Falls, Wis.; 1874; coed.; S.; †
Wisconsin State C., Stevens Point, Wis.; 1894; coed.; S.; †
Wisconsin State C., Superior, Wis.; 1896; coed.; S.; ‡
Wisconsin State C., Whitewater, Wis.; 1868; coed.; S.; †
***Wisconsin, U. of,** Madison, Wis.; 1849; coed.; S.; ‡ #
Wittenberg C., Springfield, O.; 1845; coed.; P.; ‡ #
Wofford C., Spartanburg, S.C.; 1854; men; P.; †
Woman's Medical C. of Pennsylvania, Philadelphia, Pa.; 1850; women; P.; #
Woodstock C., Woodstock, Md.; 1869; men; P.; †
Wooster, C. of, Wooster, O.; 1866; coed.; P.; †
Worcester Polytechnic Institute, Worcester, Mass.; 1865; men; P.; ‡
Wyoming, U. of, Laramie, Wyo.; 1887; coed.; S.; ‡ #

Xavier U., Cincinnati, O.; 1831; men; P.; ‡
Xavier U. of Louisiana, New Orleans, La.; 1925; coed.; P.; ‡

***Yale U.,** New Haven, Conn.; 1701; men; P.; ‡ #
Yampa Valley C. Steamboat Springs, Colo.; 1962; coed.; P.; †
Yankton C., Yankton, S. Dak.; 1881; coed.; P.; †
Yeshiva U., New York City, N.Y.; 1928; coed.; P.; ‡
***Youngstown U.,** Youngstown, O.; 1908; coed.; P.; † #

JUNIOR COLLEGES OF THE UNITED STATES

This list includes colleges, junior colleges, and lower divisions of degree-granting colleges and universities of the United States and its territories, including extension centers. These are essentially two-year schools (i.e., colleges offering freshman and sophomore programs and, frequently, conferring associate degrees).

***Abraham Baldwin Agricultural C.,** Tifton, Ga.; 1933; coed.; S.
Agricultural and Technical Institute, see **New York, State U. of.**
Alabama Christian C., Montgomery, Ala.; 1942; coed.; P.
Allan Hancock C., Santa Maria, Calif.; 1920; coed.; Dist.
Allen Military Academy, Bryan, Tex.; 1947; men; P.
All Saints' Episcopal J.C., Vicksburg, Miss.; 1908; women; P.
Alpena Community College, Alpena, Mich.; 1952; coed.; Mun.
Altus J.C., Altus, Okla.; 1926; coed.; Mun.
Alvin J.C., Alvin, Tex.; 1949; coed.; Dist.
***Amarillo C.,** Amarillo, Tex.; 1929; coed.; Mun.
American River J.C., Sacramento, Calif.; 1955; coed.; Dist.
Anchorage Community C., Anchorage, Alas.; 1954; coed.; Dist. & S.
Ancilla Domini C., Donaldson, Ind.; 1937; women; P.
Anderson C., Anderson, S.C.; 1930; women; P.
Andrew C., Cuthbert, Ga.; 1917; coed.; P.
Antelope Valley J.C., Lancaster, Calif.; 1929; coed.; Mun.
Arkansas City J.C., Arkansas City, Kan.; 1922; coed.; Mun.
***Arlington State C.,** Arlington, Tex.; 1917; coed.; part of Agricultural and Mechanical C. of Texas.
Armstrong C. of Savannah, Savannah, Ga.; 1935; coed.; Mun.
Asheville-Biltmore C., Asheville, N.C.; 1927; coed.; Mun. & Co.
Ashland County Teachers C., Ashland, Wis.; 1914; coed.; Co.
Ashland J.C., Ashland, Ky.; 1938; coed.; Mun.
Assumption J.C., Mendham, N.J.; 1953; women; P.
Auburn Community C., Auburn, N.Y.; 1953; coed.; Mun.
Augusta, J.C. of, Augusta, Ga.; 1925; coed.; Co.
Austin J.C., Austin, Minn.; 1940; coed.; Dist.
Averett C., Danville, Va.; 1914; women; P.

Bacone C., Bacone, Okla.; 1929; coed.; P.
***Bakersfield C.,** Bakersfield, Calif.; 1913; coed.; Dist.
Baltimore C. of Commerce, Baltimore, Md.; 1909; coed.; P.
Baltimore J.C., Baltimore, Md.; 1947; coed.; Mun.
Baltimore, J.C. of U. of, Baltimore, Md.; 1937; coed.; P.
Barron County Teachers C., Rice Lake, Wis.; 1907; coed.; Co.
Bay Path J.C., Longmeadow, Mass.; 1949; women; P.
Beckley C., Beckley, W.Va.; 1933; coed.; P.
Bellarmine C., Plattsburg, N.Y.; 1952; men; P.
Belleville Township J.C., Belleville, Ill.; 1946; coed.; Dist.
Bennett J.C., Millbrook, N.Y.; 1936; women; P.
Bethany Lutheran C., Mankato, Minn.; 1926; coed.; P.
Bethel C., Hopkinsville, Ky.; 1916; coed.; P.
Bismarck J.C., Bismarck, N.Dak.; 1939; coed.; Dist.
Blinn C., Brenham, Tex.; 1927; coed.; Co.
Bluefield C., Bluefield, Va.; 1922; coed.; P.
Boise J.C., Boise, Ida.; 1932; coed.; Dist.
Boone J.C., Boone, Ia.; 1927; coed.; Dist.
Boston U., J.C. of, Boston, Mass.; 1949; coed.; P.
Bradford J.C., Bradford, Mass.; 1902; women; P.
Brainerd J.C., Brainerd, Minn.; 1938; coed.; Dist.
Brevard C., Brevard, N.C.; 1883; coed.; P.
Brewton-Parker J.C., Mt. Vernon, Ga.; 1927; coed.; P.
Briarcliff C., Briarcliff Manor, N.Y.; 1933; women; P.
Broome Technical Community C., Binghamton, N.Y.; 1946; coed.; Co.
Buffalo County Teachers C., Alma, Wis.; 1902; coed.; Co.
Burdette C., Boston, Mass.; 1912; coed.; P.
Burlington C., Burlington, Ia.; 1939; coed.; Mun.

California Concordia C., Oakland, Calif.; 1918; coed.; P.
Cambridge J.C., Cambridge, Mass.; 1934; coed.; P.
Cameron State Agricultural C., Lawton, Okla.; 1927; coed.; S.
Campbell C., Buie's Creek, N.C.; 1926; coed.; P.
Campbellsville C., Campbellsville, Ky.; 1924; coed.; P.
Canal Zone J.C., Balboa Heights, C.Z.; 1933; coed.; Fed.
Caney J.C., Pippapass, Ky.; 1923; coed.; P.
Capitol Radio Engineering Institute, Washington, D.C.; 1927; men; P.
Carbon C., Price, Ut.; 1938; coed.; S.
Carver C., Charlotte, N.C.; 1949; coed.; Mun.
Casper J.C., Casper, Wyo.; 1945; coed.; Co.
Cazenovia J.C., Cazenovia, N.Y.; 1934; women; P.
Centenary C. for Women, Hackettstown, N.J.; 1929; women; P.
Centerville Community C., Centerville, Ia.; 1930; coed.; Dist.
Central Christian C., Bartlesville, Okla.; 1950; coed.; P.
Centralia C., Centralia, Wash.; 1925; coed.; Dist.
Centralia Township J.C., Centralia, Ill.; 1940; coed.; Dist.

Central Oregon Community C., Bend, Oreg.; 1949; coed.; Dist.
Central Technical Institute, Kansas City, Mo.; 1931; coed.; P.
Cerritos C., Norwalk, Calif.; 1955; coed.; Dist.
***Chaffey J.C.**, Alta Loma, Calif.; 1922; coed.; Dist.
Chamberlayne J.C., Boston, Mass.; 1915; coed.; P.
Chanute J.C., Chanute, Kan.; 1936; coed.; Dist.
Charlotte C., Charlotte, N.C.; 1946; coed.; Mun.
Chicago Academy of Fine Arts, Chicago, Ill.; 1902; coed.; P.
***Chicago City J.C.**, Chicago, Ill.; 1931; coed.; Mun.
Chipola J.C., Marianna, Fla.; 1947; coed.; Co. & S.
Chowan C., Murfreesboro, N.C.; 1935; coed.; P.
Christian C., Columbia, Mo.; 1913; women; P.
Cisco J.C., Cisco, Tex.; 1940; coed.; Mun.
Citrus J.C., Azusa, Calif.; 1915; coed.; Dist.
Clarendon J.C., Clarendon, Tex.; 1927; coed.; Dist.
Clarinda J.C., Clarinda, Ia.; 1923; coed.; Mun.
Clark C., Vancouver, Wash.; 1933; coed.; Dist.
Clarke Memorial C., Newton, Miss.; 1918; coed.; P.
Clinton J.C., Clinton, Ia.; 1946; coed.; Mun.
Coahoma J.C., Clarksdale, Miss.; 1949; coed.; S.
Coalinga C., Coalinga, Calif.; 1932; coed.; Dist.
Coastal Carolina J.C., Conway, S.C.; 1954; coed.; P.
Coffeyville C., Coffeyville, Kan.; 1923; coed.; Mun.
Cogswell Polytechnic C., San Francisco, Calif.; 1930; coed.; P.
Colby J.C., New London, N.H.; 1928; women; P.
Colorado Woman's C., Denver, Colo.; 1920; women; P.
Columbia Basin C., Pasco, Wash.; 1955; coed.; Dist.
Columbia County Teachers C., Columbus, Wis.; 1908; coed.; Co.
Community C. and Technical Institute, Benton Harbor, Mich.; 1946; coed.; Mun.
Community C. and Technical Institute of Temple U., Philadelphia, Pa.; 1947; coed.; P.
***Compton J.C.**, Compton, Calif.; 1927; coed.; Dist.
Concordia C., St. Paul, Minn.; 1905; coed.; P.
Concordia C., Portland, Oreg.; 1950; coed.; P.
Concordia C., Milwaukee, Wis.; 1881; men; P.
Concordia J.C., Bronxville, N.Y.; 1936; coed.; P.
Connecticut, J.C. of, Bridgeport, Conn.; 1927; coed.; part of U. of Bridgeport.
Connors State Agricultural C., Warner, Okla.; 1927; coed.; S.
***Contra Costa C.**, San Pablo, Calif.; 1949; coed.; Dist.
Copiah-Lincoln J.C., Wesson, Miss.; 1928; coed.; Co.
Cottey C., Nevada, Mo.; 1912; women; P.
Creston Community C., Creston, Ia.; 1926; coed.; Mun.
Cumberland C., Williamsburg, Ky.; 1917; coed.; P.
Custer County J.C., Miles City, Mont.; 1939; coed.; Co.
Cuyahoga Community C., Cleveland, O.; 1963; coed.; Co.

Daniel Payne C., Birmingham, Ala.; 1889; coed.; P.
Danville J.C., Danville, Ill.; 1946; coed.; Mun.
Dawson County J.C., Glendive, Mont.; 1940; coed.; Co.
Dean J.C., Franklin, Mass.; 1941; coed.; P.
Decatur Baptist C., Decatur, Tex.; 1897; coed.; P.
Deep Springs C., Deep Springs, Calif.; 1917; men.; P.
***Del Mar C.**, Corpus Christi, Tex.; 1935; coed.; Mun.
Devils Lake J.C., Devils Lake, N.Dak.; 1941; coed.; Dist.
***Diablo Valley C.**, Concord, Calif.; 1950; coed.; Dist.
Dixie J.C., St. George, Ut.; 1917; coed.; S.
Dodge City C., Dodge City, Kan.; 1935; coed.; Dist.
Dodge County Teachers C., Mayville, Wis.; 1925; coed.; Co.
Dominican J.C. of Blauvelt, Blauvelt, N.Y.; 1952; women; P.
Donnelly C., Kansas City, Kan.; 1949; coed.; P.
Door-Kewaunee County Teachers C., Algomo, Wis.; 1909; coed.; Co.

Eagle Grove J.C., Eagle Grove, Ia.; 1928; coed.; Mun.
East Central J.C., Decatur, Miss.; 1928; coed.; Dist.
Eastern Arizona J.C., Thatcher, Ariz.; 1921; coed.; Co. & S.
Eastern Oklahoma Agricultural and Mechanical C., Wilburton, Okla.; 1927; coed.; S.
***East Los Angeles J.C.**, Los Angeles, Calif.; 1945; coed.; Dist.
East Mississippi J.C., Scooba, Miss.; 1927; coed.; Dist.
Edward Waters C., Jacksonville, Fla.; 1930; coed.; P.
***El Camino C.**, El Camino College, Calif.; 1947; coed.; Dist.
El Dorado J.C., El Dorado, Kan.; 1927; coed.; Dist.
Elgin Community C., Elgin, Ill.; 1947; coed.; Dist.
Ellsworth J.C., Iowa Falls, Ia.; 1929; coed.; Dist.
El Reno C., El Reno, Okla.; 1938; coed.; Dist.
Ely J.C., Ely, Minn.; 1922; coed.; Dist.
Emmanuel C., Franklin Springs, Ga.; 1938; coed.; P.
Emmetsburg Community C., Emmetsburg, Ia.; 1930 coed.; Dist.
Emory J.C., Oxford, Ga.; 1929; coed.; part of Emory U.
Endicott J.C., Beverly, Mass.; 1939; women; P.
Epiphany Apostolic C., Newburg, N.Y.; 1889; men; P.
Erie County Technical Institute, Buffalo, N.Y.; 1946; coed.; Dist.
Estherville J.C., Estherville, Ia.; 1924; coed.; Dist.
Eveleth J.C., Eveleth, Minn.; 1918; coed.; Mun.
***Everett J.C.**, Everett, Wash.; 1941; coed.; Dist.

Fairbury J.C., Fairbury, Neb.; 1941; coed.; Mun.
Fairfax Hall J.C., Waynesboro, Va.; 1932; women; P.
Fashion Institute of Technology, New York City, N.Y.; 1944; coed.; Co. & S.
Felician C., Chicago, Ill.; 1953; women; P.
Ferrum J.C., Ferrum, Va.; 1936; coed.; P.
Fisher J.C., Boston, Mass.; 1952; women; P.
Flat River, J.C. of, Flat River, Mo.; 1922; coed.; Dist.
Flint J.C., Flint, Mich.; 1923; coed.; Mun.
Florida Christian C., Tampa, Fla.; 1946; coed.; P.
Foothill C., Los Altos Hills, Calif.; 1957; coed.; Dist.
Fort Dodge J.C., Fort Dodge, Ia.; 1921; coed.; Mun.
Fort Kent State Normal School, Fort Kent, Me.; 1878; coed.; S.
Fort Lewis Agricultural and Mechanical C., Hesperus, Colo.; 1927; coed.; S.
Fort Scott J.C., Fort Scott, Kan.; 1919; coed.; Mun.
Fort Smith J.C., Fort Smith, Ark.; 1928; coed.; Mun.
Fort Wayne Art School, Fort Wayne, Ind.; 1919; coed.; Mun.
Francis T. Nicholls J.C., Thibodaux, La.; 1948; coed.; part of Louisiana State U.
Franklin Technical Institute, Boston, Mass.; coed.; P.
Frank Phillips C., Borger, Tex.; 1948; coed.; Dist.
Freed-Hardeman C., Henderson, Tenn.; 1923; coed.; P.
Freeman J.C., Freeman, S.Dak.; 1927; coed.; P.
***Fresno J.C.**, Fresno, Calif.; 1910; coed.; Dist.
Friendship J.C., Rock Hill, S.C.; 1933; coed.; P.
Fullerton J.C., Fullerton, Calif.; 1913; coed.; Dist.

Gainsville J.C., Gainsville, Tex.; 1924; coed.; Mun.
Garden City J.C., Garden City, Kan.; 1919; coed.; Mun.
Gardner-Webb J.C., Boiling Springs, N.C.; 1928; coed.; P.
Garland J.C., Boston, Mass.; 1947; women; P.
Gaston Technical Institute, Gastonia, N.C.; 1952; men; S.
Georgetown Visitation J.C., Washington, D.C.; 1919; women; P.
George Washington U., J.C. of, Washington D.C.; 1930; coed.; P.
Georgia Military C., Milledgeville, Ga.; 1930; men; Mun.
Georgia Southwestern C., Americus, Ga.; 1926; coed.; S.
Glendale C., Glendale, Calif.; 1927; coed.; Dist.
Gogebic Community C., Ironwood, Mich.; 1932; coed.; Mun.
Goldey Beacom School of Business, Wilmington, Del.; 1886; coed.; P.
Gordon Military C., Barnesville, Ga.; 1928; men; Mun.
Graceland C., Lamoni, Ia.; 1915; coed.; P.
Grand Rapids J.C., Grand Rapids, Mich.; 1914; coed.; Mun.
Grand View C., Des Moines, Ia.; 1924; coed.; P.
Grays Harbor C., Aberdeen, Wash.; 1930; coed.; Dist.
Greenbrier C., Lewisburg, W.Va.; 1812; women; P.
Green County Teachers C., Monroe, Wis.; 1921; coed.; Co.
Green Mountain C., Poultney, Vt.; 1931; women; P.
Grossmont C., Spring Valley, Calif.; 1961; coed.; Dist.
Guam, Territorial C. of, Agana, Guam; 1952; coed.; Ter.
Gulf Park C., Gulfport, Miss.; 1921; women; P.
Gwynedd-Mercy J.C., Gwynedd Valley, Pa.; 1948; women; P.

Hagerstown J.C., Hagerstown, Md.; 1946; coed.; Co.
Hannibal-La Grange C., Hannibal, Mo.; 1858; coed.; P.
Harcum J.C., Bryn Mawr, Pa.; 1915; women; P.
Hartford C., West Hartford, Conn.; 1939; women; junior college division of Hartford C.
Hartnell C., Salinas, Calif.; 1920; coed.; Dist.
Henderson County J.C., Athens, Tex.; 1946, coed.; Co.
***Henry Ford Community C.**, Dearborn, Mich.; 1938; coed.; Mun.
Hershey J.C., Hershey, Pa.; 1938; coed.; Dist.
Hesston C., Hesston, Kan.; 1915; coed.; P.
Hibbing J.C., Hibbing, Minn.; 1916; coed.; Dist.
Highland J.C., Highland, Kan.; 1923; coed.; Dist.
Highland Manor J.C., West Long Branch, N.J.; 1928; women; P.
Highland Park J.C., Highland Park, Mich.; 1918; coed.; Mun.
***Hillyer C.**, Hartford, Conn.; 1937; coed.; junior college division of Hillyer C.
Hinds J.C., Raymond, Miss.; 1922; coed.; Dist.
Hiwassee C., Madisonville, Tenn.; 1908; coed.; P.
Holmes J.C., Goodman, Miss.; 1925; coed.; Co.
Holton-Arms J.C., Washington, D.C.; 1927; women; P.
Holy Cross Preparatory Seminary, Dunkirk, N.Y.; 1930; men; P.
Holyoke J.C., Holyoke, Mass.; 1946; coed.; Mun.
***Houston J.C.**, Houston, Tex.; 1927; coed.; part of the U. of Houston.
Howard County J.C., Big Spring, Tex.; 1946; coed.; Co.
Hudson Valley Community C., Troy, N.Y.; 1953; men; Co.
Hutchinson J.C., Hutchinson, Kan.; 1928; coed.; Mun.

Immaculata J.C., Washington, D.C.; 1922; women; P.
Immaculate Conception J.C., Lodi, N.J.; 1941; women; P.
Imperial Valley C., Imperial, Calif.; 1922; coed.; Mun.
Independence Community C., Independence, Kan.; 1925; coed.; Mun.
Iola J.C., Iola, Kan.; 1923; coed.; Dist.
Itasca J.C., Coleraine, Minn.; 1922; coed.; Dist.
Itawamba J.C., Fulton, Miss.; 1948; coed.; Dist.

Jackson J.C., Jackson, Mich.; 1928; coed.; Mun.
Jacksonville C., Jacksonville, Tex.; 1899; coed.; P.
Jacksonville U., Jacksonville, Fla.; 1934; coed.; P.
Jamestown Community C., Jamestown, N.Y.; 1950; coed.; Co. & S.
Jefferson City J.C., Jefferson City, Mo.; 1926; coed.; Dist.

C., College; U., University; J.C., Junior College; P., Private; S., State; Mun., Municipal; Ter., Territorial; Fed., Federal; Dist., District; Co., County; † undergraduate; ‡ undergraduate & graduate; ↓ graduate; # professional; * enrollment of 3,000 or more.

Jersey City J.C., Jersey City, N.J.; 1946; coed.; Dist.
Johnstown Center, Johnstown, Pa.; 1927; coed.; part of U. of Pittsburgh.
*__Joliet J.C.__, Joliet, Ill.; 1901; coed.; Dist.
Jones County J.C., Ellisville, Miss.; 1927; coed.; Dist.
Joplin J.C., Joplin, Mo.; 1938; coed.; Dist.

Kansas City, J.C. of, Kansas City, Mo.; 1915; coed.; Mun.
Kansas City Kansas J.C., Kansas City, Kan.; 1923; coed.; Mun.
Kemper Military School, Boonville, Mo.; 1923; men; P.
Kendall C., Evanston, Ill.; 1940; coed.; P.
Keokuk Community C., Keokuk, Ia.; 1953; coed.; Dist.
Ketchikan Community C., Ketchikan, Alas.; 1954, coed.; Dist. & S.
Keystone J.C., La Plume, Pa.; 1934; coed.; P.
Kilgore C., Kilgore, Tex.; 1935; coed.; Dist.

Lain Drafting C., Indianapolis, Ind.; 1941; coed.; P.
Lamar J.C., Lamar, Colo.; 1937; coed.; Co.
Langlade County Teachers C., Antigo, Wis.; 1906; coed.; Co.
Laredo J.C., Laredo, Tex.; 1947; coed.; Mun.
LaSalette Seminary, Altamont, N.Y.; 1953; men; P.
La Salle-Peru-Oglesby J.C., La Salle, Ill.; 1924; coed.; Dist.
Lasell J.C., Auburndale, Mass.; 1932; women; P.
Lassen J.C., Susanville, Calif.; 1924; coed.; Dist.
Lee C., Cleveland, Tenn.; 1941; coed.; P.
Lee C., Baytown, Tex.; 1934; coed.; Dist.
Lees J.C., Jackson, Ky.; 1927; coed.; P.
Lees-McRae C., Banner Elk, N.C.; 1929; coed.; P.
Leicester J.C., Leicester, Mass.; 1784; Men; P.
LeTourneau Technical Institute, Longview, Tex.; 1946; men; P.
Lincoln C., Lincoln, Ill.; 1929; coed.; P.
Lincoln County Teachers C., Merrill, Wis.; 1907; coed.; Co.
Lindsey Wilson C., Columbia, Ky.; 1923; coed.; P.
*__Long Beach City C.__, Long Beach, Calif.; 1927; coed.; Dist.
Lon Morris C., Jacksonville, Tex.; 1912; coed.; P.
Loretto J.C., Nerinx, Ky.; 1934; women; P.
*__Los Angeles City C.__, Los Angeles, Calif.; 1929; coed.; Dist.
*__Los Angeles Harbor C.__, Wilmington, Calif.; 1949; coed.; Mun.
*__Los Angeles J.C. of Business__, Los Angeles, Calif.; 1950; coed.; Dist.
*__Los Angeles Pierce J.C.__, Woodland Hills, Calif.; 1947; coed.; Mun.
*__Los Angeles Trade-Technical C.__, Los Angeles, Calif.; 1949; coed.; Mun.
*__Los Angeles Valley C.__, Van Nuys, Calif.; 1949; coed.; Dist.
Louisburg C., Louisburg, N.C.; 1915; coed.; P.
Lower Columbia J.C., Longview, Wash.; 1934; coed.; Dist.
Luther J.C., Wahoo, Neb.; 1925; coed.; P.
Lyons Township J.C., La Grange, Ill.; 1929; coed.; Dist.

Mallinckrodt C., Wilmette, Ill.; 1918; women; P.
Manitowoc County Teachers C., Manitowoc, Wis.; 1901; coed.; Co.
Manor C., Philadelphia, Pa.; 1947; women; P.
*__Marin, C. of__, Kentfield, Calif.; 1926; coed.; Dist.
Marinette County Teachers C., Marinette, Wis.; 1907; coed.; Co.
Marion C., Marion, Va.; 1913; women; P.
Marion Institute, Marion, Ala.; 1919; men; P.
Marjorie Webster J.C., Washington, D.C.; 1920; women; P.
Marshalltown J.C., Marshalltown, Ia.; 1927; coed.; Dist.
Mars Hill C., Mars Hill, N.C.; 1921; coed.; P.
Martin Branch, U. of Tennessee, Martin, Tenn.; 1927; coed.; S.
Martin C., Pulaski, Tenn.; 1870; coed.; P.
Mary Holmes J.C., West Point, Miss.; 1932; coed.; P.
Marymount C., Arlington, Va.; 1955; women; P.
Mason City J.C., Mason City, Ia.; 1918; coed.; Dist.
Maunaolu Community C., Paia, Hawaii; 1950; coed.; P.
McCook C., McCook, Neb.; 1926; coed.; Dist.
Mercy J.C., Webster Groves, Mo.; 1952; coed.; part of St. Louis U.
Mercy J.C., Tarrytown, N.Y.; 1950; women; P.
Meridian Municipal J.C., Meridian, Miss.; 1937; coed.; Mun.
Mesa County J.C., Grand Junction, Colo.; 1925; coed.; Co.
Middle Georgia C., Cochran, Ga.; 1928; coed.; S.
Midway J.C., Midway, Ky.; 1944; women; P.
Miltonvale Wesleyan C., Miltonvale, Kan.; 1909; coed.; P.
Milwaukee Institute of Technology, Milwaukee, Wis.; 1951; coed.; Mun.
Milwaukee Vocational School J.C., Milwaukee, Wis.; 1937; coed.; Mun.
Mitchell C., New London, Conn.; 1938; coed.; P.
Mitchell C., Statesville, N.C.; 1922; coed.; P.
Moberly J.C., Moberly, Mo.; 1927; coed.; Dist.
Mobile Branch, Alabama State C., Mobile, Ala.; 1936; coed.; S.
Modesto J.C., Modesto, Calif.; 1921; coed.; Dist.
Mohawk Valley Technical Institute, Utica, N.Y.; 1946; coed.; S.
Moline Community C., Moline, Ill.; 1946; coed.; Mun.
Monmouth J.C., Long Branch, N.J.; 1933; coed.; P.
Monterey Peninsula C., Monterey, Calif.; 1947; coed.; Dist.
Montgomery J.C., Takoma Park, Md.; 1946; coed.; Co.
Monticello C., Alton, Ill.; 1917; women; P.
Moody Bible Institute, Chicago, Ill.; 1886; coed.; P.
Morristown C., Morristown, Tenn.; 1923; coed.; P.
Morton J.C., Cicero, Ill.; 1924; coed.; Dist.
Mt. Aloysius J.C., Cresson, Pa.; 1939; women; P.
Mt. Mercy J.C., Cedar Rapids, Ia.; 1928; women; P.
*__Mt. San Antonio C.__, Pomona, Calif.; 1945; coed.; Dist.
Mt. St. Clare C., Clinton, Ia.; 1918; women; P.
Mt. Vernon J.C., Washington, D.C.; 1927; women; P.
Multnomah C., Portland, Oreg.; 1897; coed.; P.
Murray State Agricultural C., Tishomingo, Okla.; 1908; coed.; S.
Muscatine J.C., Muscatine, Ia.; 1929; coed.; Mun.
Muskegon Community C., Muskegon, Mich.; 1926; coed.; Dist.
Muskogee J.C., Muskogee, Okla.; 1920; coed.; Mun.

Napa C., Napa, Calif.; 1941; coed.; Dist.
Navarro J.C., Corsiciana, Tex.; 1946; coed.; Co.
Nazareth C. and Academy, Nazareth, Ky.; 1814; women; P.
New Haven YMCA J.C., New Haven, Conn.; 1926; coed.; P.
Newton J.C., Newtonville, Mass.; 1946; coed.; Mun.
New Mexico Military Institute, Roswell, N.Mex.; 1891; men; S.
*__New York City Community C. of Applied Arts and Sciences__, Brooklyn, N.Y.; 1947; coed.; Dist.
New York, State U. of, all coed.
- **Agricultural and Technical Institute**, Alfred; 1942.
- **Agricultural and Technical Institute**, Canton; 1937.
- **Agricultural and Technical Institute**, Cobleskill; 1937.
- **Agricultural and Technical Institute**, Delhi; 1937.
- *__Agricultural and Technical Institute__, Farmingdale; 1935.
- **Agricultural and Technical Institute**, Morrisville; 1908.

Nichols J.C., Dudley, Mass.; 1931; men; P.
Norfolk Division, Virginia State C., Norfolk, Va.; 1935; coed.; S.
Norfolk J.C., Norfolk, Neb.; 1942; coed.; Dist.
Norman C., Norman Park, Ga.; 1928; coed.; P.
North Dakota School of Forestry, Bottineau, N.Dak.; 1925; coed.; S.
North Dakota State School of Science, Wahpeton, N.Dak.; 1903; coed.; S.
Northeast Agricultural J.C., Sheridan, Wyo.; 1948; coed.; affiliated with U. of Wyoming.
Northeastern J.C., Sterling, Colo.; 1941; coed.; Co.
Northeastern Oklahoma Agricultural and Mechanical C., Miami, Okla.; 1919; coed.; S.
Northeast Mississippi J.C., Booneville, Miss.; 1948; coed.; Dist.
Northern Oklahoma J.C., Tonkawa, Okla.; 1920; coed.; S.
North Greenville J.C., Tigerville, S.C.; 1934; coed.; P.
North Idaho J.C., Coeur d'Alene, Ida.; 1933; coed.; Dist.
Northrup Aeronautical Institute, Inglewood, Calif.; 1942; men; P.
Northwest Community C., Powell, Wyo.; 1946; coed.; S.
Northwestern J.C., Orange City, Ia.; 1928; coed.; P.
Northwestern Michigan C., Traverse City, Mich.; 1951; coed.; Dist.
Northwest Mississippi J.C., Senatoba, Miss.; 1927; coed.; Dist.

*__Oakland City C.__, Oakland, Calif.; 1953; coed.; Dist.
Oak Ridge Military Institute, Oak Ridge, N.C.; 1933; men; P.
Oblate C. and Seminary, Bar Harbor, Me.; 1941; men; P.
Oceanside-Carlsbad C., Oceanside, Calif.; 1934; coed.; Dist.
*__Odessa C.__, Odessa, Tex.; 1946; coed.; Dist.
Ohio C. of Applied Science, Cincinnati, O.; 1919; coed.; P.
Oklahoma Military Academy, Claremore, Okla.; 1923; men; S.
Okolona C., Okolona, Miss.; 1932; coed.; P.
*__Olympic C.__, Bremerton, Wash.; 1946; coed.; Dist.
Onondaga Community C., Syracuse, N.Y.; 1962; coed.; S.
*__Orange Coast C.__, Costa Mesa, Calif.; 1947; coed.; Dist.
Orange County Community C., Middletown, N.Y.; 1950; coed.; Co.
Oregon Technical Institute, Klamath Falls, Oreg.; 1947; coed.; S.
Orlando J.C., Orlando, Fla.; 1941; coed.; P.
Otero J.C., La Junta, Colo.; 1941; coed.; Dist.
Ottumwa Heights C., Ottumwa, Ia.; 1925; women; P.
Our Lady of Hope Mission Seminary, Newburgh, N.Y.; 1946; men; P.
Outagamie County Teachers C., Kaukauna, Wis.; 1912; coed.; Co.

Pacific C., Fresno, Calif.; 1954; coed.; P.
Packer Collegiate Institute, J.C. of the, Brooklyn, N.Y.; 1919; women; P.
Paducah J.C., Paducah, Ky.; 1932; coed.; Mun.
Palm Beach J.C., Lake Park, Fla.; 1933; coed.; Co.
Palomar C., San Marcos, Calif.; 1946; coed.; Dist.
Palo Verde J.C., Blythe, Calif.; 1947; coed.; Dist.
Panola County J.C., Carthage, Tex.; 1947; coed.; Co.
Paris J.C., Paris, Tex.; 1924; coed.; Dist.
Parsons J.C., Parsons, Kan.; 1923; coed.; Dist.
*__Pasadena City C.__, Pasadena, Calif.; 1924; coed.; Dist.
Paul Smith's C., Paul Smiths, N.Y.; 1946; coed.; P.
Peace C., Raleigh, N.C.; 1917; women; P.
Pearl River J.C., Poplarville, Miss.; 1922; coed.; Dist.
Penn Hall J.C., Chambersburg, Pa.; 1926; women; P.
Pennsylvania School of Horticulture for Women, Ambler, Pa.; 1952; women; P.
Pennsylvania State U. Centers at Allentown, Altoona, Du Bois, Erie, Hazleton, McKeesport, Ogontz, Scranton-Wilkes-Barre, University Park, and Wyomissing: all coed.
Pensacola J.C., Pensacola, Fla.; 1948; coed.; Dist.
Peoria J.C., Peoria, Ill.; 1946; coed.; part of Bradley U.
Perkinson J.C., Perkinson, Miss.; 1926; coed.; Dist.
Philadelphia Bible Institute, Philadelphia, Pa.; 1913; coed.; P.

***Phoenix C.**, Phoenix, Ariz.; 1920; coed.; Dist.
Pineland C. and Edwards Military Institute, Salemburg, N.C.; 1926; coed.; P.
Pine Manor J.C., Wellesley, Mass.; 1930; women; P.
Piney Woods J.C., Piney Woods, Miss.; 1935; coed.; P.
Point Park J.C., Pittsburgh, Pa.; 1960; coed.; P.
Polk County Teachers C., St. Croix Falls, Wis.; 1905; coed.; Co.
Porterville C., Porterville, Calif.; 1927; coed.; Dist.
Port Huron J.C., Port Huron, Mich.; 1923; coed.; Mun.
Poteau J.C., Poteau, Okla.; 1942; coed.; Mun.
Potomac State C. of West Virginia U., Keyser, W.Va.; 1921; coed.; S.
Pratt J.C., Pratt, Kan.; 1938; coed.; Dist.
Prentiss Normal and Industrial Institute, Prentiss, Miss.; 1939; coed.; P.
Presbyterian J.C., Maxton, N.C.; 1929; coed.; P.
Presentation J.C., Aberdeen, S.Dak.; 1951; women; P.
Pueblo C., Pueblo, Colo.; 1937; coed.; Co.
Puerto Rico J.C., Rio Piedras, P.R.; 1949; coed.; P.
Purdue U. has junior-college extension centers at Columbus, Fort Wayne, Hammond, Indianapolis, and Michigan City: all coed.

Racine-Kenosha County Teachers C., Union Grove, Wis.; 1911; coed.; Co.
Ranger J.C., Ranger, Tex.; 1926; coed.; Dist.
RCA Institutes, Inc., New York City, N.Y.; 1909; coed.; P.
Reedley C., Reedley, Calif.; 1926; coed.; Dist.
Reinhardt C., Waleska, Ga.; 1883; coed.; P.
Richland County Teachers C., Richland Center, Wis.; 1903; coed.; Co.
***Riverside C.**, Riverside, Calif.; 1916; coed.; Dist.
Rochester J.C., Rochester, Minn.; 1915; coed.; Mun.
Roger Williams J.C., Providence, R.I.; 1948; coed.; P.

***Sacramento J.C.**, Sacramento, Calif.; 1916; coed.; Dist.
Sacred Heart J.C., Cullman, Ala.; 1940; women; P.
Sacred Heart J.C., Belmont, N.C.; 1935; women; P.
Salinas Evening J.C., Salinas, Calif.; 1935; coed.; Dist.
Salmon P. Chase C., J.C. Division, Cincinnati, O.; 1936; coed.; P.
San Angelo C., San Angelo, Tex.; 1928; coed.; Co.
***San Antonio C.**, San Antonio, Tex.; 1925; coed.; Dist.
San Benito County J.C., Hollister, Calif.; 1919; coed.; Co.
***San Bernardino Valley C.**, San Bernardino, Calif.; 1926; coed.; Dist.
***San Diego J.C.**, San Diego, Cailf.; 1914; coed.; Dist.
***San Francisco, City C. of**, San Francisco, Calif.; 1935; coed.; Mun.
***San Jose J.C.**, San Jose, Calif.; 1921; coed.; Dist.
San Luis Obispo J.C., San Luis Obispo, Calif.; 1936; coed.; Dist.
***San Mateo, C. of**, San Mateo, Calif.; 1922; coed.; Dist. & Co.
Santa Ana C., Santa Ana, Calif.; 1915; coed.; Dist.
Santa Barbara J.C., Santa Barbara, Calif.; 1946; coed.; Dist.
***Santa Monica City C.**, Santa Monica, Calif.; 1929; coed.; Mun.
***Santa Rosa J.C.**, Santa Rosa, Calif.; 1918; coed.; Dist.
Sauk County Teachers C., Reedsburg, Wis.; 1906; coed.; Co.
Sayre J.C., Sayre, Okla.; 1938; coed.; Dist.
Schreiner Institute, Kerrville, Tex.; 1923; men; P.
Scottsbluff C., Scottsbluff, Neb.; 1932, coed.; Dist.
***Sequoias, College of the**, Visalia, Calif.; 1926; coed.; Dist.
Shasta C., Redding, Calif.; 1950; coed.; Dist.
Sheboygan County Teachers C., Sheboygan Falls, Wis.; 1934; coed.; Co.
Sheldon Jackson J.C., Sitka, Alas.; 1944; coed.; P.
Shenandoah C., Dayton, Va.; 1923; coed.; P.
Shorter C., North Little Rock, Ark.; 1886; coed.; P.
Sierra C., Auburn, Calif.; 1936; coed.; Dist.
Sinclair C., Dayton, O.; 1924; coed.; P.
Skagit Valley J.C., Mt. Vernon, Wash.; 1926; coed.; Dist.
Snead J.C., Boaz, Ala.; 1935; coed.; P.
Snow C., Ephraim, Ut.; 1922; coed.; branch of Utah State. U.
Southeast Center, U. of Wyoming, Torrington, Wyo.; 1948; coed.; S.
Southern Baptist C., Walnut Ridge, Ark.; 1941; coed.; P.
Southern Seminary and J.C., Buena Vista, Va.; 1927; women; P.
Southern Union C., Wadley, Ala.; 1922; coed.; P.
South Georgia C., Douglas, Ga.; 1927; coed.; S.
South Macomb Community C., Van Dyke, Mich.; 1953; coed.; Dist.
South Texas J.C., Houston, Tex.; 1948; coed.; part of South Texas C.
Southwest Baptist C., Bolivar, Mo.; 1878; coed.; P.
Southwestern Christian C., Terrell, Tex.; 1948; coed.; P.
Southwestern C., Chula Vista, Calif.; 1961; coed.; Dist.
Southwestern J.C., Keene, Tex.; 1914; coed.; P.
Southwest Mississippi J.C., Summit, Miss.; 1927; coed.; Dist.
Southwest Texas J.C., Uvalde, Tex; 1946; coed.; Dist.
Spring Arbor J.C., Spring Arbor, Mich.; 1923; coed.; P.
Springfield J.C., Springfield, Ill.; 1929; coed.; P.
Spring Garden Institute, Philadelphia, Pa.; 1850; coed.; P.
St. Bede J.C., Peru, Ill.; 1946; men; P.
St. Bernard C., St. Bernard, Ala.; 1932; men; P.
St. Catherine J.C., Springfield, Ky.; 1931; coed.; P.
St. Charles C., Catonsville, Md.; 1926; men; part of St. Mary's Seminary and U.
St. Gregory's C., Shawnee, Okla.; 1914; men; P.
St. John's Lutheran C., Winfield, Kan.; 1922; coed.; P.
St. Joseph J.C., St. Joseph, Mo.; 1915; coed.; Dist.
St. Joseph's C., Princeton, N.J.; 1940; men; P.
St. Joseph's Seminary, Grand Rapids, Mich.; 1909; men; P.
St. Joseph's Seraphic Seminary, Callicoon, N.Y.; 1937; men; P.
St. Joseph Teacher Training Institute, St. Augustine, Fla.; 1939; women; P.
St. Lawrence Seminary, Mt. Calvary, Wis.; 1860; men; P.
St. Louis Preparatory Seminary, St. Louis, Mo.; 1900; men; P.
St. Mary's J.C., Raleigh, N.C.; 1918; women; P.
St. Mary's Seminary J.C., St. Mary's City, Md.; 1927; coed.; S.
St. Paul's C., Concordia, Mo.; 1905; men; P.
St. Petersburg J.C., St. Petersburg, Fla.; 1927; coed.; Co.
St. Philip's C., San Antonio, Tex.; 1927; coed.; affiliated with San Antonio C.
St. Thomas Aquinas C., Sparkill, N.Y.; 1952; women; P.
St. Thomas Seminary, Bloomfield, Conn.; 1897; men; P.
St. Vincent's Seminary, Philadelphia, Pa.; 1867; men; P.
State Technical Institute, Hartford, Conn.; 1946; coed.; S.
Stephens C., Columbia, Mo.; 1911; women; P.
Stockton C., Stockton, Calif.; 1935; coed.; Dist.
Stratford C., Danville, Va.; 1930; women; P.
Sue Bennett C., London, Ky.; 1922; coed.; P.
Sunflower J.C., Moorhead, Miss.; 1926; coed.; Dist.
Suomi C. and Theological Seminary, Hancock, Mich.; 1923; coed.; P.

Tacoma Catholic C., Tacoma, Wash.; 1942; women; P.
Taft C., Taft, Calif.; 1922; coed.; Dist.
Tarleton State C., Stephenville, Tex.; 1899; coed.; S.
Taylor County Teachers C., Medford, Wis.; 1911; coed.; Co.
Temple J.C., Temple, Tex.; 1926; coed.; Mun.
Texarkana C., Texarkana, Tex.; 1927; coed.; Mun.
Texas Southmost C., Brownsville, Tex.; 1926; coed.; Dist.
Thornton J.C., Harvey, Ill.; 1927; coed.; Dist.
Tiffin U., Tiffin, O.; 1924; coed.; P.
Toledo, U. of, J.C., Toledo, O.; 1938; coed.; Mun.
Trenton J.C., Trenton, Mo.; 1925; coed.; Mun.
Trenton J.C., Trenton, N.J.; 1947; coed.; S. & Mun.
Trinidad State J.C., Trinidad, Colo.; 1925; coed.; Co.
Truett-McConnell J.C., Cleveland, Ga.; 1846; coed.; P.
Tyler J.C., Tyler, Tex.; 1926; coed.; Dist.

Union J.C., Cranford, N.J.; 1933; coed.; P.
Urbana J.C., Urbana, O.; 1927; coed.; P.

Vallejo J.C., Vallejo, Calif.; 1945; coed.; Dist.
Valley Forge Military J.C., Wayne, Pa.; 1937; men; P.
Valparaiso Technical Institute, Valparaiso, Ind.; 1874; coed.; P.
***Ventura C.**, Ventura, Calif.; 1929; coed.; Dist.
Vermont C., Montpelier, Vt.; 1936; women; P.
Vernon County Teachers C., Viroqua, Wis.; 1907; coed.; Co.
Victoria C., Victoria, Tex.; 1925; coed.; Co.
Villa Julie J.C., Stevenson, Md.; 1952; women; P.
Villa Walsh J.C., Morristown, N.J.; 1948; women; P.
Vincennes U., Vincennes, Ind.; 1878; coed.; Co.
Virginia Intermont C., Bristol, Va.; 1912; women; P.
Virginia J.C., Virginia, Minn.; 1921; coed.; Mun.
Voorhees School and J.C., Denmark, S.C.; 1929; coed.; P.

Waldorf C., Forest City, Ia.; 1920; coed.; P.
Walker J.C., Jasper, Ala.; 1938; coed.; P.
Warren Wilson C., Swannanoa, N.C.; 1942; coed.; P.
Washington Hall J.C., Washington, D.C.; 1954; coed.; P.
Washington J.C., Pensacola, Fla.; 1949; coed.; Co.
Weatherford C., Weatherford, Tex.; 1921; coed.; Co.
Webber C., Babson Park, Fla.; 1927; women; P.
***Weber C.**, Ogden, Ut.; 1916; coed.; S.
Webster City J.C., Webster City, Ia.; 1926; coed.; Dist.
Wenatchee J.C., Wenatchee, Wash.; 1939; coed.; Dist.
Wentworth Institute, Boston, Mass.; 1904; men; P.
Wentworth Military Academy, Lexington, Mo.; 1923; men; P.
Wesleyan Methodist C., Central, S.C.; 1928; coed.; P.
Wesley J.C., Dover, Del.; 1942; coed.; P.
Wessington Springs C., Wessington Springs, S.Dak.; 1918; coed.; P.
Westbrook J.C., Portland, Me.; 1830; women; P.
Westchester Community C., Valhalla, N.Y.; 1946; coed.; Co.
West Georgia C., Carrollton, Ga.; 1933; coed.; S.
Wharton County J.C., Wharton, Tex.; 1946; coed.; Co.
William Woods C., Fulton, Mo.; 1890; women; P.
Wilmington C., Wilmington, N.C.; 1947; coed.; Co.
Wingate C., Wingate, N.C.; 1923; coed.; P.
Wisconsin, U. of, has junior-college extension centers at Green Bay, Kenosha, Manitowoc, Marinette, Menasha, Milwaukee, Racine, Sheboygan, and Wausau: all coed.
Wood County Teachers C., Wisconsin Rapids, Wis.; 1903; coed.; Co.
Wood J.C., Mathiston, Miss.; 1927; coed.; P.
Worcester J.C., Worcester, Mass.; 1938; coed.; P.
Worthington J.C., Worthington, Minn.; 1936; coed.; Dist.

Xaverian C., Silver Spring, Md.; 1932; men; P.

Yakima Valley J.C., Yakima, Wash.; 1928; coed.; Dist.
York J.C., York, Pa.; 1941; coed.; P.
Young L.G. Harris C., Young Harris, Ga.; 1886; coed.; P.
Yuba C., Marysville, Calif.; 1927; coed.; Dist.

C., College; U., University; J.C., Junior College; P., Private; S., State; Mun., Municipal; Ter., Territorial; Fed., Federal; Dist., District; Co., County; † undergraduate; ‡ undergraduate & graduate; ⸸ graduate; # professional; * enrollment of 3,000 or more.

CANADIAN COLLEGES AND UNIVERSITIES

This list contains the same kind of data as that given in the preceding lists with the following two additions designated by superscript numbers after the name of the college or university: ¹ indicates that the institution does not confer degrees in its own right, but by affiliation with a degree-granting institution; ² indicates that the institution confers degrees in theology only, all other degrees being conferred by affiliation with another degree-granting institution.

Acadia U., Wolfville, N.S.; 1838; coed.; P.; ‡
Agriculture, École Supérieure d'[1], Ste.-Anne-de-la-Pocatière, Que.; 1859; men; P.; affiliated with U. Laval; ‡
***Alberta, U. of**, Edmonton, Alta.; 1906; coed.; Prov.; ‡ #
Alma C., St. Thomas, Ont.; 1877; women; P.; jr. coll. affiliated with U. of Western Ontario.
Amos, C. d'[1], Amos, Que.; 1940; men; P.; affiliated with U. Laval; †
André-Grasset, C.[1], Montreal, Que.; 1927; men; P.; affiliated with U. de Montréal; †
Angèle-Mérici, C.[1], Quebec, Que.; 1936; women; P.; affiliated with U. Laval; †
Anglican Theological C.[2], Vancouver, B.C.; 1910; men; P.; affiliated with U. of British Columbia; #
Anglican Women's Training C.[1], Toronto, Ont.; 1892; women; P.; affiliated with U. of Toronto; #
Architecture, École d', Montreal, Que.; 1922; coed.; Prov.; #
Assomption, C. de l'[1], L'Assomption, Que.; 1832; men; P.; affiliated with U. de Montréal; †
Assomption, C. de l'[1], Moncton, N.B.; 1943; men; P.; affiliated with U. St.-Joseph; †
Assumption U. of Windsor, Windsor, Ont.; 1857; coed.; P.; ‡

Basile-Moreau, C.[1], St.-Laurent, Que.; 1934; women; P.; affiliated with U. de Montréal; †
Bénédictins, Monastère des, St.-Benoit-du-Lac, Que.; men; P.; #
Bibliothécaires, École de[1], Montreal, Que.; 1937; coed.; Prov.; affiliated with U. de Montréal; †
Bishop's U., Lennoxville, Que.; 1843; coed.; P.; ‡ #
Bon-Pasteur, C. du[1], Chicoutimi, Que.; 1864; women; P.; affiliated with U. Laval; †
Bourget, C.[1], Rigaud, Que.; 1851; men; P.; affiliated with U. de Montréal; †
Brandon C. Inc.[1], Brandon, Man.; 1899; coed.; P., Prov. & Mun.; affiliated with U. of Manitoba; †
***British Columbia, U. of**, Vancouver, B.C.; 1908; coed.; Prov.; ‡ #
Bruyère, C.[1], Ottawa, Ont.; 1925; women; P.; affiliated with U. d'Ottawa; †

Campion C., Regina, Sask.; 1918; men; P.; jr. coll. affiliated with U. of Saskatchewan.
Canadian Memorial Chiropractic C., Toronto, Ont.; 1945; coed.; P.; #
Canadian Services Colleges, men; Fed.; consists of three non-degree-granting, armed forces colleges, **Royal Military C.** at Kingston, Ont., **Royal Roads** at Victoria, B.C., and **C. Militaire Royal de St.-Jean** at St.-Jean, Que.
Canadian Union C., College Heights, Alta.; 1907; coed.; P.; # & jr. coll.
Carleton C., Ottawa, Ont.; 1942; coed.; P.; ‡
Charles-Garnier, C.[1], Quebec, Que.; men; P.; affiliated with U. Laval; †
Chicoutimi, Petit Séminaire de[1], Chicoutimi, Que.; 1873; men; P.; affiliated with U. Laval; †
Christ-Roi, Grand Séminaire[1], St.-Hyacinthe, Que.; 1935; men; P.; #
Christ the King, C. of[1], London, Ont.; 1955; men; P.; affiliated with U. of Western Ontario; †
Christ the King, Seminary of, Toronto, Ont.; 1931; men; P.; ⸸
Concordia C., Edmonton, Alta.; 1921; coed.; P.; jr. coll.
Cornwall C.[1], Cornwall, Ont.; 1949; men; P.; affiliated with U. d'Ottawa; †

Dalhousie U., Halifax, N.S.; 1818; coed.; P.; ‡ #
Dominicains, C. des, Ottawa, Ont.; men; P.; #

Emmanuel C., U. of[2], Saskatoon, Sask.; 1879; men; P.; affiliated with U. of Saskatchewan; #
Eudistes, C. des[1], Montreal, Que.; 1953; men; P.; affiliated with U. de Montréal; †
Eudistes, Séminaire des, Charlesbourg, Que.; men; P.; #

Fraternité Sacerdotale, Congrégation de la, Lac Supérieur, Que.; 1952; men; P.; #

Gaspé, Séminaire de[1], Gaspé, Que.; 1926; men; P.; affiliated with U. Laval; †
Gravelbourg, Le C. Catholique de[1], Gravelbourg, Sask.; 1918; men; P.; affiliated with U. d'Ottawa; †

Halifax Conservatory of Music[1], Halifax, N.S.; coed.; Prov.; affiliated with Dalhousie U.; †
Hamilton C.[1], Hamilton, Ont.; coed.; P.; affiliated with McMaster U.; †
Hauterive, C. de[1], Hauterive, Que.; 1954; men; P.; affiliated with U. Laval; †
Hautes Études Commerciales, École des[1], Montreal, Que.; 1907; coed.; Prov.; affiliated with U. de Montréal; ‡
Holy Names C.[1], Windsor, Ont.; 1934; women's college of Assumption U.; ‡
Holy Rosary Scholasticate, Ottawa, Ont.; men; P.; #
Huron C.[1], London, Ont.; 1863; men; P.; affiliated with U. of Western Ontario; † #

Immaculée Conception, Scholasticat de L', Montreal, Que.; 1885; men; P.; ⸸

Jean-de-Brébeuf, C.[1], Montreal, Que.; 1928; men; P.; affiliated with U. de Montréal; †
Jean-Jacques-Olier, C., Verdun, Que.; men; P.; †
Jésuites, C. des[1], Sudbury, Ont.; men; P.; affiliated with U. Laval; †
Jésuites, C. des[1], Quebec, Que.; 1635; men; P.; affiliated with U. Laval; †
Jesuit Seminary, Toronto, Ont.; men; P.; #
Jésus-Marie de Sillery, C.[1], Quebec, Que.; 1925; women; P.; affiliated with U. Laval; †
Jésus-Marie d'Outremont, C.[1], Outremont, Que.; 1933; women; P.; affiliated with U. de Montréal; †
Joliette, Séminaire de[1], Joliette, Que.; 1846; men; P.; affiliated with U. de Montréal; †

King's C., U. of[2], Halifax, N.S.; 1789; coed.; P.; associated with Dalhousie U.; † #
Knox C.[2], Toronto, Ont.; 1844; men; P.; a federated college of U. of Toronto; † #

Lac Mégantic, Externat Classique du[1], Lac Megantic, Que.; 1952; men; P.; affiliated with U. de Sherbrooke; †
Lakehead Technical Institute, Port Arthur, Ont.; 1948; coed.; Prov.; jr. coll.
Lassalle, Conservatoire[1], Montreal, Que.; coed.; P.; affiliated with U. de Montréal; †
***Laval, U.**, Quebec, Que.; 1852; coed.; P.; ‡ #
Lévis, C. de[1], Lévis, Que.; 1853; men; P.; affiliated with U. Laval; †
Longueuil, Externat Classique de[1], Longueuil, Que.; 1950; men; affiliated with U. de Montréal; †
Loretto C.[1], Toronto, Ont.; women's college of St. Michael's C. in U. of Toronto; †
Loyola C.[1], Montreal, Que.; 1896; men; P.; affiliated with U. de Montréal; †
Lutheran C. and Seminary[2], Saskatoon, Sask.; 1913; men; P.; affiliated with U. of Saskatchewan; #
Luther C., Regina, Sask.; 1926; coed.; P.; jr. coll. affiliated with U. of Saskatchewan.
Luther Theological Seminary[2], Saskatoon, Sask.; 1939; men; P.; affiliated with U. of Saskatchewan; #

Macdonald C.[1], Ste.-Anne-de-Bellevue, Que.; 1905; coed.; P.; a college of McGill U.; ‡
Macdonald Institute, Ontario Agricultural C.[1], Guelph, Ont.; 1903; women; Prov.; affiliated with U. of Toronto; †
Magog, Externat Classique de[1], Magog, Que.; men; P.; affiliated with U. de Sherbrooke; †
Maillet, C.[1], St.-Basile, N.B.; 1949; women; P.; affiliated with U. St.-Louis; †
Manitoba Law School[1], Winnipeg, Man.; 1914; coed.; P. & Prov.; affiliated with U. of Manitoba; #
***Manitoba, U. of**, Winnipeg, Man.; 1877; coed.; Prov.; ‡ #
Marguerite-Bourgeoys, C.[1], Montreal, Que.; 1908; women; P.; affiliated with U. de Montréal; †
Marguerite d'Youville, C.[1], Hull, Que.; 1945; women; P.; affiliated with U. Laval; †
Marguerite d'Youville, Institut[1], Montreal, Que.; 1934; coed.; P.; affiliated with U. de Montréal; †
Marianopolis C.[1], Montreal, Que.; 1943; women; P.; affiliated with U. de Montréal; †
Marie-Anne, C.[1], Lachine, Que.; 1932; women; P.; affiliated with U. de Montréal; †
Marie de France, C., Montreal, Que.; 1939; women; P.; †
Marie de l'Incarnation, C.[1], Trois Rivières, Que.; 1697; women; Prov.; affiliated with U. Laval; †
Marie-Immaculée, Séminaire Oblat de[1], Chambly, Que.; 1926; men; P.; affiliated with U. de Montréal; †
Marie-Médiatrice, C.[1], Hull, Que.; 1948; men; P.; affiliated with U. Laval; †
Marie-Médiatrice, Séminaire de[1], Montreal, Que.; 1945; men; P.; affiliated with U. de Montréal; †
Maritime Academy of Music[1], Halifax, N.S.; coed.; P.; affiliated with Dalhousie U.; †
Maritime C. of Pharmacy[1], Halifax, N.S.; 1908; coed.; P.; affiliated with Dalhousie U.; †

Maritime School of Social Work[1], Halifax, N.S.; 1941; coed.; affiliated with Acadia U., U. of King's C., and St. Francis U.; ⸸
Matane, Externat Classique de[1], Matane, Que.; 1953; men; P.; affiliated with U. Laval; †
Mathieu, C.[1], Gravelbourg, Sask.; coed.; P.; affiliated with U. d'Ottawa; †
***McGill U.**, Montreal, Que.; 1821; coed.; P.; ‡ #
McMaster U., Hamilton, Ont.; 1887; coed.; P.; ‡ #
Médecine Vétérinaire, École de[1], St.-Hyacinthe, Que.; 1886; men; Prov.; affiliated with U. de Montréal; #
Missions, Grand Séminaire des, Montreal, Que.; men; P.; #
Missions Etrangerès, Séminaire des, Pont-Viau, Montreal, Que.; 1924; men; P.; #
Montfortain, Séminaire[1], Papineauville, Que.; 1898; men; P.; affiliated with U. Laval; †
Montréal, C. de[1], Montreal, Que.; 1767; men; P.; affiliated with U. de Montréal; †
Montreal Diocesan Theological C.[1], Montreal, Que.; 1873; men; P.; affiliated with McGill U.; #
Montréal, Grand Séminaire de[1], Montreal, Que.; 1840; men; P.; affiliated with U. de Montréal; #
***Montréal, U. de**, Montreal, Que.; 1876; coed.; P.; ‡ #
Mt. Allison U., Sackville, N.B.; 1840; coed.; P.; ‡
Mt. Carmel C.[1], Niagara Falls, Ont.; coed.; P.; affiliated with St. Bonaventure U. (U.S.); †
Mt. Notre-Dame[1], Sherbrooke, Que.; 1857; women; P.; affiliated with U. de Sherbrooke; †
Mt. Royal C., Calgary, Alta.; 1910; coed.; P.; jr. coll.
Mt. St. Bernard C.[1], Antigonish, N.S.; 1883; coed.; P.; affiliated with St. Francis Xavier U.; ‡
Mt. Ste.-Anne[1], Sherbrooke, Que.; 1948; men; P.; affiliated with U. de Sherbrooke; †
Mt.-St.-Louis, C.[1], Montreal, Que.; 1892; men; P.; affiliated with universities of Laval, McGill, Montréal, and Ottawa; †
Mt. St. Vincent C., Halifax, N.S.; 1925; women; P.; †
Music Teachers' C.[1], London, Ont.; 1945; coed.; Fed.; a constituent college of U. of Western Ontario; †

Nazareth, Institut, École de Musique[1], Montreal, Que.; 1861; coed.; P.; affiliated with U. de Montréal; ‡
New Brunswick, U. of, Fredericton, N.B.; 1787; coed.; Prov.; ‡ #
Newfoundland, Memorial U. of, St. John's, Nfld.; 1949; coed.; Prov.; ‡
Nicolet, Séminaire de[1], Nicolet, Que.; 1803; men; P.; affiliated with U. Laval; †
Normale, Scolasticat-École[1], Hull, Que.; women; P.; affiliated with U. Laval; †
Normale Secondaire, École[1], Montreal, Que.; 1941; coed.; P.; affiliated with U. de Montréal; ‡
Notre Dame C., Nelson, B.C.; 1950; coed.; P.; jr. coll. affiliated with Gonzaga U. (U.S.).
Notre Dame C.[1], Ottawa, Ont.; 1932; women; P.; affiliated with U. d'Ottawa; †
Notre Dame C.[1], Wilcox, Sask.; 1927; coed.; P.; affiliated with U. d'Ottawa; †
Notre Dame d'Acadie, C.[1], Moncton, N.B.; 1949; women; P.; affiliated with U. St.-Joseph; †
Notre-Dame de Grâce, Scholasticat-École Normale[1], Hull, Que.; 1940; women; P.; affiliated with U. Laval; ‡
Notre-Dame de l'Assomption, C.[1], Nicolet, Que.; 1937; women; P.; affiliated with U. Laval; †
Notre-Dame-de-Nazareth, Abbaye de, St.-Michel-de-Rougement, Que.; men; P.; #
Notre Dame des Servites, C.[1], Ayer's Cliff, Que.; 1948; men; P.; affiliated with U. de Sherbrooke; †
Notre-Dame-de-Ste.-Croix, Scolasticat, Ste.-Geneviève-de-Pierrefonds, Que.; 1904; men; P.; ‡
Nova Scotia Agricultural C., Truro, N.S.; 1885; coed.; Prov.; jr. coll.
Nova Scotia Technical C., Halifax, N.S.; 1907; men; Prov.; ‡

Oblate Fathers' Seminary[1], Lebret, Sask.; 1927; men; P.; affiliated with U. d'Ottawa; †
Oka, Institut Agricole d'[1], La Trappe, Que.; 1893; men; P.; affiliated with U. de Montréal; ‡
Ontario Agricultural C.[1], Guelph, Ont.; 1874; coed.; Prov.; affiliated with U. of Toronto; ‡
Ontario C. of Education[1], Toronto, Ont.; 1907; coed.; Prov.; affiliated with U. of Toronto; ‡
Ontario Veterinary C.[1], Guelph, Ont.; 1862; coed.; Prov.; affiliated with U. of Toronto; ⸸ #
Optométrie, École d'[1], Montreal, Que.; 1910; coed.; P.; affiliated with U. de Montréal; #
Optometry of Ontario, C. of, Toronto, Ont.; 1925; coed.; Prov.; #
Osgoode Hall Law School, Toronto, Ont.; 1873; coed.; P.; #
Ottawa, Grand Séminaire d', Ottawa, Ont.; 1848; men; P.; #
***Ottawa, U. d'**, Ottawa, Ont.; 1848; coed.; P.; ‡ #

Pêcheries, École des[1], Ste.-Anne-de-la-Pocatière, Que,; coed.; P.; affiliated with U. Laval; †
Pédagogique, Institut[1], Montreal, Que.; 1926; women; P.; affiliated with U. de Montréal; ‡
Pédagogique, L'Institut Familiale[1], Outremont, Que.; 1942; women; Prov.; affiliated with U. de Montréal; †
Père Prévost, Petit Séminaire, Lac Supérieur, Que.; men; P.; †
Pêres Rédemptoristes, Scolasticat des[1], Aylmer, Que.; 1939; men.; P.; affiliated with U. Laval; †
Philosophie, Séminaire de, Montreal, Que.; men; P.; affiliated with U. de Montréal; #
Pine Hill Divinity Hall[2], Halifax, N.S.; 1820; coed.; P.; affiliated with Dalhousie U. and Mt. Allison U.; #
Polytechnique, École[1], Montreal, Que.; 1873; coed.; P. & Prov.; affiliated with U. de Montréal; ‡
Pontifical Institute of Mediaeval Studies[1], Toronto, Ont.; 1929; coed.; P.; affiliated with U. of Toronto; ⸸
Presbyterian C., Montreal, Que.; 1865; men; P.; #
Prince of Wales C., Charlottetown, P.E.I.; 1860; coed.; Prov.; jr. coll.
***Provincial Institute of Technology and Art**[1], Calgary, Alta.; 1916; coed.; Prov.; affiliated with U. of Alberta; †

Québec, Académie de[1], Quebec, Que.; 1862; men; P.; affiliated with U. Laval; †
Québec, Séminaire de[1], Quebec, Que.; 1663; men; P.; affiliated with U. Laval; †
Queen's C.[2], St. John's, Nfld.; 1841; men; P.; affiliated with Memorial U. of Newfoundland; † #
Queen's Theological C.[1], Kingston, Ont.; 1842; men; P.; affiliated with Queen's U.; ⸸ #
Queen's U. at Kingston, Kingston, Ont.; 1841; coed.; P.; ‡ #

Regina C., Regina, Sask.; 1911; coed.; Prov.; jr. coll. affiliated with U. of Saskatchewan.
Regina Cleri Seminary, Regina, Sask.; men; P.; #
Rimouski, Séminaire de[1], Rimouski, Que.; 1870; men; P.; affiliated with U. Laval; †
Rouyn, C. de[1], Rouyn, Que.; 1948; men; P.; affiliated with U. d'Ottawa; †
Royal Military C., see **Canadian Services Colleges.**
Royal Roads, see **Canadian Services Colleges.**
Royal Victoria C.[1], Montreal, Que.; women's college of McGill U.; ‡ #

Sacré-Coeur, C.[1], Victoriaville, Que.; 1872; men; P.; affiliated with U. Laval; †
Sacré-Coeur, C. du[1], Sudbury, Ont.; men; P.; affiliated with U. Laval; †
Sacré-Coeur, C. du[1], Sherbrooke, Que.; 1945; women; P.; affiliated with U. de Sherbrooke; †
Sacré-Coeur, École Apostolique du[1], Beauport, Que.; 1920; men; P.; affiliated with U. Laval; †
Sacré-Coeur, Scolasticat des Frères du[1], Arthabaska, Que.; 1931; men; Prov.; affiliated with U. de Sherbrooke; †
Sacré-Coeur, Séminaire du[1], St.-Victor-de-Beauce, Que.; 1910; men; P.; affiliated with U. Laval; †
Sacré-Coeur, U. du, West Bathurst, N.B.; 1899; men; P.; †
Sacred Heart C., Regina, Sask.; women; P.; jr. coll. affiliated with U. of Saskatchewan.
Sacred Heart, Convent of the, Halifax, N.S.; women; P.; jr. coll. affiliated with Dalhousie U.
Saskatchewan, U. of, Saskatoon, Sask.; 1907; coed.; Prov.; ‡ #
Sciences Domestiques, École de[1], Quebec, Que.; 1941; women; P.; affiliated with U. Laval; †
Sciences Ménagères, École des[1], Montreal, Que.; 1904; women; P.; affiliated with U. de Montréal; †
Séraphique, C., Ottawa, Ont.; men; P.; #
Sherbrooke, U. de, Sherbrooke, Que.; 1954; coed.; P.; ‡
***Sir George Williams C.**, Montreal, Que.; 1929; coed.; P.; †
St.-Alexandre, C.[1], Pointe-Gatineau, Que.; men; P.; affiliated with U. Laval; †
St.-Alphonse, Séminaire[1], Ste.-Anne-de-Beaupré, Que.; 1896; men; P.; affiliated with U. Laval; †
St. Alphonsus Seminary, Woodstock, Ont.; men; P.; #
St. Andrew's C.[2], Saskatoon, Sask.; 1913; coed.; P.; affiliated with U. of Saskatchewan; #
St. Angela's C.[1], Quebec, Que.; 1936; women; P.; affiliated with U. Laval; †
St.-Antoine, Séminaire[1], Quebec, Que.; 1903; men; P.; affiliated with U. Laval; †
St. Augustine's Seminary[1], Toronto, Ont.; 1910; men; P.; affiliated with U. of Toronto; †
St. Basil's Seminary[1], Toronto, Ont.; 1894; men; P.; affiliated with St. Michael's C. in U. of Toronto; †
St.-Boniface, C. de[1], St. Boniface, Man.; 1818; men; P.; affiliated with U. of Manitoba; †
St.-Boniface, Grand Séminaire de[1], St. Boniface, Man.; 1946; men; P.; affiliated with U. de Montréal; #
St. Chad's C.[2], Regina, Sask.; 1907; men; P.; affiliated with U. of Saskatchewan; #
St.-Charles-Borromée, Séminaire[1], Sherbrooke, Que.; 1875; men; P.; affiliated with U. de Sherbrooke; †
St.-Denis, C.[1], Montreal, Que.; 1949; coed.; P.; affiliated with U. de Montréal; †
St. Dunstan's U., Charlottetown, P.E.I.; 1855; coed.; P.; †
Ste. Anne, C., Church Point, N.S.; 1890; men; P.; †
Ste.-Anne-de-la-Pocatière, C. de[1], Ste.-Anne-de-la-Pocatière, Que.; 1827; men; P.; affiliated with U. Laval; †
Ste.-Croix, Externat Classique[1], Montreal, Que.; 1929; men; P.; affiliated with U. de Montréal; †
Ste.-Marie, C.[1], Montreal, Que.; 1848; men; P.; affiliated with U. de Montréal; †
Ste.-Marie, Séminaire[1], Shawinigan Falls, Que.; 1947; men; P.; affiliated with U. Laval; †
Ste.-Thérèse, Séminaire de[1], St.-Therese, Que.; 1825; men; P.; affiliated with U. de Montréal; †
St. Francis Xavier Seminary, Scarboro, Ont.; men; P.; #
St. Francis Xavier U., Antigonish, N.S.; 1853; coed.; P.; ‡

C., College, Collège; U., University, Université; jr. coll., junior college; P., Private; Prov., Provincial; Mun., Municipal; Ter., Territorial; Fed., Federal; † undergraduate; ‡ undergraduate & graduate; ⸸ graduate; # professional; * enrollment of 3,000 or more.

St.-François, Séminaire[1], Cap-Rouge, Que.; 1908; men; P.; affiliated with U. Laval; †
St.-Georges, Institut Pédagogique[1], Montreal, Que.; 1929; men; P.; affiliated with U. de Montréal; ‡
St.-Georges, Le Petit Séminaire de[1], St.-Georges-de-Beauce, Que.; 1946; men; affiliated with U. Laval; †
St.-Hyacinthe, Séminaire de[1], St.-Hyacinthe, Que.; 1811; men; P.; affiliated with U. de Montréal; †
St.-Jean, C.[1], Edmonton, Alta.; 1910; men; P.; affiliated with U. d'Ottawa; †
St.-Jean, C. Militaire Royal de, see **Canadian Services Colleges.**
St.-Jean Eudes, Externat Classique[1], Quebec, Que.; 1937; men; P.; affiliated with U. Laval; †
St.-Jean, Séminaire de[1], St.-Jean, Que.; 1911; men; P.; affiliated with U. de Montréal; †
St.-Jean Vianney, Séminaire[1], Montreal, Que.; 1956; men; P.; affiliated with U. de Montréal; †
St. Jerome's C.[1], Kitchener, Ont.; 1864; coed.; P.; affiliated with U. d'Ottawa; †
St. John's C.[2], Winnipeg, Man.; 1849; coed.; P.; affiliated with U. of Manitoba; † #
St.-Joseph, C.[1], St. Boniface, Man.; 1936; women's college of C. de St. Boniface; †
St.-Joseph, Maison[1], Montreal, Que.; 1856; men; P.; affiliated with U. Laval and U. de Montréal; †
St. Joseph's C.[1], Edmonton, Alta.; 1926; men; P.; affiliated with U. of Alberta; †
St. Joseph's C.[1], Toronto, Ont.; 1913; coed.; Fed.; affiliated with St. Michael's C. in U. of Toronto; †
St.-Joseph, Séminaire[1], Mont-Laurier, Que.; 1915; men; P.; affiliated with U. Laval; †
St. Joseph's Seminary, Edmonton, Alta.; men; P.; † #
St.-Joseph, U., St.-Joseph, N.B.; 1864; men; P.; ‡
St.-Laurent, C. de[1], St.-Laurent, Que.; 1847; men; P.; affiliated with U. de Montréal; †
St.-Louis, U., Edmundston, N.B.; 1947; men; P.; ‡
St. Martha's School of Nursing[1], Antigonish, N.S.; 1926; women; P.; affiliated with St. Francis Xavier U.; †
St. Mary's C., Brockville, Ont.; 1918; men; P.; jr. coll. affiliated with Assumption U.
St. Mary's C.[1], Winnipeg, Man.; 1927; women's college of St. Paul's C.; †
St. Mary's U., Halifax, N.S.; 1841; men; P.; ‡
St.-Maurice, C.[1], St.-Hyacinthe, Que.; 1935; women; P.; affiliated with U. de Montréal; †
St. Michael's C.[1], Toronto, Ont.; 1852; coed.; P.; a federated college of U. of Toronto; †
St. Patrick's C.[1], Ottawa, Ont.; 1929; coed.; P.; affiliated with U. d'Ottawa; ‡
St. Paul's C.[1], Winnipeg, Man.; 1926; coed.; P.; affiliated with U. of Manitoba; †
St. Paul, Séminaire[1], Ottawa, Ont.; 1937; men; P.; affiliated with U. d'Ottawa; ‡ #
St. Peter's C., Muenster, Sask.; men; P.; jr. coll. affiliated with U. of Saskatchewan.
St. Peter's Seminary[1], London, Ont.; men; P.; affiliated with U. of Western Ontario; #
St.-Raphaël, Externat Classique[1], Drummondville, Que.; 1946; men; P.; affiliated with U. Laval; †
St.-Sacrement, Séminaire[1], Terrebonne, Que.; 1902; men; P.; affiliated with U. de Montréal; †
Sts.-Apôtres, Grand Séminaire des, Sherbrooke, Que.; 1940; men; P.; #
Sts.-Apôtres, Séminaire des[1], Ste.-Catherine, Que.; 1946; men; P.; affiliated with U. de Montréal; †
St. Stephen's C.[1], Edmonton, Alta.; 1909; coed.; affiliated with U. of Alberta; #
St. Thomas C.[1], North Battleford, Sask.; 1932; men; P.; affiliated with U. d'Ottawa; †
St. Thomas More C.[1], Saskatoon, Sask.; 1936; coed.; P.; a federated college of U. of Saskatchewan; †
St. Thomas U., Chatham, N.B.; 1910; men; P.; ‡
St.-Viateur, Externat Classique[1], Outremont, Que,; 1951; men; P.; affiliated with U. de Montréal: †
Stanislas, C.[1], Outremont, Que.; 1938; men; P.; affiliated with U. de Montréal; †

***Toronto, U. of,** Toronto, Ont.; 1827; coed.; Prov.; ‡ #
Trinity C., U. of[2], Toronto, Ont.; 1851; coed.; P.; a federated college of U. of Toronto; † #
Trois-Rivières, Séminaire des[1], Trois-Rivières, Que.; 1860; men; P.; affiliated with U. Laval; †

Union C. of British Columbia[2], Vancouver, B.C.; 1927; coed.; P.; affiliated with U. of British Columbia; #
United C.[2], Winnipeg, Man.; 1871; coed.; P.; affiliated with U. of Manitoba; † #
United Church Training School[1], Toronto, Ont.; 1894; women; P.; affiliated with Victoria U. in U. of Toronto; †
United Theological C.[1], Montreal, Que.; men; P.; affiliated with McGill U.; #
Ursuline C. of Arts[1], London, Ont.; 1919; women; P.; affiliated with U. of Western Ontario; †
Ursulines, C. des[1], Rimouski, Que.; 1939; women; P.; affiliated with U. Laval; †

Valleyfield, Séminaire de[1], Valleyfield, Que.; men; P.; affiliated with U. de Montréal; †
Victoria C., Victoria, B.C.; 1902; coed.; Prov.; jr. coll. affiliated with U. of British Columbia.
Victoria U.[2], Toronto, Ont.; 1836; coed.; P.; a federated college of U. of Toronto; † #
Vincent-D'Indy, École[1], Outremont, Que.; 1932; women; P.; affiliated with U. de Montréal; ‡

Waterloo C.[1], Waterloo, Ont.; 1925; coed.; P. & Fed.; affiliated with U. of Western Ontario; † #
***Western Ontario, U. of,** London, Ont.; 1878; coed.; P.; ‡ #
Wycliffe C.[2], Toronto, Ont.; 1877; men; P.; a federated college of U. of Toronto; #

Xavier Junior C., Sydney, N.S.; 1951; coed.; P.; jr. coll. affiliated with St. Francis Xavier U.

FORMS OF ADDRESS

Person Being Addressed	Envelope Address	Salutation: Formal	Salutation: Less Formal	In Speaking
Ambassador (American)	The Honorable (full name), American Ambassador, (city and country)	Sir (*or* Madam):	My dear Mr. (*or* Madam) Ambassador:	Your Excellency *or* Mr. Ambassador (*or* Madam Ambassador)
Ambassador (Foreign)	His Excellency (full name), Ambassador of (country), Washington, D. C.	Sir (*or* Madam): *or* Your Excellency:	My dear Mr. (*or* Madam) Ambassador:	Your Excellency *or* Mr. Ambassador (*or* Madam Ambassador)
Archbishop (Roman Catholic)	The Most Reverend (full name), Archbishop of (city), (city and State, etc.)	Your Excellency: *or* Most Reverend Sir:	Most Reverend and dear Sir:	Your Excellency
Baron	The Right Honorable Lord (name)	My Lord: *or* Dear Sir:		Lord (name)
Baroness	The Right Honorable Baroness (name)	My Lady: *or* Dear Madam:		Lady (name)
Baronet	Sir (full name), Bt. *or* Bart.	Sir: *or* Dear Sir:		Sir (given name)
Baronet's Wife	Lady (full name)	Madam: *or* My Lady:		Lady (given name)
Bishop (Methodist)	Bishop (full name), (city and State, etc.)	Dear Bishop (surname):		Bishop (surname)
Bishop (Protestant Episcopal)	The Right Reverend (full name), Bishop of (diocese), (city and State, etc.)	Right Reverend and dear Sir:	Dear Bishop (surname):	Bishop (surname)
Bishop (Roman Catholic)	The Most Reverend (full name), Bishop of (diocese), (city and State, etc.)	Your Excellency: *or* Most Reverend Sir:	Dear Bishop (surname):	Bishop (surname)
Cabinet Officer of the U. S.	The Honorable (full name), Secretary of (the cabinet, *or* Postmaster General, etc.), Washington 25, D. C.	Sir (*or* Madam):	My dear Mr. (*or* Madam) Secretary:	Mr. (*or* Madam) Secretary
Cardinal (Roman Catholic)	His Eminence (given name) Cardinal (surname), Archbishop of (city, etc.), (city and State, etc.)	Your Eminence:		Your Eminence

Person Being Addressed	Envelope Address	Salutation		In Speaking
		Formal	Less Formal	
Common Form (Man)	Mr. (full name)	My dear Mr. (surname): *or* My dear Sir: *in plural,* Gentlemen:	Dear Mr. (surname): *or* Dear Sir:	
Common Form (Married Woman)	Mrs. (full name)	My dear Mrs. (surname): *or* My dear Madam: *in plural,* Ladies: *or* Mesdames:	Dear Mrs. (surname): *or* Dear Madam:	
Common Form (Unmarried Woman)	Miss (full name)	My dear Miss (surname): *or* My dear Madam: *in plural,* Ladies: *or* Mesdames:	Dear Miss (surname): *or* Dear Madam:	
Congressman	The Honorable (full name), House of Representatives, Washington 25, D. C.	Sir (*or* Madam):	My dear Mr. (*or* Mrs. *or* Miss) (surname):	Mr. (*or* Mrs. *or* Miss) (surname)
Consul (American or other)	(full name), Esq., American (*or* other) Consul, (city and country, or State)	Sir: *or* My dear Sir:	My dear Mr. Consul:	Mr. (surname)
Doctor (of Philosophy, Medicine, Divinity, etc.)	(full name), Ph.D., M.D., D.D., etc. *or* Dr. (full name)	My dear Dr. (surname): *or* My dear Sir:		Dr. (surname)
Duchess	To Her Grace, the Duchess of (name)	Madam:	Dear Duchess:	Duchess
Duke	To His Grace, the Duke of (name)	Sir:	Dear Duke:	Duke
Earl	The Right Honorable The Earl of (name)	My Lord:		Lord (name)
Earl's Wife	The Right Honorable The Countess of (name)	My Lady:		Lady (name)
Governor (of a State)	The Honorable (full name), Governor of (State), (capital city and State)	Sir:	My dear Governor (surname):	Governor (surname)
Judge (see also **Supreme Court**)	The Honorable (full name), (name of court), (city and State)	Sir (*or* Madam):	My dear Judge (surname):	Judge (surname)
King (or **Queen**)	His (Her) Most Gracious Majesty, King, (Queen) (name)	May it please Your Majesty:		*Initially,* Your Majesty; *thereafter,* Sir (*or* Ma'am)

Person Being Addressed	Envelope Address	Salutation: Formal	Salutation: Less Formal	In Speaking
Knight	Sir (full name), (initials of his order, if any)	Sir:		Sir (given name)
Mayor	The Honorable (full name), Mayor of (city), (city and State)	Sir (*or* Madam):	My dear Mr. (*or* Madam) Mayor: *or* My dear Mayor (surname):	Mr. (*or* Madam) Mayor
Minister (Protestant)	The Reverend (full name), (address, city, and State)	My dear Mr. (*or* Dr., *if a D.D.*) (surname):		Mr. (*or* Dr. *or, if a Lutheran,* Pastor) (surname)
Monsignor (Roman Catholic)	The Right Reverend Monsignor (full name), (city and State)	Right Reverend Monsignor (surname):		Monsignor (surname)
Nun	Sister (religious name), (initials of her order)	My dear Sister:	Dear Sister (religious name):	Sister (religious name)
President (of the United States)	The President, The White House, Washington 25, D. C.	Sir:	My dear Mr. President:	Mr. President
Priest (Roman Catholic)	The Reverend (full name), (address, city, and State)	Reverend and dear Sir:	My dear Father (surname):	Father (surname)
Prince (or Princess)	His (Her) Royal Highness, Prince(ss) (given name)	Your Royal Highness:	Sir (*or* Madam):	Your Royal Highness
Rabbi	Rabbi (full name), (address, city, and State)	My dear Rabbi (*or* Dr., *if the holder of a doctor's degree*) (surname):		Rabbi (*or* Dr.) (surname)
Representative (of a State legislature)	The Honorable (full name), Member of Assembly (or other name of the legislature), (capital city and State)	Sir (*or* Madam):	My dear Mr. (*or* Mrs. *or* Miss) (surname):	Mr. (*or* Mrs. *or* Miss) (surname)
Senator (of the United States)	The Honorable (full name), United States Senate, Washington 25, D. C.	Sir (*or* Madam):	My dear Senator (surname):	Senator (surname) *or* Mr. (*or* Madam) Senator
Senator (of a State)	The Honorable (full name), (State) Senate, (capital city and State)	Sir (*or* Madam):	My dear Senator (surname):	Senator (surname)
Supreme Court (Associate Justice)	The Honorable (full name), Associate Justice of the United States Supreme Court, Washington 25, D. C.	Sir:	My dear Mr. Justice:	Mr. Justice
Supreme Court (Chief Justice)	The Honorable (full name), Chief Justice of the United States, Washington 25, D. C.	Sir:	My dear Mr. Chief Justice:	Mr. Chief Justice
Vice President (of the United States)	The Vice President, Washington 25, D. C.	Sir:	My dear Mr. Vice President:	Mr. Vice President

TABLES OF WEIGHTS AND MEASURES

Linear Measure

1 inch			=	2.54	centimeters
12 inches	=	1 foot	=	0.3048	meter
3 feet	=	1 yard	=	0.9144	meter
5½ yards or 16½ feet	=	1 rod (or pole or perch)	=	5.029	meters
40 rods	=	1 furlong	=	201.17	meters
8 furlongs or 1,760 yards or 5,280 feet	=	1 (statute) mile	=	1,609.3	meters
3 miles	=	1 (land) league	=	4.83	kilometers

Square Measure

1 square inch			=	6.452	square centimeters
144 square inches	=	1 square foot	=	929	square centimeters
9 square feet	=	1 square yard	=	0.8361	square meter
30¼ square yards	=	1 square rod (or square pole or square perch)	=	25.29	square meters
160 square rods or 4,840 square yards or 43,560 square feet	=	1 acre	=	0.4047	hectare
640 acres	=	1 square mile	=	259	hectares or 2.59 square kilometers.

Cubic Measure

1 cubic inch			=	16.387 cubic centimeters
1,728 cubic inches	=	1 cubic foot	=	0.0283 cubic meter
27 cubic feet	=	1 cubic yard	=	0.7646 cubic meter
		(in units for cordwood, etc.)		
16 cubic feet	=	1 cord foot		
8 cord feet	=	1 cord	=	3.625 cubic meters

Chain Measure

(for Gunter's, or surveyor's, chain)

7.92 inches	=	1 link	=	20.12	centimeters
100 links or 66 feet	=	1 chain	=	20.12	meters
10 chains	=	1 furlong	=	201.17	meters
80 chains	=	1 mile	=	1,609.3	meters

(for engineer's chain)

1 foot	=	1 link	=	0.3048	meter
100 feet	=	1 chain	=	30.48	meters
52.8 chains	=	1 mile	=	1,609.3	meters

Surveyor's (Square) Measure

625 square links	=	1 square pole	=	25.29	square meters
16 square poles	=	1 square chain	=	404.7	square meters
10 square chains	=	1 acre	=	0.4047	hectare
640 acres	=	1 square mile or 1 section	=	259	hectares or 2.59 square kilometers
36 square miles	=	1 township	=	9,324.0	hectares or 93.24 square kilometers

Nautical Measure

6 feet	=	1 fathom	=	1.829 meters
100 fathoms	=	1 cable's length (ordinary) (In the U.S. Navy 120 fathoms or 720 feet = 1 cable's length; in the British Navy, 608 feet = 1 cable's length.)		
10 cables' lengths	=	1 nautical mile (6,076.10333 feet, by international agreement in 1954)	=	1.852 kilometers
1 nautical mile (Also called geographical, sea, or air mile, and, in Great Britain, Admiralty mile.)	=	1.1508 statute miles (the length of a minute of longitude at the equator)		
3 nautical miles	=	1 marine league (3.45 statute miles)	=	5.56 kilometers
60 nautical miles	=	1 degree of a great circle of the earth		

Dry Measure

1 pint			=	33.60 cubic inches	=	0.5505 liter
2 pints	=	1 quart	=	67.20 cubic inches	=	1.1012 liters
8 quarts	=	1 peck	=	537.61 cubic inches	=	8.8096 liters
4 pecks	=	1 bushel	=	2,150.42 cubic inches	=	35.2383 liters

1 British dry quart = 1.032 U.S. dry quarts.

According to United States government standards, the following are the weights avoirdupois for single bushels of the specified grains: for wheat, 60 pounds; for barley, 48 pounds; for oats, 32 pounds; for rye, 56 pounds; for corn, 56 pounds. Some States have specifications varying from these.

Liquid Measure

1 gill	=	4 fluid ounces (see next table)	=	7.219 cubic inches	=	0.1183 liter
4 gills	=	1 pint	=	28.875 cubic inches	=	0.4732 liter
2 pints	=	1 quart	=	57.75 cubic inches	=	0.9463 liter
4 quarts	=	1 gallon	=	231 cubic inches	=	3.7853 liters

The British imperial gallon (4 imperial quarts) = 277.42 cubic inches = 4.546 liters. The barrel in Great Britain equals 36 imperial gallons, in the United States, usually 31½ gallons.

Apothecaries' Fluid Measure

1 minim		= 0.0038 cubic inch	= 0.0616 milliliter
60 minims	= 1 fluid dram	= 0.2256 cubic inch	= 3.6966 milliliters
8 fluid drams	= 1 fluid ounce	= 1.8047 cubic inches	= 0.0296 liter
16 fluid ounces	= 1 pint	= 28.875 cubic inches	= 0.4732 liter

See table immediately preceding for quart and gallon equivalents.
The British pint = 20 fluid ounces.

Circular (or Angular) Measure

60 seconds (″)	= 1 minute (′)
60 minutes	= 1 degree (°)
90 degrees	= 1 quadrant or 1 right angle
4 quadrants or 360 degrees	= 1 circle

Avoirdupois Weight

(The grain, equal to 0.0648 gram, is the same in all three tables of weight)

1 dram or 27.34 grains		= 1.772 grams
16 drams or 437.5 grains	= 1 ounce	= 28.3495 grams
16 ounces or 7,000 grains	= 1 pound	= 453.59 grams
100 pounds	= 1 hundredweight	= 45.36 kilograms
2,000 pounds	= 1 ton	= 907.18 kilograms

In Great Britain, 14 pounds (6.35 kilograms) = 1 stone, 112 pounds (50.80 kilograms) = 1 hundredweight, and 2,240 pounds (1,016.05 kilograms) = 1 long ton.

Troy Weight

(The grain, equal to 0.0648 gram, is the same in all three tables of weight)

3.086 grains	= 1 carat	= 200 milligrams
24 grains	= 1 pennyweight	= 1.5552 grams
20 pennyweights or 480 grains	= 1 ounce	= 31.1035 grams
12 ounces or 5,760 grains	= 1 pound	= 373.24 grams

Apothecaries' Weight

(The grain, equal to 0.0648 gram, is the same in all three tables of weight)

20 grains	= 1 scruple	= 1.296 grams
3 scruples	= 1 dram	= 3.888 grams
8 drams or 480 grains	= 1 ounce	= 31.1035 grams
12 ounces or 5,760 grains	= 1 pound	= 373.24 grams

THE METRIC SYSTEM

Linear Measure

10 millimeters	= 1 centimeter	= 0.3937 inch
10 centimeters	= 1 decimeter	= 3.937 inches
10 decimeters	= 1 meter	= 39.37 inches or 3.28 feet
10 meters	= 1 decameter	= 393.7 inches
10 decameters	= 1 hectometer	= 328 feet 1 inch
10 hectometers	= 1 kilometer	= 0.621 mile
10 kilometers	= 1 myriameter	= 6.21 miles

Square Measure

100 square millimeters	= 1 square centimeter	= 0.15499 square inch
100 square centimeters	= 1 square decimeter	= 15.499 square inches
100 square decimeters	= 1 square meter	= 1,549.9 square inches or 1.196 square yards
100 square meters	= 1 square decameter	= 119.6 square yards
100 square decameters	= 1 square hectometer	= 2.471 acres
100 square hectometers	= 1 square kilometer	= 0.386 square mile

Land Measure

1 square meter	= 1 centiare	= 1,549.9 square inches
100 centiares	= 1 are	= 119.6 square yards
100 ares	= 1 hectare	= 2.471 acres
100 hectares	= 1 square kilometer	= 0.386 square mile

Volume Measure

1,000 cubic millimeters	= 1 cubic centimeter	= .06102 cubic inch
1,000 cubic centimeters	= 1 cubic decimeter	= 61.02 cubic inches
1,000 cubic decimeters	= 1 cubic meter (the unit is called a *stere* in measuring firewood)	= 35.314 cubic feet

Capacity Measure

10 milliliters	= 1 centiliter	= .338 fluid ounce
10 centiliters	= 1 deciliter	= 3.38 fluid ounces
10 deciliters	= 1 liter	= 1.0567 liquid quarts or 0.9081 dry quart
10 liters	= 1 decaliter	= 2.64 gallons or 0.284 bushel
10 decaliters	= 1 hectoliter	= 26.418 gallons or 2.838 bushels
10 hectoliters	= 1 kiloliter	= 264.18 gallons or 35.315 cubic feet

Weights

10 milligrams	= 1 centigram	= 0.1543 grain
10 centigrams	= 1 decigram	= 1.5432 grains
10 decigrams	= 1 gram	= 15.432 grains
10 grams	= 1 decagram	= 0.3527 ounce
10 decagrams	= 1 hectogram	= 3.5274 ounces
10 hectograms	= 1 kilogram	= 2.2046 pounds
10 kilograms	= 1 myriagram	= 22.046 pounds
10 myriagrams	= 1 quintal	= 220.46 pounds
10 quintals	= 1 metric ton	= 2,204.6 pounds

SPECIAL SIGNS AND SYMBOLS

ASTRONOMY

1. SUN, MOON, PLANETS, ETC.

☉ (1) The Sun. (2) Sunday.
☾ *or* ☽ (1) The Moon. (2) Monday.
● New Moon.
☽, ◐, *or* ☽ First Quarter.
○ Full Moon.
☾, ◑, *or* ☾ Last Quarter.
✳ *or* ✳ Fixed Star.
☿ (1) Mercury. (2) Wednesday.
♀ (1) Venus. (2) Friday.
⊕, ⊖, *or* ♁ The Earth.
♂ (1) Mars. (2) Tuesday.
♃ (1) Jupiter. (2) Thursday.
♄ (1) Saturn. (2) Saturday.
⛢ *or* ♅ Uranus.
♆ Neptune.
♇ Pluto.
☄ Comet.
①, ②, ③, *etc.* Asteroids in the order of their discovery.
α, β, γ, etc. The stars (of a constellation) in the order of their brightness; the Greek letter is followed by the Latin genitive of the name of the constellation.

2. SIGNS OF THE ZODIAC

Spring Signs

1. ♈ Aries (the Ram).
2. ♉ Taurus (the Bull).
3. ♊ *or* Π Gemini (the Twins).

Summer Signs

4. ♋ *or* ♋ Cancer (the Crab).
5. ♌ Leo (the Lion).
6. ♍ Virgo (the Virgin).

Autumn Signs

7. ♎ Libra (the Balance).
8. ♏ Scorpio (the Scorpion).
9. ♐ Sagittarius (the Archer).

Winter Signs

10. ♑ *or* ♑ Capricorn (the Goat).
11. ♒ Aquarius (the Water Bearer).
12. ♓ Pisces (the Fish).

3. ASPECTS AND NODES

☌ Conjunction;—with reference to bodies having the same longitude, or right ascension.
✱ Sextile;—being 60° apart in longitude, or right ascension.
□ Quadrature;—being 90° apart in longitude, or right ascension.
△ Trine;—being 120° apart in longitude, or right ascension.
☍ Opposition;—being 180° apart in longitude, or right ascension.
☊ Ascending Node.
☋ Descending Node.

4. SIGNS AND ABBREVIATIONS USED IN ASTRONOMICAL NOTATION

a. Mean distance.
A.R. Right ascension.
β Celestial latitude.
D. Diameter.
δ Declination.
Δ Distance.
E. East.
e Eccentricity.
h. *or* ʰ Hours: as, 5h. or 5ʰ.
i Inclination to the ecliptic.
L, l, *or* ε Mean longitude in orbit.
λ Longitude.
M. Mass.
m. *or* ᵐ Minutes of time: as, 5m. or 5ᵐ.
μ or n Mean daily motion.
+ *or* N. North.
N. P. D. North polar distance.
ν, ☊, *or* L. Longitude of ascending node.
π or ω Longitude of perihelion.
q. Perihelion distance.
ρ or R. Radius or radius vector.
— *or* S. South.
s. *or* ˢ Seconds of time: as, 16s. or 16ˢ.
T. Periodic time.
W. West.
φ Angle of eccentricity; also, geographical latitude.
° Degrees of arc.
′ Minutes of arc.
″ Seconds of arc.

BIOLOGY

○, ⊙, ① Annual plant.
②, ⊙⊙, ♂ Biennial plant.
♃ Perennial herb.
△ Evergreen plant.
⊙ Monocarpic plant, that bears fruit but once.
ƀ Shrub.
ƅ Treelike shrub.
ƅ Tree.
⌒ Climbing plant.
♂, ♁ (1) Male organism or cell. (2) Staminate plant or flower.
♀ (1) Female organism or cell. (2) Pistillate plant or flower.
☿ Perfect, or hermaphroditic, plant or flower.
○ Individual, especially female, organism.
□ Individual, especially male, organism.
♁ ♀ Unisexual; having male and female flowers separate.
♀—♁ Monoecious; having male and female flowers on the same plant.
♁ : ♀ Dioecious; having male and female flowers on different plants.
♀ ♁ ♀ Polygamous; having hermaphroditic and unisexual flowers on the same or different plants.
∞ Indefinite number, as of stamens when there are more than twenty.
0 Lacking or absent, as a part.
) Turning or winding to the left.
(Turning or winding to the right.
× Crossed with: used of a hybrid.
P Parental (generation).
F Filial (generation); offspring.
F_1, F_2, F_3, *etc.* Offspring of the first, second, third, etc. filial generation.
\+ Possessing a (specified) characteristic.
— Lacking a (specified) characteristic.
✳ Northern hemisphere.
✳ Southern hemisphere.
\|✳ Old World.
✳\| New World.
°, ′, ″ Feet, inches, lines.
′, ″, ‴ Feet, inches, lines (in European usage).

CHEMISTRY

The symbol for each of the chemical elements is formed of the initial or an abbreviation of its English, Latin, or Modern Latin name, as C for carbon, K for potassium (Mod. L. *kalium*), Mn for manganese, Au for gold (L. *aurum*). A complete list of the symbols of elements can be found on p. 469.

The formula for a chemical compound is expressed by combining the symbols of its constituent elements, with a small subscript at the right of each specifying the number of atoms of each element in a molecule of the compound. Where only one atom is involved, no subscript is used. Examples: MgO (magnesium oxide), a compound in which one atom of magnesium is combined with one atom of oxygen; H_2O (water), a compound in which two atoms of hydrogen are combined with one atom of oxygen; $NaHCO_3$ (sodium bicarbonate), a compound in which one atom each of sodium, hydrogen, and carbon, and three atoms of oxygen are combined.

Signs and Symbols

...ations, the number of molecules of the element ...mpound entering into a reaction is indicated by a ...gure placed before the symbol or formula (unless there is only one molecule), as $3O_2$, three molecules of oxygen; 2NaCl, two molecules of sodium chloride.

· separates radicals, as in $CH_3 \cdot CHO$ (acetaldehyde, C_2H_4O), or the water of crystallization, as in $CaSO_4 \cdot 2H_2O$ (gypsum, or hydrated calcium sulfate).

, indicates elements which are interchangeable; for example, (Er, Y) PO_4 means $ErPO_4$ and YPO_4 in proportions that vary.

() indicates a radical within a compound, as in $(NH_4)_2S$, ammonium sulfide, or is used to set off elements that are interchangeable, as in the example for the preceding symbol.

[] is used together with parentheses to indicate certain radicals, as in $Fe_3[Fe(CN)_6]_2$, ferrous ferricyanide, or in co-ordination formulas to indicate relationship to the central atom.

⌬ is used in structural formulas to indicate the benzene ring.

+, ++, +++, *etc.* *or* 1+, 2+, 3+, *etc.* } indicate the unit charges of positive electricity, as Al^{+++}, an aluminum ion with three positive charges.

–, – –, – – –, *etc.* *or* 1–, 2–, 3–, *etc.* } indicate the unit charges of negative electricity, as S^{--}, a sulfide ion with two negative charges.

–, =, ≡, *etc.* indicate (1) the same as the symbols immediately preceding, as S =; (2) a single, double, or triple bond, as in HC≡CH, acetylene.

·, :, ⋮, *etc.* Indicate a single, double, or triple bond, as in $C_6H_5C{:}CH$, phenylacetylene.

′, ″, ‴, *etc.* indicate (1) a valence of one, two, three, etc., as Fe‴, trivalent iron; (2) the unit charges of negative electricity, as SO_4″, a sulfate ion with two negative charges.

1–, 2–, 3–, *etc.* *or* α–, β–, γ–, *etc.* } used in names of compounds to designate one of the several possible positions of substituting groups in a parent compound, as in 2-ethylnaphthalene, γ-resorcylic acid.

– indicates levorotation, as —130°.

\+ (1) means "with the addition of, or together with," and is used in chemical equations between the formulas of the reacting substances: see example under the next symbol. (2) indicates dextrorotation as +130°.

= means "form, or result in," and is used in chemical equations between the formulas of the reacting substances and those of the reaction products. Example: $H_2SO_4 + 2NaCl = Na_2SO_4 + 2HCl$, meaning one molecule of sulfuric acid together with two molecules of sodium chloride will form one molecule of sodium sulfate and two molecules of hydrogen chloride.

→ indicates the direction of the reaction.

⇄ indicates a reversible reaction; i.e., one that can proceed in either direction, or in both directions at the same time, in a state of equilibrium.

↓ indicates that the specified reaction product (after which it is written) appears as a precipitate.

↑ indicates that the specified reaction product (after which it is written) appears as a gas.

≡ *or* ≏ means "is equivalent to" and is used in quantitative equations to indicate the quantities of specified substances that will react with each other completely, so as to leave no excess matter.

COMMERCE AND FINANCE

$ Dollar or dollars: as, $100.

¢ Cent or cents: as, 13¢.

£ Pound or pounds sterling: as, £100.

/ Shilling or shillings: as, 2/6, two shillings and sixpence.

lb Pound (in weight).

@ (1) At: as, 200 @ $1 each. (2) To: as, shoes per pr. $10 @ $15.

℘ Per.

% (1) Per cent: as, 5%. (2) Order of.

a/c Account.

B/L Bill of Lading.

B/S Bill of Sale.

c/d, C/D Carried down (in bookkeeping).

c/f, C/F Carried forward (in bookkeeping).

c/o (1) Care of. (2) Carried over (in bookkeeping).

d/a Days after acceptance.

d/s Days after sight.

L/C Letter of Credit.

\# (1) Number (before a figure): as, #5 can. (after a figure): as, 25#.

MATHEMATICS

1. NUMERATION

Arabic	*Greek*	*Roman*
0	. . .	. . .
1	α	I
2	β	II
3	γ	III
4	δ	IV *or* IIII
5	ε	V
6	ς	VI
7	ζ	VII
8	η	VIII *or* IIX
9	θ	IX *or* VIIII
10	ι	X
11	ια	XI
12	ιβ	XII
13	ιγ	XIII *or* XIIV
14	ιδ	XIV *or* XIIII
15	ιε	XV
16	ις	XVI
17	ιζ	XVII
18	ιη	XVIII *or* XIIX
19	ιθ	XIX *or* XVIIII
20	κ	XX
30	λ	XXX
40	μ	XL *or* XXXX
50	ν	L
60	ξ	LX
70	ο	LXX
80	π	LXXX *or* XXC
90	ϙ	XC *or* LXXXX
100	ρ	C
200	σ	CC
300	τ	CCC
400	υ	CD *or* CCCC
500	φ	D *or* IↃ
600	χ	DC *or* IↃC
700	ψ	DCC *or* IↃCC
800	ω	DCCC *or* IↃCCC
900	. . .	CM, DCCCC, *or* IↃCCCC
1,000	. . .	M *or* CIↃ
2,000	. . .	MM *or* CIↃCIↃ

Capital letters were sometimes used for the Greek numerals, and lower-case letters are often used for the Roman. In the Roman notation, the value of a character to the right of a larger numeral is added to that of the numeral: as, VI = V + I = 6. I, X, and sometimes C, are also placed to the left of larger numerals and when so situated their value is subtracted from that of such numerals: as, IV, that is, V – I = 4. After the sign IↃ for D, when the character Ↄ was repeated, each repetition had the effect of multiplying IↃ by ten: as, IↃↃ, 5,000; IↃↃↃ, 50,000; and the like. In writing numbers twice as great as these, C was placed as many times before the stroke I as the Ↄ was written after it. Sometimes a line was drawn over a numeral to indicate thousands: as, $\overline{C}$ = 100,000.

2. CALCULATION

\+ (1) Plus, the sign of addition; used also to indicate that figures are only approximately exact, some figures being omitted at the end: as, 2.1557+. (2) Positive.

– (1) Minus, the sign of subtraction; used also to indicate that figures have been left off from the end of a number, and that the last figure has been increased by one: as, 2.9378 = 2.94–. (2) Negative.

± *or* ∓ Plus or minus; indicating that either of the signs + or – may properly be used; also used to introduce the probable error after a figure obtained by experimentation, etc.

× Multiplied by: as, 5 × 4 = 20; multiplication is also indicated by a centered dot (5 · 4 = 20) or by placing the factors in immediate juxtaposition (2ab = 2 × a × b).

÷ Divided by; division is also indicated by the sign: (x : y), by a straight line between the dividend and the divisor $\left(\frac{x}{y}\right)$, or by an oblique (x/y).

= Is equal to; equals.

≠ Is not equal to.

\> Is greater than: as, x > y; that is, x is greater than y.

< Is less than: as, x < y; that is, x is less than y.

≮ *or* ≥ Is not less than; is equal to or greater than.

≯ *or* ≤ Is not greater than; is equal to or less than.

...ent to; applied to magnitudes or quanti-...t are equal in area or volume, but are not ... same form.

...tical with.

...gruent to.

... difference between; used to designate the ...fference between two quantities without indi-...cating which is the greater; as, $x \sim z$ = the difference between x and z.

...Varies as; is directly proportional to: as, $x \propto y$; that is, x varies as y.

... Geometric proportion: as, $\div\ x : y :: a : b$; that is, the geometric proportion, x is to y as a is to b.

: Is to; the ratio of.

: : As; equals: used between ratios.

∞ Indefinitely great: the symbol for infinity.

! *or* ⌊ The factorial of, or the continued product of numbers from one upward: as, $5! = 5 \times 4 \times 3 \times 2 \times 1$.

∴ Therefore.

∵ Since; because.

. . . And so on.

∠ Angle: as, ∠XYZ.

∟ Right angle.

⊥ The perpendicular; is perpendicular to: as, EF ⊥ MN = EF is perpendicular to MN.

|| Parallel; is parallel to: as, EF || DG.

○ Circle; circumference; 360°.

⌒ Arc of a circle.

△ Triangle.

□ Square.

▭ Rectangle.

▱ Parallelogram.

$\sqrt{}$ *or* √ Radical sign; root, indicating, when used without a figure placed above it, the square root: as, $\sqrt{9} = 3$. When any other than the square root is meant, a figure (called the *index*) expressing the degree of the required root, is placed above the sign: as, $\sqrt[3]{27} = 3$.

$^1, ^2, ^3$, *etc.* Exponents, placed above and to the right of a quantity to indicate that it is raised to the first, second, third, etc. power: as, a^2, $(a + b)^3$.

′, ″, ‴, *etc.* Prime, double (or second) prime, triple (or third) prime, etc., used to distinguish between different values of the same variable: as, x', x'', x''', etc.

‾‾	Vinculum: as, $\overline{x + y}$	These signs indicate that the quantities connected or enclosed by them are to be taken together, as a single quantity.
( )	Parentheses: as, $2(x + y)$	
[ ]	Brackets: as, $a[2(x + y)]$	
{ }	Braces: as, $b + \{2 - a[2(x + y)]\}$	

f or F Function; function of: as, $f(a)$, a function of a.

d Differential of: as, da.

δ Variation of: as, δa.

△ Finite difference, or increment.

D Differential coefficient, or derivative.

∫ Integral; integral of, indicating that the expression following it is to be integrated: as, $\int f(x)dx$ indicates the indefinite integral of $f(x)$ with respect to x.

$\int_a^b$ Definite integral, indi... ing the limits of integration: as, $\int_a^b f(x)dx$ ...es the integral of $f(x)$ with respect to x, betwe... he limits a and b.

Σ Sum; algebraic sum; whe... ed to indicate the summation of finite differ... it has a sense similar to that of the symbol ...

Π The continued product of all ... s such as (those indicated).

π Pi, the number 3.14159265+; ... tio of the circumference of a circle to its ... er, of a semicircle to its radius, and of the ... f a circle to the square of its radius.

e or ε The number 2.7182818+; th... of the Napierian system of logarithms; ... e eccentricity of a conic section.

M The modulus of a system of logarith... of the common system of logarithm... ecially equal to 0.4342944819+. ... it is

g The acceleration of gravity.

° Degrees: as, 90°.

′ (1) Minutes of arc. (2) Feet.

″ (1) Seconds of arc. (2) Inches.

h Hours.

m Minutes of time.

s Seconds of time.

MEDICINE AND PHARMACY

ĀĀ, Ā or āā [Gr. *ana*], of each.

a. c. [L. *ante cibum*], before meals.

ad [L.], up to; so as to make: as, *ad* ℥ij, so as to make two drams.

ad. [L. *adde*], let there be added; add.

ad lib. [L. *ad libitum*], at pleasure; as needed or desired.

aq. [L. *aqua*], water.

b. (i.) d. [L. *bis (in) die*], twice daily.

C. [L. *congius*], a gallon.

coch. [L. *cochleare*], a spoonful.

D. [L. *dosis*], a dose.

dil. [L. *dilue*], dilute or dissolve.

ess. [L. *essentia*], essence.

ft. mist. [L. *fiat mistura*], let a mixture be made.

ft. pulv. [L. *fiat pulvis*], let a powder be made.

gr. [L. *granum*], a grain.

gtt. [L. *guttae*], drops.

guttatim [L.], drop by drop.

haust. [L. *haustus*], a draft.

hor. decub. [L. *hora decubitus*], at bedtime.

lot. [L. *lotio*], a lotion.

M. [L. *misce*], mix.

mac. [L. *macera*], macerate.

O. *or* o. [L. *octarius*], a pint.

p.c. [L. *post cibum*], after meals.

pil. [L. *pilula(e)*], pill(s).

p.r.n. [L. *pro re nata*], as circumstances may require.

pulv. [L. *pulvis*], powder.

q. (i.) d. [L. *quater (in) die*], four times daily.

q.l. [L. *quantum libet*], as much as you please.

q. s. [L. *quantum sufficit*], as much as will suffice.

q.v. [L. *quantum vis*], as much as you like.

℞ [L. *recipe*], take: used at the beginning of a prescription.

S or Sig. [L. *signa*], write: used in prescriptions to indicate the directions to be placed on the label of the medicine.

t. (i.) d. [L. *ter (in) die*], three times daily.

℥ ounce; ℥i = one ounce; ℥ij = two ounces; ℥ss = half an ounce; ℥iss = one ounce and a half, etc.; *f*℥ = a fluid ounce.

ʒ dram; ʒi = one dram; ʒij = two drams; ʒss = half a dram; ʒiss = one dram and a half, etc.; *f*ʒ = a fluid dram.

℈ scruple; ℈i = one scruple; ℈ij = two scruples; ℈ss = half a scruple; ℈iss = one scruple and a half, etc.

♏ *or* ♍ minim.

MISCELLANEOUS

& *or* & (the ampersand) and: as A. B. Smith & Co.

&c. [L. *et cetera*], and others; and so forth.

© copyrighted.

℟ response: in religious services, used to mark the part to be uttered by the congregation in answer to the officiant.

* in Roman Catholic service books, a mark used to divide each verse of a psalm into two parts, indicating where the response begins.

℣, V', *or* V̸ versicle: in religious services, used to mark the part to be uttered by the officiant.

✠ (1) a sign of the cross used by the pope, by archbishops, and by bishops, before their names. (2) in religious services, used to mark the places where the sign of the cross is to be made.

† died: used in genealogies, etc.

× (1) by: used in dimensions, as paper 8 × 11 inches. (2) a mark representing a signature, as on a legal document, made by someone unable to write; the name is added by someone else; e.g.

his
John × *Doe*
mark